D1094697

THE OXFORD UNIVERSAL DICTIONARY

THE OXFORD UNIVERSAL DICTIONARY

ON HISTORICAL PRINCIPLES

PREPARED BY

WILLIAM LITTLE

M.A., late Fellow of Corpus Christi College, Oxford

H. W. FOWLER
M.A. Oxon.

J. COULSON
B.A. Leeds

REVISED AND EDITED BY

C. T. ONIONS

C.B.E., F.B.A.

M.A. Lond.; M.A., Hon. D.Litt. Oxon.; Hon. Litt.D. Leeds;
Hon. LL.D Birmingham; Hon. F.R.S.L.
Fellow and Librarian of Magdalen College
Sometime Reader in English Philology in the University of Oxford
Co-Editor of the Oxford English Dictionary
Corresponding Fellow of the Mediaeval Academy of America

THIRD EDITION
REVISED WITH ADDENDA

OXFORD
AT THE CLARENDON PRESS

Oxford University Press, Amen House, London E.C.4
GLASGOW NEW YORK TORONTO MELBOURNE WELLINGTON
BOMBAY CALCUTTA MADRAS KARACHI CAPE TOWN IBADAN
Geoffrey Cumberlege, Publisher to the University

FIRST PUBLISHED, FEBRUARY 1933
REPRINTED, WITH CORRECTIONS, MARCH 1933, APRIL 1933
REPRINTED 1934. SECOND EDITION 1936; REPRINTED 1939
THIRD EDITION 1944; REPRINTED, WITH CORRECTIONS, 1947
REPRINTED 1950, 1952
WITH CORRECTIONS AND REVISED ADDENDA, 1955

PRINTED IN THE UNITED STATES OF AMERICA
BY RAND McNALLY & COMPANY, CONKEY DIVISION

PREFACE

THIS Dictionary is an abridgement officially authorized by the Delegates of the Oxford University Press of *A New English Dictionary on Historical Principles*, later known as *The Oxford English Dictionary*. The need for such an abridged form of the great work was envisaged at the outset. The publication of this work is, in fact, a fulfilment of one of the provisions of the agreement entered into in the year 1879 between the Philological Society and the Oxford University Press. The relevant clause of the Indenture runs as follows:

> The Delegates may (if and whenever they think fit) prepare and publish any Dictionaries compiled or abridged from the principal Dictionary, and in such form as they may think fit, and may deal with the same in all respects at their discretion.

It was not until 1902 that the project of an abridgement was initiated. It was clear that the editors and staff engaged on the principal work had their hands too full to undertake it. A scholar from outside was found for the task in the late Mr. William Little, Fellow of Corpus Christi College, Oxford, who was asked to submit specimens in 1902, and with him negotiations were officially entered into on 24 April 1903. The work was carried on steadily by him until his death in January 1922. By this time he had prepared entirely without assistance the manuscript for the letters A to T and V, and had passed for printing about one-third of the whole dictionary.

Upon his death the materials left by him were placed in my hands for revision and completion. The gaps in the manuscript 'copy' were filled by Mr. H. W. Fowler, who abridged U and X, Y, Z, and by Mrs. E. A. Coulson, who was responsible for W. In the earlier stages of my editorship I was assisted by two experienced members of the Oxford Dictionary staff, Mr. F. J. Sweatman, M.A. Oxon., and Mr. J. W. Birt. Since 1924, when these assistants could no longer be spared for the work, the following ladies have successively taken part: Mrs. J. W. Alden (Miss A. M. Savage), M.A. Oxon., and three graduates in English of the University of Leeds, Mrs. E. A. Coulson (Miss J. Senior), Miss M. Dawn, and Miss S. M. Mills. The services rendered by all these helpers and their share in bringing the work to a successful conclusion are here gratefully acknowledged.

The aim of this Dictionary is to present in miniature all the features of the principal work. It is designed to embrace not only the literary and colloquial English of the present day together with such technical and scientific terms as are most frequently met with or are likely to be the subject of inquiry, but also a considerable proportion of obsolete, archaic, and dialectal words and uses. The Oxford Dictionary was compiled and edited from materials amounting to over five million quotations, derived from English works of literature and records of all kinds, and resulted in 15,000 large quarto pages, in which nearly half a million words are recorded with more than one and a half million illustrative quotations. This abridgement, *The Shorter Oxford English Dictionary,* presents therefore, a quintessence of those vast materials. The method reflects exactly that of the principal work. It is historical in its representation of the chronological sequence in the development of meaning. It gives the etymologies of words in such a form as to exhibit every significant stage of their history from their place of origin. The meanings are illustrated by quotations either exactly dated or assigned to their authors; the range of the texts used in these illustrations is shown in the list of Authors and Books Cited which is printed in Volume I, pp. xii–xviii. Idiomatic phrases are treated with a fullness that is unusual if not unparalleled in dictionaries of similar compass. Like the original work, this abridgement is not intended to provide a direct commentary on the peculiar vocabulary of any one author, but an attempt has been made to record the special words and meanings and even the oddities of important writers. Many provincialisms also that have some currency in standard literature or are of signal importance historically are treated here, though it may be with extreme brevity. It has been possible in many places to supplement the word-content of the original dictionary and its chronological evidence from the collections gathered by many hands during the last fifty years with a view to a grand supplement or an extensive revision of that work. It has been the aim of the compilers to keep a due proportion between the various interests, and not to exaggerate the etymological side at the expense of the semantic, and, though it has been impossible to preserve entirely the readability of the principal work, the definitions have much of their original fullness, so that the ample and leisurely character of the parent work is in a measure retained.

It is hoped that both the student and the general reader will find in this work what they may reasonably expect to find in a historical dictionary of English compressed within 2,500 quarto pages, which covers not only the history of the general English vocabulary from the days of King Alfred down to the present time, but includes also a large number of obsolete, archaic, provincial, and foreign words and phrases, and a multitude of terms of art and science. In short, it is hoped that it may be found acceptable as a lexical companion to English literature. For those who possess the great Oxford Dictionary the 'Shorter' will serve as a key to its treasures, for those who do not it will form the only possible substitute.

THE OLD ASHMOLEAN BUILDING, OXFORD. C. T. ONIONS.
December, 1932.

PREFATORY NOTE TO THE SECOND EDITION

THE several calls for reprints of this work bear testimony to its acceptability and usefulness. In the present edition an opportunity has been afforded of revising many articles and of adding many others. In all some three thousand changes have been made of one kind or another. For the great bulk of these Mr. F. J. SWEATMAN has performed the arduous task of selection, adaptation, and preparation for the printer. C. T. O.

August, 1936.

INTRODUCTION

THE following sections contain an exposition of the contents and method of this Dictionary, with directions for its use.

§ 1. The GENERAL ORDER AND ARRANGEMENT of an article is as follows (all possible features, which are of necessity not present in all or even the majority of words, being taken into account). (i) The catchword in heavy type, preceded where necessary by a diacritic mark of the status of the word († obsolete, ‖ alien), is followed by (ii) the pronunciation in phonetic transcript (§ 3), where this is not sufficiently indicated by stress-marks in the catchword itself, or unless the word is obsolete (the pronunciation being then omitted), and (iii) the notation of the part of speech (except where the word is a substantive and there is no word of another part of speech spelt in the same way). Next comes (iv) the indication of the modern currency of the word, unless already noted by a symbol, e.g. whether it is now literary, colloquial, slang, or surviving only in archaic, historical, dialectal, or other limited use. Then follows, where appropriate, (v) a statement of variant spellings or inflexional forms in heavy type with their pronunciations, if these have some special importance. The next item, which is a feature of all articles, is the indication of (vi) the earliest appearance of the word, which is shown either by the symbols OE., ME., late ME. (§ 4), or by a precise date. This is succeeded by (vii) the etymology enclosed within square brackets (§ 5); (viii) the specification of the word as belonging to some art or science (*Mus.*, *Bot.*, etc., for which see pp. xix–xxi) if it is entirely so restricted; (ix) the meanings, numbered or lettered, with specification of their status and with the date of their first appearance, or, if they are obsolete, an indication of their last known occurrence (§ 6). After each group of senses there is normally (x) a block of quotations with dates or indications of authorship, numbered according to the senses which they exemplify (§ 6). (xi) Groups of idiomatic phrases or attributive uses and combinations conclude the article, unless there are (xii) derivatives of minor importance, which are appended with an introductory 'Hence' or 'So' (§ 7).

§ 2. The VOCABULARY of this Dictionary is designed to include all words in regular literary and colloquial use, together with a selection of those which belong to the terminology of the arts and sciences and those which are current only in archaic or dialectal use, as well as of words now obsolete but of importance during some period of our literature.

The individual words of the vocabulary may be classified in various ways. In this work a broad distinction is made between *natives* and *denizens* (naturalized foreigners) on the one hand, and *aliens* (non-naturalized foreigners) on the other. *Natives* are words of Old English origin, *denizens* are borrowings from foreign languages which have acquired full English citizenship, *aliens* are words that retain their foreign appearance and to some extent their foreign sound. This last group is distinguished by the prefixing of ‖ to the catchword.

Words are also classifiable according to the sphere of their currency and usage. Where they do not belong to the language *common* to literature and everyday speech the circumstances of their use call for some characterization. Hence the necessity for such labels as, on the one hand, *obsolete* (marked by †), *literary*, *colloquial*, *slang*, *dialectal*, *local*, *archaic*, *vulgar*, and on the other, *Art*, *Natural History*, *Mathematics*, and so on. The composition of a vocabulary under these aspects may be usefully pictured in such a diagram as that devised by Sir James Murray, which is here reproduced with some modifications from Vol. I, p. xvii, of the Oxford Dictionary:

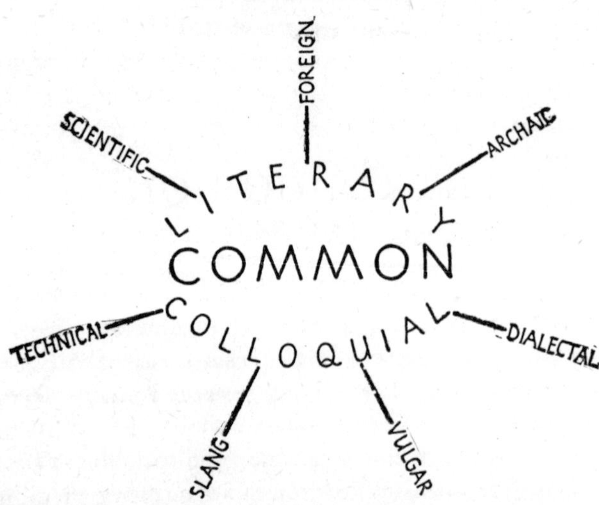

The centre is occupied by 'common' words, in which literary and colloquial usage meet. 'Scientific', 'foreign', and 'archaic' words are the specially learned outposts of the literary language; 'technical' and 'dialectal' words blend with the common language both in speech and in literature. 'Slang' touches the technical terminology of trades and occupations, as in 'nautical slang', 'University slang'; 'slang', 'vulgar' speech, and 'dialect' form a group of lower or less dignified status; 'dialectal' and 'archaic' words are allied in so far as they are outcrops of older strata of the language. In addition to and interpenetrating the common vocabulary with all its ramifications and outliers, there is a vast number of proper names, which either themselves acquire connotative value or give rise to derivatives which take their place among the ordinary words of the language.

Words created for one special occasion are here called *nonce-words.*

Where it has been found necessary to recognize variants of form having equal or nearly equal claims to be considered standard, a double, occasionally a triple, catchword indicates the diversity of usage, priority of place corresponding to priority of usage. Besides variants current in Britain, certain conventional spellings (as *honor*) of the United States have been recorded.

Exigencies of space have determined the arrangement of many compound words in groups under their first element, which usually appear in other dictionaries as 'main words'. Other linguistic elements that cannot be classed as words, viz. prefixes and suffixes, and the letters of the alphabet, are entered in their alphabetical places and receive the same historical treatment as words.

Entries of variant spellings referred to their standard form have been limited to those which are not easily recognizable, alternatives such as those between *y* and *i*, *s* and *z*, *c* and *s*, *k* and *c* being generally ignored. The word to which cross-reference is made is printed in SMALL CAPITALS.

§ 3. The PRONUNCIATION is noted within round brackets by means of a phonetic alphabet, the application of which is shown in the table printed on p. xxii of Vol. I and on p. viii of Vol. II. The chief vowel-signs of this system that diverge from or are additional to the alphabet of ordinary use are displayed at the foot of the opposite pages of every opening of the Dictionary. The additional consonant-signs are þ, ð, ʃ, ʒ, ŋ, and ɹ. Each simple sound is indicated regularly by the same single symbol. Short quantity in vowels is left unmarked, long quantity is denoted by the macron ¯; the mark generally employed to indicate short quantity ˘ is here used to denote *obscuration of quality.*

The main or primary stress is indicated by a turned period · after the vowel of the stressed syllable. Subordinate or secondary stress, where it falls otherwise than in the normal place (i.e. on the second syllable from the main stress), is marked ˑ as in *cry꞉stallizaˑtion*, *booˑkse꞉ller*. In obsolete words and in some current words, especially compounds of obvious formation or derivatives or cognates of a word that is entered with full pronunciation, the stress only is marked without further notation. Varieties in the pronunciation of a word are recorded as fully as possible, priority of position in the record being given to the variety which according to the available evidence has the more extensive currency.

In the system as a whole variation is extensively recognized, and allowance is made for local or class divergence from the standard range, but not, as a rule, for dialectal, colonial, or American varieties. Thus, the divergent pronunciations of the vowels of such words as *fast*, *bath*, and *cough*, *lost*, *soft* are shown, special symbols, (ɑ) and (ǫ́) respectively, being used to indicate that such local or individual varieties exist. Again, discrimination has been made between the vowels of *fir* (fə̄ɹ) and *fur* (fʊ̄ɹ), where south-of-England speakers make no distinction. Similarly, a difference is noted between the (ǫ) of *scotch* and the (ǫ) of *watch*, the (ǭ) of *for* and the (ǭ) of *war*, and the northerly pronunciation (ōᵊ) of vowels of words like *fort*, *port*, *mourn* is recognized, where the southerly has (ǭ), which is, on the other hand, the general sound in *form*, *short*, and *morn*. Use is made of small 'superior' letters, ⁱ and ᵘ, to express the final elements of those diphthongs which are fully developed only with certain classes of speakers, e. g. in *fate* (fēⁱt), *note* (nōᵘt), as distinguished from the generally received diphthongs of *eye* (əi), *boy* (boi), *bow* (bɑu), *few* (fiū̆). Similar recognition is given to the variation between ū̆, ū, and ⁱū̆, ⁱū which is illustrated by the pronunciation of *lieu, lure, illuminant*. A 'superior' turned e (ᵊ) is used for the vowel-element developed between ī, ē, ō, ū, ɑu, etc. and r, as in *pier* (pīᵊɹ), *pare* (pēᵊɹ), *pour* (pōᵊɹ), *poor* (pūᵊɹ), *weary* (wīᵊˑri), *scour* (skɑuᵊɹ); the modern southern development of (ūᵊɹ) to (ōᵊɹ), e.g. (ʃūᵊɹ), (ʃōᵊɹ), is not admitted, nor the monophthongal pronunciation in words like *door*, i.e. (dǭɹ) as opposed to (dōᵊɹ).

In general, 'superior' letters indicate elements that are present or absent according to individual or other usage, and are therefore used in such cases as *promptitude* (prǫˑmᵖtitiū̆d), *standstill* (stæˑnᵈstil).

An outstanding feature of the phonetic system is the recognition of the primary or ideal value of the many vowels that undergo obscuration or reduction in unstressed positions, but which may at any time revert to their full quality, as in rhetorical utterance, in singing, and in any cases of deliberate or affected precision. Examples are: *accept* (ăkseˑpt), *confer* (kǫ̆nfəˑɹ), *judgement* (dʒʊ̆ˑdʒmĕnt), *dislocate* (diˑslŏkeⁱt)—contrast *action* (æˑkʃən), *mental* (meˑntăl), *local* (lōᵘˑkăl); here the unstressed obscured vowel is in normal speech the 'mid-mixed' vowel (ə) of the second syllable of *ever* (eˑvəɹ), towards which the majority of obscured vowels tend; *mistress* (miˑstrės), *billet* (biˑlėt), *useless* (yūˑslės), where (ė) represents a 'raised' variant of (e) which approaches (i); *beauteous* (biūˑtĭəs), where (ĭ) represents a reduced form of the short vowel of *Hebe* (hīˑbĭ). In words like *fracture*, *measure*, the historical or ideal pronunciations are (fræˑktiŭɹ), (meˑʒⁱŭɹ), from which may be deduced the common colloquial forms (fræˑktʃəɹ), (meˑʒəɹ). The following equations show the general equivalents in ordinary speech, and in the majority of other phonetic systems, of the different types of obscured vowels:

ǣ ă ĕ ĭ ŏ ǫ̆ ŭ } = ə
ʊ̆ ĕ ŏ ǫ̆ ŭ }
ė ĭ = i.

§ 4. CHRONOLOGY. Every independent word and meaning is attested by an indication of its earliest known occurrence. If the record begins before the middle of the twelfth century (*c* 1150), it is regarded as falling within the Old English period and is marked OE.; if between that date and the middle of the fifteenth century (*c* 1450), it belongs to Middle English and is marked ME., the later Middle English period (*c* 1350–1450) being specified as late ME. After that period, and in exceptional instances even somewhat before 1450, dating by the year is used. The earliest known meaning of a word has no date attached, since it has already been indicated at the beginning of the article; but for each succeeding sense a date is given. Where the etymology of a word begins with OE..., (late) ME..., the date of the earliest use is considered to be sufficiently indicated and is not expressed elsewhere in the article. The latest limit of an obsolete word or sense is shown by means of the year preceded by a dash, as –1759.

§ 5. The ETYMOLOGY is given within square brackets.

(*a*) If the word is native, its form in Old English is given, and this is often referred back to a Primitive Germanic (Old Teutonic) form, which, being hypothetically reconstructed, is marked with an asterisk; cognate forms from other Germanic languages may be added, and, where the word is of Common Indo-European stock, this is shown—with a selection of related forms. The symbol :— means 'derived by organic process from', and especially 'the regular phonetic descendant of'.

'Old Teutonic' is the hypothetical prehistoric language from which were developed the Germanic languages (of which the West Germanic group comprises English, Frisian, Dutch, Low and High German, and the East Germanic Gothic and the Scandinavian tongues). 'Pre-Teutonic' is an earlier stage of this, removed only by a step from the Indo-European (Indo-Germanic, Aryan), the hypothetical original of what were ultimately differentiated as Sanskrit, Greek, Italic (Latin, etc.), Celtic, Germanic, Slavonic, etc. The designation 'Common Teutonic' is given to a form which is represented in the main Germanic languages; similarly 'Common Romance' designates a form which is represented in all the main Romance languages (Italian, Spanish, Portuguese, French, Roumanian). Popular or Vulgar Latin is that form of Latin which was disseminated in the provinces of the Roman Empire, and from which arose the distinct vernaculars known as the Romance languages. For further information the articles on the various names of languages in this Dictionary should be consulted.

(*b*) If the word is derived from a foreign language, the manner of its derivation may be indicated in any of three ways: (i) a. = adopted without change of form (or pronunciation) from the foreign word; (ii) ad. = derived by adaptation, i.e. with adjustment to English speech-habits; (iii) f. = formed on, i.e., newly shaped on the basis of, the foreign form. When the immediate etymon is identical in form with its English derivative it is not given in the etymological statement. The notation of other kinds of derivation, e.g. compositions of two existing English words or combinations of a stem with a suffix, may be reduced to the formula [f. $x + y$]. The etymology of the ulterior sources of an English word (as of French words derived from Latin, Latin from Greek, etc.) is noted by the same methods. Special observations on the later phonetic history, pronunciation, and spelling are often included in the etymological section of an article.

§ 6. MEANINGS, DEFINITIONS, QUOTATIONS, AUTHORITIES. The meanings are arranged with as strict a regard as possible for their appearance in order of time. They are liable to all the qualifications to which words themselves are liable; thus they may be marked † (obsolete), *arch.*, *dial.*, *U.S.*, *nonce-use*, and so forth, or as pertaining to some branch of science or art. In a word of long and intricate history, the meanings are usually divided into groups having roman numeral headings, within which the meanings have an independent numeration in arabic figures. For the method of dating see § 4.

Two devices are used in order to specify the application of definitions. (i) The object of a transitive verb is placed in its grammatical position in a definition, within round brackets. Such parts of a definition as are not universally applicable, as well as qualifications of its extent, are similarly treated. (ii) Additions, as of prepositions or adverbs, or an infinitive, *in italic type* indicate that the italicized words do or may enter into the construction accompanying or dependent upon the word when used in the sense defined. Examples are: *Tend*.. To watch over and wait upon (the sick or helpless); *Beat*.. To drive (a person) by blows *away*, *off*, *from*, *into*, etc.; *Force*.. To compel or constrain (a person, oneself, etc.) *to do* a thing; *Layman*.. an 'outsider' or non-expert (esp. in relation to law or medicine); *Chit*.. a (very young) child.

When the form of the catchword is used anywhere in the course of an article, it may be abbreviated for economy of space by means of the initial letter followed by a full stop.

The chief sources of the illustrative quotations, which are placed under number- or letter-headings according to the sections to which they apply, are catalogued in the list of Authors and Books Cited, printed below, pp. xii–xviii. Authors' names are printed in small capitals (e.g. SCOTT); for certain common abbreviations of these see pp. xix–xxi. Occasionally, an example of a current usage is supplied from a casual source; this is marked *mod.* (= a modern example). It has been found necessary in respect of some words or meanings whose history has been treated at considerable length in the original Dictionary, and with more detail than could be presented here, merely to refer by means of the abbreviation N.E.D. to the fuller statement there given. Modern dictionaries in general are referred to as Dicts.

§ 7. PHRASES, COMBINATIONS, and MINOR DERIVATIVES commonly form a block or blocks at the end of the article, phrases in italic or in thick type, obvious (undefined) combinations in italics. Specialized verbal phrases with adverbs or prepositions are displayed in thick type, as are also special combinations, i.e. those compound words of which the meaning cannot at once be inferred from their elements, as well as derivatives the status of which does not warrant their insertion as 'main words' of the vocabulary in their alphabetical sequence.

AUTHORS AND BOOKS CITED

Abernethy, John, 1764–1831
Academy, The (1869–99)
Adams, George, 1750–95
Adams, Thomas, fl. 1612–53
Addison, Joseph, 1672–1719
Ainsworth, William Harrison, 1805–82
Aird, Thomas, 1802–76
Akenside, Mark, 1721–70
Alcott, Louisa M., 1832–88
Alford, Henry, 1810–71
Alison, Sir Archibald, 1792–1867
Allardyce, Alexander, 1846–96
Allbutt, Thomas C., ed. *A System of Medicine*, 1896–9
Allen, Grant, 1848–99
Allingham, William, 1824–89
Andrewes, Lancelot, 1555–1626
Anglo-Saxon Chronicle, The (Thorpe, 1861; Earle and Plummer, 1892, 1899)
Anson, George, 1697–1762
Arber, Edward, ed. *An English Garner* (1877–96)
Arbuthnot, John, 1667–1735
Argyll, 8th Duke of 1823–1900
Arnold, Matthew, 1822–88
Arnold, Thomas, 1795–1842
Arnolde, Richard, d. 1521?
Ascham, Roger, 1515–68
Ashmole, Elias, 1617–92
Athenæum, The (1828–1901)
Atterbury, Francis, 1662–1732
Auckland, William Eden, 1st Baron 1744–1814
Austen, Jane, 1775–1817
Austin, Sarah, 1793–1867
Ayliffe, John, 1676–1732
Aytoun, William E., 1813–65

Bacon, Francis, Ld. 1561–1626
Bacon, Nathaniel, 1593–1660
Badham, Charles D., 1806–57
Bagehot, Walter, 1826–77
Bailey, Nathan, d. 1742
Baillie, Robert, 1599–1662
Bain, Alexander, 1810–77
Baker, Sir Richard, 1568–1645
Baker, Sir Samuel W., 1821–93
Baldwin, William, fl. 1547
Bale, John, 1495–1563
Balfour, John H., 1808–84
Bancroft, Abp. Richard, 1544–1610
Barbour, John, 1316?–95
Barckley, Sir Richard, *Discourse of the Felicitie of Man* (1598)
Barclay, James, fl. 1774
Baret, John, d. 1580?
Barham, Richard H., 1788–1845
Baring-Gould, Sabine, 1834–1924
Barlow, Joel, 1754–1812
Barlow, Peter, 1776–1862
Barlow, Bp. William, d. 1613
Barnes, Robert, 1495–1540
Barnes, William, 1801–86
Barrère and Leland, *Dictionary of Slang*, etc. (1888–90)
Barrie, Sir James M., 1860–1937
Barrow, Isaac, 1630–77
Bartlett, John R., *Dictionary of Americanisms* (1848, etc., 1876)
Baxter, Richard, 1615–91
Bayne(s), Paul, d. 1617
Beaconsfield, Earl of: see Disraeli
Beale, Francis, fl. 1656
Beattie, James, 1735–1803
Beaumont, Francis, and Fletcher, John, 1584–1616 and 1579–1625
Beckford, Peter, 1740–1811
Beckford, William, 1759–1844
Becon, Thomas, 1512–67
Bedell, Bp. William, 1571–1642
Bedwell, William, d. 1632
Beeton, Mrs. Isabella M., *Book of Household Management* (1861)
Behn, Mrs. Aphra, 1640–89
Bell, A. M., *The Principles of Speech* (1863)
Bell, William, *Dictionary of the Law of Scotland* (1838)
Ben Israel, Manasseh, 1604–57
Benlowes, Edward, 1603?–76
Bentham, Jeremy, 1748–1832
Bentley, Richard, 1662–1742
Bentley, Robert, 1821–93
Berkeley, Bp. George, 1685–1753
Berkeley, Hon. George C. G. F., 1800–81
Berkeley, Miles J., 1803–89
Berners, John Bourchier, Baron 1467–1533
Berry, Miss Mary, 1763–1802
Besant, Mrs. Annie, 1847–1933
Besant, Sir Walter, 1836–1901
Best, Thomas, *A Concise Treatise on the Art of Angling* (1787)
Beveridge, William, 1637–1705
Bewick, Thomas, 1753–1828
Bible; Wyclif's, 1382, 1388; Coverdale, 1535; Great or Cranmer's, 1539; Geneva, 1560; Bishops', 1568; Douay, 1609–10; Authorized, 1611; Revised N.T., 1881; O.T., 1884; Apocrypha, 1894. The version quoted is that of 1611, unless otherwise noted. (See p. xxi for abbreviations of titles.) See also *New Testament.*
Billingsley, Sir Henry, d. 1608
Bingham, Joseph, 1668–1723
Birch, Thomas, 1705–66
Birrell, Augustine, 1850–1933
Black, Charles C., fl. 1870
Black, William, 1841–98
Blackie, John Stuart, 1809–95
Blackmore, Richard D., 1825–1900
Blackstone, Sir William, 1723–80
Blades, William, 1824–90
Blair, Robert, 1593–1666
Blair, Robert, 1699–1746
Blake, William, 1757–1827
Blith, Walter, fl. 1649
Bloomfield, Robert, 1766–1823
Blount, Thomas, 1618–79
Blundevil, Thomas, fl. 1560
Blunt, John H., 1823–84
Bokenham, Osbern, 1393–1447?
'Boldrewood, Rolf' (T. A. Browne), 1826–1915
Bolingbroke, H. St. John, Viscount 1678–1751
Bolton, Robert, 1572–1631
Bonnycastle, John, 1750?–1821
Book of Common Prayer, The (1549, 1552, 1559, 1662)
Boorde (or Borde), Andrew, 1490?–1549
Booth, David, 1766–1846
Borrow, George, 1803–81
Boswell, James, 1740–95
Bosworth, Joseph, and Toller, T. N., *An Anglo-Saxon Dictionary* (1882–98); *Suppl.* (1908–21)
Botoner, William, 1415–1482?
Bouvier, John, *Law Dictionary of the U.S.A.* (1843–56)
Bowen, Charles S. C., Baron 1835–94
Boyle, Hon. Robert, 1627–91
Braddon, Mary E., 1837–1915
Bradley, Richard, d. 1732
Bradshaw, Henry, d. 1513
Bramhall, Abp. J., 1594–1663
Brand, John, 1744–1806
Brassey, Annie, Lady 1839–87
Brathwaite, Richard, 1588?–1673
Brent, Sir Nathaniel, 1573?–1652
Brereton, Sir William, 1604–61
Breton, Nicholas, 1545?–1626?
Brevint, Daniel, 1616–95
Brewster, Sir David, 1781–1868
Bridges, Robert, 1844–1930
Bright, John, 1811–89
Brinsley, John, fl. 1663
British Association for the Advancement of Science, Reports of the (1831–)
Brodie, Sir Benjamin C., 1783–1862
Brome, Richard, d. 1652?
Brontë, Charlotte, 1816–55
Brontë, Emily J., 1818–48
Broome, William, 1689–1745
Brougham, Henry Peter, Lord 1778–1868
Broughton, Rhoda, 1840–1920
Brown, John, 1810–82
Brown, Thomas, 1663–1704
Brown, Thomas, *Modern Farriery* (1847)
Browne, Sir Thomas, 1605–82
Browne, William, 1591–1643?
Browning, Mrs. Elizabeth Barrett, 1806–61
Browning, Robert, 1812–89
Bryant, Thomas, *Practice of Surgery* (1872)
Bryant, William Cullen, 1794–1878
Bryce, James, 1838–1922
Buchan, William, 1729–1805
Buchanan, Robert, 1813–66
Buck, Albert H., ed. *Handbook of the Medical Sciences* (1885–90)
Buckland, Francis T., 1826–80
Buckland, William, 1784–1856
Buckle, Henry T., 1821–62
Buckle, John S., *Manufacturer's Compendium* (1864)
Budgell, Eustace, 1686–1737
Bull, Bp. George, 1634–1710
Buller, Sir Francis, 1746–1800
Bulwer, John, fl. 1654
Bulwer-Lytton: see Lytton
Bunsen, Frances, Baroness 1791–1876
Bunyan, John, 1628–88
Burgon, John W., 1813–88
Burke, Edmund, 1729–97
Burnaby, Andrew, 1734?–1812
Burnet, Bp. Gilbert, 1643–1715
Burnet, Thomas, 1635?–1715
Burnett, James, Lord Monboddo, 1714–99
Burney, Frances: see D'Arblay
Burney, William, ed. *Falconer's Dictionary of the Marine* (1815)
Burns, Robert, 1759–96
Burrow, Edward J., 1785–1861
Burton, Henry, 1578–1648
Burton, Richard F., 1821–90
Burton, Robert, 1577–1640
Bury, Lady Charlotte S. M., 1775–1861
Butler, Alban, 1711–73
Butler, Bp. Joseph, 1692–1752
Butler, Samuel, *Hudibras* (1663–4,–78)
Byron, George Gordon, 6th Baron 1788–1824

Cable, George W., 1844–1925
Caine, Sir T. H. Hall, 1853–1931
Cairns, John, 1818–92

Calhoun, John C., d. 1850
Calthorpe, Sir Henry, 1586–1637
Camden, William, 1551–1623
Cameron, Lucy L., 1781–1858
Campbell, Thomas, 1777–1844
Campion, Thomas, d. 1619
Canning, George, 1770–1827
Cant, Andrew, 1590?–1663
Capgrave, John, 1393–1464
Carew, Richard, 1555–1620
Carew, Thomas, 1595?–1639?
Carey, Henry, d. 1743
Carlyle, Jane B. Welsh, 1801–66
Carlyle, Thomas, 1795–1881
Carpenter, William B., 1813–85
'Carroll, Lewis' (C. L. Dodgson), 1832–98
Carte, Thomas, 1686–1754
Cartwright, William, 1611–43
Cary, Henry F., 1772–1844
Casaubon, Meric, 1599–1671
Cassell's Encyclopædic Dictionary (1879–88)
Cassell's Supplementary Volume (1902)
Catholic Dictionary, A (1884, 1897)
Catholicon Anglicum (*c* 1483)
Caulfeild, J. M., *Seamanship Notes* (1886)
'Cavendish' (H. Jones), 1831–99
Cavendish, George, 1500–61?
Caxton, William, 1422?–91
Cayley, Arthur, 1821–95
Cecil, Robert, Earl of Salisbury, 1563?–1612
Centlivre, Susanna, 1667?–1723
Century Dictionary, The (1889–91)
— — *Supplement* (1909)
Challoner, Bp. Richard, 1691–1781
Chalmers, Alexander, 1759–1834
Chaloner, Edward, *Six Sermons* (1625)
Chaloner, Sir Thomas, 1521–65
Chambers, Sir E. K., 1866–
Chambers, Robert, 1802–71
Chambers's Cyclopædia of English Literature (1844)
Chambers's Encyclopædia (1860–68)
Chapman, George, 1559?–1634
Chapone, Hester, 1727–1801
Charles I, 1600–49
Charles II, 1630–85
Chatham, William Pitt, Earl of 1708–78
Chatterton, Thomas, 1752–70
Chatto, William A., 1799–1864
Chaucer, Geoffrey, ?1340–1400 [1773
Chesterfield, P. D. Stanhope, 4th Earl 1694–
Chesterton, Gilbert K., 1874–1936
Cheyne, George, 1671–1743
Child, Francis J., ed. *English and Scottish Ballads* (1857, 1882–98)
Chillingworth, William, 1602–44
Chitty, Sir J. W., 1828–99
Churchill, Charles, 1731–64
Churchill, John, *Voyages and Travels* (1704)
Cibber, Colley, 1671–1757
Clare, John, 1793–1864
Clarendon, Edward Hyde, 1st Earl of 1609–74
Clarke, Hyde, *New and Comprehensive Dictionary of the English Language* (1855)
Clarke, Mary Cowden, 1809–98
Cleveland, John, 1613–58
Clissold, F., *The Ascent of Mont Blanc* (1823)
Clough, Arthur H., 1819–61
Cobbett, William, 1763–1835
Cobden, Richard, 1804–65
Cockburn, Henry Thomas, Lord 1779–1854
Cockburn, John, 1652–1729
Cockeram, Henry, *The English Dictionarie* (1623)
Cocks, Richard, *Diary in Japan* (1615–22)
Cogan, Henry, fl. 1650
Coke, Sir Edward, 1552–1634
Coke, Roger, fl. 1696
Colebrooke, Henry T., 1765–1837
Coleridge, Hartley, 1796–1849
Coleridge, Samuel T., 1772–1834
Colet, John, 1467?–1519
Collier, Jeremy, 1650–1726
Collins, Mortimer, 1827–76
Collins, William, 1721–59
Colman, George (the elder), 1732–94
Colman, George (the younger), 1762–1836
Colvil, Samuel, *Whiggs Supplication* (1681)
Combe, William, 1741–1823
Conder, Eustace, *The Basis of Faith* (1877)
Conder, Josiah, 1789–1855
Congreve, William, 1670–1729
Conway, Moncure D., 1832–1907
Conybeare, Bp. John, 1692–1755
Cook, Captain James, 1728–79
Cook, Moses, *The Manner of Raising .. Forrest Trees* (1676)
Cooper, James Fenimore, 1789–1851
Cooper, Samuel, 1780–1848
Copland, Robert, fl. 1530
Corbet, John, 1620–80
'Cornwall, Barry': see Procter, Bryan W.
Cornwalleys, Henry, fl. 1693
Cornwallis, Sir William, d. 1631?
Cory, William J., 1823–92
Coryate, Thomas, 1577?–1617
Cotgrave, John, fl. 1655
Cotgrave, Randle, *Dictionarie of the French and English Tongues* (1611, 1632)
Cotton, Charles, 1630–87
Cotton, John, 1584–1652
Coues, Elliott, *Birds of the Northwest* (1873)
Coverdale, Miles, 1488–1568
Cowley, Abraham, 1618–67
Cowper, William, 1731–1800
Cox, Homersham, *The Institutions of the English Government* (1863)
Crabb, George, 1778–1851
Crabbe, George, 1754–1832
Craig, John, *A New Universal .. Dictionary of the English Language* (1849)
Craik, Mrs. Dinah M., 1826–87
Cranmer, Thomas, 1489–1556
Crashaw, Richard, 1613?–49
Crockett, Samuel R., 1860–1914
Croker, John W., 1780–1857
Cromwell, Oliver, 1599–1658
Cromwell, Thomas, Earl of Essex, 1485?–1540
Crookes, William, *Dyeing and Calico-printing* (1874)
Crowe, William, 1745–1829
Crowne, John, d. 1703?
Crozier, A. A., *Dictionary of Botanical Terms* (1892)
Cruise, William, d. 1824
Crump, Arthur, *On Banking, Currency, and the Exchanges* (1866)
Cudworth, Ralph, 1617–88
Culpepper, Nicholas, 1616–54
Curzon, Hon. Robert, 1810–73
Cussans, John E., 1837–99

Dale, Robert W., 1829–95
Dallas, Alexander J., *Reports of Cases .. Adjudged in the Courts of Pennsylvania* (1790–1807)
Dampier, William, 1652–1715
Dana, James Dwight, 1813–95
Dana, Richard H., 1787–1879
Dana, Richard H., Jr., 1815–82
Daniel, George, 1616–57
Daniel, Samuel, 1562–1619
Danneley, John F., 1786–1834? [1840
D'Arblay, Madame (Frances Burney) 1752–
Darwin, Charles R., 1809–82
Darwin, Erasmus, 1731–1802
Dasent, Sir George W., 1817–96
Daubeny, Charles G. B., 1795–1867
Davenant, Sir William, 1606–68
Davies, Sir John, 1569–1626
Davies, John (of Hereford), 1565?–1618
Davies, John (of Kidwelly) 1627?–93
Davies, Myles, 1662–1715?
Davy, Sir Humphry, 1778–1829
Day, John, fl. 1606
Dee, John, 1527–1608
De Foe, Daniel, 1661?–1731
Dekker, Thomas, 1570?–1641?
Delany, Mrs. Mary, 1700–88
De Lolme, John L., 1740?–1807
Deloney, Thomas, 1543?–1607?
De Morgan, Augustus, 1806–71
Denham, Sir John, 1615–69
Denham, Michael A., d. 1859
Dennis, John, 1657–1734
De Quincey, Thomas, 1785–1859
Derham, William, 1657–1735
Dering, Sir Edward, 1598–1644
De Vere, Sir Aubrey, 1788–1846
De Vere, Aubrey Thomas, 1814–1902
De Vere, M. Schele, *Americanisms* (1872)
D'Ewes, Sir Simonds, 1602–50
Dibdin, Charles, 1745–1814
Dibdin, Thomas Frognall, 1776–1847
Dicey, Edward, 1832–1911
Dickens, Charles, 1812–70
Digby, Sir Kenelm, 1603–65
Digges, Sir Dudley, 1583–1639
Digges, Thomas, d. 1595
Disraeli, Benjamin, Earl of Beaconsfield, 1804–81
D'Israeli, Isaac, 1766–1848
Dixon, William Hepworth, 1821–79
Dobson, H. Austin, 1840–1921
Dodsley, Robert, 1703–64
Dodwell, Henry, 1641–1711
Donne, John, 1573–1631
Doran, John, 1807–78
Douglas, Bp. Gavin, 1474?–1522
Douglas, Sir Howard, 1776–1861
Douland, or Dowland, John, 1563?–1626?
Dowden, Edward, 1843–1913
Doyle, Sir A. Conan, 1859–1930
Drayton, Michael, 1563–1631
Drummond, Henry, 1851–97
Drummond, William (of Hawthornden), 1585–1649
Dryden, John, 1631–1700
DuCange, Sieur Charles Dufresne, *Glossarium Mediæ et Infimæ Latinitatis* (ed. 1883–7)
Duff, M. E. Grant, 1829–1906
Dufton, William, *Nature and Treatment of Deafness* (1844)
Dugdale, Sir William, 1605–86
Dunbar, William, 1465?–1530?
Duncan, Archibald, *Life of Lord Nelson* (1806)
D'Urfey, Thomas, 1653–1723
Dyer, John, 1700?–58

Earle, John, 1824–1903
Eden, Richard, 1521?–76
Edgeworth, Maria, 1767–1849
Egan, Pierce, 1772–1849
Eikon Basilike (1648)
'Eliot, George' (Marion Evans), 1819–80
Elizabeth, Queen, 1533–1603
Ellis, William, d. 1758
Ellwood, Thomas, 1639–1713
Elphinstone, Mountstuart, 1779–1859
Elyot, Sir Thomas, 1499?–1546
Emanuel, Henry, *Diamonds and Precious Stones* (1865)
Emerson, Peter H., 1856–
Emerson, Ralph W., 1803–82
Encyclopædia Britannica (ed. 9) 1875–89; (ed. 10) 1902–3; (ed. 11) 1910–11; (ed. 12) 1922; (ed. 13) 1926
Encyclopædia Metropolitana (1818–45)
English Review, The, (1905–)
Erskine, John, 1695–1768
Essex, Arthur Capel, Earl of 1631–83
Etherege, Sir George, 1635?–91
Evelyn, John, 1620–1706

Faber, Frederick W., 1814–63
Faber, George S., 1773–1854

Herbert, George, 1593–1633
Herbert, Sir Thomas, 1606–82
Herrick, Robert, 1591–1674
Herschel, Sir John F. W., 1792–1871
Hervey, James, 1714–58
Hewlett, Joseph T. J., 1800–47
Hexham, Henry, 1585?–1650?
Heylin, Peter, 1600–62
Heywood, John, 1497?–1580?
Heywood, Thomas, d. 1650?
Hickeringill, Edmund, 1631–1708
Hieron, Samuel, 1576?–1617
Higden's Polychronicon, 1432–50; see also Trevisa
Higgins, John, fl. 1570–1602
Hiles, John, *A Complete Dictionary of Musical Terms* (1871)
Hill, John, 1716?–75
Hill, Thomas, fl. 1590
Hill, Thomas, d. 1653
Hitchcock, Robert, fl. 1580–91
Hobbes, Thomas, 1588–1679
Hoblyn, Richard D., 1803–86
Hoby, Sir Edward, 1560–1617
Hoccleve, Thomas, 1370?–1450?
Hogarth, George, 1783–1870
Hogg, James, 1770–1835
Holbrook, M. L., *Hygiene of the Brain and Nerves* (1878)
Holcroft, Thomas, 1745–1809
Holinshed, Raphael, d. 1580?
Holland, Josiah G., 1819–81
Holland, Philemon, 1552–1637
Holme, Randle, 1627–99
Holmes, Edward, 1797–1859
Holmes, Oliver Wendell, 1809–94
Holtzapffel, Chas. and J. J., *Turning and Mechanical Manipulation* (1843–50)
Holwell, William, 1726–98
Holyday, Barten, 1593–1661
Holyoake, Francis, 1567–1653
Home, Sir Everard, 1756–1832
Hone, William, 1780–1842
Hood, Thomas, 1799–1845
Hook, Theodore E., 1788–1841
Hook, Walter F., 1798–1875
Hooker, Sir Joseph D., 1817–1911
Hooker, Richard, 1554?–1600
Hooker, Sir William J., 1785–1865
Hooper, Bp. John, d. 1555
Hooper, Robert, 1773–1835
Hope, Alexander J. Beresford, 1820–87
Horne, Bp. George, 1730–92.
Hotten, John C., *A Dictionary of Modern Slang* (1859, etc.)
House of Commons, Journals of the (1547–)
House of Lords, Journals of the (1509–)
Housman, Alfred E., 1859–1936
Houston, Edwin J., *A Dictionary of Electrical Words* (1889)
Howell, James, 1594?–1666
Howells, William D., 1837–1920
Howitt, Mary, 1799–1888
Howitt, William, 1792–1879
Howson, Bp. John, 1557?–1632
Hoyle, Edmond, 1672–1769
Hughes, Thomas, 1822–96
Huloet, Richard, fl. 1552
Hume, David, 1711–76
Hunt, J. H. Leigh, 1784–1859
Hunt, William Holman, 1827–1910
Hunter, James, *Dictionary of Farriery* (1796)
Hussey, Robert, 1801–56
Hutchinson, Horace G., 1859–1932
Hutchinson, Lucy, fl. 1665
Hutchinson, Thomas, 1711–80
Hutton, Charles, 1737–1823
Huxley, Thomas H., 1825–95
Hyne, C. J. Cutcliffe W., 1866–1944

Imison, John, d. 1788
Index Kewensis (1893–5); *Suppl.* (1901–26)
Ingelow, Jean, 1820–97
Ingoldsby Legends by R. H. Barham
Innes, Cosmo, 1798–1874
Instructions and regulations for the formations and movements of the cavalry (1796)
Irving, Edward, 1792–1834
Irving, Washington, 1783–1859

Jackson, Benjamin D., 1846–1927
Jackson, Thomas, 1579–1640
Jacob, Giles, *A New Law Dictionary* (1729)
James VI, King of Scotland, afterwards James I of England, 1566–1625
James, Charles, d. 1821
James, George P. R., 1799–1860
James, Henry, 1843–1916
Jameson, Mrs. Anna B., 1794–1860
Jameson, Robert, 1774–1854
Jamieson, John, 1759–1838
Jefferies, Richard, 1848–87
Jefferson, Thomas, 1743–1826
Jellicoe, John Rushworth, 1st Earl 1859–
Jephson, Robert, 1736–1803
Jerrold, Douglas W., 1803–57
Jesse, E.: see Knapp, J. L.
Jevons, William Stanley, 1835–82
Jewel, John, 1522–71
Johnson, Samuel, 1709–84 (*A Dictionary of the English Language*, 1755, 1773)
Jones, John, fl. 1579
Jones, Thomas Rymer, 1810–80
Jones, Sir William, 1746–94
Jonson, Ben, 1573?–1637
Jortin, John, 1698–1770
Jowett, Benjamin, 1817–93
'*Junius*' *Letters* (1769–72)

Kames, Henry Home, Lord 1696–1782
Kane, Elisha K., 1820–57
Keatinge, Maurice B., *Travels through France and Spain* (1816)
Keats, John, 1795–1821
Keble, John, 1792–1866
Keightley, Thomas, 1789–1872
Kemble, Frances A., 1809–93
Kemble, John M., 1807–57
Ken, Bp. Thomas, 1637–1711
Kent, James, *Commentaries on American Law* (1826–30)
Ker, William P., 1855–1923
Kersey, John, fl. 1720
Key, Thomas H., 1799–1875
King, William, 1663–1712
Kinglake, Alexander W., 1809–91
Kingsley, Charles, 1819–75
Kingsley, Henry, 1830–76
Kingsmill or Kingesmyll, Andrew, 1538–69
Kipling, Rudyard, 1865–1936
Kirby, William, 1759–1850
Kirwan, Richard, 1733–1812
Klein, Edward E., 1844–1925
Knapp, John L., 1767–1845
Knight, Charles, 1791–1873
Knight, Edward H., *Dictionary of Mechanics* (1874–7); *Suppl.* (1884)
Knolles, Richard, 1550?–1610
Knox, John, 1505–72
Knox, Robert, 1791–1862
Knox, Vicesimus, 1752–1821
Kyd, Thomas, 1557?–95?

Lamb, Charles, 1775–1834
Lamb, Mary Ann, 1764–1847
Lambarde, William, 1536–1601
Landor, Walter S., 1775–1864
Lane, Edward W., 1801–76
Lang, Andrew, 1844–1912
Langhorne, John, 1735–79
Langland, William, 1330?–1400?
Lankester, Sir E. Ray, 1847–1929
Lardner, Dionysius, 1793–1859
Latham, John, 1740–1837
Latham, Robert G., 1812–88
Latimer, Hugh, 1485?–1555
Laud, Abp. William, 1573–1645
Law, William, 1686–1761
Lee, Frederick G., d. 1902
Lee, Nathaniel, 1653?–92
'Lee, Vernon' (Violet Paget), 1856–1935
Leland, John, 1506?–52
L'Estrange, Sir Roger, 1616–1704
Lever, Charles J., 1806–72
Lewes, George H., 1817–78
Lewins, William, *Her Majesty's Mails* (1864)
Lewis, John, 1675–1747
Lewis, Charlton T., and Short, Charles, *A Latin Dictionary* (1879)
Liddell, Henry G., and Scott, Robert, *A Greek-English Lexicon* (ed. 8, 1897)
Lindley, John, 1799–1865
Lingard, John, 1771–1851
Linnæus (Carl von Linné), 1707–78
Linton, Mrs. E. Lynn, 1822–98
Lithgow, William, 1582–1645?
Littleton's, Sir T., Tenures (1538)
Littré, Émile, *Dictionnaire de la langue française* (1863–77)
Livingstone, David, 1813–73
Locke, John, 1632–1704
Lockhart, John G., 1794–1854
Lockyer, J. Norman, 1836–1920
Lodge, Thomas, 1558?–1625
Longfellow, Henry Wadsworth, 1807–82
Lotze's, R. H., Logic, B. Bosanquet, tr. (1884)
Loudon, John C., 1783–1843
Lovelace, Richard, 1618–58
Lovell, Archibald, fl. 1679–87
Lover, Samuel, 1797–1868
Lowell, James Russell, 1819–91
Lower, Sir William, 1600?–62
Lowth, Bp. Robert, 1710–87
Lubbock, Sir John, 1834–1913
Ludlow, John M., 1821–1911
Lupton, Thomas, fl. 1583
'Lyall, Edna' (Ada E. Bayly), 1857–1903
Lydekker, Richard, 1849–1915
Lydgate, John, 1370?–1451?
Lyell, Sir Charles, 1797–1875
Lyly, John, 1554?–1606
Lyndesay, Sir David, 1490–1555
Lyte, Henry, tr. *Dodoens' Niewe Herball* (1578)
Lyttelton, George, 1st Baron 1709–73
Lytton, Edward G. E. L. Bulwer-Lytton, 1st Baron 1803–73

Mabbe, James, 1572–1642?
Macaulay, Thomas Babington, Lord 1800–59
McCarthy, Justin, 1830–1912
McCosh, James, 1811–94
McCulloch, John R., 1789–1864
Macdonald, George, 1824–1905
McDonogh, Felix, fl. 1820–26
McDougall, William, 1871–1938
Macfarren, Sir George A., 1813–87
Macgillivray, William, 1796–1852
Mackenzie, Sir George, 1636–91
Mackenzie, Sir Morell, 1837–92
Mackenzie, Murdoch, d. 1797
Mackintosh, Sir James, 1765–1832
Maclaren, Walter S. B., 1853–1912
Macpherson, James, 1736–96
Mahaffy, John P., 1839–1919
Maine, Sir Henry J. S., 1822–88
Maitland, Samuel R., 1792–1866
Mallock, William H., 1849–1923
Malone, Edmund, 1741–1812
Malory, Sir Thomas, fl. 1470
Malthus, Thomas R., 1766–1834
Malynes, Gerard de, fl. 1586–1641
Mandeville, Bernard, 1670?–1733
Manley, Thomas, 1628–90
Manning, Cdl. Henry E., 1808–92
Mansel, Henry L., 1820–71
Manson, George J., *The Sporting Dictionary* (1895)

Manton, Thomas, 1620–77
Manwood, John, d. 1610
Marbeck, John, d. 1585?
Markham, Gervase, 1568?–1637
Marlowe, Christopher, 1564–93
Marryat, Frederick, 1792–1848
Marshall, Alfred, 1842–1924
Marshall, John, 1818–91
Marshall, William H., 1745–1818
Marston, John, 1575?–1634
Martin, Sir Theodore, 1816–1909
Martineau, Harriet, 1802–76
Martineau, James, 1805–1900
Marvell, Andrew, 1621–78
Masefield, John, 1878–
Maskelyne, Mervin H. N. S., 1823–1911
Mason, Charlotte M. S., 1842–1923
Mason, George, 1735–1806
Mason, Jas., *The Principles of Chess* (1894)
Mason, John, fl. 1750
Massinger, Philip, 1583–1640
Masson, David, 1822–1907
Mather, Cotton, 1663–1728
Maudsley, Henry, 1835–1918
Maunder, Samuel, 1785–1849
Maundeville, Sir John, *Travels* (*c* 1400)
Maundrell, Henry, 1665–1701
Maurice, Frederick Denison, 1805–72
Maury, Matthew F., 1806–73
Max-Müller, Friedrich, 1823–1900
Maxwell, William Hamilton, 1792–1850
May, Thomas, 1595–1650
May, Sir Thomas Erskine, 1815–86
Mayhew, A. L., and Skeat, W. W., *A concise dictionary of Middle English* (1888)
Mayne, Jasper, 1604–72
Mayne, Robert G., *An Expository Lexicon of the Terms .. of Medical and General Science* (1853–60)
Medwin, Thomas, 1788–1869
Melmoth, William, 1710–99
Melville, George J. Whyte, 1821–78
Melville, Herman, 1819–91
Mendes da Costa, Emanuel, 1717–91
Meredith, George, 1828–1909
Merivale, Charles, 1808–93
Meynell, Wilfrid, 1877–1948
Miall, Louis C., 1842–1921
Middleton, Thomas, 1570?–1627
Miege, Guy, 1644–1718?
Mill, James, 1773–1836
Mill, John Stuart, 1806–73
Miller, Hugh, 1802–56
Milman, Henry Hart, 1791–1868
Milton, John, 1608–74 (*P.L.* 1667, *P.R.* 1671, *S.A.* 1671)
Minsheu, John, fl. 1617
Mirror for Magistrates, A (1559, etc.)
Mitchell, Donald G., 1822–1908
Mitford, Miss Mary R., 1787–1855
Mivart, St. George J., 1827–1900
Moir, David M., 1798–1851
Mollett, John W., *An Illustrated Dictionary of Words used in Art and Archæology* (1883)
Monboddo, James Burnett, Lord 1714–99
Monmouth, Henry Carey, 2nd Earl 1596–1661
Monro, Alexander, 1697–1767
Montagu, Elizabeth, 1720–1800
Montagu, George, 1751–1815
Montagu, Lady Mary Wortley, 1689–1762
Montagu, Bp. Richard, 1577–1641
Moore, Sir Jonas, 1617–79
Moore, Thomas, 1779–1852
More, Hannah, 1745–1833
More, Henry, 1614–87
More, Sir Thomas, 1478–1535
Morgan, Conwy Lloyd, 1852–1936
Morgan (formerly Owenson), Sydney, Lady 1783?–1859
Morier, James J., 1780?–1849
Morley, John, 1838–1923
Morley and Muir: see Watts, Henry
Morris, John, 1810–86
Morris, Sir Lewis, 1833–1907
Morris, William, 1834–96
Morse, Jedidiah, 1761–1826
Mortimer, Thomas, 1730–1810
Morton, John C., 1821–88
Moryson, Fynes, 1566–1630
'Mostyn, Sydney': see Russell, W. C.
Motherwell, William, 1797–1835
Motley, John Lothrop, 1814–77
Motteux, Peter A., 1660–1718
Moxon, Joseph, 1627–1700
Mozley, James Bowling, 1813–78
Müller, Friedrich Max-: see Max-Müller, F.
Mulcaster, Richard, 1530?–1611
Munday, Anthony, 1553–1633
Munro, Neil, *The Lost Pibroch* (1896)
Murchison, Sir Roderick Impey, 1792–1871
Murphy, Arthur, 1727–1805
Murray, David Christie, 1847–1907
Murray, Lindley, 1745–1826
Musgrave, George Musgrave, 1798–1883
Mynshul, Geffray, 1594?–1668

N. & Q. = *Notes and Queries*
Napier, Robina, ed. *Johnsoniana* (1884)
Napier, Sir William F. P., 1785–1860
Nares, Edward, 1762–1841
Nares, Robert, 1753–1829
Nashe, Thomas, 1567–1601
National Review, The (1883–)
Naunton, Sir Robert, 1563–1635
Naval accounts and inventories of the reign of Henry VII (1485–97)
Neal, Daniel, 1678–1743
Neale, John M., 1818–66
Nelson, Horatio Nelson, 1st Viscount 1758–1805
Nesse, Christopher, 1621–1705
Nevile, Thomas, fl. 1769
New Testament (versions). Tindale, 1526, 1534; Geneva, 1557; Rhemes, 1582. See also *Bible*
Newman, Edward, 1801–76
Newman, Cdl. John Henry, 1801–90
Newton, Sir Isaac, 1642–1727
Nichol, John P., 1804–59
Nichols, John, 1745–1826
Nicholson, Henry A., 1844–99
Nicholson, Peter, 1765–1844
Nicholson, William, 1753–1815
Nicol, Alexander, fl. 1739–66
Nicolas, Sir Nicholas H., 1799–1848
Nicolson, Abp. William, 1655–1727
Nightingale, Florence, 1820–1910
Noad, Henry M., 1815–77
Norris, John (of Bemerton), 1657–1711
Norris, William E., 1847–1925
North, Roger, 1653–1734
North, Sir Thomas, 1535?–1601?
Norton, Caroline E. S., 1808–77
Norton, Thomas, 1532–84
Notes and Queries (1850–)
Noyes, Alfred, 1880–
Nugent, Thomas, 1700?–72

Occleve, Thomas: see Hoccleve, T.
Ogilby, John, 1600–76
Ogilvie, John, 1797–1867
Ogilvie-Grant, William R., 1863–1924
Old English Chronicle: see *Anglo-Saxon*
Oldham, John, 1653–83
Oldys, William, 1696–1761
Oliphant, Laurence, 1829–88
Oliphant, Margaret O. W., 1828–97
Olmsted, Frederick L., 1822–1903
Opie, John, 1761–1807
Orm(in), *Ormulum* (*c* 1200)
Orrery, John Boyle, 5th Earl of Cork and 1707–62
Osborn, Hon. Mrs. Sarah, *Political and Social Letters* (1721–71)
Osborne, Dorothy (Lady Temple), 1627–95
Osborne, Francis, 1593–1659
Otway, Thomas, 1652–85
'Ouida' (Mlle L. de La Ramée), 1839–1908
Ouseley, Sir Frederick A. G., 1825–89
Overbury, Sir Thomas, 1581–1613
Owen, John, 1616–83
Owen, Richard, 1804–92
Oxford University Calendar (1810–)

Page, David, 1814–79
Paget, Francis E., 1806–82
Paley, William, 1743–1805
Palgrave, Sir Francis, 1788–1861
Palgrave, Francis T., 1824–97
Palgrave, William G., 1826–88
Palsgrave, John, d. 1554
Parker, John Henry, 1806–84
Parker, Abp. Matthew, 1504–75
Parkman, Francis, 1823–93
Parnell, Thomas, 1679–1718
Parr, Bartholomew, 1750–1810
Parr, Samuel, 1747–1825
Parry, Sir William E., 1790–1855
Paston Letters, The (1422–1509)
Pater, Walter H., 1839–94
Patmore, Coventry K. D., 1823–96
Patrick, Bp. Simon, 1626–1707
Pattison, Mark, 1813–84
Payn, James, 1830–98
Paynell, Thomas, fl. 1528–68
Peabody, Andrew P., 1811–93
Peacock, Thomas Love, 1785–1866
Peake, James, *Rudiments of Naval Architecture* (1849)
Pearce, Bp. Zachary, 1690–1774
Pearson, George, 1751–1828
Pecock, Reginald, 1395?–1460?
Peele, George, 1558?–1597?
Pegge, Samuel, 1704–96
Pembroke, Mary Herbert, Countess of 1555?–1621
Penn, William, 1644–1718
Pennant, Thomas, 1726–98
Pepys, Samuel, 1633–1703
Perkins, Charles C., 1823–86
Pettie, George, 1548–89
Petty, Sir William, 1623–87
Phillips, Edward, *The New World of Words* (1658, 1662, 1678, 1696, 1706)
Phillips, Henry, fl. 1865–81
Phillips, John, 1800–74
Phillips, William, 1775–1828
Phillpotts, Eden, 1862–
Piers Plowman: see Langland, W.
Pindar, Peter: see Wolcot, John
Pinkerton, John, 1758–1826
Piozzi, Hester Lynch (Mrs. Thrale), 1741–1821
Planché, James R., *A Cyclopædia of Costume* (1876–9)
Plat, or Platt, Sir Hugh, 1552–1611?
Playfair, John, 1748–1819
Plot, Robert, 1640–96
Pocock, Nicholas, 1814–97
Pococke, Bp. Richard, 1704–65
Poe, Edgar A., 1809–49
Pollock, Sir Frederick, 1845–1937
Pomfret, John, 1667–1702
Pope, Alexander, 1688–1744
Porson, Richard, 1759–1808
Porter, George R., 1792–1852
Potter, Christopher, 1591–1646
Potter, Humphry T., *A New Dictionary of Cant* (*a* 1790)
Powel, David, 1552?–98
Powell, John J., 1755?–1801
Prescott, William H., 1796–1859
Preston, Richard Graham, Visct. 1648–95
Price, Bonamy, 1807–88
Prichard, James C., 1786–1848
Prideaux, Humphrey, 1648–1724
Priestley, Joseph, 1733–1804

Pringle, Sir John, 1707–82
Prior, Matthew, 1664–1721
Prior, Richard C. A., *On the popular names of British Plants* (1863)
Procter, Bryan W. ('Barry Cornwall'), 1787–1874
Proctor, Richard A., 1837–88
Promptorium Parvulorum (*c* 1440, etc.)
Prynne, William, 1600–69
Pugin, Augustus W. N., 1812–52
Punch, or the London Charivari (1840–)
Purcell, John, 1674?–1730
Purchas, Samuel, 1575?–1626
Pusey, Edward B., 1800–82
Puttenham, George, d. 1590

'Q' (Sir Arthur T. Quiller-Couch), 1863–1944
Quain, Sir Richard, 1816–98
Quarles, Francis, 1592–1644
Quarterly Review, The (1809–)
Quincey, Thomas De: see De Quincey
Quincy, John, d. 1722

Radcliffe, Mrs. Ann, 1764–1823
Raffald, Mrs. Elizabeth, 1733–81
Ralegh, Sir Walter, 1552?–1618
Ramsay, Allan, 1686–1758
Ramsay, Sir Andrew C., 1814–91
Randolph, Thomas, 1605–35
Rankine, William J. M., 1820–72
Raphson, Joseph, *A Mathematical Dictionary* (1702)
Rawlinson, George, 1812–1902
Ray, John, 1627–1705
Raymond, Rossiter W., 1840–1918
Reade, Charles, 1814–84
Recorde, Robert, 1510?–58
Rees, Abraham, 1743–1825
Reid, Thomas, 1710–96
Reynolds, Bp. Edward, 1599–1676
Reynolds, Sir Joshua, 1723–92
Rhys, Sir John, 1840–1915
Rich, Barnaby, 1540?–1617
Richardson, George Fleming, 1796?–1848
Richardson, Samuel, 1689–1761
Rickman, Thomas, 1776–1841
Ridley, Bp. Nicholas, 1500?–55
Risdon, Tristram, 1580?–1640
'Rita' (Eliza M. J. von Booth, Mrs. W. D. Humphreys)
Ritchie, Anne Isabella, Lady d. 1918
Ritson, Joseph, 1752–1803
Rivers, Anthony Wydeville, Earl 1442?–83
Robertson, Frederick W., 1816–53
Robertson, William, 1721–93
Roby, Henry J., 1830–1915
Rochester, John Wilmot, 2nd Earl 1647–80
Rogers, James E. Thorold, 1823–90
Rogers, Samuel, 1763–1855
Rogers, Thomas, d. 1616
Rogers, Woodes, d. 1732
Roland, George, *A treatise on the theory and practice of the Art of Fencing* (1823)
Rolland, John, fl. 1560
Rolle, Richard, of Hampole: see Hampole
Rolleston, George, 1829–81
Rolt, Richard, 1725?–70
Romaunt of the Rose, The (lines 1–1705, Chaucer *a* 1366; lines 1706– anon. *c* 1400)
Roper, William, 1496–1578
Roscoe, Sir Henry E., 1833–1915
Roscommon, Wentworth Dillon, 4th Earl of 1633?–85
Rose, John B., fl. 1866
Ross, Sir James Clark, 1800–62
Rossetti, Christina G., 1830–94
Rossetti, Dante Gabriel, 1828–82
Rossiter, William, fl. 1871
Row, William, *Supplement to R. Blair's Autobiography* (1676)
Rowe, Nicholas, 1674–1718
Rowlands, Samuel, 1570?–1630?
Rowley, William, 1585?–1642?

Rudimentary Treatise on Navigation, A (1850) by J. Greenwood
Ruskin, John, 1819–1900
Russell, Rachel, Lady 1636–1723
Russell, William Clark, 1844–1911

Saintsbury, George E. B., 1845–1933
Sala, George A. H., 1828–96
Sale, George, 1697?–1736
Salkeld, John, 1576–1660
Salmon, George, 1819–1904
Salmon, William, 1644–1713
Sanderson, Bp. Robert, 1587–1663
Sandys, Abp. Edwin, 1516?–88
Sandys, George, 1578–1644
Sandys, William, 1792–1874
Savage, Richard, d. 1743
Sayce, Archibald H., 1846–1933
Schaff, Philip, 1819–93
Sclater, William, 1575–1626
Scoresby, William, 1789–1857
Scots Magazine, The (1739–1817)
Scott, Sir G. Gilbert, 1811–78
Scott, George Gilbert, *English Church Architecture* (1881)
Scott, Michael, 1789–1835
Scott, Sir Walter, 1771–1832
Scribner's Magazine (1887–)
Scriven, John, *A practical treatise on Copyhold Tenure* (1816)
Scrivener, Frederick H. A., 1813–91
Scrivener, S. C., *Our Fields and Cities* (1890)
Sedley, Sir Charles, 1639?–1701
Seebohm, Henry, 1832–95
Seeley, Sir John R., 1834–95
Selborne, Roundell Palmer, 1st Earl 1812–95
Selden, John, 1584–1654
Sewel, William, 1654–1720
Shadwell, Thomas, 1642?–92
Shaftesbury, Anthony Ashley Cooper, 3rd Earl of 1671–1713
Shakespeare, William, 1564–1616 (see p. xxi for abbreviations of titles)
Shand, Alexander I., d. 1907
Sharp, William, 1855–1905
Sharpe, Richard Bowdler, 1847–1909
Sharpe, Samuel, 1799–1881
Sharrock, Robert, 1630–84
Shaw, George Bernard, 1856–1950
Shaw, Vero K., *The Illustrated Book of the Dog* (1879–81)
Sheffield, John, Duke of Buckingham, 1648–1721
Shelley, Mrs. Mary Wollstonecraft, 1797–1851
Shelley, Percy Bysshe, 1792–1822
Shelton, Thomas, fl. 1612–20
Shelvocke, George, fl. 1690–1728
Shenstone, William, 1714–63
Sheridan, Richard Brinsley, 1751–1816
Sheridan, Thomas, 1719–88
Sherlock, Bp. Thomas, 1678–1761
Sherwood, Mrs. Mary Martha, 1775–1851
Shipley, Orby, 1832–1916
Shirley, James, 1596–1666
Shorthouse, Joseph H., 1834–1903
Sidney, Sir Philip, 1554–86
Simmonds, Peter L., *A Dictionary of Trade Products* (1858, 1892)
Simpson, Sir James Y., 1811–70
Sims, George R., 1847–1922
Singleton, Robert C., 1810–81
Skeat, Walter W., 1835–1912
Skelton, John, 1460?–1529
Skene, William F., 1809–92
Sloane, Thomas O'Conor, *The Standard Electrical Dictionary* (1893)
Smart, Christopher, 1722–71
Smeaton, John, 1724–92
Smiles, Samuel, 1812–1904
Smith, Adam, 1723–90
Smith, Albert R., 1816–60
Smith, Bosworth, 1839–1908

Smith, Charlotte, 1749–1806
Smith, Capt. George, *Universal Military Dictionary* (1779)
Smith, Goldwin, 1823–1910
Smith, Horatio ('Horace'), 1779–1849
Smith, James, 1775–1839
Smith, Capt. John, 1580–1631
Smith, Sydney, 1771–1845
Smith, Walter C., *Kildrostan* (1884)
Smith, Sir William, 1813–93
Smollett, Tobias G., 1721–71
Smyth, R. Brough, 1830–89
Smyth, William H., *The Sailor's Word-book* (1867)
Somerville, Alexander, 1811–85
Somerville, Mrs. Mary, 1780–1872
Somerville, William, 1675–1742
South, Robert, 1634–1716
Southey, Robert, 1774–1843
Soyer, Alexis B., 1809–58
Spectator, The (J. Addison, R. Steele, etc.), 1711–14
Speed, John, 1532?–1629
Spelman, Sir Henry, 1564?–1641
Spelman, Sir John, 1594–1643
Spence, Ferrand, fl. 1686
Spencer, Herbert, 1820–1903
Spenser, Edmund, 1552?–1599 (*F. Q.* 1590, 1596)
Spurgeon, Charles H., 1834–92
Stainer, Sir John, 1840–1901
Stanford Dictionary of Anglicised Words and Phrases, The, ed. C. A. M. Fennell (1892)
Stanhope, George, 1660–1728
Stanhope, Lady Hester L., 1776–1839
Stanhope, Philip H., 5th Earl 1805–75
Stanley, Arthur Penrhyn, 1815–81
Stanley, Sir Henry Morton, 1841–1904
Stanley, Thomas, 1625–78
Stark, John, *Elements of Natural History* (1828)
Starkey, George, d. 1665
Starkey, Thomas, 1499?–1538
Steele, Sir Richard, 1672–1729
Stephen, Sir James, 1789–1859
Stephen, Sir James Fitzjames, 1829–94
Stephen, Sir Leslie, 1832–1904
Sterne, Laurence, 1713–68
Sternhold, Thomas, d. 1549
Stevenson, Robert Louis, 1850–94
Stewart, Balfour, 1828–87
Stewart, Dugald, 1753–1828
Stillingfleet, Benjamin, 1702–71
Stillingfleet, Bp. Edward, 1635–99
Stirling, Sir William Alexander, Earl of 1567?–1640
Stirling, James H., 1820–1909
Stocqueler, Joachim H., 1800–85
Stoddart, Thomas T., 1810–80
Stonehouse, William B., *The History and Topography of the Isle of Axholme* (1839)
Stowe, Mrs. Harriet Elizabeth Beecher, 1812–96
Strafford, Thomas Wentworth, Earl of 1593–1641
Stratmann, F. H., *Dictionary of the Old English Language* (1878; ed. H. Bradley, 1891)
Strutt, Joseph, 1749–1802
Strype, John, 1643–1737
Stubbs, Bp. William, 1825–1901
Sturmy, Samuel, *The Mariners Magazine* (1683)
Suckling, Sir John, 1609–42
Sullivan, James, 1744–1808
Surflet, Richard, fl. 1600
Surrey, Henry Howard, Earl of 1517?–47
Surtees, Robert S., 1803–64
Sutcliffe, Halliwell, 1870–1932
Swainson, William, 1789–1855
Swan, Annie S. (Mrs. Burnett Smith)
Sweet, Henry, 1845–1912
Swift, Jonathan, 1667–1745
Swinburne, Algernon Charles, 1837–1909

Swinburne, Henry, 1560?–1623
Sydenham Society Lexicon of Medicine and Allied Sciences (1879–99)
Sylvester, Josuah, 1563–1618
Symonds, John Addington, 1840–93

Tate, Nahum, 1652–1715
— — and Brady, Nicholas, *A new version of the Psalms of David* (1696)
Tatler, The (R. Steele, etc.), 1709–11
Taverner, John, *Certaine Experiments concerning Fish and Fruite* (1600)
Taverner, Richard, 1505?–75
Taylor, Ann, 1782–1866, and Jane, 1783–1824
Taylor, Bayard, 1825–78
Taylor, Sir Henry, 1800–86
Taylor, Isaac, 1787–1865
Taylor, Jeremy, 1613–67
Taylor, John (Water poet), 1580–1653
Taylor, Thomas, 1576–1633
Temple, Sir William, 1628–99
Ten Brink's Early English Literature, tr. (1883)
Tennyson, Alfred, Lord 1809–92
Termes de la Ley, Les (1624)
Thackeray, Anne Isabella: see Ritchie, A. I.
Thackeray, William Makepeace, 1811–63
Theobald, Lewis, 1688–1744
Thirlwall, Bp. Connop, 1797–1875
Thomas, Joseph, 1811–91
Thompson, Francis J., d. 1907
Thompson, Silvanus P., 1851–1916
Thomson, James, 1700–48
Thomson, Thomas, 1773–1852
Thomson, Abp. William, 1819–90
Thomson, Sir William, 1st Baron Kelvin, 1824–1907
— — and Tait, P. G., *Treatise on Natural Philosophy* (1867)
Thoreau, Henry D., 1817–62
Thoresby, Ralph, 1658–1725
Thynne, Francis, 1545?–1608
Ticknor, George, 1791–1871
Tillotson, Abp. John, 1630–94
Times, The (1788–)
Timme, Thomas, d. 1620
Tindal, Matthew, 1657–1733
Tindale, William, d. 1536
Todd, Henry J., 1763–1845
Todhunter, Isaac, 1820–84
Tomlins, Sir Thomas E., Jacob's *Law Dictionary* (1797)
Tomson, Laurence, 1539–1608
Tonstall, or Tunstall, Bp. C., 1474–1559
Tooke, John H., 1736–1812
Topsell, Edward, d. 1638?
Tout, Thomas F., *History of England* (1890)
Traill, Henry Duff, 1842–1900
Trapp, John, 1601–69
Treasury of Botany, The (1866)
Trench, Abp. Richard C., 1807–86
Trevelyan, Sir George O., 1838–1928
Trevisa, John de, 1326–1412
Tristram, Henry B., 1822–1906
Trollope, Anthony, 1815–82
Trollope, Thomas A., 1810–92
Tryon, Thomas, 1634–1703
Tucker, Abraham, 1705–74
Tucker, Josiah, 1712–99
Tupper, Martin F., 1810–89
Turberville, George, 1540?–1610?
Turner, George J., ed. *Select Pleas of the Forest* (1901)
Turner, Sharon, 1768–1847
Turner, William, d. 1568
Turton, William, 1762–1835

Tusser, Thomas, 1524?–80
Tutchin, John, 1661?–1707
'Twain, Mark' (S. L. Clemens), 1835–1910
Twining, Thomas, 1735–1804
Tylor, Edward B., 1832–1917
Tyndale, William: see Tindale, W.
Tyndall, John, 1820–93
Tyrrell, James, 1642–1718
Tyrwhitt, Thomas, 1730–86
'Tytler, Sarah' (Henrietta Keddie), 1827–1914

Udall, John, 1560?–92
Udall, Nicolas, 1505–56
Underwood, Michael, 1736–1820
Ure, Andrew, 1778–1857
Urquhart, Sir Thomas, 1611–60
Ussher, James, 1581–1656

Vanbrugh, Sir John, 1664–1726
Vansittart, Henry, 1732–70
Vaughan, Henry, 1622–95
Vaughan, Thomas, 1622–66
Vaux, James Hardy, *Vocabulary of the Flash Language* (1812)
Venables, Edmund, 1819–95
Venner, Tobias, 1577–1660
Vere, Sir Francis, 1560–1609
Victoria, Queen, 1819–1901
Vigfusson, Gudbrand, *An Icelandic-English Dictionary* (1874)
Villiers, George, 2nd Duke of Buckingham, 1628–87
Vince, Samuel, 1749–1821
Vines, Sydney H., 1849–1934
Voyle, George E., and Stevenson, G. de Saint-Clair, *A Military Dictionary* (1876)

Walker, Francis A., 1840–97
Walker, John, 1732–1807
Walker, Obadiah, 1616–99
Wall, Edward J., *A Dictionary of Photography* (1889)
Wallace, Alfred R., 1823–1913
Waller, Edmund, 1606–87
Wallis, John, 1616–1703
Wallis, Thomas, *The Farrier's and Horseman's Complete Dictionary* (1764)
Walpole, Horace, 1717–97
Walton, Izaak, 1593–1683
Warburton, Rowland E. Egerton, 1804–91
Warburton, Bp. William, 1698–1779
Ward, Edward, 1667–1731
Ward, Mrs. Humphry, 1851–1920
Ward, Lester F., 1841–1913
Ward, Nathaniel, 1578–1652
Ward, Bp. Samuel, 1577–1640
Ward, William, 1769–1823
Warner, Charles Dudley, 1829–1900
Warner, Susan, 1819–85
Warner, William, 1558?–1609
Warton, Joseph, 1722–1800
Warton, Thomas, 1728–90
Washington, George, 1732–99
Waterhouse, George R., 1810–88
Waterland, Daniel, 1683–1740
Watson, Joseph Y., *British Mining* (1843)
Watson, Bp. Richard, 1737–1816
Watts, Henry, *A Dictionary of Chemistry* (1859, etc.; 1872–82; ed. Morley and Muir, 1888–94)
Watts, Isaac, 1674–1748
Waugh, Edwin, 1817–90
Weale, John, 1791–1862
Webster, John, 1580?–1625?
Webster, Noah, *A Dictionary of the English Language* (1828, etc.; 1864)

Webster's International Dictionary (1890, etc.)
— *New International Dictionary* (1911, etc.)
Weever, John, 1576–1632
Wellington, Arthur Wellesley, 1st Duke of 1769–1852
Wells, Herbert G., 1866–1946
Wesley, Charles, 1707–88
Wesley, John, 1703–91
West, Alfred S., 1846–1932
West, Gilbert, 1703–56
Westminster Gazette, The (1893–1927)
Westwood, John O., 1805–93
Weyman, Stanley J., 1855–1928
Wharton, Henry, 1664–95
Wharton, John J. S., *A Law Lexicon* (1848; ed. 5, 1872)
Whately, Abp. Richard, 1787–1863
Whewell, William, 1794–1866
Whistler, James M., 1834–1903
Whiston, William, 1667–1752
Whitaker's Almanac (1868–)
White, Gilbert, 1720–93
White, Henry Kirke, 1785–1806
White, Stewart E., 1873–
Whitgift, Abp. John, 1530?–1604
Whitman, Walt, 1819–92
Whyte-Melville, G. J.: see Melville.
Wilkes, John, 1727–97
Wilkins, Bp. John, 1614–72
Williams, Roger, 1604?–83
Willis, Nathaniel P., 1806–67
Wilson, Alexander, 1766–1813
Wilson, Sir Daniel, 1816–92
Wilson, Horace H., 1786–1860
Wilson, John, 1627?–96
Wilson, John, 1785–1854
Windham, William, 1750–1810
Wiseman, Cdl. Nicholas P. S., 1802–65
Wither, George, 1588–1667
Withering, William, 1741–99
Wolcot, John (Peter Pindar), 1738–1819
Wollaston, William, 1660–1724
Wollstonecraft (afterwards Godwin), Mary, 1759–97
Wolseley, Garnet J. W., Viscount 1833–1913
Wood, Anthony, 1632–95
Wood, Mrs. Henry, 1814–87
Wood, James, 1760–1839
Wood, John G., 1827–89
Woodbury, Walter E., *The Encyclopædia of Photography* (1892)
Woodhead, Abraham, 1609–78
Woodward, John, 1665–1728
Woolsey, Theodore D., 1801–89
Worcester, Joseph E., 1784–1865
Wordsworth, William, 1770–1850
Wotton, Sir Henry, 1568–1639
Wotton, William, 1666–1727
Wright, Thomas, 1810–77
Wyatt, Sir Thomas, 1503?–1542
Wycherley, William, 1640?–1716
Wyclif, John, d. 1384

Yarranton, Andrew, 1616–84?
Yarrell, William, 1784–1856
Yates, Edmund H., 1831–94
Yeats, William B., 1865–1939
Yellow Book, The (1894–97)
Yonge, Charlotte M., 1823–1901
Youatt, William, 1776–1847
Young, Arthur, 1741–1820
Young, Edward, 1683–1765
Young, Thomas, 1773–1829
Yule, Sir Henry, 1820–89

Zangwill, Israel, 1864–1926
Zouch, Thomas, 1737–1815

ADDENDA

Bradley, Henry, 1845–1923
Laȝamon's *Brut*, *c* 1205–*c* 1275
Murray, Sir J. A. H., 1837–1916
Percy, Thomas, 1729–1811; editor of *Reliques of Ancient English Poetry*, 1765
Robert of Gloucester's *Chronicle*, 1297

ABBREVIATIONS AND SIGNS

In this list the abbreviations are printed in the type that is normally used for them, but there are variations for special cases.

a. = ante
a. = adjective
a. (in etymologies) = adoption of
abbrev. = abbreviation, abbreviated
abl. = ablative
Abp. = Archbishop
absol. = in absolute use, absolutely
abstr. = abstract
acc(us). = accusative
act. = active
ad. (in etymologies) = adaptation of
adj. = adjective
adv. = adverb
advb. = adverbial(ly
Æol. = Æolic
AF(r). = Anglo-French
agent-n. = agent-noun
Agric. = in Agriculture
Alb. = Albanian
Alch. = in Alchemy
Alg. = in Algebra
allus. = allusively
Amer. = American
Amer. Hist. = in American History
Amer. Ind. = American Indian
Anat. = in Anatomy
Anc. (*Hist.*, etc.) = in Ancient (History, etc.)
Anglo-Fr. = Anglo-French
Anglo-Ind. = Anglo-Indian
Anglo-Ir. = Anglo-Irish
Anglo-L. = Anglo-Latin
Anthrop. = in Anthropology
aphet. = aphetic, aphetized
Apocr. = Apocrypha
app. = apparently
appos. = appositive(ly
Arab. = Arabic
Aram. = Aramaic
arch. = archaic
Arch(it). = in Architecture
Archæol. = in Archæology
Arith. = in Arithmetic
assim. = assimilated (to)
assoc. w. = associated with
Astr(on). = in Astronomy
Astrol. = in Astrology
attrib. = in attributive use, attributively
attrib. and *Comb.* = in attributive uses and combinations
augm. = augmentative
Austral. = Australian
A.V. = Authorized Version of the Bible
Bacteriol. = in Bacteriology
BEAUM. & FL. = Beaumont and Fletcher (see List of Authors)
bef. = before
betw. = between
bibl. = biblical
Biol. = in Biology
Biol. Chem. = in Biological Chemistry
B. JONS. = Ben Jonson (see List of Authors)
Boh. = Bohemian
Bot. = in Botany
Bp. = Bishop
Braz. = Brazilian
Brit. N. Amer. = British North America
Bulg. = Bulgarian
Byz. = Byzantine
c. = circa
c. = century
Camb. = Cambridge
cap. = capital (letter)
Cat(al). = Catalan
catachr. = catachrestic(ally
cc. = centuries
Cdl. = Cardinal
Celt. = Celtic
Cf., cf. = *confer*, 'compare'
Chem. = in Chemistry
Ch. Hist. = in Church History
Chor. = Chorus
Chron(ol). = in Chronology
cl. = clause
cl. L. = classical Latin
cogn. w. = cognate with
collect. = collective(ly
colloq. = in colloquial use, colloquial(ly, -ism
Com. (Rom., Teut., WGer.) = Common (Romanic, Teutonic, West Germanic)
comb. = combining
Comb. = in combination
Comm. = in Commerce
comp(ar). = comparative
Comp. Anat. = in Comparative Anatomy
compd. = compound
compl. = complement
Conch(ol). = in Conchology
concr. = concretely
conj. = conjunction, conjunctive
conjug. = conjugation
conn. w. = connected with
cons. = consonant
const. (w.) = construed with
constr. = construction
contempt. = in contemptuous use
contr. = contracted, contraction
correl. = correlative
corresp. = corresponding
corrupt. = corruption
COTGR. = Cotgrave (see List of Authors)
Cryst(all). = in Crystallography
d. = died
Da. = Danish
dat. = dative
def. = definition
def. art. = definite article
dem(ons). = demonstrative
deriv. = derivative, -ation
dial. = in dialect use, dialectally
Dict. = Dictionary
Dicts. = (in other) Dictionaries
dim. = diminutive
dist. = distinguished
distrib. = distributive
Dor. = Doric
Du. = Dutch
dub. = dubious
Eccl. = in ecclesiastical use
eccl. Gr., eccl. L. = ecclesiastical
Eccl. Hist. = in Ecclesiastical History
ed. = edited by, edition (of)
E.D.D. = The English Dialect Dictionary, ed. J. Wright
EE. = Early English
e.g. = *exempli gratia*, 'for example'
Egyptol. = in Egyptology
E. Ind. = in the East Indies
Electr. = in Electricity
Electr. Engin. = in Electrical Engineering
ellipt. = elliptical(ly
Embryol. = in Embryology
e. midl. = east midland
Eng. = English
Eng. Hist. = in English History
Engin. = in Engineering
Ent(om). = in Entomology
Epil. = Epilogue
equiv. = equivalent
erron. = erroneous(ly
esp. = especially
Ethnol. = in Ethnology
etym. = etymology
etymol. = etymological
euphem. = euphemistic(ally
exc. = except
exclam. = exclamation
f. (in cross-references, etc.) = form of
f. (in etymologies) = formed on
F. = French
fam. = familiar
fem. = feminine
ff. = forms (of)
fig. = in figurative use
fl. = floruit
Flem. = Flemish
Fo. = (First) Folio edition of Shakespeare's plays
Fortif. = in Fortification
F.Q. = Spenser's *Faerie Queene* (see List of Authors)
Fr. = French
Fr. Hist. = in French History
freq. = frequent(ly
frequent. = frequentative
Fris. = Frisian
fut. = future
G. = German
Gael. = Gaelic
Gen. = General
gen. = generally
gen(it). = genitive
Geol. = in Geology
Geom. = in Geometry
Ger. = German
GOLDSM. = Goldsmith (see List of Authors)
Goth. = Gothic
Gr. = Greek
Gram. = in Grammar
Gr. Antiq. (*Hist.*, etc.) = in Greek Antiquities (History, etc.)
Gr. Ch. = in the Greek Church
Gr.-L. = Græco-Latin
Heb. = Hebrew
Her. = in Heraldry
Herb. = with herbalists
HG. = High German
Hind. = Hindustani

Hist. = in historical use
Hort. = in Horticulture
Hydraul. Engin. = in Hydraulic Engineering
hyperbol. = (used) hyperbolically
ib., ibid. = *ibidem*, 'in the same book or passage'
Icel. = Icelandic
Ichth(yol). = in Ichthyology
id. = *idem*, 'the same name'
i.e. = *id est*, 'that is'
imper. = imperative
impers. = impersonal
impf. = imperfect
improp. = improper(ly
incl. = including
incorr. = incorrect
ind(ic). = indicative
indef. (art.). = indefinite (article)
Indo-Eur.,-Germ. = Indo-European, Indo-Germanic
inf(in). = infinitive
infl. = inflected, influenced
instr. = instrumental
int(erj). = interjection
interrog. = interrogative(ly
intr. = intransitive(ly
Ir. = Irish
Irel. = Ireland
iron. = ironical(ly
irreg. = irregular(ly
It. = Italian
J. = Johnson's Dictionary (see List of Authors)
Jam. = Jamieson's Scottish Dictionary
Jap. = Japanese
joc. = jocular(ly
Jurisp. = in Jurisprudence
L. = Latin
lang(s. = language(s
LANGL. = Langland (see List of Authors)
Law-L. = Law-Latin
Ld. = Lord
Lett. = Lettish
LG. = Low German
LINN. = Linnæus (see List of Authors)
lit. = literal(ly
lit. and *fig.* = in literal and figurative use
Lith. = Lithuanian
Liturg. = in liturgical use
LONGF. = Longfellow (see List of Authors)
LXX = Septuagint
LYDG. = Lydgate (see List of Authors)
M (in designations of languages) = Middle
Magn. = in Magnetism
Manuf. = in .. Manufacture
Marq. = Marquis
masc. = masculine
Math. = in Mathematics
MDu. = Middle Dutch
ME. = Middle English
Mech. = in Mechanics
Med. = in Medicine
med. = mediæval
Metall. = in Metallurgy
Metaph. = in Metaphysics
Meteorol. = in Meteorology
Mex. = Mexican
MHG. = Middle High German
midl. = midland
Mil(it). = in military usage
MILT. = Milton (see List of Authors)
Min. = in Mineralogy
MLG. = Middle Low German
Mme = Madame

mod. = modern
mod.L. = modern Latin
MSc. = Middle Scottish
Mus. = in Music
Myth(ol). = in Mythology
N. = North(ern
n. (of action, of agent) = noun
n. = neuter
n. (dial.) = in northern (dialects)
Nat. Hist. = in Natural History
Nat. Phil(os). = in Natural Philosophy
Nat. Sci. = in Natural Science
Naut. = in nautical use
N.E.D. = A New English Dictionary on Historical Principles
neg. = negative
neut. = neuter
next = next word or article
N.O. = Natural Order
nom. = nominative
nonce-wd. = nonce-word
north. = (in) northern (dialect)
Northumb. = Northumbrian
Norw. = Norwegian
N.T. = New Testament
num. adj. = numeral adjective
Numism. = in Numismatics
Nurs. R. = Nursery Rhyme
N.W., n.w. = North West, -western
O (in designations of languages) = Old
obj. = object
obl. = oblique
Obs., *obs.*, obs. = obsolete
obsc. = obscure
Obsol. = obsolescent
Obstet. Surg. = in Obstetrical Surgery
occ(as). = occasionally
OE. = Old English
OF(r). = Old French
OFris. = Old Frisian
OHG. = Old High German
OIr. = Old Irish
OLG. = Old Low German
ON. = Old Norse
ONF(r). = Old Northern French
ONorth. = Old Northumbrian
opp. = opposed
Org(an). Chem. = in Organic Chemistry
orig. = original(ly
Orkn. = Orkney
Ornith. = in Ornithology
OS(ax). = Old Saxon
OScand. = Old Scandinavian
OSl(av). = Old Slavonic
OSp. = Old Spanish
O.T. = Old Testament
OTeut. = Original Teutonic
Oxf. = Oxford
Palæont. = in Palæontology
PALSGR. = Palsgrave (see List of Authors)
pa. pple. = past or passive participle
pass. = passive(ly
pa. t. = past tense
Path(ol). = in Pathology
perh. = perhaps
pers. = person(al
Pers. = Persian
Peruv. = Peruvian
Petrog. = in Petrography
pf. = perfect
Pg. = Portuguese
Pharm. = in Pharmacy
Pharm. Chem. = in Pharmaceutical Chemistry
Phil(os). = in Philosophy
Philol. = in Philology
Phœn. = Phœnician
phonet. = phonetic(ally

Photogr. = in Photography
phr. = phrase(s
Phren. = in Phrenology
Phys. Chem. = in Physiological Chemistry
Physiog. = in Physiography
Phys(iol). = in Physiology
pl., pl. = plural
P.L. = Milton's *Paradise Lost*
poet. = poetical
Pol. Econ. = in Political Economy
Polit. = in Politics
pop. = popular(ly
poss. = possessive
post-Aug. = post-Augustan (Latin)
post-cl. = post-classical (Latin)
ppl. a. = participial adjective
pple. = participle
P.R. = Milton's *Paradise Regained*
Pr. = Provençal
prec. = preceding (word or article)
pred. = predicate
pred. a(dj). = predicative adjective
predic. = predicative(ly
Pref. = Preface
pref. = prefix
pre-hist. = prehistoric
prep. = preposition
pres. = present
pret. = preterite
pre-Teut. = pre-Teutonic
prim. = primitive
priv. = privative
prob. = probably
Prol. = Prologue
pron. = pronounced
pron. = pronoun
pronunc. = pronunciation
prop. = properly
Pros. = in Prosody
Prov. = Provençal
prov. = proverb
provb. = proverbial(ly
pr. pple. = present participle
Ps. = psalm
Psych(ol). = in Psychology
Qo. = Quarto edition
quot(s. = quotation(s
q.v. = *quod vide*, 'which see'
R. C. Ch. = in the Roman Catholic Church
rec. = recent
redupl. = in reduplicated form
reduplic. = reduplication of
ref. = reference
refash. = refashioned
refl. = reflexive
reg. = regular
rel. = relative
rel. to = related to
repl. = replaced
repr. = representing, representative of, represented
Rhet. = in Rhetoric
rhet. = rhetorical
Rom. = Romanic, Romance
Rom. Antiq. (*Hist.*, *Law*) = in Roman Antiquities (History, Law)
Russ. = Russian
R.V. = Revised Version of the Bible (see *Bible*, p. xii)
S. = South
S. A. = Milton's *Samson Agonistes*
S.Afr. = South African
sb. = substantive
sc(il). = *scilicet*, 'understand' or 'supply'
Sc. = Scotch, Scottish, Scots
Scand. = Scandinavian
Sc. Hist. = in Scottish History
schol. L. = scholastic Latin

Scotl. = Scotland
Sculpt. = in Sculpture
Seismol. = in Seismology
Serb. = Serbian
SHAKS. = Shakespeare (see below)
Shetl. = Shetland
sing. = singular
Sinh. = Sinhalese
Skr. = Sanskrit
Slav. = Slavonic
Sp. = Spanish
sp. = spelling
spec. = specifically
sp. gr. = specific gravity
Sport. = in Sporting use
Stock Exch. = on the Stock Exchange
str. = strong
subj. = subject, subjunctive
subord. cl. = subordinate clause
subseq. = subsequent(ly
subst. = substantival(ly
suff. = suffix
superl. = superlative
Surg. = in Surgery
s.v. = *sub voce*, 'under the word'
Sw(ed). = Swedish
S.W., s.w. = South West, -western
Syd. Soc. Lex. = The New Sydenham Society's Lexicon (see List of Authors)
synon. = synonymous
Syr. = Syriac
t. = tense
techn. = in technical use
Telegr. = in Telegraphy
Teut. = Teutonic
Theatr. = in theatrical language
Theol. = in Theology
tr. = translation of
trans. = transitive(ly
transf. and *fig.* = in transferred and figurative use
Trig. = in Trigonometry
Turk. = Turkish
Typog. = in Typography
Tyrol. = Tyrolese
ult. = ultimate(ly
unc. = uncertain
Univ. = University
unkn. = unknown
U.S. = in the English of the U.S.A.
U.S.(A.) = the United States (of America)
usu. = usually
v. = verb
var(s). = variant(s) of
var. (in 'stress var.') = variable
vb. = verb
vbl. sb. = verbal substantive
viz. = *videlicet*, 'namely'
voc. = vocative
Vulg. = the Vulgate
vulg. = vulgar(ly
W. = Welsh
W (in designations of languages) = West
w. = with
wd. = word
W. Ind(ies). = in the West Indies
wk. = weak
wk. vb. = weak verb
w. midl. = west midland
WORDSW. = Wordsworth (see List of Authors)
WS. = West Saxon
WYCL. = Wycliffe (see List of Authors)
Zool. = in Zoology

† = obsolete. ‖ = alien or not naturalized. * indicates a hypothetical etymological form. :— = regular phonetic descendant of.
The printing of a word in SMALL CAPITALS indicates that further information will be found under the word so referred to.

ABBREVIATIONS OF TITLES OF BOOKS OF THE BIBLE

Gen/esis
Exod/us
Lev/iticus
Num/bers
Deut/eronomy
Josh/ua
Judg/es
Ruth
1 Sam/uel
2 Sam/uel
1 Kings
2 Kings
1 Chron/icles
2 Chron/icles
Ezra
Neh/emiah
Esther
Job
Ps/alms
Prov/erbs
Eccl/esiastes
Song (of) Sol/omon; also Cant/icles
Isa/iah
Jer/emiah
Lam/entations
Ezek/iel
Dan/iel
Hos/ea
Joel
Amos
Obad/iah
Jonah
Micah
Nahum
Hab/akkuk
Zeph/aniah
Haggai
Zech/ariah
Mal/achi
1 Esdras
2 Esdras
Tobit
Judith
Esther (Apocr.)
Wisd/om of Solomon
Eccl(esiastic)us
Baruch
Song (of the) 3 Childr/en
Susanna
Bel & (the) Dr/agon
Prayer (of) Manasseh
1 Macc/abees
2 Macc/abees

(St.) Matt/hew
(St.) Mark
(St.) Luke
(St.) John
Acts
Rom/ans
1 Cor/inthians
2 Cor/inthians
Gal/atians
Eph/esians
Phil/ippians
Col/ossians
1 Thess/alonians
2 Thess/alonians
1 Tim/othy
2 Tim/othy
Tit/us
Philem/on
Heb/rews
Ja(me)s
1 Pet/er
2 Pet/er
1 John
2 John
3 John
Jude
Rev/elation

ABBREVIATIONS OF TITLES OF SHAKESPEARE'S WORKS

All's Well = All's Well that Ends Well
Ant. & Cl. = Antony and Cleopatra
A. Y. L. = As You Like It
Com. Err. = The Comedy of Errors
Compl. = A Lover's Complaint
Cor(iol). = Coriolanus
Cymb. = Cymbeline
Ham(l). = Hamlet, Prince of Denmark
1 *Hen. IV* = The First Part of King Henry IV
2 *Hen. IV* = The Second Part of King Henry IV
Hen. V = The Life of King Henry V
1 *Hen. VI* = The First Part of King Henry VI
2 *Hen. VI* = The Second Part of King Henry VI
3 *Hen. VI* = The Third Part of King Henry VI
Hen. VIII = The Famous History of the Life of King Henry VIII
(K.) John = The Life and Death of King John
Jul. C(æs). = Julius Cæsar
Lear. = King Lear
L. L. L. = Love's Labour 's Lost
Lucr. = The Rape of Lucrece
Macb. = Macbeth
Meas. for M. = Measure for Measure
Merch. V. = The Merchant of Venice
Merry W. = The Merry Wives of Windsor
Mids. N. (D.) = A Midsummer-Night's Dream
Much Ado = Much Ado about Nothing
Oth. = Othello, the Moor of Venice
Per. = Pericles, Prince of Tyre
Phœnix = The Phœnix and the Turtle
Pilgr. = The Passionate Pilgrim
Rich. II = The Tragedy of King Richard II
Rich. III = The Tragedy of King Richard III
Rom. & Jul. = Romeo and Juliet
Sonn. = Sonnets
Tam. Shr. = The Taming of the Shrew
Temp. = The Tempest
Timon = Timon of Athens
Tit. A. = Titus Andronicus
Tr. & Cr. = Troilus and Cressida
Twel. N. = Twelfth-Night; or, What You Will
Two Gent. = The Two Gentlemen of Verona
Ven. & Ad. = Venus and Adonis
Wint. T. = The Winter's Tale

KEY TO THE PRONUNCIATION

I. VOWELS.

ORDINARY.	LONG.	OBSCURE.
a as in Fr. *à la* mode (a la mod)	ā as in *alms* (āmz), b*ar* (bāɹ)	ă as in *a*mœb*a* (ămī·bă), flor*a*l (flōə·răl)
‖ai ... Ger. h*ai*n (hain), st*ei*n (ʃtain)		
‖au ... Ger. fr*au* (frau)		
æ ... m*a*n (mæn), f*a*shion (fæ·ʃən)		ǣ ... *a*ccept (ǣkse·pt)
ɑ ... p*a*ss (pɑs), ch*a*nt (tʃɑnt)*		
ɑu ... l*ou*d (lɑud), n*ow* (nɑu)		
ʋ ... c*u*t (kʋt), s*o*n (sʋn)	ʋ̄ ... c*u*rl (kʋ̄ɹl), f*u*r (fʋ̄ɹ)	ʋ̆ ... dat*u*m (dēɪ·tʋ̆m), papp*u*s (pæ·pʋ̆s)
e ... y*e*t (yet), t*e*n (ten)	ēə ... th*e*re (ðēəɹ), p*e*ar, p*a*re (pēəɹ)	ĕ ... mom*e*nt (mōu·mĕnt), sev*e*ral (se·vĕrăl)
‖e ... Fr. attach*é* (ataʃe)	ēɪ ... r*ei*n, r*ai*n (rēɪn), th*ey* (ðēɪ)	ĕ ... separ*a*te *adj.* (se·părĕt)
‖ɛ ... Fr. ch*e*f (ʃɛf)	‖ɛ̄ ... Fr. f*ai*re (fɛ̄r)	
	ɜ̄ ... f*i*r (fɜ̄ɹ), f*e*rn (fɜ̄ɹn), *e*arth (ɜ̄ɹþ)	
		ė ... add*e*d (æ·dėd), *e*state (ėstēɪ·t)
‖ə ... Fr. coup d*e* grace (kudəgrās)		ə ... the general obscure vowel, invariably used in the notation of -*er* (əɹ), -*ous* (əs), -*sion* (ʒən, ʃən), -*tion* (ʃən)
əi ... *I*, *eye* (əi), b*i*nd (bəind)		
i ... s*i*t (sit), m*y*st*i*c (mistik)	īə ... b*ie*r (bīəɹ), cl*ea*r (klīəɹ)	ĭ ... van*i*ty (væ·nĭti)
ɪ ... Psych*e* (səi·kɪ), r*e*act (rɪ,æ·kt)	ī ... th*ie*f (þīf), s*ee* (sī)	ɪ̆ ... r*e*main (rɪ̆mēɪ·n), b*e*lieve (bɪ̆lī·v)
o ... ach*o*r (ēɪ·koɹ), Fr. r*o*be (rob)	ōə ... b*oa*r, b*o*re (bōəɹ), gl*o*ry (glōə·ri)	ŏ ... the*o*ry (þī·ŏri)
oi ... *oi*l (oil), b*oy* (boi)		
o ... her*o* (hīə·ro), z*o*ology (zo,ǫ·lŏdʒi)	‖ō ... Fr. ch*o*se (ʃōz)	ǒ ... vi*o*let (vəi·ǒlėt), par*o*dy (pæ·rǒdi)
	ōu ... s*o*, s*ow* (sōu), s*ou*l (sōul)	
ǫ ... wh*a*t (hwǫt), w*a*tch (wǫtʃ)	ǭ ... f*ou*ght (fǭt), h*au*ghty (hǭ·ti), t*au*ght (tǭt), w*al*k (wǭk), w*a*rt (wǭɹt)	ǫ̆ ... *au*thority (ǫ̆þǫ·rĭti)
ǫ ... g*o*t (gǫt)	ǭ ... sh*o*rt (ʃǭɹt), th*o*rn (þǭɹn)	ǫ̆ ... c*o*nnect (kǫ̆ne·kt), amaz*o*n (æ·măzǫ̆n)
ǫ ... s*o*ft (sǫft) *		
‖ö ... Fr. déj*eu*ner (deʒöne), Ger. K*ö*ln (köln)	‖ȫ ... Fr. c*œu*r (kȫr)	
‖ö ... Fr. p*eu* (pö)	‖ȫ ... Ger. G*ö*the (gȫtə), Fr. j*eû*ne (ʒȫn)	
u ... f*u*ll (ful), b*oo*k (buk)	ūə ... p*oo*r (pūəɹ), m*oo*rish (mūə·riʃ)	
iu ... d*u*ration (diurēɪ·ʃən)	iū ... p*u*re (piūəɹ)	iŭ ... verd*u*re (vɜ̄·ɹdiŭɹ)
	ɪū ... l*u*re (lɪūəɹ)	ɪŭ ... meas*u*re (me·ʒɪŭɹ)
u ... *u*nt*o* (ʋ·ntu), fr*u*gality (frugæ·lĭti)	ū ... tw*o* m*oo*ns (tū mūnz)	ŭ ... alt*o*gether (ǭltŭge·ðəɹ)
iu ... Matth*ew* (mæ·þiu), virt*ue* (vɜ̄·ɹtiu)	iū ... f*ew* (fiū)	iŭ ... circ*u*lar (sɜ̄·ɹkiŭlăɹ)
	ɪū ... l*u*te (lɪūt)	
‖ü ... Ger. M*ü*ller (mü·lər)		
‖ü ... Fr. j*u*ste (ʒüst)	‖ǖ ... Ger. gr*ü*n (grǖn), Fr. p*u*r (pǖr)	

II. CONSONANTS.

b, d, f, k, l, m, n, p, t, v, z *have their usual values.*

		(FOREIGN.)
g as in *g*o (gōu)	ð as in *th*en (ðen), ba*th*e (bēɪð)	ṅ marks nasalization of the preceding vowel, as in Fr. *environ* (aṅviroṅ)
h ... *h*o! (hōu)	ʃ ... *sh*op (ʃǫp), di*sh* (diʃ)	l^y ... It. sera*gl*io (serā·l^{y}o)
r ... *r*un (rʋn), te*rr*ier (te·riəɹ)	tʃ ... *ch*op (tʃǫp), di*tch* (ditʃ), pic*t*ure (pi·ktʃəɹ)	n^y ... It. si*gn*ore (sin^{y}ō·re)
ɹ ... he*r* (həɹ), fa*r*the*r* (fā·ɹðəɹ)	ʒ ... vi*si*on (vi·ʒən), dé*j*euner (deʒöne)	χ ... Ger. a*ch* (āχ), Sc. lo*ch* (loχ, loχ^w)
s ... *s*ee (sī), *c*ess (ses)	dʒ ... *j*u*dg*e (dʒʋdʒ), ver*g*er, ver*d*ure (vɜ̄·ɹdʒəɹ)	χ^y ... Ger. i*ch* (iχ^y), Sc. ni*ch*t (nėχ^{y}t)
w ... *w*en (wen)	ŋ ... si*ng*i*ng* (si·ŋiŋ), thi*n*k (þiŋk)	γ ... Ger. sa*g*en (zā·γən)
hw ... *wh*en (hwen)	ŋg ... fi*ng*er (fi·ŋgəɹ), stro*ng*er (strǫ·ŋgəɹ)	γ^y ... Ger. le*g*en, re*g*nen (lē·γ^{y}ən, rē·γ^{y}nən)
y ... *y*es (yes), diges*ti*on (didʒe·styən)		
þ ... *th*in (þin), ba*th* (bāþ)		

* The symbols ɑ and ǫ are used to indicate respectively the local or individual variants æ, ā (e.g. in *castle*) and ǫ, ǭ (e.g. in *salt*).

Small 'superior' letters are used (*a*) to express the glide element of the diphthongs ēə, īə, ōə, ūə, ēɪ, ōu, and of the triphthongs ɑuə, əiə, iūə, (*b*) to denote an element that may or may not be present in a local or an individual pronunciation, as (lɪūt) *lute*, (wi·n^{d}mil) *windmill*, (*c*) to indicate the palatal or labial modification of certain consonants (see third column of Consonants above).

A break , is used to indicate syllabic division, or to guard against ambiguity.

' indicates that a following l, m, or n is syllabic, as in *able* (ēɪ·b'l), *rheumatism* (rū·mătiz'm), *eaten* (ī·t'n).

¶ For the notation of stress see Vol. I, pages viii, ix.

THE OXFORD UNIVERSAL DICTIONARY

A (ē̆i), the first letter of the Roman and English Alphabet (Gr. *Alpha*, Heb. *Aleph*); repr. orig. in Eng., as in L., the 'low-back-wide' vowel, formed with the widest opening of jaws, pharynx, and lips. Pl. *aes*, A's, *As*.

For its principal sounds see KEY TO THE PRONUNCIATION.

II. Besides serial order, *A* or *a* signifies *spec.* 1. *Mus.* The 6th note of the diatonic scale of C major, or the first of the relative minor scale of C. Also, the scale of a composition with A as its key-note. 2. *Naut.* See A 1 below. 3. In *Logic*: a universal affirmative. 4. In *Law, reasoning*, etc.: *any one* thing or person. 5. In *Algebra*: *a, b, c*, etc. stand for known quantities, *x, y, z* unknown.

III. *Abbreviations.* A., a., *a.* = 1. *anno*, as A.D. *anno domini*, in the year of our Lord; A.M. *anno mundi*, in the year of the world; A.U.C. *anno urbis conditæ*, in the year of the founding of the City (Rome). 2. *ante*, as a.m. *ante meridiem*, before noon; a. or *a* 1600. 3. *adjective*; *active* (verb). 4. *artium*, as A.B. (= B.A.) *artium baccalaureus*, A.M. (= M.A.) *artium magister*, Bachelor, and Master, of Arts. 5. *alto*. 6. *accepted* (of bills). 7. Associate, as A.L.S. Associate of the Linnean Society. 8. R.A. Royal Artillery, Academy, or Academician; F.B.A. Fellow of the British Academy; F.S.A. Fellow of the Society of Antiquaries. 9. A.B able-bodied seaman. 10. *ā* or *āā* in Med. ANA, q.v. 11. A.C. or a.c., alternating current.

IV. *Phrases.* 1. A per se, A by itself, *esp.* as a word; hence *fig.* (also †Apersie, †Apersey, †A per C) the first, best, or unique person or thing; = mod. *A* 1. 2. A 1. Used of ships in first-class condition, as to hull (A), and stores (1). (Lloyd's Register.) Hence *colloq. A* 1, U.S. *A No.* 1 = prime, first-class, e.g. An A number one cook MRS. STOWE.

†**A**, *adj.*[1] definite numeral. *Obs.* or *dial.* [OE. *ān*, one, later *ā* bef. a cons., became in the south *on* (*oon, one*), *o* (*oo*) and finally *one*; *an* and *a* becoming the 'indef. article'. See next wd. In the north *an(e* and *a* had both senses. See AN(E, O *a.*, and ONE.

A (toneless ă, ə; emph. ē̆i), *adj.*[2], called 'indefinite article'. Bef. a vowel-sound an (ăn, emph. æn). A weakening of OE. *ān*, 'one', which, *c* 1150, became proclitic and toneless, ăn, ă; see prec. wd. *An* is freq. bef. a cons. to 1300; bef. sounded *h* till after 1700. Now *an* is used bef. a vowel-sound or *h* mute; *a* bef. a cons., sounded *h*, and *eu-*, *u-*. But in *unaccented* syllables, many writers retain *an* bef. sounded *h*, some bef. *eu, u*, as *an historian, an university* About the 15th cent. *a* or *an* was joined with its sb. as *aman, anadder, anewt* Hence, by mistaken division, words like ADDER, NEWT. *A* is strictly *adjective*, and requires a sb. Meanings:—1. One, some, any ME 2. *A* with numeral adjectives = some, a matter of, about OE. 3. A certain, a particular ME. 4. The same 1551. 5. In each, to or for each. This was orig. the prep. *a*, OE *an, on*, defining time, as in twice *a* day; afterwards identified with the 'indef. art.', and extended from time to space, measure, weight, number. See A *prep.*[1]

1. A tree, a wish, an ice, a pouring rain (*mod.*). A Daniel SHAKS. A Poland TENNYSON. Also, following the adj. preceded by *how, so, as, too*, and in *many a, such a, what a!* Ho, such a one! *Ruth* iv. 1. Behold, how great a matter a little fire kindleth *James* iii. 5. What manner a man = *cujusmodi homo?* As fine a child as you shall see (*mod.*). Appar. bef. pl. nouns (*of* omitted): A dozen (of) men. A certayne noble knightis .. she kept LD. BERNERS. Poore a thousand crownes *A.Y.L.* I. i. 2. More than a dozen times TYNDALL. 2. A ii hundred speres LD. BERNERS. And a many merry men with him *A.Y.L.* I. i. 121. *Obs.* except in *a few, a great many, a good many*, and in dial. 3. Phr. *Once on a time.* 4. These foyles have all a length *Haml.* v. ii. 277. *Mod.* Fowls of a feather. Two at a time. 5. A peny a daye TINDALE *Matt.* xx. 2. Twentie poundes a bowe 1584. Four pieces of eight a man DE FOE. A penny a mile, sixpence a pound (*mod.*).

A, also **a'** (ǫ), *adj.*3 = ALL.

†**A** (ă), *pron. Obs.* or *dial.* [for HA = HE, HEO, HI, *he* (*Haml.* III. iii. 74), *she* (*it*), *they*, when stressless, chiefly in S. and W.] ME.

†**A**, *v.* for **ha, ha'**, worn down f. HAVE (cf. Fr. *a* = L. *habet*). Frequent in 13–17th c.; since, chiefly *colloq.* or *dial.* (TENNYSON *Northern Farmer*), and usu. spelt *ha, ha'*.

†**A**, *adv.* Also **aa, o, oo.** [OE. *á, áwa*, replaced in 13th c. by Norse *aȝ, ai, ei, ay, aye.* See AYE and O.] Ever, always.

A (ă), *prep.*[1], also **o.** [worn down proclitic f. OE. prep. *an, on.* Now repl. by *on, in*, etc., exc. in phr. like *go a begging*, etc., and in compounds like *abed*, etc.] 1. Superposition: on; as *a bed*, etc. ME. 2. Motion: on, upon, on to; as *a field*, etc. ME. 3. Juxtaposition: on, at; as in *a right* (or *left*) *half* ME. †4. Position or situation: in; as *a Rome* –1660. 5. Direction or position: towards; as *a back*, etc. ME. 6. Partition: in, into; as *a pieces* ME. †7. Position in a series: at, in; as *a first*, etc. ME. 8. Time: in, on, by; as *a night* OE. With OE. genitives *a nights, nowadays.* Esp. with advbs. of repetition: *once a day* (OE. *on dæʒe*). See A *adj.*[2] 4, and cf. Fr. *deux francs par jour.* †9. Manner: in, with, etc.; as *a this wise, a purpose* = on purpose –1695. †10. Capacity: in any one's name; esp. *a God's name* –1702. 11. State: in; as *a live*, etc. ME. 12. Process: in course of; as in *whilst these things were a doing* STOW. ME. Also in mod. *Were doing, were being done.* 13. Action; a. with *be*: engaged in; as in *They had ben a fyghtyng* LD. BERNERS. *Mod.* Been fighting. b. with vb. of motion: as in *to go a begging*, etc. ME.

†**A** (ă, ə), *prep.*[2] ME. [worn down from *of*, and once used for it in *men a war, time a day*, etc.] 1. Of, *esp.* in *a clock* = of the clock. 2. After *manner, kind, sort*, etc., *of*, in its reduced form was identified with the 'indef. art.'; thus, What manner of man? *cujusmodi homo?* became 'what manner a man?'

1. Cloth a gold *M. Ado* III. iv. 19. It's sixe a clock B. JONS. 2. No maner a person LD. BERNERS.

†**A**, *conj.* ME. 1. = And. 2. = *And, an'*, if.

†**A**, *interj.* ME. [var. O, AH.] 1. O! exclam. of surprise, admiration. 2. Ah! of grief. 3. Before proper names as a war-cry, as *A Warwick!* 4. As in *merrily hent the Stile-a* SHAKS., for metre; now burlesque. Cf. O! as in 'My Nannie, O'.

A, a- (ă, ə) *particle* or *prefix*, reduced form (now s.w. dial.) of I- *prefix*[1], Y-, the prefix of pa. pples. late ME.

An' we have all a-left the spot W. BARNES.

A-, *prefix.* 1. OE. **a-**, orig. *ar-* away, on, up, out, as in *a-rise.* Sometimes confused with OFr. *a-*:—L. *ad-, ac-, af-*, etc., as in *a(c)-curse*, etc. 2. ME. a-:—OE. *an, on*, in, on, engaged in, at, as in *asleep*, etc. See A *prep.*[1] 3. ME. a-:—OE. *of* prep. off, from, of, as in *akin*, etc. See A *prep.*[2] 4. ME. a-:—OE. *and-* against, opposite, as in *a-long.* 5. ME. a- for AT, as in *ado*, early N. Eng. *at do* = inf. *to do.* 6. a- for *i-, y-*:—*ʒe-*; see A *particle.* 7. ME. a- = Fr. pref. *a-*:—L. *ad-* to, at, expressing addition, increase, change *into.* In 15th c., as in Fr., most words from OFr. with (and some without) this prefix were treated as if formed directly from L. Cf. *a(d)dress; a(f)fect, a(c)curse* = OE. *a-* + *curse.* 8. ME. a- = Fr. *a-*:—L. *ab* off, away, from, as in *a-soil.* 9. ME. a- = Anglo-Fr. *a*, OFr. *e-, es-*:—L. *ex-* out, utterly, as in *abash.* 10. ME. a-:—Anglo-Fr. *an-*, OFr. *en-*, as in *abushment*, etc. 11. *a-*, as used by Spenser and others, is often due to vague form-association only. 12. a-, f. L. *a* = *ad*, to, reduced to *a-* bef. *sc-, sp-, st-*, as in *a-scend*, etc. See AD-. 13. a-, f. L. *a* = *ab* from, off, away; only bef. *v*, as in *avert*; see AB-. 14. a-, f. Gr. *ἀ-* used bef. a cons. for *ἀν* = *without, not, -less* as in *adamant, apetalous*, etc. In *agnostic*, etc., *a-* = *un-, non-*, and is used also with techn. words from L., as *a-sexual.*

-a, *suffix.* 1. OE. **-a** (:—early Teut. *-o*) nom. ending, as in *ox-a* = ME. *ox-e*, mod.E. *ox.* A com. ending of OE. names and titles, as *Bæda.* 2. Gr. and L. -a, nom. ending of fem. nouns (*esp.* Nat. Hist. terms, and names of women), often adopted unchanged, as *idea, soda, Diana*, etc. 3. Mod. Rom. -a, ending of fem. nouns, names of women, and occ. a sex-suffix, as *stanza*; *Eva*; *donn-a*, etc. 4. Gr. and L. -a, pl. ending of neut. nouns, occ. adopted unchanged, as *data, Mammalia*, etc.

‖**Aal** (āl). 1875. [Hind.] A species of *Morinda*, whose roots yield a red dye. Also, the dye.

‖**Aam** (ām, ǭm). 1526. [Du. *aam*, ad. (ult.) Gr. *ἄμη* a bucket.] A Du. and Ger. liquid measure, varying from 37 to 41 gallons; a cask.

‖**Aard-vark** (ā·ɹdvāɹk). 1833. [S. Afr., f. Du. *aarde* earth + *vark* pig.] An insectivorous quadruped (*Orycteropus capensis*), one of the Edentata, intermediate between Armadillos and Ant-eaters.

‖**Aard-wolf** (ā·ɹdwulf). 1833. [a. Du., f. *aarde* earth.] A S. Afr. carnivorous quadruped (*Proteles Lalandii*), intermediate between the dogs, hyenas, and civets.

Aaronic, -al (eərǫ·nik, -ăl), *a.* 1874. [f. the prop. name.] Pertaining to Aaron, Levitical, high-priestly.

Aaron's-beard (ē·ərənzbī·əɹd). [*Psalm* cxxxiii. 2.] *Herb.* A name, *esp.* of the Great St. John's wort (*Hypericum Calycinum*), and locally of other plants.

Aaron's rod. 1834. 1. [Numbers xvii. 8.] *Herb.* A name of plants, *esp.* the Great Mullein or Hag-taper (*Verbascum Thapsus*), and the Golden Rod (*Solidago Virgaurea*). 2. [Exodus vii. 9.] *Arch.* A rod with a serpent twined about it, used as an ornament.

‖**Ab** (æb). [Heb.] The 5th month of the Heb. sacred year, the 11th of the civil year. The 12th month of the Syrian year, = August.

Ab-, *pref.* repr. L. *ab*, 'off, away, from'. In rec. formations, e.g. *ab-oral, ab-* = 'position away from'.

Aba (æ·bă). 1876. A new altazimuth instrument, designed by M. d'Abbadie [and named after him] for determining latitude, etc., without the sextant.

‖**Abaca** (æ·băkă), **-ka.** The native name of the palm (*Musa textilis*) which furnishes Manilla Hemp; also, its fibre.

Abacinate (ăbæ·sinē̆it), *v. rare.* [f. med. L. *abacinare*; f. *ab* + *bacinus* a BASIN.] To blind by placing hot irons or metal plates before the eyes. Hence **Abacina·tion.**

æ (m*a*n). ɑ (p*a*ss). ɑu (l*ou*d). *v* (c*u*t). ę (Fr. ch*e*f). ə (ev*er*). əi (*I, eye*). *ə* (Fr. eau d*e* vie). i (s*i*t). *i* (Psych*e*). ǫ (wh*a*t). ǫ (g*o*t).
ö (Ger. K*ö*ln). *ö* (Fr. p*eu*). ü (Ger. M*ü*ller). *ü* (Fr. d*u*ne). *v̄* (c*u*rl). ē (ēə) (th*e*re). *ē* (ē̆i) (r*ei*n). *ę̄* (Fr. f*ai*re). ə̄ (f*i*r, f*e*rn, *ea*rth).

‖**Abaci·scus.** [L., a. Gr. ἀβακίσκος, dim. of ἄβαξ.] *Arch.* **1.** A tile or square in a mosaic pavement. †**2.** = ABACUS.

Abacist (æ·băsist). ME. [ad. late L. *abacista*, f. *abacus*.] One who uses an abacus in casting accounts; a calculator.

†**Aback.** *rare.* A square tablet or compartment.

Aback (ăbæ·k), *adv.* [OE. *on* prep. *bæc* sb. Now chiefly *Naut.*] **1.** Backwards. Also *fig.* **2.** In the rear, behind OE. Also *fig.* **3.** *Naut.* Of sails: Laid back against the mast, with the wind in front 1697. Also of the ship. Hence **To be taken aback**, to be caught in front suddenly, through a shift of wind, and driven astern; *fig.* to be disconcerted by a sudden check.

2. When tyme is, to holde thyself abacke SKELTON.

†**Abackward,** *adv.* ME. Early f. BACKWARD. Chaucer.

Abactinal (æ:b,æ̆ktəi·năl), *a.* 1857. [f. L. *ab* + ACTINAL.] *Zool.* Remote from the actinal area. See ACTINAL.

†**Aba·ctor.** 1659. [a. L., f. *abigere*.] A stealer of cattle by herds.

‖**Aba·culus.** [L., dim. of *Abacus*.] *Arch.* = ABACISCUS.

Abacus (æ·băkŭs). Pl. **-ci.** ME. [a. L. *abacus*, f. Gr. ἄβαξ.] †**1.** A board strewn with sand, for drawing figures, etc. **2.** A calculating frame, *esp.* one with sliding balls on wires 1686. **3.** The upper member of the capital of a column, supporting the architrave 1563. †**4.** = ABACK *sb.* **5.** *Gr. & Rom. Antiq.* A sideboard.

†**Abada.** *a* 1599. [Perh. Malay.] The rhinoceros. PURCHAS.

Abaddon (ăbæ·dən). ME. [Heb.] In *Rev.* ix. 11 = Gr. Ἀπολλύων, destroyer, 'the angel of the bottomless pit'. Hence the pit itself MILT. *P.R.* iv. 624.

Abaft (ăbɑ·ft). ME. [A *prep.*[1] + *bi* + *æftan*; see BAFT and AFT.] **A.** *adv.* †**1.** Backwards ME. **2.** Back ME. Usu. *Naut.* **B.** *prep.* Behind.

A. 2. Her works were rotten a. ANSON. **B.** Just a. the beam MAURY.

†**Abai·sance.** ME. [a. OFr. *abaissance*.] A low bow -1721.

Abai·ser. 1849. [mod. f. F. *abaisser*.] Burnt black or ivory black; used to lower the tones of colours in painting.

†**Abalienate** (æb,ē̆i·lienĕit), *v.* 1554. [f. L. *abalienatum, abalienare*; see ALIEN.] **1.** *Rom. Law.* To make that another's which was ours. **2.** To remove; estrange -1652. **3.** To cause aberration of (mind) -1652. Hence **Aba:liena·tion.**

Abalone (æbălōu·ni). *U.S.* 1883. [Sp.] An edible mollusc, the sea-ear.

†**Aba·nd,** *v.* 1559. [Contr. f. ABANDON.] **1.** To forsake SPENSER. **2.** To banish -1559.

†**Abando·n, -ou·n,** *adv.* ME. [a. OFr. *à bandon*; see BANDON *sb.*] Under one's control; at one's discretion.

Abandon (ăbæ·ndən), *v.* ME. [a. OFr. *abandoner*, f. *à bandon*; see prec. and cf. F. *mettre à bandon*.] †**1.** To reduce under control, subdue -1533. **2.** To give up to the control of another, surrender *to* another ME.; esp. *refl.* to surrender oneself 1564. **3.** *trans.* To relinquish a claim to underwriters (also *absol.*) 1755. **4.** To cease to hold, use, or practise; to give up, renounce ME.; to desert, leave without help 1490. †**5.** *refl.* To let oneself loose, rush headlong -1530. †**6.** To put to the ban, banish -1660.

2. To a. a place to the enemy HUME. *refl.* Abandon'd to her sorrow *Twel. N.* I. iv. 19. **3.** To a. a Ship to the Insurers 1755. **4.** Abandoning..of images 1577. To a. the Dutch war BURKE. MILT. *Sams.* 118. To a. one's own flesh and blood DE FOE, the helm of justice BURKE. **6.** Abandoned from thy bed *Tam. Shr.* Ind. ii. 112. Hence **Aba·ndoner.**

†**Abando·n, -ou·n(e,** *sb.*[1] ME. [a. OFr. *abandon*.] = BANDON. *At, in abandoun*: Recklessly.

Abandon (abæ·ndən), *sb.*[2] ? *Obs.* 1755. [f. ABANDON *v.*] The act of abandoning; *spec.* of insured property.

‖**Abandon** (aba·ndoṅ), *sb.*[3] 1850. [mod.Fr. See ABANDONMENT.] *lit.* Surrender to natural impulses; hence freedom from constraint or convention.

Abandoned (abæ·ndənd), *ppl. a.* ME. [f. ABANDON *v.*] **1.** Forsaken, cast off 1477. **2.** Self-given up *to* ME. Now always to evil. Hence (without *to*): Profligate 1692.

1. A poor, a. woman 1704. A. finery LEVER. **2.** A. to sorrow SHAKS., to despair DE FOE, to vice SCOTT. A. youth PRIOR, writings STEELE. Hence **Aba·ndonedly** *adv.* profligately; also unconventionally (f. ABANDON *sb.*[3]).

Aba:ndonee·. 1848. [f. ABANDON *v.*] One to whom anything is formally abandoned; *spec.* an underwriter.

Abandonment (abæ·ndənmĕnt). 1611. [a. Fr. *abandonnement*.] **1.** The action of abandoning, or the condition of being abandoned 1611. **2.** *Comm. Law.* Abandoning an interest or claim; *esp.* in *Marine Insurance* 1809. **3.** Self-abandonment 1860. **4.** = ABANDON *sb.*[3]

1. A. of pretences BURKE, of reason BYRON. **3.** True A...the nearest way to God VAUGHAN. **4.** A manner frank even to a. DISRAELI.

‖**Abandum.** [Med.L.] *Law.* 'Anything sequestered, proscribed, or abandoned'. TOMLINS.

†**A·banet, a·bnet.** 1707. [Heb., *Lev.* viii. 13.] A girdle of fine linen, worn esp. by Jewish priests.

†**Abanni·tion, -ation.** 1656. [f. med.L. *abannire*.] Banishment.

Abarticulation (æ:bɑ̆rti:kiŭlē̆i·ʃən). 1751. [ad. L. *ab-articulatio* = Gr. ἀπάρθρωσις GALEN; see ARTICLE.] *Anat.* Articulation allowing free motion in the joint.

Abase (ăbē̆i·s), *v.* ME. [ad. OFr. *abaissier*, f. *à* + *baissier*:—late L. **bassare*, f. *bassus*. Influenced by *base* adj.] **1.** To lower (physically). *arch.* 1477. **2.** To lower in rank, office, etc.; humiliate; degrade ME. †**3.** To lower in price or value, debase (coin) -1736.

1. To a. one's eyes SHAKS. **2.** He dyd a. hym selfe TONSTALL. To a. the proud 1762. **3.** The peece of ix pence was abaced to sixpence 1569. Hence **Aba·sedly** *adv.* **Aba·ser.**

Abased (ăbē̆i·st), *ppl. a.* 1611. [f. ABASE *v.*] **1.** In the senses of the vb. **2.** *Her.* = Fr. *Abaissé*: Turned downwards, as wings on a shield. Also said of a charge, when lowered; opp. to *enhanced.*

Abasement (ăbē̆i·smĕnt). 1561. [f. as prec.] The action of abasing, or condition of being abased.

Abash (ăbæ·ʃ), *v.* ME. [ad. Anglo-Fr. *abaïss-* = OFr. *esbaïss-*, stem of *esbaïr*, mod. Fr. *ébahir*; f. *es*:—L. *ex* utterly + *bahir* to astound, f. *bah!*] **1.** To destroy the self-possession of, to disconcert with sudden shame, consciousness of error, presumption, etc. ME. †**2.** *intr.* To stand confused, etc. -1585.

1. The lyon with his crye abassheth all other bestes W. DE WORDE. To a. the gainsayer 1863. **2.** The herte of man sholde not abasshe CAXTON. Hence **Aba·shed** *ppl. a.* put to confusion. **Aba·shedly** *adv.* **Aba·shless** *a.* unabashed BROWNING. **Aba·shment,** confusion from shame, etc.

Aba·sk, *adv.* 1866. [A *prep.*[1] 11 + BASK *v.*] Basking.

†‖**Abassi, -s.** 1753. [f. Shah *Abas* II.] A silver coin of Persia, worth about twelve-pence.

†**Aba·stard,** *v.* 1610. [ad. Fr. *abastardir*, f. *à* + *bastard*.] To render bastard; to debase -1651. var. †**Aba·stardize, -ise.**

Abate (ăbē̆i·t), *v.*[1] ME. [a. OFr. *abatre*, f. *à* + *batre*:—late L. *batere* f. cl. L. *batuere*.] **1.** *trans.* To beat down, destroy. *Obs.* exc. in *Law.* Hence, to put an end to; as (*Law*) to *abate* a nuisance, an action, a writ ME. **2.** *intr.* (through *refl.*) To become null and void 1602. †**3.** To bring down physically, socially, or mentally ME. Also †*intr.* Also with *of*: To curtail of -1637. **4.** To bring down in size, amount, value, force ME. Also *intr.* **5.** To lower in force or intensity ME. Also *intr.* **6.** To strike off, apart, deduct ME. **7.** *fig.* To bar or except 1588. **8.** With *of*: To deduct something from. *arch.* 1644. †**9.** *Falconry.* To beat with the wings; *usu.* BATE -1575.

1. Ye gates of Bruges..were abated FABYAN. **2.** Commissions shall not a. by the death of his majesty DE FOE. **3.** Abatid and defouled in helle CHAUCER. *Lear* II. iv. 161. **4.** To a. (= blunt) the edge of envy BACON, the edge of a sword HEYWOOD. The waters were abated *Gen.* viii. 3. To a. a party SCOTT. *intr.* The legacies must a. proportionately 1768. **5.** Nor (was) his naturall force abated *Deut.* xxxiv. 7. **6.** To a. something of his morning price 1866. A. me two shillings a week FRANKLIN. **7.** Abating his brutality, etc. JOHNSON. **8.** The guide abating of his pace SCOTT.

Aba·te, *v.*[2] 1528. [a. Anglo-Fr. *abatre*, earlier *enbatre* (see A- *pref.* 10) + *batre*, in phr. *se enbatre* or *abatre en*. Confused with prec.] *Law. refl.* To thrust oneself tortiously into a tenement between the death of the owner and the accession of the legal heir. Usu. *intr.*

†**Aba·te,** *sb.* ME. [f. ABATE *v.*[1]] Depression, diminution; subtraction.

Abatement[1] (ăbē̆i·tmĕnt). 1513. [a. OFr. *abatement*, f. *abatre*; see ABATE *v.*[1]] **1.** The action of abating; the being abated (see quots.). **2.** The result of abating; decrease, deduction, drawback 1624. *lit.* and *fig.*, and *techn.* in *Comm.* **3.** *Her.* A mark of depreciation 1610.

1. A. of writs PERKINS, of nuisances BLACKSTONE. *Plea in a.*, a defendant's plea, showing cause against being impleaded or sued. Much a. of my hopes CROMWELL. A. of a storm 1794, of the energies 1878. **2.** An A. to his Riches BACON. An a. out of the purchase money LD. ST. LEONARDS.

Aba·tement[2]. ME. [a. Anglo-Fr. *abatement*, f. *abatre*; see ABATE *v.*[2]] The action of abating; tortious entry.

Aba·ter[1]. 1732. [f. ABATE *v.*[1] + -ER[1].] He who or that which abates.

Aba·ter[2]. 1660. [f. ABATE *v.*[1] + -ER[4].] A plea in abatement.

Abatis (æ·bătis), **Abattis.** 1766. [a. Fr. *abatis*:—late L. **abateticius*; cf. vb. *abatre*.] *Mil.* A defence formed by placing felled trees lengthwise one over the other with their branches towards the enemy's line. Hence **A·batised** *ppl. a.*

‖**Abatjour** (abaʒū·r). [Fr.] A skylight.

Abator[1] (abē̆i·təɹ, -tǭɹ). 1592. [See ABATE *v.*[1]] **1.** One who abates a nuisance, etc. **2.** = ABATER[1]. 1592.

Aba·tor[2]. 1531. [a. Anglo-Fr., f. *abatre* = *enbatre*.] One who abates; see ABATE *v.*[2]

‖**Abattoir** (abatwā·r). 1840. [Fr. See ABATE *v.*[1]] A public slaughter-house for cattle.

Abature (æ·bătiŭr). 1575. [a. Fr. *abatture*.] The traces of a stag in the underwood.

†**Aba·ve,** *v.* ME. [? a. OFr. *abaubir*, repr. L. *ad* + *balbum*.] To put or be put to confusion. var. Abaw(e.

Aba·xial, *a.* 1857. *Bot.* = ABAXILE.

Abaxile (æb,æ·ksəil), *a.* 1854. [f. L. *ab* + *axis*.] Off the axis; eccentric.

†**Abay** (abē̆i·). ME. [a. OFr. *abai*; cf. mod.Fr. *aboi*, and see BAY *sb.*[4]] **1.** Barking; esp. when closing round the prey. The dogs then *stand at a.*, and the prey *is at a.* (mod. *at bay*). Hence **2.** To be in extremities -1670.

2. Like a wild Beast at abbay MILT.

Abb (æb). OE. [f. A- *pref.* 1 + WEB; cf. OE. *āwef, ōwef* whence WOOF.] The woof or weft in a web. Also *attrib.*

‖**Abba** (æ·bă). ME. [Aramaic.] Father. **1.** An invocation, 'Abba, father' (*Mark* xiv. 36). **2.** A title given to bishops and patriarchs in Syriac and Coptic churches.

Abbacy (æ·băsi). ME. [ABBATIE, assimilated to *prelacy*, etc. Orig. Sc.] The office, or term of office, of an abbot.

‖**Abbate** (abbā·te). [It.] An Italian abbot; = Fr. *abbé*. †**A·bbatess, A·bbotess.** OE. [f. L. *abbatissa*, fem. of *abbas*.] = ABBESS.

Abbatial (ăbē̆i·ʃăl), *a.* 1642. [a. Fr., ad. late L. *abbatialis*.] Of or pertaining to an abbacy, abbot, or abbess. var. †**Abba·tical.**

†**A·bbatie.** ME. [ad. late L. *abbatia*, f. *abbatem*.] = ABBACY.

‖**Abbé** (abe). 1780. [Fr.] The Fr. equivalent of Eng. *abbot*, but in France extended to every one who wears an ecclesiastical dress (Littré). Cf. Ital. ABBATE.

Abbess (æ·bės). [ME. *abbesse*, a. OFr. :—late L. *abbatissa*, fem. of *abbatem*.] The female superior of a nunnery.

Abbey (æ·bi). [ME. *abbeye*, a. OFr. *abeïe*, *abbaïe* (mod. *abbaye*) :—late L. *abbatia*, f. *abbatem*.] **1.** A society of *monks* governed by an *abbot*, or of *nuns* under an *abbess*. Hence—**a.** the office of an abbot. **b.** the corporation. **c.** the buildings. **2.** The Abbey Church, as *Westminster A.* 1557. Also, as in *Battle A.*, of residences which were once abbeys. **3.** *Scotl.*: The precincts of the A. of Holyrood, as a sanctuary for debtors 1709.

Abbot (æ·bət). [OE. *abbad*, *abbod*, a. *abbadem*, Rom. pronunc. of L. *abbatem*, f. *abbas*, a. Gr. ἀββᾶς, ad. Syriac; see ABBA.] The head or superior of an abbey OE. After the Reformation, occ. applied to the layman to whom the revenues were impropriated.

Ansealm a. of S. Ædmund *O.E. Chron.* The lay a. of Marney DISRAELI. *Abbat of the people*, a Genoese magistrate. †*A. of Misrule*, †*A. of Unreason*, applied ironically to the leader in mediæval revels. Hence **A·bbotcy, A·bbotship** = ABBACY.

†A·bbotric. OE. [f. ABBOT + -RIC = OE. *rice* kingdom.] An abbacy -1711.

Abbreviate (ăbrī·viₗĕt), *ppl. a.* 1530. [ad. L. *abbreviatus*, f. *abbreviare*, f. *ab* or? *ad* + *breviare*, f. *brevis*.] **A.** *adj.* †**a.** = ABBREVIATED. **b.** *Nat. Hist.* Relatively short. †**B.** *sb.* An abridgement -1716.

Abbreviate (ăbrī·viₗeit), *v.* 1450. [f. prec. Cf. ABRIDGE.] †**1.** *trans.* To shorten by omitting details -1672; to epitomize -1648; in *Math.*, to reduce to lower terms -1796; †*intr.* to speak or write briefly -1622. **2.** *trans.* To shorten by cutting off a part (see quots.).

1. It is one thing to a. by contracting, another by cutting off BACON. 2. Of time, etc.: To a. one's life BURTON, Devotions FULLER, the long way MILT. So of vowels, etc.: To make short. Of words or symbols: To contract (*the common mod. use*); Exancester abbreviated to .. Exeter DE FOE. Hence **Abbre·viated** *ppl. a.* = ABBREVIATE *ppl. a.* †**Abbre·viately** *adv.*

Abbreviation (ăbrīviₗēi·ʃən). 1460. [a. Fr. *abréviation*, ad. L. *abbreviationem*; see ABBREVIATE *ppl. a.*] **1.** The act of abbreviating 1530. **2.** The result of abbreviating 1460; an abridgement; *esp.* of a word or symbol 1727.

2. Smiffle is..an a. for Smithfield THACKERAY.

Abbreviator (ăbrī·viₗeitəɹ). 1532. [a. L.] **1.** One who abbreviates 1615. **2.** An officer who draws up the pope's briefs 1532. †**3.** A school of physicians so named 1605.

Abbre·viature. 1614. [f. L. *abbreviat-*, *abbreviare*.] †**1.** Abbreviation -1673; an abbreviated condition -1650. **2.** An abridgement 1650; a contraction 1630.

2. To write by abbreviatures SIR T. BROWNE.

A B C (ēⁱ·bī·sī·), *sb.* ME. **1.** The alphabet. [So in OFr.] †**2.** An alphabetical acrostic -1597. **3.** A spelling-book, or primer ME.; hence *fig.* the first elements (of a subject). Also *attrib.*, as in **ABC-** or **abcee-book**.

2. Chaucer's A B C, called *La Prière de Nostre Dame* SPEGHT. 3. The A B C of religion FARRAR.

‖**Abdest** (ā·bdest). [Pers.] The Mohammedan rite of washing the hands before prayer.

Abdicate (æ·bdikeit), *v.* 1541. [f. L. *abdicat-*, *abdicare*.] **1.** *trans.* To disown; *esp.* to disinherit children (= L. *abdicare filium*) 1541. †**2.** To depose *from* 1621; esp. *refl.* to divest oneself of an office (L. *abdicare se magistratu*) -1689. †**3.** To discard -1689. **4.** To give up (a right, office, etc.) either formally or by default 1633. **5.** *absol.* (by ellipsis). To renounce sovereignty, etc. 1704.

1. To a. and disinherit children MILT. 2. King James had by demise abdicated himself EVELYN. 3. To a. idolatry BP. HALL. 4. To a. thrones DE FOE, authority PRESCOTT, a power RUSKIN. Hence **A·bdicable** *a.* **A·bdicant** *adj.* abdicating; *sb.* one who abdicates. **A·bdica·tive** *a.* causing or implying abdication. **A·bdica·tor.**

A·bdicated, *ppl. a.* 1688. [f. prec.] **1.** Formally renounced (of a possession, right, etc.). **2.** Deposed (see ABDICATE 2), self-deposed 1691.

Abdication (æbdikēⁱ·ʃən). 1552. [ad. L. *abdicationem*; see ABDICATE.] **1.** The action of formally disowning. Now only techn. in Rom. Law. †**2.** Deposition 1660. **3.** Resignation (formal or virtual); *esp.* of sovereignty, etc. 1618. **4.** *Comm. Law.* Surrender of ownership to underwriters 1755.

3. A. of all power and authority BURKE. The A. of Licinius GIBBON.

A·bditory. 1658. [ad. L. *abditorium*.] A concealed repository.

Abdomen (æbdōᵘ·mĕn, æ·bdŏmen). 1541. [ad. L. *abdomen*, of unknown and much disputed origin.] †**1.** *orig.* Fat round the belly -1692. **2.** *Anat.* The belly; the lower cavity of the body from the diaphragm downwards, sometimes including the pelvic cavity; often in *Nat. Hist.* the outer surface of the belly 1615. **3.** *Zool.* In some *Arthropoda* (insects, spiders, etc.), the posterior division of the body 1788.

Abdominal (æbdǫ·minăl). 1746. [ad. mod.L. *abdominalis*, f. *abdomen*.] **A.** *adj.* **1.** *Anat.* and *Zool.* Of or pertaining to the abdomen. **2.** *Zool.* Epithet of an order of fishes; see **B.** **B.** *sb.* An abdominal fish; in *pl.* **Abdominals,** ‖**Abdominales,** an order of soft-finned osseous fishes, having the ventral fins under the abdomen and behind the pectorals.

‖**Abdominalia** (æbdǫ:minēⁱ·liă). [mod.L., pl. neut. of *abdominalis*; see ABDOMINAL: sc. *animalia*; see prec.] *Zool.* An order of the Cirripedes, having three abdominal segments bearing three pairs of cirri.

Abdominoscopy (æbdǫ:minǫ·skŏpi). [mod. f. L. *abdomen* + Gr. -σκοπία.] Examining the abdomen for disease by percussion, inspection, measurement, etc.

Abdo·minous, *a.* 1651. [f. L. *abdomen*.] Big-bellied.

Abdu·ce, *v. arch.* 1537. [ad. L. *abducere*.] = ABDUCT.

If we a. the eye into either corner SIR T. BROWNE.

Abducent (æbdiū·sĕnt), *ppl. a.* 1713. [ad. L. *abducentem*; see prec.] Drawing away or out. Chiefly *Anat.*, as *abducent* muscles, nerves. Opp. to *adducent*.

Abduct (æbdʌ·kt), *v.* 1834. [f. L. *abductum*, *abducere*; see the earlier ABDUCE.] **1.** To lead or take away illegally; to kidnap. **2.** To draw away (a limb, etc.) from its natural position 1836.

Abduction (æbdʌ·kʃən). 1626. [ad. L. *abductionem*; cf. Fr. *abduction*.] **1.** A leading away. **2.** *spec.* Carrying off or leading away illegally a wife, child, voter, etc. 1768. **3.** *Phys.* Withdrawing a limb, etc. outward from the medial line 1666. **4.** *Surg.* The separation of contiguous parts after a transverse fracture 1753. **5.** *Logic.* A syllogism, with the major premiss certain, the minor only probable; apagoge 1696.

Abductor (æbdʌ·ktəɹ). 1615. [a. mod.L. *abductor*.] **1.** *Anat.* A muscle which draws any part of the body from its normal position, or from the median line. Also *attrib.* **2.** One who abducts 1847.

A-be. *Sc.* [Prob. = *at be*, north. inf. = to be.] In *let a be*: let alone SCOTT.

Abeam (ăbī·m), *adv.* 1836. [f. A *prep.*[1] + BEAM *sb.*] *Naut.* In a line at right angles to the ship's length, opposite to its centre; abreast. Const. *of*.

Abear (ăbēᵊ·ɹ), *v.* [OE. *aberan*, f. A- *pref.* 1 + *beran*.] †**1.** To bear, carry OE. **2.** To endure, with *cannot*. *dial.* or *vulgar.* OE. †**3.** *refl.* To demean oneself 1596.

2. She couldn't a. the men DICKENS. 3. Thus did the knight himselfe a. SPENSER. Hence †**Abea·r** *sb.* **Abea·rance.** †**Abea·ring** *vbl. sb.* behaviour.

Abecedarian (ēⁱ:bīsīdē·riăn); also **ABCD-arian; abcedarian.** 1603. [f. med.L. *abecedarius* (see ABECEDARY).] **A.** *adj.* **1.** Pertaining to the alphabet; arranged alphabetically, as *A. psalms*, e. g. the 119th 1665. **2.** Pertaining to one learning the alphabet 1651. **B.** *sb.* A teacher or learner of A B C or rudiments 1603.

Abecedary (ēⁱ:bīsī·dări), *a.* and *sb.*[1] 1580. [ad. med.L. *abecedarius*, f. ABCD.] = ABECEDARIAN.

†**Abece·dary,** *sb.*[2] ME. [ad. med.L. *abecedarium*; see prec.] An ABC-book; a primer -1660.

Abed (ăbe·d), *adv.* OE. [A *prep.*[1] = OE. *on* + BED *sb.*] In bed (*arch.*); laid up 1660.

The King's a bed *Macb.* II. i. 12. A. with gout 1873. To bring a-bed: to deliver of a child. Usu. *pass.* Also *fig.*

†**Abe·de,** *v.* OE. [f. *a-* back + *bēodan*.] To announce.

Abedge, abeie, etc., obs. ff. ABYE *v.*

Abei·gh, *adv. Sc.* 1707. [?] At a shy distance, aloof.

Abele (ăbī·l, ēⁱ·bĕl). 1681. [a. Du. *abeel*, a. OFr. *abel*:—late L. *albellus*, dim. of L. *albus*.] The white poplar (*Populus alba*).

Plantations..of abeles SWIFT.

Abe·lian, A·belite, Abelo·nian. 1751. [f. *Abel*, Gen. iv. 8.] *Eccl. Hist.* One of a sect of heretics in Africa, said by Augustine of Hippo to have lived in continence after marriage, like 'righteous Abel'.

Abelmosk (ēⁱ·b'lmǫsk). [(ult.) ad. Arab. *ḥabbu-'lmisk* father of musk.] A genus of plants of the order *Malvaceæ*.

Aberdevine (æ·bəɹdĕvəi:n). 1735. [?] A bird, the Siskin (*Carduelis spinus*), closely related to the goldfinch.

Abernethy (æ·bəɹnī:þi). 1837. [?] A hard biscuit flavoured with caraway-seeds.

†**Abe·rr,** *v.* 1536. [ad. L. *aberrare*.] To go astray -1658. Also *fig.*

Aberrance (ăbe·răns). 1665. [f. ABERRANT.] The action of straying; vagary. So **Abe·rrancy,** the quality or condition of being aberrant 1646.

Aberrant (ăbe·rănt), *a.* 1830. [ad. L. *aberrantem*, *aberrare*.] **1.** Straying from the right path. *lit.* and *fig.* 1848. **2.** Deviating from the normal type; *esp.* in *Nat. Hist.* 1830.

Aberrate (æ·bĕreit), *v. rare.* 1765. [f. L. *aberrat-*, *aberrare*.] To diverge from the straight path; to produce aberration, as in optics.

Aberration (æbĕrēⁱ·ʃən). 1594. [ad. L. *aberrationem*.] **1.** The action of wandering away. *lit.* and *fig.* 1615. **2.** A wandering of the intellect 1823. **3.** Deviation from the normal type 1846. **4.** *Optics.* The non-convergence of rays of light to one focus 1753. **5.** *Astron.* An apparent displacement of a heavenly body, occasioned by the joint effect of the earth's motion and the non-instantaneous transmission of light; called also *aberration of light* 1856.

1. A comet with long aberrations CARLYLE. *fig.* The aberrations of my life BP. HALL. 2. Shades of mental a. SCOTT. 3. Aberrations of structure and of function BUCKLE. 4. *Spherical a.*, that due to the failure of a spherical mirror to cause all the rays to meet in one point. *Chromatic a.*, that due to the different refrangibilities of the coloured constituents of white light. 5. *Diurnal a.*, that due to the motion of the earth on its axis. *Annual a.*, that due to motion in its orbit. *Planetary a.*, that due to the motion of the planet while its light is passing to the earth. Hence **Aberra·tional** *a.* eccentric.

†**Aberu·ncate,** *v.* [f. *aberuncare*, erron. f. *averruncare*.] To extirpate. **Aberuncator,** erron. f. AVERRUNCATOR, an instrument for lopping trees.

Abet (ăbe·t), *v.* ME. [a. OFr. *abeter*, f. *à* + *beter* to hound on.] †**1.** To urge on -1587. **2.** *esp.* in a bad sense: To incite, instigate († *to*, or *in*) 1590. †**3.** To maintain, uphold -1725. **4.** *esp.* in a bad sense: To encourage, countenance 1779.

2. He will a. them in their damnable courses 1593. 3. To a. their opinions SIR T. BROWNE, the cause of truth WOLLASTON. 4. To a. vice and vanity JOHNSON, an invasion FREEMAN. Hence **Abe·tter;** see ABETTOR. **Abe·tting** *vbl. sb.*

†**Abet,** *sb.* ME. [a. OFr. *abet*; see prec.] **1.** Fraud -1460. **2.** Encouragement (of an offence) -1596. SPENSER.

Abetment (ăbe·tmĕnt). ME. [ad. Anglo-Fr. *abetement*; see ABET.] **1.** The action or fact of abetting (*usu.* an offence). †**2.** Deception -1586. †**3.** A bet -1615. var. **Abe·ttal.**

Abettor (ăbe·təɹ, -oɹ). Also **Abetter,** exc. in *Law.* 1514. [a. Anglo-Fr. *abettour*, f. *abeter*; see ABET.] **1.** *Law* and *gen.* One who abets an offence 1514. **2.** *gen.* A supporter, adherent 1580. Now only in a *bad* sense.

Abevacuation (æ:bĭvæ:kiu,ēⁱ·ʃən). 1851. [f. L. *ab*+EVACUATION: cf. *ab-articulation*.] *Med.* An incomplete evacuation. Also evacuation by the passage of matter from one organ into another.

Abeyance (ăbēⁱ·ăns). 1528. [a. Anglo-Fr. *abeiance*, f. *abeer, abaher* to gape after; f. *à* + *beer, baer, bader*:—late L. *badare*.] **1.** *Law.* Expectation or contemplation of law; the position of being without an owner 1528. **2.** A state of suspension; dormant condition 1660.

1. In a., that is to say alonely in the remembrance.. and consideration of the lawe *Littleton's Tenures*. **2.** His honour is in a. BURKE. Hence **Abey·ancy,** a state of abeyance. **Abey·ant** *a.* dormant.

Abhominable, abhomination, etc., the spelling of ABOMINABLE, etc., in OFr. and in Eng. to 17th c., as if f. *ab homine*, 'inhuman, beastly'. So †**Abhominal** *a.* –1659.

Abhor (ǣbhǭ·ɹ), *v.* 1449. [ad. L. *abhorrere*.] †**1.** *trans.* To shrink from with horror. *lit.* and *fig.* 1449. †**2.** To cause horror or disgust (usu. *impers.*) –1604. †**3.** *intr.* To shrink with horror *from* –1656. †**4.** To differ entirely *from* –1671.

1. *fig.* To a. all manner of meate *Ps.* cvii. 18. Which.. ye abhorre to doe MILTON. **2.** It do's abhorre me *Oth.* IV. ii. 162. **3.** The Italians abhorring from being sea men 1617. Hence **Abho·rred** *ppl. a.* detested; horrified *Haml.* v. i. 206. **Abho·rring** *vbl. sb.* = ABHORRENCE 1, 3; †*ppl. a.* repulsive.

Abhorrence (ǣbhǫ·rĕns). 1660. [f. ABHORRENT *a.*] **1.** The action of abhorring 1660. **2.** An expression of abhorrence; in *Eng. Hist.*, applied to certain addresses presented to Charles II. 1678. **3.** That which excites abhorrence 1752.

1. Out of a just Abhorrence of such a..Council, etc. *Address to Chas. II* 1680. (Hence sense 2.) **3.** Politics are my a. COWPER.

†**Abho·rrency.** 1605. [f. as prec.] **1.** The quality of being abhorrent –1709. **2.** = ABHORRENCE 3.

Abhorrent (ǣbhǫ·rĕnt), *ppl. a.* 1619. [ad. L. *abhorrentem*; see ABHOR.] **1.** Abhorring; having abhorrence *of* 1749. **2.** Opposed *to* 1619; repugnant, inconsistent 1720. **3.** Abhorred 1833.

1. A. of excess 1869. **2.** The persons most a. from blood and treason BURKE. Similars are not a. from similars 1822. Not a. to nature KEMBLE. **3.** Pride, a. as it is J. TAYLOR. Hence **Abho·rrently** *adv.*

Abhorrer (ǣbhǫ·rəɹ). 1611. [f. ABHOR *v.*] **1.** One who abhors. **2.** *Eng. Hist.* One who signed an address of ABHORRENCE 1680.

‖**Abib** (ēⁱ·bib). [Heb.; = a spike of corn.] A Jewish month, 1st of the eccl. year, 7th of the civil year, called later Nisan.

Abichite (æ·bikəit). [f. Dr. *Abich*.] *Min.* = CLINOCLASITE.

Abidance (ăbəi·dăns). 1647. [f. ABIDE *v.*] **1.** Abiding, dwelling. var. Abid[illegible]. **2.** With *by*: Conformity to 1875.

1. A. in the holy hill FULLER. **2.** A. by rules HELPS.

Abide (ăbəi·d), *v. str.* Pa. t. **abode,** also **abided.** Pa. pple. **abode, abided, abidden.** [OE. *abídan*, f. A- *pref.* 1+*bídan*; see BIDE. Orig. *intrans.* with gen. of the obj.]

I. *intr.* **1.** To wait, stay, remain OE. **2.** To reside ME. **3.** To continue to be ME. **4.** To abide *by*: to remain with, true to 1509. **5.** To stand firm 1398.

1. A. you here with the asse *Gen.* xxii. 5 Tho' much is taken, much abides TENNYSON. Their guilt..abides upon you LAW. **2.** Neither abode in any house *Luke* viii. 27. **3.** The town abode frenche LD. BERNERS. **4.** To a. by authority JUNIUS, measures EDGEWORTH, rules TYNDALL. **5.** But thou Lorde.. abydest COVERDALE.

II. *trans.* **1.** To wait for, await the issue of, endure ME. **2.** To await defiantly, to face ME. **3.** To await submissively ME. **4.** To put up with (now only in neg. and interrog. sentences) 1526.

1. Abit his tyme JAMES I. A. my removal SCOTT. The fiery lake which abideth him E. IRVING. **2.** To a. the brunt of the service CROMWELL, battle SCOTT. **3.** To abyde the lawe CAXTON. To a. thy Kingly doome *Rich. II*, v. vi. 23. **4.** I cannot a. physic 1585, the country MARTINEAU.

¶ Occas. confused with ABYE = pay for, as in *Jul. Cæs.* III. ii. 119. Hence **Abi·ding** *vbl. sb.* the action or state of one who abides; †an abode; hence **abiding-place,** place of abode; *ppl. a.* lasting, and in comb. **law-abiding,** adhering to the law. **Abi·dingly** *adv.*

Abider (ăbəi·dəɹ). 1543. [f. ABIDE *v.*] One who abides (see ABIDE *v.* I. 1, 2; II. 2).

Abietene (æ·bi,ĕtīn). 1875. [f. L. *abietem*.] A hydro-carbon distilled from the resin or balsam of the nut-pine (*Pinus sabiniana*).

Abietic (æbi,e·tik), *a.* 1864. [f. L. *abietem*.] *Chem.* Of or pertaining to fir. *Abietic acid*, a monobasic acid, $C_{20}H_{30}O_2$, the essential constituent of resin.

Abietin(e (æ·bi,ĕtin). [f. L. *abietem*.] *Chem.* A neutral resin extracted from Strasburg turpentine or Canada balsam, products of *Abies* or fir. Hence **Abieti·nic** *a.*, as *abietinic acid*, a bibasic resinous acid, $C_{44}H_{64}O_5$, obtained from species of fir.

Abietite (æ·bi,ĕtəit). [f. L. *abietem*.] *Chem.* A sugar, $C_6H_8O_3$, obtained from the needles of the silver-fir, analogous to mannite.

Abigail (æ·bigeⁱl). 1666. [f. the name of the 'waiting gentlewoman' in *The Scornful Lady* (Beau. & Fl.); also see 1 *Sam.* xxv. 24, 31.] A lady's-maid. Hence **A·bigailship.**

An antiquated A., dressed in her lady's cast clothes SMOLLETT.

†**Abiliment,** obs. f. HABILIMENT.

Ability (ăbi·lĭti). ME. [a. OFr. *ableté*:—L. *habilitatem*, f. *habilis*; see ABLE.] †**1.** Fitness –1678. **2.** Capacity in an agent. **3.** Bodily or mental power 1549. **4.** Pecuniary power *arch.* 1502. **5.** A power of the mind, a faculty. Usu. *pl.* 1587.

2. Abilite to lerne sciences CHAUCER. Habilitie to annoy HOOKER. Of a. in law to take liverie of seisin 1528. **3.** A. to lift a great stone 1576. Inferior to Condorcet in point of a. BUCKLE. **4.** Out of my leane and low a. Ile lend you something *Twel. N.* III. iv. 378. **5.** His abilities were useful rather than splendid GIBBON.

†**Abi·me.** Earliest f. ABYSM –1616.

Abiogenesis (æ:bio,dʒe·nĕsis). 1870. [f. Gr. ἄβιος (f. ἀ + βίος) + γένεσις; see GENESIS.] *Biol.* The production of living by not-living matter; 'spontaneous generation.' (Introduced by Prof. Huxley in *Brit. Assoc. Rep.* lxxvi.) Hence **A:biogene·tic** *a.* **A:biogene·tically** *adv.* **A:bio·genist,** one who believes in a. **A:bio·genous** *a.* produced by spontaneous generation. **A:bio·geny** = ABIOGENESIS.

Abiological (æ:biŏlǫ·dʒikăl), *a.* [f. Gr. ἀ not + BIOLOGICAL.] Pertaining to the study of inanimate things.

Abirritate (æb,i·riteⁱt), *v.* [f. L. *ab* + IRRITATE.] *Med.* To diminish irritation. Hence **Abi·rritant** *a.* and *sb.* a soothing agent. **Abi:rrita·tion** *Med.*, a depressed condition (opp. to irritation) of the tissues. **Abi·rritative** *a.*

Abit, obs. 3rd sing. of ABIDE *v.*

Abject (æ·bdʒĕkt), *ppl. a.* ME. [ad. L. *abjectus*. Orig. *abje·ct*, pple. and adj. Later, replaced by *abjected* as pple, *a·bject* remaining as adj. and sb.] †**1.** *pple.* Cast off, rejected –1614. **2.** *adj.* Cast down, brought low in condition, low-lying 1520. **3.** Low in regard, mean-spirited, despicable 1548. As *sb.* 1534.

2. A. fortune MILT. The a. heirs of an illustrious name MACAULAY. **3.** Seruile, a. drudges 2 *Hen. VI*, IV. i. 105. An a. liar MACAULAY. *sb.* Servants and abjects flout me G. HERBERT. Hence **A·bjectly** *adv.* **A·bjectness.**

†**Abje·ct,** *v.* 1475. [f. prec. Cf. *content* vb. from adj.] **1.** To cast off, *lit.* and *fig.* –1650; to cast down, degrade –1640. Hence †**Abje·cted** *ppl. a.*, †**Abje·ctedness.**

Abjection (ǣbdʒe·kʃən). ME. [a. Fr., ad. L. *abjectionem*; see ABJECT *a.*] †**1.** The action of casting down –1653. **2.** The condition of one cast down, degradation, low estate ME. †**3.** The action of casting off; rejection –1655. †**4.** That which is cast off; refuse. Usu. *fig.* –1534.

2. A. of mind or seruilitie HOOKER. The a. and uncivilisedness of Glasgow M. ARNOLD. **3.** A. from God 1607. **4.** These dregges and a. of all menn 1534.

Abjudge (ǣbdʒʊ·dʒ), *v. rare.* 1855. [f. L. *ab* + JUDGE *v.*] To take away by judicial decision. Opp. to *adjudge*.

Abjudicate (ǣbdʒⁱū·dikeⁱt), *v. Obs.* 1602. [f. L. *abjudicat-, abjudicare*.] **1.** To pass judgement against; reject as illegal. **2.** =ABJUDGE. Hence **Abju:dica·tion.**

†**A·bjugate,** *v.* [f. L. *abjugat-, abjugare*.] To unyoke.

†**Abju·nct,** *ppl. a.* 1610. [ad. L. *abjunctus*.] Disjoined. Hence **Abju·nctive** *a. rare.*

Abjuration (æ:bdʒurēⁱ·ʃən). 1514. [ad. L. *abjurationem*; see ABJURE.] **1.** Renunciation on oath; forswearing (*esp.* of heresies). Also *fig.* **2.** Official repudiation on oath of any principle 1650.

1. A. of his blasphemous heresies FULLER. *fig.* An a. of friendship 1842. **2.** A. of doctrines of the Church of Rome 1726. Hence *Oath of Abjuration*, i.e. disclaiming allegiance to the Pretender or any one claiming through him. *Abjuration of the realm, a town*, etc.; an oath taken to leave it for ever.

Abjure (ǣbdʒⁱū·əɹ), *v.* 1480. [a. Fr. *abjurer*, ad. L. *abjurare*.] **1.** To renounce on oath; to recant 1501. *trans.* and *absol.* †**2.** To cause to recant –1542. **3.** To disclaim solemnly; to reject upon oath 1597. Also *absol.*

1. This..Magicke I heere a. *Temp.* v. i. 51. **2.** All such must be burned, or ellis ab-Iuryd THYNNE. **3.** To a. pleasures MILT., the badges of Popery MACAULAY, the Pretender 1863. *To a. the realm*, etc.: to swear to leave it for ever. Hence **Abju·rement, Abju·rer.**

‖**Abkari** (ăbkā·ri), also **abcaree.** 1797. [Pers.] The manufacture or sale of spirits; hence, in Anglo-Ind., the excise duty on such manufacture, etc.

†**Abla·ctate,** *v. rare.* [f. L. *ablactat-, ablactare*.] To wean from the breast.

Ablactation (æblǣktēⁱ·ʃən). 1656. [ad. L. *ablactationem*; see prec.] **1.** The weaning of the young from the mother. **2.** *Hort.* Grafting by approach, inarching 1676.

†**Abla·queate,** *v. rare.* ME. [f. L. *ablaqueat-, ablaqueare* to disentangle.] To loosen or remove the soil round roots. Hence †**Ablaquea·tion.**

Ablaste·mic, *a.* 1881. [f. Gr. ἀ + βλάστημος.] Non-germinal.

†**Abla·te,** *v. rare.* 1542. [f. L. *ablat-, auferre*.] To take away.

Ablation (æblēⁱ·ʃən). 1577. [ad. L. *ablationem*; see prec.] **1.** The action of taking away. † **2.** *Med.* Subsidence of acute symptoms 1671. **3.** *Surg.* Surgical removal of any part of the body 1846. **4.** *Geol.* Surface waste of rocks or glaciers 1860.

1. Ablations of goods HAKLUYT. **2.** The a. of the disease 1671. **3.** A. of the nipple, the mamma MILLER. **4.** The a. of the ice TYNDALL.

Ablatitious (æblăti·ʃəs), *a.* 1833. [f. L. *ablatus*; see ABLATE.] Tending to take away, diminishing. *A. force* (*Astr.*), that which diminishes the gravitation of a satellite towards its planet.

Ablative (æ·blătiv), *a.* and *sb.* ME. [a. Fr. *ablatif, -ive*, ad. L. *ablativus*; see ABLATE.] **1.** *Gram.* Name of a case found in L. and other Aryan languages, but not in Gr., and expressing primarily *direction from* a place, or *time*. In L. it expressed also the *source, cause, instrument* and *agent, manner*, and sometimes *place* and *time* of an action or event. Often used as *sb.* [sc. *case*.] †**2.** = prec. –1713.

1. We learn from a fragment of Cæsar's work, *De Analogia*, that he was the inventor of the term a. in Latin MAX MÜLLER. *A. absolute*, in L. Grammar, an a. case of a noun with a participle in concord, expressing the time, occasion, etc. of a fact stated, as *sole oriente, tenebræ aufugiunt*. **2.** A. directions ..to vnteach error BP. HALL.

Abla·tor. *Surg.* Instrument used in ablation.

‖**Ablaut** (a·blaut). 1871. [mod. Germ.] *Philol.* Vowel permutation, as in *sing, sang, song, sung*, uninfluenced by a succeeding vowel (contrast *Umlaut*).

Ablaze (ăblēⁱ·z), *adv.* and *a.*, prop. **a blaze;** earlier **on blaze.** ME. [f. A *prep.*[1] + BLAZE.] In a blaze. Also *fig.* In brilliant colours 1851. In the glow of excitement 1840.

Set a. by lightning TYNDALL. *fig.* A. with gorse and broom BLACK. A. with anger J. D. LONG.

Able (ēⁱ·b'l), *a.* ME. [a. OFr. *hable, able* (mod. Fr. *habile*):—L. *habilem* 'easy to be handled', hence 'fit'. In Eng. the silent *h* was dropped, though *habile*, refash. after Fr. or L., still exists.]

I. *pass.* †**1.** Complaisant ME.; manageable

-1710. †2. Suitable -1717. †3. Liable (*to*) *Obs.* exc. *dial.* ME.

1. The Hands are the most habil members of the Body 1710. 2. To the next a. Tree with him BROME.

II. *act.* 1. Having the qualifications for, and means of, doing anything; having sufficient *power* ME. *spec.* Legally qualified 1708. †2. Strong, materially or physically, vigorous -1690; wealthy -1665. 3. Having mental power 1577.

1. Abeler þen þow To alle manere gode *c* 1450. A. to take care of myself TYNDALL. *spec. Admission*.. in Law is when .. the Bishop allows a clerk to be a. 1708. 2. Of a. bodie *All's Well* IV. v. 86. A very a. citizen in Gracious Street PEPYS. 3. A. pastours 1587, men *Ex.* xviii. 21, heads DRYDEN. An abler general 1792. *Comb.* **a.-bodied** *a.* having a body free from disability and fit for service; hence **-bodiedness.** Hence †**A·bleness.**

†Able, *v.* ME. [f. ABLE *a.* Cf. Fr. *habiller.*] 1. *trans.* To fit; make ready. (Const. *to, into, unto.*) -1583. 2. To attire 1450. 3. = ENABLE. -1693. 4. To make strong; to empower legally -1631; hence, to vouch for 1605.

3. If God shall me a. EVELYN. 4. I'll a. 'em *Lear* IV. vi. 172. Hence **A·bling** *vbl. sb.*

-able, a. Fr. *-able*:—L. *-abilem*, adj. suffix, added to vbs. in *-are*, Fr. *-er*. Orig. found only in words from OFr., but later extended to native wds., as *bearable*, etc., helped by form-association with ABLE *a.* Now always *pass.*

Ablegate (æ·blĭgeᶦt), *sb.* [ad. L. *ablegatus*; see next.] A papal envoy, who brings to a newly-appointed cardinal his insignia of office.

†A·blegate, *v. rare.* 1657. [f. L. *ablegat-, ablegare.*] To send abroad or to a distance -1665. Hence **†Ablega·tion.**

†Able·nd, *v.* OE. [f. A- *pref.* 1 + *blendan.*] To blind (temporarily). Also *fig.* -ME.

†Ablepsy, *rare.* 1652. [ad. L. *ablepsia*; a. Gr.] Blindness. *lit.* and *fig.*

†Ablesse. Coined by CHAPMAN, after *noblesse*, etc.

Ablet (æ·blėt), also **ablen.** [a. Fr. *ablette*, dim. of *able*:—late L. *abula* = *albula.*] A fish, the Bleak, *Leuciscus alburnus.*

Ablings, -ins (ēᶦ·blinz), *adv. north.* 1597. [f. ABLE *a.*] Possibly.

Abloom (ăblū̆·m), *adv.* 1855. [A *prep.*[1]] In or into bloom.

†Ablow·, *v.* OE. [f. A- *pref.* 1 + *blaw-an.*] 1. To blow upon or into. *lit.* and *fig.* -ME. 2. *intr.* and *trans.* To puff up. *lit.* and *fig.* -ME.

†Ablu·de, *v. rare.* 1612. [ad. L. *abludere.*] To differ (*from*) -1655.

Abluent (æ·bluĕnt). 1751. [ad. L. *abluentem.*] *Med.* A. *adj.* Washing away (impurities). B. *sb.* An abstergent.

Ablush (ăblɒ·ʃ), *adv.* and *a.* 1852. [A *prep.*[1]] Blushing.

†Ablu·ted, *ppl. a.* 1650. [pa. pple. of vb. **ablute*; f. L. *abluere.*] Washed away.

Ablution (æblᶦū·ʃən). ME. [ad. L. *ablutionem.*] 1. The act of washing clean: *spec.* †a. Of substances, in Alchemy and Chem. -1754. b. Of the body: as a religious rite 1533; generally 1748. c. Of chalice and paten after, and, in Rom. Ch., of the priest's hands before, during, and after, the celebration. 2. The water, etc., used in ablution; *spec.* the wine and water used to rinse the chalice and wash the priest's hands after the communion 1718. †b. A lotion 1671.

1 b. Ablutions, in the East, .. a part of religious worship STANLEY. The scanty ablutions of the morning 1859. 2. Cast the ablutions in the main POPE. Hence **Ablu·tionary** *a.*

Ably (ēᶦ·bli), *adv.* ME. [f. ABLE *a.*] In an able manner.

-ably, compd. suffix, f. ABLE + -LY, supplying advbs. to adjs. in *-able.*

Abnegate (æ·bnĭgeᶦt), *v.* 1657. [f. L. *abnegat-, abnegare.*] 1. To deny oneself (anything), to renounce (a right, etc.) 1657. 2. To abjure, as a tenet 1755.

1. To a. the personal enjoyment of life MILL. 2. To a. the very possibility of Heroism CARLYLE. Hence **A·bnega·tive** *a.* **A·bnega·tor.**

Abnegation (æbnĭgēᶦ·ʃən). 1554. [ad. L. *abnegationem*; see prec. and cf. Fr. *abnégation.*] 1. Denial; rejection (of a doctrine, etc.) 1554. 2. Self-denial; renunciation 1639; self-abnegation 1657. (*Self* now often expressed.)

1. A. of Christe KNOX, of the responsibility of choice 1875. 2. A. of the world MRS. JAMESON, of authority MOTLEY. The Pretences of Romanists to A., to a Self-denying Life PENN.

Abnormal (æbnǭ·ɹmăl), *a.* 1835. [orig. ANORMAL, refash. after L. *abnormis* (see ABNORMOUS).] Deviating from the type; contrary to rule or system; unusual 1835.

The wing of a bat is an a. structure DARWIN. A. compassion 1878. Hence **Abnorma·lity,** the quality or state of being a.; an a. feature or act. **Abno·rmally** *adv.*

Abnormity (æbnǭ·ɹmĭti). 1731. [ad. L. *abnormitas*; see next.] The quality of being abnormal; a monstrosity 1859. Usu. depreciatory.

An a...like a calf born with two heads MRS. WHITNEY.

Abnormous (æbnǭ·ɹməs), *a.* 1742. [f. L. *abnormis.* Cf. *enormous.*] 'Irregular, misshapen.' J.

A character of an a. cast 1771.

Aboard (ăbōᵊ·ɹd), *adv.* and *prep.* 1494. [f. A *prep.*[1] + BOARD, and Fr. *à bord*, the Fr. *bord* (= 1. plank; 2. ship; 3. edge) giving the uses, and ME. *shippes borde*, etc. the derivation.]

A. *adv.* 1. On board; on or on to or into a ship, etc. 1509. 2. Alongside (*hard, close*) 1494. ¶ *Catachr.* ? = abroad, adrift SPENSER.

1. Remember whom thou hast aboord *Temp.* I. i. 21. Aboord, aboord for shame *Haml.* I. iii. 56. 2. To keep the coast a. COOK. *Phrases*: **To lay** (a ship) **aboard**: to place one's own alongside of (it) 1593. **To fall aboard**: to fall foul of (a ship). Also *fig.* with *with* or *of*: to quarrel 1604. **To bring aboard**: to bring to land. **To come to aboard** (Fr. *venir, arriver à bord*): to land. **To haul the tacks aboard**: to bring their weather clues down to the chess-tree, to set the courses.

B. *prep.* [*of* omitted.] In senses A. 1, 2. ¶ *Catachr.* ? = across the breadth of SPENSER.

Is he a. the fleet? SOUTHEY. He came a. my ship DE FOE. Hard a. the shore FULLER.

Aboard, obs. f. ABORD *v.* and *sb.*

Abode (ăbōᵘ·d), *sb.*[1] ME. [vbl. sb. of ABIDE.] †1. The action of waiting -1596. †2. A temporary stay -1749. 3. Habitual residence 1576. 4. A place of habitation; house or home 1614.

1. *Without a.*, at once. Your patience for my long a. *Merch. V.* II. vi. 21. 3. The Countrey where you make a. SHAKS. 4. Paradise, Adam's a. MILT. Abodes of..pain 1767.

†Abode, *sb.*[2] 1600. [f. A-BEDE *v.*, OE. *abéodan.*] An omen.

†Abode, *v.* 1593. [f. prec.] To presage, BODE, FOREBODE. Shaks.

Abode, past tense of ABIDE.

†Abodement[1]. [f. ABODE *v.*] An omen. SHAKS.

†Abodement[2]. [f. ABODE *sb.*[1]] Abiding -1616.

†Aboding, *vbl. sb.* and *ppl. a.* [f. ABODE *v.*] Boding.

Abolish (ăbǫ·liʃ), *v.* 1490. [a. Fr. *aboliss-, abolir*:—L. *abolescere.*] To put an end to; to annul; to demolish or destroy. Now only of institutions, customs, and practices. Formerly *from, out of.*

To a. idoles *Isa.* ii. 18, the Bastille CARLYLE, pestilence KINGSLEY. Hence **Abo·lishable** *a.* **Abo·lisher. Abo·lishment** = ABOLITION.

Abolition (æbŏli·ʃən). 1529. [a. Fr., or ? ad. L. *abolitionem.*] 1. The act of abolishing; the being abolished; destruction 1529. *spec.* The abolition of the slave-trade; called familiarly 'abolition' 1788. Hence *attrib.* †2. A putting out of memory; an amnesty -1809.

1. The a. of eternal guilt JER. TAYLOR. *spec.* To promote the a. in France 1808. The A. party W. PHILLIPS, movement KEMBLE. Hence **Aboli·tionary** *a.* destructive. **Aboli·tionism,** opposition to negro slavery. **Aboli·tionist,** one who aims at a., *esp.* of negro slavery. **Aboli·tionize** *v.* to teach abolitionism. In U. S.

‖**Abolla** (ăbǫ·lă). [?] A woollen cloak worn by the soldiers and lower classes of ancient Rome.

‖**Aboma** (ăbōᵘ·mă). A large S. American serpent, *Epicratis Cenchria.*

‖**Abomasum, -us** (æbo͵mēᶦ·sŏm, -ŏs). 1706. [mod.L., f. *ab* + *omasum.*] The fourth, and true digestive, stomach of ruminants.

Abominable (ăbǫ·minăb'l), *a.* ME. [a. Fr. *abominable, abhominable*, ad. L. *abominabilis*, deserving imprecation; cf. *absit omen.* From Wyclif to 17th c. spelt *abhominable*, quasi *ab homine*, 'away from man', 'inhuman', and so in Shaks.] 1. Exciting disgust; offensive; odious. 2. *colloq.* Very unpleasant 1860. Also as *adv.*

1. Abhominable and beastly touches *Meas. for M.* III. ii. 25. A. practices BURKE. 2. The road was a. TYNDALL. As an intensive: 'A bomynable (= terrible) syght of monks' J. BERNERS. Hence **Abo·minableness,** the quality of being a. **Abo·minably** *adv.* loathsomely; *colloq.* very badly.

Abominate (ăbǫ·mineᶦt), *v.* 1644. [f. L. *abominat-, abominari*; see ABOMINABLE.] 1. To feel extreme disgust towards; to abhor. 2. *colloq.* To dislike strongly 1880.

1. The Egyptians .. abominated flesh-eaters 1728. 2. Steele .. abominated operas 1880. Hence **Abo·minate, Abo·minated** *ppl. adjs.* **Abo·minator.**

Abomination (ăbǫminēᶦ·ʃən). ME. [a. Fr., ad. L. *abominationem*; see ABOMINABLE.] 1. The feeling of disgust and hatred; loathing. †2. A state exciting disgust; pollution -1480. 3. A degrading vice ME. 4. An object that excites disgust and hatred (followed by *unto, to*); *esp.* an idol ME.

1. To have in abominacion MORE. 3. Antony, most large in his abhominations *Ant. & Cl.* III. vi. 94. An a. is committed in Israel *Mal.* ii. 11. 4. Lying lips are an a. to the Lord *Prov.* xii. 22.

†Abo·mine, *v.* [a. Fr. *abominer.*] = ABOMINATE *v.* Swift.

Aboo·n, *adv.* and *prep.* Sc. and n. form of ABOVE. Also *poet.*

Aboral (æbōᵊ·răl), *a.* 1857. [f. L. *ab* + ORAL.] *Zool.* Pertaining to the part away from the mouth.

Abord (ăbōᵊ·ɹd), *v. arch.* 1509. [a. Fr. *aborder*; see ABOARD *adv.* Cf. ACCOST *v.*] †1. To approach; to land on -1691. 2. To accost. *arch.* 1611.

†Abo·rd, *sb.* 1611. [a. Fr.] Approach, or way of approach.

Aboriginal (æbŏri·dʒinăl). 1667. [f. L. *ab origine.*] A. *adj.* 1. First or earliest known; primitive; indigenous. *spec.* Earlier than (European) colonists. 1788. 2. Pertaining to aborigines, or to native races 1851.

1. A. forests LYELL, Iberians FORD. The English are not a. STUBBS. 2. The a. fleets of ancient Caledonia D. WILSON.

B. *sb.* An original inhabitant, opp. to colonist 1767. *fig.* Of words 1858.

The thoughtless a. DARWIN. Hence **Abori·ginalism,** the due recognition of native races. **A·b-ori·gina·lity,** the quality of being a. **A·bori·ginally** *adv.* from the earliest known times.

Aborigines (æbŏri·dʒinīz, -iz). 1547. [L. At first pl. only; for sing. ABORIGINAL, aborigen, -in and esp. **aborigine** (æ·bŏri·dʒini) have been used.] 1. The inhabitants of a country (orig. of Italy and of Greece) *ab origine.* Also *fig.* 2. *spec.* The natives, as opp. to colonists 1789. 3. Used of animals and plants 1677.

1. Meere A.; that is, Homelings and not forren brought in HOLLAND. 3. An invasion of one plant over the a. DARWIN. Hence (from *sing.*) **A·bori·ginary,** an aboriginal inhabitant.

†Abo·rsement. 1540. var. f. ABORTMENT.

†Abo·rsive, *a.* 1639. [f. L. *aborsus*, var. of *abortus.*] Abortive from the first FULLER.

Abort (ăbǭ·ɹt), *v.* 1580. [f. L. *abort-, aboriri.* Cf. Fr. *avorter.*] 1. To miscarry. *trans.* and *intr.* Also *fig.* 1614. 2. *Biol.* To become sterile; to be checked in normal development, so as to remain rudimentary or to shrink away 1862. Hence **Abo·rted** *ppl. a.* born before its time; *Biol.* checked in development. **Abo·rtifa·cient** *a.* causing premature delivery; as *sb.* [sc. *drug.*] **Abo·rting** *vbl. sb.* a miscarrying; *ppl. a.* producing abortions. **†Abo·rtment,** abortion.

†Abo·rt. 1603. [ad. L. *abortus*; see prec.] A miscarriage (*lit.* and *fig.*) 1621; the offspring of a miscarriage 1603.

Abortion (ăbǭ·ɹʃən). 1547. [ad. L. *abortionem*; see ABORT.] 1. Giving untimely birth to offspring; the procuring of premature delivery so as to destroy offspring. Also *fig.* 1710. 2. *Biol.* Arrest of development of any organ (see ABORT *v.* 2) 1842. **3.** The imperfect offspring of a miscarriage; hence used *fig.* of the result of any action 1640. Hence **Abo·rtional** *a.* **Abo·rtionist,** one who procures a.

Abortive (ăbǭ·ɹtiv). ME. [a. L. *abortivus*, see ABORT.]

A. *adj.* †**1.** Pertaining to abortion; born prematurely –1664; causing abortion –1753; miscarrying –1662. **2.** Coming to nought 1593. **3.** *Biol.* Arrested in development (see ABORT *v.* 2) 1794.

1. A. be it [the child] *Rich. III*, I. ii. 21. *A. parchment*: that derived from a still-born animal. Also as *sb.* in same sense. Plunged in that a. gulf MILT. *P. L.* II. 441. **2.** A. pride 2 *Hen. VI*, IV. i. 60. An a. attempt SCOTT. **3.** Thorns..are a. branches GOOD.

B. *sb.* [The adj. used *absol.*] †**1.** An a. progeny –1760. †**2.** An a. delivery –1587. †**3.** An imperfect result of an action –1706. †**4.** An a. drug –1647.

3. My conjecture (although it is an a.) HOLLAND. Hence **Abo·rtively** *adv.* **Abo·rtiveness.**

†**Abo·rtive,** *v.* 1615. [f. prec. Cf. to *negative*.] To cause abortion –1699; *intr.* to miscarry –1692.

†**Abote,** *ppl. a.* ? = *abeaten* or *abated. Chaucer's Dreme.*

Abought, obs. pa. t. and pple. of ABYE.

Abound (ăbau·nd), *v.*[1] ME. [a. OFr. *abunder, abonder*:—L. *abundare.* Spelt later erron. *habound*, as if f. *habere.*] **1.** To overflow; to be plentiful ME. †**2.** To be rich, to have to overflowing –1765. **3.** To abound, be wealthy *in* ME.; teem *with* ME. †**4.** To go at large, expatiate ME. †**5.** To pour forth –1631.

1. To make al grace abounde in you WYCLIF. Rheumaticke diseases doe a. *Mid. N.* II. i. 105. **2.** But I have all and a. *Phil.* iv. 18. **3.** I abounde in joye WYCLIF. To a. in Teares *Wint. T.* II. i. 120. A faithfull man shall a. with blessings *Prov.* xxviii. 20. **4.** To let others **abound in their own sense** (= follow their own opinion) BURKE. Hence **Abou·nder,** one who abounds. **Abou·nding** *vbl. sb.* abundance; *ppl. a.* full-flowing, plentiful, †affluent.

†**Abou·nd,** *v.*[2] ME. [f. A- *pref.* 11, or *a-* = I-, Y- + BOUND *v.*] To limit –1627.

About (ăbau·t), *adv.* and *prep.* [OE. *onbútan*, f. *on*, in, on + *bútan* outside of.] **A.** (without obj.) *adv.* **I.** Position. **1.** Around the outside; on or towards every side; all round OE. **2.** On any side; near ME. **3.** Nearly, all but—of quantity OE.; of quality 1614.

1. Hannibal byseged hem all aboute TREVISA. *Temp.* v. i. 180. So *cast, look about.* **2.** He hangs a. doing nothing (*mod.*). **3.** A girl of a. seven 1802. A. right DICKENS, finished (*mod.*).

II. Motion. **1.** Round, in revolution OE.; in succession ME. **2.** Half round or less 1535. **3.** In circumference 1598. **4.** In a circuitous course, up and down OE.; hence, on the move, astir; prevailing (as a disease) ME.; with inf. or vbl. sb., on the point of.

1. To come a.: to revolve (as time); to come to pass. **To bring a.**: to cause to revolve; bring to pass. To twist a man's neck a. STERNE. Turn and turn a. MAYHEW. **2.** *Turn, face a. To the right a.*: in the opposite direction. *The wrong way a.*: by the wrong end or side. So *The other way a. To bring one a.* (or round), i. e. from illness, etc. *Naut.* To *make, put, go, a.*, to *go a. ship*, on the opposite tack. **3.** In the waste two yards a. *Merry Wives* I. ii. 44. The sure way (though most a.) BACON. **4.** He ledde him a. *Deut.* xxxii. 10. To move furniture a. (*mod.*). A., my Braine *Haml.* II. ii. 617. Small-pox is a. (*mod.*). *To go a. to do*: to endeavour. A. to storm 1665. A. concluding SMEATON.

B. (with obj.) *prep.* **I.** Position. **1.** On the outside of; on or towards every side of; all round OE. **2.** Somewhere near, in or near ME.; hence, in attendance on ME.; at hand 1567. **3.** Connexion: Attached to as an attribute or circumstance 1603; near so as to meddle with, concerned with ME.; touching, concerning ME. **4.** Of time, and quantity: Near, close to OE.

1. My crown a. my brows TENNYSON. To lay a. one HIERON. **2.** The meadows a. Oxford (*mod.*). Have this (herb) a. you MILT. *Comus* 647. **3.** *A. his business*: away, i. e. to attend to his own affairs. What are you a.? (*mod.*). Much Adoe a. Nothing 1599. Indifferent a. what happens HUME. **4.** Aboute prime CHAUCER, a. midnight SHAKS. A. my stature SHAKS.

II. Motion. **1.** Round (opp. to across, over, or into). *arch.* OE. **2.** To and fro in 1534; hence, frequenting 1593.

1. To beat *a. the bush.* See BUSH. To get a. the Cape DAMPIER. **2.** Cowslips dotted a. the field (*mod.*). A 'blood' or dandy a. town THACKERAY.

Comb.: **a.-sledge,** the largest hammer used by smiths; **-ward, -s** *adv.* trying, being a. to.

†**Abouts, aboutes,** *adv.* and *prep.* ME. [prob. north.] A genitival form of ABOUT, still found in HEREABOUTS, etc.

Above (ăbɒ·v). OE. [f. A *prep.*[1] + *bufan* above (cf. ODu. *boven*), f. *be* + *ufan* (cf. Germ. *oben*). North. and orig. advb.] **A.** (without obj.) *adv.* **1.** Overhead, vertically up, on high OE; in heaven ME. **2.** On the outside; covering all. ? *Obs.* ME. **3.** Higher (in various senses; see quots.). **4.** In addition 1596.

1. The clouds a. *Prov.* viii. 28. A wooden stair leading a. DICKENS. Euery perfect gift is *from above James* i. 17. **3.** Higher in place ME., position or order OE.: A. were the snowy peaks (*mod.*). *A.-written, -said*, etc. †*fig.* Thou shalt be a. and..not ..beneath *Deut.* xxviii. 13. Higher in rank, etc. ME.: A higher court, etc. Also *ellipt.* The a. will show (*mod.*). **4.** Stand indebted **over and above** *Merch. V.* IV. i. 413.

B. (with obj.) *prep.* **1.** Over; vertically up from; on the top of OE. **2.** Relatively over, covering. ? *Obs.* ME. **3.** Higher than (in various senses; see quots.). **4.** In addition to 1581.

1. The sky that hangs a. our heads SHAKS. **3.** Higher up than OE.; beyond the level or reach of ME.; and *fig.* superior to (the influence of): A. the 45th degree of N. latitude MORSE; *Above ground*: out of the grave, alive; A. the din (*mod.*); A. the anxieties of human love WORDSW. *fig.* Higher in rank or position than ME.: Abune my station SCOTT. Higher in degree or quality: *a. all*, beyond all; *a. measure*, beyond what is meet. Higher in number, quantity, etc.: Not a. once *Haml.* II. ii. 455. A. a hundred were present (*mod.*). **4.** He earns a large sum **over and above** his salary (*mod.*).

C. Elliptically (quasi-*a.* and *sb.*). **1.** By *ellipsis* of a pple. *above* stands attributively, as 'the above explanation'; or *above* may be used absol., as 'the above will show', etc. 1779. †**2.** With a possessive case, *at, to mine*, etc. *above*: something above what I am –1484.

Above-board (ăbɒ·vˌbōᵊɹd), *adv.* (and *a.*) 1616. Openly, without concealment. *lit.* and *fig.* Orig. a gambling term.

Abovesaid (ăbɒ·vˌseːd), *ppl. a. arch.* ME. Mentioned higher up; aforesaid. So **above-bounden, -cited, -found, -given, -mentioned, -named, -written.**

†**Abow,** *v.* OE. [f. OE. *abúgan*, f. A- *pref.* 1 + *búgan.*] To bend or make to bend; *fig.* to do homage, submit.

Abracadabra (æ:brăkădæ·bră). 1696. [L. First found in Q. Severus Sammonicus, 2nd c.] A cabalistic word, written in various arrangements, and used as a charm, to cure agues, etc. A spell; a mysterious word without meaning; gibberish.

The new a. of science, 'organic evolution' 1879.

Abrade (ăbrēⁱ·d), *v.* 1677. [ad. L. *abradere.*] **1.** To rub or wear off (a part *from*). **2.** To rub away. *lit.* and *fig.* 1748.

2. To a. the popularity .. of a government 1804. To a. the stomach KANE, rocks LYELL. Hence **Abra·der.**

†**Abraham, Abram,** *a.* 1599. Corrupt ff. AUBURN. *Coriol.* II. iii. 21.

Abraham-man, Abram-man. 1561. [See *Luke* xvi.] One of a class of pretended lunatics who wandered over England seeking alms, after the dissolution of the religious houses. Hence **To sham Abram**: to feign sickness.

†**Abrai·d,** *v.* OE. [f. A- *pref.* 1 + BRAID, OE. *bregdan*, to twist, hence = *retorquere.*] **1.** To wrench out (a sword) –ME. **2.** To start –1600; to startle –1596. **3.** To shout out; *trans.* and *intr.* Also *refl.* To exert oneself; to frequent LYDGATE.

†**Abraid,** *v.* and *sb.*, **-ing** *vbl. sb.*, 15th c. ff. UPBRAID, -ING, due to confusion with prec.

Abra·nchial, *a.* 1861. [f. Gr. ἀ + βράγχια.] = ABRANCHIATE. So **Abra·nchian** *a.* and *sb.*

Abranchiate (ăbræ·ŋkiĕt), *a.* 1855. [f. as prec.] *Zool.* Having no gills.

†**Abra·se,** *ppl. a.* 1600. Rubbed smooth –1688.

Abra·se, *v.* 1593. [f. L. *abras-, abradere.* Cf. *erase*, and Fr. *raser.*] To rub off or away; abrade. Hence †**Abra·sing** *vbl. sb.* **Abra·sive** *a.* having the property of abrading.

Abrasion (ăbrēⁱ·ʒən). 1656. [ad. L. *abrasionem.*] **1.** Rubbing off or away. *lit.* and *fig.* 1656. **2.** The result of rubbing off; †débris; an abraded place 1740. **3.** *Med.* Wearing away the mucus which covers the membranes by corrosive medicines. Cf. Fr. *abrasion.* 1751.

1. A. of coins CRUMP, of the skin H. M. STANLEY. **2.** A bed-sore..a simple a. BRYANT.

‖**Abraum Salts** (aːbˌraum sǫlts). 1753. [ad. Germ. *Abraum-salze.*] Mixed salts found at Stassfurt in Prussia, and also in the Isle of Wight, now used for producing chloride of potassium.

‖**Abraxas.** A cabalistic word sometimes inscribed on gems as a charm.

Abray, false f. ABRAID *v.* SPENSER.

Abrazite (æ·brăzeit). 1847. [f. Gr. ἀ ? intens. + βράζειν to boil.] *Min.* = GISMONDITE.

Abrazi·tic, *a.* [f. Gr. ἀ priv. + βράζειν.] *Min.* Not effervescing when melted before the blow-pipe.

Abreast (ăbre·st), *adv.* 1450. [f. A *prep.*[1] + BREAST.] **1.** With breasts, or fronts, in a line; side by side (in advancing) 1599. **2.** *Naut.* With the ships equally distant, and parallel 1697. **3.** *Naut.* On a parallel with the beam.

1. A breach that 16 men might enter a. 1675. *A. of*, parallel to, or alongside of something stationary. *lit.* and *fig.* A. of Millbank MARRYAT, of truth LOWELL. *A. with*, keeping up with 1655; often *fig.*

†**Abrenou·nce,** *v.* 1537. [f. L. *ab* + RENOUNCE.] To repudiate; to contradict –1656.

Many a. [theyr parentes]..and cast them of LATIMER. var. †**A·brenu·nciate** *v.*

A·brenuncia·tion. *arch.* 1641. [ad. med. L. *abrenunciationem.*] Renunciation; retractation.

†**Abre·ption.** 1681. [f. L. *abrept-, abripere.*] Snatching away; separation.

‖**Abreuvoir** (abrövwa·r). [Fr., f. *abreuver* to cause to drink:—late L. *abeverare*:—*adbiberare.*] In masonry, an interstice to be filled up with mortar or cement.

Abricock, -coct, -cot, obs. ff. APRICOT.

Abridge (ăbri·dʒ), *v.* ME. [a. OFr. *abregier, abreger*:—L. *abbreviare*; see ABBREVIATE *a.*] Always *trans.* **1.** To shorten in duration. **2.** To make shorter in words, while retaining the sense; to epitomize ME.; esp. (*Law*) to shorten a count or declaration 1691. **3.** To cut short, curtail; *esp.* rights, privileges, etc. **4.** With a person:—Constr. *of*, also *from, in.* To stint, curtail in, debar from. ME.

1. God sal abrege his days HAMPOLE. To a. a visit SMOLLETT, labour HT. MARTINEAU. **2.** Efnard.. abridged the French Psalter 1611. **3.** To a. a train FULLER, the naturall Liberty of man HOBBES. **4.** Abridged in his freedom SOUTH. Hence **Abri·dgeable, -gable** *a.* capable of, or liable to, abridgement. **Abri·dgedly** *adv.* **Abri·dger.**

Abridgement, -gment (ăbri·dʒmĕnt). 1494. [a. OFr. *abregement*, f. *abréger.*] **1.** The act of abridging; *fig.* a means of whiling away the time; the being abridged 1797. **2.** An epitome or compendium of a larger work 1523, or of a subject 1609. **3.** *Law.* Omission of parts of a plaint or demand 1641.

1. Abridgments of liberty MACAULAY. What a. (? = means of shortening) haue you for this euening *Mids. N.* V. i. 39. **2.** A mere meagre a. FREEMAN. To be Master of the Sea, is an a. of Monarchy BACON. An a. of all that was pleasant in man GOLDSM. *Retal.* 94.

Abroach (ăbrōᵘ·tʃ), *adv.* ME. [f. A *prep.*[1] + BROACH.] **1.** Broached, pierced. Also *fig.* **2.** In a state to be diffused; astir 1528.

1. A butt of strong beer a. SMOLLETT. **2.** Who set this auncient quarrell new a.? *Rom. & Jul.* I. i. 111. Phr. **To set abroach**: to pierce and leave running; to set a-foot.

†**Abroa·ch,** *v.* ME. [a. OFr. *abrochier, abrocher*, f. *à* + *brocher*; see BROACH.] To pierce (a cask, etc.). Also *fig.* –1530.

Abroad (ăbrǭ·d). ME. [f. A *prep.*[1] + BROAD. Cf. *a-long, at large.*]

A. *adv.* **1.** Widely, over a broad surface; widely scattered; widely apart, wide spread;

ӕ (man). ɑ (pass). ɑu (loud). ɒ (cut). ɛ (Fr. chef). ə (ever). əi (*I, eye*). ə (Fr. eau de vie). i (sit). *i* (Psyche). ǫ (what). ǫ (got).

hence, *Naut.* = *spread.* 2. At large; *fig.* current 1500. 3. Out of one's house ME., or home country 1450. 4. Wide of the mark; 'out' 1838.

1. The love of God is shed a. in our hearts *Rom.* v. 5. Sands [blown] like Sibels leaues a. *Tit. A.* IV. i. 106. With Dutch colours a. 1667. 2. Ther's villanie a. *L. L. L.* I. i. 190. 3. Dining a. with a friend BORROW. The badger ventures a. at dusk (*mod.*). Imported *from abroad* MACAULAY. So, I must a. (*ellipt.* for *go a.*). 4. Only a little a. DICKENS.

B. *prep.* [With place expressed.] *arch.* Throughout 1523. Also as *adj.*

A. the world BAXTER.

Abrogate (æ·brŏgĕt), *a.* and *pple.* *arch.* 1460. [ad. L. *abrogatus, abrogare.* Earlier than the vb.] Repealed.

Abrogate (æ·brŏgeᶦt), *v.* 1526. [f. prec.] 1. To repeal (a law, etc.). 2. To do away with 1588.

1. To a. a Law by the Sword MILT. To a. the pope's power FULLER. 2. Please you to a. scurilitie *L. L. L.* IV. ii. 55. Hence **A·brogable** *a.* **A·brogative** *a.* having the quality of abrogating. **A·brogator.**

Abrogation (æbrŏgēⁱ·ʃən). 1535. [ad. L. *abrogationem.*] The act of abrogating. (Not now used of persons or concrete things.)

The A. of King James by the people S. JOHNSON. A. of a right 1866.

Abroo·d, *adv.* ME. [A *prep.*[1] + BROOD *sb.*] On its brood or eggs. Also *fig.*

†**Abroo·k,** *v.* [f. A- *pref.* 11 + BROOK *v.*] To brook. 2 *Hen. VI,* II. iv. 10.

Abrupt (ăbrʋ·pt), *a.* and *sb.* 1583. [ad. L. *abruptus.*] †1. Broken away (from restraint). 2. Broken off. ?*Obs.* 1607. 3. Characterized by sudden interruption or change 1591. 4. Precipitous 1618. 5. a. *Bot.* Truncated. b. *Geol.* Suddenly cropping out. 6. As *sb.* An a. place; an abyss. (Only in MILT. *P. L.* II. 409.)

3. Your a. departure 1 *Hen. VI,* II. iii. 30. The a. style..hath many breaches B. JONS. 4. A. ravines STANLEY. Hence **Abru·ptness** (in senses 2, 3, 4).

†**Abru·pt,** *v.* 1643. [f. prec.] To break off, sever. SIR T. BROWNE. Hence **Abru·pted** *ppl. a.* **Abru·ptedly** *adv.*

Abruption (ăbrʋ·pʃən). 1606. [ad. L. *abruptionem.*] 1. A breaking off, an interruption. *arch.* 2. A sudden breaking away (of portions of a mass) 1657.

1. Sudden a. of all intercourse MILMAN. 2. Removal..by a. BRYANT.

Abruptly (ăbrʋ·ptli), *adv.* 1590. [f. ABRUPT *a.*] 1. In an abrupt manner; see ABRUPT *a.* 2, 3, 4. 2. *Bot.* As in *abruptly pinnate,* pinnate without an intermediate leaflet at the end.

Abs-, *pref.,* repr. L. *abs-,* the form of AB- off, away, from, used bef. c-, q-, t-.

Abscess (æ·bsĕs). 1543. [ad. L. *abscessus* (Celsus).] A collection of pus or purulent matter formed by a morbid process in a cavity of the body. Hence **A·bscessed** *ppl. a.*

†**Absce·ssion.** 1599. [ad. L. *abscessionem.*] 1. Departure; cessation of a pain, etc. –1659. 2. = ABSCESS. 1610.

Abscind (ăbsi·nd), *v. arch.* 1657. [ad. L. *abscindere.*] To cut off. *lit.* and *fig.*

Absciss(e (æ·bsis). Pl. **-es**; oftener as L. **abscissa** (ăbsi·sa), pl. **-æ**; also **-as.** 1698. [L. *abscissa* (sc. *linea*).] *Geom.* A line or distance cut off; *spec.* the portion of a given line intercepted between a fixed point within it, and an ordinate drawn to it from a given point without it.

Abscission (ăbsi·ʒən). 1612. [ad. L. *abscissionem*; see ABSCIND.] A cutting off (*lit.* and *fig.*); † the state of being cut off –1649. var. **Absci·sion.**

Abscond (ăbskǫ·nd), *v.* 1565. [ad. L. *abscondere.*] †1. *trans.* To hide away. *Obs.* or *arch.* 1612. Also *refl.* 2. *intr.* (refl. pron. omitted.) To hide oneself; to go away hurriedly and secretly 1565.

1. The Alps a. their heads POMFRET. 2. Some few absconded CARLYLE. Hence **Absco·ndedly** *adv.* **Absco·ndence.** **Absco·nder,** a runaway from justice.

Absee, obs. ff. A B C.

Absence (æ·bsĕns). ME. [a. Fr. *absence*:—L. *absentia.*] 1. The state of being absent or away; also the time of duration of such state. b. *poet.* An absent form or face. 2. Absence (*of mind*); inattention; abstraction 1710. 3. At Eton College, roll-call 1856.

1. Not when I was present only, but now moche more in myne a. TINDALE *Phil.* ii. 12. A. has plac'd her in a fairer light YOUNG. A. of the sonne ME. 2. Disquietude, a. of mind is on every face CARLYLE. var. †**A·bsency.**

Absent (æ·bsĕnt). ME. [a. Fr. *absent,* refash. from OFr. *ausent*:—L. *absentem.*] A. *adj.* 1. Away, not present; wanting, not existing 1718. 2. Absent-minded, paying no attention to present objects, etc. 1710. †B. *sb.* [sc. *person*] –1699.

A. 1. An a. friend 1716. Crevasses..are..totally a. TYNDALL. 2. I became a. and thoughtful SMOLLETT. Hence **A·bsently** *adv.* with absence of mind. **A·bsentness,** absentmindedness.

Comb.: **a.-minded** *a.* = ABSENT 2; **-mindedly** *adv.* = ABSENTLY; **-mindedness** = ABSENCE 2.

Abse·nt, *v.* ME. [a. Fr. *absenter,* ad. L. *absentare.*] 1. *trans.* To keep away 1530. Also *refl.* †2. *intr.* To stay away –1709. †3. *trans.* (*from* omitted). To leave 1695.

1. A. thee from felicitie awhile *Haml.* V. ii. 358. 3. To a. the kingdom LUTTRELL. Hence **Abse·nted** *ppl. a.* **Abse·nter,** one who absents himself. **Abse·nting** *vbl. sb.* being or going away. †**Abse·ntment,** staying away.

Absenta·tion. 1800. [ad. med.L. *absentationem*; cf. *Presentation.*] Absenting oneself.

Absentee (æbsĕntī·). 1537. [f. ABSENT *v.*] One who is absent on any occasion. *spec.* A landlord, etc., who lives away from his country or home. Also *attrib.*

Occasional absentees for business, health, or diversion SWIFT. A. proprietors HALLAM. In 157 benefices the incumbent was an a. HT. MARTINEAU. Hence **Absentee·ism** 1829, **Absentee·ship,** the practice or condition of being an a.

Absey, -sie, obs. f. A B C.

Absinth(e (æ·bsinþ, Fr. æbsæ̃nt). 1612. [a. Fr.] 1. The plant *Absinthium* or wormwood. 2. Essence of wormwood; also *fig.* 1865. 3. A liqueur originally distilled from wine and wormwood 1854. Hence **Absi·nthial** *a.* pertaining to wormwood; bitter. **Absi·nthian** *a.* **Absi·nthiate** *v.* to impregnate with wormwood. **Absi·nthic** *a.* belonging to a., as *absinthic acid.* **Absi·nthine** *a.* having the nature of a.; bitter. **A·bsinthism,** a disease like alcoholism, arising from a.

Absinthin (ăbsi·nþin). 1853. [f. L. *absinthium.*] *Chem.* The bitter principle of wormwood, *Artemisia Absinthium.*

Absinthium (ăbsi·nþiŏm). ME. [L.] *Bot.* The wormwood, *Artemisia Absinthium* of Linnæus, a bitter and aromatic plant.

Absinthole (ăbsi·nþǫᵘl). 1879. [f. ABSINTH + -OLE.] *Chem.* $C_{10}H_{16}O$. A liquid camphor obtained from the oil of wormwood.

Absis, obs. f. APSIS.

†**Absi·st,** *v.* 1614. [ad. L. *absistere.*] To desist.

†**Absoil, -soyle,** *v.* 1450. = ASSOIL; to absolve.

†**Absolent, -solete,** erron. ff. due to a confusion between ABSOLUTE, 'completed', and OBSOLETE.

Absolute (æ·bsŏliᵘt), *a.* ME. [a. M.Fr. *absolut,* refash. from OFr. *asolu, assolu*:—L. *absolutum, absolvere*; see ABSOLVE. The senses are mostly L.] Orig. a *pple.*; then *adj.* Formerly comp. *absoluter, -est.*

I. †1. *pple.* Detached, disengaged *from* ME. †2. Untrammelled, absorbed *in* –1483; essential ME.

II. 1. Absolute in quality or degree; perfect ME. 2. Complete, entire 1574. 3. Pure, mere 1563.

1. A. counsils 1550. Masters of the a. art of language RUSKIN. 2. An a. *Johannes fac totum* GREENE. An A. Impossibility CUDWORTH. 3. *A. Alcohol,* perfectly free from water.

III. 1. Absolute in position or relation; independent 1533. Hence, 2. Arbitrary, despotic 1612. 3. *Gram.* Detached from the usual syntactic construction, as in *ablative absolute* 1527. 4. Real, actual; opp. to *relative* and *comparative* 1666.

1. God's a. power TINDALE. A. owners 1576. 2. A. Monarchy is Tyranny; but a. Democracy is Tyranny and Anarchy both LD. BOLINGBROKE. 4. A. misery, but happiness only comparative JOHNSON.

IV. Free from condition or mental limitation. †1. Positive –1676. 2. Unqualified, unconditional (*esp.* in *Logic*) 1625. 3. *Metaph.* Existing without relation to any other being; self-existent (*mod.*). 4. *Metaph.* Capable of being known or conceived out of relation; unconditioned (*mod.*). 5. *Metaph.* Considered apart from its being subjective or objective 1809.

1. I am a. 'Twas very Cloten *Cymb.* IV. ii. 106. 2. My thoughts were sincere and a. CHARLES I. An a. proposition BOWEN. 3. By the A. is meant that which exists in and by itself, having no necessary relation to any other being MANSEL. 4. Whatever can be known (or conceived) out of relation..is the known Absolute FERRIER.

¶ In the metaph. uses the word tends to become substantival: *the Absolute,* i. e. that which is absolute.

Absolutely (æ·bsŏliᵘtli), *adv.* 1489. [f. prec.] In an ABSOLUTE manner, or degree; without condition, or limitation.

Absoluteness (æ·bsŏliᵘtnĕs). 1570. [f. as prec.] The quality of being ABSOLUTE, in various senses. (See ABSOLUTE *a.*) Also catachr. for *Obsoleteness.*

Absolution (æbsŏliū·ʃən). ME. [a. Fr., ad. L. *absolutionem.*] 1. An absolving, or formal setting free (*from* guilt, sentence, or obligation); remission (*of* sin or penance). 2. *spec.* Remission of sins declared by eccl. authority. (*The earliest use.*) ME. Also, the formula of remission 1520. 3. Forgiveness of offences generally ME. †4. *Rom. Law.* A legal acquittal 1600. †5. Delivery (of words) –1637.

1. A bull of a. from oaths..taken STUBBS. 2. Without Confession to a Priest no a. 1638. The A., ..to be pronounced by the Priest alone, standing *Comm. Prayer* (Rubric). 3. A. after the fact FREEMAN. 5. The composition [of some language] full, the a. plenteous B. JONS.

Absolutism (æ·bsŏliᵘtiz'm). 1753. [f. ABSOLUTE *a.*; after mod.Fr.] The practice of, or adherence to, the absolute. 1. *Theol.* The dogma of God's acting absolutely as to salvation; the doctrine of predestination 1753. 2. *Polit.* The practice of absolute government; despotism 1830.

Absolutist (æ·bsŏliᵘtist), *sb.* and *a.* 1830. [f. as prec.] 1. *Polit.* A partisan of absolutism in government 1830. 2. *Metaph.* One who maintains the absolute identity of subject and object 1856. 3. *adj.* Despotic 1837.

Absolutory (ăbsǫ·liᵘtəri), *a.* 1640. [ad. L. *absolutorius.*] Absolving.

Absolve (ăbsǫ·lv, ăbz-), *v.* 1535. [ad. L. *absolvere.* Cf. Fr. *absoudre, absolvant.* Replacing ASSOIL.] 1. To set or pronounce free (*from* guilt, etc.; *from the consequences of* crime or sin) 1538. 2. *spec.* To give absolution to; also with *of* or *for* 1535. 3. To remit (a sin or crime) 1592. 4. To pronounce not guilty; *esp.* in Rom. Law 1628. 5. To set free (*from,* † *of* obligations) 1649. †6. To clear up, resolve –1667. †7. To clear off (a task, etc.) –1801.

1. Absolved from any notorious crime CLARENDON. 2. To make confession, and to be absolu'd *Rom. & Jul.* III. v. 233. I dare not a. him of robbing a priest KINGSLEY. 3. The Pope for pay absolueth everything WARNER. 4. Absolves the just, and dooms the guilty POPE. 5. To a. himselfe of those ties MILT. Hence **Abso·lvable** *a.* †**Absolvatory,** erron. f. ABSOLUTORY, q.v. **Absol·ved** *ppl. a.* set free, † solved. **Abso·lver,** one who pronounces absolution, or acquits. **Abso·lving** *vbl. sb.* acquitting, † solving.

Absolvent (ăbsǫ·lvĕnt, ăbz-). 1651. [ad. L. *absolventem.*] *ppl. a.* Acquitting 1837. As *sb.* One who absolves 1651.

Absonant (æ·bsŏnănt), *a.* 1564. [f. L. *ab* + *sonantem.*] Discordant, harsh. Also *fig.* Const. *to, from.*

†**Absonous** (æ·bsŏnəs), *a.* 1622. [f. L. *absonus.*] *lit.* Out of tune; *fig.* incongruous. Const. *to.*

Absorb (ăbsǭ·ɹb), *v.* Pa. pple. **absorbed,** formerly **absorpt.** 1490. [a. Fr. *absorber,* OFr. *asorber, asorbir*:—L. *absorbere.*] I. †1. To swallow up; as water, etc.; also *fig.* –1800. 2. Hence, To incorporate 1553. 3. To engross the attention or faculties 1830.

1. To be absorpt..in a lake of fire T. BURNET. 2. *To be absorbed,* to be swallowed up, so as no longer to exist apart. Into the English nation his

own followers were gradually absorbed FREEMAN. 3. To get absorbed in a book KANE.

II. 1. To suck or drink in 1626. 2. To take up by chemical or molecular action 1707.

1. The clay refuses to a. the water. 2. It is possible to a. hydrogen in certain metals ROSCOE. Hence **Absorbabi·lity**, the quality of being absorbable. **Abso·rbable** *a.* capable of being absorbed. **Abso·rbed** *ppl. a.* swallowed up; *fig.* engrossed. **Abso·rbedly** *adv.* with engrossed attention. **Abso·rbedness**, engrossed attention. **Abso·rber**, one who, or that which, absorbs. **Abso·rbing** *ppl. a.* swallowing, imbibing; incorporating; *fig.* engrossing. **Abso·rbingly** *adv.*

Absorbency (æbsǭ·ɹbĕnsi). 1762. [f. L. *absorbentem.*] †1. The action of absorbing. 2. The quality of being absorbent 1859.

Absorbent (æbsǭ·ɹbĕnt). 1718. [ad. L. *absorbentem.*] A. *adj.* Absorbing; absorptive. B. *sb.* 1. An absorbing substance, *esp.* chalk, magnesia, etc. in *Med.*, which absorb the acidity of the stomach. Also *fig.* 2. *Physiol.* (in *pl.*) The vessels (e. g. the lacteals in animals, the extremities of the roots in plants) through which the process of absorption is carried on 1753.

1. *fig.* The country gentlemen, the absorbents of every prejudice LD. COCKBURN.

†**Absorbi·tion.** = ABSORPTION. SIR T. BROWNE.

Absorpt (æbsǭ·ɹpt), *ppl. a. arch.* 1528. [ad. L. *absorptus.*] = later ABSORBED.

A. in yellow care 1736.

Absorption (æbsǭ·ɹpʃən). 1597. [ad. L. *absorptionem.*] I. †1. The swallowing up of bodies –1753. 2. The swallowing up by inclusion in or assimilation to something else, *esp.* (*Med.* and *Path.*) of tissues or deposits 1741. 3. Engrossment of the faculties 1855.

1. The a. or burial J. KING. 2. The a. of dialects by the Latin 1860, of peasant-holdings SEELEY. 3. The a. of the English mind in the war DICKENS.

II. 1. The sucking in of fluid, light, etc. 1744. Also *attrib.* 2. *Physiol.* The imbibing of fluids by the vessels and tissues of the body, *esp.* by the lacteals of the intestine 1753.

1. A. of radiant heat TYNDALL. 2. The functions of digestion and a. CARPENTER.

Absorptive (æbsǭ·ɹptiv), *a.* 1664. [f. L. *absorpt-*, *absorbere.*] Having the quality of absorbing. *fig.* Engrossing. Hence **Abso·rptiveness. Ab sorpti·vity.**

Absquatulate (æbskwǫ·tiulēᴵt), *v.* 1830. [Of joc. U.S. origin, simulating a L. formation.] *intr.* To depart hurriedly or secretly, decamp, abscond.

Abstain (ăbstēᴵ·n), *v.* ME. [a. Fr. *abstenir*, refash. of OFr. *astenir*:—L. *abstinere.*] †1. *refl.* To keep *oneself* (*of, from*) –1535. 2. *intr.* To refrain (*from*) ME.; *esp.* from wine, etc. 1534. †3. *trans.* To keep back –1658.

1. To absteyne them selues from Idols COVERDALE. 2. Many.. nolens volens.. do asteine [from meate] BOORDE. 3. To a. men from marying MILT. Hence **Abstai·ning** *vbl. sb.* = ABSTINENCE; *ppl. a.* practising abstinence.

Abstainer (ăbstēᴵ·nəɹ). 1535. [f. prec.] One who abstains; *esp.* one who abstains from alcoholic drinks; in older writers a Nazarite.

Abstemious (ăbstī·miəs), *a.* 1610. [f. L. *abstemius.*] 1. Dispensing with wine and rich food; temperate; sparing 1624. 2. Abstinent (from other things). *rare.* 1610.

1. An absteinous life HEYWOOD. Mother and father were a. CARLYLE. The meal of the Saracens was a. SCOTT. 2. Be more a., Or else good night your vow *Temp.* IV. i. 53. Hence **Abste·mious-ly** *adv.*, **-ness.**

Abstention (ăbste·nʃən). 1521. [a. Fr., f. L. *abstent-*, *abstinere*; see ABSTAIN.] †1. The act of restraining –1653. 2. The act or state of refraining 1624. Hence **Abste·ntionist**, a partisan of a. **Abste·ntious** *a.* self-restraining.

Absterge (ăbstǝ̄·ɹdʒ), *v.* 1541. [a. L. *abstergere.*] To wipe away; to cleanse; *fig.* to purge.

Thynges yᵗ absterge or wasshe moderatly R. COPLAND. Hence **Abste·rgent** *a.* cleansing; *sb.* [sc. *substance.*] **Abste·rsion**, the act or process of cleansing or purging. **Abste·rsive** *a.* having the quality of cleansing or purging; *sb.* [sc. *agent.*] **Abste·rsiveness. Abste·rsory** *a.* abstersive.

†**Abste·rse**, *v.* 1646. [f. L. *abstersus*, cf. *asperse.*] = ABSTERGE.

Abstinence (æ·bstinĕns). ME. [a. Fr. *abstinence*, refash. on OFr. *astenance*:—L. *abstinentia.* See ABSTAIN.] 1. The action or practice of abstaining (*from*) ME. *spec.* Abstaining from hostilities, an armistice ME. 2. *absol.* Continence (the oldest sense); fasting; abstaining from alcoholic beverages, total abstinence.

1. Jewish a. from certaine kinds of meates HOOKER. The truce or a. BURTON. 2. Agayns glotonye the remedie is a. CHAUCER. A. ingenders maladies *L. L. L.* IV. iii. 259.

Abstinency (æ·bstinĕnsi). 1576. [See prec.] The quality of being abstinent; fasting; a fast. (Never used with *from.*)

Abstinent (æ·bstinĕnt). ME. [a. Fr. *abstinent*, refash. on OFr. *astenant*:—L. *abstinentem*; see ABSTAIN.] A. *adj.* Refraining; *esp.* from indulgence of appetite. B. *sb.* One who abstains, a faster. In *Eccl. Hist.* the *Abstinents* were a sect who appeared in the 3rd c. Hence **A·bstinently** *adv.*

Abstract (æ·bstrækt). ME. [ad. L. *abstractus.* Orig., pple. and adj., *abstra·ct*; later, adj. only, *a·bstract.*]

A. *pple.* and *adj.* †1. Derived –1496. †2. = ABSTRACTED 1. Const. *from.* –1765. 3. = ABSTRACTED 2. *arch.* 1509. 4. Separated from matter, practice, or particulars; ideal; abstruse. Opp. to *concrete.* 1557. 5. *absol.* 'The abstract'; the ideal 1615. Hence **A·bstract-ly** *adv.*, **-ness.**

2. The more a. from the body..the more fit [etc.] J. MORRIS. 3. Steady step and a. air 1860. A. numbers 1557, names HOBBES, substances CUDWORTH, ideas COLERIDGE, science HERSCHELL, reasoning 1870. 5. Justice in the a., is nothing 1628.

B. *sb.* 1. One thing concentrating in itself the virtues of several; a compendium 1561; *spec.* a summary or epitome 1528. Also *attrib.* 2. An abstract term 1530.

1. A man who is the a. of all faults, That all men follow *Ant. & Cl.* I. iv. 9. An a. of all that was said BURNET. **Abstract of title** (*Law*): an epitome of the evidences of ownership. 2. Substantives.. suche as the Logicians call abstractes 1530.

Abstract (æbstræ·kt), *v.* 1542. [f. ABSTRACT *ppl. a.* Pa. pple. *abstract*, later *abstracted.*] 1. *trans.* To withdraw, take away; *euphem.* to take away secretly, etc.; to purloin 1542. Also *absol.* †*Chem.* To extract –1725. 2. *trans.* To draw off; disengage *from* 1557. *absol.* To divert. 3. *refl.* To withdraw oneself, to retire *from. lit.* and *fig.* 1671. 4. To separate in mental conception; to consider apart from the concrete 1612. †5. To derive. Cf. ABSTRACT *a.* 1. 1610. 6. To epitomize 1678.

1. The brande abstracted and abjected BOORDE. Property abstracted by the Arabs LAYARD. 2. To a. the mixed people each from other SELDEN. To soothe and to a. LAMB. 3. To a. oneself from one's own interest STEELE. *Abstracting from*, withdrawing in thought from (*Obs.* or *arch.*). Abstracting from his crimes JENISON. 4. We must.. a. the notions of time, of space, and of matter GIBBON. 6. This system I..abstracted GIBBON. Hence **Abstra·cter.**

Abstracted (æbstræ·ktĕd), *ppl. a.* 1615. [f. prec.] 1. Drawn off; separate, apart *from* 1660. 2. Withdrawn from the contemplation of present objects; absent in mind 1643. †3. Separated from the concrete, ideal; abstruse (replaced by ABSTRACT *a.* 4) –1823.

1. The Evil one a. stood From his own evil MILT. 2. An a. thinker 1731, mood SCOTT. 3. A. ideas of virtue JOHNSON. Hence **Abstra·ctedly** *adv.* **Abstra·ctedness**, †abstractness; †disinterestedness; absence (of mind); ideality.

Abstraction (æbstræ·kʃən). 1549. [a. Fr., ad. L. *abstractionem.*] 1. The act of abstracting (see ABSTRACT *v.* 1). 2. *Chem.* The drawing off, or exhaling away, a menstruum from the subject it had been put to dissolve; distillation; cohobation 1753. 3. The act of separating in thought 1647. 4. The result of abstracting; a mere idea; something visionary 1644. 5. Seclusion from things of sense 1649. 6. Absence of mind 1790.

1. Justice must have..a. from all affections R. COKE. A wrongful a. of wealth from [etc.] MILL. 3. A. is thus ..a negation to one or more objects, in consequence of its [the mind's] concentration on another SIR W. HAMILTON. 4. Death is a mighty a., like Night. HAZLITT. 6. Wrapped up in grave a. BOSWELL. Hence **Abstra·ctionist**, one who deals with abstractions. †**A·bstracti·tious** *a.* resulting from a.

Abstractive (ăbstræ·ktiv). 1490. [ad. L. **abstractivus*, f. *abstractus.*] A. *adj.* Of abstracting tendency or character (see ABSTRACT *v.* 1, 4, 6). B. *sb.* Anything abstractive; *spec.* an abstract 1611. Hence **Abstra·ctively** *adv.* in the abstract; separately. **Abstra·ctiveness.**

†**Abstru·de**, *v.* 1627. [ad. L. *abstrudere.*] To thrust away.

Abstruse (æbstrū·s), *a.* 1599. [ad. L. *abstrusus*, *abstrudere.*] †1. Hidden, secret –1762. 2. Remote from apprehension; recondite 1599.

1. Hidden in the most a. dungeons SHELTON. 2. The abstruser parts of a discourse SWIFT. Hence **Abstru·sely** *adv.* **Abstru·seness. Abstru·sity** (*arch.*) abstruseness; anything abstruse.

†**Absu·me**, *v.* 1596. [ad. L. *absumere.*] To waste away –1756. Hence †**Absumption**, the process of wasting away –1661.

Absurd (æbsǝ̄·ɹd). 1557. [a. Fr. *absurde*, ad. L. *absurdus.*] A. *adj.* †1. *Mus.* Inharmonious 1617. 2. Out of harmony with reason or propriety; in mod. use, plainly opposed to reason, and *hence* ridiculous, silly 1557. †B. *sb.* [sc. *thing*] –1635. Now ABSURDITY.

2. A fault, To reason most a. *Haml.* I. ii. 103. Froward and A. men for Businesse BACON. Don't be a. BLACK. Hence **Absu·rdly** *adv.* **Absu·rdness.**

Absurdity (æbsǝ̄·ɹdĭti). 1528. [a. Fr. *absurdité*, f. L. *absurditatem.*] †1. *Mus.* Lack of harmony 1674. 2. The state or quality of being ABSURD (sense 2); folly 1528. 3. Anything absurd, e. g. a statement, action, or custom 1528.

2. The a. of delaying reformation JOHNSON. A piece of prolix a. CARLYLE. 3. An a. in Philosophy SIR T. BROWNE. Anachronisms or absurdities MCCARTHY.

Absurdum (æbsǝ̄·ɹdŏm). [L.] An absurd or illogical conclusion or condition. See REDUCTIO *ad a.*

Abthain, -thane (æ·bþēᴵn). 1535. [a. med.L. *abthania* for Gael. *Abdhaine*, abbacy.] 1. Erron. use: a 'Superior Thane'. 2. An abbacy (*Sc.*). Hence **A·bthainry, -thanrie**, an abbacy; the territory and jurisdiction of an abbot. **A·bthanage**, the jurisdiction of the supposed ABTHANE.

Abumbral (æ:bɪ̆ŏ·mbrăl), *a.* *Zool.* Short for next.

Abumbrellar (æ:bɪ̆ŏmbre·lăɹ), *a.* [f. L. *ab* + UMBRELLA, the disk of *Acalepha.*] In sea-blubbers: Pertaining to that surface of the *velum* which is turned away from the 'umbrella'; opp. to *adumbrellar.*

‖**Abuna** (ābū·nă). 1635. [Eth.; = 'our father'.] The Patriarch of the Abyssinian Ch.

Abundance (ăbŏ·ndăns). ME. [a. OFr. (*h*)*abondance*:—L. *abundantia.* Also *habundance*, as if *hab-*, f. *habere.*] 1. Overflowing state or condition; superfluity; hence, *loosely*, plentifulness ME. 2. A large quantity, or (less correctly) number ME. 3. Affluence ME.

1. The..aboundance of his love FISHER. 2. A. of good things DE FOE. A. who wa..t a morsel of bread FIELDING. Also † with nouns: Wine a. HOBBES; and † adjs.: A. better SWIFT. 3. The a. of the rich will not suffer him to sleep *Eccl.* v. 12. var. † **Abu·ndancy.**

Abundant (ăbŏ·ndănt), *a.* ME. [a. OFr. (*h*)*abundant*:—L. *abundantem.* See prec.] 1. Overflowing, more than enough; plentiful; (orig. of fluids) *c* 1450. 2. Possessing in superfluity; wealthy (*in*, †*of*) ME. Also quasi-*adv.*

1. Where synne is haboundant charity waxeth colde FISHER. 2. In labours moare aboundant TINDALE. Hence **Abu·ndantly** *adv.*

Abune, obs. north. form of ABOVE.

Aburst (ăbǝ̄·ɹst), *adv.* ME. [f. A *prep.*[1] + BURST *sb.*] †1. In a burst (of rage, etc.). 2. Bursting (*mod.*).

Abuse (ăbiū·z), *v.* ME. [a. Fr. *abuser*:—**abusare*, f. *abusus.*] †1. *Sc.* To disuse –1471. 2. To misuse; to take a bad advantage of 1413. †3. To misrepresent; to adulterate. *refl.* To make false pretensions –1749. †4. To misuse any one's confidence; to impose upon him –1776; *refl.* and *pass.* To be deceived. –1743. 5. To ill-use 1556. 6. To violate. *arch.* 1553. 7. To wrong with words; to malign 1604.

2. The liberty of the press may be abused JUNIUS. To a. an opportunity SCOTT, authority FREEMAN. 3. Abused by translators 1702. He hath been grossly

abused to you FIELDING. 4. 'The serpent me abusit' LYNDESAY. 5. To a. one's wife and family (*mod.*). 7. Of life as honest As you that thus a. me *Oth.* v. i. 123. Hence **Abu·sed** *ppl. a.* worn out; misused; deceived. **Abu·sedly** *adv.* **Abusee·**, correl. to ABUSER¹. †**Abu·sement,** a misleading. **Abu·ser¹,** one who abuses (in senses 2, 4, 6, 7).

Abuse (ăbiū·s), *sb.* 1486. [a. Fr. *abus* :—L. *abusus.*] †1. The process of using up -1539. 2. Improper use, perversion 1538; in *Rhet.* catachresis 1589. 3. An improper usage, a corrupt practice 1486. †4. Imposture, deceit -1653. †5. Ill-usage -1682. 6. Violation, defilement (now only in *self-a.*). 7. Injurious speech 1559.

2. A. of language MILL, of terms BROUGHAM, of the eyes HARLAN. 3. The abuses of the courte CAXTON. The hoary head of inveterate a. BURKE. 4. Or is it some a.? *Haml.* IV. vii. 51. 5. The a. of Falstaffe *Merry W.* v. iii. 8. 7. Treasonable abuses *Meas. for M.* v. i. 347. After exchanging a good deal of a. MACAULAY. Hence †**Abu·seful** *a.* abounding in abuse. **Abu·sefully** *adv.* abusively.

Ab-usefulness. *rare.* Used by Ruskin for, Capability of improper use.

†**Abu·ser²**. 1646. [a. Fr. *abuser.*] Illegal or wrongful use -1734.

†**Abu·sh(e, abu·sse, abu·sche,** *v.* ME. [Short for AMBUSH *v.*] To ambush -1350. Hence †**Abu·shment,** ambush.

†**Abu·sion.** ME. [a. OFr., ad. L. *abusionem*; see ABUSE *v.*] 1. Misuse, perversion -1558; *esp.* of the truth -1640; in *Rhet.* catachresis -1636. 2. Violation of law, or right, or propriety -1718. 3. Injurious language -1587.

Abusive (ăbiū·siv), *a.* 1583. [a. Fr. *abusif, -ive* :—L. *abusivus.*] Characterized by abuse: hence 1. Misapplied; in *Rhet.* catachrestic 1583. 2. Full of abuses (*arch.*) 1589. †3. Deceitful -1667. †4. Given to ill-using -1669. 5. Scurrilous 1621.

1. The a. acception..of the English word 'priest' FULKE. 2. The a. enormities of..our times NASHE. 3. Th' a. Shews of sense DANIELL. An a. treaty BACON. 5. An a. satire HOWELL. Hence **Abu·sively** *adv.* incorrectly; with foul language. **Abu·siveness.**

Abut (ăbɒ·t), *v.* ME. [repr. both OFr. *abouter*, to join two things end to end, f. *à* + *bout*; and OFr. *abuter, abutter*, to touch with an end, f. *à* + *but.* Cf. mod.Fr. *aboutir.* In Arch. *abut* = OF. *abuter, abutter.*] 1. To end at, border *on* 1463. Also *trans.* (*on* omitted). 2. To end *on*, or *against*; to lean *upon* at one end 1578. Also *trans.* (*on* omitted). 3. To cause to end *against* 1802.

1. [Selborne parish] abuts on twelve parishes WHITE. Abutting Southwark Park 1882. 2. The Chapter House abutted on the south aisle MILMAN. Hence **Abu·tter,** one who or that which abuts; *spec.* an owner of contiguous property. **Abu·tting** *ppl. a.* projecting towards; touching.

Abutilon (ăbiū·tilǫn). 1731. [mod.L., ad. Arab.] *Bot.* A genus of plants (N.O. *Malvaceæ*).

Abutment (ăbɒ·tmĕnt). 1644. [f. ABUT *v.*] 1. The meeting end to end; the place of junction. 2. The action of abutting 1870. 3. *Arch.* The solid part of a pier, wall, etc. which supports the thrust or lateral pressure of an arch 1793. 4. That upon which anything abuts or leans 1734.

1. At the abutments of four stately ways EVELYN. 3. The abutments of a bridge mean the walls adjoining the land NICHOLSON. 4. The whole scheme and a. of the..project NORTH.

Abuttal (ăbɒ·tăl). 1630. [f. ABUT *v.* (sense 1).] Abutment; *pl.* the parts in which land abuts on neighbouring lands. Hence †**Abu·ttalling** *vbl. sb.* the declaration of abuttals.

Aby, abye (ăbəi·), *v. arch.* ME. [f. A- *pref.* 1 + BUY; see BUY.] †1. To buy -1503. 2. To pay the penalty for, usu. with *sore, dearly*, etc. *arch.* ME. 3. To pay; suffer. *arch.* ME. †4. *absol.* To pay the penalty, to atone -1596. †5. *absol.* To endure, remain; = ABIDE -1596.

1. Thus dere abought is Love CHAUCER. 2. They shall a. it! SCOTT. 3. Thou wouldst a. A heavy fate MORRIS. 5. Nought that wanteth rest can long a. SPENSER.

Abysm (ăbi·z'm). ME. [a. OFr. *abisme* :—pop. L. **abyssimus*, superl. of *abyssus*; see ABYSS.] 1. a. The great deep, supposed to be *spec.*: b. a subterraneous reservoir of waters ME.; c. hell, the infernal regions 1509. 2. Any deep immeasurable space or cavity. *lit.* and *fig.* Also *attrib.*

1. b. Ocean's bed Over the a. COLERIDGE. c. Into th' Abisme of hell *Ant. & Cl.* III. xiii. 147. 2. The Abysme of Time *Temp.* I. ii. 50. Hence **Aby·smal** *a.* of, pertaining to, or resembling an abyss. *lit.* and *fig.* **Aby·smally** *adv.* unfathomably.

Abyss (ăbi·s). ME. [ad. L. *abyssus*, a. Gr. ἄβυσσος bottomless, sb. the deep. ABYSM is *arch.* or *poet.*] 1. The great deep, the primal chaos; the bowels of the earth; the infernal pit; see ABYSM. 2. A bottomless gulf; any unfathomable cavity or void space 1639. Also *fig.* 3. *Her.* The centre of an escutcheon 1753.

1. The depe bottomlesse abisse of the yerth 1534. 2. The awful a. which separates us from the stars HERSCHELL. *fig.* An abyssus of goodness BACON. Abysses of disgrace BURKE.

Aby·ss, *v.* [f. the sb.] To engulf. LOWELL.

Aby·ssal, *a.* 1691. [ad. late L. *abyssalis*, f. *abyssus.*] Unfathomable. *Abyssal Zone*, the belt of water below 300 fathoms.

‖**Abyssus** (ăbi·sɒs). [L.] Earlier f. ABYSS.

†**Ac,** *conj.* [OE. *ac.*] But -1535.

Ac-, *pref.*, assim. form of L. *ad-*, bef. *c-* (*k-*) and *qu-*. Occ., but erron., for *a-* = OFr. *an-, en-* :—*in-*, or *es-* :—*ex-*, as in EE. *acumbre*, OFr. *encombrer*, and also for *a-* = OE. *a-* or *on-*, as in *a(c)curse*, etc. Only *a-* is pronounced.

-ac, *suffix*, also **-aque, -ak(e, -ack,** repr. Gr. -ακός, -ακή, -ακόν = adj. suffix -κός, of or belonging to, w. sb. in -ια, -ιος, -ιον, as καρδιακ-ός *cardiac*, etc. Hence L. *cardiacus*, etc., whence Fr. words in *-aque.* Eng. words, e.g. *ammoniac, maniac*, etc., are adopted partly from Fr., partly from Gr. or L.; see also -ACAL.

Acacia¹ (ăkē·ʃiă). 1543. [a. Lat., a. Gr. ἀκακία, ? f. ἀκή a point.] 1. *Bot.* A genus of leguminous shrubs or trees, of the *Mimosa* tribe, yielding Gum Acacia, Gum Arabic, Catechu, etc. 2. *pop.* The North-American Locust-tree or False-Acacia (*Robinia pseud-Acacia*) 1664. 3. *Med.* The inspissated juice of the unripe fruit of species of *Acacia* and *Mimosa* 1601.

†**Aca·cia².** Something like a roll or bag, seen on medals in the hands of consuls or emperors since Anastasius. Chambers *Cycl.* 1751.

Acacine (æ·kăsin). [f. ACACIA.] Pure gum arabic.

Academe (ækădī·m). *poet.* 1588. [f. L. *Academia*; in Milton f. *Academus*; see Hor. *Ep.* II. ii. 45.] = ACADEMY 1, 3.

Our Court shall be a little Achademe *L. L. L.* I. i. 13. The olive grove of A. MILT. Hence **Acade·mial** *a.* academic. †**Acade·mian,** a disciple of Plato; an academician.

Academic (ækăde·mik). 1586. [ad. med.L. *academicus.*] A. *adj.* 1. Of the school or philosophy of Plato; sceptical 1610. 2. Of or belonging to an academy; collegiate, scholarly 1588. 3. Of or belonging to a learned society; belonging to an Academician 1879. 4. Not leading to a decision; unpractical (*mod.*).

1. A very a. faith HUME. 2. An academicke life BP. HALL. Rusticity and a. seclusion CARLYLE. 4. A purely a. discussion (*mod.*).

B. *sb.* [The adj. used *absol.*] 1. A Platonist 1586. 2. A member of a college or university 1587; *pl.* academical robes 1823. 3. = ACADEMICIAN. *rare.* 1751. 4. pl. *Academics*, the *Academica* of Cicero.

1. The schools Of academics old and new MILT. 2. The uniform habit of the academics, the square cap and gown GIBBON. Hence **Acade·micism,** a tenet of the A. philosophy.

Academical (ækăde·mikăl). 1587. [f. prec.] A. *adj.* = ACADEMIC *a.* 1, 2, 3, 4. B. *sb. pl.* Academical robes 1823. Hence **Acade·mically** *adv.* platonically; sceptically; in relation to an academy.

Academician (ăkæ:dĕmi·ʃăn). 1749. [a. Fr. *académicien*, f. med.L. *academicus.*] 1. A member of an academy, or society for promoting arts and sciences; orig. used of the Fr. Academies, and the Eng. Royal Academy 1755. 2. = ACADEMIC *sb.* 2. *rare.* 1749.

Academy (ăkæ·dĕmi). 1474. [a. Fr. *académie*, ad. L. *academia*, a. Gr. ἀκαδημία, prop. ἀκαδήμεια, f. Ἀκάδημος name of a man.] 1. The name of a garden near Athens where Plato taught 1474. 2. The school or system of Plato 1677. 3. An institution for the study of the arts and sciences, e.g. a university; *pop.* a school claiming to rank between a college and an ordinary school (a sense discredited in Eng.) 1549; †*fig.* the arts taught in an academy, or a treatise on them -1754. 4. Hence, a place of training, *esp.* in a special art, etc., as a Riding A., the Royal Military A., etc. 1570. 5. A Society for the promotion of literature, art, or science, as the French A., the Royal A., called in Eng. 'the Academy' 1691. 6. *Artists' slang.* Short for *A.-figure.* Also *attrib.*

3. The oldest A. in Scotland is that of Perth GRANT. *fig.* That living a. of love-lore my Lady Vane H. WALPOLE. 4. *A.* is particularly .. a riding-school 1751. *Comb.* **a.-figure,** a drawing, half-life-size, in crayon or pencil, from the nude. Hence †**Aca·demism,** the Academic doctrine. †**Aca·demist,** a Platonist; a sceptic; an ACADEMICIAN (sense 1); a pupil in a riding-school. **Aca·demize** *v.* (*rare*) to form into an a.

Acadialite (ăkē¹·diăləit). [f. *Acadie*, Fr. name of Nova Scotia + -LITE.] *Min.* A reddish chabazite.

Acadian (ăkē·dian), *a.* and *sb.* 1790. [f. *Acadie* (see prec.).] Of or native to Nova Scotia.

Acajou (a·kaʒu). 1725. [Fr.: see CASHEW.] 1. The Cashew or Cashew-nut. 2. A medicine yielded by the mahogany tree (Fr. *acajou*) 1879.

-acal, comp. suffix = -AC (q.v.), often used subst., + -AL, repr. L. *-alis, -ale, of the nature of* or *connected with* the *attribute* in *-ac.*

†**Acale, ak-,** *ppl. a.* ME. [?:—OE. *of-calen*, or :—lost OE. *acalen*, f. *a-* pref. intens. + *calan.*] Cold -1393.

‖**Acalepha** (ækălī·fa), *sb. pl.* 1846. [mod.L. sb. pl. (prop. adj. sc. *animalia*), f. Gr. ἀκαλήφη a nettle; also *Acalephæ* fem. pl.] *Zool.* A class of radiate marine animals, including the Jelly-fishes and Medusas, possessing the power of stinging. Occ. called sea-nettles. (Sing. *Acaleph, Acalephan.*) Hence **Acale·phan** *a.* and *sb.* **Acale·phoid** *a.*

Aca·lycine, *a.* 1858. [ad. mod.L. *acalycinus*, f. Gr. ἀ + κάλυξ.] *Bot.* Having no calyx. var. **Acaly·cinous.**

Acaly·culate, *a.* [f. Gr. ἀ + L. *calyculus*, dim. of *calyx.*] *Bot.* Having no calyculus or accessory calyx.

Acanth (ăkæ·nþ). 1662. [a. Fr. *acanthe.*] = ACANTHUS.

Acanthite (ăkæ·nþəit). [f. Gr. ἄκανθα.] *Min.* An iron-black sulphide of silver, found at Freiberg, etc.

Acantho-, ad. Gr. ἀκανθο-, combining form of ἄκανθα, with sense of 'thorn, thorny'. **acantho·ce·phalous** [Gr. κεφαλή] *a. Bot.* spiny-headed; **-cladous** [Gr. κλάδος] *a. Bot.* with spiny branches; **-logical** *a. Zool.* pertaining to the study of spines; **-phorous** [Gr. -φόρος] *a. Bot.* spine-bearing; **-pterous** [Gr. πτερόν] *a.* spiny-winged; spiny-finned = -ptery-gious; ‖ **-ptery·gii** [Gr. πτερύγιον] *sb. pl. Zool.* an order of Fishes, a group of the Osseous sub-division, having spiny rays in the dorsal fins; hence **-ptery·gian** *a.* and *sb.* [sc. *fish*], **-ptery·gious** *a.*

Acanthus (akæ·nþɒs). 1616. [L., a. Gr. ἄκανθος, f. ἄκανθα, f. ἀκή.] 1. *Bot.* A genus of herbaceous plants (monopetalous exogens, N.O. *Acanthaceæ*). *pop.* Chiefly *A. spinosus*, Bear's Breech or Brank-Ursine 1616. 2. *Arch.* A conventionalized leaf of *A. spinosus*, used in Corinthian and Composite capitals 1751.

1. Beares-breech, called of the Latines A. 1616. Hence **Acantha·ceous** *a.* of the type of the A., epithet of N.O. *Acanthaceæ.* **Aca·nthine** *a.* pertaining to the A.

Aca·psular, *a.* 1879. [f. A- *pref.* 14 + L. *capsula.*] *Bot.* Having no capsule.

Aca·rdiac, *a.* 1879. [f. Gr. ἀκάρδιος.] *Physiol.* Without a heart.

‖**Acariasis** (ækărəi·ăsis). 1828. [mod.L., f.

Gr. ἀκαρί.] *Path.* A skin-disease, caused by *Acari.*

‖ **Acaridæ** (ăkæ·ridī), *sb. pl.* 1847. [f. Acarus.] *Zool.* A family of Arachnida, comprising mites and ticks. (Sing. *Acaridan.*) Hence **Acaridan** *a.* and *sb.*

Acarpellous (ækaɹpe·ləs), *a.* 1879. [f. Gr. ἀ + mod.L. *carpellus.*] *Bot.* Having no carpels.

Acar·pous, *a.* [f. Gr. ἀ + καρπός.] *Bot.* Unfruitful.

‖ **Acarus** (æ·kărŏs). Pl. **acari.** 1658. [mod. L., f. Gr. ἀκαρί.] *Zool.* A genus of Arachnida, embracing the cheese-mite, etc.; a mite. Hence **A·caricide,** a preparation for killing *Acari.* **A·carine** *a.* **A·caroid** *a.*

†**Acast,** *v.* ME. [f. A- *pref.* 1 + Cast.] To cast away.

Acatalectic (ăkætăle·ktik), *a.* 1589. [ad. L. *acatalecticus,* ad. Gr. ἀκατάληκτος; see Catalectic.] *Pros.* Not catalectic; complete in its syllables: also as *sb.* [sc. *verse*].

Acatalepsy (akæ·tălepsi). 1605. [ad. L. *acatalepsia,* a. Gr. ἀκαταληψία.] Incomprehensibility (of the object):—a Sceptic term; correl. of Agnosticism.

Acatale·ptic, *a. rare.* 1731. [f. L. *acataleptius,* f. Gr. ἀκατάληπτος.] Relating to acatalepsy; incomprehensible.

†**Acate.** ME. [a. OFr. *acat, achat,* stem of *acater* (mod.Fr. *acheter*):—late L. *accaptare.*] 1. Purchasing. Chaucer. 2. *pl.* or *collect. sing.* Things purchased; dainties -1692. (Aphet. to Cates *c* 1460.)

Bread, wine, acates B. Jons.

†**Aca·ter, -tour.** ME. [a. Anglo-N. *acatour* (mod.Fr. *acheteur*):—late L. *accaptatorem.*] A purveyor -1637. Hence †**Aca·tery,** provisions purchased; also, the store-room for them -1751.

Acaudate (ăkǭ·deⁱt), *a.* 1879. [f. A- *pref.* 14 + Caudate.] Tailless. var. **Acaudal.**

Acaulescent (æ·kǭle·sĕnt), *a.* 1854. [f. A- *pref.* 14 + Caulescent.] *Bot.* Apparently stemless. vars. **Acau·line, Acaulo·se, Acau·lous** [all f. L. *acaulis,* Fr. *acaule*].

Accadian (ăkēⁱ·diăn). Of or belonging to Accad. See *Gen.* x. 10. A pre-Assyrian language preserved in cuneiform inscriptions.

Accede (ǣksī·d). ME. [ad. L. *accedere.*] 1. To come forward, approach -1677. 2. To arrive at, or enter upon an office, etc. Const. *to.* 1756. 3. To give one's adhesion; to assent *to* (†*unto*) ME.

1. A property, acceding, or seceding, changes its subject F. Hall. 2. To a. to the purple Burton, to a post 1879. 3. To a. to a confederacy Thirlwall. Hence **Acce·dence,** the action of acceding. **Acce·der.** *rare.*

‖ **Accelerando** (ǣkselĕræ·ndoᵘ). [It.] *Mus.* A direction: With gradual increase of speed.

†**Acce·lerate,** *ppl. a.* 1527. [ad. L. *acceleratus, accelerare,* f. *ac-* = *ad-* + *celer* swift.] Quickened.

Accelerate (ǣkse·lĕreⁱt), *v.* 1530. [f. prec.] 1. To quicken a motion or a thing in motion 1601. 2. To hasten the occurrence of 1530; hence, to antedate 1855. 3. *intr.* To become swifter 1646.

1. Every step accelerates the rapidity of the descent Junius. A. your crucible 1631. 2. The commons accelerated the grant Stubbs. Invention.. accelerated the baptism of Constantine Milman. Hence **Acce·lerated** *ppl. a.* *Accelerated motion:* motion continually increased in velocity. **Acce·leratedly** *adv.* **Acce·lerating** *vbl. sb.* and *ppl. a.* *Accelerating force:* a force that produces continually increased motion. **Acce·lerative, Acce·leratory** *adjs.* pertaining or tending to acceleration.

Acceleration (ǣkselĕrēⁱ·ʃən). 1531. [ad. L. *accelerationem;* see Accelerate.] 1. The action of accelerating, or the being accelerated; increased speed 1534. 2. The extent to which anything is accelerated; in *Nat. Phil.* the rate of increase per unit of time 1656.

1. A. of plants Cowley. With what a. I advance towards death Johnson. 2. *Uniform,* or *constant a.:* the unvarying amount per second added to the rate at which a body is moving, e. g. under the influence of gravity. *Astr.* and *Physics.* A. of the *fixed stars;* the time (3′ 55·9″) which the stars gain upon the sun in passing the meridian each day. Of the *planets,* the increased velocity of their advance from aphelion to perihelion. Of the *moon,* an increase (about 11″ per century) in the speed of the moon's mean motion. Of the *tides,* the amount by which high or low water occurs at any place before the calculated time.

Accelerator (ǣkse·lĕreⁱtəɹ). 1611. [f. Accelerate *v.*] 1. He who or that which accelerates; *spec.* certain nerves and muscles that accelerate organic functions; also, a light mail-cart used by postmen. b. An apparatus to regulate the speed of the engine in a motor-vehicle, esp. for increasing speed 1900.

†**Acce·nd,** *v.* ME. [ad. L. *accendere.*] To kindle, set on fire. *lit.* and *fig.* -1720.

†**Acce·nsed,** *ppl. a.* 1573. [f. L. *accensus.*] Kindled, set on fire -1760.

Acce·nsion. *arch.* 1646. [ad. L. *accensionem.*] Kindling or being kindled.

Accent (æ·ksĕnt), *sb.* 1538. [a. Fr. *accent,* OFr. *acent:*—L. *accentum* accus. = προσῳδία, 'song added to' speech.] 1. A prominence given to one syllable in a word, or in a phrase 1581.

Accent in Gr. (προσῳδία) and L. meant orig. variety of musical pitch in pronouncing the syllables of a word; later, stress only. The grammatical varieties of accent in Eng. are all varieties of stress.

2. a. The marks, (′) *acutus,* (‵) *gravis,* (^) *circumflexus,* indicating the nature and position of a spoken accent in a word. b. Marks (mostly ′ ‵ ^), distinguishing the qualities of sound indicated by a letter, called diacritical accents, and in Eng. ‵ to show that *-ed* is pronounced 1596. c. Marks placed over and under Heb. consonants, as signs of tone and of interpunctuation; hence *fig.* the minutest particular (of the Mosaic law) 1610. 3. The mode of utterance peculiar to an individual, locality, or nation 1600. 4. The way in which anything is said 1538. 5. *poet.* A significant tone or sound; a word; *pl.* speech 1595. 6. *Pros.* The stress laid at intervals on certain syllables of a verse, the succession constituting the rhythm 1588. 7. *Mus. Anciently:* the marks placed over words to show the notes, turns, or phrases to which they were to be sung. *Now:* stress recurring at intervals generally fixed, but variable by syncopation and cross accentuation 1609. 8. *fig.* Distinctive stress; a distinguishing mark, character or tone 1639.

1. Though we do not obserue quantitie, yet we obserue the a. very precisely Sidney. 2. b. *Accento:* an a. or point ouer anie letter to giue it a due sound Florio. c. Every pricke and a. of the law Holland. 3. A slight a., a strong provincial a., an Irish, American, etc. a. (*mod.*). 4. With like timerous a. *Oth.* I. i. 75. Mild was his a. Dryden. In broken accents Swift. 5. That any a. breaking from thy tongue Should scape.. mine eare *K. John* v. vi. 95. In State[s] vnborne, and Accents yet vnknowne *Jul. C.* III. i. 113. 6. You finde not the apostrophas, and so misse the a. *L. L. L.* IV. ii. 124. 8. These are the.. accents of honour in the German service Fuller. That which gave a. to Abraham's faith Gurnal. Hence **A·ccentless** *a.*

Accent (ǣkse·nt), *v.* 1530. [a. Fr *accenter,* f. *accent* sb.] 1. To pronounce with accent or stress; to emphasize. 2. To mark with a (written) accent. 3. To pronounce, intone 1639. 4. *fig.* To mark emphatically; to heighten 1655.

1. I can nat a. aryght in.. latyn Palsgr. 3. Sounds, accented by a thousand voices Scott. 4. Piers, accented at the cardinal points by [etc.] 1877.

Accentor (ǣkse·ntəɹ). [f. L. *ad* + *cantor.*] 1. *Mus.* One who sings the leading part. 2. A genus of birds, including the hedge-sparrow. *U. S.* The water-thrush.

Accentual (ǣkse·ntiuăl), *a.* 1610. [f. L. *accentus.*] Of or belonging to accent.

A. iambics, verses with alternate strong and weak instead of long and short syllables. Hence **Accen·tua·lity** (*rare*), the quality of being a.; in *pl.* a. particulars. **Acce·ntually** *adv.*

Accentuate (ǣkse·ntiueⁱt), *v.* 1731. [f. med.L. *accentuare;* see Accent.] 1. To pronounce or mark with an accent. 2. *fig.* To mark strongly, emphasize.

1. The French never a. their words or their feelings Hare. 2. To a. antagonism Lecky.

Accentuation (ǣkse:ntiu,ēⁱ·ʃən). 1818. [ad. med.L. *accentuationem;* see prec.] 1. The marking of accent in speech 1827. 2. The notation of accents in writing 1846. 3. Mode of pronunciation 1818. 4. *fig.* Emphasizing 1875.

†**Acce·pt,** *ppl. a.* ME. [ad. L. *acceptus.*] = Accepted. -1599.

Accept (ǣkse·pt), *v.* Pa. pple. †*accept, accepted.* ME. [? a. Fr. *accepter,* ad. L. *acceptare.*] To take or receive what is offered. Hence, 1. To take or receive with consenting mind; to receive with favour 1380. 2. To receive as adequate; hence, to admit 1530. 3. To take upon oneself as a responsibility 1524. (In senses 1–3 often with *of.*) 4. *Comm.* To accept a bill or draft: to agree or promise to pay when due 1665. Also *absol.*

1. To a. (as a prospective husband) *Merch. V.* I. ii. 102. His ring I doe a. *Ibid.* IV. ii. 9. **To accept the person** or **face of:** To favour (*esp.* on corrupt grounds). **To accept persons:** To show favouritism. [A Hebraism, in N. T. Gr. προσωποληπτεῖν, Vulg. *acceptare personam.*] 2. A fact which we may a. Freeman. To a. an apology (*mod.*). **To accept service of a writ:** to agree to consider it as validly served. 3. To a. the siege of Calais Wolsey, a post M. Pattison. Hence **Acce·pted** *ppl. a.* well-received; †acceptable. **Acce·ptedly** *adv.* **Acce·pter,** one who accepts; see sense 1, quots. **Acce·ptive** *a.* fit for acceptance; †ready to accept. **Acce·ptor** = Accepter; he who accepts a bill of exchange.

Acceptability (ǣkseptăbi·lĭti). 1660. [ad. late L. *acceptabilitatem.*] = Acceptableness.

Acceptable (ǣkse·ptăb'l, æ·ksĕptăb'l), *a.* ME. [a. Fr., ad. L. *acceptabilis.* Orig., and still poet., *a·cceptable.*] Worthy or likely to be accepted; pleasing, welcome.

What a. thynge shal I offre vnto the Lorde Coverdale *Mic.* vi. 6. Hence **Acce·ptableness. Acce·ptably** *adv.*

Acceptance (ǣkse·ptăns). 1574. [a. OFr.; see Accept.] 1. The act or fact of accepting, as a pleasure, a satisfaction of claim, or duty 1596; *esp.* favourable reception (of persons) 1596; belief 1669. 2. The state of being accepted 1649. 3. = Acceptation 3. 1716. 4. Acceptableness 1593. 5. *Comm.* (see Accept *v.* 4.) The formal engagement to pay when due; the bill itself when 'accepted'. 6. *Law.* An agreeing to the act of another by some act which binds the person in law 1574.

1. A. of the Crown Freeman. The vocalist.. sang with marked a. (*mod.*). The assertion finds a. in every rank Faraday. *Acceptance of persons:* partiality. See Accept 1, quots. 2. Holiness.. a Condition of Final A. Wesley. 3. The proper a. of the word 1857. 4. The Canon!.. A man of such a. Browning. 5. To get acceptances into circulation 1865.

Acce·ptancy. 1856. [f. Accept.] Willingness to receive. Mrs. Browning.

Acce·ptant. 1596. [a. Fr.] A. *adj.* Willingly receiving. Const. *of.* †B. *sb.* One who Accepts; *spec.* the acceptor of a bill 1596.

Acceptation (ǣk:sĕptēⁱ·ʃən). ME. [a. Fr., ad. late L. *acceptationem;* see Accept.] †1. *gen.* = Acceptance 1. -1692. 2. = Acceptance 2. *arch.* 1594. 3. The sense in which a word, etc. is accepted 1614. †4. = Acceptance 5. 1622.

3. The different acceptations of the word Knowledge Locke.

Acce·ptila·tion. 1562. [ad. L.] *Rom. Law.* The remission of a debt by an acquittance without payment. *fig.* Free remission.

†**Acception** (ǣkse·pʃən). ME. [ad. L. *acceptionem;* see Accept. Cf. Fr. *acception.*] 1. The act of accepting -1662. 2. *A. of persons* or *faces.* [A Hebraism, in Gr. προσωποληψία, L. *acceptio personæ.*] Corrupt acceptance or favouritism -1677. See Accept 1, quots. 3. = Acceptation 3 -1711.

1. Acception or takyng of money Caxton. 3. This A. of the term 1711.

Access (æ·ksĕs, ǣkse·s). ME. [In sense 4, a. Fr. *accès;* in other senses, direct f. L. *accessus.* *A·ccess* is now usual.] 1. Approaching or being approached in various senses (see quots.) ME. 2. A way or means of approach. *lit.* and *fig.* 1605. 3. A coming as an addition (replaced by Accession) 1576. 4. A (sudden) coming on of illness, anger, etc., a fit ME.; †*spec.* an ague fit -1751. Also *fig.* (mod., after Fr. *accès*).

1. = †Entrance: At our a. to the pope's presence Gardiner. = Admittance: He importunes accesse to you *A. Y. L.* I. i. 98. = Accessibility: Lord Chesterfield's easiness of a. Boswell. Opp. to *recess:* The Sunnes a. and departure Healey. The a. and recess of Parliament May. = Accession: Our a. to the

Crowne CHARLES I. 2. The Accesses of the Island MILT. Every a. to the conscience DALE. 3. I from ..thy looks receive A. in every virtue MILT. An a. of tone 1881. 4. The A. of Fevers HARTLEY. An a. of paralysis TICKNOR. *fig.* An a. of jealousy SOUTHEY. ¶Frequently written for EXCESS. Cf. sense 3. Hence †**Acce·ssive** *a.* pressing in; accessible. †**Acce·ssively** *adv.* pressingly. **Acce·ssless,** inaccessible.

Accessary (æ·ksĕsări, ækse·sări). 1480. [f. ACCESS *sb.* The *sb.* is etymologically *accessary*, the adj. *accessory*, but in use no distinction is practicable. *A·ccessary* is the hist. pronunc.] **A.** *sb.* 1. One who gives his accession (formerly *access*) to an act or undertaking. In *Law*: One who aids or abets in an offence, either before or after the fact. 2. Anything contributory or subordinate 1534.

1. There are no accessaries in Treason FINCH. 2. The attention..is distracted by the accessaries MRS. JAMESON.

B. *adj.* 1. Of persons: Acceding *to*. In *Law*: Participant, privy 1594. †2. Of things: Subordinate, adventitious; (repl. by ACCESSORY) -1691.

1. Both houses of Parliament were..made a. to the legal murders of this reign HALLAM. Hence **Acce·ssarily** *adv.* consentingly. **Acce·ssariness,** privity.

Accessible (ækse·sib'l), *a.* 1610. [a. Fr.; see ACCEDE.] 1. Capable of being used as an access (*to*). 2. Capable of being entered or reached; get-at-able 1642; *fig.* open to the influence of (const. *to*) 1818.

1. With one ascent A. from earth MILT. 2. Bold, a. coasts HOWELL. Evidence not a. to contemporaries MAY. *fig.* A. to bribery 1881. Hence **Acce·ssibi·lity.**

Accession (ækse·ʃən). 1588. [a. Fr.; see ACCEDE.] The action of going to, and its result. Hence, 1. Approach, admittance: = ACCESS 1. 1652. †2. Advance, arrival -1656. 3. Coming to a dignity, etc., *esp.* the throne 1769. 4. A coming to as an addition in various senses (see quots.) 1588; *esp.* (*Law*) Addition to property by natural growth or artificial improvement, which the owner acquires by Accession 1768. †5. A coming on of disease, etc. = ACCESS 4. -1827.

1. A. of air SIR H. DAVY, of solar light KANE. 4. = Joining: The a. of piety to patience T. ADAMS. = Assent: A. to an affair SIR J. MELVIL. *Deed of A.*, in Sc. Law, a deed by which creditors bind themselves to concur in a trust executed by their debtor for the general behoof. = Addition: A. of strength WELLESLEY. A. to a library HALLAM. 5. Accessions of folly SOUTHEY. Hence **Acce·ssional** *a.* additional.

‖**Acce·ssit.** Short for PROXIME ACCESSIT.

Accessory (æ·ksĕsəri, ækse·səri). 1549. [ad. late L. *accessorius*; see ACCEDE. For pronunc. see ACCESSARY.] **A.** *adj.* 1. Of things: Coming as an accession; additional 1618. 2. = ACCESSARY *a.* 1.

B. *sb.* 1. An accessory thing; an adjunct 1549. 2. = ACCESSARY *sb.* 1.

1. All pleasures else I accessories call HOLLAND. 2. Accessories to his bold riot MILT. Hence **Accessorial** *a.* supplementary. **Accessorily** *adv.* additionally. **Accessoriness,** secondary character.

‖**Acciaccatura** (attʃa:kkatū·ră). 1876. [It.] *Mus.* A 'grace', consisting of a small note performed quickly before an essential note of a melody; a 'crush-note'.

†**A·ccidence**[1]. ME. [a. Fr.] Hap; fortuitous circumstance -1811. Hence **Accide·ntial,** *a.* non-essential.

Accidence[2] (æ·ksidĕns). 1509. [f. L. *accidentia*, pl. neut. treated as sb. fem.] 1. That part of Grammar which treats of the Accidents or inflexions of words. 2. Hence, The rudiments of any subject 1562.

1. Aske him some questions in his A. *Merry W.* IV. i. 16. 2. The Accedence of Armorie 1562.

Accident (æ·ksidĕnt). ME. [a. Fr.:—L. *accidens.*] **I.** Anything that happens. 1. †An event; *esp.* an unforeseen contingency; a disaster ME. 2. Chance, fortune. (By a. = L. *per accidens.*) 1490. †3. *Med.* An unfavourable symptom -1671. †4. A casual appearance or effect -1765. 5. An irregularity in the landscape 1870.

1. Of mouing Accidents by Flood and Field *Oth.* I. iii. 135. *The chapter of accidents*: the unforeseen course of events. A railway a., insurance against accidents (*mod.*). 2. By a. or design FREEMAN. 4. Non a. for noon adversité Was seyn in hir CHAUCER. 5. Taking advantage of every a. of the ground 1878.

II. That which is present by chance, and ∴ non-essential. 1. *Logic.* An attribute which is not part of the essence ME. 2. Hence, any non-essential accompaniment. 3. *Her.* A note or mark that may be retained or omitted in a coat of arms 1610. †4. *Gram. pl.* (L. *accidentia.*) The changes, such as gender, number, case, etc., to which words are subject -1612. Now ACCIDENCE.

1. Whan the breed is conuerted into the..body of our lord the accidentes abyden.. whytnesse, roundenesse and sauoure CAXTON. 2. The brilliant accidents of birth, beauty [etc.] DISRAELI. Hence †**Accide·ntary** *a.* fortuitous; non-essential. †**Accide·ntarily** *adv.* **A·ccidented** *ppl. a.* characterized by accidents. (Cf. Fr. *accidenté.*)

†**A·ccident,** *a.* 1509. [ad. L. *accidentem.*] Accidental. Hence †**A·ccidently** *adv.* by chance: non-essentially.

Accidental (ækside·ntăl). ME. [? a. Fr. *accidental, -el*, ad. late L. *accidentalis*; see ACCIDENT.] **A.** *adj.* 1. Happening by, or pertaining to, chance; casual, fortuitous 1506. 2. *Logic.* Pertaining to accidents; non-essential 1553. 3. Incidental, subsidiary 1386.

1. The jury..find only a. death (*mod.*). Thy sinn's not accidentall, but a Trade *Meas. for M.* III. i. 149. 2. The propositions in which accidents were predicated of it [the subject] were called A. MILL. 3. A. benefits JOHNSON. *Accidental* sharps, flats, naturals (*Mus.*); so called only when they occur bef. particular notes, and not in the *signature* of the keys. *Accidental* colours (in *Optics*): complementary colours, due to subjective sensation. *Accidental* lights (in *Painting*): 'secondary lights; effects of light other than ordinary daylight'. Fairholt.

B. *sb.* a. A casual property, see A 2. b. *Mus.* A sharp, flat, or natural, occurring not at the commencement, but before a particular note; see A 3 (quots.). c. *Painting. pl.* Those unusual effects produced by artificial light, proceeding from a fire, candle, etc. Hence **Accide·ntalism,** in *Painting*, the effect produced by a. lights; *Med.* a system which treats disease as an a. modification of health. **A·ccidenta·lity** = ACCIDENTALNESS. **Accide·ntally** *adv.* by chance; †non-essentially. **Accide·ntalness,** the quality or fact of being a.

†**Accidie.** ME. [a. OFr. *acci·de, aci·de*, ad. med.L. *accidia*, late L. *acedia*, a. Gr. ἀκηδία.] Sloth, torpor.

The synne of Accidie CHAUCER.

Accipenser, see ACIPENSER.

†**Acci·pient,** *ppl. a.* [ad. L.] 'One who receives.' (Dicts.)

‖**Accipiter** (æ·ksipitəɹ). 1874. [a. L.] 1. *Zool.* A bird of prey, one of the *Accipitres*, or *Raptores*. 2. *Surg.* A bandage for the nose, resembling a hawk's claw. Hence **Acci·pitral** *a.* rapacious; keen-sighted. **Acci·pitrine** *a.* hawk-like.

Accise, earlier form of EXCISE; see ASSIZE.

‖**Acci·smus.** 1753. [L., a. Gr. ἀκκισμός.] *Rhet.* A feigned refusal of something desired.

†**Acci·te,** *v.* 1506. [ad. late L. *accitare*; see CITE.] 1. To summon -1674. 2. To quote -1631. 3. To excite -1637.

1. Stanislaus.. whom.. valour accited.. into the Tauric fields MILT. 3. To a. So ravenous..an Appetite B. JONS.

Acclaim (ăklēⁱ·m), *v.* ME. [Strictly two vbs.: ACCLAIM, ad. cl.L. *acclamare*, f. *ac-* = *ad-* to, at + *clamare* to shout; and *acclame*, ad. med.L. *acclamare* to claim.] †**I.** From med.L. To lay claim to -1717.

II. From cl.L. 1. To applaud 1633; to name with applause as 1749. 2. *intr.* To shout applause 1652. 3. *trans.* To shout; *spec.* to utter an ACCLAMATION 1690.

1. To a. speeches 1881. The..high Gods..Acclaimed her victress SWINBURNE. 3. Acclaiming, 'Glory be to Thee, O Lord' 1690. Hence **Acclai·m,** a shout of applause. *poet.* **Acclai·mable** *a.* **Acclai·mer.** **Accla·matory** *a.*

Acclamation (æklămēⁱ·ʃən). 1541. [ad. L. *acclamationem*; see ACCLAIM. Cf. Fr. *acclamation.*] 1. The action of acclaiming. †a. Calling to. b. Loud or eager approval, or shouting 1585. 2. An exclamation: †a. of dislike; †b. of approval. Hence c. Approbation however expressed 1541. †3. *Rhet.* A brief isolated sentence in a discourse, emphasizing what precedes it -1675.

1. To sing with a. unto the Lord ABP. SANDYS. b. The general a. of all the powers JOHNSON. [A Bill] passed *by a.* FROUDE. 2. That sad a., Blessed are the wombs which bare not 1673. The acclamations of the soldiers proclaimed him Emperor GIBBON. 3. Plain a. of Amen MILT.

Acclimata·tion. 1859. [a. Fr.] = ACCLIMATIZATION.

Acclimate (ăkləi·mĕt), *v.* 1792. [a. Fr. *acclimater.*] = ACCLIMATIZE, now more common. *lit.* and *fig.* Hence **Accli·matable** *a.* **Accli·matement** (*rare*).

Acclimation (æklimēⁱ·ʃən). 1853. [f. ACCLIMATE; cf. *narrate, narration*, etc.] = ACCLIMATIZATION.

Acclimatization (ăkləi·mătəizēⁱ·ʃən). 1830. [f. ACCLIMATIZE.] 1. The process of habituating, or being habituated, to a new climate. Also *attrib.* 2. A thing which has been acclimatized.

1. A. gardens J. BULLER. 2. The turkey..one of our best acclimatisations OWEN.

Acclimatize (ăkləi·matəiz), *v.* 1836. [f. Fr. *acclimater.* More usu. than ACCLIMATE.] To habituate, or become habituated, to a new or unusual climate. *lit.* and *fig.*

Acclimatized to unfamiliar ecclesiastical surroundings M. DAVIES. Hence **Accli·mati·zer.** **Accli·matizing** *vbl. sb.* = ACCLIMATIZATION.

Acclivity (ăkli·viti). 1614. [ad. L. *acclivitatem.*] An ascending slope. Hence **Accli·vitous** *a.*

Accli·vous, *a.* 1731. [f. L. *acclivus.*] Sloping upward.

Accloy (ăkloi·), *v. arch.* ME. [a. OFr. *encloyer* (mod. *enclouer*):—late L. *inclavare*. Later, aphet. to *cloy*. *a-* (= Anglo-Fr. *en-*) by confusion with *a*:—L. *ad* gave *accloy*.] 1. To prick with a nail, in shoeing a horse; to lame. *lit.* and *fig.* 2. To stop up an aperture as with a nail, etc.; to obstruct, clog, choke 1430. 3. To overfill ME.; to nauseate 1519; to weary 1530.

2. The laws by which the flesh Accloys the spirit BROWNING. 3. Accloyed with bribes PAYNELL, examples JEWEL. Hence **Acclo·ying** *vbl. sb.* overloading.

Accoast, *v.*; **accoasting,** *vbl. sb.* The older ff. of ACCOST, ACCOSTING, in the sense of *coast, border upon.*

†**Accoi·l,** *v.* [a. OFr. *acoillir* (mod. *accueillir*):—late L. *accolligere*; see COIL.] To collect. (Only in Spenser.) **Accoi·l,** *sb. rare.* [a. OFr. *acoil* (mod. *accueil*).] Reception.

Accolade (ækolē·d, akola·d). 1623. [a. Fr., ad. It. *accollata*, sb. f. pa. pple. of *accollare*, to embrace about the neck; see ACCOLL.] 1. prop. An embrace; the technical name of the salutation, consisting at different times of an embrace, a kiss, or a blow on the shoulders with the flat of a sword, marking the bestowal of knighthood. 2. *Mus.* A vertical line or brace, used to couple two or more staves 1882.

1. Could [the Pope] receive [the Czar] with.. an insincere a. WISEMAN. Hence **Accola·ded** *ppl. a.* knighted.

†**Acco·ll,** *v.* ME. [a. OFr. *acoler.*] To embrace -1557.

Accolled, *ppl. a.* 1723. [f. ACCOLL. Fr. *accolé* is more used.] *Her.* 1. Collared, gorged. 2. Intertwined. 3. Conjoined, united, jugate, as two shields, two lozenges, or two busts on a coin. var. **A·ccollated.**

†**Acco·mmodate,** *ppl. a.* 1525. [ad. L. *accommodatus.*] Suited; suitable, fit.

Accommodate (ăkǫ·mŏdēⁱt), *v.* 1531. [f. prec.] 1. To ascribe fittingly (a thing *to* a person) -1676; to adjust (one thing or person *to* another); †*intr.* to adapt oneself *to* -1677; to show the correspondence of one thing to another; to make consistent (const. *to*, †*unto*, †*with*) 1603. 2. To adjust, reconcile (things or persons); to bring to agreement 1597; *intr.* to come to terms 1648. †3. To fit (a thing for use); to repair (Fr. *raccommoder*) -1812; to facilitate -1703. 4. To fit or furnish a person *with* 1597; to oblige 1663; *esp.* with lodgings, etc. 1715.

1. To a. the eye to different distances BREWSTER. The intention of Poets, unto which they a. their verses HOLLAND. 2. To a. a quarrel 1677, opinions MACAULAY. I hope we shall a. with the Danes 1801. 3. Well accommodated for our lodgment HENRY. To a. a cure MASSINGER. 4. A Soldier is better accommodated, then with a wife 2 *Hen. IV*, III. ii. 72. To a. with cash for a cheque (*mod.*). The honour of accommodating [the Queen] at his house 1772. Hence

Acco·mmodable *a.* suitable. †**Acco·mmodately** *adv.* †**Acco·mmodateness.** **Acco·mmodating** *vbl. sb.* the action of the vb.; *ppl. a.* suiting; hence, *adj.* affording accommodation; pliant, conciliatory; pliable, open to corruption. **Acco·mmodatingly** *adv.* **Acco·mmodator,** he who, or that which, accommodates.

Accommodation (ăkǫmǫdēⁱ·ʃən). 1604. [a. Fr., ad. L. *accommodationem.*] 1. The action of accommodating, or the being accommodated; adaptation, adjustment 1644. 2. Adaptation of a word, expression, or system to something different from its original purpose 1724. 3. Self-adaptation; obligingness 1768. 4. An arrangement of a dispute; a settlement, compromise 1645. 5. The supplying with what is requisite. 6. Anything which supplies a want, or affords aid or refreshment; *esp.* lodgings and entertainment at an inn, etc. 1604. 7. Pecuniary aid in an emergency; a loan 1824.

1. The a. of the eye to the vision of external objects BREWSTER. 2. The adaptation or a. of a prophecy TRENCH. 3. His object in these accommodations was [etc.] HALLAM. 4. An a. between the belligerents PRESCOTT. 5. The a. of life JOHNSON. 6. Progress..is from necessaries to accommodations REYNOLDS. A. for our sick men CROMWELL. The Hummums..has good accommodations PORTER. 7. An a. of £100 from Ballantine LOCKHART.

Phrases. *Accommodation Bill*, a bill not representing an actual commercial transaction, but for the purpose of raising money on credit. *Accommodation land*: land, generally in the neighbourhood of a town or fair, having a special rental value owing to its being required by some one, to whom it is let temporarily, for the purposes of his business or property; e.g. land let to a butcher, to fatten his stock for killing, or the like. *Accommodation price*: the price, always in excess of the mere agricultural rental value, paid for such land.

Accommodative (ăkǫ·mǒdeⁱtiv), *a.* 1841. [f. *accommodat-*, *accommodare.*] Tending to accommodate. Hence **Acco·mmoda·tiveness.**

†**Acco·mpanable, -iable,** *a.* 1548. [a. Fr. *accompagnable.*] Companionable.

Accompaniment (ăkɒ·mpănimĕnt). 1744. [a. Fr. *accompagnement.*] 1. Anything that accompanies; something attending or added, by way of ornament, for symmetry, or the like 1756. 2. *Mus.* The subsidiary part or parts, instrumental or vocal, added for the sake of effect to a musical composition; *esp.* the instrumental part which sustains the voice 1744. 3. *Her.* The belt, mantlings, etc. applied about the shield, by way of ornament.

Accompany (ăkɒ·mpăni), *v.* 1460. [a. Fr. *accompagner*; see COMPANION.] 1. †To add or conjoin *to* –1587; to send (or give) *with* the addition of 1629; †*refl.* to unite oneself *with* –1650. †2. *intr.* (refl. pron. omitted.) To keep company *with*; *euphem.* to cohabit with –1760; *absol.* to combine –1577. 3. *trans.* (*with* omitted.) †To keep company with; *euphem.* to cohabit with –1660; to convoy, escort, attend *c* 1460; used *fig.* of things personified 1477. 4. To go with as an attribute or attendant phenomenon 1731. 5. *Mus.* To a. (singing, a piece, the singer): To join a singer or player by singing or playing an accompaniment.

1. With fresh souldiours to them accompanied FOXE. To a. the word with a blow (*mod.*). 3. Shee ..bid her..accompanie her solitarie father SIDNEY. The ladies accompanied the gentlemen in hunting parties STRUTT. Accompanied by his wife FREEMAN. *Déjeuner*, accompanied by half a bottle of Bordeaux HAMERTON. 4. The ejections of scoriæ were accompanied by bellowings PHILLIPS.

¶ *Accompanied* now takes *by* with personal or active agents, *with* only when the agency is secondary. Hence **Acco·mpanier.** LAMB. **Acco·mpanist, -yist.** **Acco·mpanying** *vbl. sb.* going, or acting with; or giving as an accompaniment, *esp.* in *Music*; *ppl. a.* attending; attached, appended.

†**Acco·mplement.** 1587. [f. late L. *accomplere.*] Anything that completes or perfects; see ACCOMPLISHMENT.

Accomplice (ăkǫ·mplis). 1485. [f. COMPLICE. The *ac-* is obscure.] An associate in crime or guilt. Const. *of*; also *with* the criminal, *in* the crime. Also *playfully* (*rare*).

An a. of [Catiline's] Crime DRYDEN. Our..Generall, And..his accomplices SHAKS. Hence **Acco·mpliceship** (*rare*), **Accompli·city** (*rare*), the state of being an a.

Accomplish (ăkǫ·mpliʃ), *v.* ME. [a. OFr. *accompliss-*, *acomplir*, now *accomplir*:—late L. *accomplere.* The hist. pronunc. is ăkɒ·mpliʃ.] 1. *trans.* To perform, carry out. †*intr.* –1509. 2. To complete (a work 1477, time 1574, a distance 1855). 3. To equip completely 1588. 4. To perfect in mental acquirements; to finish off 1475.

1. The desire accomplished is sweet to the soule *Prov.* xiii. 19. 2. To a. seuentie yeeres *Dan.* ix. 2, half a league or more PRESCOTT. 3. The Armourers accomplishing the Knights *Hen. V*, IV. Chor. 12. 4. Thou art a Gentleman:..well-accomplish'd *Two Gent.* IV. iii. 13. Hence **Acco·mplishable** *a.* practicable. **Acco·mplisher.**

Accomplished (ăkǫ·mpliʃt), *ppl. a.* 1475. [f. prec.] 1. Fulfilled, completed 1577. 2. Perfect; *esp.* in acquirements, etc. 1475. †3. Fully versed *in*.

1. Not yet eight years a. HOLINSHED. A. service, SOUTHEY. 2. An a. courtier *Cymb.* I. v. 103. A. speaking is an art BLACKIE.

Accomplishment (ăkǫ·mpliʃmĕnt). 1460. [a. Fr. *accomplissement.* See ACCOMPLISH.] 1. The action of accomplishing, or the being accomplished; completion. 2. The act of perfecting, or the being perfected; perfection 1561. 3. An achievement or attainment 1599. 4. Anything that completely equips, as accoutrement; in mod. use, an ornamental attainment or acquirement; occas. a superficial acquirement.

1. The A. of the Duke of York's marriage with the princess of Modena JOHNSON. 2. The finishing stroke and very A. of Virtue SHAFTESBURY. 3. A harmony—the a. of correct and vigilant judgement MRS. RADCLIFFE. 4. The externall Accomplishments of Kingly prosperity MILT. To fold and seal a letter adroitly is not the lowest of accomplishments DE QUINCEY.

Accompt, *v.* and *sb.*, arch. f. ACCOUNT. **Accomptant,** arch. f. ACCOUNTANT. **Accompter,** obs. f. ACCOUNTER.

Accord (ăkǭ·ɹd), *v.* OE. [a. OFr. *acorder*:—late L. *accordare*, refash. after L.] *lit.* To bring heart to heart. 1. †*trans.* To cause to agree, to reconcile (persons) –1702; †*refl.* and *pass.* to reconcile oneself *with* –1786; to compose (quarrels or differences) ME.; †to attune *to* –1663. 2. *intr.* (refl. pron. suppressed). To come to an agreement (see quots.) ME.; †to agree *to*, to assent or consent *to* –1674; of things: To be in harmony *with* ME.; †*impers.* to be suitable or proper (L. *convenit*) –1556. 3. *trans.* (prep. omitted). †To agree upon –1676; to agree to grant; hence, in 19th c., to grant *to*, to award.

1. We wolde gladly acorde you and hym LD. BERNERS. Musyque accordeth alle thinges CAXTON. To a. a difference LONGF. 2. Two dogges and one bone Maye never a. in one 1500. We may..a. *with* the Emperour HOLCROFT. To a. *in* common sentiments HALE. To a. *of* the time to begin H. SMITH. So *upon.* †With *subord. cl.*: I acord wel *that it ys so* CHAUCER. You, to his love must a. *A. Y. L.* v. iv. 139. His principles and practice do not a. well together (*mod.*). Do that thyng quhilk accords 1556. 3. All business being thus accorded 1676. The glimpses of eternity To saints accorded WORDSW. Hence **Acco·rdable** *a.* accordant; reconcilable. **Acco·rdancy,** agreement. **Acco·rded** *ppl. a.* reconciled; granted. **Acco·rder,** one who agrees, or bestows. **Acco·rdment,** reconcilement.

Accord (ăkǭ·ɹd). ME. [a. OFr. *acord*, *acorde*, f. *acorder*; see prec.] 1. Reconciliation; concurrence of opinion, will, or action; consent ME. 2. A formal act of reconciliation; a treaty ME. 3. *Law.* An extrajudicial arrangement 1625. 4. Harmonious correspondence, e.g. of colours and tints; *esp.* of sounds; Agreement in pitch and tone; harmony ME. †5. Assent to a proposal; permission –1602.

1. True A. is an Union of..the Will and Affections R. JONES. Family a. COWPER. A. of hands and back and forward steps WORDSW. *To be of, at a.* with: to agree with. *With* (†*of*) *one a.*: with unanimity. 2. The pees and the acord y made.. CAXTON. A general a. with Holland MOTLEY. 4. The ayres and accords of the Harpe BACON. 5. This gentle and unforced a. of Hamlet *Haml.* I. ii. 123. *Of* (†*by*, †*on*) *one's own a.*: of one's own motion.

†**Acco·rd,** *adv.* or *a.* ME. [? for *a accord*; or short f. *accorded.*] In accord. CHAUCER.

Accordance (ăkǭ·ɹdăns). ME. [a. OFr. *acordance*; see ACCORD *v.*] The state of being in accord, or the act of agreeing or granting; harmony; conformity.

The accordaunce Of..songe *Rom. Rose* 498. The degree of a. PHILLIPS. *In a. with* (rarely *to*): in conformity to.

Accordant (ăkǭ·ɹdănt), *a.* ME. [a. OFr. *acordant*; see ACCORD *v.*] 1. Conformable *to*, *with*. 2. *absol.* †Concurring in mind, agreeable –1599; agreeing in action or motion; *esp.* of sounds: harmonious 1764. †3. Appropriate, fitting –1574.

A. with reason FABYAN, with the pride of London MISS YONGE. 2. If hee found her a. *Much Ado* I. i. 14. A. strings R. LLOYD, action KINGLAKE. 3. With warrantie a. *Littleton's Ten.* Hence **Acco·rdantly** *adv.*

According (ăkǭ·ɹdiŋ), *ppl. a.* and *adv.* ME. [f. ACCORD *v.*] *ppl. adj.* †1. Corresponding *to* –1532. 2. *absol.* Agreeing in nature or action; consentient 1450. †3. Appropriate, fitting –1674. 4. *adv.* †*absol.* = ACCORDINGLY 4.

2. This a. voice of national wisdom BURKE. The a. hearts of men TENNYSON. 4. Thou [hast] a stubborne soule..And squar'st thy life a. *Meas. for M.* v. i. 487. *Phr.* According *as*: exactly or just as. According *to*: in a manner consistent with; †suitably to.

Accordingly (ăkǭ·ɹdiŋli), *adv.* ME. [f. prec.] †1. Harmoniously –1514. †2. Becomingly, suitably –1634. †3. In the order specified; respectively –1603. 4. In accordance with the premises; correspondingly 1599; in natural sequence 1688.

4. When you have seene more..proceed a. *Much Ado* III. ii. 125. *Phr.* †Accordingly *to*: conformably to. Accordingly *as*: just as.

Accordion (ăkǭ·ɹdiən). 1842. [f. It. *accordare*; cf. *clarion.*] A portable musical hand-instrument, consisting of a small pair of bellows and a range of keys, which on being pressed admit wind to metal reeds. Also as *adj.*, folding like an a. Hence **Acco·rdionist.**

Accost (ăkǫ·st), *v.* 1578. [a. Fr. *accoster*:—late L. *accostare*, to be side to side. Formerly *accoast*, after COAST.] †1. *intr.* To lie alongside –1611; *trans.* to border on –1662; to go alongside of, to COAST –1603. †2. *refl.* To accost oneself *with*, keep beside (rare); *intr.* to draw near *to* –1635. 3. *trans.* To approach for any purpose; to face; to make up to. *arch.* 1599. 4. To address 1612. 5. To solicit in the street for an improper purpose 1887.

1. *trans.* If his land accosteth the sea FULLER. 3. A. is front her, boord her, woe her, assail her *Tw. Night* I. iii. 52. 4. [They] thus..a. him soon MILT. Hence **Acco·st** *sb.* salutation. **Acco·stable** *a.* ready to accost; approachable. **Acco·sted** *ppl. a.* *Her.* placed side by side. **Acco·sting** *vbl. sb.* †a coming alongside: advance (towards intercourse), †**Acco·stment,** the action of accosting.

‖**Accouche** (akū·ʃ, ăkau·tʃ), *v.* 1867. [a. Fr *accoucher*: see A- 7, COUCH.] To act as midwife.

‖ **Accouchement** (akuʃmaṅ, ăku·ʃmĕnt, ăkau·tʃmĕnt). 1809. [Fr., f. *accoucher*; see prec.] Delivery in child-bed.

‖**Accoucheur** (akuʃö·r). 1759. [Fr., f. *accoucher*; see ACCOUCHE *v.*] A man midwife; also formerly = next.

‖**Accoucheuse** (akuʃö·z, -ö·z). 1867. [Fr. fem. of prec.] A midwife.

†**Accounsel,** *v.* ME. [a. OFr. *aconseillier.*] To COUNSEL –1649.

Account (ăkau·nt), *v.* [ME. *acunten*, a. OFr. *acunter*, *aconter*:—late L. *accomptare* for **accomputare*. Refashioned as *accompt*, after Fr.] †1. To count, count up –1582; *absol.* –1776; to calculate, reckon –1788; to reckon in –1826. Also with *to*, †*on*, †*that*. 2. *intr.* To render or receive an account ME.; *trans.* to render account of 1614; to render an account for trust moneys; to explain; to answer for (see quots.) 1679. 3. *trans.* To estimate, value, hold (a thing to be so and so). Also with *inf.* or *subord. cl.* So, to account *of*; to think *much*, etc. of a thing. ME. †4. To narrate. *trans.* and *intr.* ME.

1. He [a grocer] must be able to..a. A. SMITH. The Hejera..is accounted from the year of the flight of Mahomet..from Mecca 1788. All sorts of graces accounted *to* you D. JERROLD. 2. Ramnarain was ready to a. fairly JAS. MILL. All receipts should be accounted to a finance committee M. PATTISON. At once accounting for his deep arrears DRYDEN. To a. for the greater cold TYNDALL. The terrier accounted for one, the keeper for another THACKERAY. 3. [I] therein doe a. my selfe well paid *Merch. V.* IV. i. 417. Wee are accounted *as* sheepe *Rom.* viii. 36. They are nothing to be accounted of I. TAYLOR.

Hence **Accou·nted** *ppl. a.* reckoned. †**Accou·nter,** one who accounts or narrates. **Accou·nting** (*vbl. sb.* †computing; also *attrib.*; with *for*: answering for, explaining; *ppl. a.* †counting; that keeps accounts (*arch.*). **Accou·ntment,** the work of accounting, responsibility.

Account (ăkau·nt), *sb.* ME. [a. OFr. *acunt, acont*, later *acompt*, f. *à* + *cont*:—late L. *computum*, cl. *computum*; see prec. Refashioned *accompt* in 15th c.] **1.** Counting, reckoning, calculation ME. **2.** A statement of moneys received and paid, with calculation of the balance; also one of the heads under which accounts are kept in a ledger ME.; the preparing a statement of money transactions 1646. **3.** A reckoning in one's favour; advantage 1611. **4.** A statement of the administration of money in trust 1513; hence, a statement as to responsibilities generally; answering for conduct, e. g. on the Last Day ME.; †also in same sense pl. was used as sing. **a.** of money –1762; **b.** of responsibility or conduct –1564. **5.** *Law.* A writ or action against a bailiff, receiver, etc., who refuse to render accompt 1622. **6.** Estimation, consideration, importance ME. **7.** A relation, report or description 1614.

1. Quick at accounts (*mod.*). *To cast accounts*, to make calculations. *Money of a.*, denominations of money used in reckoning only. 2. At many times I brought in my accompts *Timon* II. ii. 142. *To open or close an a. with one. To render* or *send in an a.*: to give a statement of money due. *A. current*: a running account. *Joint a.*: one entered into by two parties not otherwise in partnership. *To keep accounts* (pl.). *To balance or square accounts*: to pay or receive the balance shown. *Cash A.*, *Suspense A.*, etc. *For the a.* (*Stock Exchange*): not for cash, but for settlement on the next settling-day. *In a. with*: in relations requiring the keeping of an a. *with*. *To place* or *pass to a.*: to debit or credit a person's a. *with*. *For a. of*: to be accounted to for. *On a.*: as an interim payment on a. of something in process. *On one's a.*: in his behalf and at his expense. *On one's own a. On a. of*: because of; †concerning. Commissioners of public a. HALLAM. 3. Wherein they expected *to find their own a.* SWIFT. A kind which cannot *be turned to any a.* HT. MARTINEAU. 4. The ordinary cannot demand accompt for them PERKINS. Claudio shall render me a deere a. *Much Ado* IV. i. 338. He has gone to his a. MARRYAT. *To give a. of*: to account for. *To give a good a. of*: to be successful with. Accompts to be made to the King LAMBARDE. We shall render an accompts for [their] lives BECON. 5. A. does not lie against an infant TOMLINS. 6. A Scholler..of good accompt B. JONS. *To make a. of.* to esteem. *To take* (*into*) *a.* (*of*): to notice. *To leave out of a. To lay one's a. with* (*on, for*): to reckon upon. (*Orig. Sc.*) 7. An accompt of my poore voyage CAMPION. He trusted nobody's a. of it DICKENS. Hence †**Accou·ntless** *a.* beyond count; irresponsible.

attrib. and *Comb.* **A.-book,** one prepared for the keeping of accounts. **A. day,** day of reckoning. **A. Sales,** a detailed account of the sale of a parcel of goods.

†**Accou·nt,** *pple.* 1548. Short f. ACCOUNTED.

Accountable (ăkau·ntăb'l), *a.* 1583. [f. ACCOUNT *v.*] **1.** Liable to be called to account; responsible (*to, for*) 1583; also simply 1642. †**2.** To be counted on –1709. †**3.** To be computed –1589; attributable *to* –1681. **4.** Explicable. (Cf. *unaccountable.*) 1665. Also with *for* 1745.

1. I am a. to no man STEELE. A. to the volunteer for the residue of the sum WELLINGTON. 4. A very a. obstinacy GEO. ELIOT. Hence **Accountabi·lity, Accou·ntableness,** responsibility (*to, for*). **Accou·ntably** *adv.*

Accountant (ăkau·ntănt). 1453. [a. Fr. *accomptant*; see ACCOUNT *v.*] †**A.** *adj.* Giving or liable to give an account –1649.

B. *sb.* **1.** One accountable or responsible. In *Law*, the defendant in action of Account 1453. **2.** One who counts; a calculator 1646. **3.** One who professionally makes up accounts; an officer in a public office who has charge of the accounts 1539. †**4.** A narrator –1655.

1. Any crown debtor or a. to the crown WILLIAMS. It is no plea by an a. that he was robbed TOMLINS. 2. He is an excellent A. STEELE. 3. *A.-General*, the superintending accountant in various public offices. Skilful accountants JEVONS. Hence **Accou·ntancy,** the art or practice of an a. **Accou·ntantship,** the office of an a.

†**Accou·ple,** *v.* 1486. [a. OFr. *acopler, acoupler*, f. *à* + *cople*.] To couple –1635. **Accou·plement.** 1483. [a. Fr.] †**1.** The action of coupling; marriage union –1594. **2.** In *Carpentry.* A tie or brace. †**Accou·pling,** *vbl. sb.* 1525. [f. ACCOUPLE.] Coupling; *esp.* union in marriage.

†**Accou·rage,** *v.* [a. Fr. *accourager*, f. *à* + *corage, courage*.] To encourage. SPENSER.

†**Accou·rt,** *v.* [f. COURT *v.* + *ac-* = *ad.*] To court. SPENSER.

Accoutre (ăkū·təɹ), *v.* 1606. [a. MFr. *accoustrer, accoutrer*; prob. f. *à* + *coustre* a sacristan, who robed the clergyman.] To equip, array.

Aptly accoustred, and armed Cap-a-pe DEKKER. He accoutred me with other necessaries SWIFT. Hence **Accou·tred** *ppl. a.* (The only part of the vb. much used.)

Accoutrement (ăkū·təɹmĕnt). 1549. [a. MFr. *accoustrement, accoutrement*; see ACCOUTRE.] **1.** Apparel, outfit, equipment. (Usu. *pl.*). *Milit.* Equipments other than arms and dress. **2.** The process of accoutring or being accoutred 1598.

Point deuice in your accoustrements *A. Y. L.* III. ii. 402. The war-contractor and the a.-maker 1858.

†**Accoy,** *v.* ME. [a. OFr. *acoier*, f. *à* + *coi*:—L. *quietum.*] To quiet; *hence*, to soothe, to silence, or daunt –1647.

With kind words accoyd SPENSER.

†**Accrea·se,** *v.* ME. [a. OFr. *accreistre*:—L. *accrescere*; see also ACCRESCE.] To increase. *trans.* and *intr.* Hence **Accrea·se** *sb.* increase.

Accredit (ăkre·dit), *v.* 1620. [a. Fr. *accréditer*, f. *à* + *crédit.*] **1.** To put into credit, to set forth as credible; to vouch for 1620. **2.** To furnish with credentials; to authorize as an envoy. Const. *to, at.* 1794.

1. His censure will (to use the new.. phrase) a. his praises COWPER. *Phr.* To a. *one* with *something*: to vouch for it as his. Mr. Bright..was accredited with having said [etc.] 1880. 2. Accredited at St. Petersburg KINGLAKE. var. †**Accre·ditate** *v.*, whence **Accredita·tion,** the action of accrediting, or being accredited. **Accre·dited** *ppl. a.* furnished with credentials; authoritatively sanctioned.

Accrementitial (æ:krĭmĕnti·ʃăl), *a.* 1879. [f. L. **accrementum*, f. *accrescere*; see ACCRESCE.] *Biol.* Pertaining to accrementition.

Accrementition (æ:krĭmĕnti·ʃən). 1879. Improp. formation after prec. Cf. *fermentation.*] *Biol.* Organic growth, by development of blastema, or by fission of cells; = ACCRETION.

Accresce (ăkre·s), *v.* 1634. [ad. L. *accrescere*. Refash. on ACCREASE from Fr.] **1.** To accrue (in Rom. Law). †**2.** *trans.* To add to 1652. Hence **Accre·scence,** continuous growth; an accretion. **Accre·scency,** an accretion. **Accre·scent** *a.* growing continuously; *Bot.* growing larger after flowering.

Accrete (ăkrī·t), *v.* 1784. [f. L. *accret-, accrescere*; see ACCRESCE.] **1.** *intr.* To grow together by adhesion; to grow *to* 1869. **2.** *trans.* To cause to grow or unite *to* 1871.

Accre·te, *ppl. a.* 1824. [ad. L. *accretus*; see ACCRESCE.] **1.** Formed by accretion; factitious. **2.** *Bot.* Grown together; said of parts normally separate 1847.

Accretion (ăkrī·ʃən). 1615. [ad. L. *accretionem*; see ACCRESCE.] **1.** Continued growth. **2.** The growing together of particles, or of parts normally separate 1655; anything so formed 1873. **3.** The process of growth by external addition 1626. **4.** The adhesion of external matter or things so as to cause increase 1713; that which so adheres, an extraneous addition 1653. **5.** *Law.* **a.** = ACCESSION. 1830. **b.** The increase of an inheritance or legacy by the addition of the share of a failing co-heir or co-legatee 1880.

1. The tendency of all power is to a. HELPS. 2. The drop, gathered by a. of minute particles, may be snow, ice, or water PHILLIPS. The Bible—an a. of casual writings H. ROGERS. 3. Inanimate Bodies ..have an A., but no Alimentation BACON. 4. The a. after *K* pure, of the palatal semivowel *y* DOUSE. The accretions of age MERIVALE.

Accre·tive, *a.* 1665. [f. L. *accret-, accrescere.*] Belonging to accretion.

†**Accri·minate,** *v.* 1655. [f. L. *ac-* = *ad-* + *criminari.*] To accuse of crime. Hence †**Accrimina·tion,** accusation of crime.

Accroach (ăkrōᵘ·tʃ), *v.* ME. [a. OFr. *acrocher* (later *accrocher*), f. *à* + *croc*; see CROOK.] *prop.* To draw with a hook; hence, **1.** To draw to oneself, acquire ME. **2.** With *to oneself*: To usurp what is not one's own 1520. **3.** *intr.* To encroach 1530.

2. They had attempted to a. to themselves royal power STUBBS. Hence **Accroa·ching** *vbl. sb.* the act of drawing to oneself; usurping sovereign power. **Accroa·chment.**

Accrual (ăkrū·ăl). [f. ACCRUE *v.*] = ACCRETION 5 b. *attrib.*, as *a. basis.*

†**Accrue** (ăkrū·), *sb.* 1577. [a. Fr. *accrue, accroître*:—L. *accrescere*; see ACCREASE.] Accession, reinforcement. (Cf. CREW.)

Accrue (ăkrū·), *v.* 1470. [f. the sb.] **1.** To fall (*to* any one) as a natural growth or increment; to come as an accession or advantage. Const. *unto, to.* **2.** To arise or spring (*from, by,* †*of*) as a natural growth or result. Used *esp.* of interest 1589. †**3.** To grow, grow up 1604. †**4.** *trans.* To collect 1594.

1. Lands left to the shore.. accrew wholly to the King 1622. 2. Interest begins to a. from the moment [etc.] MCCULLOCH. Hence **Accrue·d** *ppl. a.* accumulated by growth; *Her.* full grown. **Accrue·ment,** the action of accruing as a natural accession, or as *interest*; that which accrues or has accrued. **Accru·er** (*Law*), the action of accruing; = ACCRETION 5 b. **Accru·ing** *vbl. sb.* natural growth; *ppl. a.* arising in due course.

Accubation (æ:kiubē^i·ʃən). 1646. [ad. L. *accubationem*, var. of *accubitionem.*] †**1.** The ancient posture of reclining at table –1656. **2.** *Med.* = ACCOUCHEMENT. 1879.

Accumbent (ăkʊ·mbĕnt). 1656. [ad. L. *accumbentem, accumbere.*] **A.** *ppl. a.* **1.** Reclining at table 1727. **2.** *Bot.* Lying against anything; opp. to *incumbent.* Applied to the cotyledons of an embryo when their edges lie against the folded radicle. **B.** *sb.* One who reclines, or is, at table 1656.

†**Accu·mber,** *v.* ME. [for earlier *encombre* (A-*pref.* 10), a. OFr. *encombrer*, f. *en* + *combrer*; see CUMBER. Refash. after wds. in *a-*:—L. *ad-*.] To encumber, oppress, crush.

Accombred with the cloaked hatred of Cain *Homilies.* Hence †**Accu·mbrance,** the act of encumbering. †**Accu·mbrous** *a.* cumbrous. CHAUCER.

Accumulate (ăkiū·miŭlĕt), *ppl. a.* 1533. [ad. L. *accumulatus, accumulare*, f. *ac-* = *ad-* + *cumulare.*] Heaped up by additions. As pple. replaced by ACCUMULATED.

Accumulate (ăkiū·miŭlē^it), *v.* [f. prec.] **1.** *trans.* To heap up in a mass, to pile up; to collect. *fig.* 1529. *absol.* 1858. Occas. *lit.* (*after Lat.*) 1809. **2.** To take (*degrees*) by ACCUMULATION; also *absol.* 1691. **3.** *intr.* (from refl.) To go on increasing 1759.

1. To a. piles of wealth *Hen. VIII*, III. ii. 107, an immense debt BURKE, authorities 1798. To a. beyond our wants 1858. 3. Where wealth accumulates GOLDSMITH.

Accumulation (ăkiū·miŭlē^i·ʃən). 1490. [ad. L. *accumulationem*; see ACCUMULATE.] **1.** The action of accumulating. *lit.* and *fig.* 1606. **2.** The process of growing into a heap; *spec.* the growth of money by the addition of interest to principal 1490. **3.** The combination of several acts or exercises into one; *spec.* the taking of higher and lower degrees together, or at a shorter interval than is usual 1753. **4.** An accumulated mass; a pile 1490.

1. Quicke a. of renowne *Ant. & Cl.* III. i. 19. The instinct of a. HAMERTON. 2. The a. of ruins and rubbish from above STANLEY. 3. To say the divine offices by a. 1865. 4. An a. of knowledge JOHNSON, of capital CARLYLE, of snow HUXLEY.

Accumulative (ăkiū·miŭlĕtiv), *a.* 1651. [f. L. *accumulat-, accumulare*; see ACCUMULATE.] **1.** Arising from accumulation; cumulative. **2.** Tending to increase in amount 1857. **3.** Given to accumulate 1817. Hence **Accu·mulatively** *adv.* **Accu·mulativeness.**

Accumulator (ăkiū·miŭlē^itəɹ). 1691. [ad. L.] **1.** One who amasses 1748. **2.** One who takes degrees by ACCUMULATION 1691. **3.** Anything that accumulates. *spec.* An apparatus for accumulating electricity. 1877.

†**Accur(re,** *v.* 1555. [ad. L. *accurrere.* Cf. Fr. *accourir.*] To run to; to meet –1651. ¶Often for OCCUR.

Accuracy (æ·kiŭrĕsi). 1662. [f. ACCURATE.] The state of being ACCURATE; precision, correctness.

Experiments that require a greater a. R. WALLER. A. of singing HUXLEY.

Accurate (æ·kiŭrėt), *a.* 1612. [ad. L. *accuratus, accurare.*] †1. Executed with care –1738. 2. Of things and persons: Exact, correct, as the result of care 1612. 3. Of things: Conforming to a standard, or to truth; precise, correct 1651.

1. Acurat diaries BURTON. A. attempts 1738. 2. An a. knowledge of mineralogy SULLIVAN. An a. and learned printer DIBDIN. 3. An a. term BURKE, solution (*mod.*). Hence **A·ccurately** *adv.* with careful exactness; without error or defect. **A·ccurateness.** (Properly of a person.)

Accurse (ăkɒ̄·ɹs), *v.* *arch.* *Pa. pple.* **accursed, accurst.** ME. [f. A- *pref.* 7 + OE. *cursian* to CURSE. The *a-* in *a-curse*, appar. intens., was erron. latinized to *ac-* in 15th c.] To pronounce or imprecate a curse upon; to devote to perdition, or misery.

She had purchased a curse of the pope, to a curse all yᵉ said barons FABYAN. Accursed Above all cattle MILT. Hence **Accu·rsed, accu·rst** *ppl. a.* lying under a curse; worthy of, or bringing with it, a curse; also *absol.* **Accu·rsedly** *adv.* *arch.* **Accu·rsedness.** *arch.* †**Accu·rsing** *vbl. sb.* the act of pronouncing a curse; excommunication.

†**Accurtation.** 1583. [a. med.L. *accurtationem.*] Shortening –1594.

Accusant (ăkiū̆·zănt). 1611. [a. Fr.:—L. *accusantem, accusare.*] One who accuses.

Accusation (ækiuzēⁱ·ʃən). ME. [a. Fr., ad. L. *accusationem*, f. *accusare.*] 1. The act of accusing, or the being accused. 2. The charge, or the declaration containing it; an indictment ME.

1. Be thou constant in the a. *Much Ado* II. ii. 55. Under the a. of his country BURKE. 2. To this a. I will not plead 1862.

Accusative (ăkiū̆·zătiv), *a.* ME. [a. Fr., ad. L. *accusativus* 'of the nature of accusation' = Gr. (πτῶσις) αἰτιατική, and also 'of or pertaining to that which is caused' (τὸ αἰτιατόν).] *Gram.* In inflected languages the name of the case expressing primarily destination; hence, the case expressing the object of transitive verbs, i. e. the destination of the verbal action; applied, in uninflected languages, to the *relation* in which the object stands. Usu. sb. (*case* being omitted). †2. (From ACCUSE *v.*) Accusatory ME.

1. The fourte case is accusatif case *Gesta Rom.* (1879) 417. 2. A very a. age SIR E. DERING. Hence **Accu·sati·val** *a.* **Accu·satively** *adv.* in an a. manner; relating to the a. case.

†**Accusator, -our.** ME. [a. Fr. *accusateur*:—L. *accusatorem.*] An accuser.

Accusatorial (ăkiū̆:zătōᵊ·riăl), *a.* 1823. [f. L. *accusatorius.*] Of or pertaining to an accuser.

A. procedure, that in which the..prosecutor is..a different person from the judge BENTHAM. Hence **Accu·satorially** *adv.* by means of a formal accuser.

Accusatory (ăkiū̆·zatəri), *a.* 1601. [ad. L. *accusatorius.*] Of the nature of an accusation.

Accuse (ăkiū̆·z), *v.* ME. [a. OFr. *acuser*:—L. *accusare*, for *accausare*, f. *ac-* = *ad-* + *causare*; *a-* was refashioned as *ac-* after L.] 1. To charge with a fault; to blame; also with *as*, †*for*, or *subord. cl.* 1513. 2. To accuse *of* (†*for*, †*in*, †*upon*): To charge with the crime of ME.; also *absol.* (obj. omitted), and *intr.* 3. To betray, disclose, and *fig.* to indicate, or make known (*rare*) ME.

1. He had accused him to the king BURNET. Such frugal virtue malice may a. DRYDEN. Accused as accessary to the crime (*mod.*). 2. Atreus accused himself of murdre LYDGATE. Who is he that accuseth (*mod.*). They accusen falsely agaynste Chryste WYCLIF. 3. The distribution of the scene accuses an absence of motive or thought 1864. Hence **Accu·sable** *a.* liable to be accused; liable to the charge *of.* **Accu·sably** *adv.* **Accu·sal**, the act of accusing. †**Accu·se**, accusation 2 *Hen. VI*, III. i. 160. **Accu·sed** *ppl. a.* charged with a crime or fault. (Usu. *the accused*: the prisoner at the bar.) †**Accu·sement**, the action of accusing. **Accu·sing** *vbl. sb.* the action of accusing; *ppl. a.* blaming; reproachful. **Accu·singly** *adv.*

Accuser (ăkiū̆·zəɹ). ME. [f. ACCUSE *v.*] One who accuses or blames; *esp.* one who prosecutes in a court of justice.

Satan.., The tempter ere the a. of mankind MILT.

†**Accusor, -our.** ME. [a. Anglo-Fr.] Early ff. ACCUSER.

Accustom (ǎkɒ·stəm), *v.* 1477. [a. OFr. *acostumer*, f. *à* + *costume*:—late L. *costuma*:—*costudinem*:—cl. L. *consuetudinem* CUSTOM; *a-* was refashioned as *ac-* after L.] †1. *trans.* To make customary or familiar; to practise habitually. Freq. in pass., *to be accustomed*. –1768. †2. *intr.* To become familiar, to consort or cohabit with –1670. 3. *trans.* To habituate (*to*, †*in*, †*into*, †*for*, †*with*, or *to do*) 1478. Also *refl.* and †*intr.*

1. Such..thanks As..friends a. on the shore MARLOWE. 2. With the best man we a. openly MILTON. 3. The ear..is accustomed to stillness RUSKIN. *refl.* With servants, never a. yourself to.. passionate language CHATHAM. *intr.* Those..who..a. to wash their heads EVELYN. Hence †**Accu·stom** *sb.* habit. †**Accu·stomable** *a.* usually practising or practised. **Accu·stomably** *adv.* customarily. †**Accu·stomance,** customary use or practice. †**Accu·stomarily** *adv.* usually. **Accu·stomary** *a.* *arch.* usual. †**Accu·stomate** *ppl. a.* accustomed. **Accu·stoming** *vbl. sb.* †making oneself familiar with, consorting; habituating.

Accustomed (ǎkɒ·stəmd), *ppl. a.* 1483. [f. ACCUSTOM *v.*] 1. Made customary; habitual. †2. Frequented by customers –1772.

1. Th' a. sight of death *A. Y. L.* III. v. 4. 2. A well a. shop SMOLLETT. Hence **Accu·stomedly** *adv.* **Accu·stomedness**, the quality or fact of being a.

Ace (ēⁱs). ME. [a. Fr. *as*:—L. *as* (said to be a. Tarentine ἄς = Gr. εἷς one).] 1. *One* at dice, or the side of the die marked with one pip, and counting as one; afterwards extended to cards, dominoes, etc. *Ambs ace*, both aces; *deuce ace* (OFr.) two aces at one throw (now taken as *deuce* + *ace* = 2 and 1; so *trey ace, syce ace*, etc.). b. A point at rackets, lawn tennis, etc. 2. *fig.* Bad luck, loss (= the lowest throw); the perfection (= the best card) ME. An aviator who has brought down three enemy machines, a crack aviator 1917. 3. *fig.* A single point, a jot, particle, or atom 1528.

1. *Cymb.* II. iii. 3. 2. The a. and wale o' honest men BURNS. 3. **To bate an ace**: to make the slightest abatement. Bating him that a., he was a truly great man NORTH. **Within an ace of**: on the very point of. I was within an a. of being talked to death T. BROWN. Hence **Ace** *v.* to score an ace against an opponent (cf. 1 b above).

-acea, L. suffix, pl. neut. of *-aceus* = belonging to, etc.; see -ACEOUS. Used (in neut. pl. sc. *animalia*) to form names of classes or orders of animals, as *Crustacea*, etc.

-aceæ, L. suffix, pl. fem. of *-aceus*, as above. Used (in fem. pl. sc. *plantæ*) to form names of orders or families of plants, as *Rosaceæ*, etc.

-acean, f. L. *-aceus* + -AN. As an adj. = *-aceus*; as a sb. = sing. to collect. pls. in *-acea*.

Acediamine (æ·sĭdəi·ămein). 1877. [f. ACE[TIC] + DIAMINE.] *Chem.* An amine of composition $C_2N_2H_6$.

†**Acedy.** 1623. [f. as ACCIDIE.] Torpor.

Aceldama (ăke·l-, ăse·ldămă). ME. [Gr. Ἀκελδαμά, a. Aram. *ōkel damā* field of blood.] The name of the field near Jerusalem bought with the blood-money received by Judas Iscariot. Hence *fig.* A field of bloodshed.

fig. What an A. Sicily has been BURKE.

Acenaphthene (æ:sĭnæ·fþīn). 1877. [f. ACE[TIC] + NAPHTHENE.] *Chem.* A compound substance of the Naphthalene group, $C_{12}H_{10}$.

Acenaphthylene (æ:sĭnæ·fþilīn). 1877. [f. ACE[TIC] + NAPHTHA + -YL + -ENE.] *Chem* A compound substance of the Naphthalene group $C_{12}H_8$, having two atoms of H less than Acenaphthene.

Ace·ntric, *a.* 1852. [f. Gr. ἄκεντρος.] Without a centre.

-aceous (ēⁱ·ʃəs), suffix, f. L. *-ace-us, -a, -um*, of the nature of. Used in Nat. Hist. to supply adjs. resembling L. words in *-aceus*, to nouns in *-acea, -aceæ*; also in other words, as *cretaceous*, etc.

†**Acephal.** 1549. [a. Fr. *acéphale*, ad. late L. *acephalus*; see ACEPHALI.] **A.** *adj.* = ACEPHALOUS. **B.** *sb.* [sc. *animal*] = ACEPHALAN. 1607.

‖**Acephala** (ăse·fălă), *sb. pl.* 1847. [late L., a. Gr. ἀκέφαλα adj. neut. pl. = headless (sc. *animalia*).] One of the two great divisions of molluscs. *Sing.* ACEPHALAN, or ACEPHAL.

Acephalan (ăse·fălăn). 1856. [f. prec.] **A.** *adj.* Of or pertaining to the ACEPHALA. **B.** *sb.* [sc. *animal.*]

‖**Acephali** (ăse·făləi), *sb. pl.* 1600. [late L. pl. of *acephalus*, a. Gr. ἀκέφαλος.] 1. *Nat. Hist.* (Imaginary) men or animals without heads. 2. *Eccl. Hist.* A name of various Christian bodies, which owned either no leader, no earthly head, or no bishop 1625. †3. *Eng. Hist.* Certain Levellers of the time of K. Henry I 1721. Hence †**Acepha·lian** *a.* and *sb.* †**Ace·phalist** (*rare*); also **Ace·phalite.**

Acephalocyst (ăse·fălo,sist). 1836. [ad. mod.L. *acephalocystis*, f. Gr. ἀκέφαλος + κύστις.] A headless bladder-worm; a name for the hydatids. They are now known to be the *larva* of one of the tapeworms (*Tæniadæ*), which enlarges into a globular cyst, with the head inverted and so invisible. Hence **Ace:phalocy·stic** *a.*

Acephalous (ăse·făləs), *a.* 1731. [f. Fr. *acéphale*, or late L. *acephalus.*] 1. Headless. 2. Having or owning no leader or chief 1751. 3. *Zool.* Having no part of the body specially organized as a head, e. g. *A. Molluscs* = ACEPHALA 1741. 4. *Bot.* With the natural head aborted or cut off 1880. 5. Lacking the beginning, as an imperfect manuscript or verse 1753.

1. An a. pedigree GROTE. 2. An a. body politic was inconceivable SIR F. PALGRAVE. 5. An a. structure of sentence DE QUINCEY.

Acerate (æ·sĕrēⁱt). 1847. [f. L. *acer* maple.] *Chem.* A salt of aceric acid.

Acerb (ăsɔ̄·ɹb), *a.* 1657. [ad. L. *acerbus*; cf. Fr. *acerbe.*] Sour and bitter, as unripe fruit; also *fig.*

Acerbate (æ·səɹbēⁱt), *v.* 1731. [f. L. *acerbat-, acerbare.*] To sour or embitter; usu. *fig.* Hence **Ace·rbate** *ppl. a.* embittered.

Acerbic (ăsɔ̄·ɹbik), *a.* 1865. [f. L. *acerbus.*] Sour or harsh.

Acerbity (ăsɔ̄·ɹbĭti). 1572. [a. Fr. *acerbité*, ad. L. *acerbitatem.*] 1. Sourness of taste, with astringency 1611. 2. *fig.* Of men, their words, etc.: Sharpness and bitterness, keen harshness 1572.

2. A. of pain BARROW. The a. of political warfare DISRAELI.

Aceric (ăse·rik), *a.* 1847. [ad. mod.L. *acericus.*] Pertaining to the maple, as *aceric acid*, which is found in its sap.

Acerose (æ:sĕrōᵘ·s), *a.* 1785. [ad. L. *acerosus*, f. *acus* chaff; in sense 2 referred to *acus* needle.] 1. Like, or mixed with chaff (Dicts.). 2. *Bot.* Needle-shaped and rigid, as pine-leaves. var. **Acerous.**

Acervate (ăsɔ̄·ɹvėt), *ppl. a.* 1848. [ad. L. *acervatus.*] Heaped, growing in heaps or clusters. Hence **Ace·rvately** *adv.* **Acerva·tion,** accumulation. **Ace·rvative** *a.* tending to heaping up. **Ace·rvuline** *a.* of the form of little heaps.

Acescence (ăse·sĕns). 1765. [a. mod.Fr.; see ACESCENT.] The act of turning sour; acetous fermentation.

Acescency (ăse·sĕnsi). 1756. [f. ACESCENT.] The quality or state of turning sour; incipient or slight sourness.

Acescent (ăse·sĕnt). 1731. [ad. L. *acescentem, acescere.*] **A.** *adj.* Turning sour; or tending to turn acid; slightly sour, turned. *lit.* and *fig.* **B.** *sb.* [sc. *substance.*]

Acet-. *Chem.* In comb. = ACETIC, ACETYL bef. a vowel, as in *acet-amide*, etc.

Acetable (æ·sĭtăb'l). 1551. [ad. L. *acetabulum*, the form now used.] 1. An ancient fluid measure; a saucerful; = half a gill. 2. = ACETABULUM 2 b. 1684.

‖**Acetabulum** (æsĭtæ·biŭlŏm). ME. [L.; f. *acetum* + *-abulum* dim. of *-abrum* = a holder.] 1. *Rom. Antiq.* A cup for holding vinegar at table; hence a measure, half a gill. 2. *Animal Physiol.* A cup-shaped cavity or organ: as, a. A sucker of the cuttle-fish or other cephalopod 1661. b. The socket of the thigh-bone 1709; *Hence*, c. The socket of any joint in insects 1828. d. A placental lobe, in ruminants. 3. *Bot.* The receptacle of certain fungals. Hence **Aceta·bular** *a.* cup-like; sucker-shaped. **Aceta·buli·ferous** *a.* bearing acetabula. **Aceta·buliform** *a.* saucer-shaped.

Acetal (æ·sĭtæl). 1869. [f. ACET(IC) + AL(COHOL).] *Chem.* A colourless liquid found in preparing spirit of wine, the *diethylate of ethylidene or ethidene* CH_3–$CH(OC_2H_5)_2$.

Acetaldehyde (æsɪ̄tæ·ldɪ̄hǝid). 1877. [contr. for *Acetic aldehyde.*] *Chem.* Common or ethyl aldehyde.

Acetamide (æ·sɪ̄tămǝiːd, ăse·tămǝid). 1873. [f. as next + AMIDE.] *Chem.* The primary AMIDE in which the replacing acid radical is ACETYL; $C_2H_3O.NH_2$; a white crystalline solid, nearly neutral.

Acetanilide (æsɪ̄tæ·nilǝid). 1864. [f. ACET(YL) + ANILIDE.] *Chem.* A compound of aniline and acetyl. $C_6H_5.NH.C_2H_3O$. Erron. *acetaniline.*

†**A·cetars, a·cetaries,** *sb. pl.* 1612. [ad. L. *acetaria.*] Salad plants –1775. Hence **Aceta·rious** *a.* used in salads, as cress, etc.

Acetary (æ·sɪ̄tări). 1674. [ad. mod.L. *acetarium,* f. *acetum.*] An acid pulpy substance in the pear, etc., enclosed in a mass of calculous particles towards the base of the fruit.

Acetate (æ·sɪ̄tĕt). 1827. [f. ACET-IC.] *Chem.* A salt formed by combining acetic acid with a base; as *A. of lead.*

A·cetated, *ppl. a.* 1791. [f. *acetate* vb. (not found).] Treated with acetic acid.

Aceta·tion. 1863. [f. as prec.] = ACETIFICATION.

Acetic (ăsī·tik, ăse·tik), *a.* 1808. [f. L. *acetum.*] Of the nature of or pertaining to vinegar.
Phr. **Acetic acid**: The special acid of which vinegar is a diluted or crude form, produced by fermentation. *Chemically,* the monatomic monobasic acid of the ethyl or dicarbon series $C_2H_4O_2$. *Anhydrous acetic acid,* a synonym of *acetic anhydride. Acetic series*: The series of compound bodies containing the radical ACETYL C_2H_3O; as *A. ether, A. oxide* or *anhydride.*

Acetify (ăse·tifǝi), *v.* 1864. [f. L. *acetum.*] To subject to, or undergo, acetous fermentation. Hence **Ace:tifica·tion**, the action of converting into vinegar. **Ace·tifier,** an apparatus for producing vinegar.

Acetimeter (æsɪ̄ti·mɪ̄tǝɹ). 1875. [a. Fr. *acétimètre.*] An instrument for measuring the strength of vinegar, or other acids. Hence **A:cetime·trical** *a.* var. **Aceto·meter.**

A:ceti·metry. 1875. [f. L. *acetum* + -METRY.] The determination of the strength or sourness of vinegar or acetic acid, or the proportion of it in any substance.

Acetin (æ·sɪ̄tin). 1874. [f. ACET- + -IN(E = Gr. -ινη.] Acetic glycerin; class name of a series consisting of glycerin, in which one, two, or all the three hydrogen atoms are replaced by acetyl C_2H_3O, thus forming *mono-, di-,* or *tri-acetin.*

†**A·cetite,** earlier f. ACETATE.

A·cetize, *v.* [f. L. ACETUM.] = ACETIFY.

Aceto-. *Chem.* In comb. = ACETIC, ACETYL bef. a cons. (cf. ACET-), as in *aceto-chloride,* etc.

Acetone (æ·sɪ̄tōun). 1858. [f. ACET(IC) + Gr. -ωνη; see -ONE.] *Chem.* A colourless limpid liquid related to acetic acid, but containing less oxygen; pyro-acetic spirit. It is the acetic ketone, and is called also *Dimethyl ketone.* Hence ‖**A:cetonæ·mia,** *Med.* a morbid state, marked by the presence of a. in the blood. **A·cetonami:ne,** *Chem.* a compound amine, obtained by heating a. with ammonia. **A·cetonate,** *Chem.* a salt of acetonic acid. **Aceto·nic** *a.* derived from a. **A:cetoni·tril,** *Chem.* an alcoholic cyanide or hydrocyanic ether; the *nitril* of the acetic series, called also *Ethenyl nitril* and *Methyl cyanide.*

Acetose (æ·sɪ̄tōus), *a.* 1533. [ad. late L. *acetosus.*] Tasting like vinegar; sour. Hence **Aceto·sity,** the quality of being a. var. †**Aceto·sous** *a.*

†**A:ceto·se, -ouse.** 1547. [ad. mod.L. *Acetosa.*] The herb Sorrel or Sorrel Dock (*Rumex Acetosa*).

Acetous (æ·sɪ̄tǝs), *a.* 1778. [ad. Fr. *acéteux, -euse,* ad. late L. *acetosus.*] Of, pertaining to, or having the qualities of vinegar; sour. Also *fig.*
fig. Till all France were grown a., virulent CARLYLE. *Acetous fermentation*: The chemical reaction by which sugar or alcohol is changed into vinegar. †*Acetous acid*: A name given to vinegar in the erroneous belief that it contained less oxygen than Acetic acid.

Acetyl (æ·sɪ̄til). 1864. [f. ACET(IC) + Gr. ὕλη.] *Chem.* A monatomic radical C_2H_3O, the basis of the acetic series. Also *attrib.* and in *Comb.* Hence **Acety·lic** *a.*

Acetylene (ăse·tilīn). 1864. [f. ACETYL + -ENE.] *Chem.* A gaseous hydrocarbon, C_2H_2, used as an illuminant. Also *a. gas, lamp.*

‖**Ach** (ăχ), *int.* [G. and Celtic.] Ah!

Achænocarp (ăkī·nokāɹp). 1880. [f. Gr. ἀ + χαίνειν to gape + καρπός; cf. ACHENE.] A fruit which is an achene.

†**Acha·fe,** *v.* ME. [:–ESCHAUFE, a. OFr. *eschaufer* (*échauffer*) :—L. *ex* + *calefare* for *calefacere*; see A- *pref.* 9.] To heat; *fig.* to heat with passion –1490.

†**Acha·pe,** *v.* ME. A by-form of ESCAPE.

†**Achaque.** [Sp.] Ailment. HOWELL.

‖**Achar** (ătʃā·ɹ). *Anglo-Ind.* [a. Pers.] Pickles.

†**Acha·rne,** *v. rare.* ME. [a. Fr. *acharner* :—late L. *adcarnare.*] To thirst for blood. Hence ‖**Acha·rnement,** bloodthirsty fury.

Achate (æ·kăt), *sb.*[1] *arch.* ME. [a. OFr. *achate,* ad. L., a. Gr. ἀχάτης.] An agate.

†**Acha·te,** *sb.*[2] ME. [a. OFr. *achat.*] 1. Purchase –1691. 2. *pl.* Things purchased; CATES –1644.

†**Acha·te,** *v. rare.* 1601. [a. OFr. *achater* :—late L. *accaptare.*] To purchase.

†**Acha·tour.** ME. [a. Anglo-Fr. :—late L. *accaptatorem.*] A purchaser of provisions, *esp.* for the royal household; a purveyor –1751.

Ache, ake (ēɪk), *v.* OE. [Orig. a strong vb. like *take, shake.* Historically the vb. is *ake,* the sb. *ache,* as in *bake, batch,* etc. Both are written *ache,* but pronounced *ake,* since Johnson's erron. derivation from Gr. ἄχος; see next wd.] 1. To be in pain; *esp.* in continuous or prolonged pain; to throb with pain. †2. *trans.* To make to ache –1566.
1. Lat our hedes nevere ake CHAUCER. Thy sorrow aches in me MRS. BROWNING. Hence **A·chage** (after *breakage*) *Joc.* Aching state. **A·cher,** he who, or that which, aches. **A·chingly** *adv.*

Ache (ēɪk), *sb.*[1] [OE. *æce* is a deriv. of vb. *ac-an* to ACHE, orig. with *c* (k) palatalized to *ch* (tʃ), as in *make, match,* etc. Till 1700 the sb. was *atche* (ătʃ, ĕtʃ), pl. *atches* (ătʃĕs, ĕtʃĕs); see prec.] A pain; *esp.* a continuous or abiding pain, physical or mental.
[He] Fill all thy bones with Aches, make thee rore *Temp.* I. ii. 370. *Much Ado* III. iv. 56. Hence **A·cheless** *a.* without ache.

†**Ache** (ēɪtʃ), *sb.*[2] ME. [a. Fr. *ache* :—L. *apium,* ad. Gr. ἄπιον.] An umbelliferous plant; prop. Smallage (i.e. *Small-Ache*); also *parsley.*

Ache (ēɪtʃ), *sb.*[3] Name of the letter H, q. v.

†**Achea·t, achete,** *v.* ME. [f. A- *pref.* 9 = OFr. *es-, e-,* + CHEAT.] To escheat; to do one out of.

†**Ache·ck,** *v.* [f. A- *pref.* 11 + CHECK.] To check. CHAUCER.

†**Achee·r,** *v.* [f. A- *pref.* 11 + CHEER *v.*] To cheer –1660.

Acheilary (ăkǝi·lări), *a.* 1868. [f. Gr. ἀ + χεῖλος.] *Bot.* Wanting the lip of the corolla. Better *achilary.*

Achei·lous, *a.* 1879. [f. as prec.] *Bot.* Without a lip. Better *achilous.*

Achene (ăkī·n), also **achæne.** 1845. [ad. mod.L. *achænium,* f. Gr. ἀ + χαίνειν to gape.] *Bot.* A monospermal seed-vessel which does not open, with a separable pericarp; any small brittle seed-like fruit; a 'naked seed'. Hence **Ache·nial** *a.*

‖**Acheron** (æ·kĕrǫn). 1590. [L., a. Gr.] A fabled river of the Lower World; hence, the infernal regions. Hence **Achero·ntic, -al** *a.* of or belonging to Acheron, infernal; gloomy; waiting to cross Acheron, moribund.

†**Ache·soun.** ME. [a. OFr. *acheson, achaison* :—L. *occasionem*; refash. ENCHESOUN, ENCHEASON; aphet. to CHESOUN; see A- *pref.* 10.] Occasion, purpose.

Achieve (ătʃī·v), *v.* ME. [a. Fr. *achever,* f. *à chief* (*venir*) :—late L. *ad caput venire.*] 1. To finish, to carry out successfully, to bring to an end. *absol.* 1607. †2. *intr.* To come to an end; result, turn out –1534. 3. Of an end: To attain, to reach successfully. †4. *intr.* To attain successfully *to* –1587.
1. He that nought nassayeth, nought nacheveth CHAUCER. Bid them atchieue me, and then sell my bones *Hen. V,* IV. iii. 91. *absol.* He does atcheeue as soone As draw his sword *Coriol.* IV. vii. 23. 3. Some atchieue greatnesse *Twel. N.* V. i. 378. To a. its [the policy's] necessary ends 1882. Hence **Achie·vable** *a.* †**Achie·vance,** achievement. **Achie·ver.**

Achievement (ătʃī·vmĕnt). 1475. [a. Fr. *achèvement.* See ACHIEVE.] 1. The action of achieving. 2. Anything achieved; a feat, a victory 1593. 3. *Her.* An escutcheon or ensign armorial, granted in memory of some achievement. (In this sense corrupted to **hatchment.**)
1. Within the bounds of possible a. SOUTHEY. 2. The achievements of genius BREWSTER. 3. The Hachementes wer borne onely by Capitaynes HALL.

Achi·ll, *adv.* 1870. [A- *prep.*[1] + CHILL.] In a state of chill.

Achillean (ækilī·ăn), *a.* 1637. [f. *Achilles.*] Resembling Achilles; invulnerable, invincible.

†**Achillize,** *v.* 1672. [f. as prec.] To play Achilles with.

Achilous. [Better form of ACHEILOUS.] *Bot.* Without lips.

Achi·me, *adv.* 1860. [A- *prep.*[1] + CHIME.] Chiming.

‖**Achio·te, acho·te.** 1796. [Sp., ad. native Amer. *achiotl.*] The seeds of the Arnotto (*Bixa orellana*); the red colouring matter they yield.

Achirite (æ·kirǝit). [f. *Achir* Mahméd.] = DIOPTASE.

Achlamydate (ăklæ·midĕt), *a.* 1877. [f. Gr. ἀ + χλαμύδα.] *Zool.* Of Molluscs: Having no mantle.

Achlamydeous (æklămi·dīǝs), *a.* 1830. [f. as prec.] *Bot.* Having no envelope; without apparent calyx and corolla.

†**Acho·ke,** *v.* ME. [f. A- *pref.* 1 + CHOKE.] To choke.

Acholous (æ·kŏlǝs). [f. Gr. ἄχολος.] Lacking bile.

‖**Achor** (ēɪ·koɹ). 1585. [L., Gr. ἀχώρ.] *Med.* A scaly eruption in the hairy scalp, constituting scald-head.

Achroite (æ·kroˌǝit) [f. Gr. ἄχροος.] *Min.* Colourless tourmaline from Elba.

Achromatic (ækromæ·tik), *a.* 1766. [f. Gr. ἀχρώματος.] 1. *Optics.* Free from colour; not showing colour from decomposition in transmitting light. Also *sb.* [sc. *lens*]. 2. *Biol.* Of tissue: Uncoloured 1882.
1. The human eye is not a. TYNDALL. *sb.* An a. of four inches aperture NEWCOMB. Hence **A:chroma·tically** *adv.* so as to produce freedom from colour. **Achro·mati·city, Achro·matism,** the state or quality of being a. **Achromati·stous** *a.* (*rare*) achromatic. **Achro:matiza·tion,** the action or process of rendering a. **Achro·matize** *v.* to render a. **Achro·mato:psy,** *Med.* colour-blindness. †**Achro·mic** *a.* [improp. formed] = ACHROMATIC. **Achro·mous** *a.* (*rare*) colourless.

Achronical, -ly, incorr. ff. ACRONYCAL, -LY.

Achronism (æ·krŏniz'm). *nonce-wd.* [f. Gr. ἄχρονος.] The state of timelessness. R. LOWE. ¶ Occ. for ANACHRONISM, as if *an achronism.*

Achroö-, combining form of ACHROOUS, as in *achroödextrin,* colourless dextrin, etc.

Achroous (æ·kroǝs), *a.* 1879. [f. Gr. ἄχροος.] Colourless; achromatic.

Achylous (akǝi·lǝs), *a.* 1879. [f. Gr. ἄχυλος.] *Phys.* Without chyle.

Achy·mous, *a.* 1879. [f. Gr. ἄχυμος.] *Phys.* Without chyme.

‖**Acicula** (ăsi·kiŭlă). Pl. **aciculæ.** 1875. [L., dim. of *acus.*] *Nat. Hist.* A slender needle-like body, such as the spines or prickles of some animals and plants, or some crystals. var. **A·cicle.** Hence **Aci·cular** *a.* needle-like. **Aci·cularly** *adv.* **Aci·culate** *a.* furnished with aciculæ; marked as with needle-scratches; *improp.* = ACICULAR. **Aci·culated** *ppl. a.* marked or striated with fine lines, as if by a needle. **Aci·culiform** *a.* needle-shaped. **Aci·culine** *a.* = ACICULAR. **Aci·culite** (*Min.*) = AIKINITE, or Acicular Bismuth.

Acid (æ·sid). 1626. [a. F. *acide*, or ad. L. *acidus* (root *ac-* sharp).] **A.** *adj.* **1.** Sour, tart, sharp to the taste; tasting like vinegar. Also *fig.* **2.** *Chem.* Having the essential properties of an acid 1727. **3.** *Min.* = ACIDIC 2. 1874.

1. [Sorrel] is a cold and a. herb BACON. *fig.* In his a. manner BOSWELL, rather an a. expression of countenance DISRAELI. *A. drop*: a sweet made of sugar flavoured with tartaric acid 1836. 2. *A. salt*, a salt that retains part of the replaceable hydrogen of a dibasic acid.

B. *sb.* A sour substance; *spec.* in *Chem.* a substance belonging to a class of compounds of hydrogen with another element or elements (oxygen being generally the third element), the commonest of which are sour, and have the property of neutralizing alkalis, and of changing vegetable blues to red 1696. **A. test**: testing for gold with aquafortis; *fig.* a crucial test 1892.

Of Acids, Vitriol is the chiefest, Sea-salt next to that PHILLIPS.

Acidic (ăsi·dik), *a.* 1877. [f. ACID.] *Min.* That element in a ternary compound, which forms an oxygen, sulphur, or other salt, with a basic element, e. g. the silicon in silicate of lime 1880. **2.** Abounding in an acidic element, usu. silicon 1877.

Acidify (ăsi·difəi), *v.* 1797. [f. L. *acidum* ACID. Cf. Fr. *acidifier.*] **1.** To make acid or sour. *Chem.* To convert into an ACID. Also *fig.* **2.** *intr.* (*refl.*) To become acid.

1. *fig.* His thin existence all acidified into rage CARLYLE. Hence **Aci·difi·able** *a.* **Aci·difiant** *a.* acidifying. **Acidi·fic** *a.* (*Min.*) applied to the oxygen, sulphur, etc., which is an oxygen, sulphur, etc., salt of any basic element. **Aci·difica·tion**, the act or process of acidifying. **Aci·difier**, anything that acidifies. **Aci·difying** *ppl. a.* forming, or combining so as to form, an acid.

Acidimeter (æsidi·mĭtəɹ). 1839. [f. L. *acidum* + Gr. μέτρον.] An instrument for measuring the strength of acids. Hence **A cidime·trical** *a.* **A:cidi·metry**, the process of measuring the strength of acids.

Acidity (ăsi·dĭti). 1620. [a. Fr. *acidité*, or ad. L. *aciditātem*; see ACID.] The quality or state of being acid.

Acidosis (æsidōᵘ·sis). 1905. [irreg. f. ACID + -OSIS.] *Path.* An acid condition of the blood such as occurs in diabetes.

Acidulate (ăsi·diŭleᵗt), *v.* 1732. [f. L. *acidulus*. Cf. Fr. *aciduler.*] To make somewhat acid or sour; to flavour with an acid. Also *fig.*

fig. [No] compliment not acidulated with scorn MACAULAY.

Acidulous (ăsi·diŭləs), *a.* 1769. [f. L. *acidulus.*] Sub-acid. Also *fig.* Sour-tempered. *fig.* Gloomy and a. CARLYLE. var. **Aci·dulent.**

†**Acier.** Also **asser.** [OFr. *acer*, *acier*:— low L. *aciarium* [sc. *ferrum*], f. *acies*, edging or pointing iron.] Steel (prop. Fr.).

Acierage (æ·siĕrĕdʒ). [a. Fr. *aciérage*; see prec.] The process of plating with steel.

‖**Acies.** *Obs.* 1646. [L.] Keen attention or aim of eye, ear, etc.

A·ciform, *a.* [f. L. *acus.*] Needle-shaped.

‖**Acinaces** (ăsi·năsīz, ăki·năkīz). [L. for Gr. ἀκινάκης, orig. Pers.] *Anc. Hist.* A short sword or scimitar. Hence **A:cina·ciform**, **aci·naciform** *a.* scimitar-shaped, as in *Bot.* leaves, etc.

Acinetic (æsine·tik), *a.* 1879. [f. Gr. ἀκίνητος.] *Med.* Preventing motion. var. **Acine·sic** (improp. formation).

Acinetiform (æsinī·tifɒɹm), *a.* 1877. [f. mod.L. *acineta* (f. Gr. ἀκίνητος).] Having the form of *Acinetæ*, a genus of infusoria with suckers which are not in constant motion like the cilia or flagella of other infusoria.

‖**Acinus** (æ·sinŏs). Pl. **acini.** 1731. [L. *acinus*, a berry growing in a cluster; also a kernel.] †**1.** A berry which grows in clusters, as grapes, etc.; the cluster. **2.** *Bot.* One of the small fleshy berries or drupes which make up such fruits as the blackberry; the compound fruit itself 1830. **3.** The stones or seeds of grapes or berries 1731. **4.** *Anat.* A racemose gland; a blind end of a duct of a secreting gland, which has several lobes 1751. Hence **A·cina·ceous** *a.* consisting of acini, formed like a blackberry or raspberry. **Aci·niform, a·ciniform** *a.* clustered, or full of small kernels, like grapes. **A:cino·se** *a.* consisting of *acini*; resembling, or composed of, a cluster of small berries. **A·cinous** *a.* = ACINOSE.

-acious (-ēᶦʃəs), *suffix*, forming adjs. meaning 'given to, inclined to, abounding in'; f. L. *-aci* (nom. *-ax*) adj. ending added chiefly to vb. stems (Fr. *-ace*) + -OUS; as in *vivacious*, etc.

‖**Acipenser** (æsipe·nsəɹ). 1853. [L.] *Zool.* The sturgeon.

-acitate (-æ·siteᶦt), *suffix* = *-aci* (see -ACIOUS) + *-t-* (see -TY) + -ATE, forming vbs. on adjs. in *-aci-ous*, or sbs. in *-aci-ty*, as *capacitate*, to produce the capacity.

-acity (-æ·sĭti), *suffix.* a. Fr. *-acité*, ad. L. *-acitatem*, f. *-aci-* (see -ACIOUS) + *-tat-* (see -TY), as *voracity*, the quality of being voracious.

†**Acker.** ME. [? var. of EAGRE *sb.*, the 'bore' on tidal rivers.] †**1.** ? Flood tide; bore –1552. **2.** A ripple, or furrow on the water; a 'cat's-paw' 1808.

Acker, obs. f. ACRE.

†**Ackno·w, aknow**, *v.* OE. [f. ON, in, on, + *cnāwan*; the pref., through *o-*, *a-*, corruptly written *ac-*, after L. *ac-* bef. *c-*, *k-*, *q-*; see A- *pref.* 2.] **1.** To recognize –1430; to acknowledge, confess –1561. **2.** In pa. pple. Informed *of* –1490. **3.** To be acknown: To be (self-)recognized in relation to anything; hence, to avow (*to* a person) –1639.

3. Be not aknowne on't; I have vse for it *Oth.* III. iii. 319.

Acknowledge (ăknɒ·lĕdʒ), *v.* 1481. [f. prec.; or f. KNOWLEDGE *v.* Also pronounced -nōᵘ·lĕdʒ.] **1.** To own the knowledge of; to confess; to admit as true 1553. **2.** To recognize or confess (a person or thing to be something); or, *simply*, to own the claims of 1481. **3.** To own as genuine, or valid in law; to avow or assent to, in legal form. **4.** To own as an obligation; hence, to acknowledge (the receipt of) a letter 1667.

1. He loued .. your daughter, and meant to a. it this night *Much Ado* I. ii. 13. 2. The kingdomes that a. Christ 1 *Hen. IV*, III. ii. 111. Agents too vile to be acknowledged MACAULAY. 3. To a. a release PINKERTON. 4. But they his gifts acknowledg'd none MILT. Hence **Acknow·ledgeable** *a.* recognizable. **Acknow·ledged** *ppl. a.* recognized; admitted as true, valid, or authoritative. **Acknow·ledgedly** *adv.* **Acknow·ledger.** †**Acknow·ledging** *ppl. a.* expressing esteem or gratitude. (Fr. *reconnaissant.*)

Acknowledgement (ăknɒ·lĕdʒmĕnt). Also **acknowledgment.** 1594. [f. ACKNOWLEDGE *v.* + -MENT.] **1.** The act of acknowledging; confession, admission, avowal. †**2.** Recognition –1616. **3.** The act of recognizing the position or claims of 1611. **4.** A declaration or avowal of an act or document so as to give it legal validity 1651. **5.** The owning, or due recognition, of a gift or benefit received, or of a message 1612; hence, something given or done in return for a favour or message.

1. With this a., That God fought for us *Hen. V*, IV. viii. 124. 3. All such places as owe a. to the Dutch JAS. MILL. 4. A. of indebtedness (*mod.*). A virtual a. of the contract (*mod.*). 5. I am, with all a., etc. W. GOULD. A. of help (*mod.*). A small a. of my gratitude (*mod.*). *Comb.* **a.-money**, a sum paid at the death of a landlord, in a. of the new one.

Acla·stic, *a. rare.* 1879. [f. Gr. ἄκλαστος.] *Nat. Phil.* Not refracting.

Aclinic (ăkli·nik), *a.* 1850. [f. Gr. ἀκλινής, f. ἀ + κλίνειν.] Without inclination. Said of the magnetic equator, or *aclinic line*, where the magnetic needle lies horizontal.

A-clock, early f. **o'clock**; see A *prep.*[2] and CLOCK.

Acme (æ·kmĭ). 1570. [a. Gr. ἀκμή. First spelt as Eng. by Venner in 1620.] The highest point or pitch; the culmination or perfection; *esp.* †**a.** the period of full growth –1844; **b.** the crisis of a disease (*arch.*) 1630.

The mark and ἀκμή of our language B. JONS. In Achilles, courtesy reaches to its acmè GLADSTONE. a. One that can instruct your youth, And keepe your Acme in the state of truth B. JONS. b. The a. of a disease 1752, of frenzy CARLYLE.

Acne (æ·knĭ). 1835. [? for Gr. ἀκμή point.] *Path.* Tubercular tumours, chiefly in the face.

Acnode (æ·knōᵘd). 1873. [f. L. *acus* + NODE.] *Geom.* An isolated point belonging to a locus or curve: = *conjugate point* (CONJUGATE *a.* 6). Hence **Acno·dal** *a.* of or pertaining to acnodes.

†**A-coast**, *adv.* 1599. [A *prep.*[1] + COAST.] **1.** At one side, by the coast; see ACOST. **2.** ASHORE.

Acock (akɒ·k), *adv.* 1846. [A *prep.*[1] + COCK.] In cocked fashion; defiantly.

A-cock-bill, *adv.* 1708. *Naut.* Having the bills cocked or pointing upwards. Said of the anchor when it hangs from the cathead ready for dropping; also of the yards when placed at an angle with the deck.

A-cock-horse, *phr.*; see COCK-HORSE.

Acold (ăkōᵘ·ld), *a. arch.* ME. [prob. orig. *a-cōlod*, *a-cōled*, pa. pple.; see ACOOL.] Chilled, cold.

Tom's a-cold *K. Lear* III. iv. 59. The owl for all his feathers was a-cold KEATS.

†**Aco·ld**, *v.* [OE. *acaldian.*] To become or make cold –1440.

Aco·logy. *rare.* 1847. [f. Gr. ἄκος + -λογία.] *Med.* The doctrine of therapeutic agents.

Acolyctine (ækŏli·ktəin). [f. the plant.] *Chem.* An organic base obtained from *Aconitum Lycoctonum*; aconine.

Acolyte (æ·kŏləit). [ad. med.L. *acolitus*, *acoluthus*, a. Gr. ἀκόλουθος follower. Also aphet, COLET.] **1.** *Eccl.* One belonging to the highest of the minor orders (also, a layman) whose duties are concerned with attendance at the altar and carrying candles. **2.** An attendant; a devoted follower 1829.

1. The Acholite, which we call Benet or Cholet .. 1555. 2. The acolytes of chivalry SCOTT. Hence **A·colyteship.** vars. †**Acolouthite, Acolythist.**

†**A-co·mpass**, *adv.* 1385. [a. OFr. *à compas.*] In a circle.

Acondylous (ăkɒ·ndiləs), *a.* 1853. [f. Gr. ἀ + κόνδυλος.] *Nat. Hist.* Not jointed.

Acone·lline. 1876. [dim. f. ACONINE.] *Chem.* An organic base obtained from the root of the aconite. var. **Aconella.**

Aconic (ăkɒ·nik), *a.* 1877. [Short. f. ACONITIC.] *Chem.* In *Aconic Acid*: A nonsaturated monobasic acid, $C_5H_4O_4$. Also used in comb. as *citraconic*, etc.

Aconine (æ·kōnəin). [f. L. *aconitum.*] *Chem.* An alkaloid found in the root of aconite.

Aconite (æ·kŏnəit). 1578. [a. Fr. *aconit*, ad. L. *aconitum*, ad. Gr. ἀκόνιτον of unkn. etym.] **1.** *Bot.* A poisonous plant of the order *Ranunculaceæ*; *esp.* Monk's-hood or Wolf's-bane (*Aconitum Napellus*). **2.** An extract from *Aconitum Napellus* used in pharmacy. *poet.* Deadly poison. 1597.

1. One [sorte] is .. Aconit that baneth or killeth Panthers. The other .. Woolfs LYTE. 2. *Aconite*.. styled 'The Homœopathic Lancet' H. BUCK. Wine is A. to men COWLEY. **Winter Aconite**: *Eranthis hyemalis.* Hence **Aconi·tal** *a. rare.* **Aco·nitate**, *Chem.* a salt of Aconitic acid. **Aconi·tic** *a.*, *Chem.* in *Aconitic acid*, a basic triatomic acid $(C_6H_3O_3)'''(OH)_3$ existing in monkshood, etc.

Aconitine (ăkɒ·nitəin). 1847. [f. L. *aconitum.*] *Chem.* The essential principle of aconite, a poisonous vegetable alkaloid, with a bitter taste. var. **Aconitia.**

†**Acoo·l**, *v.* OE. [f. A- *pref.* 1 + *cōlian.*] To wax cold; *trans.* to cool.

†**Aco·p**, *adv. rare.* [A *prep.*[1] + COP.] On the top; on high. B. JONS.

Acopic (ăkɒ·pik), *a.* and *sb.* [f. Gr. ἄκοπος.] *Med.* Removing fatigue.

Acorn (ēᶦ·kɒɹn). [OE. *æcern* neut., f. *æcer*, orig. 'fruit of the open country', mast of oak, beech, etc., later, of oak only. Hence connected erron. with *oak*, OE. *āc*, north. *ake*, *aik*, as in *ake-*, *oke-corn*, *ake-*, *oke-horn*. The normal form would be *akern*, *akren*, or ? *atchern.*] †**1.** Fruit generally, or mast of trees –ME. **2.** The fruit or seed of the oak-tree; an oval nut growing in a *cupule* OE. **3.** *Naut.* A conical piece of wood fixed on the point of the spindle, above the vane, on the mast-head.

1. To slaken..hunger with acornes of okes CHAUCER. 2. His fill of pesen and oke cornes FISHER. Bearing mast or okehornes HULOET. Brused acrons [quasi a. Gr. ἄκρον top] PLAT. *Comb.* **Sea-a.** = ACORN-SHELL; **a.-barnacle** = ACORN-SHELL. Hence **A·corned** *a.* furnished with or (*Her.*) bearing acorns; fed or filled with acorns.

Acorn-shell. 1764. A multivalve Cirriped (*Balanus*), allied to the Barnacles.

‖**Acorus** (æ·kŏrŭs). 1714. [L., = Gr. ἄκορος.] A genus of plants (N. O. *Orontiaceæ*), including the Sweet Flag or Galingale (*A. Calamus*).

Acosmism (ăkǫ·zmiz'm). 1847. [f. Gr. ἀ + κόσμος.] Denial of the existence of the universe, or of a universe as distinct from God.

The a. of Spinoza and the atheism of Comte MARTINEAU. Hence **Aco·smist,** one who professes a.

†**Aco·st,** *adv.* ME. [a. OFr. *a coste* (*à côte*); later as if A *prep.*[1] + COAST, side of the land.] 1. On or by the side. 2. Ashore.

Acotyledon (akǫtilī·dən). 1819. [f. mod. L. *acotyledones*, f. Gr. ἀ + κοτυληδών, f. κοτύλη.] *Bot.* A plant which has no distinct cotyledons, or seed-lobes; as a fern, fungus, etc. Hence **Acotyle·donous** *a.*

‖**Acouchi** (ăku·ʃi). 1866. [Native name in Guiana.] *Bot. Acouchi* resin, or balsam: the balsam of *Icica heterophylla.*

Acou·chy. 1831. [a. Fr. *acouchi*, f. as prec.] *Zool.* A small rodent allied to the guinea-pig and agouti; the Surinam Rabbit.

Acoumeter (akau·mītəɹ). 1847. [improp. f. Gr. ἀκούειν + -METER.] An instrument for measuring the power of the sense of hearing. Hence **Acou·metry.**

†**Acou·nter,** *v.* ME. [f. *encounter*, a. OFr. *encontrer*; see A- *pref.* 10.] To encounter. Hence †**Acou·nter, -tre** *sb.* an encounter.

†**Acou·p(e,** *v.* ME. [a. OFr. *acoper, acolper, acoulper*, f. *à* + *coulper*:—L. *culpare* or ? for *encolper, encouper*:—L. *inculpare.* Refash. *accoup*; see Ac-.] To accuse.

Acoustic (ăkau·stik, ăkū·-), *a.* 1605. [a. Fr. *acoustique*, ad. Gr. ἀκουστικός.] 1. Pertaining to the sense of hearing, used in hearing; adapted to aid hearing; pertaining to the science of audible sounds. 2. as *sb.* A medicine or appliance which aids hearing. In *pl.*: see ACOUSTICS.

1. Acoustique Art BACON. An a. instrument 1743. *A.* or *speaking* tubes 1822. A. nerves FOSTER, telegraphy PRESCOTT. Hence **Acou·stical** *a.* of or pertaining to acoustics; promoting hearing. **Acou·stically** *adv.* in relation to the hearing of sounds. **A·cousti·cian,** one versed in acoustics.

Acoustico-, comb. f. ACOUSTIC.

Acoustics (ăkau·stiks, ăkū·-), *sb. pl.* 1683. [See ACOUSTIC, -ICS.] 1. The science of the phenomena of hearing. 2. The acoustic properties of a building 1898.

Acquaint (ăkwēⁱ·nt). *arch.* ME. [a. OFr. *acoint*:—L. *accognitum*; see ACQUAINT *v.* Repl. by ACQUAINTED.] A. *ppl. a.* = ACQUAINTED (*with*). B. *sb.* An acquaintance. CHAUCER.

Acquaint (ăkwēⁱ·nt), *v.* [ME. *acoint(e*, a. OFr. *acointer*:—late L. *adcognitare*, f. *adcognitum*; f. *ad* + *cognitum, cognoscere*, f. *co-* = *com* + *gnoscere*, incept. of **gno-ere.*] To make known. †1. *refl.* To make oneself known, become known (*to*) -1483; hence *intr.* to become acquainted, or familiar -1774. 2. *refl.* To make oneself to have, to give, or gain for, oneself acquaintance *with* any one. Now only in *pass.* ME. 3. *refl.* and *trans.* To give (oneself or any one) experimental knowledge of (a thing) 1567; †*trans.* to familiarize (const. *with*, or *inf. phr.*) -1658. 4. *trans.* To inform, make cognizant or aware (*with, that*, †*of*) 1559; *ellipt* to inform 1590; †to tell or make known -1678.

1. *intr.* Though the Choiseuls will not a. with you WALPOLE. 2. A. now thy selfe with him *Job* xxii. 21. We're acquainted now SOUTHEY. 3. Acquainting mine heart with wisedome *Eccl.* ii. 3. A. yourself with your new duties (*mod.*). *trans.* A. them to pronounce some examples BRINSLEY. 4. It were a peece of honestie to a. the King withall *Wint. T.* IV. iv. 696. *ellipt.* He begged her to a. him immediately FIELDING. Hence †**Acquai·ntable** *a.* easy to be acquainted with.

Acquaintance (ăkwēⁱ·ntăns). ME. [a. OFr. *acointance*, f. *acointer*; see ACQUAINT *v.*] 1. Knowledge of a person or thing which is more than mere recognition, and less than intimacy. 2. The state of being acquainted (const. *with*, †*of*, or *obj. gen.* as 'her', 'our' a.) 1300. 3. A person or persons with whom one is acquainted. (Orig. *collect.*, now usu. *sing.*, with pl. *acquaintances.*) ME.

1. An a. with [books] such as only..study could give BRYCE. †*To take a. of* = *mod.* **to make the a. of,** to form an a. with. 2. I shall desire you of more a. *Mids. N.* III. i. 185. Let's..drink unto Our better a. BYRON. 3. He was his a. and familyar MORE. A crowd of acquaintances GIBBON. Hence **Acquai·ntanceship** = ACQUAINTANCE 2. **Acquai·ntancy** = prec. †**Acquai·ntant** = ACQUAINTANCE 3.

Acquainted (ăkwēⁱ·ntĕd), *ppl. a.* ME. [f. ACQUAINT *v.*] 1. Familiar, through being known 1314. 2. Having mutual knowledge. Const. *with.* ME. 3. Having personal or experimental knowledge. Const. *with, of* 1480. †4. Accustomed. Const. *with, to.* -1683.

1. As things a. and familiar to us 2 *Hen. IV*, v. ii. 139. The a. sword SOUTHEY. Upon a. ground LAMB. 2. I pray you be better a. *Cymb.* I. iv. 132. 3. A. with griefe *Isa.* liii. 3, with English politics GEO. ELIOT. 4. A. only with a very moderate fortune CLARENDON. Hence **Acquai·ntedness,** the state or degree of acquaintance.

Acquest (ăkwe·st). 1613. [a. Fr. (mod.F. *acquêt*):—late L. *acquistum*, for *acquisitum, acquirere*; see ACQUIRE.] 1. A thing acquired 1622. *spec.* (*Law.*) Property gained otherwise than by inheritance. †2. = ACQUIST 1. -1787.

1. New Acquests are more Burthen, then Strength BACON. Acquests in the Study and Practice of the Law 1671. 2. In the a. of Independence J. BARLOW.

Acquiesce (ækwi,e·s), *v.* 1620. [a. MFr. *acquiescer*, f. L. *acquiescere.*] †1. *intr.* To remain at rest; to rest satisfied *in, under* -1788. 2. To agree tacitly to, concur *in*, †*to*, †*with* 1651. †3. *trans.* To bring to rest, appease -1659.

1. We were not made to a. in life and health BURKE. 2. We..a. [in the word of the Church] HOBBES. To a. in the propriety of..COWPER, the necessity of..SCOTT. var. †**Acquie·scate** *v.* Hence **Acquie·scing** *vbl. sb.* tacitly agreeing; *ppl. a.* silently compliant. **Acquie·scingly** *adv.*

Acquiescence (ækwi,e·sĕns). 1631. [a. Fr., f. *acquiescer*; see ACQUIESCE.] 1. The action or condition of acquiescing (sense 1). 2. Silent or passive assent to, or compliance with, measures or proposals. Also with *in*, †*with*, †*to.*

1. A life of worldly a. J. MARTINEAU. 2. The Chief Justice smiled a. DARWIN. A. in the charges levied ROGERS. vars. †**Acquie·scement, Acquie·scency.**

Acquiescent (ækwi,e·sĕnt). 1753. [ad. L. *acquiescentem*; see ACQUIESCE.] A. *adj.* Acquiescing; disposed to acquiesce. B. *sb.* One who acquiesces 1810. Hence **Acquie·scently** *adv.*

†**Acqui·et,** *v.* 1548. [f. L. *acquietare*; f. *ac-* = *ad-* + *quietare.*] To set at rest, quiet -1613.

Acquire (ăkwəiᵊ·ɹ), *v.* ME. [a. OFr. *aquerre, acquerre*:—L. *acquirere*, f. *ac-* = *ad-* + *quærere.* Refash. after L.] 1. To gain, or get as one's own (by one's own exertions or qualities) 1435. 2 To receive, to come into possession of 1613.

1. What w' acquire by Pains and Art BUTLER. 2. The Idler acquires weight by lying still JOHNSON. Hence **Acqui·rable** *a.* **Acquirabi·lity.** **Acqui·red** *ppl. a.* gained, opp. to *innate* or *inherited.* **Acqui·rer.** **Acqui·ring** *vbl. sb.* the action of gaining, the thing gained. †**Acqui·ry,** the process of acquiring.

Acquirement (ăkwəiᵊ·ɹmĕnt). 1630. [f. ACQUIRE *v.*] 1. The action of acquiring 1712. 2. That which is acquired; an attainment. Opp. to a (material) *acquisition*, or a natural *gift* 1630. Also *collect.* 1868.

1. Rules for the A. of a Taste ADDISON. The a. of knowledge MRS. SHELLEY. 2. His acquirements were..considerable LD. BROUGHAM. A man of ability and a. SEELEY.

†**A·cquisite,** *a.* 1532. [ad. L. *acquisitus*, *acquirere*; see ACQUIRE.] Acquired. Also as pa. pple. of ACQUIRE.

Acquisition (ækwizi·ʃən). ME. [ad. L. *acquisitionem*, f. *acquisit-, acquirere*; see ACQUIRE.] 1. The action of acquiring; see ACQUIRE *v.* 2. A thing acquired or gained 1477.

1. The a. of Wealth HOBBES. 2. The English acquisitions in Guinea R. BURTON.

Acquisitive (ăkwi·zĭtiv), *a.* 1637. [f. *acquisit-, acquirere*; see ACQUIRE.] †1. Belonging to one by acquisition -1642. 2. Able, or given, to make acquisitions 1846.

2. A. Louis Fourteenths CARLYLE. The Perceptive or A. Faculty BOWEN. Hence **Acquisiti·tious** *a.* ? *Obs.* Acquired, not *native* or *innate.* **Acqui·sitively** *adv.*

Acquisitiveness (ăkwi·zĭtivnĕs). 1826. [f. prec.] The quality of being acquisitive; desire of possession. (A faculty to which phrenologists allot a special 'organ'.)

Acquist (ăkwi·st). 1613. [var. of ACQUEST, q. v.] 1. The action of acquiring, acquisition. †2. = ACQUEST 1. -1677.

Acquit (ăkwi·t), *v.* [ME. *aquiten*, a. OFr. *aquiter, acuiter*:—late L. **acquitare*, f. *ac-* = *ad-* + **quitare* = *quietare*; see QUIT. Orig. the vowel was long as in *requite.*] To quiet a claim; hence, to satisfy the creditor; to clear the debtor.

I. 1. To discharge a claim, debt, or liability ME. †2. To perform the duties of (an office) 1530. 3. To requite (a benefit or injury). *arch.* ME. †4. To atone for (an offence) -1600.

1. To..acquite Your..promise QUARLES. To a. an obligation JUNIUS. 3. Make us that we a. not evil for evil 1535.

II. To pay off; to repay, be quits with -1599.

III. †1. To set free, release, by paying or cancelling a debt -1630. 2. To set free, release *of* or *from* a duty, obligation, or burden 1463. 3. To clear from a charge, to declare not guilty *of* ME. †4. *refl.* To deliver, rid, oneself *of* -1753. 5. To discharge oneself (*of* duty or responsibility). Hence, *simply*, To discharge one's duties, perform one's part ME.

1. Twelf pens to me, and I the wil acquite CHAUCER. 3. Three others were acquitted after..trial McCARTHY. 5. He..acquitted himself like a man (*mod.*). Hence **Acqui·t** *ppl. a. arch.* = *acquitted.* †**Acqui·t** *sb.* the act of acquitting. **Acqui·tment** (? *Obs.*), the action of acquitting; release. **Acqui·tted** *ppl. a.* exonerated. **Acqui·tter.**

Acquittal (ăkwi·tăl). ME. [f. ACQUIT.] †1. Payment, or retribution; amends -1749. 2. = ACQUITTANCE 2. *Obs.* exc. in *Law.* 1463. 3. A setting free by verdict, sentence, or other legal process 1535. 4. Discharge (of duty) 1656.

Acquittance (ăkwi·tăns), *sb.* ME. [a. OFr. *aquitance*; see ACQUIT *v.*] 1. The action of clearing off debt, or other obligation ME. 2. Hence (the result): Release, discharge ME. 3. A writing in evidence of discharge; a release, a receipt ME. Also *attrib.* †4. Release (from danger or trouble) -1631. 5. = ACQUITTAL 3. 6. = ACQUITTAL 4. *rare.*

1. This may be an a. of favours upon the turf JUNIUS. 3. You can produce acquittances For such a summe *L. L. L.* II. i. 161. Hence **Acqui·ttance** *v.* to discharge. *Rich. III*, III. vii. 233.

Acraldehyde (æ:kræ·ldĭhəid). 1869. [f. L. *acris* + ALDEHYDE.] *Chem.* One of the polymeric modifications of ALDEHYDE.

‖**Acrania** (ăkrēⁱ·niă). 1849. [mod. L. f. Gr. ἀ + κρανίον.] Absence of the skull. Hence **Acra·nial** *a.*

†**A·crasy.** 1596. [ad. med. L. *acrasia*, confusing Gr. ἀκρασία f. ἄκρατος and ἀκρασία f. ἀκρατής.] Irregularity, disorder, intemperance. Personified in Spenser.

Guyon..Doth..Acrasy defeat SPENSER *F. Q.* II. xii. *motto.*

†**Acra·ze,** *v.* 1549. [A- *pref.* 10 + CRAZE.] To weaken, impair. Hence †**Acra·zed** *ppl. a.* impaired in body, or mind.

Acre (ēⁱ·kəɹ). *Pl.* **acres.** [OE. *æcer, acer*; cogn. w. Goth. *akr-s*, L. *ager*, Gr. ἀγρός; orig. 'unenclosed land'; then, tilled, enclosed land, a piece of definite size, a land measure. In med. L. and OFr. *acra, acre*, whence *acre* for the regular *aker.*] 1. A piece of tilled or arable land, a field OE. *Obs.* exc. in *God's Acre* [from mod. Germ.] a churchyard, and prop. names, as *Long Acre*. Used *rhet.* in *pl.* for *lands*, etc. **2.** A measure of land, orig. as much as a yoke of oxen could plough in a day; later limited by statute to a piece 40 poles long by 4 broad (=4840 sq. yds.), or its equivalent.

1. Nabot .. had an Aker of a Vine yerd CAXTON. *Broad acres*, extensive lands. 2. Now would I give a thousand furlongs of sea for an a. of barren ground *Temp.* I. i. 70. Their estates were bound to the last a. BURKE. Also *loosely*: Acres of despatches CARLYLE. †An **a. length**, 40 poles or a furlong (*i.e.* furrow-length); †an **a. breadth**, 4 poles or 22 yards.

¶ Acre or Acre-fight (from L. *acram* (for *pugnam*) *committere*, where *acram* is a bad tr. of OE. *camp* combat, confused with L. *campus*, and so with *acre*) exists only in Cowel and mod. Dicts.

Hence **A·creable** *a.* per acre. **A·creage**, extent of acres; acres collectively; also *attrib.* **A·cred** *a.* possessing landed estates.

Acrid (æ·krid), *a.* 1712. [irreg. f. L. *acris* (f. root *ac-*) + -ID, perh. after *acid*, replacing *acrimonious*, *acris*, and *acrious*.] **1.** Bitter and hot to the taste; pungent, stinging, corrosive to the eyes, skin, etc. **2.** Bitterly irritating to the feelings. (Stronger than *acrimonious*.) 1781.

1. Corroded by some a. humour REID. [Sweat] turning a. MRS. BROWNING. 2. Tacitus grows more a. .. to the last MERIVALE. Hence **Acri·dity**, the quality of being a.; irritant bitterness of speech or temper. **A·cridly** *adv.* **A·cridness**, acridity. var. †**A·crious** *a.*

Acridine (æ·kridəin). 1877. [? f. ACRID *a.* + -INE = Gr. -ινη.] *Chem.* A crystalline substance, $C_{12}H_9N$, of the diphenyl group, extracted from coal-tar oil.

Acrimonious (ækrimōu·niəs), *a.* 1612. [ad. Fr. *acrimonieux*, *-euse*, ad. med.L. *acrimoniosus*; see ACRIMONY.] **1.** = ACRID 1. *arch.* **2.** Bitter and irritating in disposition or manner 1775.

1. An a. kinde of salt SIR T. BROWNE. 2. An a. contest SCOTT, expression MACAULAY. Hence **A:crimo·niously** *adv.* **A:crimo·niousness.**

Acrimony (æ·kriməni). 1542. [ad. L. *acrimonia*, f. *acris*.] **1.** The quality of being ACRID 1. *arch.* **2.** Irritating bitterness of temper 1618.

2. Cleon attacked him with great a. LANGHORNE. A. of expression WELLINGTON.

†**A·crisy.** 1721. [ad. med.L. *acrisia*, a. Gr.] **1.** A matter left undecided; also want of judgement. **2.** An undecided state or condition of a disease. var. †**Acrisia.**

‖**Acrita** (æ·krită), *sb. pl.* 1835. [mod.L., a. Gr. ἄκριτα undistinguishable, sc. *animalia*.] *Zool.* A division of the animal kingdom lacking a distinct nervous system. Hence **A·critan** *a.* and *sb.* (as sing. of prec.). **A·crite** *a.* acritan.

Acritical (ăkri·tikăl), *a.* 1864. [f. Gr. ἀ + CRITICAL.] *Med.* Not having or indicating a crisis.

Acritochromacy (æ:krito₁krōu·măsi). 1879. [mod. f. Gr. ἄκριτος + χρωματ-.] Colour-blindness, achromatopsy.

†**A·critude.** [ad. L. *acritudo*.] = ACRIDITY. -1753.

†**A·crity.** 1619. [ad. Fr. *âcreté*. Cf. *alacrity*.] Sharpness.

Acro-. Gr. ἀκρο- comb. f. ἄκρος *a.* terminal, topmost; *sb.* a tip, peak, summit.

acro·carpous [Gr. καρπός] *a.*, terminal-fruited; **-cepha·lic** [Gr. κεφαλή] *a.*, having a lofty skull, better *-cephalous*; **-ce·phaly**, loftiness of skull; **-chord** [see next], a snake of the genus *Achrocordus*, family *Hydridæ*, having a fusiform body covered with tricuspid scales; **-cho·rdon** [Gr. χορδή], a hard elongated wart; a hanging wart; **-dont** [Gr. ὀδόντ-] *sb.* and *a.*, having teeth firmly soldered to the ridge of the jaw-bones, as lizards; **-gen** [Gr. -γενης], a plant having a stem with the growing point at its extremity, opp. to *Thallogens*; hence, **-genic**, **-genous** *adjs.*; **-graphy** [Gr. -γραφία], the art of making blocks in relief, as a substitute for wood-engraving; **-lith** [Gr. λίθος], a statue with the head and extremities of stone, the trunk usu. of wood; hence, **-lithan**, **-lith·ic** *adjs.*; **-lo·gic** [Gr. λόγος] *a.*, pertaining to, or founded on, initials; **-petal** [L. *petere*] *a.*, tending towards the summit or apex; said of the order in which the parts of a plant arise; hence, **-petally** *adv.*; **-spire** [Gr. σπεῖρα], the first leaf that appears when corn sprouts, forming a developed plumule; also as *vb.*; hence, **-spired** *ppl. a.*; **-spiring** *vbl. sb.*; **-spore** [Gr. σπόρος; see SPORE], a spore produced at the apex of a hypha or cellular filament in certain fungi, a basidiospore; hence, **-sporous** *a.*

‖**A:croa·ma.** Pl. **a:croa·mata.** 1580. [Gr.] **1.** A rhetorical declamation (as opp. to an argument) 1852. **2.** *Anc. Phil.* Oral teaching heard only by the initiated; *esoteric* as opp. to *exoteric* doctrines. Hence **A:croama·tic** *adj.* orally communicated; esoteric, secret; *sb. pl.* [ellipt. after Gr. τὰ ἀκροαματικά.] Aristotle's lectures to the initiated on the esoteric parts of his philosophy. Also †**Acroama·tical** *a.*

‖**Acroasis** (ækroē¹·sis). Pl. **acroases.** 1655. [Gr.] *Anc. Hist.* A discourse listened to. Hence, **A:croa·tic** *a.* and *sb.*

Acrobat (æ·krŏbæt). 1825. [a. Fr. *acrobate*; f. Gr. ἀκρόβατος walking on tiptoe, climbing aloft.] A rope-dancer; a gymnast; a tumbler. *lit.* and *fig.* **A:croba·tic** *a.* **A:croba·tically** *adv.* **A:croba·tics** *sb. pl.* **A·crobatism.**

Acro·ck. 1615. [Fr. *à croc*.] With a prop or support.

Acrolein (ăkrōu·lī₁in). 1869. [f. L. *acris* + *olere* + -IN(E = Gr. -ινη.] *Chem.* A colourless acrid liquid (C_3H_4O''), of pungent irritating odour, formed in the destructive distillation of glycerin. It is the aldehyde of allyl.

‖**Acromion** (ăkrōu·miən). 1615. [a. Gr., or a. Fr.] *Phys.* The outer extremity of the shoulder-blade. Also *attrib.* as *a. process*. Hence **Acro·mial** *a.*

Acronarcotic (æ:kro₁naɹkǫ·tik), *a.* 1882. [improp. f. L. *acris* + NARCOTIC.] Having both acrid and narcotic qualities.

Acronych (ăkrǫ·nik), *a.* [ad. Gr. ἀκρόνυχος, f. ἄκρος + νύξ.] = next.

Acro·nychal, -ycal, *a.* 1594. [f. prec. Erron. *achronical*, f. χρόνος.] Happening in the evening or at night-fall, vespertine, as the a. rising or setting of a star. (*Not* 'rising in the evening *and* setting at sunrise'.) Opp. to *cosmical*. Hence **Acro·nychally** *adv.* var. **A·crony·ctous.**

Acroo·k, *adv.* 1480. [A *prep.*[1] + CROOK.] In a bend; crookedly.

Acrophony (ækrǫ·fŏni). 1880. [f. Gr. ἄκρο- (see ACRO-) + φωνία.] The sound of the initial; the use of the picture-symbol or hieroglyph of an object to represent phonetically the initial syllable or sound of the name of the object; *e.g.* of the symbol of an *ox*, '*aleph*,' to represent *a*. Hence **A:crophone·tic** *a.* pertaining to a.

Acropolis (ăkrǫ·pŏlis). 1662. [Gr., f. ἄκρο- (see ACRO-) + πόλις.] The elevated part, or the citadel, of a Greek city; *esp.* that of Athens. Also *fig.*

[The] A. of Man's body, the Head MORE.

Across (ăkrǫ·s), aphet. **cross.** [A *prep.*[1] + CROSS. Cf. Fr. *encroix*, Caxton's *in cross*.]

A. *adv.* **1.** In the form of a cross, crosswise, crossing 1480. **2.** Crossing the length-line, transversely; through 1523. **3.** On the other side (as the result of crossing) 1816. †**4.** Not straight; obliquely, amiss -1687.

1. A warrior frowns in stone, his legs a. 1771. 2. H'as broke my head a-crosse *Twel. N.* v. i. 178. To swim a. the Channel (*mod.*). 3. We shall soon be a. (*mod.*). 4. The squint-eyed pharisees looke a-crosse at all the actions of Christ BP. HALL.

B. *prep.* [The adv. with obj. expressed.] **1.** Direction: At right angles, or any angle, with 1626. **2.** Motion: From side to side of, not lengthwise; through, over 1591. **3.** Position: On the other side of, beyond 1750.

1. A. the theatre POTTER. [An] arch .. a. the river J. WILSON. Her bow a. her shoulder flung COLLINS. *To come across*: to come upon incidentally. 2. When my .. Falcon made her flight a-crosse Thy Fathers ground *Wint. T.* IV. iv. 15. *Across the country*: straight through between two points without regard to paths. To sweep a. one's memory G. O. TREVELYAN. 3. 'The king a. the water!' *Jacobite Toast.*

Acrostic (ăkrǫ·stik). 1587. [ad. L. *acrostichis*, a. Gr. ἀκροστιχίς, f. ἄκρο- (see ACRO-) + στίχος. Cf. *distich*.] A short poem, etc., in which the initial, the last, or the middle letters of the lines, or all of them, taken in order, spell a word, phrase, or sentence, and thus form a *single*, a *double*, or a *triple* acrostic. See also TELESTICH. **2.** An ABECEDARIAN poem 1753. †**3.** The beginning or end of a verse -1753. Hence **Acro·stic** *a.*[1] pertaining to acrostics (in senses 1, 2). **Acro·stichally, -cally** *adv.* **Acrosti·chic** *a.* **Acro·sticism,** acrostic arrangement or character.

Acro·stic, *a.*[2] 1602. [f. *acrossed* (= *acrost*).] Folded across; erratic, zigzag.

Acrostichoid (ăkrǫ·stikoid), *a.* 1882. [f. ACROSTIC(H.] An epithet of a genus of ferns, N. O. *Polypodiaceæ*, due to the peculiar distribution of the sori.

Acroteleutic (æ·kro₁tĭliū·tik). 1753. [f. Gr. ἀκροτελεύτιον.] *Eccl.* The end of a verse or psalm, or something added thereto to be sung by the people.

Acroter (ăkrōu·təɹ). 1678. [a. Fr. *acrotère*, ad. L. *acroterium*, ad. Gr. ἀκρωτήριον, f. ἄκρος.] **1.** *Arch.* In *pl.* **acroteria** or **acroters,** prop. 'The pedestals, often without bases, placed on the centre and sides of pediments for the reception of figures'. Gwilt. Also, incorr., the statues. 1706. †**2.** 'The pinnacles or other ornaments standing in ranges on the horizontal coping or parapets of a building.' Gwilt. -1759. †**3.** *Med.* The extremities of the body, the hands, feet, and head -1753. vars. **A:crote·rium, A:crote·rion.** Hence **A:crote·rial,** *a.*

Acrotic (ăkrǫ·tik), *a.* 1853. [improp. f. ἀκρότης.] *Path.* Pertaining to the outside.

Acrotism (æ·krŏtiz'm). 1853. [f. Gr. ἀ + κρότος.] *Med.* Lack of pulsation.

Acrotomous (ăkrǫ·tŏməs), *a.* [f. Gr. ἀκρότομος.] *Min.* Having a cleavage parallel with the base.

†**A-cry,** *adv.* 1593. [A *prep.*[1] + CRY.] In a cry, crying.

Acryl (æ·kril). [f. ACR(OLEIN + YL(E, Gr. ὕλη.] *Chem.* The hypothetical radical of the allyl series, C_3H_3O. Hence **A·crylate,** a salt of acrylic acid. **Acrylic** *a.* of or containing a. *Acrylic acid*, $C_3H_3O.OH$, formed by the oxidation of acrolein.

Act (ækt). ME. [*orig.* a. F. *acte*; with some meanings from L. *actus* and *actum* (pl. *acta*).] **1.** A thing done; a deed ME.; a deed implying a state 1751. †**2.** Fact or reality; opp. to intention, possibility, etc. -1677. †**3.** ? Active principle -1730. **4.** The process of doing; action, operation. (L. *actus*.) *arch.* 1494. **5.** A thing transacted in council, etc.; hence, a decree. (L. *actum*, pl. *acta*.) 1458. **6.** A record of transactions or decrees; an instrument in writing. (L. *actum*, pl. *acta*.) 1535. **7.** A 'performance' of part of a play; *hence*, One of the main divisions of a drama, completing a definite part of the action. Also *fig.* (L. *actus*.) 1613. **8.** In the Universities, a thesis publicly maintained by a candidate for a degree. Also *attrib.* 1641. †**9.** An *auto da fé*, or act of faith; a burning of heretics -1709.

1. The worthie Actes of the ancient Brytaines POWEL. An a. of bankruptcy BLACKSTONE. The a. of a madman (*mod.*). 2. If I in a., consent, or sinne of thought Be guiltie *John* IV. iii. 135. 3. God is a pure A. BEVERIDGE. 4. Wise in Conceit, in A. a very sot DRAYTON. *Act of God*: action of uncontrollable natural forces in causing an accident. *In act*: in the very doing; on the point of. (L. *in actu*.) Taken in adultery, in the very a. *John* viii. 4. 5. By new a. of Parliament 3 *Hen. VI*, II. ii. 91. A. of Attainder 1839. 6. Credit..shall be given to the public acts, records, etc. of every other state *Constit. U. S.* iv. § 1. *Acts* (*of the Apostles*). 7. Away then: our A.'s ended FLETCHER. The..first a. of our great drama FREEMAN. 8. Attendance to keep Acts GATAKER. attrib. *A. Sunday*, *A. Sermon*, *Act* (i.e. Trinity) *Term*. Hence **A·ctless** *a.* inactive.

Act (ækt), *v.* 1594. [f. L. *act-*, *agere*; prob. influenced by ACT *sb.*] †**1.** *trans.* To put in motion; actuate, animate -1748; to bring (a thing or process) into action -1791. **2.** To carry out in action. *arch.* 1610. 3. To carry out in mimic action; to perform (a play); *fig.* in a bad sense: To simulate 1594. 4. *intr.* (obj. suppressed). To perform on the stage 1598. 5. To perform on the stage of existence; to do, as opp. to *think, speak,* etc.; to comport or demean oneself 1684. Also with *for, as, on, upon, up to.* 6. Of things: To put forth energy, produce effects, exert influence, fulfil functions 1751. Also with *on.*

1. Thy senses fiue that acte thy life WARNER. Self-love.. acts the soul POPE. 2. To a. her.. abhord commands *Temp.* I. ii. 273. Acting the law we live by TENNYSON. 3. Acting her passions on our stately stage DRAYTON. Sunderland acted calumniated virtue to perfection MACAULAY. *To act a part,* or *the part of:* You have still an honourable part to a. JUNIUS. *To act (any one). lit.* and *fig.*: He that acteth another is said to beare his Person, and a. in his name HOBBES. Acting the lover SWIFT. 4. Say who acts best? J. MARSTON. 5. Acting..from..disinterested motives SIR R. PEEL. In overcoming the hostility of the West, William acted as he always did a. FREEMAN. Acting as Chaplain MACAULAY. I a. for my brother (*mod.*). To a. *on* a maxim (*mod.*). Your lordship acts up to your tenets LANDOR. 6. When several causes a. at once JEVONS. The brake refused to a. (*mod.*). Hence **A·ctable** *a.* capable of being acted (on the stage), or carried out in practice. **A·cted** *ppl. a.* carried out in action; performed (*esp.* dramatically); feigned.

Actinal (ǣktəi·năl, æ·ktinăl), *a.* 1857. [f. Gr. ἀκτῖνα.] *Zool.* Pertaining to that part of a radiate animal which contains the so-called mouth, etc.

Acting (æ·ktiŋ), *vbl. sb.* 1601. [f. ACT *v.*] 1. Execution. 2. The performance of deeds; in *pl.* doings, practices, etc. 1603. 3. The performing of plays, etc.; simulation 1664. 4. The putting forth of energy, activity, etc. 1647.

1. Betweene the a. of a dreadfull thing, And the first motion *Jul. C.* II. i. 63. 2. The great actings which are now on foot SCOTT. *Comb.* **a.-order,** *spec.* an order to act in a vacant office, pending an appointment by the ultimate authority.

A·cting, *ppl. a.* 1597. [f. as prec.] 1. Performing (dramatically). 2. Putting forth activity. 3. Performing temporary or special duties, as *Acting-Captain, -Manager,* etc.

‖**Actinia** (ǣkti·niă). Pl. **actiniæ, actinias.** 1748. [mod.L. f. Gr. ἀκτῖν-.] *Zool. prop.* A genus of the family *Actiniadæ*; *pop.,* any animal of the family; a Sea-Anemone.

Actiniform (ǣkti·nifǭɹm), *a.* 1843. [f. Gr. ἀκτῖν-.] Of a radiated form, like a sea-anemone. var. **A·ctinoid** *a.*

Actinism (æ·ktiniz'm). 1844. [f. as prec.] †1. The radiation of heat or light, or that branch of Philosophy which treats of it. 2. That property in light-rays which produces chemical changes, as in photography. Hence **Acti·nic** *a.*

Actinium (ǣkti·niŏm). 1881. [f. as next.] *Chem.* 1. A supposed chemical element, so called because light affects its salts. 2. A radioactive element. Symbol Ac. 1904.

Actino-, a. Gr. ἀκτινο- comb. f. of ἀκτίς (gen. ἀκτῖνος), a ray, a beam.

actino·che·mistry, that branch which treats of the chemical energies in solar rays; **-graph** [Gr. γράφος], an instrument for recording the variations in the power of the solar rays; **-lite** [Gr. λίθος], a bright green variety of Hornblende, occurring usu. in fasciculated crystals; var. **a·ctinote**; hence **-li·tic** *a.*; **-mere** [Gr. μέρος], a portion of the surface of a radiated animal cut off by any two meridional lines reaching from pole to pole; **-meter** [Gr. μέτρον], an instrument for measuring the intensity of the sun's heating rays; hence, **-metric(al** *a.*; **-metry** [Gr. -μετρια], the measurement of the radiation of heat from surfaces; **-morphous** [Gr. μορφή] *a.,* of radiated shape; **-phone** [Gr. -φωνος], an apparatus for the production of sound by actinic rays; hence, **-phonic** *a.*; **-phorous** [Gr. -φορος] *a.,* bearing radiating spines; **-stome** [Gr. στόμα], the mouth of a radiated animal; **-zoa** [Gr. ζῷα] *sb. pl.* a class of Radiated animals, partly *Cœlenterata,* partly *Zoophytes,* containing the sea-anemones and coral polypes; hence, **-zoal** *a.*

Action (æ·kʃən). ME. [a. Fr., ad. L. *actionem,* f. *act-, agere.*]

I. *Generally.* 1. The process or condition of acting or doing, the exertion of energy or influence; working, agency, operation ME. 2. A thing done, a deed; in *pl.* conduct. Viewed as occupying time in doing, as distinguished from ACT. 1600. 3. The thing represented as done in a drama, poem, etc. 1712. †4. *pl.* The acts or records of a court, etc. -1635. 5. Gesture, esp. in oratory; gesture and attitude in *Sculpt.* and *Painting*; trained movements of the body, etc., in animals 1579. 6. The way in which an instrument acts; also, the mechanism by which this is effected 1845.

1. A Womans thought runs before her a. *A. Y. L.* IV. i. 141. The word a. is properly applied to those exertions which are consequent on volition D. STEWART. *Quantity of a.* in *Physics*: the momentum of a body multiplied into the time. The acciouns or werkynges of Penitence CHAUCER. Chemical a. GROVE. Schemes were put *in a.* against her life HALLAM. *A. of a verb, verbal a.*: the action expressed by a verb. Submit the whole to the a. of a slow fire SOYER. 2. When our Actions do not, Our feares do make vs Traitors *Macb.* IV. ii. 3. The Actions of men [are] the best Interpreters of their thoughts LOCKE. 3. The a. of Paradise Lost ADDISON, of the Iliad CHAMBERS. 5. Sute the A. to the Word, the Word to the A. *Haml.* III. ii. 19. The roan has good knee-a. (*mod.*). 6. The a. of the air-pump 1845. The grand pianoforte with the new a. DICKENS.

II. *Specifically.* 1. The taking of legal process to establish a claim or obtain remedy; legal process; the right to raise such process ME. 2. A legal process or suit 1483. 3. Active operation against an enemy, fighting 1604; a fight 1599. †4. Acting of plays -1710; a play 1679. 5. A devotional exercise 1825. †6. A share in a joint-stock company (Fr.) 1641.

1. *To take a.*: to institute legal proceedings; hence, *gen.* to take steps. *Property in a.,* i. e. not in possession, but recoverable by legal process. (Earliest Eng. sense.) If one calls a merchant bankrupt, a. lies TOMLINS. He took prompt a. to defend his rights (*mod.*). Mr. Fang, haue you entred the A. SHAKS. 3. Cleared ship for A. 1805. A general a. WELLINGTON. 5. The a. of Thanksgiving 1855. 6. African actions fell to £30 EVELYN. Hence **A·ction** *v.* to institute a legal action against. **A·ctionable** *a.* affording grounds for an a. at law. **A·ctionably** *adv.* **A·ctional** *a.* of or pertaining to a. or actions. †**A·ctionary,** a shareholder in a joint-stock company. **A·ctioner,** an artisan who makes the ACTION (sense 6) of an instrument. **A·ctionist** (*a*) = ACTIONARY (*obs.*); (*b*) one who lays stress on (oratorical) a. **A·ctionless** *a.* void of a., inert. †**A·ctious** *a.* energetic.

†**A·ctivate,** *v.* 1626. [f. ACTIVE *a.* Cf. Fr. *activer.*] To move to activity. Cf. ACTUATE.

Active (æ·ktiv), *a.* ME. [a. Fr. *actif, active,* ad. L. *activus.*] *gen.* Characterized by action. Hence 1. Practical, *esp.* with *life,* opp. to *contemplative, speculative, theoretical* ME. 2. Originating or communicating action; spontaneous; opp. to *passive* ME. Also *absol.* sc. *qualities, forces.* 3. *Gram.* a. *prop.* An epithet of Voice in verbs used transitively; opp. to *Passive, Reflexive,* or *Middle.* That form of the vb. in which the logical subject of the action is made the grammatical subject of the assertion, as shown by inflections, position, etc. b. *Less correctly,* said of verbs themselves, either (1) by opposing *action* in Active verbs to *passion* in Passive verbs, and to the action or state which is neutral in Neuter verbs, or (2) by opposing *action* in *Active* (*Transitive* or *Intransitive*) verbs to *existence* or *state* in *Neuter* verbs. 4. Working, effective; opp. to *quiescent* or *extinct* 1640. 5. Abounding in action; energetic; diligent, brisk 1597. 6. On the credit side of the balance-sheet; opp. to *passive.* (Fr.)

1. Actyf lyf or contemplatyf LANGL. My speculative and a. instruments *Oth.* I. iii. 271. 2. The treasons of Eadwine were often passive rather than a. FREEMAN. 4. A. benevolence BOSWELL, volcanos LYELL, poison LIVINGSTONE, service FREEMAN. 5. The most a. fellow in Europe SHAKS. A. to pursue POPE. Less a. than he was COWPER. A. demand FAWCETT, markets (*mod.*). Hence **A·ctively** *adv.* †practically; spontaneously; *Gram.* in the manner of an active vb.; energetically, briskly. **A·ctiveness** = ACTIVITY 2.

Activity (ǣkti·vĭti). 1530. [a. Fr. *activité,* ad. med.L. *activitatem* = *vis agendi,* f. L. *activus*; see ACTIVE.] 1. The state of being active; the exertion of energy, action 1549. 2. Energy, diligence, liveliness 1530. †3. Physical exercise, athletics -1710. 4. Anything active, e.g. a force or operation 1646.

1. The Supreme Being (who is Activity itself) POWER. 2. The a. of France BURKE, of a volcano PHILLIPS, in the iron market (*mod.*). 4. Activities without purpose LAMB.

Acton (æ·ktən). ME. [a. OFr. *auqueton,* mod. *hoqueton,* padding; a. Sp., ad. Arab. *alqutun.*] A stuffed jerkin, worn under the mail; later, a jacket of leather, plated with mail.

Cranstoun's lance.. Through shield.. and a. past SCOTT. var. **Haqueton.**

Actor (æ·ktəɹ). ME. [a. L., f. *act-, agere.*] †1. An overseer, or factor (tr. L. *actor*). †2. He who conducts an action; a plaintiff; an advocate; a public prosecutor. *Obs.* exc. in Rom. Law. 1413. 3. One who acts, or takes part in any action; a doer 1603. 4. A stage-player 1581.

3. Condemn the fault, and not the a. of it *Meas. for M.* II. ii. 37. 4. *Rich. II,* V. ii. 24. Pitt was essentially an a. GREEN. *Comb.* **a.-manager,** a manager who is also an a. Hence **A·ctorship,** the quality of a (dramatic) actor.

Actress (æ·ktrĕs). Also **actrice.** 1589. [f. ACTOR.] †1. A female ACTOR (sense 3); replaced by ACTOR -1712. 2. A female player on the stage 1700.

Actual (æ·ktiuăl), *a.* ME. [a. Fr. *actuel,* ad. late L. *actualis*; f. *actus*; see ACT.] †1. = ACTIVE 1. -1647. 2. Existing in act or fact; real. Also *absol.* in *pl.* = actualities. 3. Existing or acting at the time; present, current 1642.

1. Walking, and other actuall performances *Macb.* V. i. 13. 2. Their own actuall miseries HOBBES. Not in a. rebellion JUNIUS. The a. proceeds JAS. MILL. 3. Their a. lord BROWNING. The a. position of affairs (*mod.*). Hence **A·ctualness.** = ACTUALITY.

Actualism (æ·ktiuăliz'm). 1860. [f. prec.] The doctrine that all existence is active, not inert or dead. HINTON.

Actuality (æ·ktiu,æ·lĭti). ME. [ad. med. L. *actualitatem,* f. *actualis*; see ACTUAL; cf. Fr. *actualité* (a neologism).] †1. Capacity of action -1677. 2. The state of being ACTUAL (sense 2); reality 1675; *pl.* actual conditions or circumstances 1665. 3. Realism in description 1850.

2. To sacrifice a truth of a. to a truth of feeling RUSKIN. *pl.* The actualities of the case M. DAVIES. 3. [Her] characters.. have a flavour of a. W. E. HENLEY. var. **A·ctualness.**

Actualize (æ·ktiuăləiz), *v.* 1810. [f. ACTUAL *a.*] 1. To make ACTUAL; to realize in action. 2. To represent realistically 1881.

1. When these possibilities are actualized DE QUINCEY. Hence **A·ctualiza·tion.**

Actually (æ·ktiuăli), *adv.* 1470. [f. ACTUAL.] †1. With deeds, actively -1660; energetically -1485. 2. In act or fact; really 1587. 3. As a present fact, at present 1663. 4. As a matter of fact; indeed; even 1762.

2. The rates of interest a. paid in business JEVONS. 3. The party a. in power (*mod.*). 4. I a. found the door standing open (*mod.*).

Actuary (æ·ktiuări). 1553. [ad. L. *actuarius,* f. *actus.*] 1. A registrar or notary, who keeps record of the acts of a court 1553. 2. An official in an insurance office who compiles tables of mortality, estimates rates of premium, etc.; or one whose profession it is to solve monetary problems depending on Interest and Probability, in connexion with life, fire, or other accidents, etc. Hence **Actua·rial, Actua·rian** *adjs.* of or pertaining to actuaries or their profession.

Actuate (æ·ktiu,eɪt), *v.* 1596. [f. med.L. *actuat-, actuare* = *ad actum redigere*; f. *actus*; see ACT.] †1. To reduce to action 1596; to render active, to excite -1751. 2. To inspire (a thing) with active properties. *arch.* 1642. Also *absol.* 3. To move to mechanical action. Also *fig.* 1645. 4. To act upon the will, as motives do 1741. †5. *intr.* To act -1657.

2. The Soul is a spirit that actuates the natural body. H. MORE. 3. To a. or put in motion the system of wheels or pinions G. ADAMS. 4. Every liberal motive that can a. an Authour BOSWELL. Hence †**A·ctuate** *ppl. a.* = ACTUATED. **A·ctuated** *ppl. a.* rendered actual, or active. **A·ctuating** *vbl. sb.*

carrying out in practice; animating; *ppl. a.* moving, inspiring.

Actuation (æ·ktiu,ēⁱ·ʃən). 1630. [f. med. L. *actuare*; see ACTUATE.] A communication of motion, a bringing into action; impulse, movement.
The best designs are spoiled by faulty a. 1879.

†A·ctuo·se, *a. rare.* 1677. [ad. L. *actuosus.*] Very active. Hence **†Actuo·sity.**

†A·cture. *rare.* 1593. [f. L. **actura.* Cf. *factura.*] Action.

Actu·rience. 1880. [f. L. *act-, agere.*] Desire to act.

Acuate (æ·kiuēⁱt), *ppl. a.* 1471. [ad. L. *acuatus, acuare,* f. *acus.*] Sharp-pointed. Hence **†A·cuate** *v.* to sharpen. *lit.* and *fig.* **A·cua·tion** (*rare*), sharpening; var. **†Acui·tion.**

Acuity (ăkiū·iti). 1543. [a. Fr. *acuité*, ad. L. *acuitatem*, f. *acus.*] Sharpness; as of a needle, an acid, wit.

Aculeate (ăkiū·liēⁱt), *a.* 1605. [ad. L. *aculeatus*, f. *aculeus*, dim. of *acus.*] 1. *Zool.* Having a sting 1661. 2. *Bot.* Set with prickles 1870. 3. *fig.* Pointed, stinging 1605.
3. Words may be a. BACON. Hence **Acu·leated** *ppl. a.* In *Nat. Hist.* Pointed; armed with prickles; also *fig.* **Acu·lea·tion,** pointedness.

Aculeiform (ăkiū·li,ifǭɹm), *a.* 1857. [f. L. *aculeus* + -FORM.] *Bot.* Like a prickle. So **Aculeolate** (ăkiū·liolēt), *a. Bot.* [f. L. *aculeolus*, dim. of *aculeus.*] Beset with small prickles.

‖**Aculeus** (ăkiū·liŏs). Pl. **aculei.** 1828. [L.] 1. *Zool.* The sting of an insect, etc. 2. *Bot.* A prickle; as in the rose 1878. Hence **†Acu·leous** *a.* aculeate. *rare.*

†Acumble, *v.* ME. [?] To benumb.

Acumen (ăkiū·mĕn). 1531. [a. L.] 1. Sharpness of wit; penetration of perception; keenness of discrimination. 2. *Bot.* A tapering point 1794.
1. The jest or a. [of epigrams] CASAUBON. Metaphysical a. REID.

Acuminate (ăkiū·minēⁱt), *ppl. a.* 1605. [ad. L. *acuminatus, acuminare.*] 1. Pointed, tapering to a point, *esp.* in *Nat. Hist.* Also quasi-*sb.* 1646. †2. Having acumen. *rare.* 1605.

Acuminate (ăkiū·mineⁱt), *v.* 1611. [f. as prec.] 1. *trans.* To sharpen; to give poignancy or keenness to. †2. *intr.* To rise or taper to a point.
1. Tones..to a. even despair COWPER. 2. Hierarchies acuminating..in a cone of Prelaty MILT. Hence **Acu·minated** *ppl. a.* pointed (*lit.* and *fig.*); made keen in discernment or attention. **Acu·minating** *ppl. a.* rising or tapering to a point. **Acu·mina·tion,** the giving point to (*lit.* and *fig.*); a tapering point; direction to a point. **Acu·mino·se** *a.* terminating in a flat narrow end. **Acu·minous** *a.* marked by acumen; acute.

Acupressure (æ·kiupre·ʃiŭɹ, -ʃəɹ). 1859. [f. L. *acu* with a needle + PRESSURE.] Prof. Simpson's method of arresting hæmorrhage from wounded arteries by the pressure of a needle passed across their mouths or tubes.

Acupunctuate (æ·kiupɒ·ŋktiu,eⁱt), *v.* 1865. [f. L. *acu* + PUNCTUATE.] To prick with a needle; also *fig.*

Acupuncture (æ·kiupɒ·ŋktiŭɹ, -tʃəɹ), *sb.* 1684. [f. L. *acu* + PUNCTURE.] Pricking with a needle; a prick so made. *spec.* The insertion of needles into living tissues for remedial purposes. Hence **A·cupu·ncture** *v.* = ACUPUNCTUATE. **A·cupu·nctura·tion,** the practice or process of a.; var. **A·cupu·nctua·tion.**

Acustom, -ance, obs. ff. ACCUSTOM, -ANCE.

Acute (ăkiū·t), *a.* 1570. [ad. L. *acutus, acuere.*] 1. Sharp at the end, coming to a point. 2. Of diseases: Coming sharply to a crisis, not *chronic.* Also *fig.* 1667. 3. Acting keenly on the senses (see quots.) 1609. 4. Of the senses or nervous system: Sensitive or responsive to impressions, finely-strung 1762. 5. Of the intellect: Discerning, penetrating, sharp-witted, shrewd, clever 1588. Aphet., *esp.* in U.S., to *cute.* Also quasi-*sb.* [sc. *accent.*]
1. An *a. angle* is that which is lesse than a right angle *Euclid.* Leaves may be a. GRAY. 3. Of pain, pleasure, etc.: Intense. The pleasure is not..a., or of great intensity BAIN. Of sounds: Shrill, high. The most a. [stave] is called the soprano OUSELEY. *A. accent*; see ACCENT 1, 2. 4. Her feelings were very a. MISS AUSTEN. 5. A most a. Iuuenal *L. L. L.* III. i. 67. An a. logician REID, observer DAVY. A cute thing (U.S.). *sb.* Marked with acutes 1824. *Comb.* **a.-angled,** having an a. angle. Hence **†Acutangular** *a.* **†Acu·te** *v.* to sharpen; to mark, etc., with an a. accent. **Acu·tely** *adv.* **Acu·tish** *a.* somewhat a.

Acuteness (ăkiū·tnĕs). 1046. [f. ACUTE *a.*] The quality of being ACUTE (in senses 1, 2, 3, 4); said of material things, of disease, of pain, etc., of sounds, of the senses or feelings, of the mental faculties.

Acuti-, a combining form of L. *acutus* sharp, in Eng. words formed on or after mod. L.; as **acutifoliate** *a.* sharp-leaved.

Acuto-, comb. advb. form of ACUTE, as in **acuto-nodose,** *acutely* nodose, or in **acuto-grave,** *acute* + grave.

-acy, *suffix* of sbs. [a branch of -CY.] Forming sbs. of quality, state, or condition. 1. as = L. *-acia*, on adjs. in *-aci-*, as 'fallacy'; 2. as = L. *-at-i-a* (med.L. *-acia*), on nouns in *-at-* (nom. *-as*), as 'abbacy'; 3. as = med. L. *-atia*, on nouns in *-atus*, as 'advocacy'; 4. repr. Gr. sbs. of state in *-ατεια*, as piracy', and in *-cracy* Gr. sbs. in *-κρατία*, as 'aristocracy'.

Ad. Colloq. abbrev. of ADVERTISEMENT.

‖**Ad,** L. prep. = 'to' in **ad hoc,** for this or the particular purpose; also *attrib.*; **ad nauseam,** to a sickening extent; **ad referendum,** subject to reference; **ad rem,** to the point or purpose. Also AD EUNDEM, etc.

Ad-, *pref.* I. repr. L. *ad* prep. 'to', with sense of motion to, change into, addition, or intensification. Assimilated bef. *c, f, g, l, n, p, q, r, s, t,* and prob. bef. *b*, as in *ab-* for *ad-breviare*; reduced to *a-* bef. *sc, sp, st.* In the 15th c. words borrowed from OFr., etc. were refash. after L., and all words since formed follow L. spelling. *Ad-* 'at', opp. to *ab-* 'away from', as in *ad-oral, ab-oral*, is recent.
2. At the same time *ad-* was substituted for *a-* where *a-* was really L. *ab*, OFr. *en* (*an*), *es*, OE. *a* (*ar*), *on*, *æt*, etc.; as in *a*(*d*)*vance*, *a*(*d*)*debted*, *a*(*c*)*curse*, *a*(*l*)*lay*, *a*(*d*)*miral*, etc.

-ad, *suffix* of sbs. I. repr. Gr. *-άδ-α* (nom. *-ás*) forming **a.** Collective numerals, as *monad*, etc. **b.** Fem. patronymics (var. *-id*), as *Dryad*, pl. *Dryades*, etc. Hence used **c.** in names of Poems, as *Iliad* the lay (*ᾠδή*) of Ilium, *Dunciad*, etc.; and **d.** to form family names of plants, as *liliad*, etc. 2. a. Fr. *-ade*, in *salad*, etc.; see -ADE.
II. suffix forming advs. and adjs. in the sense of 'towards' (the part denoted by the main element of the word), as DEXTRAD, DORSAD, LATERAD, VENTRAD, etc.

Adactylous (ădæ·ktiləs), *a.* 1858. [f. Gr. *ἀ* + *δάκτυλος.*] Without fingers, toes, or claws.

†Adad (ădæ·d), *int.* [? var. of EGAD!] Exclam. of asseveration or emphasis -1763.

Adage (æ·dēdʒ). 1548. [a. Fr. *adage*, ad. L. *adagium*, f. *ad* + **agi-*, root of *ajo* = *agio* I say.] A traditional maxim; a proverb.
The a...That Beggers mounted, runne their Horse to death 3 *Hen. VI*, I. iv. 126. Also *Macb.* I. vii. 45. Hence **Ada·gial** *a.* of the nature of an a.

‖**Adagio** (ădā·dʒ¹o). 1746. [It.] *Mus.* **A.** *adv.* A direction: Slowly. **B.** *adj.* Of movement: Slow. **C.** *sb.* A piece of music in a. time. Also *fig.*

†A·dagy, 17th c. var. of ADAGE.

Adam (æ·dăm). 1569. [Heb. *ā-dām* man.] 1. The Biblical name of the first man, the father of the human race; hence, *fig.* the unregenerate condition or character. 2. = ADAM'S ALE.
1. Whipt th'offending Adam out of him *Hen. V*, I. i. 29. *Comb.* **Adam's ale,** water (*joc.*); **-apple,** a variety of Lime (*Citrus Limetta*), of Orange or Shaddock; the projection in the neck formed by the thyroid cartilage (supposed to have been caused by a piece of the apple that stuck in Adam's throat); **-flannel,** the Great Mullein (*Verbascum Thapsus*); **-needle,** occ. name of the Shepherd's Needle (*Scandix Pecten-Veneris*); **-wine,** Sc. = ADAM'S ALE. Hence **Ada·mic, -al** *a.* like Adam; free, naked, fallen. **Ada·mically** *adv.*

Adamant (æ·dămănt). OE. [a. OFr. *adamaunt*, ad. L. *adamantem, adamas*, a. Gr., f. *ἀ* + *δαμάω*, applied to *steel*; also, by Pliny, to white sapphire, and later to the DIAMOND. In med.L. the *loadstone*, or *magnet* (an ore of iron), as if from *adamare.*] An alleged rock or mineral, of contradictory and fabulous properties. Now a poet. or rhet. name for impregnable hardness. 1. Not identified OE. Also *fig.* †2. The diamond 1393–1794. †3. The loadstone or magnet 1366–1656. Also *fig.* and *attrib.*
1. The dore was al of A. eterne CHAUCER. Gates of burning a. MILT. *fig.* The sharp a. of Fate CARLYLE. 2. A., precyowse stone *c* 1440. The a...will not be fil'd But by itself 1598. 3. As true to thee as steel to a. J. COOKE. The grace of God's spirit, like the true loadstone or a. BP. HALL. *fig.* A great A. of acquaintance BACON. *Mids. N. D.* II. i. 195. *attrib.* An a. heart 1677. A. walls B. TAYLOR. Hence **†Adama·ntive** *a.* (? misprint for *adamantine*).

†Adamante·an, *a.* [f. L. *adamanteus.*] Of adamant. MILT.

Adamantine (ædămæ·ntin), *a.* ME. [ad. L. *adamantinus*, a. Gr.; see ADAMANT.] 1. Made of, or like, adamant; unbreakable, impenetrable, impregnable. †2. Like the loadstone; magnetic -1655.
1. A state a...that is invincible HOLLAND. A. laws H. MORE, rock MILT., fortitude MACAULAY, purity of a woman RUSKIN. **A. spar,** old name of CORUNDUM.

Adama·ntoid. [f. Gr. *ἀδάμαντος* of ADAMANT; see -OID.] A form of crystal in the diamond, bounded by 48 equal triangles. DANA.

Adambulacral (æ:d,æmbiulēⁱ·krăl), *a.* 1872. [f. L. *ad* + AMBULACRA.] *Zool.* Next to the ambulacra, in echinoderms.

Adamite (æ·dămǝit). 1628. [f. ADAM.] **A.** *sb.* 1. A descendant of Adam, a human being; also, a name for the section of the human race derived from Adam 1635. 2. An imitator of Adam, an unclothed man; the name of certain sects, ancient and modern 1628. Hence **†Adami·tic** *a.* **A·damitism.** **B.** *adj.* Descended from Adam; human.

A·damite, *sb.*[2] 1837. [f. M. *Adam.*] *Min.* A zinc olivenite.

A·damsite. 1837. *Min.* = MUSCOVITE.

A-da·nce, *adv.* 1869. [A *prep.*[1] + DANCE.] Dancing.

A-da·ngle, *adv.* 1855. [A *prep.*[1] + DANGLE.] Dangling.

‖**Adansonia** (ædǎnsōu·niă). 1852. [mod. L. f. *Adanson.*] *Bot.* A genus (N.O. *Bombaceæ*) consisting of two species of gigantic trees, the Baobab, Monkey-bread, or Ethiopian Sour Gourd of W. and Central Africa, and the Cream of Tartar Tree, or Sour Gourd of N. Australia.

Adapt (ădæ·pt), *v.* 1611. [a. Fr. *adapter*, ad. L. *adaptare*, f. *ad* + *aptare*; f. *aptus*; see APT.] 1. To fit, to make suitable (*to, for*). 2. To alter so as to fit for a new use 1774.
1. The structure of the outer ear is adapted to collect and concentrate the vibrations BAIN. 2. A Comedy adapted from the French 1849. Hence **†Ada·pt** *ppl. a.* suited; fit. **Ada·pted** *ppl. a.* fitted, fit (*to, for*); altered so as to fit. **Ada·ptedness,** the quality of being adapted. **Ada·ption** = ADAPTATION. **Ada·ptive** *a.* characterized by, or given to, adaptation. **Ada·ptively** *adv.* so as to suit special conditions. **Ada·ptiveness,** the quality of being adaptive. var. **†Ada·ptate** *v.* CUDWORTH.

Adaptable (ădæ·ptăb'l), *a.* 1800. [f. ADAPT *v.*] Capable of being adapted. Hence **Adaptabi·lity** (*to, for*). **Ada·ptableness.**

Adaptation (ædæptēⁱ·ʃən). 1610. [a. Fr., ad. late L. *adaptationem*; see ADAPT.] 1. The action or process of adapting (*to*). 2. The process of modifying so as to suit new conditions 1790. 3. The condition of being adapted; anything adapted.
2. Powers of self-a. KINGSLEY. 3. The a. of immortality to our true wants J. MARTINEAU. This play is an a. from the French (*mod.*). Hence **Adapta·tional** *a.*

Ada·ptative, *a.* 1857. [f. L. *adaptat-, adaptare.*] = ADAPTIVE. Hence **Ada·ptativeness.**

Adapter, rarely **-or** (ădæ·ptəɹ). 1801. [f. ADAPT *v.*] 1. One who ADAPTS (in senses 1, 2). 2. A connecting part; in *Chem.* a tube joining two pieces of apparatus.

Ada·ptitude. 1842. [Comb. of ADAPT and APTITUDE.] Adaptedness.

‖**Adar** (ēⁱ·dăɹ). ME. [Heb.] The twelfth month of the Heb. eccl. year, the sixth of the civil year.

†Adarticula·tion. 1753. [f. L. *ad* + *articulationem*; see ARTICULATION.] *Anat.* A loose jointing of two bones. = ARTHRODIA.

‖**Adatis, -ais, addatys** (æ·dătis). 1687. Indian muslin.

†**Adau·nt,** *v.* ME. [a. OFr. *adanter* (later *addomter*).] To subdue -1597.

†**Adaw·,** *v.*[1] ME. [f. A- *pref.* 1 + DAW; cf. MHG. *ertagen.*] To awake or awaken -1530.

Til that he be adawed verrayly CHAUCER.

†**Adaw·,** *v.*[2] 1557. [?] To subdue, daunt -1654.

Adawed with some dreadfull spright SPENSER.

†**Adawe·,** *adv.* ME. [For *o dawe, of dawe* = OE. *of dazum*; see DAW(E, DAY.] Out of life. Usu. with vbs. *bring, do*: To kill -1513.

Adawn (ădǭ·n), *adv.* [A *prep.*[1] + DAWN.] Dawning.

Aday, a-day (ădē[i]·), *adv.* ME. [A *prep.*[1] + DAY = OE. *on dæze.*] †1. By day. 2. Daily 1500.

2. A peny a daye TINDALE.

Adays, a-days, *adv. phr.* ME. [A *prep.*[1] + *day's.* In OE. the gen. *dæzes* = *by day*; *a* = in, on, was added later.] †1. By day -1765. 2. **Now-a-days:** At the present day ME.

1. Pining a daies..waking a nights BURTON. 2. Reason and loue keepe little company together now-adayes *Mids. N. D.* III. i. 148.

Add (æd), *v.* ME. [ad. L. *addere*; f. *ad* + *dare.*] 1. To join or unite (a thing *to* another), so as to increase the number, quantity, or importance; to give by way of increased possession. 2. (obj. unexpressed.) To make an addition *to*; to augment 1591. 3. To say or write in addition; to go on to say, etc. ME. 4. To unite into one sum; often with *together. absol.* To perform the process of addition. So to *add up*; to *add in,* to include in a sum. 1509.

1. Lat vs..adden reuerence to suffisaunce and to power CHAUCER. To a. 3 to 5 HUTTON. All these things shall be added unto you *Matt.* vi. 33. 2. It adds to our labour (*mod.*). 3. But let me a., Sir Robert's mighty dull POPE. 4. To a. together the ideas of two days, or two years LOCKE. Hence **A·ddable** *a.* capable of being added, or added to. **A·ddible** *a.* capable of being added; whence **Addibi·lity.**

‖**Addax** (æ·dăks). 1693. [L., ad. African wd.; see Plin. *H. N.* xi. 37.] A boviform antelope, allied to the Nyl-ghau and Gnu, inhabiting N. Africa. (*Oryx nasomaculata.*)

†**Addee·m,** *v.* [f. DEEM; see A- *pref.* 11.] To adjudge. SPENSER.

‖**Addendum** (ăde·ndŏm). Pl. **addenda** (ăde·ndă). 1794. [a. L.] A thing to be added.

Adder[1] (æ·dəɹ). 1580. [f. ADD *v.*] He who adds.

Adder[2] (æ·dəɹ). [OE. *nædre.* The *n* was lost in ME., through the division of *a naddre* as *an addre.* N. dial. *nedder.*] †1. A serpent. *fig.* The old serpent, the devil. -1513. b. A dragon, or flying serpent ME. 2. A viper. *spec.* The Common Viper (*Pelias Berus*). OE. b. By extension, Applied to the *asp, basilisk, cockatrice,* etc. In mod. Zoology to species of *Clotho,* etc., as the Puff Adder and Horned Adder of Africa, Death Adder of N. Australia, etc. ME. 3. **Flying Adder,** *Adder-fly*: the Dragon-fly. 4. **Sea Adder,** *Syngnathus acus.*

1. Eue, seide he, ðat neddre bold ME. Grete addren comen flynge ME. 2. It is the bright day that brings forth the A. *Jul. Cæs.* II. i. 14. Stung with adders and Scorpions MILT. b. They are like the deafe adder [*marg.* or aspe] *Ps.* lviii. 4.

Comb.: **a.-bead,** a prehistoric, perh. Druidic, amulet; **-bolt,** a dragon-fly; **-deaf** *a.*, see 2 b, quot.; **-footed** *a.*, dragon-footed; **-pike,** the sting-fish (*Trachinus Vipera*); **-stone** = -BEAD; †**adder's fry,** brood of vipers; **-meat,** the Greater Stitchwort; **-mouth** (U.S.), plants of the genus *Microstylis*; **-spear** = ADDER'S-TONGUE.

A·dder's-grass. 1551. *Herb.* 1. The Early Spring Orchis (*O. mascula*). 2. = next.

A·dder's-tongue. 1578. *Herb.* A genus of ferns (*Ophioglossum*); also Wake Robin, Lily of the Valley, etc.

Adderwort (æ·dəɹwɔ̄ɹt). OE. Bistort.

Addice, early f. ADZE.

Addict (æ·dikt), *sb.* 1909. [f. ADDICT *v.*] One who is addicted to the habitual and excessive use of a drug or the like.

†**Addict,** *ppl. a.* 1529. [ad. L. *addictus, addicere.*] 1. Formally made over or bound *to* -1583. 2. Self-addicted, devoted *to* -1790.

Addict (ădi·kt), *v.* 1560. [f. prec.] 1. *Rom. Law.* To deliver over formally by judicial sentence *to*; *fig.* to make over, give up 1586. Also †*refl.* 2. To devote or apply habitually to a practice 1577. Also *refl.* and *pass.*

1. *fig.* The..day he addicts..to study 1670. 2. He can [not] a. his mind to..profitable business TOPSELL. *refl.* To a. themselves to Sack SHAKS., to vice PRIESTLEY.

Addicted (ădi·ktĕd), *ppl. a.* 1534. [f. prec.] 1. *Rom. Law.* Delivered over judicially; devoted. †2. Attached by one's own act (*to* a person, etc.) -1709. 3. Self-addicted *to,* prone 1561. †4. *without const.* Devoted -1652.

1. We be virgins, and a. to virginitie GREENE. 2. A. to Marius his master 1642. 3. A. to a melancholy *Twelfth N.* II. v. 222, to wine or strong drinke T. TAYLOR, stealing 1865. 4. Your Honors most a., T. B. 1594. Hence **Addi·ctedness.**

Addiction (ădi·kʃən). 1604. [ad. L. *addictionem*; see ADDICT.] 1. *Rom. Law.* A formal giving over by sentence of court; hence, a dedication to a master 1625. 2. The state of being (self-) addicted *to* 1641. †3. The way in which one is addicted; bent, inclination -1675.

2. A. to tobacco JOHNSON, to bad habits MILL. 3. *Oth.* II. ii. 6.

Additament (æ·ditămĕnt). 1460. [ad. L. *additamentum*; see ADD.] Anything added or appended.

Pretty additaments..to that main structure LAMB.

Addition (ădi·ʃən), *sb.* ME. [a. Fr., ad. L. *additionem*; see ADD.] 1. The action or process of adding (see ADD *v.*) ME. 2. That which is added; an appendix, accession, etc. ME. 3. *spec.* †a. Something added to a man's name, to distinguish him; 'style' of address -1726. †b. *Her.* Something added to a coat of arms, as a mark of honour; opp. to *abatement* -1753. †c. *Mus.* A dot placed on the right side of a note, to lengthen it by one half -1753.

1. Without a. or diminishing *Com. Err.* II. ii. 130. 2. Ireland..and other Additions to the Crown PETTY. 3. a. How do you Lieutenant? The worser, that you giue me the a. *Oth.* IV. i. 105. b. *Tr. & Cr.* IV. v. 141. Hence †**Addi·tion** *v.* to surname or style. †**Addi·tionary** *a.* additional.

Additional (ădi·ʃənăl). 1639. [f. prec.] A. *adj.* Existing in addition; added 1646. B. *sb.* something added; an addition; an 'extra' 1639. Hence **Addi·tionally** *adv.*

Addititious (æditi·ʃəs), *a.* 1748. [f. L. *addititius.*] Due to, or of the nature of, an addition. *A. force* (*Astr.*), that which increases the gravitation of a satellite towards its planet.

Additive (æ·ditiv), *a.* 1699. [ad. L. *additivus*; see ADD.] Disposed to addition; to be added. Hence **A·dditively** *adv.* var. †**A·dditory.**

Addle, (æ·d'l). [OE. *adela,* cogn. w. G. *adel,* mire; O.Swed. *adel* in *ko-adel,* cow-urine. (Not conn. w. OE. *ádl,* disease.) Since OE. only north.] A. *sb.* 1. Stinking urine or liquid filth; mire OE. 2. The dry lees of wine. (Dicts.)

B. *adj.* As in **Addle egg** (= med.L. *ovum urinæ,* cl. L. *ovum urinum,* Gr. οὔριον ᾠόν, wind-egg.). Rotten or putrid; producing no chicken ME. 2. *fig.* Empty, idle; muddled, unsound *a* 1593.

1. No more then I esteeme an a. egge *Tr. & Cr.* I. ii. 145. *Rom. & Jul.* III. i. 25. 2. A. head LYLY, epistle R. FELLOWES. His brains grow a. DRYDEN.

Comb.: **a.-brain, -head, -pate;** one whose brain is addled, a stupid bungler; **-brained, -headed, -pated** *adjs.*; **-headedness,** fatuity. Hence **A·ddleness,** putrefaction.

Addle (æ·d'l), *v.*[1] 1712. [f. ADDLE *a.*] 1. To make addle; to confuse; to make abortive. 2. *intr.* To grow addle. *lit.* and *fig.* 1812. Hence **A·ddled** *ppl. a.* **A·ddlement,** the process of addling or being addled. **A·ddling** *vbl. sb.*[1] decomposition of an egg; muddling of the wits.

†**Addle** (æd'l), *v.*[2] ME. [a. ON. *ǫðla,* f. *óðal,* property; n. dial., but not Sc.] To earn. Also *absol.* Of crops: To yield 1580. Hence †**A·ddling** *vbl. sb.*[2] earning.

†**Addoo·m,** *v.* [f. A- *pref.* 11 + DOOM *v.*] To adjudge. SPENSER.

Addorsed (ădǭ·ɹst), *ppl. a.* 1572. [f. L. *ad* + *dorsum*: cf. Fr. *adossé.*] *Her.* Turned back to back; as two animals, on a shield.

Address (ădre·s), *v.* ME. [a. Fr. *adresser*:—late L. **addrictiare,* f. *ad* + **drictiare, directiare,* f. *directum*; see DRESS and DIRECT. Refash. in 15th c.; see AD-.] I. To make straight or right, in various senses, now obs.; see quots.

†To put 'to rights', to set in order. [He] dyuers great batelles addressed LD. BERNERS. A Parlament being call'd, to addres many things MILT. We will that you..a. several Schedules Q. ELIZABETH. *intr.* Let vs addresse to tend on Hector's heeles SHAKS. †To make right or ready in attire; to clothe; to don. Addressed her selfe in Mans apparell JEWEL. To a. a frock of heavy mail BROWNING.

II. To direct. †1. To aim (*Obs.* exc. in *Golf,* 'to a. the ball') ME.; to send, refer, introduce *to* 1475; †*refl.* to betake oneself -1683. 2. To send as a written message *to*; to dedicate 1636. 3. To direct spoken words, a prepared speech, etc., *to* 1490; *refl.* to a. *oneself* in speech *to* 1665; †*intr.* to a. *to*; and *techn.* to present an address, and to 'pay addresses', to court -1765; *trans.* (*to* omitted) to speak directly to 1718.

1. Towards Eve addressed his way MILT. I addressed him to Lord Mordaunt EVELYN. Ship to be addressed to Charterers 1882. 2. To a. a letter to the public JUNIUS. *To a. a letter*: *techn.* to 'direct' it. Letters are..sometimes addressed 'London' only *P. O. Guide.* 3. To a. (*to* a person) prayers CAXTON, vows DRYDEN, discourse MACAULAY. Addressed the House of Peers MACAULAY. A. the Chair! (*mod.*).

III. †*trans.* To direct (to an object) -1591; *refl.* to apply oneself to 1393; †*intr.* (refl. pron. omitted) to set about -1725.

Hence **Addre·ssee,** the person to whom a document is addressed. **Addre·sser,** one who addresses; one who signs or delivers an address, or directs a message to any one. †**Addre·ssion,** the direction of one's course CHAPMAN. **Addre·ssor,** one who signs an address, or one who addresses a formal document.

Address (ădre·s), *sb.* 1539. [partly a. Fr. *adresse*; partly f. prec.] †1. The action of making ready or the being ready -1788; an appliance -1598; dress -1660. 2. General preparedness; skill, dexterity, adroitness 1598. 3. The action of directing or dispatching 1882. †4. The action of sending, or dedicating, a writing -1705. 5. The direction or superscription of a letter 1712. 6. †The act of addressing oneself to any one -1704; *esp.* dutiful or courteous approach, courtship. Now in *pl.* 1539. 7. Bearing in conversation 1674. 8. A formal speech of congratulation, thanks, etc.; *esp.* in reply to the Royal Speech at the opening of Parliament; a set discourse (less oratorical than a *speech,* less systematic than a *sermon*) 1751.

2. His ready a.: for no man ever resolved quicker or spoke clearer BACON. The a. of an accomplished intriguer MERIVALE. 5. This letter is to your a. (*mod.*). 6. Our addresses to Heaven NELSON. To make sham addresses to the older lady FIELDING. 7. His a...was abrupt, unceremonious CARLYLE. 8. Lord Liverpool moved the A. 1870. Short and stirring addresses (*mod.*).

Addressed (ădre·st), *ppl. a.*; also **addrest.** ME. [f. ADDRESS *v.*] †1. Erected -1595. †2. Well-ordered -1597. †3. Prepared; dressed as food -1633. 4. Arrayed. *arch.* ME. 5. Directed, sent 1598. 6. Directed as a letter. Hence †**Addre·ssedness.**

Adduce (ădiū·s), *v.* 1616. [ad. L. *adducere.*] To bring forward for consideration; to cite.

To a. authorities N. BRENT, arguments ROBERTSON, reasons BOWEN. Hence **Addu·ceable, -ible** *a.* **Addu·ced** *ppl. a.* **Addu·cer.**

Adducent (ădiū·sĕnt), *a.* 1694. [ad. L. *adducentem*; see ADDUCE.] *Phys.* Drawing towards a given point; as *adducent* muscles = ADDUCTORS. Opp. to *abducent.*

Adduct (ădʊ·kt), *v.* 1836. [f. L. *adduct-*; see ADDUCE.] *Phys.* To draw towards a common centre or median line.

Adduction (ădʊ·kʃən). 1656. [a. Fr., ad. med.L. *adductionem*; see ADDUCE.] 1. The action of adducting; see prec. 2. The action of adducing; see ADDUCE. 1764.

Adductive (ădʋ·ktiv), *a.* 1638. [f. L. *adduct-*; see ADDUCT.] Bringing to something else; *spec.* of the change wrought in transubstantiation.

Adductor (ædʋ·ktəɹ). 1746. [a. L.] *Phys.* A muscle which draws any limb, or part of the body, towards the trunk or main axis, or which folds extended parts of the body. Also *attrib.*

†**Addu·lce**, *v.* 1475. [a. MFr. *adoulcir* (mod. *adoucir*):—late L. *addulcire.*] To sweeten; to soothe.

-ade, *suff.* of sbs. 1. a. Fr. *-ade*, ad. Pr. *-āta*, fem. of pa. pple. as sb., meaning **a.** an action done, as in *blockade*; **b.** the body concerned, as in *ambuscade*; **c.** the product, as in *arcade*. The native Fr. form is *-ée*, as in *entrée*. 2. a. Fr. *-ade*, ad. Gr. -αδ-α (nom. -ας), as in *decade* (usu. *decad*). 3. ad. Sp. or Pg. *-ado*, It. *-ato*, masc. of 1, as in *brocade*, the product, and in *renegade*, the person affected.

A-dead (ăde·d), *adv.* [f. A- *pref.* 1 + DEAD.] Dead.

Adeem (ădī·m). 1845. [ad. L. *adimere*; see REDEEM.] To take away, *spec.* in *Rom. Law*, to revoke a legacy.

A-deep (ădī·p), *adv.* [A *prep.*[1] + DEEP.] Deeply. MRS. BROWNING.

‖**Adelantado** (ādelantā·do). 1599. [Sp.] A Sp. grandee; a lord-lieutenant or governor. B. JONS.

‖**Adelaster** (ædilæ·stəɹ). 1866. [f. Gr. ἄδηλος + ἀστήρ.] *Bot.* A provisional name for a plant of which the flowers and therefore its genus are unknown.

Adeling. See ATHELING.

Adelopod(e (ădī·lŏpǫd). 1847. [f. Gr. ἄδηλος + πόδα (πούς).] *Zool.* An animal whose feet are hidden.

‖**-adelphia** (ăde·lfiă), *suffix.* 1858. [Gr.] *Bot.* Collection of stamens into a bundle; as in the class-names *Monadelphia*, etc.

Adelphic (ăde·lfik), *a.* 1847. [ad. Gr. ἀδελφικός.] *Bot.* Having the stamens united into a parcel or parcels.

Adelpholite (ăde·lfŏləit). 1868. [f. Gr. ἀδελφός + λίθος.] *Min.* A Columbate of iron and manganese. DANA.

Adelphous (ăde·lfəs), *a.* 1855. [f. Gr. ἀδελφός.] *Bot.* Having the stamens grouped or united; usu. in comp. as *monadelphous*, etc.

†**Ade·mpt**, *ppl. a.* ME. [ad. L. *ademptus*; see ADEEM.] Taken away -1561.

Ademption (ăde·mʃən). 1590. [ad. L. *ademptionem*; see ADEEM.] A taking away; in *Law*, revocation of a grant or bequest.

‖**A·den.** *Obs.* Pl. **adenes.** [Gr. ἀδήν, ἀδένα.] A gland -1775.

Aden-, adeni-, adeno-, comb. forms of prec.

‖**adenalgia** (ædenæ·ldʒiă) [mod.L. *-algia*], pain, a painful swelling, in a gland; **adeniform** (ăde·nifǫɹm, æ·deni-) [L. *-formis*] *a.*, gland-like; **a·denocele** [Gr. κήλη], an adenoid tumour; **adeno·graphy** [Gr. -γραφία], description of the glandular system; **a·denoid, -al** [Gr. -ειδής] *a.*, gland-like; **a·denoids** *sb. pl.*, an overgrowth of the glandular tissue on the back of the upper part of the throat, called also *adenoid vegetations*; **adeno·logy** [Gr. -λογία], the part of Physiology which treats of the glands; hence **a:denolo·gical** *a.*; **adeno·pathy** [Gr. -παθία], disease of the glandular system; **·phorous** [Gr. -φορος] *a.*, bearing or producing glands; **a:denophy·llous** [Gr. φύλλον] *a.*, glandular-leaved; **adeno·tomy** [Gr. -τομία], dissection of or incision into a gland.

Adenose (æ·denōᵘs), *a.* 1853. [ad. mod. L. *adenosus.*] Glandulous. var. **A·denous.**

‖**Adephaga** (ăde·făgă), *sb. pl.* 1842. [a. Gr. ἀδηφάγα (sc. *animalia*), f. ἄδην + -φαγος.] A family of Beetles, also called *Carnivora.*

‖**Adeps** (æ·deps). 1657. [L.] Animal fat, lard.

Adept (ăde·pt). 1663. [ad. L. *adeptus*, *adipisci.*] **A.** *adj.* Completely versed (*in*); well-skilled 1691.

B. *sb.* [In med.L. *adeptus* used subst. = One who *has attained* the great secret of Alchemy. In Eng. the L. form *adeptus* was at first used.] Hence, One who is skilled in all the secrets of anything 1685.

Queens became adepts in Des Cartes' philosophy REID. Hence †**Ade·ptical** *a.* alchemical. †**Ade·ptist**, a skilled alchemist. **Ade·ptness**, the quality of being a. **Ade·ptship**, the condition or rank of an a.

†**Ade·ption.** 1548. [ad. L. *adeptionem*; see prec.] Attainment.

Adequacy (æ·dĭkwěsi). 1808. [f. ADEQUATE *a.*] The state or quality of being ADEQUATE.

Adequate (æ·dĭkwět), *a.* 1617. [ad. L. *adæquatus*, *adæquare.*] Const. *to*, †*with.* †1. Equal in magnitude or extent -1750. 2. Commensurate in fitness; sufficient, suitable 1617. 3. *Logic.* Fully representing 1690.

1. Not a. to the expectations JOHNSON. 2. Is language a. to describe it W. COLLINS. A. to the disease JAS. MILL. 3. A. ideas LOCKE. An a. definition MILL. Hence **A·dequately** *adv.* **A·dequateness.** **Adequa·tion**, the action of equalizing, or fact of equalling; an equivalent.

†**A·dequate**, *v.* 1599. [f. L. *adæquat-*; see prec.] To make or be equal or sufficient.

A·dequative, *a.* 1823. [ad. med.L. *adæquativus*; see prec.] = ADEQUATE 2. Scott.

Adesmy (ăde·smi). 1879. [f. Gr. ἄδεσμος.] *Bot.* Defective coherence or adherence between vegetable organs.

Adessenarian (æde:sĭnēᵊ·riăn). 1751. [f. med.L. *adessenarii*; f. *adesse.*] *Eccl. Hist.* One who held the real presence of Christ's body in the Eucharist, but not by transubstantiation.

‖**Ad eundem** (*i*,ʋ·ndem), of admission *to the same degree* in another university.

Adevism (æ·dĭviz'm). 1878. [f. Gr. ἀ + Skr. *deva.*] A denial of the legendary deities, as distinguished from *atheism*. M. MÜLLER.

Adfe·cted, *ppl. a.* 1695. [var. of AFFECTED.] Compounded. *Math.* Of equations: Containing different powers of an unknown quantity.

Adfiliate, -ation, obs. var. AFFILIATE, -ATION.

Adflu·xion. 1829. var. of AFFLUXION.

Adglu·tinate, *a.* = AGGLUTINATE.

Adhere (ædhīᵊ·ɹ), *v.* 1597. [a. Fr. *adhérer*, ad. L. *adhærere.*] 1. To stick fast, to cleave, *to* a substance, as by grasping or being glued 1651. Also *fig.* 2. To cleave *to* a person or party; to be a follower 1597. 3. To cleave *to*, continue to maintain, an opinion, practice, etc. 1656. †4. *without const.* To 'hang together'; to agree -1605. 5. *Bot.* To be adnate 1857.

1. These mouldings nearly a. to the stone RUSKIN. *fig.* Flattery adheres to power GIBBON. 2. Meane men must adheare BACON. To a. to the King's enemies LUTTRELL, to the Church of Rome MACAULAY. 3. To a. to a plan B. TAYLOR, a decision (*mod.*). 4. Nor time nor place did then a. *Macb.* I. vii. 52. Hence **Adhe·rer** (? *Obs.*), one who adheres (*to* an act, etc.). **Adhe·ring** *vbl. sb.* the act or process of sticking, etc.; *ppl. a.* clinging, etc.

Adherence (ædhīᵊ·rĕns). 1612. [a. Fr., ad. L. *adhærentia*; see ADHERE.] 1. The action of adhering (see ADHERE 1, 2, 3, 5). †2. An instance of adhering; adherent matter or circumstance -1667.

Adhe·rency. *arch.* 1582. [ad. L. *adhærentia*; see ADHERE.] 1. The quality or state of being adherent 1647. †2. That which is adherent; adhering matter, etc. -1681. †3. An adhering party; a following -1662.

1. By virtue of its a...in the flesh JER. TAYLOR.

Adhe·rent. ME. [a. Fr., ad. L. *adhærentem*; see ADHERE.] **A.** *adj.* 1. Sticking fast *to*, attached materially 1615. 2. *fig.* Attached as a circumstance 1588. †3. Attached as a partisan or follower (*to*) -1602. 4. *Bot.* Adnate 1830.

1. Vpon a rocke, and a. SANDYS. 3. To be a. to the King's enemies FULBECKE.

B. *sb.* 1. A partisan, follower, supporter (*of*) *c* 1460. †2. That which adheres -1645.

1. Luther and his adherentes MORE. Hence **Adhe·rently** *adv.*

Adhesion (ædhī·ʒən). 1624. [a. Fr., ad. L. *adhæsionem*; see ADHERE.] 1. The action of sticking *to*, by attraction, viscosity of surface, or grasping. An instance of such action. *Path.* Unnatural union of surfaces due to inflammation. 1645. Also *fig.* 2. Attaching oneself, or remaining attached, to a person, party, or tenet 1624. 3. *Psych.* Intimate and involuntary association of ideas and action 1855. 4. *Bot.* Coalescence of normally *unlike* parts; opp. to *cohesion* 1857. 5. Anything which adheres; an appendage, etc. *rare.* 1743.

1. The a. of the Finger to the Tube BOYLE. 2. A. unto authority SIR T. BROWNE, to Rome HUSSEY, to an accustomed policy KINGLAKE. *To give in one's a.*: to join as a supporter. 5. Casting off all noxious adhesions CARLYLE.

Adhesive (ædhī·siv), *a.* 1670. [a. Fr. *adhésif*, *-ive*; see prec.] 1. Sticky 1775. 2. Prepared so as to adhere, as in *adhesive envelope* 1854. 3. *fig.* Apt or tending to adhere, cling to, or persevere in 1670.

1. A plaster, moderately a. GOOCH. 3. A. to the track THOMSON (J.). Hence **Adhe·sively** *adv. rare.*

Adhesiveness (ædhī·sivnĕs). 1815. [f. as prec.] 1. The quality of being ADHESIVE. *lit.* and *fig.* 1839. 2. *Phren.* The faculty of forming and maintaining attachments to persons. *Psych.* The tendency to association of ideas. 1815.

†**Adhi·bit**, *ppl. a.* 1528. [ad. L. *adhibitus*, *adhibere.*] 1. Brought in *to* 1543. 2. Brought into application -1671.

Adhibit (ædhi·bit), *v.* 1528. [f. prec.] 1. To take or let in, admit. 2. To affix 1567. 3. To apply, use; *esp.* as a remedy 1654.

1. The witnesses adhibited MUIRHEAD. 2. We a. our seals BOSWELL. 3. Let this bolus be adhibited 1725. Hence **Adhibi·tion**, the action of adhibiting.

‖**Ad hominem** (æ:d hǫ·minem). 1748. [L.] Of arguments, etc.: Directed to the preferences or principles of the individual, not to abstract truth.

†**Adho·rt** *v.*, †**Adhorta·tion**, †**Adho·ratory**, *a.* = EXHORT, etc.

Adiabatic (æ:diăbæ·tik), *a.* 1877. [f. Gr. ἀδιάβατος.] *Physics.* Impassable (*sc.* to heat); pertaining to a condition where no heat enters or leaves a system. Hence **Adiaba·tically** *adv.*

Adiactinic (æ:diæ̆kti·nik), *a.* 1880. [f. A- *pref.* 14 + DIACTINIC.] *Chem.* Opaque to the actinic rays.

‖**Adiantum** (ædi,æ·ntǒm). 1706. [L., ad. Gr. ἀδίαντον, 'unwetted', f. ἀ + διαίνειν.] *Bot.* 1. A genus of ferns, of which True Maidenhair (*A. Capillus Veneris*) is a rare native of Britain. 2. *Herb.* and *pop.* The Black Maiden-hair (*Asplenium A.-nigrum*).

Adiaphorism (ædi,æ·fŏriz'm). 1866. [f. Gr. ἀδιάφορος + -ISM.] Theological indifference; latitudinarianism.

Adiaphorist (ædi,æ·fŏrist). 1564. [f. as prec.] **A.** *sb.* 1. An indifferentist in theology 1645. 2. *Eccl. Hist.* One of the moderate Lutherans, who held some things, condemned by Luther, to be indifferent 1564. var. **Adia·phorite.** **B.** *adj.* Theologically indifferent (*mod.*). Hence **Adiaphori·stic** *a.*, relating to adiaphorism or the *adiaphora.*

‖**Adiaphoron** (ædi,æ·fŏron), *a.* and *sb.* *arch.* Pl. **adiaphora.** 1553. [Gr., f. ἀ + διάφορος.] A thing indifferent in the eyes of the Church.

Adiaphorous (ædi,æ·fŏrəs), *a.* 1635. [f. Gr. ἀδιάφορος.] 1. Indifferent, non-essential; neutral. var. †**Adia·phoral.** †2. *Chem.* Neutral; neither alkaline nor acid -1691. 3. *Med.* Doing neither harm nor good (*mod.*).

†**Adia·phory.** [ad. Gr. ἀδιαφορία.] Indifferentism.

‖**Adiapneustia** (æ:diăpniū·stiă). 1706. [Gr.] *Med.* Defective or impeded perspiration.

Adiathermic (æ:diăþō·ɹmik), *a.* 1867. [f. Gr. ἀ + διάθερμος.] *Physics.* Impervious to heat.

Adicity (ædi·sĭti). 1882. [f. -AD 1.] *Chem.* Combining capacity of an element.

Adieu (ădiū·). ME. [a. Fr., f. à + *Dieu*, i.e. 'I commend you to God'; now a mere formula.] **A.** *int.* Good-bye! farewell! (*arch.*) *fig.* = Away! an end to. **B.** *adv.* †*To go* *adieu*: to go away -1575. *To bid or say adieu* (*to*): to take leave of ME. Hence **C.** *sb.* A leave-taking; a parting word; a farewell; esp. *to make or take adieu* ME.

A. *fig.* Adew my song ASHMOLE. A. to all ideas of nobility HUME. **C.** Too cold an a. SHAKS. His adieus were not long MISS AUSTEN.

†Adi·ght, *v.* ME. [f. A- *pref.* 1 + *dihtan*; see DIGHT.] To put in order; equip, dress -1581.

‖Ad infinitum (æ·d infinəi·tǫ̆m). 1678. [L.] Without end, for ever.

Adinole (æ·dinōul). 1837. *Min.* A variety of ALBITE.

‖Ad interim (æ·d i·ntĕrim). 1787. [L.] *adv.* Meanwhile. *adj.* Temporary 1818.

†Adinve·ntion. ME. [ad. L. *adinventionem*; see INVENT.] An invented addition -1630.

Adipe·scent, *a.* 1847. [f. L. *adipem.*] Becoming fatty.

Adipic (ădi·pik), *a.* 1877. [f. L. *adipem.*] *Chem.* In *Adipic acid*, $C_6H_{10}O_4$, a dibasic, diatomic acid, obtained by the action of nitric acid on fats.

Adipocere (æ·dipo₁sīəɹ). 1803. [a. Fr. *adipocire*; f. L. *adipem* + Fr. *cire.*] A greyish white fatty substance, chiefly *Margarate of Ammonia*, generated in dead bodies buried in moist places or submerged in water. Hence **Adipo·cerate** *v.* to convert into a. **Adipo·cera·tion,** the process of changing into a. **Adipoce·riform** *a.* **Adipo·cerous** *a.*

Adipose (æ·dipōu·s). 1743. [ad. mod.L. *adiposus.*] **A.** *adj.* Of or pertaining to adeps, or animal fat; fatty. *Adipose tissue*: the vesicular structure which contains the fat. **B.** *sb.* [sc. *substance.*] The animal fat 1865. Hence **A·dipo·seness,** the state of being fat. **Adipo·sity,** fatness; or tendency to fatness. var. (less techn.) **A·dipous.**

Adipsous (adi·psəs), *a.* 1879. [f. Gr. ἄδιψος.] *Med.* Allaying thirst.

A·dipsy (æ·dipsi). [f. as prec.] Absence of thirst.

Adit (æ·dit). 1602. [ad. L. *aditus.*] **1.** An approach; *spec.* a horizontal opening by which a mine is entered or drained. **2.** Access, entrance 1847.

1. Soughs or adits to drain them RAY. 2. A. to the executive HELPS.

Adjacency (ădʒē·sĕnsi). 1646. [ad. late L. *adjacentia*; see ADJACENT.] **1.** The quality or state of being adjacent 1805. var. **†Adja·cence** -1652. **2.** That which lies near. *pl.* Adjacent places, environs. 1646.

1. The a. of some great..river DE QUINCEY. 2. The Palais Royal and adjacencies CARLYLE.

Adjacent (ădʒē·sĕnt). ME. [ad. L. *adjacentem, adjacere.* Cf. Fr. *adjacent.*] **A.** *adj.* Lying near *to*; adjoining; bordering. (Not necessarily *touching.*)

Adjacent angles: the angles which one straight line makes with another on which it stands. Parts.. a. to London DE FOE. Hence **Adja·cently** *adv.*

B. †*sb.* That which lies near; a neighbour -1725.

†Adject. ME. [ad. L. *adjectus, adjicere.*] **A.** *ppl. a.* (adje·ct.) Joined -1612. **B.** *sb.* (a·dject.) An addition -1677.

Adject (ădʒe·kt), *v.* ME. [ad. L. *adjectare*, freq. of *adjicere.*] To add or join.

They adjected this Condition LINDSAY.

Adjection (ădʒe·kʃən). ME. [ad. L. *adjectionem*; see ADJECT *a.*] **1.** The action of adding or joining. **†2.** That which is added -1704.

1. Without a. Of your assistance B. JONS.

Adjectitious (ædʒekti·ʃəs), *a.* 1652. [f. L. *adjecticius.*] Additional.

Adjectival (ædʒektəi·văl), *a.* 1797. [f. L. *adjectivus*: a mod. substitute for ADJECTIVE *a.* in sense **1.**] Of or belonging to the adjective.

Adjective (æ·dʒektiv). ME. [a. Fr. *adjectif, -ive*, ad. L. *adjectivus*; see ADJECT *a.*] **A.** *adj.* **1.** *Gram.* Forming an adjunct to a noun substantive; dependent on as sb. as an attribute. **2.** Hence, *gen.* Dependent 1622. **3.** Of *Law*: Relating to procedure; opp. to *substantive* 1808.

1. Scotland is like a noun a. that cannot stand without a substantive ME. 2. The women were treated..as a. beings GROTE.

B. *sb.* [The adj. used *absol.*] **1.** A 'Noun Adjective', a word added to the name of a thing, and signifying an attribute of the thing 1509. **2.** Hence, *gen.* That which cannot stand alone; a dependent; an accessory 1639.

2. Those Northern Adjectives, not able to subsist without England OSBORN.

Hence **A·djective** *v.* to make adjectival. **A·djectived** *ppl. a.* made a.; used as an a. **A·djectively** *adv.* **A·djectiving** *vbl. sb.* the making adjectival.

Adjoin (ădʒoi·n), *v.* ME. [a. OFr. *ajoin-, ajoign-, ajoindre*, mod. *adjoindre*:—L. *adjungere.*] **1.** †To join on, unite, *to* or *unto* -1659; *fig.* to join on as an adjunct or supplement (*arch.*) ME. Also *refl.* and *intr.* **†2.** *intr.* To be or lie close, contiguous (*to, on, with*) -1794. **3.** *trans.* (*to* omitted.) To be contiguous to or in contact with 1745.

¶Used erron. for ENJOIN. [See A- *pref.* 10.]

1. Mortiz'd and adjoined *Haml.* III. iii. 20. 3. The head of the tomb adjoins the west wall WILSON. Hence **Adjoi·ned** *ppl. a.* †joined, united; appended or subjoined. **†Adjoi·nedly** *adv.* unitedly. **Adjoi·ning** *ppl. a.* lying next; *fig.* pertaining; connected.

†Adjoi·nant. 1494. [a. OFr. *ajoinant*; see ADJOIN.] **A.** *ppl. a.* Adjoining -1602. **B.** *sb.* One living close by 1548.

†Adjoint, *sb.*[1] ME. [a. OFr. *ajoint*:—L. *adjunctum* ADJUNCT.] A helper; an adjunct -1700.

‖Adjoint (adʒoaṅ, æ·dʒoint), *sb.*[2] [mod. Fr., pa. pple. of *adjoindre.*] A French civil officer who assists the maire; a sub-professor in a French college.

Adjourn (ădʒɝ·ɹn), *v.* ME. [a. OFr. *ajorner, ajourner*:—late L. *adjornare*, f. *ad* + *jornus*:—cl. L. *diurnus*; see JOURNAL.] **†1.** *trans.* To appoint (one) a day for his appearance; to cite, or summon for, or remand to, a stated day -1660. **2.** To defer or put off ME. **3.** To adjourn (a meeting): To put off or defer proceedings to another day 1494. **4.** *intr.* (from *refl.*) Of persons: To suspend proceedings and disperse for a time, or *sine die*. Also, to separate in order to meet elsewhere; hence *colloq.* to go in a body to another place.

2. Fro place to place to adiourne it 1559. This day a. your cares POPE. 3. To a. Parlyament FABYAN, a Court SHAKS., the Senate MIDDLETON. 4. The House..then adjourned themselves MARVELL. From the Church the people adjourned to the Hippodrome GIBBON. They thence adjourned to eat ice at a pastry-cook's MISS AUSTEN. Hence **†Adjou·rnal,** adjournment. **Adjou·rned** *ppl. a.* †cited; postponed. **Adjou·rning** *vbl. sb.* adjournment. **Adjou·rnment,** the act of adjourning; the state of being adjourned.

†Adjou·st, *v.* ME. [a. MFr. *adjouster* (mod. *ajouter*):—late L. *adjuxtare*, f. *ad* + *juxta*. Dist. from ADJUST.] **1.** To put a thing (to one); to suggest -1521. **2.** To put one thing to another, to add -1530.

Adjudge (ădʒɝ·dʒ), *v.* [ME. *aiugen*, a. OFr. *ajuger* (mod. *adjuger*):—L. *adjudicare*; see ADJUDICATE. The *a-* was refash. as *ad-* in Fr. in 14th c.] **1.** *trans.* To decide judicially ME. **2.** To pronounce or decree by judicial sentence 1563. **†3.** To determine in one's own judgement, judge -1729. **4.** To condemn ME. **5.** To award, grant, or impose judicially (*to* or *unto*) 1494.

1. And so was it adjudged in the Court of Common Pleas COKE. 2. The grant was adjudged void FULLER. 3. Divers adjudged that he was a scrivener's sone HAWARD. 4. Adjudging my family to beggary BURKE. Charles was adjudged to die P. BAYNE. 5. Hard to a. the garland SELDEN. Hence **Adju·dged** *ppl. a.* (senses 1, †2, 4, 5). **Adju·dger,** an awarder. **Adju·dging** *vbl. sb.* (senses 1, 4, 5). **Adju·dg(e)ment,** the act of adjudging.

Adjudicate (ădʒ¹ū·dikeᶦt), *v.* 1700. [f. L. *adjudicat-, adjudicare*; see JUDGE.] **†1.** *trans.* To award judicially -1731. **2.** *trans.* To try and determine judicially 1775. **3.** *intr.* To act as a judge, or court of judgement 1840.

2. Adjudicated a bankrupt 1870. 3. He ought not to a. as to his own fees 1857. Hence **Adju·dicative** *a.* having the character of adjudicating. **Adju·dicator,** one who settles a question, or awards a prize. **Adju·dica·ture,** the process of adjudicating.

Adjudication (ădʒ¹ū·dikē¹·ʃən). 1691. [ad. L. *adjudicationem*; see ADJUDICATE.] **1.** The act of adjudicating; see ADJUDICATE 1, 2. **2.** A judicial sentence or award 1782. **3.** *Law.* A decree in bankruptcy 1869. **4.** *Sc. Law.* An attachment of heritable estate as security, etc.

1. An a. in his favour PENNANT. The a. of the medal SMILES. 2. Any a. in favour of natural rights BURKE.

†A·djument. [ad. L. *adjumentum.*] Help; a helper -1663.

Adjunct (æ·dʒɝŋkt). 1588. [ad. L. *adjunctus, adjungere.*] **A.** *adj.* Joined or added; subordinate 1595.

Every humour hath his a. pleasure SHAKS. *Sonn.* xci.

B. *sb.* (Cf. Fr. *adjoint.*) **1.** Something joined to another, but subordinate, as auxiliary, or dependent upon it 1588. **2.** A person joined to another in some office or service 1639. **3.** A personal addition or enhancement 1610; a qualifying addition to a word or name 1608. **4.** *Gram.* Any word or words expanding the subject, predicate, etc., of a sentence 1589. **5.** *Logic.* Anything added to the essence; a non-essential attribute 1588.

1. Learning is but an a. to our selfe *L. L. L.* IV. iii. 314. The charters with their adjuncts STUBBS. 2. Colleagues, or rather Adjuncts, in the duties of the Office 1877. 3. The Adjuncts of a strong and subtil Capacity NAUNTON. Geographical adjuncts 'West', 'East', etc. FREEMAN. 5. To differ more in adjuncts .. than in innate quality I. TAYLOR. Hence **Adju·nctive** *a.* having the quality of contributing (*to*) or forming an a. **Adju·nctively** *adv.* as an a.

Adjunction (ădʒɝ·ŋkʃən). 1603. [ad. L. *adjunctionem*; see ADJUNCT.] **1.** The act of joining on or adding 1618. **2.** That which is joined on, etc. ? *Obs.* 1603.

Adjuration (æ·dʒ¹urē¹·ʃən). ME. [ad. L. *adjurationem*; see ADJURE.] The action of adjuring (see ADJURE 2); an earnest appeal 1611; *spec.* in exorcism ME.

An a. as vain as it was earnest FROUDE. Come, draw thy circle, speak thine a. B. TAYLOR.

Adjuratory (ădʒ¹ūə·rătəri), *a.* 1815. [ad. L. *adjuratorius*; see ADJURE.] Containing a solemn charge or appeal.

Adjure (ădʒ¹ūə·ɹ), *v.* ME. [ad. L. *adjurare.* [Cf. Fr. *adjurer.*] **†1.** To put (one) to his oath; to bind under the penalty of a curse -1643. **2.** To charge or entreat solemnly, as if under oath, or under the penalty of a curse 1483.

1. Thy father adjured the people, saying: Cursed be the man that [etc.] 1 *Sam.* xiv. 28. 2. His friends adjured him to take more care of [his] life MACAULAY. Hence **Adju·rement,** a solemn entreaty. **Adju·rer, -or,** one who adjures. **Adju·ring** *ppl. a.* charging upon oath; exorcising.

Adjust (ădʒɝ·st), *v.* 1611. [a. 16th c. Fr. *adjuster* (now *ajuster*):—med.L. *adjustare*, as if f. *ad* + *justus*. The OFr. *ajouster* (whence *ajouter*):—L. *adjuxtare* is thus refashioned in *ajuster*, after *à* + *juste*. See ADJOUST.] **1.** To arrange, compose, harmonize (differences, discrepancies, accounts) 1611. **†2.** *ellipt. intr.* To a. (*sc.* differences, or oneself): To come to terms -1733. **3.** To arrange suitably (*to, by, with*) something else 1664. **4.** To arrange suitably in relation to its parts; to regulate, systematize 1667; *esp.* of clothes, armour, etc. 1735.

1. To a. Accounts COWLEY, the preliminaries of a Treaty STEELE, a difficulty DE FOE, pretensions H. WALPOLE, the books JAS. MILL. 3. To a. the event to the prediction ADDISON, means to end BURKE, the marvellous with the probable BLAIR (J.). 4. The scientifically adjusted court precedency of France BURTON. See them..a. their clothes POPE. Hence **Adju·stable** *a.* **†Adju·stage.** *rare.* = ADJUSTMENT. Also = ADJUTAGE. **Adju·sting** *vbl. sb.* the process of arranging or disposing suitably.

Adjuster (ădʒɝ·stəɹ). 1756. [f. ADJUST.] One who adjusts; *spec.* in *average adjuster*: One who professionally assesses and apportions claims arising out of loss, etc., at sea.

Adjustment (ădʒɝ·stmĕnt). 1644. [ad. Fr. *ajustement*; see ADJUST.] **1.** The process of adjusting. **2.** The state of being adjusted; settlement 1689. **3.** An arrangement whereby things are adjusted 1736. **4.** *Comm.* The settlement among various parties of their several claims, liabilities, or payments; as the *a. of the policy*, or *of general average* in Marine Insurance.

1. The a. of the whole SIR J. REYNOLDS, of the eye

TYNDALL, of the Calendar 1881. 2. A mode of bringing [questions] to an amicable a. WELLINGTON. 3. Wheels and verniers, and delicate adjustments TYNDALL.

Adjutage, ajutage (ădʒiŭ·tĕdʒ, æ·dʒiŭtĕdʒ). 1707. [a. Fr. *ajutage*, var. *ajoutage*; see ADJUST, and ADJUSTAGE.] *lit.* An adjustment; hence in *Hydraulics*, The efflux-tube of an artificial fountain.

Adjutancy (æ·dʒiŭtănsi), 1791. [f. next; see -NCY.] 1. The office or rank of an adjutant 1820. 2. *fig.* Official order. BURKE.

Adjutant (æ·dʒiŭtănt). 1600. [ad. L. *adjutantem*, *adjutare*, freq. of *adjuvare*.] A. *adj.* Helping.

B. *sb.* 1. An assistant or helper. Now *rare.* 1622. 2. *Mil.* An officer who assists the superior officers in the details of military duty 1600. 3. *Ornith.* A gigantic species of stork (*Ciconia Argala*) native to India; so called from its gait. (Called also **a.-bird, -crane, -stork.**) 1798.

1. The Hands [and other]..adjutants of man's wit BULWER. 2. He would sit in his pavilion, and manage all by adjutants BACON.

A·djutant-ge·neral. 1. *Mil.* An officer who assists the general of an army 1645. 2. Among the Jesuits, a superintendent of a province or country, acting under the supervision of the General of the Order 1753.

A·djutator. 1647. [f. L. *adjutare*; see ADJUTANT.] *lit.* A helper. Orig. a corruption of AGITATOR, q. v.

†**Adju·te,** *v.* 1524. [a. Fr. *ajouter*; see ADJOUST.] To add –1633.

†**Adju·tor**[1]. 1531. [a. L.] A helper –1652. Occ. = ADJUTANT *sb* 2.

†**Adju·tor**[2]. 1541. [ad. Fr. *adjutoire*, ad. L. *adjutorium*.] Properly the *humerus*; also the *ulna*.

†**A·djutory.** 1541. [ad. L. *adjutorius*, neut. *-orium*, a means of help.] A. *adj.* Helping. *spec.* in *Phys.* of certain bones of the arm –1706. B. *sb.* 1. A helper 1552. 2. *Phys.* = ADJUTOR[2]. 1541. 3. Help –1678.

Adjuvant (æ·dʒiuvănt). 1609. [a. Fr., ad. L. *adjuvantem*, *adjuvare*.] *adj.* Aiding 1614. *sb.* [The adj. used *absol.*] A help, or helper 1609. *spec.* in *Med.* A substance added to a prescription to assist the action of the base.

†**A·djuvate,** *v.* 1599. [f. L. *adjuvat-*; see prec.] To aid –1708.

Adlegation (æ·dlĭgēⁱ·ʃən). 1753. [ad. L. *adlegationem*, *adlegare*. Cf. ALLEGATION.] The right claimed by the states of the old German Empire of associating their delegates with those of the Emperor in treaties, etc. relating to the common concerns of the empire. Distinguished from *legation*.

‖**Ad libitum** (æd li·bitŏm). 1705. [L.] At one's pleasure; as much as one likes. In *Music* opp. to *obbligato*. Abbrev. **ad lib.**

Admarginate (ădmā·ɹdʒineⁱt), *v.* 1834. [f. L. *ad* + *marginem*.] To add in the margin.

Admaxillary (ădmæ·ksilări), *a.* 1881. [f. L. *ad* + MAXILLARY; see AD-.] Connected with the jaw.

Admeasure (ădme·ʒiŭɹ, -ʒəɹ), *v.* [ME. *amesure*, a. OFr. *amesurer*:—late L. *admensurare.* Refash. after L.] †1. To assign a measure or limit to –1627. †2. To apply a measure to –1697. 3. To measure out to; to apportion 1641.

3. To a. and apportion [the common] TOMLINS. Hence **Admea·surer.**

Admeasurement (ădme·ʒiŭɹmĕnt, -ʒəɹ-). 1598. [a. OFr. *amesurement*; see ADMEASURE.] 1. The process of applying a measure in order to ascertain dimensions 1626. 2. Size, dimensions 1790. 3. The ascertainment and apportionment of just shares, e.g. in an inheritance or common 1598.

1. A. by acre BACON. 2. Accurate admeasurements in feet and cubits MAURICE. 3. By writ of a. of pasture BLACKSTONE. var. **Adme·nsura·tion.**

†**Admerveylle, -aylle,** *v.* 1474. [A refash. of *amerveil(le*; with *a-*:—*es-*:—L. *ex-*, confused with *a-*:—L. *ad-*; see AMARVEL.] To marvel, marvel at –1506.

Adminicle (ădmi·nik'l). Also **-cule.** 1556. [ad. L. *adminiculum*.] 1. Anything that aids or supports. 2. *Law.* Supporting or corroborative evidence. *Sc. Law.* Any writing tending to prove the existence and tenor of a lost deed. 1706. 3. *Archæol.* In *pl.* Ornaments which surround the figure on coins, etc. CHAMBERS.

1. Fasting and sackcloth .. as adminicles .. to .. prayer J. KING. 2. Only as adminicles of testimony SCOTT. Hence **A·dmini·cular** *a.* var. †**Admini·culary** *a.* and *sb.*

Adminiculate (æ:dmini·kiŭleⁱt), *v.* [f. L. *adminiculat-*, *adminiculare.*] *Sc. Law.* To support by corroboratory evidence. Hence **Adminicula·tion.**

‖**Adminiculum** (æ:dmini·kiŭlŏm). Pl. **-a.** [L.] *Entom.* In *pl.* The short spines or teeth on the abdomen of certain pupæ or grubs. KIRBY.

Administer (ădmi·nistəɹ), *v.* [ME. *amynistre*, a. OFr. *aministrer*, ad. L. *administrare.* Refash. after L.] 1. *trans.* To manage as a steward, to carry on. Also *absol.* ME. 2. *Law.* To manage and dispose of the estate of a deceased person, either under a will or under *Letters of Administration* c 1430; also *absol.* 1602. 3. *trans.* To execute or dispense 1495; to tender (an oath *to*) 1593. 4. To apply, as medicine, etc. 1541. 5. Hence *fig.* To dispense, give (anything beneficial; also (*joc.*) a *rebuke*, a *blow*, etc.) *to* 1489; *intr.* to minister *to* 1712.

1. To a. the gouernement LYDG., the secular affairs of a church HOBBES, a charity 1756, Athens GROTE, the finances of a college M. PATTISON. 3. To admynystre Ryght and Justyce FISHER. To a. the sacraments SANDYS, the Lord's Supper WESLEY, extreme unction PRESCOTT. † *To be administered*: to receive the sacrament. The Oath that we a. *Rich. II*, I. iii. 182. 5. To a. posset to the Gossips THACKERAY. Hence **Admi·niste·rial** *a.* pertaining to the administration or government. **Admi·nistrable** *a.* †**Admi·nistrer,** one who administers; fem. †**Admi·nistress.** var. **Admi·nistrate** *v.* (a sacrament, oath, medicine); hence †**Admi·nistrate** *ppl. a.* administered.

†**Admi·nister,** *sb.* [a. L.] A minister or administrator –1677.

Administrant (ădmi·nistrănt), *a.* 1602. Executive. As *sb.* An acting officer.

Administration (ădmi:nistrēⁱ·ʃən). ME. [ad. L. *administrationem*; see ADMINISTER *v.*] †1. The action of administering; service, attendance –1791; execution *of* –1611. 2. Management ME.; *ellipt.* the management of public affairs, government 1681; the executive part of the legislature, the ministry 1731. 3. *Law.* The management and disposal of the estate of a deceased person by an executor or administrator. *spec.* Authority to administer, conferred by *Letters of Administration.* 1538. 4. The action of administering something to others (see ADMINISTER *v.* 3, 4) ME.

1. [While] the Physician continues his a. HALE. The a. of an office BARCKLEY. 2. The a. of a few fields .. of a great country RUSKIN. Every measure of your grace's a. JUNIUS. A succession of weak administrations MACAULAY. 4. The a. of the sacrament ME., of war HALE, of an antidote WOOD. Hence **Administra·tional** *a.*

Administrative (ădmi·nistreⁱ:tiv), *a.* 1731. [ad. L. *administrativus*; see ADMINISTER.] 1. Pertaining to management; executive. 2. *absol.* An administrative body 1876. Hence **Admi·nistra·tively** *adv.*

Administrator (ădmi·nistreⁱ:təɹ, æ:dministrēⁱ·təɹ). 1514. [a. L.] 1. One who administers (see ADMINISTER 1) 1533; *absol.* one who has the faculty of organizing 1855. 2. One who executes or dispenses; one who applies, proffers, or gives (see ADMINISTER 3, 4, 5) 1563. 3. *Law.* a. One appointed trustee, steward, etc. during a minority or legal incapacity 1599. b. One appointed to administer an estate in default of an executor; an executor dative 1514.

1. The a. of Holstein LUTTRELL. The first of living administrators MACAULAY. 2. Administrators of Sacraments MAN, of justice MAULE. Hence **Admi·nistratorship.**

Admi·nistratrix. Pl. **-trixes** (triksĕz), **-trices** (trisīz). 1626. [a. L.] A female administrator; *spec.* a woman appointed to administer an intestate estate. Also **-tress** (*rare*).

Admirable (æ·dmirăb'l), *a.* 1596. [a. Fr.; see ADMIRE.] †1. To be wondered at –1794. Hence, 2. Exciting pleased surprise, or wonder united with approbation. In mod. usage the idea of *wonder* is lost. 1598. Also as *adv.* SHAKS.

1. Oh 'tis braue warres. Most a. *All's Well* II. i. 26. 2. A gentleman..of a. discourse *Merry W.* II. ii. 234. His wife takes a. care of him DICKENS. Hence **A·dmirableness.** **A·dmirably** *adv.* † wonderfully; excellently.

Admiral (æ·dmirăl), *sb.* ME. [a. OFr. *amiral*, fusion of Arab. *amir* and *-al-*, as in *amir-al-bahr*, Ameer (of) the Sea. Later, *am-* was treated as = Fr. *am-*:—L. *adm-*, whence *admiral*, which was then connected with med. L. *admirabilis*, etc.] †1. An emir or prince under the Sultan; any Saracen Commander –1561. 2. The commander-in-chief of a navy 1460. 3. A naval officer of the highest rank; a flag-officer c 1425. 4. The privileged commander of a fishing or merchant fleet 1708. 5. = *Admiral-ship* (cf. Fr. *le vaisseau amiral*): The ship which carries the admiral; the Flag-ship. 6. Two species of butterfly; the *Red Admiral* (*Vanessa Atalanta*), and the *White Admiral* (*Limenitis Sibylla*). 7. *Conch.* = *Admiral-shell*: a shell of the genus *Conus*.

1. Sone of the admyralle of babylone CAXTON. 2. Erle of Kente made Admyral of Englond CAXTON. *Lord High Admiral*: the full title of an officer or magistrate who had formerly the administrative duties now discharged by five *Lords Commissioners of the Admiralty*, and the judicial functions now vested in the *High Court of Admiralty*. 3. One Giles..a petty A. of four Ships MILT. *A. of the Fleet*, an officer ranking with a field-marshal; *A.*, *Vice-A.*, and *Rear-A.*, officers ranking with a general, lieutenant-general, and major-general respectively. *Admirals of the Red, White,* or *Blue*: so called from the colours hoisted by them. Hence *A. of the Blue*, (*joc.*) a *tapster* (from his blue apron): The A. of the Blue, crys, Coming Sir! 1731. 5. The mast Of some great Ammiral [It. *ammiraglia*] MILT. *Comb.* **a.-in-chief,** or **-in-general,** the supreme naval commander. Hence **A·dmiralling** *vbl. sb.* (cf. *a.-colonelling*, HUDIBRAS). **A·dmiralship,** the position of an a.; ability to perform the duties of an a.

†**A·dmiral,** *a.* [var. of ADMIRABLE, through *admirabilis*, a med.L. form of ADMIRAL *sb.*] Admirable –1650.

Admiralty (æ·dmirălti). ME. [a. OFr. *admiralté*; see ADMIRAL.] 1. The office or jurisdiction of an admiral ME. †2. The navy –1626. 3. The naval branch of the Executive; now in England the *Lords Commissioners of the A.* 1459. 4. The maritime branch of the administration of justice 1589. 5. With *the*: The building where the Lords of the Admiralty transact business 1617. 6. The command of the seas, pre-eminence on the sea. KIPLING *Seven Seas, Song of the English.*

1. His Badge or Token of the Amiraltye LELAND. 3. The admiralties of the allied powers MACAULAY. 4. *Court of A.*: the tribunal for the trial of maritime causes, formerly presided over by the Lord High Admiral, but now transferred to the Probate, Divorce, and Admiralty Division of the High Court of Justice. This judge of the A., Judge Jenkins PEPYS.

†**Admi·rance.** [a. OFr.] Admiration. SPENSER.

Admiration (ædmirēⁱ·ʃən). 1490. [a. Fr., ad. L. *admirationem*; see ADMIRE.] 1. The action of wondering or marvelling. *arch.* 1506. 2. Wonder mingled with reverence, esteem, approbation; gratified contemplation 1589. †3. Admirableness –1642. 4. An object of admiration; a marvel 1490. 5. *Note of admiration*: the mark (!).

1. A. is the daughter of ignorance FULLER. 2. The test of true a. is pleasure MOZLEY. 3. Admir'd Miranda! Indeede the top of a. *Temp.* III. i. 38. 4. Bring in the a. SHAKS. The prince..is the a. of the whole court 1716. 5. To skip over all sentences where he spied a note of a. at the end SWIFT.

Admire (ădməiə·ɹ), *v.* 1590. [a. Fr. *admirer*, refash. of OFr. *amirer*:—L. *admirari.*] 1. *intr.* To feel or express surprise or astonishment. *arch.* 2. *trans.* To view with wonder or surprise; to marvel at. *arch.* 1590. Hence 3. To gaze on with ADMIRATION (sense 2) 1594. †4. *causal.* To astonish –1650.

1. Admiring at the miracle FULLER. We may..a. that so beastly a drunkard lived so long FULLER. 2. Examples rather to be admired then imitated FULLER. 3. To a. the knowledge and promptness of [a] guide TYNDALL. Hence **A·dmira·tive** *a. rare*, characterized by admiration. **A·dmira·tively** *adv.* †**Admi·re** *sb.* admiration. **Admi·red** *ppl. a.* regarded with admiration; astonished. **Admi·redly** *adv.* in an admired manner; surprisingly. **Admi·ring** *vbl. sb.*

viewing with ADMIRATION (sense 2); *ppl. a.* full of admiration; †causing admiration. **Admi·ringly** *adv.* with admiration.

Admirer (ædmǝiǝ·rǝɹ). 1605. [f. ADMIRE *v.*] 1. One who admires (see ADMIRE *v.* 2, 3). 2. A lover 1704.

Admissible (ædmi·sib'l), *a.* 1611. [a. Fr., ad. late L. *admissibilem*; see ADMIT.] 1. Allowable, as an idea or project 1611, or (*Law*) as judicial proof 1849. 2. Worthy of being admitted to an office or relation, or to the use of a place 1775.

1. An a. supposition HALE. Parol evidence..is a. BEST. 2. A. to the English markets McCULLOCH. Hence **Admi·ssibi·lity. Admi·ssibleness.**

Admission (ædmi·ʃǝn). 1494. [ad. L. *admissionem*; see ADMIT, and distinguish from ADMITTANCE the literal action of letting in.] 1. The action of admitting to a place and its privileges, a society, or class of things. Also, the fact of being admitted, access. 1622. 2. Institution or acceptance into an office or position 1494. 3. The admitting (*of* anything) as proper, valid, or true 1538. 4. *Law*, and *gen.* A concession, an acknowledgement 1808.

1. The a. of poor suitors without fee BACON. The free a. of the light of Heaven RUSKIN. 2. This formal a. of St. Matthias into the number of the Apostles BEVERIDGE. 3. The a. of supernatural truths SULLIVAN. 4. His wife's a. that she had agreed to pay [etc.] PEAKE.

Admissive (ædmi·siv), *a.* 1778. [ad. L. *admissivus*; see ADMIT.] Characterized by admitting; tending to admit. var. **Admi·ssory** *a.*

Admit (ædmi·t), *v.* ME. [a. OFr. *amettre* :—L. *admittere*, f. *ad* + *mittere*; refash. after L.] I. As a voluntary agent. 1. To allow to enter, let in, receive; *spec.* in *Law*, into the possession of a copyhold estate. 2. *fig.* To consent to, permit ME.; to acknowledge, as lawful, etc. 1538; to concede, as true, etc. 1532. Also with *of* 1649.

1. Obsolete words are admitted JOHNSON. To a. air TYNDALL. Admitted a Commoner 1713, to benefices BURNET. Mirth, a. me of thy crew MILT. 2. She will a. no kinde of suite *Twel. N.* I. ii. 45. To a. a prayer SHENSTONE, delay JAS. MILL. To a. a title SHAKS. *John* II. i. 200, a claim to tribute WELLESLEY. To a. the outline of a story FREEMAN.

II. As an involuntary agent. 1. *trans.* To be the channel of admission to; to afford entrance 1703. 2. To have room for 1661. 3. To lie open to, be compatible with. *arch.* 1538. Also with *of* 1718.

1. This order admits the whole party (*mod.*). 2. The passage admits two abreast (*mod.*). 3. My loue admits no qualifying crosse *Tr. & Cr.* IV. iv. 9. [His] conduct admitted..of no apology MAR. EDGEWORTH. Hence **Admi·ttable** *a.* orig. = ADMISSIBLE, now lit.: Capable of being admitted to a place or as a fact; var. **Admittible. Admi·ttedly** *adv.* by general admission. **Admi·tter**, one who admits (senses I. 1, 2). †**Admi·ttie** (*rare*), admittance. B. JONS. **Admi·tting** *vbl. sb.* willing or official reception; mental assent; acknowledgement.

Admittance (ædmi·tăns). 1589. [f. ADMIT, after *assistance*, etc.] 1. The action of admitting (see ADMIT I. 1); permission to enter; the fact of being admitted 1593. †2. Admissibility -1598. †3. Admitting as valid, true, etc. -1622.

1. 'Tis Gold which buyes a. *Cymb.* II. iii. 73. A. to office in the Church HOOKER, into favor J. MORRIS. A. is the last stage..of copyhold assurances BLACKSTONE. 2. A gentleman..of great a. *Merry W.* II. ii. 235. 3. A. of a tenet J. SWAN.

Admix (ædmi·ks), *v. rare.* 1533. [f. L. *ad* + MIX :—OE. *miscan*; see ADMIXT.] To mingle with something else. *trans.* and *intr.*

Admixt (ædmi·kst), *ppl. a.* ME. [ad. L. *admixtus, admiscere*; spelt later *admixed*, as if pa. pple. of ADMIX *v.*] Mingled with.

Admixtion (ædmi·kstiǝn). ME. [ad. L. *admixtionem*: see ADMIXT.] The mingling of one thing with another.

Admixture (ædmi·kstiŭɹ). 1605. [f. L. *admixt-*; see ADMIXT.] 1. The action of mingling as an ingredient; the fact of being so mingled 1605. 2. That which is mixed with anything; an alloy 1665.

Admonish (ædmǫ·niʃ), *v.* [ME. *amonesten*, a. OFr. *amonester* :—late L. *admonestare*, f. *admonere*. The *-t* was treated as the ppl. ending, and *a-* was refash. after L.] 1. *gen.* To put in mind of duties; to counsel, to warn ME. †2. To inculcate ME. 3. To put in mind, charge, exhort, *to do* ME. 4. To put in mind, warn (*of, against, for, that*, etc.) 1541. 5. To put in mind, inform (*of, that*, etc.) 1574.

1. A. him as a brother 2 *Thess.* iii. 15. 3. Admonyst your people to do well their deuoyre LD. BERNERS. 4. He would admonest..him of his lacke in diligence ELYOT. 5. He shall be admonished of the King's pleasure BRAMHALL. Hence **Admo·nisher**, a monitor. **Admo·nishingly** *adv.*

Admonishment (ædmǫ·niʃmĕnt). ME. [a. OFr. *amonestement*; see ADMONISH.] The action of admonishing, or being admonished; an ADMONITION (sense 2).

Admonition (æ·dmŏni·ʃǝn). ME. [a. OFr. *amonition*, later *admonition*, ad. L. *admonitionem*, f. *admonere*.] 1. The action of admonishing; authoritative counsel; warning, reproof. 2. An act of admonishing; a statement of counsel or (ecclesiastical) censure 1526.

1. These things..are written for our a. 1 *Cor.* x. 11. A. or reproof JOHNSON. 2. A. is the lowest of Ecclesiasticall censures FULLER. Hence †**Admoni·tioner**, a monitor; *spec.* in *pl.* The Puritans who in 1571 presented an a. to Parliament, condemning the ceremonies of the Church of England. var. **Admo·nitor**, fem. **Admo·nitrix**; hence **Admo·nito·rial** *a.* (*rare*) = ADMONITORY.

Admonitory (ædmǫ·nitǝri), *a.* 1594. [ad. L. *admonitorius*.] Of or pertaining to an admonitor; giving admonition.

An a. glance SCOTT. A raised a. finger DICKENS.

Admortization, var. of AMORTIZATION.

†**Admo·ve**, *v.* ME. [ad. L. *admovere*.] 1. To move to or towards -1646. 2. To advance 1839. Hence **Admo·tive** *a.* characterized by motion towards.

†**Adna·scent**, *a.* 1664. [ad. L. *adnascentem, adnasci*.] Growing or produced upon something else. Hence **Adna·scence**, adhesion of parts to each other by the whole surface.

Adnate (æ·dnēɪt), *a.* 1661. [ad. L. *adnatus*; see also AGNATE.] †1. Acquired -1677. 2. *Phys.* and *Bot.* Attached congenitally by the whole surface; grown to congenitally 1661.

Adnation (ædnēɪ·ʃǝn). 1842. [f. prec.] Growth to; *esp.* in *Bot.* of different whorls of the inflorescence to each other.

Adnominal (ædnǫ·minăl), *a.* 1845. [f. L. *adnomen*.] Of or belonging to an adnoun; attached to a noun.

The adjective in [its attributive use] is a. HADLEY.

Adnoun (æ·dnaun). 1753. [f. L. *ad* + NOUN; cf. mod.F. *adnom*.] An adjective; *spec.* an adj. used substantively.

†**Adnu·mber**, *v.* [f. L. *ad* + NUMBER *v.*] To count in -1561.

Ado (ădū·), *sb.*, prop. *v. inf.* = **at do.** ME. [f. *a-* (see A- *pref.* 5) + DO.] 1. *pres. inf.* To do; *esp.* in *to have ado.* (Cf. Fr. *avoir affaire*, orig. *avoir à faire*.) 2. In doing; astir 1577. Hence, through *much ado*, etc., by taking the adverbs as adjs. qualifying *ado*: 3. *sb.* (pl. rare, *adoes, ados.*) Doing, fuss ME. 4. Labour, trouble 1485.

1. I will nowt have a. ther with SIR J. PASTON. 2. An eager bustling, that rather keeps a. than does anything EARLE. 3. *Without more ado* FREEMAN. 4. Quaking bogs, which we shall have our own ados to make..habitable CARLYLE.

†**Ado**, *pa. pple.* 1554. [for *ido, ydo, ydon*; see A- *particle*.] Done. *Dead for ado*: dead and done with. *Once for ado*: once for all. -1642.

-ado, *suffix* of sbs. 1. a. Sp. or Pg. *-ado* masc. of pa. pple., as *desperado* :—L. *desperatus*. 2. Refash. of sbs. in *-ade*, a. Fr. *-ade* fem. (= Sp. *-ada*, It. *-ata*), perh. on the erron. analogy of *renegade* = *renegado*.

‖**Adobe** (ădōᵘ·bi, ădōᵘ·b). 1834. [Sp., through U.S. from Mexico.] An unburnt brick dried in the sun. Also *attrib.*

†**Ado·d**, *int.* 1708. [for *Ah God!* cf. *adad*, etc.] -1762.

Adolescence (ædǫle·sĕns). ME. [a. Fr., ad. L. *adolescentia*; see next.] The process or condition of growing up; the growing age; youth; the period between childhood and maturity, extending from 14 to 25 in males, from 12 to 21 in females. Also *fig.*

fig. [A Disease] of National A. CARLYLE.

Adolescency (ædǫle·sĕnsi). ME. [ad. L. *adolescentia*.] The quality or state of being adolescent; *youthfulness*, as opp. to *youth*.

Adolescent (ædǫle·sĕnt). 1482. [as sb. a. Fr., ad. L. *adolescentem*; see ADULT.] A. *sb.* A person in the age of adolescence. B. *adj.* Growing from childhood to maturity 1785.

B. I see Near manhood in thy a. limbs B. TAYLOR.

†**Adon.** [a. Fr., a. L., var. of *Adonis* (q. v.).] Adonis; a fop. SHAKS.

‖**Adonai** (ădōᵘnāi, ædǫnēɪ·ǝi). 1483. [Heb.] A name of the Supreme Being; in O. T. 'Lord'; substituted by the Jews, in reading, for *Jahveh*, the 'ineffable name'.

Adonic (ădǫ·nik). 1678. [ad. Fr. *adonique*, ad. med.L. *adonicus*; cf. *Sapphicus*, etc.] A. *adj.* Of or relating to Adonis; in *Pros.* used of a metre, consisting of a dactyl and a spondee (— ◡ ◡ | — —). B. *sb.* [sc. *verse* or *line*.] 1753. var. **Ado·nian.**

Adonis (ădōᵘ·nis). 1597. [Gr., ad. Phoen. *adon* lord; a Heb. name of God.] 1. In Gr. Mythology, a youth beloved by Venus for his beauty: hence, a beau 1765. †2. A kind of wig -1775. 3. A genus of plants, N.O. *Ranunculaceæ*, including Pheasant's Eye 1597. 4. A butterfly (*Polyommatus Adonis*).

2. A fine flowing a. or white periwig 1775. Hence **Adone·an** *a.* **A·donize** *v.* to dandify. *trans.* and *intr.*

†**Ado·nist.** 1751. [f. ADONAI.] In *pl.*: A Hebrew sect, differing from the Jehovists, *esp.* as to whether the word Adonai is always read for the word Jehovah.

†**A-doors**, prop. **a doors, a door.** 1526. = both *of doors* (see A *prep.*[2]), and *at doors* (cf. *a-do*).

Cf. Driven out of doores with it *Com. Err.* IV. iv. 36. As you went in at doors MARLOWE.

†**Ado·perate**, *v.* [f. med.L. *adoperat-*; *adoperare*; see OPERATE.] To bring into operation -1681. Hence **Ado:pera·tion.**

Adopt (ădǫ·pt), *v.* 1548. [a. Fr. *adopter*, ad. L. *adoptare*.] 1. To take voluntarily into any relationship 1548; *esp.* that of a son 1604. 2. To take up from another and use as one's own 1607; *spec.* in *Philol.* To take a foreign word into use without changing its form (*mod.*). 3. To take (a course, etc.) as a matter of choice 1769. †4. *causal.* To affiliate, attach, to any one. [L. *se alicui adoptare*.] POPE. †5. To christen or rechristen -1601.

1. To a. as heyre HALL, as sonne in law BARCKLEY, as favourites JOHNSON. Rather to a. a Child, than get it *Oth.* I. iii. 191. 2. To a. a policy SHAKS., systems CHESTERFIELD, Egyptian habits FROUDE. 3. He adopted one posture H. MARTINEAU. The resolutions were adopted 1875. 4. Adopted to a foreign land POPE. Hence **Ado:ptabi·lity**, capability of being adopted; *concr.* an adoptable thing. **Ado·ptable** *a.* **Ado·ptedly** *adv.* **Ado·ptive** *a.* due to adoption; having the habit of adopting. **Ado·ptively** *adv.* by way of adoption.

†**Ado·ptant.** 1671. [a. Fr., ad. L. *adoptantem*.] One who adopts.

Adopter (ădǫ·ptǝɹ). 1572. [f. ADOPT.] 1. One who adopts, *esp.* an adoptive father. 2. One who adopts an opinion, etc. (see ADOPT *v.* 2, 3) 1829. 3. *Chem.* = ADAPTER 2.

Adoption (ădǫ·pʃǝn). ME. [ad. L. *adoptionem*, f. †*adopt-*, whence *adoptare*.] 1. The action of adopting or fact of being adopted (see ADOPT *v.* 1) ME. 2. Taking up and treating as one's own 1598; *spec.* in *Philol.* taking a foreign word into use without changing its form; a word so taken; also used *passively* 1755.

1. The friends thou hast, and their a. tride *Haml.* I. iii. 62. A. into immortal palaces LAMB. 2. The country of his own a. SEELEY. Which [words] depend for their a. on the suffrage of futurity JOHNSON. Hence **Ado·ptional** *a.* †**Ado·ptious** *a.* of or connected with a. SHAKS.

Adoptionist (ădǫ·pʃǝnist). 1847. [f. ADOPTION.] *Eccl. Hist.* One of a sect who maintained that Jesus Christ is the son of God by adoption only. Also used *attrib.*

‖**Ador.** ME. [L.] Sacrificial grain, spelt.

Adorable (ădōǝ·răb'l), *a.* 1611. [a. Fr.,

ad. L. *adorabilem*; see ADORE.] 1. Worthy of divine worship. 2. By exaggeration, said of anything to which one is passionately attached or for which one has a great regard 1710.

1. The a. wisdom of God BURKE. 2. A. places SHAFTESBURY. Hence **Adorabi·lity. Ado·rableness. Ado·rably** *a.*

Adoral (ædōə·răl), *a.* 1882. [f. L. *ad* + *or-*, mouth + -AL.] Situated at the mouth. Cf. ABORAL. Hence A·do·rally *adv.*

Adoration (ædŏrē¹·ʃən). 1543. [a. Fr., ad. L. *adorationem*; see ADORE.] 1. The act of worshipping, or paying divine honours. 2. *fig.* The exhibition of profound regard and love 1601. 3. *techn.* A method of electing a pope by a low reverence before the same candidate from two-thirds of the voters present 1599.

1. A. is .. the prostration of the Soul LIDDON. 2. How does he loue me? With adorations *Twel. N.* I. v. 274.

Adore (ădōə·ɹ), *v.* 1483. [ad. (O)F. *adorer*, replacing OF. *aourer*:—L. *adorare*: see AD- 1 and ORATE.] 1. *trans.* To make an act of the mind and will in acknowledgement of the infinite perfection of (God); to make an outward reverence expressing such an act, e.g. a bow, genuflexion, etc. b. To venerate with relative or representative honours 1582. c. To elect (a pope) by ADORATION 1670. d. *absol.* or *intr.* 1582. 2. To regard with the utmost reverence and affection 1594. ¶Confused with ADORN.

1. To preye and adoure god Almyghty CAXTON. The host, which he publicly adored SMOLLETT. 2. My soul adores judiciall schollership MARSTON. ¶The hore Congealed litle drops, which doe the morne adore SPENSER. Hence †**Ado·rative** *a.* pertaining to adoration. †**Ado·rement**, *rare.* **Ado·rer**, a worshipper; *fig.* a lover. **Ado·ringly** *adv.*

Adorn (ădǭ·ɹn), *v.* [ME. *aorne*, a. OFr. *aorner*:—L. *adornare*. Refash. after L.; see also ANORN.] 1. To be an ornament to; to beautify, add lustre to ME.; also *fig.* ME.; and hence, of persons 1534. 2. To furnish with ornaments; to deck or embellish (*with*) ME. Also *fig.* †3. To deck out speciously, dress up –1622. ¶ By confusion with ME. *adoren*: To adore 1470.

1. A Garland to adorne Her Tresses MILT. *fig.* The piety which adorns his character (*mod.*). A new Cibber shall the stage a. POPE. 2. Aourned as a king CAXTON. As a bride adorneth herselfe with her jewels *Isa.* lxi. 10. The .. vertues with which he has adorned his mind BURKE. Hence †**Ado·rn** *sb.* adornment. †**Adorna·tion**, the act of adorning, ornament. **Ado·rned** *ppl. a.* furnished with ornaments, or with qualities that give distinction. **Ado·rner. Ado·rningly** *adv.*

†**Ado·rn**, *a. rare.* [f. It. *adorno*, short f. *adornato*:—L. *adornatus*; see ADORN *v.*] Adorned.

Made so a. for thy delight the more MILT.

†**Adorna·tion.** 1597. [f. L. *adornat-*, *adornare*; see ADORN.] The act of adorning; ornament.

Adornment (ădǭ·ɹnmĕnt). 1480. [a. OFr. *aournement*, later *adornement*; see ADORN.] 1. The action of adorning. 2. That which adorns; an ornament. With *pl.* 1489.

Adosculation (ædǫskiulē¹·ʃən). 1674. [f. L. *adosculat-*, *adosculari.*] Impregnation by mere contact, without intromission.

‖**Adossée** (adose, ădǭ·si), *ppl. a.* [Fr.] *Her.* = ADDORSED.

Adown (ădau·n). *arch.* [OE. *of dúne*, L. *de monte* (see DOWN *sb.*, and cf. OFr. *à val* :—L. *ad vallem*). Soon aphet. to *dun*, *doun*, DOWN.] A. *adv.* 1. To a lower place; downward, down OE. *fig.* ME. †2. In a lower place; *esp.* on earth OE.

1. His .. collar hung a. SCOTT. 2. In this erthe adoun CHAUCER.

B. *prep.* (with obj.) Downwards upon or along ME. Also *fig.*

Adoune the staire CHAUCER. A. the sky PHILLIPS, the Pyrenees BYRON. *fig.* A. life's latter days M. ARNOLD. Hence †**Adownright** = DOWNRIGHT. †**Adow·nward** *adv.* = DOWNWARD; *prep.* = ADOWN *prep.*

Adp-, obs. f. APP-.

Adpress (ædpre·s), *v.* 1872. [f. L. *adpress-*, *adprimere.*] To press close to. Hence **Adpre·ssed** *ppl. a.* pressed close to, as hairs on stems.

‖**Adpromissor** (ædprǫmi·səɹ, -oɹ). [a. L.] *Rom. Law.* One who gives bail or security.

Adq-, obs. f. ACQ-.

Adra·d, *ppl. a. arch.* ME. [prob. weak f. *of-drad*, pa. pple. of OF-DREDE.] Frightened.

I was the less a. Of what might come MORRIS.

Adradial (ædrē¹·diăl), *a.* 1880. [f. L. *ad* + *radius.*] Situated near or beside a ray. b. *sb.* An adradial organ.

†**Adrea·d**, *v.* OE. [A- *pref.* 4.] To dread.

†**Adrea·med**, *pple.* 1556. *To be a.*, to dream.

Adrenal (ædˌrī·năl), *a.* and *sb.* 1875. [f. AD- 1 + L. *renes* kidneys.] *Anat.* = SUPRARENAL. Hence **Adrenalin** (-rī·nălin), a crystalline substance extracted from the adrenal glands, used as a hæmostatic.

†**Adre·nch**, *v.* ME. only. [f. A- *pref.* 1 + DRENCH, OE. *drencan.*] To give to drink; *trans.* to submerge, drown; *refl.* to drown (oneself); *intr.* to 'go down', as a ship. *lit.* and *fig.*

Adrift (ădri·ft), *adv.* 1624. [f. A *prep.*[1] + DRIFT. Cf. *afloat.*] Drifting, at the mercy of wind and tide. *fig.* 1690.

With all his .. trees a. MILT. *fig.* The mind .. a. YOUNG.

†**Adrip**, *adv.* 1867. [A *prep.*[1] + DRIP.] Dripping.

Adrogate (æ·drǫgē¹t), *v.* Also **arrogate.** 1649. [f. L. *adrogat-*, *adrogare.*] *Rom. Law.* To adopt a person who was at the time his own master or *sui juris.* Hence, **A·drogated** *ppl. a.* adopted when *sui juris.* **A:droga·tion.** Also **arrogation. A·droga·tor,** he who adrogates. Also **arrogator.**

Adroit (ădroi·t), *a.* 1652. [a. Fr., orig. *à droit*, OFr. *dreit*:—late L. *drictum*:—cl. L. *directum*; see DIRECT.] Possessing address or readiness of resource, either bodily or mental; dexterous, active, clever.

A. cavalry EVELYN, wrestlers 1825, intriguers MOTLEY. Hence **Adroi·tly** *adv.* **Adroi·tness**, the quality of being a.; skill and readiness, either bodily or mental.

†**Adro·p.** 1471. *Alch.* Lead; the philosopher's stone. B. JONS.

Adrostral (ædrǫ·străl), *a.* 1878. [f. L. *ad* + *rostrum.*] *Zool.* Pertaining to or at the beak or snout.

Adry·, *adv.* 1599. [f. DRY *a.*; cf. *acold*, etc.] In a dry condition; thirsty.

Ads, var. of ODS, 'minced' form of *God's*.

Adscititious (æ:dsiti·ʃəs), *a.*; also **asc-.** 1620. [f. L. *adscit-* (*ascit-*), *adsciscere.*] Assumed, adopted from without; supplemental; additional.

A. habits EVELYN. Initial vowels .. not radical, but a. M. MÜLLER. Hence **A·dsciti·tiously** *adv.*

Adscript (æ·dskript). 1822. [ad. L. *adscriptus*, *adscribere.*] A. *adj.* 1. Written after, opp. to *subscript.* 2. For med.L. *adscriptus* (*glebæ*), attached (to the soil), and therefore passing with it. Said of feudal serfs. B. *sb.* = *adj.* 2 used subst. var. **Adscri·pted** *ppl. a.* Hence **Adscripti·tious** *a.* bound by adscription.

Adscription (ădskri·pʃən). 1660. [ad. L. *adscriptionem*; see ASCRIPTION.] 1. = ASCRIPTION 1857. †2. *spec.* Circumscribing or inscribing geometrical figures –1660. 3. Attachment as an ADSCRIPT 1872.

Adsignify (ădsi·gnifəi), *v. rare.* 1798. [ad. L. *adsignificare.*] To signify an action with an addition of time, as in tenses. Hence **Adsi·gnifica·tion.**

Adsorption (ædsǭ·ɹpʃen). 1882. [f. L. *ad* + *-sorption*; see ABSORPTION.] Condensation of gases on surfaces of solids.

†**Adspira·tion.** = ASPIRATION.

Adstipulate (ădsti·piulē¹t), *v.* [f. L. *a(d)stipulat-*, *a(d)stipulari.*] *Rom. Law.* To act as second stipulant or receiving party to a bargain. Hence **Adsti·pula·tion**, the addition of, or acting as, a second stipulant. **Adsti·pula·tor**, a second stipulant who stipulates in the same terms as the first.

Adstrict, -ion, -ory, obs. vars. of ASTRICT, -ION, -ORY.

Adstringe, -ent, obs. vars. of ASTRINGE, -ENT.

‖**Adula·ria.** 1798. [f. *Adula*, Switzerland.] A variety of Orthoclase.

Adulate (æ·diulē¹t), *v.* 1777. [f. L. *adulat-*, *adulari.*] To flatter basely or slavishly. Hence **A·dula·tor.**

Adulation (æ:diulē¹·ʃən). ME. [a. OFr. *adulacion*, ad. L. *adulationem*; see ADULATE.] Servile flattery or homage; exaggerated and hypocritical praise.

Flatery and adulacioun CHAUCER. Titles blowne from a. *Hen. V*, IV. i. 271.

Adulatory (æ·diulătəri), *a.* 1611. [ad. L. *adulatorius.*] Of or belonging to an adulator; servilely or fulsomely flattering.

A. addresses BURKE. A style rather too a. HALLAM.

Adullamite (ădʋ·lăməit). ME. [f. *Adullam.*] 1. *prop.* An inhabitant of Adullam; see *Gen.* xxxviii. 12. 2. A frequenter of the cave of Adullam. *fig.* A name founded on the application by Mr. Bright of 1 *Sam.* xxii. 1, 2, to certain members of the British House of Commons who in 1866 seceded from the Liberal party on the question of Parliamentary Reform.

2. The little third party were at once christened the Adullamites McCARTHY.

Adult (ădʋ·lt, æ·dʋlt), *a.* 1531. [ad. L. *adultus*, *adolescere.*] Grown up, having reached the age of maturity. *fig.* Full-grown 1670. As *sb.* [sc. *person*] 1658.

Adult Baptism: the baptism of adults only; opp. to *Infant Baptism.* Hence †**Adu·lted** *ppl. a.* grown to maturity. *rare.* **Adu·lthood. Adu·ltness.**

†**Adu·lter.** [ME. *avouter*, a. OFr. *avoutre*, *aoutre*:—L. *adulterum* (perh. f. *ad* + *alter*); see ADULTERER.] An adulterer.

†**Adu·lter**, *v.* [ME. *avoutre*, a. OFr. *avoutrer*, *aoutrer*:—L. *adulterare*; refash. after L.] 1. To commit adultery –1775. 2. *fig.* = ADULTERATE –1651.

Adulterant (ădʋ·ltĕrănt). 1755. [ad. L. *adulterantem*; see ADULTER *v.*] A. *sb.* That which adulterates. B. *adj.* Adulterating 1881.

Adulterate (ădʋ·ltĕrĕt), *ppl. a.* 1590. [ad. L. *adulteratus*; see ADULTER *v.*] 1. Stained by adultery, either in origin or conduct; adulterous. 2. Spurious; base in origin or by intermixture 1592.

1. Possest with an a. blot *Com. Err.* II. ii. 142. Th' a. Hastings *Rich. III*, IV. iii. 69. 2. Th' a. Beauty of a falsed Cheek DANIELL. To discern between true and a. Justice HOBBES. A. copper SWIFT.

Adulterate (ădʋ·ltĕrē¹t), *v.* 1531. [f. L. *adulterat-*, *adulterare*, replacing ADULTER *v.*] †1. *intr.* = mod. *To commit adultery* –1698. †2. *trans.* To debauch –1678. 3. To render counterfeit, corrupt, debase, *esp.* by base admixture 1531.

1. She adulterates hourely with thine Vnckle Iohn SHAKS. *John* III. i. 56. 2. To murder Uriah and a. his wife MILT. 3. To a. coin with a more base metal ELYOT, scripture with false gloses MORE, our tongue with strange words ADDISON. Hence **Adulterated** *ppl. a.* = ADULTERATE *a.* 1, 2. **Adu·lterately** *adv.* **Adu·lterateness. Adu·lterator,** †an adulterer; one who debases, etc. by spurious admixture.

Adulterer (ădʋ·ltĕrəɹ). [ME. *avou-*, *avow-* *-terer*, *-trer*, f. *avouter*, ADULTER *v.* Displaced *adulter*, etc. in 17th c.] 1. One who commits adultery ME. Of a woman *c* 1550. †2. = ADULTERATOR –1650.

Adulteress (ădʋ·ltĕrĕs, -trĕs). [ME. *avoutres*, *avoutresse*, a. OFr. *avoutresse*, and fem. of ADULTER, not of prec.] A woman that commits adultery.

Adulterine (ădʋ·ltĕrəin), *a.* 1542. [ad. L. *adulterinus*, f. *adulter.*] 1. Born of adultery 1751. 2. Of or relating to adultery (*mod.*). 3. *fig.* Due to adulteration; spurious 1542. 4. Illegal, unlicensed; *esp.* in *Eng. Hist.* Adulterine castles, guilds 1640.

Adulterize (ădʋ·ltĕrəiz), *v. arch.* 1611. [f. ADULTER *sb.*] To commit adultery. Hence **Adu·lterism.** *rare.*

Adulterous (ădʋ·ltĕrəs), *a.* 1470. [f. ADULTER.] 1. Pertaining to or characterized by adultery. †2. = ADULTERINE 1. –1607. 3. Pertaining to or characterized by adulteration. *arch.* 1567.

1. A. Anthony SHAKS. An a. union (*mod.*). 3. An a. mixture SMOLLETT. Hence Adu·lterously *adv.*

Adultery (ădɒ·ltĕri). [ME. *avou-, avow--trie, -terie*, a. OFr. *avouterie, avoutrie*, f. *avoutre, aoutre*:—L. *adulter*; refash. *adultery*, as if orig. formed on L. *adulterium.*] 1. a. Violation of the marriage bed; sexual relation of a married person with one who is not his or her lawful spouse, whether unmarried (*single adultery*) or married to another (*double adultery*). In moral theology sometimes extended to irregular sexual intercourse gen.; in biblical use, idol-worship, idolatry (cf. *fornication*); *Eccl.* enjoyment by one of a benefice during the lifetime of the lawful incumbent or the translation of a bishop. †2. Adulteration -1673.

1. Of [Dame Katryne Swynford] in double Avoutry gottyn 1485. Whosoeuer loketh on a woman to lust after her, hath committed aduoutrie with her already in his hart *Matt.* v. 28 (Geneva). A. was long unknown at Sparta THIRLWALL. b. Shee..committed a. with stones and with stockes *Jer.* iii. 9. 2. Th' adulteries of Art B. JONS.

Adumbrate (æ·dɒmbrēˈt), *v.* 1581. [f. L. *adumbrat-, adumbrare.*] †1. To shade (and so complete) a sketch 1599. 2. To represent the shadow of; to outline; to sketch 1641. 3. *fig.* To represent by 'shadow' or emblem; to typify; hence, to foreshadow 1581. 4. To overshadow, darken 1670.

2. Adumbrated and obscurely indicated 1692. 3. Noah is adumbrated to us.. in Prometheus GALE. 4. Good qualities.. adumbrated by.. defects 1670. Hence Adu·mbral *a.* shady; *Zool.* = ADUMBRELLAR. Adu·mbrative *a.* having the attribute of adumbrating. Adu·mbratively *adv.*

Adumbration (ædɒmbrēˈ·ʃən). 1531. [ad. L. *adumbrationem*; see ADUMBRATE.] †1. Shading in painting -1531. 2. Representation in outline; *concr.* a sketch; a shadowy figure; a faint description 1552. 3. Symbolic representation 1622. 4. *Her.* An outline figure 1610. 5. Overshadowing; obscuration 1653.

2. Far-off hints and adumbrations LOWELL. The Prime Minister's a. of measures (*mod.*). 3. An Emblem or A. of our passage through life HARTLEY.

Adumbrellar (æ·dɪɒmbre·lăɪ), *a.* 1881. [f. L. *ad* + UMBRELLA. Cf. *adoral.*] *Zool.* Pertaining to the upper surface of the *velum*, which is turned towards the 'umbrella' or disk, in sea-blubbers; opp. to *abumbrellar.*

Adunation (ædiunēˈ·ʃən). 1555. [ad. L. *adunationem.*] Union into one.

Adunc (ădɒ·ŋk), *a.* 1626. [ad. L. *aduncus.* Hooked. Hence †Adu·ncity, hookedness. Adu·ncous *a.* hooked, incurved.

Adu·ncate, *v.* 1823. [f. med.L. *aduncat-, aduncare*; see ADUNC.] To curve inward. (Only in pa. pple.)

†Adu·re, *v.* ME. [ad. L. *adurere.*] To burn completely; to scorch, parch -1626. Hence †Adu·rent *ppl. a.* BACON.

A-du·sk, *adv.* 1856. [A *prep.*[1] + DUSK.] In dusk, dark. MRS. BROWNING.

Adust (ădɒ·st), *ppl. a.* ME. [ad. L. *adustus*; see ADURE.] 1. Scorched; burnt up; parched. Also *fig.* 1550. 2. Brown, as if scorched; sunburnt 1596. 3. *Med.* Characterized by dryness of the body, heat, thirst, burnt colour of the blood and little serum in it, etc. *Obs.* exc. in gen. sense, atrabilious, sallow, gloomy, etc. ME.

1. The Lybian air a. MILT. A. wine 1684. An a. taste HALES. 2. Here [in Spain] everything is a. and tawny FORD. 3. Choller a., and melancholie BAKER. Hence †Adu·st *v.* to burn; to dry up with heat. Also *fig.* Adu·sted *ppl. a.* = ADUST *a.* †Adu·stive *a.* fiery.

Adu·st, *adv.* and *a.* 1863. [A- *prep.*[1] + DUST.] In a dusty condition.

†Adustion. 1533. [ad. L. *adustionem*; see ADURE.] 1. The action of making ADUST -1725. 2. The state of being ADUST (senses 1, 3) -1725.

‖**Ad valorem** (æ·d vălōᵊ·rem). 1711. [L.] 'In proportion to the value'; a phrase applied to a mode of levying customs-duties upon goods when these are taxed at rates proportioned to their estimated value.

Silk goods [pay] an *ad valorem* duty of 30 per cent. 1825.

Advance (ădvɑ·ns), *v.* [ME. *auancen, avancen*, a. OFr. *avancer*:—pop. L. *abanteare*, f. *abante* (Fr. *avant*), f. *ab* + *ante*; see AD- 2, for *a-* = *ab-* becoming *ad-*.] I. To move forward *in place.* 1. To move, put, or push forward (*lit.* and *fig.*) 1509; *intr.* and *fig.* to go forward, make progress in life, etc. 1513. 2. Of a process or thing in course: To forward, help on ME.; *refl.* and *intr.* to progress towards completion 1644. 3. To put forward for notice, present 1509.

1. Brauely a. your..shields HEYWOOD. They had ..advanced about a mile DE FOE. *fig.* To a. in knowledge LOCKE, in life JOHNSON, commercially CRUMP. 2. To a. hostile preparations WELLESLEY, one's views KANE. As the work advances (*mod.*). 3. To a. arguments BENTLEY, a claim SOUTHEY.

II. To move forward *in time.* 1. To make earlier 1481. 2. To pay before due; and hence, to pay or lend on security of future reimbursement 1679.

1. The..benefits my death advances you TOURNEUR. 2. I will a. him £50 on your note-of-hand (*mod.*).

III. To move upward. 1. To raise or lift up. *lit.* and *fig. arch.* 1475. 2. To raise or promote in rank, etc., to put in a better position ME. 3. *Law.* To provide for children, *esp.* in anticipation of the provisions of a will, etc. ME. †4. *fig.* To extol; to boast -1660. 5. To raise in †amount, rate, or price 1691. *intr.* 1882. †6. To be over and above. (Cf. It. *avanzare.*) -1601.

1. The fringed Curtains of thine eyes aduance *Temp.* I. ii. 408. Advancing high The..floating Pageantry WORDSW. 2. To a. preests and clerks by prebends [etc.] 1461. To a. his family FREEMAN. 4. Praise and a. [the Lord] for ever FRITH. 5. The Bank has advanced the rate of discount to 5% (*mod.*). Rupee paper has fractionally advanced (*mod.*). Hence †Adva·nceable *a.* Adva·ncingly *adv.*

Advance (ădvɑ·ns), *sb.* 1496. [partly a. Fr. *avance*, f. *avancer*; and see prec.] I. A going forward, onward, or upward. 1. Forward motion; also *ellipt.* the order to move forward *a* 1674; *fig.* progress 1668; a step forward 1860. 2. A personal approach, an overture 1678. 3. A rise in amount, value, or price 1677.

1. The enemy's a. CLARENDON. The A. has been sounded (*mod.*). These are the days of a. TENNYSON. A very great a. DICKENS. 2. To make advances towards a reconciliation MACAULAY. 3. An a. in the..rate of discount CRUMP.

II. A putting forward. †1. = ADVANCEMENT -1696. †2. The putting forward of statements; an allegation -1699. 3. Payment in anticipation, or on security; hence, a loan 1681.

3. A weeks wages a. SWIFT. Life assurances..as security for advances CRUMP.

III. A being forward. The state of being before, to the front, or above 1668.

Much in a. of the rates of goods CHILD. Hutton was in a. of the speculation of his time HUXLEY. *In advance*: a. Of place, Ahead; b. Of time, Beforehand; c. In the position of having advanced money on account.

Comb., etc.: a.-guard, a guard before or in front of the main body of an army; -proofs, -sheets, parts of a work supplied previously to publication.

Advanced (ădvɑ·nst), *ppl. a.* 1460. [f. ADVANCE *v.*] 1. Moved forward, standing to the front 1795. 2. *fig.* Far on in life, time, etc. 1534. †3. Promoted -1681. †4. Raised (physically) -1673. 5. Raised (in amount) 1782.

1. A. guard, post, works (*Mil.*). 2. A. period of life DIGBY, beliefs SIR T. BROWNE, truths of mathematics MILL, political opinions (*mod.*).

Advancement (ădvɑ·nsmĕnt). ME. [a. Fr. *avancement*; see ADVANCE.] 1. Promotion, preferment. 2. *Law.* The promotion of children in life, *esp.* by advancing money, etc. (see ADVANCE *v.* III. 3); the money so advanced ME. †3. Vaunting -1646. 4. Furtherance of a thing in process; improvement 1551. †5. A going forward (*lit.* and *fig.*); see ADVANCE *v.* -1825. 6. Advancing or forward condition 1793. †7. Payment in advance -1649.

1. What a. may I hope from thee *Haml.* III. ii. 62. The Advancements of every Person according to his Merit MILT. 4. The Proficience and A. of Learning BACON. 6. Water-melons in good a. HAWTHORNE.

Advancer (ădvɑ·nsəɪ). 1496. [f. ADVANCE *v.*] 1. One who advances, see the vb. †2. *Rhet.* Amplification, auxesis, or climax. PUTTENHAM. 3. A second branch of a buck's horn 1496.

Advantage (ădvɑ·ntĕdʒ). [ME. *avantage*, a. Fr. *avantage*, f. *avant*, with *ad-* for *a-* = *ab-*; see ADVANCE *v.* Aphet. to *'vantage, vantage.*] I. Superior position. 1. The position, state, or circumstance of being *in advance*, or having the better of another in any respect; superiority, *esp.* in contest or debate ME. 2. In *Tennis*, the next point after DEUCE, a temporary superiority, not the game. Also *attrib.* 1641. †3. = VANTAGE-GROUND -1663. †4. A time of vantage, a chance -1667. 5. A favouring circumstance; opp. to *disadvantage* 1483.

1. The A. or Height of all the dry Land RAY. The Gauls maintained their a. GIBBON. To have, gain, get, give *a. of, over,* †*on*: superiority over. I have seen the hungry ocean gain A. on the kingdom of the shore SHAKS. To have *the a. of*: to have a personal knowledge which is not reciprocal. 2. It is but an a. to the dozen, it is no winning cast MILT. 4. Make use of time, let not a. slip SHAKS. 5. Ile use the a. of my power *Rich. II*, III. iii. 42. *To take, make one's a. of* a thing: to use any favourable condition it offers. To take an ill a. of his absence *Merry Wiv.* III. iii. 116. *To take at a.*: when the position favours the taker. *To play upon a.*: to cheat. To turn rook and play upon a. SEDLEY.

II. The result of a superior position. 1. Benefit; increased well-being ME. †2. Pecuniary profit, interest -1665. †3. Overplus, excess -1642.

1. Nailed, For our a., on the bitter Crosse SHAKS. *To a.*: Favourably. True Wit is Nature to a. dress'd POPE. 2. To lend or borrow upon a. *Merch. V.* I. iii. 71. 3. As many to th' vantage *Oth.* IV. iii. 84. Hence Advanta·geous *a.* of advantage; †over-reaching, *rare.* Advanta·geous·ly *adv.*, -ness.

Advantage (ădvɑ·ntĕdʒ), *v.* 1496. [a. Fr. *avantager, -ier*, with *ad-* for *a-* = *ab-*; see ADVANCE.] 1. To give an advantage to 1598. 2. To further the progress of 1586. †3. To add to the amount or value of -1673. 4. To benefit, profit 1526. †*absol.* -1668. †*refl.* -1693. †5. To gain -1557.

1. Advantaged in their payes BARRET. How dress advantages Women RICHARDSON. 2. To a. a cause WASHINGTON, agriculture BRIGHT. 4. To a. a statue by the addition of colour RUSKIN. What shall it avauntage a man TINDALE. They will..*a. themselves of* the wind. Hence †Adva·ntageable *a.* tending to a.

Advehent (æ·dvɪ̆hĕnt), *a.* 1836. [ad. L. *advehentem.*] Afferent.

Advene (ădvī·n), *v.* 1606. [a. MFr. *advenir* (mod. *avenir*):—L. *advenire.*] To accede or come (*to*); to be superadded. *trans.* To reach 1839.

†Adve·nient, *a.* 1594. [ad. L. *advenientem*; see prec.] Superadded; adventitious.

Advent (æ·dvĕnt). OE. [a. OFr. *advent*, literary form of *auvent*:—L. *adventus*; see ADVENE.] 1. *Eccl.* The season including the four Sundays immediately preceding the festival of the Nativity OE. 2. The Coming of Christ as Saviour of the world. Hence his Second Coming as Judge, and the Coming of the Holy Spirit. ME. 3. Any important arrival; any arrival 1742.

3. The a. of the Normans STRUTT. Expecting still his a. home TENNYSON. Hence A·dventist, one who holds millenarian views 1876. Also SECOND *A.*

‖**Adventi·tia,** *sb. pl.* 1876. [L. *adventicia*; see ADVENTITIOUS.] *Phys.* Membranous structure, covering but not belonging to an organ.

Adventitious (ædvĕnti·ʃəs), *a.* 1603. [f. L. *adventicius*; see ADVENT. Better *adventicious.*] 1. Of the nature of an addition from without; supervenient, accidental, casual. 2. *Law.* Falling to a man by mere fortune, or from a stranger; not *profectitious* 1651. 3. *Nat. Hist.* esp. *Bot.* Appearing casually or in unusual places 1676.

1. An a., no mother-language HOWELL. An a. population GROTE. 3. A. streaks, in leaves GREW, in buds GRAY, in roots OLIVER. var. †Adventi·tial *a.* Hence Adventi·tiously *adv.* Adventi·tiousness.

†Adve·ntive, *a.* 1605. [f. L. *advent-*; see ADVENE.] = ADVENTITIOUS. As *sb.* An immigrant. BACON.

†Adve·ntry. [Formed by B. JONSON on *adventer*; cf. *entry, enter.*] An adventure.

Adventure (ădve·ntiŭɪ, -tʃəɪ). [ME. *aventure, auenture*, a. OFr. *auenture*:—L. *adventura* (sc. *res*); see ADVENE. Refash. after L.] †1. That which happens without design; chance, hap, luck ME. †2. A chance occurrence.

Also in *Law*. -1727. †3. A trial of one's chance; a venture, or experiment -1790. 4. Chance of danger or loss; risk, jeopardy ME. 5. A hazardous enterprise or performance ME.; hence, a novel or exciting incident 1570. 6. A pecuniary venture, a speculation 1625. 7. Adventurous activity, enterprise ME.

1. To leave to the a. of uncertain pity HOOKER. **†Per, †by, †of a.**: by chance. **†An, †on, †in, †upon, †for a.**: In case, lest, for fear. 2. *Aventure* is a mischance, causing the death of a man, without felony BLOUNT. 3. *To give the a.*: to try the venture. *To stand in a.*: To hang in doubt. To try the faire a. of tomorrow SHAKS. *John* v. v. 22. **†At a., -s**: At hazard, recklessly. To draw a bow *at aventure* (not *at a venture*) 1 *Kings* xxii. 34. **†At all a., -s**: At random; at any risk. A mind floating at all adventures LOCKE. 4. For my sake *to put* thy life *in a.* YONG. So in *Mar. Insur.* 5. To walk alone in London seemed of itself an a. C. BRONTË. 6. My East India a. EVELYN. 7. A yearning after a. 1825. The spirit of a. BURTON. Hence **Adve·nturesome** *a.* given to running risks. **Adve·nturesomeness.**

Adventure (ădve·ntiŭɹ, -tʃəɹ), *v.* [ME. *auenture, aventure*, a. OFr. *aventurer*, f. *aventure*, ADVENTURE.] 1. *trans.* To take the chance of; to venture upon ME. 2. To risk the loss of; to imperil ME. Also *refl.* 3. *intr.* To risk oneself, to venture (*in, into, on, upon*); to dare to undertake; also *fig.* ME. †4. *intr.* To come by chance, befall. Usu. *impers.* ME.

1. I'll a. chiding FORD. 2. We had adventured our lives and liberties GODDARD. To a. themselves abroad POTTER. 3. To a. uppon the exploit SHAKS., on a shore unknown BYRON, to be sent to th' Towre SHAKS. Hence **Adve·ntured** *ppl. a.* risked; gained at a risk. **Adve·nturing** *vbl. sb.* risking; trial; *ppl. a.* venturesome.

Adventurer (ădve·ntiŭrəɹ). 1474. [a. Fr. *aventurier, adv-*, f. *aventure* ADVENTURE.] †1. A gamester 1474. 2. One who seeks adventures (see ADVENTURE *sb.* 5) 1667; *esp.* a soldier of fortune; also, a volunteer 1548. 3. One who undertakes or shares in commercial adventures; a speculator; a *Merchant Adventurer* 1609. 4. One who lives by his wits 1663.

2. Military adventurers ready to flock to any standard THIRLWALL. 3. *Adventurers* (Eng.), shareholders in a mining enterprise RAYMOND. 4. Needy adventurers were generally found in waiting GOLDSM.

Adventuress (ădve·ntiŭrės). 1754. [f. prec.] A woman who lives by her wits.

Adventurous (ădve·ntiŭrəs), *a.* ME. [a. OFr. *aventuros, -eus*; see ADVENTURE *sb.*] †1. Fortuitous ME. only. †2. Full of risk; perilous -1637. 3. Prone to incur risk, rash ME. 4. Enterprising (without *rashness*) ME.

2. To pass through this a. glade MILT. 3. A. Eve MILT. A. hypotheses WHITNEY. 4. An a. people BURKE. Hence **Adve·nturous-ly** *adv.*, **-ness.**

Adverb (æ·dvəɹb). 1530. [a. Fr. *adverbe*, ad. L. *adverbium*, Gr. ἐπίρρημα.] *Gram.* One of the Parts of Speech; a word used to express the attribute of an attribute; one that qualifies an adj., vb., or other advb. Also *attrib.*

Adverbial (ădvə̄·ɹbiăl), *a.* 1591. [ad. L. *adverbialis*; see prec.] Of or pertaining to or of the nature of an adverb 1611; given to the use of adverbs. *rare.* 1710. As *sb.* 1591. Hence **Adve:rbia·lity**, the quality of being a. **Adve·rbialize** *v.* to make an adverb of. **Adve·rbially** *adv.* **Adve:rbia·tion**, a phraseological adverb. EARLE.

†Adve·rsant, *ppl. a.* ME. [a. MFr.:—L. *adversantem, adversari*; see ADVERSE.] Opposing; adverse (*to*) -1630.

‖**Adversaria** (ædvəɹsēᵊ·riă), *sb. pl.* 1610. [L. (sc. *scripta*) things written on the side fronting us (i. e. on one side of the paper); see ADVERSE.] A commonplace book; = MISCELLANEA; also, commentaries or notes on a text, etc.

Adversary (æ·dvəɹsări). ME. [a. OFr. *aversier, adv-*:—L. *adversarius*; see ADVERSE. In Shaks. *a·dversary*, in MILT. also *adve·rsary.*] A. *sb.* 1. One who or that which takes up a position, or acts, as an antagonist; an enemy. *spec.* The Devil. 2. *pl.* = ADVERSARIA, commentaries.

1. His ancient Knot of dangerous Adversaries *Rich. III*, III. i. 182. Or shall the A. thus obtain His end MILT.

B. *adj.* Opposed. *arch.* ME. In *Law.* An a. suit: one in which an opposing party appears.

The a. Champion BOLTON. Hence **Adversa·rious** *a.* hostile. SOUTHEY.

Adversative (ădvə̄·ɹsătiv), *a.* 1533. [ad. L. *adversativus*, f. *adversat-*; see ADVERSANT.] 1. Expressive of opposition, contrariety, or antithesis. †2. Of adverse nature -1603. As *sb.* 1556. Hence **Adve·rsatively** *adv.*

Adverse (æ·dvə̄rs), *a.* ME. [a. MFr. *advers, -e*, refash. of OFr. *avers*:—L. *adversus.* Poet. *a·dverse* and *adve·rse.*] 1. Acting in opposition to, actively hostile. 2. Opposing any one's interests; hence, unfavourable, injurious, calamitous. Const. *to.* ME. 3. Opposite in position 1623.

1. Aduerse Foreyners SHAKS. A. winds DIGBY, power MILT., gales CRABBE, critics HELPS. *Adverse possession* (Law): possession of land by a person not the owner during a certain time without acknowledgement of the right of the real owner. 2. In prosperous days They swarm, but in a. withdraw their heads MILT. A. to the cause of slavery BRIGHT. 3. The a. hills BLACKIE. Hence **†Adve·rse** *v.* to oppose. **A·dversely** *adv.* **A·dverseness.**

Adversifoli-ate, -ous (ădvə̄ɹsifōᵘ·liėt, -əs), *a.* [f. L. *adversus* + *folium* + -ATE, -OUS.] *Bot.* Having leaves placed opposite to each other on the stem.

†Adve·rsion. 1647. [ad. L. *adversionem.*] Attention.

Adversity (ădvə̄·ɹsiti). ME. [a. MFr. *adversité*, refash. f. OFr. *aversite*:—L. *adversitatem*; see ADVERSE.] †1. Opposition, contrariety -ME. 2. The condition of adverse fortune; distress, trial, or affliction; an adverse circumstance; a calamity, etc. ME. †3. Perversity -1606.

2. A. findeth few friends HOLINSHED. *A. Y. L.* II. i. 12. 3. Well said, a. (= perverse one) *Tr. & Cr.* v. i. 14.

Advert (ădvə̄·ɹt), *v.* ME. [a. Fr. *avertir*:—late L. *advertēre* for cl. L. *advertĕre* (sc. *animum*). Cf. ADVERTISE, AVERT.] †1. To turn towards (*lit.* or *fig.*). *rare.* Only in ME. 2. *intr.* = ADVERTISE 1. *arch.* ME. 3. *esp.* To refer *to* in speech or writing 1777. †4. *trans.* = ADVERTISE 2. -1692. †5. To give warning of -1513. ¶ Erron. for AVERT.

2. To a. to the means of strengthening..the Nizam WELLINGTON. 3. I shall now a. to some other matters PRIESTLEY. Hence **Adve·rtent** *ppl. a.* attentive. ? *Obs.*

Advertence (ădvə̄·ɹtėns). ME. [a. MFr. *advertance, -ence*, refash. of OFr. *avertance, -ence*:—L. *advertentia*; see ADVERT.] The action of adverting or attending; occ. = ADVERTENCY.

Advertency (ădvə̄·ɹtėnsi). 1646. [ad. late L. *advertentia*; see prec.] The quality or habit of being advertent or attentive.

Advertise (æ·dvəɹtəiz, *Sc.* ædvərtəi·z), *v.* ME. [a. Fr. *avertiss-, avertir, advertir*; see ADVERT. Or? f. *advertisement.* Cf. *convertir, convert*, etc.] †1. *intr.* To take note, consider -1526. †2. *trans.* To take note of, attend to, observe -1606. 3. *trans.* To call the attention of (another); to notify, admonish, or formally warn 1490. 4. Hence (pers. obj. omitted), To give notice of, make generally known 1588; *esp.* to make publicly known, by announcement *in* a journal, by circular, etc. 1750. 5. †To give warning or information (*of*) -1765; *esp.* by public notice in a journal, by placard, etc. 1772.

3. To consider thereof and a. me timely MARVELL. Advertised by me of his design SMOLLETT. 4. Twenty things that are not to be advertised, you know MAR. EDGEWORTH. To a. a reward H. WALPOLE, a sale of slaves BURKE. Phr. *To a. for*: to ask for by public notice. Hence **Adve:rtisee·**, one advertised for, or aimed at by advertising. **A:dverti·ser**, one who advertises (senses 4, 5); a journal publishing advertisements. **A:dverti·sing** *vbl. sb.* † warning, information; a bringing into notice, *esp.* by advertisement; *ppl. a.* †adverting, attentive; issuing advertisements.

Advertisement (ădvə̄·ɹtizmėnt). 1460. [a. Fr. *avertissement, adv-*; see ADVERTISE. In U.S. ædvəɹtəi·zmėnt.] †1. Attention, heed -1651. †2. Admonition, instruction -1715. †3. Information, notification -1716. 4. A notification, a notice. *arch.* 1460. 5. A public announcement by the town-crier, in print, etc.; *spec.* a paid announcement in a newspaper 1582.

2. The advertisements came to him from..many hands BURNET. 4. An a. to the reader DIBDIN. 5. My griefs cry lowder than a. *Much Ado* v. i. 32. An a. of the particulars in the common newspapers DE FOE.

Advice (ădvəi·s). [ME. *avis*, a. OFr. *avis*:—L. **advisum*, f. *ad* + *visum, videre.* Refash. *advīs*, modified later to *advise, advice.*] †1. The way in which a matter is looked at; opinion, judgement -1651. †2. Prudence, wisdom -1523. †3. Weighing of opinions; consultation -1654. 4. Opinion given or offered as to action; used *spec.* in *Med.* and *Law.* ME. †5. The result of consultation; determination, plan -1704. †6. An act; a *senatus consultum. rare.* -1661. 7. Information given, notice; news; in *pl.* Communications from a distance. *spec.* in *Comm.* Formal notice from a party concerned. 1490. 8. = ADVICE-BOAT.

3. *To take a.*: to deliberate. Consider of it, take aduise *Judges* xix. 30. 4. *Macb.* IV. ii. 68. Ill of fever, and come only for a. PEPYS. 5. Changing aduice on the sudden SAVILE. 7. A mail from Holland, which brought me several Advices STEELE. To give a banker a. of bills becoming due CRUMP.

Comb. **a.-yacht, -boat**, one employed to bring intelligence; a dispatch-boat; see ADVISO.

Hence **†Advi·ceful** *a.* considerate; full of counsel.

Advisable (ădvəi·zăb'l), *a.* 1647. [f. ADVISE.] 1. Open to advice 1661. 2. Proper to be advised; expedient 1647.

1. An a. and teachable temper WESLEY. 2. A course Now not a. COWPER. Hence **Advi:sabi·lity**, advisableness. **Advi·sableness**, readiness to be advised; expediency. **Advi·sably** *adv.*

Advise (ădvəi·z), *v.* [ME. *auisen, avisen*, a. Fr. *aviser*:—late L. *advisare*, f. *advisum*; see ADVICE. Refash. after MFr. *adviser.*] †1. To look at, consider; also, to watch for -1603. †2. To look at *mentally*; to consider -1677; *spec.* in *Sc. Law*, to consider together ('take into *avizandum*') 1609. †3. To purpose -1586. †4. *refl.* To bethink oneself (Fr. *s'aviser*), reflect. -1656; †*intr.* to ponder, deliberate -1671. Hence 5. To consider in company, to hold a consultation 1513. 6. To offer counsel; to give advice 1375. 7. *trans.* To give counsel to, to counsel, caution ME. 8. To give (formal) notice, to inform, apprise 1591; *Comm.* to announce (an event, transaction).

4. Aduise you what you say *Twel. N.* IV. ii. 102. *intr.* A. Forthwith how thou oughtst to receive him MILT. 5. He must *a. with* his Council MISS YONGE. 7. Well use that trick no more I would a. you MARLOWE. He advised distrust SOUTHEY. 8. The States are advised that [etc.] STEELE. *Comm.* Have these drafts been advised? Hence **Advi·ser**, one who advises (senses 7, 8); †a dispatch-boat, an A(D)VISO. **Advi·sership**, the office of an adviser. **†Advi·sive** *a.* advising. **Advi·sory** *a.* having the attribute of advising.

Advised (ădvəi·zd), *ppl. a.* ME. [f. ADVISE. As adj. = Fr. *avisé.*] †1. *pple.* Having considered (*of*) -1633; hence *adj.* Deliberate, wary -1702. 2. Considered, deliberate; hence judicious ME. 3. Of persons: †determined -1483; counselled 1596; apprised 1599.

1. Are you a-uis'd o' that *Merry Wiv.* I. iii. 106. A Prince ought to be slow and a. 1702. With the *well-a.* is wisdome *Prov.* xiii. 10. 2. The more a. the deed is, the lesse a. it is FULLER. 3. The a. measures RUSKIN. *Hen. V*, II. Cho. 12. Hence **Advi·sedly** *adv.* (esp. in sense 2). **Advi·sedness**, the quality of being advised.

Advisement (ădvəi·zmėnt). ME. [a. Fr. *a(d)visement*; see ADVISE.] †1. The process of advising (see ADVISE 1, 2, 5). 2. = ADVICE 4, 5.

†Advi·so. Pl. **-oes.** 1591. [ad. Sp. *aviso*:—late L. *advisum*; see ADVICE.] 1. Intelligence. = ADVICE 7. 2. *pompously*, A suggestion 1591. 3. A dispatch- or advice-boat; var. of AVISO. 1624.

2. The honest advisoes of faith SIR T. BROWNE.

†Advisy, advisee, *ppl. a.* ME. [a. OFr. *aviset, avisé*: see ADVISE.] Well-advised; circumspect -1513.

Advocacy (æ·dvŏkėsi). ME. [a. Fr. *advocacie, -atie*, ad. med.L. *advocatia*; see ADVOCATE.] 1. The function of an advocate; pleading for or supporting. 2. = ADVOWSON, ADVOCATION 5. 1876.

Advocate (æ·dvǒkĕt), *sb.* [ME. *avocat*, a. OFr., ad. L. *advocatus*, *advocare*. Refash. after L.; see AD- 2.] 1. One who pleads the cause of any one in a court of justice; counsel. (The techn. title where Roman law is retained; also in many special tribunals.) 2. *fig.* and *gen.* One who pleads, intercedes, or speaks for another ME.; used *spec.* of Christ as the intercessor for sinners ME. 3. One who argues in behalf of a proposal or tenet. Const. *of*. 1735. †4. An ADVOWEE ME.

Faculty of Advocates: the collective bar in Scotland. *Lord Advocate*, the Scotch Attorney-General. *Judge-Advocate*, an officer who conducts the prosecution before a court-martial, the supreme officer being the *Judge-Advocate-General*. *Devil's Advocate* (*advocatus diaboli*), one who pleads against the admission of a candidate for canonization.

1. Of advocates or (as we..call them) counsel, there are two species, barristers and sergeants BLACKSTONE. 2. We have an Advocate with the Father 1 *John* ii. 1. 3. Advocates for folly dead and gone POPE, of the system of caste M. MÜLLER. Hence **A·dvocateship** (in senses 1, 2, 3).

A·dvocate, *v.*[1] 1555. [f. L. *advocat-*, *advocare*.] †1. To call (*to* oneself). 2. *Sc. Law.* To ADVOKE 1609.

Advocate (æ·dvǒkeˡt), *v.*[2] 1641. [f. the sb.] †1. *intr.* To act as advocate *for*. *arch.* †2. *trans.* To defend (by action) –1666. 3. To argue in favour of; to recommend publicly 1767.

3. The only [sensible] thing that has been advocated BURKE. To a. publication MERIVALE, a view TYNDALL. Hence **A·dvocating** *vbl. sb.* (in sense 3).

Advocation (ædvǒkēˡ·ʃən). 1474. [a. Fr. *advocacion*, ad. L. *advocationem*; see ADVOKE.] I. n. of action f. L. *advocare*. †1. A convocation –1474. 2. *Sc. Law.* The calling of an action before itself by a superior court. (See ADVOKE.) 1528. †3. The act of calling to one's aid –1753.

II. n. of office f. L. *advocatus*. †1. The function of an ADVOCATE 1, 2; advocacy –1767. †2. = ADVOCATE 4; protection of a church; = ADVOWSON. –1661.

1. Alas..My A. is not now in tune *Oth.* III. iv. 123.

Advocator (æ·dvǒkeˡtəɹ). 1482. [a. late L.] †1. A patron (saint); also = ADVOCATE 1, 2. 2. = ADVOCATE 3.

Advocatory (æ·dvǒkeˡ:təri), *a.* 1864. [f. L. *advocat-*, *advocare*.] Pertaining to the advocate.

†**A·dvocatress.** 1641. [f. *advocator* + -ESS.] A female advocate –1647. vars. †**A·dvocatrice**, †**-trix.**

†**Advo·ke**, *v.* 1533. [a. MFr. *advoquer*, ad. L. *advocare*.] To summon; *esp.* to summon a cause to a higher tribunal –1655.

Advoteresse, obs. f. ADULTERESS. **Advoulter, advouter, -er, -ess, -ous, -y**, obs. ff. ADULTER, -ER, -ESS, -OUS, -Y.

Advowee (ædvau·ī). 1691. [a. OFr. *avoué*:—L. *advocatus*; see ADVOCATE. Refash. *advoué*, whence ADVOWEE.] 1. = AVOWÉ, q.v. 2. The advocate, protector, or patron of an eccl. office. Subsequently, One who holds the advowson.

†**Advow·ry**, var. of AVOWRY.

†**Advow·sance, -ante, -sement.** [Corrupt formations on *advowson* or *advowsen* (= *advowsing*) from an imaginary *advowse*.]

Advowson (ædvau·zən, -z'n), *sb.* ME. [a. OFr. *avoëson* (in AFr. *advoeson*):—L. *advocationem*; see ADVOCATION (a doublet of *advowson*). Refash. after L. Aphet. *voweson*.] The 'patronage' of an eccl. house or office; the right of presentation to a benefice or living. (*orig.* The obligation to be its *advocate*; see ADVOWEE.)

The traffic in advowsons has never been..prevented 1865. var. †**Advow·sonage.**

Advoyer, obs. f. AVOYER.

Adward, obs. var. of AWARD *sb.* (Spenser).

†**Adwe·sch**, *v.* OE. [f. A- *pref.* 1 + *dwæscan*.] To quench.

‖**Adynamia** (ædinēˡ·mia). 1830. [mod.L. a. Gr. ἀδυναμία.] *Med.* Lack of vital power, as in some fevers. var. Adynamy.

Adynamic (ædinæ·mik), *a.* 1829. [f. prec.] 1. *Med.* Of or pertaining to adynamia; asthenic. 2. *Nat. Phil.* Characterized by the absence of force 1879.

Adytum (æ·ditʊ̆m). Pl. **adyta.** 1673. [L., a. Gr. ἄδυτον.] The innermost part of a temple; the secret shrine whence oracles were delivered; hence *fig.* A private chamber, a sanctum.

Adze, adz (ædz). [OE. *adesa* of unkn. origin.] A tool, like an ax with the blade set at right angles to the handle and curving inwards towards it; used for chipping or slicing away the surface of wood. Hence **Adze** *v.* to dress with an a.

†**Adzoo·ks.** [See ADS-.] –1841.

Æ, also **ae**, orig. a short vowel midway between *a* and *e* = *a* in *man*, replaced by *e* or *ee* in 13th c., and reintroduced for L. *æ*, Gr. αι in 16th c. Here retained only (1) in EE. words that became obs. bef. changing to *e*, as *æ* river (OE. *eá*); (2) in words directly adopted or formed from L. and Gr. which became obs. bef. changing to *e*; or which indicate ancient things, as *ægis*, or are techn. as *ætiology*. Classical scholars incline to pronounce æ long (*ī*) in all positions.

†**Æ**, *sb.*[1] [OE. *eá*, *é*, *æ*, cogn. w. L. *aqua*.] A river. Cf. EA. –1205.

†**Æ**, *sb.*[2] [OE. *æ*, *æw*, cogn. w. Skr. *ewa*.] Law; hence legal custom, rite, marriage –1200. *Comb.* **æu-breche**, adultery.

Ae (ē), Sc. form of north. ME. *a*, OE. *án*, one; see A *adj.*[1]

Æ-, *pref.* Stress form of OE. *a-* (see A- *pref.* 1) used with sbs. and adjs. Out, off, onward, away; hence priv. = *un-*, *-less*.

-æ (-ī), *pl. suffix* of L. nouns of 1st decl. in *-a*, and romanized form of Gr. -αι pl. of nouns. In all words completely popularized it yields to -s, as *arenas*, etc.

Æcern, æcirn, obs. ff. ACORN.

‖**Æcidium** (īsi·diʊ̆m). Pl. **-a.** 1867. [L. dim. of Gr. αἰκία injury.] *Bot.* The cup-shaped fruit borne on the mycelium of certain parasitic fungi.

Ædicule (e·dikiul). 1832. [ad. L. *ædicula*, dim. of *ædes*.] A small house or room; a niche.

Ædile (ī·dəil). 1580. [ad. L. *ædilis*, f. *ædes*.] *Rom. Antiq.* A magistrate in Rome, who had charge of public buildings, shows, police, etc.; hence, a municipal officer. As *adj.* 1880. Hence **Æ·dileship, Ædi·lity**, the office, or term of office, of an ædile. **Ædi·li·tian** *a.* pertaining to an ædile.

Ægemony, obs. var. of HEGEMONY.

‖**Æger** (ī·dʒəɹ), *a.* 1861. [L.] The L. word for 'sick', used at the Eng. Universities in excusing absence on account of illness; hence, a note alleging sickness.

‖**Ægilops** (e·dʒilǫps). 1601. [L., a. Gr. αἰγίλωψ, f. αἴξ + ὤψ.] 1. *Med.* An ulcer or fistula in the inner angle of the eye. †2. *Herb.* The wild-oat or other corn-weed grass –1753. 3. *Bot.* A genus of South European grasses 1872. 4. A species of Oak (*Quercus ægilops*) 1706.

Ægirite (e·dʒirəit, ī-). 1837. [f. *Ægir*.] *Min.* An ore of the Amphibole group of Bisilicates.

‖**Ægis** (ī·dʒis). 1704. [L., a. Gr. αἰγίς.] A shield, or defensive armour; *esp.* that of Jupiter or Minerva. Also *fig.* A protection 1793. *attrib.* 1793.

fig. The æ. of the laws THIRLWALL.

Ægophony (igǫ·fŏni). 1853. [f. Gr. αἴξ + φωνία.] *Path.* A tremulous resonance of the voice, like the bleating of a kid, heard in pleurisy.

†**Æ·gritude.** 1532. [ad. L. *ægritudo*.] Sickness –1647.

‖**Ægrotat** (ī·grotæt, īgrōᵘ·tæt). 1794. [L. 'he is sick'.] In Eng. Univ. use, a certificate of illness; also, a place awarded in an examination list to one who has such a certificate.

Aeipathy (eˌəi·păþi). 1853. [f. Gr. ἀεί; see -PATHY.] *Med.* An inveterate disease.

Æneid (inī·id, ī·niˌid). 1490. [ad. L. *Æneid-*, *Æneis*, f. *Æneas*; see -ID[2].] An epic poem by Virgil, with Æneas as hero; also, one of the twelve books of this poem.

Aeneous (eˌī·niˌəs), *a.* 1815. [f. L. *a(h)eneus*.] Brassy; brass-coloured.

Ænigma, -tic, etc.; see ENIGMA, -TIC, etc.

Ænigmatite, *Min.* a variety of KOELBINGITE.

Æolian (iˌōᵘ·liăn), *a.* 1789. [f. L. *æolius*, f. *Æolis* or *Æolus*.] 1. Of Æolis or Æolia, in Asia Minor; Æolic. 2. Of Æolus, god of the winds; hence of, produced by, or borne on the wind; aerial.

1. *Æolian mode* (*Mus.*): 'the ninth of the church modes.' GROVE. 2. *Æ. harp*: a stringed instrument producing musical sounds under a current of air.

Æolic (iˌǫ·lik), *a.* 1674. [ad. L. *æolicus*.] = ÆOLIAN 1.

Æolic digamma: the sixth letter of the early Greek Alphabet, surviving in the Æolic dialect. *Æ. mode*; see ÆOLIAN 1.

Æolipyle, -pile (ī·ŏlipəil, iˌǫ·lipəil). Also **eo-.** 1611. [a. Fr., ad. L. *Æoli pylæ* (= Gr. πύλαι): see *Vitruv.* i. 6.] A pneumatic instrument, illustrating the force with which vapour generated by heat in a closed vessel rushes out by a narrow aperture. First described by Hero of Alexandria.

Æolist (ī·ŏlist). [f. L. *Æolus* + -IST.] A pretender to inspiration SWIFT. Hence **Æolistic** *a.* long-winded (*mod.*).

Æolo-, combining form of *Æolus*, the impersonation of wind, as in *æolodicon*, *æolodion*, etc. names of musical wind-instruments.

Æolotropy (ī:ŏlǫ·trŏpi). 1881. [f. Gr. αἰόλος + -τροπία.] Change of physical qualities on change of position, opp. to *isotropy*; anisotropy. Hence **Æolotropic** *a.* not isotropic.

Æon, eon (ī·ǫn). 1647. [a. L., a. Gr. αἰών.] An age, or the whole duration, of the world, or of the universe; an immeasurable period of time; eternity. 2. The personification of an age. In *Platonic philosophy*, A power existing from eternity 1647.

1. Æons of æons CARLYLE. 2. The Valentinian thirty Gods and Æons CUDWORTH. Hence **Æonial, Æonian** *adjs.* everlasting.

Æquoreal (īkwōᵊ·riăl), *a.* 1838. [f. L. *æquoreus*.] Oceanic.

Ærarian (īrēᵊ·riăn), *a.* 1850. [f. L. *ærarius*, *ærarium*.] Connected with the treasury; fiscal. As *sb.* [sc. *citizen*.] A Roman citizen, unenfranchised, who paid only a poll-tax (*æra pendebat*).

Aerate (ēᵊ·əreˡt), *v.* 1794. [f. L. *aer*, perh. after Fr. *aërer*.] 1. To expose to the mechanical action of air, to supply with air 1856. 2. To expose to the chemical action of air; to oxygenate (the blood) by respiration 1794. 3. To charge with carbonic acid gas. Hence **Aerated** *ppl. a.* (in all senses).

Aeration (ēᵊərēˡ·ʃən). 1578. [a. Fr. *aération*, f. *aërer*.] †1. Exposure to the open air. 2. Supplying with fresh air; airing 1835. 3. Exposure to the chemical action of the air (see AERATE 2) 1836. 4. The charging with carbonic acid or oxygen.

Aerator (ēᵊ·əreˡtəɹ). 1861. [f. AERATE.] That which supplies or charges with air.

Aerial (ēᵊ·riăl, eˌīᵊ·riăl), *a.* and *sb.* 1604. [f. L. *aerius*, f. *aer* AIR + -AL.] 1. Composed of air; aeriform, gaseous 1664. 2. Thin as air, ethereal; unsubstantial; ideal, imaginary 1610. 3. Light as air, airy 1606. 4. Of, Pertaining to, or produced in the air; atmospheric 1604. 5. Existing, moving, or growing in the air; *spec.* with ref. to locomotion in the air 1620. 6. Placed at any airy height, elevated. Also *fig.* 1620. B. *sb.* An a. wire 1902.

2. A. bodies HOBBES, beings SCOTT, architecture (= building castles in the air) DICKENS, distinctions MILMAN. 4. Th'Eriall blew *Oth.* II. i. 39. *A. perspective* is the expression of space by any means whatever RUSKIN. 5. A. Spirits or devils BURTON, travellers DICKENS, roots for climbing GRAY. Towns a. on the waving tree POPE. 6. **A. railway**, a track consisting of overhead wires, etc. supporting carriages, usu. driven by electricity. **A. wire**, a wire supported in the air for radiating or receiving the waves of wireless telegraphy. Hence **Ae·rially** *adv.*

Aerie, aery, eyrie, eyry (ēᵊ·ri, īᵊ·ri). 1581. [ad. med.L. *aeria*, *aerea* (*aria*, *area*), prob. f. Fr. *aire*:—L. *area* an open place (Littré); or, in sense of 'stock':—L. *ager* or *atrium* (Diez).] 1. The nest of any bird of prey, *esp.* of an eagle; also of ravens, etc., which build high in the air; used *fig.* of a high-perched human dwelling or retreat. **2.** The brood in the nest; *fig.* a noble stock of children 1594.

1. And like an Eagle o're his ayerie towers SHAKS. *John* v. ii. 149. 2. fig. *Haml.* II. ii. 354.

Aeriferous (ēˑəriˑfĕrəs), *a.* 1687. [f. L. *aer* + -FEROUS.] Bearing or conveying air.

Aeriform (ēˑərifǭım), *a.* 1620. [f. L. *aer* + -FORM.] Of the form of air, gaseous 1620; *fig.* unsubstantial 1821.

Aerify (ēˑərifəi), *v. rare.* [f. L. *aer* + -FY.] **1.** *trans.* To make aeriform. **2.** = AERATE 1847. Hence **Aːerifaˑction,** the action of aerifying. **Aːerificaˑtion,** the act of becoming air; aerifaction.

Aero- (ēəˑrŏ, ēˑərŏ), repr. Gr. ἀερο-, comb. f. ἀήρ AIR.

Aerobatics (-bæˑtiks) [after *acrobatics*], evolutions performed with an aeroplane, esp. for display; so **-batic** *a.* **Aerodynaˑmics** [DYNAMICS], (*a*) the branch of pneumatics which treats of air and other gases in motion, and of their mechanical effects; (*b*) the art of moving through the air by some mechanism; the use of flying machines, aviation; so **-dynaˑmic** *a.* **Aeˑrogram,** (*a*) a message sent 'through the air', i.e. by wireless telegraphy; (*b*) a telegram conveyed partly by aeroplane. **Aeroˑgraphy** [Gr. -γραφία], description of the atmosphere. **Aerohyˑdrous** *a.* used of minerals which contain water in their cavities. **Aeroˑlogy** [Gr. -λογία], the part of science which treats of the atmosphere. **Aeˑromancy** [Gr. μαντεία], divination by air, including augury; later, weather-forecasting. **Aeroˑmeter** [Gr. μέτρον], an instrument for measuring the weight or density of air and gases; so **-meˑtric** *a.* **Aeroˑmetry** [Gr. -μετρία], the science of pneumatics. **Aeˑrophyte** [Gr. φυτόν], a plant growing wholly in the air, as epiphytal orchids, etc.; *pl.* **-phyta,** esp. lichens. **Aeˑroscepsy** [Gr. σκέψις], **-oˑscopy** [Gr. -σκοπία], the observation of the air; = AEROMANCY. **Aerosiˑderite** [Gr. σιδηρίτης], a meteorite consisting of iron ore. **Aeːrosideˑrolite** [Gr. σίδηρος + λίθος], a meteorite intermediate between stone and iron. **Aeˑrosphere** [Gr. σφαῖρα], the body of air that surrounds the earth. **b.** In various names of aeroplanes or flying machines or their parts, as *aero-biplane, -car, -engine, -surface.*

Aerobe (ēˑərōᵘb). *Biol.* 1879. [f. mod.L. *Aerobia* (Gr. βίος life).] A microbe living on free oxygen derived from air.

Aerodrome (ēəˑrŏ-, ēˑərŏdrōᵘm). 1891. [f. AERO- + Gr. δρόμος course.] †**1.** An aeroplane –1896. **2.** A course for the use of flying machines; a tract of level ground from which aeroplanes or airships can start 1902.

Aerolite (ēˑərŏləit). 1815. [var. of AEROLITH.] A mass which has fallen to the earth through the atmosphere; a meteorite. In later usage, a mass of stone, not of meteoric iron. Hence **Aeroliˑtic** *a.*

Aerolith (ēˑərŏliþ). 1819. [f. AERO- + Gr. λίθος stone. Cf. F. *aérolithe.*] = prec.

Aeronaut (ēəˑrŏnǭt, ēˑərŏnǭt). 1784. [a. F. *aéronaute,* f. Gr. ἀήρ air + ναύτης sailor.] One who sails through the air; a balloonist. *fig.* A gossamer spider 1845. Hence **Aːeronauˑtic, -al** *a.* **Aˑeronautism,** ballooning.

Aeronautics (-nǭˑtiks). 1753. [ad. mod.L. *aeronautica,* adj. pl. neut.] The science, art, or practice of aerial navigation.

Aeroplane (ēəˑrŏ-, ēˑərŏplēⁱn). 1866. [In sense 1, f. AERO- b + PLANE *sb.*³; in sense 2 ad. F. *aéroplane,* f. Gr. ἀερο-, ἀήρ AIR *sb.* + -πλανος wandering.] †**1.** A plane for aerostatic experiment; the plane of a flying machine –1905. **2.** A heavier-than-air flying machine having one or more such planes (*monoplane, biplane, triplane*) and driven by a motor. Also *attrib.* 1884.

Aerostat (ēəˑrŏstæt, ēˑərŏstæt). 1784. [adv. F. *aérostat,* f. Gr. ἀερο- + στατός standing.] **1.** Early name for a balloon or machine capable of supporting weight in the air. **2.** An aeronaut 1870.

Aerostatic (ēəːrŏstæˑtik, ēːərŏ-), *a.* 1785. [ad. F. *aérostatique,* f. as prec. + Gr. στατικός.] **1.** Pertaining to the balancing or weighing of air; pneumatic 1791. **2.** Aeronautic 1785. var. **Aːerostaˑtical** *a.*

Aerostatics (ēəˑrŏstæˑtiks), *sb. pl.* 1753. [f. AEROSTATIC *a.,* after *mathematics,* etc.] The branch of pneumatics which treats of the equilibrium and pressure of air and gases, and of bodies sustained in them; hence including AERONAUTICS.

Aerostation (ēːərŏstēⁱˑʃən). 1785. [ad. F. *aérostation,* improp. f. *aérostat,* as if = L. *-atus.*] †**1.** Aerostatics –1792. **2.** The art of raising and guiding balloons, etc., in the air; aerial navigation 1785.

‖**Æruginous** (īrūˑdʒinəs), *a.* 1605. [ad. F. *érugineux, -euse,* ad. L. *æruginosus,* f. *æruginem,* f. *æs.*] Of the nature or colour of verdigris, or copper-rust.

‖**Ærugo** (īrūˑgo). 1753. [L., f. *æs.*] The rust of copper, or brass, verdigris; the rust of any metal.

Aery (ēˑəri, ēəˑri), *a. poet.* 1586. [ad. L. *aerius.*] Aerial; hence ethereal, incorporeal.

A. tongues that syllable men's names MILT. *Comb.* **a.-light.**

Aery, var. of AERIE.

Æschynite (īˑskinəit). [f. Gr. αἰσχύνη disgrace. Named from the inability of chemical science to separate two of its (unlike) constituents.] *Min.* A blackish mineral of the tantalite group found in Russia.

Æsculapius (īskiulēⁱˑpiŏs). Also **Esc-.** 1714. [L.] The Roman god of medicine; *fig.* a physician. Hence **Æsculaˑpian** *a.* belonging to Æ.; medicinal.

Æsculetin (īskiuliˑtin). 1877. [f. L. *æsculetum*; see next.] *Chem.* A bitter crystalline substance ($C_9H_6O_4$) found in æsculin.

Æsculin (īˑskiulin). 1877. [f. L. *æsculus,* applied to the horse-chestnut.] *Chem.* A glucoside contained in the bark of the horse-chestnut, etc.; $C_{21}H_{24}O_{13}$.

Æsthesics (īsþīˑsiks, e-). 1879. [f. Gr. αἴσθησις; cf. φυσικός, f. φύσις.] An abstract science of feeling. G. H. LEWES.

‖**Æsthesis** (īsþīˑsis). 1851. [Gr.] The perception of the external world by the senses. Hence **Æstheːsiogeˑnic** *a.* producing sensation. **Æsthesioˑmeter,** an instrument for measuring the tactile sensibility of patients.

Æsthesodic (īsþīsǫˑdik), *a.* 1878. [f. Gr. αἴσθησις + ὁδός.] *Phys.* Of nerves: Providing a path for sensory impulses.

Æsthete (īˑsþīt, eˑsþīt). 1881. [ad. Gr. αἰσθητής.] One who professes a superior appreciation of what is beautiful, and endeavours to carry out his ideas in practice.

Æsthetic (īsþeˑtik, e-). 1798. [ad. Gr. αἰσθητικός, of or pertaining to αἰσθητά (as opp. to νοητά). Misapplied in Germ. by Baumgarten to 'criticism of taste', and so used in Eng. since 1830.] **A.** *adj.* †**1.** Received by the senses –1798. **2.** Of or pertaining to the appreciation or criticism of the beautiful 1831. **3.** Having or showing refined taste; in accordance with good taste 1871.

2. A wash of quite fluid Æ. tea CARLYLE. 3. He must have æ. wall-paper and a dado (*mod.*).

B. *sb.* usu. pl. **æsthetics,** as collect. sing. †**1.** The science of the conditions of sensuous perception –1803. **2.** The philosophy of taste, or of the perception of the beautiful 1833.

2. Two professors of the science [of art] and æsthetic M. PATTISON. Hence **Æstheˑtical** *a.* of or relating to æsthetics. **Æstheˑtically** *adv.* **Æsthetiˑcian,** one devoted to æsthetics. **Æstheˑticism,** the quality of being æsthetic; æsthetic doctrine; susceptibility to æsthetic influences. **Æstheˑticist,** a professor of æstheticism. **Æstheˑticize** *v.* to render æsthetic.

Æːstho-physioˑlogy. 1855. [Incorr. f. Gr. αἰσθ- or αἰσθε- perceive + PHYSIOLOGY.] The scientific study of the organs of sensation.

Æstival, estival (īˑstivăl, īstəiˑvăl, also e-), *a.* ME. [a. Fr. *estival,* ad. L. *æstivalis,* f. *æstivus.*] **1.** Of or belonging to summer, or the summer solstice. **2.** Appearing or produced in summer.

2. Vernal, æ., and autumnal garlands SIR T. BROWNE.

Æstivate (īˑstiveⁱt, e-), *v.*: also **e-.** 1626. [f. L. *æstivat-, æstivare*; see ÆSTIVE.] To spend the summer; *esp.* (Zool.) in a state of torpor. Cf. *hibernate.*

Æstivation, e- (īstivēⁱˑʃən, e-). 1625. [f. as prec.] †**1.** The spending of summer; summer retreat –1755. **2.** *Zool.* Summer-torpor; opp. to *hibernation.* Also *fig.* 1845. **3.** *Bot.* Internal arrangement of a flower-bud, before expansion; præfloration 1830.

†**Æˑstive,** *a.* Also **e-.** [ad. L. *æstivus,* f. *æstus.*] = ÆSTIVAL 1.

†**Æˑstuary.** 1706. [ad. L. *æstuarium.*] **1.** = ESTUARY. **2.** A vapour-bath.

†**Æˑstuate,** *v.* 1620. [f. L. *æstuat-, æstuare.*] To boil, to heave. Hence †**Æˑstuation,** feverish disturbance, ebullition. †**Æˑstuous** *a.* heaving. †**Æˑsture** (an irregular form), boiling. CHAPMAN.

Aetheogam (eˌīˑþĭogæm). 1845. [f. Gr. ἀήθης unusual + γάμος.] *Bot.* A cryptogam. Hence **Aetheoˑgamous** *a.* = CRYPTOGAMOUS.

Æther, -ial, etc., occas. vars. ETHER, -EAL, etc.

†**Æthiops mineral.** *Chem.* Quicksilver and sulphur ground together to a dark powder –1755.

Æˑthogen. [f. Gr. αἶθος fire + -GEN -producing.] *Chem.* Boric nitride, which gives a phosphorescent light under the blowpipe. (Dicts.)

Æthrioscope (īˑþriŏskōᵘp). 1832. [f. Gr. αἰθρία + -σκοπός, -σκοπιον.] An instrument for indicating the variations of solar radiation.

Ætiology (īti,ǫˑlŏdʒi, eˑti-). 1555. [ad. L. *ætiologia,* a. Gr. αἰτιολογία.] **1.** The assignment of a cause; also, the wherefore of a command, etc. **2.** The science or philosophy of causation; the part of any special science which deals with causes 1660; *spec.* that part of medical science which investigates the causes of disease 1684.

1. The æ. of the drinking customs (*mod.*).

†‖**Aetiˑtes.** [a. L., a. Gr. ἀετίτης prop. adj.] The eagle-stone; a hollow nodule of argillaceous oxide of iron, having a loose nucleus, fabled to be found in the eagle's nest.

†**Æviteˑrnal,** *a.* [f. L. *æviternus.*] Endless, eternal –1660. †**Æviteˑrnity,** eternity.

†‖**Æˑvum.** [L.] = ÆON. –1660.

Af-, *pref.* **1.** = L. *ad-* bef. *f-*, OFr. *a-*, refash. later with *ff,* after L. **2.** Occas. for *a-* (not = L. *af-*), as in *af(f)ray.*

Afar (ăfāˑɪ), *adv.* ME. [f. A- 2, 3 (= OF, ON) + FAR *adv.*] **1.** From far. With *see,* etc.; used of the thing seen. Now usu. with *from.* **2.** Far, at or to a distance. (In prose with *off.*)

1. To strike..thy foeman from a farre 1611. 2. In Stronds a-farre remote SHAKS. Abraham..saw the place afarre off *Gen.* xxii. 4.

†**Afeaˑr,** *v.* OE. [f. A- *pref.* 1 + *fǣran*; see FEAR, and AF- 2.] To frighten –1596.

†**Afeaˑr, afeˑre, afeiˑr.** ME. [A *prep.*¹ + FEAR.] **A.** *adv.* In fear. **B.** *conj.* Lest. (*Sc.*)

Afeard, -ed (ăfīəˑɪd), *ppl. a.* ME. [f. the vb.: freq. in SHAKS. and still dial.] Frightened.

Afer (ēⁱˑfəɪ). [L. = African.] The south-west wind. MILT.

Affability (æfăbiˑlĭti). 1483. [a. Fr. *affabilité,* f. AFFABLE.] The quality of being AFFABLE; courteousness.

A...is where a man speaketh courteysly with a sweet speech or countenance ELYOT. His usual politeness and a. THACKERAY.

Affable (æˑfăb'l), *a.* 1540. [a. Fr., ad. L. *affabilis.*] Easy of conversation or address; civil and courteous, esp. with inferiors, etc.; kindly and polite.

Raphaël, The a. archangel MILT. *P. L.* vii. 42. Gentle his look, and a. his mien 1723. Hence **Aˑffableness. Aˑffably** *adv.*

Affabrous (æˑfăbrəs), *a. rare.* [f. L. *affaber.*] Workmanlike.

Affair (ăfēəˑɪ). ME. [a. OF. *afaire* (mod. *aff-*) orig. *à faire.* Cf. ADO.] **1.** What one has to do, or has to do with; business; *more vaguely,* a concern 1611. **2.** *esp.* (in *pl.*) Ordinary pursuits of life 1484; commercial or professional business 1519; public business 1605. **3.** *sing.* Used vaguely of any proceeding which it is not desired to be precise about 1702. **4.** Loosely of material things, as a prop to an epithet 1802. †**5.** Performance –1596. †**6.** Fortune, rank. CAXTON. Cf. OFr. *de haute afaire.*

1. What is your affaire in Elsenour? *Haml.* I. ii. 174. An a. of a few days (*mod.*). 2. The affairs of mankind 1869. Men of affairs, trained to business SMILES. That in the Field; this in Affairs of State DRYDEN. 3. In our Dialect .. a lady is said to have an a. BERKELEY. An a. of honour (a duel) 1753. The a. was fiercely disputed SCOTT. 4. His wife was no

grand a. MAR. EDGEWORTH. The Plata is, in truth, a poor a. DARWIN.

†**Affa·mish**, *v.* 1568. [f. Fr. *affamer* :—L. **affamare.*] To starve. *trans.* and *intr.* Hence †**Affa·mished** *ppl. a.* **Affa·mishment.**

Affatuate (ăfæ·tiuĕt), *a.* [f. L. *ad* + *fatuus*. Cf. *infatuate.*] Infatuated. So **Affa·tuated** *ppl. a.*

†**Affe·ct**, *sb.* ME. [ad. L. *affectus.*] 1. Mental disposition (*esp.* opp. to *chere*, outward appearance, or to *effect*) –1626; desire, passion (opp. to *reason*) –1619. 2. Natural tendency –1606; *esp.* kind disposition towards –1633. 3. Bodily disposition, *esp.* disease, affection –1679.

1. The affects and Passions of the Heart and Spirits BACON *Sylva* § 97. 2. For euery man with his affects is borne *L. L. L.* I. i. 152. 3. Of great vse for the affects of the lungs 1616.

†**Affe·ct**, *ppl. a.* ME. = AFFECTED II –1538.

Affect (ăfe·kt), *v.*[1] 1483. [a. Fr. *affecter*, ad. L. *affectare.*] †1. To aim at, seek –1794. 2. To like, love. *arch.* 1550; *esp.* To like to use, frequent 1589; †*absol.* –1645; of animals and plants: To haunt 1616. 3. To assume ostentatiously 1605; with *inf.*: To profess 1720. 4. To assume falsely; to pretend 1661; with *inf.* 1603.

1. Have I affected wealth or honour *2 Hen. VI*, IV. vii. 104. To a. the skies POPE, to be made equall vnto *Ecclus.* xiii. 11. 2. She did a. me *Twel. N.* II. v. 28. Making Peace or Warre, As thou affects *Ant. & Cl.* I. iii. 71. To a. new fashions 1586, the back benches 1862. 3. To a. a saucy roughnes *Lear* II. ii. 102, a stern demeanour GIBBON. 4. He had ever affected a haughty indifference DISRAELI. To a. to be surprised 1879. Hence **Affe·cter**, -or, †a lover; an ostentatious user (*of* anything). var. †**Affectate** *v.*

Affect (ăfe·kt), *v.*[2] 1606. [f. L. *affect-*, *afficere.*] 1. To attack as a disease. †2. *Law.* To attaint *with* a crime –1726. 3. To have an effect on the feelings 1662 (cf. AFFECTED III), or on things 1631. 4. To allot specially *to* 1611.

1. The inward gangrene affected their vitals DE FOE. 2. To a. with Fraud 1726. 3. To a. the amount of the dividends 1840. 4. Affected to his special service THACKERAY. Hence **Affe·ctible** *a. rare.* **Affe·ctibi·lity.**

†**Affecta·te(d**, *ppl. a.* = AFFECTED I, 2, 3.

Affectation (æfektēⁱ·ʃən). 1548. [ad. L. *affectationem*; see AFFECT *v.*[1]] †1. An aiming at –1711; liking for –1795. Const. *of*. 2. An ostentatious fondness for, or display of 1548. 3. Artificiality of manner 1593. 4. Pretence 1581.

1. The A. of being Gay STEELE. A. of the manners ..of France GIBBON. 2. A. of eloquence 1548, of Latin 1861. 3. The essence of a. is that it be assumed CARLYLE. Mere a. 1873. Hence **Affecta·tionist.** var. **Affe·ctedness.**

Affected (ăfe·ktėd), *ppl. a.* Really *three* words.

I. Pa. pple. of AFFECT *v.*[1] 1588. †1. Aimed at –1649; loved –1705. 2. Assumed artificially 1594; pretended 1663. 3. Full of AFFECTATION (sense 3) 1588.

1. A work assigned rather than by me chosen or a. MILT. 2. I have not used any a. style MILT. Real or a. levity 1879. 3. Too spruce, too a., too odde *L. L. L.* v. i. 15.

II. adj. f. AFFECT *sb.* 1535. 1. Disposed, inclined 1587. †2. *esp.* *Well-* or *ill-*disposed (*to*) –1690. Cf. *disaffected.* †3. Of the body –1615.

1. How stands the country a. towards you BUNYAN.

III. Pa. pple. of AFFECT *v.*[2] 1579. 1. Attacked by a disease. Const. *with* or *absol.* 1619. 2. Mentally influenced (*by*), *esp.* by sorrow, or *absol.* 1626. 3. Of things: Influenced, acted upon (*by* or *absol.*) 1748. 4. Specially allotted (see AFFECT *v.*[2] 4).

1. The a. part of a city 1806. 2. Deeply a. by his own reproaches GIBBON. 3. Finances..materially a. 1783. 4. Horses a...to military purposes 1871.

Affe·ctedly, *adv.* 1596. [f. AFFECTED I.] †1. Purposely –1738; affectionately –1611. 2. Artificially 1617. 3. Hypocritically 1656.

2. A. vaine SIR T. BROWNE. The person a. described as Lupus is really [etc.] FREEMAN. 3. An a. sympathising voice, like an undertaker's 1861.

Affe·cting, *ppl. a.* 1598 [f. AFFECT *v.*[1] 1 and 4 and *v.*[2]] †1. Loving –1619. †2. Using AFFECTATION (sense 3) –1611. 3. [f. AFFECT *v.*[2]] †Impressive –1779; thrilling, touching 1720.

2. A drawling-affecting rogue SHAKS. 3. An a. farewell. Hence **Affe·ctingly** *adv.*

Affection (ăfe·kʃən), *sb.* ME. [a. Fr., ad. L. *affectionem*; see AFFECT *v.*[2]] I. The action of affecting; the being affected 1660.

1. The a. of our bodily organs from without MILL.

II. 1. An emotion of the mind ME.; †*esp.* passion, lust, as opp. to reason –1736. 2. †Mental tendency –1756; *esp.* disposition, inclination towards ME.; good disposition towards, love ME. *Esp.* in *pl.*

1. God gave them up to vile affections *Rom.* i. 26. 2. How do you know he loues her? *John.* I heard him swear his a. *M. Ado* II. i. 175. This yong Maides affections *Oth.* I. iii. 112.

III. A state of the body; *esp.* disease 1541.

It was an a. of the heart 1853.

IV. In *Metaph.* *esp.* in *pl.* [= L. *affectus.*] A property or attribute of a thing 1567.

Thought is..an a. of perishable matter 1860.

†V. = AFFECTATION –1776.

Three-pil'd Hyperboles, spruce a. *L. L. L.* v. i. 407. Hence **Affe·ctional** *a.* having affections (*mod.*). †**Affe·ctionally** *adv.* earnestly. †**Affe·ctioned** *ppl. a.* = AFFECTIONATE. †**Affe·ctious** *a.* loving.

Affe·ction, *v.* 1584. [f. the *sb.*] To love.

Can you a. the 'o-man *Merry W.* I. i. 234.

Affectionate (ăfe·kʃənĕt), *a.* 1494. [Latinized ad. Fr. *affectionné.* Cf. *ornate*, etc.] †1. Disposed mentally –1657. †2. Biased –1611. †3. Passionate –1726. †4. Eager –1750. †5. Well-affected *to* –1761. 6. Loving 1586; of things: Tender 1586.

4. I am..zealous and a. to recede as little from antiquity BACON. Their labours, however zealous or a. JOHNSON. 5. A. to the French government HUME. 6. Your most loving and a. brother JAMES VI. Your ..a. Seruant Gonerill *Lear* IV. vi. 276. An a. farewell (*mod.*). Hence †**Affe·ctionate** *v.* = AFFECTION *v.* Also *refl.* †**Affe·ctionated** *ppl. a.* = AFFECTIONATE 1, 2, 5, 6. **Affe·ctionateness**, the quality of being a.

Affectionately (ăfe·kʃənĕtli), *adv.* 1588. [f. AFFECTIONATE 2, 4, 6.] †1. Zealously –1723. 2. Lovingly 1606.

Affective (ăfe·ktiv), *a.* 1549. [a. Fr., ad. L. *affectivus.*] †1. *rare.* = AFFECTING. 2. Pertaining to the emotions, opp. to *intellectual* (see AFFECT *sb.*) 1623. Hence **Affe·ctively** *adv.*

†**Affe·ctual**, *a.* 1483. [a. OFr. *affectuel.*] 1. Earnest –1581. 2. = AFFECTIVE 2. 1655. Hence †**Affe·ctually** *adv.*

†**Affe·ctuous**, *a.* 1460. [a. Fr. *affectueux*; see AFFECT *sb.*] 1. Eager –1656; loving –1575. 2. = AFFECTIVE 2. 1674. Hence †**Affe·ctuously** *adv.*

†**Affee·ble**, *v.* 1480. [a. OFr. *afeblier.*] To enfeeble –1599.

Affee·r, *v.* 1467. [a. OFr. *afeurer* :—late L. *afforare*, f. *forum* market, -price.] 1. To assess an amercement. 2. *fig.* To confirm –1605. *Macb.* IV. iii. 34. Hence †**Affee·rance.** **Affee·rment.** **Affee·ror.**

†**Affei·r**, *v. n. dial.* ME. [a. OFr. *aferir* :—late L. *afferire*: esp. *Sc.*] To fall by right. = EFFEIR. Hence †**Affei·ring** *ppl. a.* †**Afferant** *ppl. a.* and *sb.*

Afferent (æ·fĕrĕnt), *a.* 1839. [ad. L. *afferentem*, *afferre.*] *Phys.* Conducting inwards, as *afferent nerves.* Opp. to *efferent.*

‖**Affettuoso** (affe:ttu͡ō·so), *a.* 1796. [It.] *Mus.* A direction: With feeling.

Affiance (ăfəi·ăns). ME. [a. OFr. *afiance*; see AFFY.] 1. Trust *in*, *on* 1330. †2. Confidence, assurance –1753. 3. Plighting of faith; *esp.* of troth on agreement of marriage –1809. †4. Affinity –1601.

1. My Lancelot, thou in whom I have..a. TENNYSON. 3. After a. and troth plight between them.

Affi·ance, *v.* 1523. [see prec.] To promise; *esp.* in marriage. Usu. in pass., with *to*. Hence **Affi·anced** *ppl. a.*

Affi·ant. U.S. *Mod.* [See AFFY.] One who makes an affidavit.

†**Affich(e**, *v.* ME. [a. Fr. *afficher.*] To affix.

Affidavit (æfidēⁱ·vit). 1622. [late L., = 'he has stated on oath'.] *Law.* A written statement, *sworn* by deponent, *taken* by the judge; in pop. usage *made* or *taken* by deponent. *Slang.* On my *davy.*

Affi·ed, *ppl. a. arch.* 1500. = AFFIANCED. Also *fig.*

†**Affi·le**, *v.* ME. [a. OFr. *afiler.*] To sharpen –1520.

Affiliable (ăfi·liăb'l), *a.* 1862. [f. L. *affili-*, *affiliare.*] Capable of being affiliated on or causally traced to. Const. *on*, *upon.*

Affiliate (ăfi·li͡eⁱt), *v.* 1761. [f. L. *affiliat-*, *affiliare.*] 1. To adopt as a branch, or a member of a society 1761; *intr.* (for *refl.*) to connect oneself *with* 1860. Const. *to*, *with*. 2. *Law.* To fix the paternity of an illegitimate child; hence, to ascribe a child *to* its father 1834. Also *fig.*

1. The party..that affiliates with the Republicans 1860. 2. To a. a child on a person as the..putative Father thereof 1834. Hence **Affi·liated** *ppl. a.* Usu. *fig.*

Affiliate (afi·liĕt), *a.* 1868. [see prec.] Affiliated. As *sb.* An associate 1879.

Affiliation (ăfili͡ēⁱ·ʃən). 1751. [a. mod. Fr., ad. L. *affiliationem*; see AFFILIATE.] 1. Adoption of a son 1751. 2. Adoption, by a society, of branches 1799. 3. Fixing the paternity of a child. *fig.* The fathering of a thing upon any one; also, the assignment of anything to its origin 1830.

Affi·nal, *a.* 1609. [f. L. *affinis.*] Related by marriage; from the same stock.

†**Affi·ne.** 1509. [a. Fr. *affin* :—L. *affinem.*] A. *sb.* A relation by marriage; a connexion. B. *adj.* Closely related –1657.

Affi·ned, *ppl. a.* 1597. [ad. Fr. *affiné* + -ED.] 1. Related. 2. Bound by any tie (*arch.*) 1604.

2. A. to loue the Moore *Oth.* I. i. 39.

Affi·nitive, *a.* 1651. [f. AFFINITY.] Connected by affinity.

Affinity (ăfi·nĭti). ME. [a. Fr. *af(f)inité*, ad. L. *affinitatem.*] 1. Relationship by marriage, opp. to *consanguinity*; *collect.* relations by marriage. In *R. C. Ch.*: The spiritual relationship between sponsors and their godchild. 2. Kinship generally; *collect.* kindred ME. 3. *Philol.* Structural resemblance in languages suggestive of a common stock 1599. 4. *Nat. Hist.* Structural resemblance in animals, plants, or minerals, suggestive of a common stock or type 1794. 5. *fig.* Causal relationship or connexion; family likeness 1533. †6. Vicinity –1770. 7. †Relationship by inclination; companionship –1611; hence *fig.* Any natural friendliness or attraction 1616. 8. *esp.* Chemical attraction; the tendency of certain elements or their compounds to unite and form new compounds 1753. 9. A spiritual attraction believed to exist between persons; also, the subjects of the affinity 1868.

1. Related by a. to the royal house 1849. The bar of spiritual a. FREEMAN. 2. The a. and brotherhood of mankind 1794. 5. The spiritual a. between Luther and Bunyan TULLOCH. 7. Now Jehosaphat ..joyned a. with Ahab *2 Chron.* xviii. 1. With this hath..the Spaw water great a. 1652.

Affirm (ăfɔ̄·ɹm), *v.* ME. [a. OFr. *afermer* :—L. *affirmare*: refash. after L.] †1. To make firm –1534. 2. *Law.* To confirm, ratify 1386. †3. To confirm or maintain (a statement) –1670; hence, to state positively ME.; to make a solemn AFFIRMATION (sense 5) ME. 4. *Logic* and *Gram.* To make a statement in the affirmative (as opp. to the *negative*) 1581.

2. To a. a sentence CHAUCER, a judgement COKE. 3. If my Lord affirm'd that black was white POPE. Permitted by law to a. instead of swearing 1863. 4. For Grammer sayes..two negatiues affirme SIDNEY. Hence **Affi·rmable** *a.* †affirmative; capable of being affirmed. **Affi·rmably** *adv.* **Affi·rmant** *a.* affirming; *sb.* one who affirms; var. **Affirmer.** **Affi·rmatory** *a.* assertive.

Affirmance (ăfɔ̄·ɹmăns). 1494. [a. OFr. *afermance*, f. *afermer*; see AFFIRM.] 1. A confirming 1531; in *Law*, ratification 1528. 2. A (strong) declaration 1494.

1. The a. of the decree 1808. 2. Till a. breeds a doubt COWPER.

Affirmation (æfəɹmēⁱ·ʃən). 1533. [a. Fr., ad. L. *affirmationem*; see AFFIRM.] 1. Confirmation; in *Law*, ratification. 2. The action of declaring true; *esp.* affirmative (opp. to negative) assertion 1611. 3. *Logic.* An affirmative judgement or proposition 1656. 4. That which is asserted; a statement 1593. 5. *Law.* A solemn declaration, having the value and penalties of an oath, by persons who conscientiously decline taking an oath 1695.

2. Vpon warrant of bloody a. *Cymb.* I. iv. 63. A single nod implies an a. DARWIN. 4. Paul's a., who saith..1593.

Affirmative (ăfə̄·ımătiv). ME. [a. Fr., ad. L. *affirmativus*; see AFFIRM.] A. *adj.* †1. Corroborative –1674; positive –1734. 2. *Logic.* Expressing the agreement of the two terms of a proposition 1570. 3. Hence, Asserting that the fact is so; answering 'yes'. Opp. to *negative.* 1628. †4. *Math.* Positive or real, opp. to *negative* –1789.

1. Be not confident and a. in an uncertain matter JER. TAYLOR. 3. An a. answer H. SPENCER.

B. *sb.* [sc. *mode, proposition, statement.*] 1. The affirmative mode in a proposition ME. 2. An affirmative word or proposition, opp. to a *negative* 1588. †3. An assertion –1660.

1. They all..*answered in the a.* DE FOE. 2. If your foure negatiues make your two affirmatiues *Twel. N.* v. i. 24. 3. That a. which sayes the Loadstone is poison SIR T. BROWNE. Hence **Affi·rmatively** *adv.* in an a. manner.

†Affi·rmly, Affe·rmely, *adv.* [f. Fr. *affermé.*] Firmly –1525.

Affix (ăfi·ks), *v.* 1533. [ad. med.L. *affixare*, freq. of *affigere.*] 1. To fix or fasten (*to, on, upon*) 1533. †2. *intr.* To cling or be attached *to* –1695. 3. To attach, add, as a seal, a signature, a postscript, etc. *to* 1658. Also *fig.* 1665. †4. *trans.* To fix upon –1725.

1. Affixed to a vessel 1734, *fig.* to one's studies FULLER. 3. To a. a price DIBDIN, notes 1878. *fig.* To a. ridicule to people 1734, blame FOSTER, salaries to a profession HUME. Hence **Affi·xed** *ppl. a.* attached; †fixed upon. **Affi·xer.**

Affix (æ·fiks), *sb.* 1612. [a. Fr. *affixe*, ad. L. *affixus*; see prec.] That which is attached or added 1642; *esp.* in *Gram.* An addition to a root, stem, or word; a prefix; a suffix 1612.

Affixture (ăfi·kstiŭı). 1793. [f. AFFIX *v.*] The action of affixing; the being affixed; attachment. vars. **Affixa·tion, †Affi·xion.**

Afflate (ăflē¹·t), *v. rare.* 1599. [f. L. *afflat-, afflare.*] To blow or breathe upon. Hence **Affla·ted** *ppl. a.* inspired. **Affla·tion**, inspiration.

Afflatus (ăflē¹·tŏs). 1665. [a. L.] †1. Hissing. [L. *afflatus serpentis.*] 2. The inspiration of supernatural knowledge; an overmastering impulse, poetic or other 1665. 3. *Med.* A form of erysipelas, which comes on suddenly.

2. A migratory a. LIVINGSTONE.

†Affli·ct, *ppl. a.* ME. [a. Fr. *afflict, aflit* :—L. *afflictum, affligere.*] Afflicted –1583.

Afflict (ăfli·kt), *v.* ME. [f. prec.] †1. To cast down –1667; *intr.* to become downcast ME. 2. *trans.* To trouble grievously; *refl.* to grieve 1535.

1. Reassembling our afflicted Powers MILT. 2. It is their virtues that a... him JUNIUS. Hence **†Affli·ct** *sb.* = AFFLICTION. **Affli·cter. Affli·ctingly** *adv.*

Affliction (ăfli·kʃən). ME. [a. Fr., OFr. *aflicion*, ad. L. *afflictionem*; see AFFLICT *a.*] †1. The action of inflicting grievous pain. *spec.* in religion, Self-discipline, mortification –1628. 2. The state of being afflicted ME. 3. That which afflicts; a calamity, pain, etc. 1598.

1. Feede him with bread of a., and with water of a. 2 *Chron.* xviii. 26. 2. I have seen the affliccioun of my puple WYCLIF *Ex.* iii. 7. A. of spirit *Haml.* III. ii. 324. 3. Every former a. had its charm MISS AUSTEN. Hence **Affli·ctionless** *a.*

Afflictive (ăfli·ktiv), *a.* 1611. [a. Fr., f. L. *afflict-*; see -IVE.] Tending to afflict; painful; trying. Const. *to.* Hence **Affli·ctively** *adv.*

†Afflue·, *v.* [a. Fr. *affluer*, f. L. *affluere.*] To flow towards; to flock –1521.

Affluence (æ·fluĕns). ME. [a. Fr., ad. L. *affluentia*; see prec.] 1. A flowing towards; a concourse 1600. 2. A plentiful flow; profusion 1447; *ellipt.* wealth 1603.

1. Great a. of company CARLYLE. 2. A. in rethoryk 1447, of teeres CAXTON, of all things 1633, of snows LONGF. They lived in..a. STEELE. var. **†A·ffluency** (in senses 2, 3).

Affluent (æ·fluĕnt), *a.* ME. [a. Fr., ad. L. *affluentem*; see AFFLUE.] †1. Flowing toward a place –1759. 2. Flowing freely or abundantly 1816. *fig.* Of the gifts of fortune, etc.: Plenteous 1413. 3. Hence, Wealthy. Also *fig.* Const. *in*; *of* rare. 1769. 4. *sb.* [The adj. used *absol.*] A tributary stream 1833.

1. A. blood HARVEY. 2. An a. mane SOUTHEY, fountain 1863, fortune GOLDSM. 3. An a. retreat JUNIUS. A. in expressions [etc.] 1855. 4. The.. Missouri, with its a., the Mississippi 1833. Hence **A·ffluently** *adv.*

Afflux (æ·flɒks). 1611. [ad. L. *affluxus*; see AFFLUE.] 1. A flowing towards a point; *esp.* in *Med.* of humours. 2. An accession 1661.

1. The a. of the sea 1635, of matter [to the lungs] 1661, of air 1794, of purchasers 1872. 2. An increased a. of blood 1859. var. **Afflu·xion.**

†A·ffodill. ME. [ad. med.L. *affodillus*, prob. = **asfodillus*, quasi-dim. of cl. L. *asphodilus*, a. Gr. ἀσφόδελος.] 1. Asphodel, or King's Spear (*Asphodelus*) –1615. 2. = DAFFODIL. –1611.

Afforce (ăfō̆ə·ıs), *v.* [ME. *aforce*, a. OFr. *aforcer*, var. of *efforcer*:—late L. *exfortiare*; and partly f. L. *ad* + *fortiare.*] †1. To apply force ME.; ravish ME.; attempt –1528. †2. To add force to, reinforce ME. 3. *Eng. Hist.* To strengthen by adding new members.

3. It was the practice to a. the jury HALLAM. Hence **Affo·rcement, †Afforciament,** a strengthening (sense 3); †a fort.

Afford (ăfō̆ə·ıd), *v.* OE. [f. *ge-* = *ă-* (see A- *pref.* 6), refash. *af-* + *forð-ian* to further.] †1. To further; to accomplish –ME. 2. To manage (*to do*); with *can*: To have the means, be able 1449; to spare, to bear the expense of 1833. 3. Without *can*: To give of what one has 1596. Of things: To be capable of yielding 1581; to yield naturally 1600.

2. To a. that their sons may be good for nothing SWIFT. He could a. to suffer WORDSW. To a. Another Rib MILT., beer 1833. 3. Welcome what he doth a. G. HERBERT. The world affords no law to make thee rich *Rom. & Jul.* v. i. 73. To a. an instance 1782. Olives..a. most oil when..ripe RAY. Hence **Affo·rdable** *a.* that can be afforded, spared, or yielded. **Affo·rder.**

Afforest (ăfǫ·rĕst), *v.* 1502. [ad. med.L. *afforestare*, f. *ad* + *foresta*, FOREST.] To convert into forest. Hence **Affo·resta·tion,** the action of the vb. or its result.

Affranchise (ăfræ·ntʃiz, -ʃəiz), *v.* 1475. [f. Fr. *afranchiss-*, *afranchir*, now *aff-*; see FRANK.] To free from servitude, or from a vow, etc. Hence **Affra·nchisement.**

†Affra·p, *v.* [f. FRAP, q.v.: cf. *addoom.*] To strike. SPENSER.

Affray (ăfrē¹·), *v.* ME. [a. Anglo-Fr. *afrayer, effrayer, esfreer*:—late L. *exfridare*, f. *ex* + *fridus*, ad. Teut. *friðu* peace; see AFRAID.] 1. To disturb or startle (*arch.*) ME. 2. To frighten; *esp.* in pass. (*arch.*) ME. 3. To frighten away (*arch.*) ME.

1. The kettle-drum And..clarionet a. his ears KEATS. 2. He was affrayde 1315. 3. To afray us from the euil 1610. Hence **Affray·ed** *ppl. a.* alarmed KEATS. **Affray·er.**

Affray (ăfrē¹·), *sb.* Aphet. FRAY. ME. [a. OFr. *effrei*, f. *esfreer*; see prec.] †1. An attack, or assault –1583. †2. Alarm; terror –1596. 3. †A disturbance –1810; *esp.* a breach of the peace, caused by fighting or riot in a public place 1482.

3. The tumult and a. SCOTT. An A. is a common wrong BLOUNT.

Affreight (ăfrē¹·t), *v. rare.* 1847. [ad. Fr. *affréter.*] To hire a ship to carry cargo. Hence **Affrei·ghter. Affrei·ghtment,** the hiring of a ship to carry cargo.

†Affre·t, *sb.* [?] Furious onset. SPENSER.

Affricate (æ·frikĕt). *Phonetics.* 1880. [ad. L. *affricatus*; cf. FRICATIVE.] A combination of a stop with a following fricative, as G. *pf.* Also **Affri·cative**; **A·ffricated** *a.*

†Affrie·nded, *pa. pple.* [f. AF- + FRIEND *sb.* + -ED.] Made friends. SPENSER.

†Affri·ght, *ppl. a.* OE. [See A- *pref.* 1 and FRIGHT *v.*] = next.

Affright (ăfrəi·t), *v. arch.* 1589. [f. FRIGHT *v.*, with A- *pref.* 11 (*af-*); see prec.] To frighten, to terrify. Now *poet.* for FRIGHTEN.

The Scar-Crow that affrights our children so 1 *Hen. VI*, I. iv. 43. Hence **Affri·ght** *sb.* the action of causing terror; *concr.* a cause of terror; the state of terror; whence **Affri·ghtful** *a.*, -ly *adv.* **Affri·ghten** *v.* var. of AFFRIGHT *v.* **Affri·ghter. Affri·ghtment,** †the action of frightening; the fact or state of being frightened. All *arch.*

Affrighted (ăfrəi·tĕd), *ppl. a.* 1604. [f. prec.] Struck with sudden fear; alarmed.

Th' a. Globe *Oth.* v. ii. 100. Hence **Affri·ghtedly** *adv.*

Affront (ăfrɒ·nt), *v.* [ME. *afront*, a. OFr. *afronter*:—late L. *affrontare*, f. *ad frontem.*] 1. To insult to the face or openly. 2. To put to the blush; to cause to feel ashamed ME. 3. To face in defiance; confront 1563. 4. †To meet of purpose, accost –1633; to face in position (*arch.*) 1600. †5. To set face to face –1606.

1. Not to honor vs, but to a. vs 1577. To a. the Divine Goodness GLANVILLE. 2. Lord Sandwich affronted his Grace of Grafton extremely H. WALPOLE. 3. Who, him affronting soone, to fight was readie prest SPENSER. To a. death 1856, great risk KINGLAKE. 4. To a., as 'twere by accident *Haml.* III. i. 31. What affronts our gaze BROWNING. Hence **Affro·nted** *ppl. a.* injured in one's feelings; †brazen-faced. **Affro·ntedly** *adv.* shamelessly. **†Affro·ntedness. Affro·ntee,** one who receives an affront. **Affro·nter,** †a deceiver; one who affronts. **Affro·nting** *vbl. sb.* insulting; facing; *ppl. a.* openly offensive. **Affro·ntingly** *adv.* **Affro·ntingness,** insulting manner. **Affro·ntive** *a.* of affronting character or tendency.

Affront (ăfrɒ·nt), *sb.* 1598. [f. the vb. Cf. Fr. *affront.*] 1. An open insult; a word or act of intentional disrespect. 2. Felt indignity 1662. †3. An encounter or meeting (see AFFRONT *v.* 3, 4) –1678; a position of hostility –1648.

1. Phr. *To offer an affront to, put an a. on.* 2. Candidates are .. not very susceptible of affronts COWPER.

‖Affrontee (afrọnte, ăfrɒ·ntī), *a.* 1751. [Fr. *affronté*; see AFFRONT *v.*] *Her.* 1 Front to front. 2. Looking frontwise 1766.

Affu·se, *v. rare.* 1683. [f. L. *affus-, affundere.*] To pour upon. Hence **Affu·sed** *ppl. a.*

Affusion (ăfiū·ʒən). 1615. [ad. L. **affusionem*; see prec.] A pouring on or into; e. g. of water upon the body, as (*Med.*) in fevers, or in one method of baptism. Also *fig.*

†Affy·, *v.* [ME. *afye*, a. OFr. *afier* (refash. *affier*) :—late L. *affidare.*] 1. To trust. *trans.*, *refl.*, and *intr.* Const. *to, on, in.* –1642. 2. To affirm on one's faith –1617. 3. To make fast by solemn promise; to espouse –1627; to affiance –1705. Also *fig.*

1. I do affie In thy vprightnesse *Tit. A.* I. i. 47. 3. The Prince affyes [Philippa] at the last DRAYTON. I would not a. my daughter to you ROWE. Hence **†Affy·** *sb.* trust.

†A·fgod. OE. [f. *af-* + GOD.] A false god.

Afield (ăfī·ld), *adv.* OE. [A *prep.*[1] + FIELD.] 1. On or in the field, *esp.* of labour or battle. 2. To or into the field; *hence*, to battle ME; away from home; also *fig.* ME.

1. Æneas is a. *Tr. & Cr.* v. iii. 67. 2. They a. Their cattle drive HOBBES.

Afire (ăfəi·ə·ı), *adv.* and *a.* ME. [A *prep.*[1] 11 + FIRE.] On or in fire; burning. Also *fig.*

Aflame (ăflē¹·m), *adv.* and *a.* 1555. [A *prep.*[1] 11 + FLAME.] In or into flame; in a glow. Also *fig.* 1798.

fig. All a. with curiosity W. COLLINS.

Afla·t, *adv.* ME. [A *prep.*[1] + FLAT.] In a flat position.

Aflau·nt, *adv.* 1568. [A *prep.*[1] 11 + FLAUNT.] In a flaunting state.

A-fli·cker, *adv.* [A *prep.*[1] + FLICKER.] In a flickering state. BROWNING.

Afloat (ăflō̆ᵘ·t), *adv.* and *a.* OE. [f. ON + FLOAT.] 1. In a floating condition, opp. to *aground*; at sea, opp. to *in dock, ashore* OE.; buoyed up in the air 1825. 2. In a state of overflow or submersion 1591. 3. *fig.* Unembarrassed; having one's head above water 1538. 4. Started 1559; in full swing 1604. 5. In currency 1586; *esp.* in *Comm.* of negotiable instruments (*mod.*). 6. Adrift 1714.

1. He commanded the force a. WELLINGTON. The quantity of wheat a. 1879. 2. The main deck was a. MARRYAT. 5. Various rumours were a. BRIGHT. To keep bills a. (*mod.*).

Aflow·er, *adv.* and *a.* 1876. [A *prep.*[1] II + FLOWER.] Flowering.

Aflu·tter, *adv.* 1830. [A *prep.*[1] + FLUTTER.] In a flutter.

Afoa·m, *adv.* 1849. [A *prep.*[1] + FOAM.] In a state of foam.

Afoot (ăfu·t), *adv.* ME. [A *prep.*[1] + FOOT; orig. in pl. *a* (*on*) *foten* = *on feet.*] 1. On foot, *i.e.* on one's own feet. 2. Astir, on the move 1530; hence, in active existence or operation 1601.

1. He was mounted and I a. DICKENS. 2. Mischeefe thou art a. *Jul. C.* III. ii. 265. *Comb.* **afoot-back** (after *a-horse-back*). GREENE.

Afore (ăfōᵊ·ɹ). *dial.* and *Naut.* [OE. *onforan*, influenced by *ætforan*, f. *æt* + *foran*, ME. *forn*; cf. BEFORE.] **A.** *adv.* 1. Of place: In front; in or into the forepart. 2. Of time: Before ME. **B.** *prep.* 1. Of place: Before OE. 3. Of rank, etc.: In precedence of ME. **C.** *conj.* [*ellipt.*] Sooner than ME. Still used in comb. in aforesaid 1418.

Aforehand (ăfōᵊ·ɹhænd), *adv. arch.* ME. [f. AFORE *prep.* + HAND; now BEFOREHAND.] In anticipation. †As *adj.* Prepared, provided for the future -1748.

Aforethought (ăfōᵊ·ɹþǫt). 1581. [f. AFORE *adv.* + *thought*. App. tr. of Old Law-Fr. *prepense.*] **A.** *ppl. a.* Thought before; premeditated. **B.** *sb. rare.* Premeditation 1851.

A. With malice a. COKE.

Aforetime (ăfōᵊ·ɹtəim), *adv.* 1535. [f. AFORE *adv.* + TIME.] Before in time, formerly. As *attrib.* or *sb.* rare. var. †-times.

†Afo·reward, *adv.* ME. [f. AFORE + -WARD.] First in rank; in front -1380.

‖A fortiori (ēⁱ fōᵊɹʃiōᵊ·rəi). [L. (sc. *argumento*).] With stronger reason.

Afraid (ăfrēⁱ·d), *ppl. a.* ME. [pa. pple. of *afray*, AFFRAY *v.* Not refash.] As *pple.* Alarmed, frightened; hence as *adj.*, In a state of fear, moved by fear. (As adj. it never stands bef. a noun.) Const. *of*; *inf.*; *lest, that* (with subj.); *of* with gerund = *lest* with subj.

Back they recoild affraid MILT. *P. R.* II. 739. A. of truth KINGSLEY. Willing to wound, and yet a. to strike POPE. I am a. that it is too true (*mod.*). A. of bathing.

Afreet, -it, -ite (æ·frīt). 1802. [Arab.] A demon of Mohammedan mythology.

†‖Afre·sca, *adv.* [It. *afresco.*] In fresco. EVELYN.

Afre·sh, *adv.* 1509. [A- *pref.* 3 + FRESH.] Anew, freshly.

Dead Henries wounds Open their congeal'd mouthes and bleed a. *Rich. III*, I. ii. 56.

African (æ·frikăn), *a.* and *sb.* 1564. [ad. L. *Africanus.*] Belonging to or characteristic of, a native or inhabitant of, Africa. Hence **A·fricanism** 1641, **A·fricanize** *v.* 1853.

Africander (æ·frikændəɹ). 1834. [Cape Du. (*-kaander*), f. next, after *Hollander.*] A white (esp. Dutch) native of S. Africa.

Afrikaans (æfrikā·ns). 1908. [Du. (*-aansch*).] = TAAL.

†Afro·nt, *adv.* ME. [A *prep.*[1] + FRONT *sb.* (= Fr. *de front*).] Face to face -1601; in front -1621; in a front, abreast -1621. Also as *prep.* -1622.

These foure came all a. and..thrust at me SHAKS.

Aft (ɑft), *adv.* [OE. *æftan*, f. *afta* = *af* + *ta* superl. ending.] 1. *Naut.* In or near the stern 1628; towards the stern 1678. †2. Of time: Earlier -1676.

1. *Fore and a.*: from stem to stern, lengthwise 1618.

After (ɑ·ftəɹ), *adv.* [OE. *æfter*, orig. compar. of *af*, L. *ab*, with compar. suff. *-ter*, -THER.] **A.** *adv.* Behind in place or order OE.; later in time, next following OE.

Jill came tumbling a. *Nurs. Rhyme.* That happened in the week a. (*mod.*).

B. *prep.* 1. Moving in the rear of, behind OE.; with vbs., adjs., and sbs. of action: In pursuit of, in search of OE. 2. Following in time, in succession to OE.; after the interval of OE.; subsequent to and later than OE.; subsequent to and in consequence of OE.; subsequent to and notwithstanding 1603. 3. Next to in order or importance ME. 4. According to, in harmony with OE.; in imitation of, like ME.; in a manner proportionate to (*arch.*) OE.; at (the rate of) 1530.

1. A. them, nay, before them if we can 2 *Hen. VI*, v. iii. 27. To *be after*: trying to get or do, or get into the company of. To *look, see after* (a thing gone, going, etc.): to attend to. To *call*, etc. *after*: to seek to get, etc., by calling. To enquire a. one's health SHERIDAN. Greedy a. power MACAULAY. 2. A. me cometh a man that is preferred before me *John* i. 30. Time a. time (*mod.*). A. two years' absence (*mod.*). Long a. dark 1832. I'll work a. hours DICKENS. A. his behaviour to his parents what could you expect (*mod.*). The Roman occupation was, *after all*, very superficial FREEMAN. 3. Codrus a. Phoebus sings the best DRYDEN. 4. A. our lawe he ought to dye *John* xix. 7. A. his oracle Dr. Johnson GIBBON. To dress a. HALLAM. And Corin called it a. his name cornewayle CAXTON. So to *draw, model, compose a.* Giue them a. the worke of their handes *Ps.* xxviii. 4. A. the Rate of 12*s.* per Gallon 1702.

C. *conj.* 1. Of time: with *that* (*arch.*); or *simply* ME. †2. Of manner: According as; const. *that* or *as* -1587; or *simply* -1634.

1. A. I am rysen ageyne TINDALE *Matt.* xxvi. 32 [WYCLIF A. that I schal rise aȝen].

After (ɑ·ftəɹ), *a.* [OE. *æftere*, f. *æfter* adv.; superl. *æftemest.*] Of time. †1. The second (of two) -ME. 2. Next OE.; later, *esp.* in *Comb.* 1594. 3. Of place: Nearer the rear, more aft. Chiefly *Naut.* ME. Hence †**A·fterness**, the quality of being after.

After- *in comb.* is used in many relations, in some of which the use of the hyphen indicates no more than that the grammatical relation is not that of preposition and object.

a.-band, a later band or bond after a release; **-blow** = AFTERCLAP; **-born** *ppl. a.*, born after the father's death or last will; younger; †**-brain**, the posterior lobe, the cerebellum; **-cabin**; †**-cast**, a second throw (at dice), an experimental result; **-damp**, the choke-damp left in a mine after an explosion; **-eatage** = AFTERGRASS; †**-eye**, to look after; **-growth**, an AFTERMATH; growth afterwards; **-knowledge**, knowledge after the event; **-leech**, the hinder edge (of a sail); **-liver**, survivor; **-nose**, *Entom.*, a triangular piece below the antennæ and above the nasus; **-reckoning**; **-roll**, the roll of the waves after a storm; also *fig.*; **-sails**, all those on the after-masts, and on the stays between the main and mizen masts; **-shine** = AFTERGLOW; **-sum**, the purchase money paid after the deposit; **-taste**, a taste which comes after swallowing anything; also *fig.*; **-winter**, a renewal of winter; **-wise**, wise after the event; **-world**, future generation; **-wrist**, the metacarpus; **-yards**, *Naut.* the yards in the main and mizen masts.

Afterbirth (ɑ·ftəɹbə̄ɹþ). 1587. 1. The secundine or placenta, which is expelled from the womb after the infant. Also *fig.* 2. *Rom. Law.* Birth after a father's death or last will 1875. 3. Late-born children 1871. So †**A·fter-bu·rthen, -den** (in sense 1).

Afterclap (ɑ·ftəɹklæp). ME. An unexpected stroke after the recipient has ceased to be on his guard; a surprise happening after an affair is supposed to be at an end.

Fear of afterclaps MELVILLE *Whale* xviii. 101.

†A·fterco·mer. ME. A successor; *pl.* posterity -1705.

After-course (ɑ·ftəɹkōᵊ·ɹs). 1580. †1. A later course at dinner. 2. Subsequent course. (Prop. two wds.) 1859.

Aftercrop (ɑ·ftəɹkrǫp). 1563. A second crop in one season. Hence **A·ftercrop** *v.*

†A·fterdeal. 1481. [Cf. G. *Nachtheil.*] A disadvantage -1634.

After-dinner (ɑ·ftəɹ-di·nəɹ). 1576. †1. *sb.* The time after dinner; the afternoon -1618. 2. *attrib.* Occurring after dinner; *esp.* before leaving the table 1730.

1. Upon an a. RALEIGH. 2. An a. anecdote 1826.

After-game (ɑ·ftəɹgēⁱ·m). 1631. A second game played to improve on the result of the first; *hence*, a new plan to meet a miscarriage.

Afterglow (ɑ·ftəɹglōᵘ). 1873. A glow that remains after the disappearance of any light, *esp.* that in the western sky after sunset; also *fig.*

After-grass (ɑ·ftəɹgrɑs). 1681. The grass which grows after the first crop or after harvest.

After-guard (ɑ·ftəɹgāɹd). 1826. *Naut.* The men who are stationed on the quarter-deck and poop, to work the after-sails.

†A·fterhand, *adv.* ME. [orig. *after the hand.*] Afterwards. (Now *Sc.*)

After-image (ɑ·ftəri:medʒ). 1879. The impression of a vivid sensation, retained after the external cause is withdrawn.

Afterings (ɑ·ftəriŋz), *sb. pl.* 1796. [AFTER *adv.* + -ING. Cf. *innings.*] The milk drawn last from a cow. Still *dial.*

A·fter-life. 1. A future life 1615. 2. The later period of one's life 1817.

Aftermath (ɑ·ftəɹmæþ). Also **-mowth.** 1523. Second or later mowing; the crop of grass which springs up after the mowing in early summer. Also *attrib.* and *fig.*

fig. The a. of the grest rebellion COLERIDGE.

Aftermost (ɑ·ftəɹməst, -moᵘst), *a. superl.* OE. [Orig. corrupt for OE. *æftemest*, superl. of *æftere*: in mod. use f. AFTER + -MOST.] †1. Hindmost; last in time -ME. 2. *Naut.* Most aft 1773.

Afternoon (ɑ:ftəɹnū·n). ME. [cf. L. *post meridiem.*] The time from mid-day to evening. Also *fig.* and *attrib.*

fig. In the a. of her best dayes *Rich. III*, III. vii. 186. *attrib.* A. tea 1879.

After-pain (ɑ·ftəɹpēⁱ:n). 1556. A pain which follows later; *esp.* (in *pl.*) the pains that follow child-birth. Also *fig.*

A·fterpiece. 1806. 1. A farce or short piece after the play. Also *fig.* 2. *Naut.* The heel of a rudder.

†A·fterspring. 1583. 1. Posterity -1587. 2. A second spring -1670. Also *fig.*

A·fter-su·pper. 1590. The time between supper and bed-time. *Obs.* exc. *attrib.*

Afterthought (ɑ·ftəɹþǫt). 1661. 1. A subsequent thought. 2. Reflection after the act; hence, a later explanation or evasion 1684.

Afterward (ɑ·ftəɹwəɹd), *adv.* [OE. *æfteweard*, corrupted through *æfter*, AFTER.] †1. Behind -ME.; *Naut.* aftward -1618. 2. Subsequently ME. †3. Of order: next -1581.

A·fterwards, *adv.* ME. [f. prec. + *-es*, *s* advb. gen.] At a later time.

In the a. metropolitan city NEWMAN.

After-wit (ɑ·ftəɹwi:t). *arch.* 1509. †1. Later knowledge -1680. 2. †Second thought -1607; *esp.* wisdom after the event 1579.

2. A. is everybody's wit 1736. Hence **A·fter-wi·tted** *a.* wise when too late.

A·fterwo·rt. 1725. The second run of beer.

A·ftward, *adv.* [f. AFT.] Towards the stern.

Ag-, *pref.* = L. *ad-* bef. *g*, OFr. *a-*, refash. later after L., exc. in *agree*. Occ. for *a-* not = L. *ad-*.

‖Aga, agha (ăgā·, æ·gă). 1600. [Turk.] A chief officer, military or civil, in the Ottoman empire; also, a title of distinction.

†Aga·d, *int.* = EGAD, q. v.

Agadic (ăgæ·dik), *a.* 1878. [f. L. *Agada*, HAGGADA.] Of or pertaining to the Haggada, legendary (Rabbinic).

Again (ăge·n, ăgēⁱ·n). [OE. *ongeán, ongén*; f. *on*, in + *gagn, gegn* 'direct, straight'. In 16th c. *again* became advb. only, *against* being used as *prep.* and *conj.*] **A.** *adv.* †1. Back -1480. 2. In return, in reply (*arch.*) ME. 3. Back into a former position OE.; anew, once more ME. 4. Once repeated 1593. 5. Anywhere besides (*arch.*) 1555. 6. On the other hand; besides 1533.

1. Turn a. Whittington (*arch.*). *To and a.*: to and fro. 2. I maruell why I answer'd not againe *A. Y. L.* III. v. 132. To *ring, echo*, etc., *a.*; to *creak, crack, ache, shine, gleam*, etc., *a.* 3. Here we are a. (*mod.*). To look upon his like a. *Haml.* I. ii. 188. **Now and again**: now and then. 4. Lent shall bee as long againe as it is 2 *Hen. VI*, IV. iii. 7. 5. There is not, in the world a. 1626. 6. But now a., see 1742. What a. MACAULAY.

†**B.** *prep.* = AGAINST I. 1, II. 1, 2, III. 2, 3, IV, V. 17, 18. †**C.** *conj.* Against the time that -1632.

†**Agai·n-** [the *adv.*], was formerly used in many combs., all now obs. In meaning it answered to L. *re-*, esp. in the senses of opposition, reciprocal action, and repetition.

†a.-buy *v.*, to redeem; †-buyer; †-come *v.*, to encounter; †-rise *v.*, to rebel; †-say *v.*, to say nay; to speak against; to reverse; hence †-say *sb.*, objection, †-sayer; -stand *v.*, to resist; hence †-stander; †-turn *v.*, to return.

Against (ăgen·st, ăgē·nst). ME. or late OE. [f. *aȝen, ayen* + *-es* gen. ending + *-t* parasitic, as in *amongst*, etc. Aphet. *'gainst*, poet.] A. *prep.* I. Of position. 1. Facing, in full view of (now usu. *over against*) ME.; †with (L. *apud*) -1520; *fig.* in regard to ME. 2. Near, adjoining. Still *dial.* 1531.

1. Sat backwards over a. me 1741. 'Gainst the fire SHAKS. Ageynste the Lorde ys mercy 1520. Their rights as a. each other (*mod.*).

II. Of motion. †1. Towards -1634. 2. Toward and into contact with ME.; hence, supported by 1591; having as background 1805.

2. To kyke aȝens the pricke WYCLIF. *To run a.*: to meet accidentally. Leane thine aged back a. mine Arme 1 *Hen. VI*, II. v. 43.

III. Of motion or action in opposition to. 1. Counter to ME. 2. Not in conformity with ME. 3. Towards with hostile intent (*arch.*) ME.; in active opposition to OE.; in resistance to OE.

1. To swimme a. the Tyde 3 *Hen. VI*, I. iv. 20. *A. the hair* (Fr. *à contrepoil*), *a. the grain*: opposed to the natural bent. 2. A. my general notions BURKE. 3. His hand will be a. euery man *Gen.* xvi. 12. So *to fight, speak, act a.*, a *declaration, law, protest a.*, and the like. My lectures a. pride GOLDSM. So *to be a.*, to *run, play*, etc. *a.* Proof a. their enmitie *Rom. & Jul.* II. ii. 73. Caution a. pickpockets (*mod.*).

IV. Of mutual opposition or relation. In exchange for ME.; in the opposite scale 1531.

To set off a.: to enter on the *opposite* side to a previous entry.

V. Of time. †Drawing towards -1634; *esp.* in preparation for ME.

A sermon to write a. the Assizes WESLEY.

B. *conj.* By the time that, before (*arch.*) ME. A. father comes home DICKENS.

C. *adv. rare.* = AGAIN *adv.*

†**Agai·nward**, *adv.* ME. [f. AGAIN *adv.* + WARD.] Back again -1634; in reply -1520; once more -1541; *vice versa* -1579; on the other hand -1534.

Agalactous (ægălæ·ktəs), *a.* 1879. [f. Gr. ἀ + γάλακτ- + -OUS.] *Med.* Having no milk to suckle with.

Agalaxy (æ·gălæksi). 1731. [f. mod. L., a. Gr. ἀγαλαξία = ἀγαλακτία; see prec.] *Med.* A failure of milk in a mother after child-birth. var. ‖**Agala·ctia**.

†**Aga·lloch.** 1633. [ad. L. *agallochum*, ad. Gr. ἀγάλλοχον.] The fragrant resinous heart-wood of *Aquilaria*; also called *agila-, aloes-*, eagle-wood. Lindley.

Agalmatolite (ægælmæ·tŏləit). 1832. [f. Gr. ἄγαλμα + λίθος.] *Min. prop.* The 'Figure-stone' or Pagodite; also other soft minerals, which are easily carved.

Agama (æ·gămă). 1817. [ad. Carib.] *Zool.* A genus of lizards; *pop.* one British West Indian species. Hence **Aga·mian** *a.* and *sb.* name of a sub-family of the iguanians (including the genus *A.*). **A·gamoid** *a.* resembling an agama.

†**A-ga·me,** *adv.* [A *prep.*[1] + GAME.] In sport. CHAUCER.

Agami (æ·gămĭ). 1833. [a. Fr. *agamy*, a. Guiana name.] The Trumpeter, a bird allied to the Crane.

Agamic (agæ·mik), *a.* 1850. [f. Gr. ἄγαμος; see AGAMOUS.] *Biol.* Characterized by the absence of sexual action; †*Bot.* = CRYPTOGAMIC. Hence **Aga·mically** *adv.*

†**A·gamist.** [f. Gr. ἄγαμος.] A professed celibate -1656.

Agamogenesis (æ:gămo͜dʒe·nĕsis). 1864. [f. Gr. ἄγαμος + γένεσις.] *Biol.* Generation without sexual union (as by simple division, or by buds); asexual reproduction. Hence **A:gamogene·tic** *a.* relating to a.; generating or generated without sexual union. **A:gamogene·tically** *adv.*

Agamous (æ·găməs), *a.* 1847. [f. L. *agamus*, a. Gr. ἄγαμος.] *Biol.* Asexual.

Agamy (æ·gămi). 1796. [ad. Gr. ἀγαμία.] Absence or non-recognition of the marriage relation.

Aganglionic (ăgæ:ŋgli͜ǫ·nik), *a.* 1836. [f. A- *pref.* 14.] *Phys.* Without ganglia.

‖**Aganippe.** 1630. A fountain on Mount Helicon sacred to the Muses; *fig.* poetic power or method.

Agape (ăgē·p), *adv.* 1667. [A *prep.*[1] + GAPE.] On the gape; *fig.* in wondering expectation.

A rabbit mouth that is ever a. TENNYSON.

‖**Agape** (æ·găpĭ). Pl. **agapæ**. 1696. [Gr.] A 'love-feast' held by the early Christians in connexion with the Lord's Supper.

A·gaphite. 1837. [named after *Agaphi*, a naturalist.] A kind of turquoise.

Agar-agar (ē·gar͜ē·gaɪ). 1820. [Malay.] An E. Indian seaweed from which a gelatinous substance is extracted for use in soup and for a culture medium. Also **a·gar**.

Agaric (æ·gărik, ăgæ·rik). 1533. [ad. L. *agaricum*, ad. Gr. ἀγαρικόν, f. *Agaria* in Sarmatia.] 1. *Herb.* and *Pharm.* One of various species of *Polyporus*, esp. *P. officinalis*, the 'Female Agarick', a cathartic, and *P. igniarius*, the 'Male Agarick', used as tinder, etc. *arch.* 2. *Bot.* A mushroom; *prop.* one of the genus *Agaricus* 1777. 3. = *A.-mineral.*

2. And agarics and fungi SHELLEY. A foul-flesh'd a. TENNYSON. *Comb.* **a.-mineral**, a light, spongy variety of carbonate of lime, called also Rock-milk, allied to stalactites.

Aga·sp, *adv.* 1800. [A *prep.*[1] 11 + GASP.] Gasping.

†**Aga·st, agha·st**, *v.* ME. [f. A- *pref.* 1 + *gasten*, OE. *gæstan*; see GAST. Now only in pa. pple. *agast*, erron. AGHAST.] To frighten; to take fright -1596. Hence †**Aga·sted** *ppl. a.*

Agastric (ăgæ·strik), *a.* 1836. [f. ἀ + γαστήρ.] *Zool.* Having no distinct alimentary canal.

Agate (æ·gĕt), *sb.* 1570. [a. Fr. *agathe*, ad. It. *agata*, f. L. *achates* (a. Gr. ἀχάτης).] 1. A precious stone; one of the semi-pellucid variegated chalcedonies, having the colours arranged in stripes or bands, or blended in clouds, and classed accordingly, as *moss a.*, *ribbon a.*, etc. †2. *fig.* A diminutive person, from the small figures cut in agates for seals -1599. 3. An instrument used by gold-wire-drawers for burnishing 1751. 4. *Typog.* The U.S. name of the type called in Eng. *ruby* 1871.

2. If low, an agot very vildlie cut *M. Ado* III. i. 65. Also 2 *Hen. IV*, I. ii. 19. *Comb.* **a.-shell**, one of the tropical genus *Achatina*. Hence **A·gated** *ppl. a.* marked like an a. **Agati·ferous** *a.* producing, or rich in, agates. **Aga·tiform** *a.* a.-like; var. **A·gatine**. **A·gatized** *ppl. a.* converted into a. **A·gaty** *a.* of the nature of a.

Agate (ăgē·t), *adv.* 1554. [A *prep.*[1] + GATE.] On the way; a-going.

Agathism (æ·găþiz'm). *rare.* 1830. [f. Gr. ἀγαθός.] The doctrine that all things tend towards good; opp. to *optimism*. Hence **A·gathist**.

A·gatho-, f. Gr. ἀγαθός, good, combining form.

a.-demon [Gr. δαίμων], a good genius; whence -demonic *a.*; -ka·kolo·gical *a.* composed of good and evil (*nonce-wd.*).

‖**Agave** (ăgē·vi). 1830. [L. prop. name, ad. Gr. Ἀγαυή, prop. adj. fem., illustrious.] *Bot.* A genus of plants (N.O. *Amaryllidaceæ*), including the American Aloe.

Agaze (ăgē·z), *adv.* 1430. [A *prep.*[1] + GAZE *v.*] Gazing.

†**Aga·zed, -sed**, *ppl. a.* ME. [? var. of *agast* AGHAST, affected by prec.] Affrighted -1600.

Age (ēdʒ), *sb.* ME. [a. OFr. *aäge, eäge, edage*:—late L. **ætaticum*, f. *ætatem*, contr. f. *ævitatem*, f. *ævum*; see -AGE.] I. A period of existence. 1. The time that anything has lived or existed ME. 2. The whole or ordinary duration of life 1535. 3. Such duration as ordinarily brings maturity ME.; any length of life which qualifies for anything ME. 4. A naturally distinct period or stage of life; *esp.* old age ME.; hence, the effects of age: Senility, maturity 1460.

1. Of the a. of twelue yeeres *Mark* v. 42. The *Moon's age*: the time since the occurrence of the new moon. Of what a. is the day MASSINGER. 2. The a. of man has greatly diminished 1853. 3. *Full age*, in Eng. Law, 21 years; *age of discretion*, 14 years. To come of a. (*mod.*). No limitation of a. (*mod.*). 4. One man in his time playes many parts, His Acts being seuen ages *A. Y. L.* II. vii. 143. A. with his stealing steps *Haml.* v. i. 79. When the a. is in, the wit is out *Much Ado* III. v. 37. This wine lacks a. (*mod.*).

II. A period of time. 1. The generation to which any one belongs ME. 2. A generation 1535. 3. A long but indefinite period ME.; often *loosely* in exaggeration 1590; also, a century. (Cf. Fr. *siècle*.) 1594. 4. *Hist.* A great period of human history marked by certain characters, real or mythical ME. 5. *Geol.* A great period or stage of the physical history of the Earth; an æon 1855.

1. The follies of the a. POPE. 3. Through the ages one increasing purpose runs TENNYSON. It is an a. since we met 1813. 4. The Golden, the Patriarchal, the Bronze A., the A. of the Reformation, the Middle Ages, the Prehistoric A. 5. The Ice a. or Glacial epoch KINGSLEY. Hence **Age** *v.* to grow, or make, old. **A·geing, a·ging** *ppl. a.* **A·geless** *a.* without old a. or limits of duration. **A·ge-long** *a.* long as an a. †**A·gemate**, a coeval.

-age, *suffix* of abstr. nouns, formed from names of things, or persons, or vbs. of action, as *language, baronage, wreckage*, etc. [OFr. *-age*:—late L. *-aticum*, neut. of adjs. in *-aticus*.] That which belongs or is functionally related to.

Aged (ē·dʒĕd; sense 3 ēdʒd), *ppl. a.* 1440. [f. the vb.] 1. Old. Also *fig.* 2. Belonging to old age 1588. 3. Of or at the age of 1637.

1. An a. man FREEMAN. Ag'd in vertue 1611. 2. A. wrinkles, cramps SHAKS. Hence **A·gedly** *adv.* ? *Obs.* **A·gedness**, the quality of being old, or of a stated age.

Agelast (æ·dʒĭlæst). 1877. [ad. Gr. ἀγέλαστος, f. ἀ- A- 14 + γελᾶν to laugh.] One who does not laugh.

Agen, *poet.* = southern pronunc. of AGAIN.

Agency (ē·dʒĕnsi). 1658. [ad. med.L. *agentia* = *facultas agendi*.] 1. The faculty of an agent, or of acting; action 1658; intermediation 1674. 2. Action personified 1784. 3. *Comm.* The office or function of an agent or factor 1745. 4. An establishment where business is done for another 1861.

1. The moral a. of the Supreme Being 1762. The A. of the Romish Factors with the King of Spain 1674. 2. An invisible a. arrested his progress BECKFORD. 3. The contract of a. POSTE. 4. Reuter's A. 1882.

†**Age·nd, now agendum.** Pl. †**agends, agenda.** 1629. [ad. L.: only the L. pl. *agenda* is in ordinary use.] 1. *pl.* Things to be done; opp. to matters of belief 1753. †2. *Eccl.* Matters of ritual -1775. 3. The items of business to be done at a meeting 1882.

Agenesis (ădʒe·nĕsis). 1853. [f. ἀ + γένεσις.] *Phys.* Imperfect development of the body or any part of it. var. **Agenesia.** Hence **Agene·sic** *a.*

Agennesis (ædʒenī·sis). 1847. [f. ἀ + γέννησις.] Male sterility. var. **Agennesia.**

Agent (ē·dʒĕnt). 1579. [ad. L. *agens, agere*.] A. *adj.* Acting; opp. to *patient* (*arch.*) 1620.

B. *sb.* 1. One who or that which acts; opp. to the *patient*, or the *instrument* 1600. 2. The efficient cause 1656; hence, any natural force, or substance, which produces phenomena, as *electricity, actinism, chloroform*, etc. 1756. 3. One who does the *actual work*, as opp. to the employer; a deputy, steward, emissary, etc. 1593. 4. Of things: The material cause or instrument 1579.

3. **A.-general** *spec.* the representative, under a high commissioner for the Dominion, of each of the States of Australia and of certain Provinces of Canada. 4. *Two Gent.* I. iii. 46. 5. Comb. *a.-noun*, etc. 1879. Hence †**A·gent** *v.* to act as a. in. **A·gentess.** H. WALPOLE. **Agential** (eⁱdʒe·nʃăl) *a.* of or pertaining to an a., or agency. **A·gentship** = AGENCY 3.

Ager, obs. f. EAGER *sb.*, tide, bore.

‖**Agera·sia.** 1706. [Gr.] The quality of not growing old.

Ageratum (ădʒĕ·rătŏm, *pop.* ædʒərē·tŏm). 1567. [mod.L., a. Gr. ἀγήρατον, f. ἀ + γῆρας.] †1. *Herb.* An 'everlasting' flower, known to the ancients. 2. *Bot.* A genus of plants (N.O. *Compositæ*, Div. *Eupatoriæ*) 1866.

†**Age·t**, *v.* OE. [f. A- *pref.* 1 + GET.] To seize -1490.

†**Age·te(n**, **aȝe·te(n**, *v.* OE. [A *prep.*[1] + *gēotan.*] To pour out, shed -ME.

‖**Ageu·stia.** 1853. [Gr.] *Med.* Loss of the sense of taste.

†**Aggela·tion.** *rare.* 1681. [f. L. *aggelare.*] A freezing to.

†**Agge·nerate**, *v.* 1660. [f. L. *aggenerat-*, *agg-*, *adgenerare.*] To beget as an addition. Hence †**Aggenera·tion.**

‖**Agger** (æ·dʒəɹ). ME. [L.; see AGGEST.] A mound; *esp.* in *Rom. Antiq.* the rampart of a camp.

Aggerate (æ·dʒĕreᶦt), *v. rare.* 1553. [f. L. *aggerat-*, *aggerare*; see prec.] To heap up. *lit.* and *fig.*

Aggeration (ædʒĕrē·ʃən). 1692. [ad. L. *aggerationem*; see prec.] A heaping up; in *Archæol.* the supposed raising of a mound, as an inclined plane for the erection of standing stones, etc. as at Stonehenge.

†**Agge·st**, *v.* 1655. [f. L. *aggest-*, *aggerere.*] To heap up. Hence †**Agge·stion**, accumulation.

Agglomerate (ăglǫ·mĕreᶦt), *v.* 1684. [f. L. *agglomerat-*, *agglomerare*, f. *ag-* = *ad-* + *glomerare*, *glomus*, a ball. Cf. Fr. *agglomérer.*] †1. To wind or roll into a ball. 2. To gather into a rounded mass; to heap together mechanically 1684. 3. *intr.* To collect in a mass. *lit.* and *fig.* 1730.

2. Working men .. agglomerated .. in great towns LECKY. 3. The hard agglomerating salts THOMSON. Hence **Agglo·merated** *ppl. a.* gathered into a ball; heaped loosely together. **Agglo·merating** *ppl. a.* uniting into a hard mass. **Agglo·merative** *a.*

Agglomerate (ăglǫ·mĕrĕt). 1828. [ad. L. *agglomeratus*; see prec.] A. *adj.* Gathered into a ball or cluster, or (*Bot.*) a rounded head of flowers.

B. *sb.* 1. A collection of things rudely thrown together 1831. 2. *Geol.* A mass of volcanic or eruptive fragments, united by heat; opp. to a *conglomerate.* 1830.

Agglutinant (ăglᶦū·tinănt). 1684. [ad. L. *agglutinantem*; see next.] A. *adj.* Gluing; uniting closely.

B. *sb.* 1. Any sticky substance which causes bodies to adhere together 1752. †2. *Med.* A medicine supposed to adhere to and supply the waste of tissue -1751.

Agglutinate (ăglᶦū·tinĕt), *ppl. a.* 1541. [ad. L. *agglutinatus*, *agglutinare*, f. *gluten.*] 1. United as with glue; glued together. 2. *Philol.* Consisting of root words combined by AGGLUTINATION (sense 2) 1850.

Agglutinate (ăglᶦū·tineᶦt), *v.* 1586. [f. prec.] 1. To unite as with glue; to cement. 2. *Phys.* To cause to adhere 1620. 3. To compound simple words 1830. 4. *trans.* and *intr.* To turn into glue 1869. Hence **Agglu·tinated** *ppl. a.* cemented together. **Agglu·tinating** *ppl. a.* gluing together; *Philol.* (see AGGLUTINATION 2).

Agglutination (ăglᶦū:tinē·ʃən). 1541. [ad. L. *agglutinationem*; see AGGLUTINATE *a.*] 1. The action of agglutinating; the state of being agglutinated. 2. *Philol.* The combining of simple or root words into compounds, without material change of form or loss of meaning 1830. 3. That which is agglutinated; a mass or group 1615.

Agglutinative (ăglᶦū·tineᶦ:tiv, -ĕtiv), *a.* 1634. [f. L. *agglutinat-*, *agglutinare.*] 1. Of or pertaining to agglutination; adhesive, cementing 1734. †2. *Med.* = AGGLUTINANT *sb.* 2. 1634. 3. *Philol.* Characterized by agglutination 1652.

Un-tru-th-ful-ly preserve[s] an a. character WHITNEY.

Ag(g)ra·ce, *v. arch.* [f. A- *pref.* 11 + GRACE *v.*] †1. To favour. SPENSER. 2. To grace 1825. Hence †**Aggra·ce** *sb.* favour.

Aggrandize (æ·grændəiz), *v.* 1634. [f. Fr. *agrandiss-*, *agrandir*, f. *ag-* = *ad-* + *grandire*, f. L. *grandis.*] 1. To increase, magnify, or intensify; to increase the power, rank, or wealth of. Also *refl.* 1682. 2. To make to appear greater; to exaggerate 1687; to exalt 1753. †3. *intr.* To become greater -1704.

1. To a. tortures 1634, distress 1748, the Russian Empire 1780, power RUSKIN. 2. To a. the man, and to lower the babies RICHARDSON. Hence **A·ggrandizable** *a.* **A·ggrandizer.**

Aggrandizement (ăgræ·ndizmĕnt). Also -**isement.** 1656. [a. Fr. *agrandissement*; see prec.] 1. The action of aggrandizing; the state of being aggrandized. 2. *lit.* Increase in size 1830. var. †**Aggrandiza·tion.**

†**Aggra·te**, *v.* 1591. [ad. It. *aggratare*; see AGREE.] 1. To gratify. SPENSER. 2. To thank -1633.

†**A·ggravable**, *a.* 1664. [f. L. *aggravare.*] Tending to aggravation. (Cf. *peaceable.*) -1733.

†**A·ggravate**, *ppl. a.* 1471. [ad. L. *aggravatus*, *aggravare.*] 1. Burdened. *lit.* and *fig.* -1510. 2. *Eccl.* Under censure -1481. 3. Made more serious, heightened -1733.

Aggravate (æ·grăveᶦt), *v.* 1530. [f. prec.] †1. To put weight upon; to load, *esp.* with a 'gravamen' or charge -1678. 2. †To add weight to -1698; *esp.* to make worse (things evil, offences, etc.) 1596. 3. To exasperate; *fam.* to arouse the evil feelings of 1611. 4. To add weight unduly; to exaggerate (cf. 2) 1555.

2. To introduce new mischiefs or to a...the old BURKE. Falsehood will .. a. your guilt FIELDING. 3. Threats only served to a. people THACKERAY. 4. I have not..aggravated your sense or words MARVELL. Hence **A·ggrava:tingly** *adv.* **A·ggrava:tive** *a.* and *sb. rare*, tending to a. **A·ggrava:tor.**

Aggravation (ægrăvē·ʃən). 1481. [prob. a. Fr.; see AGGRAVATE *a.*] †1. Oppression 1481. †2. Accusation -1675. 3. *Eccl.* An ecclesiastical censure 1611. 4. An increasing, or being increased, in gravity or seriousness 1615. †5. Exaggeration -1743. 6. *fam.* The action of irritating. 7. An extrinsic circumstance which increases the guilt or misery of a calamity or crime 1552.

5. Rhetorical aggravations BENTLEY. 7. An a. of their sin..that they commit it after Baptism BAXTER.

Aggregate (æ·grĭgĕt, -eᶦt), *ppl. a.* and *sb.* ME. [ad. L. *aggregatus*, *aggregare.*]

A. *ppl. a.* 1. Collected into one; formed by the collection of many units into one, collective 1659. 2. *spec.* a. *Law.* Composed of many individuals united into one association 1625; b. *Zool.* Consisting of distinct animals united into one organism 1835; c. *Bot.* Consisting of florets united within a common involucre; occ. of fruit, etc.: Collected into one mass 1693; d. *Geol.* Composed of distinct minerals, combined into one rock 1795; †e. *Gram.* Collective -1756. 3. quasi-*sb.* [sc. *state*, etc.].

1. The a. amount of labour expended..is called the cost of production ROGERS. 2. a. Each chapter is a *corporation aggregate* 1862. 3. Man *in the aggregate* RICHARDSON.

B. *sb.* 1. Sum total 1656; an assemblage of units 1650. 2. *spec.* a. *Physics.* A mass of homogeneous particles, opp. to a *compound* 1692; b. *Geol.* A mass of minerals formed into one rock 1830; c. *Build.* Material added to lime to make concrete 1881.

1. A Multitude considered as one a. HOBBES. Hence **A·ggregately** *adv.* collectively.

Aggregate (æ·grĭgeᶦt), *v.* 1509. [f. prec. Cf. Fr. *agréger.*] 1. To gather together into one whole; to mass. Also *refl* and *intr.* 1855. 2. To unite to (occ. *with*) an association, etc.; to add as a member 1651. 3. *ellipt.* [from sb.] To amount in the aggregate to (*colloq.*) 1865.

1. *intr.* We see the polar snows aggregating 1870. 2. That great..apostle, who..was aggregated to the other twelve TRENCH. Hence **A·ggregated**, orig. **A·ggregate** *ppl. a.*, collected; collective; *Zool.* = AGGREGATE *a.* 2 b; †*Bot.* = AGGREGATE *a.* 2 c. **A·ggregator**, an adherent; a compiler.

Aggregation (ægrĭgē·ʃən). 1547. [f. prec.] 1. The action of aggregating; or of adding one particle *to* an amount; the state of being aggregated (see AGGREGATE *v.* 1, 2) 1564. 2. *concr.* A whole, a mass, formed by aggregating items 1547.

1. Learning is..the a. of many mens sentences and acts 1564. His a. to the society of free-masons 1796. Their individuall imperfections .. are .. enlarged by their a. SIR T. BROWNE. 2. The Church..an a. of Believers 1638.

Aggregative (æ·grĭgeᶦ:tiv), *a.* 1644. [f. L. *aggregat-*, *aggregare.*] 1. Relating or tending to aggregation; collective. 2. Gregarious 1837.

1. Fancy, or the a. and associative power COLERIDGE. 2. His a. nature CARLYLE.

Aggregato- (ægrĭgēᶦ:to), combining form, = AGGREGATELY-.

†**Aggre·ge**, **-e·dge**, *v.* ME. [a. OFr. *agreger*, *-ier*:—late L. **aggreviare*, f. **grevis*, for *gravis*; see AGGRIEVE and AGGRAVATE.] 1. To make, or be, heavy, or dull -1393. 2. To make, become, or cause to appear, graver -1696. 3. To charge -1600.

†**Aggre·ss**, *sb.* 1678. [ad. L. *aggressus.*] Attack -1698.

Aggress (ăgre·s), *v.* 1575. [a. Fr. *aggresser*, ad. L. *aggressare*, freq. of *aggredi.*] †1. To approach. 2. *intr.* To make an attack *on*; to begin the quarrel 1714; *trans.* to attack 1775.

2. The moral law says—Do not a. H. SPENCER. Hence **Aggre·ssing** *vbl. sb.* and *ppl. a.* commencing the attack.

Aggression (ăgre·ʃən). 1611. [a. Fr. *agression*, *aggr-*, ad. L. *aggressionem*; see prec.] 1. An unprovoked attack; the first attack in a quarrel; an assault. 2. The practice of making such attacks 1704.

1. An a. upon their..liberties SCOTT. 2. A war of a. 1799.

Aggressive (ăgre·siv), *a.* 1824. [f. L. *aggress-*, *aggredi*; see AGGRESS *v.*] 1. Marked by aggression; offensive; also quasi-*sb.* [sc. *course*] 1845. 2. Disposed to attack others 1840.

1. A pleasantry SYD. SMITH. Hence **Aggre·ssively** *adv.* **Aggre·ssiveness.**

Aggressor (ăgre·səɹ). 1678. [a. L.] He who makes an aggression; he who makes the first attack in or begins a quarrel.

Aggrie·vance (ăgrī·văns). ME. [a. OFr. *agrevance*, f. *agrever*; see AGGRIEVE.] †1. That which burdens or oppresses -1664. 2. Oppression 1587. †3. Aggravation -1506.

Aggrieve (ăgrī·v), *v.* [ME. *agreve*, a. OFr. *agrever*:—L. *aggravare*, refash. after L. in 15th c.] 1. To bear heavily upon; to grieve, oppress. ? *Obs.* exc. in *pass.* †2. *intr.* To grieve -1559. †3. To make more grave or serious -1590.

1. Both were alike aggrieved MACAULAY. Hence **Aggrie·ved** *ppl. a.* †hurt in spirit, now *grieved*; injuriously affected, having a grievance; †hurt; †aggravated. **Aggrie·vedness.** **Aggrie·vement**, the action of aggrieving.

Aggroup (ăgrū·p), *v.* 1695. [a. Fr. *agrouper*, f. phr. *à groupe.* Better *agroup.*] To GROUP. *trans.* and *intr.* Hence **Aggrou·ped** *ppl. a.* **Aggrou·pment.**

‖**Aggry**, **-ri.** 1819. [?] A name for the glass beads, resembling the adder bead of the Britons, found buried in Africa.

Agha, var. AGA.

Aghast (ăgɑ·st), *ppl. a.* ME. [Pa. pple. of AGAST *v.* The *gh* is Sc.] Affrighted; *esp.* in mod. use, Seized with the physical signs of terror, or amazement. Const. *at*, †*of*, *with.* ¶ *catachrestic.* Ghastly.

With .. eyes agast MILT. A. with terror PRESCOTT. Hence **Agha·stness.**

†**A·gible**, *a.* 1613. [ad. med.L. *agibilis.*] Practicable. Also used *subst.*

Agile (æ·dʒil, -əil), *a.* 1577. [a. Fr., ad. L. *agilis.*] 1. Having the faculty of quick motion; nimble, ready. †2. Easily moved -1694.

1. His a. arme *Rom. & Jul.* III. i. 171. A robust and a. frame 1844. Hence **A·gilely** *adv.*

Agility (ădʒi·lĭti). ME. [a. Fr. *agilité*, ad. L. *agilitatem*; see AGILE.] The quality of being agile; readiness, nimbleness, activity, dexterity in motion.

The a. of their wit BACON, of youth COWPER.

Agio (æ·dʒi*o*, ē·dʒi*o*). 1682. [a. It.] 1. The percentage charged for changing paper-money into cash, or an inferior for a more valuable currency; the excess value of one currency over another. 2. *loosely*, Money-changing 1817.

2. Chabot, disfrocked Capuchin, skilful in a. CARLYLE.

Agiotage (æ·dʒiotėdʒ). 1829. [a. Fr., f. prec. The *t* is connective.] Exchange business; *loosely*, speculation in stocks and shares.

Vanity and a. are to a Parisian the oxygen and hydrogen of life LANDOR.

Agist (ădʒi·st), *v.* ME. [a. OFr. *agister*, f. *à* + *gister*, *gîter* :—L. **jacitare*, freq. of *jacere*. Cf. *à giste*.] 1. To take in cattle to remain and feed, at a certain rate; *orig.* to admit for a stated time into a forest. 2. *intr.* To remain and feed 1598. 3. To charge (lands, etc.) with a rate 1691.

3. To a. lands to keep out the sea 1691. Hence **Agi·sted** *ppl. a.* taken in to feed; of pasture, etc.: Eaten by cattle taken in at a certain rate. **Agi·sting** *vbl. sb.* and *ppl. a.* taking in to pasture; feeding on hired pasture.

Agistment (ădʒi·stmĕnt). ME. [a. OFr. *agistement*; see AGIST.] 1. The action of agisting. 2. The herbage of a forest, or the right to it 1598. 3. The rate or profit made upon agisting 1577. 4. Any rate charged upon pasture lands; esp. *agistment tithe*, paid to the vicar or rector by the occupier 1527. vars. †**Agi·stage**, †**Agista·tion**.

Agistor, -er (ădʒi·stəɹ). ME. [a. Anglo-Fr. *agistour*; see AGIST.] One who agists. *spec.* An officer of the royal forests, who took charge of cattle agisted, and accounted for the proceeds. var. †**Agista·tor**.

†**A·gitable**, *a.* 1548. [a. Fr., ad. L. *agitabilis*; see AGITATE.] Capable of being agitated –1661.

†**A·gitant**. 1670. [a. Fr.] One who stirs in, or plans, a course of action –1698.

Agitate (æ·dʒiteɪt), *v.* 1586. [f. L. *agitat-*, *agitare*, freq. of *agere*.] †1. To actuate; = ACT *v.* 1. –1748. 2. To move to and fro, shake 1599; *fig.* to perturb 1586. 3. To perturb, excite, or stir up by appeals, etc. 1822. †4. To act as an agent –1654. 5. To revolve in the mind; to contrive busily (*arch.*) 1648. 6. To discuss, or push forward 1643. 7. *absol.* To keep up an agitation (*for*) 1828.

1. Who..agitates the whole THOMSON. 2. To a. a fan SCOTT, the souls of one's hearers HOR. SMITH. 3. Each consul agitates the people in favour of his own views LEWIS. 4. Viceroyes.. to a. his State-affaires WOOD. 5. To a. desperate designs 1649. 6. Before a repeal was.. agitated BURKE. 7. *Agitate, agitate, agitate* MARQ. ANGLESEY. Hence **A·gitated** *ppl. a.* (in senses †1, 2, 6). **A·gitatedly** *adv.* **A·gitating** *vbl. sb.* the action of the vb.; *ppl. a.* acting as 'Agitators' (see AGITATOR 1); exciting. †**A·gitative** *a.* tending to a.

Agitation (ædʒiteɪ·ʃən). 1569. [a. Fr., ad. L. *agitationem*; see prec.] 1. The action of agitating, or state of being agitated (see AGITATE *v.* †1, 2, 3) 1573. 2. Mental tossing to and fro; consideration 1569. †3. Busy scheming –1626. †4. *Eng. Hist.* The action of the 'Agitators' of 1647. 5. The keeping of an object before public attention by appeals, etc.; public excitement 1828.

1. Motion or a. of the body 1711. The a. of the sea MAURY. America has been kept in continual a. In strange agitations and surprises DE FOE. 2. The business in a. FULLER. 5. The antislavery a. 1863. Hence **Agita·tional** *a.*

‖**Agitato** (adʒitā·to), *a.* [It.] *Mus.* A direction: With agitation.

Agitator (æ·dʒiteɪtəɹ). 1647. [a. L.] †1. *Eng. Hist.* An agent (see AGITATE 4); a name for the delegates of the private soldiers of the Parliamentary Army 1647–9; in which use it varied with ADJUTATOR, a corruption infl. by *Adjutant*, and *Adjutor*. 2. One who keeps up a political agitation 1780. 3. An apparatus for shaking 1871.

1. Those elective tribunes called Agitators HALLAM. 2. The great a. Daniell O'Connell. Hence **A:gitato·rial** *a.*

Aglare (ăglēᵊ·ɹ), *adv.* 1872. [A *prep.*[1]] In a glare.

Agleam (ăglī·m), *adv.* 1870. [A *prep.*[1]] Gleaming.

Aglet, ai- (æ·glĕt, ē-). ME. [a. Fr. *aiguillete*, dim. of *aiguille* :—late L. *acucula*, var. of *acicula*, dim. of *acus*.] 1. The metal tag (or *point*) of a lace 1440. 2. Hence, any metallic tag, pendent, or spangle worn as an ornament on the dress 1514; *esp.* an *aiguillette* 1843. 3. Round white stay-laces 1882. 4. *Herb.* A catkin of hazel, etc. 1578.

2. Golden aygulets, that glistred bright SPENSER *F. Q.* II. iii. 26. 4. [The willow] glints his steely aglets in the sun LOWELL.

Comb. **a.-babie**, ? a doll decked with aglets *Tam. Shr.* I. ii. 80.

A-glimmer (ăgli·məɹ), *adv.* 1860. [A *prep.*[1]] In or into a glimmering state.

Aglitter (ăgli·təɹ), *adv.* 1865. [A *prep.*[1]] In a glitter.

Aglossal (ăglǫ·săl), *a.* 1870. [f. Gr. ἄγλωσσος.] *Zool.* Tongueless.

Aglow (ăglōᵘ·), *adv.* 1817. [A *prep.*[1]] In a glow of warmth, colour, or excitement.

The Fletshorn was all a. TYNDALL. A. with delight BLACK.

Aglutition (æglᵫti·ʃən). 1847. [f. A- *pref.* 14 + L. **glutitionem*; see DEGLUTITION.] *Path.* Inability to swallow.

†**Agly·, -ey·**, *adv.* *Sc.* [A *prep.*[1] + GLEY.] Asquint, askew. BURNS.

Agminate (æ·gminėɪt), *a.* 1859. [f. L. *agmen*.] Grouped. var. **A·gminated**.

Agnail (æ·gnēɪl). [OE. *angnægl*, f. *ang-* tight, painful + *nægl* nail (of iron, etc.). *-nail*, as in *toe-nail*, and *hang-* for *ang-* in 2, 3 are etymological perversions.] †1. A corn on the toe or foot –1783. 2. A painful swelling about the toe- or finger-nail 1578. 3. A 'hang-nail' 1847.

Agname (æ·gnēɪm). 1834. [f. L. *ag-* = *ad-* + NAME.] A name in addition to the name and surname; a 'to-name', a sobriquet.

Agnate (æ·gnėɪt), *sb.* (*a.*) 1534. [a. Fr. *agnat*, ad. L. *agnatus* (*adgnatus*).] 1. A descendant by male links from the same male ancestor. 2. A descendant from a common male ancestor 1868. 3. *adj.* Related by the father's side 1860; *fig.* akin 1782. Hence **Agna·tic** *a.* related on the father's side. **Agna·tically** *adv.* **Agna·tion**, descent from a common male ancestor through male links only; descent from a common male ancestor, opp. to *cognation*; kinship by descent.

Agnathous (æ·gnăþəs), *a.* 1879. [f. Gr. ἀ + γνάθος.] *Phys.* Having no jaws.

Agnification (æ:gnifikēɪ·ʃən). *rare.* 1863. [f. L. *agnus*.] The representing (of persons) as lambs or sheep.

†**Agni·tion**. 1569. [ad. L. *agnitionem*.] Recognition, acknowledgement –1678.

Agnize (ăgnəi·z), *v. arch.* 1535. [After L. *a(d)gnos-cere*; cf. *cognize*.] 1. To recognize (*arch.*) 1611; †to own *for*, *as*, etc. –1737. 2. To recognize the existence of, confess (*arch.*) 1543.

2. I do a. A Naturall..Alacartie, I finde in hardnesse *Oth.* I. iii. 232.

Agnoiology (ægnoi,ǫ·lŏdʒi). 1856. [f. Gr. ἄγνοια.] *Philos.* The philosophy of ignorance.

Agnoites, -etes (æ·gno,əits, -īts). 1586. [ad. med.L. *agnoitæ*, ad. Gr. ἀγνοηταί.] *Eccles.* A sect who held that Christ was ignorant of some things. Hence **A·gnoetism**.

‖**Agnomen** (ægnōᵘ·men). 1753. [L.] *Rom. Antiq.* A second cognomen or fourth name, occas. assumed by the Romans, as Publius Cornelius Scipio *Africanus*; *loosely*, a 'to-name'.

His a. of Bean, or white SCOTT. Hence **Agno·minal** *a. rare.* ?*Obs.* **Agno·minate** *v. rare*, to nickname. ?*Obs.*

Agnomination (ăgnǫ:minēɪ·ʃən). Also adn-, ann-. 1588. [ad. L. *agnominationem*, f. *agnominat-*, *agnominare*.] 1. The giving of an agnomen; the agnomen. *rare.* 1775. 2. *Rhet.* Paronomasia 1588; alliteration 1595.

Agnostic (ægnǫ·stik), *sb.* and *a.* 1870. [f. A- 14 + GNOSTIC.] One who holds that the existence of anything beyond material phenomena, e.g. of a First Cause, or of noumena, cannot be known; *adj.* pertaining to agnostics or agnosticism.

The word was suggested by Thomas Henry Huxley (1825–95): it has been taken to refer to the Unknown God (Ἀγνώστῳ Θεῷ) of Acts xvii. 23.

Hence **Agno·stically** *adv.* **Agno·sticism**, the doctrine of agnostics.

‖**A·gnus**. late ME. = AGNUS DEI.

‖**Agnus Castus** (æ·gnɒs kæ·stɒs). ME. [L., a. Gr. ἄγνος, the name of the tree, confused with ἁγνός, whence *castus*.] A tree (*Vitex Agnus Castus*), called also Chaste-tree and Abraham's Balm.

‖**Agnus Dei** (æ·gnɒs dī·əi, a·gn*u*s dē·ī). ME. [L.] In *R. C. Ch.* a. A part of the mass beginning with the words *Agnus Dei*; also the music set to it. b. A figure of a lamb bearing a cross or flag 1629. c. A cake of wax stamped with such a figure and blessed by the Pope 1583.

†**Ago·**, *v.* OE. [f. A- *pref.* 1 + GO.] To go forth –ME.; to go away –1674. Of time: To pass –1550.

Ago, agone (ăgōᵘ·, ăgǫ·n). ME. [pa. pple. of prec., used as adj. with noun of time.] A. *ppl. a.* Gone by; past. (Now *follows* its noun.) B. *adv.* in *Long ago*: in time long gone, long since 1366.

A. It was ago fif year ME. Drunke.. an hour agone *Twel. N.* v. i. 204. B. So yore agoo CHAUCER. Dead and gone long ago 1833.

Agog (ăgǫ·g), *adv.* 1542. [? ad. OFr. *en gogues*, f. *gogue* fun.] In eager expectation; on the move, astir. Const. *inf.*, *on*, *upon*, *for*, *with*, *about*.

To sette on gogge 1575. A. on mischief TRAPP.

Agoing; see A *prep.*[1] 13 and Go *v.*

‖**Agon** (æ·gōᵘn). Pl. (usu.) *agones* (ăgōᵘ·nīz). 1660. [Gr., orig. 'a gathering'.] *Gr. Antiq.* A public celebration of games, a contest for the prize at the games; also *fig.*

†**A·gonal, -el**. 1610. [? Fr. *agonal* as sb.] A martyrology –1695.

Agone (ăgǫ·n), *ppl. a. arch.* and *poet.* = AGO.

Agonic (ăgǫ·nik), *a.* 1863. [f. Gr. ἄγωνος, f. ἀ + γωνία.] Having or making no angle.

Agonic line: the irregular line passing through the two magnetic poles of the earth along which the magnetic needle points directly north or south; the line of no magnetic variation.

Agonistic (ægǫni·stik), *a.* 1648. [ad. Gr. ἀγωνιστικός.] Pertaining to the ancient Greek athletic contests; *hence*, athletic. 2. *Rhet.* Polemic, combative 1660. 3. Strained, aiming at effect 1843.

2. [Dr. Parr] consumed his power in a. displays DE QUINCEY. 3. A. posture-makers CARLYLE. var. **Agoni·stical** *a.* (senses 1, 2); whence **Agoni·stically** *adv.* Hence **Agoni·stics** [pl. of adj. used *subst.*], the science of athletic combats.

Agonize (æ·gǫnəiz), *v.* 1583. [a. Fr. *agoniser*, or med.L. *agonizare*, ad. Gr. ἀγωνίζεσθαι.] 1. To torture 1583; *intr.* to suffer or writhe with agony, to be in the throes of death 1664. 2. *intr.* To contend in the arena; to wrestle. Usu. *fig.* 1711. 3. *fig.* To make convulsive efforts for effect 1865.

1. Where dying victims a. in pain FALCONER. 3. To a. after originality 1865. Hence **A·gonized** *ppl. a.* subjected to or expressing agony. **A·goni:zedly** *adv.* **A·gonizer**. **A·gonizing** *vbl. sb.* the action of the vb.; *ppl. a.* torturing; suffering or writhing with agony; in the throes of death. **A·goni·zingly** *adv.*

Agonothet(e (ăgōᵘ·nŏþīt, -þet). 1626. [ad. Gr. ἀγωνοθέτης.] A director of the public games of Greece. Hence **Ago·nothe·tic** *a.*

Agony (æ·gǒni). ME. [a. L. *agonia*, a. Gr.; see AGON.] 1. Anguish of mind, sore distress, a paroxysm of grief ME.; hence, a paroxysm of pleasure 1725. 2. *spec.* The mental anguish of Christ in Gethsemane ME. 3. The throes or pangs of death. (Now rare *simply*.) 1549. 4. Extreme bodily suffering with throes or writhing 1607. 5. A struggle or contest 1677.

1. The *agony column*: the column in a newspaper containing distressful advertisements for missing relatives, etc. An a. of confusion and despair JUNIUS. Agonies of delight POPE. 2. As cried Christ ere his a. TENNYSON. 3. Mirth cannot moue a soule in

agonie *L. L. L.* v. ii. 867. 5. The crisis, or essential a. of the Battle CARLYLE.

†**A-good**, *adv.* 1536. [A *prep.*[1] + GOOD; cf. *afresh.*] Heartily –1671.

I made her weep a. *Two Gent.* IV. iv. 170.

‖**Agora** (æ·gorǎ). 1820. [Gr.] *Gr. Antiq.* An assembly; hence, the place of assembly, *esp.* the market-place.

A:gorapho·bia. 1873. [mod.L.: see prec. and -PHOBIA.] *Path.* Morbid dislike of public places.

†**A-go·re-blood.** 1580. [A *prep.*[1]: see GORE *sb.*[1]] In or with clotted blood –1609.

Agouti, -ty (ǎgū·ti). Also **aguti.** 1731. [a. Fr., a. *aguti*, native Indian.] A genus of rodents of the Guinea-pig family.

Agrace, obs. var. of AGGRACE *v.*

Agraffe (ǎgræ·f). 1707. [a. Fr. *agrafe*, f. *agrafer* to hook.] A hook, which fastens to a ring, used as a clasp.

‖**Agraphia** (ǎgræ·fiǎ). 1871. [Gr. ἀ + -γραφία.] *Med.* Inability to write (a form of brain-disease). Hence **Agra·phic** *a.* characterized by a.

Agrarian (ǎgrē°·riǎn). 1618. [f. L. *agrarius.*] **A.** *adj.* 1. *Rom. Hist.* Relating to the land: epithet of a law (*Lex agraria*) for the division of conquered lands. 2. Hence, Connected with landed property 17..; or with cultivated land, or its cultivation 1792. 3. *Bot.* Growing wild in the fields 1843.

2. *Agrarian outrage*, one originating in discord between landlords and tenants. An a. war 1833. [Member] of the a. society 1792.

B. *sb.* 1. An agrarian law 1656. 2. One in favour of a redistribution of the land 1818.

2. An A. of three hours standing SOUTHEY.

Agrarianism (ǎgrē°·riǎniz'm). 1808. [f. prec.] 1. The principle of an equal division of lands. 2. Political agitation or dissension arising from dissatisfaction with the existing tenure of the land 1861.

Agrarianize (ǎgrē°·riǎnəiz), *v.* 1846. [f. as prec.] 1. To apportion land by an agrarian law. (Mod. Dicts.) 2. To imbue with agrarianism 1883.

†**A·gre**, *v.* [a. OFr. *agrier* (cf. *aigrir*); see EAGER.] To vex. CAXTON.

†**Agrea·t**, *adv.* 1502. [A *prep.*[1] + GREAT *a.* Cf. Fr. *en gros.*] In gross; by the lot –1632.

†**Agree·**, *adv.* ME. only. [a. Fr. *à gré*:—L. *gratum.*] Kindly, in good part. Phr. *To take a.*

Agree (ǎgrī·), *v.* ME. [a. OFr. *agreer*:—late L. **adgratare.* Aphet. as GREE.] †1. To please –1475; to accept favourably (F. *prendre à gré*) –1642. †2. To reconcile, arrange, conciliate (persons or things) –1785. Still of *accounts*, etc. To concert –1718. 3. *refl.* and *intr.* To accede, consent *to*, grant. Const. *inf.*, *to*, *absol.*, with *cl.* ME. 4. *intr.* (? for *refl.*) To come into accord or harmony; *esp.* to come to terms about the price, etc., to contract. ? *Obs.* Const. *with.* 1489. Also *on*, *as to*, †*of*, *inf.*, or with *cl.* 1523. 5. To be in harmony; to have no causes of variance. (Simply, or *together*; *with.*) 1548. To concur *with* a person *in*, *as to*, *that*, *with* an opinion 1494. 6. Of things: to accord (*simply*, or *with*) 1494; to be consistent, correspond †*to*, *with* 1526. 7. *Gram.* To be in concord; to take the same gender, number, case, or person 1530. 8. †To be suitable *to* –1671; to do well *with* (†of a person) –1697, (of food, climate, etc.) 1661.

1. The principles to be agreed by all BACON. 2. To a. the balance, the items of an account (*mod.*). Whan..this..trewse was agreed LD. BERNERS. POPE *Il.* iv. 186. 3. To a. to make a trial TYNDALL, to any couenants SHAKS., that to be law which [etc.] 1658, that a thing is so (*mod.*). 4. Did a. for a cabinet to give my wife PEPYS. To a. on terms of reconciliation FREEMAN. To a. to differ 1810, that the matter should stand over (*mod.*). 5. Two of a trade can ne'er a. GAY. One point in which they all a. JUNIUS. 6. At last..our jarring notes a. *Tam. Shr.* v. ii. 1. The beginning agreeth with the ende BARET. 8. She wondered whether the climate would a. with her THACKERAY. Hence †**Agree·** *sb.* agreement. **Agree·r**, an adherent. **Agree·ing** *vbl. sb.* a coming into or being in harmony; *ppl. a.* †conformable *to*; concurring; †suiting; † = AGREEINGLY. **Agree·ingly** *adv.* in an agreeing manner. **Agree·ingness**, the quality of agreeing.

Agreeability (ǎgrī·ǎbi·lǐti). ME. [a. OFr. *agréableté*, f. *agréable.* Obs. after Chaucer till 1778; then re-formed on AGREEABLE.] The quality of being agreeable, *esp.* in disposition.

All..a. (surely I may make words when at a loss) MISS BURNEY.

Agreeable (ǎgrī·ǎb'l), *a.*; also **agreable.** ME. [a. Fr. *agréable*, f. *agréer*; see AGREE.] 1. To one's liking; pleasant. 2. Having a liking (*to*); pleased, contented (*to do*). Now *colloq.* 1467. †3. Agreeing together –1601. 4. †Suitable, fitting –1692; †consistent (*with*) –1783; conformable (*unto*, *to*) ME. 5. *adv.* = AGREEABLY 1549. †6. *sb.* [sc. *person.*] *pl.* [sc. *things.*] Cf. *An incapable*; *eatables.* –1822.

1. An a. man—he who agrees with us DISRAELI. A. to my likynge CHAUCER. 2. If Ann's a., I say ditto THACKERAY. 4. Very a. with your general kindness BOSWELL. A. to all experience BAIN. 5. The Earl entered, a. to the Prince's summons SCOTT. Hence **Agree·ableness**, the quality of being a., pleasingness. **Agree·ably** *adv.* in a way which is pleasing, suitable *to*, or in conformity *with*; †correspondingly; †similarly; †fittingly.

Agreed (ǎgrī·d), *ppl. a.* ME. [f. the vb.] †1. Contented; made pleasing. ME. only. 2. Brought into harmony; united in feeling or sentiment ME. 3. At one in opinion 1613. 4. Settled by common consent. Now *agreed on.* 1596. 5. As a rejoinder: Consented to. = 'I agree to the proposal' 1794.

2. Can two walke together except they be a. *Amos* iii. 3. 3. Are you all a., Lords SHAKS. 4. It stands a. by all voices SHAKS. Your dowry 'greed on *Tam. Shr.* II. i. 272.

Agreement (ǎgrī·mĕnt). ME. [a. OFr. *agreement*; see AGREE.] †1. The action of pleasing –1494; consenting –1483; setting at one, atoning –1577. 2. A coming into accord; a mutual understanding; a covenant, or treaty 1400. 3. *Law.* A contract duly executed and legally binding 1536. 4. Accordance in sentiment, action, etc.; absence of dissension 1528; mutual conformity of things, affinity ME. 5. *Gram.* Concord; see AGREE *v.* 7. 6. Usu. *pl.* Agreeable qualities, etc. = Fr. *les agrémens.* 1692.

2. Were not of the a. with the King LD. BERNERS. 4. You loued better..discorde then agremente 1548. What a. hath the Temple of God with idoles 2 *Cor.* vi. 16. 6. The charms and Agreements natural to women DRYDEN. var. †**Agree·ance.**

†**Agre·st**, *a.* ME. [a. Fr. *agreste*, a. It.:—L. *agrestis.*] Belonging to the country, wild; rustic, rude –1775. As *sb.* A rustic –1480. Hence †**Agre·sted** *ppl. a.* countrified.

Agrestial (ǎgre·stiǎl), *a.* 1607. [f. L. *agrestis.*] Inhabiting the fields or open country; wild, uncouth; *spec.* in *Bot.* growing wild in cultivated land. vars. **Agre·stian** *a.* (and *sb.*) **Agre·stic** *a.*

Agricole (æ·grikōul). 1656. [a. Fr.] A husbandman. vars. †**Agri·colist**, †**A·gricultor.** Hence **Agri·colous** *a.*

Agriculture (æ·grikɒ:ltiŭr, -tʃəɪ). 1603. [ad. L. *agricultura*, i.e. *agri cultura*; see CULTURE.] The science and art of cultivating the soil; including the gathering in of the crops and the rearing of live stock; farming (in the widest sense). *spec.* Tillage (*rare*) 1862.

spec. Not fields for a., but pastures for cattle STANLEY. Hence **Agricu·ltural** *a.* of or pertaining to a. **Agricu·lturalist**, one engaged in a.; var. **Agricu·lturer** (*pop.*).

Agriculturist (ægrikɒ·ltiŭrist). 1760. [f. prec.] At first, A student of the science of agriculture; later, A farmer.

The theoretical a., and the practical farmer 1814.

†**Agrie·f**, *adv.* ME. [A *prep.*[1] + GRIEF.] In grief.

To take a.: to take it ill; opp. of *to take a-gree*, *in gree.*

Agrimony (æ·grimǝni). OE. [ad. L. *agrimonia*, Gr. ἀργεμώνη.] 1. A genus of plants (N.O. *Rosaceæ*); esp. *A. Eupatoria.* 2. A name of other plants; as Hemp A., *Eupatoria cannabina*; Water A., *Bidens*; Wild A., *Potentilla anserina* 1578.

Agrin (ǎgri·n), *adv.* 1847. [A *prep.*[1]] Grinning.

Agriologist (ægri,ǫ·lǒdʒist). 1882. [f. Gr. ἄγριος + λόγος.] One versed in the history and customs of savages.

†**A·griot.** 1611. [f. Fr. *agriote.*] A sour kind of cherry.

†**Agri·se**, *v.* OE. [f. A- *pref.* 1 + GRISE. Cf. *grisly.*] 1. To quake –1598; to abhor –1468; also *impers.* –1596; to horrify, or be horrified –1647.

‖**Agrodolce** (a·grodo·ltʃe), *a.* [It.] = AIGRE-DOUX.

‖**A·grom.** 1753. [a. Gujaráti *agrūn.*] An Indian term for a rough and cracked condition of the tongue.

Agronomic (ægrǫnǫ·mik), *a.* 1817. [f. Gr. ἀγρονόμος, f. ἀγρός + νόμος, f. νέμειν.] Of or pertaining to agronomy. vars. **Agrono·mial**, **Agrono·mical** *adjs.* Hence **Agrono·mics** [the adj. as sb. pl. or coll. sing.], the science of agronomy. **Agro·nomist**, **A·gronome** (*rare*), a student of agronomics.

Agronomy (ǎgrǫ·nǒmi). 1814. [f. Gr. *ἀγρονομία; see AGRONOMIC.] The management of land, rural economy.

†**Agro·pe**, *v.* ME. only. [f. A- *pref.* 1.] To grope out, search.

‖**Agrostis** (ǎgrǫ·stis). 1753. [L., ad. Gr. ἄγρωστις, f. ἀγρός.] *Bot.* A genus of grasses known as *Bent.*

Agrostography (ægrǫstǫ·grǎfi). 1753. [f. prec.] Description of grasses. Hence **Agro:stogra·phic**, **-al** *a.*

Agrostology (ægrǫstǫ·lǒdʒi). 1847. [f. as prec.] That part of botany which treats of grasses. Hence **Agro:stolo·gic**, **al** *a.* **Agrosto·logist**, one skilled in a.

†**Agro·te**, *v.* ME. only. [? f. A- *pref.* 1 + *grot* a particle.] To cram. (Cf. GROUT.)

Aground (ǎgrau·nd), *adv.* ME. [A *prep.*[1] + GROUND.] †1. On or to the earth –1562. 2. On or to the strand or shallow bottom of any water; opp. to *afloat* 1500. Also *fig.*

2. We run ourselves a. *Temp.* I. i. 4. Fast a. SOUTHEY.

‖**Agrypnia** (ǎgri·pniǎ). 1684. [L., ad. Gr. ἀγρυπνία.] *Med.* Sleeplessness.

Agrypnode (ǎgri·pnōud), *a.* 1879. [ad. Gr. ἀγρυπνώδης.] *Med.* Sleep-preventing.

Agrypnotic (ægripnǫ·tik), (*a.*) *sb.* 1879. [a. Fr. *agrypnotique*, f. Gr. ἄγρυπνος, after *hypnotic*: but prop. **Agrypnetic.**] *Med.* Anything which produces wakefulness.

Ague (ēⁱ·giu). ME. [a. OFr. *ague*:—L. *acuta*, used sb. in med.L. for an 'acute fever'.] †1. An acute fever –1611. 2. *esp.* A malarial fever, with paroxysms, consisting of a cold, a hot, and a sweating stage. (At first *esp.* of the hot stage, now *esp.* of the cold.) ME. 3. *fig.* Any fit of shaking or shivering 1589.

1. Brennyng Aguwes LANGL. 2. That same A. that hath made you leane *Jul. Cæs.* II. ii. 113. 3. This vain a. of the mind SCOTT. *Comb.* **a.-cake**, an enlargement of the spleen caused by a.; **-drop**, a solution of potassic arseniate, used for a.; **-grass**, *Aletris farinosa*; **-shake** *v.* to shake as with a.; **-shell**, the Hawk's-Bill; **-spell**, a charm against a.; †**-tree**, the Sassafras. Hence **A·gue** *v.* to affect as with a. (*rare*). **A·gued** *ppl. a.* affected as with a. **A·guey** *a.* = AGUISH.

†**Agui·lt.** OE. [f. A- *pref.* 1 + *gyltan*; see GUILT.] To sin –1450; to wrong –1420; to declare guilty –1530.

†**Agui·se**, *sb.* 1483. [f. GUISE + *on*, or opp. to *dis-*.] 1. Dress, array –1647. 2. as *v.* To array –1598. Hence †**Agui·sed** *ppl. a.* arrayed.

Aguish (ēⁱ·giu,iʃ), *a.* 1616. [f. AGUE *sb.*] 1. Of the character of, or tending to produce, ague 1627. 2. Subject to ague 1616. 3. *fig.* Like an ague; shivering; intermittent 1633.

1. A low a. fever 1856. A rich a. flat 1850. 3. Panics..of the a. or intermittent type. Hence **A·guishly** *adv.* **A·guishness.**

Agu·sh, *adv.* 1858. [A *prep.*[1]] Gushing.

Agynary (æ·dʒinǎri), *a.* 1879. [ad. Fr. *agynaire*, f. Gr. ἀ + γυνή.] *Bot.* Without female organs, as some double flowers. var. **Agyna·rious.**

Agynic (ădʒi·nik), *a.* 1879. [ad. Fr. *agynique*, f. as prec.] *Bot.* Having the stamens non-adherent to the ovary.

†**Agynous**, *a.* 1847. [f. Gr. ἀ + γυνή.] *Bot.* Without female organs.

Agyrate (ădʒəiə·reˈt), *a.* 1847. [f. A- *pref.* 14.] *Bot.* Not disposed in whorls or circles.

Ah (ā), *int.* ME. [perh. a. OFr. *a.* In n. dial. pronounced (ē), and occ. written *ay! eh!*, the phonetic descendant of ME. *a.*] An exclam. expressing **a.** sorrow, regret, a vain wish; **b.** surprise, admiration 1826; **c.** entreaty, appeal, remonstrance ME.; **d.** dislike, contempt, mockery ME.; **e.** opposition (*mod.*).

a. They shall not lament for him, saying Ah my brother *Jer.* xxii. 18. So *Ah me!* (north. EH ME!) **c.** Ah, Clifford, murther not this innocent child 3 *Hen. VI*, I. iii. 8. **d.** Ah thou that destroyest the Temple *Mark* xv. 29.

Aha (ăhā·, ăhā·), *int.* ME. [AH + HA.] An exclam. of †surprise, satisfaction, mockery or irony.

Aha, var. HA-HA, *sb.*, a sunk fence.

†**A hall**, *phr.* 1612. [See HALL; the *a* is perh. prep. or interj.] = 'Make room (for a dance)'.

Ahead (ăhe·d), *adv.* 1628. [A *prep.*[1]] Orig. *Naut.* Now used *fig.* in all senses. **1.** At the head, in advance (of a moving company). **2.** In the direct line of one's motion 1725. **3.** Pointing forward 1596; forward 1762. **4.** Forward or onward rapidly; headlong; also *fig.* unrestrainedly 1643.

1. The..Dolphin gets a. DRYDEN. **2.** They saw it..right a. DE FOE. **3** To fire directly a., or astern 1873. **4.** Galloping straight a. BROWNING. *Phr.* **go-a-head** *a.*; **ahead of**: away in front of.

Aheap (ăhī·p), *adv.* 1827. [A *prep.*[1]] All of a heap.

A-hei·ght. *arch.* 1605. [A *prep.*[1]] Aloft. Looke vp a height *Lear* IV. vi. 58.

Ahem (ăhem), *int.* 1763. [Lengthened f. *hem!*] An exclam. to attract attention, or gain time.

A-hey (ăhē·), *int.* 1705. [Lengthened f. HEY.] = Hey! ho!

†**A-high** (ăhəi·), *adv.* ME. [A *prep.*[1] + HIGH. Now only *on high.*] On high -1823; aloud -1489.

†**A-high-lone.** *adv. phr.* 1597. Prob. emphatic for *alone*, i. e. *all-one*, divided as *a-lone* -1664. See HIGH.

Ahi·nd, ahi·nt, *adv.* and *prep. dial.* 1768. [f. A- *pref.* 2 + HIND; cf. *afore=before.*] Behind.

†**A-ho·ld,** *adv.* [A *prep.*[1] + HOLD.] Close to the wind, so as to hold or keep to it. *Temp.* I. i. 52.

A-ho·rseback. *adv. arch.* 1490. [A *prep.*[1]] On horseback.

Ahoy·, *int.* 1751. [A *int.* + HOY.] *Naut.* A call used in hailing.

Ahull (ăhʊ·l), *adv.* 1582. [A *prep.*[1]] *Naut.* With sails furled, and the helm lashed alee; said of ships in a storm.

Ahungered (ăhʊ·ŋgəɪd), *ppl. a. arch.* ME. [Alteration of †*of hungered*:—OE. *ofhyngrod*, pa. pple. of *ofhyngrian* to HUNGER.] = ANHUNGERED. Also †**Ahungry** *a.*

A-hu·nt, *adv.* 1875. [A *prep.*[1]] On the hunt.

Ai (ā·i). 1693. [a. Braz. *aï, haï*, repr. the animal's cry.] *Zool.* A kind of Sloth (*Bradypus tridactylus*).

Aid (ēˈd), *v.* 1483. [a. OFr. *aider, -ier*:—L. *adjutare*, freq. of *adjuvare.*] **1.** To give support to; to help, assist, succour. **2.** *absol.* and with *inf.* 1601.

1. To a. with victuals, weapons, money, or ships 1 *Macc.* viii. 26. **2.** Heaven ayding *All's Well* IV. iv. 12. Hence **Ai·dable** *a.* capable of †aiding, or being aided. **Ai·dance**, aid. **Ai·ded** *ppl. a.* assisted. **Ai·der**, one who, or that which, aids.

Aid (ēˈd). 1460. [a. OFr. *aïde, aiude*:—L. *adjuta*, sb. f. pa. pple. of *adjuvare.*] **1.** Help, succour, relief 1475. **2.** *Eng. Law.* Help in defending an action, legally claimed from some one who has a joint interest in the defence 1625. **3.** Anything helpful; *esp.* in *pl.* aids and appliances 1597. **4.** *Eng. Hist.* A pecuniary grant in aid to the king; *later*, an exchequer loan 1460. **5.** A pecuniary contribution by a vassal to his lord 1590. **6.** *Fr. Hist.* (*pl.*) Customs-dues 1714. **7.** An assistant; *pl.* auxiliaries. (Cf. Fr. *aide*, and Eng. *help.*) 1569.

1. Dispatch Those Centuries to our a. *Coriol.* I. vii. 3. **2.** *To pray in aid*: to claim a. (sense 2). *Aid-prayer*: the appeal therefor. **3.** Exercise..an a. to Physick 1711. **5.** Aids, 'Pur faire fitz chiualer & pur file marier' SWINBURN. **6.** *Court of Aids*: the Court that supervised the customs-dues. Hence **Ai·dful** *a.* full of aid, helpful. **Ai·dless** *a.* †useless; unassisted.

Aidant (ēˈ·dănt), *a.* 1475. [a. OFr.: see prec.] Assisting 1483. As *sb. rare.* A helper 1475.

Aide, short for AIDE-DE-CAMP.

‖**Aide-de-camp** (e·d-də-kaṅ·, ēˈ·d-də-kǫ·ŋ). Pl. aides-de-camp. 1670. [Fr.] *Mil.* An officer who assists a general in the field, by conveying his orders, procuring him intelligence, etc.

†**Ai·el.** Also **ayle, ayel,** etc. ME. [a. OFr. *aïel, aïeul, aïol*:—late L. **aviolus*, dim. of *avus.*] A grandfather -1502.

Writ of Aile, Ayle, Ayel, Ael (Law): one which lay where a stranger had dispossessed the heir of lands of which his grandfather died seised.

Aiger, obs. f. EAGER *sb.* tidal bore.

Aiglet, obs. f. AGLET.

Aiglette, obs. f. EAGLET.

Aigre, obs. f. EAGER *a.* sour.

‖**Aigre-doux, -ce,** *a.* 1523. [Fr.] Mixed of sweet and sour.

Aigrette (ēˈ·grèt). 1645. [a. Fr.] **1.** The Lesser White Heron; see EGRET 1845. **2.** A tuft of feathers, like an Egret's; a spray of gems, etc., worn on the head 1645. **3.** In *Science* applied to the pappus of the Dandelion, etc.; the tufts on the heads of insects, etc.; rays of light from behind the moon in solar eclipses 1816.

†‖**Aigue-marine.** 1765. [Fr.] AQUA-MARINE.

Aiguille (ēˈ·gwīl, -wil). 1816. [a. Fr.] A slender, sharply-pointed peak; *esp.* those of the Alps. Hence **Ai·guille·sque** *a.* shaped like an a.

Aiguillette (ēˈ·gwile·t). 1816. [a. Fr.] = AGLET. Hence **Ai·guille·tted** *a.*

Aik, aiken, obs. north. f. OAK, OAKEN.

Aikinite (ēˈ·kinəit). 1837. [f. A. *Aikin.*] *Min.* A sulpharsenite ore, crystallizing in the ortho-rhombic system.

Ail (ēˈl), *v.* [OE. *eglan.*] †**1.** *trans.* To afflict (*rare*) ME. **2.** *impers.* To trouble, affect unusually. (Now only in *interrog., rel.*, and *indef.* sentences.) OE. †**3.** To hinder -1563. **4.** *intr.* To be ill ME.; or †in trouble -1817.

2. What ayleth the people that they wepe COVERDALE. **4.** And when he ails..he is..peevish RICHARDSON. Hence **Ai·ling** *vbl. sb.* = AILMENT; *ppl. a.* ill, suffering. **Ai·lment**, the fact of ailing; disorder.

Ail (ēˈl), *sb.*[1] ME. [f. the vb.] Trouble; affection.

†**Ail**, *sb.*[2] [OE. *egl.*] The awn of barley, etc. -1787.

‖**Ailanto, ailantus** (eˈlæ·nto, -tʊ̆s). 1845. [f. *Aylanto*, Tree of the gods, the Amboyna name; whence mod.L. *Ailantus*, corrupted in Eng. to *Ailanthus*, after Gr. ἄνθος.] *Bot.* An East Indian tree (N. O. *Simarubaceæ*), grown in S. Europe for shade, and for its leaves, the favourite food of a species of silkworm. Erron. called 'Japan Varnish'. Hence **Aila·ntery**, a grove of a. trees. **Aila·ntic** *a. Chem.* of or belonging to the A., as *ailantic acid.* **Aila·ntine**, improp. **aila·nthine** *a.* of or belonging to the A., or the A. silkworm; *sb.* silk from the A. silkworm (*Bombyx Cynthia*).

Ailette (eˈle·t). 1440. [a. Fr., dim. of *aile*:—L. *ala.*] A steel plate worn by men-at-arms on their shoulders, whence the mod. epaulette.

Aim (ēˈm), *v.* ME. [prob. f. OFr. *esmer*:—L. *æstimare* and OFr. *aesmer*:—late L. *adæstimare.*] †**1.** To esteem; to reckon; to guess -1602; to plan -1604. **2.** *intr.* To calculate or direct one's course, to attain; *fig.* to endeavour earnestly. Const. *at*; *dat. inf.*; occas. *for*, perh. after *make for.* ME. **3.** *intr.* To calculate the direction of anything about to be launched (at an object), as a missile, a blow, etc.; *fig.* to try to hit, or obtain. Const. *at.* ME. **4.** *trans.* To direct (a missile, or blow); *esp.* to direct with the eye, or point a gun, etc. (*at*); *fig.* to direct any proceeding against 1573. **5.** *absol.* To take aim; to form designs 1588.

2. A. for the Steeple *Guide Book.* **3.** A. at his breast POPE. **4.** Mrs. Bull aimed a knife at John ARBUTHNOT. **5.** I aime a Mile beyond the Moone *Tit. A.* IV. iii. 65. Hence **Aimed** *ppl. a.* †estimated; directed at a mark, etc. **Ai·mer.**

Aim (ēˈm), *sb.* [the vb. as *sb.*] †**1.** Conjecture -1625; course, direction -1679. **2.** The act of aiming ME. Also *fig.* **3.** A mark or butt (*Obs.* in lit. sense) -1632; *fig.* an object, purpose 1625.

1. Aimes and ghesses JEWEL. **2.** A certaine aime he tooke At a faire Vestall *Mids. N.* II. i. 157. †**To give aim**: to guide by informing of the result of a preceding shot. †**To cry aim**: to encourage archers by crying out '*Aim!*' Free from..selfish A. WESLEY **3.** The aym of Punishment is not a revenge, but terrour HOBBES. Hence **Ai·mful** *a.* full of purpose; whence **Ai·mfully** *adv.* **Ai·mless** *a.* purposeless; whence **Ai·mlessly** *adv.*, **Ai·mlessness.**

Ain't (ēˈnt). 1778. Later variant of AN'T, now illiterate or dial.

Air (ēəɪ). ME. [a. OFr. *air*:—L. *aerem*, a. Gr. ἀήρ, f. ἄειν. The later senses, *external manner, musical mode*, were adopted *c* 1600 from Fr. *air*, and are prob. not f. OFr. *aire*, AERIE, but are extensions of the idea of 'atmosphere'.] **I.** Atmospheric air. **1.** The gaseous substance which envelops the earth, and is breathed by all land animals; one of the four elements of the ancients, now known to be a mechanical mixture of oxygen and nitrogen, carbonic acid gas, and traces of other substances as contaminations ME. Also *fig.* †**2.** Any aeriform body, as a *gas*, a *vapour* -1819. **3.** The whole body of air *surrounding*, or (pop.) *above* the earth ME. Also *fig.* **4.** A special state of the atmosphere, as *night air*, etc. 1479; *esp.* fresh air ME.; miasma ME.; †effluvium, odour ME. **5.** Air in motion; a breeze, current, or draught 1535. †**6.** Breath; *fig.* popular applause -1821. †**7.** Hence, inspiration, whispers -1660. **8.** *fig.* (Cf. 3 and 5.) Public exposure, publicity 1601.

1. As transparent, as colourless, as invisible as the a. we breathe HUXLEY. **3.** A bird of the aire shall carry the voyce *Eccl.* x. 20. An open air meeting (*mod.*). **In the air**: **1.** *a.* In men's minds everywhere abroad; *b.* in an uncertain state. **2.** *Mil.* Protruded into the open country, with its flank unprotected. **3.** *To build (castles) in the air*: to form unsubstantial projects. **4.** The cold winter a. 1649; one's native a. POPE; change of a. 1860. Abroad to take the a. MASSINGER. Foul a. and gas fumes 1861. Hunting conies by the a. 1607. **5.** Bring with thee ayres from Heauen or blasts from Hell *Haml.* I. iv. 41. In the a. of the door (*mod.*). **8.** *To take air*: to 'get wind'. Least the deuice take a. *Twel. N.* II. iv. 144.

II. Manner, appearance. **1.** Outward appearance, look, style 1596. **2.** Of a person: Mien, gesture, manner (*arch.*) 1599; †mood -1728. **3.** An affected appearance 1660. †**4.** Stylishness -1816.

1. Seest thou not the ayre of the Court in these enfoldings *Wint. T.* IV. iv. 755. With the a. of a secret POPE, of a paradox HUME. **2.** Her a., if not her words BYRON. With a decisive a. BUTLER. **3.** Taking the a. of a supercilious mentor GEO. ELIOT. To give oneself airs FIELDING.

III. In music [= musical *mode*]. **1.** Connected succession of musical sounds; song-like music, melody 1590. **2.** *concr.* A piece of music to be sung or played as a 'solo', with or without a distinct harmonized accompaniment; a melody 1604; †a sprightly tune or song -1789. **3.** The predominant part of a harmonized composition, in part-music usu. the soprano part 1819. †**4.** A part-song 1597.

1. Any ayre of musicke *Merch. V.* v. i. 76.

Comb.: **a.-ball**, a ball inflated with a., a toy; **-bath**, an arrangement for drying chemical substances; **-bed**, one with a mattress inflated with a.; **-bladder,** (1) a sac filled with a. in an animal or plant; also, a vesicle in glass, etc.; (2) the swimming-bladder of fishes; **-bone**, a bone for the reception of a., as in birds; **-box,** (1) the AIR-CHAMBER of a fire-engine or life-boat; (2) a square wooden tube used in mining to convey a. into the face of a single drift; **-brake**, one worked by condensed a.; **-brick**, one perforated for ventilation; **-canal**; **-casing**, the casing enclosing the base of a steamer chimney, to keep heat off the deck; **-castle**, a visionary project; **-cavity**, an intercellular space in water-plants; **-cell**, any small cavity filled with a.; *esp.* (in *pl.*) small cells in the lungs of animals, forming the extremities of the ramifications of the bronchial tubes; air-cavities in plants; **-chamber**, (1) any cavity filled with a. in an animal or plant; (2) in a pump, etc., a receptacle containing a., which, when compressed, maintains a constant pressure upon the water; an air-vessel; whence **-chambered** *a.*; **-cock**, a stop-cock to let a. out or in; **-cushion**, one inflated with a.; **-drain**, a covered channel round a foundation to prevent damp; **-duct**, a passage for a., *esp.* to the air-bladder of fishes; **-engine**, one actuated by heated a.; **-fountain**, one actuated by compressed a.; **-grating**, one for the entrance of a. under floors, etc.; **-gun**, one projecting balls, etc., by compressed a.; **-hammer**, one moved by compressed a.; **-head**, **-ing**, a smaller passage in a mine, driven parallel with the gate-road, to carry a. for ventilation; **-holder**, an air-tight vessel or receiver; **-hole**, one to admit a.; *spec.* a breathing-place in the ice, in rapid rivers; the cavities in a metal casting, produced by a.; **-jacket**, one with air-tight lining, to give buoyancy in water, when inflated; **-line**, (*a*) a bee-line; (*b*) a line of aircraft; **-monger**, a visionary projector; **-pillow** (see **-cushion**); **-pipe**, one of the bronchial tubes; a ventilating pipe; **-plant**, an epiphyte, which has roots unconnected with the ground; **-poise**, an instrument for weighing a.; **-port**[1], a port-hole in a ship for ventilation; **-pump**, a machine for exhausting the a. out of a vessel by the strokes of a piston; **-root**, the root of an epiphyte, which hangs in a.; **-sac** (= **-cell**); **-scuttle** (= **-port**[1]); **-shaft**, a straight passage, *usu.* vertical, for admitting a. into a mine or tunnel; **-stone**, an aerolite; **-stove**, one which heats a. passing between its surface and its casing; **-thermometer**, one measuring temperature by the expansion of a column of a.; **-threads**, those of the gossamer spider seen floating in the a.; **-tight** *a.*, impermeable to a. 1760; whence **-tightly** *adv.*; **-trap**, one for preventing the escape of foul a. from sewers, etc.

b. In comb. relating to flying machines or aviation, as *a.-base, -fleet, -line, -liner, -mail, -pilot, -sickness*; **a. force**, that part of the forces of a country (in Great Britain, Royal Air Force, abbrev. R.A.F.) which consists of officers and men with the necessary flying machines; so **a.-commodore**, **-marshal**; **-port**[2] [PORT *sb.*[1]], a place containing an aerodrome at which flying machines start on or land from their voyages; so **-station**; **a. raid**, a raiding attack by aircraft upon an enemy; **-worthy** *a.*, in fit condition to travel through the air.

Hence **Ai·rless** *a.* void of air; stuffy; still.

Air (ēᵊɹ), *v.* 1530. [f. prec.] **1.** *trans.* To expose to the open air; to ventilate. **2.** To expose to heat, dry or warm at the fire 1610. **3.** *refl.* To expose oneself to the fresh air 1611. Also *intr.* (*arch.*) 1633. **4.** *fig.* To wear openly; and hence, to show off 1611. Also *refl.* and *intr.* 1670.

1. To a. doublet and cloak SCOTT, a room 1861. **2.** Air'd at the fire 1759. **3.** To a. myself in my native fields LAMB. **4.** I begge..leaue to ayre this jewel *Cymb.* II. iv. 98. Airing a snowy hand TENNYSON. Hence **Aired** (ēᵊɹd) *pple.* and *a.* ventilated, or dried by heat; in *comb.* having an air (said of breath, manner, mien, tune). **Ai·rer**, one who or that which airs; *spec.* a frame for airing clothes. **Ai·ring** *vbl. sb.* the action of AIR *v.* 1, 2; a walk, ride, or drive to take the air; exercising horses in the open air.

Air (ēᵊɹ), *Sc.* ēr), *adv.* (Sc. f. ERE.] †Formerly; early.

Air day or late day SCOTT.

Air|e, Sc. f. EYRE, a circuit court.

†**Air-balloo·n.** 1753. = BALLOON.

Aircraft (ēᵊ·ɹˌkrɑft). 1907. [CRAFT 8.] Flying machines collectively.

†**Aire**, *sb.*[1] 1581. [a. OF. *aire* :—L. *ara.*] An altar –1652.

†**Aire**, *sb.*[2] ME. [a. OF. *aire.*] Early f. AERIE –1706. Hence †**Aire** *v.* to build an aerie.

Airedale (ēᵊ·ɹdēl). A district in the W. Riding of Yorkshire; *A. terrier*, a breed of large rough-haired dogs.

Airily (ēᵊ·rili), *adv.* 1766. [f. AIRY *a.*] In an airy manner; thinly, lightly; with light hearts, gaily; jauntily. So **Ai·riness.**

Airman (ēᵊ·ɹmæ̆n). 1910. The pilot of an aeroplane or airship. So **Ai·rwoman.** So **Ai·rmanship** [after *seamanship*] 1864.

Airplane (ēᵊ·ɹplēⁱn). 1907. = AEROPLANE 2.

Airship (ēᵊ·ɹʃip). 1888. [After G. *luftschiff.*] A dirigible motor-driven balloon, usu. cigar-shaped.

Airt (ēᵊ·ɹt, *Sc.* ērt), *sb.* 1470. [app. a. Gael. *aird*, a height.] A quarter of the compass; a direction. Hence **Airt** *v.* to guide.

Ai·r-ve:ssel. 1676. **1.** *Nat. Hist.* Any vessel used for containing air; *esp.* the tracheæ of insects, and the spiral vessels in plants. **2.** *Hydraul.* = AIR-CHAMBER. 1819.

Airway (ēᵊ·ɹweⁱ). 1859. [f. AIR *sb.* + WAY *sb.*] **1.** A passage for air, esp. one for ventilation in a mine. **2.** The route of a service of aeroplanes or airships 1908.

Airy (ēᵊ·ri), *a.* ME. [f. AIR *sb.*] **I.** Of the atmosphere. **1.** †Atmospheric, aerial –1677; performed in the air 1624; placed high in the air, lofty; hence, heavenly (*poet.*) 1590. **2.** Exposed to the air; breezy 1596.

1. The a. voyage 1878. The aery Mountain DENHAM. A. brows MARLOWE. **2.** A more a. mode of life JOHNSON.

II. Of the substance. **1.** Composed of air, air-like, immaterial ME.; light or buoyant as air 1598; elastic 1642; sprightly 1644; delicate in imagination 1779. **2.** Unsubstantial as air; unreal 1590; superficial, flippant 1598; visionary 1667. †**3.** Assuming airs –1606; of a good air –1699.

1. Thin a. shapes ADDISON. An a. bridge, tread SCOTT. A. Songs and Galiards 1674. The fancy of Spenser; and..the a. dream that hovers over it HAZLITT. **2.** A. nothings *Mids. N.* V. i. 16. An ayrie, and meere borrow'd thing B. JONS. An a. metaphysician BURKE.

Airy, obs. and dial. f. AREA.

Aisle (əil). ME. [Orig. a. OFr. *ele, eele* :—L. *ala* wing (contr. from *axilla*). In Eng. confused with *ile, yle* island, refash., *a* 1700, as *isle*, and recently, after Fr. *aile*, as *aisle.*] **1.** A wing or lateral division of a church; the part on either side of the nave, usu. divided from it by a row of pillars. Also *fig.* †**2.** *Cross aisle*: a transept –1772. **3.** Also, **a.** Any division of a church 1762; **b.** (quasi ALLEY) A passage in a church between the rows of pews or seats 1731.

1. Long iles extend POPE. A double isle RAY. As he treads the solemn aile 1782. *fig.* Aisles of the forest 1854, of the pine B. TAYLOR. **3. b.** '*Aisle* [..to be written *aile.*] The walks in a church or wings of a quire' JOHNSON. Hence **Aisled** *adj.* furnished with aisles; *pple.* placed in an a. **Ai·sleless** *a.* unfurnished with aisles.

Ait[1] (eⁱt). [OE. *iggað, igeoð*, perh. dim. of *ieg* island. The *t* is obscure. The later *-et*, and *-ot*, are mod. after *islet*, Fr. *îlot*. See EYOT.] An islet or small isle; *esp.* one in a river.

Ait[2], **aitt**, Sc. and north. = OAT.

Aitch (the letter); see ACHE *sb.*[3] and H.

Aitch-bone (ēⁱ·tʃbōᵘn). ME. [orig. *nache-* or *nage-*bone, a. OFr. *nache, nage* :—late L. **natica* f. *natis*; see NACHE. For loss of *n*, cf. ADDER. Erron. refash. as *H-, ice-, edge-*bone.] The bone of the rump, or the cut of beef lying over it.

Aith, obs. or dial. f. OATH.

Aitiology, obs. var. of ÆTIOLOGY.

Ajar (ădʒā·ɹ), *adv.*[1] ME. [A *prep.*[1] + CHAR, OE. *cyrr* a turn.] On the turn, slightly opened, as a door. Erron. *at jar.*

The dim lattice is a. SCOTT.

Ajar, *adv.*[2] 1553. [A *prep.*[1] + JAR *sb.*; or for *at jar.*] In a jarring state, out of harmony.

A. with the world HAWTHORNE.

Ajee (ădʒī·), *adv. Sc.* and *dial.* Also **agee.** 1733. [A *prep.*[1] + JEE.] Aside; (of a gate) ajar. Also *fig.*

Ajog (ădʒǫ·g), *adv.* 1879. [A *prep.*[1]] On the jog.

Ajoint (ădʒoi·nt), *adv.* 1840. [A *prep.*[1]] On a joint or pivot. Jointed, supple.

Ake, earlier and better f. ACHE *v.*

†**Akehorne**, erron. f. ACORN.

Aker, obs. f. ACRE; var. of ACKER, tidal bore.

Aketon, -toun, obs. vars. of ACTON, HAQUETON.

Akimbo (ăki·mboᵘ), *adv.* ME. [?] The hand resting on the hips, and the elbow turned outwards.

With his arm a. 1727. Both arms a. BROWNING.

Akin (ăki·n). 1558. [contr. from *of kin.*] **A.** *adv.* **1.** Of kin, by way of blood relationship. **2.** Of things: Of nature or character, in character 1633. See also KIN 3 b.

2. To Love, Fear's neare akinne P. FLETCHER.

B. *adj.* (Only after its sb.) **1.** Of the same kin; related by blood 1586. **2.** Of things: Allied in character, etc. 1603.

1. Mother and he are a. FOOTE. **2.** The sensation was a. to giddiness TYNDALL. Hence †**Aki·nd** *a.* FULLER.

‖**Akinesia** (ækinī·siă). 1878. [a. Gr.] *Phys.* Paralysis of the motor nerves. Also **Akinesis.** Hence **Akine·sic** *a.*

Akmite (æ·kməit). 1837. [f. Gr. ἀκμή.] *Min.* A bisilicate of the Amphibole group.

Aknee (ănī·), *adv.* ME. [f. ON + KNEE.] On one's knee or knees.

Aknow, obs. f. ACKNOW *v.*

Akre [app. f. *akern* as *pl.*], obs. f. ACORN.

Al, obs. f. ALL, retained in comp. in *albeit, almighty*, etc.

Al-, *pref.*[1] = L. *ad-* bef. *l*, OFr. *a-*, refash. later after L. as *al-*. Occas. for *a-* (not = L. *al-*), as in *a(l)lay.*

Al-, *pref.*[2], the Arab. article, as in *alcohol*, etc.

-al, *suffix*[1], of adjs. and sbs. **1.** *adj.* repr. L. *-alis* = 'of the kind of, pertaining to'. In Eng. *-al* is suffixed to any L. sb., as in *bas-al*, etc.; to Gr. sbs., as in *baptismal*, etc.; to L. adjs. in *-eus, -ius, -uus, -rnus, -is*, and Gr. adjs. in *-κός, -οειδής*, as *comical, spheroidal.* **2.** *sb.* Adjs. in *-al-* used subst. in L. have been adopted in Eng.; and OFr. *-aille, -ail, -al*, f. L. *-alia* (neut. pl.) became an Eng. formative of nouns of action, as in AFr. *arrivaille* arrival.

-al, *suffix*[2] (= *al*cohol or *al*dehyde), as in *chloral, ethal.*

‖**A la** (a·la). 1646. [Fr. *à la* (sc. *mode*).] After the (specified) manner, method, or style, as *à la française*; hence *à la Reine* (= *à la mode de la Reine*), etc.

‖**Ala** (ēⁱ·lă). Pl. **alæ** (ēⁱ·lī). 1755. [L.] **1.** Any wing-like process; *esp.* (*Phys.*) a lateral cartilage of the nose; (*Bot.*) †an axil; a side petal of a papilionaceous corolla 1794. **2.** *Arch.* A side apartment of a Roman house. Cf. AISLE. 1832.

†**Alaba·ndine.** ME. [a. L. *alabandina* (sc. *gemma*), f. *Alabanda* in Caria.] **1.** = ALMANDINE –1656. **2.** = next.

Alabandite (ælăbæ·ndəit). [f. *Alabanda* (see prec.).] *Min.* A native iron-black sub-metallic sulphide of manganese, called also *manganblende.* DANA.

Alabarch (æ·lăbāɹk). 1727. [ad. L. *alabarches*, a. Gr.] Title of the chief magistrate of the Jews at Alexandria under the Ptolemies.

Alabaster (æ·lăbɑːstəɹ, æ:lăbɑ·stəɹ). ME. [a. OFr. *alabastre* (*albâtre*), ad. L., a. Gr. ἀλάβαστρος, prop. ἀλάβαστος.] **1.** A term for *sulphate* of lime or gypsum, occurring white, yellow, red, or clouded (*Modern* or *Gypseous A.*); also for the varieties of stalagmitic *carbonate* of lime used by the ancients (*Oriental* or *Calcareous A.*). **2.** A box for unguents, made of alabaster ME. †**3.** A liquid measure = half the sextary. **4.** *adj.* (*sb.* as *attrib.*) Of or like alabaster 1526.

1. Like his Grandsire cut in Alablaster *Merch. V.* I. i. 84. **4.** An a. boxe of precious oyntment TINDALE. Babes'..a. innocent arms SHAKS. vars. **Alabla·ster** (16–17th c.), ‖**Alabastri·tes.** Hence **Alaba·strine** *a.* of or like a.

‖**Alaba·strum.** 1706. *Bot.* A flower-bud.

Alablaster, obs. f. ALABASTER and ARBLASTER.

‖**A la carte** (ælakāɹt, Fr. alakart). 1826. [Fr. = by the card.] Said of meals ordered by separate items: opp. to TABLE D'HÔTE.

Alack (ălæ·k), *int.* 1480. [f. A *int.* O! + LACK *sb.*[1] used as exclam.] An exclam. of pity or shame; hence of regret or surprise. *arch., poet.*, or *dial.*

A.! our friend is gone TENNYSON. **Alack the day! alack-a-day**: shame to, woe worth, the day! Aphet. *lack-a-day*, of surprise only.

†**Ala·ck**, *adv. rare.* 1528. [A *prep.*[1] + LACK.] Lacking –1587.

†**Ala·crious**, *a.* 1602. [f. L. *alacris.*] Lively. Hence †**Ala·criously** *adv.* †**Ala·criousness.** var. **Ala·critous** (*rare*).

Alacrity (ălæ·krĭti). 1510. [a. L. *alacritatem.*] Cheerful readiness, promptitude, liveliness, sprightliness.

That meruelouse alacritee languished MORE. A. of spirit *Rich. III*, v. iii. 73. [of] Visage STEELE. Grateful a. SCOTT.

‖**Alala·**. 1675. [Dor. Gr.] A Greek battle-cry. HOBBES.

Ala·lia. 1878. [f. Gr. ἀ + λαλία.] *Med.* Loss of speech.

Alalite (æ·lălait). [f. *Ala*, in Tyrol.] A Malacolite or Diopside. DANA.

‖**Alameda** (alămē·dă). 1843. [Sp.] A public walk, shaded with trees.

†**Alami·re.** 1528. [f. *a, la, mi, re.*] *Mus.* The lowest tone but one in Aretine's scale –1760.

Alamoda·lity. 1753. [a. mod.L. *alamodalitas*, f. next.] The quality of being *à la mode.*

A.—a good and pregnant word SOUTHEY.

Alamode, ‖**à la mode** (æ·lămōud, Fr. alamo·d). 1649. [a. Fr.] 1. *phr.* In the fashion. 2. as *adj.* Fashionable 1650. †3. *subst.* A fashion or mood –1683. 4. A thin light glossy black silk 1676.

2. *A. silk*; see 4. *A. beef*: scraps of beef boiled down into a stew. 4. The alamodes of Lyons MACAULAY.

Alamort, ‖**à la mort** (æ·lămǭɹt, Fr. alamǫ·r). 1592. [Fr.; occas. *all amort*, whence AMORT.] 1. *adv.* To the death. 2. *adj.* Sick to death; dispirited.

2. What sweeting all-mort *Tam. Shr.* IV. iii. 36.

†**Alan.** ME. [a. OFr.] A wolf-hound. CHAUCER.

Aland (ălæ·nd), *adv.* ME. [A *prep.*[1] + LAND.] †In the country –1568; ashore (*arch.*); to the land ME.

Alanine (æ·lănain). 1863. [f. AL(DEHYDE) + -INE; the *-an-* is euphonic.] 1. The 'acid' monamide $C_3H_7NO_2$, derived from Lactic acid by replacement of the alcoholic hydroxyl by NH_2. 2. (in pl.) A name for the group of acid amides, derived from the lactic series.

Ala·ntin. 1847. [f. Germ. *alant* elecampane, *Inula Helenium.*] *Chem.* = INULIN.

Alar (ēi·laɹ), *a.* 1839. [ad. L. *alaris*, f. *ala.*] 1. Of or belonging to wings 1847; wing-shaped 1839. 2. *Bot.* and *Phys.* Axillary 1858.

†**Ala·rge,** *v.* ME. [a. OFr. *alargir.*] To increase –1560. Also *intr.* (OFr. *s'alargir.*)

Alarm (ălā·ɹm), *sb.* Also **alarum** (now pronounced ălēə·ɹəm, ălæ·rəm). ME. [a. OFr. *alarme*, a. It. *allarme* = *all' arme!* Mistaken in 17th c. for *all arm!*] I. As a phrase. †1. *int.* An exclam. = 'To arms' –1600. †2. quasi-*sb.* The call to arms, by crying *alarme!* or otherwise. With *cry, sound*, etc. –1594.

1. Crying al'arme, help HOLLAND. 2. Strike alarum, drummes SHAKS.

II. As *sb.* with *pl.* 1. A call to arms 1548; news of approaching hostility 1812. 2. A sound to warn of danger, or to arouse; *esp.* a sudden peal rung out by a tocsin, or a chime by a clock 1592. Also *fig.* 3. The mechanism which sounds the a.; also *fig.* Usu. *alarum.* 1586. 4. A warning of danger of any kind 1591. 5. *Fencing.* A step or stamp made on the ground with the advancing foot 1579. 6. A din (*arch.*) 1523. †7. A sudden attack; a surprise –1681. 8. A state of excitement caused by danger apprehended 1587.

1. The scouts Bring swift alarums in SOUTHEY. 2. *fig.* An alarum against Usurers LODGE. 4. Your.. benevolence *took the alarm* JUNIUS. So *to give the a.* 6. This alarum in the elements KEATS. 8. A blanket in th' Alarum of feare caught vp *Haml.* II. ii. 532.

Comb.: **alar(u)m-bell,** one rung as a signal of danger; also *fig.*; **alar(u)m-clock, -watch,** one which rings loudly at any pre-appointed hour; **alar(u)m-gauge,** an appliance to give warning of a dangerous pressure of steam or deficiency of water in a boiler; **a.-gun, -cannon,** one fired to give a.; **-post,** a post appointed for each regiment to march to in case of an a.; **-word,** a watchword. Hence **Ala·rmism,** the profession or practice of the alarmist. **Ala·rmist,** a panic-monger.

Alarm (ălā·ɹm), *v.* 1590. [f. the sb.] †1. To call to arms –1718; to rouse to action –1768. 2. To arouse to a sense of danger, to put on the alert 1651. 3. To keep in excitement 1661. 4. To excite with sudden fear or apprehension of danger 1653.

2. For the purpose of alarming the guards MACAULAY. 4. I am alarmed at the aspect of affairs (*mod.*). Hence **Ala·rmable** *a.* liable to be alarmed. **Ala·rmed** *ppl. a.* aroused, on the watch; disturbed. **Ala·rmedly** *adv.* **Ala·rming** *ppl. a.* disturbing with apprehension of danger. **Ala·rmingly** *adv.*

Alarum, var. of ALARM, now only poet., or in senses of sb. II, 2, 3.

Alary (ēi·lări), *a.* 1658. [ad. L. *alarius*, f. ALA.] Of or pertaining to wings or *alæ.*

Alas (ăla·s), *int.* ME. [a. OFr. *ha las, a las* (*hélas*), f. *ha!* = AH! + *las*:—L. *lassum.*] An exclam. of unhappiness, sorrow, pity, etc.

Alas the heauy day *Oth.* IV. ii. 42.

‖**Alastor** (ăla·stǫɹ). *rare.* 1810. [a. Gr., f. ἀ priv. + λαστ-, λαθεῖν.] A relentless spirit; a Nemesis.

Alate (ălēi·t), *adv. arch.* ME. [A *prep.*[2] + LATE.] Of late.

Alate (ēi·leit), *a.* 1668. [ad. L. *alatus*, f. *ala.*] Having wings or wing-like appendages. var. **A·lated** *a.*

Alatern(us (ælătə·ɹnǫs). 1607. [f. L. *ala* wing + *ternus* three.] *Bot.* An evergreen shrub (*Rhamnus Alaternus*) of the genus *Rhamnaceæ* or Buckthorns.

Alation (ălēi·ʃən). [a Fr., f. L. *alatus*, f. *ala.*] A winged condition; the mode in which the wings of insects are disposed.

Alaunt, var. of ALAN.

†**Alay·,** *v.* 1508. [?] Term of art: 'To carve' a pheasant.

Alb (ælb). [OE. *albe*, ad. late L. *alba* (sc. *tunica*, or *vestis*).] A tunic of white cloth, reaching to the feet, and enveloping the person; worn by priests in religious ceremonies, and occ. by consecrated kings.

[Sigismund] was buryed in his regall a. 1606.

Albacore (æ·lbăkōɹ). 1579. [a. Pg. *albacor*, f. Arab. *al bukr*, the young camel.] A fish; prop. a large species of Tunny (*Thynnus*), found in the Atlantic; also loosely, of other species. var. **Albicore** (Fr.).

Alban (æ·lbăn). 1863. [f. L. *albus.*] A white crystalline resinous substance extracted from gutta-percha on treatment with alcohol, etc.

Albata (ælbēi·tă). 1848. [a. L. *albata* adj. fem.] A white metallic composition; German silver.

†**Alba·tion.** 1612. [ad. med.L. *albationem.*] 1. *Alchem.* = ALBIFICATION. 2. Dusting; ? orig. with a white powder 1612.

Albatross (æ·lbătrǫs). 1681. [app. Pg. ALCATRAS, altered, perh. after *albus* white, the albatross being white, to *albi-*, *albe-*, *albatross.*] †1. The Frigate-bird, = ALCATRAS 2. –1753. 2. A family of birds allied to the Petrels (Order *Tubinares*), inhabiting the Pacific and Southern Oceans. The great Albatross, *Diomedea exulans*, is the largest of sea-birds.

Albe. 1697. [Eng. form of ALBUM.] *Rom. Antiq.* A register.

Albe·, *conj. arch.* Also **al be, allbe, all be.** = ALBEIT.

Albedo (ælbī·do). 1859. [L.] Whiteness; *spec.* in *Astr.* The proportion of the solar light incident upon an element of the surface of a planet, which is again reflected from it.

Albeit (ǫlbī·it), *conj.* ME. [prop. *phr.*, = *all though it be that*; see ALL *adv.*] 1. Admitting (*that*) 1460. 2. Although ME. 3. In *contr. cl.*: even if 1795.

2. All bee it he coulde not saye naye MORE. 3. A certain (a. uncertain) morrow THACKERAY.

Albert (æ·lbəɹt). In full **Albert chain.** 1883. [f. *Albert*, the Prince Consort of Queen Victoria.] A kind of watch-chain.

Albertite (æ·lbəɹtait). 1875. [f. *Albert*, New Brunswick.] *Min.* A jet-black bituminous mineral found in New Brunswick.

A·lbert-type. 1875. [f. name of inventor.] A method of printing in ink from photographic plates; also, the picture so printed.

Albescent (ælbe·sĕnt), *a.* 1831. [ad. L. *albescentem*, *albescere.*] Growing or passing into white.

Albespyne, -ine (æ·lbĕspain). ME. [a. OFr. *albespine* (mod. *aubépine*):—L. *alba spina.*] Whitethorn, hawthorn. *arch.*

†**Albeston(e.** ME. [a. OFr. *albeston*, var. *asbeston*, a. L.] = ASBESTOS –1567.

A·lbicant, *ppl. a.* 1879. [ad. L. *albicantem*; see next.] Growing white.

Albication (ælbikēi·ʃən). 1879. [f. L. *albicat-*, *albicare*, f. *albus.*] The process of growing white; *esp.* the development of light patches, bands, etc. in the foliage of plants.

Albicore, var. of ALBACORE.

†**Albifica·tion.** ME. [a. Fr., ad. L. *albificationem*; see ALBIFY.] *Alchem.* The process or art of making white –1592.

Albiflo·rous, *a.* 1879. [f. L. *albus* + *flor-* + -OUS.] *Bot.* White-flowered.

Albin(e (æ·lbin). 1817. [f. L. *albus.*] *Min.* An opaque white apophyllite found in Bohemia.

Albines (æ·lbinz), *sb. pl.* 1879. [f. L. *albus.*] *Veg. Phys.* Small colourless bodies found with aleuron grains.

Albino (ælbī·no, ælbai·no). Pl. **-os.** 1777. [a. Sp. or Pg. (orig. applied by the Pg. to white African negroes).] 1. A human being having a congenital deficiency of colouring pigment in the skin, hair, and eyes, so that the former are white, and the eyes pink. 2. Applied also to animals, as white mice, etc., and to plants lacking chlorophyll 1859. Hence **A·lbiness,** a female a. **A·lbinism, Albi·noism,** the condition of being an a.

Albite (æ·lbait). 1843. [f. L. *albus.*] *Min.* White or soda feldspar. Hence **Albi·tic** *a.* of the nature of, or containing, a.

A·lbolith. 1875. [f. L. *albus* + Gr. λίθος.] A white cement made from magnesia and silica.

‖**Albora·k.** *Obs.* 1635. [Arab.] A white mule; *esp.* that which was said to have carried Mohammed up to heaven.

‖**Albugo** (ælbiū·go). ME. [L., f. *albus.*] A disease of the eye, in which a white opaque spot forms on the transparent cornea. Hence **Albugi·nean** *a.* of or like the white fibrous tissue of the eye. **Albugi·neous** *a.* = ALBUGINEAN; albuminous. †**Albu·ginous** *a.* albuminous. †**Albu·ginousness.**

‖**Album**[1] (æ·lbǒm). Pl. **albums.** 1651. [a. L. *album*, a blank tablet; orig. used as L.] 1. *Rom. Antiq.* A tablet on which the prætor's edicts and other public matters were recorded for public information 1753. 2. A blank book in which to insert autographs, verses, drawings, stamps, etc. 1651. 3. A Visitors' Book 1775. Hence **Albumean** *a.* relating to albums; **Albumess,** a female keeper of an a. (*Nonce-wds.*) LAMB.

†‖**A·lbum**[2]. 1527. [f. L. *album.*] 1. *Path.* Leucorrhea. 2. Rent paid in white money or silver –1775.

Albumen (ælbiū·mĕn). 1599. [a. L.] 1. The white of an egg. 2. The substance which exists nearly pure in the white of an egg, and is a constituent of animal solids and fluids, and of the tuberous roots and seeds of plants; see ALBUMIN 1800. 3. *Bot.* The substance which surrounds the embryo in many seeds; the endosperm or perisperm 1677. Hence **Albu·menize** *v.* to cover, coat, or impregnate, with a. **Albu·menizer,** one who albumenizes.

Albumin (ælbiū·min). 1869. [a. Fr. *albumine*, f. L. *albumin-.*] A class of ALBUMINOIDS, comprising those soluble in water (= ALBUMEN 2), in dilute acids, and in alkalis (*acid* or *alkali albumins*). Hence **Albu·minate,** a combination of a. with certain bases, in which the a. acts as a very feeble acid. **Albu·minated** *ppl. a.* albuminized. **Albu·mini·ferous** *a.* producing a. **Albu·mini·meter,** a polarizing apparatus for measuring the a. in a liquid. **Albu·minin,** the substance of the cells enclosing the white of birds' eggs. **Albu·mini·parous** *a.* producing a. **Albu·minize** *v.* (*Biol.*) to convert into a.; whence **Albu·miniza·tion,** re-conversion of a tissue into a. ‖**Albu·mino·sis,** *Path.* a condition of the blood in which there is an excess of a.

Albumino- (ælbiū·mino), comb. f. of ALBUMEN. 1. *adv.* Albuminously, as in a.-fibrous. 2. *adj.* Albuminous, as in a.-chloride.

Albuminoid (ælbiū·minoid), *a.* 1859. [f. L. *albumin-.*] Like albumen. As *sb.* (in *pl.*)

= *Albuminoid Principles*: Organic compounds which form the chief part of the tissues of animals and plants. = PROTEIDS. 1873. Hence **Albu·minoi·dal** *a.*

Albuminose (ælbiū·minōᵘs), *a.* 1847. [ad. mod.L. *albuminosus.*] = ALBUMINOUS 1859. As *sb.* A crystalloid substance derived from albumen by the action of pepsin in weak acid solutions 1847.

Albuminous (ælbiū·minəs), *a.* 1791. [f. L. *albumin-.*] 1. Of the nature or character of albumen or albumin. 2. *Bot.* Containing albumen in the seed; see ALBUMEN 3. 3. *fig.* Insipid 1865. Hence **Albu·minousness.**

‖**Albuminuria** (ælbiū·miniūᵊ·riă). 1854. [f. L. *albumin-* + Gr. οὖρον.] *Path.* The escape of albumen in the urine.

Alburn (æ·lbɒɹn). 1753. 1. = ALBURNUM. 2. A fish; the Bleak (in L. *alburnus*).

Alburnum (ælbɒ·ɹnɒm). 1664. [a. L., f. *albus.*] The sap-wood in exogenous trees. Hence **Albu·rnous** *a.* of, or of the nature of, a.

Alcade, var. of ALCALDE; and erron. f. ALCAYDE.

Alcahest, var. of ALKAHEST.

Alcaic (ælkē·ik). Also **alch-**. 1630. [ad. L. *alcaicus*, a. Gr. ἀλκαικός, f. Ἀλκαῖος.] *adj.* Of or pertaining to Alcæus, a lyric poet of Mytilene (*c* 600 B.C.), or his metre 1637. *sb.* in *pl.* Alcaic strophes.

Alcaid, var. of ALCAYDE.

‖**Alcalde** (alka·ldė). 1615. [Sp., ad. Arab. Cf. CADI.] A sheriff or justice, in Spain and Portugal.

Alcali, etc. obs. var. of ALKALI, etc.

‖**Alca·nna, -na.** 1625. [a. Sp. *alcana*, a. Arab. *al-ḥenna*; see HENNA and ALKANET.] *Bot.* Egyptian Privet (*Lawsonia inermis*, N.O. *Lythraceæ*), or its leaves, etc., used by Orientals to dye parts of the body reddish orange; henna.

Alcargen, alcarsin; see ALK-.

‖**Alcarraza** (ælkără·ză, Sp. alkără·þă). 1818. [Sp., ad. Arab.] A porous earthenware vessel used for cooling water by evaporation.

†**A·lcatras, -ace, -ash.** 1564. [a. Sp., Pg. *alcatraz*, var. of Pg. *alcatruz* the bucket of a water-wheel, applied orig. to the Pelican, which was supposed to draw up water in its beak.] ‖1. Sp. and Pg. name of the Pelican; applied also to sea-mews, etc. †2. Eng. name for the Frigate Bird, *Tachypetes aquilus* -1692. †3. ?A kind of albatross, prob. *Diomedea fuliginosa* -1775.

‖**Alcavala** (alkăvā·lă). 1776. [Sp., ad. Arab.] A tax of ten per cent. upon sales. ADAM SMITH.

‖**Alcayde** (ælkē·d, Sp. alkai·dė). 1502. [Sp., ad. Arab.] The governor of a fortress; the warden of a prison; (in Spain, Portugal, Barbary, etc.). ¶ Occ. confused with ALCALDE.

‖**Alcazar** (alkā·þar). 1615. [Sp., ad. Arab.] A palace, fortress.

†**Alce.** 1541. [a. L. *alce.*] An elk -1753.

Alchemic, -al (ælke·mik, -ăl), *a.*; also **alchym-**. 1815. [ad. med.L. *alchimicus*; see ALCHEMY.] Of or belonging to alchemy. Also *fig.* Hence **Alche·mically** *adv.*

Alchemist (æ·lkĭmist). 1514. [a. OFr. *alquemiste, alkemiste*; see ALCHEMY.] One who studies or practises alchemy.

You are an Alcumist, make Gold of that *Timon* v. i. 117. var. †**A·lchemister.** Hence **Alchemi·stic, -al** *a.* †**A·lchemistry**, alchemy.

Alchemize (æ·lkĭməiz), *v.* 1603. [f. ALCHEMIST.] To change, as by alchemy.

Till the sunshine, striking this [*i.e.* the hair], A. its dulness MRS. BROWNING.

Alchemy (æ·lkĭmi). ME. [a. OFr. *alquimie, -kemie*, ad. med.L. *alchimia*, a. Arab. *al* + *kimia*, app. a. Gr. χημία, χημεία (transmutation), mostly explained as 'the Egyptian art', and identified with χημία 'land of *Khem*', 'black earth', i.e. Egypt. It was afterwards confused with Gr. χυμεία, f. χυ-, χέειν, to pour. Mahn thinks χυμεία was the original.] 1. The chemistry of the Middle Ages and 16th c.; limited to the pursuit of the transmutation of baser metals into gold, and the search for the alkahest, and the panacea. Also *fig.* †2. A composition, mainly of brass, imitating gold; 'alchemy gold'; also, a trumpet made of this -1812. Also *fig.*

1. It has been [said] that A. was the mother of Chemistry WHEWELL. *fig.* Guilding pale streames with heauenly alcumy SHAKS. *Sonn.* xxxiii. 2. Cherubim Put to their mouths the sounding alchymie MILT. *P. L.* ii. 516. Hence †**A·lchemy** *v.* [f. the *sb.* 2] to plate, or to alloy. Cf. to *tin, lacquer*, etc.

Alchim-; see ALCHEM-.

†**Alchitran, alkitran.** ME. [a. OFr. *alketran, alquitran*, a. Sp., ad. Arab.] The resin or pitch of fir-trees; extended to **a.** oil of cedar and juniper; **b.** mineral pitch, bitumen, etc. -1658.

Alchym-; see ALCHEM-.

Alcoate, -hate, short f. ALCOHOLATE (see ALCOHOL).

Alcohol (æ·lkŏhǫl). 1543. [a. med.L., ad. Arab. *al-koḥ'l* 'collyrium', f. Heb.; see *Ezek.* xxiii. 40.] †1. *orig.* The fine metallic powder used in the East to stain the eyelids, etc.: powdered antimony; also, occas., powdered galena -1819. †2. Any impalpable powder, produced by trituration, or esp. by sublimation -1812. †3. By extension to fluids: An essence or 'spirit', obtained by distillation -1794. *fig.* Quintessence 1830. 4. Pure spirit of wine; or (pop.) any liquor containing it 1753. 5. *Organ. Chem.* A class of compounds, of the same type as spirit of wine, composed of carbon, hydrogen, and oxygen, some of which are liquid and others solid 1850.

1. *Alcohól*: a drug called Antimonium MINSHEU. 2. *Alcohol martis*: reduced iron. The *alcohol of Sulphur* SIR H. DAVY. 3. *Alcohol of wine*: essence or spirit of wine. *fig.* The a. of egotism COLERIDGE. 4. *Absolute or anhydrous alcohol*: a. entirely free from water. Pure spirits, called a. VINCE. 5. *Common* (vinous or vinic) *Alcohol*, the best known, is a *primary, monatomic, dicarbon* or *ethyl* alcohol, $C_2H_5.OH$. Others are Methyl alcohol ($CH_3.OH$), Propyl ($C_3H_7.OH$), Butyl ($C_4H_9.OH$), Amyl ($C_5H_{11}.OH$), etc., the number being unlimited. Hence **A·lcohola·te**, a crystalline compound in which a. acts as water of crystallization. **Alcoho·lature**, an alcoholic tincture made from fresh plants.

Alcoholic (ælkohǫ·lik), *a.* 1790. [f. ALCOHOL.] 1. Of or belonging to alcohol. 2. Preserved in alcohol 1852. 3. Using alcohol 1856. As *sb. pl.* = alcoholic liquors.

1. A. strength 1836. 2. An a. specimen DANA. 3. A. thermometers 1856. Hence **Alcoho·lically** *adv.* **Alcoholi·city**, a. quality.

Alcoholism (æ·lkŏhǫli:z'm). 1852. [ad. mod.L. *alcoholismus.*] The action of alcohol upon the human system; diseased condition produced by it.

Alcoholize (æ·lkŏhǫləi:z), *v.* 1686. [ad. mod.L. *alcoholizare*; see ALCOHOL 3 and -IZE. Cf. Fr. *alcoholiser.*] †1. To sublimate -1686. †2. To rectify -1799. 3. To saturate with, or subject to the influence of, alcohol 1862. Hence **A:lcoholiza·tion.** **A·lcoholi:zing** *vbl. sb.* converting into or saturating with alcohol.

Alcoholometer (æ:lkŏhǫlǫ·mĭtəɹ). 1859. [f. ALCOHOL.] An instrument for measuring the proportion of absolute alcohol in a liquor. vars. **Alcoho·lmeter, Alcoo·meter.** Hence **Alcoholome·tric, -al** *a.* Also **Alcoometrical**, of or pertaining to alcoholometry.

Alcoholometry (æ:lkŏhǫlǫ·mĕtri). 1863. [f. ALCOHOL + Gr. μετρία.] The process of testing the proportion of absolute alcohol in a liquor. var. **Alcoo·metry.**

†‖**Alco·nde.** 1486. [Sp., f. Arab. *al* + Sp. *conde*:—L. *comitem.*] A (Spanish) Count.

A:lcoothio·nic, *a.* = ŒNOTHIONIC.

Alcoran (ælkorā·n, æ·lkorān, -æn). *arch.* ME. [a. Fr., a. Arab. *al-qorān*, the reading.] The sacred book of the Mohammedans; the Koran (now the usual form).

The Turks Alcheron, the Jews Cabala..are..to be detested GOUGE. Hence **Alcoran** *v.* to make into a Koran. †**Alcora·nal, Alcora·nic,** †**Alcora·nish** *adjs.* of or belonging to the Koran. **Alcora·nist**, one who adheres to the letter of the Koran.

‖**Alcorno·co, -que.** 1832. [Sp., f. Arab. *al* + *quern oco* spongy oak (Diez).] The cork-oak, the bark of which (*Spanish A. bark*) is used in tanning. Also *American A.*, yielding a bark formerly used in medicine.

Alcove (ælkōᵘ·v, æ·lkōᵘv). 1623. [a. Fr., ad. Sp., Pg. *alcova*, ad. Arab. *al* + *qobbah* a vault.] 1. A vaulted recess; a recess in a chamber for a bed; a recess or niche in a wall 1786. 2. A recess in a garden, orig. in the garden-wall or hedge; any bower or summer-house 1706.

2. The alcoves of box and yew COLERIDGE. Hence **Alco·ved** *ppl. a.* vaulted, arched.

Alcyon, var. of HALCYON.

Alcyon (æ·lsiǫn). *Zool.* = ALCYONIUM.

Alcyonarian (æ:lsiǫnēᵊ·riăn), *a.* 1878. [f. mod.L. *Alcyonaria.*] Belonging to the *Alcyonaria*, a sub-order of Actinoid Zoophytes; see ALCYONIUM. As *sb.* A zoophyte of that group.

‖**Alcyonium** (ælsi,ōᵘ·niǫm). 1752. [L., a. Gr. ἀλκυόνιον Bastard-sponge, said to resemble the Halcyon's nest.] *Zool.* A genus of zoophytes, giving its name to the sub-order *Alcyonaria*, forming firm fleshy masses, and including 'Dead Man's Fingers', or 'Cow's Paps'. Hence **Alcyo·nic** *a.* **A·lcyonite**, a fossil zoophyte related to *Alcyonium.* **A·lcyonoid** *a.* allied to A.; also used *subst.*

†**Ald,** *a.* Now *dial.* [OE. *ald, eald*, whence ELD.] See OLD.

†**Ald,** *sb.* ME. [var. of ELD.] Age; an age; old age -1551.

†**Alday,** *adv.* ME. [= ALL DAY.] Every day; *hence*, Always -1483.

‖**Alde·a, -dee.** *Obs.* 1698. [Pg., ad. Arab.] A Pg. village or villa -1780.

Aldehyde (æ·ldĭhəid). 1850. [= *Aldehyd.* abbrev. for *Alcohol dehydrogenatum.*] 1. A colourless volatile fluid of suffocating smell, obtained by the oxidation of Alcohol. 2. A class of compounds of the same type, each derived from its alcohol by removal of two atoms of hydrogen. (Called also *Aldides.*) 1863.

2. Thus Methyl Alcohol CH_4O, Methyl Aldehyde CH_2O. Hence **A·ldehydate**, a salt in which a. acts as a monobasic acid. **Aldehy·dic** *a.*

Alder (ǭ·ldəɹ), *sb.*[1] [OE. *alor, aler*; *d* is developed, as in *alder-best.*] A tree (*Alnus glutinosa*) related to the Birch, and common in wet places OE. 2. Extended to other shrubs or trees, as **Black Alder, A. Buckthorn** (Europ.), *Rhamnus Frangula*; Black A. (N. Amer.), *Prinos verticillatus*; White A. (N. Amer.), *Clethra alnifolia*; (S. Afr.), *Platylophus trifoliatus*; Red A. (S. Afr.), *Cunonia capensis.*

Comb. **a.-carr**, a piece of wet ground where alders grow.

†**A·lder,** *sb.*[2] [OE. *aldor, ealdor*, f. (*e*)*ald* OLD.] 1. Parent, ancestor. OE. only. 2. Chief, prince, lord -ME. (In OE. tr. L. *senior, princeps, magistratus*, etc.) Hence †**A·lderdom**, lordship.

†**Alder-**, var. of *aller-*, gen. pl. of ALL (q.v., D 2), as in *alderbest* (Chaucer), *alderliefest* (Chaucer, Shakespeare).

†**A·lderling.** 1655. [prob. f. ALDER *sb.*[1] + -LING.] A species of trout; cf. dial. *aller-trout.*

Alderman (ǭ·ldəɹmăn). [OE. *ealdormann*; see ALDER *sb.*[2], MAN *sb.*] †1. A noble or man of high rank; the governor of a district. 2. = ALDER *sb.*[2] 2. †3. The chief officer or warden of a guild 1130. 4. A municipal officer ranking next to the mayor (as still in U.S.A.), formerly (and still in the city of London) representing a ward; now, in England and Wales generally, a co-opted member of a borough or county council.

1 a. Brightnothus, aldermanne, erle, or duke of northumberlande THYNNE. b. 'Senators' or Aldermen BOLTON. 3. What an Alderman's pace he comes GAULE. An A. of Cripplegate COWPER. Hence **A·ldermanate**, the dignity of a.; the body of aldermen. **A·ldermancy**, the office of a. **Alderma·nic, †-al** *a.* of, pertaining to, or like, an a. †**Alderma·nikin**, a little a. **Alderma·nity**, (joc.) the quality of an a.; the body of aldermen. **A·ldermanlike** *a.* and *adv.* **A·ldermanly** *a.* **A·ldermanship**, the office, position, or quality of an a. **A·ldermane·ss,** †**A·lderwo·man,** †**A·ldress**, the wife of an a.

Aldermanry (ǭ·ldəɹmănri). ME. A district of a borough having its own alderman, a ward; also, the dignity of an alderman.

Aldern (ǭ·ldəɹn), *a.* OE. [f. ALDER *sb.*[1]] Of alder. As *sb.* = ALDER *sb.*[1] ME.

Aldide (æ·ldəid). *Chem.* See ALDEHYDE 2.

Aldine (ǭ·ldəin), *a.* 1802. [f. *Aldus* prop. name.] Printed or produced by Aldus Manutius, a Venetian printer in the 16th c.; the title of a modern series of books; also of certain styles of display types.

Aldol (æ·ldǫl). 1874. [f. ALD(EHYDE) + (ALCOH)OL.] A clear viscid neutral liquid, $CH_3 . CH(OH) . CH_2 . CHO$, polymerous with acetyl aldehyde.

Ale (ēl). [OE. *alu* :–**alut.*] **1.** A beverage made from an infusion of malt by fermentation, flavoured with hops, or other bitters. †**2.** In '**the ale**' (phr.), **a.** The ale-drinking; **b.** The public supply, and hence the ale-house –1617. **3.** A festival at which much ale was drunk. (Cf. *a tea.*) See also BRIDAL. OE.

Ale and *beer* were orig. synonymous; but now 'beer' is the generic name for all malt liquors, 'ale' being the name for the lighter coloured kinds.

1. Item, she brewes good Ale *Two Gent.* III. i. 304. **Buttered ale**: sugar, cinnamon, butter, and beer brewed without hops. PEPYS. 2. †**At the ale**, To goe *to the Ale* with a Christian *Two Gent.* II. v. 61. *In his Ales*: under the influence of a. *Hen. V*, IV. vii. 47. 3. There were *leet-, scot-, church-, clerk-, bed-*, and *bride-ales* SKEAT.

Comb.: **a.-barrel**, 36 (formerly 32) gallons; **-bench**, one before or in an ale-house; **-bush**, a tavern sign; **-draper**, an ale-house keeper; hence **-drapery**; **-fat** = *a.-vat*; **-firkin**, 9 (formerly 8) gallons; **-grains**, refuse malt left after brewing; **-house**, a house where a. is retailed; also *attrib.*; **-kilderkin**, a half-barrel of a.; †**-knight**, a votary of the ale-house; **-pole**, one set up as the sign of an ale-house; **-score**, **-shot**, a reckoning for a. consumed; †**silver**, a tax paid by ale-sellers within the City of London; †**-stake** = *a.-pole*; a tippler; **-tap**, prop. the tap whence ale is drawn, hence the room or place where it is kept; **-taster** = ALE-CONNER; †**-toast**, a toast in a., *fig.* a roisterer; **-vat**, one in which a. is brewed; **-wort**, the fermenting infusion of malt; **-yeast**, yeast produced in brewing ale.

Aleatory (ē·liˌătəri), *a.* 1693. [ad. L. *aleatorius.*] Dependent on the throw of a die; *hence*, dependent on uncertain contingencies, as an *aleatory contract.*

†**A·leberry.** ME. [f. ALE- + OE. *briw* brewis; cf. *bread-berry.*] Ale boiled with spice, sugar, and sops of bread –1630.

‖**A·lec.** 1520. [L.] A herring; a pickle made of small herrings. Hence **A·lecize** *v.* to dress with a. sauce.

Aleconner (ē·lkǫnəɹ). ME. An inspector of ale. Still a titular office in some boroughs.

Alecost (ē·lkǫst). 1589. [f. ALE- + COST, ad. L. *costum, -us, -os*, a. Gr. κόστος a root used as spice.] = COSTMARY, q. v.

Alectryomachy (ăleˑktriˌǫ·măki). [f. Gr. ἀλεκτρυών + -μαχία.] Cock-fighting. A Dict. wd. var. **Ale·ctoro·machy.**

Alectryomancy (ăleˑktriˌomænsi). 1684. [f. as prec. + μαντεία.] Divination by means of a cock with grains of corn. var. **Ale·ctoro·mancy.**

‖**Alectryon** (ăle·ktriˌǫ̆n). [Gr.] A cock. LONGF.

Alee (ălī·), *adv.* ME. [a. ON. *á hlé*, see LEE.] *Naut.* On or toward the lee or sheltered side of a ship; away from the wind.

The helm was *put alee* JAMES.

Ale·ft, *adv.* ME. [A *prep.*[1]] On or to the left.

Alegar (æ·lĭgăɹ, ē·lĭgăɹ). 1542. [f. ALE + *egre*, EAGER = Fr. *aigre.*] Sour ale; malt vinegar.

A. is to ale what vinegar is to wine 1881.

†**Ale·ger**, *a.* [ad. OFr. *alègre.*] Cheerful. BACON.

Ale-hoof (ē·lhūf). ME. [orig. *ale-hove*, f. OE. 'hófe, *viola*' (Ælfric); *ale-* is perh. corrupt; see HOVE.] The herb ground-ivy (*Nepeta Glechoma*). Also *hay-, hey-, horse-hove*, and HOVE.

Alei·ptic, *a. rare.* 1660. [ad. Gr. ἀλειπτικός.] Belonging to gymnastic training.

Alembic (ăle·mbik). ME. [a. Fr. *alambic*, ad. Arab. *al* the + *anbiq* a still; ad. Gr. ἄμβιξ-, ἄμβιξ cup. Aphet. *lembick.*] An apparatus formerly used in distilling, consisting of a *cucurbit* or gourd-shaped vessel, and the *cap* or *alembic* proper, the beak of which conveyed the products to a *receiver*. Also *fig.*

fig. The hot spirit drawn out of the a. of hell which in France is now so furiously boiling BURKE. Hence †**Ale·mbic**, **Ale·mbicate** *vbs.* to distil as in an a.

Alembroth (ăle·mbrǫþ). 1471. [?] *Alchem.* An old name for the double chloride of mercury and ammonium, once believed to be an alkahest.

†**Ale·ngth.** ME. [A *prep.*[1] + LENGTH.] **A.** *adv.* Lengthwise –1601. **B.** *prep.* Lengthwise to –1540.

†**Alepine, alapeen.** 1739. A mixed stuff of wool and silk, or mohair and cotton.

‖**Alerce** (äle·ɹþe). 1845. [Sp., f. L. *laricem.*] An American tree allied to the larch.

Alerion (ălīᵊ·riən). 1605. [Fr. *alérion*, med.L. *alarionem*. Of unkn. origin.] *Her.* An eagle without beak or feet.

Alert (ălə̄·ɹt). 1598. [a. Fr. *alerte*, ad. It. *all' erta* on the look-out = *alla* at the, *erta* a look-out, *lit.* something raised aloft, fem. of *erto* :—L. *erigere*. The Eng. 'on the alert' is thus etym. pleonastic.] **A.** *adv.* On the look-out; hence *adj.* (in the pred.) Watchful, wide-awake. *Mil.* 1598. *gen.* 1735. **B.** *adj.* Quick in attention and motion, lively, active 1712. **C.** *sb.* [mod.Fr. *alerte*, a military call. Cf. *alarm.*] **1.** The call to 'look out' for an attack; hence, a sudden attack 1803. **2.** **On the alert**: on the watch (replacing *alert* adv. = *all' erta*).

B. An a., joyous, and lively old soul SCOTT. C. 1. No man ever saw me drunk when an a. was expected SCOTT. 2. For ever on the a. 1882. Hence **Ale·rtly** *adv.* **Ale·rtness.**

Alethiology (ălīːþiˌǫ·lŏdʒi). *rare.* 1837. [f. Gr. ἀλήθεια.] The part of logic treating of truth.

Ale·tte. *arch.* 1816. [a. mod.Fr. *alette*, dim. of L. *ala.*] A small wing; a pilaster or buttress.

Aleuromancy (ăliūᵊ·romæːnsi). *rare.* 1656. [a. Fr., f. Gr. ἄλευρον meal + μαντεία.] Divination by means of meal or flour.

Aleurometer (æliurǫ·mĭtəɹ). 1844. [f. Gr. ἄλευρον + -(O)METER.] An instrument for measuring the quantity of gluten in flour.

Aleuron(e (ăliūᵊ·rən, -ōun). 1869. [ad. Gr.] An albuminoid or proteinous substance found in granules in seeds, etc. Hence **Aleuro·nic** *a.* of or pertaining to a.

Alevin (æ·lĕvin). 1868. [a. Fr., = *alevain*, f. OFr. *alever* to rear :—L. *adlevare.*] Young fish, fry.

†**Alew·.** *rare.* = HALLOO. SPENSER.

A·le-wife[1]. ME. [f. ALE- + WIFE = *woman.*] A woman that keeps an ale-house.

Marrian Hacket the fat A. of Wincot SHAKS.

Ale-wife[2] (ē·lwəif). Pl. **-wives.** 1867. [? Corrupt. f. *aloofe*, an Indian name.] An American fish (*Clupea serrata*) allied to the herring.

†**Alexa·nder**, *sb.* 1500. Alexandrian work; a species of striped silk.

†**Alexa·nder**, *v. nonce-wd.* To praise as an Alexander. DRYDEN.

Alexanders (ælĕgza·ndəɹs). OE. [Cf. Fr. *alexandre*, med.L. name *Petroselinum Alexandrinum.*] An umbelliferous plant (*Smyrnium Olusatrum*), called also Horse-parsley, formerly used for salads.

Alexander's Foot. 1597. A composite plant (*Anacyclus Pyrethrum*), also called Pellitory of Spain, allied to camomile.

Alexandrine (ælĕgza·ndrin), *a.* and *sb.*[1] 1589. [a. Fr. *alexandrin*, f. *Alexandre Paris*, a French poet, or from poems on Alexander written in this verse.] **A.** *adj.* Applied to a line of six feet, the Fr. heroic verse, used in Eng. to vary the heroic verse of five feet. **B.** *sb.* An A. line or verse 1667.

A needless A. ends the song That like a wounded snake, drags its slow length along POPE.

Alexandrine, *a.* and *sb.*[2] 1500. [a. Fr. *alexandrin*, ad. L. *alexandrinus*, f. *Alexandria.*] Of or belonging to Alexandria; *esp.* a kind of embroidery.

Alexandrite (ælĕgza·ndrəit). 1837. [f. Alexander I, Czar of Russia.] *Min.* A variety of chrysoberyl found in the Ural mountains.

Ale·xipha·rmic, *a.* 1671. [Modified f. ALEXIPHARMAC, Gr. ἀλεξιφάρμακον.] Having the quality or nature of an antidote against poison. As *sb.* An antidote or counterpoison 1683. vars. †**Ale·xipha·rmac**, ‖**Ale·xipha·rmacon.** Hence †**Ale·xipha·rmical** *a.*, var. †**Ale·xipha·rmacal.**

Ale·xipyre·tic, *a.* 1753. [f. Gr. ἀλεξι- + πυρετός.] Helpful against fever. Also as *sb.*

Ale·xite·ric, *a.* 1694. [f. med.L. *alexiterium*, a. Gr. ἀλεξιτήριον.] *prop.* Able to ward off contagion; but *used as* = ALEXIPHARMIC 1706. As *sb.* A preservative against contagion or poison 1694. vars. †**Ale·xite·rial** *a.*, †**Ale·xite·rical** *a.*, †**Ale·xitery** *a.* and *sb.*

‖**Alezan** (aləzaṅ·). 1848. [Fr., ad. Sp. *alazan*, of unkn. origin.] A sorrel horse.

‖**Alfa·lfa.** 1845. [Sp., ad. Arab.] Spanish, etc. name for a variety of Lucerne.

‖**Alfaqui** (alfăkī·). 1615. [Sp., ad. Arab.] A Mohammedan priest.

†**Alfe·res.** 1591. [a. OSp. and Pg., ad. Arab.] An ensign, a standard-bearer.

†**Alfet.** OE. [f. med.L. *alfetum*, latinized f. OE. *ǽl-fæt*, burning vat.] The cauldron used in the ordeal of scalding water –ME.

†**A·lfin, a·lphin.** ME. [a. OFr., f. Sp. *alfil*, a. Arab. *al-fil* the elephant.] Former name of the *bishop* in chess –1801.

†**Alfo·rge, -rja.** 1611. [Pg., ad. Arab.] **1.** A wallet, a saddle-bag –1779. **2.** The cheek pouch of a baboon –1748.

‖**Alfresco** (alfre·sko), *adv.* 1753. [It.] †**1.** = FRESCO –1764. **2.** In the open air; also *attrib.* open-air- 1753.

2. Here a. SMOLLETT. An a. emporium 1881.

‖**Alga** (æ·lgă). Pl. **algæ** (æ·ldʒī). 1551. [L.] A sea-weed; in *pl.* A division of cryptogamic plants, including sea-weeds, kindred freshwater plants, and some aerial species. var. **Alg** (*rare*). Cf. Fr. *algue.*

Algæology, -ist, bad ff. ALGOLOGY, -IST.

Algal (æ·lgăl), *a.* 1846. [f. L. ALGA.] Of the nature of an alga. As *sb.* An ally of the *algæ*. 1848.

†**Algara·d.** 1649. [a. Fr. *algarade*, ad. Sp., ad. Arab.] A raid.

†**Algarde.** ME. only. [f. name of place.] A Spanish wine formerly in repute. DRUMM. OF HAWTH.

†**Algarot, -oth.** 1706. [a. Fr., f. V. *Algarotti*, of Verona.] *Chem.* An emetic, a compound of trichloride and trioxide of antimony.

‖**Algarro·ba.** 1845. [Sp., ad. Arab.] **1.** The CAROB tree and bean. **2.** A S. Amer. mimosa with pods of like flavour.

Algate, -s, *adv.* Now *dial.* ME. [lit. *alle gate* = every way; see GATE *sb.*[2] The *-s* is analogical.] †**1.** Always –1587. †**2.** Any how –1580. †**3.** At any rate –1600. †**4.** All the way, altogether –1625. †**5.** After all –1614. **6.** Everywhere. *n. dial.* Cf. *any gate*, etc.

Algazel, early f. GAZELLE.

Algebra (æ·ldʒĭbră). 1541. [a. It. *algèbra*, ad. Arab. *al-jebr*, the redintegration of broken parts.] †**1.** The surgical treatment of fractures –1623. **2.** The part of mathematics which investigates the relations and properties of numbers by means of general symbols; a calculus of symbols combining according to defined laws 1551. A textbook of algebra (*mod.*).

2. Tell what hour o' th' day The clock does strike by A. BUTLER *Hud.* I. i. 126. Hence **Algebra·ic** *a.* of or pertaining to or occurring in a. (possessive gen.). **Algebra·ical** *a.* of or relating to a. (objective gen.). **Algebra·ically** *adv.* by algebraic processes. †**A·lgebraism, -rism**, an expression in a.; algebraic symbolism. **A·lgebra·ist, -rist**, one versed in a.; var. †**Algebri·cian.** **A·lgebraize, -rize**, to reduce to terms of or solve by a.

Algedo·nic, *a.* 1894. [f. Gr. ἄλγος + ἡδονή.] Concerned with pleasure and pain.

Algefacient (æːldʒĭfē·ʃiənt), *a.* 1879. [f. L. *algere* + *facientem.*] *Med.* Cooling.

A·lgerite. 1849. [f. F. *Alger.*] *Min.* A kind of Wernerite.

Alge·tic, *a.* 1879. [f. Gr. ἀλγέειν.] Causing or relating to pain.

Algid (æ·ldʒid), *a.* 1626. [a. Fr. *algide*,

ad. L. *algidus*.] Cold, chilly; *esp.* of one stage of an ague.

The a. breath of the desert wind BURTON. Hence **Algi·dity,** chilliness; *esp.* that due to collapse.

Algist (æ·ldʒist). 1869. [f. ALGA.] One who studies algæ.

Algodonite (ælgǫ·dŏnəit). 1837. [f. *Algodones*, place-name.] *Min.* A native arsenite of copper, Cu_3As, whitish and lustrous.

Algoid (æ·lgoid), *a.* 1874. [f. ALGA.] Like an alga.

Algology (ælgǫ·lŏdʒi). 1849. [f. L. *alga.*] The part of Botany which relates to algæ. Hence **Algolo·gical** *a.* **Algo·logist,** a student of a.

Algor (æ·lgǫ̆ɹ). ME. [a. L.] Cold, chilliness; *esp.* in the onset of fever.

Algorism (æ·lgŏriz'm). ME. [a. OFr. *augorisme, algorisme*, ad. med.L. *algorismus*, f. Arab. *al-Khowarazmi*, i.e. *native of Khiva*, surname of an Arab. mathematician. Cf. *Euclid* = plane geometry.] The Arabic, or decimal system of numeration; *hence*, arithmetic. Also *attrib.*

Corruptlye written..Augrim for algorisme, as the Arabians sounde it RECORDE. Hence **Algori·smic** *a.* arithmetical.

Algorithm, erron. refash. of ALGORISM.

Algous (æ·lgəs), *a.* 1742. [f. L. *algosus.*] Of, pertaining to, or full of sea-weeds.

‖**Alguazil** (ælgwăzi·l, Sp. algwăþi·l). 1598. [Sp., ad. Arab.] Orig. the same word as *vizier*; at first a *justice*, later a *warrant-officer*, or *serjeant*.

The gripe of the vile alguazils of Impey MACAULAY.

Algum (æ·lgɒm). 1578. [Heb., perh. f. Sanskr. *valguka.*] A Biblical tree, called also (1 *Kings* x. 11) ALMUG; prob. sandal-wood.

Algume trees 2 *Chron.* ii. 8.

‖**Alhagi** (ælhă·dʒi). 1769. [mod.L., ad. Arab.] *Bot.* A genus of leguminous plants, some of which yield a kind of manna.

Alhambra (ælhæ·mbră). [ult. ad. Arab. *al-hamrā*, i.e. the red (house).] The palace of the Moorish kings at Granada. Hence **Alhambre·sque** *a.* like the A. in style.

‖**Alha·ndal.** *Obs.* 1683. [a. Arab.] *Pharm.* The purgative extract of the Colocynth (*Citrullus Colocynthis*).

Alhenna; see ALCANNA, HENNA.

Alias (ēⁱ·liăs, æ·-). 1535. [a. L.] **A.** *adv.* Otherwise (called or named). Now *italicized.*

Violent testie magistrates (alias Fooles) *Cor.* II. i. 48.

B. *sb.* (with *pl.* **aliases.**) 1. Another name; an assumed name 1605. †2. *Law.* A second writ, containing the words *Sicut alias præcepimus*, issued after a first had failed –1809.

1. An *Aliàs* or double name CAMDEN. 2. A second [writ]..called an *alias* BLACKSTONE.

Alibi (æ·libəi), *adv.* 1727. [a. L.] Elsewhere –1777. As *sb.* The plea of having been *elsewhere* at the time of any alleged act 1774.

To prove that..he was a. ERSKINE. *sb.* An a. was set up MACAULAY.

Alible (æ·lĭb'l), *a.* 1656. [f. L. *alibilis*, f. *alere.*] Nutritive, nourishing. Hence **Alibi·lity,** nutritive quality.

Alicant (ælikæ·nt). 1500. A Spanish wine made at Alicante.

Butter'd beer, coloured with Alligant 1625. Cf. *Merry W.* II. ii. 69.

Alidad(e (ælidæ·d, æ·lidēⁱd). ME. [a. Fr. *alidade*, or med.L. *alhidada*, ad. Arab.] The index (Chaucer's *Rule*) of an astrolabe, quadrant, or other graduated instrument, carrying the sights or telescope, and showing the degrees cut off on the arc of the instrument.

Alien (ēⁱ·liĕn). ME. [a. OFr. *alien*:—L. *alienus.*] **A.** *adj.* 1. *gen.* Belonging to another person, place, or family; *esp.* to a foreign nation or allegiance. 2. Foreign in nature, character, or origin 1673. 3. Far removed from, inconsistent with ME.; repugnant, or opposed *to* 1720; *fig.* unkindly (*rare*) 1849.

1. Ruth..in tears amid the a. corn KEATS. A. domination MACAULAY. **Alien Priory:** one owing obedience to a mother-abbey in a foreign country. 2. A. pleasures BURKE. 3. His looks A. from Heaven MILT. *P. L.* iv. 572.

B. *sb.* [the adj. used absol.] 1. A stranger, a foreigner ME. Also *fig.* 2. *esp.* A resident foreign in origin and not naturalized 1330. 3. One excluded *from* (citizenship, privileges, etc.) 1549. 4. *Bot.* A plant orig. introduced from other countries 1847.

1. An a. in a strange land *Ex.* xviii. 3. *fig.* An a. from my mother's heart DICKENS. 3. Aliens from God's mercies J. H. NEWMAN.

Comb.: **a.-friend,** (-amy), **-enemy,** one owing allegiance to a country which is in alliance or at war with the country in which he resides; **aliens duty,** the special duty formerly paid by aliens on mercantile transactions; **-looking,** of foreign appearance.

Alien (ēⁱ·liĕn), *v.* ME. [a. OFr. *aliéner*:—L. *alienare.*] = ALIENATE, the later form. 1. To convert into an alien. Usu. *fig.* To estrange. 2. To transfer the property or ownership of anything. [Often written *aliene* (ēⁱlyī·n).] ME. †3. *refl.* and *intr.* To turn away, go off –1541.

1. Alien'd from their duty CLARENDON. 2. To a. the crown RALEIGH, land 1658. Hence **A·liened** *ppl. a.* = ALIENATED. **A·lienee·,** one to whom property is transferred. **A·liening** *vbl. sb.* = ALIENATING. **A·lienor,** one who transfers property to another.

Alienable (ēⁱ·liĕnăb'l), *a.* 1611. [f. prec.] Capable of being alienated. Hence **Alienabi·lity.**

Alienage (ēⁱ·liĕnĕdʒ). 1809. [a. Fr.] The state or legal standing of an alien.

†**A·lienate,** *ppl. a.* and *sb.* ME. [ad. L. *alienatus, alienare.*] 1. Estranged –1814. 2. Foreign in nature –1660. 3. *Bot.* = ALIENATED. As *sb.* An alien –1566.

Alienate (ēⁱ·liĕneⁱt), *v.* 1513. [f. prec.] 1. = ALIEN *v.* 1. 1548. 2. = ALIEN *v.* 2. 3. *fig.* To turn away, transfer 1621. †4. To alter –1587.

1. To a. colonies from the mother country BURKE. 2. To A. the Crown DRYDEN. 3. To a. capital from its natural channels 1832. 4. To a. one's purpose FOXE. Hence **A·lienated** *ppl. a.* estranged; transferred to another owner; †altered. **A·lienating** *vbl. sb.* and *ppl. a.* **A·lienator.**

Alienation (ēⁱ:liĕnēⁱ·ʃən). ME. [a. MFr. *alienacion*, ad. L. *alienationem*; see ALIEN *v.*] 1. The action of estranging, or state of estrangement. 2. The action of transferring ownership to another ME.; diversion of anything to a different purpose 1828. 3. The state of being alienated (sense 2) 1818. 4. Loss or derangement of mental faculties; insanity. (So in L.) 1482. †5. Alteration 1615.

1. The a. of the people from..the sanctuary STANLEY. 2. Prohibiting..the a. of Lands to the Church BRAMHALL. 4. A state of mental a. 1862.

Aliene, var. of ALIEN *v.*; f. ALIEN *sb.* and *a.*

Alienigenate (ēⁱ:liĕni·dʒĕneⁱt), *a.* 1855. [ad. L. *alienigenatus.*] Alien-born.

Alienism (ēⁱ·liĕniz'm). 1816. [f. ALIEN *sb.*] 1. The position of being an alien. 2. The study and treatment of mental diseases 1881.

A·lienist. 1864. [a. Fr. *aliéniste*; see ALIENATION 4 and -IST.] One who treats mental diseases.

†**A·liet.** ME. [ad. med.L. *aliætus*, a. Gr.] The osprey or sea-eagle (Wyclif); *Her.* a merlin or sparrow-hawk.

†**Ali·fe,** *adv.* [prob. f. *lief.*] In *To love a.*: to love dearly –1693.

A·liform, *a.* 1836. [ad. mod.L. *aliformis.*] Wing-shaped.

Alight (ăləi·t), *v.*[1] [OE. *alīhtan*, f. A- *pref.* 1 + *līhtan*; see LIGHT *v.*[1]] 1. To spring; to dismount *from*, †*of*, to descend *out of* OE.; †to mount –1509. 2. To land; to dismount or descend for a time; to stop ME. †3. To go or come down –1483. 4. To descend and settle (opp. to *falling*); to land on a spot by floating, flying, etc. ME. 5. To fall (*on* or *upon*) as a blow, etc. (*arch.*) ME. 6. To chance upon (*rare*) 1858.

1. To a. from a hors 1475, out of a Coach CLARENDON. 2. A-lighted at your gate *Merch. V.* II. ix. 87. To a. at an inn 1824, at a station 1872. 4. I alit upon my feet POE. 6. To a. on a collection of MSS. FROUDE. Hence †**Ali·ght** *ppl. a.* alighted, arrived.

†**Ali·ght,** *v.*[2] [?f. OE. *gelīhtan*; see A- *pref.* 6.] To lighten; to relieve –1483. var. †**Ali·ghten.**

†**Ali·ght,** *v.*[3] [OE. *on-līhtan.*] To light up; to light (a fire, etc.) –1634. var. †**Ali·ghten.**

Ali·ght, *a.* ME. [app. pa. pple. of prec.] 1. Lighted; on fire. Also *fig.* 2. Lighted up 1842. Also *fig.*

1. A Beacon..to be kept a. 1743. 2. [A] Chapel scarcely a. THACKERAY.

Align, -ment, variants of ALINE, -MENT.

Alike (ăləi·k), *a.* [mainly f. ON. *álīkr*; partly f. OE. *gelīc*, and OE. *anlīc.*] Like one another, similar or identical in form or character. (Usu. predicatively; and of things in pl.)

Male, twins, both a. *Com. Err.* I. i. 56. Hence †**Ali·kewise.**

Ali·ke, *adv.* [repr. 1. OE. *gelīce* adv. 2. ON. *álīka* adv.] In the same or like manner, equally, similarly.

Nature..kind a. to all GOLDSM.

Aliment (æ·lĭmĕnt). 1477. [a. Fr., or ad. L. *alimentum*, f. *alere.*] That which nourishes or feeds; nutriment; *fig.* that which sustains or supports 1631. 2. *Sc. Law* and *gen.* = ALIMONY 1640.

1. A., medicine, and poison BACON. 2. Some pension or a. from the Court CARLYLE. Hence **Alime·ntal** *a.* of or pertaining to a.; nutritive. **Alime·ntally** *adv.*

A·liment, *v.* 1490. [a. Fr. *alimenter*; see prec.] 1. †To nourish; *fig.* to support 1663. 2. *Sc. Law* and *gen.* To provide maintenance for 1629. Hence **A·limenter,** one who or that which affords aliment. **A·limenting** *vbl. sb.* maintenance.

Alimentary (ælime·ntări), *a.* 1615. [ad. L. *alimentarius.*] 1. Of the nature of ALIMENT; nutritious. 2. Concerned with the function of nutrition 1620. 3. Connected with maintenance 1751.

Alimentary Canal: the whole passage through the body by which food is received, digested, etc. Hence †**Alime·ntariness,** the quality of being a.

Alimentation (æ:lĭmĕntēⁱ·ʃən). 1590. [ad. med.L. *alimentationem.*] 1. The action of affording aliment 1656. 2. Process of being nourished 1605. 3. Maintenance 1590.

2. Plants..have an Accretion, but no A. BACON.

Alimentative (ælime·ntĕtiv), *a. rare.* 1881. [f. L. *alimentat-, alimentare.*] Connected with the supply of aliment. Hence **Alime·ntativeness,** better form of next.

Alime·ntiveness. 1825. [f. adj. *alimentive* (not cited).] The instinct which impels an animal to seek food, to which phrenologists assign an 'organ'.

Alimony (æ·limŏni). 1655. [ad. L. *alimonia*, f. *alere.*] 1. Nourishment; maintenance 1656. Also *fig.* 2. *esp.* The allowance made to a woman, out of her husband's estate, for her maintenance, on separation from him for certain causes 1655.

Aline, align (ăləi·n), *v.* 1693. [ad. Fr. *aligner*, f. L. *ad* + *lineare*; cf. phr. *à ligne.*] 1. To range or place in a line; to bring into line. 2. *intr.* To fall into line 1877. 3. To bring two or more points into a straight line, e.g. the sights of a rifle and the mark 1860. Hence **Ali·ner,** one who aligns. EVELYN.

Alinement (ăləi·nment). 1790. [a. Fr. *alignement*, f. *aligner.* The better Eng. spelling in the derivatives is *line* = Fr. *ligne.*] 1. Arrangement in a line or lines; used *spec.* of soldiers 1808; *concr.* a line of things arranged, a military 'line'. 2. The drawing of a straight line so that it shall pass through a particular point 1869. 3. Bringing into line; straightening 1879.

1. The alignments or stone avenues of Kermario 1881. The alignement of a battalion, of a camp JAMES.

Aliped (æ·lĭped), *a.* 1847. [ad. L. *alipedem*, f. *ala* + *pedem.*] Wing-footed, as the bat. As *sb.* A cheiropterous animal. (Dicts.)

Aliquant (æ·likwănt), *a.* 1695. [a. Fr. *aliquante*, ad. L. *aliquantum.*] *Math.* In *aliquant part*: Contained in another, but not dividing it evenly; opp. to *aliquot.* Thus 3 is an a. part of 7.

Aliquot (æ·lĭkwǫt), *a.* 1570. [a. Fr. *aliquote*, a. L. *aliquot.*] *Math.* In *aliquot part*: Contained in another, and dividing it without a remainder. Thus 2 is an a. part of 6. As *sb.* An aliquot part 1610.

‖**Alisma** (ăli·zmă). 1736. [a. L., a. Gr. ἄλισμα.] *Bot.* A genus of aquatic endogenous plants, the type of N.O. *Alismaceæ*; esp. *A. Plantago.* Hence **Alisma·ceous** *a.* of or belonging to the Alismads. **Ali·smad,** a plant of the order *Alismaceæ*. **Ali·smal** *a.* of or pertaining to alisma. **Ali·smoid** *a.* a.-like.

A·lisonite. 1837. [f. R. E. *Alison.*] A kind of COVELLITE.

Alispheno- (ælisfī·no), comb. f. of next.

Alisphenoid (ælisfī·noid), *a.* 1846. [f. L. *ala* + SPHENOID, wedge-shaped.] *Phys.* Forming the wing of the sphenoid bone at the base of the skull, or pertaining to this part. As *sb.* An a. bone 1849. Hence **A:lisphenoi·dal** *a.* pertaining to the wings of the sphenoid bone.

†**Ali·te** = *a lite*, a little; see LITE.

Alitrunk (æ·litrvŋk). 1816. [f. L. *ala* + *truncus.*] The segment of the thorax, to which an insect's wings are attached.

-ality, *comp. suffix* of sbs. = -AL + -ITY, the quality of being.

†**Ali·ve**, *v.* OE. [f. A- *pref.* 1 + LIVE, OE. *libban.*] To live.

Alive (ăləi·v), *adv.* OE. [A *prep.*[1] + ME. *live*, OE. *life*; = *on life.*] 1. In life; living. 2. (Emphatic, intensive, or expletive.) *colloq.* ME. 3. *fig.* Unextinguished, unabated, unforgotten 1602. 4. In a sentient condition; sensitive, awake, fully conscious 1732. 5. In an active condition; vivacious, brisk, quick in action 1748. 6. In a state of commotion, stirring or swarming *with* 1808.

1. Let me on-lif go 1500. A. or dead *Merch. V.* II. ii. 75. 2. Any man alive = any man in the world. Man alive! 1845. Sakes alive! (U.S.) 1860. 3. To keep discontent a. MACAULAY. 4. A. to the impression of shame BENTHAM. 5. *To look alive*: to make haste. 6. The river..a. with wherries MACAULAY.

†**Ali·ves**, *adv.* ME. [= prec. with gen. *lives* for dat. *live.*]

Ali·zarate. 1875. [f. ALIZARI.] *Chem.* A salt of alizaric acid.

‖**Alizari** (ăliză·ri). 1850. [Fr. and Sp., prob. ad. Arab.] *Comm.* The Madder of the Levant. Hence **Aliza·ric** *a.*; *esp.* in *alizaric acid* = phthalic acid.

Alizarin (ăli·zărin). 1835. [a. Fr. *alizarine*, f. ALIZARI.] *Chem.* The red colouring matter of the madder root ($C_{14}H_8O_4$).

Alkahest (æ·lkăhest). Also **alc-, alch-.** 1641. [prob. coined by Paracelsus, after Arab.] *Alchemy.* The 'universal solvent'. *fig.* An intellectual a., melting the universe into an idea 1866. Hence **Alcahe·stic, -al** *a.* all-dissolving.

Alkalamide (æ·lkălăməi:d). 1863. [f. ALKALI + AMIDE.] *Chem.* A compound ammonia in which two or more atoms of hydrogen are replaced by *acid-* and *base-* radicles.

Alkalescent (ælkăle·sĕnt), *a.* 1732. [f. ALKALI.] Becoming or tending to become alkaline. As *sb.* [sc. *substance.*] 1750. Hence **Alkale·scence**, the process of becoming, or tendency to become, alkaline; slight alkaline character; var. **Alkale·scency.**

Alkali (æ·lkăli). Pl. **alkalis**, occ. **-ies.** ME. [a. Fr. *alcali*, ad. (ult.) Arab. *al-qalīy*, f. *qalay* to roast in a pan.] 1. *orig.* A saline substance obtained by lixiviating the calcined ashes of marine plants; soda-ash. 2. *Bot.* The plant Saltwort (*Salsola Kali*) 1578. 3. Any substance having the characteristics of soda 1612. 4. *Comm.* Any form of alkaline substance, as common soda, caustic soda, caustic potash, etc., used in commerce or the arts 1822. 5. *Chem.* A series of BASES, analogous to, and including soda, potash, and ammonia, highly soluble in water, producing corrosive solutions, which neutralize strong acids, and turning vegetable yellows to brown, reds to blue, and purples to green 1813.

Comb.: **a.-metal** = ALKALINE metal; **-waste**, a by-product, sulphide of calcium. Hence †**Alka·lic** *a.* = ALKALINE. **A·lkalify** *v.* to make into or become an a., or alkaline; hence **A·lkalifi·able** *a.* †**Alkaligen**, a name for nitrogen. **Alkali·genous** *a.* generating a., or alkaline qualities. †**Alkali·meter**, an instrument for measuring the amount of a. in a solution. **Alkalime·tric, -al** *a.* **Alkali·metry**, the measurement of the strength of alkalis.

Alkaline (æ·lkăləin), *a.* 1677. [? a. Fr. *alcalin.*] Of or pertaining to or of the nature of alkalis. Also used *fig.* and *subst.* 2. **Alkaline metals**: those whose hydroxides are alkalis, *viz.* potassium, sodium, cæsium, lithium, and the hypothetical ammonium. **Alkaline earths**: the oxides of calcium, strontium, and barium. Hence **Alkali·nity**, the quality of being a. **A·lkalinize**, to make a. var. †**Alka·lious.**

†**Alka·lizate**, *ppl. a.* 1622. [ad. mod.L. *alcalizatum.*] Alkalized, alkaline -1753. Hence †**Alka·lizateness** = ALKALINITY. **Alkaliza·tion**, the action of alkalizing.

Alkalize (æ·lkăləiz), *v.* 1749. [a. Fr. *alcaliser.*] To render alkaline.

Alkaloid (æ·lkăloid). 1831. [f. ALKALI. Cf. Fr. *alcaloïde.*] *Chem.* A body resembling an alkali in properties. Applied *gen.* to all nitrogenous basic substances, or to all nitrogenous organic bases; *spec.* to the *Vegetable alkalis*, very bitter in taste, and acting powerfully on the animal system. Also *attrib.* Hence **Alkaloi·dal** *a.* of the nature of an a.

Alkanet (æ·lkănet). ME. [? ad. Sp. *alcaneta*, dim. of *alcana*; see ALCANNA. var. ORCANET.] 1. A dye-material yielding a fine red colour (see 2). 2. The plant whose root yields the dye, *Anchusa* or *Alkanna tinctoria*, N.O. *Boraginaceæ*, Orchanet, Dyer's or Sp. Bugloss, Bugloss of Languedoc 1567. 3. Applied also to: a. Common (Eng.) A. (*Anchusa officinalis*); b. Evergreen A. (*A. sempervirens*); c. Bastard A. (*Lithospermum arvense*); d. Alkanet (Amer.), (*L. canescens*).

Alkanna; see ALCANNA.

Alkargen (ælkā·ɹdʒĕn). 1877. [f. ALKAR(SIN) + (OXY)GEN.] = CACODYLIC ACID.

Alkarsin (ælkā·ɹsin). 1850. [f. ALK(ALI) + ARS(ENIC) + -IN.] *Chem.* A poisonous, spontaneously inflammable, liquid, smelling of garlic, supposed to be a mixture of cacodyl and its oxidation products; called also *Cadet's fuming liquor.*

†‖**Alkeda·vy.** 1631. [ad. Arab.] The palace of a cadi. HEYWOOD.

‖**Alkekengi** (ælkĭke·ndʒi). ME. [med.L., f. Arab.] *Bot.* A plant (*Physalis Alkekengi* Linn.) N.O. *Solanaceæ*, called also Winter-Cherry from its scarlet berries.

†**Alkermes** (ælkə̄·ɹmĭz). 1605. [a. Fr. *alkermès*, ad. (ult.) Arab.; see KERMES.] 1. The Kermes, or Scarlet Grain insect (the female of *Coccus Ilicis*) -1718. 2. A confection of which the Kermes, formerly supposed to be a berry, was an ingredient -1753.

†**A·lkin**, *a.* ME. [genitive phr., sing. or pl., *alles cynnes, alra cynna*, placed bef. the sb.; hence treated as adj., and ult. shortened to *alkin(s).*] Of every kind; every kind of -1552.

All (ǫl). OE. [Teut.; prop. adj.] **A.** *adj.* 1. with *sb. sing.* The whole amount, extent, substance, or compass of; the whole OE.; all that is possible 1594. 2. With *sb. pl.* The entire number of, without exception. (Bef. the sb., etc., exc. poet.) OE. 3. = Every. L. *omnis. Obs.* exc. with *kind*, and *manner* -1570. 4. = Any whatever (in excl. sentences and clauses) ME. Also *absol.* 5. As antecedent to relative: all *that*, all *those* OE. 6. Followed by *of*: in *sing.* The whole; in *pl.* Every individual 1800. 7. as *pl.* = All men OE. 8. as *sing.* = Everything OE.

1. All flesh is as grass 1 *Pet.* i. 24. I in all haste was sent SHAKS. All this while SHAKS. I see it all now (mod.). 2. Th' abstracts of all faults That all men follow *Ant. & Cl.* I. iv. 9. So *all these, all mine*, etc., *all we* now *we all*, or *all of us.* 3. Alle manere of marchaundises MAUNDEV. All kind of drollery (*mod.*). 4. Things without all remedie *Macb.* III. ii. 11. *Beyond all question, doubt*, etc. *To deny, disclaim, etc., all intention.* 5. All what thou commandst MILT. *P.L.* IX. 569. 6. *All of it*, etc. 7. O God, and fadir of alle WYCLIF. 8. All is not lost MILT. *P.L.* I. 105. So in **all but**: everything short of; *hence* almost. **And all**: and all the rest, *et cetera*; *hence* as well. **And all that**: and all the rest of it. **All in all**: all things in all respects. **When all comes (goes) to all**: when everything is summed up. **At all**: in every or any way (now only in neg., interrog., or hypothet. sentences or clauses). **For all**: notwithstanding. **In all**: all together; *also*, in whole. **Of all**: formerly *ellipt.* = most of all. **With all**: see WITHAL. **All and some**: distributed to each part of the whole; also, in *sing.* the sum total. So *one and all, all and sundry*, etc.

B. *sb.* 1. Everything that we have, or that concerns or pertains to us 1627. Also in *pl.* 2. Whole being, entirety, totality 1674. 3. Whole system of things, the Universe 1598.

1. Our All is at stake ADDISON. To pack up one's alls FIELDING. 2. An all of rotten Formulas CARLYLE. 3. The wide circle of the All CARLYLE.

C. *adv.* 1. *All* adj., separated from its sb., appeared to refer to the predicate, hence, to qualify it, as *adv.*: Wholly, completely, altogether, quite OE. 2. Even, just (*arch.*) 1579. 3. All through, wholly, without admixture 1705.

1. It [the City] is all full of lies *Nah.* iii. 1. It succeeded all other wise ELYOT. So †**all thing** *Macb.* III. i. 14. 2. All in the Downs the fleet was moored GAY. 3. Paces all *Lond. Gaz.*

Special constructions. 1. **All one.** Also **all a.** Quite the same. 2. Pleonastic in †**All-whole**: entire. So †**All-wholly**, †**-utterly.** 3. Emphatic in *All so, too* = Quite. 4. With adv. *the*: just so much. All the better *A.Y.L.* I. ii. 102. 5. With advbs. of place: In all directions, in every part; as **All along, All over, All round**, etc. †6. *All* emphasised the particle combined with a vb.; *esp. to-* = asunder (L. *dis*), as in *all to-broken*, quite broken in pieces; and, as **allto, alto** = wholly, was applied to other vbs., as in *all-to dirtied* LATIMER, *all-to-be-fooled* BUNYAN.

D. Obsolete uses of early inflected forms.

†1. The gen. sing. **alles**: altogether, at all -1320. †2. The gen. pl. **alra, aire, aller, alder, alther**, 'of all' -1600; esp. *absol.* bef. a superlative: Mine Alder liefest Soueraigne 2 *Hen. VI*, I. i. 28. Occ. written *all there.* Also, as in *our, your, their aller* = mod. *of us all*, etc.

E. All- in *comb.*

1. *adj.* with sb. **four(s** (sc. *extremities*). The *-s* is recent. **To be (stand) on all fours**: to be even with; **-hail**, *int., sb.*, and *v.* a salutation: *lit.* (I wish you) all health! **-might**, omnipotence; †**-night**, a service of food, fuel, or light for the whole night; **-power** = *a.-might.* 2. *adj.* with adv. ALGATE; ALWAYS; **-where** (*arch.*) everywhere; **-whither**, in every direction (*rare*). 3. *subst.* (*genit.*) with sb. = 'of all'. **-father**, *orig.* Odin; Jupiter; God. 4. *subst.* (*obj.*) with vb. inf. **-hold**, that which holds all. 5. *advb.* with sb. **-bone**, the Greater Stitchwort (*Stellaria Holostea* L.); **-heart**, the elm-tree; **-rail; -slavery; -talk; -wool.** 6. *advb.* with adj. = 'wholly, infinitely'. **-holy; -mighty; -witty**; and since 1600 with any adj. of quality, esp. *poet.*; with forms in *-ent*, and *-ive*; and with pr. pple., often as obj. of the vbl. action. 7. *advb.* with *pa. pple.* = completely; occ. = by all; freq. in SHAKS.

‖**Alla Breve** (a·lla brē·ve). 1806. [It.] *Mus. Orig.* With a breve or four minims to every bar; *now*, in quick common time, counted with two minims in the bar.

‖**A·lla Cape·lla.** 1847. [It.] *Mus.* = prec.

Allagite (æ·lădʒəit). [mod. f. Gr. ἀλλαγή.] *Min.* A carbonated variation of RHODONITE, dull-green or reddish-brown in colour.

Allagostemonous (æ:lăgo͵stī·mənəs), *a.* 1880. [f. Gr. ἀλλαγή + στήμων.] *Bot.* With stamens inserted alternately on the torus and on the petals.

Allah (æ·lă). 1702. [a. Arab., = the (true) God.] The Mohammedan name of the Deity.

Allamotti, -monti, -moth, dial. names for the Stormy Petrel.

Allan, var. of ALAN; and AULIN.

Allanite (æ·lănəit). 1843. [f. T. *Allan.*] *Min.* A brownish-black mineral, akin to Epidote, a cerium-epidote.

Allantoid (ălæ·ntoid). 1633. [ad. Gr. ἀλλαντοειδής, sausage-shaped.] *Phys.* **A.** *adj.* Of or pertaining to the allantois. **B.** *sb.* = ALLANTOIS 1667.

Allantoidian (ælæ̆ntoi·diăn). 1861. [ad. Fr.; see prec.] *Zool.* **A.** *adj.* Having the fœtus furnished with an allantois. **B.** *sb.* [sc. *animal.*]

Allantoin (ălæ·nto͵in). 1845. [f. ALLANTOIS + -IN.] *Chem.* A crystalline substance, $C_4N_4H_6O_3$, the nitrogenous constituent of the allantoic fluid.

Allantois (ălæ·nto͵is). 1646. [mod.L. in form; see ALLANTOID.] *Phys.* The fœtal membrane (named from its form in a calf) found only in mammals, birds, and reptiles, which lies under the chorion, and forms a means of communication between the fœtal and maternal blood. Hence **Allanto·ic** *a.*

Allanturic (ælæ̆ntiū·rik), *a.* 1863. [f. prec. + URIC.] Obtained from allantoin or from uric acid.

†**Alla·trate**, *v.* 1583. [f. L. *allatrare.*] To bark out. *rare.*

Allay (ălē[1]·), *v.*[1] OE. [f. A- *pref.* 1 + LAY, OE. *lęcgan*, causal of *licgan* to lie; misspelt ALLAY after words from L. in *all-* (see AD- 2). In its early forms formally identical with AL-

LEGE *v.*[1], ALLAY *v.*[2], ALLAY *v.*[3], ALLEGE *v.*[2] Hence meanings due to confusion of the vbs.] †1. To lay down, set aside; *hence*, to annul -ME.; to quell -ME.; to overthrow (a principle, etc.) -1659. 2. To put down or repress; to assuage, 'lay' a storm 1488. 3. To quell or put down; to appease ME. †4. *intr.* To subside, cease; to become mild -1723. 5. (see ALLEGE *v.*[1]) To subdue; to abate, alleviate ME. 6. (see ALLAY *v.*[2]) To temper or abate 1514; to mitigate 1603.

2. To alay (the wild waters) *Temp.* I. ii. 2. 3. To a. wrath 1600, distrusts 1623, panic 1880. 5. To a. Thir appetite MILT. *P. L.* x. 566, grief BEATTIE. 6 To a. or dim the whiteness of paper FLORIO. To a. a crime PRYNNE. Hence [f. ALLAY *v.*[1] (*v.*[2])] **Allayed** *ppl. a.* †alloyed; tempered; modified; laid (cf. *inlaid*). **Allay·er**, he who or that which allays. **Allay·ing** *vbl. sb.* †cessation; dilution; mitigation; †alloying; *ppl. a.* diluting, tempering. **†Allay·ment**, admixture with a modifying element *Cymb.* I. v. 22.

†Allay·, *v.*[2] ME. [a. ONFr. *alayer*, (*a-loyer*), var. of *alier*, *allier*, ALLY:—L. *alligare*. Replaced by ALLOY.] To mix (metals); *esp.* with a baser metal. Also *fig.* -1796.

fig. Debased and allayed with superstitious intents FULLER.

†Allay·, *v.*[3] ME. [a. OFr. *alaier*, *alleyer* :—L. *allegare*, replaced by *a(l)leguer*, ALLEGE.] To cite, allege -1470.

†Allay·, *sb.*[1] ME. [a. ONFr. *aley*, *alay*, (mod. *aloi*), f. *alayer*; see ALLAY *v.*[2]] 1. = ALLOY. *lit.* and *fig.* 2. *fig.* Alien element -1774. 3. *fig.* Composition. Cf. Fr. *de bon aloi*. -1690. 4. (f. ALLAY *v.*[1]) Dilution -1632; abatement -1758; repression -1726.

†Allay·, *sb.*[2] 1486. [a. Norm.Fr. *alais* = OFr. *eslais*, f. *eslaissier*. Cf. RELAY.] The act of laying on the hounds -1630.

Allecret; see HALECRET.

†Alle·ct, *v.* 1528. [ad. L. *allectare*, freq. of *allicere*.] To entice -1552. Hence **†Alle·ction**, enticement. **†Alle·ctive** *a.* enticing; *sb.* that which can entice.

†A·llegate, *v.* 1529. [f. L. *allegat-*, *allegare*.] = ALLEGE *v.*[2] -1639.

Allegation (ælĭgēⁱ·ʃən). 1483. [a. Fr. *allégation*, ad. L. *allegationem*; see ALLEGATE *v.*] 1. The action of alleging or making a charge before a tribunal; that which is charged. †2. An excuse -1622. 3. An assertion 1532; *esp.* a mere assertion 1635. †4. Quotation; the matter quoted -1673.

1. To sweare False allegations 2 *Hen. VI*, III. i. 181. 3. I thought their allegations but reasonable STEELE. His wild a. BOSWELL.

†Alle·ge, *v.*[1] ME. [a. OFr. *aleger* :—L. *alleviare*; cf. ABRIDGE.] = ALLAY *v.*[1] 5. -1530. Hence **†Alle·geance**[1], alleviation; var. **†Alle·gement**[1], ale-.

Allege (ăle·dʒ), *v.*[2] ME. [f. OFr. *esligier*, Norm.Fr. *alegier* :—late L. **exlitigare*. Used as = L. *allegare*, OFr. *aleier*, through *adlegiare*, latinized f. Norm.Fr. *alegier*. Replaces ALLAY *v.*[3]] 1. To declare on oath before a tribunal; hence, to plead. *Obs.* exc. *fig.* 2. To cite, quote *for* or *against* (*arch.*) ME. 3. Hence *gen.* To plead as an excuse; to adduce as reason ME. 4. To advance, as being able to prove; *hence*, to assert without proof ME.

1. The Prosecutor alleged That [etc.] STEELE. 2. They alleage Moses .. for tithes MILT. 3. To a. excuses to the contrary 1598. 4. Where much is alleged, something must be true GIBBON. Hence **Alle·geable** *a.* **†Alle·geance**[2], the action of alleging; allegation. **Alle·ged** *ppl. a.* adduced as legal ground, or as a reason; quoted; asserted as provable; asserted but not proved. **Alle·gedly** *adv.* **†Alle·gement**[2], allegation. **Alle·ger.**

Allegiance (ălī·dʒăns, ălī·dʒⁱăns). ME. [deriv. of LIEGE, q.v. The *a-* is perh. due to ALLEGEANCE[2].] †1. The relation of a liege lord ME. only. 2. The relation or duties of a liege-man to his lord; the tie of a subject to his sovereign or government ME. 3. *fig.* The recognition of the claims which any one has to our respect and duty 1732.

2. Subjects may be freed from their Allegeance HOBBES. 3. A. to a lady SCOTT, to natural science HERSCHELL. var. **Alle·giancy.** Hence **Alle·giant** *a.* loyal.

Allegoric, -al (ælĭgǫ·rik, -ăl), *a.* ME. Of or pertaining to allegory; of the nature of an allegory; constituting or containing an allegory.

What kingdom, Real or allegorick, I discern not MILT. *P. R.* iv. 389. Its chimeras, its harpies, its allegorical figures BURKE. Hence **Allego·rically** *adv.* **Allego·ricalness.** (Dicts.)

Allegorist (æ·lĭgŏrist). 1684. [f. ALLEGORIZE; cf. *baptist*.] One who writes allegories, or writes or expounds allegorically.

Bunyan .. the first of allegorists MACAULAY.

Allegorize (æ·lĭgŏrəiz), *v.* 1581. [a. Fr. *allégoriser*, ad. L. *allegorizare*, f. Gr. ἀλληγορία; see ALLEGORY.] 1. To make or treat as allegorical 1596. 2. *intr.* To expound allegorically; to construct or utter allegories 1581.

1. To a. *away* the History of the Crucifixion 1667. To a. Christ *out of* His Divinity PENN. **A·llegorizer. A·llegoriza·tion.**

Allegory (æ·lĭgŏri). ME. [ad. L. *allegoria*, *lit.* speaking otherwise than one seems to speak, a. Gr., f. ἄλλος + -ἀγορία. Cf. Fr. *allégorie*.] 1. Description of a subject under the guise of some other subject of aptly suggestive resemblance. 2. An instance of such description; an extended metaphor 1534. 3. An allegorical representation; an emblem 1639.

‖**Allegresse** (alegre·s, ælĭgre·s). 1652. [Fr.] Gaiety, gladsomeness.

‖**Allegretto** (allegre·ttǫ), *a.* 1879. [It., dim. of ALLEGRO.] *Mus.* Somewhat brisk.

‖**Allegro** (It. allē·grǫ). 1632. [It., repr. L. *alacrem*.] A. *adj.* Lively, gay MILT. B. *adv.* and *adj.* *Mus.* Brisk, lively 1721. C. *sb.* [sc. *movement*] 1777.

Alleleu (ælī·liū·). An outcry. CARLYLE.

Allelomorph (ælī·lomǭɹf). 1902. [f. Gr. ἀλλήλ- one another + μορφή form.] *Biol.* Each of a pair of mutually exclusive characters, one or the other of which is exhibited without intermixture in descendants of a cross between parental forms respectively possessing them. Hence **Alle lomo·rphic** *a.*

Alleluia (ælĭlū·iă), *int.* and *sb.*[1] ME. = HALLELUJAH. Hence **Allelu·ia·tic** *a.*

Allelu·ia, *sb.*[2] 1543. [?] The woodsorrel.

‖**Allemande** (aləmā̃·d, -ma·nd, æ·lĕmænd, æ·lmænd). 1685. [a. mod.Fr. *allemande* German (sc. *dance*); see ALMAIN.] 1. A name of various German dances 1775. 2. A piece of music forming one of the movements of the Suite 1685.

Allemontite (ælĕmǫ·ntəit). 1837. [f. *Allemont*, in Dauphiné.] A native alloy of arsenic and antimony.

Allenarly (ăle·năɹli). *north.* and *Sc.* ME. [f. ALL *adv.* + ANERLY.] 1. *adv.* Only, solely. 2. *adj.* Only, sole 1533.

Allene, = ALLYLENE.

†Alle·niate, *v.* *rare.* [f. L. *al-* = *ad-* + *lenis*.] To soften -1642.

Allerion, var. of ALERION.

†Alle·ve, *v.* 1546. [prop. *aleve*, a. OFr. *alever* :—L. *adlevare*.] To relieve. Hence **†Alle·vement.**

†Alle·viate, *ppl. a.* 1471. [ad. L. *alleviatus*, *alleviare*.] Alleviated -1671.

Alleviate (ălī·vi,eⁱt), *v.* 1528. [f. prec.] †1. To make lighter -1666. 2. To relieve, mitigate 1528. †3. To extenuate -1777.

2. To a. sorrows BP. HALL, sufferings 1871. 3. To a. a crime BLACKSTONE. Hence **Alle·viative** *a.* of an alleviating tendency. Also *sb.* **Alle·viator**, he who, or that which, alleviates. **Alle·viatory** *a.* having the attribute of relieving.

Alleviation (ălīvi,ēⁱ·ʃən). 1625. [f. ALLEVIATE.] The action of lightening weight, gravity, severity, or pain; relief, mitigation.

It [is] an a. of misery not to suffer alone JOHNSON.

Alley (æ·li). ME. [a. OFr. *alee*, mod. *allée*.] †1. A passage in or into a house -1525. Also *fig.* 2. *esp.* A walk or passage in a garden, park, etc. bordered with trees or bushes; an avenue ME. 3. A passage between buildings; hence, a lane; in *U.S.* a *Mews* 1510. 4. A long narrow enclosure for playing at bowls, skittles, etc. ME. Also *fig.* 5. A passage between the rows of pews or seats in a church 1464. In the south corruptly repl. by AISLE. 6. The space between two compositors' stands, etc. in a printing-office 1871. 7. A free space between two lines of any kind 1756.

2. A thick pleached a. in my orchard *Much Ado* I. ii. 10. Every a. green .. of this wild wood MILT. *Comus* 311. 3. *Blind Alley*: one that is closed at the end; a *cul de sac*. *The Alley*, *esp.* Change Alley, London, scene of the gambling in South Sea stocks. Hence **A·lleyed** *ppl. a.* laid out as an a., or with alleys.

Alley, var. of ALLY, a kind of marble.

All-fired (ǭ·l-fəiᵊɹd), *a.* *slang.* 1837. [*euphem.* for *hell-fired*.] Infernal. (Chiefly in U.S.) Hence **A·ll-fi·redly** *adv.*

All-flower-water. 1839. [?] Cow's urine; as a remedy.

All Fools' Day. 1712. [cf. *All Saints*, etc.] The 1st of April; pop. appropriated to practising upon people's credulity.

All fours (ǭ·l fōᵊɹz). 1707. [i. e. *all four* cards.] 1. A game of cards, played by two; called after the *four* points, *high*, *low*, *Jack* and *the game*, which make all-fours. 2. A game at dominoes, in which only four or its multiples count. See also ALL E. *comb.*

Allgood (ǭ·lgud), *sb.* 1578. The herb (*Chenopodium Bonus-Henricus*), also called English Mercury, and Good King Henry.

All-hallow, -s (ǭlhæ·loᵘz). [OE. *ealra hálgena* (*mæssedæg*) feast of all saints: see HALLOW *sb.*[1]] 1. All saints (collectively). 2. = All hallows' day, Nov. 1, or All-hallowmas (*arch.*) 1503.

Phrases *All hallows' day*: All Saints' day. *All-hallow Eve*, *Mass*, *tide*, the eve, feast, season, of All Saints; cf. HALLOW-E'EN. †*All-hallown Summer*: = *Indian Summer*, or *St. Martin's Summer*. 1 *Hen. IV*, I. ii. 178.

Alliable (ălai·ăb'l), *a.* *rare.* 1795. [a. Fr., f. *allier*; see ALLY.] Able to enter into alliance or union.

Alliaceous (æli,ēⁱ·ʃəs), *a.* 1792. [f. L. *allium*.] a. Of or pertaining to *Allium*. b. Smelling or tasting like garlic and onions.

†**A·lliage.** ME. [a. Fr. *al-*, *alliage*; see ALLY.] Alliance -1546.

Alliance (ălai·ăns), *sb.* ME. [a. OFr. *aliance*, repr. L. *alligantia*, f. *alligare*; see ALLY. In 16th c. *allia·nce*.] The state of union or combination; uniting or combining. 1. Union by marriage, affinity; consanguinity. 2. Combination for a common object; *esp.* between sovereign states ME. 3. Community in nature or qualities; affinity 1677. †4. *collect.* People united by kinship or friendship (? for *Alliants*) -1655; also, a kinsman, relation, or ally -1654. 5. *Bot.* A group of Natural Orders. LINDLEY. ¶ By confusion, for ALLEGIANCE 1581.

1. So streighte a bonde of alyaunce or consanguinitie COVERDALE. 2. The Holy Alliance SEELEY. 4. Therefore let our A. be combined *Jul. C.* IV. i. 43. Hence **Alli·ance** *v.* *rare*, to ally or ally oneself. **Alli·ancer**, one who joins or belongs to an a. *rare.*

†**Alli·ant**, *a.* 1551. [a. Fr., f. *allier*.] In league; akin. As *sb.* An ally -1656.

Allice, allis (æ·lis). 1620. [a. Fr. *alose* :—L. *alosa*.] A fish, usu. called the **allice-shad** (*Alosa Communis*)

Allicholly, joc. = MELANCHOLY. SHAKS.

†**Alli·cit**, *v.* 1725. [f. L. *allicere*.] To entice, attract. Hence (through Fr.) **†Alli·ciate** *v.* to allure. **Alli·cient** *ppl. a.* attracting; *sb.* that which attracts. **†Alli·ciency**, the quality of being attractive.

Allied (ălai·d), *ppl. a.* ME. [f. ALLY *v.*] 1. United, joined; *esp.* by kindred or affinity, or by league or treaty. 2. *fig.* Connected in nature, or qualities; akin 1603.

1. A Lady .. alide vnto the Duke *Two Gent.* IV. i. 49. 2. Great wits are sure to madness near a. DRYDEN.

Alligate (æ·ligeⁱt), *v.* ? *Obs.* 1626. [f. L. *alligare*.] †1. To tie or unite -1677. 2. To perform the operation of ALLIGATION 1671.

Alligation (æligēⁱ·ʃən). 1542. [ad. L. *alligationem*.] 1. The action of attaching; the state of being attached 1555. 2. The 'Rule of Mixtures'; the arithmetical method of solving questions concerning the mixing of articles of different qualities or values 1542.

Alligator (æ·ligeⁱtəɹ). 1568. [orig. ad. Sp. *el* or *al lagarto*, the lizard, corrupted in Eng. to *alligarter*, *allegater*, *alligator*.] 1. A genus of Saurians of the crocodile family, also called Caymans, belonging to America; pop. all large American Saurians, some of which are true crocodiles. **2.** Anything operating by jaws, as (*Mining*) **a.** A rock-breaker. **b.** A 'Squeezer' for the puddle-ball.

1. In his..shop a tortoyrs hung, An Allegater stuft [*1st Qo.* Aligarta.] *Rom. & Jul.* v. i. 43 (*1st Fol.*).

Comb.: **a. apple,** the fruit of a W. Indian tree, *Anona palustris*; **a. pear,** the fruit of a W. Indian tree, *Persea gratissima* or *Laurus Persea*; **a. tortoise,** a large marsh tortoise (*Chelydra serpentina*, fam. *Emydidæ*), called also the Snapping Turtle, found in Carolina; **a. wood,** the timber of a W. Indian tree, *Guarea Swartzii.*

Allineate (ăli·niˌeᶦt), *v. rare.* 1864. [f. L. *ad* + *lineat-*, *lineare.*] = ALINE.

Allineation, alin- (ălinɪˌēɪ·ʃən). 1837. [f. prec.] **1.** = ALINEMENT 1. 1860. **2.** = ALINEMENT 3. **3.** The position of two or more bodies in a straight line with a given point 1882.

Allision (ăli·ʒən). ? *Obs.* 1631. [ad. L. *allisionem.*] The action of dashing against.

Alli·teral, *a. rare.* 1850. [f. ALLITER(ATE), after *literal.*] Marked by alliteration.

Alliterate (ăli·tĕrēᶦt), *v.* 1816. [f. L. *al-*, *ad-* + *littera*: cf. *obliterate.*] **1.** *intr.* Of words: To begin alliteratively, to constitute ALLITERATION. **2.** To compose alliteratively 1826. Hence **Alli·terate** *ppl. a.* alliterated. **Alli·terated** *ppl. a.* composed with or marked by alliteration. **Alli·terating** *ppl. a.* producing alliteration. **Alli·terative** *a.* pertaining to or marked by alliteration. **Alli·teratively** *adv.* **Alli·terativeness. Alli·tera·tor,** one who uses alliteration.

Alliteration (ăli·tĕrēᶦ·ʃən). 1656. [f. ALLITERATE *v.*] **1.** *gen.* The commencing of two or more words in close connexion with the same letter or sound. **2.** The commencement of certain accented syllables in a verse with the same consonant or consonantal group, or with different vowel sounds, as in OE. and Teut. versification 1774.

1. Apt Alliteration's artful aid CHURCHILL. Taxation no Tyranny..was..nothing but a jingling a. MACAULAY. 2. Cf. In abit as an ermite · vnholy of werkes, Ich wente forth in þe worlde · wonders to hure *Piers Ploughman.* Hence **Alli·tera·tional** *a.* abounding in a.

Allitu·ric, *a.* [f. ALL(OXAN) + *-it-* (meaningless) + URIC.] *Chem.* In *Alliturie acid*, a product of the disintegration of alloxantin.

‖**Allium** (æ·liŏm). 1807. [L.] *Bot.* A genus of Liliaceous plants comprising garlic, onion, leek, chive, shallot, etc.

Allness (ǭ·lnės). 1652. [f. ALL.] Universality.

†**Allobro·gical,** *a.* 1640. [f. L. *Allobrogicus.*] A term applied in 17th c. to Presbyterians and Calvinists, in allusion to the fact that Geneva was anciently a town of the Allobroges.

Allocate (æ·lŏkeᶦt), *v.* 1640. [f. med.L. *allocat-*, *allocare*, f. *al-*, *ad-* to + *locare* to place. Orig. *Sc.*] **1.** To set apart for a special purpose or person; to apportion, assign. **2.** To attach locally 1842. **3.** To fix the locality of 1881.

2. Lasswade, to which..we a. ourselves DE QUINCEY.

†**A·llocate,** *sb.* 1709. [ad. med.L. *allocatum.*] A grant.

Allocation (ælokēᶦ·ʃən). 1535. [a. Fr., ad. med.L. *allocationem*; see ALLOCATE *v.*] **1.** The action of apportioning or assigning to a special person or purpose 1833; †a portion of revenue, etc. so assigned –1658. **2.** Allowing an item in an account; also, the item so allowed 1658. **3.** Disposition, arrangement 1656. **4.** Localization 1855.

1. The a. of powers under the Constitution 1876. 4. The a. of the..albuminous electric pulp in a special ..cavity OWEN.

‖**Alloca·tur.** [med.L., 'it is allowed'.] *Law.* A certificate duly given at the end of an action, allowing costs.

Allochro·ic, *a.* 1879. [f. Gr. ἀλλόχροος.] Changeable in colour.

Allochroite (ælǫ·kroˌəit). 1837. [f. as prec.] *Min.* An iron-garnet, a sub-variety of Andradite, found in Norway, etc. Dana.

Allochromatic (æ:loˌkromæ·tik), *a.* 1879. [f. Gr. ἄλλος + χρῶμα.] Of or pertaining to change of colour.

Allochroous (ælǫ·kroˌəs), *a.* 1811. [f. Gr. ἀλλόχροος.] Changing colour.

Alloclase (æ·lŏklēᶦs). 1875. [f. Gr. ἄλλος + κλάσις, cleavage.] *Min.* = next.

Alloclasite (ælǫ·klăsəit). 1868. [f. as prec.] A mineral of the pyrite division of Sulphids, containing sulphur, arsenic, bismuth, and cobalt, with traces of iron, etc.

Allocution (ælokiū·ʃən). 1615. [ad. L. *allocutionem*, f. *alloqui.*] **1.** *Rom. Antiq.* An address by a general to his soldiers; hence, in *R. C. Ch.*, by the Pope to his clergy, or to the Church 1689. **2.** *gen.* The action of addressing; hortatory address 1615.

1. The text of the a. WISEMAN. 2. This vigorous a. to..his Hareem THACKERAY.

Allod, alod (æ·lǫd). 1689. [ad. L. *a(l)lodium.*] = ALLODIUM.

†**Allo·dge.** ME. [a. Fr. *aloger*, f. *à loge.*] To lodge. Hence †**Allo·dgement.**

Allodial, al- (ălōᵘ·diăl), *a.* 1656. [ad. med.L. *al(l)odialis*; see ALLODIUM.] **1.** Of or pertaining to an allodium; or to the *a.* (opp. to the *feudal*) *system* 1747. **2.** Owning an allodium 1857. As *sb.* Allodial lands 1769; an allodial holder 1778.

2. The a. holder who held his land of no other man FREEMAN. Hence **Al(l)o·dialism,** the a. system. **Al(l)o·dialist,** an a. proprietor; var. **al(l)odiary. Al(l)o·dia·lity,** the quality of holding or being held in free ownership. **Al(l)o·dially,** *adv.*

Allo·difica·tion. 1875. [f. L. *allodium.*] *Law.* The conversion of land into allodium.

Allodium, al- (ălōᵘ·diŏm). 1628. [a. med.L. *al-*, *allodium*, f. Ger. **alôd*, *allôd*, entire property, latinized as *alodis*, f. ALL + OLG. *ôd*, estate, etc. In med.L. *al-* is usual.] An estate held, not of a superior, but in absolute ownership; opp. to *feudum* or *feud.*

For in the law of England we have not properly a. COKE, *On Litt.* 1 b.

‖**Allœo·stropha,** *a.* or *sb. pl.* [Gr. ἀλλοιόστροφα, adj. pl. neut.] Verse consisting of irregular strophes. MILT. *Sams.* Pref.

Allœotic, -al (ælɪˌǫ·tik, -ăl), *a.* [ad. Gr. ἀλλοιωτικός, f. ἀλλοιοῦν.] *Med.* Alterative.

Allogamy (ælǫ·gămi). 1879. [f. Gr. ἄλλος + -γαμία.] *Bot.* Cross-fertilization.

Allogeneous (ælodʒī·nɪˌəs), *a. rare.* [f. Gr. ἀλλογενής, f. ἄλλος + γένος + -OUS.] Diverse in kind. Hence **A·llogene·ity.**

Allograph (æ·lŏgraf). [mod. f. Gr. ἄλλος + γραφή. Cf. *autograph.*] A writing or signature made by one person for another.

Allomerism (ælǫ·mĕriz'm). [mod. f. Gr. ἄλλος + μέρος.] *Chem.* Variation in chemical constitution without change of crystalline form.

Allomerous (ælǫ·mĕrəs), *a.* [f. as prec.] Characterized by allomerism.

Allomorphite (ælomǭ·ɹfəit). [mod. f. Gr. ἀλλόμορφος, f. ἄλλος + μορφή.] *Min.* A mineral, allied to barytes or barite, having the form and cleavage of ANHYDRITE.

†**Allo·nge,** *sb.*[1] [a. Fr. *allonge*, f. *allonger.*] **1.** A lunge. (Dicts.) **2.** A long rein. J.

‖**Allonge** (alõ·ʒ), *sb.*[2] 1862. [Fr.] A slip of paper annexed to a bill of exchange, etc. to give room for more endorsements.

Allonym (æ·lŏnim). 1867. [a. Fr. *allonyme*, f. Gr. ἄλλος + -ώνυμος, f. ὄνομα. Cf. *synonym.*] **a.** The name of some one else assumed by the author of a work. **b.** A work bearing such a name. Hence **Allo·nymous** *a.*

†**Alloo·,** *v.* 1708. [for HALLOO.] To urge on with cries.

A·llopalla·dium. [mod. f. Gr. ἄλλος + PALLADIUM.] *Min.* Native palladium crystallizing under the hexagonal system.

Allopath (æ·lŏpæþ). 1830. [a. Fr. *allopathe*, f. *allopathie*; after *philosophie*, *philosophe*, and the like, but opp. to the etym.] A practitioner of allopathy.

Allopathic (ælopæ·þik), *a.* 1830. [ad. Fr. *allopathique*; after *botanie*, *botanique*, etc., and not derivable from Gr. παθικός passive.] Of or pertaining to allopathy. var. **A·llopathe·tic.** Hence **Allopa·thically** *adv.*; var. **A·llopathe·tically.**

Allopathy (ælǫ·păþi). 1842. [ad. Ger. *allopathie* (Hahnemann), f. ἄλλος + -πάθεια.] The curing of a diseased action by the inducing of another of a different kind, yet not necessarily diseased. Opp. to HOMŒOPATHY.

Allo·phanate. [mod. f. ἀλλοφανής.] *Chem.* A salt of allophanic acid.

Allophane (æ·lŏfēᶦn). 1843. [f. as prec.] *Min.* A hydrated silicate of alumina, usu. skyblue, losing its colour under the blowpipe; whence the name.

Allopha·nic, *a.* [mod. f. as prec.] Of or pertaining to anything which changes colour or appearance; as *A. acid* $C_2H_4N_2O_3$.

Allophite (æ·lŏfəit). 1880. [mod. f. Gr. ἄλλος + ὀφίτης serpentine.] *Min.* A hydrous silicate of the Margarophyllite section, inferior in hardness to serpentine.

Allophyle (æ·lŏfil). *rare.* 1577. [ad. L. *allophylus*, a. Gr. ἀλλόφυλος, f. ἄλλος + φυλή.] An alien; a Philistine. As *adj.* = ALLOPHYLIAN.

Allophylian (ælofi·liăn), *a.* and *sb.* 1844. [f. as prec.] Of a race or stock which is not Aryan or Semitic; used esp. of Asiatic and European languages; occas. = Turanian.

Allophytoid (ælǫ·fitoid). 1858. [f. Gr. ἄλλος + PHYTOID.] *Bot.* A separated vegetable bud differing from the parent plant.

Alloquial (ălōᵘ·kwiăl), *a. rare.* 1840. [f. L. *alloquium.* Cf. ALLOCUTION.] Of, or pertaining to, the action of addressing others; contrasted with *colloquial.* Hence **Allo·quiali·sm,** a phrase or manner of address.

Allot (ălǫ·t), *v.* 1547. [a. OFr. *aloter* (mod. *allotir*), f. *à* + *loter*, f. *lot* lot, a Teut. wd.] **1.** To distribute by lot, or in such way that the recipients have no choice; to assign shares authoritatively; to apportion 1574. **2.** To assign as a lot or portion *to*; to appoint (without distribution) 1547; hence, to appropriate to a special person or purpose 1574. †**3.** To appoint, destine (a person *to do*) –1677. **4.** U.S. *colloq.* To reckon (occas. with *upon*).

2. The..end that was allotted him SURREY. Ten years I will a. to the attainment of knowledge JOHNSON. 4. I a. we must economise HALIBURTON. Hence **Allo·ttable** *a.* **Allo·ttee,** one to whom an allotment is made. **Allo·tter,** one who allots. †**Allo·ttery,** allotted share *A. Y. L.* I. i. 77.

Allotheism (æ·loˌþī·iz'm). 1660. [f. ἄλλος + THEISM.] The worship of strange gods.

Allotment (ălǫ·tmĕnt). 1574. [a. Fr. *allotement*, formerly *al-*; see ALLOT.] **1.** The action of allotting. **2.** Lot in life, destiny 1674. **3.** A share or portion, *esp.* of land, allotted to a special person or purpose 1629. †**4.** *Comm.* The division of a ship's cargo into equal portions, to be distributed among purchasers by lot –1751.

2. The stinted allotments of earthly life CARLYLE. *Comb.* **a. system,** the division of land into small plots to be held for cultivation by the poorer classes at a small rent.

Allotrophic (ælotrǫ·fik), *a.* 1879. [f. Gr. ἄλλος + -τροφος.] *Med.* Variable as to nutritive properties, without any change in physical or chemical characters.

Allotropic, -al (ælotrǫ·pik, -ăl), *a.* 1849. [f. Gr. ἀλλότροπος (see ALLOTROPY) + -IC, + AL.] Of or pertaining to ALLOTROPY. Hence **Allotro·pically** *adv.* **Allo·tropi·city** (*rare*). So **A·llotrope,** an allotropic form.

Allotropism (ælǫ·trŏpiz'm). 1851. [f. as prec. + -ISM.] Allotropy as a principle or process.

Allotropize (ælǫ·trŏpəiz), *v. rare.* [f. as prec. + -IZE.] To change allotropically.

Allotropy (ælǫ·trŏpi). [mod. ad. Gr. ἀλλοτροπία, f. ἀλλότροπος, f. ἄλλος + τρόπος, f. τρέπειν.] The variation of physical properties without change of substance, first noticed by Berzelius in charcoal and the diamond.

†**A·ll ou·t,** *adv.* ME. **1.** Completely, quite –1638; esp. in *to drink a.*, to empty a bumper; cf. CAROUSE. **B.** *sb.* A bumper –1611.

A·ll o·ver, *adv.* 1577. **1.** Over the whole extent, in every part, e.g. of the body. **2.**

Finished; done for (*mod.*). 3. *adj.* (from 1) *colloq.* Indisposed all over the body 1851.

2. *It is all over with* = L. *actum est de.* Hence (from 1) **A·ll-o·verish** *a. colloq.* **A·ll-o·verishness,** general indisposition. *colloq.*

Allow (ălau·), *v.* ME. [a. OFr. *alouer* (*all-*), 1. to praise :—L. *allaudare*; 2. to bestow, assign :—L. *allocare.* Many uses blend 1 and 2.] **I.** Fr. *alouer* :—L. *allaudare.* 1. *trans.* †To praise, commend –1783; to approve of, sanction (*arch.*) ME.; *intr.* with *upon, of* 1534; to accept as satisfactory (*arch.*) ME.; †*intr.* with *of* –1748. 2. To accept as true or valid, to admit 1548; *intr.* with *of* 1528; with *subord. cl.* to concede 1643; with *compl.* to admit a thing *to be* 1593; to conclude, opine, or state as an opinion formed (*Eng.* and *Amer. dial.*) 1580. 3. *trans.* To concede, permit (an action, etc.) 1558; with *inf.* 1637; *refl.* to permit oneself to indulge *in,* †*to* 1605; *intr.* to admit *of* 1732.

1. Upon reasonable cause to be allowed by a justice of the peace BLACKSTONE. 2. It will be allowed us that marriage is a human society MILT. Allowed for law 1798. I 'lowed I'd make him sorry fur it *Scrib. Mag.* 3. Where many sorts of worship be allowed HOBBES. His .. madness Allows itself to anything *Lear* III. vii. 107.

II. Fr. *allouer* :—L. *allocare.* 1. †To assign as a right or due –1596; to give, or let any one have, as his share, or as what he needs ME.; †to portion, endow –1712. 2. †To place to one's credit, count to one –1667; hence, †to deduct from the debit, to abate –1530; *gen.* to add or deduct (so much) on account of something not formally appearing 1663.

1. The Law allowes it, And the Court awards it *Merch. V.* IV. i. 303. A. him but his plaything of a pen POPE. 2. To a. an hour for time lost in changing trains, etc. Hence **Allow·er,** one who allows (senses I. †1, 2, 3). **Allow·ment,** sanction, approval.

Allowable (ălau·ăb'l), *a.* ME. [a. Fr. *allouable*; see ALLOW and -ABLE.] †Laudable –1702; acceptable 1552; admissible, probable 1682; permissible, legitimate 1568.

Prayer for the dead is not .. a. COVERDALE. Hence **Allow·ableness. Allow·ably** *adv.*

Allowance (ălau·ăns), *sb.* ME. [a. OFr. *alouance,* f. *alouer*; see ALLOW.] The action of allowing; a thing allowed. 1. †Praise –1633; approbation, sanction, voluntary acceptance (*arch.*) 1552; †acknowledgement –1756; permission, sufferance 1628. 2. The action of placing to one's credit, admitting in an account, or allotting on account of expenses 1574; †a sum allowed in account, a consideration –1574. 3. A limited portion or sum, *esp.* of money, or food 1440. 4. Rebate, deduction, discount 1530. 5. *fig.* The taking into account of mitigating or extenuating circumstances 1676. †6. A balance –1552.

1. The a. of slavery in the South FREEMAN. 2. Illiberalite of Parents in a. towards their Children BACON. 3. They consider this A. [Pin-money] as a kind of Alimoney ADDISON. The short A., the Bread and Water of a Prison 1711. A scant a. of star-light MILT. *Comus* 308. 4. *To make allowance*: to add or deduct, in order to provide for incidental circumstances. An a. for the waste of the Timber 1663. 5. To make Allowances for Conduct STEELE.

Allowance (ălau·ăns), *v.* 1839. [f. the sb. Cf. *portion,* etc.] 1. To put upon an allowance; to limit in the amount allowed. 2. To supply in limited quantities 1840.

Allowed (ălau·d), *ppl. a.* ME. [f. ALLOW.] †1. Praised, accepted as satisfactory –1728. 2. Licensed 1589; acknowledged 1749; allotted 1440; remitted 1674.

2. An a. printer 1589, fool *Twel. N.* I. v. 101. The a. and established models of good breeding CHESTERF. Hence **Allow·edly** *adv.*

Alloxan (ælǫ·ksăn). 1853. [f. ALL(ANTOIN) + OXA(LIC).] *Chem.* An organic compound $C_4H_2N_2O_4$, one of the oxidation products of uric acid. Hence **Allo·xanate,** a salt of alloxanic acid. **Alloxa·nic** *a.*

Alloxantin (ælǫksæ·ntin). 1853. *Chem.* An organic compound $C_8H_4N_4O_7$.

Alloy (ăloi·), *sb.* 1598. [a. Fr. *aloi* :—OFr. *alei,* Norm. *alai,* whence ALLAY *sb.*[1] The Fr. *aloi* was erron. identified with *à loi.* Cf. ALLAY *sb.*[1]] 1. Fineness, standard, of gold or silver 1604; †agio of exchange –1672. 2. A baser metal mixed with a nobler, *esp.* in gold and silver coinage 1719. 3. The condition of mixture 1827. 4. An amalgam; *formerly,* a compound containing a baser metal 1656. †5. *fig.* Intrinsic quality –1674. 6. *fig.* Admixture of that which lowers in character or value; alien element 1625.

4. **Native alloy**: one of osmium and iridium occurring with native platinum. 6. A base a. of moral cowardice C. BRONTË.

Alloy (ăloi·), *v.* 1661. [a. Fr. *aloyer* :—OFr. *aleier, alier* :—L. *alligare.* Cf. ALLAY vbs.[1], [2], repl. by ALLOY.] 1. To mix with a baser metal, so as to reduce in standard 1691. 2. To mix metals 1822; *intr.* (*refl.*) to enter into combination with another metal 1839. 3. *fig.* To debase by admixture 1703. 4. *fig.* To temper, moderate 1661.

Hence **Alloy·age,** the art or process of alloying metals.

Allozooid (ælozōu·oid). 1858. [f. Gr. ἄλλος + ζῷον.] *Biol.* A separated animal bud differing in nature from the parent.

All-red, *a.* 1895. Used to indicate a telegraph-line, a trading route, etc., lying throughout in territory of the British Empire. (From the practice of colouring British and Imperial territory red in our maps.)

A·ll(-)rou·nd. 1805. **A.** *adv.* Everywhere around; affecting equally all the parts or every one in a circle or company 1871. **B.** *prep.* Around all the parts of 1805. **C.** *adj.* Including everything or every one in a given circle.

C. *An all-round man*: one who has ability in all departments. Hence **A·ll rou·nder,** he who or that which is all round, e. g. a collar.

All saints. 1580. The saints in heaven collectively. The festival, called also **All Saints' Day** (Nov. 1). Also = ALL-HALLOW *tide.*

Allseed (ǭ·lsīd). A name for various many-seeded plants. **a.** The genus *Polycarpon.* **b.** A species of Goosefoot (*Chenopodium polyspermum*). **c.** *Radiola Millegrana.* **d.** The Knot-grass (*Polygonum aviculare*).

All souls. The souls of all the pious dead. The festival on which the Ch. of Rome makes supplications on their behalf, called also **All Souls' Day** (Nov. 2). **All Souls' Eve,** the evening of Nov. 1.

Allspice (ǭ·lspəis). 1621. [f. ALL + SPICE, as combining the flavour of cinnamon, nutmeg, and cloves.] 1. An aromatic spice, Jamaica Pepper or Pimenta, the dried berry of *Eugenia Pimenta* or Allspice Tree (N.O. *Myrtaceæ*) of the West Indies. 2. A name of other aromatic shrubs: **A. Tree** or **Carolina A.,** *Calycanthus floridus*; **Japan A.,** *Chimonanthus fragrans*; **Wild A.,** *Lindera Benzoin.* Hence **A·llspi·cy** *a. nonce-wd.,* hot.

Allthing. *Obs.* or *dial.* Everything.

Allude (ălū·d), *v.* 1535. [ad. L. *alludere.*] †1. To mock –1577; to play upon words, to refer by play of words –1607; to refer by play of fancy (*trans.* and *intr.*) –1665. 2. *intr.* To have or make an indirect or passing reference **to** (not = *refer*) 1533. †3. *trans.* To refer a thing *to,* as a thing to its author –1634. †4. To hint, suggest –1677.

2. Quotations which a. to the Perjuries of the Fair STEELE. He often alluded to his poverty 1837.

‖**Allumette** (alümet). 1848. [Fr.] A match for lighting.

†**Allu·mine,** *v.* 1581. [a. Fr. *al(l)uminer,* refash. of OFr. *alumer* :—late L. *adluminare.*] To illuminate.

†**Allu·minor.** 1483. [a. Anglo-Fr. *alluminour*; see prec. Aphet. to LUMINOR and LIMNER.] An illuminator, a limner –1607.

†**Allu·rance.** 1580. [f. the vb.] Enticement. †**Allu·rant** *ppl. a.* enticing.

Allure (ăliū̆·ɹ), *v.* ME. [a. OFr. *alurer,* f. *à* + *lurer,* to LURE, orig. a term of Falconry.] 1. To attract or tempt by something flattering or advantageous; to entice; to win over. 2. To fascinate, charm 1612; †to attract, elicit –1794.

1. He .. Allur'd to brighter worlds and led the way GOLDSM. Allured by hopes of relief JOHNSON. 2. The .. Sun .. Allur'd his eye MILT. *P. L.* III. 5. 73. Hence **Allu·rer,** he who, or that which, allures. **Alluring** *vbl. sb.* the action of attracting with the prospect of advantage; †fascination; *ppl. a.* tempting, seductive; attractive, fascinating. **Allu·ring·ly** *adv.,* **-ness** (*rare*).

†**Allu·re,** *sb.*[1] 1548. [f. the vb.] = ALLUREMENT –1758.

‖**Allure** (alü·r), *sb.*[2] 1882. [Fr.] Gait; mien, air.

Allurement (ăliū̆ə·ɹmĕnt). 1548. [f. the vb.] 1. The action of alluring; enticement 1561. 2. Fascination, charm 1579. 3. That which allures; a lure, bait 1548.

1. Though Adam by his wife's a. fell MILT. *P. R.* II. 131. 3. Allurements to enlist in the army 1825.

Allusion (ăliū·ʒən). 1548. [ad. L. *allusionem*; see ALLUDE.] †1. Illusion –1618. †2. A word-play –1731. †3. A symbolical reference –1781. 4. A covert or implied reference 1612.

Allusive (ăliū·siv), *a.* 1605. [f. L. *allus-, alludere.*] †1. Punning –1656. 2. Symbolical (*arch.*) 1605. 3. Containing allusion 1607.

1. *Her. Allusive Arms,* called also *canting* or *punning* arms: those in which the charges play upon the bearer's name or title, as the martlets (OFr. *arondel*) borne by the Duke of Arundel. Hence **Allu·sive·ly** *adv.,* **-ness.** var. †**Allu·sory.**

†**All·utterly,** *adv.* ME. Wholly; absolutely –1651.

Alluvial (ăliū·viăl), *a.* 1802. [f. L. *alluvium.*] Of, pertaining to, or consisting of alluvium. var. **Allu·vian** (*rare*).

Alluvion (ăliū·viən). 1536. [a. Fr., ad. L. *alluvionem.*] 1. The wash of water against the shore, or a river-bank. 2. An inundation; a flood 1550. 3. The matter deposited by a flood 1731; *esp.* ALLUVIUM 1779. 4. *Law.* The imperceptible action of flowing water in forming new land 1751.

3. Spreading .. a ... over its meadows CATLIN.

Alluvium (ăliū·viŭm). Pl. **-ia, -iums.** 1665. [a. L., neut. of adj. *alluvius,* f. *al-* = *ad-* + *luere.*] Deposits of earth, sand, etc. left by water flowing over land that is not permanently submerged; *esp.* those left in river valleys and deltas. Also *fig.*

†**A·ll-who·le.** ME. [Cf. Fr. *tout entier.*] *adj.* Entire –1588. *adv.* Entirely –1601. Hence †**A·ll-who·lly** *adv.*

A·llwo·rk. 1830. Work, *esp.* domestic, of all kinds. *Maid of all-work*: a general servant.

Ally (ăləi·), *v.* [ME. *alie,* a. OFr. *alier* :—L. *alligare.* Cf. ALLAY *v.*[2], ALLIGATE, ALLOY.] 1. *trans.* To unite for a special object; now chiefly of marriage, association of sovereign states, and union of nature or spirit. Const. *to, with.* 2. *intr.* To enter into alliance (*arch.*) ME. †3. To mix. (Cf. *allay, alloy.*) –1500.

1. In .. mariage alied to the emperour ME. He allied himself closely to Castlemaine MACAULAY. 2. No foreign power will a. with us 1825.

Ally (ăləi·), *sb.*[1] ME. [f. the vb.] †**I.** *abstract.* Kinship –1592; alliance –1587. †**II.** *collect.* Kindred –1460. **III.** *individual.* †1. A relative –1654. 2. *fig.* Anything akin to another by structure, properties, etc. 1697. 3. One united with another by treaty or league; now usu. of sovereigns or states 1598. 4. *fig.* Anything auxiliary to another 1853.

1. This Gentleman the Princes neere Alie *Rom. & Jul.* III. i. 114. 2. The alkaline metals and their allies (*mod.*). 3. Ammon, the ancient a. of Israel STANLEY. 4. Tractarianism .. the .. a. of Rome 1853.

Ally, alley, alay (æ·li), *sb.*[2] 1720. [abbrev. of *Alabaster*; cf. *Willy,* etc.] A marble of real alabaster.

Allyl (æ·lil). 1854. [f. L. *all(ium)* + -YL = Gr. ὕλη.] *Chem.* A monovalent hydro-carbon radical, C_3H_5. Also *attrib.,* as in *allyl alcohol* C_3H_5OH, *allyl sulphide* $(C_3H_5)_2S$, etc. Hence **A·llylami·ne,** the ammonia of the a. series $C_3H_5NH_2$, also called Acrylamine. **A·llylate,** a salt of a., as *sodium allylate* C_3H_5ONa. **A·llylene,** a divalent hydro-carbon radical, C_3H_4, isomeric with acetylene. Also called *propine.* **Ally·lic** *a.* **A·llylin,** a viscid liquid, a by-product in the preparation of allyl alcohol.

Alma, almah (æ·lmă). Also ALME(H). 1814. [a. Arab. *almah,* 'learned' (in music and dancing).] An Egyptian dancing-girl.

Almacantar (ælmăkæ·ntəɹ). ME. [a. Fr. *almucantarat,* ad. Arab., deriv. of *qantarah,* a bridge.] *pl.* Circles of the sphere parallel to the horizon; parallels of altitude.

2. The name of an instrument for the determination of time and latitude 1880.

Comb. **a.-staff**, an instrument formerly used to take observations of the Sun at its rising and setting, in order to correct the compass.

Almadia (ælmădī·ă). 1681. [ad. Arab.] A river-boat. 1. An Indian boat, 80 ft. long, and very swift. 2. An African canoe, made of bark or of a hollowed trunk.

Almagest (æ·lmădʒest). ME. [a. OFr. *almageste*, ad. (ult.) Arab., ad. Gr. μεγίστη (sc. σύνταξις).] The great astronomical treatise of Ptolemy; also, other great text-books of astrology and alchemy.

‖**Alma·gra.** 1703. [Sp., a. Arab.] A deep red ochre, the *sil atticum* of the ancients, found in Spain.

†**A·lmain.** Also **-ayn, -an(e.** ME. [a. OFr. *aleman* (mod. *allemand*).] A. *adj.* German -1665. B. *sb.* 1. A German -1698. 2. A kind of dance, or dance-music. = ALLEMANDE (*arch.*) 1549.

†**A·lmaine, -any.** ME. Germany -1682.

A·lmain-ri·vets. 1530. Light armour, made flexible by overlapping plates sliding on rivets. First used in Germany.

‖**A·lma Ma·ter.** 1715. [L.] A title given by the Romans, *esp.* to Ceres and Cybele, and transferred in Eng. to Universities and schools, regarded as 'fostering mothers' to their *alumni*.

Almanac (ǭ·lmănæk). ME. [In med.L. *almanac(h*. App. f. Sp., Arab. *al-manākh*, calendar; of uncertain origin.] An annual table, or book of tables, containing a calendar of months and days, with astronomical data and calculations, ecclesiastical and other anniversaries, etc., and, in former days, astrological and astrometeorological forecasts.

Looke in the A., finde out the Moone-shine *Mids. N.* III. i. 54. Falshood and Lying..like Almanackes of the last yeare, are now gon out DEKKER. You would reduce all history to..an a. BOSWELL.

Almandine (æ·lmăndin, æ·lmăndəi:n). 1658. [a corruption of ALABANDINE. Also erron. *almondine*.] An alumina iron garnet of a violet or amethystine tint.

Turkis and agate and almondine TENNYSON.

Almandite (æ·lmăndəit). [f. prec. + -ITE.] Dana's name for almandine as a mineral, a variety of garnet.

†**A·lma·nner.** Comb. f. *all manner* used *attrib.* ME. [orig. a genitive = 'of every sort'; see MANNER and ALL.] -1526.

Alme(h; see ALMA.

‖**Almendro·n.** 1852. [Sp., augm. of *almendra* almond.] The Brazil-nut tree (*Bertholletia excelsa*).

Almery, obs. f. AMBRY.

Almes(se, obs. f. ALMS.

†**Almi·ght,** *a.* OE. [f. ALL + MIGHT, prob. pa. pple. of MAY.] = ALMIGHTY. Usu. *poet.* -1546. †**Almi·ghtful,** *a.* ME. only. [f. ALL *adv.* + MIGHTFUL.] All-powerful; var. †**Almi·ghtiful.** †**Almi·ghtin,** *sb.* and *a.* ME. only. [var. of ALMIGHTY.] Used in apposition to *God*; also alone.

Almighty (ǭlməi·ti), *a.* OE. [f. ALL *adv.* + MIGHTY. OE. *ælmeatig*.] All-powerful, omnipotent. 1. *attrib.* With *God*, etc. OE.; absol. *The Almighty* OE. Occas. in superl. 1598. 2. *gen.* All-powerful ME. ¶ *slang.* Mighty, great; exceedingly 1824.

1. I am the almightie God, walke before me *Gen.* xvii. 1. Doth the Almightie peruert justice *Job* viii. 3. 2. Almighty Sampson CHAUCER. The a. dollar (a phr. due to) W. IRVING. 'Almighty' nonsense (to speak *transatlanticè*) DE QUINCEY. vars. † **Almi·ght,** †**Almi·ghtend.** Hence **Almi·ghtily** *adv.* **Almi·ghtiness.**

Almirah, -myra (ælməi·ră). 1878. [ad. Urdu:—(through Pg.) L. *armarium*; see AMBRY.] Anglo-Ind. for a cupboard, press, chest of drawers, etc.

†**A·lmistry.** [?*joc.* for *all-mystery*.] B. JONS.

†**Almner,** var. of ALMONER.

Almoign, almoin (ælmoi·n). ME. [As *almon(e*, a. OFr. *almône* (mod. *aumône*); see ALMS.] †1. Alms; alms-chest ME. 2. Tenure by divine service, or by performing some religious duty. **Frank almoin** or *free alms* (L. *libera eleemosyna*): the tenure of lands, etc., bestowed upon God, that is, given to a religious corporation for pure and perpetual alms, free from any temporal service; perpetual tenure by free gift of charity.

†**A·lmonage.** 1655. [a. OFr. *almosnaige*, f. *almosnier*; see ALMS.] In **Frank almonage** = *frank almoin*; see ALMOIGN. -1667.

Almond (ā·mənd). ME. [a. OFr. *almande*, earlier *alemandle*, early Rom. **amendla*, *-ola*, *-ala*, f. L. *amygdala*, a. Gr. ἀμυγδάλη. The *al-* for *a-* is perh. Sp., as if *a-* were Arab. *al-*.] 1. The kernel of a drupe, the produce of the almond tree, of which there are two kinds, the sweet and the bitter. 2. The tree, *Amygdalus Communis* (N.O. *Rosaceæ*) 1697. 3. Anything made with almonds, or like almonds in shape, or almond blossom in colour; *esp.* the tonsils, called *almonds of the throat, jaws,* or *ears* (*arch.*) 1578. Also a pigeon, the Almond Tumbler 1867.

2. Mark well the flowering Almonds in the Wood DRYDEN. 3. Balls, or rather almonds, of purple marble RUSKIN. Cream colour..and a. 1879.

Comb.: **a.-butter,** a preparation of cream, whites of eggs boiled, and blanched almonds; **-kernel** (=ALMOND 1, 3); **-milk,** a preparation of sweet blanched almonds and water; **-oil,** the expressed oil of bitter almonds, or benzoic aldehyde; **a. tree,** the tree that bears almonds, also *fig.* grey hair; **a. tumbler** (see ALMOND 3); **a. willow,** *Salix amygdalina*; **-worts,** the plants of N.O. *Drupaceæ*. Hence **A·lmondy** *a.* having, or suggesting, almonds.

A·lmond-fu·rnace. 1674. [Corruption of *Allemand*, i.e. German, *furnace*.] A furnace used to separate metals from dross, and to reduce slag of litharge to lead.

Almoner[1] (ā·mənəɹ, æ·lmənəɹ). [ME. *aumoner*, ad. AF. *aumoner*, OF. *aumo(s)nier* (mod. *aumônier*), f. *aumône*, ad. pop. L. **alimosina* ALMS.] A distributor of alms on behalf of a person or a community, e.g. a sovereign, a religious house (*Hereditary High A.* and *Lord High A.* are officers of the royal household of Great Britain). b. A hospital official who has duties concerning patients' payments and their general welfare 1892. †2. An alms-giver ME.

1. Judas .. Was iesu crist aumoner ME. *fig.* The sun is the a. of the Almighty HERSCHEL. 2. An amner to the poore that helpless cry 1591.

†**A·lmoner**[2]. ME. [a. OFr. *aumosnière*:—L. **eleemosynaria*, sc. *bursa*.] An alms-purse; a bag -1460. var. **Alner.**

A·lmonership. 1847. [f. ALMONER[1] + -SHIP.] The office of an almoner.

Almonry (æ·lmŏnri). 1480. [a. OFr. *au(l)mosnerie*, f. *au(l)mosnier*; see ALMONER.] 1. A place where alms were distributed. †2. = ALMONER[2] 1536. Cf. AMBRY.

†**Almose.** 1483. [var. of ALMS.] = ALMS 1, 2. Also as sing. -1587.

Almost (ǭ·lmoust, -məst, when emph. ǭ·lmōu·st), *adv.* Aphet. **'most.** OE. [f. ALL + MOST *adv.* = *mostly*.] †1. *adj.* or *adv.* Mostly all; for the most part -1658. 2. *adv.* Very nearly, all but 1200.

1. The women..do that work a. 1658. 2. With *vb.* or *attrib.*: A. thou perswadest mee to be a Christian *Acts* xxvi. 28. Almost was never hang'd 1639. With *sb.*: You are a. come to part a. a fray *Much Ado* v. i. 113. *Almost no* = scarcely any; *Almost never* = scarcely ever, etc. †To intensify an interrog. (L. *quis fere*): Whom a. can we see who opens his arms to his enemies SOUTH.

†**Almous.** ME. Sc. **awmous.** [a. ON. *almusa*; a distinct by-form.] = ALMS 1, 2. *sing.* and *pl.*

Alms (āmz). [OE. *ælmysse*, a. pop.L. **alimosina*, perversion of *elimosina*, ad. Gr. ἐλεημοσύνη, f. ἔλεος.] 1. Charitable relief of the poor; charity; *esp.* as a religious duty. Const. with *do, make, work*; later, with *give*, etc. a. *collect.* without pl. OE. b. as *sing.* A charitable donation ME. c. as *pl.* Things given in charity 1557. †2. *fig.* A good deed, a service to God, a charity. Often *ironic.* -1623. 3. *Law.* Tenure by a., see ALMOIGN; free alms = *frank almoign*. **Reasonable alms**: a part of an intestate estate allotted to the poor.

1. a. Hir hond mynistre of fredom and almesse CHAUCER. b. To ask an a. ADDISON. c. For a. are but the vehicles of prayer DRYDEN. 2. If he be hungry it is a. to feed him SANDERSON.

Comb.: **a.-basket,** that containing the public a. *L. L. L.* v. i. 41; **-deed** = ALMS 2; †**-drink,** the remains of liquor, reserved for alms-people; **-fee,** Peter's pence or Rome-scot; **-folk,** persons supported by a.; †almsgivers; **-gift,** almsgiving, also = ALMOIGN; **-land,** land held in frank almoign. **A·lmsgi·ving.** 1690. The giving of alms. So **-gi·ver** 1630.

A·lms-house. ME. A house founded by private charity, *esp.* for the aged poor. *Formerly*, The house belonging to a monastery, where alms and hospitality were dispensed.

Almsman. OE. 1. One supported by alms; a bedesman. Also *fig.* 2. An alms-giver (*arch.*) 1483.

1. My gay Apparrell, for an Almes-mans Gowne SHAKS.

Almucantar, -urie, obs. ff. ALMACANTAR.

Almuce, early f. AMICE.

Almug (æ·lmɒg). 1611. [Heb.] An erron., but in Eng. more usual, sp. of ALGUM.

†**Almury.** [a. (ult.) Arab.] The 'denticle' or pointer on the astrolabe. CHAUCER.

†**Almu·ten.** 1625. [Corrupt f. OFr. *almutaz*, a. Arab.] *Astrol.* The ruling planet in the horoscope -1721.

Alnage (ǭ·lnėdʒ). 1477. [a. OFr. *aulnage* (mod. *aunage*), f. *aulner*, f. *alne*:—late L. *alena*, cogn. w. L. *ulna*.] 1. Measurement by the ell. *spec.* Official measurement and inspection of woollen cloth. 2. The fee for such measurement 1622.

Alnager (ǭ·lnėdʒəɹ). ME. [a. OFr. *aulnegeor*, f. *aulnage*; see prec.] A sworn officer to examine and attest the measurement and quality of woollen goods. vars. †**A·lner, Aulner.**

†**Alna·th.** ME. [Arab.] *Astrol.* The first star in the horns of Aries. CHAUCER.

Alod, -ial, -iality, etc., vars. of ALLOD, etc.

Aloe (æ·lo). [OE. *aluwan* (pl.), ad. L. *aloe*, a. Gr. ἀλόη; also as tr. Heb. = the Agalloch. Orig. always pl. in Eng.] †1. *pl.* The fragrant resin or wood of the AGALLOCH. See LIGN-ALOES. -1741. 2. A genus of plants (N.O. *Liliaceæ*, sect. *Aloinæ*) with bitter juice ME. 3. (Usu. *pl.*) A nauseous bitter purgative, procured from the inspissated juice of the plants ME. *fig.* Bitter experiences 1526. 4. *pop.* A name of other plants resembling the a., *esp.* the AGAVE or American Aloe 1682.

1. Thy garmentes are like myrre, Aloes and Cassia *Ps.* xliv. 8. 3. *fig.* The bitter aloes of the law 1617. Hence **A·loed** *ppl. a.* mixed with, or as with, or planted with, aloes.

†**Aloe·dary.** 1753. [ad. L. *aloedarium*.] 1. *Med.* A purgative, chiefly aloes. 2. *Bot.* A treatise on the Aloe.

Aloetic (ælo,e·tik). 1706. [f. Gr. ἀλόη; cf. *diuretic*.] A. *adj.* 1. *Med.* Like, or containing aloes. 2. *Chem. Aloetic Acid*: a yellow amorphous powder, 2 $C_7H_2N_2O_5.H_2O$, formed by the action of nitric acid on aloes. 1855. B. *sb.* [sc. *medicine*.] 1706.

Aloft (ălǭ·ft), *adv.* ME. [a. ON. *á lopt*, *á lopti*, to, in air, f. *lopt*, cogn. w. OHG. *luft*, OE. *lyft*. Orig. of position.] †1. Up, as a star -1577; *fig.* ruling -1601. 2. In heaven (*arch.*) ME.; high above the earth, on high ME.; †on the top -1718. Also *fig.* 3. Of direction: Into the air, up, on high; also *fig.* ME. 4. *Naut.* On or to a higher part of the ship ME. †5. *prep.* On the top of; above -1613.

2. A..cherub that sits up a. DIBDIN. Fame sits a. POPE. 3. Blow her a. DE FOE. 4. Our sayles are a loft BARCLAY. 5. I breathe again A. the flood SHAKS.

Alogian (ălōu·dʒiăn). 1675. [ad. med.L. *alogiani*, f. Gr. ἀλόγιοι; cf. *christian*.] One of a sect who denied the divinity of the 'Logos'.

Alogotrophy (ælǒgǫ·trŏfi). 1753. [f. Gr. ἄλογος + τροφή.] *Med.* Excessive nutrition, e.g. of the bones, resulting in deformity.

†**A·logy.** 1646. [ad. med.L. *alogia*, a. Gr.] Absurdity. SIR T. BROWNE.

Aloid (æ·lo,id), *a.* 1853. [f. ALOE + *-id* for -OID.] Resembling aloes.

Aloin (æ·lo,in). 1841. [f. ALOE + -IN.] *Chem.* The bitter purgative principle in aloes, $C_{17}H_{18}O_7$, which forms in crystals.

Alomancy, var. of HALOMANCY.

Alone (ălōu·n), *a.* and *adv.* ME. [orig. ALL *adv.* + ONE. Aphet. in n. dial. to LONE.] **1.** *lit.* Quite by oneself, unaccompanied; *fig.* alone of its kind, unique 1535; alone in action or feeling ME. **2.** *attrib.* Sole, unique (*rare*) 1547. **3.** Taken or acting by itself (*esp.* after, or separated from, the sb.) ME. **4.** Also of a number, in all prec. senses: By themselves ME. Subjectively. **5.** With no one else in the same case; exclusively. (Bef., after, or separated from the sb.) ME. **6.** *adv.* With vb., adj., phr., or cl.: Only, merely, exclusively ME.

1. Never less a. than when..a. HOWELL. A. on a wide sea COLERIDGE. A. in an opinion (*mod.*). So *me al-one* (or *al me one*; see ONE), *mine alone, my Lone* (now *dial.*). To let or **leave alone**: to leave to their own efforts, abstain from interfering. Let me a. for swearing *Twel. N.* III. iv. 201. 2. The a. God 1564. 3. A man lyueth not in breed aloon WYCLIF *Matt.* IV. 4. 4. They two allone ME. 5. By him a. and onely UDALL. 'Tis not a. my Inky Cloake *Haml.* I. ii. 77. Hence †**Alo·nely** *a.* and *adv.* only, sole, solitary; solely, solitarily. **Alo·neness.**

Along (ălǫ·ŋ), *a.*[1] *arch.* and *dial.* [OE. *gelang*, the pref. becoming *ă-*, or being dropped. See LONG.] In *Along of* (earlier *on*, in OE. *æt*): Pertaining, owing to; on account of. (Common in London and south. dial.)

And long of her it was That [etc.] *Cymb.* V. v. 271. A. of him and you DICKENS.

Along (ălǫ·ŋ), (*a.*[2]), *adv.* and *prep.* [OE. *and-lang*, f. *and-* facing + *lang* long. Orig. an *adj.* Cf. ENDLONG.] †**A.** *adj.* (only in OE.) Extending lengthwise, livelong. Merged in *all long*: as *all night long.* –ME.

B. *prep.* Orig. adj. with *gen.* Cf. *ahead of*, etc. Through the whole length of, from end to end of, whether *within*, or *by the side of* (often with *all*) OE.; following the line of, opp. to *across* OE.; parallel to the length of ME.

The..Tempest raves a. the plain THOMSON. Stealing ..a. the coast JOHNSON.

C. *adv.* [The prep. with obj. omitted.] **1.** In a line with the length; lengthwise. Now only with *by* and as in next. ME. **2.** With vbs. of motion: Onward in the line of motion. Also *fig.* (see quots.) ME. **3.** *ellipt.* (*with* omitted, but its force retained.) In company, with (some one) 1590. **4.** Lengthwise; at full length. Often with *all.* ME. †**5.** In full. (? = Fr. *au long.*) –1588. †**6.** Afar. (? = Fr. *au loin.*) –1580.

1. A. by the king's high way *Numb.* XX. 17. 2. *To get along*: to get on. *Get along!*: be off! *Along with*: on the way, or in company *with*; together *with*; in conjunction *with*. Then I must lug you a. with me, Says the saucy Arethusa DIBDIN. 3. The Knave..took a. his rusty Hanger 1682. *All along*: throughout. All a...a burden FREEMAN. 4. Vnder yond..Trees lay thee all a. *Rom. & Jul.* V. iii. 3. *Comb.* **a.-ships**, lengthwise to the ship.

Alongshore (ălǫ·ŋʃōᵊɹ), *adv.* 1779. [f. ALONG *prep.* + SHORE.] Along *by*, or *on*, the shore.

Alongside (ălǫ·ŋsəi·d), *adv.* 1707. [ALONG *prep.* + SIDE.] **A.** *adv.* Along or parallel to the side *of*; with *of*: side by side with; also *fig.* 1781. **B.** *prep.* [*of* omitted.] Side by side with 1793.

A. *fig.* A. of him stood his maternal uncle FREEMAN.

Alo·ngst. ME. [orig. *alonges*, advb. gen. in *-es*; corrupted to *alongest*, as if superl. Cf. *against*, etc.] **A.** *prep.* †Through the length of, opp. to *across*, etc. –1630; by the side of 1580. †**B.** *adv.* Onwards by the side of –1599; opp. to *athwart* –1737; together *with* –1817; as far as (a place indicated) –1650. *Comb.* **a.-ships** = *along-ships*; see ALONG *adv.*

Aloof (ălū·f), *adv.* 1532. [f. A *prep.*[1] + LOOF, perh. from Du. *loef*, conn. with ME. *lof*, *loof.* See also LUFF.] †**1.** *phr. Naut.* The order to keep the ship's head to the wind; now LUFF –1678. Also *fig.* **2.** *adv. Naut.* Away to the windward 1532. **3.** Hence *gen.* At a distance (*from*), apart; *esp.* with *hold, keep*, etc. 1540; from a distance 1547; also *fig.* **4.** As *compl.* or *pred.*: At a distance 1607. As †*prep.* [= *aloof from.*] (*rare*) –1667.

3. No frende draweth nere, I syt alowfe 1540. Purple cliffs, a. descried TENNYSON. *fig.* **To stand, keep, hold aloof** (*from*): to take no part in, show no sympathy with. 4. To keepe [dangers] aloofe BACON. *prep.* The great Luminarie Alooff the vulgar Constellations thick MILT. *P. L.* III. 577. Hence **Aloo·fness,** the state of being a. (*lit.* and *fig.*).

‖**Alope·cia.** ME. [L., a. Gr. ἀλωπηκία fox-mange, also baldness, f. ἀλώπηξ fox. *Med.* Baldness. Hence **Alo·pecist,** one who treats baldness.

Alorcinic (æ:lǫɹsi·nik), *a.* 1875. [f. AL(OE) + ORCIN + -IC.] *Chem.* In *Alorcinic Acid*, $C_9H_{10}O_3$, produced by melting potash upon aloes.

Alose (ălōu·s), *sb.* 1591. [a. Fr.:—L. *alosa.*] A fish (*Alosa communis*), commonly called ALLICE, or *Allice shad.*

†**Alo·se,** *v.* [a. OFr. *aloser, all-*, f. *à* + *los* :—L. **laudis* for *laus.*] To praise; also *refl.*; to report (in a bad sense). Only in ME.

‖**Alouatte** (ælu₁æ·t). 1778. [a. Fr. *alouate*, ? ad. native name.] The Howling Monkey, *Mycetes seniculus*, of S. America.

Aloud (ălau·d), *adv.* ME. [A. *prep.*[1] + LOUD *a.* Cf. *alow.*] In a loud voice; with great noise; loudly; also *fig.* (*colloq.*).

He wepte alowde *Gen.* xlv. 2.

†**Alou·t,** *v.* OE. [in form = OE. *lútian* to lurk, in sense *alútan* to stoop. The *a-* is A- *pref.* 1.] To stoop; to fall over –1480; *esp.* to bow in worship *to* –1500.

Alow (ălōu·), *adv.*[1] ME. [A *prep.*[1] + LOW *a.* Cf. *afar.*] Opp. to *aloft.* Below; downwards. Also *fig. Naut.* In or into the lower part of a vessel 1509.

Toss'd..aloft and then a. DRYDEN.

Alow (ălōu·, ălau·), *adv.*[2] *n. dial.* ME. [A *prep.*[1] + LOW.] Ablaze.

†**Alow·,** *v.*; also **all-.** 1530. [f. A- *pref.* II + LOW.] To lower. *lit.* and *fig.* –1576.

Alp[1] (ælp). 1551. [In pl. *Alps*, a. Fr. *Alpes*:—L. *Alpes*, ? = 'high' (cf. Gael. *alp*), or 'white' (cf. L. *albus*).] **1.** *pl.* The mountain range which separates France and Italy, etc. *sing.* A single peak. (In Switzerland the pasture-land on the mountain side.) **2.** Any high, *esp.* snow-capped, mountain 1598. Also *fig.*

2. O're many a Frozen, many a Fierie A. MILT. *P. L.* II. 620. *fig.* This adamantine a. of wedlock. MILT.

Alp[2] (ælp). ME. [?] A bullfinch.

†**Alp**[3]. ME. [var. of OE. *ylp.*] Elephant.

‖**Alp**[4]. 1836. [a. Ger.] A demon.

Alpaca (ælpæ·kă). 1792. [a. Sp., f. *al* Arab. art. + *paco* native name.] **1.** A Peruvian quadruped, a species of llama, having long fine woolly hair 1811. Also *attrib.* **2.** = alpaca wool 1792; also, the fabric made of it. Often *attrib.* 1838.

Alpenstock (æ·lpĕnstǫk). 1829. [mod. Ger.] A long staff, pointed with iron, used in climbing, *esp.* in the Alps.

†**Alpe·stral.** *rare.* 1664. [f. L. *alpestris* + -AL. Better *alpestrial.*] **A.** *adj.* Alpine. **B.** *sb.* An alpine species –1675.

Alpe·strian. 1861. [f. as prec. + -AN.] An Alpine climber.

Alpha (æ·lfă). ME. [a. L., a. Gr. ἄλφα, ad. Heb. *āleph*, 'ox', or 'leader', the first letter of the Heb. alphabet, formed from the hieroglyph of an ox's head.] **1.** Name of the letter A, *a*, in the Gr. alphabet 1626; hence, the beginning, *esp.* in **Alpha and Omega,** used of God. **2.** The first in numerical sequence. *esp.* **a.** *Astr.* The chief star in a constellation. **b.** *Chem.* The first of a series of isomerous modifications of a compound 1863. **c.** *Alpha rays* or *α-rays*, the first of three types of rays emitted by radio-active substances, consisting of positively-charged particles. Also *alpha* (or *α*) *particles* 1904.

1. I am alpha and oo, the bigynnyng and endyng, seith the Lord God WYCLIF *Rev.* i. 8. 2. Alpha and Beta Capricorni 1869. A. naphthol 1880.

Alphabet (æ·lfăbĕt), *sb.* 1513. [ad. L. *alphabetum*, f. *Alpha, Beta* = Ἄλφα, Βῆτα, the first two Greek letters as a name for all; cf. A B C.] **1.** *orig.* The set of letters used in writing the Gr. language; hence, any set of characters repr. the simple sounds in a language, or in speech. Also *attrib.* **2.** *fig.* The key to any study; the first rudiments 1588. †**3.** An index –1825; a series –1727.

2. I (of these) will wrest an A., And..learne to know thy meaning *Tit. A.* III. ii. 44. Hence **A·lphabet** *v.* (esp. in U.S.) = ALPHABETIZE 2. **A:lphabeta·rian,** one learning his a., a beginner; one who studies alphabets. †**A·lphabeta:ry** *a.* rudimentary; *sb.* = ALPHABETARIAN.

Alphabetic, -al (æ·lfăbe·tik, -ăl), *a.* 1642. [f. prec.; see -IC and -AL[1]. Cf. Fr. *alphabétique.*] **1.** Arranged in the order of the alphabet. **2.** Of, pertaining to, or by means of an alphabet 1736. †**3.** *fig.* Literal, strict. *rare.*

3. An alphabetical servility MILT. Hence **Alphabe·tically** *adv.*

Alphabetics (ælfăbe·tiks). 1865. [ALPHABETIC *a. pl.* used subst.] The science of the expression of spoken sounds by letters.

Alphabetism (æ·lfăbĕti:z'm). 1867. [f. ALPHABET + -ISM.] **1.** Symbolization of spoken sounds by means of an alphabet 1879. **2.** The use of certain letters of the alphabet as a signature, etc.

Alphabetize (æ·lfăbĕtəiz), *v.* 1867. [f. as prec. + -IZE.] **1.** To express by alphabetic letters; to reduce to writing. **2.** To arrange alphabetically (*mod.*).

Alphenic (ælfe·nik). 1657. [a. Fr., corrupt. f. Arab. *al* + Pers. *fānīd* refined sugar.] *Pharm.* White barley sugar.

†**Alphi·tomancy.** 1652. [ad. Fr. *alphitomantie*, f. Gr. ἀλφιτόμαντις.] Divination by barley-meal –1721.

A:lphitomo·rphous, *a.* 1879. [f. Gr. ἄλφιτον + μορφή + -OUS.] Like barley-meal in form; said of certain microscopic fungi.

Alphonsin (ælfǫ·nsin). 1751. [f. *Alphonsus* Ferrier, of Naples.] *Surg.* An instrument with three elastic branches, for extracting bullets from the body.

Alphonsine (ælfǫ·nsin), *a.* 1678. Of Alphonso the Wise, King of Castile; applied to astronomical tables invented by him, etc.

‖**Alphos** (æ·lfǫs). 1706. [L., a. Gr. ἀλφός.] *Path.* Non-contagious leprosy.

†**Alpieu·.** 1693. [a. Fr. *alpiou*, a. It. *al più.*] In the game of basset, a mark put on a card to indicate that the player doubles his stake after winning –1768.

Alpine (æ·lpəin), *a.* 1607. [ad. L. *alpinus.*] Of or pertaining to the Alps; lofty.

A. plants 1759, snows HOOK. An a. height GROTE.

Alpinist (æ·lpəinist). 1881. [a. Fr. *alpiniste.*] An alpine climber.

Alpist (æ·lpist). ? *Obs.* Also **alpia.** 1597. [a. Fr. *alpiste*, a. Sp.; ? a *Guanche* wd.] Bird-seed, *esp.* the seed of the Canary Grass (*Phalaris canariensis*).

‖**Alquifou** (ælkifū·). 1819. [Fr. *alquifoux*, ad. (ult.) Cat. *alcofol* ALCOHOL.] A lead ore, resembling antimony when broken, used by potters to make a green glaze.

Already (ǫlre·di), *adv.* ME. [ALL *adv.* + READY.] †**1.** *adj.* (*compl.*) Fully prepared –1509. **2.** *adv.* Beforehand; previously to some specified time; by this time, thus early.

2. It hath beene a. of olde time *Eccles.* i. 10. ¶ Sense 1 can still be traced in: The three Scotch regiments were a. in England MACAULAY.

Alright, frequent sp. of *all right* 1893.

†**Als.** Chiefly *north.* ME. An intermediate form between *alse* = *alswa* ALSO and AS, and used like them.

Alsatia (ælsē·ʃiă). 1688. [L. form of *El-sass*, i. e. foreign settlement, Fr. *Alsace.*] **1.** The province of Alsace, a debatable ground between France and Germany, whence **2.** Cant name for the precinct of White Friars in London, once a sanctuary for debtors and criminals; hence, an asylum for criminals. Hence **Alsatian** *a.* of or belonging to A.; *sb.* an inhabitant of A.; a debtor or criminal in sanctuary. *A.* (*wolf-dog*): see WOLF-DOG 3.

‖**Al segno** (al se·nyo). [It.] *Mus.* A direction: Go back to the sign 𝄋, and repeat.

Alsike (æ·lsik). 1852. [f. *Alsike* in Sweden.] A species of clover, *Trifolium hybridum.*

Alsinaceous (ælsinē·ʃəs), *a.* 1835. [f. L. *alsine*, a. Gr. ἀλσίνη + -ACEOUS.] *Bot.* Allied to, or like, chickweed.

Also (ǭ·lsoᵘ), *adv.* ME. [ALL *adv.* + SO (OE. *all* + *swá*). As relative, etc., shortened to As; as demonstrative weakened in force to *eke*, *too*, now the standard sense.] A. Demonstrative. †1. Wholly or quite so; in this or that very manner -ME.; in like manner, likewise -1710. 2. Further, too; replacing OE. *éac*, EKE. ME.

2. Not in Words onely, but in Woes a. 2 *Hen. IV*, II. iv. 459. Not only futile, but..a. injurious BUCKLE.

B. Correlative. *Obs.* replaced by As, So.

C. Relative and conjunctive. †As -1458; †with *subj.* As though ME.

†**Alsoo·n**, *adv.* ME. [= *als soon*, i. e. *as soon*.] 1. As soon (*as*). Cf. F. *aussitôt que*. -1579. 2. *absol.* At once. [Fr. *aussitôt*.] -ME.

Alstonite (ǭ·lstənəit). [f. *Alston* in Cumberland.] = BROMLITE.

†**Alt**[1]. 1623. [a. Fr. *alte*.] In *To make alt*: a halt -1664.

Alt[2] (ælt). 1535. [a. Pr. *alt*:—L. *altum*.] *Mus.* High tone; *spec.* in *In alt*: in the octave above the treble stave beginning with G. Also *fig.*: In an exalted frame of mind.

Altaian (ǣltē·iăn), *a.* and *sb.* 1874. [f. *Altai*; see -AN.] Belonging to the neighbourhood of the Altai Mountains. var. **Alta·ic** *a.*

Altaite (ǣltē·əit). [f. as prec. + -ITE.] *Min.* A tellurid of silver, or of lead and silver.

‖**Altaltissimo** (ɑltɑlti·simo). 1855. [It.] The very highest summit. BROWNING.

Altar (ǭ·ltəɹ). OE. [a. L. *altare*, f. *altus*. Also *aute·r*, a. OFr., till 16th c.] 1. A raised structure, with a plane top, on which to place or sacrifice offerings to a deity; also *fig.* 2. The raised structure consecrated to the celebration of the Eucharist ME.; the 'holy table' of the Eng. Prayer-book, which occupies the place of the altars removed after the Reformation 1549. 3. *fig.* A place consecrated to devotional exercises, as in *Family altar* 1693. 4. A metrical composition, written or printed in the form of an altar (*arch.*) 1680. 5. The constellation *Ara* 1556.

1. The altare of burnt offrynges *Ex.* xxxviii. 1. *fig.* The sacred a. of peace BURKE. 2. *High Altar*, the chief a. in a cathedral or church. It was not to be accounted an a. but the communion-table BRERETON. Receive this kingly sword brought now from the a. of God *Eng. Coron. Service* (where alone the word remains in authoritative use). *To lead a bride to the a.*, i. e. to the place where the marriage service in a church is concluded; whence 'hymeneal a.'

Comb.: **a.-bread**, that used in the Communion; **-cloth**, the linen cloth used at the Communion or the Mass; the silk frontal; **-fire**, the fire on an a.; *fig.* religious rite; **-front**, **-frontal**, **-facing**, a movable frame or hanging of silk, etc., placed in front of the a., the *antependium*; **-piece**, a painting or sculpture placed behind and over an a.; a reredos; **-plate**, the communion plate; **-pyx**, a pyx for holding the consecrated elements; **-rails**, those separating the sacrarium; **-screen**, the screen at the back of an a.; **-stone**, *esp.* the slab forming the top of an a.; the super-altar; **-table** = *a.-stone*; †**-thane**, a mass-priest; **-tomb**, a raised tomb resembling an a.; **-ways**, = *Altarwise*.

Hence **A·ltarage**. 1. The revenue from oblations at an a. 2. A fund to maintain an a. and a priest to say masses at it. **A·ltared** *ppl. a.* furnished with, or treated as, an a. **A·ltarist**, a vicar of a church; one who sees to what is necessary for the service of the altars. **A·ltarless** *a. poet.* **A·ltarlet**, a small a. **A·ltarwise** *adv.* after the manner, or in the position, of an a.

Altazimuth (ælt,æ·zimɒþ). 1860. [f. AL-T(ITUDE) + AZIMUTH.] An instrument for determining altitudes and azimuths.

Alter (ǭ·ltəɹ), *v.* ME. [a. Fr. *altérer*, ad. med.L. *alterare*, f. *alter*.] 1. To make otherwise or different in some respect, without changing the thing itself; to modify. 2. *intr.* (for *refl.*) To become otherwise, to undergo some change 1590. †3. To affect mentally -1674. †4. *intr.* To administer alterative medicines -1684.

1. To a. a decree *Mersh. V.* IV. i. 219, a design BURKE. 2. The law of the Medes and Persians which altereth not *Dan.* vi. 12. Hence **A·lterer**, he who or that which alters. **A·ltering** *vbl. sb.* alteration; *ppl. a.* making or becoming otherwise; †*Med.* = ALTERATIVE.

Alterable (ǭ·ltərăb'l), *a.* 1526. [a. Fr.; see prec.] †1. Liable to alter or vary -1696. 2. Capable of being altered 1574; †or of producing alteration -1594.

2. Laws..a. by Parliament 1744. Substances a. by fire PLAYFAIR. Hence **A:lterabi·lity** = ALTERABLENESS. **A·lterableness** *a.* the quality of being a. **A·lterably** *adv.*

Alterant (ǭ·ltərănt). 1626. [a. Fr.; see ALTER.] A. *adj.* Producing alteration. B. *sb.* Anything which alters 1750; *spec.* †an alterative medicine -1753.

†**A·lterate**, *ppl. a.* ME. [ad. late L. *alteratus*; see ALTER.] = ALTERED -1531.

†**A·lterate**, *v.* 1475. [f. prec.] var. of ALTER -1693.

Alteration (ǭltərē̆·ʃən). 1482. [a. Fr., ad. med.L. *alterationem*; see ALTER.] 1. The action of altering. 2. An altered condition 1532. †3. A distemper -1663. †4. *Mus.* Doubling the proper value of a note -1609.

1. He's full of a. *Lear* v. i. 3. 2. Ere long I might perceave Strange a. in me MILT. *P. L.* IX. 599.

Alterative (ǭ·ltərĕtiv). ME. [f. late L. *alterat-*, *alterare*; see ALTER, and cf. Fr. *altératif*.] A. *adj.* Tending to produce alteration; *esp.* of medicines which alter the processes of nutrition, and reduce them to healthy action 1605. B. *sb.* An alterative medicine or treatment ME.

Altercate (æ·ltəɹkeᵉt, ǭ·l-). 1530. [f. L. *altercat-*, *altercari*.] To dispute vehemently or angrily; to contend in words; to wrangle. Hence †**A·ltercative** *a.* scolding.

Altercation (æltəɹkē̆·ʃən, ǭ·l-). ME. [a. Fr., ad. L. *altercationem*; see prec.] 1. The action of altercating (see ALTERCATE); the conduct of a case by question and answer (L. *altercatio*) 1779. 2. A vehement or angry dispute, a wrangle 1552.

‖**Alter ego** (æ·ltər e·go). 1537. [L. (Cicero), 'other or second I'.] A second self; an intimate.

Alterity (ǣlte·rĭti, ǭl-). 1642. [a. Fr *altérité*.] The being different; otherness.

Altern (ǣltə̄·ɹn, ǭl-; æ·ltəɹn, ǭ·l-), *a.* 1644. [ad. L. *alternus*, every other.] 1. Alternate 1644. 2. *Cryst.* Having upper and lower faces corresponding in form, but alternate with each other in the position of their sides and angles. 3. quasi-*adv.* In turns 1677.

3. The greater to have rule by Day, The less by Night alterne MILT. *P. L.* VII. 348. *Altern base*: in oblique-angled triangles the difference or sum of the segments formed by a perpendicular falling from the vertex according as it cuts the base or base produced. Hence †**Alter·nacy**, alternate condition. †**Alte·rnal** *a.* = ALTERNATE.

Alternant (ǣltə̄·ɹnănt, ǭl-), *ppl. a.* 1640. [a. Fr., f. *alterner*, ad. L. *alternare*.] Alternating; *Min.* consisting of alternating layers (*mod.*). As *sb.* [sc. *quantity*.] 1882.

Alternate (ǣltə̄·ɹnĕt, ǭl-). 1513. [ad. L. *alternatus*, *alternare*.] A. *adj.* 1. Done or changed by turns, coming each after one of the other kind. 2. Said of a series or whole made up of such alternate members 1650. 3. Alternately taken; — about; every second 1697. 4. Alternately placed; occurring first on one side and then on the other of an axial line, *esp.* in *Bot.* of *leaves*, and in *Geom.* of *angles* 1570. 5. Reciprocal 1716. †6. Interchanged 1590. 7. quasi-*adv.* By turns 1712.

1. A. day and night (*mod.*). A. smiles and frowns, both insincere T. BROWN. 2. Smooth a. verse CRABBE. **Alternate generation**: *Biol.* genealogical succession by a. processes, as first by budding, and next by sexual reproduction; and so on. 3. He and I go on a. days, or *day about* (*mod.*). **Alternate proportion**: that obtained by comparing antecedent to antecedent and consequent to consequent 1660. 7. Wane and wax a. like the moon POPE.

B. *sb.* [the adj. used *absol.*] 1. That which alternates with something else; a vicissitude, an alternative 1718. 2. (U.S.) A second, or substitute (*mod.*).

Alternate (æ·ltəɹneᵉt, ǭl-), *v.* 1599. [f. prec.] 1. *trans.* To arrange, do, perform, or cause to occur, in alternation 1599. 2. *intr.* To succeed one another by turns, in time or space 1700. 3. *intr.* To consist of alternations. Const. *between*. 1823. 4. *intr.* To appear alternately *with* 1831.

1. Who..Hymns about the..Throne A. all night long MILT. *P. L.* v. 657. Hence **A·lterna:ting** *ppl. a.* (in senses 2, 3, 4); spec. *alternating current* (Electr.), a current which reverses its direction at regular intervals (abbrev. *A.C.* or *a.c.*). **A·lterna:tingly** *adv.*

Alternately (ǣltə̄·ɹnĕtli, ǭl-), *adv.* 1552. [f. as prec. + -LY[2].] 1. In alternate order; time about. 2. By taking the alternate terms 1695. 3. On each side in turn 1751.

Alternation (æltəɹnē̆·ʃən, ǭl-). 1611. [a. Fr., ad. L. *alternationem*; see ALTERNATE *a.*] 1. The action of two things succeeding each other by turns; alternate succession or occurrence. 2. Taking the members of a series alternately 1695. 3. Successive change in a scene or action 1633. 4. The state of being in alternate order 1830. 5. The doing of anything by two actors in turn; reading or singing antiphonally 1642. 6. *erron.* Permutation 1751.

1. The a. of pleasure and pain GOLDSM. **Alternation of generations** = *alternate generation*; see ALTERNATE *a.* 2 (quots.).

Alternative (ǣltə̄·ɹnĕtiv, ǭl-). 1590. [ad. med.L. *alternativus*, f. L. *alternat-*; see ALTERNATE *a.*] A. *adj.* 1. Stating or offering either of two things 1590. 2. Of two things: Such that one or the other may be chosen, the choice of either involving the rejection of the other. (Sometimes of more than two things.) 1861. Also (*ellipt.*) the other (of two) 1838. 3. Disjunctive 1753. †4. Alternate -1716.

2. I accept the statements as a. statements FREEMAN. The a. supposition 1838. 3. The a. conjunctions are either—or [etc.] BAIN.

B. *sb.* [the adj. used *absol.*] That which is alternative. 1. A statement or offer of two things of which either may be agreed to, but not both; permission to choose between two things 1624. ¶The only use in Johnson. 2. *loosely*, Either of two courses open to choose between. Cf. 'no other alternative'. 1814. *esp.* The remaining course. Cf. 'no alternative' (also = no choice; see 1). 1760. 3. Also, one of more than two courses which may be chosen 1848. †4. Alternation -1782.

1. The brief a. of Mahomet, death or the Koran 1853. 2. But two alternatives,.. Rome, and.. Atheism J. H. NEWMAN. There was no a. in my uncle Toby's wardrobe STERNE. 3. [I prefer] the fourth and last of these alternatives GLADSTONE. Hence **Alte·rnatively** *adv.* in a way that offers a choice between two; †by turns. †**Alte·rnativeness**, the quality of being a., or alternate.

Alte·rni-, comb. form of L. *alternus* (see ALTERN); = ALTERNATE or ALTERNATELY, as in *alterni-foliate*.

Alternity (ǣltə̄·ɹnĭti, ǫl-). *rare.* 1646. [f. L. *alternus* + -ITY. Cf. *eternity*.] †1. Alternation. 2. The counterchange of vowels, and correspondency of consonants, in certain Welsh rhymes 1856.

†**A·lternize**, *v.* [f. ALTERN + -IZE; cf. *modernize*.] To alternate. MDME. D'ARBLAY.

‖**Althæa** (ǣlþī·ă). 1669. [L., a. Gr. ἀλθαία marsh mallow, f. ἀλθεῖν to heal.] *Bot.* A genus of plants (N.O. *Malvaceæ*), including the Marsh Mallow and the Hollyhock; often extended to the genus *Hibiscus*.

‖**Althing** (ǭ·lþiŋ). [ON. *al-þing*.] The general assembly of Iceland. Hence **Althingman**, a member of the A.

Althionic (ælþi,ǫ·nik), *a.* 1858. [f. AL-(COHOL) + Gr. θεῖον.] *Chem.* In *Althionic Acid*, $C_2H_6SO_4$, produced by heating alcohol with an excess of sulphuric acid.

Although (ǭlðōᵘ·), *conj.* ME. [Now a var. of, but orig. two words and more emphatic than, THOUGH. See ALL, and THOUGH.] Even though, though..even; though; granting that, supposing that.

A. all shall be offended, yet will not I R.V. *Mark* xiv. 29.

Alti-, comb. form of L. *alto-*, *alta-*, high, and *alte* highly.

†**A·ltify**, *v.* ? *nonce-wd.* [f. L. *alti-*.] To make high. FULLER.

Alti·loquence. 1731. [f. L. *alti-* + *loquentem*.] Pompous language.

Altimeter (ǣlti·mĭtəɹ). 1847. [L., f. *alti-* + Gr. μέτρον.] An instrument for taking altitudes geometrically. Hence **Alti·metry**.

‖**Alti·ncar.** 1753. [a. (ult.) Arab.] = TINCAL.

Altisonant (ǣlti·sǒnănt), *a.* 1620. [f. L.

alti- + *sonantem.*] High-sounding, pompous, loud.

‖**Altissimo** (alti·ssimo). 1819. [It., superl. of *alto.*] *Mus.* In the phr. *In altissimo*: in the second octave above the treble stave, beginning with G.

†**Alti·tonant,** *a.* 1627. [ad. L. *altitonantem.*] Thundering from on high -1656.

Altitude (æ·ltitiud). ME. [ad. L. *altitudinem.*] 1. *gen.* Vertical extent or distance; the quality of being high or deep. 2. *Geom.* The height of a triangle, etc., measured by a perpendicular to the base or base produced 1570. 3. Height above a base (e. g. the ground, or sea-level); loftiness 1535. 4. *Astr.* Height expressed by angular distance above the horizon ME. 5. *sing.* A height; *pl.* high regions ME. 6. *fig.* High degree of any quality; high rank, power, etc. ME. †7. *fig.* in *pl.* Lofty mood, airs, phrases, etc. -1782.

1. The a. which thou hast perpendicularly fell *Lear* IV. vi. 53. 3. A toure..that in a. euened the stars 1583. 6. Euen in the a. of popedome 1596. 7. If we would see him in his altitudes NORTH. Hence **Altitu·dinal** *a.* relating to a. **A·ltitudina·rian** *a.* pertaining to the heights (of fancy, doctrine, etc.); *sb.* one given to lofty thoughts, etc.

†**A·lto,** *sb.*[1] 1591. [a. Sp., in phr. *alto hacer*, tr. Ger. *halt machen.*] A halt -1622.

Alto (a·lto), *sb.*[2] 1784. [a. It. (sc. *canto*).] *Mus.* A. *sb.* 1. The highest male voice, the counter-tenor; also, the musical part for it 1819. 2. The female voice of similar range, or the musical part sung by it, more strictly the *contralto* 1881. 3. One who has an alto voice 1784. 4. = ALT[2]. 1862. 5. A tenor violin [It.] 1833. B. *attrib.* as *adj.* Belonging to the a. 1845. **Alto clef**: the C clef when placed on the third line of the stave. **Alto-ripieno**: a tenor part, used only occ. in a grand chorus.

‖**Alto-** (a·lto), It. = high-, used in comb. 1. *Mus.*, as **a.-clarinet, -fagotto, -viola,** instruments like, but higher in pitch than, the clarinet, etc. 2. *Sculpt.* (See ALTO-RELIEVO.)

Altogether (ǫltŭge·ðəɹ). ME. [comb. of ALL and TOGETHER. Orig. a strengthening of *all*, but now advb.] A. *adj.* A strengthened form of ALL *a.* †1. The whole together; the total -1611; (*pl.* now *all together*) -1663. B. *adv.* [cf. ALL *adv.*] 1. Everything being included; in all respects; wholly, quite ME. 2. Uninterruptedly 1700. 3. **For altogether**: for all time to come, for good. Also without *for.* 1548. C. *sb.* A whole, a *tout ensemble* 1667.

B. 1. Thou wast a. born in sins *John* ix. 34. C. American fingers impart a finish and an a. (this is ..better than..*tout-ensemble*) 1865. Hence **Alto·getherness,** unity of being (*rare*).

Alto-relievo (a·lto rīlī·vo). Pl. **-os.** 1717. [It. *alto-rilievo*, occas. so spelt in Eng.] High relief; sculpture, etc., in which the figures project more than half their thickness from the background. Hence *concr.* A sculpture, etc., in high relief.

Altruism (æ·ltru,iz'm). 1853. [a. Fr. *altruisme*, formed by Comte on It. *altrui* (Fr. *autrui*) f. L. *alteri huic* 'to this other'; see -ISM.] Regard for others, as a principle of action; opp. to egoism or selfishness.

The religion of humanity, whose great moral principle is a. 1877. Hence **A·ltruist,** one who professes a. **Altrui·stic** *a.* of or pertaining to a.; benevolent. **Altrui·stically** *adv.*

†**A·ltumal,** *a.* ? *slang.* [f. L. *altum* the deep + -AL.] In *altumal cant*: maritime language.

Aludel (æ·liudel). 1559. [a. Fr., ad. Arab.] *Chem.* A pear-shaped pot of earthenware or glass, open at both ends, so that a series could be fitted one above another; used in sublimation.

Alum (æ·ləm). ME. [a. OFr.:—L. *alumen.*] A whitish transparent mineral salt, crystallizing in octahedrons, very astringent; chemically a double sulphate of aluminium potassium. In *Mod. Chem.* (with *pl.*) extended to include *Potash, Soda, Ammonia, Silver alum*, etc.; also *Iron, Manganese, Chrome, Chrome-ammonia alums*, etc.; and in *Min.* various native minerals which are chemically either alums proper, or pseudo-alums.

While chalk and a. and plaster are sold to the poor for bread TENNYSON.

Comb.: **a. cake,** a massive and porous sulphate of alumina, mixed with silica, made from fine clay; **a.-rock, -schist, -shale, -slate,** thin-bedded rocks, found in various formations, which yield a.; **-root,** the astringent roots of various plants; **-stone** = ALUNITE. Hence **A·lum** *v.* to treat with a.

‖**Alumbrado** (alumbrā·do). 1671. [Sp., f. *alumbrar*:—L. *alluminare.*] One of the Sp. *Illuminati* or Perfectionists of the 16th c.; hence, any one claiming illumination.

Alumian (ăliū·miăn). [mod. f. ALUMINA.] *Min.* A white sulphate of aluminium.

Alumina (ăliū·mină). 1790. [mod.L., f. L. *alumen*; cf. *soda*, etc., and Fr. *alumine.*] One of the earths; the only oxide (Al_2O_3) of Aluminium, the basis of alum, the chief constituent of all clays, and found crystallized as the sapphire. Hence **Alu·minate** *sb.* a compound of alumina with one of the stronger bases. **Alu·minate** *v.* to treat with alum.

Alumine (æ·liuməin). 1791. [a. F.] *Chem. arch.* = ALUMINA.

Aluminiferous (ăliūmini·fĕrəs), *a.* 1849. [f. L. *alumin-* ALUM + -(I)FEROUS.] Alum-bearing.

Aluminiform (ăliū·minifǭɹm, æ:liumi·ni-), *a.* 1864. [f. as prec. + -(I)FORM.] Having the form of an alum.

Aluminio- (æ:liumi·nio), comb. form of ALUMINIUM, as in *Aluminio-silicate.*

Aluminite (ăliū·minəit). 1868. [f. L. *alumin-* + -ITE.] *Min.* An opaque whitish native hydrosulphate of alumina; WEBSTERITE.

Aluminium (æ:liumi·niŏm). 1812. [var. and better form of ALUMINUM, ALUMIUM (Davy's names), f. ALUMINA; cf. *sodium*, etc.] A metal, white, sonorous, ductile, and malleable, very light, not readily oxidized or tarnished. In *Chem.* it has the symbol Al, is tetravalent, has *alumina* as its oxide, and the *alums* as its chief salts.

Comb. Aluminium-bronze, an alloy of a. and copper. Hence **Alumi·nic** *a.*

Aluminize (ăliū·minəiz), *v. rare.* 1857. To treat with alum; to alum.

Alumino- (ăliū·mino), comb. form of ALUMINA, ALUMINUM, implying the union of these with another element.

Alu·mino·se, *a.* 1879. [ad. L. *aluminosus.*] = ALUMINOUS. Hence **Alu:mino·sity** (*rare*).

Aluminous (ăliū·minəs), *a.* 1541. [a. Fr. *alumineux*, ad. L. *aluminosus*; see ALUM and -OUS.] Of the nature of or containing alum or alumina.

A. or clayey soils TRIMMER.

Alu·minum, U.S. var. of ALUMINIUM.

Alumish (æ·ləmiʃ), *a.* 1562. [f. ALUM.] Somewhat like alum. var. †**Alu·minish.**

†**Alu·mium**; see ALUMINIUM.

Alumniate (ălɒ·mni,ĕt). *rare.* 1879. [irreg. f. ALUMNUS; cf. *noviciate.*] The period of pupilage.

‖**Alumnus** (ălɒ·mnɒ̆s). Pl. **-i.** 1645. [L., = a foster-child; f. *alere.*] The nurseling or pupil of any school, university, etc.

Aluni·ferous, *a.* 1879. [f. Fr. *alunifère*; see -OUS.] = ALUMINIFEROUS.

Alunite (æ·liunəit). 1868. [f. Fr. *alun.*] *Min.* A mineral, also called Alum-stone and Aluminilite, consisting of common alum together with normal hydrate of aluminium.

Alunogen (ăliū·nŏdʒĕn). 1868. [f. Fr. *alun* + -GEN 'producing'.] *Min.* A hydrous sulphate of alumina, occurring as a feathery efflorescence: also called *Keramohalite, hair-salt*, and *feather-alum.*

†**A·lure.** ME. [a. OFr., now *allure*, f. *aller.*] A place to walk in; *esp.* a passage behind the parapets of a castle, or round the roof of a church; a cloister -1851.

Alutaceous (æliutē·ʃəs), *a.* 1873. [f. L. *alutacius*, f. *aluta* soft leather + -OUS.] Of the quality or colour of tawed leather.

Alveary (æ·lvi,ări). 1580. [ad. L. *alvearium* a range of bee-hives, f. *alveus*; see -ARY.] 1. A bee-hive; a title given to an early polyglot Dictionary. 2. *Anat.* The hollow of the outer ear, where the wax is found 1719.

Alveated (æ·lvi,e'tĕd), *ppl. a.* 1623. [ad. L. *alveatus.*] Hollow like a hive, vaulted, or trenched.

Alveolar (ælvī·ŏlăɹ, æ·lviŏlăɹ), *a.* 1799. [f. L. *alveolus*, a hollow, dim. of *alveus* + -AR.] 1. Of or pertaining to the sockets of the teeth, or to that part of the upper jaw, the *alveolar arch*, in which the teeth are placed. 2. Socket-shaped 1858. 3. *sb.* The alveolar processes of the maxillary bone, in which the teeth are fixed 1874.

1. The English *t* and *d* are not strictly *dental*, they are *a.* (*mod.*). var. **Alve·olary.** Hence **A·lveola·riform** *a.* shaped like cells in a honey-comb.

Alveolo- (ælvī·ŏlo), comb. form of ALVEOLUS: Of or pertaining to the sockets of the teeth or the alveolar arch, as in **alveolo-condylean plane,** that bounded by the centre of the upper alveolar arch and the base of the occipital condyles.

‖**Alveolus** (ælvī·ŏlɒ̆s). Pl. **-i.** 1706. [L., dim. of *alveus.*] A small cavity; *hence* **a.** the socket of a tooth; **b.** the cell of a honey-comb; **c.** the conical chamber of a Belemnite, or the conical body found in it. var. **A·lveole.** Hence **Alve·olate** *a.* honey-combed; pitted with small cavities. **Alve·oliform** *a.* celled like a honey-comb. **Alve·olite,** a fossil Zoophyte found in the chalk.

‖**A·lveus.** 1695. [L.] The channel of a river; the trough of the sea.

Alvine (æ·lvəin), *a.* 1754. [ad. L. *alvinus.*] Pertaining to the abdomen or its contents.

Alway (ǭ·lwe', *arch.* ǭ·lwē·), *adv.* OE. [orig. two words, in the acc. of space = *all the way*, but soon transferred to time also. Now *arch.* and *poet.*; repl. in prose by ALWAYS.] 1. Throughout all time. 2. = ALWAYS 1. ME. †3. = ALWAYS 3. -1475.

Always (ǭ·lwe'z, -wĕz), *adv.* ME. [gen. case of *all way*, prob. distrib. 'at every time'. Cf. *sometimes* and *some time.* The distinction is now lost.] 1. At all times; opp. to *sometimes*, etc. 2. = ALWAY 1; through all time; opp. to *for a time* ME. 3. Still, nevertheless, however; now, in any or every circumstance, anyway.

1. Man never is, but a. to be blest POPE *Ess. Man* I. 92. 2. To be..Had in remembrance a. with delight MILT. *P. L.* III. 704.

Aly (ē·li), *a.*; also **aley.** 1624. [f. ALE.] Of or like ale.

†**Aly·pum, -us.** 1611. [a. Gr. ἄλυπον.] An unknown plant of anodyne properties -1621.

Alyssum (ăli·sɒ̆m). 1551. [mod.L. for *alysson*, a. Gr., f. ἀ priv. + λύσσα madness.] *Bot.* 1. A genus of Cruciferous plants, including *A. Saxatile* or Gold-dust. 2. *pop.* **Sweet Alyssum** (or *A·lison*), (*Königa maritima*), A small cruciferous plant with white flowers.

Am (æm, əm, 'm, m), *v.*, 1st sing. pres. ind. of vb. BE. *Am, art, is, are*, are the only survivals in Eng. of the original substantive vb. (Skr. *as-*, Gr. ἐσ-, L. *es-*, Goth. *is-, i-*). See BE.

Amability (æmăbi·lĭti). 1604. [ad. L. *amabilitas*, f. *amabilis.* Usefully distinct from AMIABILITY.] Lovableness.

†**A·mable, -ile,** *a.* ME. [a. OFr.:—L. *amabilem.*] Lovely, lovable -1677.

Amacra·tic, *a.* [improp. f. Gr. ἅμα + κράτος.] Uniting actinic rays into one focus, as an *amacratic lens.*

‖**Amadavat** (æ:mădăvæ·t). Also **ava-.** 1777. [Indian.] An Indian song-bird (*Estrilda amandava*), brown in colour with white spots.

Amadelphous (æmăde·lfəs), *a.* 1879. [f. Gr. ἅμα + ἀδελφός brother + -OUS.] Gregarious.

Amadou (æ·mădū). 1815. [ad. F. *amadou*, a. Prov. *amadou*, prop. lover, the fungus being so named from its inflammability.] Tinder, touchwood, punk (the sterile part of the fruit body of the fungus *Fomes fomentarius*).

‖**Amah** (ā·mă). 1839. [Anglo-Ind. a. Pg. *ama.*] A wet-nurse.

Amain (ămē·n), *adv.* 1540. [f. A *prep.*[1] + MAIN, after *afoot*, etc.] 1. *lit.* In, or with, full force; vehemently, violently; in full force of numbers 1601. 2. At full speed 1563; without delay 1600. 3. Exceedingly. (Cf. L. *valde*.) 1587.

1. The blood gushed out a. HOOD. 2. They fled a. 1587. Housewives left a. Their broken tasks 1821. 3. They..thrive in wealth a. MILT. *P. R.* II. 429.

†**Amai·n(e**, *v.* 1553. [a. Fr. *amener*.] 1. To lower (*esp.* the topsail) –1627; *fig.* to abate 1578. 2. *intr.* To lower the topsail in sign of yielding; to yield 1593. 3. To conduct. (Cf. Fr. *amenée*.) *rare.* 1553.

Amalgam (ămæ·lgăm), *sb.* 1471. [? a. Fr. *amalgame*, med.L. *amalgama*, ? a perversion of L. *malagma*, a. Gr., f. μαλάσσειν.] 1. *orig.* A soft mass formed *esp.* by combination with mercury; *hence now*, any mercurial alloy. 2. By extension, An intimate mixture of any two or more substances 1626. 3. *fig.* A complete combination of various elements. Also *attrib.* 1790. 4. An alloy 1840.

1. **Native amalgam**, an a. of mercury with silver or gold, found in Columbia, etc. 2. The Body of the Wood will [become] a kind of Amalgama BACON *Sylva* § 99. 3. Custom is an a. of sense and folly HONE. 4. Quackery—a necessary .. a. for truth CARLYLE. Hence †**Ama·lgamize** *v.* to soften, *esp.* with mercury.

Ama·lgam, *v. arch.* ME. [a. Fr. *amalgamer*; see prec. Repl. by AMALGAMATE *v.*] †1. = AMALGAMATE 1, 2. 2. *trans.* To coat with amalgam 1789. 3. = AMALGAMATE 4. 1827. Hence **Ama·lgamable** *a.*

Amalgamate (ămæ·lgămĕt), *ppl. a.* 1642. [? ad. med.L. **amalgamatus*, *amalgamare*; see AMALGAM *sb.* Used as pa. pple. of AMALGAMATE *v.*] 1. Combined or alloyed 1642. 2. Coalesced; *spec.* of languages 1849.

Amalgamate (ămæ·lgămeit), *v.* 1660. [f. prec.] 1. To soften by combining with mercury; *hence*, to alloy with mercury. 2. *intr.* To combine with mercury 1751. 3. To mix so as to form a uniform compound 1821. 4. *fig.* To combine (two elements, or one *with* another) in a homogeneous whole. *trans.* 1802. *intr.* 1797.

3. Wayland..amalgamated the drugs SCOTT. 4. [The Romans] were ordained..to a. the materials of Christendom COLERIDGE. Two banks of issue had amalgamated CRUMP. Hence **Ama·lgamative** *a.* tending to or marked by amalgamation.

Amalgamation (ămæ:lgamē¹·ʃən). 1612. [f. prec.; see -ATION.] 1. The action of amalgamating (see AMALGAMATE *v.* 1). 2. *fig.* The action of combining into one uniform whole 1775. 3. The state of being united with mercury; hence, a mixture of metals generally 1753. 4. *fig.* A homogeneous union 1828.

2. The a. of the Saxons and Normans DE LOLME. 3. An a. of copper with tin 1874. 4. A close a. between ecclesiastical and civil authority GLADSTONE.

Amalgamator (ămæ·lgămeⁱtəɹ). Occ. **-er.** 1838. [f. the vb.] One who or that which amalgamates: *spec.* **a.** One who amalgamates public companies; **b.** The apparatus used for extracting silver from its ore by combining it with mercury.

Ama·lic, *a.* 1863. [f. Gr. ἀμαλός weak.] *Chem.* In *Amalic Acid*: a product of the decomposition of caffeine by chlorine, having a feeble acid reaction.

Amandin(e (ămæ·ndin). 1845. [a. Fr., f. *amande* + -IN(E.] **a.** The albumen contained in sweet almonds. **b.** A kind of cold cream made from it.

Amanitine (æmănəi·təin). 1847. [f. Gr. ἀμανῖται a sort of fungi + -INE.] The active narcotic principle of poisonous fungi.

Amanuensis (ămæ:niu͵e·nsis). Pl. **-es** (*iz*). 1619. [L. adj. used subst., f. phr. *a manu*, short for *servus a manu* + *-ensis* belonging to.] One who copies or writes from dictation.

‖**Amaracus** (ămæ·răkŏs). ME. [L., a. Gr. ἀμάρακος.] An aromatic plant, the Dittany of Crete (*Origanum dictamnus*).

Amarant(h (æ·mărænt, -ænþ). 1551. [a. Fr. *amarante*, f. L. *amarantus*, a. Gr. ἀμάραντος, prop. adj., f. ἀ not + *-μαραντος, f. μαραίνειν to fade. Also written *amaranthus*, as if + Gr. ἄνθος. Long used in L. form; *amarant* (now usu. *amaranth*) being at first poet.] 1. An imaginary flower that never fades. Also *attrib.* 1616. 2. A genus of plants (*Amarantus*, N.O. *Amarantaceæ*) with coloured foliage, including Prince's Feather and Love-lies-bleeding 1551. 3. A purple colour 1690.

1. Thir Crowns inwove with Amarant and Gold, Immortal Amarant MILT. *P. L.* III. 353. 2. Sad Amaranthus, in whose purple gore Me seemes I see Amintas wretched fate SPENSER *F. Q.* III. vi. 45. **Globe Amaranth**: *Gomphrena globosa*. Hence **A:marant(h)a·ceous** *a.* of the nature of a. **Amara·nt(h)ad**, an ally of the genus A. **Amara·nt(h)oid** *a.* and *sb.* resembling, or an ally of, a.

Amarant(h)ine (æmăræ·ntin, -þin), *a.*; amarantin MILT. 1667. [f. prec.] 1. Of or pertaining to amarant(h). 2. Fadeless, immortal 1781. 3. Amarant(h-coloured 1874.

1. Amarantin Shade MILT. *P. L.* XI. 78. 2. A. joys COWPER. 3. A. glosses HARDY.

Amarine (ămē°·rəin), *sb.* 1839. [f. L. *amarus*.] *Chem.* A bitter vegetable principle; *spec.* the alkaloid ($C_{21}H_{18}N_2$) formed by the action of ammonia on essence of bitter almonds, also called BENZOLINE.

†**Ama·ritude.** 1490. [a. OFr.:—L. *amaritudo*.] Bitterness –1666.

†**Ama·rvel**, *v.* ME. [a. OFr. *amerveillier*, earlier *ém-*, f. *es-*:—L. *ex* + *merveiller*, f. *merveille*:—L. *mirabilia*. Later ADMERVEYLLE, with *a-* erron. refash. as *ad-*.] To strike with wonder; usu. in pass. –1530.

Amaryllid (æmări·lid). 1830. [a. L. *amaryllid-*; see next.] *Bot.* A plant of the same order as the genus *Amaryllis*. Hence **Amary:llida·ceous** *a.* of or pertaining to the *Amaryllideæ*, a Nat. Ord. including Amaryllis, Narciss, and Snowdrop; var. **A:maryl·li·deous.**

‖**Amaryllis** (æmări·lis). 1794. [L., a. Gr. Ἀμαρυλλίς, name of a country-girl in Theocritus, etc.] *Bot.* A genus of bulbous plants, typical of the N.O. *Amaryllidaceæ*; applied also to allied genera.

Here and there, on sandy beaches A milky-bell'd a. blew TENNYSON.

Amass (ămæ·s), *v.* 1481. [a. Fr. *amasser*, f. *à* + *masser*, f. *masse*.] 1. *gen.* To collect into a mass or masses, pile up 1594; *intr.* to assemble (*arch.*) 1572. 2. *esp.* To accumulate as one's own. (The earliest, now the usual sense.) 1481.

1. To a. [things] into one 1644, balls 1694. 2. To a. grete tresours CAXTON, stores of knowledge 1712, gold POPE, materials SMILES. Hence **Ama·ssable** *a. rare.* **Ama·sser**, one who amasses.

Amassment (ămæ·smĕnt). 1665. [a. OFr. *amassement*; see prec.] The action or result of amassing.

That famous a. of troops KINGLAKE.

Ama·te, *v.*¹ *Obs.* or *arch.* ME. [a. OFr. *amater*, f. *à* + *mater*, f. *mat* dejected.] To cast down.

A half-blown flow'ret which cold blasts a. KEATS.

†**Ama·te**, *v.*² 1596. [f. A- *pref.* + MATE *v.*] To be a mate to; to equal –1642.

Amateur (æmătə̄·ɹ, æ·mătiū°ɹ). 1784. [a. Fr., ad. L. *amatorem*. Occ. pronounced as Fr.; often with (ə̄) for Fr. *eu*; also *-iū°·ɹ*.] 1. One who loves, is fond *of*, or has a taste for, anything. 2. One who cultivates anything as a pastime; hence occas. = dabbler 1803. 3. *attrib.* Done by amateurs 1848.

1. Amateurs of a superficial philosophy CHALMERS. 2. Not amateurs..but professional men DE QUINCEY. 3. A. theatricals 1849. A. running records 1882. Hence **Amateu·rish** *a.* suggesting an a., having the faults of a. work. **Amateu·rish-ly** *adv.*, **-ness.** **A·mateurism**, the characteristic practice of an a. **A·mateurship**, the quality or character of an a.

Amative (æ·mătiv), *a.* 1636. [f. L. *amat-*, *amare*.] Disposed to loving. Hence **A·mativeness** *Phren.* propensity to love, or sexual passions 1815.

Amatol (æ·mătǫl). 1918. A high explosive compounded of *am*monium nitrate and trinitro*tol*uene.

Amatorial (æmătō°·riăl), *a.* 1603. [f. L. *amatorius*.] 1. Of or pertaining to a lover, or love-making. 2. Epithet of the oblique muscles of the eye, which assist in *ogling* 1751.

Amatory (æ·mătəri). 1599. [ad. L. *amatorius*.] **A.** *adj.* Of or pertaining to a lover, love-making, or sexual love. **B.** *sb.* A philtre 1635.

A. An a. poem 1772, poet 1846, sentiment THACKERAY. Hence †**Amato·rious** *a.*

‖**Amaurosis** (æmǫrōᵘ·sis). 1657. [mod.L. a. Gr. ἀμαύρωσις, f. ἀμαυρόειν.] *Med.* Partial or total loss of sight, from disease of the optic nerve, usu. without external change in the eye.

An A. or Gutta Serena 1704. Hence **Amauro·tic** *a.* affected with a.

†**Amay·**, *v.* ME. [a. ONFr. *amaier* = OFr. *esmaier*, f. *es-*:—L. *ex* + *-magare*; see DISMAY.] To dismay –1485.

Amaze (ămē¹·z), *v.* ME. [OE. *āmasian*: cf. MAZE.] †1. To craze –1642; to perplex –1642; to fill with panic –1706. 2. To overwhelm with wonder; to astound or greatly astonish 1592; *intr.* to be astounded (*arch.*) 1589; †*refl.* to bewilder oneself –1678.

2. Crystal eyne, Whose full perfection all the world amazes *Ven. & Ad.* 634. I amaze me MILT.

Amaze (ămē¹·z), *sb.* Also *a maze.* ME. [f. the vb.] †1. = AMAZEMENT †1. 2. Extreme wonder. (Chiefly poet.) 1579.

2. With pleasure and a., I stood transported ADDISON. Hence †**Ama·zeful** *a.* amazing; amazed.

Amazed (ămē¹·zd), *ppl. a.* [f. AMAZE *v.*] In the senses of the vb.

I am a. at your passionate words *Mids. N.* III. ii. 220. Hence **Ama·zedly** *adv.* **Ama·zedness.**

Amazement (ămē¹·zmĕnt). 1595. [f. as prec.] *orig.* Loss of one's wits. †1. Mental stupefaction, frenzy –1746; bewilderment –1722; consternation –1756. 2. Overwhelming wonder 1602.

1. Behold, destraction, frenzie, and a., Like witlesse Antickes, one another meete *Tr. & Cr.* v. iii. 85. This A. of the Magistrates DE FOE. Amazements and panick terrors MILT. 2. Wonder and a. *Acts* iii. 10.

†**Amazia** (ămē¹·ziă). 1874. [mod.L., repr. Gr. *ἀμαζία, f. ἀ + μαζός breast.] *Med.* Non-development of the breasts in a female.

Amazing (ămē¹·ziŋ). 1530. [f. the vb.] 1. *vbl. sb.* The action of causing AMAZEMENT. †2. *ppl. a.* Causing AMAZEMENT –1781. 3. Astounding, great beyond expectation 1704. 4. quasi-*adv.* Wonderfully 1824.

2. Let thy blowes.. Fall like a. thunder on the Caske Of thy amaz'd, pernicious enemy SHAKS. 3. A. generosity 1704. An a. assertion BURKE. Hence **Ama·zingly** *adv.* (Now often hyperbol. in colloq. use for: Very.)

Amazon (æ·măzǫn). Pl. **-ons**; also 4–7 **-ones.** In 6–7 *amā·zon.* ME. [a. L., a. Gr. Ἀμαζών, as if f. ἀ + μαζός a breast, but?] 1. *pl.* A race of female warriors alleged to exist in Scythia. 2. Hence, A female warrior (*lit.* and *fig.*) 1578. 3. *transf.* A strong, tall, or masculine woman 1758.

2. Belike she minds to play the A. 3 *Hen. VI*, IV. i. 106.

Comb.: **a.-ant**, a species of red ant, of which the neuters capture and enslave the young of other species; also, the neuters alone; **-stone**, a bright verdigris-green variety of orthoclase, worn as an amulet.

Amazonian (æmăzōᵘ·niăn), *a.* 1594. [f. L. *amazonius*.] 1. Of or pertaining to the Amazons; warlike, or masculine, as a woman 1594. 2. Of the river Amazon, or its basin 1863. 3. *sb.* An Amazon (fabulous) 1704.

Amazonite (æ·măzǫnəit). 1601. [f. AMAZON.] †1. An Amazon –1630. 2. *Min.* = AMAZON-STONE.

Ambage (æ·mbĕdʒ). Pl. **ambages** (æ·mbĕdʒĕz, *or as L.* æmbē¹·dʒīz). ME. [a. Fr. *ambages*, a. L. *ambages*, f. *amb-* + *agere*. Naturalized in 16th c., but latterly treated as L.] I. Of language (from Fr.; pron. *a·mbages*; with *sing.*). 1. Equivocation, deceitful ambiguities (*arch.*). †2. Obscure language –1713; circumlocutions –1678. †3. *Rhet.* (in *sing.*) Periphrasis 1589.

1. Ambages, and treacherous Counsels NORTH.

II. Of paths, ways. [From, or as L. *ambā·ges*.] 1. Circuitous paths, windings (*arch.*) 1615; *fig.* indirect proceedings; delaying practices 1546. †2. Dark ways of action. (Cf. Livy I. 56.) –1797.

1. *fig.* He shall, by Ambages of diets, bathings, etc. prolong life BACON. Hence **Ambagio·sity**, circuitousness (*rare*). **Amba·gious** *a.* full of ambages: **a.** circumlocutory; **b.** circuitous. **Amba·giously** *adv.* **Amba·giousness**, the quality of being ambagious (*rare*). †**Amba·gitory** *a.* ambagious. (Badly coined by SCOTT.)

Ambassade, em- (æ·m-, e·mbăsā¹d). *Obs.* or *arch.* ME. [a. Fr.:—L. **ambactiata*, **ambactiare*, f. *ambactia*, f. *ambactus* a servant

(? vassal). Cf. AMBASSY, EMBASSY; also AMBASSIATE. In SHAKS. and subseq. *ambassa·de* or *a·mbassade.*] 1. = AMBASSY 1. 1450. 2. = AMBASSY 3. 1450. 3. = AMBASSY 2. 1560.

Ambassador, em- (ǣm-, ĕmbæ·sădəɹ). ME. [a. Fr. *ambassadeur*; see AMBASSADE. Of the variants *embassador*, with *embassy*, was common in 17–18th c., and is still used in U.S.] 1. An official messenger sent by or to a sovereign or public body; *esp.* a minister of high rank sent by one sovereign or state on a mission to another, an *A. Extraordinary*. 2. (= *Ordinary* or *Resident A.*, formerly *A. Leger.*) A minister of the highest rank who permanently represents his sovereign or country at a foreign court, and has a right to a personal interview with the foreign sovereign or chief magistrate 1603. 3. An appointed or official messenger (now only *fig.*) 1483. 4. *A. Plenipotentiary*: one with full power to sign treaties, and act for his sovereign 1603.

2. Intends you for his swift A., Where you shall be an everlasting Leiger *Meas. for M.* III. i. 58. 3. An Embassador of loue *Merch. V.* II. ix. 92. Hence **Amba·ssado·rial** *a.* of or pertaining to an a. **Amba·ssadorship,** the office, position, or function of an a.; var. †**Amba·ssadry.**

Ambassadress (ǣmbæ·sădrĕs). 1594. [f. prec.] 1. A female ambassador or messenger; var. **ambassadrix.** 2. The wife of an AMBASSADOR (*leger*) 2; var. †**amba·ssadrice.**

Ambassage, em- (æ·m-, e·mbăsĕdʒ). Also **imb-**. [Orig. *am-*, *emba·ssage*, but *e·m-* in SHAKS. Of Eng. formation, ? on OFr. *ambasse* (:—L. *ambactia*), or by taking *ambass-* as a vb.-stem; see -AGE. Usu. spelt EMBASSAGE.] †1. = AMBASSY 1. –1640. 2. = AMBASSY 2. 1548. 3. = AMBASSY 3. 1605. See also EMBASSAGE.

†**Amba·ssiate.** ME. [ad. med.L. *ambassiata*; see AMBASSADE.] 1. The business of an ambassador –1548. 2. An embassy –1580. 3. A single envoy –1535.

Ambassy, em- (æ·m-, e·mbăsi). 1588. [a. OFr. *ambassée* :—L. **ambactiata*, (not :—L. *ambactia*, whence OFr. *ambasse*); see AMBASSADE. Usu. spelt EMBASSY.] 1. The mission, function, or office of an ambassador 1600. 2. The message brought by an ambassador 1606. 3. A body of men sent as ambassadors; an ambassador and his suite or surroundings 1732.

‖**Ambe** (æ·mbi). 1711. [Gr. ἄμβη, Ion. for ἄμβων a projecting edge.] 1. *Surg.* An apparatus for reducing dislocations of the shoulder. 2. *Anat.* A superficial crest of a bone 1879.

Amber (æ·mbəɹ), *sb.*¹ ME. [a. Fr. *ambre*, a. Arab. *'anbar*, 'ambergris'.] †1. *orig.* = AMBERGRIS (*greece of amber, gris, gray amber*. –1718. Also *attrib.* †2. **White Amber:** Spermaceti –1611. 3. A yellowish fossil resin, used for ornaments, etc., which when rubbed becomes *electric* (f. ἤλεκτρον its Gr. name). †4. An amulet made of a. –1691. 5. *fig.* Amber-coloured 1735. 6. An alloy of four parts of gold with one of silver (L. *electrum*, Gr. ἤλεκτρον) ME. 7. = LIQUIDAMBAR 1569. 8. (*local*) St. John's-wort. 9. *adj.* [cf. Fr. *ambré.*] Amber-coloured.

1. [Perfuming] the air with a., aloes-wood, etc. 1718. 3. Thicke A., or Plum-Tree Gumme *Haml.* II. ii. 200. Like a fly in a. 1847. †*Spirit of amber*: succinic acid. 6. Out of the midst thereof as the colour of a. [WYCLIF electre] *Ezek.* i. 4. 9. Robed in flames and a. light MILT. *L'Alleg.* 61.

Comb.: **a. Fauna,** the animals whose remains are found in a.; **a. Flora,** the plants found in a.; **a.-forest,** the primeval forest the trees of which yielded a.; **-pear,** an AMBRETTE; **-seed,** the seeds of *Abelmoschus moschatus*, musk-seed, Ambrette, used as a perfume; **-tree,** a name of the genus *Anthospermum*; **-varnish,** copal varnish. Hence **A·mbering** *vbl. sb.* giving a scent of a. **A·mbery** *a.* of the nature or colour of a.

†**A·mber,** *sb.*² OE. [perh. ad. L. *amphora*, assim. to Teut.] A dry measure of four bushels.

Amber, *sb.*³, obs. f. AMBRY.

Amber (æ·mbəɹ), *v. rare.* 1616. [f. the sb.] 1. To perfume with ambergris 1616. 2. To make amber-coloured 1809. 3. To preserve in amber 1882.

Amber-days; see EMBER-DAYS.

Ambergris (æ·mbəɹgrīs). 1481. [a. Fr. *ambre gris*. Orig. called AMBER in Eng.; now used for *amber* proper, as opp. to *resin*, or succin: the *gris* was pop. rationalized as *grease*, *Greece*, etc.] A wax-like substance of ashy colour, found floating in tropical seas, and as a morbid secretion in the intestines of the sperm-whale. Used in perfumery, and formerly in cookery.

In pastry built, or from the spit, or boiled, Gris-amber-steam'd MILT. *P. R.* II. 341. Praise is like a.; a little whiff of it..is very agreeable POPE.

Ambidexter (æ:mbide·kstəɹ). 1532. [a. med.L., f. *amb(i)-* + *dexter*. In 17th c. *ambodexter.*] A. *adj.* 1. *lit.* Right-handed on both sides, able to use both hands equally well 1646. 2. Double-dealing 1613. 3. Two-sided 1806.

1. Only man is a. SIR T. BROWNE. 2. A. Lawyers 1705. 3. An a. controversialist 1839.

B. *sb.* 1. [sc. *man.*] Also *fig.* 1598. 2. *Law.* One who takes money on both sides 1532. 3. A double-dealer 1555.

3. Ambidexters, or..such as can shift on both sides 1555. Hence **A:mbidexte·rity,** the power of using both hands alike; manysided resourcefulness; double-dealing. **A:mbide·xtral** *a.* belonging to both sides.

Ambidext(e)rous (æ:mbide·kstrəs), *a.* 1646. [f. med.L. *ambidexter* + -OUS.] = AMBIDEXTER. Hence **A:mbide·xt(e)rously** *adv.* **A:mbide·xtrousness.**

Ambient (æ·mbiĕnt). 1596. [ad. L. *ambientem*, *ambire.*] A. *adj.* †1. Revolving –1620. 2. Circling about (something). *rare.* 1655. 3. Lying round, surrounding, encompassing 1596; *esp.* as a fluid; circumfused 1605. ¶ Misused for 'limpid', of the air.

1. A. years CHAPMAN. 2. A. Winds, That course about the quarters of the globe DISRAELI. 3. Opening to the a. light MILT. *P. L.* VI. 481.

B. *sb.* [The adj. used *absol.*] †1. A canvasser 1649. 2. An encompassing circle or sphere 1624. 3. *Astrol.* The ambient air or sky 1686.

Ambigenal (ǣmbi·dʒĕnal), *a.* 1727. [f. (by Newton) L. *ambigenus* + -AL¹.] Of two kinds, hybrid. (Used to describe a kind of hyperbola.)

Ambigenous (ǣmbi·dʒĕnəs), *a.* 1850. [f. as prec.] Of two kinds; *spec.* applied to a multifoliate calyx, externally leaf-like and internally petaloid.

†**Ambigu.** 1688. [a. Fr.: prop. adj. = AMBIGUOUS.] A banquet at which a medley of dishes are set on together –1753.

Ambiguity (æmbigiū·ĭti). ME. [a. Fr. *ambiguité*, ad. med.L. *ambiguitatem*; see AMBIGUOUS.] †1. Subjectively: Hesitation, doubt –1590; *concr.* an uncertainty –1658. 2. Objectively: Double or dubious meaning ME.; *concr.* an equivocal expression 1591.

2. To clear the..laws..from a. MACAULAY. Without ambages or ambiguities DRYDEN.

Ambiguous (ǣmbi·giuˌəs), *a.* 1528. [f. L. *ambiguus*, f. *ambigere*, f. *amb-* + *agere* + -OUS.] I. Objectively. 1. Doubtful; not clearly defined 1528. 2. Open to more than one interpretation; equivocal. (The common use.) 1532. 3. Of doubtful position or classification 1603.

1. A. shadows 1800, distances RUSKIN. 2. Answers ..dark, A., and with double sense deluding MILT. *P. R.* I. 435. 3. Mungrell and a. shapes FLORIO.

II. Subjectively. †1. Hesitating, doubtful –1649. 2. Of doubtful issue 1612; hence, not to be trusted 1756. 3. Of oracles, etc.: Using words of doubtful or double meaning 1566.

1. Doubtfull and a. in all thir doings MILT. 2. A. paths 1850. 3. Antinous .. thus a. spoke POPE. Hence **Ambi·guously** *adv.* **Ambi·guousness.**

Ambilævous, -levous (æ:mbilī·vəs), *a. rare.* 1646. [f. L. *amb(i)-* + *lævus* + -OUS.] Left-handed on both sides; clumsy.

Ambi·parous, *a.* 1879. [f. L. *amb(i)-* + *-parus.*] *Bot.* Of a bud: Containing both flowers and leaves.

Ambit (æ·mbit). ME. [ad. L. *ambitus.*] 1. A circuit, compass, or circumference 1597; *esp.* a space round a house, castle, etc., the liberties, verge. 2. The limits of a district 1845; *fig.* the compass of actions, words, etc. 1691.

2. The a. of the manor DIGBY, of legislation 1882.

Ambition (ǣmbi·ʃən), *sb.* ME. [a. Fr., ad. L. *ambitionem*, f. *ambire*; cf. AMBIT.] 1. The eager or inordinate desire of honour or preferment. †2. Ostentation; pride of state –1631. 3. A strong desire *of*, (occ. *for*), *to be* or *do* anything creditable, etc. 1607; the object of such a desire 1602. †4. Canvassing. (L. *ambitio.*) 1531.

1. Cromwel, I charge thee, fling away A., By that sinne fell the Angels SHAKS. 3. The pitiful a. of possessing..more acres BURKE. Their a. is in heaven RUSKIN. 4. I..used no a. to commend my deeds MILT. *Sams.* 246. Hence **Ambi·tionist,** one ruled by a. **Ambi·tionless** *a.*

Ambition (ǣmbi·ʃən), *v.* 1628. [a. Fr. *ambitionner*; cf. *raisonner.*] †1. *trans.* To move to ambition. 2. To desire strongly. (Const. *simple obj.*, *inf.*, or *cl.*) 1664.

Ambitious (ǣmbi·ʃəs), *a.* ME. [ad. Fr. *ambitieux*; see AMBITION and -OUS.] 1. Full of AMBITION (sense 1). 2. Strongly desirous *of*, †*for*, *to be*, or *do* 1513. 3. *fig.* As if aspiring; swelling, towering 1601. 4. Of works of art, etc.: Aspiring or pretentious 1751. †5. quasi-*sb.* [sc. *man.*] –1563.

1. With a. aim Against the Throne and Monarchy of God MILT. *P. L.* I. 41. 2. I am a. for a motley coat *A. Y. L.* II. vii. 43. A. of long words 1855. 3. I haue seene Th'a. Ocean swell *Jul. C.* I. iii. 7. 4. An a. attempt ended in failure (*mod.*). Hence **Ambi·tious-ly** *adv.* in an a. manner; **-ness.**

Amble (æ·mb'l), *v.* ME. [a. Fr. *ambler* :—L. *ambulare.*] 1. *intr.* Of horses, etc.: To move by lifting the two feet on one side together, alternately with the two feet on the other; hence, to move at a smooth or easy pace. 2. To ride at an easy pace ME. 3. Hence, to walk, dance, etc., like an ambling horse, or *fig.* of any easy motion 1596.

1. I will tell you who time ambles withal *A. Y. L.* III. ii. 328. [The mare] ambles most 1690. 2. To a. the circuit with the Judges WYCHERLEY. 3. The skipping King, hee ambled vp and downe 1 *Hen. IV*, III. ii. 60. How fast your thoughts a. H. WALPOLE. Hence **A·mbler,** a horse, mule, etc., or person that ambles. **A·mbling** *vbl. sb.* motion in an amble; *ppl. a.* moving in an amble. **A·mblingly** *adv.*

Amble (æ·mb'l), *sb.* ME. [a. Fr., f. *ambler*; see prec.] 1. The pace described in prec. (sense 1), and *loosely*, an easy pace. 2. Of persons: A movement suggesting an amble 1607.

1. A fine easy a. B. JONS. The usual pace of [mules] is an a. JEPHSON. 2. His Antick a. 1607.

Ambleocarpus (æ:mblīˌoˌkā·ɹpəs), *a.* 1847. [f. Gr. ἀμβλώσκειν to miscarry + καρπός.] *Bot.* Having the seeds entirely, or largely, abortive.

‖**Amblosis** (ǣmblōu·sis). 1706. [Gr., f. ἀμβλίσκειν.] *Med.* Abortion. Hence **Amblo·tic** *a.* causing abortion; *sb.* [sc. *medicine.*]

Amblygon (æ·mbligǫn); also **ambligon.** 1570. [a. Fr. *amblygone*, ad. Gr. ἀμβλυγώνιος, f. ἀμβλύς + γωνία.] †A. *adj.* Obtuse-angled –1796. B. *sb.* [sc. *figure*, esp. *triangle.*] 1570. Hence **Ambly·gonal** *a.* (*rare*); vars. †**Amblygo·nial,** †**Ambly·gonous. Ambly·gonite** (*Min.*) a typical greenish white translucent mineral, occurring in obtuse-angled rhombic prisms, and consisting of alumina, lithia, potash, soda, iron, and fluoric acid.

‖**Amblyopia** (æmbliˌōu·piă). 1706. [mod. L., a. Gr. ἀμβλυς + ὤψ.] *Path.* Impaired vision, due to defective sensibility of the retina, etc.; the early stage of *amaurosis.* var. **A·mblyopy.** Hence **Amblyo·pic** *a.*

Ambo (æ·mbo). Pl. **ambos** (-ōuz), also L. ambones. 1641. [a. late L. *ambo*, ad. Gr. ἄμβων; see AMBON.] The pulpit or reading-desk in early Christian churches; an oblong enclosure with steps at both ends.

Ambodexter, etc., obs. f. AMBIDEXTER, etc.

Ambo·lic, *a.* 1879. [ad. Gr. ἀμβολικός.] Abortifacient.

Ambon (æ·mbǫn). 1725. [a. Gr. ἄμβων, prob. f. ἀνα-βα-.] †1. = AMBO –1794. 2. *Anat.* The margin of the sockets of the large bones. (So in Galen.) 1811.

Amboyna (wood) (ǣmboi·nă). 1866. [f. *Amboyna.*] The wood of the *Pterospermum indicum* (N.O. *Sterculiaceæ*).

Ambreate (æ·mbriˌeʹt). 1839. [f. med. L. *ambre* + -ATE⁴.] *Chem.* A salt of Ambreic acid.

Ambreic (ǣmbrī·ik), *a.* 1831. [f. as prec.

+-IC; see next.] *Chem.* Of or pertaining to ambrein or ambergris, as *Ambreic Acid.*

Ambrein (æ·mbrīˌin). 1832. [a. Fr. *ambréine*, f. *ambre*; see -IN.] *Chem.* A crystalline fatty substance, the main constituent of ambergris.

Ambrette (ambre·t). 1725. [a. Fr., dim. of *ambre*; see -ETTE.] 1. A pear with an odour of musk. 2. The seeds of *Hibiscus Abelmoschus*, used in perfumery 1858.

Ambrite (æ·mbrəit). [f. AMBER + -ITE; ad. Ger. *ambrit* 1861.] *Min.* A yellowish-grey, sub-transparent fossil resin found in New Zealand.

Ambrology (ǣmbrǫ·lŏdʒi). 1879. [f. mod. L. *ambra* + -(O)LOGY.] The natural history of amber.

Ambrose (æ·mbrouz). ME. [a. Fr. *ambroise*:—L. *ambrosia* (see next).] 1. *Herb.* An English plant: the Wood Sage (*Teucrium Scorodonia*); also *Chenopodium Botrys.* †2. = AMBROSIA 1. –1621.

Ambrosia (ǣmbrōu·ziă, -ʒiă) 1567. [a. L., a. Gr. ἀμβροσία, fem. adj. f. ἀ not + μβροτός mortal.] 1. *Gr. Myth.* The fabled food (1590), drink (1567), or unguent (1667), of the immortals. Also *fig.* 2. *transf.* Water, oil, and fruits mixed as a libation; also a perfumed draught 1685. 3. *fig.* Something divinely sweet to taste or smell 1731. 4. Bee-bread 1609. 5. *Herb.* A name of plants; see AMBROSE 1597. 6. *Mod. Bot.* A genus (N.O. *Compositæ*) of weeds allied to Wormwood. *A. artemisifolia* is the Oak of Jerusalem.

1. Drinkes Nectar, eates diuine A. MARSTON. His dewie locks distill'd A. MILT. *P. L.* v. 57. 3. The a. of her lips DE QUINCEY. Hence †**Ambro·siac** *a.* ambrosial. †**Ambro·siate** *a.* formed or furnished with a. var. †**A·mbrosie, -y.**

Ambro·sia·ceous, *a.* 1879. [f. prec.] *Bot.* Akin to the genus *Ambrosia.*

Ambrosial (ǣmbrōu·ziăl, -ʒiăl), *a.* 1596. [f. L. *ambrosius*, a. Gr. ἀμβρόσιος + -AL[1]; see AMBROSIA.] 1. Immortal, celestial; *orig.* belonging to or worthy of the gods 1596; *transf.* belonging to heaven 1637; *fig.* divinely fragrant; occas., divinely beautiful 1667. 2. Of pollen, or bee-bread (*rare*) 1816.

1. A. food POPE, locks 1866, oil 1870. A. fruits, fetched from the tree of life, And from the fount of life a. drink MILT. *P. R.* IV. 586. The broad a. aisles of lofty lime TENNYSON. Hence **Ambro·sially** *adv.* **Ambro·sian** *a.*[1] = AMBROSIAL.

Ambrosian (ǣmbrōu·ziăn), *a.*[2] 1609. [ad. L. *Ambrosianus*, f. *Ambrosius* (same word as in prec.) bishop of Milan.] 1. Of, pertaining to, or instituted by St. Ambrose. 2. Of the Ambrosian Library at Milan 1724.

1. *A. rite or office*: one used in the A. church of Milan. *A. chant*: a chant now merged in the Gregorian. 2. The A. manuscript 1724.

Ambrosin (æ·mbrosin). 1753. [ad. med. L. *ambrosinus* (sc. *nummus*); see AMBROSIAN *a.*[2]] A coin bearing the figure of St. Ambrose on horseback.

Ambrosine (æ·mbrosin). 1872. [f. L. *ambrosius* + -INE; or ? f. *amber.*] *Min.* A resinous mineral of eocene age, related to amber, found near Charleston, S.C.

Ambrotype (æ·mbrŏtəip). 1855. [? f. AMBER + TYPE.] U.S. name for a photograph on glass, with lights given by the silver, and shades by a dark background showing through.

Ambry, aum- (a·mbri). ME. [ad. L. *armarium* (in med.L. also *almarium*), f. *arma* + *-arium* depot; the *b* is adscititious. As *almery*, confused with *almonry*. In Anglo-Ind. ALMIRAH.] 1. *gen.* A repository; a cupboard; a locker, a press; †*fig.* = treasury –1628. 2. *spec.* A place for keeping victuals (*arch.* and *dial.*) ME.; a locker, or recess in the wall of a church, for sacramental vessels, etc. (*arch.*) ME.; †archives –1775. ¶ Corruptly for ALMONRY (*Almry* or *Ambry Close*, Westminster, was orig. *Almonry Close*).

Ambs-ace (æ·mz ē·s). ME. [a. OFr. *ambes as*:—L. *ambas as*; see ACE.] *lit.* Double ace, the lowest throw at dice; hence *fig.* bad luck; worthlessness ME.; next to nothing 1679. ? *Obs.*

I had rather be in this choise, than throw Ames-ace for my life *All's Well* II. iii. 85.

‖**Ambulacrum** (æmbiulēi·krǒm, -æ·krǒm). Pl. -a. 1837. [L.; f. *ambulare.*] An avenue or double row of pores for the protrusion of the tube-feet, as in an echinoderm. Hence **Ambula·cral** *a.* of or pertaining to the ambulacra of echinoderms. ‖**Ambulacra·ria, -aire,** a series of the perforated coronal pieces in an echinus. **Ambula·criform** *a.* having the shape of ambulacra.

Ambulance. 1819. [a. Fr. (formerly *hôpital ambulant*), f. L. *ambulantem*; see -ANCE.] Not in gen. use bef. the Crimean war. 1. A moving hospital, attending an army as it moves, so as to succour the wounded without delay. Often *attrib.* 1819. 2. An ambulance waggon or cart for conveying the wounded off the field, etc. 1854.

1. *attrib.* A. waggons 1860, men 1864.

Ambulant (æ·mbiŭlănt), *a.* 1654. [ad. L. *ambulantem.*] 1. Walking, moving about. 2. Shifting, unfixed (*rare*) 1810.

1. An a. 'Revolutionary Army' CARLYLE.

Ambulate (æ·mbiŭlēit), *v. rare.* 1623. [f. L. *ambulat-*, *ambulare.*] To walk, move about. Hence **A·mbulative** *a.* always moving. ? *Obs.*

Ambulation (æmbiŭlēi·ʃən). 1541. [ad. L. *ambulationem.*] 1. The action of walking, moving about 1574. †2. The spreading of a gangrene –1751.

Ambulator (æ·mbiŭlēitəɹ). 1652. [a. L.] 1. One who walks about. 2. An instrument for measuring distances on the road, also called *perambulator* 1859.

Ambulatory (æ·mbiŭlătəri), *a.* 1622. [ad. L. *ambulatorius*, f. *ambulator.*] 1. Of or pertaining to a walker, or walking. 2. Adapted for walking 1835. 3. Unfixed in abode; movable 1622. 4. *fig.* Shifting, temporary, mutable. (So in Fr.) 1631.

1. A. exercise 1622, life 1796. 3. Many [schools] are a. 1845. 4. A man's will..is a., or alterable, untill death 1651. They..think virtue and vice a. MRS. PIOZZI. var. **A·mbulato·rial** (in senses 1, 2).

A·mbulatory, *sb.* 1623. [ad. med.L. *ambulatorium*; see -ORY.] A place (open or *esp.* covered) for walking in; an arcade, a cloister.

†**A·mbuling,** *ppl. a.* [refash. of AMBLING after L. *ambulans.*] In *Ambuling Communion*, an observance of the Lord's Supper while moving about –1655.

Amburbial (ǣmbv̄·rbiăl), *a.* 1656. [f. L. *amburbialis*, f. *amb-* + *urbs*; see -AL[1].] *Rom. Antiq.* Connected with the city; *esp.* with the expiatory procession round Rome.

Ambury, var. of ANBURY.

Ambuscade (æ·mbǒskē·d), *sb.* 1582. [a. Fr. *embuscade*, ad. It. *imboscata*, f. *imboscare*; see AMBUSH *v.* In 17th c. AMBUSCADO.] 1. = AMBUSH 1 (and now more formal). 2. = AMBUSH 2. 1674. 3. *fig.* = AMBUSH 4. 1794.

2. The lurking a. 1814. 3. The a. of a fallacy 1844.

Ambuscade (æmbǒskē·d), *v.* 1592. [f. the sb.] To lie, or conceal, in ambush. Hence **Ambusca·ded** *ppl. a.* placed in ambuscade; ambushed. **Ambusca·der,** one who lies in ambush.

Ambusca·do, *sb. arch.* Pl. **os,** †**-oes,** †**o's.** 1592. [refash. of AMBUSCADE after Sp.; see -ADO[2]. Usual in 17th c.] 1. = AMBUSCADE 1. †2. = AMBUSCADE 2. –1726. 3. *fig.* 1640.

1. Of cutting Forraine throats, of Breaches, Ambuscados, Spanish Blades *Rom. & Jul* I. iv. 84. Hence †**Ambusca·doed** *ppl. a.* ambuscaded.

Ambush (æ·mbuʃ), *sb.* 1489. [a. OFr. *embusche*, f. *embuscher*; see AMBUSH *v.* The *am-* is obscure; ? due to *ambages.*] 1. *strictly.* A military disposition consisting of troops concealed in a wood, etc., in order to surprise an enemy. (See AMBUSCADE 1.) †2. The force (*pl.* troops) so disposed –1653. 3. Any persons (or person) lying in wait 1573. 4. *fig.* 1592. ¶ Confused with AMBAGES 1602.

1. Then Ionathans men that lay in a. rose vp 1 *Macc.* ix. 40. *To make, construct, lay an a.* 2. The Ambushes rose, and put themselves [etc.] 1653. 3. Once I did lay an a. for your life *Rich. II*, I. i. 137. 4. The ambushes of envy JOHNSON.

Ambush (æ·mbuʃ), *v.* ME. [a. OFr. *embuscher*:—late L. **inboscare*, f. *in* + *boscus* BUSH. For *am-* see prec. *Ambu·sh* till 17th c.] 1. To place in ambush, in order to surprise an enemy. *Obs.* or *arch.* 2. *intr.* (refl. pron. omitted) To lie down in ambush; lie in wait 1626. 3. *trans.* To waylay, attack from an ambush 1631.

2. The archest chin Mockery ever ambush'd in M. ARNOLD. 3. This party were ambushed .. and defeated 1780. Hence **A·mbushed** *ppl. a.* placed or lying in ambush; also *fig.*

Ambushment (æ·mbuʃmĕnt, formerly embu·ʃ-). *arch.* ME. [a. OFr. *embuschement*, f. *embuscher*; see AMBUSH *v.* and -MENT.] 1. = AMBUSH 1. †2. = AMBUSH 2. ME. †3. A surprise party –1655. †4. *fig.* Devices to entrap –1641.

Ambu·stion. 1623. [ad. L. *ambustionem.*] A burn, a scald. ? *Obs.*

Amebean, var. of AMŒBÆAN.

‖**Ameer** (ămīᵊ·ɹ). Also **amír.** 1614. [a. Arab. *amir* commander, EMIR. The spelling *Amir, Ameer* is mod.] †1. = EMIR –1679. 2. The title of various Mohammedan rulers in Scinde and (*esp.*) in Afghanistan 1803. Hence **Amee·rship,** the position of an A.

†**A·mel,** *sb.* ME. [a. AFr. **amail* (see A- *pref.* 9), OFr. *esmail*, med.L. *smaltum*; acc. to Diez, f. Teut. **smaltjan* to SMELT. Replaced by ENAMEL.] Enamel. Also *attrib.* –1625. Hence †**A·mel** *v.* to enamel; **A·meled, a·melled** *ppl. a.*; †**A·meling** *vbl. sb.*

Amelanchier (æmĕlæ·nʃiəɹ). 1741. [ad. Savoy *amelancier* the medlar.] *Bot.* A genus of small trees, allied to the Medlar.

Amelcorn (æ·mĕlkǫɹn). 1578. [a. Ger. *amelkorn*, f. L. *amylum* + CORN.] An inferior wheat, the Larger Spelt (*Triticum vulgare dicoccum*); French Rice.

†**A·m(e)let.** 1761. [a. OFr. *amelette*, now *om-*.] = OMELET.

Ame·liorable, *a.* 1807. [f. AMELIORATE.] Capable of amelioration.

Ameliorate (ămī·liŏrēit), *v.* 1767. [f. Fr. *améliorer*, OFr. *ameillorer*, f. *à* + *meillorer* :—L. *meliorare.*] 1. To make better, improve. 2. *intr.* To grow better 1789.

1. In every human being there is a wish to a. his own condition MACAULAY. Hence **Ame·liora·tive** *a.* tending to a. **Ame·liora·ter.**

Amelioration (ămīˌliŏrēi·ʃən). 1659. [a. Fr. *amélioration.*] 1. The action of making better; the being made better; improvement. 2. *concr.* An improvement 1776.

1. In a course of a. BURKE. 2. Buildings .. and other ameliorations A. SMITH.

Amen (ē·me·n, *often* ā·me·n). OE. [a. L. or Fr., a. Gr. ἀμήν, a. Heb. *āmēn* certainty, truth; adopted in Gr. by the LXX, whence in N.T., and in early Christian use, in Gr. and L.] **A.** *int.* or *adv.* 1. (from L.) = Finis. 2. After a prayer or wish: Be it so really! ME. 3. After a statement, confession of faith, etc.: It is so in truth OE. 4. As retained in the Bible from Gr. or Heb.: Truly, verily ME.

2. But delyuere vs fro yuel. Amen *that is so be it* WYCLIF *Matt.* vi. 13.

B. *sb.* 1. The concluding word *Amen!* ME. 2. An expression of assent or belief 1579. 3. *transf.* Conclusion 1677. 4. A title of Christ (*Rev.* iii. 14); = The faithful one.

1. No better word to say, then A. 1597. 2. False doctrine strangled by its own a. MRS. BROWNING. 3. The A. of my life HALE.

Amen (ē·me·n), *v.* 1854. [f. the sb.] To say Amen to; to ratify solemnly, say the final word to.

Amenable (ămī·năb'l), *a.* 1596. [app. a. AFr. *amenable*, f. *amener*, f. *à* + *mener*:—L. *minare* to drive cattle by minatory shouts.] 1. Liable to answer (*to* a tribunal, etc., or *absol.*); responsible. 2. Of things: Liable to the legal authority of 1768. 3. *loosely*, Liable (*to* a charge, etc.) 1863. 4. *fig.* Capable of being tested by. Const. *to.* 1845. 5. Responsive *to*; tractable 1803.

1. Not amesnable to Law SPENSER. 3. A. to an imputation 1876. 4. A. to the touch, but invisible to the eye BUCKLE. 5. [Not] a. to discipline WELLINGTON. Will..is a. to habit MILL. Hence **Ame·nabi·lity,** the quality of being a. (senses 1, 5). **Ame·nableness,** the quality or state of being a. **Ame·nably** *adv.*

†**Amena·ge,** *v. rare.* [a. OFr. *amenager.*] To domesticate. SPENSER.

†**Amenance, -aunce.** 1591. [a. OFr. *amenance.*] Conduct, bearing –1739.

Amend (ăme·nd), *v.* ME. [a. OFr. *amender* :—L. *emendare*, f. *e*=*ex*+*mendum*, *menda*. Aphet. to MEND in 14th c.] **1.** To free from faults, correct, convert; to rectify (*arch.*); *esp.* to emendate 1483. *intr.* To reform oneself ME. **2.** To make alterations (in a bill before Parliament) (see AMENDMENT 2) 1777. **3.** To repair; to restore (*arch.*). Now usu. MEND. ME. †**4.** To heal (the sick); to cure (a disease) –1804; *intr.* to recover –1611. **5.** To improve. *trans.* ME. *intr.* (*rare*) 1530. †**6.** To better, surpass –1500. †**7.** To make amends for an offence. (Cf. MEND.) –1635.

1. If here One Sinner doth a. Strait there is Joy H. VAUGHAN. To a. his civil government BURKE. A *mandamus* may not be amended after return TOMLINS. 3. Dame Gurton these breeches amended 1575. 4. *intr.* Th affliction of my mind amends *Temp.* V. i 115. 5. To punish you by the heeles, would a. the attention of your eares SHAKS. Hence **Ame·nd** *sb.*; see AMENDS. **Ame·ndable** *a.* capable of being amended. **Ame·ndableness. Ame·ndatory** *a.* of or pertaining to amendment; tending to amend (U.S.). **Ame·nder** (usu. with *of*), one who or that which amends.

‖**Amende-honorable** (amäṅ·d onora·bl'). 1670. [Fr. = honourable compensation (see AMENDS). Treated as Eng. in 18th c., now usu. as Fr. Occas. without *honorable*. Orig. a public and humiliating acknowledgement of crime, now *fig.*] Public apology and reparation to one who has been injured or offended in his honour. Cf. AMENDS 2.

Amendment (ăme·ndmĕnt). ME. [a. OFr. *amendement*, f. *amender*; see AMEND and -MENT.] The action or result of amending. **1.** Removal of faults or errors, reformation; esp. (*Law*) in a writ or process 1607. **2.** The alteration of a bill before Parliament; hence *concr.* a proposed alteration (which if adopted may even defeat the measure) 1696. *In a Public Meeting*: A proposed alteration submitted as a resolution for adoption; occas., a counter-motion. †**3.** Repair –1682. **4.** Improvement ME.; *esp.* in health 1526. †**5.** Reparation ME. only.

1. I see a good a. of life in thee: from Praying, to Purse-taking 1 *Hen. IV*, I. ii. 114. A. of the law GOLDSM. 2. A Bill .. was agreed to with some amendments 1710. 4. What hope is there of his maiesties a.? He hath abandon'd his Physitions, Madam *All's Well* I. i. 12.

Amends (ăme·ndz). ME. [a. OFr. *amendes*, pl., f. *amender* to AMEND.] Used as a collect. sing. with sing. vb., *amende* being rare in Eng.] †**1.** A fine (= L. *pœnæ*) –1618. **2.** Reparation, compensation, satisfaction. *pl.* in form ME. †*sing.* –1668. †**3.** Improvement *esp.* in health –1709.

2. *To make amends* we have many .. ballads COWPER. To make an honourable Amends ADDISON. To make amend in time MARVELL. 3. But here I feel a. MILT. *Sams.* 9. Hence †**Ame·ndsful** *a. rare*, making compensation.

Amene (ămī·n), *a.* ME. [a. OFr. *amene, ad. L. *amœnum*. Freq. in 15th c., and still occas.] Agreeable. var. †**Ame·nous.**

Amenity (ămī·nĭti, ăme·nĭti). ME. [? a. Fr. *aménité*, or ad. L. *amœnitatem*.] **1.** The quality of being pleasant or agreeable. **2.** *pl.* †Pleasant places 1644; pleasant ways or manners 1841; the pleasurable features of an estate 1928.

1. The a. of the climate PRESCOTT, of Erasmus DIBDIN. 2. The amænities of nature H. WALPOLE. Amenities of authors D'ISRAELI, of home life 1866.

‖**Amenorrhœa** (ăme:norī·ă). 1804. [mod. L. f. ἀ + μήν + -ροια. Cf. Fr. *aménorrhée*.] *Med.* Absence or suppression of the menstrual discharge. Hence **Amenorrhœ·al** *a.*

Ament (ame·nt). 1791. [ad. L. *amentum*.] *Bot.* = AMENTUM.

Amental (ăme·ntăl), *a.*[1] (and *sb.*) 1847. [f. L. *amentum* + -AL.] *Bot.* Bearing catkins.

Ame·ntal, *a.*[2] *nonce-wd.* 1877. [f. ἀ + MENTAL; cf. *atheistic*.] Denying or dispensing with the existence of mind.

‖**Amentum** (ămentǒm). Pl. **-a.** 1770. [L. Cf. AMENT.] A catkin. Hence **Amenta·ceous** *a.* of the nature of, or bearing, catkins. **Amenti·ferous** *a.* bearing catkins. **Ame·ntiform** *a.* catkin-shaped.

†**Ame·nty.** 1623. [ad. L. *amentia* (now used in *Path.*), f. *a*+*mentem*.] *Path.* Madness.

†**Amenuse,** *v.* ME. [a. AFr. *amenuser*, f. *à*+*menuisier* :—late L. **minutiare*, f. *minutus*. Refash. (ult.) as AMINISH.] *trans.* To make less –1554. *intr.* –1481.

Amerce (ămɔ̄·ɹs), *v.* ME. [orig. *amercy*, a. AFr. *amercier*, f. *à* + *merci* :—L. *mercedem*. From *estre à merci* came *estre à mercié*, whence *amercier*.] **1.** To fine arbitrarily; *fig.* and *loosely*, to exact something from; to punish 1570. **2.** Also with the penalty expressed (see quots.) 1500.

1. To be amerced to the Crown 1863. To be amerced for sins unknown BYRON. 2. To be amerc'd a Supper 1725. He would a. him in half his wages SCOTT. A. him with the loss of his Kingdom MILT. Amerced of heaven MILT. *P. L.* I. 604. Hence **Ame·rciable** *a.*; also †**ame·rceable,** liable to be amerced. **Ame·rcing** *vbl. sb.* mulcting. var. †**Ame·rciate.**

Amercement (ămɔ̄·ɹsmĕnt). [ME. *amerciment*, a. AFr., f. *amercier*; see AMERCE. In 15th c. also AMERCIAMENT.] **1.** The infliction of a penalty or fine at the 'mercy' of the inflicter (orig. one lighter than the fixed fines) 1513. **2.** The fine itself ME. Also *fig.*

1. Liable to an a. from the Crown for raising a false accusation BLACKSTONE. 2. Yt is necessary to .. levie the sayd amerciments 1483.

Amerciament (ămɔ̄·ɹsiămĕnt). ME. [Refash. of prec., after med.L. *amerciamentum*. More freq. than prec. as techn. term.] = AMERCEMENT (in both senses).

Amerced, and by the A. affeered to 10s. SCROGGS.

American (ăme·rikăn). 1578. **A.** *adj.* **1.** Belonging to the continent of America. **2. a.** †Belonging to the British colonies in North America –1775. **b.** Belonging to the United States.

2. b. *A. cloth*, an enamelled oilcloth used chiefly for covering tables, chairs, etc.

B. *sb.* **1.** An aborigine of the American continent; now called an 'American Indian' 1578. **2.** A native of America of European descent, *esp.* a citizen of the United States 1765.

1. Worse Than ignorant Americans MASSINGER. 2. We Americans are terribly in earnest about making ourselves HOWELLS.

Americanism (ăme·rikăni:z'm). 1794. [f. prec. + -ISM.] **1.** Attachment to the United States 1808. **2.** Anything peculiar to the United States; *esp.* a word or phrase (the usual, and earliest, Eng. use) 1794.

1. The leaven of A. 1861. 2. I hate this shallow A. which hopes to get rich by credit EMERSON.

Ame·ricanist. 1881. [f. as prec. + -IST.] One who makes a special study of subjects pertaining to America, as its ethnology, etc.

Americanize (ăme·rikănəi:z), *v* 1816. [f. AMERICAN *a.* + -IZE.] **1.** *strictly*, To make American; *esp.* to naturalize as a citizen of the United States 1816. **2.** *loosely*, To make American in character. (A dyslogistic term of Eng. party politics.) 1830. **3.** *intr.* To become American in character, etc. 1875.

2. They say we must not .. A. our institutions BRIGHT. Hence **Ame·ricaniza·tion**, the process of Americanizing. **Ame·ricanized** *ppl. a.* made American, or like the American.

Americo-, comb. form of America, as in Americo-mania, a craze for what is American.

Ames-ace, obs. f. AMBS-ACE.

Amess, obs. f. AMICE.

‖**Ametabola** (æ:mĭtæ·bǒlă), *sb. pl.* 1870. [mod.L. adj. pl. neut. (sc. *insecta*), a. Gr. ἀμετάβολα, f. ἀ + μετάβολος.] *Zool.* A subclass of insects, e.g. Lice, etc., which do not undergo metamorphosis. Hence **Ame:ta·bo·lian** *a.* belonging to the *Ametabola*; *sb.* [sc. *insect*.] **Ame:tabo·lic, Ameta·bolous** *adjs.*, not undergoing metamorphosis.

Ame·tallous, *a.* 1879. [f. Gr. ἀ + μέταλλον + -OUS.] Non-metallic.

Amethyst (æ·mĭþist). [ME. *ametist*, a. OFr. *ametiste*, ad. L. *amethystus*, a. Gr. ἀμέθυστος, f. ἀ + μέθυ.] **1.** A precious stone of a clear purple or bluish violet colour, consisting of quartz coloured by manganese, or by a compound of iron and soda. Also *fig.* **2.** *Her.* The colour of the A., purple violet 1572. Also *attrib.* = AMETHYSTINE 2. 1601.

1. The amethist staieth drunkennesse LODGE. **Oriental Amethyst**: a rare violet variety of sapphire. *fig.* Towers of a. KEATS.

Amethystine (æmĭþi·stin), *a.* 1670. [ad. L. *amethystinus*; see prec. and -INE.] **1.** Of, or containing, amethyst. **2.** Amethyst-coloured; violet-purple 1671.

2. A. flowers 1671, wings DISRAELI, ether 1870.

‖**Ametropia** (æmĭtrōᵘ·piă). 1875. [mod.L. f. ἄμετρος + ὤψ + -ια abst. ending.] *Path.* Any abnormal condition of the refraction of the eye. Hence **Ametro·pic** *a.*

Ametrous (ămī·trəs), *a.* 1879. [f. ἀ + μήτρα + -OUS.] *Path.* Having no uterus.

†**Ami, amy(e.** ME. only. [a. OFr. :—L. *amicus*.] A friend, a lover.

Amiability (ēᶦmiăbi·lĭti). 1807. [f. next.] **1.** The quality of being AMIABLE. **2.** Lovableness (better AMABILITY, q. v.) 1869.

Amiable (ēᶦ·miăb'l), *a.* ME. [a. OFr. *amiable* :—L. *amicabilem*, f. *amicus*; subseq. confused with OFr. *amable* :—L. *amabilem*. Occas. comp. *-er, -est*.] **1.** (= L. *amicabilem*.) †Friendly; kind –1491; kindly disposed (? U.S.) 1875; of conduct, temper, mood, etc.: Friendly ME. †**2.** (= L. *amabilem*.) Lovable –1788; of things (*arch.*) ME. **3.** Having pleasing qualities of heart (a fusion of senses 1 and 2) 1749.

1. Lay an a. siege to the honesty of this Ford's wife *Merry W.* II. ii. 243. In no a. temper MACAULAY. †**Amiable numbers**: see AMICABLE. 2. We are a. or odious in the Eyes of our great Judge ADDISON. This a. home of the dead M. ARNOLD. 3. The a. temper of pity FIELDING. Hence **A·miableness,** (*a*) = AMABILITY; (*b*) = AMIABILITY. **A·miably** *adv.* †amicably; †lovably; good-temperedly.

Amiant(h (æ·mi₁ænt, -ænþ). ME. [a. Fr. *amiante*; see next.] = next. Now *poet.*

‖**Amiant(h)us** (æmi₁æ·ntǒs, -þǒs). 1668. [L., a. Gr. ἀμίαντος undefiled. The (*h*) is after *polyanthus*.] *Min.* **1.** A variety of asbestos, splitting into fibres, which have been woven into a fabric. **2.** A fibrous kind of greenish chrysolite 1862.

1. Here is amianthus, as fine and soft as any cotton thread RUSKIN. Hence **Amia·nt(h)iform** *a.* of the structure of a. **Amia·nt(h)ine** *a.* of the nature of a. **Amia·nt(h inite,** a variety of actinolite. **Amia·nt(h)oid** *a.* a.-like; *sb.* [sc. *mineral*] = ASBESTOID; whence **Amiant(h)oi·dal** *a.* a.-like.

Amic (æ·mik), *a.* 1863. [f. AM(MONIA) or AM(IDE) + -IC.] *Chem.* Of or pertaining to ammonia, of the nature of an amide; *esp.* in *Amic acid*, an acid amide; e.g. *lactamic* acid.

Amicable (æ·mikăb'l), *a.* 1532. [ad. L. *amicabilis*, f. *amicus*. Earlier AMIABLE.] **1.** *gen.* Friendly. **2.** *esp.* Of arrangements: Done with mutual goodwill; harmonious 1609. †**3.** Kindly, genial –1691.

1. Each a. guest POPE. 2. An a. settlement of all differences 1794. *Amicable suit*: a friendly action instituted by agreement between the parties, in order to secure a judicial decision on a point of law. 3. **Amicable** (or *amiable*) **numbers**: numbers which are mutually equal to the whole sum of each other's aliquot parts, e.g. 284 and 220. Hence **A:mica·bi·lity,** the quality of being a.; *concr.* friendly relations. **A·micableness. A·micably** *adv.*

†**Amical,** *a.* 1652. [a. Fr. Cf. *inimical*.] Friendly –1691.

Amice[1] (æ·mis). [ME. *amyse*. Earlier *amyt* AMIT(E, a. OFr. *amit* :—L. *amictus*. Perh. confused with next, whence the *s*.] †**1.** *gen.* A loose wrap ME. **2.** *Eccl.* An oblong or square piece of white linen, worn by clerics about the neck and shoulders, and originally also covering the head 1532. **3.** *Loosely* of other garments 1641.

2. As the Jewes dyd fyrst couer Chrystes face .. so hath the Priest .. an Amise put vpon his head BP. WATSON. var. †**Ami·ct.**

Amice[2] (æ·mis). ME. [ad. OFr. *aumuce*, med.L. *almutia*, of obscure origin (cf. Ger. *mutse, mütze*). Confused with prec., and since 17th c. known only as the *grey amice*.] **1.** A cap, a hood or hooded cape, later a badge, made of, or lined with, grey fur, worn by the clergy. †**2.** The fur of the marten or grey squirrel, used as in 1. –1598.

1. Morning fair .. in a. gray MILT. *P. R.* IV. 427.

Amid (ămi·d). OE. [orig. *on middan*, dat. sing. of *midde* adj. Cf. L. *in medio* and Gr. ἐν μέσῳ, also used subst. Subseq. treated as a prep. with, later without, *of*.] †**A.** *adv.* In the midst –1581.

B. *prep.* **1.** In the middle *of*. Now only *poet.* OE. **2.** *more loosely*, Near the middle of, surrounded by (with *sing.* or *pl. sb.*). Chiefly *poet.* ME. 3. *esp.* In relation to the circumstances of an action 1513.

1. Ruth..in tears a. the alien corn KEATS. 3. A. the broil SCOTT, general shouts of dissent FREEMAN.

Amid-, comb. form of AMIDE, used instead of AMIDO- bef. vowels.

A·midated, *ppl. a.* 1878. *Chem.* Converted into an amide.

Amide (æ·maid, ămai·d in comb.). 1850. [f. AM(MONIA) + -IDE.] *Chem.* †1. *orig.* A name given to derivatives of ammonia (NH_3) in which one atom of H was exchanged for a metal or organic radical, acid or basic, these being viewed as compounds of the *metal*, etc. with *amidogen* (NH_2). 2. *Mod. Chem.* Generic name of the compound ammonias in which one or more atoms of hydrogen are replaced by an *acid* radical 1863. 3. Extended to ALKALAMIDES. 4. *Acid amide*: AMIC ACID, or ALANINE. Hence **Ami·dic** *a.* of or derived from an a.

Amidide (æ·midəid). 1854. [f. AMIDE + -IDE.] *Chem.* A simple compound of amidogen with another element or complex radical.

Amidin (æ·midin). 1833. [f. *amid-* (as in Fr. *amidon*), f. L. *amylum* + -IN.] *Chem.* 1. The soluble matter in the granules of starch. 2. Starch in solution 1839.

Amidmost (ămi·dmoust, -əst). [mod. f. *amid* or *midmost*; cf. AMIDST.] *adv.* In the very middle. *prep.* In the very centre of. MORRIS.

Amido- (ămai·do), comb. form of AMIDE, used also in phrases as *amido compounds*, etc.

Amidogen (ămai·dŏdʒen). 1850. [f. AMIDO- + -GEN.] *Chem.* The hypothetical radical (NH_2) of the primary amides and amines (equal to ammonia minus one of its hydrogen atoms).

Amidships (ămi·dʃips), *adv.* 1692. [= in the ship's middle, f. AMID, with gen., and therefore an old phr.] In, *occas.* to or towards, the middle of a ship.

Amidst (ămi·dst). ME. [f. AMID, *amidde*, with gen. *-s*, subseq. corrupted to *-st*. Cf. *amongst*, etc. Aphet. MIDST. Used more distributively than *amid*.] A. *adv.* In the middle.

B. *prep.* 1. In or into the middle of (with *sing.* or *pl. sb.*) ME. 2. Amongst, in the course of (with *sing.* or *pl. sb.*) ME.

1. The fruit of this fair tree a. The garden MILT. *P. L.* ix. 661. Lost, Amids the moving waters CHAPMAN. 2. To smile a. adversity 1756. A. his ascetic follies 1849.

Amidulin (ami·diŭlin). 1879. [f. Fr. *amidon* + -ULE + -IN.] *Chem.* A soluble preparation of starch.

†**Ami·dward.** ME. [f. AMID + -WARD, after *downward*, etc.] *adv.* Towards or near the middle -1513. *prep.* Towards or near the middle of ME. only.

‖**Amildar** (æ·məldāɹ). 1799. [a. Pers.] A native factor in India; *esp.* a collector of revenue.

†**Ami·nded,** *pa. pple.* 1578. [f. A = *ge-* + MINDED.] Minded -1640.

Amine (æ·main, ămai·n in comb.). 1863. [f. AM(MONIA) + -INE.] *Chem.* Generic name of the *compound ammonias*, in which one or more atoms of hydrogen are replaced by alcohol or other base-radicals.

†**Ami·nish,** *v.* 1477. [Refash. of AMENUSE; cf. *diminish.*] To diminish -1530.

Amir, var. of AMEER.

Amiral, -el, -eld, obs. ff. ADMIRAL.

Amiss (ămi·s). ME. [A *prep.*[1] + MISS *sb.*] A. *adv.* Away from the mark. 1. Erroneously, missing its object ME. 2. Defectively, falling short of its object; faultily ME. 3. *euphem.* Wrongly ME.

1. Our Archyers shet neuer arowe amys CAXTON. 2. I cannot be lodged amisse in this house 1579. 3. Apt to see wrong, and speak a. H. MARTINEAU.

Phrases. 1. **To come** or **happen amiss:** to happen out of order or untowardly. 2. **To do, deal,** or **act a.:** to err; *euphem.* to do wrong. 3. **To take** (a thing) **a.:** *orig.* to miss its meaning (i. e. (*a*)*mis-take*); *now*, to misinterpret its motive and take offence at it. So **To think a.**

B. quasi-*adj.* [Never *attrib.*] Out of order; deficient, faulty ME.; *esp.* negatively, *Not amiss*: not beside the mark 1513; not bad 1860.

What is amisse? You are, and doe not know't *Macb.* II. iii. 102. It is likewise not a. to hope JOHNSON.

C. †*sb.* [The *adv.* or *adj.* used subst.] An error or fault; hence *euphem.* an evil deed -1700. *Haml.* IV. v. 18.

Amissible (ămi·sĭb'l), *a.* 1672. [a. Fr., ad. L. *amissibilem*, f. *amiss-*, *amittere*.] Liable to be lost. Hence **Ami·ssibi·lity,** possibility of being lost or losing. So †**Ami·ssive** *a.* tending to or marked by loss.

Amissing (ămi·siŋ), *ppl. a.* 1634. [= *a-missing* (see A *prep.*[1] 12, 13); chiefly Sc.] = MISSING.

†**Ami·ssion.** 1623. [a. Fr., ad. L. *amissionem.*] Loss.

†**Ami·t,** *v.* 1525. [a. L. *amittere.*] To lose. Occ. with *of.* -1756.

†**Amit(e,** *sb.* ME. [a. OFr. *amit* (now *amict*):—L. *amictum*; see AMICT and AMICE.] 1. = AMICE[1] 1, 2. 2. = AMICE[2]. ME.

Amity (æ·mĭti). 1474. [a. Fr. *amitié*:—pop. L. **amicitatem* (= L. *amicitiam*).] Friendship, friendliness; friendly relations, *esp.* of a public character between states or individuals.

Treaties of a. and commerce G. DUFF. Ancient amities DISRAELI.

‖**Amma** (æ·mă). 1706. [med.L. for Gr. ἅμμα.] *Surg.* A band or truss.

Ammelide (æ·mĭləid). 1846. [f. AM(MONIA) + MEL(AM) + -IDE.] *Chem.* A white powder, $C_6N_9H_9O_3$, produced by concentrated sulphuric acid acting on melam; regarded as acid amide of cyanuric acid.

Ammeline (æ·mĭləin). 1846. [f. as prec. + -INE.] *Chem.* A white powder, $2\,CyH_2N\,.\,CyH\,.\,O$, produced by boiling melam with dilute sulphuric acid, etc.; an amic base of cyanuric acid.

Ammeter (æ·mĭtəɹ). 1882. [f. AM(PÈRE) + -METER.] An instrument for measuring electric current.

Ammi (æ·mi). 1551. [a. L., a. Gr. ἄμμι.] *Bot.* Bishop-weed. var. †‖**A·mmeos** (Gr. gen. taken as nom.).

Ammiral, -ant, obs. ff. ADMIRAL.

†‖**Ammi·tes, am-.** 1750. [a. Gr. ἀμμίτης, f. ἄμμος sand.] *Min.* OOLITE.

Ammo-, comb. form of AMMONIUM, implying conjunction of that basyl with an element, as in *Ammopalladium*.

Ammodyte (æ·mŏdəit). 1607. [ad. L. *ammodytes*, a. Gr., f. ἄμμος + δύτης.] *Zool.* †1. A venomous snake of S. Europe, the Sand Natter -1774. 2. The sand-eel, *Ammodytes* 1698.

Ammonia (ămōu·niă). 1799. [a. mod.L., invented as a name for the gas obtained from *Sal-ammoniac*; see next.] 1. A colourless gas with pungent smell and strong alkaline reaction, NH_3, called also *Spirit of Hartshorn*, and *Volatile* or *Animal Alkali*. 2. *pop. Ammonia*, or spec. *Liquid Ammonia*: a solution of a. in water 1850. 3. *Chem.* Applied to a series of compounds in which one or more hydrogen atoms of NH_3 are replaced by an acid radical 1863.

Ammoniac (ămōu·niæk). ME. [a. Fr., ad. L. *ammoniacum*, a. Gr. ἀμμωνιακόν, f. Ἄμμων, Gr. name of *Amun* Egyptian god. Also *armoniac*, by confusion with ἁρμονία.] A. *adj.* 1. In *Sal Ammoniac*, i. e. Salt of Ammon, a hard white opaque crystalline salt, chemically called Ammonium Chloride, formerly *Muriate of Ammonia*. (Supposed to have been prepared from the dung of camels near the shrine of Jupiter Ammon.) 2. in *Gum Ammoniac*, i. e. gum of Ammon, a gum-resin, of peculiar smell and bitterish taste, the inspissated juice of an umbelliferous plant (*Dorema Ammoniacum*) found wild from N. Africa to India. Used in medicine, and as a cement. 1627. 3. Ammoniacal 1646.

B. *sb.* 1. = Gum Ammoniac. Also ammoniacum. 1420. †2. = Ammonia. [mod. Fr. *ammoniaque.*] -1802.

Ammoniacal (æmŏnəi·ăkăl), *a.* 1732. [f. prec. + -AL.] Of, pertaining to, or of the nature of ammonia.

Ammoniaco- (æmŏnəi·ăko), comb. form of AMMONIAC or AMMONIACAL; also = AMMONIA +, as in *a.-magnesian phosphate*.

Ammoni·acum; see AMMONIAC *sb.* 1.

†**Ammo·niate.** 1844. [f. AMMONIA + -ATE[4].] *Chem.* A combination of ammonia and a metallic oxide. Hence **Ammo·niated** *ppl. a.* combined with ammonia.

Ammonic, -al (ămǫ·nik, -ăl), *a. rare.* 1869. [f. as prec. + -IC, + -AL.] Of or derived from ammonia or ammonium.

Ammonio- (ămōu·nio), comb. form of AMMONIUM, indicating the presence of that basyl or its salts in a compound.

Ammonite (æ·mŏnəit). 1706. [f. mod.L. *ammonites*, f. on med.L. *Cornu Ammonis*, 'Ammon's horn', which the fossil resembles. Orig. as L., with pl. *Ammonitæ.*] 1. A fossil genus of Cephalopods, with whorled chambered shells; once thought to be coiled snakes petrified, and called *Snake-stones*. (SCOTT *Marmion* II. xiii.) †2. = AMMITES, i.e. oolite -1753. Hence **A·mmoniti·ferous** *a.*

Ammonium (ămōu·niŏm). 1808. [a. mod. L. f. (by Berzelius) on AMMONIA.] *Chem.* The radical, NH_4, supposed to exist in the salts of ammonia, which behaves in composition as a monatomic alkaline metal, replacing sodium and potassium. *attrib.* in **a. alum** (see ALUM); **a. amalgam,** an amalgam of a. and mercury.

†**Ammo·niuret.** 1839. [f. AMMONIA + -URET.] *Chem.* = AMMONIATE. Hence **Ammo·niuretted** *ppl. a.* combined with ammonia (or ammonium). ? *Obs.*

Ammo·philous, *a.* 1879. [f. Gr. ἄμμος + φίλος.] Sand-loving.

Ammunition (æmiuni·ʃən), *sb.* 1626. [a. Fr. *a(m)munition*, vulg. *amonition*, *la munition* being prob. taken as *l'amonition*. Now vulg. in Fr.; retained in Eng. with *amm-*, after L. *imm-*, *comm-*, etc.] 1. Military stores or supplies; *orig.* of all kinds; *now*, powder, shot, shell; and, in extension, offensive missiles generally. Also *fig.* 2. *attrib.* as *a.-boots*, *-bread*, etc., those supplied as equipment or rations.

Ammuni·tion, *v.* 1644. [f. the sb.] To supply with ammunition. Hence **Ammuni·tioned** *ppl. a.*

Amnemonic (æmnĭmǫ·nik), *a.* 1879. [f. Gr. ἀ + μνημονικός; see MNEMONICS.] *Path.* Marked by loss of memory.

‖**Amnesia** (æ̆mnī·siă). 1878. [mod.L., a. Gr.] *Path.* Loss of memory. Hence **Amne·sic** *a.*

Amnestic (æ̆mne·stik), *a.* 1879. [f. Gr. ἀμνηστία.] *Med.* Causing loss of memory.

Amnesty (æ·mnĕsti), *sb.* 1580. [a. Fr. *amnestie*, or ad. L., a. Gr. ἀμνηστία.] 1. Forgetfulness; an intentional overlooking 1592. 2. An act of oblivion, a general overlooking or pardon of past offences, by the ruling authority 1580.

1. Reconcilement..by an a., and passing over that which is past BACON. 2. An act of a. and indulgence BURKE. Hence **A·mnesty** *v.* to give a. to; proclaim a.

Amnion (æ·mniǫn). 1667. [a. Gr. ἀμνίον the caul, dim. of ἀμνός lamb.] *Phys.* The innermost membrane enclosing the fœtus before birth. Also *attrib.*

Amnios (æ·mniǫs). 1657. [non-Gr. var. of AMNION.] 1. *Phys.* = AMNION. 2. *Bot.* The fluid produced within the sac which receives the embryo-rudiment 1816.

‖**Amniota** (æmni,ōu·tă), *sb. pl.* 1879. [mod. L., formed anomalously after next.] The vertebrates, including reptiles, birds, and mammals, which possess an amnion.

Amniotic (æmni,ǫ·tik), *a.* 1822. [mod. f. non-Gr. AMNIOS (prob. Fr.); see -OTIC.] Of, pertaining to, or characterized by, an amnion; as *Phys.* the *a. liquid*, *Bot.* the *a. sac*. var. **A·mnic** (*rare*).

Amœba (ămī·bă). Pl. **-bæ, -bas.** 1841. [ad. Gr. ἀμοιβή.] *Zool.* A microscopic animalcule (class *Protozoa*) having no constant form. Hence **Amœ·biform** *a.* amœba-like; proteiform. var. **Amœboid.**

Amœbæan (æmĭbī·ăn), *a.*; also **amebean.** 1658. [f. L. *amœbæus* (a. Gr., f. ἀμοιβή) + -AN.] Alternately answering; responsive.

Amoibite (ămoi·bəit). [f. (Ger. 1844) Gr. ἀμοιβή + -ITE.] *Min.* A variety of Gersdorffite.

†**Amoi·nder,** *v. rare.* 1601. [a. Fr. *amoindrir.*] To diminish -1631.

†**Amo·lish,** *v.* 1624. [a. Fr. *amoliss-*, *amolir*, ad. L. *amoliri.*] To remove forcibly -1640. Hence †**Amoli·tion,** displacement.

†**Amo·llish**, *v.* 1474. [a. OFr. *amoliss-*, *amolir*, f. *à* + *molir*:—L. *mollire*.] To soften, appease -1483. Hence †**Amo·llishment.**

‖**Amomum** (ămōᵘ·mŏm). ME. [L., ad. Gr. ἄμωμον.] *Bot.* A genus of aromatic plants (N.O. *Zingiberaceæ*), including the species which yield Cardamoms and Grains of Paradise. Hence **Amo·meous** *a.*

Among (ămɒ·ŋ). OE. [orig. *on gemang* (see MENG), then *onmang*, whence *amang*, *among*. *gemang* gave IMONG, MONG. Aphet. *'mong* by mod. poets.] **A.** *prep.* In the crowd of, *hence* associated with. **1.** Surrounded by (occ. = *in*) OE. **2.** In company or association with or beside; in the house, city, or country of. (= L. *apud*, Fr. *chez*, Ger. *bei*.) ME. **3.** In the number or class of ME.; *esp.* pre-eminent among ME. †**4.** During, in course of -1691. **5.** With or by (the members of a group) generally ME. **6.** Divided between ME.; by the joint action of 1597; reciprocally between ME.

1. 'Mong Boyes, Groomes, and Lackeyes *Hen. VIII*, v. ii. 18. Amonge a basket ful of roses CHAUCER. 2. The Cananites dwelt a. them at Gaser *Judg.* i. 3. Amonge all elementes water is prouffytablest TREVISA. He is a Saul a. the people (*mod.*). 5. Vsed emonge marchantes CAXTON. Popular a. the Irish SYD. SMITH. 6. What are they a. so many *John* vi. 9. You haue a. you kill'd a sweet and innocent Ladie *Much Ado* v. i. 194. They quarrelled a. themselves ADDISON.

B. *adv.* [The prep. used *ellipt.*] †**1.** During this (period), at the same time -1598. †**2.** Betweenwhiles -1606. †**3.** Of place: Together, among *something else* -1624.

Amongst (ămɒ·ŋst), *prep.* ME. [f. AMONG, with gen. *-es*, corrupted to *-st* after superlatives; cf. *against*, etc.] = AMONG in all senses exc. 4, but less usual in the primary local sense, and, when so used, generally implying dispersion, intermixture, or shifting position.

‖**Amontillado** (amǫntilʸā·do). 1825. [Sp.; f. *Montilla*, a town in Spain + *-ado* -ATE [2].] Formerly, a specially dry sherry; now, sherry of a matured type. **b.** *attrib.* in fig. sense 1862.

Amoral (ēⁱ,mǫ·răl), *a.* 1882. [A- *pref.* 14 + MORAL *a.*] Non-moral. Hence -ism, etc.

†**A·moret.** ME. [a. OFr. *amorete*, *-ette*, dim. of *amour*:—L. *amorem*.] **1.** An amorous girl; a paramour -1794. **2.** = AMORETTO -1598. **3.** A love-knot -1423. **4.** A love sonnet -1594. **5.** *pl.* Love-glances; dalliances -1651. Cf. AMOURETTE.

‖**Amoretto** (æmore·to, It. amore·tto). 1596. [It., dim. of *amore*; pl. †*amorettoes*, †*amoretto's*, now as It., *amoretti*.] †A lover; †a love-sonnet; †a love-trick; a cupid.

‖**Amorino** (amorī·no). Pl. **-i.** [It., dim. of *amore*.] A cupid.

Amorist (æ·mŏrist). 1581. [f. L. *amor* or Fr. *amour*.] One who professes (usu. sexual) love. Hence **Amori·stic** *a. rare.*

†**A-mo·rnings**, *adv.* ME. [f. A *prep.*[1] + MORNING with gen. *-s*; cf. 'of a morning'.] In the morning; every morning -1633.

†‖**Amoro·sa.** 1634. [It.] A female lover; a wanton.

†‖**Amoro·so.** 1616. [It.] A lover -1706

Amorous (æ·mŏrəs), *a.* ME. [a. OFr. *amorous* (mod. *amoureux*):—L. *amorosum*, f. *amor*.] **1.** Habitually inclined to love. Also *fig.* of things. **2.** In love, enamoured, fond. Also *fig.* of things. (Const. *absol.*; or with *on*, *of*, †*in*.) ME. **3.** Showing love or fondness (sexual or general) ME. **4.** Of or pertaining to (sexual) love ME. †**5.** *passively.* Lovable, lovely -1611.

2. Our..Musitian groweth a. *Tam. Shr.* III. i. 63. A. on Hero *Much Ado* II. i. 161. Amerous of that lady 1450. 3. His eyen gray and a. LD. BERNERS. 4. Fful is the place..Of songis amerous CHAUCER. 5. O mother of God moste .. a. 1557. Hence **A·morously** *adv.* in the way of love. **A·morousness**, the quality of being a.; var. †**Amoro·sity.**

Amorpha (ămǭ·ɹfă). 1753. [f. Gr. ἄμορφος.] *Bot.* A genus of N. American deciduous shrubs, with long spiked clusters of purple flowers.

Amorphism (ămǭ·ɹfiz'm). 1852. [f. as prec. + -ISM.] Want of regular form; *esp.* want of crystalline structure.

Amorpho- (ămǭ·ɹfo), comb. f. AMORPHOUS.

Amorphophyte (ămǭ·ɹfǒfəit). 1879. [f. AMORPHO- + φυτόν.] *Bot.* A plant having flowers of irregular or anomalous form.

Amorphous (ămǭ·ɹfəs), *a.* 1731. [f. mod. L. *amorphus*, a. Gr. ἄμορφος + -OUS.] **1.** Having no determinate shape; unshapely; belonging to no type. **2.** *Min.* and *Chem.* Uncrystallized 1801. **3.** *Geol.* Without definite parts 1830. **4.** *Biol.* Without definite structure 1848. **5.** *fig.* Unorganized, ill-digested 1837.

1. An a. hat D'ISRAELI. 5. An a. Sansculottism taking form CARLYLE. var. **Amo:rpho·se** *a.* (*rare*). Hence **Amo·rphous-ly** *adv.*, **-ness.**

‖**Amorphozoa** (ămǭ:ɹfo,zōᵘ·ă), *sb. pl.* 1857. [mod.L. f. AMORPHO- + Gr. ζῷα.] *Zool.* Protozoa, e.g. sponges, which have no regular form. Hence **Amorphozo·ary**, a compound amorphozoic organism. **Amorphozo·ic** *a.*

Amo·rphy. 1704. [ad. Gr. ἀμορφία.] Shapelessness. (Used in jest by Swift.)

†**A-morrow**, *adv.* OE. [A *prep.*[1] + MORROW.] In the morning; next morning -1480.

Amort (ămǭ·ɹt), *adv.* and *pred. a.* 1590. [f. *à la mort*, as *all amort*, by omission of *all*. See ALAMORT.] In the state or act of death; inanimate; *fig.* spiritless.

All a. [*obpressam*] for feare HOLLAND. Halfe a-mort 1619. Now a., alive now BROWNING.

Amortization, -isation (ămǭ:ɹtizēⁱ·ʃən). 1672. [ad. med.L. *a(d)mortizationem*; see next.] **1.** The act of alienating lands in mortmain, i.e. to a community having perpetual existence. **2.** The extinction of a debt, *esp.* by means of a sinking fund. *concr.* The money thus paid 1864. var. **Amo·rtizement, -ise-.**

Amortize, -ise (ămǭ·ɹtiz), *v.* ME. [orig. a. Fr. *amortiss-*, *amortir*:—of late L. **admortire*, f. *ad* + *mortem*; see -IZE [2].] †**1.** *trans.* To deaden -1656; *intr.* to droop 1480. **2.** To alienate (lands) in mortmain, i.e. to a corporation ME. **3.** To extinguish a debt, etc., usu. by means of a sinking fund 1882.

2. To render inalienable or..a. the crown lands STUBBS. 3. To a. the Egyptian Debt 1882. Hence **Amo·rtizable, -isable** *a.* extinguishable. **Amo·rtized, -ised** *ppl. a.* †destroyed; held in, or as in, mortmain; held in commission.

Amotion (ămōᵘ·ʃən). *arch.* 1641. [ad. L. *amotionem*; see AMOVE *v.*[2]] **1.** The action of removing; ousting; *esp.* removal of a person from office. **2.** Deprivation of possession 1653.

Amount (ămau·nt), *v.* ME. [a. OFr. *amonter*, f. *amont*, lit. *à mont*:—L. *ad montem*. Occas. aphet. to *mount*. See MOUNT.] †**1.** *intr.* To go up, mount -1631; to mount up -1706. **2.** To come up to (a number or quantity); †*trans.* with simple, or quasi-advb. obj. -1480; *intr.* with *to* 1546. †**3.** *intr.* To result -1650. **4.** †*trans.* To mean, signify -1460; *intr.* with *to*: To be tantamount *to* ME. †**5.** *causal.* To cause to rise, to raise -1655.

2. *intr.* Which doth a. to three odde Duckets more *Com. Err.* IV. i. 30. 4. *intr.* The proofs..do not a. to a demonstration ADDISON. Hence **Amou·nting** *ppl. a.* †resulting; with *to*: Equalling in sum or effect.

Amount (ămau·nt), *sb.* 1710. [f. the vb.] **1.** The sum total to which anything mounts up; *spec.* the sum of the principal and interest 1796. **2.** *fig.* The full value, effect, or significance 1732. **3.** A quantity or sum viewed as a total 1833.

1. The A. of the said Drawback 1710. 2. The whole a. of that enormous fame POPE. 3. The a. of resistance which William met with FREEMAN.

Amour (ămūᵊ·ɹ, Fr. amu·r). ME. [a. OFr. *amur*, *amour*:—L. *amorem*. In 15–17th c. accented *a·mour* as Eng. (cf. *ena·mour*); later, treated as a euphem. use of mod. Fr.] †**1.** *gen.* Love, affection -1742; *pl.* the tender affections (L. *amores*, Fr. *amours*) -1727. **2.** A love-affair, love-making. (Now only joc. of honourable love-making.) 1567. **3.** *usually*, An intrigue 1626.

1. †*In amours* (with): in love (*with*). 3. Intrigue, that's an old phrase; ..a. sounds better DRYDEN.

Amourette (amure·t). 1865. [a. mod.Fr. for obs. Eng. AMORET.] **1.** A petty amour. **2.** The Love-grass (*Briza media*) 1866.

‖**Amour-propre** (amur,pro·pr'). 1818. [Fr.] Sensitive self-love; self-esteem.

†**Amo·ve**, *v.*[1] ME. [a. OFr. *amover*:—L. *admovere*; cf. also OFr. *esmover*:—L. *exmovere*.] **1.** To set in motion, excite -1590; *esp.* to move the feelings of (Fr. *émouvoir*) -1596. **2.** To arouse. SPENSER.

Amove (ămū·v), *v.*[2] 1494. [ad. L. *amovere*.] **1.** To remove from a position; to dismiss (a person) from an office. (Now only in *Law*.) †**2.** To remove (things immaterial) -1664. Hence **Amo·vable** *a.*, also **amovible**, removable. †**Amo·val**, removal.

Ampassy. *dial.* See AMPERSAND.

Ampelideous (æmpĭli·dĭəs), *a.* 1879. [f. mod.L. *ampelideæ* (f. Gr. ἄμπελος + OUS; see -IDEOUS.] *Bot.* Of the vine family.

Ampelite (æ·mpĭləit). 1751. [ad. L. *ampelitis*, a. Gr., in ἀμπελῖτις γῆ, an earth sprinkled on the vine.] *Min.* A bituminous earth; perh. cannel coal. Hence **Ampeli·tic** *a.*

Ampelography (æmpĭlǫ·grăfi). 1879. [a. Fr. *ampélographie*, f. Gr. ἄμπελος + -γραφία.] The scientific description of the vine.

A·mper. OE. A tumour; a blemish. (Cf. ANBURY.) Now *dial.*

Ampère (ăṅpe·r, æmpēᵊ·ɹ). 1881. [a. *Ampère*, the Fr. electrician.] *Electr.* The unit of current; the current that one volt can send through one ohm.

Amperometer (æmpĕrǫ·mĭtəɹ). 1882. [f. prec. + -(O)METER.] *Electr.* = AMMETER.

Ampersand (æmpəɹsæ·nd). 1837. Also **ampassy-, ampussy-, ampus-.** Corruption of '*and* per se—*and*', = the character &; i.e. '& by itself = and'. Found in all dial. glossaries.

Of all the types in a printer's hand Commend me to the A. *Punch* 17 Apr. 1869.

Amphi-, *prefix*, a. Gr. ἀμφι- both, of both kinds, on both sides, about, around. Used in derivatives, etc.

Amphiarthrosis (æ:mfi,aɹþrōᵘ·sis). 1836. [f. AMPHI- + ARTHROSIS.] *Anat.* A form of jointing combining diarthrosis and synarthrosis, in which the bones are united by an elastic cartilage, admitting of a certain amount of movement; as in the carpus, etc. Hence **A:mphiarthro·dial** *a.* characterized by a.

‖**Amphibia** (ămfi·biă), *sb. pl.* 1609. [L., a. Gr. ἀμφίβια (sc. ζῷα); *sing.* †**amphibion**, †**-ium**, now AMPHIBIAN; in sense 3.] **I.** *sing.* *-um*, *-on*, pl. *-a*, *-ums.* **1.** A being that is equally at home in water or on land. **2.** *fig.* A being of ambiguous or double position 1645.

2. Ask these a. what names they would have. What ..papists? no..protestants? no 1645.

II. *pl.* only. *Zool.* †**a.** Reptiles (including mod. Amphibia). LINNÆUS. **b.** Mammals (including seals, etc.). CUVIER. **c.** Since Macleay, the fourth division of Vertebrata, intermediate between reptiles and fishes, whose young have gills like fishes, as frogs, newts, etc.

Hence **Amphi·bial** *a.* and *sb.* (*rare*) = AMPHIBIAN. **Amphi·bian** *a.* of double or doubtful nature; of or pertaining to the A.; *sb.* one of the A. **Amphi·biolite, -lith**, the fossil remains of an amphibian.

Amphibiology (ămfi:bi,ǫ·lŏdʒi). 1840. [f. prec. + -(O)LOGY.] A scientific treatise on the Amphibia; the part of zoology which treats of Amphibia. Hence **Amphi:biolo·gical** *a.*

Amphibious (ămfi·biəs), *a.* 1643. [f. as prec. + -OUS.] **1.** Living both on land and in water 1654. **2.** Of, pertaining to, suited for, or connected with, both land and water 1646. **3.** Combining two lives, positions, classes, qualities, etc. 1643.

1. Th' a. Otter 1735. The a. tribe as willow, osier, etc. 1813. 2. A floating island, an a. spot WORDSW. 3. I have considered this a. Pope CARLYLE. Hence **Amphi·bious-ly** *adv.*, **-ness.** (Dicts.)

Amphibium, (L.) sing. form of AMPHIBIA.

Amphibole [1] (æ·mfibōᵘl). 1606. [a. Fr., ad. L. *amphibolum*, a. Gr. ἀμφίβολον, f. ἀμφί on both sides and βάλλειν to throw.] †**1.** An ambiguity; = AMPHIBOLY -1668. **2.** Hornblende. So named by Haüy 1801, in allusion to the great variety in composition, etc., assumed by the genus. Dana includes under it Actinolite, Asbestos, Hornblende, Tremolite, etc. (The pronunc. ămfi·bŏli is erron.) 1833. Hence **Amphibo·lic**, †**-al** *a.* equivocal; of, or of the nature of, the mineral amphibole; var. **Amphi·boline.** **Amphi·bolite, -yte**, = Hornblende-rock or Diabase.

‖**Amphibole** [2] (ămfi·bŏlĭ). 1854. [Gr.] *Gr. Antiq.* A casting-net.

Amphibology (æmfibǫ·lŏdʒi). ME. [a. Fr. *amphibologie*, ad. late L. *amphibologia*, for *amphibolia* (Cic.), a. Gr., after *tautologia*, etc.] 1. = AMPHIBOLY 1. 2. = AMPHIBOLY 2. 1589. Hence **Amphi·bolo·gical** *a.* ambiguous, *prop.* of a sentence or phrase; equivocating. **Amphibo·logism**, an amphibolous construction or phrase (*rare*).

Amphi·bolosty·lous, *a.* 1879. [f. Gr. ἀμφίβολος + στῦλος.] *Bot.* Having a non-apparent style.

Amphi·bolous, *a.* 1641. [f. L. *amphibolus*; see AMPHIBOLE.] †1. Of double or doubtful character or sense -1660. 2. *Path.* Spreading on both sides 1880.

Amphiboly (æ̆mfi·bŏli). 1588. [a. OFr. *amphibolie*, ad. L., a. Gr. ἀμφιβολία; see AMPHIBOLE.] 1. Ambiguous discourse; a quibble. (AMPHIBOLOGY is earlier and more pop.) 1610. 2. *Logic.* Ambiguity arising from uncertain construction, where the individual words are unequivocal. In pop. use confused with equivocation. 1588.

Amphibrach (æ·mfi͵bræk). Also **-us, -ys, -ee.** 1589. [ad. L. *amphibrachus*, *-ys*, a. Gr. ἀμφίβραχυς, short at both ends. The *-ee* is prob. after *spondee*, etc.] *Gr. and L. Pros.* A foot consisting of a long between two short syllables, as *ămātă*. Occas. now with reference to accent, as *drama·tic*.

So Prior: 'As Chlŏē cāme īntŏ thĕ rōom t'ŏthĕr dāy' GRAY.

Amphi·bryous, *a.* 1866. [f. Gr. ἀμφί + βρύειν to swell + -OUS.] *Bot.* Growing by additions all over the periphery.

Amphica·rpus, *a.* 1866. [f. Gr. ἀμφί + καρπός.] *Bot.* Having fruit of two kinds, or at two times.

Amphichro·ic, *a.* 1876. [f. Gr. ἀμφί + -χροος.] Having a double action on test colours in chemistry.

Amphicœ·lous, *a.* 1869. [f. Gr. ἀμφί + κοῖλος.] *Phys.* Concave on both sides, double concave, as vertebræ. So **Amphicœ·lian.**

†**A·mphicome.** [f. Gr. ἀμφί + κόμη.] A kind of figured stone, round, but rugged, once used in divination (Chambers).

Amphictyonic (æmfi:kti͵ǫ·nik), *a.* 1753. [ad. L. *amphictyonicus*, a. Gr.; see next and -IC.] Of the Amphictyons; also *transf.*

Amphictyons (æ̆mfi·kti͵ǫ̆nz), *sb. pl.* 1586. [ad. Gr. ἀμφικτύονες, orig. ἀμφικτίονες, they that dwelt round.] *Gr. Hist.* Deputies from the states of ancient Greece composing a council.

Amphictyony (æmfi·kti͵ǫ̆ni). 1835. [ad. Gr. ἀμφικτυονία, f. prec.] *Gr. Hist.* A confederation of Amphictyons; a league of neighbouring states for the common interest.

†**Amphid(e** (æ·mfid). 1842. [f. Gr. ἀμφί + -IDE.] *Chem.* An obs. name for salts viewed by Berzelius as compounds of two oxides, sulphides, selenides, or tellurides, as distinct from the *haloid* salts.

A·mphidisc. 1867. [f. Gr. ἀμφί + δίσκος.] *Zool.* Asteroid spicules, resembling two toothed wheels united by an axle, which form a layer surrounding the gemmules of sponges.

†**Amphidro·mic, -al**, *a.* 1658. [f. Gr. ἀμφιδρομία + -IC, + -AL.] Pertaining to the Amphidromia (an Attic festival at the naming of a child, when friends carried it round the hearth, and then named it).

Amphigam (æ·mfi͵gæm). 1845. [a. Fr *amphigame*, f. Gr. ἀμφί + γάμος.] *Bot.* A name of plants having no distinct sexual organs, also called *Agamæ*. Hence **Amphi·gamous** *a.* of or pertaining to Amphigams.

‖**Amphigastria** (æmfi͵gæ·striă), *sb. pl.* 1842. [mod.L., f. Gr. ἀμφί + γαστρ- (γαστήρ).] *Bot.* Scale-like leaves developed on the under side of some Liverworts.

Amphigean (æ̆mfi·dʒī·ăn), *a. rare.* 1864. [f. Gr. ἀμφί + γῆ + -AN.] Extending all over the earth from the equator to both poles.

Amphigen[1] (æ·mfi͵dʒen). 1879. [a. Fr. *amphigène*, f. Gr. ἀμφί + -γενής.] *Bot.* = THALLOGEN.

†**A·mphigen**[2]. 1842. [f. Gr. ἀμφί + -GEN.] *Chem.* An element, as oxygen, sulphur, selenium, tellurium, capable of forming, in combination with metals, both acids and bases (Berzelius).

Amphigene (æ·mfi͵dʒīn). 1803. [a. Fr. *amphigène*; see AMPHIGEN[1].] *Min.* = LEUCITE. (Rejected by Dana.) Hence **Amphi·genite, -yte**, a lava containing a., or leucite.

Amphigenous (æ̆mfi·dʒĕnəs), *a.* 1835. [f. AMPHIGEN + -OUS.] 1. *Bot.* Growing all round a central point. 2. *Chem.* Of the nature or class of an amphigen 1879.

Amphigony (æ̆mfi·gŏni). 1876. [f. Gr. ἀμφί + -γονία.] Sexual reproduction. Hence **Amphigo·nic** *a.* pertaining to a.; bisexual. **Amphi·gonous** *a.* pertaining to both parents.

‖**Amphigouri, -gory** (æ·mfigūᵊri, æ·mfi͵gŏri). 1809. [mod.Fr.; ? f. Gr. ἀμφί + γῦρος circle, or -αγορία, cf. *allegory*.] A burlesque writing without sense, as a nonsense-verse.

Amphilogism (æ̆mfi·lŏdʒiz'm). *rare.* 1866. [f. Gr. ἀμφίλογος + -ISM.] A circumlocution.

†**Amphi·logy.** [ad. Gr. ἀμφιλογία.] Ambiguity. (Dicts.)

Amphimacer (æ̆mfi·măsəɹ). 1589. [ad. L. *amphimacrus*, a. Gr. ἀμφίμακρος long at both ends.] *Gr. and L. Pros.* A foot consisting of a short between two long syllables, as *cārĭtās*, or (mod.) *multitude*, etc.

‖**Amphioxus** (æmfi͵ǫ·ksŏs). 1836. [mod. L. f. ἀμφί + ὀξύς tapering at both ends.] *Zool.* A genus (containing one species) of fishes, called also the Lancelet, the lowest of the vertebrates.

We cannot regard A. as a fish *Athenæum*.

Amphipneust (æ·mfi͵pniūst). Pl. **-s**, or collect. **amphipneusta.** 1841. [f. Gr. ἀμφί + -πνευστος.] *Zool.* An Amphibian having both lungs and gills, as the Proteus and Siren.

Amphipod (æ·mfi͵pǫd). 1835. [f. next.] *sb.* One of the *Amphipoda*. *adj.* = AMPHIPODOUS. 1852.

‖**Amphipoda** (æmfi·pŏdă), *sb. pl.* As sing. AMPHIPOD. 1837. [mod.L. (sc. *animalia*), f. Gr. ἀμφί + -ποδα (πούς).] *Zool.* An order or sub-order of the sessile-eyed Crustacea, having feet of two kinds, as the common sand-hopper. Hence **Amphi·podan** *a.* of or pertaining to the A.; var. **Amphi·podous.** **Amphipo·diform** *a.*

Amphiprostyle (æ̆mfi·prŏstəil). 1706. [a. Fr., ad. L., a. Gr. ἀμφιπρόστυλος, f. ἀμφί + πρόστυλος PROSTYLE.] *Arch.* A temple having a portico in the rear as well as the front, but without columns at the sides.

‖**Amphisa·rca.** 1854. [mod.L. f. ἀμφί + σάρκα.] *Bot.* A hard-rinded berry, succulent within and woody without, as a calabash.

‖**Amphisbæna** (æmfisbī·na). ME. [L., a. Gr. ἀμφίσβαινα, f. ἀμφίς + βαίνειν. Cf. Fr. *amphisbène*.] 1. A fabled serpent, with a head at each end, and able to move in either direction: now a poet. conception. 2. *Zool.* A worm-like genus of lizards, having head and tail scarcely distinguishable 1833.

1. Complicated monsters head and taile, Scorpion, and Asp, and A. dire MILT. *P. L.* x. 524. Hence **Amphisbæ·nian** *a.* **Amphisbæ·nic** *a.* of the nature of an a. **Amphisbæ·nous** *a.* walking equally in opposite directions.

Amphiscians (æ̆mfi·ʃiănz), *sb. pl.* 1622. [f. med.L. *Amphiscii* (also used), a. Gr. ἀμφίσκιοι (f. ἀμφί + σκιά) + -AN.] Inhabitants of the torrid zone, whose shadows at one time fall northward, at another southward.

Amphistome (æ·mfi͵stōᵊm). 1880. [ad. mod.L. *amphistoma*, f. Gr. ἀμφί + στόμα.] *Zool.* A genus of worms, having suckers at both ends of the body. Hence **Amphi·stomoid** *a.* like or akin to the Amphistomes.

Amphistylic (æmfi͵stəi·lik), *a.* 1876. [f. Gr. ἀμφί + στῦλος + -IC.] Having piers supporting both upper and lower mandibular arches, as the skulls of certain sharks.

Amphitheatre, -ter (æ·mfi͵þī·ătəɹ). 1546. [ad. L. *amphitheatrum*, a. Gr., f. ἀμφί + θέατρον. The 17–18th c. spelling *-ter* is common in U.S.] †1. *etymol.* A double theatre -1807. 2. Hence, An oval or circular building, with seats rising behind and above each other, around an open space or arena 1546. 3. A place of public contest, an arena 1640. 4. A semicircular rising gallery in a theatre 1882. †5. *fig.* Surrounding scene -1711. 6. *transf.* A level surrounded by rising slopes 1772. 7. *Hort.* An arrangement of shrubs and trees resembling an a. 1753.

2. The students gathered in the a. to see a painful operation 1883. 4. A. stalls DICKENS. Hence **A·mphithe·atred** *ppl. a.* formed into, or provided with, an a. **A·mphithea·tric, -al** *a.* of or pertaining to or resembling an a. **A·mphithea·trically** *adv.*

Amphithere (æ·mfi͵þīᵊɹ). 1859. [ad. mod. L. amphitherium (also in use), f. Gr. ἀμφί + θηρίον.] *Palæont.* An extinct genus of small marsupials.

Amphi·tropal, *a.* 1847. [f. Gr. ἀμφί + τρόπος + -AL.] *Bot.* Of an embryo: So curved as to have both apex and radicle presented to the hilum. var. **Amphi·tropous.**

‖**Amphitryon** (æ̆mfi·tri͵ǫ̆n). 1862. [f. Molière's *Amphitryon* III. v.] A host, a dinner-giver.

Amphodarch (æ·mfŏdāɹk). 1878. [ad. Gr. ἀμφοδάρχης.] *Gr. Ant.* One governing a quarter of a town.

‖**Amphora** (æ·mfŏră). Pl. **-æ.** 1465. [L., ad. Gr. ἀμφορεύς, short for ἀμφιφορεύς.] 1. *Cl. Antiq.* A two-handled vessel, for holding wine, oil, etc. 2. A liquid measure, Greek, = about 9 gals.; or Roman (also called quadrantal), = 6 gals. 7 pts. 3. *Bot.* The lower part of a pyxis 1821. var. †**Amphore** (in senses 1, 2). Hence **A·mphoral** *a.* of, pertaining to, or like an a.

Amphoric (æmfǫ·rik), *a.* 1839. [ad. mod.L. *amphoricus*, f. prec.; see -IC.] 1. = AMPHORAL (*rare*). 2. *Med.* Like the sound produced by blowing or speaking into an amphora, etc., as in *a. cough*, etc. Hence **Amphori·city**, a. quality.

Amphoteric (æmfote·rik), *a. rare.* 1849. [f. Gr. ἀμφότερος + -IC.] Both acid and alkaline.

Ample (æ·mp'l), *a.* 1481. [a. Fr.:—L. *amplus*. Compar. *-r*, *-st*, also with *more*, *most*.] 1. Extending far; broad, wide, spacious. (Now always *eulogistic*.) 1548. 2. Roomy, capacious; copious 1596. 3. Of things immaterial: Large in extent or amount 1481; *esp.* full, complete 1592; liberal, unstinted 1536. 4. Of a writing, etc.: Copious 1592.

1. This a. third of our faire kingdome *Lear* I. i. 82. Ruling in large and a. Emperie SHAKS. 2. That a. hous SPENSER *F. Q.* III. xi. 49. 3. A more a. and large commission 1542. A. justice JUNIUS, provision 1834. 4. An ampler description 1670. Hence **A·mpleness** (*arch.*). **A·mply** *adv.* in an a. manner.

†**A·mple, amply**, *v.* ME. = AMPLIFY -1533.

†**Ample·ct**, *v.* 1525. [ad. L. *amplecti*.] To embrace -1657. var. †**Ample·x.**

Amplexation (æmplĕksēⁱ·ʃən). *rare.* 1615. [f. L. *amplexat-*, *amplexari*.] †1. Embracing. 2. *Surg.* A method of treating fracture of the clavicle.

Amplexicaudate (æ̆mple:ksi͵kǭ·deⁱt), *a.* 1879. [f. L. *amplexus* + *cauda*.] *Ent.* Having the tail enveloped in the interfemoral membrane.

Amplexicaul (æ̆mple·ksikǫl), *a.* 1760. [ad. mod.L. *amplexicaulis* (Linn.).] *Bot.* Embracing the stem, said of sessile leaves. var. **Ample:xicau·line.**

Amplexifoliate (æ̆mple·ksi͵fōᵘli͵ĕt), *a.* 1879. [f. mod.L. *amplexifolius*, after L. *foliatus*.] *Bot.* Having leaves which clasp the stem.

†**A·mpliate**, *v.* 1513. [f. L. *ampliat-*, *ampliare*. Cf. AMPLE *v.*] To enlarge; to amplify -1686. Hence **A·mpliate**, †**A·mpliated** *ppl. adjs.* enlarged, amplified.

Ampliation (æmpli͵ēⁱ·ʃən). *arch.* 1509. [a. Fr., ad. L. *ampliationem*; see AMPLIATE *v.*] 1. Enlarging; amplification. 2. That which is added in enlarging; an enlargement or extension 1590. 3. *Law.* Deferring of judgement for further consideration 1656.

Ampliative (æ·mpliĕtiv), *a.* 1842. [f. L. *ampliat-*; see AMPLIATE *v.*] *Logic.* Enlarging a simple conception by predicating of it something which is not directly implied in it.

Amplification (æ·mplifikēⁱ·ʃən). 1546. [ad. L. *amplificationem*; see AMPLIFY.] The action of amplifying. 1. Enlargement. *concr.* That which is added. 2. Augmentation in extent, importance, significance, etc. *concr.*

An enlarged representation. 1569. *esp.* Extension of meaning 1551. 3. *Rhet.* The extension of a simple statement by rhetorical devices; making the most of a thought, etc. 1553. 4. Additions made; statement as amplified 1567.

2. *Amplification of the predicate* (in *Gram.*) = extension of the predicate. 3. A. is the spinning-wheel of the *bathos*, which draws out and spreads it POPE. No a. at all, but a positiue and measured truth BACON.

A·mplifica:tory, *a. rare.* [mod. f. L. *amplificator.*] Of the nature of enlargement.

Amplifier (æ·mplifəi,əɹ). 1546. [f. next.] One who or that which amplifies or enlarges. b. *spec.* An apparatus for increasing the strength of wireless signals; also, a loud speaker used for making a voice more audible.

Amplify (æ·mplifəi), *v.* ME. [a. Fr. *amplifier*, f. L. *amplificare*, f. *amplus.*] †1. To enlarge in space or capacity -1636; in volume or amount -1626. Also *intr.* (*refl.*) -1600. 2. Of things immaterial: To extend in amount, importance, etc. 1549. 3. To expand (a story, etc.) ME. 4. *intr.* To enlarge, expatiate 1590. 5. To magnify, exaggerate 1561.

1. To a. states 1636, sounds BACON. 2. To a. one's jurisdiction 1767. 3. Instead of saying .. Turnus died, he amplifies his death 1751. 4. He would a. so much, he would often lose his way 1670.

Amplitude (æ·mplitiud). 1549. [a. Fr., ad. L. *amplitudo*, f. *amplus.*] The quality of being AMPLE. 1. Extension in space; *chiefly* width, breadth 1599. 2. Of things immaterial: Width, breadth, fullness; copiousness 1605. 3. Wide (mental) range 1575. 4. Excellence, splendour 1549. 5. *Astr.* Angular distance at rising or setting from the eastern or western point of the horizon 1627. 6. Extent of motion in space; *esp.* (in *Physics*), *A. of a vibration*: the distance a particle moves from side to side in one vibration 1837.

1. An a. of form and stature, answering to her mind LAMB. 2. The a. of the divine charity 1850. 3. As for the A. of his Lordship's mynde 1575. 4. The state and a. of their Empire FULLER. 5. *Magnetic Amplitude*: The a. reckoned from the eastern and western points as shown by the compass.

‖**Ampu·lla.** Pl. -æ. ME. [L. ? f. *amb-* + *olla* pot, or dim. of *amphora* quasi *ampholla.*] 1. *Rom. Antiq.* A small globular flask or bottle, with two handles. 2. A vessel for holding consecrated oil, etc. 1598. 3. *Biol.* Any vessel shaped like an ampulla; the dilated end of any canal, duct, etc. in an animal; the spongiole of a root 1821. var. †**A·mpul** (in senses 1, 2). Hence **Ampulla·ceous** *a.* like an a.; bottle-shaped, inflated. **A·mpullar, A·mpullary** *adjs.* of the form or character of an a. **A·mpullate** *a.* furnished with, or shaped like, an a.; bellied; var. **A·mpullated** *ppl. a.* **Ampu·lliform** *a.* flask-shaped, bulging.

Ampullosity (æmpŏlǫ·sĭti). *rare.* 1868. [f. med.L. *ampullosus* (f. *ampulla*) + -ITY.] Inflated inanity; bombast. BROWNING.

Ampus-and, ampussy; see AMPERSAND.

Amputate (æ·mpiuteⁱt), *v.* 1638. [f. L. *amputat-*, *amputare.*] 1. *gen.* To lop off or prune. *Obs.* exc. as *fig.* 2. *spec.* To cut off a limb, or any projecting part of the body. Also *absol.* 1639. Hence **A·mputated** *ppl. a.* cut off, as a limb, etc. **A·mputating** *vbl. sb.* amputation. **A·mputator**, one who amputates. *lit.* and *fig.*

Amputation (æmpiutēⁱ·ʃən). 1611. [ad. L. *amputationem* (or a. Fr.).] 1. The operation of amputating (see AMPUTATE). Also *attrib.* 2. *fig.* Excision, *e.g.* of sentences, etc.; pruning 1664.

2. 'Twas he..Made those that represent the nation Submit and suffer a. BUTLER *Hudibr.* II. i. 364.

‖**Ampyx** (æ·mpiks). [Gr. ἄμπυξ.] *Gr. Antiq.* A broad metal band worn on the forehead of ladies of rank; also, the headband of horses.

‖**Amrita** (æmrī·tă). Also **Amreeta.** 1810. [ad. Skr. (= Gr. ἄμ(β)ροτος). The *i* is erron. lengthened.] Immortal, ambrosial.

The A.-cup of immortality SOUTHEY.

†**A·msel, amzel.** 1705. [app. a. Ger., cogn. w. OE. *ósle*, now *ousel.*] The Blackbird, or the Ring Ousel.

†‖**Amtman** (a·mtmăn). 1587. [Ger.; cf. AMBASSADE.] One in charge; a bailiff, steward, magistrate, etc.

Amuck (ămɒ·k), *a.* and *adv.*; also **amock, amok.** 1663. [ad. Malay.] 1. Orig. *adj.* or *sb.* A frenzied Malay. 2. To run amuck: to run viciously, frenzied for blood. (Here orig. *adj.*) 1672. 3. *fig.* Wild, or wildly. (Usu. with *run.*) Const. *on, at, against,* (*with, of*). 1689. ¶ Erron. treated as *muck* sb.

3. Too discreet To run a muck, and tilt at all I meet POPE. ¶Runs an Indian muck at all he meets DRYDEN.

Amulet (æ·miŭlĕt). 1601. [ad. L. *amuletum* (Pliny), of unkn. origin.] 1. Anything worn as a charm against evil, disease, witchcraft, etc. Also *fig.* 1621. †2. *Med.* A medicine whose virtue or mode of operation is occult -1753.

1. Amulets against agues SIR T. BROWNE. *fig.* He is our A., our Sun BURTON. Hence †**Amule·tic** *a.* of or pertaining to amulets; *sb.* [sc. *medicine.*]

Amuse (ămiū·z), *v.* 1480. [a. OFr. *amuser*, f. *à* causal + *muser* to stare stupidly. Not in SHAKS.] †1. *intr.* To gaze in astonishment -1681; *trans.* to cause to muse or stare, to puzzle -1741. †2. To occupy the attention of. Const. *upon, with, about, to.* (esp. *refl.* and *pass.*) -1734. 3. To divert the attention of; to beguile, mislead. (The usual sense in 17-18th c.) *arch.* 1480. 4. To keep in expectation, in order to gain or waste time (*arch.*) 1639; †to keep up for a purpose -1693. 5. To divert the attention of from serious business; *hence*, to divert; *esp.* to tickle the fancy of. Const. *with, by, in, at.* 1631. 6. To beguile, while away 1771.

1. To .. stupify, fluster, and a. the senses SWIFT. 2. Amused and engrossed by the things of sense WATTS. 3. Tools of the Devil, to cheat and a. the world DE FOE. Their Fleet was to a. ours whilst they cross from Leghorn NELSON. 4. Amused with vain expectations 1777. 5. To a. himself with trifles 1687. 6. He did this to a. their concern 1771. Hence **Amu·sable** *a.* capable of being amused. **Amusee·**, the person amused. **Amu·ser. Amu·singly** *adv.*, **-ness.**

Amusement (ămiū·zmĕnt). 1611. [a. Fr., f. *amuser*; see AMUSE and -MENT.] The action of amusing, or a thing done to amuse. †1. Musing -1712; bewilderment -1699. 2. The action of amusing (sense 3). *arch.* 1692. †3. A diversion to gain or waste time -1710. 4. The action of amusing (sense 5) 1698. 5. *concr.* A pastime, play, game, etc. (Orig. *depreciatively.*) 1673.

1. Useless a. and dispute LOCKE. 4. A. is the happiness of those that cannot think POPE. When men are rightly occupied, their a. grows out of their work RUSKIN. 5. Plays and other amusements 1753.

†**Amusette** (æmiuze·t). 1761. [a. Fr., dim. f. *amuse.*] A light field-cannon, invented by Marshal Saxe.

Amusive (ămiū·ziv), *a.* 1728. [f. AMUSE *v.* after *abusive*, etc.; see -IVE.] Such as to amuse. †1. Illusive -1760; recreative -1753. 2. Interesting; *esp.* fitted to make one smile or laugh 1760. 3. Tending to amusement 1781. Hence **Amu·sively** *adv.* **Amu·siveness.**

A-mu·tter, *adv.* 1856. [A *prep.*[1]] Muttering. MRS. BROWNING.

†**Amu·zle**, *v. rare.* 1795. [? dim. of *amuse.*]

Amyctic (ămi·ktik), *a.* 1853. [ad. L. *amycticus*, a. Gr., f. ἀμύσσειν.] *Med.* Excoriating, irritating, vellicating.

†**A·mydon, -oun.** ME. [a. Fr. *amidon* :—late L. *amydum*, for cl. *amylum*; see AMYL.] Finest flour -1616.

Amyelencephalic (ăməi:ĕlensĭfæ·lik), *a.* 1875. [f. Gr. ἀμύελος + ἐγκέφαλος + -IC.] *Phys.* Having the central nervous system wanting.

Amyelotrophy (ăməi:ĕlǫ·trŏfi). 1879. [f. Gr. ἀ + μυελός + -τροφία.] *Path.* Atrophy of the spinal cord.

Amyelous (ămǝi·ĕlǝs), *a.* [f. Gr. ἀμύελος + -OUS.] *Phys.* Wanting the spinal cord.

Amy·gdal. ? *Obs.* OE. [ad. L. *amygdala*, a. Gr. ἀμυγδάλη.] †1. An almond -ME. 2. *pl.* The tonsils; also, the almonds of the ear 1541. Hence **Amy:gdala·ceous** *a. Bot.* akin to the almond. **Amy·gdalate** *a.* made of almonds; †*sb.* = *almond-milk* (see ALMOND); *Chem.* a salt of Amygdalic acid. **Amygda·lic** *a. Chem.* of or pertaining to almonds. *Amygdalic Acid*, $C_{20}H_{26}O_{12}$, derived from amygdalin by boiling with an alkali. **Amygdali·neous** *a.* belonging to the almond tribe.

Amygdalin (ămi·gdălin). 1651. [f. as prec. + IN.] *Chem.* $C_{20}H_{27}NO_{11} + 3\ H_2O$; a GLUCOSIDE found crystalline in almonds, etc., and amorphous in cherry-laurel leaves, etc.

‖**Amygdalitis** (-əi·tis). 1876. [f. as prec. + -ITIS.] *Med.* Inflammation of the tonsils.

Amygdaloid (ămi·gdăloid), *a.* 1791. [f. Gr. ἀμυγδάλη + -OID. Cf. Fr. *amygdaloïde.*] Almond-shaped; having almond-shaped nodules 1836. As *sb. Geol.* An igneous rock, usually trappean, containing almond-shaped nodules or geodes of agate, chalcedony, calcspar, etc. Hence **Amygdaloi·dal** *a.*

Amygdule (ămi·gdiul). 1877. [f. L. *amygd(ala)* + -ULE.] *Geol.* An agate pebble.

†**A·myl**[1]. 1572. [ad. L. *amylum*, a. Gr. ἄμυλον.] Starch; finest flour -1601. Cf. AMYDON.

Amyl[2] (æ·mil). 1850. [f. L. *am(ylum* starch + -YL(E = Gr. ὕλη. An inappropriate name. See N. E. D.] *Chem.* The monatomic alcohol radical of the pentacarbon series C_5H_{11}, also called *Pentyl* or *Quintyl.*

attrib. =amylic: as in **Amyl alcohol**, CH_2CH_3. $(C_2H_4)OH$, a burning acrid oily liquid, the chief constituent of Fusel oil; **Amyl hydride**, =*pentane*; **Ethyl-amyl-acetate**, the essence of jargonelle pears. Hence **A·mylami·ne**, an amine in which one hydrogen atom of ammonia is replaced by amyl. **A·mylate**, a salt of the radical amyl, in which amyl replaces the oxygenated group in a metallic salt. **A·mylene**, the diatomic hydrocarbon, or olefine, of the pentacarbon series, C_5H_{10}, formed by the removal of one atom of water from amyl alcohol; it has anæsthetic properties. **Amy·lic** *a.* of or pertaining to amyl; = AMYL *attrib.*

Amylaceous (æmilēⁱ·ʃəs), *a.* 1830. [f. L. *amylum* + -ACEOUS. Cf. Fr. *amylacé.*] Of the character or nature of starch; starchy.

Amylo-, comb. form of AMYL [1], [2]. Hence: **amylo·ce:llulo·se** [L. *cellulosus*], a supposed constituent of starch granules, which is colour-ed copper-red by iodine; **-gen**, soluble starch; **-ly·tic** [Gr. -λυτικός] *a.*, converting starch into dextrine and sugar; **-meter** [Gr. μέτρον], an instrument for testing the amount of starch, in potatoes, etc.; **-sy·nthesis** [Gr. σύνθεσις], the formation of starch by assimilation.

Amyloid (æ·miloid). 1857. [f. L. *amylum*, Gr. ἄμυλον + -OID.] A. *adj.* Starch-like. B. *sb.* 1. Any non-nitrogenous starchy food 1872. 2. A starch-like substance forming the cell-walls in the cotyledons of various plants. 3. An albuminoid developed in diseased degeneration of various animal organs. Also *attrib.* Hence **Amyloi·dal** *a.*

Amylose (æ·milōᵘs). 1877. [f. as prec. + -OSE. *Chem.* A subdivision of the *Carbohydrates.* The Amyloses are dextrin, starch, inulin, glycogen, cellulose, tunicin, and gum, all having the composition $C_6H_{10}O_5$, or a multiple thereof.

Amyosthenic (ăməi,ǫspe·nik). 1879. [f. Gr. ἀ + μῦς, μυός + -σθένεια + -IC.] *Med.* A medicine which depresses muscular action.

Amyo·trophy. 1879. [f. Gr. ἀ + μῦς, μυός + -τροφία.] *Path.* Atrophy of muscle. Hence **Amyotro·phic** *a.*

A·myous, *a.* 1879. [f. Gr. ἄμυος.] *Path.* Wanting in muscle.

‖**Amyris** (æ·miris). 1865. *Bot.* A genus of tropical trees and shrubs, yielding resinous products.

Amzel, var. of AMSEL.

†**An**, *adj.*[1] Earlier form of the numeral ONE; retained in the north. See ANE, A *adj.*[2], and ONE.

An (toneless ăn, ən; emph. æn), *adj.*[2], *indef. article.* The older and fuller form of *a*, now retained only bef. a vowel sound, by most writers bef. *h*, and by some bef. *eu*, *ū* (= *yū*), in unaccented syllables. For its history, and signification, see A *adj.*[2]

An, an' (ăn, ən, 'n), *conj.* [weakened from AND.] 1. = AND, *conj. co-ordinate.* (L. *et.*) OE. Rare after 1500, exc. in dial. as *an'*, and in common pronunc. 2. = AND, *conj. conditional.* = *if.* (L. *si.*) *arch.* and *dial.* Rare bef. 1600; exc. in *an't* (= *an it*), occurring only once in the 1st Folio of SHAKS. Mod. writers make *an'* for 'and', L. *et*, dial. or illiterate, but *an'* or *an* for 'and', L. *si*, arch. Dialectally both are *an'*; the intensified *and if, an if*, still exists in s.w. dial. as *nif.*

2. There, an't shall please you *L. L. L.* v. ii. 584. Nay then two treyes, an if you grow so nice *Ibid.* v. ii. 232.

†**An**, *prep.* The orig. form of ON, in Anglo-Saxon also absorbing *in*. After 11th c. *on* prep. occ. became *ăn* bef. vowels, as *an edge*, etc. (see A *prep.*[1]), but later again this became *on*, or *in*, exc. in go *an* (now *a*) hawking, twice *an* hour. See AN- *pref.* 1, and A *prep.*[1]

Each particular haire to stand an end *Haml.* I. v. 19. Set my pugging tooth an edge *Wint. T.* IV. iii. 7.

An-, *prefix.* 1. OE. and ME. **an-** = AN *prep.* (see prec.) Cf. A- *pref.* 2. *Obs.*, exc. as in *anon, anent*, etc. 2. ME. **an-**, reduced f. OE. *and-*, against; see AND-. †3. ME. **an-**:—OE. *ān* one. 4. ME. **an-** = Anglo-Norm. *an-*, OFr. *en-*:—L. *in-* = in, into, as ANOINT (L. *inunctum*), etc. 5. ME. **an-**, for earlier *a-* = OE. *a-* (A- *pref.* 1), or OFr. *a-*:—L. *ab-*, *ad-*, *ex-*, *ob-*, as *a(n)s-aumple*, refash. *example*, or changed to *ensample*. 6. ME. **an-**, earlier *a-*, = OFr. *a-*:—L. *an-* = *ad-* 'to', bef. *n-*, as in *a(n)nounce*. See AD-. 7. **an-**, repr. L. *an-* = *ad-* bef. *n-*, as in *annul*, etc. 8. **an-**, repr. L. *an-* bef. certain cons., for *am-*, *amb-*, *ambi-* on both sides, about. 9. **an-**, repr. Gr. ἀν- for ἀνά up, back, etc. (see ANA-) bef. a vowel; also in *anchor*[2], *anchoret*. 10. **an-**, repr. Gr. ἀν-, not, without (bef. cons. ἀ; see A- *pref.* 14); esp. in scientific words.

-an, *suffix.* I. Derivative. 1. repr. L. *-anus*, *-ana*, *-anum*, of or belonging to. Orig. in ME. *-ain*, or (after *i*) *-en*, after OFr., but later refash. *-an*. *Esp.* added to proper names; 'belonging to a place', as *Oxonian*, etc.; 'following a founder', or 'a system', as *Lutheran, Anglican*, etc.; and (*Zool.*) 'belonging to a class or order', as *crustacean*, etc. Prop. these are all adjs., but many are used subst. as in L. In L. this termination was added to others, as *-ius*, in *-ianus*, whence -IAN, which is in use merely a euphonic var. of *-an*; cf. *Corinthian, Roman*. 2. in *Chem.* for *-ane*, as in *azotan* (obs.).

†II. Inflectional. †1. In OE. *pl.* ending = ME. *-en*, as *ox-en*:—OE. *ox-an*. Hence (dat. or loc. sing.) in advb. or prep. forms, as *beforan*. †2. In OE. pres. inf. ending, = ME. *-en*, *-e*, as OE. *writan*, ME. *write(n*; now *write*.

Ana (ē¹·nă, ā·nă). 1727. [a. L. *-ana* in neut. pl. of adjs. in *-anus* (see -AN *suffix* 1), as in (*Dicta*) *Virgiliana*. Used in Fr. as sb. sing. *un ana*.] A. *suffix.* Sayings of a person, literary trifles, gossip, etc., of a place; anecdotes of, notes about, or publications bearing upon 1741.

Shakespeariana 1863.

B. *sb.* 1. *collect. sing.* (with *pl.*) A collection of the sayings or table talk of any one 1727. 2. *collect. pl.* Clever sayings or anecdotes of any one; notes, etc. relating to a person or place; literary gossip ? 1755.

1. Boswell's Life of Johnson..the *Ana* of all *Anas* SOUTHEY. 2. Ere days that deal in ana TENNYSON.

‖**Ana** (æ·nă), *adv.* Often written *āā* or *ā*. 1500. [med.L. a. Gr. ἀνά (see next) as advb.] In prescriptions: Throughout, of each, of every one alike: *hence* formerly, 'an equal quantity or number'.

Ana of each does the just Mixture make COWLEY.

Ana-, *pref.*, repr. Gr. ἀνά up, in place or time, back, again, anew, in words and derivatives from Gr.

Ana, var. of ANNA, Indian money.

Anabaptism (ænăbæ·ptiz'm). 1577. [ad. L. *anabaptismus*, a. Gr., f. ἀνά+βαπτισμός.] 1. Re-baptism. (The orig. sense in L.) Also *transf.* 1645. 2. The doctrine of the Anabaptists; also, occas., of modern Baptists (see next). 1577. So †**Anaba·ptistry.**

Anabaptist (ænăbæ·ptist). 1532. [ad. mod. L. *anabaptista*; see prec. Cf. Fr. *anabaptiste*.] 1. *lit.* One who baptizes over again (whether *frequently*, or *once*). Hence 2. *Ch. Hist.* Name of a sect which arose in Germany in 1521. 3. Applied (invidiously) to the Baptists; and occas. (loosely) to other non-Anglicans 1586. Also *attrib.*

3. Baptists never called themselves *ana*baptists; as they did not admit that immersion .. was *baptism* [without] an intelligent concurrence..on the part of the recipient DR. J. ANGUS. *attrib.* An.. a. preacher SWIFT. Hence **A·nabapti·stic, -al** *a.* connected with or attributed to Anabaptists; **-ly** *adv.*

Anabaptize (æ:năbæ̆ptəi·z), *v.* 1637. [ad. med.L. *anabaptizare*, ad. Gr. ἀναβαπτίζειν.] To re-baptize, re-christen; *hence*, to re-name.

Marvell..now anabaptized Dr. Turner as Mr. Smirke H. COLERIDGE.

‖**Anabas** (æ·nābæs). 1845. [mod.L. (Cuvier), a. Gr. ἀναβάς, ἀναβαίνειν.] A genus of acanthopterygian fishes, which sometimes leave the water, and even climb trees.

‖**Anabasis** (ănæ·băsis). 1706. [a. Gr., f. ἀναβαίνειν; cf. βάσις.] 1. A going up, a military advance; *esp.* that of Cyrus the younger into Asia, as narrated by Xenophon. †2. *Med.* The course of a disease to its climax 1706.

1. General Sherman's great a. 1864.

†‖**Ana·bathrum.** 1623. [L., a. Gr. ἀνάβαθρον.] A raised platform; a pulpit -1759.

Anabatic (ænăbæ·tik), *a.* 1811. [ad. Gr. ἀναβατικός.] *Med.* Of or belonging to ANABASIS (sense 2); increasing (as a fever).

Anabiotic (æ:năbəi,ǫ·tik), *a.* 1879. [f. Gr. ἀνά + βιωτικός.] *Med.* Stimulant or tonic.

†‖**Anabro·sis.** 1721. [Gr., f. ἀναβρω-, ἀναβιβρώσκειν.] *Med.* Corrosion of the soft parts of the body. Hence †**Anabro·tic** *a.*

‖**Anaca·mpsis.** 1879. [Gr., f. ἀνακάμπτειν.] Reflection; reaction. Hence **Anaca·mptic, -al**, *a.* causing or suffering reflection; chiefly of echoes. **Anaca·mptically** *adv.* by way of a. †**Anaca·mptics,** (*a*) = *Catoptrics* (see CATOPTRIC); (*b*) the branch of Acoustics, that relates to reflection of sound.

Anacard (æ·năkāɹd). 1541. [a. Fr. *anacarde*, ad. mod.L. *anacardium*, f. Gr. ἀνά + καρδία, from its shape. Now used in L. form.] The nut of the Cashew (*Anacardium occidentale*); also, any plant of N.O. *Anacardiaceæ* (Lindley). Hence **Anaca·rdate.** *Chem.* See ANACARDIC. **Anaca·rdia·ceous** *a. Bot.* belonging to the *Anacardiaceæ*, as the Cashew, and the trees that produce mangos, pistachios, etc.

Anacardic (ænăkā·ɹdik), *a.* 1863. [f. mod. L. *anacardium* + -IC.] Of the Cashew-nut; as in *anacardic acid*, $C_{44}H_{64}O_7$, extracted from it by the action of ether. Its salts are **anacardates.**

Anacathartic (æ:nă,kăþā·ɹtik). 1696. [f. Gr. ἀνά + CATHARTIC.] *Med. adj.* Causing *anacatharsis*, i. e. vomiting or expectoration. *sb.* [sc. *drug*, etc.] Now written ANOCATHARTIC.

‖**A:nacephalæo·sis.** *rare.* 1696. [Gr.; see next.] Recapitulation.

Anacephalize (ænăse·făləiz), *v.* ? *Obs.* 1654. [f. Gr. ἀνά + κεφαλή + -IZE.] To recapitulate.

‖**Anacharis** (ănæ·kăris). 1848. [mod.L. f. Gr. ἀνά + χάρις.] A N. American water-weed (*A. Alsinastrum* or *Elodea Canadensis*), which appeared unaccountably in Britain in 1842, and rapidly filled canals, ditches, and ponds, all over the country.

Anachoret(e, anachorite, var. ANCHORET.

Ana·chorism. *nonce-wd.* [f. Gr. ἀνά + χωρίον, to match *anachronism*; see -ISM.] Something foreign to the country. LOWELL.

Anachronic, -al (ænăkrǫ·nik, -ăl), *a.* 1807. [f. Gr. ἀνά + χρόνος; cf. *chronic.*] Erroneous in date or order; marked by anachronism. Hence **Anachro·nically** *adv.*

Anachronism (ănæ·krŏniz'm). 1646. [a. Fr. *anachronisme*, ad. L. *anachronismus*, a. Gr., f. ἀναχρονίζειν.] 1. An error in computing time, or fixing dates; reference of an event, etc., to a wrong date. Used *etymologically* of a date which is too early (*prochronism*), but also of too late a date (*parachronism*). 2. Anything done or existing out of date; *hence*, any former thing, which is, or would be, out of harmony with the present; a *practical a.* 1816.

2. A pilgrimage now seems an a. 1859. Hence **Ana·chronist,** one who commits an a. (DE QUINCEY.) **Ana·chroni·stic** *a.* of the nature of, or involving, a. **Ana·chronize** *v.* to transfer to a wrong time. (LOWELL.) **Ana·chronous** *a.* involving a.; **-ly** *adv.*

†**Anack.** 1615. Oatmeal bread -1750.

Anaclastic (ænăklæ·stik), *a.* 1753. [f. Gr. ἀνάκλαστος, f. ἀνακλαίειν + -IC.] 1. *Opt.* Pertaining to, or produced by, refraction 1796. 2. Springing back with a crackling sound 1753. As *sb.* (*pl.*) [Cf. *acoustics.*] = Dioptrics 1696.

1. *Anaclastic curves*: certain apparent curves seen at the bottom of a vessel full of water, etc., caused by refraction. 2. *Anaclastic glasses*: low phials, with very thin, slightly convex, bottoms, which become concave, and again convex, with a crackling noise, as the air in the phials is sucked out or returned.

Anaclete (æ·năklīt). *rare.* 1817. [ad. Gr. ἀνάκλητος, f. ἀνακαλέειν; cf. *paraclete.*] The Recalled; a name given to Julian the Apostate.

Anacœnosis (æ:nă,sīnō͞u·sis). 1589. [med. L. a. Gr. ἀνακοίνωσις, f. ἀνά + κοινόειν, f. κοινός.] *Rhet.* A figure, by which the speaker applies to his hearers or opponents for their opinion upon the point in debate.

‖**Anacoluthia** (æ:năkol'iū·þiă). 1856. [L., a. Gr.] A want of grammatical sequence; the passing to a new construction before the original one is completed.

‖**Anacoluthon** (æ:năkol'iū·þǫn). Pl. **-a** (-ons). 1706. [a. L., a. Gr., f. ἀν priv. + ἀ copul. + κέλευθος.] *Gram.* An instance of anacoluthia. Hence **A·nacolu·thic** *a.* of or pertaining to anacoluthia; lacking grammatical sequence; **-ally** *adv.*

Anaconda (ænăkǫ·ndă). Also **-o.** 1768. [?] Orig. A large Ceylonese snake (? *Python reticulatus*, or *P. molurus* Gray); *spec.* applied (erron.) to a large S. American Boa (*Eunectes murinus* Gray), called in Brazil *sucuriuba*; *loosely*, any large snake which crushes its prey.

Anacreontic (ănæ:kri,ǫ·ntik), *a.* 1656. [ad. L. *anacreonticus*, f. Gr. Ἀνακρέων prop. name.] Of, or after the manner of, the Greek poet Anacreon. As *sb.* [sc. *poem.*] 1656. Hence **Ana:creo·ntically** *adv.*

Anacrotism (ănæ·krŏtiz'm). 1879. [f. Gr. ἀνά + κρότος.] *Phys.* A secondary oscillation or notch in the upward portion of the curve obtained in a sphygmographic tracing. Hence **Anacro·tic** *a.* (More fully *anadicrotic.*)

‖**Anacru·sis.** 1833. [L., repr. Gr. ἀνάκρουσις.] *Pros.* A syllable at the beginning of a verse, before the just rhythm.

Anadem (æ·nădĕm). *poet.* 1604. [ad. L. *anadema*, a. Gr., f. ἀναδεῖν.] A wreath for the head; a chaplet, a garland.

Anadems of flowers DRAYTON.

†**A·nadesm.** 1658. [ad. Gr. ἀναδέσμη.] A bandage for wounds.

Anadicro·tic, fuller f. ANACROTIC.

‖**Anadiplosis** (æ:nă,diplō͞u·sis). 1589. [L., a. Gr., f. ἀνά + διπλόειν.] *Rhet.* Reduplication; the beginning of a sentence, line, or clause with the concluding, or any prominent, word of the preceding.

As thus: Comforte it is for man to haue a wife, Wife chast, and wise..*Anadiplosis* PUTTENHAM.

Anadrom (æ·nădrǫm). 1859. [a. Fr. *anadrome*, ad. Gr. ἀνάδρομος.] An anadromous fish.

Anadromous (ănæ·drŏmǝs), *a.* 1753. [f. Gr. ἀνάδρομος.] 1. *Zool.* Ascending rivers to spawn. 2. *Bot.* Of ferns: Having their lowest secondary branches on the anterior side of the pinnæ 1881.

‖**Anæmia** (ănī·miă). 1836. [mod.L., a. Gr. ἀναιμία, f. ἀν + αἷμα.] *Path.* Lack of blood, or of red corpuscles in the blood. Hence **Anæ·mial, Anæ·mic** *adjs.* bloodless; of or pertaining to a.

Anæmo·tropy. 1860. [f. Gr. ἀν + αἷμα + -τροφια.] *Path.* Deficient nourishment of the blood.

Anære·tic. 1879. [f. Gr. ἀναιρετικός.] *Med.* An agent which tends to destroy tissue.

Anaerophyte (ănē·ərо,fəit). 1876. [f. Gr. ἀν + ἀήρ, ἀέρος + φυτόν.] *Bot.* A plant which does not need a direct supply of air.

‖**Anæsthesia** (ænesþī·siă, ænīs-). 1721. [mod.L., a. Gr. ἀναισθησία, f. ἀν + αἴσθησις. Cf. Fr. *anesthésie*. The *æ* is by some pronounced (*ī, i, ĭ*) according to place of accent.] Loss of feeling or sensation; insensibility. Also *fig.* var. †**Anæsthe·sis.** Hence **Anæsthe·siant** *adj.* producing a.; *sb.* an anæsthetic. **Anæ:sthesi·meter,** an instrument for measuring the amount of an anæsthetic administered.

Anæsthetic (ænesþe·tik, -þī·tik), *a.* 1847. [a. Gr. ἀναίσθητος, f. ἀν + αἰσθητός. Cf. Fr. *anesthétique*, and ÆSTHETIC.] 1. Insensible 1848. 2. *fig.* Unfeeling (*rare*) 1860. 3.

Producing, or connected with the production of, insensibility 1847. 4. *sb.* [sc. *agent.*] 1848.

1. An a. state SIMPSON. 2. A cold a. temperament 1860. 3. An a. agent, operation SIMPSON. Hence **Anæsthe·tically** *adv.* as, or in the way of, an a.; so as to produce anæsthesia.

Anæsthetize (ăne·sþītəiz, ănī-), *v.* 1848. [f. as prec. + -IZE.] To render insensible. Hence **Anæsthe·tist,** one who administers anæsthetics. **Anæ·sthetiza·tion,** the process of rendering insensible; subjection to anæsthetics.

‖**Anagennesis** (ænăˌdʒēnī·sis). 1879. [Gr.] A reproduction of structure.

Anaglyph (æ·năglif). 1651. [ad. Gr. ἀναγλυφή, f. ἀνά + γλύφειν. Cf. Fr. *anaglyphe.*] 1. An ornament worked in low relief. 2. A superimposed stereogram 1909. Hence **Anagly·phic** *a.*; *sb.* (*pl.*) = ANAGLYPTICS.

Anaglyptic (ænăgli·ptik), *a.* 1656. [ad. L., a. Gr. ἀναγλυπτικός; see prec.] Of or pertaining to ANAGLYPHS. As *sb.* (*pl.*) The art of carving in low relief, chasing, embossing, etc. 1662.

Anaglyptograph (ænăgli·ptǒgraf). 1876. [f. Gr. ἀνάγλυπτος + -γραφος.] A machine for producing representations in relief, of coins, medals, etc. Hence **Anaglypto·graphy,** the art of engraving such representations.

‖**Anagnorisis** (ænăgnǫ·risis). 1800. [L., a. Gr.] Recognition; the *dénouement* in a drama.

Anagnost (æ·năgnǫst). ? *Obs.* 1601. [ad. L. a. Gr. ἀναγνώστης.] A reader, a prelector; the reader of the lessons in church.

‖**Anagoge** (ænăgōu·dʒi). 1706. [L., a. Gr. ἀναγωγή, f. ἀνάγειν.] †1. Spiritual elevation, esp. to understand mysteries. 2. Mystical or spiritual interpretation 1849. var. **A·nagogy** (a better Eng. form). Hence **Anago·gic** *adj.* of or pertaining to a.; mystical, spiritualized; *sb.* one skilled in explaining the Scriptures; *sb. pl.* anagogic studies, or practices. **Anago·gical** *a.* Of words, etc.: mystical, spiritual, allegorical; *catachr.* of persons. **Anago·gically** *adv.* with a hidden spiritual sense.

Anagogy, better form of ANAGOGE.

Anagram (æ·năgræm). 1589. [ad. mod. L. *anagramma,* f. Gr. ἀναγράφειν, to write up, back, or anew.] 1. A transposition of the letters of a word, name, or phrase, whereby a new one is formed. †2. *loosely* or *fig.* A transposition, a mutation –1678.

1. This *Gustavus* (whose a. is *Augustus*) was a great Captain HOWELL.

†**A·nagram,** *v. rare.* 1630. [f. the sb.] To ANAGRAMMATIZE. *trans.* and *intr.* –1751.

Anagrammatic, -al (æ:năˌgrămæ·tik, -ăl), *a.* 1605. [f. mod. L. *anagrammat-, anagramma* (see ANAGRAM) + -IC, + -AL. Cf. Fr. *anagrammatique.*] Of or pertaining to an anagram; performed or produced by transposition of letters. Hence **A:nagramma·tically** *adv.*

Anagrammatize (ænăgræ·mătəiz), *v.* 1591. [ad. Gr. ἀναγραμματίζειν; cf. Fr. *anagrammatiser.*] To transpose so as to form an ANAGRAM.

Others..a. it from *Eva* into *væ*, because (they say) she was the cause of all our woe 1637. Hence **Anagra·mmatism,** the formation of anagrams; var. †**Anagra·psis. Anagra·mmatist,** a maker (or book) of anagrams; var. †**A·nagrammist** (*rare*).

†**A·nagraph.** [ad. Gr. ἀναγραφή.] An inventory. (Dicts.)

Anal (ē·năl), *a.* 1769. [ad. mod.L. *analis.*] 1. Of or pertaining to the anus 1836. 2. Situated near the anus 1769.

Analcite, -ime (ănæ·lsəit, -əim). [mod. f. Gr. ἀν + ἄλκιμος, for which Dana substituted ἀναλκής + -ITE, weak (in electric power).] *Min.* One of the Zeolite section of Hydrous Silicates, occurring in trap rocks.

Analects (æ·nălekts), *sb. pl.* 1623. [ad. L. *analecta,* a. Gr., f. ἀνά + λέγειν. Freq. in L. form.] †1. Crumbs; gleanings –1721. 2. Literary gleanings. (Usu. as a title.) 1658.

1. No trencher-a. 1643. 2. The Confucian A. 1861.

‖**Analemma** (ænăle·mă). 1652. [L., 'the pedestal of a sun-dial', a. Gr. ἀνάλημμα a prop, f. ἀναλαμβάνειν.] †1. *orig.* A sort of sun-dial. (? in Eng.) 2. An orthographical projection of the sphere, made on the plane of the meridian; used in dialling, etc. 1652. 3. A gnomon or astrolabe, having the projection on a plate of wood or brass, with a horizon or cursor fitted to it, formerly used in solving problems 1667. 4. A scale of the sun's daily declination drawn from tropic to tropic on artificial terrestrial globes 1832.

A·nalepsy. ? *Obs.* ME. [ad. med.L. *analepsia* (also used), f. Gr. ἀνάληψις.] *Med.* 1. Epilepsy arising from stomachic disorder. 2. The support given in the treatment of a fractured limb 1860.

Analeptic (ænăle·ptik), *a.* 1661. [ad. mod. L. *analepticus,* a. Gr., f. ἀναλαμβάνειν; see ANALEMMA.] *Med.* Restorative, strengthening. As *sb.* [sc. *medicine* or *aliment.*] 1671. var. †**Anale·ptical.**

‖**Analgesia** (ænældʒī·siă). 1706. [mod.L., a. Gr. ἀναλγησία.] *Med.* Insensibility to pain; opp. to *anæsthesia,* total insensibility. Hence **Analge·sic** *a.* tending to remove pain; *sb.* [sc. *drug.*] (Better *analgetic.*)

Anallagmatic (æ:nălægmæ·tik), *a.* 1869. [f. Gr. ἀν + ἄλλαγμα(τ-), f. ἀλλάττειν.] *Math.* Not changed in form by inversion, as the sphere.

†**Ana·logal,** *a.* 1631. [f. L. *analogus.*] = ANALOGOUS. (Freq. in 17th c.)

Analogic (ænălǫ·dʒik), *a.* 1677. [ad. L. *analogicus,* a. Gr., f. ἀναλογία; see ANALOGY. Cf. Fr. *analogique.*] Of or belonging to, or †constituted by, analogy.

Analogical (ænălǫ·dʒikăl), *a.* 1570. [f. as prec. + -AL[1].] †1. *Math.* Proportional 1570. 2. Of the nature of analogy 1609. 3. Expressing an analogy, metonymic; as the *apple* of the eye 1623. †4. Figurative 1638. 5. = ANALOGIC 1854. 6. = ANALOGOUS (*arch.*) 1644.

2. A. or inductive reasoning PRICE. 3. When a country which has sent out colonies is termed the mother country, the expression is a. MILL. Hence **Analo·gically** *adv.* **Analo·gicalness,** the quality of being a.; fitness for illustration. *rare.*

†**Ana·logism.** *rare.* 1656. [ad. Gr. ἀναλογισμός proportionate calculation; see ANALOGON.] 1. *Math.* The constitution of a proportion –1667. 2. An argument from cause to effect; *a priori* reasoning 1656. 3. *Med.* Diagnosis by analogy –1753.

Analogize (ănæ·lŏdʒəiz), *v.* 1655. [f. ANALOGY, or f. Fr. *analogiser.*] 1. *intr.* To employ analogy; *orig.* to reason by proportion. 2. *trans.* To figure 1743; to make, or show to be, analogous 1802. 3. *intr.* (for *refl.*) To be in general harmony 1733.

3. Exceptions..a. with special providences in the mundane order F. HALL. Hence **Ana·logist,** one who seeks, or argues from, analogies. **Ana·logi·stic** *a.* of or pertaining to (linguistic) analogists. **Ana·logizing** *vbl. sb.* the perception of analogies, analogical reasoning.

‖**Ana·logon.** Pl. **-a.** 1810. [a. Gr., f. ἀνά + λόγος.] = ANALOGUE.

Analogous (ănæ·lŏgəs), *a.* 1646. [f. L. *analogus,* a. Gr. ἀνάλογος; see prec.] 1. Having analogy; similar in attributes, circumstances, relations, or uses; *esp.* in *Nat. Hist.* 1664. Const. *to.* 2. = ANALOGICAL 3 (*rare*) 1671.

1. We are in a state of trial..a. or like to our moral and religious trial BUTLER. The bristles and quils in other Animals..are a. to the hairs in a man 1664. 2. Nouns are either Univocal, Equivocal, or A. ABP. THOMSON. Hence **Ana·logous-ly** *adv.*, **-ness.**

Analogue (æ·nălǫg). 1826. [a. Fr., f. Gr. ἀνάλογον ANALOGON, which was earlier.] 1. An analogous word or thing 1837. 2. *esp.* in *Nat. Hist.* a. A part of an animal or plant representative of a different part in another. Strictly said of organs of different origin. 1826. b. A species or tribe in one region, or at one period, which represents a different species or tribe elsewhere or at a different epoch 1830. c. A representative in a different class or group 1835.

1. 'Renard the Fox' has its a. among the Kafirs SAYCE. 2. The fossil shells with their recent analogues LYELL. The fishes, marine analogues of flying creatures G. ALLEN.

Analogy (ănæ·lŏdʒi). 1536. [ad. L. *analogia,* a. Gr., f. ἀνάλογος; see ANALOGON. Cf. Fr. *analogie.*] 1. *Math.* Proportion; agreement of ratios 1557; hence, †due proportion –1774. 2. Equivalency or likeness of relations. Const. *to, with, between.* 1550. 3. *more vaguely,* Similarity 1605. †4. A simile or similitude –1651. 5. = ANALOGUE 1646. 6. *Logic.* a. Resemblance of relations or attributes as a ground of reasoning. b. Presumptive reasoning based on the assumption that if things have some similar attributes, they will have other similar attributes 1602. 7. *Language.* Similarity of formative or constructive processes. (*Form-association* is the term now used where the *forms* only of words are considered.) 1659. 8. *Nat. Hist.* Resemblance of form or function without identity of essence 1814.

2. Which three parts active [experimental, philosophical, magical] have a correspondence and a. with the three parts speculative BACON. 3. Places, Persons..which bear a Resemblance, or at least some remote A., with what we find represented ADDISON. 5. The child is the a. of a people yet in childhood LYTTON. 6. A. is of weight..towards determining our Judgment BUTLER. A., however, is not proof, but illustration STUBBS.

†**A·nalyse,** *sb.* 1638. [a. Fr., f. med.L. *analysis.*] = ANALYSIS –1730.

Analyse, -ze (æ·nălǝiz), *v.* 1601. [a. mod. Fr. *analyser* (= *faire l'analyse*), f. *analyse* ANALYSIS; see prec. On Gr. analogies the vb. would have been *analysize,* whence ANALYZE, the Eng. spelling.] *Prim. sign.* To take to pieces. To make an ANALYSIS of; to separate, distinguish, or ascertain the elements of anything complex, as a material collection, chemical compound, light, sound, a miscellaneous list, account, or statement, a sentence, phrase, word, conception, feeling, action, process, etc. See ANALYSIS.

To a. the process of inference MILL, the sensations of pleasure and pain DARWIN, the nature of Jacobinism COLERIDGE, limestone SMEATON, samples of water (*mod.*), a poem MOORE, lines into syllables JOHNSON, light BREWSTER. Hence **A·naly:sable, -zable** *a.* capable of being analyzed. **A:nalysa·tion, -za·tion,** analysis. **A·nalysed, -zed** *ppl. a.* resolved or reduced to its elements.

Analyser, -zer (æ·nălǝizǝr). 1627. [f. prec.] 1. He who or that which analyzes. 2. In the polariscope, the part which exhibits the fact that the light has been polarized 1863.

1. Bacon—the great a. of common sense 1869.

Analysis (ănæ·lisis). Pl. **analyses** (-īz). 1581. [a. med.L., a. Gr. ἀνάλυσις, f. ἀνά + λύειν.] 1. The resolution of anything complex into its simple elements, opp. to *synthesis*; the exact determination of its components. *Obs.* of things material. 2. *concr.* A tabular statement, a synopsis or conspectus, of the results of the above process 1668. Specifically. 3. *Chem.* The resolution of a chemical compound into its *proximate* or *ultimate* elements; the determination of its elements, or of the foreign substances which it may contain 1655. 4. *Opt.* The resolution of light into its prismatic constituents 1831. 5. *Literature.* The critical examination of any production, so as to exhibit its elements in simple form 1644. 6. *Gram.* The ascertainment of the elements composing a sentence, or any part of it 1612. 7. *Math.* *Ancient a.*: the proving of a proposition by resolving it into simpler propositions already proved or admitted. *Modern a.*: the resolving of problems by reducing them to equations. 1656. 8. *Logic.* The tracing of things to their sources; the discovery of general principles underlying concrete phenomena 1680.

1. A. is not the business of the Poet. His office is to portray, not to dissect MACAULAY. 2. A. of.. In Memoriam (*title*). 3. *Qualitative analysis* determines *what* the elements of a chemical compound are, *quantitative* in what quantity each is present, by weight (*gravimetrical*) or by volume (*volumetrical*) N.E.D. 5. Such, in brief a., was the memorable Declaration of Elizabeth MOTLEY. 6. *Logical, Syntactic, or Sentence Analysis*: the resolution of the sentence into elements having definite relations to the whole sentence and to each other, as *subject* and *predicate* with their respective *enlargements.* 8. A. finds out causes by their effects WATTS.

Analyst (æ·nălist). 1656. [a. Fr. *analyste,* f. *analyser,* after vbs. in *-iser,* whence *-iste* (Eng. -IST). See ANALYSE. Cf. *latiniser, latiniste.*] One who makes an ANALYSIS, *esp.* in *Math.* 1656; and *Chem.* (the common use now) 1800.

Analytic (ænăli·tik), *a.* 1590. [ad. med.L. *analyticus,* a. Gr.; see ANALYSIS. Cf. Fr. *ana-*

lytique.] A. *adj.* 1. Of, pertaining to, or in accordance with ANALYSIS; resolving compounds into their elements 1601. 2. Addicted to analysis; analytical 1805.

B. *sb.* mostly *pl.* analytics, tr. L. *analytica*, a. Gr. ἀναλυτικά, adj. pl. neut. used subst. as title of Aristotle's treatises on Logic. 1. *gen.* The science and art of ANALYSIS 1641. 2. *spec.* That part of Logic which treats of analysis 1590; †the application of Algebra to geometry -1751.

Analy·tical, *a.* 1525. [f. as prec.] 1. Of or pertaining to analytics; employing the analytic method; *Lang.* expressing the elements of a proposition or complex notion by distinct words, instead of combining several into one word, as *with a sword* for *gladio* 1873. 2. = ANALYTIC *a.* 1. 1656. Hence **Analy·tically** *adv.*

‖**Anamnesis** (ænămnī·sis). 1657. [Gr.] The recalling of things past; reminiscence.

The doctrine of A., in Plato, according to which the soul had pre-existed in a purer state, and there gained its ideas 1876. Hence **Anamne·stic** *a.* recalling to mind; aiding the memory; †*sb.* [sc. *medicine* or *symptom.*]

Anamorphism (ænămǭ·ɹfiz'm). 1836. [f. Gr. ἀνά + μορφή + -ISM.] 1. Distorted projection. 2. Progression from a lower to a higher type 1852. Hence **Anamo·rphous** *a.* distorted (*rare*).

Anamorphose (ænămǭ·ɹfōus, -ōs), *v. rare.* [f. next; cf. METAMORPHOSE.] To represent by ANAMORPHOSIS.

Anamorphosis (ænămǭ·ɹfŏsis). 1727. [a. Gr. ἀναμόρφωσις, f. ἀνα + μορφόειν. Also *anamorphō·sis.*] 1. A distorted projection or drawing of anything, which, when viewed from a particular point, or by reflection from a suitable mirror, appears regular and properly proportioned; a deformation. 2. *Bot.* Abnormal transformation, due to degeneration or change in the habit of a plant 1830. 3. = ANAMORPHISM 2. 1852.

Anan, obs. f. ANON.

Anan (ănæ·n), *int. Obs.* or *dial.* 1553. Same wd. as ANON *adv.* orig. in answer to a call, 'Presently,' and later = 'I beg your pardon! Sir? Eh?' See 1 *Hen. IV*, II. iv. 71.

Ananas (ănē·năs, -ā·năs). Also **anana.** 1613. [f. Peruv. *Nanas.*] 1. The pine-apple plant (*Ananassa sativa*) or fruit. 2. An allied West Indian fruit (*Bromelia Pinguin*).

Anandrious (ǣnæ·ndri,əs), *a.* 1879. [f. Gr. ἀνανδρία.] *Med.* Without virility; impotent.

Anandrous (ǣnæ·ndrəs), *a.* 1847. [f. Gr. ἄνανδρος, f. ἀν + ἀνδρ- + -OUS.] *Bot.* Having no stamens, as the females of diœcious, or the female flowers of monœcious plants.

Ana·ntherous, *a.* 1866. [f. AN- *pref.* 10.] *Bot.* Destitute of anthers. var. **Ana·ntherate.**

Ana·nthous, *a.* 1866. [f. Gr. ἀνανθής + -OUS.] *Bot.* Flowerless.

Ana·nthropism. [f. Gr. ἀν + ἀνθρωπισμός.] A lack of humanity. SEELEY.

Ananym (æ·nănim). *rare.* 1867. [loosely f. Gr. ἀνά + ὄνυμα, ANONYM having another meaning.] The real name written backwards.

Anapæst (æ·năpest, -pīst). 1678. [ad. L. *anapæstus*, a. Gr. ἀνάπαιστος, f. ἀνά + παίειν.] *Pros.* 1. A reversed dactyl, a metrical foot, consisting of two short syllables followed by a long one. 2. A verse composed of, or containing, such feet 1846.

1. For your *anapestus*..ye haue..*mānĭfōld, mōnĭlēsse*, etc. PUTTENHAM.

Anapæstic (ænăpe·stik, -ī·stik), *a.* 1699. [ad. L. *anapæsticus*; see prec.] Composed of anapæsts. As *sb.* Verses containing anapæstic feet 1699.

sb. Where an a. is terminated by a trochee BENTLEY. Hence **Anapæ·stical** *a.* **Anapæ·stically** *adv.* in a. rhythm (*rare*).

Anapa·ganize, *v. rare.* [f. Gr. ἀνά + PAGANIZE.] To make pagan again. SOUTHEY.

Anapeiratic (æ:năpəiræ·tik), *a.* 1879. [irreg. f. Gr. ἀναπειράεσθαι.] *Path.* Resulting from the habitual use of certain muscles for a long time, as *writer's paralysis.*

†**A-na·pes.** 1575. In *Fustian a napes* = O Napes, of Naples -1627.

‖**Anaphora** (ănæ·fŏră). 1589. [L., a. Gr., f. ἀνά + φέρειν.] *Rhet.* The repetition of the same word or phrase in several successive clauses. See *Heb.* xi. 24.

Anaphrodisiac (ǣn,æ:frodi·ziăk), *a.* 1823. [f. Gr. ἀν + ἀφροδισιακός.] That diminishes sexual appetite. As *sb.* [sc. *drug.*] An antaphrodisiac 1865.

Anaphroditic (ǣn,æ:frodi·tik), *a.* 1879. [f. Gr. ἀναφρόδιτος + -IC. Cf. Fr. *anaphroditique.*] *Biol.* Developed without concourse of sexes.

Anaphroditous (ǣn,æ:frodəi·təs), *a.* 1879. [f. as prec. + -OUS.] Without sexual appetite.

Anaplasty (æ·năplasti). 1879. [a. Fr. *anaplastie*, f. Gr. ἀνάπλαστος, f. ἀναπλάσσειν, to form anew.] *Surg.* Reparation of external lesions by the use of adjacent healthy tissue. Hence **Anapla·stic** *a.* of or pertaining to a.

‖**Anaplerosis** (æ:năplirōu·sis). 1680. [mod. L., a. Gr.] The filling up of a deficiency. Hence **A:naplero·tic** *a.* tending to supply deficiencies of tissue; *sb.* (in *pl.*) an anaplerotic substance.

Anapnograph (ănæ·pnŏgrɑf). 1870. [f. Gr. ἀναπνοή + -γραφος.] An instrument for registering the movements and amount of expiration and inspiration.

Anapno·ic, *a.* 1879. [f. as prec. + -IC.] Pertaining to respiration.

Anapnometer (ænăpnǫ·mĭtəɹ). 1860. [f. as prec. + μέτρον.] A spirometer.

Anapodeictic (ǣn,æ:podəi·ktik), *a. rare.* [f. Gr. ἀν + ἀποδεικτικός.] Undemonstrable.

Anapophysis (ænăpǫ·fisis). 1854. [f. Gr. ἀνά + ἀπόφυσις.] *Phys.* A small bony process, projecting backward from the neural arch of the vertebræ. Hence **A:napophy·sial,** of or pertaining to an a.

Anaptotic (ænăptǫ·tik), *a.* 1850. [f. Gr. ἀν(ά) + ἄπτωτος; see APTOTIC.] Falling back from inflection, as *a. languages.*

Anarch (æ·năɹk), *sb.* 1667. [ad. Gr. ἄναρχος; cf. *monarch*, etc.] An author of anarchy; a leader of revolt. As *adj.* Without government; anarchical (*rare*) 1822.

The A. old MILT. *P. L.* II. 988. Lo! the great Anarch's ancient reign restor'd POPE. Hence **Ana·rchal** *a.* (*rare*) = ANARCH *a.*

Anarchic (ănā·ɹkik), *a.* 1790. [f. Gr. ἄναρχος + -IC; after ἀρχικός.] Of or belonging to anarchy; lawless.

Anarchical (ănā·ɹkikăl), *a.* 1597. [f. as prec. + -AL.] 1. = prec. 2. Connected with, tending to, or involving anarchy 1649.

1. That..a. little commonwealth MOTLEY. 2. A. doctrines 1797, efforts 1847. var. **Ana·rchial.** Hence **Ana·rchically** *adv.*

Anarchism (æ·năɹkiz'm). *rare.* 1642. [f. as prec. + -ISM.] The principles or practice of anarchy, or anarchists.

Anarchist (æ·năɹkist). 1678. [f. as prec. + -IST.] One who admits of no ruling power; an advocate of anarchy; one who upsets settled order. quasi-*adj.* 1812.

Anarchize (æ·năɹkəiz), *v.* 1800. [f. as prec. + -IZE; cf. *monarchize.*] To reduce to anarchy; to destroy the settled order of.

Anarchy (æ·năɹki). 1539. [ad. Gr. ἀναρχία, or med.L. *anarchia*; cf. Fr. *anarchie.*] 1. Absence of government; a state of lawlessness due to the absence or inefficiency of the supreme power; political disorder. 2. *transf.* Absence or non-recognition of authority in any sphere 1667; moral or intellectual disorder 1656.

1. This unleful lyberty or lycence of the multytude is called an Anarchie TAVERNER. A Polity without an Head..would..be..Anarchy H. MORE. 2. The waste Wide Anarchie of Chaos MILT. *P. L.* x. 283. An a. of thought,—a perpetuity of mental revolutions W. GROVE. Hence **Ana·rchial** *a.*

†**Ana·reta.** 1647. [Incorr. f. *anæreta*, Lat. ad. Gr. ἀναιρέτης.] *Astrol.* The planet that destroys life -1819.

Anarthrous (ǣnā·ɹþrəs), *a.* 1808. [f. Gr. ἀν + ἄρθρον + -OUS.] 1. Of Greek sbs.: Used without the article. 2. *Phys.* Jointless; or apparently so 1879. Hence **Ana·rthrously** *adv.* without the (Gr.) article. **Ana·rthrousness.**

Anasarca (ænăsā·ɹkă). ME. [f. Gr. ἀνὰ + σάρξ (σάρκα); perh. orig. a phr.] *Path.* A dropsical affection of the subcutaneous cellular tissue of a limb, etc. Also *transf.* and *fig.* 1807. Hence **Anasa·rcous** *a.* of the nature or showing signs of a.

Anasei·smic, *a.* 1881. [f. Gr. ἀνά + σεισμός + -IC.] Of an earthquake shock: Moving vertically.

†**Anasta·ltic,** *a.* 1775. [ad. Gr. ἀνασταλτικός, f. ἀνά + στέλλειν.] Styptic. As *sb.* Restringent medicines.

Anastatic (ænăstæ·tik), *a.* 1849. [f. Gr. ἀνάστασις + -IC.] Of the nature of revival; *spec.* of a printing process, in which facsimiles are produced by a transfer process from zinc plates.

Anastomose (ănæ·stŏmōuz), *v.* 1697. [a. Fr. *anastomoser*; see ANASTOMOSIS.] †*trans.* To connect by ANASTOMOSIS. *intr.* To inosculate. Said of blood-vessels, rivers, branches of trees, etc. Hence **Ana·stomosed** *ppl. a.* connected by anastomosis. **Ana·stomosing** *vbl. sb.* = ANASTOMOSIS; *ppl. a.* inosculating; var. **Anastomo·sant.**

‖**Anastomosis** (anæ:stŏmōu·sis). Pl. **-o·ses.** 1615. [mod.L., a. Gr., f. ἀναστομόειν.] Intercommunication between two vessels, channels, or branches, by a connecting cross branch. Orig. of the cross connexions between the arteries and veins, etc.; now of those of any branching system.

The African name..Tanganyika, signifying an a., or a meeting-place R. BURTON.

Anastomotic (ănæ·stŏmǫ·tik). 1657. [ad. L., a. Gr. ἀναστομωτικός; see prec.] †1. (As in L.) Of medicines: Designed to open the mouths of vessels. (Occ. also, *anastomatic.*) -1721. 2. Pertaining to or forming ANASTOMOSIS 1836.

‖**Anastrophe** (anæ·strŏfī). 1577. [Gr.] *Rhet.* Inversion or unusual order of words or clauses, as 'All Italy about I went'.

Anatase (æ·nătēⁱs). 1843. [a. Fr., ad. Gr. ἀνάτασις, f. ἀνά + τα-, stem of τείνειν.] *Min.* Haüy's name for OCTAHEDRITE.

†**A·nathem,** *sb.* 1555. [a. Fr. *anathème*, ad. L. *anathema*; see next. Rhymes with *them* (1598), and *dream* (1630).] 1. = ANATHEMA 1. *rare.* 2. = ANATHEMA 2. -1648.

Anathema (ănæ·þĭmă). Pl. **anathemas;** also, in sense 3, **anathe·mata.** 1526. [a. L. *anathema*, a. Gr. ἀνάθεμα, orig. 'a thing devoted', later 'an accursed thing' (see *Rom.* ix. 3). Orig. var. of ἀνάθημα an offering. Cf. ANATHEME.] 1. Anything accursed, or consigned to damnation. Also quasi-*adj.* 2. The formal act, or formula, of consigning to damnation; *spec.* the great curse of the Church, excommunicating a person; or denouncing a doctrine or practice as damnable 1590. Hence *gen.*, Any imprecation 1691. 3. [= ἀνάθημα, better pron. ænăþī·mă.] A thing devoted to divine use 1581.

1. Paul wished to become a. himself, so he could thereby save his brethren TUCKER. 2. The Pope ..has condemned the slave trade—but no..heed is paid to his a. GLADSTONE. 'Confound the man!' was my mental a. LYTTON. Hence **A:nathema·tic** *a.* of the nature of, or pertaining to, an offering (*rare*). †**Ana:thema·tical** *a.* of the nature of an a.; *sb.* = ANATHEMA. †**Ana·thematism,** an ecclesiastical denunciation.

Anathema Maranatha (mærănē·þă). 1526. [Gr. ἀνάθεμα; Μαρὰν ἀθά = Syriac *māra·n ethā·* 'the Lord has come'. The pronunc. should be *măræ:n,āthā·.*] Taken erron. as a portentously intensified *Anathema. Maran atha* forms a distinct sentence.

Let him be Anathema. Maranatha. 1 *Cor.* xvi. 22.

Anathematize (ănæ·þĭmătəiz), *v.* 1566. a. Fr. *anathématiser*, ad. L. *anathematizare*, f. Gr. ἀναθεματίζειν; see prec.] 1. *trans.* To pronounce an anathema against (see ANATHEMA 2). 2. *absol.* To curse 1837. var. **Ana·themize.** Hence **Ana:thematiza·tion,** the action of anathematizing; var. †**Ana:themiza·tion. Ana·thematizer.**

Anatheme (æ·năþīm). 1654. [a. Fr., ad. L. *anathema*, a. Gr.; see ANATHEMA 3.] An offering dedicated to God.

†**Anati·ferous,** *a. rare.* 1646. [f. L. *anas* (*anati-*) + *-ferus* + -OUS.] Producing ducks or geese; *i. e.* producing barnacles, once sup-

posed to grow on trees, and dropping off into water, to turn to Tree-geese (Pennant II. 238).

Anatocism (ănæ·tŏsiz'm). *arch.* 1656. [ad. L. *anatocismus*, a. Gr., f. ἀνά + τοκίζειν, f. τόκος.] Compound interest.

Anatomic, -al (ænătǫ·mik, -ăl), *a.* 1586. [a. L. *anatomicus*, a. Gr., f. ἀνατομή; see ANATOMY and -IC, -AL.] Of or pertaining to the study or practice of anatomy. **2.** Of anatomy; structural; also *transf.* 1627. Hence **Anato·mically** *adv.*

Anato·mico-, comb. form of ANATOMIC.

Ana·tomiless, *a. rare.* [f. ANATOMY.] Devoid of anatomy. RUSKIN.

Anatomism (ănæ·tŏmiz'm). 1860. [a. Fr. *anatomisme*; see ANATOMIZE.] **1.** Analysis or display of anatomic structure (*mod.*). **2.** The doctrine that the phenomena of life are explained by the anatomical structure of living organisms. (Cf. ANIMISM.) 1860.

Anatomist (ănæ·tŏmist). 1569. [a. Fr. *anatomiste*; see ANATOMIZE.] **1.** One skilled in (*esp.* human) anatomy 1594. Also *fig.*

Anatomize (ănæ·tŏməiz), *v.* 1541. [ad. med.L. *anatomizare*, f. *anatomia*; see ANATOMY.] **1.** To dissect; to cut up an animal or vegetable body in order to lay open the position, structure, and relations of its various parts. Also *absol.* 1870. **2.** *fig.* To lay open minutely; to analyze 1553.

1. A. me into atomies 1596. 2. To a. wit GREENE, a town or country HOWELL, the doctrine of free government BURKE. Hence **Ana·tomiza·tion**, dissection; †anatomic structure. **Ana·tomi·zer.**

Anatomy (ănæ·tŏmi). 1528. [a. Fr. *anatomie*, ad. L., a. Gr. ἀνατομία, abstr. sb. = ἀνατομή, f. ἀνά + τεμ-, τομ-. By erron. division *anatomy* gave *a natomy, an atomy*; see ATOMY.] **1.** The artificial separation of the parts of an organized body, in order to discover their position, structure, and economy; dissection 1541; †with *quick, live*: Vivisection –1668. †**2.** *concr.* A body, or part, anatomized; a subject for dissection –1751. **3.** A model of the body, as dissected 1727. **4.** *pop.* A skeleton 1594; a skeleton with the skin left, a mummy 1586; a living being reduced to skin and bone 1590; also *transf.* and *fig.* 1605. Cf. ATOMY. **5.** The bodily frame 1592. **6.** The science of the structure of organized bodies, divided into *Animal A.* or *Zootomy*, *Vegetable*, *Human*, and *Comparative* 1541; a treatise on the science 1528. **7.** Anatomical structure 1579. **8.** Detailed examination or analysis 1569. †**9.** Chemical analysis –1686.

2. They must ha' dissected, and made an Anatomie o' me B. JONS. 4. Death..Thou fell A. SHAKS. *John* III. iv. 40. More like an a. than a living person SOUTHEY. One Pinch: a hungry leane-fac'd Villain, A meere Anatomie *Com. Err.* v. 238. 5. In what vile part of this Anatomie Doth my name lodge *Rom. & Jul.* III. iii. 106. 8. The Anatomy of Melancholy: what it is [etc.] BURTON (*title*). var. †**A·natome** (3 syllab.).

Anatopism (ănæ·tǫpiz'm). *rare.* 1812. [f. Gr. ἀνά + τόπος + -ISM.] A putting of a thing out of its proper place.

Anatreptic (ænătre·ptik), *a.* 1655. [ad. Gr., f. ἀνατρέπειν.] Overturning; a subdivision of Platonic Discourse.

Anatripso·logy. 1839. [f. Gr. ἀνάτριψις.] *Med.* The doctrine of the use of friction.

Anatri·ptic, *a.* 1879. [f. Gr. ἀνάτριπτος (f. ἀνατρίβειν) + -IC.] *Med.* Belonging to, or characterized by, friction, as a medicine.

†**Anatron.** 1706. [a. Sp., ad. Arab. *an-* (= *al*) *natrūn*.] Native carbonate of soda; see NATRON.

Anatropous (ănæ·trŏpəs), *a.* 1847. [f. mod.L. *anatropus* (f. ἀνά + -τροπος, f. τρέπειν) + -OUS.] *Bot.* Having its nucleus inverted, opp. to *orthotropous*: said of the ovule of phanerogamous plants. var. **Ana·tropal.**

Anatta, anatto (ănæ·tă, -o). Also **annatto**, annotto. 1682. [? native Amer.] An orange-red dye, procured in Central America from the pulp surrounding the seeds of the *Bixa orellana*; used to colour cheese, etc.

†**Anau·nter.** Still *dial.* ME. [= AN + *aunter*, early f. ADVENTURE.] In peril; lest.

Anaxagorean (ænæksægōrī·ăn), *a.* 1586. [f. *Anaxagoras.*] Of or pertaining to Anaxagoras, a Greek philosopher who taught that matter was eternal, but was combined into bodies by a supreme intelligence. Also as *sb.*

Anaxa·gorize, *v.* [f. as prec.] To hold the principles of Anaxagoras. CUDWORTH.

Anaxima·ndrian, *a.* 1678. [f. *Anaximander* + -IAN.] Adhering to the tenets of Anaximander. Also as *sb.*

Anbury, amb- (æ·nbəri, æ·m-). 1598. [*Ambury*, phonetic var. of *anbury*, perh. = *ang-berry*, f. OE. *ang-* pain. Not f. OE. *ampre* AMPER. Cf. ANGLEBERRY.] **1.** A soft tumour or spongy wart on horses and oxen. **2.** A diseased affection of the roots of turnips, etc.; called also 'finger and toe' 1750.

-ance, *suffix*; a. Fr. *-ance*:–L. *-antia, -ēntia, -entia.* Since 1500 various words orig. in *-ance* from Fr. have been altered back to *-ence* after L., and more recent words have taken *-ence* or *-ance* according to the L. vowel. Hence much inconsistency, as in *dependance, -dence, resistance, subsistence.* As a living formative *-ance* has occas. been added to native vbs., as *forbear-ance, ridd-ance*, etc.

Ancestor (æ·nsĕstəɹ). [ME. *ancestre*, a. OFr. *ancestre*, nom.:—L. *antecessor*, and *ancesor*, acc. :—L. *antecessorem*, f. *ante* + *cedere*. A combination of (late AFr.) *-our* and *-s-* from later Fr. *auncestre* gave *auncestour, -or* (16th c.), now *ancestor*. See also ANTECESSOR.] **1.** One from whom a person is descended, either by the father or mother; a forefather (usu. one more remote than a grandfather). Also, of animals, and *fig.* **2.** *Biol.* An organized being of a lower type, whence others of a later type are inferred to have been developed 1863.

1. Tyme, that eldith our auncessours ME. When I am sleeping with my Ancestors 2 *Hen. IV*, IV. iv. 61. *fig.* Eldest Night and Chaos, ancestors of Nature MILT. *P. L.* II. 894. The institutions, the wisdom, of our ancestors BURKE. 2. The a. of the African elephant RAMSAY. Hence **Ancesto·rial** *a.* = ANCESTRAL. **Ancesto·rially** *adv.* by inheritance from one's ancestors.

Ancestral (ænse·străl), *a.* 1523. [a. OFr. *ancestrel*, f. *ancestre*; see prec. and -AL[1].] **1.** Of, belonging to, or inherited from ancestors 1579; *esp.* in *Law* 1523. **2.** *Biol.* Of, pertaining to, or constituting the original, or an earlier, type (see ANCESTOR 2) 1862. var. **Ance·strial** (*rare*).

Ancestress (æ·nsĕstrĕs). 1580. [f. ANCESTOR + -ESS.] A female ancestor.

Ancestry (æ·nsĕstri). ME. [Eng. modification (due to *ancestre*) of OFr. *anceserie*; see ANCESTOR.] **1.** The relation or condition of ancestors; progenitorship; *hence*, distinguished or ancient descent. **2.** *collect.* The line or body of ancestors. (Cf. *tenantry*, etc.) ME.

1. Som worthy blood of Auncetrye CHAUCER. A son, whose Death disgraced his a. DRYDEN. 2. Our a., a gallant Christian race COWPER.

Anchithere (æ·ŋkiþiᵊɹ). 1879. [ad. mod. L. *anchitherium* (also used), f. Gr. ἄγχι + θηρίον.] *Palæont.* A fossil Eocene and Miocene animal having three toes on each foot; regarded as an ancestor of the horse.

Anchoic (æ̃ŋkōu·ik), *a.* 1863. [f. Gr. ἄγχειν (+ *o*) + -IC.] *Chem.* In *Anchoic acid*: a dibasic acid, $C_9H_{16}O_4$, emitting suffocating fumes.

Anchor (æ·ŋkəɹ), *sb.*[1] [OE. *ancor*, a. L. *ancora* (erron. *anchora*), ? cogn. w. Gr. ἄγκυρα, f. stem αγκ-, whence *angle*. The current spelling follows *anchora*.] **1.** An appliance for holding a ship, etc., fixed in a particular place, by mooring it to the bottom of the sea or river; a heavy iron, composed of a long shank, with a ring at one end for the cable, and at the other two arms or flukes, tending upwards, with barbs on each side. **2.** *fig.* That which gives stability or security ME. **3.** *transf.* Any contrivance or instrument which holds fast or gives security; also, an anchor-shaped appendage, as the spicules on Holothuroids 1855. **4.** *Arch.* An ornament shaped like an anchor or arrow-head; used with the egg ornament 1663.

The largest anchor is the SHEET-anchor; next are the BOWER-anchors; the smallest is the KEDGE-anchor. 1. The a. is foul, that is, the Cable has got about the Fluke 1692. Anchors of rusty fluke TENNYSON. 2. Which hope we haue as an anker of the soule *Heb.* vi. 19. Say Warwicke was our A.: what of that 3 *Hen. VI*, v. iv. 13. This sheet-anchor of happiness, Religion CHATHAM.

Phrases (from sense 1). *lit.* and *fig.* **1. At (an, the,** *obs.*) **anchor,** in OE. *on ancre*: anchored. **2. To come to (an) anchor:** = ANCHOR *v.* 2, 4. **3. To cast anchor:** to drop the a.; *hence*, to take up a position. Also of the ship: *she* cast a. **4. To weigh anchor:** to take up the a., so as to sail away. **5. The anchor comes home:** *i.e.* is dragged from its hold. So, a ship *drags her a.* *To slip the a.*, to let it go by letting the cable slip.

Comb.: **a.-frost,** the clogging of a mill-wheel with ice below the water-surface; **-ice,** ground-ice; **-lining** = *bill-boards* (see BILL *sb.*[3]); **-plate,** a heavy piece of timber or metal, serving as a point of support (*e.g.* for the cables of a suspension-bridge); **-ring,** the great ring for attaching the cable; **-shackle,** an iron loop used instead of an a.-ring; **-stock,** a bar which crosses the top of an a., at right angles to the shank, and also to the plane of the arms; also as *v.*; **-tow,** the cable of an a.; **-watch,** a part of a crew kept on duty while the ship lies at a.

†**A·nchor,** *sb.*[2] [OE. *ancra*, for *ancora*, shortened f. L. *anachoreta*; see ANCHORET. App. *án(cora*, after *án* 'one, alone', by pop. etym. The wd. occurs last in SHAKS.] **1.** An ANCHORET. **2.** An ANCHORESS –1466.

1. And anchors cheere [*i.e.* chair] in prison be my scope *Haml.* III. ii. 229 (2nd Qo.). 2. *Ancren Riwle*, the 'Rule of Nuns'.

Anchor (æ·ŋkəɹ), *v.* ME. [? a. Fr. *ancrer*, f. *ancre*; cf. med.L. *ancorare.*] **1.** To secure with an anchor; to place at, or bring to, anchor. **2.** *intr.* To cast or come to anchor. (Said of crew or ship.) 1578. **3.** *fig.* To fix as with an anchor 1594. **4.** *fig. refl.* and *intr.* To fix oneself, one's attention, etc. 1581.

3. Till that my Nayles were anchor'd in thine eyes *Rich. III*, IV. iv. 231. 4. Whilst my Inuention .. anchors on Isabell *Meas. for M.* II. iv. 4.

Anchorage[1] (æ·ŋkərėdʒ). 1516. [f. prec. + -AGE.] **1.** The action of anchoring; lying at anchor 1611. **2.** Conditions admitting of anchoring, *esp.* anchorage-ground 1706. **3.** *transf.* A position of support, a hold 1860. **4.** *fig.* A stay for the mind or feelings 1677. **5.** Anchorage-dues 1516. **6.** A ship's anchors 1588.

4. The Church a., ..the new a. in the Bible FROUDE. 6. The Barke..Returnes..From whence..she weigh'd her A. *Tit. A.* I. i. 73.

A·nchorage[2]. 1593. [f. ANCHOR *sb.*[2]] The retreat of an anchoret.

Anchored (æ·ŋkəɹd), *ppl. a.* 1611. [f. the vb.] **1.** With the anchor dropt; held fast by the anchor; firmly fixed, at rest. **2.** Furnished with anchors; or, *esp.* in *Her.*, with anchor-like appendages 1611.

Anchoress, ancress (æ·ŋkŏrĕs, æ·ŋkrĕs). ME. [f. *ancre*, ANCHOR *sb.*[2]] A female anchoret.

Yef ho were ankeras or nonne 1450.

Anchoret, -ite (æ·ŋkŏrĕt, -əit). 1460. [f. *anachoret(e* (a. L. *anachoreta*, ad. Gr. ἀναχωρητής), influenced by earlier Eng. *ancre* (ANCHOR *sb.*[2]).] **1.** One who has withdrawn or secluded himself from the world, usu. for religious reasons; a recluse, a hermit. *masc.* and *fem.* Also *attrib.* 1847. **2.** *Ch. Hist.* The recluses of the East. (Often *anachoret.*) 1553. **3.** *fig.* Any one of secluded habits 1616.

1. The severity of an a. JOHNSON. 3. Th' anachorit of love DRUMM. OF HAWTH. Hence **Anchore·tic, -al** *a.* of, pertaining to, or like an a. **A·nchore·tish, -i·tish** *a.* hermit-like. **A·nchoretism, -it-,** the practice of an a.

Anchoring (æ·ŋkəriŋ), *vbl. sb.* 1593. [f. the vb.] **1.** The action or state of lying at anchor; anchorage. **2.** *transf.* Fixing securely 1767. **3.** *ppl. a.* Coming to or lying at anchor; holding firm 1605.

1. Good a., cleane ground R. HAWKINS. *Comb.*: **a.-ground, -place,** one suited for anchoring; **-room,** space for anchoring; **-stone,** one used instead of an anchor.

Anchorite,-itish, vars. of ANCHORET,-ISH.

†**A·nchoritess.** *arch.* = ANCHORESS. FULLER.

A·nchorless, *a. rare.* 1863. [f. ANCHOR *sb.*[1] + -LESS.] Without an anchor; *fig.* drifting.

Anchovy (æ̃ntʃōu·vi, occ. æ·ntʃŏvi). 1596. [a. Sp., Pg. *anchova*; ? ad. Basque *anchoa*, as if 'dried fish'.] A small fish of the Herring family (*Engraulis encrasicholus*), found esp. in the Mediterranean, and pickled for exportation.

Item, Anchoues, and Sacke after supper ijs. vid. 1 *Hen. IV*, II. iv. 588. *Comb.*: a.-pear, a West Indian fruit, eaten like the mango; also the tree (*Grias cauliflora*) which bears it; -toast.

‖**Anchusa** (æŋkiū·sā). [L.] A hairy-stemmed plant of the genus so named, such as alkanet and bugloss. Hence **Anchu·sic** *a.* in *A. acid* (1863) = **A·nchusin**, the colouring matter of alkanet, a dark-red amorphous powder 1863.

Anchylose, ank- (æ·ŋkilōuz), *v.* 1787. [f. ANCHYLOSIS; cf. *metamorphose.*] 1. To effect anchylosis in; *usu.* in *pass.* to be solidly united bone to bone. 2. *intr.* To grow stiff. Of two bones: To grow together. 1833. Hence **A·nchylosed, ank-** *ppl. a.* grown together; stiffened; *fig.* cramped.

‖**Anchylosis, ank-** (æŋkilōu·sis). 1713. [Gr., f. ἀγκυλόειν, f. ἀγκύλος; *ch* or *k* repr. κ, instead of the reg. *c.* Cf. Fr. *ankylose.*] The formation of a stiff joint by consolidation of the articulating surfaces; the coalescence of two bones originally distinct. Also *fig.* Hence **Anchylo·tic, ank-** *a.* of or pertaining to a.

†**A·nciency.** 1548. [corrupt f. ANCIENTY, as if f. *ppl. adj.* in -ENT.] The quality of being ancient -1759.

Ancient (ēi·nʃĕnt), *a.* and *sb.*[1] ME. [a. Fr. *ancien*:—late L. *antianum*, for **anteanum*, f. *ante*, by form-assoc. with ppl. forms in *-nt*, whence *-t.*] A. *adj.* Of date. 1. Belonging to time past (*arch.*) 1490; †whilom, *ex-* -1718; *esp.* belonging to times *long* past, old ME. 2. *spec.* Belonging to the period before the fall of the Western Roman Empire; opp. to *modern*, and *mediæval* 1605. ** Of duration. 3. Of early origin, going far back 1475; hence, time-worn, hoary 1586. 4. Of living beings: Old, of great age (*arch.*) ME.; having the wisdom, etc., of age, venerable (*arch.*) 1460; old-fashioned (*rare*) 1598; veteran, senior (now *old*) ME. 5. *Law.* In *Ancient tenure, Tenure of ancient demesne*: that existing in those manors which belonged to the crown in the reigns of Edward the Confessor and William the Conqueror.

1. Thy antient kindness BUNYAN. They mourned their a. leader lost POPE. (Cf. Fr. *ancien gouverneur.*) A. weapons of war 1777, civilisation 1836. 2. The antient languages 1808. A. art 1846, literature 1875. 3. O thou awncient Israel *Baruch* iv. 5. Contending ..for a. rights 1855. These times are the a. times, when the world is a. BACON. This a. city, Memphis YOUNG. 4. Farewell, auncient Lady *Rom. & Jul.* II. iv. 150. The precepts of a. experience JOHNSON. An a. ditty, long since mute KEATS. Respect to be had to graue and a. souldiers 1598.

B. *sb.* 1. One who lived in ancient times. Usu. in *pl. The Ancients*: *esp.* the Greeks, Romans, etc. 1541; *esp.* the ancient classics 1615. 2. *The Ancient of Days*: the Almighty. *Dan.* vii. 9. 3. An aged man (or animal); a patriarch 1502. †4. An ancestor (*rare*) -1649; a senior (usu. *his ancient*) -1659. 5. An Elder (*arch.*) 1534. 6. A senior member of the Inns of Court or of Chancery. (*Obs.* in use.) 1563.

1. If Mr. Shakespear had not read the ancients HALES. The same Ancient [Plutarch] 1763. 4. Reinolds was..bred up in the same college..with Jewel his a. and R. Hooker his contemporary FULLER.

Ancient (ēi·nʃĕnt), *sb.*[2] *arch.* 1554. [corrupt f. ENSIGN. Also by pseudo-etym. **antesign.**] 1. An ensign, or standard: *pl.* insignia, colours. 2. A standard-bearer, an 'ensign' (in full †ancient-bearer). 1596.

1. A red a., on the mizen-top DE FOE. 2. Hee is call'd aunchient Pistoll *Hen. V*, III. vi. 20.

Anciently (ēi·nʃĕntli), *adv.* 1502. [f. ANCIENT *a.* + -LY[2].] 1. In ancient times; †formerly -1774. 2. †Of long standing -1686; like something old HAWTHORNE.

Ancientness (ēi·nʃĕntnĕs). 1537. [f. as prec. + -NESS.] The quality of being ANCIENT (now *antiquity*); †ancient condition -1657; †seniority -1628.

Ancientry (ēi·nʃĕntri). *arch.* 1580. [f. as prec.; cf. *pageantry.*] 1. The quality or estate of being ANCIENT. †2. Ancestry SPENSER; *collect.* elders -1611. 3. Antiquity 1755; *pl.* or *collect.* antiquities 1866.

1. I allow my a. H. WALPOLE. 2. The Auncientry of the Parish 1589. 3. I love those tales of a. 1839.

†**A·ncienty.** ME. [a. AFr. *ancienté*, for OFr. *ancienneté*, f. *ancien*; cf. ANCIENCY.] 1. Antiquity -1602; *concr.* the ancients 1556. 2. Old standing -1623; agedness -1569; seniority -1775.

‖**Ancile** (ænsəi·lĭ). 1600. [L., pl. *ancilia.*] The sacred tutelary shield of Rome, said to have fallen from heaven.

Ancillary (æ·nsilări), *a.* 1667. [ad. L. *ancillarius*, f. *ancilla.*] 1. Subservient, subordinate (*to*). 2. *lit.* (after L.) Of or pertaining to maid-servants (*rare* and *affected*) 1852.

1. Rather a. than essential H. TAYLOR. 2. The a. beauty THACKERAY.

†**Ancille.** ME. [a. OFr. *ancelle*:—L. *ancilla.*] A handmaid -1500. var. ‖**Anci·lla.** [L.]

Ancipital (ænsi·pitāl), *a. rare.* 1794. [f. L. *ancipit-* (*anceps*) two-headed (f. *an* (= *ambi*) both + *capit-*) + AL.] Having two sharp edges. vars. **Anci·pitate, Anci·pitous.**

Anci·stroid, *a.* 1879. [f. Gr. ἄγκιστρον + -OID.] Hook-shaped.

Ancle, var. of ANKLE.

†**A·ncoly.** 1561. [a. Fr. *ancolie*, for *accolie*, f. L. *aquilegia.*] Columbine -1578.

A·ncome. *Obs.* or *dial.* ME. [? var. of *on-come.*] A boil forming unexpectedly; also, later, a whitlow.

‖**Ancon** (æ·ŋkǫn). Pl. **anco·nes.** 1706. [L., a. Gr. ἀγκών.] 1. *Phys.* The elbow. 2. *Arch.* The corner or quoin of a wall, etc. 1706. Also, a truss or console supporting a cornice at the flank 1823.

Ancon sheep: A race with long bodies, and short legs, the fore-legs crooked; bred from a single lamb so born in 1791. Hence **A·nconal** *a.* of or pertaining to the elbow; vars. **Anco·neal, Anco·neous. A·nconoid,** elbow-like.

†**A·ncony.** 1674. A bloom, perh. *Ancona* (Italy) which was an iron-work centre -1825.

Ancor, obs. form of ANCHOR.

†‖**Ancora.** 1712. [It.] = Fr. ENCORE.

Mr. Froth cried out *Ancora* ADDISON.

Ancoral (æ·ŋkŏrăl), *a. rare.* 1852. [ad. L. *ancoralis*; see ANCHOR.] *Zool.* Of or pertaining to an anchor; anchor-like, as the feet of some parasitic crustacea.

-ancy, *suffix.* [ad. L. *-antia*, forming abstr. sbs. on ppl. adjs. in *-antem* (see -ANT).] Mod. Eng. var. of -ANCE, expressing *quality, state*, or *condition*, as opp. to *action* (Fr. *-ance*). Many words orig. in *-nce* have been refash. accordingly, as *constancy, infancy*, etc.

Ancyroid (ænsəi·roid), *a.* 1839. [ad. med. L. *ancyroides*, a. Gr. ἀγκυροειδής; see ANCHOR. Occas. *ankuroid.*] *Phys.* Anchor-shaped, as the coracoid process of the scapula; also, the middle cornu of the lateral ventricle of the brain.

And (ænd, ənd, *famil.* ən, 'n), *conj.*[1] formerly *prep.* [repr. (1) OE. *and, ǫnd*, prep. 'against'; (2) OE. *ęnd*, conj.; cf. L. *ante*, Gr. ἀντί. See also AN *conj.*] †A. *prep.* (with *dat.*) Before; besides. OE. only.

B. *conj. co-ordinate.* Side by side with, along with, in addition to. I. Connecting words. 1. Simply connective OE. 2. Expressing continuous repetition (of groups, or indefinite) OE. 3. Emphatic. a. opp. to *or* (mod.); b. = and other (expressing a difference of quality) 1569. 4. Connecting an adj. adverbially with another which follows, esp. *famil.* after *nice, fine* 1592. †5. Bef. both words: = Both — and —. (A Latinism.) -1520. 6. When many notions, etc., are connected, *and* is now expressed only with the last, exc. rhetorically ME.

1. One and twenty; (cf. twenty-one). (*And* is used also to connect fractions to wholes, pence to shillings, etc., but not different denominations of weights and measures, nor in 'railway time'.) **And all**: see ALL. 2. Yea, two and two, Newgate fashion 1 *Hen. IV*, III. iii. 104. Higher still and higher SHELLEY. 3. b. Alack, there be roses and roses, John! BROWNING. (Cf. Molière's 'il y a fagots et fagots' 1666, as against 1569.) 4. His slow and mouing finger *Oth.* IV. ii. 56. Nice and warm (*mod. fam.*).

II. Connecting co-ordinate clauses or sentences. 1. Simply connective. a. additive OE. b. adversative OE. 2. Introducing a consequence, actual or predicted OE. 3. Introducing an amplificative clause OE. 4. Connecting two vbs. in the sense of *to* with the inf., *esp.* after *go, come, send, try* 1671.

1. b. Hee said, I goe sir, and went not *Matt.* xxi. 30. 2. A pretty young woman, and I did kiss her PEPYS. This do, and thou shalt liue *Luke* x. 28. 3. Scrooge signed it: and Scrooge's name was good upon 'Change DICKENS. 4. To try and teach the erring soul MILT. *P. R.* I. 224.

III. Introductory. 1. Continuing the narration OE.; occ. = 'Yes! and' 1847. 2. In expressing surprise at, or asking the truth of, what one has heard 1788. As quasi-*adv.* 3. Also; even. (A Latinism.) ME. *Obs.* or *arch.*

1. You are now to obey me. And I will KINGSLEY. 2. And are you really going (*mod.*). 3. She brought to him her beauty and truth, But and broad earldoms three LOWELL.

C. *conj. conditional*, = If. [Prob. elliptical; cf. *so*; or conn. w. the introductory *and*. Others write *an*, as in *an't = and it* (*c* 1600). See AN *conj.*] 1. If; also 'and if', 'an' if' ME. 2. Concessive: Even if, although ME. †3. = as if -1606; whether, L. *an* (*illiterate* or *dial.*) -1602. ¶Also used *subst.* 1638.

1. And you will not, sir, Ile take my heeles *Com. Err.* I. ii. 94. But and yf that evill servaunt shall say TINDALE *Matt.* xxiv. 48. 3. I will roar you an 'twere any Nightingale *Mids. N.* I. ii. 86. *subst.* Absolutely, and without any ifs and ands CUDWORTH.

†**And,** *conj.*[2] *after comparatives.* 1463. [erron. expansion of '*an*, 'than', confused w. an'; see prec.]

A made a finer end..and it had beene any Christome child *Hen. V*, II. iii. 12.

And, *sb.*; see ANDE.

†**And-,** *pref.* Against, in return, toward. In OE. it remained only in sbs. and adjs.; and now as *an-* in *answer*. When proclitic, as in vbs., it became *ǫn-*, and later *a-* as in *along* (see A *pref.* 4).

-and, *suffix.* repr. OE. *-ende*, later ME. and mod. *-ing*. Ppl. adjs. from Fr. in *-ant*, *-aunt* often changed to *-and* in 15th c.; cf. *warrant, warrand, merchant, marchand*, etc.

†**Anda·batism.** 1630. [f. L. *andabata*, a Roman gladiator who fought mounted, in a helmet without eyeholes; ? ad. Gr. ἀναβάτης.] The practice of a hoodwinked gladiator; contention in the dark DRUMM. OF HAWTH.

Andalusite (ændăl[i]ū·səit). 1837. [f. *Andalusia* + -ITE.] *Min.* A hard silicate of alumina, in rhombic crystals of various colour, first found in Spain.

‖**Andante** (anda·nte, ændæ·nti). 1742. [It., pr. pple. of *andare.*] *Mus. adj.* Of movement: Moderately slow and distinct. Also as adv. *sb.* [sc. *movement* or *piece.*] 1784.

‖**Andantino** (andantī·no). 1819. [It., dim. of prec.] *Mus. adj. orig.* Rather slower than andante; but freq.: With less of andante, *i.e.* rather quicker. *sb.* [sc. *movement* or *piece.*] 1845.

†**And(e,** *sb.* [OE. *anda*, in the south after 1200 ONDE. Still north. dial. as *and, aand, aynd, aind.*] 1. (from OE.) Emotion against, animus -ME. 2. (from ON. *andi.*) Breath -1536. Hence †**Ande,** *v.* to breathe, blow.

Andean (æ·ndĭ,ăn), *a.* 1839. Of, pertaining to, or like the Andes.

Andesine (æ·ndĭzin). 1862. *Min.* = next.

Andesite (æ·ndĭzəit). 1850. [f. *Andes* + -ITE.] *Min.* A silicate of alumina, lime, and soda, found in the Andes and elsewhere. Hence **Andesi·tic** *a.*

Andiron (æ·ndəi·əɹn). ME. [a. OFr. *andier* (mod. Fr. *landier*, i. e. *l'andier*), cf. med.L. *andena, anderia*, etc. The ME. *-yre* (*aundyre*) was erron. taken for *yre, yren* iron, hence the spellings *and-, hand-iron.*] A horizontal bar, one of a pair, sustained on short feet, with an upright pillar, usually ornamental in front, placed at each side of the hearth, to support burning wood.

‖**Andou·ille.** ? *Obs.* 1605. [Fr.:—L. *inductilia* things put in.] A kind of sausage.

‖**Andouille·t.** ? *Obs.* 1706. [a. Fr., dim. of prec.] Minced veal and bacon, etc., or chopped fish, rolled into a paste.

Andrana·tomy. ? *Obs.* 1811. [f. Gr. ἀνδρ- (ἀνήρ) + ANATOMY.] The dissection of the human (*esp.* male) body.

A·ndrew. 1618. †1. A broad-sword, an Andrea Ferrara (*rare*). †2. A valet. CONGREVE. 3. See MERRYANDREW.

Andro-, comb. f. Gr. ἀνήρ, a man, a male. **andro·dice·cious** [Gr. διά + οἰκία], *a. Bot.* with flowers on one plant hermaphrodite, and on the other staminate only; **-dy·namous** [Gr.

δύναμις] *a.*, *Bot.* having stamens and petals unusually developed; -**mo·rphous** [Gr. -μορφος] *a.*, having the form of a male; -**pe·tal** [+PETAL], *Bot.* a petal produced from a stamen; -**pe·talar**, -**pe·talous** *adjs.*, *Bot.* made double by having the stamens changed into petals; -**phagous** [Gr. -φαγος] *a.*, man-eating, anthropophagous; -**phore** [Gr. φόρος (φερ-)], *Bot.* the column formed by the united filaments in monadelphous plants; *Zool.* the male gonophore of some *Physaphoridæ*; -**sphinx** [+SPHINX], a sphinx whose human portion is male; -**spore** [Gr. σπόρος], *Bot.* the zoospore which in some *Algæ* produces the male reproductive organs; -**tomous** *a.*, *Bot.* having the filaments of the stamens divided into two parts; †-**tomy** = ANTHROPOTOMY.

‖**Andrœ·cium.** 1839. [mod.L., f. Gr. ἀνδρο- + οἰκίον.] *Bot.* The male organs of a flower collectively.

Androgyne (æ·ndrǒdʒin). 1552. [a. Fr., ad. L. *androgynus* (also used), a. Gr. ἀνδρόγυνος, f. ἀνδρο- + γυνή.] 1. A being of both sexes; a hermaphrodite. †2. An effeminate man; a eunuch (*rare*) –1742. 3. *Bot.* An androgynous plant 1785. Hence **Andro·gynal** *a.* = ANDROGYNOUS. **Andro·gynally** *adv.* **Andro·gynary** *a.* having both stamens and pistils developed into petals, as the double narcissus. **Andro·gyny**, hermaphroditism.

Androgynism (ǣndrǫ·dʒiniz'm). 1869. [f. prec. + -ISM.] *Bot.* Change from the diœcious to the monœcious condition.

Androgynous (ǣndrǫ·dʒinəs), *a.* 1628. [f. as prec. + -OUS.] 1. Uniting the (physical) characters of both sexes; hermaphrodite 1651. †2. Hence, effeminate 1628. 3. *Astrol.* Of planets: Both hot and cold 1652. 4. *Bot.* Bearing both stamens and pistils in the same flower, or on the same plant 1793.

1. Many of the rabbins are of opinion that Adam was created a. 1751.

Android (æ·ndroid). *rare.* 1727. [mod. L *androides* (also used), f. Gr. ἀνδρο- + εἶδης.] An automaton resembling a human being. Hence **Androi·dal** *a.*

†**A·ndrolepsy.** *rare.* An Athenian custom whereby, if a citizen were killed abroad, and his death unatoned for, three subjects of the offending country were seized as reprisals.

Andromed(e (æ·ndrǒmėd). 1876. *Astr.* A system of meteors radiating from a point in Andromeda.

Andromeda (ǣndrǫ·mīdă). 1706. [Gr., prop. name.] 1. A constellation of the northern hemisphere. 2. *Bot.* A genus of shrubs (N.O. *Ericaceæ*), native to Britain and N. America 1794.

-androus, *Bot. suffix* of adjs., f. mod.L. *-andrus* (a. Gr. -ανδρος adj. ending). = 'having .. male organs or stamens', as *triandrous*, etc.

†**Ane**, *a.* [OE. *án*, ONE.] 1. *án-e*: repr. inflections of *án* 'one'; and after the sb. = 'only'; see ONE –ME. 2. In ME., n. dial., var. of *an* (*ane*=*ān*), as def., or indef. article, according to the stress. See AN *adj.*[1] 3. In 16th c. *literary Sc.*=One, an, a. 4. In mod. Sc. and n. dial., *absol.*=one; the adj. form being *a*, *æ*.

-ane, *suffix.* 1. Occas. Eng. ad. L. *-anus*, esp. in words that have also a form in *-an*, as *humane*. 2. *Chem.* Hofmann's formative of the names of the saturated hydrocarbons of comp. C_nH_{2n+2}, also called *paraffines*, as *Methane*, etc.

Anear (ănīᵊ·ɹ). 1608. [cf. *afar.*] *adv.* Well-nigh; near, opp. to *afar* 1798. *prep.* Near, near to 1732.

adv. The lady..well a-near Does fall SHAKS. Now ..far, and now a-near SCOTT. *prep.* A. a bank (*mod.*).

Ane·ar, *v. arch.* 1534. [f. A- *pref* 11 + NEAR *v.*] †1. *intr.* To draw near *to* –1583; to be near 1583. 2. *trans.* To approach 1586.

Aneath (ănī·þ, *Sc.* ăne·þ), *prep.* 1801. [f. A *prep.*[1] + NEATH; cf. *afore.*] Beneath.

Anecdotage (æ·nekdoutėdʒ). 1823. [f. ANECDOTE + -AGE.] 1. Anecdotes; anecdotic literature. 2. *joc.* Garrulous old age [after *dotage*] 1835.

2. A man who has reached his a.—to use a pun .. conveyed from Wilkes M. COLLINS.

Anecdote (æ·nėkdout). 1676. [a. Fr., or med.L. *anecdota* (also used), a. Gr. ἀνέκδοτα.] 1. *pl.* Secret, or hitherto unpublished narratives or details of history. 2. The narrative of an interesting or striking incident or event. (*At first*, An item of gossip.) 1761. Also *collect.*

1. Anecdotes of Florence, or the secret history of the House of Medicis F. SPENCE (*title*). 2. An after-dinner a. (*mod.*). Hence **A·necdotal** *a.* **A·necdoted** *ppl. a.* made the subject of an a. (*rare*). **Anecdo·tic**, **-al** *a.* = *anecdotal*; addicted to anecdote. **Anecdo·tically** *adv.* **Anecdotist** (æ·nėkdoutist, ăne·kdŏtist), a relater of anecdotes or *anecdota*.

Anelace (**anelate** in Blount), var. ANLACE.

Anele (ănī·l), *v. arch.* ME. [orig. *anelien*, f. AN- *pref.* 1 + *elien*, f. OE. *ele*:—**oli*, ad. L. *oleum*. Cf. ANOIL.] 1. To anoint; *esp.* to give extreme unction to ME. Hence **Ane·led** *ppl. a.* †**Ane·ler**. **Ane·ling** *vbl. sb.*

Anelectric (ænīle·ktrik), *a.* 1830. [f. AN- *pref.* 10 + ELECTRIC.] †a. Non-electric. b. Parting rapidly with electricity. As *sb.* †a. A body which does not become electric when rubbed. b. A metal, etc., which being a good conductor parts rapidly with electricity 1863.

Anelec·trode. 1864. [f. ἀνά + ELECTRODE.] The positive pole of a galvanic battery.

‖**Anelectrotonus** (ænīlektrǫ·tǒnǒs). 1873. [f. ἀνά + ἤλεκτρον + τόνος.] *Phys.* A state of depressed irritability produced in a nerve near the positive pole of an electric current which traverses it. Hence **Anele·ctroto·nic** *a.*

Anelytrous (ăne·litrəs), *a.* 1847. [f. Gr. ἀν- + ἔλυτρον + -OUS.] *Ent.* Not having elytra or wing-cases.

Anemious (ănī·miəs), *a. rare.* 1879. [f. Gr. ἀνέμιος + -OUS.] Windy, growing in windy places.

Anemo- (ăne·mǒ, ænīmǫ·), comb. f. Gr. ἄνεμος wind.

anemo·cracy [Gr. κρατεία], *nonce-wd.*, a government by the wind; -**gram** [Gr. γράμμα], a prepared sheet marked by an anemograph; -**graph** [Gr. -γραφος], an instrument for recording on paper the direction and force of the wind; -**graphic** *a.*; -**graphy** [Gr. -γραφία], (*a*) description of, or a treatise on, the winds; (*b*) the art of recording the direction and force of the wind; -**logy** [+-LOGY], the science of the winds; -**logical** *a.*; -**philous** [Gr. φίλος] *a.*, wind-loving, wind-fertilized; -**scope** [Gr. -σκοπος], an instrument for showing the direction of the wind, or foretelling a change of weather.

Anemometer (ænīmǫ·mītəɹ). 1727. [f. Gr. ἄνεμος + -(O)METER.] 1. An instrument for measuring the force of the wind. 2. An apparatus for indicating the wind-pressure in an organ 1876. Hence **Ane·mome·tric**, **-al** *a.* **Ane·mome·trograph** = *anemograph*; see ANEMO-. **Anemo·metry**, the measurement of the force or velocity of the wind.

Anemone (ăne·mǒni, *Bot. L.* ænīmōᵘ·nī). 1551. [a. L., a. Gr. ἀνεμώνη, daughter of the wind, f. ἄνεμος.] 1. *Bot.* A genus of plants (N. O. *Ranunculaceæ*), of which one (*A. nemorosa*), the wind-flower, is common in Britain. Also *attrib.* 2. *Zool.* **Sea Anemone**: pop. name of various Actinoid Zoophytes 1773.

1. Woods with anemonies in flower till May M. ARNOLD. Hence **Anemo·nic** *a. Chem.* derived from the a. **Ane·monin**, *Chem.* an acrid crystalline substance, obtained from the a. *var.* **Anemony.**

Anencephalous (ænense·faləs), *a.* 1836. [f. Gr. ἀν + ἐγκέφαλος + -OUS. Cf. Fr. *anencéphale.*] *Phys.* Brainless; wanting the brain. var. **Ane·ncepha·lic.** Hence **Anence·phaloid** *a.* partially, or tending to be, a.

An-e·nd. *arch.* ME. [See AN *prep.*, and END.] †1. At last. 2. To the end; continuously (*arch.*) ME. 3. On end (*arch.*) 1593.

2. †*Most an end*: almost uninterruptedly, mostly. 3. Mine haire be fixt an end 2 *Hen. VI*, III. ii. 318.

Anent (ăne·nt), *prep.* [OE. *on efen, on efn, on emn*, = on even (ground) with. By 1200 a final *-t* occurs, dat. *-te*, gen. *-tes*, and in 14th c. the final *-s* becomes *-st*, whence *anentist, anentst, anenst* (midl.). The north. form is *anent*. Cf. *again, against.*] †1. In a line with, beside (OE. only); on a par with –ME.; in the company of, by (L. *apud*, Fr. *chez*) –ME. (Still *dial.*) 2. Fronting, over against (*arch.* or *dial.*) ME. 3. In respect or reference to, concerning. (*Sc.* and affected by Eng. writers.) ME. 4. *adv.* (obj. understood). Opposite (*dial.*) 1520.

Ane·nterous, *a.* 1847. [f. Gr. ἀν+ἔντερα + -OUS.] *Zool.* Having no intestine.

Ane·piplo·ic, *a.* 1879. [f. Gr. ἀν+ἐπίπλοον+ -IC.] *Phys.* Having no epiploon, or omentum.

†**A·nerly**, *adv. north.* ME. [f. ANE; cf. ALLENARLY.] Only; only just –1513.

Aneroid (æ·nĕroid), *a.* 1848. [a. Fr. *anéroïde*, f. Gr. ἀ + νηρός.] Of a barometer, in which the pressure of the air is measured, not by the aid of a fluid, as mercury, but by its action on the elastic lid of a box exhausted of air. As *sb.* [Short for 'Aneroid barometer'.] 1849.

Anes, earlier f. ONCE. *Sc.*

‖**Anesis** (æ·nīsis). 1811. [Gr.] *Med.* The abatement of symptoms.

Anesthetic, var. of ANÆSTHETIC.

Anet (æ·net). ME. [a. Fr. *anet, aneth*:—L. *anethum*, a. Gr. ἄνηθον (ἄνισον). See ANISE.] The herb Dill (*Anethum graveolens*). *Comb.* anetseed, the seed of a. **A·nethated** *ppl. a.* prepared or mixed with dill.

Anethene (æ·nīþīn). 1874. [f. L. *anethum* + -ENE.] *Chem.* The most volatile part of the essential oil of dill, fennel, etc.; $C_{10}H_{16}$.

Anethol (æ·nīþǫl). 1863. [f. L. *anethum* + -OL.] *Chem.* An essential principle of the oils of anise, fennel, etc.; $C_{10}H_{12}O$.

Ane·tic, *a.* 1853. [ad. L., a. Gr. ἀνετικός; see ANESIS.] *Med.* Assuaging, soothing.

Aneuch, north. f. ENOUGH.

Aneurysm, -ism (æ·niuriz'm). 1656. [ad. Gr. ἀνεύρυσμα, f. ἀνά + εὐρύνειν, f. εὐρύς; *-ysm* follows the etym., but *-ism* is more freq.] *Path.* A morbid dilatation of an artery, due to disease, or to a tumour caused by rupture, of the arterial coats. Hence **Aneury·smal**, **-i·smal** *a.* marked or affected by a.; var. †**Aneurysma·tic**, **-al.**

Anew (ăniū·), *adv.* OE. [*A-new*, earlier *o-new*, prob. for *of new*; see A- *pref.* 3; and cf. Fr. *de nouveau, à nouveau, à neuf.*] 1. Once more, afresh, as a new action. 2. In a new way ME. †3. Newly, opp. to *of old* –1728; freshly –1582.

†**Anew·**, *v.* OE. [? f. OE. *ed* again + NEW.] To renew –1690.

†**A·nfract.** *rare.* 1567. [ad. L. *anfractus* (also used).] A winding –1611.

Anfractuose (ǣnfræ:ktiu,ōᵘ·s), *a. rare.* 1691. [ad. L. *anfractuosus*; see ANFRACTUOUS.] Winding, sinuous.

Anfractuosity (ǣnfræ:ktiu,ǫ·sĭti). 1596. [a. Fr., f. as prec.] 1. *lit.* Sinuosity; usu. *concr.* in *pl.* winding crevices, channels, etc.; *spec.* the sinuous depressions separating the convolutions of the brain 1687. 2. *fig.* Involution, intricacy; *concr.* in *pl.* 1652.

2. The anfractuosities of the human mind JOHNSON. var. **Anfra·cture.**

Anfractuous (ǣnfræ·ktiu,əs), *a.* 1621. [ad. L. *anfractuosus*, f. *anfranctus* a winding.] Sinuous; circuitous; spiral.

Angary (æ·ngări). 1880. [ad. F. *angarie*, ad. L. *angaria* forced service, ult. Gr., f. ἄγγαρος courier.] The right of a belligerent to use and destroy neutral property.

Angel (ē^i·ndʒĕl). [ME., a. OF. *-ele*, repl. OE. *engel*:—**angil-*, Com. Teut. loan, a. L. *angelus*, Gr. ἄγγελος messenger.] 1. A ministering spirit or divine messenger; one of an order of spiritual beings superior to man in power and intelligence, who are the attendants and messengers of the Deity OE.; hence b. one of the fallen spirits, who rebelled against God OE.; c. a guardian or attendant spirit (*lit.* and *rhet.*) ME.; d. *fig.* a person who resembles an angel in attributes or actions 1592. 2. Any messenger of God, as a prophet or preacher (a Hellenism) ME.; a pastor or minister of a Church ME.; *poet.* a messenger ME.; *fig.* in *angel of death* 1574. 3. *transf.* A conventional figure with wings 1536. 4. An old Eng. gold coin, orig. called ANGEL-NOBLE, having as its device the archangel Michael and the dragon. Its value varied from 6*s.* 8*d.* to 10*s.* 1488. **5.** *attrib.* = ANGELIC 1611.

1. Thou hast maad hym a litil lesse than aungels WYCLIF *Ps.* viii. 6. Angels are bright still, though the brightest fell *Macb.* IV. iii. 22. b. The deuill and his angels *Matt.* xxv. 41. c. There is no euill Angell but Loue *L. L. L.* I. i. 78. d. O, speake againe, bright Angell *Rom. & Jul.* II. ii. 26. 2. To the aungel of the chirche of Smyrna, wrijte thou WYCLIF *Rev.* ii. 8. The dear good a. of the spring, The nightingale B. JONS. 4. His stripes washed off With oil of angels MASSINGER.

Comb.: **†a.-bed**, an open bed without bed-posts; **-cornice**, one decorated with figures of angels; **angels' eyes**, the plant, germander speedwell; **-fish**, one of the *Squalidæ* or Shark family, named from the wing-like expansion of its pectoral fins, the Monk-fish, Tiddle-fish, Shark-ray; **†-gold**, standard gold; **-like**, *adv.*; **-noble**, see ANGEL 4; **†-proof**, the gold standard of the a.; **-shot** (Fr. *ange*), a kind of chain-shot, made of the (2 or 4) segments of a bullet, attached by chains to a disk; **†-water** [for Angelica-water], a perfume, orig. consisting chiefly of Angelica, subseq. of ambergris, rose, myrtle, and orange-flower waters.

Hence **A·ngelhood,** the condition of an a.; a brotherhood of angels. **†Ange·lify** *v.* (*rare*), also **A·ngelize** *v.* (*arch.*), to make into or like an a. **Angelo·latry,** angel-worship. **Angelo·logy,** that part of theology which treats of angels; doctrine as to angels. **Angelo·phany,** the visible manifestation of angels.

A·ngelate. 1863. [f. ANGELIC *a.*²] *Chem.* A salt of angelic acid.

Angelet (ē·ndʒĕlĕt). 1481. [a. OFr. = It. *angeletto*, dim.; cf. *eaglet.*] †1. A gold coin; a half-angel. 2. A little angel; *fig.* a pretty child 1823.

Angelic (ændʒe·lik), *a.*¹ 1485. [ad. Fr. *angelique*, ad. L. *angelicus*, a. Gr.; see ANGEL.] 1. Of or pertaining to angels; of angel kind. 2. Like an angel; *hence*, of superhuman intelligence, innocence, purity, sweetness, etc. 1510.

1. The angelyk visyon CAXTON. *Angelic Salutation*, the *Ave Maria* (Luke i. 28). Th' a. guards MILT. [Satan's] Wit and Angelick Faculties STEELE. 2. Fair a. Eve MILT. *P. L.* v. 74. *Angelic doctor* (i. e. spiritual as an angel): Thomas Aquinas.

Ange·lic, *a.*² 1863. [f. next.] *Chem.* Of or derived from angelica; as in *Angelic acid* $C_5H_8O_2$, occurring in the root of *A. archangelica*, etc.

‖**Angelica** (ændʒe·likă): 1578. [med.L. = *herba angelica* 'root of the Holy Ghost'.] 1. An aromatic umbelliferous plant (*A. archangelica*, or *A. officinalis*), used in cookery and medicine; the genus, of which the prec. plant is the type. Also *attrib.* 1641. 2. Short for a. Angelica water (cf. *Angel-water*). b. Candied angelica root 1653.

Ange·lical, *a.* 1509. [f. ANGELIC + -AL.] 1. = ANGELIC 1 (*arch.*). 2. = ANGELIC 2. 1577. 3. Of or pertaining to a divine messenger or pastor. Cf. ANGEL 2 (*rare*) 1678. Hence **Ange·lically** *adv.* **†Ange·licalness** (*rare*).

Angelina (ændʒĕlī·nă). 1663. [f. ANGEL; see -INA.] *Bot.* A genus of *Leguminosæ*, native esp. to tropical America.

Angelot (æ·ndʒĕlǫt). *arch.* 1525. [a. Fr., dim. of OFr. *angele*:—L. *angelus.*] †1. A Fr. gold coin struck by Louis XI, bearing the image of St. Michael and the dragon; also an Eng. piece coined at Paris by Henry VI. †2. A cheese, made in Normandy [and stamped with the coin. Littré.] –1719. 3. A musical instrument 1678.

‖**Angelus** (æ·ndʒĕlǫs). 1727. [L., '*Angelus* domini nuntiavit Mariæ'.] 1. A devotional exercise commemorating the Incarnation, in which the Angelic Salutation is thrice repeated, said by Roman Catholics, at morning, noon, and sunset, at the sound of a bell. 2. Short for *Angelus-bell* 1847.

2. Softly the A. sounded LONGF.

Anger (æ·ŋgəɹ), *sb.* ME. [a. ON. *angr*, f. root *ang* straitened; cf. OE. *ang-* in Comb., and L. *angere.*] †1. That which pains or afflicts, or the feeling which it produces; trouble, vexation, sorrow –1475. 2. The active feeling provoked against the agent; passion, rage; wrath, ire ME. 3. Inflammatory state of any part of the body; physical pain. (Still *dial.*) ME.

1. Syknesses and angres LANGL. *P. Pl.* 2. A., which is a desire of revenge; Hatred, which is inveterate a. BURTON. A. is the executive power of justice MANNING. 3. Where the greatest a. and soreness still continued TEMPLE (J.). Hence **A·ngerless** *a.* **A·ngerly** *adv.* (*arch.*) † painfully; †furiously; = ANGRILY; also as adj.: angry.

Anger (æ·ŋgəɹ), *v.* ME. [a. ON. *angra*, f. *angr*; see prec.] †1. To distress, vex, hurt –1440. 2. Hence, to make angry, enrage ME.; *intr.* (refl. pron. omitted.) *rare.* ME. †3. To irritate or inflame a sore –1760.

2. You have both pleased and angered me JOHNSON. 3. Itch most hurts when angerd to a sore POPE. Hence **A·ngered** *ppl. a.* provoked to wrath (*lit.* and *fig.*); inflamed; flushed as with rage.

†A·ngild. [OE., f. AN- *pref.* 1 + *gildan* to pay.] In OE. law, compensation for injury. (Erron. taken later as 'single payment'.)

‖**Angina** (ændʒină, ǣndʒəi·nă, f. supposed L. *angīna*). 1590. [L.; cf. *angere*, and Gr. ἀγχόνη.] *Path.* 1. Quinsy. 2. (In full *Angina pectoris.*) A dangerous disease, marked by sudden and severe pain in the lower part of the chest, with a feeling of suffocation; called also *breast-pang, heart-stroke*, and *spasm of the chest* 1772. Hence **A·nginous** *a.* (sense 2).

Angio-, a comb. form, repr. Gr. ἀγγεῖον a vessel. Occ. spelt *angeio-*; but Roman *ī* = Gr. ει. Exc. in ændʒi,ǫ· (stress on *o*), pronunc. should be ændʒəi·o, but æ·ndʒi,o is common. **angio·ca·rpian** [Gr. καρπός], *Bot.* an angiocarpous plant; **-ca·rpous** *a.*, *Bot.* having the fruit in an envelope not constituting part of the calyx; **-graph** [Gr. -γραφος], a kind of sphygmograph; **-graphy** [Gr. -γραφία], a description (*a*) of vessels, instruments, etc., used by any nation, (*b*) of the blood-vessels; **-logy** [Gr. -λογία], the part of anatomy which treats of the blood-vessels; **-monospe·rmous** [+ MONOSPERMOUS] *a.*, *Bot.* bearing solitary seeds each in its own pod; **-scope** [Gr. -σκοπος], an instrument for examining the capillary vessels of animals and plants; **-sperm** [Gr. -σπερμος, f. σπέρμα], *Bot.* a plant which has its seeds enclosed in a seed-vessel; opp. to *gymnosperms*; **-spe·rmal, -spe·rmatous, -spe·rmous** *adjs.*; **-sporous** [Gr. σπόρος] *a.*, *Bot.* having spores enclosed in a hollow receptacle, as the puff-ball, etc.; **-stomous** [Gr. -στομος, but cf. L. *angere* for sense] *a.*, *Conch.* having a narrow opening, as some univalve shells; **-te·nic** [Gr. τεν- stem of τείνειν] *a.*, *Med.* tending to stretch the blood-vessels: applied to inflammatory fevers; **-tomy** [Gr. -τομία], the anatomy of the blood-vessels.

†A·ngiport. *rare.* 1647. [ad. L. *angiportus*, f. *angere* + *portus.*] A narrow entrance, or opening in a wall –1652.

Angle (æ·ng'l), *sb.*¹ *arch.* [OE. *angul*:—**angulr*; cf. L. *uncus, angulus*, and *ank-*.] 1. A fishing-hook; often also the line and rod OE. †2. *fig.* A person or thing that catches like a hook –1598. 3. [f. the vb.] An act of angling 1874.

1. Giue me mine A., weele to th' Riuer *Ant. & Cl.* II. v. 10. 2. A woman, . is a very a., hir hert is a net *Ecclus.* vii. 26. *Comb.* **a.-worm,** a worm for bait.

Angle (æ·ŋg'l), *sb.*² ME. [a. Fr.:—L. *angulum*, dim. of **angus*; cf. Gr. ἄγκος, L. *angere* and *ank-*.] 1. The space included between two meeting lines or planes; hence in *Geom.* the degree of inclination of two lines to each other. 2. The meeting-point of two lines not in the same direction. Also *fig.* 1605. 3. A corner, viewed (*a*) as a retreat, (*b*) as a projection. Also *fig.* ME. 4. An outlying spot, a nook. Also *fig.* (*arch.*) ME. 5. A sharp projection; *hence*, an angular fragment. Also *fig.* 1684. 6. *Astrol.* Any of the four 'houses', at the cardinal points of the compass ME.

The inclination of two lines in the same plane is a plane angle, formed either by straight lines (*rectilineal*), or curved (*curvilineal*); if on the surface of a sphere it is a *spherical* angle; the space included by more than two plane angles meeting at a point is a *solid* angle. From measurement by angle in physics, mechanics, etc., come such phrases as *angle of application, depression, deviation, elevation, incidence, inclination, position, reflection, refraction, repose, rest, traction, vision*; and *To take the angle.*

1. *At angles with*: so placed as to form an a. with, opp. to *parallel. On the angle*: obliquely. 3. For truth will seek no angles 1655. No bonch nor a. PUTTENHAM. 4. Whom I left. . In an odde A. of the Isle *Temp.* I. ii. 223. 5. The fractured angles of upturned ice KANE.

Comb.: **a.-bar,** the upright bar at the a. of a polygonal window; also = *a.-iron*; **-bead,** a vertical bead fixed to an exterior a., flush with the surface of the plaster; **-brace,** a piece of timber fixed to the adjacent sides of a quadrangular framing; **-iron,** an L-shaped piece of iron, used to secure or strengthen framework; **-meter,** an instrument for measuring angles, *esp.* a CLINOMETER; **-staff** = *a.-bead*; **-tie** = *a.-brace*; **-wise,** *adv.*

Angle (æ·ŋg'l), *sb.*³ OE. [ad. L. *Anglus*, pl. *Angli*, a. OTeut. **angli-*, in OE. *ęngle* (occ. *Angle*), the people of *Angul, -ol, -el* (= ANGLE *sb.*¹) in Holstein, so called from its shape; subseq. the 'English' race.] *pl.* A Low-German tribe that settled in Britain, formed the kingdoms of Northumbria, Mercia, and East Anglia, and finally gave their name to the 'English' people.

Angle (æ·ŋg'l), *v.*¹ 1496. [f. ANGLE *sb.*¹; cf. to *hook.*] 1. To fish with a hook and bait. Const. *for*, †*to*. Also *trans.* (*rare.*) 1866. 2. *fig.* To use artful or wily means to catch a person or thing; to 'fish'. Const. *for*. 1589. †Also *trans.* –1683.

1. It is but a sory lyfe and an yuell to stande anglynge all day to catche a few fysshes 1530. 2. Shee . . did a. for mee, madding my eagernesse with her restraint *All's Well* v. iii. 212. Shooes which . . angled their Charity, that pass'd along OLDHAM.

A·ngle, *v.*² 1575. [f. ANGLE *sb.*²] †1. *intr.* To run into a corner. 2. *refl.* To move in angles 1876. Hence **A·ngled** *ppl. a.* †driven into, or stationed in, a corner; placed at angles; having an angle or angles; also **-angled** in comb.

Angleberry, anle-. 1600. [? var. of ANBURY, or *ang-berry.*] A fleshy excrescence resembling a strawberry, found growing on the feet of cattle, etc.

Angler (æ·ŋgləɹ). 1552. [f. ANGLE *v.*¹] 1. One who angles (*lit.* and *fig.*). 2. *Zool.* A British fish (*Lophius piscatorius* Linn.), so named from its preying on small fish, which it attracts by moving certain wormlike filaments attached to the head and mouth. Called also Sea Devil, Frog or Toad Fish, and Fishing Frog. 1766.

Anglesite (æ·ŋglĭsəit). 1837. [f. *Anglesea* (where first found) + -ITE.] *Min.* The native sulphate of lead, lead vitriol.

Anglian (æ·ŋgliăn), *a.* and *sb.* 1726. [f. L. *Angli* (see ANGLE *sb.*³) + -AN.] Of or pertaining to the Angles. *East Anglian*, of East Anglia or the East Angles. var. **A·nglic** *a.*

Anglican (æ·ŋglikăn), *a.* 1635. [ad. med. L. *Anglicanus*, f. *Anglicus*; see prec.] 1. Of or peculiar to the English ecclesiastically; of the reformed Church of England, and other churches in communion with it. Also opp. to *Roman*; moderate High Church. 2. English 1860. 3. *sb.* An adherent of the reformed Church of England; *esp.* one holding High Church principles 1797.

1. A. orders GLADSTONE, doctrine and discipline MACAULAY. 3. Whether Catholicks, Anglicans, or Calvinists BURKE.

A·nglicanism. 1846. [f. prec.] Adherence to the doctrine and discipline of the Anglican, as the genuine representative of the Catholic, Church.

Anglicism (æ·ŋglisiz'm). 1642. [f. ANGLICIZE; see -ISM.] 1. Anglicized language; *hence*, an idiom specially English. †2. An English fashion 1787. 3. English political principles or methods 1873.

1. Dr. B. has abundance of pure Anglicisms in his Latin BENTLEY.

Anglicize (æ·ŋglisəiz), *v.* 1748. [f. L. *Anglicus* + -IZE.] To make English in form or character; to English. Also *intr.* (*rare*). Hence **A·nglicіza·tion,** the making English.

Anglify (æ·ŋglifəi), *v.* 1751. [f. L. *Angli* + -FY.] = prec. (Rather out of use.) Hence **A·nglifica·tion.**

Angling (æ·ŋgliŋ), *vbl. sb.* 1496. [f. ANGLE *v.*¹] The action or art of fishing with a rod. Also *fig.* 1674.

Uncertain anglings for distinction CARLYLE.

A·nglish, *a. rare.* = ANGLIAN. CARLYLE.

Anglo- (æ·ŋglǫ), comb. form of L. *Anglus* English. For history see ANGLO-SAXON. 1. a. English, of England: as in ANGLO-CATHO-

LIC, -SAXON; **a.-Danish,** pertaining to the Danes in England; **-French,** the French retained and separately developed in England; **-Latin,** Anglicized Latin; *a.-Judaic, -Jewish, -Norman.* **b.** Of English race, origin, descent, as *Anglo-American*, etc. **2.** English *and*; English in connexion with; as *Anglo-Russian*, etc.

Anglo-Ca·tholic. 1841. [see ANGLO-.] **A.** *adj.* Catholic of the Anglican communion. **B.** *sb.* **1.** *Hist.* An Englishman who, without wishing to sever the English from the Catholic Church, was in favour of its national independence 1858. **2.** *Modern.* A member of the Church of England who maintains its 'catholic' character 1849. Hence **Anglo-Catholicism,** catholicism of the Anglican type.

Anglo-Indian (æ·ŋglo,i·ndiăn), *a.* and *sb.* 1861. [ANGLO- 1 b.] (A person) of British birth, now or formerly resident in India; also, of mixed European and Indian parentage, Eurasian.

A·ngloman, -e. *rare.* 1860. [a. Fr. *angloмane*; see ANGLOMANIA.] Anglomaniac.

Anglomania (æŋglo,mē·niă). Occas. **anglomany.** 1787. [f. ANGLO- + Gr. μανία, after Fr. *anglomanie.*] A mania for what is English. Hence **Angloma·niac** *sb.* a rabid partisan of what is English (*rare*).

Anglophobe (æ·ŋglŏfōᵘb). 1866. [a. Fr.] One afflicted with ANGLOPHOBIA.

Anglopho·bia. 1816. [f. ANGLO- + Gr. -φοβία.] Intense fear or hatred of England. **Anglopho·bic** *a.* (*rare*). **Anglopho·bist** (*rare*) = ANGLOPHOBE.

Anglo-Saxon (æ:nglo,sæ·ksən), *sb.* and *a.* [Prob. ad. L. *Anglo-Saxones, -Saxonicus,* in which *Anglo-* is advb. Hence = English Saxons, opp. to *Ald-Seaxan*, or Old-Saxons of the continent. Orig. *Angli Saxones* (two words), whence *Angli-*, and finally *Anglo-Saxones.* In OE. use, rare in the Eng. form.] **1.** English Saxon, Saxon of England; opp. *orig.* to the 'Old Saxons' of the continent. Hence, opp. also to the Angles. **A.** *sb.* (the only contemporary use) OE. **B.** *adj.* In N.E.D. and in this Dictionary, the language of England bef. 1100 is called OE.; *Anglo-Saxon* when used = the Saxon (as opp. to the Anglian) *dialects* of OE. **2.** Extended to the entire Old English people and language before the Norman Conquest. (This use dates from Camden. Subseq. the word was explained as = *Angle + Saxon*, a union of Angle and Saxon, whence ANGLO- 2, q. v.) **A.** *sb.* 1610. **B.** *adj.* (*absol.* The Old English language.) 1610. **3.** Used rhet. for *English* in its ethnological sense. **A.** *sb.* 1853. **B.** *adj.* 1840. Hence **Anglo-Sa·xondom,** the Anglo-Saxon domain; the Anglo-Saxons collectively; rhet. for Great Britain and the United States. **Anglo-Sa·xonism. a.** Anything peculiar to the Anglo-Saxon race; *esp.* a word, phrase, or habit of speech belonging to the Old English. **b.** The sentiment of being Anglo-Saxon (sense 3) ethnologically; a belief in the Anglo-Saxon race.

Angola (ǣŋgōᵘ·lă). 1827. A corruption of ANGORA; the fabric made of Angora wool.

Angor (æ·ŋgŏɹ). ME. [a. OFr.:—L. *angorem.* Now only *Med.*] †**1.** Anguish -1711. **2.** *spec.* A feeling of anxiety and constriction in the precordial region; cf. *angina* 1666.

Angora (ǣŋgōᵊ·ră). 1833. [mod. f. Ἄγκυρα Ancyra.] **1.** A town in Asia Minor, giving its name to a goat, and to its silk-like wool; also to a cat, etc. **2.** The fabric ANGOLA 1867.

Angostura; see ANGUSTURA.

Angry (æ·ŋgri), *a.* ME. [f. ANGER *sb.* + -Y¹; cf. *hungry.* Compar. *-er, -est.*] †**1.** Full of trouble actively, troublesome -1667; affected by trouble, vexed -1485. **2.** Feeling or showing resentment against the agent or cause of trouble; enraged, wrathful. Const. *at, about* the occasion; *at, with* the person. ME. **3.** Moved or excited by anger 1509. **4.** Looking or acting as if in anger ME.; red (*rare*) 1632. **5.** Habitually under the influence of anger, choleric, passionate (*arch.*) ME. **6.** Inflamed, smarting 1579. **7.** Sharp, keen (*rare*) ME.

2. A. letters to his angrier mistress (*mod.*). A. with you *Hen. V*, IV. i. 217, at him *Timon* III. iii. 13. 3. The a. trade of war COTTON. 4. Now..Doth..warre bristle his a. crest SHAKS. *John* IV. iii. 149. An angrie countenance *Prov.* xxv. 23. A. masses of cloud TYNDALL. Sweet rose, whose hue angrie and brave [etc.] G. HERBERT. 5. Honour, this busie, a. thing ROWE. 7. I never ate with angrier appetite TENNYSON. Hence **A·ngrily** *adv.* **A·ngriness.**

Ångström (unit). 1921. [The name of A. J. *Ångström*, a Swedish physicist.] A hundred-millionth of a centimetre, used in expressing short wave-lengths (abbrev. A.U.).

Anguiform (ǣ·ŋgwifǭɹm), *a.* 1800. [f. L. *anguis* + -FORM.] Snake-shaped.

†**Anguille, anguelle.** 1500. [a. Fr.:—L. *anguilla,* dim. of *anguis.*] A sort of small worms cast up by sick hawks. Hence **Angui·lliform** *a.* eel-shaped.

Anguillule (ǣŋgwi·liul). 1860. [f. L. *anguilla.*] A small eel-shaped creature; *esp.* one of the *Anguillulidæ* or eels found in sour paste or vinegar.

Anguine (æ·ŋgwin), *a.* 1657. [a. L. *anguinus,* f. *anguis.*] Of or resembling a snake or serpent.

Anguineous (ǣŋgwi·nĭəs), *a. rare.* 1656 [f. as prec.; see -EOUS.] Snake-like; as in Newton's *Anguineous Hyperbola.*

Anguish (æ·ŋgwiʃ), *sb.* [ME. *anguise, angoise,* a. OFr. *anguisse, angoisse*:—L. *angustia,* f. root *angu-* in *ang(u)ere.*] Formerly with *pl.* Excruciating or oppressive bodily or mental suffering; pain, or grief.

Anguysshes as of the child berere WICLIF *Jer.* iv. 31. One paine is lesned by anothers a. *Rom. & Jul.* I. ii. 47. I wil speake in the a. of my spirit *Job* vii. 11.

Anguish (æ·ŋgwiʃ), *v.* ME. [a. OFr. *anguissier, angoissier*:—L. *angustiare*; see prec.] To distress with severe pain or grief, excruciate. Also *intr.* (refl. pron. omitted.) Hence **A·nguished** *ppl. a.* sorely distressed; expressing pain.

A·nguishous, *a. Obs.* or *dial.* ME. [a. OFr. *anguissus,* later *-oisseux*:—late L. *angustiosum*; see ANGUISH *sb.*] Tormenting -1554; distressed -ME.; anxious -1503.

Angular (æ·ŋgiŭlăɹ), *a.* 1597. [ad. L. *angularis*; see ANGLE.] **1.** Having an angle or angles, sharp-cornered 1598. **2.** Constituting, placed in or at, an angle 1597; measured by angle 1674. **3.** Having the joints and bones prominent. Of action: Jerky, abrupt, awkward. 1850. **4.** Stiff and formal; unaccommodating; cantankerous 1840.

1. A. handwriting 1863. 2. An a. aperture of 60°. 3. The a. female in black bombazine HOLMES. Many bows and a deal of a. politeness HAWTHORNE. Hence **A·ngularly** *adv.* in or with angles; at (acute) angles; in an a. manner; see ANGULAR 3.

Angularity (æŋgiulæ·riti). 1642. [f. L. *angularis* + -ITY.] **1.** The quality or state of being ANGULAR. *concr.* in *pl.* Angular outlines, sharp corners 1853. **2.** Want of rounded outline. Of manner: Crankiness. 1848.

Angulate (æ·ŋgiŭlĕt), *a.* 1794. [ad. L. *angulatus, angulare,* f. *angulus.*] Formed with corners; angled. Hence **A·ngulate** *v.* to make cornered. **A·ngulately** *adv.* with angles or corners. **Angula·tion,** a making angulate; angular formation or position.

Angulato- (æŋgiŭlē·to), comb. f. L. *angulatus* used advb. Angulately.

Angulo- (æŋgiŭlo), comb. f. L. *angulus* (see ANGLE *sb.*²) used advb., as in *a.-dentate,* angularly toothed.

Angulo·meter. *rare.* 1859. [f. prec.] An instrument for measuring external angles.

A:ngulo·se, *a. rare.* = ANGULOUS.

Anguloso- (æŋgiulōᵘ·so), comb. f. L. *angulosus,* used advb., as in *a.-gibbous,* gibbous with the curved sides almost forming angles.

Angulous (æ·ŋgiŭləs), *a.* ? *Obs.* 1656. [a. Fr. *anguleux,* ad. L. *angulosus.*] Having angles or corners; angular.

‖**Anguria** (ǣŋgiūᵊ·riă). 1611. [L., f. Gr. ἀγγούριον.] *Bot.* A plant of the gourd family; also its fruit.

†**Angu·st,** *a.* 1599. [a. Fr. *anguste,* ad. L. *angustus,* f. *angere.*] Strait, compressed -1661.

Angu·state, *a.* 1847. [ad. L. *angustatus*; see prec.] Narrowed, as leaves at the base. Hence **Angusta·tion,** contraction.

Angusti- (ǣŋgɒ·sti), comb. f. L. *angustus* narrow; as in *angustifoliate, -ous* narrow-leaved, *angustirostrate,* with narrow beak.

†‖**Angu·stia.** *rare.* [L.] Straits. SIR T. BROWNE.

Angustu·ra, or **Angostura.** 1791. A town on the Orinoco, now Ciudad Bolivar. It gives its name to a bark, the produce of *Galipea* or *Cusparia febrifuga,* a febrifuge and tonic.

†**Anha·ng,** *v.* ME. only. [var. AHANG:—OE. *ahōn.*] To hang. *trans.* and *intr.*

Anharmonic (æ:nhaɹmǫ·nik), *a.* 1863. [ad. Fr. *anharmonique,* f. Gr. ἀν- + -ἁρμονικός.] *Math.* Not harmonic. Applied to the *section* of a line by four points A, B, C, D, when their mutual distances are such that $\frac{AB}{CB}$ is unequal to $\frac{AD}{CD}$; the ratio between these two quotients is called the *anharmonic ratio* of AC.

Anhelation (ænhĭlē·ʃən). *arch.* 1623. [a. Fr., ad. L. *anhelationem*; see next.] **1.** A difficulty with breathing, panting; asthma. **2.** *fig.* Panting, aspiration (*after*) 1631.

†**Anhe·le,** *v.* ME. [a. OFr. *aneler, anheler*:—L. *anhelare.*] **1.** ? To blow, puff ME. only. **2.** *fig.* To pant *for,* aspire *to* -1536.

†**Anhe·lous,** *a.* 1661. [f. L. *anhelus* + -OUS.] Short of breath, panting -1684.

Anhidrotic (ænhidrǫ·tik), *a.* 1880. [f. Gr. ἀν + ἱδρωτικός, f. ἱδρώς.] *Med.* Tending to check perspiration. As *sb.* [sc. *medicine.*]

Anhistous (ænhi·stəs), *a.* 1880. [f. Gr. ἀν + ἱστόν + -OUS; cf. Fr. *anhiste.*] *Biol.* Of tissue: Without recognizable structure.

Anhungered (ǣnhɒ·ŋgəɹd), *ppl. a. arch.* ME. [Alteration (cf. ENHUNGERED) of †*of hungered*: see AHUNGERED. Cf. AN- 1.] **1.** Overcome with hunger, hungry. **2.** *fig.* Eagerly desirous 1848.

†**An-hu·ngry,** *a. rare.* 1607. [var. of *a-hungry* (see A-HUNGERED).] Hungry -1681.

Anhydride (ænhəi·drəid). 1863. [f. Gr. ἄνυδρος + -IDE.] *Chem.* A compound formed by the union of oxygen with another element, without hydrogen, but which, on exposure to water, absorbs hydrogen and becomes an acid. Also called *anhydrous acids,* because produced by expelling the water from oxy-acids.

Anhydrite (ænhəi·drəit). 1831. [f. as prec. + -ITE.] *Min.* Anhydrous gypsum or sulphate of lime.

Anhydro- (ænhəi·dro), combining form of next, as in *anhydro-borate,* etc.

Anhydrous (ænhəi·drəs), *a.* 1819. [f. Gr. ἄνυδρος + -OUS.] **1.** *Chem.* Having no water in its composition: said of *salts, crystals,* destitute of water of crystallization, etc. **2.** *transf.* Sapless, dried up 1872. var. **Anhy·dric.**

‖**A·nicut, ann-.** 1784. [Anglo-Ind. ad. Tamil.] The dam constructed across a river to fill, and regulate the supply of, the irrigating channels.

Anidioma·tic, -al, *a. rare.* Landor's substitutes for *unidiomatic, -al.*

†**Anie·ntise, -ish,** *v.* ME. [a. OFr. *anientiss-, anientir,* f. *à* + *nient,* mod. *néant*:—late L. **neëntem*; see ENTITY and -ISH.] **1.** To bring to naught, annul, destroy -1483. **2.** To bring low, reduce -1530. var. **Anie·nte.** Hence †**Anie·ntisement,** annihilation.

Anigh (ănəi·). 1773. [f. NIGH; intended as arch. Cf. *near, anear.*] *adv.* Nigh 1868. *prep.* Near to 1773.

Anight (ănəi·t), *adv. arch.* [OE. *on niht* (*a* for proclitic *on*).] By night, at night.

They mete neuer but a nyght ME.

Anights (ănəi·ts), *adv. arch.* 1440. [fusion of *on niht,* and *nihtes* advb. gen.] = prec., though *-s* is occas. taken as pl.

Such [men] as sleepe a-nights *Jul. C.* I. ii. 193.

Anil (æ·nil). 1581. [a. Fr. or Pg. ad. (ult.) Arab.] **1.** The Indigo shrub 1712. **2.** The indigo dye 1581. **3.** Formative of names of aniline compounds and derivatives; as **anilamic** = PHENYLAMIC, **chloranil** $C_6Cl_4O_2$.

Anile (æ·nəil), *a.* 1652. [ad. L. *anilis,* f. *anus.*] Of or like an old woman; weak-minded.

Anilic (ăni·lik), *a.* 1863. [f. ANIL.] **1.** Of or pertaining to anil; as in *Anilic* (or *Indi-*

gotic) Acid 1868. 2. -anilic in comb. = of aniline.

Anilide (æ·nilǝid). 1863. [f. ANIL + -IDE, = *Anil(ine am)ide.*] *Chem.* A species of alkalamide related to aniline as amides to amines: hence called *phenylamide.*

Aniline (æ·nilǝin). 1850. [f. ANIL + -INE.] *Chem.* A chemical base yielding many beautiful dyes; obtained orig. by distilling indigo with caustic potash, now from coal-tar, etc. It is a colourless, oily, aromatic, volatile liquid, $C_6H_5(NH_2)$, which may be viewed as ammonia in which one hydrogen atom is replaced by the compound radical phenyl C_6H_5, hence also called *Phenylamine.* Also *attrib.* 1864.

Anility (ăni·lĭti). 1623. [ad. L. *anilitatem*; see ANILE.] The state of being an old woman; dotage. In fig. use stronger than *senility.*

†**A·nimadve·rsal.** [f. ANIMADVERT, after *reversal.*] The faculty of perceiving; consciousness. MORE.

Animadversion (ænimădvǝ̄·ɹʃǝn). 1599. [ad. L. *animadversionem*; see ANIMADVERT.] †1. The action or the faculty of noticing –1795; (with *pl.*) notice, monition, warning –1712. 2. The action of taking judicial cognizance of offences, and of inflicting punishment; *concr.* with *pl.* a penal visitation (*arch.*) 1646. 3. The utterance of criticism or reproof 1599; *concr.* a criticism, *esp.* one implying censure 1599.

2. A power whose lightest measure of a. would be banishment ALISON. 3. [A temper] of a. and cavil M. PATTISON. 3. Some sharp animadversions HALLAM.

†**A·nimadve·rsive,** *a.* 1642. [See ANIMADVERT and -IVE.] Percipient –1685.

Animadvert (ænimădvǝ̄·ɹt), *v.* 1637. [ad. L. *animadvertere*, orig. two words *anim(um advertere.*] †1. *trans.* To turn the mind to, observe –1679. 2. *intr.* To take note, remark, bethink oneself. Const. *simply*, or with *that* (*arch.*) 1642. 3. *intr.* To take judicial cognizance of; *hence*, to proceed by way of punishment or censure (*arch.*) 1671. 4. To comment critically (*on*) 1665.

3. The law will a. hereon as an injury BLACKSTONE. 4. To a. on defects HALLAM. Hence **A·nimadve·rter**, also **-ve·rsor**, one who animadverts (*arch.*)

Animal (æ·nimăl). 1541. [a. L. *animal*, for *animale* adj. neut. f. *anima.* As sb. hardly in Eng. bef. end of 16th c.; not in Bible 1611.]

A. *sb.* 1. A living being, endowed with sensation and voluntary motion, but in the lowest forms distinguishable from vegetable forms only by evident relationship to other animal forms 1602. 2. One of the lower animals; a brute or beast, as distinguished from man. (Often limited *pop.* to quadrupeds, and *fam.* to those used by man.) 1600. 3. A human being in whom the animal nature has the ascendancy. Cf. *creature.* 1588. 4. *slang.* var. for 'hog' in 'go the whole hog' 1838. †5. *ellipt.* in *pl.* Animal spirits –1647.

1. What a piece of work is a man!.. the Parragon of Animals *Haml.* II. ii. 20. When an organism receives nutritive matter by a mouth..it is called an a. OWEN. 2. He..feasts the a. he dooms his feast POPE. We fastened our animals to trees round the camp-fire (*mod.*). 3. He is onely an a., onely sensible in the duller parts *L. L. L.* IV. ii. 27.

B. *adj.* [orig. = Fr. *animal*, ad. L. *animalis.* Like L. *animalis*, treated in med. Eng. occas. as a deriv. of *anima*, occas. of *animus*, but in mod. use connected with the sb. *animal* only.] †1. Connected with sensation, innervation, and will; opp. to *vital* and *natural.* Occas. = psychical. See ANIMAL SPIRITS. –1668. 2. Of or pertaining to the functions of animals; opp. to *intellectual* and *spiritual* 1651. 3. Carnal; opp. to *moral*, *spiritual* 1633. 4. = sb. used *attrib.*; opp. to *vegetable* 1646.

1. Motions proceeding from sense..called a. motions HOBBES. 2. The A. Œconomy 1718. The mere a. courage of the soldier FREEMAN. 3. The a. nature ..the a. appetites FROUDE.

Comb. and *phrases*: **a. charcoal**, that formed by charring a. substance; **a. electricity**, that developed in certain animals, as the torpedo and electric eel; **a. food**; **a. flower**, one of the actinozoa, as the sea-anemone; **a. heat**, the constant temperature maintained within the bodies of living animals; **a. kingdom**, the whole species of animals viewed scientifically, as one of the three great divisions of natural objects; **a. magnetism** = MESMERISM; **a. myth**, one founded upon the habits of animals; **a. painter, painting, piece**; **a. plant**, a zoophyte or polype, as coral; **a. world.**

Hence **Anima·lic** *a. rare.* †**A·nimalish** *a.* of the nature of an a. CUDWORTH.

Animalcula, *sb. pl.*; see ANIMALCULE.

Animalcular (ænimæ·lkiŭlăɹ), *a. rare.* 1753. Of or pertaining to animalcules 1765, or †animalculism –1807. var. **Anima·lculine.**

Animalcule (ænimæ·lkiŭl). 1509. [ad. L. *animalculum*, dim. of *animal.* Often used in the L. form, with pl. *animalcula* (which pl. is occ. made a sing. with pl. *animalculæ*).] †1. A small or tiny animal, as a mouse, or any invertebrate –1831. 2. A microscopic animal: *esp.* of the *Rotifera* and *Infusoria* 1677.

1. The basest of created animalcules, the Spider CARLYLE.

Animalculism (ænimæ·lkiŭliz'm). 1874. [f. as prec. + -ISM.] *Phys.* or *Path.* The theory that animalcules are (1) the germs of life, and (2) the cause of diseases, and thus explain phenomena. Hence **Anima·lculist**, an adherent of A.; one who makes a study of animalcules.

†**Animali·llio.** [dim. of ANIMAL after It.] A tiny animal. HOWELL.

Animalism (æ·nimăliz'm). 1831. [f. as prec. + -ISM.] 1. Animal activity; sensuality. 2. The doctrine which views men as mere animals 1857. 3. A merely sensual being (*rare*) 1868.

1. Healthy a. KINGSLEY. A face..without a vestige of a. 1868. 3. Girls, Hetairai, ..Hired animalisms TENNYSON.

Animalist (æ·nimălist). 1837. [f. as prec. + -IST.] 1. One who takes the 'animal' side of a discussion. 2. An adherent of ANIMALISM 2; a sensualist 1851. 3. = ANIMALCULIST 1874.

Animality (ænimæ·lĭti). 1615. [a. Fr. *animalité*, f. *animal* adj.; see -ITY. Cf. *humanity.*] 1. The sum of the animal qualities and functions; vital power. 2. The merely animal nature, as opp. to the moral and spiritual; animalhood 1646. 3. Animal nature, life; opp. to *vegetable* or *inorganic* 1647. 4. The animal series 1770.

2. Ignorance and a. (*mod.*). A. and primitive barbarism (*mod.*).

Animalize (æ·nimălǝiz), *v.* 1741. [f. ANIMAL + -IZE.] †1. To represent in animal form. 2. To convert into animal substance 1770. 3. To reduce to animal nature; to sensualize 1806.

3. Has sensualized and animalized its character ARNOLD. Hence **A·nimaliza·tion**, the act of animalizing (senses 2, 3); ‖distribution of animal existence, animal population. [Fr.]

Animally (æ·nimăli), *adv.* 1600. [f. as prec. + -LY [2].] †1. Psychically, in respect of the *anima*, animal soul –1678. 2. Physically, opp. to *intellectually* 1866.

Animal spirits (formerly, **spirit**). [see ANIMAL, *adj.* 1.] †1. *orig.* The supposed 'spirit' or principle of sensation and voluntary motion; answering to nerve fluid, nerve force, nervous action –1777. †2. Nerve, animal courage –1719. 3. *coll. pl.* Nervous vivacity, healthy animalism 1739.

3. She had high animal spirits MISS AUSTEN.

†**A·nimant**, *a. rare.* 1677. [ad. L. *animantem*; see ANIMATE.] Having life; animated 1678. As *sb.* [sc. *creature.*] 1677.

†**Anima·stic**, *a.* 1651. [ad. med.L. *animasticus.* A hybrid; cf. *onomastic.*] Spiritual, opp. to *material*; occ. = ANIMATE –1855. †As *sb.* Psychology. SIR W. HAMILTON.

Animate (æ·nimĕt), *ppl. a.* and *sb.* 1546. [ad. L. *animatus*, *animare*, f. *anima.*] A. *pple.* and *adj.* †1. *pple.* Animated, inspired –1640. 2. *adj.* Endowed with life 1605. 3. Lively 1801. 4. Pertaining to animals 1828.

2. Phylosophers..have affirmed the..loadstone to be a. 1605.

B. †*sb.* A living thing –1669.

Animate (æ·nimeⁱt), *v.* 1538. [f. prec.] 1. To give life to, quicken, vivify 1542. 2. To give the appearance of life to (*arch.*) 1612. 3. To impart vividness or interest to, enliven 1670. 4. To fill with boldness, inspirit 1538; †*intr.* to become animated –1782. 5. To inspire, incite 1583. 6. To actuate, or put in motion 1646.

2. Poetry..which..animates matter JOHNSON. 3. To a. a play FLECKNOE, the song POPE. 4. The shouting animates their hearts DRYDEN. 5. Animated by religious zeal MARLOWE. 6. Motion..which animates the bullet TYNDALL. Hence **A·nimatingly** *adv.* **A·nimative** *a.* having the faculty of animating. **A·nimator, -er**, he who or that which animates.

Animated (æ·nimeⁱtĕd), *ppl. a.* 1532. [f. prec. + -ED.] 1. Endowed with life 1534; *fig.* appearing alive 1711. 2. Full of activity; spirited; vivacious 1585. 3. Inspired, actuated, encouraged 1532. †4. Pertaining to animated beings 1753.

1. *Animated Nature*: that portion which is alive; the animal world. A. waters 1827. Heroes in a. marble frown POPE. 2. The discussion was a. PRESCOTT. 3. Our newly a. common enemies MILT. 4. A. pathology 1753. Hence **A·nimatedly** *adv.*

Animation (ænimē̆ⁱ·ʃǝn). 1597. [ad. L. *animationem*; see ANIMATE.] 1. The action of animating (see ANIMATE *v.*); quickening. 2. The state of being alive, animateness (*arch.*) 1615. 3. Vivacity, sprightliness 1790. †4. Inspiration –1664; *esp.* encouragement –1680.

1. The fourth act that goeth to make man, is called A. HOWELL. 2. Suspended a. 1837. 3. Johnson.. talked with great a. BOSWELL. 4. A great a. of my ..endeavours 1616.

‖**Animé** (a·nime, æ·nimi), *sb.* 1577. [Fr., ? = 'alive' with insects; or a native name.] A name for resins, *esp.* that obtained from a West Indian tree (*Hymenæa Courbaril*).

‖**Animé** (a·nime), *a.* 1731. [Fr.] *Her.* In action and showing a desire to fight; having the eyes, etc. of a different tincture from the animal itself.

Animine (æ·nimǝin). 1863. [f. ANIM(AL + -INE.] *Chem.* An organic base obtained from bone-oil, etc.

Animism (æ·nimiz'm). 1832. [f. L. *anima* + -ISM.] 1. The doctrine of the *anima mundi* (Stahl 1720); the doctrine that the phenomena of animal life are produced by an immaterial *anima*, or soul, distinct from matter. 2. The attribution of a living soul to inanimate objects and natural phenomena 1866. 3. By extension: Spiritualism; the belief in the existence of soul or spirit apart from matter 1880.

2. Polytheism..takes very largely the form of a. 1877. Hence **A·nimist**, an adherent of a. **Animi·stic** *a.* of or belonging to a. or animists.

Animosity (ænimǫ·sĭti). ME. [a. Fr. *animosité*, f. L. *animositatem*, f. *animosus.*] †1. Spiritedness, courage –1670. 2. Excitement of feeling against any one; active enmity 1605.

1. Confirming his wavering hand unto the a. of that attempt SIR T. BROWNE. 2. The more affinity there is between theological parties, the greater commonly is their a. HUME.

†**A·nimous**, *a. rare.* 1620. [a. Fr. *animeux*, ad. L. *animosus*, f. ANIMUS.] Spirited; also, hot-tempered.

Animus (æ·nimŏs). No pl. 1831. [a. L.] Actuating feeling, bias, animating (usu. hostile) temper; *hence*, animosity.

Anion (æ·niǫn). 1834. [a. Gr. ἀνιόν a thing going up, f. ἀνιέναι.] *Electr.* Faraday's term for an ion carrying a negative charge of electricity by virtue of which it is attracted, on electrolysis, to the anode. Cf. CATION.

Anis-, *Chem.* comb. form of L. *anīsum*, anise, forming names of compounds derived from oil of anise, as **A·nisal**, short for *anisic aldehyde*, etc.

Anisanthous (ænǝisæ·nþǝs), *a.* 1880. [f. Gr. ἄνισος + ἄνθος + -OUS.] *Bot.* Having perianths of different form.

Anisated (æ·niseⁱtĕd), *ppl. a.* 1880. [cf. Fr. *anisé.*] Mixed or flavoured with aniseed.

Anise (æ·nis). [ME. *anys*, *-eys*, *-ese*, a. Fr. *anis*:—L. *anisum*, a. Gr. ἄνισον; see ANET.] 1. An umbelliferous plant (*Pimpinella Anisum*), a native of the Levant, anciently confused with the Dill (*Anethum graveolens*), prob. the anise of the Bible of 1611. 2. *fig.* See *Matt.* xxiii. 23. 1741.

Aniseed (æ·nisīd). ME. 1. The seed of the anise. Also *attrib.* 1698. 2. = ANISETTE (*rare*) 1756.

‖**Anisette** (anize·t). 1837. [Fr., in full *Anisette de Bordeaux*, f. ANISE + *-ette* dim.] A liqueur flavoured with aniseed.

Anisic (æni·zik), *a.* [mod. f. ANISE + -IC.] Of or derived from anise, as in *a. series, acid*, etc.

Aniso-, comb. form of Gr. ἄνισος unequal,

a formative *esp.* of negatives of corresponding terms in Iso-.

a·niso·-**bryous** [Gr. βρύειν] *a.*, *Bot.* = *anisodynamous*; -**dacty·lic** [Gr. δάκτυλος] *a.*, *Zool.* unequal-toed (said of those insessorial birds called *Anisodactyles*); -**dy·namous** [Gr. δύναμις] *a.*, *Bot.* growing more strongly on one side of the axis than on the other; -**gynous** [Gr. γυνή] *a.*, *Bot.* having the carpels not equal in number to the sepals; -**me·ric** [Gr. μέρος] *a.*, *Chem.* not composed of the same proportions of the same elements; -**merous** [see prec.] *a.*, not having equal, or the same number of, parts, unsymmetrical; *esp.* in *Bot.* having unequal numbers of parts in different whorls; -**me·tric** [Gr. μέτρον] *a.*, of unequal measurement, consisting of unequal or non-symmetrical parts; -**metro·pia** [Gr. μέτρον + ὤψ, ὦπα], *Path.* inequality in the refractive power of the two eyes; -**metro·pic** *a.*; -**pe·talous** [Gr. πέταλον] *a.*, *Bot.* with unequal petals; -**phy·llous** [Gr. φύλλον] *a.*, *Bot.* with unequal leaves; -**pterous** [Gr. πτερόν] *a.*, having unequal wings; *esp.* in *Bot.* of fruit, flowers, etc.; -**ste·monous** [Gr. στήμων] *a.*, *Bot.* having the stamens unequal in number to the petals or sepals; -**sthe·nic** [Gr. σθένος] *a.*, of unequal strength; -**stomous** [Gr. στόμα] *a.*, *Bot.* having unequal mouths, as in a calyx unequally divided; -**tropal**, -**tropous** *a.* = ANISOTROPIC; -**tropy** [Gr. -τροπία], the quality of being anisotropic, æolotropy.

Anisotropic (ænəi:sotrǫ·pik), *a.* 1879. [f. Gr. ἄνισος + τροπικός, f. τρόπος.] Possessing the power both of right- and left-handed polarization; æolotropic.

Anker (æ·ŋkəɹ); also **ankor, anchor.** 1673. [a. Du. (and Ger.), of unkn. origin.] **1.** A liquid measure used in various parts. That of Rotterdam, once used in England, holds 10 old wine or $8^1/_3$ imperial gallons. **2.** A cask or keg of the above capacity 1750.

Ankerite (æ·ŋkərəit). 1843. [f. Prof. *Anker* of Styria.] *Min.* A mineral closely allied to Dolomite, with the magnesia largely replaced by iron, with or without magnesia.

Ankle, ancle (æ·ŋk'l). [Two forms: (1) OE. *anclēow*; (2) mod. *ankle, ancle*, earlier *ankyl*, prob. ME. from Norse. The latter, f. root *ank-*, L. *ang-*, is the orig. Teut. form.] The joint which connects the foot with the leg; the slender part between this and the calf.

His stockings..downe giued to his Anckle *Haml.* II. i. 80. Hence **A·nkled** *ppl. a.* furnished with ankles (*rare*).

Anklet (æ·ŋklėt). 1832. [f. prec. + -LET, after *bracelet*.] An ornament or fetter for the ankle.

Ankylose, -osis, vars. of ANCHYLOSE, -OSIS.

Anlace (æ·nlăs, -ės). *arch.* ME. [?] A short two-edged knife or dagger, broad at the hilt, and tapering to a point, formerly worn at the girdle. (Obs. bef. 1500. Used loosely by mod. poets.)

†**A·nlet.** 1557. [a. OFr. *anelet*, dim. of *anel* :—L. *anellus*, dim. of *anulus*.] A small ring –1660.

Anna (æ·nă). 1727. [a. Hind.] An East Indian money of account; the 16th part of a rupee.

¶ In Anglo-Indian speech 'a 6-anna share' = $^6/_{16}$, '4 annas of dark blood' = a quadroon, etc.

Annabergite (ænăbə·ɹgəit). 1852. [f. *Annaberg*, in Saxony; see -ITE.] *Min.* A hydrous arsenate of nickel, apple-green in colour, occurring in capillary crystals, or as an earthy mass.

A·nnal, *sb.* sing. form of ANNALS. Hence †**A·nnal** *v.* to compose annals, chronicle (*rare*). **A·nnalism**, annal-writing (*rare*). **A·nnalist**, a writer of annals; also *ellipt.* and *transf.* **A·nnalistic** *a.* of or proper to the annalist or annals. †**A·nnalize** *v.* to chronicle.

Annals (æ·nălz), *sb. pl.* 1536. [ad. L. *annales* (sc. *libri*).] **1.** A narrative of events written year by year 1563; *sing.* the record of a single year, or a single item, in a chronicle 1699; also *attrib.* **2.** Historical records generally 1581. **3.** Masses said for the space of a year 1536.

1. Annals..contain the mere jottings down of unconnected events STUBBS. The annal of that year BENTLEY. *attrib.* The annal Text MILT. **2.** The short and simple annals of the poor GRAY.

†**A·nnary.** [f. L. *annus* + -ARY; cf. *diary*.] An annual record. FULLER.

Annates (æ·neⁱts, -ėts). 1534. [a. Fr. *annate*, ad. med.L. *annata*, whence *année*.] **1.** The first-fruits, or one year's revenue, paid to the Pope by bishops, etc., of the R.C. Church on their appointment to a see or benefice.

The annates of English benefices, transferred to the Crown at the Reformation, were given up in the reign of Queen Anne to form the fund known as Queen Anne's Bounty.

2. *Sc. Law.* A half-year's salary, in addition to the stipend, which is legally due to the executors of a deceased minister 1571.

Anneal (ănī·l), *v.* OE. [f. AN- *pref.* 1 + OE. *ǣlan* to burn, perh. modified (in sense 3) by OFr. *neeler, nieler* to enamel :—L. *nigellare*, f. *nigrum*.] †**1.** To set on fire, kindle (*lit.* and *fig.*) –ME. †**2.** To subject to the action of fire; to fire, bake, fuse, glaze –1668. **3.** To burn in colours upon glass, earthenware, or metal, to enamel by encaustic process (*arch.*) 1580. **4.** To toughen after fusion by exposure to continuous and slowly diminished heat, as glass, steel, etc. 1664. Also *fig.*

3. When thou dost a. in glasse thy storie G. HERBERT. **4.** *fig.* The mind to strengthen and a. SCOTT. Hence **Annea·ler**, he who or that which anneals (*rare*).

†**Anne·ct**, *v.* 1531. [ad. L. *annectere*.] = ANNEX –1737.

Annectent (ăne·ktėnt), *a.* 1826. [ad. L. *annectentem*; see prec.] Joining on, connecting. Transitional or a. characters OWEN.

Annelid(e (æ·nėlid). 1834. [a. Fr. *annélide*, f. as next.] *Zool. sb.* One of the *Annelida*. *adj.* Of or pertaining to the *Annelida* 1855. vars. **Anne·lidan** *a.* and *sb.*, **Anneli·dian** *a.*

‖**Annelida** (ăne·lidă), *sb. pl.* 1834. [mod. L. f. Fr. *annelés* (Lamarck 1801), ringed, f. OFr. *annel* :—L. *annellus*, dim. of *anulus*.] *Zool.* A class of animals (*Articulata* Cuvier) comprising the Red-blooded worms with bodies composed of annular segments.

Anne·lidous. *rare.* 1845. [f. as prec. + -OUS.] Of the nature of an annelid.

Anneloid (æ·neloid). 1869. [f. as prec. + -OID.] *Zool.* An animal resembling the *Annelida*.

Annex (ăne·ks), *v.* ME. [a. Fr. *annexer*, f. *a(n)nexe* :—L. *annexum, annectere*, f. *ad* + *nectere*: with sense 3 cf. ANNEXATION.] **1.** To join (*to*) (*arch.*). **2.** To unite materially, as an accessory (*arch.*) 1605. **3.** To join as an addition to existing possessions 1509. **4.** To append 1450. **5.** To affix (a seal, or signature) (*arch.*) 1603. **6.** To attach as an attribute ME., condition 1588, or consequence 1538.

2. Ye a... Periwiges and counterfeite Haire PRYNNE. **3.** Julius Cæsar annexed Brittaine to the Romaine emperie 1534. **6.** It is annexed to the Soveraignty, to be Judge HOBBES. Salvation is not annexed to a right knowledge of geometry M. ARNOLD. Hence **Anne·xable** *a.* †**A·nnexary**, an adjunct. **Anne·xed** *ppl. a.*; also **annext. Anne·xer**, one who annexes (territory). **Anne·xment**, an adjunct (*rare*). *Haml.* III. iii. 21.

Annex(e (ăne·ks), *sb.* 1540. [a. Fr. *annexe* :—L. *annexum*; see prec. Obs. bef. 1700, but lately re-adopted.] †**1.** An adjunct, accessory –1686. **2.** *Sc. Law.* An appurtenance 1540. **3.** An appendix 1647. **4.** From mod. Fr. *annexe*: A supplementary building; a wing 1861.

3. The annex to the Anglo-Turkish convention of 1878 (*mod.*). **4.** Newnham and Girton, and .. the Woman's Annex at Harvard 1883.

Annexation (ænėksēⁱ·ʃən). 1611. [ad. med. L. *annexationem, annexare*; see ANNEX *v.*] **1.** The action of annexing (see ANNEX *v.* 1, 3, 6) 1634. †**2.** The thing annexed 1611.

1. France..by the a. of Piedmont, had overstepped the Alps BRYCE. The a. of punishment to vicious acts 1833.

Annexa·tionist. 1845. [f. prec.] One who advocates annexation (of territory). Also *attrib.* or *adj.* 1852.

Used in *U.S.* (1845) of the 'annexation' of Texas.

Annexion (ăne·kʃən). *arch.* 1600. [ad. L. *annexionem*; see ANNEX *v.*] **1.** = ANNEXATION 1. 1611. †**2.** The thing annexed; an adjunct –1748.

2. With the annexions of fair gems enrich'd. SHAKS. Hence **Anne·xionist** = ANNEXATIONIST.

†**Anni·hil**, *v.* 1490. [a. Fr. *annihiler*, ad. late L. *annihilare*, f. *ad* + *nihil*.] = ANNIHILATE –1595.

Annihilable (ănəi·hĭlăb'l), *a.* 1677. [f. L. *annihilare*; see prec.] Capable of being annihilated.

Annihilate (ănəi·hĭlėt), *ppl. a. arch.* ME. [ad. L. *annihilatus*; see ANNIHIL. Displaced by *Annihilated*.] **1.** Reduced to nothing. †**2.** Made null and void –1587.

Annihilate (ănəi·hĭleⁱt), *v.* 1525. [f. prec., displacing ANNIHIL.] **1.** To reduce to nothing, blot out of existence 1586. **2.** To make null and void, cancel, abrogate 1525; to treat as non-existent (*arch.*) 1542. **3.** To extinguish virtually 1630. **4.** To destroy the collective or organized existence of anything 1808.

1. Ye Gods! a. but space and time, And make two lovers happy POPE. **2.** To a. arguments 1665, rights JUNIUS, law 1836, exploits SMOLLETT. **3.** Thou who with thy frown Annihilated senates BYRON. **4.** To a. an army WELLINGTON, the fleet of Napoleon 1879. Hence **Anni·hilated** *ppl. a.* utterly destroyed. **Anni·hilative** *a.* such as to a.; crushing. **Anni·hilator**, he who, or that which, utterly destroys.

Annihilation (ănəi:hĭlēⁱ·ʃən). 1638. [a. Fr.; see ANNIHIL and -ATION.] **1.** The action of annihilating (see ANNIHILATE *v.* 1, 2, 4). **2.** The state of being annihilated 1677.

1. Suppose the a. of all matter PRIESTLEY. An a. of credit 1796, of an army 1796. **2.** Political a. 1851.

Annihilationism (anəi:hilēⁱ·ʃəniz'm). 1881. [f. prec. + -ISM.] *Theol.* The doctrine of the total annihilation of the wicked after death. Hence **Anni·hila·tionist.**

A·nnist. A partisan of Queen Anne. SWIFT.

Anniversarily (ænivə̄·ɹsărĭli), *adv.* 1631. [f. as next.] By annual return.

Anniversary (ænivə̄·ɹsări). ME. [ad. L. *anniversarius* returning yearly, f. *annus* + *versus*; see -ARY. Orig. eccles. and in med.L. used subst., as *anniversaria* (sc. *dies*).] **A.** *adj.* **1.** Returning at the same date yearly; annual 1552; †*loosely*, repeated each year –1738. †**2.** Completed in a year –1704. **3.** [*attrib.* use of *sb.*] Of or pertaining to an anniversary 1654.

B. *sb.* [sc. *day, service*, etc.] **1.** The yearly return of any remarkable date, the day on which some interesting event is annually celebrated ME. **2.** The celebration which takes place on such a date; *orig.* a mass in memory of some one on the day of his death ME. †**3.** *R. C. Ch.* The commemorative service performed daily for a year after a person's death –1753.

‖**Anno Domini** (æ·no dǫ·minəi). 1579. [L.; usu. written A.D.] In the year of the Lord in the year of the Christian era; **b.** *jocular colloq.* as *sb.* Advanced or advancing age 1885.

Annominate (ănǫ·mineⁱt), *v. rare.* 1765. [var. of *agnominate* (see AGNOMEN).] To call by some epithet or title.

Annomination (ănǫ·minēⁱ·ʃən). 1753. [var. of AGNOMINATION.] **1.** Paronomasia. †**2.** Alliteration 1775.

‖**Annonce** (anǭ·s). *rare.* 1807. [Fr.] = ANNOUNCEMENT.

Annotate (æ·nǒteⁱt), *v.* 1733. [f. L. *annotat-, an-* (*ad-*) *notare*; see NOTE.] **1.** To add notes to (a work or author) 1755. **2.** *intr.* To add or make notes. Const. *on, upon.* 1733.

2. It was Coleridge's habit to a. with a pencil 1882. var. †**Anno·te.** Hence **A·nnotated** *ppl. a.* furnished with notes. **A·nnotative** *a.* of the nature of annotation.

Annotation (ænotēⁱ·ʃən). 1460. [ad. L. *annotationem*; see prec.] **1.** The action of annotating 1570. †**2.** Chronological reckoning –1669. **3.** *concr.* (usu. *pl.*) A note, by way of explanation or comment 1528.

3. The minute..with annotations in the margin 1528.

Annotator (æ·nǒteⁱtəɹ). 1663. [a. L.; see ANNOTATE.] One who annotates; a commentator. Hence **Anno·tatory** *a.* of or pertaining to an a., or his work.

†**A·nnotine.** *rare.* [ad. L. *annotinus*, f. *annus*.] *Bot.* A tree of which the fruit does not ripen in a single season; *e.g.* the fig. Hence **Anno·tinous** *a.* a year old.

Annotto, var. of ANATTA.

Announce (ănau·ns), *v.* 1483. [a. OFr. *anoncer* :—L. *adnuntiare*, f. *ad* + *nuntiare*, f. *nuntius*.] **1.** To deliver news; to make public or official intimation of; to proclaim 1485. **2.** *ellipt.* To intimate the approach or presence of 1761. **3.** To make manifest to the senses, or mind 1781.

1. Who..publish laws, a. Or life or death PRIOR. The angel..announced to them that he was rysen CAXTON. 2. Dinner was announced 1802. 3. His feeble efforts announced his degenerate spirit GIBBON. Hence **Annou·ncer** 1611; *spec.*, in broadcasting, a person who announces the subjects of a programme and the items of news (1922).

Announcement (ănau·nsmĕnt). 1798. [a. Fr. *annoncement*; see -MENT.] The action of announcing; public or official notification.

Annoy (ănoi·), *sb.* Aphet. to NOY. [ME. *anui, anoy(e,* a. OFr. *anoi, anui, enui* (mod. *ennui*), f. L. phr. *in odio* (Diez), whence *inodio* as sb. For double *n*, see AN- *pref.* 6. Now mostly poet. Cf. ANNOYANCE.] **1.** A disturbed or ruffled feeling arising from impressions, etc., which one dislikes. Orig. = mod. Fr. *ennui*; now active discomfort. **2.** That which causes the feeling; annoyance ME.

1. His *ennui* amounted to a. 1812. *To work, †do, annoy*: to cause trouble, to molest. Hence †**Annoy·ous** *a.* disturbing; troubled. †**Annoy·ously** *adv.*

Annoy (ănoi·), *v.* Also aphet. to NOY. [ME. *anuien, anoien,* a. OFr. *anuier,* as if f. Romanic *inodiare* (found in OIt.), f. *inodio*; see prec.] †**1.** *intr.* To be odious, or a cause of trouble (*to,* or *dat.*); *trans.* to trouble, bore (= Fr. *ennuyer*) -1534. **2.** *trans.* To affect so as to ruffle, trouble, vex. (Refers to the feeling, rather than the action; hence freq. in pass.) ME. †*intr.* (refl. pron. omitted.) -1555. **3.** To molest, injure; *esp.* in *Mil.* ME. *absol.* ME. †**4.** To derange, affect injuriously -1721.

1. Ye all are anoyed and wery of all goodness LD. BERNERS. 2. She will not be annoy'd with suters *Tam. Shr.* I. i. 189. 3. The works on the hills would a. the town NELSON. When fears a. BLAKE. Hence **Annoy·er. Annoy·ing-ly** *adv.*, **-ness.**

Annoyance (ănoi·ăns). ME. [a. OFr. *anuiance,* f. *anuier*; see prec.] **1.** The action of annoying; molestation. **2.** The state of feeling caused by what annoys; vexation 1502. **3.** Anything annoying, a nuisance 1592.

2. A. and trouble of mind MILT. 3. *Jury of Annoyance*: one appointed to report upon public nuisances. Hence **Annoy·ancer,** he who, or that which, annoys. [Cf. *conveyancer.*]

Annual (æ·niuăl). ME. [a. OFr. *annuel,* ad. late L. *annualem* (= cl. *annalem*).] **A.** *adj.* Of, belonging to, or reckoned by, the year; yearly. **2.** Recurring once every year 1548. **3.** Repeated yearly and occupying the whole year 1635. **4.** Lasting for a year only ME.

1. Three thousand Crownes in Annuall fee *Haml.* II. ii. 73. Annual Register 1650. 2. So stears the..crane Her a. Voiage MILT. *P. L.* VII. 431. 3. The a. course of the sun FROUDE. 4. A. parliaments STUBBS, plants BACON. Hence **A·nnually** *adv.* yearly.

B. *sb.* **1.** In *R.C.Ch.* A mass said either daily for a year after, or yearly on the anniversary of, a person's death; *also,* the payment for it. **2.** A yearly payment, tribute, allowance, etc. *Obs.* exc. in *Sc. Law,* where *annual*=quit-rent. 1622. **3.** Anything that lasts only for a year; *esp.* an annual plant (perpetuating itself by seed) 1710. **4.** A book published once a year; a year-book 1689.

3. Oaths are the children of fashion; they are..almost annuals SWIFT. Like an a. in a garden, which must be raised anew every season DE FOE. Hence **A·nnualist,** a contributor to an a. **A·nnualize** *v.* to write for an a. SOUTHEY.

Annuary (æ·niuări). 1550. [ad. Fr. *annuaire,* f. *annus.*] †*adj.* = ANNUAL *a.* -1651. *sb.* †**1.** A priest who says annual masses 1550. **2.** = ANNUAL *sb.* 4. 1856.

†**Annueller.** ME. [See ANNUAL *sb.* 1.] A priest who celebrates ANNUALS -1528.

A·nnuent, *a.* 1727. [ad. L. *annuentem, annuere.*] Nodding; *spec.* of the muscles which nod the head.

†**Annui·sance.** ME. [a. AFr. *anuisance*; cf. *anuier.*] Nuisance, injury -1751.

Annuitant (ăniu·itănt). 1720. [f. next, after *accountant,* etc.] One who holds, or receives, an annuity. Also *fig.*

Annuity (ăniu·iti). ME. [a. Fr. *annuité*:—med.L. *annuitatem,* f. *annuus.*] **1.** A yearly allowance, or income. **2.** *Law.* The grant of an annual sum for a term of years, for life, or in perpetuity, chargeable primarily upon the grantor's person, and his heirs if named; opp. to *rentcharge* ME. **3.** An investment of money, entitling the investor to receive a series of equal annual payments, made up of both principal and interest, except in the case of perpetual annuities; *also,* the annual sum thus paid 1693.

In *perpetual annuities* the payments cease only on repayment of the principal; in *deferred* or *reversionary annuities* they commence after some specified time or event.

Annul (ănv·l), *v.* ME. [a. OFr. *anuller* (mod. *annuler*):—late L. *annullare,* f. *an-* = *ad-* + *nullum.*] **1.** To reduce to nothing, extinguish. **2.** To put an end to (an action, etc.); to abolish, cancel ME. **3.** To destroy the force of; to render void in law ME.

1. Light..to me is extinct, And all her various objects of delight Annulled MILT. *Sams.* 70. 2. Intellect annuls Fate EMERSON. 3. To a. a pardon SELDEN, a contract 1786, statutes MACAULAY. Hence **Annu·llable** *a.* (*rare*). †**A·nnullate** *v.* = ANNUL. †**Annulla·tion,** the act of annulling, or being annulled. **Annu·ller.**

Annular (æ·niŭlăr), *a.* 1571. [ad. L. *annularis,* f. *annulus.* Cf. Fr. *annulaire.*] **1.** Of or pertaining to a ring or rings; ring-like; ring-formed, ringed; *esp.* in *Phys.* of ringed or ring-like structures 1691. **2.** = ANNULARY 2. 1648.

1. An a. body like a Wasp 1664. 2. His a. finger 1648. *Phrases. Annular space,* that between an inner and an outer ring or cylinder. *A. ligament* (*Phys.*), a muscular band girding the wrist and ankle. *A. process* or *protuberance* (in the brain), the *Pons Varolii,* a ring-like process of the medulla oblongata. *A. Eclipse* of the sun (*Astr.*), when the dark body of the moon is seen projected upon the sun's disk, leaving a ring of light visible all round. *A. vault* (*Arch.*), a vaulted roof over an annular space between two concentric walls. Hence **Annula·rity,** a. quality or form. **A·nnularly** *adv.* after the manner or form of a ring or rings.

Annulary (æ·niŭlări), *a.* 1623. [ad. L. *annularius,* f. *annulus.*] †**1.** = ANNULAR 1. -1691. **2.** Bearing the ring. (Said of the fourth finger of the left hand.) Also as *sb.* [sc. *finger.*] 1623.

‖**Annulata** (æniulē¹·tă), *sb. pl.* 1847. [L. adj. pl. neut. (sc. *animalia*).] = ANNELIDA (the commoner name); occ. = ANNULOSA; see ANNULATE 2.

Annulate (æ·niŭlĕt), *a.* 1830. [ad. L. *annulatus.*] **1.** Furnished or marked with a ring or rings; *esp.* in *Bot.* **2.** = ANNULATED 3. 1852.

Annulated (æ·niŭle¹tĕd), *ppl. a.* 1668. [f. prec.] **1.** That wears rings. **2.** Furnished with rings; marked with ring-like lines, ridges, or grooves 1668; *Her.* having an annulet. **3.** Composed of rings, or a series of ring-like segments united so as to form a tube 1748.

Annulation (æniulē¹·ʃən). 1829. [f. ANNULATE; see -ATION.] The formation of rings or ring-like divisions; *concr.* a ring.

Annulet (æ·niŭlĕt). 1572. [f. L. *annulus* + -ET.] **1.** A little ring 1598. **2.** *Her.* A small circle worn as a charge 1572. **3.** *Arch.* A small fillet encircling a column 1727.

Summer annulets and winter rings 1647.

Annulment (ănv·lmĕnt). 1491. [f. ANNUL + -MENT.] The act of reducing to nothing, or declaring void. var. †**Annu·llity.** [? after *nullity.*]

Annuloid (æ·niŭloid), *a.* 1855. [f. L. *annulus* + -OID.] Ring-like. In *Zool.* applied by Huxley to the *Annuloida*; see next.

‖**Annuloida** (æniuloi·dă), *sb. pl.* 1851. [prop. mod. L. *annuloidea* (sc. *animalia*); see prec.] *Zool.* The Annuloid animals, a modification of the *Annulosa,* placed between them and the *Infusoria* (Huxley).

‖**Annulosa** (æniulōu·să), *sb. pl.* 1855. [mod. L. (sc. *animalia*).] *Zool.* The ANNULOSE animals, including the higher *Articulata.* Hence **Annulo·san,** one of the *Annulosa.*

Annulose (æniulōu·s), *a.* 1826. [f. mod.L. *annulosus*; see ANNULUS and -OSE.] **1.** Ringed or ring-like. **2.** *Zool.* Having the body formed of a series of ring-like segments 1835.

‖**Annulus** (æ·niŭlŏs). Pl. **-i.** 1563. [L., erron. for *anulus,* dim. of *anus* a rounding.] **1.** A ring, or ring-like body. **2.** *Geom.* A ring, or solid formed by the revolution of a circle about a straight line exterior to its circumference as an axis, and in the plane of the said circle 1802. **3.** *Bot.* In ferns: The ring of cells round the sporangia. In mosses: The elastic external ring of epidermal cells with which the brim of the sporangium is furnished. In fungi: The portion of the veil which remains like a collar round the stalk. 1830. **4.** *Astr.* A ring of light, as in an annular eclipse 1871.

Annum, [L.] year, in *per annum*; see PER.

†**Annu·merate,** *ppl. a.* ME. only. [ad. L. *annumeratus.*] Reckoned in. Hence †**Annu·merate** *v.* †**Annu:mera·tion.**

Annunciade (ănvnsi₁ē¹·d). 1706. [a. Fr. *annonciade,* ad. It. *annunciata*:—L. *annuntiare*; see -ADE.] **a.** A military order, thus re-named in 1439, in honour of the Annunciation of the angel Gabriel; **b.** A female religious order founded by Queen Jane of France; a nun of that order.

¶ The Eng. forms of wds. derived from L. *annuntiare* follow the erron. med. spelling *annunciare.*

†**Annu·nciate,** *ppl. a.* ME. [ad. L. *annunciatus*; see ANNOUNCE.] Announced (*esp.* beforehand) -1509.

Annunciate, -tiate (ănv·nʃi₁e¹t), *v.* 1536. [f. prec.] **1.** To proclaim = ANNOUNCE 1. **2.** To proclaim as coming, ready, etc. 1652.

2. They who did a. unto the blessed Virgin the conception of the Saviour PEARSON. Hence †**Annu·nciable** *a.* (*rare*). **Annu·nciative** *a.* characterized by or proper to annunciation (*rare*).

Annunciation (ănv:nsi₁ē¹·ʃən). ME. [a. Fr. *annonciation,* ad. L. *annuntiationem*; see ANNOUNCE and -TION.] **1.** The action of announcing; the matter so announced, announcement 1563. **2.** *esp.* The intimation of the incarnation, made by the angel Gabriel to the Virgin Mary ME. **3.** The church festival commemorating that event; Lady-day (March 25) ME.

2. No subject has been more frequently treated..than that of the A. RUSKIN.

Annunciator (ănv·nʃi₁e¹tər). 1753. [ad. L. *annuntiator.*] He who, or that which, announces; *spec.* **a.** an officer of the Gr. Ch., who gave notice of holy days; **b.** an indicator, used in hotels, etc., to show where attendance is desired.

Ano- (ē¹·no), comb. f. L. *anus,* as in *anoperinæal,* pertaining to anus and perinæum.

Ano- (æ·no), *pref.* a. Gr. ἄνω adv. 'upward'.

Anocarpous (ænokā·rpəs), *a.* 1880. [f. Gr. ἄνω + καρπός + -OUS.] *Bot.* Of ferns: Bearing fructification on the upper part of the frond.

Anocathartic (æ:no₁kăþā·ɹtik), *a.* and *sb.* 1853. [f. Gr. ἄνω + CATHARTIC; formerly *ana-.*] Emetic.

Anode (æ·nōud). 1841. [ad. Gr. ἄνοδος, way up.] *Electr. strictly*: The path by which an electric current leaves the positive pole, and enters the electrolyte, on its way to the negative pole (Faraday). *loosely*: The positive pole. In both senses opp. to *cathode.*

Anodic (ænǫ·dik), *a.* 1853. [f. as prec. + -IC.] *Med.* Of nerve force: Proceeding upwards.

Anodon(t (æ·nŏdǫn, -ǫnt). 1847. [mod.L. *anodonta* (also used), f. Gr. ἀν + ὀδόντα.] *Zool.* A genus of bivalve molluscs, without teeth on the hinge of their shell; e.g. fresh-water mussels.

Anodyne (æ·nŏdəin). 1543. [ad. L. *anodynus,* a. Gr., f. ἀν priv. + ὀδύνη.] **A.** *adj.* Having the power of assuaging pain; also *fig.* var. †**Ano·dynous. B.** *sb.* [So Gr. ἀνωδύνον, L. *anodynum* (also used).] **1.** A medicine or drug which alleviates pain 1543. **2.** *fig.* Anything that soothes the feelings 1550.

2. Time..the only a. of sorrow BREWSTER.

Anoetic (æno₁e·tik), *a. rare.* [f. Gr. ἀ + νοητός + -IC.] Unthinkable. FERRIER.

Anogenic (æno₁dʒe·nik), *a.* 1878. [f. Gr. ἄνω + -γενης + -IC.] Developed up- or inwardly.

†**Anoi·l,** *v.* ME. [var. of ENOIL, a. OFr. *enuiler* (mod. *enhuiler*), perh. affected by ANELE.] To anoint with oil; *spec.* to administer extreme unction -1688.

†**Anoi·nt,** *ppl. a. etc.* ME. [a. OFr. *enoint*:—L. *inunctum, inungere,* with *an-* var. of *en-.* Now *anointed.*] Anointed -1450.

Anoint (ănoi·nt), *v.* ME. [f. prec. Treated as if *a*+*noint,* and aphet. to NOINT, and occ. spelt *annoint.*] **1.** To smear or rub over with oil or unguent; to oil, grease, apply ointment to. **2.** *spec.* To apply or pour on oil, etc., as a religious ceremony, as at baptism or on consecration ME. †3. *fig.* To besmear with flattery -1483. 4. To moisten or rub with any substance ME; hence, *ironically*: To beat soundly, to 'baste' 1500.

1. A. thine eyes with eye salue, that thou mayest see *Rev.* iii. 18. Fragrant oils the stiffen'd limbs a. DRYDEN. 2. All kynges of fraunce ben enoynted at Raynes CAXTON. 4. Jesus made clay, and anointed mine eyes *John* ix. 11. Hence **Anoi·nter**, one who anoints; *spec.* one of a 17th c. sect, who anointed people before admitting them. **†Anoi·ntment**, the action of anointing; ointment.

Anointed (ănoi·ntėd), *ppl. a.* ME. [f. prec. + -ED.] 1. Smeared or rubbed with oil, etc., *esp.* as a sacred rite; *fig.* consecrated (*rare*) 1597. 2. *absol.* A consecrated one. *The Lord's Anointed*: Christ or the Messiah; also, a king by divine right 1529.

Anointing (ănoi·ntiŋ). ME. [f. as prec. + -ING¹.] 1. The action of oiling the body. 2. *fig.* The application of oil on consecration to an office ME. †3. Ointment -1561. Also *attrib.*

Anoli, -is (ănōu·li, -is). 1706. [a. native name.] *Zool.* A genus of lizards of the Iguana family, found in the West Indies.

†Ano·mal, *a.* 1569. [a. Fr., ad. L. *anomalus*, a. Gr. ἀνώμαλος, f. ἀν + ὁμαλός.] Irregular, anomalous -1681. As *sb.* [sc. *thing*.] -1665.

Anomaliped (ănǫ·măliped), *a. rare.* 1847. [f. L. *anomalus* (see ANOMAL) + *ped-* (*pes*).] Having an anomalous foot; having the middle toe united to the exterior by three phalanges, and to the interior by one only. As *sb.* [sc. *bird*.]

Anomalism (ănǫ·măliz'm). *rare.* 1668. [f. Gr. ἀνώμαλος (see ANOMAL) + -ISM.] Anomalousness; an example of irregularity.

Anomalist (ănǫ·mălist). *rare.* 1860. [f. as prec. + -IST.] One who held that language was conventional or arbitrary in its origin.

Anomalistic, -al (ănǫ:măli·stik, -ăl), *a.* 1727. [f. as prec. + -IC, + -AL.] 1. Of or pertaining to an anomaly, or anomalist. 2. *Astr.* Pertaining to the anomaly or angular distance of a planet from its perihelion.

2. *Anomalistic year*: the time occupied by the earth (or other planet) in passing from perihelion to perihelion, which is 365 d. 6 h. 13′ 49·3″. *Anomalistic month*: the time occupied by the moon in passing from perigee to perigee, etc.

Anomalo- (ănǫ·mălo), comb. form of Gr. ἀνώμαλος irregular; as in **Anomalogo·natous** [Gr. γονατ- (γόνυ)] *a.*, *Zool.* of or belonging to the *Anomalogonati*, an order of birds lacking the *rectus femoris* muscle.

Anomalous (ănǫ·mălǝs), *a.* 1646. [f. L. *anomalus* (see ANOMAL) + -OUS.] 1. With *to*: Unequal, unconformable, incongruous (*arch.*) 2. *simply*: Unconformable to the common order; irregular; abnormal 1655.

2. A. Feavers 1667, structure DARWIN, Nouns 1706. Hence **Ano·malous·ly** *adv.*, **-ness.**

Anomaly (ănǫ·măli). 1571. [ad. L. *anomalia*, a. Gr., f. ἀνώμαλος; see ANOMAL.] 1. Unevenness, inequality, of condition, motion, etc. 2. Irregularity, deviation from the common or natural order, exceptional condition or circumstance. *concr.* An anomalous thing or being. 1664. 3. *Astr.* The angular distance of a planet, etc., from its last perihelion or perigee; so called because the first irregularities of planetary motion were discovered in the discrepancy between the actual and the computed distance 1669. 4. *Mus.* A small deviation from a perfect interval, in tuning instruments with fixed notes 1830.

2. Time changes a. into system HALLAM. There is no greater a. in nature than a bird that cannot fly DARWIN. The anomalies or irregularities of the [English] tongue WATTS.

Anomo- (æ·nŏmo, ănǫ·mŏ), comb. form of Gr. ἄνομος without law, f. ἀ + νόμος.

a.-bra·nchiate [Gr. βράγχια], *Zool. adj.* having gills of irregular structure; *sb.* [sc. *crustacean*]; **-ca·rpous** [Gr. καρπός] *a.*, *Bot.* bearing unusual fruit; **-dont** [Gr. ὀδοντ-] *a.* and *sb.*, *Zool.* having irregular or no teeth, applied to a genus of fossil reptiles; **-phy·llous** [Gr. φύλλον] *a.*, *Bot.* having leaves irregularly placed; **-rho·mboid** [Gr. ῥομβο-ειδής], *Cryst.* a name given to varieties of crystalline spars, which always fracture into irregular rhomboids; **-rhomboi·dal** *a.*

Anomœo·mery. *rare.* [f. Gr. ἀνομοιομερής.] The theory that the ultimate atoms of matter are dissimilar. CUDWORTH.

Anomouran, -muran (ænǫmū·răn), *a.* 1877. [f. *Anom(o)ura* (mod.L. f. Gr. ἄνομος + οὐρά) + -AN.] *Zool.* Of the *Anomoura* or stalk-eyed crustacea, which have no regular type in the abdomen or tail. As *sb.* One of the *Anomoura*. Hence **Anom(o)u·ral** *a.* having the character of the *Anomoura.* var. **Anomou·rous** *a.*

†A·nomy. 1591. [ad. Gr. ἀνομία.] Disregard of (divine) law; lawlessness -1755.

Anon (ănǫ·n). [OE. *on ān* into one, *on āne* in one.] †1. In one course, straight on, even -ME. †2. *strictly*, Straightway, at once. (Occ. revived by mod. writers.) -1611. 3. By misuse: Soon, in a little while 1526. 4. Now or here again 1588. 5. A response by a servant, etc.: 'Presently, coming', and later = 'Beg your pardon! Sir! Eh?' See ANAN.

1. *Anon to*: even to; = L. *usque ad.* 2. He that heareth the word, & a. with ioy receiueth it *Matt.* xiii. 20. †*Anon so* or *as*: as soon as ever (Fr. *aussitot que*). †*Anon after, after anon*: directly after. 3. †*Till anon*: until by and by. Thou do'st me yet but little hurt; thou wilt a. *Temp.* II. ii. 84. 4. Now for this Cardinal, a. for another 1670. *Ever and anon*: every now and then *L.L.L.* v. ii. 102.

Anonaceous (ænonēi·ʃǝs), *a.* [See below and -ACEOUS.] Of or pertaining to the family *Anonaceæ*, typified by the genus *Anona* (custard-apple, alligator-apple, sour-sop, sweet-sop).

Anonad (ănōu·năd). 1847. [f. as prec. + -AD 1.] *Bot.* A plant of the N.O. *Anonaceæ.*

Anonym (æ·nŏnim). 1812. [a. Fr. *anonyme* (also used), ad. Gr. ἀνώνυμος ANONYMOUS.] 1. A person who remains nameless. 2. A pseudonym 1866. Hence **†Ano·nymal** *a.* anonymous (*rare*). **Anony·mity**, the state of being anonymous. (Used of an author or writings.) 1829.

Anonymous (ănǫ·nimǝs), *a.* 1601. [f. Gr. ἀνώνυμος (f. ἀν + ὄνομα, in Æol. ὄνυμα) + -OUS.] 1. Nameless; of unknown name. Also *subst.* 1603. 2. *transf.* Of unknown or unavowed authorship 1676. 3. Illegitimate (*rare*) 1881.

1. A. correspondents STEELE, altars PALEY. 2. An a. book EVELYN, pamphlet MORSE, attack BREWSTER. Hence **Ano·nymous·ly** *adv.*, **-ness.** **Ano·nymu·ncule** [after L. *homunculus*], a petty a. writer.

Anophyte (æ·nŏfǝit). 1850. [ad. mod.L. *anophytum*, f. Gr. ἄνω + φυτόν.] *Bot.* A name of the non-vascular acrogens, or mosses, etc.

Anoplothere (ănǫ·plŏþīǝr). 1815. [a. Fr., f. Gr. ἄνοπλος + θηρίον. Also **anoplotherium.**] *Palæont.* A Middle Eocene pachydermatous quadruped, having no apparent means of defence. Hence **Anoplothe·roid** *a.* like an a.; also used *subst.*

Anopluriform (ænǫplīū·rifǭɹm), *a.* 1816. [f. mod.L. *anoplura* (f. Gr. ἄνοπλος + οὐρά) + -(I)FORM.] *Zool.* Of the form of the *Anoplura* (insects having no tail appendage); louse-like.

†A·nopsy. 1646. [f. Gr. ἀν + ὄψις; as if ad. Gr. ἀνοψία, not so used.] Want of sight.

Anorexy (æ·nore:ksi). 1598. [ad. mod.L. *anorexia* (also used), a. Gr., f. ἀν + ὀρέγειν.] *Path.* Want of appetite. Hence **Anore·ctous** *a.* without appetite.

Anorgano·logy. 1876. [f. Gr. ἀνόργανος + -(O)LOGY; neg. form of ORGANOLOGY.] The part of Natural Science relating to inorganic objects.

†Anormal (ănǭ·ɹmăl), *a.* 1835. [a. Fr. *anormal*, var. of *anomal*. In Eng. taken as f. L. *a* + *norma*, referred to L. *abnormis*, and refash. later ABNORMAL.] = ABNORMAL.

†Ano·rn, *v.* [ME. *aourne*, a. OFr. *aörner, aöurner*:—L. *adornare*, with A- *pref.* 2 (*an-*) for A- *pref.* 7. Confused also with *anourn*, inf. of vb. ANOURE.] To deck, dress; = ADORN -1558. To worship. (See ANOURE.) WYCLIF. Hence **†Ano·rnament**, adornment.

Anorthic (ănǭ·ɹþik), *a.* 1864. [f. Gr. ἀν + ὀρθός + -IC.] *Cryst.* Irregular in crystallization; called also *triclinic*, etc.

Anorthite (ănǭ·ɹþǝit). 1833. [f. as prec. + -ITE.] *Min.* Lime-feldspar, a mineral occurring in small triclinic glassy crystals.

‖**Anortho·pia.** 1849. [mod.L., f. Gr. ἀν + ὀρθός + -ωπία. f. ὤψ.] *Path.* Obliquity of vision.

Anorthoscope (ănǭ·ɹþoˌskōup). 1842. [f. as prec. + -σκοπος.] An optical toy for viewing distorted figures drawn on a rotating disk.

‖**Ano·smia.** 1811. [mod.L., f. Gr. ἀν priv. + ὀσμή.] *Path.* Loss of the sense of smell.

Another (ănʌ·ðǝɹ), *a.*, and *pron.* ME. [orig. *an other* (often *a nother*, occas. *a other*). In OE. *ōðer* was used alone. See OTHER.] 1. One more; orig. *a second* of two; subseq. *an additional.* (Pl. *other*: with sb. understood, *others.*) *fig.* A second in effect; a counterpart to 1577. 2. A different; different in effect (const. *than, from* catachr.) ME. 3. Contrasted with *one.* (Esp. in sense 2.) ME.

1. Clarence hath not a. day to liue *Rich. III*, I. i. 150. 'You are a.,' cries the sergeant FIELDING. *Such another*: another of the same sort. *fig.* Another Nelson (*mod.*). 2. Let a. man praise thee, and not thine owne mouth *Prov.* xxvii. 2. Of persons (with *poss.* **another's**; *pl.* **others**): Arte thou he that shall come: or shall we loke for a. *Matt.* xi. 3. Another's knowledge BACON. He is nowe become a. man 1588. 3. One man's meat is a. man's poison *Provb.* Of two things only (now *the other*): Let's go hand in hand, not one before a. *Com. Err.* v. i. 425. *One with another*: (*a*) all together; (*b*) taken on the average. *One another*: a compound reciprocal pron. with poss. *one another's* (now *each other's*). Said of two or more.

†Ano·ther-gates, *a.* 1594. [orig. gen. case; see GATE.] Of another sort -1693. var. **†Ano·ther-gaines.**

Ano·therguess, *a. arch.* 1625. [reduction of *anothergets* for ANOTHER-GATES; *-guess* is misleading.] = prec.

I wish you anothergets wife than Socrates had HOWELL. var. **†Ano·therguise.**

Anotta, anotto, vars. of ANATTA.

†Anou·r, *sb.* ME. only. [var. of *onour, honour.* See ANOURE *v.* and HONOUR.] Honour, worship.

Anou·ra. [f. Gr. ἀν + οὐρά.] *Zool.* An order of tailless Amphibians; see ANOUROUS.

†Anou·re, *v.* ME. [repr. 1. OFr. *anorer*:—L. *honorare.* 2. *aörer*:—L. *adorare.* See ADORE, ANORN.] To adore, worship, or honour. To deck (see ANORN). Hence **†Anou·rement** = ADORNMENT.

Anourous (ănūǝ·rǝs, anau·-), *a.* 1838. [f. Gr. ἀν + οὐρά + -OUS.] *Zool.* Tailless, as the frog and toad, or (less correctly) the crab.

Anp-, freq. earlier spelling of AMP-.

‖**Ansa** (æ·nsă). *Pl.* **ansæ.** Formerly **anse, -s.** 1665. [L.] A name applied to the apparent ends of Saturn's ring seen projecting like two handles beyond the disk.

Anserated (æ·nsĕrēⁱtėd), *ppl. a.* 1678. *Her.* Of a cross: Having the extremities cleft and terminated in the heads of serpents, eagles, etc.

Anserine (æ·nsĕrǝin), *a.* 1839. [ad. L. *anserinus*, f. *anser.*] 1. Of, pertaining to, or of the nature of, a goose. 2. Stupid; as the goose is erron. supposed to be. So **A·nserous** *a.* 1858.

‖**Anspessa·de.** 1751. [Fr. *l'anspessade*, erron. ad. It. *lancia spezzata*, broken lance; applied orig. to a cavalier, who, on his horse being killed under him, was made a petty officer in the foot.] An officer in the foot below a corporal.

Answer (ɑ·nsǝɹ), *sb.* [OE. *a·ndswaru*, f. *and-* against + **swarā-* swearing.] 1. A reply made to a charge; a defence. *spec.* in *Law.* The counter-statement made in reply to a complainant's bill of charges ME. 2. A reply to an objection; a reply in writing or debate, setting forth arguments opposed to those previously advanced 1534. 3. A reply to a question. (The common use.) OE. 4. A reply to an appeal, address, remark, letter, etc.; a response, rejoinder ME. 5. The solution of a problem 1592. 6. A practical reply; anything done in return. In *Fencing*, the return hit. 1535. 7. *Mus.* A re-echoing or reproduction of sounds 1869.

1. To dampne a man with-oute answere CHAUCER. 2. An a. to the Protest of the Free Church 1846. 3. Grim andswaru *Beowulf.* I will bee a foole in question, hoping to bee the wiser by your a. *All's Well* II. ii. 42. 4. I called my seruant, and he gaue me no answere *Job* xix. 16. There must be a. to his doubt TENNYSON. 6. The a. was..a volley of musketry DARWIN. Hence **A·nswerless** *a.* having no a., having no possible a. (*rare*).

Answer, *v.* [OE. *andswarian*, deriv. of sb. *andswaru* (see prec.). For sense-development cf. Gr. ἀποκρίνεσθαι and L. *respondere.*] I.

To answer to a charge. 1. *intr.* To speak in reply to a charge, defend oneself OE.; with *for*: To answer charges in regard to ME. 2. *intr.* To speak or undertake responsibility *for* ME. To guarantee. Const. *for.* 1728. 3. *trans.* To make a defence against; *hence*, to justify (*arch.*) 1552. 4. To reply to, meet an objection or argument ME. 5. To meet practically, atone for; esp. *intr.* Const. *for.* ME. 6. To satisfy a pecuniary claim, pay; *hence*, to be sufficient for (a liability) 1581. 7. To repay, recoup 1587. 8. To fulfil (wishes, etc.) 1653; to suit 1714. 9. *intr.* (*ellipt.*). To serve the purpose, succeed. Also: To turn out (well or ill). 1783.

1. To a. at the bar of public opinion (*mod.*). We that haue good wits, haue much to a. for *A. Y. L.* v. i. 13. 2. When Miss Browning 'answered for it' Miss Phoebe gave up doubting MRS. GASKELL. 3. To a. the stealing of a cup MARLOWE. 4. To a. an argument 1526, Forgeries 1635, a protest (*mod.*), Locke (*mod.*). 5. Grievouslie hath Cæsar answered for it *Jul. C.* III. ii. 85. 6. His fortunes cannot a. his expense 1608. To a. a fine 1770. 8. I shall .. a. your hopes WALTON, expectations 1878. 9. It answered..as a speculation FROUDE.

II. To answer a question, etc. 1. To speak or write in reply to a question, remark, etc.; *also*, To reply to an implied question OE. 2. Coupled with *say*. (A Hellenism of the N.T.) *arch.* OE. 3. *trans.* or *absol.* To solve a problem put as a question in an examination. 4. **To answer to a name:** to answer when addressed by the name; to have the name of 1599. 5. To say or sing antiphonally 1611. 6. To make a responsive sound, as an echo ME. 7. To reply favourably. Cf. I. 8. 1593. 8. To reply to a knock, bell, or other practical request or signal 1597.

1. To a. their question directly DE FOE. No man was able to a. him a word *Matt.* xxii. 46. 4. I a. to that name *Much Ado* v. iv. 73. 6. The woods shall a., and their echo ring POPE. 7. Doubt not ye the Gods have answer'd TENNYSON.

III. To correspond. 1. *trans.* To act in conformity with, to obey; *esp.* of a ship: *To answer the helm.* 1610. 2. *intr.* To act in sympathy with 1684; *trans.* to repeat 1599. 3. To give back in kind 1576. 4. *intr.* To correspond with (in any respect). Const. *to.* ME. †*trans.* To come up to –1789.

1. I come, to a. thy best pleasure *Temp.* I. ii. 190. 2. Fire answers fire SHAKS. 3. Able to answere feast with feast 1601. 4. I wish she had answered her picture as well SHERIDAN.

Answerable (ɑ·nsərăb'l), *a.* 1548. [f. ANSWER *v.* and *sb.* + -ABLE.] 1. Liable to be called to account; responsible. 2. Such as responds to demands, etc.; suitable (*arch.*) 1571. 3. Corresponding, accordant (*arch.*) 1580; proportional, commensurate (*to*) 1617; equivalent, adequate *to* (*arch.*) 1581. 4. *pass.* Able to be answered (*rare*) 1697.

1. He was a. with his head, if [etc.] 1781. A. to the power which appointed him FREEMAN, for what we do NEWMAN. 2. Her treatment..was not a. to her merits RICHARDSON. 3. With a thickness a. to their height EVELYN. Revenue..not a. to its necessary expenditure WELLINGTON. Hence **A·nswerableness,** correspondency (*arch.*); responsibility. **A·nswerably** *adv.* in an answerable manner (*absol.* or with *to*).

Answerer (ɑ·nsərəɹ). 1511. [f. ANSWER + -ER[1].] 1. One who replies to a charge, argument, etc. 1533. 2. One who replies to a question or appeal 1556. †3. One responsible –1539.

Ant (ænt). Pl. **ants.** [OE. *ǣmete, ǣmete*; whence *amete, amte, ante* (cf. *account* for *accompte*), *ant*; also *emete*, EMMET. *Ant* is the more literary form.] 1. A small social insect of the Hymenopterous order, celebrated for its industry; an emmet, a pismire. 2. **White ant:** A destructive social insect of the Neuropterous order, also called Termite 1729.

Goe to the Ant [*Wycl.* ampte, amte, *Coverd.* Emmet], thou sluggard *Prov.* vi. 6. *Comb.*: **a.-bear,** the great ant-eater, *Myrmecophaga jubata*; **-catcher**= ANT-THRUSH; **-eggs, ants' eggs,** the larvæ of ants (a favourite food of young pheasants); **-fly,** a winged ant; **-heap, -hill, -hillock,** the mound raised over an ant's nest; **-rice,** the grains of *Aristida oligantha*, harvested by ants; **-worm,** the larva of the ant.

Ant, obs. form of AUNT, and of AND.

An't (ānt), contraction of *are n't, are not* 1706; colloq. for *am not*; also illiterate or dial. for *is not, have* or *has not*. Cf. AIN'T.

†**An't** (ănt). Var. of *on't*, prop. 'on it', but freq. = *o't* 'of it'. 1589. See ON.

Ant-, *pref.*, short f. ANTI- 'against', bef. vowels, and *h-*.

-ant[1], *suffix*, a. Fr. *-ant* :—L. *-entem, -āntem, -ēntem*, pres. pple. ending (see -ENT); sometimes ad. *-āntem* only. Fr. words in *-ant*, repr. some L. *-ănt*, some L. *-ent, -ēnt*, became after adoption in Eng. *-au·nt*, and again *-ant* with change of stress. Some have since been refash. with *-ent* after L., as *pendant, -ent*, etc. Hence, much inconsistency and uncertainty in the spelling.

-ant[2], a corruption of *-an*, due to confusion of *-an, -and, -ant*, as in *pheasan(t, truan(t, tyran(t*, etc.

‖**Anta** (æ·ntă). Usu. in pl. **antæ.** 1751. [L. (pl. only), ? f. *ante.* Cf. ANTES.] *Arch.* A square pilaster on either side of a door, or at the corner of a building.

Antacid (æntˌæ·sid), *a.* 1732. [f. ANT- + ACID.] Corrective of acidity, *esp.* in the stomach. As *sb.* A remedy for, or preventive of, acidity. var. **Antiacid.**

Antacrid (æntˌæ·krid), *a.* 1853. [f. ANT- + ACRID.] Corrective of acridity in the secretions.

Antæ; see ANTA.

Antagonism (æ̆ntæ·gŏniz'm). 1838. [ad. Gr. ἀνταγώνισμα; see ANTAGONIZE.] 1. The mutual resistance of two opposing forces, physical or mental; active opposition to a force. Const. *between* two things; *to, against, with* a thing. 2. An opposing force or principle 1840.

2. As if resulting from mighty and equal antagonisms DE QUINCEY. var. †**Anta·gony.** MILT.

Antagonist (æ̆ntæ·gŏnist). 1599. [ad. L. *antagonista*, ad. Gr. ἀνταγωνιστής, f. ἀνταγωνίζεσθαι; see ANTAGONIZE.] 1. One who contends with another in any contest; an opponent, an adversary; an impersonal agent acting in opposition 1711. 2. *Phys.* A muscle which counteracts another 1706. 3. Used *attrib.* as sb., or adj.: = ANTAGONISTIC 1671.

1. Satan..A. of Heaven's Almightie King MILT. *P. L.* x. 387. Marke what good vse our A. makes of this conclusion PRYNNE. Fire and air act as antagonists in boiling 1794.

Antagonistic, -al (æ̆ntæ:gŏni·stik, -ăl), *a.* 1632. [f. prec. + -IC, + -AL.] Of the nature of an ANTAGONIST 1, 2. Hence **Antagoni·stically** *adv.*

Antagonize (æ̆ntæ·gŏnəiz), *v.* 1634. [ad. Gr. ἀνταγωνίζεσθαι, f. ἀντί+ἀγών; see AGON.] †1. *trans.* To compete with, rival. 2. To act in antagonism to, to contend with, oppose actively 1742; in U.S. used of forces not of the same kind, e.g. a person may antagonize (i.e. oppose) a bill 1882. 3. *Phys.* To counteract the action of; hence, to neutralize 1833. 4. *intr.* To act in antagonism 1861. 5. *trans.* To render antagonistic 1882. Hence **Anta·gonized** *ppl. a.* (sense 5). **Anta·gonizer,** *Phys.* (*rare*) = ANTAGONIST 2. **Anta·gonizing** *ppl. a.* acting in opposition; mutually opposing.

Antalgic (æ̆ntˌæ·ldʒik), *a.* 1753. [f. ANT- + Gr. ἄλγος + -IC.] *Med.* Tending to prevent or mitigate pain 1775. As *sb.* = ANODYNE.

Antalkali (æntˌæ·lkăli). 1834. [f. ANT- + ALKALI.] *Med.* Anything which counteracts the action of an alkali, *esp.* in the system. Hence **Anta·lkaline** *a.* and *sb.*

Antambulacral (æ:ntˌæmbiulĕ̄·krăl, -æ·krăl), *a.* Also **anti-amb-.** 1870. [f. ANT- + AMBULACRAL.] *Zool.* Opposite to what is ambulacral, as the upper side of a star-fish.

‖**Antana·clasis.** ? *Obs.* 1646. [L., a. Gr. ἀντανάκλασις, f. ἀντί + ἀνακλάειν.] *Rhet.* 1. Repeating a word in a different or even contrary sense 1657. 2. 'A returning to the matter after a parenthesis' (J.) 1646.

1. 'That Abraham against hope believed in hope'.. is an a. MANTON.

†**Antanago·ge.** 1589. [f. ANT- + Gr. ἀναγωγή.] *Rhet.* Retorting a charge when unable to answer it. (Now only in Dicts.)

Antaphrodisiac (æ:ntˌæfrodi·ziæk), *a.* 1742. [f. ANT- + Gr. ἀφροδισιακός, f. 'Αφροδίτη.] Tending to counteract venereal desire. As *sb.* [sc. *medicine*, etc.] 1753.

Antaphroditic (æ:ntˌæfrodi·tik), *a.* 1706. [f. ANT- + Gr. 'Αφροδίτη + -IC.] Of use against venereal disease 1755. *sb.* 1. [sc. *medicine.*] †2. = ANTAPHRODISIAC 1719.

Antapoplectic (æ:ntˌæpople·ktik), *a.* 1697. [f. ANT- + APOPLECTIC.] *Med.* Tending to prevent or cure apoplexy. †*sb.* [sc. *medicine.*] 1753.

†**A·ntarchy.** *rare.* 1656. [ad. mod.L. *antarchia*, f. Gr. ἀντί + -αρχία, f. ἀρχ- in ἄρχειν.] Opposition to government.

Antarctic (æ̆ntā·ɹktik), *a.* [ME. *antartyk*, a. OFr., ad. L. *antarticus*, a. Gr. ἀνταρκτικός, f. ἀντί + ἀρκτικός, f. ἄρκτος the Bear. Also æ̆ntā·ɹtik, after the orig. Eng. spelling.] 1. Opposite to the arctic; pertaining to the south polar regions; southern. †2. *fig.* Contradictory, antipodean –1711. As *sb.* [The adj. used *ellipt.*] The south pole, or the regions adjacent ME.

1. *Antarctic Pole*, the South Pole of earth or heavens. *A. Circle*, the parallel of 66° 32′ South. A. flora 1881.

Antarthritic (æntˌăɹþri·tik), *a.* 1706. [f. ANT- + ARTHRITIC.] *Med.* Tending to prevent or relieve gout 1775. *sb.* [sc. *medicine.*] 1706.

Antasthmatic (æntˌæ̆sþmæ·tik), *a.* 1681. [f. ANT- + ASTHMATIC.] *Med.* Tending to prevent or relieve asthma. As *sb.* [sc. *medicine.*]

Antatrophic (æntˌătrǫ·fik), *a.* 1811. [f. ANT- + ATROPHIC.] *Med.* Tending to counteract atrophy. Also as *sb.*

Ante, obs. f. ANT, AUNT. See also *ANTE.

Ante-, L. *prep.* and *adv.*, used in composition with vbs., vbl. sbs., other sbs., and adjs. derived from phrases, as *ante-mundane*, f. *ante mund(um* + *-ane*.

A. *sbs.* (Main stress on *a·nte*: *a·ntechapel.*) 1. Of position: usu. = A smaller introductory —; as **a. -portico; -stomach;** also **-bath,** an apartment opening into the bath; **-church**=ANTE-CHAPEL; **-nave,** the western part of a divided nave; **-number,** the preceding number. (Since 1600.) 2. Of time or order: = A previous —, *or* A something previous to —; **-predicament; -taste;** also **-eternity,** the quality of having existed from all eternity; **-noon,** the forenoon. (Since 1600.)

B. *adjs.* (Main stress not on *ante*: *ante-nu·ptial, ante-wa·r.* Usu. of 19th c.) 1. Of position: = Before, in front of —; **a. -cæcal,** before the *cæcum*; **-initial,** prefatory; **-pectoral,** in front of the breast. 2. Of time or order: = Occurring or existing in the time before (a fact etc. implied or expressed); a. with adj. ending: **-baptismal; -Christian; -historic; -jentacular,** before breakfast; **-judiciary,** taking place before judgement; **-Mosaic; -Norman; -nuptial; -patriarchal,** existing before the patriarchs; **-posthumous,** posthumous (professedly), but written before; **-reformational.** b. with sb., forming attrib. phr. *-communion, -reformation, -war.* In this sense *ante-* varies with *pre-*.

Ante-, freq. earlier spelling of ANTI-.

†**A·nte-a·cted,** *ppl. a. rare.* 1607. [f. L. *ante-act-, ante-agere* (a questionable compound).] Previously done or spent –1620.

Anteal (æ·ntĭăl), *a. rare.* 1852. [f. L. *ante.*] Pertaining to what is in front.

†‖**Ante-a·mbulo.** 1609. [L., f. *ante* + *ambulare.* Freq. in 17th c.] One whose business it is to walk in front, an usher.

A·nt-ea·ter. 1764. 1. A group of the *Edentata* having long thread-like viscous tongues. They comprise the Ant-eaters proper (*Myrmecophaga*) of S. America, the Scaly Ant-eaters (*Manis*), and the Aardvark (*Orycteropus*). 2. The Aculeated, or Porcupine Ant-eater (*Echidna*), found in Australia 1868. 3. A bird, the ANT-THRUSH 1827.

A·nteceda·neous, *a.* 1630. [f. med.L. **antecedaneus*, f. *antecedere*; see -ANEOUS.] Preliminary or previous.

Antecede (æntǐsī·d), *v. arch.* 1624. [ad. L. *antecedere*, f. *ante* + *cedere.*] 1. To go before, in time, place, or rank; to surpass. 2. *intr.* To go or come before 1628.

Antecedence (æntǐsī·dĕns). 1535. [f. L. *antecedentia*; see next.] 1. The action or fact of going before, priority 1651. †2. That which goes before, *spec.* an antecedent, a premiss 1535. 3. *Astr.* A motion from east to west; retrograde motion 1669.

Antecedency (æntǐsī·dĕnsi). 1598. [ad. L. *antecedentia*, f. *antecedentem*; see ANTECEDE.] 1. The quality or condition of being antecedent. †2. An antecedent state of things; in *pl.* = ANTECEDENT 5. –1748.

Antecedent (æntǐsī·dĕnt), *sb.* ME. [a. Fr. *antécédent* (see next). Cf. L. *antecedens.*] 1. A thing or circumstance which goes before in time or order; often also implying causal relation with its *consequent* 1612. Hence **2.** *Logic.* (Opp. to *consequent.*) The statement upon which any consequence logically depends; hence, the premisses of a syllogism (*obs.*); the first part of a conditional proposition ME. **3.** *Gram.* The substantive to which a following (*esp.* a relative) pronoun refers ME. **4.** *Math.* The first of two terms between which a ratio is expressed; the first and third in a series of four proportionals 1570. **5.** *pl.* The events of a person's past history; also used of institutions, etc. 1841. †**6.** *lit.* = ANTE-AMBULO –1632.

1. Circumstances..governed by a long chain of antecedents BUCKLE. 2. You have shewn us the a., now let us have the *ergo* 1587. 5. They will..sift what the French call their antecedents 1841.

Antecedent (æntĭsī·dĕnt), *a.* 1543. [a. Fr., ad. L. *antecedentem*; see ANTECEDE.] **1.** Preceding, in time or order. Also with *to*, †*unto*, and quasi-*advb.* **2.** *ellipt.* Previous to investigation; presumptive, *à priori* 1794.

1. A period a. to all contemporary..records 1878. 2. The a. improbability of miracles. 1859. Hence **Antece·dently** *adv.* before in time or causality; *à priori.*

†**Antece·ll,** *v. rare.* 1635. [ad. L. *antecellere.*] To excel –1642.

Antecessor (æntĭse·sɔɹ, æntĭ-). ME. [a. MFr. *antécesseur*, refash. of *ancesseur*, after L. *antecessorem*; see ANCESTOR.] **1.** One who goes before (*esp.* in office); a predecessor; †an ancestor –1660. †**2.** A professor of civil law 1751. †**3.** *pl.* One of the advanced guard of an army 1753.

1. Our fathers and Antecessours of olde tyme LD. BERNERS.

Antechamber (æ·ntĭ,tʃē·mbəɹ). Improp. **anti-.** 1656. [a. Fr. *antichambre*, f. *anti* for *ante* + *chambre*, after It.] **1.** A room leading to the chief apartment, in which visitors wait; *orig.* the room admitting into the (royal) bed-chamber. Also *fig.* and *transf.*

Ante-chapel (æ·ntĭ,tʃæpĕl). 1703. [f. ANTE + CHAPEL.] A University term for the outer part at the west end of a chapel.

Antedate (æ·ntĭdēᶦt), *sb.* 1580. [f. ANTE + DATE *sb.*] A date affixed or assigned, earlier than the actual date. †**2.** *fig.* Anticipation 1624.

Antedate (æntĭdēᶦ·t), *v.* 1587. [f. prec. *sb.*; cf. *date.*] **1.** To affix or assign an earlier than the true date to. **2.** To carry back to an earlier time 1600. **3.** To accelerate 1640. **4.** To precede in date 1664. **5.** To anticipate 1611.

1. To a. a letter 1858, a vow 1631. 2. By Reading a Man does as it were A. his Life J. COLLIER. 3. A fright of his Mother..antedated his nativity FULLER. 5. Antedating My Lord's command 1611.

Antediluvial (æ·ntĭdilⁱū·viăl), *a. rare.* 1823. [f. ANTE + L. *diluvium* + -AL [1].] Older than the Flood. Hence **A·ntedilu·vially** *adv.*

Antediluvian (æ·ntĭdilⁱū·viăn), *a.* 1646. [f. as prec. + -AN.] **1.** Existing before the Noachian deluge 1657. **2.** Referring to the period before the Flood 1646. **3.** Of the sort which obtained before the Flood 1698. **4.** Very antiquated. (Disparaging.) 1726. **5.** *sb.* [The adj. used *absol.*] One who lived before the Flood; *fig.* one who is very old 1684.

1. The a. language HARTLEY. 3. An a. lease of life 1846. 4. A sorry a. makeshift of a building LAMB.

†**A·ntefact.** *rare.* 1623. [ad. L. *antefactum.*] A thing done before.

Confession was of antefacts, not post facts FULLER.

Antefix (æ·ntĭfiks). Usu. in *pl.* 1832. [ad. L. *antefixum* (also used, pl. -a).] Ornaments on the eaves and cornices of ancient buildings, to conceal the ends of the tiles; also ornamental heads, etc., making the spouts from the gutters. Hence **Antefi·xal** *a.*

A·nteflexed, *ppl. a. rare.* 1872. [f. ANTE + L. *flex-*, *flectere* + -ED.] Bent forward; *spec.* of the uterus. Hence **Antefle·xion,** a bending forward; *spec.* of the uterus (*rare*).

‖**Antefurca** (æntĭfɜ̄·ɹkă). 1826. [mod.L., f. L. *ante* + *furca.*] *Ent.* In cockroaches, an internal forked projection from the sternal wall of the anterior somite of the thorax.

†**Antela·tion.** *rare.* 1553. [ad. med.L. *antelationem.*] Precedence –1623.

Antelope (æ·ntĭlo͡ʊp). ME. [a. OFr. *antelop*, ad. L. *ant(h)alopus*, Gr. ἀνθόλοψ, of unkn. origin and meaning.] Any species of the deer-like ruminant genus *Antilope* (Pallas), characterized by cylindrical, annulated horns, and the possession of a lachrymal sinus, and grouped as *True* Antelopes, *Bush* A., *Capriform* A., and *Bovine* A. The name is now pop. associated with the first. Also *attrib.*

The Gr., L., and OFr. antelope was a creature haunting the banks of the Euphrates, very savage, hard to catch, and having long saw-like horns. This is the heraldic animal.

The a. and wolfe both fiers and fell SPENSER *F. Q.* I. vi. 26. To the group of true Antelopes also belongs the Gazelle CARPENTER.

Antelucan (æntĭlⁱū·kăn), *a.* 1654. [ad. L. *antelucanus*, f. *ante* + *luc-* (*lux*).] Of or pertaining to the hours before dawn.

Antemeridian (æ:ntĭ,mĕri·diăn), *a. rare.* 1656. [f. L. phr. *ante meridiem*; see -AN.] Of or belonging to the forenoon.

Antemetic (ænt,ĭme·tik), *a.* 1706. [f. ANT- + EMETIC.] Tending to check vomiting. Also as *sb.* [sc. *medicine.*]

Antemundane (æntĭmɒ·ndēᶦn), *a.* 1731. [f. ANTE- + L. *mundus*, after *mundane.*] Existing or occurring before the creation of the world.

Antemu·ral. ?*Obs.* 1774. [ad. L. *antemurale*, f. *ante* + *murus.*] A strong high wall with turrets, called also the barbican.

Antenatal (æntĭnēᶦ·tăl), *a.* 1817. [f. ANTE- + NATAL.] Happening or existing before birth.

‖**Antenna** (ænte·nă). Pl. **-æ,** occas. **-as.** 1698. [a. L. *antenna* a sail-yard, used as tr. Gr. κεραῖαι 'horns' of insects by Theod. Gaza (died 1478).] *Zool.* A sensory organ, occurring in pairs on the heads of insects and crustacea; pop. called *horns* or *feelers.* **2.** *Bot.* Two long processes in the male flower of certain orchids, which when touched eject the pollinium from the flower 1862. **3.** A wireless aerial 1902.

1. The antennæ are organs of touch HUXLEY. Hence **Ante·nnal, Ante·nnary** *adjs.* of, relating to, or of the nature of antennæ. **Antenni·ferous** *a.* bearing antennæ. **Ante·nniform** *a.* of the form of antennæ.

Antennule (ænte·niūl). 1845. [dim. of ANTENNA.] *Zool.* A tiny organ of the nature of an antenna. Hence **Ante·nnular, -y** *a.* of the nature of small antennæ.

Ante-orbital (æntĭō·ɹbităl), *a.* Also **ant-.** 1839. [f. ANTE- + ORBIT.] *Phys.* Situated in front of the eyes.

Antepagment (æntĭpæ·gmĕnt). 1678. [ad. L. *antepagmentum* (also used, *pl.* -a), f. *ante* + *pangere.*] *Arch.* One of the jambs or moulded architraves of a door.

Antepa·schal, *a. rare.* 1660. [f. ANTE + L. *pascha* + -AL [1].] Coming before the Passover, or before Easter.

A·ntepast. Also **anti-.** 1590. [f. ANTE- + L. *pastus*, f. *pascere*; cf. *repast.*] †A whet taken before a meal; also, a foretaste.

An a. of the odium they were to incur H. WALPOLE.

‖**Antependium** (æntĭpe·ndiŏm). Often **anti-.** 1696. [L., f. *ante* + *pendere.*] A covering for the front of the altar, used in R.C. and some Anglican churches; occas. used for FRONTAL.

Antepenult (æ:ntĭ,pĭnɒ·lt), *a.* and *sb.* 1585. [abbrev. of next.] = ANTEPENULTIMATE.

‖**Antepenultima** (æ:ntĭ,pĭnɒ·ltimă). 1581. [L. (sc. *syllaba*), f. *ante* + *pænultima* last but one. Formerly with Eng. pl. in *-s.*] *Pros.* The last syllable but two of a word.

Antepenultimate (-ɒ·ltimĕt), *a.* 1727. [f. L. *antepænultimus*, after *ultimate.*] The last but two. Orig. of syllables; but extended to order in place or time. 1730. Also as *sb.* 1727.

Antephialtic (æ:nt,efi,æ·ltik), *a.* 1853. [ad. mod.L. *antephialticus*, f. Gr. ἀντί + ἐφιάλτης nightmare.] *Med.* Good against the nightmare. Also as *sb.*

Antepileptic (æ:nt,epile·ptik), *a.* 1656. [f. ANT- + EPILEPTIC.] *Med.* Good against epilepsy. Also as *sb.*

†**A·nteport.** *rare.* 1644. [ad. It. *antiporta*, f. *anti* = L. *ante* + *porta.*] **1.** An outer gate or door. **2.** A hanging in front of a door –1669.

Anteposition (æntĭpozi·ʃən). *rare.* 1753. [f. L. *anteponere*; cf. *position.*] The placing of anything in front; *esp.* (*Gram.*) of a word which normally follows.

Antepra·ndial, *a.* 1847. [f. ANTE- + *prandium.*] Before-dinner.

Anterior (æntī͡ə·riəɹ), *a.* 1611. [a. L., f. *ante*; cf. Fr. *antérieur.*] **1.** Of place: Fore, more to the front; opp. to *posterior.* **2.** Of time, etc.: Preceding, former, earlier 1794. Also with *to.* (Thus *anterior* is comparative in sense, but not in const.) 1728. Hence **Anterio·rity,** the quality of being a. **Ante·riorly** *adv.*

A·ntero-, Eng. comb. f. assumed L. **anterus*, positive of ANTERIOR; = Front, fore.

a.-frontal, pertaining to the front part of the forehead; **-parietal,** belonging to the front of the parietal or side plates of the skull; **-posterior,** front and back, forward and backward.

Ante-room (æ·ntĭrūm). 1762. [after Fr. *antichambre.*] A room before, or forming an entrance to, another.

Antes (æ·ntīz), *sb. pl.* 1789. [cf. Fr. *antes*, ad. L. *antas.*] *Arch.* = ANTÆ.

A·ntescript. *rare.* 1831. [after *postscript.*] A note written in front or on the top of a letter, etc.; *also*, The whole letter before the postscript.

†**Antestature.** 1706. [a. Fr., f. L. *ante* + *statura*, f. *stat-*, *stare.*] A small intrenchment, raised in haste, to dispute the rest of the ground, when the enemy has gained part.

Ante-temple (æ·ntĭtemp'l). 1703. [ad. med. L. *antetemplum*, tr. Gr. πρόναος PRONAOS.] The portico of a church or of an ancient temple; occas. = *ante-nave* (see ANTE-).

†**A·ntethem(e.** 1494. [f. THEME, a. Fr. *thème*:—L. *thema*, a. Gr. θέμα + ? ἀντί or L. *ante.* Not found in med.L. or OFr.] The text prefixed to a sermon as its theme or motto –1561.

Antetype (æ·ntĭtəip). 1612. [f. ANTE- + TYPE.] A preceding type; an earlier example.

Anteversion (æntĭvɜ̄·ɹʃən). 1853. [ad. L. *anteversionem.*] = ANTEFLEXION.

Antevert (æntĭvɜ̄·ɹt), *v.* 1649. [ad. L. *antevertere*, f. *ante* + *vertere.*] †**1.** To avert beforehand –1677. **2.** To turn forward 1870. Hence **Anteve·rted** *ppl. a.* = ANTEFLEXED.

Anth-, Gr. ἀνθ, comb. form of ἀντί (see ANTI-) bef. an aspirate. Often in mod. scientific wds. *anti-*, as in *anthelix*, *anti-helix.*

Anthelion (ænþī·liŏn, ænt,h-). Pl. **-a.** 1670. [late Gr. ἀνθήλιον, neut. for ἀντήλιον, f. ἀντί + ἥλιος.] A luminous ring or nimbus seen surrounding the shadow of the observer's head projected on a cloud or fog-bank opposite the sun.

Anthelix; see ANTI-HELIX.

Anthelmintic (ænþĕlmi·ntik), *a.* 1684. [f. ANTH- + Gr. ἑλμινθ- (ἕλμινς) + -IC.] *Med.* Of use against intestinal worms. Also as *sb.* 1706.

Anthem (æ·nþĕm), *sb.* [OE. *antefn(e*, a. Rom. **antefna*:—late L. *antifona*, for *antiphona*, a. Gr. ἀντίφωνα; see ANTIPHON. The development in Eng. was *ante·fne*, *ante·vne*, *ante·mne*, *a·ntemn*, *a·ntem*, *a·nthem.*] **1.** A composition, in prose or verse, sung antiphonally; an ANTIPHON. *Obs.* or *arch.* OE. **2.** A composition in unmeasured prose (usu. from the Scriptures or Liturgy) set to music for sacred use ME. **3.** *loosely* in poetry: Any song of praise or gladness. Also used of the Eng. National Anthem (techn. a *hymn*). 1591.

1. Continuing .. untill an Anthymne was sung LESTRANGE. 2. For my voice, I haue lost it with hallowing and singing of Anthemes SHAKS. 3. Thy plaintive a. fades Past the near meadows KEATS.

Anthem (æ·nþĕm), *v.* 1628. [f. the sb.; cf. to *chant*, etc.] *trans.* To celebrate in an anthem.

Anthemy (æ·nþĭmi). *rare.* 1880. [f. Gr. ἀνθε- (ἄνθος). Also as L. *anthemia.*] *Bot.* A flower-cluster of any kind.

Anther (æ·nþəɹ). 1791. [a. Fr. *anthère*, and mod.L. *anthera*, in cl. L. 'a medicine extracted from flowers', a. Gr. ἀνθηρά fem. of ἀνθηρός, f. ἀνθ- (ἄνθος).] *Bot.* That part of the stamen containing the pollen, which when mature is shed forth for the fertilization of the ovary.

Comb.: **a.-dust,** pollen; **-valve,** the opening by which the pollen is shed. Hence **A·ntheral** *a.* **Antheri·ferous** *a.* a.-bearing. **Anthe·riform** *a.* a.-shaped. **A·ntherless** *a.* without anthers. **Anthero·genous** *a.* produced or developed from anthers, as petals in a double rose. **A·ntheroid** *a.* anther-like in appearance or functions.

‖**Antheridium** (ænþĕri·diŏm). 1854. [mod.

L. f. *anthera.*] *Bot.* Oblong or globular sperm cells found in Cryptogams, answering to the anthers of flowering plants. Hence **Antheri·dial** *a.* pertaining to, or of the nature of, an a.

†**A·ntherine.** Also **anterne.** 1710. [? f. Gr. ἀνθηρός.] A kind of poplin –1739.

A:ntherozo·oid, -zo·id. 1854. [f. L. *anthera* + ZOOID.] *Bot.* One of the minute moving bodies in the antheridia of cryptogams. Hence **A:ntherozooi·dal, -zoi·dal** *a.*

‖ **Anthesis** (ænþī·sis). 1835. [Gr., f. ἀνθέ-ειν.] Full bloom.

†**A·nthine,** *a.* 1656. [ad. L. *anthinus*, a. Gr., f. ἄνθος.] Derived from or flavoured with flowers. As *sb.* (= L. *anthinum mel.*) Honey, oil, or wine flavoured with flowers.

Antho- (ænþo, *-o, -ŏ, -ǫ*), comb. form, f. Gr. ἄνθος flower.

antho·bian [Gr. βίος] *a.*, *Ent.* an animal (*esp.* a beetle) living in or feeding on flowers; **-ca·rpous** [Gr. -καρπος] *a.*, *Bot.* of or pertaining to the *Anthocarpi* (Lindley), fruits composed of flowers and fruit proper blended into a mass, as in the pine-apple; **-ce·phalous** [Gr. -κέφαλος] *a.*, having a flower-like head; **-cy·anin(e** [Gr. κύανος], also **-cyane, -kyan,** the blue colouring matter in plants; **-graphy** [Gr. -γραφία], *Bot.* the scientific description of flowers; **-lite** [Gr. λίθος], *Geol.* a name for certain fossil plants resembling flowers; *Min.* a variety of Amphibolite; ‖**-lysis** [Gr. λύσις], *Bot.* a retrograde metamorphosis of a flower, in which parts normally combined are separated; **-ma·nia** [Gr. μανία], an extravagant passion for flowers; **-phore** [Gr. -φορος], *Bot.* the stalk which in some flowers raises the receptacle above the calyx; **-phorous** [see prec.] *a.*, flower-bearing; **-si·derite** [Gr. σιδηρίτης], *Min.* a hydrous silicate of iron occurring in feathery flowers; **-sperm** [Gr. σπέρμα], *Bot.* a little coloured concretion scattered in the tissue of certain Fucoids; **-taxy** [Gr. -ταξία], *Bot.* arrangement of flowers according to their inflorescence; **-xa·nthin(e** [Gr. ξανθός], now called *xanthophyll.*

A·nthoid, *a.* 1859. [f. Gr. ἄνθος + -ειδής.] Flower-like.

Anthology (ænþǫ·lŏdʒi). 1640. [ad. L. *anthologia*, a. Gr., f. ἄνθος + -λογια, f. λέγειν.] **1.** A collection of the flowers of verse, i. e. small choice poems, *esp.* epigrams; orig. applied to the Gr. collections so called. **2.** Any other literary collection 1856. **3.** 'A collection of flowers' (J.) 1755. **4.** A hymnal [= Gr. ἀνθολόγιον] 1775. †**5.** A treatise on flowers. [Cf. *zoology*, etc.; also in Fr.] –1706.

1. Anthologies are sickly things 1851. Hence **Antholo·gical** *a.* †treating of flowers; of or relating to a literary a. **Antho·logist,** the compiler of an a.

Anthony (**St.**), the patron saint of swineherds, to whom one of each litter was usually vowed. Hence, *pop.* **Anthony** = the smallest pig of a litter. **Anthony's** or **St. Anthony's fire,** a popular name of erysipelas (from the tradition that those who sought his intercession recovered from that distemper in 1089).

He will follow him like a St. Anthony's Pig FULLER.

Anthood (æ·nt,hud). 1879. [f. ANT + HOOD.] Ant nature; ants collectively.

Anthophyllite (ænþofi·ləit, -ǫ·filəit). 1843. [f. mod.L. *anthophyllum* clove.] *Min.* A variety of hornblende, so called from its colour. Hence **Anthophylli·tic** *a.*

†**A·nthos.** 1585. [a. Gr.] Rosemary, 'the flower' *par excellence.*

‖ **Anthozoa** (ænþozō·ă), *sb. pl.* ? *Obs.* 1851. [mod.L., f. Gr. ἄνθος + ζῷα.] *Zool.* Another name for Actinozoa, including sea-anemones, coralline, polypes, etc. Hence **Anthozo·ic** *a.*

Anthozo·oid. 1877. [f. Gr. ἄνθος + ZOOID.] *Zool.* An individual animalcule of a compound Zoophyte.

Anthra-. *Chem.* Abbrev. of *Anthrac-*, stem of ANTHRACENE, forming compound names of Anthracene derivatives, as **anthraqui·none,** $C_{14}H_8O''_2$, obtained by oxidation of anthracene, crystallizing in pale yellow needles. It is the source of artificial alizarin.

Anthracene (æ·nþrăsīn). 1863. [f. Gr. ἄνθρακ- (-αξ) coal + -ENE.] *Chem.* A complex hydrocarbon, $C_{14}H_{10}$, obtained from coal-tar. It belongs to the Benzol group. Also *attrib.*, as in *Anthracene Red*, artificial alizarine. var. **Anthracin.**

Anthracic (ænþræ·sik), *a.* 1881. [f. as prec. + -IC.] Of or pertaining to anthrax. Hence **Anthra·ciform** *a.* having the form or appearance of anthrax; so **A·nthracoid** *a.*

Anthracite (æ·nþrăsəit). 1601. [ad. L. *anthracites*, a. Gr., f. as prec.] †**1.** A stone described by Pliny, perh. hydrophane –1750. **2.** The non-bituminous variety of coal, called also Glance Coal, Blind Coal, and Stone Coal. Also *attrib.* 1812. Hence **Anthraci·ferous** *a.* yielding a. **Anthraci·tic** *a.* of, pertaining to, or resembling, a. **A·nthraciti·sm,** the anthracitic condition (of coal). **A·nthracitous** *a.* containing or characterized by a.

Anthracometer (æ:nþrăkǫ·mĭtəɪ). 1847. [f. Gr. ἄνθρακ- (ἄνθραξ) + -(O)METER.] An instrument for measuring the carbonic acid in a mixture. Hence **A:nthracome·tric** *a.*

Anthraconite (ænþræ·kŏnəit). 1843. [f. as prec. + -ITE.] *Min.* Von Moll's name for common black marble and the black bituminous limestones called swinestones or stinkstones.

Anthracothere (æ·nþrăko,þīəɪ). 1833. [ad. mod.L. *anthracotherium* (also used), f. as prec. + θηρίον.] A pachyderm quadruped whose remains occur in Tertiary lignites and coal.

Anthracoxen(e (æ·nþrăkǫksīn). 1863. [f. as prec. + ξένος. So called as being a foreign substance in coal.] *Min.* A brownish-black resin-like substance, occurring in amorphous masses which alternate with layers of coal, in the coal-beds of Bohemia.

Anthrax (æ·nþræks). ME. [a. L., a. Gr. ἄνθραξ coal, a carbuncle.] **1.** A carbuncle, or malignant boil. **2.** 'Splenic fever' in sheep and cattle, caused by minute organisms introduced into the blood, which multiply rapidly. Also 'malignant pustule', caused in man by infection from animals so affected. 1876.

Anthropic, -al (ænþrǫ·pik, -ăl), *a. rare.* 1859. [ad. Gr. ἀνθρωπικός, f. ἄνθρωπος.] Of or belonging to a human being; human.

Anthropo-, repr. Gr. ἀνθρωπο-, stem and comb. form of ἄνθρωπος man.

Anthropocentric (ænþrō:po,se·ntrik), *a.* 1863. [f. prec. + Gr. κέντρ-ον + -IC.] Centring in man; regarding man as the central fact of the universe, to which all surrounding facts have reference.

Anthropogeny (ænþropǫ·dʒĕni). 1839. [f. as prec. + Gr. -γένεια.] The investigation of the origin of man.

Anthropoglot (ænþrō·pǫglǫt). 1847. [f. as prec. + Gr. γλῶττα.] An animal with a tongue like a man's, *e.g.* a parrot.

Anthropography (ænþropǫ·grăfi). 1570. [f. as prec. + Gr. -γραφία.] †**1.** A description of the structure of man –1839. **2.** The branch of anthropology which treats of the geographical distribution of the races of mankind, and their local variations; ethnography 1834.

Anthropoid (æ·nþrǒpoid, ænþrō·po,id), *a.* 1832. [ad. Gr. ἀνθρωπο-ειδής.] Of human form, man-like 1837. As *sb.* **a.** A being that is human in form only. **b.** An anthropoid ape 1832. Hence **Anthropoi·dal** *a.*

Anthropolatry (ænþropǫ·lătri). *rare.* 1658. [ad. Gr., f. ἄνθρωπος + λατρεία.] Man-worship.

Anthropolite, -lith (ænþrō·pǒləit, -liþ). 1848. [f. ANTHROPO- + Gr. λίθος; see -LITE.] A petrified man.

Anthropological (-lǫ·dʒikal), *a.* 1825. [f. ANTHROPOLOGY + -IC + -AL.] Of, pertaining to, or connected with, anthropology; relating to the nature of man, or the natural history of mankind. So **Anthropolo·gic** (*rare*). Hence **Anthropolo·gically** *adv.*

Anthropologist (ænþropǫ·lŏdʒist). 1805. [f. next; see -IST.] One who pursues the science of anthropology.

Anthropology (-ǫ·lŏdʒi). 1593. [f. Gr. ἄνθρωπος + -λογία.] **1.** The science of man, or of mankind, in the widest sense. (The orig Eng. meaning.) 1593. **b.** The science of the nature of man, embracing Human Physiology and Psychology. (The restricted sense current to *c* 1860.) 1706. **c.** The study of man as an animal 1861. †**2.** A speaking in terms of men; anthropomorphic language –1751.

Anthropomancy (ænþrō·pomæ:nsi). 1618. [f. ANTHROPO- + Gr. μαντεία.] Divination by the entrails of men.

Anthropometry (ænþropǫ·mĕtri). 1839. [f. ANTHROPO- + Gr. -μετρία.] The measurement of the human body with a view to determine its average dimensions, etc., at different ages and in different races or classes. Hence **Anthro:pome·tric, -al** *a.* of, belonging to, or skilled in, a. **Anthro:pome·trically** *adv.* in regard to a.

Anthropomorphic, -al (ænþrō:pomǭ·ɪfik, -ăl), *a.* 1827. [f. Gr. ἀνθρωπόμορφος + -IC, + -AL.[1]] Of the nature of anthropomorphism. **a.** Treating the Deity as having a human form and character. **b.** Attributing a human personality to anything impersonal or irrational 1858.

a. The a. language of the Pentateuch WESTCOTT. b. The a. abstractions which we call nations BLACK. Hence **Anthro:pomo·rphically** *adv.*

Anthropomorphism (-mǭ·ɪfiz'm). 1753. [f. ANTHROPOMORPHIZE; see -ISM.] **1.** Ascription of a human form and attributes to the Deity, or of a human attribute or personality to anything impersonal or irrational. **2.** The use of terms applicable to men in speaking of God 1833.

1. The a. of the vulgar GIBBON. 2. The strong a. of the Hebrew Scriptures COLERIDGE. Hence **Anthro:pomo·rphist,** one who uses a.

Anthropomorphite (-mǭ·ɪfəit). 1561. [ad. L. *anthropomorphitæ*, a. Gr.; see ANTHROPOMORPHOUS and -ITE.] **1.** One ascribing (as an article of religious belief) a human form to God; *spec.* applied to **a.** A sect that arose in Egypt in the 4th c.; **b.** A party in the Western Church in the 10th c. **2.** *attrib.* or as *adj.* = ANTHROPOMORPHITIC 1662. Hence **Anthropomorphi·tic, -al** *a.* of or proper to anthropomorphites 1662.

Anthropomorphitism (-mǫ·ɪfitiz'm). 1664. [f. prec. + -ISM.] **a.** The doctrine of anthropomorphites. **b.** Anthropomorphism.

Anthropomorphize (-mǭ·ɪfəiz), *v.* 1845. [f. Gr. ἀνθρωπόμορφος + -IZE.] *trans.* To render, or regard as, anthropomorphous. Also *absol.*

Anthropomorphology (-mǫɪfǫ·lŏdʒi). [f. as prec. + Gr. -λογία.] = ANTHROPOMORPHISM 2. Hence **Anthropomorpholo·gically** *adv.*

Anthropomorphosis (-mǫɪfō·sis, -mǭ·ɪfŏsis). 1863. [f. Gr. ἀνθρωπομορφό-ειν; see next.] Transformation into human shape.

Anthropomorphous (-mǭ·ɪfəs), *a.* 1753. [f. Gr. ἀνθρωπόμορφος (f. ἄνθρωπος + μορφή) + -OUS.] **1.** Having the form of a man. **2.** = ANTHROPOMORPHIC 1858. Hence **Anthropomo·rphously** *adv.* (*rare*).

Anthropono·mical, *a.* ? *Obs.* 1734. [f. Gr. ἄνθρωπος + νόμος + -ICAL.] Concerned with the laws which regulate human action.

Anthropopathy (-pǫ·păþi). 1647. [ad. med. L. *anthropopatheia*, a. Gr., f. ἄνθρωπος + πάθος.] Ascription of human feelings and passions (to the Deity, etc.).

Expressions which spoke of God by what is called a.—that is, as subject to wrath, repentance, and other human emotions FARRAR. var. **Anthropo·pathism.** Hence **Anthropopa·thic** *a.*, **-ally** *adv.*

‖**Anthropophagi** (-pǫ·fădʒəi), *sb. pl.* 1552. [L., a. Gr., f. ἄνθρωπος + φαγεῖν.] Man-eaters, cannibals. Rarely in sing. *anthropophagus.*

The Canibals that each others eate, The Anthropophague *Oth.* I. iii. 144. Hence **Anthro:popha·gic, -al** *a.* of, connected with, or relating to anthropophagy. †**Anthropophagi·nian.** *rare.* [app. after *Carthaginian.*] Used as sing. to *Anthropophagi Merry W.* IV. v. 9. **Anthropo·phagism,** cannibalism. **Anthropo·phagist, Anthropo·phagite,** a habitual cannibal. **Anthropo·phagistic** *a.*

Anthropo·phagous, *a.* 1831. [f. L. *anthropophagus* + -OUS.] Man-eating, cannibal. Hence **Anthropo·phagously** *adv.* (*rare*).

Anthropophagy (ænþropǫ·fădʒi). 1638. [ad. Gr. ἀνθρωποφαγία; see above.] The eating of men, cannibalism.

Anthropopho·bia. *nonce-wd.* [f. ANTHROPO- + Gr. -φοβία.] Aversion to man.

Anthropophuism (ænþropǫ·fiu,iz'm). 1858. [f. Gr. ἀνθρωποφυής (f. ἄνθρωπος + φυή) + -ISM.]

The ascription of a human nature to the gods. Hence **Anthropophui·stic** *a.* ascribing a human nature to the gods; having such a nature ascribed.

Anthroposophist (ænþrǫpǫ·sǒfist). [f. ANTHROPO- + Gr. σοφιστής.] One furnished with 'the wisdom of men'. (Cf. 1 *Cor.* ii. 5, 13.) KINGSLEY.

Anthroposophy (-pǫ·sǒfi). 1742. [f. as prec. + Gr. σοφία.] The knowledge of the nature of man. *Also*, Human wisdom.

Anthropotomy (ænþrǫpǫ·tǒmi). 1855. [f. Gr. ἄνθρωπος + -τομία, f. τομ- (τέμνειν).] Anatomy of the human body. Hence **Anthro:po·to·mical** *a.* **Anthropo·tomist**, one who studies human anatomy.

Anthropu·rgic, *a. rare.* 1838. [f. Gr. ἀνθρωπουργός + -IC; cf. θεουργός.] *prop.* Man-making; also used as: Acted upon by man.

Anthypnotic, anthysteric: see ANTI-HY-.

‖**Anthypophora** (ænþipǫ·fǒră). Also **antihyp-**. 1589. [L., a. Gr., f. ἀντί + ὑποφορά allegation.] *Rhet.* Counter-inference or allegation. Hence **Anthypophore·tic** *a.*

Anti-, *prefix*[1]; repr. Gr. ἀντί-, ἀντ-, ἀνθ- (see ANT-, ANTH-), 'opposite, against, in exchange, instead, representing, rivalling, simulating'; in Eng. used in compounds already formed in Gr., or others modelled on them. Also as a living formative, with sbs. expressed, or implied in adjs., and in the derivatives of these, after *antichrist*, *antichristian*, and *antipope*, the only examples in use bef. 1600. Shakspere has no *anti-* combinations.

Combinations. I. Sbs. in which *anti-* attributively qualifies a sb. The main stress is on *a·nti* (a·nti‚ki·ng). 1. Formed on the type of ANTICHRIST; = 'Opposed, in opposition, opponent, rival', whence 'pretended, spurious, pseudo-': as *anti-bishop*, *-Cæsar*, *-Messiah*, etc. b. The opposite or reverse of; an opponent of: as *anti-hero*, *-Paul*, etc. 2. With names of things: a. = Opposed, opposing, opposite, opposition-, counter-; as *anti-Bartholomew*, *-decalogue*, *-endowment*, *-parliament*, *-Rome*, etc. b. = The opposite, contrary, or reverse of; as ANTICLIMAX, *-poison*, etc. II. Adjs. and attrib. phrases, with sb. expressed, as *anti-zealot*, or implied in an adj., as *anti-national*. The stress is *not* on *anti-* (anti‚ca·tholic). 3. Adjs., formed on the type of ANTICHRISTIAN = Opposed to Christ, Christians, or what is Christian: as *anti-national*, or (rarely) *anti-church-ian*, etc. Occ. *anti-* simply reverses the sense of the adj.: as *anti-grammatical*, *-warlike*, etc. 4. Attrib. phrases, consisting of *anti-*governing a sb., where *anti-* may be considered as a preposition = *against*. Examples are: **anti-aircraft** (defence, gun 1914); **anti-court** party (perhaps the earliest *c* 1650); **Anti-combination** (laws), **Anti-Corn-Law** (league), **Anti-rent** (agitation), **Anti-slavery** (society), **Anti-state-church** (association), **Anti-vaccination** (league). III. Sbs. uniform with, or formed on the preceding adjs. and attrib. phrases. Stress not on *anti-* (anti-ca·lvinist). 5. Combs. in which *anti-* is prefixed to a personal appellation: as *anti-Arminian*, *-Calvinist*, *-episcopist*, *-missionary*. 6. Combs. chiefly in -IST, as *anti-alcoholist*, etc. 7. Names a. of systems, as *anti-slavery*, etc.; b. of material agents or appliances, as **anti-ferment**; **anti-erysipelas**, a plant so named from its use; **anti-huff**, a substance used to adulterate cheese, etc. 8. Abstract sbs., chiefly in *-ism*, as *anti-negroism*, etc.

Anti-, *pref.*[2] Var. of ANTE- 'before', being the form in It., OFr., and occ. in L., hence sometimes in Eng. words from these, as *antichamber*, etc.

Anti-acid, -aphrodisiac, -apoplectic, -arthritic, -asthmatic; see ANTACID, etc.

‖**Antiæ** (æ·nti‚ī), *sb. pl.* 1874. [L. (sc. *comæ*), f. *antius.*] *Zool.* Forelocks.

‖**Antiar** (æ·ntʃăɹ, æ·ntiăɹ). [a. Jav. *antjar*, *antshar.*] The Upas tree of Java, *Antiaris toxicaria*; also, the poison obtained from it. Hence **A·ntiarin**, the poisonous principle of the Upas tree.

Anti-attrition (æ:nti‚ătri·ʃən). 1833. [ANTI- 7.] That which resists attrition. *spec.* Any compound applied to machinery to resist the effects of friction; as black lead mixed with grease, etc. Also *fig.*

‖**Antibacchius** (æ:nti‚băkəi·ŭs). 1589. [L., a. Gr. ἀντιβάκχειος; see BACCHIUS.] *Pros.* A reversed bacchius, a foot of two long and one short syllable. Hence **Antiba·cchic** *a.*

Antibi·lious, *a.* 1835. [ANTI- 3.] Of use against biliousness.

Antibio·tic, *a. rare.* 1860. [f. ANTI- 3 + Gr. βιωτικός.] Opposed to a belief in the presence or possibility of life.

†**Anti-Birmingham.** 1681. [ANTI- 5.] *Eng. Hist.* An anti-Whig, a Tory; a nickname given to the opponents of the Exclusion Bill in 1680; its supporters were nicknamed by Tories 'Birmingham (= counterfeit) Protestants'.

Antibody (æ·nti‚bǫdi). 1901. [tr. G. *antikörper*: ANTI- 2 a.] *Biol. Chem.* A body formed in the blood, etc. to attack a toxin, etc.

Antibrachial (ænti‚bræ·kiăl), *a.* 1836. [f. med.L. *antibrachium* (f. *ante* + *brachium*) + -AL.[1]] *Anat.* Of or pertaining to the forearm.

Antiburgher (æ:ntibǖ·ɹgəɹ). 1766. [ANTI- 5.] A section of the Secession Church in Scotland, which held it unscriptural to take the Burgess Oath: see BURGHER.

Antic (æ·ntik). 1529. [app. ad. It. *antico*, but used as = *grottesco*; see GROTESQUE. Not developed in Eng. from ANTIQUE.] A. *adj.* 1. *Arch.* and *Decorative Art.* Grotesque, in composition or shape; bizarre 1548. 2. Absurd from incongruity, grotesque, in gesture, shape, or attire 1590. †3. Grinning, like 'antics' in architecture -1697.

1. Whether *Grotesca* (as the Italians) or Antique worke (as wee call it) should be receiued WOTTON. 2. An Anticke disposition *Haml.* I. v. 172. Antick shapes 1642. To be sung in an a. Cope MILT. 3. Your mimick mouthes, your antick faces QUARLES.

B. *sb.* †1. *Arch.* and *Decorative Art.* A monstrous, fantastic, or incongruous representation of objects of the animal or the vegetable kingdom, as in tracery, or sculpture -1830. 2. A grotesque gesture, posture, or trick; also *fig.* of behaviour. (Usu. in *pl.*) 1529. †3. A grotesque theatrical representation -1673. 4. A performer who plays a grotesque part, a clown, mountebank, etc. 1564. Also *transf.* and *fig.*

1. Woven with antickes and wyld ymagery SPENSER. Gargils or Antiques HOLLAND. 3. Some .. show, or pageant, or anticke, or fire-worke *L. L. L.* v. i. 119. 4. Jugglers and dancers, antics, mummers, mimics MILT. *Sams.* 1325. *Rich. II*, III. ii. 162.

Antic (æ·ntik), *v.* 1589. [f. prec.; cf. to *caper* and *capers.*] †1. *trans.* To make antic or grotesque 1606. 2. *intr.* To perform antics 1589.

Anticachectic (æ:nti‚kăke·ktik), *a.* 1719. [f. ANTI- 3 + Gr. καχεκτικός; see CACHECTIC.] *Med.* Used against cachexy. Also as *sb.*

†**Antica·mera.** 1625. [a. It.] An antechamber -1670.

Anticatarrhal (æ:nti‚kătā·răl), *a.* 1753. [ANTI- 3.] Of use against catarrh. Also as *sb.*

Antica·tholic, *a.* 1819. [ANTI- 3.] Opposed to what is catholic. Also as *sb.*

Anticausotic (æ:nti‚kǭsǫ·tik), *a.* 1753. [f. ANTI- 3 + Gr.*καυσωτικός, f. καυσόεσθαι.] *Med.* Of use against a burning fever. Also as *sb.*

Anticeremonial (æ:nti‚serĭmōu·niăl), *a.* 1655. [ANTI- 3 or 4.] Opposed to ceremonies. var. †**Anticeremo·nian.**

†**Anti-chamber**, var. of ANTECHAMBER.

Antichlor(e (æ·nti‚klōəɹ). 1869. [f. ANTI- 7 + CHLOR(INE.] *Chem.* A substance used to remove the last traces of chlorine in bleaching.

Antichrist (æ·nti‚krəist). ME. [a. OFr. *antecrist(e*, ad. L. *antechristus*, a. Gr. ἀντίχριστος (1 John ii. 18).] 1. An opponent of Christ. 2. The title of a great personal opponent of Christ and His kingdom, expected to appear before the end of the world ME.

1. The first Antichrist, Simon Magus PUSEY. 2. God shal make shorte the tyme of Antecryst FISHER. The question, whether the Pope be A. HOBBES.

Antichristian (ænti‚kri·stiăn), *a.* 1531. [f. prec., after *Christian*; often treated as f. ANTI- + CHRISTIAN, and in 17–18th c. hyphened.] A. *adj.* 1. Of or pertaining to Antichrist 1532. 2. Opposed to what is Christian or to Christianity. (Often *anti-christian.*) 1587.

1. Tindales antichristen heresyes MORE. 2. Shelley's a. opinions 1870.

B. *sb* †1. A follower of Antichrist -1753. 2. An opponent of Christianity 1621.

2. Toland, the great oracle of the anti-christians SWIFT. Hence **Antichri·stianism**, the system of Antichrist; the quality of being opposed to Christianity; anything a.; var. †**A:ntichristia·nity.** †**Antichri·stianize** *v.* to oppose Christ. **Antichri·stianly** *adv.*

†**Anti·chronism.** 1612. [ad. Gr. ἀντιχρονισμός.] Contradiction of true chronology; anachronism -1728.

‖**Antichthon** (ǣnti·kþǒn), *pl.* †**-chthones** (-·kþǒnīz). 1601. [Gr., prop. adj. (sc. γῆ), f. ἀντί + χθών.] 1. A (supposed) second Earth on the opposite side of the sun 1655. †2. *pl.* The inhabitants of the opposite side of the earth -1684.

Anticipant (ǣnti·sipănt), *a.* 1626. [ad. L. *anticipantem*; see ANTICIPATE *a.*] 1. Operating in advance. 2. Apprehending beforehand, expectant 1798. 3. As *sb.* One who anticipates 1854.

2. Wakening guilt, a. of Hell SOUTHEY. 3. O meek a. of that sure pain [etc.] M. ARNOLD.

†**Anticipate**, *ppl. a.* 1549. [ad. L. *anticipatus*, *anticipare*, f. *ante* + *-cipare*, deriv. f. *capere.*] Anticipated.

Anticipate (ǣnti·sipeᵗt), *v.* 1532. [f. prec.] †1. To seize beforehand -1783. 2. To use or spend in advance 1674. 3. To deal with (a thing) or perform (an action) before another; to forestall 1605; to be before (another) in acting 1682. 4. To observe or practise or cause to happen, earlier than the due date 1534. 5. †*intr.* To occur earlier -1646; *trans.* to precede (*rare*) 1855. 6. To take into consideration before the due time; also *absol.* 1532. 7. To realize beforehand (a certain future event) 1643; to look for (an uncertain event) as certain. Const. *simple obj.* or *subord. cl.* 1749.

2. To a. one's income 1883. 3. To a. the vengeance of heaven GOLDSM. To be anticipated by one's predecessors 1877. 4. To a. a payment 1751. 6. He is to a. consequences and provide for the future 1796. 7. My fears A. thy words SMOLLETT. Those, not in the secret, anticipated an acquittal 1839. Hence †**Anti·cipately** *adv.*

Anticipation (ænti:sipēᵗ·ʃən). 1548. [ad. L. *anticipationem*; see ANTICIPATE *a.*] 1. The action of anticipating (see ANTICIPATE 1, 2); the using of money before it is at one's disposal; the sum so used. 2. Prior action that 'prevents', provides for, or precludes the action of another 1553. 3. Assignment to too early a time; *hence*, observance in advance 1774. 4. Occurrence in advance of the due time; *ellipt.* the amount of such earlier occurrence. *Obs.* in gen. sense. -1697. b. *Mus.* The introduction in advance of part of a chord which is to follow 1819. 5. Intuitive preconception; *à priori* knowledge; presentiment 1549. †6. The formation of opinions before examining the evidence, prepossession, prejudice -1711. 7. The action of realizing a thing before it occurs 1711. 8. Expectation 1809.

1. Restrained from a. by the settlement LD. ST. LEONARDS. 2. So shall my a. preuent your discovery *Haml.* II. ii. 304. 6. Men give themselves up to the first anticipations of their mind LOCKE. 7. And when the thoughts on evil pore, A. makes it more 1764. 8. The a. of many readers COLERIDGE.

Anti·cipative, *a.* 1559. [f. L. *anticipat-* + -IVE.] 1. Having the faculty or habit of anticipating. 2. Of the nature of anticipation 1664. Hence **Anti·cipatively** *adv.*

Anti·cipator. Also **-er.** 1598. [a. L.] One who anticipates. Hence **Anti·cipatory** *a.* of or pertaining to an anticipator; of the nature of anticipation. **Anti·cipatorily** *adv.*

Anticivic (ænti‚si·vik), *a. rare.* 1805. [ad. Fr. *anticivique*; see ANTI- 3 and CIVIC.] Opposed to citizenship, *esp.* to the Fr. doctrine of citizenship of 1789.

Anticivism (ænti‚si·viz'm). *rare.* [a. Fr. *anticivisme*; see ANTI- 8 + CIVISM.] Opposition to citizenship (as in prec.). CARLYLE.

A·nticize, *v. rare.* [f. ANTIC *sb.*] To play antics. BROWNING.

Anticlastic (ænti‚klæ·stik), *a.* 1879. [f. Gr. ἀντί + κλάειν.] Applied to a surface having two curvatures, transverse to each other, in opposite directions, as the surface of a saddle.

Anticlimax (æ:nti‚kləi·mæks). 1727. [ANTI- 2.] 1. *Rhet.* The opposite of climax; the addition of a particular which suddenly lowers the effect. 2. A descent in contrast to a previous rise 1858.

1. And thou Dalhoussy the great God of war, Lieutenant colonel to the Earl of Mar POPE. 2. [His] later years.. were only an a. MCCARTHY.

Anticlinal (ænti‚kləi·năl), *a.* 1833. [f. Gr.

ἀντί + κλίνειν + -AL.] 1. *Geol.* Forming a ridge, in which strata lean against each other, and whence they dip in opposite directions. Opp. to *synclinal.* 2. *Anat.* (A vertebra) having an upright spine, towards which the spines on both sides incline 1870. As *sb.* [sc. *fold, axis, crest,* or *line.*] 1849.

Anticline (æ·nti͵kləin). 1861. [f. as prec., after *incline.*] An anticlinal fold.

A·nticly, *adv. arch.* 1556. [f. ANTIC *a.*] Grotesquely.

Go antiquely, and show outward hideousnesse *Much Ado* v. i. 96. So †**A·nticness,** oddity (*rare*).

Anticonvellent (æ:nti͵kǫnve·lĕnt), *a.* 1876. [f. ANTI- 3 + L. *convellentem, convellere.*] *Med.* Of use against convulsions. Also as *sb.* So **A:nticonvu·lsive** *a.* and *sb.*

Anticor (æ·nti͵kōə:r). 1607. [f. ANTI- + L. *cor.*] A swelling which breaks out in the breast of a horse, etc., over against the heart.

Anticorrosion (ænti͵kǒrōu·ʒən). 1851. [ANTI- 7.] A substance which prevents corrosion.

Anticous (ǣntəi·kəs), *a.* 1870. [f. L. *anticus* (f. *ante*) + -OUS.] *Bot.* Fronting the axis of the whorl to which it belongs.

Anticyclone (æ·nti͵səi:klǫun). 1877. [ANTI- 2.] *Meteor.* The rotatory outward flow of air from an atmospheric area of high pressure; also, the whole system of high pressure and outward flow.

Anticyclonic (æ:nti͵səiklǫ·nik), *a. Meteor.* 1. [f. ANTI- 3 + CYCLONIC.] Opposed to cyclones or cyclonic theories 1860. 2. [f. ANTICYCLONE.] Of or pertaining to an anticyclone 1871. Hence **Anticyclo·nically** *adv.* after the manner of an anticyclone.

Antidicoma·rianite. 1625. [ad. med.L., ad. Gr., f. ἀντίδικος + Μαρία.] *pl.* Adversaries of Mary; Oriental Christians of the 4th c., who denied the perpetual virginity of the mother of Jesus. So **Antidicoma·rian** *a.* and *sb.*

†**Anti·dotary,** *a.* 1541. [ad. med.L. *antidotarius,* f. *antidotum;* see next.] Of the nature of an antidote -1657. As *sb.* 1. [sc. *application.*] 1583. 2. A book describing antidotes; occas. = A dispensary -1727.

Antidote (æ·ntidǫut). 1543. [(? a. Fr.) ad. L. *antidotum,* a. Gr. ἀντίδοτον, prop. neut. sing. Also used as Gr. or L., with pl. *-a.*] A medicine given to counteract the action of poison, or an attack of disease. Const. *against, for, to.* Also *fig.*

Where are poysons, antidots are most G. HERBERT. His very mirth is an a. to all gaiety GOLDSM. Hence **A·ntidotal** *a.* of, pertaining to, or of the nature of an a. **Antido·tally** *adv.;* also †**Antido·tically.**

Antidote (æ·ntidǫut), *v.* 1630. [f. the sb.] †1. *trans.* To furnish with an antidote; fortify against poison. Also *fig.* -1703. 2. To apply an antidote to, counteract. Also *fig.* 1661.

Antidromous (ǣnti·drǒməs), *a.* 1878. [f. Gr. ἀντί + -δρομος + -OUS.] Running in an opposite direction round an axis. var. **Anti·dromal.**

Antidysenteric (æ:nti͵disĕnte·rik), *a.* 1853. [ANTI- 3.] *Med.* Of use against dysentery. Also as *sb.*

Antidysuric (æ:nti͵disiūᵊ·rik), *a.* [f. ANTI- 3 + Gr. δυσουρικός, f. δυσουρία.] *Med.* Of use against dysury.

Anti-emetic, -ephialtic, vars. of ANTEMETIC, etc.

Anti-ethnic (ænti͵e·þnik), *a.* 1861. [f. ANTI- 3 + Gr. ἐθνικός, f. ἔθνος.] Against the Gentiles, or non-Jewish nations.

Antifebrile (ænti͵fe·bril, fī-), *a.* 1661. [ANTI- 3.] *Med.* Of use against fever. As *sb.* [sc. *substance.*] 1661. var. **Antifebri·fic** (erron. *-febritick*).

Antifriction (ænti͵fri·kʃən). 1837. [ANTI- 7.] That which prevents friction. Also *fig.* Oil of flattery, the best patent a. known CARLYLE.

Antigalactic (ænti͵gălæ·ktik), *a.* 1847. [f. ANTI- 3 + Gr. γαλακτικός, f. γάλακτ-.] Of use in preventing the secretion of milk. Also as *sb.*

Anti-Ga·llican, *a.* 1755. [f. ANTI- 3 + L. *Gallicus.*] Opposed to what is French 1765. *sb* One opposed to the French 1755. var. **Anti-Ga·llic.** Hence **Anti-Ga·llicanism.**

Anti-god (æ·nti͵gǫd). 1684. [ANTI- 1.] He who or that which is opposed to God. *Hence* b. A rival deity; c. An evil demon.

Antigorite (ǣnti·gŏrəit). 1862. [f. *Antigorio* in Piedmont.] *Min.* A variety of serpentine.

Antigro·pelos. 1848. [f. Gr. ἀντί + ὑγρός + πηλός (which gives *anthygropē·los*) !] Waterproof leggings.

Anti-guggler (æntigʊ·gləɪ). 1794. [f. ANTI- 6 + *guggle* = GURGLE + -ER [1].] A siphon inserted into carboys, etc., in drawing off liquor, so as to admit the air without gurgling.

Antihelix, anthelix (ænti͵hī·liks, æ·nþī·liks). 1721. [a. Gr. ἀνθέλιξ, f. ἀντ(ί + ἕλιξ.] *Anat.* The curved elevation within the helix or outer rim of the ear.

Antihydropic (æ:nti͵həidrǫ·pik), *a.* 1742. [f. ANTI- 3 + Gr. ὑδρωπικός, f. ὕδρωψ.] *Med.* Of use against dropsy. Also as *sb.*

Antihypnotic (æ:nti͵hypnǫ·tik), *a.* Also anthypn-. 1681. [f. ANTI- 3 + Gr. ὑπνωτικός.] *Med.* Tending to prevent sleep. Also as *sb.*

Antihysteric (æ:nti͵histe·rik), *a.* 1747. [ANTI- 3.] *Med.* Of use against hysteria. Also as *sb.*

Anti-icteric (æ:nti͵ikte·rik), *a.* 1853. [f. ANTI- 3 + Gr. ἰκτερικός, f. ἴκτερος.] *Med.* Of use against jaundice. Also as *sb.*

Anti-Jacobin (ænti͵dʒæ·kǒbin), *a.* 1809. [ANTI- 3.] Opposed to the party called Jacobins in France in 1789; hence, opposed to the French Revolution, and to those who sympathized with democratic principles, who were nicknamed *Jacobins* by Mr. Pitt's followers. As *sb.* One opposed to the Jacobins, etc.; also, name of a weekly paper started in 1797. Hence **Anti-Ja·cobinism.**

A·ntilibra·tion. *rare.* 1858. [f. ANTI- + L. *librationem.*] Counterpoising.

Antilithic (ænti͵li·þik), *a.* 1853. [f. ANTI- 3 + Gr. λιθικός, f. λίθος.] *Med.* Of use against stone in the bladder. Also as *sb.*

Antilogarithm (ænti͵lǫ·gărĭþ'm). 1675. [ANTI- 2.] *Math.* †1. The complement of the logarithm of a sine, tangent, or secant; or the difference between that and the logarithm of 90 degrees -1796. 2. The number to which the logarithm belongs 1675. Hence **Antiloga·ri·thmic** *a.*

Antilogy (ǣnti·lŏdʒi). 1614. [ad. Gr. ἀντιλογία.] A contradiction in terms, or ideas.

Speculation ends in a series of insoluble antilogies SIR W. HAMILTON.

Antilopine (ǣnti·lǒpəin), *a.* Also **ante-.** 1827. [ad. mod.L. *antilopinus;* see ANTELOPE.] Of or pertaining to the antelope.

Antilyssic (ænti͵li·sik), *a.* [f. ANTI- 3 + Gr. λύσσα + -IC.] *Med.* Of use against hydrophobia. Also as *sb.*

Antimacassar (æ:nti͵măkæ·səɪ). 1852. [f. ANTI- 7 + *macassar,* proprietory name of hair-oil.] A covering thrown over sofas, chairs, etc., to protect them from grease in the hair, etc., or as an ornament.

†**Antimagistra·tical,** *a.* 1645. [ANTI- 3.] Opposed to the power or claims of civil magistrates -1669. var. †**Antimagi·strical** *a.* (*rare*).

Antima·son. [ANTI- 5.] One professing opposition to freemasonry. (U.S. politics.) Hence **Antimaso·nic,** *a.* **Antima·sonry,** opposition to freemasonry.

Antimasque, -mask (ænti͵mɑ·sk). 1613. [ANTI- 2.] A grotesque interlude between the acts of a masque. (Occ. made *Antic-masque.*) Hence **A·ntima·squer, -ker,** a performer in an a.

Antimere (æ·ntimīᵊɪ). 1877. [f. Gr. ἀντί + μέρος.] *Biol.* Usu. pl. *antimeres,* or as L. *antimera:* Opposite divisions or halves. Hence **Antime·ric** *a.*

‖**Antimetabole** (æ:nti͵mĭtæ·bǒli). 1589. [L., a. Gr., f. ἀντί + μεταβολή.] *Rhet.* Repetition of words or ideas in inverse order.

‖**Antimetathesis** (æ:nti͵mĭtæ·þĭsis). [L., a. Gr., f. ἀντί + μετατιθέναι.] *Rhet.* Inversion of the members of an antithesis.

Antimeter (ǣnti·mĭtəɪ). 1819. [f. Gr. ἀντί + μέτρον.] An obsolete instrument, called also *Reflecting Sector,* for measuring small angles.

Antimona·rchical, *a.* 1625. [ANTI- 3.] Opposed to monarchy. vars. †**Antimona·rchial, Antimona·rchic.** Hence **Antimonar·chically** *adv.*

Antimo·narchy. 1648. [ANTI- 7.] Opposition to monarchy. Hence **Antimo·narchist.**

Antimonate (æ·ntimonēᵊ:t, -mǭᵘ·neᵊt). 1854. [f. ANTIMONY + -ATE [4].] *Chem.* A salt of Antimonic acid.

Antimonial (æntimǭᵘ·niăl), *a.* 1605. [ad. mod.L. *antimonialis;* see ANTIMONY.] 1. Of or pertaining to antimony. 2. Containing antimony in combination 1771. 3. *sb.* A medicine containing antimony 1727.

1. *Antimonial cups:* cups made of glass of antimony, to communicate emetic qualities to wine. 2. *Antimonial wine:* sherry containing tartarated antimony. A. arsenic, copper, etc. (*mod.*).

Antimo·niate. 1801. = ANTIMONATE. Hence **Antimo·niated** *ppl. a.* treated with antimony.

Antimonic (æntimǫ·nik), *a.* 1834. [f. L. *antimonium* + -IC.] Of or pertaining to antimony. In *Chem.* applied to compounds in which antimony combines as a pentad; as *Antimonic acid* (prop. *A. oxide*), or *Antimony pentoxide* Sb_2O_5.

Antimonide (æ·ntimonəi:d, -mǭᵘ·nəid). 1863. [f. as prec. + -IDE.] *Chem.* A compound of antimony with hydrogen, a metal, or an organic radical. Also called STIBIDE, and formerly ANTIMONIURET.

A·ntimonio·so-, comb. f. ANTIMONIOUS.

Antimonious (æntimǭᵘ·niəs), *a.* 1833. [f. L. *antimonium* + -OUS.] Of the nature of, or containing, antimony. In *Chem.* applied to compounds in which antimony combines as a triad; as *Antimonious Chloride* $SbCl_3$, etc. var. **Antimo·nous.**

Antimonite (æ·ntimonəi:t, -mǭᵘ·nəit). 1834. [f. as prec. + -ITE.] 1. *Chem.* A salt of antimonious acid. †2. = STIBNITE.

Antimo·niuret. 1841. [f. as prec. + -URET.] *Chem.* See ANTIMONIDE. Hence **Antimo·niuretted** *ppl. a.* combined with antimony (in a gaseous state).

Antimony (æ·ntiməni). 1477. [ad. med.L. *antimonium,* prob. ad. Arab. In pop. etym. = *anti-moine* (monks'-bane).] A brittle metallic elementary body, of bright bluish-white colour and flaky crystalline texture. Symbol Sb (*Stibium*). a. *Alchem.* and *Pharm.* Orig. applied to the native trisulphide (called also *gray antimony,* or *Stibnite*), the στίμμι, *stibium* of the ancients, and *al-koh'l* of the Arabs (see ALCOHOL); the *antimonium, proteus, leo ruber,* etc., of the alchemists. b. *Chem.* The simple element. (Called earlier *Regulus of Antimony.*) 1788.

Combs., etc.: **Antimony blende** = Red A.; **A. bloom** = White A.; **A. glance** = Gray A. (see a); **A. ochre,** *Cervantite;* **A. vermilion,** a red pigment precipitated from an antimonial solution; **Butter of A.,** an old name of the trichloride, a translucent fatty mass; **Crocus of A.,** an impure sulphide of a. and sodium; **Glass of A.,** an oxy-sulphide fused; **Red A.** = *Kermesite;* **Saffron of A.** = Red A.; **Tartarated A.,** tartar emetic.

Antinational (ænti͵næ·ʃənăl), *a.* Opposed to one's own nation, or to a national party.

Antinephritic (æ:nti͵nĭfri·tik), *a.* 1678. [f. Gr. ἀντί + νεφρῖτις + -IC. *Med.* Of use against disease of the kidneys. Also as *sb.*

Antinomian (æntinǭᵘ·miăn). 1645. [f. med.L. *Antinomi,* the name of the sect (f. Gr. ἀντί + νόμος).] A. *adj.* Of or pertaining to the antinomians. B. *sb.* One who maintains that the moral law is not binding upon Christians, under the law of grace 1645. *spec.* One of a sect alleged to hold this opinion, which arose in Germany in 1535. var. †**Anti·nomist** *sb.* Hence **Antino·mianism,** †**Anti·nomism,** the doctrine or practice of antinomians. †**Antino·mianize** *v.* to teach antinomianism.

Antinomy (ǣnti·nŏmi). 1592. [ad. L., a. Gr. ἀντινομία, f. ἀντί + νόμος.] 1. A contradiction in a law, or between two equally binding laws. †2. A contradictory law, statute, or principle; an authoritative contradiction -1656. 3. A contradiction between conclusions which seem equally logical, reasonable, or necessary; a paradox; intellectual contradictoriness 1802.

1. The antinomies or contradictions of the Code and Pandects GIBBON. 2. His own a., or counterstatute

Milt. var. A·ntinome (*rare*). Hence Antino·mic, -al *a.* of, pertaining to, or characterized by a.

Anti-odontalgic (æ:nti,odǫntæ·ldʒik), *a.* 1817. [Anti- 3.] *Med.* Of use against toothache. Also as *sb.*

Anti-orgastic (æ:nti,ǫɪgæ·stik), *a.* 1880. [f. Anti- 3 + Gr. *ὀργαστικός, f. ὀργά-ειν.] *Med.* Allaying excitement, sedative.

Antiparallel (ænti,pæ·rălĕl). *rare.* 1660. †1. Parallel but opposed. 2. *Geom. pl.* Two lines which make with two other lines angles equal each to each, but contrary ways, one being exterior and the other interior 1796.

Antiparalytic, -al (æ:nti,pærăli·tik, -ăl), *a.* 1755. [Anti- 3.] *Med.* Of use against paralysis. Also as *sb.*

Antiparliame·ntary, *a.* 1643. [Anti- 3.] 1. Opposed to (the Long) Parliament or the parliamentary party. *Obs.* or *Hist.* vars. †**Antiparliame·ntal, Antiparliame·ntarian.** 2. Against parliamentary usage 1656.

†**Antiparliamentee·r.** 1643. [Cf. *pamphleteer.*] A writer or speaker against (the Long) Parliament.

Antipathetic, -al (æ̆ntipăþe·tik, -ăl), *a.* 1601. [ad. Gr. *ἀντιπαθητικός, f. ἀντιπαθέ-ειν; cf. παθητικός.] Having an antipathy or constitutional aversion; opposed in nature or tendency (*to*). Hence **Antipathe·tically** *adv.* var. †**Anti·pathous.**

Antipathic (ænti,pæ·þik), *a.* 1830. [ad. Fr. *antipathique*; see Antipathy.] Of or belonging to antipathy; of contrary nature or character (*to*); *spec.* in *Med.* having or producing the contrary symptoms.

Antipathist (æ̆nti·păþist). *rare.* 1817. [f. Antipathy + -ist.] One possessed by an antipathy; a natural enemy.

Antipathize (æ̆nti·păþəiz), *v.* ? *Obs. rare.* 1633. [f. Antipathy + -ize; the opposite of *sympathize.*] 1. *intr.* To feel the opposite. 2. *trans.* To render antipathetic 1667.

Antipathy (æ̆nti·paþi). 1601. [ad. L. *antipathia*, a. Gr., f. ἀντιπαθής, f. ἀντί + πάθος.] †1. Contrariety of feeling, disposition, or nature; natural incompatibility. Opp. to *sympathy.* –1692. 2. Feeling against; constitutional or settled aversion 1606. 3. *concr.* That which is †contrary in nature, or the object of antipathy 1622.

1. No contraries hold more a., Then I, and such a knaue *Lear* II. ii. 93. 2. A Sect, whose chief Devotion lies In odd perverse Antipathies Butler.

Antipendium, incorr. form of Ante-.

Antiperiodic (æ:nti,piəri,ǫ·dik), *a.* 1861. [Anti- 3.] *Med.* Destroying the periodicity of diseases that run a typical course.

Antiperistaltic (æ:nti,peristæ·ltik), *a.* 1706. [Anti- 3.] *Phys.* Contrary to peristaltic motion; acting upwards.

Antiperistasis (æ:nti,pĕri·stăsis). *arch.* 1598. [L., a. Gr., f. ἀντί + περίστασις.] Opposition or contrast of circumstances; resistance or reaction roused against any action.

Having their penury doubled by the a. of others plenty Fuller. Hence **A:ntiperista·tic, -al** *a.* heightened by contrast, **-ally** *adv.* (*rare*).

Antipestilential (æ:nti,pestile·nʃăl), *a.* 1683. [Anti- 3.] *Med.* Of use against the plague, etc. Also as *sb.*

A. pills De Foe.

Antipha·rmic, *a.* 1853. [f. Anti- 3.] *Med.* = Alexipharmic.

Antiphlogistian (æ:nti,flodʒi·stiăn), *a.* 1788. [Anti- 3 + Gr. φλογιστόν + -ian.] Opposed to the theory of phlogiston, or the existence of an element of pure fire. As *sb.* An opponent of this theory.

Antiphlogistic (æ:nti,flodʒi·stik), *a.* 1744. [f. as prec. + -ic; cf. *phlogistic.*] 1. = prec. adj. 1788. 2. *Med.* Counteracting inflammation 1769; also *fig.* (*rare*) 1840. As *sb.* [sc. *medicinal agent.*] 1744.

2. *fig.* A cooling a. speech Hood.

Antiphlogistin (æ:nti,flodʒi·stin). 1901. [f. as prec. + -in [1].] A proprietary preparation used as an anodyne, antiseptic, and antiphlogistic.

Antiphon (æ·ntifǒn). 1500. [ad. med.L. *antiphona*, as sb. fem. sing. repr. Gr. τὰ ἀντίφωνα, neut. pl., f. ἀντί + -φωνος, f. φωνή. See Anthem.] 1. A versicle or sentence sung by one choir in response to another 1652. 2. = Anthem 1. 1500. 3. *techn.* A short piece of plain-song introduced before a psalm or canticle, the meaning of which it illustrates and enforces 1775. 4. *transf.* A response, answer 1651.

Antiphonal (æ̆nti·fǒnăl), *a.* 1691. [a. OFr., ad. ? med.L. *antiphonalis*; see prec.] 1. Of the nature of an antiphon; sung alternately 1719. 2. Responsive in sound, or (*transf.*) other effect 1848. As *sb.* = Antiphonary 1691.

1. A. singing was first brought into the church of Milan Bingham. Hence **Anti·phonally** *adv.* So **Antipho·nic** *a.* mutually responsive. **Antipho·nically** *adv.*

Antiphonary (æ̆nti·fǒnări). 1681. [ad. med. L. *antiphonarium*; see Antiphon.] A book of antiphons. vars. †**Anti·phonar, Anti·phoner** (the earliest word).

Antiphony (ænti·fǒni). 1592. [f. Gr. *ἀντιφωνία, after συμφωνία. Confused with Antiphon in use.] 1. Opposition of sound; or harmony produced by it 1603. 2. = Antiphon 1. 1592. 3. Antiphonal singing. Also *fig.* 1753. 4. *concr.* = Antiphon 2. 1868. †5. = Antiphon 3. –1753. 6. *transf.* A response or echo 1657.

3. Life answering life across the vast profound In full a. Mrs. Browning. 6. The eccho or a., which these..exclaimers hope..to draw..from their audience Shaftesbury.

‖**Antiphrasis** (æ̆nti·frăsis). 1533. [L., a. Gr., f. ἀντιφράζειν.] *Rhet.* Use of words in a sense opposite to their proper meaning.

You are pastors, but it is by an a., *a minime pascendo* Cromwell. Hence **Antiphra·stic** *a.*, **-ally** *adv.*

Antiphthisic (ænti,ti·zik), *a.* 1853. [Anti- 3.] *Med.* Tending to check phthisis. Also as *sb.*

Antiplastic (ænti,plæ·stik), *a.* [f. Anti- 3 + πλαστικός, f. πλάσσειν.] *Med.* Unfavourable to the process of healing or granulation. Also used of medicines which impoverish the blood.

Antipleuritic (æ:nti,pluri·tik), *a.* 1712. [Anti- 3.] Of use against pleurisy. Also as *sb.*

Antipodagric, -al (æ:nti,podæ·grik, -ăl), *a.* 1712. [Anti- 3.] *Med.* Of use against gout. Also as *sb.*

Antipodal (æ̆nti·pǒdăl), *a.* 1646. [f. Antipodes.] 1. Of or pertaining to the Antipodes. 2. *transf.* Directly opposite (*to*) 1664.

Antipodean (æ̆nti:pǒdī·ăn), *a.* 1651. [irreg. f. Antipodes, perh. after *European.*] 1. Of or pertaining to the opposite side of the world; *esp.* Australasian 1861. 2. *joc.* Having everything upside down 1852. 3. *fig.* Diametrically opposed (*to*) 1651. var. †**Antipo·dian** (better).

Antipodes (æ̆nti·pǒdīz), *sb. pl.* ME. [a. L., a. Gr. (οἱ) ἀντίποδες, those having the feet opposite. Sing. *-pod, -pode*, quite regularly, f. *antipod(e)s* (trisyllabic); also †*antipos.*] †1. Those who dwelt directly opposite to each other on the globe, as it were feet against feet –1837. †2. *fig.* Those who in any way resemble the dwellers on the opposite side of the globe 1605. 3. Places on the surface of the earth directly opposite to each other, or the place which is directly opposite to another (*esp.* to our own region) 1549. 4. *transf.* The exact opposite of a person or thing. (With sing. *antipode.*) 1641. †5. As adv. (sb. in apposition) in *To walk antipodes to*, etc. –1718.

2. He will neuer be one of the A., to tread opposite to the present world Bacon. 3. I will goe on the slightest arrand now to the Antypodes *Much Ado* II. i. 273. 4. Fools..are a. unto the wise Sir T. Browne. *At antipodes*: in direct opposition. Hence **Anti·podist**, a believer in the antipodes (when the belief was heresy); as *adj.* = Antipodal. †**Anti·podite**, an inhabitant of the antipodes.

Antipole (æ·nti,pōᵘl). 1822. [Anti- 2.] The opposite pole. *fig.* The direct opposite.

Antipope (æ·nti,pōᵘp). 1579. [orig. a. Fr. *antipape*, ad. med.L. *antipapa*, after *antichristus.*] A pope elected in opposition to one held to be canonically chosen; *spec.* of those who resided at Avignon during 'the great schism of the West'. (So called by adversaries.)

Antipruritic (ænti,pruri·tik), *a.* 1876. [f. Anti- 3 + L. *pruritis* + -ic.] *Med.* Tending to relieve itching.

Antipsoric (æntipsǫ·rik), *a.* 1853. [f. Anti- 3 + Gr. ψώρα + -ic.] *Med.* Of use against the itch. Also as *sb.*

‖**Antipto·sis.** 1657. [med.L., a. Gr., f. ἀντί + πτῶσις.] *Gram.* The use of one case for another.

Antipyic (ænti,pəi·ik), *a.* 1853. [ad. Fr. *antipyique*, f. Gr. ἀντί + πύον; see -ic.] *Med.* Tending to prevent suppuration. Also as *sb.*

Antipyretic (æ:nti,pire·tik), *a.* 1681. [f. Anti- 3 + Gr. πυρετός; cf. *pyretic.*] *Med.* Tending to prevent fever. Also as *sb.*

Antipyrotic (æ:nti,pirǫ·tik), *a.* 1839. [f. Anti- 3 + Gr. πυρωτικός.] *Med.* Of use against burns. As *sb.* Anything so used.

Antiquarian (ænti,kwēᵊ·riăn), *a.* 1610. [f. L. *antiquarius* (see Antiquary) + -an.] 1. Of or connected with the study of antiquities 1771. 2. Applied to a large size of drawing paper 1875. 3. As *sb.* [The adj. used *absol.*] An antiquary 1610.

1. A. researches Freeman. Hence **Antiqua·rianism**, the profession, etc., of the a. **Antiqua·rianize** *v. colloq.* to play the a. **Antiqua·rianly** *adv.* (*rare*).

‖**Antiqua·rium.** *rare.* 1881. [L., neut. of adj.] A repository of antiquities.

Antiquary (æ·nti,kwări). 1563. [ad. L. *antiquarius*, f. *antiquus*; see Antique.] **A.** *adj.* Of antiquity; ancient (*rare*) 1606.

Here's Nestor Instructed by the A. times *Tr. & Cr.* II. iii. 262.

B. *sb.* [sc. *man, thing.*] †1. A man of great age –1635. †2. An official custodian or recorder of antiquities. (A title bestowed by Hen. VIII upon Leland.) –1763. 3. A professed student, or collector, of antiquities. (*Orig.* a student of early history, *now* opp. to *archæologist.*) 1586.

3. Antiquaries, who hold everything worth preserving, merely because it has been preserved 1762.

Antiquate (æ·nti,kwĕt), *ppl. a. arch.* 1537. [ad. L. *antiquatus, antiquare*; see Antique.] = Antiquated.

Antiquate (æ·nti,kweᶦt), *v.* 1596. [f. prec.] 1. To make old, or obsolete; to abolish as out of date. 2. To give an antique colour or appearance to 1821.

1. He [the Pope] antiquates the precepts of Christ Marvell. Hence **Antiqua·tion**, the action of making, or state of being, antiquated; abolition; the production of an appearance of age.

Antiquated (æ·nti,kweᶦtĕd), *ppl. a.* 1623. [f. prec.] 1. Grown old, inveterate 1670. 2. Obsolete 1623. 3. So old as to be unworthy to survive; often 'old-world' 1692. 4. Old-fashioned, as surviving from, or as imitating, earlier usage 1675. 5. Of persons: Very old, superannuated. Also *fig.* 1678.

1. A. prejudices Burke. 2. Reviving a. laws 1695. 3. Deride..the a. folly Bentley. 4. A. phraseology Freeman. 5. [An] a. Sybil Addison.

Antique (æ̆ntī·k, æ·ntik). 1530. [ad. L. *antiquus, anticus*, f. *ante*, or immed. f. Fr. Antic is a parallel form, distinct in sense. In senses 1, 2 (æ·ntik) is still used in poetry; 4–6 are always, 3 usually (æ̆ntī·k). See Antic.] **A.** *adj.* 1. Ancient, olden. (Now usu. rhet. = of the 'good old times'.) 1541. 2. Having existed since olden times; aged, venerable (*arch.*) 1536. 3. Old-fashioned; out of date. 1647. 4. Of, belonging to, or after the manner of the ancients (of Greece and Rome) 1734; or of any ancient time, archaic 1753. 5. *Bookbinding.* See Antique *v.* 6. *Typogr.* Of a type in which all the lines are of uniform thickness 1871.

1. The anticke world Spenser. The Senatours of th' antique Rome *Hen. V*, v. Prol. 26. 2. In place of things of antick use Butler *Hud.* II. i. 792. Antique walls Gibbon. 4. A group that's quite a., Half naked, loving, natural, and Greek Byron.

B. *sb.* [The adj. used *ellipt.*; sc. *man, thing.*] †1. A man of ancient times; *pl.* the Ancients –1598. 2. A relic of ancient art, or of the past 1530. 3. *The antique*: ancient work in art, antique style 1751.

2. Pictures, medals, intaglios, and antiques of all kinds Goldsm. 3. Drawing from the a. 1859. Hence **Anti·quely** *adv.* †anciently; in an a. manner. **Anti·queness.** **Anti·quish** *a.* (*rare*).

Antique, occ. sp. of Antic in 16–17th c.

Antique (æ̆ntī·k), *v.* 1753. [f. the adj.] To bind (books) after an antique manner, by ornamenting the edges with ramifications, etc.

Antiquist (æ·ntikwist, æ̆ntī·kist). *rare.* 1784. [f. ANTIQUE.] †An antiquary; a collector or connoisseur of antiques.

Antiquitarian (æntiˌkwitēᵊ·riăn). 1641. [f. ANTIQUITY; cf. *humanitarian.*] One attached to the practices or opinions of antiquity.

Antiquity (æ̆nti·kwĭti). ME. [a. Fr. *antiquité*, ad. L. *antiquitatem*; see ANTIQUE.] 1. The quality of being ancient; long standing 1450. †2. Old age (of human life); seniority –1677. 3. Ancient character 1850. **Elliptical senses. 4. The time of antiquity; *esp.* the time of the ancient Greeks and Romans ME. 5. The people (or writers, etc.) of ancient times collectively; the Ancients 1538. 6. (Now *pl.* or *collect.*) Matters, customs, precedents, etc., of earlier times; ancient records 1557. 7. (Now usu. *pl.*) Relics, or monuments of antiquity 1513. Also *attrib.*

2. Is not your voice broken?..and euery part about you blasted with A. 2 *Hen. IV*, I. ii. 208. 3. [An] air of a. M. MÜLLER. 4. A. is like fame, *caput inter nubila condit* BACON. 5. That indigested heap, and frie of Authors, which they call A. MILT. 7. Antiquities are history defaced, or some remnants of history which have escaped the shipwreck of time BACON.

Antirachitic (æ:ntiˌrăki·tik), *a.* 1853. [f. ANTI- 3 + Gr. ῥαχῖτις + -IC.] *Med.* Tending to cure spinal disease.

Antirrhinum (æntĭrəi·nŏm). Pl. **-s.** 1551. [a. L., a. Gr. ἀντίρρινον, f. ἀντί + ῥίς.] *Bot.* A genus of Scrophulariaceous plants, also called Snapdragon.

A. or Calves-snout 1741.

Antisabbatarian (æ:ntiˌsæbătēᵊ·riăn), *a.* 1645. [ANTI- 3, 5.] Opposed to the observance of the Sabbath by Christians. Also as *sb.*

‖**Antiscii** (æ̆nti·siˌəi, -i·ʃiˌəi), *sb. pl.* 1706. [L., a. late Gr., f. ἀντί + σκιά.] Those who live on the same meridian, but on opposite sides of the equator, so that their shadows fall at noon in opposite directions. Hence **Anti·scian** *a.* of or pertaining to the Antiscii; *sb.* (*pl.*) = ANTISCII.

Antiscion (æ̆nti·ʃiɒn). 1658. [f. as prec.] *Astrol.* Applied to signs of the Zodiac equidistant on opposite sides from Cancer and Capricorn.

Antiscolic (æntiˌskɒ·lik), *a.* 1880. [irreg. f. ANTI- 3 + Gr. σκώληξ + -IC.] *Med.* = ANTHELMINTIC.

Antiscorbutic (æntiˌskɒɪbiū·tik), *a.* 1696. [ANTI- 3.] Of use against scurvy. Also as *sb.*

Antiscriptural (æntiˌskri·ptiŭrăl), *a.* 1677. [ANTI- 3.] Opposed to Holy Scripture.

Antiscrofulous (æntiˌskrɒ·fiŭləs), *a.* 1880. [ANTI- 3.] *Med.* Of use against scrofula.

Antisepalous (æntiˌse·păləs), *a.* 1879. [f. Gr. ἀντί + SEPAL + -OUS.] *Bot.* Placed opposite to the sepals.

‖**Antisepsis** (æntiˌse·psis). 1875. [mod.L., f. Gr. ἀντί + σῆψις.] *Med.* The principle of antiseptic surgical treatment.

Antiseptic (æntiˌse·ptik), *a.* 1751. [f. ANTI- 3 + σηπτικός, f. σήπειν.] Counteracting putrefaction; *fig.* preventing moral decay 1820. Also as *sb.* (*lit.* and *fig.*).

A. bandages TYNDALL. *fig.* Not divine men, yet useful a. products of their generation CARLYLE. Hence **Antise·ptically** *adv.* **Antise·pticist**, one who believes in ANTISEPSIS.

Antisocial (æntiˌsōᵘ·ʃăl), *a.* 1797. [ANTI- 3.] 1. Opposed to society or companionship. 2. Opposed to the principles on which society is constituted 1849.

Antispasmodic (æ:ntiˌspæzmɒ·dik), *a.* 1681. [ANTI- 3.] Good against spasms. Also as *sb.*

Antispast (æ·ntiˌspæst). 1706. [ad. Gr. ἀντίσπαστος, f. ἀντισπά-ειν.] *Pros.* A metrical foot composed of an iambus and a trochee, as Ἀλέξανδρος.

Antispastic (æntiˌspæ·stik), *a.* 1541. [ad. Gr. ἀντισπαστικός; see prec.] 1. *Med.* Tending to divert. 2. *Pros.* Consisting of, or containing, antispasts 1811. 3. As *sb. Med.* An a. agent 1719.

Antisplenetic (æ:ntiˌsplĭne·tik), *a.* 1734. [ANTI- 3.] *Med.* Good against disease of the spleen. Also as *sb.*

‖**Antistrophe** (æ̆nti·strŏfĭ). 1605. [L., a. Gr., f. ἀντιστρέφειν.] 1. The returning movement, from left to right, in Greek choruses and dances, answering to the strophe; the lines of choral song recited during this movement; any choral response 1619. 2. An inverse correspondence 1605. 3. *Rhet.*, etc. a. Repetition of words in inverse order. b. The figure of retort, or turning an opponent's plea against him 1625.

2. An inverse correspondence with the Nile (north and south, therefore, as the a. of south and north) DE QUINCEY. Hence **Antistro·phic** *a.* of or pertaining to antistrophes; *sb.* (*pl.*) the lyrical part of Greek dramas. **Antistro·phically** *adv.* (*rare*). **Anti·strophize** *v.* (*rare*), to form an a.

‖**Antistrophon** (æ̆nti·strŏfŏn). 1611. [Gr., neut. sing., f. as prec.] *Rhet.* An argument that is retorted upon an opponent.

Antistruma·tic. 1676. [see next.] *Med. adj.* = next. *sb.* A remedy for scrofula.

Antistrumous (æntiˌstrū·məs), *a.* 1861. [f. ANTI- 3 + L. *struma* + -OUS.] *Med.* Tending to cure scrofula.

Antisyphilitic (æ:ntiˌsifĭli·tik), *a.* 1830. [ANTI- 3.] Of use against syphilis. Also as *sb.*

Antitetanic (æ:ntiˌtĭtæ·nik), *a.* 1875. [ANTI- 3.] *Med.* Good against tetanus. Also as *sb.*

Antithalian (æntiˌþēᵊ·liăn), *a.* [f. ANTI- 3 + *Thalia*, the Grace of festivities.] Opposed to festivity.

Antitheism (æntiˌþī·iz'm). 1833. [ANTI- 8.] The doctrine of antitheists.

Antitheist (æntiˌþī·ist). 1860. [ANTI- 5.] One opposed to belief in the existence of a God. Hence **A:ntithei·stic** *a.*

Antithesis (æ̆nti·þĭsis). Pl. **antitheses.** 1529. [a. L., a. Gr., f. ἀντί + τιθέναι. Already in Gr. a term of Logic, etc.] 1. *Rhet.* An opposition or contrast of ideas, expressed by using in contiguous sentences or clauses, words which are strongly contrasted with each other; as '*thou* shalt *wax*, and *he* shall *dwindle*'. 2. The second of two such opposed clauses; a counter-thesis 1533. 3. By extension: Direct opposition (between two things); contrast. Const. *of, between,* †*with.* 1631. 4. The opposite. Const. *of, to.* 1831.

1. All arm'd with points, antitheses, and puns POPE. 3. The a. of natural and revealed religion KINGSLEY. 4. The very a. to a great dramatist MACAULAY. Hence **Anti·thesize** *v.* to form antitheses or put into a. (*rare*). **Anti·thesizer** (*rare*).

Antithet (æ·ntiþet). 1580. [ad. L. *antitheton*, a. Gr., neut. of adj.; see prec. Long used in Gr. and L. form, pl. -a (erron. -as).] †1. = ANTITHESIS 1. –1610. 2. An antithetic statement 1605.

Antithetic (æntiþe·tik), *a.* 1610. [ad. Gr. ἀντιθετικός; see prec. and -IC.] That is of the nature of antithesis, *esp.* in *Rhet.*; directly opposite 1864. 2. Consisting of two opposites 1842.

2. The dual or a. character of force involved in the term polarity W. GROVE. So **Antithe·tical** *a.* connected with, containing, or using antithesis; marked by direct opposition 1583. **Antithe·tically** *adv.*

Antitoxin (æntitɒ·ksin). 1892. [ANTI- 2 b.] A substance having the property of counteracting a toxin.

Anti-trade (æ·ntiˌtrē¹d), *attrib. phr.* and *sb.* 1853. [ANTI- 2.] A wind that blows steadily in the opposite direction to the trade-wind.

‖**Antitragus** (æ:ntiˌtrē¹·gŏs). 1842. [ANTI- 2.] *Anat.* The thicker part of the antihelix, opposite to the tragus.

Antitrinitarian (æ:ntiˌtrinĭtēᵊ·riăn). 1641. [ANTI- 3.] *adj.* Opposed to the doctrine of the Trinity 1665. *sb.* One who rejects that doctrine 1641. Hence **Antitrinita·rianism.**

Antitropal (æ̆nti·trŏpăl), *a.* 1855. [f. Gr. ἀντί + -τροπος + -AL¹.] *Bot.* Of an embryo: Inverted, so as to have the radicle at the extremity of the seed, opposite to the hilum. So **Anti·tropous.**

Antitype (æ·ntiˌtəip). 1635. [ad. med.L. *antitypus*, a. Gr. ἀντίτυπος, f. ἀντί + τύπος.] That which is represented by the type or symbol. Hence **A·ntitypal** *a.* (*rare*). **Antity·pical** *a.* of the nature of or pertaining to an a.

†**Anti·typous**, *a. rare.* 1678. [f. Gr. ἀντίτυπος; see prec.] Resisting force; material, solid.

Antitypy (æ̆nti·tĭpi). *rare.* 1605. [ad. Gr. ἀντιτυπία.] Resistance of matter to force of penetration, compression, or motion.

Antivariolous (æ:ntiˌvărəi·ŏləs), *a.* 1880. [ANTI- 3.] *Med.* Good against small-pox.

Antivenereal (æ:ntiˌvĭnīᵊ·riăl), *a.* 1676. [ANTI- 3.] *Med.* Of use against venereal disease.

A:ntivermi·cular, *a.* 1717. [ANTI- 3.] = ANTIPERISTALTIC.

Antizymic (æntiˌzi·mik), *a.* 1804. [f. ANTI- 3 + Gr. ζύμη + -IC.] Opposing fermentation. *sb.* An a. substance.

Antizymotic (æ:ntiˌzimɒ·tik, -zəimɒ·tik). 1875. [f. ANTI- 3 + Gr. ζυμωτικός.] *adj.* = prec. *sb.* A substance that prevents fermentation.

Antler (æ·ntləɹ). [ME. *auntolier, auntelere*, a. OFr. *antoillier*:—late L. **ant(e)ocularem* (*ramum*); cf. Ger. *augensprosse.* An earlier **antoglier*, later OFr. *andoillier*, gave *andouiller.*] 1. *orig.* The lowest (forward-directed) branch of the horn of a stag, etc.; later, any branch, the lowest being then the *brow-antler*, and the next *bes-antler.* 2. Hence *pop.*: The branched horn of a stag, etc. 1829.

1. Huge stags with sixteen antlers MACAULAY. 2. A vaulted apartment garnished with stags' antlers SCOTT. Hence **A·ntlerless** *a.* without antlers.

Antlered (æ·ntləɹd), *ppl. a.* 1818. [f. prec + -ED².] 1. Bearing antlers; adorned with stags' horns 1828. 2. *transf.* 1870.

1. An a. stag BRYANT, hall SCOTT. 2. A. fern DISRAELI.

‖**Antlia** (æ·ntliˌă). 1828. [L., a. Gr. ἀντλία bilge water, ἀντλίον a bucket.] *Ent.* The proboscis or haustellum of insects, with which they suck up juices. Hence **A·ntliate** *ppl. a.* furnished with an a.

A·nt-li:on. 1815. [tr. Gr. μυρμηκο-λέων, in the LXX.] A neuropterous insect, or genus of insects (*Myrmeleon*), the larva of which lies in wait for and devours ants.

Anto·cular, *a. rare.* 1870. [f. L. *ante* + *ocularis.* Cf. ANTLER.] Placed in front of the eye.

‖**Antœci** (æntī·səi), *sb. pl.* 1622. [L., a. Gr. ἄντοικοι, f. ἀντί + -οικος.] The dwellers under the same meridian, on opposite sides of the equator, and equally distant from it. Hence **Antœ·cian** *a.* of or belonging to the opposite latitude; *sb.* (*pl.*) = ANTŒCI.

‖**Antonomasia** (æ:ntŏnomē¹·ziă, æ̆ntɒ·no). 1589. [L., a. Gr., f. ἀντονομάζειν.] The substitution of an epithet, etc., or the name of an office or dignity, for a person's proper name, as *the Iron Duke* for Wellington. Also, conversely, the use of a proper name to express a general idea, as in calling a wise judge *a Daniel.* Hence **Antonoma·stically** *adv.* (*rare*).

Antonym (æ·ntŏnim). 1870. [f. Gr. ἀντωνυμία.] A term which is the opposite of another, a counter-term.

Antorbital, var. ANTE-ORBITAL.

Antozone (æntˌōᵘ·zōᵘn). 1862. [f. ANT- + OZONE.] *Chem.* A gaseous product, once supposed to be a permanently positive variety of oxygen, but now shown to be hydrogen dioxide H_2O_2. Hence **Anto·zonide.**

Anto·zonite. 1868. [f. prec. + -ITE.] *Min.* A dark violet-blue Fluorite.

Antral (æ·ntrăl), *a. rare.* 1880. [f. L. *antrum* + -AL¹.] Of the nature of, or pertaining to, a cavity.

Antre (æ·ntəɹ). 1604. [a. Fr.:—L. *antrum*, a. Gr. ἄντρον.] *poet.* A cave, a cavern.

Antars vast, and Desarts idle *Oth.* I. iii. 140.

Antrorse (æntrɒ̄·ɹs), *a.* 1858. [ad. mod.L. *antrorsus*, f. L. **antero-* + *versus*, after *extrorsus*, etc.] Bent forward or upward.

Antroversion (æntrovɔ̄·ɹʃən). 1880. [f. *antro-*, for *antero-* (see prec.) + L. *versionem.*] = ANTEVERSION.

Antrove·rt, *v. rare.* 1854. [f. as prec. + L. *vertere.*] To turn or bend forward.

‖**Antrum** (æ·ntrŏm). Pl. **-a.** ME. [L., a. Gr. ἄντρον.] A cavern; *spec.* in *Phys.* of cavities in the body.

‖**Antrustion** (æ̆ntrv·stiən). 1848. [a. Fr., or med.L. *antrustionem*, f. OHG. *trôst*, latinized as *trustis* + AND- prob. 'toward'.] A voluntary follower of Old Frankish princes at the period of the national migrations. Hence **Antru·s·tionship.**

A·ntsigne. 1576. Obs. f. ENSIGN, as if f. *ante* + *signum*.

A·nt-thru·sh. 1863. [ANT *sb.*] A bird of the Thrush family, which lives on ants, etc.

Anura, -ous, vars. of ANOURA, -OUS.

Anury (æ·niūri). 1876. [ad. mod.L. *anuria* (also used), f. Gr. ἀν + οὖρον. Cf. Fr. *anurie.*] *Path.* Absence or lack of urine.

‖**Anus** (ē¹·nɒs). 1658. [L.] **1.** The posterior opening of the alimentary canal, through which the excrements are ejected. **2.** An opening at the base of a flower 1730.

Anvil (æ·nvil), *sb.* [OE. *ǫnfilti*, f. *an, on*, perh. + **filtan* to weld. Cf. SILVER.] **1.** The block (usually of iron) on which the smith hammers and shapes his metal; also *fig.* **2.** *transf.* Anything like a smith's anvil in shape or use; esp. (*Phys.*) one of the bones of the ear, the incus 1687.

1. Bitwene þe anfelde and þe hamoure ME. Him that smote the anuill *Isa.* xli. 7. *fig.* Hammering me vpon the anvild CAMDEN. *On* or *upon the anvil*: in preparation, in hand; He has now on the a. another scheme BURKE.

Comb.: **a.-proof**, the standard of hardness of an a.; **-rock**, a kind of Sandstone, so named from the form of two masses of it in Kentucky.

A·nvil, *v.* 1607. [f. the sb.] **1.** *trans.* To fashion on an anvil; usu. *fig.* **2.** *intr.* To work at an anvil 1882.

Anxiety (æ̃ŋzəi·ěti). 1525. [ad. L. *anxietatem*; see ANXIOUS.] **1.** The quality or state of being ANXIOUS; solicitude, concern. **2.** Strained or solicitous desire (*for*, or *to effect*) 1769. **3.** *Path.* A condition of agitation and depression, with a sensation of tightness and distress in the præcordial region 1661.

1. There dyed he without grudge, without anxietie MORE. 2. A...for the general welfare JUNIUS.

Anxious (æ·ŋkʃəs), *a.* 1623. [f. L. *anxius*, f. *angere.*] **1.** Troubled in mind about some uncertain event; being in disturbing suspense; concerned, solicitous. Const. †*of, for, about* 1711. **2.** Fraught with trouble, distressing, worrying. (*Obs.* exc. as transf. use of 1.) 1667. **3.** Full of desire and endeavour (*to effect*) 1742.

1. A., and cast down 1636. A. for their own safety MACAULAY. 2. A. cares MILT. *P. L.* viii. 185. 3. A. to please BLAIR. Hence **A·nxious·ly** *adv.*, **-ness** (*rare*).

Any (e·ni), *a.* and *pron.* [OE. *ænig*, f. *án* one (in umlaut *ǽn*) + *ig, -ig*, adj. ending, here perh. dim.; cf. L. *ullus*:—**unulus.* The ME. forms, *eny, ei*, were south., *any* midl., *ony* midl. and north. Fem. and pl. forms in *-e* also existed in ME. The living mod.Eng. word is *eny.*] *Primarily adj.* **1.** *gen.* In *sing.* = A — no matter which, or what. In *pl.* = Some — no matter which, of what kind, or how many. **a.** Used primarily in interrog., hypothet., and condit. forms of speech OE. **b.** With a preceding neg.: = None at all, of any kind, etc., not even one OE. **c.** In affirm. sentences: = (constructively) *Every* one of the sort named ME. **2.** Quantitative: = A quantity or number however great or small 1526. **3.** Qualitative: Of any kind or sort whatever; = earlier ANY-KYNS. Occas. *depreciatory*: Any, however imperfect 1866. **4.** *absol.*, esp. after a sb. already expressed, or bef. *of* ME. †**5.** Either (of *two*). Still dial., esp. north. -1585. **6.** *pronominally.* = Any one, anybody; in *pl.* any persons OE. **7.** *adverbially*, esp. with comp. adjs., as *any sooner*, etc.: In any degree, at all ME. **8.** **Any one. a.** as *adj.* (e·ni wɒ·n) Any single; **b.** *absol.* as in 'any one of them'; **c.** *pron.* (e·ni,wɒn) Any person. ME. **9.** In *comb.* with interrog. wds., which then become indefinite.

1. a. Who wil shew vs any good *Ps.* iv. 6. b. Not to be done at any time BURKE. c. Any time these three hundred yeeres *Merry W.* I. i. 11. *At any rate, in any case*: whatever the circumstances may be. 2. Haue ye here eny meate *Luke* xxiv. 41. 4. If there be any of him left, Ile bury it *Wint. T.* III. iii. 136. 5. Anie of them both THYNNE. 6. Please they any, That serue many 1562. 7. Any longer SHAKS. more 1680, farther STEELE, the worse 1875.

Anybody (e·ni,bǫdi, -bǫ̆di), *sb.* or *pron.* 1490. **1.** comb. of ANY and BODY in the sense of *person*: Any person. See ANY *a.* 1. Formerly two words. **2.** Qualitative. **a.** In interrog. or hypothet. expressions, *laudatory*: a person of some importance. **b.** In affirm. expressions, *depreciatory*: an ordinary person. 1826.

1. If he doe..finde any body in the house *Merry W.* I. iv. 4. 2. Everybody was there who is a. DISRAELI. Two or three anybodies J. BRIGHT.

Anyhow (e·ni,hau). 1740. [see ANY 9.] **1.** *adv.* In any way or manner whatever. **2.** *advb. conj.* In any case, at least 1825.

1. Done a., no profitable one CARLYLE. 2. Any how, it must be acknowledged [etc.] NEWMAN.

†**Any-kyn, -s.** ME. only. [Orig. genitive phr. = 'of any kind', afterwards, with loss of *-s*, looking like an adj. = 'any kind of'.] Any kind or manner.

Anything (e·ni,þiŋ), *pron.*, *sb.*, *adv.* OE. **1.** *pron.* A comb. of ANY and THING, in the widest sense of the latter. See ANY *a.* Orig. always two words; now rarely exc. when stress is upon *thing.* **2.** *sb.* Thing of any kind 1596. **3.** *adv.* Any whit, in any measure OE.

1. If ye shall ask any thing in my name, I will do it *John* xiv. 14. 2. She is my house..my oxe, my asse, my a. *Tam. Shr.* III. ii. 234. 3. Yf my lady your wyf come ony thyng nyghe yowe CAXTON. Hence **A·nythinga·rian** [after *trinitarian*, etc.], one who professes no creed in particular. (A contemptuous term.)

Anyway (e·ni,weⁱ), *adv.* and *conj.* 1570. [cf. ANYWAYS, and *always, alway.*] **1.** *adv.* In any way or manner, anyhow; in any measure. **2.** *advb. conj.* In any case 1859.

1. Anything that sauoureth any way of newnesse BIBLE *Transl.* Pref. 1.

Anyways (e·ni,weⁱz). 1560. [ANY + *ways*, advb. genitive, as in ALWAYS.] = prec. 1, 2.

Anywhen (e·ni,hwe·n), *adv.* 1831. [see ANY 9.] At any time, ever. *Rare* in literature.

†**A·nywhence,** *adv. rare.* 1613. [see ANY 9.] From anywhere.

Anywhere (e·ni,hwēᵊɹ, -hwē̆ɹ). ME. [see ANY 9. Preceded by *owhere, aywhere* -1485.] In any place. Formerly two words.

Anywhither (e·ni,hwi:ðəɹ), *adv. arch.* 1611. [see ANY 9. Preceded by *owhither.*] To or towards any place.

Anywise (e·ni,waiz), *adv.* OE. [for *in any wise* (also used); OE. *ǽniȝe wisan.*] In any manner, way, or case; at all.

Any law or usage to the contrary hereof in a. notwithstanding 1775.

Aonian (e,ōᵘ·niăn), *a.* 1607. Of or belonging to Aonia, a region of ancient Bœotia, containing the mountains Helicon and Cithaeron, sacred to the Muses or 'Aonian maids'.

Above th' Aonian mount MILT. *P. L.* I. 15.

Aorist (ē·ŏrist), *a.* 1581. [ad. Gr. ἀόριστος, f. ἀ + ὁριστός, f. ὁρίζειν.] *Gram.* One of the past tenses of the Gr. verb, which denotes a simple past occurrence, with none of the limitations of the other past tenses. Hence **Aori·stic** *a.* undefined; of or pertaining to the aorist tense. **Aori·stically** *adv.*

Aorta (e,ǭ·ɹtă). 1594. [a. mod.L., a. Gr. ἀορτή, *lit.* that which is hung, f. ἀείρειν.] *Phys.* The great artery or trunk of the arterial system, from its origin in the left ventricle of the heart to its division into the two iliac arteries. Hence **Ao·rtal, Ao·rtic** *adjs.*

Ap-, *pref.*[1] = L. *ad-* bef. initial *p-*. In OFr. *ad-, ap-* became *a-*, and in this form the Fr. wds. were adopted in Eng., as *a-part, a-ply*, etc. Later the *p* was again doubled, after L. See AD- *pref.* 2, A- *pref.* 10.

Ap-, *pref.*[2] = Gr. ἀπ', short for ἀπό off.

Ap-, *pref.*[3] [Welsh *ap*, f. *map* son; cf. *Mac.*]

Apace (ăpē¹·s), *adv.* ME. [orig. phr. *a pace*, like *afoot*, etc., f. A *prep.*[1] + PACE, formerly *pas.*] *lit.* At a pace, *i.e.* at a good pace (orig. of the pace of men); *hence*, With speed; swiftly; †immediately -1723.

He commeth to hym apaas CHAUCER. Kings of armies did flee a. *Ps.* lxviii. 12. Like water yᵗ runneth a pace. Hoording wealth a. 1604. An ill weed growes a. 1611.

Apache (ăpæ·ʃ). 1902. [Fr., a. name of a warlike tribe of Amer. Indians.] A type of robber and assassin frequenting Paris, etc.; *gen.* a ruffian.

‖**Apagoge** (æpăgōᵘ·dʒi). 1727. [Gr., abduction, f. ἀπάγειν. A term of Aristotelian logic.] †**1.** *Logic.* = ABDUCTION. **2.** A demonstration which proves a thing by showing the impossibility or absurdity of denying it; a *reductio ad absurdum* 1753. †**3.** *Math.* The passage from one proposition, which has been demonstrated, to the proof of another 1753. Hence **Apago·gic, -al** *a.* of, pertaining to, or of the nature of a. **Apago·gically** *adv.*

Apaid (ăpē¹·d), *ppl. a. arch.* ME. [f. APAY *v.*] **1.** Satisfied, pleased. †**2.** Repaid -1748.

Apair, Apale, Apall; see APP-.

Apaise, apayse, obs. ff. APPEASE.

Apanage, app- (æ·pănėdʒ). 1602. [a. Fr., f. *apaner*:—L. **appanare*, f. *ad* + *panis*; see -AGE. Both forms are equally common.] **1.** The provision made for the maintenance of the younger children of kings, princes, etc.; orig. a province, jurisdiction, or office. **2.** *loosely*, A perquisite 1835. **3.** A dependent territory or property; a dependency 1807. **4.** *transf.* A specially appointed, or natural accompaniment, endowment, or attribute 1663.

2. The diplomatic service..the a. of the wealthy FREEMAN. 3. Ireland..the..appanage of our empire SYD. SMITH. 4. Had he thought it fit, That wealth should be the appenage of wit SWIFT. Hence **A·panaged** *ppl. a.* endowed with an a.

Apanthropy (æp,æ·nþrǒpi). *rare.* 1753. [ad. Gr. ἀπανθρωπία, f. ἀπ(ό) + ἄνθρωπος; cf. Fr. *apanthropie.*] A form of melancholy characterized by a dislike to society.

Apar-; see later APPAR-.

‖**A·parithme·sis.** 1753. [Gr.] *Rhet.* A figure: Enumeration.

Apart (ăpā·ɹt), *adv.* ME. [Fr. *à part*; like *a-side*, etc., in form, but the senses follow the Fr.] **1.** To one side, aside, to a place removed from the general body. **2.** Apart from each other; asunder ME. **3.** Separately in thought, or consideration 1577. **4.** Separately in action or function; individually ME. Also (with ellipsis of *standing*, etc.) = Separate. (Cf. Fr. *c'est un homme à part.*) 1786. **5.** *fig.* Aside, away from all employment, etc. (Fr. *mettre, laisser à part.*) (*arch.*) 1477. Also *absol.* as 'jesting apart' (Fr. *raillerie à part*) = Laid aside 1732. **6.** Away from common use for a special purpose 1604. Const. *from* (in all senses) 1617. *Rarely* prepositional (*from* omitted) 1615.

1. Get thee a-part and weepe *Jul. C.* III. i. 282. Judas being a. with the Elders 2 *Macc.* xiii. 13. 2. The Spartans lived in villages a. 1728. 3. Let us view each ingredient a. 1756. 4. Power..exercised either collectively, or a. and severally SELDEN. A class a. MACAULAY. 5. Lay a. all filthinesse *James* i. 21. 6. Places *set apart* for the worship of God 1680. A. this city, in the harbour CHAPMAN. Hence **Apa·rt** *v.* to set aside. **Apa·rtness,** aloofness.

Apartment (ăpā·ɹtmĕnt). 1641. [a. Fr. *appartement*, ad. med.L. *appartimentum*, f. *appartire*, f. L. *ad* + *partire.*] **1.** A suite of rooms in a house or building allotted to the use of an individual or party (*arch.*). **2.** A single room in a house; with pl. *apartments* in sense 1. 1715. †**3.** Quarters -1719. †**4.** A compartment -1727.

1. My a. consisted of three elegant..rooms GIBBON. 2. I stole..to the window of my a. SCOTT. 3. My Appartment in the tree DE FOE *Crusoe* 54. Hence **Apa·rtme·ntal** *a.* (*rare*).

†**Apa·ss,** *v.* ME. [a. OFr. *apasser*, f. *à* + *passer.*] To pass on or by. Rarely *trans.*

Apathaton, corrupt f. *epitheton.* SHAKS.

Apathetic, -al (æpăþe·tik, -ăl), *a.* 1744. [f. APATHY, after PATHETIC, + -AL.] Of, or pertaining to, apathy; unemotional; indifferent. Hence **Apathe·tically** *adv.*

Apathist (æ·păþist). *rare.* 1640. [See APATHY and -IST.] One addicted to apathy.

A·pathize, *v. rare.* [mod. f. as prec. + -IZE.] To render insensible.

Apathy (æ·păþi). 1603. [a. Fr. *apathie*, ad. L. *apathia*, a. Gr. ἀπάθεια, f. ἀπαθής, f. ἀ + παθε- (πάθος).] **1.** Freedom from, or insensibility to, suffering, passion, or feeling; passionless existence. **2.** Indolence of mind, indifference to what normally excites emotion or interest 1733. Also *transf.* (of the markets, etc.) 1881.

1. A. was considered by the Stoics as the highest condition of Humanity LEWES. 2. A certain a., or sluggishness in his nature PRESCOTT.

Apatite (æ·pătait). 1803. [f. Gr. ἀπάτη + -ITE; from the deceiving forms of the mineral.] *Min.* A native crystallized phosphate of lime, varying in colour from white to green, blue, violet, brown; transparent, translucent, or opaque. Also *transf.*

Apay (ăpēⁱ), *v. arch.* ME. [a. OFr. *apayer*, f. late L. **adpacare*, f. *ad*+*pacare* (cf. APPEASE and PAY). Refash. as *appay*; see AP- *pref.* 1.] **1.** To satisfy, content (*arch.*). †**2.** To repay –1631.

Ape (ēⁱp), *sb.* [OE. *apa* m., *ape* f.; prob. an adopted word in OTeut.] **1.** An animal of the monkey tribe (*Simiadæ*); the generic name before 'monkey', and still occas. so used, esp. with reference to their resemblance to, and mimicry of, men. **2.** *spec.* A member of the *Simiadæ*, having no tail nor cheek-pouches; as the gorilla, chimpanzee, orang-outan, and gibbons 1699. **3.** *fig.* One who plays the ape; an imitator, a mimic. Usu. contemptuous. ME. †**4.** *transf.* A fool –1741. †**5.** as *adj.* Foolish –1509.

1. Apes With foreheads villanous low *Temp.* IV. i. 249. 2. An a., properly so called, is without a tail 1764. 3. O sleepe, thou A. of death *Cymb.* II. ii. 31. 4. *God's ape*: a natural born fool. The titled a., her husband RICHARDSON.

Phrases: *To play the ape*: to imitate (badly). †*To make any one his ape, to put an ape in his hood*: to befool or dupe him. CHAUCER. *To lead apes in hell*: the supposed consequence of dying an old maid. *To say an ape's paternoster*: to chatter with cold.

Comb., etc.: †**a.-bearer, -carrier**, a strolling buffoon, who carried a monkey about; †**-leader**, an old maid, see Phrases; **Sea Ape**: the fish *Squalus Vulpes*, Sea Fox, or Thresher. Hence **A·pedom** (*rare*). **A·pehood.**

Ape (ēⁱp), *v.* 1632. [f. the sb.] To imitate, *esp.* absurdly.

To a. the sprightliness of wit JOHNSON. Art..doth a. nature 1663. Hence **Aped** *ppl. a.* counterfeit. **A·per** (*rare*).

A-peak (ăpīˑk), *adv.* (*a.*) 1596. [a. Fr. *à pic*; see PEAK, PIKE.] *Naut.* In a vertical position; vertical. Also *fig.*

A *ship* drawn directly over the anchor is *apeak*; the *anchor* is *apeak* when the cable has been sufficiently hove in to bring the ship over it. *Oars apeak*: held vertically.

Apel-; see later sp. APPEL-.

Apelles (ăpeˑlīz). 1630. A Gr. painter in the time of Alexander the Great; occas. (connotatively) = a master artist.

Apen-; see later sp. APPEN-.

Apepsy (ăpeˑpsi). 1678. [ad. mod.L. *apepsia* (also used), a. Gr., f. ἀ + πέπτειν.] *Med.* Lack of digestive power.

Aper-; see later sp. APPER-.

‖**Aperçu** (apersüˑ). 1882. [Fr.] A summary exposition, a conspectus.

Aperient (ăpīᵊˑriĕnt), *a.* 1626. [ad. L. *aperientem, aperire* (orig. *ăperire*), f. *ā* = *ab* + *par(i)ere* to get; cf. Eng. *undo.*] *Med.* Opening the bowels; laxative. Also as *sb.*

‖**Aperitif** (aperitīf). 1894. [F. *apéritif*:—L. *aperitivus*, f. *aperire* to open.] An alcoholic drink taken before a meal as an appetizer.

Aperitive (ăpeˑrĭtiv), *a.* and *sb.* 1582. [var. of *apertive*; see APERT.] = APERIENT *a.* and *sb.*

A per se, apersee; see A (the letter).

Apert (ăpēˑɹt). *arch.* ME. [a. OFr.:—L. *apertum, aperire*; see APERIENT. Aphet. PERT.] *adj.* Open, public ME.; †evident –1674; †expert –1483; †outspoken, insolent (cf. PERT) –1688. †*adv.* Openly, plainly, publicly –1556. Hence †**Ape·rtion**, the action of opening; an opening. **Ape·rtive** *a.* †open; also = APERIENT. **Ape·rtness**, the quality of being open; †plainness of speech.

Ape·rtly, *adv.* ? *Obs.* ME. [f. prec. + -LY ².] Openly; evidently; boldly.

Aperto·meter. 1880. [f. L. *apertus* + (-o)-METER.] An appliance attached to a microscope for measuring the angular aperture of object-glasses.

Aperture (æˑpəɹtiŭɹ). 1649. [ad. L. *apertura.*] †**1.** The process of opening –1708. **2.** An opening; a gap, cleft, chasm, or hole 1665. **3.** *Opt.* The space through which light passes in any optical instrument. Also *attrib.* 1664. **4.** *Geom.* The space included within two right lines which meet in a point and make an angle 1706.

Apery (ēⁱˑpəri). 1616. [f. APE *sb.*, or APER.] **1.** The practice of an aper, aping 1616; a silly or apish action 1851. **2.** A collection or colony of apes 1862.

2. More apish than all the apes of all aperies KINGSLEY.

Apet-; see later sp. APPET-.

Apetaloid (ăpeˑtăloid), *a.* 1870. [f. as next + -OID.] *Bot.* Of apetalous form.

Apetalous (ăpeˑtăləs), *a.* 1706. [f. mod.L. *apetalus* (a. Gr., f. ἀ + πέταλον) + -OUS.] *Bot.* Without petals.

Apex (ēⁱˑpĕks). Pl. **apices** (ēⁱˑpisīz, æˑp-), **apexes.** 1603. [a. L. *apex*, perh. f. *ap-* to fit to (cf. *vertex*, f. *vertere*).] **1.** (*As in L.*; see quot.) *rare.* 1603. **2.** The tip, top, peak, or pointed end of anything, as of a mountain, spire, shell, leaf, etc.; the vertex of a triangle or cone 1610. Also *fig.* **3.** A horn on a Hebrew letter (=κεραία *Matt.* v. 18 in Vulg.); hence †*fig.* A tittle, a jot –1680.

1. A hat of..wool, whose top ended in a cone, and was thence called an a. B. JONSON. 2. The a. of the dome 1848. *Apex* (U.S. *Min.*), the end or edge of a vein nearest the surface 1881. 3. Every a. or tittle JACKSON. Hence **A·pexed** *ppl. a.* pointed.

Aph-, repr. Gr. ἀφ', var. of ἀπό 'off, away from', bef. an aspirated vowel.

Aphæresis (ăfīᵊˑrĭsis). Also **aphe-**. 1611. [a. L., a. Gr., f. ἀφ' = ἀπό + αἱρέ-ειν.] *Gram.* The taking away of a letter or syllable at the beginning of a word. Hence **Aphære·tic** *a.* (*rare*).

Apha·nesite. [badly f. Gr. ἀφανής.] *Min.* = CLINOCLASITE.

‖**Aphaniptera** (æfăniˑptĕră), *sb. pl.* 1835. [mod.L., f. Gr. ἀφανής + -πτερος.] *Zool.* A small order of insects, having only rudimentary scales for wings. Hence **Aphani·pterous** *a.*

Aphanite, -yte (æˑfănəit). 1862. [f. Gr. ἀφανής + -ITE.] *Min.* A compact dark-coloured hornblende rock, uniform in texture and showing no distinct grains (whence its name); also called *Corneine.* Hence **Aphani·tic** *a.*

Aphanozygous (æfănǫˑzigəs), *a.* 1871. [f. Gr. ἀφανής + ζυγόν (for ζύγωμα) + -OUS.] *Anthrop.* Having the cheek-bones invisible from above.

‖**Aphasia** (ăfēⁱˑziă). 1867. [mod.L., a. Gr., f. ἀ + φάναι (cf. φάσις).] *Path.* Loss of the faculty of speech, as a result of cerebral affection.

Aphasic (ăfæˑzik), *a.* 1867. [f. prec. + -IC.] Suffering from aphasia. *sb.* One suffering from aphasia; var. **Apha·siac** (the better form).

Aphelion (ăfīˑliǫn). Pl. **aphelia.** 1656. [Græcized f. mod.L. *aphelium* (used earlier), f. Gr. ἀφ' = ἀπό + ἥλιος; formed (by Kepler) after *apogæum*, ἀπόγαιον. Cf. PARHELION.] *Astr.* That point of a planet's or comet's orbit at which it is farthest from the sun. Also *fig.*

Apheliotropic (ăfīˑliˌǫtrǫˑpik), *a.* 1880. [f. Gr. ἀφ' = ἀπό + ἥλιος + -τροπικός.] Turning away from the sun; said of leaves, etc. Hence **Aphe:liotro·pically** *adv.* **Aphe·lio·tropism**, the habit of bending away from the light.

‖**Aphemia** (ăfīˑmiă). 1864. [mod.L. f. Gr. ἀ + φήμη; but Gr. ἄφημος = unknown.] *Path.* Loss of power of articulation; *spec.* a form of APHASIA, in which words are still understood and conceived. Hence **Aphe·mic** *a.* and *sb.*

Aphesis (æˑfĭsis). 1880. [a. Gr., f. ἀφιέναι. Suggested by Sir J. A. H. Murray.] The gradual and unintentional loss of a short unaccented vowel at the beginning of a word; as in *squire* for *esquire*, etc. It is a special and frequent form of *Aphæresis.* Hence **Aphe·tic** *a.* pertaining to, or resulting from, a. **Aphe·tically** *adv.* by way of a. **A·phetism**, a word resulting from a., as *squire*, etc. **A·phetize** *v.* to shorten by aphesis.

‖**A·pheta.** 1647. [L., ad. Gr. ἀφέτης, a starter in races.] *Astrol.* The giver of life in a nativity. Hence **Aphe·tic, -al** *a.* life-giving.

Aphidian (ăfiˑdiăn). 1855. [f. *aphid-*, stem of mod.L. APHIS.] *adj.* Of or pertaining to aphides. *sb.* One of the aphides.

Aphilanthropy (æfilæˑnþrǫ̆pi). ? *Obs.* 1753. [f. Gr. ἀφιλάνθρωπος; see A- *pref.* 14 and PHILANTHROPY.] **1.** 'Want of love to mankind'. J. **2.** *Med.* A form of melancholy in which solitude is preferred; anthropophobia.

‖**Aphis** (æˑfis). Pl. **aphides** (æˑfidīz). 1771. [mod.L. (Linn.); etym. unkn.] A family of minute insects, also called *plant-lice*, which are very destructive. They are prodigiously prolific, multiplying by parthenogenesis; and are tended by ants for the honey-dew which they yield, whence occas. called *ant-cows.*

Comb. **a.-lion**, *Chrysopa perla.* Hence **Aphidi·phagous, Aphidi·vorous** *adjs.*, feeding on aphides, like the lady-bird. **Aphido·logist**, a student of the *Aphides.*

Aphlogistic (æflodʒiˑstik), *a.* 1831. [f. Gr. ἀφλόγιστος + -IC.] Without flame.

Aphlogistic or *Flameless Lamp*: Sir H. Davy's lamp, in which a coil of platinum wire is kept in a state of flameless ignition by spirit.

Aphonic (ăfǫˑnik), *a. rare.* 1827. [f. Gr. ἄφωνος + -IC.] Having no vocal sound.

Aphony (æˑfŏni). 1684. [ad. mod.L. *aphonia* (oftener used), a. Gr., f. ἀ + φωνή.] Inability to produce vocal sound, or voice.

Aphorism (æˑfŏriz'm). 1528. [a. Fr. *aphorisme*, ad. med.L. *aphorismus*, a. Gr. ἀφορισμός; see APHORIZE. From the 'Aphorisms of Hippocrates'.] **1.** A 'definition' or concise statement of a principle in any science. **2.** Any principle or precept expressed shortly and pithily; a maxim 1590.

1. Knowledge, while..in aphorisms and observations ..is in growth BACON. 2. Is not thy common talk found aphorisms MARLOWE. 'Tis an old Aphorisme *Oderunt omnes quem metuunt* HOWELL. Hence **A:phorisma·tic** *a.* [irreg. f. Gr. ἀφόρισμα.] aphorismic or aphoristic. †**A·phorismer**, a dealer in aphorisms (MILT.). **Aphori·smic** *a.* having the form of aphorisms. **A·phori·sming** *ppl. a.* dealing in aphorisms (*rare*).

Aphorist (æˑfŏrist). 1713. [f. APHORIZE.] One who writes or utters aphorisms. Hence **Aphori·stic** *a.* of or pertaining to an aphorist; of the nature of an aphorism. **Aphori·stically** *adv.* pithily.

Aphorize (æˑfŏrəiz), *v. rare.* 1669. [ad. Gr. ἀφορίζειν, f. ἀφ' = ἀπό + ὁρίζειν, f. ὅρος.] To write or speak in aphorisms; to make terse general reflections.

Aphrite (æˑfrəit). 1868. [f. Gr. ἀφρός + -ITE; = *foam-stone.*] *Min.* A carbonate of lime or calcite.

Aphrizite (æˑfrizəit). [f. Gr. ἀφρίζειν + -ITE.] *Min.* Black tourmaline from Krageröe in Norway.

Aphrodisiac (æfrodiˑziæc), *a.* 1719. [ad. Gr. ἀφροδισιακός, f. ἀφροδίσιος; see next.] Venereal; having a venereal tendency 1830. *sb.* A drug, etc., inducing venereal desire 1719. Also *fig.*

Aphrodisian (æfrodiˑziăn), *a.* 1860. [f. Gr. ἀφροδίσιος, f. Ἀφροδίτη + -AN.] Belonging to Venus, devoted to sensual love.

‖**Aphrodite** (æfrodəiˑtī), *sb.*¹ 1658. [Gr.; = *foam-born.* Formerly æˑfrodəit.] **1.** The Grecian Venus. **2.** *Zool.* A genus of marine worms with bristles of iridescent hues; also called *Sea-mouse* 1857.

Aphrodite (æˑfrodəit), *sb.*² 1837. [f. prec., taken as 'foam-stone' from its ending -ITE; cf. APHRITE.] *Min.* A soft opaque milk-white mineral, consisting mostly of bisilicate of magnesium, allied to Sepiolite or meerschaum.

A·phronitre. ? *Obs.* ME. [ad. L. *aphronitrum*, f. Gr. ἀφρὸς νίτρου.] Foam of nitre; saltpetre.

Aphrosi·derite. 1847. [f. Gr. ἀφρός + σίδηρος + -ITE.] *Min.* A soft ferruginous dark olive-green mineral, a variety of Prochlorite.

‖**Aphtha** (æˑfþă). 1657. [L., a. Gr. ἄφθα, mostly in pl.; ? conn. w. ἅπτειν.] *Path.* The infantile disease 'thrush', and, in the plural, the small white specks on the mouth and tongue which characterize it. Hence **A·phthous** *a.* of the nature of, or characterized by, a.

Aphthitalite (æfþiˑtăləit). 1835. [f. Gr. ἄφθιτος + λίθος, because unalterable in the air.] *Min.* A native sulphate of potash found upon lava; called also Vesuvian salt, Aphthalose, Arcanite, and Glaserite.

Aphthong (æˑfþǫŋ). 1847. [ad. Gr. ἄφθογγον.] A letter which is not sounded in the pronunciation of a word; a mute.

Aphthonite (æˑfþŏnəit). [f. Gr. ἄφθονος plentiful + -ITE.] *Min.* A steel-grey ore, resembling, or identical with, tetrahedrite. Corruptly *Aftonite.*

Aphyllous (ăfi·ləs), *a.* 1830. [f. mod.L. *aphyllus* (a. Gr., f. ἀ + φύλλον) + -OUS.] *Bot.* Naturally leafless.

Apiaceous (ēⁱpiˌēⁱ·ʃəs), *a.* 1839. [f. mod.L. *Apiaceæ*, f. *apium*; see -ACEOUS.] *Bot.* Of the N.O. *Apiaceæ* or *Umbelliferæ*; umbelliferous.

Apian (ēⁱ·piăn), *a.* 1862. [ad. L. *apianus*, f. *apis*.] Of or belonging to bees.

Apiary (ēⁱ·piări). 1654. [ad. L. *apiarium*, f. *apis*.] A place where bees are kept. Hence **Apia·rian** *a.* pertaining to bee-hives or bee-keeping; *sb.* = next (*rare*). **A·piarist,** one who keeps an a.

Apical (æ·pikăl, ēⁱ·pi-), *a.* 1828. [f. L. *apicem* (see APEX) + -AL[1].] Of, belonging to, or at an apex, summit, or tip. Hence **A·pically** *adv.* **A·picifi:xed** *ppl. a.* fixed to the apex. **Apicilar, Apici·llary** = APICULAR.

Api·cial, incorr. var. of APICAL.

Apician (ăpi·ʃăn), *a.* 1699. [f. *Apicius*, a Roman epicure + -AN.] Of or pertaining to epicures or to luxurious diet.

A pick a back, apickaback; see PICK-A-BACK.

Apicular (ăpi·kiŭlăɹ), *a. rare.* 1854. [f. mod.L. *apiculus*.] Of or belonging to a little apex.

Apiculate (ăpi·kiŭlĕt), *a.* 1830. [ad. mod. L. *apiculatus*, f. *apiculus*.] Having a minute apex. So **Api·culated** *ppl. a.*

Apiculture (ēⁱ·piˌkɒ:ltiŭr, -tʃəɹ). 1864. [f. L. *apis* + *-cultura*.] Bee-keeping or -rearing.

‖**Apiculus** (ăpi·kiŭlŏs). 1863. [mod.L. dim. of APEX.] A minute point or tip.

Apiece (ăpī·s), *adv.* ME. [orig. two words, *a piece*; but the connexion with *piece* is not now retained.] For each piece, thing, or (*colloq.*) person; each, for each, to each; severally, individually.

Six waterpottes of stone..contaynynge two or thre fyrkins a pece TINDALE *John* ii. 6.

†**A-pie·ces,** *advb. phr.* 1560. [A *prep.*[1] + *pieces*; see PIECE *sb.*] In pieces, to pieces –1678. *fig.* –1663.

A-pi·nch, *advb. phr.* [A *prep.*[1]] So as to pinch. MRS. BROWNING.

Apiocrinite (æpiˌǫ·krinəit). 1830. [f. Gr. ἄπιον + κρίνον, after *encrinite*.] *Palæont.* The pear-encrinite, a stalked echinoderm of the Oolite, so called from its shape.

Apiol (ēⁱ·piˌǫl). 1872. [f. L. *apium*.] *Chem.* and *Med.* Parsley-camphor, obtained by distilling parsley seeds with water.

Apio·logist. *rare.* [f. L. *apis*+(-O)LOGIST.] A scientific student of bees. EMERSON.

Apish (ēⁱ·piʃ), *a.* 1532. [f. APE *sb.*] **1.** Like an ape 1570. **2.** Ape-like in manner; befitting an ape; affected, silly, trifling 1532. **3.** Foolishly imitative 1579.

1. Two devilish apes, or a. devils RUSKIN. **2.** He bowed with a thousand a. congees SMOLLETT. **3.** We are but too a., apt to be led much by examples SANDERSON. Hence **A·pishly** *adv.* **A·pishness.**

A·pism. [f. APE.] The practice of aping. CARLYLE.

Apjohnite (æ·pˌdʒǫnəit). 1847. [f. *Apjohn*, its first analyzer.] *Min.* Manganese alum; a double sulphate of potash and manganese, occurring in fibrous or asbestiform masses, white, and lustrous.

†**Apla·ce,** *advb. phr.* ME. [f. A- *pref.* 14 + PLACE *sb.*; cf. Fr. *en place*.] Into this place, in place –1637.

Aplacental (æplăse·ntăl), *a.* 1857. [f. A- *pref.* 14 + PLACENTAL.] *Zool.* Having no placenta.

Aplanatic (æplănæ·tik), *a.* 1794. [f. Gr. ἀπλάνητος (f. ἀ+πλανά-ειν) + -IC.] Free from (spherical) aberration, as a compound lens. Hence **Apla·natism,** a state or condition.

Aplastic (ăplæ·stik), *a.* 1839. [f. Gr. ἄπλαστος + -IC, after πλαστικός.] Characterized by, or tending to, irregularity or absence of organic structure (techn. *aplasia*).

‖**Aplomb** (aˌplǫṅ·). 1828. [Fr., f. *à plomb* 'according to the plummet'.] **1.** The perpendicular; perpendicularity 1872. **2.** Confidence, self-possession 1828. Also *attrib.*

Aplotomy (ăplǫ·tŏmi). 1852. [f. Gr. ἁπλός + -τομη, f. τέμνειν.] *Surg.* Simple incision.

‖**Apnœa** (æpnī·ă). 1719. [mod.L., a. Gr. ἄπνοια.] *Path.* Suspension or cessation of breathing.

Apo-, *pref.*; repr. Gr. ἀπό- off, from, away; quite. In mod. scientific words = 'detached', as *apo-carpous*.

Apocalypse (ăpǫ·kălips). ME. [ad. L. *apocalypsis*, a. Gr., f. ἀποκαλύπτειν.] **1.** The revelation of the future granted to St. John in the isle of Patmos; also the book of the New Testament containing it. **2.** Any revelation or disclosure ME.

1. He who saw Th' Apocalyps MILT. *P. L.* IV. 2. **2.** The A. of all State-arcana SWIFT.

Apocalypst (ăpǫ·kălipst). *rare.* 1829. [irreg. = *apocalypt*, or *apocalyptist*.] A revealer of the unknown.

Apocalypt (ăpǫ·kălipt). *rare.* 1834. [ad. Gr. *ἀποκαλύπτης, f. ἀποκαλύπτειν.] = APOCALYPTIST.

Apocalyptic (ăpǫ·kăli·ptik), *a.* (*sb.*) 1629. [ad. Gr. ἀποκαλυπτικός; see APOCALYPSE.] **1.** Of or pertaining to the Apocalypse of St. John 1663. **2.** Of the nature of a revelation 1683. †**3.** Of persons: Dealing with the Apocalypse, or with prophetic revelations generally –1690. **4.** *sb.* The writer of the Apocalypse, St. John the Divine; also = APOCALYPST 1629. Hence **Apo:caly·ptical** *a.* = APOCALYPTIC *a.* 3. **Apo:caly·ptically** *adv.* after the manner, or by means, of revelation or of the Apocalypse; (*joc.*) so as to reveal what should be concealed.

Apocalyptist (ăpǫ·kăli·ptist). *rare.* 1864. [f. Gr. ἀποκαλύπτειν + -IST.] The writer of the Apocalypse.

Apocarpous (æpokā·ɹpəs), *a.* 1830. [f. Gr. ἀπό + -καρπος.] *Bot.* Having the carpels distinct.

‖**Apocatastasis** (æ:poˌkătæ·stăsis). *rare.* 1678. [L., a. Gr., f. ἀποκαθιστάναι.] **1.** Restoration, re-establishment. **2.** *Path.* Return to a previous condition 1753. **3.** *Astr.* Return to the same apparent position. (So in Gr.) 1822.

Apocathartic (æ:poˌkăþā·ɹtik), *a.* 1859. [ad. Gr. ἀποκαθαρτικός, f. ἀποκαθαίρειν.] *Med.* Purging. Also as *sb.*

Apocopate (ăpǫ·kŏpĕt, -ĕ¹t), *ppl. a.* 1850. [ad. mod.L. *apocopatus*, f. APOCOPE.] Cut short by apocope.

Apocopate (ăpǫ·kŏpeⁱt), *v.* 1851. [f. as prec.] To cut off (*esp.* the last letter or syllable of a word). Hence **Apo:copa·tion,** the action of apocopating; apocopated state.

‖**Apocope** (ăpǫ·kŏpĭ). 1591. [L., a. Gr. ἀποκοπή.] The cutting off or omission of the last letter or syllable of a word. Hence **Apoco·pic** *a.*

Apocrisiary (æpokri·ziări). Also **apo·crisary.** ME. [ad. med.L. *apocrisiarius*, f. Gr. ἀπόκρισις.] A person appointed to give and receive answers; *spec.* a papal nuncio.

Apocrustic (æpokrɒ·stik), *a.* Also **apocroustic.** 1706. [ad. mod.L. *apocrusticus*, a. Gr. ἀποκρουστικός, f. ἀποκρούειν.] *Med.* Having power to repel, astringent. Also as *sb.*

Apocrypha (ăpǫ·krifă). ME. [neut. pl. (sc. *scripta*) of late L. *apocryphus*, a. Gr. ἀπόκρυφος, f. ἀποκρύπτειν. As sb. prop. treated as pl., with sing. *apocryphon*; but in common usage as sing., with pl. *apocryphas*.] †**A.** *adj.* Of unknown authorship; spurious; uncanonical (see *sb.*); false –1690.

B. *sb.* **1.** A writing of doubtful authorship or authenticity; *spec.* those books included in the Septuagint and Vulgate, which were not originally written in Hebrew and not counted genuine by the Jews, and which, at the Reformation, were excluded from the Sacred Canon by the Protestant party. Also *attrib.* 1539. **2.** [As in Gr.] Hidden things (*rare*) 1839.

1. What's now apocrypha, my wit, In time to come may pass for holy writ POPE. var. †**Apocryph(e, †-crif(e.**

Apocryphal (ăpǫ·krifăl), *a.* 1590. [f. as prec. + -AL.] **1.** Of doubtful authenticity; spurious, false, mythical; *spec.* Of or belonging to the Jewish and early Christian uncanonical literature 1615. **2.** Sham, counterfeit 1610.

1. If but one word be true..In all th' a. romance BUTLER *Hud.* III. i. 492. **2.** A whoreson, upstart a. captain B. JONSON. Hence **Apo·cryphalist,** one who supports the inclusion of the Apocrypha in the Bible (*rare*). **Apo·cryphally** *adv.* (*rare*). **Apo·cryphalness** (*rare*).

†**Apo·cryphate,** *a.* 1486. [f. APOCRYPHA.] Of apocryphal origin; spurious –1655.

Apocynaceous (ăpǫ:sinēⁱ·ʃəs), *a.* 1883. [f. mod.L. *apocynaceæ*, f. *Apocynum*, ad. Gr. ἀπόκυνον.] *Bot.* Of or belonging to the N.O. *Apocynaceæ*, or Dog-banes. var. **Apocy·neous.**

Apod(e (æ·pǫd, æ·poᵘd). 1601. [f. Gr. ἄπους, ἀποδ-, f. ἀ + πούς; after mod.L. *Apodes, Apoda*.] *Zool. adj.* Footless 1816. *sb.* (usu. *pl.* = mod.L. *Apodes, Apoda*.) Term applied to birds, fish, and reptiles, in which feet or ventral fins are either absent or only rudimentary. Hence **A·podal** *a.* lacking feet or ventral fins.

Apodeme (æ·pŏdīm). 1852. [ad. mod.L. *apodema* (also used), f. Gr. ἀπό + δέμας.] *Zool.* One of the processes on the exoskeleton of the thorax of *Arthropods*, which serve as attachment for muscles, etc. Hence **Apo·demal** *a.* of or pertaining to an a.; var. **Apode·matal.**

Apodiabolosis (æ:poˌdəiăbŏlōᵘ·sis). *rare.* 1827. [f. Gr. διάβολος, after *apotheosis*.] A making or treating as diabolical.

Apodictic, -deictic (æpodi·ktik, -dəi·ktik), *a.* 1652. [ad. L. *apodicticus*, a. Gr. ἀποδεικτικός, f. ἀποδεικνύναι. The analogical sp. is *-dict-*.] Of clear demonstration; established incontrovertibly. (By Kant applied to a judgement enouncing a necessary and hence *absolute* truth.) var. **Apodi·ctical, -dei·ctical** (*arch.*). Hence **Apodi·ctically, -dei·ctically** *adv.*

‖**Apodio·xis.** ? *Obs.* 1657. [L., a. Gr. ἀποδίωξις.] *Rhet.* A figure: Rejecting an argument or objection with indignation as absurd.

‖**Apodixis, -deixis** (æpodi·ksis, -dei·ksis). ? *Obs.* 1623. [L., a. Gr. ἀπόδειξις.] Demonstration, absolute proof.

‖**Apodosis** (ăpǫ·dŏsis). 1638. [L., a. Gr., f. ἀποδιδόναι.] *Rhet.* The concluding clause of a sentence (opp. to *protasis*); now usu. the consequent clause in a conditional sentence, as 'If thine enemy hunger, *feed him*'.

Apodous (æ·podəs), *a.* 1816. [f. Gr. ἀποδ- (see APODE) + -OUS.] *Zool.* Footless, apod.

‖**Apodyterium** (æpoˌditī·riŏm). 1695. [L., a. Gr. ἀποδυτήριον, f. ἀποδύειν.] A dressing-room; *orig.* one in which clothes were deposited by those preparing for the bath or *palæstra*.

Apogæic, -gaic (æpodʒī·ik, -gēⁱ·ik), *a.* 1839. [f. Gr. ἀπόγαιος (see APOGEE) + -IC.] = APOGEAN. So **Apoge·al** *a.*

Apogean (æpodʒī·ăn), *a.* 1644. [f. as prec. + -AN.] **a.** Proceeding off from the earth or land. **b.** Of or pertaining to apogee.

Apogee (æ·podʒī). 1594. [a. Fr. *apogée*, f. L. *apogæum*, a. Gr. ἀπόγαιον (also ἀπόγειον), adj. neut., but used absol. by Ptolemy (sc. διάστημα). The Gr. and L. forms were also used.] *Astr.* **1.** The point in the orbit of the moon, etc., at which it is farthest from the earth; also, the greatest distance of the sun from the earth in *aphelion*. (A term of the Ptolemaic astronomy which viewed the earth as the centre of the universe.) †**2.** The meridional altitude of the sun on the longest day –1646. **3.** Hence *fig.* **a.** The most distant spot. **b.** The highest point, climax. 1600.

1. A., if the sun be supposed to revolve, Aphelion, if the earth WOODHOUSE. **3.** The trade of the Netherlands..had by no means reached its a. MOTLEY.

Apogeotropic (æ:poˌdʒīˌotrǫ·pik), *a.* 1880. [f. (by Darwin) Gr. ἀπό + γεο- (γῆ) + -τροπικός.] *Bot.* Turning away from the ground. Hence **A:pogeotro·pically** *adv.*

Apogeotropism (æ:poˌdʒīˌǫ·trŏˌpiz'm). 1880. [f. as prec. + -ISM.] The tendency of leaves, etc., to turn away from the earth.

Apograph (æ·pograf). 1601. [ad. Gr. ἀπόγραφον, f. ἀπογράφειν.] An exact transcript.

Apoious (ăpoi·əs), *a. rare.* 1880. [f. Gr. ἄποιος.] Having no active qualities; neutral; *e.g.* water.

Apojove (æ·poˌdʒōᵘv). 1867. [a. Fr., ad. mod.L. *apojovium*, f. Gr. ἀπό + L. *Jov-*; cf.

apogee.] *Astr.* The point in the orbit of a satellite of Jupiter at which it is farthest from the planet.

Apolar (ăpōu·laɪ), *a.* 1859. [f. A- *pref.* 14 + POLAR.] *Biol.* Having no poles or fibrous processes, as certain nerve-cells.

Apolaustic (æpǫlǭ·stik), *a.* 1871. [ad. Gr. ἀπολαυστικός.] Given to enjoyment; self-indulgent.

The lordly, a., and haughty undergraduate 1880.

Apollinarian (ăpǫ·linēᵊ·riăn), *a.* 1586. [f. L. *Apollinaris* of Apollo; also proper name + -AN.] **1.** Sacred to or in honour of Apollo 1753; var. †**Apo·llinar.** **2.** Of or pertaining to Apollinaris of Laodicea (4th c.), who held heretical opinions on the Incarnation 1659. As *sb.* An adherent of Apollinaris 1586; var. **Apollina·rist** (? *obs.*).

Apollonian (æpǫlōu·niăn), *a.* 1663. [f. L. *Apollonius*, a. Gr.; also proper name + -AN.] **1.** Pertaining to or resembling Apollo, the sun-god of the Greeks and Romans, the patron of music and poetry; var. **Apollo·nic.** **2.** Of Apollonius of Perga, a geometer and investigator of conic sections 1727.

Apollo·nicon. 1834. [f. Gr. ἀπολλώνιος, after *harmonicon*, etc.] A chamber-organ of great power, first exhibited in 1817.

‖**Apollyon** (ăpǫ·liǫn). ME. [L., a. Gr. ἀπολλύων, f. ἀπολλύειν.] The destroyer; a name given to the Devil. (See Rev. ix. 3–11.) Hence **Apollyonist**, a subject of Apollyon.

†**Apo·loger.** 1621. [f. Gr. ἀπόλογος + -ER[1].] A fabulist –1653.

Apologetic (ăpǫ·lǒdʒe·tik). 1605. [a. Fr. *apologétique*, ad. L. *apologeticus*, a. Gr.; see APOLOGY.] **A.** *adj.* **1.** Of the nature of a defence; vindicatory 1649. **2.** Regretfully acknowledging or excusing fault or failure 1855.

2. A subdued and a. tone MACAULAY.

B. *sb.* **1.** A formal apology for a defence of a person, doctrine, course, etc. 1605. **2.** *pl.* or *collect. sing.* The defensive method of argument; often *spec.* The argumentative defence of Christianity 1733.

2. The science of apologetics..was unknown till the attacks of the adversaries of Christianity assumed a learned and scientific character 1834. Hence **Apo·loge·tical** *a.* = APOLOGETIC *a.*; **-ly** *adv.*

†**Apolo·gical,** *a.* 1607. [f. Gr. ἀπολογία, or ἀπόλογος + -ICAL.] Of the nature of an apology, or of an apologue –1665.

Apologist (ăpǫ·lǒdʒist). 1640. [a. Fr. *apologiste*, f. Gr. ἀπολογία; see APOLOGY and -IST.] One who apologizes for, or defends by argument; a literary champion.

Mr. Hume, the staunch a. .. of all the Stuarts LD. BROUGHAM.

Apologize (ăpǫ·lǒdʒəiz), *v.* 1597. [f. APOLOGY + -IZE; cf. ἀπολογέ-εσθαι: ἀπολογίζεσθαι is a deriv. of ἀπόλογος APOLOGUE.] **1.** *intr.* To make or serve as an APOLOGY; to offer defensive arguments; to make excuses. Also in mod. usage: To acknowledge and express regret for a fault without defence. Const. *for.* †**2.** *trans.* (*for* omitted.) (*rare*) 1733.

1. They had very little wine, which the governor apologised for DE FOE. **2.** T' apologise his late offence SWIFT. Hence **Apo·logi·zer,** one who apologizes; earlier = APOLOGIST.

Apologue (æ·pǒlǫg). Also 6–7 **-logy.** 1552. [a. Fr., ad. L., a. Gr. ἀπόλογος.] An allegorical story intended to convey a useful lesson. (*Esp.* a fable in which the actors or speakers are animals or inanimate things.)

To teach the people in apologies, bringing in how one beast talketh with another LATIMER.

Apology (ăpǫ·lǒdʒi), *sb.* 1533. [ad. L. *apologia* (also used), a. Gr., f. ἀπό + -λογία.] **1.** The pleading off from a charge or imputation; defence or vindication from accusation or aspersion. **2.** Justification, explanation, or excuse 1588. **3.** A frank acknowledgement, by way of reparation, of offence given, or an explanation that offence was not intended, with expression of regret for any given or taken 1594. **4.** A poor substitute 1754.

1. Apologie of Syr Thomas More, Knyght; made by him, after he had geuen ouer the Office of Lord Chancellor of Englande MORE (*title*). An A. for the Bible BP. WATSON. **2.** His *enter* and *exit* shall bee strangling a Snake; and I will haue an Apologie for that purpose *L. L. L.* v. i. 142. **3.** In her face excuse Came Prologue, and Apologie to prompt MILT. *P. L.* IX. 854. **4.** Gibbon..had no nose at all, only an a. for one C. MATHEWS. Hence †**Apo·logy** *v.* to apologize (*rare*).

A·pomeco·meter. 1869. [f. Gr. ἀπό + μῆκος + μέτρον.] An instrument for measuring the distance of objects.

A·pomeco·metry. 1570. [f. as prec. + -μετρία.] The art or science of measuring the distances of objects.

Apomorphia (æpomǭ·ɹfiă). 1869. [f. Gr. ἀπό + MORPHIA.] *Chem.* A white crystalline powder, $C_{17}H_{17}NO_2$, obtained by heating morphia with an excess of hydrochloric acid: also **Apomorphine.** It is a prompt emetic.

‖**Aponeurosis** (æ:po₁niurōu·sis). Pl. **-es.** 1676. [L., a. Gr., f. ἀπονευρό-ειν to change into a tendon.] *Phys.* A white, shining, fibrous membrane, serving as the sheath of a muscle, or forming the connexion of a muscle and a tendon. Hence **A:poneuro·graphy,** the description of aponeuroses. **A:poneuro·logy,** the science of aponeuroses. **A:poneuro·tic** *a.* **A:poneuro·tomy,** dissection of the aponeuroses.

A-poo·p, *adv.* 1809. [A *prep.*[1]] On the poop, astern.

Apopemptic (æpope·mptik). *rare.* 1753. [ad. Gr. ἀποπεμπτικός, f. ἀποπέμπειν.] *adj.* Pertaining to dismissal; valedictory. *sb.* [sc. *hymn.*]

Apopetalous (æpope·tăləs), *a.* 1875. [f. Gr. ἀπό + πέταλον + -OUS.] *Bot.* Having the petals distinct or free.

‖**Apophasis** (ăpǫ·făsis). 1657. [L., a. Gr.] *Rhet.* A figure in which we feign to deny or pass over what we really say or advise.

†**A:pophlegma·tic, -al,** *a.* 1727. [mod. formation, not on Gr. analogies; cf. ἀποφλεγματίζειν and PHLEGMATIC.] *Med.* Promoting the removal of phlegm. Also as *sb.* [sc. *agent.*] var. **Apophlegma·tizant** (prob. f. mod.L.).

†**Apophle·gmatism.** 1615. [ad. Gr. ἀποφλεγματισμός, f. ἀποφλεγματίζειν.] *Med.* **1.** The action of purging phlegm from the head. **2.** An apophlegmatic agent or treatment.

Apophthegm, apothegm (æ·pǒþem). 1553. [ad. Gr. ἀπόφθεγμα, f. ἀπό + φθέγγεσθαι. The sp. *apophthegm*, preferred by Johnson, is now the more usual form in England. Cf. Fr. *apophthegme*, It. *apotegma.*] A terse, pointed saying, embodying an important truth in few words; a pithy or sententious maxim.

Johnson suddenly uttered..an a., at which many will start: 'Patriotism is the last refuge of a scoundrel' BOSWELL. Hence **A·pophthegma·tic, -al, apothegm·** *a.* of, pertaining to, or of the nature of, an a.; addicted to the use of apophthegms; sententious, pithy. **A·pophthegma·tically, apothegm·** *adv.* **Apophthe·gmatist, apothegm-,** a professed maker of apophthegms. **Apophthe·gmatize, apothegm·** *v.* to write or speak in apophthegms.

Apophyge (ăpǫ·fidʒi). 1563. [a. Gr. ἀποφυγή, f. ἀποφεύγειν. In L. *apophygis*, Fr. *apophyge*; hence better æ·pofidʒ.] *Arch.* The part of a column where it springs out of its base, or joins its capital, usually moulded into a concave sweep or cavetto.

Apophyllite (ăpǫ·filəit, æpofi·ləit). 1810. [f. Gr. ἀπό + φύλλον + -ITE; so named because it exfoliates under the blow-pipe.] *Min.* A zeolitic mineral, a hydrated silicate of lime and potash, with a trace of fluorine; occurring in glassy square prisms or octahedrons, or laminated masses, with a pearly lustre.

Apophyllous (æpofi·ləs), *a. rare.* 1875. [f. as prec. + -OUS.] *Bot.* Having the sepals free.

‖**Apophysis** (ăpǫ·fisis). Pl. **-es.** Also **apophyse.** 1611. [Gr., f. ἀπό + φύσις.] **1.** *Phys.* A natural protuberance or process, arising from, and forming a continuous part of, a bone. **2.** *Bot.* A dilatation of the base of the theca or spore-case in some mosses 1794. Hence **Apo·physate** *a.* furnished with an a. (*rare*). **Apophy·sial** (less correctly **apophysal**) *a.* belonging to, or of the nature of, an a.; var. **Apo·physary.**

Apoplectic, -al (æpople·ktik, -ăl), *a.* 1611. [ad. Fr. *apoplectique*, or L., a. Gr. ἀποπληκτικός, f. ἀποπλήσσειν; see APOPLEXY and -IC, -AL[1].] **1.** Of, pertaining to, or causing apoplexy. **2.** Suffering from, or showing signs of, apoplexy. Also *fig.* 1721. †**3.** = ANTAPOPLECTIC –1753. **4.** *sb.* One liable to, or suffering from, apoplexy 1670.

1. One of your stiff-starched a. cravats DICKENS. **2.** A short-necked a. sort of fellow MISS AUSTEN. **3.** A. balsam ADDISON. Hence **Apople·ctically** *adv.* **Apople·ctiform** *a.* having the form of apoplexy.

A·poplex. *arch.* 1533. [ad. L. *apoplexis*, a. Gr. ἀπόπληξις.] = APOPLEXY.

A·poplex, *v. arch.* 1602. [f. prec. sb.] To strike with apoplexy, benumb.

Sure, that sense Is apoplex'd *Haml.* III. iv. 73.

Apoplexy (æ·po₁pleksi). ME. [a. Fr. *apoplexie*, ad. L. *apoplexia* (occ. used), a. Gr. ἀποπληξία, f. ἀπό + πλήσσειν.] A malady, sudden in its attack, which arrests the powers of sense and motion; usually caused by an effusion of blood or serum in the brain, and preceded by giddiness, partial loss of muscular power, etc. Also *transf.* or *fig.* **2.** Occas. applied to the effusion of blood in other organs 1853.

1. This Apoplexie is (as I take it) a kind of Lethargie, a sleeping of the blood, a horson Tingling *2 Hen. IV*, I. ii. 126. The Apoplexie or falling euill in Hawkes MARKHAM. **2.** *A. cutaneous*, a sudden determination of blood to the skin MAYNE.

†**Apore·tic, †-al,** *a. rare.* 1605. [a. Fr. *aporetique*, ad. Gr. ἀπορητικός, f. ἀπορέ-ειν; see -AL[1].] Full of doubts and objections –1688.

‖**Aporia** (ăpōᵊ·riă, -ǫ·riă). 1589. [L., a. Gr., f. ἄπορος; see prec.] *Rhet.* A figure: Doubt.

Aporose (æ:porouˑs), *a.* 1865. [f. Gr. ἀ + mod.L. *porosus*, f. L. *porus*, a. Gr.; see POROUS.] Not porous; *spec.* of the corals of the sub-order *Aporosa.*

†**Aporrhœ·a.** 1646. [mod.L., a. Gr., f. ἀποῤῥέ-ειν.] An emanation, effluvium –1681.

A-port (ăpōᵊ·ɹt), *adv.* 1626. [A *prep.*[1] + PORT.] On or towards the port side of the ship, the left side when looking forward. *To put the helm a-port* (= 'to port the helm'): to move the rudder to the starboard side, making the ship turn to the right.

Apose·palous, *a.* 1875. [f. Gr. ἀπό + SEPAL + -OUS.] *Bot.* Having free sepals.

‖**Aposiopesis** (æ:po₁səi₁opī·sis). 1578. [L., a. Gr.] *Rhet.* A figure, in which the speaker suddenly halts, as if unable or unwilling to proceed.

A., an excellent figure for the ignorant, as 'What shall I say?' when one has nothing to say POPE. Hence **A·posiope·tic** *a.*

Aposi·tic, *a.* 1853. [ad. Gr. ἀποσιτικός, f. ἀπό + σῖτος.] *Med.* Tending to diminish appetite; causing *apositia* or distaste for food.

Apostasy (ăpǫ·stăsi). Also **-acy.** ME. [ad. L. *apostasia*, a. later Gr. ἀποστασία = ἀπόστασις.] **1.** Abandonment or renunciation of one's religious faith or moral allegiance. **b.** *R. C. Ch.* The action of quitting a religious order or renouncing vows without legal dispensation 1532. **2.** The abandonment of principles or party generally 1579.

1. Raphael..had forewarned Adam by dire example to beware Apostasie MILT. *P. L.* VII. 44. **2.** A. from every good principle 1773.

Apostate (ăpǫ·stĕt). ME. [a. Fr., and L. *apostata*, ad. Gr. ἀποστάτης. The L. *apostata*, with pl. *apostata(e)s*, was the commoner form till 1650.] **A.** *sb.* **1.** One guilty of APOSTASY **1**; a pervert. **b.** *R. C. Ch.* One who renounces a religious order without legal dispensation ME. **2.** A turncoat, a renegade ME.

1. High in the midst..Th' A. in his Sun-bright Chariot sate MILT. *P. L.* vi. 100. **2.** Apostates, to their own Country, and Cause 1687.

B. *adj.* **1.** Guilty of APOSTASY; renegade, infidel; rebellious ME. **2.** Deserting principles or party; perverted 1671.

1. So spake th' Apostate Angel MILT. **2.** Those a. abilities of men STEELE. Hence †**Apo·state** *v.* = APOSTATIZE. **Aposta·tic** *a.* (*rare*) = APOSTATE *a.* **1.** **Aposta·tical** *a.* of the nature of apostates or apostasy; †withdrawing, retrograde. **Apo·statism,** the practice of apostatizing.

Apostatize (ăpǫ·stătəiz), *v.* 1552. [ad. late L. *apostatizare*, for earlier *apostatare*, f. *apostata.*] **1.** To be guilty of APOSTASY (*from*, *to*) 1611. **2.** To abandon a principle, desert a party 1648.

2. He apostatized from your cause CROMWELL.

†**A·postem(e, -tume, -thume.** ME. [a. Fr., ad. L. *apostema*, a. Gr., *spec.* separation of

purulent matter into an abscess, f. ἀποστα-, ἀποστῆναι (cf. *abs-cess*). Corruptions are, in OFr. *apostume* (as if f. L. *postumus*), changed later to *empostume*; hence Eng. *impostume*, IMPOSTHUME (cf. *posthumous*), in 18th c. the only form. Accented *a·postem* by Johnson.] A gathering of purulent matter in any part of the body; an abscess. Also *fig.* Hence **†Apo·stemate, -umate** *a.* formed into an a.; festering; *sb.* = APOSTEM. **†Apo·stemate, -umate** *v.* to be affected with an a.; *intr.* to fester. **†Apo:stema·tion,** etc., the formation of an a.; =APOSTEM. **Aposte·matous** *a.* of the nature of an a.; characterized by abscesses.

‖**A posteriori** (ē̆ pǫste:ri,ōᵊ·rəi, ā poste:riō·ri), *advb.* (and *adj.*) *phr.* 1710. [L., opp. to *a priori.*] A phrase used to characterize reasoning from effects to causes, from experience and not from axioms; empirical, inductive; inductively.

Knowledge *a posteriori* is a synonym for knowledge empirical or from experience SIR W. HAMILTON.

Aposthume, -ation, etc.; see APOSTEME.

Apostil, -ille (ăpǫ·stil), *sb.* 1527. [a. Fr. *apostille,* of unkn. origin; see POSTIL. ?conn. with OF. *apost* :—L. *appositum.*] A marginal note, comment, or annotation.

The world..was to move upon protocols and apostilles MOTLEY. Hence **Apo·stil** *v.* to write marginal notes to (*rare*).

Apostle (ăpǫ·s'l). [Two forms: 1. OE. *apostol,* (ME. *apostel, -yl*), ad. L. *apostolus* (a. Gr. ἀπόστολος, f. ἀποστέλλειν. 2. the current *apostle* (*c* 1225), a. OFr. *apostle* (later *apostre,* mod. *apôtre*). In 16th c. the OFr. spelling prevailed. The pop. form in ME. was †*postel.*] †1. (As in Gr.) One sent, a messenger; applied in N.T. to Jesus Christ –1611. 2. Any of the twelve witnesses whom Jesus Christ sent forth to preach his Gospel; also, later, Barnabas (Acts xiii. 2, xiv. 14), and Paul, the Apostle of the Gentiles OE. 3. One who in any way imitates or resembles the Apostles ME.; *esp.* the missionary who first plants Christianity in any region ME.; the chief advocate of a new principle or system 1810. †4. The Acts and Epistles of the Apostles –1794. †5. A letter dimissory; *pl.* in *Rom. Law.* A short statement of the case, sent up by a lower to a higher court, when an appeal is made –1753.

1. Neither is an a. greater then he that sent him *Rhem.* John xiii. 16. 2. The glorious company of the Apostles praise Thee *Te Deum.* 3. The king's booted apostles BURTON. Boniface has gained the title of the A. of Germany 1844. M. Comte is..an a. of science 1870.

Comb., etc.: **a. skulls,** very long and narrow skulls LAING; **A. spoons,** old-fashioned silver spoons, the handles of which end in figures of the Apostles. Hence **Apo·stlehood,** the office or position of an a. (*arch.*). So **Apo·stleship. Apo·stolize** *v.* (*rare*), *trans.* to proclaim (a message); *intr.* to act as or like an a.

†Apostoi·le. ME. only. [a. OFr. *apostolie,* later *-oile* :—late L. *apostolicus,* prop. adj. APOSTOLIC.] The pope.

Apostolate (ăpǫ·stŏleⁱt). 1642. [ad. L. *apostolatus*; see APOSTLE.] The office or position of an apostle; leadership in a propaganda.

I no otherwise assume the A. of England .. than I assume the A. of all Europe WESLEY.

Aposto·lian. = APOSTOLIC *sb.* (heretic).

Apostolic (æpŏstǫ·lik). 1477. [a. Fr. *apostolique,* ad. late L., a. Gr. ἀποστολικός; see APOSTLE, -IC.] A. *adj.* 1. Pertaining to or contemporaneous with the Apostles 1549. 2. Of the nature or character of the Apostles 1549. 3. Of or pertaining to the pope as successor of St. Peter; papal 1477.

1. And a. statues climb To crush the imperial urn BYRON. 2. A. charity COWPER, devotion to the service of the poor DE QUINCEY. 3. Dependent on the A. See LINGARD. Hence **Aposto·licism,** profession of, or claim to, apostolicity. **Apo:stoli·city,** the quality of being a. in character or origin.

B. *sb.* A heretical sect, who imitated the Apostles, in wandering about without staves, shoes, money, or bags 1580.

Aposto·lical, *a.* (*sb.*) 1546. [a. OFr., f. as prec. + -AL[1].] 1. Connected with or relating to the Apostles, or to what is apostolic 1577. 2. Of the Apostolic See 1546. 3. Formerly (and still occas.) = APOSTOLIC 1548. 4. *sb.* One who maintains the doctrine of apostolical succession 1839.

1. *Apostolical succession* (*Eccl.*), an uninterrupted transmission of spiritual authority through a succession of bishops from the Apostles downwards. Hence **Aposto·lically** *adv.* **Aposto·licalness.** ?*Obs.*

Apostrophe[1] (ăpǫ·strŏfi). Also †**-phy.** 1533. [a. L., a. Gr. ἀποστροφή, f. ἀπό + στροφή.] 1. *Rhet.* A figure, in which a speaker or writer suddenly stops in his discourse, and turns to address pointedly some person or thing, either present or absent; an exclamatory address. (Not confined, as occas. stated, to a person *present* (Quintilian), and the *absent,* or *dead.*) 2. *Bot.* The aggregation of protoplasm and chlorophyll-grains on the cell-walls adjacent to other cells; opp. to *epistrophe* 1875.

1. The a. to light at the commencement of the third book [of *Paradise Lost*] COLERIDGE.

Apostrophe[2] (ăpǫ·strŏfi). Also †**-phus.** 1588. [a. Fr. *apostrophe,* ad. L. *apostrophus,* a. Gr. ἡ ἀπόστροφος (sc. προσῳδία). Prop. trisyllabic, as in Fr., but ignorantly confused with prec.] †1. The omission of one or more letters in a word –1642. 2. The sign (') used to indicate the omission of a letter, as in *o'er*; and as a sign of the mod. Eng. genitive or possessive case, as in *boy's, men's, Moses',* etc. 1588.

It orig. marked merely the omission of *e* in writing, as in folio's=*folioes* nom. pl., but was gradually disused exc. in, and extended to all, possessives.

You finde not the apostrophas [?apostrophus], and so misse the accent *L. L. L.* IV. ii. 123.

Apostrophic (æpo,strǫ·fik), *a.* 1795. [f. prec. + -IC.] 1. Of, pertaining to, or given to the use of, rhetorical apostrophe 1820; var. **Apo·strophal.** 2. Of or pertaining to the grammatical apostrophe 1795.

Apostrophize (ăpǫ·strŏfəiz), *v.* 1611. 1. f. APOSTROPHE[1]. *Rhet.* To address in an apostrophe 1725. Also *absol.* 2. f. APOSTROPHE[2]. To omit one or more letters of a word; to mark with the sign (') the omission of letters 1611. Hence **Apo·strophized** *ppl. a.* (in both senses).

Apostume, -ation, etc.; see APOSTEME, etc.

Apotactite (æpotæ·ktəit). 1727. [a. med.L. *apotactita,* ad. Gr. ἀποτακτίτης, f. ἀπότακτος (cf. Luke ix. 61).] One of an early Christian sect, who renounced all their possessions in imitation of the early church in Jerusalem.

†Apo·telesm (ăpǫ·tĭlezm). *rare.* 1636. [ad. Gr. ἀποτέλεσμα, f. ἀποτελέ-ειν.] 1. (as in Gr.) The result, the sum and substance. 2. *Astrol.* The casting of a horoscope 1651. Hence **Apotelesma·tic** *a.* of or pertaining to the casting of horoscopes.

†Apo·thec. 1591. [a. OFr. *apotheque,* ad. L. *apotheca,* a. Gr. ἀποθήκη.] A shop, or storehouse; *esp.* for drugs. Also *fig.* –1657.

Apothecary (ăpǫ·þĭkări). ME. [a. OFr. *apotecaire* :—late L. *apothecarius*; see APOTHEC.] †1. *orig.* One who kept a store or shop of non-perishable commodities, spices, drugs, comfits, preserves, etc. 2. *spec.* The earlier name for: One who prepared and sold drugs for medicinal purposes; now called a druggist or pharmaceutical chemist. The modern apothecary is a general medical practitioner, by licence of the Apothecaries Company; but in pop. usage the term is archaic. ME. †3. [cf. OFr. *apotecarie,* and late L. *apothecaria.*] Drugs collectively; a store of drugs; medical treatment by drugs –1621. 4. *attrib.* 1562.

2. *Apothecaries' Weight*: that by which drugs are compounded. O, true Appothecary: Thy drugs are quicke *Rom. & Jul.* v. iii. 119. 4. A. shops 1601.

‖**Apothecium** (æpoþī·ʃiŏm). Pl. **-a.** 1830. [mod.L., a. Gr. *ἀποθήκιον, dim. of ἀποθήκη.] The shield or spore-case, containing the fructification in lichens.

Apothegm, -them, vars. of APOPHTHEGM.

Apothem (æ·pŏþėm). [mod. f. Gr. ἀποτιθέναι, after θέμα; cf. Fr. *apothème.*] 1. *Math.* In a regular polygon: The perpendicular dropped from the centre upon one of the sides. Cf. *off-set.* 2. The insoluble brown deposit which forms in vegetable extracts exposed to the air (Berzelius).

Apotheosis (æpoþī·ŏsis, ăpǫ:þi,ōᵘ·sis). 1605. [a. L., a. Gr. ἀποθέωσις, f. ἀπό + θεό-ειν to make a god of. The second pronunc. is now more usual.] 1. The action of ranking, or fact of being ranked, among the gods; deification; divine status. 2. The exaltation of any person, principle, practice, etc.; the canonization of saints; a deified ideal 1651. 3. *loosely,* Ascension to glory, release from life; resurrection 1649.

1. That which the Grecians call *Apotheosis*..was the supreme honour which a man could attribute unto man BACON. 2. The a. of Milton 1739, of familiar abuses COLERIDGE. 3. His Majesties Speech upon the Scaffold, and His Death or A. 1649.

Apotheosize (æpoþī·ŏsəiz, ăpǫ·þi,osəi:z), *v.* 1760. [f. prec. + -IZE.] To elevate to, or as if to, the rank of a god; to exalt. var. **Apo·theose.**

‖**Apothesis** (ăpǫ·þĭsis). 1811. [L., a. Gr., f. ἀποτιθέναι.] 1. (As in Gr.) The setting of a fractured or dislocated limb. 2. *Arch.* = APOPHYGE.

Apotome (ăpǫ·tŏmi). Also **-tomy.** 1571. [a. Gr., f. ἀποτέμνειν.] 1. *Math.* The difference of two quantities, commensurable only in power (*i.e.* in their squares, etc.); as between $\sqrt{2}$ and 1, which is the difference between the diagonal and side of a square. 2. *Mus.* A variety of semitone 1696.

Apo·tropous, *a.* 1880. [f. Gr. ἀπότροπος (f. ἀποτρέπειν) + -OUS.] *Bot.* Turned away.

Apozem (æ·pŏzėm). *arch.* Also †**-zeme.** 1603. [a. Fr. *apozème,* ad. late L. *apozema,* a. Gr. ἀπόζεμα, f. ἀπό+ζέ-ειν.] *Med.* A decoction or infusion. Hence **†Apoze·mical** *a.*

†Appai·r, apai·r, *v.* [ME. *ampayr-i,* ad. OFr. *empeirer, amp-* (mod. *empirer*), f. *em-* = *en-* + **peirer* :—L. *pejorare,* f. *pejor-.* The prefix *am-,* treated as native *an-* bef. a cons., was reduced to *a-,* and later erron. spelt *ap-*; see AP- *pref.*[1] *Empeyr, empair* in 16th c. was refash. after L. as IMPAIR, the form now current.] 1. *trans.* To IMPAIR –1643. 2. *intr.* (refl. pron. omitted) To deteriorate –1581.

Appal, appall (ăpǭ·l), *v.* ME. [? a. OFr. *apalir, apallir,* later *ap(p)alir* to wax pale; also *trans.* to make pale. This etym. accounts for the *senses* better than for the *forms.* See also the simple PALL *v.,* and PALE *v.* and *a.* The better sp. is *appall,* as in the derivatives.] †1. *intr.* To wax pale or dim ME. only; *fig.* to fail, decay –1596; to lose savour, etc., to become flat or stale (cf. PALL *v.*) –1568. †2. To lose heart, become dismayed 1450. †3. *trans.* To make pale –1583; *fig.* to cause to fade or fail, to impair –1616. †4. To quell (anger, pride, etc.) (*rare*) –1598. 5. To cause the heart of (any one) to sink, to dismay 1532. Also *absol.*

5. A man..that dare looke on that which might appall the Diuell *Macb.* III. iv. 59. *absol.* Thoughts that awe but not appal KEBLE. Hence **†Appa·l, appall** *sb.* the act of appalling; dismay (*rare*). **Appa·lled** *ppl. a.* †made pale or faint; made flat or stale (cf. PALLED); bereft of courage, etc. by sudden terror, dismayed; also *fig.* **Appa·llingly** *adv.* **Appa·lment,** consternation (*rare*).

†Appale, apale (ăpēⁱ·l), *v.* 1500. [? (1) ad. Fr. *appalir,* (2) assim. of *appall* to PALE *a.* or *v.,* or (3) new formation on PALE *a.* or *v.* See prec. vb.] 1. *intr.* =APPAL *v.* 1. –1598. 2. *trans.* =APPAL *v.* 3, 5. –1686.

2. Make mad the guilty and apale the free *Haml.* II. ii. 590. Hence **†Appa·lement,** the action of dismaying; dismay.

‖**Appa·lto.** [It., f. *appaltare.*] A monopoly. DISRAELI.

Appanage, var. of APANAGE.

Apparail, -ment, obs. f. APPAREL, etc.

†Apparance. *rare.* 1546. [a. OFr. *aparance* :—L. *adparantem.*] Preparation –1594.

†A·pparate. *rare.* 1600. Anglicized f. APPARATUS.

†Appara·tion. 1533. [ad. L. *apparationem.*] Preparation –1657.

Apparatus (æpărēⁱ·tŏs). Pl. (*rare*) **-atus, -atuses.** 1628. [a. L., f. *apparare,* f. *ad* + *parare.*] †1. The work of preparing; preparation –1722. 2. The things collectively in which preparation consists, and by which its processes are maintained; equipments, material, machinery; material appendages or arrangements 1628. 3. *esp.* The mechanical requisites for scientific experiments or investigations 1727; the organs by which natural processes are carried on 1718; materials for the critical study of a document 1727.

1. An a. and necessary introduction thereunto 1638.

2. The gaudy a. of female vanity 1767. 3. The whole a. of vision BUTLER.

Apparel (ăpæ·rĕl), *v. arch.* ME. [a. OFr. *apareiller* (mod. *app-*) :—Rom. *adpariculare, f. *ad* + *pariculum, dim. of *par*. For *app-* see AP- *pref.*[1] In inflexions *-l* is usu. doubled in G. Brit., single in U. S.] Usually *trans.* or *refl.* †1. *trans.* To make ready or prepare (*for*) -1631. 2. To furnish with things necessary ME.; †to equip for fighting -1672. 3. To array with proper clothing; to attire. (The ordinary sense, but now *arch.*, and not in spoken use.) ME. Also *fig.* (*arch.*)

1. Ryal shippes..ful wel arayd and enparelled and enarmed CAXTON. 3. They which are gorgeously apparelled *Luke* vii. 25. *fig.* When thou wert appareld in thy flesh TOURNEUR. Apparelled in celestial light WORDSW. Looke sweet, speake faire..Apparell vice like vertues harbenger *Com. Err.* III. ii. 12. Hence **Appa·relment,** †preparation; *concr.* equipment, apparel (*rare*).

Apparel (ăpæ·rĕl), *sb.* [ME. *aparail*, a. OFr. (mod. *appareil*), f. vb. *apareiller*; see APPAREL *v.*] †1. The work of fitly preparing -1485; *concr.* materials, requisites, apparatus -1725; furniture, appendages (as of a house, gun, etc.) -1535. 2. The outfit of a ship (*arch.*) ME. 3. Personal outfit or attire; clothing, raiment (*arch.*) ME. †4. Aspect -1526. 5. †Ornament ME. (only); *esp.* ornamental embroidery on certain eccles. vestments (*revived*) 1485.

1. Socrates sayde That women ben thapparayles to cacche men CAXTON. 2. Tackle, A., Provisions, etc. *Charter-party*. 3. The Apparell oft proclaimes the man *Haml.* I. iii. 72. Style (the apparell of matter) 1610. 5. The Albe..should be made..with apparells PUGIN.

†**Apparence, -ance.** ME. [a. OFr. *aparence, -ance*. Subseq. refash. as APPEARANCE by assim. to the vb. *appear*.] 1. = APPEARANCE (in all senses) -1686. 2. The position of being heir apparent -1628.

Apparency (ăpēə·rĕnsi, ăpæ·r-). *arch.* ME. [ad. L. *apparentia*, f. *apparentem*; see APPARENT. Cf. *transparency*.] †1. Appearance -1684. 2. The quality of being apparent; visibility; show of reason 1604. 3. The position of being heir apparent 1741.

Apparent (ăpēə·rĕnt, ăpæ·r-), *a.* ME. [a. OFr. *aparant, -ent* :—L. *apparentem*, *apparere*, subseq. refash.; see APPEAR.] 1. Meeting the eyes, showing itself; visible, plainly seen (*arch.*). †2. Conspicuous -1603. 3. Manifest to the understanding; evident, obvious; palpable ME. †4. Likely so far as appearances go -1754. 5. Seeming, as distinct from (though not necessarily opposed to) what really *is*. Contrasted with *real*. (The commonest sense now.) 1645. †6. *sb.* [by ellipsis.] An heir apparent. Also *fig.* -1646.

1. An Owl-eyed buzzard that..sees not things apparent WITHERS. 3. The mind is repelled by useless and a. falsehood JOHNSON. In *Heir apparent*, etc.: Manifest, evident; applied to one who will undoubtedly inherit, if he survive the present possessor; opp. to heir *presumptive*. 4. The three a. candidates are Fox, Pitt, and Murray H. WALPOLE. 5. His real merit, and a. fidelity GIBBON. 6. Next to thy selfe, and my young Rouer, he's Apparant to my heart *Wint. T.* I. ii. 178. Hence †**Appa·rent** *v.* to make a. (*rare*). **Appa·rentness** (*rare*).

Appa·rently, *adv.* ME. [f. prec. adj. + -LY[2].] †1. Evidently; visibly -1651. 2. Evidently to the understanding; clearly 1553. 3. Seemingly; contrasted with *really*. (See APPARENT 5.) 1566. 4. So far as one can judge 1846.

1. The Prophets .. who saw not God a. like unto Moyses HOBBES.

Apparition (æpări·ʃən). 1481. [a. Fr., ad. L. *apparitionem*; see APPEAR. The senses are late L. and Fr. In etym. and sense-development = APPEARANCE, but now in use mainly in sense 7.] 1. The action of appearing, or becoming visible 1525. 2. *Astr.* The first appearance of a star, etc., after disappearance or occultation 1556. †3. The manifestation of Christ; the Epiphany; the season commemorating it. -1703. 4. *Astr.* Visibility, *esp.* of a star, planet, or comet 1601. †5. Semblance -1667; form or aspect -1660. 6. That which appears; an appearance, *esp.* if remarkable or unexpected; a phenomenon 1481. 7. *spec.* An immaterial appearance as of a real being; a spectre, phantom, ghost. (The sense now current.) 1601. Also *transf.* or *fig.* †8. An illusion, a sham -1679.

1. A sudden a. of the foul fiend SCOTT. The a. of a new public body in the state M. ARNOLD. 4. The circle of *perpetual apparition*, between which and the elevated pole the stars never set HERSCHEL. 6. The steamer was such a terrible a. to them LIVINGSTONE. 7. I thinke it is the weakenesse of mine eyes That shapes this monstrous A. *Jul. C.* IV. iii. 277. Hence **Appari·tional** *a.* spectral, subjective.

Apparitor (ăpæ·ritəɪ). 1528. [a. L., f. *apparere*, to appear as an attendant; see APPEAR.] 1. The servant or attendant of a civil or eccles. officer. 2. *spec.* a. (*Rom. Antiq.*) A general name for the public servants of the Roman magistrates 1533. b. A beadle in a University, etc., who carries the mace 1727. 3. *gen.* A herald, pursuivant, usher (*lit.* and *fig.*) 1561. 4. One who appears 1843 (*rare*).

1. All the hell pestering rabble of Somners and Apparitors MILT. 2. a. Six hundred apparitors, who would be styled at present either secretaries, or clerks, or ushers, or messengers GIBBON.

†**Appa·ssionate,** *ppl. a.* 1580. [ad. It. *appassionato*.] Impassioned -1609. Hence †**Appa·ssionate** *v.* to impassion.

†**Appa·st.** 1580. [a. Fr. (mod. *appât*), f. *à* + *past* :—L. *pastus*, f. *pascere*.] Food, bait -1633.

‖**Appaumé** (apōme), *ppl. a.* 1864. [Fr., f. *à* + *paume* :—L. *palma*.] *Her.* With the hand open, so as to display the palm.

Appay, late sp. of APAY *v.*

†**Appea·ch,** *v.* [ME. *apeche*, repr. *anpeche (see A- *pref.* 10, AN- *pref.* 4), Eng. or AFr. f. *enpescher* :—L. *impedicare*, f. *im* + *pedica*, f. *pedem*. Displaced by IMPEACH, latinized f. *enpeche*, subseq. re-introduced.] 1. To impede, delay 1460. 2. To impeach -1650. 3. To asperse (honour, character, etc.) -1700. 4. To inform against (a crime, etc.) -1658. 5. *intr.* To 'peach'. *All's Well* I. iii. 197. Hence †**Appea·cher,** one who impeaches; an informer. †**Appea·chment,** a criminal charge.

Appeal (ăpī·l), *v.* [ME. *apele*, a. OFr. *apeler* :—L. *app-*, *adpellare*, f. *adpellere*. See AP- *pref.*[1] The change of *-e-* to *-ea-* was a 16th c. 'reform'.] I. *trans.* To appeal a person. *Obs.* or *Hist.* 1. To call (one) to answer before a tribunal; in *Law*: To accuse of a crime which the accuser undertakes to prove. *spec.* a. To impeach *of* treason. b. To turn 'approver', and accuse an accomplice of treason or felony. c. To accuse of a heinous crime, in respect of which the accuser demands reparation. *Obs.* exc. *Hist.* 2. To challenge (*arch.*) ME. †3. To claim as judge (*rare*) ME. only; to call to witness (*rare*) -1649.

1. To appeale a man is as much as to accuse him COKE. 3. To a. Cesar WYCLIF *Acts* xxv. 12, the testimony of God MILT.

II. *intr.* Const. *to.* 1. To remove a case from an inferior to a higher court; also *fig.* ME. 2. To call upon an authority for sanction or decision in one's favour ME.; also *fig.* ME. 3. To call *to* a witness, etc., for corroboration ME. 4. To make entreaty, or earnest request, *to* a person *for* a thing 1540. 5. To address oneself *to* some principle, faculty, class, etc., in expectation of support 1794.

1. They appeale from custome to reason HOBBES. *fig.* To a. from Philip drunk to Philip sober. *Provb. phr.* *To appeal to the country* (sc. *from parliament*): to dissolve parliament after an adverse vote in the House of Commons, in order to take the sense of the constituencies on the question. 2. *fig.* To a. to the sword MACAULAY. 3. I a. to the judicious observers for the truth, etc. STEELE. 4. I appell to your Highnes for mercy CROMWELL. 5. He appealed to their sense of feudal honour FREEMAN. Pictures a. to the eye, arguments to the reason (*mod.*).

III. *trans.* To appeal a thing. To remove to a higher tribunal 1481.

To a. a case of taste to a court of final judicature LOWELL. Hence **Appea·lable** *a.* that can be appealed against, or *to*. **Appea·ler,** one who makes an appeal, or brings an accusation. **Appea·lingly** *adv.* imploringly. **Appea·lingness.**

Appeal (ăpī·l), *sb.* ME. [a. OFr. *apel* (mod. *appel*), f. *apeler*; see APPEAL *v.*] 1. A calling to account before a legal tribunal; in *Law*: A criminal accusation made by one who undertook under penalty to prove it. See APPEAL *v.* I. *Obs.* exc. *Hist.* †2. A challenge -1700. 3. The transference of a case from an inferior to a higher court; the application for such transference; the transferred case ME. *transf.* as *an appeal to the country* 1799. 4. The call to an authority for vindication, or to a witness for corroboration. Cf. APPEAL *v.* 5, 6. 1626. 5. A call for help, etc.; an entreaty 1859. 6. Language addressed *to*, or likely to influence, some particular principle, faculty, class, etc. 1833.

1. Aumerle is guiltie of my true Appeale *Rich. II*, IV. i. 79. An a. of treason TOMLINS, of felony COX. 3. *Court of Appeal*: a court for re-hearing cases previously tried in inferior courts. 4. They saw no hope but in an a. to arms FREEMAN.

Appear (ăpīə·ɪ), *v.* [ME. *apere*, a. *aper-*, stem of OFr. *apar-eir, -oir* :—L. *adp-*, *apparere*. Later *appere*, APPEAR. See AP- *pref.*[1], and for *-ea-* cf. APPEAL *v.* Orig. rhymed with *bear*.] 1. To come forth into view, as from concealment, or from a distance; to become visible. 2. To be in sight, be visible ME. 3. To present oneself formally before a tribunal; *hence*, to act as counsel ME. 4. To come before the public in any character or capacity; to come out 1607. 5. To be plainly set forth in a document; to be declared; to occur 1531. 6. To be plain, manifest ME; *impers.* ME. 7. To be in one's opinion; to seem. Also *impers.* ME. 8. To seem, as distinguished from *to be*; to be to the superficial observer 1599.

1. The Dutch begin to a. again near Gravesend MARVELL. Aperede an ongel of heuene in here slepe ME. 3. Mr. —— appeared for the prosecution (*mod.*). 4. To a. at St. James's Coffee House ADDISON, in print POPE. 5. As more large apperyth in for-sayde autoryte 1531. 6. It doth appeare, you are a worthy Judge *Merch. V.* IV. i. 236. 8. That they may appeare vnto men to fast *Matt.* vi. 16. Hence †**Appea·r** *sb.* appearance (*rare*). **Appea·rer** (senses 1, 3). **Appea·ringly** *adv.* seemingly.

Appearance (ăpīə·răns). [ME. *aparaunce*, orig. a. Fr. *aparance, -ence* :—L. *apparentia* f. *apparentem*, *apparere*. Subseq. assim. to the vb. *appere*, APPEAR. Cf. APPARENCE, -ENCY, -ENT.] 1. The action of appearing (see APPEAR 1). 2. The action of appearing formally; *esp.* in a court to answer or prosecute a suit or charge; called *making* or *putting in* an appearance ME. 3. The action of coming before the public, etc., in any character 1671; the coming out of a book 1882. 4. Occurrence in a document 1868. 5. Show, parade 1591. 6. Appearing or seeming to be; semblance ME.; †likelihood -1793; †*subjectively*, perception -1627. 7. Apparent form, look, aspect ME.; *pl.* the general 'look' of things 1677. 8. *esp.* as opp. to *reality*: Outward look or show ME. 9. *concr.* That which appears, or meets the view; *esp.* a natural phenomenon 1666; an apparition 1470.

1. The a. of the fleet was unlooked for FREEMAN. 2. All men must put in a personal a. at the last Assize SPURGEON. 3. The gravity of my behaviour at my very first a. in the world ADDISON. 5. All who pretend to make an A. STEELE. 6. *To all appearance*: so far as appears to any one. With the a. of safety SMEATON. 7. Thou hast a grim apparence *Coriol.* IV. v. 66. *pl.* Appearances are all in your favour (*mod.*). 8. To preserve an a. of consistency PALEY. *To save* or *keep up appearances*: to maintain artificially the outward signs. 9. Natural appearances COWPER. Whose.. sword Had three times slaine th' a. of the King *2 Hen. IV*, I. ii. 128. var. †**Appea·rency.**

Appeasable (ăpī·zăb'l), *a.* 1549. [a. OFr. *apaisable*; see APPEASE and -ABLE.] Capable of being appeased.

Appease (ăpī·z), *v.* [ME. *apese*, a. OFr. *apeser*, *apaisier* (mod. *apaiser*), f. *à* + *pais* (mod. *paix*) :—L. *pacem*. See AP- *pref.*[1], and for *-ea-* cf. APPEAL *v.*] 1. To bring to peace, settle (strife, etc.); †to calm (persons) -1774. Also *fig.* 2. To pacify (anger, etc.); also *fig.*; to propitiate (him who is angry) ME. 3. To assuage, allay, or relieve ME. 4. To pacify, by satisfying demands (*lit.* and *fig.*) 1548. Also †*refl.* and †*intr.* in all senses.

1. To a. a mutiny BACON, a disordred city KNOLLES. 2. To a. enmity by blandishments and bribes JOHNSON, the incensed Father MILT. *P. L.* v. 846. 3. To a. anxiety 1828. 4. To apease mennes bodyly thruste CAXTON. Bacchus appeased him [Vulcan] with wine NEWTON. Hence **Appea·ser,** one who or that which appeases. †**Appea·sive** *a.* tending to appease (*rare*).

Appeasement (ăpī·zmĕnt). ME. [a. OFr. *apaisement*; see APPEASE.] 1. The action or process of appeasing. 2. Pacification, satisfaction 1586. var. †**Appea·se** (*rare*).

Appellant (ăpe·lănt). 1480. [a. Fr., f. *appeler*; see APPEAL *v.* and -ANT.]

A. *adj.* 1. *Law* and *gen.* Appealing: a. accusing, challenging; b. appealing to a higher tribunal; c. asking or crying for aid. 1593. 2. *Law.* Appellate 1818.

B. *sb.* 1. One who appeals another of treason, etc.; see APPEAL *v.* 1. *Obs.* exc. *Hist.* Hence, †A challenger –1671. 2. One who APPEALS (senses 4, 5, 6) 1611. b. *Ch. Hist.* in pl. The Jansenists and others who appealed to a general council against the 'Unigenitus' bull 1753. 3. One who APPEALS (senses 7, 8) 1704.

1. Answer thy a... Who now defies thee thrice to single fight MILT. *Sams.* 1220. 3. An humble..a. for the laurel SWIFT.

Appellate (ăpe·lět). 1726. [ad. L. *appellatus*; see APPEAL *v.*] *ppl. a.* Appealed to; taking cognizance of appeals 1768. †*sb.* One who is appealed against (*rare*) 1726.

Appellate (æ·pĕlēit), *v. rare.* 1765. [f. L. *appellat-*; see APPEAL *v.*] To call, designate.

Appellation (æpĕlēⁱ·ʃən). ME. [a. Fr., ad. L. *appellationem*; see APPEAL *v.*] †1. (f. OFr. *apeler.*) = APPEAL *sb.* 3 (–1679); the action of appealing or calling on –1671. 2. (f. Fr. *appeler*, or L. *appellare.*) Calling by a name, nomenclature 1581. 3. A designation or name given to a person, thing, or class ME.

3. Stenny, an a. he always used of and towards the Duke CLARENDON. Hence **Appella·tional** *a.*

Appellative (ăpe·lătiv). 1520. [ad. L. *appellativus*, f. *appellat-*; see APPEAL.] A. *adj.* 1. Designating a class; *common* as opp. to *proper.* †2. Of the nature of an APPELLATION (sense 3) –1654. 3. Of or pertaining to the giving of names 1860.

B. *sb.* 1. A common noun, or name applicable to each member of a class 1591. 2. A designation, or descriptive name 1632.

2. Wily Will justified his a. SCOTT. Hence **Appe·llatively** *adv.* as a common noun.

†Appe·llatory, *a.* 1553. [ad. L. *appellatorius*, f. *appellator-*; see APPEAL and -ORY.] Pertaining to an appellant or an appeal –1726.

Appellee (æpĕlī·, ăpe·lī·). 1531. [a. Fr. *appelé*, pa. pple. of *appeler* to APPEAL.] *Law.* 1. One who is appealed against. (See APPEAL *v.* 1, 2.) †2. The defendant in an appeal; now called the *respondent.* COTGR.

Appellor (ăpe·lǭɹ, æ:pelǭ·ɹ). ME. [a. AFr. *apelour*:—OFr. *apeleor*:—L. *appellatorem*; see APPEAL.] One who accuses of crime, challenges, or informs against an accomplice.

Appenage, obs. f. APANAGE.

†Appe·nd, *v.*¹ ME. [a. OFr. *apendre*, to pertain:—L. *appendĕre*, for *appendere*, f. *ap-* = *ad-* + *pendere.* Not conn. (in Eng.) with APPEND *v.*²] *intr.* To belong, pertain, or be proper *to* –1470. Hence **Appe·nding** *ppl. a.* = APPENDANT.

Append (ăpe·nd), *v.*² 1646. [a. L. *appendĕre*; see APPEND *v.*¹] *trans.* 1. To hang on, attach as a pendant 1646. 2. To attach as an accessory 1779, or as an appendix 1843.

2. Some additional remarks .. are appended MILL.

Appendage (ăpe·ndĕdʒ). 1649. [f. prec. + -AGE; cf. *apanage* (in 17th c. *appennage*).] 1. That which is attached as if by being hung on; a subsidiary, but not an essential, adjunct 1713; *esp.* an addition to territory or property 1667; *Nat. Hist.* a subsidiary organ 1785. Also *transf.* of persons 1838.

1. Dwelling-houses and their appendages DIGBY. Antennæ and other appendages used for feeling 1874. The dance..being..merely an a. to the Song 1763. Hence **Appe·ndaged** *ppl. a.* having an a.

Appendance, -ence (ăpe·ndĕns). 1523. [a. Fr., f. *a(p)pendre*; see APPEND¹.] †1. A dependent possession –1662. †2. An extraneous adjunct or concomitant –1677. 3. *Law.* The fact of being appendant 1832.

†Appe·ndancy, -ency. 1615. [f. APPENDANT.] 1. The quality or state of being appendant 1641. 2. = APPENDANCE 2. –1669.

Appendant, -ent (ăpe·ndĕnt). 1509. [a. Fr., pr. pple. of *appendre*. Orig. conn. with APPEND *v.*¹, but influenced by APPEND *v.*²]

A. *adj.* Const. *to, on.* 1. *Law.* Attached or belonging as an additional but subsidiary right 1523. 2. Attached in a subordinate relation; adjunct 1577. 3. Attendant, consequent 1509. 4. *lit.* Hanging attached (*to*) 1576.

1. Those tenantes that haue commen appendaunt FITZHERB. Liberties..a. to manors SELDEN. 3. A pleasure embased with no a. sting SOUTH. 4. The seal a. by a silken cord 1874.

B. *sb.* [the adj. used *absol.*] *arch.* 1. *Law.* A lesser right or property attached by prescription to one more important 1525. 2. An appendage; a dependency 1587; also *transf.* of persons 1641. 3. A consequent quality, property, principle, etc. 1587. 4. An appendix; a pendant 1570.

3. The numerous corollaries or appendents COLERIDGE.

Appe·ndical, *a.* 1850. [f. L. *appendicem* + -AL¹.] Of the nature of an appendix.

†Appe·ndicate, *v. rare.* 1677. [f. as prec.] To append. Hence **†Appe·ndica·tion,** addition by way of appendix (*rare*).

†Appe·ndice, *v. rare.* 1661. [f. *appendice* sb.; see APPENDIX.] To add as an appendix –1702. *intr.* To form an appendix. Hence **Appe·ndicing** *ppl. a.* appendant.

Appendicitis (ăpendisəi·tis). 1886. [f. L. *appendic-, -ix* + -ITIS.] *Med.* Inflammation of the vermiform appendix of the cæcum.

Appendicle (ăpe·ndik'l). 1611. [ad. L. *appendicula*, dim. of APPENDIX.] A small appendix or appendage. Hence **Appendi·cular** *a.* belonging to, or of the nature of, an a. **Appendi·culate** *a.* furnished with appendicles; forming an a.; var. **Appendi·culated** *ppl. a.*

Appendicularian (æpĕndi:kiŭlēᵊ·riăn), *a.* 1880. [f. mod.L. *Appendicularia* (see prec.) + -AN.] *Zool.* Pertaining to the *Appendicularia*, a family of minute ascidian molluscs, with long tail-appendages. Also as *sb.*

Appendix (ăpe·ndiks), *sb.* Pl. **-ices** (-isīz) and **-ixes.** 1542. [a. L., f. *appendĕre*; see APPEND. A sing. *appendice* after Fr. occurs in 17th c.] = APPENDAGE, but more restricted in use. 1. A subsidiary extraneous adjunct; a dependency. *Obs.* exc. as in 2. 1592. †*transf.* of persons –1692. 2. An addition subjoined to a document or book, having some contributory value, but not essential to completeness 1549. 3. *Biol.* A small process developed from the surface of any organ 1615. †4. A subsidiary accompaniment; an accessory –1699.

1. Normandy, once an A. of the Crown of England HOWELL. My children .. are but the Appendixes of me 1692. 2. Towards the end whereof is an A. or Postscript 1638. 4. Idleness is an a. to nobility BURTON.

Appendix (ăpe·ndiks), *v. rare.* 1755. [f. the sb.] To add as an appendix. Hence **Appe·ndixed** *ppl. a.*

Appennage, obs. f. APANAGE.

Appense (ăpe·ns), *a. rare.* 1829. [f. L. *appensus*, *appendĕre* to APPEND.] *Bot.* Hung up, pendulous.

†Appe·ntice. *rare.* 1616. [a. Fr. *appentis*, OFr. *apentis*, f. *apendre*, 3 sing. *apent*, after adjs. in *-tis, -tif*; cf. APPRENTICE. Hence aphet. PENTICE, corrupted to PENTHOUSE.] A lean-to building, a penthouse.

†Appercei·ve, *v.* ME. [a. OFr. *aperceveir*:—late L. **appercipĕre*, for **appercipĕre*, f. *ap-* = *ad-* + *percipere* to PERCEIVE. See AP- *pref.*¹] To perceive, recognize, notice –1614.

Apperception (æpəɹse·pʃən). 1753. [ad. Fr. *aperception*, f. *apercevoir*; see prec.] *Metaph.* 1. The mind's perception of itself as a conscious agent; self-consciousness. 2. Mental perception, recognition 1839.

1. A.. by which we are conscious of our own existence, and conscious of our own perceptions REID.

†Appe·ril. *rare.* 1607. [f. PERIL *sb.* See A- *pref.* 11.] Peril –1632.

Faith, I will bail him, at mine own a. B. JONS.

Appertain (æpəɹtēⁱ·n), *v.* ME. [a. OFr. *apartenir, aper-*:—late L. *adpertinere*, f. *ad* + *pertinere.* See AP- *pref.*¹] 1. *intr.* To belong as parts to the whole, or as members to a family or class, and hence, to the head of the family; to be related, akin *to* 1450. 2. To belong, or be suited, proper, or appropriate *to* ME. 3. To pertain, relate ME. †*impers.* –1623. †*absol. As appertains*: as is proper –1611. †4. *trans.* (*to* omitted.) To belong to, befit –1601.

1. All the men that appertained unto Korah *Numb.* xvi. 32. 2. Do all rites, That appertaine unto a buriall *Much Ado* IV. i. 210. Hence **†Appertai·nance,** var. of APPURTENANCE. **†Appertai·nment** (*rare*) *Tr. & Cr.* II. iii. 87. **Appertinance, -ence,** obs. ff. APPURTENANCE. **Appe·rtinent,** var. of APPURTENANT, esp. in the non-legal sense.

†Appertise, -yse. 1480. [a. OFr., f. *apert*; see APERT.] Evidence of skill, *esp.* in arms.

†Appe·te, *v.* ME. [a. Fr. *appéter*, ad. L. *appetere.*] To seek after, desire –1685.

Appetence (æ·pĭtĕns). 1610. [a. Fr., ad. L. *appetentia*; see next.] The action of seeking for; appetite, desire.

Appetency (æ·pĭtĕnsi). 1627. [ad. L. *appetentia*, f. *appetentem*; see next.] 1. *strictly*, The state of longing for, desiring; appetite, passion. Also = APPETENCE. Const. *of, for, after.* 1631. 2. Instinctive inclination or propensity 1802. 3. Of things inanimate: Natural tendency, affinity 1627. 4. *Metaph.* Suggested by Sir W. Hamilton as a term including both desire and volition 1836.

1. Brutish appetencies 1652. An a. after literary distinction MASSON.

Appetent (æ·pĭtĕnt). ME. [ad. L. *appetentem, appetere.*] 1. Longing, eagerly desirous. Const. *after, of.* 2. *Metaph.* Connected with desire and volition 1837.

1. A. after glory and renown 1646.

Appetible (æ·pĭtib'l), *a.* 1471. [ad. L. *appetibilis*, f. *appetere.*] *adj.* †1. Attractive. 2. Worthy of being sought after; desirable 1622. †Also as *sb.* SOUTH.

2. The a. fruit 1847. Hence **A:ppetibi·lity.** ?*Obs.*

†Appeti·sse, *v.* [a. Fr. *appetisser*, f. *à+petit.*] To make small. CAXTON.

Appetite (æ·pĭtəit), *sb.* ME. [a. OFr. *apetit*, ad. L. *appetitus*, f. *appetere.*] Const. *for*; formerly *to, of,* and *inf.* 1. Bent of the mind; desire, inclination, disposition. 2. *vaguely*, Inclination, preference, liking, fancy (*arch.*) 1490. 3. *esp.* The determinate desire to satisfy the natural necessities, or fulfil the natural functions, of the body; one of those instinctive cravings which secure the preservation of the individual and the race ME. 4. *spec.* Craving for food, hunger. Also *fig.* ME. 5. Capacity for, or feeling as regards, food; relish ME. †6. Of things: Natural tendency towards –1667. 7. The object of desire (*arch.*) ME. 8. A whet. (So in Fr.) 1693.

1. Obeying without reflection the a. of the moment GROTE. Such an a. for consolation SHERIDAN. 2. *To* or *after one's appetite*: just as one pleases. 3. The most violent Appetites in all Creatures are Lust and Hunger ADDISON. 4. Now good digestion waite on A., And health on both *Macb.* III. iv. 38. 5. I have seen a Man in Love..lose his A. ADDISON. Hence **†A·ppetite** *v.* to have an a. for; to satisfy. **A·ppetited** *ppl. a.* furnished with an a.

Appetition (æpĭti·ʃən). 1603. [ad. L. *appetitionem*, f. *appetit-*; see prec.] The direction of desire towards an object or purpose; seeking after.

Appetitive (æ·pĭtəitiv, ăpe·tĭtiv), *a.* 1577. [a. Fr. *appetitif, -ive*, ad. L. **appetitivus*, f. *appetit-*; see APPETITE *sb.* and -IVE.] 1. Characterized by appetite. 2. Giving an appetite; attractive (*rare*) 1864.

Appetize (æ·pĭtəiz), *v. rare.* [f. Fr. *appétissant*, **appetissier* as if:—L. **adpetitiare*; assim. to vbs. in -IZE. In Eng. perh. only colloq.] To give appetite, to cause relish for food. Hence **A·ppetized** *ppl. a.* furnished with an appetite. **A·ppetizement,** hunger (*rare*). **A·ppetizer,** a whet or stimulant to appetite. **A·ppetizing** *ppl. a.* exciting a desire, *esp.* for food; stimulating the appetite. **Appeti·zingly** *adv.*

Applaud (ăplǭ·d), *v.* 1536. [ad. L. *applaudere*, f. *ap-* = *ad-* + *plaudere.*] 1. *intr.* To clap the hands in expression of approbation; *hence*, to express approval loudly 1598. †2. To applaud *to*: To give approbation *to* –1685; to express agreement with –1635. 3. *trans.* To express approval of audibly, or in any way 1591.

1. Caps, hands, and tongues, a. it to the clouds *Haml.* IV. v. 107. 3. I would a. thee to the very Eccho, That should a. again *Macb.* V. iii. 54. O that our Fathers would a. our loues *Two Gent.* I. iii. 48. Hence **†Applau·d** *sb.* applause. **Applau·ded** *ppl. a.* loudly approved. **Applau·der.** **Applau·dingly** *adv.*

Applause (ăplǭ·z), *sb.* 1596. [ad. L. *applausus*, f. *applaudere*; see prec.] 1. Approbation loudly expressed 1596; marked approval or commendation 1601. †2. Agreement or assent. Cf. APPLAUD *v.* 2. *rare.* 1612. †3. The object of applause 1623.

1. Hearing a. and vniversall shout *Merch. V.* III. ii. 144. The Censures and Applauses of Men 1714. 3. The applause! delight! the wonder of our stage B.

JONS. Hence †**Applau·sible** *a.* worthy to be applauded (*rare*).

Applausive (ăplǭ·siv), *a.* 1605. [f. L. *applaus-, applaudere* + -IVE.] 1. Loudly expressive of approbation 1609; approbative 1628. †2. Worthy of applause -1607. Hence **Applau·sively** *adv.*

Apple (æ·p'l). [Com. Teut.: OE. *æppel.* Origin unknown.] 1. The round firm fleshy fruit of a Rosaceous tree (*Pyrus Malus*), found wild, as the Crab-apple, in Europe, etc., and cultivated in innumerable varieties all over the two Temperate Zones OE.; short for APPLE-TREE 1626. 2. Any fruit, or similar vegetable production; esp. such as in some respect resemble the Apple OE.; *Bot.* any fruit of the structure of the Apple; a pome 1729. 3. Hence forming part of many names of fruits; as †**Apple Punic**, the pomegranate; **Apple of Sodom**, or *Dead Sea Fruit*, of fair appearance externally, but turning, when grasped, into smoke and ashes; supposed by some to be the fruit of *Solanum Sodomeum*, by others of *Calotropis procera*; *fig.* any hollow disappointing thing ME.; **Apple of Adam** = ADAM'S APPLE; **Apple of Love** = LOVE APPLE. 4. The fruit of the 'forbidden tree' (Milton) OE. 5. Anything like an apple in form or colour, as *Golden Apple*: the Orb in the British Regalia OE.

1. A goodly a. rotten at the heart *Merch. V*, I. iii. 102. There's small choise in rotten apples *Tam. Shr.* I. i. 139. 2. The fruit or apples of Palm-trees TOPSELL. 5. A round bal or hollow a. of glasse 1601.

Phrases: **Apple of discord**: the golden a. inscribed 'For the fairest', thrown by Eris, the personification of discord, into the assembly of the gods, and contended for by Juno, Minerva, and Venus; whence, any subject of dissension. **Apple of the eye**: the pupil, which was supposed to be a globular solid body. Used as a symbol of that which is most cherished.

Combs.: **a.-aphis**, the insect (*Lachnus lanigerus*) which produces **a.-blight**, a cottony substance found on trees; **-brandy**, a spirit distilled from cider; **-corer**; **-eating** *a.*, *fig.* easily-tempted; †**-fallow** *a.*, yellowish-red, bay; **-fly**, a small green fly found sometimes within an apple; †**-garth**, an orchard; †**-gray** *a.*, streaky in colour like an a.; **-jack**, U.S. name for *a.-brandy*; **-moth**, *Tortrix pomana*; **-shell**, **-snail**, a family of Gasteropods, so named from their shape; †**-squire**, a pimp; **-tree**; **-wife**, **-woman**, one who keeps a stall for the sale of apples; **-worm**, the maggot bred in apples; †**-yard** = *-garth.*

To upset the apple-cart: see UPSET *v.*

Apple (æ·p'l), *v. rare.* OE. [f. the sb.] 1. To form or turn into apples; to bear apples. 2. *intr.* To gather apples 1799.

A·pple-John. Also **John-Apple.** 1597. [f. S. John's Day, when it is ripe.] An apple said to keep two years, and to be ripe when much withered.

A dish of Apple-Iohns 2 *Hen. IV*, II. iv. 5.

Apple-pie. 1590. A pie made with apples; *transf.* the Willow-herb.

Apple-pie bed: a bed in which, as a practical joke, the sheets are so folded that a person cannot get his legs down. *Apple-pie order*: complete order. [Explained as '*Cap-a-pie order*', but this phr. is not found.]

†**Appli·able**, *a.* 1499. [f. APPLY *v.*; earlier than APPLICABLE.] 1. Ready to apply oneself *to*; docile, well-disposed -1699. 2. Capable of being APPLIED; having reference -1679. Hence †**Appli·ableness.** †**Appli·ably** *adv.*

Appliance (ăplai·ăns). 1561. [f. APPLY *v.* + -ANCE.] †1. Compliance; subservience -1603. 2. The action of applying 1561. 3. A thing applied as means to an end; apparatus 1597.

1. Too noble, to conserue a life In base appliances *Meas. for M.* III. i. 89. 2. Acted-on..by the a. of birch-rods CARLYLE. 3. Aske God for Temp'rance; that's th' a. onely which your disease requires *Hen. VIII*, I. i. 124. Hence **Appli·ancy**, adaptability, pliancy (*rare*).

†**Appli·ant**, *a.* ME. [a. OFr. *apliant, aplier*; see APPLY.] Pliant; diligent; pertinent *to* (*rare*).

Applicable (æ·plikăb'l), *a.* 1563. [f. L. *applicare* + -ABLE; cf. Fr. *applicable.* Repl. *appliable.*] †1. = APPLIABLE 1. -1674. 2. Capable of being applied; having reference. (See APPLY *v.*) 1660. 3. Fit or suitable 1835. Hence **A·pplicableness** (*rare*) = APPLICABILITY.

Applicant (æ·plikănt), *a.* (*sb.*) 1485. [ad. L. *applicantem, applicare*; see APPLY *v.*] †1. Pliant, docile (*rare*). 2. Applying (*rare*). 3. *sb.* One who applies or makes request 1485.

Applicate (æ·plikeit, -ĕt). 1534. [ad. L. *applicatus*; see APPLY *v.*] A. *adj.* †1. Closely adapted, suited; inclined towards 1652. 2. Put to practical use; applied, concrete 1796.

2. A. number = concrete HUTTON.

B. *sb.* 1. In Conic Sections: An ordinate 1706. 2. An applied department; an application 1855.

2. Geometry and its applicates 1855.

†**A·pplicate**, *v.* 1531. [f. L. *applicat-.*] By-form of APPLY.

Application (æplikēi·ʃən). 1493. [a. Fr., ad. L. *applicationem*; see APPLY.] The action of applying; the thing applied. 1. The action of putting a thing to another 1632; *esp.* in *Geom.* 1727. 2. The putting on of a medicament; the remedy so applied 1601. 3. The bringing of anything to bear practically upon another; *spec.* in *Theol.* of 'the redemption purchased by Christ' 1647. 4. The putting of anything to a use or purpose; employment 1538. 5. The bringing of a general or figurative statement to bear upon a particular case, or upon matters of practice; the moral of a fable 1493; the capacity of being thus used; relevancy 1842. 6. The action of applying one's self closely *to* a task, diligence 1605; the object of such diligence 1734. †7. Obsequiousness 1605. 8. *Astr.* The action of approaching. ? *Obs.* 1594. 9. The action of making an †appeal, request, or petition *to* a person; the request so made 1647.

1. The place of a. of a force 1879. 2. Application Of Medicines to th' Imagination BUTLER *Hud.* II. iii. 287. 3. A sufficient a. of legal penalties MILL. 4. The a. of the loadstone to navigation 1794. 5. The a. of the Law to the present case HOBBES. A parable, related without any a. or moral BUTLER. This has no a. to present circumstances (*mod.*). 6. A. for ever so short a time kills me LAMB. 9. Frequent applications to God in prayer BURNET.

Applicative (æ·plikeitiv, -ĕtiv), *a.* 1638. [f. L. *applicat-* (see APPLICATE) + -IVE.] Characterized by being put into actual contact with anything 1680; practical 1638. Hence **A·pplicatively** *adv.* practically.

Applicator (æ·plikeitər). *rare.* 1659. [a. L. **applicator*; see APPLY.] He who (*obs.*) or that which applies.

Applicatory (æ·plikatŏri), *a.* 1540. [f. L. *applicat-* (see APPLICATE) + -ORY.] Having the property of applying to practical use; †applicable 1649; †making application or request -1673. †As *sb.* A means of applying to practical use -1667. Hence **A·pplicato·rily** *adv.* by way of application or request.

Applied (ăplai·d), *ppl. a.* 1500. [f. APPLY *v.* + -ED.] †1. Folded (*rare*). 2. Put to practical use; practical, as opp. to *abstract* or *theoretical* 1656. Hence †**Appli·edly** *adv.* (*rare*).

Appli·er. 1565. [f. APPLY *v.* + -ER[1].] He who, or that which, applies.

†**Appli·que, -i·ke**, *v.* 1483. [a. Fr. *appliquer.*] By-form of APPLY *v.*

‖**Appliqué** (aplīke), *sb.* 1841. [Fr., pa. pple. used as sb.] Work applied to or laid on another material; *spec.* a trimming cut out in outline and laid on another surface. Also in metal work. Hence **Appliquéd.**

Applot (ăplǫ·t), *v.* 1647. [f. PLOT; cf. *lot, allot.*] To divide into plots or parts; to apportion. Hence **Applo·tment**, apportionment.

Apply (ăplai·), *v.* [ME. *aplie*, a. OFr. *aplier*:—L. *applicare*, f. *ap-* = *ad-* + *plicare.* Cf. APPLIQUE.] I. To put a thing into practical contact with another. 1. *trans.* To bring into contact; to put close *to*; *esp.* in *Geom.* 1660. †2. *intr.* To come into, or be in, contact -1793. 3. *trans.* To place (a plaster, etc.) in contact with the body; *hence*, to administer any remedy 1541; *fig.* to bring (a thing) to bear upon 1596. 4. To appropriate *to* 1460; to put to use, dispose of 1502. 5. To use (a word) in special reference *to* (a thing) 1628. 6. To bring (a law, test, etc.) into contact with facts, to put into practical operation 1586. 7. To refer (a general or figurative statement) *to* a particular instance ME. 8. *intr.* To have a valid reference *to* 1790. †9. *trans.* To refer, ascribe -1709; to compare, liken -1661.

1. He shal applie to hym hooli men WYCLIF *Numb.* xvi. 5. To a. light, heat, a foot-rule *to* (*mod.*). 3. A. the iuyce to any wound 1579. To a. comfort to him who is not..ready for it FULLER. 4. To a. the Poll money to the use of the warre MARVELL. 6. The Difficulty is how to a. this Rule SHERLOCK. 7. I leave you to a. the remark FORDYCE. 8. It will a. no less to our own case.

II. To bring oneself into close contact with a pursuit. 1. To give or devote (any faculty) assiduously *to*, or *to do* 1450; also *refl.* and *intr.* †2. *trans.* To handle vigorously; to wield, practise. Replaced by PLY. -1667. †3. To keep at (a person) *with.* See PLY. -1594.

1. That we may applie oure hertes vnto wyssdome *Ps.* lxxxix. 12. Let your remembrance a. to Banquo *Macb.* III. ii. 30. 2. The birds thir quire a. MILT.

III. To bend, conform, or adapt *to. trans.*, †*refl.*, and †*intr.* ME.

Wholy applyinge himselfe to the Kings humour 1533.

IV. To bend or direct *to.* (Cf. L. *applicare navem*, and ACCOST, ADDRESS.) †1. To bring (a ship) to land; to direct or steer (her course, one's course, etc.) -1613; *intr.* to land; to steer, go -1819. †2. *trans.* To address or direct (words) to -1744. 3. *intr.* with *to.* †a. To appeal to. b. To address oneself for information or aid. Also *refl.* 1642.

3. b. Exiles, who had come..to a. for succour MACAULAY. Hence **Apply·ing** *vbl. sb.* application; plying. †**Apply·ment** = APPLICATION, APPLIANCE.

‖**Appoggiatura** (appǫ:ddʒatū·ră). 1753. [It. Cf. Fr. APPUI.] *Mus.* A grace-note or passing tone prefixed as a support to an essential note of a melody. *transf.* A prop, a point of support.

Appoint (ăpoi·nt), *v.* [ME. *apoint(e*, a. OFr. *apointer, -ier*, f. *à point*; see POINT. Sometimes refash. after med.L. *appunctare.*] I. To come, or bring matters, to a point. 1. *intr.* (and *pass.*) †To arrange definitely -1660; to make an appointment (*arch.*) 1509; *trans.* to arrange (*arch.*) 1588; to make an appointment for a meeting with 1528. 2. †*refl.* and *pass.* To make up one's mind -1586; *intr.* to resolve (*arch.*) 1440.

1. Apointed to be playd to Morowe night 1604. 2. The Lord had appointed to defeate the good counsell of Ahithophel 2 *Sam.* xvii. 14.

II. To determine authoritatively. 1. *trans.* To fix (a time, *later* a place) for any act ME.; to fix a. *that* it shall be, b. a thing 1538. †2. To grant authoritatively -1764. 3. *Law.* To declare an appointment under a power. (See APPOINTMENT 5.) 1601. 4. To ordain, devote, destine (a person or thing) *to* or *for* (*arch.*); *to do* or *suffer* (*arch.*) 1496. 5. To ordain, set up, nominate 1460.

1. The time appointed for execution DE FOE. T'a. Who should attend on him *Hen. VIII*, I. i. 74. 4. The Creator..has appointed every thing to a certain Use BUDGELL. Appointed to be tried DE FOE. 5. Who appointed you then (*mod.*). To a. a Committee ADDISON.

III. (Cf. Fr. *en bon point.*) †To put in order, make ready -1615; *esp.* to equip completely, to furnish. *Obs.* exc. in pa. pple. 1490.

Lodgings..well-appointed 1660. Thus appointed.. he was in readiness to depart SCOTT.

IV. After Fr. and L. †1. To point to or at, to point out -1556. †2. To arraign -1674 (*rare*).

2. A. not heavenly disposition, father MILT. *Sams.* 373. Hence **Appoi·ntable** *a.* (?*Obs.*) capable of being, or proper to be, appointed. **Appoi·ntee**, one who is nominated to an office, or one in whose favour a power of APPOINTMENT is exercised. **Appoi·nter**, one who ordains, or nominates. (See also APPOINTOR.)

Appoi·nt, *sb.* 1555. [f. the vb. Cf. Fr. *appoint.*] †1. Agreement -1565. †2. Equipment 1592. 3. *Comm.* Settlement *per appoint*: Exact and independent settlement, *i.e.* not by payments on account, etc.

Appointed (ăpoi·ntĕd), *ppl. a.* 1535. [f. as prec.] 1. Fixed beforehand 1585; fixed by authority 1535. 2. With *well, ill*, etc.: Fitted out, equipped 1535.

‖**Appointé** (apwănte), *a.* 1753. [Fr.] *Her.* When things are placed touching each other at the points or ends.

Appointment (ăpoi·ntmĕnt). ME. [a. OFr. *apointement*; see APPOINT *v.*] †1. The action of agreeing; a pact, contract -1745; *spec.* the act of capitulating; terms of capitulation -1605. 2. *spec.* An agreement for a meeting; engagement, assignation 1530. †3. Purpose -1606. 4. The action of ordaining what is to be done; direction, ordinance 1440. 5. *Law.* The act of declaring the destination of any specific property, in exercise of a power conferred for that purpose 1601. 6. The action of nominating to, or placing in, an office; the office itself 1658. 7. Equipment, outfit, furniture, or any article thereof. Now usu. *pl.* 1575. †8. An allowance paid, *esp.* to a public officer -1761.

2. For missing your meetings and appointments *Merry W.* III. i. 92. 3. No certain purpose or a. MORE. 4. According to a natural order or a. BUTLER. 5. An a...to a charitable use BLACKSTONE. 6. A poor baronet, hoping for an a. GEO. ELIOT. 7. I have not one a... which I set so much store by, as I do by these jack-boots STERNE. 8. He had the appointments of an ambassador BURNET.

Appointor (ăpoi·ntǫ̆r). 1882. [repr. ME. *appointour*:—OF. *apointeor*; see APPOINT.] *Law.* The legal form of APPOINTER: The person who exercises a power of appointment.

†**Appo·rt**, *sb.* ME. [a. OFr. *aport*, f. *aporter*; see AP- *pref.*[1]] 1. Demeanour -1606. 2. *pl.* Things brought; offerings; revenues -1530. So †**Appo·rt**, *v.* to bring; *intr.* to arrive *at*.

Apportion (ăpōə·ɹʃən), *v.* 1574. [a. OFr. *apportionner*, f. *à* + *portionner*, f. *portion*.] 1. To assign (*to*) as a proper portion; to allot 1587. 2. To portion out, to share 1574. 3. To proportion (*arch.*) 1615.

1. His guardians had apportioned to him an allowance DISRAELI. 2. To a. the expenses of production between the two MILL. Hence **Appo·rtionable** *a.*

†**Appo·rtionate**, *v.* 1523. [f. med.L. *apportionat-*, *apportionare*. Occurs first as pa. pple.] = APPORTION *v.*

Apportionment (ăpōə·ɹʃənmĕnt). 1628. [f. APPORTION *v.* + -MENT.] 1. The act of distributing or allotting in proper shares. 2. The state or fact of being thus distributed 1681.

†**Appo·se**, *v.*[1] ME. [orig. a var. of OPPOSE, ME. *oposen* and *aposen* = OFr. *oposer* and *aposer*, used in med.L. sense of *opponere* 'to argue against'. In senses which suggested *apponere*, as if 'to put it to one', the form *appose* prevailed. Aphet. to POSE, the mod. repr. See next.] 1. To confront with objections or hard questions; to examine -1615. *absol.* and *intr.* -1581. 2. *spec.* To examine as to accounts, to audit -1738. 3. = OPPOSE.

1. Thus beginneth the Master to a. his Scholar 1553. I would I might a. CAMPION. Hence †**Appo·sal**, a posing question; legal examination of accounts. †**Appo·ser**, an examiner; an Exchequer officer who audited the sheriffs' accounts (till 1833).

Appose (ăpōᵘ·z, emphatic æ·pōᵘ·z), *v.*[2] 1593. [repr. L. *apponere*, after *compose*, etc., formed on OFr. *poser*:—L. *pausare*, but treated as repr. L. *ponere* (see PAUSE, POSE).] 1. To put one thing *to* another, as a seal to a document; to put (food) before. 2. To place in apposition or juxtaposition 1800.

1. Atrides..food sufficient Appos'd before them, and the peers appos'd their hands to it CHAPMAN.

Apposite (æ·pŏzit), *a.* 1621. [ad. L. *appositus*, *app-*, *ad-ponere*.] 1. Well put or applied; appropriate (*to*). †2. Of persons: Ready with apt remarks -1788. 3. See OPPOSITE.

1. Her language is not copious but apposit HABINGTON. Hence **A·pposite·ly** *adv.*, **-ness**.

Apposition[1] (æpozi·ʃən). 1659. [a. OFr. *aposicion*, *apposition*, var. of *opposition*, in med. L. sense of *opponere*; see APPOSE *v.*[1]] A public disputation by scholars; a formal examination by question and answer; still applied to the Speech Day at St. Paul's School, London.

Apposition[2] (æpozi·ʃən). ME. [ad. L. *appositionem*, f. *apponere*; see APPOSITE.] 1. The action of apposing (see APPOSE[2] 1); application 1541; †that which is apposed, an addition -1655. 2. The placing of things in contact, or side by side 1660; the being so placed, juxtaposition, parallelism 1606. †3. *Rhet.* The addition of a parallel word, etc., by way of explanation or illustration of another -1638. 4. *Gram.* The placing of a word beside, or in syntactic parallelism with, another; *spec.* the addition of one sb. to another, or to a noun clause, as an attribute or complement; the position of the sb. so placed 1440.

1. By the A. of a Publick Seal 1726. 2. The cut surfaces and edges of the wounds are to be brought into a. T. BRYANT. 4. In various forms of a., especially that of the word to the sentence JOWETT. Hence **Appo·si·tional** *a.* of or belonging to a.; -ly *adv.*

Appositive (ăpǫ·zitiv), *a.* 1693. [f. L. *apposit-* (see APPOSITE) + -IVE.] Of, pertaining to, or standing in apposition. Also as *sb.* Hence **Appo·sitively** *adv.* in construction.

Appraisal (ăprē̆ⁱ·zăl). 1817. [f. next.] The act of appraising; the setting of a price. Also *fig.*

Appraise (ăprē̆ⁱ·z), *v.* 1535. [f. PRAISE *v.*, which it replaces in this sense. Cf. APPRIZE.] 1. To fix a price for; *esp.* as an official valuer. 2. *transf.* To estimate the amount, or worth of. Also *refl.* 1841.

1. All this morning at Pegg Kite's..appraising her goods that her mother has left PEPYS. 2. Appraised his [the infant's] weight TENNYSON. Hence **Apprai·sable** *a.* **Apprai·singly** *adv.*

Appraisement (ăprē̆ⁱ·zmĕnt). 1642. [f. as prec. + -MENT.] 1. The action of appraising; valuation by an official appraiser. 2. Estimated value 1703. 3. *transf.* Estimation of worth generally 1858.

Appraiser (ăprē̆ⁱ·zəɹ). 1529. [f. as prec. + -ER[1].] One who appraises: *spec.* a licensed valuer. Also *transf.*

The appraisers sworn to appraise goods sold under distress for rent 1857.

†**A·pprecate**, *v. rare.* 1631. [f. L. *apprecat-*, *apprecari*, f. *ad* + *precari*, f. *precem*.] To pray for, devoutly wish, *to* -1674. Hence †**Apprecation**. †**A·pprecatory** *a.* intercessory.

Appreciable (ăprī·ʃiˌăb'l), *a.* 1818. [f. L. *appretiare*, later *appreciare* + -BLE; cf. Fr. *appréciable*.] 1. Capable of being appreciated, valued, or recognized by the mind. 2. Perceptible, sensible 1820.

1. An a. interest 1818. Hence **Appre·ciably** *adv.*

Appreciate (ăprī·ʃiˌeⁱt), *v.* 1655. [f. L. *appretiat-*, *appretiare*, f. *ap-*, *ad-*, + *pretium*. Not in Johnson.] 1. *trans.* To form an estimate of worth, quality, or amount 1769. 2. To estimate aright 1798; *esp.* to be sensitive to, or sensible of, any delicate impression or distinction 1833. 3. To esteem adequately or highly 1655. 4. To raise in value; opp. to *depreciate* 1779; *intr.* (esp. in U. S.) 1789.

1. The..want of candour..with which Priestley appretiated Hume 1817. 2. A blind man is able to a. sound, touch, etc., but not colours F. HALL. 3. To a. Homer GLADSTONE. 4. Gold has been steadily appreciating in value 1882. Hence **Appre·ciated**, adequately valued; enhanced in exchangeable value. **Appre·ciatingly** *adv.*

Appreciation (ăprīʃiˌē̆ⁱ·ʃən). [a. Fr., f. *apprécier*, L. *appretiare*; see APPRECIATE and -TION. Found once *c* 1400; then not till 17th c.] 1. The action of setting a money value upon; appraisement (*rare*) 1799. 2. The action of estimating; deliberate judgement 1604. 3. Perception, *esp.* of delicate impressions or distinctions ME. 4. Adequate or high estimation 1650. 5. Rise in exchangeable value. See APPRECIATE 4. 1789.

2. A. of the condition of things 1880. 3. A. of the intricacies of a country 1879. 4. A. of scenery 1870. 5. A considerable a. in the value of Gold GOSCHEN.

Appreciative (ăprī·ʃiˌĕtiv), *a.* 1850. [f. L. *appreciat-* + -IVE. Cf. Fr. *appréciatif*.] Showing APPRECIATION (senses 3, 4).

Kindly a. words 1850. Hence **Appre·ciative·ly** *adv.*, **-ness**.

Appreciator (ăprī·ʃiˌeⁱtəɹ). 1842. [f. L. *appretiare*, after L. analogies.] One who values adequately or highly.

Appreciatory (ăprī·ʃiˌătəri), *a.* 1819. [f. prec.; see -ORY.] Of or befitting an appreciator; appreciative. Hence **Appre·ciatorily** *adv.*

Appredicate (æ̆pre·dikeⁱt). 1837. [ad. mod. L. *appraedicatum* (= Gr. προσκατηγορούμενον); see PREDICATE.] The copula, considered as not included in the predicate.

Apprehend (æprĭhe·nd), *v.* ME. [a. Fr. *appréhender*, ad. L. *app-*, *adprehendere*, f. *ad* + *prehendere*. The earlier contracted form *apprendere* had taken the sense of 'learn', and later 'teach, inform'; cf. Fr. *apprendre*, Eng. APPRISE.] I. Physical. 1. To lay hold upon, seize (*lit.* and *fig.*) *arch.* 1572. 2. To seize in name of law, arrest 1548. †3. To take possession of -1652; to embrace (an offer, etc.) -1633.

2. To fynde sum occasion..to attache and apprehende him UDALL.

II. Mental. †1. *gen.* To learn. Also *absol.* -1680. 2. To become or be conscious by the senses of 1635; †to feel -1670. 3. To lay hold of with the intellect; to see; to catch the meaning of; also *absol.* 1577. 4. To understand (a thing *to be*); to take as; also *absol.* 1614. 5. To anticipate (*mostly* things adverse) 1603. 6. To anticipate with fear 1606.

1. Thereby they provoke many to a. virtue ELYOT. 2. To a. a voice from heaven HOBBES. 3. Each man ..avails him of what worth He apprehends in you BROWNING. As soone..apprehended as read 1631. Cousin, you a. passing shrewdly *Much Ado* II. i. 84. 4. They apprehended it a great courtesy done unto them FULLER. In general, I a., the later French critics have given the preference to Racine HALLAM. 5. A man that apprehends death no more dreadfully, but as a drunken sleepe *Meas. for M.* IV. ii. 149. 6. Which makes me much a. the end of those honest Worthies SIR T. BROWNE. Hence **Apprehe·nded** *ppl. a.* arrested; conceived; dreaded. **Apprehe·nder**, one who seizes, or arrests; one who feels, or understands. **Apprehe·ndingly** *adv.* by apprehending.

Apprehensible (æprĭhe·nsib'l), *a.* 1631. [ad. L. *apprehensibilis*, f. *apprehens-*, *apprehendere*.] Capable of being APPREHENDED (see APPREHEND II. 5, 6). Const. *by*, *to*. Hence **Apprehe·nsibi·lity**. **Apprehe·nsibly** *adv.* (*rare*).

Apprehension (æprĭhe·nʃən). ME. [ad. (? through Fr.) L. *apprehensionem*; see APPREHEND and -ION.] *gen.* The action of seizing upon, seizure. The mental senses are the earliest. I. Physical. 1. The action of laying hold of; prehension (*rare*) 1646. 2. *Law.* The action of taking manual possession 1832. 3. Seizure or arrest in the name of justice or authority 1577.

1. [A lobster's claw is] a part of a. SIR T. BROWNE. 3. A warrant for his a. was obtained 1881.

II. Mental. 1. †*gen.* The action of learning -1641; sensible perception (*arch.*) 1590. †2. Sympathetic perception -1644. 3. The action of grasping with the intellect; conception, intellection 1597. 4. The apprehensive faculty; understanding 1570. 5. The product, or the abiding result, of grasping mentally; a conception; a view, notion, or opinion 1579. 6. Anticipation; *chiefly* of things adverse 1603. 7. Dread 1648.

2. Dark night..The eare more quicke of a. makes *Mids. N.* III. ii. 178. 3. The love and a. of duty BACON. 4. Simple a. denotes..the soul's naked intellection of an object GLANVILL. O the quick a. of women DEKKER. 5. Which, according to vulgar a., swept away his legs JOHNSON. 6. The sence of death is most in a. *Meas. for M.* III. i. 78. 7. I looked about with some a. 1709.

Apprehensive (æprĭhe·nsiv), *a.* ME. [ad. med.L. *apprehensivus*, f. *apprehens-*; see APPREHEND and -IVE.] †1. In the habit of seizing, ready to embrace (an opportunity, etc.) -1641. 2. Pertaining to, or apt for, the laying hold of sensuous or mental impressions ME. 3. Of faculties: Showing apprehension; intelligent 1621. 4. Of persons, etc.: Perceptive; *hence*, quick to learn. Const. *of*. 1601. 5. Having an apprehension or notion; conscious, sensible. Const. *of* or *subord. cl.* (*arch.*) 1611. 6. Anticipative of something adverse. (The usual sense.) Const. *simply*, with *of*, or *subord. cl.*, *from*, *for*. 1633. †7. Apprehensible 1692.

1. A. of occasions wherein [etc.] LD. STRAFFORD. 2. My a. tenderest parts MILT. *Sams.* 623. 3. A sense so a. and discriminant NEWMAN. 4. More fond of Miracles, than a. of Truth MILT. 6. Noah's niece, being a. of the deluge, set out for Ireland H. WALPOLE. He was a. an operation would be necessary 1802. Hence **Apprehe·nsively** *adv.* with anticipation, *esp.* of danger. **Apprehe·nsiveness**, fearfulness.

†**Appre·nd**, *v. rare.* 1567. [See APPREHEND.] To seize; to grasp mentally -1642.

Apprentice (ăpre·ntis), *sb.* [ME. *aprentys*, a. OFr. *aprentis*, nom. of *aprentif*, f. *aprendre* (see APPREHEND), 3rd sing. *aprent*, after wds. in *-tis*, *tif*:—L. *-tivus*. (In mod.Fr. *apprentis* is pl. with sing. *apprenti*.) Cf. APPENTICE. The aphet. PRENTICE was long more usual.] 1. A learner of a craft; one who is bound by legal agreement to serve an employer for a period of years, with a view to learn some handicraft, trade, etc., in which the employer is reciprocally bound to instruct him. 2. A barrister-at-law of less than 16 years' standing. *Obs.* exc. *Hist.* ME. 3. By extension: A beginner, a tyro 1489. 4. *adj.* or *attrib.* ME.

2. Barristers (first stiled apprentices)..who answered to our bachelors BLACKSTONE. 3. As yet they were apprentices to piracy FULLER.

Apprentice (ăpre·ntis), *v.* 1631. [f. the sb.] To bind as an apprentice; to indenture. Hence **Appre·nticement** (*rare*).

Apprenticeship (ăpre·ntisʃip). 1592. [f. APPRENTICE *sb.* + -SHIP; repl. *Apprenticehood*.] 1. The position of an apprentice (see APPRENTICE 1); service as an apprentice; also *transf.* or *fig.* 1592. 2. The period for which an apprentice is bound 1667. 3. *Hence*: A period of seven years 1780.

1. *Serving his apprenticeship* in the military art MACAULAY. [An] a. in Sanskrit grammar M. MÜLLER. 3. Three 'prenticeships have passed away..Since I

was bound to life HOOD. vars. †**Appre·nticeage**, †**Appre·nticehood.**

Appress (æpre·s), *v.* 1791. [f. L. *appress-, apprimere.*] = ADPRESS.

†**Appre·st.** ME. [a. Fr. *appreste* (mod. *apprêt*), f. *à* + *prest* (mod. *prêt*):—L. *præstus.*] Provision; *esp.* pecuniary provision, loan -1570.

Appre·ve, *v.*, pa. pple. **approven.** *Obs.* or *dial.* ME. [ad. OFr. *a(p)preuve*, north. equiv. of APPROVE *v.*[1]] = APPROVE *v.*[1]

Apprise (ăprəi·z), *v.*[1]; also **apprize.** 1694. [f. Fr. *apprendre* (OFr. *aprendre*), (pa. pple. *appris, -ise*), after *comprise*, etc. *A(p)prendre* had taken the special sense of 'teach, inform'; see APPREHEND.] 1. To impart information to; acquaint. Hence in *pass.* To be aware 1712. 2. To notify, advise (*rare*) 1817.

1. The adjoining cell, as the reader is apprised, was occupied by Gurth SCOTT.

Apprize, -ise (ăprəi·z), *v.*[2] *arch.* ME. [a. OFr. *apriser*, perh. f. *à pris*, as if *mettre à prix*. In Eng. APPRAISE is more common.] 1. *Sc. Law.* To put up for sale at a set price, appraise 1533. 2. To value, appreciate ME. Hence †**Appri·zement,** appraisement. **Appri·zer, -ser,** one who appraises; *Sc. Law,* a creditor for whose behoof an appraisal is made.

Appro. (æ·pro), abbrev. of *approbation* or *approval*, in *on a.*, said of goods sent for a customer's examination with a view to purchase.

Approach (ăprōu·tʃ), *v.* [ME. *aproch(e,* a. OFr. *aprochier* (mod. *approcher*):—late L. *adpropiare*, f. *ad* + *propius*, f. *prope*. For *app-* see AP- *pref.*[1] The *oa* is phonetic (*c* 1600).] 1. *intr.* To come nearer, or draw near, in space. Const. *simply*, or with *to*. *trans.* To come near to ME. Also *fig.* 2. *trans.* Of lines, etc.: To be so situated in space that the parts lie successively nearer to a given point or line 1598. 3. To come near to a person: *i. e.* into personal relations. *intr.* with *to* (*arch.*) ME. *trans.* ME. 4. *euphem.* Of sexual relations 1611. 5. Of time, etc.: To draw nigh ME. 6. To come near, be nearly equal. *intr.* with *to* ME. *trans.* 1698. 7. *Mil.* To make approaches to (see APPROACH *sb.* 6). 8. *causal.* To bring near locally; approximate (*arch.*) 1541. Also *fig.*

1. A., thou Beacon to this vnder Globe *Lear* II. ii. 170. Approch the Chamber *Macb.* II. iii. 76. 2. Here the boundary approaches, but does not quite reach the river (*mod.*). 3. I cannot a. her without Awe STEELE. 5. When now the Nuptial time Approaches DRYDEN. 6. He.. thought even to have approached Homer TEMPLE. 7. Ground..easy to A., and as..dangerous to Storm CLARENDON. 8. So saying he approached to the fire a three-footed stool SCOTT. Hence **Approa·cher.** **Approa·ching** *vbl. sb.* the action of drawing near; *spec.* in *Mil.* and *Hort.* = APPROACH *sb.* 6, 7; *ppl. a.* drawing or coming near (*lit.* and *fig.*). **Approa·chment,** †approach; affinity.

Approach (ăprōu·tʃ), *sb.* 1489. [f. the vb.; cf. Fr. *approche.*] 1. The act of approaching (see APPROACH *v.* 1) 1555; †*spec.* nearer advance of an enemy -1652. 2. *pl.* Movements towards personal relations; advances 1642. 3. Access (*arch.*) 1563; an access 1633. 4. A drawing near in time or circumstance 1593. 5. A coming near in quality or character 1750. 6. *Mil.* Entrenchments, etc., by which the besiegers draw closer to the besieged; also *fig.* 1633. 7. *Hort.* The bringing of the branch of one tree close to that of another for grafting; called also ablactation or inarching 1658.

1. The a. of a Comet to the Earth WHISTON. 2. What Approaches, Smiles, Shrugs, Habits, are..requirable from them 1654. 3. Honour hath in it..the a. to kings 1626. The station and its approaches 1878. 4. Death's a. 2 *Hen. VI*, III. iii. 6. Signs of the a. of a reaction SEELEY. Hence **Approa·chless** *a. poet.* unapproachable.

Approachable (ăprōu·tʃăb'l), *a.* 1571. [f. APPROACH *v.* + -ABLE.] Capable of being approached; accessible (*lit.* and *fig.*) 1611.

This Truth.. a. by most CARLYLE. Hence **Approa·chabi·lity.** **Approa·chableness.**

†**A·pprobate,** *ppl. a.* ME. [ad. L. *approbatus, approbare*, f. *ap-* = *ad-* + *probare*, f. *probus.*] Approved formally, or authoritatively -1577.

Approbate (æ·prŏbeⁱt), *v.* 1470. [f. prec.] 1. To approve expressly; to sanction authoritatively. Obs. in England, but in use in U.S., often as simply = *approve.* 2. *Sc. Law.* To approve as valid. Also *transf.* 1836.

2. *To approbate and reprobate*: to take advantage of the parts of a deed which favour one, and repudiate the rest. Hence **A·pprobated** *ppl. a.* = APPROVED. **A·pprobator** (*rare*), one who sanctions; an approver. ? *Obs.* **A·pproba·tory** *a.* of the nature of or tending to approbation or sanction. (Orig. in phr. *letter approbatory.*)

Approbation (æprobēⁱ·ʃən). ME. [a. Fr., ad. L. *approbationem*; see prec.] †1. The action of proving true; confirmation -1718. 2. The action of declaring good or true; sanction 1502. 3. Approval expressed or felt 1548. b. *On approbation*: see APPRO. †4. Probation -1654.

1. Would I had put my Estate..on th' a. of what I haue spoke *Cymb.* I. iv. 134. 2. Received the royal a. 1839. 3. Nods of A. BUDGELL. 4. This day, my sister should the Cloyster enter, And there receiue her a. *Meas. for M.* I. ii. 183.

Approbative (æ·prŏbeⁱtiv), *a. arch.* 1611. [a. Fr., ad. L. *approbativus*; see APPROBATE and -IVE.] Expressing approbation or approval. Hence **A·pproba·tiveness,** the quality of being a.; in *Phrenol.* love of approbation.

†**Appro·mpt,** *v. rare.* [f. L. *ap-* = *ad-* + *promptus* PROMPT.] To make ready; stimulate. BACON.

Approof (ăprū·f). *arch.* ME. [a. OFr. *aprove*, f. *aprover*:—L. *approbare*; see APPROBATE and APPROVE. Cf. *proof.*] 1. The act of proving; trial. 2. Sanction, approbation 1439.

1. A Souldier..and of verie valiant approofe *All's Well* II. v. 3. 2. *Meas. for M.* II. iv. 174.

Appropinquate (æpropi·ŋkweⁱt), *v. arch.* 1623. [f. L. *appropinquat-, appropinquare*, f. *ap-* = *ad-* + *prope.*] To come near *to.* †*trans.* To bring near (*rare*) 1646. Hence **A:ppropinqua·tion,** the action of coming or bringing near; approach. **Appropi·nquity,** nearness (*rare*). So †**Appropi·nque** *v.* BUTLER, *Hud.* I. iii. 590.

†**Appro·pre, appro·prie.** ME. [a. OFr. *aproprier*:—late L. *appr-, adpropriare*, f. *ad* + *proprius*. Replaced in 17th c. by the latinized APPROPRIATE.] = APPROPRIATE 1, 2, 3, 5.

Appropriable (ăprōu·pri,ăb'l), *a.* 1646. [f. L. *appropriare* + -BLE; see prec.] Capable of being appropriated.

†**Appro·priament.** 1633. [f. as prec. + -MENT.] A characteristic.

Appropriate (ăprōu·pri,ĕt), *ppl. a.* 1525. [ad. L. *appropriatus*, f. as prec.] *pple.* or *adj.* 1. Annexed or attached (*to*), as a possession; appropriated. *spec.* in *Eccl.* Annexed as a benefice to a religious corporation 1599. †2. Selfish 1627; individual 1796. 3. Attached as an attribute, quality, or right; peculiar, own. Const. *absol.*, *to.* 1525. 4. Specially suitable, proper. Const. *to, for.* 1546. Also as †*sb.* [sc. *thing*, or *attribute.*] -1642.

3. Honour, a. to the Soveraign only HOBBES. 4. Prayers..a. for the great solemnity FREEMAN. Hence **Appro·priate-ly** *adv.*, **-ness.**

Appropriate (ăprōu·pri,eⁱt), *v.* 1528. [f. prec. Repl. APPROPRE.] 1. †To make over to any one as his own; to set apart -1723. Const. *to oneself*; = next. 1583. 2. *ellipt.* To take for one's own, or to oneself 1635. 3. *Eccl.* To annex (a benefice) to some religious corporation as its property 1528. 4. To assign to a special purpose. Const. *to, for.* 1605. 5. To assign or attribute specially or exclusively *to* (*arch.*) 1533. 6. To make, or select as, appropriate *to*; to suit (*arch.*) 1594.

1. The name 'priesthood'..was never appropriated by the apostles to themselves 1876. 4. After appropriating £18,424 for the payment of interest on debentures 1882. 5. The word presumption I a. to the internal feeling COLERIDGE. Hence **Appro·priated** *ppl. a.* (in senses 1, 4, 5, 6, repl. APPROPRIATE as pple.).

Appropriation (ăprōu·pri,ēⁱ·ʃən). ME. [ad. L. *appropriationem*; see prec.] 1. The making of a thing private property, *esp.* one's own; taking to one's own use; *concr.* the thing so appropriated. 2. *Eccl.* Transference to a religious corporation of the tithes and endowments intended for the maintenance of religious ordinances in a parish; *concr.* the benefice or tithes so appropriated ME. 3. Assignment of anything to a special purpose; *concr.* the thing (*esp.* money) so assigned -1690. †4. Special attribution; a special attribute -1690.

1. The rapacious a. of the abbey lands M. PATTISON. 3. *Appropriation Bill*: a Bill in Parliament, allotting the revenue to the various purposes to which it is to be applied. 4. Hee makes it a great a. to his owne good parts, that he can shoo him [his horse] himselfe *Merch. V*, I. ii. 46.

Appropriative (ăprōu·pri,ĕtiv), *a.* 1655. [f. L. *appropriat-* (see APPROPRIATE) + -IVE.] Of appropriating character or tendency. Hence **Appro·pria·tiveness.**

Appropriator (ăprōu·pri,eⁱtəɪ). 1726. [a. L. **appropriator.*] 1. One who appropriates 1840. 2. The religious corporation that owns the fees and endowments of a benefice 1726; var. †**Appropri·etary** [irreg. f. APPROPRIATE, after PROPRIETARY] (*rare*).

Approvable (ăprū·văb'l), *a.* 1449. [f. APPROVE *v.*[1] + -ABLE.] Able to be approved; worthy of approval. Hence **Appro·vableness.**

Approval (ăprū·văl). 1690. [f. APPROVE *v.*[1] + -AL. Rare bef. 1800; now usual.] The action of approving; sanctioning approbation.

Mankind had stamped its a. upon certain actions MILL. *On approval*: see APPRO.

Approvance (ăprū·văns). *arch.* 1592. [a. OFr. *aprovance*; see APPROVE *v.*[1] and -ANCE.] = APPROOF, APPROVAL.

Approve (ăprū·v), *v.*[1] [ME. *aprove*, a. OFr. *aprover* (mod. *approuver*):—L. *app-, adprobare*, f. *ad* + *probare*, f. *probus*. Cf. APPREVE, and its pa. pple. APPROVEN; also, in part, Fr. *éprouver.*] I. [= Fr. *approuver.*] †1. To make good; to prove, demonstrate -1677. †2. To attest with some authority, to confirm -1781. 3. To demonstrate practically, display, make proof of. Also *refl.* 1551. 4. To confirm authoritatively. *Hence* techn. for confirming the sentence of a court-martial ME. 5. To pronounce to be good, commend ME. *intr.* Const. †*on, of.* 1658. 6. *trans.* To recommend oneself, one's qualities, etc., as worthy of approval; to commend *to* 1611.

1. One thing..which must approue thee honest *Cymb.* V. v. 245. 2. What damned error, but some sober brow Will..approue it with a text *Merch. V*, III. ii. 79. 3. Opportunities to a. his stoutness and worth EMERSON. 'Tis an old lesson; Time approves it true BYRON. He ..approved himself a very vile person 1656. 5. I entirely a. that precaution WELLINGTON. Would his grandfather a. of what he had done KINGSLEY. 6. Without approving the heart to God CROMWELL.

II. [= Fr. *éprouver.*] †1. To put to the proof; to try -1770. †2. To find by experience -1651.

1. Nay, taske me to my word: approue me Lord 1 *Hen. IV*, IV. i. 9. Hence **Appro·vingly** *adv.*

Appro·ve, approw·, *v.*[2] 1483. [a. OFr. *aproer*, f. *à* + *pros*, obj. *prode, pro, prou, preu* 'profit', as if a Romanic subst. use of *pro* or *prod* in *prodest.* The Eng. form ought to be *approw* (cf. *allow*).] *Law.* To make profit to oneself of (*e. g.* land), by increasing the value or rent. *esp.* Said of a lord of a manor enclosing common land, as permitted by the Statute of Merton (20 Hen. III. c. iv.). Cf. IMPROVE.

Approved (ăprū·vd), *ppl. a.* ME. [f. APPROVE *v.*[1]] 1. Proved by experience, tried; †convicted -1635. 2. Pronounced good; sanctioned, esteemed 1667.

1. The old a. mode BURKE. To knit my soul to an approued wanton *Much Ado* IV. i. 45. 2. *Approved-of*: regarded with commendation. Hence **Appro·ved-ly** *adv.*, **-ness** (*rare*).

Approvement [1] (ăprū·vmĕnt). 1615. [a. OFr. *aprovement*, later *app-*, f. *aprover*; see APPROVE *v.*[1]] 1. The proving guilty, or convicting, by becoming 'approver' 1768. 2. †Approbation -1665; that which is approved 1673.

The doctrine of a. has been obsolete now for 150 years 1824.

Appro·vement [2], **approw·ment.** 1475. [a. OFr. *aproement*; see APPROVE *v.*[2]] 1. The action of approving (see APPROVE *v.*[2]). Cf. IMPROVEMENT. †2. The profits themselves 1489.

Approver [1] (ăprū·vəɪ). ME. [f. APPROVE *v.*[1] + -ER[1].] 1. One who proves or offers to prove (another) guilty; *hence*, an informer. Now restricted to: One who confesses a felony and turns king's (queen's) or state's evidence. †2. One who tests -1691. 3. One who confirms or commends 1548.

1. An A., while he is in that service, hath a Peny a day 1679.

†**Appro·ver** [2], **approw·er.** ME. [a. AFr. *aprouour*; see APPROVE *v.*[2] Ought to be written *apprower.*] One who looks after the profit of an employer; a steward or bailiff; an agent -1758.

Approximate (ăprǫ·ksimĕt), *a.* (*sb.*) 1646. [ad. L. *approximatus, approximare*, f. *ad* + *proximus.*] 1. Very near; nearly resembling. 2. *Phys. Sc.* Set very close together 1839. 3.

ellipt. Reasonably or nearly correct 1816. 4. *sb.* An approximate result or quantity (*rare*) 1784.

1. Three a. faunas DARWIN. 3. A. uniformity 1853.

Approximate (ăprǫ·ksimeˈt), *v.* 1660. [f. prec.] 1. *trans.* To bring close or near, to cause to approach (*to*). Rarely of physical motion. 2. *intr.* To come near or close (*to*). Rarely of physical motion; commonly of conceptions to which ideas of space are transferred. 1789. 3. *trans.* [the prep. omitted.] To come close to, approach closely 1789.

1. Shakespeare approximates the remote, and familiarizes the wonderful JOHNSON. 2. The shores gradually a. SIR J. ROSS. 3. Rentals approximating £4,000 per annum 1883. Hence **Appro·ximated** *ppl. a.* brought close; nearly reached; approximate. **Appro·ximately** *adv.* nearly; *ellipt.* with near approach to accuracy. **Appro·ximator.**

Approximation (ăprǫksimēˈ·ʃən). 1646. [f. L. *approximare*]. 1. The action of approximating (see APPROXIMATE *v.*); approach, proximity (*lit.* and *fig.*) †b. *spec.* in *Med.* Communication of a disease by contact –1753; †c. in *Hort.* = APPROACH *sb.* 7. 1765. 2. A coming or getting near to identity in quantity, quality, or degree; an approach to a correct estimate or conception. *concr.* The result of such a process. 1660. 3. *Math.* A process of solving problems, wherein a continual approach is made to the exact quantity 1695.

1. The world's decay and a. to its period 1664. An a. of feeling among those whom opinions have divided SOUTHEY.

Approximative (ăprǫ·ksimētiv), *a.* 1830. [f. L. *approximat-*; see APPROXIMATE *a.*] Of approximate character; nearly reaching accuracy. Hence **Appro·xima·tive·ly** *adv.*, **-ness.**

‖**Appui** (apü̆i, ăpwī·), *sb.* 1573. [F.; see next. At one time naturalized.] †1. Support, stay, prop –1601. 2. *Mil.* Defensive support. Also *fig.* 1809. 3. *Horsemanship.* The reciprocal sense of the action of the bridle between the horse's mouth and the horseman's hand 1727.

2. *Point of appui*: Any fixed object or marker upon which a body of troops is directed to commence its formation into line.

Appui, appuy, *v.* 1656. [a. Fr. *appuyer*, OF. *apoier*:—late L. *appodiare*, f. *ap-* = *ad-* + *podium*, a. Gr. πόδιον, f. πούς.] To prop or stay; *spec.* in *Mil.* to post (troops) near some point which affords support.

The enemy have their right appuied upon these mountains 1813.

Appulse (ăpɒ·ls). 1626. [ad. L. *appulsus*, f. *ap-* = *ad-* + *pellere*. Some pronounce æ·pɒls.] 1. A driving toward or against. †*spec.* The running of a ship towards a point. Also *fig.* 1642. 2. *Astr.* The arrival of a star or planet at the meridian or other point; the coming into conjunction of two heavenly bodies –1668.

1. The continual a. of fresh sap GREW.

†**Appu·nctuation.** *rare.* [f. med.L. *appunctuat-*, *appunctuare*, f. *ad* + *punctum*; see APPOINT.] The action of defining; determination.

Appurtenance (ăpɒ̄·ɹtĭnăns). [ME. *apurtena(u)nce*, a. AF. *apurtenance*:—late L. *appertinentia*; see APPERTAIN. The second vowel has varied, as *a*, *e*, *o*, *u*, but *u* is now accepted. Formerly often unchanged in the pl.] 1. *Law* and *gen.* A thing that belongs to another, a belonging; a minor property, right, or privilege, belonging to another as principal, and passing with it; an appendage. 2. A contributory adjunct, an accessory ME; *esp.* in *pl.* the mechanical accessories employed in any function or system; apparatus, gear. Also *fig.* ME. 3. The fact or state of appertaining 1846.

2. The a. of Welcome is Fashion and Ceremony *Haml.* II. ii. 388. The Pope, with his appertinences the Prelats MILT. All the appurtenances of a great establishment 1840. Hence †**Appu·rtenanced** *ppl. a.* furnished with, as an a.

Appurtenant (ăpɒ̄·ɹtĭnănt), *a.* (*sb.*) ME. [a. OFr. *apartenant*, *aper-*:—L. *appertinentem*; see prec. In sense 2 often refash. as *appertinent.*] 1. Belonging as a property or right (*to*); *spec.* in *Law*, constituting an APPURTENANCE (sense 1). 2. Appertaining as if by right (*to*); appropriate to; pertinent ME. 3. *sb.* A belonging 1483.

1. Villeins a. to the soil of the master HALLAM. 2. Euery thing, That to the feste was apertinent CHAUCER. 3. All the appertinents Belonging to his Honour *Hen. V*, II. ii. 87.

Apricate (æ·prikeˈt), *v. rare.* 1697. [f. L. *apricat-*, *apricari*, f. *apricus.*] 1. *intr.* To bask in the sun. 2. *trans.* To expose to sunlight 1851. Hence **Aprica·tion.**

Apricot (ēˈ·prikǫt). 1551. [orig. ad. Pg. *albricoque*, or Sp., but subseq. assim. to Fr. *abricot*. Cf. also OSp. *albarcoque*, ad. (through Arab.) Gr. πραικόκιον, prob. ad. L. *præcoquum*, var. of *præcox*, 'early ripe'. The *apr-* was perh. due to false etymol.; cf. '*in aprico coctus*' (Minsheu), and *abricoct.*] 1. A stone-fruit allied to the plum, of an orange colour, roundish-oval shape, and delicious flavour. 2. The tree which bears this fruit (*Prunus Armeniaca*) 1573. Also *attrib.*

1. Yond dangling Apricocks *Rich. II*, III. iv. 29.

April (ēˈ·pril). ME. [a. OFr. *avrill*:—L. *aprilis* (sc. *mensis*). Soon refash. after L. At first accented *apri·l(e.)*] The fourth month of the year. *attrib.* 1579. Also *fig.* (in reference to April showers, etc.) and *attrib.*

Half-opening buds of A. TENNYSON. The vncertaine glory of an Aprill day *Two Gent.* I. iii. 85. *fig.* The Aprill's in her eyes, it is Loue's spring *Ant. & Cl.* III. ii. 43. And hopes and light regrets that come Make April of her tender eyes TENNYSON. *Comb.*: **a.-fool**, one who is sportively imposed upon, on the first of April, or *April-fool-day*; †-**gentleman**, a newly-married husband; **-gowk** (i. e. *cuckow*), north. for **-fool.**

‖**A priori** (ēˈ prī,ōˈ·rəi), *advb.* (and *adj.*) *phr.* 1710. [L.; cf. *a posteriori.*] 1. A phrase used to characterize reasoning from causes to effects, from abstract notions to their consequences, from assumed axioms (and not from experience); deductive; deductively. 2. Hence *loosely*, Previous to any special examination, presumptively 1834. 3. *Metaph.* Prior to experience; innate in the mind 1841.

1. Nor can we *a priori* determine the value of any new instrument SMEATON. 2. An *a priori* conjecture FARRAR. 3. The term *a priori* is now..employed [by the Kantian school] to characterise those elements of knowledge which..as native to, are potentially in, the mind antecedent to the act of experience SIR W. HAMILTON. Hence **Aprio·rity**, the quality of being innate in the mind; practice of *a priori* reasoning.

Aproctous (ăprǫ·ktəs), *a.* 1870. [f. Gr. ἀ + πρωκτός + -OUS.] *Phys.* Having no anus.

Apron (ēˈ·prən, ēˈ·pəɹn), *sb.* [ME. *naperoun*, *napron*, a. OF. *naperon*, dim. of *nape*, *nappe*:—L. *mappa* table-napkin. For L. *m* = Fr. *n* cf. *matta*, *natte*, etc. For *a napron* becoming *an apron* see A *adj.*²] 1. An article of dress, orig. of linen, worn in front of the body, to protect the clothes from dirt or injury, or simply as a covering. 2. A similar garment worn officially by bishops, deans, Freemasons, etc. 1704. 3. Anything like an apron in shape or function, *esp.* the leather covering for the legs in a gig, etc. 1875. 4. Technical uses:

a. A platform placed at the bottom of a sluice or entrance to a dock, so as to intercept the fall of water. b. in *Gunnery*, A square piece of lead laid over the touch-hole. c. in *Ship-building*, A kind of false or inner stem, fayed on the aftside of the stem, to strengthen it. d. in *Plumbing*, A strip of lead which conducts the drip of a wall into the gutter. e. in *Mech.* The piece that holds the cutting tool in a planing machine. f. *Theatr.* The stage-area in front of the curtain.

5. *Apron of a roast goose or duck*: the skin covering the belly, which encloses the stuffing 1755.

1. A Napron of worsted 1569. Where is thy Leather A., and thy Rule *Jul. C.* I. i. 7. 2. *Green apron*: a lay preacher (contemptuous).

Comb. etc.: **a.** †-**man**, a mechanic; †-**rogue** = **-man**; **-squire** = APPLE-SQUIRE. Hence **A·pronful**, the quantity that can be held in an a. **A·pronless** *a.*

Apron (eˈ·prən), *v.* 1865. [f. the sb.] To cover with, or as with, an apron. Hence **A·proned** *ppl. a.* having an apron (usu. in *comb.*); formerly: Mechanic. †**Apronee·r**, one who wears an apron; a shopman or mechanic. (Used of the Parliamentary party during the Civil Wars.) †**A·proner**, one who wears an apron; a barman, waiter.

A·pron-string. 1542. The string with which an apron is tied on.

Apron-string hold or *tenure*: tenure in virtue of a wife, or during her life-time only. *Tied to the apron-strings of* (a mother, etc.): unduly controlled by.

‖**Apropos** (aprǫpō·). 1668. [Fr. f. *à* + *propos*, f. L. *propositum.*] Const. *to*, *of*. A. *adv.* 1. To the purpose; opportunely. 2. With regard *to*, as suggested by. (Fr. *à propos de.*) *absol.*: By the way 1761. B. *adj.* To the point or purpose; pertinent, happy 1691. C. *sb.* †A pertinent occurrence 1783; pertinency 1860.

1. [They] arrived very apropos ADDISON. 2. But a-propos! Hast thou seen the girl SMOLLETT. B. A tale extremely a. POPE. C. To describe with a. 1860.

Apse (æps). Pl. **apses** (æ·psīz). 1822. [ad. L. *apsis*; cf. *basis*, *base*, etc. See APSIS.] 1. *Arch* A semi-circular or polygonal recess, arched or dome-roofed in a building, *esp.* at the end of the choir, aisles, or nave of a church. Cf. APSIS 3. 1846. 2. *Astr.* = APSIS 2. 1822.

†**A·psid.** Also **abside.** 1670. [a. It. *abside*, ad. L. *absidem* or *apsidem.*] = APSE, APSIS –1743.

Apsidal (æ·psidăl), *a.* 1846. [f. L. *apsidem* + -AL¹.] 1. *Astr.* Of or belonging to the apsides 1859. 2. *Arch.* Of the form or nature of an apse 1846.

‖**Apsis** (æ·psis). Pl. **apsides** (æpsəi·dīz, usu. in Eng. æ·psidīz). 1601. [L., a. Gr. ἀψίς, ἁψίς, f. ἅπτειν.] †1. Circumference; orbit of a planet –1706. 2. *Astr.* One of the two points in the elliptic orbit of a planetary body at which it is respectively at its greatest and least distance from the body about which it revolves; the aphelion or perihelion of a planet, the apogee or perigee of the moon 1658. 3. *Arch.* = APSE 1. Hence (*a*) The bishop's throne in ancient churches. (*b*) A reliquary.

2. *Line of apsides*: the line joining the apsides.

Apsychical (ăpsəi·kikăl), *a. rare.* 1678. [f. Gr. ἀ + ψυχικός (f. ψυχή) + -AL¹.] 1. Unspiritual. 2. Not controlled by the mind 1878.

Apt (æpt), *a.* ME. [ad. L. *aptus*, *_apere_, to fasten.] Const. *to*, *for*, or *inf.* 1. Fitted (materially), fitting (*rare*) 1791. 2. Suited, fitted, adapted (†*to*, or *for*): fit (*arch.*) ME. 3. *ellipt.* Suited to its purpose; becoming, appropriate 1563; *esp.* of language, thoughts, etc.: Expressive, apposite 1590. 4. Having an habitual tendency (*to* do); habitually liable; prone 1528. 5. Susceptible to impressions; ready to learn. Mod. const. *at.* 1535.

2. Places apte to make cites ME. A. for any bodily exercise 1700. 3. Pray the good woman take some apter time DEKKER. In all the play There is not one word a. *Mids. N.* V. i. 65. The prompt reply or the a. retort DISRAELI. 4. For fat is wondrous a. to burn BUTLER *Hud.* III. i. 1048. So a. to quarell *Rom. & Jul.* III. i. 34. 5. The aptest scholar that ever was DE FOE.

†**Apt,** *v.* 1540. [f. the adj.: cf. *fit*, to *fit.*] 1. To make fit, adapt (*to*) –1672. 2. *intr.* (for *refl.*) To suit 1602. 3. *trans.* To incline, dispose *to* –1641.

1. A song wel apted too a melodious noiz LANEHAM. 2. Here occasion apteth, that [etc.] 1602.

Apteral (æ·ptĕrăl), *a. rare.* 1833. [f. Gr. ἄπτερος + -AL¹.] 1. Wingless; *Zool.* = APTEROUS. 2. *Arch.* Having no columns along the sides.

A·pteran, *a.* 1852. [f. as prec. + -AN.] *Zool.* Wingless. As *sb.* One of the *Aptera*.

A·pteroid. 1836. [f. as prec. + -OID.] *Zool.* A bird having the wings merely elementary.

A·pterous, *a.* 1775. [f. as prec. + -OUS.] 1. *Zool.* Wingless; *esp.* belonging to the *Aptera*, a sub-order of Insects including lice and springtails. 2. *Bot.* Of seeds, etc.: Having no membranous expansions; opp. to *alate* 1830.

Apteryx (æ·ptĕriks). 1813. [f. Gr. ἀ + πτέρυξ.] *Ornith.* A New Zealand bird, about the size of a goose, with merely rudimentary wings and no tail, called by the natives Kiwi.

Aptitude (æ·ptitiūd). 1548. [a. Fr., ad. med.L. *aptitudo*, f. *aptus*; see APT *a.* Cf. ATTITUDE.] 1. The quality of being fit for a purpose or position, or generally; fitness, suitableness 1643. 2. Natural tendency or propensity 1633. 3. Natural capacity *for* any pursuit 1789; *esp.* intelligence, quick-wittedness 1548.

1. That sociable and helpful a...between man and woman MILT. 2. [The] nature and aptitudes [of children] LOCKE. 3. A. for mechanical inventions MORSE. The general idea..he had acquired with great a. DICKENS.

Aptly (æ·ptli), *adv.* 1525. [f. APT *a.* + -LY².] In an apt manner (see APT 1, 3, 5).

Aptness (æ·ptnes). 1538. [f. as prec. + -NESS.] The state or quality of being apt (see APT 3, 4, 5).

A scholar of any a. 1612.

Aptote (æ·ptōˈt). 1589. [ad. L. *aptotum*, a. Gr. ἄπτωτον, f. ἀ + πτωτός.] *Gram.* A noun that has no distinction of cases; an indeclinable noun. Hence **Apto·tic** *a.* uninflected. (Applied to languages without inflexions.)

Apulmo·nic, *a. rare.* 1874. [f. A-*pref.* 14 + PULMONIC.] Having no lungs.

Apyre·tic, *a.* 1842. [f. Gr. ἀ + πυρετός + -IC.] *Path.* Free from fever.

Apyrexy (æ·pireksi). 1656. [ad. mod.L. *apyrexia* (also used), a. Gr., f. ἀ + πυρέσσειν.] *Path.* The period of intermission in a fever. Hence **Apyre·xial** *a.* (*rare*).

Apyrous (ăpəi·rəs, æ·pirəs), *a.* 1782. [f. Gr. ἄπυρος (f. ἀ + πυρ-) + -OUS. Cf. Fr. *apyre.*] Not altered by exposure to fire.

‖**Aqua** (ē·kwă, æ·kwă). ME. The Latin word for *water*, used in Pharmacy and Chemistry, with sense of: Liquid, solution.

‖**Aquafortis** (ēkwă,fǭ·ɹtis). 1601. [L.] The early scientific, and still the pop. name of the Nitric Acid of commerce, a powerful solvent and corrosive. †Also of other powerful solvents –1607. Also *fig.* Hence **A·quafo·rtist,** one who makes etchings or engravings by means of a.

Aquamarine (ē:kwă,mărī·n). 1727. [ad. L. *aqua marina*; earlier AIGUE MARINE from Fr.] 1. A bluish-green variety of beryl. 2. Hence as *adj.* and *sb.* Bluish-green (colour); sea-colour(ed 1846.

†‖**A·qua mira·bilis.** 1741. [L.] 'The wonderful water, prepared of cloves, galangals, cubebs, mace, cardomums, nutmegs, ginger, and spirits of wine, digested twenty-four hours, then distilled.' J. –1818.

Aquapuncture (ē:kwă,pɒ·ŋktiūr). 1876. [f. L. *aqua* + PUNCTURE.] *Med.* Puncture of the skin by means of a fine jet of water from a force-pump.

‖**Aqua regia** (ē:kwă,rī·dʒiă). Also **aqua regis.** 1610. [L.] A mixture of nitric and hydrochloric acids, so called because it can dissolve the 'noble' metals, gold and platinum.

‖**Aquarelle** (ækwăre·l). 1869. [Fr., ad. It. *acquerella*, dim. of *acqua* :—L. *aqua.*] A kind of painting or illuminating with Chinese ink and thin transparent water-colours. Also, the design so produced. Hence **Aquare·llist,** an artist in a.

Aquarian (ăkwēə·riăn). 1586. [f. L. *aquarius* (in pl. masc. *Aquarii* name of a heretical sect) + -AN.] **A.** *adj.* Of, or pertaining to, an aquarium (*rare*) 1865. var. **Aqua·rial. B.** *sb.* 1. One of a sect of early Christians, who used water instead of wine in the Lord's Supper 1586. 2. One who keeps an aquarium 1857.

Aquarium (ăkwēə·riɒm). Pl. **-iums, -ia.** 1854. [L. adj. neut. sing.; cf. cl. L. *aquarium* a watering-place for cattle.] An artificial pond, or a tank (usu. with glass sides), in which aquatic plants and animals are kept alive for observation and study. Also, recently, a place of entertainment, containing such aquariums.

‖**Aquarius** (ăkwēə·riɒs). ME. [L. = water-carrier, subst. use of *aquarius* adj.] *Astr.* A constellation, giving its name to the eleventh sign of the zodiac, which the sun enters on the 21st of Jan.

Aquarius is the butlere of goddes and yeuyth them a water potte ME.

A-quarter (ăkwǭ·ɹtəɹ), *advb. phr.* 1849. [A *prep.*[1]] *Naut.* On the quarter, *i.e.* 45° abaft the beam.

Aquatic (ăkwæ·tik). 1490. [a. Fr. *aquatique*, ad. L. *aquaticus*, f. *aqua.*] **A.** *adj.* †1. Watery, rainy –1686. 2. Living or growing in or near water 1642. 3. Of pastimes: Taking place in or upon the water 1866.

B. *sb.* 1. An aquatic plant or animal (*arch.*); one given to aquatic pastimes 1669. 2. A water-drinker (*rare*). FRANKLIN. 3 *pl.* Pastimes conducted in or upon the water 1865.

Hence †**Aqua·tical** *a.* of aquatic nature; having to do with water. **Aqua·tically** *adv.*

Aquatile (æ·kwătil, -əil). *arch.* 1622. [ad. L. *aquatilis*, f. *aqua.*] *adj.* = AQUATIC *a.* 2. *sb.* = AQUATIC *sb.* 1. 1638.

Aquatint (æ·kwă,ti·nt), **aqua-tinta** (æ:kwă,ti·ntă), *sb.* 1782. [a. Fr. *aqua-tinte*, and It. *acqua tinta* :—L. *aqua tincta* (*tingere*).] Engraving on copper by the use of a resinous solution and nitric acid, which produces effects resembling those of Indian-ink or water-colour drawing; also, the design so produced. Also *attrib.* Hence **Aquatint,** *v.* to engrave in a. **Aquati·nter.**

Aquavalent (ăkwæ·vălĕnt). 1881. [f. L. *aqua* + *valentem*; cf. *equivalent.*] *Chem.* The molecular proportion between an anhydrous salt and the water of its cryohydrate.

‖**Aqua-vitæ** (ē:kwa,vəi·tī). 1471. [L.; cf. Fr. *eau de vie*, Ir. *uisge bheatha*, '*usquebaugh*'.] 1. A term of alchemy applied to unrectified alcohol; occ. applied, in commerce, to ardent spirits of the first distillation. 2. Hence, *pop.* Any form of ardent spirits taken as a drink, as brandy, etc. 1547. 3. *attrib.* 1634.

2. That curst restriction On Aquavitæ BURNS.

Aqueduct (æ·kwĭdɒkt). 1538. [ad. L. *aquæductus, aquæ ductus*, f. *ducere*. Cf. Fr. *aquéduc.*] 1. An artificial channel for the conveyance of water from place to place; a conduit; *esp.* an elevated structure of masonry so used. Also *fig.* 2. The similar structure (also called *aqueduct-bridge*) by which a canal is carried over a river, etc. 1791. 3. *Phys.* Name of small canals, chiefly in the head of mammals 1709.

3. The facial nerve..traversing..a canal termed the Aqueduct of Fallopius MIVART.

†**Aqueity.** [See AQUEOUS.] The watery principle. B. JONS.

†**Aque·nch,** *v.* [OE. *acwęncan*, f. A-*pref.* 1 + *cwęncan* to QUENCH.] 1. To quench, put out –1482; to satisfy ME. *intr.* To go out –1485. 2. *fig.* To put an end to –1578.

Aqueo- (ē:kwĭ,o), comb. f. AQUEOUS; as in *aqueo-igneous*, by the action of super-heated water.

Aqueous (ē·kwĭ,əs), *a.* 1643. [as if f. L. **aqueus* + -OUS. Cf. Fr. *aqueux* (:—L. *aquosus*).] 1. Of, or of the nature of, water; watery; diluted with water 1646. 2. Connected with, or relating to water 1731. 3. *Geol.* Produced by the action of water 1802.

1. *Aqueous humour* of the eye, a fluid, nearly pure water, contained in the space between the cornea and the lens. 3. The a. rocks, sometimes called the sedimentary LYELL. Hence **A·queously** *adv.* in, or by means of, water (*rare*).

†**Aquerne.** [OE. *ácweorna*, later *ácwern*, of unknown origin.] A squirrel –ME.

Aquiferous (ăkwi·fĕrəs), *a.* 1836. [f. L. *aqui-*, comb. f. *aqua* water: see -FEROUS.] Conveying or yielding water.

†**A·quilege.** 1599. [ad. med.L. *aquileja.*] Columbine.

Aquilegia (ækwilī·dʒiă). [mod.L., of unc. origin: cf. prec.] A genus of ranunculaceous plants having pentamerous flowers with spurred petals; = COLUMBINE *sb.*[2]

Aquiline (æ·kwilin, -əin), *a.* 1646. [ad. L. *aquilinus*, f. *aquila.*] 1. Of or belonging to an eagle 1656. 2. Eagle-like; *esp.* of the nose: Curved like an eagle's beak, hooked 1646.

Terribly arch'd, and a. his nose COWPER.

†**Aquilon.** ME. [a. OF., ad. L. *aquilonem.*] The north or north-north-east wind. SHAKS.

A-qui·ver, *adv.* 1883. [A *pref.*[1]] In a quiver, trembling.

Aquo·se, *a. rare.* 1727. [ad. L. *aquosus.*] Watery.

Aquosity (ăkwǫ·sĭti). 1528. [ad. med.L. *aquositatem*, f. *aquosus.*] Moist or watery quality; †*concr.* moisture, humour –1720.

What better philosophical status has 'vitality' than a. HUXLEY.

Ar (āɹ). Name of the letter R.

Ar, obs. f. ARE (see BE *v.*), and EAR *v.*

†**Ar-,** *pref.*[1] The orig. WGer. form of the prefix, reduced in OE. to *a-*. See A-*pref.* 1 and Æ-*pref.* Cf. ARISE.

Ar-, *pref.*[2] = L. *ad-* bef. *r-*, reduced in OF. to *a-*, and later often re-spelt *ar-* after L., and so in Eng. Hence most words from OF. in *ar-* are now written *arr-*, e. g. *arrange*, etc. See also AD- 2.

-ar [1], *suff.* 1. of *adjs.* repr. L. *-arem* (*-aris*, *-are*) 'belonging to', cogn. w. *-alem*, and used where *l* preceded. See -AL. In Eng. words adopted from OF. orig. *-er*, but later assim. to L. with *-ar*, e. g. L. *scholarem*, OF. *escolier*, AFr. *escoler*, ME. *scoler*, now *scholar*. 2. of *sbs.* repr. L. *-are*, *-ar*, neut. of adjs. in *aris*, meaning 'thing pertaining to'.

-ar [2], *suff.*, occas. repr. of L. *-arius*, *-arium* (usu. repr. by -ER, -ARY). Generally, a refash. of *-er* from OFr. *-ier*, after the prec., or after mod.Fr. in *-aire*, as *bursar*, ME. *burser*, F. *boursier*, and *vicar*, F. *vicaire*. The Sc. *notar*, etc., are from the F. forms in *-aire*.

-ar [3], *suff.*, occ. var. of -ER, -OR, suffix of agent, and -ER suffix of comparative. Common in n. dial., and in mod.Eng. in *beggar*, *liar*, etc.

Arab (æ·răb). 1634. [a. Fr. *Arabe*, ad. L. adj. *Arabem* (nom. *Arabs*), a. Gr. Ἄραψ.] 1. A native of Arabia. 2. An Arab horse 1880. 3. (orig. *City, street Arab.*) A homeless little wanderer; a child of the street 1848. 4. *adj.* Of or pertaining to Arabia or the Arabs 1816.

3. City Arabs..are like tribes of lawless freebooters 1848. 4. The delicate A. arch of her feet TENNYSON.

‖**Araba** (ără·bă). Also **aroba.** 1845. [a. Arab.] A wheeled carriage used in the East.

Arabesque (æräbe·sk). 1656. [a. Fr. *arabesque* Arabian.] **A.** *adj.* 1. Arabian, Arabic 1842; *esp.* carved or painted in arabesque (see *sb.* 2) 1656. 2. *fig.* Strangely mixed, fantastic 1848.

B. *sb.* [the adj. used *absol.*] †1. The vulgar Arabic language –1796. 2. Mural or surface decoration in colour or low relief, composed in flowing lines of branches, leaves, and scroll-work fancifully intertwined. Also *fig.* 1786.

The arabesques of Raphael and the Renascence, founded on Græco-Roman work, include representations of living creatures, and to this variety the term is now usually applied. Moorish and Arabic work is distinguished as Moorish Arabesque, or Moresque. 2. *fig.* His manner of writing is—a wild complicated Arabesque CARLYLE. Hence **Arabe·squed** *ppl. a.* ornamented in a. **Arabe·squely** *adv.* in the style of the Arabs, or of arabesques.

Ara·bia. The country so named; *fig.* Spices 1711.

Arabian (ărē·biăn). ME. [f. prec. + -AN.] **A.** *adj.* Belonging to Arabia 1606.

Arabian bird: the phœnix, *fig.* a unique specimen. Oh Anthony, oh thou A. bird *Ant. & Cl.* III. ii. 12.

B. *sb.* A native of Arabia; also, one of an Arabian sect (3rd c.) holding that the soul died and rose with the body ME.

Arabic (æ·răbik), *a.* ME. [a. OF., ad. L. *Arabicus.*] 1. Of or pertaining to Arabia or its language 1650; *esp.* in *Gum arabic*, exuded by certain species of Acacia, and *Arabic acid*, obtained from it. 1616. 2. *absol.* The language of the Arabs ME.

1. *Arabic numerals*: the figures 1, 2, 3, 4, etc. 2. Those English (or rather European) nouns..derived from Arabic, as *alchemy*, *alcohol*, etc. EARLE. Hence **Ara·bical** *a.* **Ara·bicism,** an Arabic idiom or peculiarity. **Ara·bicize** *v.* to make like Arabic.

Arabin (æ·răbin). 1840. [f. ARAB-IC + -IN.] *Chem.* The pure soluble principle in gum arabic and the like. Hence **Arabino·se,** sugar derived from a. **Arabi·nic, Arabino·sic** *a.*

‖**Arabis** (æ·răbis). 1706. [med.L. *Arabis.*] *Bot.* A genus of cruciferous plants, named prob. from growing on sandy or stony places.

Arabist (æ·răbist). 1753. [f. ARAB + -IST; cf. Fr. *arabiste.*] A student of Arabic, or follower of the medical system of the Arabs.

Arable (æ·răb'l), *a.* 1576. [ad. L. *arabilis*, f. *arare*. Earlier, *erable*, *earable*, from the obs. vb. *ere* EAR.] Capable of being ploughed; fit for tillage; opp. to *pasture-* or *wood-land*. Also quasi-*sb.* Arable land 1576.

If the tenant conuert arable land into wood COKE *On Litt.* 536. Errable land *Ibid.* 85 b.

Araby (æ·răbi). ME. [a. OFr. *arabi*, *arrabi.*] **A.** *adj.* Arabian, Arabic (*arch.* and *poet.*) 1502. **B.** *sb.* †1. An Arab –1587. †2. An Arab horse. ME. only. 3. [a. F. *Arabie.*] Arabia ME.

†**Ara·ce,** *v.* ME. [a. AF. *aracer*, OFr. *aracier*, f. *arachier.*] To pull up by the roots; to tear away –1530. var. †**Ara·che.**

Araceous (ărē·ʃəs), *a.* [f. mod.L. *Araceæ*, f. *arum*, a. Gr. ἄρον; see -ACEOUS.] *Bot.* Belonging to the N.O. *Araceæ*, as the Cuckoo-pint or Wake-robin (*Arum maculatum*).

Arach; see ORACH.

‖**A·rachis.** [mod.L., ad. Gr. ἄραχος, or ἀρακίς, some leguminous weed.] *Bot.* A genus of leguminous plants, including one known as the Ground Nut. Hence **Arachidic,** as in *Ara-*

chidic Acid ($C_{20}H_{40}O_2$), obtained from the oil of the Ground Nut.

Arachnean (ærækn*ī*·ăn), *a. rare.* 1854. [f. Gr. ἀραχναῖος, f. ἀράχνη + -AN.] Like a spider's web, gossamer.

Arachnid (ăræ·knid). 1869. [f. Gr. ἀράχνη; cf. Fr. *arachnide.*] *Zool.* A member of the *Arachnida.* ‖**Ara·chnida**, *sb. pl.* [mod.L.], a class of the *Arthropoda*, comprising spiders, scorpions, and mites; distinguished by having eight legs, by lacking wings and antennæ, and by breathing by means of tracheal tubes or pulmonary sacs. Hence **Ara·chnidan** *a.* of or belonging to the *Arachnida*; *sb.* an arachnid. **Arachnidean, -ian** *a.* and *sb.* = prec. **Arachni·dial** *a.* [f. next] of or pertaining to the *Arachnidium.* ‖**Arachni·dium** [mod.L.], the apparatus by which the spider produces its web. **Ara·chnidous** *a.* of the nature of the *Arachnida.*

Arachnoid (ăræ·knoid). 1836. [ad. mod. L. *arachnoides*, a. Gr. ἀραχνο-ειδής.] **A.** *adj.* **1.** *Bot.* Covered with or formed of cobweb-like hairs or fibres 1857. **2.** *Phys.* Of or pertaining to the arachnoid. (See B.) 1836. **3.** *Ent.* Resembling the *Arachnida* 1852.

B. *sb.* The delicate serous membrane or membranous sac lining the *dura mater*, and enveloping the brain and spinal cord 1839.

Hence **Arachnoi·dal** *a.* of the nature of, or pertaining to, the arachnoid. **Arachnoideal, -ean, -eous** *a.* unnecessary vars. of ARACHNOID, -AL.

Ara:chnolo·gical, *a.* Of, or pertaining to, arachnology. **Arachno·logist**, a student of, or proficient in, arachnology. **Arachno·logy** [f. Gr. ἀράχνη + -(O)LOGY], the department of Zoology relating to spiders, or to the *Arachnida.*

Arad (ē°·răd). 1853. [f. AR-UM + -AD.] *Bot.* An araceous plant, as the Wake-robin.

Aræometer, areo- (ē°ri͵ǫ·mītəɹ). 1706. [mod.f. Gr. ἀραιός thin+μέτρον. App. through F. *aréomètre*: whence the prevalent sp., as if f. AREA, or AREO-, of Mars.] An instrument for measuring the specific gravity of fluids; a hydrometer. Hence **Aræ:ome·tric, -al** *a.* of or pertaining to aræometry. **Aræo·metry** [Gr. μετρία], the art or science of estimating the specific gravity of fluids by the use of the a.

Aræostyle (ărī·ostəil). Also **areo-**. 1706. [ad. L. *aræostylus*, a. Gr., f. ἀραιός rare, few + στῦλος; cf. Fr. *aréostyle.*] *Arch.* **A.** *adj.* Of columned buildings: Having the distance between the columns equal to four or more diameters of the column. **B.** *sb.* A building, or style of building, in which the columns are so arranged.

Aræosystyle (ărī:osi·stəil). 1834. [a. Fr. *aréosystyle*, f. as prec.+σύστυλος; see SYSTYLE.] *Arch.* An alternately very wide and very narrow intercolumniation.

†**Aræo·tic**, *a.* 1634. [ad. late L. *aræoticus*, a. Gr., f. ἀραιό-ειν.] Tending to make thin the humours of the body. Also as *sb.*

†**Ara·ge**, *v.* 1470. [a. OF. *arager*, f. *à* + *rage.*] To enrage -1568.

Aragonite, arr- (æ·răgŏnəit). 1803. [f. *Aragon* or *Arragon* in Spain.] *Min.* A carbonate of lime, crystallizing in orthorhombic prisms and many derived forms.

Aragonspath, Aragon Spar, = prec.

‖**Araguato.** 1852. [See ALOUATTE.] The 'howling monkey'.

‖**Araignée** (are·nʸe). 1706. [Fr.; = spider's web.] *Mil.* A military mine constructed with branching galleries.

Arain. *Obs.* exc. *dial.* ME. [a. OF. *araigne* :—L. *aranea.*] A spider.

†**Arai·se**, *v.* ME. [A- *pref.* 1; cf. *rise, arise.* Cf. also AREAR.] **1.** To raise, lift up -1557; to raise from the dead -1601; to raise (money, troops, a siege, etc.) -1548. **2.** To arouse -1494.

1. A medicine..powerfull to a. King Peppin SHAKS.

Arak, var. of ARECA, and obs. f. ARRACK.

A-rake (ărē·k), *adv.* 1883. [A *prep.*¹] On the rake; inclined.

Aramæan (ærămī·ăn), *a.* 1834. [f. L. *Aramæus*, Gr. Ἀραμαῖος.] Belonging to the country or language of Aram; Syrian, Syriac. As *sb.* A native of Aram.

Aramaic (ærămē·ik), *a.* 1834. [f. as prec.; see -IC.] Of Aram; *spec.* applied to the northern branch of the Semitic family of languages, including Syriac and Chaldee. Often used *absol.* sc. *language.* vars. †**A·ramite**, †**Arami·tic.** Hence **Arama·ism**, an A. idiom or peculiarity.

Araneidan (ærănī·idăn), *a.* 1835. [f. mod. L. *Araneida*, the typical family of *Arachnida*, f. L. *aranea.*] *Zool.* Of or belonging to the *Araneida* or spiders. As *sb.* A spider. **Arane·iform** *a.* having the shape of a spider. **Araneo·logist** = *arachnologist.*

Araneose (ărē¹·ni͵ōu·s), *a.* 1880. [ad. L. *araneosus*, f. *aranea.*] = ARACHNOID. var. **Ara·neous.**

‖**Arango** (ăræ·ŋgo). Pl. **-oes.** 1715. A bead made of rough carnelian, formerly imported from Bombay for re-exportation to Africa.

†**A-ra·nk**, *adv.* ME. [A *prep.*¹] In a rank or row -1570.

Araphoro·stic, arapho·stic, *a.* 1828. [Incorr. f. Gr. ἄρραφος, f. ἀ + ῥάπτειν.] Unsewed, seamless, as shoes, etc.

†**Ara·se**, *v.* 1523. [a. OF. *araser*, f. *à ras*, f. *ras* :—L. *rasus.* Cf. *erase.*] To raze, level with the ground. Also (? erron.) to erase. -1553.

Aration (ărē¹·ʃən). *arch. rare.* 1663. [ad. L. *arationem.*] Ploughing; tillage.

Araucaria (ærǫkē°·riă). 1833. [f. *Arauco*, name of a province, whence *Araucania*, south of Chili.] *Bot.* A genus of lofty coniferous trees, native to the southern hemisphere, one species of which (*A. imbricata*, called also 'Monkey-puzzler') is now cultivated in Great Britain. Hence **Arauca·rian** *a.* of or belonging to the genus Araucaria; *sb.* a species of this or an allied genus.

A·rbalest, -balist, -blast. *Obs.* exc. *Hist.* OE. [a. AFr. **arb(e)leste*, OF. *arbaleste* :—L. *arcuballista*, f. *arcus* + *ballista.* See also ARCUBALIST.] **1.** A cross-bow, consisting of a steel bow fitted to a wooden shaft, furnished with special mechanism for drawing and letting slip the bowstring, and discharging arrows, bolts, stones, etc. **2.** = *Arbalester* 1450. **3.** A mathematical instrument, formerly used to take the altitude of the stars 1816.

1. A quarel..shotte out of Arbalaste CAXTON. Unbend thy arblast, and come into the moonlight SCOTT. Hence **A·rbalester, -balister, -blaster**, a soldier armed with an a.; a cross-bowman (*Obs.* exc. *Hist.*). †**A·rbalestre, -ter, -blaster**, = ARBALEST; also, the missile shot from the a. **Arbale·strier, alblastrer** (*Obs.* exc. *Hist.*) = *Arbalester.* **A·rbalestry**, the art or practice of shooting with an a.

†**A·rber, e·rber.** ME. [a. Fr. *herbière*; cf. *herbier* in Littré.] The windpipe or weasand; occ. extended to the whole 'pluck'. *To make the erber* (hunting phr.): to take out the 'pluck', the first stage in disembowelling. (See Sir W. Scott in Notes to *Sir Tristram*, p. 268, where it is wrongly explained.)

Arbiter (ā·ɹbitəɹ). 1502. [a. L. (? f. *ar-* = *ad-* + *betere, bitere*, to go, 'one who goes to see'). Cf. ARBITRATOR, ARBITRER.] **1.** *gen.* One whose opinion or decision is authoritative in a matter of debate; a judge. **2.** *spec.* One who is chosen by the parties in a dispute to decide the difference between them; an arbitrator, an umpire 1549. Also *transf.* or *fig.* **3.** One who has a matter under his sole control 1628.

1. The late Mr. Fox (no mean a. in literary taste) DIBDIN. 2. *fig.* Twilight..short A. Twixt Day and Night MILT. *P. L.* IX. 50. 3. Use..which is the a. of language REID.

†**A·rbitrable**, *a.* 1531. [f. L. *arbitrari* + -BLE.] Subject to the decision of an arbiter -1650.

Arbitrage (ā·ɹbitrėdʒ). 1480. [a. Fr.; see ARBITRE *v.* and -AGE.] **1.** Exercise of the functions of an arbitrator; decision by arbitration (*arch.*). **2.** Authoritative decision or determination (*arch.*) 1601. **3.** *Comm.* The traffic in Bills of Exchange drawn on sundry places, and bought or sold in sight of the daily quotations of rates in the several markets (see ARBITRATION of Exchange). Also, the similar traffic in Stocks. [In this sense from mod.F. and pronounced (arbitra·ʒ).] 1881. Hence **A·rbitragi:st**, one who transacts arbitrage business.

Arbitral (ā·ɹbitrăl), *a.* 1609. [a. Fr., ad. late L. *arbitralis*, f. *arbiter*; see -AL.] **1.** *Sc. Law.* Of or pertaining to arbiters or arbitration. **2.** Subject to the exercise of will 1662.

Arbitrament, -ement (aɹbi·trămĕnt). ME. [a. OF. *arbitrement*, f. *arbitrer*; see ARBITRE *v.*: latinized as *arbitrament*, since *c* 1830 the more usual form.] †**1.** Free choice -1810. **2.** The power to decide for others; absolute control (*Obs.* exc. as fig. of 3.) 1534. **3.** The deciding of a dispute by an ARBITRATOR. Also *fig.* and *transf.* 1549. **4.** The award of an arbitrator; sentence accepted as authoritative ME. †**5.** Friendly agreement, compromise -1625.

1. To stand or fall Free in thine own A. it lies MILT. *P. L.* VIII. 641. 2. I committe to your charge and a., that thing LD. BERNERS. 3. *fig.* The a. of Swords *Hen. V*, IV. i. 168, of Time 1863, of war 1870. 4. To renounce their a. and sentence 1642.

Arbitrary (ā·ɹbitrări), *a.* (*sb.*) 1574. [ad. L. *arbitrarius*, f. *arbiter.*] **1.** Dependent upon will or pleasure. (*Obs.* in gen. use.) -1768. **2.** *Law.* Relating to, or dependent on, the discretion of an arbiter; discretionary, not fixed 1581. **3.** Based on mere opinion or preference; *hence*, capricious 1646. **4.** Unrestrained in the exercise of will, absolute; *hence*, despotic 1642. **5.** *sb.* [sc. *number, term*, etc.] 1879.

1. The same things were a., and might have been otherwise WHITGIFT. 2. The fines on admission.. even if a., must be reasonable SCRIVEN. 3. Our estimation of birth is entirely a. and capricious JOHNSON. 4. Acts of Will and Tyranny, which make up an A. Government 1642. var. †**Arbitra·rious.** Hence **A·rbitrarily** *adv.* capriciously; despotically; var. †**Arbitra·riously.** **A·rbitrariness**, capriciousness; despotism.

Arbitrate (ā·ɹbitreᶦt), *v.* 1590. [f. L. *arbitrat-*, *arbitrari*; see ARBITER. Cf. earlier ARBITRE, through Fr.] **1.** *gen.* To decide. *Obs.* or *arch.* **2.** *trans.* To give an authoritative decision with regard to, determine (*arch.*) 1605. **3.** To act as arbitrator or umpire (*in, between*) 1619. **4.** *trans.* To settle by, or submit to, arbitration 1592.

2. But certaine issue stroakes must a. *Macb.* V. iv. 20. An equal poise of hope and fear Does a. the event MILT. *Comus* 411. 4. Let them a. the differences 1647. Hence **A·rbitrated** *ppl. a.* settled by arbitration; *spec.* determined by 'Arbitration of Exchange'.

Arbitration (āɹbitrē¹·ʃən). ME. [a. OF. *arbitracion, -tion*, ad. L. *arbitrationem*; see prec.] †**1.** Uncontrolled decision -1651. **2.** The settlement of a question at issue by one to whom the parties agree to refer their claims in order to obtain an equitable decision 1634.

1. The a. of War, and Peace HOBBES. 2. *Arbitration-bond*..a bond entered into by two or more parties to abide by the decision of an arbitrator BLACKSTONE. *Arbitration of Exchange* (cf. F. *arbitrage*): The determination of the rate of exchange to be obtained between two countries or currencies, when the operation is conducted through a third or several intermediate ones, in order to ascertain the most advantageous method of drawing and remitting bills.

Arbitrator (ā·ɹbitreᶦtəɹ). ME. [a. OF. *arbitratour, -eur*, ad. L. *arbitratorem*; now the legal term.] **1.** = ARBITER 2. †**2.** Hence *fig.* of that which brings about a definite issue -1606. **3.** = ARBITER 3. 1579.

2. That old common A., Time, Will one day end it *Tr. & Cr.* IV. iii. 225. 3. God is the a. of success in war WHISTON. Hence **A·rbitra:torship.**

†**A·rbitre**, *v. rare.* 1494. [a. F. *arbitrer.*] Earlier f. ARBITRATE -1548.

†**A·rbitrer, -or.** ME. [a. AFr. *arbitrour.*] Earlier f. ARBITRATOR -1814.

Arbitress (ā·ɹbitrĕs). ME. [a. OF. *arbitresse*, fem. of *arbitre.*] A female ARBITER (senses 2, 3).

While over head the Moon Sits A. MILT. *P.L.* I. 784. var. **Arbitra·trix.**

†**Arbitry.** ME. [Two words: **1.** *Arbitre* (*e* mute), a. OF. *arbitre* :—L. *arbitrium*; **2.** *Arbitrie, -y*, later ad. L. *arbitrium.*] **1.** Power to choose or act -1649. **2.** Arbitration -1609. **3.** Decision, award -1615.

Arblast, -er, vars. of ARBALEST, -ER, -RE.

Arbor¹ (ā·ɹbəɹ). 1659. [a. F. *arbre* tree, also axis, assim. later to L. *arbor.*] *Mech.* **a.** The main support or beam of a machine (*e.g.* of a crane); **b.** The axle or spindle on which a wheel revolves. (Cf. *axle-tree.*)

‖**Arbor**² (ā·ɹbǫɹ). 1669. L. for 'tree', used as part of names in *Bot., Chem.*, etc.; as in *Bot.* **arbor Judæ**, the Judas tree (*Cercis siliquastrum*); in *Chem.* **arbor Dianæ**, the arborescent appearance formed on introducing mercury into a solution of nitrate of silver; **arbor Saturni**, the similar precipitate formed by putting zinc into a solution of acetate of lead.

Arbora·ceous, *a.* 1848. [f. ARBOR[2] + -ACEOUS.] Tree-like or wooded.

A·rbor Day. 1872. [ARBOR[2].] A day set apart, orig. in Nebraska, U.S.A., for the planting of trees.

Arboreal (aɪbōə·riăl), *a.* 1667. [f. L. *arboreus* + -AL[1].] **1.** Pertaining to, or of the nature of, trees; vars. **A·rboral, A·rborary, Arbo·rical** (*rare*). **2.** Connected with, haunting, or inhabiting trees 1834; var. **Arbo·rean.**

Arboreous (aɪbōə·riəs), *a.* 1646. [f. as prec. + -OUS.] **1.** Abounding in trees 1664. **2.** = ARBOREAL 1646. **3.** = ARBORESCENT 1753.

Arborescence (āɪbore sĕns). 1856. [f. next.] Tree-like formation. Also *fig.*

Arborescent (āɪbore·sent), *a.* 1675. [ad. L. *arborescentem*; see prec.] **1.** Tree-like in growth or size; having a woody stem. **2.** Branching like a tree 1679; *spec.* in *Arch.* 1849.
1. A. grass, very like a bamboo DARWIN. Hence **Arbore·scently** *adv.*

Arboret[1] (āɪbŏret). *arch.* 1596. [f. L. *arbor.*] A little tree, a shrub.

†**A·rboret**[2]. 1604. [ad. L. *arboretum.*] A shrubbery; arbour.

‖**Arboretum** (āɪborī·tŏm). Pl. **-a.** 1838. [L.] A place devoted to the cultivation and exhibition of rare trees; a tree-garden.

Arbo·ricole, *a. rare.* 1874. [f. L. *arbor* + *-cola.*] Inhabiting or haunting trees.

Arboriculture (āɪbŏri,kɒltiŭr). 1834. [f. L. *arbor* + *cultura.*] The cultivation of trees and shrubs for use and ornament. Hence **A·rboricu·ltural** *a.* **A·rboricu·lturist.**

A·rboriform, arbo·-, *a.* 1848. = ARBORESCENT 2.

Arborist (āɪbŏrist). 1578. [orig. a. F. *arboriste*, now *herboriste*; later f. L. *arbor.*] †**a.** A keeper of a 'herber', a herbalist. **b.** A scientific student or cultivator of trees.

Arborization (āɪbŏrəizē·ʃən). 1794. [f. next.] The production of a tree-like appearance, as (*Min.* and *Chem.*) in dendritic silver ore, or the markings of agates, etc.; (*Anat.*) by the distension or injection of capillary vessels.

Arborize (āɪbŏrəiz), *v.* 1847. [f. L. *arbor.*] To make tree-like. Perh. only in **Arbori·zed.**

Arborous (āɪbŏrəs), *a.* [f. L. *arbor* + -OUS.] Of, belonging to, or consisting of trees. MILT.

†**A·rbor vine** (J.), **arbor** (? *arbour*) **wind.** 1551 The Sarsaparilla.

‖**Arbor vitæ** (āɪbɒɪ vəi·tī). 1664. [L.] **1.** *Bot.* An evergreen shrub of the genus *Thuja*, N O. *Coniferæ*. **2.** *Phys.* The arborescent appearance of a longitudinal section of the cerebellum 1800.

†**A·rbory.** 1600. [after wds. in -ORY, or -RY.] = ARBOUR -1695.

Arbour, -or (āɪbəɪ). ME. [orig. (*h*)*erber*, a. AF., OF. (*h*)*erbier*:—L. *herbarium*, f. *herba*. *Erber* became *arber* by a change freq. with *-er* bef. a cons. (cf. *harbour, carve*, etc.); and *arber* in 16th c. was written *arb-our, -or* (vars. of *-er*), and connected with L. *arbor.*] †**1.** A garden lawn, or green; a garden of herbs or flowers -1578. †**2.** An orchard. [Cf. *orchard*, and F. *verger*. Orchards were usu. formed on grass.] -1580. †**3.** Trees or shrubs, trained on trelliswork; espaliers -1648. **4.** A bower or shady retreat, usu. of lattice-work covered with climbing shrubs and plants ME.; †**a** covered alley or walk -1712.
4. A litel herber that I have, That benched was on turves fressh ygrave CHAUCER. Those hollies of themselves a shape As of an a. took, A close, round a. COLERIDGE. Yon flourie Arbors, yonder Allies green, Our walks at noon, with branches overgrown MILT. *P. L.* IV. 626. Hence **A·rboured** *ppl. a.* embowered; furnished with arbours.

Arbuscle (āɪbɒs'l). 1657. [ad. L. *arbuscula*, dim. of *arbos.*] **a.** A dwarf tree, a tree-like shrub. **b.** A tuft of feathery cilia. Hence **Arbu·scular** *a.* of or pertaining to arbuscles; tufted.

†**Arbu·st.** *rare.* [a. F. *arbuste*, ad. L. *arbustum.*] A dwarf tree, a shrub. EVELYN. Hence †**Arbu·stive** *a.* shrubby; trained to a tree.

Arbute (āɪbiūt). *arch.* or *poet.* 1551. [ad. L. *arbutus.*] = ARBUTUS.
The thin-leav'd A. Hazle Graffs receives DRYDEN.

‖**Arbutus** (āɪbiutɒs). 1551. [L.] A genus of evergreen shrubs and trees (N.O. *Ericaceæ*), including the species *Arbutus Unedo*, or Strawberry Tree, cultivated for ornamental purposes.

Arc (āɪk). ME. [a. OF.:—L. *arcum* (*arcus*).] **1.** Part of a curve; also *transf.* or *fig.* 1570. **2.** *spec.* in *Astr.* The part of a circle which a heavenly body appears to pass through above (*diurnal arc*) or below (*nocturnal arc*) the horizon. The earliest use in Eng. Also *fig.* ME. **3.** A band contained between parallel curves, or anything of this form, e. g. the rainbow (F. *arc-en-ciel*), the arc of a quadrant, etc. 1642. †**4.** An arch. (Cf. Fr. *arc de triomphe.*) -1731. **5.** *Electr.* The luminous bridge formed between two carbon poles, when they are separated by a small air space, and a current of electricity is sent through them. Also *attrib.* in *a. lamp, light* 1821. **6.** *transf.* in *Phys.* Circuit 1855.
2. Parfourmed hath the sonne his ark diourne CHAUCER. **4.** Turn arcs of triumph to a garden-gate POPE.

Arc, obs. f. ARK.

‖**Arcabucero** (āɪkăbuþē·ro). [Sp.] = HARQUEBUSIER. LONGF.

Arcade (aɪkē¹·d), *sb.* 1731. [a. Fr., ? ad. med.L. *arcata*, f. *arcus.*] †**1.** An arched opening or recess in a wall -1823. **2.** 'A continued arch' (J.); a passage; a walk formed by a succession of arches having a common axis, and supported on columns or shafts. Also used of an avenue of trees, etc.; and of any covered avenue, *esp.* one with rows of shops, etc., on one or both sides 1731. **3.** *Arch.* A series of arches on the same plane, either open or closed: In mediæval architecture, an ornamental dressing to a wall, consisting of colonnettes supporting moulded arches. Gwilt. (= F. *arcature.*) 1795.
1. A small a. or receptacle for holy water WARTON. **2.** A garden, with trim lawns, green arcades and vistas of classic statues THACKERAY.

Arcade (aɪkē¹·d), *v.* 1805. [f. the sb.] To furnish with, or form into, an arcade. Hence **Arca·ding** *vbl. sb.* arcades as ornament.

Arcadian (aɪkē¹·diăn), *a.*[1] and *sb.* 1590. [f. L. *Arcadius* (f. Gr. Ἀρκαδία in the Peloponnesus).] **A.** *adj.* Belonging to Arcadia, taken as the ideal region of rural felicity; ideally rural or rustic 1667. **B.** *sb.* An ideal rustic. Hence **Arca·dianism,** pastoral simplicity. **Arca·dianly** *adv.*

Arca·dian, *a.*[2] 1870. [f. ARCADE.] Of, pertaining to, or furnished with arcades.

Arcady (āɪkădi). *poet.* 1590. [ad. L. *Arcadia.*] See ARCADIAN.

Arcane (aɪkē¹·n), *a.* 1547. [ad. L. *arcanus.*] Hidden, secret.
The A. Mysteries of Atheism CUDWORTH.

‖**Arcanum** (aɪkē¹·nɒm). Usu. in pl. **-a.** 1599. [L. In 17–18th c. the pl. was occ. treated as sing. with pl. *arcanas.*] **1.** A hidden thing; a profound secret. **2.** *Alchem.* One of the great secrets of nature; *hence*, a marvellous remedy, an elixir 1646.
1. The mysterious arcana of political intrigue BURTON. **2.** The Philosophers stone, potable gold, or any of those Arcana's SIR T. BROWNE. Hence **Arca·nal** *a.*

‖**Arc-boutant** (āɪ,butaṅ·). 1731. [Fr.] *Arch.* An arched or flying buttress.

Arch (āɪtʃ), *sb.* ME. [a. OF. *arche*:—L. *arca*; also, confused in OF. with *arc*:—L. *arcum* (see ARC).] **I.** = L. *arcus.* †**1.** = ARC 1, 2. -1831. **2.** A curved structure of firm material, either bearing weight or merely ornamental ME. **3.** *transf.* Anything having the curves or structures of 1, 2; *esp.* the rainbow 1590. **4.** Curvature in the shape of an arch 1855. **5.** An arched roof, a vault; *fig.* the heavens 1606. **6.** **Court of Arches,** or briefly *Arches*: the eccles. court of appeal for the province of Canterbury, formerly held at the church of St. Mary-le-Bow (or 'of the Arches'), so named from the arches that supported its steeple 1297.
1. An A. of the Horizon SIR T. BROWNE. **2.** 'Tis the last keystone That makes the a. B. JONS. **3.** The circled arches of thy brows GREENE. The Queene o'th Skie, whose watry A., and messenger, am I *Temp.* IV. i. 71. **4.** The delicate Arab a. of her feet TENNYSON. **5.** This vaulted A. *Cymb.* I. vi. 33. **6.** Cited to appear in the Arches at Bow Church FOXE.

II. *pl.* (= L. *arca.*) Archives 1600.
Comb. etc.: **a.-brick, -stone,** a wedge-shaped brick or stone used in the construction of arches; **-buttress** = ARC-BOUTANT; **archways** = ARCHWISE; **-work,** structure consisting of arches.

Arch (āɪtʃ), *v.* ME. [a. OFr. *archer*; cf. mod.F. *arquer.*] **1.** To furnish with an arch. **2.** To form into an arch, to curve. *trans.* 1625. *absol.* and *intr.* 1732. Also with *over.* †**3.** To put *together* so as to be mutually supporting, like the stones of an arch. So *to arch up*, -1662. **4.** *trans.* To overarch 1795.
2. Arched like the back of a frightened Cat BUCKLAND. Build on the wave, or a. beneath the sand POPE. **4.** The blue blocks that a. the source of the Arveiron TYNDALL.

Arch (āɪtʃ), *a.* (*sb.*) 1547. [ARCH- *pref.* used as a separate wd.; see next.] **1.** Chief, prime, pre-eminent. (Now rare without the hyphen.) **2.** [From assoc. with *wag, knave*, etc., and hence with *fellow, face*, etc.] Clever, cunning, waggish. Now usu. of women and children: Slily saucy, pleasantly mischievous 1662. **3.** quasi-*sb.* A chief (one) 1605.
1. We cannot helpe it though we can, which is the A. infirmity in all morality 1647. **2.** The archest chin Mockery ever ambush'd in M. ARNOLD. **3.** The Noble Duke. . My worthy A. and Patron *Lear* II. i. 61.

Arch- (āɪtʃ; exc. in *archangel*), *prefix*; repr. Gr. ἀρχι-, comb. f. ἀρχός chief. In OE. at first translated by *héah-* high, but later adopted from L. as *arce-, ærce-, ęrce-*, ME. *erche-, arche-*. From these *arch-* later became a living formative. (In mod. literary words from Gr. the prefix is ARCHI- q. v.) In pronunciation established compounds tend to have the main stress on *arch-*, *esp.* when prefixed to a name, as *A·rchbishop Cra·nmer*. **1.** In titles: meaning, 'Chief, principal, -in-chief; superior, -master'; as ARCHBISHOP, ARCHDEACON, ARCHDUKE; *esp.* in titles of offices in the Holy Roman or German empire, as *arch-chamberlain*, etc. 1693. **2.** In descriptive appellations: meaning, 'One pre-eminent as; greatest, chief, leading', as *arch-mystagogue*, etc. In mod. use *esp.* with terms of odium: meaning, 'Out-and-out, worst of, ringleader of'; as *arch-agitator*, etc., often with a specific reference to the Devil. 1548. **3.** As prec., with sense of 'First in time, original', as *arch-father*. Mostly *arch.* 1541. **4.** Of things: with senses: **a.** 'Chief, main, prime', as *arch-mock* (*Oth.* IV. i. 71); **b.** 'Primitive, original', as †*arch-christendom*. *spec.* **a.-house,** archducal house (of Austria); †**-sea,** archipelago; **-see,** archiepiscopal see. **5.** Adjectives: as †*arch-chemic*. MILT. *P. L.* III. 609.

Archæan (aɪkī·ăn), *a.* 1881. [f. Gr. ἀρχαῖος + -AN.] *Geol.* Of or belonging to the earliest geological period.

Archæo- (āɪki,o), ad. Gr. ἀρχαιο-, comb. f. ἀρχαῖος ancient, primitive (f. ἀρχή). Formerly, and still occas., spelt *archaio-*.
archæo-geology, that of ancient periods of the world's history; **-li·thic** [Gr. λίθος] *a.*, of or pertaining to the most ancient stone implements used by prehistoric man; **-sto·matous** [Gr. στόμα] *a.*, having the primitive orifice of invagination of the wall of the embryo persistent as a mouth; **-zo·ic** [Gr. ζωή] *a.*, pertaining to the era of the earliest living beings on our planet.

Archæography (āɪki,ǫ·grăfi). 1804. [f. ARCHÆO- + Gr. -γραφία.] Systematic description of antiquities. Hence **A·rchæogra·phical** *a.*

Archæologic (āɪki,o,lǫ·dʒik), *a.* 1731. [ad. Gr. ἀρχαιολογικός; see ARCHÆOLOGY and -IC.] Of or pertaining to archæology. Hence **A·rchæolo·gical** *a.* **A·rchæolo·gically** *adv.*

Archæo·logist. 1824. [f. next; see -IST.] A professed student of archæology. vars. **Archæo·loger, A·rchæolo·gian.**

Archæology (āɪki,ǫ·lŏdʒi). 1607. [ad. Gr. ἀρχαιολογία, f. ἀρχαῖος + -λογία.] **1.** Ancient history generally; systematic description or study of antiquities. **2.** *spec.* The scientific study of the remains and monuments of the prehistoric period.
2. A. displays old structures and buried relics of the remote past TYLOR.

‖**Archæopteryx** (āɪki,ǫ·ptěriks). 1859. [f. ARCHÆO- + Gr. πτέρυξ.] *Palæont.* The oldest known fossil bird, having a long vertebrate tail.

Archaic (aɹkē·ik), *a.* 1832. [ad. Gr. ἀρχαϊκός, f. ἀρχαῖος.] Marked by the characteristics of an earlier period; primitive, antiquated 1846; *esp.* of language: Belonging to an earlier period, though still retained by individuals, or for special purposes, poetical, liturgical, etc. 1832. Hence **Archa·ical** *a.* (*rare*), **-ly** *adv.*

Archaism (ā·ɹke₁iz'm). 1643. [ad. Gr. ἀρχαϊσμός, f. ἀρχαΐζειν. Cf. F. *archaïsme.*] **1.** The retention or imitation of what is old or obsolete; archaic style. **2.** An archaic word or expression 1748. Hence **A·rchaist,** an antiquary; one who employs archaism. **Archai·stic** *a.* of or pertaining to an archaist; imitatively archaic; affectedly antique.

Archaize (ā·ɹke₁əiz), *v.* 1850. [ad. Gr. ἀρχαΐζειν.] To imitate the archaic; to render archaistic.

Archangel (ā·ɹk₁ē¹ndʒĕl; see ARCH-). OE. [a. OF., or ad. L. *archangelus*, a. Gr. ἀρχάγγελος (see ANGEL), the pref. remaining hard bef. *a.*] **1.** An angel of the highest rank. Also *fig.* **2.** *Herb.* **a.** Name of several species of Dead-Nettle and allied plants (*Lamium, Galeopsis, Galeobdolon, Stachys*); **b.** formerly of the Black Stinking Horehound (*Ballota nigra*). 1551. **3.** A fancy pigeon 1867.

1. The feast of S. Michael the Ark-angell PERKINS. Hence **Archange·lic, -al** *a.* **Archa·ngelship.**

Archbishop (ā·ɹtʃ₁bi·ʃəp; see ARCH-). OE. [prob. a substitution of *arch-* for *heah* in OE. *heah-biscop.*] The chief bishop; the highest dignitary in an episcopal church, superintending the bishops of his province; a metropolitan.

We shall see him For it, an Arch-byshop *Hen. VIII*, III. ii. 74. Hence **Archbi·shopess** (*nonce-wd.*), the wife of an a. **Archbi·shophood, Archbi·shopship. Archbi·shopling. Archbi·shoply** *a.*

Archbi·shop, *v.* 1692. [f. prec.] To make or call archbishop. In phr. *To archbishop it*: to act as archbishop.

Archbi·shopric. OE. [cf. *bishopric.*] The see, jurisdiction, rank or office, of an archbishop.

Arch-buttress; see ARCH *sb.*

Arch-butler, -chamberlain, etc.; see ARCH- 1.

A·rch-cha·nter. *Hist.* ME. [ad. med.L. *archicantor* (also used).] A precentor.

Archdeacon (ā·ɹtʃ₁dī·kən; see ARCH-). [OE. *arce-, ærce-diacon*, ad. L. *archidiaconus*, a. Gr.; see ARCHI- 1 and DEACON.] The chief deacon; *orig.* the chief of the attendants on a bishop, whose duties gradually placed him next in rank to the bishop. In *Eng. Ch.* the archdeacon is appointed by the bishop, superintends the rural deans, and holds the lowest eccl. court, with the power of spiritual censure.

Which archdeacons are termed in law the bishops eies HARRISON. Hence **Archdea·conate,** the position of a. **Archdea·coness,** the wife of an a. **Archdea·conry,** the jurisdiction, rank, office, or residence, of an a. **Archdea·conship.**

A·rchdea·n. *Hist.* ME. [See DEAN.] The chief of the deans. Sc. for ARCHDEACON. –1646. Hence †**Archdea·nery,** the jurisdiction, rank, or office of an a.

Archdiocese (ā·ɹtʃ₁dəi·ŏsīs). 1844. [ARCH- 4.] The see or jurisdiction of an archbishop.

Archduchess (ā·ɹtʃ₁dʊ·tʃĕs). 1618. [ad. F. *arche-, archiduchesse*; see ARCH- 1 and DUCHESS.] The wife of an archduke; or *spec.* a daughter of the Emperor of Austria.

Archduchy (ā·ɹtʃ₁dʊ·tʃi). 1680. [ad. earlier F. *archeduché*:—L. **archiducatus*; see ARCH- 4 and DUCHY.] The territory subject to an archduke. var. **Archdu·kedom.**

Archduke (ā·ɹtʃ₁diū·k, ā·ɹtʃ₁diū·k; see ARCH-). 1530. [a. OF. *archeduc*, now *archiduc*:—Merovingian L. *archiducem*; see ARCH- 1 and DUKE.] The chief duke: *formerly* title of the rulers of Austrasia, Lorraine, Brabant, and Austria; *now* titular dignity of sons of the Emperor of Austria. Hence **Archdu·cal** *a.*

†**Arche.** ME. [a. OF. *arche*:—L. *arca*; cf. ARK.] = ARK *sb.* 2, 3. Also *transf.* –1532.

Arched (āɹtʃt, -tʃĕd), *ppl. a.* 1581. [f. ARCH *v.* + -ED.] Furnished with, formed into, or consisting of, an arch or arches 1598. †**b.** A. **viol,** a musical instrument somewhat resembling a hurdy-gurdy (PEPYS *Diary* 5 Oct. 1664).

1. The right arched-beauty of the brow *Merry W.*

Archegay (ā·ɹtʃĭgāi). *Hist.* 1523. [a. Fr. *archegaie*, var. of *arcigaye*, a. (ult.) Arab: now called in Eng. (from Pg.) *assagai, assegai.* (Erron. disyllabic in W. Morris.)] An iron-pointed wooden dart; an assagai.

‖**Archegonium** (āɹkĭgōᵘ·niʊ̆m). Pl. **-a.** 1854. [mod.L., dim. of Gr. ἀρχέγονος, f. ἀρχε- = ἀρχι- (see ARCHI-) + γόνος. Occ. **archegon.**] *Bot.* The female organ in Cryptogams, corresponding to the pistil in flowering plants. Hence **Archego·nial** *a.*

Archelogy (aɹke·lŏdʒi). 1856. [ad. mod.L. *archelogia*, f. Gr. ἀρχή + -LOGY.] The scientific study of principles.

†**A·rchemastry.** 1477. [?f. ARCHI- + MASTERY, or corruption of *alchemistry*; cf. ARCHYMIST.] Supreme skill; mastery of applied science, or applied mathematics –1594. Hence †**A·rchemaster,** a supreme master.

A·rch-e·nemy. 1550. [ARCH- 2.] A chief enemy; *spec.* the arch-fiend Satan.

Archer (ā·ɹtʃəɹ). ME. [a. AFr. *archer*, OF. *archier*:—L. *arcarium*, f. *arcus.*] **1.** One who shoots with bow and arrows, *esp.* in war; a bowman. Also *fig.* and *attrib.* †**2.** An arrow. (Cf. *arbalester.*) –1485. †**3.** Name of the bishop in Chess 1656. **4.** The ninth zodiacal constellation, *Sagittarius* 1594. **5.** *Ichthyol.* A fish (*Toxotes jaculator* Cuvier), which shoots water at insects resting near.

1. If wee can doe this, Cupid is no longer an A. *Much Ado* II. i. 401. Hence **A·rcher·ess, -ship.**

Archery (ā·ɹtʃəri). ME. [a. OF. *archerie*, f. *archier.*] **1.** The practice or art of shooting with bow and arrow; skill as an archer. Also *fig.* **2.** *collect.* An archer's weapons; bows, arrows, etc. 1440. **3.** *collect.* A company of archers 1465. †**4.** A feudal service; (see quot.) 1691.

1. Sir Boy let me see your Archerie *Tit. A.* IV. iii. 2. 4. *Archery* was a Service of keeping a Bow for the Use of the Lord [etc.] BLOUNT.

Arches (ā·ɹtʃĭz). 1626. [Cf. *arch-sea*, ARCH- 4.] A seamen's term for the Archipelago.

Arches-court; see ARCH *sb.* 6.

Archetypal (aɹke·tipăl, ā·ɹkĭtəipăl), *a.* 1642. [f. L. *archetypum* ARCHETYPE + -AL [1].] Of the nature of, constituting, or pertaining to, an archetype; primitive, original.

(In Platonic philosophy, *archetypal* is applied to the idea or form as present in the divine mind prior to creation, and still cognizable by intellect, independently of the *ectypal* object.)

A. forms of language FARRAR. Hence **Archety·pally** adv. var. †**Archety·pical.**

Archetype (ā·ɹkĭtəip). Also †**archi-,** †**arch-.** 1605. [ad. L. *archetypum*, a. Gr. ἀρχέτυπον, f. ἀρχε- = ἀρχι- + τύπος.] **1.** The original pattern from which copies are made; a prototype. **2.** *spec.* **a.** in *Minting.* A coin of standard weight. ? *Obs.* **b.** in *Compar. Anat.* An assumed ideal pattern of the fundamental structure of each great division of organized beings 1849.

1. The House of Commons, the a. of all the representative assemblies which now meet MACAULAY. 2. The vertebrated a. MURCHISON.

Archetypist (ā·ɹkĭtəipist). 1881. [f. as prec. + -IST.] One who studies early typography.

‖**Archeus** (aɹkī·ʊ̆s). *Hist.* 1641. [mod.L. *archæus*, f. Gr. ἀρχαῖος.] The Paracelsian immaterial principle which produces and regulates the activities of the animal and vegetable economy; vital force. Also *attrib.* 1798. Hence †**Arche·al** *a.*

Arch-fiend (ā·ɹtʃ₁fī·nd). 1667. [ARCH- 2.] A chief of fiends; Satan.

Arch-flamen (ā·ɹtʃ₁flē¹·men). ME. [ad. med. L. *archiflamen* = *archiepiscopus*; see ARCHI- and FLAMEN.] A chief flamen or priest; an archbishop.

Bishop Valentine! thou venerable A. of Hymen LAMB.

Arch-foe (ā·ɹtʃ₁fōᵘ·). 1615. [ARCH- 2.] Arch-enemy; *spec.* the Devil.

A·rch-he·retic. 1528. [ARCH- 1, 2.] A chief or first heretic; a founder or leader of heresy. So **Arch-heresy,** fundamental or extreme heresy.

Archi- (ā·ɹki-), *pref.*, a. L. *archi-*, Gr. ἀρχι-; see ARCH-. The form used in words taken in modern times from Gr. or L., in compounds modelled on these, and occ. in adjs. whose sbs., being of earlier date, have *arch-*, as *archdeacon, archidiaconal.*

1. = ARCH-; chief, first in authority or order. **a.** in *sbs.*, as ‖**archidida·scalus** [Gr. ἀρχι-διδάσκαλος], head-master of a school; whence **archididasca·lian, -ine** *a.*; **archi-master,** see *Archemaster*; **archi-typo·grapher** [mod. L. *architypographus* in Laudian Statutes], chief printer, superintendent of printing office. **b.** in *adjs.*, as ARCHIDIACONAL, etc. **2.** In *Biol.* and *Anthrop.*, meaning 'archetypal' or 'primitive': as **a·rchiblast,** the epiblast; **archine·phron,** the primitive kidney, whence **archine·phric** *a.*; **archiptery·gium,** the primitive fin or wing, whence **archiptery·gian** *a.* Also **archili·thic, archizo·ic;** see ARCHÆO-.

Archiater (āɹki₁ē¹·təɹ). 1634. [a. F. *archiatre*, ad. L. *archiatrus*, a. Gr., f. ἀρχι- + ἰατρός.] The chief physician, *esp.* the king's or court physician.

†**A·rchical,** *a.* 1651. [f. Gr. ἀρχικός, f. ἀρχή + -AL [1].] **1.** Governmental –1692. **2.** Of the nature of a first principle. CUDWORTH.

Archidiaconal (ā·ɹki₁dəi₁æ·kŏnăl), *a.* 1651. [f. L. *archidiaconus* + -AL [1].] Of, pertaining to, or holding the position of, an archdeacon. So **Archidia·conate,** the office or order of archdeacons (*rare*).

†‖**Archido·xis.** 1643. [mod.L. f. Gr. ἀρχι- + δόξις.] A work of Paracelsus; a collection of philosophical secrets.

Archiepiscopacy (ā·ɹki₁ĭpi·skŏpăsi). 1642. [f. late L. *archiepiscopus*, a. Gr.] **a.** The system of church government by archbishops. †**b.** = *archiepiscopate* 1662. So **A·rchiepi·scopal** *a.* of, pertaining to, or of the nature of, an archbishop. **Archiepi·scopalship. A·rchiepi·scopa·lity,** archiepiscopal character. **A·rchiepi·scopate,** an archbishop's tenure of office; also = ARCHBISHOPRIC.

Archi·gony. 1876. [f. ARCHI- 2 + Gr. -γονία.] = ABIOGENESIS.

Archil (ā·ɹtʃil, ā·ɹkil). 1483. [corruption of ORCHIL, a. OF. *orchel, orcheil*, ad. It. *orchello.* Earlier *oricello.* Origin uncertain.] A name of various species of lichens, also called Orchil and Orchilla-weed (*Roccella tinctoria*, etc.), which yield a violet dye, and the chemical test substance litmus. Also, the colouring-matter prepared from these lichens.

Archilochian (āɹkilōᵘ·kiăn), *a.* 1751. [f. L. *Archilochius*, f. Gr. Ἀρχίλοχος.] Pertaining to, or derived from, Archilochus, the alleged inventor of iambic metre.

Archimage (ā·ɹkimē¹dʒ). 1553. [f. ARCHI- + L. *magus*, ad. Gr. Formerly also *archimagus, archimago.*] A chief magician; a great wizard.

Dismiss..the false a., Dissimulation SCOTT.

Archimandrite (āɹkimæ·ndrəit). 1591. [ad. med.L. *archimandrita*, ad. late Gr., f. ἀρχι- (see ARCHI-) + μάνδρα an enclosed space, a monastery.] In *Gr. Ch.* The superior of a monastery, or the superintendent of several; an *abbot*, or *father provincial.*

Archimedean (āɹkimī·dĭăn, -mĭdī·ăn), *a.* Also **-ian.** 1813. [f. L. *Archimedeus* (f. next) + -AN.] Of, pertaining to, or invented by Archimedes.

Archimedean Screw or *Archimedes' Screw*: an instrument for raising water, formed by winding a tube into the form of a screw around a long cylinder.

‖**Archimedes** (āɹkimī·dīz). Also **Archimede** (ā·ɹkimīd). 1630. [Gr. proper name.] A Syracusan mathematician, famous for discoveries in applied mechanics, etc., and for the saying that with a point to stand upon he could move the world. (Used connotatively.)

Archimime (ā·ɹkiməi·m). Also **arch-.** 1658. [ad. L. *archimimus*, a. Gr.; see ARCHI- and MIME.] A chief buffoon or jester; the chief mimic who in Roman funeral processions imitated the deceased.

Arching (ā·ɹtʃiŋ), *vbl. sb.* 1598. The action of the vb. ARCH; *concr.* structure consisting of arches; arched curve. *ppl. a.* Forming an arch, or arched curve 1677.

Archipelago (āɹki₁pe·lăgoᵘ). Pl. **-os, -oes.** 1502. [ad. It. *arcipelago*, f. *arci-* (ARCH- 4) + *pelago*:—L. *pelagus*, a. Gr. πέλαγος sea. No such word occurs in ancient or med.Gr. Cf. ARCHES.] **1.** The Ægean Sea, between Greece and Asia Minor. *Hence* 2. Any sea or sheet of water, studded (like the Ægean) with many islands; *transf.* a group of islands 1600.

2. These broken lands and Islands being very many in number, do seeme to make there an Archipelagus HAKLUYT. var. †Archipe·l. Hence A·rchipela·gian, A·rchipela·gic *adjs.*

†Archisy·nagogue. 1582. [ad. L. *archisynagogus*, a. Gr. (in N.T.).] The ruler of a synagogue -1753.

Architect (ā·ɹkitekt). 1563. [? a. Fr. *architecte*, ad. L. *architectus*, f. Gr. ἀρχιτέκτων, f. ἀρχι- (see ARCHI-) + τέκτων, with some derivatives as if f. L. *tectus, tegere.*] 1. A master-builder. *spec.* One whose profession it is to prepare plans of edifices, and exercise a general superintendence over their erection. *Naval Architect*: One who takes this part in the construction of ships. 2. One who designs and frames any complex structure; *esp.* the Creator 1659. 3. One who so plans or constructs, as to achieve a desired result; a builder-up 1588; *transf.* of things 1835.

1. One pulls down his house and calls architects about him JOHNSON. 2. The great A. of nature CHALMERS. The a. of the Iliad GROTE. 3. Chiefe A. and plotter of these woes *Tit. A.* v. iii. 122. Hence A·rchitective *a.* pertaining to architecture; fitted for construction. †A·rchitector = ARCHITECT 1; a superintendent. A·rchitectress, a female a.

Architectonic, -al (ā·ɹki,tektǫ·nik, -ăl). 1595. [ad. L. *architectonicus*, a. Gr.; see ARCHITECT and -IC, -AL.] A. *adj.* 1. Of or pertaining to architecture; serviceable for construction 1608. 2. Constructive 1595. 3. Directive, controlling. (So in Gr.) 1678. 4. *esp.* in *Metaph.* Pertaining to the systematization of knowledge 1801.

1. A. skill [of birds] G. WHITE. 4. The a. impulse of reason, which seeks to refer all science to one principle CAIRD. Hence A·rchitecto·nically *adv.* in relation to architectonics; with architectural fitness.

B. *sb.* Architectonic(s: the science a. of architecture 1660; b. (*Metaph.*) of the systematic arrangement of knowledge 1838.

Architectural (āɹkite·ktiŭrăl), *a.* 1762. [f. ARCHITECTURE + -AL [1].] Of, relating to, or according to, architecture. Hence Archite·cturali·st, a professed student of, or connoisseur in, architecture. Architecturaliza·tion, adaptation to the purposes of architecture. Archite·cturali·ze *v.* to adapt to architectural purposes or design. Archite·cturally *adv.*

Architecture (ā·ɹkitektiŭr), *sb.* 1563. [a. Fr., ad. L. *architectura*, f. *architectus*; see ARCHITECT.] 1. The art or science of constructing edifices for human use, specialized as *Civil, Ecclesiastical, Naval,* and *Military.* Occas. regarded merely as a fine art. (See quots.) 2. The action or process of building (*arch.*) 1646. 3. *concr.* Architectural work; structure 1611. 4. A special method or style of structure and ornamentation 1703. 5. *transf.* or *fig.* Construction generally 1590.

1. Marine A. 1800. A., as distinguished from mere building, is the decoration of construction G. SCOTT. 3. The ruins of their a. are the schools of modern builders JOHNSON. 4. Many other architectures besides Gothic RUSKIN. Hence A·rchitecture *v.* to design as architect. KEATS.

Architrave (ā·ɹkitrēⁱv). 1563. [? a. Fr., f. ARCHI- + *trave* :—L. *trabem* (*trabs*).] *Arch.* 1. The lowest division of the entablature, the main beam that rests upon the abacus on the capital of a column; the epistyle. 2. Collective name for the parts (lintel, jambs, and their mouldings) that surround a doorway or window. Also *attrib.* 1663. 3. Ornamental moulding round the exterior of an arch. Also *attrib.* 1849.

1. Doric pillars overlaid With Golden A. MILT. Hence A·rchitraved *ppl. a.* furnished with an a.

†Architricline. ME. [a. Fr. *architriclin*, ad. L., a. Gr. ἀρχιτρίκλινος (in N. T.), f. ἀρχι- + τρίκλινος.] The ruler of a feast -1493.

Archive (ā·ɹkəiv, -kiv). 1603. [a. Fr. *archif, -ive*, ad. late L. *archium, archivum*, a. Gr. ἀρχεῖον, f. ἀρχή.] 1. A place in which public records or historic documents are kept. Now only in *pl.* 1645. 2. A historical record or document so preserved. Chiefly in *pl.* 1638. 3. *transf.* and *fig.* in both senses 1603.

1. Lubeck, wher the Archifs of their ancient Records is still HOWELL. 2. Some rotten a., rummaged out of some seldom-explored press LAMB. 3. So expert was he, a living a. in that business CARLYLE. Hence A·rchival *a.* A·rchivist, a keeper of archives.

Archivolt (ā·ɹkivǭult). 1731. [ad. It. *archivolto, arcovolta*, f. *arco* :—L. *arcus* + *volta.*] *Arch.* The under curve of an arch, from impost to impost; the band of mouldings which ornaments this curve.

A·rchlet. 1862. [f. ARCH *sb.*] A little arch.

Archlute (ā·ɹtʃ,liū·t). 1727. [ad. Fr. *archiluth*; see ARCH- and LUTE.] A long and large lute, having its bass strings lengthened, and each row doubled either with a little octave or a unison.

Archly (ā·ɹtʃ,li), *adv.* 1662. In an arch manner (see ARCH *a.*).

A. the maiden smiled LONGF.

Archness (ā·ɹtʃ,nės). 1709. The quality of being arch (see ARCH *a.*).

With a provoking a. in her looks RICHARDSON.

Archology (aɹkǫ·lŏdʒi). 1825. [f. Gr. ἀρχή + -(O)LOGY.] a. Doctrine of the origin of things. b. Science of government.

Archon (ā·ɹkǫn). 1659. [a. Gr. ἄρχων, f. ἄρχειν.] 1. The chief magistrate, or, after the time of Solon, one of the nine chief magistrates, of Athens. 2. A ruler or president 1735. 3. A power subordinate to the Deity, held by Gnostics to have made the world 1751.

2. We might establish a Doge, a lord A., a regent BOLINGBROKE. Hence A·rchonship, the office, or tenure of office, of an a.; so A·rchontate. Archo·ntic *a.* of or pertaining to an a.; *sb.* one of the Gnostics, who held that the world was created by *archontes* (ἄρχοντες); see ARCHON 3.

A·rch-pre·late. 1594. [ARCH- 1.] Chief prelate; archbishop.

A·rch-pre·sbyter. Also archi-. 1562. [See ARCHI- and PRESBYTER.] = ARCHPRIEST. Hence †A·rchpre·sbytery, full-blown presbyterianism. MILT.

Archpriest (ā·ɹtʃ,prī·st). 1485. [a. Fr. *archeprestre* :—L. *archipresbyter.*] A chief priest; *spec.* a kind of vicar to the bishop, acting also as dean of the cathedral; *later*, a rural dean. Hence †Archprie·sthood, †Archprie·stship, the position or office of an a.

Arch-sea, Arch-see; see ARCH- 4.

A·rch-trai·tor. 1539. [ARCH- 2.] Chief traitor; *spec.* Satan, Judas Iscariot.

A·rch-vi·llain. [ARCH- 2.] Chief villain, ringleader of villany. *Meas. for M.* v. i. 57.

Archway (ā·ɹtʃ,weⁱ). 1802. [f. ARCH *sb.* + WAY.] 1. An arched passage. 2. An arched entrance 1808.

†A·rchwife. [ARCH- 2.] A masterful wife. CHAUCER.

A·rchwise, *adv.* 1577. [f. ARCH *sb.* + WISE.] In the form of an arc, arch, or vault.

Arcifinious (āɹsifi·niəs), *a. rare.* 1859. [f. L. *arcifinius* (f. *arc-* (*arx*), or *arcere* + *finis*) + -OUS.] Having a frontier which forms a natural defence.

Arciform (ā·ɹsifǫɹm), *a.* 1839. [f. L. *arcus* + -(I)FORM.] Bent like a bow, bow-shaped, as certain nerve-fibres.

Arcograph (ā·ɹko,grɑf). 1822. [f. L. *arcus* + -GRAPH.] An appliance for drawing an arc of a circle without using a central point; a cyclograph.

Arctation (āɹktēⁱ·ʃən). 1656. [f. L. *arctare*; see ART *v.*[1]] *Med.* The action of drawing close together; constriction.

Arctic (ā·ɹktik). [ME. *artik*, a. OF. *artique*, ad. L. *articus, arcticus*, a. Gr. ἀρκτικός, f. ἄρκτος the constellation *Ursa Major.* Refash. since 17th c.] A. *adj.* 1. Of or pertaining to the north pole, or north polar regions; northern. 2. *fig.* with reference to extremeness or cold 1670.

1. *Arctic pole*: the north pole of the heavens or earth. *Arctic Circle* of the earth: the fixed parallel of 66° 32′ North, which separates the North Temperate and North Frigid Zones. In the latitude in which astronomy was first cultivated, the great bear just swept the sea, and did not set, whence the boundary circle [= *Arctic Circle* of the heavens (*obs.*)] obtained its name 1834.

B. *sb.* [the adj. used *absol.*] The north pole or north polar regions; the arctic circle. Also *fig.* 1569.

Arctitude (ā·ɹktitiud). 1828. [ad. med.L. *arctitudo*, f. *ar(c)tus.*] Tightness, straitness; cf. ARCTATION.

Arctogæal (āɹkto,dʒī·ăl, -gī·ăl), *a.* 1870. [f. mod.L. *Arctogæa* (f. Gr. ἄρκτος + γαῖα) + -AL [1].] Of or belonging to the *Arctogæa*, or arctic regions of the earth.

‖Arcturus (āɹktiūᵊ·rɒs). ME. [L., a. Gr. ἀρκτοῦρος, f. ἄρκτος + οὖρος guardian.] The brightest star in Bootes; formerly, the whole constellation, and occ. the Great Bear itself.

Canst thou guide A. with his sons *Job* xxxviii. 32.

Arcuate (ā·ɹkiu,ėt), *a.* 1626. [ad. L. *arcuatus, arcuare*, f. *arcus.*] Curved like a bow, arc-shaped, arched. So A·rcual, A·rcuated *adjs.* Hence A·rcuately *adv.*

Arcuation (āɹkiu,ēⁱ·ʃən). 1696. [ad. late L. *arcuationem*; see ARCUATE *a.*] 1. A curving into the shape of an arch; incurvation. 2. *Hort.* A method of raising trees, by bending down twigs and pegging them into the ground to take new root. ? *Obs.* 1727. 3. The use of the arch in building; arched work 1856.

A·rcubalist, -ister, = ARBALEST, -ESTER.

Arcubos, -use, obs. ff. HARQUEBUS.

-ard, *suffix*, a. OF. *-ard, -art*, a. Ger. *-hart, -hard*, 'hardy'. In ME. in words from OFr., as *bastard*, and names of things, as *placard*; later, an Eng. formative, as in *drunkard*, etc., meaning 'one who does to excess, or does what is discreditable'. In some words it has replaced *-ar, -er*, as in *stander, standard* (tree). Occ. now written *-art*, as in *braggart.*

‖Ardass. ? *Obs.* 1701. [a. Fr. *ardasse*, f. Pers.] A very fine sort of Persian silk. Hence Ardassine, a fabric made from it.

‖A·rdeb. 1861. [Arab.] An Egyptian dry measure (185 litres).

†‖Ardelio, -on. 1621. [a. L., f. *ardere.*] A busybody -1653.

Ardency (ā·ɹdĕnsi). 1549. [f. next.] 1. Burning quality 1634. 2. *fig.* Warmth of feeling or desire; intense eagerness, zeal. 1549.

2. With a great a. of spirit, he pierced Gods ear LATIMER.

Ardent (ā·ɹdĕnt), *a.* [ME. *ardaunt*, a. OF. *ardant* :—L. *ardentem, ardere*, assim. to L. later.] 1. Burning, red-hot; fiery, parching. 2. Inflammable. *Obs.* exc. in *ardent spirits*, with reference to their fiery taste. 1471. 3. Glowing like fire; flaming, fierce 1603. 4. *fig.* Glowing with passion or desire; eager, zealous ME.

1. A. feuers HOLLAND. 2. Spirits of wine, or any a. spirit BREWSTER. 3. A. eyes POPE. 4. Ardaunt in auarice CHAUCER. *Ardent*, said of a vessel when she ..comes to the wind quickly SMYTH. Their .. ryght ardaunt courage CAXTON. Hence A·rdently *adv.*

†A·rder. 1524. [Prob. a. ON. *arðr* plough, ? ad. L. *aratrum.*] 1. Ploughing; *esp.* the fallowing -1688. 2. Land ploughed up and left fallow -1668.

Ardour, ardor (ā·ɹdəɹ). ME. [a. OF. *ardour*, earlier *ardor, -ur*, mod. *ardeur* :—L. *ardorem*, f. *ardere.* The sp. *ardor*, assim. to L., has been in use since 16th c.] 1. Fierce or burning heat; *concr.* fire, flame 1645. †2. *poet.* An effulgent spirit. (Cf. *Heb.* i. 7.) 1667. 3. *fig.* Heat of passion or desire; warmth of emotion, eagerness, enthusiasm. Const. *for.* (Formerly used of evil passions, but now only of generous impulses.) ME.

1. The excessive ardours of the sun COTTON. 2. The winged saint .. from among Thousand Celestial ardors .. up springing light MILT. *P. L.* v. 249. 3. The Ardeur and brennyng of lecherye CAXTON. A martial ardor 1769. The bright ardours of boyhood J. WILSON.

Arduous (ā·ɹdiu,əs), *a.* 1538. [f. L. *arduus* + -OUS.] 1. High, steep, difficult to climb; also *fig.* 1713. 2. Hard to achieve; difficult, laborious, severe 1538. 3. Of the activity: Strenuous, energetic, laborious 1753.

1. To forgive is the most a. pitch human nature can arrive at STEELE. 2. An a. battle POPE, task 1775, enterprise MACAULAY. 3. An a. climber TYNDALL. Hence A·rduous-ly *adv.*, -ness.

A·rdurous, *a. rare.* [? for *ardorous.*] Ardent. CARY.

†Are, A re (ā·rē), *sb.*[1] 1450. [A + RE *sb.*[1]] *Mus.* Name of the note A in Aretino's 1st, 4th, and 7th hexachords, in which it coincided with the second lowest note, sung to the syllable *re.*

Are to plead Hortensio's passion *Tam. Shr.* III. i. 74.

‖Are (ar), *sb.*[2] 1819. [Fr., ad. L. *area.*] The unit of superficial measurement in the Fr. metric system; a square of which the side measures ten metres, equal to 119.6 sq. yards.

Are (āɪ, ăr, 'r, ɪ), *v.* Pl. pres. Ind. of BE. Part of the orig. substantive vb.; cf. AM.

Area (ēᵊ·riă). Pl. **areas**, occ. **areæ**. 1538. [a. L.] **1.** A level piece of ground not built over or occupied; a clear space within a building, as the arena of an amphitheatre, etc. **2.** An enclosed court, *spec.* a sunken court, which gives access to the basement of dwelling-houses; often *attrib.* 1649. **3.** Superficial extent. (Formerly also of cubic content.) 1570. **4.** A particular extent of (*esp.* the earth's) surface; a region, tract 1845; *Biol.* a limited part of the surface of any organism 1851. **5.** *fig.* Scope, range, extent 1627. †**6.** A bed or border in a garden. (So in L.) -1669. **7.** A bald place on the head. (So in L.) 1706.

1. A floor or a. of goodly length 1651. The a. or platform of the old stage CIBBER. Comfortable a. seats (*Theat. Advt.*). 2. Windows which opened to the a. below STEELE. *Area-sneak*: a thief who steals into kitchens through area-gates. 3. The a. of a triangle 1570. 4. The a. over which a language is spoken LATHAM. The germinative a. 1880. 5. The whole a. of life 1852.

†**Area·ch**, *v.* [OE. *arǣcan*, f. A- *pref.* 1 + *rǣcan*, to REACH.] **1.** *trans.* To reach, get at (*esp.* with a weapon) -1513; *fig.* to obtain -1596; to hand, deliver -1530. **2.** *intr.* To reach, extend (*to*). Also *fig.* -1541.

Aread, arede, areed (ărī·d), *v. arch.* [OE. *arēdan*, f. A- *pref.* 1 + *redan*; see READ. The reg. conjugation is *area·d, are·d, are·d.*] †**1.** *trans.* To divine -1600; to make known, utter -1642. **2.** To guess (*arch.*) ME. **3.** To interpret, solve (*arch.*) OE. ** Later senses formed on READ. **4.** *trans.* To counsel 1559. Also *intr.* or *absol.* **5.** To decide, adjudge 1593.

2. Rightly he ared the Maid's intent SOUTHEY. 3. So is thy dream areded W. MORRIS. 4. I arede therfore..all people to be wise 1559. 5. We may best areede who is most credible 1593.

†**Area·d**, *sb.* 1590. [f. the vb.] Counsel -1601.

†**Area·dy**, *a.* ME. [f. READY; see A- *pref.* 6.] Prepared; in readiness -1480. Hence †**Area·dily** *adv.* †**Area·diness.**

Areal (ēᵊ·riˌăl), *a.* 1676. [ad. L. *arealis*, f. *area.*] Of, pertaining to, or of the nature of, an area. Hence **Area·lity**, condition in respect of area.

†**Area·r**, *v.* [OE. *arǣran*, f. A- *pref.* 1 + *rǣran* to REAR.] **1.** To raise, set up -1627; also *fig.* **2.** To raise (a person) *against* -1611. **3.** *refl.* and *intr.* -ME.

A-rea·r, *adv.* [A *prep.*[1] + REAR *sb.*] In the rear.

†**Area·son.** ME. [a. OFr. *ares-*, *araisoner*, mod. *arraisonner*:—late L. *adrationare*, f. *ad* and *rationem*; see REASON.] By-form of ARRAIGN *v.*; to address words and *esp.* questions to; to call to account -1594.

‖**Areca** (æ·rĭkă). 1599. [a. Pg., ad. (ult.) Tamil.] Name of the tree and fruit of a genus of palms, of which *A. Catechu* yields a nut which the natives roll up in betel-leaves and chew.

A-ree·k, *adv.* [A *prep.*[1]] Reeking. SWIFT.

Arefaction (ærĭfæ·kʃən). ? *Obs.* 1576. [f. *arefacere*; see next.] The action or process of drying; dried condition.

Arefy (æ·rĭfəi), *v.* ? *Obs.* 1542. [irreg. ad. L. *arefacere*, f. *arere* + *facere*. Cf. *satisfy.*] *trans.* and *intr.* To dry up, parch.

Arena (ărī·nă). Pl. **arenas.** 1627. [a. L., prop. *harena*, sand.] **1.** The central part of an amphitheatre, in which the combats take place; orig. strewn with sand. Also, the whole amphitheatre. *fig.* A battle-field 1814. **2.** Any sphere of public or energetic action 1798. **3.** *Med.* Sand or gravel deposited from the urine 1706.

1. The thronged a. shakes with shouts for more BYRON. The a. of controversy H. ROGERS. 2. The a. of authorship H. REED.

Arenaceo- (ærĭnē¹·ʃiˌo), comb. f. L. *arenaceus* (see next); =sandy, as in *a.-argillaceous*, of the nature of sandy clay.

Arenaceous (ærĭnē¹·ʃəs), *a.* 1646. [f. L. *arenaceus*, f. *arena*; see -ACEOUS.] Having the appearance of sand; sandy; largely composed of sand or quartz grains. Also *fig.*

‖**Arenaria** (ærĭnēᵊ·riă). 1806. [L., fem. of *arenarius.*] The Sandwort; a genus of small herbs (N.O. *Caryophyllaceæ*) allied to chickweed.

Arena·rious, *a.* ? *Obs.* 1758. [f. L. *arenarius*; see -ARIOUS.] =ARENACEOUS.

Arenation (ærĭnē¹·ʃən). ? *Obs.* 1717. [ad. L. *arenationem.*] *Med.* Application of hot sand to the body as a remedy.

Are·ndalite. 1868. [f. *Arendal* in Norway + -ITE.] *Min.* = EPIDOTE.

Arendator; see ARR-.

Arenicolite (ærĭni·kŏləit). 1864. [f. mod. L. *arenicola* (f. *arena* + *-cola*) + -ITE.] A worm-hole made orig. in sand, and preserved in a sandstone rock.

Arenicolous (-ŏləs), *a.* 1851. [f. as prec + -OUS.] Inhabiting sand.

Arenilitic (ăre:nili·tik), *a.* 1799. [f. **arenilite* (f. L. *arena* + Gr. λίθος) + -IC.] Of or pertaining to sandstone.

Arenose (æ:rĭnōᵘ·s), *a.* 1731. [ad. L. *arenosus.*] Sandy. var. †**A·renous.**

Areno:so-, comb. f. L. *arenosus*, Eng. *arenose.*

Areo-, f. Gr. Ἄρεος of Ares or Mars; *esp.* in *Astr.*; as **A:reoce·ntric** *a.*, having Mars as centre. **Areo·graphy**, description of the physical features of Mars; whence **Areo·grapher, Areo·graphic** *a.* **Areo·logy**, scientific investigation of the substance of Mars.

‖**Areola** (ărī·ŏlă). Pl. **areolæ.** 1664. [L., dim. of *area.*] A very small area. **1.** A small space marked out on a surface by intersecting lines, as the space between the veins of a leaf or the nervures of an insect's wing. **2.** An interstice in the tissue of any organized substance 1848. **3.** A circular spot; the coloured circle about a nipple, or a vesicle, or pustule 1706. **4.** *Biol.* **a.** A slightly depressed spot on any surface 1872. **b.** The cell-nucleus of a plant 1862. Hence **Are·olar** *a.* consisting of areolæ; *spec.* in *areolar* (or *connective*) *tissue*: the mixture of fibrous and elastic tissue, which underlies the skin. Also, of or pertaining to a small area. **Are·olate, Are·olated** *ppl. adjs.* marked by, or consisting of, areolæ. **A:reola·tion**, division into areolæ. **Are·olet**, a small areola. var. **A·reole.**

Areometer, var. of ARÆOMETER.

Areo·pagist, rare var. of next.

Areopagite (æriˌǫ·păgəit). ME. [ad. L. *areopagites*, a. Gr. ἀρειοπαγίτης; see AREOPAGUS.] A member of the court of Areopagus.

Areopagi·tic. 1649. [ad. L. *Areopagiticus*, a. Gr.; see prec. and -IC.] **A.** *adj.* Of or pertaining to the Areopagus or its court. **B.** *sb.* A speech imitating the oration of Isocrates addressed to the court of Areopagus. So **Areopagi·tical** *a.*

‖**Areopagus** (æriˌǫ·păgŏs). 1642. [L., a. Gr. Ἄρειος πάγος the hill of Ares.] A hill at Athens where the highest judicial court held its sittings; *hence*, the court itself, and *transf.* any important tribunal.

Areo·pagy. 1646. [f. L. *Areopagus* + -Y.] A secret tribunal.

Areostyle, -systyle, areotic; see ARÆ-.

Arere, obs. var. of AREAR *v.*; earlier f. ARREAR.

Arest, obs. f. ARREST, and ERST.

†**Are·t, are·tt(e**, *v.* ME. [a. OFr. *areter*, *aretter*, f. *à* + *reter*:—L. *reputare*; see REPUTE. Erron. latinized as *arrectare*, whence the sp. *arect, arrect.*] **1.** *trans.* To reckon -1485; to ascribe *to* -1549; to charge *upon* -1602. **2.** To indict a person (*of*) -1641. ¶ **3.** To commit a charge to. (A false use of Spenser's.) -1625.

Aretaics (ærĭtē¹·iks), *sb. pl.* [f. Gr. ἀρετή.] The science of virtue. J. GROTE.

‖**Arête** (arēt). 1862. [Fr.:—OF. *areste*, L. *arista* ear of corn, fish-bone or spine.] A sharp ascending ridge or edge of a mountain. The local name in Fr. Switzerland, now technical with climbers.

Arew(e, obs. f. ARROW, AROW, and ARUE.

Arfvedsonite. 1837. [f. *Arfvedson* a chemist + -ITE.] *Min.* A ferruginous variety of hornblende, occurring in black crystals; soda-hornblende.

Argaile, argal, obs. vars. of ARGOL.

A·rgal, *conj. adv.* 1602. Perversion of L. *ergo* 'therefore'; hence *subst.* a clumsy piece of reasoning.

He drownes not himselfe, A., he..shortens not his owne life *Haml.* v. i. 21. Mr. Buckle's argument is as absurd an a. [etc.] 1861.

‖**Argala** (ā·ɪgălă). Better **argee·lah.** 1754. [Hind.] The adjutant-bird (*Ciconia Argala*).

‖**Argali** (ā·ɪgăli). 1779. [Mongol.] *Zool.* The wild or rock sheep of Asia.

‖**Argan.** 1809. [a. Arab.] An evergreen tree (N.O. *Sapotaceæ*), found in Morocco, furnishing an oil from its seeds.

Argand (ā·ɪgænd). 1790. A lamp invented by Aimé Argand about 1782, having a cylindrical wick, which allows air to pass to both inner and outer surfaces of the flame; also, a ring-shaped gas-burner made on the same principle.

‖**Argema** (ā·ɪgĭmă). 1661. [L., a. Gr. ἄργεμα, -μον, f. ἀργός; cf. ALBUGO.] *Med.* A small white ulcer or speck on the margin of the cornea. var. **Argemon.**

Argent (ā·ɪdʒĕnt). 1500. [a. Fr., ad. L. *argentum.*] **A.** *sb.* **1.** The metal silver (*arch.* or *poet.*) 1530. †**2.** Silver coin; hence *gen.* cash -1742. **3.** *Her.* The silver of a coat of arms; the white colour in armorial bearings 1562.

1. *Spume of a.* (L. *argenti spuma*): litharge of silver. 3. Called Siluer, and blased by the name of A. 1562.

B. *adj.* Of, or resembling, silver; silvery white 1590; *esp.* in *Her.* 1591.

The a. moon H. COLERIDGE. The a. Eagle that he bare HARINGTON. Hence **Arge·ntal** *a.* of silver; as in *Argental Mercury*, the *Amalgam* of Dana. **Arge·nteous** *a.* silvery. **Argenti·ferous** *a.* yielding silver. **Argenti·fic** *a.* producing silver. **Arge·ntify** *v.* to turn into silver.

Argentan (ā·ɪdʒĕntæn). 1857. [a. Fr., f. L. *argentum.*] An alloy of nickel, copper, and zinc; German silver.

Argentate (ā·ɪdʒĕntē¹t), *sb.* 1880. [f. L. *argentum* + -ATE[4].] *Chem.* A combination of a base with argentic oxide, as in *A. of Ammonia*, fulminating silver.

Argentate, *a.* 1880. [ad. L. *argentatus*; cf. Fr. *argenté.*] Silvery, or shining white with a tinge of grey.

Argentic (aɪdʒe·ntik), *a.* 1868. [f. L. *argentum* + -IC.] *Chem.* Containing silver in chemical composition; as *A. Chloride*, AgCl, etc.

Argentine (ā·ɪdʒĕntəin). 1537. [a. Fr. *argentin*, ad. L. *argentinus.*] **A.** *adj.* Of, made of, or containing silver. **2.** Silvery 1578.

1. An antick deaurate with letters a. 1537. 2. Celestial Dian, goddess a. *Per.* v. i. 251.

B. *sb.* **1.** A material simulating silver: **a.** Electro-plate. **b.** The silvery lamellæ on the scales of fish, used in making artificial pearls 1839. **2.** *Zool.* A genus of small fishes, of the family *Salmonidæ*, with silvery scales; see 1 b. Also used of the *Scopelus Pennanti*, now called the Pearlside. 1769. †**3.** *Herb. Argentine Thistle*, the Cotton Thistle (*Onopordium Acanthium*) 1578. **4.** *Min.* Slate-spar 1794.

Argentite (ā·ɪdʒĕntəit). 1837. [f. L. *argentum* + -ITE.] *Min.* Silver-glance or argyrose, a native sulphide found traversing granite, etc.

Arge·nto-, comb. f. L. *argentum*; = 'Having silver as a constituent'.

Argento·meter. 1879. [f. L. *argentum* + -METER.] An instrument for measuring the strength of silver solutions.

Argentous (aɪdʒe·ntəs), *a.* 1869. [f. L. *argentum* + -OUS.] *Chem.* Containing silver in composition (in twice the proportion contained in the compounds called argentic), as *A. Chloride*, Ag_2Cl; *A. Oxide*, Ag_4O.

Argentry (ā·ɪdʒĕntri). 1622. [ad. F. *argenterie*; cf. L. *argentaria* (sc. *vasa*, etc.); see ARGENT.] Silver plate. *Obs.* exc. *fig.*

Pawning his own a. and jewels HOWELL.

†**A·rgent-vi·ve.** 1453. [a. F.:—L. *argentum vivum.*] Quicksilver -1662.

Argh, *a.* [Com. Teut.] **1.** Cowardly, fearful. (Still in north. dial.) OE. **2.** Inert, lazy, reluctant. (Still in north. dial.) OE.

Argh(e, *v.* ME. [f. prec.] To be timid; to hesitate from fearfulness. (Still in Sc.)

Argil (ā·ɪdʒil). 1530. [a. F. *argille* (mod. *argile*), ad. L. *argilla* (formerly used), a. Gr.

ἄργιλλος, f. ἀργής.] Clay, *esp.* potter's clay. Proposed at one time as a name for alumina.

Argilla·ceo-, comb. f. next.

Argillaceous (ā̆ɹdʒilē¹·ʃəs), *a.* 1731. [f. L. *argillaceus* + -OUS.] Of the nature of clay; largely composed of clay; clayey.

Argilli·ferous, *a.* 1800. [f. L. *argilla*+-(I)-FEROUS.] Yielding clay.

Argillite (ā̆·ɹdʒiləit). 1795. [f. as prec. + -ITE.] *Min.* Argillaceous schist, clay slate. Hence **Argilli·tic** *a.*

Argillo- (aɹdʒi·lo), comb. f. ARGILLOUS, as in **a.-calcareous** *a.* calcareous with an admixture of clay; **-calcite**, a clayey lime.

Argillous (aɹdʒi·ləs), *a. rare.* ME. [a. OFr. *argillus* (mod. *argileux*):—L. *argillosum.*] Clayey. var. †**A·rgillo·se.**

†**Argin**(e. *rare.* 1589. [a. It. *argine*:—pop. L. **argerem*, for **adgerem*, *aggerem* (Diez).] An embankment or rampart in front of a fort.

A·rgle, *v.* Still *dial.*; also in **argle-bargle**, **argol-bargol.** 1589. [prob. a perversion of *argue*; or cf. *haggle.*] **1.** To dispute about. **2.** *intr.* To bandy words, wrangle 1823.

Argol[1] (ā̆·ɹgǫl). ME. [?] The tartar deposited from wines, and adhering to the sides of the casks as a crust; crude bitartrate of potassium, which, when purified, becomes *cream of tartar.*

‖ **Argol**[2], **-al** (ā̆·ɹgəl). 1856. [Mongol.] Dried cow-dung used as fuel in Tartary.

Argon (ā̆·ɹgǫn). 1895. [n. of Gr. ἀργός idle (ἀ- not, ἐργ- WORK).] *Chem.* An inert gas occurring in very small quantity in the air.

Argonaut (ā̆·ɹgŏnǫt). 1596. [ad. L. *Argonauta*, ad. Gr. Ἀργοναύτης.] **1.** One of the legendary heroes who sailed with Jason in the Argo in quest of the Golden Fleece. **2.** Name of a genus of cephalopod molluscs of the octopod type, *esp.* of the 'paper nautilus', formerly believed to sail on the surface of the sea 1835. Hence **Argonau·tic** *a.* of or pertaining to the Argonauts; *sb.* an Argonaut; a poem concerning the Argonauts.

†**Argosi·ne.** *rare.* 1559. [prob. ad. It. *Ragusino*; see next.] ? A Ragusan –1645.

Argosy (ā̆·ɹgŏsi). 1577. [app. ad. It. *Ragusea*, i.e. *una* (*nave* or *caracca*) *Ragusea*. Ragusa appears in 16th c. Eng. as *Arragosa*, etc.; whence, doubtless, the transposition in *argosea*, etc. The early uses show no reference to the Argo.] *Hist.* and *Poet.* A merchant-vessel of the largest size and burden; *esp.* those of Ragusa and Venice. Also *transf.* and *fig.*

Argosies with portly saile Like Signiors and rich Burgers on the flood *Merch. V.* I. i. 9.

†**A·rgot**[1]. Also **argo.** ME. [a. Fr., mod. *ergot.* Cf. ERGOT.] **a.** The spur of a cock; the analogous part on the feet of other animals. **b.** A spur left in pruning a tree –1708.

‖ **Argot**[2] (argo). 1860. [Fr., of unkn. etym.] The jargon, slang, or peculiar phraseology of a class, *orig.* that of thieves and rogues. Hence **Argo·tic** *a.*

Argue (ā̆·ɹgiu), *v.* ME. [a. OFr. *arguer*:—L. *argutare*, freq. of *arguere*, and now taken as the equivalent of *arguere.*] **I.** †**1.** To convict. Const. *of.* –1660. †**2.** *trans.* To accuse, call in question. Const. *of.* –1692. **3.** To prove or evince; to indicate 1494.

1. Which of you shal a. me of sinne *John* viii. 46. 2. Nor would we a. the definitive sentence of God SIR T. BROWNE. 3. Not to know mee argues your selves unknown MILT. *P. L.* IV. 831. So bad a death, argues a monstrous life 2 *Hen. VI*, III. iii. 30.

II. 1. *intr.* To bring forward reasons in support of or against a proposition; to discuss; to reason; *hence*, to raise objections, dispute. Const. *with*, *against* an opponent; *for*, *against* a proposition; †*of*, *about* a matter. ME. **2.** *trans.* To discuss the pros and cons of; to examine controversially 1494. **3.** To maintain, by adducing reasons, *that* [etc.] 1548. **4.** To use as an argument (*arch.*) 1626.

1. His philosophy and faculty of arguing GLANVILL. More ready to a. than to obey BACON. Of good and evil much they argu'd then MILT. *P. L.* II. 562. 2. The sayd causes warre well and sufficiently argued 1494. Phrases. *To a. away, off*, etc.: to get rid of by argument 1713. *To a. into* or *out of*: to persuade by argument into, or out of, a course of action, etc. Hence **A·rguable** *a.* capable of being argued. **A·rguer.** **A·rguing** *vbl. sb.* †accusation; argument.

Argufy (ā̆·ɹgiufəi), *v. colloq.* 1751. [illiterate f. ARGUE. Cf. *speechify.*] **1.** *intr.* To prove something; *hence*, to signify. **2.** To dispute, wrangle 1800. **3.** *trans.* To worry with argumentation 1771.

†**Argu·itively**, *adv. rare.* 1665. [f. L. *arguit-*, *arguere* + -IVE + LY[2].] In a way that proceeds by argument.

Argument (ā̆·ɹgiumĕnt). ME. [a. Fr., ad. L. *argumentum* (also used); see ARGUE.] **1.** Proof, token. (Passing from *clear proof* to *proof presumptive*; cf. ARGUE 3.) (*arch.*) **2.** *Astr.* and *Math.* The angle, arc, etc., on which the calculation of another quantity depends ME. **3.** A statement or fact advanced to influence the mind, or to support a proposition; *spec.* in *Logic*, the middle term of a syllogism. Also *fig.* Const. †*to*, *for*, and later *against*. ME. (In certain phrases borrowed from the schools the L. form *argumentum* is used, *esp.* in *argumentum ad hominem*). **4.** A connected series of statements intended to establish (or subvert) a position; a process of reasoning; argumentation ME. **5.** Statement of the pros and cons of a proposition; discussion; debate 1494; †*transf.* subject of contention –1614. **6.** Theme, subject (*arch.*) 1570. **7.** The summary of the subject-matter of a book; *fig.* the contents 1535.

1. It is..no great a. of her folly *Much Ado* II. iii. 242. 3. To pleade my cause before him, and to fyll my mouth with argumentes *Job* xxiii. 3. The arguments for and against..trial by jury COX. 4. The successive steps of the a. 1877. 5. In a. with men a woman ever Goes by the worse MILT. *Sams.* 903. Sheath'd their swords for lack of a. *Hen. V*, III. i. 21. 6. It would be a. for a weeke 1 *Hen. IV*, II. ii. 100. He grew the A. of all Tongues CLARENDON. 7. If I would ..try the a. of hearts, by borrowing *Timon* II. ii. 187. Hence †**Argume·ntal** *a.* argumentative. †**A·rgumenti·ze**, to conduct an a.

†**A·rgument**, *v.* ME. [a. Fr. *argumenter*, ad. L. *argumentari*; see prec.] **1.** *intr.* To argue –1637; to furnish proof *that* 1558. **2.** *trans.* To make the subject of argument 1746. Hence †**Argume·ntable** *a.* that may be argued; argumentative. **A:rgumenta·tor**, a reasoner.

Argumentation (ā̆ɹgiumĕntē¹·ʃən). 1491. [a. Fr., ad. L. *argumentationem*; see ARGUMENT *v.*] **1.** The action of inferring a conclusion from propositions premised; methodical employment or presentation of arguments; formal reasoning. **2.** Interchange of argument, debate 1538. **3.** =ARGUMENT 4. 1548.

1. The eloquence and a. of the bar SCOTT. 2. But what a. can a man hold with him CLARENDON. 3. What a misfashioned a. is this 1548.

Argumentative (ā̆ɹgiume·ntătiv), *a.* 1642. [a. Fr. *argumentatif*, *-ive*, f. L. *argumentat-*, *argumentari.*] †**1.** Of the nature of an argument (*for*); of weight as evidence (*of*) –1691. **2.** Controversial, logical 1647. **3.** Addicted to argumentation; capable of arguing 1667.

3. A strong, capacious, a. mind GIBBON. Hence **Argume·ntative·ly** *adv.*, **-ness.**

‖**Argumentum**; see ARGUMENT.

Argus (ā̆·ɹgŏs). ME. [L., a. Gr. Ἄργος.] **1.** A mythological person fabled to have had a hundred eyes. *Hence*, a very vigilant watcher. (After the death of Argus, his eyes were transferred by Hera to the tail of the peacock.) **2.** A genus of pheasants, natives of Asia, esp. *A. giganteus*, which is as large as a turkey 1768. **3.** A butterfly of the genus *Polyommatus* 1827.

1. Fayre pecocks .. full of A. eyes SPENSER.

Comb.: **a.-eyed** *a.*, watchful or sharp-sighted; **-shell**, a species of porcelain-shell; **-snake**, one marked by rows of round ocellated red spots.

†**Arguta·tion.** 1641. [ad. L. *argutationem*; see ARGUE.] Cavilling, cavil –1681.

Argute (aɹgiū·t), *a.* ME. [ad. L. *argutus*; see ARGUE.] †**1.** Of taste: Sharp. **2.** Shrill 1719. **3.** Of persons, etc.: Quick, keen, subtle, shrewd, *esp.* in small matters 1577. Hence **Argu·te·ly** *adv.*, **-ness.**

Argyll (aɹgəi·l). 1822. [f. proper name.] A vessel of metal, like a small coffee-pot, for serving up gravy hot.

Argyr-, argyro- (ā̆·ɹdʒir-, -ro), repr. Gr. ἀργυρο- comb. f. ἄργυρος silver.

Argyra·nthemous, Argyra·nthous [Gr. ἄνθος, ἀνθεμίς] *a.*, *Bot.* having silvery white flowers. **Argyra·spid** [L. *argyraspides*, Gr. ἀργυράσπιδες], in *pl.* the silver-shielded; a corps of the Macedonian army. ‖**Argu·ria**, *Med.* silver-poisoning. **Argy·ric** [Gr. ἀργυρικός] *a.*, *Chem.* = ARGENTIC. **A·rgyrite, Argyro·se**, *Min.* = ARGENTITE. **Argyroce·phalous** [Gr. κεφαλή] *a.*, having a shining white head. **Argyroce·ratite** [Gr. κέρατ-], *Min.* = CERARGYRITE.

Arh-; see ARRH-.

‖ **Aria** (ā̆·riˌă). 1742. [It.] *Mus.* An air, melody, or tune; *esp.* a more elaborate accompanied melody sung by a single voice in the older operas, etc., as dist. from simple airs or songs.

Arian, -ize. *Ethnol.* See ARYAN.

Arian (ē°·riăn), *a.* 1532. [ad. L. *arianus*, f. *Arius*, *Arīus*, Gr. Ἄριος, Ἄρειος, prop. name.] Of, pertaining to, or holding the doctrine of, Arius, a presbyter of Alexandria in the 4th c., who denied that Christ was *consubstantial* with God 1642. As *sb.* One holding this doctrine.

Our first Teutonic version of the Scriptures was by an A. missionary, Ulfilas STANLEY. Hence **A·rianism**, the A. doctrine or heresy. **A·riani·ze** *v.* to follow the doctrine of Arius; to convert to Arianism. **A·riani·zer.**

-arian (ē°·riăn) *suffix*, f. L. *-arius* + -AN, first appearing in the 16th c., as in names of sects (*Disciplinarian*) and holders of religious tenets (*Trinitarian*); hence gen. (*humanitarian*).

Aricine (æ·risəin). 1847. [f. *Arica* in Peru + -INE[5].] *Chem.* An alkaloid.

Arid (æ·rid), *a.* 1652. [ad. L. *aridus*; perh. through Fr. *aride.*] **1.** Dry, parched, withered. *Hence*, barren, bare 1656. **2.** *fig.* Uninteresting, jejune 1827. Hence **A·ridly** *adv.*, **-ness.**

1. A. sands BAKER. 2. A. studies 1846.

Aridity (ări·dĭti). 1599. [ad. L. *ariditas*; see ARID.] **1.** Arid state or quality, parched condition, dryness, barrenness: *spec.* (*Med.*) of the body. **2.** *fig.* Lack of interest; in the theological sense, want of unction or tenderness 1692.

2. The excessive a. of scholasticism LECKY.

†**Ariel**[1]. ME. A word from the Vulgate (after Ἀριήλ of the LXX, etc.). rendered 'altar'.

(Generally in O.T. the word occurs as a man's name; also an appellation of Jerusalem = 'lion of God'; in Milton as the name of an angel, in Shaks. of 'an Ayrie spirit'; in *Astron.* of a satellite of Uranus.)

Ariel[2] (ē°·riˌĕl). 1832. [a. Arab.] A species of the gazelle found in Western Asia and Africa.

‖ **Aries** (ē°·riˌīz). ME. [L.] The ram; a zodiacal sign, which the sun enters on the 21st of March.

Arietation (æ:ri-, ē°:riˌĕtē¹·ʃən). *arch.* 1625. [ad. L. *arietationem*, f. *arietare.*] **1.** The action of butting like a ram; *hence*, the striking with a battering-ram, etc. **2.** *transf.* and *fig.* Battering, clashing, concussion 1625.

‖ **Arietta** (ɑriˌe·ttă). 1742. [It.; dim. of ARIA.] *Mus.* A short air. var. ‖**Arie·tte.** [Fr.]

Aright (ărəi·t), *adv.* OE. [A *prep.*[1] + OE. *riht.*] **1.** In a right manner; justly, correctly. †**2.** Straightway. (Cf. RIGHTS.) –1460. **3.** Right: Exactly (*arch.*) ME. †Straight –1611. **4.** On the right (hand) (*arch. rare*) 1795.

1. A generacion that set not their herte a. *Ps.* lxxvii. 8. 4. A., aleft, The..foemen scatter SOUTHEY. Hence †**A·ri·ght** *v.* to make right. **Ari·ghtly**, †**Ari·ghts** *advs.*

Aril (æ·ril). 1794. [ad. mod.L. *arillus* (also used), f. med.L. *arilli*, Sp. *arillos*, raisins.] *Bot.* (See quot.)

The..arillus is an accessory seed-covering, more or less incomplete, formed between the time of fertilization and the ripening of the seed, by a growth from the apex of the funiculus, at or just below the hilum GRAY. Hence **A·rillary** *a.* of or pertaining to the a. **A·rillate, A·rillated, A·rilled** *ppl. adjs.* furnished or covered with an a. **Ari·lliform** *a.* **A·rillode**, a false a., originating at or near the micropyle.

†**A·riolate**, *v. rare.* 1652. [f. L. *ariolat-*, prop. *hariolat-*, *hariolari.* (The *h-* is rare in Eng.)] To divine, foretell from omens. Hence †**Ariola·ter, -or**; vars. †**A·riole**, †**A·rioler**, †**A·riolist.** †**Ariola·tion.**

Ariose (ɑriˌōᵘ·s), *a.* 1742. [ad. It. *arioso*; see next.] *Mus.* Melodious; song-like.

‖ **Arioso** (ɑriˌōᵘ·so), *a.* 1742. [It.; = *airy*, f. *aria.*] *Mus.* Ariose, melodious. Used of instrumental music, it describes a sustained vocal style; of vocal music, an air of the character both of air and recitative, which requires rather to be *said* than *sung*. Hence used *advb.* as a direction, and *subst.* as a piece of such music.

A-ri·ot, *adv.* 1851. [A *prep.*[1]] In riot.

-arious, *comp. suffix*, forming adjs., f. L. *-arius, -a, -um* 'connected with' + -OUS (as if ad. L. *-ariosus*; cf. *cariosus*). The reg. Eng. repr. of *-arius* is -ARY[1].

A-ri·pple, *adv.* 1855. [A *prep.*[1]] In a ripple.

Arise (ărəi·z), *v.* *Pa. t.* **arose**; *Pa. pple.* **arisen.** OE. [f. A- *pref.* 1 + RISE; = to 'rise up', intensive of *rise*. Almost replaced by RISE, in all senses, exc. those in III.] **I. 1.** To get up from sitting or kneeling, to stand up (*arch.*); †hence *transf.* and *fig.*: To adjourn (as a court), to stand on end (as hair) –1649. **2.** To get up †from a fall –1667; from sleep or rest (*arch.*) OE. **3.** To come above the horizon (of the sun, etc.); *transf.* of the day, morning. Now *arch.* and *poet.* OE. **4.** To rise from the dead. Now *poet.* OE. **5.** To rise from inaction; *esp.* in hostility or rebellion (*against*). Now *poet.* OE. **6.** To rise in agitation, to boil up. Now *poet.* OE. **7.** *transf.* Of sounds: To come up so as to be audible ME.

1. A., let us go hence *John* xiv. 31. 2. Awake, a., or be for ever fall'n MILT. *P. L.* I. 330. A., a.! the morning is at hand KEATS. 3. A. faire Sun and kill the enuious Moone *Rom. & Jul.* II. ii. 4. 4. Many bodies of the saints which slept arose *Matt.* xxvii. 52. 5. Aryse o Lorde God, lift vp thine honde *Ps.* ix. 12. 6. A wind arose and rush'd upon the South TENNYSON. 7. And there arose a great cry *Acts* xxiii. 9.

II. To go or come higher. **1.** To go or come up, ascend on high, mount. Now *poet.* OE. †**2.** To rise with its summit or surface; to grow higher, to swell up –1664; to rise in rank, etc. –1756; in price or amount –1714; to attain to, reach –1798.

1. The duste arose with the wynde 1450.

III. To spring up, come above ground, into existence. **1.** †To spring forth from its source. *transf.* To take its rise, originate. OE. **2.** To be born, come into the world of action OE. **3.** Of things: To spring up, be raised, built, etc. (*poet.* or *rhet.*) OE. **4.** To spring, originate, or result *from*, †*of* ME. **5.** *gen.* To come into existence or notice OE.

2. There arose no prophet more in Israel like vnto Moses *Deut.* xxiv. 10. 4. Some sodaine mischiefe may a. of it SHAKS. Comfort arose from the reflection 1793. 5. Questions which arose in the Privy Council MACAULAY. Those Thoughts which a.. in the Mind of Man ADDISON. Hence †**Ari·se** *sb.* arising.

‖**Arista** (ări·stă). Pl. **-æ.** 1691. [L.] The awn or beard of grain or grasses; *hence* used of similar bristle-like processes. Hence **Ari·state** *ppl. a.* awned, bearded.

Aristarch (æ·ristāɹk). 1621. [ad. L., a. Gr. Ἀρίσταρχος, a severe Greek critic of the Homeric poetry.] A severe critic. Hence **Arista·rchian** *a.* severely critical.

†**Aristi·ppus.** 1627. [Name of a luxurious Gr. philosopher.] A cant name for canary wine –1703.

Aristo- (æ·risto), comb. f. Gr. ἄριστος best; as in *a.-democratical*, having a democratic constitution limited by aristocratic elements.

Aristocracy (æristǫ·krăsi). 1561. [ad. L. *aristocratia*, a. Gr., f. ἄριστος + -κρατία. Cf. Fr. *aristocracie* (14th c.).] Contrasted earlier with *monarchy*; now with *democracy*. **1.** *lit.* The government of a state by its best citizens. Also *fig.* **2.** That form of government in which the sovereign power lies with those who are most distinguished by birth and fortune; oligarchy 1577; a state so governed 1603. **3.** An oligarchy 1611. *Hence* **4.** The class to which such a ruling body belongs; the nobles; *pop.* all those who by birth or fortune rank distinctly above the rest of the community. Also *fig.* 1651. **5.** = *aristocraticism* 1822.

1. A truer A., or Government again by the Best CARLYLE. 2. The republic of Venice is an a. 1751. 4. Our a. and gentry date, on the whole, from the days of Henry the Eighth ROGERS.

Aristocrat (æ·ristokræ:t, ări·stǒkræt). 1789. [a. Fr. *aristocrate* (not after Gr.), f. *aristocratie, -ique*. A pop. formation of the Fr. Revolution.] A member of an aristocracy; *strictly*, one of an oligarchy; *hence*, one of a patrician order, a noble; *occ.* one who favours an aristocratic form of government (opp. to *democrat*).

Their excellencies, the *aristocrats* of Venice A. YOUNG. In came that fierce A., Our pursy woollen-draper COLERIDGE.

Aristocratic (æristo,kræ·tik), *a.* 1602. [a. Fr. *aristocratique*, ad. Gr. ἀριστοκρατικός; see ARISTOCRACY.] **1.** Of or pertaining to an aristocracy; attached to or favouring aristocracy. **2.** Befitting an aristocrat; grand, stylish 1845.

1. The so-called a. party, the landlords G. DUFF. 2. The principal tradesmen..deemed it more 'aristocratic' DISRAELI. Hence **A:ristocra·tical** *a.* oligarchical; of or belonging to the higher classes; *sb.* a partisan of aristocracy. **A:ristocra·tically** *adv.* **A:ristocra·ticalness**, a. quality or style. **A:ristocra·ticism**, adherence to a. principles or custom. **A·ristocra:tism**, haughty exclusiveness. **Aristo·cratize** *v.* to make a.; to favour aristocracy.

‖**Aristolochia** (æ:ristolǒu·kiă). ME. [a. med. L. *aristologia*, ad. L. *aristolochia*, a. Gr., f. ἀριστόλοχος (as promoting child-birth).] *Bot.* A genus of shrubs, including *A. Clematitis*, the Common Birthwort.

Aristo·logy. 1835. [f. Gr. ἄριστον breakfast + -λογία.] The art or science of dining. Hence **A:ristolo·gical** *a.* **Aristo·logist.**

Aristotelian (æ:ristotī·liăn). 1607. [f. L. *Aristoteles*, Gr. Ἀριστοτέλης + -IAN; cf. *Christian*.] *adj.* Of or pertaining to Aristotle, the Greek philosopher, or to his system. *sb.* One who follows, or is skilled in, the philosophy of Aristotle. var. **A:ristotele·an.** [f. L. *Aristoteleus*, Gr. Ἀριστοτέλειος.] Hence **Aristote·lianism**, the system or any doctrine of Aristotle. **A:ristote·lic**, †**-al** *a.* = ARISTOTELIAN. **Aristo·telism** = *Aristotelianism*. **Aristo·telize** *v.* to lean towards or teach the system of Aristotle.

Aristulate (ări·stiŭlėt), *ppl. a.* [f. mod.L. *aristula*, dim. of *arista* + -ATE[2].] *Bot.* Bearing a diminutive awn.

Arithmancy (æ·riþ,mænsi). 1577. [contr. f. *arithmomancy* (see ARITHMO-).] Divination by numbers. Hence **Arithma·ntical** *a.*

Arithmetic (ări·þmĕtik), *sb.* ME. [orig. a. OFr. *arismetique*, for L. *arithmetica*, a. Gr. ἡ ἀριθμητική (sc. τέχνη), f. ἀριθμέ-ειν, f. ἀριθμός. In ME. erron. referred to L. *ars metrica*; see ARSMETRY.] **1.** The science of numbers; the art of computation by figures. **2.** Arithmetical knowledge, computation 1607. **3.** A treatise on computation 1623.

1. These roguish Arsmetrique gibbets or flesh-hookes, and cyphers or round oos NASHE. 2. But now 'tis oddes beyond Arithmetick *Cor.* III. i. 245.

†**Arithme·tic**(k. 1652. [a. Fr. *arithmétique*.] *adj.* = ARITHMETICAL. –1767. *sb.* An arithmetician –1711.

Arithmetical (æriþme·tikăl), *a.* 1543. [f. L., a. Gr. ἀριθμητικός (see ARITHMETIC) + -AL.] Of, pertaining to, or connected with arithmetic; according to the rules of arithmetic. As *sb.* A number in an a. progression 1798. Hence **Arithme·tically** *adv.*

A. progression, series: one of which the terms differ by a constant difference, positive or negative. So *a. proportion.*

Arithmetician (ări:þmĭti·ʃăn, æ:riþ-). 1557. [a. Fr., f. L. *arithmetica*; see ARITHMETIC and -ICIAN.] One skilled in arithmetic.

Arithmo-, comb. f. Gr. ἀριθμός number. **arithmo·cracy** [Gr. -κρατία], rule by a mere numerical majority; whence **-cra·tic** *a.*; **-gram** [Gr. γράμμα], a number expressed by the letters of a word, name, or phrase; **-graphy** [Gr. -γραφία], representation of a number by letters; **-lo·gical** [Gr. -λογικός] *a.*, pertaining to the scientific treatment of numbers; **-logy** [Gr. -λόγια], a treatise on numbers, or statement bearing on them; **-ma·ncy** [Gr. -μαντεία], divination by numbers; arithmancy; **-meter** [Gr. -μέτρον], an instrument for working out arithmetical problems.

-arium, *suffix* of sbs., a. L. *-arium* 'thing connected with or employed in, place for', orig. neut. of adjs. in *-arius*. The reg. Eng. repr. of *-arium* is *-ary*; see -ARY[1].

Ark (āɹk), *sb.* [Com. Teut.: OE. *arc*, acc. *arce*, prob. a. L. *arca*; see ARCHE.] **1.** A chest, coffer, close basket, etc.; *esp.* in *north. dial.* a bin for meal, etc. OE. **2.** *spec.* in *Jew. Hist.* The wooden coffer containing the tables of the law, kept in the Holiest Place of the Tabernacle. Also called *Ark of the Covenant*, *Ark of Testimony*. See ARCHE. OE. Also *fig.* **3.** The large floating covered vessel in which Noah was saved at the Deluge; hence *fig.* a place of refuge OE. **4.** *transf.* A ship, boat, etc.; *spec.* in U.S., a large flat-bottomed river boat used to transport produce 1475. †**5.** An enclosure for catching or confining fish.

1. She toke an arke of bul-rushes *Ex.* ii. 3. 2. There-in an A., and in the A. his Testimony MILT. *P. L.* XII. 251. *To touch* or *lay hands on the ark*: to treat irreverently what is held to be sacred (2 *Sam.* vi. 6). 3. There is sure another flood toward, and these couples are comming to the Arke *A. Y. L.* v. iv. 36. *Comb.*: **a.-full**; **-net**, a kind of fish-trap (cf. *eel-ark*); **-shell**, a species of bivalve mollusc. Hence †**Ark**, *v.* to shut up in an ark.

Arkansite. *Min.* A variety of BROOKITE.

Arkite (ā·ɹkəit). 1774. [f. ARK.] *adj.* Of or pertaining to Noah's ark. *sb.* An inmate of the ark.

Arkose (aɹkǭu·s). 1839. *Geol.* A sandstone containing felspar and quartz.

Arksutite (ā·ɹksutəit). 1868. [f. *Arksut* in Greenland + -ITE.] *Min.* A white, vitreous fluoride of lime, soda, and alumina.

Arle (āɹl), *v. north.* 1609. [f. ARLES. Cf. Fr. *arrher*.] To give earnest-money to or for.

Arles (āɹlz). *north. dial.* ME. [app. a. OF. *erle, *arle :—L. *arrhula dim. of ARRHA. A pl., but occ. used as sing.] Money given to bind a bargain; *esp.* that given when a servant is hired; earnest-money 1540; *fig.* an earnest, a foretaste ME. var. **Arles-penny.**

†**A·rling.** [OE. *eorðling*, f. *eorðe* earth.] A bird; the wheatear –1753.

Arm (āɹm), *sb.*[1] [Com. Teut.; cogn. w. L. *armus*; cf. Gr. ἁρμός, f. *ar-* to join.] **I.** The limb. **1.** The upper limb of the human body, from the shoulder to the hand; the part from the elbow downwards being the *fore-arm*. **2.** *fig.* Might, power, authority OE.; a prop, a stay ME.; and generally 1597. **3.** The fore limb of an animal 1607; in *Falconry*, the leg of a hawk from the thigh to the foot 1575; the flexible limbs or other appendages of invertebrate animals 1822. **4.** A sleeve 1797.

1. Smot him þoru þe riht arum ME. She stript it from her Arme *Cymb.* II. iv. 101. 2. I haue broken the arme of Pharaoh *Ezek.* xxx. 21. *Secular arm*: the authority of a temporal (opp. to an eccl.) tribunal. Sir Lancelot, my *right arm* (= main stay) TENNYSON. I saw the new moon, late yestreen, Wi' the auld moon in her a. *Sir Patrick Spens.* 4. The right a. lined with fur H. WALPOLE.

II. Things resembling arms. **1.** A narrower portion of anything projecting from the main body, as an *arm of the sea*, of a machine, etc. OE. **2.** One of the branches into which a main trunk divides, as an arm of a tree, a river, a nerve, etc. ME. **3.** One of two lateral (and usu. horizontal) parts, which answer to each other, as (*Naut.*) the parts of an anchor which bear the flukes; the parts of the yard extending on either side of the mast (see YARD-ARM); in machines, the parts of the balance; in levers, the part from the fulcrum to the point of application of the power or weight 1659. **4.** One of the two rails of a chair, sofa, etc., on which the sitter's arms may rest. See ARM-CHAIR. 1633.

1. That a. of the sea..now called the Humber DE FOE. Phrases. **a. Arm-in-arm** (improp. *arm-and-arm*): said of two persons, when one interlinks his arm with the other's; hence *fig.* in close communion. **To give** or **offer one's arm** (to): to allow *or* invite a person to walk arm-in-arm with one, or lean on one's a. **A child** or **infant in arms**: one too young to walk. **With open arms**: with eager welcome. **b. At arm's** †**end, length**: as far away from one as the arm can reach; *hence*, away from familiarity, at a distance; *spec.* in *Law*, without fiduciary relations. **To work at arm's length**: awkwardly or disadvantageously.

Comb.: **a.-bone**, the *humerus*; **-coil**, an armlet; †**-gaunt** *a.*,? with gaunt limbs; †**-great** *a.*, as large round as an a.; †**-labour**, manual labour; **-piece**, armour to protect the a.; **-strong**, *a.*, strong of a.

Arm, *sb.*[2] Usu. in *pl.* **Arms** (āɹmz). ME. [a. F. *armes* :—L. *arma* (no sing.), f. *ar-* to fit. The sing. *arm* is rare and late.] **I.** *pl.* Things used in fighting. **1.** Defensive covering, etc., for the body; armour, mail. Now *poet.* **2.** Instruments of offence used in war; weapons ME.; *sing.* a particular kind of weapon 1861.

2. *Fire-arms*: those for which gunpowder is used. *Small-arms*: those not requiring carriages, opp. to

artillery. *Stand of arms*: a complete set for one soldier. A well-balanced a. 1877. *Man of arms*, later *man-at-arms*: one practised in war; a fully-armed knight.

II. Elliptical senses. (Only *pl.* exc. in 4.) 1. The exercise of arms; fighting, war, etc. ME. 2. The practice or profession of arms 1450. 3. Deeds or feats of arms. Now *poet.* ME. 4. *sing.* and *pl.* Each kind of troops of which an army is composed; the infantry, cavalry, artillery, and engineers; orig. the two first 1798.

1. Success in arms 1780. *To appeal to arms*; see APPEAL *v.* 2. Since first I follow'd Armes SHAKS. 3. Arms and the man I sing DRYDEN. *A passage, assault, of* (or *at*) *arms*; see PASSAGE, ASSAULT. 4. About 12,000 of all arms GLEIG.

III. Transf. and fig. senses. (Usu. *pl.*) 1. in *Law*. Anything that a man, in his anger, takes into his hand to cast at, or strike another 1641. 2. Instruments of defence or attack possessed by animals; the ARMATURE or ARMOUR of plants 1711. 3. *fig.* (from 2) of things immaterial ME.

3. The intellectual arms of Reason SIR T. BROWNE.

IV. Heraldic Arms. Heraldic insignia or devices, borne originally on the shields of knights or barons to distinguish them (hence called ARMORIAL bearings), which later became hereditary. Also the ensigns of countries, corporations, etc. ME. *collect.* as *sing.* 1590.

The lawful holder of Arms has in them a true estate in fee BOUTELL. *In arms with*: quartered with. *To bear arms*: to show armorial bearings. Also *to grant* or *assign arms*. *Coat of Arms*: see ARMOUR *sb.* *College of Arms*: the Heralds' College, where armorial bearings are granted. *King at Arms*: a chief herald.

Phrases: **To arms!** take to your arms, be ready to fight. **In arms**: armed, ready to fight; also *fig.* **To take up arms**: to arm oneself, rise in hostility; also *fig.* **To bear arms**: to serve as a soldier. **To turn one's arms against**: to make war upon. **To lay down arms**: to surrender. **Under arms**: in battle array; so, **to lie upon their arms. Stand to your arms!** i.e. in order of battle with arms presented.

Arm (āɹm), *v.*[1] ME [a. F. *armer*:—L. *armare*, f. *arma*; see ARM *sb.*[2]] 1. *lit.* To furnish with arms, *esp.* (in early use) with armour; *now*, with weapons. 2. Hence, *transf.* and *fig.*: To *arm* a. with tools or appliances; b. with qualities, offensive or defensive ME; c. (an animal) with natural organs of offence or defence 1607; d. (a thing) with necessary appendages, etc. 1534; e. to prepare (for action, etc.) 1590. 3. *intr.* for *refl.* To arm oneself ME. 4. *trans.* To plate (*with*), or furnish with a protective covering ME. 5. To furnish (a magnet) with an armature 1664.

1. To a. a man of war 1716, the population GLEIG, the heels of fighting cocks STRUTT. 2. b. Arme me, Audacitie, from head to foote *Cymb.* I. vi. 19. d. First you must a. your hook WALTON. e. Arme your selfe To fit your fancies to your Fathers Will *Mids. N.* I. i. 117. 3. Arme, arme, and out *Macb.* V. v. 46.

Arm (āɹm), *v.*[2] 1538. [f. ARM *sb.*[1]] †1. To put one's arms or arm round (*rare*) 1611. 2. To give one's arm to 1612. †3. *intr.* To project like an arm 1538.

‖**Armada** (aɹmē·dă). 1533 (**-ado**). [a. Sp. *armada*:—L. *armata*: see ARMY.] 1. A fleet of ships of war. 2. *spec.* The 'Invincible Armada' sent by Philip II of Spain against England 1588. 3. An armament 1728.

3. Nor was the naval unworthy of the land a. LYTTON. Hence **Armadi·lla**, a small fleet of ships of war; a small war-vessel.

Armadillo (āɹmădi·lo). 1577. [a. Sp., dim. of *armado*:—L. *armatus*, *armare*. Pl. formerly **-oes**, now **-os**.] 1. Name of several species of burrowing animals (order *Edentata*), peculiar to South America; encased in bony armour, within which they roll themselves into a ball when attacked. 2. *transf.* A genus of small terrestrial Crustacea (order *Isopoda*), having the power of rolling themselves into a ball 1847.

Armageddon (āɹmăge·dǫn). 1811. [Rev. xvi. 16.] The site of the last decisive battle on the Day of Judgement; hence, a final contest on a grand scale.

Armament (ā·ɹmămĕnt). 1699. [ad. L. *armamentum*, *armare*: prob. after F. *armement*.] 1. A force (*esp.* naval) equipped for war. Also *fig.* 2. Munitions of war; *spec.* the great guns on board a man-of-war 1721. 3. Equipment for resistance or action of any kind 1870. 4. The process of equipping for war 1813.

1. That boundless A. of Mechanisers and Unbelievers threatening to strip us bare CARLYLE. 4. With the a. of the navy, Hawkins had not much to do 1868.

†**Armame·ntary.** *rare.* 1731. [ad. L. *armamentarium*, f. prec.] An armoury, an arsenal; *transf.* (in L. form) a case of (surgical) apparatus.

Armature (ā·ɹmătiŭɹ). 1542. [ad. L. *armatura*, f. *armat-*, *armare*. The same L. word (through OF.) is now ARMOUR.] 1. Arms, armour (*esp.* defensive) 1669. b. *fig.* esp. in Theol. lang. 1542. †2. Armed troops. (So in L.) –1765. 3. The art of protecting with armour, etc. 1611. 4. *transf.* Protective covering of animals or plants; *occ.* apparatus of attack 1662. 5. a. *Magnetism.* A piece of soft iron or steel placed in contact with the poles of a magnet, which preserves and increases the magnetic power 1752. †b. The coatings of tinfoil on a Leyden jar. 6. Iron framing used to consolidate a building 1846. 7. *Electr.* That part of a dynamo or electric motor carrying the conductors, consisting usually of a number of separate coils of wire on a laminated core of soft iron. Also *attrib.* and *Comb.* 1884.

1. *fig.* Not the armour of Achilles, but the A. of St. Paul SIR T. BROWNE.

A·rm-chair. Also **armed-chair.** 1633. [f. ARM *sb.*[1] q. v.] A chair with arms.

Armed (āɹmd, ā·ɹmĕd), *ppl. a.*[1] ME. [f. ARM *v.*[1]] 1. *lit.* Furnished with arms or armour. 2. *transf.* and *fig.* Furnished (see ARM *v.*[1] 2, 5) 1585. 3. *Her.* Having the claws or talons of a different tincture from that of the adjoining parts; *also*, represented with claws, teeth, etc. 1572.

1. *Armed demonstration, neutrality*, when the power making the demonstration or remaining neutral is fully equipped for war. *Armed to the teeth* (intensive phr.) COBDEN.

Armed, *ppl. a.*[2] 1625. [f. ARM *sb.*[1]] Having, or fitted with, arms.

Armenian (aɹmī·niăn). 1598. [f. L. *Armenia*.] *adj.* Of or pertaining to Armenia or the Armenians 1727. *sb.* A native of Armenia; an adherent of the Armenian Church 1598.

1. *Armenian bole*: a pale red earth from Armenia. *Armenian stone*: a blue carbonate of copper, formerly used as an aperient, etc. var. †**Arme·niac** *a.*; whence, by corruption, *bole ammoniac*.

Armer (ā·ɹməɹ). 1611. [f. ARM *v.*[1] + -ER[1].] One who arms.

Armet (ā·ɹmĕt). 1507. [a. F., also in OF. *armette*, dim. of *arme*.] A globular iron helmet, with visor, beaver, and gorget, which replaced the basinet in 15th c.

Armful (ā·ɹmful). 1579. [f. ARM *sb.*[1]] As much as both arms, or one, can hold; a heap.

A·rm-ho·le. ME. [f. ARM *sb.*[1]] 1. An armpit (*arch.*). Also *fig.* 2. The similar cavity in other animals (*arch.*) 1607. 3. The hole in a garment through which the arm is put 1775.

Armiger (ā·ɹmiˌdʒəɹ). 1762. [a. L.; in med. L. a squire.] An esquire; *orig.* one who attended a knight to bear his shield, etc.; later, one entitled to bear (heraldic) arms. Hence **Armi·geral** *a.* of squires. **Armi·gerous** *a.* entitled to bear (heraldic) arms.

Armil (ā·ɹmil). 1480. [a. OF. *armille*:—L. *armilla*; partly ad. *armilla*.] 1. = ARMILLA 1. 2. One of the insignia of royalty, put on at the coronation 1485. 3. = ARMILLA 4. 1837.

‖**Armilla** (aɹmi·lă). 1706. [L., f. *armus*.] 1. A bracelet; now *esp.* in *Archæol.* 2. A coronation garment 1721. 3. An iron ring, hoop, or brace, in which the gudgeons of a wheel move 1706. 4. An ancient astronomical instrument, consisting of a circular hoop fixed in the plane of the equator (*Equinoctial A.*), sometimes crossed at right angles by another in the plane of the meridian (*Solstitial A.*) 1797.

Armillary (ā·ɹmilări, aɹmi·lări), *a.* 1664. [f. L. *armilla*; cf. F. *armillaire*. See -ARY.] Of or pertaining to bracelets or hoops. As *sb.* = ARMILLA 4. 1841.

Armillary Sphere: a skeleton celestial globe, consisting merely of metal rings representing the equator, ecliptic, tropics, arctic and antarctic circles, and colures, revolving on an axis, within a wooden horizon.

†**A·rming,** *sb.* [OE.; f. *earm*, poor; see -ING[1].] A poor or miserable creature –1605.

Arming (ā·ɹmiŋ), *vbl. sb.* ME. [f. ARM *v.*[1]] 1. The action of arming; †*concr.* arms, armour. 2. Any defensive or protective covering; *spec.* on a ship 1466. 3. The equipment of anything with that which strengthens, or fits for a purpose; *concr.* the part thus furnished; *spec.* the tallow at the bottom of the sounding-lead; the armature of a magnet. Often *attrib.* 1552. 4. Furnishing with heraldic devices 1598.

4. *attrib.* in **arming-press**, a bookbinder's machine used in stamping and lettering the covers of books.

Arminian (aɹmi·niăn), *a.* 1618. [f. *Arminius*, Latinized f. *Harmensen*.] Of, belonging to, or following the doctrine of, James Arminius or Harmensen, a Dutch Protestant theologian, who opposed Calvin, *esp.* on predestination. Arminius died in 1609. As *sb.* An adherent of the doctrine of Arminius 1618.

The A. . . is condemn'd for setting up free will against free grace MILT. The Arminians believe it [predestination] is conditional; the Calvinists, that it is absolute WESLEY. Hence **Armi·nianism**, the A. doctrines, or adherence to them. **Armi·nianize** *v.* to make A.; to teach Arminianism; whence **Armi·nianizer**, one who teaches Arminianism.

Armipotent (aɹmi·pǫtĕnt), *a.* ME. [ad. L. *armipotentem*.] Mighty in arms: orig. of Mars. Hence **Armi·potence** (*rare*).

Armistice (ā·ɹmistis). 1707. [ad. mod.L. *armistitium*, f. *arma* + *-stitium*, f. *sistere*, as in *solstitium*, etc.] A cessation from arms; a short truce. Also *fig.* 1841.

A·rmless, *a.*[1] ME. [f. ARM *sb.*[1] + -LESS.] Without arm or branch.

A·rmless, *a.*[2] 1619. [f. ARM *sb.*[2]] Without weapons, unarmed.

Armlet (ā·ɹmlĕt). 1535. [f. ARM *sb.*[1]] 1. An ornament, etc., worn round the arm. (Cf. *bracelet*, worn at the wrist.) 2. A small arm of the sea or of a river (see ARM *sb.*[1] II. 1) 1538. 3. Armour for the arm 1706.

‖**Armoire** (arˌmwar). 1571. [a. F.] An AMBRY.

Armoniac, obs. f. AMMONIAC.

Armor(e, Armorer, obs. ff. ARMOUR, -ER.

Armorial (aɹmōə·riăl), *a.* 1576. [f. ARMORY + -AL.] Pertaining to heraldic arms. As *sb.* A book containing coats of arms 1753.

‖**Armorica** (aɹmǫ·rikă). ME. [L.] Name of the part of Gaul now called Bretagne or Brittany. **Armo·ric** *a.* of Armorica or its people, *absol.* its language. **Armo·rican** *a.* = *Armoric*; *sb.* an inhabitant of Armorica.

Armoried (ā·ɹmŏrid), *ppl. a.* 1866. [f. ARMORY + -ED[2].] Decked with escutcheons.

Armorist (ā·ɹmŏrist). 1586. [f. ARMORY + -IST.] One skilled in heraldry, or in blazoning arms.

Armory (ā·ɹmŏri). 1489. [a. OF. *armoierie*, f. *armoier* = It. *armeggiare*, f. *arma*. See also ARMOURY.] 1. Heraldry. 2. Armorial bearings (*arch.*) 1500. †3. Ensigns of war 1523.

Armour (ā·ɹməɹ). ME. [a. OF. *armeüre*:—L. *armatura* ARMATURE. Etymologically the sp. should be as in *vest-ure*.] 1. *collect. sing.* Defensive covering for the body; mail. †2. (with a *pl.*) A suit of mail –1751. 3. *collect. sing.* with *pl.* The whole apparatus of war, offensive and defensive. (*Obs.* exc. in *Law.*) ME. †Often = *arms* in obs. phrases –1577. †4. = ARM *sb.*[2] II. 1. –1602. 5. *fig.* now only from sense 1. ME. 6. *transf.* in *Naut.* †a. = ARMING *vbl. sb.* 2. b. The steel or iron sheathing of a ship of war. See ARMOUR-PLATE. 1466. 7. A diver's water-tight suit; (cf. 2.) 1822. 8. *Nat. Hist.* Protective or defensive covering of animals or plants; †*abst.* protection, etc. 1605. 9. Heraldic insignia ME. ¶For ARMER or ARMOURER 1550.

1. Arms on A. clashing MILT. *P. L.* VI. 209. 3. The people..were up in a. against the King HOLINSHED. 5. Let vs put on the Armoure of lyght TINDALE *Rom.* xiii. 12. 6. A belt of a...to protect broadside guns 1870. 9. *Coat armour* = 'coat of arms', orig. a vest of silk, etc., embroidered in colours, worn over the armour of a knight, to distinguish him. Cf. ARM *sb.*[2] IV.

Comb.: **a.-bea·rer**, one who carried a warrior's armour; a squire; see 1 *Sam.* xiv. 14; **-fish**, *Cataphractus Americanus*; **-proof**, as impenetrable as a., or ? proof against arms; **-wise**, *adv.* Hence **A·rmour** *v.* to put a. on. **A·rmoured** *ppl. a.* clad in a.; also *transf.*, esp. of war-vessels; cf. ARMOUR-CLAD. **A·rmourless** *a.*

A·rmour-cla·d, *ppl. a.* 1869. [f. prec.] Clad in, or protected by, armour. *Ellipt.* as *sb.* A war-ship protected by a sheathing of iron or steel. Cf. *ironclad*.

Armourer (ā·ɹməɹəɹ). ME. [a. AF. *armurer*, f. *armeüre* ARMOUR.] 1. A maker of armour; now, a manufacturer of arms. 2. One who equipped men-at-arms in their mail. Also *fig.* Now *Hist.* ME. 3. An official who has charge of the arms of a ship, regiment, etc. 1753. ¶Confused with *armure* by CHAUCER.

2. The Armourers accomplishing the Knights *Hen. V*, IV. Cho. 12. The A. of my heart *Ant. & Cl.* IV. iv. 7.

A·rmour-pla·te. 1864. One of the metal pieces or plates of which armour is composed; *esp.* one of the plates of iron or steel used to cover the sides of war-ships. Hence **A·rmour-pla·ted** *ppl. a.* **A·rmour-pla·ting** *vbl. sb.* (used *concr.* for 'armour-plates').

Armoury, -ory (ā·ɹməri). ME. [Perh. orig. a. OF. *armoierie.* But soon referred to ARMOUR, and spelt like it. In 16th c. referred to L. *armarium*, and spelt *armary.* From the sp. *armor* (16th c.) *armory* was also common. Cf. ARMORY.] 1. Armour collectively (*arch.*). †2. An armed force –1532. 3. A place where arms are kept, an arsenal. Also *fig.* 1538. 4. The workshop of an armourer; a place where arms are manufactured (U.S.) 1841. 5. The craft of the armourer 1718.

1. Celestial Armourie, Shields, Helmes, and Speares MILT. *P. L.* IV. 553. 3. The goodliest weapons of his armorie *Tit. A.* IV. ii. 11. *fig.* A book of Apothegms is an a. of thought SELDEN.

Armozeen (āɹmŏzī·n). 1599. [a. F. *armoisin, -ine.* (Of uncertain origin.)] A stout plain silk, usu. black, used for clerical gowns, etc.

A·rmpi·t. ME. [f. ARM *sb.*[1]] 1. The hollow under the arm where it is jointed to the trunk. 2. The analogous cavity in other animals. Cf. ARM-HOLE. (*arch.*) 1601. †3. *fig.* The axil of a plant 1601.

Armure, -rer, -rie, obs. ff. ARMOUR, etc.

Army (ā·ɹmi). ME. [a. F. *armée*:—L. *armata, armare, lit.* 'act of arming, armed force'. The concr. sense is late in Fr. and Eng., and occurs first in reference to a *naval* force; cf. ARMADA.] †1. An armed expedition by sea or land –1525. 2. *gen.* An armed force (by sea or land); a host. *Obs.* exc. as in *land-army*, etc. 1460. 3. *spec.* †a. A naval armament, an armada, a fleet –1786. b. A land force; a body of men armed for war, and organized in divisions and regiments under officers, and a commander-in-chief or general 1557. 4. *transf.* A vast assemblage, a host 1500. *fig.* (from 3.) A marshalled host 1593. 5. (*fig.* or *transf.* from 2, 3, 4.) A body of men organized, or striving for the advancement of a cause, as the *Salvation Army*, the *Blue Ribbon Army* 1543.

2. He sent a navall armie etc. KNOLLES. 3. a. A true Discourse of the Armie [*i. e.* 'Spanish Armada']..assembled in the hauen of Lisbon 1588. b. *Standing Army*: an army of professional soldiers kept permanently on foot, not raised on each special occasion. *The Army*: the whole military service of a state (first so named *c* 1647). 4. The whole a. of waiters (*mod.*), of words COKE. Armies of Pestilence *Rich. II*, III. iii. 87. 5. The noble armye of Martyrs do prayse the 1543. *Comb.*: **a.-corps**, a main division of an a. in the field; **-list**, an official list of all the commissioned officers of the Army; **-worm**, the larva of the cotton-moth.

Arn(e. Now *dial.* 1791. [? = *allern*, var. of ALDERN.] The alder tree.

Arnatto, var. of ANATTA.

†A·rnement. ME. [? conn. w. OF. *arrement*:—L. *atramentum.*] Ink, or materials for making it –1586.

Arnica (ā·ɹnikă). 1753. [mod.L. of unknown origin.] 1. A genus of Composite plants, including *A. Montana* or Mountain Tobacco, which has medicinal properties. 2. A medicine (*esp.* a tincture) prepared from the plant 1788.

2. Stiffish cock-tail, taken in time, Is better for a bruise than a. BROWNING. Hence **A·rnicin,** *Chem.* the bitter active principle of a. **A·rnicine,** an alkaloid found in a.

Ar'n't, contr. for *are not*; cf. AIN'T, AN'T.

Arnotto, var. of ANATTA.

Arnut, obs. f. EARTH-NUT.

A-roa·r, *adv.* 1461. [A *prep.*[1]] In a roar.

Aroid (ēͤ·roid). 1830. [f. ARUM + -OID. The N.O. *Araceæ* is also called *Aroideæ.*] *Bot.* A plant allied to the Arum; an arad. Hence **Aroi·deous** *a.*

Aroint, aroynt (ăroi·nt). 1605. [?] 1. In *Aroint thee!* (? verb in the imperative, or interjection): Avaunt! Begone! 2. Used by Mr. and Mrs. Browning as a vb.: To drive away with an execration 1850.

1. Aroynt thee, witch *Macb.* I. iii. 6. Also *Lear* III. iv. 129. (The orig. sources of the word.) 2. That Humbug, whom thy soul aroints BROWNING.

Arolla (ărǫ·lă). 1881. [ad. F. *arolle.*] French Swiss name for the *Pinus cembra.*

Aroma (ărōͧ·mă). ME. [a. OF. *aromat* (now *aromate*), ad. L. *aromata*, pl. of *aroma*, a. Gr. Pl. **aromas,** occas. now **aromata.**] †1. Spice; usu. in *pl.* –1753. 2. The distinctive fragrance of a spice, plant, etc.; *gen.* an agreeable odour 1814. 3. *fig.* A subtle pervasive quality or charm 1851.

3. The pure Parisian a. TROLLOPE.

Aromatic (ærŏmæ·tik), *a.* ME. [a. Fr. *aromatique*, ad. L. *aromaticus*; see prec.] 1. Yielding aroma; spicy, fragrant, sweet-smelling. 2. *Chem.* Epithet of a group of organic compounds, consisting of benzene and its homologues 1869. 3. *sb.* 1494.

1. Die of a rose in a. pain POPE. 3. While Ma'am the Aromatics blended, To gain the scent which she intended COMBE. Hence **Aroma·tical** *a.*, **-ly** *adv.*

Aromatization (ărōͧ:mătəizēͥ·ʃən). 1603. [ad. med.L. *aromatizationem*; see next.] The action or process of rendering aromatic; aromatic flavouring.

Aromatize (ărōͧ·mătəiz), *v.* 1480. [a. F. *aromatiser*, ad. L. *aromatizare*, ad. Gr. ἀρωματίζειν, f. ἀρωματ- AROMA.] To render aromatic or fragrant; to flavour or season with spice. Also *fig.* Hence **Aro·matizer.**

†A-roo·m, *adv.* ME. [orig. *on rúm, on rúme*; see A *prep.*[1] and ROOM.] To or at a distance; aside, off –1530.

A-roo·t, *adv.* [A *prep.*[1]] On root; *hence* firm. CHAUCER.

Aroph. 1657. [Said to be a contr. for *aroma philosophorum.*] Name of various Paracelsian medicinal preparations.

Arose (ărōͧ·z), pa. t. of ARISE.

Around (arau·nd). ME. [A- *pref.* 2; cf. *across.* Rare bef. 1600; not in SHAKS., nor Bible 1611.] A. *adv.* (Often with *all.*) †1. In circumference; in a round –1596. 2. On or along the circuit (of a globular body) 1596. 3. *gen.* On every side ME. 4. In U.S.: = ROUND. 5. In U.S.: = ABOUT. a. All about, at random. b. Somewhere near. B. *prep.* 1. On or along the circuit ME. 2. So as to surround; about 1816. 3. On all sides of 1667. Also *fig.* 4. In U.S.: At random through, about.

A. 3. The signs of the time were all a. BUCKLE. 4. Enough to go a. 1883. 5. a. To fool a. b. To stand a. (*mod.*). B. 1. Nor war nor battle's sound was heard the world a. MILT. 2. With his martial cloak a. him WOLFE. 4. To travel a. the country (*mod.*).

Arousal (ărau·zăl). 1854. [f. next + -AL [2].] The action of arousing, or being aroused.

Arouse (ărau·z), *v.* 1593. [A- *pref.* 11; cf. *rise, arise*, etc.] 1. To raise or stir up from sleep or inactivity. 2. To stir into activity (emotions, etc.) 1728. 3. *intr.* (for *refl.*) To wake up 1822.

1. Grasping his spear, forth issu'd to a. His brother COWPER. 2. No suspicion was aroused MERIVALE. Hence **Arou·se** *sb.* an alarum (*rare*). **Arou·ser. Arou·sing** *ppl. a.*

A-row·, *adv.* ME. [A *prep.*[1]] 1. In a row, rank, or line. †2. In succession –1598.

1. Till home they walk arowe SIDNEY.

‖**Arpeggio** (arpe·ddʒiǫ). 1742. [It., f. *arpa* harp.] *Mus.* The employment of the notes of a chord in rapid succession instead of simultaneously; a chord thus treated. Hence **Arpe·ggio** *v.* to play or sing as an a.

‖**Arpent.** 1580. [a. F.:—L. *arepennis* = *semijugerum*, according to Columella a Gallic word. Formerly naturalized as ā·ɹpĕn(t, ā·ɹpin; now arpaṅ, as Fr.] An obs. Fr. measure of land, a hundred square perches, varying with the value of the perch from about an acre and a quarter to about five-sixths of an acre. Hence ‖**Arpenteu·r** (Fr.), a land-surveyor. A. YOUNG.

Arquated, obs. var. of ARCUATED.

Arquebus, etc.; see HARQUEBUS.

Arquerite (ā·ɹkwĕrəit). [f. (1842) *Arqueros* in Chili.] *Min.* A native amalgam of silver.

Arquifoux, var. of ALQUIFOU.

Arr, *sb.* ME. [a. ON. *örr, ör.*] A wound, scar. Still north. dial.

†Arr, *v.*[1] ME. [?] To anger, vex, worry –1651.

†Arr, *v.*[2] 1483. [Echoic.] To snarl as a dog –1603.

‖**Arracacha** (æräkā·tʃă). 1823. [native Indian.] *Bot.* A genus of umbelliferous plants, with tuberous roots, including *A. Esculenta*, which is used for food.

Arrach, obs. f. ORACH.

Arrack (ăræ·k, æ·răk). 1602. [Ult. Arab. meaning 'sweat, juice'. In use in all Mohammedan countries. See also RACK.] In Eastern countries any spirituous liquor of native manufacture; *esp.* that distilled from the fermented sap of the coco-palm, or from rice and sugar, fermented with the coco-nut juice. Also *attrib.*

Arragonite; see ARA-.

Arrah (æ·ră), *int.* 1705. [Irish.] An expletive, expressing emotion or excitement.

Arraign (ărēͥ·n), *v.*[1] [ME. *arayne*, a. AF. *arainer*, OF. *arais-*:—L. *adrationare*, f. *ad* + *rationare*, f. *rationem.*] †1. *trans.* To call to account; to interrogate, examine –1447. 2. *esp.* To call to answer on a criminal charge; to indict. Hence *gen.* To accuse, charge with fault. ME. 3. To impeach, call in question, find fault with (actions, measures, etc.) 1672. Also *absol.*

2. Thou art here accused and arraigned of High Treason *Wint. T.* III. ii. 14. 3. To a. the abuses of public and private life GIBBON. Hence **Arrai·gn** *sb.* arraignment. **Arrai·gner.**

†Arrai·gn, *v.*[2] 1528. [a. late AFr. *arraigner, arainer*, mis-spelling of *aramer*:—late L. *adhramare*, f. *ad* + **hramire*, perh. to hang up.] *Law.* To appeal to, claim, demand; in phr. *arraine* (i. e. *arrame*) *an assize.*

Arrand, obs. f. ERRAND, ARRANT.

Arraignment (ărēͥ·nmĕnt). 1548. [a. OF. *araisnement*; see ARRAIGN *v.*[1]] 1. The act of arraigning, or being arraigned; accusation before a tribunal, indictment, charge. 2. Hostile criticism 1595.

1. The a. of the prisoners 1864. 2. An a. of their proceedings 1722.

Arrange (ărēͥ·ndʒ), *v.* [ME. *araynge*, a. OF. *arangier*, f. *à* + *rangier*, f. *rang* RANK. Rare till mod. times; not in BIBLE 1611, SHAKS., MILT., or POPE.] 1. To draw up in ranks or in line of battle. 2. To put (the parts) into order; to adjust 1802; *refl.* to prepare oneself 1865. 3. *Mus.* To adapt (a composition) for instruments or voices for which it was not written 1838. 4. To place in some order, dispose 1791; *intr.* to fall into place 1805. 5. To settle (claims, differences, etc.), to adjust 1837. 6. *intr.* To come to an agreement or understanding 1796. 7. To plan, or settle details, beforehand 1786. 8. *intr.* (*simply*, or with *inf.* or *subord. cl.*) To settle details with other persons concerned 1849.

1. Arranged in supreme regimental order CARLYLE. 2. A mechanism previously arranged PALEY. 4. The parts in the two dramas were differently arranged FREEMAN. 5. The quarrel..was arranged SEELEY. 6. We cannot [now] a. with our enemy BURKE. 7. Every step..was calculated and arranged 1837. 8. To a. about my passport HAWTHORNE. Hence **Arra·nger.**

Arrangement (ărēͥ·ndʒmĕnt). 1727. [a. F., f. *arranger*; see -MENT.] 1. The action of arranging (see ARRANGE *v.* 2). 2. Arranged condition, order 1743; style or mode of disposition 1785. 3. *concr.* A structure or combination of things for a purpose, etc.; hence loosely, like *affair*, etc. 1800. 4. *Mus.* The act of arranging a composition (see ARRANGE *v.* 3); *concr.* a piece so arranged 1849. 5. A settlement of mutual relations, claims, or matters in dispute 1855; *euphem.* an affair of gallantry 1751. 6. Disposition of measures for a particular purpose 1786.

2. In my new a., I ought to have placed this piece [etc.] WARTON. 3. That lace a. which you call a cap 1881. 5. An a. that would please everybody MACAULAY. 6. The arrangements for the flight MACAULAY.

Arrant (æ·rănt), *a.* ME. [var. of ERRANT, which, from its use in *arrant thief*, etc., became an intensive, 'notorious, downright'. For the vowel-change cf. *arrand* = *errand*, etc.] †1. Wandering, itinerant; *esp.* in *knight, bailiff arrant*, now ERRANT. –1647. 2. In *arrant thief* [= robber]: *orig.* an outlawed robber roving about the country, a highwayman; *hence*, a public, notorious, professed robber, a common thief ME. 3. Hence, notorious, downright, unmitigated ME.; *transf.* of things 1639. 4.

Without opprobrious force: Thorough, genuine, 'regular' 1570. †4. Good-for-nothing, rascally -1761.

2. Every servant an a. thief as to victuals and drink SWIFT. 3. A. dunce GREENE, knaue SHAKS., asse BURTON, cowards DE FOE, Atheism BENTLEY, nonsense RICHARDSON, trifling BUCKLE. 4. With the air of an a. old bachelor W. IRVING. 5. So a. a critic of the modern Poets as..to damn them without a hearing POPE. Hence **A·rrantly** *adv.* abominably.

Arras (æ·răs). ME. [a. *Arras* in Artois.] 1. A rich tapestry fabric, in which figures and scenes are woven in colours. 2. A hanging screen of this formerly placed round the walls of rooms 1598. Also *fig.* Also *attrib.*

1. My suit of A. with the story of the Nativity and Passion BACON. 2. I will ensconce mee behinde the A. *Merry W.* III. iii. 97. *attrib.* Our dim a.-picture of these University years CARLYLE. Hence **A·rrased** *ppl. a.* covered with a.

Arrasene (ærăsī·n). 1881. [f. ARRAS.] A material of wool and silk, used in embroidery.

‖**Arrastre** (ărɑ·stre). 1881. [Sp., f. (ult.) L. *rastrum.*] An apparatus for grinding ores by dragging a heavy stone round on a circular bed.

Arras-wise, erron. f. *arris-wise*; see ARRIS.

Array (ărēⁱ·), *v.* [ME. *aray(e,* a. AF. *arayer* = OF. *areyer,* f. *a, ad* + **redo* (OF. *rei, rai, roi*), 'preparation, order'.] 1. To set or place in order of readiness, *esp.* for battle. Also *fig.* 2. *Law.* To array a panel, a jury 1591. †3. To put in order for a purpose; prepare -1485; *spec.* of food -1513; of a house, etc. -1450. 4. To furnish the person with raiment (= arrayment), to attire; *now,* to dress up with display ME. 5. *transf.* and *fig.* To attire ME.; to adorn, set off 1652. †6. *ironically,* To give a dressing to, thrash; rout -1530; to put into a plight, afflict -1600; to disfigure, dirty -1575.

1. This place is..fit..to a. an host of men upon 1576. *fig.* To a. themselves against Science BUCKLE. 4. Take vp thy chyldren and aray them 1523. I drinke, I eate, a. my self, and liue *Meas. for M.* III. ii. 26. 5. Arraye youe withe iustice EARL RIVERS. Pearld dew arraies As yet the virgin-meads 1652. Hence **Array·er,** one who arrays; *spec.* in *Hist.* (= *Commissioner of Array.*) **Array·ment,** accoutrement; RAIMENT.

Array (ărēⁱ·), *sb.* [ME. *arai, aray(e,* a. AFr. *arai* = OF. *arei* (*aroi, arroi*); see prec.] 1. Arrangement in line or ranks, *esp.* martial order. Also *fig.* †2. A display of military force -1553. 3. The calling forth of a military force, as the militia, etc. 1640. 4. *concr.* A military force. *Hist.* The militia of a county or city. 1643. 5. An imposing series 1814. 6. *Law.* The order of impanelling a jury; the panel 1579. 7. A state of special preparation, as for war, festivities, etc. Now *poet.* ME. †8. Plight; state of affairs -1568. 9. Outfit, attire. Now *poet.* ME. Also *fig.* and *transf.*

1. Place thy men-at-arms In battle 'ray GREENE. Wedged together in the closest a. GIBBON. 3. The form of the *Commission of Array* was settled in parliament *anno* 5 Hen. 4. TOMLINS. 4. The whole a. of the city of London was under arms MACAULAY. 5. An a. of powerful Doric cities GROTE. 6. The Jurors names are ranked in the pannel one vnder another, which..ranking..is called the a. COKE. 7. To be redy in their moost defensible arraye 1484. *In evil array*: in a bad condition. 9. Thou Wolfe in Sheepes a. SHAKS. Hence **Array·al,** muster of a force; array.

†**Arrea·r,** *adv.* [ME. *arere,* a. OF. *arere* (mod. *arrière*):—Merovingian L. *ad retro.*] Backward -1591; behind -1600; overdue (now *in arrear*) -1768.

Arrear (ărīᵊ·ɹ), *sb.* ME. [The prec. adv. used *absol.*: 'that which is behind'.] I. *In arrear.* 1. Backward. *In arrear of*: behind 1845. 2. Behind in the discharge of duties or liabilities. Cf. ARREARAGE. 1621. So *In arrears.*

2. I am two or three letters in a. A. KNOX.

II. Without *in.* 1. The rear, *esp.* of a train or procession (*arch.*) 1627. †2. A portion held back 1768. 3. That wherein one has fallen behind; *esp.* a debt remaining unpaid 1658; in *pl.* outstanding liabilities; debts 1648.

3. To you..I owe a long a. of thanks DICKENS. To pay the late Arrears of the Army 1648. Hence †**Arre·ar** *v.* to keep back; *intr.* to fall back, retreat.

Arrearage (ărīᵊ·rėdʒ). [ME. *arer-,* a. OF. *arerage,* f. *arere*; cf. *avant-age* ADVANTAGE.] †1. Indebtedness, debt -1637. With pl. *In ar-rearages*: in arrears -1642. 2. *gen.* State of being in arrear 1576. 3. *concr.* That which is in arrear; an outstanding balance 1466; something still in reserve 1594. 4. *pl.* = ARREAR 3. ME.

†**Arrea·r-guard,** and ‖**Arrière-guard.** 1489. [a. Fr. *arrière-guarde*; naturalized in 16–17th c., but now spelt partly as Fr. Aphet. as *ryere-, rere-* REAR. See also next.] = REAR-GUARD.

†**Arrea·r-ward.** 1589. [f. ARREAR *adv.* + WARD, North. F. *warde,* = Central Fr. *guarde, garde.*] = prec.

Arrect, later corrupt f. †ARET *v.* to impute.

†**Arre·ct,** *v.* 1529. [f. L. *arrect-, arrigere.*] To set upright; to direct upwards, lift up -1556.

Arrect (ăre·kt), *ppl. a.* 1646. [ad. L. *arrectus*; see prec.] Set upright, pricked up (as the ears of a horse); *fig.* intent, on the alert.

†**Arre·ctary.** [ad. L. *arrectarius,* f. *arrectus.*] An upright post. BP. HALL.

‖**Arrenda·tor.** [med.L. f. *arrendare* = *arrentare,* f. F. *arenter, arr-*; see ARRENT.] One who rents or farms at a yearly rent.

Arrenotokous (ærĭnǫ·tŏkəs), *a.* 1877. [f. Gr. ἄρρην + -τόκος.] Used of the parthenogenetic females which produce male young. Hence **Arreno·toky.**

Arrent (ăre·nt), *v.* 1598. [a. F. *arrenter,* f. *à* + *rente* RENT.] To let out or farm at a rent; *spec.* to allow the enclosure of forest land 'with a low hedge and small ditch' under a yearly rent. Hence **Arre·ntable** *a.* **Arrenta·tion,** the action, or privilege, of arrenting.

†**Arre·ption.** *rare.* 1612. [f. L. *arrept-, arripere.*] A sudden carrying off -1633.

†**Arrepti·tious,** *a.* 1641. [f. L. *arrepticius,* f. *arreptus.*] 1. Liable to raptures, ecstatic, mad -1656. 2. Hastily caught up; hurried 1653.

1. Odd arrepititious frantic extravagancies HOWELL.

Arrest (ăre·st), *v.* ME. [a. OF. *arester*:—late L. *adrestare.*] †1. *intr.* To stop -1483; to stay, rest -1538. 2. *trans.* (and *refl.*) To cause to stop; to stop the course of (a person or animal, a thing in motion, motion, etc.) ME. †3. *refl.* To stop (Fr. *s'arrêter*); to tarry -1563. †4. *trans.* and *refl.* To keep our minds, ourselves, fixed upon -1667. 5. *gen.* To catch, lay hold upon (*Obs.* exc. *fig.*) 1481. 6. *esp.* To lay hold upon, or apprehend by legal authority ME.; *transf.* of property (now only in Sc. and Admiralty Law) 1598. 7. *fig.* To take as security 1588. 8. *trans.* To catch and fix (the sight, attention, etc.) 1814; to catch and fix the attention of (a person) 1835. ¶ *catachr.* To wrest 1593.

2. In the pursuit of greatness he was never arrested by the scruples of justice GIBBON. Its progress is arrested 1879. *To arrest judgement*: to stay proceedings, after a verdict, on the ground of error. 4. We may a. our thoughts upon the divine mercies JER. TAYLOR. 5. We cannot a. sunsets RUSKIN. 6. I A. thee of High Treason *Hen. VIII,* I. i. 201. The Roecliff was arrested in a cause of collision 1869. 7. We a. your word *L.L.L.* II. i. 160. *Meas. for M.* II. iv. 134. 8. Arrested and held by the interest of the story MACREADY. Hence **Arre·stable** *a.* **Arresta·tion,** stopping; apprehension by legal authority (more or less Fr.). **Arre·sted** *ppl. a.* stopped; seized by legal warrant. **Arre·stee,** the person in whose hands property is attached by arrestment (see ARRESTMENT 3). **Arre·ster,** he who or that which arrests, *esp.* by legal authority; *Sc. Law,* one who uses ARRESTMENT (more formally ARRESTOR). **Arre·sting** *vbl. sb.* stopping; apprehending by legal authority; *ppl. a.* that arrests the attention. **Arre·stingly** *adv.*

Arrest (ăre·st), *sb.*[1] ME. [a. OF. *areste* stoppage, and *arest* act of arresting.] †1. The act of standing still; stoppage, halt, delay -1598; continuance; abiding-place ME. only. 2. The act of stopping anything in its course; stoppage, check ME. 3. The act of laying hold of; seizure (*lit.* and *fig.*) ME. 4. *spec.* The apprehending of one's person, in order to be forthcoming to answer an alleged or suspected crime 1440. 5. Custody, imprisonment. Also *fig.* ME. *transf.* Of a ship 1848. †6. A judgement, decree, order, or sentence (*prop.* Fr.; now *arrêt*). Also *fig.* -1721.

1. †*In arrest*; in rest, as a lance. †*At arrest*: at attention. 2. Some Checke or A. in their Fortunes BACON. An a. of the vital processes (*mod.*). *Arrest of Judgement*: see ARREST *v.* 2 (quots.). 3. The first arrests of sleep LAMB. 5. The Forty hath decreed a month's a. BYRON. *Under (an) arrest*: under legal restraint, arrested. 6. He sends out Arrests On Fortinbras, which he (in breife) obeys *Haml.* II. ii. 67.

Arrest, *sb.*[2] ? *Obs.* 1639. [a. F. *areste*:—L. *arista*; see ARÊTE.] 1. Mangy tumours on the hind-legs of a horse; called also *rat-tails.* 2. in *pl.*: The small bones of a fish.

Arrestive (ăre·stiv), *a.* 1850. [f. ARREST *v.* + -IVE.] 1. Tending to arrest, arresting. 2. *Gram.* Used of conjunctions such as *but* 1863.

Arrestment (ăre·stmĕnt). 1474. [a. OF. *arestement* (*arrêtement*); see ARREST *v.* and -MENT.] 1. The action of stopping; *concr.* the result of stopping 1836. 2. Apprehension of a person by legal authority. (Chiefly *Sc.*) Also *fig.* 1474. 3. Seizure of property by authority of law; attachment. *Esp.* in *Sc. Law.* 'A process by which a creditor may attach money or moveable property, which a third party holds for behoof of his debtor' 1581.

‖**Arrêt** (ărē·, ăre·t). 1650. [Fr.:—OF. *arest,* f. *arester,* now *arrêter.*] = ARREST *sb.*[1] 6.

‖**Arrha** (æ·ră). Pl. **-æ.** 1573. [L. *arr(h)a,* also *arr(h)abo,* a. Gr. ἀρραβών. See Liddell and Scott. Cf. ARLES.] Earnest-money, a part of the purchase-money given to bind a bargain; *fig.* a pledge. Hence **A·rrhal** *a.*

Arrhizal (ărəi·zăl), *a.* Also **arh-.** 1880. [f. Gr. ἀ + ῥίζα.] *Bot.* Rootless. var. **Arrhi·zous.**

Arrhythmic, -al (ări·þmik, -ăl), *a.* Also **arh-.** 1880. [A-*pref.* 14.] Not rhythmic; *spec.* in *Path.* of the pulse. Hence **Arrhy·thmically** *adv.* var **Arrhy·thmous.**

Arrhythmy (æ·riþmi). 1844. [ad. Gr. ἀρρυθμία.] Want of rhythm or measure.

Arride (ărəi·d), *v.* 1599. [ad. L. *arridere.*] †1. To smile at, laugh at, scorn -1656. 2. To gratify. ? *Obs.* 1599.

2. His humour arrides me exceedingly B. JONS. Hence †**Arri·dent** *a.* smiling; gratifying.

‖**Arrière** (aryḗ·r). Mod. Fr. form of ARREAR (OF. *arere*), used in combs., partly refash.

arriere-band [cf. ARRIÈRE-BAN], a rear-division of an army; **-fee** or **fief,** a sub-fief; **-supper** (also REAR-SUPPER), a late supper; †**-tenant,** the tenant of a mesne lord, a sub-tenant; †**-vassal,** the holder of an arriere-fief.

‖**Arrière-ban** (æ·riəɹ-bæ·n, aryḗr-bañ·). 1523. [a. F., for **ari-ban, hari-ban,* f. OHG. *hari* host + *ban* order under penalty. In pop. etymol. *ari-* became *ariere, arrière,* variously interpreted. In Eng. perverted to *arrear-, rear-band, arrear-van.*] *prop.* The order of a (Frankish or French) king summoning his vassals to the military service due by holders of fiefs; the body of vassals thus summoned or liable to be summoned. *Corruptly,* the summoning of the *arrière-vassals.*

‖**Arrière-pensée** (aryḗrpañse). 1824. [F., 'behind thought'.] Mental reservation.

Arris (æ·ris). 1677. [Corrupt f. F. *areste* (mod. *arête*); see ARÊTE.] The sharp edge formed by the angular contact of two plane or curved surfaces; *e.g.* the edges of a prism, or those that separate the flutings in a Doric column. var. **Aris,** *dial.* **Arridge.**

Comb.: **a.-fillet,** a piece of timber of a triangular section, used to raise the slates against a chimney-shaft or a wall; **-gutter,** a V-shaped wooden gutter fixed to the eaves of a building; **-ways, -wise** *adv.* ridge-wise.

Ar(r)ish (æ·riʃ). Also **ersh.** 1597. [Dial. var. of EDDISH.] Stubble; a stubble-field.

†**Arrivage.** ME. [a. OF. *arivage*:—late L. *arribaticum* for *adripaticum,* f. *adripare*; see ARRIVE *v.* Orig. accented *arriva·ge.*] 1. Landing, arrival -1627; a landing-place -1542. 2. That which befalls one 1603.

Arrival (ărəi·văl). ME. [a. AF. *arrivaille,* f. *arriver*; see ARRIVE *v.*] 1. The coming to shore, landing. 2. *gen.* The act of arriving (see ARRIVE *v.* 4) 1518; *transf.* of things 1712. 3. The coming to a position, state of mind, etc. 4. One that arrives or has arrived 1847.

1. They set apart the sixth day of August, after their a., for fasting and prayer C. MATHER. 2. Demand of yonder Champion The cause of his arriuall heere in Armes *Rich. II,* I. iii. 8. 2. *For arrival*: (a cargo) to be delivered when the ship arrives.

†**Arri·vance.** 1604. [f. ARRIVE *v.*] The act or fact of arriving; arrivals -1646.

Arrive (ărəi·v), *v.* ME. [a. OF. *ariver,* cogn. w. late L. *arribare*:—*adripare* = *ad ripam appellere.*] 1. To †bring, or come to shore or into port; to land. *intr.* Of things 1755. **2.** *trans.* (by omission of prep.) To come to, reach (*arch.*) 1587. †**3.** To bring, convey -1667. **4.** *intr.* To come to the end of a journey, to some definite place, upon the scene. Const. *at, in, upon,* †*into,* †*to.* ME. *transf.* Of things 1651. **5.** *trans.* (by omission of prep.) To come to, reach (*arch.*) 1647. **6.** *intr.* To come to as the result of continuous effort; to attain, achieve, compass. Const. †*to, at,* †*inf.* ME. **7.** *intr.* To come to by growth, lapse of time, etc.; to reach. Const. †*to, at.* 1599. Of time and temporal states: To come, so as to be present 1748. **8.** To come about, happen 1633; †*trans.* to happen to -1659.

1. The schype arryvyth at the haven purposyd 1538. *Sold to arrive*: (a cargo) sold for delivery on arrival in port. 2. Ere he a. the happy Ile MILT. *P. L.* II. 409. 4. Before Harold could actually a. GEO. ELIOT. A policeman arrived upon the scene (*mod.*). The ladder now arrived TYNDALL. 6. To a. at any employment 1671, at a knowledge of a law of nature 1850, at a conclusion H. SPENCER. 7. Arrived at years of discretion ADDISON. At length the hour arrived SMOLLETT. 8. What they had long hoped would a. TRENCH. Hence †**Arri·ve** *sb.* landing, arrival. **Arri·ver.**

‖**Arroba** (ărōᵘ·bă). 1598. [Sp., ad. Arab.] **1.** A weight used in Spain and Sp. America, of the standard value of 25 Sp. or 25·36 Eng. pounds, but varying locally. **2.** A Sp. liquid measure, varying from 2·6 to 3·6 gallons 1633.

Arrogance (æ·rŏgăns). ME. [a. F., ad. L. *arrogantia*; see ARROGANT.] The taking of too much upon oneself as one's right; undue assumption of dignity, authority, or knowledge; aggressive conceit, presumption, or haughtiness.

Their a. was soon humbled by misfortune GIBBON.

Arrogancy (æ·rŏgănsi). 1529. [ad. L. *arrogantia*; see ARROGANT.] The quality or state of being arrogant; †a piece of arrogance -1649.

Arrogant (æ·rŏgănt), *a.* (*sb.*) ME. [a. F., ad. L. *arrogantem*; see ARROGATE.] **1.** Making or implying unwarrantable claims to dignity, authority, or knowledge; aggressively conceited or haughty, overbearing. †**2.** *sb.* [sc. *person.*] -1668. Hence **A·rrogant·ly** *adv.*, **-ness** (*rare*).

Arrogate (æ·rogeᵉit), *v.* 1530. [f. L. *arrogat-, adr-, arrogare.* See also ADROGATE.] **1.** *Rom. Law.* To adopt as a child. (See ADROGATE.) 1649. **2.** To claim and assume as a right that to which one is not entitled; to appropriate without just reason, or through self-conceit, insolence, or haughtiness. Const. *to* and *refl. pron.*, or *simple obj.* 1537. **3.** To assume without foundation 1563. **4.** To ascribe *to* (another) without just reason 1605.

2. To themselves all glory a., to God give none MILT. *P. R.* IV. 315. And a. a praise that is not ours ROWE. 4. To antiquity we a. many things, to ourselves nothing COLERIDGE. Hence **A·rroga·tingly** *adv.* **A·rrogator**, one who adrogates; one who advances pretentious claims.

Arrogation (ærogēⁱ·ʃən). 1590. [ad. L. *arrogationem*; see ARROGATE.] **1.** = ADROGATION. **2.** Unwarrantable assumption 1594.

‖**Arrondi** (arondi), *ppl. a.* 1727. [Fr.] *Her.* Rounded (by shading), as parts of a coat of arms.

‖**Arrondissement** (arondisₗman). 1807. [Fr., f. *arrondiss-, arrondir.*] **1.** The action of rounding off an outline (*rare*) 1815. **2.** An administrative sub-division of a French department 1807.

†**Arrou·nd**, *v.* 1625. [AR- *pref.*¹] To flow round -1652.

†**Arrou·se**, *v.* 1480. [a. F. *arrouser*, mod. *arroser*:—L. *adrorare*, f. *ad* + *ros, ror-* (Brachet).] To bedew, sprinkle, water -1635.

Arrow (æ·roᵘ), *sb.* [OE. *earh* for *arh* :— OTeut. *arhwo-* neut., and *arwe* for *arhwe* :— **arhwôn* weak fem.; prob. 'the thing belonging to the bow', *arhw* being cogn. w. L. *arquus, arcus.* Rare in OE.] **1.** A slender pointed missile shot from a bow, usu. feathered and barbed; occ. used of a *bolt*, or *quarrel*. Also *fig.* **2.** *Surveying.* An iron pin (orig. a real arrow) used to stick in the ground at the end of a chain 1753. **3.** Anything arrow-shaped 1834. **4.** The constellation *Sagitta* 1727. †**5.** *Geom.* The *sagitta*, or versed sine of an arc -1751. **6.** The leading shoot of a plant or tree 1580. **7.** *Fortif.* A work in communication with the covert-way, placed at the salient angle of the glacis 1816.

1. I will shoot three arrowes..as though I shot at a marke 1 *Sam.* XX. 20. *fig.* The Slings and Arrowes of outragious Fortune *Haml.* III. i. 58. 3. The spire is surmounted by an a. (*mod.*). 6. The cane-fields then in a. 1833.

Comb.: **a.-loop, -slit**, a narrow loop-hole or slit for shooting through; **-plant**, a species of pine; **-smith**, a maker of iron arrow-heads; **-snake**, *Acontias jaculus*; **-stitch**, the triangular stitch used in securing the ends of whalebone in stays; †**-stone**, a belemnite; **-wise**, *adv.* **Broad Arrow**, *lit.* one having a broad arrow-head; the arrow-head-shaped mark, used by the British Board of Ordnance, and placed on government stores; in *Her.* = PHEON. Hence **A·rrow** *v.* to shoot arrows (*rare*); to shoot into blossom, as the sugar-cane. **A·rrowed** *a. poet.* made into an a.; provided with arrows.

Arrow, vulgar corruption of *e'er a, ever a.*

A·rrow-grass. 1792. Eng. name of the endogenous genus *Triglochin*, referring to the 3-barbed appearance of the burst capsule.

A·rrow-head. 1483. **1.** The pointed part of an arrow, made separately from the shaft; *esp.* those of flint, jade, etc., as *elf-arrows*, found among prehistoric remains. **2.** Broad arrow-head. **a.** *prop.* a kind of arrow-head. **b.** *transf.* = *Broad Arrow.* **c.** *fig.* Any mark like these 1865. **3.** A direction-mark 1836. **4.** *Bot.* The genus *Sagittaria*, of which *S. sagittifolia* has arrow-head-shaped leaves 1597. *attrib.* 1875. Hence **A·rrow-hea·ded** *a.* shaped like an arrow-head; *spec.* = CUNEIFORM.

A·rrow-root. 1696. [So named because used to absorb poison from wounds made by poisoned arrows.] **1.** *Bot.* A plant; orig. *Maranta arundinacea*, a herb with fleshy tuberous rhizomes, found in the West Indian Isles; also, other species of *Maranta.* **2.** *Comm.* A pure nutritious starch, prepared from the tubers of *Maranta* (and from many other plants) 1811. **3.** The food prepared from this starch 1848.

A·rrow-wood. 1848. An American name for species of *Viburnum* (*V. dentatum, pubescens,* etc.) with long straight stems used by the Indians for the shafts of their arrows.

Arrowy (æ·roᵘₗi), *a.* 1637. [f. ARROW + -Y.] Consisting of, or abounding in, arrows 1671. **2.** Like an arrow, in shape, motion, etc. 1637.

1. Sharp sleet of a. showers MILT. *P. R.* III. 324. 2. A. minarets 1877, Rhone BYRON. A. words, each one hitting its mark GEO. ELIOT.

‖**Arroyo** (ăroi·o). 1850. [Sp.:—OSp. *arrogio*, med.L. *arrogium.*] A rivulet or stream; *hence*, the bed of a stream, a gully. (*in U.S.*)

'Arry (æ·ri). 1874. [Vulgar for *Harry.*] Used humorously for: A low-bred fellow (who 'drops his *h*'s') of lively temper and manners. Hence **'A·rryish** *a.* vulgarly jovial.

Arse (āɹs). *Obs.* in polite use. [Com. Teut.: cogn. w. Gr. ὄρρος, *ὄρσος.] The fundament, buttocks, or rump of an animal OE.; *transf.* or *fig.* the bottom; the fag end, tail ME.

Phr. *Arse upwards*: in good luck.

Comb.: †**a.-foot**, a dabchick, or penguin; **-gut**, the rectum, also *fig.*; **-smart**, the plant Water-pepper (*Polygonum Hydropiper*); †**-ward** *adv.* and *a.* backward; perverse, perversely; whence †**-wardly** *adv.*

A·rsedine. 1472. [?] A gold-coloured alloy of copper and zinc; 'Dutch gold'.

Arsen- (ā·ɹsĕn), short for ARSENIC, used **1.** in *Comb.*, as in *Arsen-dimethyl*, $As_2(CH_3)_4$. **2.** in derivatives, with var. **Arseni-** (aɹsī·ni).

A·rsenate or **Arse·niate**, a salt of arsenic acid, e.g. *Sodium arsenate.* **A·rsenetted** *ppl. a.* combined chemically with arsenic. **Arse·niate** *a.* mixed or treated with arsenic (*rare*). **Arse·niated** *ppl. a.* = *arseniate.* **A·rsenide**, a primary combination of arsenic with another element, or an organic radical. **A·rsenite**, a salt of arsenious acid, as *Arsenite of lead*, etc.; *Min.* = *arsenolite* (*see* ARSENO-).

Arsenal (ā·ɹsĭnăl). 1506. [a. It. *arze- arsenale.* The original is Arab. *dār aççinā'ah*, workshop, represented by Rom. *darsena*, whence *arsena* (with *d* dropped). The final *-ale, -al* is It. or Sp.] **1.** A dock equipped for the reception, construction, and repair of ships; a dockyard. *Hist.* **2.** A public establishment for the manufacture and storage, or for the storage alone, of arms and ammunition 1579. Also *fig.*

Arsenate, -etted, -iate, etc.; see ARSEN-.

Arsenic (ā·ɹsnik), *sb.* ME. [a. OF., ad. L. *arsenicum*, a. Gr. ἀρσενικόν (ἀρρενικόν), adj. neut. 'masculine, male', used subst.] **1.** Name of a chemical element, and of some of its compounds, which are strong poisons. †**a.** orig. *Yellow Arsenic* or ORPIMENT, the trisulphide of arsenic (As_2S_3) -1634. †**b.** *Red Arsenic* or REALGAR, the *disulphide* (As_2S_2), the σανδαράκη of the Greeks -1751. **c.** in pop. use: *White Arsenic*, the trioxide of arsenic (As_2O_3), native (as arsenolite) and manufactured 1605. **d.** *Chem.* and *Min.* The element: a brittle semi-metallic substance, steel-grey, crystallizing in rhombohedrons, and volatilizing without fusion, with an odour of garlic. It links metals and non-metals. Symbol As. 1812. *fig.* Poison 1598. **2.** *attrib.* = Of arsenic, arsenical. *Arsenic bloom*, a. trioxide in native crystals. *Arsenic glass*, the same in a vitreous mass obtained from the powder by re-sublimation.

1. c. *Flowers of a.*: the trioxide of a. sublimed.

Arsenic (aɹse·nik), *a.* 1801. [f. the sb.] *Chem.* Of or belonging to arsenic; in *Chem.* combining as a pentad. *Arsenic anhydride* = arsenic pentoxide.

Arsenic- (aɹse·nik), in derivation; as in **Arse·nicane**, Davy's name for arsenious chloride. **Arse·nicate** *v.* to mix or treat with arsenic. **Arse·nicated** *ppl. a.* **Arse·nicism**, disease produced by arsenic, also called *Arseni·asis.* **Arse·nicite**, *Min.* = PHARMACOLITE. **Arse·nicized** *ppl. a.* treated or impregnated with arsenic. **Arsenico·phagy**, *Med.* the eating of arsenic, as by the Tyrolese.

Arsenical (aɹse·nikăl), *a.* 1605. [f. L. *arsenicum* + -AL¹.] Of, of the nature of, or containing arsenic; pertaining to or effected by arsenic.

Arsenide, -ite; see ARSEN-.

Arsenio- (aɹsī·nio), comb. form of next, as in **arse·nio-si·derite**, a fibrous yellowish-brown mineral, containing arsenic acid, sesquioxide of iron, and lime.

Arsenious (aɹsī·niəs), *a.* 1818. [f. ARSEN(IC) + -IOUS.] Of the nature of, or containing, arsenic; in *Chem.* applied to compounds in which arsenic combines as a triad, as *Arsenious oxide.* var. **A·rsenous.**

Arseniuret (aɹse·niŭrĕt). 1834. [cf. *sulphuret.*] *Chem.* Replaced by ARSENIDE. Hence **Arse·niuretted** *a.* combined with arsenic, chiefly in *Arseniuretted hydrogen*, for which Watts uses *arsenetted* (see ARSEN-).

Arseno- (ā·ɹsĕno), comb. f. ARSENIC, *arsenous* (see ARSENIOUS), in comps. and derivs. **A·rsenocro·cite** = *arseniosiderite* (see ARSENIO-). **Arse·nolite** [Gr. λίθος], white arsenic as a native mineral (Dana). **A·rsenopy·rite** [Gr. πυρίτης], native arsenio-sulphide of iron, called also Mispickel (Dana).

‖**Arsheen** (āɹʃī·n). 1734. [Russ.] A measure of length used in Russia and Turkey.

Arsine (ā·ɹsəin). [f. ARS(ENIC) + -INE, after *amine.*] *Chem.* A compound having the structure of an amine, with arsenic instead of nitrogen; i. e. *Arseniuretted hydrogen* (AsH_3), and any derivative such as *Trimethyl arsine* $(CH_3)_3As$. Hence **Arsi·nic** *a.*

‖**Arsis** (ā·ɹsis). ME. [L., a. Gr. ἄρσις, f. αἴρειν. Explained variously: in Gr., 'the raising of the foot in beating time' (Liddell and Scott); or perh. 'the raising of the voice to a higher pitch' (A. J. Ellis). In Latin, the raising of the voice on the first syllable of a metrical foot.] **1.** (See above.) **2.** In mod. use: The strong syllable in Eng. metre, the strong note in barred music; thus identical with the mod. meaning of L. *ictus* 1834. ‖**3.** In Mus. *Per arsin*: By descent of voice or sound from higher to lower pitch. ? *Obs.* 1706.

Arsmetik, -tric, -trik, obs. ff. ARITHMETIC.

†**A·rsmetry.** 1594. Corruption of *arsmetrick*, after *geometry.*

†**A·rson**¹. ME. [a. OF. *arçun* (also *archon*) :—late L. *arcionem*, f. *arcus.*] **1.** A saddle-bow -1623. **2.** Occ., a saddle -1460.

Arson (ā·ɹsən). 1680. [a. OF.:—late L. *arsionem*, f. *ars-, ardere.*] The act of wilfully and maliciously setting fire to another man's house, ship, forest, etc.; or to one's own, when insured, with intent to defraud the insurers.

A·rsy-ve·rsy. *Obs.* in polite use. 1539. [f. ARSE *sb.* + L. *versus.*] *adv.* Backside foremost;

perversely, preposterously. *adj.* Contrary, preposterous 1659.

Art (ɑ̄ɹt), *sb.* ME. [a. OF.:—L. *artem*, prob. f. *ar-* to fit. The OF. *ars*, nom. (sing. and pl.), was also used.] **I.** Skill. Sing. *art*; no pl. **1.** *gen.* Skill as the result of knowledge and practice. **2.** Human skill (opp. to *nature*) ME. **3.** The learning of the schools; see II. 1. †**a.** *spec.* The *trivium*, or any of its subjects -1573. **b.** *gen.* Learning, science (*arch.*) 1588. †**4.** *spec.* Technical or professional skill -1677. **5.** The application of skill to subjects of taste, as poetry, music, etc.; *esp.* in mod. use: Perfection of workmanship or execution as an object in itself 1620. **6.** Skill applied to the arts of imitation and design, *Painting, Architecture*, etc.; the cultivation of these in its principles, practice, and results. (The most usual mod. sense of *art* when used simply.) 1668.

1. Golde, or siluer, or stone grauen by arte, and mans deuice *Acts* xvii. 29. 2. A. may err, but nature cannot miss DRYDEN. 3. b. So vast is a., so narrow human wit POPE. *Words* or *terms of art*: words peculiar to a particular art or pursuit. 5. A. more frequently appears in fiddling and dancing, then in noble deeds 1675. We mean by a...also a law of pure and flawless workmanship M. ARNOLD. 6. Sacred and Legendary A. MRS. JAMESON (*title*).

II. Anything wherein skill may be attained. Sing. *an art*; pl. *arts*. **1.** Chiefly in pl. Certain branches of learning, which are of the nature of instruments for more advanced studies, or for the work of life. Applied in the Middle Ages to the *trivium* (containing *grammar, logic*, and *rhetoric*), and the *quadrivium* (containing *arithmetic, geometry, music*, and *astronomy*); called also the *free* or *liberal* arts. Hence the 'faculty' of arts in the Universities, and the degrees of 'Bachelor' and 'Master of Arts'. †*sing.* Any one of these subjects. ME. only. **2.** A body of rules for practice. Often opp. to *science*. 1489. *esp.* A craft, business, or profession ME.; a guild of craftsmen 1832. **3.** An occupation in which skill is employed to gratify taste or produce what is beautiful 1597. **4.** An acquired faculty of any kind; a knack 1637.

1. He being a Master in all the seuen liberall Arts, is not so ignorant in grammar FULKE. 2. So that the Arte and Practique part of Life must be the Mistresse to this Theorique *Hen. V*, I. i. 51. 3. *The Arts* (specifically) = the Fine Arts.

III. Conduct. Studied conduct or action; address; artfulness 1600; an artful device; wile, trick, etc. (chiefly in *pl.*) 1597.

Phrases: *Art and part* (*Sc. Law* and *gen.*): orig. *to be concerned in* (*either*) *by art* (in contriving it), *or by part* (taken in executing it): whence, *to have* art or (and) part in; corruptly *To be* art or part in (*be* for *have*, or = to be *of* art, etc. in); *To be* art and part in: to be accessary in both ways, or, *loosely*, to be accessary. *Industrial, mechanical, useful arts*: those in which the hands and body are more concerned than the mind. *Fine Arts*: see FINE ART.

Comb. **1.** passing into adj. **a.** = produced by an artist, composed with conscious artistry: said esp. of poetry and music, opp. to *popular* or *folk*, as *a. ballad, song*. **b.** = designed to produce an artistic effect, as *a. china, needlework, pottery*. **2. a. union**, an association for promoting the arts, esp. the arts of design.

†**A·rt**, *v.*[1] ME. [ad. L. *artare*, f. *artus*.] To cramp, limit -1496; to constrain *to do* -1553.

†**Art**, *v.*[2] 1602. [f. ART *sb.*] **1.** To instruct in arts, or in an art 1660. **2.** To artificialize (*rare*) 1627. **3.** To obtain by art (*rare*) 1602. **4.** phr. *To art it*: to use art or artifice -1655.

Art (ɑ̄ɹt, ăɹt, 'ɹt), *v.*[3] 2nd sing. pres. ind. of BE, part of the orig. substantive vb.; cf. AM.

Artemisia (ɑ̄ɹtǐmi·ziă). ME. [L., a. Gr. ἀρτεμισία, f. Ἄρτεμις.] *Bot.* A genus of plants (N.O. *Compositæ*), of bitter or aromatic taste, including the Common Wormwood, Mugwort, and Southernwood.

†**A·rter.** 1622. [a. OF. *artre*.] A wood-worm.

†**Arte·riac.** 1661. [ad. L. *arteriacus*, Gr. ἀρτηριακός; see ARTERY.] *adj.* Of or pertaining to the windpipe. *sb.* A remedy for disease of the windpipe.

Arterial (ɑɹtīə·riăl), *a.* 1541. [a. F. *artérial*, mod. *artériel*; see ARTERY.] **1.** Of, or of the nature of, an artery. **2.** Resembling an artery in having a main channel and branches; esp. of main roads or lines of transport 1831.

1. The scarlet blood is commonly known as a. HUXLEY. 2. *Arterial drainage*: a system of drains ramifying like an artery. (A term objected to on the ground of the direction of the flow.) var. **Arte·rious.** Hence **Arte·rialize** *v.* to convert venous into a. (blood) by exposure to oxygen in the lungs; to furnish with an a. system. **Arte·rializa·tion**, arterializing.

Arterio- (ɑɹtīə·rio) [a. Gr. ἀρτηριο-], comb. f. ARTERY, ARTERIAL.

arterio·graphy [Gr. -γραφία], systematic description of the arteries; **-logy** [Gr. -λογία], scientific study of, or a treatise upon, the arteries; **-tomy** [Gr. -τομία], cutting into or opening an artery, esp. for blood-letting; that part of anatomy which treats of the dissection of arteries; whence **-tomist.**

Arte·riole. 1839. [ad. mod. L. *arteriola*, dim. of *arteria*.] A minute or ultimate artery.

‖**Arteritis** (ɑ̄ɹtĕrəi·tis). 1836. [f. L. *arteria* + -ITIS.] *Path.* Inflammation of an artery.

Artery (ā·ɹtəri), *sb.* ME. [ad. L. *arteria*, a. Gr., prob. f. αἴρειν (cf. AORTA); at one time referred to ἀήρ.] †**1.** The trachea or windpipe. (L. *arteria aspera*.) -1661. **2.** One of the tubes forming part of the system of vessels by which the blood is conveyed from the heart ME. Also *attrib.* Also *fig.* **3.** *transf.* A main channel in a ramifying system of communication 1860. †**4.** A ligament -1658.

Among the ancients, the arteries were regarded as air-ducts, ramifying from the trachea. Mediæval writers supposed them to contain 'spiritual blood', or 'vital spirits' (cf. ANIMAL SPIRITS), an error which survived Harvey's discovery for some time.

1. [The Lungs]..through the Artire, throat and mouth, maketh the voice BACON *Sylva* § 199. 3. The great arteries of inland commerce MAURY. Hence **A·rtery** *v.* to furnish with, or as if with, arteries.

Artesian (ɑɹtī·zăn), *a.* 1830. [ad. F. *artésien*, f. OF. *Arteis*, now *Artois*.] Of or pertaining to Artois, or resembling the wells first made there, in which a perpendicular boring into a synclinal fold of the strata produces a constant supply of water rising spontaneously.

Artful (ā·ɹtful), *a.* 1613. [f. ART *sb.*] †**1.** Learned, wise -1681. **2.** Having practical skill; dexterous, clever (*arch.*) 1697. **3.** Skilful in adapting means to ends, adroit; *whence*, wily; crafty, deceitful 1739. **4.** Performed according to the rules of art; artistic (*arch.*) 1615. **5.** Produced by art, artificial (opp. to *natural*) 1706. **6.** Of actions, etc.: Skilfully adapted for a purpose; *whence*, cunning, crafty 1705.

2. A. hands POPE. 3. A. and designing men BEWICK. 4. Thyrsis! whose a. strains have oft delayed The huddling brook MILT. *Comus* 494. 5. The a. distresses of a romance 1779. 6. This is a very a. dodge DICKENS. Hence **A·rtfully** *adv.* with skill; craftily; **-ness.**

Arthritic (ɑɹþri·tik), *a.* (*sb.*) [ME. *artetyke*, orig. a. OF. *artetique*, corrupt ad. L. *arthriticus*, a. Gr., f. ἄρθρον.] **1.** Of or pertaining to diseased joints; *spec.* gouty. †**2.** Good against gout, etc. -1752. **3.** *sb.* †**a.** Gout. **b.** A gouty person. ME.

Arthri·tical, *a.* (*sb.*) ? *Obs.* 1528. [f. prec.] **1.** = prec. †**2.** Of the nature of a joint 1646. †**3.** *sb.* A remedy for affections of the joints 1671.

‖**Arthritis** (ɑɹþrəi·tis). 1544. [a. Gr., f. ἄρθρον.] *Path.* Inflammation of the joints; *spec.* gout. Hence **A·rthritism**, the disposition in which affections of the joints are liable to occur.

Arthro-, comb. f. Gr. ἄρθρον joint.

Arthro·dy·nic [Gr. ὀδύνη] *a.*, *Path.* of or pertaining to *Arthrodynia*, i. e. pain in the joints, chronic rheumatism; **-graphy** [Gr. -γραφία], systematic description of the joints; **-pathy** [Gr. -πάθεια], painful affection of the joints; ‖**-sia** [mod.L.] = ARTHRITIS; **-sis** [L., a. Gr.], connexion by a joint; **-stome** [Gr. στόμα], the mouth of the *Arthropoda* (L. Agassiz); **-zoic** [Gr. ζωικός] *a.*, *Zool.* the sixth series of the *Metazoa* (Huxley).

‖**Arthrodia** (ɑɹþrōᵘ·diă). 1634. [mod.L., a. Gr., f. ἀρθρώδης.] *Phys.* Articulation in which the surfaces of the bones are either plane, or but slightly convex and concave respectively; *e. g.* the shoulder-joint. Hence **Arthro·dial**, **Arthro·dic** *adjs.*

Arthrology (ɑɹþrǫ·lŏdʒi). 1644. [f. Gr. ἄρθρον + -λογία.] **1.** A scientific treatise on the joints 1859. †**2.** Finger speech 1644.

‖**Arthropoda** (ɑɹþrǫ·pŏdă), *sb. pl.* 1870. [mod.L., f. Gr. ἄρθρον + πούς (ποδ-). Sing. **arthropod**; also pl. **-pods.**] *Zool.* Animals with jointed feet; a name for the more highly organized *Annulosa* or *Articulata*, comprising Insects, Spiders, Crustacea, and Myriapoda, in respect of their antennæ, wings, or legs. Hence **Arthro·podal, Arthro·podous** *adjs.* of or belonging to the *Arthropoda*.

Artiad (ā·ɹti,ăd). 1870. [f. Gr. ἄρτιος.] *Chem.* An element or radical of even equivalence, *e. g.* a dyad or tedrad.

Artichoke (ā·ɹti,tʃoᵘk). 1531. [ad. north. It. *articiocco, arciciocco*, ad. OSp., a. Sp. Arab. *al-kharshōfa* = Arab. *al-kharshūf*.] **1.** A composite plant (*Cynara Scolymus*), allied to the thistles; its eatable parts are the fleshy bases of the involucral leaves or scales of the flower, and its receptacle when freed from the bristles, etc. Also *fig.* **2. Jerusalem Artichoke**: a species of Sunflower (*Helianthus tuberosus*), having edible tuberous roots 1620.

2. From this *girasol* (i. e. in the It. name *Girasole Articiocco*) we have made Jerusalem, and from the Jerusalem a. we make Palestine soup PEACOCK.

Article (ā·ɹtik'l), *sb.* ME. [a. F., ad. L. *articulus*, dim. of *artus*, f. *ar-* to join; cf. ARM, ART.] †**1.** A joint -1693. **2.** A nick of time which joins two periods, a juncture; the critical moment ME. **3.** [cf. L. *articulus*, the parts jointed on; whence *transf.* the component parts.] The separate clauses of any summary of faith ME.; of a statute 1523; each count of an indictment ME. **4.** Each head or point of an agreement or treaty; hence **a.** in *pl.* a formal agreement ME. **b.** Terms, conditions (*arch.*) 1650 †**5.** A clause in a will; a legacy -1761. **6.** *gen.* A paragraph, section, or distinct item ME. **7.** A literary composition *in* a journal, magazine, encyclopædia, etc., but treating a topic independently 1712. †**8.** A particular piece of business, a matter, or concern; a subject -1793; an item in an account, list, etc. -1774. **9.** A distinct part or portion; a piece, a particular 1741. **10.** *ellipt.* (= article of trade, etc.): A commodity; a piece of goods or property, etc. 1804. †**11.** *Arithm.* The number 10; each round number between units and hundreds -1751. **12.** *Gram.* A name for the adjs. *a, an, the* 1530.

2. In the A. of the Setting of the Sun 1665. *In the article of death* BP. NEWTON. 3. The Thirty-nine Articles [of the Church of England] BROUGHAM. The famous act of the six articles in the Year, 1539 C. M. *Let. to Curat.* **Lords of the Articles**: *Sc. Hist.* a standing committee of the Scottish Parliament, who drafted and prepared the measures submitted to the House. **The Articles of War**: regulations made for the government of the military and naval forces of Great Britain and the United States. And charge him with what articles they lusted FOXE. 4. a. Articles of Separation FIELDING, of capitulation WELLINGTON. *Articles of Apprenticeship*: terms of agreement between an apprentice and his employer. *Articles of Association*: rules, conditions, etc., upon which a commercial agreement is founded. 7. Charles Lamb's articles, signed 'Elia' 1822. Leading articles THACKERAY. 8. A soul *of great a.* (= moment) *Haml.* v. ii. 122. Wealth, which is the great A. of Life STEELE. *In the article of*: under the head of. 9. *An article of*: a thing coming under the head of. 10. Lady Selina was just the a. he wished for 1856.

Article (ā·ɹtik'l), *v.* 1447. [f. prec.] †**1.** *trans.* To formulate in articles, specify; with *cl.*, to state *that* -1592. **2.** To set forth in articles *against* 1494; *absol.* to bring charges *against* 1530. **3.** *absol.* To indict 1604. †**4.** To arrange by treaty, or stipulations. *trans.* -1682; *intr.* with *subord. cl.* or *inf.* -1762; also *with* (a person), *for* (a thing) -1770. **5.** To bind by articles of apprenticeship 1820. **6.** To furnish with articles (of faith) (*rare*) 1826.

2. All his..follies were articled against him JER. TAYLOR. The Lords..began..to a. against the Protector 1611. 3. Articled for an ecclesiastical offence 1868. 4. I will a. with them to do so WESLEY. 5. Articled to an attorney 1820. Hence **A·rticled** *ppl.a.* (in senses 1, 5, 6). **A·rticler**, one who draws up articles or charges.

Articular (ɑɹti·kiŭlăɹ), *a.* ME. [ad. L. *articularis*, f. *articulus*; see ARTICLE.] **1.** Of, or pertaining to, the joints. var. **Arti·culary.** **2.** *Gram.* Of the nature of an ARTICLE (*sb.* 12) 1750. Hence †**Arti·cularly** *adv.* article by article.

‖**Articulata** (ɑɹti·kiŭlēᵊ·tă), *sb. pl.* 1834. [L., adj. pl. neut. (sc. *animalia*).] *Zool.* Cuvier's third great sub-kingdom of animals, embracing invertebrate animals with an external skeleton, having the body and limbs composed of segments jointed together, as Insects, Crustacea, etc. (Cf. ANNULOIDA, ARTHROPODA.)

Articulate (ɑɹti·kiŭlėt), *a.* (*sb.*) 1569. [ad. L. *articulatus*; see ARTICLE.] **1.** United by a joint 1610; composed of jointed segments 1607; *Zool.* of the type of the ARTICULATA 1855. **2.** Distinctly jointed or marked 1664. **3.** Of sound: Divided into distinct and significant parts; *fig.* speaking intelligibly 1586. **4.** Hence *transf.*: Distinct 1626. †**5.** Formulated, set forth in articles -1726. †**6.** Consisting of tens. See ARTICLE *sb.* II. -1646. **7.** *sb. Zool.* One of the ARTICULATA 1874.

3. Beasts..created mute to all articulat sound MILT. *P. L.* IX. 557. *Articulate-speaking*: using articulate speech. 4. A. hearing 1626, Apparitions H. MORE, Thoughts CARLYLE. var. **Arti·culated** *ppl. a.* (exc. in sense 6.) Hence **Arti·culate·ly** *adv.*, **-ness.**

Articulate (ɑɹti·kiŭleⁱt), *v.* 1553. [f. prec.] **1.** To attach by a joint. (Usu. in *pass.*) 1616. **2.** To connect by, or mark with, apparent joints. (Usu. *pass.*) 1644. **3.** *intr.* (for *refl.*) To form a joint *with* 1832. **4.** *trans.* To divide (vocal sound) into distinct and significant parts 1594; to pronounce distinctly, express in words, utter 1691; *intr.* to utter words; to speak distinctly; *often* to pronounce 1642. **5.** To formulate or specify in an article or articles. ? *Obs.* 1562. †**6.** *trans.* and *intr.* To charge *against* -1603. †**7.** To arrange by articles or conditions -1676. †**8.** To come to terms, capitulate -1643.

2. Reticulated or articulated 1879. 4. To interpret and a. the deep dumb wants of the people CARLYLE. He had..so great a weakness in his tongue, that he could not a. COTTON.

Articulation (ɑɹti:kiŭlēⁱ·ʃən). 1541. [a. F., ad. L. *articulationem*, f. *articulare*.] **1.** The action of jointing; the state of being jointed; mode of jointing or junction 1597. **2.** A joint: **a.** The structure whereby two bones, or parts, are connected, whether stiffly, or so that one moves in or on the other 1615. **b.** *Bot.* The place at which a leaf, etc., separates from the plant; *also*, a knot or joint 1658. **3.** A segment of a jointed body 1664. **4.** Articulate voice 1615; utterance, speech 1711; an articulate sound, *esp.* a consonant 1764. **5.** Articulate quality (*rare*) 1785.

2 a. To form a kind of ball and socket a. KIRBY. 4. Overgreat distance confoundeth the a. of sounds BACON *Sylva* § 194. 5. The definiteness and a. of imagery COLERIDGE. Hence **Articula·tionist**, one who teaches deaf-mutes.

Articulator (ɑɹti·kiŭleⁱtəɹ). 1777. [f. L. *articulare*.] **1.** One who articulates words. **2.** *techn.* One who articulates bones, and mounts skeletons 1865. Hence **Arti·culatory** *a.* (sense 1). Occ. = ARTICULAR **1.**

‖**Arti·culus.** 1877. [L.] Occas. scientific term for *joint.* Pl. articuli.

Artifact (ā·ɹtifækt). Also **arte-.** *rare.* 1834. [f. L. *arti-* + *factus.*] An artificial product.

‖**Artifex** (ā·ɹtifeks). 1657. [L.] Artificer.

Artifice (ā·ɹtifis). 1534. [a. F., ad. L. *artificium.*] †**1.** The action of an artificer, construction, workmanship, *esp.* mechanic art -1682. †**2.** The product of art -1688; an artificial substance 1677. †**3.** Mode or style of workmanship -1756. †**4.** Constructive skill -1777. **5.** Human skill 1857. **6.** Skill in expedients; address, trickery 1618. **7.** An ingenious expedient, a manœuvre, device, trick. (The ordinary sense now.) 1656.

1. The skill of A. or Office mean MILT. *P. L.* IX. 39. 4. Does it not counterwork the a. of nature HUME. 7. He condemned Rhetorick, as being used rather as an A., than an Art 1660.

Artificer (ɑɹti·fisəɹ). ME. [app. an AF. or ME. formation on ARTIFICE; cf. *officer.*] **1.** One who makes by art or skill; *esp.* a craftsman. **2.** *Mil.* A soldier mechanic attached to the ordnance, artillery, and engineer service 1804. †**3.** *gen.* Maker, manufacturer -1751. **4.** *transf.* Contriver, inventor. (Cf. ARCHITECT.) 1605. †**5.** One who practises any art; a savant. (Cf. ARTIST.) 1635. †**6.** An artful person; a trickster -1621.

1. A base a. NASHE. 4. A. of fraud..the first That practised falshood under saintly shew MILT. *P. L.* IV. 121. Hence **Arti·ficership**, workmanship.

Artificial (ārtifi·ʃăl). ME. [a. F. *artificiel*, ad. L. *artificialis*, f. *artificium*; see ARTIFICE and -AL.] **A.** *adj.* **I.** Opp. to *natural.* **1.** Made by or resulting from art or artifice; not natural. **2.** Made by art in imitation of, or as substitute for, what is natural or real 1577. **3.** Factitious; *hence*, feigned, fictitious 1650. **4.** Affected 1598.

1. To give an a. stimulus to population MCCULLOCH. A. Teares SHAKS., hunger 1834, light 1879. 2. A list of a. flies F. FRANCIS. 4. Frivolous and a. 1849.

†**II.** Displaying art or skill. (All *Obs.*) **1.** Skilfully made -1738; skilful -1682. **2.** Scholarly -1628. **3.** Workmanlike -1656. **4.** Artful, deceitful -1702.

1. The a. structure of the eye 1738. 2. Scholastique and artificiall men DONNE.

†**III.** Of or pertaining to art. (All *Obs.*) **1.** According to the rules of art -1753. **2.** Technical -1809.

B. *sb.* [the adj. used *absol.* in *pl.*] Artificial things; products of art 1611.

Phrases: *Artificial horizon*: a level reflecting surface, such as that of a fluid at rest, or a mirror laid horizontally on the earth's surface, used in taking altitudes. *Artificial grasses*: such as do not grow spontaneously in a locality, but are sown. *Artificial lines*: lines on a sector representing the logarithmic sines and tangents. *Artificial numbers*: logarithms. *Artificial system* or *classification* (in *Nat. Hist.*): a system based on arbitrary, limited, and unimportant characters, and serving chiefly as an index.

Hence **Artifi·cialism**, an a. principle or practice. **Artifi·cialize** *v.* to make a. **Artifi·cially** *adv.* **Artifi·cialness**, the quality of being a., opp. to naturalness.

Artificiality (ā:ɹtifiʃi,æ·lĭti). 1763. [f. prec.] **1.** The quality or state of being artificial. **2.** with *pl.* An artificial thing or characteristic.

†**Artifi·cious**, *a.* 1530. [a. F. *artificieux*:— L. *artificiosus*; see ARTIFICE and -OUS.] Displaying constructive skill; affected; artful -1679. Hence †**Artifi·ciously** *adv.*

†**A·rtilize**, *v.* 1744. [ad. F. *artialiser.*] To make artificial -1778. Cf. ARTIZE.

†**Arti·ller**, *sb.* ME. [a. OF. *artiller, -ier*, also in OF. *articulier*; cf. OF. *artill(i)er*:—L. *articulare*; app. f. late L. *articula*, dim. of *ars.*] A maker of artillery; *spec.* a bowyer -1483.

Artillerist (ɑɹti·lĕrist). 1778. [f. ARTILLERY.] One who studies the principles of gunnery; a gunner.

Artillery (ɑɹti·lĕri), *sb.* ME. [a. OF. *artillerie*; see ARTILLER.] †**1.** Warlike munitions, implements of war -1794. **2.** Engines for discharging missiles; formerly, catapults, slings, arbalests, bows, etc. 1476; now, large guns, ordnance 1533. †**3.** Missiles discharged in war (*arch.*) -1867. **4.** The science and practice of Gunnery (formerly of Archery) 1545. **5.** That branch of an army which manages the cannons in war 1786. **6.** *fig.* (with reference to 1, 2, 3.) 1599. **7.** Thunder and lightning (*poet.*) 1596.

2. Ionathan gaue his a. vnto his ladde 1 *Sam.* xx. 40. Artillerie, th' infernall instrument, New brought from hell to scourge mortalitie With hideous roaring and astonishment DANIEL. 7. Heauen's Artillerie SHAKS.

Comb.: **a.-company**, a company †of archers, or of a. (sense 5); **-park**, the place in which the a. is encamped, or collected; **-train**, a number of pieces of ordnance mounted on carriages and fitted out for marching. Hence **Arti·llerying** *vbl. sb.* firing of a. CARLYLE. **Arti·lleryman**, one who serves a gun; one who belongs to the a. **Arti·lleryship**, the skilful management of cannon; artillery practice.

Artiodactyl(e (ā:ɹti,o,dæ·ktil). 1849. [f. Gr. ἄρτιος + δάκτυλος.] *Zool. adj.* Having an even number of toes. *sb.* [sc. *ungulate animal.*]

Artisan (āɹtizæ·n). 1538. [a. F., ad. It. *artigiano*:—late L. **artitianus*, f. *artitus*, *artire* to instruct in arts (Diez). Cf. *partisan.*] †**1.** One who practises or cultivates an art; an artist -1795. **2.** One occupied in any industrial art; a mechanic, handicraftsman, artificer 1538. Also *fig.* Also *attrib.* 1859.

2. The meanest a...contributes more to the accommodation of life than the profound scholar JOHNSON.

Artist (ā·ɹtist). 1581. [a. F. *artiste*, a. It. *artista*:—late L. *artista*, f. *ars.*] **A.** *sb.* **I.** †**1.** A learned man, a Master of Arts (see ART *sb.* II. 1) -1753. †**2.** *gen.* One who pursues some practical science 1677; *spec.* a medical practitioner -1761; an astrologer or alchemist; *later*, a chemist -1686.

2. The Tuscan A. [*i.e.* astronomer] MILT. *P. L.* I. 288.

II. †**1.** A follower of a pursuit in which skill comes by study or practice; *hence*, a proficient; a practical man, opp. to a *theorist* -1793. †**2.** A follower of a manual art; a mechanic, etc. -1815. **3.** One who makes his craft a 'fine art'. Cf. ARTISTE. 1849.

1. I will give you more directions concerning fishing; for I would fain make you an A. WALTON. 3. A famous pilau, made by my a. [*i.e.* cook] CURZON.

III. 1. *gen.* One who cultivates one of the fine arts, which please by perfection of execution. (Formerly extended to all the *arts* presided over by the *Muses.*) 1581. **2.** *spec.* One skilled in †**a.** music -1712; **b.** dramatic art (see ARTISTE) 1714; **c.** now *esp.* one who practises the arts of design; or, pop. and more usually, one who cultivates painting as a profession 1747.

1. The true poet is always a true a. 1855. 2. He judged her [the actress] as a woman, not an a. C. BRONTË. She's a perfect Hebe; and if I were an a., I would paint her GEO. ELIOT.

†**IV.** One who practises **artifice**; a schemer -1813.

B. *adj.* Artistic, skilful 1603.

Hence **A·rtistdom**, the class or estate of artists. **Artist-like** *adj.* artistic; *adv.* artistically; var. **A·rtistly** *adv.* **A·rtistry**, the occupation or characteristics of an a.; artistic ability.

Artiste (arti·st). 1832. [Fr.; see ARTIST; re-introduced in consequence of the limited sense now given to *artist.*] = ARTIST II. 3, III. 2 a, b.

A·rtistess. A female artist. H. WALPOLE.

Artistic, -al (ɑɹti·stik, -ăl), *a.* 1753. [ad. F. *artistique*; see ARTIST and -IC, -AL[1].] Of or pertaining to artists or art; befitting an artist. Hence **Arti·stically** *adv.* tastefully; from an a. point of view.

†**A·rtize**, *v.* [f. ART *sb.*] *intr.* To exercise an art. *trans.* To artificialize. FLORIO.

Artless (ā·ɹtlės), *a.* 1589. [f. ART *sb.* + -LESS.] **1.** Devoid of art or skill, unpractised, ignorant; devoid of the fine or liberal arts, uncultured 1599. **2.** Constructed, or designed, without art; clumsy; inartistic 1695. **3.** Unartificial, natural, simple 1672. **4.** Simple-minded, sincere, ingenuous 1714.

1. The artlesse tongue of a tedious dolt NASHE. A shadowy life—a., joyless, loveless RUSKIN. 2. Brogues, a kind of a. shoes JOHNSON. 3. Such A. beauty lies in Shakespears wit DRYDEN. 4. Imitation is a kind of a. flattery BUDGELL. Hence **A·rtless-ly** *adv.*, **-ness.**

Art-like. 1630. *adj.* In accordance with, or resembling, art 1651. *adv.* According to the rules of art 1630.

†**A·rtly**, *adv.* 1576. [f. ART *sb.*] With art; skilfully -1662.

Artocarpad (āɹtokā·ɹpăd). 1834. [f. mod. L. *artocarpus*, f. Gr. ἄρτος + καρπός.] *Bot.* A tree belonging to the *Artocarpeæ*, or Bread-fruit group. **Artoca·rpeous, -pous** *a.* of or pertaining to this group.

†**Arto·latry.** 1626. [ad. Gr. ἀρτολατρεία.] The worship of bread -1658.

Arto·phagous, *a. rare.* 1816. [f. Gr. ἀρτοφάγος.] Bread-eating.

Artotyrite (āɹtotəi·rəit). 1586. [ad. med.L. *artotyrita*, f. Gr. ἀρτότυρος bread and cheese; see -ITE.] *Eccl. Hist.* One of a sect who celebrated the Eucharist with bread and cheese.

Artou, artow, obs. contr. of *art thou.*

A·rts-man. *arch.* 1551. [f. *art's* + MAN; cf. *craftsman*, etc.] One skilled in an art or in arts.

†**A·rts-ma·ster.** 1589. [f. as prec. + MASTER.] **1.** (Also *art-master.*) A teacher of art, or of an art or craft -1740. **2.** One who is master of a craft; a chief artificer -1624.

Arty (ā·ɹti), *a. colloq.* 1901. [-Y[1].] Contemptuous or joc.: Of artistic pretensions.

‖**Arum** (ēə·rŏm). Pl. **-s.** 1551. [L., a. Gr. ἄρον (also used).] **1.** *Bot.* A genus of plants (N.O. *Araceæ*), with a large spathe, enclosing a fleshy spadix, as the Wake-robin, Cuckoo-pint, or Lords and Ladies (*A. Maculatum*). **2.** *attrib.*, as in **Arum lily** (*Richardia æthiopica*) 1599.

Arundinaceous (ărʊndinēⁱ·ʃəs), *a.* 1657. [f. L. *arundinaceus*, f. *(h)arundo*; see -ACEOUS.] Reed-like, reedy. var. **Arundi·neous** (*rare*).

Aruspex, and derivatives; see under HAR-.

A·rval, -el, -ill. Now *dial.* 1459. [App. ad. Norse; cf. ON. *erfi-öl*, f. *arfr* (OE. *erfe*) + *öl* ALE.] A funeral feast. Also *attrib.*

Arval (ā·ɹvăl), *a.* 1656. [ad. L. *arvalis*, f. *arvum.*] Of or belonging to ploughed land:

esp. in *Arval Brethren* (= L. *Fratres Arvales*), a college of priests in Ancient Rome, who offered sacrifice to the field-Lares to secure good crops.

-ary[1], *suffix* of adjs. and sbs., ad. L. *-arius*, *-arium*. In ME. *-arie*, later *-arye*. **A.** *adjs.* repr. (or after) L. *-arius* 'connected with, pertaining to'; as *arbitrary*. **B.** *sbs.* **1.** repr. (or after) L. *-arius* 'a man (or male) belonging to or engaged in'; as *adversary*, *January* (mensis). **2.** repr. (or after) L. *-arium* 'a thing connected with or employed in, a place for'; as *aviary*, *granary*. **3.** repr. L. *-aria* (Fr. *-aire*); as *fritillary*.

-ary[2], *suffix* of adjs.; occas. ad. L. *-aris* 'of the kind of, belonging to', as *military*. The reg. Eng. repr. is -AR[1].

Aryan, Arian (ēᵊ·riăn, ā·riăn). 1601. [f. Skr. *ārya* 'noble', and earlier a national name 'comprising the worshippers of the gods of the Brahmans' (Max Müller); cf. mod. Pers. *Irân*. *Aryan* is recent, but distinguishes the word from ARIAN in *Eccl. Hist.*] **A.** *adj.* Applied to the family of languages, which includes Sanskrit, Zend, Persian, Greek, Latin, Celtic, Teutonic, and Slavonic; also called *Indo-European*, *Indo-Germanic*, and occ. *Japhetic*; or restricted to the Asiatic portion of these, as the only members of the family known historically to have called themselves by the name. *absol.* The original Aryan language 1847.

B. *sb.* A member of the Aryan family; one belonging to, or descended from, the ancient people who spoke the parent Aryan language 1851.

The region of the Arianes, all scorched and senged with the parching heate of the Sunne HOLLAND.

Aryanize (ēᵊ·riănəiz, ā·riăn-), *v.* 1858. [f. prec.] To make characteristically Aryan. Hence **Aryanized** *ppl. a.* made Aryan in language (though not of Aryan race).

Aryteno- (æritī·no), comb. form of next.

Arytenoid (æritī·noid). 1727. [ad. mod.L. *arytænoides*, ad. Gr. ἀρυταινοειδής, f. ἀρύταινα funnel + -ειδής.] *Phys. adj.* Funnel-, pitcher-shaped: applied *spec.* to two pyramidal cartilages of the larynx which regulate the vocal chords, and to parts connected with them. As *sb.* [sc. *cartilage, muscle.*] 1849. var. **Arytæ·noid.** Hence **A·rytenoi·dal** *a.* belonging to the a. cartilages, etc.

As (æz, ǣz, əz), *adv.* (*conj.* and *rel. pron.*) OE. [Worn-down f. *all-so*, OE. *all-swá* 'wholly so', which remains disyllabic in the demonstrative ALSO. The phonetic series (Midl.) is *alswá, alswo, also, alse, ase, as, æz.*] **A.** In a main sentence, as Antecedent or Demonstrative Adverb. †**1.** *As* . . . *so*: In that quantity . . . (in which) . . . –1532; in that way . . . (in which) . . . ME. only. **2.** *As* . . . *as*: In that degree . . . (in which) . . . Expressing the *Comparative of Equality*: as good *as* gold, etc. ME. **3.** With relative cl. elliptically absent: *as*=*equally* ME.

2. He was as covetous as cruel W. WOTTON. **3.** I hear quite as well as I am (*mod.*). *As lief*, *as soon* (as not).

B. In a subord. sentence, as a Relative or Conjunctive Adverb, introducing a clause:

I. Of quantity or degree. (Preceded by *adj.* or *adv.*) **1.** With antecedent *as*: . . . In which degree (expressing the *Comparative of Equality*; cf. A. 2); As if, as though (*arch.*) ME. **2.** With antecedent *so* in the same sense as **1.** ME. **3.** With antecedent *as* (*so*) suppressed: Emphatic ME.; Concessive=Though, however ME. †**4.** After comparatives = Than –1824.

1. Will serve as well as I were present there MARLOWE. **2.** No country suffered so much..as England MACAULAY. **3.** Momentarie as a sound *Mids. N.* I. i. 144. Bad as his Actions were..would there not [etc.] 1742. **4.** I rather like him as otherwise SCOTT.

II. Of quality or manner. (Preceded by a *verb.*) * *With antecedent expressed.* †**1.** With antecedent *as*: . . . in the way that ME. only. **2.** With antecedent *so*, or *such, same*, etc.: . . . in the manner that . . . (*arch.*) ME. **3.** With the clauses transposed for emphasis; *as* . . . *so*: in the way that . . . (in that manner) ME.; even as, just as; both . . . and (*arch.*) 1602. ** *With antecedent not expressed.* **4.** =with antecedent *so* omitted: . . . in the manner that . . . ; to the same extent as; even as; . . . as on the other hand; whereas; whilst 1523. **5.** = mod. As if, as though (*arch.*) ME. **6.** With the subord. cl. abbreviated: As if, as it were OE. †With numbers = About –1523. **7.** With subj. or obj. repr. subord. cl.: The same as, like ME.; in the character, capacity, or *rôle* of 1523. **8.** Used to introduce elliptical or parenthetical clauses, e.g. *as a rule*, etc. ME. **9.** Introducing clauses used to attest a statement, or to adjure any one by his faith, hopes, etc.: In such a manner as befits the prayer, †wish, belief, etc. that . . . ME.

2. So doe, as thou hast said *Gen.* xviii. 5. **3.** As she brews so let her bake 1614. **4.** General amicable *As-you-were* between Austria and Bavaria CARLYLE. The oath, *as it stands*, is [etc.] 1882. If I had been present, as I was not, I should [etc.] (*mod.*). **5.** I heard the wrack As earth and sky would mingle MILT. *P. R.* IV. 447. *As it were*: As if it were so, in some sort; She has thought fit, as it were, to mock herself STEELE. **6.** God dealeth with you as with sonnes *Heb.* xii. 7. **7.** Yee shall bee as Gods, knowing good and euill *Gen.* iii. 5. The fact is assumed as a hypothesis 1837. *As who*: Like one who, as if one (*arch.*); †as being he who –1583. **8.** This war was, *as usual*, no less feeble in its operations than [etc.] HUME. **9.** This sweares he, as he is a Prince SHAKS.

III. Of time and place. **1.** When, while, whenever ME. †**2.** Where ME. only.

1. They wander, grazing as they go DRYDEN.

IV. Of reason. It being the case that; inasmuch as; since ME.

As you are not ready, we must go without you (*mod.*).

V. Of result or purpose. †**1.** With finite vb. (Now repl. by *that*, through *as that*.) So . . . as: in such manner . . . that –1777; *Such* . . . *as*: of that kind . . . that –1671. **2.** With inf. (Still in use.) 1590. * *With* so *wanting, or conjoined with* as *in the subord. cl.* †**3.** =mod. *so that* (through *so as that*) –1797.

2. To be so good as to come (*mod.*).

VI. Introducing an attrib. cl.; after *such*, *same*, etc. **1.** After *such* (OE. *swylc* containing *swá, so*), and after *same* (an adv. followed by *swá* in OE.) *as* = That, which, who ME. **2.** With *such* omitted, or replaced by *that, those*, 'as' becomes a relative pron. = That, who, which. Still in dial. use. ME. **3.** In parenthetic clauses, affirming or commenting on a word 1550; also=A thing or fact which 1552. **4.** =Such as, of the kind of; for instance. (App. ellipt. = *such* as . . . *is.*) ME. †**5.** Added to *there, then, thither*, etc. (earlier to *where, when*, etc.) to make them conjunctive –1808.

1. Such a one as was the glory of the land of Israel A.V. *Transl. Pref.* **3.** I haue vs'd thee (Filth as thou art) with humane care *Temp.* I. ii. 346. Yff..we shoulde warre with them (as God defende) 1552. **4.** A prelat, as an abott or a priour WYCLIF.

VII. Introducing dependent sentences or clauses. **1.** A noun sentence, after *say, know*, etc. Also *as that, as how*. (Replaced by *that.*) 1483. †**2.** Contracted interrog. sentences: *As how?* (arch.) *As why?* (illiterate.) –1801. †**3.** Formerly bef. an inf. cl., where now a pple. is used, as in 'Speaking of volcanoes, I [etc.]'.

1. I believe as how your man deals with the devil SMOLLETT.

VIII. Prefixed to preps. and advs. **1.** With preps. = *as far as, so far as*. (In *as in, as by, as after*, etc., *as* was pleonastic.) ME. **2.** With advs. and advb. phrases. Of time: in *as then, as now*, etc., *as* is restrictive. In literary Eng. *as yet* (still in use)=up to this time ME. †Of place: *as here*, etc. –1532.

1. My only doubt was as to the mode HELPS. **2.** He could not get John punished as then 1653.

Phrases: **1.** *As much* has the special sense of: The same; what practically amounts to that, so; as in 'I thought as much'. **2.** *As well* has the special senses: **a.** (with following *as*) Just as much..as; equally..with; in the same way..as; both..and; like; in addition to, besides. **b.** (*ellipt.*) Just as much, no less; also. **c.** (*absol.*) As well as not; *hence* (deferentially) better. **3.** *As good as*: Practically.

‖**As** (æs), *sb.* 1601. [L.] A Roman copper coin, originally weighing twelve ounces, after the first Punic war reduced to two ounces, during the second to one, and by the *Lex Papiria* (B.C. 191) to half an ounce.

As, obs. f. ACE, ASS, and ASH.

As-, *prefix*[1], assim. f. L. *ad-*, bef. *s-*. Orig. adopted from OF. as *a-*; but refash. later.

As-, *prefix*[2], var. of OF. *es-*:–L. *ex-*, as in *as-cape* (now *es-cape*), *as-tonish* (still used).

‖**Asafœtida** (æsăfe·tidă). ME. [med.L.: *asa*, latinized f. Pers. + *fœtida* adj. fem.] A concreted resinous gum, with a strong alliaceous odour, procured from the *Narthex asafœtida*, etc.; used in cookery, and as an antispasmodic in medicine. Also, the plant itself 1607.

A-sa·le, *adv.* 1553. [A *prep.*[1]] On sale, for sale.

‖**Asarabacca** (æ:sărăˌbæ·kă). 1551. [f. L. *asarum*, a. Gr. ἄσαρον plant name + *bacca.*] *Herb.* The plant *Asarum Europæum*, used now as an ingredient in cephalic snuffs.

Asarin (æ·sărin). 1834. [f. L. *asarum* (see prec.) + -IN.] *Chem.* A crystallizable, aromatic, camphor-like substance obtained from the root of asarabacca; also called *Camphor of Asarum*. var. **A·sarone.**

Asbestos, asbestus (ǣzbe·stǫs, -ɒs). ME. [a. L. *asbestos*, a. Gr., f. ἀ + σβεστός, f. σβεννύναι.] †**1.** The unquenchable stone. (A distorted reference to the action of cold water on quick lime.) –1750. †**2.** An (alleged) incombustible flax (see 3) –1734. **3.** A mineral of fibrous texture, capable of being woven into an incombustible fabric; AMIANT or AMIANTUS. In *Min.* applied to all fibrous varieties of Hornblende or Amphibole, and of Pyroxene, as well as to *Amiantus*. 1607. Also *fig.* Also *attrib.* var. **Asbest** (*arch.*). Hence **Asbe·stic** *a.* of the nature of a. **Asbe·stiform** *a.* having the form or appearance of a. **Asbe·stine, Asbe·stous** *a.* of, pertaining to, or having the properties of a.; incombustible. **Asbe·stoid** *a.* resembling a.; *sb.* (*Min.*) = BYSSOLITE; so **Asbestoi·dal** *a.*

Asbolan, asbolite (æ·zbolæn, -əit). 1837. [f. Gr. ἀσβόλη soot; see -AN[2] 2, -ITE.] *Min.* A kind of wad containing oxide of cobalt; also called *Earthy Cobalt*.

Asboline (æ·zbələin). 1863. [f. as prec. + -INE[4].] An acrid volatile oil obtained from soot.

Ascan (æ·skăn), *a.* 1876. [f. mod.L. *ascus*, Gr. ἀσκός.] *Bot.* Of or belonging to an *ascus*, as *ascan spores*.

†**Asca·pe**, *v.* ME. form of ESCAPE –1523.

‖**Ascarides** (ăskæ·ridīz), *sb. pl.* ME. [mod. L., a. Gr. ἀσκαρίδες, pl. of ἀσκαρίς. Occas. sing. ascarid.] *Zool.* A genus of intestinal worms; thread-worms.

†**Asce·nce.** 1450. [a. OF. *ascense.*] Earlier equiv. of ASCENT, ASCENSION.

Ascend (ăse·nd), *v.* ME. [ad. L. *ascendere*, f. *ad* + *-scendere* = *scandere*. Occas. conjugated with *be* in perfect tenses.] **1.** *intr.* (occas. with *up*) To go or come up; to mount, soar; to rise, be raised 1514. **2.** Of planetary bodies, etc.: **a.** *spec.* To come above the horizon. **b.** *gen.* To move towards the zenith. **3.** To rise by growth or construction. Only *poet.* 1667. **4.** To slope upwards 1832. **5.** *trans.* To walk up, climb; *hence*, to reach the top of ME. **6.** To go up into or get up on; to mount. *Obs.* exc. *poet.*, and in 'to ascend the throne'. 1593. **7.** *intr.* To proceed from the inferior to the superior; to rise in thought, feeling, station, etc. 1549. **8.** To rise in pitch 1597. **9.** To go back in time, or in genealogical order 1574.

1. Voice always ascends, the vibration moving most naturally upwards DE FOE. **2.** All mild ascends the Moon's more sober light POPE. **3.** Where Apennine ascends GOLDSM. **5.** *To ascend* a river: to go along it towards its source. **9.** Inheritance may..not lyneally a. 1574. Hence **Asce·ndable** *a.* (*rare*), that may be ascended. **Asce·nder.**

Ascendancy, -ency (ăse·ndĕnsi). 1712. [f. ASCENDANT; see -ANCY.] The state or quality of being in the ascendant; paramount influence, domination. Constr. *over*. (The spellings are equally common.)

He would not submit to the a. of France MACAULAY. var. **Asce·ndance, -ence.**

Ascendant, -ent (ăse·ndĕnt). ME. [a. OF., ad. L. *ascendentem*; see ASCEND and -ANT. The prevalent sp. is now *-ant.*] **A.** *adj.* **1.** *gen.* Rising; tending upwards 1591; *spec.* in *Phys.* and *Bot.* = ASCENDING *ppl. a.* 3. 1611. **2.** *Astr.* Rising towards the zenith; *spec.* in *Astrol.* Just above the eastern horizon 1594. **3.** *fig.* Superior; predominant 1634.

1. Rooted and a. strength like that of foliage RUSKIN. **3.** To make a. all that is rational..in us 1806.

B. *sb.* [the adj. used *absol.*] **1.** *Astrol.* The point of the ecliptic, or degree of the zodiac, which at any moment (*esp.* at the birth of a child) is just rising above the eastern horizon;

the horoscope ME. Hence *fig.* 1654. **2.** *gen.* = ASCENDANCY. Const. *over.* 1596. **3.** †An upward slope; a flight of steps. Also *fig.* –1641. †**4.** One who ascends –1701. †**5.** A summit or peak –1676. **6.** One who precedes in genealogical order; an ancestor; a relative in the ascending line 1604.

1. Min ascendent was Taur, and Mars therinne CHAUCER. *The house of the ascendant*: 5 degrees of the zodiac above and 25 below the ASCENDANT (B. 1). *The lord of the ascendant*: any planet within the house of the ascendant. **2.** Strong minds have undoubtedly an a. over weak ones CHESTERF. **In the ascendant**: supreme, dominant. (Erron.: Rising, ascending.) Hence **Ascende·ntal** *a.* of the nature of ascent (*rare*).

Asce·ndible, *a. rare.* [ad. L. *ascendibilis.*] = *Ascendable* (see ASCEND *v.*).

Ascending (ăse·ndiŋ), *vbl. sb.* 1482. [f. ASCEND *v.*] The action of the vb. ASCEND; ascent, ascension.

attrib. in *Ascending Latitude*: the latitude of a planet when ascending. *A. Node*: the point in a planet's orbit where it crosses the ecliptic in ascending.

Asce·nding, *ppl. a.* 1616. [f. as prec.] **1.** Rising, mounting up 1667. **2.** Sloping upwards; acclivitous 1616. **3.** Directed upwards: *spec.* in *Phys.* of structures that pass, or serve as a passage, from a lower to a higher part of the body; and in *Bot.* of a stem which gradually curves to an erect position 1713. **4.** Going backwards in genealogical order 1703. Hence **Asce·ndingly** *adv.* with upward motion.

Ascension (ăse·nʃən). ME. [ad. L. *ascensionem*; see ASCEND. Exc. in **2**, **3**, ASCENT is now usual.] **1.** *gen.* The action of ascending (see ASCEND *v.*) 1574. **2.** *spec.* The ascent of Jesus Christ to heaven on the fortieth day after His resurrection. Occ. = *Ascension-day.* ME. **3.** *Astr.* The rising of a celestial body ME. †**4.** *Alch.* Distillation, evaporation; *concr.* a fume –1817. **5.** Upward slope (*arch.*) 1447.

2. *Ascension-day*: the day on which the ascension into heaven took place, and on which it is commemorated; Holy Thursday. **3.** *Right Ascension* of the sun or a star: the degree of the equinoctial or celestial equator, reckoned from the first point in Aries, which rises with it in a right sphere, or which comes with it to the meridian; the arc of the equator intercepted between this degree and the first point of Aries; celestial longitude. *Oblique Ascension* of a star: the arc of the equator intercepted between the first point of Aries and the point of the equator which rises with the sun or star in an oblique sphere.

Ascensional (ăse·nʃənăl), *a.* 1594. [f. prec. + -AL.] Of or belonging to ascension, or ascent.

A. Difference in *Astr.*: the difference between the right and oblique ascension of the sun or a star.

Asce·nsionist. 1863. [f. as prec. + -IST.] One who makes ascents.

Ascensive (ăse·nsiv), *a.* 1646. [f. L. *ascens-* (*ascendere*) + -IVE.] **1.** Given to moving upwards; rising, progressive. **2.** *Gram.* Augmentative, intensive 1857. var. †**Asce·ntive.**

Ascent (ăse·nt). 1600. [(Not in Fr.) f. ASCEND *v.*, after *descent.*] **1.** *gen.* The act of ascending; upward movement 1614. Also *fig.* (see ASCEND 7) 1607. **2.** *esp.* The act of climbing or travelling up 1753. Also *fig.* **3.** A going back in time or in genealogical order; †*concr.* a single step backward in genealogy 1628. **4.** Method or way of ascending 1600; *concr.* a way up; upward slope; a flight of steps, etc. 1611. †**5.** An eminence –1742.

1. To him with swift a. he up return'd MILT. *P. L.* x. 224. **2.** The a. of the Simplon DICKENS. **4.** With one a. Accessible from Earth MILT. *P. L.* v. 545.

Ascertain (æsəɹtē̆·n), *v.* [ME. *acertein,-ain*, a. OF. *acertaine-, acertener* (late AF. *asser-*), f. *à* + *certain* CERTAIN. In Eng. assim. to *certain*, and orig. pronounced ăsə̄·ɹtĕn. The prefix *as-* for *ac-* is etym. erron.] †**1.** *trans.* To make (a person) certain; to assure; *loosely*, To inform, apprise. Const. *simply*, with †*of*, or †*subord. cl.* –1789. *refl.* To make oneself certain –1731. **2.** *trans.* To make (a thing) certain to the mind (*arch.*) 1494; †to establish as a certainty –1810. **3.** To find out or learn for a certainty; to make sure of, get to know. (The only current use.) 1794. †**4.** To ensure, secure (*to* a person) –1823. †**5.** To bring or deliver certainly, destine or doom (a person) *to* –1667. †**6.** To make (a thing) certain, or definite; to decide, fix, limit –1789.

1. Who may .. Be ascertained that Two and Two make four CHURCHILL. **2.** [This] would a. it not to be the production of Johnson BOSWELL. **3.** Legal measures for ascertaining the culprit GEO. ELIOT. **6.** Some effectual method for correcting, enlarging, and ascertaining our language SWIFT. Hence **Ascertai·nable** *a.* that may be ascertained (senses 3, 6). **Ascertai·nableness. Ascertai·nably** *adv.* **Ascertai·ned** *ppl. a.* †fixed; known. **Ascertai·ner.**

Ascertainment (æsəɹtē̆·nmĕnt). 1657. [f. ASCERTAIN *v.* + -MENT.] The process or result of ascertaining. **1.** Reduction to certainty; exact determination (*arch.*). **2.** Finding out, discovery 1799.

Ascescent, -ency, erron. vars. ACESCENT, -ENCY.

Ascetic (ăse·tik). 1646. [ad. Gr. ἀσκητικός, f. ἀσκητής a monk or hermit, f. ἀσκέ-ειν to exercise; see -IC.] **A.** *adj.* **1.** Of or pertaining to the Ascetics, or to the exercise of rigorous self-discipline; severely abstinent, austere. **2.** = ASCETICAL 1. 1822.

1. A. discipline BURKE, gloom TENNYSON.

B. *sb.* **1.** *Eccl. Hist.* One of those who in the early church retired into solitude, to exercise themselves in meditation and prayer, and in the practice of rigorous self-discipline by celibacy, fasting, and toil 1673. **2.** *gen.* One who is extremely rigorous in self-denial 1660. **3.** *pl.* An ascetical treatise 1751.

1. The Ascetics, who obeyed and abused the rigid precepts of the gospel GIBBON.

Asce·tical, *a.* 1617. [f. prec. + -AL.] **1.** Pertaining to, or treating of, the spiritual exercises by which perfection and virtue may be attained, as in *Ascetical Theology.* **2.** = ASCETIC *a.* 1. 1836. Hence **Asce·tically** *adv.*

Asceticism (ăse·tisiz'm). 1646. [f. ASCETIC + -ISM.] The principles or practice of the Ascetics.

Ascham (æ·skăm). 1860. [f. *Ascham*, author of *Toxophilus.*] A sort of cupboard or case to contain implements of archery.

Ascians (æ·ʃiănz), *sb. pl.* 1635. [f. med.L. *Ascii* (also used), a. Gr. ἄσκιοι, f. ἀ + σκιά.] Inhabitants of the torrid zone, who twice a year have the sun directly overhead, and then cast no shadows.

Ascidian (ăsi·diăn), *a.* 1835. [f. mod.L. *Ascidia* (see ASCIDIUM) + -AN.] *Zool.* Of or pertaining to the Ascidia (or Ascidiæ), a group belonging to the tunicate Mollusca 1856. As *sb.* [sc. *animal.*] Hence **Asci·dia·rium,** the aggregate mass of organisms in compound Ascidians. **Asci·dioid** *a.* resembling the Ascidia. **Asci·diozo·oid,** one of the organisms forming an ascidiarium.

‖**Ascidium** (ăsi·diŏm). Pl. **-a.** 1766. [mod. L., ad. Gr. ἀσκίδιον, dim. of ἀσκός.] **1.** *Zool.* (Also *Ascidia*, pl. *-æ.*) A genus of tunicate molluscs, having the enveloping tunic elastic and leathery. **2.** *Bot.* A pitcher-shaped leafy appendage 1830. Hence **Asci·diate, Asci·diform** *adjs.* shaped like an a.

Ascigerous (ăsi·dʒĕrəs), *a.* 1829. [f. mod. L. *ascus* + -(I)GEROUS.] *Bot.* Bearing or producing asci (see ASCUS).

Ascitan (ăsəi·tăn, æ·sităn). 1727. [f. mod. L. *Ascitæ*, a. Gr. Ἀσκῖται, f. ἀσκός; see -ITE, -AN.] *Eccl. Hist.* One of a heretical sect (2nd c.), who used to dance round an inflated wine-skin, in reference to *Matt.* ix. 17.

†**Asci·te,** earlier f. ACCITE *v.*

‖**Ascites** (ăsəi·tīz). ME. [L., a. Gr. ἀσκίτης (sc. ὕδρωψ), f. ἀσκός.] *Path.* A collection of serous fluid in the peritoneal cavity; dropsy of the abdomen. Hence **Asci·tic, -al** *a.*

Ascititious (æsiti·ʃəs), *a.* 1628. [f. L. *ascit-* = *adscit-*, *adsciscere* + -ITIOUS.] = ADSCITITIOUS (now more common).

Asclepiad[1] (ăsklī·piæ̆d). 1656. [ad. L. *Asclepiadeus*, a. Gr., f. Ἀσκληπιάδης.] *Gr. and L. Pros.* A verse, invented by Asclepiades, consisting of a spondee, two (or three) choriambi, and an iambus. Also *attrib.* Hence **Asclepiade·an** *a.*

Ascle·piad[2]. 1859. [f. next.] *Bot.* A plant of the order *Asclepiadaceæ*; see next. Hence **Asclepiada·ceous** *a.* of or belonging to this order. **Asclepiade·ous** *a.* of the genus *Asclepias.*

‖**Asclepias** (ăsklī·piæs). 1578. [mod.L., a. Gr., f. Ἀσκληπιός Æsculapius.] *Bot.* A genus of plants, giving its name to a N.O., including the Milkweed, Swallow-wort, etc.

Asco- (æ·sko), comb. f. ASCUS, used in *Bot.*: **asco·go·nium** [cf. *archegonium*], the spirally-coiled organ from which the asci are produced; **-myce·tal, -myce·tous** *a.* of or belonging to the *Ascomycetes*, or fungi, in which spores are formed asexually in the interior of asci; **-phorous** [Gr. -φορος] *a.*, producing asci; **-spore,** a spore developed in an ascus.

Ascribe (ăskrəi·b), *v.* [ME. *ascrive*, a. OF. *ascriv-, ascrire* :—L. *ascr-, adscribere.* Altered to *ascribe* after L. in 16th c.] †**1.** *trans.* To annex or add in writing, to subscribe –1649; to dedicate *to* –1563; to enroll in a class –1680; to appoint –1624. **2.** To enter *to*, or to the credit of, in an account; to assign, impute, refer, as due *to* ME. **3.** To reckon or count *to*, as a characteristic, etc. (*rarely* as a material possession); to claim for ME. †**4.** To count –1601. †**5.** with *compl.* To consider as. *refl.* To pretend *to be.* –1580.

2. We usually *ascribe* good, but *impute* evil JOHNSON. Others ascribed the whole disaster to the use of small notes HT. MARTINEAU. **3.** Ascribing .. All 'holiness unto the Lord' 1880. Hence **Ascri·bable** *a.* that may be ascribed; attributable.

†**Ascri·pt,** *ppl. a.* 1564. [ad. L. *ascriptus*: see ASCRIBE. Cf. ADSCRIPT.] Enrolled; appointed –1610.

Ascription (ăskri·pʃən). 1597. [ad. L. *ascriptionem*; see ASCRIBE. Cf. ADSCRIPTION.] †**1.** The act of ascribing (see ASCRIBE 1, 2, 3). **2.** *concr.* The declaration thus made 1845.

1. The theoretical a. of English law to immemorial unwritten tradition MAINE.

Ascriptitious (æskripti·ʃəs), *a. rare.* 1652. [f. L. *ascriptitius*; see ASCRIPT and -ITIOUS Cf. *adscriptitious.*] †**1.** Appended to a list 1658. **2.** Merely ascribed to. (Cf. *fictitious.*) 1652.

†**Ascry·,** *v.* [ME. *ascrie*, a. AF. **ascrier*, a. OF. *escrier* (mod. *écrier*), f. *es* :—L. *ex* + *crier.* Aphet. SCRY.] **1.** To call forth, out, or upon –1450; *esp.* to challenge –1523. **2.** *intr.* To shout, exclaim –1528. **3.** *trans.* = DESCRY; *hence* to espy; inform upon –1559. Hence †**Ascry·** *sb.* outcry, clamour.

‖**Ascus** (æ·skŏs). Pl. **-i.** 1830. [mod.L., a. Gr. ἀσκός.] *Bot.* A membranous tubular cell, *esp.* the sac-like cell at the end of the branches of the hyphæ in certain fungi, etc., in which the reproductive sporules or sporidia develop.

A-sea (ăsī·), *adv.* 1858. [A *prep.*[1]] On the sea; to the sea.

A-see·the, *adv.* 1879. [A *prep.*[1]] Seething.

A-seity (ēⁱsī·ĭti, ăsī·ĭti). 1691. [f. L. *a se* + -ITY; cf. Fr. *aséité.*] *Metaph.* Underived or independent existence.

Aselline (ăse·ləin), *a. rare.* 1855. [f. L. *asellus* + -INE.] Of or pertaining to a little ass, or to the two stars in Cancer called *Aselli.*

Aseptic (ēⁱse·ptik), *a.* 1859. [f. A- 14 + Gr. σηπτικός: cf. Gr. ἄσηπτος, and see ANTISEPTIC.] Not liable to putrefy; preventing putrefaction. Also as *sb.* Hence **Ase·pticism.**

Asexual (ēⁱse·ksiuăl), *a.* 1830. [A- 14.] *Biol.* Not sexual, without sex. In *Bot.* formerly of cryptogams; cf. AGAMIC. Hence **Ase:xua·lity,** a. condition, absence of sex.

†**Asfa·st, as fast,** *adv. phr.* ME. only. Formerly in the special sense of: As fast as might be, straightway (Fr. *aussitôt*).

Ash (æʃ), *sb.*[1] [Com. Teut.: OE. *æsc.*] **1.** a. A forest tree, indigenous to Europe, Western Asia, and North Africa; having silver-grey bark, pinnate foliage, a peculiar winged seed or samara called the 'ash-key', and tough close-grained wood valuable for implements. **b.** The tribe of trees *Fraxineæ*, N.O. *Oleaceæ*, including the Common Ash (*Fraxinus excelsior*) and the Manna or Flowering Ashes (*Ornus Europæa* and *rotundifolia*). OE. **2.** The timber of the ash-tree ME. †**3.** The ashen shaft of a spear; a spear –1700.

1. The warlike beech; the a. for nothing ill SPENSER *F. Q.* I. i. 9. **3.** My grained A. *Cor.* IV. v. 114.

Comb.: **a.-key,** the winged two-celled seed or samara of the ash-tree; **-leaf,** an early potato with leaves like ash-leaves. **Ground Ash,** an ash sapling; an umbelliferous herb with pinnate leaves, *esp.* the ASHWEED, and Wild Angelica. **Mountain Ash,** the Rowan-tree or Quickbeam (*Pyrus Aucuparia*); occas. the

Aspen (*Populus tremula*), called also **Quaking Ash, Wild Ash**, occas. the Mountain Ash; also the *Ornus*.

Ash (æʃ), *sb.*² ; commonly in *pl.* **ashes** (æ·ʃéz). [Com. Teut.: OE. *asce, axe.*] **1.** The powdery residue, chiefly earthy or mineral left after the combustion of any substance. *pl.* OE. *collect. sing.* ME. *simple sing.* ME. Also *transf.* or *fig.* **2.** That which remains of a human body (*orig.*) after cremation or (*transf.*) total decomposition; hence *poet.* for 'mortal remains' ME. **3.** Dust of the ground. (Hence applied to man's mortal constitution.) OE. **4.** Death-like pallor; the colour of wood ashes ME. **5.** A symbol of grief or repentance OE.

1. Sprinkle sordid ashes all around DRYDEN. A charring ember, smouldering into a. 1868. My heart is within me As an a. in the fire SWINBURNE. *Volcanic ash*: the powdery matter ejected from volcanoes. *Black ash*: a mixture of carbonate of soda and sulphide of calcium formed in manufacturing soda from salt. *To lay in ashes*: to burn to the ground; Whole kingdoms laid in ashes ADDISON. **2.** I commende.. thy body to the grounde,..asshes to asshes, dust to dust *Bk. Com. Pr.* E'en in our ashes live their wonted fires GRAY. **b.** *The Ashes*: the symbolical remains of English cricket taken back to Australia. N.E.D. Suppl. **3.** Lord, what shall Earth and Ashes do? WESLEY. **4.** The lip of ashes, and the cheek of flame BYRON. **5.** Repents..not in ashes, and sackecloath, but in new Silke, and old sacke 2 *Hen. IV*, I. ii.

Comb.: **a.-bin**, a receptacle for ashes, etc.; **-fire**, a low fire of ash and cinders; **-furnace**, one used in glass-making; **-heap**; **-hole**; **-leach**, a hopper or tub in which wood-ashes are placed that the alkaline salts may be dissolved from them; **-like** *a.*; **-oven** (= *-furnace*); **-pan**; **-pit**; **-tub** (= *-bin*).

Ash (æʃ), *v.*¹ *dial.* [f. ASH *sb.*¹] To flog with an ash-stick. Cf. *To birch.*

Ash (æʃ), *v.*² 1645. [f. ASH *sb.*²] To strew with ashes.

†**Asha·ke**, *v.* [OE. *asceacan.*] To shake off; *fig.* to dispel –ME.

A-sha·ke, *adv.* 1856. [A *prep.*¹] Shaking.

Ashame (ăʃē¹·m), *v.* OE. [f. A- *pref.* 1 + OE. *sc(e)amian.*] †**1.** *intr.* To feel shame –1566. **2.** *trans.* To put to shame 1591.

Ashamed (ăʃē¹·md), *pred. a.* OE. [pa. pple. of prec.] **1.** Affected with shame; abashed or put to confusion; disconcerted. Const. *of*, †*on*, †*for* ME.; with *subord. cl.* ME.; with *inf. phr.* 1647. **2.** With *inf. phr.*: Reluctant through fear of shame *to*. With a negative: Prevented by fear of shame from. ME. Rarely *attrib.*

1. In Milton, the Devil is never described a. but once ADDISON. A. of sitting idle JOHNSON, to be seen TENNYSON. **2.** I am aschamyd to begge WYCLIF *Luke* xvi. 3. Hence **Asha·medness.**

Ashen (æ·ʃĕn), *a.*¹ ME. [f. ASH *sb.*¹ + -EN.] **1.** Of or pertaining to an ash-tree 1562. **2.** Made of the wood of an ash ME.

Ashen (æ·ʃĕn), *a.*² 1808. [f. ASH *sb.*² + -EN.] **1.** Of ashes. Also *fig.* 1850. **2.** Ash-coloured, deadly pale 1808.

2. The a. hue of age SCOTT.

Ashery (æ·ʃĕri). 1859. [f. ASH *sb.*² + -ERY.] **a.** A place where potash or pearlash is manufactured. **b.** An ash-pit.

Ashet (æ·ʃĕt). *north. dial.* 1552. [a. Fr. *assiette.*] A dish, or platter.

A-shi·ne, *adv.* 1840. [A *prep.*¹] Shining.

A-shi·pboard, *adv.* 1598. On board ship.

A-shi·ver, *adv.* 1840. [A *prep.*¹] In a shiver.

Ashlar (æ·ʃlǝɹ). ME. [a. OF. *aiseler, aisselier*:—L. *axillaris*, f. *axilla*, dim. of *axis, assis*, 'axle', also 'board, plank'. The use of wood preceded that of stone.] **1.** A square hewn stone for building purposes or for pavement (?so called as resembling a wooden beam); also used as a missile. Called also *Ashlar-stone.* **2.** Masonry of hewn stone, usu. in thin slabs, used as a facing to rubble or brick wall. Also *attrib.* 1681.

1. A. stones of the Bastille continue thundering through the dusk CARLYLE. *Ashlar-work*: masonry constructed of square hewn stones; opp. to *rubble-work*. *Ashlar-rafter, -piece* = *ashlaring.* Hence **A·shlared** *ppl. a.* covered with a.; cf. 2. **A·shlaring** *vbl. sb.* the short upright quartering fixed in garrets between the rafters and the floor, to cut off the angles formed by the rafters. Also, ashlar masonry.

Ashling (æ·ʃliŋ). 1883. [f. ASH *sb.*¹] An ash sapling.

Ashore (ăʃōǝ·ɹ), *adv.* 1586. [A *prep.*¹] **1.** To the shore; to land. **2.** On shore, on land 1631.

1. I must be getting a. now BLACK. **2.** He behaves himself a. as if he were still on board STEELE.

Ash-We·dnesday. ME. [f. ASH *sb.*² + WEDNESDAY.] The first day of Lent; so called from the custom introduced by Pope Gregory the Great of sprinkling ashes on the heads of penitents on that day.

Ashweed (æ·ʃwīd). 1578. [f. ASH *sb.*¹] *Herb.* The Goutweed (*Ægopodium Podagraria*).

Ashy (æ·ʃi), *a.* ME. [f. ASH *sb.*²] **1.** Consisting of ashes 1483. **2.** Covered or sprinkled with ashes ME. **3.** Ash-coloured, deadly pale 1541. **4.** quasi-*adv.* 1592.

Eyebrows..you can see are a.-blond CARLYLE.

Asian (ē¹·ʃiăn). *arch.* 1563. [ad. L. *Asianus.*] = ASIATIC.

Asiarch (ē¹·ʃi,āɹk). 1753. [ad. L. *Asiarcha*, ad. Gr. Ἀσιάρχης, f. Ἀσία + -αρχης.] Director of religious rites, etc. in Asia Minor under the Romans. (Cf. *Acts* xix. 31.)

Asiatic (ē¹ʃi,æ·tik), *a.* 1631. [ad. L. *Asiaticus*, a. Gr., f. Ἀσία.] Of or pertaining to Asia or its inhabitants; formerly applied to literary style. As *sb.* A native of Asia. Hence **Asia·tically** *adv.* in A. manner, in accordance with A. customs. **Asia·ticism**, an A. phrase or practice. **Asia·ticize** *v.*, improp. **A·siatize**, to make A., to conform to A. customs.

It is A. prose, as the Ancient Critics would have said; prose somewhat barbarously rich M. ARNOLD.

Aside (ăsǝi·d). ME. [orig. *on side*; see A *prep.*¹ (In U.S. often = Eng. *apart.*)] **A.** *adv.* **I.** Of motion. **1.** To one side; out of the way, away. **2.** Into seclusion or privacy, apart 1450. **3.** Away from one's person; off, down 1596. **4.** Out of thought or use 1440.

1. To..slip a. from difficulty BURKE. **2.** But soft, a.; heere comes the King *Haml.* v. i. 240. **3.** Let us lay a. every weight *Hebr.* xii. 1. **4.** *To lay or set a.*: (*fig.*) to put away, dismiss; He often laid a. decorum 1798. *Law. To set a.* (a verdict, etc.): to quash it.

II. Of direction. **1.** Off from the direct line ME. **2.** Sidewise, obliquely ME.; var. †**Asi·den.**

1. They are all gone a., they are together become filthy *Ps.* xiv. 3.

III. Of position. †**1.** On one side, off –1610. **2.** Apart from the general company; in privacy ME. **3.** *A. from*: besides 1818 *U.S.*

2. *To speak a., i. e.* apart, so as to be (supposed) inaudible to the general company, or, on the stage, to the other players.

B. *prep.* [by omission of *of.*] **1.** At the side of 1615. †**2.** Past, beyond –1663.

C. *sb.* [the *adv.* used *attrib.*] **1.** Words spoken aside, or in an undertone, so as to be (supposed) inaudible to some person or persons present 1727. **2.** An indirect or side effort (*mod.*).

2. The asides of many writers possess a more lasting ..influence than their deliberate..labours 1877.

A-si·mmer, *adv.* 1849. [A *prep.*¹] On the simmer.

†**Asine·go.** 1606. [a. Sp. *asnico*, dim. of *asno.*] **1.** A little ass –1685. **2.** A fool, dolt –1714.

2. An Asinico may tutor thee; Thou..Asse SHAKS.

Asinine (æ·sinǝin), *a.* 1610. [ad. L. *asininus*, f. *asinus.*] **1.** Of or pertaining to asses 1624. **2.** Like an ass; obstinate, stupid 1610.

1. Her a. dayrie 1624. **2.** A. employ COWPER. Hence **Asini·nity**, stupidity.

Asiphonate (ăsǝi·fǝnē¹t), *a.* 1859. [f. A- *pref.* 14 + SIPHONATE.] *Zool.* Having no respiratory siphon. As *sb.* An acephalous mollusc so characterized.

-asis, *suff.*, L. *-āsis*, Gr. -ᾱσις, forming names of diseases, really nouns of state or process, as *elephantiasis, psoriasis*, etc.

‖**Asitia** (ăsi·ʃiă). 1853. [mod.L., a. Gr. ἀσιτία, f. ἀ + σῖτος.] *Path.* Loathing, or, more correctly, a want, of food.

Ask (ask), *v.* [Com. Teut.: OE. *ásćian, ácsian*. Till *c* 1600 *ax* was, but *ask* is now, the literary form.] †**I.** *trans.* To call for –ME.

II. 1. To call upon for information or an answer: **a.** *trans.* With the thing asked as object OE.; †*at* (still *dial.*), †*to*, *of* a person ME.; **b.** With the person asked as object OE.; with the thing asked as second object OE.; *of* (arch.), *about* (a matter), *after* or *for* (a person) OE. **2.** With no object expressed: To inquire †*of, about, after* (a thing or person), *for* (a person) OE.

1. a. To a. what I wanted STEELE. To a. a question, the price, a name (*mod.*). A farmer of whom I asked the way (*mod.*). **b.** Aske my dogge *Two Gent.* II. v. 36. Aske mee if I am a Courtier *All's Well* II. ii. 38. To a. a person the way, his name, etc. (*mod.*), of his early life TENNYSON. **2.** To ask *for* a person; to ask to see; formerly = to ask *after*. A. for this great Deliverer now, and find him Eyeless in Gaza at the Mill with slaves MILT. *Sams.* 40.

III. 1. To make request for: **a.** *trans.* With the thing asked as object; *simply* ME.; *of, from* a person ME.; *to do* or *be done to* ME.; **b.** *trans.* With the person asked as object ME.; *to do* or *for* (a thing) ME. **2.** To make request: With no object ME.; *for* (a thing) ME.

1. a. I axe no more 1570. *To a. a price*: to a. so much as the price. To a. another favour of [anyone] BURNS. **b.** I a. Mr. Blifil pardon FIELDING. I asked him to accompany me TYNDALL. I might aske you for your Commission *A. Y. L.* IV. i. 138. **2.** Aske and it shalbe giuen you *Matt.* vi. 7. I'll .. a. for leave DICKENS. *To ask for*: to act so as to incur.

IV. Pregnant senses and special uses. †**1.** To investigate –1612. **2.** To ask as by right, call for, demand; *esp.* in *To ask an account* ME. **3.** To make proclamation in church, etc., calling on any who have claims or objections to put them forward; *esp.* in *To ask* (now *To publish*) *the banns* 1450. **4.** *ellipt.* To ask to come, invite (*mod.*). **5.** *fig.* Predicated of things: Need, call for ME.

4. We ought to a. him to dinner (*mod.*). **5.** To give a Milton birth ask'd ages more COWPER.

Ask (ask), *sb.* ME. [app. worn down from OE. *áđexe* newt.] A newt or eft; *Sc.* and *north.* occ. also the lizard. See also ASKER ².

Askance (ăska·ns), *adv.* 1530. [app. later f. ASKOY(N)E infl. by ASKANCE(S.] **1.** Sideways, askew, asquint; with a side meaning 1876. **2.** *ellipt.*, quasi-*adj.* Turned sideways 1593.

1. To look at, eye, view askance: to look at with disdain, envy, jealousy, and now *esp.* with mistrust. **2.** Whom the grand foe, with scornful eye a., Thus answerd MILT. *P. L.* VI. 149.

†**Aska·nce**, *v.* [f. prec.] To turn aside. SHAKS. *Lucr.* 637.

†**Aska·nce(s**, *conj. adv.* late ME. [app. f. As *adv.* + OF. *quanses* as if:—pop.L. **quam si* (whence MDu. *quansijs*, Du. *kwansuis*).] **1.** As though –1580. **2.** *ellipt.* As if saying –1572.

Askant (ăska·nt), *adv.* 1695. [app. var. of ASKANCE, after ASLANT, etc.] = ASKANCE. ¶ In SHAKS. *Haml.* (Qos.) IV. vii. 167 *ascaunt* is read, but the folios have *aslant.*

†**A·skapart.** ME. Name of a race of warriors living near Arabia; also of a giant assailed by Sir Bevis of Southampton –1735.

Asker ¹ (a·skǝɹ). ME. [f. ASK *v.*] **1.** One who asks (questions, favours, gifts, alms, etc.). †**2.** A prosecutor; an exactor, oppressor –1483.

A·sker ². *dial.* 1674. [f. ASK *sb.*] A newt.

Askew (ăskiū·). 1573. [Related to SKEW *v.*, *a.*, and *adv.* But cf. ASCOYE (Lydg.).] **A.** *adv.* Obliquely, to one side, awry. **B.** *adj.* Made or standing awry; skew 1859. **C.** †*sb.* A sidelong glance 1655.

adv. Lattice blinds all hanging a. DICKENS. *To look askew*: i. e. sidelong, out at the corners of one's eyes; *fig.* to look as if pretending not to see; to reflect *upon*. *adj.* A. arches 1859, bridges 1862.

Asking (a·skiŋ), *vbl. sb.* OE. [f. ASK *v.*] **1.** The act of putting a question; †a question –ME. **2.** Praying, begging ME.; a petition, a prayer, etc. (*arch.*) ME. †**3.** A price asked –1637. †**4. a.** A calling for justice. **b.** Exaction. –1480. **5.** The publication of banns of marriage. *fam.* 1727. Hence **A·skingly** *adv.*

Askle·nt, ascle·nt, *adv.* Sc. f. ASLANT.

†**Askoye·, askoy·ne**, *adv.* ME. [*skoyne* is app. Du. *schuin* sidewise. But see ASQUINT, ASKEW, and note on ASKANCE.] Sidewise, askance. (Always with *look.*) –1552.

Aslake (ăslē¹·k), *v.* [OE. *aslacian*; see SLAKE *v.*] †**1.** *intr.* To become slack; to grow less –1587. **2.** To cool (*arch. rare*) 1810. **3.** To mitigate, assuage, abate (*arch.*) ME.

Aslant (ăsla·nt). ME. [f. ON (see A *prep.*¹) + SLANT.] *adv.* On the slant, in a sloping direction, obliquely. quasi-*adj.* Slanting 1790. *prep.* Across in a slanting direction 1602.

prep. There is a Willow growes a. a Brooke SHAKS.

Asleep (ăslī·p), *adv.* and *pred. a.* ME. [f. A *prep.*¹ 11 + SLEEP.] **1.** In a state of sleep; *fig.* at rest, dormant, idle 1590. **2.** Into a state of sleep ME.; *fig.* of inactivity or quiescence 1545. **3.** *fig.* Dead ME. **4.** *transf.* Of the limbs:

Benumbed. Formerly also=Stunned. ME. **5.** *Naut.* The sail just bellying out (opp. to *flapping*) 1867.

1. *fig.* Their pride and mettall is asleepe SHAKS. 2. By whispering winds soon lull'd a. MILT. *L'Alleg.* 116. 3. David..fell on sleepe and was laide vnto his fathers *Acts* xiii. 36. 4. Leaning long upon any part maketh it numme, and, as wé call it, asleepe BACON.

Aslope (ăslō̆u·p), *a.* and *adv.* ME. [prob. f. OE. *aslopen* pa. pple.; or f. *slope* + A- *pref.* 2, though *aslope* is earlier.] *adj.* Inclined, slanting. *adv.* On the incline, aslant, crosswise, athwart. Also *fig.*

While the first drizzling show'r is borne a. SWIFT.

A-slu·g, *adv.* 1619. [A *prep.*[1]] Sluggishly.

A-smea·r, *adv.* 1861. [A *prep.*[1]] Smeared.

A-smou·lder, *adv.* 1880. [A *prep.*[1]] Smouldering.

A-sno·rt, *adv.* 1850. [A *prep.*[1]] Snorting.

A-soa·k, *adv.* 1609. [A *prep.*[1]] Soaking.

Asomatous (ăsō̆u·mătəs), *a.* 1731. [f. L., a. Gr. ἀσώματος.] Unembodied, incorporeal.

A-sou·th, *adv.* 1809. [A *prep.*[1]] In the south.

Asp[1] (asp). [Com. Teut.: OE. *æspæ, æspe, æps=æsp.* See ASPEN.] **1.** A poplar (*Populus tremula*), with greyish bark and spreading branches, the leaves of which are especially tremulous. Also *attrib.* OE. **2.** The wood of this tree 1551.

1. Cherry and quaking a... belted the little brook 1848.

Asp[2] (asp). ME. [ad. L. *aspis* (formerly used, with pl. *aspisses*), a. Gr. ἀσπίς. See also ASPIC[1].] *Zool.* **1.** A small, venomous, hooded serpent, found in Egypt and Libya; the *Naje Haje.* **2.** Also a species of Viper (*Vipera Aspis*), and *poet.* any venomous serpent 1712.

1. The venym of eddris, *that ben clepid aspis,* vndur her lippis WYCLIF *Rom.* iii. 13.

‖**Aspalathus** (ăspæ·lăþʊ̆s). 1601. [L., a. Gr. ἀσπάλαθος.] A genus of African shrubs (N.O. *Leguminosæ*); the fragrant wood of some.

A sweete smell like cinamon, and a. *Ecclus.* xxiv. 15.

‖**Aspalax** (æ·spălæks). 1860. [L., a. Gr. ἀσπάλαξ, usu. σπάλαξ.] *Zool.* A genus of Rodentia, resembling the mole.

Asparagine (ăspæ·radʒəin). 1813. [f. ASPARAGUS + -INE.] *Chem.* A nitrogenous crystallizable compound contained esp. in asparagus. It is primary malic diamide $C_4H_4O_3(NH_2)_2$.

Asparaginous (æspăræ·dʒinəs), *a.* 1832. [f. prec.] Allied to or like asparagus.

Asparagus (ăspæ·răgəs). OE. [L., a. Gr. ἀσπάραγος, prop. ἀσφ-, of doubtful origin. In med.L. often *sparagus*, whence Eng. *sperage* (16th and 17th c.), displaced subseq. by *asparagus*, aphet. *'sparagus*, whence *spara-, sparrow-grass* (18th c.). Now *asparagus* is the polite form.] A plant (*Asparagus officinalis*, N.O. *Liliaceæ*), the vernal shoots of which form a delicacy of the table. *Bot.* The genus of which this is a species.

I will have Sparagus every meale all the yeare long BROME. A hundred of Sparrowgrass PEPYS.

Comb. **a.-beetle**, a small beetle (*Crioceris Asparagi*), that feeds upon the foliage of the a.

Aspara·mic, Aspa·ramide = ASPARTIC, ASPARAGINE.

A-spa·rkle, *adv.* 1840. [A *prep.*[1]] Sparkling.

Aspartic (ăspā·ɹtik), *a.* 1847. [f. (arbitrarily) *asparagus.*] *Chem.* Of or pertaining to asparagine; *esp.* in *Aspartic acid*, $C_4H_7NO_4$.

Aspect (æ·spekt). ME. [ad. L. *aspectus*, f. *a-, ad-spicere.* Still occas. *aspe·ct*, as in Shaks., Milt., etc.] **I. 1.** †The action of looking at; contemplation; gaze, view –1810; a look, a glance (also *fig.*) 1590. †**2.** Mental looking; regard, respect– 1673.

1. That the basilisk killeth by a. BACON. Some other Mistresse hath thy sweet aspects *Com. Err.* II. ii. 113.

II. 1. *Astrol.* The relative positions of the planets as they appear to an observer on the earth's surface at a given time. (*prop.* The way in which, from their relative positions, they look upon each other.) ME. **2.** A looking, facing, or fronting, in a given direction; exposure 1667; the side or surface which fronts in any direction 1849. **3.** Bearing; reference *to* 1509. **4.** A phase 1824. **5.** *Gram.* A verbal form used to express action or being in respect of its inception, duration, or completion 1853.

1. Frendly aspectys of planetes CHAUCER. Aspects In Sextile, Square, and Trine, and Opposite MILT. *P. L.* x. 658. 2. The setting Sun..with right a. Against the eastern Gate of Paradise MILT. *P. L.* IV. 541. 3. Divers things..which I hope have a public a. CROMWELL. 4. Two aspects of one..thought 1870.

III. 1. The look which one wears; countenance, face 1590. **2.** The appearance presented to the eye 1594; to the mind 1704. †**3.** *concr.* A thing seen; an appearance –1722.

1. Thy martial face and stout aspect MARLOWE. Of ..vinegar a. SHAKS. 2. The physical a. of the country GREEN. The superficial aspects of Buddhism 1883. Hence **Aspe·ctable, -ible** *a.* (now *rare*), visible; fit or fair to look upon. †**Aspe·ctful** *a.* benignant.

†**Aspe·ct**, *v.* 1548. [ad. L. *aspectare*, freq. of *aspicere.* Cf. *respect*, etc.] **1.** To look for, expect –1584. **2.** To look at, behold; watch –1698. **3.** Of a planet: To look upon another in one of the 'Aspects' –1671. **4.** To look on with favour (*rare*) 1663. **5.** *intr.* To look; to have a bearing –1651. Hence **Aspe·ctant** *a.* *Her.* facing each other. **A·spected** *ppl. a.* †**1.** (*aspe·cted*). Looked at. †**2.** *pple.* or *adj.* Looked at by a planet. **3.** *adj.* Having an aspect.

†**Aspe·ction.** 1646. [ad. L. *aspectionem.*] The act of looking at, watching –1652.

Aspen (a·spĕn). ME. [f. ASP[1]; cf. *ashen.*] *adj.* **1.** Of or belonging to the asp; see ASP[1]. **2.** *fig.* Tremulous; timorous ME. *sb.* = ASP[1] 1596.

1. Lyk an a. leaf he quok for ire CHAUCER. 2. A. fear CHAPMAN.

†**A·sper, a·spre,** *a.* ME. [a. OF. *aspre* (mod. *âpre*):—L. *asper.*] **1.** Rough, rugged –1681. **2.** Harsh in sound or taste –1639. **3.** Harsh to the feelings; cruel –1578. **4.** Of persons: Harsh –1630. **5.** Hardy; mettled, savage –1503.

‖**Asper** (æ·spəɹ), *sb.*[1] [L. *asper* (sc. *spiritus*); see prec.] *Gr. Gram.* The rough breathing; the sign (ʽ) above an initial vowel, or over ρ, = Roman *h*; thus ὥς = *hōs*, ῥάβδος = *rhabdos.*

Asper (æ·spəɹ), *sb.*[2] 1589. [a. Fr. *aspre*, ad. Byzantine Gr. ἄσπρον, f. ἄσπρος white (said to be ad. L. *asper*).] A silver Turkish coin (120 aspers = 1 piastre); now a 'money of account.'

Asperate (æ·spĕrĕt), *ppl. a.* 1623. [ad. L. *asperatus.*] Roughened, rough. Hence **A·sperate** *v.* to make rough, rugged, or harsh.

Asperge (ăspə̄·ɹdʒ), *v.* 1547. [a. F. *asperger*, ad. L. *aspergere.*] To sprinkle, besprinkle.

Aspe·rge, *sb.* 1579. [f. prec. or next.] †A sprinkling of holy water; also, an aspergillum.

Asperges (ăspə̄·ɹdʒiz). 1553. [a. L. *asperges*, in *Asperges me, Domine, hyssopo et mundabor*, the opening words of the mass. Cf. F. *aspergès.*] *R.C.Ch.* = prec.

Aspergill (æ·spəɹdʒil), and ‖**Aspergillum** (æspəɹdʒi·lŏ̆m). 1649. [f. L. *aspergere* + *-illum* dim. suffix; cf. *vexillum.*] *R.C.Ch.* A kind of brush used to sprinkle holy water; see ASPERGES. (The L. form is the more usual.) Hence **Aspergi·lliform** *a.* shaped like an a., as the stigmas of some grasses.

‖**Aspergi·llus.** 1847. *Biol.* A genus of microscopic fungi, resembling the holy-water sprinkler in appearance.

Asperifoliate, -ous (æ:spĕrifō̆u·liĕt, -liəs), *a.* 1686. [f. mod.L. *asperifolius* (f. *asper* + *folium*) + -ATE, -OUS.] *Bot.* Having rough leaves; formerly *spec.* of the *Boragineæ.*

Asperity (ăspe·rĭti). [ME. *asprete*, a. OF. *asprete* (mod. *âpreté*):—L. *asperitatem*; assim. to the L. word.] **1.** Unevenness of surface, roughness; *concr.* in *pl.* sharp or rough excrescences 1491. **2.** Roughness of savour, tartness (*arch.*) 1620. **3.** Harshness of sound (*arch.*) 1664. **4.** Of style: Lack of polish, ruggedness (*arch.*) 1779. **5.** *fig.* Harshness to the feelings; *hence*, hardship, difficulty. (The earliest sense; *arch.* exc. in **b.** Bitter coldness, rigour.) ME. **6.** Harshness of temper; crabbedness, acrimony; in *pl.* harsh, embittered feelings 1664.

1. The asperities of the Moon H. MORE. 3. Our language, of which the chief defect is ruggedness and a. JOHNSON. 5. The nakedness and a. of the wintry world JOHNSON. 6. A. of reply JOHNSON.

†**A·sperly,** *adv.* ME. [f. ASPER *a.*] Harshly; fiercely, bitterly –1531.

Aspermous (ăspə̄·ɹməs), *a.* 1853. [f. Gr. ἄσπερμος + -OUS.] *Bot.* and *Phys.* Without seed. var. **Aspe·rmatous.** Hence **Aspe·rmatism,** lack of seed, impotence.

†**Aspe·rn(e,** *v. rare.* 1513. [ad. L. *asperna-ri.*] To spurn.

†**A·sperness.** [f. ASPER *a.*] Bitterness. CHAUCER.

A·sperous, *a.* 1547. [f. L. *asper* + -OUS. Cf. *dexterous*, etc.] **1.** Rough, rugged. (Now techn.) †**2.** Rough-tasted 1670. †**3.** Cruel –1653. Hence **A·sperously** *adv.* (*rare*).

Asperse (ăspə̄·ɹs), *v.* 1490. [f. L. *aspers-, aspergere*; see ASPERGE.] **1.** To besprinkle, bespatter *with.* **2.** To sprinkle, scatter 1607. †**3.** To intermingle –1607. **4.** To bespatter *with* damaging imputations, etc. In 17th c.: Injuriously and falsely to charge *with.* 1611. **5.** To slander, defame, traduce, vilify 1647.

1. She dide a. the place with the waters CAXTON. 4. The calumnies with which the Jews had aspersed him PALEY. 5. A libel tending to a. or vilify the house of Commons JUNIUS. To a. a man's character 1868. Hence **Aspe·rsed** *ppl. a.* 1. Besprinkled; *spec.* in *Her.* strewed or powdered with small charges. 2. Calumniated, defamed. †**Aspe·rsive** *a.* defamatory; †**-ly** *adv.*

Aspersion (ăspə̄·ɹʃən). 1553. [ad. L. *aspersionem*; see ASPERSE.] **1.** The action of besprinkling, or of sprinkling or scattering. **2.** That which is sprinkled 1610. **3.** The action of casting damaging imputations, or false and injurious charges; defamation 1633. **4.** A damaging report; a calumny, slander 1596.

1. A. may answer the true end of baptism BURNET. 3. Who by aspersions throw a stone At the head of others, hit their own G. HERBERT. 4. The a. of his being a great usurer FULLER.

‖**Aspersoir** (asperswar). 1851. [Fr.] An aspergillum.

‖**Aspersorium** (æspəɹsō̆ə·riŏ̆m). 1861. [med. L. f. *aspers-*; see -ORIUM.] A vessel for holding the holy water used in ceremonial sprinkling.

Asphalt (æ·sfælt, æsfæ·lt). Also **asphaltum,** esp. in scientific use. ME. [ad. late L. *asphalton, -tum*, a. Gr. ἄσφαλτον, var. of ἄσφαλτος, of foreign origin. The familiar use of asphalt pavement gave *a·sphalt.*] **1.** A smooth, hard, brittle, black or brownish-black resinous mineral, a mixture of different hydrocarbons; called also *mineral pitch, Jews' pitch*, and in the O.T. *slime* ME. Also *attrib.* **2.** A composition of bitumen, pitch, and sand, or made from natural bituminous limestones, used to pave streets and walks, etc. Mostly *attrib.* 1847.

1. Cressets fed With Naphtha and Asphaltus MILT. *P. L.* I. 729. A whole lake of a. is said to exist in.. Trinidad KIRWAN. 2. *Artificial asphaltum*: a mixture of coal-tar with sand, chalk, or lime. Hence **Aspha·lt** *v.* to cover or lay with a. **Aspha·lter,** one who lays down a. **Aspha·ltic** *a.* of the nature of, or containing, a., as in *Asphaltic Pool*: the Dead Sea MILT. **Aspha·ltite** *a.* asphaltic.

Asphaltene (æ:sfæltīn). 1837. [a. mod.F *asphaltène*, f. ASPHALT + -ENE.] *Chem.* An oxygenated hydro-carbon, supposed to be the solid constituent of asphalt.

Asphe·terism. 1794. [f. Gr. ἀ + σφέτερος, after σφετερισμός.] The doctrine that there ought to be no private property; communism. **Asphe·terize** *v.* to practise aspheterism (*rare*).

Asphodel (æ·sfŏdĕl). 1597. [ad. L., a. Gr. ἀσφόδελος, of unkn. origin. Earlier AFFODIL, whence DAFFODIL.] *Bot.* **1.** A genus of liliaceous plants, including the White Asphodel or King's Spear. **b.** By the poets made an immortal flower, and said to cover the Elysian meads. (Cf. Homer *Odyss.* XI. 539.) 1634. *attrib.* (occ. = 'Elysian'.) 1831. **2.** With qualifications: **a.** Bog, English, or Lancashire A. (*Narthecium Ossifragum*), common on moorlands. **b.** False A., in America, a species of Tofieldia. **c.** Scotch A. (*Tofieldia palustris*), a British subalpine plant.

1. b. The dead are made to eat Asphodels about the Elysian meadows SIR T. BROWNE. The a. meadows of their youth RUSKIN. Hence **Asphode·lian** *a.*

‖**Asphyxia** (æsfi·ksiă). 1706. [mod.L., a. Gr. ἀσφυξία, f. ἀ + σφύξις (whence *asphyxis*, also used). See ASPHYXY.] **1.** *lit.* Stoppage of the pulse. **2.** The condition of suspended animation produced by a deficiency of oxygen in the blood; suffocation. Also *fig.* 1778.

[In asphyxiated animals the pulse beats long after respiratory action has ceased.]

2. Lingering a. of soul O. W. HOLMES. Hence **Asphy·xial** *a.* of, pertaining to, or characterized by, a.

Asphyxiate (æsfi·ksi,ē̆it), *v.* 1836. [f. prec.]

To affect with asphyxia, to suffocate. Hence **A-sphy·xia·tion**, the action of producing asphyxia, or condition of being asphyxiated.

Asphyxiator (æsfi·ksi,eˡtəɹ). 1882. [f. as prec.; see -ATOR.] An asphyxiating agent; an apparatus for extinguishing fire by the agency of carbonic acid gas, etc.

Asphyxy (æsfi·ksi). 1784. [ad. F. *asphyxie*.] = ASPHYXIA. Hence **Asphyxy** *v.* to asphyxiate. (Chiefly in pa. pple.)

Aspic[1] (æ·spik). 1530. [a. F. *aspic*, a. Pr., unexplained deriv. of L. *aspidem*, *aspis*; see ASP[2].] 1. By-form of ASP[2], chiefly *poet.* Also *attrib.* Also *fig.* 1649. 2. *transf.* A piece of ordnance which carries a 12-pound shot. (? Fr.)

1. Showing the aspic's bite TENNYSON. A. poison LAMB. The Aspicke of invadeing feare 1649.

Aspic[2] (æ·spik). 1604. [a. F. *aspic* (in *huile d'aspic*) for *spic*, ad. It. *spigo* = OF. *espic* :—L. *spicus*, collateral form of *spica*.] The Great Lavender or Spike (*Lavandula Spica*).

Aspic[3] (æ·spik). 1789. [a. F. *aspic*, as in 'froid comme un aspic'. Littré.] A savoury meat jelly, made of and containing meat, fish, game, hard-boiled eggs, etc. Also *attrib.*

Aspidistra (æspidi·stră). 1822. [mod.L., f. Gr. ἀσπιδ-, ἀσπίς shield, after *tupistra*.] A plant of the liliaceous genus so named (of China and Japan), kept in dwelling rooms.

Aspirant (ăspəiə·rănt, *occas.* æ·spirănt). 1738. [a. F. and ad. L. *aspirantem*; see ASPIRE *v.*] *adj.* = ASPIRING 1814. *sb.* One who aspires; one who, with steady purpose, seeks advancement, privilege, or advantage 1738.

sb. The way to greatness was left clear to a new set of aspirants MACAULAY. The A. to the Mysteries WARBURTON.

Aspirate (æ·spirĕt). 1669. [ad. L. *aspiratus*; see ASPIRE *v.* Cf. Fr. *aspiré*.] **A.** *ppl. adj.* Aspirated.

B. *sb.* 1. A consonantal sound which is followed by or blended with the sound of H 1727. 2. The simple sound of the letter H, or its equivalent the *spiritus asper* (ʽ). *Esp.* applied to the initial *h-*. 1725.

1. That the aspirates.. are real mutes or contact sounds.. is beyond question WHITNEY. 2. A Middlemarch mercer of polite manners and superfluous aspirates GEO. ELIOT.

Aspirate (æ·spireˡt), *v.* 1700. [f. L. *aspirat-*; see prec. Cf. F. *aspirer*.] 1. To pronounce with a breathing; to prefix H to a vowel, or add H or its supposed equivalent to a consonant sound. Also *absol.* 2. To draw out a gas or vapour from a vessel; cf. ASPIRATOR 1880.

1. Our *w* and *h* aspirate DRYDEN. ¶ Erron. *asperate*, after *spiritus asper*.

Aspiration (æspireˡ·ʃən). ME. [ad. L. *aspirationem*; see ASPIRE.] I. (From ASPIRE.) †1. Inspiration –1535. 2. The action of breathing; a breath, sigh. *techn.* The drawing in of air in, or as in, breathing. 1607. 3. The action of aspiring; steadfast desire for something above one 1606.

3. That spirit of his In a. lifts him from the earth *Tr. & Cr.* IV. v. 16.

II. (From ASPIRATE.) 1. The action of aspirating; see ASPIRATE *v.* ME. 2. An aspirated sound or letter; the letter H or its equivalent; the breathings (ʽ) and (ʼ) in Greek; = ASPIRATE *sb.* 1550.

2. What is no substantial letter but a bare a. FULLER. ¶ Erron. *asperation*; see prec. ¶.

Aspirator (æ·spireˡtəɹ). 1863. [f. L. *aspirare*. Cf. F. *aspirateur*.] He who or that which aspirates, breathes, or blows upon; *spec.* **a.** an apparatus for drawing a stream of air or gas through a tube; **b.** an instrument for evacuating pus from abscesses by means of an exhausted receiver; **c.** a kind of winnowing machine. Hence **Aspi·ratory** *a.* of or pertaining to aspiration (*rare*).

Aspire (ăspəiə·ɹ), *v.* 1460. [ad. L. *asp-*, *adspirare*.] †1. *trans.* To breathe *to* or *into*, to inspire –1633; *intr.* to exhale (*rare*) –1750. 2. *intr.* To have a fixed desire or ambition for something at present above one; to seek to attain, to pant, long. Const. *to*; *after*, *at*, †*for*; with *inf.*; *absol.* 1460. †*trans.* To be ambitious of, aim at –1816. 3. *intr.* To rise up, as smoke, etc.; hence *gen.* to mount up, tower, rise high, become tall. Also *fig.* 1585. †*trans.* To mount up to, reach, attain. Also *fig.* –1596.

2. Woman oght to be repressed..if she a. to any dominion KNOX. Wilt thou a. to guide the heauenly Car *Two Gent.* III. i. 153. 3. Orgilio sees the golden pile a. JOHNSON. *trans.* That gallant spirit hath aspir'd the clouds *Rom. & Jul.* III. i. 122.

Aspirin (æ·spĭrin). 1899. [G.] A sedative drug composed of acetyl and salicylic acid; a dose of this.

Aspiring (aspəiə·riŋ). 1565. [f. prec.] *vbl. sb.* Aspiration 1584; †upward tapering 1634. *ppl. a.* 1. Of lofty aim, ambitious 1577. 2. Rising, tapering upward 1565. *fig.* 1579.

1. Two able and a. prelates. Hence **-ly** *adv.*, **-ness.**

A·spish, *a.* 1608. [f. ASP[2] + -ISH.] Of or pertaining to asps.

Asplenium, *Bot.*; see SPLEENWORT.

Asport (æspōə·ɹt), *v.* 1621. [ad. L. *asportare*, f. *as-* = *abs-* = *ab-* + *portare*.] To carry away, remove feloniously.

Asportation (æspoɹteˡ·ʃən). 1502. [ad. L. *asportationem*; see prec.] The action of carrying off; in *Law*, felonious removal of property.

A-spou·t, *adv.* 1870. [A *prep.*[1]] Spouting.

A-spraw·l, *adv.* 1878. [A *prep.*[1]] Sprawling.

A-sprea·d, *adv.* 1879. [A *prep.*[1]] Spread out.

Asprete, obs. f. ASPERITY.

A-sprou·t, *adv.* 1880. [A *prep.*[1]] Sprouting.

†**Aspy·**, *sb.* ME. [a. AF. **aspie* = OF. *espie*.] = SPY *sb.* –1467.

A-squa·t, *adv.* 1748. [A *prep.*[1]] Squatting.

Asquint (ăskwi·nt), *adv.* (and *a.*). ME. [? f. A *prep.*[1] + a word like Du. *schuinte* 'slant'. Aphet. to *squint* adv., whence *squint* vb. and sb.] 1. (To look) to one side; obliquely, out at the corners of the eyes ME. Also *transf.* and *fig.* 2. (To look) with suspicion, askance (*arch.*) ME.; with bias (*arch.*) 1605; furtively (*arch.*) 1727; †to cast a passing glance –1650. 3. *esp.* (To look) obliquely through defect in the eyes, so that they look in different directions ME. Also *fig.* 4. With other verbs (*rare*). Off to one side. ? *Obs.* 1645. 5. quasi-*adj.* (Only in pred. or after the sb. *eye*.) 1643.

A-squi·rm, *adv.* 1866. [A *prep.*[1]] Squirming (U.S.).

Ass (æs). [OE. *assa* m., perh. dim. of Old Northumbrian *asal*, *assal*, *assald*, from the Celtic, evidently ad. L. *asinus*, displacing *ęsol* for *ęsel*, the common Teut. form. The L. and Gr. names are prob. of Semitic origin.] 1. A quadruped of the horse kind, but smaller, with long ears, tuft at end of tail, and black stripe across the shoulders. Called also *donkey* in familiar use (in Scotland *cuddie*). **b.** *fig.* 'Beast of burden' 1614. **c.** In fables and proverbs, the type of clumsiness, ignorance, and stupidity. 2. Hence *transf.* An ignorant fellow, a conceited dolt 1578.

1. He shall but beare them, as the Asse beares Gold *Jul. C.* IV. i. 21. A braying a. COWPER. **c.** An unlettered king is a crowned a. FREEMAN.

Phrases: 1. *To make an ass of*: to treat as an ass, stultify. *To make an ass of oneself*: to behave absurdly. 2. *Asses' Bridge* or *Pons Asinorum*: a name given to the fifth proposition of the first book of Euclid's Elements. 3. *Astr.* The *Two Asses*: the stars γ and δ of the constellation Cancer, on either side of the nebula *Præsepe* (the *Crib*).

Ass, *v. nonce-wd.* To call ass 1592; to act the ass 1647.

Assafœtida, var. of ASAFŒTIDA.

Assagai, assegai (æ·săgai). 1625. [a. F. *azagaye*, or Pg. *azagaia*, a. Arab. *az-zaghāyah*, i. e. *az-* = *al-* the, *zaghāyah* native Berber word; *assegai* is newspaper spelling.] A slender spear or lance of hard wood, usu. pointed with iron, used in battle. Orig. the native name of a Berber weapon adopted by the Moors; in English use commonly the missile weapon of the South African tribes. **b.** *attrib.* **Assagai tree, wood,** a large South African tree (*Curtisia faginea*, N.O. *Cornaceæ*). Hence **A·ssagai, asse-** *v.* to pierce with an a.

‖**Assai** (assāi·), *adv.* [It.] *Mus.* A direction: Very; as in *adagio assai* = very slow.

Assail (ăseˡ·l), *v.* [ME. *asaile*, *assaile*, a. OF. *asalir*, *asaillir* (mod. *assaillir*):—late pop. L. *adsalire*, f. *ad* + *salire*. Refash. with *ass-* in 15th c., and in some senses influenced by ASSAY *v.*] To leap upon or at. 1. To attack **a.** by physical means; **b.** with hostile action or influence 1564; **c.** by speech or writing 1593. 2. To address with reasoning or argument 1440. 3. To approach with the intention of mastering (anything arduous) 1680. *fig.* Of states physical, emotional, or mental ME. 4. Of things: To dash against, encounter 1667. †5. To tempt, try –1564; to woo –1611. 6. *absol.* quasi-*intr.* in prec. senses ME. †7. To venture on, ASSAY –1595; *intr.* to endeavour, ASSAY –1606.

1. To a. one another like brute Beasts STEELE. **b.** Virtue may be assail'd, but never hurt MILT. *Comus* 589. Let crowds of Critics now my verse a. POPE. She assailed her husband on the subject of taking work 1833. 3. New pangs of mortal fear our minds a. DRYDEN. 4. No rude noise mine ears assailing COWPER. 5. Beauteous thou art, therefore to be assail'd SHAKS. *Sonn.* xli. 6. Though troubles a. NEWTON. Hence **Assai·l** *sb.* assault (*arch.*). **Assai·lable** *a.* open to assault, or hostile criticism. †**Assai·lableness. Assai·ler**, one who assails. **Assai·lment**, the action of assailing; power of assailing.

Assailant (ăseˡ·lănt). 1532. [a. F. *assaillant*; see prec.] *adj.* Assailing (*arch.*) 1592. *sb.* 1. He who, or that which, assails or attacks 1532. 2. A hostile critic 1665.

1. So shall we passe along, And neuer stir assailants SHAKS. 2. The assailants of the syllogism MILL.

Assamar (æ·sămāɹ). 1863. [f. L. *assus* + *amarus*.] *Chem.* Reichenbach's name for the bitter substance produced when gum, sugar, starch, gluten, meat, bread, etc. are roasted in the air till they turn brown.

Assapanick. 1706. [Amer. Ind.] *Zool.* The flying squirrel of Virginia and Maryland.

Assart (ăsā·ɹt), *v.* 1523. [a. AF. *assarter*, OF. *essarter*:—late L. *exsartare*, f. *ex* + **sartare*, freq. of *sar(r)ire* to hoe, weed.] *Law.* To grub up trees and bushes from forest-land, so as to make it arable. Also *absol.*

Assart (ăsā·ɹt), *sb.* 1598. [a. AF., OF. *essart*, perh. formed in Fr. on prec. vb. See also ESSART.] 1. A piece of land converted into arable by assarting 1628. 2. The action of assarting 1598. Also *attrib.* So †**Assa·rtment.**

A·ssary. 1727. [ad. Gr. ἀσσάριον, or L. *assarius* = As.] A Roman copper coin, translated by 'farthing' in N.T.

Assassin (ăsæ·sin). 1531. [a. F., or ad. It. *assassino*, ad. Arab. *ḥashshāshīn*, lit. 'hashish-eaters'. The European form is from the Arab. pl., as in *Bedouin*. Still accented *a·ssassin* in 1679.] 1. *lit.* A hashish-eater. *Hist.* (in *pl.*) Certain Moslem fanatics in the time of the Crusades, who were sent forth by their Sheikh, the 'Old Man of the Mountains', to murder the Christian leaders 1603. 2. Hence: One who undertakes to put another to death by treacherous violence. (Used chiefly of the murderer of a public personage.) 1531. Also *fig.* Also *attrib.*

1. The assassins..before they attacked an enemy, would intoxicate themselves with..an inebriating electuary, called *hashish* J. WOLFF. 2. *fig.* Lord Byron was the a. of his own fame DIBDIN. *attrib.* The a. spear DISRAELI. var. †**Assa·ssinant.**

†**Assa·ssin(e**, *v.* 1647. [a. F. *assassiner*; see prec.] To assassinate. Also *fig.* –1788.

†**Assa·ssinate**, *sb.* 1600. [In sense 1, app. a. F. *assassinat*, ad. med.L. *assassinatus*; sense 2 is unexplained.] 1. Assassination. Also *fig.* –1755. 2. = ASSASSIN 2. Also *fig.* –1737.

Assassinate (ăsæ·sineˡt), *v.* 1618. [f. med. L. *assassinat-*, *assassinare*; see ASSASSIN.] 1. To kill by treacherous violence. Also *absol.* †2. To attack by an assassin –1706. 3. *fig.* To destroy or wound by treachery 1626.

1. Brutus and Cassius..conspired to a. him 1618. 3. Your rhimes a. our fame DRYDEN. Hence †**Assa·ssinacy**, assassination. **Assa·ssinative** *a.* disposed to a. (*rare*). **Assa·ssinator**, an assassin. **Assa·ssinatress**, a female assassin. †**Assa·ssinous** *a.* of the nature of assassins MILT.

Assassination (ăsæ:sineˡ·ʃən). 1605. [f. ASSASSINATE; see -TION.] The action of assassinating; the taking the life of any one by treacherous violence, *esp.* by a hired emissary, or volunteer. Also *fig.*

If th' A. Could trammell vp the Consequence, and catch With his surcease, Successe *Macb.* I. vii. 2.

Assa·tion. ? *Obs.* 1605. [a. F., f. L. *assare.*] Roasting or baking.

Assault (ăsǭ·lt), *sb.* [ME. *asaut*, a. OF. *asaut* (later *assaut*) :—late pop. L. **adsaltus*, f. *saltus*; cf. ASSAIL. Altered to *assault* (after L.) *c* 1530.] **1.** *gen.* An onset with hostile intent; an attack with blows or weapons. **2.** The sudden charge of an attacking force against the walls of a city or fortress; a storm ME. **3.** An unlawful attack upon the person of another. (In *Law* a menacing word or action may constitute an *assault*; the term *battery* being added when an actual blow is inflicted.) 1447. **4.** An attack upon institutions, opinions, or customs 1449. **5.** *transf.* and *fig.* 1508. **6.** *esp.* An attack by spiritual enemies. (The earliest use in Eng.) ME. †**7.** A wooing –1611.

1. In which a., we lost twelue hundred men SHAKS. **Assault** (of or **at arms**): an attack made upon each other by two fencers, etc., as an exercise or trial of skill; a display of hand-to-hand military exercises. 2. *To make, give, a., to win, gain, take, carry by a.* 3. If one lifts up his cane, or his fist, in a threatning manner at another; or strikes at him, but misses him; this is an a. BLACKSTONE. 4. Assaults upon the prerogative of parliament CLARENDON. 5. The sharpe assautes of deth FISHER. 7. Inuincible against all assaults of affection *Much Ado* II. iii. 120.

Assault (ăsǭ·lt), *v.* 1450. [a. OF. *asauter*, f. L. *ad* + *saltare*, which replaced *ad-*, *as-sultare*, freq. of *adsalire*. Cf. prec. and ASSAIL.] **1.** To make a violent hostile attack by physical means upon; to commit an assault upon the person of (see ASSAULT *sb.* 3). Also *fig.* or *transf.* **2.** = ASSAIL *v.* 3. (*arch.* or *Obs.*) 1551. **3.** = ASSAIL *v.* 5. 1667. **4.** To come upon, attack, invade, as disease. (*arch.* or *Obs.*) 1594. **5.** To tempt, try. (*arch.* or *Obs.*) 1529. **6.** *absol.* chiefly in sense 1. 1489.

1. Naked as I am I will a. thee *Oth.* V. ii. 258. Assaulting the constable DE FOE. *To a. a city* or *fortress*: to storm it. 5. Satan ceaseth not to a. our faith ABP. SANDYS. Hence **Assau·ltable** *a.* **Assau·lter.**

†**Assau·t,** *adv.* (*adj.*) ME. [a. F. *à saut.*] In phr. *To go* or *be assau(l)t*: to seek the male, to rut –1601.

Assay (ăsē¹·), *sb.* Also aphet. SAY, and refash. ESSAY, q.v. ME. [a. OF. *assai*, *assay*, var. of *essai*, *essay* :—L. *exagium* 'weighing', f. *exagere*, *exigere*, to weigh, examine, test, etc. Replaced since 1600 by ESSAY.] **1.** The trying, in order to test the virtue, fitness, etc. (of a person or thing). *Obs.* exc. as fig. of 3. †**2.** 'Trial', tribulation –1671; experiment –1768; experience ME. only. **3.** *spec.* The trial of metals, by touch, fire, etc.; the determination of the quantity of metal in an ore or alloy; or of the fineness of coin or bullion ME. **4.** The substance to be assayed 1837. **5.** The trial of weights, measures, quality of bread, etc. by legal standard. Now *Hist.* 1601. **6.** Tasting (*arch.*) 1477; †*fig.* a foretaste –1605. **7.** The act of tasting the food or drink before giving it to an exalted personage. Now *Hist.* 1547. **8.** An endeavour (*arch.*) ME.; †best effort –1797. †**9.** An assault –1705; a first tentative effort –1677; a sample –1675. **10.** †**a.** Approved quality, proof, etc. of metal, etc. –1596. **b.** Standard of fineness in the precious metals 1820.

1. A great a. of the human soul RUSKIN. 2. My way must lie Through many a hard a. MILT. *P. R.* I. 263. 7. *Cup of assay*: a small cup with which a. of wine, etc. was taken. 8. A. of disobedience BACON. 9. Galling the gleaned Land with hot Assayes SHAKS. Phr.: **At all assays.** (Also *at all, every, assay.*) †At every trial, or time of need; hence: At all events; always –1658. †(Armed, ready) *at all assays*: ready for every event –1603. *Comb.*: **a.-master,** the master of an assay-house; **-ton,** a weight of 29166⅔ grams.

Assay (ăsē¹·), *v.* ME. [a. OF. *as(s)ayer*, *as(s)aier* :—late L. **exagiare*, f. *exagium*; see ASSAY *sb.* Now archaic for ESSAY.] **1.** To put to the proof, try; to test. *Obs.* exc. as fig. of 3. †*intr.* To make trial (*of*) –1576. †**2.** To try by touch (*lit.* and *fig.*) ME. **3.** To make an assay (see ASSAY *sb.* 3) 1440. Also *fig.* **4.** With *of.* To try by tasting; *spec.* to taste first (see ASSAY *sb.* 7). Now *Hist.* ME. †**5.** To practise by way of trial –1725. †**6.** To examine for the sake of information –1622; to inquire –1664; to learn or know by experience –1597. †**7.** To try with afflictions –1596, temptations –1614, force –1676. †**8.** To assail with words, or arguments –1603; with love-proposals –1598. **9.** To attempt, try to do ME.; *intr.* †to set oneself (*to do*) –1669; to do one's best, endeavour ME.; †to venture –1678.

1. I shall..his strength as oft a. MILT. *P. R.* II. 233. 2. Crist..bad him [Seynt Thomas] assaye his woundes ME. 3. To a. it for lead 1818. 5. Let him tempt and now a. His utmost subtlety MILT. *P. R.* I. 143. 9. The King's strength was failing, but he assayed to show himself in the usual kingly state FREEMAN. Hence **Assay·able** *a.* **Assay·ing** *vbl. sb.* the action of proving or trying; *spec.* the trial of metals; †*Mus.* a preliminary flourish.

Assayer (ăsē¹·əɹ). ME. [a. AF. *assaior*, *-our*, f. *assayer* to ASSAY.] **1.** One who tries, or finds out by trial. **2.** One who assays metals 1618. **3.** An officer who tastes food before it is served to a prince or lord (L. *prægustator*). (In this sense prob. confused with ASSEOUR, 'he who sets the table'.) ME.

†**Assea·l,** *v.* ME. [Later form of *asseele*, for earlier **ansele*, *ensele*, a. OF. *enseeler* :—late L. *insigillare* (see ENSEAL).] To set one's seal to –1492; to seal up. Also *fig.* ME. only.

†**Assecu·re,** *v.* 1594. [ad. med.L. *assecurare*, f. L. *as-* = *ad-* + *securus.*] To make secure; to assure –1597. Hence †**Assecu·rance.** †**Assecura·tion.**

†**Assecu·tion.** 1630. [f. L. *assecut-*, *assequi.*] The action of obtaining, acquirement –1726.

Assegai, recent var. of ASSAGAI.

†**Assei·ze,** *v. rare.* [*as-* = A- *pref.* II.] To seize. MARLOWE.

Asself (ăse·lf), *v.* 1632. [As- *pref.*] To take to oneself, appropriate.

Assemblage (ăse·mblėdʒ). 1704. [a. F., f. *assembler*; see ASSEMBLE *v.*¹ and -AGE.] **1.** A bringing or coming together; the state of being collected 1730. **2.** The joining of two things. *Obs.* exc. in *Carpentry.* 1727. **3.** A number of persons gathered together. (Less formal than *assembly.*) 1741. **4.** A collection of things 1704.

1. The first a. of the thegns at York FREEMAN. 3. An a. of all ages and nations H. WALPOLE. 4. An a. of bare poles 1833. var. †**Assembla·tion.**

†**Asse·mblance**¹. 1485. [a. F. :—late L. *assimulantia*; see ASSEMBLE *v.*¹] Assemblage, assembling –1596.

†**Asse·mblance**². 1485. [a. F. in sense of ASSEMBLE *v.*²] Semblance, show –1597. var. †**Asse·mblant.**

Assemble (ăse·mb'l), *v.*¹ ME. [a. OF. *a(s)sembler* :—L. *ad-*, *assimulare*, f. *ad* + *simul.*] Occ. strengthened by *together.* **1.** To bring together into one place, company, or mass; to collect, convene; †*formerly*, to heap up ME. †**2.** To unite (*to* or *with*) –1483; to couple (sexually) ME. only. **3.** *intr.* To come together into one place or company; to congregate, meet ME. †**4.** *esp.* To meet in fight –1513.

1. To a. on yche side soudiours ynoch ME. These proverbs..I assembled FRANKLIN. 3. The Parliament assembled in November 1860. *refl.* All the men of Israel assembled themselves unto king Solomon 1 *Kings* viii. 2.

†**Asse·mble,** *v.*² 1483. [a. OF. *a(s)sembler*, perh. confused w. *ressembler*; see RESEMBLE.] To compare; to resemble –1550.

Asse·mble, *sb.* 1883. [ASSEMBLE *v.*¹ 3, in the imperative.] *Mil.* The second beat of the drum, or other signal, ordering soldiers to strike tents and stand to arms. Cf. ASSEMBLY.

†**Asse·mblement.** 1470. [a. OF., f. *assembler*; see ASSEMBLE *v.*¹ and -MENT.] An assembly, assemblage –1645.

Assembler (ăse·mbləɹ). 1635. [f. ASSEMBLE *v.*¹] **1.** One who collects or convenes. **2.** One who takes part in an assembly, *e.g.* in the Westminster Assembly of Divines 1647.

Assembly (ăse·mbli). ME. [a. OF. *a(s)semblee*, sb., f. fem. pa. pple. of *assembler*; see ASSEMBLE *v.*¹ Cf. *army.*] **1.** = ASSEMBLAGE 1. †**2.** The coming together of two persons or things –1483; hostile meeting, attack –1535. **3.** A gathering of persons, a concourse, throng ME. **4.** *esp.* A gathering of persons for deliberation and decision; a deliberative body, a legislative council ME. **5.** A congregation 1600. **6.** A social gathering, either private, as a modern 'reception' or 'at-home', or public, as in the 18th century 1590. †**7.** = ASSEMBLAGE 4. –1699. **8.** A military call by drum or bugle. Cf. ASSEMBLE *sb.* 1727.

3. If there bee any in this A., any deere Friend of Cæsar's *Jul. C.* III. ii. 19. 4. *Assembly* or *General Assembly*: the name given to the legislature in some of the United States of America. *General A.* of the Church of Scotland: the representative body which meets annually to direct its affairs. *National A.* of France: the popularly-elected branch of the legislature. *Westminster A.* of Divines, appointed by the Long Parliament in 1643, to aid in settling the government and liturgy of the Church of England (whence *The Assembly's Catechism*). 6. He will find admittance into all the crowded Balls and Assemblies FOOTE. *Comb.*: **a.-man,** a member of an A. (sense 4); **-room,** a room in which assemblies (sense 6) were formerly held, and in which balls, etc. are now given.

Assent (ăse·nt), *v.* ME. [a. OF. *a(s)senter* :—L. *assentare* (*-ari*), irreg. freq. of L. *assentire* (*-iri*), f. *as-* = *ad-* + *sentire*, whence also mod.F. *assentir.*] **1.** *intr.* To give the concurrence of one's will, to agree *to*, to comply with (*arch.*, exc. as said of the sovereign *assenting* to a measure, or as in 4). Replaced by *consent.* †*trans.* (ellipt.) To agree to –1675. †**2.** *intr.* To agree together, determine. Const. *to*, *into.* –1470. *trans.* To agree upon (a thing) –1591. †**3.** *intr.* To submit, yield (*to*) –1636. **4.** To give or express one's agreement with a statement or matter of opinion. Const. *to*, †*with*, †*unto.* (The mod. use as distinguished from CONSENT.) ME. †**5.** *refl.* in prec. senses –1485.

1. The Lords passed a resolution to which the King assented 1863. 4. Assenting to the premises, we reject the conclusion F. HALL. Damn with faint praise, assent with civil leer POPE. Hence †**Asse·ntant** (repl. by ASSENTIENT) *ppl. a.* assenting; agreeing; *sb.* one who assents or consents to. **Asse·nter,** one who assents or consents. **Asse·ntingly** *adv.* **Asse·ntive** *a.* inclined to assent. **Asse·ntiveness.**

Assent (ăse·nt), *sb.* ME. [a. OF. *a(s)sent*, f. *assenter*; see prec.] **1.** The concurrence of the will, compliance with a desire (*arch.* and repl. by *consent*, exc. as in next). **2.** Official, judicial, or formal sanction; the action or instrument that signifies such sanction ME. †**3.** Accord –1718. †**4.** Opinion –1559. **5.** Agreement with a statement, or matter of opinion; mental acceptance. (The mod. use as distinguished from CONSENT.) 1534.

2. I will nothyng graunt withowt the under shreves a. I. PASTON. 3. Made kyng by a. of the britons CAXTON. Phr. *By* or *with one assent, common assent.* 5. Our a. to the conclusion being grounded on the truth of the premises MILL. The deliberate *assent and consent* of a parliament STUBBS. var. **Asse·ntment** (*arch. rare*).

†**Asse·nt,** *pa. pple.* [f. SEND.] Sent forth; sent for. GOWER.

Assenta·neous, *a.* [f. late L. *assentaneus* + -OUS.] Inclined to assent, deferential. LANDOR.

Assenta·tion. 1481. [a. F., ad. L. *assentationem*; see ASSENT *v.*] The (obsequious or servile) expression or act of assent.

Abject flattery and indiscriminate a. degrade CHESTERF. Hence **Assenta·tious** *a.*

Assentator (æsĕntē¹·təɹ). 1531. [a. L.] One who assents to or connives at. Hence **Asse·ntato·rily** *adv.* (*rare*).

Assentient (ăse·nʃĕnt). 1851. [ad. L. *assentientem.* Replaces *assentant.*] *ppl. a.* Assenting, accordant. *sb.* An assenter 1859.

Assentor (ăse·ntǫɹ). 1880. [See -OR.] An assenter; *spec.* used of those who, in addition to the proposer and seconder, subscribe the nomination-paper of a candidate in an election.

†**Asseour.** ME. only. [OF., f. *asseoir.*] An officer who used to set the king's table for dinner. Cf. ASSAYER 3 and ASSEWER.

Assert (ăsō·ɹt), *v.* 1604. [f. L. *assert-*, *asserere*, to put one's hand on the head of a slave, either to set him free or claim him. Cf. also med.L. *assertare.*] †**1.** To set free (*rare*). (Cf. L. *asserere in libertatem.*) –1699. †**2.** To take the part of; to champion, protect. Cf. 4. –1814. **3.** To claim as belonging *to* (*arch.*) 1652; †to lay claim to –1791. **4.** To vindicate a (disputed) claim to (anything) 1649. **5.** To declare formally and distinctly, aver, affirm 1604. †**6.** To affirm the existence of –1724; to bespeak (*rare*) –1823; to state –1677.

2. That I may a. th' eternal Providence, And justifie the wayes of God to men MILT. *P. L.* I. 25. 4. To a. one's rights JUNIUS. *To assert oneself*: to insist upon the recognition of one's rights or claims, and take means to secure them. 5. It is not directly asserted, but it seems to be implied FREEMAN. Common sense asserts the existence of a reality H. SPENCER. Hence †**Asse·rt,** assertion (*rare*). **Asse·rtable, -ible** *a.* capable or worthy of being asserted. **Asse·rtative** *a.*

(*rare*) = ASSERTIVE. **Asse·rted** *ppl. a.* claimed, maintained; affirmed. **Asse·rter.**

Assertion (ăsə̄·ɹʃən). 1449. [ad. L. *assertionem*; see ASSERT.] †1. The action of setting free –1707. 2. The action of maintaining or defending a cause; vindication (*arch.*) 1532. 3. Insistance upon a right or claim 1660. 4. The action of positively stating; declaration, averment 1449; a positive statement, a declaration 1531.

2. Flinching from the a. of his daughter's reputation SCOTT. 3. An a. of her right of arbitrary taxation GREEN. The haughty and defiant *self-assertion* of Dante LOWELL. 4. Looseness of a. CHURCH. A sweeping, unqualified a. HAZLITT.

Assertive (ăsə̄·ɹtiv), *a.* 1562. [f. ASSERT *v.*] Of the nature of, or characterized by, assertion; declaratory, affirmative; dogmatic, positive. Hence **Asse·rtive·ly** *adv.*, **-ness.**

Assertor (ăsə̄·ɹtǫɹ, -əɹ). 1566. [a. L.; see ASSERT *v.*] †1. (In L. senses) One who liberates, or lays claim to, a slave –1678. 2. A champion, vindicator, advocate 1647. 3. One who makes a positive statement 1646.

Assertorial (æsəɹtō°·riăl), *a.* 1863. [f. prec.] *Logic.* Of the nature of assertion, affirming that a thing *is*; opp. to *problematical*, and *necessary* or *apodictical*. var. **Asserto·rical.** Hence **Asserto·rially** *adv.*; var. **Asserto·rically.**

Assertory (ăsə̄·ɹtəri), *a.* 1617. [f. as prec.] 1. Assertive, affirmative 1639. 2. *Logic.* = ASSERTORIAL 1837.

1. *Assertory oath*: one taken in support of a present statement, as opp. to a *promissory oath*.

Asservilize (ăsə̄·ɹviləiz), *v. rare.* 1877. [f. As- *pref.*[1] + SERVILE.] To make servile. var. †**Asse·rvile.**

Assess (ăse·s), *v. Aphet.* CESS, SESS. 1447. [a. OF. *assesser*:—late L. *assessare*, freq. of *assidere*, f. *ad-* + *sedere*. Cf. mod. Fr. *asseoir*, and ASSIZE.] 1. To fix the amount of (taxation, fine, etc.) to be paid by a person or community. 2. To determine the amount of and impose *upon* 1495. 3. To impose a fine or tax upon; to tax, fine. Const. *in*, *at* the amount. 1494. Also *fig.* 4. To estimate officially the value of (property or income) for taxation 1809.

2. A forced loan was assessed upon the whole kingdom GREEN. 3. John Hampden was assessed twenty shillings COX. 4. To a. a person's annual income 1842. Hence †**Asse·ss(e** *sb.* = ASSESSMENT. **Asse·ssable, -ible** *a.* capable of being assessed, liable to assessment. **Asse·ssably** *adv.* ratably.

Assessed (ăse·st), *ppl. a.* 1552. [f. ASSESS *v.* + -ED.] 1. Fixed by assessment 1796. 2. Subject to taxation, taxed, fined 1552.

1. *Assessed taxes*: those on inhabited houses, male servants, carriages, dogs, hair-powder, armorial bearings, and game.

Assession (ăse·ʃən). 1447. [ad. L. *assessionem*; see ASSESS.] 1. A sitting beside or together; a session 1560. †2. = ASSESSMENT ME. only. Hence **Asse·ssionary** *a.* pertaining to a. or assessors. ? *Obs.*

Assessment (ăse·smĕnt). 1540. [f. ASSESS *v.* + -MENT.] The action of assessing; the amount assessed. 1. The determination of the amount of taxation, etc., to be paid 1548. 2. The scheme of charge or taxation 1700. 3. The amount of charge so determined upon 1611. 4. Official valuation of property or income for the purposes of taxation; the value assigned to it 1540. 5. *fig.* Estimation 1626. 6. *attrib.* 1870.

1. The assessement of..fines 1548. 5. In the comparative a. of Hellenic forces GROTE.

Assessor (ăse·səɹ). ME. [a. OF. *assessour* (mod. *assesseur*):—L. *assessorem*; see ASSESS *v.*] 1. One who sits beside; *hence*, one who shares another's position, rank, etc. 1667. 2. One who sits as assistant or adviser to a judge or magistrate; *esp.* an assistant skilled in technical points of law, commercial usage, navigation, etc. [The earliest sense in Eng.] ME. 3. One who assesses taxes; one who assesses income or property for taxation 1611. 4. *transf.* or *fig.* in prec. senses 1625.

1. Whence to his Son, Th' A. of his Throne, he thus began MILT. *P. L.* VI. 670. 2. The body of unlearned assessors, termed..Jurymen BENTHAM. Hence **Assesso·rial** *a.* of or pertaining to an a. or assessors; var. †**Asse·ssory.** **Asse·ssorship**, the office, position, or function of an a.

†**Asse·th(e**, *sb.* ME. [a. OF. *a(s)set* (pronounced *ase·þ*), orig. the same word as *assez* adv. :—late L. *ad satis*. The word had no connexion in Eng. with *assets*.] Satisfaction; amends –1494. Hence †**Asse·the** *v.* to satisfy.

Assets (æ·sĕts). 1531. [a. late AF. *assets*:—late pop. L. *ad satis* 'to sufficiency', as in *aver assetz* 'to have sufficient'. Orig. sing., but now treated as pl., with sing. *asset.*] 1. *Law.* Orig.: Sufficient estate or effects; *esp.* 'Goods enough to discharge that burthen, which is cast upon the executor or heir, in satisfying the testator's or ancestor's debts and legacies' (COWELL). 2. Extended to: Any property or effects liable to be applied as in sense 1. (Now a *collective plural.*) 1583. 3. *Law* and *Comm.* Effects of an insolvent debtor or bankrupt, applicable to the payment of his debts; and by extension: All the property of a person or company which may be made liable for his or their debts. (In this sense used as *pl.*, with sing. *asset.*). Also *fig.* 1675.

1. Unlesse that he hath A. by discent in Fee simple 1574. 2. *Assets in hand*: effects in the hands of executors which are applicable to discharge the testator's debts. He left not assids enough to bury him COLLIER. 3. A very doubtful asset (*mod.*).

Assever (ăse·vəɹ), *v. arch.* 1581. [ad. L. *asseverare*, f. *as-* = *ad* + *severus.*] To asseverate. Hence †**Asse·vering** *ppl. a.* solemnly affirmative.

Asseverate (ăse·vĕrēˡt), *v.* 1791. [f. L. *asseverat-*; see prec.] To affirm solemnly, assert emphatically, avouch, aver.

They asseverated that they saw no child 1791. Hence †**Asse·verantly** *adv.* **Asse·vera·tingly** *adv.* **Asse·verative, Asse·veratory** *adjs.* of, pertaining to, or characterized by asseveration.

Asseveration (ăse·vĕrē·ʃən). 1556. [ad. L. *asseverationem.*] 1. The action of asseverating 1564. 2. That which is asseverated; a solemn or emphatic declaration or assertion 1556. 3. Emphatic confirmation; an oath 1602.

1. With more or lesse a., as they [things] stand.. prooued more or lesse BACON. 3. With many choice asseverations DICKENS.

†**Assew·er.** 1478. [? Used as identical with ASSEOUR, and also as if a compound of SEWER. Cf. also ASSAYER 3.] An officer who used to set the table for a banquet, or who himself carried in and arranged the dishes; a sewer –1483.

A·ss-head. 1550. [See ASS 2 and HEAD.] A stupid fellow. Hence **A·ss-hea·ded** *a.* stupid.

Assibilate (ăsi·bilēˡt), *v.* 1844. [f. L. *assibilat-*, *ads-*, *assibilare.*] To give a sibilant sound to. Hence **Assi·bila·tion**, pronunciation with a sibilant sound.

Assidæan, -ean, -ian (æsidī·ăn). ME. [f. Gr. Ἀσιδαῖοι (ad. Heb. *ḥăsīdīm*, saints) + -AN.] a. orig.: One of the Jews who, under the leadership of Mattathias, opposed the attempts of Antiochus Epiphanes to introduce idolatry among them. (1 *Macc.* ii. 42.) b. later: A member of a Jewish sect professing peculiarly intimate communion with God; more usu. *Chasidim*.

†**A·ssident.** 1753. [ad. L. *assidentem*; see ASSESS *v.*] *adj.* Usually, but not always, accompanying (a disease). *sb.* [sc. *symptom.*] Hence †**A·ssidence** (*rare*).

†**Assi·dual**, *a.* ME. [a. OF. *assiduel*, f. L. *assiduus*; see -AL[1].] 1. = ASSIDUOUS 1. –1651. 2. = ASSIDUOUS 3. –1678. Hence †**Assi·dually** *adv.* constantly.

†**Assi·duate**, *a.* 1494. [f. *assiduat-*, *assiduare*, f. *assiduus* ASSIDUOUS.] Constantly exercised –1658. Hence †**Assi·duately** *adv.*

Assiduity (æsidiū·iti). 1605. [ad. L. *assiduitatem*, f. *assiduus.*] Constant or close attention to the business in hand, unremitting application, perseverance. 2. Persistent endeavour to please (*arch.*) 1630; *esp.* in *pl.* constant attentions 1683. †3. Frequency –1668.

1. To fail in a purpose for want of a. GEO. ELIOT. 2. The obsequiousnesse and a. of the Court 1630.

Assiduous (ăsi·diuˌəs), *a.* 1538. [f. L. *assiduus* (f. *assidere*; see ASSESS *v.*) + -OUS.] 1. Constant in application to the business in hand, persevering, sedulous 1660. 2. Obsequiously attentive (*arch.*) 1725. 3. Of actions: Unremitting, persistent 1538.

1. To be a. in our prayers JER. TAYLOR. 2. Few can be a. without servility JOHNSON. 3. To wearie him with my a. cries MILT. *P. L.* XI. 310. Hence **Assi·duously** *adv.* **Assi·duousness**, assiduity.

†**Assie·ge**, *v.* [ME. *asege*, a. OF. *asegier* (mod. *assiéger*):—late L. *assediare*, f. *as-* = *ad-* + *sedium* (cf. *obsidium*).] To besiege, beset. Hence †**Assie·ge**, **Assie·gement** *sbs.* a siege.

Assientist (æsiˌe·ntist). 1713. [f. next + -IST.] A party to an Assiento contract; a shareholder in an Assiento company.

‖**Assiento, asiento** (ăsye·nto, æsiˌe·nto). 1714. [Sp.] A contract, or convention between the King of Spain and other powers, for furnishing the Spanish dominions in America with negro slaves. *spec.* That made between Great Britain and Spain at the peace of Utrecht.

‖**Assiette** (asye·t). 1869. [Fr. = seat, site.] *Bookbinding.* A composition laid on the cut edges of books before gilding them.

A·ssify, *v.* 1804. [f. ASS.] To make an ass of (*joc.*).

Assign (ăsəi·n), *v.* ME. [a. OF. *a(s)signer*:—L. *ad-*, *assignare*, f. *ad* + *signare*, f. *signum.*] I. 1. To allot (*to*); to appoint, apportion, make over. 2. To transfer or formally make over to another. In *Eng. Law* the appropriate word to express the transference of *personal* property. ME. 3. To allot or appoint *to* a person, or for a purpose ME. †4. To prescribe (a course of action) –1607. 5. To appoint, designate, for an office, duty, or fate. *Obs.* exc. in *Law.* ME. 6. To settle or authoritatively determine (a time or period) ME. 7. To lay down as a thing ascertained 1664.

1. The work which here God hath assign'd us MILT. 3. The Lords assigned us five very worthy lawyers BP. HALL. 5. If the founder has..assigned any other person to be visitor BLACKSTONE. 6. A hell to the duration of which no period is assigned 1883.

II. To point out exactly, designate, specify ME.; *spec.* in *Law* 1672.

The special locality which Jewish tradition has assigned for the place STANLEY.

III. To ascribe, attribute, or refer 1541; to ascribe (a reason) *to* or as accounting *for* 1489; to allege, suggest (as a reason, etc.) 1665.

To a. a motive to behaviour JUNIUS, a supposition of forgery PALEY. Hence **Assi·gner**, one who assigns; see the vb.

†**Assign**, *sb.*[1] 1. [f. ASSIGN *v.*] Command 1633. 2. [f. SIGN *sb.*] A sign, portent 1601.

Assign (ăsəi·n), *sb.*[2] 1450. [ME. *assigne* (trisyllabic), a. F. *assigné*, has given *assign* and *assignee*, ME. *-e* becoming mute in the former in the 15th c. Cf. ASSIGNEE.] †1. = ASSIGNEE 1. –1714. 2. = ASSIGNEE 2. Esp. in *heirs and assigns*. 1450. †3. An appurtenance SHAKS.

Assignable (ăsəi·năb'l), *a.* 1659. [f. ASSIGN *v.*] 1. That may be assigned 1809, specified 1659, referred as belonging *to* 1673, alleged as accounting for 1659. Hence **Assi·gnabi·lity. Assi·gnably** *adv.*

‖**Assignat** (æ·signæt, asinʸā·). 1790. [Fr., ad. L. *assignatum.*] Paper money issued by the revolutionary government of France, on security of the state lands. Cf. ASSIGNATION 4.

Assignation (æsignē·ʃən). ME. [a. OF. *assignacion*, ad. L. *assignationem*; see ASSIGN *v.* and -ATION.] 1. The action of allotting; apportionment 1600. 2. The action of legally assigning (see ASSIGN *v.* 2). Also a. formal declaration of transference; b. the transferred interest. (Now usu. ASSIGNMENT.) 1579. †3. The setting apart of certain revenue to meet a claim. Also a. the mandate granting the money; b. the amount set apart. –1747. 4. Paper currency; a bill, an *assignat* 1674. †5. Appointment to office –1656; prescription, order –1605. 6. The arrangement of a particular time and place (*esp.* for an interview); an appointment, tryst 1660. 7. Attribution as belonging or due *to* 1603.

1. Not a Matter of Choice, but of divine A. 1716. 6. Compelled to make assignations with as much secrecy as two young lovers 1854.

Assignee (æsinī·). ME. [See ASSIGN *sb.*[2] Here final *-e*, preserved through law French, has been refash. as *-ee*. (Cf. *avowee.*)] *ppl. a.* Assigned, appointed 1494. *sb.* 1. One who is appointed to act for another; a deputy, agent, or representative ME. 2. One to whom a right of property is legally transferred 1467.

2. *Assignees in bankruptcy*: those to whom the management, realization, and distribution of a bankrupt's estate is committed, on behalf of the creditors. Hence **Assignee·ism**, the practice of appointing assignees. **Assignee·ship.**

Assignment (ăsəi·nmĕnt). ME. [a. OF.

assignement, ad. late L. *assignamentum*; see ASSIGN *v.*] **1.** The action of appointing as a share, allotment 1460. **2.** Legal transference of a right, etc. (cf. ASSIGN *v.* 2); the document effecting or authorizing it 1592. †**3.** = ASSIGNATION 3. –1678; **b.** = ASSIGNATION 4. –1708. **4.** The allotting of convicts as unpaid servants to colonists 1843. †**5.** Appointment to office; setting apart for a purpose –1600; appointment, command –1744. **6.** = ASSIGNATION 7. 1704. **7.** Statement (of a reason) 1651; specification 1646.

1. A. of lands to the veterans MERIVALE. **6.** By his a. of definite functions to definite organs LEWES.

Assignor (æsinǭ·ɹ). 1668. [f. ASSIGN + -OR.] *Law.* One who assigns a right or property. (Correlative with *assignee.*)

Assimilable (ăsi·milăb'l), *a.* 1646. [ad. late L. *assimilabilis*; see ASSIMILATE.] **1.** That may be appropriated as nourishment 1667. **2.** That may be likened *to* 1847. Also as *sb.* 1646. Hence **Assi:milabi·lity.**

†**Assi·milate.** 1671. [ad. L. *assimilatus.*] *ppl.* Likened. *sb.* That which is like.

Assimilate (ăsi·milēⁱt), *v.* 1578. [f. L. *assimilat-, assimilare*, f. *ad-* + *similis.*] **I.** To make or be like. **1.** To cause to resemble 1628. Const. *with.* (Influenced by II.) 1849. To make alike 1785. **2.** *intr.* To be or become like *to* 1837; also with *with.* (See 1.) 1768. **3.** To adapt *to* (*arch.*) 1664. *intr.* (for *refl.*) To conform *to* (*arch.*) 1792. **4.** To liken, compare, class. Const. *to, with.* 1616. †**5.** To be like, take after –1661.

1. To a. our law in this respect to the law of Scotland BRIGHT. **2.** Which revenues..do always a., or take the same nature, with the antient revenues BLACKSTONE. **4.** Marcus Aurelius mournfully assimilated the career of a conqueror to that of a simple robber LECKY.

II. To absorb and incorporate. **1.** To convert into a substance of its own nature; to absorb into the system, incorporate. Also *fig.* 1578. **2.** *intr.* To become absorbed or incorporated into the system. Also *fig.* 1626. ¶Occas. for ASSIMULATE, q. v.

1. Aliment that is easily assimilated, and turned into blood ARBUTHNOT. **2.** *fig.* I am a foreign material, and cannot a. with the Church of England J. H. NEWMAN. Hence **Assi·milative** *a.* of, characterized by, or tending to assimilation; that may be or has been assimilated. **Assi·milator,** he who or that which assimilates. **Assi·milatory** *a.* assimilative. vars. †**Assi·mile, Assi·milize.**

Assimilation (ăsi:milēⁱ·ʃən). Also **-ulation.** 1605. [ad. L. *assimilationem*, f. *assimilare.*] **1.** The action of making or becoming like; the state of being like; similarity, likeness. **2.** Conformity *with* (*arch.*) 1677. **3.** Comparison 1855. **4.** Conversion into a similar substance; *esp.* the conversion by an animal or plant of extraneous material into fluids and tissues identical with its own. (By some restricted to the final stage.) Also *fig.* 1626.

1. Wisdom..is..an a. to the Deity 1660. **4.** A...is the ultimate term of nutrition TODD. *fig.* Which, by a bland a., incorporated into politics the sentiments which beautify and soften private society BURKE.

†**Assi·mulate,** *v.* 1630. [f. *assimulat-, assimulare*, var. of *assimilare* in sense of *simulare*; see ASSIMILATE *v.*] = ASSIMILATE –1652.

Assinego, var. of ASINEGO.

†**Assinuate,** *v.* Corrupt f. INSINUATE.

‖ **Assise** (asī·z). 1882. [mod.Fr. = layer; see ASSIZE.] *Geol.* A formation consisting of parallel beds of rock agreeing in their organic remains.

Assish (æ·siʃ), *a. rare.* 1587. [f. ASS.] Stupid. Hence **A·ssishness.**

Assist (ăsi·st), *v.* 1514. [a. F. *assister*, ad. L. *assistere*, f. *ad-, as-* + *sistere.*] †**1.** *intr.* To take one's stand *to* or towards; *fig.* to stand *to* (an opinion) –1646. *trans.* To stand near, or by; to attend –1650. †**2.** *trans.* To join. Also *absol.* –1610. **3.** *intr.* To be present (*at*) as a spectator (now treated as Fr.), or as taking part 1626. **4.** To aid, help; to second, to succour, to promote 1547. *absol.* and *intr.* 1514. Const. †*to, in,* or *inf.*

2. The King, and Prince, at prayers, let's a. them *Temp.* I. i. 57. **3.** To a. at a solemn Masse 1626. The dinner at which we have just assisted THACKERAY. **4.** To a. the rebellious Gauls 1683, a friendless person STEELE, digestion (*mod.*). To a. in the murder of her husband BROOME. Hence **Assi·ster, -or** (legal var.), he who assists (senses 3, 4). **Assi·stful** *a.* ?*Obs.* **Assi·sting** *ppl. a.* †bordering; †attendant; giving aid. **Assi·stless** *a. poet.* helpless.

Assistance (ăsi·stăns). ME. [a. F., f. *assister*; see ASSIST *v.* and -ANCE.] **1.** Presence, attendance (*Obs.* exc. as Fr.) 1520. **2.** *collect.* (rarely *pl.*) Persons present, bystanders. (*Obs.* exc. as re-adopted from Fr.) 1491. **3.** The action of helping or aiding; *also*, the help afforded, aid, relief. Formerly often in *pl.* ME. †**4.** *collect.* (rarely *pl.*) A body of helpers; see ASSISTANT *sb.* 3. –1692.

1. His sumptuous burial..solemnized with so great an a. of all the University MILTON. **3.** By the..assystence of almyghty god TREVISA. **4.** After them the Court of A. 1692.

Assistant (ăsi·stănt). ME. [a. F., ad. L. *assistentem.* The sp. follows the Fr.] **A.** *adj.* †**1.** Standing or remaining by, present –1677. **2.** Present to help; auxiliary (*to*) ME.

2. Animals a. to man 1858. The Assistant-Surgeon's Tent 1844.

B. *sb.* †**1.** One who is present; one who takes part. Usu. in *pl.* –1781. **2.** A helper; a promoter; *also*, a means of help, an aid 1541. **3.** *spec.* **a.** A deputy-judge. **b.** An official auxiliary to the Father-General of the Jesuits. **c.** *Court of Assistants*: certain senior members who manage the affairs of the City of London Companies 1611.

2. Numbers and rhymes..as assistants to memory MRS. CHAPONE. Hence **Assi·stantship.**

Assith, -ment, obs. ff. ASSYTH, -MENT.

Assize (ăsəi·z). [ME. *asise, assyse*, a. OF. *asise, assise*, subst. use of pa. pple. fem. of *asseoir*:—L. *assidere*; cf. ASSESS. In the sense of 'assessment' corrupted to *acise, accise*, now corruptly EXCISE. Also aphet. as SIZE.] †**1.** A sitting of a consultative or legislative body. **2.** The decree or edict made at such a sitting. Now *Hist.* ME. †**b.** Hence *gen.* Ordinance, regulation –1523. †**3.** *esp.* Ordinances regulating weights and measures, and the weight and price of articles of general consumption (*assisæ venalium*); rule of trade ME. **4.** The statutory regulation of the price of bread and ale by the price of grain 1447. **5.** The standard so ordained; *hence*, customary or prescriptive standard ME. †**6.** *Hence*: Measurement. (Now SIZE.) –1624. Extent (of things immaterial) –1655. **7.** Orig. used of: All legal proceedings of the nature of inquests or recognitions ME.; hence, an action to be so decided; also the writ by which it is instituted 1574. **8.** Hence (usu. in *pl.*): The sessions held periodically in each county of England, for the purpose of administering civil and criminal justice, by judges acting under certain special commissions. ME. Also *attrib.* ME. **9.** In Scotland: A trial by jury ME.; the jury or panel 1513. †**10.** Judgement, sentence –1643. **11.** With *great, last*, etc.: The Last Judgement ME. †**12.** *transf.* The office of judge, censorship –1675. †**13.** Fixation of imposts. (See EXCISE.) 1642.

2. By..the a. of arms, it was provided that every man's armour should descend to his heir BLACKSTONE. †*Rent of assise*: a fixed rent. **3.** The act of 51 Henry III. (1266) is called the a. of bread and of ale 1821. **5.** Convicted for selling bread under the a. LUTTRELL. **7.** The *Grand* or *Great Assize*, the assizes of *Mort d'ancestre*, *Novel disseisin*, etc. **11.** Till summon'd to the last a. COMBE.

†**Assi·ze,** *v.* ME. [a. AF. *assiser*, f. *assise* ASSIZE.] **1.** To place ME. only. **2.** To ordain, decide ME. only; to assess –1624. **3.** To regulate according to a standard –1638. Hence **Assi·zement,** the action of assizing; statutory inspection.

Assizer, -or (ăsəi·zəɹ). [ME. *assisour*, a. AF., f. as prec.] **1.** *Eng. Hist.* One of those who constituted the assize or inquest. **2.** *Sc. Law.* A juryman. (*Obs.* exc. *Hist.*) ME. **3.** An officer who had charge of the Assize of Weights and Measures, or who fixed the Assize of Bread and Ale 1751.

†**Asso·bre,** *v.* [? A- *pref.* 11.] To make or become sober. GOWER.

Associable (ăsōᵘ·ʃiăb'l), *a.* 1611. [a. F., f. *associer* to ASSOCIATE; see -ABLE.] †**1.** Companionable COTGR. **2.** That may be associated in thought (*with*) 1855. **3.** *Phys.* Liable to be affected by sympathy with other parts. Hence **Asso:ciabi·lity. Asso·ciableness.**

Associate (ăsōᵘ·ʃi,ĕt). ME. [ad. L. *associatus, as-, ad-sociare*, f. *ad* + *socius.*] **A.** *ppl. a.* = ASSOCIATED. **1.** Joined in companionship, function, or dignity. **2.** Allied, confederate 1600. **3.** United in the same group or category; concomitant 1750.

1. A president and six a. judges BROUGHAM. **3.** The Mouth..Jaws, and A. Parts 1880.

B. *sb.* [the adj. used absol.] **1.** One who is united to another by community of interest, etc.; a partner, comrade, companion 1533. **2.** A companion in arms, ally 1548. **3.** One who shares an office or position of authority with another; a colleague, coadjutor. *spec.* One of the officers of the Superior Courts of Common Law in England, formerly directed by *writ* to *associate* themselves with the judges in taking the assizes. (Abolished in 1879.) 1552. **4.** One who is frequently in company with another, on equal and intimate terms; a companion, mate 1601. **5.** One who belongs to an association with a status subordinate to that of a full member or 'Fellow' 1812. **6.** A thing placed or found in conjunction with another 1658.

4. No mean Cumrades, no base associates WEEVER. **5.** Associates of the Academy of Sciences BREWSTER. Hence **Asso·ciateship.**

Associate (ăsōᵘ·ʃi,ēⁱt), *v.* ME. [f. prec.] **1.** *trans.* To join, join *with, in*; to link together, unite, confederate; to elect as ASSOCIATE (see the *sb.* 5) 1806. **2.** *trans.* To join (things together, or one *with* another). (Mostly *refl.* or *pass.*) 1578. **3.** *intr.* **a.** To combine for a common purpose, to join or form an association 1653. **b.** To have intercourse (*with*) 1644; to make oneself a partner in (a matter) 1881. †**4.** To escort, attend –1657; to consort with –1590; of things: (cf. 2) to accompany –1691.

1. None but Papists are associated against him SWIFT. **2.** Faults..associated with transcendent merit JOHNSON. To a. rose-leaves with hell-fires M. CONWAY. **3.** When bad men combine, good men must a. BURKE. A. with men much older than yourself CHATHAM. *refl.* I a. myself with that answer (*mod.*). Hence **Asso·ciative** *a.* of, pertaining to, or characterized by association. **Asso·ciatively** *adv.* **Asso·ciator, -er,** he who or that which joins in association. **Asso·ciatory** *a.* having the quality of associating.

Asso·ciated, *ppl. a.* 1611. [f. prec. + -ED.] **1.** Joined in companionship, action or purpose, dignity or office, allied. **2.** Connected in thought 1748. **3.** Combined (*with*); occurring in combination 1830.

3. *A. movements*: those coincident or consensual, but unconnected, with the essential act calling them forth.

Association (ăsōᵘ·ʃi-, ăsōᵘ:si,ēⁱ·ʃən). 1535. [ad. L. *associationem*; see ASSOCIATE.] **1.** The act of associating, or the being associated (see ASSOCIATE *v.* 3); confederation, league 1535. **2.** A body of persons associated for a common purpose; the organization formed to effect their purpose; a society; *e.g.* the British Association for the Advancement of Science, etc. 1659. †**3.** A document setting forth the common purpose of a number of persons, and signed by them –1855. **4.** Fellowship, intimacy 1660. **5.** Conjoining one person or thing with another 1774. **6.** *Law.* The appointment of additional legal colleagues; the writ appointing them. (Cf. ASSOCIATE *sb.* 3.) 1613. **7.** The mental connexion between an object and ideas (*e.g.* of similarity, contrariety, contiguity, causation). (*Association of ideas.*) 1690. **8.** An idea linked in the mind with some object of contemplation, and recalled in connexion with it 1810.

1. *Deed of a.*: the document setting forth the particulars of a proposed limited liability company. **4.** The nobility would be profaned by my a. SMOLLETT. **7.** Words being arbitrary must owe their powers to a. JOHNSON. **8.** Pleasant associations with a place 1862. **A. football,** the kind played (according to the rules of the Football Association, 1863) with a round ball, which must not be handled. Cf. SOCCER.

Associationism (ăsōᵘ:ʃi,ēⁱ·ʃəniz'm). 1882. [f. prec. + -ISM.] The doctrine that mental and moral phenomena may be accounted for by association of ideas. var. **Asso:cia·tionalism. Asso:cia·tionist, -alist,** one who belongs to an association; one who holds the doctrine of association of ideas.

Assoil (ăsoi·l), *v.* ME. [f. OF. *a(s)soille* pres. subj., *a(s)soil* pres. indic. of *a(s)soldre*, *a(s)soudre* :—L. *absoluere=absolvere.* Subseq. refash. as ABSOIL, leading to ABSOLVE, from the L.] 1. To absolve from sin, pardon. Const. *of*, *from* (*arch.*) ME. b. from purgatory (*arch.*) 1483. †2. To absolve from any ecclesiastical sentence –1691. 3. To set free (*of, from* obligations, etc.) –1650. 4. To pronounce not guilty. Const. *of, from* (*arch.*) 1528. 5. To release; to discharge. Const. *of, from* (*arch.*) ME. †6. To unloose the knot of, solve. (Cf. SOIL *v.*) –1696. †7. To refute –1721. 8. To purge, atone for (*arch.*) 1596. †9. To discharge (an obligation) (*rare*) 1596. †10. To get rid of (a thing) (*rare*) 1596. ¶ 11. *Catachr.* for SOIL, *sully* 1845.

1. 'God assoilzie her!' ejaculated old Elspeth SCOTT. 4. The houses did a. the army from all suspicion CROMWELL. 5. Death's mild curfew shall from work a. MRS. BROWNING. Hence †**Assoi·l** *sb.* solution (*rare*). **Assoi·ler**, absolving (from excommunication). **Assoi·lment**, the action of assoiling, or being assoiled; †discharge (of a duty); †solution, reconciliation (of conflicting statements). ¶ *Catachr.* for: Defilement.

Assoilzie (ăsoi·lyi, asoi·li, retaining Fr. *l mouillé*), Scotch f. ASSOIL *v.*

†**Assoi·n(e**, *sb.* ME. only. [var. of ESSOIN.] An excuse put in for non-appearance.

†**Assoi·n(e**, *v.* ME. [var. of ESSOIN *v.*] To put in an excuse for non-appearance of –1646; *intr.* to excuse oneself, decline –1470.

Assonance (æ·sŏnăns). 1727. [a. F., f. L. *assonare*, f. *as-=ad-+sonare.*] 1. Correspondence of sound between words or syllables. 2. *Pros.* The correspondence or riming of one word with another in the accented vowel and those which follow, but not in the consonants, as in OFr., Sp., and other versification 1823. 3. A word or syllable answering to another in sound 1882. 4. *transf.* Rough correspondence 1868.

2. In the Roland such assonances occur H. NICOL. 4. A. between facts seemingly remote LOWELL. var. **A·ssonancy** (sense 1). ? *Obs.*

Assonant (æ·sŏnănt). 1727. [a. F., ad. L. *assonantem*; see prec.] *adj.* Characterized by assonance. *sb.* [sc. *word.*] 1862. Hence **Assona·ntal, Assona·ntic** *adjs.* of or pertaining to assonance.

Assonate (æ·sŏneit), *v.* 1656. [f. L. *assonat-*; see ASSONANCE.] To correspond in sound, *esp.* in vowel-sound.

As soon, assoo·n, *adv.* ME. See AS, and SOON. *Assoon* had also the special meaning: Immediately. (Fr. *aussitôt.*) –1585.

Assort (ăsǭ·ɹt), *v.* 1490. [a. OF. *assorter* (mod. *assortir*), f. *à+sorte.*] 1. To distribute (things, *rarely* persons) into groups, as being of like nature or intended for the same purpose; to classify. 2. To group *with* 1833. 3. *intr.* To fall into a class; to be of a sort, match *well* or *ill with* 1800. 4. *intr.* To consort *with* 1823. 5. To furnish with an assortment 1611.

1. Assorting some parcels on the counter 1803. 2. He would..a. it with the fabulous dogs..as a monstrous invention DICKENS. 3. His *muse* assorts ill with the personages of the Christian mythology 1800. 4. To a. with fisher-swains LAMB. Hence **Asso·rtedness.**

Assortment (ăsǭ·ɹtmĕnt). 1611. [f. ASSORT *v.*; cf. Fr. *assortiment.*] 1. The action of assorting; assorted condition; classification. 2. A group of things of the same sort 1759. 3. An assorted set, whether of varieties of the same thing, or of different things 1791.

3. Such as the sample is, will the entire a. be 1869.

†**Asso·t**, *v.* ME. [a. OF. *a(s)soter*, f. *à+sot.*] To become or act like a fool; to become infatuated. *trans.* To make a fool of –1741. Hence †**Asso·te** *pa. pple.* SPENSER.

Assua·de, *v. rare.* 1806. [f. As- *pref.*[1] + L. *suadere.*] To present as advice.

Assuage (ăswē·dʒ), *v.* [ME. *aswage, asuage*, a. OF. *a(s)souager, -agier*, f. L. type **assuaviare*, f. *ad+suavis.* Cf. *abridge* (L. *abbreviare*).] *trans.* 1. To soften, mitigate, appease, allay (passion, pain, disease, appetite). 2. To pacify (the excited person) ME. 3. *gen.* To abate (*esp.* anything swollen) (*arch.*) ME. *intr.* †4. To become less violent –1722. 5. *gen.* To grow less; to abate, subside ME.

1. To a. religious animosities BUCKLE, human misery MILMAN, hunger DRYDEN, thirst COMBE. 2. Kindling pity, kindling rage At once provoke me, and asswage ADDISON. 4. His sorwe gan aswage CHAUCER. 5. As the deluge assuaged MOTLEY. Hence **Assua·gement.** 1. The action of assuaging; or the being assuaged. 2. An assuaging medicine or application. **Assua·ger**, he who, or that which, assuages.

Assuasive (ăswē·siv). ? *Obs.* 1708. [f. As- *pref.*[1] + *-suasive*; confused in sense with ASSUAGE.] *adj.* Soothingly persuasive. *sb.* [sc. *medicine* or *application.*] 1829.

Music her soft a. voice applies POPE.

Assubjugate (ăsʊ·bdʒŭgeit), *v.* 1606. [*as-* = A- *pref.* 11.] To reduce to subjection. So †**Assubje·ct.**

†**Assuefa·ction.** 1644. [ad. L. **assuefactionem*, f. *assuefacere*, f. *assuetus + facere.*] The action of accustoming; becoming or being used to a thing; habituation –1682.

Forget not how a. unto anything minorates the passion from it SIR T. BROWNE. So †**A·ssuetude.**

Assume (ăsiū·m), *v.* 1436. [ad. L. *as-, adsumere.* The early pa. pple. was ASSUMPT.] 1. To take to be with one; to adopt, take 1581. *esp.* To receive up into heaven. (The earliest use in Eng.; cf. ASSUMPTION 1.) (*arch.*) †2. To adopt, elect, to some position. (So in L.) –1670. †3. To take into the body (food, etc.). (So in L.) –1657. 4. To take upon oneself (a garb, etc.) 1447. 5. To take to oneself formally (the insignia of office, etc.); to undertake (an office) 1581. 6. To lay claim to, usurp 1548. 7. To pretend to possess; to simulate 1602; (with *inf.*) to pretend 1714. 8. To suppose 1598. 9. *Logic.* To add the minor premiss to a syllogism 1628.

1. To a. as a partner in business 1868. 4. Then should the Warlike Harry.. A. the Port of Mars *Hen. V*, Prol. 6. 5. Mr. Speaker assumed the Chair 1640. 6. Murray assumed to himself the praise of all that was done BURNET. 7. A. a vertue, if you haue it not *Haml.* III. iv. 160. Sage saws assuming to inculcate content LAMB. 8. Assuming the truth of the history PALEY. Hence **Assu·mable** *a.* that may be assumed. **Assu·mably** *adv.* **Assu·med** *ppl. a.* usurped; pretended; taken for granted. **Assu·medly** *adv.* presumably. **Assu·mer. Assu·ming** *vbl. sb.* assumption; pretension. **Assu·mingness.**

†**A·ssument.** *rare.* 1731. [ad. L. *assumentum*, f. *assuere.*] Something tacked on.

†**Assu·mmon**, *v.* 1450. [? A- *pref.* 11.] To summon –1607.

Assumpsit (ăsʊ·msit). 1612. [L. = 'he has taken upon himself'.] 1. An undertaking; *spec.* in *Law.* a. A promise or contract, oral or in writing not sealed, founded upon a consideration; b. An action to recover damages for breach or non-performance of such a contract. †2. An assumption 1628.

†**Assu·mpt.** 1447. [ad. L. *assumptus, assumere.*] *pa. pple.* Used as pa. pple. of the vb. ASSUME –1587. *sb.* An assumption –1638.

†**Assu·mpt**, *v.* 1530. [f. prec.] 1. = ASSUME *v.* 1, 2. –1629. 2. To put on, assume –1611.

Assumption (ăsʊ·mʃən). ME. [ad. L. *assumptionem*; see ASSUME *v.* The eccl. use was the earliest in Eng.] 1. The action of receiving up into heaven; ascent to or reception into heaven 1577; *esp.* the reception of the Virgin Mary into heaven, with body preserved from corruption (*R. C. Ch.*); the feast held annually on the 15th of August in honour of the event. 2. Incorporation, inclusion; adoption (*arch.*) 1617. †3. The taking of food, etc., into the body –1645. 4. The taking upon oneself of a form or character; taking of office or position 1646; the form or character assumed 1871. 5. *Law.* A promise or undertaking, either oral or in writing not sealed 1590. 6. Appropriation 1754. 7. Unwarrantable claim, usurpation 1647; arrogance 1606. 8. The taking of anything for granted as the basis of argument or action 1660; a supposition, postulate 1628. 9. *Logic.* The minor premiss of a syllogism 1588.

1. The A. of Elias 1627. 4. The a. of the Bachelor's degree ROGERS. 6. *Arms of assumption = assumptive arms.* The a. of the whole legislative authority MACKINTOSH. 7. His usual air of haughty a. SCOTT. 8. Hold! says the Stoick, your assumption's wrong DRYDEN. Hence **Assu·mptious** *a.* given to a. (*rare*). **Assu·mptiousness.**

Assumptive (ăsʊ·mtiv), *a.* 1611. [ad. L. *assumptivus*; see ASSUMPT and -IVE.] 1. Characterized by being assumed. 2. Of the nature of an assumption 1650. 3. Apt to assume; appropriative; arrogant 1829.

1. *Assumptive arms* in *Her.*: those assumed by any one, formerly with, now without, sanction. Hence **Assu·mptively** *adv.*

Assurance (ăʃūə·răns). ME. [a. OF. *asseürance* (mod. *assurance*), f. *asseürer* to ASSURE. Cf. ASSECURANCE.] 1. A promise making a thing certain; an engagement, pledge, or guarantee. *esp.* Terms of peace. *Obs.* exc. *Hist.* 1513. †2. A marriage engagement –1641. 3. A declaration intended to give confidence 1609. 4. *Law.* The conveyance of lands or tenements by deed; a legal evidence of the conveyance of property 1583. 5. The action of insuring or securing the value of property in the event of its being lost, or of securing the payment of a specified sum in the event of a person's death; insurance. (Techn., life-*assurance* is now differentiated from fire- and marine-*insurance.*) 1622. †6. = *Assuredness* –1603. 7. Security 1559. 8. Subjective certainty; in *Theol.* certainty of salvation; confidence, trust ME. 9. Self-confidence; steadiness, intrepidity 1594. 10. Hardihood, presumption, impudence 1699.

1. Plight me the full a. of your faith *Twel. N.* I. v. 192. 3. He was..sincere in the assurances he..gave MCCARTHY. 4. The Touchstone of Common Assurances and Conveyances SHEPPARD (*title*). 7. To sende ..unto a place of most assuraunce all..prisoners 1576. 8. But yet Ile make a. double sure *Macb.* IV. i. 83. 10. Quote authors they had never read, with an air of a. BENTLEY. Hence †**Assu·rancer**, one who makes great professions. **Assu·rant**, one who takes out a policy of insurance. †**Assu·rantly** *adv.* confidently.

Assure (ăʃūə·ɹ), *v.* ME. [a. OF. *aseürer* (mod. *assurer*) :—late L. *adsecurare*; see ASSECURE, SECURE, and SURE.] 1. †To render safe; to secure –1614; †to make sure of –1674; to make safe *from* or *against* risks. esp. *To assure life.* (Cf. ASSURANCE 5.) ME. 2. To establish securely 1474. †3. To make sure the possession or reversion of; to convey by deed –1670. †4. To betroth –1581. 5. To ensure (an event) 1622; to make certain (a thing doubtful) (*arch.*) 1682. †6. To guarantee. Const. *to* a person, †*absol.*, or with *subord. cl.* ME. 7. To give confidence to, encourage ME. †*refl.* and †*intr.* To have confidence –1641; to venture –1513. 8. To make (a person) sure or certain (*of*, or *that*) ME. *refl.* and *pass.* To feel certain 1484. 9. To tell (a person) confidently as a thing that he may trust (*that*, or *of*) 1513. †10. To state positively –1677.

1. If they could be assured against any unpleasant consequences 1884. 2. As weak States each other's Pow'r a. DRYDEN. 3. And with my proper blood A. my soul to be great Lucifers MARLOWE. 5. Yet is not the Success for Years assur'd DRYDEN. 7. Youre humanité Assureth us and giveth us hardynesse CHAUCER. 8. Thy words a. me of kind success MARLOWE. A. yourself, sir..that [etc.] SCOTT. 9. He assured us of his own willingness to go (*mod.*). Hence †**Assu·re** *sb.* assurance. **Assu·ringly** *adv.*

Assured (ăʃūə·ɹd). ME [f. prec.+-ED.] *ppl. a.* †1. Made safe; secure –1614. 2. Made certain ME. †3. Pledged –1672; betrothed –1590. 4. Certified 1574; satisfied, confident 1523. 5. Self-possessed; in a bad sense: Presumptuous 1475. As *sb.* (occ. with pl. in -s). A person whose life or goods are insured 1755. Hence **Assu·redness**, assurance.

Assuredly (ăʃūə·rĕdli), *adv.* ME. [f. prec. + -LY [2].] 1. Certainly; in very truth. 2. With confidence 1508.

1. It will almost a. rain 1758. Yours a., W. Burleigh 1578. 2. Trust thereto a. 1557.

Assurer (ăʃūə·rəɹ). 1607. [f. ASSURE *v.* + -ER [1].] 1. He who, or that which, gives assurance. 2. = ASSUROR 1827. 3. One who insures his life. (A recent use.) 1865.

†**Assu·rge**, *v.* 1556. [ad. L. *assurgere.*] To arise –1670.

Assurgent (ăsʊ̄·ɹdʒĕnt), *a.* 1578. [ad. L. *assurgentem*; see prec.] Ascending; in *Bot.* rising obliquely. 2. Seeking ascendancy 1881. As *sb.* He who, or that which, rises up 1791. Hence **Assu·rgency.**

Assuror (ăʃūə·rǫɹ). 1622. [f. ASSURE *v.*; see -OR.] One who assures or insures any one's life or property; an underwriter. (A legal form of ASSURER.)

Assyrian (ăsi·riăn). 1591. [See -AN.] *adj.* Of Assyria; *absol.* its language. *sb.* A native of Assyria 1815. var. †**Assy·riac** *a.*

Assyriology (ăsi:riǫ·lŏdʒi). 1865. [See -(O)LOGY.] The study of the language, history, and antiquities of Assyria. Hence Assyriological *a.* pertaining to A. **Assyrio·logist, As·sy·riologue,** a student of A.

Astacian (ăstē¹·ʃiăn). [f. L. *astacus*, Gr. ἀστακός lobster + -IAN.] *Zool.* A crustacean of the lobster kind. **A·stacite, Asta·colite,** a fossil crustacean, resembling a lobster or crayfish.

A-starboard (ăstā·ɹbōᵊɹd), *adv.* 1627. [A *prep.*[1]] *Naut.* On or towards the starboard side. *To put the helm a-starboard*: to bring the rudder to the port side, making the vessel turn to the left.

A-sta·re, *adv.* 1855. [A *prep.*[1]] Staring; prominent.

†**Asta·rt,** *v.* ME. [A- *pref.* 1.] **1.** *intr.* To start up -1596; to start into existence (*orig.* with *dat.* of person); hence *trans.* to befall -1579; to start off, escape -1541. **2.** *trans.* (*orig.* with *dat.*) To escape, avoid -1575.

A-sta·rt, *adv.* 1721. [A *prep.*[1]] With a start, suddenly.

†**Asta·te,** early var. of ESTATE.

Astatic (ăstæ·tik), *a.* 1832. [f. Gr. ἄστατος + -IC.] *Electro-Magn.* Having no tendency to remain in a fixed position.

Astatic needle: one so situated as to be unaffected by the earth's magnetism. Hence **Asta·tically** *adv.*

A-stay (ăstē¹·), *adv.* 1867. [A *prep.*[1]] *Naut.* Used of an anchor when, in heaving in, the cable is at an acute angle, in a position like that of one of the ship's stays. Cf. A-PEAK.

†**A-stay·s,** *adv.* 1622. = ABACK -1671.

Astee·r, *adv. Sc.* 1535. [A *prep.*[1] + *stere*, var. of STIR.] Stirring; in commotion.

Asteism (æ·stiˌiz'm). 1589. [ad. L. *asteismus*, a. Gr., f. ἀστεῖος, f. ἄστυ.] *Rhet.* Genteel irony, polite and ingenious mockery.

A·stel. ME. [a. OF. *astelle*:—late L. *hastella*, dim. of *hasta*.] †**1.** A slip of wood; a splinter; split wood -1472. **2.** *Mining.* A board, or ceiling of boards, over the men's heads in a mine, to protect them (Weale).

Aster (a·stəɹ). 1603. [a. L., a. Gr. ἀστήρ.] †**1.** A star. *Obs.* as Eng. -1706. **2.** *Bot.* A large genus of the N.O. *Compositæ*, with radiated flowers, including the indigenous British Sea Starwort or Michaelmas Daisy (*A. Tripolium*) 1706. **3.** China Aster: a flower (*Callistephus chinensis*) resembling the asters proper 1794. Hence **Astera·ceous** *a.*

-aster (æstəɹ), a. L. *-aster*, suffix of sbs. and adjs., expressing incomplete resemblance, hence generally pejorative (Diez); in Eng. used only in words from L. or Rom., e. g. *poetaster.*

‖**Aste·ria.** 1646. [L.] A precious stone mentioned by Pliny; either the *Asteriated sapphire* or Cymophane.

†**Aste·rial,** *a.* 1686. [f. Gr. ἀστέριος + -AL.] **a.** Of or connected with the stars 1708. **b.** Star-like; asteriated.

‖**Asterias** (ăstīᵊ·riæ̆s). Pl. **-æ.** 1794. [mod. L., a. Gr. ἀστερίας, f. ἀστήρ. A sing. **asteria** occurs.] *Zool.* A genus of Echinoderms, containing the common Five-rayed Star-fish, with allied species. **Aste·rialite,** a fossil star-fish. **A·sterid, Asteri·dian,** an animal belonging to the *Asteridæ* or star-fish family.

Asteriated (ăstīᵊ·riˌeⁱtĕd), *ppl. a.* 1816. [f. Gr. ἀστέριος + -ATE + -ED.] Radiated; with rays diverging from the centre, as in a star.

‖**Asterion** (ăstīᵊ·riǫn). OE. [mod.L., a. Gr. ἀστέριον, f. ἀστήρ.] †**a.** *Herb.* Name of an unknown plant. **b.** in *Phys.* The point behind the mastoid process, where the parietal, occipital, and temporal bones meet.

Asterisk (æ·stĕrisk). 1612. [ad. L. *asteriscus*, a. Gr. ἀστερίσκος, dim. of ἀστήρ.] **1.** A little star 1682. **2.** *transf.* Anything shaped or radiating like a star; *spec.* in *Eastern Ch.* a star-shaped instrument placed above the chalice and paten to prevent the veil from touching the elements 1708. **3.** *esp.* The figure of a star (*) used in writing and printing **a.** as a reference to a footnote, **b.** to indicate an omission, **c.** to mark words and phrases as conjectural, obscure, etc., **d.** as a dividing mark, etc. 1612.

3. The A. divides each verse of a Psalm into two parts 1824. Hence **A·sterisk** *v.* to mark with an a.

Asterism (æ·stĕriz'm). 1598. [ad. Gr. ἀστερισμός, f. ἀστήρ.] **1.** A cluster of stars; a constellation. †**2.** *loosely,* A star, or anything star-shaped -1743. **3.** Three asterisks placed thus (⁂) to direct attention to a particular passage. *Rarely,* a single asterisk so used. 1649. **4.** *Min.* (Also *asterismus.*) An appearance of light in the shape of a six-rayed star, as in star sapphire 1879. Hence **Asteri·smal** *a.* of or pertaining to asterisms. †**Asteri·stic** *a.* starry (*rare*).

†**A·sterite.** ME. [ad. L. *asterites* (also used), a. Gr.] A gem known to the ancients; cf. ASTERIA, ASTRION.

Astern (ăstə̄·ɹn), *adv.* (*prep.*). 1627. [A *prep.*[1]] *Naut.* **1.** In or at the stern 1675; hence, in the rear 1627. **2.** Of motion: To the rear, backward; stern foremost 1681. **3.** *prep.* At the stern of (a ship) 1675.

Asternal (ăstə̄·ɹnăl), *a.* 1847. [f. A- *pref.* 14 + L. *sternum*, ad. Gr. στέρνον + -AL[1].] Not joined to the breast-bone.

Asteroid (æ·stĕroid). 1802. [ad. Gr. ἀστεροειδής, f. ἀστήρ.] **A.** *adj.* Star-shaped, star-like 1854. **B.** *sb.* **1.** One of the numerous minute planetary bodies revolving round the sun between the orbits of Mars and Jupiter; called also *planetoids* and *minor planets* 1802. †**2.** A meteor -1849. **3.** Hence, a kind of fire-work 1875. Hence **Asteroi·dal** *a.*; var. †**Asteroi·dical.**

Asterophyllite (æ:stĕroˌfi·ləit). 1847. [f. Gr. ἀστήρ + φύλλον + λίθος.] *Palæont.* A fossil plant, with leaves arranged in whorls, found in the coal formations of Europe and America.

‖**Asthenia** (æsþīnəi·ă). Occ. **a·stheny.** 1830. [mod.L., a. Gr. ἀσθένεια, f. ἀ + σθένος.] *Path.* Lack of strength, diminution of vital power, debility. **Astheno·logy,** scientific consideration of diseases arising from debility. **Asthe·no·pia** [Gr. ὤψ, ὦπα], weakness of sight. Hence **Asthe·nic, -al** *a.* of, pertaining to, or characterized by a.

Asthma (æ·sþmă, æ·smă). ME. [a. Gr. ἆσθμα, f. ἄζειν, f. ἄειν.] Difficulty of breathing; *spec.* a disease of respiration, marked by intermittent paroxysms of difficult breathing, with a wheezing sound, constriction in the chest, cough, and expectoration.

Asthmatic (æ̆sþmæ·tik), *a.* (*sb.*) 1542. [ad. L. *asthmaticus*, a. Gr.; see ASTHMA and -IC.] **1.** Affected with or suffering from asthma. **2.** Of or pertaining to, or good against, asthma 1620. **3.** *fig.* Wheezy 1853. **4.** *sb.* One suffering from asthma 1610. Hence **Asthma·tical** *a.*, **-ly** *adv.*

Astigmatic (æstigmæ·tik), *a.* 1849. [f. Gr. ἀ + στίγμα, -ματ-, + -IC.] *Phys.* Pertaining to or characterized by astigmatism.

Astigmatism (ăsti·gmătiz'm). 1862. [f. as prec + -ISM.] A structural defect in the eye, viz. unequal curvature of the cornea, which prevents the rays of light from being brought to a common focus on the retina.

†**Asti·pulate,** *v.* 1548. [f. L. *astipulat-*, *a(d)stipulari.*] *intr.* To make an agreement or stipulation; to assent (*to*) -1652; *trans.* to assent to 1658. Hence †**Asti:pula·tion,** bargain; assent; a confirming statement.

†**Asti·r,** *v.* [OE. *astyrian*; see STIR.] To stir up, move -1567.

Astir (ăstə̄·ɹ), *adv.* 1823. [A *prep.*[1] Perh. f. Sc. ASTEER, q.v. Not in any 18th c. Dict.] Stirring; *esp.* out of bed; *gen.* in motion; in excitement.

All kings and kinglets..are a.; their brows clouded with menace CARLYLE.

†**Astite, as tite,** *adv.* Chiefly *north.* ME. See As and TITE. It had also the special sense: Immediately (Fr. *aussitôt*). -1674.

Astomatous (ăstǫ·mătəs), *a.* 1855. [See next.] Having no mouth; as in *Zool.* the *Astomata*, a division of the Protozoa, comprising the *Gregarinidæ* and *Rhizopoda.*

Astomous (æ·stŏməs), *a.* 1857. [f. Gr. ἄστομος (f. ἀ + στόμα) + -OUS.] Having no mouth; as in *Bot.* those Mosses in which the urn does not open by the detachment of the operculum.

†**Astone, astun** (ăstʊ·n), *v.* ME. [app. a. OF. *estoner* (now *étonner*):—L. **extonare*, f. *ex* + *tonare*. See STUN, later and perh. aphet. f. *astun*. Cf. G. *staunen*, *erstaunen*.] **1.** To stun -1612; to daze (the eyes) CHAUCER. **2.** To strike mute with amazement; to astonish -1677. **3.** *intr.* To be amazed. (Cf. G. *erstaunen*.) ME. only. Hence †**Astoned, Astunned** *ppl. a.* †**Asto·ning** *vbl. sb.* = ASTONISHING.

Astonied (ăstǫ·nid), *ppl. a.* ME. [var. of *astoned.* Sometimes derived from *stony*, and used as = *petrified.*] †**1.** Stunned; made insensible, benumbed, paralysed -1611. Of the teeth: set on edge ME. **2.** Dazed (*arch.*); dismayed (*arch.*); amazed (*arch.*) ME.

Astonish (ăstǫ·niʃ), *v.* 1530. [Later var. of *astony.*] †**1.** To stun; to deprive of sensation, as by a blow -1635; to set the teeth on edge -1656. †**2.** To stun mentally; to drive stupid, bewilder -1600. †**3.** To dismay -1601. **4.** To amaze, surprise greatly 1611.

1. I astonysshe with a stroke upon the head 1530. 3. Such dreadfull Heraulds to a. *Jul. C.* I. iii. 56. 4. The people were astonished at his doctrine *Matt.* vii. 28. Hence †**Asto·nishable** *a.* calculated to a. **Asto·nishedly** *adv.* **Asto·nisher.**

Astonishing (ăstǫ·niʃiŋ), *vbl. sb.* 1530. [f. prec.] †Deprivation of sensation; dismaying (*arch.*); surprised wonder. Hence **Asto·nishing-ly** *adv.*, **-ness.**

Asto·nishment. 1576. [f. as prec.] †**1.** Insensibility -1656. †**2.** Loss of sense or wits; mental prostration -1725. **3.** Loss of presence of mind, coolness, or courage (*arch.*) 1586. **4.** Amazement due to the sudden presentation of anything unlooked for or unaccountable 1594. **5.** An object of such amazement 1611.

2. *Wine of astonishment*: stupefying wine *Ps.* lx. 3. 3. They stricken were with great a., And their faint hearts with senselesse horror queld SPENSER. 4. Thou in our wonder and a. Hast built thy selfe a livelong monument MILT. *On Shaks.* 5. Thou shalt become an a., a prouerbe, and a by-worde *Deut.* xxviii. 37.

Astony (ăstǫ·ni), *v. arch.* ME. [var. of ASTONE.] **1.** *trans.* = ASTONE -1646. **2.** *intr.* (? or *absol.*) (*rare*). MRS. BROWNING.

Astoo·p, *adv.* 1644. [A *prep.*[1]] In an inclined position.

Astound (ăstau·nd), *ppl. a. arch.* ME. [Phonetic development of ASTONED, *astun'd.*] †**1.** Stunned -1596. **2.** Confounded; amazed (*arch.*) 1440. Hence †**Astou·ndedness.**

Astound (ăstau·nd), *v.* [f. *c* 1600 from prec. as contracted form of a pa. pple. *astounded.*] †**1.** To deprive of consciousness, stupefy -1727. **2.** To shock with alarm, surprise, or wonder 1634.

2. These thoughts may startle well, but not a. The virtuous mind MILT. *Comus* 210. Hence **Astou·ndingly** *adv.* **Astou·ndment.**

†**A·stracism.** *rare.* 1590. [? Cf. ASTERISK, etc.] An asterism; an asterisk -1695.

A-stra·ddle, *adv.* 1703. [A *prep.*[1]] In a straddling position. *A-straddle of*: bestriding.

Astragal (æ·străgăl). 1563. [ad. L., a. Gr. ἀστράγαλος.] **1.** *Phys.* The ball of the ankle-joint; the huckle-bone; = ASTRAGALUS 1. Hence in *pl.* (as in Gr.): Dice, which were orig. huckle-bones 1727. **2.** *Arch.* A small moulding, of semicircular section, placed round the top or bottom of columns. Also *attrib.* 1563. **3.** *Gunnery.* A ring or moulding encircling a cannon about six inches from the mouth 1656.

Astragalomancy (ăstræ·găloˌmæːnsi). 1652. [f. ASTRAGALUS + -MANCY.] Divination by means of dice or huckle-bones.

‖**Astragalus** (ăstræ·gălŏs). 1541. [L., a. Gr.; see ASTRAGAL.] **1.** *Phys.* The ball of the ankle-joint, the upper bone of the foot, on which the tibia rests. **2.** *Bot.* An extensive genus of leguminous plants, including *A. verus*, which produces gum tragacanth, and three British species known as Milk-vetch 1548.

†**Astrai·n,** *v.* ME. [a. OF. *astreign-*, *astreindre*:—L. *astringere* to ASTRINGE.] To bind -1594.

A-strai·n, *adv.* 1856. [A *prep.*[1]] On the strain.

Astrakhan (æstrăkæ·n). 1766. The skin of still-born or very young lambs from Astrakhan in Russia, the wool of which resembles fur.

Astral (æ·străl), *a.* (*sb.*) 1605. [ad. L. *astralis*, f. *astrum.*] **1.** Of, connected with, or proceeding from the stars. **2.** Star-shaped, star-like 1671. **3.** *sb.* An astral lamp 1860.

1. A. showers SIR F. PALGRAVE. *Astral spirits*

those formerly supposed to live in the heavenly bodies, represented as fallen angels, souls of dead men, etc. **2.** *A. lamp*: one resembling an Argand lamp, with the oil in a flattened ring, and so contrived that uninterrupted light is thrown upon the table below it.

A-stra·nd, *adv.* 1810. [A *prep.*[1]] Stranded.

†**Astray·,** *v.* ME. [var. of ESTRAY (see A- *pref.* 9), a. OF. *estraier*:—L. **extravagare*, f. *extra* + *vagare*. Cf. ASTRAY *adv.*, and STRAY.]

Astray (ăstrē·), *adv.* or *a.* ME. [perh. the OF. pa. pple. *estraié* (see prec.), with *-e* lost. As adj. STRAY is now used; cf. *alive, live.*] **1.** Out of the right way, wandering. **2.** Away from the right 1535.

1. And lead these testie Riuals so a. *Mids. N.* III. ii. 358. **2.** They go astraie and speake lyes *Ps.* lxii. 3.

‖**Astre.** 1500. [a. OF. *astre, aistre*, of unkn. origin.] A hearth, a home. Hence **Astrer,** a peasant householder, residing at the hearth where he was bred.

†**Astre·an,** *a. rare.* [f. Gr. ἀστραῖος + -AN.] Of or belonging to the stars. HOWELL.

Astrict (ăstri·kt), *v.* 1513. [f. L. *astrict-, astringere.*] **1.** To bind up, compress; *hence*, to render costive 1548. **2.** To bind by moral or legal obligation 1513. **3.** To restrict, limit *to* 1588. **4.** *Sc. Law.* To restrict in tenure.

3. The mind is thus astricted to certain necessary modes or forms of thought SIR W. HAMILTON. Hence **Astri·cted** *ppl. a.* confined, restricted; *spec.* in *Sc. Law* of lands held on such terms that the tenant must take grain grown upon them to be ground at a particular mill, paying a toll called *multure* or *thirlage*.

Astriction (ăstri·kʃən). 1536. [ad. L. *a(d)strictionem*. Cf. F. *astriction.*] **1.** The action of binding, or drawing close together, *esp.* the soft organic tissues; the state of being thus bound; constriction; constipation 1568. †**2.** Astringency –1750. †**3.** Obligation, bond –1643. **4.** Restriction; *spec.* in tenure; see prec. 1619.

4. In Norway there is no a. to mills S. LAING.

Astrictive (ăstri·ktiv), *a.* (*sb.*) 1555. [f. L. *astrict-* (see ASTRICT *v.*) + -IVE.] †**1.** Binding (*lit.* and *fig.*) –1659. **2.** Astringent, styptic 1562. **3.** *sb.* An astringent 1657. Hence **Astri·ctively** *adv.*

Astride (ăstrəi·d). 1664. [A *prep.*[1]] **1.** *adv.* With the legs stretched wide apart, or so that one leg is on each side of some object between. Also *transf.* and *fig.* **2.** *prep.* Bestriding 1713.

1. The way in which the impudent little beggar stands a., and sticks his little feet out THACKERAY.

Astringe (ăstri·ndʒ), *v.* 1523. [ad. L. *a-, ad-stringere.*] **1.** To bind together, draw close; to constrict; *hence*, to constipate 1562; †*intr.* to become constricted. HOLLAND. †**2.** To bind morally or legally; to oblige –1752.

2. Your Grace is not astringed or bounden to any charge 1523.

Astringency (ăstri·ndʒĕnsi). 1601. [f. ASTRINGENT; see -ENCY.] **1.** Astringent quality. †**2.** Astricted state 1669. **3.** *fig.* Harshness 1823.

1. The a. of tea is due to the tannin present 1881.

Astringent (ăstri·ndʒĕnt). 1541. [a. F., ad. L. *astringentem*; see ASTRINGE.] *adj.* **1.** Having power to draw together or contract the organic tissues; binding, constrictive, styptic. **2.** *fig.* Severe, stern 1820. †**3.** Constipated 1662. **4.** *sb.* [sc. *medicine* or *substance.*] 1626.

4. Blood is stanched .. by astringents BACON *Sylva* § 66. Hence **Astri·ngently** *adv.*

Astringer, var. of AUSTRINGER.

‖**A·strion.** ME. [L., dim. of Gr. ἀστήρ.] A kind of precious stone; perh. the star sapphire. Cf. ASTERIA, ASTROITE.

Astro- (æ·strŏ), repr. Gr. ἀστρο-, comb. f. ἄστρον.

astro-a·lchemist, one who mingled astrology and alchemy; **-chronolo·gical** *a.*, pertaining to the chronology of the heavenly bodies; **-litho·logy,** the scientific study of meteoric stones; **-ma·gical** *a.*, pertaining to star-divination; †**-phano·meter** [Gr. φανός], = ASTROMETER; †**-phile,** a lover of the stars; **-photo·meter,** an apparatus for measuring the intensity of a star's light; **-photome·trical** *a.*; **-phy·llite** [Gr. φύλλον], an orthorhombic mineral of yellow colour and micaceous composition, occurring sometimes in stellate groups; **-phy·sical** *a.*, relating to stellar physics; **-theo·logy,** that part of theology which may be deduced from a study of the stars; a religious system based upon the observation of the heavens.

Astrognosy (ăstrǫ·gnŏsi). 1871. [ad. mod. L. *astrognosia*, f. Gr. ἀστρο- + γνωσία = γνῶσις.] Knowledge of the stars, *esp.* the fixed stars.

Astrogony (ăstrǫ·gŏni). 1869. [f. ASTRO- + Gr. -γονία.] The doctrine of the generation of the stars. var. **Astro·geny.** Hence **Astrogo·nic** *a.*

Astrography (ăstrǫ·grăfi). 1740. [f. ASTRO- + Gr. -γραφία.] The science of describing the stars; the mapping of the heavens.

Astroite (æ·strǫ|əit). 1601. [ad. L. *astroites* (Pliny), f. Gr. ἀστρο-.] **1.** = ASTRION. †**2.** Any star-shaped mineral or fossil –1728. **3.** *Zool.* A species of madrepore 1708.

Astrolabe (æ·strŏlēb). ME. [a. OF. *astrelabe*, and ad. med.L. *astrolabium*, f. Gr. ἀστρολάβον, orig. adj. 'star-taking'.] An instrument formerly used to take altitudes, and to solve other problems in astronomy.

The chief types of the astrolabe were: *a.* A portable ARMILLA. *b.* A planisphere. *c.* A graduated brass ring, with movable index turning upon the centre. His almagest .. his astrylabe CHAUCER. Hence **Astrola·bical** *a.*

Astrolatry (ăstrǫ·lătri). 1678. [f. ASTRO- + Gr. λατρεία.] The worship of the stars.

†**A·strologe.** ME. [a. OF., corruption of *aristoloche.*] The herb ARISTOLOCHIA –1706.

Astrologer (ăstrǫ·lŏdʒəɹ). ME. [f. ASTROLOGY. Cf. ASTRONOMER.] †**1.** An observer of the stars, a practical astronomer. (Orig. distinguished from *astronomer* as *practical* from *speculative.*) –1676. †**2.** The cock ME. only. **3.** One who professes (judicial) astrology (see ASTROLOGY 1 b) 1601.

1. An A. expert in his art, foretelleth an eclipse of the Sunne 1625. **2.** The cok, commune a. CHAUCER. vars. †**A·strolog, -logue; Astro·logaster** ? *Obs.*; †**Astrolo·gian.**

Astrologic (æstrolǫ·dʒik). 1569. [Ult. ad. Gr. ἀστρολογικός; see ASTROLOGY.] **1.** *adj.* Of or belonging to astrology or astrologers 1648. †**2.** *sb. pl.* Matters or facts of astrology –1671. Hence **Astrolo·gical** *a.* astronomical; pertaining to astrology; var. **Astro·logous. Astrolo·gically** *adv.*

Astro·logize, *v.* 1733. [f. Gr. ἀστρολόγος + -IZE.] To examine by astrology; *intr.* to practise or study astrology (*rare*).

Astrology (ăstrǫ·lŏdʒi). ME. [a. F. *astrologie*, ad. L. *astrologia*, a. Gr., f. ἀστρολόγος, f. ἄστρον + -λογος. In OF. and ME. *astronomie* was the earlier and general word, *astrologie* coming in later for the art or practical application of astronomy. Not in SHAKS.] **1.** *gen.* Practical astronomy; the application of astronomy, *esp.* (in later usage) to the prediction of events natural and moral. It was of two kinds: †**a.** *Natural A.*: the calculation and foretelling of natural phenomena, as tides and eclipses, etc. (*Obs.* since 17th c.). **b.** *Judicial A.*: the art of judging of the occult influences of the stars upon human affairs; astromancy. (The only meaning since 17th c.) †**2.** = ASTRONOMY –1807.

1. Naturall A., when it keepes it selfe within its due bounds is lawfull BP. HALL. Judicial A. judicially condemned W. ROWLAND (*title*).

Astromancy (æ·stromæ:nsi). *rare.* 1652. [ad. med.L., a. Gr. ἀστρομαντεία.] Divination by the stars; astrology (in mod. sense). Hence **A·stroma:ncer** (*rare*). **Astroma·ntic** *a.* of or pertaining to a.; *sb.* an astromancer.

Astro-meteorology (æ:stro|mī:tiŏrǫ·lŏdʒi). 1862. [f. ASTRO- + METEOROLOGY.] The investigation of the (alleged) influence upon the weather, climate, etc. of planetary phenomena, such as sun-spots, comets, planetary conjunctions, etc.; also, the (pretended) prognostication of the weather. Hence **A:strome:teorolo·gical** *a.* **A:strome:teoro·logist.**

Astrometer (ăstrǫ·mītəɹ). 1830. [f. ASTRO- + Gr. μέτρον.] An instrument for measuring the apparent relative magnitude of the stars.

Astronomer (ăstrǫ·nŏməɹ). ME. [f. ASTRONOMY.] One who studies astronomy. †**b.** An astrologer –1611.

A. Royal: official title of the a. who has charge of one of the royal, or national, observatories of Great Britain. **b.** Astronymers and enchaunteris..that disseyven mennus wittis WYCLIF 2 *Chron.* xxxiii. 6.

Astronomic (æstronǫ·mik), *a.* 1712. [a. F. *astronomique*, ad. L. *astronomicus*, a. Gr.; see ASTRONOMY.] Of or belonging to astronomy.

Astronomical, *a.* 1556. [f. prec.] Connected with, bearing upon, dealing with astronomy. (Cf. an *Astronomical* Society with an *astronomic* fact.) Also *ellipt.* as *sb. pl.* 1706.

Astronomical year: one determined by a. observations, apart from conventional reckoning. *ellipt.* A. Numbers or Astronomicals. (See Sexagesimal Fractions.) Hence **Astrono·mically** *adv.*

†**Astronomien, -an.** ME. [a. F.; cf. *chrestien*, etc.] Early word for ASTRONOMER (including *astrologer*).

Astronomize (ăstrǫ·nŏməiz), *v.* 1682. [f. ASTRONOMY; see -IZE.] *intr.* To pursue astronomy; to act or speak astronomically.

Thales..astronomising as he walked H. ROGERS.

Astronomy (ăstrǫ·nŏmi). ME. [a. OF. *astronomie*, ad. L. *astronomia*, a. Gr., f. (ult.) ἄστρον + νέμειν. In OF. and early Eng. *astronomie* was used before *astrologie*, and included it; subseq. *astrologie* was differentiated as the *art* or *practice* of *astronomy*, and by the 17th c. both words took their current senses.] The science which treats of the constitution, relative positions, and motions of the heavenly bodies, including the earth. †**b.** Astrology –1728.

Astronomye, whiche is of all clergye the ende CAXTON. **b.** Not from the stars do I my judgment pluck, And yet methinks I have astronomy SHAKS. *Sonn.* xiv.

†**A·strophel.** [? corruption of *astrophyllum.*] Name of an unknown plant. SPENSER.

Astroscope (æ·strŏskoup). 1675. [f. ASTRO- + Gr. -σκοπος.] An old instrument composed of two cones, having the constellations, etc., delineated on their surface. Hence †**Astro·scopy.**

†**Astru·ctive,** *a. rare.* [f. L. *astruct-* (*a(d)struere*) + -IVE.] Constructive. BP. HALL.

A-strut (ăstrʊ·t), *adv.* ME. [A *prep.*[1]] **1.** Sticking out; puffed up (*arch.*). †**2.** Stubbornly –1460. **3.** On the strut, strutting.

Astucious (ăstiū·ʃəs), *a.* Also **-tious.** 1823. [ad. F. *astucieux*, f. L. *astutus* ASTUTE.] Astute. Hence **Astu·ciously** *adv.* **Astu·city,** astuteness.

Astute (ăstiū·t), *a.* 1611. [(? a. F. *astut*) ad. L. *astutus*, lengthened f. *astus.*] Of keen penetration, *esp.* as to one's own interests; subtle, sagacious; wily.

The a. fickleness of a barbarian BOSW. SMITH. Hence **Astu·tely** *adv.* **Astu·teness** (occ. *astutia*).

Astylar (ăstəi·lăɹ), *a.* 1842. [f. Gr. ἀ + στῦλος + -AR.] Without columns or pilasters.

Asty·llen. 1849. *Mining.* A small dam in an adit or level.

A-su·dden, *adv.* 1875. [A *prep.*[1]] Of a sudden.

Asunder (ăsʊ·ndəɹ), *adv.* [OE. phr. *on sundran*; see A *prep.*[1] and SUNDER.] †**1.** In or into a position apart –1548. **2.** Of two or more things: Apart from each other in position, direction, or thought ME. **3.** Of one thing: In two, in pieces; *esp.* with *break, rend*, etc. 1450.

2. Wide a. as pole and pole FROUDE. My Chaffe And Corne shall flye a. SHAKS. Freres and feendes been but litel a. CHAUCER. Hence **Asu·nderness.**

†**Asu·nder,** *v.* [f. A- *pref.* 1 + OE. *sundrian.*] To put asunder, divide –1593.

A-swa·rm, *adv.* 1882. [A *prep.*[1]] Swarming.

†**A-swa·sh,** *adv.* 1530. [A *prep.*[1] + ?] **1.** Crosswise, aslant –1611. **2.** With scorn –1611.

A-sway·, *adv.* 1858. [A *prep.*[1]] Swaying.

A-swea·t, *adv.* 1879. [A *prep.*[1]] Sweating.

A-swi·m, *adv.* 1663. [A *prep.*[1]] Swimming.

A-swi·ng, *adv.* 1876. [A *prep.*[1]] Swinging.

†**Aswi·the, as swithe,** *adv.* ME. only. As quickly. Also, immediately. Cf. ASSOON, etc.

A-swoon (ăswū·n), *adv.* ME. [perh. for *aswown* = *iswowen*, OE. *geswōgen*; see ASWOUGH and SWOON *sb.*] In a swoon or faint. Hence **Aswoo·ned** *ppl. a.* **A-swou·nd** *adv.* (*arch.*).

†**Aswou·gh, aswow(e,** *adv.* (or *ppl. a.*) OE. [perh. = *iswowe*:—*iswowen*:—OE. *geswōgen* senseless.] = A-SWOON –1460.

†**Asy·le.** Early f. ASYLUM (in senses **1, 2, 3**).

Asyllabical (æsilæ·bikăl), *a.* 1751. [A- *pref.* 14.] Not constituting a syllable.

Asylum (ăsəi·lŏm). Pl. **-ums** (also, exc. in

sense 3, -a). ME. [a. L., a. Gr. ἄσυλον, neut. of adj., f. ἀ + σύλη. Cf. ASYLE.] 1. A sanctuary for criminals and debtors, from which they cannot be forcibly taken without sacrilege. 2. *gen.* A secure place of refuge or shelter 1642. 3. *abstr.* Inviolable shelter; protection 1725. 4. A benevolent institution affording shelter and support to some class of the afflicted, the unfortunate, or destitute; *esp.* (pop.) a 'lunatic asylum' 1776.

1. Romulus..set up a sanctuarie or lawlesse church, called A. HOLLAND. 2. The *A.* for superstition SIR E. DERING. 3. The Right of A. 1725. 4. Asyla for [lepers] PENNANT.

Asymbo·lic, -al, *a.* 1660. [A- *pref.* 14.] Not symbolic(al.

†**Asy·mmetral,** *a.* 1630. [f. Gr. ἀσύμμετρος + -AL[1].] a. Incommensurable. b. ASYMMETRICAL.

Asy·mmetra·nthous, *a.* [f. as prec. + Gr. ἄνθος + -OUS.] *Bot.* Having asymmetric flowers.

Asymme·tric, -al, *a.* 1690. [Gr. ἀ + SYMMETRIC(AL.] Not symmetrical, with the parts not arranged correspondingly. var. †**Asy·mmetrous** (*rare*). Hence **Asymme·trically** *adv.*

Asymmetroca·rpous, *a.* [f. Gr. ἀσύμμετρος + καρπός + -OUS.] Having asymmetric fruit.

Asymmetry (ăsi·mĕtri). 1652. [ad. Gr. ἀσυμμετρία: see SYMMETRY.] 1. *Math.* The relation of two quantities which have no common measure. ? *Obs.* 2. Want of symmetry or proportion 1664.

Asymptote (æ·simtǭut). 1656. [ad. (ult.) Gr. ἀσύμπτωτος.] *Math.* A line which continually approaches a given curve, but does not meet it within a finite distance. A rectilinear asymptote may be considered as a tangent to the curve when produced to infinity. Also *fig.* and *attrib.* **Asy·mptosy,** the quality of being asymptotic. HOBBES. Hence **Asympto·tic(al** *a.* **Asympto·tically** *adv.*

Asynartete (ăsi·naɹtīt). 1830. [ad. Gr. ἀσυνάρτητος (also used *subst.*).] *Pros.* 1. *adj.* Not connected; consisting of two members having different rhythms. 2. *sb.* [sc. *verse.*] Hence **Asy·narte·tic** *a.*

Asynchronism (ăsi·ŋkrŏniz'm). 1875. [A- *pref.* 14.] Non-correspondence in time. **Asy·nchronous** *a.* not coinciding in time.

‖**Asyndeton** (ăsi·ndĭtǫn). 1589. [L., a. Gr. τὸ ἀσύνδετον, subst. use of adj.] *Rhet.* A figure which omits the conjunction. **Asynde·tic** *a.* not connected by conjunctions.

A...as thus: I saw it, I said it, I will sweare it PUTTENHAM.

Asyntactic (æsintæ·ktik), *a.* 1880. [f. Gr. ἀσύντακτος + -IC (after *syntactic*).] Loosely put together, ungrammatical.

‖**Asystole** (ăsi·stŏlĭ). 1870. [mod.L.; see SYSTOLE.] *Path.* Cessation of the functional contraction of the heart. **Asy·stolism** [= Fr. *asystolie*], the symptoms of a.

At (æt, ăt), *prep.* [Com. Teut.: OE. *æt*, usu. governing *dat.* Lost in mod.G. and Du., and replaced by *to* (G. *zu*, Du. *toe*), as in s. w. Eng. dialects.] **I.** Local position. 1. Expressing primarily the relation of a thing to a point of space which it touches; hence, indefinitely, the *place* where it is, in the sense of *close to, near, by, in,* etc. OE. 2. With proper names of places, *esp.* of towns (exc. one's own town, or capital), and small islands OE. 3. *At* a person (L. *apud*): In contact with, *esp.* (*ellipt.*) applying to, pestering, assailing ME. Also (*ellipt.*) with possessive case: At a person's (house). Fr. *chez*, G. *bei*. 1562. 4. Expressing some practical connexion: e. g. *at* school (cf. *in* school) OE. 5. Assisting or present at OE. 6. Expressing the point or part, side or direction, where anything is, or is applied OE. 7. Of distance: e. g. *at* arm's length 1526. 8. Referring an attribute to a particular part: e. g. out *at* elbows OE. 9. Defining the point *at* which anything enters or issues, and hence = *through* or *by* OE. 10. Determining the source *at* which we seek anything; e. g. *to ask*, etc., at. *Obs.* or *dial.* (repl. by *of, from*) exc. in *at the mouth* or *hands of.* OE. 11. With verbs of motion: †*to* -1601; †*esp.* into personal contact with -1678; even to, as far as: e. g. *to come* (arch.), *arrive, land* at ME.; to reach (through obstacles), *esp.* in *to come, get* at 1530. 12. Hence, of motion *towards*; often *against* ME. 13. Of motion to attain or acquire (*lit.* and *fig.*) 1590.

1. To deliver..materials at the spot 1787. 2. At St. Helena, at the Lakes, (formerly also *at*, now *in*, London, Ireland). 3. They are at me for a subscription (*mod.*). We met at her father's (*mod.*). 5. He had been at the battle THACKERAY. 6. With a dog at his heels (*mod.*). An infant at the breast (*mod.*). 9. He entered at the front door (*mod.*). 11. He..commanded None should come at him *Wint. T.* II. iii. 32. Stooping down to get at his ear DICKENS. 12. *To run, rush, go, have, throw, shoot, etc.* at; *to stare, shout, swear, etc.* at; *to hint, etc.* at. 13. Drowning men catch at straws *Provb.* Setting your cap at him MISS AUSTEN.

II. Of action, position, state, condition, manner. 1. With things put for the activities of which they are the objects, centres, or instruments: e. g. *at meat* = eating; *at the bar*; *at sword's point*; *assault-at-arms*, etc. OE. 2. With actions, as *at work* 1440; *at it*: hard at work 1606. 3. After many verbs of action: *to work, toil* at; *to tear* at, etc. ME. 4. Connecting adjs. of occupation and proficiency, or their sbs., with a thing or action OE. 5. Of posture, position: *at gaze, at bay* 1535. 6. Of state, or condition of existence: e. g. *at peace, at a loss*, etc. ME. 7. Of mutual relations: e. g. *at one, at daggers drawn* ME. 8. Of manner, measure, extent, etc.: e. g. *at large, at random* ME. 9. Of conditioning circumstance: e. g. *at peril, at a disadvantage*, etc. ME. 10. Of relation to some one's will or disposition: e. g. *at his discretion*, etc. ME.

4. In agility and skill at his weapons MACAULAY.

III. Of relative position in a series, degree, rate, value. 1. Defining special point in a series at which one begins, stops, etc.; *esp.* with superlatives ME. 2. Of rate or degree, *at* which a thing is done ME. 3. Of price or value ME. 4. = *according to* ME.

1. Johnson at his very best TREVELYAN. 2. She.. worked at high pressure 1882. 3. To set at nought their counsel (*mod.*). 4. By land or by water at their choice MACAULAY.

IV. Of time, order, occasion, cause, object. 1. Introducing the time or occasion ME.; the age *at* which one is ME.; distance in time, interval ME. 2. Of the number of times, turns, etc. ME. 3. Of order: e. g. *at first*, etc. OE. 4. Introducing the occasion, and *hence* the cause of a fact, action, or emotion ME.

1. Late at Night DRYDEN. At the Restoration Hyde became chief minister MACAULAY. At riper years MARLOWE. At three Months after date 1716. 2. To complete the business at two sittings (*mod.*). 4. They bee caryed aboute like babes at euery blast of doctrine 1574. Impatient at the delays KANE.

V. Phr. See *at* ALL, *at any* RATE, *at* STAKE, AT HOME, AT ONE, AT ONCE.

VI. †With the infinitive mood: e. g. nothing *at* do, nothing ADO -1470.

VII. †1. With preps. -1594. 2. With advbs. *Obs.* or *dial.* 1440.

At, 'at (ăt). ME. [Worn-down f. *that*; rare after 1500, but still *dial.*] 1. *adv.* or *conj.* = 'that'. 2. *rel. pron.* That; who, which; what ME.

At-, *pref.*[1]:—OE. *æt-*. The prep. AT in composition, 'at, close to, to', freq. in OE., and occas. in ME., but now lost exc. in *atwi·te*, surviving as *twit.*

†**At-,** *pref.*[2]:—OE. *æt-*. Repr. earlier OE. *oþ-, oð-*, 'away, from'.

At-, *pref.*[3]; assim. f. L. *ad-*, bef. *t.* Erron. refash. of *a-* in many non-Latin words, as *a(t)tame*, etc. See AD- *pref.*[2]

‖**Atabal** (atăba·l). 1672. [a. Sp., a. Arab. *at*, i. e. *al* + *tabl* the drum.] A kettle-drum or tabour used by the Moors.

Atacamite (ătæ·kămait). 1837. [f. *Atacama* in Chili + -ITE.] *Min.* A bright green ore, an oxychloride of copper.

Atactic (ătæ·ktik), *a.* 1842. [f. Gr. ἄτακτος + -IC.] Of language: Not syntactic.

Ataghan (æ·tăgan). 1813. var. of YATAGHAN, q. v.

†**Ata·ke,** *v.* ME. only. [A- *pref.* 1.] To overtake; get at.

†**Atala·ntis.** 1709. Brief title of a romance [cf. Bacon's *New Atlantis*] satirizing the movers of the Revolution of 1688; hence *gen.* a secret or scandalous history -1789.

†**Ata·me,** *v.* Also att-. [A- *pref.* 1; for OE. *atemian.*] To tame, subdue -1530.

Ataraxy (æ·tăræksi). Also in L. form **ataraxia.** 1603. [ad. Gr. ἀταραξία, f. ἀ + ταράσσειν.] Freedom from disturbance of mind or passion; stoical indifference.

Ataunt (ătǭ·nt), *adv.* ME. [a. F. *autant.*] †1. As much as possible, thoroughly -1520. 2. *Naut.* With all sails set. (Also *ataunto, all-a-taunto.*) 1622.

Atavic (ătæ·vik), *a.* 1866. [ad. F. *atavique*, f. L. *atavus*; see next and -IC.] Of or pertaining to a remote ancestor. var. **Atavi·stic.**

Atavism (æ·tăviz'm). 1833. [a. F. *atavisme*, f. L. *atavus.*] Resemblance to more remote ancestors rather than to parents; tendency to reproduce the ancestral type in plants and animals. b. *Path.* Recurrence of the disease or constitutional symptoms of an ancestor after the intermission of one or more generations.

Some mysterious a.—Some strange recurrence to a primitive past BAGEHOT.

Ataxy (ătæ·ksi, æ·tæksi). Also in sense 2 as L. *ataxia.* 1615. [ad. Gr. ἀταξία, f. ἀ + τάξις.] †1. Irregularity, disorderliness -1733. 2. *Path.* Irregularity of the animal functions, or of the symptoms of disease.

1. A mere a., or confused chaos 1634. 2. *Locomotor ataxy*: inability to co-ordinate the voluntary movements. Hence **Ata·xic** [not on Gr. analogies] *a.* characterized by a. *Ataxic fever*: malignant typhus.

Atchison (æ·tʃisən, ēⁱ·tʃi-). *Obs.* exc. *Hist.* 1605. [Sc. pronunc. of Atkinson, assay-master of the Edinburgh Mint in James VI's reign.] A copper coin, coated with silver = two-thirds of an English penny, or eight pennies Scots -1773.

‖**Ate** (ēⁱ·tī). 1587. [L., a. Gr. ἄτη.] Infatuation; personified by the Greeks as goddess of mischief and rash destruction.

Not by myself but vengeful Ate driven POPE.

Ate (et, *occas.* ēⁱt), pa. t. of EAT *v.*

-ate, *suffix*[1], formerly *-at*, forming sbs. derived from L. sbs. in *-atus* (*-ato-* and *-atu-*), *-atum, -ata.* 1. In OFr., L. *-atus, -atum* became *-é*, refash. later, and adopted in Eng., as *-at*, with *-e* added in Eng., after 1400, to mark the long vowel. In meaning words in *-ate* are chiefly: a. Sbs. denoting office or function, or the persons performing it, as *episcopate, syndicate.* b. Participial nouns, as *legate* 'one deputed', *mandate* 'a thing commanded'. c. Chemical terms, denoting salts formed by the action of an acid on a base, as *nitrate*, etc. 2. In some words *-ate* = F. *-ate*, ad. L. or It. *-ata*, as in *pirate*, etc.

-ate, *suffix*[2], formerly *-at*, forming ppl. adjs. from L. pa. pples. in *-atus, -ata, -atum* by dropping the termination, e. g. *desolatus, desolat*, subseq. *desolate.* Hence many causative verbs, to which, for a time, the ppl. adjs. served as pa. pples., afterwards becoming obs. or simple adjs. (But cf. *situate* = *situated.*) 2. L. ppl. adjs. in *-atus* were also formed on nouns, etc., when no other part of the vb. was required. Hence *caudate, insensate, apiculate*, etc. 3. Words like *delegate, reprobate*, etc., orig. adj., are also used subst.; see -ATE[1].

-ate, *suffix*[3], a verbal formative, used to English L. vbs. in *-are*, and to form Eng. vbs. on other L. words or elements. This use originated in the formation of vbs. from the ppl. adjs. in *-ate* mentioned under -ATE[2]. Cf. *separate, fascinate, isolate, felicitate, capacitate*, etc.

-ate, *suffix*[4], in *Chem.*; see -ATE[1] 1 c.

Atechnic (ăte·knik). 1869. [A- *pref.* 14; cf. Gr. ἄτεχνος.] *adj.* Not having technical knowledge. *sb.* [sc. *person.*]

‖**Ate·knia.** 1874. [mod.L., a. Gr.] Childlessness.

Atelectasis (ætĭle·ktăsis). 1859. [mod.L., f. Gr. ἀτελής + ἔκτασις.] *Path.* Imperfect dilatation, *esp.* of the lungs of newly-born children.

Atelene (æ·tĭlīn), *a.* 1859. [f. Gr. ἀτελής.] *Crystallog.* Imperfect; wanting regular forms in the genus.

‖**Atelier** (a·təlye·). 1840. [F.: cf. ASTEL.] A workshop; an artist's or sculptor's studio.

Atellan (ăte·lăn). Also Att-. 1647. [ad. L. *Atellanus*, f. *Atella* in Campania.] 1. *adj.* Of or pertaining to Atella, or its licentious farces;

hence, farcical, ribald. **2.** *sb.* A dramatic composition of this kind.

Atelo- (æ·tĭlo), comb. f. Gr. ἀτελής imperfect, as **atelo·glo·ssia**, malformation of the tongue; **-gna·thia**, of the jaws; **-mye·lia**, of the spinal marrow; **-sto·mia**, of the mouth.

A-temporal (ăte·mpŏrăl), *a.* 1870. [A- *pref.* 14.] Timeless.

Ater-; see ATTER-.

Athalamous (ăþæ·lăməs), *a.* 1847. [f. Gr. ἀ + θάλαμος + -OUS.] *Bot.* Of lichens: Having no conceptacles on the thallus.

Athamantin (æþămæ·ntin). 1863. *Chem.* A crystalline substance, $C_{24}H_{30}O_7$, of rancid soapy odour and bitter taste, procured from the roots and seeds of *Athamanta oreoselinum.*

Athamaunte, obs. f. ADAMANT.

Athanasian (æþănē·ʃiăn). 1586. [f. *Athanasius*, archbishop of Alexandria in the reign of Constantine.] *adj.* Of or pertaining to Athanasius. *sb.* An adherent of the doctrines of Athanasius. **Athana·sianism,** the principles or doctrines of the Athanasian Creed. **Athana·sianist,** an adherent of this Creed.

Athanasian Creed: that beginning '*Quicunque vult*', which has been attributed to Athanasius.

Athanasy (ăþæ·năsi). 1870. [ad. L., a. Gr. ἀθανασία.] Deathlessness, immortality.

Athanor (æ·þănǭɹ). 1471. [ad. Arab. *at-tannūr*, the furnace.] *Alch.* A digesting furnace used by the alchemists, in which a constant heat was maintained by means of a self-feeding apparatus. Also *fig.*

Atheism (ē·þiˌiz'm). 1587. [a. F. *athéisme*, f. Gr. ἄθεος.] Disbelief in, or denial of, the existence of a God. *Also*, Godlessness (*practical* atheism).

A little or superficial knowledge of philosophy may incline the mind of man to a. BACON.

Atheist (ē·þiˌist). 1571. [a. F. *athéiste*; see prec.] **1.** One who denies or disbelieves the existence of a God. **2.** One who denies God morally 1577. **3.** *attrib.* Atheistic, impious 1667.

1. The Atheistes which say..there is no God GOLDING. **2.** When the Priest Turns A., as did Ely's Sons MILT. *P. L.* I. 495. **3.** The A. crew MILT. Hence **Athei·stic, -al** *a.* of or befitting an a.; involving atheism; of the nature of an a., godless, impious. **Athei·stically** *adv.* **Athei·sticalness.** ? *Obs.*

Atheize (ē·þiˌaiz), *v.* 1678. [f. Gr. ἄθεος.] **1.** *intr.* To speak, write, or act as an atheist. **2.** *trans.* To render atheistic. Hence **A·theizer.**

†**A·thel,** *sb.*[1] [OE. *æðel-u*, f. root **aþ*.] Ancestry; *spec.* noble ancestry; *hence*, honour, might -ME.

†**A·thel,** *a.* and *sb.*[2] [Com. Teut.: OE. *æðele, ędele*; see prec. Cf. L. *generosus*, f. *genus*.] *adj.* Noble, illustrious -ME.; excellent, fine -ME. *sb.*[2] One who is noble; a lord, chief -1515.

Atheling (æ·þĕliŋ). *Obs.* exc. *Hist.* [OE., f. *æðel.* (In med.L. *adal-, adelingus*.)] A member of a noble family, a prince, lord, baron; in OE. poetry often used in pl. for 'men'; later restricted to a prince of the blood royal, *esp.* the heir apparent to the throne.

‖**Athenæum** (æþĭnī·ŏm). Also **-eum.** Mod. pl. **-æums.** 1727. [a. L., a. Gr. Ἀθηναῖον, (the temple) of Ἀθήνη.] **1.** *Gr. Antiq.* The temple of Athene in ancient Athens, in which professors taught, and orators and poets rehearsed their compositions. (Similar institutions were established at Rome and Lyons.) **2. a.** A literary or scientific club 1864. **b.** A literary club-room, reading-room, etc. 1822. **c.** A periodical devoted to literature, art, etc., e.g. *The Athenæum*, published in London (*mod.*).

Atheological (ēːþiˌoˌlǫ·dʒikăl), *a.* 1641. [A- *pref.* 14.] Opposed to theology. **Atheolo·gian,** one destitute of theology. **Atheo·logy,** opposition to theology.

Atheous (ē·þiˌəs), *a.* 1612. [f. Gr. ἄθεος + -OUS.] †**1.** Atheistic -1792. **2.** Not dealing with the existence of a God; opp. to the negative *atheistic* 1880.

1. Suffers the Hypocrite or a. Priest To tread his Sacred Courts MILT. *P. R.* I. 487.

Atherine (æ·þĕrəin). 1770. [ad. mod.L. *atherina*, a. Gr. ἀθερίνη.] Name of various species of smelt.

Athermancy (ăþǝ·ɹmănsi). 1863. [f. Gr. ἀθέρμαντος; see next.] Athermanous quality.

Athermanous (ăþǝ·ɹmănəs), *a.* 1863. [f. Gr. ἀ + θερμαν-, θερμαίνειν, f. θέρμη + -OUS.] *Physics.* Not permeable by radiant heat.

‖**Atheroma** (æþĕrōu·mă). 1706. [L., a. Gr. ἀθήρωμα, f. ἀθήρη = ἀθάρη groats.] *Path.* **a.** An encysted tumour containing matter resembling oatmeal-gruel. **b.** Fatty degeneration of the arterial coats. Hence **Athero·matous** *a.*

†**Athe·ticize,** *v. rare.* [irreg. f. Gr. ἀ + θετικός.] To set aside. BEVERLEY.

†**Athi·nk,** *v.* ME. only. [Worn-down f. OF-THINK.] impers. *It athinks me*; it repents me.

Athirst (ăþǝ·ɹst), *ppl. a.* [Worn-down f. OE. *ofþyrst*, for *ofþyrsted*. Cf. A-HUNGERED.] Suffering from, or oppressed by, thirst; *fig.* eager, longing (*for*) 1480.

fig. My soule is a thurste for God *Ps.* xlii. 1.

Athlete (æ·þlīt). 1528. [ad. L. *athleta*, ad. Gr. ἀθλητής, f. ἆθλος, ἆθλον. Bef. 1750 always, and still occas., in L. form.] **1.** A competitor in the physical exercises that formed part of the public games in ancient Greece and Rome. **2.** One who by special training has acquired great physical strength; one who exhibits feats of strength and activity; a physically powerful man 1827. *fig.* 1759.

2. *fig.* Athletes of debate LOWELL. Hence **A·thletism.**

Athletic (æþle·tik). 1605. [ad. L. *athleticus*, Gr. ἀθλητικός: see prec. and -IC.] **A.** *adj.* **1.** Pertaining to an athlete, or to the contests in which an athlete engages. Also *fig.* 1636. **2.** Of the nature of, or befitting, an athlete; muscular, robust 1659.

†**B.** *sb.* **a.** = ATHLETICS. **b.** An athlete -1817.

a. Art of Activity, which is called a. BACON. var. **Athle·tical.** ? *Obs.* Hence **Athle·tically** *adv.* **Athle·ticism,** the practice of, or devotion to, athletic exercises; training as an athlete.

Athle·tics. 1727. [ATHLETIC *a.* used in pl. Cf. L. *athletica*.] The practice of physical exercises by which muscular strength is increased.

Athlothete (æ·þloˌþīt). 1850. [ad. Gr. ἀθλοθέτης.] The awarder of prizes, judge, or steward in the public games.

At home, at-home (ætˌhōu·m). OE. [See AT and HOME.] *advb. phr.* **1.** At one's home; prepared to receive visitors 1829. **2.** (As opp. to ABROAD): **a.** Near at hand. **b.** In one's own country OE. **3.** At ease, as if in one's own home. Hence *fig.* Thoroughly conversant *with*, practised *in* 1840. **4.** *sb.* A reception of visitors during certain stated hours, when the visitors may call and leave as they please 1745.

1. The President makes it a point to be 'at home' on Sunday afternoons 1883. **2. a.** No newes so bad abroad as this at home *Rich. III*, I. i. 134. **3.** Never ..at home in our island MACAULAY.

A-thri·ll, *adv.* 1879. [A *prep.*[1]] Thrilling.

A-thro·b, *adv.* 1857. [A *prep.*[1]] Throbbing.

A-throng (ăþrǫ·ŋ), *adv.* ME. [A *prep.*[1]] In a throng; thronged.

Athwart (ăþwǭ·ɹt). 1470. [A *prep.*[1]] **A.** *adv.* **1.** Across from side to side, transversely; usu. in an oblique direction 1611. *Naut.* From side to side of a ship 1762. **2.** Across the course (of anything) 1594; *fig.* perversely, awry 1596.

B. *prep.* [the adv. with obj. expressed.] **1.** From side to side of, transversely over, across 1470. †**2.** To and fro over, all over. (Only in north. dial.) -1662. **3.** *Naut.* Across or transversely to the course of 1693. **4.** Across the direction of; hence *fig.* into the notice of 1622. **5.** Across the course of 1667; *fig.* in opposition to 1644.

1. Nor neuer lay his wreathed arms a. His louing bosome *L. L. L.* IV. iii. 135. **3.** *To run athwart*: to run into sidewise. **4.** Ye sweep a. my gaze COLERIDGE. *Comb.*: **a.-hawse,** said of a ship's position across the stem of another ship at anchor; **-ship** *a.*, **-ships** *adv.*, from side to side of the ship; **-wise,** athwart.

Athymy (æ·þimi). 1853. [ad. Gr. ἀθυμία.] *Path.* Despondency.

-atic, *suffix*, forming adjs., (= Fr. *-atique*) ad. L. *-aticus*, a case of the suffix *-icus*, 'of, of the kind of' (see -IC), appended to pa. ppl. stems of verbs; as in *erratic*; also used with sbs., e.g. *aquatic*, etc. Cf. -AGE.

-atile, *suffix*, forming adjs. (= mod.F. *-atile*), ad. L. *-atilis*, consisting of the suffix *-ilis* (see -ILE) 'denoting possibility or quality', appended to ppl. stems of *-at-* of vbs. in *-are*, as *volatile*; also with sbs. as *aquatile*.

Ati·lt, *adv.* 1562. [A *prep.*[1] (perh. AT).] **1.** Tilted up, and just ready to fall over. Also *fig.* **2.** In phr. *To run* (or *ride*) a-tilt: i. e. in an encounter on horseback with the thrust of a lance. Now usu. *fig.* Const. *at, with, against*. [*a-* is here obscure.] 1591.

2. Breake a Launce, and runne a-Tilt at Death 1 *Hen. VI*, III. ii. 51.

Atimy (æ·timi). 1847. [ad. Gr. ἀτιμία.] Public disgrace; *spec.* deprivation of civil rights.

A-ti·ngle, *adv.* 1855. [A *prep.*[1]] Tingling.

-ation (-ē·ʃən), the form of the compound suffix -T-ION (*-s-ion, -x-ion*), which forms nouns of action from L. pples. in *-atus* of vbs. in *-are*, Fr. vbs. in *-er*, and their English representatives. See -TION. In Eng., nouns in *-ation* number more than 1500 in modern use. A few have no Eng. vb., e. g. *constellation*, etc.; the great majority have a vb. in *-ate*, e. g. *cre-ate, -ation*, etc.; some are formed on Gk. vbs. in -IZE (= L. *-izare*, Fr. *-iser*), e. g. *organize, -ation*, etc.; the remainder have a vb. without suffix, derived through Fr., e. g. *alter-ation, caus-ation*, etc. The latter are pop. referred to the Eng. vbs. *alter, cause*, etc.; and *-ation* thus becomes a living Eng. suffix, and is applied to words not of Fr. origin, as in *starvation*, etc. Words in which *-ation* is merely added to the vb. are synonymous with the vbl. sb. in *-ing*, and tend to replace it, as *vexation, vexing*, etc.

A-tiptoe (ăti·ptōu), *adv.* 1576. [A *prep.*[1]] On the tips of one's toes.

-ative, ad. Fr. *-atif, -ative*, L. *ativus*, consisting of *-ivus* (see -IVE) appended to ppl. stems in *-at-* of vbs. in *-are*, e. g. *demonstrative*, and by extension *talkative*; also *authoritative*, from the sb. AUTHORITY.

Atlantad (ǣtlæ·ntăd), *adv.* 1825. [f. as next + *-ad* (? after Gr. -δε towards).] *Phys.* Towards the atlas (vertebra); towards the upper part of the body.

Atlantal (ǣtlæ·ntăl), *a.* 1803. [f. Gr. ἀτλαντ-, ἄτλας (see ATLAS *sb.*[1]) + -AL[1].] *Phys.* Of or belonging to the atlas; belonging to the upper part of the body.

Atlantean (ætlǣntī·ăn), *a.* 1667. [f. L. *Atlanteus*, f. *Atlant-*; see prec. and -EAN.] Pertaining to, or having the strength of, Atlas.

With A. shoulders MILT. *P. L.* II. 306.

‖**Atlantes** (ǣtlæ·ntīz), *sb. pl.* 1706. [L., a. Gr.; see ATLAS *sb.*[1]] *Arch.* Figures or half-figures of men used instead of columns to support an entablature.

Atlantic (ǣtlæ·ntik), *a.* (*sb.*) ME. [ad. L. *Atlanticus*, a. Gr., f. Ἀτλαντ-; see ATLAS *sb.*[1]] Of or pertaining to Mount Atlas in Libya (see ATLAS). Hence applied to the sea near the western shore of Africa, and later to the whole ocean lying between Europe and Africa on the east and America on the west. 1601. *fig.* Far-reaching, distant; *transf.* in U. S.: Eastern 1650. †**2.** = ATLANTEAN -1652. †**3.** Of the size of an atlas JOHNSON. **4.** *sb.* The Atlantic ocean; also *fig.* ME.

4. Down on the Earth it in Atlanticks rain'd KEN.

Atlanto- (ǣtlæ·nto), comb. f. ATLAS *sb.*[1] (sense 2), as in *atlanto-axial*.

Atlas (æ·tlăs), *sb.*[1] Pl. **atlases.** 1589. [a. L., a. Gr. Ἄτλας, -αντα; name of a god, who was supposed to hold up the pillars of the universe, also of the mountain in Libya that was fabled to support the heavens. Hence the fig. uses.] **1.** One who supports a great burden; a mainstay. **b.** *Arch.* (See ATLANTES.) **2.** *Phys.* The uppermost cervical vertebra, which supports the skull, being articulated above with the occipital bone. (So in Gr.) 1699. **3.** A collection of maps in a volume. [This use, found first in Mercator, is said to be derived from a representation of Atlas supporting the heavens forming a frontispiece to early atlases.] 1636. **4.** A similar volume containing illustrative plates, etc., or a conspectus of a subject arranged in tabular form; *e. g.* 'an anatomical atlas', 'an ethnographical atlas' 1875. **5.** A large square folio resembling a volume of maps; an *a.-folio*. **6.** A large size of drawing-paper 1712.

1. The A., and sustainer of the whole state of Holland 1618. **3.** Atlas; or a Geographic Description of the World, by Gerard Mercator and John Hondt (*title*) 1636. *Comb.* a.-beetle, a gigantic olive-green lamellicorn beetle (*Chalcosoma Atlas*).

Atlas (æ·tlăs), *sb.*[2] ? *Obs.* 1687. [a. (ult.) Arab. Cf. It. *raso*, shaved, satin.] A silk-satin made in the East.

Atlas (æ·tlăs), *v.* 1593. [f. ATLAS *sb.*[1]] To prop up, like Atlas.

A·tlo-, atloi·do-, comb. ff. ATLAS, formed on imperfect analogy; see ATLANTO-. So **Atloide·an** *a.* = ATLANTAL.

Atmido·meter. 1830. [f. Gr. ἀτμίς; see -(O)METER.] = ATMOMETER.

Atmology (ætmǫ·lŏdʒi). 1837. [f. Gr. ἀτμός; see -(O)LOGY.] *Physics.* The science of the laws and phenomena of aqueous vapour. Hence **Atmo·logist**, one skilled in a. **Atmolo·gical** *a.*

Atmolysis (ætmǫ·lisis). 1866. [f. as prec. + λύσις; cf. *analysis.*] *Physics.* The (partial) separation of gases of unequal diffusibility. **A·tmolyse, -ze** *v.* to perform a. **A·tmolyser, -zer**, an instrument for effecting it.

Atmometer (ætmǫ·mĭtəɪ). 1815. [f. Gr. ἀτμός + μέτρον.] *Physics.* An instrument for measuring evaporation from a moist surface.

Atmosphere (æ·tmŏsfīəɪ), *sb.* 1638. [ad. mod.L. *atmosphæra*, f. Gr. ἀτμός + σφαῖρα.] **1.** The spheroidal gaseous envelope surrounding any of the heavenly bodies. **b.** *esp.* The whole body of terrestrial air. **2.** *transf.* A gaseous envelope surrounding any substance 1863. **3.** †A supposed outer envelope of effective influence surrounding various bodies –1750. **b.** *Magnetic Atmosphere*, the sphere within which the magnet acts. **c.** *fig.* Mental or moral environment 1797. **4.** The air in any particular place, *esp.* as affected by heat, cold, purifying influences, etc. 1767. **5.** A pressure of 14·7 lb. on the square inch, which is that of the atmosphere on the earth's surface 1830.

1. There is an Atmosphæra, or an Orb of Gross Vaporous Air immediately encompassing the Body of the Moon WILKINS. 3. c. He lives in a perfect a. of strife, blood, and quarrels SCOTT. 4. The suffocating a...of a small apartment 1767. Hence **A·tmosphere** *v.* to surround like, or as with, an a.

Atmospheric, -al (ætmŏsfe·rik, -ăl), *a.* 1661. [f. prec.; see -IC, -ICAL.] **1.** Of the nature of, or forming, the atmosphere 1664. **2.** Existing, taking place, or acting in the air 1666. **3.** Caused, produced, or worked by the action of the atmosphere 1661.

2. Small a. tides 1835. 3. The a. engine of Newcomen 1822. *Atmospheric engine*, a steam-engine in which the piston was forced down by the pressure of the atmosphere, after the condensation of the steam that caused it to rise. *Atmospheric line*, the equilibrium-line on the indicator-card of a steam-engine. *Atmospheric pressure*: see ATMOSPHERE 5. *Atmospheric railway*, one worked by the propulsive force of compressed air or by the formation of a vacuum; a pneumatic railway. Hence **Atmosphe·rically** *adv.*

Atmosphe·rics, *sb. pl.* 1913. [pl. of prec.] Interfering sounds in aerial communication due to electric disturbance in the atmosphere.

‖**Atoll** (ătǫ·l, æ·tǫl). 1625. [prob. = Malayalam *aḍal* 'uniting' (Col. Yule).] A coral island consisting of a ring-shaped reef enclosing a lagoon. *Comb.* and *attrib.* 1842.

Such sunken islands are now marked by rings of coral or atolls standing over them DARWIN.

Atom (æ·təm). ME. [a. F. *atome*, ad. L. *atomus*, a. Gr. ἄτομος adj. used subst., f. ἀ + -τομος, τέμνειν. Also (in 16th c.) *atomus, atomos*, with pl. *atomi.*] * Scientific. **1.** A hypothetical body, so small as to be incapable of further division; and thus held to be one of the ultimate particles of matter 1477. **2.** In Nat. Phil. *Physical Atoms*: the supposed ultimate particles in which matter actually exists (without reference to divisibility) 1650. **3.** *Chemical Atoms*: **a.** The smallest particles in which the elements combine, or are known to possess the properties of a particular element 1819. **b.** The smallest known quantity of a chemical compound 1847. ** In popular use. **4.** A particle of dust, or a mote in the sunbeam (*arch.*) 1605. **5.** A very minute portion, a particle, a jot 1630. **6.** Anything relatively very small; an atomy 1633. Also *attrib.* *** Of time. [In Gr. ἄτομος [1 Cor. xv. 22) = 'twinkling of an eye'.] †**7.** The smallest mediæval measure of time = $^{15}/_{94}$ of a second ME. only.

1. That the universe was formed by a fortuitous concourse of atoms SWIFT. 2. Atoms are endowed with powers of mutual attraction TYNDALL. 4. Rays of light Peopled with dusty atoms BYRON. 5. There was not an a. of water SIR J. ROSS. *To smash, shiver*, etc., *to* or *into atoms*. Casting atomes of Scripture, as dust before mens eyes HOBBES. 6. The smallest ant or a. HERBERT. Hence †**A·tom** *v.* to atomize. **Atoma·re**, an area supposed to be formed by a combination of ultimate atoms. **A·tomecha·nics**, the mechanics of atoms. **A·tomless** *a. poet.* without leaving an a.

Atomic (ătǫ·mik), *a.* (*sb.*) 1678. [f. prec.] **1.** Of or pertaining to atoms 1692. **2.** Concerned with atoms 1678. **3.** Adhering to the atomic philosophy 1691. **4.** Minute 1809. **5.** Simple, elemental 1881. †**6.** *sb.* An adherent of the atomic philosophy. CUDWORTH.

1. *Atomic weight* in *Chem.*: the weight of an atom of an element (or radical), as compared with that of an atom of hydrogen, taken as unity; also the sum of the weights of the atoms of a compound. *A. volume* of a body: the space occupied by a quantity of it proportional to its atomic weight. 2. *A. philosophy*: the doctrine taught by Leucippus, Democritus, and Epicurus: see ATOMISM. *A. theory* in *Chem.*: the doctrine that elemental bodies consist of aggregations of indivisible atoms of definite relative weight; that the atoms of different elements unite with each other in fixed proportions; and that the latter determine the fixed proportions in which elements and compounds enter into chemical combination with each other. 4. A. globules 1809. Changes almost a. ROGERS. var. **Atoma·tic** *a.* (*rare*). Hence **Ato·mical** *a.*, **-ly** *adv.*

Atomicity (ætŏmi·sĭti). 1865. [f. prec. + -ITY.] *Chem.* The combining capacity of an element (or radical), *i.e.* the number of atoms of hydrogen, or other monovalent element, with which one of its atoms normally combines. Now usu. called *valency.*

Atomism (æ·tŏmiz'm). 1678. [f. ATOM + -ISM.] **1.** Atomic philosophy; the doctrine of the formation of all things from indivisible particles endued with gravity and motion; var. †**Ato·micism.** **2.** Individualism 1836.

Atomist (æ·tŏmist). 1610. [f. as prec. + -IST.] **1.** One who holds the principles of atomism; var. **Atomi·cian** (*rare*). **2.** A student or exponent of the *atomic theory* (see ATOMIC *a.* 2) 1869. Hence **Atomi·stic, -al** *a.* of or pertaining to atomists or atomism; consisting of separate atoms. **Atomi·stically** *adv.*

Atomization (æ·tŏməizēⁱ·ʃən). 1871. [f. ATOMIZE.] The process of reducing to minute particles, *spec.* in *Med.* of reducing liquids to a fine spray.

Atomize (æ·tŏməiz), *v.* 1678. [f. ATOM + -IZE.] †**1.** To hold the atomic philosophy. **2.** To reduce to atoms, or to an atom; to belittle 1845. Hence **A·tomizer**, *spec.* an instrument for reducing liquids to a fine spray.

Atomology (ætŏmǫ·lŏdʒi). 1678. [f. Gr. ἄτομος + -λογία.] The science of atoms.

Atomy[1] (æ·tŏmi). 1597. [f. ANATOMY, taken as *an atomy*; cf. *natomy.* Now mostly joc.] **1.** An anatomical preparation; *esp.* a skeleton 1728. **2.** An emaciated or withered living body 1597. *fig.* or *transf.* of things 1848.

You starved bloodhound!..Thou a., thou! SHAKS.

Atomy[2] (æ·tŏmi). 1591. [f. *atomi*, pl. of *atomus* (see ATOM), treated as Eng. sing.] **1.** An atom, a mote 1595. **2.** A mite, a pigmy 1591.

1. To count Atomies SHAKS. 2. Drawne with a teeme of little Atomies Ouer mens noses *Rom. & Jul.* I. iv. 57.

Atonal (ǣ-, eⁱtōᵘ·năl), *a.* 1922. [A- 14.] *Mus.* Having no reference to a key or tonic.

At once (ăt₁wɒ·ns), *advb. phr.* ME. [AT *prep.* and ONCE, ME. *anes, ones*, gen. of ONE, 'one time, once'.] †**1.** At one stroke, etc.; once for all; in (or into) one heap; together –1579. **2.** At one and the same time ME. **3.** In one and the same act, position, etc.; equally, both 1588. **4.** Immediately 1531.

At one (ăt₁wɒ·n), *adv.* (passing into *adj.*) *phr.* [ME. *at on(e)*, *aton* (from the 13th c.), i.e. AT *prep.* II. 6 and absol. use of ONE, prob. after OF. *à un* (:—Rom. **ad ūnum* to or into one thing). Cf. ATONEMENT, ATONE *v.*] **1.** In concord or friendship; opp. to *at variance*, etc. Sometimes = Reconciled (*arch.*). ME. **2.** Into a state of harmony or unity of feeling, as *to bring, make*, etc., *at one* (*arch.*) ME. **3.** Of one mind ME. †**4.** Together. SPENSER.

1. So beene they both atone SPENSER *F. Q.* II. i. 29. *Comb.* at-oneness (*rare*).

Atone (ătōᵘ·n), *v.* 1555. [Back-formation from ATONEMENT. Not used in A.V., though *atonement* was used by Tindale (see next, sense 3).] **1.** *trans.* To set at one, reconcile. *Obs.* exc. as etymol. archaism 1593. †**b.** To compose (differences) –1702. †**2.** *intr.* To come into unity or concord –1607. **3.** *trans.* To reconcile, to appease 1617. **4.** *absol.* To make reconcilement or propitiation **a.** *for* the offender 1682; **b.** *for* the offence (= to make amends) 1665. **5.** *trans.* (*for* omitted) To expiate 1665. †**6.** *trans.* To join in one –1672. *fig.* To harmonize 1691. *intr.* 1649.

1. The king and parliament will soon be atoned MILT. To a. a broil 1565. 2. He and Aufidius can no more a. Then violent'st contrariety *Cor.* IV. vi. 72. 3. So heaven, atoned, shall dying Greece restore POPE. 4. b. Nothing can a. for the Want of Modesty STEELE. 5. To a. sin BARROW. 6. *fig.* To a. our ideas with our perceptions HARE. Hence **Ato·nable, ato·neable** *a.* that may be atoned for. **Ato·ne** *sb.* †reconciliation; expiation (*arch.* with mod. sense). **Ato·ner.**

Atonement (ătōᵘ·nmĕnt). 1513. [f. AT ONE + -MENT, after earlier ONEMENT.] †**1.** The condition of being *at one* with others; concord, agreement –1623. †**2.** The action of setting at one, or being set at one, after discord; reconciliation –1685; appeasement –1622. **3.** *spec.* in *Theol.* Reconciliation or restoration of friendly relations between God and sinners 1526. **4.** Propitiation by reparation of wrong or injury; amends, expiation 1611; *Theol.* propitiation of God by expiation of sin 1611. ¶*Atonement* is variously used by theologians in the sense of *reconciliation, propitiation, expiation.* (Not so applied in any version of the N. T.)

1. What a. . is there betwixt light and darkness PHILPOT. 2. He desires to make attonement Betweene the Duke of Glouster, and your Brothers *Rich. III*, I. iii. 36. 3. The office to preache the a. TINDALE 2 *Cor.* v. 18. 4. The best A. he can make for it ADDISON. The High-Priest..having made an A. for the Sins of the People ADDISON. *Comb.* a.-money, money paid in expiation of sins. Hence **Ato·nementist**, one who holds the Calvinistic doctrine of the atonement.

Atonic (ătǫ·nik). 1727. [ad. med.L. *atonicus*, f. Gr. ἄτονος, f. ἀ + τόνος, f. τείνειν; see -IC.] **A.** *adj.* *Pros.* Unaccented; *usu.* not bearing the stress or syllabic accent 1878. **2.** *Path.* Wanting tone, or nervous elasticity 1792.

2. We live in..an a. age 1861.

B. *sb.* **1.** *Pros.* A word or element of speech not having an accent. (Used *spec.* in Gr. Gram. of ὁ, ἡ, οἱ, αἱ, ἐν, ἐς, εἰς, ἐκ, ἐξ, εἰ, οὐ, ὡς.) 1727. **2.** *Med.* A remedy having power to allay excitement 1864.

Atony (æ·tŏni). 1693. [a. F. *atonie*, ad. med.L. *atonia*, a. Gr.; see ATONIC.] *Path.* Want of tone; enervation, languor. Also *fig.*

Ennui is..an intellectual a. 1847.

Atop (ătǫ·p). 1655. [A *prep.*[1]] **1.** *adv.* On or at the top 1658; with *of* 1672. **2.** *prep.* [*of* omitted.] On the top of 1655.

1. A black mass a-top, and a metallic mass at bottom 1779.

†**Atou·r**, *sb.* ME. [a. OF. *aturn, -ourn, -ur, -our* (mod. *atour*); see ATURN.] **1.** Attire, array –1475. **2.** Military equipment or preparation –1480.

Atour (ătōᵘ·r). ME. [App. f. AT *prep.* + *our, ower*, Sc. f. OVER.] **A.** *prep.* **1.** Over. **2.** In defiance of (an obstacle, etc.) 1535.

1. *By and atour*: in addition to; By and attour her gentle havings SCOTT.

B. *adv.* Over and above, besides ME.

Atrabilarian (ætrăbilēə·riăn). 1678. [f. med.L. *atrabilarius*; see ATRABILE.] *adj.* = ATRABILARIOUS. *sb.* A hypochondriac.

Atrabila·rious, *a.* 1684. [f. as prec. + -OUS.] **1.** Of or pertaining to black bile. **2.** Atrabilious, hypochondriacal; acrimonious. vars. †**A·trabilar**, †**-ai·re**, †**Atrabila·ric**, †**Atrabi·lary.**

†**A·trabile.** 1594. [a. F., ad. L. *atra bilis* (also used), tr. Gr. μελαγχολία.] *lit.* Black bile, an imaginary fluid, supposed anciently to be the cause of melancholy; *hence*: Melancholy, spleen.

Atrabi·liary, *a.* 1725. [ad. mod.L. *atrabiliarius*; see ATRABILE and -ARY.] **1.** Of or pertaining to black bile; applied to the renal or suprarenal glands, and to the arteries supplying them. **2.** = ATRABILIOUS.

Atrabilious (ætrăbi·liəs), *a.* 1651. [f. L. *atrabilis* (see ATRABILE), after *biliosus.*] Affected by black bile or 'choler adust'; melancholy; splenetic.

My a. censures CARLYLE. vars. **Atrabi·liar, †Atrabi·lous.** Hence **Atrabi·liousness.**

Atrament (æ·trămĕnt). ME. [ad. L. *atramentum*, f. **atrare*, f. *ater.*] Blacking, ink; any similar black substance. Hence **Atrame·ntal** *a.* ink-. **Atrame·ntous** *a.* inky, black.

†Atre·de, *v. rare.* [f. AT-*pref.*^{2}+*rede* READ.] To outdo in counsel. CHAUCER.

A-tre·mble, *adv.* 1856. [A *prep.*^{1}] Trembling.

†Atre·n, *v.* ME. [f. AT-*pref.*^{2} + OE. *rennan.*] *intr.* To run away (with *dat.* = from).

Men may the wise atrenne, and nought atrede CHAUCER.

‖**Atresia** (ătrī·ʃiă). 1866. [mod.L., f. Gr. ἄτρητος not perforated.] *Path.* Occlusion of a natural channel of the body.

A·trial, *a.* 1869. [f. L. *atrium* (see ATRIUM) + -AL ^{1}.] *Phys.* Of or belonging to the *atrium.*

A-trip (ătri·p), *adv.* 1626. [A *prep.*^{1}] *Naut.* 1. Of yards: Swayed up, ready to have the stops cut for crossing. Of sails: Hoisted from the cap, sheeted home, and ready for trimming. 2. Of an anchor: Just raised perpendicularly from the ground in weighing 1796.

‖**Atrium** (ēi·triŏm). 1577. [L.] I. A court. a. The central hall of a Roman house. b. A portico in front of the principal doors of churches, etc. 2. *Phys.* a. That part of the auricle into which the veins pour the blood. b. In the Tunicata: A large cavity into which the intestine opens. 1870.

Atro- (æ·tro), comb. f. L. *ater* black, as in *atrosanguineous* of a dark blood-red colour.

†Atro·ce, *a.* [a. F., ad. L. *atrocem.*] Atrocious. NORTH.

Atrocious (ătrōu·ʃəs), *a.* 1669. [f. L. *atroci-* (*atrox*), f. *ater* + -OUS.] 1. Excessively and wantonly savage or cruel; heinously wicked. †2. Stern, fierce; extremely violent –1733. 3. *colloq.* Very bad, execrable (*mod.*).

1. A. criminals 1772, acts DARWIN. 2. A. Symptoms CHEYNE. 3. An a. pun (*mod.*). Hence **Atro·ciously** *adv.* **Atro·ciousness.**

Atrocity (ătrǫ·sĭti). 1534. [(? a. Fr.,) ad. L. *atrocitatem*, f. *atrox.*] 1. Savage enormity, horrible wickedness. 2. Fierceness, sternness, implacability (*arch.*) 1635. 3. An atrocious deed 1793. 4. *colloq.* A very bad blunder, violation of taste or good manners, etc. 1878.

3. The deeds..known as 'the Bulgarian atrocities' McCARTHY. 4. Atrocities in spelling 1878.

A·trophous, *a.* 1877. [f. Gr. ἄτροφος + -OUS.] Characterized by atrophy. var. **Atro·phic.**

Atrophy (æ·trŏfi), *sb.* 1620. [a. F. *atrophie*, ad. L. *atrophia*, a. Gr., f. ἄτροφος, f. ἀ + τροφή.] A wasting away of the body, or any part of it, through imperfect nourishment; emaciation.

Pining a. MILT. *fig.* By fatal a. of purse 1782.

Atrophy (æ·trŏfi), *v.* 1865. [f. prec. sb.] *lit.* and *fig.* 1. *trans.* To starve. 2. *intr.* To become atrophied or abortive 1865. Hence **A·trophied** *ppl. a.*; var. **Atro·phiated.**

Atropine (æ·tropəin). 1842. [f. *atropa* deadly nightshade, f. Gr. Ἄτροπος, one of the Fates.] *Chem.* and *Med.* A poisonous alkaloid found in the Deadly Nightshade and the seeds of the Thorn-apple. var. **Atro·pia. Atro·pic** *a.* of or pertaining to a., as in *Atropic acid.* **A·tropini·sm, A·tropism,** poisoning by a. **A·tropini·zed** *ppl. a.* poisoned by a.

Atropous (æ·trŏpəs), *a.* 1839. [f. Gr. ἄτροπος (f. ἀ + τρόπος) + -OUS.] *Bot.* Of ovules: Not inverted, erect. var. **A·tropal.**

Atrous (ēi·trəs), *a. rare.* [f. L. *ater, atro-* + -OUS.] *Nat. Hist.* Jet-black.

A-try (ătrəi), *adv.* 1611. [? A *prep.*^{1}] *Naut.* Of a ship in a gale: Kept by a judicious balance of canvas with her bows to the sea.

Attach (ătæ·tʃ), *v.* ME. [a. OF. *atachier* (mod. *attacher*), f. *à* + a radical conn. w. Bret. *tach*, Sp., Pg. *tacha*, a TACK, q. v. Thus *lit.* 'to tack to'. Cf. F. *détacher.*]

The sense development was: 1. In OF. 'to fasten' (recently adopted in Eng.). 2. To '*attach* by some tie to the control of a court', hence to 'arrest, seize'. 3. F. *attacher*, subseq. *attaquer*, after It. *attaccare*, gave Eng. ATTACK, and occas. (in 17th c.) *attach.*

I. 1. *Law.* To place or take under the control of a court; to arrest or seize by authority of a writ of attachment: a. a person; b. property, goods ME. †2. To accuse –1653. †3. To seize, lay hold of. Also *fig.* –1681.

1. Euery shiriffe..shall attache the saide offenders 1531. He was attached of heresy BURNET. b. France ..hath attach'd Our Merchants goods at Burdeux SHAKS. 3. Attach'd with weariness *Temp.* III. iii. 5.

†II. To attack –1666.

III. 1. To tack on; to fasten or join (*to*) by tacking, tying, sticking, etc. 1802. 2. To join on (e. g. a person *to* a company, etc.). Often *refl.* 1700. 3. To join in sympathy or affection *to.* Often in pass. *To be attached to.* 1765. b. *esp.* To win the attachment of 1811. 4. To fix *to*, as a name, description, or other adjunct 1812; *refl.* to fasten itself on, stick *to* 1861. 5. To attribute 1837.

1. The means of attaching the doublet to the hose SCOTT. 2. A Bedouin who had attached himself to us 1873. 3. How she attached her little brothers to her 1833. b. Incapable of attaching a sensible man MISS AUSTEN. 4. The liability which English law attaches to contracts SIR C. BOWEN. 5. The importance they attached to their own services PRESCOTT.

IV. *intr.* (for *refl.*) 1. To fall, or come *upon*, and adhere to 1780. 2. To be incident *to*, †*on* 1791. 3. To come into legal operation in connexion with anything 1818.

3. The wife's right to dower accordingly attached WILLIAMS. Hence **†Atta·ch** *sb.* arrest; *fig.* an attack of disease, etc.; an attachment; a thing attached. **Atta·cher,** one who attaches.

Attachable (ătæ·tʃăb'l), *a.* 1579. [f. prec + -ABLE.] 1. Liable to arrest or seizure. 2. Capable of being tacked on as an adjunct *to* anything 1856. 3. Capable of attachment 1865.

‖**Attaché** (ătæ·ʃe). 1835. [Fr.] A junior official attached to the staff of an ambassador, etc.; a naval or military representative of his government in a foreign country. b. *A. case*, a small leather case for carrying papers 1904.

Attached (ătæ·tʃt), *ppl. a.* 1552. [f. ATTACH *v.* + -ED.] 1. Arrested 1611; †seized (with sickness, etc.) –1619; joined functionally 1859; joined by taste, affection, or sympathy *to*, affectionate 1793; incident *to* 1852. 2. Fastened by a material union *to* 1841; *Zool.* stationary, as opp. to 'free' 1854. *Arch.* joined to a wall, etc., not 'detached' 1879. Hence **Atta·chedly** *adv.*

Attachment (ătæ·tʃmĕnt). 1447. [a. F. *attachement*; see ATTACH *v.*] 1. The action of attaching (see ATTACH *v.* 1); now *esp.* of arrest for contempt of court; the writ commanding it 1468. 2. The taking of property into the actual or constructive possession of the judicial power 1592. †3. Arrest, confinement –1606. 4. The action of fastening on, or being fastened on or to; connexion 1817. 5. Affection, devotion, fidelity 1704. 6. A fastening, tie, or bond 1801. 7. An adjunct 1797.

1. If he does not appear, an a. is issued against him DE LOLME. 2. *Foreign attachment*: 'legal seizure of the goods of foreigners, found in some liberty (*e. g.* the City of London) to satisfy their creditors within such liberty'. 5. The lover's eye discovered the object of his a. SCOTT. 7. The Eolian a. to the pianoforte (*mod.*).

Attack (ătæ·k), *v.* 1600. [a. F. *attaquer*, ad. It. *attaccare*; see ATTACH *v.* Not in Shaks.] *trans.* in all senses. 1. To fasten or fall upon with force or arms; to assail, assault. (The common military term.) Also *absol.* 2. To set upon with hostile action or words, so as to overthrow, injure, or bring into disrepute 1643. 3. To assail with temptations 1673. 4. To enter upon a work of difficulty 1871. 5. Of disease: To seize upon, begin to affect 1677. 6. To begin to act upon destructively, to begin to waste, decompose, or dissolve 1842.

1. The strong towns he successively attacked GIBBON. 2. Who attacks the liberty of the press JUNIUS. 5. Rheumatism..attacks indiscriminately the young and old KEMBLE. 6. White ants .. often attacking the wood-work of houses 1842. Hence **Atta·ckable** *a.* assailable. **Atta·cker.**

Attack (ătæ·k), *sb.* 1667. [f. the vb., or a. F. *attaque.* Not in Shaks.: once in Milt.] 1. The act of attacking (see ATTACK *v.* 1). The common military term; opp. to *defence.* b. *ellipt.* for: Point of attack, attacking force 1709. 2. *fig.* The offensive part in any contest; *e. g.* the bowling in *Cricket*, etc. 1822. 3. An assault with hostile or bitter words 1751. 4. *fig.* The commencing of operations on a work of difficulty. So (*joc.*) upon dinner, etc. 1812. 5. An access of disease; a fit or bout of illness 1811. 6. The commencement of destructive or dissolving action by a physical agent 1842. 7. *Mus.* [after It. *attacca.*] The action or manner of beginning a piece, passage, or phrase, in respect of precision and clarity; also *gen.*, brilliance of style, courageous rendering 1880.

1. The dire a. Of fighting Seraphim MILT. *P. L.* VI. 248. 3. The a. upon a rising character JOHNSON. 5. Attacks of overpowering giddiness SEELEY.

Attain (ătēi·n), *v.* [ME. *ateyn(e, ateine*, a. OF. *ataign-, ateign-, ateindre*:—L. *attingere*, f. *ad-* + *tangere.*] †I. *trans.* 1. To touch, hit –1475; to touch upon, treat of –1448. †2. To catch in an offence, convict, condemn, ATTAINT.

II. *trans.* †1. To overtake, come up with, catch –1622. 2. To reach by motion, gain (a point aimed at) 1585; (an age or time) 1826. 3. To reach, arrive at, by continuous effort ME. 4. To come into the possession of (not now used of a material thing) (*arch.*) ME. †5. To 'get at', find out –1666.

2. We quickly shall a. the English shore 1585. To a. one's sixteenth year (*mod.*). 3. Reason is not..borne with us..but attayned by Industry HOBBES. 4. He attained the Crowne and Scepter of the Realme MORE.

III. *intr.* 1. To get (*to*) ME. 2. To live on (*to* a time or age) 1535. 3. To succeed in reaching. Cf. II. 3, 4. ME. †4. = II. 5, but with *to, unto* –1628.

1. Nor nearer might the dogs a. SCOTT. 2. He has attained to years of discretion (*mod.*). 3. Infallibility..being what no man can a. vnto PRIDEAUX.

†IV. (cf. L. *attinere.*) To stretch, reach (*to*) –1530; to pertain *to* (ME. only).

Hence **Attai·nable** *a.* **Attai·nableness. Attai·ner. Attai·ning** *vbl. sb.*

†Attai·n, *sb.* 1599. = ATTAINMENT –1665.

Attainder (ătēi·ndəɹ). 1473. [Subst. use of OF. *ataindre, ateindre*:—L. *attingere*, erron. associated later with F. *taindre, teindre*:—L. *tingere* to TINGE, TAINT.] 1. The action or process of attainting: *orig.* as in ATTAIN *v.* I. 2; later, the legal consequences of judgement of death or outlawry, in respect of treason or felony, viz. forfeiture of estate real and personal, corruption of blood, so that the condemned could neither inherit nor transmit by descent, and generally, extinction of all civil rights and capacities. From the false derivation referred to above, the second of these was looked upon as the essence of ATTAINDER. b. Act of Attainder 1587. †2. *fig.* Condemnation; dishonouring allegation –1593; stain of dishonour –1752.

1. *Bill* or *Act of Attainder*: one introduced or passed in the English parliament (first in 1459) for attainting any one without a judicial trial. All attainders are now abolished WILLIAMS. 2. Th' Attaindor of his sland'rous Lippes *Rich. II*, IV. i. 24. vars. **†Attai·ndrie** COKE, **†Attai·ndure.**

Attainment (ătēi·nmĕnt). ME. [f. ATTAIN *v.* + -MENT.] 1. The action or process of attaining, reaching, or acquiring by effort (no *pl.*) 1549. 2. That which is attained; *esp.* a personal accomplishment 1680.

1. Dost thou ayme at the a. of wisedome HEALEY. 2. A man of good attainments 1736. A low standard of a. PATTISON.

Attainor (ătēi·nəɹ, -ǭ·ɹ). [a. AF. *atteignour* = OF. *atteigneur*; see ATTAIN *v.*] *Law.* One of the twenty-four jurors in the process of ATTAINT.

†Attai·nt, *ppl. a.* ME. [a. OF. *ateint, ataint*, mod. *atteint, a(t)teindre* to ATTAIN, formed like *teindre*, and not from L. *attactus.* Erron. referred to L. *tinctus* stained.] 1. Convicted, attainted. Used *orig.* as pa. pple. of ATTAIN, subseq. of ATTAINT *v.*; also as adj. –1768. 2. Affected with sickness, passion, etc.; infected –1500. 3. Exhausted. [Cf. F. *éteint.*] –1485.

Attaint (ătēi·nt), *v.* ME. [f. ATTAINT *ppl. a.* (cf. *to convict*), used as pa. pple. before *attainted.* Its senses are thus due partly to *attain*, partly also to later association with TAINT *v.*^{1}, L. *tingere*; cf. the aphetic TAINT.] †1. = ATTAIN *v.* I. 1, II. 5. –1530. †2. To convict –1768. †3. *Old Law.* To convict a jury of having given a false verdict; to bring an action to reverse a verdict so given –1667. 4. To subject to ATTAINDER (sense 1) ME. 5. To accuse *of* crime or dishonour (*arch.*) 1586. 6. To touch, strike, or affect, as a disease, or other bodily or mental affection 1534. †7. (Cf. TAINT.) To infect -1631. 8. (=TAINT.) To infect with corruption, poison, etc. 1580; *fig.* to sully 1596.

4. To be attainted is, that his Blood be held in Law as stained and corrupted HOBBES. 5. Rebecca..being attainted of sorcery..doth deny the same SCOTT. 7. Attaynted With coveytous and ambycyon SKELTON. 8. When secret Vlcers shall a. thy breath QUARLES. Lest she with blame her honour should a. SPENSER. Hence **Attai·ntment**, conviction, attainder. **Attai·nture** = ATTAINDER; *fig.* stain.

Attaint (ătē̆·nt), *sb.* 1523. [a. OF. *ateinte, atainte* pa. pple. fem. used subst.; see ATTAINT *ppl. a.*] 1. The act of touching; *spec.* a hit in tilting (*arch.*) 1525; †*fig.* a dint (of misfortune, etc.) 1655. 2. *Vet. Surgery.* A blow on the leg of a horse caused by over-reaching 1523. 3. *Old Law.* The conviction of a jury for giving a false verdict; a legal process for reversing the verdict and convicting the jurors. (This was done by a grand jury of twenty-four.) 1528. 4. =ATTAINDER 1603. 5. *fig.* Imputation or touch of dishonour; stain 1592.

1. Both the others failed in the a. SCOTT. Thou..maiest without a. o're-looke The dedicated words SHAKS.

†**Attal**, var. of ETTLE *v.*

†**Atta·me**, *v.* [ME. *atame*, a. OF. *atamer*:—L. *attaminare*, f. *at-* = *ad-* + *-tamen* = **tagmen*, f. *tangere.*] 1. *trans.* To cut into -1494; to broach (a cask, etc.) -1440. 2. To attack, meddle with -1450; to begin (ME. only).

Attar (æ·tăɹ). Also **atar**, and OTTO. 1798. [a. Pers., ad. Arab.] A fragrant, volatile, essential oil obtained from the petals of the rose; fragrant essence (of roses). The full Pers. *Attar-gul* 'essence of roses' is occas. used.

†**Atta·sk**, *v.* [A- *pref.* 11 (*at-*).] To blame. *Lear* I. iv. 366.

†**Atta·ste**, *v.* ME. [a. OF. *ataster*, f. *at-* = *ad-* + **taxitare*; see TASTE.] To taste, experience. *trans.* -1559. *absol.* -1460.

Atte, obs. f. AT; also = ME. *at þe*, at the.

Atteal (æ·tīl). 1600. *Ornith.* A kind of duck of the Orkney and Shetland isles.

Attemper (ăte·mpəɹ), *v.* ME. [a. OF. *atemprer* (mod. *attremper*):—L. *attemperare*, f. *at-* = *ad-* + *temperare.*] 1. To qualify, modify, or moderate by admixture; to temper. 2. To modify the temperature of ME. 3. To moderate, assuage (passion or harshness); to soothe, appease (persons) ME. 4. To restrain. Also *refl.* ? *Obs.* ME. 5. To regulate ME. 6. To make fit or suitable *to*. Also *refl.* ME. 7. To attune 1579. 8. To temper (metal) 1869.

1. The love attempered the sorow CAXTON. 2. A. the air with a fire of charcoal EVELYN. 6. God often attempers Himself..to the condition of men PUSEY. 7. High airs, attemper'd to the vocal strings POPE. Hence **Atte·mperament, -perment**, the bringing to a proper temper; mixture in due proportions.

†**Atte·mperance.** ME. [a. OF. *atemprance*; see prec.] 1. Moderation -1560. 2. =*Attemperament* (see ATTEMPER) -1555. 3. Harmony 1481. 4. Natural constitution. CHAUCER.

†**Atte·mperate**, *ppl. a.* ME. [ad. L. *attemperatus*; see ATTEMPER.] Temperate; well-regulated; well-proportioned -1534. Hence †**Atte·mperately** *adv.*

Attemperate (ăte·mpĕrĕ'ɪt), *v.* 1561. [f. prec.] †1. =ATTEMPER 5, 6. -1711. 2. = ATTEMPER 2. 1605. Hence **Atte·mpera·tion**, the action of attempering or regulating. **Atte·mperator**, that which attempers; *spec.* in *Brewing*, an arrangement for regulating the temperature of the fermenting wort, etc. †**Atte·mperature**, attempered condition.

†**Atte·mpre**, *a.* ME. [a. OF. *atempré.*] Temperate, mild -1555. Hence †**Atte·mprely** *adv.*

Attempt (ăte·mt), *v.* 1513. [a. OF. *attempter* (*attenter*):—L. *attemptare, attentare*, f. *at-*, *ad-*, + *tentare*, freq. of *tendere*. See also ATTENT.] I. 1. To make an effort or endeavour to do or accomplish some action. 2. *ellipt.* To try to accomplish or attain (any action or object of activity, *esp.* one attended with risk or danger); to venture upon 1534. †3. To try to use or in use -1770.

1. Him he attempts with studied arts to please DRYDEN. To a. the conversion of the English GREEN. 2. Courage and Hardiness to a. the Seas RAY.

II. †1. To try with afflictions -1650. 2. To try to seduce, or entice; to tempt (*arch.*) 1513. †3. To try to obtain or attract -1749. †4. To try to move (by entreaty, etc.) -1673.

2. God..Hinder'd not Satan to a. the minde of Man MILT. *P. L.* x. 8. 4. Deare sir, of force I must a. you further, Take some remembrance of vs as a tribute *Merch. V*, IV. i. 421.

III. †1. *intr.* (with *indirect pass.*) To make an attack, or assault *upon*. Fr. *attenter sur. Obs.* (Now 'to make an attempt upon' or as 2.) -1697. 2. *trans.* To try to take by force, master, or overthrow; to attack: a. an enemy, fortress, etc.; also *fig.* and *transf.* (*arch.*) 1562; †b. to try to ravish or seduce -1741.

1. We look to be attempted upon euery day CROMWELL. †*To a. nothing upon* = Fr. *rien attenter sur.* 2. b. The Judges..who attempted Susanna 1610. *To a. the life of*: to try to take the life of. Hence **Atte·mpter**, one who attempts anything; †an assailant; †one who attempts the virtue of a woman; †a tempter. **Atte·mptingly** *adv.*

Attempt (ăte·mt), *sb.* 1534. [f. prec. vb.] 1. A putting forth of effort to accomplish what is uncertain or difficult; a trial, endeavour; enterprise, undertaking 1548; *esp.* futile endeavour 1605. †2. The thing attempted, aim -1790. 3. †a. An attack, onset -1665. b. A personal assault on a person's life, a woman's honour, etc. (Now usu. 'an attempt upon the life of', etc.) 1593. †4. Temptation, seduction -1667.

1. If God be favourable vnto our attemptes UDALL. They haue awak'd, And 'tis not done: th' a., and not the deed, confounds vs *Macb.* II. ii. 11. *To make an a.*: to try (*to do*). 3. a. Hee Prepares for some a. of Warre *Macb.* III. vi. 39. b. The Maid will I..make fit for his a. *Meas. for M.* III. i. 267. var. †**Attempta·tion.** **Atte·mptless** *a.* without attempting.

Attemptable (ăte·mtăb'l), *a.*; in 7 **-ible.** 1611. [f. ATTEMPT *v.* + -ABLE.] That may be attempted. Hence **Atte·mptabi·lity.**

†**Atte·mptive**, *a. rare.* 1603. [irreg. f. ATTEMPT *v.* + -IVE.] Given to attempts; venturous. This great nation..A., able, worthy, generous DANIEL.

Attend (ăte·nd), *v.* Aphet. TEND. [ME. *atende*, a. OF. *atendre*:—L. *at-*, *adtendere*, f. *ad-* + *tendere.*] To stretch to; *hence*, to direct the mind or energies to; to watch over; to wait for, expect. I. 1. To turn one's ear to, listen to. *trans.* (*arch.*) ME. *intr.* (Const. *to, unto.*) 1447. 2. To turn the mind to, regard, consider. †*trans.* -1775. *intr.* with *to* 1678. 3. To turn the energies to, look after. †*trans.* -1798. *intr.* with *to*, †*upon*, †*inf.*, or †*subord. cl.* ME.

1. My tale A. SCOTT. O Lord, a. vnto my crie *Ps.* xvii. 1. 2. To a. to the justice of the case only McCULLOCH. 3. To a. tasks POPE, to one's work 1833.

II. 1. To direct one's care to; to TEND, guard. *trans.* (*arch.*) ME. *intr.* with *to* 1796. 2. *trans.* To apply oneself to the care or service of; *esp.* to minister to (the sick), to pay professional visits to (a patient) 1572. 3. To wait upon 1469; *intr.* to be in waiting 1514; with *on, upon*, †*of* 1499. 4. To follow, escort, or accompany, for the purpose of rendering services. (Used *spec.* in relation to royal personages.) *trans.* 1653. *intr.* with *on, upon*; and *absol.* 1591. 5. *Mil.* and *Naut.* To follow closely upon for hostile purposes. (*trans.*, and *intr.* with *to.*) 1674. 6. Of things: To follow closely upon, to accompany. (Now only of things immaterial.) *trans.* 1615. *intr.* with *on, upon* 1606. †7. *causal.* To follow up, conjoin -1775. 8. To present oneself at a meeting, etc., in order to take part in the proceedings. *trans.* e. g. to *attend* church, a *place* of worship 1646. *intr.* Const. *at* the place. 1660.

1. They a. their lamps KANE. To a. to all the services NELSON. 2. Hired nurses who attended infected people DE FOE. 3. Summoned to a. the King MACAULAY. 4. The Portuguese infanta..was attended by a numerous train of nobles PRESCOTT. Trip Audry, I a. *A. Y. L.* v. i. 66. 5. If this is so, a force is necessary to a. [the Enemy] NELSON. 6. Our food was attended with some ale FIELDING. Destruction and misery a. on wicked doings 1847. 7. I have..attended them with brief observations BACON. 8. To a. lectures 1770, a funeral, school, at the City Temple (*mod.*).

III. 1. *trans.* To look out for, await 1475; †*ellipt.* with *cl.* to wait to see or learn -1699. †2. *fig.* Of things: To be reserved for, await -1734. †3. To expect -1692. †4. *intr.* To tarry, wait -1768.

1. Here I a. The king—and lo! he comes SMOLLETT. They must a. the moving of the waters 1642. Attended what would be the Issue TEMPLE. Hence **Atte·ndedness** (*rare*).

Attendance (ăte·ndăns). ME. [a. OF. *atendance*; see ATTEND *v.* and -ANCE.] †1. = ATTENTION 1. -1790. †2. = ATTENTION 2. -1674. 3. The action or condition of attending (see ATTEND II. 4); ministration, assiduous service ME. 4. Waiting the leisure, convenience, or decision of a superior 1461. 5. The action or fact of being present at a meeting, etc., or when summoned 1460. †6. Waiting -1664; expectation -1641. †7. A body of attendants, retinue -1779. 8. The body of persons present at any proceedings 1835.

3. Phr. *In attendance.* Reputation for..good a. on his customers DE FOE. 4. *To* †*wait, dance, a.* = 'to attend' (usu. contemptuous). 5. The number of attendances recorded (*mod.*). *Comb.* **a.-officer**, one whose duty it is to see that children attend school.

†**Atte·ndancy.** Also **-ency.** 1594. [f. prec.; see -NCY.] 1. Attention 1679. 2. The giving of attendance 1594. 3. =ATTENDANCE 7. 1586. 4. Attendant relation 1626. 5. An adjunct 1654. 6. Expectation 1646.

Attendant (ăte·ndănt). ME. [a. OF. *attendant*; see ATTEND.] A. *adj.* †1. Attentive -1649. 2. Waiting upon, in order to do service; ministrant 1485. Const. †*to, on, upon.* ME. †3. *Law.* Dependent on; owing service to -1641. 4. Accompanying; closely consequent. Const. *on, upon.* 1617. 5. Present at meeting, etc. (see ATTEND II. 8) 1588.

2. Other Suns..With thir a. Moons thou wilt descrie MILT. *P. L.* VIII. 149. 4. *Attendant Keys* in *Mus.*: the keys or scales on the fifth above, and fifth below (or fourth above) any key-note or tonic, considered in relation to the key or scale on that tonic. A. circumstances (*mod.*).

B. *sb.* 1. One who attends (see ATTEND II. 4); a servant, satellite, companion 1555. *transf.* or *fig.* 1667. 2. 'One that waits the pleasure of another' (J.) 1684. 3. An accompaniment, close consequent 1607. 4. One who is present at a meeting, etc. (see ATTEND II. 8) 1641. 5. *Law.* (See *adj.* 3.)

1. Sin..and her black a., Death MILT. *P. L.* VII. 547. 3. The laugh, the jest, attendants on the bowl POPE. Hence **Atte·ndantly** *adv.*

Attender (ăte·ndəɹ). 1461. [f. ATTEND *v.*] 1. One who gives heed; an observer 1660. 2. He who (or that which) waits upon, *esp.* to render service 1461. 3. =ATTENDANT *sb.* 4. 1704. **Atte·ndress**, a waitress. FULLER.

†**Atte·ndment.** *rare.* ME. [a. OF. *atendement.*] 1. Sense, meaning. 2. A thing that attends; *pl.* surroundings 1646.

Attent (ăte·nt), *ppl. a.* 1482. [ad. L. *attentus.*] Intent, attentive (*to, upon*).

Myne eares shall be attente vnto prayer 2 *Chron.* vii. 15. Hence **Atte·ntly** *adv.*

†**Atte·nt**, *sb.* [ME. *atent(e*, a. OF. *atente*, now *attente*:—L. **attenta* sb., f. fem. of pa. pple. *attentus*. In OF. confused w. *entente*, whence sense 2.] 1. Attention; heed -1652. 2. Intention, aim -1450. Hence †**Atte·ntful** *a.*

Atte·ntat(e. ? *Obs.* 1622. [var. of ATTEMPTATE; cf. F. *attentat.*] †1. A criminal attempt or assault -1721. 2. An attempt to gain an unauthorized advantage in law, e. g. after an inhibition is decreed.

Attention (ăte·nʃən). ME. [ad. L. *attentionem*; see ATTEND. Used by Chaucer in transl. from L., then not till *c* 1600.] 1. The action, fact, or state of attending or giving heed; earnest direction of the mind, consideration, or regard. The mental faculty of attending. 2. Practical consideration, notice 1741. 3. Attending to the comfort and pleasure of others; ceremonious politeness, courtesy. Often in *pl.* 1752. †4. A consideration (*rare*) 1784. 5. *Mil.* A cautionary word used as a preparative to any particular exercise or manœuvre 1820.

1. The tongues of dying men Inforce a. *Rich. II*, II. i. 6. A. is that state of mind which prepares us to receive impressions. *To pay* or *give a.* *To attract, call, draw, arrest, fix*, etc. *a.* 2. They have a. to everything, and always mind what they are about CHESTERF. 3. *To pay a.* or *one's attentions to*: to court. 5. *To come to a.*: to assume a prepared military attitude; so *to stand at a.*

Attentive (ăte·ntiv), *a.* 1570. [a. F. *attentif, -ive.*] 1. Steadily applying one's mind, or energies; intent, heedful, observant 1577. 2. Giving watchful heed to the wishes of others; polite, courteous 1570.

1. Diligent and a. at their workes 1622. 2. Very a. to the ladies (*mod.*). Hence **Atte·ntive-ly** *adv.*, **-ness.**

Atte·nuable, *a.* ? *Obs.* [f. L. *attenuare.*] That may be attenuated. SIR T. BROWNE.

Attenuant (ăte·niu,ănt), *a.* 1603. [a. F., ad. L. *attenuantem*; see next.] Having the property of thinning; *spec.* in *Med.* of thinning the secretions. As *sb.* [sc. *drug, agent.*] 1725. var. †**Atte·nuative.**

Attenuate (ăte·niu,eit), *v.* 1530. [f. L. *attenuat-, attenuare*, f. *at-* = *ad-* + *tenuare*, f. *tenuis.*] **1.** To make thin or slender (*e.g.* by natural or artificial shaping, starving, physical decay, etc.). **2.** To make thin in consistency, to separate the particles of a substance, to rarefy 1594. *spec.* in *Med.* To make thinner (the humours or concretions of the body) 1533. **3.** *fig.* To reduce in intensity, force, amount, or value; †to extenuate 1530. **4.** *intr.* To become slender, thinner, or weaker 1834.

1. They crucifie the soul of man, a. our bodies BURTON. 2. Salt, for example, may a. earth 1762. 3. To a. power 1530, numbers 1645, authority 1850, appetites LECKY. Hence †**Atte·nuater, -or** = ATTENUANT *sb.*

Attenuate (ăte·niu,ět), *ppl. a.* 1626. [ad. L. *attenuatus*; see prec.] **1.** Slender, thin; tapered, reduced to thinness 1848. **2.** Rarefied; refined 1626.

1. The a. hands 1864. 2. Such a rare and a. substance, as is the spirit of living creatures BACON.

Attenuation (ăte:niu,ē·ʃən). 1594. [ad. L. *attenuationem*; see ATTENUATE.] **1.** The making thin or slender; diminution of thickness; emaciation 1631. **2.** Diminution of density 1594. **3.** The process of weakening, as if by dilution 1868.

3. The gradual 'attenuation' of disease germs 1882.

A·tter, *sb.* [Com. Teut.: OE. *átr, átor, attor.*] †**1.** Venom, *esp.* that of reptiles –ME. †**2.** Gall; also *fig.* –ME. **3.** Corrupt matter, pus. Still in *Sc.* and *north. dial.* ME. Hence †**A·tter** *v.* to envenom; also *fig.*; to mix with gall.

A·ttercop. [OE. *attorcoppa*, f. *attor* poison + *coppa*, deriv. of *cop* top, or *cop* cup. Cf. COBWEB, formerly *cop-webbe.*] †**1.** A spider –1691. **2.** *fig.* A venomous person 1505. **3.** Misapplied to: A spider's web 1530.

Atte·rmine, *v.* ? *Obs.* ME. [a. OF. *aterminer*, ad. L. *atterminare.*] To settle the term of; *esp.* to adjourn payment of (a debt) till a day fixed.

†**Atte·rr**, *v.* 1598. [a. F. *atterrer*, f. *à* + *terre.*] To bring to the ground, humble –1614.

†**A·tterrate**, *v.* 1673. [f. It. *atterrare*, f. *a* + *terra.*] To fill up with (*esp.* alluvial) earth –1757. Hence †**Atterra·tion.**

A·ttery, a·ttry, *a.* OE. [f. ATTER *sb.*] †**1.** Venomous –ME. †**2.** Mixed with gall (*lit.* and *fig.*) –ME. †**3.** Malignant –1535. **4.** Purulent 1868.

Attest (ăte·st), *v.* 1596. [a. F. *attester*, ad. L. *attestari*, f. *at-* = *ad-* + *testari*, f. *testis.*] **1.** *trans.* To bear witness to, affirm the truth or genuineness of; to testify, certify. **b.** formally by signature or oath 1665. **2.** *transf.* Of things: To be evidence of, vouch for 1599. **3.** *intr.* To testify *to* 1672. **4.** *trans.* To call to witness (*arch.*). (So in Fr.) 1606. **5.** To put (a man) on his oath, or solemn declaration 1685.

1. The merit of the English bowmen .. is strongly attested by Froissart 1875. b. I will assert nothing here, but what I dare a. SWIFT. 4. But I a. the gods, your full consent Gaue wings to my propension *Tr. & Cr.* II. ii. 132. Hence **Atte·stable** *a.* **Atte·ster, -or**; var. **Attesta·tor. Atte·stive** *a.* furnishing evidence (*rare*). **Atte·stment**, testimony (*rare*).

Attest (ăte·st), *sb.* 1606. [f. prec. vb.] **1.** Evidence, testimony. **2.** Attesting signature, attestation 1649.

1. Th' a. of eyes and eares *Tr. & Cr.* V. ii. 122.

Attestant (ăte·stănt). 1880. [ad. L. *attestantem*; see ATTEST *v.*] *ppl. adj.* Bearing witness. *sb.* One who attests (by signature).

Attestation (ætestē·ʃən). 1547. [a. F., ad. L. *attestationem*; see ATTEST *v.*] **1.** The act of bearing witness; the testimony borne; evidence, proof 1598. **b.** Formal confirmation by signature, oath, etc.; *esp.* the verification of the execution of a deed or will by signature in the presence of witnesses 1674. †**2.** The act of calling to witness –1741. **3.** The administration of an oath, *e.g.* of the oath of allegiance to a recruit 1812.

1. b. The last requisite to the validity of a deed is the a., or execution of it in the presence of witnesses BLACKSTONE.

Atte·stative, *a.* 1832. [f. L. *attestat-*; see -ATIVE.] Of the nature of, or pertaining to, attestation.

Attic (æ·tik), *a.* and *sb.*[1] 1599. [ad. L. *Atticus*, Gr. Ἀττικός.] **1.** Of or pertaining to Attica, or to its capital Athens; Athenian. *Formerly* = Greek. **2.** Having characteristics peculiarly Athenian; *hence*, of style, etc.: Pure, classical 1633. **3.** *sb.* A native of Attica, an Athenian (author) 1699.

1. No Atticke eloquence is so sweete DEKKER. 2. Well, but Addison's prose is A. prose M. ARNOLD. *Attic salt* or *wit* (L. *sal Atticus*): refined, delicate, poignant wit. *Attic faith*: inviolable faith. *Attic base* in *Arch.*: a base consisting of an upper and lower torus divided by a scotia and two fillets, used for Ionic, Corinthian, and occ. for Doric columns. *Attic order*: a square column of any of the five orders. vars. †**A·ttical, -an**, *adjs.* (*rare*).

Attic (æ·tik), *sb.*[2] (orig. *adj.*). 1696. [a. F. *Attique*, ad. L. *Atticus*; see prec.] **1.** A small order (column and entablature) placed above another order of much greater height constituting the main facade. (Usually an Attic order, with pilasters; whence the name.] **2.** *attrib.* quasi-*adj.* in *Attic storey*: orig. the space enclosed by such a structure; *hence*, the top storey of a building, under the beams of the roof, where there are more than two storeys 1724. **3.** The highest storey of a house, or a room in it; a garret. Hence *joc.* the brain. 1817.

2. The Rustic and A. Stories are 12 feet high each DE FOE. 3. A small lodging in an a. MACAULAY.

†**Atti·ce**, *v.* 1450. [a. OF. *atisier, -icier* (mod. *attiser*):—late L. **attitiare*, f. *at-* = *ad-* + *titio* brand. Cf. ENTICE.] To stir up, instigate; to gain over, entice –1557.

Atticism (æ·tisiz'm). 1612. [ad. Gr. Ἀττικισμός.] **1.** Siding with, or attachment to, Athens 1628. **2.** The peculiar style and idiom of Greek as used by the Athenians; *hence*, refined, elegant Greek, and *gen.* a refined amenity of speech, a well-turned phrase 1612.

Atticist (æ·tisist). 1835. [ad. Gr. Ἀττικιστής.] One who affected Attic style.

Atticize (æ·tisəiz), *v.* 1610. [ad. Gr. Ἀττικίζειν.] **1.** *intr.* To side with or favour Athens 1753. **2.** To affect Attic style; to conform to Athenian (or Greek) habits, modes of thought, etc.

†**Atti·nge**, *v.* 1639. [ad. L. *attingere.* Cf. ATTAIN.] To touch upon, come in contact with –1742. Hence †**Atti·ngency**, effective contact.

‖**Attirail, attiral.** *Obs.* 1611. [F., f. *attirier* + *-ail*] Apparatus, gear –1790.

Attire (ătəi·ɹ), *v.* See also aphet. TIRE *v.*[2] [ME. *atire*, a. OF. *atirer*, earlier *atirier*, formed on *à tire* (*tiere*), of uncertain origin; see TIER.] †**1.** To put in order. †**2.** To prepare, fit out –1440. **3.** To equip: †**a.** for war: To arm –1593. **b.** with dress, etc.: To dress, adorn. (Now only literary and usu. *refl.* and *pass.*) ME. **c.** To dress (the head, *mostly* of women) (*arch.*) ME.

3. a. A palfray of prise, prudly atyrit ME. b. To greet her thus attired TENNYSON. c. Shee painted her face, and tyred her head, and looked out at a window 2 *Kings* ix. 30. Hence **Atti·red** *ppl. a.*; *spec.* in *Venery* and *Her.* furnished with horns. **Atti·rement**, outfit, dress; †furniture, †decoration.

Attire (ătəi·ɹ), *sb.* ME. [f. ATTIRE *v.*[1]; cf. APPAREL, ARRAY.] †**1.** Equipment for war –1440. †**2.** Personal adornment. Also (with *pl.*) an ornament. –1642. **3.** Dress, apparel; †(with *pl.*) a dress ME. †**4.** Head-dress; *spec.* of women. Also aphet. TIRE. (Erron. conn. w. *tiara.*) –1611. **5.** *Venery* and *Her.* The 'head-gear' of a deer 1562. **6.** *fig.* Anything which clothes or adorns; the external surroundings of anything immaterial 1610. †**7.** In plants: The parts within the corolla, as the stamens, and the florets of the disk in Composite flowers –1751.

3. Having neither..nor attyre to clothe their backes 1553. 5. The Heralds call the Horns of a Stag..his A. BRADLEY. 6. Earth in her rich a. MILT. *P. L.* VII. 501.

Attiring (ătəi·riŋ), *vbl. sb.* ME. **1.** The action of fitting out, accoutring, dressing. **2.** Dress, trappings; head-dress; personal ornament. Also *fig.* 1552. **3.** = ATTIRE *sb.* 5. 1678. *Comb.*: †**A.-house, -room** = *Tiring-house, -room*, the room where players dress themselves for the stage; **a.-room**, a dressing-room, generally.

Attitude (æ·titiud). 1668. [a. F., ad. It. *attitudine*:—med.L. *aptitudinem*; see APTITUDE. Orig. a techn. term of the Arts of Design, taking the place of *aptitude c* 1710; thence extended into general use.] **1.** In *Fine Arts*: The disposition of a figure in statuary or painting; *hence*, the posture given to it. (Now merged in 2.) **2.** A posture of the body proper to or implying some action or mental state 1725. Also *fig.* **3.** Settled behaviour or manner of acting, as representative of feeling or opinion 1837. **4.** *Attitude of mind*: habitual mode of regarding anything 1862.

1. Though we retain the words, *Action* and *Posture* ..the tearm *Aptitude* (F. *attitude*) is more expressive J. EVELYN. 2. *To strike an a.*: to assume it theatrically. *fig.* The mien and attitudes of truth JOHNSON. 4. The allegorical a. of mind 1881. Hence **Attitu·dinal** *a.* pertaining to attitudes. **A:ttitudina·rian**, one who studies or practises attitudes. **A:ttitudina·rianism**, the excessive use of attitudes.

Attitudinize (ætitiū·dinəiz), *v.* 1784. [f. It. *attitudine* + -IZE.] *intr.* To study or practise attitudes excessively; to pose. Also *fig.*

Don't attitudinise JOHNSON. *fig.* In every line that he wrote Cicero was attitudinising for posterity FROUDE. Hence **Attitu·diniza·tion**, the practice of attitudes. **Attitu·dinizer.**

Attle (æt'l). 1849. [? Cf. ADDLE.] *Mining.* 'Refuse; impure off-casts in the working of mines' (Weale).

Attollent (ătǫ·lĕnt). 1713. [ad. L. *attollentem, attollere.*] *adj.* Lifting up; *spec.* of certain muscles. (Usu. in L. form, *attollens*). *sb.* [sc. *muscle.*]

Attomy, Attonce, Attone, obs.; see ATO-.

Attorn (ătv̄·ɹn), *v.* 1458. [a. OF. *atorner, atourner*, f. *à* + *tourner*. The sp. follows med. L. *attornare.*] **1.** *trans.* To turn over to another; to assign, transfer 1649. **2.** *intr.* (for *refl.*) In *Feudal Law*: To transfer oneself (*i. e.* one's homage and allegiance) from one lord to another; to do homage to, as lord. Also *fig.* 1611. **3.** *Mod. Law.* To agree formally to be the tenant of one into whose possession the estate has passed 1458. So *to attorn tenant.* 1844.

1. To a. a vassal's service to some other 1649, one's allegiance 1691. 3. Tenant who attorns under any mistake may defend against lessor WHARTON.

Attorney (ătv̄·ɹni), *sb.*[1] [ME. *aturne, atorne*, a. OF. *atorné*, pa. pple. masc. of *atorner*, 'one appointed', *not*, as erron. in law dicts., 'one who acts *in the turn* of another'. See ATTORN.] †**1.** One appointed to act for another; an agent, deputy, commissioner. In later times only *fig.* –1642. **2.** (*Attorney in fact, private attorney.*) One duly appointed or constituted (by *Letter* or *Power of Attorney*) to act for another in business and legal matters, either *generally*, or in some *specific* act 1466. Also *fig.* **3.** (*Attorney-at-law, public attorney.*) A properly-qualified legal agent practising in the courts of Common Law (as a *solicitor* practised in Chancery); one who conducts litigation in these courts, preparing the case for the barristers, who plead in open court. (Often used as almost = knave, or swindler. In U.S. the distinction between *attorney* and *counsel* does not exist. The title was abolished in England by the Judicature Act of 1873.) ME. **4.** *transf.* An advocate, mediator. ? *Obs.* 1537. **5.** Specific title of the law officer, or clerk, of various courts or councils 1494.

1. I will attend my husband..And will haue no atturney but my selfe *Com. Err.* V. i. 100. 2. None may appear in Gods service by an Atturney FULLER. 3. Johnson observed, that 'he did not speak ill of any man behind his back, but he believed the gentleman was an a.' BOSWELL. 4. Be the Atturney of my loue to her SHAKS. 5. *The King's Attorney*: now ATTORNEY-GENERAL. *Mr. Attorney*, the style used in speaking to or †*of* him.

Attorney-general. †**1.** *gen.* A legal representative acting under a general power of attorney; opp. to *a. special* or *particular*. Pl. *attorneys general*. –1717. **2.** *spec. Attorney-General, Attorney General*: a legal officer of the state empowered to act in all cases in which the state is a party. In England, Ireland, etc., and in U.S., the first ministerial law-officer of the government. In the duchies of Lancaster and Cornwall, and county palatine of Durham, the title of his or her Majesty's attorney. Pl. (better): *Attorney-Generals*. 1533. Hence **Attorney-generalship.**

Atto·rney, *sb.*[2] 1461. [a. OF. *atournée*,

attornée = L. **attornata* (but in med.L. *attornatio, attornatus*).] †1. The action of appointing a legal representative, procuration. (? *Hence*, 'by attorney'.) -1635. Now only used in, **2.** *Letter* or *Warrant of Attorney*: a legal document by which a person appoints one or more persons to act for him as his attorney or attorneys. *Power of A.*: the authority so conferred, the document itself.

Atto·rney, *v.* [f. the sb.] To perform by attorney. *Wint. T.* I. i. 30.

Atto·rneydom. 1881. The body of attorneys collectively. (*Contemptuous.*)

Atto·rneyism. 1837. The practice of the 'rascally attorney'. (*Vituperative.*)

Atto·rneyship. 1591. **1.** The acting as an attorney for another; proxy. **2.** The profession and practice of an attorney; also = *Attorney-generalship* 1611.

Attornment (ătɒ̄·ɹnmĕnt). 1531. [a. OF. *atournement*; see ATTORN.] **1.** A turning over; transference or assignment 1650. **2.** *spec.* The transference of his homage, etc., by a tenant to a new feudal lord; *hence*, legal acknowledgement of the new landlord 1531.

†Attour, var. of ATOUR *adv.* and *prep.*

†Attou·rne, *v.* ME. = RETURN -1470.

Attract (ătræ·kt), *v.* 1540. [f. L. *attract-*, *attrahere*, f. *at-*, *ad-* + *trahere*. After the earlier *abstract*, etc.] Only *trans.* †1. To draw in; to absorb -1652; to inhale -1667. †2. To pull, drag in -1677. **3.** To draw to itself by invisible influence: **a.** Said of physical forces 1627. **b.** Said of influencing the will and action of men and animals 1568. **c.** Said of presenting conditions favourable, *e.g.* to parasites, disease, criticism, etc. 1771. **4.** Hence, without material movement: **a.** To excite towards oneself the pleasurable emotions of a person, who thus 'feels drawn' to one 1601. **b.** To draw forth, and fix upon oneself the attention, or notice, of others 1692.

3. a. Jet and amber attracteth straws SIR T. BROWNE. b. A great capital attracts great talent HELPS. c. Conditions which a. fever (*mod.*). 4. a. Adornd..and lovely to a. Thy love MILT. *P. L.* x. 152. b. A wife.. Made to a. his eyes, and keep his heart DRYDEN. Hence **†Attra·ct** *sb.* attraction; chiefly in *pl.* charms. **Attra·ctable** *a.* capable of being attracted; whence **Attra·ctabi·lity, Attra·ctableness. Attra·ctingly** *adv.*

Attraction (ătræ·kʃən). 1533. [ad. L. *attractionem*; see ATTRACT *v.* and -TION.] †1. Absorption; the taking in of food -1621. †2. Inhalation -1638. †3. *Med.* The action of drawing humours, etc.; *concr.* an application that so draws, a poultice, etc. -1656. †4. Pulling -1578. **5.** The action of a body in drawing to itself, by some physical force, another to which it is not materially attached; the force thus exercised 1607. *fig.* Personal influence, figured as magnetic 1750. **6.** The action of causing men or animals to come to one by influencing their appetites, etc. 1742. **7.** The action of drawing forth interest, affection, sympathy; the power of so doing 1767. **8.** An attracting quality 1608. **9.** A thing or feature which 'draws' people; *esp.* any interesting or amusing exhibition 1862.

5. The Sunnes a Theefe, and with his great a. Robbes the vaste Sea *Timon* IV. iii. 439. *Magnetic attraction*: the action of a magnet in drawing and attaching iron to itself. *Electric a.*: the similar action of electrified bodies upon other substances. *A. of gravity* or *gravitation*: that which exists between all bodies, and acts at all distances, with a force proportional to their masses, and inversely proportional to the square of their distance apart. *Molecular a.*: that which takes place between molecules, and acts only at infinitely small distances. *A. of cohesion*: that by which the particles composing a body are kept together. *A. of adhesion*: that by which certain substances, when brought into contact, stick together. *Capillary a.*: that whereby a liquid is drawn up through a hair-like tube. *Chemical a.* = AFFINITY. 6. The a. of the disaffected to his standard (*mod.*). 8. She had new Attractions every time he saw her STEELE. Hence **Attra·ctionally** *adv.* **†Attra·ctionist**, one who accounted for phenomena by a theory of a. **Attra·ctionless** *a.*

Attractive (ătræ·ktiv). 1540. [a. F. *attractif, -ive*, f. as if repr. L. **attractivus*; see ATTRACT *v.* and -IVE.] **A.** *adj.* †1. Absorptive -1713. †2. *Med.* Drawing humours -1786. **3.** Having the property of ATTRACTION (sense 5). Also *fig.* 1602. **4.** Having the quality of ATTRACTION (sense 6) 1590. **5.** Having the quality of attracting attention, etc.; interesting, engaging, pleasing, alluring. (Now the most frequent use.) 1602.

5. Interesting and a. for those who love to hear an old man's stories of a past age SCOTT. Hence **Attra·ctively** *adv.* **Attra·ctiveness.**

B. *sb.* †1. *Med.* A medicament which 'draws' -1786. †2. That which draws like a magnet. Also *fig.* -1652. †3. An ATTRACTION (sense 9) -1765. †4. A quality that attracts; *esp.* an attractive personal quality. (Now repl. by ATTRACTION.) -1805.

Attractor (ătræ·ktəɹ). 1641. [f. ATTRACT.] **1.** That which attracts 1646. **2.** One who draws by sympathy, etc. 1641.

Attrahent (æ·trăhĕnt). 1661. [ad. L. *attrahentem*; see ATTRACT *v.*] *adj.* That attracts, attracting. *sb.* [sc. *agent.*]

The motion of steel to its a. GLANVILL.

†Attra·p, *v.*[1] 1524. [a. F. *attraper*, f. *à* + *trappe*.] To catch in, or as in, a trap -1681.

†Attra·p, *v.*[2] 1580. [f. A- *pref.* 11 + TRAP *v.*] Usu. in pa. pple. **attrapped.** Furnished with trappings -1693.

†Attrecta·tion. 1615. [ad. L. *attrectationem*.] Touching, handling -1663.

Attributable (ătri·biŭtăb'l), *a.* 1665. [f. ATTRIBUTE *v.* + -ABLE.] Capable of being attributed, *esp.* as owing **to**, produced **by**.

How much is a. to that cause MILL.

†A·ttribute, *ppl. a.* ME. [ad. L. *attributus*, *attribuere*; now *attributed*.] Attributed; assigned, given. -1599.

Attribute (æ·tribiŭt), *sb.* ME. [prob. subst. use of prec., through L. *attributum* (Theol.); cf. F. *attribut.*] **1.** A quality ascribed to any person or thing, one which is in common usage assigned to him; hence, *occas.*, an epithet or appellation in which the quality is ascribed. †2. Distinguished quality or character; credit, reputation. (Cf. *quality*, etc. in 'a person of *quality*', i. e. '*quality* worth naming'.) -1690. **3.** A material object recognized as symbolic of any office, or actor; *spec.* in *Painting*, etc.: A conventional symbol added to identify the personage represented 1596. **4.** An inherent or characteristic quality 1836. (Sir W. Hamilton's distinction (*Metaph.* viii. (1870) I. 151) is hardly historical.) **b.** in *Logic*, That which may be predicated of anything; *strictly* an essential and permanent quality 1785. **5.** *Gram.* An attributive word; a predicable. *esp.* in *Sentence Analysis*: = Attributive adjunct, *i.e.* an adj., or a word, phr., or cl. equivalent to an adj.

1. Mercy is..an a. to God himselfe *Merch. V*, IV. i. 195. 2. It takes From our achievements..The pith and marrow of our a. *Haml.* I. iv. 22. 3. The club is an a. of Hercules 1727. *Merch. V*, V. iv. 191. 4. The attributes and acts of God, as far as they are revealed to man BACON. Beauty was an a. of the family SCOTT. b. Every a. is..an universal REID.

Attribute (ătri·biŭt), *v.* 1523. [f. the prec. ppl. adj. The poets down to Dryden and Scott show *attribu·te, a·ttribute.*] **1.** To assign, give, concede *to* any one, as his right (*arch.* or *Obs.*). **b.** To ascribe in praise 1563. **2.** To ascribe *to* as belonging or proper 1538. **3.** To ascribe as an attribute belonging, proper, or inherent 1534; as an effect *to* the cause 1530. **4.** To ascribe *to* an author as his work 1599. **5.** To assign in one's opinion to its proper time and place 1567.

2. God attributes to place No sanctity, if none be thither brought By men MILT. *P. L.* XI. 836. †*To attribute* (*much*), etc.: to ascribe great importance *to*. 3. To a. folly to God 1611. I cannot a. this honour to any desert in me 1626. Hence **Attri·buter** (*rare*).

Attribution (ætribiū·ʃən). 1467. [a. F., ad. L. *attributionem*; see ATTRIBUTE *a.*] **1.** Bestowal (in fact) (*arch.* or *Obs.*). **2.** Ascription in statement 1649. **3.** The assigning of a quality as belonging or proper to anything 1651. **4.** The ascribing of an effect to a cause, of a work to its (supposed) author, date, place, or of date and place to a work 1665. †5. *Rhet.* Giving of epithets 1589. **6.** *Logic.* Predication of an attribute 1860. **7.** Anything ascribed in one's opinion, *e.g.* appellation, credit, sense of a word, etc. ? *Obs.* 1596. †8. An attribute 1589. **9.** Authority or function granted (to a ruler, delegate, etc.). (From mod.Fr.) 1796.

3. The a. of sexes to plants WHEWELL. 7. Such a. should the Dowglas haue, As not a Souldiour..Should go so generall currant through the world 1 *Hen. IV*, IV. i. 3. 9. Trials for homicide were only a small part of its attributions GROTE.

Attributive (ætri·biŭtiv). 1606. [a. F. *attributif, -ive*, f. L. *attribut-*; see ATTRIBUTE *a.*] **A.** *adj.* †1. Characterized by attributing. SHAKS. **2.** *Logic.* That assigns an attribute to a subject 1849. **3.** *Gram.* That expresses an attribute 1840. **4.** So-assigned, so-ascribed. Cf. *putative*, and ATTRIBUTION 4. 1866. **B.** *sb.* A word that denotes an attribute. (Now usu. limited to adjs. and their equivalents.) 1750. Hence **Attri·butive·ly** *adv.*, **-ness** (*rare*).

Attrist (ătri·st), *v.* ? *Obs.* 1680. [a. F. *attrister*, f. *à* + *triste*:—L. *tristis*.] To sadden.

Attrite (ătrəi·t), *ppl. a.* 1625. [ad. L. *attritus*, *atterere*, f. *at-* = *ad-* + *terere*.] **1.** Ground down by friction. ? *Obs.* 1654. **2.** Having ATTRITION (sense 4) 1625. Hence **Attri·ted** *ppl. a.* worn down by friction. Also *fig.* **Attri·tive** *a.* characterized by attrition (*rare*). **Attri·tor. Attri·tus,** matter produced by attrition.

Attrition (ătri·ʃən). ME. [ad. L. *attritionem*, f. *attrit-*; see ATTRITE.] **1.** The act or process of rubbing one thing against another 1601. Also *fig.* **2.** Rubbing away, wearing or grinding down, by friction 1601. **3.** *Surg.* **a.** Excoriation, abrasion. **b.** Comminuted fracture 1543. **4.** An imperfect sorrow for sin, not amounting to *contrition* or utter crushing, and having its motive, not in love of God, but in fear of punishment. (*Scholastic Theol.*) ME.

2. Contact with English society exercises a constant a. on the system of castes M. MÜLLER.

Attroopment (ătrū·pmĕnt). *rare.* 1795. [a. F. *attroupement*, f. *attrouper*, f. *à* + *troupe*.] A tumultuous troop or crowd.

Attune (ătiū·n), *v.* 1596. [AT- *pref.*[3]; prob. suggested by ATONE.] **1.** To bring into musical accord. Const. *to.* Also *fig.* **2.** To bring (a musical instrument) to the right pitch; to tune. Also *fig.* 1728. **3.** To make tuneful 1667.

1. *fig.* The mind attuned to grace FREEMAN. 3. Joy lift her spirit, joy a. her voice COLERIDGE. Hence **Attu·ne** *sb.* harmony (*rare*). **Attu·nement.**

A-tu·mble, *adv.* 1881. [A *prep.*[1]] In tumbling condition.

A-twain (ătwē·n), *adv. arch.* ME. [A *prep.*[1] Cf. A-TWO.] **1.** In two. **2.** Asunder 1870.

Atwee·l, *phr. Sc.* 1768. ? Contr. f. *wat weel* = 'wot well'; aphet. '*tweel.*

Atween (ătwī·n). *arch.* and *dial.* ME. [f. A *prep.*[1] + *-tween*, stem of BE-TWEEN, after *afore*, etc.] *prep.* Between. †*adv.* Between whiles -1596.

†Atwi·nd, *v.* [f. AT- *pref.*[2] + OE. *windan.*] To escape (with *dat.* = from) -ME.

A-twi·st, *adv.* 1754. [A *prep.*[1]] Twisted, askew.

†Atwi·te, *v.* [f. AT- *pref.*[1] + OE. *witan.* Aphet. TWIT, formerly *twite.*] To reproach, blame, taunt, twit -1530.

A-twi·tter, *adv.* 1833. [A *prep.*[1]] In a twitter.

Atwixt (ătwi·kst), *prep. arch.* or *dial.* ME. [A-*pref.* 2 + *-twix(t*, stem of *betwixt*; cf. *atween.* Aphet. 'TWIXT.] Between.

A-two (ătū·), *adv. arch.* and *dial.* [OE. *on tú, on twá*; see A *prep.*[1] The regular prose form is *in two.*] **1.** In or into two parts (*arch.*). †2. Apart, asunder -1450.

Atypic (ăti·pik), *a.* [A- *pref.* 14.] Not typical, not conformable to the ordinary type.

‖**Aubade** (obā·d). 1678. [Fr., ad. Sp. *albada*, f. *alba* dawn.] A piece of music to be played or sung at dawn; an open-air morning serenade; hence, any morning concert.

The crowing cock..Sang his a. LONGF.

‖**Aubain** (obæ̃n). 1882. [Fr.; med.L. *Albanus*; ?] A non-naturalized foreigner subject to the right of *aubaine*.

‖**Aubaine** (obē·n). 1727. [Fr.: see prec.] A right of French kings, whereby they claimed the property of every non-naturalized stranger who died in their country. Abolished in 1819.

Aube, obs. f. ALB.

‖**Auberge** (obɛ·rʒ). 1615. [Fr.:—*alberge*, 11th c. *herberge*, a. MHG., OHG. *heri-berga*, lit. 'army-shelter'; cf. HARBOUR.] An inn. Hence ‖**Aubergi·ste,** keeper of an a. **†Aube·rgical** *a.*

‖ **Aubergine** (*o*berʒi·n). 1794. [Fr.] The fruit of the Egg-plant, *Solanum Esculentum.*

‖ **Aubin** (*o*beṅ). 1753. [Fr., = *hobin*, f. Eng. HOBBY (Diez).] A kind of broken gait, between an amble and a gallop.

Auburn (ǭ·bɒɹn), *a.* ME. [a. OF. *alborne, auborne*:—L. *alburnus* whitish. In 16–17th c. written *abron, abrune, abroun,* which suggested deriv. from *brown*, and modified the meaning.] *orig.* Of a yellowish- or brownish-white colour; *now*, of a golden- or ruddy-brown colour. quasi-*sb.* 1852.

Abourne or blounde CAXTON. The rays..lit up her pale red hair to a. GEO. ELIOT.

Au·chlet. *Sc.* 1796. [f. *aucht*, EIGHT + -LET *dim.*, or LOT, a part.] The eighth part of a boll; cf. *firlot*, the fourth part.

Aucht, Sc. form of AUGHT and EIGHT.

†**Au·ctary.** 1580. [ad. L. *auctarium*, f. *auct-, augere.*] Augmentation –1653.

Auction (ǭ·kʃən), *sb.* 1595. [ad. L. *auctionem* 'a sale by increase of bids'.] †1. Increase, growth –1696. **2.** A public sale in which each bidder offers more than the last previous bid, the article put up being sold to the highest bidder. Called in Scotl. and north of Engl. a *roup.* (In U. S. 'to sell or put up *at* auction' is common; in Engl. the const. is 'to sell *by*' or 'put up *to*' auction.) 1595. **3.** A public sale of analogous character 1673. †4. The property put up to auction 1732.

2. **Auction bridge**: see BRIDGE *sb.*[2] 3. *Dutch auction*: one in which property is offered at a high price, the price being gradually lowered till some one buys it. Hence **Au·ction** *v.* to sell by a. 1807.

Auctioneer (ǭkʃəniə·ɹ), *sb.* 1708. [f. prec.] One who conducts sales by auction. Hence **Auctionee·r** *v.* to sell by auction.

‖ **Auctor** (ǭ·ktǫɹ). 1875. [L.] *Rom. Law.* The person who warrants the right of possession; *hence*, a vendor.

Auctor, obs. f. AUTHOR.

†**Aucto·rizate, autor-.** 1548. [ad. med.L. *auctorizatus.*] *pa. pple.* Authorized. *adj.* Of established authority 1558.

Aucuba (ǭ·kiŭbă). 1819. [Jap.] *Bot.* A hardy evergreen diœcious shrub (*A. Japonica*, N.O. *Cornaceæ*), with laurel-like leaves usually blotched with pale yellow.

A...introduced by Mr. John Grœfer in 1783 REES.

Aucupate (ǭ·kiŭpeit), *v.* ? *Obs.* 1630. [f. L. *aucupat-, aucupari*, f. *aucupem*, f. *avis* + *capere.*] *lit.* To go a bird-catching; *fig.* (as in L.) to lie in wait for, gain by craft.

Audacious (ǭdēⁱ·ʃəs), *a.* 1550. [f. L. *audac(i-, audax*, f. *audere*; see -ACIOUS. Cf. Fr. *audacieux.*] **1.** Daring, confident, intrepid. *transf.* of things 1609. **2.** Unrestrained by, or defiant of, decorum and morality; presumptuously wicked, shameless 1591.

1. Big was her voice, a. was her tone:—The maid becomes a youth DRYDEN. A. Ornaments B. JONS. 2. Like an a. profligate, as he was 1825. Hence **Auda·ciously** *adv.* **Auda·ciousness,** boldness; reckless daring; effrontery.

Audacity (ǭdæ·siti). ME. [f. L. *audacem*; see prec. and -ACITY.] **1.** Boldness, intrepidity; confidence. **b.** Daring originality 1859. **2.** Boldness combined with recklessness; venturesomeness 1531. **3.** Open disregard of decorum or morality; effrontery, shamelessness 1545.

1. b. Happy a. of language 1878. 2. The desperate a. of his [Clive's] spirit MACAULAY. 3. His Excellency was shocked at her a. LIVINGSTONE.

Audible (ǭ·dib'l), *a.* (*sb.*) 1529. [ad. med.L. *audibilis*, f. *audire.*] *adj.* **1.** Able to be heard. †**2.** Able to hear (*rare*) 1603. **3.** *sb.* [the adj. used *absol.*] A thing capable of being heard 1626.

1. The ioyes of heauen are .. to mans eares not a. MORE. Hence **Audibi·lity, Au·dibleness,** audible capacity. **Au·dibly** *adv.* so as to be heard, aloud.

Audience (ǭ·diĕns). ME. [a. F. *audience*, refash. of OF. *oiance*:—L. *audientia*, f. *audientem.*] **I.** Audience (*abstractly*). *No pl.* **1.** The action of hearing. **2.** The state of hearing, or being able to hear; hearing ME. **3.** Judicial hearing ME. **4.** Formal hearing, reception at a formal interview; see II. 1. ME.

1. *To give audience*: to give ear. 2. †*In* (*open, general*) *a.*: so that all may hear. He said, in open a.: 'This is your place' MALORY. 3. *Court of Audience* or *A. Court*: an eccl. court, at first held by the Archbishop, afterwards by his auditors. That of Canterbury is now merged in the Court of Arches. 4. The ambassador had a. of her majesty (*mod.*).

II. An audience. *With pl.* **1.** A formal interview granted (*esp.* by a sovereign) to an inferior for conference or the transaction of business. Const. *of, with.* 1514. **2.** The persons within hearing; an auditory ME.; *transf.* the readers of a book 1855. **3.** A court, either of government or justice, in Sp. America; also, the territory administered by it. (Sp. *audiencia.*) 1727.

1. *Audience of leave*: farewell interview. 2. Fit a. find, though few MILT. *P. L.* VII. 31.

†**Au·diencer, -ie·r.** 1611. [a. F. *audiencier*: see prec.] 'An Officer in the Chancerie, that examines .. all letters patents, etc. .. receives the fees of the seale', etc. (Cotgr.) –1752.

Audient (ǭ·diĕnt). 1612. [ad. L. *audientem*; see AUDIENCE.] *adj.* Listening 1839. *sb.* A listener; *spec.* (in *Eccl. Hist.*) a hearer of the gospel, not yet a member of the church.

Audiometer (ǭdi,ǫ·mĭtəɹ). 1879. [f. L. *audire* + Gr. μέτρον.] An application of the telephone for measuring minute differences of hearing.

Audiphone (ǭ·difoᵘn). 1880. [f. L. *audire* + Gr. φωνή. Improp. formed after *telephone*, f. Gr. -φωνος sounding.] An instrument which, placed against the upper teeth, enables the deaf to hear more distinctly.

Audit (ǭ·dit), *sb.* ME. [ad. L. *auditus*, f. *audire.*] **1.** *gen.* A hearing; *esp.* a judicial hearing of complaints, a judicial examination (*arch.*) 1598. **2.** Official examination of accounts with verification by reference to witnesses and vouchers. (Accounts were orig. *oral*; cf. Matt. xxv. 19–30; Luke xvi. 2–7.) ME. *fig. Esp.* the Day of Judgement 1548. **3.** A periodical settlement of accounts between landlord and tenant; *hence*, receipts, revenue 1489. **4.** A balance-sheet as prepared for the auditor (*arch.*) 1550.

1. With his orisons I meddle not, for hee appeals to a high a. MILT. 2. *fig.* One who..is hasting continually to his final a. HERVEY. 3. A Nobleman that had the greatest Audits, of any Man in my Time BACON. 4. An auditt of the time I have spent 1619.

Comb.: **a. ale,** ellipt. *audit*, ale of special quality brewed (at certain Colleges in the English Universities), orig. for use on the day of a.; **-house, -room,** a building or room appendant to a cathedral, used for the transaction of business.

Audit (ǭ·dit), *v.* 1557. [f. prec. sb.] **1.** *trans.* To make an official systematic examination of (accounts). †**2.** *gen.* To calculate –1667. †**3.** *intr.* To draw up an account –1712.

1. Auditors generall..to Audite..thaccompts of all other officers 1557. 3. Let Hocus a.; he knows how the money was disbursed ARBUTHNOT. Hence **Au·dited** *ppl. a.* submitted to audit.

Audition (ǭdi·ʃən). 1599. [ad. L. *auditionem.*] **1.** The action, power, or faculty of hearing; listening. **b.** A trial hearing of an applicant for employment as a vocalist, etc. 1908. **2.** Something heard; cf. *vision* 1762.

1. Quite beyond his limit of a. TYNDALL.

Auditive (ǭ·ditiv), *a.* 1611. [a. F. *auditif, -ive*, f. L. *audit-, audire.*] = AUDITORY *a.* 1.

Auditor (ǭ·ditəɹ). ME. [a. AF. *auditour* = Fr. *auditeur*, ad. L. *auditor.*] **1.** A hearer, listener ME. **2.** One who learns by oral instruction; a disciple; in *Eccl. Hist.* a catechumen; cf. AUDIENT *sb.* **3.** An official whose duty it is to receive and examine accounts of money in the hands of others, who verifies them by reference to vouchers, and has power to disallow improper charges ME. **4.** One who listens judicially and tries cases, as in the Audience Court (see AUDIENCE 3) 1640.

1. What, a Play toward? Ile be an a. *Mids. N.* III. i. 81. 3. Call me before th' exactest Auditors, And set me on the proofe *Timon* II. ii. 165.

Auditorial (ǭditōᵊ·riăl), *a.* 1859. [f. L. *auditorius* + -AL[1].] **1.** = AUDITORY *a.* **2.** Of or pertaining to auditors or an audit 1883. Hence **Audito·rially** *adv.* by means of hearing or listening.

Auditorium (ǭditōᵊ·riɒ̆m). 1727. [a. L. *auditorium*, adj. neut. used subst.; see AUDITORY.] **1.** The part of a public building occupied by the audience; in ancient churches, the nave. ‖**2.** The reception room of a monastery 1863.

Auditorship (ǭ·ditəɹʃi:p). 1779. The office or position of an auditor.

Auditory (ǭ·ditəri), *a.* 1578. [ad. L. *auditorius*, f. *auditor.*] **1.** Pertaining to the sense or organs of hearing; received by the ear. **2.** Belonging to the AUDITORIUM 1740.

1. Three small bones in the A. Organ..Incus, Malleus, and Stapes SIR T. BROWNE. var. **Audi·tual.**

Auditory, *sb.* ME. [ad. L. *auditorium* (see above).] **1.** An assembly of hearers. **2.** A place for hearing; an AUDITORIUM 1548. †**3.** A philosophical school –1774. †**4.** The office of an auditor of accounts 1611.

Auditress (ǭ·ditrĕs). 1667. A female auditor.

Adam relating, she sole a. MILT. *P. L.* VIII. 51.

‖ **Au fait** (*o* fē·), *advb. phr.* 1748. [Fr.] In phr. *To be au fait in* or *at*: to be well instructed in, thoroughly conversant with. *To put a person au fait of* (= F. *mettre au fait de*): to instruct thoroughly in.

†**Auf(e.** 1621. [a. ON. *álfr* (cogn. w. OE. *ælf*).] An elf's child, a changeling left by the fairies; *hence*, a misbegotten, deformed, or idiot child. The earlier form of OAF. –1750.

†**Auge,** *sb.* 1594. [a. OF., a. Arab. *awj* height.] **1.** = APOGEE 2, 3. –1679. **2.** = APOGEE 1. 1594. **3.** = APSIS 1. 1601.

Augean (ǭdʒī·ăn), *a.* 1599. [f. L. *Augeas*, Gr. Αὐγείας; see -AN.] Abominably filthy; *i.e.* like the stable of Augeas, King of Elis, which contained 3,000 oxen, and had been uncleansed for 30 years, when Hercules, by turning the river Alpheus through it, purified it in one day.

Augelite (ǭ·dʒĭləit). 1868. [f. Gr. αὐγή + λίθος.] *Min.* A hydrous phosphate of alumina.

Auger (ǭ·gəɹ). [OE. *nafu-gár*, f. *nafu* + *gár*, lit. 'nave-borer'. Cf. OE. *hafoc*, now *hawk*; the *n-* has been lost, as in *adder.*] **1.** A carpenter's tool for boring holes in wood, etc., having a long pointed shank with a cutting edge and a screw point, and a handle fixed at right angles to the top of the shank, by means of which the tool is worked round with both hands. **2.** An instrument for boring in the earth, having a stem which may be lengthened as the perforation extends 1594.

1. Item three naugers 1572. Your Franchises..confin'd Into an Augors boare *Cor.* IV. iv. 87. *Comb.*: **a.-hole,** the hole drilled by an a.; **-shell,** the shell of the molluscous genus *Terebra.*

‖ **Auget, -ette** (*o*ʒe, ǭdʒe·t). 1816. [Fr., dim. of *auge*:—L. *alveus.*] **a.** A wooden pipe containing the powder used in exploding a mine. **b.** The priming tube used in blasting 1881.

Augh! (ǭχ), *int. Sc.* = faugh!

Aught, *sb.*[1] [Com. Teut.: OE. *ǽht.* In Sc. *aucht* (āuχt) is still in use.] **1.** Possession; property OE. †**2.** *esp.* Live stock –ME.

Aught (ǭt), *sb.*[2] (*pron.*), *adv.*, *adj.* [f. OE. *á, ó* + *wiht*; *lit.* 'e'er a whit'. Hence also ME. *ōht, ōght*, mod. *ought*, the sp. now reserved for the vb. In Shaks., Milt., Pope, *ought* and *aught* occur indiscriminately.] **1.** *sb.* (*pron.*) Anything whatever; anything. †**2.** *adj.* (Attrib. use of prec. Cf. *naught* = worthless.) Anything worth, something worth; worthy, doughty –ME. **3.** *adv.* [The accus. of the sb. used advb.] To any extent, in any respect, at all ME.

1. For aught I know GOLDSM. 3. Nor aught suspect the doom COWPER.

Augite (ǭ·dʒəit). 1804. [ad. L. *augites* (Pliny), a. Gr., f. αὐγή; see -ITE.] *Min.* An aluminous variety of PYROXENE, greenish, brownish, or pure black in colour, consisting chiefly of silica, magnesia, iron, and lime, and occurring mostly in volcanic rocks. Hence **Augi·tic** *a.* of, pertaining to, or characterized by, a.

Augment (ǭ·gmĕnt), *sb.* ME. [a. F., ad. L. *augmentum*, f. *augere.*] †**1.** Increase, augmentation –1696. **2.** *Gram.* The prefixed vowel (in Skr. *ă*, in Gr. ε) which marks the past tenses of the vb. in early Aryan languages. (Occ. used of other prefixes, *e. g.* the *ge-* of German pa. pples.)

In Gr., the ε, when separate, is called the *syllabic augment*; when it goes to form a long vowel or diphthong, the *temporal augment.* Hence **Au·gmentless** *a.*

Augment (ǭgme·nt), *v.* ME. [a. F. *augmenter*, earlier *aumenter*:—L. *augmentare*; see prec.] **1.** *trans.* To make greater in size, number, amount, degree, etc.; to increase 1460. **2.** *intr.* To become greater in size, etc. ME. †**3.** *trans.* To add to the resources of –1601. †**4.** *trans.* and *refl.* To raise in estimation or dignity

-1655. 5. *Her.* (*trans.*) To make an honourable addition to (a coat of arms) 1655. †6. To multiply (mathematically) -1593.

1. Hou our Navye may be mayntaynyd, and augmentyd 1460. 2. The rains a. DRYDEN. 5. The Armes of London were augmented with the addition of a Dagger FULLER. Hence **Augme·ntable** *a.* capable of †increasing, or being increased. **Augme·ntedly** *adv.* **Augme·nter,** he who or that which augments; *spec.* a magnifying glass.

Augmentation (ǫgmĕntē·ʃən). 1463. [a. OF. *aument-, augmentacion* (mod. *-tion*), ad. late L. *augmentationem*; see AUGMENT *v.*] 1. The action or process of augmenting (see AUGMENT *v.* 1, 2, †4). 2. Augmented state or condition; increase 1533. 3. That by which anything is augmented; an addition 1576. 4. *Her.* An honourable addition to a coat of arms 1662. 5. *Med.* 'The period between the commencement and height of a fever' (Mayne). 6. *Mus.* The repetition of a subject (*esp.* in fugues) in notes double or quadruple those of the original 1597. 7. *Sc. Law.* Increase of clerical stipend obtained by an action (*Process of A.*) in the Court of Teinds 1653.

1. To the avmentacion of his lif loode 1463. The excessive a. of their numbers MCCULLOCH. 2. The result was an a. of the revenue 1825. 3. The new Mappe, with the a. of the Indies *Twel. N.* III. ii. 85.

Augmentation Court, Court of Augmentation(s, or ellipt. *The Augmentation*: a court established by 27 Hen. VIII, so called because, by the suppression of monasteries, it augmented the revenues of the Crown. Dissolved by 1 Mary, sess. 2, cap. 10. **Augmenta·tioner,** an officer of this court.

Augmentative (ǫgme·ntătiv), *a.* (*sb.*) 1502. [a. F. *augmentatif, -ive,* f. L. *augmentat-*; see AUGMENT *v.* and -IVE.] 1. Having the property of augmenting; in Metaph. = AMPLIATIVE. 2. *Gram.* Augmenting in force the idea conveyed, said of suffixes, etc., of derivative words, and words with augmentative *affixes* 1641. 3. *sb.* An augmentative formative or word 1804.

2. For the word *wizard*, from *witch*, see the Section on A. forms LATHAM. var. **Augme·ntive** (less usual). Hence **Augme·ntatively** *adv.*

Augrim(e, -isme, -ym(e, obs. ff. ALGORISM.

Augur (ǭ·gəɹ), *sb.* 1549. [a. L.; perh. f. *avis* + *-gar*, conn. w. *garrire*; or f. *augere* (Fick).] 1. *Rom. Hist.* A religious official, who interpreted omens derived from the flight, singing, and feeding of birds, the appearance of the entrails of sacrificial victims, etc., and advised upon the course of public business in accordance with them. 2. Hence: A soothsayer, diviner, or prophet generally 1593.

1. Augures, that by observation of the birds of the air..made men believe they knew things to come HOOPER. 2. A. accursed! denouncing mischief still POPE. vars. †**Au·gurer,** †**Au·gurist.** Hence **Au·gurate, Au·gurship,** the office, or term of office, of an a. **Au·gurous** *a.* presaging (*rare*).

Augur (ǭ·gəɹ), *v.* 1549. [f. prec. sb.] 1. *trans.* To prognosticate from signs or omens; to divine, forebode, anticipate 1601. Of things: To portend, give promise of 1826. 2. *intr.* (or with *subord. cl.*) To take auguries; to conjecture from signs and omens 1808. 3. *trans.* (also with *in*) To usher in with auguries; to inaugurate 1549.

1. It seems to a. genius SCOTT. 2. Do we a. from them [cock-sparrows], as the Romans did from chickens 1840. To a. *well* or *ill*: to have *good* or *bad* anticipations *of, for*; Of things: to give *good* or *bad* promise. All augured ill for Alpine's line SCOTT. var. †**Au·gurize.**

Augural (ǭ·giŭrăl), *a.* 1513. [ad. L. *auguralis*; see AUGUR *sb.*] 1. Of or pertaining to augurs or augury. 2. Significant of the future; lucky or ominous 1600.

1. The a. gate 1598, staff of Romulus 1770. 2. Aristotle saith that sternutation was an a. signe GALE.

†**Au·gurate,** *v.* 1623. [f. L. *augurat-, augurari*, f. *augur.*] 1. *intr.* To perform the duties of augur 1678. 2. = AUGUR *v.* 1. 1652. 3. = AUGUR *v.* 3. 1623. Hence †**Augura·tion,** augury; *gen.* prognostic, token.

†**Au·gure.** By-form of AUGURY.

Augurial (ǫgiūᵊ·riăl), *a.* 1513. [ad. L. *augurialis* (synonym of *auguralis*).] Pertaining to augury.

Augury (ǭ·giŭri). ME. [a. OF. *augurie*, ad. L. *augurium.*] 1. The art of the augur; divination. 2. An augural observation, or rite 1742. 3. An omen drawn by augury; a significant token of any kind 1612. 4. *fig.* Presentiment, anticipation 1783; presage, promise 1797.

1. We defie Augury..If it be now, 'tis not to come; if it bee not to come, it will bee now *Haml.* v. ii. 230. 2. The priests..took the auguries and gave the signal for onset STUBBS. 4. He resigned himself..with a docility that gave little a. of his future greatness PRESCOTT. var. †**Au·gurism.**

August (ǫgʊ·st), *a.* 1664. [ad. L. *augustus*, prob. f. *augur*, as if 'auspicious'; perh. influenced by *augere*. Cf. F. *auguste.*] 1. Inspiring mingled reverence and admiration; magnificently impressive; stately, solemnly grand; venerable, revered 1664. 2. Venerable from birth or position; dignified, eminent, majestic. (Occas. perfunctory.) 1673.

1. The funeral was..the saddest and most a. that Westminster had ever seen MACAULAY. 2. And made obeisance to that a. Assembly 1720. var. †**Augu·stious.** Hence **Augu·st-ly** *adv.*, **-ness.**

August (ǭ·gɒ̆st), *sb.* OE. [f. L. *augustus* (see prec.).] The eighth month of the year, named after Augustus Cæsar, the first Roman emperor. Hence **Au·gust** *v.* to ripen.

†**Augu·stal,** *a.* 1658. [ad. L. *Augustalis*, f. *Augustus.*] Of or pertaining to the emperor Augustus, or to his worship; imperial -1730.

Augustan (ǫgʊ·stăn, ǭ-, ǒ-), *a.* (and *sb.*) 1645. [ad. L. *Augustanus*, f. *Augustus.*] 1. Connected with the reign of Augustus Cæsar, the palmy period of Latin literature 1704. 2. Hence, Of the palmy period of purity and refinement of any national literature; and *gen.* Classical 1819. 3. Of Augsburg (Augusta Vindelicorum), where in 1530 Luther and Melanchthon drew up their confession of Protestant principles 1645. 4. *sb.* A writer of the Augustan age (of any literature) 1882.

2. The reign of queen Anne is often called the A. age of England 1819. 3. Som embracing..the Augustane and som the Helvetian Confession HOWELL. var. †**Auguste·an** *a.* CUDWORTH.

Augustin(e (ǫgʊ·stin, ǭ·gɒ̆stin), *sb.* (and *a.*) ME. [ad. L. *Augustinus*, name of the Latin father.] An Augustinian monk. See also AUSTIN.

Augustinian (ǫgʊsti·niăn), *a.* (and *sb.*) 1602. [f. L. *Augustinus* (see prec.) + -IAN.] 1. Of or pertaining to St. Augustine or his doctrines, chief of which were immediate efficacy of grace and absolute predestination. *sb.* An adherent of his doctrines 1674. 2. Belonging to (*sb.* one of) the order of Augustines 1602. 3. Adhering to (*sb.* an adherent of) Augustine the Bohemian 1645. Hence **Augusti·nianism, Augu·stinism,** the doctrines of St. Augustine and his followers.

Auh (ǫh), *int.* expressing disgust 1732.

Auk (ǭk). 1678. [cogn. w. Sw. *alka*, Da. *alke*:—ON. *álka.*] A northern sea-bird, with short wings used only as paddles; strictly applied to the Great A. (*Alca impennis*), Little A. (*Mergulus melanoleucus* or *alle*), Razor-bill (*Alca torda*); but dial. also to the guillemots.

Auk(e, -ly, -ness, -ward, obs. ff. AWK, etc.

Aularian (ǭlēᵊ·riăn). 1695. [f. late L. *aularius*, f. *aula*, Gr. αὐλή.] *adj.* Of or belonging to a hall. *sb.* A member of a hall at Oxford or Cambridge. var. **Au·lary** *a.* (*rare*).

Auld (ǭld, *Sc.* āld), *a. dial.* [mod. Sc. and north Eng., f. OE. *ald.*] = OLD; as in *auld lang syne*, 'old long-since' (used subst.); *Auld Reekie*, 'Old Smoky', a sobriquet of Edinburgh; *auldfarrand*, 'favouring' the old, having the manners or sagacity of age; *auld-warld.*

Aulete (ǭ·līt). 1850. [ad. Gr. αὐλητής.] A flute-player. Hence **Aule·tic** *a.*

Aulic (ǭ·lik). 1701. [ad. F. *aulique*, L. *aulicus*, a. Gr., f. αὐλή.] A. *adj.* Of or pertaining to a court; courtly.

Aulic Council: in the old German Empire the personal council of the Emperor; it heard appeals from Germanic states, and was dissolved, with the Empire, in 1806. Now the name of a council at Vienna, managing the war-department of the Austrian Empire.

B. *sb.* The ceremony observed in the Sorbonne in granting the degree of doctor of divinity, when, after a harangue from the Chancellor, the new doctor received his cap and presided at a disputation. Hence †**Au·licism,** a courtly phrase.

Auln-, ault- (in various words); see AL-.

Aum (ǭm). 1502. Mod. Eng. var. of AAM.

Aumail (ǭmē·l). *rare.* [Refash. of AMEL *sb.*, after Spenser's *aumayld*; see *Ameled.*] Enamel.

Aumbry(e, -brie, arch. spellings of AMBRY.

‖**Aumil** (ǭ·mil, ā·mil). 1800. [Urdū (prop. Arab.)] A native collector of revenue in India; also called *amaldar*, AMILDAR. Hence by confusion **Aumildar** (with same sense).

‖**Aumônière.** 1834. [Fr.] = ALMONER 2.

†**Au·ncel.** ME. [a. AF. *aunselle, auncelle*, app. for *launcelle* (l- taken as the article), ad. It. *lancella*, dim. of *lance* balance:—L. *lanx*. Prob. contrasted with the 'Balancia domini regis' or *King's Beam.*] A kind of balance and weight formerly used in England -1691.

Aunc-, aund- (in various words); see AN-.

‖**Aune** (ōn). 1706. [Fr.; see ALNAGE.] An ell; an obs. Fr. cloth measure.

Aunt (ānt). ME. [a. OF. *aunte, ante*:—L. *amita*. In Eng. *mine aunt* by erron. division gave *my naunt*; cf. *nuncle*, and *adder*, etc.] 1. The sister of one's father or mother. Also, an uncle's wife, *aunt-in-law*. b. (in U.S.) Any benevolent and generally helpful woman; cf. Sp. *tia* 1861. †c. A title for the 'sister university', used by alumni of Oxford or Cambridge -1701. †2. An old woman; a gossip 1590. †3. A procuress; a prostitute -1678.

1. *Merry W.* IV. ii. 76. c. PEPYS *Corr.* 1701. Hence **Au·nthood, Au·ntship,** the relationship of a. **Au·ntly** *a.*

Aunt Sally: a game in which the figure of a woman's head with a pipe in its mouth is set up, and the player, throwing sticks from a certain distance, tries to break the pipe.

†**Au·nters,** *adv.* ME. [f. *aunter, aventure*, ADVENTURE; the *-s* (orig. wanting) may be genitival; cf. *per adventure* and *per-hap-s.*] In any case; perhaps -1807.

Auntie, aunty (ā·nti). 1792. Familiar f. *aunt*. In U.S.: A term often used in accosting elderly women.

‖**Au pair** (*o* pē̆r). 1928. [Fr., = on equality.] Applied to an arrangement between two parties by which mutual services are rendered without consideration of money payment.

‖**Aura** (ǭ·ră). ME. [L., a. Gr. αὔρα.] 1. A gentle breeze, a zephyr. 2. A subtle emanation from any substance, *e.g.* the odour of flowers 1732. Also *fig.* 3. *Electr.* †a. = Electrical ATMOSPHERE. b. The current of air caused by the discharge of electricity from a sharp point, *e.g.* from those of the electrical whirl 1863. 4. *Path.* A sensation, as of a current of cold air rising from some part of the body to the head, a premonitory symptom in epilepsy and hysterics 1776.

Hence **Au·ral** *a.*[1]

Aural (ǭ·răl), *a.*[2] 1847. [f. L. *auris* + -AL[1].] 1. Of or pertaining to the organ of hearing. 2. Received or perceived by the ear. **Au·rally** *adv.*

Aurantiaceous (ǭræ:nti,ē·ʃəs), *a.* 1837. [f. mod. L. *aurantiaceæ*, f. *aurantium*, latinized ad. ORANGE; see -ACEOUS.] Of or belonging to the N.O. *Aurantiaceæ*, including the orange, etc.

‖**Aurata** (ǭrē·tă). 1520. [a. L., pa. pple. fem. of *aurare* (used subst.).] A gold-coloured fish; prob. the Golden Maid, a variety of Wrasse.

Aurate (ǭ·reᵗt). 1838. [f. L. *aurum* + -ATE[4].] *Chem.* A compound of auric acid with a base.

Aurated (ǭ·reᵗted), *ppl. a.*[1] 1864. [f. L. *auratus* (see AURATA) + -ED.] Like or containing gold; gold-coloured, gilded. †In *Chem.* Combined with auric acid.

Au·rated, *ppl. a.*[2] 1843. [Badly f. L. *auritus*. *Conchol.* Having ears, as in the pecten.

Aureate (ǭ·ri,ĕt), *a.* ME. [ad. L. *aureatus*, f. *aureus.*] Golden, gold-coloured 1450. †Also *fig.* var. †**Au·real.**

Aureity (ǭrī·iti). 1824. [f. L. *aureus* + -ITY.] The properties peculiar to gold.

Aurelia (ǭrī·liă, ǭ-, ǒ-). 1598. [a. It., from fem. of *aurelio*, f. *aurum*; thus = *chrysalis*, Gr. χρυσαλλίς, f. χρυσός.] 1. *Ent.* The chrysalis of an insect, *esp.* of a butterfly. (Now *rare.*) 1607. †2. The Gold-flower (*Heliochrysum Stœchas*) 1598. 3. *Zool.* A genus of phosphorescent marine animals of the class *Acalephæ* 1876.

Aure·lian. 1778. [f. prec. + -AN.] *adj.* Of or pertaining to an aurelia; *gen.* golden 1791. *sb.* A lepidopterist 1778.

‖**Aureola** (ǭrī·ŏlă). 1483. [Lat., adj. fem. (sc. *corona*), dim. of *aureus*. In sense 1 = *coronula.*] 1. *Mediæval* and *R.C.Ch.* The celestial crown won by a martyr, virgin, or doctor, as victor over the world, the flesh, or the devil; the several degrees of glory of these. **2.** = AUREOLE 2. 1727. **3.** = AUREOLE 3. 1871.

Aureole (ǭ·rĭ,ōul). ME. [ad. L. *aureola*; see prec.] **1.** = AUREOLA 1. **2.** *Art.* Properly: The gold disk surrounding the head (or ? figure) in early pictures; *hence*, applied by some to **a.** The radiant circle of light depicted around the head 1848; by others to **b.** The oblong glory, or *vesica*, with which divine figures are surrounded 1851. **c.** *fig.* A glorifying halo 1852. **3.** *transf.* An actual halo of radiating light; *esp.* that seen in eclipses; also in wider sense 1842.

2. c. The a. of young womanhood O. W. HOLMES. **3.** An inseparable a. of sweet sound MRS. BROWNING.

Aureolin (ǭ·rĭŏlin, ǭrī·ŏlin). 1879. [f. L. *aureolus* (see above) + -IN.] A transparent yellow pigment.

‖**Au revoir** (o:rəvwā·r). 1694. [Fr., = lit. 'to the seeing again'.] Good-bye till we meet again.

Auric (ǭ·rik), *a.* 1838. [f. L. *aurum* + -IC.] Of or pertaining to gold. In *Chem.* used of compounds in which gold is trivalent.

Aurichalcite (ǭrikæ·lsəit). 1844. [f. *aurichalcum*, erron. sp. of L. *orichalcum*, a. Gr ὀρείχαλκον. So called, because when reduced it yields brass.] *Min.* A cuprous hydrozincite, of pale green, verdigris, or sky-blue colour.

Auricle (ǭ·rik'l). 1653. [ad. L. *auricula*, dim. of *auris.*] **1.** The external ear of animals. Formerly limited to the lower lobe of the human ear. *transf.* An 'ear' or ear-hole 1859. **2.** An ear-shaped process; a lobe; *esp.* in *Bot.* and *Conch.* (Cf. AURICULATE.) 1665. **3.** Name of the two upper cavities of the heart which receive blood from the veins and lungs respectively 1664. **4.** A kind of ear-trumpet 1864.

Auricomous (ǭri·kŏməs), *a.* 1864. [f. L. *auricomus* (f. *auri-* + *coma*) + -OUS.] Of or pertaining to golden hair.

‖**Auricula** (ǭri·kiŭlă). 1655. [L.; see AURICLE.] **1.** = AURICLE 1. 1691. **2.** (See quot.). **3.** *Bot.* A species of Primula, also called Bear's-ear, named from the shape of its leaves 1655. **4.** A genus of pulmoniferous molluscs, found chiefly in brackish swamps 1843.

2. In the Echinoida, ambulacral plates of the oral margin of the corona are produced into five perpendicular perforated processes, which arch over the ambulacra and are called the auriculæ HUXLEY.

Auricular (ǭri·kiŭlăɹ). 1542. [ad. med.L. *auricularis*; see prec.] **A.** *adj.* **1.** Of or pertaining to the ear 1649. **2.** Perceived by the ear; audible 1579; †earsay -1626. **b.** *esp.* (in *auricular confession*): Told privately in the ear 1542. **3.** Pertaining to the auricle of the heart 1870. **4.** Shaped like an auricle 1857.

2. You shall..by an A. assurance haue your satisfaction *Lear* I. ii. 99. A. traditions BACON. The practice of a. confession brought with it an entire science of casuistry HALLAM. *Auricular witness* (F. *témoin auriculaire*): one who relates what he has heard. Hence **Auri·cularly** *adv.* in one's ear, in a whisper; by means of auricles.

B. *sb.* An auricular organ or part. *spec.* **a.** A tuft of feathers covering the orifice of a bird's ear. **b.** The little finger, as the one most easily inserted in the ear: Fr. *doigt auriculaire* 1797.

Auriculate (ǭri·kiŭlĕt), *ppl. a.* 1713. [f. L. *auricula* + -ATE [2].] Furnished with auricles or earlike appendages. **1.** *Bot.* Of leaves: Having at the base a pair of small, blunt, ear-shaped projections. **2.** *Conch.* Having an ear-shaped process on one or both sides of the *umbones*, as in certain bivalves 1854. var. **Auri·culated.** Hence **Auri·culately** *adv.*

Auriculo- (ǭri·kiŭlo), comb. f. AURICLE, as in *a.-temporal*, *-ventricular*, etc.

Auri·culoid, *a.* 1856. [f. L. *auricula* + -OID.] Shaped like an auricula or auricle.

Auriferous (ǭri·fĕrəs), *a.* 1727. [f. L. *aurifer* + -OUS.] Containing or yielding gold. *lit.* and *fig.* Hence **Auri·ferously** *adv.*

‖**Au·rifex.** 1862. [L.] A worker in gold.

Aurific (ǭri·fik), *a.* 1667. [f. L. *auri-* + *-ficus.*] Producing gold.

Aurification (ǭ:rifikē·ʃən). 1881. [f. AURIFY; see -ATION.] Working in gold; *spec.* the stopping of a tooth with gold.

Auriform (ǭ·rifǭɹm), *a.* 1816. [f. L. *auris* + -FORM.] Shaped like an ear.

Aurify (ǭ·rifəi), *v.* 1652. [f. L. *auri-* + -FY, L. *-ficare.*] *trans.* and *intr.* To turn into gold.

‖**Auriga** (ǭrəi·gā). ME. [L.] A charioteer. †**a.** *fig.* Leader. **b.** *Astr.* The Wagoner. †**c.** *Phys.* The fourth lobe of the liver. †**d.** *Med.* A bandage for the sides. **Auriga·tion,** the action or art of driving a chariot.

†‖**Auri·go.** ME. [L., var. of *aurugo.*] Jaundice -1795.

Aurigraphy (ǭri·grăfi). [ad. med.L. *aurigraphia*, f. *auri-* + Gr. -γραφία.] A writing or graving in gold (Dicts.).

Aurilave (ǭ·rilēv). 1874. [f. L. *auris* + *lav-*, *lavare.*] An instrument for cleansing the ear.

Aurin (ǭ·rin). 1869. [f. L. *aurum* + -IN.] *Chem.* A red colouring matter produced by heating phenol with certain acids.

Auriphrygiate (ǭrifri·dʒĭ,ĕt), *ppl. a.* 1814. [ad. med.L. *auriphrygiatus*, f. *auriphrygium.*] Embroidered or fringed with gold. SOUTHEY.

†**Auripi·gment.** ME. [ad. L. *auripigmentum* (also used).] Now ORPIMENT -1741.

Auriscope (ǭ·riskoup). 1853. [f. L. *auris* + Gr. -σκοπος.] *Med.* An instrument for examining the ear. **Auri·scopy,** the use of the a.

Aurist (ǭ·rist). 1678. [f. L. *auris* + -IST.] *Med.* A specialist in regard to diseases of the ear.

Aurited (ǭrəi·tĕd, ǭ·ritĕd), *ppl. a.* [f. L. *auritus* (f. *auris*) + -ED. Furnished with ears or auricles; auriculate.

Aurivorous (ǭri·vŏrəs), *a.* 1783. [f. L. *auri-* + *-vorus.*] Gold-devouring.

Auro- (ǭ·ro), comb. f. L. *aurum*, as in **a.-ce·phalous** *a.*, having a gold-coloured head; **-chlo·ride,** a chloro-aurate; **-plumbi·ferous** *a.*, containing lead mixed with gold; **-tellu·rite,** SYLVANITE.

‖**Aurochs** (au·rǫks, ǭ·rǫks). 1766. [a. Ger., obs. f. *auerochse* :—MHG. *ûr-ochse*, f. *ur* = OE. *úr*, OTeut. **ûrus* the *Urus* + G. *ochs.*] Historically and properly, an extinct species of Wild Ox (*Bos Urus* Owen, *B. primigenius* Boj.) described by Cæsar as *Urus*. Since this became extinct, the name has been erron. applied to the European Bison (*Bos Bison* Gesn., *B. bonasus* Linn.), still extant in Lithuania.

Aurora (ǭrōə·ră). 1483. [L. Occas. in Fr. form *aurore.*] **1.** The rising light of the morning; the dawn. **2.** *personified*, The (Roman) goddess of the dawn, rising with rosy fingers from the saffron-coloured bed of Tithonus 1587. **3.** *fig.* The early period; *poet.* 'rise', 'dawn', 'morn' 1844. **4.** A luminous atmospheric phenomenon, now ascribed to electricity, occurring near, or radiating from, the earth's northern or southern magnetic pole, and visible from time to time by night over more or less of the earth's surface; pop. called the Northern (or Southern) Lights, merry-dancers, streamers, etc. (Now the ordinary prose meaning of *Aurora*, which is used generically, with Eng. pl. *auroras*, without any thought of 'dawn'.) 1621. **5.** A rich orange colour, as of the sky at sunrise 1791. **6.** Name of a monkey (*Chrysothrix sciurea*), a sea-anemone, and of various flowers 1774.

2. Zephyr with A. playing MILT. *L'Alleg.* 19. **4.** Lit up by auroræ and long lingering twilights LOCKYER. *Comb.* etc.: **A. australis, borealis, septentrionalis:** the Southern and Northern Lights, the latter orig. described by Gassendi under the appellation of 'northern dawn' (see sense 4). **A.-parrot,** *Psittacus Aurora*; **-pole,** one of the two points on the earth's surface which form the centres of the luminous circles of the aurora borealis and australis; **-snake.**

Auroral (ǭrōə·răl), *a.* 1552. [f. prec. + -AL.] **1.** Of or pertaining to the dawn, eastern; *fig.* of the first period of anything. **2.** Like the dawn; dawning, roseate, rosy 1827. **3.** Of or pertaining to the aurora (borealis) 1828. **4.** Like the aurora in its coruscations 1871.

1. The French a. 'biscuit de Rheims' BADHAM. **2.** The a. light of Tasso CARLYLE. **4.** A. flashings of wit PALGRAVE. Hence **Auro·rally** *adv.* (senses 2, 4).

Aurorean (ǭrōə·rĭăn), *a.* 1819. [f. AURORA + -EAN.] Belonging to dawn, or like it in hue. At tender eye-dawn of a. love KEATS.

Aurous (ǭ·rəs), *a.* 1862. [f. L. *aurum* + -OUS.] Of or containing gold; *Chem.* of compounds in which gold is univalent, e.g. aurous iodide, AuI.

Aurulent (ǭ·riŭlĕnt), *a.* 1731. [ad. L. *aurulentus*, f. *aurum.*] Gold-coloured.

‖**Aurum** (ǭ·rŏm). 1500. [L.] Gold.

a. fulminans = FULMINATE of gold; **a. mosaicum** or **musivum**, bisulphide of tin, known also as *bronze-powder*; †**a. potabile,** 'drinkable gold', gold held in a state of minute subdivision in some volatile oil, formerly taken as a cordial.

Auscultate (ǭ·skɒltēit), *v.* 1881. [f. L. *auscultat-*, *auscultare*, f. *aus-* = *aur-* in *auris* + ?.] *trans.* To listen to; *spec.* in *Med.* to examine by auscultation. var. **Auscu·lt.**

Auscultation (ǭskɒltē·ʃən). 1634. [ad. L. *auscultationem*; see prec.] **1.** The action of listening or hearkening. **2.** *Med.* The action of listening, with ear or stethoscope, in order to judge by sound the condition of heart, lungs, or other organs 1833.

2. The whole doctrine of a. as a means of diagnosis J. FORBES. **Auscu·ltative** *a.* of the nature of, or pertaining to, a. **Auscu·ltatory** *a.* of or pertaining to listening, or (*Med.*) to a.

Auscultator (ǭ·skɒltēitəɹ). 1831. [a. L.; see prec.] **1.** *Med.* One who practises auscultation 1833. ‖**2.** Title formerly given in Germany to a young lawyer who has passed his first public examination, and is thereupon employed by Government, but without salary or fixed appointment. (Now *referendar.*)

‖**Auspex** (ǭ·speks). Pl. **auspices.** 1598. [L., contr. for *avispex*, f. *avis* + *-spex*, *specere.*] *Rom. Antiq.* One who observed the flight of birds, to take omens thence; *hence*, a director, protector.

†**Au·spicate,** *a.* 1603. [ad. L. *auspicatus*, *auspicare*, *-ari*; see prec.] Started with good auspices; fortunate -1657.

Auspicate (ǭ·spikēit), *v.* 1603. [f. prec.] †**1.** *trans.* To give omen of, prognosticate. **2.** *intr.* To augur, predict 1848. **3.** *trans.* To initiate with an auspicious ceremony; to give a fortunate start to 1611. **4.** To handsel, signalize (one's entrance upon) 1652. **5.** *trans.* and †*intr.* To begin 1652.

3. To a. his Temporall affaires with Spirituall deuotions SPEED. **4.** The..acts, by which [this new Government] auspicated its entrance into function BURKE. Hence †**Auspica·tion,** the taking of auspices (*rare*).

Auspice (ǭ·spis), now usu. in pl. **auspices** (ǭ·spisĕz). 1533. [a. F. *auspice*, ad. L. *auspicium*; see AUSPEX.] **1.** An observation of birds for omens; a sign or token given by birds. **2.** *gen.* Any divine or prophetic token; prognostic; *esp.* indication of a happy future 1660. **3.** Prosperous lead; patronage, favouring direction; *esp.* in phr. *Under the auspices of* 1637.

2. A life which had opened under the fairest auspices MACAULAY. **3.** Under the auspices of religion and piety BURKE. Hence **Auspi·cial** *a.* of or pertaining to auspices or augury; auspicious.

Auspicious (ǭspi·ʃəs), *a.* 1601. [f. L. *auspicium.*] **1.** Ominous, *esp.* of good omen, betokening success 1614. Of persons: Predicting good 1702. **2.** Favouring, conducive to success 1610. Of persons: Propitious, kind 1601. **3.** Favoured by fortune, prosperous 1616.

1. A. planets YOUNG. **2.** Calme Seas, a. gales *Temp.* v. i. 314. **3.** For five a. years 1804. Hence **Auspi·ciously** *adv.*, **-ness.**

†**Au·spicy.** 1603. [ad. L. *auspicium.*] The drawing of omens from birds -1687.

‖**Auster** (ǭ·stəɹ). ME. [L.] The south wind; *hence*, the south.

Austere (ǭstīə·ɹ), *a.* ME. [a. OF. *austere*, ad. L., a. Gr. αὐστηρός, f. αὔειν to dry.] **1.** Sour or bitter and astringent; harsh to the taste 1541. **2.** Harsh to the feelings generally; stern; rigorous, judicially severe ME.; grim in warfare ME. **3.** Severe in self-discipline, strict, abstinent ME. **4.** Grave, sober 1667. **5.** Severely simple; without any luxury 1597.

1. Sloes a. COWPER. **2.** They would be gentle, not a. BROWNING. **3.** An a. life PRIESTLEY. **4.** Eve.. With sweet austeer composure thus reply'd MILT. *P. L.* IX. 272. **5.** This a. repast HOOKER. Hence **Auste·rely** *adv.*, **-ness.**

Austerity (ǭste·rĭti). ME. [a. OF. *austerité*, ad. late L. *austeritatem*; see AUSTERE.] **1.** Harshness to the taste, astringent sourness 1634. **2.** Harshness to the feelings; stern or severe treatment or demeanour; judicial severity ME.; *transf.* rugged sternness (*arch.*) 1713. **3.** Severe self-discipline; abstinence, asceticism

1590; *esp.* in *pl.* ascetic practices 1664. **4.** Severe simplicity; lack of luxury 1875.

2. Notwithstanding the a. of the Chair BURKE. **3.** To protest For aie, a., and single life *Mids. N.* I. i. 90. The austerities of an anchorite 1851.

Austin (ǭ·stin). ME. [Syncopated f. *Augustin, Au·gstin.*] = AUGUSTINIAN. var. †**Au·stiner.**

Austral (ǭ·străl), *a.* ME. [ad. L. *australis*, f. *Auster*; see -AL[1].] Belonging to the south, southern; *also*, influenced by the south wind, warm and moist.

A. magnetism is the imaginary magnetic matter which prevails in the southern regions of the Earth MAXWELL. *Austral signs*: the six signs of the zodiac from *Libra* to *Pisces*.

Australasian (ǭstrălē·ʃăn). 1766. [f. *Australasia*, ad. F. *Australasie* (f. L. *Australis* + *Asia*); orig. a name for one of 3 divisions of the *Terra Australis* (De Brosses): now = Australia and its adjoining islands.] *adj.* Of or belonging to Australasia. *sb.* A native or colonist of Australasia.

Australene (ǭ·strălīn). 1863. [f. L. *australis* + -ENE.] *Chem.* The chief constituent of English turpentine-oils, prepared from the turpentine of *Pinus australis*; also called *austraterebenthene.*

Australian (ǭstrē¹·liăn). 1693. [ad. F. *australien*, f. L. *australis*, in *Terra Australis*, now *Australia.*] *sb.* †**1.** A native of the *Terra Australis*, including Australasia, Polynesia, and 'Magellanica'. **2.** A native of, *later*, also, a colonist or resident in, the island-continent of Australia. *adj.* Of or belonging to Australia 1814. Hence **Austra·lioid** *a.*, also **Au·straloid,** of the ethnological type of the aborigines of A.

†**Au·strian,** *a. rare.* [f. L. *Austr-*, *Auster.* (To be distinguished from *Austrian*, of *Austria* = Ger. *Oesterreich.*)] Southern. QUARLES. var. †**Au·strine.**

Austringer (ǭ·strindʒəɹ). Also **astr-, ostr-.** 1486. [Corrupt f. *ostregier*, a. OF. *ostruchier* :— late L. **austurcarius*, f. *austurcus*, the goshawk. For intrusive *n* cf. *messenger*, etc.] A keeper of goshawks. See also OSTREGER.

Austromancy (ǭ·stromænsi). 1656. [f. L. *Auster* + Gr. μαντεία.] Divination from observation of the winds.

†**Autæ·sthesy.** 1642. [f. Gr. αὐτ(ο- + αἴσθησις.] Self-consciousness –1652.

Autantitypy (ǭtæ̆nti·tĭpi). [f. Gr. αὐτ(ο + ANTITYPY.] Ultimate incompressibility in body. SIR W. HAMILTON.

Autarch (ǭ·taɹk). 1865. [ad. Gr. αὔταρχος, f. αὐτ(ο- + ἀρχός.] = AUTOCRAT.

Autarchy[1] (ǭ·tăɹki). 1691. [ad. Gr. αὐταρχία; see prec.] **1.** Absolute sovereignty, despotism 1692. **2.** Self-government 1691.

Autarchy[2] (ǭ·tăɹki). (Better **-arky,** or **-arcie.**) 1643. [ad. Gr. αὐτάρκεια, f. αὐτ(ο + ἀρκέ-ειν.] Self-sufficiency.

†**Autexousy.** *rare.* [ad. Gr. αὐτεξουσία.] Free-will. Hence †**Autexou·sious** *a.* exercising free-will. CUDWORTH.

Authentic (ǭþe·ntik). ME. [a. OF. *autentique*, ad. L., a. Gr. αὐθεντικός, f. αὐθεντία, and αὐθέντης 'one who does a thing himself'.] **A.** *adj.* †**1.** Of authority, authoritative; entitled to obedience or respect –1849. †**2.** Legally valid –1723. Of persons: Legally or duly qualified –1610. **3.** Entitled to belief, as being in accordance with, or as stating fact; reliable, trustworthy, of established credit. (The prevailing sense; often opp. to, occas. identified with, *genuine.* See sense 6.) ME. †**4.** Original, first-hand; opp. to *copied* –1822. **5.** Real, actual, genuine. (Opp. to *pretended.*) (*arch.*) 1490. **6.** Really proceeding from its reputed source or author; genuine. (Opp. to *counterfeit, forged*, etc. Cf. note, sense 3.) 1790. †**7.** Own, proper –1649. **8.** *Mus.* **a.** Of eccl. modes: Having their sounds comprised within an octave from the final; also of a melody: composed in an authentic mode 1730. **b.** Of a cadence: Having the tonic chord immediately preceded by the dominant 1873. Opp. to PLAGAL.

1. The bible, Whiche is a booke autentyke and credible ME. An a. writer 1710. **2.** Under autenticke seales 1466. **3.** If some stanch Hound, with his authentick Voice Avow the recent Trail SOMERVILLE. Some of the authentickest annalists HOWELL. **4.** Joves a. fire MILT. *P. L.* IV. 719. **5.** A faint a. twilight CARLYLE. **7.** [For justice] to put her own a. sword into the hands of an unjust..man MILT. var. **Authe·ntical** *a.* Hence **Authe·ntically** *adv.* †**Authe·nticly** *adv.*

B. *sb.* †**1.** An authoritative document –1602; an original document –1655. **2.** The *Authentics*: a collection of the New Constitutions of Justinian (translated authentically from the Gr.) 1614. †**3.** An authority (*rare*) 1713. †**4.** *Mus.* = Authentic mode (see A. 8); var. †**Au·thent.** 1609.

Authenticate (ǭþe·ntikeˡt), *v.* 1653. [f. med.L. *authenticat-*, *authenticare*, f. *authenticus.*] **1.** *trans.* and *refl.* To invest with authority 1733; to give legal validity to; establish the validity of 1653. **2.** To establish the title to credibility of a statement, or of a reputed fact 1654. **3.** To establish the genuineness of 1852.

1. They want antiquity to a. their ceremonies NORTH. **2.** To a. a hypothesis 1664, a conclusion 1856. Hence **Authe·nticator.**

Authentication (ǭþe:ntikē¹·ʃən). 1788. [f. prec.] The action of authenticating; the condition of being authenticated.

The use of seals for the a. of contracts C. ADDISON.

Authenticity (ǭþĕnti·sĭti). 1657. [f. AUTHENTIC.] The quality of being authentic, **1.** as being authoritative or duly authorized. **2.** as being true in substance 1762. **3.** as being genuine; genuineness 1760. **4.** as being real, actual; reality 1851.

3. With regard to the a. of these fragments of our Highland poetry HUME. vars. †**Authe·nticalness,** †**Authe·nticness** (senses 1, 2, 3).

¶ Some writers, esp. on the Christian evidences, confine *authenticity* to sense 2, and use *genuineness* in sense 3.

Author (ǭ·þəɹ). ME. [a. AF. *autour*, OF. *autor*, later *auteur*, ad. L. *auctor*, f. *augere.* The sp. *auth-* appeared in Eng. *c* 1550 as a scribal variant of *aut-* (cf. *rhetor, rethour*).] **I.** *gen.* The person who originates or gives existence to anything: **a.** An inventor, constructor, or founder. Now *obs.* of things material; exc. as in b. ME. **b.** (*of all*, etc.) The Creator ME. **c.** He who gives rise to an action, event, circumstance, or state of things ME. †**d.** The prompter or instigator –1656. **2.** *spec.* One who begets; a father, an ancestor. (Still used in *Author of his being*; cf. 1 c.) ME. **3.** *esp.* and *absol.* One who sets forth written statements; the writer or composer of a treatise or book. (Now usu. includes *authoress.*) ME. *ellipt.* An author's writings 1601. **4.** An authority, an informant. (Usu. with *poss. pron.* 'my author'.) ? *Obs.* ME. **5.** *attrib.* 1711.

1. a. One Robert Creuequer, the authour of the Castle 1576. **b.** A. and maker of all thynges FISHER. **c.** The..A. of their variance *Ant. & Cl.* II. vi. 138. **2.** Old Walter Plumer (his reputed a.) LAMB. **3.** No a. ever spar'd a brother GAY. I will read politicke Authours *Twel. N.* II. v. 175. **4.** I wold se a better a. therof than such an heretyque as Luther MORE. Hence †**Au·thor** *v.* to originate, cause; to declare, say. **Autho·rial, auto·** *a.* pertaining to an a. of books. **Autho·rially** *adv.* **Au·thoring** *vbl. sb.* book-writing. (FIELDING.) **Au·thorish** *a.* (*rare*). **Au·thorism,** the position or character of a writer of books. **Au·thorling,** a petty a. **Au·thorly** *a.*

Authoress (ǭ·þŏrĕs). 1478. [f. AUTHOR + -ESS. Not in Fr.] A female author: **a.** an originator, causer; **b.** a leader; **c.** a mother; **d.** *esp.* a female literary composer. (Now used only when sex is emphasized; see AUTHOR 3.)

Authoritarian (ǫþǫ·ritē³·riăn), *a.* 1879. [f. AUTHORITY + -ARIAN; cf. *trinitarian.*] Favourable to the principle of authority. As *sb.* One who supports this principle 1883.

Authoritative (ǫþǫ·riteˡ:tiv), *a.* 1605. [f. as prec.] **1.** Of authority, exercising or assuming power; imperative, dictatorial. **2.** Possessing authority; entitled to obedience or acceptance 1653. **3.** Proceeding from a competent authority 1809.

1. He was diligent and in acting a. NORTH. **2.** An a. canon of faith J. TAYLOR. **3.** An a. declaration of pardon 1853. Hence **Autho·rita·tive-ly** *adv.*, **-ness.**

Authority (ǫþǫ·rĭti, ǭ-, ǫ̆-). ME. [a. F. *autorité*, ad. L. *auctoritatem*, f. *auctor.* The Fr. was spelt *authorité* in 16th c.] **1.** Power or right to enforce obedience; moral or legal supremacy; the right to command, or give an ultimate decision. **2.** Derived or delegated power; authorization ME. **3.** Those in authority. (Formerly in *sing.* = Government; now usu. abst. in *sing.*, concr. in *pl.*) 1611. **4.** Power to influence the conduct and actions of others; personal or practical influence ME. **5.** Power over the opinions of others; authoritative opinion; intellectual influence ME. **6.** Title to be believed; authoritative statement; weight of testimony. Occas.: Authorship, testimony. ME. **7.** The quotation or book acknowledged, or alleged, to settle a question or give conclusive testimony ME. **8. a.** The author of an accepted statement. **b.** An expert in any question. 1665.

1. Proud man, Drest in a little briefe authoritie *Meas. for M.* II. ii. 118. *In authority*: in a position of power. **2.** By what auctorite dost thou these things, and who gaue the this auctorite COVERDALE *Mark* xi. 28. **3.** A. has thought fitt..to prosecute the offenders LUTTRELL. The Mozambique authorities LIVINGSTONE. **4.** With your Lordship's Interest and A. in England ADDISON. **5.** The auctority of the ancients CAXTON. **6.** On the a. of the evening papers (*mod.*). **7.** By turning o'er authorities SHAKS. **8.** Historians in a season of faction are not the best authorities PRESCOTT. A great utilitarian a. BLACKIE.

Authorization (ǭ:þŏrəizē¹·ʃən). 1610. [f. AUTHORIZE.] The conferment of legality; formal warrant or sanction.

A. does away the fraud: what is authorized is legalized BENTHAM.

Authorize (ǭ·þŏrəiz), *v.* ME. [a. F. *autoriser*, ad. med.L. *auctorizare.* See AUTHOR. In 16th c. *aucto·rise.*] **I.** †**1.** To set up or acknowledge as authoritative –1620. †**2.** To give legal force to –1692. **3.** To give formal approval to; to sanction, countenance ME.; to justify 1603. †**4.** To vouch for –1646.

3. The gentlest..of philosophers..authorised the persecution of Christianity MILL. If Human Strength might a. a Boast COWLEY. **4.** A womans story, at a Winters fire, Authoriz'd by her Grandam SHAKS.

II. 1. To endow with authority; to commission 1494. **2.** †*refl.* To found one's authority *upon* 1581. **3.** To give legal or formal warrant to (a person) *to do*; to empower, permit authoritatively 1571. **4.** Of things: To give satisfactory ground to 1794.

1. Did manyfestly auctoryse his sonne UDALL. **3.** We..by warrant herof authoriss you to procede LD. BURLEIGH. **4.** Past experience authorises us to infer.. MILL. Hence **Au·thori·zable** *a.* †having the faculty of authorizing; capable of being authorized. **Au·thorizer,** one who authorizes.

Authorized (ǭ·þŏrəizd), *ppl. a.* ME. [f. prec.] **1.** Possessed of authority; thoroughly established; highly esteemed. **2.** Placed in (*obs.*) or endowed with authority 1483. **3.** Legally or duly sanctioned or appointed 1480.

1. Received and a. opinions COLERIDGE. **3.** *Authorized Version* of the Bible: a popular appellation of the version of 1611, which has never claimed to be 'authorized'.

Authorless (ǭ·þəɹlĕs), *a.* 1713. [f. AUTHOR *sb.*] **1.** Anonymous. **2.** Without originator; uncreated 1862. **3.** Void of authors 1879.

Authorship (ǭ·þəɹʃip). 1710. [f. as prec. + -SHIP.] **1.** Occupation or career as a writer of books. **2.** The dignity of an author 1782. **3.** Literary origin or origination 1825. **4.** *gen.* Origination of an action, state of affairs, etc. 1884.

1. The trade of a. COLERIDGE. **4.** The a. of the riots at Aston Park 1884.

‖**Auto** (au·to). 1727. [Sp. and Pg. :—L. *actus.*] **1.** A play 1779. **2.** = AUTO-DA-FÉ 1727.

Auto (ǭ·to), short for AUTOMOBILE *sb.*, after Fr. 1899.

Auto- (ǭ·to), repr. Gr. αὐτο- 'self, one's own, by oneself, independently', comb. f. αὐτός self. In Eng., to a certain extent, a living element, prefixable esp. to scientific terms denoting action or operation, and occas. to others, in combs. which are virtually nonce-words.

auto-ca·rpous [Gr. καρπός] *a.*, *Bot.* '(a fruit) consisting of pericarp alone having no adnate parts' (Gray); var. **-ca·rpian; -ce·phalous** [Gr. κεφαλή] *a.*, *lit.* having a head or chief of its own; independent or archiepiscopal or patriarchal jurisdiction; **-clave** [L. *clavus* nail or *clavis* key], a French stew-pan with a steam-tight lid; **-dida·ct** [Gr. -δίδακτος], one who is self-taught; **-dyna·mic** [Gr. -δύναμος] *a.*, *Physics*, operating by its own power, as the *Autodynamic elevator*, a machine for raising weights, worked by a falling column of water; **-facture,**

self-making; **-gamy** [Gr. -γαμία], *Bot.* self-fertilization; **-ga·mic** *a.*, characterized by, or fit for, autogamy; **-genous** [Gr. -γενής], self-produced, independent; *spec.* **a.** in *Phys.* of parts of the skeleton developed from independent sources of ossification; **b.** in *Path.* of the essential elements of morbid tissues; **c.** of a process of soldering, by melting and so joining the ends of metal; vars. **-ge·neal, -ge·nic**; **-geny, -gony,** a mode of spontaneous generation, opp. to *plasmogeny*; **-latry** [Gr. λατρεία], self-worship; **-logy,** scientific study of oneself; **-math** [Gr. -μαθής], *rare,* an autodidact; **-metry** [Gr. -μετρία], self-measurement, self-estimation; measurement of the parts of a figure in terms of its entire height; **-metric** *a.*; **-molite** [f. Gr. μολεῖν], *Min.* a variety of GAHNITE; **-mo·rphic** [Gr. -μορφος] *a.*, characterized by automorphism; **-mo·rphically** *adv.*; **-mo·rphism,** the ascription of one's own characteristics to another; **-noe·tic** [Gr. νοητικός] *a.*, self-perceiving; **-nym** [Gr. ὄνυμα = ὄνομα], a book published under the author's real name; **-pa·thic** [Gr. παθικός] *a.*, of or pertaining to disease inherent in a living being itself; **-phagous** [Gr. -φαγος, f. φαγεῖν] *a.*, self-devouring; **-phagy,** sustenance of life by absorption of the tissues of the body; **-phoby** [Gr. -φοβία], *rare,* fear of referring to oneself; **-phony** [Gr. -φωνία], *Med.* observation of the resonance of the practitioner's own voice in auscultation; **-phonic** *a.*; **-ophtha·lmoscope** [Gr. ὀφθαλμός + σκοπός], = *Autoscope*; **-plasty** [Gr. -πλαστος], *Surg.* repair of wounds, etc., by means of tissue taken from other parts of the same body; **-pla·stic** *a.*; **-psorin** [Gr. ψώρα], *Med.* a patient's own virus administered homœopathically in cases of itch, smallpox, etc.; **-sche·diasm** [ad. Gr. αὐτοσχεδίασμα], something extemporized or done off-hand; **-schedia·stic, -al** *a.*; **-sche·diaze** *v.*; **-scope** [Gr. -σκοπος], an instrument for the self-examination of the eye; **-scopy,** the use of the autoscope; **-sty·lic** [Gr. στῦλος] *a.*, *Phys.* of skulls having the mandibular arch suspended by its own proper pier, the quadrate; **-suggestion** = SELF-SUGGESTION 1890; **-tomic** [Gr. -τομός] *a.*, self-intersecting. **b.** Used in names of self-acting mechanisms, as *a.-coherer* 1885. **c.** Short for AUTOMOBILE in *autobus, -car* 1895.

Autobiographer (ǭ:toˌbəiǫ·grăfəɹ). 1829. [See AUTO-.] One who writes the story of his own life.

Autobiographic (ǭ:toˌbəiˌǒgræ·fik), *a.* 1850. [See AUTO-.] **1.** Of the nature of autobiography. **2.** Of the character of an autobiographer 1864. Hence **Au·tobiogra·phical** *a.* (1829) belonging to autobiography; also = AUTOBIOGRAPHIC **1, 2.** **Au·tobiogra·phically** *adv.*

Autobiography (ǭ:toˌbəiˌǫ·grăfi, -biˌǫ·g-). 1809. [f. AUTO- + BIOGRAPHY.] The writing of one's own history; the story of one's life written by himself.

What would we give for such an A. of Shakspeare CARLYLE.

Autochthon (ǭtǫ·kþǫ̆n, -ōun). Pl. **autochthons,** or L. **autochthones** (ǭtǫ·kþǒnīz). 1646. [a. Gr. αὐτόχθων, f. αὐτο- + χθών land.] **1.** One sprung from the soil he inhabits; a 'son of the soil'. **2.** Hence in *pl.*: The earliest known dwellers in any country; aborigines 1741. **3.** Original inhabitants or products 1837.

1. There was therefore never any A...but Adam SIR T. BROWNE. Hence **Auto·chthonal, Autochtho·nic, Auto·chthonous** (1805), *adjs.* native to the soil, aboriginal; in *Path.* remaining confined in the part in which it first arose, as a thrombus. **Auto·chthonism,** birth from the soil of a country, or aboriginal occupation of it.

Autochthony (ǭtǫ·kþǒni). 1846. [f. as prec.] Autochthonous condition.

Autocracy (ǭtǫ·krăsi). 1655. [ad. Gr. αὐτοκράτεια: see AUTOCRAT. Cf. F. *autocratie*.] †**1.** Self-sustained power -1755. Of states: = AUTONOMY. **2.** Absolute government 1855. Also *transf.* **3.** *Med.* The controlling influence of the vital principle on disease 1864.

2. The religious a. of the Pope MILMAN. The a. of philosophic bodies 1860.

Autocrat (ǭ·tǒkræt). 1803. [a. F. *autocrate,* ad. Gr. αὐτοκρατής, f. αὐτο- + κράτος.] A monarch of uncontrolled authority; an absolute, irresponsible governor. (*Autocrat of all the Russias,* a title of the Czar.)

The Russian noble is..a serf to his a., and an a. to his serf H. SPENCER. Hence **Autocra·tic, -al,** *a.* despotic, absolute. **Autocra·tically** *adv.* **Au·tocratship.**

Autocrator (ǭtǫ·krătǫɹ). ? *Obs.* 1789. [a. Gr.] = AUTOCRAT. †**Autocrato·ric, -al** *a.*

Autocratrix (ǭtǫ·krătriks). 1762. [Latinized fem. of prec.] A female autocrat; the title of empresses of Russia, first assumed by Catherine II.

‖**Auto-da-fé, -de-fé** (au·toˌdăˌfē··, dĕˌfē··). Pl. **autos-da-fé**; improp. **auto-da-fés.** 1723. [Pg. *da* of the, Sp. *de* of; = judicial sentence or act of (the) faith. Cf. ACT *sb.*] **1.** A judicial 'act' or sentence of the Inquisition. **2.** The execution of the sentence; *esp.* the public burning of a heretic 1727.

Autogiro (ǭ:toˌdʒəiə·ro). 1925. Also **-gyro.** [f. AUTO- b + It., Sp. *giro* GYRE.] Trade-name of a type of flying machine that can descend vertically by means of a windmill revolving freely on its own shaft.

Autograph (ǭ·tǒgraf). 1640. [ad. L. *autographum,* Gr. αὐτόγραφον, adj. neut. (used subst.), f. αὐτο- + -γραφος.] **1.** That which is written in one's own handwriting; one's own manuscript. *abstr.* One's own handwriting 1858. **2.** A person's own signature. Hence *attrib.* 1791. **3.** A copy produced by autography 1868. *adj.* Written in the author's own handwriting 1832; var. †**Auto·graphal** *a.*

Au·tograph, *v.* 1818. [f. prec. sb.] **1. a.** To write with one's own hand. **b.** To reproduce by autography. **2.** To write one's autograph on or in 1837.

Autographic, -al (ǭtogræ·fik, -ăl), *a.* 1868. [f. AUTOGRAPH; see -IC, -AL.] Of or pertaining to autography; of the nature of an autograph; written in the author's own handwriting. Hence **Autogra·phically** *adv.* in autograph, by means of autography.

Autography (ǭtǫ·grăfi). 1644. [f. AUTOGRAPH.] **1.** The action of writing with one's own hand; the author's own handwriting. **2.** Reproduction of the form of anything by an impression of the thing itself; nature printing; *esp.* a process in lithography by which a writing or drawing is transferred from paper to stone 1864. †**3.** = AUTOBIOGRAPHY 1661. **4.** Autographs collectively 1788.

1. Every expert would here detect the a. of the son of Jesse SPURGEON.

†**Autoki·nesy.** [ad. Gr. αὐτοκινησία.] Spontaneous motion. CUDWORTH. Hence †**Au·tokine·tical** *a.*

†**Au·toma.** 1625. Erron. sing. of *automata* (see AUTOMATON) -1669.

†**Au·tomate.** 1649. [a. Fr., ad. L. *automaton, -um.*] *sb.* = AUTOMATON -1751. *adj.* = AUTOMATIC 1818. var. †**Auto·matary** *a.*

Automatic, -al (ǭtǒmæ·tik, -ăl), *a.* 1586. [f. Gr. αὐτόματος; see AUTOMATON, and -IC, -AL.] Of the nature of, or pertaining to, an automaton. **1.** *lit.* Self-acting, having the power of motion or action within itself 1812. **2.** Going by itself; *esp.* of machinery and its movements, which produce results otherwise done by hand, or which simulate human or animal action 1802. **3.** Of animal actions: Not accompanied by volition or consciousness, mechanical 1748. **4.** Not characterized by active intelligence 1843. **5.** Relating to automatons 1860.

1. In the universe, nothing can be said to be a. SIR H. DAVY. 2. A Sewing Machine with a. tension (*mod.*). 3. The winking of the eyes is essentially a. BAIN. 4. Mechanical and a. acts of devotion MILMAN. Hence **Automa·tically** *adv.* **Auto·mati·city,** a. condition or nature.

Automatism (ǭtǫ·mătiz'm). 1838. [f. AUTOMATON.] **1.** The quality of being automatic, or of acting mechanically only; involuntary action. *Hence,* the doctrine attributing this quality to animals. **2.** Mechanical, unthinking routine 1882. **3.** The faculty of independently originating action or motion. (From the orig. sense of *automaton.*) 1876. Hence **Auto·matist,** one who holds the doctrine of a. (sense 1).

Auto·matize, *v. rare.* 1837. [a. Fr. *automatiser*; see next.] To reduce to an automaton.

Automaton (ǭtǫ·mătǫ̆n). Pl. **-ata, -atons.** 1611. [a. Gr. αὐτόματον, adj. neut., adopted in L. as *automaton, -atum.* See also AUTOMA.] **1.** *lit.* Something which has the power of spontaneous motion or self-movement 1625. Thus applied to: **2.** A living being viewed materially 1645. **3.** A piece of mechanism having its motive power so concealed that it appears to move spontaneously; now usu. applied to figures which simulate the actions of living beings, as clock-work mice, etc. 1611. **4.** A living being whose actions are purely involuntary or mechanical 1678. **5.** A human being acting mechanically in a monotonous routine 1796.

1. [It] doth move alone, A true a. BEAUM. & FL. 2. These living Automata, Human bodies BOYLE. 3. Another a. strikes the quarters EVELYN. 5. [Slaves]..a set of scarcely animated automatons 1796.

Automatous (ǭtǫ·mătəs), *a.* 1646. [f. Gr. αὐτόματος (see prec.) + -OUS.] **1.** Acting spontaneously; having power of self-motion 1769. **2.** Of the nature of an automaton 1646.

1. I am not a.: I need to be wound up 1808.

Automobile (ǭtomōu·bil, -mǒbī·l). Chiefly *U.S.* 1886. [a. F.] **A.** *adj.* Self-propelling. **B.** *sb.* A motor vehicle. Also as vb.

Autonomic, -al (ǭtonǫ·mik, -ăl), *a.* 1659. [f. AUTONOMY + -IC, -ICAL.] Self-governing.

Reason is thus ever autonomic; carrying its own law within itself 1854. Hence **Autono·mically** *adv.*

Autonomist (ǭtǫ·nŏmist). 1865. [f. as prec. + -IST.] An advocate of autonomy. Also *attrib.*

Autonomize (ǭtǫ·nŏməiz), *v.* 1878. [f. as prec. + -IZE.] To make autonomous.

Autonomous (ǭtǫ·nŏməs), *a.* 1800. [f. Gr. αὐτόνομος (f. αὐτο- + νόμος) + -OUS.] **1.** Of or pertaining to an autonomy. **2.** Possessed of autonomy; self-governing. In *Metaph.*: see AUTONOMY **1** c. 1804. **3.** *Biol.* **a.** Conforming to its own laws only. **b.** Independent, *i.e.* not a mere form or state of some other organism. 1861.

2. If the [Irish] nation was to become a. 1804. 3. The view that they [lichens] are a. organisms T. DYER.

Autonomy (ǭtǫ·nŏmi). 1623. [ad. Gr. αὐτονομία; see prec.] **1.** Of a state, institution, etc.: The right of self-government, occ. specialized as political, local, or administrative. **b.** Personal freedom 1803. **c.** *Metaph.* Freedom (of the will); the Kantian doctrine of the self-determination of the will, apart from any object willed; opp. to *heteronomy* 1817. **2.** *Biol.* Autonomous condition (see AUTONOMOUS **3**) 1871. **3.** A self-governing community 1840.

3. All those autonomies wherewith the world was filled..one after another, stoop and disappear 1840.

Autopsy (ǭ·tǫpsi, -ǫ·psi). 1651. [ad. mod. L. *autopsia* (also used), a. Gr., f. αὐτοπτος; cf. F. *autopsie.*] **1.** Seeing with one's own eyes; personal observation. **2.** Dissection of a dead body, so as to ascertain by actual inspection *esp.* the cause or seat of disease; post-mortem examination 1678. Also *fig.*

1. The defect of a. may be compensated by sufficient testimony of a multitude DE QUINCEY. 2. *fig.* This a. of a fine lady's poem MISS BRADDON.

Autoptic, -al (ǭtǫ·ptik, -ăl), *a.* 1651. [ad. Gr. αὐτοπτικός; see prec. and -IC, -AL [1].] Of, or of the nature of, an eyewitness; based on personal observation. Hence **Auto·ptically** *adv.* **Autopti·city,** a. quality or nature.

Autor, -ial, -ity, etc., obs. ff. AUTHOR, etc.

Autotheism (ǭtoþī·iz'm). 1582. [f. Gr. αὐτόθεος (f. αὐτο- + θεός) + -ISM.] **1.** The doctrine of God's self-subsistence, *esp.* that of the Second Person of the Trinity. **2.** Self-deification 1619.

1. Calvin's a. signifies..That God the Son is not *Deus de Deo,* God from God BLOUNT. So **Autothe·ist** (in both senses).

Autotype (ǭ·tǒtəip). 1853. [f. AUTO- + τύπος, after *prototype,* etc.] **1.** A 'type' or true impress of the thing itself; a reproduction in facsimile. **2.** A process of permanent photographic printing, which reproduces works of art in monochrome; a facsimile produced by it. Also *attrib.* or as *adj.* 1869.

1. The outward and visible a., of the spirit which animates it [the utterance] KINGSLEY. Hence **Au·totype** *v.* to reproduce by a. process.

Autotypography (ǭ·toˌtipǫ·grăfi). [f. AU-

TO- + TYPOGRAPHY.] A process by which drawings made on gelatine are transferred to soft metallic plates, which may be used for printing.

Autumn (ǭ·tə̆m). ME. [a. OF. *autompne* (mod. *automne*), ad. L. *autumnus*, of doubtful etym.] 1. The third season of the year, or that between summer and winter, reckoned astronomically from the descending equinox to the winter solstice; i. e. in the northern hemisphere, from September 21 to December 21. Pop., it comprises, in Great Britain, August, September, and October; in North America, September, October, and November; in the southern hemisphere it corresponds in time to the northern spring. *poet.* The fruits of autumn, harvest 1667. 2. *fig.* A season of maturity, or of incipient decay 1624.

1. Though she chide as loud As thunder, when the clouds in Autumne cracke *Tam. Shr.* I. ii. 96. On [Thir Table's] ample square..All A. pil'd MILT. *P. L.* v. 394. 2. The.. of a form once fine LANGHORNE.

Comb.: A.-bells, *Gentiana Pneumonanthe*; -fly, *Conops Calcitrans* Linn.

Autumn (ǭ·tə̆m), *v.* 1771. [ad. L. *autumnare.*] To bring or come to maturity.

Autumnal (ǭtɒ·mnăl), *a.* 1574. [ad. L. *autumnalis*, f. *autumnus* AUTUMN.] 1. Of, belonging or peculiar to, autumn 1636. 2. Maturing or blooming in autumn 1574. 3. *fig.* Past the prime (of life) 1656.

1. *Autumnal Equinox*: the time when the sun crosses the equator as it proceeds southward. *A. point*: the point at which the celestial equator is intersected by the ecliptic as the sun proceeds southward; the first point in Libra. *A. signs*: *Libra*, *Scorpio*, and *Sagittarius*. *A. star*: Sirius. Thick as A. Leaves MILT. *P. L.* I. 302. 3. Melissa..verged on the a. DICKENS. So †Autu·mnian. Hence Autu·mnally *adv.*

Autumnity (ǭtɒ·mnĭti). ? *Obs.* 1599. [ad. L. *autumnitatem.*] Autumn quality or conditions. Au·tumnize *v.* to make autumnal (in appearance) (*rare*).

Autunite (ǭ·tɒnəit). 1868. [f. *Autun* in France + -ITE.] *Min.* A hydrous phosphate of lime and uranium, of citron or sulphur-yellow colour; also called *lime-uranite*.

Au·turgy. Also -ergy. 1651. [ad. Gr. αὐτουργία.] Self-action; working with one's own hand.

‖**Auxesis** (ǭksī·sis). 1577. [L., a. Gr., f. αὐξάνειν.] *Rhet.* Amplification; hyperbole.

By this figure, the orator doth make..of thistles, mighty oaks PEACHAM. Hence Auxe·tic, †-al *a.* amplifying. Auxe·tically *adv.*

Auxiliar (ǭgzi·liăɹ). *arch.* 1583. [ad. L. *auxiliaris.*] *adj.* AUXILIARY, helpful (*to*). *sb.* An AUXILIARY; something which helps 1670.

adj. A. to divine [purposes] WORDSW.

Auxiliary (ǭgzi·liări). 1601. [ad. L. *auxiliarius*, f. *auxilium.*] A. *adj.* Const. *to.* 1. Helpful, assistant, giving support or succour 1603. b. in *Grammar*: see B. 3. Formerly applied to any subordinate or formative elements of language, *e.g.* prefixes, prepositions. 1677. 2. Subsidiary to the ordinary 1687.

1. Calling upon the a. name of Jesus 1686. A. cohorts MERIVALE. 2. A. Seamen, are such as have another Trade besides, wherewith to maintain themselves, when they are not employed at sea PETTY. *Auxiliary scales* in *Mus.*: the six keys or scales, consisting of any key major, with its relative minor, and the relative keys of each WEBSTER.

B. *sb.* A helper, assistant, confederate, ally; *also*, that which is a source or means of help 1656. 2. *Mil.* (usu. in *pl.*) Foreign or allied troops in the service of a nation at war 1601. 3. *Gram.* A verb used to form the tenses, moods, voices, etc. of other verbs 1762. 4. *Math.* A quantity introduced to simplify or facilitate some operation, as in equations, etc.

1. He Rains and Winds for Auxiliaries brought COWLEY. 2. The third [sort of soldiers] are Auxiliaries, which serue for pay 1601. 3. After the verb *to be*, the next in importance among the auxiliaries is the verb *to have* 1835. var. †Auxi·liatory *a.* and *sb.*

†**Auxi·liate**, *v.* 1656. [f. L. *auxiliat-*, *auxiliari*; see above.] To help.

Av-. From the Norman Conquest to *c* 1625, the letter *u* had the phonetic value of both *u* and *v*, and *v* was merely the initial *shape* of *u*. Hence *Au-* was commonly written for *Av-*. Such words are here entered under Av-.

Ava, ava' (ăvā·), *phr. Sc.* 1768. [Worn-down f. *of all.*] Of all; at all.

‖**Ava** (ā·vă), *sb.* 1831. Native name in the Sandwich Islands of a species of Cordyline yielding an intoxicating liquor; the liquor itself; and *gen.* any intoxicant spirit.

Avadavat. Corrupt f. AMADAVAT. [Itself a corruption of *Ahmadabad*. Yule.]

Avail (ăvē̆·l), *v.* ME. [App. f. VAIL *v.* (ad. F. *vaille*, *valoir*:—L. *valere*) taken as an aphetic form.] 1. *intr.* To have efficacy for the accomplishment of a purpose; to be of use, afford help. 2. To be of value, or advantage ME. 3. *trans.* (at first with *dat.*) To be of use or advantage to; to profit; to help ME. 4. esp. *To avail oneself of* (in Shaks., ellipt., *To avail of*): a. to profit by 1603. b. to use 1768. 5. *causal.* To give (a person) the advantage of; hence, *ellipt.* to inform, assure *of.* (Only in U.S.) 1785. †6. *intr.* To do well, profit -1563. †7. *trans.* To be equivalent to -1598.

1. This labor..too no great purpose avayleth 1583. 2. Whilst counsel auayled 1583. 3. What avails it me to oppose them RICHARDSON. 4. a. I..availed myself of my position to [etc.] TYNDALL. 5. To a. government of information T. JEFFERSON. Hence Avai·ler. Avai·lment, the fact of being beneficially effective.

Avail (ăvē̆·l), *sb.* ME. [f. prec. vb.] 1. Beneficial effect; advantage. *arch.* or *Obs.* exc. as in quots. 2. Assistance, aid. *Obs.* exc. as in quots. 1450. 3. Value, estimation. *Obs.* or *arch.* 1513. 4. *concr.* (chiefly *pl.*) Profits or proceeds; remuneration or perquisites. Cf. VAILS. (Still common in U.S.) 1449.

1. Taking a. of the cover 1871. †*To have at avail*: i. e. at an advantage. 2. *Of a.*: of advantage in accomplishing a purpose, effectual. *Of no a.*, *without a.*: ineffectual. *Of little a.*: to little purpose. 3. The Marchaunt..Doth ioy for gaine of his auailes 1568. Hence †Avai·lful *a.* of much a. (A desirable word.)

Availability (ăvē̆i:lăbi·lĭti). 1803. [f. next.] 1. Available quality. b. *spec.* in U.S. That qualification in a candidate which makes his success probable, apart from substantial merit 1848. 2. *concr.* That which is available 1867.

1. b. He was..nominated for his a.,—that is, because he had no history LOWELL.

Available (ăvē̆·lăb'l), *a.* 1451. [f. AVAIL *v.* + -ABLE.] 1. Capable of producing a desired result (*arch.* or *Obs.*) 1502. b. *Law.* Valid 1451. 2. Of advantage (*to*, *unto*) (*arch.*) 1474. 3. Capable of being turned to account; *hence*, at one's disposal, within one's reach 1827.

1. And all charges by him lawfully made..shall be good and a. in law BLACKSTONE. 3. Lenders..wish..to have their assets as a. as they can ROGERS. Hence Avai·lableness, †efficacy; = AVAILABILITY 1, 1 b. Avai·lably *adv.*

‖**Aval.** 1880. [F., f. *à val*; see AVALE *v.*] An endorsement (*lit.* a writing 'at the bottom') on a bill, etc., guaranteeing payment of it.

Avalanche (æ·vălɑnʃ, ævălɑ·nʃ). 1789. [a. F., dial. f. *avalance* 'descent'; see AVALE *v.*] 1. A large mass of snow, mixed with earth and ice, loosened and descending swiftly down a mountain side. Also *transf.* and *fig.* Also *attrib.*

Ye avalanches, whom a breath draws down BYRON. Such an a. of forgeries CARLYLE.

†**Ava·le**, *v.* ME. [a. OF. *avaler*, f. *à val*:—L. *vallem*; cf. AMOUNT *v.*] 1. *intr.* To come, go, or get down; to dismount, alight -1596. 2. Of things: To sink, flow, or sail down -1596. 3. *trans.* To cause to descend, fall, or sink; to lower; to send downwards -1770. 4. To lower (the visor of a helmet); *hence*, to doff (hat, etc.) -1557. Also *fig.*

3. Phœbus gan auaile His weary waine SPENSER. Hence †Ava·ling, descent; declivity.

Avance, obs. f. ADVANCE.

‖**Avania** (avănī·ă). 1687. [?] An imposition by the (Turkish) government; *spec.* (as applied by Christians) an extortionate exaction or tax levied by the Turks. See also AVENY. Hence Avanious *a.* extortionate.

Avant, obs. f. AVAUNT.

‖**Avant-** (ăvɑ·nt, avañ). 1600. [F.:—L. *abante*, f. *ab* + *ante*. See AVAUNT. In early words worn down to *vant-*, *van-*, and occ. to *vaw-*, *va-*.] In a few combs., partly French, partly hybrid:

†ava·nt-, avaw·mbrace (oftener VAMBRACE), armour for the front of the arm; -courier, one who runs or rides before; a herald; *esp.* (in *pl.*) the scouts, skirmishers, or advance-guard of an army; -fosse [Fr.], the ditch on the outer side of a counterscarp, dug at the foot of the glacis; -gua·rd, *Obs.* and -garde [Fr.], the vanguard or van of an army; †-lay, the laying on of fresh hounds to intercept a deer already chased by others; †-mu·re, the outer wall of a fortress, etc.; †-wa·rd, aphet. VAWARD (common in Shaks.), VANWARD, = *avant-garde*.

Avantage, obs. f. ADVANTAGE.

Avant-courier, *v.* [f. the sb.] To herald.

†**Ava·nters, avancers**, *sb. pl.* ME. [?] Part of the numbles of a deer -1486.

Avanturine, var. AVENTURINE.

Avarice (æ·văris). ME. [a. OF., ad. L. *avaritia*, f. *avarus.*] Inordinate desire of getting and hoarding wealth; cupidity. Also *fig.*

To me a. seems not so much a vice, as a deplorable piece of madnesse SIR T. BROWNE. *fig.* The worst a. is that of sense POPE.

Avaricious (ævări·ʃəs), *a.* 1474. [a. F. *avaricieux*, *-euse*, f. *avarice.*] Immoderately desirous of wealth; grasping. Also *fig.*

Queen Elizabeth was a. with pomp H. WALPOLE. var. †Ava·rous. Hence Avari·ciously *adv.*; var. †Ava·rously. Avari·ciousness.

Avast (ăvā·st), *phr.* 1681. [prob. worn-down f. Du. *hou'vast*, *houd vast*, hold fast.] *Naut.* Hold! stop! stay! cease!

'A. heaving,' said Gascoigne MARRYAT.

Avatar (ɑvătā·ɹ, æ·vătāɹ). 1784. [ad. Skr. *avatāra* descent.] 1. *Hindoo Myth.* The descent of a deity to the earth in an incarnate form. 2. Incarnation 1815. 3. Manifestation or presentation to the world as a ruling power or object of worship 1859. 4. *loosely*, Manifestation, phase 1850.

1. The ten Avatars or descents of the deity, in his capacity of Preserver SIR W. JONES. 2. A third a. of this singular emanation of the evil principle [Bonaparte] SCOTT. 3. The a. of Mathematics MASSON, of art 1883. 4. Wit and sense are but different avatars of the same spirit L. STEPHEN.

†**Avau·nt**, *sb.*[1] ME. [f. AVAUNT *v.*[1]] A vaunt; boasting, vain-glory -1553. *To make avaunt*: to boast; = AVAUNT *v.*[1]

†**Avau·nt**, *sb.*[2] [The adv. used subst.; cf. *alarm*, etc.] The order to be off -1711.

To give her the a. SHAKS.

†**Avau·nt**, *v.*[1] ME. [a. OF. *avanter*, f. *à* + *vanter*:—late L. *vanitare*, freq. of **vanare*, f. *vanus*. Mostly *refl.*] 1. *trans.* To boast of (an action); to praise (a person) -1556. 2. *refl.* To vaunt oneself -1580. *intr.* in same sense -1576. Hence †Avau·nter. †Avau·ntry, boasting.

†**Avau·nt**, *v.*[2] ME. [f. AVAUNT *adv.* and *int.*] 1. *intr.* To advance -1596. 2. *trans.* To raise, ADVANCE -1605. 3. To be off, depart -1601.

Avaunt (ăvǭ·nt, ăvā·nt), *adv.*, *int.*, etc. ME. [a. F. *avant*:—L. *ab ante* used in late L. for *ante.*] †A. *adv.* Forward, to the front -1440. B. *int.* orig. and lit.: Onward! go on! *Hence*, Begone! away! 1485. C. *prefix.* Fore-. See AVANT-, VANT-, VAN-.

int. A., she cried, offensive to my sight POPE.

Ave (ē̆·vi). ME. [a. L., f. *avere.*] A. *int.* Hail!—Farewell! B. *sb.* 1. A shout of welcome, or farewell 1603. 2. Short for AVE MARY, q. v. ME. 3. a. The time of ringing the Ave-bell. b. The beads on a rosary, one for each Ave repeated. 1463.

A. And 'Ave, Ave, Ave,' said, 'Adieu, adieu' for evermore TENNYSON. B. 2. *Ave-bell*: that rung at the hours when Aves are to be said.

†**Ave·ll**, *v.* 1530. [ad. L. *avellere.*] To pull up or away -1651.

Avellan (ăve·lăn, æ·vĕlăn). ME. [ad. L. *Avellanus* of Avella in Campania.] *adj.* Of Avella; filbert-, hazel-; cf. L. *Avellana nux*. *sb.* A filbert- or hazel-nut ME. *attrib.* in *Her.* of a cross like four filberts joined together 1611.

Ave Maria. [L. and It.], and **Ave Mary** (ē̆ˈvi,mēᵊri). ME. [See AVE.] The *Hail Mary!* the angelic salutation to the Virgin (*Luke* i. 28), combined with that of Elizabeth (*v.* 42), used devotionally, with the (more recent) addition of a prayer to the Virgin, as Mother of God; so named from its first two words. b. = AVE *sb.* 2, 3 a. 1599.

The Eng. pronunc. of the L. is ē̆·vi,mărai·ă, but ā·ve,mārī·ă, after It., is common; some poets have mā·rī,ā after L.

Avenaceous (ævĭnēˑʃəs), *a.* 1775. [f. L. *avenaceus*, f. *avena*; see -ACEOUS.] Of the nature of, or belonging to, oats; in *Bot.* belonging to the *Avenæ* or Oat-grasses, including the cultivated oats.

†**Aˑvenage.** 1594. [a. F., f. *aveine, avoine* :—L. *avena*.] A payment in oats made to a landlord.

†**Aˑvenant.** ME. only, exc. 2. [a. OF., pr. pple. of *avenir* :—L. *advenire*.] *adj.* 1. Convenient. 2. Comely; pleasant -1481. *sb.* That which suits one; convenience, purpose.

Aveˑner. *Obs.* exc. *Hist.* ME. [a. OF. *avenier* :—L. *avenarius*.] A chief officer of the stable, who had charge of the provender for the horses. Hence †**Aveˑnary, -ery,** the office of the a.

Avenge (ăveˑndʒ), *v.* ME. [a. OF. *avengier*, f. *à* + *vengier* :—L. *vindicare*; see VINDICATE.] 1. To take vengeance, inflict retributive punishment, exact satisfaction, or retaliate, on behalf of (a person, a right, etc.); to vindicate. Const. *on, upon, of* (arch.), †*against*, †*over* the offender; *of, against* the offence (*arch.*). *intr.* (refl. pron. omitted) To take vengeance 1535. 2. *trans.* To take vengeance, etc., on account of (a wrong or injury, or the feelings caused by it) ME. †3. To take vengeance upon -1666.

1. A., O Lord, thy slaughtered saints MILT. Thou shalt a. thy right NEALE. 2. To a. even a look that threatened her with insult BURKE. Hence **Aveˑnge** *sb.* execution of vengeance (*arch.*). †**Aveˑngeance, Aveˑngement,** vengeance. **Aveˑngeful** *a.* vengeance-taking, full of vengeance. **Aveˑngingly** *adv.*

¶ At no period is *avenge* absolutely restricted to the idea of just retribution, as distinguished from *revenge*, although the restriction is largely prevalent.

Avenger (ăveˑndʒəɪ). ME. [f. prec. vb.] 1. He who avenges (the injured or the injury) 1535. †2. He who takes vengeance on (the offender). Cf. AVENGE *v.* 3. -1667.

1. Time, the a. BYRON. 2. With fury driv'n By his A. MILT. *P. L.* x. 241. Hence **Aveˑngeress.**

Aveˑniform, *a.* [f. L. *avena*.] Oat-like.

Avenin (ăvīˑnin). 1863. [f. as prec.] The nitrogenous principle of the oat.

Avenous (ăvīˑnəs), *a.* 1881. [A- *pref.* 14 + L. *vena*. *Avenious* is bad.] Veinless.

Avens (æˑvĕnz). ME. [a. OF. *avence*; origin unkn.] *Herb.* Pop. name of the Wood A., or Herb Bennet (*Geum urbanum*), and Water A. (*Geum rivale*); also applied to the Mountain A. (*Dryas octopetala*).

Aventail, -ayle (æˑvĕntēl). ME. [a. AF. **aventail* = OF. *esventail*; see prec.] The mouthpiece of a helmet.

Aventine (æˑvĕntəin). 1625. [ad. L. *Aventinus* (sc. *mons*) one of the seven hills of Rome.] *fig.* A secure position (*obs.*).

†**Aveˑntre,** *v.* [? The form suggests F. *à* + *ventre*. Meaning unkn.] SPENSER.

He dressed his shelde, and they auentred their speres 1557.

†**Aveˑnture.** 1672. [a. OF. (see ADVENTURE *sb.*), used spec. in Eng. law-books of death by accident pure and simple; opp. to *mesaventure*.]

Aventurine, -in (ăveˑntiūrin). Also **avant-.** 1811. [a. F., ad. It. *avventurino*; so called from its accidental discovery.] 1. A brownish-coloured glass flecked with gold-coloured spangles, manufactured first at Murano. Also called *Artificial a., A. glass, Gold flux.* 2. *transf.* A variety of quartz, spangled with yellow scales of mica 1858.

A. felspar or **sunstone,** a mixture of oligoclase and orthoclase spangled with yellowish crystals.

Avenue (æˑvĭniu), *sb.* 1600. [a. F. *avenue* sb., from. fem. pa. pple. of *avenir* :—L. *advenire*. Occas. in 18th c. *aveˑnue*.] †1. The action of coming to 1639. 2. *gen.* A way of approach; a passage or path of entrance or exit. (Formerly a military term.) Now chiefly *fig.* 1600. 3. The chief approach to a country-house, usu. bordered by trees; *hence* any broad roadway marked by objects at regular intervals. Occ. of the trees alone. (The current literal sense.) 1654. 4. A fine wide street (*esp.* in U.S.) 1858. 5. The ambulacrum in sea-urchins 1841.

2. To watch.. this a. to India 1800. *fig.* New avenues of wealth GREEN. 3. Let them read for *avenue*, the principal walk to the front of the house EVELYN. 4. Northumberland A. (*mod.*). Hence **Aˑvenue** *v.* to make into an a.; to form avenues in.

†**Aˑveny.** 1676. Anglicized f. AVANIA.

Aver (ēˑvəɪ), *sb.*[1] [OE. *eafor* app. (horse) transport, ME. *aver, eaver* cart-horse; perh. cogn. with L. *opus* work.] A draught-horse; now *Sc.* and *north. dial.* old horse, nag.

An auld jaded aver to ride upon SCOTT.

†**Aver,** *sb.*[2] ME. [a. AF. *aver*, OF. *aveir* (later *avoir*), subst. use of *aveir* (:—L. *habēre*) to have.] Possessions, property, estate; farm-stock, cattle.

Aver (ăvəˑɪ), *v.* ME. [a. F. *avérer* :—late L. **adverare*, f. *ad* + *verus*.] †1. *trans.* To declare true -1646. †2. To prove true, confirm -1678. 3. *Law.* To prove or justify a plea; to offer to justify an exception pleaded; to make an averment 1490. 4. To assert as a fact 1509. 5. To assert the existence or occurrence of 1611.

4. What one author avers upon the subject, another denies 1839. Which .. I do averr to be a Calumny BENTLEY. 5. Chronicles auer many stranger accidents MILT. Hence **Aveˑrrable** *a.* capable of being †verified, or asserted. †**Aveˑrral,** averment.

Aver-, in some compound terms pertaining to feudal usage, appears to be connected with AVERAGE *sb.*[1]:

†**aver-corn,** ? corn paid as a feudal due or in lieu of service; †**averland,** ? land subject to average; †**averpenny,** ? money paid in lieu of average; †**-silver,** ? = *averpenny*.

Aˑverage, *sb.*[1] 1489. [In OF. *average*, med. L. *averagium*, app. = *avera* in Domesday Book, 'one day's work which the King's tenants gave to the sheriff' (Spelman). In *Sc.* worn down to *arriage*. Orig. unkn. Referred to OF. *ovre, œvre*; also to *aver* (Skene), and Danish *hoveri* (Wedgwood).] *Old Law.* Some kind of service due by tenants to the feudal superior. Explained in Law Dicts., since Sir J. Skene, as 'service done by the tenant with his beasts of burden'.

Average (æˑvĕrēdʒ), *sb.*[2] 1491. [Formed after *primage*, etc. The orig. meaning is *duty* charged on goods; deriv. uncertain. ? f. It. *avere*, OF. *aveir*, goods.] *Maritime. †1. *orig.* A duty charged upon goods; a customs-duty or the like -1760. 2. Any charge over and above the freight incurred in the shipment of goods, and payable by their owner. (Still in *petty average*.) 1491. 3. *spec.* The expense or loss to owners, arising from damage at sea to the ship or cargo 1622. 4. The incidence of any such charge, expense, or loss; *esp.* the equitable distribution of such expense or loss among all the parties interested 1598. **Transf. 5. The determination or statement of an arithmetical mean; a medial estimate. (Now only in *at, on, an a.*) 1735. 6. The arithmetical mean so obtained; the medium amount, the ruling quantity, rate, or degree; the 'common run' 1755.

4. *Particular average* is the incidence of the partial loss or damage of ship, cargo, or freight, through *unavoidable accident*, upon the individual owners (or insurers) of the interests affected. *General a.* is apportionment of loss caused by *intentional* damage to ship, or sacrifice of cargo, etc., and of expense incurred, to secure the general safety of ship and cargo; in which case contribution is made by the owners, etc. in proportion to the value of their respective interests. 5. Earthquake-shocks occur, on an a., about three times a week HUXLEY. 6. The month's a. of wrecks has been.. three a day MAURY. The hotel is.. above the a. 1867.

Comb.: **a.-adjuster, -stater,** one whose profession it is to adjust claims and liabilities in a case of General Average, and to make up an **a.-statement** showing the same. Hence **Aˑverager,** an a.-adjuster.

†**Average,** *sb.*[3] 1537. [Cf. ARRISH.] The pasturage of arable land after harvest.

Average (æˑvĕrēdʒ), *a.* 1770. [attrib. use of AVERAGE *sb.*[2], in sense 5.] 1. Estimated by average. 2. Equal to what would be the result of taking an average; medium, ordinary; of the usual standard 1803.

1. The a. price of corn 1770. 2. A modern drawing of a. merit RUSKIN. Hence **Aˑverageiy** *adv.*

Average (æˑvĕrēdʒ), *v.* 1821. [f. AVERAGE *sb.*[2] in sense 5; cf. to *square*, etc.] 1. *trans.* To estimate, by dividing the aggregate of a series by the number of its units (*at*); to form an opinion as to the prevailing standard of 1831. 2. *ellipt.* for: To average itself at; to be on an average 1821. 3. *ellipt.* for: To do, take, etc., on an average 1822.

2. The sale of the book.. averaged a thousand copies a year MASSON. 3. So much this surgeon averaged upon each day for about twenty years DE QUINCEY.

Averin (ēˑvərĕn). *Sc.* 1768. [?] The cloudberry or knoutberry (*Rubus chamæmorus*).

Aˑverish, *v. dial.* [f. AVERAGE *sb.*[3]] To consume the eddish, arrish, or average.

Averment (ăvəˑɪmĕnt). ME. [a. F. *averement*; see AVER *v.*] 1. The action of proving, by argument or evidence. 2. *Law.* Formal offer to prove or justify a plea; the proof or justification offered, verification 1514. 3. Assertion, affirmation 1633. 4. A positive statement, assertion, or declaration 1629.

2. *Averment*.. general.. concludes every plea, etc., .. with these words, *and this he is ready to verify* TOMLINS. 3. Noise and bold a. SCOTT.

Avern (ăvəˑɪn). 1599. [a. F. *Averne* 'the pit of hell', ad. L. *Avernus* (sc. *lacus*), = Gr. ἄορνος (λίμνη), f. ἀ + ὄρνις.] A lake in Campania, the effluvium from which was said to kill birds flying over it. b. The infernal regions.

Avernal (ăvəˑɪnăl). 1578. [a. F. *Avernal*, ad. L. *Avernalis*; see prec.] *adj.* Of the nature of, or belonging to, Avernus; infernal. *sb.* An inhabitant of Avernus, a devil. var. **Aveˑrnian** *a.*

Averroist (ævĕrōuˑist). Also **Averrh-.** 1753. One of a sect of peripatetic philosophers who appeared in Italy before the restoration of learning, and adopted the leading tenets of Ibn Roshd or Averrhoes, an Arabian philosopher born at Cordova, viz. that the soul is mortal, or that the only immortal soul is a universal one, from which particular souls arise, and into which they return. Hence **Averroˑism.**

Averruncate (ævĕrvˑŋkeᶦt), *v.* ? *Obs.* 1623. [f. L. *averruncat-*, *averruncare*, f. *a, ab* + *verruncare* to turn. Erron. in 17th c. f. *eruncare* to weed out.] 1. *prop.* To avert, ward off 1663. 2. *improp.* To root up, to prune 1623. Hence **Averruncaˑtion** (in both senses).

Averruncator (ævĕrvŋkeᶦˑtəɪ). 1842. [f. prec. in sense 2.] A pair of pruning shears, or a knife-blade working within a hook, mounted on a pole and worked by a string or wire; used for cutting off the higher branches of trees.

Aversation (ævəɪsēˑʃən). *arch.* 1600. [ad. L. *aversationem*.] †1. The act of turning away -1673. †2. Estrangement -1659. 3. = AVERSION 4 (*arch.*) 1613. 4. = AVERSION 5. 1730.

3. Auersation towards Society BACON.

Averse (ăvəˑɪs), *a.* 1597. [ad. L. *aversus*, *avertere* to AVERT.] †1. Turned away or in the reverse direction, averted -1703; quasi-*adv.* -1814. †2. Lying on the opposite side 1667. †3. Behind 1646. 4. Turned away in mind or feeling; actuated by repugnance; habitually opposed, disinclined 1597. Const. *from, to.* (The use of *to*, condemned by Johnson, is explained by the analogy in sense to words like *hostile*, etc. Shaks. does not use the word.) With *inf.* Unwilling 1646. †5. Of things: Adverse -1683. †6. *sb.* The hinder part (so L. *aversum*); the reverse of a coin -1658.

1. The tracks a. a lying notice gave DRYDEN. 4. That Law.. which leads the Willing, and compels the A. HARRIS. As men auerse from war *Micah* ii. 8. What Cat's a. to fish GRAY. A. to declare herself openly 1777. Hence †**Aveˑrse** *v.* to turn away. **Aveˑrsely** *adv.* in the reverse direction; backwardly; with aversion. **Aveˑrseness** = AVERSION 4.

Aversion (ăvəˑɪʃən). 1596. [ad. L. *aversionem*; see AVERSE.] †1. The action of turning away oneself, one's eyes, etc.; in *Rhet.* = APOSTROPHE [1] 1. -1668. †2. The action of averting -1684. †3. Estrangement (*from*) -1691. 4. An averted state of mind or feelings; a mental attitude of opposition or repugnance; an antipathy 1651. Const. †*towards*, †*against*, *from*, *to* (*for*), *infin.* See AVERSE 4. 1626. 5. An object of dislike or repugnance 1678.

4. There are among Brute Creatures many natural Aversions and Antipathies STEELE. Nature.. has put into Man a desire of Happiness, and an a. to Misery LOCKE. A. from war 1771. 5. 'The Excursion', Writ in a manner which is my a. BYRON.

Avert (ăvəˑɪt), *v.* ME. [a. OF. *avertir* :—late L. *avertere* (cl. *avertĕre*), f. *a* = *ab* + *vertere*. OF. *avertir* represented also *advertere* to ADVERT, q. v.] 1. *trans.* To turn away. *fig.* To estrange (*arch.*) 1532. 2. *intr.* (refl. pron. omitted.) To turn away (*arch.*) 1483. 3. *trans.* To turn away (the face, eyes, thoughts) 1578. 4. To turn away anything about to befall, *esp.* things threatened; to ward off 1612. †5. To oppose -1667. ¶ 6. *catachr.* for EVERT and REVERT.

1. *fig.* Appease Zeus and the averted Gods L. MORRIS.

3. Therefore beseech you T'auert your liking a more worthier way *Lear* I. i. 214. 4. Any expedient which might a. the danger MACAULAY. Hence **Ave·rted** *ppl. a.*, turned aside; unpropitious (*arch.*). **Ave·rtedly** *adv.* **Ave·rter.** **Ave·rtible, -able** *a.*

Avertiment, obs. f. ADVERTISEMENT.

Avian (ē̆ⁱ·viăn), *a.* 1870. [f. L. *avis* + -AN.] Of or pertaining to birds. var. **A·vine.**

Aviary (ē̆ⁱ·viări). 1577. [ad. L. *aviarium*, f. *avis.*] A large cage, house, or inclosure, in which birds are kept.

Lincolnshire may be termed the a. of England, for the wild fowl therein FULLER. Hence **A·viarist.**

Aviation (ē̆ⁱviˌē̆ⁱ·ʃən). 1887. [ad. F., irreg. f. L. *avis* + -ATION.] Flying in an aeroplane. So **A·viator,** †(*a*) a flying machine 1891, (*b*) the pilot of an aeroplane 1896 (so **-tress, -trix**).

‖**Avicularium** (ăvikiulēᵊ·riŏm). Pl. **-a.** 1856. [mod.L., f. as prec.] *Zool.* A small, snapping, prehensile process, shaped like a bird's head with a movable mandible, found on the cells of many Polyzoa. **Avicula·rian** *a.*

Aviculture (ē̆ⁱ·vikŏltiŭr). 1880. [f. L. *avis* + *cultura.*] Rearing of birds; bird-fancying.

Avid (æ·vid), *a.* 1769. [ad. F. *avide*, ad. L. *avidus*, f. *avere.*] Greedy. Const. *of, for*, etc.

The human heart is a. of pleasure and gain 1769. vars. **Avi·dious,** †**A·vidous.** Hence **A·vidly** *adv.*, var. **Avi·diously.**

Avidity (ăvi·dĭti). 1449. [ad. F. *avidité*, ad. L. *aviditatem*; see AVID.] 1. Extreme eagerness, greediness. *transf.* of things 1646. 2. *ellipt.* Greediness of gain, graspingness 1662.

1. To read with a. TYNDALL.

†**A-vie·**, *adv.* 1509. [f. A *prep.*[1] + VIE *sb.*] In emulation -1644.

†**Aview·**, *v.* 1494. [Cf. f. *aveuer*, f. *à* + *vue*, and see VIEW *sb.* and *v.*] To view officially; to reconnoitre; in Spenser = to view -1596.

Avifauna (ē̆ⁱ·viˌfǭ·nă), *sb.* 1874. [f. L. *avis* + FAUNA.] The Fauna of a district so far as concerns birds.

Avignon Berry (ăvi·nyǫ̃n). 1727. [f. *Avignon* in France.] The fruit of the *Rhamnus infectorius*, etc., used for dyeing yellow, and for making *sapgreen.*

†**Avi·le**, *v.* ME. [a. OF. *aviler* (= mod. *avilir*) :—Rom. **advilare*, f. *ad* + *vilis.*] To make vile; degrade; hold cheap; vilify -1670. Hence †**Avi·lement.**

‖**Avion** (avyoṅ). 1898. [ad. F., f. L. *avis* + *-on*, after *ballon.*] A (French) aeroplane.

Avis(e, etc., obs. f. ADVICE, ADVISE, etc.

†**Avi·sion.** ME. [a. OF., app. f. *à* + *vision*, after *aviser*, etc.] A dream; a monition (given in a dream) -1525.

Aviso (ăvəi·zo). Pl. **-os,** †**-o's.** 1634. [a. Sp. *aviso* :—late L. *advisum*; see ADVICE, the Eng. cogn.] †1. Intelligence; a notification -1654. 2. An ADVICE-BOAT 1714.

Avital (ăvəi·tăl, æ·vităl), *a.* ? *Obs.* 1611. [f. L. *avitus* + -AL[1].] Ancestral, ancient.

Avives (ăvəi·vz), *sb. pl.* ? *Obs.* 1616. [a. F. (also *vives*), ad. (ult.) Arab. lit. the she-wolf.] A swelling of the parotid glands in horses; the strangles; also called VIVES.

‖**Avizandum, avis-** (ævizæ·ndŏm). 1861 [gerund. of med.L. *avizare, avisare.*] Consideration. *To take a case into* or *to a.* is for a judge to take it for consideration out of court.

‖**Avocado** (ævokā·do). 1697. [Sp. *avocado* advocate, substituted pop. for the Aztec *ahuacatl* (Tylor).] The fruit of a W. Indian tree (*Persea gratissima*); a large pear-shaped fruit, called also *Alligator Pear.*

Avocat(e, obs. f. ADVOCATE.

†**A·vocate**, *v.* 1543. [f. L. *avocat-*, *avocare.* In sense 2, f. F. *avoquer*, ad. L. *advocare*; see ADVOKE, ADVOCATE *v.*[1]] 1. To call away, withdraw (*from*) -1752. 2. To call to a higher tribunal; = ADVOCATE *v.*[1] 2. -1679.

1. Avocated and called away from sin BECON. 2. Seeing now . . the cause avocated to Rome 1649. Hence **Avo·cative** *a.* calling off or away; *sb.* anything which calls away.

Avocation (ævokē̆ⁱ·ʃən). 1529. [ad. L. *avocationem.* In sense 5, f. AVOCATE *v.* 2.] I. (= L. *avocatio.*) 1. The calling away (of a person) from an employment; diversion of the thoughts (*arch.*) 1617. 2. The condition of being called away; distraction 1646. 3. That which calls one away from an occupation. *Hence*, A minor occupation, a by-work (πάρεργον). 1642. 4. *improp.* Ordinary employment, usual occupation, vocation, calling 1660.

1. I could be larger, but for a sudden auocation to business HOWELL. 3. Heaven is his vocation, and therefore he counts earthly employments avocations FULLER. 4. Found, even in the midst of his most pressing avocations, time for private prayer MACAULAY. The common avocations of life 1761.

II. (= L. *advocatio.*) = ADVOCATION 2. 1529. His unjust a. of the cause to Rome FROUDE.

Avocatory (ăvǫ·kătəri), *a.* (*sb.*) 1666. [ad. med.L. *avocatorius*; see AVOCATE.] 1. Recalling, that recalls. 2. *sb.* (in L. form) Avocatory letter or mandate 1689.

Letters avocatory: letters by which a sovereign recalls his subjects from a foreign state with which he is at war, or bids them desist from illegal proceedings.

Avocet, -set (æ·vose:t). 1766. [a. F. *avocette*, ad. It. *avosetta.*] One of the Wading birds (*Grallatores*), allied to the Snipes and Stilts, distinguished by its flexible upturned beak.

Avoid (ăvoi·d), *v.* ME. [a. AF. *avoider* = OF. *esvuidier*, f. *es* + *vuidier*, f. *vuide*; see VOID *v.* and *a.* Cf. EVACUATE.] Formerly strengthened with *out, away.* I. †1. *trans.* To make void or empty; to free or rid (*of*) -1601. 2. To make void or of no effect. In *Law*, to defeat (a pleading); to invalidate (a sentence, etc.). ME. †3. *intr.* (for *refl.*) Of benefices: To become void, or fall vacant -1726.

1. A-voyd þou thi trenchere 1500. 2. To a. a feoffment COKE, a deed BLACKSTONE, a purchase 1858.

II. †1. To empty out, remove -1641; to eject by excretion, to void -1691; to get rid of, put an end to -1685. †2. To get rid of, send away (a person *from, out of* a place) -1643. †3. *intr.* To move or go away, withdraw; to retire, retreat -1763. Const. *from, out of, forth of* -1611. †4. *trans.* To depart from, quit (a place); to dismount from (a horse) -1660.

1. To a. and end controversies BAXTER. 2. *refl.* A. thee, Fiend SCOTT. 4. Ye commaunded them to auoyde your Court CAXTON.

III. 1. To leave alone; to have nothing to do with. (The usual current sense—cf. II. 4.) ME. 2. To escape, evade; to keep out of the way of 1530. †3. To prevent, obviate -1831.

1. Never have to do with hym, if thou mayst avoyde hym PALSG. Avoiding Scylla, he fell into Charybdis (*mod.*). 2. T'auoid the Censures of the carping World *Rich. III*, III. v. 68. Hence †**Avoi·d** *sb.* the withdrawal of dishes after meals. **Avoi·dable** *a.* liable to be made or become void (? *Obs.*); †to be avoided; capable of being avoided. **Avoi·dably** *adv.* **Avoi·der,** one who avoids. **Avoi·dless** *a.* (*poet.*) inevitable; indefeasible.

Avoidance (ăvoi·dăns). ME. [f. prec. + -ANCE.] †1. The action of emptying a vessel, etc.; *hence*, a clearing away, removal; ejection, excretion -1661; an outlet -1625. 2. Voidance, invalidation. (*Esp.* in *Law.*) 1628. †3. The action of vacating a benefice, etc. 1642. 4. The becoming vacant, vacancy; also *ellipt.* the right to fill up the vacancy 1462. †5. Dismissal, removal -1650. †6. Withdrawal, exit -1635. 7. The action of avoiding anything unwelcome, or shunning a person 1610.

1. Fountaines, Running . . from the Wall, with some fine Auoidances BACON. 2. The a. of the marriage MILMAN. 4. A learned Vintner and worthie to haue the next auoydance of Bacchus his chaire PLAT. 7. Some things may be yeelded for the . . a. of others misconstruction BP. HALL.

Avoirdupois (æ·vəɹdəpoi·z). ME. [Corrupt sp. of *avoir-de-pois*, f. OF. *avoir*, property, AVER, *de* of, *pois, peis* (= It. *peso*) :—L. **pesum, pensum*, weight. The best mod. sp. is 17th c. *averdepois*; in any case *de* ought to be restored.] †1. Merchandise sold by weight -1691. 2. (In full *avoirdupois weight*) The standard system of weights used, in Great Britain, for all goods exc. the precious metals, precious stones, and medicines 1485. 3. Weight. (U.S.) 1597.

The A. pound contains 7000 grains. The cwt. contains in U.S. 100, in G.B. 112 lb., and the ton of 20 cwt. differs accordingly. In the pound, ounce, and dram there is no difference.

3. The weight of an hayre will turne the Scales betweene their Haber-de-pois 2 *Hen. IV*, II. iv. 276.

†**Avo·ke**, *v.* 1529. [In sense 1, ad. L. *avocare*, after *revoke*, etc. In sense 2, a. MF. *avoquer*, ad. L. *advocare.*] 1. To call away (*rare*) -1639. 2. = ADVOKE, ADVOCATE *v.*[1] 2. 1529.

†**A·volate**, *v.* 1673. [f. L. *avolat-*, *avolare.*] To fly off, escape, exhale, evaporate -1709. Hence †**Avola·tion.**

Avolitional (ævoli·ʃənăl), *a.* 1855. [A- *pref.* 14.] Not volitional.

Avoset, var. of AVOCET.

Avouch (ăvau·tʃ), *v.* ME. [a. OF. *avochier*, ad. L. *advocare.* A more technical synonym of *avow.* Cf. VOUCH.] †1. To appeal or refer for confirmation to some warrant or authority -1718; to certify by reference to vouchers 1540; to establish upon testimony -1678. 2. To give one's own warrant; to guarantee. *intr.* 1532. *trans.* 1548. 3. To declare as a thing one can prove, or upon which one offers his own express testimony as a personal witness; to affirm, assert. (Formerly also of matters of inference or opinion.) 1494. 4. To acknowledge (or claim) solemnly as one's own, AVOW (*arch.*) 1579. 5. To acknowledge an act of a subordinate agent (*arch.*) 1553; to own to (any act) as one's own (*arch.*) 1606. 6. To acknowledge (a charge), confess, avow 1649. 7. To acknowledge and support or justify (combining 4 with 2); to make good (*with*) 1599.

1. †*To avouch a thing upon one*: to call or cite him as warrant for it. Auouching of him [God] as a witnesse vnto their lye 1619. 2. I can a. for her reputation DE FOE. 3. Loe how plainly Saint Augustine auoucheth Purgatorie BEDELL. 4. Thou hast auouched the Lord this day to be thy God *Deut.* xxvi. 17. 5. He for whom thou dost this villanie . . will not a. thy fact DANIEL. 6. To a. oneself a coward SCOTT. 7. And will a. his saying with the sword MARLOWE. Hence †**Avou·ch** *sb.* (*arch.*) guarantee. *Haml.* I. i. 57. **Avou·chable** *a.* able to be avouched. **Avou·ched** *ppl.a.* vouched for; avowed. **Avou·cher. Avou·chment**, guarantee; declaration.

‖**Avoué** (avuˌe). 1851. [F. :—L. *advocatus*; = Eng. AVOWÉ, ADVOWEE.] A patron.

†**Avou·r(e**, *sb.*[1] *rare.* ME. [erron. for *avourie*, AVOWRY.] = AVOWRY 2.

†**Avou·re**, *sb.*[2] [for AVOWER.] (Legal) Avowal. SPENSER.

Avouter(e, etc., obs. f. ADULTER, etc.

Avow (ăvau·), *v.*[1] ME. [a. OF. *avouer*, *avoer*:—L. *advocare.* Semi-latinized to *advow*, whence ADVOWSON. Cf. AVOUCH.] 1. To own or acknowledge (a person) as one's own. †2. To own (the deeds of an agent); to sanction -1651. 3. To declare (as a thing one can vouch for); to affirm, maintain ME. 4. To own, admit, or confess (facts, etc., that one might conceal or deny). Const. as in 3. ME. 5. *refl.* and *pass.* To confess one's identity 1465. 6. *Law.* To justify or maintain (*spec.* a distress) 1528.

1. His Father . . avowed him for his Son NORTH. †*To a.* (*oneself*) *on* or *upon*: to claim the authority of. 3. De Clerieux . . aduowed his report to be true for them both 1596. 4. Many a man thinks, what he is ashamed to a. JOHNSON. 5. A. yourself, and prove the charge 1769. Hence †**Avow·** *sb.*[1] avowal (*rare*). **Avow·able** *a.* **Avow·ableness. Avow·er,** one who avows. †**Avow·ment,** avowal.

†**Avow** (ăvau·), *v.*[2] ME. [a. ? OF. *avouer*, 1. *à* + *vouer*:—late L. *votare*, freq. of *vovere, votum.*] 1. *trans.* To put (one) to a vow or oath (*to* or *to do*); to dedicate by a vow (*to*) -1583. 2. *intr.* (from *refl.*) To take a vow (*to* or *to do*) -1603. Hence **Avow** *sb.*[2] a vow; †a votive offering.

Avowal (ăvau·ăl). 1732. [f. AVOW *v.*[1]] Acknowledgement; unconstrained admission.

A plain a. of his sentiments PRESCOTT.

Avowance (ăvau·ăns). 1603. ? *Obs.* [See AVOW *v.*[1]] 1. The action of the avowant 1642. 2. Public acknowledgement.

Avowant (ăvau·ănt). 1529. [a. F., pr. pple. (used subst.) of *avouer*; see AVOW *v.*[1]] In *Law*, A challenger; a person making AVOWRY or cognizance.

†**Avowé.** ME. [a. OF. *avoué*:—L. *advocatus*; see ADVOCATE *sb.*] An advocate, or patron; *esp.* a patron saint -1490.

Avowed (ăvau·d), *ppl. a.* ME. [f. AVOW *v.*[1]] 1. Acknowledged, owned. 2. Self-acknowledged 1651.

1. A. brutality 1659. 2. An a. enemy to American independency 1792. Hence **Avow·ed-ly** *adv.*, **-ness.**

Avowry (ăvau·ri). [ME. *avoerie*, a. OF. f. *avouer* (see AVOW *v.*[1]). In 16th c. Eng. *advowry*, esp. when = *advowson*, but *avowry* is the current form.] †1. The function of an *avoué*, ADVOWEE, advocate or patron; patronage, protection. 2. Advocacy, protection or authority *personified*: a protector, a patron; *esp.* a patron saint. (Occ. *attrib.*) ME. †3. Advowson 1660. 4. (From AVOW *v.*¹, in its legal sense): The avowal of an act done; *esp.* the plea whereby one who distrains for rent *avows* the act and justifies it 1531. †5. (Due to both vbs. AVOW): A vowing, solemn declaration, or oath –1593.

4. He is said to make *avowry* if he justifies in his own right..and to make *cognisance* if he justifies in the right of another DIGBY.

Avowter(e, -trie, -tresse, etc., obs. ff. ADULTER, etc.

†Avoy·, *int.* ME. only. [a. OF.] Exclam. of surprise, fear, remonstrance.

‖**Avoyer** (avwaˌye, ăvoi·əɹ). 1586. [F.] Till 1794, the Fr. title of the chief magistrate of some of the Swiss Cantons.

Avulse (ăvʊ·ls), *v.* 1765. [f. L. *avuls-, avellere.*] To pluck off, tear away.

Avulsion (ăvʊ·lʃən). 1622. [ad. L. *avulsionem*; see prec.] 1. The action of plucking out or tearing away; forcible separation. 2. A part torn off 1678. 3. *Law.* The sudden removal of land, by change in a river's course, or by the action of flood, to another person's estate; distinguished from *alluvion* 1864.

1. By a. or division of the Sea..Sicily was..severed from Italy PEACHAM.

Avuncular (ăvʊ·nkiŭlăɹ), *a.* 1831. [f. L. *avunculus*, dim. of *avus* + -AR.] Of, belonging to, or like, an uncle. (*joc.*) Of a pawnbroker; see UNCLE 1859.

Love..Paternal or a. LANDOR.

Avu·nculize, *v.* [f. as prec. + -IZE.] To act like an uncle. FULLER.

Avys(e, -ness, etc., obs. ff. ADVICE, -ISE, etc.

Aw- was frequently written in ME. for Au-, and in Sc. for Av-. For such forms see Au-, Av-.

Aw, obs. f. AWE, OWE, OUGHT.

Awa, Sc. f. AWAY.

Await (ăwē¹·t), *v.* ME. [a. ONF. *awaitier* (OF. *aguaitier*), f. *à* + *waitier* (mod. *guetter*); see WAIT *v.* Cf. ATTEND *v.*] †1. To keep watch, watch for; *esp.* to waylay –1671. †2. *trans.* To watch for a chance of doing, contrive, plot (harm) *to* ME. †3. To look at, notice ME.; *intr.* to take note ME. †4. *intr.* with *on, inf. phr.*, or *subord. cl.* To keep watch, take care, endeavour –1603. †5. To attend. *trans.* –1641. *intr.* with *on, upon*, or *absol.* –1742. †6. *intr.* To wait *upon* to do business –1489. 7. To wait for (an event or person). *trans.* ME. (This and 8 are the only current senses.) †*intr.* To wait –1821; with *for* –1608. 8. To be in store, be reserved, for 1593.

5. On whom three hundred gold-capt youths a. POPE. 7. Gabriel sat..awaiting night MILT. *P. L.* IV. 550. 8. What fates a. the Duke of Suffolke 2 *Hen. VI*, I. iv. 35. Hence †**Awai·t** *sb.* ambush; a snare; watch, watchfulness; caution. **Awai·ter,** †one who lies in wait; †an attendant. **Awai·ting** *vbl. sb.* †ambush; †attendance; waiting, expectation (*arch.*).

Awake (ăwē¹·k), *v.* Pa. t. **awo·ke,** formerly also **awa·ked.** Pa. pple. **awo·ke** and **awa·ked.** [From two vbs.: 1. OE. *awæcnan, awoc, awacen*, compound of *wæcnan*. Hence mod.E. *awaken, awakened*. 2. Late OE. *awacian, awacode*, a compound of *wacian*, identical in sense with *awæcnan*. Hence *awake, awaked*. Later, *awoke* and its pa. pple. were referred to AWAKE as strong equivalents of *awaked*. The tendency to restrict the strong pa. t. and pa. pple. to the orig. intrans. sense, and the weak inflexion to the trans., has never been fully carried out.] I. *intr.* 1. To come out of the state of sleep; to cease to sleep. Cf. AWAKEN 1. 2. *fig.* To rise from a state resembling sleep, as death, indifference, inaction; to become active or vigilant 1450. 3. To be or keep awake (*rare*) 1602.

1. Hee awoke out of his sleepe *Judg.* xvi. 20. And Jacob awaked out of his sleepe *Gen.* xxviii. 16. 2. A.! A.! English Nobilitie! Let not slouth dimme your Honors 1 *Hen. VI*, I. i. 78. My Lute a. WYATT. *To awake to*: to become alive to.

II. *trans.* (replacing ME. AWECCHE.) 1. To arouse from sleep ME. 2. *fig.* To rouse from a state resembling sleep; to make active ME.

1. No dreadful Dreams awak'd him with affright DRYDEN. His disciples..awoke him *Matt.* viii. 25. 2. He will a. my mercie *John* IV. i. 26. Hence **Awa·ker** = *Awakener*.

Awake (ăwē¹·k), *pred. a.* ME. [Short for *awaken*, orig. pa. pple. of AWAKE *v.*] 1. Roused from sleep, not asleep ME. 2. *fig.* In activity; vigilant, on the alert 1618.

1. She still beheld Now *wide awake*, the vision of her sleep KEATS. 2. Grudge his own rest, and keep the world a. DRYDEN. He was *awake to* the dangers FROUDE.

Awaken (ăwē¹·k'n), *v.* [OE. *awæcnan*, earlier *on-wæcnan*, f. A- *pref.* 2 + *wæcnan*. See AWAKE. We still prefer *awaken* to *awake* in sense 4 (now the most frequent).] 1. *intr. lit.* = AWAKE *v.* I. 1. 2. *transf.* and *fig.* = AWAKE *v.* I. 2. 1768. 3. *trans. lit.* To rouse from sleep 1513. 4. *transf.* and *fig.* To rouse into activity; to stir up; kindle (desire, anxiety, etc.); in *Theol.* to arouse to a sense of sin 1603.

2. Just awakening, and darkly feeling after God WESLEY. 3. Satan..his next subordinate Awak'ning MILT. *P. L.* v. 672. 4. To a... their Piety and Industry HOBBES. Hence **Awa·kenable** *a.* **Awa·kener,** he who or that which awakens. **Awa·kening** *vbl. sb.* a rising or an arousing from sleep or its semblance; *ppl. a.* rising as if from sleep; fitted to arouse; rousing. **Awa·kenment.**

Awalt (ā·wəlt), *adv. Sc.* 1799. [?] Of a sheep: Lying helplessly on its back.

A-wane (ăwē¹·n), *adv.* ME. [A *prep.*¹] †In want; on the wane.

Awanting (ăwǫ·ntiŋ), *ppl. a.* 1661. [Erron. for the phr. *a wanting* (see A *prep.*¹ 12, 13). Cf. *amissing.*] Wanting.

Award (ăwǭ·ɹd), *v.*¹ ME. [a. AF. *awarder*, central F. *esguarder*, to observe:—Rom. **exwardare, -guardare*, f. *ex* + *wardare, guardare*, ad. OLG. **wardēn* (mod.G. *warten*) to watch. Cf. WARD, GUARD.] †1. *trans.* To decide after deliberation –1725. 2. To determine upon and appoint by judicial sentence 1533. 3. To adjudge (*to* a person) 1523. †4. To sentence, appoint (*to do*) –1650. †To sentence, consign (*to* custody, etc.) –1648.

2. An umpire..awarded that the local board should pay..200*l.* 1884. 3. A pound of that same marchants flesh is thine, The Court awards it, and the law doth give it *Merch. V*, IV. i. 300. Hence **Awa·rdable** *a.* rightly or lawfully to be awarded. **Awa·rder.** †**Awa·rdment** = AWARD *sb.* †**Awa·rdship,** the action of an awarder, arbitration.

†**Awa·rd,** *v.*² 1534. [f. A- *pref.* 14 + WARD *v.*] 1. To guard. 2. To ward off –1783.

Award (ăwǭ·ɹd), *sb.* ME. [a. AF. *award, -airt, agard* = OF. *ewart, eswart, esguart*, f. *eswarder, esguarder*; see AWARD *v.*¹] 1. A sentence or decision after examination, *esp.* that of an arbitrator or umpire; the document embodying it. 2. That which is awarded or assigned, as payment, penalty, etc. 1596. †3. Custody, wardship. (Cf. WARD *sb.*) –1570.

1. Sette attone by the adward off the Kyng PASTON. 2. The balance of the Geneva A. 1882.

Aware (ăwē·ɹ), *pred. a.* [OE. *gewær*, f. *ge* (see A- *pref.* 6) + *wær*; see WARE.] †1. Watchful, on one's guard –1542. 2. Informed, cognizant, conscious, sensible ME. †3. *ellipt.* with *be* omitted. (Be) on your guard, (be)ware. (Cf. *Soft!* Quick!) –1590.

1. *To be a. of* to be on one's guard against. Are you all a. of..evil-speaking WESLEY. 2. Arnan loked, and was a. of Dauid 1 *Chron.* xxii. 21. Are you a. that your friends are here (*mod.*). Hence **Awa·redom.** H. WALPOLE. **Awa·reness,** the quality or state of being a. †**Awa·ring** *vbl. sb.* perception.

†**Awa·rn,** *v.* [A- *pref.* 11.] To warn. SPENSER.

A-wash (ăwǫ·ʃ), *adv.* (*pred. a.*) 1833. [A *prep.*¹] 1. Flush with the surface of the water, so that it just washes over. 2. Washing about, at the mercy of the waves 1870.

2. The rising water set everything a. READE.

A-wa·ste, *adv.* [A *prep.*¹] Wasting. MRS. BROWNING.

A-wa·tch, *adv.* [A *prep.*¹] On the watch. MRS. BROWNING.

A-wa·ve, *adv.* [A *prep.*¹] On the wave, waving. BROWNING.

Away (ăwē¹), *adv.* [In OE. a phr. ON *prep.*, and *weg*, later *a-weg*; in ME. and mod. dialects reduced to *'way.*] I. Of motion in place, removal. 1. On (his or one's) way; on. 2. From this (or that) place, to a distance OE. 3. Off, aside; also *fig.* as in to *fall away* ME. 4. Out of one's possession; *e.g.* with *put, give, take, throw*, etc. ME. 5. From existence; to death, to an end, to nothing ME. 6. Hence used with trans. vbs., as '*boil, kiss* away', and '*explain, analyse* away'; also with intr. vbs., as 'to sigh away one's life', making them trans. 1661.

1. Come a. death *Twel. N.* II. iv. 55. 2. The bride's going-away dress 1884. A. went Gilpin COWPER. 3. To lay work a. LONGF. 5. Man dieth, and wasteth a. *Job* xiv. 10.

II. Of action. [From I.] 1. Onward in time, on, continuously, e. g. *to work away* 1562. 2. Straightway, without hesitation or delay; chiefly colloq., as in *Fire away! Say away!* and U.S. and Eng. dial. *Right away* 1535.

III. Of position. [From senses I. 2 to 5.] 1. In the other direction ME. 2. Added to *where, there, here,* = about. (Now *dial.*) 1564. 3. In another place; at a distance; off 1712. 4. Gone (from a place); absent; wanting ME. 5. Gone (from existence); destroyed, consumed; dead; fainted. (Now chiefly *dial.*) ME.

1. I turned a. from this despicable troop STEELE. 3. I shall not be able to stay a. *Spect.* 4. I called and found him a. (*mod.*).

IV. Elliptical (vb. suppressed). 1. = Go away ME. 2. = Go or get away *with*, take away 1526. 3. = Get on or along *with*, put up with 1477. 4. *And away* (= and going away again), in *once and away* (now *once in a way*) = once but not continuously 1583. ¶ 5. Formerly erron. for WAY.

1. A., get thee downe *Ex.* xix. 24. 2. Awaye with him, crucify him *John* xix. 15. 3. That saucy fleer I cannot a. with RICHARDSON. 4. Short hints and a., may please a Scholar 1655. var. †**Away·s** (with advb. gen. *-s*). Hence †**Away·ward** *adv.* turned away; away; var. **-wards**; quasi-*adj.* averted, wayward. *Comb.* **a.-going** *ppl. a.*

Awe (ǭ), *sb.*¹ [a. ON. *agi*, repr. an OTeut. **agon-*; but in EE. f. OE. *ege*:—OTeut. **agiz*, Goth. *agis*; both f. *agan* to fear, and treated as dial. variants of the same word.] †1. Terror, dread –1784. 2. Dread mingled with veneration, as of the Divine Being OE. 3. Solemn and reverential wonder, tinged with latent fear, inspired by what is sublime and majestic in nature 1756. 4. Power to inspire fear or reverence OE. †5. Anger, fierceness, rage –ME. †6. A cause of dread; a restraint –1657.

1. His voice Shook the delinquent with such fits of a. COWPER. 2. There is an a. in mortals' joy, A deep mysterious fear KEBLE. 3. She pointed with a. to a mighty object HT. MARTINEAU. 4. Shall Rome stand vnder one mans a. *Jul. C.* II. i. 52.

Comb.: †**a.-bound** *a.* bound by a.; submissive, obedient; **-struck** *a.* struck with, or overwhelmed by, a.

Phrases. *To stand in awe of*: to dread; *later*, to entertain a profound reverence for. (Orig. 'Awe stood to men', later, 'Awe stood men (*dat.*)', inverted into 'men stood awe', 'men' being erron. taken as a nom. case; 'in' was inserted to restore the sense.) *To hold* or *keep in awe* (*of*): to restrain or control by fear (of). *Haml.* v. i. 238.

Hence **Awe·less, aw·less** *a.* without dread, undaunted; irreverent; †that inspires no awe. **Awe·lessness. Awe·some, aw·some** *a.* reverential; inspiring awe, appalling, weird. (Chiefly *Sc.*)

Awe, *sb.*² 1503. [Etym. and orig. form unkn.] One of the float-boards of an undershot water-wheel, on which the water acts.

Awe (ǭ), *v.* ME. [f. AWE *sb.*¹; OE. had *égan*; cf. AWE *sb.*¹ 6.] 1. To inspire with dread, terrify, daunt; to control by the influence of fear. (Orig. *impers.*) 2. To influence or control by profound respect or reverential fear 1611. 3. To inspire with reverential wonder combined with latent fear 1753. †4. To reverence (*rare*) 1632.

1. Shall quips, and sentences..awe a man from the careere of his humour *Much Ado* II. iii. 250. 2. He was not awed by the sanctity of the place GIBBON. Hence **Aw·ed** *ppl. a.* awe-struck; †dreaded. **Awing, aweing** *vbl. sb.* and *ppl. a.*

Awearied (ăwī³·rid), *ppl. a.* 1604. [A- *pref.* 11.] Wearied, weary.

Aweary (ăwī³·ri), *pred. a.* 1552. [A- *pref.* 11.] Tired, weary. Const. *of.*

I ginne to be a. of the Sun *Macb.* v. v. 49.

A-weather (ăwe·ðəɹ). 1599. [A *prep.*¹] *Naut. adv.* Towards the weather or windward side, in the direction from which the wind blows; *esp.* in *helm a-weather*; opp. to *a-lee. prep.* Short for *a-weather of.*

†**Awe-band.** 1536. [f. AWE *sb.*¹] A curb, check, restraint; 'a band for tying black cattle to the stake' (Jamieson).

A-week (ăwī·k), *adv.* 1547. [A *prep.*¹ 8; cf. *a-day.*] In every week, weekly.

Aweel (ăwī·l), *conj. adv. Sc.* 1800. [weakened f. *ah well!* cf. Fr. *eh bien.*] Well!

Aweigh (ăwē¹·), *adv.* 1627. [A *prep.*¹]

Naut. Of an anchor: Just raised perpendicularly from the ground; = *a-peak, a-trip.*

A-we·st, *adv.* 1809. [A *prep.*[1]] In the west; westward.

Awe-strike (ǭ·ˌstrəi·k), *v.* 1832. [f. AWE-STRUCK by analysis.] To strike with awe. Hence **Awe·-stri·cken** *ppl. a.* = AWE-STRUCK.

Awe-struck (ǭ·ˌstrʊ·k), *ppl. a.* 1634. [f. AWE *sb.* + *struck* pa. pple.] Struck with awe.

Awful (ǭ·ful), *a.* OE. [f. AWE *sb.*[1], continuing the sense of OE. *egefull.* Occas. comp. *awfuller, -est.*] **1.** Causing dread; terrible, appalling. **2.** Worthy of, or commanding, profound respect or reverential fear OE. **3.** Solemnly impressive; sublimely majestic 1660. **4.** *slang.* Frightful, very ugly, monstrous; and *hence* as a mere intensive = Exceedingly great, bad, etc. 1834. †**5.** Terror-stricken; timorous –1748. **6.** Profoundly respectful or reverential 1593.

1. A. massacres GREEN. **2.** Cato's character..is rather a. than amiable ADDISON. **4.** An a. scrawl 1870, dufter 1873, time (*mod.*). **5.** A weak and a. reverence for antiquity WATTS. Hence **Aw·fully** *adv.* dreadfully; sublimely, majestically; *slang,* very (cf. Gr. δεινῶς); with a feeling of awe. **Aw·fulness,** the quality of inspiring awe; the being full of awe (*arch.*).

†**Awha·pe,** *v.* ME. [?] To amaze –1591.

†**A-whee·ls,** *adv.* [A *prep.*[1]] On wheels. B. JONS.

A-whe·t, *adv.* [A *prep.*[1] (On imperfect analogy.)] In act of whetting. CONINGTON.

Awhile (ăhwəi·l), *adv.* [OE. *āne hwīle*: usu. written together since 13th c.] (For) a short time, (for) a little.

A. she paused, no answer came SCOTT.

¶ Improp. written together, when *while* is purely a sb.

After awhile they seemed [etc.] OUIDA.

†**A-whiles, a wiles,** *advb. phr.* [A- *pref.* 11 (or A *prep.* 1).] At times 1546.

A-whi·r, *adv.* 1865. [A *prep.*[1]] Whirring.

A-whi·rl, *adv.* 1883. [A *prep.*[1]] Whirling.

†**Awi·de,** *adv.* 1609. [f. WIDE, after *afar,* etc.] Wide, widely –1642.

A-wi·ng, *adv.* 1823. [A *prep.*[1]] On the wing.

A-wi·nk, *adv.* 1883. [A *prep.*[1]] Winking.

†**Awk** (ǭk), *a.* ME. [prob. a. ON. *afug,* 'turned the wrong way', f. *af* away. Cf. *hafoc, hawk.*] **1.** In the wrong direction, backhanded –1634. **2.** Untoward, perverse –1655. **3.** Awkward to use, clumsy –1674. **4.** *adv.* –1694. **5.** *sb.* –1674. Hence †**Aw·kly** *a.* perverse. †**Aw·kly** *adv.* in the wrong direction; *hence,* unluckily; perversely, awkwardly. †**Aw·kness.**

Awkward (ǭ·kwəɹd), *adv.* and *a.* ME. [f. AWK *a.* + -WARD, *i.e.* 'in an awk direction'; cf. *forward.* The adjectival use is later.] †**A.** *adv.* In the wrong direction, or way. **a.** Upside down; hindside foremost. **b.** In a backward direction, with a back stroke. **c.** Asquint. **d.** Occ. = AWALT, q.v. –1589.

B. *adj.* **1.** Turned the wrong way, back-handed; not straightforward, oblique. Still *dial.* 1513. †**2.** Froward, perverse –1755. †**3.** Untoward, unfavourable (*lit.* and *fig.*) –1663. **4.** Of things: Ill-adapted for use; clumsy in operation 1695. Of persons: Clumsy in action, bungling 1530. **5.** Ungraceful, ungainly; uncouth 1606. **6.** Of things: Embarrassing, inconvenient 1709. Of persons: Embarrassed 1713. **7.** Of things: Not easy to deal with; *euphem.* for 'rather dangerous' 1860. Of persons: Dangerous to meddle with 1863.

2. I haue an aukward pride in my nature FIELDING. **3.** With a. winds and with sore tempests driven MARLOWE. **4.** A., unmanageable instruments 1783. Clumsy, aukward, unhandy people SWIFT. **5.** Vulcan with aukward grace his office plies POPE. The son an aukward booby GOLDSM. **6.** He was beginning to feel a. with his Whig friends L. HUNT. **7.** There is an a. step here 1881. An 'awkward customer' 1863. Hence **Aw·kwardish** *a.* **Aw·kwardly** *adv.* †wrongly; clumsily; in a bungling way; inelegantly; embarrassingly; dangerously. **Aw·kwardness.**

Awl (ǭl). [OE. *æl,* cogn. w. OHG. *ala,* mod.G. *ahle,* ON. *alr* (cf. Skr. *ārā*). For *nall,* due to wrong division, cf. ADDER.] **1.** A small tool, having a slender, tapering, sharp-pointed blade, with which holes may be pierced; a piercer, pricker, bodkin. **2.** *esp.* That used by shoemakers. Cf. also BRADAWL (used by carpenters). OE. Also *fig.* **3.** *transf.* A sharp spine, or boring organ ME.

2. The Cobler kept him to his nall B. JONS. *To pack up one's awls*: cf. ALL *sb.* (Perh. a pun.)

Comb.: **a.-bird,** the Green Woodpecker (*Picus Viridis*); **-shaped** *a.,* subulate; **-wort,** a plant (*Subularia aquatica*) so named from its leaves.

Awm(e, obs. f. AAM, AUM, AIM.

Awmbrie, -y, awmery, obs. ff. AMBRY.

Awmous, Sc. f. ALMOUS.

Awn (ǭn), *sb.* ME. [app. a. ON. *ǫgn,* pl. *agnar.* The OE. form does not occur.] The spinous process, or 'beard' that terminates the grain-sheath of barley, oats, etc.; extended in *Bot.* to any similar growth. Hence **Aw·ned** *ppl. a.*[1] furnished with an a. **Aw·nless** *a.* without awns. **Aw·ny** *a.* bearded, bristly (*rare*).

Awn (ǭn), *v.*[1] 1807. [f. prec. sb.] To get rid of the awns. Cf. *to shell* (peas).

Awned, *ppl. a.*[2] 1881. [badly f. AWN-ING + -ED[2].] Awninged.

Awning (ǭ·niŋ). 1624. [Obscure; orig. nautical. Prob. f. F. *auvent,* 'a penthouse of cloth, etc. before a shop window, etc.' (Wedgwood). Less prob. f. LG. *havenung,* f. *haven* (E. Müller); or f. Pers. *āwan, āwang,* anything suspended (Skeat).] **1.** A roof-like covering of canvas, etc., used as a shelter from sun, rain, etc.; *esp.* above the deck of a vessel. **2.** *transf.* **a.** *Naut.* That part of the poop-deck which is continued forward beyond the bulk-head of the cabin. **b.** *gen.* A shelter. 1764. Hence **Aw·ninged** *ppl. a.* furnished with an a. **Aw·ningless** *a.*

A-wo·bble, *adv.* 1881. [A *prep.*[1]] Wobbling.

†**Awo·nder,** *v.* ME. [prob. worn-down f. OE. *ofwundrian*; cf. *athirst.*] **1.** *impers.* It astonishes (one). **2.** *intr.* To be astonished –1513. **3.** *pa. pple.* Amazed –1513.

A-work (ăwɜ̄·ɹk), *adv.* ME. [A *prep.*[1]] At work, in activity.

Maystres..to set them awerke CAXTON.

†**Awo·rry,** *v.* [OE. *awyrgan*; see WORRY *v.*] To strangle; to worry –ME.

†**Awo·rth,** *adv.* ME. [A *prep.*[1]] In *To take a.*: to take (a thing) in honour, or at its worth; *hence,* to bear patiently, to disregard –1537.

A-wrack (ăræ·k), *adv.* 1627. [A *prep.*[1]] In a state of wreck.

†**A-wrea·k,** *v.* [OE. *awrecan*; see WREAK.] **1.** To punish (an offence, etc.) –1481. **2.** To condemn –ME. **3.** To avenge or revenge –1586.

A-wreck (ăre·k), *adv.* 1878. [A *prep.*[1]] In a wrecked condition.

Awrong (ărǫ·ŋ), *adv.* ME. [A *prep.*[1]] Wrong, in a wrong way.

Awry (ărəi·). ME. [A *prep.*[1]; cf. *aright,* etc.] **A.** *adv.* **1.** Away from the straight; to one side; unevenly, crookedly, askew ME. **2.** *fig.* Out of the right course or place; amiss 1494.

1. *To look awry*: to look ASKANCE or ASQUINT. **2.** Much of the Soul they talk, but all awrie MILT. *P. R.* IV. 313. *To go, run, step, tread, walk awry*: (of persons) to do wrong; (of things) to go wrong. *To tread the shoe awry*: to fall from virtue. Cf. F. *faux pas.* Where he trod his holy sandals a. FULLER.

B. *adj.* (usu. *pred.* Cf. WRY.) **1.** Out of the right course or position; disordered, disarranged; crooked, distorted 1658. **2.** *fig.* Perverted, wrong 1581. *ellipt.* quasi-*vb.* 1613.

2. Nothing more *awry from* the Law of God..then that a Woman should give Laws to Men MILT.

Ax, obs. or dial. f. ASK *v.*

Axal (æ·ksăl), *a.* 1823. = AXIAL.

Axe (æks), *sb.*[1] Also **ax.** [Com. Teut.: OE. *æx,* akin to Gr. ἀξίνη, and prob. to L. *ascia.*] **1.** A tool for hewing, cleaving, or chopping trees, wood, ice, etc.; consisting of a squarish head, now usu. of iron with a steel edge, fixed by means of a socket upon a handle or helve of wood. Also called (*esp.* when light) a *hatchet.* OE. **b.** PICK-AXE, q.v. **2.** In olden warfare: A battle-axe ME. **3.** The headsman's axe. Hence *fig.* execution. 1450. **b.** *The a.*: the cutting down of expenditure in public services; a body for doing this 1922. **4.** In *Archæol.* applied to double-edged or wedged-shaped stone implements 1851.

2. The Lochaber ax is only a slight alteration of the old English bill JOHNSON. The two-handed axe of Harold FREEMAN. **3.** Gave to the cruel ax a darling son YOUNG. **b.** The Geddes axe 1923.

Comb.: **a.-man,** a woodman; a warrior armed with a battle-axe; **-stone,** a greenish variety of jade or nephrite, used in S. America, etc., for making stone hatchets.

Phrases. *To put the axe in the helve*: to solve a doubt. *To send the axe after the helve* (= the better *To send the helve after the hatchet*). *To have axes to grind* (U.S. politics): to have private ends to serve. [In ref. to a story told by Franklin.]

Axe, *sb.*[2] *Obs.* exc. *dial.* = AXLE, AXIS.

Axe, *v.* Also **ax.** 1677. [f. AXE *sb.*[1]] **1.** To shape or trim with an axe. **2.** To remove (officials, etc.) to save expenditure; to cut down (expenditure) by means of 'the axe' 1923.

1. The..stretchers in returns, which are not axed, are dressed upon the rubbing-stone. **2.** Under the Geddes recommendations fifteen hundred officers had been axed 1923.

Axed (ækst). 1830. [f. AXE *v.* or *sb.*[1]] **1.** *ppl. a.* Shaped or dressed with an axe. **2.** *adj.* Furnished with an axe or axes 1879.

2. The axed fasces of the lictors FARRAR.

†**Axes, axesse, axez, axis, axys,** obs. ff. ACCESS, 'attack, fit, ague'.

This axes hath made hym so weake PALSGR.

Axial (æ·ksiăl), *a.* 1849. [f. L. *axis.*] **1.** Forming, or of the nature of, an axis. **2.** Of, or belonging to, an axis 1859. **3.** Round, or about, an axis 1862.

1. A true or a. root HENFREY. **2.** A. inclination [of the planets] PROCTOR. **3.** The earth's a. rotation TYNDALL. Hence **Axia·lity,** a. quality. **A·xially** *adv.* in the direction of the axis, from pole to pole.

Axiferous (æksi·fĕrəs), *a.* 1842. [f. L. *axis* + *-fer* + -OUS; cf. F. *axifère.*] *Bot.* Consisting of an axis only, without leaves or appendages.

A·xiform, *a.* 1847. [f. as prec. + -FORM.] In the shape of an axis.

Axifugal (æksi·fiŭgăl), *a.* 1740. [f. as prec. + L. *fugere* + -AL[1].] = CENTRIFUGAL; in *a. force*: tendency to fly from the axis of rotation.

Axil (æ·ksil). 1794. [ad. L. *axilla*; see below.] *Bot.* The upper angle between a leaf or petiole and the stem from which it springs; also that between a branch and the trunk.

Axile (æ·ksəil), *a.* 1845. [f. as if ad. L. **axilis,* f. *axis.*] Belonging to the axis. Used in *Bot.* of an embryo having the same direction as the axis of the seed.

‖**Axilla** (æksi·lă). Pl. **-æ.** 1616. [L., = armpit; dim. of **axula,* whence *ala.*] **1.** An armpit. **2.** = AXIL 1830.

Axillar (æ·ksilăɹ), *a.* (*sb.*) 1541. [a. F. *axillaire,* ad. L. **axillaris,* f. *axilla*; see prec.] **1.** = AXILLARY 1. 1651. **2.** = AXILLARY 2. 1831. **3.** *sb.* An axillary vein 1541.

Axillary (æ·ksilări), *a.* 1615. [f. as prec.; see -ARY[2].] **1.** Pertaining or adjacent to the armpit. **2.** *Bot.* Situated in, or growing from, the axil.

1. The a. artery 1791. A. feathers DARWIN. **2.** A. leaves REES.

Axin (æ·ksin). 1873. *Chem.* An oleaginous and waxy product, yielded by the large Mexican cochineal (*Coccus axinus*), and used as an ointment. Hence **Axi·nic** *a.*

Axine (æ·ksəin). 1826. [f. AXIS[2].] *Zool. adj.* Of or pertaining to the group of stags of which the Spotted Axis is typical. *sb.* One of this group.

Axi·niform, *a.* 1852. [f. Gr. ἀξίνη + -(I)-FORM.] Shaped like an ax-head.

Axinite (æ·ksinəit). 1802. [f. as prec.] *Min.* One of Dana's epidote group of unisilicates, consisting chiefly of silica, alumina, lime, and iron, with acute-edged crystals somewhat like an ax-head.

Axinomancy (ǣksi·noˌmænsi). 1601. [ad. L. *axinomantia,* a. Gr., f. ἀξίνη + μαντεία.] Divination by means of an ax-head.

Axiolite (æ·ksiˌoləit). 1879. [f. L. *axis* + Gr. λίθος.] *Min.* Elongated lenticular and curved zones of brownish glass, exhibiting crystallization or fibrous structure at right angles to a median line, as in a rhyolite. **A:xioli·tic** *a.*

Axiom (æ·ksiəm). 1485. [a. F. *axiome,* ad. L. *axioma,* a. Gr., f. ἀξιό-ειν, f. ἄξιος.] **1.** A proposition that commends itself to general acceptance; a well-established or universally-conceded principle; a maxim, rule, law. In Bacon An empirical law 1626. †**2.** *Logic.* A proposition (true or false) –1742. **3.** *Logic* and *Math.* A self-evident proposition, not requiring demonstration, but assented to as soon as stated 1600.

1. Which A., though received by most, is yet certainly false HOBBES. Empirical rules (Bacon would call them *axioms*) SIR W. HAMILTON. 3. The a. that the whole is greater than its part H. SPENCER.

Axiomatic (æksiŏmæ·tik), *a.* 1797. [ad. Gr. ἀξιωματικός; see prec. and -ATIC.] 1. Of the nature of an AXIOM (sense 3); self-evident. 2. Characterized by axioms; axiomatical 1812. 3. Full of maxims, aphoristic 1834.

1. A. truths H. SPENCER. 2. He gave an a. form to the Science SIR H. DAVY. 3. The most a. of English Poets SOUTHEY.

A·xioma·tical, *a.* 1588. [f. as prec.] †1. *Logic.* Pertaining to, or of the nature of, an AXIOM (sense 2) –1679. 2. Of or relating to AXIOMS (sense 3) 1676. 3. = AXIOMATIC 1. 1678. 4. = AXIOMATIC 3. 1738. Hence **A·xioma·tically** *adv.*

Axis[1] (æ·ksis). Pl. **axes** (æ·ksīz). 1549. [a. L. *axis*, cogn. with OE. *eax*; see AX *sb.*[2]] I. Axis of rotation. 1. The axle of a wheel. ? *Obs.* 1619. *fig.* The 'pivot' on which a matter turns. 2. *Phys.* A tooth or process on the second cervical vertebra, upon which the head is turned; the vertebra itself 1694. 3. The imaginary straight line about which a body (*e.g.* the earth) rotates; the prolongation of that of the earth on which the heavens appear to revolve 1549. †4. *fig.* A central prop, which sustains any system –1646. 5. The geometrical line, by the revolution of a superficies about which, globes, cylinders, cones, etc. are said to be generated 1571.

1. The a. of the revolt was the religious question MOTLEY. 4. The Atlas or maine a., which supported this opinion, was daily experience SIR T. BROWNE.

II. Axis of symmetry. 1. The straight line about which the parts of a body or system are symmetrically arranged 1796. 2. *Geom.* Any line in a regular figure which divides it into two symmetrical parts; in a conic section, the line from the principal vertex or vertices, perpendicular to the tangent at that point; in a curve, a straight line which bisects a system of parallel chords (called *principal axis* when it cuts them at right angles) 1734. 3. *Cryst.* An imaginary line drawn between the centres of opposite faces or edges, or the apices of opposite angles 1817. 4. *Optics.* A ray passing through the centre of the eye or of a lense, or falling perpendicularly on it; the line which passes through the centres of the lenses in a telescope; the straight line from the eye to the object of sight 1701. 5. *Phys.* and *Zool.* (With 5, 6, and 7 cf. III.) The central core of an organ or organism; the central skeleton or nervous cord; the central column of a whorled shell. 1741. 6. *Bot.* a. The central column of the inflorescence. b. The main stem and root. 7. *Physiogr.* and *Geol.* A central ridge; the central line in a valley 1830.

1. *Axis of a balance*: the line upon which it turns. *A. of oscillation* (of a pendulum, etc.): a horizontal line passing through the centre of the oscillation, and perpendicular to its plane. *A. of polarization*: the central line round which the prismatic rings or curves are arranged. *Neutral a.* (of a girder): the line where there is neither compression nor tension (Brewster). 2. *Transverse a.* (in the ellipse and hyperbola): that which passes through the two foci; *conjugate a.*: that which bisects the transverse one at right angles. (The axes of an ellipse are also called *major* and *minor.*) 4. *A. of incidence*: the line passing through the point of incidence perpendicularly to the refracting surface. *A. of refraction*: the continuation of the same line through the refracting medium. *A. of double refraction*: the line on both sides of which double refraction takes place, but along which it does not exist. 7. *Anticlinal a.*: the line along which two opposite planes of stratification meet in a ridge. *Synclinal a.*: the line along which they meet in a depression.

III. A straight line from pole to pole (cf. I. 3), or from end to end, of any body. 1. *gen.* e. g. *Axis of the equator*: the polar diameter of the earth; see I. 3. *Axis of the ecliptic, of the horizon*: a diameter of the sphere passing through these circles at right angles 1796. 2. *spec.* An imaginary line uniting the two poles of a magnet 1664. 3. A main line of motion, growth, extension, direction 1818.

IV. Axis of reference. *Analyt. Geom.* Each of the two intersecting lines, by reference to which the position of a *locus* is determined 1855.

Comb. **a.-cylinder** (or **-band**), the central fibre of a nerve tube.

Axis[2] (æ·ksis). 1601. [L. (Pliny.)] *Zool* Buffon's name for an Indian deer (*Cervus axis*) known by sportsmen as the Hog-deer.

Axle (æ·ks'l). 1596. [Not in OE.; found in 13th c. in *axle-tree* (synonymous with the native AX-TREE), f. ON. *öxull* masc.; thence taken and used in place of OE. *eax*, *eax*; see AX *sb.*[2]] 1. The centre-pin or spindle upon which a wheel revolves, or which revolves along with it. (In carriages, used to include the axle-tree or axle-bar.) 1634. *fig.* (Cf. 'pivot'.) 1635. 2. The imaginary line about which a planet, etc. (or, anciently, the heaven) revolves. Also *poet.* the pole, the sky or heaven. (Cf. AXLE-TREE 3 b.) *Obs.* exc. *poet.* (Replaced by AXIS.) 1596.

1. The gilded car of day His glowing a. doth allay In the steep Atlantic stream MILT. *Comus* 96. *fig.* Mov'd..as upon the a. of discipline MILT. 2. Since earth on a. ran MRS. BROWNING.

Comb.: **a.-bar,** an iron bar serving the purpose of an axle-tree; **-box,** in a locomotive engine or railway carriage, the box, usu. of cast iron, within which the ends of the axles revolve; **-guards,** the part of the frame in which the a.-box slides up and down as acted on by the springs; **-journal, -neck,** the polished end of the a. which revolves under the bearing in the a.-box; **-nail, -pin,** one of the two nails or pins used to fasten a cart to the axle-tree; **-shaft,** a driving shaft forming an extension of the a. of a wheel. Hence **A·xled** *a.* furnished with an a.

†A·xle-too·th. 1483. [a. Da. *axel* molar + TOOTH.] A molar tooth, a grinder.

Axle-tree (æ·ks'l,trī). [ME. *axel-tre*, a. ON. *öxul-tré*; see AXLE[2].] (Now restricted to sense 1.) 1. The fixed bar, etc., on the rounded ends of which the opposite wheels of a carriage revolve. †2. The spindle or AXLE of any wheel; the 'axle' in the *Wheel-and-axle* –1664. *fig.* (Cf. *pivot*, *axis.*) –1674. †3. = AXLE 3. –1633.

1. *Axle-tree arms*: the ends which project beyond the wheels. 3. Strong as the A. In which the Heauens ride *Tr. & Cr.* I. iii. 65. Hence **A·xletreed** *a.* furnished with an a.

Axminster (æ·ksminstəɹ). 1818. [Name of a town in Devonshire.] Used attrib. in *A. carpet* or *rug*, and absol.: a seamless carpet formerly made at A., having a thick soft pile.

Axoid (æ·ksoid). 1876. [f. AXIS + -OID.] A curve generated by the revolution of a point round an advancing axis, *e.g.* the cycloid.

Axoide·an, *a.* 1840. [f. AXIS, on imperfect analogy.] = AXIAL.

Axolotl (æ·ksŏlǫt'l). 1786. [Aztec.] *Zool.* A batrachian reptile (*Siredon pisciforme*, family *Proteidæ*) found in Mexican lakes, resembling the salamander in appearance, but retaining through life the gills of its young state.

Axonometry (æksǫ·ǫ·mėtri). 1865. [f. Gr. ἄξον- (ἄξων) + -μετρία.] Measurement of axes.

Axophyte (æ·ksŏfəit). 1857. [f. Gr. ἄξων axis + φυτόν plant.] *Bot.* A plant that has an axis or stem. var. **Axo·nophyte.**

Axotomous (ǣksǫ·tŏməs), *a.* 1834. [f. as prec. + Gr. τομ-, -τέμνειν + -OUS.] *Min.* Having a cleavage perpendicular to the axis.

Axunge (æ·ksɒndʒ). 1541. [a. F. (mod. *axonge*), ad L. *axungia* (also used), f. *axis* + *ungere*.] The internal fat of the kidneys, etc.; *esp.* goose-grease, lard; also *gen.* fat, grease. Hence **Axu·ngious** *a.* lard-like.

Ay-, formerly interchangeable with *ai-* in many words: e. g. *ayd(e*, etc. For such see AI-. It also interchanged with EI-, EY-; and occ. with A-, EA-, E.

Ay, aye (ē¹), *adv.* [Early ME. *aȝȝ*, *ai*, *ei*: a. ON. *ei*, *ey*, cogn. with OE. *á*, ME. *o*, *oo*, mod.G. *je*, Goth. *aiw*:—OTeut. **aiwo·z*, cogn. w. L. *ævum*. Cf. Gr. ἀεί, αἰϝεί 'ever', and αἰϝών 'age'. Exc. in poetry, *ay* is northern. Etymology, phonology, and analogy favour the sp. *ay*. The word rimes with *bay*, etc. See AYE.] 1. a. Ever, continually; b. on all occasions. (Now only in *Sc.* and *north. dial.*). 2. With *comp. degree.* (Still in *Sc.*) –ME.

1. And ay the ale was growing better BURNS. Phrases. *For ay*: for ever. Also *for ever and ay*; in ME. *for ay and o.* (Only *poet.* in Eng.). †*In aye*: for ever.

Ay (ē¹), *int.* (*sb.*) ME. [prob. a natural ejaculation.] 1. = Ah! O! (Northern exclam. of surprise, invocation, earnestness.) 2. *Ay me!* = Alas! Ah me!—an exclam. of regret, sorrow, pity 1591. 3. *sb.* 1607.

2. Ay me! how dread can look the Dead MRS. BROWNING.

Ay, var. of AYE, yes.

‖ **Ayah** (ai·ă) 1782. [Anglo-Ind., a. Pg. *aia*, fem. of *aio* a tutor.] A native Indian nurse or lady's maid.

Aye, ay (ai, əi), *interj.* (*adv.*), *sb.* 1576. [Origin unkn. At first written I. Perh. a dial. form of AY *adv.* (cf. *aye but*); less probably a phonetic var. of *ya* 'yea'. The sp. *aye* is preferable.] *int.* (*adv.*?) 1. An affirmative response to a question: Yes, even so. Common in dial. and nautical language; the formal word used in voting 'yes' in the House of Commons; but arch. for 'yes' in mod. educated language. 2. Indicating assent to a previous statement, and preliminary to a further one 1598. 3. *sb.* An affirmative answer or vote; in *pl.* (ellipt.) those who so vote 1589.

1. If you say I, syr, we will not say no 1576. 2. I, so I do B. JONS. I; but you doe us wrong 1640. 3. The ayes proved 138 and the noes 129 MARVELL.

Aye, var. of AY *adv.* ever.

A-year, *phr.* = in the year, per annum; see A *prep.*[1]

Aye-aye (ai·ai·). 1781. [a. Fr., a. Malagasy; prob. from its cry.] *Zool.* A quadrumanous animal (*Cheiromys Madagascariensis*), of the size of a cat, found only in Madagascar; it is classed with the Lemurs, but in many points approaches the Rodentia.

A-yelp (ă,ye·lp), *adv.* [A *prep.*[1]] Yelping. MRS. BROWNING.

Ayen(e, etc., obs. f. AGAIN, etc.

†Aye·nbite. ME. [f. *ayen* + BITE; ME. tr. of L. *remorsus.*] Remorse.

Ay-green (ē¹·grīn). 1562. [= *Evergreen*; see AY *adv.*] *Herb.* The house-leek.

†Ayie·ld, *v.* [OE. *agieldan*; see YIELD.] To yield up –1450.

Ayme, obs. f. *Ay me!*

†Ayne, *a.* 1483. [a. OF. *ainé*, f. *ains né*.] First-born, eldest, EIGNE.

Ayo·nd, ayo·nt, *prep. dial.* 1724. [A-*pref.* 2; cf. *beyond*. (*Ayont* is Sc. and north. dial.)] Beyond, on the other side of.

Ayre, -ie, -y, obs. ff. HEIR, AERIE.

Ayrshire (ē³·ɹʃəɹ), *a.* and *sb.* 1856. A breed of horned cattle named from the shire of Ayr, and esteemed for dairy farming.

Azalea (ăzē¹·liă). Pl. **-as.** 1753. [a. mod. L. (Linn.), a. Gr. ἀζαλέα, adj. fem. 'dry'.] *Bot.* A genus of shrubby plants (N.O. *Ericaceæ*), growing in sandy soil, and blooming profusely, with showy and mostly fragrant flowers. The one British species (*A. procumbens*) is by some made a distinct genus, *Loiseleuria*.

Azarole (æ·zărōᵘl). 1658. [a. F. *azerole*, ad. (ult.) Arab.] The fruit of the Neapolitan Medlar, a species of Hawthorn (*Cratægus azarolus*); also, the tree itself, occ. called, after Fr., **Azerolier.**

Azedarac (ăze·dăræk). 1753. [a. Fr., a. Pers.] *Bot.* 1. A lofty tree (*Melia Azedarach*), with bipinnate leaves, a native of the East Indies; called also Bead-tree, Pride of India, False Sycamore, and Holy-tree. 2. *Pharm.* The bark of the root of this tree, used in medicine 1853.

†A·zimene, *a.* 1647. *Astrol.* Weak and lame degrees –1819.

Azimuth (æ·zimɒþ). ME. [a. F. *azimut*, ad. Arab. *as-sumūt*, f. *as* = *al* the + *sumūt*, pl. of *samt* way. Cf. ZENITH.] 1. An arc of the heavens extending from the zenith to the horizon which it cuts at right angles; the quadrant of a great circle of the sphere passing through the zenith and nadir, called an *azimuth circle*. 2. The angular distance of any such circle from a given limit, *e.g.* a meridian 1626. 3. *transf.* and *fig.* Horizontal angle, or direction; point of the compass 1667.

2. *Magnetic azimuth*: the arc intercepted between the magnetic meridian and the great circle. *A. compass*: a minutely divided mariner's compass, fitted with vertical sights, used for taking the magnetic a. of a heavenly body. *A. dial*: one whose gnomon is perpendicular to the plane of the horizon. *A. mirror*: an instrument placed on the glass cover of a mariner's compass and used for taking azimuths.

Azimuthal (æzimiū·þăl), *a.* 1654. [f. prec.] 1. Of or pertaining to the azimuth; used in taking azimuths. 2. In azimuth, in a horizontal circle.

2. *Azimuthal error* (of a transit instrument): its

deviation in azimuth from the plane of the meridian. Hence **Azimu·thally** *adv.*

Azo- (æ·zo-). *Chem.* Short comb. f. AZOTE, nitrogen. Used **1.** *gen.* of compounds containing nitrogen; **2.** *spec.* of compounds in which nitrogen is substituted for another element; and *particularly*, of compounds derived from the aromatic hydrocarbons, which contain nitrogen combined in a peculiar way, constituting the *azo-* and *diazo-* compounds, or *azo-* derivatives.

1. Azohu·mic, nitrogenized humic (acid); **Azoli·tmin,** the principal colouring matter of litmus; **Azole·ic,** an acid formed by treating oleic with nitric acid. **2. Azopa·raffins,** formed from the paraffins by substituting 1 atom of nitrogen for 3 of hydrogen: as *azo-methane*, etc.; **Azobenzene, azotoluene.**

Azoic (ăzōu·ik), *a.* 1854. [f. Gr. ἄζωος (f. ἀ + ζωή) + -IC.] Having no trace of life; in *Geol.*, Containing no organic remains, as *Azoic period.*

Azonic (ăzǫ·nik), *a.* 1795. [a. Gr. ἀζωνικός (f. ἀ + ζώνη) + -IC.] Not confined to a zone.

Azoology (æ:zoǫ·lŏdʒi). 1817. [f. Gr. ἄζωος + -λογία.] The science of inanimate nature.

Azorite (æ·zorəit). 1868. [f. *Azores* + ITE.] *Min.* A white mineral crystallizing in minute octahedrons, occurring in albitic rock.

Azote (æ·zōᵘt). 1791. [a. F., irreg. f. Gr. ἀ- 14 + ζώειν to live, ζωή life.] Lavoisier's name for *nitrogen*, as unable to support life.

Hence: †**A·zotane,** Davy's name for Chloride of Nitrogen. **A·zotine,** a residuum of melted wool, rich in nitrogen, resulting from the action of superheated steam on cotton and woollen rags. †**A·zotite,** a nitrite. †**Azo·tous** *a.* nitrous. †**Azo·turet,** a nitride. **Azoto·meter,** an apparatus for measuring nitrogen.

A·zoth. 1477. [Arab. *az-zāūq.*] *Alch.* **a.** Mercury. **b.** The universal remedy of Paracelsus.

Azotic (ăzǫ·tik), *a.* 1791. [f. AZOTE.] *Chem.* Of, pertaining to, or chemically compounded with, azote. †*A. air* or *gas*: nitrogen. †*A. acid*: nitric acid. *fig.* Deadening.

Azotize (æ·zŏtəiz), *v.* 1804. [f. as prec. + -IZE.] To nitrogenize; *hence*, to deprive of oxygen. **A·zotized** *ppl. a.* nitrogenous.

Aztec (æ·ztek). 1787. An Indian of the Nahuatian tribe, which founded the empire of Mexico.

‖**Azulejo** (aþulē·ho). 1854. [Sp., f. *azul* blue.] A kind of Dutch glazed tile painted in colours.

A·zuline. 1864. [? f. as prec. + -INE.] A shade of blue.

Azure (æ·ʒəɹ, ē¹·ʒiŭɹ). ME. [a. OF. *azur*, ad. (ult.) Pers. *lājward, lāzhward*, lapis lazuli. The *l-* is dropped, as if it were the article.] **A.** *sb.* **1.** The precious stone lapis lazuli. **2.** A bright blue pigment or dye; *ellipt.* a fabric dyed of this colour ME. **3.** *Her.* Blue, represented in engravings by horizontal lines ME. **4.** The clear blue of the unclouded sky 1481. **5.** The unclouded vault of heaven 1667.

1. A broche of golde and asure CHAUCER. **4.** The colour of Asure lyke unto the heuen whan it is pure and clere CAXTON. **5.** Not like those steps On Heavens A. MILT. *P. L.* I. 297.

B. *adj.* **1.** *Her.* Blue 1450. **2.** Coloured like the unclouded (southern) sky; cerulean 1505. **3.** *fig.* Clear, cloudless 1827.

2. Her a. veins SHAKS. He rides his a. Carr DRYDEN. *Comb.*: **a.-spar,** lazulite; **-stone,** the lapis lazuli or lazulite. Hence **A·zure** *v.* to dye, or colour a. vars. **Azu·rean** *a.* (*rare*); **A·zured** *ppl. a.* (*arch.*). **Azu·reous** *a.* (*rare*). †**A·zurn** *a.* MILT.

Azurine (æ̆·ziŭrəin,-in). 1600. [a. F. *azurin*; see -INE[1].] **1.** *adj.* Blue; pale blue, inclining to grey (Littré). **2.** *sb.* The blue Roach (*Leuciscus cæruleus*) 1832.

Azurite (æ·ziŭrəit). 1868. [f. AZURE + -ITE.] *Min.* Blue carbonate of copper, an ore allied to malachite.

Azury (æ·ʒəri, ē¹·ʒiŭri), *a.* 1600. [f. as prec. + -Y[1]; cf. F. *azuré.*] Blue, bluish. ? Hence †**A·zury** *sb.* azure hue or colour.

Azygos, -ous (æ·zigəs). 1646. [(a. or) f. Gr. ἄζυγος, f. ἀ + ζυγόν; see -OUS.] **1.** *adj.* Fellowless, unpaired; used techn. of organic parts not existing in pairs. **2.** *sb.* [sc. *organic part.*] Hence **A·zygously** *adv.* singly.

Azyme (æ·zim, -əim). 1582. [ad. L., a. Gr. ἄζυμος, -μα, f. ἀ + ζύμη.] The Jewish passover cake of unleavened bread; also, in *pl.* the feast of unleavened bread. Hence **A·zymous** *a.* unleavened.

Azymite (æ·ziməit). 1727. [ad. L. *azymita*, ad. Gr. ἀζυμίτης, f. ἄζυμος; see prec.] One who administers the Eucharist with unleavened bread; a name given by the Gr. Ch. to the Roman Catholics and others.

B

B (bī). The second letter of the Roman alphabet, corresponding to, and in form derived from, the Gr. *Beta*, and Heb. *Beth*; repr. the sonant labial mute, or lip-voice stop consonant. *Pl.* Bees, B's, *Bs.*

II. Used to indicate serial order, with the value of *second*, as (b., *b.*) the left-hand page or *verso* of a leaf, the second column of a page. Also *spec.*: **1.** *Mus.*: In England the 7th note of the scale of C major, called H in Germany, where B means the English B flat (=B♭, Fr. *B rond*), a semitone lower than B. **2.** In *Law*, etc., B is put for a second or another person or thing. **3.** *Alg.* (see A. II).

III. *Abbreviations.* **1.** B. (*Mus.*) Bass, Basso. B. (*Chem.*) Boron. b., *b.*, born. B. (in *Academical degrees*) Bachelor, or L. *baccalaureus*, as B.A. (or A.B.) Bachelor of Arts, etc. B. (b.) in *Cricket* 'Byes', b. bowled by. B.B.C. British Broadcasting Corporation (*orig.* Company); B.C. Before Christ; B. and S. Brandy-and-soda; B.V. (M.), the Blessed Virgin (Mary), (*Beata Virgo Maria*).

2. *B.* or *B. flat*), joc. for *bug* (*Cimex lectularius*).

†**Ba,** *v. rare.* ME. [Cf. OF. *baer, beer*, to gape.] To kiss, as a child -1529.

Baa (bā), *v.* 1586. [Echoic.] To bleat.

He's a Lambe indeed, that baes like a Beare *Cor.* II. i. 12. Hence **Baa** *sb.* the bleat of a sheep or lamb. **Baa-lamb,** a lamb (nursery-word).

‖**Baal** (bē¹·ăl). Pl. **Baalim.** ME. [Heb. *ba'al* lord.] The chief male deity of the Phœnician and Canaanitish nations; *transf.* false god.

Peor and Baalim Forsake their temples dim MILT. Hence **Ba·alish** *a.* of or belonging to B.; idolatrous. **Ba·alism,** the worship of B.; idolatry. **Ba·alist,** a worshipper of B.; *transf.* a worshipper of false gods or idols; var. **Ba·alite** *a.* (All applied in 17th c. to the R.C. worship.)

Bab, earlier f. BABE (now dial.).

Bab, dial. f. BOB, a bait for eels.

Ba·ba[1], var. of *pa·pa*, papa.

‖**Ba·ba**[2]. 1864. [Fr.] A light plum-cake.

Ba·bacoote. 1880. [ad. Malagasy.] A species of lemur (*Lichanotus brevicaudatus*).

Babbie, babby, Sc. and n. dial. f. BABY.

Ba·bbit, *v.* 1875. [See next.] To line with Babbit-metal. Hence **Ba·bbiting,** a fitting of Babbit-metal.

Babbit-metal. 1875. [Also *Babbit's metal*; f. inventor's name.] A soft alloy of tin, antimony, and copper, used in journal-bearings, etc., to diminish friction.

Babblative (bæ·blătiv). 1583. [f. BABBLE *v.* + -ATIVE.] Given to babbling.

Babble (bæ·b'l), *v.* ME. [prob. f. the infantile *ba, ba* (with freq. suffix *-le*); cf. *prattle*, and F. *babiller*. Perh. affected in sense by *Babel.*] **1.** *intr.* To utter inarticulate or indistinct sounds, like a child. **2.** To talk childishly, to prattle; to talk incoherently, or foolishly; to utter meaningless words ME. **3.** To talk excessively; to chatter 1510. Also *transf.* of streams, birds, hounds, etc. **4.** *trans.* To utter with meaningless iteration; to prate ME. **5.** To reveal by chattering. Cf. *blab.* 1562.

2 A long tongu'd babling Gossip *Tit. A.* IV. ii. 150. **3.** Echo babling by the mountain's side SIR W. JONES. **5.** Who heareth all, And all bableth 1562. Hence **Ba·bblement,** †**Ba·blery,** idle or unseasonable chatter. **Ba·bblingly** *adv.* **Ba·bblish** *a.* full of idle talk; var. **Ba·bbly.**

Babble (bæ·b'l), *sb.* 1460. [f. the vb. Cf. F. *babil.*] **1.** Inarticulate speech, as of infants 1688. **2.** Idle, foolish, or unseasonable talk 1460. **3.** Confused murmur, as of a stream 1616.

1. The babes, their b. TENNYSON. **3.** This Sack has fill'd my head so full of bables, I am almost mad BEAUM. & FL.

Babbler (bæ·bləɹ). 1530. [f. the vb.] **1.** A foolish or idle talker, a chatterer. **2.** A prating gossip; a blabber 1580. **3.** A hound that gives tongue too freely 1732. **4.** Name for the Long-legged Thrush, on account of its note 1839.

2. For who will open himselfe to a Blab or a B. BACON. var. †**Ba·belard.**

Babe (bē¹b). ME. [? short for †*baban.* Superseded in ordinary use by BABY. *Babe*, not *baby*, is used in the Bible.] **1.** An infant. †**2.** =BABY *sb.* 2. -1595. **3.** *fig.* =BABY *sb.* 5. 1526.

3. *Babes in Christ*: newly-made converts to Christianity. Even babes in Christ are in a sense perfect WESLEY. Hence **Ba·behood,** infancy. **Ba·belet,** a tiny babe. †**Ba·beship. Ba·bish** *a.* infantile, silly (*arch.*). †**Ba·bishly** *adv.* †**Ba·bishness.**

Babel (bē¹·bĕl). ME. [a. Heb. *bābel*, Babylon; assoc. in Genesis with the idea of 'confusion'. It has no known Semitic root.] **1.** The city and tower, described in *Gen.* xi, where the confusion of tongues took place; hence **a.** a lofty structure; **b.** a visionary scheme. **2.** A scene of confusion; a confused assemblage 1625. **3.** A confused turbulent medley of sounds 1529.

1. Therfor was callid the name of it B., for there was confoundid the lippe of all the erthe WYCLIF *Gen.* xi. 9. **2** The whole b. of sectaries joined against the church SWIFT. Hence **Ba·beldom,** noisy confusion. †**Ba·belish** *a.* noisily confused. **Ba·belism,** noisy confusion of speech; strange utterance. **Ba·belize** *v.* to make a b. of.

Ba·bery. ME. [? orig. f. *babwynrie*, BABOONERY; in later use, f. BABE, BABY *sb.* 4.] Grotesque ornamentation in architecture and books; grotesque absurdity.

‖**Babillard** (babilʸā·r, bæ·bilaɹd). 1802. [F., f. *babiller*; cf. BABBLER 4.] The CHATTERER, a small bird.

Babingtonite (bæ·biŋtŏnəit). 1837. [f. Dr. *Babington.*] *Min.* A bisilicate of iron and lime, with manganese and magnesia, found in greenish-black crystals in Norway, and elsewhere.

†**Ba·bion.** 1599. [a. F., formed on 'a radicle *bab* found in *babiole*' (Littré). App. identified in Eng. with *baboon.*] A baboon; an ape; applied to persons -1624.

Babiroussa, -russa (bābirŭ·să). 1696. [f. Malay *bābi* hog + *rūsa* deer.] *Zool.* A species of wild hog (*Babirussa alfurus*) found in the islands of Eastern Asia. The upper canine teeth, in the male, pierce the lip and grow upwards and backwards like horns. Also called Hog-deer, Indian Hog, Horned Hog.

†**Ba·bish,** *v.* 1460. [? f. OF. *baubiss-, baubir*; perh. influenced by *babish* adj.] To scoff at, scorn; to treat as mere children -1549.

Bable, old sp. of BABBLE.

‖**Baboo** (bā·bu). 1782. [Hindi.] *orig.* = our *Mr.* or *Esquire*; hence, A native Hindoo gentleman; also, a native clerk who writes English; occas. used of a Bengali, with a superficial English education.

Baboon (băbŭ·n). ME. [a. F. *babuin*, mod. *babouin*, or ad. med.L. *babewynus.* Of unknown origin.] †**1.** A grotesque figure (? of a *baboon* in sense 2) used in architecture, etc. -1592. **2.** A member of one of the divisions of the *Simiadæ* or Monkeys, distinguished by a long dog-like snout, large canine teeth or tusks, capacious cheek-pouches, and naked callosities on the buttocks; they are mostly inhabitants of Africa ME. **3.** *fig.*; cf. *ape* 1500.

2. His forehead low as that of a b. MACAULAY. *Comb.* **b.-bird,** *Threnœdus Militaris*, with a note like that of a b. Hence **Baboo·nery,** a colony of baboons (cf. *rookery*); baboonish condition, or behaviour. **Baboo·nish** *a.* baboon-like.

‖**Babouche** (băbŭ·ʃ). 1695. [a. F., ad. (ult.) Pers., f. *pā* foot + *pōsh* covering.] A Turkish or oriental slipper.

‖**Babui·na.** 1882. [fem. of mod.L. *babuinus*, = F. *babouine.*] A female baboon.

Baby (bē¹·bi), *sb.* ME. [Dim. of BABE, which it has superseded in familiar use.] **1.** An infant of either sex. (Formerly = *child*; now, usually, an infant 'in arms'.). †**2.** A doll, puppet -1721. †**3.** The small image of oneself reflected in the pupil of another's eye; hence, *to look babies* -1682. **4.** *pl.* Pictures in books: cf. BABERY. Still in *n. dial.* 1598. Also *fig.*

Comb. **1.** passing into *adj.* = young; small or diminutive of its kind, as *b. car, grand, jib* 1873. **2. b.-farmer,** one who takes infants to nurse for payment, whence *baby-farming*, etc.; **-house,** a doll's house; **-jumper,** a frame suspended by an elastic attachment, so that a young child secured in it may exercise its limbs; **-like** *a.* infantile; *adv.* as a baby does. Hence **Ba·byhood,** the period or condition of infancy; babies collectively; babyishness. So **Ba·bydom** (*rare*). **Ba·byish** *a.* childish, simple, silly. **Ba·byish-ly** *adv.*, **-ness. Ba·byism,** babyhood; babyishness; babyish phrase or action. **Babyo·latry** (*nonce-wd.*).

baby-worship. Ba·byship, *babyhood*; the personality of a baby.

Baby (bē¹·bi), *v.* 1742. [f. prec.] To treat as a baby.

Babylon (bæ·bilən), *sb.* ME. [a. L., Gr. Βαβυλών, Heb. *Bābel*.] The capital of the Chaldee Empire; also, the mystical Babylon of the Apocalypse; whence, used polemically of the papal power, and rhetorically of any great and luxurious city.

The approach.. to mighty Babylon [= London] BYRON. Hence **Babylo·nic** *a.* = BABYLONIAN *a.* †**Babylo·nical** *a.* of or belonging to B.; hence *fig.* **a.** Romish, popish; **b.** Babel-like, tumultuous. †**Babylo·nically** *adv.* **Ba·bylonism**, †*fig.* Popery; a Babylonian word or phrase. **Ba·bylonize** *v.* to make Babylonian.

Babylonian (bæbilōᵘ·niăn). 1564. [f. L., Gr. Βαβυλώνιος.] **1.** *adj.* Of or belonging to Babylon; hence *fig.* **a.** huge; †**b.** popish; **c.** (cf. *Rev.* xvii. 4) scarlet. **2.** *sb.* An inhabitant of Babylon; hence *fig.* †**a.** papist; **b.** astrologer.

Babylonish (bæbilōᵘ·niʃ), *a.* 1535. **1.** Of, belonging to, or made at Babylon. **2.** *fig.* †**a.** Popish; **b.** Babel-like, confused in language.

1. A costly Babilonish garment *Josh.* vii. 21. 2. A B. dialect, Which learned pedants much affect BUTLER.

‖**Bac** (bæk). 1672. [Fr.] **1.** A flat-bottomed French ferry-boat; a ferry. **2.** In *Brewing* and *Distilling*; see BACK *sb.*[2]

‖**Bacalao** (bækălā·o). 1555. [a. Sp. *bacallao* cod-fish.] Cod-fish.

Baccalaurean (bækălǭ·rĭăn), *a.* 1845. [f. med.L. *baccalaureus* + -AN.] Befitting a bachelor.

Baccalaureate (bækălǭ·rĭ,ĕt). 1625. [ad. med.L. *baccalaureatus*, f. as prec.] **1.** The University degree of bachelor. **2.** = BACHELOR 1696. **3.** quasi-*adj.* in *B. sermon*: a farewell discourse to a graduating class. (U.S.) 1864.

‖**Baccara, -at** (bakără). 1866. [a. F.] A game at cards played for money between a banker and punters.

Baccate (bæ·ke¹t), *a.* 1830. [ad. L. *baccatus*.] **1.** Bearing berries; bacciferous 1836. **2.** Berry-like 1830. So **Ba·ccated** *ppl. a.* †set with pearls; berry-bearing.

Bacchanal (bæ·kănăl). 1536. [ad. L. *bacchanalis*, also *bacca-*, *baca-*, f. *Bacchus*, Gr. Βάκχος.] **A.** *adj.* **1.** Of or pertaining to Bacchus or his worship 1550. **2.** Riotously drunken, roystering 1711.

B. *sb.* **1.** A devotee of Bacchus; a Bacchant or Bacchante 1590. **2.** A drunken reveller 1812. **3.** (Usu. *pl.*) A festival in honour of Bacchus. [L. *Bacchanalia*.] 1616. **4.** An orgy 1536. **5.** A dance or song in honour of Bacchus 1606. **6.** A scene of revelry painted or sculptured 1753.

1. The riot of the tipsie Bachanals *Mids. N.* v. i. 48. 4. At their debauches and bacchanals BURKE. 5. Shall we daunce now the Egyptian Backenals SHAKS.

‖**Bacchanalia** (bækănē¹·liă), *sb. pl.* 1633. [L.; see prec. Formerly treated in Eng. as sing., with pl. *-as*.] **1.** The festival held in honour of Bacchus 1753. **2.** Drunken revelry; an orgy 1633. †**3.** A drinking-song; cf. BACCHANAL *sb.* 5. 1651. †**4.** = BACCHANAL 6. 1662.

Bacchanalian (bækănē¹·liăn), *a.* (*sb.*) 1565. [f. L. *bacchanalis*, BACCHANAL + -AN.] **1.** Of, connected with, or relating to Bacchanals 1622. **2.** Marked by, connected with, or given to drunken revelry 1565. **3.** *sb.* A drunken reveller, a tippler 1617.

2. B. writers JOHNSON, tones H. STANLEY. Hence **Bacchana·lianism**, **Ba·cchanalism**, b. practices, drunken revelry. **Bacchana·lianly** *adv.*

Bacchanalize (bæ·kănăləiz), *v.* 1656. [a. F. *bacchanaliser*; see BACCHANAL and -IZE.] **1.** *intr.* To indulge in revelry. **2.** *trans.* To turn into drunken revelry.

Bacchant (bæ·kănt). 1699. [ad. L. *Bacchantem*, sb. (in L. fem. only), f. *bacchari*, ad. Gr. βακχά-ειν.] **1.** *sb.* A priest, priestess, or votary of Bacchus; *hence*, a drunken reveller. **2.** *adj.* Bacchus-worshipping, wine-loving 1800. Hence **Baccha·ntic** *a.* of or pertaining to the bacchants.

Bacchante (băka·nt, bæ·kănt, băkæ·ntī). 1797. [a. F. *bacchante*, ad. L. *Bacchantem*; see prec. The first pronunc. is after Fr.; the third after It., favoured by the frequent pl. (of both genders) *Bacchantes* (-æ·ntīz) after L.] **1.** *sb.* A priestess or female votary of Bacchus. **2.** *attrib.* as *adj.*; cf. BACCHANT 1821.

Bacchar, baccar (bæ·kăɹ). 1551. [a. L. *bacc(h)ar*, *bacc(h)aris* (also used), a. Gr. βάκκαρις, βάκχαρις ('a Lydian wd.').] *Bot.* A plant variously identified. (*Baccharis* is now applied to an American genus of *Compositæ*.)

Baccharis.. in englishe sage of hierusalem TURNER.

Bacchic (bæ·kik), *a.* 1669. [ad. L. *Bacchicus*, a. Gr.] **1.** Of or pertaining to Bacchus or his worship. **2.** Frenzied like a votary of Bacchus; riotously drunken, jovial 1699. †**3.** (*absol.* as) *sb.* A drinking-song 1676. †**Ba·cchical** *a.*

‖**Bacchius** (băkəi·ɒs). 1589. [L., a. Gr. Βακχεῖος (sc. πούς).] A metrical foot of three syllables, one short and two long.

‖**Bacchus** (bæ·kɒs). 1496. [L., a. Gr. Βάκχος.] The god of wine; *hence*, wine.

Bacciferous (bæksi·fĕrəs), *a.* 1656. [f. L. *baccifer*, f. *bacca*; see -FER and -OUS.] Berry-bearing, producing berries.

Bacciform (bæ·ksifǭɹm), *a.* 1839. [ad. mod. L. *bacciformis*; see -FORM.] Berry-shaped.

Baccivorous (bæksi·vŏrəs), *a.* 1661. [f. L. *bacca* + *-vorus* + -OUS.] Berry-eating.

Baccy (bæ·ki). 1833. *colloq.* f. *bacca*, *bacco*, clipped forms of TOBACCO; see -Y[6].

Bacharach (ba·χăraχ, bæ·kăræk). 1620. A town on the Rhine giving its name to a wine formerly esteemed. var. **Back-rac(k**.

†**Bache.** OE. [?] The vale of a stream or rivulet –1494.

Bachelor (bæ·tʃĕləɹ). ME. [a. OF. *bacheler* :—L. type **baccalaris*, prob. conn. w. *baccalaria*, ? a grazing farm, f. *bacca* for *vacca*; thus *baccalarius* would be one employed on it.] **1.** A young knight who followed the banner of another; a novice in arms. [Hence the suggested derivation from *Bas Chevalier*.] Hence, **b.** *Knight Bachelor*, a simple knight; the full title of a gentleman who has been knighted 1609. †**2.** A junior member, or 'yeoman', of a trade-guild, or City Company –1809. **3.** A man or woman who has taken the first degree at a university. [In this sense latinized as *baccalarius*, and altered by a pun to *baccalaureus*.] ME. **4.** An unmarried man (of marriageable age) ME. †**5.** A single woman. B. JONS.

4. His wife!..I haue heard him sweare he was a bachiler DEKKER.

Comb. **Bachelor's** or **Bachelors' Buttons**: *Herb.* any of various flowers of round or button-like form; orig. the double variety of *Ranunculus acris*; also the Tansy.

Hence **Ba·chelordom**, the estate or body of bachelors collectively. **Ba·chelorhood**, the state or quality of a b. **Ba·chelori·sm**, a habit or peculiarity of a b. **Ba·chelorly** *a.* bachelor-like.

Ba·chelorshi·p. 1591. **1.** The state of being a bachelor, *i. e.* unmarried. †**2.** The state or position of a knight bachelor 1611. **3.** The standing of a Bachelor of Arts, etc. 1656.

†**Ba·chelry.** ME. [a. OF. *bachelerie*, f. *bacheler*; see BACHELOR.] **1.** The quality of a young knight; prowess. **2.** Bachelors collectively: **a.** Young knights as a class. (Cf. *chivalry*.) –1656. **b.** A body of unmarried men –1615.

Bacillary (bæ·silări), *a.* 1865. [ad. mod. L. *bacillarius*, f. L. *bacillus* little rod. Cf. F. *bacillaire*.] Of, pertaining to, or consisting of little rods. So **Baci·lliform** *a.* rod-shaped.

‖**Bacillus** (băsi·lɒs). Pl. **bacilli.** 1883. [late L. (in Isidore), dim. of *baculus*, var. of *baculum*.] *Nat. Hist.* A genus of *Schizomycetæ*, microscopic vegetable organisms of the lowest grade among what were called *Infusoria*. Dist. from *Bacterium* by its larger size and mode of reproduction. First described by Müller *ante* 1850.

Bacin, bacinet, obs. ff. BASIN, BASINET.

Back (bæk), *sb.*[1] [Com. Teut.: OE. *bæc* (neut.) :—OTeut. **bako-(m)*. Cf. RIDGE.] **I.** **1.** *properly*. The convex surface of the body of man and vertebrated animals which is adjacent to the spinal axis, and opposite to the belly. It extends from the neck and shoulders to the extremity of the backbone. **2. a.** In man, the hinder surface of the body, that which is turned upon those who are left behind OE. **b.** that part of the body which is the special recipient of clothing ME. **c.** the part which bears burdens OE. **d.** In animals, the upper surface opposite to that on which they move or rest ME.

2. The Army broken, And but the backes of Britaines to be seen *Cymb.* v. iii. 6. Borrow..of thy backe and thi belly LATIMER. Wrongs more then our backe can beare *Tit. A.* IV. iii. 48.

II. *transf.* **1.** That side or surface of any object which is opposite to the face or front, or side approached or contemplated; *e.g.* the convex side of the hand; the under side of a leaf; the convex part of a book; the thick edge of a knife ME. **2.** The side of any object away from the spectator, the other or farther side 1645.

1. He put his name at the b. of a bill SHERIDAN. 2. Passing by the b. of the Goodwin Sand 1704.

III. Parts of things having relation, or analogous in position, to the back. †**1.** *pl.* Clothes –ME. †**2.** A back-plate –1695. Also *fig.* **3.** The hind part; *e.g.* of a garment, a chair, etc. 1530. **4.** The rear of an armed force (*arch.*) 1597. †**5.** A following; backing –1662.

3. A chair without a b. 1670. 4. He leaues his backe vnarm'd 2 *Hen. IV*, I. iii. 79.

IV. **1.** *fig.* The surface of a river, the waves, etc., as bearing burdens 1610. **2.** The ridge of a hill, †of the nose 1615. **3.** The keel and kelson of a ship 1692.

1. I saw him beate the surges vnder him, And ride vpon their backes *Temp.* II. i. 115. 3. A..ship with her b. broken 1883.

Phrases: **a.** With preps. *At the b. of*: behind, close behind, as in supporting, pursuing, etc. *Behind the b. of*: (*emphatic for*) behind; in the absence of **b.** With verbs. *To break the b. of*: (*fig.*) to overburden; to finish the hardest part of. *To put* or *set up the b.*: to arch it as angry cats do; to anger. *To turn the b.*: to flee; *to turn the b. upon*: to abandon. *To be* or *lie on one's b.*: to be laid up, to be afflicted.

attrib.: **ba·ckache**, pain in the back 1601.

Back (bæk), *sb.*[2] 1682. [a. Du. *bak* trough, a. F. *bac* (see BAC).] A tub, trough, vat; *esp.* as used by brewers, etc.

Back (bæk), *a.* 1490. [BACK *sb.*[1] used attrib.; also partly BACK *adv.* used ellipt.; cf. BACK-.] **1.** Situated at the back, behind, or away from the front; remote, as in *b. blocks* (Australia), *settlement*; mean, obscure, as in *b. slum*. (¶The superl. BACKMOST is still in use.) **2.** In arrear; behindhand 1525. **3.** Reversed, as in *b. current*, *b. smoke* 1857.

Back (bæk), *v.* ME. [f. BACK *sb.*[1]] **1.** To cover the back; to put a back to 1793; to form the back of 1826. **2.** (Cf. BACK *sb.*[1]) To support physically, materially (*esp.* by a bet), or morally 1548; in *Sporting*, of dogs: To follow the lead of a dog that points 1860. **3.** To mount, ride on (a horse) 1592. **4.** To write at the back of (a bill, cheque, etc.) 1768; to print on the back. **5.** *trans.* To set, lay, or incline back; *esp.* by reversing the action; as, to back a boat, a locomotive engine, etc. 1707. **6.** *intr.* To move back, or in the reverse direction, as the wind 1486. **7.** To lie with the back *on* 1891.

1. To b. a book (*mod.*). The chalk cliffs which b. the beach HUXLEY. 2. A troup of Demi-lances to b. them 1548. Phr. *To b. an anchor, rope*, or *chain*: to reinforce with another. Which Godly course Augustine backeth 1612. *To b. a horse* 1699. *To b. the field*: to bet on the rest of the horses, against the favourite. To b. one's opinion with a wager BYRON. Phr. *To b. up*: to support or second; esp. in *Cricket*, of a fielder or batsman. 5. *To b. a sail, a yard*: to lay it aback so that the wind may retard the ship. Phr. *To b. the oars*. 6. Phr. *To b. out*: to move out backwards without turning; *fig.* to retreat out of a difficulty. *To b. down*, to descend as one does from a ladder. Also *fig.*

Back (bæk), *adv.* ME. [Aphet. f. ABACK, OE. *on bæc* = into or in the rear.] **1.** Toward the rear (often with the vb. omitted); away from the front, or from the actual or ordinary position ME. **2.** Away from an engagement or undertaking 1783. **3.** Backward in time 1711. **4.** In the reverse direction, so as to return to a former place, or condition 1535; in reversal of action or change of any kind (often with AGAIN) 1607. Also *ellipt.* **5.** In return, requital, retaliation 1599. **6.** At a point or distance behind ME. **7.** In a state of check 1535. **8.** In time past, ago 1796. **9.** Behindhand, in arrear 1875.

1. B. with that leg 1590. B., beardless boy SCOTT. The angel of the Lord rolled b. the stone *Matt.* xxviii. 2. To force b. a bolt (*mod.*). 2. To go b. from one's word MACAULAY. 3. B. to the days of Solomon STEELE. 4. The whole country fell b. into heathenism FREEMAN. *ellipt.* To be b. = Fr. *être de retour*. 5. To

answer b. (*mod.*). Hence *b.-answer, -chat, -talk*, implying rudeness or insolence. 7. The Lord hath kept thee b. from honour *Numb.* xxiv. 11. 8. Dug up, a few years b. SOUTHEY.

Phrases. *B. and forth*: backwards and forwards, to and fro. *Back of*: back from, behind. (In U.S.)

Back-, *in comb.* is used in many relations, substantive, adjective, and adverbial (rarely verbal), and the combs. are usually self-explanatory. The use of the hyphen is often optional, especially when *back* can be viewed as an adj.

Special Combs.: **b.-bar**, a bar in the chimney to hang a vessel on; **-casing** *Mining*, a temporary shaft-lining of bricks, in front of which the permanent lining is built; **-chain**, a chain that passes over a cart-saddle to support the shafts of a cart; **-draught**, a draught of air backward, a hood for producing this in a fire; **-flap, -fold** (= *back-shutter*); **-hair**, the long hair at the back of a woman's head; **-lining**, in *Archit.*, the piece of a sash-frame parallel to the pulley-piece and next to the jamb on either side; **-links**, the links in a parallel motion which connect the air-pump rod to the beam; **-painting**, the method of painting mezzotinto prints, pasted on glass, with oil colours; **-pater-noster**, the Lord's Prayer repeated backwards as a charm, *fig.* a muttered curse; **-pressure**, in the steam-engine, the resistance of the atmosphere or waste-steam of the piston; **-rest**, a guide attached to the slide-rest of a turning-lathe, to steady the work; **-rope** (of a horse) = BACKBAND; *Naut.*, one leading inboard from the martingale; **-shift**, in *Coal-Mining*, the second shift or set of hewers for the day; **-shutter**, the part of a shutter which folds up behind; **-stop**, in *Cricket* = LONG-STOP; **-sweep**, in *Shipbuilding*, that which forms the hollow of the top-timber; **-swimmer**, the hemipterous insect *Notonecta*; **-tack** (*Sc. Law*), a lease of land given by the mortgagee of it to the mortgagor on condition of payment of rent till redeemed; **†-timber** (*joc.* for) clothing; **†-trick**, ? a caper backwards in dancing (*Twel. N.* I. iii. 131); **-word** (in *Lancs.*), withdrawal from a promise or from an accepted invitation, also *dial.* a rude answer; **-wort** (*Herb.*), old name for the Comfrey (*Symphytum officinale*).

†Backare, baccare, *interj. phr.* 1553. [perh. joc. f. BACK *adv.* + *-are*, L. inf. ending.] Back! give place! *Tam. Shr.* II. i. 72.

Backband (bæ·kbænd). 1523 [f. BACK *sb.* + BAND.] A broad leather strap, or iron chain, passing over a cart-saddle, and serving to support the shafts.

†Ba·ckbear, *sb.* 1598. [f. BACK *sb.*[1] 2 c + BEAR *v.*] In *Forest Laws*: The act of carrying on the back venison killed illegally. -1667.

†Ba·ck-berend, *adj.* (*pr. pple.*) [OE. *bæc-berende*, f. *bæc* + *beran*; see prec.] Bearing on the back: long used as a law-term to describe a thief caught thus carrying off stolen property.

Backbite (bæ·kbəit), *v.* ME. [f. BACK *adv.* + BITE *v.*] To detract from the character of, to traduce, speak ill of. Also *absol.* or *intr.*

People will b. one another to any extent rather than not be amused HELPS. Hence **Ba·ckbi·ter**, a secret calumniator.

†Ba·ckblow. 1642. [f. BACK *sb.*[1] and *adv.* + BLOW *sb.*] A blow struck at the back or from behind. Also *fig.* (Cf. AFTER-CLAP.)

fig. So many back-blows of fortune 1649.

Back-board (bæ·kbōᵊɹd). OE. [f. BACK *sb.*[1]] †1. = LARBOARD. Only in OE. 2. A board placed at, or forming, the back of anything, *e.g.* of a cart 1761. 3. A board attached to the rim of a water-wheel, to prevent the water from running off the floats into the interior of the wheel 1864. 4. A board held or strapped across the back to straighten the figure 1794. Hence **Ba·ckboa·rd** *v.* to subject to the use of a b.

Backbone (bæ·kbōᵘn). ME. [f. BACK *sb.*[1] 1 + BONE. Still occas. hyphened.] 1. The vertebral column, the spine. 2. *transf.* A main support or axis, or chief substantial part, *e.g.* the b. of a bicycle 1684. 3. *fig.* The main element; mainstay 1849. 4. Strength of character, stability of purpose, firmness 1865.

1. Phr. *To the backbone*: completely; English to the b. 1864. 2. The Cordilleras, or b. of America TYLOR. 3. The b. of our subject EARLE. 4. A character destitute of b. 1865.

Ba·ckcast, *sb. n. dial.* 1818. [f. BACK *adv.* + CAST *sb.*] A throw back; a reverse.

Ba·ck-cast, *ppl. a.* 1580. [f. BACK *adv.* + CAST *pple.*] Cast backwards.

Back-door (bæ·k₁dōᵊɹ). 1530. [f. BACK *a.* + DOOR.] 1. A door at the back of a building, etc.; a secondary or private entrance. 2. *fig.*; also *attrib.* = Unworthily secret 1611.

2. The backe doore.. Of the vnguarded hearts SHAKS.

Backed (bækt). ME. [f. BACK *sb.* and *v.*] 1. *adj.* Having a back, background, or backing; *esp.* in *comb.*, as *broad-backed.* 2. *pple.* and *a.* Supported at the back, etc. (See the vb.) 1589.

Backen (bæ·k'n), *v.* 1649. [f. BACK; cf. *lessen.*] To put, keep, or throw back; to retard. Now *rare.* †2. *intr.* To draw back 1748.

Back-end (bæ·k₁e·nd). 1617. [f. BACK *a.* + END. Cf. FORE-END.] 1. The hinder of two ends. 2. The later part of a season; (*absol.*) of the year: The late autumn 1820.

Backer (bæ·kəɹ), *sb.* 1583. [f. BACK *v.*] 1. A supporter; *esp.* one who bets on a horse or event, or supports by money or credit. 2. *Archit.* A narrow slate at the back of a broad square one where it begins to get narrow 1823.

†Ba·cker, *a. compar.* 1564. [f. BACK *a.*] Farther back, hinder. So *superl.* **†Ba·ckermost.**

Backet (bæ·kėt). *Sc.* 1789. [a. F. *baquet*, dim. of *bac*, BACK *sb.*[2]] Shallow wooden trough.

Backfall (bæ·kfǭl). 1676. [f. BACK *adv.* and *sb.*] †1. A grace in old English music. 2. A fall on the back in wrestling. Often *fig.* 1838. 3. A lever in the coupler of an organ 1880.

Back-fire (bæ·kfəiᵊɹ), *sb.* 1897. [BACK *adv.*, BACK-.] A premature explosion in the cylinder of a gas or oil engine, tending to drive the piston in a direction reverse to that in which it should travel. Also as *vb.*, and said of the engine. So **Ba·ck-firing** *vbl. sb.*

Back-forma·tion. 1887. [BACK *adv.*] Formation of a seeming root-word from a word which might be (but is not) a derivative of it, as *burgle* from *burglar.*

Backfriend (bæ·kfre:nd). 1472. [f. BACK *sb.* or *adv.*] †1. A pretended friend; an unavowed enemy -1827. 2. A backer 1599.

Backgame (bæ·kgē¹:m). 1718. = next.

Backgammon (bækgæ·mən). 1645. [App. = *back-game, -play* (ME. *gamen*), because the pieces are often obliged to go *back.*] 1. A game played on a board consisting of two tables (usu. hinged together), with draughtsmen whose moves are determined by throws of the dice. 2. *spec.* A victory in which the winner has borne all his men off, before the loser has carried all his men to his own table 1883.

Background (bæ·kgraund). 1672. [f. BACK *a.*] 1. The ground or surface lying behind the objects which occupy the *foreground*; *esp.* as represented in any of the Arts of Design 1752. Also *fig.* 2. Retirement, obscurity 1779.

1. Ranger retires to the b. WYCHERLEY. 2. Keep your madness in the b. SHERIDAN. Hence **Ba·ckground** *v.* to form a b. to. MRS. BROWNING.

Back-hand (bæ·k₁hæ·nd). 1657. [f. BACK *adv.*] A. *sb.* 1. The hand turned backwards in making a stroke, as (at *Tennis*) in taking balls at the left hand, *hence* the left-hand play or court. Hence *fig.* 2. Handwriting with the letters sloped backwards (*mod.*). B. *attrib.* = BACK-HANDED 1695.

Back-handed (bæ·khæ·ndėd), *a.* 1813. [f. the *sb.*] 1. With the back of the hand. 2. Directed backwards, or with the hand or arm crossing the body, as a sword-cut; sloping backwards, as handwriting. 3. *fig.* †a. Backward, remiss; b. Indirect 1817.

3. A back-handed reminder DICKENS. Hence **Back-ha·ndedness.**

Back-hander. 1836. [f. as prec.] 1. A blow with the back of the hand. Also *fig.* 2. An extra glass of wine out of turn, the bottle being passed back 1854.

2. I will take a b., as Clive don't seem to drink THACKERAY.

Backing (bæ·kiŋ), *vbl. sb.* 1596. [f. BACK *v.*] The action of BACK *v.* 1. The action of supporting at the back. 2. The mounting of a horse; the breaking in of a colt to the saddle 1607. 3. Retardation 1649. 4. Motion backward, *esp.* of the wind 1686. 5. *techn.* a. *Printing.* 'Perfecting' a sheet by printing it also on the back. b. *Bookbinding.* Preparing the back with glue, etc. before putting on the cover. 6. That which backs; a body of supporters; that which forms a back or hinder part 1793.

1. Call you that b. of your friends? a plague vpon such b. SHAKS.

Back-lash (bæ·klæʃ). 1863. *Mech.* The jarring reaction or striking back of a wheel or set of wheels in a piece of mechanism, when the motion is not uniform or when sudden pressure is applied. var. **Ba·ck-lashing.**

Back-log (bæ·k₁lǫ·g). 1684. [BACK *a.*] A large log placed at the back of a wood fire to keep it in. Also *fig.* Something in reserve 1883.

Backmost (bæ·kmŏst), *a. superl.* 1782. [f. BACK *a.*; after *foremost*, etc.] Most to the back, hindmost. var. **Ba·ckermost.**

Back-piece (bæ·kpīs). 1586. [f. BACK *sb.* or *a.*] 1. A piece of armour protecting the back. Also *fig.* 2. The piece which forms the back 1838.

Back-plate (bæ·kplē¹t). 1656. [f. as prec.] 1. A plate of armour for the back. 2. A plate placed at or forming the back 1772.

†Ba·ck-ra·cket. 1608. [f. BACK *adv.*] The return of a ball in tennis; *fig.* a 'tu quoque'.

Backs, *sb.* (*pl.*) 1535. *Leather-trade.* The thickest and best-tanned hides.

Back-set (bæ·kset), *sb.* 1721. [f. BACK *adv.*] 1. A setting back; a reverse, relapse. (orig. Sc.) 2. An eddy or counter-current 1882.

Ba·ckse·t, *v.* 1573. [f. as prec. + SET *v.*] †1. To set upon in the rear. 2. (in U.S.) To re-plough in the autumn prairie-land ploughed in the spring 1883.

Ba·ck-se·ttler. 1809. [f. *back-settlement*; see BACK *a.* 1.] One who lives in the back settlements of a colony or new country.

Backsheesh, var. of BAKSHEESH.

Backside. 1489. [f. BACK *a.* Now pronounced as two words, exc. in sense 3.] 1. The hinder or back part; the back, the rear. 2. The back premises; also, the privy. Now *dial.* 1541. 3. (bæ·ksəid). The posteriors or rump 1500. †4. = BACK *sb.* II. 1. -1720. †5. *fig.* The reverse side; the opposite -1695.

5. Just the very b. of Truth CONGREVE.

Backsight (bæ·k₁səi·t). 1860. [f. BACK *adv.*] a. In *Surveying*, a sight or reading taken backwards, or towards the point of starting. b. The sight of a rifle nearer the stock.

Back-slang (bæ·k₁slæ·ŋ). 1860. [f. BACK *adv.*] Slang in which every word is pronounced backwards; as *yynep* for *penny.*

Backslide (bæ·ksləi·d), *v.* 1581. [f. BACK *adv.* + SLIDE *v.*] To *slide back*, in a fig. sense; to fall away, *esp.* in religious faith and practice; to relapse. Hence **Ba·cksli·der**, an apostate.

†Ba·ck-sta·ff. 1627. [f. BACK *sb.*] A quadrant for taking altitudes at sea, so named because the observer turned his back to the sun.

Backstairs (bæ·kstēᵊɹs). 1627. [f. BACK *a.*] 1. Stairs at the back of a house; a secondary staircase 1654. 2. *esp.* The private stairs in a palace, used for other than state visitors 1627; also *fig.* 3. *attrib.* Of, pertaining to, or employing underhand intrigue at court. (Occ. *backstair.*) 1697.

3. A b. influence and clandestine government BURKE.

Backstay (bæ·kstē¹). 1626. [f. BACK *a.* or *sb.*] 1. *Naut.* (often *pl.*) Long ropes, slanting a little abaft, extending from the upper mastheads to the sides of the ship; used to second the shrouds in supporting the masts. Cf. A-STAYS. 2. *gen.* A stay or support at the back; *e.g.* in *Printing*, a leather strap to check the carriage of a printing-press 1864.

Backster (bæ·kstəɹ). 1867. A flat piece of wood or cork, strapped on the feet for walking over loose beach.

Backster, obs. f. BAKER. Hence **†Ba·ckstress**, a female baker.

Back-stitch (bæ·kstitʃ). 1611. [f. BACK *adv.*] A method of sewing in which, for every new stitch, the needle enters behind, and comes out in front of, the end of the previous one. Hence **Backstitch** *v.* to sew thus.

Back-stroke (bæ·k₁strōᵘk). 1674. [f. BACK *adv.*] A stroke in return; a recoil; also, a back-handed stroke.

Back-sword (bæ·k₁sōᵊɹd). *arch.* 1611. [f. BACK *sb.*] 1. A sword with only one cutting edge. 2. A single-stick; *hence* b. fencing exercise with it 1699. 3. A fencer with backsword or single-stick 1672. Hence **Back-swo·rding. Back-swo·rdman.**

†Ba·ck-wa·rd, *sb.* ME. Rear-guard, rear-ward -1580.

Backward (bæ·kwəɹd). ME. [orig. aphet.

f. ABACKWARD; later referred to BACK.] **A.** *adv.* **1.** In the direction of one's back, as with *lean, push*, etc.; **b.** With the face to the rear, as with *go, ride, walk* ME. †**2.** Of position: Toward the back of a place (*arch.*); commonly *back, to, at, the back* –1812. **3.** In the direction which is ordinarily behind one, or from which one is moving (*arch.*); commonly *back, behind* ME. **4.** In the direction from which one has come. (Not properly used of persons or animals.) ME. **5.** In the direction of retreat. (Usu. *back.*) ME. **6.** *fig.* Towards a worse state. (More usu. *back.*) 1583. **7.** Towards or in the past (*arch.*; commonly *back*) 1562. **8.** In the reverse direction or order 1520; *fig.* the wrong way 1552.

3. *To look, turn the head b.* 4. Like as an arowe.. returneth not bacwarde 2 *Esdras* xvi. 16. *B. and forward*: to and fro; also *fig.* 5. Let them be driuen b., and put to shame *Isa.* i. 4. 8. What is Ab speld b. with the horn on his head *L. L. L.* v. i. 50. Phr. *To ring the bells b.*: to ring them beginning with the bass bell, in order to give the alarm, etc.

B. *adj.* [attrib. (often ellipt.) use of the *adv.*] **1.** Directed to the rear 1552. **2.** Directed in the opposite way; of or pertaining to return 1604. **3.** Reversed 1725. †**4.** Perverse, unfavourable –1605. †**5.** Placed towards or at the back –1819. **6.** Turning or hanging back from action; reluctant; shy, bashful 1599. **7.** Behindhand, late; *esp.* of the season or crops 1616. **8.** Reaching into the past 1650.

2. Their b. course *Oth.* I. iii. 38. 6. Perish the man, whose mind is b. now *Hen. V*, IV. iii. 72. 7. A very b. scholar HUME. Hence **Ba·ckward-ly** *adv.*, **-ness.**

C. *sb.* †**1.** *lit.* The hinder part of the body 1627. **2.** *poet.* The past portion (of time) 1610.

2. The dark b. and abisme of Time *Temp.* I. ii. 50.

†**Ba·ckward,** *v.* 1594. [f. the adj.] To put or keep back, retard –1660.

Backwardation (bækwəɹdēⁱ·ʃən). 1850. [f. prec. vb., after *retardation*, etc.] *Stock Exchange.* The percentage paid by a seller of stock for the privilege of postponing delivery till the next account or to any other future day. So †**Backwardiza·tion.**

Backwards (bæ·kwəɹdz). 1513. [f. BACKWARD with advb. gen. *-s.*] **A.** = BACKWARD *adv.* †**B.** = BACKWARD *a.* (*rare*) –1683.

Backwash (bæ·kwǫʃ), sb. 1876. [f. BACK *adv.*] The motion of a receding wave; a backward current.

Ba·ckwash, *v.* 1775. [cf. prec. sb.] **1.** To affect with backwash 1882. **2.** To clean the oil from wool after combing.

Backwater (bæ·kwǭːtəɹ). ME. [f. BACK *a.* or *adv.*] †**1.** Water flowing in from behind –1577. **2.** Water dammed back in its course, or that has overflowed in time of flood 1629. **3.** Water dammed back for any purpose 1792. **4.** A piece of water without current, parallel to a river, and fed from it at the lower end by a backflow 1863. **5.** A creek or arm of the sea parallel to the coast, separated by a narrow strip of land from the sea, and communicating with it by barred outlets 1867. **6.** A backward current of water 1830. **7.** The swell of the sea thrown back from contact with a solid body; *e.g.* with the paddles of steamboats. Also *attrib.* 1838.

6. A kind of b., or eddying swirl CARLYLE. 7. The b. cast from the paddles 1865.

Back-way (bæ·kwēⁱ). 1577. [f. BACK *a.*] A way at, or to the back; *hence*, a bypath.

Backwoods (bæ·kwu·dz). 1834. [f. BACK *a.*] Wild, uncleared forest land; *e.g.* that of North America. Also *attrib.* Hence **Backwoo·dsman,** a settler in the backwoods.

Bacon (bēⁱ·kən). ME. [a. OF. *bacon, -un* (= med.L. *baconem*), a. OHG. *bacho* :—OTeut. **bakon-* cogn. w. **bako-z* BACK *sb.*[1]] **1.** The back and sides of the pig, cured by salting, drying, etc. Formerly also = *pork.* †**2.** The carcase of a pig; *rarely* a live pig –1768. †**3.** A rustic, a chaw-bacon 1596.

3. On Bacons, on, what ye knaues? Yong men must liue 1 *Hen. IV*, II. ii. 93.

Phr. *To save one's b.*: to escape bodily injury or loss. Hence **Ba·coner,** a pig fit for being made into b.

Baconian (beⁱkōᵘ·niăn), *a.* and *sb.* 1812. [f. Lord *Bacon* + -IAN.] **1.** Pertaining to, an adherent of, the experimental and inductive system of philosophy taught by him. **2.** Pertaining to, an advocate of, the theory that Lord Bacon wrote the works attributed to Shakespeare 1886. Hence **Baco·nianism.**

Bacony (bēⁱ·kəni), *a.* 1878. [f. BACON + -Y[1].] Like bacon; fatty; *esp.* in a state of fatty degeneration, as *b. liver.*

Bacterial (bæktīᵊ·riăl), *a.* 1871. [f. BACTERIUM + -AL[1].] *Biol.* Of or pertaining to bacteria. vars. **Bacte·rian, Bacte·ric.**

Bactericidal (bæktīᵊrisəi·dăl), *a.* [f. as prec. + L. *-cida.*] *Biol.* Destructive to bacteria.

Bacteriology (bæktīᵊriǫ·lŏdʒi). 1884. [f. BACTERIUM + -(O)LOGY.] The science of bacteria. Hence **Bacte:riolo·gical** *a.* 1886. **Bacte:rio·logist,** a student of b. **Bacte:rio·scopy,** microscopic investigation of bacteria.

Bacterium (bæktīᵊ·riŭm). Pl. **-a.** 1847. [mod.L., ad. Gr. βακτήριον, dim. of βάκτρον.] A genus of *Schizomycetæ*, microscopic unicellular rod-shaped vegetable organisms, found in all decomposing animal and vegetable liquids. Hence **Bacteri·tic** *a.*, marked by the (morbid) presence of bacteria. **Ba·cteroid** (better *bacterioid*), of the nature of, or allied to, bacteria.

Bacule, var. of BASCULE.

Baculine (bæ·kiŭləin), *a.* 1710. [f. L. *baculum* + -INE.] Of or pertaining to the stick, or to punishment by caning, etc.

Baculite (bæ·kiŭləit). 1822. [f. as prec. + -ITE.] *Palæont.* A genus of fossil cephalopods, with chambered cylindrical shells.

Baculo·metry. [f. as prec. + Gr. -μετρία.] Measurement of distances or lines by means of a staff or staves. (Dicts.)

Bad (bæd), *a.* (and *sb.*). [ME. *badde* (prob. repr. OE. *bæddel* hermaphrodite). Compared *badder, baddest* to 18th c.; though Shaks. has only *worse, worst*, taken over from *evil, ill*, after *bad* acquired that sense.] **A.** *adj.* **I.** In a privative sense. **1.** Of defective quality or worth. **2.** Incorrect 1688. **3.** *Law.* Not valid 1883. **4.** Unfavourable; that one does not like ME.

1. Mete and drynke..it was ful poure and badde CHAUCER. A b. correspondent 1873. *B. air* 1884. *B. coin*: debased, false coin. *B.* (i. e. irrecoverable) *debts. To go b.*: to decay. *With b. grace*: unwillingly. 2. To speak b. French 1767. B. form (*mod. slang*). *B. shot*: a wrong guess. 3. The claim is b. 1883. 4. The good fortune as the badde GOWER. In a b. sense 1751.

II. In a positive sense. **1.** Immoral, wicked ME. **2.** Offensive, disagreeable 1515. **3.** Injurious, dangerous. Const. *for.* 1653. **4.** In ill health, in pain 1748.

1. Corrupted by b. books 1767. 2. B. colour 1515, weather NELSON, temper MACAULAY. *B. blood*: angry feeling. 3. B. for his eyes ADDISON. A b. fall 1855. 4. B. with my gout RICHARDSON.

B. quasi-*sb.* **1.** *absol.* That which is bad 1591. **2.** *sb.* (with *pl.*) A bad thing or (*rarely*) person 1592.

1. T'exchange the b. for better *Two Gent.* II. vi. 13. (To go) *to the b., i. e.* to ruin; (to be, etc.) *to the bad, i.e.* in deficit. Hence **Ba·ddish** *a.* rather bad.

Bad, badd, obs. ff. BADE, BODE.

Badder, obs. compar. of BAD.

Badderlocks. *Sc.* 1789. [perh. for *Balderlocks*, f. BALDER.] An edible sea-weed (*Alaria esculenta*).

Bade, pa. t. of BID *v.*; obs. f. BODE *sb.* and *v.*

Badge (bædʒ), *sb.* ME. [?] **1.** A distinctive device, emblem, or mark, orig. = *cognizance* in *Her.*, but now worn as a sign of office, employment, membership of a society, etc. **2.** *gen.* A distinguishing sign 1526. Also *transf.* and *fig.* **3.** *Naval Arch.* A sort of ornament near the stern of small vessels, containing either a sash or the representation of one 1769.

1. B. of a gentylman PALSGR. 2. For suffrance is the b. of all our Tribe *Merch V.* I. iii. 111. *Comb.* b.-man, a licensed beggar or almsman. Hence **Ba·dgeless** *a.* without b. or cognizance.

Badge (bædʒ), *v.*[1] ME. [f. prec. sb.] To mark with, or distinguish by, a badge.

†**Badge,** *v.*[2] 1552. [?Cf. BADGER *sb.*[1]] To deal as a badger (see BADGER *sb.*[1]); *hence*, to regrate –1772.

Badger (bæ·dʒəɹ), *sb.*[1] 1500. [agent-n. f. BADGE *v.*[2]] One who buys corn and other commodities and carries them elsewhere to sell; a cadger, hawker, or huckster. Still *dial.* (Explained in 17th c. as a 'forestaller'.)

Badger (bæ·dʒəɹ), *sb.*[2] 1523. [prob. f. BADGE *sb.* + -ARD, from the white mark borne like a badge on its forehead. Cf. BALLARD.] **1.** A plantigrade quadruped (*Meles vulgaris*) intermediate between the weasels and the bears; it is a nocturnal, hybernating animal, digging for itself a burrow, which it defends fiercely against attack. Called earlier *brock* and *bauson*; also *gray.* **2.** (in *U.S.*) Nickname of inhabitants of Wisconsin 1856. **3. a.** An artificial fly (for angling); **b.** a brush (for painting or shaving) made of badger's hair.

1. *Cape-* or *Rock-b.*: the daman (*Hyrax Capensis*). *Honey-b.*: the ratel (*Ratellus mellivorus*). *Badger* (in Australia): the wombat.

Comb.: **b.-baiting, -drawing,** the sport of setting dogs to draw out a b. from its (artificial) hole; hence *badger-baiter*; **-dog** (= Ger. *dachshund*); **-fly** = (BADGER 3 a); **-legged** *a.*, having legs of unequal length, as the b. was thought to have. Hence **Ba·dgerly** *a.* badger-like; greyish-haired.

Badger (bæ·dʒəɹ), *v.* 1794. [f. prec. sb.] **1.** To bait like a badger; *hence*, to subject (one who cannot escape from it) to persistent worry or persecution. **2.** *dial.* [f. BADGER *sb.*[1]] To beat down in price 1875. Hence **Ba·dgerer,** a badger-dog; *dial.* a cheapener. **Ba·dgering** *vbl. sb.* persecution; *dial.* beating down the cost.

‖**Badiaga** (bădyā·gă, bædiˌāgă). 1753. [Russ. = 'river-sponge'.] A species of alga, the powder of which takes away the livid marks of bruises.

‖**Badian** (bā·diăn). 1847. [a. F. *badiane*, a. (ult.) Urdū *bādyān.*] The Chinese or Star Anise; see ANISE.

Badigeon (bădi·dʒən). 1753. [a. F.; etym. unkn.] A mixture of plaster and freestone ground together, used by builders, etc., or of sawdust and glue, used by joiners, for filling up defects in their work, or giving a surface to it.

‖**Badinage** (badina·ʒ, bæ·dinėdʒ). 1658. [a. F., f. *badiner.*] Light raillery, or humorous banter. Hence **Badinage** *v.*, to banter playfully.

†**Badiner,** *v.* 1697. [a. F. Irreg. adopted in inf.] To banter. Hence ‖**Badi·nerie·,** raillery. †**Badineu·r,** one who banters.

†**Ba·dling.** [OE. *bædling*, f. *bæddel* (see BAD).] A womanish man –1600.

Badly (bæ·dli), *adv.* ME. [f. BAD *a.* + -LY[2].] **1.** Defectively. **2.** Unsuccessfully ME. **3.** Incorrectly 1836. **4.** Immorally, improperly 1440. **5.** So as to cause pain, danger, disgrace, or harm 1799. **6.** *colloq.* with 'need, want' = Much, greatly (*mod.*). **7.** *dial.* Unwell 1783.

‖**Badmash, bud-** (bɒdmaˑʃ). 1843. [Pers. and Urdū.] One following evil courses; a 'bad lot'.

Badminton (bæ·dmintən). 1853. [The Duke of Beaufort's country seat.] **1.** A kind of claret-cup. **2.** A game resembling lawn-tennis, played with shuttle-cocks 1874.

Badness (bæ·dnės). ME. [f. BAD *a.* + NESS.] **1.** Inferior quality or condition; incorrectness; invalidity 1539. **2.** Evil quality or condition; wickedness; noxiousness ME.

Bæ- in OE. and EE. words; see BA-.

Bætyl (bī·til). *rare.* [ad. L., a. Gr. βαίτυλος.] A sacred meteoric stone.

Baff, *sb. Sc.* 1800. [?a. OF. *baffe*; or echoic.] A blow with anything flat or soft, *e.g.* the palm of the hand, a soft ball, etc. Also vb. 1858.

†**Baff,** *v.* ME. [?f. Du. *baffen*; or echoic.] To bark or yelp; also *transf.* –1599.

Baffle (bæ·f'l), *v.* 1548. [Etym. uncertain. Perh. three distinct words. Cf. Sc. *bauchle*, for senses 1–2. Cf. also F. *beffler* (Cotgr.) 'to gull', etc., and *bafouer* 'to hoodwinke..; *also* to baffle, abuse', etc.; the first, if not both, f. OF. *befe*, *beffe* mockery.] †**1.** To subject (*esp.* a perjured knight) to public disgrace or infamy –1660. †**2.** *gen.* To treat with contumely –1693. †**3.** To gull, cheat –1726. †**4.** *intr.* To juggle –1733. †**5.** To bewilder, confound –1704. †**6.** To bring to nought –1812. **7.** To defeat any one in his efforts; to frustrate, to foil 1675. **8.** *intr.* To struggle ineffectually 1860.

1. He by the heels him hung upon a tree And baffu'd so, that all which passed by The picture of his punishment might see SPENSER *F. Q.* VI. vii. 27. 3. To cheat and b. the poor man DE FOE. 6. To b. Reproach with Silence STEELE. 7. b. To check, turn, or disperse in its course, by an opposing force or obstacles 1748. Hence **Ba·ffled** *ppl. a.* disgraced MILT.; foiled. **Ba·fflement,** the action of baffling; being baffled. **Ba·ffling-ly** *adv.*, **-ness.**

Baffle (bæ·f'l), *sb.* 1628. [f. prec. sb.] †1. Affront –1692. †2. A shuffle 1783. †3. Discomfiture –1745. 4. Baffled state 1843. 5. = *baffle-plate* 1881.
attrib.: *b.-plate*, = BAFFLER 3; also, a plate hindering or regulating the passage of fluid through an outlet or inlet, or the direction of sound.

Baffler (bæ·fləɹ). 1606. [f. BAFFLE *v.*] †1. A juggler; a trifler –1677. 2. He who or that which BAFFLES (in various senses) 1677. 3. A contrivance used in stoves and furnaces, for changing the direction of the heated air 1861.

Baffy (bæ·fi). 1888. [f. BAFF *sb.*] *Golf.* A short wooden club for lofting. Also *b. spoon*.

Baft. 1598. [Prob. a. Pers. *baft* woven.] A coarse and cheap fabric, usually of cotton.

Baft (bɑft). [OE. *beæftan*, f. *be* by, at + *æftan* behind. Cf. AFT.] A. *adv.* 1. Behind; now only *Naut.*: Astern, aft, abaft (*arch.*). †2. Of time: After (*rare*) ME. B. †*prep.* [orig. the adv. with dat. of reference.] Behind, to the rear of –ME.

Bag (bæg), *sb.* [Early ME. *bagge*, ? f. ON. *baggi* 'bag' (not elsewhere in Teut.).] 1. *gen.* A receptacle of flexible material open only at the top (where it can be closed); a pouch, a small sack. 2. *spec.* = Money-bag, purse ME. †3. *poet.* in *pl.* Bagpipes –1790. 4. A silken pouch to hold the back-hair of a wig; cf. BAG-WIG 1702. 5. A measure of quantity, varying with the commodity 1679. 6. = Mail-bag; mail 1702. 7. *Sporting.* = Game-bag; *hence*, the quantity killed on one occasion 1486. Also *fig.* 8. *transf.* An udder, a dug 1579. 9. A sac (in the body of an animal) containing honey, poison, etc. (Usu. *fig.*) 1529. 10. *pl.* The stomach. (*N. dial.* and *Sc.*) 11. *Coal-Min.* A cavity filled with gas or water 1733. 12. *fig.* Clothes that hang loosely; (*vulg.*) trousers 1860.
2. *John* xii. 6. 9. *Mids. N.* III. i. 171.
Phrases. *B. of bones*: an emaciated living person. *To give* (one) *the b. to hold*: to engage any one while slipping away, to leave in the lurch. *To let the cat out of the b.*: to disclose the secret. **B. and baggage**: all belongings; *orig.* as in *to march out* (*with*) *b. and baggage*, i. e. without surrender of anything; now used to express the completeness of the departure.
Comb.: **b.-fox**, a fox brought alive in a bag to be turned out before the hounds; **-muff**, a muff containing a pouch; **-rod**, a fishing-rod which can be carried in pieces in a case; **-sleeve**, one tight at the wrist and baggy above; **-wolf** (cf. *-fox*). Hence **Ba·gful.**

Bag (bæg), *v.*[1] ME. [f. the sb.] I. *intr.* To bulge; *Naut.* to sag 1440; to hang loosely, as clothes 1824. †2. *intr.* To be pregnant –1603. 3. *trans.* To cause to swell or bulge 1583. 4. To put into a bag or bags 1573. 5. To put game killed into a bag; *also*, to kill game 1814. 6. *colloq.* To catch, seize, steal 1818.
1. Bagging to leeward MARRYAT. 4. To b. Hops 1711. 6. Led up..for bagging fowles HUGHES. Hence **Ba·gger**, †*spec.* a miser.

Bag, *v.*[2]; also **badge.** 1697. [?Cf. BATCH.] To cut corn, pease, or beans, with a bagging or badging hook. Hence **Ba·gging** *vbl. sb.* reaping corn, pease, and beans thus.

‖**Bagasse** (băgæ·s). 1854. [a. F., ad. Sp. *bagazo*, perh. var. of *bagage*; cf. BAGGAGE 4.] The refuse products in sugar-making. Hence **Baga·sse-bu·rner**, a furnace for burning b.

Bagatelle (bægăte·l). 1637. [a. F., ad. It. *bagatella*, prob. f. *baga*; see BAGGAGE. Now scarcely naturalized in sense 1; sense 2 is purely Eng.] 1. A trifle, a thing of no value or importance 1645. b. A piece of verse or music in a light style 1827. 2. A game played on a table having a semicircular end at which are nine numbered holes. The balls are struck from the other end with a cue. 1819.

Baggage (bæ·gėdʒ). ME. [a. OF. *bagage*, f. *baguer* 'to tie or truss up', or f. the sb. *bagues* 'bundles', pl. of *bague* = It. and late L. *baga*; cf. BAG.] Usually *collective* in senses 1–4 (formerly occas. with pl.). 1. The collection of property in packages that a traveller takes with him on a journey; luggage. (The regular term in U.S.; in Great Britain usu. called 'luggage'.) 2. *spec.* The portable equipment of an army; = L. *impedimenta* 1489. †3. *fig.* Burdensome matters –1757. †4. Rubbish, refuse –1661; pus –1610; *fig.* trash, 'rot' –1579. †5. A worthless or vile fellow –1601. 6. A good-for-nothing woman, a strumpet 1596. 7. Used joc. of any young woman, *esp.* with *artful*, *pert*, etc. 1672.
1. Indians..to cary b. 1578. 2. *Bag and b.*: see BAG. 4. To read such beastly b. FULKE. 7. I believe the b. loves me CONGREVE.
†B. *adj.* (from attrib. use of the sb. in sense 4; cf. *trumpery*.) †1. Rubbishy –1625. †2. Trashy, despicable –1640. †3. Good-for-nothing, scurvy –1670. †4. Purulent –1597.
Comb.: **b.-check**, a ticket for luggage on U.S. railways; **-man**, or **-master**, one who has charge of the b.; **-room**, a luggage-office; **-smasher** (*joc.*), railway-porter (U. S.).
Hence **Ba·ggaged** *ppl. a.* (*nonce-wd.*), packed up BYRON. †**Ba·ggagely** *adv.* rubbishy. **Ba·ggager**, one who carries or has charge of b.

†**Bagge**, *v.* ME. only. [?] To look askew; to leer, ogle.

Bagged (bægd), *ppl. a.* ME. [f. BAG *v.*] †1. Big with young –1616. 2. Enclosed in, or as in, a bag; encysted 1572. 3. Hanging slack, or in bags 1618. 4. Having bags 1861.

Ba·gging, *sb.*[1] 1750. [?orig. a vbl. sb.] Used in n. dial. for food eaten between meals; now, *esp.* in Lancs. a substantial afternoon tea.

Bagging (bæ·giŋ), *sb.*[2] 1732. [f. BAG *sb.*[1] cf. *sacking*, etc.] Coarse woven fabric out of which bags are made.

Baggit (bæ·git). 1848. [?Sc. form of BAGGED (sense 1).] A salmon that has just spawned.

Baggy (bæ·gi), *a.* 1831. [f. BAG *sb.* + -Y.] 1. Puffed out; hanging loosely. 2. *fig.* Of language: Inflated 1866. Hence **Ba·ggily** *adv.* **Ba·gginess**, baggy state.

†**Ba·gle.** ME. [a. ON. *bagall*, ad. L. *baculum*.] The staff or crozier of a bishop –1557.

Bagman (bæ·gmæ̆n). 1531. [f. BAG *sb.* + MAN.] 1. One who carries a bag 1531. 2. *spec.* A commercial traveller, who shows samples and solicits orders for his principal, etc. (*Depreciatory.*) 1765. 3. A bag-fox 1875.

‖**Bagne** (banʸ). 1863. [mod.F., ad. It. *bagno*.] = BAGNIO 2.

Bagnio (bæ·nyo). 1599. [a. It. *bagno*:—L. *balneum*.] †1. A bath, a bathing-house; *esp.* one with appliances for sweating, cupping, etc. –1820. 2. An oriental prison for slaves 1599. 3. A brothel. (Cf. STEW.) 1624.

Bagpipe (bæ·gpəip), *sb.* ME. [f. BAG *sb.*[1] + PIPE.] 1. A musical instrument of great antiquity, consisting of an air-tight wind-bag, and one or more reed pipes into which the air is pressed by the performer. Now often in *pl.*
Formerly a favourite rural Eng. instrument; now chiefly used in the Scottish Highlands, and in Ireland. The Highland bagpipe is a greased leathern bag covered with flannel, inflated through a valved mouth-tube, and having three *drones* or bass pipes, and a *chanter* for the tenor or treble.
2. *fig.* A wind-bag; a long-winded speaker 1603. Hence **Ba·gpi·per.**

Ba·gpipe, *v.* 1769. [from the shape the sail assumes.] *Naut.* Of the mizzen: To lay it aback, by bringing the sheet to the mizzen-shrouds.

†**Ba·gpu·dding.** 1598. [f. BAG *sb.*[1]] A pudding boiled in a bag –1817.

Bag-reef (bæ·gɹīf). 1867. *Naut.* A fourth or lower reef of fore-and-aft sails.

Baguette (băge·t). 1727. [a. F.; in *Archit.* ad. It. *bacchetta*, dim. of *bacchio*:—L. *baculum*.] A small moulding of semicircular section, like an astragal.

Bag-wig (bæ·gˌwi·g). (Also as two wds.) 1717. An 18th c. wig, with the back-hair enclosed in a bag.

Bah (bā), *int.* 1817. [? after mod.F. *bah!*] An exclam. of contempt.

‖**Bahar, barr(e** (băhā·ɹ). 1753. [Arab.] A measure of weight used in India and China, varying in different places from 223 to 625 lbs.

‖**Bahu·t.** [a. F. *bahutte*.] A dress for masquerading. MISS BERRY.

Baign(e, obs. f. BAIN.

‖**Baignoire** (be·nwar, -wɐ̄ɹ). 1873. [F., lit. 'a vessel for bathing in'.] A box at the theatre on the same level as the stalls.

Bail (bēˑl), *sb.*[1] ME. [In senses 1 and 2, a. OF. *bail*, f. *baillier* (see BAIL *v.*[1]). The other senses are Eng.] †1. Custody, jurisdiction –1596. †2. Delivery ME. only. †3. The friendly custody of a person otherwise liable to be kept in prison, upon security given for his appearance at a time and place assigned –1809. †4. Temporary release from imprisonment on finding sureties or security to appear for trial; *also*, release –1768. 5. Security so given 1495; also *fig.* 6. The person or persons who thus become sureties 1593. Also *fig.*
1. His body is undyr your bayle ME. 3. *Admitted to b.* if the offences were bailable SELDEN. So *let to b.* 5. Put to sufficient baill 1495. *To give leg b.* (joc.): to be beholden to one's legs for release, to run away. 6. I'll go b. for that THACKERAY. *Comb.*: **b.-bond**, the bond entered into by a b.; **-piece**, a slip of parchment containing the recognizance which is handed to the court.

Bail, *sb.*[2] [ME. *beyl*, prob. a. ON. *beygla*, f. *beygja* = OE. *bēgan*, *bygan* to bend.] 1. A hoop; a half-hoop for supporting the cover of a wagon, the tilt of a boat, etc. 1447. 2. The hoop-handle of a kettle, etc. 1463.

Bail, bayle (bēˑl), *sb.*[3] [ME., a. OF. *bail*, *baille*, ? vbl. sbs. of *baillier* to enclose; see BAIL *v.*[3] Cf. BAILEY. The deriv. from L. *baculum* is without evidence.] 1. *pl.* Outer line of fortification, formed of stakes; palisades 1523. 2. The wall of the outer court of a feudal castle; *hence*, the courts themselves. See BAILEY. †3. *pl.* The bulwarks of a boat –1603. 4. A bar or pole to separate horses in an open stable 1844.

Bail, *sb.*[4] 1575. [? same as prec. wd.] †1. A cross-bar. 2. In *Cricket*, each of the two pieces of wood laid across the stumps 1770.

†**Bail**, *sb.*[5] 1466. [a. F. *baille* a bucket, prob. :—late L. *bacula*, dim. of *baca* BACK *sb.*[2]] *Naut.* A bucket or scoop for bailing water from a boat.

Bail (bēˑl), *v.*[1] 1548. [a. OF. *baillier*, *bailler* :—L. *bajulare* 'to carry', later 'to manage', and 'to be guardian'.] 1. 'To deliver (goods) in trust, upon a contract expressed or implied that the trust shall be faithfully executed on the part of the bailee'. Blackstone. [See BAILMENT, BAILOR, BAILEE.] 1768. 2. To admit to bail, to liberate on bail. Said of the magistrate (*arch.*). 1548. Also †*fig.* and *gen.* 3. To procure the liberation of (any one) by becoming bail for him. Also *fig.* 1587. 4. *fig.* To be security or pledge for 1587.
1. If cloth be..bailed to a taylor to make a suit of cloathes BLACKSTONE. 3. I offer to b. the fellow out 1859. Hence **Bailed** *ppl. a.* released on bail.

Bail, *v.*[2] 1600. [related to OF. *bail*, *baille*, BAIL *sb.*[3] ? as deriv. or source.] 1. To confine (*rare*). 2. *To bail up* (in Australia): a. To secure a cow's head in a bail while she is milked; b. (Said of bushrangers) To 'stick up' and disarm before robbing; also *intr.* To disarm oneself by throwing up the arms 1880.
1. My friends heart let my poore heart bale SHAKS.

Bail, *v.*[3] 1613. [f. BAIL *sb.*[5]] To lade water out of a boat, etc., with buckets (formerly called bails), or other vessels. a. To b. *the water* (out). b. To b. *the boat* (out) 1840. c. *absol.* 1624.

†**Bai·lable**, *a.*[1] 1502. [a. OF. *baillable*.] Deliverable.

Bailable (bēˑ·lăb'l), *a.*[2] 1554. [f. BAIL *v.*[1] and *sb.*[1]] 1. Entitled to be released on bail. 2. Admitting of bail, as a *b. offence* 1649.

Bailage (bēˑ·lėdʒ). 1753. [f. BAIL *v.*[1]] A duty upon delivery of goods.

†**Bai·l-dock, ba·le-dock.** 1624. [? f. BALE *sb.*[3] barrier; see DOCK.] At the Old Bailey, London, (formerly) 'a small room taken from one of the corners of the court, and left open at the top; in which, during the trials, are put some of the malefactors' (*Scots Mag.*) –1823.

†**Baile, bayle**, *int.* 1529. [perh. imper. of Fr. *bailler* 'Deliver (blows)!'] A call to combatants to engage –1530.

Bailee (bēˑlī·). 1528. [f. BAIL *v.*[1]] One to whom a BAILMENT (sense 1) is made.

Bai·ler[1]. 1883. [f. BAIL *v.*[4]] He who or that which bails water out, *esp.* a machine to lift and throw out water from a pit, etc.

Bai·ler[2]. 1881. [f. BAIL *sb.*[4]] *Cricket.* A ball that hits the bails.

Bailey (bēˑ·li). [ME. var. of *bayle*, BAIL *sb.*[3]: possibly f. med.L. *balium*, *ballium*; cf. *vetus Ballium* = Old Bailey. Not in Fr.] 1. The external wall of a feudal castle; more widely, any circuit of walls which surrounded the keep. 2. Later: The outer court of a feudal castle; also, any court within the circuits of walls. Hence *outer*, *inner* 1845. **3.** Retained in proper names: e.g. the *Old Bailey* in London, the seat of the Central Criminal Court, so called from the ancient *bailey* of the city wall between Lud Gate and New Gate, within which it lay 1570.

Bailie (bē̆·li). [ME. *bailli*, a. OF., later form of *baillis*, *baillif*, BAILIFF.] *Obs.* in England. †**1.** = BAILIFF 1. -1662. **2.** *In Scotland.* †**a.** *formerly*, The chief magistrate (= sheriff) of a barony -1754; **b.** *now*, A municipal magistrate (= Eng. alderman) 1484. †**3.** = BAILIFF 2. -1668. †**4.** = BAILIFF 3. -1730. Hence **Bai·liery, -ary,** = BAILIWICK 1, 2. So **Bai·lieship,** the office of b.

Bailiff (bē̆·lif). [ME. *baillif*, a. OF., obj. case of *baillis*:—late L. *bajulivus*, f. *bajulus* manager; see BAIL *sb.*[1] and cf. BAIL *v.*[1]] **1.** One charged with administrative authority in a certain district, the chief officer of a hundred; the 'chief magistrate', as in High B. of Westminster, a 'custodian', as in B. of Dover Castle. **2.** A sheriff's deputy, who executes writs, etc., distrains, and arrests ME. **3** An agent who collects rents, or a steward who manages an estate, for the landlord; one who superintends the husbandry of a farm for its owner or tenant 1531.

1. The quene sent in hast to the Baillifs of wynchestre CAXTON. **2.** Then a Processe-seruer (a Bayliffe) *Wint. T.* IV. iii. 102. Hence **Bai·liffry** (*rare*), a *Bailiery*. **Bai·liffship,** the office of b. **Ba·lival** *a.* of or pertaining to a b. or his office.

†**Bai·liffwick.** 1509. [f. prec. + -WICK.] **1.** The district under the jurisdiction of a bailiff -1766. **2.** = BAILIFFSHIP. -1570. **3.** Stewardship 1605.

Bailiwick (bē̆·li,wik). 1460. [f. as prec.] **1.** A district under a bailie or bailiff. In *Eng. Hist.* it includes *sheriffdom*; also *transf.* **2.** = prec. (sense 2). *Hist.* †**3.** = prec. (sense 3). -1601. var. **Bailliage.**

†**Baillie, bailly.** [ME. *baillie*, a. OF.:—late L. *bajulia*, f. *bajulus*.] **1.** The jurisdiction, or office of a BAILIE or BAILIFF; delegated authority; stewardship -1738. **2.** *gen.* Jurisdiction, charge -1475. **3.** A BAILIWICK ME. only.

Bailment (bē̆·lmĕnt). 1554. [a. OF. *baillement*.] **1.** Delivery for a specific purpose; delivery in trust, upon a contract expressed or implied, that the trust shall be faithfully executed 1602. **2.** The action of bailing a person accused. Also the record of the same.

‖**Bailo** (bai·lo). Occ. **baile.** 1682. [It.:—L. *bajulus*. See BAIL *sb.*[1] and BAILIFF.] The Venetian 'Resident' at the Ottoman Porte.

Bailor (bē̆·lǭ·ɪ). 1602. [f. BAIL *v.*[1] + -OR; cf. *bailee*.] *Law.* One who makes a BAILMENT (sense 1).

Bailsman (bē̆·lzmæ̆n). 1862. [f. BAIL *sb.*[1]] One who gives bail for another, a bail.

Bain (bē̆n). Now *dial.* ME. [a. ON. *beinn* direct; also, hospitable.] **A.** *adj.* **1.** Willing -1674. **2.** Limber -1674. **3.** Direct; short (*n. dial.*) 1864. **B.** as *adv.* **1.** Willingly -1513. **2.** Near, 'handy' (*n. dial.*) 1700.

†**Bain,** *sb.* 1475. [a. F.:—L. *balneum*.] **1.** A quantity of water, etc. placed in a vessel, in which one may bathe -1641; the vessel itself -1543; *abstractly*, a bath -1563. **2.** = BAGNIO 1. -1693. **3.** A hot or medicinal spring -1655. **4.** in *pl.* Stews -1599. **5.** *Chem.* An apparatus for heating gradually through the medium of water, sand, etc. Cf. BATH. -1657.

†**Bain,** *v.* ME. [a. F. *baigner*:—L. *balneare*.] **1.** To bathe; to drench -1602. Also *fig.* **2.** *intr.* To bathe oneself (*lit.* and *fig.*) -1573.

‖**Bain-marie** (bæ̃nmarī). 1822. [Fr.; ad. L. *balneum Mariæ*, app. = Gr. κάμινος Μαρίας 'furnace of Maria' (Jewish alchemist).] A flat vessel to hold hot water, in which other vessels are placed for heating food, etc.

‖**Bairam** (bairā·m, bai·răm). 1599. [Turk. and Pers.] The name of two Mohammedan festivals—the *Lesser B.*, lasting three days, which follows the fast of Ramadan, and the *Greater B.*, seventy days later, lasting four days.

Bairn (bēᵊɹn, in Sc. bern). [Com. Teut.: OE. *bearn*:—OTeut. **barno-(m)*, f. *beran* to bear. Lost in southern English.] A child; a son or daughter. (Expressing relationship.)

Mercy on's, a Barne?.. A boy or a childe I wonder *Wint. T.* III. ii. 70. Hence **Bai·rnie,** little child. **Bai·rnish** *a.* childish. **Bai·rnishness, Bai·rnliness,** childishness. **Bai·rnly** *a.* childish; child-like; also, †as *adv.* **Bai·rn-team, -time,** also **Barmteam,** brood of children, offspring; posterity.

†‖**Baisemain.** 1656. [Fr.] A kiss of the hands; in *pl.* respects -1748.

Bait (bē̆t), *v.*[1] [ME. *beȝȝten*, *beyten*, a. ON. *beita*, causal of *bíta* to BITE.] †**1.** To set on to bite or worry (*lit.* and *fig.*). **2.** To set on dogs to bite or worry a chained or confined animal; †to hunt with dogs ME. Also *fig.* **3.** To attack with endeavour to bite or tear 1553. Also *absol.* **4.** *fig.* To harass with persistent attacks ME. **5.** *trans.* To give food and drink to (a horse, etc.), *esp.* on a journey ME. Also (*refl.* and) *intr.* **6.** *intr.* Of travellers: To stop at an inn for rest and refreshment; *hence*, to make a short stay ME. Also *fig.* †**7.** *intr.* (and *refl.*) To feed -1633. Also †*fig.* **8.** To furnish (a hook, etc.) with a bait ME. Also *fig.* **9.** To lay (a place) with bait 1623. **10.** To offer bait to; to tempt 1590.

2. Are these thy Beares? Wee'l bate thy Bears to death 2 *Hen. VI*, v. i. 148. **4.** To b. a Secretary of State MACAULAY. **6.** To b. here a few days longer SHERIDAN. *fig.* For evil news rides post, while good news baits MILT. *Sams.* 1538. Hence **Bai·ted** *ppl. a.* (senses 2, 9). **Bai·ter. Bai·ting** *vbl. sb.* and *ppl. a.*

Bait, *v.*[2] *Falconry.* See BATE *v.*[1]

Bait (bē̆t), *sb.* ME. [a. ON. *beit* (neut.) pasture, *beita* (fem.) food, cogn. w. OE. *bát*; in part f. BAIT *v.*[1]] **1.** Food placed on a hook or in a trap, in order to allure fish or other animals ME.; worms, fish, etc. to be thus used 1496. Also *fig.* **2.** Food, refreshment; *esp.* a feed for horses, or slight repast for travellers, upon a journey. Still *dial.* a snack taken between meals. Also †*fig.* 1570. **3.** A halt for refreshment or rest 1579. **5.** Setting dogs to worry other animals 1450.

1. Let your b. fall gently upon the water WALTON. *fig.* A doore without locke, is a baite for a knaue TUSSER. Hence **Bai·tless,** without food (*rare*).

Baize (bē̆z), *sb.* 1578. [a. F. *baies*, pl. fem. used subst. of adj. *bai*:—L. *badius* BAY, prob. its original colour. The pl., treated as a collect. sing., gave *bayze*, *baize*.] **1.** A coarse woollen stuff, having a long nap. Also *attrib.* **2.** A curtain, table-cover, etc. of baize 1862. Hence **Baize** *v.* to cover or line with b.

‖**Bajocco** (ba,yǫ·kko). Pl. **-cchi.** 1547. [It., f. *bajo* brown.] A small Italian copper coin (now obs.) worth about a halfpenny.

†**Ba·julate,** *v. rare.* 1613. [f. L. *bajulat-*, *bajulare*, f. *bajulus*.] To carry, *esp.* as a BADGER *sb.*[1] FULLER.

Bake (bē̆k), *v.* [Com. Teut.: OE. *bacan*. Orig. a str. vb. The weak pa. pple. *baked* appeared in 16th c., and is alone used by Shaks.] **1.** To cook by dry heat acting by conduction and not by radiation, as in an oven, etc., or on a heated surface; primarily used of preparing bread. (In transf. uses not sharply separated from *roast*.) **b.** *fig.* To ripen with heat 1697. **2.** To harden by heat ME. **3.** To harden as frost does 1572. †**4.** To cake -1684. **5.** *intr.* (for *refl.*) To undergo baking 1665.

3. Th' earth When it is bak'd with frost *Temp.* I. ii. 256. **5.** These apples b. badly (*mod.*).

Comb., *bake* (= *baking* vbl. sb.) attrib., as **b.-board; -house; -stone.** Hence **Bake** *sb.* In *Sc.* A biscuit; the act, process, or result, of baking. **Ba·ken** *ppl. a.* (*arch.*). **Ba·king** *vbl. sb.* attrib. *b.-powder*, a substitute for yeast, used in making bread.

Bakelite (bē̆·kĕlait). 1913. [ad. G. *bakelit*, f. the name of L. H. *Baekeland* its inventor + -ITE [1].] A proprietary name of a synthetic resin formed by the condensation of phenols and formaldehyde, used as a plastic and for insulating purposes.

†**Ba·ke-meat.** ME. [f. *bake* = *baken*; also *baken*, *baked m.*] Pastry, a pie -1700.

Baker (bē̆·kəɹ). [OE. *bæcere*, f. *bacan*.] **1.** One who bakes; *spec.* one whose business it is to make bread. **2.** A small portable tin oven. In U.S. **3.** An artificial salmon fly 1867.

Comb.: **b.-feet, -legs, -knees, baker's knee,** names of deformities incident to bakers; **-legged, -kneed,** *a.*; **baker's salt,** a name for commercial carbonate of ammonia, used instead of yeast. Phr. *Baker's dozen*: thirteen. Hence **Ba·kerdom,** condition of a b. **Ba·kership,** skill as a b. **Ba·kery,** craft or business of baker: a baker's establishment.

‖**Baksheesh, bakhshish** (bæ·kʃīʃ). 1755. [Pers.; = 'present'.] Oriental for a 'tip'. Hence **Ba·ksheesh** *v.* to 'tip'. Also *absol.*

Bal. 1600. [a. Cornish *bal* 'collection of mines'.] A mine. Also *attrib.*, as in *b.-girl*, etc.

Balaam (bē̆·lăm). 1648. **1.** Name of the prophet (*Numb.* xxii–xxiv), used connotatively. Hence **Balaam** *v.* to make a B. of. **Ba·laamite,** one who follows religion for gain; **Balaamitical** *a.* **2.** (In journalistic slang) Trumpery paragraphs reserved to fill up the columns of a newspaper, etc. **B.-box** (or **-basket**), a receptacle for such matter.

‖**Balachong** (bæ·lătʃǫŋ). 1697. [a. Malay.] A condiment for rice, made of putrid shrimps or small fishes pounded up with salt or spices, and then dried.

Balaclava (bælăklā·vă). [Site of Crimean battle in 1854.] *B. helmet* (*cap*), a woollen covering for the head and shoulders worn esp. by soldiers on active service 1892.

Baladine (bæ·lădīn). 1599. [a. F., f. OF. *balade* (mod. *ballade*) dancing-song; see BALLAD.] †**1.** A theatrical dancer; a mountebank -1676. **2.** A female public dancer BROWNING. †**3.** A ballad-maker or -singer 1604.

Balalaika (bælălai·kă). 1788. [Russ.] Instrument of guitar kind, used esp. in Russia.

Balance (bæ·lăns), *sb.* ME. [a. Fr.:—late L. **bilancia*, f. L. *bilanx adj.*, f. *bi-* twice + *lanx* scale. Occ. confused with BALLAST.] **1.** An apparatus for weighing, a beam poised so as to move freely on a central pivot, with a scale pan at each end. †**2.** *sing.* One scale of a balance; *pl.* scales. (The *pl.* was occ. *balance*. See *Merch. V.* IV. i. 255.) -1655. **3.** **a.** The constellation *Libra*. **b.** The seventh sign of the Zodiac ♎, into which the sun enters at the autumnal equinox 1488. **4.** Any apparatus used in weighing 1829. **5.** *Watchmaking.* A contrivance which regulates the speed of a watch, etc. 1660. **6.** *Naut.* The operation or result of reefing with a *balance-reef*; see below 1762. **7.** *fig.* The balance of reason, justice, or opinion ME.; †one scale of the balance -1635. **8.** The wavering balance of Fortune or chance ME. †**9.** *Hence*, Hesitation, doubt -1683; risk -1685. **10.** Power to decide ME. **11.** A weight which produces equilibrium; a counterpoise. Also *fig.* 1601. **12.** Equilibrium 1642. **13.** General harmony between the parts of anything; *esp.* in the Arts of Design 1732. **14.** **a.** Physical equipoise 1667; **b.** Equipoise of mind, etc.; sanity 1856. **15.** The preponderating weight; the net result 1747. **16.** The process of finding the difference, if any, between the Dr. and Cr. sides of an account; the tabular statement exhibiting this; the result 1588; *gen.* a comparative reckoning (*rare*) 1719. **17.** An equality between the total of the two sides of an account. Cf. 12. 1652. **18.** The difference between the Dr. and Cr. sides of an account 1622. **19.** *Comm. slang*: The remainder 1864.

1. He had a b. in his hand R.V. *Rev.* vi. 5. **2.** A pair of Ballance FULLER. **7.** A Moth wil turne the ballance, which Piramus which Thisby is the better *Mids. N.* v. 324. **8.** Mens lives hang in the ballance 1612. **10.** Henry viii held the b. with .. a stronger hand 1760. **12.** **Balance of power** (*in Europe*): such an adjustment of power that no single state is in a position to interfere with the independence of the rest. **14.** If my mind had retained its b. KANE. **15.** The b. of evidence appears in favour of the due execution BROUGHAM. **16.** *To strike a b.*: to determine the exact difference, if any, between the two sides of an account (*lit.* and *fig.*). **Balance of trade**: the estimation of the difference of value between the exports and imports of a country; the difference in favour of, or against, the country. **18.** *B.* (*of indebtedness*): the difference between the amounts which two parties mutually owe each other. *B.* (*in hand*): the sum remaining over after realizing all assets and discharging all liabilities. *B.* (*due*): the sum still outstanding on an account.

Comb.: **b.-beam,** the beam of a b., *also* the beam keeping a drawbridge balanced aloft; **-bob,** a heavy lever ballasted at one end, and attached at the other to the pump-rod; **-fish,** *Squalus zygæna*; **-knife,** a table-knife with a handle which keeps the blade from touching the cloth; **-master, -mistress,** an acrobat; **-reef,** the closest reef of a lower fore-and-aft sail, used to steady the ship in stormy weather, whence *balance-reefed*; **-sheet**, a tabular statement of assets and liabilities; **-step** (= GOOSE-STEP); **-yard** = *balance-beam*.

Balance (bæ·lăns), *v.* 1579. [a. F. *balancer*, f. *balance* sb. (Like the sb., occas. confused with *ballast*.)] **1.** *trans.* To weigh (a matter); to ponder 1694. **2.** To weigh two things, considerations, etc., against each other 1596. **3.** To counterpoise one thing *by*, *with*, or *against* another 1624. **4.** To bring to or keep in equilibrium 1634. **5.** To poise, keep steady or erect 1840; also *refl.* and *intr.* **6.** *trans.* To equal in weight, counterpoise. Also *absol.* to balance (each other) 1727. **7.** *Hence*: To neutralize the effect of, make up for 1593. **8.** *intr.* To waver, deliberate 1655. **9.** *Dancing*: To *set to* a partner 1775. **10.** *trans.* To add up the Dr. and Cr. sides of an account, and ascertain the difference, if any, between their amounts 1588. **11.** To equalize the two sides of an account by making proper entries; hence b. accounts are said (intr.) *to b.* (i. e. themselves); or an entry is said *to b. the account*, or an opposite entry 1622. **12.** *Hence*: To settle (an account) by paying an amount due 1740. **13.** *Naut.* To reef with a balance-reef; see BALANCE *sb.*

2. Truth is determined by balancing probabilities 1875. 5. Strong men..balancing chests of drawers.. upon their heads DICKENS. 6. Do these scales b. (*mod.*). 7. To ballance the Protestants, the Jesuits were set on foot FULLER. 8. A disposition to b. and temporize MERIVALE. 10. To compute and b. my gain and my loss SWIFT. 12. A cheque for £30 to b. his account 1877. Hence **Ba·lanceable** *a.* **Ba·lanced** *ppl. a.*, poised; in equipoise; well arranged or disposed. **Ba·lancement** (*rare*), equipoise.

Balancer (bæ·lănsəɹ). ME. [f. prec.] †**1.** One who weighs with a balance (*rare*) –1611. **2.** An acrobat 1510. **3.** One who maintains the balance of power 1731. **4.** Something which helps to preserve the balance; *spec.* the *halteres* or *poisers* in two-winged flies 1753.

‖**Bala·ndra.** 1845. [Sp.] A small coasting vessel.

Balanid (bæ·lănid). 1836. [f. BALANUS + -ID.] *Zool.* A member of the *Balanidæ* or Acorn-shells.

Balaniferous (bælăni·fĕrəs), *a.* 1881. [f. as prec. + -(I)FEROUS.] Acorn-bearing.

Balanite (bæ·lănəit). 1598. [ad. L., a. Gr. βαλανίτης, f. βάλανος.] †**1.** A kind of precious stone. **2.** A fossil balanid 1835.

Balanoid (bæ·lănoid). 1869. [ad. Gr. βαλανοειδής.] *adj.* Acorn-shaped. *sb.* A balanid.

Balas (bæ·lăs). ME. [a. OF. *balais*, *balai*, f. (ult.) Pers. *Badakhshān* near Samarcand, where found.] A delicate rose-red variety of the spinel ruby. Now usu. *b.-ruby*.

†**Ba·latron, -oon.** *rare.* 1623. [ad. L. *balatronem* (= *blateronem*).] A buffoon –1678. Hence **Balatro·nic** *a.*

‖**Balausta** (bălǭ·stă). 1842. [mod.L. (Linn.).] *Bot.* The fruit of the pomegranate.

Balaustine (bălǭ·stin). Also **-in, -ian.** 1671. [ad. Gr. βαλαύστιον.] The flower of the wild pomegranate, used when dried as an astringent. var. †**Balau·sty.**

Balbu·tient, *a.* 1642. [ad. L. *balbutient-em*.] Stammering.

‖**Balbuties** (bælbiū·ʃiˌīz). 1655. [mod.L., f. *balbutire*.] *Med.* Stuttering; lisping.

†**Balcon.** *rare.* 1635. [a. F.] = BALCONY –1665.

Balcone·tte. 1876. [f. BALCONY.] A miniature balcony.

Balcony (bæ·lkŏni). 1618. [a. It. *balcone*, f. *balco*, a. OHG. *balcho* (= Eng. *balk*) a beam. Till *c* 1825 bælkōᵘ·ni, though bæ·lkŏni occurs once in Swift.] **1.** A platform projecting from the wall of a house or room, supported by pillars, brackets, or consoles, and enclosed by a balustrade. **2.** The similar structure at the stern of large ships 1666. **3.** In theatres: †A stage-box; *now*, The open part above the dress circle 1718.

1. The Maids to the Doors and the Balconies ran, And said, lack-a-day! he's a proper young man SWIFT. Hence **Ba·lconied** *ppl. a.* furnished with a b.

Bald (bǭld), *a.* [ME. *balled*, of unkn. origin. Prob. f. BALL *sb.*[3] (Cf. also BALLARD.)] †**1.** ? Rotund ME. only. **2.** Lacking hair on some part of the head where it naturally grows ME.; also *fig.* **3.** Without hair (feathers, etc.) on other parts of the body ME. Also *transf.* (see quots.) **4.** Streaked or marked with white. [Cf. Welsh *ceffyl bâl* (F. *cheval belle-face*).] 1690. **5.** *fig.* Bare of meaning or force ME. **6.** Bare of ornament and grace 1589. **7.** Undisguised 1854.

2. His heed was ballid, and schon as eny glas CHAUCER. Occasion's b. behind; Slip not thine opportunity MARLOWE. 4. Now Ierkin, you are like to lose your haire, & proue a b. Ierkin *Temp.* IV. 238. Thy b., awful head, O sovran Blanc 1817. 5. Balde sermons 1593, some b. truism COLERIDGE. 6. B. Latine 1693, prose 1851, the b. street TENNYSON. 7. A b. egotism 1870.

Comb.: *b.-faced*, *-nosed* (sense 4). Also **b.-coot**, the Coot (*Fulica atra*), so called from its white frontal plate, destitute of feathers: *fig.* = *bald-head*; **-head**, one who has a b. head; *transf.* a kind of pigeon: whence *bald-headed*; **-pate**, one who has a b. head; *transf.* a kind of duck; also used *attrib.* = BALD *a.*; whence *bald-pated*; **-rib**, a joint of pork cut nearer the rump than the spare-rib; (*joc.*) a lean bony person. Hence †**Bald** *v.* to make b. (*lit.* and *fig.*). **Ba·ldly** *adv.*

Bald, early and north. f. BOLD.

Baldachin, -quin. 1598. [a. F., Sp. *baldaquin*, in med.L. *baldakinus*, f. *Baldacco*, It. form of *Bagdad*, where the stuff was made. Cf. BAUDEKIN.] **1.** A rich stuff, orig. woven with woof of silk and warp of gold; rich brocade. **2.** A structure in the form of a canopy, either borne on columns, suspended from the roof, or projecting from the wall, placed above an altar, throne, or doorway; orig. made of the stuff described in sense 1. 1645.

Ba·lden, *v.* 1883. [f. BALD *a.*] To make or become bald.

Balder, -ur. [ON. *Baldr*, cogn. w. OE. *baldor* hero, f. *bald*; see BOLD.] A Scandinavian deity, whose name occurs in: **B.-herb** (*Amaranthus hypochondriacus*); **B. Brae, Balder's Brae, Baldeyebrow** (*Anthemis Cotula*). See also BALDMONEY and BADDERLOCKS.

Balderdash (bǭ·ldəɹdæʃ), *sb.* 1596. [?] †**1.** ? Froth –1599. †**2.** A jumbled mixture of liquors, *e.g.* of milk and beer, beer and wine, etc. –1693. **3.** *transf.* A senseless jumble of words; trash 1674.

2. Beer or buttermilk, mingled together..To drink such b. B. JONSON. [App. the primary sense is 1 or 2.]

Baldmoney (bǭ·ldmʊni). ME. [Etym. unkn. Not = *Balder's Money*.] *Herb.* †**1.** Gentian –1597. **2.** Mew (*Meum alhamanticum*) 1598.

Ba·ldness. ME. [f. BALD *a.* + -NESS.] **1.** Absence of hair, *esp.* from the head. Also *fig.* **2.** *transf.* Lack of natural covering 1863. **3.** Poverty of style; lack of ornament; bareness 1774.

Baldric (bǭ·ldrik). ME. [Obscure L. *balteus* (OHG. *balz*, Eng. *belt*) does not account for *bald-*.] **1.** A belt or girdle, often richly ornamented, worn pendent from one shoulder across the breast, and used to support a sword, bugle, etc. **2.** *fig.* The zodiac, as a gem-studded belt 1596. †**3.** A necklace –1577. †**4.** The leather-gear, etc., for suspending the clapper of a church bell –1742. Hence **Baldric-wise** *adv.*

†**Bale,** *a.* [Com. Teut.:—OTeut. **balwoz*.] **1.** Actively evil –ME. **2.** Sorrowing –ME.

Bale (bēˡl), *sb.*[1] [Com. Teut.: OE. *balu*, *bealu*:—OTeut. **balw-o(m)*, neut. of prec. adj. Usu. *poet.* Marked obs. *c* 1600, and rare thence till 19th c.] **1.** Evil, *esp.* as active; fatal, dire, or malign, quality or influence; woe, mischief, harm, injury; in early use often = death, infliction of death. **2.** Evil as suffered; torment, pain, woe ME. **3.** Misery, grief ME.

Bale, *sb.*[2] [Com. Teut.: OE. *bǣl* and ON. *bál* great fire:—OTeut. *bal-o(m)*. Mostly north., and app. f. ON. *bal*. Latterly mixed up with prec. wd. Cf. also BALE-FIRE.] †**1.** *gen.* A great consuming fire; a bonfire –1600. **2.** *spec.* **a.** A funeral pile or pyre. (*Obs.* exc. in W. MORRIS.) OE. **b.** A signal- or beacon-fire. *Sc.* (*arch.*) 1455. **3.** *fig.* 1568.

Bale (bēˡl), *sb.*[3] [ME. *bale*, perh. a. OF. *bale*, *balle*, ? ad. OHG. *balla* (BALL *sb.*[1]), or Gr. πάλλα. Or perh. f. Flemish *bale* 'bale', adopted from F. *Bale* and *ball* are distinct in Eng.] **1.** A large bundle or package, orig. more or less round in shape; now, *spec.* one closely pressed, done up in canvas, etc., and corded or hooped, for transportation. **2.** A varying measure of quantity 1502. †**3.** The set of dice –1822.

Comb. **b.-goods**, merchandise in bales: opp. to *case-goods*. Hence **Bale** *v.*[1] to make up into a bale or bales.

†**Bale,** *v.*[2] *rare.* ME. only. [a. OF. *baler*, *baller*:—late L. *ballare*.] To dance.

Bale, *v.*[3] 1692. Erron. sp. of BAIL *v.*[3]

Bale, obs. sp. of BAIL *sb.* and *v.*; improp. f. BAIL *sb.*[2]

†**Baleare,** *a.* 1576. [f. L. *Balearis*.] = *Balearic*. Hence **Balea·rian** *a.* and *sb.*, and **Balea·ric** *a.* [L. *Balearicus*] of or pertaining to, *sb.* a native of, Majorca, Minorca, Iviça, etc. (= L. *Baleares Insulæ*), in the Mediterranean Sea. *Balearic Crane*: the Crowned Crane.

Baleen (bălī·n). [ME. *baleyne*, a. OF. *baleine*:—L. *balæna*.] †**1.** A whale –1601. **2.** ? The Sea-bream ME. **3.** Whalebone. Also *attrib.* ME.

Bale-fire (bēˡ·lfəiəɹ). OE. [f. BALE *sb.*[2] (occas. confused with BALE *sb.*[1]) + FIRE. Till lately Sc. only. Cf. BELTANE.] **1.** A great fire in the open air. In OE. *spec.* the fire of a funeral pile. **2.** A signal- or beacon-fire. (App. first used by SCOTT.) 1805. **3.** A bonfire, *feu de joie* 1800.

1. The fires of death, The bale-fires flash on high BYRON.

Baleful (bēˡ·lful), *a.* [OE. *bealu-full*, f. BALE *sb.*[1] Chiefly literary.] **1.** Full of active evil. **2.** *subjectively*: †**a.** Full of pain or suffering –1579. **b.** Unhappy; sorrowful (*arch.*) ME.

1. B. weedes SHAKS., Envy SMOLLETT, prejudices 1863. 2. B. spirits barr'd from realms of bliss 1812. Hence **Ba·leful-ly** *adv.*, **-ness.**

Ba·leless, *a. arch.* [OE. *bealulēas*; see BALE *sb.*[1] and -LESS.] Harmless, innocent.

†**Baleys,** *sb.* ME. [a. OF. *baleis*, nom. sing. (or acc. pl.) of *balei* (mod. *balai*).] A rod; also, a birch, as used in flogging –1517. Hence **Baleys** *v.* to flog (still *dial.*).

†**Balinger** (bæ·lindʒəɹ). *Hist.* ME. [a. AF. *balengier* = OF. *baleinier* a whale-ship, f. *baleine*.] A kind of sloop; acc. to Adm. Smyth, without forecastle.

†**Bali·ster, -ester.** 1489. [a. OF. *balestier*:—L. *ballistarius*.] A crossbow-man –1613.

‖**Balistraria** (bælistrēᵊ·riă). 1845. [med.L., fem. of adj. *ballistrarius*.] *Archit.* **a.** A cruciform opening in the walls of a fortress, through which arbalests were discharged. **b.** A room in which arbalests were kept.

‖**Balize** (bălī·z). 1847. [F. *balise* = Sp. *valiza*; of unkn. origin.] A pole, surmounted by a barrel, or the like, raised as a beacon at sea.

Balk, baulk (bǭk), *sb.* [Com. Teut.: OE. *balca* ridge, also OE. *bolca* gangway of a ship. The orig. sense was perh. 'bar'. *Balk* is the analogous spelling; but *baulk* is common, and in Billiards usual.] †**1.** A ridge, or mound –ME. †**2.** An isthmus; a bar of sand, etc. –1633. **3.** A ridge between two furrows (L. *porca*), or a strip of ground left unploughed OE. **4.** A piece missed in ploughing ME. †**5.** *fig.* A blunder –1717; †an omission –1775. †**6.** A stumbling-block, obstacle –1747. **7.** *fig.* A check or defeat 1660; a disappointment 1733. **8.** *transf.* The part of a billiard table behind a transverse line (the 'baulk-line') near one end, within the D or half-circle of which a player whose ball is in hand must place it to make his stroke 1800. **9.** A roughly squared beam of timber ME. **10.** A tie-beam of a house. A loft above was called 'the balks'. Now chiefly *north.* ME. **11.** The beam of a balance. Now *dial.* ME. **12.** *dial.* Stakes surrounded by netting or wicker work for catching fish 1836. **13.** The stout rope by which fishing nets are fastened one to another in a fleet. (In Cornw. *balch.*) 1847.

3. Narrow balks that intersect the fields 1821. 5. *To make a balk*: to blunder. 7. There cannot be a greater b. to the tempter SOUTH. 8. *To make a baulk*: to bring one's own and the red ball within the baulk, when the opponent's ball is in hand. 11. Unto the tubbes hangyng in the balkes CHAUCER.

Balk (bǭk), *v.*[1] ME. [f. prec. sb.] †**1.** *trans.* (and *absol.*) To make balks in ploughing –1611. **2.** To miss or omit intentionally; †to pass by –1783; to ignore 1440; to refuse (*e.g.* drink offered) 1587; to avoid (a duty, etc.) 1631; to let slip 1601. **3.** *intr.* To stop short, swerve. *Esp.* of a horse: To jib, refuse to go on, to shy. 1481. **4.** *trans.* To miss unintentionally -1710. **5.** To place a balk in the way of; to check 1589; to disappoint 1590; to frustrate 1635. †**6.** *trans.* and *absol.* To quibble, chop logic, bandy words -1653.

2. I never..balked an invitation out to dinner JOHNSON. To b. an opportunity DRYDEN. **3.** If he balked, I knew I was undone DE FOE. His horse balked at a leap 1862. **5.** An enemy who is baulked and defeated, but not overcome DE FOE. Balk'd of his prey POPE. Hence **Balked** *ppl. a.* †ridged; †? heaped up (1 *Hen. IV*, I. i. 69); checked; disappointed. **Ba·lker**[1], one who balks, or makes or frequents balks. **Ba·lkingly** *adv.*

Balk, *v.*[2] ? *Obs.* 1603. [prob. a. Du. *balken*, cogn. w. OE. *bælcan* to shout (which would itself give *balch*).] To signify to fishing-boats, by shouting or signals from the heights, the direction taken by shoals of herrings or pilchards. Hence **Ba·lker**[2], one who does this; a huer, hooer, or conder.

†**Ba·lkish,** *a.* 1577. [f. BALK *sb.* + -ISH[1].] In ridges; uneven.

Balky (bǭ·ki), *a.* 1856. [f. as prec. + -Y[1].] Given to balking (as a horse).

Ball (bǭl), *sb.*[1] [ME. *bal*, a. ON. *böllr*:—OTeut. **balluz.* No OE. form is known. Error. derived from F. *balle* 'ball' and 'bale'. See BALE *sb.*[3]] **1.** *gen.* A globular body. **2.** *spec.* Any planetary body, *esp.* the earth, the globe ME. †**3.** The golden orb borne together with the sceptre -1715. **4.** A globular body to play with, as in foot-ball, tennis, golf, cricket, etc. (Perh. the earliest Eng. sense.) ME. **b.** A game played with a ball ME. **c.** A throw, toss, or delivery of the ball, *esp.* in *Cricket* 1483. **5.** A missile (orig. spherical) projected from an engine of war. In artillery, a solid as dist. from a hollow projectile. ME. **6.** *Pyrotechny* and *Mil.* A globular case filled with combustibles; e. g. *fire-, smoke-, stink-balls* 1753. **7.** A small globe of wood, etc. used in voting by BALLOT 1580. **8.** *Ball of the eye*: **a.** orig. the pupil; **b.** now, the eye itself within the socket ME. **9.** A rounded mass of any substance ME. **10.** *Med.* A bolus. Now only in *Vet. Med.* 1576. **11.** (f. F. *balle*) A BALE 1583. **12.** A kind of small cushion used by printers for inking the type 1611. **13.** Any rounded protuberant part of the body; *esp.* of the thumb and great toe 1483. **14.** The central hollow of the palm of the hand or sole of the foot (*obs.*); the central part of an animal's foot 1601.

1. He rolleth vnder foot as dooth a bal CHAUCER. **2.** This Terrestrial b. *Rich. II*, III. iv. 41. **3.** The Scepter, and the B. *Hen. V*, IV. i. 277. **4.** *No ball*, one unfairly bowled. *Wide ball*, one not properly within the batsman's reach. **5.** Mineral and stone.. to found their Engins and their Balls Of missive ruin MILT. *P. L.* vi. 518. To load with b. MACAULAY. **7.** One black b. in three excludes DICKENS. **8.** His sightless balls SCOTT. **9.** Balls of cowslips HERRICK.

Phrases, etc. *fig.* from games:—*To catch* or *take the b. before the bound*: to anticipate opportunity. *To have the b. at one's foot* or *before one*: to have a thing in one's power. *To keep the b. up* or *rolling*: to keep the conversation, etc., from flagging. *To take up the b.*: to take one's turn in conversation, etc. *The b. is with you*: it is your turn. **B. and socket**: a joint formed of a rounded end partly enclosed in a cup or socket, which is strong and yet moves freely. *Three (golden) balls*: the sign of a pawnbroker; supposed by some to be taken from the ensign of the Medici family.

Comb.: **b.-bear·ing(s,** a contrivance for lessening friction by means of small loose metal balls, used for the bearings of axles; **-cartridge,** a gun- or pistol-cartridge containing a bullet; **-clay,** very adhesive clay, as that brought up in lumps sticking to a ship's anchor; **-cock,** a self-regulating cistern-tap turned on and off by the rising or falling of a hollow floating ball; **-flower** (*Arch.*), an ornament like a ball within three or four petals of a flower, often inserted in a hollow moulding; **-mine,** iron-ore found in nodules; **-stamp,** an American ore-crushing machine; **-stone,** a rounded lump of ironstone or limestone; **-tap** (= *ball-cock*); **-thistle,** the Globe Thistle, also a species of Echinops; **-valve,** one opened or closed by the rising or falling of a valve which fits a cup-shaped opening in the seat; †**-vein,** iron ore in nodules; **-weed,** *Centaurea nigra.*

Ball (bǭl), *sb.*[2] 1632. [a. F. *bal*, f. *baler* BALE *v.*[2]] †**1.** A dance or dancing 1633. **2.** A social assembly for the purpose of dancing 1632. Also *attrib.*, as *ball-room* (1752).

2. Balls .. the perdition of precious houres JER. TAYLOR. Phr. *To give, go to, a b.* *To open the b.*: (*fig.*) to commence operations.

†**Ball,** *sb.*[3] 1523. [prob. f. Celtic.] **1.** A white streak or spot; ? a bald place. **2.** ? A white-faced horse; hence, a horse's name 1573.

Ball (bǭl), *v.* 1593. [f. BALL *sb.*[1]] **1.** *trans.* To round or swell out. **2.** To make or wind into a ball 1658. **3.** *intr.* To gather (itself) into a ball 1713. **4.** To clog, or become clogged, with balls (of snow, etc.) 1828.

4. The pony stumbled through the..snow..getting its feet balled 1863.

Ballad (bæ·lăd). 1492. [ME. *balade*, a. OF. *balade* (mod. *ballade*):—late L. *ballare* to dance: cf. BALE *v.*[2] In 16th and 17th c. *-ad* became *-at(e, -et* (cf. *salad, sallet*), and in Sc. *-ant.* Cf. BALLET. See also BALLADE.] †**1.** A song to accompany a dance -1616. **2.** A light, simple song of any kind; now *spec.* a sentimental or romantic composition, each verse of which is usu. sung to the same melody 1492. †**3.** A popular song, often scurrilous or personal -1825. †**4.** A posy. (Cf. L. *cantilena.*) -1601. **5.** A simple spirited poem in short stanzas, narrating some popular story. (This sense is mod.) 1712.

2. We do nought togyder, But prycked balades synge 1500. **3.** Who makes a ballet for an ale-house doore 1602. **4.** Spend, and god shall send .. saith tholde ballet J. HEYWOOD. **5.** The grand old b. of Sir Patrick Spence COLERIDGE.

Comb.: **b.-monger,** one who sells ballads; *contemptuously*, ballad-maker (Shaks); **-farce, -opera,** a play into which popular songs are introduced.

Hence **Ba·llader,** a writer of ballads or †scurrilous verses. **Balla·dic,** †**-al** *a.* of the nature of, or pertaining to, ballads. †**Balladie·r,** a street b.-singer. **Ba·lladism,** the characteristic quality of ballads. **Ba·lladist,** a ballader. **Ba·lladize** *v.* to make, or turn into, a b. **Ba·lladry,** b. poetry; composition in the b. style. (Formerly *depreciative.*)

Ba·llad, *v.* ? *Obs.* 1592. [f. prec. sb.] **1.** To write or compose ballads. **2.** *trans.* To make the subject of (scurrilous) ballads 1606.

Ballade (bălā·d). ME. [Early (also mod. F.) sp. and pronunc. of BALLAD, now technical.] **1. a.** *strictly*, A poem consisting of one or more triplets of seven- or (later) eight-lined stanzas each ending with the same line as refrain, and (usu.) an envoy. **b.** A poem divided into stanzas of equal length, usu. of seven or eight lines. †**c.** *occas.* One of these stanzas. **2.** *collect.* Poetry of this form ME. **3.** *Mus.* **a.** A composition of poetic character, usu. for piano. **b.** = BALLAD **2. c.** Kind of tone-poem for orchestra.

Ballan (bæ·lăn). 1769. *Zool.* A kind of Wrasse (*Labrus maculatus*).

Ballarag, obs. f. BULLYRAG.

†**Ba·llard.** ME. [app. f. BALL *sb.*[3] Cf. BALD.] A bald-headed person.

Ballast (bæ·lăst), *sb.* 1530. [? f. LG. *ballast* 'bad lading' (see BALE *a.*); or f. ODa. *barlast* 'bare load'; both found bef. 1400.] **1.** Any heavy material, as gravel, sand, etc., placed in a ship's hold, to sink her to such a depth as to prevent her from capsizing when in motion. **2.** *fig.* That which tends to give stability in morals, politics, etc. 1612. †**3.** *transf.* Load, freight -1646. **4.** Gravel, broken stone, slag, etc. used to form the bed of a railroad. Also applied to burnt clay. 1837.

1. *In ballast*: **a.** in the hold. **b.** Of ships: Laden with b. only. **c.** Of materials: In the capacity of b. **2.** Solid and sober natures, have more of the b., then of the saile BACON. *Comb.*: **b.-ports,** square holes cut in the sides of merchantmen for taking in b.; **-shovel** (*Min.*), a round-mouthed shovel.

Ballast (bæ·lăst), *v.* 1538. [f. prec. sb.] **1.** To furnish (a ship) with ballast. **2.** *transf.* To steady 1596; also *fig.* †**3.** To load (*with* cargo) -1666. **4.** *transf.* and *fig.* To weight (*arch.*) 1566. **5.** To fill in or form with BALLAST (sense 4) 1864. ¶ **6.** Confused w. BALANCE *v.* 1611.

2. Deliberation..to b. the impetuosity of the people A. YOUNG. **4.** To b. my purse SCOTT. Hence **Ba·llastage,** toll paid for the privilege of taking ballast. **Ba·llaster,** one who supplies ships with ballast. **Ba·llasting** *vbl. sb.*; *concr.* and *fig.* = BALLAST *sb.*

Ballat, -ry, obs. ff. BALLAD, -RY.

Ballatoo·n. 1828. A Russian lumber-boat.

Balled (bǭld), *ppl. a.* 1591. [f. BALL *v.*[1] and *sb.*[1]] **a.** Formed into a ball. †**b.** Cleared of lumps; cf. *shelled peas.*

Baller (bǭ·ləɹ). 1668. [f. BALL *v.*[1] and *sb.*[2]] **1.** One who forms into balls 1865. †**2.** One who goes to balls. PEPYS.

Ballerina (bælərī·nă). 1792. [It.] A danseuse, esp. one in a leading rôle.

‖**Ballet** (ba·le, *rarely* bæ·lėt). 1667. [a. F., dim. of *bal*; see BALL *sb.*[2] In 17th c. confused w. BALLAD.] **1.** A theatrical representation, consisting of dancing and pantomime, originally employed to illustrate foreign dress and manners, but now mainly an exhibition of skill in dancing. †**2.** A dance -1829.

1. Not a Balette or Masque, but a play DRYDEN. *Comb.*: **b.-master, -mistress,** one who arranges and directs the dancing of the b.

Ballet (bæ·lėt), *sb.*[2] 1727. [f. BALL *sb.* + -ET dim. suffix; cf. OF. *balette.*] *Her.* A little ball.

Ballet, -ette, obs. ff. BALLAD.

Balling (bǭ·liŋ), *vbl. sb.* 1713. [f. BALL *v.*[1] + -ING[1].] **1.** Formation into a ball or balls; occas. *attrib.*, as in *b.-machine* (for winding twine), etc. **2.** The throwing of (snow-) balls 1865.

†**Ba·llised,** *ppl. a.* 1624. [? for *pallised*, ad. F. *palissé.*] Surrounded with a railing or balustrade. WOTTON.

Ba·llist. *rare.* ME. [ad. L. *ballista.*] = next.

‖**Ballista** (bălĭ·stă). Also (less well) **balista.** Pl. **-æ,** occas. **-as.** 1598. [L., f. (ult.) Gr. βάλλειν.] An ancient military engine, resembling a bow stretched with cords and thongs, used to hurl stones, etc.; in med.L. also for: Arbalest.

Balli·stic, *a.* 1775. [f. prec.] Of or pertaining to the throwing of missiles; projectile.

The b. power of our weapons 1879. *Ballistic pendulum*: an instrument for determining the relative velocity of projectiles.

Balli·stics, *sb. pl.* 1753. [f. prec.; cf. *athletics*, etc.] The science of projectiles.

‖**Ballium** (bæ·li,ŏm). 1798. [med.L., f. F. *bail.*] = BAIL *sb.*[3] 2, and BAILEY.

Ba·llock. *Obs.* in polite use. OE. [prob.:—Teut. *ball-* (see BALL *sb.*[1]).] A testicle.

†**Ballon.** *rare.* 1753. [a. F. *balon*, f. *bale*, BALE *sb.*[3]] A bale, as of paper.

Balloon (bălū·n), *sb.* 1634. [ad. It. *ballone* great ball, f. *balla.* Cf. F. *ballon.*] †**1.** A large inflated leather ball, struck to and fro by the arm protected by a bracer of wood -1801. †**2.** The game played with this -1820. †**3.** *Pyrotechny.* = *shell* or *bomb* -1753. **4.** *Archit.* A globe crowning a pillar, pier, etc. 1656. **5.** *Chem.* A large globose glass vessel, with one or more short necks, used to receive the products of distillation, etc. 1727. **6.** An air-tight envelope of silk, etc., usually globose or pear-shaped, which, when inflated with light gas, rises in the air; *esp.* one with a car attached to carry human beings for purposes of observation, etc. 1783. *fig.* Anything inflated and empty 1812. **7.** *Hort.*: **a.** A method of training fruit trees in which the branches form the shape of a balloon. **b.** A balloon-shaped trellis. **8.** The outline containing words represented in comic papers as issuing from the mouth of any one.

2. That wondrous match at ballon SCOTT. **6.** The hollow b. of popular applause CARLYLE.

Comb.: **b.-brasser** (cf. F. *brassart*, the wooden bracer worn by b.-players); **-fish,** one of the Diodontes, so named because they distend their bodies with air.

Hence (besides nonce-words): **Balloo·ner,** an aeronaut; *Naut.* a b.-like sail. **Balloo·nery, -nry. Balloo·ning** *vbl. sb.* aeronautics. **Balloo·nist,** an aeronaut.

Ballot (bæ·lət), *sb.*[1] 1549. [ad. It. *ballota* 'a rounde bullet . . a voice or lot' (Florio), dim. of *balla* BALL *sb.*[1]] **1.** A small ball used for secret voting; hence, a ticket, etc. so used. **2.** The method of secret voting; orig. by means of small balls placed in an urn or box; an instance of this; the votes thus recorded 1549. **3.** A method of drawing lots by taking small balls, etc., from a box; hence *gen.* lot-drawing 1680.

1. To convey each Man his bean or b. into the Box MILT. **2.** To try the result of a b. MACAULAY. **3.** The b. for the militia WELLINGTON. *Comb.*: **b.-box,** a box used for the balls in a b.; *fig.* secret voting; **-paper,** the voting-paper used in a b. Hence **Ba·llotage,** in France, the second b., to decide between the two candidates that have come nearest to a legal majority. **Ballotee·r,** an advocate of the b. †**Ba·llotin,** an officer in charge of a b.-box. **Ba·llotist,** an advocate of the b.

Ba·llot, *sb.*[2] 1865. [a. F., dim. of *balle* BALE *sb.*[2]] A small bale, of 70 to 120 lbs.

Ballot (bæ·lət), *v.* 1549. [a. It. *ballottare*, f. *ballota*; see BALLOT *sb.*[1]] †**1.** *trans.* To vote upon secretly, as by depositing small balls in an urn or box -1691. 2. *intr.* To give a secret vote (*for, against*) 1580. 3. To select by the drawing of lots 1785.

2. *To b. for*: to select, elect, or reject, by secret voting. 3. *To b. for*: to select by lot. To b. for another day for one's resolution 1884. Hence †**Ballota·tion**, voting by ballot. **Ba·lloter.**

†**Ballo·te.** 1551. [a. F., ad. L., a. Gr. βαλλωτή.] *Herb.* The Black Stinking Horehound.

‖**Ballottement** (bălǫ·tmĕnt). 1839. [F.] *Med.* A mode of diagnosing pregnancy.

†**Ba·llow,** *sb.* [Only in loc. cit.] = BATON 1.

Ice try whither your Costard or my B. be the harder *Lear* IV. vi. 247. (Fo. 1623.)

Bally (bæ·li), *a.* and *adv. slang.* 1887. A euphemism for *bloody* (BLOODY A. 8, B. 2), used as a vague intensive of general application.

Ballyhoo (bæ·lihū), orig. *U.S.* 1901. [?] A barker's speech; advance publicity; blarney.

Balm (bām), *sb.* [ME. *basme, bame*, a. OF. :—L. *balsamum*; see BALSAM. Refash. after L. *bal-*.] 1. An aromatic substance, exuding naturally from various trees of the genus *Balsamodendron*. †2. An aromatic preparation for embalming the dead -1618. 3. Fragrant oil or ointment 1447; also *fig.* 4. Aromatic ointment used for soothing pain or healing wounds (*arch.*) ME. Also *transf.* or *fig.* 5. A tree yielding balm; one of the genus *Balsamodendron*, N.O. *Amyridaceæ* ME. 6. Name of some fragrant garden herbs (N.O. *Labiatæ*); esp. Balm Gentle or Balm-mint (*Melissa officinalis*) and Bastard Balm (*Melittis melyssophyllum*). Also Field Balm (*Calamintha Nepeta*). 1440.

4. As B. to fester'd wounds MILT. *Sams.* 186. 5. Let not their precious balms break my head *Ps.* cxli. 5. *Phrases*: **Balm of Gilead** (also *Balm of Mecca*), a gold-coloured oleo-resin exuded from the tree *Balsamodendron Gileadense*, or perh. *B. Opobalsamum*, once esteemed as an antiseptic and vulnerary. **b.** *American B. of G.*: a resin obtained from the *Icica carana*. (The Heb. word *tsŏri* (see *Gen.* xxxvii. 25) was identified with *resin* by the Vulg. 'Balm' began with Coverdale.) **Balm of Gilead Fir**: the N. American species yielding Canada Balsam.

Balm (bām), *v. arch.* ME. [app. f. prec. sb.] 1. To embalm (*arch.*). 2. †To anoint, or mix, with balm, etc. -1600; to smear with something sticky 1530. 3. To soothe, alleviate (pain, etc.) (*arch.*) ME.

Balm-apple: see *Balsam-apple* in BALSAM *sb.*

Ba·lm-cri·cket. 1783. [app. a mistr. of G. *baum-grille* tree-cricket.] The cicada.

The balm-cricket carols clear In the green that folds thy grave TENNYSON. (Taken by Tennyson from Dalzel *Analec. Maj.* II. 187.)

Balmoral (bælmǫ·răl). 1864. [f. *Balmoral* Castle.] Name for: **a.** A variety of Scotch cap. **b.** A kind of figured woollen petticoat. **c.** A kind of boot lacing in front.

Balmy (bā·mi), *a.* 1500. [f. BALM *sb.* + -Y[1].] 1. Yielding balm 1667. †2. Resinous 1782. 3. Fragrant 1500. 4. *fig.* Soft and soothing 1604. 5. Of wind, air, weather, etc. (combining 3 and 4): Deliciously mild, fragrant, and soothing 1704. 6. Of healing virtue 1746. 7. *slang.* Soft, weak-minded, idiotic 1851. Also BARMY 1896.

3. B. breath *Oth.* v. ii. 16, firs 1824. 4. B. slumbers *Oth.* II. ii. 259, sleep YOUNG. 5. The b. zephyrs POPE. Hence **Ba·lmify** *v.* **Ba·lmily** *adv.* **Ba·lminess.**

Ba·lneal, *a.* 1645. [f. L. *balneum* + -AL[1].] Of or pertaining to a (warm) bath or bathing.

Balneary (bæ·lnĭări). 1646. [ad. L. *balnearium.*] A bath or bathing-place; a medicinal spring.

Balnea·tion. ? *Obs.* [f. med.L. *balneare.*] Bathing.

Balneo·graphy. [f. L. *balneum* + Gr. -γραφία.] A description of, or treatise upon, baths. **Balneo·logy** [see -LOGY], scientific medical study of bathing, etc.; whence **Ba:lneolo·gical** *a.* **Balneothe·rapy** [Gr. θεραπεία], treatment of disease by baths or medicinal springs.

‖**Balneum** (bæ·lnĭǒm). 1471. [L.] 1. A bath or bathing 1652. 2. *Alch., Chem.*, and *Cookery.* = BAIN MARIE. (Occas. *balneo.*)

†**Balow·, baloo·.** 1611. [app. a nursery word.] 1. *int.* An utterance used in lulling to sleep 1724. 2. *sb.* **a.** A lullaby. **b.** A song and tune containing this word. 1611.

‖**Balsa** (bæ·lsă). 1778. [Sp.] A raft or fishing-float, used chiefly on the Pacific coasts of S. America.

Balsam (bǭ·lsăm), *sb.* OE. [ad. L. *balsamum.* Between OE. and *c* 1600 replaced by *basme, baume* from F. (see BALM), and *spec.* by the L. form, or the It. *balsamo.*] 1. = BALM *sb.* 1. 2. An aromatic oily or resinous medicinal preparation, for healing wounds or soothing pain 1579. Also *fig.* †3. *transf.* in *Alch.* A healthful preservative essence, oily and softly penetrative, conceived by Paracelsus to exist in all organic bodies -1753. †4. = BALM *sb.* 2; *fig.* a preservative -1753. 5. *Chem.* Compounds, insoluble in water, consisting of resins mixed with volatile oil 1673. 6. = BALM *sb.* 7. OE. 7. A flowering plant of the genus *Impatiens*, esp. *I. Balsamina*; also *I. Noli-tangere* 1741.

1. *True Balsam*, or *B. of Mecca* (the earliest known sort): *Balm of Gilead*, q.v. The discovery of America ..gave also *B. of Acouchi*, *of Copaiba*, *of Peru*, *of Tolu*, and *Canada B.* 2. Is this the Balsome, that the vsuring Senat Powres into Captaines wounds *Timon* III. v. 10. 4. Noble Acts are the Balsom of our Memories SIR T. BROWNE.

Comb.: **B. Apple** (or *Balm Apple*): name of species of *Momordica* (*M. Balsamina*, *M. Charantia*), gourd-like plants with highly coloured fruits, also called *Apple of Jerusalem*, and Male B. Apple. Also used, improp., of the common garden B. ('Female' B. Apple).

Hence **Balsama·tion,** the process of embalming. **Balsami·ferous** *a.* yielding b. **Ba·lsamy** *a.* balmy.

Balsam (bǭ·lsăm), *v.* 1666. [f. prec. sb.] 1. To anoint with balsam; to heal, salve. Also *intr.* (for *refl.*) 2. To embalm (*rare*) 1855.

Balsamic (bǫlsæ·mik, bæl-). 1605. [f. Gr. βάλσαμον + -IC.] **A.** *adj.* 1. Of the nature of, or yielding, balsam 1676. 2. Balmy 1714. 3. Soothing, restorative 1605. 4. Of, pertaining to, or full of, BALSAM (sense 3) 1644. 5. *fig.* Soothing, healing, balmy 1667. **B.** *sb.* = BALM *sb.* 4, BALSAM *sb.* 2. 1713. Hence **Balsa·mical** *a.* **Balsa·mically** *adv.* var. **Ba·lsamous** *a.*

†**Ba·lsamine.** 1578. [a. F., ad. Gr. βαλσαμίνη, f. βάλσαμον.] Book name for: **a.** *Balsam Apple*; **b.** the plant *Impatiens Balsamina*.

‖**Ba·lsamum.** OE. [a. L., a. Gr. βάλσαμον (prob. f. Semitic).] 1. = BALM *sb.* 1. 2. = BALM *sb.* 2-4. ME. 3. *Alch.* = BALSAM *sb.* 3. ME. 4. = BALSAM *sb.* 6. ME. Also *attrib.*

Balter, bolter (bǭ·ltəɹ, bǭᵘ(l)təɹ), *v.* Now *dial.* ME. [prob. Scand.; cf. Da. *baltre, boltre* tumble, gambol.] †1. To tumble about, *e.g.* in dancing -1500. 2. *trans.* To tread clumsily (*dial.*). 3. To mat (the hair) 1693. 4. *intr.* (for *refl.*) To form tangled knots or clots 1601. Hence **Ba·lter** *sb. dial.* a clot.

Baltimore (bǭ·ltimōᵊɹ). Also **B.-bird, -oriole.** An American bird (*Icterus Baltimorii*) of the Starling family; so named because its colours (orange and black) are those of the coat of arms of Lord Baltimore, formerly proprietor of Maryland.

Baluster (bæ·lǒstəɹ). 1602. [a. F. *balustre*, ad. It. *balaustro*; so named from It. *balausta*, *balaustra* 'blossom of the wild pomegranate' (L. *balaustium*, Gr. βαλαύστιον), which a baluster resembles in shape. In Eng., corrupted to (ult.) BANISTER.] 1. A short pillar of circular section, slender above and bulging below; usu. one of a series called a *balustrade*. Also, a similar pillar used in a window. 2. A slender upright post supporting a rail; in *pl.* a railing, a balustrade 1633. 3. (Usu. in *pl.*) The uprights which support the handrail of a staircase; also, the whole structure. Now usu. BANISTER(S. 1732. 4. *collect. sing.* A balustrade (*arch.*) 1644. 5. *Class. Arch.* 'The lateral part of the volute of an Ionic capital' (Gwilt). Hence **Ba·lustered** *ppl. a.* furnished with, or enclosed by, balusters.

Balustrade (bæ·lǒstrēⁱ·d). 1644. [a. F., f. *balustre*; see prec.] A row of balusters surmounted by a rail or coping. Hence **Ba·lustra·ded** *ppl. a.* **Ba·lustra·ding**, b.-work.

Bam (bæm), *v. slang.* 1707. [conn. w. BAMBOOZLE; ? as abbrev., or source.] To hoax, cozen 1738. Also *absol.* or *intr.* Hence **Bam** *sb.* a hoax or imposition.

‖**Bambino** (bambī·no). 1761. [It., dim. of *bambo* silly.] A child, a baby; *spec.* an image of the child Jesus in swaddling clothes.

Bambocciade. 1868. [ad. F. *bambochade*, It. *bambocciata*, f. *bamboccio*, f. *bambo* (see prec.); a nickname of the painter Peter de Laer.] A painting of rustic and grotesque scenes.

Bamboo (bæmbū·). 1598. [? Malay *bambu* or Canarese *bănbŭ*. Cf. Du. *bamboes*.] A genus of giant grasses (genus *Bambusa*), common in tropical countries. Also the stem of any of these used as a stick, etc. *Comb.* **b.-coolie**, one that carries loads suspended on bamboos. Hence **Bamboo·** *v.* to beat with a b.

Bamboozle (bæmbū·z'l), *v.* 1703. [prob. of cant origin. Cf. BAM.] 1. To deceive by trickery, hoax, cozen. Also *absol.* or *intr.* 2. To mystify 1712.

1. Certain Words invented by some pretty Fellows, such as Banter, Bamboozle..some of which are now struggling for the vogue SWIFT *Tatler* No. 230 ¶ 7. Hence **Bamboo·zle** *sb.* bamboozling. **Bamboo·zlement**, mystification. **Bamboo·zler.**

Bambusa; see BAMBOO.

Ban (bæn), *v.* [OE. *bannan* to summon:—OTeut. **bannan* to proclaim under penalty, f. root *ba-*, cogn. w. Gr. φα-, L. *fa-*, speak. Cf. BAN *sb.*] †I. [from OE.] To summon by proclamation. (Chiefly, to arms.) -ME.

II. [f. ON. *banna*, ? and med.L. *bannum.*] 1. To curse, imprecate damnation upon (*arch.*) ME. Also *intr.* 2. *trans.* and *absol.* To chide, address with angry language (*dial.*) ME. 3. To anathematize (*arch.*) ME. 4. To interdict, proscribe 1816.

1. And some men b. the, & some men blesse 1460. 4. To whom the goodly earth and air Are bann'd and barr'd BYRON.

Ban (bæn), *sb.*[1] ME. [partly a. OF. *ban*, influenced by med.L. *bannum*; partly f. BAN *v.* F. *ban* was :—late L. *bannum*, ad. Teut. *bann*, *ban* sb., f. *bannan*; see prec. The simple sb. *bann* does not occur in OE.] 1. A summons by public proclamation, chiefly to arms; an edict. ‖2. **a.** The gathering of the (French) king's vassals for war; the whole muster; orig. = *arrière-ban*. **b.** In France now the *ban* is the younger part of the population liable to serve, the *arrière-ban* the reserve; in Prussia, the first and second *bans* are the two divisions of the Landwehr. ME. ‖3. Sentence of banishment; whence 'to keep', or 'break his b.' 1873. 4. Proclamation of marriage; always in *pl.*, now spelt BANNS, q. v. 5. A formal eccl. denunciation; anathema, interdict 1481. Also *fig.* 6. *gen.* A curse, supposed to have supernatural sanction and power to harm 1602. 7. An imprecation of a curse 1596. 8. A formal and authoritative prohibition; an interdict 1667. 9. Sentence of outlawry; *esp.* 'Ban of the (Holy Roman) Empire' 1674. 10. *fig.* Practical outlawry, denunciation by society or public opinion 1839.

4. Beneath the b. of Pope and Church SCOTT. 6. With Hecats B., thrice blasted, thrice infected *Haml.* III. ii. 269. 8. To taste it under banne to touch MILT. *P. L.* IX. 925. 10. Opinions which are under the b. of society MILL.

‖**Ban** (bæn), *sb.*[2] 1614. [Pers. 'lord'; introduced by the Avars who ruled in Slavonic countries subject to Hungary.] The viceroy of certain military districts in Hungary, Slavonia, and Croatia, who takes the command in time of war. Hence, **Banate, Bannat**, the district under the jurisdiction of a b. **Banal** *a.* of or pertaining to a b.; *sb.* a Banate.

Banal (bē·năl, bæ·-), *a.* 1753. [a. F., f. *ban*:—med.L. *bannum*; see BAN *sb.*[1] and -AL[1].] 1. Of or belonging to compulsory feudal service. 2. (From the intermediate sense of, Open to the use of all the community): Commonplace, trivial 1864.

Banality (bănæ·lĭti). 1861. [ad. F. *banalité*; see prec.] 1. Anything trite or trivial; a commonplace. 2. Triteness, triviality 1878.

Banana (bănā·nă). 1597. [a. Pg. or Sp., given as the native name in Guinea (Congo).] 1. A tree (*Musa sapientum*) cultivated largely in tropical countries; it grows to a height of 20 feet 1697. 2. The fruit of this tree, growing in clusters of angular, finger-like berries containing a highly nutritious pulp 1597. Also *attrib.*

Comb. **b.-bird**, a gregarious West Indian bird (*Xanthornus icterus*).

Banausic (bănǭ·sik), *a. rare.* 1876. [ad. Gr. βαναυσικός, f. βαῦνος forge.] Proper for a mechanic.

Banbury. A town in Oxfordshire, England, once noted for its Puritan zeal, now for its cakes.

‖**Banc** (bæŋk). 1727. [AF. = 'bench'; see BANK *sb.*] *Law.* Bench; in phr. *in banc* = in BANCO.

‖**Banco** (bæ·ŋko), *a.* [It.; = bank.] The bank money of account in certain places, as dist. from (depreciated) *currency.* Retained in calculating exchanges with foreign countries.

‖**Banco** (bæ·ŋko), *sb.* 1768. [L., abl. of *bancus*; see BANK *sb.*² and cf. BANC.] In L. phr. *in banco* = on the bench: used of sittings of a superior Court of Common Law as a full court.

Band (bænd), *sb.*¹ [ME. *band, bond,* a. ON. *band* neut.:—OTeut. **bando-(m),* f. *band-* stem of *bindan.* Not in OE.; see BEND *sb.*¹ *Band* and *bond* were orig. only phonetic variants (cf. *land, lond,* etc.).] **1.** Anything with which a person is bound; a shackle, chain, fetter, manacle (*arch.*). Also *fig.* **2.** A string or tie with which any loose thing is bound ME.; in *Bookbinding,* one of the cords or straps crossing the back of a book, to which the quires or sheets are attached 1759. **3.** A hinge of a door or gate ME. **4.** A connecting piece by which the parts of a whole are held firmly together ME. **5.** A leading-string, strap, or chain (*lit.* and *fig.*) ME. †**6.** *Logic.* The copula (*rare*) -1628. **7.** An obligation which operates as a tie, restraint, or bond ME. **8.** A uniting force or influence (now BOND) 1483. **9.** An agreement, or promise, binding on him who makes it (now BOND) ME. **10.** Security given; a deed legally executed, binding on him who delivers it (now BOND) 1521. †**11.** A league -1649. †**12.** Binding quality or power -1619. †**13.** A state of union 1631.

1. Euery one's bands were loosed *Acts* xvi. 26. *fig.* Bunden faste With bandes of syn HAMPOLE. 4. The bands of life *Rich. II,* II. ii. 71. 7. To joyne in Hymens bands *A. Y. L.* v. iv. 136. 10. His word is as good as his b. FULLER.

Band (bænd), *sb.*² [Late ME. *bande,* a. F., 'flat strip, edge, side'; in OF. also *bende,* a. OHG. *bindâ*:—OTeut. **bindôn,* f. *bindan.* The var. BEND, f. OF. *bende,* is retained in *Her.*] **1.** A strip of any material flat and thin, used to bind together, clasp, or gird 1483. **2.** *esp.* A flat strip of a flexible substance (*e.g.* leather, india-rubber, etc.), used to bind round an object 1611. **3.** A flat strip or strap used to confine a dress at the waist, etc., or to encircle and confine a hat, cap, or other article of apparel 1552. **4.** *spec.* **a.** The neck-band or collar of a shirt, orig. used to make it fit closely round the neck. Hence, a collar or ruff. 1568. Hence, **b.** A pair of strips (now called *bands*) hanging down in front, as part of clerical, legal, or academical dress 1700. **5.** A strip of linen, etc., to swathe the body; a bandage 1568. **6.** *Mech.* A flat strap, belt, etc., passing round two wheels or shafts, by which motion is communicated from the one to the other 1705. †**7.** A side or flitch (of bacon). [The earliest use in Eng., f. OF. *bande* side] ME. **8.** Anything having the appearance of a band in sense 1. 1823. **9.** A more or less broad stripe crossing a surface 1470; **b.** (*pl.*) a fault in flannel and serge cloth, when stripes occur across the piece. **10. a.** *Ent.* A transverse stripe of colour, also called *fascia*; **b.** A space between two elevated lines or ribs; also called *vitta.* 1841. **11.** *Geol.* A stratum with a band-like section 1837.

Comb.: **b.-case** = BANDBOX; **-collar** (cf. 4 above); **-fish,** a fish of the genus *Cepola*; **-pulley,** a flat-faced wheel, fixed on a shaft and driven by a b.; **-saw,** an endless saw, consisting of a steel belt with a serrated edge running over wheels; **-string,** a string for fastening bands (see above, 4); **-wheel,** one to which motion is communicated by a band running over it.

Band (bænd), *sb.*³ 1490. [Late 15th c. *bande,* a. F., app. ad. Teut.; see BAND *sb.*¹, and BEND *sb.*¹ See also BEND *sb.*³] **1.** An organized company; a troop. **2.** A confederation of persons having a common purpose 1657. **3.** A company of persons or animals in movement 1601. **4.** A company of musicians; now usu. of players upon various wind and percussion instruments; applied also to various sections of an orchestra, as *the string b.,* etc., and sometimes loosely to the entire orchestra 1660.

1. The 'black bands' who still Ravage the frontier BYRON. *Trained* or *train-band*; see TRAIN-BAND. 3. Hee diuided the..camels into two bands *Gen.* xxxii. 7. *Comb.*: **b.-master,** the leader of a b. of musicians; **-stand,** a structure for the use of a b. of musicians.

Band (bænd), *sb.*⁴ 1513. [? Cf. BAND *sb.*², BANDE = bound; also Welsh *bant* 'height'.] A ridge of a hill; in the Lake district, *esp.* a long narrow sloping offshoot from a higher hill.

Band (bænd), *v.*¹ 1488. [a. F. *bander,* f. *bande* BAND *sb.*¹ and ².] **1.** To bind with a band or bands. †**2.** To furnish or cover with a band or bandage -1855. **3.** To mark with stripes 1853. **4.** To join or form into a company 1530.

4. Certaine of the Iewes banded together *Acts* xxiii. 12. Hence **Ba·nded** *ppl. a.*; *spec.* in *Her.* with a band differing in colour from the garb. **Ba·nder,** a confederate.

†**Band,** *v.*² 1580. [perh. short f. BANDY *v.*] = BANDY *v.*

†**Band(e.** 1420. [var. of *bonde,* ME. form of BOUND *sb.*] = BOUND, limit -1523.

Bandage (bæ·ndėdʒ), *sb.* 1599. [a. F., f. *bande* BAND *sb.*²; see -AGE. Orig. a term of surgery.] **1.** *Surg.* A strip of woven material used to bind up a wound, sore, etc. **b.** *abst.* = *Bandaging vbl. sb.* **2.** A strip of flexible material used for binding or covering up, *esp.* the eyes 1715. **3.** A strip of material used to bind together any structure (*arch.*) 1766.

2. Tie the controversy with bandages of argument MAURICE. Hence **Ba·ndage** *v.* to tie or bind up with a b. (*lit.* and *fig.*). **Ba·ndager. Ba·ndaging** *vbl. sb.* the action or art of applying bandages; material for bandages. **Ba·ndagist,** a maker of bandages.

†**Bandalore.** 1790. A toy containing a coiled spring, which caused it, when thrown down, to rise again to the hand -1864.

Bandanna, -ana (bændæ·nă). 1752. [Cf. Hind. *bāndhnū* a mode of dyeing in which the cloth is tied in places to prevent the parts tied from receiving the dye; ?through Pg.] A coloured silk handkerchief with spots left white or yellow by this process. Now used also of cotton handkerchiefs, in which the pattern is produced by chemical agency. Also *attrib.*

Bandbox (bæ·ndbǫks). 1631. [f. BAND *sb.*² + BOX.] A slight box of card-board or thin chip, for collars, hats, caps, and millinery; orig. made for the bands or ruffs of the 17th c.

‖**Bandeau** (bæ̆ndō·). Pl. **-eaux.** 1790. [F.:—OF. *bandel,* dim. of *bande* BAND *sb.*²; cf. BANDORE ².] **a.** A narrow band or fillet for the hair. **b.** A bandage for the eyes. **c.** A fitting-band inside a woman's hat 1908.

That b...was worn by every woman at court 1790.

†**Ba·ndel, bandle.** 1598. [a. OF. *bandele*; see prec.] A swaddling-band -1603. Hence **Ba·ndelet,** a small band, streak, or fillet; in *Archit.* small flat moulding, encircling a column.

‖**Banderilla** (banderī·lʸă). [Sp., dim. of *bandera.*] A little dart, ornamented with a banderole, which bull-fighters stick into the neck and shoulders of the bull. Hence **Ba·nderille·ro,** the bull-fighter who uses banderillas.

Banderol(e, bandrol, bannerol (bæ·ndĕrǒl, -ōᵘl, bæ·nĕrǒl). 1562. [a. F., dim. of *bandière, bannière,* prob. after It. *banderuola.*] **1.** A long narrow flag or streamer. **2.** A ribbon-like scroll bearing a device 1622. **4.** *Archit.* A flat band with an inscription. **5.** = BANNEROL.

1. The..lances bore gay bandaroles W. IRVING.

Bandicoot (bæ·ndikūt). 1789. [corrupt f. Telegu *pandi-kokku* 'pig-rat'.] **1.** An Indian rat (*Mus malabaricus* or *giganteus*), as big as a cat, and very destructive. **2.** A genus of insectivorous Australian marsupials (*Parameles*), resembling the above 1831.

Banding (bæ·ndiŋ), *vbl. sb.* 1575. [f. BAND *v.*¹] **1.** Combining in parties. **2.** Formation of, or marking with, bands or stripes 1859.

Banding-plane: one used for cutting out grooves and inlaying strings and bands.

Bandit (bæ·ndit). Pl. **banditti** (the more usual), **ba·ndits.** 1593. [a. It. *bandito,* in pl. *banditi* sb., pa. pple. of *bandire* = med.L. *bannire* to proscribe; see BAN *sb.* and *v.,* and cf. BANISH. The pl. *banditti,* after DITTO, It. *detto,* occurs also as a collect. sing.; and in 17th c. as sing., with pl. *-is, -ies.*] *lit.* One who is proscribed or outlawed; *hence,* a lawless desperate marauder. *collect. sing.* A company of bandits 1706. Also *attrib.*

The banditti do you call them?..I am sure we call them plain thieves in England 1602. An adventurer had assembled a banditti WELLINGTON.

Bandle (bæ·nd'l). 1623. [ad. Irish *bannlamh,* f. *bann* measure + *lamh* arm.] An Irish measure of two feet in length.

Bandlet (bæ·ndlėt). 1727. [syncop. f. *Bandelet.*] A small band, fillet, or streak; in *Arch.* = *Bandelet.*

†‖**Ba·ndo.** 1598. [a. It. (and Sp.).] A public proclamation -1642.

Bandog (bæ·ndǫg). ME. [f. BAND *sb.*¹ 5 + DOG.] *orig.* A (ferocious) dog tied or chained up; hence, a mastiff, bloodhound. Also *fig.*

To speak b. and Bedlam: i. e. furiously and madly.

Bandoleer, -ier (bændǒlīᵊ·ɹ). 1577. [a. F. *bandouillere,* f. It. *bandoliera,* f. *bandola* dim. of *banda* BAND.] †**1.** A broad belt, worn over the shoulder and across the breast, by which a wallet might be suspended -1767. **2.** *esp.* A belt of this kind worn by soldiers; *orig.* to support the musket, and carry cases containing charges for it; *later,* a shoulder-belt for cartridges 1596. **3.** By transference: in sing. One of the cases; hence used in *pl.* as = prec.

Bandoline (bæ·ndǒlin). 1856. [? f. *band* or *bandeau.*] A gummy preparation for fixing the hair.

†**Ba·ndon, -oun,** *sb.* ME. [a. OF. *bandon, bandun,* f. late L. *bandum* = *bannum*; see BAN *sb.*¹] Jurisdiction, dominion, control -1611.

†**Ba·ndon,** *v.* ME. Aphet. f. ABANDON *v.*

Bandore ¹ (bæ̆ndōᵊ·ɹ, bæ·-). 1566. [ad. Sp. or Pg., f. L., a. Gr. πανδοῦρα, πανδουρίς. Hence, by corruption, BANJO.] A guitar- or lute-like instrument, used as a bass to the cithern. Cf. PANDORA ², PANDORE.

†**Bando·re** ². 1712. [corruption of F. *bandeau.*] A widow's head-dress -1719.

Bandsman (bæ·ndzmæ̆n). 1842. **a.** A member of a (musical) band. **b.** *Mining.* A man having to do with the band or flat rope by which coal, etc. is hoisted 1852.

Ba·ndster. 1794. [f. BAND *sb.*¹; cf. *maltster.*] One who binds sheaves.

‖**Bandu·rria.** [Sp.] = BANDORE ¹. LONGF.

Bandy (bæ·ndi), *v.* 1577. [? Cf. F. *bander* (in Tennis), perh. f. *bande* side; and with senses 6, 7 cf. F. *bander* in *se bander contre.* Cf. BAND *v.*¹ The terminal *-y* is unexplained.] **1.** To throw or strike to and fro, as balls in tennis, etc. (Usu. *fig.*) Also *absol.* †**2.** To toss aside or away -1667. **3.** To toss from side to side 1596. **4.** To toss about 1600; to discuss from mouth to mouth 1642. **5.** To give and take; to exchange 1589. †**6.** To band together, league. *trans.* and *intr.* -1818. **7.** *intr.* To contend 1588.

1. Kingdoms..be no balles for me to bandie HOLINSHED. 4. Bandied about thus from pillar to post BARHAM. 5. Phr. *To b. words*: to argue pertinaciously. Do you b. lookes with me *Lear* I. iv. 92. 7. That Law may b. with nature..was an error MILT.

Bandy (bæ·ndi), *sb.*¹ 1578. [App. f. the vb.] †**1.** A way of playing tennis, no longer known -1607. †**2.** A stroke with a racket, a ball so struck; a return at tennis -1655. **3.** = HOCKEY. 1693. **4.** A club curved at its lower end, used in this game 1629. var. (sense 3), **Bandy-ball.**

Bandy (bæ·ndi), *sb.*² 1761. [a. Telugu.] A carriage, buggy, or cart, used in India.

Bandy (bæ·ndi), *a.* 1552. [see the senses.] **1.** Of legs: Curved laterally with the concavity inward. [perh. attrib. use of BANDY *sb.*¹ 4.] Also short for *bandy-legged.* 1687. **2.** Marked with bands; cf. BAND *sb.*² 9 b. 1552. **3.** Full of bands [f. BAND *sb.*³ 4.] Hence **Ba·ndiness. Ba·ndy-legged** *a.* (both from sense 1).

Bane (bē̆ⁱn), *sb.* [Com. Teut.: OE. *bana, bona*:—OTeut. **banon-.* Cogn. w. Gr. φόνος, etc.] †**1.** A slayer or murderer -1691. **2.** That which destroys life; *esp.* poison. (Now only *fig.,* referred to 4; and in *comb.,* as HENBANE, etc.) ME. †**3.** Murder, death, destruction -1655. **4.** That which causes ruin or woe; the curse. (Now the usual sense.) 1577. **5.** Ruin, harm, woe. Chiefly *poet.* ME. **6.** The rot in sheep 1859.

1. Let Rome herselfe be b. vnto herselfe *Tit. A.* v.

iii. 73. 2. B. and antidote ADDISON. 4. Theoretic plans..the b. of France BURKE.

Bane, *v. arch.* 1578. [f. BANE *sb.*] †1. To kill: said *esp.* of poison –1596. 2. To harm, hurt, poison 1587.

2. For what shall heal, when holy water banes KEBLE.

Baneberry (bēⁱ·nberi). 1755. [f. BANE + BERRY.] A plant, *Actæa spicata* (N.O. *Ranunculaceæ*); also, its fruit.

Baneful (bēⁱ·nful), *a.* 1579. [f. BANE *sb.*[1]] 1. Life-destroying; poisonous 1593. 2. Pernicious 1579.

1. The old serpent's b. breath 1593. 2. B. superstition 1832. Hence **Ba·neful-ly** *adv.*, **-ness**.

Banewort (bēⁱ·nwɒɹt). 1578. [f. BANE + WORT.] Any poisonous plant (*dial.*); *spec.* the Lesser Spearwort (*Ranunculus Flammula*), reputed to poison sheep; also, the Deadly Nightshade.

Bang (bæŋ), *v.*[1] 1550. [Cf. ON. *banga* to hammer; also LG. *bangen, bangeln.*] 1. To strike violently with a resounding blow; to thump, thrash. 2. *intr.* To strike violently or noisily; to bump or thump. Of a door: To slam. 1713. 3. Hence: To make a violent noise 1840. 4. To knock about; to drub, defeat. *lit.* and *fig.* 1604. b. *Comm.* To beat down 1884. 5. *colloq.* To outdo 1808. 6. Used advb. *esp.* with *come, go,* in the senses of: a. with a violent blow; b. with a sudden clap; c. all of a sudden (F. *tout d'un coup*).

1. An..anvil bang'd With hammers TENNYSON. *To b. off* (a gun, a tune, etc.), *To b.* (a door). 4. To b. the market by heavy sales 1884. 5. This bangs Bannagher *Irish Provb.* Hence **Ba·nger**, he who or that which bangs; *slang*, an astounding lie. **Ba·nging** *vbl. sb.* and *ppl. a.*; *fig.* (*colloq.*) 'thumping'.

Bang, *v.*[2] 1882. [f. BANG *sb.*[2]] To cut (the front hair) square across.

Their hair banged low over their foreheads (*mod.*).

Bang (bæŋ), *sb.*[1] 1550. [f. BANG *v.*[1]] 1. A heavy resounding blow. 2. A sudden violent or explosive noise 1855. 3. Impetus, go 1774.

2. The steps..were let down with a b. THACKERAY.

Bang (bæŋ), *sb.*[2] 1880. [= hair cut bang off; cf. BANG-TAIL.] The front hair cut square across the forehead. (Orig. in U.S.)

Bang, *sb.*[3], obs. f. BHANG.

Ba·ngle, *v.* Now *dial.* 1567. [?] 1. Orig. of hawks: To beat about in the air, instead of making direct for the quarry. 2. *intr.* To flap, hang loosely 1622.

1. *To bangle* (*away*): to fritter away. 2. **Bangled** (also **bangle**) **ear**, one hanging loosely, like a spaniel's. Hence †**Ba·ngling** *vbl. sb.* squabbling.

Bangle (bæ·ŋg'l). 1787. [a. Hind. *bangrī*, orig. a coloured glass ring worn on the wrist.] A ring-bracelet or anklet. Hence **Ba·ngled** *ppl. a.* wearing bangles.

†**Ba·ngster.** Now *dial.* 1570. [f. BANG *v.* + -STER.] A bully; a winner –1824.

Ba·ng-tai·l. 1870. [Cf. BANG *v.* 6 c.] A (horse's) tail cut horizontally across; hence **Bang-tailed** *ppl. a.*

Ba·ng-up, *adj. slang.* Also **banged-up.** 1812. [Cf. *slap-up.*] Quite up to the mark.

Banian (bæ·niăn). 1599. [a. Pg., prob. a. Arab., ad. Gujerati *vāniyo*, f. Skr. *vanij* merchant.] 1. A Hindoo (*esp.* Gujerati) trader. 2. In Bengal: A native broker attached to a firm or the like: now called *sircar* 1687. 3. A loose gown, jacket, or shirt of flannel. (Orig. *attrib.* from sense 1.) 1725. 4. **Banian-** or **Banyan-tree**, now often **Banyan**: the Indian Fig Tree (*Ficus religiosa* or *Indica*), the branches of which drop shoots to the ground, that take root and support their parent branches; thus, one tree will often cover much ground. [The appellation was orig. given by Europeans to an individual tree of this species growing near Gombroon on the Persian Gulf, under which the Banian settlers had built a pagoda.]

1. The religion of the Banians not permitting them to eat any thing that hath had life 1676. *Comb.* **b.-day** (*Naut.*), one on which no meat is served out (see prec. quot.).

Banish (bæ·niʃ), *v.* ME. [a. OF. *baniss-*, *banir* (mod. *bannir*):—late L. *bannire*; see BAN.] †1. *orig.* To proclaim as an outlaw. 2. To condemn by public edict or sentence to leave the country; to exile ME. 3. *gen.* To send or drive away, expel, dismiss 1450. †4. To empty. Cf. AVOID *v.* –1573.

1. Sycorax..from Argier..was banish'd *Temp.* I. ii. 266. 3. To die, is to be banisht from my selfe *Two Gent.* III. i. 171. B. squint suspicion MILT. *Comus* 413. Hence **Ba·nisher**, he who or that which banishes.

Banishment (bæ·niʃmĕnt). 1507. [f. prec.] 1. The action of banishing; a state of exile. 2. *gen.* Enforced absence; dismissal 1535.

1. The B. of that worthy Coriolanus *Cor.* IV. iii. 22.

Banister (bæ·nistəɹ). Also **bannister.** 1667. [Corruption of BALUSTER, q.v.] = BALUSTER 3. Also as *collect. sing.*

He comes down stairs..thumping the banisters all the way SHERIDAN.

Banjo (bæ·ndʒo). Also **banjore, banjer.** 1790. [Corruption of BANDORE, through Negro slave pronunc.] A stringed musical instrument, played with the fingers, having a head and neck like a guitar, and a body like a tambourine. **Ba·njoist**, one who plays a b.

Banjulele (bændʒŭlēⁱ·li). 1925. [f. prec., after UKULELE.] A stringed musical instrument of a type between a banjo and a ukulele.

Bank (bæŋk), *sb.*[1] [ME. *banke*, prob. a. ON. :—OTeut. **bankon-*; see BANK *sb.*[2] and BENCH. The primary sense of *bank-* is prob. 'shelf'.] 1. A raised shelf or ridge of ground. 2. A high ground, fell. Still *n. dial.* ME. b. *Hence*, A hillside, a brae; a 'hanger' ME. †3. An earthwork, an embankment –1611. 4. A shelving elevation in the sea or the bed of a river. Also, a bed of oysters or the like. 1605. 5. A long flat-topped mass: *e.g.* of cloud, snow, etc. 1626. 6. *Mining.* a. 'The face of the coal at which miners are working' 1862. b. 'An ore-deposit or coal-bed worked by drifts above water-level' 1881. 7. The sloping margin of a river or stream; the ground bordering upon a river ME. Also *fig.* †8. The sea-coast or shore –1592. 9. A raised edge of a pond, lake, etc.; also *Mining*, the ground at the pit-mouth. ME. 10. Lateral inclination when rounding a curve. Cf. BANK *v.*[1] 7. 1913.

1. I know a banke where the wilde time blowes *Mids. N.* II. i. 249. 4. But here, vpon this Banke and Schoole of time Wee'ld iumpe the life to come *Macb.* I. vii. 7. 5. A b. of clouds BACON, of mist R. DANA, of fog 1848. 7. Tyber trembled vnderneath her bankes *Jul. C.* I. i. 50. 8. From Englands banke Droue backe againe 2 *Hen. VI*, III. ii. 83.

Comb.: **Bank cress** (*Herb.*), the Hedge-mustard (*Sisymbrium officinale*; **b.-engine**, the engine at a pit's mouth; **-fish**, cod from Newfoundland Bank, whence *-fishing*, *-fishery*; **-hook**, a large fishing-hook attached by a line to the b. of a stream; **-jug**, the Willow Warbler, or Willow Wren; **-manager**, the superintendent at a pit's mouth; **-martin, -swallow**, the Sand-martin; **-smack**, a Newfoundland fishing-smack.

Bank (bæŋk), *sb.*[2] [ME. *baunk, banck*, app. a. OF. *banc*:—late L. *bancus*, ad. Teut. *bank, banc*:—OTeut. **banki-z* BENCH; cogn. w. prec.] †1. A long seat for several, a bench; a platform. (Cf. *mountebank.*) –1680. †2. A seat of justice; = BENCH. Cf. BANCO *sb.* –1768. 3. The bench occupied by rowers of each oar in a galley 1599. 4. *catchr.* A rank of oars 1614. 5. *Printing.* The table on which the sheets are laid 1565.

2. *Bank-royal*: King's Bench. *Common Bank*: Common Pleas.

Bank (bæŋk), *sb.*[3] 1474. [Early mod.E. *banke*, a. F. *banque*, ad. It. *banca* fem. (the masc. *banco* was also used); ad. Teut. *bank, banc*; see prec. wd. The orig. meaning 'shelf, bench' was extended in It. to that of 'counter, money-changer's table', whence 'money-shop, bank', and passed, with banking, into other countries.] 1. The table of a dealer in money. Now *Hist.* 1567. †2. The place of business of a money-dealer –1649. †3. A sum of money, an amount (It. *monte*) –1758. 4. In games of hazard, the amount which the banker has before him 1720. †5. A joint stock or capital –1790. †6. A capital so contributed for lending to the poor; a loan-bank; whence the pawnbroker's establishment (Fr. *mont-de-piété*) –1633. 7. In modern use: An establishment for the custody of money received from, or on behalf of, its customers. Its essential duty is to pay their drafts on it; its profits arise from the use of the money left unemployed by them. *fig.* 1642.

Banks (in England) are—a. *Private Banks*, carried on by one or not more than ten persons in partnership. Cf. sense 2. b. *Joint-Stock Banks*, of which the capital is subscribed by many shareholders. Cf. sense 5. Of these the greatest is.. c. *The Bank of England*, shortly 'The Bank', which manages the service of the public debt, receives and accounts for the revenue when collected, and issues legal tender notes to an amount automatically regulated. Its banking business does not differ from that of other banks.

4. He had seen his friend..break the b. three nights running THACKERAY. 5. No Banke or Common Stocke, but euery Man..Master of his owne Money BACON. 7. I defined a b. to be an institution for the transfer of debts B. PRICE. †*In bank*: at one's banker's; *fig.* in store.

Comb.: **B. annuities**, a techn. term for certain British government funds; usu. 'consols'; **b.-cheque**, an order to pay issued on a b.; **-court**, the weekly meeting of the Governor and Directors of a joint-stock b.; *also*, the general court of proprietors; **-credit**, a credit opened for any person at a bank, so that he can draw for the amount; **-money** (cf. BANCO *a.*); *also*, money in the b.; **-paper**, bank-notes in circulation; bills of exchange accepted by a banker; **-post**, a kind of writing-paper used in foreign correspondence; **-rate**, the rate per cent. per annum at which the Bank of England will discount bills of exchange having not more than 95 days to run; **-stock**, the capital stock of the Bank of England, orig. £1,200,000, now £14,553,000. **B. of deposit**, one that receives lodgements of money. **B. of issue** or **circulation**, one which issues its own notes or promises to pay. **Savings-b.**, one to take charge of the savings of the poor, or of small sums of money.

Bank (bæŋk), *v.*[1] 1590. [f. BANK *sb.*[1]] 1. To border, edge, hem in as a bank; †*intr.* to border *upon* 1598. 2. To confine within a bank. Also *fig.* 1622. 3. *Watch-making*: a. To confine the movement of the escapement. b. *intr.* To impinge against the banking-pins. †4. To coast. SHAKS. 5. *trans.* To pile *up* 1833; *intr.* (for *refl.*) to rise *up* into banks 1870. 6. To cover up (a fire) with fresh fuel, so as to make it burn slowly 1860. 7. *trans.* To incline (an aeroplane or car) laterally in rounding a curve. Also *intr.* 1911.

Bank, *v.*[2] 1727. [f. BANK *sb.*[3]] 1. *intr.* To keep a bank. 2. *intr.* To keep an account with a banker 1833. 3. *trans.* To deposit in a bank. Also, to convert into current money. 1864. 4. *intr.* To form a bank at a gaming-table 1826.

3. If Parliament were to b. this whole estate 1868. 4. b. To count or rely *upon* 1883. Hence **Ba·nkable** *a.* receivable at a bank, as 'bankable securities'.

Bank-bill. 1696. [see BANK *sb.*[3] and BILL.] a. In U.S., and formerly in England, a BANK-NOTE. b. A bill drawn by one bank on another; a *banker's draft.* c. *Bank Post Bill*: a bill, usu. at seven days' sight, issued by the Bank of England for transmission by post.

Bank-book. 1714. [see BANK *sb.*[3]] A book furnished by a banker to each customer, containing a transcript of his account; a *Pass-book.* (Also called *Banker's book.*)

†**Ba·nker**[1]. ME. [a. AF. **banker* = ONF. *bankier*, f. *banc.*] A covering for a bench or chair –1660.

Banker[2] (bæ·ŋkəɹ). 1534. [f. BANK *sb.*[3] + -ER, after F. *banquier* (also used).] 1. One who keeps or manages a BANK *sb.*[3]; in *pl.* a joint-stock banking company. 2. One who keeps the bank in a gambling-house; the dealer, in some games of chance 1826. 3. A gambling game of cards 1891.

1. *Bankers' Books*, Books of Account, etc., extracts from which are evidence in a British Court of Law. Hence **Ba·nkerdom**, the banking interest. **Ba·nkeress**, a female b.; a banker's wife.

Banker[3] (bæ·ŋkəɹ). 1666. [f. BANK *sb.*[1] + -ER[1].] 1. A ship employed in cod-fishing on the Bank of Newfoundland. (Cf. F. *banquier.*) 2. A labourer who makes banks of earth, ditches, etc. 1795. 3. *Hunting.* A horse which can jump on and off banks too wide to be cleared. (Cf. *fencer.*) 4. (*Australia*). A river full to the brim.

Ba·nker[4]. 1677. [f. BANK *sb.*[2]] a. A wooden bench for dressing bricks. b. A stone bench used by masons. c. (*Local.*) A pile of Purbeck stone from the quarry.

Banket (bæ·ŋkĕt). 1886. [a. Du. *banket*, sweetmeats, etc., ad. F. *banquet*; cf. Du. *banketbakker* confectioner.] *South African Mining.* (See quot.) Also *attrib.*, as *b.-reef*, etc.

What is known as the *Main Reef Series* comprises half-a-dozen parallel beds of conglomerate—locally called 'Banket' from its resemblance to the sweetmeat known in English as 'almond-rock' T. REUNERT.

Ba·nk-full, *a.* 1581. Full to the bank.

Bank ho·liday. 1871. [see BANK *sb.*[3] + HOLIDAY.] A day on which banks are legally closed. (Bills payable on these days are paid next day.)

Banking (bæ·ŋkiŋ), *vbl. sb.* 1735. [f. BANK in various senses.] **1.** The business of a banker. Also *attrib.* **2.** The construction of banks 1753. **3.** Embankment 1853. **4.** Fishing on the Newfoundland (or other) Bank 1842. **5.** In *Watch-making*: Limitation of the motion of the balance, by the *banking-pins* or *screw* 1870. **6.** *B.-ground* (in U.S.): a place where logs are brought to a river bank 1880.

Ba·nking-house. 1809. A mercantile firm engaged in banking.

Bank-note. 1695. [See BANK *sb.*[3], and NOTE.] A promissory note given by a banker: *formerly*, one payable at a fixed date and to a specified person; *now*, one payable to bearer on demand, and circulating as money.

Bankrupt (bæ·ŋkrɒpt), *sb.* 1533. [In 16th c. *banke rota, banqueroute*, a. It. *banca rotta*, with *-rupt* assim. to L. *ruptus*. The transference to the agent (in sense 2) is Eng. only.] †**1.** = BANKRUPTCY. Chiefly in the phrase 'to make b.' (Fr. *faire banqueroute*). –1712. **2.** Any person, whose effects, on his becoming insolvent, are administered and distributed for the benefit of all his creditors, under the Bankruptcy Laws. **b.** *pop.* One who is unable to meet his liabilities, whether he is in the Bankruptcy Court or not 1580. **3.** *transf.* One without resources 1586.

Formerly only a trader could be made a *bankrupt*; other persons became *insolvent*. The distinction was abolished in 1869.

2. †*To play the bankrupt*: to become insolvent; *often*, to play false with the money of others, and *fig.* to prove false to a trust. These modern languages will, at one time or other, play the b. with books BACON. Hence †**Ba·nkruptly** *adv.*

Ba·nkrupt, *v.* 1552. [App. f. the sb. (in sense 1). Not in It. or F.] †**1.** To fail; = the early phr. 'to make bankrupt'. See BANKRUPT *sb.* 1. –1689. **2.** *trans.* To make (any one) bankrupt 1616. †**3.** To beggar, exhaust the resources of (*lit.* and *fig.*) –1748.

3. Make rich the ribs, but bankerout the wits SHAKS.

Ba·nkrupt, *a.* 1566. [conn. w. the sb. in sense 2; in Eng. only.] **1.** Under legal process because of insolvency; insolvent 1570. **2.** *fig.* †Discredited –1612; at the end of one's resources 1589; stript bare *of*, or now wanting *in* (a property or quality) 1589.

2. To be out of fashion, is to bee banquerupt 1601. I shall make your wit b. *Two Gent.* II. iv. 42. B. of intelligence 1651.

Bankruptcy (bæ·ŋkrɒpsi). 1700. [f. BANKRUPT + -CY, with *-t* retained. Successively termed *bankrupting, bankruptism, bankrupture, bankruptship*, and finally *bankruptcy*.] **1.** The state of being, or fact of becoming, bankrupt. Also *attrib.* **2.** *fig.* Utter wreck, or loss of (a quality) 1761.

2. A general b. of reputation BURKE.

‖**Ba·nkshall.** 1673. [prob. Bengali *bankaśālā* 'hall of trade'.] **a.** A warehouse. **b.** The office of a harbour master, or port authority.

Banksia (bæ·ŋksiă). 1803. [f. name of Sir Joseph *Banks*; see -IA[1].] An Australian genus of shrubs with dense spikes of flowers.

Ba·nk-si·de. 1596. [f. BANK *sb.*[1]] **1.** The sloping side of a bank. **2.** The margin of †sea, lake, or river 1618.

Ba·nksman. 1598. [f. BANK *sb.*[1]] An overlooker above ground at a coal mine.

Ba·nky, *a.* Now *dial.* 1601. [f. as prec. + -Y[1].] Full of banks; of or pertaining to, or inclined like, a bank; hilly.

Banner (bæ·nəɹ), *sb.* ME. [a. OF. *banere, baniere*, f. late L. *bandum, bannum* standard, f. Goth. *bandwa, bandwo* 'signum', perh. f. root *band, bind.*] **1.** *prop.* A piece of stout taffeta or other cloth, attached by one side to the upper part of a staff, and used as a standard. (Chiefly *Hist.*) Also *fig.* **2.** An ensign or flag bearing some device, carried in a procession. (Sometimes restricted to an ensign other than an ordinary flag.) ME. Also *fig.* **3.** *transf.* The company ranged under a banner. Now *Hist.* ME. †**4.** = BANDEROLE 2. *Hen. V*, IV. ii. 60. **5.** *Bot.* The vexillum of a papilionaceous flower 1794.

1. Terrible as an armie with banners *Sol. Song* vi. 4. Our glorious *semper eadem*, the b. of our pride MACAULAY. The star-spangled b. KEY. **2.** A b. with the strange device, Excelsior LONGF.

Comb.: **b.-cry**, a cry summoning men to join a b., a slogan; **-screen**, a fire-screen hung by its upper edge.

Banner (bæ·nəɹ), *v.* 1667. [f. BANNER *sb.*] To furnish, or decorate, with banners.

A Bannered Host, Under spread ensigns marching MILT. *P. L.* II. 885. Hence **Ba·nnered** *ppl. a.* furnished with, or blazoned on, a banner.

Ba·nnerer. Now *Hist.* ME. [a. AF. *banerer*; see BANNER.] **1.** A standard-bearer. **2.** = BANNERET. 1484.

Banneret (bæ·nĕrĕt). [ME. *baneret*, a. OF., f. *baniere*.] **1. a.** Orig., a knight able and entitled to bring vassals into the field under his own banner; commonly used as a title of rank. (This sense was mainly Fr.) **b.** Subseq., a title and rank conferred for deeds done in the king's presence on the field of battle; thus, a rank and order of knighthood 1548. Hence *knight-banneret*, opp. to *knight-bachelor* 1475. **2.** An official in Swiss cantons and Italian republics 1689. **3.** Confused with BANNERER 1494.

1 b. Sir Ralph Sadleir..the last Knyht B. of England 1635.

Bannerette (bænĕre·t). Also **banneret.** ME. [a. OF. *banerete, -ette*, dim. of *baniere*; see BANNER.] A small banner.

Ba·nnerman. *Sc. arch.* 1500. [f. BANNER *sb.*[1]] A standard-bearer.

Bannerol (bæ·nĕrōu·l, -ŏl). 1548. Var. of BANDEROLE; *esp.* A banner borne at the funerals of great men, and placed over the tomb.

†**Banni·tion.** 1644. [ad. med.L. *bannitionem.*] Banishment, expulsion –1758.

Bannock (bæ·nək). OE. [a. Gael. *bannach*, ?ad. L. *panicium*, f. *panis*.] In Scotland and north of England, a large cake, usually of barley- or pease-meal, round or oval in form, and flattish, but thicker than 'scon' or oat-cake.

Comb. **b.-fluke** (also *bannet-*), *Sc.* the turbot.

Banns (bænz), *sb. pl.* ME. [= BAN *sb.*[1] 'proclamation' in a specific use. The sing. occurs in 15th c.] **1.** Public notice given in church of an intended marriage, in order that those who know of any impediment thereto may lodge objections 1440. †**2.** Proclamation or prologue of a play –1609.

1. Our bans thrice bid GAY. Phrases. *To †bid, ask, publish, put up the b. To forbid the b*: to make a formal objection to the intended marriage. Also *fig.*

Banquet (bæ·ŋkwĕt), *sb.* 1483. [a. F. *banquet*, dim. of *banc* bench; cf. It. *banchetto*, dim. of *banco*; cf. also *table, board*, in sense of 'meals'.] A sumptuous entertainment of food and drink; now usu. a ceremonial or state feast, followed by speeches. Also *transf.* and *fig.* 1495. †**2.** A slight repast between meals. Occas. called *running b.* –1657. **3.** A course of sweetmeats, fruit, and wine; a dessert. *Obs.* in gen. use. 1523. †*collect.* Sweetmeats –1700. †**4.** A wine-drinking carousal –1719. See also BANQUETTE.

1. The Lord Mayor..gave a b. to her Majesty's Judges 1885. **2.** Besides the running B. of two Beadles [*i.e.* a whipping] *Hen. VIII*, v. iv. 69.

Banquet (bæ·ŋkwĕt), *v.* 1514. [a. F. *banqueter*, f. as prec.] **1.** *trans.* To entertain at a banquet 1538. **2.** *intr.* To take part in a banquet; to carouse; also *fig.* 1514. **3.** To take a BANQUET (senses 2, 3) 1564.

2. Born but to b., and to drain the bowl POPE. The minde shall b., though the body pine *L. L. L.* I. i. 25.

Banquetee·r. 1821. = BANQUETER 2.

Banqueter (bæ·ŋkwĕtəɹ). 1542. [f. BANQUET *v.*] †**1.** The giver of a banquet –1637. **2.** A guest at a banquet 1549.

‖**Banquette** (bañke·t). 1629. [Fr., ad. It. *banchetta*, dim. of *banca*. Formerly **banket, -quet.**] **1.** A raised way running along the inside of a parapet, or bottom of a trench, on which soldiers stand to fire at the enemy. **2.** A raised footway or side-walk 1842. **3.** The long low bench behind the driver in a French 'diligence' 1859.

Banshee (bæ·nʃī). 1771. [Phonetic sp. of Ir. *bean sídhe* 'female of the elves'.] A supernatural being supposed by the Scotch and Irish peasantry to wail under the windows of a house where one of the inmates is about to die.

Banstickle (bæ·nstik'l). 1450. [prob. f. OE. *bán* bone + *sticels* prick.] The Three-spined Stickleback.

Bant, *v.*; see BANTING.

Bantam (bæ·ntăm). 1749. [perh. f. *Bantam* in Java.] A small variety of the domestic fowl; the cocks are spirited fighters; also *fig.* in reference to size or 'cockiness' 1782.

B. battalion, a battalion of men below normal standard. *B.-weight*, a boxer from 8 st. 6 to 8 st.

Banter (bæ·ntəɹ), *sb.* 1690. [Of unkn. etym. Treated as slang in 1688.] **1.** Wanton or humorous ridicule; *now usually*, good-natured raillery, pleasantry 1702. **2.** A jest (*arch.*) 1700.

1. I have done my utmost for some years past to stop the progress of *Mobb* and *Banter* SWIFT.

Banter (bæ·ntəɹ), *v.* 1676. [see prec.] **1.** To make fun of; to ridicule; to rally, chaff. Now usually of good-humoured raillery. **2.** To impose upon, orig. in jest; to cheat, bamboozle (*arch.*) 1688. **3.** *absol.* or *intr.* (in prec. senses) 1688.

1. B. him, b. him, Toby. 'Tis a conceited old Scarab D'URFEY. Hence **Ba·nterer. Ba·nteringly** *adv.*

Banting (bæ·ntiŋ). 1864. Name of a London cabinet-maker, given to his method of reducing obesity by avoiding fat, starch, and sugar in food. Hence **Bantingism, Bantingize** *v.*, and, humorously, **Bant** *v.*

Bantling (bæ·ntliŋ). 1593. [?f. BAND, swathe; or corrupt f. Ger. *bänkling* bastard, f. *bank* bench; cf. BASTARD.] A young or small child, a brat. (Formerly = *bastard.*) Also *fig.*

Lo their precious Roman b., lo the colony Camulodune TENNYSON.

Banxring (bæ·ŋksriŋ). 1824. [Javanese.] A squirrel-like insectivore.

Banyan, the prevailing spelling of BANIAN 4.

‖**Banzai** (bænzəi·). 1904. [Jap. '10,000 years'.] A cheer used in greeting the emperor, etc.

Baobab (bā·o̦bæb). 1640. [app. central African.] A tree (*Adansonia digitata*), with an enormously thick stem, found throughout tropical Africa, and long naturalized in India. Called also Monkey-bread, and Ethiopian Sour Gourd. The fibres of the bark are used for ropes and cloth.

Baphomet (bæ·fomet). 1818. [a. F.] **a.** A mediæval form of Mahomet. **b.** Alleged name of the idol which the Templars were accused of worshipping. Hence **Baphome·tic** *a.*

Baptism (bæ·ptiz'm). [ME. *bapteme*, a. OF. *baptesme*, mod. *baptême*, ad. L. *baptismus*, a. Gr., f. βαπτίζειν. Refash. after L. and Gr.] The action or ceremony of baptizing; application of water to a person by immersion, pouring, or sprinkling, as a religious rite, symbolical of purification or regeneration, and betokening initiation into the Church. Also *fig.* (in various senses.)

Name of b.: see *Baptismal name*. The b. of bells and ships ABP. SANDYS. The b. of blood in martyrdom [*i. e.* death by violence of unbaptized martyrs] 1860. var. †**Baptiza·tion.**

Baptismal (bæpti·zmăl), *a.* 1641. [ad. med. L. *baptismalis*; see prec.] Of, pertaining to, or connected with baptism.

Baptismal name: the Christian name given at baptism. Hence **Bapti·smally** *adv.*

Baptist (bæ·ptist). ME. [a. OF. *baptiste*, ad. L. *baptista*, ad. Gr. βαπτιστής, f. βαπτίζειν.] **1.** One who baptizes; *esp.* John, the forerunner of Christ. **2.** One who immerses himself, or is immersed (*rare*) 1775. **3.** One of a body of Protestants holding that baptism ought to be administered only to believers, and by immersion; at first called, by opponents, ANABAPTISTS 1654. Also *attrib.*

1. *Baptist's day*: the 24th of June.

Baptistery, -try (bæ·ptistəri, -tri). 1460. [a. OF. *baptisterie*, mod. *baptistère*, ad. L. *baptisterium*, a. Gr., f. βαπτίζειν.] **1.** That part of a church (or, earlier, a building contiguous to the church), in which baptism is administered. **2.** A receptacle, in Baptist places of worship, containing water for the baptismal rite 1835. **3.** = BAPTISM. 1851.

Bapti·stic, *a.* 1884. [ad. Gr. βαπτιστικός.] = BAPTIST *attrib.* Hence †**Bapti·stical** *a.* of or belonging to baptism (*rare*).

Baptize (bæptəi·z), *v.* ME. [a. F. *baptiser*, *-izer*, ad. L. *baptizare*, ad. Gr. βαπτίζειν, f. βάπτειν.] **1.** To administer baptism to; to christen. Also *absol.* Also *fig.* (in reference to initiation, spiritual agency, etc.) **2.** To give a name to, as in baptism 1549.

1. *fig.* Sorrow had baptized her O. W. HOLMES. 2. Ile be new baptiz'd; Hence foorth I neuer will be Romeo *Rom. & Jul.* II. ii. 50. Hence **Bapti·zer.**

‖**Baquet** (bake). 1786. [Fr., dim. of *bac* BACK *sb.*²; cf. BACKET.] A small tub or trough.

Bar (bāɹ), *sb.*¹ [ME. *barre*, a. OF. :—late L. *barra*, of unkn. origin.] I. 1. A piece of wood, metal, or other rigid material, long in proportion to its thickness, and frequently used as a barrier, fastening, or obstruction. 2. A narrow four-sided block of metal or material as manufactured, *e.g.* of iron or soap; an ingot 1595. 3. A small slip of silver fixed transversely below the clasp of a medal 1864. 4. A straight strip or stripe, narrow in proportion to its length, a broad line; *e.g.* of colour ME. 5. *Her.* An honourable ordinary, formed like the fess, but narrower, and including the fifth part or less of the field 1592. 6. *Farriery.* a. (usu. *pl.*) The transverse ridges of a horse's palate. b. The recurved ends of the crust of a horse's hoof, meeting in the centre of the sole 1617.

1. *Bar*, a drilling or tamping-rod RAYMOND. The b. of a gate, door, hatch, etc. The b. of a fence, grating. 5. *B. sinister*: pop., but erron., the heraldic sign of illegitimacy: see BATON, BEND.

II. 1. That which forms an enclosure, or obstructs entry or egress ME. 2. A barrier closing the entrance to a city; *subseq.*, the gate replacing this, as in *Temple Bar*, etc. ME. 3. A bank of sand, silt, etc., across the mouth of a river or harbour, which obstructs navigation 1586. 4. *Mus.* A vertical line (now commonly called the *bar-line*) drawn across the stave to mark the metrical accent; hence, that which is included between two bars 1665. b. = BASS-BAR, FRET *sb.*³ 5. *Law.* A plea which arrests an action or claim at law 1495; also *fig.*

2. A house without the Barres at Aldgate 1645. 4. Phr. *Double b.*: two parallel vertical lines, marking the close of a section. 5. *In b.* (*of*): as a sufficient reason (against).

III. 1. *Law.* The barrier or wooden rail at which prisoners are stationed for arraignment, trial, or sentence ME.; *fig.* a tribunal, *e.g.* that of public opinion ME. 2. Hence: a. Court; *esp.* in *At (the) b.*: in open court ME. b. A (particular) court of law, as, the Exchequer b. 1559. 3. *In the Inns of Court.* A partition separating the seats of the benchers from the rest of the hall, to which students, after they had attained a certain standing, were 'called'. *Obs.* (After 1600, *bar* was assumed to mean the b. in a court of justice, within which King's Counsel and Sergeants-at-Law have places, but not ordinary barristers.) 4. Barristers collectively, or *spec.* those practising in a particular court, circuit, or county 1559. 5. The profession of a barrister 1632. 6. *In legislative assemblies.* The rail dividing from the body of the house a space near the door to which non-members may be admitted for business purposes 1577. 7. *In an inn, etc.* A counter, over which drink or food is served out to customers; *also*, the space behind this, and sometimes the whole apartment 1592.

1. When self is at the b., the sentence is not like to be impartial GLANVILL. 2. *Trial at b.*: a trial before the full court in which the action is brought; in England, the Queen's Bench Division. 3. *To be called to the b.*: to be admitted a barrister. *To be called within the b.*: to be appointed King's Counsel. 6. A deputation..heard at the b. of the Commons 1849.

Comb.: **b.-boat**, one marking the position of a b.; **-diggings**, shallows of a stream worked for gold; **-iron**, iron wrought into bars; **-keeper**, one who keeps a b., or keeps guard at a barrier; **-line** (see II. 4 above); **-shot**, a shot consisting of two half cannon-balls joined by an iron bar; **-silver**, silver in bars; so **-tin**; **-tracery**, Gothic window-tracery, resembling a b. of iron twisted into various forms; **-ways**, **-wise** *adv. Her.* horizontally across the field.

Bar, *sb.*² 1724. [a. F.] A fish, *Sciæna aquila*, the *maigre*.

Bar, *sb.*³ (= Ger. *berg*); see BARMASTER, BARMOTE.

Bar (bāɹ), *v.* Pa. t. and pple. **barred.** [ME. *barren*, a. OF. *barrer*, f. *barre* BAR *sb.*¹] 1. To make fast by a bar or bars; to fasten up with bars. 2. To fasten in by means of bars. Also *transf.* and *fig.* 1460. 3. To close by some barrier 1596. 4. To obstruct; to arrest or stop 1578. 5. To hinder, prohibit *from*; to debar *of* 1551. 6. To stop, hinder 1559. 7. To exclude from consideration 1481. 8. To object to 1611. 9. To mark with a bar or bars ME. 10. To make into bars 1712.

1. Shut the doores and barre them *Neh.* vii. 3. 4. What villaine Boy, bar'st me my way in Rome *Tit. A.* I. i. 291. To b. a person from his action 1726. To b. dower, a right 1884. 7. Nay but I barre tonight *Merch. V.* II. ii. 208. 8. †*To b. the dice*: to declare the throw void. 10. *To b. a vein (Farriery)*: to tie it above and below a part which is to be operated on.

Bar (bāɹ), *prep.* 1714. [f. BAR *v.*; prob. after *except*, etc.; cf. BARRING.] Excluding from consideration, except.

‖**Baragouin** (ba·ragwe·ṅ, -gwin). 1613. [a. F., f. Breton *bara* bread + *gwîn* wine (Littré, q. v.), or *gwenn* white.] Unintelligible speech; jargon, double-Dutch. Hence **Baragoui·nish** *a.*

Baralipton (bærăli·ptǫn). 1653. A mnemonic wd. representing the first indirect mood of the first syllogistic figure, in which a particular affirmative conclusion is drawn from two universal affirmative premisses.

‖**Barathrum** (bæ·răþrɒm). 1520. [L., a. Gr. βάραθρον.] A pit, gulf. Hence a. A pit at Athens, into which criminals condemned to death were thrown 1849. b. The abyss, hell 1520. c. An insatiable extortioner or glutton (so in It.) 1609.

Barb (bāɹb), *sb.*¹ ME. [a. F. *barbe*:—L. *barba.*] †1. The beard of a man (*rare*) –1618. 2. A similar appendage in animals 1468. 3. A piece of white plaited linen, worn over or under the chin, as by nuns ME. 4. *Veter. Surg.* in *pl.* Folds of the mucous membrane under the tongue of horses and cattle, protecting the orifices of the ducts of the submaxillary glands; the disease caused by their inflammation 1523. 5. *Her.* A sepal (*pl.* the calyx) of a flower 1572. 6. One of the lateral processes from the shaft of a feather, which bear the barbules 1836. 7. Little ridges produced in metal-working, *e.g.* by engravers; bur 1842. 8. A sharp process curving back from the point of a weapon (*e.g.* a fish-hook), rendering its extraction difficult ME. Also *fig.* 9. *Bot.* A hooked hair 1864.

8. *fig.* The malice of a good thing is the b. that makes it stick SHERIDAN.

†**Barb**, *sb.*² 1566. [Corrupt f. BARD ².] A covering for the breast and flanks of a war-horse –1630.

Barb (bāɹb), *sb.*³ 1636. [a. F. *barbe*, f. *Barbarie.*] Occas. *attrib.* 1. A horse of the breed imported from Barbary and Morocco, noted for speed and endurance. Also called BARBARY. 2. A black or dun pigeon, orig. introduced from Barbary 1725.

Barb (bāɹb), *v.* 1483. [a. F. *barber*, f. *barbe.*] †1. To shave or trim the beard of –1693. Also *absol.* or *intr.* (for *refl.*) 2. *transf.* To clip; to mow 1483. Also †*fig.* 3. To furnish with barbs 1611. Also *fig.* 4. To pierce with, or as with, a barb 1803.

3. Arrows barbd with fire MILT. *P. L.* VI. 546. She barbs with wit those darts too keen before SHERIDAN.

Barbadoes (baɹbē·douz). Name of an island, in the West Indies, referred to Pg. *las barbadas* 'bearded', epithet of the Indian fig-tree growing there; formerly 'the Barbadoes'.

Phrases, etc. **B.-cherry**, the tart fruit of the *Malpighia urens*. **B. leg**, a form of elephantiasis incident to hot climates. **B. nuts**, the purgative seeds or fruit of the *Jatropha Curcas*, or *Curcas purgans*. **B. pride**, a plant (*Poinciana pulcherrima*), used for fences. **B. tar**, a greenish petroleum. **B.-water**, a cordial flavoured with orange- and lemon-peel. Also †**Barbadoes** *v.* to transport to B.

Barbal (bā·ɹbăl), *a.* 1650. [f. L. *barba* + -AL ¹.] Of or belonging to the beard.

†**Ba·rbar.** ME. [a. F. *barbare*, ad. L. *barbarus.*] A. *sb* = BARBARIAN –1723. B. *adj.* = BARBAROUS –1726.

Barbara (bā·ɹbără). 1589. A mnemonic term designating the first mood of the first syllogistic figure, in which both premisses and the conclusion are universal affirmatives.

Barbaresque (bāɹbăre·sk), *a.* 1804. [a. F. *barbaresque* (= It. *barbaresco*) belonging to Barbary. See BARBAR and -ESQUE, and cf. BARBARY.] 1. Of or pertaining to Barbary 1824. 2. Barbarous in style, *esp.* in reference to art 1823. 3. as *sb.* A native of Barbary 1804.

2. Architecture .. b., rich in decoration, at times colossal in proportions, but unsymmetrical DE QUINCEY.

Barbarian (baɹbē·riăn). 1549. [a. F. *barbarien*, f. F. *barbarie*, on L. type **barbarianus*. See BARBAROUS.] A. *sb.* 1. *orig.* A foreigner. 2. *Hist.* a. A non-Hellene. b. A non-Roman. c. A non-Christian. d. A non-Italian. 3. A rude, wild, uncivilized person 1613. 4. An uncultured person 1762. †5. A native of Barbary. [See BARBARY.] –1709.

1. I shall be vnto him that speaketh, a B., and he that speaketh shal be a B. vnto me 1 *Cor.* xiv. 11. 2. I would they were Barbarians..not Romans *Cor.* III. i. 238. 4. Cromwell, though himself a b., was not insensible to literary merit HUME.

B. *adj.* 1. Non-Hellenic, non-Roman (*most usual*), non-Christian 1549. 2. Uncivilized, savage, rude 1591. †3. Of or belonging to Barbary –1699.

1. Bought and solde..like a B. slaue *Tr. & Cr.* II. i. 51

Barbaric (baɹbæ·rik), *a.* 1490. [a. OF. *barbarique*, ad. L., a. Gr. βαρβαρικός, f. βάρβαρος.] 1. = BARBARIAN *a.* 2. 1490. 2. Pertaining or proper to barbarians or their art 1667. 3. = BARBARIAN *a.* 1. 1849.

2. B. Pearl and Gold MILTON. Hence **Barba·rically** *adv.*

Barbarism (bā·ɹbăriz'm). 1579. [a. F. *barbarisme*, ad. L. *barbarismus*, a. Gr., f. βαρβαρίζειν to speak like a foreigner.] 1. The use of words or expressions not in accordance with the classical standard of a language; *hence*, rudeness of language. b. A foreign or non-classical word or idiom 1589. 2. Barbarous social or intellectual condition; opp. to *civilization* 1584. Also with *a* and *pl.* (Only in Eng.) 1645. †3. BARBARITY –1665.

1. A b., then, is a fault of style originating in rudeness and ignorance; but a solecism is [one] originating in affectation and over-refinement 1801. 2. Plundering and other barbarismes HOWELL.

Barbarity (baɹbæ·rĭti). 1570. [f. L. *barbarus* + -ITY; not in L. or Fr.] †1. = BARBARISM 2. –1819. 2. Barbarous cruelty; inhumanity. (The usual sense.) 1685. Also with *a* and *pl.* 3. = BARBARISM 1. ? *Obs.* 1706. 4. Barbarism of style in art. Also with *a* and *pl.* 1644.

2. With breach of faith, with cruelty and b. DE FOE.

Barbarize (bā·ɹbărəiz), *v.* 1644. [partly ad. Gr. βαρβαρίζειν; partly f. L. *barbarus* + -IZE.] 1. *intr.* To speak or write like a barbarian. 2. *trans.* To render barbarous 1648. 3. *intr.* To fall into barbarism 1824.

2. The hideous changes which have since barbarized France BURKE.

Barbarous (bā·ɹbărəs), *a.* 1526. [f. L. *barbarus*, a. Gr., prob. with a primary reference to speech. Cf. L. *balbus* stammering.] 1. Of language: a. *orig.* Not Greek; *subseq.* not Greek nor Latin; *hence*, not classical or pure. Hence, b. Unpolished; pertaining to an illiterate people. 2. Of people: Foreign in speech; *orig.* non-Hellenic; *then*, not Roman; *occas.* not Christian 1542. 3. Uncultured, unpolished; rude, savage. (Opp. to *civilized.*) 1538. 4. Cruelly savage, or harsh 1588. 5. Harsh-sounding, coarsely noisy 1645. †6. = BARBARIC 2. –1700.

2. The b. people shewed vs no little kindnesse *Acts* xxviii. 2. 3. *Twel. N.* IV. i. 52. 4. The b. aspect of war MOZLEY. 5. A b. noise MILT. 6. B. gold DRYDEN. Hence **Ba·rbarous-ly** *adv.*, **-ness.**

Barbary (bā·ɹbări). ME. [I. a. OF. *barbarie*, ad. L. *barbaria*, *barbaries*, f. *barbarus*. In II. ult. f. Arab. *Barbar*, *Berber*.] I. †1. Foreign nationality; heathenism. *concr.* Non-Christian lands. *attrib.* = Paynim. –1629. †2. Barbarity –1635. †3. Uncultivated speech. Also *attrib.* –1608. II. The Saracen countries along the north coast of Africa. (The surviving sense.) 1596. Also *attrib.*, esp. in **Barbary ape, horse**, etc. Also †*ellipt.* = BARB *sb.*³

Barbastel(le (bāɹbăste·l, bā·ɹbăstel). 1791. [a. F.] A dark brown bat (*Plecotus barbastellus*), found in France and Germany.

Barbate (bā·ɹbeɪt), *a.* 1853. [ad. L. *barbatus.*] Bearded; furnished with a small hairy tuft or tufts.

†**Ba·rbated**, *a. rare.* 1782. [f. as prec. + -ED.] Barbed, as an arrow; barbate –1802.

Barbecue (bā·ɹbĭkiū), *sb.* 1697. [ad. Sp. *barbacoa*, a. Haitian.] 1. A rude framework, used in America for sleeping on, and for smoking or drying meat over a fire. 2. An ox, hog, etc., roasted whole 1764. 3. (in U.S.) An open-air social entertainment, at which animals are roasted whole 1809. 4. An open floor on which coffee-beans, etc. may be dried 1855.

1. His Couch or Barbecu of Sticks DAMPIER. 3. I am invited to dinner on a barbicu FOOTE.

Barbecue (bā·ɹbĭkiū), *v.* 1661. [f. prec. sb.] 1. To dry or cure on a barbecue; see the sb. 1, and 4. 2. To broil or roast (an animal) whole on a huge gridiron.

2. B. your whole hogs to your palate LAMB.

Barbed (bāɹbd), *ppl. a.*[1] 1526. [f. BARB *v.*, *sb.*[1] + -ED.] †1. Bearded (*rare*) 1693. †2. Wearing a BARB (sense 3) –1601. 3. *Her.* Having a calyx 'coloured proper' 1611. 4. Furnished with a barb or barbs 1611.

4. Can'st thou fill his skinne with b. yrons *Job* xli. 7.

Barbed (bāɹbd, bā·ɹbĕd), *ppl. a.*[2] 1509. [f. BARB *sb.*[2] + -ED.] Barded (see BARD *v.*[1]).

Barbel (bā·ɹbĕl). ME. [a. OF. *barbel*, mod. *barbeau* :—late L. *barbellus*, dim. of *barbus* (the fish), f. *barba*.] 1. A large European fresh-water fish (*Barbus vulgaris*), named from the fleshy filaments which hang from its mouth. 2. A fleshy filament hanging from the mouth of certain fishes 1601. Hence **Ba·rbelled, -eled,** *ppl. a.* furnished with barbels. **Ba·rbelling, -eling** *vbl. sb.* fishing for b.

†**Ba·rbeled, -bled,** *ppl. a.* ME. [f. OF. *barbelé*.] Barbed –1480.

Barbellate (bā·ɹbĕlĕ't), *a.* 1847. [f. mod.L. *barbella*, dim. of *barbula*.] *Bot.* Furnished with *barbellæ* or short stiff hairs.

Barbellulate (baɹbe·liŭlĕ't), *a.* 1847. [f. mod.L. *barbellula*, dim. of *barbella*; see prec.] *Bot.* Furnished with *barbellulæ* or minute conical spines.

Barber (bā·ɹbəɹ), *sb.* [ME. *barbour*, OF. *barbeor* :—L. type *barbatorem*, f. *barba*. The terminal *-er* is partly after F. *barbier*.] a. One whose business it is to shave or trim the beard, and cut and dress the hair. (Now usu. *hair-dresser*.) Formerly the barber was also a surgeon and dentist. b. *fig.* A curtailer. B. JONS. Also *attrib.*, as in †**b.-monger,** a frequenter of the barber's shop, a fop.

For Barbers they use their women CAPT. SMITH.

Phrases. *Barber's chair*, one common to all his customers, †*fig.* a drab. *Barber's music*, discordant music, like that formerly produced by waiting customers in a barber's shop. *Barber's pole*, a pole painted spirally with red and white stripes, used as a barber's sign. Hence **Ba·rber** *v.* (*rare*) to trim.

Barberry, berberry (bā·ɹbĕri, bɜ·ɹbĕri). ME. [ad. med.L. *barbaris, berberis*, of unkn. origin.] *Bot.* 1. A shrub (*Berberis vulgaris*), with spiny shoots, and pendulous racemes of small yellow flowers, succeeded by oblong, red, sharply acid berries; the bark yields a bright yellow dye. Also the genus *Berberis*. 2. The berry of this tree 1533. Also *attrib.*

Barbery (bā·ɹbəri). ME. [a. F. *barberie*, f. *barbier*.] †1. A barber's shop. 2. The barber's art or craft 1540.

Barbet (ba·ɹbĕt). 1753. [a. F. *barbet*, prob. OF. ppl. adj. = *barbu*.] 1. A little dog with long curly hair 1780. †2. Name of a worm with tufts of white filaments, which feeds on aphides 1753. 3. A family of birds, found in warm countries, having a short conical bill, with tufts of bristles at its base. (In F. *barbu*.) 1824.

‖**Barbette** (baɹbe·t), *sb.* 1772. [Fr., dim. of *barbe*.] A platform within a fortification, on which guns are raised for firing over the parapet. *Guns en barbette, b. gun* or *battery*: those so mounted as to fire over the parapet; similarly in ironclad ships. Hence *attrib.*, as in *b.-cruiser, -turret.*

Barbican (bā·ɹbikæ̆n). ME. [a. F. *barbacane*, perh. f. Arab. or Pers.] An outer defence to a city or castle, *esp.* a double tower erected over a gate or bridge. †2. A temporary wooden tower. CAXTON. †3. A loophole in the wall of a castle or city 1600.

Ba·rbicanage. 1691. [ad. med.L. *barbicanagium*, f. prec.] Tribute paid for the maintenance of barbicans.

Barbicel (bā·ɹbisĕl). 1869. [ad. mod.L. *barbicella*, dim. of *barba*; cf. PEDICEL.] One of the minute hooked filaments which interlock the barbules of a bird's feathers.

Barbi·gerous, *a.* 1731. [f. L. *barbiger* + -OUS.] Bearded.

‖**Ba·rbiton, -os.** 1545. [L., a. Gr.] A many-stringed instrument; a lute or lyre. Hence †**Ba·rbitist,** a player on the b.

Barble, obs. f. BARBEL.

Barbotine (bā·ɹbŏtin). 1865. [a. F., f. *barboter*.] A paste of kaolin clay used to ornament pottery.

Barbre, obs. f. BARBARY.

‖**Barbula** (bā·ɹbiŭlă). 1688. [L., dim. of *barba*.] 1. A small beard. ?*Obs.* 2. The inner row of fringes in the peristome of mosses 1866.

Barbule (bā·ɹbiŭl). 1835. [ad. L. *barbula*; see prec.] 1. = BARBEL 2. 2. One of the processes fringing the barbs of a feather 1835. 3. *Bot.* = BARBULA 2. 1881.

Barcarole, -olle (bā·ɹkărōul). 1779. [ad. It. *barcaruolo*; in sense 2 a. F. *barcarolle*, It. *barcaruola*; f. BARCA.] ‖1. An Italian boatman 1854. 2. A song sung by Venetian gondoliers; a piece of music composed in imitation of such songs 1799.

†**Barcelo·na.** 1795. [f. *Barcelona*, in Spain.] A handkerchief or neckerchief of soft twilled silk –1833.

‖**Barco·ne.** [It., augment. of BARCA.] A vessel used for freight in the Mediterranean. var. **Barcon** (Webster).

Bard (bāɹd), *sb.*[1] ME. [a. Gael. and Ir. *bàrd* :—OCelt. **bardos* (whence Gr. βάρδος, L. *bardus*). Orig. a term of contempt, but idealized by Scott.] 1. An ancient Celtic order of minstrel-poets, who composed and sang (usually to the harp) verses celebrating the achievements of chiefs and warriors. In Welsh *spec.* A poet who has been recognized at the Eisteddfod. 2. In early Lowland Scotch: A strolling musician or minstrel 1449. 3. Used of the Old English *gleeman*, Scandinavian *scald*, etc. 1623. 4. *poet.* A 'singer'. (Chiefly after Lucan.) 1667.

2. Feinzied fooles, bairdes, rynners about .. after sundrie punishments, may be hanged SKENE. The last of all the bards was he Who sung of Border minstrelsy SCOTT. 4. That wild rout that tore the Thracian b. In Rhodopè MILT. *P. L.* VII. 34.

Bard, *sb.*[2] Now *Hist.* 1480. [a. F. *barde* horse-armour, perh. f. (ult.) Arab. *al-barda'ah*, 'the stuffed pack-saddle for ass or mule'. Erron. called BARB, q. v.] 1. (Usu. *pl.*) A covering of armour for the breast and flanks of a war-horse; occas. an ornamental covering of velvet or the like. 2. *pl.* Plate armour, as formerly worn by men-at-arms 1551.

Bard (bāɹd), *sb.*[3] 1725. [a. F. *barde*, transf. from prec.] A thin slice of bacon used to cover a fowl, etc.

Bard (bāɹd), *v.*[1] 1521. [a. F. *barder*, f. *barde* BARD *sb.*[2] and [3].] 1. To arm or caparison with bards. (Chiefly in pa. pple.) 2. To cover with slices of bacon 1665.

†**Bard,** *v.*[2] 1641. [app. by confusion of BARB *v.* and BEARD.] = BARB *v.* 2. –1693.

†**Barda·sh.** 1548. [a. F. *bardache*.] A catamite –1721.

†**Barde·l(le.** *rare.* 1603. [a. F.; see BARD *sb.*[2]] A pack-saddle –1753.

Bardic (bā·ɹdik), *a.* 1775. [f. BARD *sb.*[1] + -IC.] Of, pertaining to, or of the character of, bards. So **Bardish** (bā·ɹdiʃ) *a.* of or belonging to bards. (*Somewhat depreciatory.*) **Bardism** (bā·ɹdiz'm), the system, doctrine, or principles of bards. **Ba·rdling,** an inexperienced poet; a poetaster; var. **Ba·rdlet.**

‖**Bardocucu·llus.** 1611. [L.] A Gallic peasant's cloak, with a hood, worn also by monks.

Ba·rdship. 1787. [f. BARD *sb.*[1] + SHIP.] The office, dignity, or personality of a bard.

Bare (bēəɹ). [Com. Teut.: OE. *bær*:—OTeut. **baz-oz* barefoot.] A. *adj.* 1. Without covering, naked. 2. = BAREHEADED (*arch.*) ME. 3. *fig.* Open to view OE. 4. Of natural objects: Without the covering which they have at other times OE. 5. Stripped of hair, wool, flesh, etc.; bald ME. 6. Unfurnished, uncovered, unarmed ME. †7. Defenceless –1551. †8. Desolate –1642. 9. Destitute, needy; scantily furnished ME. Hence, 10. a. Empty ME.; b. †Worthless –1596; c. Bald, unadorned ME.; †d. Simple, unpolished –1603. 11. Without addition, mere; — only ME. †12. Sheer, absolute, very –ME.

1. Make b. the legge *Isa.* xlvii. 2. In his b. shirt 1866. 3. B. in thy guilt MILT. *Sams.* 902. 4. The Country .. being eaten b. 1720. 6. To lie upon b. boards 1722. One's b. hands *Oth.* I. iii. 175. B. Liueries SHAKS. *Bare poles* (Naut.): masts with no sails set. 8. SHAKS. *Lucr.* 1741. 9. As b. as Job BALE. B. of saintliness 1883. 10. A b. treasury DRYDEN. B. excuses SHAKS. 11. The b. Necessaries of Life ADDISON. A b. majority 1844. *B. contract* (Law): an unconditional promise or surrender.

B. *adv.* With numeral adjs.: BARELY (*arch.*) –1716.

†C. *sb.* †1. A naked part of the body. Also *fig.* –1611. †2. A bare space or place –1706.

Comb. **b.-bone,** a lean skinny person.

Bare (bēəɹ), *v.* [OE. **barian*, f. *bær* BARE *a.*] 1. To make or lay bare, expose to view; to unsheathe. 2. *fig.* To disclose, make manifest ME. 3. To strip. Const. *of, from* 1440.

1. Have bar'd my Bosome to the Thunder-stone *Jul. C.* I. iii. 49. 3. To b. a garden LIVINGSTONE.

Bareback (bēə·ɹbæk), *a. adv.* 1562. = BAREBACKED 2.

Bare-backed (bēə·ɹbækt), *a.* 1628. [see BARE *a.* 6.] 1. With the back bare 1831. 2. Without saddle; also with *ride* as *adv.*

‖**Bareca, -ka** (barē·kă). 1773. [a. Sp.] A small cask or keg, a BREAKER.

Barefaced (bēə·ɹfēɪst), *a.* (in use occas. advb.). 1590. 1. With the face uncovered: *hence* a. beardless, also *fig.*; b. without mask. 2. Avowed, open 1605. 3. Hence: Audacious, shameless 1674.

2. B. and open tyranny 1766. 3. A b. orphan DICKENS, lie MRS. STOWE. Hence **Ba·refaced-ly** *adv.*, **-ness.**

Barefoot (bēə·ɹfut). [OE. *bærfōt*. See BARE *a.*] With the feet bare: a. as *adj.*, passing (with vbs. of motion) into b. *adv.*

b. Who waitth for dead men shoen, shall go long barefoote *Prov.* Hence **Ba·re-foo·ted** *a.*

‖**Barége** (bare·ʒ). 1811. [Fr.; f. *Barèges* in the Pyrenees.] 1. A gauze-like, silky dress-fabric, orig. made at Baréges 1851. 2. A mineral water obtained at Baréges. Hence **Barégin(e,** a glairy organic substance found in many mineral waters after exposure to the air.

Ba·rehead, *a.* and *adv. arch.* ME. = next.

Bare-headed (bēə·ɹhe·dĕd), *a.* and *adv.* 1530. [f. prec.; cf. *barefoot(ed.*] With the head uncovered, *esp.* as a token of respect. Hence **Bare-headedness.**

Barely (bēə·ɹli), *adv.* OE. [f. BARE *a.* + -LY[2].] 1. Nakedly 1483. 2. Without concealment or disguise OE. †3. Unconditionally; wholly; positively –ME. 4. Merely, only (*arch.*) 1577. 5. Only just; *hence*, not quite, with difficulty 1494. 6. Scantily; baldly 1535.

2. To put a question b. before any one 1875. 4. Not b. in word, but truly in deed HANMER. 5. B. time to get out of the way 1805.

Ba·reness. 1552. [f. BARE *a.* + -NESS.] 1. Nakedness. 2. Destitution, scantiness; baldness (*lit.* and *fig.*) 1580; †leanness –1596.

Baresark (bēə·ɹsāɹk). 1840. [lit. = 'bare shirt'; see BERSERKER.] 1. *sb.* (also *attrib.*) A BERSERKER. 2. *adv.* In a shirt only, without armour.

†**Ba·rful,** *a.* [f. BAR *sb.*] Full of hindrances. *Twel. N.* I. iv. 41.

Bargain (bā·ɹgĕn), *sb.*[1] ME. [a. OF. *bargaine*. See BARGAIN *v.*] †1. Discussion between two parties as to terms; chaffering –1596. 2. An agreement between two parties settling the part of each in a transaction between them; a compact ME. b. Occas., the compact in relation to one of the parties only, *e.g.* a 'bad b.' 1502. 3. That which is acquired by bargaining; a purchase qualified as *good*, etc.; *without qualification*, an advantageous purchase ME. 4. *transf.* A (bad or unfortunate) 'business' (*arch.*) ME. †5. Contention for the mastery; battle. *north.* –1606. Also *fig.*

1. †*To beat a (the) b.*: to haggle. 2. So clap hands, and a bargaine *Hen. V*, V. ii. 134. 3. Picked up as a b. 1882.

Phrases. **B. and sale** (*Law*): a kind of conveyance, in which the legal owner agreed with the purchaser for the sale to him of his interest, and the purchaser paid, or promised to pay, the money for the land. *Dutch* or *wet b.*: one concluded by the parties drinking together. *Into*, †*to, the b.*: over and above what is agreed; besides. †*To sell any one a b.*: to make a fool of him SHAKS. *To strike* (†*up*) *a b.*: to come to terms over a purchase. *To make the best of a bad b.*: to make the best of adverse circumstances.

Hence **Ba·rgainee·**, the party with whom an agreement of bargain and sale of land is made. **Ba·rgainer,** one who bargains; †=*Bargainor.* **Ba·rgaino·r,** the party making an agreement of bargain and sale of land.

Ba·rgain, *sb.*[2] Now *dial.* 1602. [?same wd. as prec.] A small farm-holding.

Bargain (bā·ɹgėn), *v.* ME. [a. OF. *bargaigner*:—late L. **barcaneare*, ?f. *barca* (Diez).] **1.** *intr.* To haggle over terms, negotiate. **2.** To arrange terms; to strike a bargain *with* (a person) *for* 1483. **3.** *trans.* To agree to buy or sell; to contract for. *Obs.* exc. in *To bargain and sell.* 1488. †**4.** *Sc.* To contend –1513.

1. Judas bargaining with the priests 1859. **2.** I.. have bargained to be landed in France P. JONES. Phr. *To bargain for*: *fig.* to arrange for beforehand; to count on, expect.

Bargander, obs. f. BERGANDER.

Barge (bāɹdʒ), *sb.* ME. [a. OF.:—L. type *barga*; or ?**barica* (Diez). As to *barga* see BARK *sb.*[2]] **1.** A small sea-going vessel with sails; *spec.* one next in size above a BALINGER. Now *Hist.* **2.** A flat-bottomed freight-boat or *lighter*, chiefly for canal- and river-navigation 1480. †**3.** *vaguely*, A rowing-boat; *esp.* a ferry-boat. (Used for L. *linter.*) –1601. **4.** *spec.* The second boat of a man of war; a long narrow boat for the use of the chief officers 1530. **5.** A vessel of state, propelled by oars (or towed); an ornamental house-boat 1586. **6.** (in *U.S.*) A large carriage 1881.

4. A b. properly never rows less than ten [oars] FALCONER. **5.** *Ant. & Cl.* II. ii. 196. *Comb.*: **Barge-man,** one who has charge of, or rows in, a b. **Barge-master,** the owner of a b. **Barge-pole,** esp. in colloq. phr. *would not touch with a b.-p.*, regard with loathing. Hence **Barge** *v.* to carry by b.; also *intr.* (*slang*) to lurch or bump heavily *into*, *against*, etc., to intrude *in* 1888.

Ba·rge-board. 1833. [see next.] A board running along the edge of the gable of a house, to conceal the barge-couples, etc.

Ba·rge-cou·ple. 1562. [With *barge-* cf. med.L. *bargus* gallows = L. *furca.*] *Archit.* Two beams mortised and tenoned together to increase the strength of a building.

Bargee (bāɹdʒī·). 1666. [f. BARGE *sb.* + -EE (irreg.).] A bargeman.

Ba·rge-course. 1668. [see prec.] A portion of the roof of a house carried slightly beyond the wall at the gable-end, to keep out rain, etc.

Ba·rge-stone. 1833. [see BARGE-COUPLE.] In *pl.*: Stones forming the sloping line of a gable.

Bargh (bāɹf). *dial.* 1674. [mod. north. f. BARROW, ME. *bergh.*] **1.** A detached low ridge 1823. **2.** A road up a steep hill 1674. **3.** A mine 1693.

Barghest (bā·ɹge·st). 1732. [perh. ad. Ger. *berg-geist*; or f. Ger. *bahre* bier (Scott), or Ger. *bär.*] A goblin, in the shape of a large dog, fabled to portend death or misfortune.

†**Ba·r-goose.** 1598. [app. short f. *barnacle-goose.*] The barnacle-goose –1647.

†**Ba·ria.** Also **barya.** 1812. [f. BARIUM.] *Chem.* = BARYTA –1819.

Baric (bēᵊ·rik), *a.*[1] 1869. [f. BARIUM + -IC.] *Chem.* Of barium; containing barium in composition.

Baric (bæ·rik), *a.*[2] 1881. [f. Gr. βάρος + IC.] Of or pertaining to weight, *esp.* that of the air; barometric.

Barilla (bări·lă, bări·lʸa). 1622. [a. Sp.] **1.** A maritime plant (*Salsola Soda*) growing largely in Spain, Sicily, and the Canary Islands. **2. a.** An impure alkali produced by burning dried plants of this and allied species; used in making soda, soap, and glass. **b.** Also, an impure alkali made from kelp.

Baring (bēᵊ·riŋ), *vbl. sb.* 1601. [f. BARE *v.* + -ING[1].] **1.** The action of laying bare. **2.** That which is removed in this process; the top soil.

Barish (bēᵊ·riʃ), *a.* 1661. [f. BARE *a.* + -ISH[1].] Somewhat bare.

Barite (bēᵊ·rəit). [f. BARIUM + -ITE.] *Min.* Dana's name for BARYTES.

Baritone: see BARYTONE. The spelling with *i* is now usual, esp. when applied to the voice.

Barium (bēᵊ·riŏm). 1808. [f. BARYTA; cf. *soda, sodium.*] *Chem.* A white metallic element, not found native, but as the basis of baryta.

Bark (bāɹk), *sb.*[1] ME. [a. Scand. *bark-*:—OTeut. **barkuz.*] **1.** The rind or outer sheath of the trunk and branches of trees; *spec.* that used in dyeing, tanning, etc., spent bark, tan. †**2.** The rind, husk, or shell of fruit and grains –1661. **3.** *gen.* An outer covering or husk. Now *dial.* 1601. **4.** *dial.* and *slang.* The skin 1758. **5.** *fig.* Outside (*arch.*) ME. **6.** *spec.* in *Med.* (also *Jesuits'* or *Peruvian Bark*): The bark of the Cinchona tree, from which quinine is procured 1704.

1. He is no friend to the tree, that strips it of the b. FULLER. *Comb.*: **b.-bed,** a hot-bed made of spent b.; **-bound** *a.*, hindered in growth by tightness of the b.; **-heat,** that of a b.-bed; **-louse,** a kind of aphis, infesting the b. of trees; **-pit,** a pit filled with b. and water in which hides are steeped; **-worm** = *bark-louse.*

Bark, barque (bāɹk), *sb.*[2] 1475. [a. F. *barque*, ad. It. *barca* :—L. *barca.* Possibly from Celtic.] **1.** *orig.* Any small sailing vessel; now rhet. or poet. for any sailing vessel; = BARGE 1. Also *fig.* **2.** A rowing boat; now only poetically and vaguely 1598. **3.** *spec.* A sailing vessel of particular rig; in 17th c. used of the *barca-longa*; *now* of a three-masted vessel with fore- and main-masts square-rigged, and mizen-mast fore-and-aft rigged. (Freq. spelt *barque.*) 1601.

1. The skarfed barke puts from her natiue bay *Merch. V.* II. vi. 15. My spirit's b. is driven, Far from the shore SHELLEY.

Bark (bāɹk), *sb.*[3] 1562. [f. BARK *v.*[1]] **1.** The sharp explosive cry of dogs; also, that of foxes, squirrels, etc. **2.** *transf.*; *e.g.* the sound of cannon-firing; *colloq.* a cough. 1871.

Bark (bāɹk), *v.*[1] [OE. *beorcan*, str. vb., repr. an earlier *bercan*, **berkan*; cogn. w. OE. *borcian.* According to some, a var. of BREAK, OE. *brecan* :—OTeut. **brekan.*] **1.** *intr.* To utter a sharp explosive cry. (Orig. of dogs, hence of other animals.). **2.** *fig.* To speak or cry out angrily or aggressively ME. **3.** *mod. colloq.* To cough. †**4.** *trans.* To utter with a bark; to break out with –1644.

1. Harke, harke, bowgh, wawgh; the watch-Dogges barke *Temp.* I. ii. 383. **2.** Phr. *To bark against* (or *at*) *the moon*: to clamour to no effect.

Bark (bāɹk), *v.*[2] ME. [f. BARK *sb.*[1]] **1.** *intr.* (with *over*) To form a bark. **2.** *trans.* To treat with bark; to tan ME. **3.** To strip off the bark from 1545. Also *fig.* **b.** *transf.* To scrape the skin (*esp.* from the shins and joints) 1850. **4.** To enclose with or as with bark 1633.

3. *fig.* Would barke your honor from that trunke you beare, And leaue you naked *Meas. for M.* III. i. 72. Phr. *To b.* (a squirrel, etc.): to shoot at the bark beneath it and kill it by concussion.

†**Ba·rkary.** 1594. [ad. med.L. *barcarium, bercarium, bercaria*, for *berbicaria*, f. *berbica* sheep = cl. L. *berbex*; cf. F. *bergerie.*] A sheep-fold –1641.

Barkentine, var. of BARQUENTINE.

Barker (bā·ɹkəɹ), *sb.*[1] ME. [f. BARK *v.*[1] + -ER[1].] **1.** One who or that which barks; a dog. **2.** *fig.* A noisy assailant 1483. **b.** One who cries wares at a cheap shop or show; now chiefly *U.S.* 1700. **3.** The Spotted Redshank (*Totanus fuscus*) 1802. **4.** *slang.* A pistol 1815.

Ba·rker, *sb.*[2] ME. [f. BARK *v.*[2] + -ER[1].] †**1.** A tanner –1609. **2.** One who barks trees 1611.

Ba·rkey. *colloq.* 1847. [f. BARK *sb.*[2] + -EY = -Y[4].] A little bark.

Barking (bā·ɹkiŋ), *vbl. sb.*[1] ME. [f. BARK *v.*[1] + -ING[1].] **1.** The utterance of barks; *transf.* harsh coughing 1813. **2.** *fig.* Angry outcry 1549.

Ba·rking, *vbl. sb.*[2] ME. [f. BARK *v.*[2] + -ING[1].] **1.** Tanning 1440. **2.** Cutting off the bark from trees; ring-barking 1545.

2. *Barking-irons*: tools used for barking trees.

Ba·rking, *ppl. a.* 1552. [f. BARK *v.*[1]] The action of BARK *v.*[1] Also *transf.* and *fig.*

Barking-bird, the *Pteroptochus Tarnu*, so named from its voice; **b.-iron** (*slang*), a pistol. Hence **Ba·rkingly** *adv.*

Barky (bā·ɹki), *a.* 1590. [f. as prec.] Covered with, or of the nature of, bark.

1. The b. fingers of the Elme *Mids. N.* IV. i. 48.

Barley (bā·ɹli). [OE. *bærlīc*, ? f. OTeut. **baroz-*, **bariz-* 'barley' + *-līc* (see -LY[1]).] A hardy awned cereal (genus *Hordeum*); used for food, and for making malt liquors and spirits. **a.** The plant ME. **b.** The grain. *French, Pearl, Pot barley.* OE.

Comb.: **b.-bird,** name given locally to the wryneck, siskin, greenfinch, and occas. the nightingale, which appear about the time of barley-sowing; **-bree, -broth,** strong ale; **-candy** (=*barley-sugar*); †**-hat** (cf. BARLEY-CAP, -HOOD); **-milk,** a gruel of b., or b.-meal; **-mow,** a stack of b.; †**-sick** *a.* intoxicated; **-straw** (*fig.*), a trifle; **-sugar,** a confection made from sugar, formerly by boiling in a decoction of b.; **-water,** a demulcent drink, made by the decoction of pearl b.

Ba·rley, *int. Sc.* and *n. dial.* 1814. [perh. corrupt f. F. *parlez*, Eng. *parley.*] Parley, truce; a term used in children's games.

Barley-break (bā·ɹli,brēɪk). 1557. [Of unkn. etym.] An old country game, resembling *Prisoner's Bars*, played by six persons (three of each sex) in couples; one couple had to catch the others, who were allowed to 'break', and change partners, when hard pressed.

†**Ba·rley-ca·p.** 1598. [f. BARLEY.] In phr. *To have on*, etc., *a barley-cap*: to be tipsy; hence *barley-cap* = tippler.

Barley-corn (bā·ɹli,kǭɹn). ME. [See CORN.] **1.** = BARLEY. **b.** Personified as *John Barleycorn*; esp. as providing malt liquors 1620. **2.** A grain of barley 1588. **3.** A grain of barley as a measure of length, ⅓, formerly also ¼, of an inch 1607. **4.** *Building.* A little planed cavity between the mouldings of joiner's work 1753.

1. John Barleycorn, Thou king o' grain BURNS.

Ba·rley-hoo·d. 1529. [cf. BARLEY-CAP.] A fit of drunkenness, or of ill humour brought on by drinking.

†**Ba·rling.** 1611. [a. Sw. *bärling* pole.] A pole. DE FOE.

†**Barm,** *sb.*[1] [Com. Teut.: OE. *barm*:—OTeut. **barmoz*, f. *beran* to bear.] A bosom, a lap OE.

Barm (bāɹm), *sb.*[2] [OE. *beorma*; prob. Com. Teut.] The froth that forms on the top of fermenting malt liquors; used to leaven bread, and to ferment other liquors; yeast, leaven. Also *transf.* or *fig.* Hence **Barm** *v.* (*arch.*) to leaven; to rise in fermentation.

Barmaid (bā·ɹmēɪd). 1772. [f. BAR *sb.*[1]] A female who serves at a tavern or hotel bar.

Barman (bā·ɹmæ̆n). 1714. [f. BAR *sb.*[1]] **1.** One who prepares (metal) bars. **2.** One who serves at the bar of a public-house 1837.

Barmaster (bā·ɹmā·stəɹ). 1662. [Earlier *barghmaster*, ad. Ger. *bergmeister*, f. *berg-* mining-.] A local judge among miners.

Barmecide (bā·ɹmĭsəid). 1713. Patronymic of a family of princes at Bagdad, one of whom put a succession of empty dishes before a beggar, pretending that they contained a sumptuous repast—a fiction which the beggar humorously accepted. (See 'Arabian Nights'.) Hence one who offers imaginary food or illusory benefits. Often *attrib.* Hence **Barmeci·dal** *a.*

Ba·rming. *Sc. rare.* 1823. [? f. BARM *v.*] The formation of barm on a fermenting liquor; *fig.* the accruing of interest on money.

Barmkin (bā·ɹmkin). *north. arch.* ME. [? confused with BARBICAN.] The battlement of the outer fortification of a castle; a turret or watchtower on the outer wall.

Barmote (bā·ɹmōᵘt). 1653. [Earlier *barghmote*, f. Ger. *berg-* mining- + MOTE; cf. *barmaster.*] A local court amongst miners.

Barmy (bā·ɹmi), *a.* 1535. [BARM *sb.*[2]] Full of barm. Also *fig.* Also = BALMY *a.* 7.

Like b. beer HOGG.

Barn (bāɹn), *sb.* [OE. *bęre-ern* lit. 'barley-place', f. *bęre* + *ærn, ern*, reduced in ME. to *bern*, mod. *barn.*] A covered building for the storage of grain; also of hay, straw, flax, etc.

Comb. etc.: **b.-floor,** the floor of a b., *hence* what is there stored; **-gallon,** two imperial gallons (of milk); **barn(s)man,** a thresher; **-owl,** a bird of prey (*Strix flammea*), also called White, Church, and Screech Owl; **-stormer,** a strolling player; **-swallow,** the common house-swallow; **-yard,** the enclosure round a b., a farm-yard. Hence †**Barn** *v.* to garner.

Barn(e, obs. f. BAIRN.

Barnabite (bā·ɹnăbəit). 1706. [f. *Barnabas* the apostle.] A member of a religious order named from the Church of St. Barnabas at Milan.

Barnaby (bā·ɹnăbi). 1595. [a. F. *Barnabé*, ad. L. *Barnabas*.] By-form of Barnabas; whence **B.-day, B. bright, or long B.**, St. Barnabas' Day, June 11, in Old Style reckoned the longest day; **B.-thistle**, the *Centaurea solstitialis*, which flowers about June 11.

Barnacle (bā·ɹnăk'l), *sb.*[1] [ME. *bernak*, a. OF. *bernac* 'camus'; of which *bernacle* is app. a dim.] **1.** A kind of bit or twitch for the mouth of horse or ass; later, *spec.* an instrument consisting of two hinged branches placed on the nose of a restive horse. **2.** An instrument of torture similarly applied. Also *fig.* 1625. **3.** *colloq.* in *pl.* = SPECTACLES. [Prob. from their bestriding the nose.] 1571. Hence **Ba·rnacle** *v.*[1] to apply a barnacle to (a horse) 1861.

Barnacle (bā·ɹnăk'l), *sb.*[2] [ME. *bernekke*, *bernake*, OF. *bernaque*, med.L. *bernaca*. Cf. mod.L. *bernicla*, *-acula*, and mod.F. *bernicle*, *barnacle*. The name was orig. applied to the *bird*, not to the *shell*.] **1.** A species of wild goose (*Anas leucopsis*), allied to the Brent Goose, found in the arctic seas (where alone it breeds), and visiting the British coasts in winter. (Formerly fabled to be produced out of the fruit of a tree, or to grow upon the tree attached by its bill (whence called *Tree Goose*), or to be produced out of a shell. **b.** Now often *Bernacle Goose* 1768. **2.** Name of the pedunculate genus of Cirripides, which attach themselves to objects by a long fleshy foot-stalk. Occas. used of sessile Cirripides; see ACORN-SHELL. (From this the B. Goose was supposed to be produced.) 1581. **3.** *fig.* A companion that is difficult to shake off 1607. Hence **Ba·rnacle** *v.*[2] to affix strongly 1863.

Barnacled (bā·ɹnăk'ld), *ppl. a.* 1691. **a.** Covered with barnacles. **b.** *colloq.* Wearing spectacles.

†Ba·rnage. ME. [f. *barn*, var. of BAIRN + -AGE.] Infancy –1513.

†Ba·rnard. 1532. [app. var. of late ME. *berner*, one who waited with hounds to intercept a hunted animal.] A swindler's decoy; a lurking scoundrel –1608.

Barn dance. 1892. orig. *U.S.* A dance danced in a barn; *spec.* a dance in which partners advance side by side and then dance a waltz or schottische step.

Barn-door. 1547. The large door of a barn. (Used joc. of a target too large to be missed, and, in *Cricket*, of a player that blocks every ball.) *attrib.* Reared at the b.-door 1685.

Ba·rney. 1865. **a.** Cheating (*slang*). **b.** *Mining.* A small car attached to a rope and used to push cars up a slope.

Barnumize (bā·ɹnəməiz), *v.* 1851. [f. *Barnum*, showman.] To exhibit with a lavish display of puffing advertisements. **Ba·rnumism**, boastful 'tall talk'.

Barograph (bæ·rǫ̆graf). 1865. [f. Gr. βάρος + -γραφος; cf. *telegraph*.] A barometer, actuating mechanism which records automatically the atmospheric pressure. **Ba·rogram**, the record traced by a b.

Baroko, -oco (bărōᵘ·ko). 1581. *Logic.* A mnemonic word, repr. the fourth mood of the second syllogistic figure, in which a particular negative conclusion is drawn from a universal affirmative major premiss and a particular negative minor.

Barology (bărǫ·lŏdʒi). 1859. [f. Gr. βάρος + -λογία.] The science of weight.

Ba:romacro·meter. 1847. [f. Gr. βάρος + μακρός + μέτρον.] An instrument for taking the weight and length of new-born infants.

Barometer (bărǫ·mĭtəɹ). 1665. [f. Gr. βάρος + μέτρον.] An instrument for measuring the weight or pressure of the atmosphere, and hence for forecasting the weather, ascertaining the height of an ascent, etc. Also *fig.*

(The common barometer is a straight glass tube, 34 inches long and closed at the top, filled with mercury, and inverted in an open cup of the same liquid. The *siphon barometer* is a curved tube, with the mercury in the shorter limb exposed to the air; it is adapted as the *wheel barometer* by putting on the mercury in the shorter limb a float with a cord attached, which passes over a pulley, and moves an index.)

fig. Interest is the true b. of the state HUME.

Comb. **Barometer-gauge:** an appliance resembling a b., attached to the receiver of an air-pump, to indicate the rarity of the air within. Hence **Barome·tric, -al** *a.* of the nature of, pertaining to, or indicated by, a b. **Barome·trically** *adv.*

Ba:rome·trograph. 1847. [f. as prec. + -γραφος.] = BAROGRAPH. **Ba:rometro·graphy**, the part of science which treats of the barometer.

Barometry (bărǫ·mĕtri). 1713. [f. BAROMETER.] The art or science of barometric observation.

Barometz (bæ·rŏmets). 1791. [app. ad. Russ. *baranets*, dim. of *baran* ram.] The creeping root-stock and frond stalks of a woolly fern (*Cibotium barometz*) turned upside down; once thought to be half-animal, and called the Scythian Lamb.

Baron (bæ·rən). [Early ME. *barun*, *-oun*, a. OF. *barun*, *-on*, acc. of *ber*:—late L. *baro* man, of unkn. origin.] **1.** *Hist.* Orig., one who held, by military or other honourable service, from the king, or other superior; subseq. restricted to the *King's barons*, and later to the *Great Barons*, who were summoned by writ to Parliament; *hence*, a lord of Parliament; a peer. **2.** The lowest rank or order of nobility ME. **†3.** Formerly applied to the freemen of London, York, etc.; applied till the 18th c. to the freemen of the Cinque Ports, and, till 1832, to the burgesses returned by these ports to Parliament. **4.** Title of the judges of the Court of Exchequer ME. **5.** *Law* and *Her.* (conjoined with *feme*, *femme*): Husband 1594. **6.** A foreign title (giving no rank in England), *e.g.* Baron Rothschild. ‖**7.** In foreign use applied in respect to any man, also to Christ and the saints ME.

2. Boþe knizt and barun..erl..and king ME. 3. Foure Barons Of the Cinque-Ports *Hen. VIII*, IV. i. 48. 4. Barons of the Exchequer..because Barons of the realm were used to be employed in that office 1751. 7. Ioseph, þat god barune 1300.

Phr. *Baron of Beef* [orig. unkn.]: two sirloins left uncut at the backbone. *Comb.* **b.-court:** see COURT-BARON.

Hence **Ba·ronism** (*rare*), feudalism. **Ba·ronist** (*rare*), an adherent of the Barons' party. ‖**Baronne·tte**, a baron's daughter; occ. a baronet's wife. **Ba·ronship**, the position of a b.

Baronage (bæ·rŏnėdʒ). [ME. *barnage*, a. OF.:—L. type **baronaticum*, f. *baronem*.] **1.** The barons collectively; the nobles, lords, peerage. **b.** *ellipt.* A list of the barons; a 'Peerage'. **†2.** A barony –1480. **3.** The dignity of a baron 1614.

1. The Judges..were the B. of England SELDEN.

Baroness (bæ·rŏnės). ME. [a. OF. *barnesse*, *baronnesse*; see BARON.] **a.** The wife of a baron. **b.** A lady holding the title in her own right.

Baronet (bæ·rŏnėt), *sb.* ME. [dim. of BARON.] **†1.** *orig.* A word meaning *young*, *little*, or *lesser baron*. Used of gentlemen, not barons by tenure, summoned to the House of Lords by Edward III. In Ireland, the holder of a small barony. Often = BANNERET. –1662. **2.** *now*, A titled order, the lowest that is hereditary, ranking next below a baron, having precedence of all orders of knighthood, except that of the Garter. A baronet is a commoner. 1614.

They consist of *Baronets of England* (now of *Great Britain*) instituted in 1611; *Baronets of Scotland* (or of *Nova Scotia*) instituted in 1625; *Baronets of Ireland* instituted in 1619. Of the two latter there have been no new creations since 1707 and 1801 respectively.

Hence **Ba·ronete·ss**, the wife of a b. **Barone·tical** *a.*

Baronet (bæ·rŏnet), *v.* Pa. t. and pple. -eted. 1733. [f. prec. sb.] To raise to the rank of baronet. (Usu. in *pass.*)

Baronetage (bæ·ronėtėdʒ). 1720. [f. BARONET *sb.* + -AGE.] **1.** The rank of baronet 1760. **2.** The order of baronets 1876. **b.** A book giving a list of the order, with other particulars 1720.

Baronetcy (bæ·rŏnėtsi). 1812. [f. as prec. + -CY.] A baronet's rank or patent. So **Ba·ronethood, Ba·ronetship.**

Baronial (bărōᵘ·niăl), *a.* 1767. [f. BARONY + -AL[1].] Of or pertaining to a baron or the barons; befitting the rank of a baron.

Barony (bæ·rŏni). ME. [a. OF. *baronie*:—late L. **baronia*; see BARON.] **1.** The domain of a baron. **b.** In Ireland: A division of a county 1596. **c.** In Scotland: A large freehold estate (even though owned by a commoner). 1843. **†2.** The baronetage –1596. **3.** The rank or dignity of baron; baronship 1788. var. **Ba·ronry** (in senses 1, 3). ? *Obs.*

Baroque (bărǫ·k), *a.* 1818. [a. F., ad. Pg. *barroco* rough pearl; of unkn. origin.] Irregularly shaped; grotesque, odd; *spec.* of a florid style of late Renaissance architecture prevalent in the 18th c. Also *ellipt.* as *sb.*

Baroscope (bæ·rŏskoᵘp). 1665. [f. Gr. βάρος + -σκοπος.] **1.** A kind of barometer. **2.** An instrument designed to show that bodies in air lose as much weight as that of the air they displace 1881. Hence **Barosco·pic, -al** *a.*

Barouche (bărū·ʃ). 1813. [ad. dial. Ger. *barutsche*, ad. It. *barrocio*, f. L. *birotus* two-wheeled, perh. after *carroccio*. Not in Fr. (exc. as taken from Eng.)] A four-wheeled carriage with a half-head behind which can be raised or let down, having a seat in front for the driver, and seats inside for two couples to sit facing each other.

Barque (bāɹk). Var. of BARK *sb.*[2]

Barquentine, bark- (bā·ɹkĕntīn). 1693. [f. BARK *sb.*[2] after BRIGANTINE.] A small bark; *spec.* now: A vessel having the fore-mast square-rigged, and the main- and mizen-masts fore-and-aft-rigged.

†Barr, *v.* 1653. [var. of BARY *v.* (= L. *barrire*).] To utter the cry of an elephant.

Barrable (bā·răb'l), *a.* 1788. [f. BAR *v.* + -ABLE.] That can be legally stayed.

†Ba·rracan. 1638. [a. F., a. Arab., f. Pers.] A fabric: orig. coarse camlet; still in Spain 'a water-proof cloth of coarse wool or goat's hair' (Marsh). Used vaguely by European writers.

Barrace (bæ·răs). *Obs.* exc. *Hist.* ME. [a. OF. *barras*, f. *barre*.] **1.** A barrier or outwork in front of a fortress. **2.** The lists 1513. **3.** Hence: Contention (cf. BARRAT) 1470.

Barrack (bæ·răk), *sb.* 1686. [a. F. *baraque*, ad. It. *baracca* a tent, etc. Origin unkn.] **1.** A temporary hut or cabin. Still in *n. dial.* **b.** A straw-thatched roof, sliding on four posts, under which hay is kept. (In U.S.) 1848. **2.** A set of buildings used as a place of lodgement or residence for soldiers. Properly in *pl.* (collect.) 1697.

1. He lodged in a miserable hut or b. GIBBON.

Barrack (bæ·răk), *v.*[1] 1701. [f. prec. sb.] **1.** To provide with or locate in barracks. **2.** *intr.* To lodge in barracks 1834.

Ba·rrack, *v.*[2] 1890. [orig. Austral., f. native *borak* chaff, banter.] *intr.* To shout derisively so as to disconcert players. Also *transf.*

Barracoon (bærăkū·n). 1851. [a. Sp. *barracon* (?), augm. of *barraca*; see BARRACK *sb.*] An enclosure, in which negro-slaves, etc., are temporarily detained.

Barracuda, -coota, -couta (bærăkū·dă, -ū·tă). 1678. [? Sp.] A voracious fish (*Sphyræna barracuda*) found in West Indian seas.

Ba·rragan, -on. 1787. A kind of fustian.

Barrage (bā·rėdʒ). 1859. [a. F., f. *barre* BAR *sb.*[1]; see -AGE.] **1.** The action of barring; the formation of an artificial bar in a river, etc., to increase the depth of water; the bar thus formed. **2.** (bæ·rāʒ, -ėdʒ). A barrier of continuous artillery or machine-gun fire concentrated on a given area; also *creeping* or *moving b.*, and *b. fire.*

‖**Barranca** (băræ·ŋkă). 1884. [Sp., used in U.S.] A deep ravine with precipitous sides.

Barrandite (bæ·rāndəit). 1868. [f. name of *Barrande*, a geologist.] *Min.* A phosphate of alumina and iron occurring in spheroidal concretions in Bohemia.

†Ba·rras. 1640. A coarse linen fabric, orig. from Holland –1714.

†Ba·rrat. ME. [a. OF. *barat* (nom. *baras*), also OF. *barate* fem. deceit, fraud, trouble, etc. Origin unkn.] **1.** Deception, fraud –1503. **2.** Trouble –1552. **3.** Contention –1496. Hence **†Ba·rrat** *v.* to quarrel.

Barrator, -er (bæ·rătəɹ). ME. [a. AF. **baratour* = OF. *barateor*, *-eeur* f. *barat*; see BARRAT.] **1.** [f. AF. *baratour.*] One who buys or sells eccles. preferment, or offices of state. **2.** A judge who takes bribes 1864. **3.** A ship's master who commits BARRATRY (sense

3) 1847. †4. [f. BARRAT *sb.*] One who fights; *esp.* a hired bully -1583. †5. A brawler -1714. 6. One who vexatiously raises, or incites to, litigation ME. Hence †**Ba·rratous** *a.* quarrelsome.

Barratrous (bæ·rătrəs), *a.* 1842. [f. BARRATRY + -OUS.] In *Marine Law*: Of the nature of barratry. **Ba·rratrously** *adv.*

Barratry (bæ·rătri). ME. [a. OF. *baraterie*; see BARRAT.] 1. The purchase or sale of eccles. preferment, or of offices of state. 2. *Sc. Law.* The acceptance of bribes by a judge 1773. 3. *Marine Law.* Fraud, or gross and criminal negligence, on the part of the master or mariners of a ship, to the prejudice of the owners, and without their consent 1622. 4. The offence of habitually moving or maintaining lawsuits or quarrels 1645.

Barred (bāɹd), *ppl. a.* ME. [f. BAR *v.* and *sb.*[1]] 1. Secured or shut with bars 1593. 2. Having, or furnished with, a bar or bars 1571. 3. Ornamented with bars, as *b. owl* ME.

Barrel (bæ·rĕl), *sb.* ME. [a. F. *baril*; of unkn. origin.] 1. A cylindrical wooden vessel, generally bulging in the middle and of greater length than breadth, formed of curved staves bound together by hoops, and having flat ends; a cask. 2. A measure of capacity both for liquids and dry goods, varying with the commodity ME. 3. By metonymy: Intoxicating liquor. Cf. 'the bottle'. ME. †4. *abst.* Brand, quality. See HERRING. -1789. 5. A revolving cylinder or drum, round which a chain or rope is wound; as, the b. of a windlass; the b. of a watch, containing the mainspring; the revolving b. of a musical box, barrel-organ, etc. 1500. 6. A (usually hollow) cylinder forming part of various objects; *e.g.* of a pump, engine-boiler, bell, feather 1629. 7. The metal tube of a gun, through which the shot is discharged. Hence in *single b.*, etc., of the whole weapon 1648. 8. The belly and loins of a horse, ox, etc. 1703. 9. *Phys.* The cavity of the ear situated within the tympanic membrane 1706.

Comb.: **b.-bird**, dial. name of the Long-tailed Tit; **-bulk**, a measure equal to five cubic feet; **-drain**, a cylindrical brick drain; **-ful**; **-head**, (either) flat end of a b.; **-organ**, orig., a musical instrument of the organ type, with a pin-studded revolving barrel or cylinder acting mechanically on the keys; now, an instrument in which the notes are produced by metal tongues struck by pins fixed in the barrel; also as vb.; **-pen**, one with a split cylindrical shank to take a wooden holder; **-sewer** (cf. *-drain*); **-vault**, one with a semi-cylindrical roof; whence **-vaulted**.

Barrel (bæ·rĕl), *v.* 1466. [f. prec. sb.] 1. To put or pack in a barrel or barrels. 2. *gen.* To store up 1589.

Barrelled, -eled (bæ·rĕld), *ppl. a.* 1494. [f. BARREL + -ED.] 1. Packed or stowed away in a barrel or barrels. 2. Shaped like a barrel 1853. 3. Having a barrel or barrels; chiefly in *comb.*, as *single-b.* 1704.

Barren (bæ·rĕn). Comp. *barrener*, *-est*. ME. [a. OF. **barain*, *brahain*, of unkn. origin. If *barain* was the original form, then f. *bar* 'man, male' (L. type **baraneus*), according to Diez. But ?] A. *adj.* 1. Of a woman: Bearing no children. 2. Of animals: Not pregnant at the usual season ME. 3. Of plants, etc.: Without fruit or seed ME. 4. Of land: Unproductive. So of mines, etc. ME. 5. Void of vital germs 1871. 6. *fig.* Bare of interest, arid ME. 7. Unprofitable 1549. 8. Of persons: Unresponsive, dull 1590. 9. *Const.* in all prec. senses with *of*.

1. To live a b. sister all your life *Mids. N.* I. i. 72. 4. B. mines 1776, soil MILL. 6. A list of b. names GROTE. 7. B. praise DRYDEN. 8. B. Spectators *Haml.* III. ii. 46. 9. Hearts b. of kindness STEELE. Hence †**Ba·rren**, †**Ba·rrenize** *vbs.* to make b. or sterile. **Ba·rrener**, a cow not in calf for the year. **Ba·rrenly** *adv.*, **-ness**.

B. *sb.* [the adj. used *absol.*] †1. [sc. *woman* or *animal*.] ME. 2. A tract of barren land; *spec.* a. in N. America, plains on which grow small trees and shrubs, but no timber, as *oak-barrens*, etc.; b. in Kentucky, certain really fertile tracts; c. in Nova Scotia and New Brunswick, open marshy spaces in the forest.

Barrenwort (bæ·rĕnwɒɹt). 1597. [f. BARREN + WORT.] *Herb.* Name of the genus *Epimedium*, esp. of *Epimedium alpinum* (N.O. *Berberidaceæ*).

Barret (bæ·rĕt). 1828. [a. F. *barrette*; see BIRETTA.] A little flat cap; *esp.* the BIRETTA.

Barricade (bærikēⁱ·d). 1642. [a. F. *barricade*, or refash. of BARRICADO.] 1. = BARRICADO 1. 2. *transf.* and *fig.* Any barrier obstructing passage 1735. 3. *Naut.* = BARRICADO 4. 1769.

1. The world has heard of the Barricades of Paris 1670.

Barrica·de, *v.* 1592. [f. prec.] 1. To block with a barricade. Also *transf.* and *fig.* 2. To shut in with or as with a barricade 1657.

1. B. al the streets 1592. 2. B. mee with these Bulwarkes against myne enemyes 1657.

Barricado (bærikēⁱ·do), *sb.* Pl. **-oes, -os.** 1590. [ad. F. *barricade* (see -ADO), f. *barrique*, the first *barricades* being composed of casks filled with earth, stones, etc. Now usu. BARRICADE in prose.] 1. A hastily formed rampart of barrels, wagons, stones, or anything at hand, thrown up to obstruct an enemy's advance. 2. *transf.* and *fig.* = BARRICADE 2. 1611. †3. A natural frontier MILT. 4. *Naut.* A strong wooden rail, supported by stanchions, and extending, as a fence, across the foremost part of the quarter-deck (Falconer) 1675.

1. Many were drowned in the river, which proved a b. to the French LUTTRELL.

Barricado (bærikēⁱ·do), *v.* 1598. [f. prec. sb.] 1. To close or block with (or as with) a barricade 1611. 2. To fortify or defend with barricades. Also *fig.* 1601. 3. To shut up, bar in securely (*lit.* and *fig.*) 1598. 4. To preclude *from* (*lit.* and *fig.*) 1611.

3. I barricado'd myself round with the chests 1719.

Barrico (bărī·ko). Pl. **-oes.** 1607. [ad. Sp. *barrica*.] A keg.

Barrier (bæ·riəɹ), *sb.* [ME. *barrere*, a. AF., OF. *barrière*:—late L. *barraria*, f. *barra* BAR.] 1. *gen.* A material obstruction of any kind which bars advance or prevents access. a. *orig.* A palisade or stockade erected to defend a gate, etc. b. *transf.* a fortress, etc., which commands the entrance into a country 1600. c. A fence or railing to prevent access to any place 1570. d. The *carcer* or starting-place in the ancient race-course 1600. e. In continental towns: The gate at which custom duties are collected 1825. f. *Coal-mining.* A breadth of coal left against an adjoining royalty, for security against water or foul air 1851. 2. *spec.* in *pl.* The palisades enclosing the ground where a tournament, etc., was held; the lists. Also, a low fence running down the centre of the lists. 1581. 3. Any natural obstacle which bars access 1703. 4. Anything immaterial that keeps separate and apart 1702.

2. At length the barriers were opened, and five knights advanced slowly into the area SCOTT. 4. He ..erects a b. between himself and his reader GODWIN.

Comb.: **b.-gate**, a heavy gate closing the opening through a b.; **-reef**, a wall of coral rock, separated from the land by a deep channel; **-treaty**, one fixing the frontier of a country, *esp.* 'The Treaty of the Barriers' signed at Antwerp in 1715. Hence **Ba·rrier** *v.* to close or shut with a b. **Ba·rriered** *ppl. a.* furnished with or confined by a b. or barriers.

Barring (bā·riŋ), *vbl. sb.* ME. [f. BAR *v.*] The action of BAR *v.*

Barring-out: shutting the school-room against the master, etc., a mode of schoolboy rebellion.

Barring (bā·riŋ), *prep.* 1481. [f. BAR *v.* 8; cf. *saving*, etc.] Excluding from consideration, except.

Barrister (bæ·ristəɹ). 1532. [f. BAR *sb.*[1] + ?.] A student of law, who has been called to the bar, and practises as advocate in the superior courts of law. Formally *barrister-at-law*.

Revising barrister: one appointed to revise the list of persons qualified to vote for Members of Parliament. Hence **Barriste·rial** *a.* **Ba·rristership. Barrista·tion**, the action of a b. (*nonce-wd.*)

Barrow (bæ·roᵘ), *sb.*[1] [Com. Teut.: OE. *beorg* (:—*berg*):—OTeut. **bergo-z*. Obs. bef. 1400, exc. in dial. *bargh*, *barf*, and *barrow*, revived in connexion with the 'barrows' of Salisbury Plain, etc.] 1. A mountain, hill, or hillock. (Still in local use, as in Cadon B. in Cornwall, Whitbarrow in Lancs., etc.) 2. A grave-mound, a tumulus OE. 3. *dial.* A mound or heap 1869.

3. Grassy barrows of the..dead TENNYSON.

Barrow (bæ·roᵘ), *sb.*[2] [Com. Teut.: OE. *bearg* (:—*barg*):—OTeut. **bargu-z*; known only in Teut.] 1. A castrated boar. Still *dial.* †2. A badger (*rare*). (? mispr. for *bauson*) 1552.

Barrow (bæ·roᵘ), *sb.*[3] [ME. *barewe*, f. OE. **bearwe*, OTeut. **barwâ*, f. *beran* to BEAR. Cf. BIER.] 1. A contrivance for the carrying of a load; a frame, having shafts or trams by which it is carried, and sometimes four legs; a stretcher; a bier; a hand-barrow ME. 2. A modification of this, having a wheel or wheels; a wheel-barrow; a costermonger's barrow ME. b. The contents of a barrow 1598. 3. *Salt-making.* A conical basket for draining wet salt 1686.

Comb.: **b.-man, -woman**, one employed in wheeling a b.; **-tram**, the shaft of a b.; **-way** (*Mining*), a tram-way on which the barrow-men put the tubs of coal. Hence **Ba·rrow** *v.* to transport in a b.

Ba·rrowist. 1589. *Hist.* A follower of Henry Barrowe, one of the founders of Congregationalism, executed for nonconformity in 1593.

Barrulet (bæ·riŭlĕt). Also **-ette.** 1562. [dim. of **barrule*, dim. of F. *barre*.] *Her.* The fourth part of a *bar*.

Barruly (bæ·riŭli), *a.* 1562. [ad. AF. *barrulée*; see prec.] *Her.* Crossed by barrulets. var. **Ba·rrulety** *a.* (Dicts.)

Barry (bā·ri), *a.* 1486. [a. F. *barré*.] *Her.* (A field) Divided horizontally into equal parts by bars of two colours alternating.

Barse. Still *dial.* [Com. Teut.; OE. *bærs*, *bears* (:—*bars*), f. root **bars-*, *bors-*, whence Sc. *birse* bristle.] Name of a fish, subseq. corrupted to BASE and BASS(E.

Bart., abbrev. of BARONET, written after the name, and supplementary to the prefixed *Sir*, also given to a Knight.

Barter (bā·ɹtəɹ), *v.* ME. [app. f. *barat*, BARRAT *v.*, but **barater* has not been found.] 1. To give (a commodity) for something (not being *money*) taken as of equivalent value. Const. *for*, †*with* a thing, *with* a person 1440. 2. *fig.* a. To exchange 1602. b. To dispose of for a consideration, usu. an unworthy one 1664. 3. *intr.* To trade by exchange of commodities 1485.

1. To b. ware for ware PALSGR. 2. To b. blowes 1602. E'en liberty itself is barter'd here GOLDSM. Hence **Ba·rterer. Ba·rtering** *vbl. sb.*

Barter (bā·ɹtəɹ), *sb.* 1592. [f. prec. vb.] 1. The act or practice of trafficking by exchange of commodities; truck. Also *fig.* 2. Goods to be bartered 1740. 3. *Arith.* The computation of the comparative values of different commodities; the method of computing this. var. †**Ba·rtery** (in senses 1, 2).

Barth. Still *dial.* 1573. [? See BERTH.] A sheltered place for cattle.

Bartholomew (bɑɹþǫ·lŏmiū). Also **Bartlemy** (bā·ɹt'lmi), **Bartelemy, Bart'lemy.** 1552. [ad. L. *Bartholomæus*; partly a. F. *Barthélemy*.] a. Name of one of the twelve apostles, whose festival is held on the 24th of August (*B.-day*, *-tide*). b. On this day, in 1572, took place the massacre of the Protestants in France. c. On the same day, in 1662, the English Act of Uniformity (*B. Act*) came into force. d. Used of a fair (*B. Fair*) held annually from 1133 to 1855, at West Smithfield; and hence of articles sold at it, e. g. *B.-baby*, *-boar*, *-pig*, etc.

Bartisan, bartizan (bā·ɹtizæn). *Hist.* or *Arch.* 1801. [A seventeenth-century form of BRATTICING revived by Sir Walter Scott.] A battlemented parapet at the top of a castle or church; *esp.* a battlemented turret projecting from an angle at the top of a tower, etc.

Barton (bā·ɹtən). [OE. *bęre-tún*, f. *bęre* barley + *tún* enclosure; see TOWN.] †1. A threshing-floor OE. only. 2. A farm-yard. (The regular mod. sense.) 1552. 3. A demesne farm 1587. †4. A pen for poultry -1783.

Bartram, obs. f. BERTRAM.

‖**Bartsia** (bā·ɹtsiă). 1753. [f. *Bartsch* of Königsberg.] *Bot.* A genus of *Scrophulariaceæ*, including *B. Odontites*.

Ba·rvel, -ell. 1878. [? corrupt f. *barm-fell*.] A leather apron.

Barwood (bā·ɹwud). 1788. [Cf. *logwood*.] The red wood of *Baphita nitida*, imported from the Gaboon, etc., used chiefly for dyeing purposes, and also for violin bows, etc.

Baryce·ntric, *a.* [f. Gr. βαρύς + κέντρον + -IC.] Of or pertaining to the centre of gravity.

Baryphony (bări·fŏni). [f. as prec. + φωνή]. *Med.* Difficulty of speech.

Baryta (bărəi·tă). 1809. [f. next.] *Chem.* †Barium monoxide; barium hydroxide, $Ba(OH)_2$. avr. †Ba·ryt 1794 [F. *baryte*].

Barytes (bărəi·tīz). 1789. [f. Gr. βαρύς; see -ITES.] †1. = BARYTA. (Occas. *attrib.*) -1854. 2. Native sulphate of barium, heavy spar, BARITE. 1789. Hence **Bary·tic** *a.* of, pertaining to, or containing baryta or barium.

Barytine, Barytite, synonyms of BARITE.

Baryto- (bărəi·to), comb. f. BARYTA, as in **B.-ca·lcite**, a carbonate of barium and calcium. **B.-cele·stite**, a sulphate of barium and strontium.

Barytone, -itone (bæ·ritōun). 1609. [a. F. *barytone*, ad. Gr. βαρύτονος, f. βαρύς + τόνος.] A. *sb.* 1. The male voice of barytone compass, ranging from lower A in the bass clef to lower F in the treble clef. 2. A singer having such a voice 1821. 3. A musical instrument of deep sound: †a. a kind of bass viol; b. the smaller bass saxhorn in B♭ or C. 1685. 4. *Gk. Gram.* A barytone word: see B. 2.

B. *adj.* 1. Of the voice: Having a compass intermediate between bass and tenor. b. Suited for a barytone voice. c. Possessing a barytone voice. 1729. 2. *Gr. Gram.* Not having the acute accent on the last syllable 1828.

Basal (bēi·săl), *a.* (*sb.*) 1828. [f. BASE *sb.*] 1. Pertaining to, situated at, or forming the base. 2. *fig.* Fundamental 1865. 3. *sb.* A basal part; *spec.* one of the basal plates encircling the stem of the crinoids 1877.

1. *Basal plane* and *cleavage* in *Crystallog.*: one parallel to the lateral or horizontal axis. Comb. *b.-nerved*, with nerves all springing from the base of the leaf. Hence **Ba·sally** *adv.*

Basalt (băsǭ·lt, bæ·sǫlt). 1601. [ad. L. *basaltes* (also used); orig. an African word (Pliny).] *Min.* A kind of trap rock; a greenish- or brownish-black igneous rock, composed of augite or hornblende containing titaniferous magnetic iron and crystals of feldspar, often lying in columnar strata, as at the Giant's Causeway in Ireland, etc. (Pliny's *basaltes* was prob. Syenite.) Also *attrib.* 2. A black porcelain invented by Wedgwood 1832.

The B. is only Lava, which has flowed beneath the sea DARWIN. Hence **Basa·ltic, †Basa·ltine** *adjs.* of, consisting of, of the nature of, or resembling b. **Basa·ltiform, Basa·ltoid** *adjs.* having the form of b. **†Basa·ltin(e,** *Min.* a kind of basaltic hornblende.

Basan, bazan (bæ·zăn). 1714. [a. F. *basane*, prob. ad. (ult.) Arab. *bitānah* lining; cf. BASIL.] Sheep-skin tanned in bark; distinguished from *roan*, which is tanned in sumach.

Basanite (bæ·sănəit). 1794. [ad. L. *basanites* (*lapis*), f. Gr. βάσανος.] A velvet-black siliceous quartz, used for testing the purity of gold, etc., by means of the mark left after rubbing the metal upon it.

†‖Bas bleu (bā,blö). 1801. [F. tr. of Eng. BLUE-STOCKING.] A blue-stocking, a literary lady -1821.

Basculation (bæskiulēi·ʃən). 1881. [f. F. *basculer*; see next.] *Surg.* The movement by which retroversion of the uterus is remedied.

Bascule (bæ·skiūl). 1678. [a. F. *bascule* a see-saw, f. *battre*, or *bas* + *cul.*] An apparatus acting on the principle of the lever, whereby one end is raised when the other is depressed; *esp.* in **Bascule-bridge**, a drawbridge balanced by a counterpoise which rises or falls as the bridge is lowered or raised.

Base (bēi·s), *sb.*[1] ME. [a. F. *base*:—L. *basis*, a. Gr., f. βα- 'go'.] 1. The bottom of any object, considered as its support, or that on which it rests. 2. *fig.* Fundamental principle, foundation 1500. 3. *Archit.* a. The plinth and mouldings between the bottom of the shaft and the top of the pedestal, or between the shaft and the pavement ME. b. The plinth and mouldings which project at the bottom of the wall of a room. c. The lowest course of masonry in a building. 4. A pedestal 1440. 5. *Gunnery*, The protuberant rear-portion of a cannon, between the knob and the base-ring. 6. *Bot.* and *Zool.* That extremity of a part or organ by which it is attached to the trunk 1831. 7. *Her.* The lower part of a shield 1611. 8. *Geom.* That line or surface of a plane or solid figure on which it is considered to stand 1570. 9. *Fortification.* The imaginary line which connects two salient angles 1721. 10. *gen.* The principal ingredient 1471. 11. *Dyeing.* A substance used as a mordant, by which colours are fixed 1791. 12. *Mod. Chem.* The electro-positive compound body which combines with an acid to form a salt, the correl. of ACID, including, but wider than ALKALI 1810. 13. *Gram.* The form of a word to which suffixes are attached 1875. 14. a. The line from which runners start, or which serves as a goal, in a race. b. The fixed line or goal in hockey, etc. c. The fixed points or stations in rounders or base-ball. 1695. 15. *Mil.* The line or place relied upon as a stronghold and magazine, and from which the operations of a campaign are conducted. Also *transf.* 1860. 16. *Surv.* A line on the earth's surface or in space, of which the exact length and position are accurately determined, and which is used as a base (sense 8) for observations and computations 1834. 17. *Math.* The number from which a system of numeration or logarithms proceeds 1874.

1. The extent of the b. of the great pyramid JOHNSON. 15. The territory on which these resources are spread is called the 'base of operations' KINGLAKE.

Comb.: **b.-burner**, a furnace or stove in which the fuel is supplied to the fire automatically from a hopper as the lower stratum is consumed; **-line**, *Mil.* that on which all magazines and means of supply for an army are established (cf. 15, 16); in *Gunnery*, a line traced round a cannon at the rear of the vent; **-ring**, a moulding on the breech of a cannon between the b. and the first reinforce.

Base (bēis), *sb.*[2] Also **prisoner's base.** 1440. [f. BASE *sb.*[1], or ? a corruption of *bars* (cf. BAR *sb.*[1]).] A game played by two sides, who occupy contiguous 'bases' or 'homes'; any player running out from his base is chased by one of the other side, and, if caught, made a prisoner.

†*To bid base*: to challenge SHAKS. *Ven. & Ad.* li.

†Base (bēis), *sb.*[3] *Hist.* 1548. [app. BASE *sb.*[1] 'bottom'.] * *sing.* 1. ? The housing of a horse -1667. ** pl. *bases* (cf. *skirts*). 2. A plaited skirt, appended to the doublet, and reaching from the waist to the knee; also an imitation of this in mailed armour -1821. 3. The skirt of a woman's outer petticoat or robe -1697. 4. An apron -1663.

†Base, *sb.*[4] 1450. *Mus.* The spelling of BASS *sb.*[5], till the 19th c.

Base, *sb.*[5] Now *dial.* 1440. [corruption of OE. *bærs* BARSE, now BASS.] = BASS *sb.*[1]

†Base, *sb.*[6] 1544. [app. a corruption of F. *barce, berche*, in same sense.] The smallest kind of cannon used in 16–17th centuries -1692.

Base (bēis), *a.* ME. [a. F. *bas*:—late L. *bassus.*] 1. Low; of small height (*arch.*). In *Bot.* denoting lowly growth; e. g. *B. Broom, B. Rocket.* 1578. †2. Low-lying; *esp.* geographically or topographically -1851. 3. Of sounds: Not loud; deep, BASS 1450. 4. *fig.* Of lowly condition, plebeian (*arch.*) 1490. 5. Illegitimate. ? *Obs.* exc. in BASE-BORN. 1570. 6. Low in the natural scale 1534. 7. Low in the moral scale; reprehensibly cowardly, selfish, or mean; opp. to *high-minded* 1535. 8. Degraded or degrading, menial 1594. 9. *Law.* Servile, as opp. to *free* 1523. 10. Of inferior quality; mean, poor, shabby, etc. 1561. Of language: Debased 1549. 11. Worthless 1607. 12. Debased, counterfeit, as coin, etc. 1528.

2. B. Egypt watered .. with Nilus HOLLAND. 4. Borne of basse parentage CAXTON. 6. Ciuet is of a baser birth then Tarre *A. Y. L.* III. ii. 69. B. vermine, such as Rats 1680. 7. B., fearefull, and despayring Henry 3 *Hen. VI*, I. i. 178. A most b. piece of flatterie RALEIGH. 9. *B. tenure, estate, fee*: *orig.* tenure by *b. service*, such as a villain owed to his lord; *later*, such tenure in fee simple as may determine on the fulfilment of a contingent qualification or limitation. See also B.-COURT. 11. *B. metals*: those not classed as *noble* or *precious*. 12. B. money MACAULAY.

†Base, *v.*[1] ME. [partly aphet. f. ABASE *v.*; partly a. F. *baisser*:—late L. *bassare*; see BASE *a.*] 1. To lower -1626. 2. To lessen in amount or value; to debase (metals) -1626.

Base (bēis), *v.*[2] 1587. [f. BASE *sb.*[1]] 1. To make a foundation for. 2. To place *on* or *upon* a foundation or logical basis; to secure. (So F. *baser.*) 1841.

2. These [bank-]notes were based on gold ROGERS.

Base-ball (bēi·sbǭl). 1850. [f. BASE *sb.*[1] 14.] The national field-game of the United States; so called from the bases or bounds (usu. four in number) which mark the circuit to be taken by each player of the in-side after striking the ball. Also, the ball used in the game.

Base-born (bēi·s,bǭɹn), *a.* 1591. [f. BASE *a.* 4, 5, 6.] 1. Of humble birth, plebeian 1593. 2. *fig.* Of base origin or nature 1591. 3. Illegitimate 1645.

1. Ten-thousand base-borne Cades SHAKS.

Base-court (bēi·s,kōəɹt). 1491. [f. BASE *a.* 2 + COURT; in sense 1 f. F. *basse-court* (mod. *basse-cour*).] 1. The lower or outer court of a castle or mansion, occupied by the servants; the court in the rear of a farm-house, containing the out-buildings. 2. A court of justice that is not of record; *e.g.* a court baron 1542.

Basedow's disease; see BRONCHOCELE.

†Ba·selard. ME. [a. AF. *baselard(e*; prob. a deriv. of late L. *badile, badillus* a bill-hook (P. Meyer); *z* (*s*) for *d* is Provençal.] A dagger or hanger, worn at the girdle -1788.

Baseless (bēi·slės), *a.* 1610. [f. BASE *sb.*[1]] a. Without base or foundation; groundless. b. *Mil.*; cf. BASE *sb.*[1] 15. 1862.

The baselesse fabricke of this vision *Temp.* IV. i. 151. Hence **Ba·selessness.**

‖Basella (băse·lă). 1761. [mod.L., ? dim. of L. *basis.*] *Bot.* A genus of climbing plants (N.O. *Chenopodiaceæ*); the Malabar Nightshade.

Basely (bēi·sli), *adv.* 1500. [f. BASE *a.* + -LY[2].] †1. In a low tone -1577. 2. In humble rank of life; illegitimately (? *Obs.*) 1583. 3. Dishonourably, disingenuously 1550. †4. At small value or esteem -1651.

Basement (bēi·smėnt). 1730. [f. BASE *sb.*[1] or *v.*[2] + -MENT.] 1. The lowest or fundamental portion of a structure 1793. 2. *fig.* Groundwork; *attrib.* = fundamental 1818. 3. *spec.* The lowest storey (not a cellar) of a building, *esp.* when sunk below the ground level 1730. 4. The action of basing; the being based; cf. *debasement* 1836.

1. *Basement-membrane*: a fine transparent layer lying between the epithelium and the fibro-vascular layer of mucous membranes.

Baseness (bēi·snės). 1552. [f. BASE *a.* + -NESS.] The quality or condition of being BASE; an instance of this 1598.

I once did hold it .. A basenesse to write faire *Haml.* V. ii. 34. We alledged .. the b. of his metal SWIFT.

Basenet, -ette, vars. of BASINET.

†Bash, *v.*[1] ME. [Aphet. f. ABASH *v.*] 1. *trans.* To disconcert, dismay, abash -1594. 2. *intr.* To be daunted; to be abashed -1610.

Bash (bæʃ), *v.*[2] 1641. [Chiefly north.; echoic.] To strike with a smashing blow 1790.

†Basha·lic(k. 1682. Early f. PASHALIK -1703.

Bashaw (bāʃǭ·). 1534. [a. Turk., var. of *pāshā*, prob. f. *bāsh* head.] 1. The earlier form of PASHA. 2. *fig.* A grandee; a haughty imperious man 1593.

1. With all the insolence of a basha FIELDING.

Bashful (bæ·ʃfŭl), *a.* 1548. [f. BASH *v.*[1] + -FUL.] †1. Wanting in self-possession, daunted -1709. 2. Shrinking from publicity, shy; sensitively modest; excessively self-conscious, sheepish 1548. 3. Of things, etc.: Characterizing or characterized by extreme sensitiveness or modesty 1595.

2. I pity b. men COWPER. 3. Hence bashfull cunning *Temp.* III. i. 81. Hence **Ba·shfully** *adv.*

Ba·shfulness. 1534. [f. prec. + -NESS.] †1. *Bashfulness of*: a timid or reverential shrinking back from -1674. 2. The quality of being BASHFUL (sense 2) 1539.

2. Haue you no modesty, no maiden shame, No touch of bashfulnesse *Mids. N.* III. ii. 286.

‖Bashi-bazouk (bæ:ʃi,băzū·k). 1855. [Turk.; lit. 'one whose head is turned'.] A mercenary soldier belonging to the irregular troops of the Turkish army; notorious for their lawlessness and savage brutality. Also *fig.*

†Ba·shless, *a.* 1578. [f. BASH *v.*[1] + -LESS.] Shameless; bold.

†Ba·shment. ME. [Aphet. f. ABASHMENT.] Discomfiture, shame -1610.

Bashyle; see BASYLE.

Basi- (bēi·si), comb. f. BASE, BASIS, in sense of 'pertaining to, situated at, or forming, the base of'; e. g. **b.-branchial, -cranial, -facial, -hyal, -temporal,** pertaining to, situated at, or forming, the base or posterior part of, the branchial arch (in fishes), the skull, the face, the hyoid bone, the temples. Often used *ellipt.*; e. g. the *basihyal* (bone).

Basial (bē̆·ziăl), *a.* [f. L. *basium* + -AL [1].] Of or pertaining to kissing.

Basic (bē̆·sik), *a.* 1842. [f. BASE *sb.*[1] + -IC.] 1. Of, pertaining to, or forming a base: *spec.* in *Archit.* and *Chem.* 2. Having the base in excess 1854. **a.** *Chem.* (A salt) Having the amount of the base atomically greater than that of the acid, or exceeding in proportion that of the related neutral salt. **b.** *Min.* (An igneous rock) Having relatively little silica. **c.** Applied to a process of steel manufacture, in which phosphorus is eliminated by the use of non-siliceous materials for the lining of the converters; hence, the steel thus produced 1880.

See also MONOBASIC, BIBASIC, TRIBASIC.

Basicerite (beⁱsi·sĕrəit). 1877. [f. Gr. βάσις + κέρας + -ITE.] *Anim. Phys.* The second segment of the antenna of an Arthropod.

Basicity (beⁱsi·sĭti). 1849. [f. BASIC *a.* + -ITY.] *Chem.* The power of combining with bases possessed by an acid, dependent on the number of atoms of hydrogen replaceable by a metal which are contained in it.

‖**Basidium** (băsi·diŏm). 1858. [mod.L. dim., f. Gr. βάσις + -ιδιον dim. ending.] *Bot.* Name given to the cells of the fructification in some fungi, which bear the spores. Hence **Basi·diospore**, *Bot.* a spore borne at the extremity of a b.

Basifugal (beⁱsi·fiugăl), *a.* 1875. [f. L. *basis* + *-fugus* + -AL [1].] *Bot.* Tending away from the base, as *b. growth* (of a leaf, etc.). Hence **Basi·fugally** *adv.*

‖**Basigynium** (bēⁱsi,dʒi·niŏm). 1880. [mod. L., f. Gr. βάσις + γυνή + -IUM, repr. Gr. dim. -ιον.] *Bot.* The pedicel or stalk bearing the ovary.

Basil [1] (bæ·zil). 1481. [a. OF. *basile*, ad. L. *basilisca*, f. *basiliscus* BASILISK; in Gr. βασιλικόν 'royal', whence *basilicum*, supposed to be an antidote to the basilisk's venom, and app. confused in L. with *basiliscus*.] *Herb.* 1. Popular name of a genus (*Ocymum*, N. O. *Labiatæ*) of aromatic shrubby plants, including the culinary herbs Common or Sweet B. (*O. basilicum*), and Bush or Lesser B. (*O. minimum*). 2. A book-name for: Wild B. (*Calamintha Acinos*, or *C. Clinopodium*), Field or Cow B. (*Saponaria Vaccaria*); also B.-balm, -thyme 1578.

†**Ba·sil** [2]. *rare.* 1565. [a. OF. *basile*; see prec.] 1. = BASILISK 2. 1565. †2. An iron round the ankle of a prisoner. (Perh. a distinct wd.) -1755.

Basil [3], **bazil** (bæ·zil). 1674. [App. corrupt f. Fr. *basane*.] = BASAN, q. v. Also *attrib.*

Basil, *sb.*[4] and *v.*, corrupt f. BEZEL.

Basilar (bæ·silăı), *a.* 1541. [ad. mod.L. *basilaris*, irreg. f. *basis*; see BASE *sb.*[1]] Of, pertaining to, or situated at the base, *esp.* at that of the skull. So **Ba·silary.**

Basilic, -al (băsi·lik, -ăl), *a.* 1541. [a. F. *basilique*, ad. L. *basilicus*, a. Gr.] 1. Kingly (*rare*) 1728. 2. *Phys.* Specific epithet of the large vein of the arm starting from the elbow and discharging into the axillary vein. [So called from its supposed importance.] 1541.

Basilic (bæ·sĭlik), *sb. arch.* 1703. [a. F. *basilique*, ad. L. *basilica*.] = BASILICA 1, 2.

Basilica (băsi·likă). Pl. **-as**, *rarely* **-æ.** 1541. [a. L. *basilica*, Gr. βασιλική (sc. οἰκία, στοά), adjs. fem., f. (ult.) βασιλεύς.] 1. *Anc. Hist.* Orig., a royal palace; thence, an oblong building or hall, with double colonnades and a semicircular apse at the end, used for a court of justice and place of public assembly. 2. A building of this type, used for Christian worship; improp. applied to churches generally. In Rome applied spec. to the seven principal churches founded by Constantine. 1563. †3. The basilic vein; see BASILIC *a.* 2. -1751. 4. (*neut. pl.*) = BASILICS, q. v.

2. The application of the name of B. to the small burial-chapels in the Catacombs is a mistake PARKER. Hence **Basi·lical** *a.*[2], **Basi·lican** *a.* of, pertaining to, or resembling a b. **Basi·licanism,** adherence to the basilican type of church. **Basi·licate** *a.* shaped like a b.

†**Basilicock.** ME. = BASILISK 1. -1583.

Basi·licon, -um. 1541. [L. *basilicum*, Gr. βασιλικόν (sc. φάρμακον), adj. neut.] Name of ointments supposed to possess sovereign virtues. ¶ See also BASIL *sb.*[1]

Basilics (băsi·liks), *sb. pl.* 1751. [ad. L. *basilica* (also used), a. Gr., adj. neut. pl.] A digest of the laws of Justinian, etc., translated from Latin into Greek, by command of the emperors Basil and Leo.

Basilidian (bæsili·diăn). 1586. [f. L. *Basilides* + -IAN.] 1. *adj.* Of, pertaining to, or derived from Basilides, an Alexandrian Gnostic of the 2nd century. 2. *sb.* One of his followers.

Basili·scan, *a. rare.* 1600. [f. L. *basiliscus.*] Pertaining to a basilisk. So **Basili·scine.**

Basilisk (bæ·zilisk, bæ·s-). Also (from Sp.) basilisco. ME. [ad. L. *basiliscus*, a. Gr. βασιλίσκος, dim. of βασιλεύς.] 1. A fabulous reptile, also called a *cockatrice*, alleged to be hatched by a serpent from a cock's egg; its breath, and even its look, was said to be fatal. [So called from a crown, 'combe or coronet', on its head.] Also *fig.* (often *attrib.*) 2. *transf.* A large brass cannon, throwing a shot of about 200 pounds weight. (Cf. SHAKS. *Hen. V*, v. ii. 17.) 1549. 3. *Zool.* A small American lizard of the family *Iguanidæ*, having on its head a hollow crest which can be inflated at will 1813. †4. The Golden-crested Wren or Kinglet (*Regulus cristatus*) 1753. †5. The star Regulus in Leo -1751.

1. Make me not sighted like the Basilisque *Wint. T.* I. ii. 389. 2. The Basilisks, That, roaring, shake Damascus turrets down MARLOWE. 3. The green and golden b. SHELLEY. Hence **Basili·skian** *a.*

Basin (bē̆·s'n). [ME. *bacin*, a. OF., mod. *bassin*:—late L. *bachinus*, f. ?.] 1. A circular vessel of greater width than depth, used for holding water for washing and other liquids. **b.** The quantity held by a basin 1834. 2. A similar dish for any purpose 1525. 3. The scale-dish of a balance ME. †4. *pl.* ? Cymbals -1609. 5. *spec.* A concave tool used in the manufacture of convex glasses 1727. †6. *Phys.* **a.** The pelvis; **b.** A funnel-shaped cavity situated between the anterior ventricles of the brain. -1771. 7. A hollow depression, natural or artificial, containing water 1712. 8. A dock constructed in a tidal river or harbour, in which by means of flood-gates the water is kept at a constant level 1709. Also *transf.* 9. A land-locked harbour; a bay 1725. 10. *Phys. Geog.* The tract of country drained by a river, or which drains into a particular lake or sea 1830. 11. *gen.* A circular or oval valley or hollow 1854. 12. *Geol.* A circumscribed formation in which the strata dip inward from all sides to the centre; the deposit, *esp.* of coal, lying in such a depression 1821.

1. Basons and ewers, to laue her dainty hands *Tam. Shr.* II. i. 350. A b. of soup (*mod.*). 7. And in a b. black and small Receives a lofty waterfall WORDSW. 9. The harbor of Quebec .. a b. two miles across THOREAU. 10. The hydrographical b. of the Thames LYELL. Hence **Ba·sined** *ppl. a.* placed or contained in a b. **Ba·sinful,** the content of a b.

Basinet, basnet (bæ·sinĕt, bæ·snĕt). Now *Hist.* ME. [a. OF. *bacinet*, dim. of *bacin* BASIN.] A small, light, steel headpiece, in shape somewhat globular, and closed in front with a ventail or visor.

Basiophthalmite (bē̆:si,ǫfþæ·lməit). 1877. [f. Gr. βάσις + ὀφθαλμός + -ITE.] *Anim. Phys.* The lowest joint of the eye-stalk of Crustacea.

Basipodite (beⁱsi·pŏdəit). 1870. [f. Gr. βάσις + ποδ- (πούς) + -ITE.] *Anim. Phys.* The second segment of the leg of an Arthropod.

Basis (bē̆·sis). Pl. **bases.** 1571. [ad. L. *basis*, a. Gr.; see BASE *sb.*[1]] 1. (Literal senses, now rarely used.) = BASE *sb.*[1] 1, †3, 6, †8. †2. A pedestal -1686. 3. The main constituent 1601. 4. A foundation, support (of anything immaterial) 1605. 5. That on which anything is reared, and by which its constitution or operation is determined 1601. 6. = BASE *sb.*[1] 15 (*lit.* and *fig.*) 1833.

2. Cæsar.. That now on Pompeyes B. lye[s] along *Jul. C.* III. i. 115. 3. Salt, the B. of all Natural Productions 1665. 4. Great Tyranny, lay thou thy b. sure *Macb.* IV. iii. 32. 5. The b. of Exchange MALYNES, of mutual compensation BURKE.

Basi·solute, *a.* 1847. [f. L. *basis* + *solutus.*] *Bot.* Of leaves: Prolonged at the base below the point of origin.

Bask (bask), *v.* ME. [app. for **bathask*, a. ON. *baðask*, refl. of *baða* to bathe. Cf. *or* from *other*, etc.] †1. *intr.* (also *refl.*) To bathe, *esp.* in warm water, etc., whence *transf.* to swim in blood, etc. -1530. 2. *trans.* Chiefly *refl.*; = 3. 1600. 3. *intr.* To expose oneself to, or disport oneself in a flood of warmth; to lie enjoying the heat 1697. Also *fig.*

2. A foole, Who laid him downe, and bask'd him in the Sun *A. Y. L.* II. vii. 15. 3. Basking in the sunshine of unmerited fortune BURKE.

†**Bask,** *a.* ME [a. ON. *beisk* bitter.] Bitter, acrid -1808.

†**Baske,** *v.* 1642. Var. of BASH *v.*[2]

Basket (ba·skĕt), *sb.* ME. [Origin unkn. Not in Teut. or Rom.] 1. A vessel of wickerwork, made of plaited osiers, cane, rushes, etc. **b.** taken as the type of daily provisions; also, of alms 1535. 2. A basketful 1725. 3. A wickerwork guard for the hilt of a sword-stick; *ellipt.* a basket-hilt sword or stick 1773. 4. The overhanging back compartment on the outside of a stage coach (*arch.*) 1773. 5. *Mil.* A gabion 1753. 6. The vase of a Corinthian capital, with its foliage, etc. (Gwilt) 1753. 7. A wickerwork or wire screen used in hat-making.

1. Looke, heere is a b...he may creepe in heere *Merry W.* III. iii. 137. **b.** Blessed shal be thy baszkett, & thy stoare COVERDALE *Deut.* xviii. 5. *To be left in the b.*: to remain unchosen (like the worst apples, etc.). *The pick of the b.*: *i. e.* of the lot. 4. It has shook me worse than the b. of a stage-coach GOLDSM.

Comb.: **b.-beagle,** a small dog used to hunt a b.-hare; **-boat,** a boat of b.-work; in India, a circular b., covered with skins; **-button,** a metal button with a basket-pattern on it; **-fish,** a star-fish of the genus *Astrophyton*, with five rays divided into curled filaments; **-hare,** one turned out of a b. to be coursed; **-hilt,** a b.-shaped hilt of a sword; hence **b.-hilted**; **-osier,** the *Salix Forbyana*; **-work,** structure composed of interlaced osiers, twigs, etc., or carved in imitation of this. Hence **Ba·sketful, Ba·sketing.** (Cf. *matting.*) **Ba·sketry,** b.-work, or -ware.

Basket (ba·skĕt), *v.* 1583. [f. prec. sb.; cf. *to bag.*] 1. To put into, or hang up in, a basket. Also *fig.* 2. To throw into the waste-paper basket; also *fig.* 1867.

Ba·sket-ba:ll. 1893. A game played with a large inflated ball, the object being to score by casting it into a basket fixed ten feet above the ground at one's opponents' end.

Ba·sking, *ppl. a.* 1742. [f. BASK *v.*] That basks or suns himself.

Basking-shark: the largest species of shark (*Selachus maximus*), called also Sun-fish; so named from its habit of lying on the surface of the water.

Basnat, -et, -ette, -ite, vars. of BASINET.

Bason, var. of BASIN.

Bason (bē̆·s'n), *sb.* 1727. [Origin unkn.] *Hat-making.* A bench with a plate of iron or stone flag fitted in it, and a little fire underneath, on which formerly the first part of the felting process was performed. Hence **Ba·son** *v.* to harden the felt on the b.

Basque (bask). 1817. [a. F. *Basque*:—late L. *Vasco* an inhabitant of Vasconia.] **A.** *sb.* 1. A native of Biscay; name of the ancient race inhabiting both slopes of the Western Pyrenees, who speak a language of non-Aryan origin 1835. 2. The language of this race 1860. 3. The continuation of a lady's bodice, forming a kind of short skirt. (? A distinct wd.) 1860. **B.** *adj.* Of or pertaining to the Basques 1817. Hence **Basqued** *ppl. a.* (sense 3). †**Ba·squish** *a.* and *sb.* Basque (language).

Basquine (baskī·n). 1819. [a. F., f. *basque*; see prec.] A rich outer petticoat worn by Basque and Spanish women.

Bas-relief, Bass-relief (ba:s,rĭlī·f, bā:rĭlī·f). 1667. [a. F., ad. It. *basso-rilievo* low RELIEF. Cf. BASSO-RELIEVO.] 1. Low relief; sculpture or carved work in which the figures project less than one half of their true proportions from the background 1696. 2. *concr.* A sculpture, etc. in low relief 1667.

Bass, basse (bæs), *sb.*[1] ME. [corruption of BARSE; cf. BASE *sb.*[5]] 1. The Common Perch (*Perca fluviatilis*), or an allied freshwater species 1440. 2. A voracious European marine fish (*Labrax lupus*) of the Perch family; called also Sea-wolf and Sea-dace. Also an allied species (Sea-bass) caught off N. America. 1530.

1. *Black Bass*: a Perch (*Perca huro*) found in Lake Huron.

Bass (bæs), *sb.*² 1691. [corruption of BAST *sb.*¹] 1. The inner bark of the lime or linden; *loosely*, any similar fibre. Also *attrib.* b. A fibre obtained from certain palms used for brushes, ropes, etc. 1881. 2. *ellipt.* A mat, a hassock, a flat plaited bag, etc., made of this 1706.

Bass (bæs), *sb.*³ 1686. [perh. for *bas-* or *base-coal.*] *Mining.* Shale stained dark by vegetable matter.

Bass (bæs), *sb.*⁴ 1849. Ale or beer (India Pale Ale or Bitter Beer) made by Messrs. Bass and Co. of Burton-on-Trent.

Bass (bēⁱs), *a.* and *sb.*⁵ [ME. *bas, base*; spelt after *basso*, but pronounced *base.*] A. *adj.* †1. Low in sound, soft –1513. 2. Low in the musical scale 1533. 3. Of, pertaining to, or suited to the bass part (see B. 1) 1552. Hence in *comb.*, as BASS-VIOL, etc.

3. *B. voice*: that ranging from E♭ below the b. stave to F above it. *B. clef*: see CLEF¹.

B. *sb.* 1. The lowest part in harmonized musical composition; the deepest male voice, or lowest tones of an instrument, which sound this part 1450. Also = THOROUGHBASS. 2. A singer or instrument (or a string) having such a voice, part, or compass; *spec.* a bass tuba (see TUBA), BASS-VIOL, DOUBLE-BASS 1591.

1. *Comb.*: **b.-baritone**, a voice higher than bass, yet of bass and not tenor quality; a singer having such a voice.

Bass, *v. nonce-wd.* [f. BASE *sb.*⁵] To utter with bass sound.

The Thunder..did base my Trespasse *Temp.* III. iii. 99.

Bass-bar (bēⁱ·sbāɹ). 1838. [f. BASS *sb.*⁵] *Mus.* An oblong piece of wood fixed lengthwise within violins, etc., to resist the pressure of the left foot of the bridge.

Basset (bæ·sėt), *sb.*¹ 1616. [a. F., dim. of *basse*; see BASE *a.*] A short-legged dog used in unearthing foxes and badgers.

†**Basset** (bæ·sėt), *sb.*² 1645. [(a. F. *bassette*), ad. It. *bassetta*, f. *bassetto*, dim. of *basso*; see BASE *a.*] A game at cards, resembling Faro. Hence **B.-table**. **Ba·sset** *v.*¹ to play at b.

Basset (bæ·sėt), *sb.*³ 1686. [? See BASSET *sb.*¹] *Geol.* The edge of a stratum showing at the surface of the ground; an outcrop. Also *attrib.* Hence **Ba·sset** *v.*² to crop out at the surface. **Ba·sseting** *vbl. sb.* the outcrop.

Basset-horn (bæ·sėt,hǭɹn). 1835. [tr. It. *corno di bassetto*; see BASSETTO.] *Mus.* A tenor clarinet of extra compass.

‖**Bassette** (base·t) [Fr., ad. It. *bassetto*], and **Bassetto** (basse·tto). [It., dim. of *basso*; see BASE *a.*, BASS *a.*] *Mus.* A small bass-viol.

Bass-horn. [See BASS *a.* 3.] *Mus.* A modification of the bassoon, much deeper in its tones.

‖**Bassia** (bæ·siă). 1863. [mod.L.; f. *Bassi*, an Italian botanist.] *Bot.* A genus of tropical trees (N.O. *Sapotaceæ*), from the seeds of which a butter-like oil is pressed. Hence **Ba·ssic** *a.*

Bassinet. Also **bassinette.** 1578. [a. F., dim. of *bassin*; see BASINET.] 1. (bæ·sinėt.) Var. of BASINET. †2. *Herb.* Name of species of Ranunculus and Geranium, and of the Marsh Marigold –1727. 3. (bæ:sine·t.) An oblong wickerwork basket, hooded at one end, used as a cradle for babies, or a perambulator 1854.

‖**Basso** (bα·sso). 1817. [It.] *Mus.* = BASS *a.* 3, *sb.*⁵ 1, 2. Hence **b. cantate**, a high bass voice, between b. profundo and baritone; **b. continuo** = THOROUGHBASS; **b. ostinato** = GROUND-*bass*; **b. profondo**, usu. **profundo**, a deep bass voice, having a compass of about two octaves above D below the bass stave; also, a singer having such a voice; **b. ripieno**, a bass part used only occ. in a grand chorus.

Bassoon (băsū̆·n). 1727. [ad. F. *basson*, augment. f. *bas.*] *Mus.* 1. A wooden double-reed instrument, with a compass of about three octaves, used as a bass to the oboe. 2. An organ-stop similar in tone to a b. **Bassoo·nist.**

‖**Ba·sso-relie·vo, -rilie·vo.** Pl. **-os.** 1676. [ad. It. *basso-rilievo* (ba·sso rīlyē·vo).] = BAS-RELIEF.

Bassorin (bæ·sŏrin). 1830. [f. *Bassora* + -IN.] A chemical principle found in Bassora and other gums, insoluble but swelling to a gelatinous state in water.

Bass-viol (bēⁱ·s,vəi·əl). 1590. [See VIOL.] A viol da gamba for playing the bass part in older concerted music; a violoncello.

Bass-wood (bα·s,wud). 1824. [f. BASS *sb.*²] The American Lime or Linden (*Tilia americana*); also, its wood. Also *attrib.*

Bast (bαst), *sb.*¹ [Com. Teut.: OE. *bæst*. Ult. origin unkn. See BASS *sb.*²] The inner bark of the lime or linden; also, any flexible fibrous bark (cf. BASS *sb.*²). Also *attrib.* 2. A rope, mat, etc. made of bast; cf. BASS *sb.*² 1450.

†**Bast,** *sb.*² and *a.* ME. [a. OF. *bast* (mod. *bât*, med.L. *bastum*) pack-saddle (used as a bed by muleteers), in phr. *fils de bast*, lit. 'pack-saddle child'; cf. BASTARD, BANTLING.] A. *sb.* Bastardy –1494. B. *adj.* Bastard –1572.

†‖**Basta** (bα·stă). *int.* 1596. [a. It.] Enough!

Bastard (bα·stăɹd). ME. [a. OF., mod. *bâtard* = *fils de bast*; see BAST *sb.*²] A. *sb.* 1. One begotten and born out of wedlock; an illegitimate or natural child. Also *fig.*

By the civil and canon laws, a child born out of wedlock is legitimated by the subsequent marriage of the parents; and by the law of England, and of some of the United States, the subsequent marriage of the parents of a bastard legitimates the child.

†2. A mongrel –1602. 3. A sweet Spanish wine, resembling muscadel; any sweetened wine. *Hist.* ME. †4. Anything of inferior quality or unusual make; *e. g.* a kind of cloth –1523; a cannon –1753; a size of paper –1774. 5. A large sail used in the Mediterranean. (So F. *bâtard.*) 1753. 6. *Sugar-refining.* A coarse brown sugar made from the refuse syrup of previous boilings; also, a mould into which sugar is drained. (So F. *bâtard.*) 1859.

1. Fame being a b. or *filia populi*, 'tis very hard to find her father FULLER. 3. Anon sir, Score a Pint of B. in the Halfe Moone 1 *Hen. IV*, II. iv. 30.

B. *adj.* 1. Born out of wedlock ME. 2. Mongrel, hybrid. ? *Obs.* ME. 3. *fig.* Illegitimate, unauthorized 1558. 4. *fig.* Not genuine; spurious; debased 1552. 5. Having the appearance of; an inferior kind of; as, *b. diamonds*, *B. Alkanet*, etc. 1530. 6. Of abnormal shape or irregular (*esp.* large) size; *spec.* applied: a. to a file intermediate between the coarse and fine cuts 1677; b. in *Printing*, to (*a*) a fount of type cast on a larger or smaller body than that to which it usually belongs, (*b*) an abbreviated title on the page preceding the title-page of a book; †c. to swords, guns, etc. –1753.

3. Usurie..is the B. use of money BACON. *B. branch* or *slip*: one springing of its own accord from the root of a tree, or where not wanted. 5. *B.-wing*: *Zool.* three or four quill-like feathers placed at a small joint in the middle of a bird's wing, taken as the analogue of the thumb in mammals.

†**Ba·stard,** *v.* 1549. [f. prec. sb.] *trans.* To BASTARDIZE –1658. Also *fig.*

†**Ba·stardice, -ise.** 1579. [a. F., mod. *bâtardise.*] Bastardy; falsity –1611.

Bastardism (bα·stăɹdiz'm). ? *Obs.* 1589. [f. BASTARD *sb.* + -ISM.] = BASTARDY 1.

Bastardize (bα·stăɹdəiz), *v.* 1587. [f. BASTARD + -IZE.] 1. *trans.* To declare or stigmatize as bastard 1611. †2. To beget bastard issue (*Lear* I. ii. 144). 3. To deteriorate 1587. Also *intr.* Hence **Ba:stardiza·tion.**

†**Ba·stardly,** *a.* 1552. [f. BASTARD *sb.* + -LY¹.] 1. Of bastard sort; unauthorized; counterfeit; debased –1785. 2. = BASTARD *a.* 5. –1610.

Bastardy (bα·stăɹdi). 1486. [a. OF. *bastardie*, f. *bastard*; see -Y.] 1. The condition of a bastard; illegitimate birth. Also *fig.* 2. Begetting of bastards, fornication; also *fig.* 1577.

Baste (bēⁱst), *sb.* Also **bast.** 1850. *Card-playing.* Var. of BEAST.

Baste (bēⁱst), *v.*¹ ME. [a. OF. *bastir* (mod. *bâtir*); f. Rom. *bastire* to put together (Diez).] *trans.* To sew together loosely; hence †a. To quilt; b. To tack together temporarily with long loose stitches. Also *transf.* or *fig.*

fig. To b. up a story hastily or clumsily SCOTT.

Baste (bēⁱst), *v.*² 1509. [?] 1. To moisten (a roasting joint, etc.) with melted fat, gravy, etc. Also *transf.* or *fig.* †2. To perfuse as with a liniment –1735. 3. To mark (sheep) with tar (*north.*).

Baste (bēⁱst), *v.*³ 1533. [Perh. a fig. use of prec.] *trans.* To beat soundly, cudgel. Also *fig.*

Baste (bēⁱst), *v.*⁴ 1850. [f. BASTE *sb.*] *Card-playing.* Var. of BEAST *v.*

Bastel-house (bæ·stĕlhaus). 1544. [f. *bastel*, var. of BASTILE.] A fortified house.

Basten (bæ·stĕn), *a.* [OE. *bæsten*; see BAST *sb.*¹] Made of bast.

‖**Bastide** (bα·stid, bastī·d). 1523. [a. OF., ad. Pr. *bastida* sb., f. *bastir* to build.] 1. *Obs.* exc. *Hist.* A fortlet. ‖2. A country-house in southern France.

Bastille, -ile (bαstī·l, bα·stil), *sb.* ME. [a. F.:—late L. *bastilia* pl., f. *bastire.* Refash. after Fr.] 1. A tower or bastion of a castle; a small fortress. 2. *spec.* In siege operations: a. A wooden tower on wheels. b. One of a series of huts, defended by entrenchments, for the accommodation of the besieging troops. ME. 3. Name of the prison-fortress built in Paris in the 14th and destroyed in the 18th century 1561. 4. Hence: A prison 1790.

3. That rock-fortress..which they name B., or Building, as if there were no other building CARLYLE.

Bastille, -ile (bαstī·l, bα·stil), *v.* 1480. [f. OF. *bastiller*, f. *bastille*; see prec.] †1. To fortify (a castle) –1500. 2. [f. prec. sb.] To confine in a bastille 1742.

Basti·llion. *Hist.* 1549. [a. OF. *bastillon*, dim. of *bastille.*] A small fortress or castle; a fortified tower.

†**Ba·stiment.** 1598. [partly ad. Sp. *bastimiento*, partly a. F., both f. Rom. *bastire*, to put together, build.] 1. Military supplies –1622. 2. A building, a wall 1679.

Bastinade, -onade (bæstinēⁱ·d, -ŏnēⁱ·d). *sb.* (*arch.*) 1660. [Eng. ad. BASTINADO, after Fr.] = BASTINADO *sb.* 1–3.

Bastina·de, -ona·de, *v. arch.* 1601. [f. prec. sb.] To BASTINADO.

Bastinado (bæstinēⁱ·do), *sb.* 1577. [a. Sp. *bastonada*, f. *baston* stick.] 1. A blow with a stick or cudgel; *esp.* one upon the soles of the feet. 2. A cudgelling (*arch.*) 1594. 3. *spec.* An Eastern method of punishment, by beating with a stick the soles of the culprit's feet 1726. 4. A stick, staff, truncheon, etc. 1598.

Bastina·do, *v.* Also **-onado.** 1614. [f. prec. sb.] 1. To beat with a stick (*arch.*). 2. *spec.* To beat or cane on the soles of the feet 1688.

Bastion (bæ·stiən). 1598. [a. F., ad. It. *bastione*, f. *bastire* of uncertain origin.] A projecting part of a fortification, consisting of an earthwork in the form of an irregular pentagon, having its base in the main line, or at an angle, of the fortification; its 'flanks' are the two sides which spring from the base, and are shorter than the 'faces' which meet in the frontal angle. Also *transf.* and *fig.* Hence **Ba·stioned** *ppl. a.* furnished with or defended by a b. or bastions. **Ba:stione·t,** a small b.

Ba·stite, 1837. [f. *Baste* in the Harz Mountains + -ITE.] *Min.* A bronze- or greenish-coloured impure foliated serpentine; Schiller-spar.

Basto (bα·sto). 1675. [a. Sp.] The ace of clubs in quadrille or ombre.

†**Baston.** ME. [a. OF., mod. *bâton*, f. late L. **bastonem.* See BATOON and BATON.] 1. A staff or stick used as a weapon or as a symbol of office –1756. 2. A stanza or verse. (Transl. of *staff, stave.*) ME. only. 3. *Her.* = BATON 3. –1660. 4. *Old Law.* One of the Warden of the Fleet's men, who attended the king's courts with a red staff, to take into custody such as were committed by the court. (Cf. *tip-staff*, etc.) –1671. 5. *Archit.* A torus. (So F. *bâton.*) –1847.

Bastonite. [f. *Bastoigne* in Luxembourg + -ITE.] *Min.* A variety of LEPIDOMELANE.

Basyl(e (bēⁱ·sil, bæ·sil). 1863. [f. Gr. βάσις + ὕλη.] *Chem.* A body that unites with oxygen to form a base. Hence **Ba·sylous** *a.*

Bat (bæt), *sb.*¹ 1575. [Replaces ME. *bakke*, app. from Scand.; cf. Da. *aften-bakka* 'evening-bat', etc.] A member of the Mammalian order of *Cheiroptera*, and *esp.* of the family *Vespertilionidæ*; consisting of mouse-like quadrupeds (whence the names *Rere-mouse*, *Flitter-mouse*) having the fingers extended to support a thin membranous wing which stretches from the side of the neck by the toes of both pairs of feet to the tail; they were formerly classed as birds. They are all nocturnal.

The curious formation of a b., a mouse with wings BOSWELL.

Comb.: **b.-shell**, a species of volute; **b.-tick**, an insect parasitical on bats. Also in many adjs., as **b.-blind, -eyed, -minded**, etc.

Bat (bæt), *sb.*² ME. [? a. OF. *batte*, referred to *battre*; or = OE. **bat*, perh. f. Celt.; or echoic (cf. *pat*). Possibly two or three distinct wds.] **1.** A stick, a club, a staff for support or defence (*arch.*). †**2.** ? A balk of timber –1686. **3.** The wooden implement with rounded handle and flattened blade used in cricket. (The most common mod. sense.) 1706. **b.** Short for *batter, batsman* 1859. **4.** Harlequin's sword of lath. [From F.] 1859. †**5.** A lump, piece ME. only. **6.** *esp.* A piece of a brick having one end entire 1519. **7.** Shale interstratified between seams of coal, etc. Cf. BASS *sb.*⁴ 1686. **8.** A felted mass of fur, etc., in hat-making; often spelt BATT 1836. **9.** A sheet of cotton wadding for quilts; batting. **10.** A blow. Cf. BAT *v.* ME.

1. Make you ready your stiffe bats and clubs *Cor.* I. i. 165.

‖**Bat, bât** (bā, bāt, bæt), *sb.*³ ME. [a. F. *bât* pack-saddle, OF. *bast*:—late L. *bastum*, ? conn. w. Gr. βαστάζειν.] **1.** A pack-saddle. Only in *comb.*, as †**b.-needle**, a packing-needle; **bât-horse** (F. *cheval de bât*), a sumpter-beast; **bât-mule**. **2.** In *bat-money*: An allowance for carrying baggage in the field. Occas. confused w. BATTA. 1793.

Bat (bæt), *v.*¹ ME. [f. BAT *sb.*²] **1.** To strike with or as with a bat; to cudgel, beat. **2.** To hit a ball with a bat. Also *absol.* 1773.

Bat, *v.*² 1615. [var. of BATE *v.*¹ and ².] **1.** *intr.* To bate or flutter as a hawk. **2.** *trans.* (*dial.* and in U.S.) *To b. the eyes*: to wink 1847.

†**Ba·table**, *a.* 1453. [Short f. DEBATABLE; cf. BATE *sb.*¹] Debatable –1610.

‖**Batardeau** (batardo·). 1767. [Fr.: formerly *bastardeau*, dim. of *bastard* 'a dike' (Littré).] **a.** A coffer-dam. **b.** A wall built across the moat or ditch surrounding a fortification.

Batata (bătā·tă, bătē·tă). 1577. [a. Sp. a. Haitian.] A plant (*Batatas edulis*, N. O. *Convolvulaceæ*), called also Spanish or Sweet Potato.

Batavian (bătē·viăn). 1598. [f. L. *Batavia*, f. *Batavi*, a people who dwelt on Betawe, an island between the Rhine and the Waal. See -AN.] **A.** *adj.* Of or pertaining to the ancient Batavi. **b.** Pertaining to Holland or the Dutch. 1796. **B.** *sb. pl.* **a.** The ancient Batavi. **b.** The Dutch or Netherlanders (*rare*). 1598.

Batch (bætʃ). [ME. *bache, bacche*, repr. OE. **bæcce*, f. *bacan* to BAKE; cf. *wake, watch*, etc.] †**1.** The process of baking –1551. **2.** *concr.* A baking; the quantity produced at one baking 1461; †*ellipt.* the bread itself 1648. Also *fig.* †**3.** *fig.* and *transf.* Sort, lot –1705. **4. a.** The quantity of dough for one baking. **b.** The quantity of corn sent at one time to the mill. 1549. **5.** *transf.* A quantity produced at one operation, *e. g.* a brewing (*arch.*) 1713. **6. a.** An instalment 1833. **b.** A set 1598.

2. Thou crusty b. of Nature, what's the newes *Tr. & Cr.* V. i. 5. **3.** One..o' your owne b. B. JONS. **5.** A b. of beer 1713, of soup 1878. **6.** A b. of prize-money 1833, of visitors 1793.

Bate (bēt), *v.*¹ ME. [a. OF. *batre* (mod. *battre*):—late L. *battere* for cl. L. *batuere*.] †**1.** To contend with blows or arguments –1440. **2.** *Falconry.* To beat the wings impatiently and flutter away from the fist or perch. (F. *se battre*.) ME. Also †*fig.* **b.** To flutter downwards 1590.

2. *fig.* Come, civil night..Hood my vnman'd blood, bayting in my Cheekes *Rom. & Jul.* III. ii. 14. Hence **Ba·ter**, a hawk that bates.

Bate (bēt), *v.*² ME. [aphet. f. ABATE *v.*¹] †**1.** To beat down or away –1601. **2.** To lower, let down; *fig.* to cast down, humble ME. Also †*intr.* **3.** To beat back or blunt the edge of (*lit.* and *fig.*) 1535. †**4.** To reduce –1691; †*intr.* to decrease –1596. **5.** To lessen in force or intensity. Now chiefly in *To b. one's breath.* ME. **6.** To strike off or take away (a part of) 1440; *ellipt.* to deprive (a person) *of* 1823. †**7.** To omit, except –1704.

1. B. the earth from about the roots of olives HOLLAND. **2.** Bating nor heart nor hope S. ROGERS. (Cf. 6.) **3.** Which shall b. his sythes keene edge *L.L.L.* I. i. 6. **4.** These greefes and losses have so bated mee *Merch. V.* III. iii. 32. **6.** I will not b. a penny 1602. *To bate an ace*; see ACE 3. Phr. †*To bate of*: to make a lessening of. †**Ba·teless** *a.*

Bate (bēt), *v.*³ 1875. [?] *Tanning.* To steep in bate; see BATE *sb.*⁴

†**Bate**, *sb.*¹ ME. [f. BATE *v.*¹; or short f. DEBATE *sb.*] Contention, discord –1690.

At (*the*) *b.*: at strife. Hence †**Ba·teful** *a.* full of strife.

Bate (bēt), *sb.*² *dial.* 1450. [f. BATE *v.*²] †**1.** Depression 1686. **2.** Deduction, abatement 1450.

Bate (bēt), *sb.*³ *n. dial.* 1664. [?] The grain of wood or stone.

Bate (bēt), *sb.*⁴ 1804. [Cf. G. *beisse*, f. *beissen* to BAIT *v.*¹] *Tanning.* An alkaline lye, used to make the hides supple; a vat containing it; the process of steeping in it.

‖**Bateau** (bato). Pl. **bateaux** (batōz). [Fr. :—OF. *batel*; cf. med.L. *batellus*, prob. f. Teut. *bátr*, OE. *bát*, BOAT.] A light river-boat; *esp.* the long tapering boats with flat bottoms used by the French Canadians. erron. **Batteau.**

Batell (bæ·tl), var. of BATTEL.

†**Batement.** 1677. Aphetic of ABATEMENT.

Bat-fowl (bæ·tˌfau·l), *v.* 1440. [app. f. BAT *sb.*² + FOWL *v.*] **1.** To catch birds at night by dazing them with a light, and knocking them down or netting them. †**2.** *slang.* To swindle, to victimize the simple –1608. Hence **Ba·t-fow·ler, Ba·t-fow·ling** *vbl. sb.* (in both senses).

†**Ba·tful**, *a.* 1549. [f. *bat-* (see BATTEN *v.*); freq. in Drayton.] = BATTABLE –1612.

Bath (baþ), *sb.*¹ Pl. **baths** (bāðz). [OE. *bæð*:—OTeut. **baþom*, neut., f. OTeut. **baþo-* to foment (cf. mod.G. *bähen*) cogn. w. L. *fovere*.] **1.** The action of immersing the body, or a part of it, in, or surrounding it with, water, vapour, hot air, mud, or the like. Also *transf.* **2.** A quantity of water or other liquid for bathing OE. **3.** *fig.* and *transf.* Any enveloping medium producing effects analogous to those of bathing ME. **4.** A receptacle, apartment, or building containing a series of apartments, for bathing; (the latter usu. *pl.*) 1591. **5.** A place for undergoing medical treatment by bathing, etc. Usu. in pl. Cf. BATH ² 1. 1562. **6.** *Chem.* A contrivance for producing a steady heat at high temperature, or at a temperature not exceeding that of boiling point, as a sand-b., a water-b. 1599. **7.** *Photography.* A solution in which photographic plates or prints are immersed; the vessel holding the solution 1861. **8.** *Metallurgy.* A mass of molten material in a furnace 1881. **9. Order of the Bath:** a high order of British knighthood. (So called from the bath which preceded installation.) 1603.

1. *transf.* His head all over in a b. of sweat MANDEVILLE. **3.** A b. of blisse CHAUCER, of sunshine 1871. Sleepe..sore Labors B. *Macb.* II. ii. 38. **4.** The Lambeth Baths (*mod.*). **5.** Matlock Bath (*mod.*).

Bath (baþ), *sb.*² OE. [Same word as prec., orig. a dat. pl. *baðum*, whence as an indecl. sb. *Baðum, Baðon* (latinized *Bathonia*), reduced through *Baþen, Bathe*, to *Bath* in 17th c.] A city in the west of England, so called from its hot springs. Also *attrib.*

Comb. etc.: **B.-brick**, a preparation of calcareous earth moulded in form of a brick, made at Bridgwater; used for cleaning polished metal. **B. bun**, a large fruit bun with sugared top. **B.-chair**, a large chair on wheels for invalids. (Both these are often written without a capital B.) **B.-metal**, an alloy, consisting of 3 or 4 oz. of zinc to one pound of copper. **B. oolite, B.-stone**, a building stone from the oolite formation near Bath. **B.-post**, a sort of letter-paper.

Bath (bæþ), *sb.*³ ME. [a. Heb.] A Hebrew liquid-measure, about six and a half gallons.

Bath (baþ), *v.* 1660. [f. BATH *sb.*¹; cf. to *tub*, etc.] To subject to a bath. Different from *bathe* in having a distinct reference to a vessel for bathing, and in being always literal.

To London and saw the bath-ing..of the Knights of the Bath EVELYN.

Bathe (bēið), *v.* [Com. Teut.: OE. *baðian* :—OTeut. *baþ-ōn*, f. *baþo-(m)* BATH *sb.*¹] **1.** *trans.* To immerse, as in a bath; to plunge or dip ME. **2.** To apply liquid so as to wet or moisten copiously; to lave, perfuse, suffuse OE. **3.** To envelop, or encompass, like the air, etc. 1816. **4.** *intr.* To take a bath; earlier also, to bask OE. Also in transf. and fig. uses 1576.

1. The moder batheth the chylde TREVISA. **2.** To b. the eye with vinegar and water 1877. The river bathed the foot of the walls GIBBON. Bathed in sweat 1746, in tears BURKE. Phr. *To bathe in blood*: usu. *fig.* to express the great quantity shed. **3.** The babe ..Lies bathed in joy EMERSON. Hence **Bathe** *sb.* an act of bathing (intr.) 1831. **Ba·ther**, one who takes a bath, esp. in sea or river. So **Ba·thing** *vbl. sb.*; also, the conditions of this (1880); *attrib.* in *bathing dress*, MACHINE (1b), etc.

Bathetic (băþe·tik), *a.* 1834. [irreg. f. *bathos*, erron. after *pathetic*.] Characterized by bathos; absol. *The b.* = BATHOS.

Bathometer (băþǫ·mĭtəɹ). 1875. [f. Gr. βάθος + μέτρον.] A spring balance for ascertaining the depth of water without measuring the sounding line.

Bathos (bē·þǫs). 1727. [a. Gr. βάθος. First made Eng. in sense 2 by Pope.] **1.** Depth; bottom 1758. **2.** *Rhet.* Ludicrous descent from the elevated to the commonplace; anti-climax 1727. **3.** Hence *gen.* A come-down 1814.

Bathukolpian (bæþiukǫ·lpiăn), *a. rare.* 1825. [f. Gr. βαθύς + κόλπος.] Deep-bosomed. var. **Bathuko·lpic.**

‖**Bathybius** (băþi·biŏs). 1868. [mod.L., f. Gr. βαθύς + βίος.] *Zool.* Huxley's name for a gelatinous substance found at the bottom of the Atlantic Ocean, and at first supposed to be a formless mass of living protoplasm, but now regarded as an inorganic precipitate.

Bathymetric, -al (bæþime·trik, -ăl), *a.* 1862. [f. Gr. βαθύς + μετρικός, + -AL; cf. BATHOMETER.] Of or pertaining to the measurement of depth, *spec.* to the vertical range of distribution of plants and animals in the sea. Hence **Bathyme·trically** *adv.*

Bathymetry (băþi·mĕtri). [f. as prec. + -μετρια.] The art or science of measuring depths (in the sea). WEBSTER.

Bating (bē·tiŋ), *prep.* 1568. [pr. pple. of BATE *v.*² 7 used absol.; cf. *barring*, etc.] Leaving out of account.

Batiste (bătī·st). 1697. [a. F. *batiste* = *Baptiste*, its original maker, of Cambray (Littré).] The French word for *cambric*; applied in commerce to a fabric of the same texture, made of cotton as well as linen. Often *attrib.*

†**Ba·tler**, in mod. edd. of SHAKS. **Batlet.** *rare.* [f. BATTLE *v.*⁴; or ? dim. f. BAT *sb.*²] A beetle for battling clothes. *A. Y. L.* II. iv. 49.

‖**Batman**¹ (bæ·tmăn). 1599. [Turk.] An oriental weight varying according to the locality.

Batman² (bæ·tmæn, †bā·mæn). 1809. [f. BAT *sb.*³] **1.** A man in charge of a bat-horse and its load. **2.** An officer's servant.

‖**Baton** (bæ·tən, ‖batoṅ). 1548. [a. F. *bâton* :—OF. *baston*, whence BASTON. Cf. BATOON.] **1.** A staff or stick used as a weapon –1829; also *gen.* a stick 1801. **2.** A staff of office; *e.g.* a Marshal's b. 1590. **3.** *Her.* An ordinary, in breadth the fourth part of a BEND, broken off short at each end, so as to have the figure of a truncheon; used in Eng. coats of arms only in the form of the *baton sinister*, the badge of bastardy (pop. *bar sinister*) 1816. **4.** *Mus.* The wand used in beating time. (Often pronounced as Fr.) 1867. **5.** See BATTEN.

4. Phr. *Under* ——*'s baton*, conducted by ——. Hence **Ba·ton** *v.* to strike with a b.; formerly, to cudgel. **Ba·toned** *ppl. a.* furnished with, or bearing, a b.; in *Her.* marked with, or bearing, the b. of bastardy.

Batoon (bătū·n), *sb. arch.* 1562. [Now superseded by BATON.] = BATON 1, 2, 3, 5. Hence **Batoo·n** *v.* (*arch.*) = BATON *v.*

‖**Batrachia** (bătrē·kiă), *sb. pl.* 1847. [prop. *batrachia*, mod.L., a. Gr. βατράχεια (sc. ζῷα), adj., neut. pl., f. βάτραχος.] *Zool.* **a.** One of Brongniart's four orders of Reptiles. **b.** Now, restricted to an order of the class Amphibia, containing those animals only, as frogs and toads, which subsequently discard the gills and tail of their larval state. (The sing. is BATRACHIAN.) Hence **Batra·chian** *a.* of or pertaining to the B., *esp.* frogs and toads; *sb.* an animal of the order B.

Batrachite (bæ·trăkəit). 1837. [ad. L., a.

Gr. βατραχίτης (λίθος).] **a.** A stone resembling a frog in colour. **b.** A fossil batrachian.

Batracho-, comb. f. Gr. βάτραχος frog: **Ba·trachoid** *a.*, frog-like. **Ba·trachomyo·machy** [ad. Gr., f. βάτραχος + μῦς + -μαχία], the battle of the frogs and mice, a mock heroic poem, possibly of the Homeric age. **Batracho·phagous** [Gr. -φάγος] *a.*, frog-eating. **Ba·trachopho·bia** [Gr. -φοβία], dread of or aversion to frogs, toads, etc.

Batsman (bæ·tsmæn). 1756. [f. *bat's* (BAT *sb.*[2]).] One who handles the bat at cricket.

Batt, var. of BAT *sb.*[2] 8.

‖**Batta**[1] (bæ·tă). 1680. [a. Indo-Pg. *bata*, prob. ad. Canarese *bhatta* rice.] *Anglo-Ind. orig.* Subsistence money. Hence, extra pay during a campaign, and *spec.* An extra allowance, which became a constant addition to the pay of officers serving in India.

‖**Batta**[2] (bæ·tă). 1680. [a. Urdu.] *Anglo-Ind.* In Indian Banking, agio; discount on coins not current, or of short weight.

†**Ba·ttable**, *a.*[1] 1570. [f. *bat-* (see BATTEN *v.*) + -ABLE.] Fattening; fertile in pasture –1641.

†**Battable**, *a.*[2] 1601. [a. OF., f. *battre.*] That may be beaten out, malleable.

†**Battailant**. 1591. [a. F. *bataillant.*] **1.** *adj.* Combatant SPENS. **2.** *sb.* A combatant SHELTON.

Battailous (bæ·tĕləs), *a. arch.* ME. [a. OF. *bataillos* (*-eus*), f. *bataille.*] Fond of fighting, ready for battle.

Battalia (bătā·lyă). *arch.* 1594. [a. It. *battaglia.* Doublet of BATTLE.] **1.** *Mil.* Order of battle. (Usu. with *in, into.*) 1613. †**2.** = BATTLE *sb.* 6, 7. (Cf. BATTALION **1.**) –1750. Also *fig.* (cf. 'host').

1. Friedrich draws out in b. CARLYLE.

Batta·lia pie. 1664. [ad. F. *béatilles*, med.L. *beatillæ*, 'small blessed articles', as samplers worked by nuns, etc., dim. of L. *beatus. Battalia* is due to pop. etym.] 'Tit-bits, as cocks' combs, sweetbreads, etc. in a pie'.

Battalion (bătæ·liən). 1589. [a. F. *bataillon*, ad. It. *battaglione*, augm. or dim. of *battaglia.* (Cf. BATTALIA.)] **1.** *gen.* A large body of men in battle array; one of the large divisions of an army. †**b.** = BATTLE 7. –1656. **2.** *spec.* A body of infantry (or engineers) composed of several companies, and forming part of a regiment. (The number of battalions in a regiment varies greatly.) 1708.

1. Providence is on the side of the strongest battalions *Provb.* Hence **Batta·lion** *v.* (*rare*) to form into a b.

Battel, batell (bæ·t'l), *sb.* 1594. [First recorded in L. pl. form *batelli* (15th cent.); of unkn. origin, but perh. f. BATTLE *v.*[3]] Now only in *pl.* **battels, batells**, except attrib. In the University of Oxford (and formerly elsewhere), a provision of food taken by a member of a college; hence, the accounts of the costs of such provisions, and other college charges, for an individual; also, such college accounts in general.

Ba·ttel, *v.* 1570. [see prec., and cf. BATTLE *v.*[3]] **1.** In Univ. of Oxford: To have a kitchen and buttery account in college. †**2.** (?) To put into a common stock –1606.

Ba·tteler. *Obs.* exc. *Hist.* 1604. [f. BATTLE *v.*] One who battels in college; formerly, an order of students in Oxford below Commoners.

Batten (bæ·t'n), *sb.*[1] 1658. [var. of BATON *sb.* in techn. use.] **1.** *Carp.* and *Build.* A piece of squared timber, not more than 7 inches broad and $2^1/_2$ inches thick, used for flooring, etc.; a scantling. **2.** *spec.* A bar or strip nailed or glued across parallel boards, to hold them together, or prevent warping; a ledge, a clamp 1663. **3.** *Naut.* A narrow strip nailed to the masts and spars to prevent them from chafing; one used to fasten down the edges of the tarpaulin fixed over the hatchways; also, a wooden bar from which hammocks are slung 1769.

Comb. **b.-door**, a door formed of narrow boards, held together by battens. Hence **Ba·ttening** *sb.* the application of, or a structure formed with, battens.

Batten (bæ·t'n), *sb.*[2] 1831. [corrupt f. F. *battant.*] A movable bar in a silk-loom which closes the weft.

Batten (bæ·t'n), *v.*[1] 1591. [app. a. ON. *batna*, f. *bati* improvement. Cf. BATTLE *v.*[3]] **1.** *intr.* To improve in condition; *esp.* (of animals) to thrive, grow fat by feeding. **b.** To glut oneself *on*; to gloat *in* 1602. **c.** *fig.* To thrive (*esp.* to the detriment of another) 1605. **2.** To grow fertile (as soil); to grow rank (as a plant) 1855. †**3.** *trans.* To improve, fatten up. (The pa. pple. *battened* belonged orig. to the intr. sense; cf. *well-read*, etc.) –1790.

1. It makes her fat you see. Shee battens with it B. JONS. *fig.* Battening vampyre-like on a People next door to starvation CARLYLE. Hence **Ba·ttener.**

Batten (bæ·t'n), *v.*[2] 1775. [f. BATTEN *sb.*[1]] To furnish or strengthen with battens.

To b. down (chiefly *Naut.*): to fasten down with battens.

Batter (bæ·təɹ), *v.*[1] ME. [f. *bat-* 'beat', as in OF. *batre*, Eng. BAT *v.* etc.; cf. *stutter*, etc.] **1.** *trans.* (and *absol.*) To strike with repeated blows so as to bruise or shatter. **2.** *transf.* and *fig.* To subject (persons, etc.) to crushing or persistent attack 1578. **3.** To beat out of shape, as (in *Printing*) the surface of type 1697. †**4.** [f. BATTER *sb.*[1]] To beat into a batter –1622. †**5.** *Sc.* To paste, to fix (as with paste) –1756.

1. Or with a logge B. his skull *Temp.* III. ii. 98. The Ramme that batters downe the wall *Tr. & Cr.* I. iii. 206. **3.** Boats..battered by exposure to ice and storm KANE. Hence **Ba·tterable** *a.* **Ba·tterer.**

Batter (bæ·təɹ), *v.*[2] ME. [? conn. w. F. *abattre.*] *Archit. intr.* Of walls, etc.: To incline from the perpendicular.

Batter (bæ·təɹ), *sb.*[1] 1546. [prob. f. BATTER *v.*[1]] **1.** A mixture of two or more ingredients beaten up with a liquid for culinary purposes. Also *transf.* **2.** *Sc.* Flour and water made into paste 1530. **3.** A heavy bruising blow (*rare*) 1823. **4.** A cannonade of heavy ordnance 1859. **5.** *Printing.* A bruise on the face of printing type, etc. (Cf. BATTER *v.*[1] 3.) 1824. Also *attrib.*

Ba·tter, *sb.*[2] 1743. [f. BATTER *v.*[2]] The slope of a wall, terrace, or bank from the perpendicular.

Batter-rule, an instrument consisting of a plumb-line and a frame, used for setting a wall, etc. at the proper slope or b.

Ba·tter, *sb.*[3] 1824. [f. BAT *v.*[1]] One who bats, *esp.* in *Cricket.*

Battering (bæ·təriŋ), *vbl. sb.* 1542. [f. BATTER *v.*[1]] **1.** The action of the vb., *esp.* in *Mil.* **2.** Bruising or defacement thus caused 1558.

Comb.: **b.-charge**, the full charge of powder for a cannon; **-engine** = RAM; **-train**, a number of cannon intended for siege purposes.

Battering-ram. 1611. [f. prec. + RAM. Cf. L. *aries* ram.] An ancient military engine employed for battering down walls, consisting of a beam of wood, with a mass of iron at one end, sometimes shaped like a ram's head.

Battery (bæ·təri). 1531. [a. F. *batterie*, f. *battre*; see -ERY.] **1.** The action of battering or assailing with blows; also *transf.* or *fig.*; *spec.* in *Law*, an unlawful attack upon another by beating, etc., including technically the least touching of another's person or clothes in a menacing manner. †**b.** A bruise –1639. **2.** A number of guns placed in juxtaposition for combined action; in *Mil.*, the smallest division of artillery for tactical purposes 1555. **3.** The platform or fortified work, on or within which artillery is mounted (sometimes including the artillery there mounted) 1590. Also *transf.* or *fig.* **4.** *Mining.* The set of stamps that work in one mortar of a stamp-mill 1881. **5.** (from 2) A combination of simple instruments. **6.** *Electr.* A number of Leyden jars so connected that they may be charged and discharged simultaneously 1748. Also *fig.* **7.** *Galvanism.* A series of cells, each containing the essentials for producing voltaic electricity, connected together. Also used of a single voltaic cell. 1801. **8.** *Optics.* A combined series of lenses or prisms 1867. **9.** Apparatus for preparing or serving meals. [= F. *batterie de cuisine*; ? from next sense.] 1819. **10.** Metal, or articles of metal, wrought by hammering 1502. **11.** *Mining.* **a.** A bulkhead of timber. **b.** The plank closing the bottom of a coal-chute. (Raymond.) **12.** *Mus.* The percussion section of an orchestra.

1. Ile haue an action of B. against him *Twel. N.* IV. i. 36. **2.** *Horse batteries*, those in which the gunners are carried partly on the carriages, partly on horses; *Field Batteries*, those in which they are carried wholly on the carriages. *Garrison batteries*, bodies of artillerymen serving heavy guns in forts, etc.

Phrases, etc. *B.-wagon*: one carrying tools and materials for repair of the b. *Cross-batteries*: two batteries playing upon the same point from different directions. *Enfilading b.*: one which sweeps the whole line attacked. *Floating b.*: a heavily armed and armoured vessel for bombarding fortresses. *In b.*: (a gun) projecting in readiness for firing through an embrasure or over a parapet. *Masked b.*: one screened from the enemy's view.

Batting (bæ·tiŋ), *vbl. sb.* 1611. [f. BAT *v.*[1], *sb.*[2]] **1.** The action of using or striking with a bat: †**a.** in *Laundry-work* –1798. **b.** in *Cricket* 1773. **c.** in cleaning raw cotton by hand 1819. **2.** Cotton fibre prepared in sheets for quilts, etc.; cf. BAT *sb.*[2] 9. 1875.

Battle (bæ·t'l), *sb.* [ME. *batayle, -aile, -aille*, a. OF.:—Vulgar L. *battalia*, corrupt f. late L. *battualia*, adj., neut. pl., f. late L. *battuere* (perh. Celt.).] **1.** A hostile encounter between opposing forces; a fight. **2.** A single combat, a duel ME. Also applied to animals. **3.** (Without article or pl.): Fighting, war ME. †**4.** A war –1557. **5.** *fig.* Strife, struggle for victory ME. **6.** An army, or one of its main divisions, in battle array; = BATTALION (*arch.*) ME. †**7.** The main body of an army or naval force; = BATTALIA 2, BATTALION 1 b. (More fully 'great' or 'main b.') –1596. †**8.** = BATTALIA 1. –1596.

1. *Pitched b.*, one of which the ground has been chosen beforehand by both sides. *Soldier's b.*, one which is decided by the courage and energy of the soldier. **2.** *Trial by b.*: the legal decision of a dispute by single combat. **B. royal**, a fight (*spec.* a cock-fight) in which several combatants engage; a general engagement; hence *fig.* a general squabble. The race is not to the swift, nor the b. (= victory) to the strong *Eccles.* ix. 11. **5.** Their mouthes are softer then butter, and yet haue they batell in their mynde COVERDALE *Ps.* lv. 21. **6.** What may the Kings whole Battaile reach vnto 1 *Hen. IV*, IV. i. 129. **7.** A Vanguard..a Battaile of 400..ships, and a Reare RALEIGH.

Phrases. *To offer, refuse, accept b.*; *to join b.*; also, *to do b.*; *to give b.*, to attack. *Line of b.*: the position of troops drawn up in b. array; the line formed by ships of war in an engagement. Hence *line-of-battle ship*, one large enough to take part in a main attack; formerly, one of 74 guns and upwards.

Comb.: **b.-cry, -word**, a war-cry, a slogan; **-field, -ground**, the field or ground on which a b. is fought; **-piece**, a painting of a b., a passage describing a b.; **-wise** *adv.* in manner or order of b.

Battle, battel (bæ·t'l), *a. Obs.* exc. *dial.* 1513. [? f. **bat* repr. ON. *bati*; see BATTEN *v.*[1]] **1.** Of grass, etc.: Improving to sheep and cattle; fattening. **2.** Hence, of land: Rich, productive (prop. in pasture) 1540.

Battle (bæ·t'l), *v.*[1] ME. [a. F. *batailler.*] **1.** *intr.* To fight. (Now usu. *fight.*) **b.** *fig.* To maintain a (defensive) struggle, e. g. *with* or *against* bigotry, etc. 1502. †**2.** *trans.* and *refl.* To embattle ME. only. **3.** To assail in battle. Also *fig.* ME.

1. Whiles Lyons Warre, and battaile for their Dennes SHAKS. His virtues battling with his place SWIFT. They *b. it* beyond the wall BYRON. Hence **Ba·ttled** *ppl. a.*[1] ranged in battle-array; *poet.* fought.

†**Ba·ttle**, *v.*[2] ME. [a. OF. *bataillier, -eillier* to furnish with *batailles* 'battlements'; see also BATTLEMENT.] To fortify or furnish with battlements. (Usu. in *pass.*) –1618. Hence **Ba·ttled** *ppl. a.*[2] embattled; †crenelated. **Ba·ttling** *vbl. sb.* embattling; *concr.* battlements.

†**Battle, battel** (bæ·t'l), *v.*[3] 1548. [? deriv. of BATTLE *a.*] *trans.* †**1.** *trans.* To feed, or nourish –1662. †**2.** To fertilize –1662. †**3.** *intr.* To grow fat, to thrive –1721. †**4.** To become fertile –1578. Hence †**Ba·ttled** *ppl. a.*[3] fattened; manured.

†**Battle**, *v.*[4] 1570. [? freq. of BAT *v.*[1], or var. of BEETLE.] To beat (clothes) with a wooden beetle during washing, or when dried.

Battle-ax, -axe (bæ·t'l,æks). ME. **1.** A kind of ax used as a weapon of war in the Middle Ages. **2.** A halberd or bill 1709.

Battledore (bæ·t'ldōəɹ), *sb.* ME. [Perh. ad. Pr. *batedor* 'beater'; cf. Sp. *batidor*, f. *batir*. But the historical connexion is not shown.] **1.** A beetle used in washing, also for mangling linen clothes; hence applied to other similarly shaped instruments. **2.** An instrument like a small racket used in playing with a shuttlecock 1598. **b.** The game of *b. and shuttlecock* 1719. **3.** A horn-book; so called from its usual shape. *Obs.* exc. *dial.* 1693.

Phrase. **Battledore barley**: a cultivated barley (*Hordeum zeocriton*) with short broad ears. Hence [f. sense 2] **Ba·ttledore** *v.* to toss or fly to and fro.

Battlement (bæ·t'lmĕnt), *sb.* [ME. *bateill-, batayle-, batelment*, a. OF. **bateillement*, f. *batailler*.] **a.** An indented parapet at the top of a wall, orig. used for purposes of defence, subseq. for architectural decoration. The raised parts are *cops* or *merlons*, the indentations *embrasures* or *crenelles*. **b.** *loosely* for 'embattled roof'. 1595. **c.** *fig.* The towering summits of the mountains, the roof of the heavens 1667.

Thrown by angry Jove Sheer o're the Chrystal Battlements MILT. *P. L.* I. 742. Hence **Ba·ttlement** *v.* to furnish or decorate with battlements. **Ba·ttlemented** *ppl. a.* having battlements.

Battler[1] (bæ·tləɪ). [ME. *batelur*, a. OF. *batailleor, -eur*, f. *bataillier*; in mod. Eng. f. BATTLE *v.*] One who fights; a fighter.

†**Ba·ttler**[2]. *rare.* 1650. [f. BATTLE *v.*[4]] **1.** One who beats with a bat or battledore -1720. **2.** A small bat for playing at ball. **3.** = BATLER.

Battleship (bæ·t'lʃip). 1884. Short for *line-of-battle ship* (1705): see BATTLE *sb.* phr.

Battology (bætǫ·lŏdʒi). 1603. [ad. Gr. βαττολογία, f. Βάττος- (see Herod. iv. 155) + -λογία.] A needless repetition in speaking or writing. Hence **Battolo·gical** *a.* **Batto·logist. Batto·logize** *v. trans.* and *intr.*

‖**Battue** (batü·). 1816. [F., pa. pple. fem. of *battre* used subst.] **1.** The driving of game from cover (by beating the bushes, etc.). **2.** *transf.* **a.** A thorough beat up or search. **b.** Wholesale slaughter, *esp.* of unresisting crowds.

‖**Batture** (‖batü·r, bătiū·ɪ). 1856. [a. F.] A river- or sea-bed elevated to the surface.

‖**Battuta** (battū·tă). 1819. [It.] *Mus.* The beating of time.

Batty (bæ·ti), *a.* 1590. [f. BAT *sb.*[1] + -Y[1].] **1.** Belonging to a bat. **2.** *slang.* Crazy 1922.

Batz (bæts). 1625. [Ger.; prob. taken as a pl., whence *bat* 17–18th c.] A small coin worth four kreuzers, formerly current in Switzerland and South Germany.

Baubee, -ie, vars. of BAWBEE.

Bauble (bǭ·b'l). ME. [From (1) OF. *babel*, also *baubel* 'child's toy', of uncertain etym. (2) ME. *babyll, babulle, bable*, conn. w. '*bablyn* to oscillate, *librillare*'.] †**1.** A stick with a mass of lead fixed or hung at one end, used for weighing, etc. -1570. †**2.** A child's toy -1814. **3.** A showy trinket, or gewgaw ME. **4.** The baton of the Court Fool or jester ME. **5.** *transf.* or *fig.* A foolish matter, or †person 1579; a paltry thing 1634.

3. Paltrie cap..a b. *Tam. Shr.* IV. iii. 82. 4. Such is a fole and well worthy a babyll 1509. That fooles bable, the Mace 1676. Hence †**Bau·bling** *a.* paltry.

Bauch, baugh (bāχ, bāχʷ, bāf), *a. Sc.* 1560. [perh. ON. *bagr* poor.] Weak, poor, pithless; sorry, shaky. ¶The north. Eng. dial. is *baff*, as in *baff week*, 'hard-up week'.

Bauchle, bachle (bā·χʷ'l). *Sc.* 1787. [?] **1.** An old shoe worn down at the heel. **2.** A shambler, a ne'er-do-well.

Baud(e, obs. f. BAWD. So †**Baudery**, bawdry.

Baudekin, baudkin (bǭ·dĭkin, bǭ·dkin). *Obs.* exc. *Hist.* ME. [a. OF.:—med.L. *baldakinus*, f. *Baldacco*, It. f. Bagdad.] = BALDACHIN I.

†**Bau·dery.** [a. F. *bauderie*, f. *baud*.] Gaiety, mirth. CHAUCER.

Baudrons (bǭ·drənz). *Sc.* 1450. [perh. Celt.; cf. Ir. *beadrac* frolicsome, etc.] Sc. name for the cat.

†**Bau·frey.** *rare.* 1639. [perh. = BELFRY.] A beam.

‖**Bauge** (bǭʒ). 1847. [mod. Fr.] A drugget made at Bauge in Burgundy.

Bauk, obs. f. BALK.

Bauld, dial. f. BOLD.

Baulk, var. of BALK, *esp.* in Billiards.

Bauson (bǭ·sən). *arch.* [ME. *bausen*, a. F., see next. But in Fr. never applied to the badger.] **1.** *sb.* A badger; see BADGER *sb.*[2] **b.** A fat or pertinacious person 1607. **2.** *adj.* = BAUSOND 1587.

Bau·sond, *a. Obs.* or *dial.* ME. [a. OF. *bausant*, also *bauchant*, and *bauzan*, etc., piebald; of doubtful etym. Cf. F. *balzan*.] Of animals: Having white spots on a black or bay ground; *esp.* (now) having a white patch on the forehead, or a white stripe down the face.

Bauxite. 1872. [F. (1821).] Var. BEAUXITE.

‖**Bavardage** (bavardā·ʒ). 1835. [F., f. *bavarder*, f. *bavard*, f. *bave* saliva.] Idle talk.

†**Ba·varoy.** 1714. [prob. ad. F. *bavarois*.] A surtout -1788.

Bavian, obs. f. BABION.

Bavin (bæ·vin), *sb.* 1528. [?] **1.** A bundle of brushwood, etc., bound with only one withe; in *Mil.* a fascine. **2.** Impure limestone. (? a different wd.) 1839.

1. *attrib.* **b. wits**, wits having a quick and short-lived blaze 1 *Hen. IV*, III. ii. 61. Hence †**Ba·vin** *v.* to bind up into bavins.

Bawbee (bǭbī·). *Sc.* 1542. [prob. from the name of a mint-master, the laird of *Sillebawby*; cf. ATCHISON, and perh. BODLE.] A Scotch coin of base silver, orig. three, later six, pennies of Scotch money, or a half-penny English; *hence*, a half-penny, a copper.

Bawble, obs. f. BAUBLE.

Bawcock (bǭ·kǫk). 1599. [a. F. *beau coq*, for *bewcock*.] Fine fellow, good fellow.

Good B. bate thy rage *Hen. V*, III. ii. 25.

Bawd (bǭd), *sb.*[1] ME. [Of uncertain origin. OF. *baud* 'bold, gay' differs in sense from *bawd* and is not found as a sb. Perh. an abbrev. of BAWDSTROT.] A procurer or procuress; since *c* 1700 only fem., and applied to a woman keeping a place of prostitution. Also *fig.* Hence **Baw·dily** *adv.* **Baw·diness**, †dirtiness; lewdness. **Baw·dship.** (Cf. *lordship*.)

†**Bawd**, *sb.*[2] *dial.* 1592. [? same wd. as *badde*, BAD *sb.*; cf. *puss*.] A hare.

†**Bawd**, *v.*[1] 1529. [f. BAWDY *a.*[1]] To dirty.

Bawd, *v.*[2] *arch.* or *Obs.* 1651. [f. BAWD *sb.*[1]] To pander; also *fig.*

Bawdry (bǭ·dri). *arch.* ME. [f. BAWD *sb.*[1] + -RY.] **1.** The practice of a bawd. †**2.** *gen.* Unchastity -1651. **3.** Lewdness in speech or writing; obscene talk, etc. 1589.

†**Bawdstrot.** ME. [OF. *baudetrot*, suggesting earlier OF. *baldestrot, baudestrot*, f. *bald, baud* 'bold, gay' (see BAUDE) + ? Teut. *strutt* STRUT.] A BAWD, male or female -1483.

†**Baw·dy**, *a.*[1] ME. [Etym. unkn. Cf. F. *boue*.] Soiled, dirty -1621. Hence †**Baw·dy** *v.* to make dirty.

Bawdy (bǭ·di), *a.*[2] 1513. [f. BAWD *sb.* + -Y.] **1.** Of, pertaining to, or befitting a bawd. (Usu. of language.) **2.** quasi-*sb.*, esp. in *To talk b.*: Lewd language, obscenity. *Comb.* **b.-house**, a brothel.

Bawhorse, obs. f. *bât-horse*: see BAT *sb.*[3]

Bawke. *dial.* 1880. [? var. of BACK *sb.*[2]] *Mining.* A bucket for raising coal.

Bawl (bǭl), *v.* 1556. [Prob. ad. med.L. *baulare* to bark as a dog. But cf. Icel. *baula*, Sw. *böla* to low like a cow.] †**1.** *intr.* To bark or howl as a dog -1753. **2.** *gen.* To shout protractedly at the top of one's voice; to bellow. Often with *out*. 1570. **3.** *trans.* To utter with bawling 1597.

1. At my blunte behauour barke ye or ball ye J. HEYWOOD. 3. To b. out, My Beloved; and the Words Grace! Regeneration! Sanctification! *Tatler* No. 66 ¶ 1. Hence **Bawl** *sb.* a loud prolonged rough cry. **Baw·ler**, one who bawls, *esp.* a preacher. **Baw·ling** *vbl. sb.*; *spec.* in *Hunting*, the giving tongue too loudly.

Bawn (bǭn). 1537. [ad. Ir. *bábhun*, of unkn. deriv.] A fortified enclosure; the fortified court or outwork of a castle.

1. Our Englishe men assauted the..baon of the castell 1537.

†**Baw·rel, baw·ret.** 1706. [?] The female and male of a kind of hawk. (Dicts.)

Bawsint, bawson, etc., var. BAUSON, -OND.

Ba·xter. *Obs.* exc. *dial.* [OE. *bæcestre*, fem. of *bæcere*, f. *bacan* to BAKE. A true fem.; but in later use only masc.] A baker: fem. ME.; masc. or fem. OE.

Bay (bēɪ), *sb.*[1] ME. [a. OF. *baie*:—L. *baca* berry.] †**1.** A berry, *esp.* that of the laurel or bay-tree -1866. **2.** Short for *Bay-tree* or *Bay Laurel* (*Laurus nobilis*), called also Sweet Bay; also applied to other laurels 1530. **b.** (Cf. BAY *sb.*[2] 3.) **3.** Usu. in *pl.* Leaves or sprigs of this tree, *esp.* as a wreath for a conqueror or poet; hence *fig.* the fame attained by these 1564.

2. I have seen the wicked in great power, spreading himself like a green bay tree *Ps.* xxxvii. 35. 3. A poet's garland made of bays GREENE. *Comb.* **b.-rum**, an aromatic liquid, obtained by distilling rum in which bay-leaves have been steeped.

Bay (bēɪ), *sb.*[2] ME. [a. F. *baie*:—late L. *baia*.] **1.** An indentation of the sea into the land with a wide opening. **2.** A recess in a range of hills, etc. 1853. **3.** in U.S.: **a.** An arm of a prairie extending into, and partly surrounded by, woods. **b.** A piece of marshy ground covered with Bay-trees 1848.

1. My affection hath an vnknowne bottome, like the B. of Portugall *A. Y. L.* IV. i. 211.

Comb.: **b.-duck**, (east Eng.) name of the Sheldrake; **-floe, -ice**, new-formed ice, such as first appears in sheltered water; **Bay-state**, pop. name (in U.S.) for the State of Massachusetts.

Bay (bēɪ), *sb.*[3] ME. [a. F. *baie*, OF. *baée* (L. type *badata*), f. *bayer* to gape.] **1.** An opening in a wall; *esp.* the space between two columns. **2.** 'The division of a barn or other building, generally from fifteen to twenty feet in breadth' (Gwilt). Of a house: The space lying under one gable, or between two party-walls. 1557. **3.** Applications of 'recess': e. g. *horse-bay*, the stall for a horse; *sick-bay*, part of the forepart of a ship's main-deck, used as a hospital 1582. **4.** = Applications of 'intervening space', as *bay* in plastering, of joists, of roofing 1823. **5.** An internal recess formed by causing a wall to project outwardly, for the reception of a window, etc.

Bay (bēɪ), *sb.*[4] ME. [In *to hold at b.*, a. OF. *bay*, It. *bada* suspense (f. late L. *badare*); in *to stand at b.*, aphet. f. ABAY, a. OF. *abai* barking. See BAY *v.*[1]] **1.** The deep prolonged barking of a dog when hunting 1530. **2.** *esp.* The chorus raised by hounds in conflict with the quarry; *hence*, the final conflict with the quarry ME. **3.** Used of the position of a hunted animal, when obliged to turn and defend itself: *To stand, be at, turn to, b.* ME.; also *fig.* **4.** Of the action of the hunted animal: *To hold or keep at (a) b.* (the hounds) 1532.

1. Dogs..all bristle and b. C. BRONTË. 3. To fight to the last and die at b. FROUDE. 4. By Riding..keep Death as it were at a B. 1711.

Bay (bēɪ), *sb.*[5] 1440. [?] †**1.** Obstacle. **2.** An embankment or dam 1581.

Bay (bēɪ), *sb.*[6] 1863. [short for *bay-antler*, earlier *be-* or *bes-antlier*, f. OF. *bes* second + ANTLER.] The second branch of a stag's horn.

Bay (bēɪ·), *sb.*[7] *Obs.* exc. *Hist.* 1581. [a. F. *baie* the colour BAY; see BAIZE.] Baize. Usu. in pl., whence BAIZE, q. v.

Bay (bēɪ), *a.* (and *sb.*) ME. [a. F. *bai*:—L. *badius*.] **1.** A reddish brown colour; used esp. of horses. **2.** as *sb.*, *ellipt.* for 'bay horse' 1535.

Bay (bēɪ), *v.*[1] ME. [a. OF. *bayer*, with deriv. *abayer* (see Littré s. v. *aboyer*); but influenced by BAY *sb.*[4]] **1.** To bark, prop. of a hound or mastiff. **2.** *fig.* (see quots.) ME. **3.** To assail with barking ME. Also *fig.* **4.** To utter by baying 1591. **5.** To pursue, or drive to bay, with barking 1590. **6.** To bring to bay, hold at bay 1575.

2. What moves Ajax thus to b. at him *Tr. & Cr.* II. iii. 99. 3. I had rather be a dog, and b. the moon Than such a Roman *Jul. C.* IV. iii. 27. 4. To b. a welcome KANE.

Bay (bēɪ), *v.*[2] 1649. [f. the sb. in 'at bay'; see BAY *sb.*[4]] **1.** *intr.* To turn to, stand at, bay. **2.** *trans.* To stand at bay against (*rare*) 1848.

Bay (bēɪ), *v.*[3] 1598. [conn. w. BAY *sb.*[5], ? as source or (prob.) as deriv.] To obstruct, dam (water).

‖**Bayadère** (bāyădē·r, -dīə·ɪ). 1598. [F., ad. Pg. *bailadeira*; cf. *bailar* to dance.] A Hindoo dancing girl.

The southern Bayadère, who differ considerably from the nâch girls of northern India HEBER.

Bayard (bēɪ·ăɪd), *a.* and *sb.*[1] *arch.* ME. [a. OF. *baiard*, f. *bai*; see BAY *a.*[1]] **1.** Bay-coloured; *absol.* a bay horse. **2.** Name of the bay-coloured magic horse given by Charlemagne to Rinaldo; *whence* **a.** Mock-heroic for any horse ME. **b.** Taken as the type of blindness, or blind recklessness ME. 3. *Hence*: A self-confident ignoramus 1529.

2. Who is so blind as Bold Bayarde 1609. 3. Being a b., who never had the soul to know, what conversing means MILT. Hence †**Bay·ardism**, ignorant presumption. †**Bay·ardly** *a.* bayard-like (sense 3).

†**Bay·ard**, *sb.*[2] 1642. [a. F. *bayard*, in same sense.] A hand-barrow used for heavy loads.

Bayberry (bē¹·beri). 1578. [f. BAY *sb.*[1] 2.] 1. The fruit of the bay-tree. 2. In U.S., the fruit of the Wax-myrtle (*Myrica cerifera*); also, the plant 1860. 3. In Jamaica, the fruit of the Bayberry Tree, *Eugenia acris*, a species of Pimento 1756.

Bayed (bēd), *ppl. a.* 1848. [f. BAY *sb.*[3] + -ED.] Having a bay, formed as a bay or recess.

Bayness (bē·nės). 1570. [f. BAY *a.*[1] + -NESS.] The quality of being bay-coloured.

Bayonet (bē·ŏnet). 1692. [a. F. *baïonnette*, ? f. *Bayonne*, as first made or used there; or dim. of OF. *bayon*, *baion* shaft of a cross-bow.] †‖1. A short flat dagger –1707. 2. A stabbing instrument of steel for fixing to the muzzle of a musket or rifle. See also *Sword-bayonet*. 1704. b. *abst.* Military force 1774. 3. *pl.* Soldiers armed with bayonets 1780. 4. *Mech.* A pin which plays in and out of a hole, and serves to engage and disengage portions of machinery, a clutch 1798.

2. Under the rule of the b. 1879. 3. On the demand of 40,000 Irish bayonets BURKE. *Comb.*, etc.: *Spanish Bayonet*, a species of Yucca, found in N. America; **b.-clutch**, a clutch with two prongs for engaging and disengaging machinery; **-joint**, one in which the two parts cannot be separated by a simple longitudinal movement 1812. Hence **Bay·oneted** *ppl. a.* armed or fitted with a b.

Bayonet (bē·ŏnet), *v.* 1700. [f. prec. sb.] 1. To stab with a bayonet. 2. To drive or coerce at or as at the point of the bayonet 1790.

2. To sabre and to b. us into a submission BURKE.

Bayou (bəi·ū). 1766. Also **bayeau**, **bio**. [Amer.-F., ad. Choctaw *bayuk*.] In southern U.S., a stream or channel with little current, often forming an inlet or outlet to a river or lake.

Bay-salt (bē·sǫlt). 1465. [prob. f. BAY *sb.*[2]] Salt, obtained in large crystals by slow evaporation; orig., from sea-water by the sun's heat.

Bay-window (bē·wi·ndoᵘ). ME. [f. BAY *sb.*[3]] A window forming a bay in a room, and projecting outwards from the wall; often called a *bow*-window.

Baywood (bē·wud). 1869. Mahogany from the Bay of Campeachy.

Bayz, var. of BAIZE.

Bazaar, bazar (băzā·ɹ). 1599. [Ult. a. Pers. *bāzār* market.] 1. An Oriental market-place or market, usually consisting of ranges of shops or stalls. 2. A fancy fair for the sale of useful and ornamental articles, usually in behalf of a charitable or religious object 1816.

2. *Soho Bazaar* 1816. A b. is the clergyman's.. ultimate hope 1876.

Bdellatomy (delæ·tŏmi). 1868. [f. Gr. βδέλλα + -τομία.] *Med.* The practice of cutting leeches to empty them of blood while still sucking.

‖**Bdellium** (de·liŏm). ME. [a. L., ad. Gr. βδέλλιον; used in Gr. versions later than the LXX as tr. Heb. *b'dōlakh*, rendered in *Gen.* by ἄνθραξ 'carbuncle', in *Num.* by κρύσταλλος 'crystal', and explained by the Rabbins as 'pearl, pearls'.] 1. Name of several trees or shrubs of the N.O. *Amyridaceæ*, chiefly of the genus *Balsamodendron*, yielding a gum-resin resembling impure myrrh. 2. The gum-resin itself 1585. 3. As tr., in the Eng. Bible, of Heb. *b'dōlakh*; see above ME.

3. Ther is foundun bdelyum and the stoon onychyrus WYCLIF *Gen.* ii. 12. Cf. *Num.* xi. 7.

Bdellometer (delǫ·mĭtəɹ). 1839. [ad. F. *bdellomètre*, f. Gr. βδέλλα + μέτρον.] *Med.* An instrument proposed as a substitute for leeches, and showing the amount of blood drawn.

Be (bī), *v.* [OE. *béon*, f. stem **beu-**.

An irreg. and defective vb., the full conjugation of which is made up of the surviving inflexions of three vbs., viz. (1) the original Aryan subst. vb. with stem **es-**, Skr. *as-*, Gr. ἐσ-, etc.; (2) the vb. with stem **wes-**, Skr. *vas-* to remain; (3) the stem **beu-**, Skr. *bhu-*, Gr. φυ-, L. *fu-*, OE. *béon* to become. Of the stem *es-*, OE. possessed only the present tenses, all the other parts being supplied from the stem *wes-*, pa. t. *wæs*. *Beon*, *be*, meaning to 'become, come to be', at first served merely as a future tense to the vb. *am-was*, thus constituted, but as parts of *am-was* became obs., it took their place, and now it gives its name to the whole verb *am-was-be*. In OE. the pres. Indic. of *am* had two pl. forms, (1) *sind*, *sindon*, and (2) *earon*, *aron*. Of these *sind*, *-on* was replaced in southern Eng. bef. 1250 by *beth*, *ben*, *be*; while *aron*, *aren*, *are* survived in the north, and spread south, till early in 16th c. *are* appeared in standard Eng. *Be* was in concurrent use till the end of the century (see Shaks., and Bible of 1611), and still occurs as an archaism. But the regular mod. Eng. pl. is *are*.

For the history of the inflexions see N.E.D. s.v.]

1. To have place in the realm of fact, to exist; *also*, to live. 2. To come into existence, come about, happen, take place OE. 3. To be the case or the fact, *esp.* in *So be*, *Be it that* = suppose that ME. 4. To continue, remain ME. 5. With adv. or prepositional phrase: stating *where* or *how*, i. e. in what place or state a thing is. [=Sp., Pg. *estar* as dist. from *ser*.] OE. 6. To belong, pertain, befall: with *dat.* or *to* = have. Now only in exclams. or wishes (with *be* often omitted). ME. 7. With adj., sb., or adjective phrase; acting as simple copula: stating *of what sort* or *what* a thing is. a. To exist as the subject of some predicate OE. b. To exist as the thing known by a certain name; to be identical with OE. c. To signify, amount to, mean ME. d. *ellipt.* To be good for, 'stand'. *Obs.* or *dial.* 1749. 8. With pples. and infins., serving as an auxiliary and forming periphrastic tenses. a. With *pa. pple.*: in *trans. vbs.*, forming the passive voice OE.; in *intr. vbs.*, forming perfect tenses (now largely displaced by *have*) OE. b. With the present pple.: with *active* signification OE.; with *passive* signification, as 'our house was building' (= mod. 'was being built') 1551. c. With the dat. infin., making a future of appointment or arrangement; hence of necessity, obligation, or duty (now replaced by *have*) ME. (The same constr. is used in the sense 'to be proper or fit (to)'.)

1. Troy is no more DRYDEN. God is, nay alone is CARLYLE. 2. When is it to be (*mod.*). 3. And be it indeed that I haue erred *Job* xix. 4. 4. Phr. *Let be* (arch.): leave as it is; leave off; *Sc.* omit. Ile.. not be all day neither *All's Well* II. i. 94. Don't be long (*mod.*). 5. Your book is here (*mod.*). There is a cow in the garden (*mod.*). I had been to see Irving (*mod.*). To be off; to be in debt, at one's ease (*mod.*). Is your father well *Gen.* xliii. 27. 6. O well is the, happie art thou COVERDALE *Ps.* cxxvii. 2. Success (be) to your efforts (*mod.*). 7. a. Then are they glad *Ps.* cviii. 30. b. My selfe am Naples *Temp.* I. ii. 434. c. Is it nothing to you, all ye that passe by *Lam.* i. 12. I'le tell you what it is, you must leave (*mod.*). 8. a. Mony ben calle(d ME. They are rested in their batayls LD. BERNERS. b. Leat vs be trudgeing 1562. c. Uneasy.. about their being to go back again DE FOE. †*To be to seek*: to have to seek. They are not to compare with these (*mod.*).

Phrases. *I were better* (*best, as good*), orig. *me were better* = it were better for me. Now *had better* is used, after *had rather*, etc. Cf. HAVE, RATHER. *He came here Monday was a week*, i. e. he came here on the Monday a week before Monday last. Here the phrase became a mere adjectival clause. *Was* is now generally omitted: I was in town Monday (was) three weeks. *To be about to*: see ABOUT. *What one would be at*: what one aims at. *To be for*: a. to be bound for; b. to be on the side of; c. to desire (*dial.*).

Be-, *prefix*:—OE. *be-*, weak form of the prep. and adv. *bī-* (*big*) BY. The original meaning was 'about', weakened in preps. and advs. into *at* or *near*. Still (*esp.* in senses 2, 6, 7) a living element.

1. Forming derivative vbs., with sense of 'around': a. on all sides, as in BESET, BESMEAR, etc.; b. from side to side (within a space), in or through all its parts, thoroughly, as in BESTIR, *bejumble*, etc. 2. Forming intensive vbs., with sense of 'thoroughly, soundly, conspicuously, to excess, ridiculously', as in *bemuzzle*, *bewidow*, etc. 3. Forming derivative vbs. with privative meaning 'off, away', as in BEDEAL, BEREAVE. 4. Making vbs. trans., by adding a prepositional relation: primarily 'about', whence *against*, *at*, *for*, *to*, *on*, *upon*, *over*, as in BESPEAK, speak about (or for, to), BEMOAN, moan about (or over), etc. 5. Forming trans. vbs. on adjs. and sbs., taken as complements of the predicate, meaning To make: as BEFOUL, BEDIM, BEFOOL, BESOT. In mod. use, nearly all contemptuous. b. To style, dub, etc., as in *bemadam*, *be-Roscius*, etc. 6. Forming trans. vbs. on sbs. used in an instrumental relation; the primary idea being: a. To surround, cover, or bedaub with, as in BECLOUD, BEDEW. Thence b. To affect in any way, as in BENIGHT, BEGUILE, BEFRIEND. In both sets there is often the notion of 'thoroughly, to excess'. c. In sense of 'bereave of', as in BEHEAD, BELIMB, etc. (No longer in living use.) 7. Forming ppl. adjs., which unite the prec. senses, esp. 6 and 2, in the notion of 'covered or furnished with', usu. in an overdone way. In mod. use (e. g. with Carlyle) *be-* is often merely rhet., expressing depreciation, raillery, etc.; cf. *booted* and *bebooted*, etc. This is now the most freq. use of *be-*.

Beach (bītʃ), *sb.* 1535. [?] 1. (Usu. *collect.*, formerly occas. with *pl.*): The water-worn pebbles of the sea-shore; shingle. 2. The shore of the sea, the strand; *spec.* the part lying between high- and low-water-mark. (This is prob. Shakspere's sense.) Also *transf.* In *Geol.* An ancient sea-margin. 1596.

1. Rowling pebble stones, which those that dwell neere the sea do call Bayche GERARD. 3. The Pibbles on the hungry b. *Cor.* v. iii. 58.

Comb.: **b.-comber**, a long wave rolling in from the ocean (U. S.); also, a settler on the Pacific islands, living by pearl-fishery, etc., or loafing about wharves and beaches (whence *beach-combing* ppl. a.); **-grass**, a reedy grass (*Arundo arenaria*) growing on the seashore; **-man**, one who earns his living on the b.; **-master**, an officer in charge of the disembarkation of troops; **-wagon**, a light open wagon, with two or more seats. Hence **Bea·chless** *a.* **Bea·chy** *a.* covered with shingle.

Beach (bītʃ), *v.*[1] 1840. [f. prec. sb.] *trans.* To haul or run up on the beach.

†**Beach**, *v.*[2] 1571. [? aphet. f. ABECHE, a. OF. *abechier*, f. *à* + *bec*.] To give a beakful to (a young bird); hence *spec.* in *Falconry*, to give a little as a whet to appetite.

Beached (bī·tʃėd, bītʃt), *a.* and *pple.* 1590. [f. BEACH *sb.* and *v.*] 1. Having a beach; in early use, Covered with shingle. 2. Driven or dragged up on the beach (*mod.*).

1. The b. margent of the sea *Mids. N.* II. i. 82.

Beacon (bī·kən), *sb.* [OE. *béacn* (neut.):—OTeut. **baukno(m)*. Only Teut.] †1. A sign, a portent. †2. An ensign –1483. 3. A signal; *spec.* a signal-fire ME. 4. Hence *gen.* A signal station, watch-tower 1611. 5. A conspicuous hill, on which beacons were (or might be) lighted; *e. g.* Dunkery B. on Exmoor, etc. 1597. †b. A division of a wapentake; prob. a district or bound to furnish a beacon 1641. 6. Any conspicuous object, as a lighthouse, etc., placed upon the coast or at sea, to warn or direct ME. Also *fig.*

4. Therefore was the name of it called.. Mizpah [*marg.* that is a b. or watchtower] *Gen.* xxxi. 49. 6. Modest Doubt is cal'd The B. of the wise SHAKS.

Beacon (bī·kən), *v.* 1644. [f. prec. sb.] †1. *trans.* *To beacon up*: to kindle as a beacon –1651. 2. To light up, as a beacon-fire does 1803. Also *fig.* 3. To furnish, or mark the position of, with a beacon or beacons. Occas. with *off*, *out*. 1821. 4. *intr.* To shine like a beacon 1821.

2. To b. the dale with midnight fires SCOTT. 3. To b. out a boundary 1883. 4. The soul of Adonais, like a star, Beacons from the abode where the Eternal are SHELLEY. Hence **Bea·coned** *ppl. a.* furnished with a beacon.

Beaconage (bī·kənėdʒ). 1607. [f. as prec. + -AGE.] a. Toll paid for the maintenance of beacons. b. A system of beacons.

Bead (bīd), *sb.* [ME. *bede*, pl. *bedes*, *beden*, aphetic f. *ibed*, OE. *ȝebed* prayer (f. root of BID *v.* B).] †1. Prayer; *pl.* devotions –1554. 2. One of a string of small perforated balls forming the *rosary* or *paternoster*, used for keeping count of the number of prayers said ME. 3. Hence: A small perforated body, of glass, amber, metal, wood, etc., used as an ornament ME. b. In *pl.* (†occas. in *sing.*) A string of beads for the neck 1500. 4. *transf.* a. A drop of liquid or of molten metal 1596. b. A bubble of foam; *spec.* the foam or head upon certain beverages 1753. c. The small knob which forms the front sight of a gun 1841. d. A string of sponges 1885. 5. *Archit.* a. A small globular ornament, usu. applied in a row like a string of beads. b. A narrow moulding of semi-circular section.

1. *To bid a b.*: to offer a prayer. Also *To say one's beads*. 2. *To tell* or *count one's beads*: to say one's prayers. 3. *fig.* You minimus.. You b., you acorne *Mids. N.* III. ii. 329. 4. a. Beds of sweate 1 *Hen. IV*, II. iii. 61. The b. of impure silver 1854. b. Swimming about among the foam-beads below KINGSLEY. c. *To draw a b. upon*: to take aim at (U. S.).

Phrase. *Baily's beads*: a phenomenon observed in total eclipses of the sun, in which, before the beginning and after the end of complete obscuration, the sun's crescent appears as a band of brilliant points, resembling a string of beads.

Comb. I. (f. sense 2, mostly arch., and now often spelt *bede*): **b.-folk**, people (often pensioners) who pray for a benefactor; **-house** (Welsh *Bettws*), *orig.* a house of prayer, *hence* an alms-house, in which prayers are to be offered for the soul of the founder; **-woman** (cf. *b.-folk*). **II. -proof** *a.* (of alcoholic spirits), such that a crown of bubbles (see 4 b) formed by shaking will stand for some time (a fallacious test of strength); **-sedge**, the Bur-reed (*Sparganium ramosum*); **-snake**, a small American snake (*Elaps fulvus*); **-stone**, one used as a bead, or of which beads are made; **-tree**, the AZEDARAC. Hence **Bea·ded** *ppl. a.* worked with beads; edged with bead-like protuberances; furnished with or wearing beads; formed into or like beads; covered with bubbles. **Bea·der**, a tool used in silver chasing to make a b. pattern. **Bea·diness**, beady quality. **Bea·ding**, the formation of beads; bead-work, in trimming, etc.; a bead moulding, etc.; a preparation used to make liquor form beads. **Bea·dy** *a.* beadlike; (of eyes) small, round and glittering; covered with beads (of sweat, etc.); frothy; *Archit.* having a b. moulding.

Bead (bīd), *v.* 1577. [f. prec.] **1.** To furnish with beads, a bead, or beading. **2.** *intr.* To form into a bead or beads 1873. **3.** To string like beads; also *fig.* 1883.

1. Dew, which beaded the webs of the spiders 1856.

†**Bea·d-hook.** [? f. OE. *beadu* war.] A kind of boat-hook. CHAPMAN.

Beadle (bī·d'l), *sb.* [orig. OE. *bydel*:—OTeut. **budilo-z*, deriv. of *biudan*, in OE. *béodan* to offer, announce, command. In ME. superseded by the Fr. form *bedel*. The arch. forms *beadel, bedel, bedell* are in use in spec. senses.] †**1.** One who makes a proclamation –1644; the crier of a law-court; a town-crier –1691. **2.** A messenger or under-officer of justice OE. **3.** An apparitor or precursor; **a.** *spec.* in the Eng. Universities (conventionally spelt *bedel, -ell*), the name of certain officials, with duties which are now chiefly processional ME.; **b.** the apparitor of a trades guild ME. **4.** An inferior parish officer appointed to keep order in church, punish petty offenders, give notices of vestry meetings, etc. etc. 1594.

4. The unlucky boys with toys and balls were whipped away by a b. STEELE. Hence **Bea·dledom**, stupid officiousness. **Bea·dlehood, Bea·dleism**, the state or dignity of a b. †**Bea·dlery, Bea·dleship**, the office or jurisdiction of a b.

Bead-roll (bī·dˌrōul). 1500. [f. BEAD *sb.* + ROLL *sb.*] **1.** *orig.* A list of persons to be specially prayed for (*arch.*). **2.** *transf.* A string of names; a catalogue; a pedigree; a long series 1529. **3.** A rosary 1598.

2. Dan Chaucer.. On fames eternall b. worthie to be fyled SPENSER *F. Q.* IV. ii. 32.

Beadsman (bī·dzmæn). [ME. *beodeman*, f. BEAD *sb.*[1]: with *beadsman* cf. *townsman*, etc.] **1.** *lit.* A man of prayer; one who prays for the soul of another. **2.** One paid or endowed to pray for others; a pensioner bound to pray for the souls of his benefactors 1528. Hence, later: **a.** An inmate of an almshouse; **b.** in Scotland: A licensed beggar 1788. **3.** A petitioner (*arch.*) 1600. †**4.** = the mod. 'humble servant'. (Cf. 'your petitioners will ever pray'.) –1645.

1. His friend and bedesman, Abbot Eadwine FREEMAN. 2. The very Beads-men learn to bend their Bowes *Rich. II*, III. ii. 116.

Beagle (bī·g'l). 1475. [? f. F. *bégueule*, f. *béer* to gape + *gueule*.] **1.** The smallest English hound, used for hare hunting when the field follows on foot. **2.** *fig.* A spy or informer; a constable 1559. Hence **Bea·gling** *vbl. sb.* 1889.

1. A physiological peculiarity.. enables the B. to track its prey by the scent HUXLEY.

Beak (bīk), *sb.* ME. [a. F. *bec*, of Gaulish origin. The lengthened vowel originated in the pl. *bekes, beekes, beaks*.] **1.** The horny termination of the jaws of a bird, consisting of two pointed mandibles; a bird's bill. **2.** The (often horny) extremities of the mandibles of other animals; *e.g.* the turtle, octopus, etc. 1822. †**3.** The snout of quadrupeds –1607. **4.** The elongated head, proboscis, or sucker mouth of certain insects; *e.g.* the weevil, cochineal 1658. **5.** *joc.* The human nose 1854. **6.** *transf.* A beak-shaped projection; a peak 1440. **7.** The projection at the prow of ancient vessels, *esp.* of war galleys; *now* = BEAK-HEAD 1550. **8. a.** A prolongation of the shell of a univalve beyond the aperture, containing the canal. **b.** The projecting apex or *umbo* of each valve, in a bivalve 1851. **9.** *Bot.* A sharp projecting process, as in the seeds of Crane's-bill, etc. 1820. **10.** The spout of a retort, still, etc. 1641. **11.** *spec.* **a.** in *Forging* (see BEAK-IRON). **b.** in *Carpentry*, the crooked end of a holdfast. **c.** in *Gas-fitting*, a gas-burner with a circular hole $^1/_{28}$ of an inch in diameter 1676. **12.** *Archit.* A little pendent fillet left on the edge of the larmier, forming a canal behind to prevent the water from running down the lower bed of the cornice 1734. Hence **Bea·kful**, as much as can be held in a bird's b. **Bea·kless** *a.* **Bea·ky** *a.* furnished with a b.

Beak (bīk), *sb.*[2] *slang.* 1845. [?] A magistrate.

Beak (bīk), *v.* ME. [a. OF. *bequer*, f. *bec* BEAK *sb.*[1]] **1.** *trans.* To strike or seize with the beak; to push the beak into. Also *intr.*; occas. *fig.* **2.** *intr.* To project with or as with a beak (*rare*) ME.

Beaked (bīkt), *ppl. a.* 1572. [f. BEAK *sb.*[1]] **1.** Furnished with a beak 1589. **2.** *spec.* **a.** in *Her.* used when the beak of the fowl is of a different tincture from the body 1572. **b.** in *Bot.* Rostrate 1841. **3.** Pointed or hooked 1590.

2. Three herons arg...b. and legged or BOUTELL. 3. Each b. promontory MILT. *Lycidas* 94.

Beaker (bī·kəɹ). [ME. *biker*, ad. ON. *bikarr*:—OTeut. type **bikarjo-(m)*, ? a. L. *bicarium*, referred by Diez to Gr. *βῖκος*, drinking-bowl. Sc. *bicker*. The Eng. form is assim. to BEAK.] **1.** A large drinking vessel with a wide mouth, a goblet. (Now literary.) **b.** The contents of a beaker 1819. **2.** An open-mouthed glass vessel, with a lip for pouring, used in scientific experiments 1877.

1. Stimulated by .beakers of Badminton DISRAELI.

Beak-head (bī·kˌhed). 1580. [f. BEAK *sb.*[1]] **1.** *Naval Arch.* **a.** = BEAK 7. **b.** A small platform at the fore part of the upper deck. **c.** The part of a ship in front of the forecastle, fastened to the stem, and supported by the main knee. **2.** *Archit.* An ornament shaped like a bird's beak used in Norman mouldings 1849.

Bea·k-iron. 1667. [corrupt f. BICKERN (= F. *bigorne*, It. *bicornia*, an anvil with two pointed ends), altered by pop. etym.] The pike of a blacksmith's anvil.

†**Beal**, *sb.*[1] ME. [var. of BOIL *sb.*] A pustule –1783.

‖**Beal** (bēl, bīēl), *sb.*[2] [Gael. *béul* mouth.] The mouth of a river or valley. SCOTT.

Beal, *v.* Now *Sc.* or *dial.* 1611. [f. BEAL *sb.*[1]] To gather, suppurate.

Be-all (bī·ǫl), *sb. phr.* 1605. That which constitutes the whole. *Macb.* I. vii. 5.

Beam (bīm), *sb.* [Com. Teut.: OE. *béam* 'tree', 'plank' = Ger. *baum*:—West Ger. **baumo-z*. The original meaning and the connexion of sense 15 are doubtful.] †**1.** A tree; only in OE., exc. in HORNBEAM, etc. †**2.** The roodtree or cross. (Cf. *Acts* v. 30.) –1720. **3.** A large piece of squared timber, long in proportion to its breadth and thickness; *orig.* the squared timber of a whole tree. The current sense. OE. Also *fig.* (see *Matt.* vii. 3). **4.** The wooden cylinder in a loom, on which the warp is wound before weaving; also called *fore-b.* The similar roller on which the cloth is wound as it is woven; also called *back-b.* OE. **5.** The great timber of the plough, to which all the other parts of the plough-tail are fixed OE. **6.** The transverse bar of a balance, from the ends of which the scales are suspended; also, the balance. Often *fig.* ME. †**7.** The pole of a chariot –1697. †**8.** A large bar of metal –1613. **9.** The shank of an anchor. **10.** In the steam-engine, etc.: A heavy iron lever, having a reciprocating motion on a central axis, one end of which is connected with the piston rod from which it receives motion, and the other with the crank or wheel-shaft; also called *working-* and *walking-beam* 1758. **11.** The main trunk of a stag's horn which bears the antlers 1575. **12.** *Naut.* One of the horizontal transverse timbers holding a ship together 1627. **13.** *Hence*, The greatest breadth of a ship 1627. **14.** Hence designating the side of a vessel or sideward direction 1628. **15.** A ray or pencil of light; also *fig.* OE. **b.** In full *wireless b.*, wireless waves sent as a beam, i.e. undispersed, by reflection from a parabolic mirror 1924.

3. A rush will be a beame To hang thee on *John* IV. iii. 129. 4. The shaft of his speer was as the beem of websters WYCLIF 1 *Sam.* xvii. 7. 6. Deceivable and untrue Beams and Scales 1503. *The common b.*, the *King's b.* (*Hist.*): the public standard balance kept by the Grocers' Company of London. *To kick* or *strike the b.*: (of one scale of a balance) to be greatly outweighed. 14. *Lee* or *weather b.*: the side away from *or* towards the wind. *On the* (*starboard or larboard*) *b.*: at some distance on the (right *or* left) side of a ship, at right angles to the keel. *Abaft* or *before the b.*: behind *or* before an imaginary line drawn across the centre of the ship. *B. sea*: one rolling against the ship's side. **B.-ends**, the ends of a ship's beams. *To be*, or *be laid, on the b.-ends*: to have them touching the water, so that the vessel is in danger of capsizing; *fig.* to be utterly at a loss, hard up. 15. How farre that little candell throwes his beams *Merch. V.* v. i. 90. A B. of truth 1674, of comfort 1742.

Comb.: **b.-bird** (*dial.*), the Spotted Flycatcher; **-centre**, the central pin on which the b. of a steam-engine works; **-compass**, an instrument consisting of a b. with sliding sockets, for drawing large circles; **-line**, that which shows the junction of the upper sides of the beams with the ship's sides; **-trawl** *v.* to fish with a trawl-net kept open by a b.

Hence **Beamed** *ppl. a.* having a horn of the fourth year, as a stag. **Bea·mer**, one who works with a b. **Bea·mful** *a.* luminous. **Bea·mily** *adv.* radiantly. **Bea·miness**, radiance. **Bea·mish** *a. arch.* shining brightly. **Bea·mless** *a.* without beams; also *fig.* **Bea·mlet**, a little b.; var. †**Bea·mling.**

Beam (bīm), *v.* ME. [?:—OE. *béamian*, f. BEAM *sb.*] **1.** *trans.* To throw out or radiate (beams of light); to emit in rays. Also *fig.* **2.** *intr.* To shine radiantly (*lit.* and *fig.*) 1640. **3.** To stretch (cloth) over a beam; to use a beam in *Tanning* 1605. **4.** To smile radiantly 1893.

1. The genial Sun.. Beams forth ungentle influences SHENSTONE. 2. Her.. countenance beamed with smiles W. IRVING. Hence **Bea·ming** *vbl. sb.* radiance; the use of a beam. **Bea·mingly** *adv.*

Bea·m-tree. 1800. [Short f. *Whitebeam* (tree), so called from the white under-surface of its leaves.] A tree (*Pyrus Aria*) related to the Apple, Pear, and Wild Service.

Beamy (bī·mi), *a.* ME. [f. BEAM *sb.* + -Y [1].] **1.** Emitting beams of light; radiant. **2.** Massive as a (weaver's) beam 1698. **3.** Antlered 1697. **4.** Of a ship: Broad in the beam 1882.

1. B. eyes SHELLEY. 2. Lords of the biting axe and b. spear HEBER. 3. B. stags DRYDEN.

Bean (bīn). [Com. Teut.: OE. *béan* (fem.) = Ger. *bohne*:—OTeut. **baunâ* (str. fem.).] **1.** A smooth, kidney-shaped, laterally flattened seed, borne in long pods by a leguminous plant, *Faba vulgaris*. **2.** The plant that bears this seed OE. **3.** The plant and seed of the allied genus *Phaseolus*, including the French, Kidney, or Haricot Bean (*P. vulgaris*), and Scarlet Runner (*P. multiflorus*) 1548. **4.** Name of the seeds of other plants resembling the common bean ME. **5.** Any object like a bean in shape; e.g. small coals 1561. **6.** In literary and proverbial uses (see quots.) ME.

1. Beanes.. are harde of digestion, and make troblesum dreames TURNER. 3. *Navy b.*: the dried haricot. *Pea b.*: a small variety of it. 4. **Egyptian or Pythagorean B.**, the seed of the Lotus (*Nelumbium speciosum*); **B. of St. Ignatius**, seed of *Strychnos amara*. See also COFFEE 3, TONKA 1. 6. No rich man.. dredeth God The worth of a b. ME. To convey each man his b. or ballot into the box MILT. Alwaie the bygger eateth the beane 1562. 7. *slang.* (A piece of) money; *not a b.*, no money whatever 1903.

Slang phrases. *To be full of beans*, to be full of energy and in high spirits (cf. BEANY *a.*). *To give* (a person) *beans*, to deal severely with, punish heavily; so *to get beans*. *Old b.*: familiar form of address.

Comb.: **b.-brush**, the stubble of beans; **-caper**, Eng. name of the S. Afr. genus *Zygophyllum*, plants with flower-buds used as capers; **-crake**, the corn-crake; **-dolphin**, the aphis of the bean; **-fly**, a pale purple insect, found on beans; **-goose**, a goose (*Anser segetum*), so called from the aspect of its bill; **-mouse**, the Long-tailed Field-mouse; **-pole, -stick**, *fig.* a lanky fellow; **-stalk**, the stem of the b.-plant; **-straw**, the dried stems of the b.-plant; **-tree**, a name of various trees bearing podded seeds, as the carob, laburnum, catalpa, etc.; **-trefoil**, a bushy shrub, *Anagyris fœtida*: also, the laburnum; **-vine**, *Phaseolus diversifolius*.

Hence **Bea·ny** *a. slang*, spirited, fresh.

Bea·n-feast. 1806. [From *beans* being a prominent dish.] An annual dinner given by employers to their work-people. Hence **Bea·no** (*slang*, orig. Printers' abbrev.), also, a merry time or spree.

Bear (bēəɹ), *sb.*[1] [OE. *bera* = Ger. *bär*:—OTeut. **beron-*. Connected by Fick with L. *ferus*.] **1.** A heavily-built, thick-furred plantigrade quadruped, of the genus *Ursus*, belonging to the *Carnivora*, but having teeth partly adapted to a vegetable diet.

The best-known species are the Brown Bear of Europe (*U. arctos*), the White or Polar B. (*U. maritimus*), the Grizzly B. (*U. horribilis* or *ferox*), and Black B. (*U. Americanus*) of N. America, and the Syrian B. (*U. Syriacus*), mentioned in the Bible. There are fossil remains of larger species.

2. *fig.* A rough, unmannerly, or uncouth person 1579. **3.** *Astr.* Name of two constellations, the 'Great Bear' and 'Lesser Bear' ME. **4.** In New South Wales, the *Phaseolarctos*, a Marsupial animal, called by the natives *Koala* or 'Biter' 1847. **5. Sea-bear:** a species of seal 1847. **6.** A rough mat for wiping boots on; a block covered with shaggy matting for scrubbing decks 1795. **7.** A machine for punching holes 1869. **8.** *Stock Exchange.* A speculator for a fall; *i.e.* one who sells stock for future delivery expecting that meanwhile prices will fall. *Formerly,* The stock so contracted to be delivered. 1709.

1. You must not sell the skin till you have shot the b. 1858. 2. *To play the b.*: to behave rudely and roughly. 8. *To sell a B.*, to sell what one hath not BAILEY.

Comb.: **bear('s)-breech**, Brank-ursine; **b.-dog**, one used in hunting or baiting bears; **bear's-ear**, the AURICULA; **b.-garden**, a place set apart for the baiting of bears, etc., *fig.* a scene of strife and tumult; **bear's-garlic**, *Allium Ursinum* or Ramsons; **-grease**, the fat of the b., used esp. in cosmetic preparations; **b.-hound** (= *-dog*); **-leader**, a travelling tutor, cf. sense 2; **-play**, rough tumultuous behaviour; **-warden** = BEARWARD.

Hence **Bea·rish** *a.* b.-like; rough; surly; *Stock Exchange*, belonging or tending to a fall in prices. **Bea·rish-ly** *adv.*, **-ness. Bea·r-like** *a.* and *adv.* after the manner of a b.

Bear (bīᵊɹ), *sb.*² [OE. *bere* (masc.):—OTeut. **bariz* (neut.).] Barley: the orig. Eng. name, retained only in the north; hence *spec.* the six- (or four-) rowed variety (*Hordeum hexastichon* or *tetrastichon*), till lately chiefly grown there.

Bear (bēᵊɹ, bīᵊɹ), *sb.*³ *Obs.* or *dial.* [ME. *bere*, cogn. w. LG. *büre*, mod.Ger. *bühre*.] A case for a pillow.

Bear (bēᵊɹ), *v.*¹ *str.* Pa. t. **bore.** Pa. pple. **borne** (bōᵊɹn), **born** (bǭɹn). [Com. Teut. and Aryan: OE. *beran* :—OTeut. stem *ber-* = L. *fer-*, Gr. φερ-, Skr. *bhar-*. The pa. t. was in OE. *bær, bǣron*, whence (ult.) *bare*, the literary form. *Bore* was not general till after 1600; the A. V. has only *bare*.]

I. 1. To support and remove; to carry; now restricted in prose to the carrying of something weighty. Also *fig.* **2.** *refl.* To carry oneself; behave, acquit oneself ME. **3.** To carry about with or upon one, to wear; to have OE. **4.** To wield (power, sway, etc.); to hold (an office) ME. **5.** *fig.* To entertain (a feeling) ME.

1. Boren aboute wiþ windis WYCLIF. Borne senseless from the lists SCOTT. *fig.* To b. tale or tidynges HULOET. Phr. *To b. in mind. To b. witness, record, testimony. To b. away, off*: to carry off as a winner. *To b. out*: to back up, confirm. *To b. (any one) company, a hand*: to bring, give, lend it. †*To b. in hand*: to maintain (a statement); to pretend (*Cymb.* v. v. 43); to delude (*Much Ado* IV. i. 305). †*To b. it*: to carry the day. 3. Apt to b. arms G. FERRERS. To b. a fair face 1550, seven per Cent. Interest 1710, a firm front SOUTHEY, a very high rental ROGERS. 5. One beryth malyce agayn another STARKEY.

II. 1. *trans.* To sustain, support (a weight or strain) OE. Also *absol.* or *intr.* Also *fig.* (Formerly also *b. out.*) **2.** To sustain successfully; *fig.* to stand (a test, etc.); to admit of 1523. Also †*intr.* (for *refl.*) **3.** To sustain (anything painful or trying); to endure; to tolerate OE. **4.** To hold (*up*), to support, keep *up* ME. †**5.** *trans.* To uphold (any one in a course of action). Also *refl.* and *intr.* –1697. **6.** To hold up, hold on top or aloft ME. **7.** To have written or inscribed upon it 1503. **8.** *fig.* To purport (*that*) (*arch.*) ME.

1. Proportionate.. to the stress it was likely to b. SMEATON. *fig.* There shall no poore neighbour.. bere no losse MORE. Phr. *To b. a part*: to take a part in. 2. To b. criticism DRYDEN, ornament RUSKIN. 3. The wrongs I b. from Atreus' son POPE. This Railer is not to be born 1704. I cannot b. antimacassars (*mod.*). Phr. *To b. hard, or heavily* (L. *ægre ferre*): to endure with a grudge. *To b. with*: to put up with. 4. *To b. a rein up*: to hold in check by means of a bearing rein. A manly voice.. Bare burthen to the music well SCOTT. 5. Phr. *To b. up*: to uphold (a principle); to keep up the spirits of (a person); also *intr.* (for refl.). 7. A Pillar.. bare this inscription, *Sacred to Diana* STANLEY. To b. an effigy 1853.

III. 1. *trans.* To move onward by pressure; to push, force, drive; *esp.* in phr. *To b. down*: to overthrow, vanquish ME. **2.** *intr.* To press (laterally) *on*, to come with force against (*arch.*) 1450. **3.** Transferred to downward pressure; with *down, on* 1674. **4.** *intr.* To exert or transmit pressure *upon, on, against*; to rest *upon*; also, to thrust (as an arch against its piers) 1677. **5.** To tend to affect; to have reference to, touch 1672. **6.** To thrust, pierce *through* –1485. **7.** *intr.* To press; to move with effort or with persistence in some direction. Also with *back, away, on, down*, etc. 1593. **8.** To extend in a particular direction 1601. **9.** Chiefly *Naut.*: To lie off in a certain direction from a given point. (Cf. BEARING.) 1594. **10.** Of cannon: To lie so as to cover 1692.

1. Borne backward Talbot turns SOUTHEY. His.. zeal bore down all opposition MACAULAY. 5. To point out how the argument bears on the general question PALEY. Phr. *To bring to b.*: to cause to act (*against, upon*, etc.). *To b. in*, pass. *to be borne in*: to be forced in *upon* (the mind). 7. Stand backe; roome, beare backe *Jul. C.* III. ii. 172. B. a little to the right (*mod.*). Phr. *Naut. To b. away*: to sail away. *To b. down* (*upon* or *towards*): to sail with the wind (towards). *To b. off*: to sail so as to keep clear (of land, etc.). *To b. up*: to put the helm up so as to put the ship before the wind. *To b. up for* (a place): to sail towards. *To b. down upon*: to proceed (*esp.* with force) against. 8. Possession Bay bore due west SIR J. ROSS. 9. Our after-guns ceased to b. NELSON.

IV. 1. To bring forth, produce, yield OE. Also *absol.* **2.** To give birth to OE. Also *absol.*

¶ Since *c* 1775 the pa. pple. *born* is used only in sense IV. 2, and there only in the pass., when not followed by *by* and the mother. In all other cases *borne* is used.

1. The Oakes beare Mast *Timon* IV. iii. 422. India, black Ebon and white Ivory bears DRYDEN. *absol.* An apple that bears well (*mod.*). 2. Sarray non childre ne bar ME.

Bear (bēᵊɹ), *v.*² 1842. [f. BEAR *sb.*¹] *intr.* To speculate for a fall on the Stock Exchange. *trans.* To produce a fall in the price of (stocks, shares, or commodities).

Bearable (bēᵊ·răb'l), *a.* 1550. [f. BEAR *v.*¹ + -ABLE.] That may be borne; endurable. Hence **Bea·rableness. Bea·rably** *adv.*

Bea·rance. 1725. [f. BEAR *v.*¹ + -ANCE.] **1.** Endurance (*arch.*). **2.** A bearing (in mechanism) 1834.

Bea·r-baiting, *vbl. sb.* 1475. [f. BEAR *sb.*¹] The sport of setting dogs to attack a bear chained to a stake; also *fig.*

An old way of Recreating, Which learned Butchers call Bear-Baiting BUTLER.

Bearberry (bēᵊ·ɹberi). 1625. [f. BEAR *sb.*¹] **a.** A procumbent shrub, *Arctostaphylos Uva-ursi* (Family *Ericaceæ*), bearing astringent berries; also *A. alpina* (Black Bearberry). **b.** (occas. The Arbutus. †**c.** (erron.) = BARBERRY.

Bearbine, -bind (bēᵊ·ɹbəin). 1732. [f. OE. *bere* BEAR *sb.*² + *bindan*.] **a.** The Lesser Field Convolvulus; **b.** the hedge convolvulus; **c.** a species of Polygonum (*P. Convolvulus*).

Beard (bīᵊɹd), *sb.* [Com. Teut.: OE. *beard* = Ger. *bart* :—OTeut. **bardo-z* (not known in Gothic). Kinship to L. *barba* is doubtful.] **1.** The hair that grows upon the chin, lips, and adjacent parts of a man's face; now usu. excluding the moustache. **2.** The similar growth on the face of other animals; *e.g.* the goat, lion, etc. ME. **3.** *Zool.* **a.** The appendages to the mouth of some fishes. **b.** The rows of gills in some bivalves, *e.g.* the Oyster. **c.** The byssus of certain shell-fish, *e.g.* the *Pinna*. **d.** Two small processes situated above the antlia of moths and butterflies; the similar part in some *Diptera*, *e.g.* the Gnat. 1753. **4.** *Ornith.* **a.** The bristles at the base of the beak in the Barbet (*Bucco*), etc. **b.** The vane of a feather. 1802. **5.** Specific name of: The freshwater Shrimp, the Hake, and a kind of pigeon 1611. **6.** *Bot.* The awn of grasses; prickles, bristles, or hair-like tufts found on plants; also quasi-*fig.* 1552. †**7.** The barb of an arrow, fish-hook, etc. –1793. **8.** *Printing.* **a.** That part of the type above and below the face, which allows for ascending and descending letters. **b.** The horizontal bases and tops added to the letters. 1823. **9.** *Obs.* or *dial.* The brim or margin of a vessel. [f. ON. *barð*.] ME.

1. †*In spite of or maugre any one's b.*: in defiance of his purpose. *To one's b.*: to one's face, openly. *Comb.* **b.-grass**, the genus of grasses *Polypogon*; **-moss**, a British lichen (*Usnea barbata*); **-tree**, the Hazel. Hence **Bea·rdless** *a.* without a b.; *fig.* immature. **Bea·rdlessness. Bea·rdlet**, a tiny awn. **Bea·rdy** *a.* bearded.

Beard (bīᵊɹd), *v.* ME. [f. prec. sb.] †**1.** To become bearded –1672. **2.** *trans.* To cut or strip off the beard of (*e.g.* oysters) ME. **3.** To oppose openly and resolutely; to set at defiance, thwart, affront. [Partly from the idea of taking a lion by the beard.] 1525. **4.** To furnish with a beard ME.

3. To b. the lion in his rage SMOLLETT.

Bearded (bīᵊ·ɹdėd), *ppl. a.* ME. [f. BEARD *sb.* or *v.*] **1.** Having a beard; *spec.* in B. Eagle, Tit, Titmouse, etc. 1530. Also *transf.* **2.** Of a comet, etc.: Having a train (*arch.* or *poet.*)

Beardie (bīᵊ·ɹdi). 1828. [f. BEARD *sb.*] Chiefly *Sc.* The Loach (*Cobitis barbatula*).

Bearer (bēᵊ·rəɹ). ME. [f. BEAR *v.*¹ + -ER ¹.] **1.** *gen.* He who or that which bears, carries, or brings; a carrier, messenger, etc. **b.** One who helps to carry a corpse to the grave; a pall-bearer 1633. **c.** In India: A palanquin-bearer 1766; also, a body-servant 1811. **2.** The actual holder or presenter of a cheque, draft, or order to pay money 1683. **3.** *Her.* One who bears heraldic arms 1610. **4.** The possessor or holder of rank, office, or of any personal quality 1597. **5.** That in, or by means of, which anything is carried; *e.g.* a bier 1847. **6.** He who or that which supports or sustains 1483; *spec.* in *Printing*, a kind of packing used to lessen the pressure of the types 1846. **7.** She who, or that which, brings forth or produces; *spec.* a fruit-yielding tree. ME.

1. Bearers of burdens 2 *Chron.* ii. 18. In behalf of this young man, the b. PEPYS. 7. The Tree is a great Bearer 1719.

†**Bea·rherd.** 1589. [f. BEAR *sb.*¹ + HERD.] The keeper of a bear, who leads him about for exhibition –1860. vars. **Bearard, Berard, Beareheard, Berrord** (all in Shaks.).

Bearing (bēᵊ·riŋ), *vbl. sb.* ME. [f. BEAR *v.*¹ + -ING ¹.] **1.** (f. BEAR *v.*¹ I.) The action of the vb. **2.** The carrying of oneself (with reference to the manner); deportment; demeanour ME. **3.** *Her.* A single charge or device 1562. †**4.** (f. BEAR *v.*¹ II.) Upholding –1552. **5.** Supporting, endurance 1526. **6.** A material support; a supporting surface; supporting power ME. **7.** *Carpentry.* The length of a beam between two supports, span 1677. **8.** (f. BEAR *v.*¹ III.) A straining in any direction; thrust, pressure 1591. **9.** Tendency to exert influence; aspect 1785. **10.** *Mech.* (usu. in *pl.*) Those parts of a machine which bear the friction; the block or supports on which a shaft or axle turns, and also the part of the shaft or axle resting on these supports 1791. **11.** The direction in which any point lies from a point of reference, *esp.* as measured in degrees from a quarter of the compass. In *pl.* the relative positions of surrounding objects. 1635. **12.** The direction of any line on the earth's surface in relation to a meridian 1802. **13.** *Naut.* The widest part of a vessel below the plank-shear 1627. **14.** (f. BEAR *v.*¹ IV.) The action of bringing forth; birth. Also in comb. *child-bearing*. ME. **15.** The action of producing leaves, flowers, and *esp.* fruit 1583. **16.** A crop 1838.

1. The b. of Armes 1598, a grudge (*mod.*). 2. His b. towards women 1873. 5. Insolent beyond b. 1815. 9. The legal bearings of the case 1867. 11. Phr. *To take one's bearings*: to determine one's position with reference to surrounding objects; also *fig.* 16. Rich mellow bearings WORDSW.

Comb.: †**b.-cloth**, a child's christening robe; **-door** (*Coal-Mining*), one of the main doors for ventilation.

Bearing (bēᵊ·riŋ), *ppl. a.* ME. [f. BEAR *v.*¹] **1.** That bears (see the vb.) 1500. †**2.** Of food: Sustaining –1633. **3.** Bringing forth ME.

Comb. **b.-rein**, a short fixed rein which passes from the bit to the saddle, and keeps the horse's head up and its neck arched; also *fig.*

†**Bea·rleap, -lep(e.** ME. [f. ME. *beren* + LEAP basket.] A carrying basket –1677.

Bear's-foot. 1551. [f. BEAR *sb.*¹] *Herb.* **1.** Pop. name of species of Hellebore, *esp.* of the Black Hellebore (*H. fœtidus*). **2.** Also of Bear's-breech or Acanthus, of Lady's Mantle, and of Monkshood 1552.

Bearskin (bēᵊ·ɹ,skin). 1677. [f. as prec.] **1.** The skin of a bear used as a wrap or garment.

Also *fig.* 2. The tall cap worn by the Guards in the British Army 1863. 3. A shaggy woollen cloth used for overcoats. 4. See BEAR *sb.*[1] 8.

4. *Bearskin jobber*, early name of the 'bear' on the Stock Exchange (prob. in allusion to the proverb 'To sell the bear's skin before one has caught the bear').

Bearward (bēᵊ·ɹwǭɹd). ME. [f. as prec.] 1. The keeper of a bear, who leads it about for exhibition; also *fig.* †2. The constellation Bootes, or its chief star Arcturus, just behind *Ursa Major* -1577.

Beast (bīst), *sb.* ME. [a. OF. *beste* :—L. *bestia.*] 1. A living being, an animal. (Used as tr. Gr. ζῷον, or L. *animal.*) 2. A quadruped, as dist. from man, and also from birds, reptiles, fishes, etc. (The current literary use.) ME. 3. A domesticated animal, used as part of the farm stock or cattle [F. *bestiaux, bétail*] ME. b. An animal used in riding, driving, etc.; a draught animal ME. 4. *fig.* A human being swayed by animal propensities ME. 5. A brutal, savage, irrational man. (Now expressive of disgust, or merely aversion.) ME. 6. In *Card-playing.* [orig. *beste* as in 17th c. Fr. Mod.F. *bête.*] An obs. game, resembling *Nap.* b. A penalty at this game; also at Ombre and Quadrille. -1751.

1. Þe nedder..was mast wis of ani best ME. 2. Beasts, Birds, Fishes, and Insects RAY. *Wild b.*: an animal not domesticated, formerly esp. a beast of the chase, now esp. a ferocious animal from abroad. b. *The Beast*: Antichrist (*Rev.* xiii. 18). 3. *Luke* x. 34. 5. Also of things. Phr. *a beast of*..a beastly 1862.

Comb. **b.-fly**, the gad-fly. Hence **Bea·sthood**, the rank, condition, or nature of beasts. **Bea·stie** (orig. *Sc.*), an endearing form of BEAST. **Bea·stily** [as if f. *beasty* adj.] *adv.* bestially SHELLEY. †**Bea·stish** *a.* = BEASTLY. †**Bea·stlihead** = BEASTHOOD, BEASTLINESS (Spenser). **Bea·stlike** *a.* and *adv.*

Beast (bīst), *v.* 1646. [f. prec. sb.] See also BASTE *v.*[4] †1. To treat as a beast. 2. *pass.* To fail to win at Ombre, or to incur a forfeit 1653.

Beastliness (bī·stlinės). ME. [f. BEASTLY + -NESS.] Beastly quality; resemblance to a beast; *concr.* = 'beastly stuff'.

Beastlings, var. of BEESTINGS.

Beastly (bī·stli), *a.* ME. [f. BEAST + LY[1].] †1. Of the nature of a BEAST (sense 1) -1526. 2. Of the nature of a BEAST (sense 2) (*arch.*) ME. †3. Brutish, irrational -1703. 4. Like a beast in conduct ME. 5. Abominable; disgusting, or offensive, *esp.* from dirtiness 1603.

2. See more of this b. fable BEDWELL. 4. The b. vice of drinking to excess SWIFT. 5. That b. hole, London MISS BROUGHTON.

Beastly, *adv.* ME. [f. as prec. + -LY[1].] †1. In a beastly manner -1652. 2. Added to an adj.: Abominably, offensively. (In society slang, often merely = Exceedingly.) 1561.

Beat (bīt), *v.*[1] *str.* & *wk.* Pa. t. **beat** (bīt). Pa. pple. **beaten** (bī·t'n), **beat.** [Com. Teut.; OE. *bēatan* :—OTeut. **bautan*, not found in Gothic.] I. 1. To strike with repeated blows. 2. *intr.* To strike repeated blows (*on, at*) ME. 3. Said of the action of the feet upon the ground in walking, etc. Often *fig.* OE. 4. To punish by beating; to thrash OE. †5. To batter, bombard -1664. 6. Of physical agents: To dash against, strike violently, assail (*poet.*) OE. Also *intr.* with *on, upon, against*; also *absol.* OE. †7. Said of the impact of sounds -1677. †8. To hammer at (a subject), to thresh out; to discuss, reason about -1659. †9. *intr.* To insist with iteration *on* or *upon* -1633. 10. To overcome, to conquer in any contest, *at* doing anything; to master, to excel. (Cf. *thrash.*) 1611. Also *absol.* †11. To strike *together* the eyelids (= BAT), or the teeth; also *intr.* -1617. 12. To flap (the wings) *with force*; also *intr.* (*absol.*) ME. 13. *intr.* Of the heart: To strike against the breast; *hence*, to throb, pulsate. (Said also of the pulse, etc. and *fig.* of passions.) ME. 14. *intr.* Hence a. Of a watch, etc. b. *Mus.* To sound in pulsations; see BEAT *sb.*[1] 4. 1614.

1. *To b. the breast*: i. e. in sign of grief. *To b. the air, the wind*: to fight to no purpose or against no opposition. 3. *To b. the streets*: to walk up and down. *To b. a path* or *track*: to tread it hard or bare by frequent passage; *hence*, to open up a way. 6. The Sunne beat vpon the head of Ionah *Jonah* iv. 8. 10. 'This beats me altogether', mused the lawyer J. PAYN. You may *b.* the Latine *into their heads* 1612.

II. 1. *trans.* To force or impel (a thing) by striking, hammering, etc. 1607. Also *fig.* 2. To drive by blows (a person) *away, off, from, into,* etc. ME. 3. To break, crush, or overthrow by hard knocks; to batter 1570. †4. = ABATE, or BATE. Now only in *b. down.* -1785. 5. *Naut.* (*intr.*) To strive or make way against wind or current 1677. Said *trans.* of the ship or of the mariners. 6. *Venery.* (*intr.*) a. To run hither and thither. b. To take to the water, and go up stream; also *trans.* 1470. 7. To affect the state or condition of by beating: a. to hammer, forge ME.; b. to pound, pulverize ME.; to mix; to make into a batter; to switch or whip (an egg, etc.). Also with *up.* 1486. 8. To strike (cover) in order to rouse or drive game; to scour (a wood) in hunting ME. Also *intr.* or *absol.* Also *fig.* esp. with *about.* 1709. 9. Of a drum: a. *intr.* = To sound when beaten 1656; b. *trans.* To express by its sound when beaten 1636; c. *intr.* = To be beaten 1816.

1. *fig. To b.* (a thing) *into one's head, mind,* etc. 2. He's beat from his best ward *Wint. T.* I. ii. 33. 5. *To b. about*: to tack against the wind. 7. *To b. a carpet* (mod.). They shall beate their swords into plough-shares *Isa.* ii. 4. 8. To b. the jungle BAKER. fig. *To b. about the bush*: *lit.*, as in I. 12; *fig.* to make a cautious or roundabout approach. *To b. up* (*for*) *recruits, to beat up the town for recruits,* etc. *To b. up the quarters of*: to visit unceremoniously (*colloq.*). 9. The Drums beat to Arms 1758. The drums of Limerick beat a parley MACAULAY. Before the assembly beats THACKERAY. Phr. *To b. time*: to mark musical time by beating a drum, by tapping, by striking the air with a baton, etc.; also *fig.* to keep time with.

Comb. With adverbs. **B. about**: (see II. 5). **B. away**: a. *intr.* to go on beating; b. *trans.* to drive away by blows. **B. back**: a. to force back by beating; b. to drive back by force; c. to cause to rebound. **B. down**: a. to drive downward by beating; b. to break down by heavy blows; c. *fig.* to overthrow (an institution, opinion, etc.); d. to force down by haggling (cf. II. 4); e. *intr.* to come down with violence, like rain, the sun's rays, etc.; f. (see II. 4); g. to reduce by beating. **B. in**: a. to knock in by beating; b. to drive in by force; c. to smash or batter in by blows; d. to inculcate; e. (see II. 4). **B. off**: a. to drive away from by blows, attacks, etc.; b. (see II. 4). **B. on**: (see I. 2). **B. out**: a. to trace out a path by treading it first (cf. II. 3); b. to knock or force or shape out by beating; c. to drive out by force or fighting; d. to hammer out into a bulge, to extend by hammering; e. to thresh (corn); f. to hammer out, or get to the bottom of (a matter, laboriously); g. (in U. S.) to exhaust; h. to measure out by beats. **B. up**: a. to tread up by much trampling; b. to bring to equal consistency by beating; c. *to b. up quarters,* etc. (see II. 8).

Phrases. *To b. the bounds*; to trace out the boundaries of a parish, striking certain points with rods, etc.

Beat (bīt, bēit), *v.*[2] 1534. [conn. w. BEAT *sb.*[3], q.v.] To slice off the rough sod from uncultivated or fallow ground: cf. BEAT *sb.*[3]

Beat (bīt), *sb.*[1] 1615. [f. BEAT *v.*] I. A stroke or blow. 2. *Fencing.* A particular blow struck upon the adversary's sword or foil 1753. 3. A stroke upon a drum, the striking of a drum with the sound produced; the signal thus given; also in *drum-b.* Occas. *fig.* 1672. 4. The movement of the hand or baton, by which the rhythm of a piece of music is indicated; also, the different divisions of a bar or measure with respect to their relative accent 1880. 5. A recurring stroke; a measured sequence of strokes or blows, or sounds thereby produced 1795. 6. A throbbing or undulating effect taking place in rapid succession when two notes not quite of the same pitch are sounded together 1733. 7. *Mus.* Name given to a melodic grace or ornament of uncertain identity 1803. 8. The round of a watchman, etc. on duty. [prob. f. BEAT *v.*[1] I. 3.] 1825. 9. A tract ranged over in pursuit of game 1875. 10. In sailing: One of the transverse courses in beating to windward 1880. 11. *Physics* and *Wireless Telegr.* Each of the pulsations of amplitude produced when two oscillations of different frequencies occur simultaneously in the same system 1918.

5. Phr. *In* or *out of b.*, *off the b.*: making a regular or irregular succession of strokes. 11. *Comb.*: **b.-note,** a note whose frequency equals the difference in the frequencies of two oscillators.

Beat (bīt, *dial.* bet), *sb.*[2] 1450. [? f. BEAT *v.* = 'a quantity to be beaten at once'. Cf. *stack,* etc.] A bundle of flax or hemp made up ready for steeping.

Beat (bīt, bēit), *sb.*[3] [In Devonsh. *bait, bate, beat,* pronounced (bēt). But historically *beat(e* is the proper form. See BEAT *v.*[2]] The rough sod of moorland, or the matted growth of fallow-land, which is sliced off and burned before plowing the land.

Comb. **b.-ax** (in Devonsh. *dial.* bidax, bidix), the ax or adze used in paring off b.

Beat (bīt), *ppl. a.* ME. Short f. BEATEN; as *adj.*: Overcome by hard work or difficulty; common in *dead-b.* (*lit.* and *fig.*)

Beaten (bī·t'n), *ppl. a.* ME. Used adjectively in many senses of BEAT *v.*, q.v. 1. Trodden, hard, bare, or plain. Often *fig.* 1477. †2. Trite -1756. †3. Inured *to* -1700. 4. Worked by hammering ME.; whence, pure gold being most malleable: Fine, of pure quality; also *fig.* 1535. 4. Conquered 1562. 5. Exhausted 1681. 6. Scoured for game (*mod.*).

Beater (bī·təɹ). 1483. [f. BEAT *v.* + -ER[1].] 1. A person who beats (see BEAT *v.*); *spec.* a man employed in rousing and driving game 1825. 2. An instrument for beating; used in many specific senses 1611.

Beath (bīð), *v.* Still *dial.* [OE. *beðian* to foment :—OTeut. **baþian*; see BATH.] 1. To foment. 2. To heat unseasoned wood in order to straighten it 1496.

Beatific, -al (bīˌăti·fik, -ăl), *a.* 1605. [ad. L. *beatificus* (f. *beatus*), + -AL[1].] Making blessed; imparting supreme happiness.

Beatific vision: a sight of the glories of heaven. Hence **Beati·fically** *adv.*

Beatification (biˌæ:tifikē·ʃən). 1502. [a. F., f. L. *beatificat-*, *beatificare.*] 1. The action of making, or the being made, blessed. 2. *R. C. Ch.* An act of the Pope, declaring a deceased person to be in the enjoyment of heavenly bliss, and granting a form of worship to him (the first step towards canonization) 1626.

Beatify (bīˌæ·tifəi), *v.* 1535. [a. F. *béatifier*, ad. L. *beatificare.*] 1. To make supremely happy or blessed. 2. To declare supremely blessed 1677. 3. *R. C. Ch.* To pronounce to be in enjoyment of heavenly bliss; see BEATIFICATION 2. 1629.

2. To b. wealth BARROW. var. **Beati·ficate.**

Beating (bī·tiŋ), *vbl. sb.* ME. [f. BEAT *v.*] 1. The infliction of repeated blows; *spec.* punishment by blows; the dashing of waves against the shore; the flapping of wings; rousing of game, etc. 2. A defeat in a contest (*mod.*). 3. *Naut.* Sailing against the wind (*mod.*). 4. A pulsating or throbbing movement 1601.

5. The b. of a watch 1801, of the heart HUXLEY.

Beatitude (bīˌæ·titiūd). 1491. [a. F., ad. L. *beatitudo*, f. *beatus.*] 1. Supreme blessedness or happiness. 2. An ascription of special blessedness; *esp.* (in *pl.*) those pronounced by Christ in the Sermon on the Mount 1526. 3. = BEATIFICATION 2. (*lit.* and *fig.*) 1837.

Beau (bōᵘ), *a.* and *sb.* ME. [a. late OF. *beau, biau*, earlier *bel* :—L. *bellus.* The adj., in ME. quite naturalized, and pronounced as in *beauty, Beaulieu* (biū·li), is now obs. The sb. is a reintroduction from mod. F., whence its pronunc.] †A. *adj.* 1. Beautiful. 2. Used in addressing relations, friends, etc.: = 'fair' (fair sir), 'dear' (dear sir), etc. -1513.

B. *sb.* Pl. **beaux, beaus** (bōᵘz). 1. A man who attends excessively to dress, mien, and social etiquette: a fop, a dandy 1687. 2. The attendant or suitor of a lady 1720.

1. You're a perfect Woman, nothing but a b. will please you T. BROWN. Hence **Beau** *v.* to act the b. to. **Beau·ish** *a.* after the manner of a b.; dandified.

†**Beauclerk** (bōᵘ·klāɹk). ME. [a. F. *beau* + *clerc* :—L. *clericus*; see CLERK.] A scholar. (Surname of Henry I.) -1856.

Beaufet, Beaufin; see BUFFET, BIFFIN.

‖**Beau garçon** (bo garsoṅ). 1665. [F.] An exquisite, a fop.

Beau-ideal (bōᵘ·əidī·ăl). 1801. [a. F. *beau idéal* the ideal Beautiful. In Eng. *ideal* tends to be taken as the sb.] †1. The Beautiful, or beauty, in its ideal perfection -1801. 2. That type of beauty or excellence in which one's ideal is realized, the perfect type or model 1820.

‖**Beau-monde** (bo·mōṅ·d, bōᵘˌmǫ·nd). 1714. [a. F.] The fashionable world, society.

†**Beau·pe·re.** ME. [f. OF. *beau + père*, or in

sense 2 *per, peer* (mod. *pair*) equal. See BEAU. In OF. used politely of every one whom one called 'father'; but about 16th c. distinctive for 'father-in-law' or 'step-father'. See also BEL.] **1.** A term of courtesy, used *esp.* to or of an eccles. 'Father' -1599. **2.** Good fellow, fellow, companion -1610.

†**Beau·pers, bewpers.** 1592. [? f. *Beaupreau*, a town of France.] A fabric, app. linen; used for flags -1720.

Beau-pot (bōu·pǫt). 1761. [? erron. sp. of BOUGH-POT.] A vase for cut flowers.

†**Beausire.** ME. [a. F. *beau sire*; see BEAU, BEAUPERE.] Fair sir, a form of address -1513.

Beauteous (biū·tĭəs), *a.* 1440. [f. *beaute*, BEAUTY *sb.* Cf. *plenteous*.] Distinguished by beauty, beautiful. (*Literary*.)

England is beauteuous..flour of londes all aboute CAXTON. Hence **Beau·teous-ly** *adv.*, **-ness.**

Beautification (biū·tifikēi·ʃən). 1640. [f. BEAUTIFY.] The action of beautifying; embellishment.

Beautiful (biū·tiful), *a.* 1526. [f. BEAUTY *sb.* Occ. comp. with *-er, -est*, usu. with *more, most.*] **A.** Full of beauty, possessing the qualities which constitute beauty; pleasing to the senses or intellect. Used colloq. of anything that a person likes very much, *e.g.* a b. ride.

Beautifull for situation, the ioy of the whole earth is mount Sion *Ps.* xlviii. 2. B. weather HAWTHORNE. A b. operation in surgery (*mod.*).

B. quasi-*sb.* **1.** = Beautiful one 1535. **2.** That which is beautiful. *The beautiful*: beauty in the abstract.

Hence **Beau·tiful-ly** *adv.*, **-ness.**

Beautify (biū·tifəi), *v.* 1526. [f. as prec. + -FY.] To render, or grow, beautiful.

To beautifie the house of God HIERON. Hence **Beau·tifier.**

Beauty (biū·ti). [ME. *bealte, beute*, a. OF. *bealte, beaute*, earlier *beltet*, mod. *beauté*:—late L. **bellitatem*, f. *bellus*.] **1.** That quality or combination of qualities which affords keen pleasure to the senses, *esp.* that of sight, or which charms the intellectual or moral faculties. **2.** The abstract quality personified 1667. **3.** A beautiful person or thing; *esp.* a beautiful woman. (Often ironical.) 1483. **b.** *collectively*, The beautiful women, etc. 1611. **4.** A beautiful feature or trait; an ornament, grace 1563.

1. Beauties ensigne yet Is Crymson in thy lips *Rom. & Jul.* v. iii. 94. We ascribe b. to that which is simple; which has no superfluous parts; which exactly answers its end EMERSON. **2.** Such a lord is Love, And B. such a mistress of the world TENNYSON. **3.** A celebrated B. ADDISON. **b.** The b. of Israel is slaine vpon thy high places 2 *Sam.* i. 19. **4.** The concealed beauties of a writer ADDISON.

Comb.: with reference to face massage, etc., as *b. doctor, parlour* (orig. *U.S.*), *specialist*; **b.-sleep**, the sleep secured before midnight; **-spot**, (*a*) a patch placed on a lady's face to heighten its beauty 1657; (*b*) a locality conspicuous for its beauty 1919.

Hence **Beau·tiless** *a.* void of b.

Beau·ty, *v. arch.* ME. [f. prec. sb.] To render beautiful.

Beauxite (bōu·zəit). 1868. [f. *Beaux* or *Baux* in France.] *Min.* A hydrous oxide of alumina and iron, used as a source of aluminium.

Beaver[1] (bī·vəɹ). [Com. Aryan: OE. *beofor*, earlier *befor* (= *bevor*):—OTeut. **bebru-z*:—OAryan **bhebhrú-s*, reduplicated deriv. of *bhru-* brown.] **1.** An amphibious rodent, with a broad, oval, flat, scaly tail, palmated hind feet, coat of soft fur, and hard incisor teeth with which it cuts down trees; remarkable for its skill in constructing huts for its habitation, and dams for preserving its supply of water. **2.** The fur of the beaver ME. Also *fig.* and *attrib.* **3.** A hat made of beaver's fur, or some imitation of it 1528. **4.** A felted cloth, used for overcoats, etc. 1756. **5.** A kind of glove 1816.

3. Mr. Holden sent me a bever, which cost me £4 5*s*. PEPYS. *In beaver* (Univ. slang): in a tall hat, etc., not in cap and gown.

Comb.: **b.-rat**, the musquash or MUSK-RAT; **-stones**, the two small sacs in the groin of the b., from which the substance 'castor' is obtained. Hence **Bea·vered** *ppl. a.* wearing a b. (hat). **Bea·vertee·n**, a cotton twilled cloth, in which the warp is drawn up into loops, forming a pile, which is left uncut; cf. *velveteen*. **Bea·very**, a place in which beavers are kept.

Beaver[2] (bī·vəɹ). *Obs.* exc. *Hist.* [ME. *baviere*, a. OF. *bavière*, orig. a child's bib, f. *bave* saliva.] The lower portion of the face-guard of a helmet, when worn with a visor; but occas. serving the purposes of both. Also *fig.*

Then saw you not his face? O yes, my Lord, he wore his b. up *Haml.* I. ii. 230.

†**Beba·r**, *v.* ME. [See BE- 1.] To bar about; to debar -1649.

‖**Bebeeru, bibiru** (bĭbī·ᵊrū). 1851. [native name.] The Greenheart Tree of Guiana (*Nectandra Rodiæi* or *leucantha*). **Bebee·ria, Bebee·rine**, also **beber-, bibir-**, an alkaloid resembling quinine, yielded by this tree.

Beblee·d, *v. arch.* ME. [See BE-.] To cover with blood, make bloody.

Beble·ss, *v.* 1598. [f. BE- 2.] To bless profusely.

Bebli·ster, *v.* 1575. [f. BE- 1.] To blister badly.

Bebloo·d, *v.* 1580. = BEBLEED.

†**Beblo·t**, *v.* ME. [f. BE- 2.] To blot all over; also *fig.* -1580.

Beblu·bbered, *ppl. a.* 1583. [See BE-.] Befouled with tears; also †with blood.

Becall (bĭkǭ·l), *v.* ME. [See BE- 4.] †**1.** To challenge -1500. **2.** To call names 1683.

Becalm (bĭkā·m), *v.* 1559. [See BE- 2.] **1.** To make calm; to quiet; *fig.* to assuage, tranquillize 1613. **2.** *Naut.* To shelter from, or deprive (a ship) of, wind; usu. in pass. 1595.

1. What power becalms the innavigable seas POPE. **2.** The fleet was becalmed off the Godwin Sands MACAULAY.

Because (bĭkǭ·z, -kǫ·z), *adv.* and *conj.* ME. [f. BY *prep.* + CAUSE *sb.* Orig. a phrase, often followed by a subord. clause introduced by *that* or *why*. *That* was at length omitted. *For* was occas. prefixed in nearly all constructions.] **A.** *adv.* **1.** Followed by *that* or *why*: For the reason that (*arch.*). **2.** Followed by *of* and subst.: **a.** By reason *of*, on account *of* ME. †**b.** For the sake *of*, for the purpose *of* -1523. †**3.** Followed by *to* with inf. = In order *to* -1546.

B. *conj.* [from A. 1.] **1.** For the reason that; inasmuch as, since ME. **2.** In order that, so that, that. (Common *dial.*) 1485.

1. We wonder we are ignorant and we fear b. we are weak BUCKLE.

‖**Be:ccabu·nga.** 1706. [med.L., f. Ger. *bachbunge*, f. *bach* brook + *bunge*:—OHG. *bungo* bulb.] *Bot.* The BROOKLIME, q.v.

‖**Beccaccia** (bekka·ttʃa). [It.] A woodcock. BROWNING.

‖**Beccafico** (bekkăfī·ko). 1621. [It.; lit. 'fig-pecker'.] A small migratory bird of the genus *Sylvia*, much esteemed as a dainty in the autumn, when it has fattened on figs and grapes.

†**Becco.** 1604. [a. It. *becco* a goat.] A cuckold -1623.

‖**Bechamel** (be·ʃămel). 1796. [f. the Marquis de *Béchamel*, steward of Louis XIV.] *Cookery.* A fine white sauce thickened with cream.

Bechance (bĭ₁tʃa·ns), *v.* 1527. [See BE-.] **1.** *intr.* To happen, chance. **2.** (with dat. obj.) To befall (a person) 1530.

1. All happinesse b. to thee in Millaine SHAKS.

†**Becha·nce**, *adv.* 1548. [f. BY *prep.*] By chance -1570.

Becharm (bĭ₁tʃā·ɹm), *v.* ME. [See BE-.] To hold by a charm.

‖**Bêche-de-mer** (bę̄ʃ də mę̄r). 1814. [Quasi-Fr. of Eng. origin, alteration of Pg. *bicho do mar* 'sea worm'.] The Trepang.

Bechic (be·kik, bī·kik). 1661. [ad. F. *béchique*, ad. L. *bechicus*, a. Gr., f. βήξ.] **A.** *adj.* Tending to cure or relieve a cough 1678. **B.** *sb.* [sc. *medicine*.] 1661.

Beck (bek), *sb.*[1] ME. [a. ON. *bekk-r*:—OTeut. **bakki-z* masc.; cogn. with **baki-z*, whence OE. *bęce* masc. Only Teut.] A brook or stream; *spec.* a brook with a stony bed or rugged course.

Beck (bek), *sb.*[2] ME. [f. BECK *v.*] **1.** A nod, or other mute signal, indicating assent, command, etc. Also *transf.* **2.** A bow, a curtsey, a nod, etc. Chiefly *Sc.* ME.

1. With a b. of the head or hand, as we beckon to servants DE FOE. Phr. *To be at the b. and call of.*

Beck (bek), *sb.*[3] 1828. [? corrupt f. BACK *sb.*[2]] = BACK *sb.*[2]

Beck (bek), *v.* ME. [short f. BECKON *v.*] **1.** *intr.* To make a mute signal, or significant gesture, as by nodding, etc. *trans.* To express by a beck 1821. **2.** *trans.* (obj. orig. *dat.*) To make a mute signal to; to beckon 1486. **3.** *intr.* To nod, bow; to curtsey. Chiefly *Sc.* 1535.

2. When gold and siluer becks me to come on SHAKS.

Be·cker, becket. *dial.* 1602. Sea-bream.

Becket (be·kėt), *sb.* 1769. [?] *Naut.* A contrivance, usu. a loop of rope with a knot on one end and eye at the other, or a large hook, or a wooden bracket, used for confining ropes, tackle, oars, spars, etc., and also for securing the tacks and sheets of sails. Hence **Be·cket** *v.* to fasten by or furnish with beckets.

Beckon (be·k'n), *v.* [OE. *bīecnan*:—OTeut. **bauknjan*, f. *baukno-*, in OE. *béacn* BEACON. Also OE. *béacnian*.] **1.** *intr.* To make a mute signal with the head, hand, finger, etc.; now *esp.* in order to bid a person approach. **2.** *trans.* (obj. orig. *dat.*): To make a significant gesture of head or hand to; hence, to summon or bid approach ME.

1. I beckon'd with my Hand to him, to come back DE FOE. **2.** Iago becons me: now he begins the story *Oth.* IV. i. 134. **Be·ckon** *sb.* a significant gesture of head, hand, etc., *esp.* one indicating assent or command.

†**Becla·p**, *v.* ME. [See BE-.] To catch or lay hold of suddenly -1530.

Beclaw·, *v.* 1603. [See BE-.] To scratch or tear all over with claws or nails.

Beclip (bĭkli·p), *v.*[1] *arch.* [OE. *beclyppan*, f. BE- 1 + *clyppan*; see CLIP *v.*] †**1.** To embrace -1669. **2.** To wrap round, encircle OE. †**3.** To lay hold of; to catch, overtake -1557.

Beclog (bĭklǫ·g), *v.* ME. [See BE-.] To encumber with a sticky substance.

†**Beclo·se**, *v.* [Orig. OE. *beclýsan*, f. BE- + *clýsan*; see CLUSE; subseq. CLOSE after Fr.] To shut up or in; to imprison -1677.

Beclothe (bĭklōu·ð), *v.* Pa. t. and pple. **beclothed, beclad.** 1509. [See BE- 1.] To clothe about.

Becloud (bĭklau·d), *v.* 1598. [See BE- 6.] To cover or obscure with clouds. Also *fig.*

To b. unpleasant facts GEO. ELIOT.

Become (bĭkʋ·m), *v.* Pa. t. **became**; Pa. pple. **become.** [Com. Teut.: OE. *becuman* = Goth. *biquiman*, f. *bi-* BE- 1 + *quiman*, in OE *cuman* to COME.] †**1.** *intr.* To come (to a place), to arrive; later, to go -1737. Also †*transf.* †**2.** To happen; to befall -1655. **3.** To come to be (something or in some state) ME. **4.** To come into being 1598. **5.** To accord with; to befit (obj. orig. *dat.*) ME. **6.** *impers.* (now usu. with *it*). †**a.** (*absol.*, with *to*, *for*, or *clause*.) Replaced by 'it is becoming'. -1591. **b.** with *object*. (orig. *dat.*) To befit ME. **7.** Hence, To look well (on or with), to set out ME.; *hence*, To look well in (a dress, etc.) 1660.

1. *transf.* It becomes to be loved on its own account SYD. SMITH. **3.** His wife looked backe..she became a pillar of salt *Gen.* xix. 26. **5.** Soft stilnes and the night Become the tutches of sweet harmonie *Merch. V.* v. i. 57. **6.** Fonder of hunting than became an Archbishop FREEMAN. **7.** She will b. thy bed *Temp.* III. ii. 112. To b. a gown HELPS. Phr. *B. of* (after 'what'): *orig.* = 'come out of, result from'; *now*, replaces 'where is it become', etc. (= 'where went it, has it gone') in reference to the later locality, position, or fate of a thing.

†**Beco·med**, *ppl. a.* [f. BECOME (sense 7) + -ED[1].] Befitting. *Rom. & Jul.* IV. ii. 26.

Becoming (bĭkʋ·miŋ), *vbl. sb.* (and *ppl. a.*) 1600. [f. BECOME *v.*] **1.** The action of befitting; that which befits or graces (*rare*). **2.** A coming to be 1853. **3.** *ppl. a.* Befitting 1565.

Within the limits of b. mirth *L. L. L.* II. i. 67. *The becoming*: decorum; that which is coming into existence (FERRIER). Hence **Beco·ming-ly** *adv.*, **-ness.**

Becripple (bĭkri·p'l), *v.* 1660. [See BE- 2 or 5.] To make lame.

Becrow·n, *v.* 1583. [See BE- 2.] To crown.

Becu·rl, *v.* 1614. [See BE- 2.] To cover or deck out with curls.

Bed (bed), *sb.* [Com. Teut.: OE. *będd, będ*, neut., Goth. *badi*:—OTeut. **badjo-(m)* neut. Referred by Franck to Aryan **bhodh*, whence L. *fod(i-* to dig.] **I.** The sleeping-place of men or animals. **1.** A permanent structure or arrangement for sleeping on or for the sake of rest. It consists for the most part of a sack or mattress, stuffed with something soft or springy, often raised upon a bedstead, and covered with sheets, blankets, etc. The name is given both to the whole structure, and to the stuffed sack or mattress. Also *fig.* 2. *transf.* As the place of conjugal union, and of procreation and child-birth ME. 3. Any sleeping place ME. 4. *fig.* The grave ME.

1. He was in his b. and a slepe on a fethyr bedde CAXTON. *B. and board*: entertainment with lodging and food. Of a wife: full connubial relations. 2. False to his B. *Cymb.* III. iv. 42. George..the eldest son of this second b. CLARENDON. 4. As we hollowed his narrow b. WOLFE.

II. 1. A level or smooth piece of ground in a garden, usu. somewhat raised; also the plants which grow in it OE. 2. The bottom of a lake or sea, or of a watercourse 1586. 3. An extended base, a matrix 1633. 4. A level surface on which anything rests, *e.g.* the level surface in a printing press on which the form is laid 1846. 5. Hence *techn.*:

a. *Gunnery.* The portion of a gun-carriage on which the gun rests. b. *Archit.* and *Building.* The surface of a stone, or brick, which lies in the mortar; the under side of a slate. c. *Mech.* Any solid foundation, framework, or support, upon which to rest a superstructure. d. *Carpentry.* A support or rest, *e.g.* for a ship on the stocks, etc. e. *Railway-making.* The layer of stone, etc. upon which the rails are laid.

1. Beds of violets blue MILT. 2. The b. of the Adriatic LYELL.

III. 1. A layer or stratum; a horizontal course; *spec.* in *Geol.* 1616. 2. A layer of reptiles, shell-fish, etc. covering a space or tract of ground 1608.

1. The lowest 'bed' of the Lias LYELL. 2. A b. of oysters 1688.

Phrases, etc. *To bring to b.*, formerly = put to b.; now usu. pass., to be delivered of a child; also *fig.* (See ABED.) *To die in one's b.*: to die at home or of natural causes. *To keep one's b.*: to remain in b. through sickness, etc. So *To leave one's b.*: to recover. *To make a b.*: to put one in order after use. *To lie* or *sleep in the b. one has made* (cf. prec.): to accept the natural results of one's own conduct. *To make up a b.*: to extemporize sleeping accommodation. *To take to one's b.*: to become confined to b. through sickness or infirmity.

Comb., etc.: **b.-key**, an iron tool for screwing and unscrewing the nuts and bolts of a bedstead; **-moulding** (*Archit.*), 'the mouldings under a projection, as the corona of a cornice' (Gwilt); **-pan**, a warming-pan; a chamber utensil constructed for use in b.; **-piece**, **-plate** (*Mech.*), the foundation or support of any mechanical structure; **-post**, a post of a b.; **-rock** (*Geol.*), the solid rock underlying superficial formations; also *fig.* bottom, lowest level; **-screw**, one used for holding together the posts and beams of a wooden bedstead; also, a machine for lifting heavy bodies, often used in launching vessels; **-sore**, a soreness of the skin produced by long lying in b.; **-stone**, a large heavy stone used as the foundation and support of girders, etc. in building; also, the lower stone in an oil-mill, on which the runners roll; **†-swerver**, one unfaithful to the marriage-bed (*Wint. T.* II. i. 93); **†-vow**, promise of fidelity to the marriage-bed; **-way** (*Geol.*), an appearance of stratification in granite; **-wrench**, = *bed-key*; **†-work**, work that is or can be done in bed, easy work *Tr. & Cr.* I. iii. 203.

Bed, *v.* Pa. t. and pple. **bedded.** [OE. *beddian* f. *bed(d)*, BED.] †1. *intr.* To prepare a bed –ME. 2. To put to bed; to furnish with a bed ME. 3. To take (a wife) to bed (*arch.*) 1548. 4. *intr.* To go to bed ME. 5. To provide (animals) with litter 1480. 6. *intr.* Of an animal: To make its lair 1470. 7. To plant in or as in a garden bed 1671. 8. To EMBED 1586; *intr.* to rest *on* 1875. 9. *Building.* To lay (bricks, etc.) in position in cement or mortar 1685. 10. *Masonry.* To dress the face of a stone (cf. BED *sb.* II. 5b) 1793. 11. To spread with a bed of anything. Cf. *to carpet.* 1839. 12. To lay (*e.g.* oysters) in a bed or beds 1653. 13. *intr.* To form a compact layer 1615.

4. O then we'll wed, and then we'll b. CAREY. 5. To rub, feed, and b. a horse WESLEY. Phr. *To bed up*: to lie up in strata *against.*

Bedabble (bĭdæ·b'l), *v.* 1590. [See BE- 1.] To wet with dirty liquid, or so as to make dirty.

Bedad (bĭdæ·d), *int. Irish.* 1710. [= *By dad*, or *by God* (cf. *begad*).] An asseveration.

†**Beda·ff**, *v.* [f. BE- 5 + DAFF *sb.*] To befool. CHAUCER.

†**Beda·ggle**, *v.* 1580. [f. BE- + DAGGLE.] To bemire the bottom of (dress) –1660.

Bedangled (bĭdæ·ng'ld), *ppl. a.* 1601. [See BE- 1.] Beset with things dangling about one.

Bedarken (bĭdā·ɹk'n), *v.* [See BE- 1.] To involve in darkness. Also *fig.*

Bedash (bĭdæ·ʃ), *v.* 1564. [See BE- 1.] a. To dash against. b. To injure by dashing. c. To cover with dashes of colour, etc.

Bedaub (bĭdǭ·b), *v.* 1553. [See BE- 1.] 1. To daub over, to plaster 1558. Also *fig.* 2. To bedizen 1581. Also *fig.*

1. They all bedawbed their faces with mire 1683.

Bedawee·, -wi, -wy, pl. **bedawee·n, -win**, forms of BEDOUIN, -S.

Bedazzle (bĭdæ·z'l), *v.* 1596. [See BE- 2.] To dazzle thoroughly. So **Beda·zzlement.**

Bedchamber (be·dˌtʃē¹:mbəɹ). ME. [f. BED *sb.* + CHAMBER.] A room intended for holding a bed; *arch.*, and displaced by *bedroom*, exc. in reference to the royal bedchamber.

The Ladies of the Bed-chamber 1702.

Bed-clothes (be·d-klōuðz), *sb. pl.* (The sing. is obs.) ME. [f. BED *sb.* + CLOTHES.] Sheets, blankets, etc., for a bed.

Bedder (be·dəɹ). 1612. [f. BED *v.* or *sb.*] 1. One who puts to bed; one who litters cattle. 2. An upholsterer. Now *dial.* 1803. 3. The lower stone in an oil-mill 1611. 4. A bedding-out plant 1862.

Bedding (be·diŋ), *vbl. sb.* OE. [f. BED.] 1. (conn. w. BED *sb.*) The articles which compose a bed, *esp.* the mattress, etc., and the bed-clothes. b. Anything used to sleep on or in (*arch.*) ME. c. Litter 1697. 2. A foundation 1611. 3. Arrangement of rocks, etc. in beds or layers 1860. 4. (conn. w. BED *v.*) A putting to bed; *esp.* of a bride 1859. 5. Planting flowers in beds; bedding out 1862.

Comb.: **b.-moulding** = *Bed-moulding*; **-stone**, a straight piece of marble used to try the rubbed side of a brick.

Bede, *sb.*[1] ME. form of BEAD *sb.*, prayer. Now *arch.* So **bedehouse, bedesman**, etc.

Bede (bīd), *sb.*[2] A miner's pickaxe. RAYMOND.

Bedeck (bĭde·k), *v.* 1566. [See BE- 1.] To deck about, to cover with ornament.

So bedecked, ornate, and gay MILT. *Sams.* 712.

Bedeguar (be·dĭgāɹ). Also **-gar, -gaur.** 1578. [a. F., ad. (ult.) Pers. *bādāwar*, lit. 'wind-brought'. In sense 2 taken as if f. Pers. *bād* wind + Arab. *ward* 'rose'.] †1. A white spiny plant, perh. the Milk Thistle (*Silybum Marianum*) –1601. 2. A kind of gall on rose-bushes produced by an insect *Cynips rosæ* 1578.

Bedel, bedell, archaic forms of BEADLE, q. v. So **Bedelry**, etc.

†**Bede·lve**, *v.* [OE. *bedelf-an*, f. BE- + *delf-an* to DELVE.] 1. To dig about OE. only. 2. To bury –1513.

Bedeman, obs. f. BEADSMAN.

Bede·ne, *adv.* Now *dial.* [ME. *bidene*, f. ? + ME. *æne, ene*, OE. *æne* once.] = ANON; occ. a mere expletive, or a rime word.

Bedevil (bĭde·v'l), *v.* 1768. [See BE- 5, 6.] 1. To treat diabolically. 2. To possess with, or as with, a devil 1831. 3. To torment, worry 1823. 4. To 'play the devil with'; to transform mischievously or bewilderingly 1800.

1. My poor..Muse..be-deviled with their..ribaldry BYRON. 4. To b. the registration DISRAELI. Hence **Bede·villed, -iled** *ppl. a.* **Bede·vilment.**

Bedew (bĭdiū·), *v.* ME. [See BE-.] *pass.* To be wetted with dew; hence *active*, To cover with or as with dew. Also *transf.* and *fig.*

The moisture which bedews a cold metal or stone when we breathe upon it HERSCHEL.

Bedfellow (be·dfe:lou). 1478. [f. BED + FELLOW.] One who shares a bed with another; also *fig.*

†**Bed-fere, -ifere.** ME. [cf. BED + IFERE, and FERE:—OE. *gefera* fellow.] = prec. –1656.

Bedfordshire (be·dfōɹdʃəɹ). 1665. Name of an English county; joc. for *bed.*

Be·dgown. 1762. [See GOWN.] 1. A woman's night-gown. 2. A kind of jacket worn by working women in the north 1827.

Be·d-hea·d. ME. [See HEAD.] The upper end of a bed.

Bedight (bĭdəi·t), *v. arch.* Pa. pple. **bedight, -ed.** ME. [f. BE- + DIGHT.] To equip, array, bedeck. (Now *poet.*)

Bedim (bĭdi·m), *v.* 1566. [See BE-.] To make dim.; *esp.* the eyesight 1583. Also *fig.*

Bedi·p, *v.* [OE. *bedyppan. Obs.* after 12th c. till *c* 1600.] To dip, immerse.

Bedizen (bĭdəi·z'n, -di·z'n), *v.*; also **bediz-zen.** 1661. [f. BE- + DIZEN. All Eng. orthoepists have (əi).] To dress out, *esp.* with vulgar finery; also *fig.* Hence **Bedi·zenment.**

Bedlam (be·dləm). [ME. *Bedlem* = *Bethlem*, *Bethlehem.*] †1. Bethlehem in Judea –1616. 2. The Hospital of St. Mary of Bethlehem, used since 1547 as an asylum for the insane. 3. Hence, A madhouse 1663. Also *fig.* †4. An inmate of a lunatic asylum, a madman; *spec.* one of the discharged, but often only half-cured, patients, licensed to beg, wearing as a badge a tin plate on their left arm –1701. Also *attrib.*, and *adj.* 1535.

2. Phr. *Jack or Tom o' B.*: a madman. 3. 'Twas both an hospital and b. 1699. 4. She roar'd like a B. SWIFT. Plaine b. stuffe MILT. Hence **Be·dlamite** *sb.* an inmate of B.; a lunatic; *adj.* lunatic.

Be·d-ma·ker. 1465. [f. BED *sb.* + MAKER.] 1. One who constructs beds 1500. 2. One who makes beds after they have been slept in 1465.

†**Bedo·te**, *v.* ME. [See BE- 3.] To cause to dote, befool –1583.

Bedouin (be·duˌīn), *sb.* (and *a.*) ME. [a. F., a. Arab. *badāwīn*, pl. of *badawīy*, f. *badw* desert.] An Arab of the desert. b. *transf.* A gipsy. (Cf. *City Arab.*) 1863. Also *attrib.* Hence **Be·douinism.**

Bedrabble (bĭdræ·b'l), *v.* 1440. [See BE- 2.] To make dirty with rain and mud.

Bedraggle (bĭdræ·g'l), *v.* 1727. [See BE-.] a. To wet (skirts, etc.) so that they drag or hang limp. b. 'To soil clothes by suffering them, in walking, to reach the dirt' (J.).

Bedral, bederal (be·d(ĕ)răl). *Sc.* 1815. [App. corrupt f. BEADLE.] A church officer, often acting as clerk, sexton, and bell-ringer.

Bedrench; see BE-.

Bedrid (be·drid), *a.*, orig. *sb.* [OE. *bedreda, -rida*, f. *bed* + *rida*, f. *rīdan* to ride.] 1. Confined to bed through sickness or infirmity. Now usu. *Bedridden.* 2. *fig.* Worn out 1621.

1. To her decrepit, sicke, and b. Father *L. L. L.* I. i. 139. var. **Be·dri·dden**, the *-en* being due to the analogy of ppl. adjs.

†**Be·drip.** [OE. *bed-rip*, f. *bed-* (see BEAD) + *rip*: lit. 'reaping by request'; called also *bēn-rip*, f. *bēn* prayer.] A service which some tenants owed to their lord, viz. at his request to reap his corn at harvest-time –ME.

Bedroom (be·drūm). 1590. [See ROOM.] 1. Room in bed (*Mids. N.* II. ii. 51). 2. A room used to contain a bed; a sleeping apartment. (Replacing BEDCHAMBER.) 1616. Hence **Be·d-roomed** *a.* having a b.

Bedrop (bĭ¦drǫ·p), *v.* ME. [See BE- 4.] 1. To wet with drops. 2. *pa. pple.* Sprinkled as with drops; *fig.* interspersed ME.

Bedside (be·dsəi:d). ME. [For *bed's side.*] Place or position by a bed; *esp.* by way of attendance on one confined to bed (so *b. manner* of a doctor 1869).

Bedspread (be·dspred). orig. *U.S.* 1848. [SPREAD *sb.* II. 2; cf. Du. *bed(de)sprei.*] A light thin covering to spread over the clothes on a bed.

†**Bedstaff** (be·dstaf). Pl. **staffs, staves.** 1576. A stick used in some way about a bed. Formerly handy as a weapon; hence, prob., the phr. *in the twinkling of a b.* –1845.

Say there is no virtue in cudgels and bedstaves BROME.

Bedstead (be·dsted). 1440. [See STEAD.] Strictly, the place occupied by a bed; but long ago transferred to the framework of a bed.

Be·dstock. *n. dial.* 1483. [See STOCK.] A BEDSTEAD, or its front and back parts.

Be·dstraw. ME. [See STRAW.] †1. The straw formerly used as bedding –1637. 2. A genus of plants (*Galium*, N.O. *Rubiaceæ*), one of which (*G. verum*) is known as *Our Lady's B.* 1527.

Bedtick (be·dtik). 1569. [See TICK.] A bag or case, into which feathers, etc. are put to form a bed. Hence **Be·dti·cking**, the materials of which bedticks are made; also *attrib.*

Bedtime (be·dtəim). ME. [See TIME.] The hour for going to bed. Also *fig.*

Between our after supper, and bedtime *Mids. N.* v. i. 34.

Bedub (bĭdʊ·b), *v.* 1657. [See BE- 2.] †a. To adorn. b. To denominate.

Bedull, bedung, bedust; see BE- *pref.*

Bedward, -wards (be·dwǫɹd, -z), *adv.* ME. [See -WARD(S: orig. *to bedward.*] Towards bed or †bedtime.

Bedwarf, bedye; see BE- *pref.*

Bee [1] (bī). [Com. Teut.: OE. *bēo*:—OTeut. **bīôn-* or *biôn*; f. root *bi-*, perh. = Aryan *bhi-* 'to fear', in the sense of 'quivering' or 'buzzing'.] **1.** A genus of insects of the Hymenopterous order, living in societies composed of one queen, or perfect female, a few males or 'drones', and an indefinite number of undeveloped females or 'neuters' (which are the workers), all having four wings; they produce wax, and collect and store up honey. **2.** Applied to a group of allied insects, e. g. Humble B., Mason B., Carpenter B., etc. OE. **3.** (orig. in U. S.): A meeting of neighbours to unite their labours for the benefit of one of their number; as a *quilting-b.*, etc. *Hence*: A gathering for some object, e. g. a *spelling-b.* 1809.

2. The Humble Bees are larger than the Bees 1861. **4.** I made a b.; that is I collected .. the most expert .. of the settlers to assist at the raising GALT.

Phr. To have *a b. in one's bonnet*: *i. e.* a craze on some point, a screw loose. (Cf. *maggot.*) *Comb.*: **b.-bird,** the Spotted Fly-catcher, also a humming-bird; **-cell,** one of the cells of the comb; **-cuckoo,** an African bird (*Cuculus Indicator*), which indicates the nests of wild bees; **-eater,** a genus of birds (*Merops*) which devour bees; **-fly,** a two-winged fly resembling a b., *esp.* certain of the *Bombylidæ* and *Syrphidæ*; **-glue,** the substance with which bees fill up crevices, and fix the combs to the hives, propolis; **-gum,** U.S. local name for a b.-hive; **-hawk,** the Honey Buzzard; also a clear-wing hawk-moth (*Sesia furciformis*); **-line,** a straight line between two points on the earth's surface, such as a b. was supposed to take in returning to its hive; **-master,** a keeper of bees; so **-mistress; -nettle,** species of Dead-nettle much visited by bees; **-orchis,** a plant (*Ophrys apifera*) with a flower in part resembling a b.; **-tree,** one in which bees have hived; **-wine,** nectar of a flower.

Bee [2] (bī). [Com. Teut.: OE. *bēag, bēah*:—OTeut. **baugo-z* ring, f. **bug-, baug-* to bow. *Bee* is the northern type.] †**1.** A ring or torque of metal -1552. **2.** *Naut.*: *bee,* a hoop of metal; *bee-block,* a piece of hard wood, bolted to the outer end of the bowsprit, to reeve the fore-mast stays through.

Bee·brea:d. OE. [f. BEE + BREAD. The mod. wd. is prob. a new combination.] †**1.** *orig.* In OE.: Honeycomb with the honey in it. **2.** Pollen, or honey and pollen, consumed by the nurse-bees 1657. **3.** Used of plants yielding nectar, as the White Clover and Borage.

Beech (bītʃ). [OE. *bēece, bēce,* from OTeut. **bōkā*, cogn. w. L. *fagus* beech, and Gr. φαγός, φηγός 'esculent oak', f. root of φαγεῖν.] **1. a.** A forest tree indigenous to Europe and Western Asia, having fine thin smooth bark, and glossy oval leaves, and bearing triquetrous nuts (called *mast*); it has several varieties, as the Purple, Copper, and Fern-leaved Beech. **b.** The genus *Fagus*, N.O. *Corylaceæ*, including the Common Beech (*F. sylvatica*). **c.** The wood of this tree. Often *attrib.* 1607. **2.** Applied to other trees resembling the beech of Europe.

Comb.: **b.-drops,** a North American plant, *Epiphegus*, N.O. *Orobanchaceæ*, parasitic upon the roots of the b.; **-fern,** *Polypodium Phegopteris*; **-finch,** local name of the Chaffinch; **-marten,** see MARTEN; **-mast,** the fruit of the b.; **-oil,** oil extracted from b.-mast; **-owl,** local name of the Tawny Owl; **-wheat** = BUCKWHEAT.

Beechen (bī·tʃĕn), *a. arch.* and *poet.* [OE. *bēcen*:—*bōecen*:—OTeut. **bōkino-z*; see prec.] **1.** Of, pertaining to, or derived from the beech. **2.** Made of the wood of the beech 1663. ¶ Replaced by BEECH *attrib.*

A b. bowl, A maple dish WORDSW.

Beechy (bī·tʃi), *a.* 1612. [f. BEECH + -Y.] Of characterized by, or abounding in, beeches.

Beef (bīf), *sb.* Pl. **beeves,** in U.S. **beefs.** ME. [a. OF. *boef* (= mod.F. *bœuf*):—L. *bovem*, acc. of *bos*, cogn. w. Gr. βοῦς, Skr. *go-*, Eng. Cow.] **1.** The flesh of an ox, bull, or cow, used as food. **2.** *transf.* (see quots.) 1661. **3.** An ox, or any animal of the ox kind; *esp.* a fattened beast, or its carcase. Usu. in *pl.* (*arch.* or *techn.*) ME.

1. What say you to a peece of Beefe and Mustard *Tam. Shr.* IV. iii. 23. **2.** Ling.. is counted the beefe of the Sea LOVELL. Chelmsford.. showed less b. about him 1862.

Comb.: †**b.-brained** *ppl. a.* thick-headed; **-head,** a thick-head; **-tea,** the juice extracted from b., used as a food for invalids; **-witted** *a.* (= *beef-brained*); hence **-wittedness.** Hence **Bee·finess,** beefy quality; also *transf.* **Bee·fing, bee·fin** (*dial.*), an ox for slaughter. **Bee·fy** *a.* abounding in, or like, b.; fleshy; stolid.

Bee·fea:ter. 1610. [f. BEEF + EATER; cf. OE. *hlāf-æta*, lit. 'loaf-eater', a menial servant. Not conn. w. *buffet.*] **1.** An eater of beef; *contemptuously*, a well-fed menial. (Properly *beef-eater.*) **2.** One of the Yeomen of the Guard; also of the Warders of the Tower of London 1671. **3.** *Ornith.* A genus of African birds (*Buphaga*), called also Ox-peckers 1836.

Beefing, var. of BIFFIN, a kind of apple.

Beef-steak (bī·fˌstēi·k). 1711. A thick slice of beef, cut from the hind-quarters of the animal. Also *attrib.*

Beef-steak Club, a society founded by Lord Peterborough; the members wear a gridiron upon their buttons.

Beef-wood (bī·fwud). 1756. [f. BEEF + WOOD.] **1.** The timber of an Australian tree (*Casuarina*), so called from its red colour 1836. **2.** Also applied to other trees, e. g. in N. S. Wales to *Stenocarpus salignus*; in Queensland to *Banksia Compar* (both N.O. *Proteaceæ*), etc.

Beehive (bī·həiːv). ME. [f. BEE *sb.*[1] + HIVE *sb.*] A receptacle used as a home for bees; usually made of thick straw work in the shape of a dome.

Beele. Now *dial.* 1671. [app. a var. of BILL.] A pick-ax with both ends sharp. Hence **Beeleman.**

Beelzebub (biˌe·lzǐbɒb). OE. [a. L., used in the Vulgate both for the N.T. Gr. βεελζεβούβ, and the Heb. *ba'al-z'būb*, 'fly-lord'. See 2 Kings i. 2. Milton made Beelzebub one of the fallen angels.] The Devil; a devil; also *transf.*

Been, *pa. pple.* of BE *v.* Also, obs. f. *be*, pres. infin., and pres. indic. pl.

Been, obs. pl. of BEE *sb.*[1] var. of BEIN *a.*

Beënt (bī·ĕnt), *a.* 1865. [f. BE *v.* + L. *suffix* -ENT.] *Metaph.* That is or exists; existing (in the most abstract sense); also used subst. (tr. Ger. *seiend* = the Hegelian *pure being.*)

Beer (bīᵊɹ), *sb.*[1] [Com. WGer.: OE. *bēor.* Etym. uncertain.] **1.** An alcoholic liquor obtained by the fermentation of malt (or other saccharine substance), flavoured with hops or other bitters. Formerly distinguished from *ale* by being hopped; but now generic, including ale and porter. See ALE. **2.** Applied to other fermented liquors, as *nettle beer*, etc. OE.

1. **Buttered beer:** see ALE. **Small beer:** weak b.; *fig.* small things, as in *To think no small b. of oneself.* Phr. *To be in b.*: to be intoxicated.

Comb.: **b.-faucet,** a machine for aerating flat b.; **-float,** a hydrometer for ascertaining the density of b.-wash; **-garden,** one attached to an inn for the consumption of b.; **-house,** one licensed for the sale of b. only; **-money,** an allowance to servants instead of b.; **-vinegar,** vinegar made from b. (cf. BEEREGAR). Hence **Bee·riness,** beery quality or condition. **Bee·rishly** *adv.* in beery fashion.

†**Beer** (bī·əɹ), *sb.*[2] *rare.* ME. [f. BE *v.*] One who is; *spec.* the Self-existent, the great *I Am* -1602.

Beer, *sb.*[3] 1712. [The same wd. as BIER.] *Weaving.* A (variable) number of ends in a warp.

Beeregar (bīᵊ·rĭgăɹ). ? *Obs.* 1500. [f. BEER *sb.*[1] + *egre*, EAGER = F. *aigre*; after *vinegar*, etc.] Sour beer; vinegar made from beer.

Beery (bīᵊ·ri), *a.* 1861. Belonging to, or abounding in beer; affected by beer; beer-like.

Beest (bīst). [Com. Teut.: OE. *bēost.*] The first milk drawn from a mammal, *esp.* a cow, after parturition.

Beestings (bī·stiŋz). [OE. **bīesting*, *bȳsting*, as if f. **biestan*, f. *bēost*; see prec. Now usu. in pl.] **1.** = prec. †**2.** A disease caused by imbibing beestings. L. *colostratio.* 1607.

Bees-wax (bī·zˌwæːks). 1676. [f. BEE [1] + WAX.] The wax secreted by bees as the material of their combs. Hence **Bee·swax** *v.* to rub or polish with b.

Beeswing (bī·zˌwiŋ). 1860. [f. BEE + WING.] The second crust, consisting of shining filmy scales of tartar, formed in port and some other wines after long keeping; so called from its appearance; *ellipt.*, old wine showing beeswing. Hence **Bee·s-winged** *a.* so old as to show b.

Beet (bīt). [OE. *bēte*, ad. L. *beta.* Common in OE.; then lost till *c* 1400.] **1.** A plant or genus of plants (N.O. *Chenopodiaceæ*), having a root used for food, and also for yielding sugar. There are two species, the Common or Red (*Beta vulgaris*), and the White (*B. cicla*). Formerly used chiefly in pl. 'beets', like *beans*, etc.

Comb.: †**B.-raves** [a. F. *bette-rave* 'beet', lit. 'beet-turnip'], the small red b.; **-root,** the root of the b.; also *attrib.*

Beet, bete (bīt), *v.* Now *dial.* [Com. Teut.: OE. *bēetan, bētan*:—OTeut. **bōtjan* to advantage, f. *bōtâ-*, in OE. *bōt* BOOT.] **1.** *trans.* To mend, make good. **2.** To relieve ME. **3.** To make, kindle, put on (a fire) OE. **4.** To mend (a fire). Still in *Sc.* See also BOTE. ME.

4. Nyght and day greet fuyr they under betten CHAUCER.

Beetle (bī·t'l), *sb.*[1] [OE. *bietel*, in Anglian **bētel*:—OTeut. **bautilo-z*, f. *bautan*, in OE. *bēatan* to beat.] **1.** An implement with a heavy head, and a handle or stock, used to drive wedges, ram paving stones, etc.; a mall. Also *fig.* **2.** The type of heavy dullness 1520.

1. *Three-man b.*: one that requires three men to lift it. See 2 *Hen. IV*, I. ii. 255. **2.** Tendre wyttes.. be made as dull as a betell 1520. *Comb.* **b.-head,** the monkey of a pile-driving engine.

Beetle (bī·t'l), *sb.*[2] [OE. *bitula, bitela*, f. an adj. **bitul, bitol*, f. *bītan* to BITE. Confused in fig. use with BEETLE *sb.*[1]] **1.** The class name for coleopterous insects, having the upper pair of wings converted into hard wing-cases (elytra) that close over the back, and protect the lower or true wings. **2.** In pop. use applied *esp.* to those which are large and black, and including the **Black-beetle** or COCKROACH, which is not a beetle OE. **3.** A type of blindness; whence *fig.* 1548.

1. The poore B. that we treade vpon *Meas. for M.* III. i. 79. **2.** Beetles blacke approach not neere *Mids. N.* II. ii. 22. **3.** They that had charge to guyde other, were poore blinde betels themselves TOMSON.

Beetle (bī·t'l), ? *a.* ME. [prob. one of the two sbs. BEETLE, according to the meaning.] **1.** In **Beetle-browed:** 'Having prominent brows', Johnson (but *brow* in ME. was always = eyebrow, not = forehead); having 'black and long' (1782), or 'shaggy, bushy, or prominent' eyebrows (ME.) Usu. reproachful, and occas. simply = Lowering, scowling. Cf. *supercilious.* Also *fig.* **2. a.** (qualifying *brows*) 1532. **b.** Of the brow of a mountain: Prominent, or perh. tree-clad 1580.

2. I rather would a husband wed With a beetill brow than a beetell hed *Prov.* var. **Bee·tled** *a.* (in sense 2).

Beetle (bī·t'l), *v.*[1] 1602. [f. BEETLE *a.* 2 b. App. used as a nonce-wd. by SHAKS.] **1.** *intr.* To 'lift up beetle brows' (Sidney), scowl; in mod. use, 'to overhang'; but prob. used by Shaks. with some reference to eyebrows. **2.** *fig.* To hang threateningly 1859.

1. The dreadfull summit of the Cliffe, That beetles o'er his base into the Sea *Haml.* I. iv. 71.

Beetle (bī·t'l), *v.*[2]; also (*Sc.*) **bittle.** 1608. [f. BEETLE *sb.*[1]] To beat with a beetle, in order to thresh, crush, or flatten; also, *techn.*, to emboss fabrics by pressure from figured rollers.

Beeves (bīvz). Pl. of **BEEF**; now usu. poet. for 'oxen'.

Befall (bǐfǭ·l), *v.* Pa. t. **befell** (-fel). Pa. pple. **befallen.** [OE. *bef(e)all-an* f. BE- 2 + *f(e)allan* to fall.] †**1.** *intr.* To fall. (Chiefly *fig.*) -1649. **2.** To fall *to*; to pertain; be fitting ME. **3.** To happen ME. †**4.** To become *of* -1590.

2. '*Reddite Caesari*,' seide god, 'þat to cesar byfalleþ' LANGL. **3.** Lest peraduenture mischiefe b. him *Gen.* xlii. 4. So b. my soule, As this is false *Com. Err.* V. i. 208. Phr. †*Fair, foul befall.*

Befeather, Befetter, etc.: see BE- *pref.*

†**Befile,** *v.* [OE. *befȳlan*, f. BE- 1 + *fȳlan* to FILE. Repl. by BEFOUL.] To make foul; to defile -1532.

Befit (bǐfi·t), *v.* 1460. [See BE- 2.] **1.** *trans.* To be fit for; to agree with; to become. **2.** To be proper to, as a duty or task; to be right for 1602. †**3.** To fit out *with* -1759.

1. Any businesse that We say befits the houre *Temp.* II. i. 289. **2.** It us befitted To beare our hearts in greefe *Haml.* I. ii. 2. Hence **Befi·ttingly** *adv.*

Befla·tter, Beflower, Befoam, Befog, †**Befold;** see BE-.

Befool (bǐfū·l), *v.* ME. [See BE- 5.] **1.** To dupe. **2.** To treat as a fool, call fool 1612.
1. The old Rumpers were befoold by Cromwel 1673. 2. Who is hee, whom Salomon doth so often be-foole in his Prouerbs HIERON.

Before (bǐfōᵊ·ɹ). [OE. *beforan*, f. *bi-*, BE-by + *foran* adv. :—OTeut. **forana* from the front, advb. deriv. of *fora*, FOR. Primarily an adv.] **A.** *adv.* **1.** Of motion: Ahead, in front. **2.** Of position or direction: In front, in or on the fore side ME. **3.** In time previous, earlier, sooner; *hence*, beforehand; in the past ME.
1. I am sent with broome b. *Mids. N.* v. i. 397. 2. Had he his hurts b.? *Macb.* v. vii. 75. 3. When the But is out we will drinke water, not a drop. b. *Temp.* III. ii. 2. Phr. *Long b.*, *the week b.*, etc.

B. *prep.* **1.** Of motion: Ahead of OE.; driven in front of 1598; *hence*, with causal force 1535. **2.** Of position or direction: In front of OE. **3.** In front of so as to be in the sight of; under the cognizance of OE. **4.** In the (mental) view of (*arch.*) OE. **5.** Open to the knowledge of ME. **b.** Claiming the attention of 1711. **6.** In front of one; in prospect. **a.** Open to ME. **b.** Awaiting 1807. **7.** Preceding in order of time OE. **8.** Earlier than (a date or event) ME. **9.** Previous to the expiration of a future space of time 1865. **10.** In precedence of; in advance of ME. **11.** In preference to ME. **12.** In comparison with 1711.
1. Theyr gyde..to go b. them 1526. The leaf b. the wind KINGSLEY. Our enemies shall falle b. us 2 *Hen. VI*, IV. ii. 37. 2. When many meats are set b. me HOOKER. *B. the mast*: used of common sailors who are berthed in the forecastle in front of the foremast. 3. The proceedings b. the police court (*mod.*). 4. Though this be not theft b. the world 1583. 5. *B. God!* = As God knows. b. The problem b. us BUCKLE. 6. a. The World was all b. them, Where to choose, Their place of rest MILT. *P. L.* XII. 646. 7. Brave men were living b. Agamemnon BYRON. 9. Some day b. long TROLLOPE. 11. They would die b. yielding (*mod.*). 12. So shows..My spirit b. Thee TENNYSON.

C. *Conj.* or *conjunctive adv.* **1.** Of time: Previous to the time when ME. **2.** Rather than 1596.

D. 1. quasi-*adj.* = Anterior ME. **2.** quasi-*sb.* 1850.
1. Punisht for b. breach of the King's Lawes SHAKS.

Beforehand (bǐfōᵊ·ɹhænd), *adv.* (*a.*) ME. [Orig. two wds. Cf. L. *præ manu*, *manibus* 'at hand, in readiness', used in ME. as = 'beforehand'.] **1.** In advance; *spec.* in reference to payment in advance. †**2.** Before this or that –1520. †**3.** *adj.* Prepared (*rare*) 1704.
1. To pay a yeere or two yeeres rent before hande 1583. *To be b. with*: to anticipate; to forestall in action. *To be b. with the world*: to have money in hand for future contingencies (*arch.*).

Befo·resaid, *ppl. a.* ME. Now *arch.* = AFORESAID.

Befo·retime, *adv.* ME. [cf. *aforetime.*] In former time. Hence †**Beforetimes** *adv.*

Befo·rtune, *v. rare.* 1591. [See BE-.] *intr.* To befall.
As much, I wish all good b. you *Two Gent.* IV. iii. 41.

Befoul (bǐfau·l), *v.* ME. [See BE- 5.] To make foul, cover with filth.

Befriend (bǐˌfre·nd), *v.* 1559. [See BE- 2.] To act as a friend to, to help, favour; to further.

Befringe (bǐˌfri·ndʒ), *v.* 1611. [See BE- 1.] To furnish or adorn with (or as with) a fringe.
Befringed with gold FULLER.

Befur (bǐfɒ̄·ɹ), *v.* 1859. [f. BE- + FUR *v.* and *sb.*] To cover with furs.

Beg (beg), *v.* ME. [? f. OF. *begart*, *begard*, *begar*, med.L. *begardus* = BEGHARD, q. v. Not conn. w. BAG.] **1.** *trans.* To ask (bread, money, etc.) in alms; *intr.* to ask alms; *esp.* to live by asking alms ME. **2.** To ask as a favour: *intr.* to ask humbly or supplicatingly, entreat ME. **3.** In *B. pardon, excuse, leave*, etc.: often a courteous mode of asking what is expected, or even of taking as a matter of course 1600. **4.** To take for granted without warrant; *esp.* in *To b. the question* 1581.
1. Yet haue I not seene the righteous forsaken, nor his seede begging bread *Ps.* xxxvii. 25. They which begge must not choose 1617. 2. I have three favours to b. of you H. WALPOLE. I must..begge for pardon 1649. He begg'd of me to steale 't *Oth.* v. ii. 229. 3. *Mod.* In reply to your letter I b. leave to say..; hence *ellipt.* I beg to say...
Phrases. †*To beg a person*: to petition the Court of Wards for the custody of a minor, an heiress, or an idiot, as feudal superior, etc.; hence also *fig.* *To b.* (any one) *for a fool*. to set him down as a fool. *To b. off* (trans. and intr. for refl.): to obtain by entreaty the release of (any one) from a penalty, etc. Hence **Be·ggable** *a.* capable of being begged.

†**Beg,** *sb.* 1686. [a. Osmanli *beg* 'prince, governor', now pronounced as *bey*; see BEY, and cf. BEGUM.] A bey. *Beg beg* = BEGLERBEG.

Begad (bigæ·d), *int. colloq.* 1742. Minced form of *by God*. So †**Begar** (bigā·ɹ) SHAKS.

Begem (bǐˌdʒe·m), *v.* 1800. [See BE-.] To set about or stud with gems.

Beget (bǐge·t), *v.* Pa. t. **bego·t**, *arch.* **bega·t.** Pa. pple. **bego·tten.** [Com. Teut.: OE. *begit-an*. See GET.] †**1.** To acquire (usu. by effort) –1602. **2.** To procreate, generate; occas. said of both parents ME. †**b.** = GET (with child) –1611. **3.** *Theol.* Applied to the relationship of the Father to the Son in the Trinity ME. **4.** *fig.* and *transf.* To call into being 1581.
1. *Haml.* III. ii. 8. 2. He that begetteth a foole, doth it to his sorrow *Prov.* xvii. 21. 4. His eye begets occasion for his wit *L. L. L.* II. i. 69. Hence **Bege·ttal** (*rare*). **Bege·tter,** a procreator; also *fig.*

†**Bege·t,** *sb.* ME. only. [f. BEGET *v.*] **1.** The action of acquiring; *concr.* gain; spoils of war. **2.** Procreation; *concr.* progeny.

Beggar (be·gəɹ), *sb.* ME. [See BEG *v.* In 15–17th c. usu. *begger.*] **1.** One who asks alms, *esp.* habitually. **2.** *transf.* One in needy circumstances ME. †**3.** One who begs a favour; a suppliant. (The regular form of this and 4 would be *begger.*) –1601. †**4.** One who begs the question –1694. **5.** = BEGHARD ME. **6.** = Mean or low fellow ME. Also used playfully (cf. *rogue*, etc.) 1833.
1. A certaine begger named Lazarus *Luke* xvi. 20. *Sturdy b.*: an able-bodied man begging without cause, and often with violence. 6. A good-hearted little b. HUGHES.
Comb.: †**beggar's bush,** a bush under which a b. finds shelter (name of a tree near Huntingdon, formerly a rendezvous for beggars), *fig.* beggary; **beggar's-lice,** the plant called Clivers, also (in U.S.) certain boraginaceous plants, whose fruit or seeds stick to the clothes; **b.-tick** (in U.S.), the plant *Bidens frondosa*; **b.-weed,** a name of several plants, so called because they indicate poverty of soil, or beggar the land.
Hence **Be·ggardom,** mendicancy; mendicants as a body. **Be·ggarhood,** the condition of a b.; people in this condition. **Be·ggarism,** practice characteristic of a b.; extreme poverty.

Beggar (be·gəɹ), *v.* 1528. [f. prec. sb.] **1.** To make a beggar of; to impoverish. Also *fig.* **2.** To exhaust the resources of, outdo 1606.
1. [Conscience] beggars any man that keepes it *Rich. III*, I. iv. 145. 2. Phr. *To b. description, compare*, etc. *Comb.* **Beggar-my-neighbour:** a game at cards. Hence **Be·ggarer.**

Beggarly (be·gəɹli), *a.* 1526. [f. BEGGAR + -LY[1].] **1.** In the condition of, or befitting a beggar; indigent, mean 1545. **2.** *fig.* Destitute of meaning or value 1526. **3.** Sordid 1577.
1. Ragged, old, and beggerly *Tam. Shr.* IV. i. 140. 2. B. Arguments CLARENDON. 3. Beggerly thankes *A. Y. L.* II. v. 29. Hence **Be·ggarliness.** So **Be·ggarly** *adv.* indigently; suppliantly.

Beggary (be·gəri). ME. [f. BEGGAR.] **1.** The condition of a beggar; extreme poverty. Also *fig.* †**2.** The action or habit of begging –1764. **3.** *concr.* Beggars as a class; a place where they live 1615. †**4.** Beggarly stuff –1644.
1. Nought But beggery, and poore lookes *Cymb.* v. v. 10. 4. The Jewish b. of old cast Rudiments MILT.

†**Be·gged, -eth.** [f. BEG *v.* Orig. *beggeth*, after 'a hunteth', from OE. *huntað* sb. 'hunting' Skeat.] In phr. *To go a-begged*: to go a-begging. CHAUCER.

Begging (be·giŋ), *vbl. sb.* ME. [f. BEG *v.*] **1.** The action or habit of asking earnestly; *spec.* of asking alms. **2.** *To go* (or *have been*) *a begging*: **a.** to go about begging 1535; **b.** *fig.* (said of offices, etc., in need of men to fill them; things finding no purchaser; and the like.) 1593.
2. Benefices went a begging HOWSON.

Beghard (be·gāɹd). [ad. med.L. *beghardus*, either directly, or through *béguine*, f. Lambert *Bègue*.] A member of one of the lay brotherhoods which arose in the Low Countries in the 13th c., in imitation of the female BEGUINES. Many were simply idle mendicants: see BEGGAR *sb.* 5.

Be-gi·ft, *v.* ME. [See BE- 6.] †**1.** To entrust. **2.** To present with gifts 1590.

Begi·ld, *v.* 1594. [See BE-.] To cover with, or as with, gold.

Begin (bǐgi·n), *v.* Pa. t. **began** (bǐgæ·n), pa. pple. **begun** (bǐgɒ·n). [Com. WGermanic or OTeut.: OE. *bi-*, *beginnan*, f. *bi-* BE- about + **ginnan*, perh. to open, open up (a rare instance of the simple verb occurs in OE.). An alternative pa. t. *begun* was current till early 19th c.] **1.** *intr.* To set oneself *to do* something, commence or start OE.; also *absol.* and with preps., as *at*, *by*, *from*, *with* ME. **b.** To start speaking 1563 (esp. *poet.*). **c.** *To b. on, upon*: to set to work upon, start to deal with 1808. **2.** *trans.* To set about doing, start upon OE. **3.** To start (a thing) on its course, bring into being or action, be the first to do or practise ME. **4.** *intr.* To enter upon its career, come into existence, arise, start ME.
1. Then began men to call vpon the Name of the Lord *Gen.* iv. 26. You alwaies end ere you b. *Two Gent.* II. iv. 32. *To b. with*, (†*withal*), advb. phr.: at the outset. 2. Proud Nimrod first the savage chace began POPE. 3. And than a newe [world] shal beginne GOWER. Phr. *To b. the world*: to start in life.

Beginner (bǐgi·nəɹ). ME. [f. prec. vb. + -ER[1].] **1.** One who begins; an originator, founder. **2.** *spec.* One beginning to learn; a tyro 1470.
2. A band of raw beginners BYRON.

Beginning (bǐgi·niŋ), *vbl. sb.* ME. [f. as prec. + -ING[1].] **1.** The action or process of entering upon existence or upon action, or of bringing into existence; commencing, origination. **2.** The point of time at which anything begins; *absol.* the time when the universe began to be ME. **3.** Origin, source, fount ME. **4.** The first part ME. **5.** The rudimentary stage; the earliest proceedings. Often in *pl.* ME.
1. A line hath his b. from a point 1570. 2. In the bigynnyng God made of nouȝt heuene and erthe WYCLIF *Gen.* i. 1. 4. Who hast safely brought us to the b. of this day *Bk. Com. Pr.* 5. Great fortunes acquired from small beginnings A. SMITH. Hence **Begi·nningless** *a.* uncreate.

Begird (bǐgə̄·ɹd), *v.* Pa. t. and pple. **begirt.** [OE. *begyrdan*, f. *bi-*, BE- 1 + *gyrdan* :—OTeut. **gurdjan* to GIRD.] **1.** To gird about or round. Also *fig.* **2.** To encompass *with*. Also *fig.* OE. †**3.** *spec.* To besiege –1791.

Begirdle (bǐgə̄·ɹd'l), *v.* 1837. [See BE- 1.] To encompass like a girdle.

Begirt (bǐgə̄·ɹt), *v.* 1608. [See BE- 1. A secondary form of GIRD, from the pa. pple. *girt*, or f. *girt*, obs. f. GIRTH *sb.*] To surround, enclose.

‖**Beglerbeg** (be·gləɹbeg). 1594. [a. Turk. 'bey of beys'; cf. BEG (of which *begler* is the pl.).] The governor of a province of the Ottoman Empire, in rank next to the grand vizier.

Begloom (bǐˌglū·m), *v.* 1799. [See BE-.] To render gloomy.

Begnaw (bǐnǭ·), *v.* Pa. pple. **begnawn.** [OE. *begnagan*, f. BE- 1 + *gnagan* to GNAW.] To gnaw at; to corrode; to nibble.

Bego·, *v.* *Obs.* exc. in *pa. pple.* **begone.** [Com. Teut.: OE. *begān*, f. *bi-*, BE- about + *gangan*, *gân* to GO.] †**1.** To go about, inhabit; to cultivate –ME. †**2.** To go about hostilely; to beset, overrun –1602. †**3.** To dress –1513. **4.** To beset as an environment. Now only in *woe-begone*, and the like. (Orig. 'him was wo begone', i. e. to him woe had closed round.) ME.

†**Bego·d,** *v. rare.* 1576. [See BE- 6.] To make a god of –1716.

Begone (bǐgǫ·n), *ppl. a.*; see BEGO 4.

Begone (bǐgǫ·n), *v. arch.* ME. [orig. consisting of the imper. of BE and the pa. pple. of GO.] Go away, depart, take yourself off. Later established as one word and sometimes const. as an inf. (cf. *beware*).
Angrily ordered to b. CARLYLE.

Begonia (bǐgōᵘ·niă). 1751. [f. Michel *Begon*, a French promoter of botany.] A genus of plants, having flowers without petals, but with coloured perianths, and often richly-coloured foliage, cultivated as ornamental plants.

Begorra (bǐgǫ·ră), *int.* 1839. Ir. var. of BEGAD, BEGAR.

Begotten (bǐgǫ·t'n), *ppl. a.* ME. [pa. pple. of BEGET *v.*] †**1.** Gotten –1523. **2.** Procreated. (Usu. with *only-*, *first-*.) Also *absol.* ME.

Begrace (bǐˌgrēⁱ·s), *v.* 1530. [See BE- 5.] To address as 'your grace'.

†**Begra·ve,** *v.* [Com. Teut.: OE. *bi-*, *be-*

grafan, f. BE- + *grafan* (= OHG. *graban*) to dig.] **1.** To bury -1528. **2.** To engrave ME.

Begrease, begrim, begroan, etc.; see BE- *pref.*

Begrime (bǐˌgrəi·m), *v.* 1553. [See BE- 6.] To blacken or soil with grime.

My name..is now begrim'd and blacke As my own face *Oth.* III. iii. 387.

†**Begri·pe,** *v.* [Com. WGer.: OE. *begrīpan*, f. BE- + *grīpan* to GRIPE.] **1.** To catch hold of; to seize and hold fast -1485. **2.** To take in, contain ME.

Begrudge (bǐˌgrʊ·dʒ), *v.* [f. BE- + GRUDGE, ME. *grucchen* to murmur.] To grumble at; *esp.* to envy (one) the possession of; to give reluctantly, to be reluctant.

To begrutch the cost of a school C. MATHER.

Begru·tten, *ppl. a. Sc.* 1805. [f. BE- 4 + *grutten*, pa. pple. of GREET *v.*] Swollen in face by much weeping.

†**Be·gster.** Also **beggestere.** [f. BEG *v.*] A beggar. CHAUCER.

†**Begua·rd,** *v.* 1605. [See BE- 6.] To adorn with 'guards' or facings -1640.

Beguile (bǐgəi·l), *v.* ME. [See BE- 2.] **1.** To over-reach with guile. Also *absol.* **2.** To deprive *of* by fraud, to cheat out *of* ME. †**3.** To cheat (hopes, etc., or a person in them); to disappoint, to foil -1670. **4.** To win the attention of by wiling means; to charm; to wile on, or into any course 1593. **5.** To divert attention in some pleasant way from; to wile away 1588.

1. To b. this crafty fish WALTON. **2.** Let no man b. you of your reward *Col.* ii. 18. **3.** Thou hast beguil'd my hopes *Two Gent.* v. iv. 37. **5.** By sports like these are all their cares beguil'd GOLDSM. Hence **Begui·lement. Begui·ler. Begui·lingly** *adv.*

Beguine (begi·n, be·gin). 1483. [a. F. *béguine*, f. Lambert *Bègue* or *le Bègue* ('the Stammerer'), a priest of Liège, the founder of the order.] A name for members of certain lay sisterhoods which began in the Low Countries in the 12th c., who devoted themselves to a religious life, but took no vows, and might go away and marry. They are still represented in the Netherlands. Hence **Be·guinage,** an establishment of, or house for, beguines.

‖**Begum** (bī·gɒm). 1634. [Urdū (Pers.) *begam*, ad. East. Turk. *bigim*, fem. of *big*, *bik* prince (cf. BEG, BEY).] A Mohammedan queen, or lady of high rank in Hindustan.

Begun (bǐgʊ·n), *ppl. a.* 1483. [f. BEGIN *v.*] That has begun, or has been begun.

Begunk (bǐgʊ·ŋk), *v. Sc.* 1821. To delude, take in. Hence **Begu·nk** *sb.* a befooling trick.

Behalf (bǐˌhā·f). ME. [BIHALVE, orig. a phr., *be healfe*, and subseq. a prep., became a sb., by the mixture of *on his halve* and *bihalve him*, both meaning 'by or on his side', in *on his bihalve*; see HALF.] **1.** *On b. of*: †**a.** (*lit.*) On the side of -1502; (*fig.*) On (one's own) part or side -1538. **b.** On the part of (another). (With the notion of official agency.) ME. †**c.** As concerns. Also, *on this b.*, etc. -1674. ¶In recent use *on b. of* is often found, improp., in the sense of *in b. of* 2 b. **2.** *In b. of*: †**a.** In the name of -1606. **b.** In the interest of. (With the notion of interposition.) 1598. **c.** *In this* or *that b.*: in respect of this or that; in this or that matter, or aspect (*arch.*). Cf. 1 c. 1458.

1. b. Things which a servant may do on b. of his master BLACKSTONE. **2. a.** And rob in the behalfe of charitie *Tr. & Cr.* v. iii. 22. **b.** Speaking in B. the Trading Interest 1719. **c.** More could be said in that b., but [etc.] 1658.

Beha·ng, *v. Obs.* exc. in *pa. pple.* **Behung.** [OE. *behón*, f. BE- + *hón* (:—*hanhan*) to HANG.] To hang (a thing) about *with*.

†**Beha·p(pen,** *v.* 1450. [See BE- 2.] To befall. With *dat. obj.* -1714.

Behave (bǐˌhē·v), *v.* Pa. t. **behaved.** 1440. [f. BE- 2 + HAVE, to *have* (in a specified way), *esp.* in refl. = Ger. *sich behaben*. Not conn. w. OE. *behabban* 'to contain, detain'.] **1.** *refl.* To bear, comport, or conduct oneself; to act: **a.** with *adv.* or phr. (Formerly a dignified expression, but now usually as in b.) **b.** Without qualification: To conduct oneself with propriety. (Now chiefly said of children.) 1691. Also *transf.* of things. †**2.** To handle, conduct, regulate -1607. **3.** *intr.*: in same senses as 1 a. and b. 1719.

1. To b. oneself with gallantry STEELE, with insolence 1715. **b.** B. yourself (*mod.*). **2.** *Timon* III. v. 22. **3.** He behaved like a man of sense MACAULAY. *To b. towards* or *to*: to act in regard *to*. Hence **Beha·ved** *ppl. a.* (usu. with *adv.*, as *well-*, etc.). **Beha·ving** *vbl. sb.* conduct.

Behaviour (bǐˌhē·viəɹ), *sb.* 1490. [f. BEHAVE *v.*, after HAVOUR, form of AVER *sb.*; really OF. *aveir, avoir*, affiliated in Eng. to *have*, and spelt *haver, havour*, etc. See HAVOUR.] **1.** Manner of conducting oneself; bearing, manners. †**b.** 'Person'. *John* I. i. 3. **c.** *absol.* Good manners 1591. **2.** Conduct; course of action *towards* or *to* others 1515. †**3.** Handling, disposition *of* (anything); bearing (*of* body) -1589. **4.** *transf.* Of things 1674.

1. In clennes of lyfe and in a gentyll behauer BALE. **c.** Strong aversion to b. DE FOE. **2.** *To be* (or *stand*) *on* or *upon one's b.*, or *one's good b.*: to be placed on a trial of conduct or deportment; hence, to behave one's best. **4.** The b. of the vessel during her maiden voyage 1882. Hence †**Beha·vioured** *a.* mannered.

Behaviourism (bǐhē·vyəriz'm). *Psychol.* 1913. [f. prec. sb. + -ISM.] A theory and method of psychological investigation based on the objective study of behaviour. Hence **Beha·viourist,** one who practises this method; **-i·stic** *a.*

Behead (bǐˌhe·d), *v.* [OE. *behéafdian*, f. BE- 3 (priv.) + *héafod* HEAD.] *trans.* To deprive of the head or top part. Also *fig.*

To bee byhedded at Pountfreit MORE. Hence **Behea·dal.**

Behemoth (bǐhī·mǫþ, -ǭþ). ME. [Heb. *b'hēmōth*, used in Job xl. 15. Usu. taken as an Egyptian word *p-ehe-mau* 'water-ox'.] An animal: prob. the hippopotamus; also a general term for one of the largest and strongest animals. Cf. LEVIATHAN.

Lo! that I made with thee bemoth WYCLIF *Job* xl. 15. B. biggest born of Earth MILT. *P. L.* VII. 471.

Behest (bǐˌhe·st), *sb.* [OE. *behǽs*, repr. of OTeut. **bihait-ti-*, abst. sb. f. *bihait-an*, in OE. *behátan* to BEHIGHT; thence, early ME. *bihese*, whence *bihes-te*, after wds. in *-te*, OE. *-t*. See HEST.] †**1.** A vow, promise -1634. **2.** A command, injunction ME.

1. Breken his biheste CHAUCER. **2.** Us he [God] sends upon his high behests MILT. *P. L.* VIII. 238. Hence †**Behe·st** *v.* to vow, promise.

†**Behi·ght,** *v.* [OTeut.: OE. *bi-, behátan*, f. *bi-*, BE- + OE. *hátan* = Goth. *háitan* to call. The Past *behight* (*behite*) was ultimately taken as present, with pa. t. and pple. *behighted*. See HIGHT *v.*] **I. 1.** To vow, promise -1621. **2.** To hold out hope of (life, etc.) -1571. **3.** To assure (one) of the truth of a statement. (Cf. mod. *I promise you.*) -1513.

1. The trayteresse..That al behoteth, and nothing halt CHAUCER. **3.** Litel whil it last, I you biheete CHAUCER.

II. Improper uses by the archaists. **1.** *trans.* To grant, deliver. SPENSER. **2.** To bid, ordain. SPENSER. **3.** To call, to name -1652. **4.** To bespeak 1615. Hence †**Behi·ght** *sb.* a promise.

Behind (bǐhəi·nd), *adv. prep.* (*sb.*) [OE. *bi-, behindan*, f. *bi-*, BE- + *hindan*, f. root *hind-* in HINDER, HINDMOST, with advb. suffix *-ana*, orig. meaning direction *from*. The use as prep. originated in an OE. dat. of reference, *behindan him* 'in the rear *as to him*'.] **A.** *adv.* **1.** In a place whence the others have gone; *fig.* in the position, condition, or state which a person or thing has left ME. **b.** In the past 1526. **2.** In the rear of anything moving; following ME. **3.** *fig.* (from 1.) In reserve; still to come ME. **4.** *fig.* (from 2.) **a.** Of progress; *hence* of rank, order, etc. ME. **b.** *esp.* In arrear ME. **5.** At the back; in the rear ME. Also *fig.* **6.** Backwards ME. **7.** To the back, into the rear ME.

1. We shall abyde bihynde ME. To leave this world behinde DONNE. **b.** As in the winters left b. TENNYSON. **2.** *To come b.*: to follow. *To fall b.*: to fall into the rear. **3.** But stronger evidence is b. MACAULAY. **4. a.** B. with no one in kind speeches MISS BURNEY. **b.** B. with my landlord 1614. **6.** Run, Nor look b. 1692. **7.** Go b. and look (*mod.*).

B. *prep.* **1.** In a place, or (*fig.*) condition, state, or time left by (one) ME. **2.** In the rear of (one moving); after ME. **b.** Inferior to, in progress, order, etc. 1526. **3.** Later than (the set time) 1600. **4.** In the space lying to the rear of, on the back side of ME. Also *fig.* **5.** On the farther side of; beyond ME.; *fig.* hidden by 1866. **6.** Backward from (oneself) ME. **7.** To the back side of ME. Also *fig.*

1. He left b. him myself and a sister *Twel. N.* II. i. 20. **2. b.** B. her years LAMB. **4.** *B. fortifications*, etc.: inside of, so as to be defended by them. **5.** B. the Mountain DRYDEN. *B. the scenes*: in the rear of the scenery of a theatre; *hence*, out of sight, in private. **7** Get thee b. mee, Satan *Matt.* xxvi. 23. *To go b.*: to press an inquiry into what is not avowed. Phr. *B. (one's) back*: emphatic for *b. (one)* in all senses, *esp.* 'in one's absence'.

C. as *sb.* (*colloq.* and *vulgar*): The back side (of the person or of a garment); the posteriors.

Behindhand (bǐhəi·ndˌhænd), *adv.* (and *a.*) 1530. [f. BEHIND *prep.* + HAND, prob. after *beforehand*.] **1.** In arrears financially, in debt. (Const. *with*.) **2.** Behind time, late, too late; behind the times 1549. **3.** In a state of backwardness (*in*); ill prepared (*with*) 1542. **4.** *attrib.* Backward, tardy. *Wint. T.* v. i. 151.

1. Something b. with the world SWIFT. **3.** B. in politeness STERNE.

†**Behi·ther,** *adv.* and *prep.* 1521. [See BE-, and cf. *behind*, etc. (A word worth reviving.)] **A.** *prep.* **1.** On this side of. (L. *cis, citra*.) -1711. **2.** Short of, save -1671. **B.** *adv.* On the nearer side 1650.

1. A..seat 2 miles b. Cliefden EVELYN.

Behold (bǐhōu·ld), *v.* [OE. *bihaldan*, f. *bi-*, BE- + *haldan* to HOLD. The sense of watching is Eng. only.] †**1.** *trans.* To hold by, retain -1525. †**2.** *intr.* To hold on *by*, belong *to*; *trans.* to concern -ME. †**3.** To regard (with the mind), consider; *intr.* to have regard *unto*, *to* -ME. **4. a.** To hold in view, to watch (*arch.*) OE. Hence **b.** To see: the current sense ME. †**5.** *intr.* To look -1795. †**6.** *intr.* To look or face; *trans.* to face -1677. †**7.** To look upon *as* -1662.

4. a. From far B. the field POPE. **b.** I neuer yet beheld that speciall face, Which I could fancie *Tam. Shr.* II. i. 11.

Beho·ld, *int.* 1535. Imper. of prec. vb.; = Lo!

B., I will send my messenger *Mal.* iii. 1.

Beholden (bǐhōu·ld'n), *ppl. a.* ME. [Orig. pa. pple. of BEHOLD *v.*] **1.** Attached or obliged (*to* a person). †**2.** In duty bound (*to do* something) -1502.

1. The more b. is the lorde unto hym CAXTON. †**Beholdenness,** a mistake for *Beholdingness*, q. v.

Beholder (bǐhōu·ldəɹ). ME. [f. BEHOLD *v.* + -ER[1].] One who beholds, a watcher, spectator.

Beholding (bǐhōu·ldiŋ), *vbl. sb.* ME. [f. as prec. + -ING[1].] **1.** The action of looking at; sight; †consideration. **2.** The thing beheld (*arch.*) ME. ¶ Johnson's sense 'Obligation' is a blunder.

Beho·lding, *ppl. a.* 1483. [f. as prec. + -ING[2].] †**1.** Under obligation. (Orig. an error for BEHOLDEN.) In late use: Dependent. -1719. **2.** Gazing 1593. Hence †**Beho·ldingness,** obligation; dependence.

Behoof (bǐhū·f). [OE. **bihóf* 'utility', f. *bi-*, BE- + *hafjan*, OE. *hębban*, pa. t. *hóf* 'to HEAVE'.] **1.** Use, benefit. Chiefly in *to, for, on (the) b. of.* (*In, on b. of*, are due to confusion with *behalf*.) *pl.* rare. ME. †**2.** Duty (*rare*) 1594. †**3.** ? A douceur SPENSER.

1. To the use and b. of A and his heirs BLACKSTONE.

Behove, behoove (bǐhū·v, -hōu·v), *v.* [OE. *bi-, behófian*; see BEHOOF. Lit. 'to be of behoof'. Historically, it rimes with *move*, not with *grove*, as now.] †**1.** *trans.* To have use for or need of -1670. **2.** †To be physically of use or needful *to*; (only in 3 *pers.*) -1667; to be incumbent ME.; to befit, be due *to*; to belong 1470. **3.** quasi-*impers.* (the subject being a clause). Now ordinarily with *it* (*arch.*). ME. **4.** As a personal verb: = must needs, ought, have. (Due to confusion of acc. and nom. Now only *Sc.*) ME.

3. It behooves the more weakly..to be more cautious 1756. It behoveth, that the son of man must die TINDALE. Hence †**Beho·vable** *a.* useful, incumbent. **Beho·veful, -hoo·veful** *a.* (*arch.*) useful; expedient; needful. †**Beho·vefully** *adv.* †**Beho·vely** *a.* of use.

Beige (bēʒ). 1858. [a. F.] A fine woollen dress-material, originally left in its natural colour but now dyed. **b.** A yellowish-gray shade, like that of unbleached wool. Also *adj.* and *Comb.*

Beild, var. of BIELD *sb.* and *v.*

Bein (bīn), *a.* and *adv.* Now *dial.* ME. [?] **A.** *adj.* †**1.** Pleasant, kindly; nice. (L. *amœnus*, *almus, benignus.*) -1513. **2.** Comfortable 1533. **3.** Well-to-do 1548. **B.** *adv.* Pleasantly ME.

Being (bī·iŋ), *vbl. sb.* ME. [f. BE *v.*] **1.** Existence, material or immaterial; life 1596. **2.** Existence in some relation of place or condition 1526. †**b.** Standing (in the world) -1818. †**c.** Livelihood -1731. **3.** Substance, constitution, nature ME.; essence 1530. **4.** *gen.* That which exists or is conceived as existing 1628; (with qualifications) God 1600; a human being 1751.

1. The house had no corporate b. FREEMAN. A legacy to a person in b. POWELL. **2.** During his b. a Bishop BURNET. **3.** Our very b. is none of ours 1659. **4.** Beings that had no other existence but in their own minds LOCKE. The Supreme B. SCRIVENER. This mean, incorrigible b. MAR. EDGEWORTH. Hence **Be·ingless** *a.* non-existent.

Being (bī·iŋ), *ppl. a.* 1458. [f. BE *v.*] **1.** Existing, present; *esp.* in *The time b.* **2.** *absol.* = It being the case that, seeing.

†**Bei·sance.** 1556. Aphet. f. OBEISANCE, ABAISANCE -1650.

†**Beja·de,** *v.* 1620. [See BE-.] To tire out -1641.

Bejan (bī·dʒən). *Sc.* 1642. [a. F. *béjaune*, f. *bec jaune.*] A 'yellow beak' or freshman: a term adopted from the University of Paris.

†**Beja·pe,** *v.* ME. [See BE- 2.] To play a trick on; to befool -1500.

Beje·suit. 1644. [See BE- 5.] To work upon by, or subject to, Jesuits.

Bejewel (bĭdʒiū·ĕl), *v.* 1557. [See BE- 6.] To deck with or as with jewels; to spangle.

Beknave (bĭnē·v), *v.* 1525. [See BE- 5.] To call 'Knave'.

†**Beknow·,** *v.* ME. [See BE- 2.] To recognize -1560; to confess -1580.

Phr. *To be beknown*: to be aware *of*; *hence*, to confess. Hence **Beknow·n** *ppl. a.* (*arch.*) known.

‖**Bel,** *a.* ME. [a. F.:—L. *bellum, -am.* Naturalized in ME.] †Fair, fine, beautiful -1678. Used also as a formative prefix in *belsire, belfader*, etc. Cf. *good* in *goodsire*, etc., and mod.F. *bonpapa*, etc.

Belabour (bĭlē·bəɹ), *v.* 1596. [See BE- 4.] †**1.** To labour at; to ply -1686. **2.** To buffet with all one's might 1600. Also *fig.*

1. To b. the earth with culture BARROW. **2.** The tempest which belaboured him 1600.

†**Bel-accoil, -accoyle.** ME. [a. OF. *bel acoil*; cf. ACCOIL.] Kindly greeting, welcome -1596.

Belace (bĭlē·s), *v.* 1648. [See BE-.] **1.** To adorn with lace. †**2.** To beat with stripes.

Bela·ce, *v.* '*Sea Term.* To fasten; as to belace a rope'. Johnson. [A mistake for BELAGE, made first in Bailey's folio, 1730.]

†**Bela·ge,** *v.* 1678. [ME. *belegge*, obs. f. BELAY, or ad. Du. *beleggen.*] *Naut.* To make fast any running rope.

Belam, *v.* 1595. [f. BE- + LAM *v.*] To thrash.

†**Belamou·r.** 1595. [f. F. *bel* + *amour.*] **1.** A loved one of either sex -1603. **2.** A look of love 1610. **3.** Name of some flower. SPENSER.

†**Be·lamy.** ME. [a. F. *bel ami.*] Fair friend (*esp.* as a form of address) -1689.

†**Bela·p,** *v.* ME. [See BE- 1.] To clasp; to surround -1562.

Belate (bĭlē·t), *v.* 1642. [See BE- 5.] To make late, delay.

Belated (bĭlē·tĕd), *ppl. a.* 1618. [f. prec. + -ED [1].] **1.** Overtaken by lateness of the night; *hence*, benighted. **2.** Coming or staying too late; behind date 1670.

1. B. shepherd swains 1789. **2.** Who contested this b. account BURKE. Hence †**Bela·tedness.**

Belaud (bĭlǭ·d), *v.* 1849. [See BE- 2.] To load with praise.

Belay (bĭlē·), *v.* [OE. *bi-, belęcgan*, f. *bi-*, BE- + *lęcgan* (= OTeut. *lagjan*) to LAY. For the naut. use cf. BELAGE.] †**1.** *trans.* To surround, enclose, etc. (a thing) *with* -1606. †**2.** *spec.* To beset with armed men; to beleaguer -1698; to waylay -1760. **3.** *Naut.* To coil a running rope round a cleat, belaying pin, or kevel, so as to secure it. (The only current sense.) 1549. Also *transf.*

3. Mak fast and b. 1549. *B. there*, stop! (Smyth). Hence **Belaying** *vbl. sb.*; chiefly *attrib.*, as in *belaying-cleat, -pin.*

Belch (beltʃ, belʃ), *v.* [OE. *bealcian.* See BELK.] **1.** *intr.* To void wind noisily from the stomach, to eructate. (Now *vulgar.*) **2.** To ejaculate; to vent with vehemence (L. *eructare*). In later use confined to the utterance of offensive things, or to furious vociferation. OE. **3.** To emit by belching. Also *fig.* 1561. **4.** To vomit (*lit.* and *fig.*) 1558. **5.** To eject, throw out; *esp.* of volcanoes, and *hence* of cannons, etc. 1580.

2. To b. out blasphemies against God 1612. **3.** Belching the soure crudities of yesterdayes Poperie MILT. **5.** Aetna hill doth belke forth flakes of fire 1580.

Belch, *sb.* 1513. [f. prec. vb.] An eructation 1570. Also *fig.* 1513. **b.** *slang.* Poor beer 1706.

Belcher (be·lʃəɹ). 1812. [f. Jim *Belcher*, a pugilist.] Any particoloured handkerchief, *esp.* one with blue ground and white spots, worn round the neck.

Beldam, -dame (be·ldəm). 1440. [f. *bel-* (see BEL) + *dam*, earlier *dame* 'mother'.] †**1.** A grandmother (or more remote ancestress). Also *fig.* -1863. **2.** An aged woman. (In 16th c. used in addressing nurses.) 1580. **3.** *esp.* A hag; a witch; a virago (of any age) 1586.

1. To show the beldame daughters of her daughter SHAKS. *Lucr.* 953. **3.** That accursed b. whom she caused to work upon me SCOTT.

Beleaguer (bĭlī·gəɹ), *v.* 1589. [a. Du. *belegeren*, f. *be-* + *leger* CAMP; see LEAGUER.] To surround (a town, etc.) with troops so as to prevent ingress and egress, to invest. 1590. Also *transf.*

Antwerpe..then by him beleaguered 1598. Hence **Belea·guerer. Belea·guerment.**

†**Belea·ve, -eve,** *v.* [OE. *belǣfan*: OTeut. *bilaibjan*, f. *bi-*, BE- + *laibjan*, in OE. *lǣfan* to LEAVE.] **1.** *trans.* To let or cause to remain behind, to abandon -1627. **2.** *intr.* [taking place of BELIVE: = Ger. *bleiben.*] To remain behind, survive, continue -ME. Hence †**Belea·ving** *vbl. sb.* that which is left.

†**Belee,** *v. rare.* [See BE- 6.] To place (a ship) so that the wind is cut off from her.

fig. I..must be be-leed and calmed *Oth.* I. i. 30.

Belemnite (be·lĕmnəit). 1646. [f. mod L. *belemnites* (also used), f. Gr. βέλεμνον a dart (cf. AMMONITE).] *Palæont.* A fossil common in rocks of the Secondary formation; a straight, smooth, cylindrical object, a few inches long, convexly tapering to a point, formerly known, from its shape and supposed origin, as *thunderbolt, thunderstone*, etc. It is the internal bone of an animal allied to the cuttle-fish. Also, this extinct animal. Hence **Belemni·tic** *a.*

†**Bele·per,** *v.* 1623. [See BE- 5.] To afflict with or as with leprosy -1649.

‖**Bel-esprit** (be·lesprī·). 1638. [Fr.] A clever genius, a brilliant wit.

A beauty and a bel esprit MAR. EDGEWORTH.

Beletter (bĭle·təɹ), *v.* 1655. [See BE- 6.] †**1.** To serve with letters. **2.** *nonce-wd.* To decorate with letters (e. g. F.R.S., etc.) 1883.

†**Be·lfather.** 1440. [See BEL.] Grandfather -1483.

Belfry (be·lfri). [ME. *berfrey, -ay*, a. OF. *berfrei, -ai, -ay*, pointing to a late L. *berefrēdus*, ad. Teut. *bergfrid 'defensive place of shelter'.] †**1.** A wooden tower, usually movable, formerly used in besieging fortifications. Prob., at first, a mere shed or pent-house. -1530. **2.** A shed to shelter cattle, carts, produce, etc. 1553. **3.** A bell-tower 1440. **b.** The room of the church tower in which the bells are hung 1549. †**c.** The part of the floor under the tower, where the ringers stand -1659. **4.** *Naut.* An ornamental framing, with a covering, under which the ship's bell is hung 1769.

‖**Belga** (be·lgă). 1926. [L., fem. of *Belgus* Belgian (sc. *pecunia*).] A Belgian unit of exchange (= five Belgian francs).

†**Belga·rd.** [ad. It. *bel guardo.*] A loving look. SPENSER.

Belgium (be·ldʒǒm). 1602. **a.** Latin name of the territory occupied by the Belgæ; **b.** a name for the Netherlands; **c.** title of the new kingdom established by the separation of the provinces watered by the Meuse and Scheldt from the kingdom of the Netherlands. **Belgia** = prec. **b. Belgian** (be·ldʒăn) *a.* of or pertaining to Belgium; as *sb.* †**a.** one of the ancient Belgæ of southern England; †**b.** a Low German; **c.** a native of modern Belgium; **d.** a kind of canary. **Belgic** (be·ldʒik) *a.* of or pertaining to the Netherlands; *sb.* a Low German.

Belial (bī·liăl). ME. [a. Heb., f. *b'lī* without + *ya'al* use; hence lit. 'worthlessness', and 'destruction'; but later treated as a proper name = ὁ πονηρός Satan.] The spirit of evil personified; used by Milton as the name of one of the fallen angels. Also *attrib.*

B. came last, then whom a Spirit more lewd Fell not from heaven MILT. *P. L.* I. 490.

Belibel; see BE- 2.

†**Belie** (bĭləi·), *v.*[1] [OE. *bi-, be-licgan*, f. *bi-*, BE- + *licgan* = OHG. *ligan* to LIE.] **1.** To lie around, encompass -1627; *spec.* to beleaguer -ME. **2.** To lie near; to pertain or belong *to* -1522.

Belie (bĭləi·), *v.*[2] [OE. *belēogan*, f. *bi-*, BE- + *lēogan* = Goth. *liugan* to LIE, tell lies.] Always *trans.* †**1.** To deceive by lying. **2.** To tell lies about; *esp.* to calumniate by lies ME. †**3.** To allege falsely -1659. **4.** To misrepresent 1601; †to disguise -1810. †**5.** To contradict as a lie or a liar -1649. **6.** To be false or faithless to 1698. **7.** To show to be false; to falsify (expectations, etc.) 1685. †**8.** ? To fill with lies. *Cymb.* III. iv. 38.

2. To b. the subjects of the King HUME. **3.** To belye divine Authority MILT. **4.** A declar'd Papist, If his own letter to the Pope belye him not MILT. **6.** He grossly belied his faith FREEMAN. Hence **Beli·er.**

Belief (bĭlī·f). [Early ME. *bileafe*, f. *bi-*, BE- + *leafe*:—OE. *lēafa*, shortened from *gelēafa* 'belief':—OTeut. type *galaubon-, f. *galaub-* 'dear, esteemed'; see BELIEVE.] **1.** The mental action, condition, or habit, of trusting to or confiding in a person or thing; trust, confidence, faith. (*Faith*, orig. = fidelity, fealty, used in 14th c. to translate L. *fides*, has ultimately superseded 'belief' in this sense.) **b.** *absol.* Trust in God; the virtue of faith (*arch.*) ME. **2.** Mental assent to or acceptance of a proposition, statement, or fact, as true, on the ground of authority or evidence; the mental condition involved in this assent 1533. **3.** The thing believed; in early use, *esp.* a religion. Now often = opinion, persuasion. ME. **b.** Intuition, natural judgement 1838. **4.** A creed. *The B.*: the Apostles' Creed (*arch.*) ME.

1. A stedfast byleue of God FISHER. **b.** The war of B. against Unbelief CARLYLE. **2.** My only defence shal be beleefe of nothing SIDNEY. We talked of b. in ghosts BOSWELL. Statements unworthy of b. (*mod.*). Phr. *B. in* (a thing): persuasion of its existence. **3.** It is my b. that.. 1714. Hence †**Belie·fful** *a.*

Believable (bĭlī·văb'l), *a.* ME. [f. BELIEVE *v.*] Capable of being believed. Hence **Believabi·lity. Belie·vableness.**

Believe (bĭlī·v), *v.* [Early ME. *bileven*, f. *bi-*, BE- + *leven*:—OE., Anglian *lēfan*, short f. *gelēfan*, a Com. Teut. vb.:—OTeut. *galaubian to believe, f. *galaub-* 'dear, pleasing'; cf. Goth. *liuban*, Teut. root *lub-, Aryan *lubh-*, to hold dear, whence also LOVE, LIEF. The hist. form is *beleeve*. *Believe* is prob. after *relieve* (from Fr.).] **I.** *intr.* **1.** To have confidence or faith *in*, and consequently to rely upon. Const. *in*, and (in theol. lang.) *on*. Also *absol.* †**2.** To give credence *to*. Repl. by II. 1, 2. -1647. **3.** *ellipt.* To believe *in* (a person or thing), i. e. in its existence or occurrence 1716.

1. I Beleue in God the father almightie *Bk. Com. Pr.* To b. in human nature MOZLEY, universal suffrage (*mod.*). *absol.* Be not afraid, onely beleeue *Mark* v. 36. **3.** To b. in ghosts, the sea serpent (*mod.*).

II. *trans.* **1.** To give credence to (a person in making statements, etc.). Obj. orig. *dat.* ME. **2.** To give credence to (a statement) ME. **3.** With cl. or inf. phrase: To hold it as true *that*.., to think ME. †**4.** To hold as true the existence of. (Now expressed by I. 3.) -1732.

1. A man..who deserves to be believed CLARENDON. **2.** Beleeving lies Against his Maker MILT. *P. L.* X. 42. **3.** Our Conqu'ror whom I now Of force b. Almighty MILT. *P. L.* I. 144. **4.** To b. a God SWIFT. Hence **Belie·ving** *vbl. sb.* the having faith; confidence; the acceptance of a statement as true; *ppl. a.* that believes, or has faith. **Belie·vingly** *adv.*

Believer (bĭlī·vəɹ). 1549. [f. prec. + -ER [1].] One who believes. **a.** One who has faith in the doctrines of religion; *esp.* a Christian. **b.** *gen.* One who believes *in* (or *of*) anything 1600.

Thou diddest open the kyngdome of heauen to all

beleuers *Bk. Com. Pr.* A b. in the rights and power of the crown GREEN.

Beli·ght, *v.* Now *dial.* ME. [See BE-.] To light up.

Belike (bǐləi·k). 1533. [? f. *be* = BY + LIKE *a.* or *sb.*; ? 'By what seems'.] **A.** *adv.* To appearance, probably; possibly. var. †**Beli·kely.** †**B.** *adj.* Like, likely (*to do* something) -1805.

†**Beli·me,** *v.* 1555. [See BE- 6.] To cover, or entangle, as with bird-lime -1674.

Belittle (bǐli·t'l), *v.* 1796. [See BE-. Orig. *U. S.*] 1. To diminish in size. 2. To dwarf 1850. 3. To depreciate 1862.

3. The *Times* in 1809 belittled the victory of Talavera 1881. Hence **Beli·ttlement.**

†**Beli·ve, bilive, blive,** *v.* [OE. *bi-*, *belīfan* :—OTeut. **biliƀan*, f. *bi-*, BE- + **līƀan* 'to remain'. Cf. mod.G. *bleiben*, and its Eng. repr. LEAVE.] *intr.* To remain -1483.

Belive (bǐləi·v), *adv.* [Orig. in ME. *bi, be life, be live,* f. *be, bi,* BY *prep.* + *life, live,* dat. of *līf* LIFE; lit. 'with life'; cf. QUICK, and mod. *look alive.*] 1. With speed, eagerly. (Still *Sc.*) ME. †2. At once -1563. Hence 3. Soon; anon. (Still *Sc.*) 1616.

†**Belk,** *v.* Dial. form of BELCH; *esp.*, To boil, to throb.

Bell (bel), *sb.*[1] [Com. LG.: OE. *belle*, perh. from root of BELL *v.*[4] to make a loud noise.] 1. A hollow body of cast metal, usu. of the form of an inverted deep cup with a recurving brim, which rings, by the vibration of its whole circumference, when struck by a clapper, or hammer suspended within. 2. *spec.* A bell rung to tell the hours; the bell of a clock ME. b. *Naut.* The bell which is struck on shipboard, every half-hour, to indicate the number of half-hours of the watch which have passed; a period of half-an-hour thus indicated 1836. 3. *transf.* Applied to any object or part shaped like a bell; hence BLUE-B., HAREBELL, etc. 1610. 4. *Archit.* The naked vase or corbeille of the Corinthian or Composite capitals 1848. 5. *Mus.* (usu. in *pl.*) An instrument consisting of a number of long metal bars or tubes of various lengths, which when struck with a hammer give out sounds resembling those of different-sized bells. = CARILLON 3.

Phrases. *To bear the b.*: to take the first place (cf. BELL-WETHER). *To bear* or *carry away the b.*: to carry off the prize (perh. a golden or silver bell given as a prize in races, etc.). The two phrases have been confused. *By b. and book, book and b.* (*i.e.* those used in the service of the mass): a mediæval oath. *To curse by b., book, and candle*: referring to a form of excommunication which ended 'Doe to the book, quench the candle, ring the b.!' Also used as a summary of the terrors of excommunication; and *joc.* of the accessories of a religious ceremony. For *b. the cat* see BELL *v.*[5] *As sound as a b.*: see SOUND *a.*

Comb., etc.: **b.-animalcules, -animals,** the *Vorticellidæ*, infusoria having a b.-shaped body on a long flexible stalk; **-binder,** the large Wild Convolvulus or Bindweed; **-boat,** one with a b. which rings as the vessel is moved by the waves, and thus gives warning; so **-buoy**; **-crank,** a kind of lever for communicating motion from one bell-wire to another lying at right angles to it; also *attrib.*; **-founder,** a caster or maker of bells; **-gable,** one in which bells are hung; **-glass,** a b.-shaped glass, used to protect plants; **-hanger,** one whose busines it is to put up bells, bell-wires, etc.; **-heather,** the cross-leaved heath, *Erica tetralix*; **-jar,** a b.-shaped glass jar used in chemical and physical laboratories; **-moth,** a group of the family *Tortricidæ*, named from their outline when at rest; **-pepper,** a species of Capsicum (*C. grossum*), named from the shape of the fruit; **-polype** (= *bell-animalcule*); **-pull,** a handle or cord attached to a b.-wire; **-ringer,** one who rings a church or town b.; **-roof,** one shaped like a b.; **-rope,** the rope by which a b. is rung; **-stone,** the part of a column between the shaft and the abacus (cf. 4); **-tent,** one resembling a t. in shape; **-tower**; **-trap,** a bell-shaped stench-trap.

Bell, *sb.*[2] 1594. [? A transf. use of prec., from its shape.] The strobile of the hop plant. So **Bell** *v.*[1], to be, begin to be, in b. 1574.

Bell, *sb.*[3] Now chiefly *Sc.* and *dial.* 1483. [Cf. mod. Du. *bel.*] A bubble.

Bell, *sb.*[4] 1510. [f. BELL *v.*[4]] The cry of a stag or buck at rutting time.

†**Bell,** (bel), *v.*[2] Pa. pple. **bollen.** ME. [App. repr. OE. *belgan* to swell.] *intr.* To swell up (like a boil) -1664. Also *fig.*

Bell, *v.*[3] Now *dial.* 1598. [Goes with BELL *sb.*[3]] *intr.* To bubble.

Bell (bel), *v.*[4] [OE. *bellan* to bellow; cf. BELLOW.] 1. *intr.* To bellow, roar. 2. *spec.* Of the cry of deer in rutting time 1486. 3. *trans.* To bellow forth 1596.

Bell, *v.*[5] 1721. [f. BELL *sb.*[1]] 1. *trans.* To furnish with a bell 1762. 2. To cause to bulge out 1870.

1. *To b. the cat*: to hang a bell round the cat's neck, so as to be warned of its approach, as the mice proposed to do in the fable, and *esp.* to undertake the perilous part in any movement.

‖**Belladonna** (be:lăˌdǫ·nă). 1597. [mod.L.; a. It. 'fair lady'.] 1. *Bot.* The specific name of the Deadly Nightshade (*Atropa B.*), occas. used as Eng. 2. *Med.* The leaves and root of this plant, and the drug thence prepared, the active principle of which is *atropine* 1788.

1. Bella-donna..so called because the Italian ladies make a cosmetic from the juice PULTNEY. **Belladonna Lily,** *Amaryllis Belladonna*, a native of the Cape of Good Hope.

Bellarmine (be·lāɹmīn). Now *Hist.* 1719. A glazed drinking-jug with capacious belly and narrow neck, orig. designed as a burlesque likeness of Cardinal Bellarmine.

Jugs, Mugs, and Pitchers, and Bellarmines of State D'URFEY.

Bell-bird (be·lbəɹd). 1848. [f. BELL *sb.*[1]] A name given to two birds, the *Procnias carunculata* or Campanero of Brazil, and the *Myzantha melanophrys* of Australia, both having a bell-like note.

Belle (bel). 1622. [a. mod.F., OF. *bele* :— L. *bella*, fem.; see BEAU, BEL.] **A.** *adj.* †1. Handsome 1668. 2. In Fr. phrases, occas. used in Eng., as *b. assemblée* brilliant gathering; *b. dame* belle; *b. passion* the tender passion 1698. **B.** *sb.* A handsome woman; a reigning beauty 1622.

sb. The b. of all Paris last winter O. MEREDITH.

Belled (beld), *ppl. a.* 1833. [f. BELL *sb.* or *v.*] 1. Furnished with a bell or bells. Often in comb. 2. Bell-flowered. Often in comb. 1850.

Belleric, beleric (bele·rik), *a.* and *sb.* 1757. [a. F., ad. (ult.) Arab. *balīlaj.*] The fruit of *Terminalia Bellerica*, or Bastard Myrobalan, imported from India for use as a dye.

‖**Belles-lettres** (be:l le·tr), *sb. pl.* 1710. [Fr.; 'fine letters', parallel to *beaux arts*; embracing grammar, rhetoric, and poetry.] Elegant literature or literary studies; formerly = 'the humanities', *literæ humaniores.* Now = 'literature'; and *esp.* applied to light literature, or the æsthetics of literary study. Hence **Belle·trist, -lettrist,** one devoted to belles-lettres. **Belletri·stic** *a.* of or pertaining to belles-lettres.

Bell-flower (be·lˌflauəɹ, -flauᵊɹ). 1578. [f. BELL *sb.*[1]] Any plant of the genus *Campanula*, having bell-shaped blossoms.

Be·ll-house. *arch.* and *dial.* OE. [f. BELL *sb.*[1]] = BELFRY 4.

†**Be·llibone.** *rare.* 1579. [? corrupt f. F. *belle et bonne*, or perversion of BONNIBEL.] A bonny lass.

†**Be·llic, -al,** *a.* 1513. [a. F. *bellique*, ad. L. *bellicus.*] Of or pertaining to war; warlike -1680.

Bellicose (be:likōᵘ·s), *a.* ME. [ad. L. *bellicosus.*] Inclined to war or fighting; warlike.

Our godis aboue..In Albione hes plantit..The perfite pepill, bald and bellicois STEWART. Hence **Be·llico·sely** *adv.* **Bellico·sity.** var. †**Be·llicous.**

Bellied (be·lid), *ppl. a.* 1475. [f. BELLY *v.* or *sb.*] 1. Having a belly. Often in comb., e. g. *big-b.* b. Corpulent 1532. Also *fig.*

1. The Colt..Sharp headed, Barrel belly'd, broadly backed DRYDEN. B. monks 1532.

Belligerence (beli·dʒĕrĕns). 1814. [f. BELLIGERENT *a.*] The carrying on of hostilities; also = next.

Belli·gerency. Also **-ancy.** 1863. [f. as prec.] The position or status of a belligerent.

Belligerent (beli·dʒĕrĕnt). 1577. [The earlier *belligerant* was ad. L. *belligerantem*, *belligerare.* The current sp. is erron.; but cf. *magnificent.*] **A.** *adj.* 1. Waging regular recognized war. Also *fig.* or *transf.* 1809. 2. *attrib.* Of or pertaining to belligerents 1865. **B.** *sb.* A nation, party, or person waging regular war 1811. Also *fig.* or *transf.* 1839.

Belling (be·liŋ), *vbl. sb.* 1440. [f. BELL *v.*[4] + -ING[1].] 1. The roaring of animals. 2. *spec.* The cry of deer in rutting time; hence *ellipt.* the rutting season. Occas. *attrib.* 1513.

Belli·potent, *a.* 1635. [ad. L. *bellipotentem.*] Mighty in war. (*Obs.* in serious use.)

Bellman (be·lmæn). ME. [f. BELL *sb.*[1]] 1. A man who rings a bell; *esp.* a town-crier. (Formerly a bellman also acted as night-watchman, and called the hours.) †2. He who 'bears the bell'; the best (*rare*) 1617.

1. The b. came by..and cried 'Past one of the clock, and a cold, frosty, windy morning' PEPYS.

Be·ll-me·tal. 1541. An alloy of about 4 parts of copper to one of tin, of which bells are made. Also *attrib.*

Bell-metal ore, stannite, which has the appearance of bell-metal.

Bellon (be·lən). 1794. Lead-colic.

Bellona (belōᵘ·nă). 1605. [L., f. *bellum.*] 1. Name of the goddess of war; also *transf.* 2. One of the asteroids.

Bellona's Bridegroom, lapt in proofe *Macb.* I. ii. 54.

Belloot, belote (bĕlū·t, bĕlōᵘ·t). 1866. [ad. Sp. *bellota* acorn.] The edible acorn of *Quercus Ballota*, in N. Africa and Spain. **Bellote Oak:** the tree which bears it.

Bellow (be·lōᵘ), *v.* [OE. *bylgian*, ME. *belwen*, of uncertain etym. Cf. BELL *v.*[4]] 1. *prop.* To roar as a bull. 2. Used of other animals 1486. 3. Of human beings: To cry in a loud and deep voice; to roar (*depreciative* or *joc.*); also to roar from pain 1602. Also *trans.* 4. Of thunder, cannon, etc.: To make a loud hollow noise; to roar ME. Also with *obj.* 1706.

1. Iupiter Became a Bull, and bellow'd *Wint. T.* IV. iv. 28. 2. The croaking Rauen doth b. for Reuenge *Haml.* III. ii. 264. 3. Not fit for that liberty which.. they bellowed for MILT. *trans.* To b. out blasphemies 1581. 4. A soun As lowde as beloweth wynde in helle CHAUCER. Hence **Be·llower.**

Be·llow, *sb.* 1779. [f. prec. vb.] The roar of a bull. Also *transf.* of human beings, cannon, thunder, a storm, etc.

Bellows (be·lōᵘz, be·ləs), *sb.* OE. [Now used only in the pl. In OE. *blæst-bęl(i)g* 'blowing-bag', reduced later to *bęlg, bylg, bylig*, whence ME. *beli, bely, buly*, the same wd. as BELLY, q. v. In the 16th c. the northern form *belu, belw*, with pl. *belwes, belowes, bellows*, became established as the lit. form.] An instrument or machine constructed to furnish a strong blast of air. In its simplest form, it consists of an upper and lower board joined by flexible leather sides, enclosing a cavity, and furnished with a valve opening inwards, through which air enters, filling and expanding the cavity, and with a nozzle, through which the air is forced out when the machine is compressed. Used to blow a fire, to supply air to an organ, etc. Often, with reference to the two halves or handles, called *a pair of b.*, rarely, as sing., *a bellows.* Also *fig.* 2. The expansible part of a camera 1884. 3. *Hydrostatic Bellows*; see HYDROSTATIC.

1. Thou..like a b., swell'st thy face DRYDEN. *fig.* My voice is not a b. unto ire KEATS.

Comb. **b.-fish,** *Centriscus Scolopax*, from its shape.

†**Be·llows,** *v. rare.* 1605. [f. prec.] To blow (with bellows) -1748.

†**Bellrags.** 1548. *Herb.* A water plant, *Nasturtium amphibium* (Britten).

Bell-tongue; see BILTONG.

†**Be·lluine,** *a.* 1618. [ad. L. *belluinus*, f. *bellua.*] Pertaining to or characteristic of beasts; brutal -1731.

The animal and b. life ATTERBURY.

Bell-wether (be·lwe:ðəɹ). ME. [f. BELL *sb.*[1]] 1. The leading sheep of a flock, on whose neck a bell is hung 1440. 2. *fig.* A leader. (Mostly *contemptuous.*) ME.

Bellwort (be·lwɒɹt). 1884. [f. BELL *sb.*[1]] Any plant of the N.O. *Campanulaceæ*. Also, in U. S., a name for the genus *Uvularia.*

Belly (be·li), *sb.* [ME. *bali, beli* :-OE. *bæl(i)g, bęl(i)g*, 'bag, skin', Goth. *balgs* :— OTeut. **balgi-z*, f. *belgan*, pa. t. *balg*, to be inflated. See also BELLOWS. The sense 'belly' is Eng. only.] †1. A bag, purse, pod, husk OE. only. †2. The body -ME. 3. That part of the human body which lies between the breast and the thighs, and contains the bowels; the abdomen. (The ordinary mod. sense.) ME. 4. The under part of the body of animals 1440.

5. That part of the body which receives food; the stomach with its adjuncts ME. 6. The bowels ME. 7. The womb 1440. 8. The 'inside' of the body 1491. 9. The interior (of things material and immaterial) 1535. 10. The bulging part, *e.g.* of a bottle, a vein of ore, a muscle, etc. 1591. 11. A concave surface, *e.g.* the belly of a sail 1607. 12. The front, inner, or lower surface of anything, as opp. to the *back*; e.g. the upper plate of the sounding box of a violin, etc.; the sound-board of a piano 1790.

3. The Iustice in faire round b. *A. Y. L.* II. vii. 154. 4. A..Serpent on his b. prone MILT. *P. L.* x. 514. 5. The b. is not filled with fair words *Prov.* Whose God is their bely *Phil.* iii. 19. Evyll beastes, and slowe belies *Tit.* i. 12. To work for the Backs and Bellies of the People 1719. 8. Ionas in the bely of the fysh *Jonah* ii. 1. 9. Out of the bely off hell I cried *Jonah* ii. 2.

Comb.: **b.-ache**, the colic in the bowels; **-bound** *a.*, constipated; **-brace**, a cross-brace passing beneath the steam-boiler of a locomotive; **†-cheat** (*slang*), food; also, an apron; **†-doublet**, one covering the b.; **-fretting**, pain in a horse's b.; also, the galling of a horse's b. with a girth; **-gut**, a slothful glutton; **-guy** (*Naut.*), a tackle applied half-way up sheers; **-pinched** *a.*, pinched with hunger; **†-slave**, a glutton; **-stay** (*Naut.*), a stay used half-mast down.

Belly (be·li), *v.* 1606. [f. prec.] 1. To cause to swell out. 2. *intr.* To bulge or swell out 1624. †3. To become corpulent -1772.

3. I begin to b., I think SHADWELL.

Be·lly-band. 1523. [f. BELLY *sb.*] 1. The band which passes round the belly of a horse in harness, to check the play of the shafts. 2. *Naut.* A strip of canvas stitched across a sail, to strengthen it 1860. 3. The piece of string on the face of a kite to which the ball of twine is attached.

†Be·lly-cheer, *sb.* 1549. [f. as prec.] 1. The gratification of the belly -1650. 2. *concr.* Viands -1699. **†Be·lly-cheer** *v. intr.* to feast.

Belly-ful (be·li₁ful). 1535. [f. as prec.] 1. One's fill of food 1573. 2. A sufficiency; as much as one cares to take. (Now *coarse.*)

1. I never once had my b., even of dry bread SMOLLETT. 2. Bellyfulls of Sermons 1705.

Belly-god (be·li₁gǫd). 1540. [f. as prec.] One who makes his belly his god; a glutton.

†Be·lly-piece. 1591. [f. as prec.] 1. The peritoneum -1659. 2. An apron 1689. 3. The piece forming the belly of a violin, etc. 1609.

Be·lly-ti·mber. 1607. [f. as prec.] Food. (Not now in serious use.)

†Belo·ck, *v.* [See BE- 2.] Intens. of LOCK. *Meas. for M.* v. 210.

Belomancy (be·lomænsi). 1646. [f. Gr. βέλος + μαντεία.] Divination by means of arrows.

Belong (bǐlǫ·ŋ), *v.* [ME. *bi-*, *belongen*, app. intensive of *longen*; see LONG *v.*[2]] 1. *intr.* To go along with, as an adjunct, function, or duty; to pertain *to*. Also *impers.* or with subject *it*. 2. To pertain, concern, or relate *to* (*arch.*) ME. 3. To be the rightful possession of. Const. *to*; occas. w. *indirect obj.* ME. b. To be a property or attribute of 1662. 4. To be connected with; to form a part or appendage of ME.

1. Wee know what belongs to a Watch *Much Ado* III. iii. 40. Here..it doth not well b. To speak KEATS. 2. All that belongs to this *Cymb.* v. v. 147. 3. Property belonging to another state 1852. If motion doth b. to it 1662. 4. To b. to a parish CAXTON, to the Lady Oliuia SHAKS., to a period 1875, to the rank and file 1884.

Belonging (bǐlǫ·ŋiŋ), *vbl. sb.* 1603. [f. prec. + -ING[1]. Perh. the pl. *belongings* was orig. taken from pr. pple., = 'things belonging'.] Usu. in *pl.* only. 1. Circumstances connected with a person or thing. 2. Goods, effects 1817. 3. Relatives 1852. 4. A thing forming a part, appendage, or accessory of another 1863.

1. Thy selfe and thy belongings Are not thine owne so proper *Meas. for M.* I. i. 30. 2. Collecting their belongings 1871. 3. To be trouble enough to one's belongings DICKENS.

Belonite (be·lǒnəit). 1879. [f. L. *belone*, a. Gr.] *Min.* A mineral variety occurring in microscopic needle-shaped crystals.

Belo·rd, *v.* 1586. [See BE- 5.] 1. To address as 'my lord'. 2. To act the lord over.

Belove (bǐlʊ·v), *v.* [ME. *biluven*, *-loven*. Cf. Ger. *belieben*.] †1. *intr.* To be pleasing ME. only. 2. To love. Now only in *pass.* ME.

Beloved (bǐlʊ·vėd, -lʊ·vd). ME. [f. prec. + -ED[1].] A. *ppl. adj.* Loved. (Often *well-*, etc.).

Dearly b. brethren *Bk. Com. Pr.*

B. *sb.* (cf. *dear.*) One who is beloved 1526.

What is thy beloued more then another beloued *Song* v. 9.

Below (bǐlōᵘ·). [f. BE *prep.* + LOW *a.* (in ME. *loȝ*, *loogh*). Rare (and only as adv.) in ME. App. a var. of *a-lowe* ALOW, parallel to *an-high* (now *on high*); cf. *a-fore*, *be-fore*.] A. (without obj.) *adv.* 1. *gen.* In or to a lower position, lower down; also *fig.*; *hence*, later in a book or writing; at the foot of the page 1694. 2. a. Under heaven; on earth (*arch.* or *poet.*) 1574. b. Under the earth; in Hades, in hell 1610. c. On a lower floor; in or into the cabin or hold of a ship 1598.

1. The child..leaped..into the flood b. GOLDSM. *fig.* The judgment of the Court b. 1834. 2. Man wants but little here b. GOLDSM. Or Phœbus Steeds are foundered Or Night kept chain'd b. *Temp.* IV. i. 31.

B. (with obj.) *prep.* 1. Lower in position than 1575. Also *fig.* 2. Lower on a slope than; farther down a valley or stream than; nearer (what is considered) the bottom of a room than 1603. 3. Deeper than. Also *fig.* 1849. 4. Underneath 1605. 5. Lower in a graduated scale than; hence *fig.* lower in rank, dignity, or station than 1601; inferior to 1711. 6. = BENEATH 1637.

1. B. the snow-line 1849. *B.-stairs* (now usu. *downstairs*): on or to the floor b., *esp.* the ground-floor. 2. B. the gangway sat a strong Radical party 1885. 3. At a small depth b. the surface 1849. 5. B. par 1788, Zero 1849, the average 1884. *fig.* To dress b. oneself LAMB. 6. A compiler..who thinks no fact b. his regard HALLAM.

†Be·lsire. ME. [f. BEL + SIRE; cf. *beldame.*] A grandfather; an ancestor -1631.

†Be·lswagger. Also **belly-.** 1592. [? a contr. of *belly-swagger.*] A swaggering gallant or bully; a whoremonger, pimp -1775.

Belt (belt), *sb.* [Com. Teut.: OE. *bęlt*, prob. :—OTeut. **baltjo-z*, ad. L. *balteus.*] 1. A broadish flat strip of leather, etc., used to gird the person, and to support articles of use or ornament; b. *esp.* one worn as a mark of rank or distinction ME. Also *fig.* 2. *transf.* A broadish strip or stripe, or a continuous series of objects, engirdling something 1664. 3. *Mech.* A broad flat strap, passing round two wheels or shafts, and communicating motion from one to the other 1795. 4. A broadish flexible strap. (The idea of girdling here begins to be lost.) 1672. 5. A tract or district long in proportion to its breadth 1808. b. *Arch.* 'A course of stones projecting from the naked, either moulded, plain, or fluted' (Gwilt). c. *Naval Arch.* A series of thick iron plates running along the water-line in armoured vessels 1885.

1. The champion's b. THACKERAY. *fig.* Within the b. of rule *Macb.* v. ii. 17. Phr. *To hit below the b.*: *fig.* to act unfairly in any contest. 2. A b. of ice SOUTHEY, of Scotch firs 1834. The body of Jupiter is surrounded by several parallel faint substances called Belts 1787. 5. A range or b. about forty degrees broad, across the old continent 1808. *Great* and *Little Belts*: two channels leading to the Baltic.

Comb.: **b.-lacing**, thongs for lacing together the ends of machine belts; **-saw** (= *band-saw*; see BAND *sb.*[2]); **-wise** *adv.* in the manner of a b.

Belt (belt), *v.* ME. [f. BELT *sb.*[1]] 1. To gird with or as with a belt; to fasten on with a belt. Also *refl.* 2. To thrash with a belt. Cf. *to strap.* 1649. 3. To shear, as the buttocks and tails of sheep 1523.

1 *transf.* They b. him round with hearts undaunted WORDSW. 3. Belting of sheep, is the dressing of them from filth HOLME.

Beltane (be·ltě̆n). ME. [Lowland Sc. f. Gael. *bealltainn*, the first of May.] 1. The first day of May (reckoned since 1752 according to Old Style); Old May-day. The quarter-days anciently in Scotland were Hallowmas, Candlemas, Beltane, and Lammas. ‖2. An ancient Celtic anniversary celebration on May-day, when great bonfires were kindled on the hills 1772.

2. For him thy b. yet may burn BYRON. *attrib.* The shepherd lights his b. fire SCOTT.

Belted (be·ltėd), *ppl. a.* 1483. [f. BELT *v.*, *sb.*] 1. Wearing, or girded with, a belt; *spec.* as the cincture of an earl or knight; fastened on by means of a belt. 2. Furnished with a belt or belts; marked by bands of colour 1785.

1. A prince can mak a b. knight BURNS. 2. B. cruisers 1884. *B. cattle*: a Dutch breed of black cattle with a broad band of white round the middle.

Belting (be·ltiŋ), *vbl. sb.* 1567. [f. BELT *v.*, *sb.*] 1. The action of the vb. 2. *concr.* Belts collectively, or the material for making them; also, a belt.

†Belue. *rare.* 1474. [a. OF., ad. L. *belua*, *bellua.*] A great beast; *spec.* a whale -1572.

‖Beluga (bǐlū·gă). 1591. [In sense 1, a. Russ. *bělúga*; in sense 2, a. Russ. *bělú·χa*; both f. *bělo-* white.] 1. The Great or Hausen Sturgeon (*Acipenser huso*), found in the Caspian and Black Seas. 2. The white Whale (*Delphinapterus leucas*), an animal of the Dolphin family, found in herds in the Northern Seas.

Belute (bǐlⁱū·t), *v.* 1760. [f. BE- + LUTE, ad. L. *lutum.*] To cover with mud.

Belvedere (belvǐdīᵊɹ). 1596. [a. It., f. *bel*, *bello*, beautiful + *vedere* sight. The Eng. pronunc. perh. follows the Fr. *belvédère.*] 1. *Archit.* A raised turret or lantern on the top of a house, or a summer-house erected on an eminence, commanding a fine view. 2. *Hort.* A plant, *Kochia scoparia* (N.O. *Chenopodiaceæ*), also called *Summer Cypress* 1597.

1. Apollo B., a..statue of Apollo..placed..in the B. of the Vatican 1834.

Belzebub, var. of BEELZEBUB.

‖Bema (bī·mă). 1683. [a. Gr. βῆμα, lit. 'a step' (f. βα- go); hence, a raised place to speak from; whence, the apse or chancel of a basilica.] 1. *Eccles. Antiq.* The altar part or sanctuary in ancient churches; the chancel. 2. *Gk. Antiq.* The platform from which Athenian orators spoke 1820.

Bemad (bǐmæ·d), *v.* 1605. [See BE- 2.] To make mad.

Unnatural and bemadding sorrow *Lear* III. i. 38.

Bemangle, bemask, bemaster, bemaul, bemazed, etc.; see BE-.

†Beme, *sb.* [OE. *bēme.*] A trumpet -1500. Hence **†Beme** *v.* to blow on a trumpet; also *transf.*

†Bemea·n, *v.*[1] ME. [f. *bi-*, BE- 2 + MEAN *v.*, OE. *mǣnan.*] To signify -1502.

Bemean (bǐmī·n), *v.*[2] 1651. [See BE- 5.] To render mean, to abase.

†Bemee·t, *v.* 1605. [See BE- 2.] To meet with. *Lear* v. i. 20.

†Beme·te, *v.* [OE. *bemetan*; prob. recoined by Shaks.] To measure. *Tam. Shr.* IV. iii. 113.

Bemire (bǐməiᵊɹ), *v.* 1532. [See BE- 6.] To befoul with, or plunge in, mire; *pass.* to sink in the mire (*lit.* and *fig.*).

I was filthily bemired SWIFT. Doubt..bemires the soul WESLEY.

Bemist (bǐmi·st), *v.* 1598. [See BE- 6.] To involve in, or as in, mist.

Bemoan (bǐmōᵘ·n), *v.* [OE. *bi-*, *bemǣnan*; see MOAN.] To lament (*trans.* and *intr.*).

The children of Israel..bemoaning the ruines of Sion WALTON.

Bemo·ck, *v.* 1607. [See BE- 2.] To flout.

To gird the Gods—Bemocke the modest Moone *Cor.* I. i. 261.

†Bemoi·l, *v.* 1596. [See BE-.] To bemire. *Tam. Shr.* IV. i. 77.

†Bemol. ME. [a. F. (med.L. *B mollis*).] 1. Name given to B♭, when first introduced into the scale. 2. By extension: a. A flat 1609. b. A semitone 1626.

Bemonster (bǐmǫ·nstəɹ), *v.* 1605. [See BE- 5.] 1. To make monstrous. 2. To regard as, or call a monster 1692.

†Bemou·rn, *v.* [OE. *be-*, *bimurnan.*] To lament (*trans.* and *intr.*) -1622.

Bemouth, bemud, bemuddle, bemuffle, etc.; see BE-.

Bemuse (bǐmiū·z), *v.* 1735. [See BE- 2.] To make utterly muddled, as with drink. ¶ *joc.* To devote entirely to the Muses. POPE.

A parson much be-mus'd in beer POPE.

Ben (ben). *Sc.* and *north.* ME. [A dial. var. of ME. *binne* BIN 'within':—OE. *binnan*, cogn. w. Ger. *binnen.*] A. *adv.* Within, towards the inner part; *esp.* in or into the parlour, etc. from the kitchen. (The words *but* and *b.* had reference originally to houses with only one outer door, opening into the kitchen.) b. *But and b.*: in the outer and inner apartment, in both (or all) parts of the house ME. B. *prep.*

In or into the inner part of 1684. **C.** *adj.* Inner 1774. **D.** *sb. ellipt.* The inner room 1791.

‖**Ben** (ben), *sb.*² 1788. [Gael. *beann*:—OCelt. **benno-*, **bendo-* 'peak, horn'.] A mountain-peak, *e.g.* Ben Nevis.

Ben (ben), *sb.*³ 1559. [a. Arab. *bān* 'the ben-tree'.] The winged seed of the Horse-radish tree (*Moringa pterygosperma*); also called *b.-nut.* Hence *Oil of B.* 1594.

Ben, obs. pres. indic., subj. pl., and inf. of BE *v.*

†**Bena·me,** *v. Obs.* (*arch.* in pa. pple.) Pa. t. and pple. benamed, benempt, benempted. [OE. *benęmnan*; cf. mod.G. *benennen.*] †**1.** To declare solemnly –1615. †**2.** To name. SPENSER. **3.** To name, describe as 1580.

Bench (benᵗʃ), *sb.* [OE. *benc*:—OTeut. **bankiz*; cf. BANK *sb.*¹ and *sb.*² **1.** A long seat, usually of wood or stone, with or without a back. **2.** The seat on which judges sit in court; the judge's seat or seat of justice; hence, the office of a judge, the judicial status (as opp., e.g., to *bar*) ME. **b.** The place where justice is administered as †*The* (*Court of*) *Common B.*, (*The Court of*) *King's or Queen's B.* (since the Judicature Act of 1873, a division of the High Court of Justice). **c.** A court of justice 1589. **d.** The judges or magistrates collectively, or the judge or magistrate sitting in the seat of justice 1592. **3.** A seat where persons sit side by side in some official capacity 1742. **b.** *transf.* The dignity of occupying such a seat. **c.** The persons collectively who occupy such a seat 1600. **4.** Anything similar in form to a long seat (sense 1): †**a.** a footstool; **b.** the table at which carpenters, etc. work; **c.** a banker's counter ME. **5.** *transf.* A collection of dogs as exhibited at a show on benches (*mod.*). **6.** = BANK *sb.*¹ 1. 1450. **7.** Any conformation of earth, stone, etc. which has a raised and flat surface 1730. **8.** *Law.* See FREE-BENCH.

1. Thy benches of Yuorie *Ezek.* xxvii. 6. 2. To be raised to the b. (*mod.*). **d.** The b...smiled 1592. 3. The b. of bishops 1771, the Treasury b. 1812. 6. Vpon a b. couered with greene torves we satte 1551. 7. A b. or layer of coal RAYMOND.

Comb.: **b.-clamp**, a vice with sliding side used to force together the parts of work; **-holdfast, -hook**, an iron hook, sliding in a socket, by which a plank may be gripped; **-plane**, a joiner's plane for working on a flat surface; **-shears**, shears used by copper- and zinc-workers; **-show** (see 5); **-stop, -strip**, a strip of wood or metal fixed on a carpenter's b. to rest his work against; **-table**, a low stone seat on the inside of walls, or round the bases of pillars, in churches, cloisters, etc.; **-warrant**, one issued by a judge, as opp. to a *justice's* or *magistrate's warrant*.

Hence **Be·nchlet**, a little b., a stool.

Bench (benʃ), *v.* ME. [f. prec. sb.] **1.** *trans.* To furnish with benches. **2.** To seat on a bench. Also *refl.* and *intr.* 1605.

1. I-benchede newe with turvis CHAUCER. 2. Whom I..Haue bench'd, and rear'd to Worship SHAKS.

Bencher (be·nʃəɹ). 1534. [f. as prec.+-ER¹.] **1.** One who sits on a bench (or thwart). **2.** *esp.* A magistrate, judge, assessor, senator, alderman, etc. (*arch.*) 1571. **3.** *spec.* One of the senior members of the Inns of Court 1582.

1. O, the benchers phrase: *pauca verba* B. JONS. Hence **Be·nchership**, the position of a b. in an Inn of Court.

Be·nch-mark. 1864. A surveyor's mark, cut in rock, or other durable material, to indicate the starting or other point in a line of levels for the determination of altitudes over the face of a country. It consists of a broad arrow with a horizontal bar through its apex, thus ⩚. When below sea-level, the mark is inverted.

Bend (bend), *sb.*¹ [Com. Teut.: OE. *bęnd* str. fem. (pl. *bęnda*):—OTeut. **bandjā-*, f. *band-* stem of *bindan* to BIND. The orig. Eng. wd., now replaced by BAND *sb.*¹, BOND, exc. in naut. use.] †**1.** A band, bond, fetter. *pl. collect.* Bonds, imprisonment. –ME. †**2.** =A clamp; a connecting piece –1596. **3.** *Naut.* A knot, used to unite one rope to another, or to something else, as the *cable b.*, *fisherman's b.*, etc. (The only extant sense.) 1769.

Bend (bend), *sb.*² OE. [App. originally Eng., as a sense of the prec. wd. Later, identified w. OF. *bende* (mod. Fr. *bande*); see BAND *sb.*²] †**1.** A thin flat strip adapted to bind round. *Archit.* a scroll or riband –1743. **2.** *Her.* An ordinary drawn from the dexter chief to the sinister base of the shield, containing the fifth, or, if charged, the third, part of the field in breadth. *B. sinister*: a similar ordinary drawn in the opposite direction: one of the marks of bastardy. Cf. BATON. ME. **3.** A shape or size in which ox- or cow-hides are tanned into leather, forming half of a 'butt'.

2. *In b.*: placed bendwise. *Parted per b.*: divided bendwise. 3. **B.-leather** (orig. *north.*): the leather of a b., *i.e.* the stoutest kind of leather; sole-leather. Hence **Be·ndlet**, var. †**Be·ndel**, a smaller b. †**Be·ndly, Be·ndwise**, *advs.* in the position or direction of a b.

†**Bend,** *sb.*³ 1475. [a. F. *bende* (also used), var. of *bande.*] = BAND *sb.*³ –1611.

Bend (bend), *sb.*⁴ 1529. [Late deriv. of BEND *v.*] **1.** The action of the vb. BEND; bending; bent condition. †**2.** Inclination of the eye in any direction 1601. **3.** Turn of mind, bent 1591. **4.** *concr.* A thing of bent shape; the bent part, *e.g.* of a river, a road 1600. **5.** *Naut.* (*pl.*) The wales of a ship 1626.

1. A wave just on the b. HAWTHORNE. 2. That same eye whose b. doth awe the world *Jul. C.* I. ii. 123. 4. The perfection of fishhooks in shank, b. [etc.] 1883.

Bend (bend), *v.* Pa. t. and *pple.* **bended, bent.** [OE. *bęndan*, prob. = ON. *benda* 'to join, strain, bend', OTeut. **bandjan*, f. *bandjā* 'string, band', in OE. *bęnd.* In OE. used only in the senses of 'to confine', and 'to bend a bow', *i.e.* to hold it in restraint with the string.] †**1.** To put in bonds OE. only. **2.** *spec.* To bring into tension by a string (a bow, etc.). Also *fig.* OE. **3.** *Naut.* To tie, fasten on, make fast ME. †**4.** To bring into the shape of a bow; to arch –1655. **5.** To bow, curve, crook, inflect. Used only of things which possess some rigidity. Now the main sense. ME. **6.** *intr.* To assume or receive a curved form, or one in which one part is inclined at an angle to the other ME. **7.** *spec.* Of persons: To bend the body, to stoop, *e.g.* in submission; to bow ME. Also *fig.* **8.** *trans.* To cause to bow, stoop, incline, or relent 1538. **9.** *trans.* To turn away from the straight line; to deflect, turn 1513. Also *fig.* **10.** *intr.* To incline in any direction; to trend 1572. †**11.** *trans.* To direct, aim, bring to bear *against*, *upon*, *at* –1801. Also †*fig.* **12.** *fig.* (*intr.*) To direct oneself, turn (*arch.*) ME.; *trans.* to direct or turn (one's steps, etc.) 1579. **13.** To direct, turn, or incline (the eyes, or ears), in the direction of anything seen or heard 1581.

2. Sone there were good bowes ibent 1500. *fig.* They b. their tongue like their bow for lies *Jer.* ix. 3. I am settled, and b. up Each corporal agent to this terrible feat *Macb.* I. vii. 79. 3. *To b. the cable*: to fasten it to the ring of the anchor. *To b. a sail*: to make it fast to its proper yard or stay. 4. *To b. the brows*: (*orig.*) to arch the eyebrows; (*later*) to knit the brow; to scowl. 5. On knees down bent GOWER. 6. Their knees b. so, that they are apt to trip 1815. 7. I bent down to go in SWIFT. The sonnes also of them that afflicted thee, shall come bending vnto thee *Isa.* lx. 14. 8. The spirit of the rustic gentry was not to be bent MACAULAY. *To b. the head or face*: to lower it by bending the neck. 11. They bent their guns at the frigate CROMWELL. *To be bent*: to be intent, determined. 12. Thence we came: And..Thither we b. againe *All's Well* III. ii. 57. 13. And to my cries.. Thine ear with favor b. MILT.

Hence **Be·ndable** *a.* **Be·nded** *ppl. a.* the orig. pa. pple., now semi-arch., and used chiefly in *on bended knees*, etc. **Be·ndsome** *a.* flexible.

†**Be·nded,** *a.* ME. [f. BEND *sb.*²] *Her.* = BENDY –1572.

Bender (be·ndəɹ). 1496. [f. BEND *v.*] **1.** He who or that which bends. **2.** A pair of pliers. †**3.** A flexor muscle –1668. **4.** *slang.* A sixpence 1836.

†**Be·nding,** *vbl. sb.* [f. BEND *sb.*²] Decoration with bends or stripes. CHAUCER.

Bendy (be·ndi), *a.* 1486. [ad. OF. *bendé*; see BEND *sb.*²] *Her.* Of a shield: Divided into an even number of bends, coloured alternately.

†**Bene.** [OE. *bēn, ben*:—OTeut. **bōni-z*; perh. f. root *ba-* 'cry'; see BAN.] Prayer, boon; *esp.* prayer to God –ME.

Beneaped (bĭnī·pt), *ppl. a.* 1692. [BE- 6 b.] Left aground by a neaping spring tide.

Beneath (bĭnī·þ). [OE. *biniðan, beneoðan*, f. *bi-*, BE- + *niðan, neoðan*, f. OTeut. *niþar* 'lower, down'; see NETHER + *-ana* 'from'. Orig. an adv.] **A.** *adv.* **1.** *gen.* In a lower position; =BELOW *adv.* **1.** ME. **2.** =BELOW *adv.* 2 a, b. ME. **3.** Directly below, underneath ME.

2. Hell from b. is mooued for thee *Isa.* xiv. 9. 3. It droppeth as the gentle rain from heaven Upon the place b. *Merch. V.* IV. i. 186.

B. (with obj.) *prep.* (Now usu. *under*, or *below*, exc. in sense 7, and fig. uses of 4.) †**1.** *gen.* In a position lower than. Now usu. BELOW *prep.* **1.** OE. **2.** Directly down from; under, underneath ME. **3.** Immediately under; underneath; hence, concealed by 1611. **4.** Under, as overborne by pressure; often *fig.* ME. †**5.** =BELOW *prep.* 2. –1704. **6.** *fig.* =BELOW *prep.* 5. OE. **7.** Unworthy of. Better BELOW. 1849.

2. Lands that lye b. another Sun DRYDEN. 3. The waters b. the earth *Deut.* v. 8. 4. Our Country sinks b. the yoake *Macb.* IV. iii. 39. 7. So farre b. your soft and tender breeding *Twel. N.* V. i. 332.

‖**Benedicite** (benĭdəi·sitĭ). ME. [L.; 2nd pl. imper. of *benedicere.* Also *bendicite, benste.*] **A.** *interj.* **1.** Bless you! **2.** Bless us! Good gracious! ME. **B.** *sb.* **1.** Invocation of a blessing 1610. **2.** *esp.* The blessing asked at table. (The earliest sense in Eng.) ME. **3.** The canticle in the Book of Common Prayer, known also as 'The Song of the Three Children' 1661.

Benedict (be·nĭdikt). 1576. [ad. L. *benedictus*; see prec.] †**A.** *adj.* Blessed, benign; *spec.* in *Med.* mildly laxative –1693. †**b.** *Priest b.*: = BENET, exorcist. **B.** *sb.* Also **benedick.** A newly married man; *esp.* an apparently confirmed bachelor who marries. [From the character of that name. See *Much Ado* V. iv. 100.]

Benedictine (benĭdi·ktin). 1602. [a. F. *bénédictin*, f. L. *benedictus.*] **A.** *adj.* Of or belonging to St. Benedict or the order founded by him 1630. **B.** *sb.* **1.** One of the order of monks, also known, from their dress, as 'Black Monks', founded by St. Benedict about the year 529. 1602. **2.** A kind of liqueur 1882.

Benediction (benĭdi·kʃən). ME. [ad. L. *benedictionem.*] **1.** The utterance of a blessing; solemn invocation of blessedness upon a person; devout expression of a wish for the happiness, prosperity, or success of a person or an enterprise: **a.** *gen.* ME.; **b.** as officially pronounced, *esp.* at the consecration of an abbot 1638; **c.** as pronounced at the conclusion of divine worship 1549; **d.** as an expression of thanks; *spec.* as grace before or after meals 1671; **e.** as a service in the R. C. Ch. 1812. **2.** Blessedness 1483.

1. **a.** Hold your hand in b. o're me *Lear* IV. vii. 58. **d.** The thought of our past years in me doth breed Perpetual b. WORDSW. 2. As if my Trinkets had.. brought a b. to the buyer *Wint. T.* IV. iv. 614. Hence **Benedi·ctional**, a book of forms of b.; var. **Benedi·ctionary. Benedi·ctory** *a.* of or pertaining to the utterance of b.

Benedictive (benĭdi·ktiv), *a.* 1660. [f. L. *benedict-*, *benedicere* + -IVE.] **1.** Tending to bless. **2.** *Gram.* A form of the Optative Mood in Skr., also called the 'precative' 1841.

‖**Benedi·ctus.** 1552. [L.; see above.] **1.** The fifth movement in the service of the Mass, beginning with the words 'Benedictus qui venit' 1880. **2.** The hymn of Zacharias (Luke i. 68), used as a canticle in the Book of Common Prayer 1552.

Benedi·ght. *Obs.* or *arch.* ME. [ad. L. *benedictus.*] Blessed.

Benefaction (benĭfæ·kʃən). 1662. [ad. L. *benefactionem*; see BENEFIT.] **1.** A doing good, beneficence; a benefit or blessing. **2.** *esp.* The bestowal of money for a charitable purpose; a gift, bounty, endowment 1674.

2. She was liberal in her benefactions to convents and colleges PRESCOTT.

Benefactor (benĭfæ·ktəɹ). 1494. [a. L.; see BENEFIT.] **1.** One who renders aid to others, or to a cause or institution. **2.** A well-doer 1603.

1. A b. of learning BACON. 2. *Meas. for M.* II. i. 50. Hence **Benefa·ctorship**, the office or action of a b. **Benefa·ctory** *a.* of or pertaining to a b.; beneficial. **Benefa·ctress**, a female b.

Benefic, -al (bĭne·fik, -ăl), *a.* 1600. [ad. L. *beneficus*, + -AL.] **1.** *Astrol.* Of favourable influence. **2.** *gen.* Beneficent, kindly 1641.

Benefice (be·nĭfis). ME. [a. OF., ad. L. *beneficium.*] †**1.** A kindness, favour; a grace or indulgence –1677. **2.** Favourable influence or operation; advantage, protection. Now *Hist.* ME. †**3.** Beneficial property or action (as of natural causes) –1652. **4.** Land granted in feudal tenure; a fief. (Only as tr. L. *beneficium.*) 1753. 5. *esp.* An ecclesiastical living ME.

2. *B. of clergy*; see BENEFIT 3 b. 4. Benefices.. were grants of Roman provincial land to be holden.. on condition of military service MAINE. 5. Then he dreames of another b. *Rom. & Jul.* I. iv. 81. Hence Be·nefice *v.* to endow or invest with a church living. Be·neficed *ppl. a.* holding a b.

Beneficence (bǐne·fǐsěns). 1531. [ad. L. *beneficentia.*] 1. Doing good, active kindness. 2. *concr.* A benefaction 1654.

1. Law itself is only b. acting by a rule BURKE.

†Bene·ficency. 1576. [See prec.] The quality of being beneficent -1682.

Beneficent (bǐne·fisěnt), *a.* 1616. [f. L. *beneficent-*, whence *beneficentior*, compar. of *beneficus*. Cf. *magnificent.*] Doing good, performing kind deeds. (Replacing *beneficial* in this sense.)

A b. genius 1879. That b. luminary the Sun 1772. So Bene·fice·ntial *a.* of or pertaining to beneficence. Bene·ficently *adv.*

Beneficial (benǐfi·fǎl), *a.* 1494. [a. F., ad. L. *beneficialem*, f. *beneficium.*] †1. = BENEFICENT -1658. 2. Of benefit 1494. 3. *Law.* a. Of or pertaining to a benefice; beneficed. Now *Hist.* 1592. b. Of or pertaining to the usufruct of property; enjoying the usufruct 1844.

2. These beneficiall Newes *Oth.* II. ii. 7. 3. b. A b. owner J. WILLIAMS, interest KEBLE. Hence Bene·fi·cial·ly *adv.*, -ness.

Beneficiary (benǐfi·ʃiǎri). 1611. [ad. L. *beneficiarius*; cf. F. *bénéficiaire.*] A. *adj.* Holding, held as, or pertaining to the holding of a benefice: *spec.* feudatory 1626.

B. *sb.* 1. The holder of a fief; a feudatory 1611. 2. The holder of an eccles. living 1641. 3. A debtor to another's bounty 1662.

2. Your Beneficiaries the Priests MILT. 3. Content to be a b. of society—to receive favors and confer none HOLLAND.

Beneficiate (benǐfi·ʃiě̀t), *v.* 1871. [f. Sp. *beneficiar* to benefit from a mine.] *Min.* To reduce (ores). Hence Beneficia·tion.

[**Beneficience, -ficiency, -ficient**, erron. ff. of BENEFICENCE, etc., orig. misprints.]

Benefit (be·nǐfit), *sb.* [ME. *benfet*, a. AF., = Fr. *bienfait*:—L. *benefactum.*] †1. A thing well done; a good deed -1811. 2. A kind deed; a favour, gift (*arch.*) ME. 3. Advantage, profit, good. (The ordinary sense.) 1512. b. *Law.* The advantage of belonging to a privileged order which was exempted from the jurisdiction or sentence of the ordinary courts of law: in *B. of Clergy, B. of Peerage*; see CLERGY, PEERAGE. 1488. c. Pecuniary profit 1592. 4. Hence a. A theatrical performance the receipts from which are given to a particular actor, etc. 1709. †b. A prize in a lottery; a winning ticket -1715. †c. A BENEFICE (sense 5), an endowment -1719. d. The pecuniary assistance, etc. to which an insured person is entitled 1911.

2. Her [Fortune's] benefits are mightily misplaced *A.Y.L.* I. ii. 37. 3. To labour for the b. of mankind JOHNSON. The b. of the doubt (*mod.*), of the contract 1885. 4. She was going to have a b. and appear as Ophelia THACKERAY.

Benefit (be·nǐfit), *v.* 1549. [f. prec. sb.] 1. *trans.* To do good to, to be of advantage or profit to; to improve, help forward. 2. *intr.* (for *refl.*) To receive benefit 1613.

1. A system..which injures our interests without benefiting those of the colonies LUBBOCK. Hence Be·nefiter, he who confers, or derives benefit.

†Bene·me, *v.* [OE. *bi-*, *benǣman*, deriv. of *bineman*, pa. t. *benam*. Or ? var. of BENIM.] To deprive (with *gen.*); to take away -1562.

Benempt, obs. pa. t. and pple. of BENAME.

†Beneplacit. *rare.* 1643. [ad. late L. *beneplacitum.*] Good pleasure, gracious purpose.

Benet (be·nět), *sb.* ME. [a. OF. *beneit* (mod. F. *bénit*):—L. *benedictus*; see BENEDICT.] The third of the four lesser orders in the R.C.Ch., one of whose functions was the exorcizing of evil spirits.

Benet (bǐne·t), *v.* 1602. [See BE- 6.] To cover as with, or catch in, a net. Usu. *fig.*

†Beneurous, *a.* [a. OF. *beneureus* (mod. *bienheureux*).] Happy, blessed. CAXTON.

Benevolence (bǐne·vǒlěns). ME. [a. OF. *benivolence*, ad. L. *benevolentia*; see BENEVOLENT.] 1. Disposition to do good, kindness, generosity, charitable feeling (towards mankind). †2. Affection, goodwill (towards another) -1817. 3. *concr.* An act of kindness; a gift of money; a charitable contribution ME. 4. A sum of money, disguised as a gift (*donum*), demanded by the sovereign from his subjects without the consent of parliament 1473.

1. Sauer of vs by thy beneuolence CHAUCER. 2. †*To ao one's b.*: to lend one's friendly offices. I..will be glad to do my b. *Merry W.* I. i. 32. 4. The B. proves ..an occasion of so much discontent..that it had better it had never been set up PEPYS 1661.

†Bene·volency. 1540. [See prec.] The quality of being benevolent; also *concr.* a gift of money -1766.

Benevolent (bǐne·vǒlěnt), *a.* 1482. [a. OF. *benivolent, benvolent*, ad. L. *bene volentem.*] 1. Desirous of the good of others, of a kindly disposition, charitable, generous. 2. Well-wishing *to, unto* (= L. *bene volens*) 1502.

1. Beloued old man! b. as wise POPE. *transf.* The b. Heat of the Sun HALE. Hence Bene·volently *adv.* †Bene·volous *a. Astrol.* auspicious.

Bengal (bengǭ·l). Name of a province of Hindustan. Hence 1. Applied to piece goods imported from Bengal in the 17th c. 1680. 2. *Comb.* etc., as **B. light**, a firework producing a steady and vivid blue-coloured light, used for signals; **B. root**, the root of the Yellow Zedoary; **B. silk, B. stripes**, striped ginghams formerly imported from Bengal; **B. tiger**, the tiger proper, which abounds in Lower Bengal.

Bengali, Bengalee (bengǭ·lī). 1613. [a. native *Bangālī.*] A. *adj.* Of or belonging to Bengal. B. *sb.* A native of Bengal; the language of Bengal.

Be·nic, *a.* 1873. [f. BEN.] *Chem.* Obtained from oil of ben.

Benight (bǐnəi·t), *v.* 1560. [See BE- 6.] 1. To be overtaken by, or (*active*) to involve in, the darkness of night. Also *refl.* 1654. 2. To involve in darkness, to cloud (*lit.* and *fig.*) 1610. 3. To blind 1621.

1. I am like to be benighted, for the day is almost spent BUNYAN. 2. Whom Error doth b. 1692.

Benign (bǐnəi·n), *a.* ME. [a. OF. *benigne, benin*:—L. *benignus*, prob. for *benegenus*, f. *bene* + *-genus*. Cf. *malignus*; for the sense L. *gentilis*, Eng. *gentle.*] 1. Of a kind disposition, gracious; †meek. 2. Exhibiting or manifesting kindly feeling; bland, gentle, mild ME. Also *transf.* of things. 3. *Med.* †a. Of medicines: Gentle in operation -1735. b. Of diseases: Not malignant 1743.

1. Charity is benyngne WYCLIF. 2. *transf.* fful lusty was the weder and benigne CHAUCER. Hence Beni·gnly *adv.*

Benignancy (bǐni·gnǎnsi). 1876. [f. next; see -ANCY.] Benignant quality or manner.

Benignant (bǐni·gnǎnt), *a.* 1782. [Formed on BENIGN, or L. *benignus*, after *malignant*. Not in Johnson.] Cherishing or exhibiting kindly feeling towards inferiors or dependants; gracious, benevolent (with a suggestion of condescension). Also *transf.* of things.

1. Your b. sovereign BURKE. The b. or malignant character of our natal star 1844. Hence Beni·gnantly *adv.*

Benignity (bǐni·gnǐti). [ME. *benignete*, a. OF. *benignité*, ad. L. *benignitatem.*] 1. Kindly feeling; kindness of disposition, or of manner. (Now attributed to superiors or those who are venerable.) b. *concr.* A kindly or generous deed 1534. 2. Of things (*arch.*) See BENIGN 2, 3.

1. O God..Thow be my sheld, for thy benignite CHAUCER. b. Ample grants and benignities 1590.

†Beni·m, *v.* [Com. Teut.: OE. *bi-, be-niman*, f. *bi-*, BE- + *niman*, OTeut. **neman* to take; see NIM.] 1. *trans.* To take away -1494. 2. To deprive; (without constr.) to rob; to spoil, ravish -1480.

2. Euer he that was strengest bynome hym that was feblyst CAXTON.

Benison (be·nisən). [ME. *beneysun*, a. OF. *beneiçun*:—L. *benedictionem*. Now poetic or quaint for *benediction.*] 1. Blessing, beatitude. 2. Benediction ME.

1. The bountie, and the benizon of Heauen *Lear* IV. vi. 228. Her patriot Dead have b. MRS. BROWNING. 2. I have slept sound under such a b. SCOTT.

Benjamin[1] (be·ndʒǎmin). 1580. [Corrupt f. *benjoin*, earlier f. BENZOIN, assim. to Benjamin.] 1. Gum benzoin. 2. **Benjamin tree**: a. *Styrax Benzoin*, which yields benzoin; b. *Benzoin odoriferum* or *Lindera benzoin*, a N. American shrub with tonic bark; called also *Benjamin-bush*, and in U.S. *Benjamin*; c. *Ficus Benjamina*. 1640.

Be·njamin[2]. 1817. [f. a tailor's name.] A form of overcoat for men. (Still slang or joc.)

Bennet[1] (be·nět). [ME. *herbe beneit*, tr. L. *herba benedicta*, said to put the devil to flight.] In Herb Bennet, the common Avens, *Geum urbanum* (N. O. *Rosaceæ*). Used also of the Hemlock, and the Wild Valerian.

Be·nnet[2]. Earlier f. BENT; see BENT *sb.*[1] 2.

†Be·nnet[3]. A fish of the African seas -1784.

Benorth (bǐnǭ·ɹþ). [OE. *be northan*, f. BE- prep. and pref. + *norþan* adv. from the north; cf. *biforan.*] A. †*adv.* To the north -1535. B. *prep.* North of. Now only *Sc.* ME.

Benshi, -shie, var. of BANSHEE.

Bent (bent), *sb.*[1] ME. [In the sense of 'stiff-grass' = OE. *beonet-*:—earlier **binut*, mod.G. *binse* 'rush, reed', etc.:—WGer. **binut* of unknown etym.] 1. A name given to grass of a reedy habit; also to various grass-like reeds, rushes, sedges, etc. With *pl.* 'bents'. Also *collect.* 2. The stiff flower-stalk of grasses. (Also *bennet.*) 1577. 3. The name of the genus *Agrostis*. More fully *B. grass*. 1796. 4. A place covered with grass, as opp. to a wood; a bare field, unenclosed pasture-land, a heath. In ME. the stock poetic wd. for 'field' (of battle), L. *campus*. ME. 5. ?A hill-side, slope. (Only in southern writers.) ME.

4. [Three lords] upon the b. did breathlesse bide *Flodden F.* ix. 84. *To flee, go, take to the b.*: to escape to the open country.

Bent (bent), *sb.*[2] 1521. [f. BEND *v.*; prob. after L. or Fr.; cf. *descend, descent*, F. *rendre, rente.*] 1. A curved position or form; curvature. Also *fig.* (Now *rare.*) 1541. †2. A curved part, a bend; a bow -1677. †3. Bowing, stooping -1713. 4. The condition of being deflected in some direction; a turn, twist, inclination; cast (of the eye); set (of a current), etc. Usu. *fig.* 1534. b. *esp.* Mental inclination; propensity, bias. The usual mod. sense. 1586. †5. That towards which an action, etc. is directed; aim, purpose -1798. †6. Impetus. F. *élan*. -1742. 7. Degree of tension of a bow; *hence* limit of capacity, etc. Now only in *To the top of one's b.*, or the like. 1594.

4. They weare their faces to the b. Of the King's lookes *Cymb.* I. i. 13. Bents, and Propensities, and Inclinations, will not do the Business SOUTH. The whole b. of their actions MILT. 7. They foole me to the top of my b. *Haml.* III. ii. 401.

Bent (bent), *ppl. a.* ME. [f. BEND *v.*] 1. Constrained into a curve, as a strung bow; deflected from the straight line. †2. Wound up for action; couched for a spring; levelled as a weapon -1675. †3. Determined, devoted, set -1740. 4. Directed in a course, bound 1697.

1. The Bente Mone CHAUCER. *B. brow*: tan arched eyebrow; a knit brow. 4. Saylors homeward b. DRYDEN. *Comb.* b.-lever, a lever whose arms form an angle with each other.

Benthamism (be·nþǎmiz'm). 1840. The philosophical system of Jeremy Bentham, 1748–1832, who taught that the aim or end of life is happiness, identified by him with pleasure, and that the highest morality is the pursuit of the greatest happiness of the greatest number. So Bentha·mic *a.* of or according to Bentham. Be·nthamite *sb.* an adherent of B.; *a.* = prec.

Benthos (be·nþǫs). *Biol.* 1891. [Gr. = depth of the sea.] The flora and fauna of the bottom of the sea. Hence Be·nthic, -o·ic, -o·nic *adjs.*

Be·ntinck. [f. Captain *Bentinck.*] 1. *pl.* Triangular courses, now superseded by storm stay-sails; also used in U.S. as try-sails. 2. B.-boom, one which stretches the foot of the foresail in many small square-rigged merchantmen. **B. shrouds**: shrouds extending from the weather-futtock staves to the opposite lee-channels; not now used.

Benting (be·ntiŋ), *vbl. sb.* 1672. [f. BENT *sb.*[1] + -ING[1].] 1. The going after bents. *B.-time*: the time when pigeons, etc. are reduced to feed on bents; also *transf.* 2. The seeding stalks of the plantain (herb) 1807.

Benty (be·nti), *a.* 1597. [f. BENT *sb.*[1] + -Y[1].] 1. Of, of the nature of, or pertaining to BENT. 2. Covered with BENT 1700.

†**Benu·mb**, *ppl. a.* ME. [Orig. *benomen*, f. *beniman* 'to deprive', in phr. 'to be benome(n the power of one's hands', and subseq. used elliptically. Replaced by *benumbed*. See also BENIM.] –1530.

Benumb (bĭnʊ·m), *v.* 1485. [f. prec.; a bad sp. of *benum*, after *dumb*, etc.] **1.** To make insensible, torpid, or powerless; *occas.* to stupefy or stun 1530. **2.** To deaden (the mental powers, will, feelings) 1485. Also *fig.*

Hence Benu·mbed *ppl. a.* (replacing *benome(n)*). **Benu·mbedness. Benu·mbment.**

Benzene (benzī·n, be·nzīn). 1835. orig. -ine. [f. BENZOIC + -ENE.] *Chem.* An aromatic hydrocarbon, phenyl hydride, C_6H_6, a colourless liquid obtained from coal-tar oil: = BENZOL **1.**

attrib. **b. ring,** the arrangement of the six carbon atoms in the formula of the b. molecule.

Benzine (benzī·n, be·nzīn). 1885. [f. as prec. + -INE.] An inflammable liquid, petroleum ether, prepared from natural petroleum, and used as a solvent. Hence as vb., to clean with b.

Benzo-, bef. a vowel **benz-**. [f. BENZOIC.] A formative of the names of substances belonging to, or derived from, the benzene series.

Be·nzamide, C_7H_7NO, the amide of benzoic acid. **Be·nzil, -ile,** a yellowish crystalline substance, $C_{14}H_{10}O_2$, formed by the action of oxidizing agents on benzoin. **Benzi·lic** acid, $C_{14}H_{12}O_3$; a salt of which is **Be·nzilate. Be·nzin(e,** earliest name of BENZENE. **Be·nzoate,** a salt of benzoic acid; hence **Be·nzoated** *a.* **Be·nzone,** the ketone of benzoic acid (diphenyl ketone). **Benzoyl** (be·nzoɪil), the hypothetical radical, C_7H_5O, of benzoic acid, etc.; hence **Benzoy·lic** *a.* **Be·nzyl,** the hypothetical radical $C_6H_5.CH_2$, contained in *Benzyl alcohol*, etc; hence **Benzy·lic** *a.* **Be·nzylene,** a hypothetical diatomic radical, C_7H_6, found in chlorobenzyl; hence **Benzyle·nic** *a.*

Benzo·ic, *a.* 1791. [f. BENZO-IN + -IC.] *Chem.* Of or derived from benzoin; as **B. acid,** $C_7H_6O_2$, a monobasic acid of the Aromatic series, existing in large quantity in gum benzoin.

Benzoin (be·nzoɪin, -zoin). 1558. [In 16th c. *benjoin*, a. F., repr. Sp. *benjuy*, Pg *beijoim*, It. *benzoi*, for **lo-benjuy*, etc, a. Arab. *lubān jāwī*, 'frankincense of Iāwā' (Sumatra). The *lo-*, app. taken for the article, was dropped in Romanic.] **1.** A resinous substance obtained from the *Styrax benzoin*, a tree of Sumatra, etc.; now termed for distinction *Gum b.*; also, by pop. corruption BENJAMIN. **2.** *Bot.* A genus of *Lauraceæ*, including the Benzoin Laurel 1866. **3.** *Chem.* Bitter-almond-oil camphor: a constituent of gum-benzoin; it is a ketone, $C_{14}H_{12}O_2$, of the di-phenyl group, and crystallizes in shining prisms 1863. Hence **Be·nzoinate** *v.* to impregnate with b.

Benzol, -ole (be·nzǫl, -zōᵘl). 1838. [f. BENZOIC + the -OL of ALCOHOL. The sp. -OLE prob. refers to L. *oleum*.] **1.** *Chem.* (Benzol) Liebig's name for *benzine*, now replaced by Hoffmann's BENZENE. Also in comb. 1869. **2.** *Min.* Dana's name for native benzene or benzol.

Benzoline (be·nzŏlīn, -lin). 1874. [f. BENZOL + -INE.] **1.** *Chem.* Earlier name for AMARINE. **2.** A commercial name for impure benzene, and often for other inflammable liquid hydrocarbons, *esp.* coal-tar naphtha. Also, for a light hydrocarbon obtained from petroleum, and used to burn in lamps.

Bepaint (bĭpēⁱ·nt), *v.* 1555. [See BE- **1.**] To paint over; to paint obtrusively; to colour.

Else would a maiden blush b. my cheeke SHAKS.

Bepelt, bepinch, beplaster, etc.; see BE-.

Beplumed (bĭɪplū·md), *ppl. a.* 1582. [See BE- **7.**] Furnished with feathers.

Bepommel, bepowder, bepraise, beprose, bepuff, etc.; see BE-.

Bequeath (bĭɪkwī·ð), *v.* [OE. *bi-*, *becweðan*, f. BE- 4 + *cweðan* to say; see QUOTH. An old word, kept alive in wills.] †**1.** To say; to mean –ME. †**2.** To assign, give as an attribute –1674. **3.** †**a.** To make over, assign –1611. **b.** To leave by will. (The only surviving sense.) OE. Also *fig.* †**4.** To commit *to*, *unto*; to commend –1718. †**5.** *gen.* To give, yield –1674.

3. a. B. to Death your numnesse *Wint. T.* v. iii. 102. **b.** Bequeathing it as a rich Legacie Vnto their issue *Jul. C.* III. ii. 141. **4.** The judges to the common urn b. Their votes DRYDEN. **5.** A niggards purse shall scarce b. his master a good dinner 1608. Hence **Bequea·thable** *a.* **Bequea·thal,** the action of bequeathing. **Bequea·ther. Bequea·thment,** the action of bequeathing; a bequest.

†**Bequea·th**, *sb.* [ME. *byquide*:—OE. *bicwide*, f. *bi-*, BE- + *cwide* a saying:—OTeut. **qidi-z*, f. *qiþan*.] **1.** Byword, proverb. (Only in OE.) **2.** Bequest, testament –1642. Also *fig.*

Bequest (bĭɪkwe·st). [ME. *biquyste*, *biqueste*, prob. for **bicwis*, *bi-cwiss(e*, f. *bi-*, BE- + *cwis*, *cwiss(e* 'saying':—OTeut. **qissi-z*:—**qiþ-ti-z*, f. *qiþan*. Cf. BEHEST.] **1.** The action of bequeathing; gift by will, etc. **2.** *concr.* A legacy 1496.

1. B. in a primitive state of society, was seldom recognized MILL. Hence †**Beque·st** *v.* to bequeath.

Beqwete, -qweth(e, etc. obs. ff. BEQUEATH.

†**Berai·n**, *v.* ME. [See BE- 4.] **1.** To rain upon –1582. **2.** To besprinkle as with rain –1567.

Berate (bĭrēⁱ·t), *v.* 1548. [See BE- 2. *Obs.*, exc. in U.S.] To rate vehemently; to scold.

†**Bera·ttle**, *v.* 1553. [See BE- 4.] To rattle away upon, or at; to fill with din –1602.

Beray·, *v. arch.* 1530. [f. BE- 2 + RAY *v.* (aphet. f. ARRAY). By mod. writers usu. misspelt BEWRAY.] **1.** To disfigure, defile (with dirt, etc.). **2.** *fig.* To asperse 1576.

Berber (bə·ɹbəɹ). 1842. [See BARBARY.] **A.** *sb.* An Arab name for the aboriginal people west and south of Egypt; now applied to any member of the great N. African stock to which belong the aboriginal races of Barbary and the Tuwariks of the Sahara. **B.** *adj.* Of or pertaining to the Berbers or their language; applied (often *absol.*) to one of the three great subdivisions of the Hamitic group 1854.

†**Be·rber.** *Sc.* 1440. [a. OF. *berbere*, in med. L. *berberis*.] = BARBERRY.

From *Berberis* (*berberid-*) also; **Be·rberal** *a. Bot.*, of or related to the Barberry, or genus *Berberis*. **Berberida·ceous,** belonging to the N O. *Berberidaceæ*, of which the barberry is the type. **Berberi·deous,** belonging to the tribe *Berberideæ*, which includes the barberry. **Berbe·ria, Be·rberine,** a yellow bitter principle, obtained from the barberry, etc.

Berberia = BERIBERI, a disease.

Berceaune·tte. 1885. [Tradesman's pseudo-etymological perversion of *bassinette*, which has no connexion with F. *berceau*.]

†**Be·rcelet.** ME. [Corruption of OF. *berseret*, dim. of *bersier* huntsman, f. *berser*, *bercer*, orig. to shoot with the bow. Thence It. *bersaglio* an archer's butt, whence *bersagliere* rifleman.] A hunting dog –1679.

Berdash, var. of BURDASH.

Bere, obs. f. BEAR, BEER, BIER, BIRR, BOAR.

Bereave (bĭrī·v), *v.* [Com. Teut.: OE. *bi-*, *berêafian*:—OTeut. **biraubōjan*, f. *bi-*, BE- + **raubōjan*, in OE. *rêafian* to rob; see REAVE *v.*] **1.** To deprive, rob, strip, dispossess *of*. Since *c* 1650 mostly of immaterial possessions, *life*, *hope*, etc., exc. in reference to the loss of relatives. (In the former case *bereft*, in the latter *bereaved*, is more usual.) **2.** To rob, plunder (a possessor); to leave destitute, orphaned, or widowed ME. †**3.** To remove by violence –1718.

1. Madam, you have bereft me of all words *Merch. V.* III. ii. 177. The accident which had bereaved the father of his child D'ISRAELI. All joy was bereft me SCOTT. **3.** Thy life, Echechus! next the sword bereaves POPE. Hence **Berea·ved,** occ. **Berea·ven** (poet.), *ppl. a.*, *spec.* deprived by death of a near relative, etc. **Berea·vement,** the state or fact of being bereaved. **Berea·ver.**

Bereft (bĭre·ft), *ppl. a.* 1531. [f. BEREAVE.] **1.** Forcibly deprived *of*; void *of* 1586. †**2.** Taken away 1531. **3.** Deprived of a near relation, bereaved (*rare*) 1828.

Berenice's hair (berĕnəi·sĭz hēᵊɹ). 1601. [f. *Berenice*, wife of Ptolemy Euergetes, king of Egypt, *c* 248 B.C., whose hair, stolen from the temple of Venus, was said to have been afterwards placed in heaven as a constellation.] The name of a small constellation situated near the tail of Leo; formerly of the star Canopus.

Beresite (be·rĭsəit). 1849. *Min.* A fine-grained granite from Beresowsk in the Ural.

‖**Beret, berret** (berę, be·rĕt). 1850. [Fr., :—late L. *birretum* cap; see BIRETTA.] A round flat cap worn by the Basque peasantry; also a clerical biretta, and a cap named from it.

Berg (bəɹg). 1823. [Short for ICEBERG, a. Ger. *eisberg*.] A (floating) mountain or mass of ice. Hence **Be·rgy** *a.*

Berg, obs. f. BARROW *sb.*[1]

Be·rgamask. 1590. [ad. It. *Bergamasco*.] †**1.** *B. dance*: a rustic dance, framed in imitation of the people of Bergamo in Italy. *Mids. N.* v. 360. **2.** A native of Bergamo 1602.

Bergamot[1] (bə̄·ɹgămǫt). 1696. [f. *Bergamo*, in Italy.] **1.** A tree (*Citrus Bergamia*); from the rind of the fruit a fragrant oil is prepared, called Essence of Bergamot. Also *attrib.* **2.** The essence itself 1766. †**3.** Snuff scented with bergamot –1785. **4.** A kind of mint (*Mentha citrata*). **Wild B.** (in U.S.), *Monarda fistulosa*. 1858. **5.** A woven tapestry of mixed flock and hair, first produced at Bergamo 1882.

Bergamot[2] (bə̄·ɹgămǫt). 1616. [a. F. *bergamotte*, ad. It. *bergamotta*, perversion of Turk. *beg-armūdi*, 'prince's pear'; cf. Ger. *Fürstenbirne*.] A fine kind of pear. Also *attrib.*

Be·rga·nder. 1544. [? f. ME. *berȝ* shelter + GANDER; cf. the synonym *burrow-duck*. But cf. Ger. *berg-ente* 'mountain-duck'.] *Ornith.* An old name of the Sheldrake, *Tadorna vulpanser*, which breeds in rabbit-holes or burrows.

Be·rgeret. ME. [a. F. *bergerette*.] A pastoral.

‖**Bergfall** (be·rχᵞfal, bə̄·ɹgfǫl). 1856. [Ger.] The ruinous fall of a mountain peak, an avalanche of stones.

Bergmannite (bə̄·ɹgmănəit). 1811. [f. *Bergmann*, a mineralogist + -ITE.] *Min.* A Natrolite, red or white in colour, found in Norway.

Bergomask, = BERGAMASK.

Bergylt, berguylt (bə·ɹgilt). 1809. [? f. ON *berg* rock.] **1.** The name of a fish, the Black Goby, in Shetland. **2.** The Norwegian haddock or Sea Perch (*Sebastes Norvegicus*) 1838.

‖**Be·ribe·ri.** 1879. [Cingalese, redupl. of *beri* weakness.] *Med.* An acute disease, prevalent in India, generally presenting dropsical symptoms, with paralytic weakness of the legs.

Berime, berhyme (bĭrəi·m), *v.* 1589. [See BE- 4.] To compose rimes about; often, to lampoon. *A. Y. L.* III. ii. 186.

Berkeleian (bə̄ɹklī·ăn). [f. *Berkeley*, Bishop of Cloyne (died 1753), who denied the objective existence of the material world.] **A.** *adj.* Of or originating with Berkeley. **B.** *sb.* A follower of Berkeley. Hence **Berkelei·anism, Be·rkeleyism,** the philosophical opinions held by Berkeley and his followers.

Berlin (bə̄·ɹlin, bəɹli·n). 1731. [The name of the capital of Prussia, used *attrib.*, and transferred to things coming thence.] **1.** An old-fashioned four-wheeled covered carriage, with a seat behind covered with a hood. [Also *Berline* from Fr.] **2.** Short for 'Berlin wool' 1881. **3.** Short for 'Berlin Glove': A knitted glove (of Berlin wool) 1836.

Comb., etc.: **B. black,** a black varnish used for coating the better kinds of ironware; **B. blue** = PRUSSIAN BLUE; **B. castings,** ornamental objects of **B. iron,** a very fusible quality of iron, suitable for casting figures and delicate objects; **B. warehouse,** a shop for B. wool, etc.; **B. wool,** a fine dyed wool used for knitting, tapestry, etc.; **B. work,** worsted embroidery.

Berlin, -ling, var. of BIRLINN. SCOTT.

†‖**Berli·na, -ino.** [It.] Pillory. B. JONS.

Berm (bə̄ɹm). 1729. [a. F. *berme*, a. MDu. and Ger. *berme*; prob. cogn. w. ON. *barmr* brim.] **1.** A narrow space or ledge; *esp.* in *Fortif.* a space, from 3 to 8 feet wide, sometimes left between the ditch and the base of the parapet. **2. Berm-bank,** the bank of a canal opposite the towing path. [? Only in U.S.] 1854.

Bermuda (bəɹmū·dă, -miū·dă). 1640. A group of islands in the N. Atlantic; *hence*, a variety of cigar, or rolled tobacco. **B. grass,** name in U.S. of *Cynodon Dactylon*.

Bernacle, -icle, bernak(e, vars. of BARNACLE.

Bernardine (bə̄·ɹnăɹdin), *a.* (*sb.*) 1676. **1.** Of or pertaining to St. Bernard (abbot of Clairvaux in 1115), or to the Cistercian order, patronized by him. **2.** *sb.* A monk of this order.

†**Berne.** [OE. *beorn*, earlier *biorn* (:—**bern*)

'warrior', hence 'man', *vir*, ἀνήρ.] A warrior; later, poet. for 'man' –1528.

Bernoo, bernous, vars. of BURNOUS.

Bero·b, *v.*; see BE- 2.

‖**Beroe** (be·ro,ī). 1769. [a. L., Gr. βερόη, a daughter of Oceanus.] *Zool.* A genus of small, gelatinous, marine animals classed by Huxley among the Cœlenterata.

†**Bero·gue,** *v.* 1673. [See BE- 5.] To call (one) a rogue –1733.

Berret, berretta, obs. ff. BERET, BIRETTA.

Berried, *a.* 1794. [f. BERRY *sb.*] 1. Bearing berries. 2. Formed as or consisting of a berry; baccate 1824. 3. Bearing eggs; 'in berry', as a hen lobster carrying her eggs 1868.

1. Red-berried holly 1871.

Berry (be·ri), *sb.*[1] [Com. Teut.: OE. *berie*, pointing to an OGer. **bazjo-m*, referred conjecturally to **bazo-z* BARE, also to Skr. *bhas-* to eat.] 1. Any small globular, or ovate juicy fruit, not having a stone; in OE. *esp.* the grape; in Sc. and n. Eng. the gooseberry. b. *loosely*, A coffee bean 1712. 2. *Bot.* A many-seeded inferior pulpy fruit, the seeds of which are scattered throughout the pulp, as the grape, gooseberry and currants 1809. 3. The eggs in the roe of a fish; the eggs of a lobster 1768.

Be·rry, *sb.*[2] [f. OE. *beorg* hill: a var. of BARROW *sb.*[1]] A mound, hillock, or barrow. Now *dial.*

†**Be·rry,** *sb.*[3] 1486. [See BURROW.] 1. A (rabbit's) burrow –1685. Also *transf.*

Be·rry, *v.*[1] Now *dial.* [ME. *berien, bery*, ad. ON. *berja* to strike. Cogn. w. L. *ferire.*] 1. To beat, thrash. 2. To thresh (corn, etc.) 1483. 3. To beat (a path, etc.).

Berry (be·ri), *v.*[2] 1865. [f. BERRY *sb.*[1]] 1. *intr.* To come into berry; to swell. 2. To go gathering berries 1871.

Berserk, -er (bɔ̄·ɹsəɹk, -əɹ). 1822. [Icel. *berserkr*, acc. *berserk*, pl. *-ir*, prob. = 'bear-coat'. Cf. BARESARK.] A wild Norse warrior, who fought on the battle-field with a frenzied fury known as the 'berserker rage'; often a lawless bravo. Also *fig.* and *attrib.*

Berskin, obs. f. BEARSKIN.

Berstel, obs. f. BRISTLE.

Berth (bɔ̄ɹþ). 1622. [Prob. f. BEAR *v.* in its naut. senses; cf. *bear off.*] 1. *Naut.* Convenient sea-room. Also *transf.* and *fig.* 2. Hence, The place where a ship lies when at anchor or at a wharf 1706. 3. *Naut.* 'A place on board a ship for a mess to put their chests, etc.'; whence, A room where any number of the officers or ship's company mess and reside 1706. b. *fig.* (*Naut.*) Proper place (for a thing) 1732. c. *transf.* An allotted place in a barracks, a coach, etc. 1813. 4. A situation, a place, an appointment. (Usu. a 'comfortable' one.) 1720. 5. A sleeping-place in a ship; a long box or shelf on the side of a cabin, or of a railway carriage, for sleeping in 1796.

1. Giving the apparent phantom what seamen call a wide b. SCOTT. 3. The best b. in the coach SCOTT. 4. An officer's b. R. DANA. You have a good warm b. here MISS BURNEY. *Comb.* **b.-deck,** the deck on which the passengers' berths are arranged.

Berth (bɔ̄ɹþ), *v.*[1] 1667. [f. prec. sb.] 1. To moor or place (a ship) in a suitable position. Also *refl.* of the ship or sailors. 2. To allot a berth to. Usu. in *pass.* 1845. 3. To provide with a situation 1865.

3. Comfortably berthed in the City Chamberlainship 1865.

Berth, *v.*[2] 1574. [perh. f. Icel. *byrði* board.] To cover or make up with boards. (Chiefly in Ship-building.)

Bertha, berthe (bɔ̄·ɹþă, bɔ̄ɹþ). 1856. [a. F. *berthe*, englished as *bertha*, from the proper name.] A deep falling collar, attached to the top of a low-necked dress.

Berthage (bɔ̄·ɹþėdʒ). 1881. [f. BERTH *v.*[1] + -AGE.] Accommodation for mooring vessels.

Berthierite (bɔ̄·ɹþiərəit). 1827. [f. *Berthier*, a naturalist.] *Min.* A sulphide of antimony and iron, occurring native in elongated masses.

Berthing (bɔ̄·ɹþiŋ), *vbl. sb.*[1] 1800. [f. BERTH *v.*[1]] The action of placing a ship in a berth.

Be·rthing, *vbl. sb.*[2] 1706. [f. BERTH *v.*[2]] The upright planking of the sides, etc. of a ship; *esp.* that outside above the sheer-stroke.

‖**Bertillonage** (bęrtiyonā·ʒ). 1892. [f. name of Fr. criminologist.] A system of identifying criminals by measurements, finger prints, etc.

†**Be·rtram.** 1578. [a. Ger., corruption of L. PYRETHRUM.] Pellitory of Spain.

†**Beru·n,** *v.* [Com. Teut.: OE. *berinnan.*] To run or flow round –1515.

Beryl (be·ril). ME. [a. OF. *beryl*:—L. *beryllus*, a. Gr. βήρυλλος.] A. *sb.* 1. A. transparent precious stone of a pale-green colour passing into light-blue, yellow, and white; distinguished only by colour from the emerald. Varieties are the *aquamarine*, which is of pale bluish-green, and the chrysoberyl, and perh. the chrysoprase, which are yellow. So *beryl-stone.* Also †*fig.* 2. *Min.* A mineral species including not only the beryl, but also the emerald, a variety of the beryl, distinguished by the presence of oxide of chromium. Beryl is a silicate of aluminium and glucinum. 1837. †3. *transf.* A fine kind of crystal or glass –1625. †4. A mirror –1576. 5. The colour of the beryl (pale sea-green) 1834.

B. *attrib.* and as *adj.* 1. Of beryl; also *formerly*, Of crystal 1594. 2. *adj.* Beryl-like in colour, clear pale green 1857. Hence **Be·ryl-line** *a.* b.-like.

Beryllia (běri·liă). 1873. [f. BERYLLIUM; cf. *magnesia.*] *Chem.* The oxide of beryllium or glucinum; GLUCINA.

Beryllium (běri·liǒm). 1863. [f. BERYL + -IUM.] *Chem.* A metallic element formerly called GLUCINUM. Symbol Be.

Berylloid (be·riloid). [f. L. *beryllus* + -OID.] *Crystallog.* A geometrical solid consisting of two twelve-sided pyramids put base to base, as in the beryl.

Berzelianite (bəɹzī·liănəit). [f. *Berzelius*, chemist and mineralogist.] *Min.* A native selenide of copper, silver white with metallic lustre. **Berze·liite,** an anhydrous arsenate of lime and magnesia; Kühnite.

Bes-, repr. OF. *bes-*:—L. *bis* 'twice, in two ways, doubly'; in Romanic, 'secondarily, in an inferior way'; whence, 'improperly, unsymmetrically, not right or straight, awry, aslant'. Found in Eng. as *bes-, be-, bez-*.

Besai·el, besaile. *Obs.* exc. *Law.* ME. [a. OF. *besayel, besaiol* (mod. *bisaïeul*), f. *bes*:—L. *bis* + *ayel, aiol, aieul* (see AIEL).] A great-grandfather. b. *Law.* In *Writ of besaile*, a writ which formerly lay for the heir where his great-grandfather died seised of land in fee-simple, and a stranger entered the day of his death, or abated after his death.

Besai·nt (bǐsēⁱ·nt). 1603. [See BE- 5.] To make a saint of.

Besand(e, -saunt(e, obs. ff. BEZANT.

Bes-antler, var. of BEZ-ANTLER.

Bescatter (bǐ,skæ·təɹ), *v.* 1574. [See BE- 1.] a. To besprinkle *with.* b. To scatter about.

Bescratch, -scrawl, -screen, -scribble, -scumber, etc.; see BE-.

Besee·, *v. arch.* [Com. Teut.: OE. *biséon, beséon*, f. *bi-*, BE- + *séon*, in OTeut. **sehwan* to SEE.] I. †1. *intr.* To look about; to see; also *fig.* –ME. †2. To see to; *hence*, to use (*well* or *ill*) –1596. †3. To provide, arrange ME. only. II. Later uses of the pa. pple. **Beseen.** †1. Seen; as in *well-beseen*, good looking –1542. 2. Appearing; furnished ME.

Beseech (bǐsī·tʃ), *v.* Pa. t. and pple. **besought** (bǐsǭ·t). ME. [f. *bi-*, BE- 2 + ME. *secen, sechen, seken* to SEEK.] †1. To seek after, try to get. 2. To beg earnestly for ME. 3. To supplicate ME. 4. To ask earnestly (*arch.*) ME.

2. I b. your worship's name *Mids. N.* III. i. 183. 3. I b. thee, shew me thy glory *Ex.* xxxiii. 18. I pray and b. you..to accompany me *Bk. Com. Pr.* 4. To b. for food SOUTHEY. Hence †**Besee·ch** *sb.* (*rare*) beseeching. **Besee·cher,** a petitioner, *esp.* to the king or his courts. **Beseeching·ly** *adv.*, **-ness. Besee·chment,** beseeching.

Beseek(e, obs. f. BESEECH.

Beseem (bǐsī·m), *v.* ME. [See BE- 2.] †1. To seem, look. (Mostly in 3rd pers.) –1779. Also *impers.* 2. To suit in appearance; to become, befit ME. 3. *absol.* To be seemly ME.

2. A prison may well b. his holiness MARLOWE. Sad pause and deep regard b. the sage SHAKS. *Lucr.* 277. 3. To treat thee as beseems MILT. Hence **Besee·mingly** *adv.*, **-ness. Besee·mly** *a.* seemly; whence **Besee·mliness.**

Beset (bǐse·t), *v.* Pa. t. and pple. **beset.** [Com. Teut.: OE. *bi-, besettan*, f. *bi-*, BE- + *settan* (Goth. *satjan*) to SET, causal of *sitjan* to SIT. *Beset* is thus causal to BESIT.] I. *trans.* 1. To set about, surround *with.* Now only in pa. pple. 2. To surround with hostile intent; to assail (a person); to invest (a place); to occupy (a road, passage, etc.) ME. Also *fig.* 3. *gen.* To close round; hem in 1534.

1. A tiara beset with pearls DE QUINCEY. 2. The lioness..beset by men and hounds POPE. *fig.* The sinne which doth so easily b. us *Heb.* xii. 1. Beset with contradictions FREEMAN. 3. Completely beset [by ice] KANE.

II. To set (in fig. sense), to bestow. All *trans.* †1. To set or place (one's mind, trust, etc.) *on* or *upon*; = SET *v.* –1627. †2. To employ (one's wit, money, etc.). Cf. *bestow.* –1560. †3. To bestow (*esp.* in marriage), to allot, transfer –1599. †4. To set in order –1500. †5. To become. Cf Sc. *set*, Fr. *seoir.* –1598.

1. This worthi man ful wel his witte bisette CHAUCER. Hence **Bese·tter. Bese·tting** *ppl. a.* (*esp.* in *besetting sin*).

Besetment (bǐse·tmĕnt). 1830. [f. prec.] 1. The fact of besetting; *concr.* that which besets one. 2. A condition of being beset 1853.

†**Besew, beshade, beshadow, beshame, beshear,** etc.; see BE-.

Beshine (bǐʃəi·n), *v.* [Com. Teut.: OE. *bi-, bescīnan*, f. *bi-*, BE- 1 + *scīnan* (OTeut. *skīnan*) to SHINE.] To shine about or upon; to illumine. Obs. bef. 1600, but revived by Carlyle. Hence **Besho·ne** *ppl. a.*

Beshrew (bǐ,ʃrū·), *v. arch.* ME. [See BE- 2.] †1. To make wicked; to deprave –1556. †2. To curse, or blame greatly, as the cause of misfortune –1682. b. Now only in *Beshrew me, thee*, etc.: 'Devil take, hang'; also, 'plague on', and often playful. [Perh. ellipt. Cf. (*I*) *thank you.*]

Beshroud, †beshut, etc.; see BE-.

Beside (bǐsəi·d). [ME. *bi siden, bisiden*:—OE. *be sīdan* (dat. sing.). In OE. only as two wds. Cf. BIHALVE.] A. *adv.* 1. †By the side, by one's side; hard by (*arch.*). 2. In addition. (Now usu. BESIDES.) ME. 3. Otherwise, else. (Now usu. BESIDES.) 1588. †4. On or to one side. (Now ASIDE.) –1604. †5. By, past. *To go b.*: to pass on one side, to miss. –1592.

1. Some on horsys and some besyde ME. 2. My selfe, and diuers Gentlemen b. SHAKS. 3. We talk'd Of thee and none b. 1816.

B. *prep.* 1. *lit.* By the side of; *hence*, hard by ME. b. *fig.* Side by side with in rank, or for comparison 1513. 2. In addition to (Now usu. BESIDES.) ME. 3. Other than, else than. (Now usu. BESIDES.) ME. †4. Outside of, out of, away from, past –1663. Also *fig.*

1. The thefe that honge on the crosse besyde our lorde 1526. Seint Gyles b. Holbourne ME. *fig.* Besyde Latyne our langage is imperfite 1513. 4. *To go b.*: to pass by, miss. *To look b.*: to overlook, miss. (*fig.*) *B. oneself*: out of one's wits; cf. F. *hors de soi*, Ger. *ausser sich.* Enough to put him quite b. his patience SHAKS. B. the purpose MORE, my Scope RAY, the real issue FROUDE. At Durham, b. all expectation, I met an old friend JOHNSON.

Besides (bǐsəi·dz). ME. [f. BESIDE + *s* of the advb. gen., prob. a northern substitute for the southern *-en* of *besiden.*] A. *adv.* †1. = BESIDE A 1. –1450. 2. In addition, as well 1564; moreover 1596. 3. Other than that mentioned, else 1596. †4. Now ASIDE 1611.

2. Hast thou here any b. *Gen.* xix. 12. B., they were indemnified for it BURKE. 3. Robbers, who break with all the world b., must keep faith among themselves BURKE.

B. *prep.* †1. = BESIDE B 1. –1677. 2. Over and above, in addition to, as well as. (This and 3 are the ordinary current senses.) 1535. 3. Other than, else than: in neg. and interrog. sentences = 'except, excluding' ME. †4. = BESIDE B 4. –1702. Also *fig.*

2. Besydes all this, betwene you and us there is a great gulfe set *Luke* xvi. 26. 3. The Jews..for ever unsainting all the world b. themselves SOUTH.

Besiege (bǐsī·dʒ), *v.* [ME. *bi-, by-, besege(n*, f. BE- 1 + *sege(n*, aphet. f. *asege(n*, ASSIEGE.] To sit down before (a town, etc.) with armed forces in order to capture it; to lay siege to, beleaguer, invest. Also *fig.* and *transf.*

Antigonus besieged the city for ten months THIRLWALL. When forty winters shall b. thy brow SHAKS. *Sonn.* ii. To b. the doors of the bakers 1789. To b. Heaven with supplications 1867. Hence †**Besie·ge** *sb.* siege. **Besie·ged** *ppl. a.* invested by hostile forces; *absol.* the people besieged. **Besie·gement**, the action of besieging; the being besieged. **Besie·ger. Besie·gingly** *adv.* (*rare*).

Besilver, besing, etc.; see BE-.

†**Besi·t**, *v.* [OE. *besittan*, f. BE I + *sittan* to SIT; see BESET.] **1.** To encamp about, besiege ME. only. **2.** To sit properly upon (as a dress); to fit, suit. Cf. F. *seoir.* -1614.

Beslabber, var. of BESLOBBER.

Beslave (bĭ,slēⁱ·v), *v.* 1615. [See BE- 5.] To make a slave of; to call 'slave'; to pollute with slavery.

Beslaver (bĭ,sla·vəɹ), *v.* 1589. [See BE- I; cf. BESLOBBER.] **1.** To slaver upon or over. **2.** To cover with fulsome flattery 1861.

Beslobber (bĭ,slǫ·bəɹ), *v.* ME. [See BE- I.] To wet or befoul with saliva (= to BESLAVER), or with liquid food escaping from the mouth; to kiss like a drivelling child; *fig.* = prec. 2.

Beslubber (bĭ,slʋ·bəɹ), *v.* ME. [f. BE- I + SLUBBER *v.*] To wet and soil with a thick liquid; to bedaub.

Besmear (bĭ,smīᵊ·ɹ), *v.* [OE. *bismierwan*, f. *bi-*, BE I + *smierwan*:—OTeut. **smerwjan*, f. **smerwo-(m)*, in OE. *smeoru*, grease.] To smear over or about; to cover (and soil) *with* any greasy or sticky substance. Also *fig.*

Besmering and dawbing eche other with dirte and myer 1535.

Besmirch (bĭ,smɔ̄·ɹtʃ), *v.* 1602. [See BE- I.] To soil, discolour, as with smoke, soot, or mud; *fig.* to dim the lustre of.

Besmoke (bĭ,smōᵘ·k), *v.* ME. [See BE- 4.] To fill, or act on, with smoke, to fumigate.

†**Besmo·ttered**, *ppl. a.* [?] Bespattered as with mud. CHAUCER.

Be-smut (bĭ,smʋ·t), *v.* 1610. [See BE- I.] To blacken with smut; also *fig.*

Be-smu·tch, *v.* 1831. [See BE- I.] To besmirch.

Besnow (bĭ,snōᵘ·), *v.* [OE. *besniwian.*] To cover with or as with snow.

†**Beso·gne.** 1615. [a. F., ad. It. *bisogno*, cf. BESONIO.] **a.** A raw recruit. **b.** = BEZONIAN. -1658. So †**Beso·gnier.**

Besoi·l, *v.* ME. [See BE- I.] To sully; also *fig.*

Besom (bī·zəm), *sb.*[1] [Com. WGer.: OE. *besema, besma*:—OTeut. **besmon-*.] †**1.** A bundle of rods or twigs used for birching -ME. **2.** An implement for sweeping, usu. a bunch of broom, etc. tied round a handle; a broom. (In lit. Eng. 'broom' is now the generic name, 'besom' specific.) OE. **3.** *fig.* Any agent that sweeps away or cleanses ME.

3. Swepe thy soul clene wyth the besome of the drede of God ME.

Besom, *sb.*[2] *Sc.* 1816. A low woman.

Be·som, *v.* ME. [f. BESOM *sb.*[1] Cf. *to brush.*] †**1.** *intr.* To sweep with violence ME. only. **2.** To sweep (*away, out*, etc.) 1791. Hence **Be·somer**, one who uses a besom.

†**Beso·nio, beso·gnio.** 1603. [var. of BISOGNIO, a. It. *bisogno*, applied to soldiers who landed in Italy from Spain ill found and in want of everything. Cf. BESOGNE.] **a.** A raw soldier. **b.** (term of contempt) A needy beggar; a base worthless fellow. See BEZONIAN. -1820.

†**Beso·rt**, *v.* [See BE-.] To assort or match with; to befit. *Lear* I. iv. 272. ? Hence †**Beso·rt** *sb.* suitable company. *Oth.* I. iii. 238.

Besot (bĭsǫ·t), *v.* 1581. [f. BE- + SOT; cf. ASSOT.] **1.** *trans.* To cause to dote *on*; to infatuate *with.* **2.** To stupefy in mind or morally 1615. **3.** To make a sot of. (Said of narcotics.) Also *absol.* 1627.

2. Besotted with words HAZLITT. **3.** Pleasure..has an opiate in it; it stupefies and besots YOUNG. Hence **Beso·tted-ly** *adv.*, **-ness.**

Besought (bĭsǭ·t), pa. t. and pple. of BESEECH.

Besouth (bĭsau·þ), *prep.* Now *Sc.* ME. [See BE-.] On or to the south of.

Bespangle (bĭ,spæ·ŋg'l), *v.* 1593. [See BE- 6.] To besprinkle with or as with spangles. var. **Bespa·nkle.**

[Stars] to..b. a canopy over our heads WOLLASTON.

Bespatter (bĭ,spæ·təɹ), *v.* 1644. [See BE- I.] **1.** To spatter over or about 1674. **2.** *fig.* To asperse (*with* abuse, etc.). Usu. in a bad sense. 1644. **3.** *spec.* To slander 1653.

1. Bespattered with mud THIRLWALL.

†**Bespaw·l**, *v.* 1602. [See BE- I.] To bespatter with saliva; also *fig.* -1647.

Bespeak (bĭ,spī·k), *v.* Pa. t. **bespoke,** and (*arch.*) **-spake.** Pa. pple. **bespoken, bespoke.** [Com. WGer.: OE. *bi-, besprecan*, f. *bi-*, BE- + *sprecan* (*specan*) to SPEAK.] †**1.** *intr.* To call out, complain *that* OE only. †**2.** To exclaim: orig. by way of remonstrance; later, simply, to speak -1791. †**3.** *trans.* To speak against -ME. †**4.** To speak about; to discuss -1489. **5.** To speak for; to arrange for, engage beforehand; to order (goods) 1583. **6.** To address (a person). Now *poet.* 1590. **7.** To speak of, indicate 1628; to augur 1719.

2. Until their Lord himself bespake, and bid them go MILT. **5.** To b. a lodging 1602, a play STEELE, one's custom 1712, a friendly reception for oneself COBBETT. **7.** But her house Bespake a sleepy hand of negligence WORDSW. Circumstances that b. war HAWTHORNE. Hence **Bespea·k** *sb.* a bespeaking; *esp.* of a play; *hence*, a benefit night, when the actor's friends, etc. choose the play. **Bespea·ker.**

Bespecked, bespeckle, bespew, bespeed, etc.; see BE-.

†**Bespe·te**, *v. arch.* [ME. *bespeten*, f. BE- + *speten*, OE. *spǣtan* to spit.] = BESPIT. CHAUCER.

Bespice, bespill; see BE-.

Bespi·t, *v. arch.* ME. [See BE- I.] *trans.* To spit upon. Rarely *intr.* with *upon.*

Besplash, bespot; see BE-.

Bespou·t, *v.* 1575. [See BE-.] To besprinkle by spouting (*lit.* and *fig.*).

Woe for the age,.. quack-ridden, bespeeched, bespouted CARLYLE.

Bespread (bĭ,spre·d), *v.* [ME. *bi-, bespred(en*, f. *bi-*, BE- + *spreden* to SPREAD.] **1.** To spread *with.* **2.** Of things: To spread over 1641. **3.** To spread out 1557.

2. Mats bespreading the floor 1779.

Bespre·ng, *v.* *Obs.* exc. in pa. pple. **besprent.** [OE. *besprengan*, f. BE- I + *sprengan*:—OTeut. *sprangjan*, causal of *springan* to SPRING.] **1.** *trans.* To sprinkle over; to strew *with* -1606. **2.** To sprinkle (things) about -1820. var. †**Bespri·ng.**

Besprent (bĭ,spre·nt), *ppl. a.* ME. [f. prec.] **1.** Besprinkled, strewed *with.* **2.** Scattered about 1567.

1. Knot-grass dew-b. MILT. *Comus* 542. Flower-b. meadows WORDSW.

Besprinkle (bĭ,spri·ŋk'l), *v.* [ME. *besprengil*, **besprenkel*, f. BE- I and 4 + *sprenkel*, freq. of *sprengen* to asperse.] *trans.* To sprinkle all over *with.* Also *fig.*

The walls were besprinkled with holy water GIBBON. Hence **Bespri·nkler.**

†**Bespurt,** †**bespurtle, besputter,** †**besquirt**; see BE- 4.

Bessemer (be·sĭməɹ). 1856. [f. the inventor, Sir H. *Bessemer.*] **B. process**: a process for decarbonizing and desiliconizing pig-iron so as to convert it into steel or malleable iron, by passing air through the molten metal. Hence **B. iron, steel,** briefly *Bessemer*; also *attrib.*

Best (best), *a.* and *adv.* [Com. Teut.: OE. (adv.) *bętst*, earlier *bętest, bętost* = OTeut. **batist*, superl. f. comp. **batiz* BETTER. The *t* has been assimilated to following *s* in all mod. Teut. langs.] **A.** *adj.* Superl. of GOOD. Most good (*Goodest* is not an OTeut. form.) **I. 1.** Excelling all others in quality. **2.** Of persons: Most kind. Of persons and things: Most advantageous; most appropriate. OE. **3.** Largest, most; *esp.* in *best part* 1538.

1. Of many good, I thinke him b. *Two Gent.* I. ii. 102. The b. people in the town (*mod.*). **2.** Which of your brothers is b. to you (*mod.*). *I, you*, etc. *had b.* (formerly *me were b.*, later *I were b.*): it would be b. for me, etc. See BETTER.

II. *absol.* (rarely passing into a *sb.*) **1.** *pl.* The best people OE. **2.** *sing.* The best thing, point, circumstance, element ME. **3.** With possessive. *One's best*: **a.** The best one can (do) ME. **b.** Best state, point, or condition 1571. **c.** Best clothes 1790.

2. Bad is the b. 1693. All these I better in one generall b. SHAKS. *Sonn.* xci. **3.** He did his b. to seem to eat POPE. It exhibits man at his b.

Phrases, etc. *To put one's b. foot* or *leg foremost*: to do one's b. to get on. With *verbs*: *To have the b. of it*: to have the advantage in a contest, or a transaction, and *hence*, the least possible loss; so *To make the b. of it.* With *preps.*: †*At the b., at b.*: in the best possible manner or condition. *At b.*: (taken) in the most favourable aspect, making every allowance. *For the b.*: aiming at, tending to, the b. result. *To the b.*: to the utmost effort or extent (of one's power, etc.).

B. *adv.* Superl of WELL. **1.** With *vbs.* In the most excellent way, in the highest degree; in the most suitable manner, with the greatest advantage, to the fullest extent OE. **2.** With *adjs.* and *pples.* written with the hyphen, as *b.-bred, b.-conditioned*, i.e. *best condition* + *-ed* ME. **3.** With *agent-nouns*, as *b.-wisher.*

1. Who b. bear his mild yoke, they serve him b. MILT. **2.** The b.-laid schemes o' mice an' men BURNS. The b.-natured fellow alive 1863.

Best, *v. colloq.* 1863. [f. prec.: cf. *to worst.*] To get the better of.

†**Bestad, -stadde,** *v.* 1579. Earlier f. BESTED *pa. pple.* Used only in pass.; but by Spenser made a pa. t. and active pple. = BESET.

Bestain (bĭ,stēⁱ·n), *v.* 1559. [See BE- I.] To mark with stains.

†**Besta·nd**, *v.* [Com. Teut.: OE. *bestanden* = Goth. (and OTeut.) *bistanden*, f. *bi-*, BE- + *standan* to stand.] **1.** To stand by or near; *esp.* to stand by (the dead), to mourn for. Also *absol.* -ME. **2.** To stand round in hostility, to beset -1485.

Bestar (bĭ,stā·ɹ), *v.* 1612. [See BE-.] To spangle or adorn as with stars. Hence **Besta·rred** *ppl. a.*; *spec.* decorated with the star of an order.

Bestead (bĭ,ste·d), *v.* Pa. t. **besteaded.** Pa. pple. **bested, bestead.** 1581. [f. BE- 2 + STEAD *v.* to prop.] **1.** *trans.* To assist. **2.** To avail 1589.

1. Better able by his purse..to b. his neighbours, than they him 1627. **2.** Thou vain Philosophy! Little hast thou bestead CLOUGH.

†**Bestea·l**, *v.* [OE. *bestelan*, f. BE- + *stelan* to STEAL.] *intr.* (and *refl.*) To steal or move stealthily (*away* or *on*) -1597.

Bested, bestead (bĭste·d), *pa. pple.* [ME. *bistad*, f. *bi-*, BE- 2 + *stad*, later *sted* 'placed'; see STED *v.* and *pa. pple.* The sp. *bestead* is merely analogical. Cf. BESTAD.] †**1.** Placed ME. only. †**2.** Settled ME only. **3.** Beset *by*, †*with* ME. **4.** Situated, circumstanced (with *ill*, etc.) ME. †**b.** (Without an adv.) Hard pressed -1587.

3. Bestad with dethe on euery syde 1493. **4.** I never saw a fellow worse bestead 2 *Hen. VI*, II. iii. 56.

Bestial (be·stiăl), *sb.* [Two forms: *a.* ME. *bestaile*, a. OF. *bestaille* (sing. fem.):—L. *bestialia* 'cattle'; *β.* mod. Eng. and Sc. *bestial*, a. OF. *bestial*, sing. of mod. F. *bestiaux*, subst. use of *bestial* adj., ad. L. *bestialis.*] **1.** A collective term for domestic animals, kept for food or tillage. Since 17th c. displaced in Eng. by *cattle*, but in Sc. still in use. **2.** A single beast; (with *pl.*) ME.

Bestial (be·stiăl), *a.* [ME.: a. OF. *bestial*, ad. L. *bestialis.*] **1.** Of or belonging to the lower animals, *esp.* quadrupeds. **2.** *transf.* Like a beast; brutish, irrational; barbarous ME. **3.** *esp.* Like a beast in indulging the animal instincts; depraved, lustful, cruel, brutal, beastly, obscene 1447.

1. A Satyr; of Shape, part Humane, part B. STEELE. **2.** Bestiall ignorance 1615. **3.** Thy faythfull felowe is bestiall dronkennes BARCLAY. Hence **Be·stialism**, the condition of beasts. **Be·stially** *adv.*

Bestiality (bestiæ·lĭti). [ME. *bestialite*, a. F. *bestialité*; see BESTIAL.] **1.** The state or quality of being BESTIAL. †**2.** Unnatural connexion with a beast -1765.

Bestialize (be·stiăləiz), *v.* 1684. [f. BESTIAL *a.* + -IZE.] To change into the form or nature of a beast; to brutalize, debase.

He bestializes man and humanizes beasts 1845.

†**Be·stian**, *a.* 1652. [f. L. *bestia* + -AN.] Of or belonging to the 'Beast' of the Apocalypse (cf. BEAST) -1701. **Be·stianism**, the power of the Beast. **Be·stianize**, to be a follower of the Beast.

Bestiary (be·stiări). 1625. [ad. L. *bestiarius*, and *bestiarium*; see -ARY.] †**1.** A beast-fighter in the Roman amphitheatre. **2.** A treatise on beasts, as written during the Middle Ages 1840.

Besti·ck, *v.* 1623. [f. BE- 1 and 4.] **1.** To cover all over. Also *fig.* **2.** To transfix 1667.

Bestill; see BE- 1.

Bestir (bǐ₁stɔ̄·ɪ), *v.* [OE. *bestyrian*, f. BE- 2 + *styrian.*] To stir up. **a.** *refl.* To busy oneself ME. **b.** *trans.* To rouse into activity 1549.

B. the and hardiliche fight ME. Bestyre youre werye handes COVERDALE.

Best man (be·st mæ·n). 1814. [orig. Sc.] The groomsman at a wedding.

Bestorm (bǐ₁stǭ·ɪm), *v.* 1651. [See BE- 1.] To storm on all sides.

Bestow (bǐ₁stōᵘ·), *v.* [ME. *bistowen*, f. *bi-*, BE- 2 + *stowen* to STOW.] **1.** To place, locate; to dispose of (*in* some place) (*arch.*). **2.** To stow away (*arch.*) ME. **3.** To lodge, put up (*arch.*) 1577. Also *refl.* †**4.** To settle or give in marriage. Also *refl.* –1714. **5.** To apply, to employ (*in* an occupation); to devote *for* a purpose ME.; *esp.* †to lay out (money) –1631; †*refl.* to acquit oneself –1606. **6.** *trans.* (and *absol.*) To confer as a gift 1535.

1. How should I b. him? Shall I put him into the basket againe *Merry W.* IV. ii. 48. **5.** The boy..bestowes himselfe Like a ripe sister *Two Gent.* III. i. 87. **6.** In bestowing, madam, he was most princely *Hen. VIII*, IV. ii. 56. The importance that wealth can b. MAR. EDGEWORTH. Hence **Bestow·able** *a.* capable of being bestowed. **Bestow·al,** location; gift. **Bestow·ed** *ppl. a.* (often with *well-*, *ill-*). **Bestow·er. Bestow·ment,** bestowal; a gift.

Bestraddle, bestraw, etc.; see BE- *pref.*

†**Bestrau·ght,** *v.* and *ppl. a.* 1547. [f. BE- *intens.* + STRAUGHT. *Bestract* is not found.] **1.** as *pa. t.* Distracted, bereft (*of* wits) 1580. **2.** *pa. pple.* and *adj.* Distraught 1547.

Bestreak, bestream; see BE-.

Bestrew (bǐ₁strū·), *v.* Also **bestrow** (bǐ₁strōᵘ·). Pa. pple. **bestrewed; bestrewn, bestrown.** [OE. *bi-*, *bestréowian*, f. *bi-*, BE- 1 + *stréowian* to STREW.] **1.** To strew *with.* Also *transf.* and *fig.* **2.** To strew or scatter about 1667. **3.** To lie scattered over 1718.

1. The dewy turf with flowers bestrewn WORDSW. **2.** So thick bestrown Abject and lost lay these, covering the Flood MILT. *P. L.* I. 311. Hence **Bestrew·ment** (*rare*).

Bestride (bǐ₁strəi·d), *v.* Pa. t. **bestrode;** also **bestrid.** Pa. pple. **bestridden;** also **-strid, -strode.** [OE. *bi-*, *bestrīdan*, f. *bi-*, BE- 4 + *strīdan* to STRIDE.] **1.** To sit upon or across with or as with the legs astride. **2.** To stand over with the legs astride. Also *fig.* 1601. Also *transf.* of things (e. g. a rainbow, bridge). **3.** To stride across. Also *fig.* 1600.

1. The pressed nostril, spectacle-bestrid COWPER. **2.** He doth b. the narrow world like a Colossus *Jul. C.* I. ii. 135. When I bestrid thee in the warres, and tooke Deepe scarres to saue thy life *Com. Err.* V. i. 192.

Bestrow, -n, vars. of BESTREW, -N.

†**Bestr·ut,** *ppl. a.* 1603. [Cf. ASTRUT, etc.] Swollen –1648.

Bestuck, pa. t. and pple. of BESTICK.

Bestu·d; see BE- 1.

‖**Bestuur** (bĕstǖ·r). 1885. [Du.; f. *besturen* to govern.] Administration; i. e. in the Dutch-speaking parts of S. Africa.

Bet (bet), *sb.* 1592. [? aphet. f. ABET *sb.*] The staking of money or other value on the event of a doubtful issue; a wager; also, the sum of money or article staked.

An even b. (fig.): a balance of probabilities.

Bet (bet), *v.* Pa. t. and pple. **bet;** also **betted.** 1597. [?f. prec.] To stake or wager in support of an affirmation or on the issue of a forecast. Also *absol.*

Iohn of Gaunt..betted much Money on his head 2 *Hen. IV.* III. ii. 50. He enjoys it [gambling] that looks on and bets not EARLE. *You b.* (*slang*, U.S.): certainly.

†**Bet,** *adv.* (and *a.*) [Com. Teut.: OE. *bęt*:—OTeut. **batiz* adv. *Bet(e)re*, the neut. of the adj., finally superseded *bet* about 1600.] *adv.* **1.** The earlier form of BETTER –1586. **2.** As predicate after *be* –1643. **3.** *absol.* and quasi-*sb.* *The bet*: the advantage –1592.

†**Bet,** *adv.*[2] ME. [? = go better, i.e. quicker (Skeat).] In *Go b.* –1617.

Beta (bī·tă). ME. [a. L., Gr. βῆτα.] **1.** The second letter of the Greek alphabet Β, β. **2.** Used to mark: *esp.* **a.** *Astron.* The second star in a constellation. **b.** *Chem.* The second isomerous modification of an organic compound. **c.** *Beta rays* or *β-rays*, the second of three types of rays emitted by radioactive substances, with great penetrative power 1904.

Betaine (bī·te₁əin). 1879. [irreg. f. *beta* BEET *sb.*] *Chem.* A base ($C_5H_{11}NO_2$) found in beet and mangold-wurzel.

Betake (bǐtē̆·k), *v. str.* Pa. t. **betook.** Pa. pple. **betaken.** [ME. *be-*, *bitake(n.* Confused early with *betæche* BETEACH.] †**1.** = BETEACH 2, 3, 4. –1649. **2.** *refl.* To commit oneself, have recourse *to* any kind of action 15... **3.** *refl.* To resort, turn one's course, go 1612.

1. Nowe to the Devil I the b. SKELTON. **2.** That defence thou hast, b. the too't *Twel. N.* III. iv. 240. *To b. oneself to one's heels*: to run away. **3.** Whither shall I b. me, where subsist? MILT. *P. L.* X. 922.

†**Betea·ch,** *v.* [OE. *betǣc(e)an*, f. BE- 2 + *tǣc(e)an* to show. Cf. BETAKE.] **1.** To point out OE. only. **2.** To hand over, give up, yield –1513. **3.** To entrust, give in charge *to* –1513. **4.** To commit or commend *to* (God, the Devil, etc.) –1685. **5.** To TEACH –ME.

†**Beteela.** 1598. [app. = Pg. *beatilha*, ? = med.L. *beatilla*, dim. of *beata* a nun; cf. BATTALIA.] A kind of East Indian muslin –1727.

†**Beteem,** *v.* 1565. [app. f. BE- 2 + TEEM to think fit. Cf. Du. *betamen.*] **1.** To think fit –1647. **2.** To grant, concede –1674. **b.** To allow *Haml.* I. ii. 141.

Betel (bī·t'l). 1553. [Prob. a. Pg. *betel*, ad. Malayâlam *veṭṭila*; cf. Skr. *vīṭi.*] The leaf of a plant, which is wrapped round parings of the areca nut and a little lime, and chewed in India, etc. as a masticatory 1585. **b.** Also the shrubby plant (*Piper betle*, or *Chavica betel*, N.O. *Piperaceæ*) which yields the leaf 1553.

Betel nut: the nut of the Areca Palm (see ARECA); so misnamed because chewed with the b. leaf. Hence *b.-tree*, Areca Catechu.

†**Bete·ll,** *v.* [OE. *betęllan.*] To speak for; to declare; to lay claim to; to calumniate –1567.

Bête noire (bē̆t nwār). 1850. [Fr. = black beast.] An insufferable person or thing.

Beth(e, = shall be, is, are, be (ye); see BE *v.*

Bethel (be·þĕl). 1617. [Heb., 'house of God'.] **1.** A place where God is worshipped; the pillar that marks it. (See *Gen.* xxviii. 17.) **2.** *transf.* A chapel or meeting-house 1840.

Bethink (bǐþi·ŋk), *v.* Pa. t. and pple. **bethought** (bǐþǭ·t). [Com. Teut.: OE. *biþęncan* :—OTeut. **biþankjan*, f. *bi-*, BE- + *þankjan* to THINK.] **1.** *trans.* To think of or about; to recollect. *Obs.* exc. w. cl. †**2.** To conceive –ME.; to consider –1647; to contrive –1593. †**3.** To regret, grudge –1696. †**4.** *refl.* To take thought; to recollect oneself –1649. **5.** To reflect; *also*, to call to mind ME. **6.** To resolve. (Fr. *s'aviser.*) ME. **7.** *intr.* To reflect, think (*arch.*) ME. **8.** *pass.* *To be bethought*: to bethink oneself (in senses 4, 5, 6) ME.

3. I can never b. any pains..in the service of my country LOCKE. **4.** If they shall bethinke themselues ..and repent 1 *Kings* viii. 47. **5.** I will bethinke me: come againe to morrow *Meas. for M.* II. ii. 145. **6.** It may be I shall otherwise bethinke me *Jul. C.* IV. iii. 251. Hence †**Bethou·ght** *pple.* and *a.* purposed; minded (with *ill-*, etc.).

Bethlehem, Bethlem; see BEDLAM.

†**Be·thlehemite.** Also **Bethlemite.** One of an order of monks existing in England in the 13th c.; they wore a five-rayed star, in memory of the star of Bethlehem. BAILEY.

Bethumb, bethump, bethwack; see BE-.

Bethwine (be·þwəin). 1609. [? a perversion of *bind-with.*] Local name of: **a.** The Great Hedge Convolvulus (*C. sepium*). **b.** The Bearbind (*Polygonum Convolvulus*). **c.** The Traveller's Joy (*Clematis Vitalba*).

Betide (bǐtəi·d), *v.* [ME. *bitide-n*; see TIDE *v.*] **1.** *intr.* To happen, befall. Only in 3rd pers. and often *impers.* Also, with *dat. obj.*; occas. *to*, *unto* ME. †**2.** To become *of* (rarely *on*) –1675. †**3.** To fall to as a possession –1587. †**4.** To befit (any one) –1566. ¶*catachr.* To bode 1799.

1. B., b., whatever b., Haig shall be Haig of Bemerside *Pop. Rime.* But woe b. the wandering wight SCOTT.

†**Beti·me, bitime,** *v.* ME. only. [f. *bi-*, BE- + *time(n* to happen; see TIME *v.*] *intr.* To betide. In *L.L.L.* IV. iii. 382 *be time* should be read, as in the Folio of 1623.

†**Beti·me,** *adv.* [ME. *bi-*, *by-time*, i. e. *by time.*] In good time; early in the day –1630.

To businesse that we loue, we rise b. *Ant. & Cl.* IV. iv. 20.

Betimes (bǐtəi·mz), *adv.* ME. [f. BETIME + genitival *-s*; cf. *besides.*] **1.** At an early time, period, or season. **2.** *spec.* Early in the morning 1481. **2.** In good time ME. **3.** In a short time, speedily ME.

1. He must learn b. to love truth HELPS. **2.** Not to bee a bedde after midnight, is to be vp b. *Twel. N.* II. iii. 2. **3.** He tyres b., that spurs too fast b. SHAKS.

Betitle, betoil; see BE-.

Betoken (bǐtōᵘ·k'n), *v.* [ME. *bitacnien*, later *bitok(e)nen*, f. *bi-*, BE- + *tácnian* to signify, f. *tácn* TOKEN.] †**1.** To signify; to express in words –1612. †**2.** To be a type of –1667. **3.** To be a sign, or omen of; to presage ME. **4.** To point to, indicate 1486.

2. In the Cloud a Bow..Betok'ning peace from God and Cov'nant new MILT. *P. L.* XI. 867. **3.** Like a red morn, that ever yet betoken'd Wreck to the seaman SHAKS. *Ven. & Ad.* 453. **4.** With looks Betokening rage CARY. Hence **Beto·kener.**

‖**Beton** (be·toṅ, be·tən). 1819. [Fr., OF. *betun*, a. Pr.:—L. *bitumen.*] A concrete, composed of sand, lime, and hydraulic cement.

Beto·ngue, *v.* 1639. [See BE- 6.] To flout.

Betony (be·təni). ME. [a. F. *betoine*, ad. late L. **betonia* for *betonica*, in Pliny (*N. H.* XXV. 46) *vettonica.*] *Bot.* **1.** *prop.* A plant (*Stachys Betonica*), formerly credited with medicinal and magical virtues. **b.** Applied also to: **St. Paul's B.** (*Veronica serpyllifolia*); **Water-B.** (*Scrophularia aquatica*).

†**Beto·rn,** *ppl. a.* ME. [See BE- 1.] Torn; tattered –1599.

Betoss; see BE- 1.

†**Betraise, -traish,** *v.* ME. [f. BE- 2 + *traïss-*, *trahiss-*, stem of F. *trahir.*] A by-form of BETRAY, chiefly north. **1.** = BETRAY 1. –1558. **2.** To deceive (the trustful) –1501; to entrap (the unsuspecting) –1583.

Betrap (bǐ₁træ·p), *v.*[1] [OE. *betręppan*, *-træppan*, f. BE- 1 + *tręppan* to TRAP.] To catch in a trap, circumvent, enclose. Also *fig.*

†**Betra·p,** *v.*[2] 1509. [f. BE- 1.] To furnish with trappings (*lit.* and *fig.*) –1597.

Betray (bǐ₁trē̆·), *v.* [ME. *bi-*, *betraien*, f. *bi-*, BE- 2 + *traien*, a. OF. *traïr* :—L. *tradere.*] **1.** To give up to, or place in the power of an enemy by treachery. **2.** To be or prove false to (a trust or him who trusts one); to disappoint the hopes or expectations of ME. Also *fig.* †**3.** *loosely*, To disappoint –1704. **4.** To lead astray, as a false guide; to mislead, seduce, deceive (the trustful) ME. **5.** To reveal with breach of faith (a secret) 1735. **6.** To reveal against one's will the existence, identity, real character of (a person or thing desired to be kept secret) 1588. **7.** To reveal incidentally; to exhibit, show signs of (a thing which there is no attempt to keep secret) 1697.

1. Verely I saye vnto you, that one of you shall betraye me *Matt.* xxvi. 21. **2.** To b. a cause BURKE. **4.** Pride and self-confidence b. man to his fall PUSEY. **5.** To b. a patient's confidence 1798. **6.** I do b. my selfe with blushing *L. L. L.* I. ii. 138. **7.** A temple..which betrayed great antiquity BRYANT. Hence **Betray·al** (senses 1, 2, 6). **Betray·er. Betray·ment** = *Betrayal.*

Betread, betrend, betrim; see BE-.

Betroth (bǐ₁trōᵘ·ð, -trǭ·þ), *v.* [ME. *bitreuðien*, f. *bi-*, BE- 6 + ME. *treuðe*, *treowðe*, TRUTH *sb.* The hist. and analogical pronunc. is as in *clothe*, *loathe.*] **1.** To engage (a woman) in contract of marriage, to plight one's troth to (*arch.*). **2.** To affiance (usu. the woman to the man) 1566. **3.** *fig.* Said of God and his Church or people. Also, of the relation of a bishop to a church before consecration. 1611. †**4.** *transf.* **a.** To pledge –1670. **b.** To espouse (a cause) –1674.

1. If a man wish to b. a maiden LINGARD. **2.** The lovers were soon after betrothed 1798. **3.** I will b. thee vnto me for euer *Hosea* ii. 19. **4.** What is hee for a foole that betrothes himselfe vnto vnquietnesse *Much Ado* I. iii. 49. Hence **Betro·thal,** the act of betrothing; the being betrothed; affiance. **Betro·thment** = *Betrothal.*

†**Betru·st,** *v.* 1440. [See BE- 2.] To trust (a person); to entrust -1748.

†‖**Be·tso.** 1641. [It.] A small brass coin in Venice.

Better (be·təɹ), *a.*, (*sb.*), and *adv.* [Com. Teut.: OE. (sing. masc.) *bętera* = Goth. *batiza* :—OTeut. **batiz-on-*, used as compar. of *gôdo-z* GOOD, but itself pointing to an unkn. stem. The root *bat-* was prob. related to *bôt-*; see BEET *v.* and BOOT *v.*] **A.** *adj.* The compar. of GOOD, q. v.: more good. **1.** Of superior quality. **2.** Of persons: Kinder. Of persons and things: More profitable, useful, or suitable for a purpose; more desirable ME. **3.** More; larger, greater 1580.

1. I could haue b. spared a b. man 1 *Hen. IV*, v. iv. 104. People of the b. Sort DE FOE. 2. Some b. Messenger *Two Gent.* I. i. 159. Oh excellent deuise, was there euer heard a better *Two Gent.* II. i. 145. 3. Vntill nine and b. 1630. The b. half of his estate SWIFT. *B. half*: orig. *my b. half*, the more than half of my being; said of a very close friend; *esp.* (after Sidney) used for 'my husband' or 'wife'; now, joc. appropriated to the latter. *I, we, you, he*, etc. *had b.* (orig. *me, us*, etc. *were betere* (or *bet*) = it would be more advantageous for me, etc. Now replaced by *I had b.* = I should have or hold it better, to do, etc. See HAVE. *To be b. than one's word*: to do more than one has promised.

II. *absol.* **1.** Something better; that which is better 1635. **2.** *sb.* with possessive pron.: One's superior ME.

1. I never look'd for b. at his hands SHAKS. 2. His b. doth not breath vpon the earth SHAKS. Who cals? Your betters Sir *A. Y. L.* II. iv. 68. Prudence got the b. of his pride THIRLWALL.

B. *adv.* [The orig. form was BET, q. v.] **1.** In a more excellent way ME. **2.** In a superior degree ME. †**b.** Rather -1801. **3.** In the predicate, after *be*, the adv. and adj. run together. **4.** With *adjs.* and *pples.*, usually written with the hyphen, as *b.-advised, b.-humoured*, i. e. (*better humour*) + *-ed*, etc. 1609.

1. I drinke b. than I syng 1530. 2. Where-by it [sage] prospereth the b. 1577.

Phrases. *To be b.*: to be improved in health, *esp.* after an illness. (In north. use, to be well again.) *To get b.*: to amend, recover. *To think b. of*: **a.** (a thing): to reconsider it and decide more wisely. **b.** (a person): to form a better opinion of him. *B. off*, comp. of *well off*: see OFF.

Better, -or (be·təɹ), *sb.* 1609. [f. BET *v.* + -ER [1].] One who makes bets.

Better (be·təɹ), *v.* [ME. *bet(e)re(n* :—OE. **bet(e)rian* :—OTeut. **batizojan*, f. **batiz*- BETTER.] **1.** To make better; *esp.* morally, or in health or worldly condition 1581. **2.** To do better than 1548. **3.** *intr.* To grow better, improve 1832.

1. Love betters what is best WORDSW. Girls marry merely to 'b. themselves' 1792. 2. Each day still b. others happinesse SHAKS. Hence **Be·ttering** *vbl. sb.* making better; becoming better.

Betterment (be·təɹmĕnt). 1598. [f. as prec. + -MENT.] **1.** Making or becoming better; being better; improvement. **2.** *spec.* Improvement of property. (In U.S.) 1809. †**3.** = BETTERNESS 1. 1678.

Betterness (be·təɹnĕs). ME. [f. BETTER *a.* + -NESS.] **1.** The quality of excelling; superiority. **2.** *spec.* Fineness of the precious metals above the standard 1530.

Betting (be·tiŋ), *vbl. sb.* 1599. [f. BET *v.* + -ING [1].] The making of bets, wagering.

Comb., as **b.-book**, a book in which bets are entered; **-man**, a better, *usually* a professional gambler.

‖**Bettong.** 1839. A species of kangaroo rat, about the size of a hare.

Bettor. †**1.** Aphet. f. ABETTOR 1671. **2.** Var. of BETTER *sb.*

Betty (be·ti), *sb.* [dim. of *Bet*, abbrev. of *Elizabet, -beth.*] **1.** A female familiar name, now chiefly rustic or homely. Hence, **2.** Given in contempt to a man who occupies himself with a woman's duties. (So MOLLY.) **3.** A pear-shaped bottle covered with straw; called by chemists a *Florence flask*. (? Only in U.S.) 1725. **4.** Cant name for a short crowbar; called now a *Jemmy* 1700.

4. Ruffians, who, with Crows and Betties, Break Houses 1707. Hence (sense 2), **Be·tty** *v.* to fuss about (*colloq.*).

Betulin (be·tiŭlin). 1879. [f. L. *betula.*] *Chem.* A resinous substance extracted from the bark of the birch-tree (*Betula alba*).

†**Betu·mbled,** *ppl. a.* [See BE- 2.] Disordered. SHAKS. *Lucr.* 1037.

Between (bĭ̆twī·n), *prep.* and *adv.* [Combines two forms: *a.* OE. *bi-, betwéonum*, etc., ME. *bitwenen, -twene*; *β.* OE. *bi-, betwéon*, etc., ME. *bitwēn*; see BE-. The second elements of both forms answer ult. to cases of the Goth *tweih-nai* 'two each', a deriv. of *twa* TWO. After 1400 both forms coalesced in *betwene* (= betwēn), whence mod. *between.*]

A. *prep.* **1.** Of a point: In the space which separates two points; in the direct line which joins two points. Also *fig.* ME. **2.** Of time, quantity, or degree: Intermediate to two others OE. **3.** Expressing the relation that motion along a line bears to two points on opposite sides of it ME. **4.** Expressing the relation of the continuous space which separates or connects two points ME. **5.** Hence *transf.* of objective relations uniting two (or more) parties; also, of subjective relations involving comparison ME. **6.** Expressing motion from one body or place to another 1598. **7.** Expressing reciprocal action or relation between two agents OE. **8.** Used of relation to two (or more) things or parties acting conjointly or participating in action OE. **9.** Expressing the relation of a line to two spaces which it separates ME. Also *transf.* OE. **10.** The only word expressing the relation of a thing to many surrounding things severally and individually OE.

1. I lie b. that sun and thee SHAKS. *fig.* B. hope and fear BURTON. *B. wind and water*: along the line where anything is submerged in water, etc., *esp.* on the load-line of a ship. 2. B. one and two in the morning BOSWELL, Forty and Fifty ADDISON, frost and thaw MISS AUSTEN. 3. The salt rheume that ran betweene France and it *Com. Err.* III. ii. 132. 4. The lang Scots miles That lie b. us and our hame BURNS. 5. A marriage, an alliance, a coalition b. [etc.]. 7. I will put enmitie betweene thee and the woman *Gen.* iii. 15. 8. To take the bit b. his teeth DRYDEN. *B. ourselves*: as a matter not to be communicated to others. We brought home six brace b. us MISS AUSTEN. They had it b. them (*mod.*). 9. There was but a ston wal hem be-tweene CHAUCER. Phr. *B. the bark and the tree.* 10. B. the prior, the boatmen, and a little offering to St. Patrick, he had not as much money left [etc.] SOUTHEY.

B. *adv.* (Mostly the prep. with obj. understood.) **1.** Of place: In an intermediate position or course (*lit.* and *fig.*) OE. **2.** Of time: In the interval, at intervals ME.

1. *To go b.*: to act as a medium or mediator: see GO-BETWEEN.

C. quasi-*sb.* **1.** Anything occupying an intermediate position; an interval of time 1611. **2.** An intermediate size of sewing-needle 1862.

Between-decks (bĭ̆twī·nˌdeks), *adv.* and *sb.* 1725. [f. BETWEEN *prep.* + DECK.] **A.** *adv.* In the space between the decks of a ship. **B.** *sb.* The space itself 1769.

Betwee·nity. 1760. [Formed playfully by H. Walpole, after *extremity*, etc.] Intermediateness of kind, quality, or condition; anything intermediate.

Between-whiles (bĭ̆twī·nˌhwəilz). 1678. At intervals.

Betwixt (bĭ̆twi·kst), *prep.* and *adv.* [ME. *betwix* :—OE. *betweohs, -tweox, -twux, -twyx, -tux*. The terminal *-t* is without significance.] **A.** *prep.* **1.** = BETWEEN. Still in dial. use. OE. **2.** Of more than two: in early use = AMONG OE.

†*B. and* (prob. ellipt. for *b. this and..*) *n. dial.*: between this (or that) and.., until. ME.

B. *adv.* = BETWEEN 1, 2. ME.

B. and between (colloq.): in an intermediate position; neither one thing nor the other.

Beudantite (biū·dăntəit). [f. *Beudant*, French mineralogist.] *Min.* A mineral occurring in modified acute rhombohedrons, containing sesquioxide of iron and oxide of lead, with phosphoric or arsenic acid, or both.

‖**Beurré** (bŏ̈re). 1741. [Fr., 'buttered, buttery'.] A mellow variety of pear. Also *attrib.*

Bevel (be·vĕl). 1562. [App. a. OF. **bevel*, implied in F. *beveau* (Boiste), *biveau* (Littré), *buveau* (Cotgr., etc.); of unkn. etym.] **A.** *adj.* **1.** *Her.* Of a line: Broken so as to have two equally acute alternate angles, thus ⌐_/‾. **2.** Oblique; *esp.* at more than a right angle; sloping, slant 1600.

2. I may be straight though they themselues be beuel SHAKS. *Sonn.* cxxi.

B. *sb.* **1.** A common joiner's and mason's tool, consisting of a flat rule with a moveable tongue stiffly jointed to one end, for setting off angles 1611. **2.** A slope from the right angle, an obtuse angle; a slope from the horizontal or vertical; a surface or part so sloping. (Occ. used techn. for *b.-angle.*) 1677.

2. The brethren o' the mystic level May hing their head in waefu' b. BURNS.

Comb., etc.: **b.-angle**, any angle exc. 90° or 45°; **-gear, -gearing,** gear for conveying motion by means of b.-wheels from one shaft to another at an angle with it; **-joint,** a sloping joint for uniting pieces of timber end to end; **-wheel,** a toothed wheel whose working face is oblique with the axis.

Be·vel, *v.* 1677. [f. prec. sb.] **1.** *trans.* To cut to a slope; to reduce (a square edge) to a more obtuse angle; often with *off, away*, etc. **2.** *intr.* To recede in a slope from the right angle; to slant 1679.

2. Their houses are very ill built, the walls b., without one right angle in any apartment SWIFT.

Bevelled, beveled (be·vĕld), *ppl. a.* 1757. [f. the vb.] **a.** Made or cut to a bevel; sloped off. **b.** *spec.* in *Archit.*; in *Crystallog.*: Replaced by BEVELMENT; in *Her.* = BEVEL A 1.

Be·velling, beveling, *vbl. sb.* 1769. [f. as prec.] A cutting to an oblique angle; the slant so given; a bevelled portion: *esp.* in *Shipbuilding*. Used also in comb., as **b.-board** (*Shipbuild.*), **-machine** (*Bookbind.*).

Be·velment. 1804. [f. as prec. + -MENT.] The process of bevelling; *spec.* in *Crystallog.*, the replacement of the edge of a crystal by two similar planes equally inclined to the adjacent faces.

Be·ver (bī·vəɹ), *sb.* 1451. [a. OF. *beivre* (now *boire*), subst. use of pres. inf.:—L. *bibere.*] †**1.** Drink. †**2.** A potation; a time for drinking -1626. **3.** A small repast between meals. Chiefly *dial.* (in *pl.* at Winchester) 1500. Hence †**Be·ver** *v.*[1] to partake of b.

Bever (be·vəɹ), *v.*[2] Now *dial.* 1470. [Freq. f. OE. *beofian.*] To tremble, shake.

Beverage (be·vĕrĕdʒ). [ME. a. OF. *bevrage* (mod.F. *breuvage*), f. the sb. *bevere* (in OF. *beivre*, see BEVER sb.): L. type **biberaticum.*] **1.** Drink; *esp.* a liquor which is in common use. †**2.** Drinking, a draught -1697. **3.** *spec.* A name applied locally to various drinks; as, lemonade, small cider, etc. 1721. **4.** A drink, or drink-money. Now *dial.* 1721.

1. Tea..that elegant and popular b. BOSWELL.

Bevil(e, bevilled, vars. of BEVEL, -ELLED.

‖**Bevue** (bevü). 1716. [Fr., f. *bé-, bes-* pejorative + *vue.*] An error of inadvertence.

Bevy (be·vi). ME. [Of unkn. etym. In form = OF. *bevee, buvee*, 'drink, drinking'.] **1.** The proper term for a company of maidens or ladies, of roes, of quails, or of larks. **2.** *transf.* A company; *rarely*, a collection of objects 1603.

1. A Beavie of fair Women, richly gay MILT. *P. L.* XI. 582. 2. What a beavy of beaten slaves are here BEAUM. & FL.

Bewail (bĭ̆wēɪ·l), *v.* ME. [See BE- 4.] **1.** *trans.* To wail over, *esp.* over the dead. Also *refl.* **2.** To lament loudly, mourn. Also *refl.* ME. **3.** *intr.* To utter lamentations ME.

2. Bewaylynge ay the day that they were borne CHAUCER. Hence **Bewai·lable** *a.* proper to be bewailed. **Bewai·led** *ppl. a.* lamented; †expressed by wailing. **Bewai·ler. Bewai·lingly** *adv.* **Bewai·lment.**

Beware (bĭ̆wēə·ɹ), *v.*[1] ME. [For *be ware*, OE. *wær* adj., ME. *war, ware*, used only (exc. for a time) in those parts of the vb. where *be* is found, viz. the imper., infin., and pres. subj. (the indic. being *I am ware*, etc.). See WARE.] **1.** To be cautious or on one's guard; to take heed. Const. *simply*; with *of*, †*from*, †*with*; †with infin.; with cl.; with simple obj. †**2.** To have a care of. Const. with *of*; with simple obj.; with infin. or cl. (*arch.*). -1713. †**3.** To take warning by -1605. **4.** As an inflected vb. 1598.

1. B. of all, but most b. of Man POPE. Since I am a dog, b. my phangs *Merch. V.* III. iii. 72. 2. Now, bishop, b. thy purse 1600. 4. I had bewar'd if I had foreseen MILT. We b. to ask only for high things EMERSON.

†**Bewa·re,** *v.*[2] ME. [f. BE- 2 + WARE *v.* to spend (north.).] To lay out (money, etc.) -1472.

Bewash, bewed; see BE-.

Beweep (bĭ̆wī·p), *v.* [OE. *bewepan*; see WEEP.] **1.** To weep for, weep over. **2.** To wet with or as with tears 1420. †3. *intr.* To weep ME. only.

1. I all alone beweepe my out-cast state SHAKS.

†Bewe·nd, *v.* [Com. Teut.: OE. *bewęndan. Bewend* is the causal of BEWIND.] *trans.* To turn round or away. Also *refl.*, and *intr.* (for *refl.*). -ME.

Bewest (bĭwe·st). [OE. *be westan.*] *adv.* and *prep.* On or to the west (of). Now only *Sc.*

Bewet; see BE-.

Bewet, bewit (biū·ėt), *sb.* 1486. [dim. of OF. *beue*:—L. *boia*, in pl. *boiæ* collar for the neck.] *Falconry.* A ring or slip of leather for attaching the bell to a hawk's leg.

†Bewho·re, *v.* 1604. [See BE- 5.] To call whore; to make a whore of -1623.

†Bewie·ld, *v.* [ME. *biwelden*; see WIELD.] To hold in hand, handle, wield. *refl.* To use one's limbs. -1577.

Bewig (bĭwi·g), *v.* 1774. [See BE- 6.] To furnish with a wig. Hence **Bewi·gged** *ppl. a.* **a.** Wearing a wig. **b.** Ruled by red-tape.

A paltry Baden, a bewigged Prussia 1851.

Bewilder (bĭwi·ldəɹ), *v.* 1684. [f. BE- 2 + WILDER.] 1. *lit.* To lose in pathless places (*arch.*) 1685. 2. *fig.* To perplex, confound; to cause mental aberration 1684.

1. Bewildered in the enormous extent of the town JOHNSON. 2. The bewilder'd soul BEATTIE. Hence **Bewi·ldered** *ppl. a.* at a loss for a way; *fig.* confused mentally; *transf.* pathless. **Bewi·ldered-ly** *adv.*, **-ness**. **Bewi·lderingly** *adv.*

Bewilderment (bĭwi·ldəɹmĕnt). 1820. [f. prec. + -MENT.] 1. Bewildered state. 2. An inextricable confusion or medley of objects 1844.

1. Thought was arrested by utter b. GEO. ELIOT.

Bewit (*Falconry*), var. of BEWET.

Bewitch (bĭwi·tʃ), *v.* [ME. *bewicchen*, f. *bi-*, BE- 2 + *wicchen*:—OE. *wiccian*, f. *wicca* masc., *wicce* fem., WITCH.] 1. To affect (*esp.* to injure) by witchcraft or magic. Occ. with *into*, etc. 2. *fig.* To influence as if by witchcraft; to fascinate, charm. Now usu. of pleasing influences. 1526.

1. Looke how I am bewitch'd *Rich. III*, III. iv. 70. 2. I am bewitcht with the rogues company 1 *Hen. IV*, II. ii. 18. Hence **Bewi·tcher**. **Bewi·tchery** = BEWITCHMENT. **†Bewi·tchful** *a.* having power to b. **Bewi·tching** *vbl. sb.* fascination; *ppl. a.* fascinating. **Bewi·tching-ly** *adv.*, **-ness**.

Bewi·tchment. 1607. [f. prec. + -MENT.] 1. The fact or power of bewitching. 2. The being bewitched 1810.

1. I will counterfet the b. of some popular man *Cor.* II. iii. 108.

†Bewo·nder, *v.* 1580. [See BE-. Cf. Ger. *bewundern.*] 1. *trans.* To fill with wonder -1600. 2. To wonder at, admire -1628.

†Bewo·rk, *v.* Pa. pple. **bewrought**. [OE. *bewyrcan*; see WORK. Cf. Ger. *bewirken.*] 1. To work round about. 2. To embroider -1637.

Bewrap (bĭræ·p), *v.* [ME.; see WRAP *v.*] To wrap up, cover. Also *fig.*

Bewray (bĭrē·), *v. arch.* [ME. *bewreien*; see WRAY. Now *expose.*] †1. To accuse, malign ME. only. †2. To expose (a person) by divulging his secrets, etc. *Hence*, To reveal (the doer of an act). -1603. 3. To divulge (secrets) prejudicially ME. †4. To reveal, make known -1611. †5. To betray (a fugitive) -1628. 6. = BETRAY 6. 1535. †7. = BETRAY 7. -1763.

3. None shulde issue out to b. their enterprice LD. BERNERS. 4. Write downe thy mind, b. thy meaning so *Tit. A.* II. iv. 3. 6. Thy speach bewrayeth the *Matt.* xxvi. 73. Hence **Bewray·er** (*arch.*). **†Bewray·ingly** *adv.* **†Bewray·ment**.

Bewray, erron. f. BERAY.

†Bewrea·k, *v.* [ME. *bewreke*; see WREAK *v.*] To avenge; to wreak -1586.

Bewrought, pa. pple. of BEWORK.

†Bewry·, *v.*[1] [OE. *bewrēon*; see WRY *v.*[1]] To cover up or over -1513.

†Bewry, *v.*[2] [See WRY *wk. v.*] To distort.

Bey (bē), *sb.* 1599. [a. Osmanli, 'prince, governor'; see BEG *sb.*] A Turkish governor of a province or district; also a title of rank.

Bey, *v.* [Com. Teut.: OE. Anglian *bēgan*. Still *dial.*] *trans.* and *intr.* To bend.

‖**Beylic, -lik** (bē·lik). 1733. [a. Osmanli *beglik, beylik.*] The jurisdiction of a bey.

Beyond (bĭ,yǫ·nd), *adv.* and *prep.* [OE. *begeondan*, f. *bi-*, BE- + *geondan*:—OTeut. **jandana*, f. **jand* (in OE. *geond*) across, through, beyond. *Lit.* 'on yon side, on the farther side'.] **A.** *adv.* 1. On the farther side, farther away. 2. In addition (*rare*) 1886.

1. B., a line of heights TENNYSON.

B. *prep.* 1. On the farther side of OE.; past, further on than ME. 2. To the farther side of, past OE. Also *fig.* 3. Towards the farther side of, past. (With *look*, etc.) 1597. 4. Of time: Past, later than 1597. 5. *fig.* Outside the limit or sphere of, past 1535. 6. More than, in amount or degree 1500. 7. In addition to; in neg. and interrog. sentences almost = Except. Cf. BESIDES. 1449.

1. *B. seas*: out of the country; abroad. 2. B. your depth POPE, the line of rectitude WASHINGTON. †*To go b.*: to circumvent. 3. *To look b.*: to misconstrue; you looke b. him quite 2 *Hen. IV*, IV. iv. 67. 4. Which shall..remain B. all date SHAKS. 5. B. the reach of mercie SHAKS. So, *b. belief, doubt, endurance, question*, etc. *To be b. a person* (colloq.): to pass his comprehension. 6. An amount..b. their value 1885. Delight b. the bliss of dreams MILT. *Comus* 813. *B. measure* (advb. phr.): excessively. 7. Somewhat b. and above all this HOOKER.

C. quasi-*sb.* That which lies on the other side or farther away; that which lies beyond our present life or experience 1581.

They are the All, with no b. MARTINEAU. *The back of b.*: any very out of the way place.

†Beza·n, *sb.* [a. Du. *bezaan*, ad. It. *mezzana* mizen.] App. a small sailing vessel. PEPYS.

Bezant, byzant (be·zănt, bĭza·nt). ME. [a. OF. *besan* (pl. *besanz*):—L. *byzantius* (sc. *nummus*); cf. *Byzantine.*] 1. A gold coin first struck at Byzantium, and in England varying in value between the sovereign and half-sovereign, or less. There were also silver Bezants worth from a florin to a shilling. Used by Wyclif to translate both *talentum* and *drachma*. 2. The gold offered by the kings of England at the sacrament, or at festivals 1667. 3. *Her.* A gold roundel representing the above coin plain and unstamped. Also *attrib.* 1486.

Bez-antler (bē-, bē,zæ·ntləɹ). Also **bay antler**. 1598. [f. *bez-*, BES- secondary + ANTLER.] The second branch of a deer's horn.

Bezanty (bĭza·nti), *ppl. a.* Also **bezantee**. 1486. [a. F. *besantée*; see BEZANT.] *Her.* Charged with or formed of bezants.

Bezel (be·zĕl). 1611. [a. OF. **besel*, **bezel*, in mod. F. *biseau, bizeau*, also *basile*; ? dim. of *bis, ber.* Cf. BEVEL.] 1. A slope, a sloping edge or face; *esp.* that of a chisel, etc. (usu. *basil*). 2. The oblique sides or faces of a cut gem 1839. 3. 'The groove and flange by which the crystal of a watch or the stone of a jewel is retained in its setting' 1616. Hence **Be·zel** *v.* to grind or cut to an edge; to bevel.

‖**Bezesteen** (be·zĕstīn). 1656. [a. Turk. *bazistān*, orig. Pers. for 'clothes-market'.] An exchange, bazaar, or market-place in the East.

‖**Bezetta** (bĭze·ta). 1863. [Corrupt f. It. *pezzetta*, dim. of *pezza* a PIECE of cloth.] A pigment prepared by dipping linen rags in certain colouring matters.

Bezique (bĕzī·k). 1861. [Corrupt f. F. *besigue, besy*; of unkn. etym.] A game of cards, in which the knave of diamonds and queen of spades together form 'Bezique'.

Bezoar (bī·zo₀əɹ, be·zo₀aɹ). 1477. [ad. Arab. *bāzahr* or *bādizahr*, ad. Per. *pād-zahr* counter-poison; f. *zahr* poison. The sp. *bezoar* is app. of mod.L. origin.] †1. *gen.* An antidote -1750. 2. *spec.* **a.** A calculus or concretion found in the stomach or intestines of some animals, chiefly ruminants, formed of layers of animal matter deposited round some foreign substance. Often called *b.-stone.* (The ordinary current sense.) 1580. †**b.** Other alleged stones or concretions -1634. †**c.** Various medicinal preparations -1807. †3. *transf.* The wild goat of Persia, the best-known source of the calculus (2 a) -1781; var. **b.-goat**; so **b. antelope**.

Bezoardic, -artic (bezo₀ā·ɹdik, -ā·ɹtik). 1670. [ad. mod.L. *bezoardicus, -articus*; a. F. *bezoard, bezoart*, BEZOAR.] **A.** *adj.* Of the nature of, or pertaining to, bezoar. **B.** *sb.* An antidote 1671.

†Bezonian (bĭzōu·nian). 1592. [f. It. *bisogno* + ?-AN.] = BESONIO -1843.

Be·zzle, *v.* Now *dial.* [Late ME. *besil*, a. OF. *besiler, besillier*, shortened f. *embesillier*; see EMBEZZLE.] *trans.* To make away with (drink, one's money, the property of others); *intr.* to guzzle, to revel 1604.

‖**Bhang, bang** (bæŋ). 1598. [An Eastern wd., f. Skr. *bhangā* hemp. *Bhang* is the better spelling.] Indian Hemp, the leaves and seed-capsules of which are chewed or smoked, or eaten in sweetmeats, or sometimes an infusion of them is drunk. The name is occas. given to *hashish* (see HASHISH).

‖**Bheesty, bheestie** (bī·sti). 1781. [Urdū *bhīstī*, a. Pers. *bihishtī*, f. *bihisht* paradise; prob. joc.] In India, the servant who supplies an establishment with water, which he carries in a skin slung on his back.

Bi- *pref.*[1], the early OE., and the ordinary ME., form of the prefix BE-, q. v.

Bi- *pref.*[2], a. L. *bi-* (earlier *dui-*, cogn. w. Gr. δι-, Skr. *dvi-*) 'twice, doubly, having two, two-', which is in Latin a prefix of adjs., occas. of sbs., rarely of vbs. *Bi-* is used in Eng. to form:—

I. Adjs., with the sense:—1. Having or furnished with two —, two- —, as **bi-angular, -ate, -ated, -ous**, having two angles; **bibracteate**, having two bracts; **bicallose, -ous**, having two callosities; **†bicapited, bicapitate; bicapsular; bicavitary**, having two cavities; **bicentral; bichord; bicilate; bicoloured, biconsonantal; bicorporal, -ate, -ated, -eal**, having two bodies; **bifacial; biglandular; bimarginate, bimembral, bimuscular; binodal**, having two nodes; **binuclear**, having two nuclei; **biovulate, bipetalous; bipupillate**, having two pupil-like markings; **biradiate; birainy**, having two rainy seasons; **bispinous, bistipuled; bitentaculate; bituberculate, -ated; bivaulted.** 2. Doubly —; — in two ways or directions; on both sides; as **biconic, -al**, conical in two directions; **biconvex**, etc. 3. *Bot.* and *Zool.* Twice over, re-; *i.e.* having characteristically divided parts which are themselves similarly divided, as BILACINIATE, etc. 4. Lasting for two —; occurring or appearing every two —; as BIENNIAL, **bi-hourly, -monthly, -weekly.** **b.** Occurring or appearing twice in a —; as in **bi-diurnal, -monthly, -quarterly, -weekly, -winter, -yearly.** (*Semi-* would avoid the ambiguous usage; *e.g. semi-monthly*; cf. *half-yearly.*) 5. Joining two —; as BI-ACHROMIAL, etc. 6. Occ. as in **bimanual**, employing two hands; BISERIATE, etc.

II. Advbs., vbs., and sbs.; *esp.* sbs. formed after L. analogies, in which *bi-* = 'double, two'; as **bimillionaire**, the man who is worth two millions of money; **binomenclature; biprong.**

III. *Chem.* Sbs. and adjs., in which *bi-* = having two equivalents of the acid, base, etc. named; as *bicarbonate of soda*, etc. Now superseded by *di-*.

Biacid (bəi,æ·sid), *a.* 1864. [see BI- *pref.*[2] III.] *Chem.* Of a base: Capable of combining with an acid in two different proportions.

Biacuminate (bəi,ăkiū·minĕt), *a.* 1880. [see BI- *pref.*[2] I. 1, 2.] *Bot.* Two-pointed.

Biannual (bəi,æ·niuăl). 1877. [See BI- *pref.*[2] I. 4, 4 b.] **A.** *adj.* Half-yearly. **B.** = BIENNIAL *sb.*

Biarticulate; see BI- *pref.*[2] I. 1.

Bias (bəi·ăs). 1530. [a. F. *biais*, 'oblique, obliquity'; of unkn. etym. With pl. *biases.*] **A.** *adj.* †1. Oblique -1688. **b.** *spec.* in dress (cf. B 1): Cut across the texture 1883. 2. Swelled as the bowl on the biased side. *Tr. & Cr.* IV. v. 8.

1. *On the b.*: diagonally.

B. *sb.* 1. An oblique or slanting line. Now only of a gore, cut across the texture of a woven fabric. 1530. 2. *Bowls.* The construction or form of the bowl causing it to swerve when rolled; the curved course in which it runs; the allowance made for this deviation 1570. Also *fig.* 3. *transf.* An inclination, leaning, bent; predisposition *towards*; predilection; prejudice 1572. †4. Set course -1799. 5. A swaying influence, impulse, or weight 1587.

2. A bowl may lie still for all its Byass SOUTH. *fig.* Which set a B. vpon the Bowle, of their owne Petty Ends BACON. 3. Our natural b. to evil HARE. 4. *To put out of* or *off one's b.*: to put out, disconcert. 5. The Bribery and Byass of Sense and Flesh STANHOPE.

C. *adv.* 1. Obliquely, aslope. *Obs.* exc. of dress. 1575. †2. Off the straight, awry -1633.

Bias (bəi·ăs), *v.* 1622. [f. prec. sb. In inflexions, often spelt *biasses, biassed*, etc.; but the single *s* is more regular; cf. the sb.] 1. To give bias to (a bowl) 1662. Also *transf.* and *fig.* †2. *intr.* To swerve from the right line -1687.

1. Men whom no Advantages can byass BURNET. Such exercises as..biased the mind to military pursuits STRUTT.

Bias(s)ed (bəi·ăst), *ppl. a.* 1611. [See prec.] Having a bias; *esp.* unfavourably inclined.

Bib (bib), *v.* ME. [perh. ad. L. *bibere.*] *trans.* and *intr.* To drink; tipple.

Folks kept bibbing beer BROWNING. Hence **Biba·tion**, bibbing. **Bi·bber** (freq. in comb., as *wine-b.*).

Bib (bib), *sb.*[1] 1580. [prob. f. BIB *v.*] **a.** A cloth placed under a child's chin for cleanliness, *esp.* at meals. **b.** A similar cloth worn by adults, often as the upper part of an apron 1687.

Best b. and tucker: best clothes (of girls, women, or men).

Bib (bib), *sb.*[2] 1674. [f. BIB *sb.*[1]] The whiting-pout (*Gadus luscus*).

Bibacious (bi-, bəibēⁱ·ʃəs), *a.* 1676. [f. L. *bibaci-* (nom. *bibax*).] Given to drinking; bibulous. So **Biba·city**, addiction to drinking.

Bibasic (bəibēⁱ·sik), *a.* 1847. [See BI- *pref.*[2] I. 1.] *Chem.* Having two bases.

B. acid: one which contains two atoms of displaceable hydrogen, and can therefore form two series of salts. Now usu. DI-BASIC.

Bibb (bib). 1779. [var. of BIB *sb.*[1]] *Naut.* A bracket under the trestle-tree of a mast, resembling in position a child's bib.

Bibble (bi·b'l), *v.* 1529. [freq. of BIB.] †1. *trans.* and *intr.* To keep drinking –1583. 2. a. *intr.* To dabble with the bill like a duck. b. *trans.* To drink with a dabbling noise. 1552. Hence **Bi·bbler.**

Bibble-babble (bi·b'l,bæ·b'l). 1532. [Redupl. of BABBLE; cf. *tittle-tattle*, etc.] Idle talk; prating.

Bibitory (bi·bitəri), *a. rare.* 1696. [ad. mod.L. *bibitorius*, f. *bibit-* stem of *bibere.*] Of or pertaining to drinking; *spec.* in *B. muscle* = 'rectus internus oculi'.

Bible (bəi·b'l). [a. F. *bible*, 13th c.:–late L. *biblia*, fem. sing. for earlier *biblia* neut. pl., a. Gr. τὰ βιβλία, lit. 'the books', later *spec.* 'the canonical books, the Scriptures'.

The Gr. βιβλία was pl. of βιβλίον, dim. of βίβλος, the inner bark of the papyrus, paper, the ordinary wd. for 'book'. The Scriptures were regarded as one work. In OE. *bibliopéce* alone occurs as a name for the Scriptures.]

1. The Scriptures of the Old and New Testament. (Occas. used for the Old Testament.) ME. b. A copy of the Scriptures 1468. 2. Hence *fig.* A textbook, an authority; a sacred book 1804. †3. *transf.* A large book, a tome –1629. 4. A library. [Cf. *bibliotheca* in sense of *biblia.*] ME.

1. As þe bibul sais ME. Certaine bookes which we call the B. or Olde Testament GOLDING. b. License ..for the sale of his Bibles COVERDALE. The 'Breeches B.' (see (Genev.) *Gen.* iii. 7), the 'Vinegar B.' 2. The poets who have contributed to the B. of existing England sentences of guidance EMERSON. 3. Men myght make of hem a b. xx^{ti}. foote thykke CHAUCER.

Comb.: **B.-oath**, one taken upon the B.; **-reader, -woman**, one employed to read the B. from house to house. Hence **Bi·blic, -al** *a.* of, relating to, or contained in, the B. **Bi·blically** *adv.* **Bi·blicism**, adherence to the letter of the B. **Bi·blicist**, one who adheres to the letter of the B. **Bi·blicize** *v.* to subject to the B. **Bi·blism**, adherence to the B. as the sole rule of faith; whence **Bi·blist.**

Bible-Chri·stian. 1766. 1. A Christian according to the Scriptural standard. 2. One of a sect founded in 1815 by W. O. Bryan, a Wesleyan preacher in Cornwall 1860.

Bible-cle·rk. 1626. a. A student of the Bible. b. *spec.* One of a class of students in certain colleges at Oxford, having the duty of reading the lessons in chapel, and of saying grace in Hall.

Biblico- (bi·bliko), comb. f. BIBLIC, -AL, as in **b.-literary** *a.*, relating to the literature of the Bible; **b.-poetic**, etc.

Biblio- (bi·bli,o), repr. Gr. βιβλίο-, stem and comb. f. βιβλίον book.

Biblio·cla·sm [Gr. -κλασμος], destruction of books, or of the Bible; so **-cla·st**; **-gno·st** [Gr. γνώστης], one who knows books and bibliography; **-gony** [Gr. -γονία], the production of books; **-klept** [Gr. -κλέπτης], a book-thief; **-kle·ptoma·niac**, a book-thief regarded as insane; **-latry** [Gr. -λατρεία], book-worship; excessive reverence for the mere letter of the Bible; so **-later, -latrist, -latrous** *a.*; **-mancy** [Gr. μαντεία], divination by books, or by verses of the Bible; **-ma·nia** [Gr. μανία], a rage for collecting books; so **-ma·ne, -ma·niac** *sb.* and *a.*, **-mani·acal** *a.*, **-ma·nian** *a.* and *sb.*, **-manism, -manist**; **-pegy** [Gr. -πηγία, f. πηγνύναι], bookbinding as a fine art; so **-pe·gic** *a.*, **-pegist, -pegi·stic(al** *a.*; **-phagist** [Gr. -φάγος], a devourer of books; so **-pha·gic** *a.*; **-pho·bia** [Gr. -φοβία], aversion to books; **-po·esy** [Gr. ποιησία], the making of books; **-taph** [Gr. τάφος], one who buries books under lock and key; so **-ta·phic** *a.*, **-taphist.**

Bibliographer (bibli,ǫ·grăfəɹ). 1656. [f. Gr. βιβλιογράφος + -ER[1].] †1. One who writes or copies books –1761. 2. One who writes about books, their authorship, printing, publication, etc. var. **Bi·bliograph.**

Bibliographic, -al (bi·bliogræ·fik, -ăl), *a.* 1802. [f. as prec. + -IC, + -AL.] Of, relating to, or dealing with bibliography. Hence **Bi·bliogra·phically** *adv.*

Bibliography (bibli,ǫ·grăfi). 1678. [a. Gr. βιβλιογραφία.] †1. The writing of books. 2. The systematic description and history of books, their authorship, printing, publication, editions, etc. 1814. 3. A book containing such details 1838. 4. A list of the books of a particular author, printer, country; the literature of a subject 1869. Hence **Biblio·graphize** *v.* to write a b. of.

Bibliology (bibli,ǫ·lŏdʒi). 1807. [f. BIBLIO- + -LOGY.] a. Book-lore; bibliography. b. Biblical literature, doctrine, or theology 1859. Hence **Bi·bliolo·gical** *a.*, of or pertaining to b. **Biblio·logist**, a student of b.

Bibliophil(e (bi·bli,ofil). 1824. [a. F. *bibliophile.*] A lover of books; a book-fancier; also as *adj.* **Bi·bliophi·lic** *a.* of or pertaining to a b. **Biblio·philism**, the principles and practice of a b. **Biblio·philist**, a b. **Biblio·philous** *a.* addicted to bibliophily. **Biblio·phily**, love of books, taste for books.

Bibliopole (bi·bli,opōul). 1775. [ad. L. *bibliopola*, Gr. βιβλιοπώλης, f. βιβλίον + πώλης.] A dealer in books, a bookseller. **Bibliopo·lar, -po·lic, -po·lical** *a.* of or belonging to booksellers; hence **Bi·bliopo·lically** *adv.* **Biblio·polism**, the principles or trade of bookselling. **Biblio·polist**, a bookseller; whence **Bi·bliopoli·stic** *a.* **Biblio·poly, Bi·bliopo·lery**, bookselling.

Bibliothec (bibli,ǫ·þek), *a.* and *sb.* 1641. [f. next.] Belonging to a library or librarian; *sb.* a librarian.

‖**Bibliotheca** (bi·bli,o,þī·kă). [L., ad. Gr. βιβλιοθήκη, f. βιβλίον + θήκη repository: used by Jerome for the BIBLE: hence OE. *bibliopéce*, the BIBLE.] a. (in OE.) The Scriptures, the Bible. b. *mod.* A collection of books, a library. c. A bibliographer's catalogue. Hence **Bi·bliothe·cal** *a.* belonging to a library. **Biblio·thecary** *sb.* †a library; a librarian; *adj.* of or belonging to a library or librarian. So **Biblio·theca·rian** *a.* and *sb.*

‖**Bibliothèque.** 1549. [a. F.; formerly naturalized, but now treated as Fr. (bibliⁱo,tę·k).] = BIBLIOTHECA b.

‖**Biblus, -os** (bi·blǫ̆s, -ǫ̆s). 1656. [L., a. Gr. βίβλος.] The papyrus; its inner bark.

Bibulous (bi·biŭləs), *a.* 1675. [f. L. *bibulus.*] 1. Absorbent of moisture. 2. Addicted to drinking 1861. 3. Relating to drink 1858.

1. B. paper 1827. Hence **Bi·bulously** *adv.*

Bicalcarate (bəikæ·lkărēⁱt), *a.* 1876. [f. BI- *pref.*[2] I. 1 + CALCARATE, f. L. *calcar.*] Furnished with two spurs.

Bicameral (bəikæ·mĕrăl), *a.* 1832. [See BI- *pref.*[2] I. 1.] Having two (legislative) chambers. So **Bica·merist**, an advocate of two chambers.

Bicarbide, -onate, -uret, etc.: see BI- *pref.*[2] III.

Bicarinate (bəikæ·rinēⁱt), *a.* 1872. [See BI- *pref.*[2] I.] *Bot.* Furnished with two keels or axial ridges.

Bicaudal; see BI- *pref.*[2] I.

†**Bi·cched,** *ppl. a.* ME. [? f. BITCH + -ED.] Cursed –1533. *B. bones*: dice.

Bice (bəis). ME. [a. F. *bis*; of unkn. etym.] †A. *adj.* Brownish grey. B. *sb.* (also *attrib.*) 1. Short for *blewe bis* 'blue b.': a dull blue, often loosely identified with azure ME. 2. The pigment which yields this colour, prepared from smalt; also a green pigment (*green b.*) made by adding yellow orpiment to smalt 1548.

Bicentenary (bəise·ntīnări, -sentī·nări). 1862. [See BI- *pref.*[2] I, and CENTENARY.] A. *adj.* Consisting of or relating to two hundred (*years*, as if confused with *bicentennial*). B. *sb.* Used for: The two hundredth anniversary.

Bicentennial (bəisĕnte·niăl). 1883. [See BI-*pref.*[2] I. 4, and CENTENNIAL.] A. *adj.* Occurring every two hundred years; lasting two hundred years. B. *sb.* = BICENTENARY (and etymologically more correct).

Bicentral; see BI- *pref.*[2] I.

Biceps (bəi·sĕps). 1634. [a. L., f. *bi-* + *-ceps* = *caput.*] A. *adj.* Having two heads or summits; *spec.* of muscles. B. *sb.* A muscle with two heads or tendinous attachments; *spec.* the flexor muscle on the front of the upper arm (often taken as the type of physical strength); also, that of the thigh.

Bichlo·ride. 1810. [See BI- *pref.*[2] III.] *Chem.* A compound in which two equivalents of chlorine are combined with a metal, etc.

Bichromate (bəi,krōu·mĕt). 1854. [See BI-*pref.*[2] III.] *Chem.* A salt containing two equivalents of chromic acid, *e.g. B. of potash*; whence **Bichro·mated, -matized** *ppl. a.*

Bicipital (bəisi·pităl), *a.* 1646. [f. L. *bicipit-, biceps* + -AL[1].] 1. = BICEPS *a.* 2. Of or pertaining to the biceps (muscle) 1831.

Bici·pitous, *a.* 1646 [f. as prec.] Having two heads or terminal extremities, as *b. serpents.*

Bicker (bi·kəɹ), *sb.*[1] 1458. [Sc. f. BEAKER.] A (wooden) bowl or dish for containing liquor Formerly, a drinking cup.

Bicker (bi·kəɹ), *sb.*[2] [ME. *biker*, of unkn etym.] 1. Skirmishing; an encounter; exchange of blows. 2. *Sc.* A street or school fight with stones, etc. 1470. 3. Quarrel; angry altercation ME. 4. Noise as of contention, rattle of light guns, sound of a stream brawling over stones, etc. 1870. b. *Sc.* A short rapid run. BURNS.

Bicker (bi·kəɹ), *v.* [ME. *bikeren*, of unkn. etym.] 1. To skirmish; to fight. †2. *trans.* To attack with repeated strokes –1550. 3. *intr.* To quarrel, wrangle 1450. 4. *transf.* Applied to the making of any rapidly repeated noisy action, such as the brawling of a stream over stones, the pattering of rain, etc. 1748. b. *Sc.* To make a short quick run 1792. 5. *poet.* Of flame and light in quick movement: To flash, quiver, glisten. Cf. *flicker.* 1667.

3. Though their Merchants b. in the East Indies MILT. 4. At the crook of the glen, Where bickers the burnie SCOTT. 5. She saw Dust, and the points of lances b. in it TENNYSON. Hence **Bi·ckerer**, a skirmisher. **Bi·ckerment**, bickering.

Bickern (bi·kəɹn). 1547. [a. F. *bigorne*:– L. *bicornia* pl., f. *bi-* + *cornu.*] *orig.* An anvil with two projecting taper ends; *later* (see BEAK-IRON) used of: One such taper end of an anvil.

Bicolligate (bəikǫ·ligēⁱt), *a.* 1847. [See BI-*pref.*[2] I. 2.] *Ornith.* Of the anterior toes of birds: United by a basal web.

Biconjugate (bəikǫ·ndʒ'ŭgĕt), *a.* 1847. [See BI- *pref.*[2] I. 2.] Twice paired: applied *e.g.* in *Bot.* to a petiole that forks twice.

Bicorn (bəi·kǫɹn). 1823. [ad. L. *bicornis.*] A. *adj.* Having the horns or horn-like processes. B. *sb.* [sc. *animal.*] vars. **Bi·corned, Bico·rnous, Bi·cornu·te** *a.*

Bicrenate (bəi,krī·nēⁱt), *a.* 1835. [See BI-*pref.*[2] I. 3.] *Bot.* Of (leaf-) margins: Crenate or scolloped, with the scollops themselves crenate.

Bicrescentic, -cristate; see BI- *pref.*[2] I. 2.

Bicru·ral, *a.* 1847. [See BI- *pref.*[2] I.] Two-legged.

Bicuspid (bəikʊ·spid). 1836. [f. L. *bi-* + *cuspidem.*] A. *adj.* Having two cusps or points. B. *sb.* A premolar tooth in man. var. **Bicu·spidate** *a.*

Bicycle (bəi·sik'l), *sb.* 1868. [a. Fr., f. BI-*pref.*[2] II + Gr. κύκλος.] A machine for riding, consisting of a saddle-seat surmounting two wheels, to which the rider communicates motion by means of pedals. Hence Bicy·clic *a.* of or connected with bicycles. Bi·cyclism, the practice or art of bicycling. Bi·cyclist, one who rides a b. Bicy·cular *a.* of the nature of a b. or pertaining to bicycling.

Bi·cycle, *v.* 1869. [f. prec.] To ride on a bicycle. Hence Bi·cycler, Bi·cycling.

Bid (bid), *v. str.* Pa. t. **bad, bade** (bæd), **bid.** Pa. pple. **bidden, bid.** [Orig. two vbs.; viz. A. OE. *béodan*:—OTeut. **beudan* 'to stretch out, reach out, offer', hence, 'to communicate, proclaim, command'; pre-Teut. **bheudh*, cogn. w. Skr. *budh* to present, and perh. w. Gr. πυθ- (for φυθ-) in πυθέσθαι. See BODE. B. OE. *biddan*:—OTeut. **bidjan*, assigned to a pre-Teut. **bhedh*- 'to press', whence 'to ask pressingly, require, command'. In lit. Eng., the forms of *biddan, bid* survive, with senses from both vbs.]

A. Senses from OE. *béodan*, ME. *bede*. **1.** *trans.* To offer. *Obs.* in gen. sense. **2.** *trans.* To offer (a certain price) *for* ME.; *intr.* (*ellipt.*) to make an offer (*for* a thing) 1611. Often *fig.* †**3.** To proclaim, announce, threaten –1603.

1. That spirit which had bidden defiance to .. the House of Valois MACAULAY. 2. Who bids five shillings for this lot (*mod.*). Phr. *To b. against*: to compete with in offers. To b. for the Irish vote (*mod.*). Phr. *To b. up*: to raise the price by successive bidding. *To b. fair* (intr.): to offer with reasonable probability, seem likely. 3. *To b. the banns*: to proclaim them (but cf. B. 1). To b. a truce to thought SOUTHEY.

B. Senses from OE. *biddan*. **1.** *trans.* To ask pressingly, beg, entreat, pray OE.; also †*intr.* –1458. **2.** To ask (any one) to come, to invite (*to* a feast, etc.) (*arch.* but common *dial.*) ME. **3.** To command, enjoin, order. (Still literary and colloq. in the north; but in the south expressed by *tell.*) OE. †**4.** To bid not to do, forbid –1622.

1. I bidde god I neuere mot haue Ioye CHAUCER. To haue of God what yᵗ he bedde ME. Phr. To b. a *bene, bede, prayer*, etc.: *orig.* to pray; *later* 'to move the people to join in prayer', as in BIDDING PRAYER. *To b. welcome, adieu, farewell, good-bye, good morning.* (Now used without analysis, 'bid' being merely = 'say, utter, express'.) 2. I made a feast; I bad him come TENNYSON. 3. Thou..bad'st me bury Loue *Rom. & Jul.* IV. v. 83. He will not stand when he is bidden *Much Ado* III. iii. 32.

Hence **Bid** *sb.* the offer of a price, the amount offered; *spec.* at an auction. **Bi·ddable** *a.* ready to do what is bidden, docile. **Bi·ddance**, invitation. **Bi·dder**, one who bids (*esp.* in senses A. 2, B. 2, 3).

†**Bi·d-ale.** 1462. [See BID *v.* B. 2 and ALE.] An 'ale' for the benefit of some person, to which a general bidding was given –1733.

Bi·dcock. The Water-rail. DRAYTON.

Bidden, pa. pple. of BID and BIDE.

Bidding (bi·diŋ), *vbl. sb.* ME. [f. BID *v.* + -ING¹.] **1.** A bid. †**2.** Request, entreaty ME. only. †**3.** Praying; prayer –1440. **4.** Invitation, summons 1810. **5.** A command, order, injunction ME.

3. *Bidding of beads, beads-bidding; bidding of prayers, bidding prayer.* The orig. sense was 'praying of prayers', *i. e.* praying; cf. BID *v.* B. 1. In the 16th c., when *bid* in the sense of 'pray' was becoming obsolete, the 'bidding of prayers' became 'the directing or injoining of prayers'. Hence 'the form of bidding prayers' or 'prayer' (= *precationem hortandi*), whence, by a later misunderstanding, 'the bidding-prayer', as if this exhortation were itself a kind of prayer qualified by 'bidding'.

Biddy¹ (bi·di). [abbrev. of BRIDGET.] Used in U.S. for an Irish maid-servant.

Bi·ddy². *Obs.* exc. *dial.* [?] A chicken, a fowl. *Twel. N.* III. iv. 128.

Bide (bəid), *v.* [Com. Teut.: OE. *bīdan*:—OTeut. **bīdan* to wait. Now mostly ABIDE, exc. in north. Eng. and Sc.] **1.** *intr.* To remain in expectation, to wait. (Chiefly north., and *poet.*) **2.** To remain or continue *in* some state or action (*arch.*) OE. **3.** To stay (*esp.* when others go) (*arch.*) OE. **4.** Of things: To remain, be left ME. **5.** To sojourn, dwell (*arch.*) ME. **6.** *trans.* To await. Now only in *To b. one's time.* OE. **7.** To await in resistance, to face, encounter. Cf. ABIDE. ME. **8.** To endure, suffer, undergo. Cf. ABIDE. Now *dial.* ME. **9.** To tolerate, put up with. Cf. ABIDE. ME.

1. 'B. a wee, b. a wee,' said Cuddie SCOTT. 3. Who bides at home, nor looks abroad EMERSON. 5. The spirit who bideth by himself In the land of mist and snow COLERIDGE. 9. I never could b. the staying still in ae place SCOTT.

Bident (bəi·dĕnt). 1675. [ad. L. *bidentem, bidens.*] **1.** An instrument or weapon with two prongs. **2.** A two-year-old sheep (*rare*) 1881. So **Bide·ntal** *a.* belonging to a b. **Bide·ntate, -tated** *a.* having two teeth or tooth-like processes; var. †**Bide·nted. Bide·ntial** *a.* two-pronged.

‖**Bide·ntal,** *sb.* 1692. [L.] A place struck by lightning, consecrated, and enclosed. Also *fig.*

Bidet (bi·dē, bide·t). 1630. [a. F., of unkn. etym.] **1.** A small horse. **2.** 'A vessel on a low narrow stand, which can be bestridden' for bathing purposes.

Bidigitate: see BI- *pref.*² I.

Biding (bəi·diŋ), *vbl. sb.* ME. [f. BIDE *v.*] **1.** Expectation; tarrying. **2.** Stay, dwelling ME. †*concr.* A dwelling –1687.

2. I'll lead you to some b. *Lear* IV. vi. 228. *Comb.* b.-place.

‖**Bidri, bidree, bidry** (bi·dri). 1794. [Urdū *bidrī*, f. *Bidar* or *Bedar* a town in India.] An alloy of copper, lead, tin, and zinc, used as a ground for inlaying with gold and silver, in the manufacture of *Bidri-* or *Biddery-ware*.

†**Bi·dstand.** A highwayman. B. JONS.

Bield (bīld), *sb.* Now *dial.* [Com. Teut.: OE. *beldo*, f. *bald, beald* (OTeut. **balþo-z*), BOLD. Conn. w. mod. Sc. *bield, beild* through sense 3.] **1.** Boldness. **2.** Confidence; *hence*, comfort ME. **3.** Help; defence ME. **4.** Cheer, sustenance. (Only Sc.) 1513. **5.** Shelter; a place of shelter. (Only Sc. and n. dial.) 1450.

5. Better a wee bush than nae b. BURNS.

Bield (bī·ld), *v.* Now *dial.* [Com. Teut.: OE. *beldan, bieldan, byldan*, f. OTeut. **balþo-z* BOLD. Cf. prec.] **1.** To make bold. **2.** *intr.* To have confidence ME. **3.** To defend, shelter. *Sc.* and *n. dial.* ME. **4.** *intr.* To find refuge or protection; to lodge, dwell ME.

3. That..bielded me as if I had been a sister SCOTT.

Biennial (bəi,e·niăl). 1621. [f. L. *biennis, biennium.*] **A.** *adj.* **1.** Existing or lasting for two years; *esp.* of plants. **2.** Taking place once in every two years 1750. **B.** *sb. Bot.* A plant which springs from seed and vegetates one year, and flowers, fructifies, and perishes the next 1770. Hence **Bie·nnially** *adv.*

‖**Bienséance** (byæn,se,āns). 1788. [Fr., f. *bien* + *séant*, f. *seoir* to befit.] Decorum.

†‖**Bienvenue.** ME. [Fr. (byænvənü).] Formerly as freq. in Eng. use as *adieu*.] **1.** Welcome –1629. **2.** A fee exacted from a new workman 1793.

Bier (bīᵊɹ). [Com. Teut.: OE. *bǽr, bér* = OTeut. **bêrâ* f. *beran* to bear. The sp. is after F. *bière*.] **1.** A framework for carrying; a handbarrow; a litter, a stretcher. Now *Hist.* **2.** The movable stand on which a corpse is placed before burial; that on which it is carried to the grave OE. **3.** *transf.* A sepulchre 1513.

Comb.: †**b.-balk**, a balk in a field where there is a right of way for funerals; †**-right**, an ordeal in which a person, accused of murder, was required to approach the corpse, and clear himself on oath.

Bifacial, bifanged; see BI- *pref.*² I.

Bifarious (bəifē·ᵊriəs), *a.* 1656. [f. L. *bifarius.*] **1.** Twofold, ambiguous (*arch.*). **2.** *Bot.* Ranged in two rows 1846. Hence **Bifa·riously** *adv.*

Bifer (bəi·fəɹ). [a. L., f. *bi-* + *-fer.*] A plant which produces flowers or fruit twice a year. So **Bi·ferous** *a.*

Biffin (bi·fin). 1794. [A dial. pronunc. of *beefing*, f. BEEF, in reference to the colour of the apple.] **1.** A (Norfolk) cooking apple. **2.** A baked apple, flattened in the form of a cake 1822. vars. Beefen, -in, -ing, beaufin (a fabricated spelling, as if f. F. *beau* + *fin*).

Bifid (bəi·fid, bi·fid), *a.* [ad. L. *bifidus.*] Divided into two parts by a cleft or notch. **Bi·fidly** *adv.* **Bi·fidate** *a.* (a bad var.). **Bifi·dity.**

Bifilar (bəifəi·lăɹ), *a.* 1870. [f. BI- *pref.*² I + FILAR, f. L. *filum.*] Fitted with two threads; *spec.* applied to apparatus for measuring minute distances or angles, minute forces, etc.

Gauss's b. magnetometer 1870.

Bifistular (bəifi·stiŭlăɹ), *a.* 1870. [See BI- *pref.*² I.] Having two tubes.

Biflorous (bəi,flōᵊ·rəs), *a.* 1794. [f. mod.L. *biflorus* + -OUS.] Bearing two flowers or blooms. var. **Biflo·rate.**

Bifold (bəi·fōᵘld), *a.* 1609. [See BI- *pref.*² I.] Double, twofold.

Bifoliate, bifoliolate; see BI- *pref.*² I.

Biforate (bəifōᵊ·rĕt, bi·fŏreᵗt), *a.* 1842. [f. BI- *pref.*² I.] Having two perforations.

Biforine (bi·fŏrəin). 1842. [f. L. *biforis* + -INE.] *Bot.* An oval sac found in the pulpy part of some leaves, which discharges its contents by an opening at each end.

Biforked (bəi·fǭɹkt), *a.* 1578. [See BI- *pref.*² I.] Having two forks, branches, or peaks.

Biform (bəi·fǭɹm), *a.* 1816. [ad. L. *biformis.*] Having, or partaking of, two forms. var. **Bi·formed.** Hence **Bifo·rmity.**

Bifront (bəi·frɒnt), *a.* 1598. [ad. L. *bifrontem.*] Having two faces or aspects; double; *absol.* = Janus. vars. **Bifro·ntal, Bifro·nted.**

Bifurcate (bəi·fɔ̄ɹkeᵗt), *v.* 1615. [f. med.L. *bifurcatus*; at first only in the pa. pple.] To divide into two forks, branches, or peaks. *trans.* and *intr.* So **Bifu·rcate** *a.* = BIFORKED. **Bifurca·tion**, division into two forks or branches; the point of division; the branches, or one of them.

Big, *sb. Obs.* exc. *dial.* 1573. [?] **1.** A teat. **2.** A boil 1601.

Big (big), *a.* [ME. *big, bigg, bigge*: perh. Norse.] †**1.** Of great strength or power. L. *validus, potens.* –1599. †**2.** Of things: Strong; stiff; forceful; violent, vehement –1604. **3. a.** Of great size, bulk, or extent; large 1552. **b.** *esp.* Grown, grown up 1552. **c.** 'Having comparative bulk, greater or less' 1547. **4.** Far advanced in pregnancy. Const. *with*, occas. *of.* 1535. Also *transf.* and *fig.* **5.** Loud 1581. **6.** Important. (Colloq. or joc. for *great.*) 1577. **7.** Pompous; *esp.* in *To talk, look b.* 1570.

1. Bigge Mars SHAKS. 2. Farewell the bigge Warres *Oth.* III. iii. 349. 3. The biggest and the fattest Bishoprick MILT. Ile run away Till I am bigger *Cor.* V. iii. 128. Statues..bigger than life HOGARTH. 4. Their women bygg with childe *Hos.* xiii. 16. B. with the fate Of Cato and of Rome ADDISON. 6. Pompey surnam'd the b. *L. L. L.* V. ii. 555. 7. Nay, looke not b., nor stampe, nor stare *Tam. Shr.* II. ii. 230.

Comb.: **b.-bellied** *a.* corpulent; pregnant; **-horn**, a species of sheep inhabiting the Rocky Mountains. Also in various collocations with specific force, as **b. drum, game, toe; b. daisy**, the Ox-eye daisy, etc.; **b. dog**, a watch-dog; also *fig.*; **b. trees**, the Sequoias or Wellingtonias of the Sierra Nevada.

Big, bigg (big), *v. Obs.* exc. *n. dial.* [ME. *biggen, bygge*, a. N. *byggja* to inhabit.] *trans.* To build. Also *transf.* and *fig.*

God..sal..bigge þe cites of Jude *E. E. Ps.* lxviii. 36. Hence **Bi·gging** *vbl. sb.* †dwelling; building; a building. *n. dial.*

Big, var. of BIGG barley.

‖**Biga** (bəi·gă). 1850. [L.] *Rom. Antiq.* A two-horsed chariot.

†**Bi·gam(e.** ME. [a. OF. *bigame*, ad. med. L. *bigamus*, f. *bi-* + Gr. -γαμος.] **A.** *adj.* Having at the same time two wives or husbands. **B.** *sb.* One so married. In *Eccl. Law* applied to one who marries a second time. –1502. var. ‖**Bi·gamus.**

Bigamist (bi·gămist). 1631. [f. as BIGAMY.] A man or woman living in BIGAMY (senses 1, 2).

Bigamous (bi·gămǝs), *a.* 1864. [f. med.L. *bigamus* (see BIGAM(E) + -OUS.] Living in bigamy; involving bigamy. Hence **Bi·gamously** *adv.* so as to commit or involve bigamy.

Bigamy (bi·gămi). ME. [a. F. *bigamie*, f. *bigame*; see BIGAM(E.] **1.** The crime of having two wives or husbands at once. Also *fig.* 1635. **2.** *Eccl. Law.* Marriage of, or with, a widow (*or* widower). Now *Hist.* ME.

1. Lamech, that broute in first bigamie CAPGRAVE. 2. Our laws certainly allow [b.] FIELDING.

Bigarreau, -roon (bi·gărōᵘ, -rū·n). 1675. [a. F., f. *bigarré.*] The large white heart-cherry, which has one side yellow, and the other red.

†**Bi·gate,** *a.* (*sb.*) 1600. [ad. L. *bigatus.*] (A coin) bearing the figure of a biga.

Bigeminal (bəi,dʒe·minăl), *a.* 1836. [See BI- *pref.*² I. 6.] Existing or arranged in pairs; *spec.* in *Phys.* of the *corpora quadrigemina* of the brain. var. **Bige·minate** *a.* Also **Bige·minated** *ppl. a.* (Chiefly in *Bot.*)

Bigener (bəi·dʒĭnəɹ). 1835. [a. L., f. *bi-* + *gener-* (nom. *genus*).] A cross between two genera. Hence †**Bige·nerous** *a.* hybrid.

Bigential (bəi,dʒe·nʃăl), *a.* 1846. [See BI- *pref.*[2] I.] Composed of or containing two races or peoples.

Bigg, big (big). *Sc.* and *dial.* 1450. [a. ON. *bygg* barley = OE. *béow* grain:—OTeut. **beowo-m*, f. OAryan root **bheu* (whence BE; cf. Gr. φύω, Skr. *bhū*).] The four-rowed barley. (*Barley* is generic; *bear* interchanges locally, now with *barley*, now with *bigg*.)

Biggen (bi·g'n), *v.* Now *dial.* 1643. [f. BIG *a.*] **1.** To make or become big. **2.** To recover strength after confinement (*dial.*) 1674.

Bi·gger, *a.*, compar. of BIG. Also *sb.* One who is bigger.

Biggin[1] (bi·gin). 1530. [a. F. *béguin*, from the cap worn by BEGUINES.] **1.** A child's cap; *fig.* infancy 1609. **2.** A hood for the head, a night-cap; the coif of a Serjeant-at-law 1562.

2. Hee whose Brow (with homely Biggen bound) Snores out the Watch of Night 2 *Hen. IV*, IV. v. 27.

Biggin[2]. 1803. [f. the inventor's name.] A kind of coffee-pot with a strainer.

Bi·ggish, *a.* 1626. [f. BIG *a.*] Rather big.

Bi·ggonet. *Sc.* 1725. [Dim. of BIGGIN.] A woman's cap or headdress.

Bight (bəit). [OE. *byht* bend:—OTeut. **buhti-z*, f. *bugan* to BOW. Cf. Ger. *bucht*. See also BOUGHT *sb.*] **1.** A bending or bend; *esp.* an angle, hollow, or fork in the human or animal body; a corner. **2.** *esp.* The loop of a rope, as opp. to the ends 1622. **3.** *Geog.* An indentation in a coast line, a recess of a bay, a bend in a river, etc. 1481. Also *fig.* **4.** The space between two headlands, a slightly-receding bay; *spec.* in the Bights of Benin and Biafra; also *transf.* a bay-like segment 1555.

1. B. of the Elbow RAY. 4. A b. of meadow STEVENSON.

†**Bi·gly,** *a.* ME. [f. BIG *v.* + -LY[1].] Habitable; pleasant -1803.

Bigly (bi·gli), *adv.* ME. [f. BIG *a.* + -LY[2].] †**1.** With force or violence -1556. **2.** Loudly, boastfully, pompously 1532.

Bigness (bi·gnės). 1494. [-NESS.] **1.** Large size or bulk; also *fig.* **2.** Size, bulk 1529.

1. B. with the bulk of mankind is the nearest synonym for greatness HARE. 2. The b. of a large pea 1826.

‖**Bignonia** (bignōu·niă). 1835. [f. Abbé *Bignon*, librarian to Louis XIV.] *Bot.* A genus of plants, N.O. *Bignoniaceæ*, with showy trumpet-shaped flowers. Hence **Bignonia·ceous, Bigno·nial** *adjs.*

Bigot (bi·gət, -ŏt). 1598. [a. F., of unkn. etym.] †**1. a.** A hypocrite. **b.** A superstitious person -1664. **2.** A person obstinately and unreasonably wedded to a creed, opinion, or ritual 1661. Also *transf.* **3.** as *adj.* or *attrib.* 1623.

2. A dogmatist in religion is not a long way off from a b. WATTS. 3. Old b. zeal against Christians 1844.

Bigoted (bi·gətėd), *a.* 1645. [f. prec. (In 17th c. *bigo·tted*.)] Obstinately and blindly attached to some creed, opinion, or party, and intolerant towards others.

A b. Jacobite 1759. So nursed and b. to strife BYRON. Hence **Bi·gotedly** *adv.* var. †**Bigo·tic** *a.* So †**Bigo·tical** *a.*, whence **Bigo·tically** *adv.*

Bigotry (bi·gətri). 1674. [a. F. *bigoterie*, f. *bigot*.] The condition of a bigot; obstinate and blind attachment *to* a creed, etc.; *concr.* a specimen of bigotry 1715. var. †**Bi·gotism.**

Bigwig (bi·gwig). 1792. [f. BIG + WIG, from the large wigs formerly worn by people of importance.] A man of high official standing, or of note or importance. (*humorous* or *contemptuous*.) Hence **Bi·gwigged** *ppl. a.*; **Bigwi·ggedness, Bigwi·ggery, Bigwi·ggism,** official display of importance.

†**Biha·lve, -en, -es,** *adv.* and *prep.* [OE. *be healfe* 'by (the) side'.] Beside -ME.

‖**Bijou** (bi·ʒu). Pl. **bijoux.** 1838. [F.: prob. a. Breton *bizou* 'ring with a stone' f. *biz, bez* finger.] A jewel, a trinket; a 'gem' among works of art. Also *attrib.* Hence ‖**Bijou·terie,** bijoux collectively.

Bijugate (bəi·dʒ'ugeˈt), *a.* 1725. [See BI- *pref.*[2] I.] **1.** Of a coin: Bearing two heads side-facing, one overlapping the other. **2.** Two-paired. var. **Bi·jugous.**

Bike (bəik), *sb.*[1] *n. dial.* ME. [?] **1.** A nest of wasps, hornets, or wild bees. **2.** *fig.* A swarm of people; a 'crew' 1552.

Bike, *sb.*[2], *v.* Colloq. abbrev. of BICYCLE.

‖**Bikh.** 1830. [Hindī:—Skr. *visha* poison.] The poison of various Aconites, esp. *Aconitum ferox*; also the root or plant.

Bilabiate (bəilē̆ˈbi,ĕt), *a.* 1794. [See BI- *pref.*[2] I.] Two-lipped. var. **Bila·bial.**

Bilaciniate (bəilăsi·ni,ĕt), *a.* [See BI- *pref.*[2] I.] *Bot.* Of leaves: Doubly laciniate.

Bilamellate, -ated (bəilæ·meleˈt, -ē̆tėd), *a.* 1846. [See BI- *pref.*[2] I.] Having or consisting of two small thin plates. var. **Bila·mellar.**

Bilaminate, -ated (bəilæ·mineˈt, -ētėd), *a.* 1839. [See BI- *pref.*[2] I.] Having or consisting of two thin plates. var. **Bila·minar.**

Biland, var. of BYLAND *Obs.* peninsula.

Bilander (bi·lăndəɹ, bəi·-). 1656. [ad. Du. *bijlander*, f. *bij* BY + *land* LAND.] A kind of hoy with a trapezoidal mainsail; used in Holland for coast and canal traffic.

Like bilanders to creep Along the coast DRYDEN.

Bilateral (bəilæ·tėral), *a.* 1775. [See BI- *pref.*[2] I. 6.] Of, pertaining to, or affecting two sides; disposed on opposite sides of an axis. *Law.* Pertaining to or affecting two parties 1818. Hence **Bila·terally** *adv.* on both sides. **Bila·terism, Bilatera·lity, Bila·teralness, b.** condition.

Bilberry, bill- (bi·lbėri). 1577. [Cf. Da. *böllebær*, f. *bölle* (of unkn. etym.) + *bær* BERRY.] **1.** The fruit of a dwarf hardy shrub (*Vaccinium Myrtillus*); the berry, called also WHORTLEBERRY and BLAEBERRY, is of a deep blue black. Also the plant. Used also *attrib.* **2.** Used of other species of *Vaccinium*; e. g. the Great B. (*V. uliginosum*) 1640.

1. There pinch the Maids as blew as Bill-berry *Merry W.* v. v. 49. Hence **Bi·lberrying** *vbl. sb.* gathering bilberries.

Bilbo[1] (bi·lboᵘ). 1592. [f. *Bilbao* in Spain, long called in Eng. *Bilboa*. Cf. *Toledo blade*.] A sword noted for the temper of its blade. Now *Hist.* 1598. **b.** A humorous term for the sword of a bully 1676. Also *attrib.*

At drawn b. SCOTT.

Bilbo[2]. Pl. **bilboes** (bi·lboᵘz). 1557. [?] A long iron bar, with sliding shackles to confine the ankles of prisoners, and a lock to fasten one end of the bar to the floor.

Me thought I lay Worse then the Mutines in the Bilboes *Haml.* v. ii. 6.

Bilboquet (bilbǫke·t). 1616. [a. F., in OF. *bille-boquet*, of unkn. origin.] †**1.** A cord with two sticks fastened to it, used by gardeners to square out beds -1688. **2.** The plaything called Cup-and-ball; also, the game 1743.

Bilcock (bi·l,kǫk). 1678. The Water-rail.

Bile (bəil). 1665. [a. F., ad. L. *bilis*.] **1.** The fluid secreted by the liver, and poured into the duodenum, as an aid to the digestive process. It is bitter, yellowish or green in colour, and of a complex structure. (Formerly called *choler*, and in early physiology one of the 'four humours'.) **b.** Excess or derangement of the bile 1803. **2.** *fig.* Anger, peevishness. Cf. CHOLER, GALL, SPLEEN. 1836.

1. **Black b.**: see ATRABILE. b. I am..quite free both from gout and b. PITT. *Comb.* **b.-stone,** a calculus formed in the gall-bladder.

Bile, obs. f. BOIL tumour.

†**Bi·lewhit,** *a.* OE. [prob. f. OTeut. **bili-*, found in mod.G. *billig* + WIT.] Mild, clement; innocent -ME.

Bilge (bildʒ), *sb.* 1513. [corrupt f. BULGE, ad. OF. *boulge* = mod.F. *bouge*.] **1.** The bottom of a ship's hull, on which the ship would rest if aground; also the lowest internal part of the hull. **b.** Bilge-water 1829. **c.** *slang.* Nonsense, 'rubbish' 1921. **2.** The belly of a cask, etc. 1513.

Comb.: **b.-free** *a.* (of a cask), stowed so that the b. does not come in contact with the floor; **-piece** = BILGE-KEEL; **-pump,** a pump to draw off the b.-water; **-ways,** cradles, placed under the bottom, to conduct the ship into the water whilst launching. Hence **Bilged** *ppl. a.* broad-bottomed. **Bi·lgy** *a.*

Bilge, *v.* 1557. [f. the sb.] **1.** *trans.* To stave in a ship's bottom. **2.** *intr.* (for *refl.*) To suffer fracture in the bilge; to spring a leak. Also *fig.* 1728. **3.** *trans.* and *intr.* To bulge 1807.

Bi·lge-keel. 1850. The timber fastened under the bilge of boats, etc., to keep them upright when on shore, or to reduce rolling.

Bi·lge-water. 1706. The foul water that collects in the bilge of a ship.

Bili- (bəili), comb. f. L. *bilis* bile, used esp. in the names of bile-pigments; as *bili-cyanin, -rubin, -verdin*, etc. Hence also **Bilia·tion,** the secretion of bile. **Bili·ferous** *a.* †**Bi·lifica·tion,** making bile. †**Bi·lify** *v.* to form bile.

Bi·liary, *a.* 1731. [ad. F. *biliaire*.] **1.** Of or pertaining to the bile. **2.** = BILIOUS 2. 1837.

1. The b. duct 1731. B. organs CARLYLE.

‖**Bilimbi** (bili·mbi). 1772. [Tamul.] An Indian tree (*Averrhoa Bilimbi*, N.O. *Oxalidaceæ*), which yields a juice used in the cure of skin-diseases; also its fruit.

†**Bi·liment.** 1553. [aphet. f. ABILIMENT, HABILIMENT.] **1.** *gen.* = HABILIMENT -1790. **2.** *spec.* in 16th c.: Attire or ornaments for a woman's head or neck. So *B. lace.*

Bilin (bəi·lin). 1849. [f. BILE + -IN.] A gummy pale yellow mass, once considered to be the principal constituent of the bile.

Bilinear (bəili·niăɹ), *a. rare.* [See BI- *pref.*[2] 6.] Of, pertaining to, or contained by, two (straight) lines. MANSELL.

Bilingual (bəili·ŋgwăl), *a.* 1847. [f. L. *bilinguis* + -AL[1].] **1.** Having, or characterized by two languages 1862. **2.** *spec.* Of inscriptions, etc.: Inscribed simultaneously in parallel versions in two languages. Also quasi-*sb.*

2. The inscriptions were b., in Assyrian characters as well as Greek GROTE. Hence **Bili·ngually** *adv.* **Bili·nguist,** one who speaks two languages. vars. **Bili·nguar, Bili·nguous.**

Bilious (bi·liəs), *a.* 1541. [ad. F. *bilieux*:—L. *biliosus*, f. *bilis*.] †**1.** = BILIARY 1. -1697. **2.** Affected by, or arising from excess or derangement of the bile 1651. **3.** Choleric, peevish, ill-tempered 1561.

2. Rise in the morning as b. as a Bengal general DISRAELI. 3. The outpouring of a b. cynicism 1866. Hence **Bi·liously** *adv.* **Bi·liousness,** bilious quality or condition; *fig.* ill-temper.

Biliteral (bəili·tėrăl), *a.* 1787. [See BI- *pref.*[2] I.] Consisting of two letters; as quasi-*sb.* a linguistic root consisting of two letters.

The so-called biliterals are..the result of phonetic decay SAYCE. Hence **Bili·teralism,** a b. condition of language.

Bilk (bilk), *sb.* 1633. [? Cf. *balk*.] **1.** *Cribbage.* A balking or spoiling of an adversary's score in his crib 1791. †**2.** A statement having nothing in it -1733. **3.** A 'take in' 1664. **4.** A person who bilks; a cheat 1790.

2. Bilk! what's that? Why, nothing: a word signifying Nothing; and borrowed here to express nothing B. JONS. 4. Johnny W—lks, Thou greatest of bilks SHERIDAN.

Bilk (bilk), *v.* 1651. [? f. the sb.] **1.** *Cribbage.* To balk any one's score in his crib. **2.** To balk (hope, etc.); to cheat, deceive, betray 1672. **3.** To 'do out' *of*; to defraud; to evade payment of 1672. **4.** To elude, evade, give the slip to 1679.

2. Hopes often bilkt OLDHAM. 3. His skill..In bilking tavern bills COWPER.

Bill (bil), *sb.*[1] [Com. WGer.: OE. *bil, billes* neut., sword:—OTeut. **biljo-(m*, ?conn. w. Skr. *bhil* to cleave.] †**1.** A kind of sword mentioned in OE. poetry. **2.** An obsolete weapon carried by soldiers and watchmen, varying in form from a concave blade with a long wooden handle, to a kind of concave ax with a spike at the back and its shaft ending in a spear-head; a halberd ME. **3.** Short for BILLMAN 1495. **4.** An implement having a long blade with a concave edge (cf. BILL-HOOK), used for pruning, cutting wood, etc. OE. †**5.** A pickax -1483.

2. Wer't with the Speare, or Browne B., or the Pike DRAYTON. The watchmans browne bil 1589. 3. A strong guard of bills and bows SCOTT.

Bill, *sb.*[2] [OE. *bile*, prob.:—OTeut. **bili-*, ? f. same root as prec. sb.] **1.** The horny BEAK of certain birds, *esp.* when slender or weak. †**2.** *transf.* The beak, muzzle, or snout of other animals (cf. BEAK) -1625. **3.** A beak-like projection, as in *Portland B., Selsea B.* ME. **4.** *Naut.* The point of the fluke of an anchor 1769.

2. How she holds vp the Neb, the Byll to him *Wint.*

T. I. ii. 183. 4. **B.-board,** a board for the b. of the anchor to rest upon. *Comb.* **B.-fish** (*Belone truncata*), a sea-fish of N. America. Also called Sea-pike Silver Gar-fish, etc.

Bill (bil), *sb.*[3] [ME. *bille*, AngloL. *billa*, altered f. med.L. *bulla* 'a seal', whence *transf.* 'a sealed or formal document'.] **1.** A written document (orig. sealed); a letter, note, memorandum (cf. BILLET *sb.*). *Obs.* exc. in *Law* and *Comm.* †**b.** A papal 'bull' -1500. †**c.** A lampoon -1587. †**d.** A deed -1613. †**2.** A (written) petition to a person in authority -1728. **3.** The draft of an Act of Parliament submitted to the legislature for discussion and adoption as an 'Act'. (*Private bills* are still introduced in the form of petitions.) 1512. †**4.** *Law.* A written statement of a case; a pleading (*esp.* by a plaintiff), e. g. a *b. of complaint* in Chancery; an indictment -1788. **b.** *Sc. Law.* Any summary application by way of petition to the Court of Session. †**5.** A written list, an inventory -1605. †**b.** *Med.* A prescription -1754. **c.** *Naut.* A list of persons appointed to duties 1830. **d.** *Typog.* A list of the quantities of each letter required for a fount 1824. **6.** A note of charges for goods delivered or services rendered; a *b. of parcels* ME. †**7.** A label. *A. Y. L.* I. ii. 131. **8.** A poster, a *handbill* 1480. **9.** (More fully **B. of Exchange**) A written order by the drawer to the 'drawee' to pay a certain sum on a given date to the drawer, or to the 'payee' 1579. †**b.** Loosely used for: A promissory note. Cf. BANK-BILL, EXCHEQUER-BILL. -1721.

3. We knew..that the B. must remain a B., and could never become an Act of Parliament GLADSTONE. 4. *To find a true b., to ignore the b.*, said of a Grand Jury, in criminal Assizes, finding that there is, or is not, sufficient evidence for the case to go before the judge and an ordinary jury. 5. c. Like him that took the Doctor's B. And swallow'd it instead o' th' Pill BUTLER *Hud.* I. i. 603. 6. Well, now, Master Snip, let me see your b. B. JONS. 8. He set vp his bils here in Messina, and challenged Cupid at the flight *Much Ado* I. i. 39. 9. *Accommodation B.*: see ACCOMMODATION.

Phrases: **B. of fare,** a list of dishes to be served at a banquet, or which may be ordered (at stated prices) at a restaurant; often *fig.* a programme; **b. of health,** an official certificate given to the master of a vessel, stating whether at the time of sailing any infectious disease existed on board or in the port (hence a *clean b., suspected* or *touched b., foul b.*); **b. of lading,** an official detailed receipt given by the master of a vessel to the person consigning goods, by which he makes himself responsible for their safe delivery to the consignee; †**b. of mortality,** an official return, published periodically, of the deaths (later, also of the births) in a certain district; **b. of sale,** a written instrument effecting a transfer of personal property; *spec.* a document given as security for money borrowed, authorizing seizure of the property on default; **b. of sight,** permission from the custom-house officers to land goods for inspection in their presence, when it is not possible to enter them accurately; **b. of store,** a custom-house licence for a vessel to carry stores for a voyage custom-free; also, for British goods to be brought back into the United Kingdom within five years from the time of exportation. Also *b. of attainder, attorney* (= letter of attorney), *credit, exceptions, indictment, review, rights*, etc., see these words.

Comb. **b.-head** (sense 6), paper ruled for a tradesman's bills, having his name, etc. printed at the top.

Bill, *sb.*[4] *rare.* [For *beel, beeal*, dial. f. BELL, BELLOW.] Bellowing; the boom of the bittern.

Bill (bil), *v.*[1] 1440. [f. BILL *sb.*[1]] *trans.* To work at or on with a bill; to hoe, hack, chop, lop.

Bill, *v.*[2] ME. [f. BILL *sb.*[2]] †**1.** *intr.* To peck -1678. **2.** To stroke bill with bill (as doves) 1592. **3.** *transf.* To caress 1606.

2. Like two silver doves that sit a-billing SHAKS. 3. What, billing againe *Tr. & Cr.* III. ii. 60.

Bill, *v.*[3] ME. [f. BILL *sb.*[3]] †**1.** *trans.* To enter (in a bill, book, etc.) -1656. †**2.** To enter in a list -1633. †**3.** To make the subject or object of a bill; to lampoon; to indict; to petition -1728. **4.** To announce by bill 1694. **5.** To plaster over or crowd with bills 1851.

4. At the Opera to-night Flick and Flock is 'billed' 1871. 5. To b. a town 1884.

Bi·llage, *sb.* and *v.* A var. of BILGE.

Bi·llard. *Obs.* or *dial.* 1661. [?] The Coal-fish; cf. BILLET *sb.*[3]

Billbe·rgia, bilbe·rgia. 1858. [f. *Billberg*, botanist.] A genus of epiphytes (N.O. *Bromeliaceæ*), natives of S. America.

Billed, *ppl. a.* ME. [f. BILL *sb.*[1] and [2].] Furnished with a bill; having a beak, spike, etc. (Usu. in comb., as *broad-b.*, etc.)

Billet (bi·lėt), *sb.*[1] [ME. and AF. *billette*, AngloL. *billetta*, dim. of *billa, bille*, BILL *sb.*[3]] †**1.** A short written document -1555; a note 1579; †a pass -1823. **2.** *Mil.* An official order requiring the addressee to board and lodge the soldier bearing it. **b.** The quarters so assigned 1858. **c.** *fig.* A post, berth 1870.

1. The Lady..writ this B. to her Lover STEELE. 2. **B.-master,** the official who makes out billets. Phr. *Every bullet has its b.* (*i. e.* its appointed destination): only those are killed whose death Providence has ordained.

Bi·llet, *sb.*[2] 1440. [a. F. *billette*, and *billot*, dims. of *bille* 'trunk of a tree'; of unkn. etym.] **1.** A piece of wood cut to a proper length for fuel; billet-wood. **2.** A (thick) stick used as a weapon 1603. **3.** A small bar of metal 1670. **4.** *Archit.* A Norman moulding, consisting of short cylindrical pieces placed lengthwise at intervals in a hollow moulding. Also *attrib.* 1835. **5.** *pl.* The excrements of a fox. ¶Senses belonging doubtfully to this or the prec. wd. **6.** *Her.* A bearing of the shape of a rectangle placed on end 1592. **7.** *Saddlery.* **a.** A strap which enters a buckle. **b.** A loop which receives the end of a buckled strap. 1481.

2. Or they shall beat out my braines with billets *Meas. for M.* IV. iii. 58. *Comb.*: **b.-head,** a piece of wood at the bow of a whale-boat, round which the harpoon line runs; **b.-moulding** = BILLET *sb.*[2] 4.

Bi·llet, *sb.*[3] 1769. [? corrupt f. BILLARD.] A coal-fish, when one year old.

Billet (bi·lėt), *v.* 1599. [f. BILLET *sb.*[1]] †**1.** *trans.* To enter in a list; to enroll -1629. **2.** To assign quarters to; *spec.* to quarter (troops) by billet *in, at, on, upon, with.* 1599.

2. Go where thou art Billited *Oth.* II. iii. 386.

‖**Billet-doux** (bi·ledū·). 1673. [Fr.] A love-letter. (Now *joc.*)

He..writes the billets doux to a miracle DRYDEN.

Billeté, -etté, -etty (bi·lėti). 1572. [a. F., f. *billet*; see BILLET *sb.*[2] 6.] *Her.* Charged with billets.

Bill-hook (bi·l,huk). 1611. [f. BILL *sb.*[1]] A heavy thick knife or chopper with a hooked end, used for pruning, etc.

Billiards (bi·lyădz), *sb. pl.* Sing. only in comb. 1591. [a. F. *billard*, the game; named from *billard* 'a cue', dim. of *bille* stick. In Eng. made pl. as in *draughts, skittles*, etc.] A game played with balls on a rectangular table having a smooth cloth-covered horizontal surface, the balls being knocked about, according to rules, by means of cues.

Let it alone, let's to billards *Ant. & Cl.* II. v. 3. *Comb.*: **b.-cloth,** fine green woollen cloth used for covering billiard-tables; **-marker,** a person who marks the scores in b.; *also*, an apparatus for registering results; **-table,** the table on which the game is played; in England usu. 12 ft. by 6, covered with b.-cloth, surrounded by a cushioned ledge, and provided with six pockets at the corners and sides.

Billingsgate (bi·liŋsgėt). ME. [prob. f. *Billing*, personal name.] **1.** A gate of the city of London; the fish-market near it, noted for vituperative language. Also *attrib.* **2.** Violent abuse 1676. †**3.** A foul-mouthed person, a scold -1790.

2. Philosophers and Divines, who..write in learned Billinsgate SHAFTESB.

Billion (bi·lyən). 1690. [a. F. *billion*, f. BI- *pref.*[2] + (MI)LLION, the second power of a MILLION. Eng. retains the orig. use. Subseq. changed in France; see 2 below.] **1.** In Great Britain: A million millions. (= Fr. *trillion.*) **2.** In U. S. (as in France, where the system of numeration is based on groups of threes, not of sixes): A thousand millions. Hence **Billionai·re,** the possessor of property worth a b. of money. **Bi·llionth** *a.* the ordinal adj. corresponding to 'billion'; *sb.* the billionth part.

Billman (bi·lmæn). 1530. [f. BILL *sb.*[1]] A soldier or a watchman armed with a bill; a labourer using a bill.

Billon (bi·lən). 1727. [a. F., 'debased metal', orig. 'mass', f. *bille*, BILLET of wood, etc.; cf. BILLOT.] An alloy of gold or silver with copper, tin, or other base metal, in which the latter predominates.

Billot (bi·lət). [a. F. *billot* a wooden block.] **1.** Obs. f. BILLET *sb.*[2] **2.** Bullion in the bar before being coined 1846. (Dicts.)

Billow (bi·lo^u), *sb.* 1552. [App. a. ON. *bylgja*, f. com. Teut. *belgan* to swell; see BELL *v.*[1]] †**1.** The swell produced on the sea, a river, etc. by wind or tide -1614. **2.** *prop.* A great swelling wave of the sea; often used as = WAVE, and hence poetically for 'the sea'. 1552. Also *fig.* and *transf.*

2. Why now blow winde, swell B., And swimme Barke SHAKS. *transf.* Billows of armed men 1854.

Bi·llow, *v.* 1597. [f. prec. sb.] *intr.* To rise in billows; to surge, swell. Also *fig.*

A laugh..billowed and broke through the whole school 1865.

Billowy (bi·loui), *a.* 1615. [f. BILLOW *sb.*] **1.** Characterized by billows. **2.** Of, pertaining to, or of the nature of billows 1791. Also *transf.*

1. Crests and troughs of a b. sea GEIKIE.

Billy (bi·li). 1795. [f. *Billy*, for *Willie*, pet form of *William.*] A name for: **a.** a slubbing machine; **b.** a highwayman's club; **c.** an Australian bushman's tea-pot. Cf. JACK, JEMMY, etc.

Billyboy (bi·liboi). 1855. [?] 'A Humber or East-coast boat, of river-barge build, and a try-sail'. SMYTH.

Billycock (bi·likǫk). 1862. [prob. f. name of *William Coke*, for whom it was made.] A kind of bowler hat.

Billy-goat (bi·ligō^ut). 1861. [f. *Billy* (a male name) + GOAT.] A male goat (*colloq.*).

Bilobed (bəilō^u·bd), *ppl. a.* 1756. [See BI- *pref.*[2] I.] Having, or divided into, two lobes. vars. **Bilo·bate, Bi·lobated.**

Bilo·bular, *a.* 1859. [See BI- *pref.*[2] I.] Having, or divided into, two small lobes.

Bilocation (bəilokē^i·ʃən). 1858. [See BI- *pref.*[2] II.] The fact or power of being in two places at the same time.

Bilocellate (bəilǫ·sėlėt), *a.* 1880. [See BI- *pref.*[2] I.] Having two minute cells.

Bilocular (bəilǫ·kiŭlăı), *a.* 1783. [f. BI- *pref.*[2] I + LOCULAR.] Having, divided into, or consisting of two cells. var. **Bilo·culate.**

Biloquist (bi·lǒkwist). 1810. [See BI- *pref.*[2] II.] One who can speak with two different voices. So **Bilo·quial** *a.*

‖**Biltong** (bi·ltǫŋ). 1815. [S. Afr. Du., f. *bil* buttock + *tong* tongue.] (Tongue-like) strips of lean meat dried in the sun.

Bima·culate, -ated, *a.* 1769. [See BI- *pref.*[2] I.] Marked with two spots.

‖**Bimana** (bi·mănă, bəi-), *sb. pl.* 1839. [mod. L. neut. pl. of **bimanus* (sc. *animalia*), Buffon's *bimane*, f. L. *bi-* + *manus.*] *Zool.* Two-handed animals: Cuvier's name for an order of Mammalia, of which man is the only species. Hence **Bi·manal, Bi·manous** *adjs.* two-handed; of or belonging to the *B.* **Bi·mane,** one of the *B.*

Bimarginate, bimembral; see BI- *pref.*[2] I.

Bimedial (bəimī·diăl), *a.* (and *sb.*) 1570. [f. BI- *pref.*[2] I + MEDIAL.] *Geom.* The sum of two medial lines; a medial line being the geometric mean between two lines commensurable only in power.

Bimestrial (bəime·striăl), *a.* 1846. [f. L. *bimestris* (f. *bi-* + *mensis*) + -AL[1].] Lasting two months; occurring every two months.

Bimetallic (bəimĭtæ·lik), *a.* 1876. [ad. F. *bimétallique*, f. *bi-* + *métallique*: first used by M. Cernuschi in 1869.] Of, pertaining to, or using a double standard of currency, i. e. one based upon the two metals gold and silver, as opp. to a monometallic currency.

In point of fact the world is already b.; but it is an unregulated and haphazard bimetallism which prevails among us H. H. GIBBS.

Bimetallism (bəime·tăliz'm). 1876. [f. as prec. + -ISM.] The system of allowing the unrestricted currency of two metals (*e. g.* gold and silver) at a fixed ratio to each other, as coined money. So **Bime·tallist,** an advocate of b. Also *attrib.* or as *adj.*

Bimillenary (bəimi·lĭnări). 1850. [f. BI- *pref.*[2] II + MILLENARY.] Properly an adj.: Of or pertaining to two thousand, two thousand strong; but taken to express: A space of two thousand years (better *bimillennium*).

Bimodulus (bəimǫ·diŭlǒs). 1881. [See BI-

*pref.*² II.] *Math.* The double of the modulus of a system of logarithms. Hence Bimo·dular *a.*

Bimonthly, bimuscular; see Bi-*pref.*² I. 4.

Bin (bin), *sb.* [OE. *binn(e* str. fem. 'manger, crib, hutch', etc., ? f. a root *ben-, *bun- to twist, plait, common to Celt. and Teut.] 1. *gen.* A receptacle (*orig.* of wicker- or basket-work) 1570. †2. *spec.* A manger -ME. 3. A hutch, for corn, meal, bread, etc. Also, later, for dust, coal, etc. ME. 4. A partitioned stand for storing wine in bottle; *transf.* wine from a particular bin 1758.

3. A little b. best fits a little bread. 4. A b. reserved for banquets Tennyson. Hence **Bin** *v.* to stow in a b.

Bin, obs. and dial. f. *been*, pa. pple. etc. of Be *v.*

Bin-, *pref.*, treated as euphonic f. Bi- *pref.*², used before vowels. Not L.: app. it originated in Fr. *binocle*, prob. formed from L. *bini*. Thence extended in Eng., esp. to chemical compounds (see Bi- *pref.*² III), as *binacetate*, etc.

Binal (bəi·năl), *a.* 1658. [mod.L. *binalis*, f. L. *bini*.] Twin, double, twofold.

Binary (bəi·nări). 1460. [ad. L. *binarius*, f. *bini*.] **A.** *adj.* Of, pertaining to, characterized by, or compounded of, two; dual 1597.

B. system (of classification): one by which each group or sub-group is divided by dichotomy till individuals (or genera) are reached. In *Mus. B. measure*: that which has two beats to a bar. *B. form*: the form of a movement which is divided into two sections. In *Astron. B. stars* or *system*: two stars or suns, one of which revolves round the other, or both of which revolve round a common centre. In *Chem.* and *Min. B. compound*: one consisting of two elements. *B. theory*: that which considers all acids as compounds of hydrogen with a radicle, and all salts as similar compounds with a metal replacing hydrogen. In *Math. B. arithmetic*: a method of computation in which the b. scale is used. *B. scale*: the scale of notation whose radix is 2, in which, therefore, 1 of the denary scale is 1, 2 is 10, 3 is 11, 4 is 100, etc. *B. logarithms*: a system for use in musical calculations, in which 1 is the logarithm of 2, and the modulus is 1·442695.

B. *sb.* 1. A combination of two things; a pair, 'two'; duality. ? *Obs.* 1460. 2. *Astron.* A binary star or system. Cf. A.

Binate (bəi·neɪt), *a.* 1807. [ad. mod.L. *binatus*, f. L. *bini*.] Arranged in couples. **Bina·tely** *adv.* in pairs.

Binaural (bino̧·răl), *a.* 1881. [f. Bin- (or L. *bini*) + Aural, f. L. *auris*.] Of, pertaining to, or used with both ears, as the *b. stethoscope*.

Bind (bəind), *v.* Pa. t. and pple. **bound.** [Com. Teut.; OE. *bindan*, pa. t. *band*, pl. *bundon*, pple. *bunden*; cogn. w. Skr. *bandh*:— Aryan *bhendh to bind.] 1. *trans.* To make fast with a tie; to tie up ME. Also *fig.* 2. *esp.* To make fast with bonds; to make a captive OE. Also *fig.* 3. To tie (a knot *obs.*); hence *fig.* to conclude (a bargain), to make (any contract) fast or sure ME. 4. To make costive 1597. 5. To bandage (the body, etc. *with* something) OE. 6. To cover with dressings and bandages. Usu. with *up*. ME. 7. To fasten round, to gird, wreathe, encircle OE. 8. To secure with a border; also *fig.* ME. 9. To tie so as to hold together; to fasten together; to unite OE. Also *fig.* Also *intr.* (for *refl.*) To cohere 1674. 10. To tie or restrain, *e.g.* by a covenant, oath, etc ME. 11. To constrain with legal authority 1463. 12. To subject to a specific legal obligation 1462. 13. To attach *to*, by ties of duty, gratitude, etc. 1530.

1. Fast binde fast finde J. Heywood. *fig.* To b. men to their kind 1866. 2. To open the preson to them that are bounde *Isa.* lxi. 1. To b. the conscience 1634. 3. To b. the bargain *Act Frauds* xvii. 6. B. vp my Wounds *Rich. III*, v. iii. 177. 9. Hee that bindeth sheaues *Ps.* cxxix. 7. To b. the loose sand (*mod.*). Phr. *To b. up*: i.e. together into one volume. *transf.* To b. the chariot to the swift beast *Micah* i. 13, a rug across the shoulders 1720, two countries together 1855. 12. To b. over to keep the peace Dickens. *I dare*, or *will be bound*: I feel certain. *To be bound*: to be under obligation, moral or legal, *to do*. As marriage binds *A. Y. L.* v. iv. 59.

Bind (bəind), *sb.* OE. [f. Bind *v.*] 1. Anything used to bind; a band or tie; *spec.* in *Mus.*, a straight (or curved) line placed under (or over) notes of the same pitch, to indicate that the sound is to be sustained. Cf. Tie *sb.* 6 b. 2. A twining or climbing stem, *esp.* of the hop-plant. b. = Bine. ME. 3. Hence, †a. Honeysuckle or Wood-bine. b. = Bindweed (*Convolvulus* and *Polygonum*). 1440. 4. Indurated clay 1799. 5. A measure of quantity in salmon and eels 1477. 6. Capacity, limit. *Sc.* 1551.

†**Bind-days.** 1664. = Boon-days.

Binder (bəi·ndəɹ). OE. [f. Bind *v.* + -er¹.] 1. *gen.* One who binds. (See the vb.) 2. *spec.* a. A bookbinder 1556. b. One who binds sheaves 1611. 3. Anything used to bind; a band, bandage, etc. Also *fig.* 1695. 4. A connecting piece; *esp.* in *Carpentry*, a tie-beam or binding joint; in *Ship-building*, a principal part of a ship's frame, such as keel, transom, stem, etc. 1642. 5. In various techn. uses: *esp.* a. A band of straw, etc. for binding sheaves; b. A detachable cover for unbound magazines, etc. †6. *Med.* Anything which Binds the bowels -1678. †7. A cement -1751.

Bindery (bəi·ndəri). 1828. [f. prec.] A bookbinder's workshop. (Orig. U.S.)

Binding (bəi·ndiŋ), *vbl. sb.* ME. [f. as prec.] 1. The action of the vb. Bind in various senses. 2. The state of being bound ME. 3. *concr.* A bond, band, bandage; a fastening ME. 4. *spec.* a. The strong cover of a book, which holds the sheets together, etc. 1647. b. A protective covering for the raw edges of a fabric; braid, etc. 1598. c. *Archit.* & *Shipbuilding.* A band of masonry and brickwork; a connecting timber, etc. 1626.

Bi·nding, *ppl. a.* ME. [f. as prec.] 1. That binds together or up; causing or tending to cohere; astringent, styptic. 2. *fig.* Obligatory, restrictive, coercive 1611.

1. Byndynge frost and colde, blesse ȝe to the Lord Wyclif *Dan.* iii. 69. *Comb.*: **b.-joist**, a joist resting on the wall-plates and carrying other joists; **-plate**, one of the iron plates used to strengthen a puddling-furnace; **-screw**, a screw used in various instruments for clamping or adjustment. Hence **Bi·nding·ly** *adv.*, **-ness.**

Bindweed (bəi·ndˌwīd). 1548. [f. Bind *v.* + Weed. (? Occ. for Bindwith.)] *Bot.* 1. Name for the species of the N.O. *Convolvulus*; as *C. sepium*, *C. arvensis*, etc. 2. Used also vaguely of species of *Smilax*, *Honeysuckle*, *Tamus*, etc. 3. **Black, Corn,** or **Ivy B.,** *Polygonum Convolvulus*; **Blue B.,** Bittersweet or Woody Nightshade.

Bindwith (bəi·ndˌwiþ). 1797. [f. Bind + With(e.] *Clematis Vitalba* or Traveller's Joy.

Bine (bəin). 1727. [Dial. f. Bind *sb.*] A flexible shoot of a shrub, a climbing stem; *esp.* of the hop, whence *White-b.*, etc.

Binervate (bəinə̄·ɹveɪt), *a.* 1842. [See Bi-*pref.*² I.] Having two nerves (in *Bot.* and *Ent.*).

Bing (biŋ), *sb.*¹ ME. [a. ON. *bing-r* masc. 'heap'.] 1. A heap or pile 1513. 2. *spec.* A heap of metallic ore, of alum; 8 cwt. of lead ore 1815. 3. = Bin. Now *dial.* ME. 4. The kiln of a furnace in which charcoal is burnt in metal-smelting 1658.

1. Potato-bings Burns. 2. *B. ore*, or *b.*: the best lead ore. Hence **Bing** *v.* to pile or put up in a b.

†‖**Bing,** *sb.*² 1701. [Chinese.] A kind of tea.

Binge (bindʒ), *sb.* 1854. [Cf. dial. *binge* to soak.] *slang.* A drinking-bout; a spree. Also vb.

Bi·ngo. 1861. [App. joc. f. B. (cf. B. and S.) + Stingo.] Brandy (*slang*).

Bink (biŋk). *Sc.* and *n. dial.* [Later f. ME. *benk* = Bench *sb.*] 1. = Bench 1, 2, 6, 7. 2. A shelf; also, a dresser 1535.

Binnacle (bi·năk'l). 1622. [Corrupt f. earlier *bittacle*, app. ad. Sp. *bitacula* 'a place where the compasse or light is kept in a ship', cogn. w. F. *habitacle*:—L. *habitaculum*.] A box on the deck of a ship near the helm, in which the compass is placed. Also *attrib.*

Binny (bi·ni). *Ichthyol.* The barbel of the Nile (*Barbus bynni*).

Binocle (bi·nǒk'l). 1696. [a. F., f. L. *bini* + *oculi*.] A field- or opera-glass having tubes for both eyes.

Binocular (binǫ·kiŭlăɹ). 1713. [f. L. *bini* + *oculi*.] **A.** *adj.* 1. Having two eyes? *Obs.* So **Bino·culate** *a.* 2. Performed by or adapted to both eyes 1738. **B.** *sb.* (Short for *b. glass*.) A Binocle. Also, applied to a microscope. 1871. Hence **Bino·cula·rity**, b. quality; simultaneous employment of both eyes. **Bino·cularly** *adv.*

Binomial (bəinōu·miăl). 1557. [f. late L. *binomius*; see Binomy.] **A.** *adj.* 1. *Math.* Consisting of two terms; see B. 2. = Binominal.

1. *B. theorem*: the formula by which any power of a binomial may be found without performing the successive multiplications.

B. *sb.* An algebraic expression consisting of two terms joined by + or − (formerly only +).

Binominal (bəinǫ·minăl), *a.* 1880. [f. L. *binominis*, f. *bi-* + *nomin-* (*nomen*).] Having two names, *esp.* those of genus and species in scientific nomenclature.

Binominated (bəinǫ·mineɪtėd), *a.* 1857. [f. L. *bi-* + *nominatus*.] Having two names. So **Bino·minous** *a.*

†**Bi·nomy.** 1571. [ad. mod.L. *binomium* (also used).] = Binomial *sb.* -1670.

Binotonous (bəinǫ·tŏnəs), *a.* 1802. [f. L. *bini* + *tonus*; ? after *monotonous*.] Consisting of two notes, as a *b. cry*.

Binous (bəi·nəs), *a.* 1832. [f. L. *bini*.] = Binate.

Binoxalate, Binoxide; see Bin-.

Binuclear, -ate; see Bi- *pref.*² I.

Bio- (bəi·o, bəiˌǫ·). Gr. βιο-, comb. f. βίος 'life, course or way of living' (as opp. to ζωή 'animal life, organic life'). In mod. scientific wds. extended to mean 'organic life'.

Bio-bibliogra·phical *a.*, dealing with the life and writings of an author. **Bioblast** [Gr. βλαστός], *Biol.* a minute mass of amorphous protoplasm having formative power. **Bioce·ntric** *a.*, treating life as a central fact. **Bioche·mic, -al** *a.*, pertaining to the chemistry of life. **Biodyna·mic, -al** *a.*, of or relating to biodynamics. **Biodyna·mics**, the doctrine of vital force, or of the action of living organisms. **Bi-ogen,** the substance of the soul, the 'od' of Reichenbach. **Bio·gnosy**, generic term for the life-sciences. **Biokine·tics**, the doctrine of the successive changes through which organisms pass in development. **Bioly·tic** *a.*, life-destroying. **Biomagne·tic** *a.*, of or pertaining to animal magnetism. **Bioma·gnetism**, animal magnetism. **Bio·meter**, a measurer of life. **Bio·metry**, the calculation of the average duration and expectation of life. **Biophysio·logist**, an investigator of the physiology of living beings. **Bi·oscope**, a view of life; that which affords it. **Biosta·tic, -al** *a.*, of or pertaining to biostatics. **Biosta·tics**, the doctrine of structure as adapted to act, as opp. to *biodynamics* or *biokinetics*.

Biocellate (bəiˌǫ·seleɪt), *a.* 1847. [f. Bi-*pref.*² I + Ocellate.] Marked with two small eye-like spots, as a wing, etc.

Biogenesis (bəioˌdʒe·nėsis). 1870. [f. Gr. βιο-, Bio- + γένεσις.] The theory that living matter always arises by the agency of pre-existing living matter. Hence **Bioge·nesist,** one who holds the theory of b.

Biogeny (bəiǫ·dʒĭni). 1870. [f. Gr. βιο-, Bio- + -γενεια.] 1. The history of the evolution of living organisms 1879. Hence **Biogene·tic** *a.* of or pertaining to b. **Bio·genist.** 2. = Biogenesis.

Bi·ograph. 1897. [U.S. trade name; see -graph.] An earlier form of cinematograph.

Biographer (bəiǫ·grăfəɹ). 1715. [f. Biography + -er, replacing *biographist*.] A writer of biographies, or of a life. var. **Bio·graphist.**

Biographic, -al (bəiˌogræ·fik, -ăl), *a.* 1738. [f. Biography: see -ic, -ical.] Of, or of the nature of biography. **Biogra·phically** *adv.*

Biographize (bəiˌǫ·grăfəiz), *v.* 1800. [f. as Biography.] To write a biography of.

Biography (bəiǫ·grăfi). 1661. [ad. mod.L. *biographia* or late Gr. βιογραφία; see Bio-, -graphy.] 1. The history of the lives of individual men, as a branch of literature. 2. A written record of the life of an individual 1791. Also *transf.* of an animal or plant.

1. In all parts of B... Plutarch equally excell'd Dryden.

Biologic, -al (bəiˌolǫ·dʒik, -ăl), *a.* 1859. [f. Biology + -ic, + -al.] Of, relating to, or of the nature of biology. Hence **Biolo·gically** *adv.*

Biologist (bəiˌǫ·lŏdʒist). 1813. [f. as prec.] One who studies biology.

Bio·logize, *v.* 1862. [f. as prec.] †1. To

mesmerize -1874. 2. To cultivate biology; to deal with biologically. *intr.* and *trans.*

Biology (bəiǫ·lŏdʒi). 1813. [mod. f. Gr. βίος + -λογία. See Littré.] †1. The study of human life and character. 2. The science of physical life, dealing with organized beings or animals or plants, their morphology, physiology, origin, and distribution; occas. = PHYSIOLOGY 1819. †3. = ELECTRO-BIOLOGY -1874.

Bioplasm (bəi·o͵plæzm). 1872. [f. BIO- + Gr. πλάσμα.] *Biol.* Prof. Beale's term for: The germinal matter of all living beings; living protoplasm. Hence **Biopla·smic** *a.*

Bioplast (bəi·o͵plæst). 1877. [f. BIO- + Gr. πλαστός.] *Biol.* A small separate portion of Bioplasm generally less than the thousandth of an inch in diameter. Hence **Biopla·stic** *a.*

Biordinal (bəiǭ·ɹdinăl). 1853. [f. BI- *pref.*² II + ORDINAL.] *Math.* **A.** *adj.* Of the second order. **B.** *sb.* A linear differential equation of the second order; see ORDINAL 1881

Biotaxy, etc.; see BIO- *pref.*

Bio·tic, *a. rare.* 1600. [ad. L., a. Gr. βιωτικός, f. βίος.] †1. Of or pertaining to (common) life, secular. 2. Of animal life; vital. So **Bio·tical.** 1874.

Biotite (bəi·ŏtəit). 1862. [f. *Biot*, French mineralogist.] *Min.* Hexagonal or magnesia mica.

Bipalmate, biparietal; see BI- *pref.*²

Bi·parous, *a.* 1731. [f. BI- *pref.*² 2 + L. *-parus* (*parĕre*).] Producing two at once (in time or place).

Bipartible (bəipā·ɹtib'l), *a.* 1847. [f. L. *bipartire*, after *partibilis.*] Divisible into two parts. var. **Bipa·rtile.**

Bipartient (bəipā·ɹtiĕnt). 1678. [ad. L. *bipartientem*, f. as prec.] **A.** *adj.* That divides into two parts. **B.** *sb.* A number which divides another into two equal parts 1819.

Bipartite (bəipā·ɹtəit), *a.* 1506. [ad. L. *bipartitus*, pa. pple. of *bipartire.*] 1. Divided into or consisting of two parts 1574. b. Divided between or shared by two 1618. c. *Bot.* Divided into two parts nearly to the base 1864. 2. *Law.* Drawn up in two corresponding parts, one for each party 1506. var. **Bipa·rted.** Hence **Bipa·rtitely** *adv.* **Biparti·tion**, division into two parts (action or result).

Bipe·ctinate, -ated, *a.* 1836. [f. BI- *pref.*² I + PECTINATE.] Having two margins toothed like a comb.

Biped (bəi·pĕd). 1646. [ad. L. *bipedem*, f. *bi-* + *pedem* (*pes*).] **A.** *sb.* A two-footed animal. **B.** *adj.* Two-footed 1793.

Bipedal (bəi·pĭdăl), *a.* ME. [ad. L. *bipedalem*, f. as prec.] †1. Two feet long ME. only. 2. Biped 1607. 3. Of, pertaining to, or caused by a biped 1833. Hence **Bipeda·lity**, the quality of being two-footed.

Bipe·ltate, *a.* 1846. [f. BI- *pref.*² I + PELTATE.] Having a defence like a double shield.

Bipennate, -ated (bəipe·nĕ'it, -e'itĕd), *a.* 1713. [f. BI-*pref.*² I + PENNATE.] Two-winged.

Bipinnate (bəipi·nĕ'it), *a.* 1794. [ad. mod. L. *bipinnatus*; see PINNATE.] 1. Doubly or subordinately pinnate. So **Bipi·nnated** *a.* 2. *Zool.* Having feathery appendages in opposed pairs 1856.

Bipinnatifid (bəipinæ·tifid), *a.* 1830. [f. BI- *pref.*² I. 3 + PINNATIFID.] *Bot.* Of leaves: Pinnatifid, with the pinnæ themselves similarly divided. So **Bipinnatiparted, -partite, -sect, -sected.**

Biplane (bəi·plĕ'n). 1908. [BI-², PLANE *sb.*³] An aeroplane having two planes or main supporting surfaces, one above the other.

Bipolar (bəipōu·lăɹ), *a.* 1810. [f. BI- *pref.*² I + POLAR.] Having two poles or opposite extremities. Also *fig.* Hence **Bipola·rity.**

Bi·pont, bipo·ntine, *a.* [ad. L. *Bipontinus*, f. *Bipontium.*] Of editions of the classics, etc.: Printed at Zweibrücken (*Bipontium*) in Bavaria, in the late 18th c.

Bipunctate (bəipɒ·ŋktĕ'it), *a.* 1864. [ad. mod.L. *bipunctatus.*] Having or marked by two punctures or points. var. **Bipu·nctual.** (Dicts.)

Biquadrate (bəi͵kwǫ·drĕ'it). 1706. [f. BI- *pref.*² + QUADRATE.] *Math.* The square of the square (power or root); = BIQUADRATIC. Hence **Biqua·drate** *v.* to raise to the fourth power.

Biquadratic (bəi͵kwǫdræ·tik). 1661. [f. BI- *pref.*² + QUADRATIC.] *Math.* **A.** *adj.* Pertaining to the biquadrate, or fourth power of a number 1668. **B.** *sb.* **a.** The fourth power of a number. **b.** A biquadratic equation.

B. equation: an equation in which the unknown quantity is raised to the fourth power. *B. parabola*: a curve of the third order, having two infinite legs tending the same way. *B. root*: the square root of the square root.

Biquintile (bəi͵kwi·ntəil, -il). 1647. [f. BI- *pref.*² I + QUINTILE.] *Astrol.* An aspect of the planets, when they are distant from each other twice the fifth part of a great circle,—that is, 144 degrees.

Biradiate, -ated; see BI- *pref.*² I.

Bira·mous, *a.* [f. BI- *pref.*² I + L. *ramus.*] Two-branched. HUXLEY.

Birch (bɔ̄ɹtʃ), *sb.* [In OE.: (1) *berc, beorc*:—OTeut. **berkâ-* str. fem.; (2) *bierce, byrce, birce*:—OTeut. **birkjôn-* wk. fem., a deriv. of **berkâ-*. An Indo-Germanic tree name. (2) gave ME. *birche*, mod. *birch*; *birk* is northern; cf. CHURCH, KIRK.] 1. A genus of hardy northern forest trees (*Betula*), having smooth tough bark and slender branches. **a.** *esp.* The common European species (*B. alba*); also called Lady Birch, Silver B., White B. The Weeping or Drooping B. (*B. pendula*) is a variety. **b.** **Dwarf-B.** (*B. nana*); **Paper B.** or **White B.** of America (*B. papyracea*); **Cherry B.** (*B. lenta*), also called **Sweet Mahogany** or **Mountain B.** **c.** The wood of this tree ME. **d.** The pl. *birks* in the north signifies a grove of birches 1724. 2. A bunch of birch-twigs used for flogging; a birch-rod 1648. 3. A canoe made of the bark of *B. papyracea* 1864.

1. Byrche..serueth..for betynge of stubborne boyes TURNER. Shadows of the silver birk Sweep the green that folds thy grave TENNYSON.

Comb.: **b. camphor**, a resinous substance obtained from the bark of *B. nigra*; **b. oil**, an oil extracted from the bark of the b., and used in the preparation of Russia leather, to which it gives its smell; **b.-rod** = BIRCH 2; **b.-water**, the sap obtained from the b. in spring; **b.-wine**, wine prepared from b.-water. Hence **Birch** *v.* to punish with a b.-rod; to flog.

Birchen (bɔ̄·ɹtʃ'n), *a.* 1440. [f. prec.] Of or pertaining to BIRCH 1, 2; composed of birch.

Canoe-men, in their b. vessels 1865.

Bird (bɔ̄ɹd). [ME. *byrd, bryd*:—OE. *brid* masc. (pl. *briddas*), used only of the young of birds. Found only in Eng.] 1. *orig.* The young of the feathered tribes; a chicken, eaglet, etc.; a nestling. Still in n. dial. Also †*transf.* and *fig.* b. A maiden, a girl. [At first confused with *burde* BURD; but later taken as fig. sense of 1 or 2.] ME. 2. Any feathered vertebrate animal; a member of the second class (*Aves*) of the great Vertebrate group. (Now used generically in place of FOWL.) ME. 3. *Sport.* A game bird; *spec.* a partridge. Also *fig.* 1596. 4. *fig.* (See quots.) 1588.

1. He..cheryssheth vs, as the egle her byrdes 1526. b. The B. is dead That we haue made so much on *Cymb.* IV. ii. 197. 2. The bryddes of the aier have nestes TINDALE *Matt.* viii. 20. 3. Am I your B., I meane to shift my bush *Tam. Shr.* v. ii. 46. Reports say the birds are very wild (*mod.*). 4. *Arabian b.* = phœnix. A little b. has whispered a secret to me 1833. There must be such queer birds however B. TAYLOR.

Phr. *Birds of a* (= *one*) *feather*: those of like character. *To get the* (*big*) *b.*, to be hissed.

Comb.: 1. With defining word, as **b. of Jove**, the eagle; **b. of Juno**, the peacock; **b. of paradise**, one of the family *Paradiseidæ*, remarkable for the beauty of their plumage; **B. of passage**, any migratory b.; **b. of Washington**, the American Eagle (*Falco leucocephalus*); **b. of wonder**, the phœnix. 2. †**b.-bolt**, a blunt-headed arrow, used for shooting birds; **-call**, an instrument for imitating the note of birds, in order to attract them; **B-** (or **bird's**) **cherry**, a wild fruit tree or shrub (*Prunus Padus*); **-fly**, a fly (*Ornithomyia*) which lives under the plumage of birds; **-mouthed** *a.*, having a mouth like a b.; *hence*, unwilling to speak out (*obs.*); **-organ**, a small organ used in teaching birds to sing; **-pepper**, kinds of capsicum; **-seed**, canary-seed, hemp, millet, plantain, etc.; **-spit**, a spit for roasting birds on, †*fig.* a rapier; **-witted** *a.*, lacking the faculty of attention. 3. (Comb. of *bird's*): *a. gen.* as **bird's-beak moulding**, one which in section forms an ovolo or ogee with or without a fillet under it followed by a hollow; **-mouth**, an interior or re-entrant angle cut out of the end of a piece of timber. **b.** *esp.* in plant-names; *e.g.* **Bird's bread**, the small Yellow Stone-crop (*Sedum acre*); **Bird's eggs**, the Bladder Campion; **Bird's tare**, a species of Arachis; **Bird's tongue**, the Greater Stitchwort (*Stellaria holostea*), the Common Maple, Scarlet Pimpernel, Ornithoglossum, etc. (from the shape of their leaves); also the fruit of the ash-tree. Hence **Bi·rdikin, Bi·rdlet, Bi·rdling**, a little b.

Bird (bɔ̄ɹd), *v.* 1576. [f. prec.] *intr.* To catch or shoot birds.

Bird-cage (bɔ̄·ɹd͵kĕ'dʒ). 1490. [f. BIRD *sb.* + CAGE *sb.*] 1. A cage for a bird or birds. 2. *Sporting.* The paddock at Newmarket 1884.

1. The Bird-Cages in St. James's Park. [Hence *Birdcage Walk.*] 1691.

†**Birde.** [App. short f. **ȝebirde*:—OE. *gebyrd*(*o* 'birth'.] 1. Birth; offspring -ME. 2. Family, nation -ME.

Birder (bɔ̄·ɹdəɹ). 1481. [f. BIRD *v.* + -ER¹.] †1. A fowler -1622. 2. A breeder of birds 1827. 3. A wild cat (*local*) 1864.

Birdie (bɔ̄·ɹdi). 1792. [f. BIRD *sb.* + -IE, -Y⁶.] 1. A dear little bird. 2. *Golf.* The fact of doing a hole in one under the par score (chiefly *U.S.*) 1921.

Bi·rd-lime. *sb.* 1440. A glutinous substance spread upon twigs, by which birds may be caught. Also *fig.* and *transf.* Also *attrib.*

Hence **Bi·rd-lime** *v.* to smear or catch with (or as with) b. **Bi·rd-limy** *a.*

Bird's-eye. Also **bird-eye.** 1597. **1.** *sb.* A name of several plants with small round bright flowers, as the *Bird's-eye Primrose* (*P. farinosa*), Germander Speedwell, species of *Adonis* (usu. *Pheasant's eye*), Robert's Geranium, etc. 2. A manufactured tobacco in which the ribs of the leaves are cut along with the fibre 1861. 3. *attrib.* Of or belonging to a bird's eye; as in *Bird's-eye view*: a view of a landscape from above, such as a bird would have; *fig.* a résumé of a subject 1762. 4. *attrib.* Marked as with bird's eyes; spotted; as *Bird's-eye limestone, maple*, etc. 1665.

Bi·rd's-foot, bi·rd-foot. 1578. Applied to objects having the shape of a bird's foot, as **a.** A small yellow vetch (*Ornithopus*); **b.** A small fern (*Cheilanthes radiata*); **c.** = Bird's-foot Trefoil.

Bird's-foot Trefoil or *Lotus*: a yellow leguminous plant (*Lotus corniculatus*), a native of Britain. *Bird's-foot star, sea-star*: an echinoderm related to the star-fish.

Bi·rd's-nest, bird-nest, *sb.* 1597. 1. (Usu. two wds.): The nest of a bird; *spec.* the edible nest of certain species of swallow found in the Chinese Sea. Also *attrib.* 1599. 2. A CROW'S NEST, q. v. 1867. 3. A name of plants: **a.** The Wild Carrot; **b.** *Monotropa Hypophitys*; **c.** = Bird's-nest Orchid.

Bird's-nest fern, a name given to some exotic ferns from their habit of growth; **Bird's-nest Orchid** (*Neottia Nidus-avis*), a plant, wild in Britain, entirely of a brown feuillemort colour. Hence **Bi·rd's-ne·sting, bird-nesting** *vbl. sb.* the action or occupation of searching for bird's-nests; whence **Bi·rd's-ne·st** *v. intr.*

Bireme (bəi·rīm). 1600. [ad. L. *biremis*, f. *bi-* + *remus.*] **A.** *adj.* Having two banks of oars. **B.** *sb.* [sc. *galley.*]

Biretta (bire·tă). Also **beretta, birretta.** 1598. [a. It. *berretta* and Sp. *birreta*:—late L. *birretum* cap, f. *birrus* (*byrrhus*), prob. ad. Gr. πυῤῥός flame-coloured.] The square cap worn by clerics of the R.C.Ch.; that of priests being black, of bishops purple, of cardinals red.

Birgand(**er**, obs. f. BERGANDER.

Birk, -en, -in, north. ff. BIRCH, BIRCHEN.

Birkie (bɔ̄·ɹki, *Sc.* be·rkie). 1724. [?] **A.** *sb.* Joc. term for a man 'with a mind of his own'; occas. = 'strutting fellow', often simply = 'fellow', 'carle'. 2. *Cards.* = 'Beggar-my-neighbour' 1777. **B.** *adj.* Mettlesome 1821.

Birl (bɔ̄ɹl, *Sc.* bir'l), *v. Sc.* 1724. [App. echoic.] To revolve or cause to revolve rapidly and with characteristic noise; to spin.

Birle (bɔ̄ɹl), *v. Obs.* exc. *dial.* [OE. *byrelian*, f. *byrele*, of doubtful etym.] 1. To pour out (drink, *to* or *for* any one). 2. To ply *with* drink ME. 3. *intr.* To carouse; *trans.* to drink and pass (the cup). (Pseudo-*arch.*) 1800.

Bi·rlie, bi·rley. *Sc.* 1609. Corrupt f. BYRLAW, used in comb. (See also BURLEY-.)

‖**Birlinn** (bī·ɹlin). 1595. [Gael.] A large rowing boat, used by the chieftains in the Western Islands of Scotland.

Birmingham (bɔ̄·ɹmiŋhæm). A town in Warwickshire, in England. See ANTI-BIRMINGHAM. Also **Birminghamize** *v.*, to make up artificially. Cf. BRUMMAGEM.

Birostrate, -ated, Birotate; see BI- *pref.*[2] I.

Birr (bɔ̄ɪ, *Sc.* bėrr). ME. [a. ON. *byrr* favouring wind :—OTeut. **burjo-z*, f. *beran* to bear. Sense 3 is prob. echoic.] †1. A strong (carrying) wind ME. only. 2. Momentum, impetus; rush OE.; emphatic utterance 1825. 3. An energetic whirring sound 1837.

2. What the Scotch call the B... the emphatic energy of his pronunciation LD. COCKBURN. 3. The b. of the moorcock SMILES. Hence Birr *v.* to emit a b.

Birretta, var. of BIRETTA.

Birse (bəɪs, *Sc.* bėrs), *sb.* [OE. *byrst* bristle. Now only Sc.] = BRISTLE. Also *fig.*

Birsle (bə·ɪs'l, *Sc.* bė·rs'l), *v. Sc.* 1513. [?] To toast hard; also *fig.*

†**Birt, burt.** 1552. [?] A Turbot -1783.

Birth (bɔ̄ɪþ), *sb.* [Early ME. *byrþ(e, burð(e, birþ(e*, f. (ult.) stem of *beran* to BEAR.] 1. The bearing of offspring. a. Giving birth ME. b. The being born, nativity ME. Also *fig.* of things. 2. That which is born; offspring; young (of animals) (*arch.*) ME. Also *fig.* of things. 3. Parentage, lineage, descent ME. *spec.* Noble lineage 1595. †4. Nature, kind, sex -1592. 5. Conditions involved in birth ME. †6. *Astrol.* Nativity SHAKS. 7. *Theol.* in *New b.*: regeneration 1535.

1. a. Two children at one b. 2 *Hen. VI*, IV. ii. 147. b. The birthe of Cryst our thraldom putte vs fro CHAUCER. Phr. *To give b. to*: to bear (offspring). The b. of an idea 1875. 2. *fig.* Innouations, which are the Births of Time BACON. 3. She is no equall for his b. *Much Ado* II. i. 172. 5. An Athenian by b. JOWETT. 7. Baptism confers a new b. MANNING.

attrib.: **b. control**, the artificial restriction of esp. the use by married persons of contraceptive methods; **b. mark**, a mark on the skin dating from b.; **b. rate**, the ratio of the number of births to the population. Hence †**Bi·rthdom**, birthright.

Bi·rth, *v. rare.* ME. [f. prec.] *intr.* To have birth.

Birth, obs. f. BERTH.

Birthday (bɔ̄·ɹþdēɪ). ME. [f. BIRTH + DAY.] 1. The day on which any one is born; *transf.* that of origin or commencement 1580. 2. The anniversary of the day of birth; occas. *spec.* of that of the sovereign ME. Also *attrib.*

1. The Anniversary of the B. of this Glorious Queen STEELE. 2. This is my B.; as this very day was Cassius born *Jul. C.* V. i. 72. *B. suit*: bare skin.

Birthnight (bɔ̄·ɹþnəit). 1628. [f. as prec. + NIGHT.] 1. The night on which any one is born 1671. 2. The night annually kept in memory of any one's birth 1628. †3. *spec.* The evening of a royal birthday -1730. *attrib.*

1. The Angelic Song in Bethlehem field, On thy birth-night MILT. *P. R.* IV. 506.

Birthplace (bɔ̄·ɹþplēɪs). 1607. [f. as prec. + PLACE.] The place where a person (or *fig.* a thing) is born.

The b. of valour BURNS *Farew. Highlands.*

Birthright (bɔ̄·ɹþ,rəit). 1535. [f. as prec. + RIGHT.] Right by birth; the rights, privileges, etc. to which one is entitled by birth. *spec.* The rights of the first-born. Also *fig.*

Sell me this daye thy byrth-right *Gen.* XXV. 31. The laws of the land are the b. of every native COLERIDGE.

Birthwort (bɔ̄·ɹþ,wɒɹt). 1551. [f. as prec. + WORT.] *Bot.* The genus of shrubs ARISTOLOCHIA.

‖**Bis**, *adv.* 1819. [Fr. and It., a. L.] Encore, again: used a. in *Mus.* as a direction to repeat a phrase or passage. b. Twice; to call attention to the occurrence of a number, word, etc., twice, as 'p. 175 (*bis*)'.

Bis-, *pref.*[1] The prec. adv. used occas. bef. *s*, *c*, or a vowel, in place of BI- *pref.*[2], as in *bis-alternate*, etc.

Bis-, *pref.*[2], *Chem.* abbrev. of BISMUTH, used in comb.

Bis; see BICE, BYSS.

Bisaccate; see BI- *pref.*[2] I.

†**Bisa·nnual**, *a.* and *sb.* = BIENNIAL.

‖**Biscacha** (bis,ka·tʃă). Also **biz-, vis-**. 1837. [a. Sp. *biscacho.*] *Zool.* A species of the *Chinchillidæ*, a burrowing rodent of S. America.

Biscayan (bi·skēɪăn), *a.* 1634. [f. *Biscay* + -AN.] Belonging to, or characteristic of the province of Biscay; also as *sb.*, an inhabitant or native of Biscay. So Biscayen [ad. F. *biscaïen*], a. A long heavy musket, first used in Biscay; b. One of its balls.

†**Bi·scot**, *sb.* 1662. [f. SCOT = payment.] A fine formerly imposed on owners of marsh-lands for failure to repair banks, ditches, etc. -1790.

†**Biscotin.** 1727. [a. F.; cf. BISCUIT.] A sweet biscuit made of flour, sugar, eggs, etc.

Biscuit (bi·skėt). ME. [a. OF. *bescoit, bescuit*, mod. *biscuit*, on L. type **biscoctum* (*panem*), bread 'twice baked'. From 16th to 18th c. spelt *bisket*, as still pronounced.] 1. A kind of crisp dry bread more or less hard, made generally in thin flat cakes. The essential ingredients are flour and water, or milk, without leaven. In U.S., a small soft cake, usually fermented. 2. *Pottery.* Pottery-ware fired once, but not glazed, or embellished; also *fig.* 1791.

1. As drie as the remainder bisket After a voyage *A. Y. L.* II. vii. 39. var. **B. bread.** Hence **Bi·scuiting** *vbl. sb.* (sense 2).

Biscutate (bəi,skiū·tēɪt), *a.* 1838. [f. BI- *pref.*[2] I. 6 + SCUTATE.] Having two shields; resembling two bucklers.

‖**Bise** (bīz, bīz). ME. [a. F., of unkn. etym.] A keen dry N. or NNE. wind, prevalent in Switzerland and its neighbourhood.

Bise, obs. f. BICE.

Bisect (bəise·kt), *v.* 1646. [mod. f. *bi-, bis-* + *sect-, secare.*] 1. To cut into two equal parts. (The usual sense.) 2. To divide into any two parts 1789. 3. *intr.* To fork 1870.

1. Borneo is nearly bisected by the equator 1879.

Bisection (bəise·kʃən). 1656. [f. prec., after L. *sectionem.*] 1. Division into two (usually equal) parts. 2. Forking 1870. Hence **Bise·ctional** *a.*, **-ly** *adv.*

Bisector (bəise·ktəɪ, -tǭɪ). 1864. [f. BISECT *v.*] One who bisects; a bisecting line.

Bisectrix (bəise·ktriks). 1854. [f. prec.] = prec.; *spec.* in biaxial polarization, the line bisecting the angle between the two axes of polarization (= *linea bisectrix*).

Bisegment (bəise·gmėnt). 1847. [f. BI- *pref.*[2] II + SEGMENT.] One of the two equal parts into which a line, etc., is divided.

Biseptate, biserial, biseriate, biserrate; see BI- *pref.*[2]

‖**Biset** (bizę, bi·zėt). 1834. [a. Fr., f. *bis* dark-grey.] The wild rock-pigeon.

Bisetous (bəisī·təs), *a.* 1842. [f. BI- *pref.*[2] I + L. *sæta* + -OUS.] Having two *setæ* or bristles. var. **Biseto·se.**

†**Bi·sexed**, *a.* 1606. [See BI- *pref.*[2] I + SEX.] Of both sexes -1646. So **Bise·xous** *a.*

Bisexual (bəise·ksiuăl, -ʃuăl), *a.* 1824. [See BI- *pref.*[2] I.] Of two sexes; *spec.* having both sexes in the same individual.

The .. tradition .. that the original man .. was b. COLERIDGE.

Bish, var. of BIKH.

Bishop (bi·ʃəp), *sb.* [OE. *biscop, bisceop, biscep*, a. vulgar L. (*e*)*biscopus* :—L. *episcopus*, a. Gr. ἐπίσκοπος 'overseer': a Common Germanic loanword.] 1. A spiritual superintendent or overseer in the Christian Church. a. In N. T. versions, tr. ἐπίσκοπος, used either descriptively, or as a title. In Acts xx. 28 (where applied to the πρεσβύτεροι of Ephesus) replaced in some versions by 'overseers'. Also applied to Christ. (Occas. used in non-episcopal churches of the pastor or chief elder.) ME. b. *spec.* In the episcopal churches: A clergyman consecrated for the spiritual government of a diocese, ranking next below an archbishop (where these exist). (The sense in which the wd. passed into all the Teut. langs.) OE. †2. *transf.* Any chief priest, *e.g.* a *pontifex maximus*, Mohammedan caliph, etc. -1647. 3. One of the pieces in the game of chess, having the upper part shaped like a mitre; formerly called *archer* 1562. 4. The Lady-bird 1674. 5. A sweet drink, compounded of wine, oranges or lemons, and sugar; mulled and spiced port 1738. 6. a. A bustle (*U.S.*) 1860. b. A child's smock (*n. dial.*) 1874.

1. a. In the language of the New Testament the same officer in the Church is called indifferently 'bishop' ἐπίσκοπος and 'elder' or 'presbyter' πρεσβύτερος LIGHTFOOT. b. *Bishop in partibus (infidelium)* in R. C. Ch., a titular bishop, whose diocese is in the possession of infidels. Bischops .. shulden not amersy pore men WYCLIF. 5. That liquor called b., which Johnson had always liked BOSWELL.

Comb.: **Bishop's Bible**, the version published in 1568 under the direction of Abp. Parker; **bishop's length** (*Painting*), a certain size of canvas. b. Plant-names: **bishop's cap**, the genus *Mitella* or Mitrewort; **bishop's elder** = *bishop-weed*; **bishop's hat**, *Epimedium alpinum*; **bishop's leaves**, Water Figwort (*Scrophularia aquatica*); **bishop's weed**, **b.-weed**, the genus AMMI; also *Ægopodium*; **bishop('s wort**, Wood Betony, *Stachys betonica*; also Devil-in-a-bush, *Nigella damascena*.

Bi·shop, *v.*[1] *arch.* [OE. *bisceopian.*] 1. To administer confirmation to; to confirm (*arch.* or *Obs.*). 2. To make a bishop of 1549. 3. To let (milk, etc.) burn while cooking. In allusion to the proverb 'The bishop has put his foot into it'. (*n. dial.*) 1863.

[If the porage be burned..we say the bishop hath put his foote in the potte..because the bishops burn who they lust TINDALE.]

Bi·shop, *v.*[2] 1727. [f. *Bishop*, personal name.] 1. To file down the teeth of (a horse) so as to make him look young. 2. To murder by drowning (cf. BURKE *v.*) 1840.

Bishopdom (bi·ʃəpdəm). [OE. *bisceopdōm.*] †1. = BISHOPHOOD -1635. 2. Episcopal order; *concr.* bishops collectively 1641.

Bi·shopess. 1672. The wife of a bishop (*nonce-wd.*); a she-bishop (*joc.*) 1854.

Bishophood (bi·ʃəphud). [OE. *bisceophād.*] The office, dignity, or rank of a bishop.

Bishoplike (bi·ʃəp,ləik). A. *adj.* Like a bishop; †episcopal OE.; var. **Bi·shoply** *a.* B. *adv.* After the manner of a bishop 1555.

Bishopric (bi·ʃəprik). [OE. *bisceoprīce*, f. *bisceop* + *rīce* realm.] 1. The province of a bishop; a diocese. 2. The office or position of a bishop ME. †3. Overseership. (tr. Gr. ἐπισκοπή.) -1592.

3. His Bishopricke [*marg.* office: or, charge] let another take *Acts* i. 20.

Bishopstool (bi·ʃəp,stūl). [OE. *bisceopstōl*; see STOOL.] The throne, seat, or see of a bishop. *Obs.* since 13th c., but revived by historians.

Bisie, obs. f. BUSY.

Bisk (bisk), *sb.* 1647. [a. F. *bisque* crayfish soup.] A rich soup made by boiling down birds, etc.; *spec.* crayfish soup.

Bisk, var. of BISQUE[1].

Bismar (bi·smăɪ). 1805. [a. Da. *bismer*, ON. *bismari* steelyard.] 1. A steelyard used in Orkney, Shetland, etc. 2. The fifteen-spined stickleback (*Gasterosteus spinachia*), from its supposed resemblance to the steelyard 1805.

†**Bisme.** 1513. [aphet. f. *abisme.*] A deep pit -1663.

†**Bi·smer**, *sb.* [WGer.: OE. *bīsmer, -or*, = OHG. *bīsmer* ridicule, f. *bi-*, BY + *-smer*, ? conn. w. MHG. *smieren* to smile.] 1. Disgrace; mockery; scorn -1460. 2. A person worthy of scorn; a pander or bawd -1535. Hence †**Bi·smer** *v.* to treat with scorn.

Bismethyl; see BIS- *pref.*[2] *Chem.*

‖**Bismillah.** 1813. [Arab.] In the name of Allah; a Mohammedan exclam.

Bismite (bi·smait, biz-). [f. BISM(UTH + -ITE.] *Min.* The native oxide of bismuth; bismuth-ochre.

Bismite, bismoke, etc.; see BE-.

Bismuth (bi·smɒ̆þ, biz-). 1668. [a. Ger. *bismuth*; now *wismuth* or *wismut.* Of unkn. deriv.] One of the elementary bodies; a reddish white metal, found native, and also in combination. (Chemically, a triad and a pentad, used in the arts and in medicine. Symbol Bi.)

Comb.: **b.-blende** = EULYTITE; **-glance** = *Bismuthinite*; **-ochre** = BISMITE; **-silver**, Ag_6Bi = CHILENITE. Hence **Bismuthal** *a.* of or pertaining to b. **Bi·smuthate**, a salt of bismuthic acid. **Bismuthic** *a.* combined with b. as a pentad, as *bismuthic oxide* Bi_2O_5. **Bi·smuthide** (*Chem.*), a primary compound of b. with another element or an organic radical; (*Min.*) a family of minerals of the b. type. **Bi·smuthine**, a compound of b. having the structure of an amine; also = **Bismu·thinite** (*Min.*), native sulphide of b., or *b.-glance*, a lead-grey lustrous mineral, isomorphous with stibnite. **Bi·smuthous** *a.* combined with b. as a triad, as *bismuthous oxide* Bi_2O_3. **Bi·smutite, Bismuthite** (*Min.*), the native hydrous carbonate of b., Bi_2C, of various forms and colours.

Bison (bəi·sən, bi·sən, bi·zən). ME. [ad. L. *bison* (pl. *bisontes*), ad. OTeut. *wisand, in OE. *wesend*, the native name. Etymologically bi·sən is correct, but bəi·sən is usual.] 1. *orig.* A European Wild Ox (*Bos Bison* Gesn., *B. Bonasus* Linn.), still existing in Lithuania. (Occas., but erron., called the *Aurochs.*). 2. The N. American species *B. Americanus*, pop. 'Buffalo', now found chiefly in the region of the Rocky Mountains 1774.

‖**Biso·gnio, bisogno,** early ff. BESONIO, BEZONIAN.

Bispinose, -ous; see BI- *pref.*[2] I.

Bisque[1] (bisk). 1656. [a. F.; of unkn. origin.] *Tennis.* Odds given to a player in the form of a point to be scored once during the set at any time he may elect. In *Croquet*: An extra turn allowed to a weaker player.

Phr. *To give one fifteen*, etc. *and a b.*: to give him long odds, to 'leave him nowhere'.

Bisque[2]. 1664. [f. BISCUIT.] 1. ? BISCUIT (bread). 2. In *Pottery*, = BISCUIT 2; also, unglazed white porcelain.

Bisque, var. of BISK, soup.

†**Bisse·xt.** ME. [ad. L. *bi(s)sextus (dies)*, f. *bis* + *sextus.*] *prop.* The intercalary day in leap-year (see next); also = BISSEXTILE. -1618.

Bissextile (bise·kstil). 1581. [ad. L. *bi(s)sextilis (annus)*, *i.e.* (the year) of the *bissextus*; see prec.] A. *adj.* Containing the *bissextus* which the Julian calendar inserts every fourth year after the *sixth* day before the calends of March, or 24th of February 1594. *B. day* (= L. *bissextus dies*; see above). B. *sb.* Leap-year.

†**Bi·sson,** *a.* [OE. (Northumb.) *bisene.* See Skeat.] 1. Blind -1559. *Occas.*, purblind -1607. 2. ? Blinding. *Haml.* II. ii. 529.

Bist, obs. or dial. = *art*; see BE *v.*

Bistipuled; see BI- *pref.*[2] I.

Bistort (bi·stɔ̄ɹt). 1578. [ad. L. *bistorta* fem. pa. pple.] 1. A species of Polygonum (*P. bistorta*) having a root twisted upon itself; also called *Snakeweed.* See ADDERWORT. 2. *Surgery.* = BISTOURY 1655.

Bistoury (bi·stəri, bi·sturi). 1490. [ad. mod. F. *bistouri*; of unkn. origin.] *Surgery.* A scalpel; made in three forms, straight, curved, or curved and probe-pointed.

Bistre (bi·stəɹ). Also **bister.** 1727. [a. F. *bistre*, of unkn. etym.] A brown pigment prepared from soot; the colour of this. Also *attrib.* **Bi·stred** *ppl. a.* stained with or as with b.

†**Bi·sulc.** 1650. [ad. L. *bisulcus*, f. *bi-* + *sulcus.*] A. *adj.* Cleft in two; *spec.* having a cloven hoof 1661. B. quasi-*sb.* A cloven-hoofed animal 1693. So **Bisu·lcate, Bisu·lcated, Bisu·lcous** *adjs.* in same sense.

Bit (bit), *sb.*[1] [Com. Teut.: OE. *bite* str. masc.:—OTeut. *biti-z str. masc., f. *bītan* to BITE. In OE. *bite* 'act of biting', and *bita* 'piece bitten off' (see BIT *sb.*[2]), were distinct, but both are now *bit.*] †1. The act or action of biting; a BITE -1653. Also *fig.* and *transf.* 2. What one bites, victuals 1719. 3. The biting part of anything; the blade, edge, or cutting end of a tool; *spec.* the movable boring-piece of a drill, or a similar tool for use with machines, etc.; the cutting-iron of a plane, the jaws of tongs, pincers, etc. 1594. 4. The part of a key which engages with the levers of the lock 1644. 5. The mouthpiece of a horse's bridle, consisting of the metal *b.-mouth*, and adjacent parts, to which the reins are attached ME.

1. An idle servant..good at b., and nothing else 1635. 2. A b. and a sup KINGSLEY. 5. *To draw b.*: to stop one's horse by pulling at the reins; *fig.* to slacken speed. *To take the b. in his teeth* (of a horse): *i.e.* so that it cannot hurt the mouth; hence, to be beyond restraint; also *fig.* Hence **Bi·tted** *ppl. a.* (sense 5).

Bit, *sb.*[2] [Com. Teut.: OE. *bita* wk. masc., morsel:—OTeut. *biton- wk. masc., f. *bītan* to bite. See BIT *sb.*[1] For 'piece bitten off' BITE is now used.] †1. A bite or mouthful -1665. Hence 2. Morsel (of food) ME. 3. A small piece, a fragment 1606. 4. A small portion, a little (of anything) 1740. 5. *colloq.* A jot, a whit. Also *advb.* 1675. 6. Of money: a. *Thieves' slang.* Money 1607. b. In the Southern States of N. America, etc., a small silver coin forming a fraction of the Spanish dollar, or of its value in current money 1683. c. *colloq.* A small piece of money. In slang = fourpence. 1829.

2. Dainty bits make rich the ribs *L. L. L.* I. i. 26. 3. Bits of linen 1718, glass or china 1838. *By bits* 1624. 4. *A b. of one's mind* (colloq.): see PIECE *sb.* 2. An interesting b. 1879. To stop for a b. GODWIN. 'Bits of children' = poor little children. A b. of a coward 1885. *To do one's b.*: to do one's proper share, orig. in the war of 1914–18. 5. It isn't changed a b. TROLLOPE.

†**Bit,** *sb.*[3] [OE. *byt(t*, ad. med L. *buttis, butta*, of unkn. etym. Cf. BUTT, BOTTLE.] A leathern bottle; the uterus; a fire-bucket -1467.

Bit (bit), *v.* 1583. [f. BIT *sb.*[1]] To put the bit into the mouth of; to accustom to the bit. Also *fig.*

Bit, pa. t. and pple. of BITE *v.*

Bitake, etc. ME. f. BETAKE, etc.

Bitch (bitʃ), *sb.*[1] [OE. *bicce.* Cf. ON. *bikkja.*] 1. The female of the dog; also of the fox, wolf, and occas. of other beasts. 2. Applied to a (lewd) woman. Not now in decent use. ME.

Bitch, *sb.*[2] 1747. *Mining.* = BECHE.

†**Bitch,** *v.* 1675. [f. BITCH *sb.*[1] 2.] To frequent lewd women.

Bite (bəit), *v.* Pa. t. **bit.** Pa. pple. **bitten;** also **bit** (*arch.*). [Com. Teut.: OE. *bītan*:—OTeut. *bītan, cogn. w. Skr. *bhid-*, L. *fid-* (*findere*) to cleave. Orig. inflected like *write.*] 1. *trans.* To cut into, pierce, or nip with the teeth (incisors or canines). Also *intr.* or *absol.* 2. To wound or lacerate with the teeth OE. Also *fig.* Also *absol.* and *intr.* ME. 3. To sting as a serpent, or an insect that sucks blood ME. †4. To nibble, to eat. *trans.* and *intr.* or *absol.* -1640. 5. *intr.* To seize or snap *at* (bait) 1653. Also *fig.* 6. To cut into or penetrate, as a sharp-edged weapon. Also *fig.* Also *absol.* OE. 7. To cause a sharp smarting pain (to): as a blister, etc. ME. 8. *trans.* and *absol.* To affect painfully or injuriously with intense cold. Cf. *frost-bitten.* 1552. 9. To corrode, or eat into 1623. 10. *trans.* and *intr.* To grip or take hold, either by penetration or friction: used of the action of a plough, an anchor, a skate on ice, etc. 1523. Also *fig.* †11. *trans.* To speak sharply or injuriously against (cf. *backbite*). Also *intr.* -1683. 12. (*colloq.*) To 'take in'. Now only in *pass.* 1709.

1. The appulle that Adam bett 1500. 2. The dog.. went mad, and bit the man GOLDSM. 3. Saynt machaire Kylde a flee that bote hym CAXTON. 6. I haue a Sword; and it shall b. vpon my necessitie *Merry W.* II. i. 136. 8. Freize, freize, thou bitter skie that dost not bight so nigh as benefitts forgot *A. Y. L.* II. vii. 184. 9. *To b. in* in *Engraving*: to eat out etched lines with an acid. 12. 'The biter bit' (*mod.*).

Phrases. *To b. the dust, ground*, etc.: to fall in death, to die. *To b. the lip*: to restrain the expression of anger or mirth. So †*To b. one's tongue.* †*To b. the thumb at*: to put the thumb nail into the mouth, and with a jerk make it to knack (Cotgr.); to give the 'fico', to insult.

Bite (bəit), *sb.* 1499. [f. BITE *v.* Replacing BIT *sb.*[1] and [2] in various senses.] 1. The act or action of cutting, piercing, or wounding, with the teeth; also *transf.* and *fig.* b. The corrosive action of acid upon the metal plate in etching 1875. 2. The biting of food; *concr.* food to eat, as in *b. and sup* 1562. 3. *Angling.* The seizure of the bait by the fish 1653. 4. A piece bitten off (usu. to eat); a mouthful 1535. 5. A wound made with the teeth 1736. 6. The grip or hold of an edge surface in mechanical contrivances. Also *fig.* 1865. 7. *Typogr.* A blank left in printing through the accidental covering of the form by the frisket 1677. †8. *slang.* a. A deception; a 'sell'. (Cf. BITER 2.) -1726. b. A sharper -1846.

1. His bark is worse than his b. *Mod. Provb.* 4. Never make two bites of a cherry SCOTT. †8. a. What were then called bites and bams, since denominated hoaxes and quizzes SCOTT. Hence **Bi·teable, bi·table** *a.* (*rare*). **Bi·teless** *a.* that does not bite.

Biter (bəi·təɹ). ME. [f. BITE *v.*] 1. One who or that which bites. 2. *spec.* A hoaxer, a sharper. (*Obs.* exc. in 'the biter bit'.) 1680.

Bite·rnate; see BI- *pref.*[2] 3.

†**Bite-sheep.** 1553. [Cf. Ger. *beissschaf.*] A pun upon *bishop* -1683.

Your Bishops are bite-Sheep 1683.

Bitheism; see BI- *pref.*[2] II.

Biting (bəi·tiŋ), *vbl. sb.* ME. [f. BITE *v.* + -ING[1].] 1. The action of the vb. Also *fig.* †2. The wound made by a bite; the part bitten -1669. 3. *Biting in* (cf. BITE *v.* 9).

Bi·ting, *ppl. a.* ME. [f. BITE *v.* + -ING[2].] 1. That bites. 2. That causes pain or smart (*lit.* and *fig.*). In names of plants: Acrid, pungent 1597.

2. B. weather DICKENS. Too bitter, too byting, too satiricall 1611. So b. a calamity FIELDING. Hence **Bi·tingly** *adv.*

Bi·tless. 1605. [f. BIT *sb.*[1] 8.] Not having a bit.

Bi-tri- (bəiˌtrəi), *pref.* compounded of BI- *pref.*[2] and TRI-, expressing a possibility of either conformation specified; as in **bitripartite,** divided into two or three parts.

Bitt, usu. in *pl.* **bitts** (bits). 1593. [? Teut., f. root of *bītan* to bite.] *Naut.* One of the posts fastened in pairs in the deck or decks of a ship, for fastening cables, belaying ropes, etc.

The chief pair, the *riding bitts*, are used for fastening the cable while the ship rides at anchor; others are the *topsail-sheet bitts, carrick-bitts, windlass bitts*, etc. Hence **Bitt** *v.* to coil or fasten (a cable) upon the bitts.

Bittacle, obs. f. BINNACLE.

Bitten (bi·t'n), *ppl. a.* 1599. [f. BITE *v.*] 1. Cut into, pierced, or wounded with the teeth; *fig.* infected 1613. Often in comb. †2. *actively.* Biting. (Cf. *fair-spoken.*) (*rare*) 1616.

Bitter (bi·təɹ), *a.* and *sb.*[1] [Com. Teut.: OE. *biter*, prob. f. root of *bītan* to BITE, but now no longer even 'biting', or 'acrid' in taste.] A. *adj.* 1. Obnoxious, or irritating to the gustatory nerve; having the characteristic taste of wormwood, quinine, or the like; the opposite of *sweet*; causing 'the proper pain of taste' (Bain). Also *fig.* 2. *transf.* Attended by pain or suffering; grievous OE. 3. Hence, of a state: Full of affliction; mournful, pitiable 1485. 4. Expressing or betokening intense grief, or misery ME. †5. Causing suffering; cruel, severe -1635. 6. Virulent OE. 7. Of words (or the person who utters them): Stinging, harsh, cruelly reproachful, virulent ME. 8. Of wind, weather, etc.: Keen, cutting, bitingly cold 1600.

1. When I was sick, you gaue me b. pils *Two Gent.* II. iv. 149. B. truths COLERIDGE. 2. A b. moment SCOTT. *To the b. end*: to the last extremity, to death. But see BITTER *sb.*[2] 3. All our b. griefe *Tit. A.* v. iii. 89. 4. Esau..cried with a great and exceeding b. cry *Gen.* xxvii. 34. 6. A b. partisan MACAULAY. 7. A b. Foole *Lear* I. iv. 150. In b. terms ADDISON. 8. Freize, freize, thou b. skie *A. Y. L.* II. vii. 184.

B. quasi-*sb.* 1. That which is bitter; bitterness (*lit.* and *fig.*) OE. 2. A bitter medicinal substance: now usu. BITTERS, q. v. 1711. Hence †**Bi·tterful** *a.* full of bitterness. **Bi·tterish** *a.* somewhat b. **Bi·tterly** *adv.*

Bitter (bi·tər), *adv.* [OE. *bitere, bitre*, f. BITTER *a.*] = Bitterly (*arch., poet.*, and *dial.*).

Bitter-, *a.* and *adv.* in *comb.*

1. Advb. and parasynthetic, as *b.-pungent, -tasted*, etc. 2. (*adj.*) In names of plants and other productions, denoting a. a bitter variety of the plant, etc., as **b. almond, b. beer;** b. a distinct plant or substance, as **b.-apple** (= *bitter-gourd*); **-cress,** a book-name for the genus *Cardamine*, and esp. *C. amara*; **-cucumber** or **-gourd,** the Colocynth (*Citrullus Colocynthus*); **b. earth,** magnesia; **-fitch** (= *bitter-vetch*); **b. herb,** *Erythræa Centaurium*; **-king,** a tree, *Soulamea amara*, of the Eastern Archipelago; **-nut,** the Swamp Hickory, *Carya amara*, of North America; †**-salt,** Epsom salts; **-spar,** *Min.* a variety of dolomite; **-vetch,** a book-name for species of *Lathyrus* and *Vicia* formerly *Orobus*; †**-weed,** species of poplar, also a N. American species of wormwood; **-wood,** the timber of an American genus of trees *Xylopia*, also the trees; **-wort,** species of gentian, esp. *G. Amarella.*

Bitter, *sb.*[2] 1627. [f. BITT + -ER.] *Naut.* A turn of the cable round a bitt.

When a..rope is paid out to the bitter-end, no more remains to be let go SMYTH. (Hence perh. *bitter end*; but cf. BITTER *a.* 2.)

Bitter (bi·təɹ), *v.*[1] [ME. *bitt(e)re(n.*] *trans.* To make bitter; also †*fig.*

Bitterbump, var. of BUTTERBUMP, bittern.

Bi·ttering, *sb.* 1864. = BITTERN *sb.*[2] 2.

Bittern (bi·təɹn), *sb.*[1] [ME. *botor*, a. OF. *butor*, ? conn. w. rare L. *butionem* in same sense. The *-n* is prob. analogical. The zool. name *botaurus* points to a fanciful deriv. from *bos taurus*, the bittern being called *taureau d'étang, bœuf de marais*, etc.] 1. A genus of gralla-

torial birds (*Botaurus*), allied to the herons, but smaller. *spec.* The species *B. stellaris*, a native of Europe. It utters a 'boom' during the breeding season, whence its names *mire-drum*, and *bull of the bog*. See also *botaurus* above.
As a Bitore bombleth in the Myre CHAUCER.

Bittern (bi·tən), *sb.*² 1682. [perh. dial. f. *bittering*.] **1.** The lye which remains after the crystallization of common salt from sea-water, etc. Also *attrib.* **2.** An old trade name for a mixture of quassia and other drugs employed in adulterating beer; called also *bitterin(g)* 1775.

Bitterness (bi·tənės). [OE. *biternys.*] The quality or state of being bitter: **a.** to taste; **b.** to the mind or feelings; **c.** anguish of heart; **d.** animosity, acrimony; **e.** intensity of cold. †*concr.* Anything bitter –1790.
In the bitternesse of my soule *Isa.* xxxviii. 15. The bittrenesse of the aloe tre 1477. The bitternesse..of the Winter MARKHAM.

Bitters (bi·təɹz), *sb. pl.* 1713. [f. BITTER *sb.*¹] Bitter medicines generally, as quinine, etc.; *spec.* alcoholic (or other) liquors, impregnated with the extract of gentian, quassia, orange peel, or the like, and used as stomachics, etc. (Also in *sing.*)

Bitter-sweet (bi·təɹ,swīt). ME. **A.** *adj.* Sweet with an admixture or aftertaste of bitterness; also *fig.* **B.** *sb.* **1.** A thing which is bitter-sweet (*lit.* and *fig.*) ME. **2.** A kind of apple ME. **3.** *Herb.* The Woody Nightshade, *Solanum Dulcamara* 1568.

†**Bi·tter-swee:ting.** [f. prec.] The Bitter-sweet Apple. *Rom. & Jul.* II. iv. 83.

Bi·ttock. *n. dial.* 1802. [dim. of BIT *sb.*²] A little bit.

Bittor, -our, obs. ff. BITTERN, the bird.

Bitts, *sb. Naut.*; see BITT *sb.*

†**Bitume,** *v.* [f. *bitume*, obs. f. BITUMEN.] To smear or spread with bitumen. SHAKS.

Bitumen (bitiū·mėn, bitiū·mėn). 1460. [a. L., stem *bitumin-*.] **1.** Orig., a kind of mineral pitch found in Palestine and Babylon, used as mortar, etc.; Jew's pitch. **2.** Generic name of native hydrocarbons more or less oxygenated, including naphtha, petroleum, asphalt, etc. **3.** A pigment prepared from asphalt 1855. Also *attrib.* Hence **Bitu·minate** *v.* to cement with b.; to convert into or impregnate with b. **Bitu:mini·ferous** *a.* yielding b. **Bitu·minize** *v.* to convert into, or impregnate with, b.; to varnish with b.; whence **Bitu:miniza·tion.** **Bitu·minoid** *a.* resembling b.

Bituminous (bitiū·minəs), *a.* 1620. [a. F. *bitumineux*, ad. L. *bituminosus.*] **a.** Of the nature of, consisting of, or containing bitumen. **b.** *spec.* as in *b. coal, limestone, schist, shale; cement, mastic* 1830. Also *fig.*
1. The Plain, wherein a black b. gurge Boiles out from under ground, the mouth of Hell MILT. *P. L.* xii. 41.

Bivalent (bi·vălėnt), *a.* 1869. [f. BI- *pref.*² III + *-valent*, ad. L. *valentem*, *valere.*] *Chem.* Combining with two atoms of an element or radicle; also *divalent*. Hence **Bi·valency,** the property of being b.

Bivalve (bəi·vælv). 1661. [f. BI- *pref.*² I + VALVE.] **A.** *adj.* †**1.** Having two folding parts 1677. **2.** *Zool.* Having two shells united by a hinge 1661. **3.** *Bot.* Having two valves 1737. vars. **Bi·valved, Biva·lvous, Biva·lvular. B.** *sb.* **1.** *pl.* Folding-doors. *Hist.* 1832. **2.** *Zool.* A mollusc having a shell consisting of two halves joined together by an elastic ligament at the hinge, so as to open and shut like a book; e.g. the oyster, mussel, etc. Also the shell of such animal. 1683. **3.** *Bot.* A bivalve seed-vessel.

Bivaulted; see BI- *pref.*² I.

Biventer (bəive·ntəɹ). 1706. [See BI- *pref.*² II.] *Phys.* A muscle having two bellies; *esp.* the digastric muscle. Hence **Bive·ntral** *a.*

Bive·rb. *rare.* 1831. [See BI- *pref.*² II.] A name composed of two words. **Bive·rbal** *a.* relating to two words; punning (*rare*).

Bivial (bi·viăl), *a.* 1877. [f. BIVIUM + -AL¹.] *Phys.* Of or pertaining to the *bivium*.

Bivious (bi·viəs), *a.* 1644. [f. L. *bivius*, f. *bi-* + *via*.] Having or offering two ways.

‖**Bivium** (bi·viŏm). 1877. [a. L.; see prec.] The two hinder ambulacra of Echinoderms.

Bivocal (bəivōᵘ·kăl). 1813. [f. BI- *pref.*² II + VOCAL.] A combination of two vowels, a diphthong. **Bivo·calized** *ppl. a.* placed between two vowels.

Bivouac (bi·vwæk, bi·vu,æk). 1706. [a. F. *bivouac, bivac*, prob. from dial. (Swiss) Ger. *beiwacht*, a patrol of citizens added to assist the town watch by night.] **1.** *Mil.* Orig., a night-watch by a whole army under arms, to prevent surprise; now, a temporary encampment under improvised shelter or none; also, the place of this. **2.** A camping out 1853.

Bivouac, *v.* 1809. [f. prec.] *Mil.* Of troops: To remain, *esp.* during the night, in the open air, without tents, etc. Also *transf.*
1. The Carrousel, where about 2000 Prussians are bivouacked 1815.

Biw-; see BEW-, BYW-.

‖**Bixa** (bi·ksă). 1879. [Central Amer.] A genus of small trees, from the fruits of one of which (*B. orellana*) the dye anatta is prepared. **Bixin,** the colouring principle of anatta.

Biz. 1865. Colloq. abbrev. BUSINESS.

Bizant, Bizantine, obs. ff. BEZANT, BYZANTINE.

Bizarre (bizā·ɹ, as F. biza·r'), *a.* 1648. [a. F. *bizarre* 'odd', formerly 'soldier-like'; cf. Sp. and Pg. *bizarro* 'handsome, brave'.] Eccentric, whimsical, odd; grotesque, irregular.
Her attire seemed as bizarre as her person LD. HERBERT. B. tulips 1843. Hence ‖**Biza·rrerie,** b. quality.

Bizcacha, var. of BISCACHA.

Bizel, obs. f. BEZEL.

Bizygomatic (bəi:zigəmæ·tik), *a.* 1878. [f. BI- *pref.*² I. 5 + ZYGOMATIC.] Joining the two zygomatic arches.

Blab (blæb), *sb.*¹ ME. [? echoic. Not the source of *blabber* v., which is earlier. Cf. *labbe* 'blabber' (Chaucer), and BABBLE.] **1.** One who does not control his tongue; a babbler, or tell-tale; used also of the tongue. **2.** Loose chatter ME. Also in *comb.*
1. To be..avoided as a b. MILT. *Sams.* 491.

Blab, *sb.*² *Obs.* exc. *dial.* 1656. [var. of BLEB, BLOB.] A bubble; a blister. Hence **B.-lipped** = Blabber-lipped.

Blab, *v.*¹ 1535. [App. f. *blabbe*, BLAB *sb.*¹] †**1.** *trans.* To utter with open mouth; usually with *out*. Also *absol.* –1598. **2.** *trans.* To open one's mouth about; to reveal indiscreetly 1583. **3.** *intr.* To talk indiscreetly, to betray secrets 1601. **4.** *trans.* (*transf.*) To bewray 1597.
2. Ile blabb all, and not sticke to tell 1589. To b. out a secret 1869. **3.** Mum's the Word, I never b. 1747. **4.** Beaufords red sparkling eyes b. his hearts mallice 2 *Hen. IV*, III. i. 154. Hence **Bla·bber** *sb.*

†**Blab,** *v.*² 1601. [f. BLAB *sb.*²] To make swollen (the cheeks) –1719.

†**Bla·bber,** *a.* 1483. [First in comb. *blabyrlypped*. Cf. BLOB, BLUBBER, BUBBLE.] Swollen, protruding; said of the lips and cheeks –1800.

†**Blabber,** *v.* [ME. *blaberen*: cf. BABBLE. See also BLAB.] **1.** *intr.* To make sounds with the lips and tongue as an infant (cf. sense 3); to babble, mumble –1800. **2.** *intr.* To chatter –1483. Also *trans.* **3.** To move the tongue between the lips in mockery –1629. Hence †**Bla·bberer.**

Black (blæk), *a.* [OE. *blæc, blac* (def. *blace*) = OHG. *blah-, blach-* (in comb.). In OE. often confused w. *blac* shining, white:—OTeut. **blaiko-* (see BLAKE). For conjectural Teut. types see N. E. D. In Eng. *black* has ousted SWART.] **1.** As a colour pertaining to objects, even in full light: Absorbing all light; 'of the colour of night' (J.); 'of the colour of soot or coal'; 'of the darkest possible hue'; swart. **b.** Having a very dark skin, as negroes or negritos; *loosely*, swarthy OE. **c.** *fig.* Of or pertaining to the negro race 1852. **2.** Characterized in some way by this colour OE. **3.** Characterized by absence of light ME. **4.** Soiled, dirty ME. **5.** *fig.* Having dark purposes, malignant; deadly; baneful, disastrous, sinister 1583. **6.** *fig.* Foul, iniquitous, atrocious 1581. **7.** *fig.* Dismal, gloomy, sad 1659. **b.** Of the countenance, the 'look' of things: Clouded with anger; threatening, boding ill 1709. **8.** *fig.* Indicating disgrace, censure, etc. Cf. BLACK BOOKS, LIST, etc. 1612.
1. B. velwet 1536, Chimney-sweepers SHAKS., hair 1611, port-wine 1859. **c.** The b. blood..in my veins STEVENSON. **2.** The blak dowglass BARBOUR. How if she be Blacke and Witty *Oth.* II. i. 133. **3.** The blacke winter night GOWER. The heauen was blacke with cloudes 1 *Kings* xviii. 45. **5.** That b. Name, Edward, b. Prince of Wales *Hen. V*, II. iv. 56. A b. augury BYRON. **6.** B. ingratitude 1738. A. b. lie 1839. **7.** B. despair 1809, looks 1840. *To look b.*: to look angrily (*at* or *upon*).
Phrases. **B. and blue**: discoloured by beating, etc., so as to have b. and blue or livid bruises. **B. and tan** (of a terrier dog): having the back b., and tan (yellowish brown) upon the face, flank, and legs. Also *ellipt.* as *sb.* **B. and white**: **a.** *adj.* Having a surface diversified with b. and white. **b.** *sb.* Black characters upon white paper; writing. Phr. *In b. and white*: in writing or in print. **c.** *Art.* (A sketch, etc. in) black tint on white paper, or with white colour used.
Comb. (For such as **b. cattle, coal, draught,** etc. see CATTLE, COAL, etc.) **b.-band,** an earthy carbonate of iron found in the coal measures, and containing coaly matter; †**b. canon,** a canon regular of St. Augustine; **b. character** = BLACK-LETTER; **-coat,** parson (*depreciative*); **B. Country,** a name given to parts of Staffordshire and Warwickshire blackened by the coal and iron trades; **b.-fellow,** an Australian aboriginal; **-heart** (for *black* HEART-CHERRY), a dark sort of cultivated cherry; **b. note** *Mus.*, a note with a solid (black) head, as a crotchet (opp. to *white note*); **b. quarter,** a disease of cattle (= BLACK-LEG 1); **b. rent,** black mail, an illegal tribute; **-seed,** the b. Medick; **b. strap** (or **stripe**), an inferior port wine, also a mixture of rum and treacle; **b. sugar** (*Sc.*), liquorice juice; **B. Watch**: see WATCH *sb.* II. 8; **-wort,** the Comfrey. Hence **Bla·ckish** *a.* somewhat b. **Bla·ckly** *adv.*

Black, *sb.* ME. [The adj. used absol.] **1.** Black colour or hue. Also in pl. **2.** A black paint, dye, or varnish, as *lamp b., Brunswick b.*, etc. 1573. **3.** A black speck; *spec.* the smut in wheat, a flake of soot, etc. ME. †**4.** The dark spot in the centre of the eye –1648. **5.** Black fabric or material; as black clothing, funereal hangings, etc. 1608. **6.** = Black man or woman: **a.** A negro, negrito, etc. 1625. †**b.** One of a band of poachers who went about their work with blackened faces. *attrib.* in *black-act* (9 Geo. I. xxii). –1809.
1. Knowe what whyte is, and it is soone perceyued what blacke is 1526. **3.** If you see a b. on my nose, tell me so DICKENS. **5.** Neither are all that weare blackes his mourners 1636. **6. a.** The mouth of the Riuer [Gambra] where dwell the Blackes, called Mandingos PURCHAS.

Black (blæk), *v.* ME. [f. BLACK *a.*] †**1.** *intr.* To be or become black –1460. **2.** *trans.* To make black; now *esp.* to put black colour on ME.; to clean and polish with BLACKING 1557. **3.** *fig.* To sully; to defame. (Usu. *blacken.*) 1440.
2. Causing his shoos to be blacked 1684. The Russian censor who blacks out all matter that is displeasing to the Government GEN. GORDON.

Blackamoor (blæ·kămūᵊɹ, -mōᵊɹ). 1547. [= *Black Moor* (also used); the connecting *a* is unexplained. Cf. *black-a-vised.*] **1.** A Negro; any very dark-skinned person. (Now a nickname.) Also *attrib.* **2.** *attrib.* Quite black 1813.
1. The Negro's, which we call the Blacke-Mores RALEIGH. **2.** Some b. rook 1856.

Black art. 1590. [Prob. 'black' = 'dark and secret', or 'devilish'; but the name is also associated with med.L. *nigromantia*, corrupt f. *necromantia.*] **1.** Magic, necromancy †**2.** *Thieves' slang.* Lock-picking –1608.

Black-a-vised (blæ·kăvəi:st), *a. n. dial.* Also **-viced, -vized.** 1758. [f. BLACK *a.* and F. *vis* face; ? *black-à-vis*, or *black o' vis.*] Dark-complexioned.

Black-ball, bla·ckball, *sb.* 1847. **1.** A composition used by shoemakers, etc., and also for taking rubbings of brasses and the like; a *heel-ball.* **2.** A black ball of wood, etc., dropped into the urn to express an adverse vote; *hence*, an adverse secret vote 1869.

Blackball (blæ·kbǫl), *v.* 1770. [See prec.] **1.** To exclude from a club, etc. by adverse votes, recorded by placing black balls in the ballot-box, or in other ways. **2.** To exclude from society, taboo 1840. **3.** To blacken with black-ball 1818.
1. I shall make a note to b. him at the Athenæum DISRAELI. Hence **Bla·ckballer.**

Blackberry (blæ·kberi). OE. **1.** The fruit of the bramble (*Rubus fruticosus*), and its varieties. Also *attrib.* **2.** The bramble 1579. **3.** Now, in the north, the Black Currant (*Ribes* *nigrum*), formerly in some localities the Bilberry 1567.

1. If Reasons were as plentie as Black-berries [etc.] 1 *Hen. IV*, II. iv. 265. Hence **Bla·ckbe·rrying** *vbl. sb.* the gathering of blackberries. Cf. NUTTING.

Blackbird (blæ·kbəɹd). 1486. [The only BIRD in an earlier sense (before crows and rooks were included) which is *black.*] **a.** A species of thrush (*Merula turdus*, L.). In N. America the name is given to other birds, e. g. the *Gracula quiscala*, and *Oriolus* (*Agelaius*) *phœniceus.* **b.** *loosely* = Songster.

Black board, bla·ckboard. 1823. A large wooden board, or the like, painted black, and used in schools, etc. to draw or write upon with chalk.

Black book. 1479. **1.** An official book bound in black 1624. **2. a.** *Black Book of the Exchequer*: a book kept in the Exchequer Office, containing an official account of the royal revenues, etc. (? *c* 1175). **b.** *Black book of the Admiralty*: an ancient code of rules for the government of the navy, compiled in the reign of Edw. III. **3.** An official return prepared in the reign of Henry VIII, containing the reports of the visitors upon the abuses in the monasteries 1581. **4.** A book recording the names of persons who have incurred censure or punishment 1592. **5.** A book of necromancy 1842.

4. *To be in* (*any one's*) *black books*: to be out of his favour.

Black-browed, *ppl. a.* 1590. Having a dark brow or front; frowning, scowling.

Black cap, bla·ck-cap, bla·ckcap. **1.** *Black cap*: spec. that worn by English judges when in full dress, and assumed when passing sentence of death upon a prisoner 1838. **2.** One who wears a black cap 1856. **3.** *Blackcap*: A bird having the top of the head black, as the Blackcap Warbler, *Curruca* (or *Motacilla*) *atricapilla*. Also, in U.S., *Parus atricapillus*, the Blackcap Tit or Chickadee. 1678.

Blackcock (blæ·k,kǫk). 1427. The male of the Black Grouse or BLACK GAME.

Black death; see DEATH.

Black dog. 1706. †**1.** A cant name for a base silver coin –1724. **2.** *fig.* Depression of spirits; ill-humour 1826.

Black drop. 1823. **1.** *Med.* A dark-coloured medicine, chiefly opium, with vinegar and spices. **2.** *Astron.* A dark drop-like appearance observed at solar transits of Venus and Mercury 1869.

Blacken (blæ·k'n), *v.* [ME. *blakne*(*n*, *blakone*(*n*, f. BLACK *a.*] **1.** *intr.* To become black (*lit.* and *fig.*). **2.** *trans.* To make black or dark (*lit.* and *fig.*) 1552.

1. To b. into cynicism MORLEY. 2. Calumnies, tho' they do not burn, yet b. DRUMM. OF HAWTH. The Birds.. blackening all the air KINGSLEY. Hence **Bla·ckener.**

Black eye. 1604. **1.** An eye of which the iris is very dark-coloured 1667. Hence **Black-eyed** *a.* **2.** A discoloration of the flesh around the eye produced by a blow 1604.

Bla·ck-face. 1844. A black-faced sheep or other animal.

Bla·ck-faced, *a.* 1592. **1.** Having a black or dark-coloured face. Also *fig.* 1594. **2.** Of things: Dark, gloomy.

Black fish. 1754. **1.** A name of several varieties of Eng. and Amer. fishes; *e.g.* the Black Ruff (a kind of perch), *Centrolophus pompilus* (a kind of mackerel), *Tautoga Americana* (a species of wrasse). **2.** A small species of whale 1796. **3.** A name given to salmon just after spawning; whence **Black-fisher. Black-fishing,** the taking of these; in Scotland, *esp.* by torchlight at night 1808.

Black flag. 1593. A flag of black cloth, used with reference to death or deadly purpose; *e.g.* as a sign that no quarter will be given or asked, as the ensign of pirates, and as a signal of the execution of a criminal. Also in *pl.* used of the pirates of the Chinese Sea, etc.

Black foot. 1842. One of a tribe of N. Amer. Indians.

Black friar. 1500. One of the Dominican friars, so called from the colour of their dress. Hence in *pl.*, the quarters of these friars, in London or elsewhere. 1583.

Black game. 1678. Black Grouse (*Tetrao tetrix*), of which the male is called BLACKCOCK, and the female *grey hen.*

Blackguard (blæ·gǟɹd). 1532. [lit. *Black Guard*, of uncertain application.] **A.** *sb.* †**1.** The scullions and kitchen-knaves of a royal or noble household, who had charge of pots and pans, etc. –1678. †**b.** The servants and camp-followers of an army. Also *fig.* –1702. †**2.** A guard of attendants, black in person, dress, or character –1705. †**3.** The vagabond or criminal class of a community –1768; *esp.* the shoeblacks –1736. †**4.** A guard black in person, dress, or character. Also *fig.* Cf. 2. –1745. †**5.** A street shoe-black; a 'city Arab' –1785. **6.** One of the criminal class; hence, an unprincipled scoundrel. (A highly opprobrious term.) 1736. **7.** A kind of snuff. Also called *Irish b.* 1792.

1. Ye have lyen among the Pots, black and sooty, as the black guard of an army TRAPP. 4. Satan..placed his Black Guards there 1696. 5. The little b. who gets very hard His halfpence for cleaning your shoes SWIFT. 6. And cheat like ony unhang'd b. BURNS.

B. *attrib.* or *adj.* †**1.** Of or pertaining to the shoe-black or street Arab class –1822. **2.** Blackguardly 1784.

2. I have heard him use language as b. as his action BYRON.

Hence **Bla·ckguardism,** blackguardly conduct or language. **Bla·ckguardly** *adj.* characteristic of a b., ruffianly, low; *adv.* after the manner of a b. **Bla·ckguardry** (*rare*) = BLACKGUARD *sb.* 3.

Blackguard (blæ·gaɹd), *v.* 1786. [f. prec. sb.] **1.** *intr.* To act the blackguard (senses 3, 6). **2.** *trans.* To treat as a blackguard; to abuse or revile in scurrilous terms 1823.

Black-head (blæ·khed). 1658. **1.** A name of certain black-headed birds. **2.** Acne 1885.

Black-hole, Black Hole. 1758. (Beside obvious application to any black hole:) **1.** *Mil.* The punishment cell in a barracks; the guard-room. (The name has become historic in connexion with the Black Hole of Fort William, Calcutta, into which 146 Europeans were thrust for a whole night in 1756, of whom only 23 were alive next morning.) **2.** *gen.* A place of confinement for punishment 1831.

Blacking (blæ·kiŋ), *vbl. sb.* 1571. [f. BLACK *v.*] **1.** The action of making black 1609. †**2.** Lamp-black 1594. **3.** Any preparation for making black; *esp.* for giving a shining black surface to boots and shoes 1571.

Black Jack, bla·ck-jack. 1513. **1.** A large leather beer-jug, coated with tar. ? *Obs.* 1591. **2.** Mining term for zinc sulphide or blende 1747. **3.** *U.S.* A kind of oak (*Quercus nigra*) 1856. †**4.** *Sc.* A black leather jerkin; see JACK –1820. **5.** The mustard beetle 1886.

Black lead, black-lea·d, bla·cklead. 1583. †**1.** A black ore of LEAD. **2.** Name of the mineral plumbago or graphite, consisting of almost pure carbon with a little iron; it is chiefly used in the form of pencils, and as a polish for iron-work. (The name preceded the knowledge of its composition.) 1583. **b.** A pencil of this substance 1656. Also *attrib.* Hence **Black-lea·d** *v.* to colour or rub with, or draw in, black-lead.

Bla·ck-leg, -legs. 1722. **1.** A disease in cattle and sheep which affects the legs. (Better *black-legs.*) **2.** A turf swindler; a sharper generally 1771. **3.** Opprobrious term for: A workman willing to work for a master whose men are on strike 1865. Hence **Bla·ck-leg** *v.*, to take the place of a worker on strike. **Black-le·ggery, -le·gism,** profession or practice of a b.

Bla·ck-letter, black letter, bla·ckletter. **1.** A name (dating from *c* 1600) for the type used by the early printers, a form of which is still in regular use in Germany, and, as 'Gothic' or 'Old English', in occasional use in England. **2.** Anything printed in this type 1811. **3.** *attrib.* (Usu. w. hyphen, or as one wd.) 1791.

1. The Seven champions in the black-letter ARBUTHNOT. *Black letter day*: an inauspicious day; as distinguished from *e.g.* a saint's-day, marked in the calendar with red letters.

Black list. 1692. **1.** A list of persons who have incurred suspicion, censure, or punishment; cf. BLACK *a.* 8. **2.** *fig.* A list of bad cases 1853. **Bla·ck-list** *v.* to enter in a black list.

Black mail. 1552. Also **black-mail, blackmail.** [f. MAIL = rent, tribute.] **1.** *Hist.* A tribute formerly exacted from small owners in the border districts of England and Scotland, by freebooting chiefs, in return for immunity from plunder. **2.** Hence, Any payment extorted by intimidation 1840. †**3.** *Law.* Rent reserved in labour, produce, etc., opp. to 'white rents', reserved in white money or silver –1768.

1. The boldest of them will never steal a hoof from any one that pays black-mail to Vich Ian Vohr SCOTT. Hence **Black-mai·l** *v.* to levy black mail upon; to extort money by the unscrupulous use of an official or social position, or of political influence or vote. **Black-mai·ler.**

Black Maria. 1874. A prison van for the conveyance of prisoners.

Black mark. 1845. A mark made against the name of a person who has incurred censure, penalty, etc. Also *fig.*

Black Monday; see MONDAY.

Black Monk. ME. See MONK.

Black moor, more; see BLACKAMOOR.

Bla·ck-mouth. 1642. A black-mouthed person or animal; *fig.* a slanderer. So †**Black-mou·thed** *a.* having a black mouth; also *fig.*

Bla·ck-neb. *dial.* 1802. [See NEB, beak.] **1.** Name for black-billed birds, as the Crane and the Common Crow. †**2.** *Sc.* A person of democratic sympathies at the time of the French Revolution –1864.

Bla·ckness. ME. [f. BLACK *a.* + -NESS.] The quality or state of being black.

The spots of Heauen, More fierie by nights Blacknesse *Ant. & Cl.* I. iv. 13.

Black nob, ox; see NOB, OX.

†**Bla·ck-pot.** 1590. A beer-mug (cf. BLACK-JACK); a toper –1818.

Black Prince. 1563. **1.** A name given to the eldest son of Edw. III. [The explanations current are guess-work.] †**2.** The prince of darkness, the devil 1589.

Black pudding. (Also hyphened.) 1568. A sausage made of blood and suet.

Black Rod. 1632. Short for *Gentleman Usher of the Black Rod*, so called from his symbol of office. The chief Gentleman usher of the Lord Chamberlain's department of the royal household, and also usher to the House of Lords, and to the Chapter of the Garter. Also, a similar office in colonial legislatures.

Black salts. 1880. Impure potassium hydrate. Hence **Bla·ck-salter,** a maker of this.

Black sheep; see SHEEP *sb.* 2 c.

Bla·ckshirt. 1923. [tr. It.] = FASCIST.

Blacksmith (blæ·ksmiþ). 1483. A smith who works in iron or black metal, as opp. to a 'whitesmith' who works in tin.

Black-snake. 1688. **1.** A name for dark-coloured snakes; as in U. S. the *Coluber constrictor* and *C. Alleghaniensis*; in Jamaica the *Natrix atra.* **2.** *U. S.* A long whip-lash 1883.

Bla·ck-tail. 1661. †**1.** An unkn. sea fish; the *melanurus* of ancient writers. **2.** A name for varieties of the perch 1734.

Bla·ck-thorn. ME. **1.** A common thorny shrub, bearing white flowers before the leaves and very small dark purple plums; the Sloe (*Prunus spinosa*). **b.** A walking-stick made of the stem of this 1849. Also *attrib.* **2.** *U.S.* A hawthorn (*Cratægus tomentosa*) 1864.

Bla·ck-wash. 1818. **1.** *Med.* A lotion of calomel and lime-water. **2.** Any composition used for washing over and blackening 1861. Hence **Bla·ckwash** *v.* to wash with a black liquid; *fig.* to calumniate.

Bla·ckwater. †**1.** A dark-coloured stream 1678. **2.** A disease of cattle 1800. **3.** *B. fever*, a tropical disease characterized by dark-coloured urine 1884.

Bla·ck-wood, blackwood. 1631. A name given to various trees and their dark-coloured timber.

Blacky (blæ·ki), *sb. colloq.* Also **-ie, -ey.** 1815. A black, negro. Cf. *darky.*

Bla·cky, *a.* 1594. [f. BLACK *a.*] Blackish.

Blad, *sb.*[1] *Sc.* 1715. [f. BLAD *v.*] A firm flat blow.

Blad, *sb.*[2] *Sc.* Also **blaud.** 1527. [? f. as prec.] A fragment, piece, lump.

Blad, *v. Sc.* 1524. [? echoic.] To slap heavily.

Bladder (blæ·dəɹ). [Com. Teut.: OE. *blǣdre, blǣdre* :—OTeut. **blǣ-drôn-*, f. stem *blǣ-* to BLOW + *-drôn*, cogn. w. Gr. -τρα, -τρον.] **1.** *orig.* The musculo-membranous bag which receives the urinary fluid; the *urinary b.* **b.** Any membranous bag in the animal body; usu. defined, as *gall-, air-, swimming-b.* 1661. †**2.** A boil, blister, pustule –1607. **3.** The prepared bladder of an animal, used as a float, as part of a bagpipe, etc. ME. **4.** A vesicle, a bubble 1702. **5.** *fig.* Anything inflated and hollow; a 'wind-bag' 1579. **6.** *Bot.* An inflated pericarp 1578; a hollow vesicle, as in various seaweeds 1789. Also *attrib.*

3. Boyes that swim on bladders *Hen. VIII*, III. ii. 359. 5. Prick the b. of our pride SANDERSON. Them that are..bladders full of winde 1579.

Comb.: **b.-campion**, *Silene inflata*, named from the inflated calyx; **-fern**, a fern of the genus *Cystopteris*; **-green**, a pigment obtained from the Common Buckthorn, sap-green; **-kelp**, = *bladder-wrack*; **-nose**, a species of seal; **-nut**, the fruit of *Staphylea pinnata*, contained in b.-like pods; also the shrub; **-pod**, the *Physolobium*, a species of *Leguminosæ*; the American B.-pod is *Vesicaria Shortii*; **-seed**, the *Physospermum*, named from the loose outer coating of the undeveloped fruit; **-senna**, the *Colutea arborescens*, with distended pods; **-tangle**, **-weed**, = *bladder-wrack*; **-wort**, a genus of water-plants, *Utricularia*, with small bags on roots, stems, and leaves, filled with air; **-wrack**, a species of sea-weed (*Fucus vesiculosus*), with air-bladders in the fronds. Hence **Bla·dderet** (*Phys.*), a small b.; a vesicle. **Bla·ddery** *a.* of the nature of a b. (*lit.* and *fig.*); abounding in bladders or vesicles.

Bladder, *v.* 1440. [f. prec.] †**1.** *intr.* To swell out like, or into, a bladder –1543. †**2.** *trans.* To inflate –1649. **3.** To put into a bladder, as 'bladdered lard'.

Blade (blēɪd). [Com. Teut.: OE. *blæd*, neut.:—OTeut. **blado(m*, perh. f. OTeut. stem **blô-*, see BLOW *v.*[2], cogn. w. L. *flos.* In OE. *blæd* for 'leaf' or 'foliage' occurs only once; in ME. not at all.] **1.** The leaf of a herb or plant; *esp.* the leaves of grass and cereals; also, the whole plant before the ear appears. Cf. 2. 1450. **2.** *Bot.* The broad, thin, expanded part of a leaf or petal; the lamina 1835. **3.** The broad, flattened part of any instrument or utensil, as a spade, bat, paddle, oar OE. **4.** The thin cutting part of an edged tool or weapon; often put poetically for the whole weapon, etc. ME. Also *fig.* **5.** The *shoulder-blade* or scapula ME. **6.** *Archit.* The principal rafter of a roof 1851. **7.** A gallant, a free and easy fellow; 'fellow'. (Now colloq. or slangy: in lit. use, a reminiscence of last century.) 1592.

1. First the b., then the eare, after that the full corne in the eare *Mark* iv. 28. Phr. *In the b.*: i. e. not yet in the ear. 4. The haft also went in after the b. *Judges* iii. 22. And by his syde he baar a rusty b. CHAUCER. 7. A b. whom I took for a decent tailor COBBETT. A knowing b. DICKENS. A keen Yorkshire b. 1882. *Comb.*: **b.-bone**, the shoulder-b., the corresponding bone of animals and 'joint' of meat; **-fish**, a Ribbon-fish (*Trichiurus lepturus*). Hence **Bla·dy** *a.* characterized by a b., or blades; blade-like.

Blade (blēɪd), *v.* 1440. [f. prec. sb.] **1.** To take off the BLADES (sense 1). *dial.* **2.** To provide with a (cutting) blade. **3.** *intr.* To put forth blades 1601.

Bladed (blēɪ·dĕd), *ppl. a.* 1578. [f. as prec.] **1.** Lanceolate. **2.** Having a blade or blades 1590. **3.** ? Not yet in full ear *Macb.* IV. i. 55. **4.** Stripped of the blades 1611. **5.** *Min.* Having a structure characterized by long narrow plates.

Blae (blē, bliə, blī), *a.* (*sb.*) Now *Sc.* and *n. dial.* [ME. *blo*, n. dial. *bla*, a. ON. *blá*, dark blue, livid :—OTeut. **blaw* :—**blǣwo-z* blue.] **A.** *adj.* **1.** Blackish blue; livid; also, bluish grey, lead-coloured. **2.** Bleak, sunless 1513. **B.** *sb.* A kind of soft slate 1724.

Blaeberry (blē·beri, bliə·-). 1562. [f. BLAE + BERRY.] Sc. and north. name of the BILBERRY, fruit and plant.

‖**Blague** (blag), *sb.* 1837. [Fr.] Humbug. Hence ‖**Blague** *v.* to tell lies.

Blain (blēɪn). [OE. *blegen* = Du. *blein.*] **1.** A blister, botch, pustule. Cf. CHILBLAIN. **2.** A bladder growing on the root of the tongue of beasts against the windpipe 1727. Hence **Blain** *v.* to affect with blains.

Blake, *a. Obs.* exc. *dial.* ME. [prob. f. OE. *blác* pale = OTeut. **blaiko-z*, f. root of *blīkan* to shine, BLIKE. See BLACK.] **1.** Pallid, wan; of a sickly hue. **2.** Yellow (*local*) 1691. Hence †**Blake** *v.* to become pale.

Blame (blēɪm), *v.* ME. [a. OF. *blâmer, blasmer* :—late L. *blasphemare*, ad. Gr. βλασφημεῖν to BLASPHEME.] **1.** *trans.* To find fault with. †**2.** To reprove –1559. †**3.** To bring into disrepute –1611. †**4.** To accuse (*of, with*) –1649. **5.** To lay the blame on ME.

1. Goe girle, I cannot b. thee now to weepe *Tam. Shr.* III. ii. 27. 5. She has nobody to b. for it but herself ADDISON. Phr. *To b.*: in 16–17th c. *to* was taken as *too*, and *blame* as = blameworthy. The King mine Vnkle is too b. for it *Rich. III*, II. ii. 13. Hence **Bla·meable, bla·mable** *a.* **Bla·meably, bla·mably** *adv.* **Bla·mer.**

Blame (blēɪm), *sb.* ME. [a. OF. *blâme, blasme*; see prec.] **1.** The action of censuring; imputation of demerit on account of a fault; reproof; reprehension. †**2.** A charge –1581. **3.** Blameworthiness; fault (*arch.*) ME. **4.** Responsibility for anything wrong ME.

1. The contrary to Fame and Applause, to wit, B. and Derision 1709. 3. Holy and without b. *Ephes.* i. 4. 4. He took all the b. on himself MORLEY. Hence **Bla·meful** *a.* blaming, fully meriting b. **Bla·mefully** *adv.*, **-ness.** **Bla·meless** *a.* uncensured; undeserving of b. **Bla·melessly** *adv.*, **-ness.** **Bla·meworthy. Bla·meworthiness.**

Blancard (blæ·ŋkāɹd). 1848. [a. F. (also *blanchard*), f. *blanc* + -ARD.] A linen cloth woven in Normandy, the thread of which is half bleached before it is woven.

Blanch (blɑnʃ), *sb.* 1601. [f. BLANCH *a.*, and *v.*] †**1.** White paint (esp. for the face) –1610. †**2.** A white spot on the skin –1609. **3.** *Min.* 'Lead ore mixed with other minerals'. Raymond.

Blanch, *a. Obs.* exc. *Hist.* ME. [a. OF. *blanche*, fem. of *blanc*: see BLANK.] †**1.** White, pale, as *b. sauce*, etc. –1586. **2.** *Her.* White, argent 1697. **3.** *Blanch*, Sc. *blench*; more fully *b. farm, blench ferme*: Rent paid in silver; in Sc. writers any nominal quit-rent 1602. As *adv.* = In blench.

Blanch (blɑnʃ), *v.*[1] ME. [a. F. *blanchir*, f. *blanc*. Cf. also BLANK *v.*] **1.** To make white, whiten: now chiefly by depriving of colour; to bleach; *spec.* to make (metals) white. Also *fig.* **2.** *Cookery.* To whiten almonds, etc. by taking off the skin; *hence*, to scald in order to remove the skin ME. **3.** To whiten plants by depriving them of light 1669. **4.** To palliate, to 'whitewash'. (Now only with *over.*) 1549. **5.** *intr.* To turn white; to bleach; to pale 1768.

1. Age had blanched his hair MERIVALE. The famine blanches your lips RUSKIN. 4. To b. and varnish her deformities MILT. 5. As when the rolling breakers boom and b. on the precipices TENNYSON. Hence **Bla·ncher**[1].

Blanch, *v.*[2] 1572. [var. of BLENCH, q.v.] †**1.** To bilk –1602. †**2.** To blink (a fact); to pass without notice –1671. **3.** *intr.* To start back (*arch.*) 1572. **4.** *trans.* To turn off, aside, away; to head back (deer) 1592

3. 'Tis no time to b. 1572. Hence **Bla·ncher**[2], one who heads back (deer), etc.

†**Blanch**, *v.*[3] 1572. [Worn down f. *blandish.*] *intr.* = BLANDISH *v.* 2. –1612.

Bookes will speake plaine, when Counsellors B. BACON.

Blanchimeter (blɑnʃi·mɪtəɹ). 1847. [f. BLANCH + -METER.] An instrument for measuring the blanching power of chloride of lime and potash; a chlorometer.

Blancmange, -manger (blămā·nʒ, -mɒ·nʒ, -mā·nʒ). [In 14th c. *blancmanger*, a. OF. *blancmanger*, 'white eating'. The pronunc. is that of the 18th c. *blomange, blamange.*] †**a.** Formerly: A dish of fowl minced with cream, rice, almonds, sugar, eggs, etc. **b.** Now: A sweetmeat made of dissolved isinglass or gelatine boiled with milk, etc., and forming an opaque white jelly. Also *fig.* (cf. *flummery.*)

ffor blankmanger that made he with the beste CHAUCER.

Bland (blænd), *sb.* 1703. [a. ON. *blanda*, a mixture of fluids.] In Orkney and Shetland, a beverage made of buttermilk and water.

Bland (blænd), *a.* 1661. [ad. L. *blandus.*] **1.** Smooth and suave; mildly soothing or coaxing; gentle. **2.** Of things: soft, mild; genial, soothing; not irritating; not stimulating 1667.

1. With b. words at will MILT. *P. L.* ix. 855. 2. The air was b. 1872. Hence **Bla·ndly** *adv.*, **-ness.**

†**Blanda·tion.** *rare.* 1605. [f. BLAND *a.* + -ATION.] Flattery; an illusion.

Blandi·loquence. *rare.* 1656. [ad. L. *blandiloquentia.*] Smooth speech, flattering talk. So **Blandi·loquent, -loquous** *adjs.* (*rare*).

Blandish (blæ·ndiʃ), *v.* ME. [a. F. *blandiss-*, stem of *blandir* :—L. *blandiri*, f. *blandus.*] **1.** To flatter gently by words or actions, to coax; to cajole. **2.** *intr.* (*absol.*) To use blandishments ME. †**3.** *trans.* To offer blandly (cf. *to smile thanks*) –1638.

3. Though they [flowers] sometime b. soft delight DRUMM. OF HAWTH. Hence **Bla·ndisher.**

Blandishment (blæ·ndiʃmĕnt). 1591. [f. as prec. + -MENT.] **1.** Gently flattering speech or action; cajolery. **2.** *fig.* Attraction, allurement. *concr.* Anything that pleases or allures. 1594.

1. Strange .. blandishments of words BACON.

Blank (blæŋk), *a.* ME. [F. *blanc* :—OTeut. **blanko-z* shining.] **1.** †White; pale, colourless –1821. **2.** Of paper: Left white; not written upon, or marked; said also of orders, cheques, and documents left with an empty space for special signature or instruction 1547. **3.** *gen.* Empty, without contents, void 1748. **4.** *fig.* Void of interest, result, or expression 1553. **5.** (Looking) non-plussed; as in *To look b.* 1542. **6.** Of emotions: Prostrating the faculties 1634. **7.** *gen.* Pure, downright, sheer, absolute (with neg. or priv. force) 1839.

1. The blanc Moone MILT. *P. L.* x. 656. 2. A b. Passport 1708. Bills drawn *in b.* (*i. e.* without names specified) 1861. 3. B. darkness HOOD, space 1856. 4. A b. day 1832. 5. Upon this I looked very b. ADDISON. 6. Countenances of b. dismay DICKENS. 7. B. atheism 1871. *B. verse*: verse without rime; *esp.* the iambic pentameter or unrimed heroic 1589.

Comb., etc. (in sense 2): **b. acceptance, cheque**, one not having the amount filled in; **b. bar**, a plea in bar, to compel the plaintiff in an action of trespass to assign the certain place where the trespass was committed; **b. charter**, a document given to the agents of the crown in Richard II's reign, with power to fill it up as they pleased; hence *fig.* liberty to do as one likes; **b. indorsement**, a bill in which the indorsee's name is omitted. Also (in sense 3): **b.-cartridge**, one containing no ball; **-door** (*Archit.*), an imitation-door; **-tire**, a tire without a flange; **-tooling** = blind-blocking; see BLIND; **-window**, an imitation-window. Hence **Bla·nkly** *adv.*, **-ness.**

Blank (blæŋk), *sb.* ME. [f. prec.] †**1.** A small French coin, orig. of silver, later of copper, worth 5 deniers; also a silver coin of Henry V, current in the parts of France then held by the English –1629. **2.** The white spot in the centre of the target; hence *fig.* anything aimed at, the range of such aim 1554. **b.** 'Level line mark for cannon, as point-b., equal to 800 yards' (Smyth). †**3.** A nonplus –1580. **4.** A lottery ticket which does not gain a prize, as *to draw a b.* 1567. **5.** A blank space in a document 1570. **b.** Provisional words printed in italics (instead of blank spaces) in a bill before Parliament 1817. †**6.** A blank form (*e.g.* a blank charter) –1780. **b.** An empty form; nothing at all 1700. **7.** *fig.* A vacant space, place, or period 1601. **8.** Blank verse 1589. **9.** *Mech.* A piece of metal, cut and shaped, and ready for finishing; *esp.* in *Coinage*, the disc of metal before stamping 1596. **10.** The $^1/_{230400}$ of a grain 1680. **11.** A domino without points on either or both of its divisions. **12.** A dash written in place of an omitted letter or word. Cf. DASH.

2. As level as the cannon to his b. Transports his poisoned shot *Haml.* IV. i. 42. Also *Oth.* III. iv. 128. 4. When one has drawn a b. W. IRVING. 7. And what's her history? A blanke, my lord SHAKS.

Blank (blæŋk), *v.* 1483. [f. prec.] †**1.** *trans.* = BLANCH *v.*[1] –1652. **2.** To nonplus. Cf. BLANK *a.* 5. (*arch.*) 1548. **3.** To frustrate, disconcert (plans, etc.) (*arch.*) 1566. †**4.** To turn away. (Cf. BLANCH *v.*[2] 4.) –1659. **5.** To render blank or void; to veil from sight 1763. **b.** To indicate by a dash (——) 1789. ¶ **c.** Blank (printed ——, but read 'blank') = 'damn', or the like 1873. †**6.** *intr.* To blench; to shrink back –1642.

2. Which fairly blanked the bold visage of Adam Woodcock SCOTT. 5. Night..blank'd half the Globe CHURCHILL. c. B. him! that is just like him C. READE.

Blanket (blæ·ŋkėt), *sb.* ME. [a. OF. *blankete, blanquette*, dim. of *blanc*. Cf. BLUNKET.] †1. An undyed woollen stuff used for clothing –1440. 2. A large oblong sheet of soft loose woollen cloth, used chiefly as a bed-covering; also for throwing over a horse, and, by savages, for clothing ME. Also *fig.* 3. *Printing.* A woollen cloth used to deaden and equalize the pressure of the platten 1824. 4. *transf.* A layer of blubber in whales 1885.

2. A rascally Slaue, I will tosse the Rogue in a B. *2 Hen. IV*, II. iv. 241. *fig.* The B. of the darke *Macb.* I. v. 54. *A wet b.*: a person or thing that throws a damper over everything. *Born on the wrong side of the b.*: i. e. illegitimate.

Bla·nket, *v.* Pa. t. and pple. **-eted.** 1605. [f. the sb.] 1. To cover with or as with a blanket. 2. *Yachting.* To take the wind out of the sails of a yacht by passing to windward of it 1884. 3. To toss in a blanket 1609. Hence **Bla·nketed** *ppl. a.* covered with or as with a blanket; in U.S. used *spec.* of cattle having a broad belt of white round the middle.

†**Blanketee·r.** 1755. [f. BLANKET + -EER.] **a.** One who uses a blanket. **b.** *pl.* A body of operatives who met at the Blanket Meeting in Manchester, on 10th March, 1817, provided with blankets, etc., in order to march to London and call attention to their grievances. –1833.

Blanketing (blæ·ŋkėtiŋ), *sb.* 1577. [f. as prec.] 1. Material for blankets; supply of blankets 1677. 2. The action of the vb. (senses 2, 3) 1577.

Blare (blēᵊɹ), *v.* 1440. [? Echoic. Cf. MDu. *blaren*, etc.] 1. *intr.* To roar with prolonged sound in weeping, as a child; to bellow as a calf. Now *dial.* 2. To sound a trumpet, to trumpet. (Now the ordinary wd. in this sense.) 1782. 3. *trans.* To utter in blaring 1859.

2. Blairing like trumpeters at a fair COWPER. Hence **Blare** *sb.*[1] the weeping of a child, the bellowing of calves; the noise of trumpets, etc.

Blare, *sb.*[2] 1867. A paste of hair and tar for caulking the seams of boats.

Blarney (blā·ɹni), *sb.* 1819. [f. *Blarney*, a village near Cork. The saying is that whoever kisses the 'Blarney stone' in the castle will ever after have a cajoling tongue and the art of flattery.] Smoothly flattering or cajoling talk (*colloq.*). Hence **Bla·rney** *v.* (*trans.*) to assail with b.; (*intr.*) to use flattering speech.

†**Blas.** [In ME. var. of BLAST, f. OE. *blǣsan, ON. *blása*.] 1. A blast, breath. ME. only. 2. A supposed flatus or influence of the stars, producing changes of weather 1662.

‖**Blasé** (bla·ze), *a.* 1819. [Fr.] Exhausted by enjoyment, disgusted with it; used up.

Blason, obs. f. BLAZON.

Blaspheme (blɑsfī·m), *v.* [ME. *blasfeme-n*, a. OF. *blasfemer*, ad. L. *blasphemare*, ad. Gr. βλασφημέειν, f. βλάσφημος evil speaking. Transferred to L. in the Vulgate. See BLAME.] 1. *intr.* To talk profanely. 2. *trans.* To utter impiety against (God or anything sacred) ME. 3. *gen.* To speak evil of, revile, calumniate ME.

2. Blaspheming God, and cursing men on earth *2 Hen. VI*, III. ii. 372. 3. So they b. the muse TENNYSON. Hence **Blasphe·mer.**

†**Blasphe·me,** *a.* and *sb.*[1] ME. only. [a. F. *blasphème*, ad. L. *blasphemus*, ad. Gr.; see prec.] A. *adj.* Blasphemous. Hence †**Blasphemely** *adv.* B. *sb.* A blasphemer.

†**Blasphe·me,** *sb.*[2] ME. [a. F. *blasphème*:–L. *blasphemia*.] Early f. BLASPHEMY –1583.

In b. of the goddis CHAUCER.

Blasphemous (bla·sfīməs), *a.* 1535. [f. L. *blasphemus* (see BLASPHEME *a.*) + -OUS. In Marlow and Milton *blasphē·mous*, after L.] 1. Uttering profanity. †2. Abusive, defamatory –1610.

1. O argument b., false and proud MILT. *P. L* v. 809. 2. You bawling, b., incharitable dog *Temp.* I. i. 43. Hence **Bla·sphemous-ly** *adv.*, **-ness.**

Blasphemy (bla·sfīmi). [ME. *blasfemie, blasphemie*, a. OF., ad. L. *blasphemia*, a. Gr., f. βλάσφημος. In Spenser *blasphe·my*. Cf. BLASPHEME *sb.*[2]] 1. Profane speaking of God or sacred things; impious irreverence. Also *fig.* 1605. †2. *gen.* Evil speaking, defamation –1656. †b. *transf.* A thing evil spoken of 1609.

1. B. against the Almighty BLACKSTONE, *fig.* against learning BACON.

Blast (blɑst), *sb.* [Com. Teut.: OE. *blǣst*:–OTeut. *blǣs-tu-z, f. *blǣsan to blow; see BLAZE *v.*[2] Cf. L. *fla-tu-s*.] 1. A blowing or strong gust of wind. 2. A puff of air through the mouth or nostrils; a breath (*arch.*) ME. 3. The blowing of a trumpet or other wind-instrument; hence, the sound so produced; any similar sound. Also *fig.* ME. 4. A strong current of air produced artificially 1618. b. *spec.* That used in iron-smelting, etc. 1697. †5. The sudden stroke of lightning –1751. 6. A sudden infection (formerly attributed to the breath of a malignant power, foul air, etc.). a. Blight; also an insect which causes it. b. *transf.* and *fig.* Any blasting influence, a curse 1547. c. A flatulent disease in sheep. 7. An explosion 1635; the quantity of explosive used 1885. 8. *Sc.* A smoke (of tobacco). Cf. *Counterblast.*

1. Snows, and Bitter Blasts DRYDEN. 2. The b. of thy nostrils *Ex.* xv. 8. 3. Loud as the trumpet's b. HAN. MORE. Phr. †*At one b.* (L. *uno flatu*): at the same time. 4. To give very strong and lasting Blasts for Iron Forges 1697. *In b., at* or *in full b.*: at work. *Out of b.*: stopped. 6. b. Resistless as the blasts of pestilence JOHNSON.

Comb.: **b.-fan,** a fan for producing a b. of air; **-hearth,** a hearth for reducing lead-ore; **-hole,** the hole by which water enters a pump; **-pipe,** in a locomotive, a pipe conveying the steam from the cylinders into the funnel and so increasing the draught.

Blast (blɑst), *v.* ME. [f. the sb.] 1. †*intr.* To blow violently –1768; †*trans.* to blow (*out, forth, abroad*); to proclaim –1631. †2. a. *intr.* To blow (on a trumpet, etc.). b. *trans.* To blow (a trumpet, etc.). c. To din or denounce (any one) by trumpeting. –1858. 3. To blow (up), inflate. Also *intr.* (for *refl.*) *Obs.* exc. *dial.* 1578. 4. To blow up by explosion 1758. 5. To blow or breathe on balefully, to blight 1532. Also *transf.* and *fig.* †6. To wither under a blight –1630. 7. To curse. Often in imprecations. 1640. Also *absol.*

5. O fairest flower, no sooner blown but blasted MILT. Blasted or stricken with a planet 1580, with lightning 1634. To b. the Memory..of King William STEELE. He saw; but blasted with excess of light, Clos'd his eyes in endless night GRAY. 6. Tell Beauty how she blasteth RALEIGH. 7. Calling on their Maker to curse them .. b. them, and damn them MACAULAY. Hence **Bla·sted** *ppl. a.* a low expression of reprobation and hatred. **Bla·ster,** one who or that which blasts.

-blast [ad. Gr. βλαστός sprout, shoot, germ], used techn., esp. in Biology, in sense of 'germ, embryo', as in *epiblast, mesoblast*, and *hypoblast*.

‖**Blastema** (blæstī·mă). Pl. **blaste·mata.** 1849. [a. Gr., f. vbl. stem βλαστε-, βλαστα- to sprout.] 1. *Biol.* The primary formative material of plants and animals; protoplasm. Now *spec.*: The initial matter out of which any part is developed. 2. *Bot.* The budding or sprouting part of a plant 1880. Hence **Blaste·mal, Blastema·tic** *adjs.* of or pertaining to b.

Bla·st-fu·rnace. 1706. A furnace in which a blast of air is used; *spec.* the common furnace for iron-smelting.

Bla·stide. 1880. [f. Gr. βλαστός + εἶδος.] *Biol.* 'The clear space in each segment of a dividing impregnated ovum, which precedes the appearance of a nucleus'. (*Syd. Soc. Lex.*)

Blasting (bla·stiŋ), *vbl. sb.* 1460. [f. BLAST *v.* + -ING[1].] †1. The production of blasts; flatulence –1579. 2. Withering or shrivelling up caused by atmospheric, electric, or unseen agency 1535. 3. Blowing rocks to pieces; also its result 1824. var. **Bla·stment** (sense 2).

Blasto- (blæsto), repr. Gr. βλαστο-, stem and comb. form of βλαστός sprout, germ. Used techn. in the sense of 'germ' or 'bud'.

Blastoca·rpous [Gr. καρπός] *a.*, *Bot.* of the nature of a seed which germinates before escaping from the pericarp. **Bla·stocele** [Gr. κηλίς spot], the germinal spot. **Bla·stocheme** [Gr. ὄχημα vehicle], a Medusa in which a generative body is developed in the radiating canals. **Bla·stochyle** [Gr. χυλός juice], the mucilaginous fluid in the embryonal sac of plants. **Bla·stocœle** [Gr. κοῖλος], the central cavity which forms in the ovum after segmentation. **Blastoco·lla** [Gr. κόλλα glue], *Bot.* the gummy substance which coats certain buds. **Bla·stocyst** [Gr. κύστις bladder], **Blastocy·stinx** [Gr. κύστιγξ little bladder] = BLASTODERM. **Bla·stodisc,** the germinal disc of the ovum of birds. **Blastoge·nesis,** reproduction by buds. **Blasto·geny,** Haeckel's term for the germ-history of persons. **Blasto·graphy,** the scientific description of the buds of plants. **Bla·stomere** [Gr. μέρος], each of the segments into which the impregnated ovum at first divides. **Bla·stophor** [Gr. -φορος], a portion of the spermatophore which remains to carry spermatoblasts; whence **Blasto·phoral** *a.* **Bla·stophore,** *Bot.* Richard's name for the part of the embryo with a large radicle which bears the bud. **Blasto·phyly** [Gr. φυλή tribe], Haeckel's name for the tribal history of persons. **Bla·stopore** [Gr. πόρος passage], the orifice produced by the invagination of a point on the surface of a blastule, or blastosphere, to form the enteron. **Bla·stosphere,** a name for the impregnated ovum, when, after segmentation, it has acquired a blastocœle and blastoderm. **Blastostro·ma** [Gr. στρῶμα a stratum], the germinal area. **Bla·stostyle** [Gr. στῦλος pillar], a stalk upon which gonophores are developed in the Hydrozoa.

Blastoderm (blæ·stodǝɹm). 1859. [f. BLASTO- + Gr. δέρμα.] *Embryol.* A disk of cells found in the early segmentation of a fertilized ovum (as differentiated from *blastula*, a hollow ball of cells, and *morula*, a solid ball). Hence **Blastoderma·tic, Blastode·rmic** *adjs.*

Bla·stule. 1882. [dim. (on L. type) f. Gr. βλαστός.] A small germ; a blastophore.

Blasty (bla·sti), *a.* 1583. [f. BLAST *sb.* + -Y[1].] Characterized by blasts of wind. †2. Causing blight 1667.

Blatant (blēi·tănt), *a.* Also **blattant.** [App. coined by Spenser as an epithet of calumny, 'the blat(t)ant beast', with a thousand tongues. Cf. L. *blattire* to babble.] 1. In 'the blat(t)ant beast' (cf. *F. Q.* v. xii. 37, 41 and *passim*): see above 1596. 2. *fig.* Noisy; offensively or vulgarly clamorous; bellowing 1656; clamorous 1790. 3. Loud-voiced 1791; loud 1816.

1. 'The blattant beast,' quoth he, 'I doe pursew' SPENSER *F. Q.* VI. i. 7. 2. Up rose a b. Radical BAGEHOT. Not the less Hear I the b. appetite demand Due sustenance COWPER. Hence **Bla·tancy. Bla·tantly** *adv.*

Blate (blēit, *dial.* blĕt, bliᵊt), *a.* *Sc.* and *n. dial.* [Found in Sc. late in 15th c. Phonetically = OE. *blát* livid, pale.] †1. Pale, ghastly. (In OE.) †2. Void of feeling –1548. †3. Spiritless –1560. 4. Undiscerning 1513. 5. Bashful, backward, sheepish 1600.

5. When I was beardless, young, and b. BURNS.

Blate (blēit), *v. rare.* [?f. BLEAT (sense 2 b), and BLATANT.] To babble, prate. PEPYS.

Blatera·tion (blætǝrēi·ʃǝn). Also **blatt-.** 1656. [ad. late L. *blaterationem*. Cf. BLATTER *v.*] Babbling chatter.

†**Blateroo·n.** Also **blatt-.** 1645. [ad. L. *blateronem*.] A babbler.

Blather; see BLETHER.

Blatherskite; see BLETHERSKATE.

‖**Bla·tta.** 1601. [L.] 1. Generic name of the Cockroach. 2. Purple; purple silk 1658. Hence †**Bla·ttean** *a.* purple.

Blatter (blæ·tǝɹ), *v.* 1555. [ad. L. *blaterare*, and partly echoic.] *intr.* To speak or prate volubly. Also *trans.*

1. Noe matter tho' Ignorance b. folly DANIEL. Hence **Bla·tter** *sb.* a volley of clattering words, or sound of rapid motion. **Bla·tterer.**

†**Blau·nner.** ME. [app. = *blaundemere*, which suggests a Fr. *blanc de mer, of unkn. application.] A species of (? white) fur used to line hoods, etc. –1460.

‖**Blauwbok** (blāu·bǫk). 1786. [Du. *blaauwbok*, f. *blaauw* blue + *bok* buck.] *S. Afr.* A large Antelope (*A. leucophæa*), with bluish hair.

Blay, bley (blēi). Also (*rare*) **blea.** [OE. *blæge*:—OTeut. *blaijôn.] A fish, the bleak.

†**Blayk(e,** *a.* [ME. *bleik*, a. ON. *bleikr*, cogn. w. OE. *blác*:—OTeut. *blaiko-z, f. the stem of *blîkan* to shine. Cf. BLAKE, BLEAK, BLOKE.] a. Pale. b. Yellow. –1570.

Blaze (blēiz), *sb.*[1] [OE. *blase, blæse* (OTeut. type *blasôn-).] †1. A torch –1535. 2. A bright glowing flame or fire OE. Also *fig.* 3. Brilliant light; a glow of colour 1564. 4. *fig.* a. Splendour, brilliant display 1579. b. Clear or full light 1748.

2. *In a b.*: in flames. *Blazes* pl.: referring to the flames of hell, used in: *The blazes! Like blazes*: furiously. *To (the) blazes*: to the deuce. His rash fierce b. of Ryot *Rich. II*, II. i. 33. **3.** Dark, amid the b. of noon MILT. *Sams.* 80. **4.** A b. of jests JOWETT. The b. of publicity LECKY.

Blaze (blēiz), *sb.*[2] 1639. [Not in OE. or ME. But = ON. *blesi* 'white star on a horse's forehead', f. stem *blas-*, *blaz-* shining, white.] **1.** A white spot on the face of a horse or ox. **2.** *transf.* A white mark made on a tree, *esp.* by chipping off bark; also, a track indicated by such marks. (First in U. S.) 1737.

Blaze (blēiz), *v.*[1] ME. [f. BLAZE *sb.*[1] Not in OE., or any other Teut. lang.] **1.** *intr.* To burn with a bright fervent flame. Also *fig.* **2.** *trans.* To cause to blaze (*rare*) 1485. **3.** *intr.* To shine like flame or fire. Also with *forth*. ME. Also *trans.* with cognate obj. 1667. **4.** *intr.* To shine or be conspicuous. Also with *out*. ME.

1. *To b. up*: to flash into a blaze. *fig.* Stein..blazed up, and there was an exchange of hot words SEELEY. *To b. out*: to exhaust in a blaze of excess (*arch.*); *intr.* to go out with a flare. **3.** Eyes That sparkling blaz'd MILT. *P. L.* I. 194. Phr. *To b. away*: to fire continuously with guns, etc.: *fig.* to work enthusiastically (*colloq.*). Cf. *fire away*. Hence **Bla·zer**[1], one who or that which blazes; a jacket, usually of wool and bright-coloured, often with a badge, worn esp. at sports. **Bla·zing** *ppl. a.*; in *Venery*: Of scent, very strong; as opp. to a *cold scent*. **Bla·zingly** *adv.*

Blaze (blēiz), *v.*[2] ME. [In sense 1 = ON. *blása* to blow:—OTeut. **blǣs-an*, f. root **blǣ-* (Aryan **bhlē-*, L. *fla-re*; see BLOW) with suffixal *-s-* taken into the root. Confused later with BLAZON.] †**1.** To blow (e. g. with a musical instrument); to puff –1535. **2.** *trans.* To proclaim (as with a trumpet), to make known 1450. **b.** with *abroad*. (The prevalent use.) 1552. †**3.** To BLAZON –1628. **4.** (Mixing senses 2 and 3.) †**a.** To celebrate –1635. †**b.** To portray –1642.

2. b. Fearing..that I should b. it abroad in his lifetime BOSWELL. **3.** What Herald [can] b. their Arms without a blemish F. GREVILLE. Hence **Bla·zer**[2], one who proclaims.

Blaze, *v.*[3] 1812. [f. BLAZE *sb.*[2]] To mark (trees) with white by chipping off bark, etc. Also to indicate (a spot or path) by such marks.

Blazed (blēizd), *a.* 1685. [f. BLAZE *sb.*[2]] Having a blaze on the face.

Blazing star. 1460. †**1.** A comet –1762. **2.** *fig.* Cynosure, 'star' (*arch.*) 1460. †**3.** = BLAZE *sb.*[2] 1. 1705. **4.** Pop. name of three N. Amer. plants: *Alteris farinosa, Chamælirium luteum*, and *Liatris squarrosa*.

Blazon (blēi·z'n), *sb.* ME. [a. F. *blason* (found in other Romanic langs.). Orig. = 'shield', and thus not conn. w. BLAZE *sb.*[1] or [2] or Ger. *blasen* (BLAZE *v.*[2]).] †**1.** A shield used in war. ME. only. **2.** *Her.* A shield in heraldry; coat of arms; a banner bearing the arms. **3.** Heraldic description or representation of armorial bearings 1610. **4.** (cf. BLAZE *v.*[2]) A description or record, *esp.* of virtues or excellencies 1577. **5.** Divulgation, publication 1602.

2. St. George's b. red SCOTT. **3.** The earliest b. of a Royal Banner..occurs in the Roll of Caerlaverock BOUTELL. **4.** The b. of sweet beauties best SHAKS.

Blazon (blēi·zən), *v.* 1513. [f. prec.; see BLAZE *v.*[2]] **1.** To describe in proper heraldic language. Also *absol.* 1586. **2.** To depict according to the rules of heraldry 1570; *fig.* to illuminate 1699. **3.** To adorn as with blazonry 1813. Also *fig.* **4.** = BLAZE *v.*[2] 4. 1513. **5.** To publish boastfully 1534. **6.** = BLAZE *v.*[2] 2. Also with *forth, out*. Often in a bad sense. 1577.

1. To b. the arms painted in the glass windows WARTON. **2.** Having his armes verie excellentlie blazoned in fine coulored glasse 1593. **3.** Walls..blazoned all with feats of pride SCOTT. **4.** To b. the kingly attributes and virtues 1863. **5.** I wold neuer blasen loue with my tongue LD. BERNERS. **6.** To b. out their blames SPENSER. Hence **Bla·zoned** *ppl. a.* (senses 2, 6). **Bla·zoner,** a herald; one who records with commendation; one who proclaims. **Bla·zonment,** blazoning; proclaiming.

Blazonry (blēi·zənri). 1622. [f. as prec.] **1.** The description or depicting of heraldic devices. **2.** Armorial bearings 1649. Also *fig.* **3.** *fig.* Brilliant or artistic display 1814.

2. The old impresa or arms, b. of the house and family DRUMM. OF HAWTH. var. †**Bla·zure.**

-ble, a. OF. *-ble*:—L. *-bilem*, nom. *-bilis*, suffix forming verbal adjs., with the sense 'given to, tending to, like to, fit to, able to'. The most numerous of the *-ble* words are those in *-able*. In Fr., all pres. pples. in *-ant* (now the universal form of pres. pple.) may give rise to an adj. in *-able*. But in Eng. *-ible* is preferred wherever there was or might be a L. *-ibilis*; while *-able* is used for words of distinctly Fr. or Eng. origin. Hence the distractions of English usage. See -ABLE, -IBLE. An *e* mute before *-able must* be retained after *c, g*, as *peaceable, changeable*, etc., and it is usually retained in monosyllables, as *tameable*, etc.; otherwise its retention is more or less optional. In words from Eng., a final consonant is usu. doubled before *-able*, when doubled in the pres. pple., as *clubbable*, etc.

Adjs. in *-bili-, -ble*, were orig. active (and neuter) as well as passive; but the majority of the former remain only (if at all) with a passive force, as in *credible, audible*, which is also the only use of *-able* as a living formative, e. g. *eatable, likeable*, etc.

Blea (blī), *sb. rare.* 1730. [?] The young wood of a tree under the bark; the alburnum.

Blea, *v. Obs.* exc. *dial.* 1568. [Prob. echoic. Cf. Gr. βληχάομαι, βληχή bleating. (Pronunc. blē, bliə, blī.)] *intr.* To bleat as a lamb; to cry piteously as a child.

Bleach (blītʃ), *sb.*[1] OE. [Cf. OE. *blǣco*, f. *blac, blǣc* pale.] †**1.** A disease of the skin. Cf. OE. *blǣce* leprosy. 1601. **2.** An act of bleaching.

†**Bleach,** *sb.*[2] 1486. [From BLACK. See N.E.D.] Any substance used for blacking –1611.

†**Bleach,** *a.* [ME. *bleche*, OE. *blǣc, blac* white, pale.] = BLEAK *a.* 1, 2.

Bleach (blītʃ), *v.*[1] [Com. Teut.: OE. *blǣc(e)an*:—OTeut. **blaikjan* to bleach, f. **blaiko-z, blaiki-z* white; see BLAKE *a.*] **1.** To whiten (linen, etc.) by washing and exposure or by chemical processes ME. Also *fig.* **2.** To blanch, *esp.* by exposure 1583. **3.** *intr.* To become white or colourless 1611. Also *fig.*

1. When..Maidens b. their summer smockes *L. L. L.* V. ii. 916. **3.** Bones of travellers bleaching amongst the yellow sand 1865. Hence **Blea·cher,** one who or that which bleaches. **Blea·chery,** a place where bleaching is done.

†**Bleach,** *v.*[2] 1611. [f. BLEACH *sb.*[2]] To blacken.

Bleak (blīk), *sb.* 1496. [? f. ON. *bleikja*:—OTeut. **blaikjōn-*, f. **blaiko-* white.] A small river-fish, called also the Blay (*Leuciscus alburnus*); also an allied sea-fish.

Bleak (blīk), *a.* 1538. [Parallel form of *bleche* (*bleach*), *bleyke, blake, bloke*. Cf. BLAKE, BLEACH, BLEYKE *a.*] **1.** Pallid, wan; of a sickly hue. Still *dial.* 1566. **2.** Bare of vegetation; exposed; now often wind-swept 1538. **3.** Cold, chilly 1595. **4.** *fig.* Cheerless 1719.

2. Our lodgings, standing b. upon the sea *Per.* III. ii. 14. **3.** The b. air MILT. *P. R.* II. 72. Hence **Blea·kish** *a.* **Blea·k-ly** *adv.*, **-ness.** So **Blea·ky** *a.*, inclining to b. (in senses 2, 3).

†**Bleak** (blīk), *v.* ME. [Three formations.] I. **1.** = BLEACH *v.*[1] 1, 2. –1612. **2.** *intr.* = BLEACH *v.*[1] 3. 1606. II. To chill or ? make livid with cold 1605. III. = BLEACH *v.*[2] 1611.

Blear (bliəɹ), *a.* [ME. *blere*, epithet of the eyes, of unkn. origin.] **1.** Of the eyes or sight: Dim from water or other superficial affection. Also *fig.* **2.** *transf.* Dim, misty, indistinct in outline 1634.

1. Her eyes grew watery and b. THACKERAY. **2.** To cheat the eye with b. illusion MILT. *Comb.*: **b-eyed** *a.* having b. eyes, or wits; **-witted,** having the mental faculties dimmed. Hence **Blea·rness,** blearedness (of the eyes). **Blea·ry** *a.* more or less b.

Blear (bliəɹ), *v.*[1] ME. [perh. f. prec.] †**1.** *intr.* To have watery or inflamed eyes. (Said also of an albino.) –1570. **2.** *trans.* To dim (the eyes) with tears, rheum, or inflammation ME. **b.** To blur (the face) as with tears ME.

2. He..bleared his eyes with books LONGF. **b.** The Heaven weeps and blears itself, in sour rain CARLYLE. Phr. (*fig.*) *To b. the eyes*: to deceive, hoodwink *Tam. Shr.* V. i. 120. Hence **Blea·redness. Blea·ring** *vbl. sb.* being bleared; the action of making blear; *transf.* the guttering of a candle.

†**Blear,** *v.*[2] ME. [Cf. BLARE *v.*] *intr.* To protrude the tongue in mockery –1605.

Bleat (blīt), *v.* [Com. WGer.: OE. *blǣtan*:—WGer. *blǣtan*, echoic; see BLEA *v.*] **1.** *intr.* To cry as a sheep, goat, or calf. Also *trans.* (with cognate obj.) 1719. **2.** *transf.* Used contemptuously of the human voice 1563.

1. Lambs, that did..b. the one at th'other *Wint. T.* I. ii. 68. Hence **Blea·ter.**

Bleat (blīt), *sb.* 1505. [f. the vb.] The cry of a sheep, goat, or calf; *transf.* any similar cry. A Calfe..Much like to you, for you haue iust his b. *Much Ado* V. iv. 51.

Bleb (bleb), *sb.* 1607. [app. like BLOB and BLUBBER, from the action of making a bubble with the lips.] **1.** A small swelling on the skin; also on plants. **2.** A bubble of air in water, glass, etc. 1647. **3.** A vesicular body 1775. Hence **Bleb** *v.* to furnish with blebs. **Ble·bby** *a.* full of blebs or bubbles.

Bleck, *sb.* Now *dial.* [ME. *blek(e* = ON. *blek* ink, OTeut. type **blakjo(m*, f. **blak-* BLACK.] **1.** Black fluid substance; *spec.* †ink; †shoemakers' black; black grease round an axle, etc. **2.** Soot or smut, a smut 1590. Hence **Bleck** *v.* (now *dial.*) to blacken; also *fig.*

Blee (blī). *arch.* [OE. *blēo*:—OTeut. **blijo-(m* colour, hue. An obs. poet. wd., used once or twice lately.] **1.** Hue (*arch.*). **2.** Complexion; visage (*arch.*) ME.

1. Eyes so grey of b. MRS. BROWNING. **2.** His daughter bright of b. 1834.

Bleed (blīd), *v.* Pa. t. and pple. **bled.** [OE. *blēdan*:—OTeut. **blōdjan*, f. **blōdo(m* BLOOD.] **I.** *intr.* **1.** To emit, discharge, or lose blood. **2.** To lose blood from wounds; to die by bloodshed ME. Also *fig.* **3.** Of plants: To emit sap when wounded 1674. **4.** Said of blood, etc.: To drop, ooze forth ME. **5.** With cognate obj.: To emit as blood ME. Also *fig.*

1. Least he should bleede to death *Merch. V.* IV. i. 258. *fig.* O my heart bleedes To think oth' teene that I haue turn'd you to *Temp.* I. ii. 63. **2.** Cæsar must b. for it *Jul. C.* II. i. 171. *To b. well*: Of corn, etc.: to give a large yield (*dial.*). Of persons: to lose or part with money to an extent that is felt. **5.** Shee did ..I would faine say, b. Teares *Wint. T.* V. ii. 96.

II. *trans.* **1.** To draw or let blood from, *esp.* surgically ME. **2.** To extort money from (*colloq.*) 1680.

2. By Jove, sir, you've bled that poor woman enough THACKERAY. Hence **Blee·der,** one who draws blood; *Med.* a person subject to hæmophilia.

Bleeding (blī·diŋ), *ppl. a.* ME. [f. prec.] **1.** In senses of the vb. **2.** *fig.* and *transf.* Said of nations devastated by war, etc. 1668.

1. Whose sonnes lye scattered on the b. ground SHAKS. With b. hearts HOOKER. **2.** Greece, b. and exhausted 1863.

Comb.: **b.-heart,** pop. name for plants; *e.g.* the Wallflower, *Dicentra formosa*, and a variety of Cherry; **b. root** = BLOOD-ROOT.

Blei·nerite. *Min.* = BINDHEIMITE.

Blemish (ble·miʃ), *v.* ME. [a. OF. *blemiss-*, *blemir*, f. *blême*, of unkn. origin.] †**1.** To hurt, damage, deface –1607. †**2.** To dim (the eye-sight) –1677. **3.** To mar, injure the working of ME. **4.** To impair the perfection of 1460. **b.** To impair morally; to sully ME. **c.** To discredit, disable. *Obs.* exc. in *Law.* ME.

3. To b. the peace 1625. **4. b.** To b. reputation 1735. **c.** To b. oneself by pleading one's own insanity BLACKSTONE. Hence **Ble·misher. Ble·mishment,** damage; flaw; impairment.

Blemish (ble·miʃ), *sb.* 1526. [f. the vb.] **1.** Physical defect or disfigurement, *e.g.* the scar of a broken knee in a horse; a stain 1535. **2.** *transf.* A defect or flaw generally 1555. **3.** *fig.* A moral defect; a fault, blot, slur 1526.

1. Speaking thicke (which Nature made his b.) *2 Hen. IV*, II. iii. 34. **3.** Some stain or b. in a name of note TENNYSON. Hence **Ble·mishless** *a.*

Blemmatrope (ble·mătrōup). 1876. [f. Gr. βλέμμα + τρόπος, f. τρέπειν.] An apparatus for illustrating the various positions of the eye.

†**Blench,** *sb.* [f. BLENCH *v.*[1]] **1.** A trick. ME. only. **2.** A side glance. SHAKS.

Blench, *a.* Sc. form of BLANCH *a.*

Blench (blenʃ), *v.*[1] OE. [In sense 1:—OE. *blęncan* = ON. *blekkja*. The north. form was BLENK, q.v.] †**1.** To deceive, cheat –ME. **2.** *intr.* To start aside, so as to elude anything; to shy; to flinch ME. **3.** *trans.* To elude; to flinch from; to blink ME. †**4.** To disconcert, turn aside –1640. **5.** *intr.* Of the eyes: To lose firmness of glance, to quail 1775.

2. Sometimes you doe b. from this to that *Meas. for M.* IV. v. 5. **5.** That..influence at which the eyes of eagles have blenched BURKE. Hence **Ble·ncher,** he who or that which turns or frightens away, *e.g.* a scarecrow; one who flinches.

Blench, *v.*² var. of BLANCH *v.*¹, q.v.

Blencorn, var. of BLEND CORN; see BLEND(E.

†**Blend,** *v.*¹ [Com. WGer.: OE. *blęndan*:—OTeut. type **blandjan*; see BLIND.] To make blind; to dazzle. Also *fig.* -1600.

Blend (blend), *v.*² [ME. *blenden*, prob. ad. ON. *blanda*; see BLAND *v.*] **I.** *trans.* **1.** To mix, to mingle; *esp.* to mix (spirits, teas, wines, etc.), so as to produce a certain quality. †**2.** To mix or stir up (a liquid); hence occas., to render turbid, spoil; occas., to agitate, trouble; to disturb (joy, peace, beauty, weather) -1596. **3.** To mingle closely *with* 1591. **4.** To mix (components) so that their individuality is obscured in the product; now the most frequent *trans.* use 1601.

3. To b. realty with personalty 1788. 4. Rider and horse,—friend, foe,—in one red burial blent BYRON.

II. *intr.* **1.** To mix, mingle; *esp.* so as to form a uniform mixture ME. **2.** To pass imperceptibly into each other, *esp.* in reference to colour 1812.

1. All motions, sounds, and voices..B. in a music of tranquillity WORDSW. Hence **Blend** *sb.* a blending. **Ble·nder,** one who or that which blends. **Ble·nding** *vbl. sb.* and *ppl. a.*

†**Blend(e.** Also **bland.** ME. Obs. pa. pple. of BLEND *v.*² As *adj.* = BLENDED -1679. *Comb.*: **blend corn, blencorn,** wheat and rye sown and grown together; **b.-water,** a urinary disease of cattle.

Blende (blend). 1683. [a. Ger. *blende*, f. *blenden* to deceive; called also *pseudogalena*, because it yields no lead.] *Min.* Sulphide of zinc. Hence **Ble·ndous, Ble·ndy** *adjs.* pertaining to or containing b.

Blenheim (ble·nĕm, -im). Name of the Duke of Marlborough's house, near Woodstock; used in a. *Blenheims*, a breed of spaniels 1851; b. *B. Orange*, a golden-coloured apple 1879.

†**Blenk,** *v.* OE. **1.** = BLENCH *v.*¹ 1, 2, 4. -ME. **2.** To blanch. Cf. BLENCH *v.*² -1600. **3.** = BLINK 1, 3, 4. -1625.

†**Blenk,** *sb. north.* Earlier f. BLINK.

Blennioid (ble·niˌoid). 1865. **A.** *adj.* Allied to the BLENNY. **B.** *sb.* [sc. *fish.*]

Blenno-, blenn-, a. Gr. βλέννος, βλέννα, mucus, comb. form.

Blennoge·nic, Blenno·genous *a.*, generating mucus. **Ble·nnoid** *a.* resembling mucus. **Blennorrha·gia, Blenno·rrhœa,** discharge of mucus; hence **-rrha·gic, -rrho·ic** *a.*

Blenny (ble·ni). 1774. [ad. L. *blennius* (in Pliny), f. Gr. βλέννος slime, mucus.] A genus of small spiny-finned fishes, the scales of which are coated with mucus.

Blent, *ppl. a.* [f. BLEND *v.*²] Mingled.

Blepharo- (ble·făro), a. Gr. βλέφαρον eyelid, comb. form.

Blephari·tis, inflammation of the eyelids. **Ble·pharopla·sty,** the operation of supplying any deficiency caused by wound or lesion of the eyelid; hence **Ble pharopla·stic** *a.* **Ble·pharospasm,** spasm of the orbicular muscle of the eyelids. **Ble·pharostat,** an instrument for fixing the eyelid during operations.

Blere, obs. f. BLEAR.

‖**Bles-bok** (ble·sbǫk). 1824. [Du., f. *bles* BLAZE *sb.*² + *bok* goat.] A South African antelope, the *Gazella albifrons*.

Bless (bles), *v.*¹ [OE. *blœ̄dsian, blēdsian, blētsian*, f. *blōd* blood. Not in other Teut. langs. The orig. meaning was thus 'to mark or consecrate with blood'. (See *Exod.* xii. 23.) But the word was chosen at the Eng. conversion to render L. *benedicere* 'to praise', which was itself used as tr. Heb., in the sense 'to bend the knee, worship'.

The pa. t. and pple. are usu spelt *blessed*, though pronounced (blest), exc. occas. in verse, or liturgical reading. As an adj. *blest* is now archaic, but is frequent in verse, and traditional phrases.]

1. To consecrate by a spoken formula or charm, or, later, by a prayer. **2.** *spec.* To sanctify (and protect) by making the sign of the cross. esp. *refl.* and *absol.* To cross oneself (*arch.*) OE. †**3.** To guard, keep *from* (evil) -1650. Also †*refl.* **4.** To call holy; to adore (God) as holy OE. **5.** To pronounce words that confer divine favour OE.; to invoke blessings upon ME. **6.** To confer well-being upon; to make happy, to prosper; *orig.* said of God OE. **7.** *refl.* To account or call themselves supremely happy *with, in, that* 1611. ¶ In ME. *bless to*, app. after *benedicere alicui*. **8.** Exclamatory uses: **a.** in sense 3, as *God b. me!* ellipt. *b. me!* *b.* (also *save*) *the mark* (see MARK). **b.** in sense 7, as (*God*) *b. you!* ¶ **9.** In many senses *bless* is euphemistic or ironical for curse, etc. 1812.

1. Phr. *To b. food*, to ask God's blessing upon it (cf. 5). 2. *Not to have a penny to b. oneself with*: in allusion to the cross on the silver penny (cf. Ger. *Kreutzer*), or to the practice of crossing the palm with a piece of silver. 3. The bellmans drowsy charm To b. the doors from nightly harm MILT. *Pens.* 83. 4. Then God be blesst, it is the blessed Sunne *Tam. Shr.* IV. v. 18. 5. Then shal the Busshop blisse the children, thus saying *Bk. Com. Prayer*. The Fatherless..and the Stranger b. his unseen Hand in their prayers STEELE. 6. It [mercy] is twice blest, It blesseth him that giues, and him that takes *Merch. V.* IV. i. 186. 7. The nations shall blesse themselues in him *Jer.* iv. 2. 8. B. us! What a word on A title-page is this MILT. *Sonn.* xi. 5. *To b. oneself*: to ejaculate 'God b. me!', etc. Hence **Ble·sser.**

†**Bless,** *v.*² 1526. [a. F. *blesser*; cf. BLECHE.] To wound; to thrash -1612.

Tarry, thou knave..I shall make these hands b. thee 1575.

†**Bless,** *v.*³ 1596. [Mainly Spenserian; ? a use of prec.] To brandish; also to brandish round (an object *with* a weapon).

Blessed, blest (ble·sĕd, blest), *ppl. a.* ME. [f. BLESS *v.*¹ See note under BLESS *v.*] **1.** Consecrated, holy. **2.** Adorable ME. **3.** Happy, fortunate ME.; beatified 1475. Also *absol.* The beatified saints ME. **4.** Pleasurable, blissful 1458. **b.** Of plants and herbs: Endowed with healing virtues, as *b. thistle, Carduus benedictus* 1563. **5.** = 'cursed' or the like (cf. BLESS *v.* 9) 1806. As quasi-*adv.* Blessedly 1600.

1. The B. Sacrament 1688. 2. Oure blessyd lorde Iesu 1493. **c.** She desires no isles of the blest, no quiet seats of the just TENNYSON. 4 b. The blest infusions That dwell in vegetives *Per.* III. ii. 35. Hence †**Ble·ssedful** *a.* full of blessing. †**Ble·ssedhede,** beatitude. **Ble·ssedly, ble·stly** *adv.* **Ble·ssedness,** the state of being blessed, *esp.* with divine favour, as in *single blessedness* *Mids. N.* I. i. 78; hence used *joc.* for the unmarried state.

Blessing (ble·siŋ), *vbl. sb.* OE. [f. BLESS *v.*¹ + -ING¹.] †**1.** The action of the vb. (senses 1, 2) -1563. **2.** Authoritative declaration of divine favour; benediction; and hence **b.** Invocation of divine favour. **3.** Favour and prospering influence of God. (So now 'to ask a b.') OE. **4.** Anything that makes happy or prosperous; a boon ME. †**b.** A present (tr. Heb.) -1611. **5.** Grateful adoration ME.

2. All the blessings Of a glad father, compasse thee about *Temp.* v. i. 179. 3. With God's B. he will recover 1881. 4. Eminence, Wealth, Soueraignty; which, to say sooth, are Blessings SHAKS. b. I pray thee, take a b. of thy seruant 2 *Kings* v. 15.

Blest, pa. t. and pple. of BLESS *v.*¹

Blet (blet), *v.* 1835. [ad. (by Lindley) F. *blettir*, f. *blet.*] *intr.* To become 'sleepy' as an over-ripe pear.

Blether, blather (ble·ðəɹ, blæ·-), *v.* *Sc.* and *n. dial.* [ME. *blather*, a. ON. *blaðra*, f. *blaðr* nonsense. In U. S. *blather*, the etymological form, is usual.] **1.** *intr.* To talk nonsense loquaciously 1524; *trans.* to babble 1810. **2.** *intr.* To cry loudly (*dial.*) 1863. Hence **Ble·ther, bla·ther** *sb.* voluble nonsense.

Ble·therskate, bla·therskite. *dial.* and *U.S. colloq.* 1650. [f. BLETHER *v.* + SKATE in Sc. used contemptuously. Popularized in U.S. by the Sc. song *Maggie Lauder*, during the War of Independence.] A talker of blatant nonsense.

Jog on your gait, ye bletherskate *Maggie Lauder* i.

Ble·tonism. 1821. [f. M. *Bleton.*] The supposed faculty of perceiving subterraneous springs and currents by sensation.

Blewits (bl¹ū·ˌits). 1830. [prob. f. BLUE.] An edible mushroom.

†**Bleymes.** 1725. [a. F. *bleime* = *blême* adj.; see BLEMISH.] An inflammation in the foot of a horse between the sole and the bone.

Blick (blik). 1881. [a. Ger. *blick* sheen.] The brightening or iridescence appearing on silver or gold at the end of the cupelling or refining process (Raymond).

Blight (bləit), *sb.* 1611. [?] **1.** *gen.* Any atmospheric or invisible influence that suddenly blasts, nips, or destroys plants, or affects them with disease; a diseased state of plants so originating 1669. **2.** *spec.* **a.** Diseases in plants caused by fungoid parasites, as mildew, rust, or smut 1611. **b.** An aphis, destructive to fruit-trees 1802. **3.** *fig.* Anything which withers hopes or prospects, or checks prosperity 1852.

3. The withering b. of Turkish rule 1884.

Blight (bləit), *v.* 1695. [f. prec.] **1.** *trans.* To affect with blight. **2.** *fig.* To affect balefully, nip in the bud 1712.

2. Deprivation of rank..which blights so many prospects LEWIS. Hence **Bli·ghtingly** *adv.*

Blighter (bləi·təɹ). 1822. [f. prec. + -ER¹.] **1.** A thing that blights. **2.** A contemptible fellow; sometimes *joc.* 1896.

Blighty (bləi·ti). *Army slang.* 1915. [ad. Hind. *bilāyatī* foreign, f. Arab. *wilāyat* VILAYET.] England, home; in the war of 1914–18, a wound that secured return to England.

†**Blin,** *v.* [OE. *blinnan* = **belinnan*: see BE-, LIN *v.*] *intr.* and *trans.* To leave off, stop -1765.

Blind (bləind), *a.* [Com. Teut.: OE. *blind* :—OTeut. **blindo-z*; cf. Lith. *blĕndzas.*] **1.** Without the sense of sight. **b.** *absol.* A blind person, *esp.* as *pl.* The blind as a class OE. **c.** (*attrib.* of prec.) Of, pertaining to, or for the use of the blind as a class: as *b. asylum* (mod.). **2.** *fig.* and *transf.* Lacking in intellectual, moral, or spiritual perception OE. **3.** *fig.* Undiscriminating; inconsiderate, heedless, reckless ME. **b.** Purposeless 1873. **4.** *fig.* Acting without intelligence or consciousness 1692. **5.** *transf.* Dark, obscure (*arch.*) OE.; †having its light cut off -1705. **6.** Dim; indistinct ME.; of a letter, indistinctly or imperfectly addressed 1864. **7.** Out of sight, secret, obscure. With *b. alley* cf. 10. **b.** Of a way or path: Difficult to trace 1593. **8.** Covered from sight 1513. **9.** Having no openings for light or passage 1603. **10.** Closed at one end. So *b. alley*; cf. 7. 1668. **11.** Of plants: Without buds or eyes, or without a terminal flower.

1. Galileo, frail and b. 1859. **b.** If the blinde lead the blinde, both shall fall into the ditch *Matt.* xv. 14. 2. Blynde jugement of men WYCLIF. *B. side*: the unguarded, also, formerly, the unpresentable side. 3. B. prejudice HAZLITT, speed DICKENS, fury MACAULAY. 4. B. chance BENTLEY. 5. *B. lantern*: a dark lantern. 6. *B. man, officer, reader*, a post-office official who deals with 'b. letters'. 7. To..some b. change-house SCOTT. **b.** The b. mazes of this tangled wood MILT. *Comus* 181. 9. A b. wall, hedge, window, door (*mod.*). Phr. *B. story*, one without point.

Comb.: **b. area** (*Archit.*), a clear space around the basement wall of a house; **b.-axle** = *dead-axle*; **-beetle,** a name for beetles which fly against people, esp. by night; also, a small beetle found in rice; **-blocking** (*Bookbinding*), impressions on book-covers produced by heated blocks, etc., without gold-leaf; **-coal,** non-bituminous coal which burns without flame; **-fish,** the *Amblyopsis spelæus*; **-gallery** (see Blind *a.* 10); **-hazard, -hookey,** games at cards; **-level** (*Mining*), one not yet connected with other workings; **-shaft,** a winze; **-shell** (*Artillery*), one containing no powder, also one that fails to explode; **-spot,** the spot on the retina which is insensible to light; **-story** (*Archit.*), a triforium below the clerestory of a cathedral, admitting no light; **b. tooling** = *blind-blocking*. Hence **Bli·ndish** *a.* **Bli·ndling** *sb.* a b. person. **Bli·ndly** *adv.* in a b. way; without an opening. **Bli·ndness** (*lit.* and *fig.*).

Blind (bləind), *v.* [f. BLIND *a.*, first in ME.; phonetic var. of BLEND *v.*¹] **1.** To make blind; to render insensible to light or colour. Also *fig.* **2.** To hide; to make difficult to trace ME. **3.** To deprive (things) of light 1643. **b.** To eclipse 1633. **4.** *Gunnery.* To provide with blindages 1850. **5.** *intr.* To be or become blind or dim ME.

1. Blinded of one eye 1875. This great light blyndeth my sight PALSGR. *fig.* How jealousy blinds people SHERIDAN. 3. **b.** Thy sweet eyes..b. the stars. Hence **Bli·nded** *ppl. a.* (senses 1, 4); having the window-blinds drawn down. **Bli·nder,** he who or that which blinds; a blinker for a horse. (U. S.) **Bli·ndingly** *adv.*

Blind (bləind), *sb.* 1535. [f. BLIND *v.* or *a.*] **1.** Anything which obstructs the light or sight; *esp.* a screen for a window made of woven material mounted on a roller 1702. **2.** A blinker for a horse. **3.** A blindage 1644.

†4. Any means or place of concealment -1697. 5. *fig.* A pretence, a pretext, to conceal one's real design 1664.

2. *Venetian blinds*: those made of light laths fixed on strips of webbing. 5. Her constant care of me was only a b. STEELE. Hence **Bli·ndage**, a screen or the like used in fortification, sieges, etc. to protect from the enemy's firing; a mantelet. **Bli·ndless** *a.*

Blindfold (bləi·ndfōᵘld), *v.* [ME. *blindfelle(n*, f. *fellen* to FELL. The assoc. with *folding* is a 16th c. perversion.] †1. To strike blind -1440. 2. To cover the eyes, *esp.* with a bandage ME. 3. *fig.* To darken the mind 1581.

Blindfold, *a.* 1450. [see prec.] 1. Having the eyes bandaged so as to prevent vision 1483. 2. *fig.* With the mind blinded; without forethought, reckless. Cf. BLIND *a.* 3.

2. The b. blows of ignorance DRYDEN. Hence **Bli·ndfold** *sb.* a bandage over the eyes (*lit.* and *fig.*). **Bli·ndfoldly** *adv.* (*rare*).

Blind gut. 1594. [See BLIND *a.* 10.] The *cæcum.*

†**Bli·nd-head.** 1662. A cover for a retort; a retort with such a cover -1743.

†**Blindman.** ME. Now written as two wds. *Much Ado* II. i. 205.

Blind-man's-buff (bləi·nd mænz bʊ·f). 1590. [f. BLIND-MAN + BUFF = buffet, blow.] A game in which one player is blindfolded, and tries to catch and identify any one of the others, who, on their part, push him about. Also *fig.*

fig. Government by Blind-man's-buff CARLYLE.

Blind man's holiday. The time just before candles are lighted.

Bli·nd-nettle. OE. [f. BLIND *a.* II, as wanting sting.] *Herb.* The Dead-nettle; also the Hemp-nettle and Hedge Nettle.

Blind-worm (bləi·nd,wɔ̄ɹm). 1450. [Cf. Da. *blindorm*; so called from the smallness of its eyes.] The Slow-worm (*Anguis fragilis*). Formerly used also of the Adder.

Blink (bliŋk), *v.* [In ME. only as occas. var. of BLENK. Since 1575 exclusively mod. Eng. Cf. Ger. *blinken.* Of unkn. origin.] †1. To deceive (*rare*). [For ME. BLENCH *v.*[1] 1.] †2. *intr.* = BLENCH *v.*[1] 2 (*rare*) ME. only. 3. To twinkle with the eye or eyelids; to glance; to look with glances; to wink for an instant 1590. 4. To cast a sudden or momentary gleam of light; to shine unsteadily or dimly 1786. 5. To shut the eyes to; to shirk, pass by, ignore: *orig.* a sporting phrase 1742. 6. To turn (milk, beer, etc.) slightly sour 1616. *intr.* 1648. ¶7. To cause to blink. LANDOR. (Pseudo-arch.)

3. On him she..blinkit bonnilie 1729. A..setter..blinking at the blaze 1863. 4. Ev'ry star that blinks aboon BURNS. 5. Dogs b. their coveys BYRON. Hence **Blinked** *ppl. a.* affected with a blink. **Bli·nking** *vbl. sb.*; *spec.* in *Brewing*: giving a sharp taste to beer by letting the wort stand; *ppl. a.*, winking, etc.; also (*slang*) used as a substitute for a strong expletive.

†**Blink,** *sb.*[1] ME. [f. BLINK *v.* 1.] 1. A trick; = BLENCH *sb.* ME. only. 2. *pl.* Boughs thrown to turn aside deer from their course; also feathers, etc. on a thread to scare birds -1625.

Blink (bliŋk), *sb.*[2] ME. [f. BLINK *v.* 3-4.] 1. A momentary gleam of light; a slight flash; a twinkling gleam; also *poet.* glimmer 1717. Also *fig.* 2. A (bright) glance; a glimpse. (Chiefly *Sc.*) 1594. 3. *transf.* An instant, the twinkling of an eye; = Ger. *Augenblick.* (Chiefly *Sc.*) 1813. 4. = ICE-BLINK: a shining whiteness about the horizon produced by reflection from distant masses of ice. Also, loosely, a large mass or field of ice. 1772.

1. Like blue-bottle flies in a b. of sunshine SCOTT. 3. Bide a b. SCOTT. 4. The b. from packs of ice, appears of a pure white 1818. Hence **Blinks** *sb. Herb.* Blinking Chickweed, *Montia fontana.*

Blink (bliŋk), *a.* 1590. [Cf. BLINKED.] 1. Of the eyes: Habitually blinking. Hence **Blink-eyed** *a.* 2. Of milk: Slightly sour 1883.

Blinkard (bli·ŋkǎrd). 1510. [f. BLINK *v.* + -ARD.] 1. One who habitually blinks or winks. 2. *fig.* One who lacks mental perception 1523. 3. *attrib.*, or *adj.*, usu. *fig.* 1529.

Blinker (bli·ŋkəɹ). 1636. [f. as prec. + -ER[1].] 1. One who blinks; a purblind person. 2. *pl.* Spectacles for directing the sight in one direction only, so as to cure squinting, or to protect the eyes; = GOGGLES 1732. b. Leather screens attached to a horse's bridle on each side to prevent his seeing in any direction except straight ahead 1789. 3. The eye (*slang.*) 1816.

2. Bigots who but one way see Through blinkers of authority M. GREEN. Hence **Bli·nker** *v.* to put blinkers on; *fig.* to hoodwink.

Blirt (blɔ̄ɹt), *v. n. dial.* 1721. [? echoic.] To burst into tears; disfigure with tears. Hence **Blirt** *sb.* a gust of wind and rain. *Naut.*

Bliss (blis), *sb.* [OE. *bliðs*:—OTeut. type **blīþsjā-*, f. **blīþi-s*, OE. *blīðe* blithe. Cf. BLESS *v.*[1] 7.] †1. Blitheness of aspect. (Only in OE.) 2. Blitheness; gladness; enjoyment; *esp.* the beatitude of heaven. Hence, paradise. *concr.* A cause of delight. OE.

2. Blisse of þe bodi WYCLIF. O only blest, and Author of all b. DRUMM. OF HAWTH. Far other once beheld in b. MILT. *P. L.* i. 607. *concr.* Womman is mannes Ioye and al his blis CHAUCER.

Blissful (bli·sful), *a.* ME. [f. BLISS *sb.* + -FUL.] 1. Full of or fraught with bliss. †2. Beatified; sacred -1534. †3. Having power to bless 1598.

1. B. bride of a b. heir TENNYSON. The b. Seat MILT. Hence **Bli·ssful-ly** *adv.*, **-ness.**

Bli·ssom, *a.* 1668. [a. ON. *blæsma*, in same sense.] Of a ewe: In heat.

Bli·ssom, *v.* ME. [f. as prec.] 1. *trans.* Of a ram: To tup. In *pass.* said of the ewe. 2. *intr.* To be lustful ME.

Blister (bli·stəɹ), *sb.* [ME. *blester, blister*, ? a. OF. *blestre* ('tumeur' Godef.), and ON. *blāstr*, f. *blāsa* to blow. Not in OE.] 1. A thin vesicle on the skin, containing serum, caused by friction, a burn, a vesicatory, or the like. 2. A swelling, containing fluid or air, on a plant, metal, a painted surface, etc. 1597. 3. *Med.* Anything applied to raise a blister 1541.

Comb.: **b.-beetle, -fly,** an insect used for raising blisters, *spec.* the Spanish fly (*Cantharis vesicatoria*); **-copper,** copper having a blistered surface, obtained during smelting; **-plant,** a name for *Ranunculus acris, R. sceleratus*, etc.; **-steel,** steel having a blistered surface, obtained during the process of converting iron into shear-steel, etc. Hence **Bli·stery** *a.*

Blister (bli·stəɹ), *v.* 1496. [f. prec.] 1. *trans.* To raise blisters on. Also *fig.* and *transf.* Also *absol.* 1541. 2. *intr.* To be or become covered with blisters 1496.

1. Bled, cupped, or blistered SCOTT. *fig.* This tyrant whose sole name blisters our tongue *Macb.* IV. iii. 12.

Blite (bləit). ME. [ad. L. *blitum*, a. Gr. βλίτον.] *Herb.* Name for plants of the N.O. *Chenopodiaceæ*: esp. Wild Spinach (*C. Bonus-Henricus*), *Amaranthus blitum*, species of *Atriplex*, and the genus *Blitum* (STRAWBERRY BLITE). Formerly also for Garden Spinach.

Blithe (bləið), *a.* (*sb.* and *adv.*) [Com. Teut.: OE. *blīðe*:—OTeut. **blīþi-z*; ? f. stem **blī-* to shine.] A. *adj.* †1. Exhibiting kindly feeling to others -1570. 2. Jocund, gay, sprightly, merry. (Now mostly of things.) OE. 3. Of men: Joyous, cheerful; glad, happy, well-pleased. Since 16th c. chiefly *poet.* OE.

2. Buxom, b., and debonair MILT. *Allegro* 24. B. sounds of festal music 1855. 3. Bardolph, be blythe SHAKS. **Bli·the-ly** *adv.*, **-ness.** **Bli·thesome** *a.*

B. *sb.* †1. A blithe one; cf. *fair.* 1548. †2. Compassion, good-will; mirth, delight -1585. Hence **Bli·theful** *a.* **Bli·thefully** *adv.*

C. *adv.* †a. Benignantly. b. Blithely. OE.

Blithering (bli·ðəriŋ), *ppl. a. colloq.* 1889. [f. *blither*, var. BLETHER.] Senselessly talkative; as an intensive, 'consummate', and hence, contemptible.

Blizzard (bli·zǎɹd). orig. *U.S.* 1829. [prob. echoic; cf. dial. *blizzer, blizzom*, said of blazing, blasting, or dazzling things.] 1. A sharp blow or knock; a shot. Also *fig.* 2. A furious blast of frost-wind and blinding snow 1870.

2. Those fearful blasts known as 'blizzards' which send the..dry snow whirling in icy clouds 1881.

Bloat (blōᵘt), *a.*[1] [ME. *blote*, ? = ON. *blaut-r* 'soaked, wet'; or from a parallel form **blōt.* With sense 2 cf. ON. *blautr fiskr*, i.e. 'soft fish'.] †1. ? Soft with moisture. ME. only. 2. *B. herring*: a bloater: see BLOAT *v.*[1] -1661.

Bloat (blōᵘt), *a.*[2] [ME. *blout, blowt* = ON. *blautr*- soft. See also BLOAT *a.*[1]] †1. *Blowte, bloute*: ? Soft, flabby; puffy -1603. 2. *Bloat*: Puffed, swollen, *esp.* with self-indulgence. (In mod. writers an echo of Shaks.: see quot.) 1638.

1. Let the blowt king tempt you againe to bed *Haml.* III. iv. 182. [So all the Quartos, exc. Q 1.]

Bloat, *v.*[1] 1611. [app. f. BLOAT *a.*[1]] *trans.* To cure (herrings) by a process which leaves them soft and only half-dried. (*Bloated* herrings are opposed to *dried* or *red* herrings.) Hence **Bloa·ted** *ppl. a.*[1] half-dried in smoke.

Bloat, *v.*[2] 1677. [app. f. BLOAT *a.*[2]] 1. To blow out, swell, make turgid. Also *absol.* 2. *intr.* To swell 1735.

Bloa·ted, *ppl. a.*[2] 1664. [f. prec. + -ED.] 1. Swollen, puffed up, *esp.* with self-indulgence; of things, overgrown, of excessive size. 2. Swollen with pride; puffed up, pampered 1731.

1. B. wassailers KEATS, armaments DISRAELI. 2. A b. aristocracy 1868. Hence **Bloa·tedness.**

Bloa·ter. 1832. [f. BLOAT *a.*[1], after *deader*, etc.] A bloat or bloated herring.

Blob (blǫb), *sb.* 1536. [See BLEB.] 1. A bubble. Now *n. dial.* 2. A pimple. *n. dial.* 1597. 3. A globule of liquid or viscid substance 1725. 4. A small rounded mass of colour 1863.

3. A honey b. [yellow gooseberry] GALT. A b. of ink 1857, jelly 1866. Hence **Blo·bby** *a.*

Blobber (blǫ·bəɹ), *a.* 1593. [var. of BLABBER, perh. influenced by BLOB.] Of the lips: Thick, swollen, protruding. Hence **b.-lipped** *a.*

Hanging b. lips but pout for Kisses DRYDEN.

Blobber, obs. and dial. f. BLUBBER *sb.* and *v.*

Block (blǫk), *sb.* [Partly ME. adoption of F. *bloc*, a. OHG. *bloh* (mod. Ger. *block*), of unkn. origin; partly taken directly from BLOCK *v.*] 1. A log of wood; part of the trunk of a tree. Often used in similes as a type of inertia or stupidity. 2. A large solid piece of wood: a. One of which the top or surface is used for various operations: *e.g.* for chopping on, *esp.* by butchers; for beetling or hammering on; for mounting, or dismounting from, a horse, etc. 1485. b. The piece of wood on which the condemned were beheaded 1541. c. A falcon's perch 1844. 3. A piece of wood or other substance on which something is moulded or shaped: *spec.* a. A mould for a hat 1575. Hence b. *fig.* Shape, fashion (of hat) 1580. 4. *Mech.* A pulley or system of pulleys mounted in a case; used to increase the mechanical power of the ropes running through them; employed esp. for the rigging of ships, and in lifting great weights 1622. 5. A piece of wood which acts as a support 1801. 6. A piece of wood on which lines, letters, or figures are engraved, in order to be printed from it, or to be stamped by pressure 1732. 7. *gen.* Any solid mass of matter with an extended surface 1530. b. A large quantity of anything dealt with at once. Hence *In b.*: wholesale; = Fr. *en bloc.* 1876. 8. A lump of wood, stone, etc. that bars one's way; *fig.* an obstacle. Now only in *stumbling-b.* 1500. 9. *spec.* A mass of rock or stone in its unhewn state 1847. b. A piece prepared for building purposes; also, the bricks which children build with 1854. 10. A compact mass of buildings, with no intervening spaces; (*esp.* in U.S. and Canada) the quadrangular mass of buildings included between four streets, etc. b. A space of ground bounded by four streets. 1851. 11. *fig.* A blockhead; a hard-hearted person 1553. 12. (from BLOCK *v.*) A blocking up, *e.g.* of traffic or progress 1864. 13. *Cricket.* The position in which a batsman blocks balls; the *centre* of the wicket; hence *b.-hole* (or *b.*) a mark made in the ground to indicate the *centre.* 14. *attrib.* or *adj.* Taken in the block 1864.

1. Sitting patient on a big b.—huge stump of a tree-root FROUDE. 2. He laid down his head upon the b. CLARENDON. 3. We have blockes for all heads DEKKER. *Barber's b.*: a wooden head for a wig. 7. A b. of tin 1758, of masonry 1813, of ice TYNDALL. b. Large blocks of the Stock for future delivery 1876. 9. *Erratic b.*: a boulder transported by physical agencies far from its native site. 10. American towns are built in blocks FREEMAN. 11. You Blockes, you stones, you worse than senslesse things *Jul. C.* I. i. 40. *A chip of the* (*same* or) *old b.*: a piece of the same stuff; a descendant taking after a parent or ancestor. *As deaf* (etc.) *as a b.*: see 1. *To cut blocks with a razor*: (any incongruous application of abilities or means). **B. system** (on *Railways*): a system in which the line is divided into sections, with signals, so worked that no train is allowed to pass into any section till it is wholly clear.

Comb.: **b.-battery,** in gunnery, a wooden battery for two or more small pieces mounted on wheels; **-furnace** = *Bloomery*; **-letters,** printing-types cut out of wooden blocks; **-printing,** printing from wooden blocks, as in the BLOCK-BOOKS, now also used for printing calico, etc.; so **-printed** *a.*; **-ship,** a ship

moored to block the entrance to a harbour; -tin, see TIN.
Hence **Blo·ckage**, a blocked (up) state. **Blo·ckish** *a.* of the nature of a b.; obtuse; roughly blocked out, rude. **Blo·ckish-ly** *adv.*, -ness.

Block (blǫk), *v.* 1570. [a. F. *bloquer*, f. *bloc* BLOCK *sb.*] 1. *trans.* To obstruct or close with obstacles (a passage). Also *fig.* 1645. 2. To shut *up* or *in* by obstructing ingress or egress 1630. 3. *spec.* To blockade (usu. with *up*) 1591. 4. To obstruct the course of 1865. 5. *Cricket.* To stop (a ball) with the bat; also *absol.* 1773. 6. *Parliament.* To prevent or postpone the passage of a bill; *spec.* to give notice of opposition to a bill, so that it cannot be taken after half-past twelve (midnight) 1884. 7. *trans.* To shape on, or stamp with, a block 1622. 8. To mark out roughly; to plan. Now usu. with *out*; also *in.* 1585. 9. To cut *out* into blocks, *e.g.* coal 1863. 10. To support or fit with blocks of wood 1881.
2. Our little harbor was..blocked in by heavy masses [of ice] KANE. 6. The term 'blocking' is a colloquial expression recognized in this House MR. SPEAKER 1884. 8. Pictures blocked in roughly 1884.

Blockade (blǫkē¹·d). ? 1680. [f. BLOCK *v.*, after Fr. wds. in -ADE.] 1. The shutting up of a place, blocking of a harbour, line of coast, frontier, etc., by hostile forces or ships, so as to stop ingress and egress 1693. 2. *transf.* A party of blockade-men. 3. *fig.* 1742.
1. *Paper b.*: one declared by a belligerent to exist, but not effective. *To raise a b.*: to withdraw the investing forces, or compel them to withdraw. *To break a b.*: to enter a blockaded port by force. *To run a b.*: to enter or leave a blockaded port by eluding the blockading force.
Comb.: b.-man, a coastguardsman; -runner, a vessel which attempts to run into a blockaded port; the owner, master, or one of the crew of such a vessel.

Blocka·de, *v.* 1680. [f. prec. sb.] 1. *trans.* To subject to a blockade as an incident of war. 2. *transf.* and *fig.* To obstruct 1732.
2. Huge bales of British cloth b. the door POPE. Hence **Blocka·der**, one who blockades; a blockading vessel.

Blo·ck-book. 1727. †a. A book of wooden tablets. b. A book printed from engraved wooden blocks.

Blo·cker. 1609. [f. BLOCK *v.*] One who blocks; *spec.* in *Shoemaking* and *Bookbinding*.

Blockhead (blǫ·khĕd). 1549. [f. BLOCK *sb.*] †1. A wooden head, a wooden block for hats or wigs –1698. 2. Hence, an utterly stupid fellow 1549. †3. as *adj.* Blockheaded, stupid –1719.
2. Block-heads and dull-pated Asses 1668. Hence **Blo·ckhea·ded** *a.* stupid, obtuse. **Blo·ckhea·dedness. Blo·ckhea·dish** *a.* **Blo·ckheadism.** †**Blo·ckheadly** *a.*

Blockhouse (blǫ·khaus). [Common since *c* 1500: of uncertain history. App. earlier in Eng. than in Ger., Du., or Fr.] a. *orig.* A detached fort blocking a strategical point. b. Later: An edifice constructed chiefly of timber, loopholed and embrasured for firing. 1512. c. *slang.* A prison 1624. d. A house of squared logs of timber 1857. Also *transf.* and *fig.*
a. The b. of Tilberie GERARD. d. The Backwoodsman who begins by building a b. 1878.

Blo·cking, *vbl. sb.* 1585. [f. BLOCK *v.* or *sb.*] 1. The action of the vb. BLOCK 1637. 2. The product of this action 1585. 3. *Carpentry.* See BLOCK *v.* 10. 1823.
Blocking course (or **blocking**): the plain course of stone which surmounts the cornice at the top of a Greek or Roman building; also a projecting course of stone or brick at the base of a building.

†**Blo·ckwood.** = LOGWOOD –1667.

Bloke (blōᵘk), *sb. slang.* 1851. [?] Fellow.

†**Blok(e, bloc,** *a.* [repr. of OE. *blāc*:—OTeut. **blaiko-z*, f. stem of *blīkan, blaik* to shine; or f. OE. *blæc*, (*blac-*) BLACK. Cf. BLAKE.] Pale; also black, dark. ME. only.

†**Blo·man.** ME. only. [f. *blo* adj. blackish blue + MAN.] A black man, negro.

Blond, blonde (blǫnd). 1481. [a. F.:—med. L. *blondus* yellow, of unkn. origin. Revived as Fr. in 17th c.; whence the final *e* when applied to a woman.] A. *adj.* Prop. (of the hair): Light auburn; *loosely*, light-coloured, fair. b. *Blond(e lace*: see B 2. B. *sb.* 1. A person with blond hair; one with 'fair' hair and complexion; *esp.* a woman, in which case spelt *blonde* 1822. 2. (More fully *blonde lace*): A silk lace of two threads, twisted and formed in hexagonal meshes; orig. of unbleached silk, but now white or black. Usu. written *blonde*, as in Fr. (sc. *dentelle*). 1755. Also *attrib.*
Comb. b-metal, a clay ironstone of the coal measures. Hence **Blo·ndness.**

Blood (blʊd). [Com. Teut.: OE. *blōd*:—OTeut. **blôdo-m*, found only in Teut.] I. 1. The red liquid circulating in the arteries and veins of man and the higher animals; extended, later, to the corresponding liquid, coloured or colourless, in animals of lower organization. 2. *fig.* and *transf.* Applied to liquids or juices in some way resembling it; e.g. to a blood-like juice; to the sap of plants, etc. ME. 3. Blood shed; hence, bloodshed; manslaughter, murder, death OE. b. The guilt of bloodshed OE.
1. *Flesh and b.*: = 'humanity', as opp. to 'deity or disembodied spirit'. See FLESH. †*To let b.* (in Surg.): to bleed; also *transf.* to shed the b. of. †*God's b.!* †*Christ's b.!* †*'S blood!* †*Blood*: forcible ejaculations not now in use. 2. Go, sucke the subtle b. o' th' Grape *Timon* IV. iii. 432. 3. An Affront that nothing but B. can expiate ADDISON. b. His b. be on vs, and on our children *Matt.* xxvii. 25.
II. †1. The vital fluid; *hence*, the vital principle; life –1740. 2. The supposed seat of emotion, passion; whence, Passion, temper, mood, disposition; *emphatically*, mettle, anger ME. 3. The supposed seat of animal appetite; hence, the fleshly nature of man 1597.
2. When you perceiue his b. enclin'd to mirth *2 Hen. IV*, IV. iv. 38. Phr. *To breed bad* (or *ill*) *b.* *In cold b.*: not in the heat of passion. 3. The strongest oathes, are straw To th' fire ith' b. *Temp.* IV. i. 53. *In b.*: full of life; *out of b.*: not vigorous. (Hunting phrases.)
III. 1. The typical part of the body which children inherit from their parents and ancestors ME. 2. Hence, Blood-relationship, and *esp.* parentage, lineage, descent; also: Family, kin, race, stock, nationality ME. 3. *concr.* Persons of any specified blood or family collectively; blood-relations, kindred, family, race ME. 4. *esp.* Offspring, child, near relative, one dear as one's own offspring ME. 5. Blood worth mention, good blood; good parentage or stock. Cf. BIRTH (*sb.*¹) ME. Also *attrib.*
1. *Blue blood*: tr. Sp. *sangre azul* claimed by certain families of Castile, as being uncontaminated by Moorish, Jewish, or other admixture; prob. founded on the blueness of the veins of people of fair complexion. *Fresh b.*: a new strain or stock not related by b. to the family; also *fig.* [God] hath made of one b. all nations of men *Acts* xvii. 26. 2. *B. royal* or *the b.*: royal race or family. *Whole b.*: race by both father and mother, as opp. to *half-b.*, by one parent only. Hence concr. *half-b.*: one whose b. is half of one race and half of another. B. is thicker than water *Provb.* 3. By that one Deed Enobles all his B. DRYDEN. *To run in the* (†*a*) *b.*: *i.e.* in a family or race. 4. (*Own*) *flesh and b.*: near kindred. See FLESH. 5. The highest pride of b. MACAULAY. In horses..there is nothing like b. 1846. *To restore in* or *to b.*: to re-admit to forfeited privileges of birth and rank those under sentence of 'corruption of b.'; see ATTAINDER.
IV. †1. A living being –ME. 2. 'A hot spark' (J.); a 'fast' or foppish man. *arch.* 1562. b. *Univ.* and *Public School slang.* One of those who are held to set the fashion in dress and manners.
2. A..celebrated 'b.' or dandy about town THACKERAY. *Young b.*; now, a youthful member of a party, who brings to it youthful vigour.
†V. A disease in sheep and in swine –1787.
Comb.: b.-baptism, the martyrdom of early Christians who had not been baptized; -bath, a bath in warm b.: also, a massacre; †-boltered *ppl. a.*, clotted with b.; *esp.* having the hair matted with b.; [see BALTER]; -fine, one paid as whole or part compensation for murder; -flower, genus *Hæmanthus*; †-hunter, one who tracks murderers; -pudding, a black pudding; -ripe *a.*, (of fruit) so ripe that the juice has become b.-coloured, hence -ripeness; -sausage, a black pudding; -tree (Bot.), *Croton gossypiifolium*; -vein, a moth (*Bradyepetes amataria*); -wood, name of several trees, *e.g.* in Jamaica *Gordonia hæmatoxylon*, in Australia various species of Eucalyptus, etc.
Hence †**Bloo·ding** *sb.* a black pudding. **Bloo·dless** *a.* without b., *hence* lifeless; pallid from want of b.; unattended by bloodshed. **Bloo·dless-ly** *adv.*, -ness. **Bloo·d-like** *a.* like b.; like a blood (horse).

Blood (blʊd), *v.* 1593. [f. prec.] 1. *trans.* To cause blood to flow from; *esp.* in *Surg.* to BLEED 1633. 2. To wet or smear with blood. ? *Obs.* 1593. 3. *Venery.* To give a hound its first taste, or sight and smell of the blood of the game it is to hunt. Also *fig.* 1781. †4. To raise the blood of, *i.e.* to exasperate; *esp.* soldiers at the beginning of a fight –1677.
1. They had scruples about eating an animal not blooded in their own way LIVINGSTONE. 2. To b. the points of spears DRYDEN. 3. Blooded to fox BECKFORD.

Blooded (blʊ·dĕd), *a.* ME. [f. BLOOD *v.* or *sb.* + -ED.] †1. Stained with blood –1637. 2. Having (*hot, cold*, etc.) blood 1805. 3. Of horses: Of good breed 1858.

Bloo·d-guilty, *a.* 1597. [f. BLOOD + GUILTY.] Responsible for bloodshed. Hence **Blood-guiltiness.** So **Blood-gui·ltless** *a.*

Bloo·d-hea·t. 1812. The ordinary heat of blood in the healthy human body, viz. 98·6° Fahr. Also *fig.*

Bloo·dhound. ME. A large, very keen-scented dog (*Canis sanguinarius*), formerly much used in tracking large game, stolen cattle, and fugitives. Also *fig.* of men. Also *attrib.*

Bloo·d-le·tter. [OE. *blōd lǣtere.*] He who or that which lets blood. So **Bloo·d-letting,** phlebotomy; also *fig.*

Bloo·d-mo·ney. 1535. a. A reward for bringing about the death of another; *e.g.* money paid to a witness who gives evidence leading to conviction on a capital charge. b. Money paid the next of kin as compensation for the slaughter of a relative.

Blood-red, Bloo·d-re·d, *a.* ME. Red like blood.

Bloo·d-rela·tion. 1846. [See RELATION.] A person related by birth; a kinsman. var. **Bloo·d-re·lative.** HAWTHORNE.

Bloo·d-root. 1578. Pop. name of plants: *esp.* the Tormentil; Crimson Crane's Bill, and Red Puccoon (*Sanguinaria canadensis*) of N America.

Bloodshed (blʊ·dˌʃed), *sb.* (*a.*) 1500. [f. the phr. *to shed blood.*] 1. The shedding of blood; slaughter 1536. †2. An act of blood-shedding. (With *pl.*) –1677. 3. The shedding or parting with one's own blood; *orig.* said of the death of Christ. ? *Obs.* 1500. †4. = BLOOD-SHOT *sb.* and *adj.* –1702.
1. The long b. of the Civil Wars GREEN. Hence **Bloo·dshe·dder.**

Bloodshot (blʊ·dˌʃǫt). 1607. [Shorter f. BLOOD-SHOTTEN.] A. *adj.* Of the eye: Overshot or suffused with blood 1618. Also *fig.* and *transf.* 1851. †B. *sb.* [The adj. used *absol.*] 1. An effusion of blood, caused by inflammation of the conjunctiva –1671. 2. Any effusion of blood 1611.

†**Blood-shot** (blʊ·dʃǫt), *v.* 1578. [f. BLOOD-SHOT *a.*] To make bloodshot –1643.

Bloo·d-sho·tten, *a.* (*sb.*) *arch.* 1507. [Instrumental comb. f. *shotten* pa. pple. of SHOOT *v.*] A. *adj.* Earlier f. BLOODSHOT: now *arch.* †B. *sb.* = BLOOD-SHOT *sb.* 1578.

Blood-spavin; see SPAVIN.

Bloo·d-stain, *sb.* 1838. [f. BLOOD and STAIN *sb.*] A stain made by blood. So **Bloo·d-stained** *a.* stained with blood (*lit.* and *fig.*).

Blood-stone (blʊ·dstōᵘn). 1551. 1. A name given to certain precious stones spotted or streaked with red; esp. the mod. HELIOTROPE; also the *heliotrope* of Pliny. 2. Hematite. (Dicts.)
1. The bloodstone stoppeth blood 1551.

Bloo·d-strange. 1578. [? corrupt f. ME. *streng* 'string, tie'; or of Ger. or Du. origin. Cf. Ger. *harnstrenge* morbid retention of urine.] *Herb.* An obs. name of the Mousetail (*Myosurus minimus*).

†**Bloo·d-suck,** *v.* 1541. [f. BLOOD *sb.* + SUCK *v.*] *trans.* To suck blood from; said of leeches. Also *fig.* –1592.

Blood-sucker (blʊ·dsʊ·kəɹ). ME. [cf prec.] 1. An animal which sucks blood; *esp.* the leech. †2. One who draws or sheds the blood of another –1659. 3. *fig.* An extortioner; a sponger 1668.
3. While there is a silver sixpence left, these blood-suckers will never be quiet SWIFT.

Bloodthirsty (blʊ·dþɔ̄ːɹsti), *a.* 1535. Thirsting for blood; eager for bloodshed.

Blood-vessel (blʊ·dveˑsĕl). 1694. One of the tubes (veins or arteries) which convey the blood throughout the animal system.

Bloo·d-warm, *a.* 1577. As warm as blood; see BLOOD-HEAT. Also *fig.*

Blood-wite (blʊ·dwəit). Also (erron.) **-wit.** [OE. *blōdwīte*, f. *blōd* blood + *wīte* punishment.]

A penalty for bloodshed: **a.** in *O. E. Law*, A fine to be paid to the alderman or king, in addition to the *were-gild* ME. **b.** *gen.* A penalty for murder 1881.

Blood-worm (blɒ·dwɒɹm). 1741. **a.** A small bright-red earth-worm used by anglers. **b.** The scarlet larva of a genus of crane-flies (*Chironomus*) found in rain-water cisterns, etc.

Blood-wort (blɒ·dwɒɹt). ME. A name of plants having red roots or leaves, or supposed to stanch or to draw blood; *e.g.* the Bloody Dock (*Rumex sanguineus*), the Dwarf Elder (*Sambucus Ebulus*); also Burnet (*Sanguisorba officinalis*), and genus *Hæmodorum*.

Bloody (blɒ·di). [Com. Teut.: OE. *blōdig* :—OTeut. *blōđago-z; see BLOOD.] **A.** *adj.* **1.** Of the nature of, composed of, resembling, or pertaining to blood. **2.** Covered, smeared, stained, with blood; bleeding OE. **3.** Of animals: Having blood in the veins ME. **4.** Accompanied by or involving bloodshed; sanguinary ME. **5.** Of thoughts, words, etc.: Concerned with, portending, decreeing bloodshed ME. **6.** Bloodthirsty; blood-guilty 1563. **7.** Blood-red 1591. **8.** In low Eng., an epithet expressing detestation; often merely intens., *esp.* with a neg., as 'not a b. *one*'. [Prob. from the advb. use.] 1840.

1. In great agony he swet blody droppes 1526. 2. Dirty b. spots H. MORE. *B. grave*: the grave of one who has been murdered. †*B. hand* in *Forest-law*: one kind of trespass in the King's forest, in which a man is found there in any way imbrued with blood; cf. RED-HAND(ED); in *Her.*, the armorial device of Ulster, borne by baronets. 4. A b. deed *Macb.* II. iv. 23, battle ADDISON. 5. I do begin to haue b. thoughts *Temp.* IV. i. 220. 6. B. Queen Mary DICKENS. Hence **Bloo·dily** *adv.* **Bloo·diness.**

B. *adv.* †**1.** Bloodily ME. **2.** As an intensive: Very . . . and no mistake; abominably, desperately. Colloq. to *c* 1750; now low Eng., and usu. printed 'b—y'.

[Probably f. *blood*, *'sblood* (see BLOOD *sb.* I. 1)+-Y[1]; cf. WOUNDY *adv.*, f. WOUNDS.]

2. The doughty Bullies enter b. drunk DRYDEN. This is a b. positive old fellow FIELDING.

Comb.: **a.** †**b. flux** (formerly *flix*), dysentery; **b. nose beetle**, *Timarcha*; †**b.-water**, *hæmaturia*. **b.** In names of plants, as **b. finger**, the Foxglove; **b. man's finger**, the same; also the Arum or Wake-Robin; **b. dock** (*Rumex sanguineus*); **b. twig**, the Dogwood (*Cornus sanguinea*).

Bloody (blɒ·di), *v.* 1530. [f. the adj.] *trans.* To make BLOODY; also *fig.*

Bloody-bones (blɒ·di,bōᵘnz). Formerly -bone. 1550. Usu. in *Rawhead and Bloody-bone(s*, as the name of a bugbear to terrify children; also *fig.* 'bugbear, terror'.

Bloom (blūm), *sb.*[1] [ME. *blom*, *blome*; a. ON. *blóm* neut. 'a flower, bloom', and *blómi* masc. 'bloom, prosperity':—OTeut. *blōmon-m., f. the stem *blō- 'blow'.] **1.** The blossom or flower of a plant. (Expressing florescence as the culminating beauty of the plant.) **b.** *collect.* Blossom, flowers ME. Also *transf.* of persons (cf. 'flower'). **2.** *fig.* Prime, perfection ME. **3.** The crimson tint of the cheek; flush, glow. Also *fig.* 1752. **4.** The delicate powdery deposit on fruits like the grape, plum, etc., when fresh-gathered, and on certain plant-leaves. (? from prec.) 1639. **b.** *fig.* Freshness, delicate beauty 1777. **c.** In various special senses: *e.g.* the yellowish deposit on well-tanned leather, the powdery appearance on newly struck coins, etc. 1825. **5.** A fine variety of raisin 1841.

1. The fruytes of the holy goost..be more lyke..to be called blomes and floures than fruytes 1526. Sight of vernal b. MILT. *P. L.* III. 43. *In b.*: in flower, flowering. **b.** He was Engelondes blome ME. 2. His Maie of youth, and bloome of lustihood *Much Ado* v. i. 76. 3. Miss Bath had..recovered..her b. FIELDING. 4 **b.** *To take the b. off*: to deprive (a thing) of its first freshness or beauty. Hence **Bloo·mless** *a.* **Bloo·my** *a.*

Bloom (blūm), *sb.*[2] [:—OE. *blōma* in same sense. No examples known between OE. and the end of 16th c.] **1.** A mass of iron after having undergone the first hammering. *spec.* An ingot of iron or steel, or a pile of puddled bars, brought into the form of a thick bar, and left for further rolling when required for use 1674. ¶ **2.** Improp. The ball or mass of iron from the puddling furnace 1865. Hence **Bloomery, -ary,** the first forge in an iron-works through which the metal passes after melting, and in which it is made into blooms.

Bloom (blūm), *v.*[1] [ME. *blomen*, f. BLOOM *sb.*[1]] **1.** *intr.* To bear flowers; to blossom. **2.** *fig.* and *transf.* To come into, or be in, full beauty or vigour; to flourish ME. **3.** *trans.* To bring into bloom; to cause to flourish. Chiefly *fig.* (*arch.*) 1592. **4.** *intr.* To glow 1860. **5.** *trans.* To give a BLOOM to 1821. **6.** *techn.* To cloud a varnished surface 1859.

2. The daughter begins to b. before the mother can be content to fade JOHNSON. 3. The Tree of Life.. blooming Ambrosial Fruit MILT. *P. L.* IV. 219.

Bloom, *v.*[2] 1875. [f. BLOOM *sb.*[2]] To hammer or squeeze the ball or mass of iron from the puddling-furnace into a bloom; to shingle.

Bloomed (blūmd, *poet.* -ėd), (*ppl.*) *a.* 1505. [f. BLOOM *sb.* and *v.*] In bloom. Also *fig.*

Bloomer[1] (blū·məɹ). 1730. [f. BLOOM *v.*[1]] **1.** A plant that blooms (in some way). **2.** A floriated letter 1899. **3.** [= *blooming* error.] A bad mistake (*slang*) 1889.

Comb. **b.-pit,** a tan-pit in which hides are treated with a strong infusion of tanning liquor.

Bloomer[2]. *Hist.* 1868. [f. Mrs. Amelia Jenks *Bloomer* of N.Y.] More fully *B. costume, dress*: A style of female dress consisting of a short skirt and long loose trousers gathered closely round the ankles. **b.** Loose trousers or knickerbockers worn by women cyclists, etc.; 'rational dress' 1896. Hence **Bloo·merism,** the principles of Mrs. Bloomer as to female dress.

Bloo·ming, *ppl. a.* ME. [f. BLOOM *v.*[1]] **1.** That blooms 1664. **2.** *fig.* In the bloom of health, beauty, youth; flourishing ME. **b.** Bright, shining 1513. ¶ **3.** *slang.* Full-blown; often = BLOODY (sense 8) or the like. Cf. BLESSED (5). 1882.

2. His b. bride 1774. **b.** Her b. mantle torn TENNYSON. 3. Oh, you b. idiot 1882. Hence **Bloo·mingly** *adv.*

Blooth, var. of BLOWTH, bloom.

Blore (blōᵊɹ), *sb. arch.* 1440. [app. conn. w. *blow*, *blast*; perh. partly echoic (an 'expressive word', J.).] **a.** A violent blowing; also *fig.* **b.** *transf.* The air. CHAPMAN.

Blore, *v.* Now *dial.* 1440. Var. of BLARE, q.v.

Blossom (blɒ·səm). [OE. *blōstm*, *blōstma*, *blósma*, referred to the same root as BLOOM (*blō*-).] **1.** 'The flower that grows on any plant, previous to the seed or fruit'. (J.) Orig. the generic wd. for 'flower'. See BLOOM, FLOWER. **a.** A single flower (with *pl.*) OE. **b.** *collect.* The mass of flowers on a fruit-tree, etc. ME. Also *fig.* (by *simile.*) 1789. **2.** *fig.* Anything compared to the preceding ME. **3.** *techn.* **a.** *Mining.* The decomposed outcrop of a vein or a coal-bed. **b.** The colour of a horse whose hairs are white mixed with sorrel or bay, peach-colour; a horse so coloured.

1. **a.** The braunches ful of blosmes softe CHAUCER. *fig.* He prest the b. of his lips to mine TENNYSON. 2. The bloosme of comely courtesie SPENSER. My babe, my b. TENNYSON. Nipt in the blossome BP. HALL.

Comb. **b.-faced** *a.* having a red bloated face; so **-nosed.** Hence **Blo·ssomless** *a.* **Blo·ssomy** *a.*

Blossom (blɒ·səm), *v.* [OE. *blōstmian*, ME. *blosme(n*, f. prec.] *intr.* To put forth blossoms, bloom, flower. Also *transf.* and *fig.*

Fruites that blossome first, will first be ripe SHAKS.

Blot (blɒt), *sb.*[1] ME. [Only in Eng.; ?] **1.** A spot or stain of ink, mud, etc. **b.** An obliteration 1704. **c.** *transf.* Any dark patch; also, a blemish or disfigurement 1578. **2.** *fig.* A moral stain; a disgrace, a fault ME. **b.** Imputation of disgrace 1587.

1. Inky blottes and rotten Parchment bonds *Rich. II*, II. i. 64. 2. O dignity, O b. To honour and religion MILT. *Sams.* 411. Hence **Blo·tless** *a.*

Blot, *sb.*[2] 1598. [? a. Da. *blot* uncovered.] **a.** In *Backgammon*: An exposed piece, liable to be taken; also, the action of exposing a piece. **b.** *fig.* An exposed point in one's procedure; a fault or failing; also, a mark, butt 1649.

a. *To hit a b.*: to take an exposed piece. **b.** Here the critic has hit a b. (*mod.*).

Blot (blɒt), *v.* 1440. [f. BLOT *sb.*[1]] **1.** *trans.* To spot or stain with ink, tears, etc.; to blur. Also *absol.* **b.** *intr.* To become blotted 1860. **2.** To cover with worthless writing; to disfigure (*arch.*) 1494. **b.** To paint coarsely 1844. **3.** *fig.* **a.** To cast a blot upon; to tarnish (*arch.* or *Obs.*) 1566. †**b.** To stigmatize, calumniate -1611. **4.** To obliterate, efface. (Usu. with *out.*) 1530. **5.** *fig.* To efface, obscure, eclipse 1592. **6.** To dry with blotting-paper 1854.

1. Evene as he [my pen] goth he doth b. 1447. 2. The vnpleasant'st words That euer blotted paper *Merch. V.* III. ii. 253. 3. Vnknit that thretaning vnkinde brow..It blots thy beautie *Tam. Shr.* v. ii. 139. 4. My name be blotted from the booke of Life *Rich. II*, I. iii. 202. Repent yee..that your sins may be blotted out *Acts* iii. 19.

Blotch (blɒtʃ). 1604. [Eng. only. App. echoic f. BLOT. With sense 1 cf. BOTCH.] **1.** A discoloured patch on the skin; a pustule, boil, or botch. **2.** A large irregular spot or blot of ink, colour, etc. 1768. Also *fig.* and *transf.* **3.** = BLOT (of ink). *north.* and *Sc.* 1863.

2. The snow fell in large blotches 1807. Hence **Blo·tchy** *a.*

Blotch (blɒtʃ), *v.* 1604. [f. prec.] **1.** *trans.* To mark with blotches. **2.** = BLOT *v.*[1] *north.*

†**Blote, blot.** 1657. [? Conn. w. *blow* in *fly-blown*, etc.] The egg or larva of flies, etc.

Blotter (blɒ·təɹ). 1591. [f. BLOT *v.*] **1.** One who or that which blots, *esp.* a sorry writer 1601. **2.** A thing used for drying wet ink-marks, as a blotting-pad 1591. **3.** *Comm.* A waste-book; also, a rough copy of a letter. CRAIG.

Blottesque (blɒte·sk), *a.* 1880. [f. BLOT *v.*, after *grotesque*, etc.] **a.** Of painting: Characterized by blotted touches heavily laid on. **b.** quasi-*sb.* A daub 1882. Hence **Blotte·squely** *adv.* with b. effect.

Blotting (blɒ·tiŋ), *vbl. sb.* 1440. [f. BLOT *v.*] The action of the vb.; *concr.* a blot, smear, obliteration.

Phr. *B. out*: obliteration of writing, etc.; also, effacement, destruction.

Comb.: **b.-book,** a book consisting of leaves of b.-paper; also, a waste-book; **-case,** a cover enclosing b.-paper; **-pad,** a pad consisting of sheets of b.-paper joined at the edges; **-paper,** a bibulous unsized paper, used to absorb superfluous ink.

Blouse (blauz). 1828. [a. Fr. (blūz), of unkn. etym.] A short loose garment of cotton or silk, resembling a shirt, worn on the upper part of the body; prop. applied (as an alien term) to the blue blouse of the French workman. **2.** *transf.* A French workman 1865. Hence **Bloused** *ppl. a.* wearing a b.

Blow (blōᵘ), *v.*[1] Pa. t. **blew.** Pa. pple. **blown.** [OE. *blāwan* :—Goth. type *blaian, *baiblō, OTeut. ?*blǣjan, cogn. w. L. *flare*.] **I. 1.** *intr.* The proper verb naming the motion or action of the wind, or of an aerial current. **2.** To send out a strong current of air, *e.g.* from the mouth, or from bellows OE. **3.** To breathe hard, pant, puff ME. **4.** Of whales, etc.: To eject water and air from the blow-holes; to spout 1725. **5.** To utter noisy breath; to brag (chiefly *dial.*); to storm (chiefly *colloq.*) ME. ¶ *dial.* To smoke a pipe. **6.** (causal of 2.) ME. **7.** (causal of 3.) To cause to pant: usu. of horses 1651. **8.** *trans.* To emit (a current of air, breath, etc.) with the mouth; also to force (a current of air) *through*, *into*, *upon*, by other means. Also *fig.* ME. **b.** To smoke (tobacco); also *intr.* (*dial.*) 1808. †**9.** To utter; also with *out.* Usu. in a bad sense: To utter boastfully, angrily, etc. -1652. **10.** *trans.* To drive or carry by means of a current of air; also *fig.* ME. **b.** *intr.* To be driven or carried by the wind 1842. **11.** *trans.* (*fig.*) To proclaim, blaze *abroad*, †*out*, etc. ME.

1. Heark how it rains and blows WALTON. *To b. great guns*: to blow a violent gale. *To b. up*: to rise, increase in force. 2. *To b. hot and cold*: to be inconsistent or vacillating. (See Æsop's Fables.) 5. He brags and he blaws o' his siller BURNS. 6. To blowe smithes bellowes 1577. 7. To be well blown in the pursuit 1859. 8. Good thoughts are blown into a man by God HOBBES. *To b. off*: (*trans.*) to allow (steam, etc.) to escape forcibly with a blowing noise; also *fig.* to get rid of in a noisy way; *intr.* (for *refl.*) of steam, gas, etc.: to escape forcibly. 10. What winde blew you hither, Pistoll 2 *Hen. IV*, v. iii. 90. *To b. over*: (of storms, etc.) to pass over a place without descending upon it; to come to an end; also *fig.* of misfortune, danger, etc.

II. 1. To make (a wind-instrument) sound by blowing air into it OE. **b.** To sound (a blast) *on* or *with* an instrument ME. **c.** To sound the signal of (an advance, etc.) *on* an instrument ME. **d.** Predicated of the instrument 1593. **2.** *intr.* Of a wind-instrument: To give forth a sound by being blown ME. Of the blower: To sound a blast ME. Of the blast: To sound 1599. **3.**

To direct a current of air against so as to cool, warm, or dry ME. 4. *esp.* To direct a current of air into (a fire), in order to make it burn. Also with *up.* ME. †5. *fig.* To excite, inflame, fan (passion, discord, etc.). Usu. with *up.* -1776. 6. *trans.* To clear of matter by sending air through 1532. 7. *trans.* To inflate, puff up; to shape by inflation. Const. *up, out.* ME. †8. *fig.* To puff *up* with pride or vanity. Also *absol.* -1718. Also †*fig.* 9. *trans.* To shatter, destroy, etc. by means of explosion. Const. with adverbs of direction, esp. *up.* 1599. 10. *intr.* To undergo explosion; to erupt. Usu. with *up.* 1694.

1. B. ye the cornet in Gibeah *Hosea* v. 8. *To b. one's own trumpet*: to brag. d. Sonorous mettal blowing Martial sounds MILT. *P. L.* I. 540. 2. Trumpet, b. loud *Tr. & Cr.* I. iii. 256. Let the mournful martial music b. TENNYSON. 4. *To b. the coals* or *the fire* (fig.): to fan the flame of discord. *To b. out*: to extinguish by a current of air; also *intr.* The glass blew in, the fire blew out TENNYSON. In *Metallurgy. To b. in, out*: to put a blast furnace in, out of, operation. 6. To b. the nose 1532. So *to b. eggs, gaspipes,* etc. 7. To b. bladders A. YOUNG, soap-bubbles TYNDALL. 8. Kunnynge blowith, charite edifieth WYCLIF 1 *Cor.* iv. 19. 9. To b. up mines 1599. *To b. any one's brains out*: to shoot him through the head (with fire-arms). *To b. up* (fig.): †to destroy; to scold (*colloq.*). 10. *To b. out* (Mining): to go off like a gun, but without shattering the rock.

III. 1. To expose, inform upon. Now *slang.* 1575. Also *absol.* 2. Said of flies, etc.: To deposit their eggs. [App. old natural history, unconnected with the notion of blowing or inflating meat.] †*trans.*, and †*absol.* or *intr.* -1771. b. *trans.* To fill (a place) with eggs. Cf. FLY-BLOWN. 1588. 3. To curse, 'confound', 'hang'. *vulgar.* (With pa. pple. *blowed.*) 1835.

1. D—n me, if I don't blow..I'll tell Tom Neville L. HUNT. 2. b. These summer flies Haue blowne me full of maggot ostentation *L.L.L.* v. ii. 409.

Phr. **To blow upon**: To take the bloom off; to make hackneyed; to defame; also to inform upon.

Blow (blōu), *v.*[2] Pa. t. **blew.** Pa. pple. **blown.** [OE. *blōwan*, f. OTeut. **blōjan*, from root *blō-*, cogn. w. L. *flos, florem*, etc.; cf. BLOOM.] 1. *intr.* = BLOSSOM *v.* 1. 2. *fig.* To bloom; to attain perfection 1610. 3. To cause to blossom (*lit.* or *fig.*) ? *Obs.* 1645.

1. I know a banke where the wilde time blows *Mids. N.* II. i. 249. 2. Wit in Northern Climates will not b. DRYDEN.

Blow (blōu), *sb.*[1] 1460. [?] 1. A stroke; a violent application of the fist or of any instrument to an object. Also *fig.* Cf. 'stroke'. 1605. 2. *fig.* A severe disaster; a sudden and severe shock 1678. 3. 'An act of hostility' (J.). Usu. in *pl.* 1593.

1. Well strooke, there was b. for b. *Com. Err.* III. i. 56. A most poore man, made tame by Fortunes blows *Lear* IV. iv. 225. 3. Their controversie must either come to blowes, or be undecided HOBBES.

Phrases. *At a (one) b.*: by one stroke; suddenly; at once. *To strike a b.* (fig.): to take vigorous action.

Blow (blōu), *sb.*[2] 1660. [f. BLOW *v.*[1] Later than BLOW *sb.*[1]] 1. A blowing; a blast. a. of the wind. b. of whales 1851. c. of a wind-instrument; of the nose 1723. 2. *fig.* A boast; boastfulness 1684. 3. The oviposition of flesh-flies, etc. 1611. 4. *Metallurgy.* A single *heat* of the Bessemer converter; the quantity of metal dealt with at one time 1883.

1. *To get a b.*: to expose oneself to the action of a fresh breeze.

Blow-, in *comb.*

1. With adverbs, denoting actions; as **b.-out**, a quarrel; also, a 'good feed' (*slang*); **-up**, an explosion; *fig.* a disturbance. 2. With sb., qualified by *blow-* (= 'blowing', or 'that blows', or 'is blown'); as **b.-ball**, the globular seeding head of the dandelion, etc.; also *fig.*; **-cock**, a tap by which to blow off steam; **-gun** = BLOW-PIPE 2; **-line** (*Angling*), a fishing-line of the lightest floss silk, used with the living fly; **-post**, a system of conveying letters, etc. by pneumatic tubes; **-tube** = BLOW-PIPE 2; also a tube used in glass-blowing; **-valve**, the shifting valve of a condensing engine. 3. With sb., as object after *blow* (= 'one who blows'); as **b.-bottle**, **-bowl**, a sot; †**-point**, a game.

Blow (blōu), *sb.*[3] 1710. [f. BLOW *v.*[2]] 1. A state of blossoming; bloom 1759. Also *fig.* 2. A display of blossoms, or (*fig.*) of anything brilliant 1710. 3. Manner, style, or time of blossoming. Also *fig.* 1748. 4. Blossom 1797.

1. The wood-anemone was in b. 1759. 2. A b. of tulips ADDISON. 3. Flowers of richer..b. H. MILLER.

Blo·wen. *slang.* Also **blowing.** 1812. A wench, trull.

Blower[1] (blōu·əɹ). [OE. *blāwere*, f. *blāwan* to BLOW[1].] 1. *gen.* One who or that which blows. 2. *spec.* A marine animal which blows (see BLOW *v.*[1] I. 4); *e.g.* a whale 1854. 3. A contrivance for producing a current of air; *e.g.* a plate of metal fixed before a fire 1795. 4. An escape of gas through a fissure in a coal-mine; the fissure itself; a current of air escaping through a fissure in a glacier 1822. 5. *fig.* A boaster (*dial.* and in *U.S.*) 1863.

1. The best b. of horn ME. 5. General Grant..is not one of the 'b.' generals 1863.

Blo·wer[2]. 1796. [f. BLOW *v.*[2] + -ER[1].] A plant which blooms.

Blowess, var. of BLOWSE.

Blow·-fly. 1852. Pop. name of the Flesh-fly.

Blow-hole (blōu·hōul). 1691. [See BLOW *v.*[1] I. 4.] 1. Each of the two holes (constituting the nostrils) at the top of the head in cetaceans, through which they breathe or blow 1787. †2. = AIR-HOLE 2. 1691. 3. A hole through which air or gas escapes; *spec.* for the escape of steam or foul air from underground passages, etc. 1875. 4. A hole in the ice to which whales and seals come to breathe.

1. The blow-holes are two in number in many, but in others only one HUNTER.

Blowing (blōu·iŋ), *vbl. sb.*[1] OE. [f. BLOW *v.*[1]] 1. *gen.* The action of the vb. 2. Breathing; hard breathing; *esp.* of animals ME. 3. The oviposition of flesh-flies; †*concr.* the egg of a flesh-fly or other insect. 1558. 4. **Blowing up**: an explosion; *colloq.* a scolding.

Comb.: **b.-cylinder**, the air-cylinder of a blast-engine; **-engine** = *blowing-machine*; **-furnace**, a blast-furnace used in glass-working; **-iron**, **-pipe**, **-tube** (*Glass-working*), an iron tube used in blowing glass; **-machine**, any machine for producing a blast of air.

Blow·ing, *vbl. sb.*[2] ME. [f. BLOW *v.*[2]] The action of the vb. †A bloom or blossom. Also *fig.*

Blow·ing, *ppl. a.*[1] ME. [f. BLOW *v.*[1]] That blows; *esp.* windy.

B. adder, snake, a snake of Virginia, that extends and inflates the surface of its head before it bites.

Blow·ing, *ppl. a.*[2] OE. [f. BLOW *v.*[2]] In bloom, blossoming.

Blown (blōun), *ppl. a.*[1] ME. [f. BLOW *v.*[1]] 1. Fanned, driven or tossed by the wind 1552. 2. Out of breath 1674. †3. Stale; tainted -1640. 4. Whispered, hinted. *Oth.* III. iii. 182. 5. Inflated; formed by inflation ME. Also *fig.* (*arch.*) 1483.

Blown, *ppl. a.*[2] OE. [f. BLOW *v.*[2]] In bloom; that has blossomed. Cf. FULL-BLOWN.

Blow-pipe, blowpipe. 1685. [f. BLOW *v.*[1]] 1. A tube through which a current of air, etc. is blown into a flame to increase the heat, for the purpose of fusing metals, etc.; esp. employed in chemical experiments, analysis, etc. Also *attrib.* b. *Glass-blowing.* A tube by which the molten glass is blown into shape. 2. A long tube through which American Indians propel arrows or darts by force of the breath 1825.

Blowse, -sed, -sy; vars. of BLOWZE, etc.

Blowth. Now *dial.* 1602. [f. BLOW *v.*[2]; cf. *growth.*] Blowing; blossom, bloom.

Blowy (blōu·i), *a.* 1830. [f. BLOW *v.*[1] + -Y[1].] Windy.

Blowze (blauz). 1573. [? f. root of BLUSH. In some uses influenced by BLOW *v.*[1] Perh. orig. a cant term. Cf. BLOWEN.] †1. A beggar's trull; a wench -1719. 2. 'A ruddy fat-faced wench' (J.).

1. Calls his b., his queene HERRICK. Hence **Blow·zy** *a.* like a b.; coarse, rustic; of hair, etc., frowzy, slatternly.

Blowzed (blauzd), *a.* 1748. [As if pa. pple. of *to blowze* = 'to make blowzy'; cf. prec.] Rendered blowzy in the face. So **Blow·zing** *a.* tending to be blowzy.

†**Blub**, *v.* 1559. [var. of dial. *blob* vb.; cf. BLOB *sb.*] †1. To swell, puff out. *trans.* and *intr.* -1684. 2. = BLUBBER *v.* 3. 1873. Hence †**Blub** *a.* swollen, protruding; chiefly in *Comb.*

Blubber (blɒ·bəɹ), *sb.* [ME. *blober, bluber.* Prob. echoic; cf. BLEB, and BLABBER.] †1. The boiling of the sea. ME. only. 2. A bubble upon water. Now *dial.* ME. 3. A jelly-fish or Medusa 1602. 4. The fat of whales, etc., from which train-oil is obtained 1664. 5. The action of blubbering 1825.

4. In a large whale the b. will weigh thirty tons YEATS. 5. All in a b. of tears CARLYLE.

Comb.: **b.-guy**, a guy, suspended between the fore and main masts of a whaler, to assist in securing and supporting the carcase of a whale; **-lamp**, one which burns b.-oil; **-spade**, a spade-like knife used by whalers. Hence **Blu·bbery** *a.* (sense 4).

Blu·bber, *a.* 1667. [var. of earlier BLABBER, BLOBBER.] Swollen, protruding; *esp.* said of the lips. (Often hyphened, as b.-lipped, etc.)

Blubber (blɒ·bəɹ), *v.* [ME. *blubren, blober.* See the sb.] †1. *intr.* To bubble, bubble up; to make a bubbling noise -1750. 2. *trans.* To utter or cry *out* with copious tears and sobs 1590. 3. *intr.* To weep effusively. (Much used in ridicule for 'weep'.) ME. 4. To wet profusely or disfigure with weeping. Also *fig.* 1584.

2. She..sobbing, blubbers forth her sins GAY. 3. Phœbe Mayflower blubbered heartily for company SCOTT. Hence **Blu·bbered** *ppl. a.* flooded with tears; said of the eyes, cheeks, face; also, later, swollen with weeping. **Blu·bberer.** **Blu·bberingly** *adv.*

Blu·cher. 1831. [f. Field-Marshal von *Blücher* (blüχᵊ̆ər), but pop. pronounced (blu·tʃəɹ) or (blū·kəɹ).] A strong leather half-boot.

Bludgeon (blɒ·dʒən). 1730. [?] A short stick or club, with one end loaded or thicker than the other, used as a weapon. Hence **Blu·dgeon** *v.* to strike with a b.

Blue (blū, blⁱū), *a.* [ME. *blew*, a. OF. *bleu*, a Com. Rom. wd.:—OTeut. *blǣwo-z* blue, whence also ON. *blá-*, ME. *bla, blo*, now BLAE. The pronunc. (blⁱū) belongs to dictionaries.] 1. Of the colour of the sky and the deep sea, or a hue resembling it. b. Of a flame or flash without red glare; *esp.* in phr. *To burn b.*, as a candle is said to do as an omen of death, or as indicating the presence of ghosts or of the Devil 1594. c. Taken as the colour of constancy. Hence *true b.* (fig.) 1500. 2. Livid, leaden-coloured ME. 3. *fig.* Affected with fear, discomfort, anxiety, etc.; low-spirited; *esp.* in *To look b.* 1550. 4. *transf.* Belonging to the political party which has chosen blue for its colour. (In England usu. the Conservative party.) 1835. 5. Of women: Learned, pedantic. See BLUE-STOCKING. (Usu. *contemptuous.*) 1788. 6. *fig.* As the colour of plagues and things hurtful. Cf. BLUE DEVIL 1742. 7. *colloq.* Obscene 1840.

1. The b. sky bends over all COLERIDGE. The skyish head Of blew Olympus *Haml.* v. i. 277. His b. blade 1809. The b. distance DICKENS. Heere My blewest vaines to kisse *Ant. & Cl.* II. v. 29. 2. B. meagre hag MILT. *Comus* 434. 3. *B. funk* (slang): extreme nervousness. 4. To vote *b.* 1868. *True b.*: (see above 1 c) spec. used of the Scottish Presbyterian or Whig party, in contradistinction to the royal *red.* 5. They are all so wise, so learned, and so b. MAR. EDGEWORTH.

Phrases (*colloq.*). *Till all is b.*: said of the effect of drinking on the eyesight. *By all that's b.*; cf. Fr. *parbleu* (euphem. for *pardieu*).

Comb. 1. Used descriptively and distinctively, in forming the names of a. *Animals*, as **b.-back**, a species of bird; **-breast**, the Blue-throated Redstart, **b. bull**, the Nyl-gau or Nhilgai of India; **b. cat**, a Siberian cat valued for its fur; **b. cocks**, the *Salmo albus*; **b. fox**, a variety of the Arctic fox, and its fur; **b. hawk**, (*a.*) the Peregrine Falcon; (*b.*) the Ring-tailed Harrier (*Circus cyaneus*), also called *b glede* and *b. kite*; **b.-head**, a worm used as bait; **b. poker**, a duck, the Pochard; **b.-poll** = *blue cocks*; **-rock**, a kind of pigeon; **-throat**, a bird, the *Sylvia suecica*; **b. tit** = BLUE-CAP 4; **b.-wing**, a genus of ducks. b. *Plants*, as **b.-berry**, various species of *Vaccinium*; **-blaw**, **-cup** = BLUEBOTTLE 1; **b. chamomile** or **b. daisy**, the Sea Starwort, etc.; **b.-gage**, a kind of plum; **-grass** (*U.S.*), various species of *Carex*; also WIRE-GRASS; **b. gum** (tree), the *Eucalyptus globulus* of Australia; **b.-hearts**, *Buchnera americana*; **b. rocket**, *Aconitum pyramidale*; **b. tangles**, *Vaccinium frondosum*; **b.-weed**, Viper's Bugloss, *Echium vulgare.* c. *Minerals*, as **b. asbestos** = CROCIDOLITE; **b.-billy**, the residuum of cupreous pyrites after roasting with salt; **b. copper**, **b. malachite**, = AZURITE; **b. copperas**, **b. stone**, **b. vitriol**, sulphate of copper (see VITRIOL); **b. felspar**, **b. spar**, = LAZULITE; **b. iron** = VIVIANITE; **b. slipper**, Gault clay (*local*).

2. Special combs. or phrases. †**b. apron**, one who wears a b. apron, a tradesman; **b. blanket**, the banner of the Edinburgh craftsmen; *fig.* the sky; **b. blood** (see BLOOD 7, quots.); **b. dahlia**, anything rare or unheard of; **b. disease**, *Cyanosis*; **b. fire**, a b. light used on the stage for weird effect; hence *attrib.* sensational; **b. heat**, a heat of about 550° Fahr., at which ironwork assumes a bluish tint; **b. jacket**, a sailor (*esp.* as opp. to a marine); **b. jaundice** = *blue disease*; **b. laws**, severe Puritanic laws said to have been enacted in the 18th c. at New Haven, Connecticut, U.S.; **b. light**, a pyrotechnical composi-

tion which burns with a b. flame, used also at sea as a night-signal; **b. line** (in *Tennis*), the service-line (so coloured); **b. mantle,** dress, and title, of one of the four pursuivants of the English College of Arms; **b. Monday,** (*a.*) the Monday before Lent; (*b.*) a Monday spent in dissipation by workmen; **b. moon** (*colloq.*), a rarely recurring period; **b.-mould,** the mould on cheese so coloured, consisting of a fungus, *Aspergillus glaucus*. **b. ointment,** mercurial ointment; **Blue Peter,** a b. flag with a white square in the centre, hoisted as the signal of immediate sailing; hence, in *Whist*, the signal or call for trumps; **b. pill,** a mercurial antibilious pill; **b. point** (see POINT); **b. pot,** a black-lead crucible; **b. ruin** (*slang*), (bad) gin; **b. water,** the open sea.

Blue, *sb.* ME. [the adj. used absol. or ellipt.] **1.** Blue colour. (With *pl.*) **2.** A pigment of a blue colour, usually defined, as *cobalt*, etc. *b.* 1862. **b.** *spec.* A powder used by laundresses 1618. **3.** Blue clothing or dress 1482. **4.** Ellipt., for blue animals, objects, or substances, indicated by the context 1787. **5.** The sky; the sea 1647. **6.** = *Blue Squadron*, one of the three 17th c. divisions of the English fleet 1703. **7.** *pl.* Applied to companies of troops, wearing blue 1766. **8.** The colour worn by a party, faction, or class; hence, *transf.* a member of such party, etc. Also *true b.* See BLUE *a.* 1 c, 5. 1755. **9.** Short for 'blue-stocking' 1788. **10.** *Archery.* The second ring from the centre of the target 1882.

1. The b. of distance, however intense, is not the b. of a bright blue flower RUSKIN. 4. The potatoes were salmons and blues 1845. Bits of old Nankin 'blue' 1884. 5. Where one may float between b. and b. GEO. ELIOT. 8. *Dark Blues*: Oxford men or Harrow boys. *Light Blues*: Cambridge men or Eton boys. *To win his b., to be a B.*: to be chosen to represent his University (or School) in rowing, cricket, etc. *An old B.*: one who has figured in an inter-University contest. *Blue-coat boy*: a scholar of Christ's Hospital.
Phr. *The blues* (for '*blue devils*'): depression of spirits (*colloq.*).

Blue, *v.* 1606. [f. the adj.] **1.** To make blue. **2.** To treat (linen) with BLUE (see BLUE *sb.* 2 b) 1862. †**3.** *intr.* To blush (*slang*). SWIFT. Hence **Blu(e)ing** *vbl. sb.* a making blue; in U.S. laundresses' blue.

Bluebeard (blūˑbiəɹd). 1822. A personage of popular mythology, so called from the colour of his beard. References are frequent in literature to the locked turret-chamber, in which hung the bodies of his murdered wives.

The B. chamber of his mind, into which no eye but his own must look CARLYLE.

Blue bell, blue·-bell. 1578. [See BELL *sb.*¹] **1.** A species of *Campanula* (*C. rotundifolia*). Called also the 'hair-bell' or 'hare-bell'. (Usu. blū,beˑl, or as two wds.) **2.** In the south of Eng.: (blūˑbel) a bulbous-rooted plant, *Scilla nutans* (*Hyacinthus non-scriptus* Linn.) 1794.

Blue·-bird. 1688. **1.** A small perching bird (*Motacilla sialis* Linn., *Sylvia sialis* Wilson), common in U.S. in early spring. Its upper part is sky-blue. **2.** ? A species of albatross (*Diomedea fuliginosa*) 1731.

Blue-black. 1823. **A.** *adj.* Black or dark with a tinge of blue 1853. **B.** *sb.* A pigment of this colour.

Blue bonnet, -bo·nnet. 1682. [Cf. BLUE-CAP.] **1.** *spec.* A broad round flat cap of blue woollen material, formerly in general use in Scotland. **2.** *transf.* A blue-bonneted peasant or soldier 1818. **3.** Sc. name of species of *Centaurea*, as the Bluebottle 1863. **4.** *dial.* = BLUE-CAP 4.

Blue book, blue·-book. 1715. A book bound in blue; now *spec.* one of the official reports of Parliament and the Privy Council, issued in a blue paper cover. **b.** *U.S.* A printed book, containing the names, places of birth, salaries, etc. of all persons holding office under the government.

Blue·bottle. 1551. **1.** The Blue Corn-flower (*Centaurea cyanus*). Also used of other blue flowers. **2.** A nickname for a beadle or a policeman 1597. **3.** *B. fly*: a fly (*Musca vomitoria*) with a large bluish body: the Blow-fly.

Blue·-cap. 1596. [Cf. BLUE-BONNET.] **1.** A cap of blue material; the 'blue bonnet' of Scotchmen. Also *attrib.* 1674. †**2.** *transf.* A Scotchman –1663. **3.** *dial.* A salmon in its first year; so called because it has a blue spot on its head 1677. **4.** The Blue Titmouse (*Parus cæruleus*) 1804. **5.** = BLUE BONNET 3. 1821.

Blue coat, blue·-coat. 1593. **1.** Formerly the dress of servants, etc.; hence of almoners and charity children 1600. **2.** One who wears a blue coat; *e.g.* an almsman, a beadle; a soldier or sailor 1593. Also *attrib.* **3.** (= *Blue-coat boy*): A scholar of a charity school wearing the almoner's blue coat; *esp.* a scholar of Christ's Hospital 1665. Hence **Blue·-coated** *a.*

Blue devil. 1616. **1.** A baleful demon (cf. BLUE *a.* 3, 7). **2.** *fig.* in pl. *Blue devils*: **a.** Depression of spirits 1787. **b.** The apparitions seen in *delirium tremens* 1822.

Blue eye. 1552. †**a.** = BLACK EYE 2. †**b.** A blueness round the eye from weeping, etc. **c.** An eye of which the iris is blue. Hence **Blue·-eyed** *a.*, now in sense c.

Blue-eyed grass: *Sisyrinchium Bermudianum.*

Blue·-fish. 1734. **a.** A species of *Coryphæna*, found about the Bahamas, etc. **b.** *Temnodon saltator*, a salt-water fish of the mackerel order, but larger.

Blue gown, blue·-gown. 1787. †**1.** The dress of an almoner, in Scotland of a king's bedesman or licensed beggar. BURNS. **2.** One who wears this dress. Also *attrib.* 1816.

Blu(e)ism. 1822. The characteristics of a blue-stocking.

Blue·-John. 1672. †**1.** = AFTER-WORT. Hence *fig.* –1683. **2.** The blue fluor-spar found in Derbyshire 1772.

Blue·ly, *adv.* 1647. [f. BLUE *a.* + -LY ².] **1.** With a blue colour or tinge. †**2.** Badly; only in *To come off b.* –1783.

Blueness (blūˑnės). 1491. [f. BLUE *a.* + -NESS.] The quality of being BLUE (senses 1, 2, 6, 7).

Blue·-nose. (Chiefly in U.S.) 1837. **1.** A purplish potato grown in Nova Scotia. **2.** A nickname for a Nova Scotian 1837. **3.** A kind of clam shell-fish 1883.

Blue ri·bbon, riband. 1651. **1.** A ribbon of blue silk worn as a badge of honour; *esp.* the blue ribbon of the order of the Garter. **2.** The greatest distinction, the first place or prize 1848. **3.** A small strip of blue ribbon, worn as a distinctive badge by certain teetotallers 1878.

3. *Blue Ribbon Army*: the association of such teetotallers. Hence **Blue-ribboner, -ism, -ist, -ite.**

Blue-stocking (blūˑstǫkiŋ). [First found in the 17th c. (see 1 a). In its transferred sense, it dates from the assemblies which met at Montagu House in London about 1750 in order to substitute for card-playing literary conversation, etc., etc. At these a principal attendant was Mr. Benjamin Stillingfleet, who habitually wore blue worsted instead of black silk stockings. In reference to this the coterie was dubbed by Admiral Boscawen 'the Blue Stocking Society'.] **1.** *attrib.* Wearing blue worsted stockings; *hence*, not in full dress, in homely dress. (*contemptuous.*) **a.** Applied to the 'Little Parliament' of 1653. **b.** Applied depreciatively to the assemblies at Montagu House, their frequenters, etc. 1757. **c.** Hence, Of women: Having or affecting literary tastes; learned 1804. **2.** *sb.* = *Blue Stocking Lady.* (Now obsolescent) 1790. **3.** The American Avocet (*Recurvirostra americana*). BARTLETT.

1. a. That Blew-stocking Parliament, Barebone Parliament 1683. b. He [Mr. Stillingfleet] has left off his old friends and his blue stockings MRS. MONTAGUE (1757). Hence **Blue-stockingism.**

Bluet, -ett. ME. [2 wds.: **1.** a. F. *bluette*, fem. dim. of *bleue*; **2.** a. F. *bleuet, bluet*, masc. dim. of *bleu*.] †**1.** A bluish woollen cloth. **2.** The Corn Bluebottle (*Centaurea cyanus*). In U.S., *Oldenlandia cærulea*, also a Bilberry (*Vaccinium angustifolium*). 1727.

Blueth. *nonce-wd.* Blueness. H. WALPOLE.

Blue-wa·ter school. A school of naval opinion which holds that the possession of a predominant fleet would make the British islands practically (*i. e.* in all probability) impervious to invasion, though not to the landing of even large raiding parties. (Sir J. K. Laughton, March 18, 1909, in the *Times*.)

Bluey (blūˑi). 1802. [f. BLUE *a.* + -Y ¹.] **A.** *adj.* More or less blue; also as *adv.* **B.** *sb.* (in Australia): A bushman's bundle, generally wrapped in a blue blanket.

Bluff (blɒf), *a.* 1627. [Of unkn. origin.] **1.** Presenting a broad flattened front. **2.** *fig.* **a.** 'Big, surly, blustering' (J.); later, rough, blunt 1705. **b.** Good-naturedly blunt 1808.

1. B. headland COWPER, bows [of a steamer] 1861. 2. a. I maul'd you when you look'd so b. SWIFT. b. B. downright honesty. Hence **Blu·ff-ly** *adv.*, **-ness.**

Bluff (blɒf), *sb.*¹ 1737. [f. prec.] A cliff or headland with a broad precipitous face. (First used in U.S.)

Bold bluffs, that mark the limits of an ancient shore GEIKIE. Hence **Blu·ffy** *a.* full of bluffs; rather bluff.

Bluff, *sb.*² Now *dial.* 1777. [conn. w. BLUFF *v.*] **1.** A blinker for a horse. **2.** *slang.* An excuse; ? a blind. **3.** The action of bluffing in the game of *poker*; see BLUFF *v.*¹ *Hence*, challenging or confident language or demeanour, 'tried on' in the hope of intimidating an opponent. (First used in U.S.) 1848.

3. The offer was only a b. 1884.

Bluff, *v.* 1674. [conn. w. BLUFF *sb.*² 1, prob. as source. Of unkn. etym. Prob. a cant Restoration term. Recent users seem to connect with BLUFF *a.* or *sb.*¹, and make it mean 'to hoodwink by assuming a fictitious bold front'.] **1.** *trans.* To blindfold or hoodwink. **2.** In the game of *poker*: To impose upon (an opponent) as to the strength of one's hand, by betting heavily upon it, or the like, so as to induce him to throw up the game. (Of U.S. origin.) Hence *transf.* 1864. **3.** *intr.* To attempt the imposition described in **2.** 1882.

2. *To b. off*: to frighten off by bluffing. Hence **Blu·ffer.**

Bluish (blūˑiʃ), *a.* ME. [f. BLUE *a.* + -ISH ¹.] Somewhat blue; *esp.* in comb., as *b.-green*, etc. Hence **Blu·ish-ly** *adv.*, **-ness.**

Blunder (blɒˑndəɹ), *v.* [ME. *blondren*; ? freq. of *blond*, BLAND *v.*, to mix (cf. the trans. senses), or ? f. Icel. *blonda* to doze (see the intr. senses). Perh. two distinct verbs.] **I.** †**1.** *trans.* To mix up confusedly; to derange; to make (water) turbid –1638. **2.** To confound (in one's mind) stupidly 1699.

II. 1. *intr.* To move blindly or stupidly; to flounder, stumble. Often with *on, into, against*. ME. Also *fig.* †**2.** *intr.* To deal blindly and stupidly –1471. **3.** *trans.* To utter thoughtlessly, stupidly, or by a blunder. Usu. with *out*. 1483. **4.** *intr.* To make a stupid and gross mistake in doing anything 1711. **5.** *trans.* To mismanage, make a blunder in 1805.

1. The horses had to b. their way along a bright rushing river 1880. *To b. upon*: to come upon by a 'fluke'. 4. The soldier knew some one had blunder'd TENNYSON. 5. To b. a siege WELLINGTON. Hence **Blu·nderer. Blu·nderingly** *adv.*

Blunder (blɒˑndəɹ), *sb.* ME. [app. f. the vb.] †**1.** Confusion, clamour –1774. **2.** A gross mistake 1706.

2. Another mistake, not to call it a b. DE FOE.

Blunderbuss (blɒˑndəɹbɒs). 1654. [ad. Du. *donderbus*, f. *donder* thunder + *bus* gun (orig. box, tube); perverted after *blunder*.] **1.** A short gun with a large bore, firing many slugs, and doing execution at short range without exact aim. (No longer used in civilized countries.) **2.** *transf.* A blustering noisy talker (*obs.*); a blunderhead 1685. Also *attrib.*

Blu·nderhead. 1697. [? an alteration of *dunderhead*: cf. BLUNDERBUSS.] A blundering muddle-headed fellow. Hence **Blu·nderhea·ded** *a.*, **Blu·nderhea·dedness.**

Blunge (blɒndʒ), *v.* 1830. [app. echoic.] *Pottery.* To mix (clay, etc.) up with water.

Blunger (blɒˑndʒəɹ). 1830. [f. prec.] An appliance for blunging; formerly a wooden instrument, with a cross handle at the top; now an apparatus driven by power.

†**Blu·nket.** 1440. [? ad. OF. *blanquet.*] **A.** *adj.* Grey, greyish blue –1783. **B.** *sb.* [sc. *fabric.*] ? = BLANKET *sb.* 1. –1600.

Blunt (blɒnt). ME. [?] **A.** *adj.* **1.** Dull; said orig. of the sight, whence of the perceptions, etc. **2.** Not sharp; without edge or point. (Now the leading literal sense.) ME. **b.** *transf.* to the effect 1656. Also *fig.* †**3.** Barren, bare –1599. **4.** Rude, unpolished (*arch.*) 1477. †**b.** Unfeeling, unsparing. SHAKS. **5.** Abrupt of speech or manner; plain-spoken; curt 1590.

1. Ill can your blunter feelings guess the pain CAMPBELL. 2. If the yron be b. *Eccles.* x. 10. A b. pencil 1753, hatchet 1885. b. A b. stroke COWLEY. 5. By

his b. bearing he will keepe his word *Hen. V*, IV. vii. 185. Hence **Blu·ntish** *a.* **Blu·nt-ly** *adv.*, **-ness.**

B. *sb.* †1. A foil for fencing –1694. 2. A make of needles 1833. 3. *slang.* Ready money 1812.

Blunt, *v.* ME. [f. BLUNT *a.*] 1. To dull, or make less sharp. Also *intr.* 2. To make dull (the feelings or faculties) 1597.

1. Cupid now..blunts the point of ev'ry dart SWIFT. 2. B. not his Loue..By seeming cold SHAKS.

Blur (blɒ̄ɪ), *sb.* 1548. [Obscure.] 1. A smear which partially obscures 1601. 2. *fig.* A moral stain, a blemish 1548. 3. An indistinct blurred appearance 1860.

1. He that clenses a blot with blotted fingers makes a greater blurre QUARLES. 2. This b. to youth SHAKS. *Lucr.* 222. 3. The..nebulous b. of Orion EMERSON. Hence **Blu·rry** *a.*

Blur (blɒ̄ɪ), *v.* 1581. [See prec.] 1. To obscure or sully by smearing with ink, etc. b. *intr.* To make blurs 1622. 2. *fig.* To stain, sully, blot, or blemish; to disfigure, befoul 1593. 3. To make indistinct or dim. Also *fig.* 1611. 4. *transf.* To dim (the senses, etc.) 1620.

1. A full paper blurred over with falsehoods FULLER. 2. Such an Act That blurres the grace and blush of Modestie *Haml.* III. iv. 41. 3. One low light..Blurr'd by the creeping mist TENNYSON. 4. Feare..blurres your senses 1620.

Blurb (blɒ̄ɪb). orig. *U.S.* 1924. [?] A publisher's commendatory advertisement of a book.

Blurt (blɒ̄ɪt), *v.* 1573. [app. echoic.] 1. *intr.* To emit the breath eruptively from the mouth; to snort in sleep. Also *trans.* with *out.* Now *dial.* 1611. †2. *intr.* To puff in scorn, to pooh –1654. Also *trans.* 3. *trans.* (usu. with *out*): To utter abruptly, or impulsively; to burst out with 1573. *absol.* MILT.

2. All the world will b. and scorn at us 1596. 3. To b. out the broad staring question of, Madam will you marry me GOLDSM.

Blurt (blɒ̄ɪt), *sb.* 1580. [f. the vb.: cf. BLIRT.] †1. An eruptive emission of breath from the mouth, *esp.* in contempt –1611. 2. An abrupt impulsive outburst 1865.

†**Blurt,** *int.* 1592. [The vb.-stem used without const.] 'Pooh!' 'a fig for!' –1606.

Blush (blɒʃ), *v.* Pa. t. and pple. **Blushed, blusht.** [ME. *blusche, blosche, blysche,* app. f. a stem **blŭsi-* from root **blŭs-* 'burn, glow, be red'. Its history is obscure.] †1. *intr.* To shine forth; also, to cast a glance. (in allit. ME. poetry.) 2. *intr.* To become red in the face, (usu. from shame or modesty); to colour up 1450. b. *trans.* To exhibit, make known by blushing. Chiefly *poet.* 1592. c. To turn *into, out of,* by blushing 1636. 3. *fig.* To be ashamed 1530. 4. *transf.* To become or be red, or roseate 1679. 5. *trans.* To make red 1593.

2. She changed coloure and blussyd as rudy as a rose LD. BERNERS. b. Ile b. you Thanks *Wint. T.* IV. iv. 595. 3. I do not b. to own, that I am out of fashion BOLINGBR. 5. Ne're returneth, To b. and beautifie the cheeke againe 2 *Hen. VI,* III. ii. 167. Hence **Blu·sher. Blu·shingly** *adv.*

Blush (blɒʃ), *sb.* (*a.*) ME. [f. the vb.] †1. A gleam –1661. 2. A glance. *Obs.* exc. in *at, on,* etc. (*the*) *first b.* ME. 3. A look, appearance. Now *dial.* 1620. 4. The reddening of the face, caused by shame, modesty, etc. 1593. 5. *transf.* A rosy colour or glow; a flush of light or of colour 1590. 6. *adj.* Of the colour of a blush 1633.

2. Vidimus. And that not..'at a b.', passing by; but had a full sight BP. ANDREWES. 3. Without any b. of absurdity 1620. 4. Put off your Maiden Blushes *Hen. V,* v. ii. 253. *To put to the b.*: to put to shame. 5. Light's last blushes ting'd the distant hills LYTTELTON. *Comb.* **b.-rose,** a rose of a very delicate pink. Hence †**Blu·shet,** little blusher. B. JONS. **Blu·shful** *a.* full of blushes; blush-coloured, rosy. **Blu·shfully** *adv.*, **-ness. Blu·shless** *a.* unblushing. **Blu·shy** *a.* blush-coloured; suffused with blushes.

Bluster (blɒ·stəɪ), *v.* [? Two vbs. Perh. echoic; in II., conn. w. BLOW, BLAST, etc.; cf. ON. *blástr* sb. 'blast, blowing, hissing'.]

†I. The ME. vb. *intr.* To wander blindly or aimlessly. Cf. BLUNDER *v.* 3.

II. The mod. vb. 1. *intr.* To blow boisterously or with stormy violence: said of wind. Also said of water agitated by wind or flood 1530. Also *fig.* b. To blow about, dishevel (*rare*) 16.. †2. *intr.* To breathe hard 1530. †3. *trans.* To utter with stormy violence and noise. Usu. with *out* or *forth.* –1604. 4. *intr.* To storm or rage boisterously; to hector 1494. b. *trans.* To force, or drive, by blustering 1661.

1. When to land B. the winds and tides the selfsame way TENNYSON. 4. Boswell blustered, but nothing could be got JOHNSON. Hence **Blu·sterer,** one who or that which blusters. **Blu·steringly** *adv.*

Bluster (blɒ·stəɪ), *sb.* 1583. [f. prec. vb.] 1. Boisterous blowing; a rough and stormy blast. Also *fig.* 2. The boisterous blast of a wind instrument, etc. 1724. 3. Boisterous inflated talk 1704.

1. The skies..threaten present blusters SHAKS. 3. Mirabeau has much more of b.; a noisy, forward, unresting man CARLYLE. Hence **Blu·sterous, -strous** *a.* boisterous, stormy; truculent. **Blu·stery** *a.* boisterously blowing; noisily self-assertive.

†**Bo,** *a.* (*pron.*) [OE. *bégen, bá, bú,* the stem being a Goth. *ba-*, OTeut. *bo-*, found in Gr. ἄμ-φω, L. *am-bo,* etc.] The earlier word for BOTH.

†**Bo,** *conj.* ME. The common form of prec. used with *and.*

Bo, boh (bōᵘ), *int.* ME. [Cf. L. *bo-are,* Gr. βοάειν.] An exclam. to surprise or frighten.

Phr. *To say* or *cry 'bo' to a goose,* (also occas.) *a battledore* to open one's mouth, speak.

Boa (bōᵘ·ă). Pl. **boas** (occas. in L. form boæ). ME. [a. L. *boa,* of unkn. origin.] 1. *Zool.* A genus of large non-venomous serpents native to tropical S. America, which kill their prey by constriction. Pop. any large serpent of similar habits, *e.g.* the Python of the Old World. 2. A snake-like coil of fur worn by ladies round the neck 1836.

Boa-constrictor (bōᵘ·ă kǫnstri·ktǫɪ). 1809. [f. prec. + L. *constrictor.*] A large Brazilian serpent of the genus *Boa,* erron. supposed by Linnæus to be the largest species; pop., any great crushing snake, whether a Boa or a Python. Also *fig.*

fig. A great logical boa constrictor 1848.

‖**Boanerges** (bōᵘănɔ̄·ɪdʒīz), *proper name.* ME. [a. Gr. βοανεργές (*Mark* iii. 17), prob. repr. Heb. *b'nēy regesh* 'sons of thunder'.] The name given by Christ to the two sons of Zebedee. Hence, as a sing. (pl. *-es, -esses*), a loud vociferous preacher or orator.

Boanthropy (boˌæ·nþrǫpi). 1864. [f. Gr. βοάνθρωπος.] A form of madness in which a man believes himself an ox (see *Daniel* iv. 33).

Boar (bōᵊɪ). [Only in WGer.: OE. *bár,* on OTeut. type **bairo-z.*] The male of the swine, whether wild or tame (but uncastrated). b. The flesh of the animal 1460. c. *spec.* **Wild Boar**: usual name of the wild species (*Sus Scrofa*). ME. d. *fig.* applied to persons ME.

Comb.: **boar's ears** (corruption of *bear's ears*): see AURICULA; **boar's foot,** a plant, *Helleborus viridis.*

†**Boar,** *v.* 1528. [f. prec.] Of swine: To be in heat –1607.

Board (bōᵊɪd), *sb.* [(1) OE. had *bord*[1] 'board, plank, shield, ? table', a Com. Teut. str. neut. sb.:—OTeut. **bord-o(m,* repr. an Aryan **bhr̥dhom,* Skr. **br̥dham*; see BRED *sb.* (2) OE. had *bord*[2] 'border, rim, side, ship's side', also a Com. Teut. sb., orig. str. masc., but also neut.:—OTeut. **bord-oz* side, border, rim. The two were associated and confused at an early date. (3) The WGer. *bord*[2] masc. 'border, edge, coast, ship, ship's side', adopted in Romanic, has, as F. *bord,* reacted on the Eng.] I. A board of wood, etc. [OE. *bord*[1].] 1. A piece of timber sawn thin, usually rectangular, and of greater length than breadth; a thin plank. (A *board* is thinner than a *plank,* and is generally less than 2½ inches in thickness.) b. *spec.* in *pl.* The stage of a theatre. Cf. STAGE. 1779. 2. A tablet, *e.g.* a *black b., paste-b., spring-b., notice-b.,* etc. ME. b. *spec.* One on which games are played, as *chess-b., backgammon-b.,* etc.; also the frame used for scoring at cribbage. Often *fig.* 1474. 3. A kind of thick stiff paper, formed by pasting or squeezing layers of paper together, as *pasteboard, cardboard, mill-b.,* etc. 4. *Bookbinding.* Pieces of strong pasteboard covered with paper and used for the covers of books. So *In cloth boards*: in boards covered with cloth. 1533.

1. Ships are but boords *Merch. V.* I. iii. 32. b. To go upon the boards GARRICK. 2. b. *To keep one's name on the boards*: to remain a member of a college (at Cambridge). There is scarce any thing but pawns left upon the b. CLARENDON. 4. The bookseller..had not one in boards LOCKHART.

II. A table. [Cf. ON. *borð.*] †1. *gen.* A table –1470. 2. *spec.* A table used for meals; now, always, one spread for a repast. Chiefly *poet.*; but see BED 1. ME. 3. *transf.* Food served at the table; daily meals provided according to stipulation; the supply of daily provisions; entertainment. Often joined with *bed* or *lodging.* ME. 4. A table at which a council is held; *hence* a council-meeting 1575. b. Hence: The persons who meet at a council-table, as *B. of Control, B. of Trade, B. of Guardians,* etc. 1613. 5. Any piece of furniture resembling a table, as *sideboard* a side table ME.

1. *Above b.*: open, openly; cf. I. 2 b, and see ABOVE-BOARD. *To sweep the b.* (at cards): to take all the cards, to pocket the stakes. 2. †*God's b.*: the Communion table in a church. Fful ofte tyme he hadde the bord bigonne (*i.e.* taken precedence at table) CHAUCER. 3. He payth for hys borde wykely xx*d.* MARG. PASTON. 4. b. 'Bow to the b.,' said Bumble. Oliver..seeing no b. but the table, fortunately bowed to that DICKENS.

†III. [OE. *bord*[2].] A shield –1535.

IV. [OE. *bord*[2]; lost in ME. and replaced by F. *bord.*] A hem, an edge, a coast. *Obs.* exc. in *seaboard.* OE.

V. A ship's side. [OE. *bord*[2]: reinforced by OF. *bord.*] 1. *Naut.* The side of a ship. (See ABOARD.) Now only in phrases, as *over* (*the*) *b., weather-b.,* etc. OE. †2. (*poet.* in OE.) A ship –ME. 3. *Naut.* Sideward direction (in reference to the ship's course); the course of a ship when tacking. Cf. TACK. 1533.

1. They came within b. MALORY. *By the b.*: (down) by the ship's side, overboard, as *To slip by the b. To come, go,* etc. *by the b.*: to fall overboard, to go for good and all. *To try by the b.*: to try boarding. Also *fig. On b.*: on one side, close alongside (*of* a ship or shore); also as *prep.,* short for *on b. of.* Also, in common use: On or in a ship, boat, etc.; into or on to a ship. (Ellipt. for *on ship-b.*) Also *transf.* (in U.S.). In or into a railway train, tram-car, etc. *To lay* (*a ship*) *on b.*: to place one's own ship alongside of (it). *To run on b.* (*of*), *to fall on b.* (*of*): *lit.* to run against, fall foul *of* (a ship); *fig.* to make an attack, fall, *upon* (a person or thing). *B. on b.,* (corruptly) *b. and b., b. by b.*: side by side. [*On b.* is app. an expansion of ABOARD, taken from Fr. *à bord,* short for *au bord du vaisseau,* in which *bord* 'ship's side' comes to be equal to 'ship' itself.] 3. *To make boards*: to tack. *To make short boards*: to tack frequently.

Comb.: **b.-measure,** superficial measure applied to boards; **-money** = BOARD-WAGES; **-nail,** a spike or large brad; **-rule,** a scale for finding the superficial area of a b. without calculation.

Board (bōᵊɪd), *v.* 1460. [f. prec. sb.: cf. ABORD and F. *border.*] 1. *trans.* a. To come close up to or alongside (a ship), usually for the purpose of attacking. b. In later use, To go on board of or enter (a ship), usually in a hostile manner. Also *absol.* (in sense b.) 1494. 2. *trans.* To go on board of 1597. *transf.* (in U.S.) To enter (a railway train, etc.); to enter in a hostile way 1879. 3. *fig.* To approach, address, assail; to make advances to. Cf. ACCOST. 1547. 4. *intr.* Of a ship: To tack 1627. †5. *trans.* To border on; *intr.* to lie close *by* –1636. 6. To cover or furnish with boards 1530. 7. To provide with daily meals; now generally to provide with both food and lodging at a fixed rate 1599. 8. *intr.* To be supplied with food, or food and lodging, at a fixed rate; to live with a family as one of its members for a stipulated charge 1556. 9. *causal.* To place at board. Also with *out.* 1655.

1. b. In boarding the San Nicholas..we lost about seven killed NELSON. 6. The floors were roughly boarded over HOWELLS. To have books boarded BUCKLE. 8. He had engaged to b. with the family W. IRVING. Hence **Boa·rdable** *a.* that can be boarded, as a ship; *fig.* approachable. (Dicts.)

Boarder (bōᵊ·ɪdəɪ). 1530. [f. BOARD *v.*] 1. One who has his food, or food and lodging at the house of another, or lives with a family as one of its members, at a fixed rate. *spec.* A boy who boards and lodges at a school. 2. One who boards an enemy's ship 1769.

Boa·rding, *vbl. sb.* 1546. [f. BOARD *v.* + -ING[1].] 1. *Naut.* The action of coming close up to, or of entering (a ship), usually in a hostile manner. 2. The action of covering with boards; boards collectively, a structure of boards 1552. 3. *Currying.* The treatment of leather with a graining-board 1870.

Comb.: **b.-house,** one in which persons board; **-out,** the obtaining of stated meals at another person's house; the placing of destitute children in families where they are treated as members; **-school,** one in which pupils are boarded as well as taught.

†**Boa·rd-school.** 1. A boarding-school 1740. 2. A school under the management of a School-board, as established by the Elementary Education Act of 1870. Also *attrib.* -1903.

Boa·rd-wages, board wages. 1539. Wages allowed to servants to keep themselves in victual.

Boar-fish (bōə·ɹfiʃ). 1836. A fish (*Capros aper, Zeus aper*) akin to the Mackerel, having a turned-up snout.

Boarish (bōə·riʃ), *a.* 1550. [f. BOAR *sb.*] Of, pertaining to, or resembling, a boar; sensual; cruel. (Formerly often confused with *boorish.*)
A grosse and borish opinion MILT. Hence **Boa·rish·ly** *adv.*, **-ness.**

Boast (bōᵘst), *sb.* [ME. *bōst* sb., of unkn. origin.] †1. Loud noise of the voice, outcry. ME. only. †2. Speaking big, menace -1637. 3. Proud or vain-glorious speech; vaunt, brag ME. †b. Pomp, vain-glory -1440. 4. 'A cause of boasting, an occasion of pride, the thing boasted' (J.) 1593.
4. It is my b., that I was the first Minister who looked for it [merit] W. PITT. Hence **Boa·stful** *a.* full of boasting; given to boasting. **Boa·stful·ly** *adv.*, **-ness.** †**Boa·stive** *a.* (*rare*) boastful. **Boa·stless** *a.* (*rare*).

Boast (bōᵘst), *v.*¹ [ME. *bōsten*, of unkn. origin.] †1. To threaten. *intr.* and *trans.* -1756. 2. *intr.* To vaunt; to brag *of, about,* glory *in* ME. Also *refl.* ME. 3. *trans.* To extol; to brag of ME. 4. To display vaingloriously or proudly (*arch.*) 1590. 5. *fig.* To possess as a thing to be proud of 1697.
2. B. not thy selfe of to morrow *Prov.* xxvii. 1. 3. Who boast'st release from hell MILT. *P. R.* I. 409. We .. but b. we know POPE. 4. Would steer too nigh the Sands, to b. his Wit DRYDEN. Hence **Boa·sted** *ppl. a.* vaunted. **Boa·ster**¹, one who BOASTS. **Boa·stingly** *adv.*

Boast, *v.*² 1823. [?] 1. *Masonry.* To pare stone with a broad chisel and mallet. 2. *Sculpture.* To shape roughly before putting in details. Hence **Boa·ster**², a broad chisel for boasting.

Boat (bōᵘt). [OE. *bát*, app. f. OTeut. **baito-*, found also in ON. *beit.* From OE. *bát*, adopted in ON. as *bát-r*, the word prob. passed into LG. and Du. as *bôt, boot.*] 1. A small open vessel, usually propelled by oars, though sometimes by a sail. b. Extended to fishing vessels, mail packets, and small steamers. (Sometimes also to large ocean steamers.) 1571. 2. A vessel or utensil like a boat in shape, as a *sauce-b.*, an *incense-b.* 1684.
1. To hazard our liues in one small B. 1 *Hen. VI*, IV. vi. 33. White Star Line .. the Boats are uniform and vary little in point of speed 1880.
Phrases. *To take b.*: to embark in a b. *To be in the same b.* (fig.): to be in the same case. *To sail in the same b.* (fig.): to act together.
Comb.: **b.-cloak,** a large cloak worn by officers on duty at sea; **-hook,** an iron hook and spike fixed at the end of a pole, used in pulling a boat towards, or pushing it off from, any fixed object; **-house,** a house communicating with the water, in which boats are kept; **-insect,** the BOAT-FLY; **-shell,** the genus *Cymba* of molluscs; **-slide,** a double inclined plane (with rollers) over which a boat may be drawn, thus avoiding the lock; **-tail,** a genus of birds, *Quiscalinæ*; **-train,** a railway train timed to meet a b.

Boat (bōᵘt), *v.* 1610. [f. prec. sb.] 1. To place, or carry, in a boat 1613. †2. *intr.* To take boat 1610. 3. To go in a boat, to row; to conduct a freight-boat (*U.S.*) 1673.
1. *To b. the oars*, is to cease rowing and lay the oars in the boat SMYTH. 3. We boated to Antwerp RAY. Hence **Boa·table** *a.* navigable by boat. (Orig. U.S.) **Boa·tage,** carriage by boat; a charge paid on such carriage; †boats, etc. collectively. **Boa·ter,** a canal-boat man; one who boats for pleasure; a hard straw hat worn by men.

Boa·t-bill. 1776. [See BILL *sb.*²] A genus of birds (*Cancroma*) belonging to the Heron tribe; esp. *C. cochlearia*, so called from the shape of its bill.

Boa·t-fly. 1753. A water-bug (*Notonecta glauca*), whose body resembles a boat.

Boatful (bōᵘ·tful). Pl. **boatfuls,** formerly **boatsful.** 1652. [f. BOAT *sb.* + -FUL.] The quantity or number which fills a boat.

Boating (bōᵘ·tiŋ), *vbl. sb.* (and *ppl. a.*) 1610. [f. BOAT *sb.* and *v.*] †1. Boats collectively. Cf. *shipping.* 1610. 2. The action of going by boat, or of rowing; now *esp.* rowing as an amusement 1788. Also *attrib.* †3. A punishment in ancient Persia, in which the offender was tied in a boat, and left to perish 1753. 4. *ppl. a.* Addicted to boating 1884.

†**Boa·tion.** 1646. [f. L. *boare.*] Bellowing.
[To] assist this mugiency or b. SIR T. BROWNE.

Boatman (bōᵘ·tmæn). 1513. 1. A man who manages a boat. 2. = BOAT-FLY. 1841. Hence **Boa·tmanship,** the art of managing a boat.

†**Boa·tsman.** 1549. 1. A boatswain -1622. 2. = BOATMAN 1. -1684.

Boatswain (bōᵘ·tswēⁱn, usu. bōᵘ·s'n). 1450. [f. BOAT + SWAIN, a. ON. *sveinn* boy, servant.] 1. An officer in a ship who has charge of the sails, rigging, etc., and whose duty it is to summon the men to their duties with a whistle. 2. The Arctic Skua (*Cataractes parasiticus*) 1835.
Comb.: **boatswain's-mate,** a boatswain's deputy or assistant; **b.-bird,** a tropical bird (*Phaeton æthereus*) so called from its whistle.

Boa·t-woman. 1843. A woman who manages a boat.

Bob (bǫb), *sb.*¹ ME. [?] 1. A bunch or cluster. *north.* Still Sc. for a nosegay. †2. A rounded mass at the end of a rod, etc.; a knob -1659. *spec.* The weight on a pendulum, a plumb-line, the arm of a steelyard (*dial.*); a beam, etc. in a pumping engine (*dial.*). 1752. †3. A pendant; an ear-drop -1773. 4. A knot or bunch of hair; also, a short bunch or curl; cf. *bob-curl.* Often short for **b.-peruke, -periwig, -wig,** a wig having the bottom locks turned up into bobs or short curls. 1685. 5. A horse's tail docked short 1711. 6. A knob, knot, or bunch of coloured ribbons; a weight on the tail of a kite 1761. 7. A bunch of lob-worms threaded on worsted, used to catch eels 1660. 8. A knob-like body 1615. †9. a. The larva of a beetle used as bait for fish. b. A beetle: chiefly in *comb.*, as *black-b., blind-b.* (also *fig.*) -1792. 10. The refrain of a song (? as if a pendant to each stanza) 1606.
3. My cousin Con's necklaces, bobs, and all GOLDSM. 4. A decent powdered doctor's b. MAR. EDGEWORTH. 10. *To bear a b.*: to join in the chorus.
Comb.: **b.-curl,** ? a short curl like a tassel; **-jerom,** a bob-wig; **-pendulum, -balance,** one with a b. or bobs; **-periwig, -peruke, -wig**: see 4.

†**Bob,** *sb.*² 1528. [f. BOB *v.*¹] A trick; a bitter jest -1682.

Bob (bǫb), *sb.*³ 1571. [f. BOB *v.*²] †1. A blow with the fist -1721. †2. *fig.* A rap; often a bitter jibe -1734. 3. A tap 1611.
Dry b.: a blow that does not break the skin (*lit.* and *fig.*).

Bob (bǫb), *sb.*⁴ 1550. [f. BOB *v.*³] 1. An act of bobbing. 2. Sc. name of some dances 1550. 3. A curtsy 1825.

Bob (bǫb), *sb.*⁵ 1671. [perh. conn. w. BOB *sb.*⁴] *Bell-ringing.* A term for certain changes in the working of the methods by which long peals of changes are produced. (See Grove *Dict. Music* s.v. *Change.*)

Bob (bǫb), *sb.*⁶ 1879. An apparatus for polishing burnished metal surfaces, consisting of a disc or discs of leather or cloth, revolving rapidly on a spindle.

Bob (bǫb), *sb.*⁷ 1721. A pet form of *Robert.* Hence, perh. **dry-bob,** a boy (at Eton) who takes to land-sports; **wet-b.,** one who takes to boating; **light-b.,** a soldier of the light infantry, etc.

Bob (bǫb), *sb.*⁸ *slang.* 1812. [?] A shilling.

Bob, *a.* 1709. [*Bob* in *bobtail* taken as an adj.; cf. BOBBISH.] 1. Cut short (as a horse's tail). 2. *slang.* ? Lively, 'nice' 1721.

†**Bob,** *v.*¹ [ME. *bobben*, a. OF. *bober* to befool.] 1. To make a fool of, deceive, cheat -1725. b. To take by deception *Oth.* V. i. 16. 2. To mock, flout. ME. only.
1. *To b.* (*out*) *of*: to cheat (out) of; You shall not b. vs out of our melody *Tr. & Cr.* III. i. 75.

Bob (bǫb), *v.*² [ME. *boben, bobben*; perh. echoic.] †1. To buffet -1605. 2. To strike with anything knobbed ME. 3. To rap or tap 1745. 4. To cause to rap or bounce *against, at,* etc. 1612.

Bob (bǫb), *v.*³ ? ME. [App. echoic, expressing short jerking or rebounding motion.] 1. *intr.* To move up and down; *hence*, to dance; to move to and fro. 2. *intr.* To move up or down with a bob or slight jerk; *spec.* to curtsy. With cognate obj., *To b. a curtsy.* 1794. 3. *trans.* To move (a thing) up or down with a slight jerk. Cf. BOB *v.*² 4. 1685.
1. A postilion .. bobbing up and down on the off-horse HAWTHORNE. *To b. for apples, cherries*, etc.: to snatch with the mouth at apples, etc. floating on water, or dangling from a string. 2. The end of the pole bobbed up and struck me (*mod.*). *Comb.* **b.-fly,** in angling, a second artificial fly that bobs on the water, to indicate the position of the end-fly.

Bob (bǫb), *v.*⁴ 1614. [f. BOB *sb.*¹ 7.] *intr.* To fish (*for* eels) with a bob. Also *fig.*

Bob, *v.*⁵ 1822. [BOB *sb.*¹ 5.] 1. *trans.* To dock (a horse's tail). 2. To cut (the hair) short so that it hangs level above the shoulders 1918.

Bob (bǫb), *adv.* 1673. The stem of BOB *v.*² or ³, used to denote sudden action.

‖**Bobac** (bōᵘ·băk). 1774. [Pol.] A burrowing squirrel, the Polish Marmot. var. **Boback.**

Bobadil (bǫ·bădil). 1771. A thrasonical character in Ben Jonson's *Every Man in Hum.*; hence, a braggart who pretends to prowess. Hence **Bobadi·lian, Bo·badilish** *adjs.*, **-ism.**

†**Boba·nce.** ME. [a. OF.] Boasting -1534.

Bobbed (bǫbd), *a.* 1658. [f. BOB *sb.*¹ + -ED².] Furnished with a BOB (in various senses); formed into a bob; cut short.

Bobber (bǫ·bəɹ). 1837. [f. BOB *v.*³, ⁴ + -ER¹.] 1. He who or that which bobs up and down or in and out; *spec.* a float used in angling, also the *bob-fly.* 2. One who bobs for eels 1882. 3. *dial.* and *slang.* A mate or chum 1860.

Bobbery (bǫ·bəri). *slang.* 1816. [Anglo-Ind. repr. Hindī *Bāp re!* O father!, an exclam. of surprise or grief.] Noisy disturbance, row.

Bobbin (bǫ·bin), *sb.* 1530. [a. F. *bobine*, of unkn. origin.] 1. An article round which thread or yarn is wound, for use as required, in weaving, sewing, etc. a. A small pin of wood, with a notch, used in lace-making. b. A wooden or metal cylinder, perforated so as to revolve on a spindle, having a flange at one or both ends, used in the processes of spinning, warping, weaving, etc. c. A small spool, placed within the shuttle, in some sewing machines. d. An ordinary reel or spool. e. A reel round which wire is coiled in electrical instruments 1870. 2. A fine cord or narrow braid in haberdashery 1578. 3. A rounded piece of wood attached to a latch-string 1820.
Comb.: **b.-lace,** lace made on a pillow with bobbins; **-winder,** a contrivance for winding thread, etc. on a b. Hence **Bo·bbin** *v.* to wind on bobbins.

Bobbinet, var. of BOBBIN-NET.

Bo·bbing, *vbl. sb.* 1526. [f. BOB *v.* + -ING¹.] 1. Beating, striking; also *fig.* giving a rap. (See BOB *sb.*³ 2.) 2. Movement up and down, etc.; dancing, curtsying. (See BOB *v.*³) 1776. 3. Fishing for eels with a bob 1653.

Bobbin-net, bobbinet (bǫ·binˌneˑt, bǫ·binet). 1832. [f. BOBBIN + NET.] A kind of machine-made cotton-net, originally imitating bobbin-lace.

Bobbish (bǫ·biʃ), *a. dial.* and *slang.* 1813. [Cf. BOB *a.*, BOB *v.*³] Well; in good spirits. Hence **Bo·bbishly** *adv.*

Bobby (bǫ·bi), *sb.* 1. Pet form of *Bob.* (See BOB *sb.*⁷) 2. [Hence, after Mr. (later Sir) *Robert* Peel, who introduced the new Police Act in 1828.] A slang nickname for a policeman. See also PEELER. 1851.

Bob-cherry. A children's game; see BOB *v.*³ 1 (quots.).

†**Bobet,** *sb.* ME. [f. BOB *sb.*³ or *v.*³; cf. *buffet.*] A cuff -1530.

Bobolink (bǫ·bǫliŋk). Also **boblincoln,** etc. 1796. [app. *Bob Lincoln*, or *Bob o' Lincoln*, echoic of the bird's call.] A North American singing-bird (*Dolichonyx oryzivorus*). Called also *Reed-bird* and *Rice-bird.*

Bob-sled, Bob-sleigh. 1848. A sled or sleigh, made of two short sleds or sleighs coupled together; used in drawing logs, etc. (U.S.) Now also a long sleigh used in Alpine sport by a 'crew' of tobogganers.

Bobstay. 1758. [f. BOB (? sense) + STAY *sb.*] *Naut.* A rope used to draw down the bowsprit of a ship and keep it steady. Also *attrib.*

Bob-tail. 1577. [f. BOB *sb.*¹ + TAIL.] A. Two words (bǫ·b tēⁱ·l): The tail (of a horse) cut short. B. *attrib.* (bǫ·btēⁱl). Having a bobtail 1605. C. *sb.* (bǫ·bteⁱl). 1. [sc. *horse*, or *dog*.] 1676. †b. An arrow 'big toward the hede'. ASCHAM. †2. *transf.* A contemptible fellow 1619. 3. *collect. Tag-rag and bob-tail*, or *tag, rag, and bob-tail*: the rabble 1659.

Bobtail (bǫ·btēⁱl), *v.* 1577. [f. prec.] To dock the tail of; *fig.* to curtail. Hence **Bob-tailed** *a.* with tail cut short.

Bob-white (bǫ·bˌhwəit). 1864. The common partridge of N. America (*Odontophorus Virginianus*), so called from its note.

Bob-wig; see BOB *sb.*¹ 4.

Boc, boc-land, etc.; see BOOK *sb.*

‖**Bocage.** 1644. [F. *bocage* (bokaˑʒ):—OF. *boscage*.] Woodland; var. of BOSCAGE.

‖**Bocal** (bokaˑl, bōᵘˑkăl). 1847. [mod.F. and Sp.] A glass bottle or jar with a short wide neck. (Dicts.)

Bocardo, bokardo (bokāˑɹdo). 1509. 1. *Logic.* A mnemonic word, representing a mood of the third syllogistic figure in which a particular negative major premiss (O), and a universal affirmative minor (A), give a particular negative conclusion (O). †2. The name of the prison in the old North Gate of the city of Oxford, pulled down in 1771. †3. A prison –1709.

1. B., which..was the opprobrium of the scholastic system of reduction SIR W. HAMILTON. 2. Wee haue set Dunce [Duns Scotus] in B. 1535.

Bocasin (bǫ·kăsin). 1485. [a. Sp. *bocací*, a. Turk. *bōghāsī* cotton cloth.] A fine buckram.

‖**Bocca** (boˑkkă, bǫˑkă). 1799. [It.; = 'mouth'.] 1. A circular opening in a glass-furnace, through which the melting-pots are inserted and withdrawn. 2. The mouth of a volcano 1881.

‖**Boccarella** (bokkăreˑllă, bǫkareˑlă). 1799. [dim. of prec.] A smaller opening on each side of the bocca in a glass-furnace.

‖**Boche** (bǫʃ). 1914. [Fr. slang, = rascal, German, of unc. etym.] French soldiers' name for: German.

Bock, bock-land, etc.; see BOOK *sb.*

†**Bo·ckerel, bo·ckeret.** 1653. [?] Names of the male and female of a long-winged hawk.

Bockey (bǫ·ki). 1860. [?dim. of Du. *bokaal*.] A bowl made from a gourd. (New York.)

Bocking (bǫ·kiŋ). 1759. [f. *Bocking* in Essex.] A coarse woollen drugget or baize.

†**Bo·cstaff, -stave.** [OE. *bōcstæf*. Cf. Goth. **bôkastafs*, f. *bok* book + *staf-* staff, letter, orig. 'beech-staff'; but see BOOK. Replaced in 13th c. by *letter*. Cf. Ger. *buchstabe*.] A letter (of the alphabet).

Bodd-; see BOD-.

Bode (bōᵘd), *sb.*¹ [Com. Teut.: OE. *boda* :—OTeut. **bodon-*, f. *bod-* stem of *beudan*; see next.] One who proclaims; a herald, a messenger. Resuscitated from 12th c. by some recent writers on OE. history.

Bode (bōᵘd), *sb.*² [Com. Teut.: OE. *bod* :—OTeut. **gabodo(m*, f. *bod-* pa. ppl. stem of *beudan*; see BID *v.*] †1. Behest –ME. †2. Message –1637. †3. Premonition, omen –1632. 4. Foreboding (*arch.*) 1587. 5. A bid. Still in n. dial. ME.

†**Bode,** *sb.*³ ME. [? aphet. f. ABODE.] Biding, tarrying, delay. *But b.*: without delay. –1593.

Bode (bōᵘd), *v.* [OE. *bodian*, f. *boda* messenger.] †1. To proclaim; *absol.* to preach (the gospel) –ME. †2. To decree, command (a person) *that* –ME. 3. To announce beforehand, predict, presage (*arch.*) OE. 4. Of things: To portend ME.; *esp.* (with *well* or *ill*) To give *good* or *bad* promise 1700. 5. To forebode (usu. *evil*) 1740.

3. There are croakers in every country, always boding its ruin FRANKLIN. 4. This boades some strange erruption to our State *Haml.* I. i. 69. Hence **Bo·der**, one who or that which bodes. **Bo·dingly** *adv.* var. †**Bo·den.**

Bode = **behoved,** pa. t. of BUS *v.*

Bodeful (bōᵘˑdful), *a.* 1813. [mod.; f. BODE *sb.*² + -FUL.] Full of presage, ominous.

‖**Bodega** (bodīˑgă). 1876. [Sp.:—L., a. Gr. ἀποθήκη.] A wine-shop in Spain; adopted as a name for a cellar or shop for the sale of wines only.

Bodement (bōᵘˑdmĕnt). 1605. [f. BODE *v.*¹ + -MENT.] 1. An omen, presage. 2. Foreboding 1642. 3. Prediction, prognostication 1826.

2. Bodements sweet of immortality COLERIDGE.

Bo·den, *ppl. a. Sc.* Also **bodin.** ME. [?] †1. Accoutred, armed. See FEIR. –1828. 2. Fitted out, prepared; dressed. Usu. with *well* or *ill*. ME.

1. Bodin in effeir of war SCOTT.

Bo·deword. Now *n. dial.* ME. [f. BODE *sb.*²] †1. Behest. ME. only. †2. Message –1700. 3. Presage 1832.

Bodge, *sb.*¹ 1589. [f. BODGE *v.*; cf. BOTCH *sb.*²] A clumsy patch; a botched piece of work. Now *dial.*

†**Bodge,** *sb.*² A measure of oats; app. about half a peck. B. JONS.

Bodge, *v.* 1552. [Altered f. BOTCH *v.*; cf. *grudge* from *grutch*.] To patch clumsily. Now *dial.* Hence **Bo·dger**¹.

Bo·dger². 1736. [? = BADGER *sb.*¹] ? A pedlar. Now *dial.*

Bodice (bǫ·dis). 1566. [var. of *bodies* (see BODY II. 2), retaining the old sound of final *-s*.] 1. *Formerly*, An inner garment for the upper part of the body, strengthened with whalebone; a corset, stays; freq. called *a pair of bodies* (*bodice*) = 'a pair of stays' 1618. Also *fig.* 2. The upper part of a woman's dress, a tight-fitting outer vest (cf. BODY *sb.*); also, an inner vest worn over the stays. Also *attrib.*

1. A pair of new blewish Bodice 1706. 2. Nothing but her vpper bodies FLETCHER.

Bodied (bǫ·did), *ppl. a.* 1547. [f. BODY + -ED.] 1. Having a body or trunk; usu. in comb., as *big-b.*, etc. b. Having substance, strength, etc. 1611. 2. Made corporeal or material; embodied 1646.

1. Ill-fac'd, worse b., shapelesse euery where *Com. Err.* IV. ii. 20. 2. Like the b. heaven in clearness BROWNING.

†**Bo·dikin, Bodikie.** Also **bodkin.** 1598. [dim. of BODY.] 1. A diminutive body, a particle 1668. 2. (*God's, ods*) *bodikins! bodkins!* (*bodlikins!*) An oath: God's dear body! –1753.

Bodiless (bǫ·dilės), *a.* ME. [f. BODY + -LESS.] 1. Having no body; incorporeal, unsubstantial. 2. Wanting the trunk 1587.

1. This Bodilesse Creation extasie Is very cunning in *Haml.* III. iv. 138.

Bo·dilize, *v. nonce-wd.* [after *spiritualize*.] To make material. SOUTHEY.

Bodily (bǫ·dĭli), *a.* ME. [f. BODY + -LY¹.] †1. Of the nature of body; corporeal, physical; as opp. to *spiritual* –1674. 2. Of or belonging to the body or physical nature of man ME. †b. Real, actual *Cor.* I. ii. 5. †3. Solid; of or pertaining to a solid –1601.

2. The fear .. of corporeall hurt, which we call *B. Fear* HOBBES. †*B. oath*: = CORPORAL OATH. Hence **Bo·diline·ss.**

Bodily (bǫ·dĭli), *adv.* ME. [f. as prec.] †1. In the manner of, or with regard to, the body; (often = 'unspiritually') –1685. 2. In the flesh; in person 1440. 3. *transf.* 'Body and all'; all together, in one mass, as a whole 1793.

2. Christ..b. present 1640. 3. A. portrait..cut out b. from the walls 1877.

Bodken, -kin, obs. vars. of BAUDEKIN.

Bodkin (bǫ·dkin). ME. [?] †1. A short pointed weapon; a dagger, lancet, etc. –1657. 2. A small pointed instrument used for piercing holes in cloth, etc. 1440. 3. A long pin used by women to fasten up the hair 1580. 4. An instrument with a knobbed point, having a large eye, for drawing tape or cord through a hem, loops, etc. 1714. 5. *Printing.* An awl-like tool used to pick out letters from set-up type 1846. 6. *transf.* (*colloq.*) A person wedged in between two others where there is room for two only; *esp.* in *To ride* or *sit b.* 1798.

1. When he himselfe might his Quietus make With a bare B. *Haml.* III. i. 76. 6. While the pressed b., punched and squeezed to death, Sweats in the mid-most place 1798. Hence **Bo·dkin, Bo·dkinize** *v.* to squeeze in as a b. (sense 6).

Bodkin (*Ods bodkins!*), var. of BODIKIN.

Bodkin, bodkin-work, var. of BAUDEKIN.

Bodle (bǫ·d'l). *Sc.* 1650. [? f. a mint-master *Bothwell*.] A Scotch copper coin = one-sixth of an English penny; the smallest coin.

Not that I cared a brass b. for his benison SCOTT.

Bodleian (bǫdlīˑăn, bǫ·dliˌăn). 1663. [f. Sir Thomas *Bodley*, who in 1597 refounded the Library.] A. *adj.* Of or pertaining to Sir T. Bodley or the Library bearing his name. B. quasi-*sb.* The Oxford University Library; also colloquially called **Bodley.** Also *fig.* and *transf.*

†**Bo·drag(e.** 1537. [prob. Ir.; cf. *buaidhreadh* molestation.] A hostile incursion –1596.

Body (bǫ·di). [OE. *bodig* neut.] I. 1. The physical or material frame of man or of any animal; the whole material organism. (In *Biol.* occas. used of plants.). 2. Short for 'dead body', corpse ME. 3. Used symbolically of the bread in the sacrament of the Lord's Supper ME.

1. He shold come fyght with hym b. for b. CAXTON. Difficult to keep b. and soul together (*mod.*). 2. The lyon stode by the b. 1 *Kings* xiii. 24.

II. 1. The main portion of the animal frame; the trunk OE. b. The main stem, trunk, stock of a plant or tree 1523. Also *fig.* 2. The part of a dress which covers the body; also the part of a woman's dress above the waist, as dist. from the loose skirt 1585. 3. The main, central, or principal part OE. b. *Naut.* The hull of a ship; various sections of this 1691. 4. The main portion of a collection or company; the majority; the bulk of anything 1599. †5. A retort. (With some reference to *spirit*.) –1800. 6. *Type-founding.* The breadth of the shank of the type, as opp. to its thickness; hence, size of type 1824.

1. All heade and veri litel b. 1600. Phr. *The B. of Christ* (*fig.*): the Church of which Christ is the head. 3. The b. of a land SHAKS., of a tree DE FOE, of true religion BURKE. 4. The b. of a discourse *Much Ado* I. i. 287, the Empire 1678.

III. Personal being, individual. 1. The material being of man, taken for the whole; the person. Chiefly legal. ME. 2. An individual, of either sex. (Now familiar, with a tinge of compassion.) ME

1. A warrant..to bring without delay the b. of the same prisoner 1652. *Heir of the b.*: an heir who is a direct descendant. 2. It shall be given away to some poor b. WALTON.

IV. 1. *Law.* An artificial 'person' created by law; a corporation. Always with defining adj., as *b. corporate*, etc. 1461. 2. A society, association, league, fraternity 1689. 3. An organized collection of fighting men; a force. (The most general term so applied.) 1597. 4. (loosely) A collective mass of persons or things 1593. 5. A pandect (cf. L. *corpus juris*); a textbook 1593.

1. The king is a b. politick, for that a b. politique never dieth MILT. (*B. politic* means also an 'organized society'.) The b. politic: the nation in its corporate character; the state. (Orig. with reference to the *headship* of the sovereign.) 3. A b. of horse 1769. 4. The entire b. of the Scripture HOOKER. A b. of opinion (*mod.*). 5. A b. of laws BENTLEY.

V. Transferred to matter generally. 1. A material thing ME. 2. *Geom.* A solid 1570. 3. Amount; bulk; quantity 1650. 4. *Chem.* and *Min.* Any kind of 'substance', simple or compound, solid, liquid, or gaseous 1594. 5. *abstractly.* Matter 1668. †6. Reality, as opp. to shadow, etc. –1702. 7. Substance or substantial quality 1645. Also *fig.* 8. Fundamental constituent 1787. †9. *Metaph.* An entity; an agent or cause of phenomena –1660.

1. *Heavenly bodies*: *now*, the masses of matter that exist away from the earth, the sun, moon, planets, comets, etc.; *orig.* the seven 'bodies celestial' of the astro-alchemists, viz. the sun, moon, and five old planets, to which answered seven ancient metals, called 'the seven bodies terrestrial'. A b...may be defined, the external cause to which we ascribe our sensations MILL. 3. A b. of igneous rock MURCHISON, of air HUXLEY. 4. Crystallized bodies, such as nitre BREWSTER. *Simple bodies*: the chemical elements; *Compound bodies*: the substances formed by their combination. 6. The verie Age and Bodie of the Time *Haml.* III. ii. 26. 9. Night and Day are bodies 1660. Voice is a B., for it maketh that which is heard; in a word, whatsoever is, is a B. and a Subject STANLEY.

Comb.: **b.-chamber,** the outer and largest chamber of a shell occupied by the b. of the animal; **-cloth,** a cloth to cover horses, etc.; **-coat,** one fitting closely to the body, †a dress-coat; **-colour,** a colour that has b., as opp. to a tint or wash; a colour rendered opaque by the addition of white; **-hoop,** one securing the arris pieces of a made mast; **-lifter** = *body-snatcher*; **b.-line bowling** (*Cricket*), fast bowling delivered persistently on the leg side; **-louse,** a species of louse (*Pediculus corporis*) which infests the body of the uncleanly; **-plan,** in *Shipbuilding*, an end elevation of a ship, showing the breadth, contour of the sides, timbers, etc.; **-snatcher,** one who secretly disinters dead bodies for the purpose of dissection; **-tube,** the main tube forming the body of an organ-pipe; **-whorl**, the last and largest whorl of a shell, containing the b. of the mollusc.

Body (bǫ·di), *v.* 1449. [f. prec.] *trans.* 1. To furnish with a body; to embody. †2. To give body to (*lit.* and *fig.*) –1657. †3. To draw up or form (troops, etc.) into a body. (Also *intr.* for *refl.*) –1653.

Phr. *To b. forth*: to represent to oneself as in bodily form; to exhibit in outward reality; to typify.

Body-guard (bǫ·diˌgāːɹd). 1735. [cf. F. *garde du corps.*] 1. A guard for the person (*esp.* of a sovereign); a retinue or escort. 2. A soldier of the body-guard 1861.

Bodyhood (bǫ·dihud). 1674. [f. BODY *sb.*] The quality of having a body or of being body.

Bœhmenism (bǒ·mĕniz'm). 1656. The doctrines taught by Jacob Bœhme, a German mystic and theosophist (1575–1624); so **Bœhmenist, Bœhmenite.** var. **Behmenism.**

Bœ·otarch. 1822. [ad. Gr. Βοιωτάρχης.] A chief magistrate of the Bœotian league.

Bœotia (biˌōu·ʃiă). 1786. A district of ancient Greece proverbial for the stupidity of its inhabitants; hence *fig.* **Bœ·otize** *v.* to become or make Bœotian.

Bœotian (biˌōu·ʃăn). 1598. [f. prec.] A. *adj.* Of Bœotia; dull, stupid; var. **Bœo·tic.** B. *sb.* A native of Bœotia; a thick-head 1649.

‖**Boer** (būəɹ). Formerly **boor.** 1824. [Du. *boer* 'farmer', the same word as BOOR.] A Dutch colonist in S. Africa engaged in agriculture or cattle-breeding.

Bog (bǫg), *sb.*[1] 1505. [ad. Ir. or Gael. *bogach*, f. *bog* soft.] A piece of wet spongy ground, consisting chiefly of decayed moss and other vegetable matter, too soft to bear the weight of any heavy body upon its surface; a morass or moss. b. (without *pl.*) Bog-land, boggy soil 1687. Also *fig.* (Cf. *fog.*) 1614.

That Serbonian B... Where Armies whole have sunk MILT. *P. L.* II. 592. A b. of uncertainty DICKENS.

Comb. a. In names of plants growing in bogs: as *B. Asphodel, Cinquefoil, Pimpernel*, etc.; **b. bean, b. nut,** or **b. trefoil,** also called BUCKBEAN; **b. berry,** the Cranberry; **b. moss,** various species of Sphagnum; **b. myrtle,** Sweet Gale (*Myrica Gale*); **b. orchis,** *Malaxis paludosa*; **b. pink,** Lady's Smock (*Cardamine pratensis*); **b. rush,** *Schœnus nigricans*; **b. violet** = BUTTERWORT (*Pinguicula*). b. Special comb.: **b.-blitter, -bluiter, -bumper,** the Bittern; **-butter,** a fatty hydrocarbon found in the peat-bogs of Ireland; **-earth,** earth composed of, or largely mixed with, peat; **b. fir** = *bog-pine*; **b. iron, b. iron ore,** a brittle porous variety of brown hæmatite found in bogs; **-jumper,** (*local*) the Bittern; **-land,** marshy land; *joc.*, Ireland, hence **-lander**; **b. manganese,** the hydrated peroxide of manganese; **-mould** = *bog-earth*; **b. oak,** the wood of oak preserved in a black state in peat-bogs, etc.; **b. ore** = *bog iron ore*; **-pine,** pine-wood found in peat-bogs; **-spavin,** an encysted tumour on the inside of the hock of a horse; **-timber, -wood,** the trunks of trees found in peat-bogs. Hence **Bo·gginess,** boggy quality. **Bo·ggy** *a.* of the nature of, or characterized by, b.; swampy; *transf.* flabby.

†**Bog, bogge,** *sb.*[2] 1527. [? var. of *bugge* BUG.] A bugbear, a source of dread –1676.

Bog (bǫg), *v.* 1603. [f. BOG *sb.*[1]] 1. To sink or entangle in a bog. Also *fig.* 1641. 2. *intr.* (for *refl.*) To sink and stick in a bog 1800.

1. Bogged up to the saddle-girths SCOTT.

Bogey (bōu·gi). 1892. Also **bogy, bogie.** [f. (Colonel) *Bogey*, an imaginary partner (see N.E.D., Suppl.).] *Golf.* The score that a good player should do a hole or a course in. (Cf. PAR *sb.*[1] 4.)

Bogey, var. of BOGIE, BOGY.

Boggard, -art (bǫ·găɹd, -ăɹt). 1570. [A north. and midl. word related to BOGGLE, BOGLE, and BOG *sb.*[2]] 1. = BOGLE. †2. An object at which a horse boggles –1725.

Boggle (bǫ·g'l), *v.* 1598. [app. f. *boggle*, var. of BOGLE. Assoc. later w. *bungle.*] 1. *intr.* To start with fright, shy; to be startled *at.* 2. To raise scruples, stickle (*at, about, over*, etc., or *to do*) 1638. 3. 'To play fast or loose' (J.); to palter 1613. 4. To bungle 1853.

1. You b. shrewdly, euery feather starts you *All's Well* v. iii. 232. 2. To b. at an oath 1876. 3. Are ye not afraid to b. thus with God Almighty DRUMM. OF HAWTH. 4. To b. at a lock 1853. Hence **Bo·ggler.**

Boggle (bǫ·g'l) *sb.* 1660. [f. prec.] 1. The act of boggling; scruple (1667); a bungle (1834).

Boggle, dial. var. of BOGLE.

Bo·g-house. *dial.* and *vulg.* 1705. A privy, 'a house of office' J.

Bogie (bōu·gi). Also **bogy, bogey.** 1817. [A n. dial. word, of unkn. etym. Not conn. w. BOGY.] 1. *n. dial.* A low strong truck upon four small wheels, also called *trolly.* Hence, *gen.* the truck used by platelayers on a railway. 2. A low truck running on two or more pairs of wheels and attached to the fore-part of a locomotive engine or the ends of a long railway-carriage by a central pivot, on which it swivels freely in passing curves 1844. Also *attrib.*

Bogie, var. of BOGEY, BOGY.

Bogle (bōu·g'l). *north. Eng.* **boggle.** 1505. [Of uncertain etym.: ? f. *bogge* BOG *sb.*[2], var. of *bugge* BUG; perh. a. Welsh *bwg.*] 1. A phantom causing fright; a goblin, bogy, or spectre. 2. *fig.* and *transf.* A bugbear (not a phantom); a mere phantom 1663.

Bo·g-trot, *v.* 1734. [f. next.] *intr.* To trot over, or live among, bogs.

Bog-trotter (bǫ·g-trǫːtəɹ). 1682. [f. BOG *sb.* + TROTTER.] †1. One accustomed to trot over bogs –1755. 2. *spec.* Applied to the wild Irish in the 17th c. 1682.

Bogus (bōu·gəs), (*sb.*[1]) *a.* 1827. [A cant word of U.S. Perh. related to BOGY, etc.] †1. *sb.* An apparatus for counterfeit coining 1827. 2. *adj.* Counterfeit, spurious, sham 1852.

2. B. transactions 1857. A b. Company..instead of paying dividends..goes into Liquidation GIFFEN.

Bogus (bōu·gəs). *sb.*[2] *U.S.* [? same wd. as prec.] A liquor made of rum and molasses.

Bogy, bogey (bōu·gi). Also **bogie.** Pl. **bogies.** 1836. [Cf. BOGLE, etc.] 1. As quasi-proper name: The devil. 2. A bogle 1857. 3. *fig.* A bugbear; an object of terror 1865.

1. The people are all naughty and Bogey carries them all off THACKERAY. See also BOGEY, BOGIE.

Bohea (bohī·). 1701. [ad. Chinese *Wu-i-(shan)* the *Wu-i* hills in north of Fuhkien. The Fuhkien dialect uses *b* for *w* or *v* (Edkins).] A. *adj.* Of the Wu-i hills, whence black tea first came to England; applied also to similar tea grown elsewhere 1704. B. *sb.* 1. = *B. tea.* The name orig. of the finest kinds of black tea, now of the poorest. 1701. 2. An infusion of this tea 1706.

2. Richardson's goddess who fed on muffins and b. THACKERAY.

Bohemia (bohī·miă). 1449. 1. A kingdom of central Europe, forming part of the Austrian empire. 2. Gipsydom; see BOHEMIAN *sb.* 2. 1871. 3. The community of social Bohemians, or their district. So F. *la bohême.* [f. BOHEMIAN *sb.* 3.] 1861.

3. B. had no name in Philip's young days THACKERAY.

Bohemian (bohī·miăn). 1579. [f. prec. The transf. senses are taken from French.] A. *sb.* 1. A native of Bohemia 1603. b. A Bohemian Protestant or Hussite. FULKE. 2. A gipsy. [F. *bohême, bohémien.*] 1696. 3. A gipsy of society; *esp.* an artist, literary man, or actor, who leads a vagabond or irregular and unconventional life. (Used with much latitude, with or without reference to morals.) 1848.

3. She was of a wild, roving nature, inherited from father and mother, who were both Bohemians, by taste and circumstances THACKERAY.

B. *adj.* 1. Of or belonging to Bohemia. 2. Of or pertaining to the gipsies 1848. 3. Of, or characteristic of, social Bohemians 1861.

Comb.: **B. chatterer,** or **waxwing,** a bird of passage (*Ampelis* or *Bombycilla garrula*); **B. glass,** a fine kind of glass, orig. made in Bohemia, in which potash is the alkali used. Hence **Bohe·mianism,** the conduct and manners of a B.

†**Boiette.** [? = 16th c. F. *boëtte, boëte*, var. of *boîte.*] A casket. LD. BERNERS.

‖**Boiguacu.** [Tupi; = 'big serpent'.] Native name of the Boa Constrictor or other large boa.

Boil (boil), *sb.*[1] [OE. *býl*: com. Teut.:– OTeut. *bûljâ-*, from root *bûl-* in Goth. *uf-bauljan* to blow up. The ME. form was *bile.* Cf. BEAL.] A hard inflamed suppurating tumour; a furuncle. *transf.* A blister on a painted surface 1840. Also *fig.*

Holy Job healed of his biles 1737.

Boil (boil), *sb.*[2] 1440. [f. BOIL *v.*] 1. An act of boiling. 2. The state of boiling, or being at boiling point; also *transf.* and *fig.* 1813. 3. That which is boiled 1755.

2. The coffee was near the b. 1870. 3. I put the linen..into a b. of soap 1755.

Boil (boil), *v.* [ME. *boille-n, boile-n*, a. OF. *boillir*:—L. *bullire.*] 1. *intr.* Of a liquid: To bubble up in agitation through the action of heat upon the lowest portions of the liquid, which become gaseous and escape; also said of the vessel containing the liquid. b. To reach the boiling point, to turn from the liquid into the gaseous state ME. 2. *transf.* To move with an agitation like that of boiling water; to bubble, to seethe ME. 3. *fig.* Said of passions, persons in a passion, etc. ME. 4. *trans.* To cause to bubble with heat (see 1); to bring to the boiling point; *esp.* said of food, said also of the containing vessel ME. Also *intr.* (for *refl.*) 5. To subject to, cook, cleanse, produce, etc. by, boiling ME. Also *intr.*

1. The fire causeth the waters to boyle *Isa.* lxiv. 2. Phr. *To b. over*: to bubble up and run over the side of the vessel. 2. The billows b. POPE. 3. Resentment was boiling in his sullen, unsociable mind HUME. 5. A Cook they hadde..To boille the chiknes with the Marybones CHAUCER. Martyrs..were stoned..or boiled in oil TENNYSON. *To b. away* (intr.): to evaporate in boiling. *To b. down*: to lessen the bulk of by boiling; *fig.* to condense.

Phr. *To b. the pot*: to supply one's livelihood. So *to keep the pot boiling*: also = to keep anything going. Cf. POT. Hence **Boiled** *ppl. a.* brought to the state of ebullition; subjected to, cooked, cleansed, etc. by, boiling. (In *Cymb.* I. vi. 125 *boiled stuff* = harlots.) *ellipt.* Boiled beef or mutton. *colloq.*

Boiler (boi·ləɹ). 1540. [f. prec.] 1. One who boils (anything). 2. A vessel in which any liquid is boiled 1725. b. *spec.* In a steam-engine, the large vessel, usually of wrought-iron plates riveted together, in which the water is converted into steam; the tank attached to a kitchen grate; the vessel in which clothes are boiled 1757. 3. What makes anything boil, as in *pot-b.*, a piece of work done *to boil the pot.* 4. A vegetable, etc. suited for boiling 1812.

Comb. etc. (in sense 2 b) as **b.-alarm,** an apparatus for indicating lowness of water in a b.; **-feeder,** an apparatus for supplying a b. with water; **-float,** one which by its rising or falling turns the feed-water off or on; **-iron, -plate,** rolled iron of ¼ to ½-inch thickness, used for making steam-boilers, etc.; **-man,** one who attends to a b.; **-protector,** a coating to prevent the escape of heat from a b.; **-tube,** one of the tubes by which heat is diffused through the water in a b.

Boilery (boi·ləri). 1628. [a. F. *bouillerie.*] A place for boiling anything, *e. g.* salt or sugar. Usu. in comb., as *sugar-b.*

Boiling (boi·liŋ), *vbl. sb.* ME. [f. BOIL *v.* + -ING[1].] 1. The action of the vb. (senses 1–5). 2. That which is boiled or being boiled, a decoction; a quantity boiled at one time; hence *the whole b.* (slang): 'the whole lot'. 1674.

Comb.: **b.-furnace,** a reverberatory furnace sometimes employed in the decarbonization of cast iron; **-house,** a boilery; **-heat, -point, -temperature,** the temperature at which anything boils; *spec.* that at which water boils (at the sea-level 212° Fahr., 100° Cent.); *fig.* a high degree of excitement, etc. Hence **Boi·lingly** *adv.*

Boist, *sb.* [ME. *boiste*, a. OF. *boiste*, in Pr. *bostia*, repr., through late L. *bossida, boxida*, L. *pyxida*, a. Gr. πυξίδα (πυξίς) a box (Brachet).] †1. A box, a casket (= BOX *sb.*[2] 1) –1633. 2. A rude hut (*dial.*) 1840.

Boisterous (boi·stərəs), *a.* 1474. [app. var. of *boisteous, boistuous*, BOISTOUS.] †1. Rough, coarse, as *e. g.* food. CAXTON. †2. Of rough, strong, or stiff texture; unyielding –1700. †3. Bulky, big and cumbrous –1642. †4. Painfully rough *Rom. & Jul.* I. iv. 26. †5. Coarse-growing, rank. MILT. *Sams.* 1164. †6. Acting roughly; violent 1695. 7. Rough, as opp. to 'calm' 1576. 8. Of persons and actions: †a. Violently fierce, truculent –1791. b. Too rough or clamorous. (Orig. in a bad sense.) 1568. c. Abounding in rough but good-natured activity bordering upon excess 1683.

2. The leathern out-side, boistrous as it was, Gave way DRYDEN. 3. His boystrous club SPENSER. 6. A b. and bestial strength MILT. 7. The boyst'rous Seas DRAYTON. 8. c. Their b. Mirth STEELE. Hence **Boi·sterous-ly** *adv.*, **-ness.**

†**Boi·stous,** *a.* ME. [Of unkn. etym. Welsh *bwystus* 'ferocious' (14th c.) may be a deriv. of **bwyst*:—L. *bestia*, or it may be the ME. *buystous.*] 1. Of persons, etc.: Rough, unpolished –1547. 2. = BOISTEROUS 2, 3, 6, 7, 8. –1578. Hence †**Boi·stous·ly** *adv.*, †**-ness.**

Boke, *v.* Now *dial.* 1601. [Cf. POKE *v.*] *intr.* and *trans.* To butt, to poke.

Bolar (bōᵘ·lăɹ), *a.* 1676. [f. BOLE *sb.*] Consisting of, or of the nature of, bole. var. †**Bo·lary.**

‖**Bolas** (bōᵘ·las), *sb. pl.*; also as sing. with *pl.* bolases. 1843. [Sp.: pl. of *bola* ball.] A missile, used by the Patagonians and others, consisting of two or more balls or stones connected together by strong cord; these are swung round the head and discharged so as to wind round and entangle cattle, etc.

†**Bolbanac, bolbonac.** 1578. *Herb.* The plant 'Honesty' (*Lunaria biennis*) -1640.

†**Bold,** *sb.* [OE., prob. for *bodl, *boðl, *boþl :—OTeut. *boþlo-, f. *bu-, bo-* dwell + *-tlo* instrumental suffix (Sievers).] A dwelling -ME.

Bold (bōᵘld), *a.* [Com. Teut.: OE. *bald*:—OTeut. **balþo-z*. Only in Teut.] **1.** Stout-hearted, daring, fearless. Often = *brave. absol.* A bold man. Now only pl. *the b.* ME. quasi-*adv.* Boldly 1593. **2.** Of words, actions, etc.: Showing or requiring courage ME. **3.** In bad sense: Audacious, presumptuous; opp. to 'modest' ME. **4.** †Strong, big. Of grain, etc.: Well-filled ME. †**5.** Confident (*in*), sure (*of*) -1616. **6.** *fig.* Showing daring, vigour, or licence of conception or expression 1667. **7.** Striking to the eye; firmly marked, pronounced 1678. **8.** *Naut.* Of a coast: Rising steeply from water; used also of the deep water close to such a shore; also, generally, of any broad, steep, or projecting rock. Of a ship: Broad and bluff in the bows. 1628. Also in *comb.*

1. The righteous are bolde as a lyon *Prov.* xxviii. 1. B.-following where your fathers led BURNS. 2. A b. design MILT., task POPE, belief JOWETT. *To make (so) b., to be (so) b.*: to venture, presume so far as (*to do* a thing). 3. Ane deuill of hell, Is na compair to the iniquitie, Of bald women DOUGLAS. A b. young woman (*mod.*). 5. Be b. in vs, weele follow where thou lead'st *Tit. A.* V. i. 13. 6. A b. expressive phrase POPE. 7. A good b. hand SHERIDAN. 8. At Honfleur ..they can ride in b. water 1787. Hence **Bo·ld-ly** *adv.*, **-ness.**

†**Bold,** *v.* [OE. *bealdian*; see prec.] **1.** *intr.* To be or become bold -1706. **2.** *trans.* To make bold, encourage -1605.

†**Bold-beating,** *a.* Confusion of *bold-faced* and *brow-beating*. *Merry W.* II. ii. 28.

Bo·lden, *v.* Now *dial.* 1526. [f. BOLD *a.*] **1.** To make bold, encourage. *refl.* To make bold (*to do*). **2.** *intr.* To take courage 1864.

1. These..b. us likewise and spur us on KENNET.

Bold-face (bōᵘ·ld,fēˈs). 1692. One who has a bold face; an impudent person; also *attrib.*

A Sauce-box, and a Bold-face RICHARDSON. Hence **Bo·ld-faced** *ppl. a.*

Bole[1] (bōᵘl). ME. [a. ON. *bolr, bulr.*] The trunk of a tree. *transf.* Anything of a cylindrical shape like the trunk of a tree, as a roll, a pillar, etc.

The shadow of the b. of the tree FISHER.

Bole[2] (bōᵘl). ME. [ad. med.L. *bolus*, a. Gr. βῶλος clod of earth; first used in Eng. in *b. armeniac.*] **1.** The name of several kinds of fine, compact, earthy, or unctuous clay, usually coloured yellow, red, or brown by the presence of iron oxide 1641. **b.** *spec.* **B. armeniac,** †*armoniak*, etc.: an astringent earth brought from Armenia, and formerly used as an antidote and styptic ME. †**2.** A large pill, a BOLUS; also *fig.* -1725.

Bole[3] (bōᵘl). *Sc.* 1728. Also **boal.** [?] **a.** A small square recess in the wall of a room for holding articles. **b.** An unglazed aperture in a wall for admitting air or light; sometimes closed with a shutter.

Open the b. wi' speed, that I may see if this be the right Lord Geraldin SCOTT.

Bole[4]. 1670. A place where in ancient times lead ores were smelted -1785.

Bolection (bolе·kʃən). 1708. [?] *Archit.* A moulding which projects before the face of the work decorated, as a raised moulding round a panel.

‖**Bolero** (bolēᵊ·ro, -iᵊ·ro). 1787. [Sp.] A lively Spanish dance; also the music for it.

Boletus (bolī·tŏs). 1601. [a. L., ad. Gr. βωλίτης, perh. f. βῶλος; see BOLE[2].] *Bot.* A large genus of fungi, having the under surface of the pileus full of pores. Hence †**Bole·tic** *a. Chem.* Of or pertaining to B., as *Boletic acid.*

Bolide (bǫ·laid). 1852. [a. F., ad. L., a. Gr. βολίς missile.] A large meteor; usually one that explodes; a fire-ball.

Bolk, *v.* Now *dial.* [ME. *bolken*, f. same root as BELCH.] **1.** = BELCH 1-3. **2.** *intr.* To vomit; to retch ME.; also *trans.* **3.** *fig.* and *transf.* To eject (as a volcano) 1513. **4.** *intr.* To heave or throb, like a confined gas, etc. 1561. **5.** To flow in gulps 1550. Hence †**Bolk** *sb.* a belch.

Boll (bōᵘl), *sb.*[1] ME. [var. of BOWL *sb.*[1]:—OE. *bolla*; see BOWL.] †**1.** Earlier f. BOWL *sb.*[1], q.v. †**2.** A bubble. ME. only. **3.** *spec.* A rounded seed-vessel or pod, as of flax or cotton 1500. †**4.** A round knob -1660. †**5.** The Adam's apple; see THROAT-BOLL.

Comb. **b.-worm,** an insect that destroys the cotton b. or pod.

Boll (bōᵘl), *sb.*[2] ME. [? a. ON. *bolli* = OE. *bolla* BOWL.] A measure of capacity for grain, etc., containing in Scotland 6 imperial bushels, but in the north of England varying from the 'old b.' of 6 to the 'new b.' of 2 bushels. Also a measure of weight = 140 pounds.

Bollandist (bǫ·lăndist). 1751. [f. *Bolland*, a Flemish Jesuit (17th c.) + -IST.] *pl.* The Jesuit writers who continue the *Acta Sanctorum*, begun by John Bolland.

Bollard (bǫ·lăɹd). 1844. [? f. BOLE *sb.*[1] + -ARD.] *Naut.* A wooden or iron post, on a ship, a quay, etc., for securing ropes to. Also *attrib.*, as in *b.-timber*, one of two large oak timbers bolted to each side of the stem, and supporting the bowsprit.

†**Bo·llen,** *ppl. a.* ME. [f. BELL *v.*[1]] Swollen; puffed up -1609.

Here one, being thronged, bears back, all b. and red SHAKS. *Lucr.* 1417. vars. †**Boln, bolne.**

Bolling (bōᵘ·liŋ), *sb.* 1691. [f. BOLE[1].] A pollard (tree).

‖**Bolli·to.** 1753. [It. = 'boiled'.] The calcined materials for glass-making, frit.

Bologna (bǒlōᵘ·nʸă). 1563. A town in Italy, anciently called Bononia. Hence **Bolo·gnan, Bono·nian** *a.*; also **B. bottle, flask, phial,** an unannealed bottle, which may be dropped upon a brick floor without breaking, but will burst in pieces if scratched; **B. phosphorus,** a phosphorescent preparation of B. stone and gum; **B. sausage,** a large kind of sausage first made at B.; **B. spar, stone,** native sulphate of baryta found near B., having phosphorescent properties.

Bolometer (bolǫ·mǐtəɹ). 1881. [f. Gr. βολή beam of light + μέτρον.] An electrical instrument of great sensitiveness for measuring radiant heat. Hence **Bolome·tric** *a.*

Bolshevik (bǫ·lʃǐvik), *sb.* and *a.* 1917. [a. Russ. *bol'shévik*, compar. of *bol'shoy* big.] A member of the extreme wing of the Russian Socialist Party (later, the Communist Party), which seized the supreme power in Russia after the revolution of March 1917; first applied to the party advocating the maximum socialist programme in 1903; *transf.* an extreme revolutionary. (Cf. MAXIMALIST, MENSHEVIK.) So **Bo·lshevist** *sb.* and *a.* 1917 (abbrev. **Bo·lshy, -ie** 1920); whence **Bo·lshevism, Bo·lshevize** *v.*

Bolster (bōᵘ·lstəɹ), *sb.* [Com. Teut.: OE. *bolster*:—OTeut. **bolstro-z*, f. OTeut. root **bŭl* to swell.] **1.** A long stuffed pillow or cushion used to support the sleeper's head in a bed; now restricted to the under-pillow. **2.** Applied to things of the nature of a pad: †**a.** A surgical pad or compress -1813. †**b.** A ridge of padding on a saddle -1753. †**c.** A padding in a garment -1753. **d.** *Naut.* in *pl.* Small cushions of tarred canvas, also pieces of timber, used to prevent chafing between ropes and other parts of the ship 1769. **3.** Applied to parts of mechanism which form a support or base: **a.** A block of wood fixed on a siege-gun carriage, on which the breech rests during transport. **b.** The transverse bar over the axle of a wagon. Also, the principal cross-beam of a railway-truck or carriage body. 1686. **c.** The part of the pier on which a truss-bridge rests. **d.** The spindle-bearing in the rail of a spinning-frame 1825. **e.** A horizontal cap-piece laid upon the top of a post or pillar, to shorten the bearing of the beam of a string-piece supported by it. **f.** In the centering of an arch, each of the transverse pieces which lie across the ribs and support the voussoirs. **g.** The plate or block of a punching-machine on which the metal to be punched is laid 1677. **4.** Applied to things of the nature of a supporting or strengthening ridge: **a.** The projecting shoulder of a knife, chisel, etc. which abuts upon the handle 1827. **b.** The metallic end of the handle of a pocket-knife. **c.** A raised ridge on the wrestplank of a piano to give bearing to the strings by raising them. **5.** *Archit.* One of the rolls forming the sides of an Ionic capital; cf. BALUSTER 1876.

Bolster (bōᵘ·lstəɹ), *v.* 1508. [f. prec. sb.] **1.** *trans.* To support with a bolster 1610. **2.** *transf.* and *fig.* To prop *up* 1508. **b.** *fig.* To uphold or bear out (evil doers, crime, etc.). Also with *up.* 1523. **c.** Now usually: To give fictitious support to. Usually with *up*, occas. *out.* 1581. **3.** To pad, or stuff out with padding. 1530. Also *fig.* †**4.** *spec.* in *Surg.* To furnish with a pad or compress. Also *fig.* -1766. **5.** ? *intr.* To lie on the same bolster. *Oth.* III. iii. 399. **6.** To belabour with bolsters 1871.

1. Bolstered up in bed 1873. 2. c. To b. up the credit of the government WELLINGTON. 3. Revenues bolstered out with secular dignities 1616. Hence **Bo·lstered** *ppl. a.* **Bo·lsterer,** a supporter. (Usu. in a bad sense.) **Bo·lstering** *vbl. sb.* the action of the vb.; *concr.* padding; in *Surg.* a pad.

Bolt (bōᵘlt), *sb.*[1] [OE. *bolt*, a cross-bow bolt. Etym. unkn.] **1.** An arrow; *esp.* a stout and short arrow with thickened head, called also *quarrel.* Often *fig.* **2.** A thunderbolt 1535. **3.** An appliance for fastening a door, viz. a cylindrical or other piece of iron, etc. moving longitudinally through staples on the door, so that its end can be shot or pushed into a socket in the door-post or lintel. **b.** That part of a lock which springs out and enters the staple. ME. †**4.** An iron for fastening the leg; a fetter -1688. **5.** A stout metal pin with a head, used for holding things fast together. See CLINCH, RING, etc. 1626. **6.** *transf.* A roll of woven fabric, usually of a definite length, as 30 yards, 28 ells, 40 feet. ME. **7.** A bundle (of osiers, reeds, etc.) of a certain size 1725. **8.** Wood in special size for cleaving into laths 1688. **12.** Name of the Globe-flower, and Marsh Marigold 1597; also of species of Buttercup 1640.

2. *A b. from the blue* (BLUE *sb.* 5): a complete surprise. 3. Forc't Vertue is as a b. overshot; it goes neither forward nor backward MILT. **c.** In breech-loading rifles, a sliding part resembling a door-bolt which is moved back and forth to open and close the bore; a corresp. part in a Lewis gun.

Comb.: **b.-cutter,** one who cuts bolts; a machine for cutting bolts, or threads on bolts; **-hole,** a hole through which a b. passes; **-iron,** round bar iron; **-strake** (*Naut.*), certain strakes of plank which the beam fastenings pass through; **-threader,** a machine for cutting screw-threads on bolts.

Bolt (bōᵘlt), *sb.*[2] 1550. [f. BOLT *v.*[2]] **1.** A sudden spring or start. **2.** The act of breaking away; breaking away from a political party. (*U.S. colloq.*) 1835. **3.** Bolting food 1835.

†**Bolt, boult,** *sb.*[3] ME. [f. BOLT *v.*[1]] A flour-sieve, a boulter -1611.

Bolt, boult (bōᵘlt), *v.*[1] ME. [a. OF. *bulter* (now *bluter*) :—OF. *buleter*, for **bureter* = It. *burattare*, f. *bura, bure*, a kind of cloth (Diez). The historical spelling is *boult.*] **1.** To sift; to pass through a sieve or bolting-cloth. Also *transf.* and *fig.* **2.** *fig.* To examine by sifting; to search and try ME.

1. To b. the bran From the pure flour POPE. The fan'd snow, that's bolted By th' Northerne blasts *Wint. T.* IV. iv. 375. 2. I must first b. myself before I can censure them BURKE.

Bolt (bōᵘlt), *v.*[2] ME. [f. BOLT *sb.*[1]] †**1.** To spring back; to spring or start *up, upright* (*arch.*) **2.** To spring suddenly †*upon, in, into* 1666; to dart *forth, forward, out* 1513. **3.** To dart *off* or *away* 1611; *spec.* Of a horse: To break away from the rider's control 1820; **b.** *transf.* To break away from a political party (*U.S. politics*) 1884. **4.** To discharge like a bolt; to shoot; to expel ME. **5.** To blurt *out* or *forth* 1577. **6.** *colloq.* To swallow hastily and without chewing, to gulp *down* 1794. **7.** *trans.* = *bolt from* in sense 3. (*U.S. politics.*) 1884. †**8.** To fetter; also *fig.* -1606. **9.** To secure (a door, etc.) with a bolt 1580. 10. To fasten together or furnish with bolts 1727.

2. I think to b. upon you at Bath JOHNSON. Forth he bolted from the bush 1834. 3. My donkey bolted about every five minutes 1877. 5. The Rudest Head will b. a Paraphrase DANIEL. 6. He bolted the alcohol SCOTT. 8. To b. vp change *Ant. & Cl.* v. ii. 6. 10. I have ordered her [a ship] to be new bolted NELSON.

Bolt, *adv.* ME. [The sb. (BOLT[1]) and stem of the vb. (BOLT[2]).] 1. In †*b. up, b. upright* the sb. = 'as a bolt'. Hence **Bolt-upri·ghtness.** 2. The vb. stem used *advb.* = 'bolting, with one bolt, straight'. 1845.

Boltel (bōu·ltĕl). 1463. [?] A plain round moulding; a shaft of a clustered pillar.

Bolter[1], **boulter** (bōu·ltəɹ). 1440. [f. BOLT *v.*[1] + -ER[1].] 1. One who sifts meal, etc. 2. A piece of cloth used for sifting; a sieve; a bolting-machine. Also *fig.* Also, the fabric thus used. 1530.

Bo·lter[2]. 1840. [f. BOLT *v.*[2] + -ER[1].] 1. One that bolts or runs; *esp.* a horse that bolts. 2. One who bolts from his party (*U.S.*) 1883.

2. To whom a 'scratcher' or a 'b.' is more hateful than the Beast 1883.

Bolt-head, bolt's-head. 1475. [f. BOLT *sb.*[1]] 1. The head of a BOLT (senses 1, 5). 2. *Chem.* A globular flask with a long cylindrical neck, used in distillation 1610.

Bo·lt-hole. 1839. [BOLT *v.*[2]] 1. *Mining.* A short connecting heading or opening. 2. = *bolting-hole* (BOLTING *vbl. sb.*[2]) 1851.

Bolting, boul- (bōu·ltiŋ), *vbl. sb.*[1] ME. [f. BOLT *v.*[1]] 1. The act of sifting, *lit.* and *fig.*; *concr.* siftings. †b. The private arguing of law cases for practice -1670.

2. Means for the b. out of the truth SANDERSON.

Bo·lting, *vbl. sb.*[2] 1692. [f. BOLT *v.*[2]] The action of the vb., in various senses. *Comb.* b.-hole, a hole by which to bolt; *fig.* a means of escape.

Bo·ltless, *a.* Without a bolt or bolts, as *b. lightning* (*poet.*).

Bo·ltonite. *Min.* A unisilicate mineral, a variety of Forsterite, found near Bolton, Mass.

Bolt-rope (bōu·lt,rōup). 1626. [f. BOLT *sb.*[1]] *Naut.* A rope sewn all round the edge of the sail, to prevent it from tearing.

Boltspreet, -sprit, obs. var. of BOWSPRIT.

Bolus (bōu·lŏs). Pl. **boluses.** 1603. [a. mod.L., a. Gr. βῶλος clod.] 1. *Med.* A large pill. (Often contemptuous.) 2. A small rounded mass of anything 1782. 3. = BOLE[2] 1. 1682.

1. Physic him to death with pills and boluses 1832. Your Home Rule b. BLACK.

‖**Bom, boma.** 1864. Native name in Congo, W. Africa, of a huge non-poisonous snake, in Brazil applied to the largest boas.

Bomb (bǫm), *sb.* 1588. [a. F. *bombe*, ad. It. *bomba*, f. L. *bombus* humming. In the British army (bʋm) was formerly usual.] †1. tr. Sp. *bomba de fuego* 'a ball of fire' 1588. 2. A hollow iron projectile, usually spherical, charged with an explosive fired by concussion or a fuse; formerly = SHELL *sb.* III. 2 b; now usu. a hand-grenade (e. g. *Mills b.*) or an explosive shell dropped by aircraft 1684. b. *Whale-fishery.* A harpoon with an explosive charge in its head 1883. †3. A small war-vessel carrying mortars for throwing bombs. More fully *b.-ketch, -vessel,* etc. -1804.

Volcanic b.: a roundish mass of lava thrown out of a volcano. *Comb.* b.-lance = 2 b.

Bomb (bǫm), *v.* 1688. [f. prec.] Formerly, to bombard; now, to attack with bombs.

†**Bo·mbace, -ase.** 1553. [a. OF. *bombace*:— late L. *bombacem, bombax*, corrupt f. L. *bombyx*, a. Gr. βόμβυξ silkworm, silk.] 1. Raw cotton -1609. 2. Cotton-wool; *fig.* padding -1662.

Bombard (bǫ·m-, bʋ·mbăɹd), *sb.* ME. [a. OF. *bombarde*, in med.L. *bombarda*, prob. f. L. *bombus*; see BOMB.] 1. The earliest kind of cannon, usually throwing a stone ball or a very large shot. 2. = BOMB *sb.* 3. †3. A leather jug for liquor; a black-jack -1635. †*fig.* A toper 1617. 4. An early variety of bassoon. Also BOMBARDO. ME.

1. Springalles, bombardes, bowes, and other artillary LD. BERNERS. 3. That huge B. of Sacke 1 *Hen. IV*, II. iv. 497. *Comb.*: †b.-man, a pot-boy; †b.-phrase (tr. L. *ampulla*), bombast.

Bombard (bǫmbā·ɹd), *v.* 1598. [f. F. *bombarder*; see prec.] †1. *intr.* To fire off bombards -1695. 2. *trans.* To batter with shot and shell. Also *fig.* 1686. 3. *Cookery.* To stuff (a fillet of veal) 1769.

2. *fig.* Milton..bombarding Salmasius with foul epithets M. PATTISON. Hence **Bomba·rdment,** continuous attack upon a place with shot and shell.

Bombardier (bǫm-, bʋmbăɹdīə·ɹ). 1560. [a. F.; see BOMBARD.] 1. A soldier in charge of a bombard; an artilleryman (*arch.*) 2. *spec.* †a. Formerly: One of the master-gunner's men, employed about the mortars and howitzers -1769. b. Now: A non-commissioned officer in the artillery 1844. †3. A bomb-ship 1686.

Comb. b. beetle, a genus of beetles (esp. *Brachinus crepitans*) which when irritated eject fluid with a sharp report and blue vapour.

‖**Bomba·rdo.** [It.] = BOMBARD *sb.* 4.

Bo·mbardon, -o·ne. 1856. [a. It. *bombardone*, augmentative f. prec.] *Mus.* A brass instrument of the trumpet-kind, in tone resembling an ophicleide; also a brass reed-stop on the organ.

Bombasine (bǫm-, bʋ·mbăzī·n). 1555. [a. F. *bombasin*, ad. late L. *bombasinum*, f. *bombyx* silk, and later 'tree-silk' or cotton.] †1. = BOMBACE 1. -1580. 2. A twilled dress-material, composed of silk and worsted, cotton and worsted, or worsted alone. In black, much used in mourning. 1572. Also in *comb.*

In Sorrow's dismal crape or bombazeen 1789.

Bombast (bǫ·m-, bʋ·mbăst), *sb.* 1568. [var. of BOMBACE, *bombase*, the *t* being perh. phonetic. Contemporary usage favours bǫm-.] †1. Raw cotton; cotton-wool -1665. Also *attrib.* 2. Cotton-wool used as padding or stuffing for clothes, etc. *Obs.* exc. *Hist.* 1572. Also †*fig.* 3. *fig.* Inflated or turgid language; fustian 1589. Also *transf.*

2. Iacks quilted with b. to resist arrowes 1601. 3. Another soars, inflated with b. BYRON. Hence **Bomba·stic, -al** *a.* of the nature of b.; turgid; given to the use of bombastic language. **Bomba·stically** *adv.* †**Bo·mbastry,** bombastic composition SWIFT.

Bombast, *v. arch.* 1565. [f. prec., q.v.: in the vb. stress is oftener on the last syllable.] †1. To stuff or pad with cotton-wool, etc. -1820. 2. *fig.* and *transf.* To stuff, inflate, *esp.* with bombastic language 1566.

2. That doth..bumbast his labours with high swelling and heaven-disembowelling words FLORIO.

Bo·mbast, *ppl. a.* 1575. [f. BOMBACE *v.*; later = sb. used *attrib.*] †1. Stuffed, padded, puffed out -1656. 2. *fig.* Puffed, empty, inflated. Of language: Bombastic. 1604.

2. A bumbast circumstance, Horribly stufft with Epithites of warre *Oth.* I. i. 13. Forty b. lines GIBBON. So †**Bombastly** *adv.* H. WALPOLE.

Bombax (bǫ·mbæks). 1834. [Altered f. L. *bombyx*; see BOMBACE.] A genus of tropical trees (N.O. *Sterculiaceæ*), which bear a fruit containing seeds surrounded by a silky fibre; esp. *B. Ceiba*, the Silk-cotton tree of W. Indies.

Bombazeen, -zin(e, var. of BOMBASINE.

Bombed (bǫmd, bǫ·mbĕd), *ppl. a. rare.* [ad. F. *bombé.*] Rounded, convex. BROWNING.

Bombic (bǫ·mbik), *a.* 1816. [f. L. *bombyx* (see BOMBYX) and -IC.] Of or pertaining to the silk-worm; as in *b. acid*, an acid secreted by the silk-worm.

Bombilate (bǫ·mbileit), *v.* [f. reputed L. **bombilare* for *bombitare.*] *intr.* To hum, buzz. So **Bombilation.**

Bo·mbinate, *v.* 1880. [f. L. *bombinare*, a corrupt var. of *bombitare.*] To buzz. Hence **Bombin·ation.**

[RABELAIS II. vii, Questio subtilissima, utrum chimera in vacuo bombinans possit comedere secundas intentiones.]

†**Bo·mb-ketch.** 1693. [See BOMB and KETCH.] A small ketch-rigged vessel, carrying one or two mortars for bombarding -1830.

Bo·mb-proof. 1755. [See PROOF.] **A.** *adj.* Strong enough to resist bombs or shells. **B.** *sb.* [sc. *shelter* or *structure.*] 1809.

Bo·mb-shell. 1708. = BOMB 2. Also *fig.*

‖**Bombus** (bǫ·mbŏs). 1753. [L.] 1. *Med.* A humming noise in the intestines, ears, etc. 2. *Entom.* The genus containing the humble-bees.

†**Bombycine** (bǫ·mbisin), *a.* 1599. [ad. L. *bombycinus*, f. *bombyx.*] 1. Silken, silk; as *sb.*, a silk fabric -1736. 2. Of cotton, of paper made of cotton, as a *b. MS.* 1886.

†**Bombycinous** (bǫmbi·sinəs), *a.* 1656. [See prec. and -OUS.] 1. Made of silk, silken (Dicts.) 2. Of a pale yellow colour, like the silk-worm before it spins -1820.

†**Bomby·lious,** *a.* 1713. [f. L., a. Gr. βομβυλιός a humble-bee, etc., now made the generic name of the Humble-bee Fly.] Buzzing, humming, like a large bee.

‖**Bombyx** (bǫ·mbiks). ME. [L., a. Gr. βόμβυξ.] 1. The silk-worm. †2. Raw silk. ME. only. 3. *Entom.* A genus of moths, including the Silk-worm moth (*Bombyx mori*). Occas. any moth of the sub-order *Bombycina.* 1847.

‖**Bon** (boṅ), *a.* Fr. = 'good'; adopted in ME. in the form *bon, bone*, BOON, q. v.; also used in several Fr. phrases.

Bon-accord (bǫnăkǭ·ɹd). *Sc.* Agreement, good-fellowship; an expression of good will. **Bon-chrétien** (boṅ-krẹtyæṅ). [Fr. = 'good Christian'.] A name given to one or two kinds of pears. **Bon mot** (boṅ mo, pl. mōz). [Fr. = 'good saying'.] A clever or witty saying. **Bon-ton** (boṅ-toṅ). *arch.* Good style, good breeding; polite society; the fashionable world. **Bon-vivant** (boṅ vivaṅ); *fem.* **bonne vivante** (bǫn vivāṅt). One fond of good living; a gourmand. Cf. BONNE.

‖**Bona fide.** 1542. [L. = 'with good faith'. Commonly anglicized as (bōu·nă fəi·di).] **A.** *adv.* In good faith; genuinely.

The same to procede bona fide, without fraude 1542.

B. *adj.* (orig. with agent nouns.) Acting or done in good faith; genuine 1788.

A bona fide purchaser for valuable consideration 1788. The bona fide poor 1882.

‖**Bona fides** (bōu·nă fəi·dīz). 1845. [L.] Good faith, freedom from intent to deceive.

†**Bonaght.** 1568. [Irish.] A tribute formerly levied by Irish chiefs for the maintenance of soldiers -1827.

The barbarous practices of coshering and b. HALLAM

†**Bonair(e,** *a.* ME. [a. F. *bonnaire*, short f. *debonnaire.*] 1. Well-bred, courteous, complaisant -1696. As quasi-*adv.* = *bonairly*. Hence †**Bonairly** *adv.*, courteously, meekly. †**Bonairness,** †**Bonairty,** gentleness, courtesy.

†**Bonally, bonaillie** (bonæ·li, -*e*·li). *Sc.* 1470. [ad. F. *bon aller.*] Good speed, farewell; as in 'to drink his b.'

‖**Bonanza** (bonæ·nsă). *U.S. colloq.* 1878. [Sp.; = fair weather, prosperity, f. L. *bonus.*] 1. *Mining.* A body of rich ore. Used *esp.* of the great silver mines on the Comstock lode. Also *fig.* 2. *attrib.* as in **b. farm,** one which is 'a mine of wealth'; one on a large scale with all modern appliances; so **b. farmer** 1883.

1. The 'boss', the 'railroad king', and the b. Crœsus *N. Amer. Rev.*

Bonapartism (bōu·năpaɹti·z'm). 1815. Attachment to the government and dynasty founded in France by Napoleon Bonaparte.

Bonapartist (bōu·năpaɹtist). Also **Buonapartist.** 1815. **A.** *sb.* An adherent of Bonapartism. **B.** *adj.* Adhering to Bonaparte or Bonapartism 1869.

‖**Bo·na-ro·ba.** 1597. [a. It. *buonaroba.*] A wench; a wanton.

‖**Bona·sus, bona·ssus.** 1572. [a. L., a. Gr. βόνασος bison.] *Zool.* The BISON. See also AUROCHS.

†**Bonave·nture.** 1500. [app. ad. It. *buonaventura.*] 1. A kind of boat or ship -1614. 2. 'The old outer mizen, long disused.' Smyth.

‖**Bon-bon** (bo·ṅ,bo·ṅ, bǫ·n,bǫ·n). 1818. [Fr.; cf. *goody.*] 1. A confection made of sugar. †2. A dainty -1842. Hence ‖**Bonbonnière,** a small fancy box to hold sweets.

Bonce (bǫns). 1862. [? conn. w. BOUNCE.] A large marble; a game played with such marbles.

†**Bonchief.** ME. [f. F. *bon* + *chef* (see CHIEF); opp. to MISCHIEF.] Good fortune -1563.

Bond (bǫnd), *sb.*[1] [ME. *bond*, a phonetic var. of BAND *sb.*[1], preserving more the connexion with *bind, bound.*] 1. That with which one is bound; a shackle, chain, fetter, manacle (*arch.*) (and only in *pl.*). *abstr.* Imprisonment, custody. (Latterly only in *pl.*) (*arch.*) ME.

2. That with which a thing is tied down, or together; e.g. the withe which ties up a fagot, etc. Cf. also 9. ME. †**b.** Formerly, 'string, band, tie' –1674. †**3.** A bandage –1670. **4.** A restraining force; a uniting tie ME. **5.** An agreement or engagement binding on him who makes it. **b.** A covenant between two or more persons ME. **6.** *Eng. Law.* A deed by which A (the *obligor*) binds himself, his heirs, executors, or assigns to pay a certain sum to B (the *obligee*), or his heirs, etc. 1592. **b.** *Sc. Law.* A mortgage 1862. **7.** A document of this nature issued by a government or public company borrowing money: now = *debenture* 1651. **8.** Surety 1632. **9.** Techn.: **a.** *Bricklaying* and *Masonry.* A method of disposing the bricks or stones in a wall, etc., by which the whole is bound into one compact mass; also a brick or stone placed lengthways through a wall to bind and strengthen it, a binder. **b.** *Carpentry.* The jointing of two or more pieces of timber together; also in *pl.* the timbers used for strengthening the wall of a building. **c.** *Slating.* The distance between the lower edge of an upper slate and the nail of the one below it. 1677.

1. Altogether such as I am, except these bonds *Acts* xxvi. 29. †*Our Lady's bonds*: pregnancy; accouchement. 4. The tight bonds of an old order MORLEY. The b. of right or law 1592. Charitie, the verie bonde of peace and all vertue *Bk. Com. Prayer.* Phr. *Bond(s of wedlock, matrimony.* 5. O Kingis word suld be a kingis bonde 1500. *To put under bonds*: to order to find bail. 6. †*Single* or *simple b.*: one by which the obligor binds himself to a payment absolutely and unconditionally. *Penal b.*: one with a condition attached that the deed shall be made void by some stated performance or observance, the sum named being only a penalty in case of default. Goe with me to a Notarie, seale me there Your single b. *Merch. V.* I. iii. 146. 7. Bonds of turnpike commissioners POWELL. 9. **a.** *English b.*, the method in which the bricks are placed in alternate courses of headers (bricks laid endwise towards the face of the wall) and stretchers (bricks laid lengthwise); *Flemish b.*, that in which each course consists of alternate headers and stretchers.

Phrases. *In b.*: (goods liable to customs-duty) stored in bonded warehouses, till it suits the importer to pay the duty and take possession. The importer on entering the goods pledges himself by b. to redeem them. So *to take out of b.*, *release from b.*

Comb.: (sense 4) *b.-friend*; (sense 6) *b.-creditor*, *-debt*; (sense 9) *b.-piece*; **b.-stone** = BONDER¹; **b.-timber**, horizontal pieces, built in walls, to strengthen them. See also under BAIL *sb.*¹, CAUTION, CORROBORATION, etc. Hence **Bo·ndless** *a.*

Bond (bǫnd), *sb.*² and *a.* [Early ME. *bonde* :—OE. *banda*, *bunda*, a. ON. *bonde* (*-i*), contr. of *bóande*, *búande*, ppl. sb. f. *búa*, *bóa* to dwell, L. *colere*, and thus = Ger. *bauer*.] **A.** *sb.* †**1.** Householder; husband. (Only in OE.) †**2.** Peasant, churl (ranking below *burgess*) –1450. †**3.** Base vassal, serf [tr. med.L. *nativus*]; a slave; also *fig.* –1618.

2. When I soughte silver..Of baron, burges, or of bande 1450. 3. I liue her b., which neither is my foe, Nor frend T. WATSON.

B. *adj.* **1.** In a state of serfdom or slavery; in bondage (*to*). Also *fig.* (*arch.*) ME. †**2.** Of or pertaining to slaves; servile –1567.

1. Whether wee bee b. or free 1 *Cor.* xii. 13.

‖**Bond**, *sb.*³ 1884. [Du., = 'league' (Ger. *bund*), f. *binden* to bind.] In reference to the Dutch-speaking population of S. Africa: A league or confederation. Hence **Bondsmen.**

Bond (bǫnd), *v.* 1677. [f. BOND *sb.*¹] **1.** *trans.* in *Building*: To bind together so as to give solidity; to hold together by bond-stones, clamps, etc. **2.** *intr.* To hold together so as to give solidity 1836. **3.** *trans.* To encumber with bonded debt; to mortgage 1883. **4.** To put into bond (see BOND *sb.*¹) 1809.

3. They said the road..was too heavily bonded 1883.

Bondage (bǫ·ndėdʒ). [ME. *bondage*, ad. Anglo-L. *bondagium*, f. BOND *sb.*² Influenced later by BOND *sb.*¹] †**1.** Tenure in villenage; the service rendered by a *bonde* or BOND –1651. **2.** The condition of a serf or slave; servitude, serfdom, slavery ME. **b.** *transf.* The condition of being bound or tied up; that which binds (*poet.*) 1597. **3.** *fig.* Subjection to some bond, binding power, influence, or obligation 1450. †**b.** Binding force. *Cymb.* II. iv. 111.

2. To love B. more than Liberty MILT. *Sams.* 270. 3. The b. of sin and vice COVERDALE. Hence †**Bo·ndage** *v.* to reduce to b.

Bondager (bǫ·ndėdʒəɹ). *Sc.* 1837. [f. prec.] In Scotland and Northumberland, a female outworker, supplied by each cotter on a farm, as a condition of his tenancy.

Bonded (bǫ·ndėd), *ppl. a.* 1597. [f. BOND *sb.*¹ + -ED.] **1.** Held, pledged, or confirmed by bond. **2.** Put into bond. (See BOND *sb.*¹) 1809.

1. That strong b. oth SHAKS. 2. **B. store, warehouse**, one in charge of Custom-house officials, in which goods may be kept in bond.

Bonder¹ (bǫ·ndəɹ). 1845. [f. BOND *v.* + -ER.] **1.** *Building.* A binding stone or brick. **2.** A person who puts goods into bond, or owns goods in bond.

‖**Bonder**² (bǫ·ndəɹ). [Erron. formation from Norweg. *bonde*, pl. *bönder*.] A Norwegian peasant farmer or petty freeholder. **Bonderman.**

Bo·ndhold. *Obs.* exc. *Hist.* 1611. [Cf. *copyhold*, etc.] Tenure in bond service, or of bond-land; a sort of *copyhold*.

Bo·ndholder¹. *Obs.* exc. *Hist.* 1539. [f. prec.] A tenant in bond service, or of bond-land.

Bondholder² (bǫ·ndhōᵘ:ldəɹ). 1844. [f. BOND *sb.*¹ 9.] A person who holds a bond or bonds granted by a private person or by a public company or government.

Bonding (bǫ·ndiŋ), *vbl. sb.* 1677. [f. BOND *v.*] **1.** The action of the vb. **2.** The storing of goods in bond; hence **b.-house, -warehouse.**

Bond-land. [OE. *bondeland*, f. *bonda* BOND *sb.*²] Land held by bondage tenure; a form of copyhold land.

Bondmaid, -maiden (bǫ·ndmeᶦd, -mēᶦd'n). *arch.* 1526. [See next.] A slave girl. So **-servant, -service.**

Bondman (bǫ·ndmǣn). *arch.* ME. [f. BOND *sb.*² (cf. *husband*); but subseq. influenced by BOND *sb.*¹] **1.** = BOND *sb.*² **2.** *Obs.* exc. *Hist.* **2.** A villein; a serf, slave ME. Hence **Bo·ndmanship.** So **Bo·ndwoman.**

Bo·ndslave. 1561. = BONDMAN, -WOMAN.

Bondsman (bǫ·ndzmǣn). 1735. [f. BOND *sb.*¹, with genitival *'s*; in sense 2 used as a var. of BONDMAN.] **1.** One who becomes surety by bond 1754. **2.** = BONDMAN 2.

‖**Bonduc** (bǫ·ndɒk). 1696. [a. F., a. Arab. *bunduq*, now 'hazel-nut'.] A tropical leguminous shrub of two species (*Guilandina Bonduc* and *G. Bonducella*) bearing respectively yellow and lead-coloured seeds, also called Nicker-nuts.

Bone (bōᵘn), *sb.* [Com. Teut.: OE. *bán* :— OTeut. **baino(m.*] **1.** The general name for each of the distinct parts which unitedly make up the skeleton of vertebrate animals; differentiated as, *ankle-*, *blade-*, *jaw-b.*, etc. **2.** *pl.* The bones of the body collectively, the skeleton; hence, the bodily frame, body, person (*joc.*) ME. **b.** = 'mortal remains' OE. **3.** The bony substance of the body. (Used as *collect. sing.*) OE. Also *fig.* **4.** The material of the bones, which consists of animal matter, *ossein*, and salts of carbonate and phosphate of lime in varying proportions 1471. Also *transf.* (see WHALEBONE). **5.** Anything made of bone, ivory, etc. **a.** *pl.* Dice ME. **b.** *pl.* Pieces of bone struck or rattled, to make rude music 1590. **c.** *pl.* Bobbins made of trotter bones, for weaving bone-lace. *Twel. N.* II. iv. 46. **d.** A strip of whalebone used in stays, etc.; also *attrib.* 1595. **6.** A bone (or part of one) with flesh on it, a fragment of meat. Often in comb. as *aitch-b.*, etc. ME. Also *fig.* **7.** *transf.* A callous growth on the legs of horses, becoming as hard as bone; as in *b.-spavin*, etc. **8.** *fig.* The hard framework of anything, e.g. of a ship 1634. **9.** *Min.* The slaty matter intercalated in coal-seams 1880.

1. Fie how my bones ake *Rom. & Jul.* II. v. 27. By these tenne bones (*i.e.* the fingers) 2 *Hen. VI*, I. iii. 193. Phr. *Hard*, or *dry*, *as a b.* 2. Night hangs vpon mine eyes, my Bones would rest *Jul. C.* V. v. 41. She'll never live to make old bones 1873. **b.** Cvrst be he yᵗ moves my bones *Inscr. over Shakspere's Grave.* 3. Art thou not of my b., and of my flesh 2 *Sam.* xix. 13. *To the b.*: through the flesh, so as to touch the bone; *fig.* to the inmost part. So *In the b.* 5. **b.** *Mids. N.* IV. i. 33.

Phrases. (sense 6) *A b. to pick* or *gnaw*: something to occupy one as a bone does a dog; a 'nut to crack'. *To have a b. to pick with one*: to have something disagreeable to settle with a person. *B. of contention*, *discord*, etc.: some thing that causes contention, discord, etc. Cf. 6. *To make bones of* or *about*: to make objections or scruples about. So *Without more bones*, etc., referring to bones found in soup, etc. as an obstacle to its being swallowed.

Comb. etc.: **b.-ash**, the mineral residue of bones burnt in contact with air, chiefly phosphate of lime; **-bed** (*Geol.*), a stratum abounding with bones of animals; **-black**, animal charcoal; **-breaker**, a name of the Osprey (L. *ossifraga*, Ger. *beinbrecher*); also *attrib.*; **-brown**, a pigment obtained by roasting bones, etc. till uniformly brown; **-cave**, one in which are found bones of animals; **-charcoal** = *bone-black*; **-dog**, a kind of Dog-fish; **-dust**, bones ground for manure; **-earth** = *bone-ash*; **-fever**, phlegmonous inflammation of the hand and arm, often seen in workers in b.; **-fish**, a species of whale, valued for its whalebone; **-manure** = *bone-dust*; **-nippers** (*Surg.*), cutting forceps used in the removal of b.; **-shaker**, the bicycle as originally made (*joc.*); **-spavin**, a bony excrescence on the inside of a hock of a horse's leg; **-spirit**, a crude ammoniacal liquor obtained from b.; †**-work**, work done with b.-bobbins. Hence **Boned** *ppl. a.* having bones; chiefly in comb., as *big-b.*, etc.; manured with b.; stiffened with whalebone; deprived of the bones. **Bo·neless** *a.* without bones; destitute of b.; *fig.* wanting backbone.

Bone (bōᵘn), *v.*¹ 1494. [f. BONE *sb.*] †**1.** *intr.* ? To throw out spicules of bone. PEPYS. **2.** *trans.* To take out the bones from; also *fig.* 1494. **3.** To manure with bones; to stiffen with whalebone 1871.

Bone (bōᵘn), *v.*² *slang.* 1819. [?] *trans.* To take into custody; to lay hold of; to steal.

Bone, *v.*³ See BONING *vbl. sb.*²

†**Bone-ace.** 1611. [? conn. w. F. *bon, bonne.*] A game at cards in which the player who turns up the highest of the third cards dealt obtains the 'bone' or half the stake; also, the ace of diamonds, the highest card in this game –1726.

Bone-lace. 1574. [f. BONE *sb.* 5 c.] Lace, usually of linen thread, made by knitting upon a pattern, with bobbins originally made of bone.

Boneset (bōᵘ·nse·t). 1670. [prob. f. BONE + SET *v.*] †**a.** The Common Comfrey, *Symphytum officinale* (*rare*). **b.** A North American plant, *Eupatorium perfoliatum*, valued for its medicinal properties; thorough-wort.

Bone-setter (bōᵘ·nse·təɹ). 1470. One who sets broken or dislocated bones; a surgeon; now *spec.* one who makes a calling of treating fractures, without being a surgeon. So **Bone-setting** *vbl. sb.* and *ppl. a.*

Bonetta, var. of BONITO.

†**Bo·ne-wort.** [OE. *bánwyrt.*] Name of plants supposed to be bone-healing, as the common Daisy, Golden-Rod, etc. –1736.

Bonfire (bǫ·nfəiəɹ), *sb.* 1483. [f. BONE *sb.* 1 + FIRE. In Sc. *bane-fire.*] †**1.** A great fire in which bones were burnt in the open air –1684. †**2.** A funeral pyre. (tr. L. *pyra, rogus* in 16–17th c.) –1658. **3.** A fire in which heretics or proscribed books were burnt 1581. **4.** A large fire kindled in the open air: **a.** (orig.) on certain anniversaries. These were orig. *bone-fires* in sense 1. 1493. **b.** (In mod. use) in celebration of a victory or the like, or for amusement, or combined amusement and utility 1530.

1. Ere I die, those foul idolaters Shall make me bonfires with their filthy bones MARLOWE. 4. **b.** Celebrate the victorie with bonefiers in euerie town RALEIGH. Hence **Bo·nfire** *v.* (*rare*) to illuminate with bonfires; *intr.* to make bonfires.

†**Bo·ngrace.** 1530. [a. F. *bonnegrace*, f. *bonne grace.*] **1.** A shade worn on the front of women's bonnets to protect the complexion –1636. **2.** A broad-brimmed hat (*arch.*) 1606.

‖**Bonhomie** (bǫnomī). Also **bonhommie.** 1803. [F.] Good nature; the quality of being a good fellow.

‖**Bonhomme** (bǫnoᵊm). 1526. [Fr.] †**1.** A member of an order of begging friars who came over to England in the 13th c. –1697. †**2.** A name given to the Albigenses 1751. ‖**3.** A peasant. *Jacques B.*: the French peasant. 1851.

Boniface (bǫ·nifeᶦs). 1803. [Proper name.] Name of the jovial innkeeper in Farquhar's *Beaux' Stratagem* 1707; thence generic as the proper name of innkeepers.

Boniform (bǫ·nifǫɹm), *a.* 1677. [ad. mod. L. *boniformis*, used as tr. Plato's ἀγαθοειδής.] Having the form of good; akin to the Good Used by H. More to denote a faculty cognizant of moral goodness.

Bonify (bǫ·nifəi), *v.* 1603. [ad. F. *bonifier.*] †**1.** To benefit. **2.** To make good, turn into good 1678. So Bonifica·tion, †bettering; the paying of a bonus.

Boning (bōu·niŋ), *vbl. sb.*[1] 1495. [f. BONE *v.* + -ING[1].] **1.** The removing of bones from meat, fish, etc. **2.** The applying of bones to land as manure 1875.

Bo·ning, *vbl. sb.*[2] 1785. *Surveying*, etc. The process of judging of the straightness of a surface or line by the eye, as by looking along the tops of two straight edges, or along a line of poles; also *attrib.*, as in *b. rod*, etc.

Bonitarian (bǫnitēə·riăn), *a.* 1861. [f. late L. *bonitarius* (cited only in Gr. spelling), f. L. *bonus* or *bonitas.*] Beneficial; having beneficial possession without legal title. So **Bo·nitary.**

‖**Bonito** (bǫnī·to). 1599. [a. Sp., of unkn. origin.] The striped tunny; a fish about three feet long, common in tropical seas. Also *transf.* var. **Bone·ta.**

†**Bo·nity.** 1585. [ad. L. *bonitas* 'goodness', a sense lost from BOUNTY.] Goodness –1790.

Bon mot; see BON.

‖**Bonne** (bǫn). 1529. [F., fem. of *bon* good; as sb. a nurse.] †**A.** *adj.* Good. **B.** *sb.* A (French) nursemaid 1771.

Phrases. **Bonne-bouche** (bǫn buʃ). *Pl.* **bonnes bouches.** In Fr. 'A pleasant taste in the mouth': in Eng. = 'dainty morsel'. †**Bonne mine** (bǫn min). Good appearance. *To make a bonne-mine* (Mil.): to show oneself in force.

†**Bo·nnering,** *vbl. sb.* 1613. [f. Bishop *Bonner.*] Burning for heresy –1627.

Bonnet (bǫ·nėt), *sb.* [ME. *bonet*, a. OF. *bonet, bounet, bonnet*, short for *chapel de bonet*, in med.L. *bon(n)etum*, a material.] **1. a.** A head-dress of men and boys. In Eng. replaced by *cap*, but retained in Sc.; hence, occas. = 'Scotch cap'. **b.** A head-dress of women out of doors; usually without a brim, and covering no part of the forehead 1499. **c.** *Her.* The velvet cap within a coronet. **2.** *Naut.* An additional piece of canvas laced to the foot of a sail to catch more wind ME. **3.** *Fortif.* A portion of the works at any salient angle, raised to protect from enfilade fire and ricochet 1700. **4.** The second stomach of ruminants 1782. **5.** *techn.* Applied to a protective covering or defence: **a.** The cowl at the top of a lighthouse, chimney, etc. **b.** A wire covering over the chimney of a locomotive engine or steamer (chiefly in U. S.); **c.** A covering over the cage in mines; **d.** A cap for a safety lamp; **e.** An iron plate covering the openings in the valve-chambers of a pump. 1862. **f.** The protecting hood over the machinery of a motor vehicle 1902. **6.** = BLUE-BONNET 3. **7.** A thing or person used to put a good face on underhand proceedings. Also *fig.* 1833.

1. Off goes his b. to an Oyster-wench *Rich. II*, I. iv. 31. *To vail* (or *vale*) *the b.*: to take it off in respect. **7.** His look and bearing are..those of a b. at a fashionable hell 1833.

Phr. *To have a bee in one's b.*: see BEE[1].

Comb.: **b.-headed** *a.* (*Archit.*), of a window in which the outside of the arch is more splayed than the jambs; **-limpet,** a gasteropodous mollusc, so called from the shape of the shell; **-macaque, -monkey,** a monkey (*Macacus Sinicus*), so called from the arrangement of the hairs on its head; **-piece,** a gold coin of James V of Scotland, on which the king is represented wearing a b.; **-shape,** the frame-work of a b. Hence **Bo·nnetless** *a.*

Bonnet (bǫ·nėt), *v.* 1607. [f. the sb.] †**1.** *intr.* To take the bonnet off in respect. SHAKS. **2.** To put a bonnet on 1858. **3.** To crush down a person's hat over his eyes 1837.

3. The Students hustled and 'bonnetted' a new Professor 1882.

Bonnibel (bǫ·nibe·l). *arch.* 1579. [?f. F. *bonne et belle*; cf. BELLIBONE.] Fair maid.

†**Bo·nilass(e.** 1546. Now two wds.: Bonny lass –1579.

Bonny (bǫ·ni), *a.* 1529. [Of uncertain origin; app. connected in some way with OF. *bon, bone*, or ME. *bon(e)* BOON *a.*] **1.** Pleasing to the sight, comely, expressing homely beauty. Now Sc. and n. and midl. Eng. **2.** †**a.** Of fine size 1600. **b.** Looking well, plump (*dial.* and *colloq.*) 1749. †**3.** Smiling, bright –1820.

1. Honest men and b. lasses BURNS. **3.** Then sigh not so, but let them goe And be you blithe and bonnie SHAKS. Hence **Bo·nnily** *adv.* **Bo·nniness.**

†**Bonny,** *sb.* 1671. [? Cf. BUNNY.] *Mining.* A bed of ore, not forming, nor communicating with, a vein.

Bonny-clabber (bǫ·ni,klæ·bəɹ). *Anglo-Irish.* 1631. [a. Ir. *bainne* milk, *claba* thick.] Milk naturally clotted on souring; = Sc. *loppert* or *lappert* milk.

Bonspiel (bǫ·nspīl, -spėl). *Sc.* 1565. [? a. Du. **bondspel*, f. *bond* and *spel.*] †**1.** A set match. **2.** *spec.* A 'grand curling-match' between two clubs or districts 1772.

‖**Bontebok** (bǫ·ntĕbǫk). 1786. [Du.: f. *bont* pied + *bok* buck.] A S. African Antelope (*Damalis Pygarga*, Gray) also called Pied Antelope.

Bon-ton; see BON.

Bonus (bōu·nǒs). 1773. [? orig. Stock Exchange slang: L. *bonus* used for *bonum.*] A boon or gift over and above what is normally due. **a.** A premium for services rendered or expected; occas. = *douceur, bribe.* Also *fig.* and *attrib.* **b.** An extra dividend paid out of surplus profits; a portion of the profits of an insurance company distributed 'pro rata' to the policy-holders 1808.

Bon-vivant; see BON.

Bonxie (bǫ·ŋksi). 1802. Shetland name of the Skua Gull.

Bony (bōu·ni), *a.* 1535. [f. BONE *sb.*] **1.** Of, pertaining to, of the nature of, bone or bones; consisting or made of bones. **2.** Abounding in bones; having large or prominent bones 1598. *Comb.* **b.-pike,** an American ganoid fish. Hence **Bo·niness.**

Bonze (bǫnz). 1588. [a. F., ad. Pg. *bonzo*, prob. ad. Jap. *bonzô* or *bonzi*, ad. Chin. *fan seng* 'religious person'.] A term applied by Europeans to the Buddhist clergy of Japan, and occas. of China, etc. Hence **Bo·nzery,** a Buddhist monastery.

Boo, booh (bū). *int.* (*sb.*) 1801. [Echoic.] An expression of contempt or aversion.

Boo (bū), *v.* 1816. [f. prec.] To low as a cow; to utter 'boo!'; to hoot.

Boob. *U.S. slang.* 1912. = BOOBY 1.

Booby (bū·bi), *sb.* 1599. [prob. ad. Sp. *bobo* 'fool' and 'booby' (the bird).] **1.** A dull, heavy, stupid fellow, *esp.* a dunce. Also *attrib.* **2.** A species of Gannet, esp. *Sula fusca* 1634.

Comb.: **b.-hatch** (*Naut.*), a smaller kind of companion which lifts off in one piece; **-hutch** (*dial.*), a small clumsy cart; **-prize,** a prize (of no value) awarded to the last or lowest scorer; **-trap,** a kind of practical joke in vogue among schoolboys and others. Hence **Boo·byish** *a.* awkwardly silly. **Boo·byism.**

Boodh, boodha, etc.: see BUDDHA, etc.

Boodle (bū·d'l). *U.S.* 1833. [perh. ad. Du. *boedel* property, possessions.] **1.** Crowd, lot: often *whole kit and boodle.* **2. a.** Counterfeit money 1858. **b.** Money or means for corrupt dealing in public affairs 1884.

2. b. 'Sinews of war'..'soap' and other synonymes for campaign b. are familiar 1884.

Boohoo·, *int.* and *sb.* 1525. A word imitative of noisy weeping or laughter. Also as vb.

Book (buk), *sb.* [Com. Teut.: OE. *bōc* (pl. *bēc*), f. OTeut. **bōks.* The orig. meaning was 'writing-tablet': in pl. tablets, hence book, a sense subseq. extended to the sing. Generally connected with OE. *bōc, bēce*, BEECH, q. v.] **1.** A writing; a written charter or deed. *Obs.* exc. *Hist.* †**2.** A (written) narrative, record, list, register –1681. **3.** *gen.* A collection of sheets of paper or other substance, blank (cf. 8), written, or printed, fastened together so as to form a material whole; *esp.* such a collection fastened together at the back, and protected by covers; also, a literary composition long enough to make one volume, as dist. from a *tract, pamphlet, essay*, etc. Also *fig.* ME. †**4.** 'Benefit of clergy' –1710. †**5.** Book-learning, scholarship, lessons, reading. In later use only *pl.* –1680. **6.** A main subdivision of a large treatise ME. **7.** The libretto of an opera, etc. 1768. **8.** A volume in which to keep records of commercial transactions, minutes, etc. Also, one containing such records. 1498. **9.** *Betting.* A betting-book 1856. **10.** *Whist.* The first six tricks taken by either side. **11.** A packet of gold-leaf.

1. The witnesses, that subscribed the booke of the purchase *Jer.* xxxii. 12. **2.** This is the booke of the generations of Adam *Gen.* v. 1. **3.** Books, as well printed as in Manuscript TINDAL. *fig.* Our life.. Findes..bookes in the running brookes *A. Y. L.* II. i. 16. The b. of Knowledge MILT., of Heauen, Fate, Bookes of Memory SHAKS. **5.** My sonne profits nothing..at his Booke *Merry W.* IV. i. 15. **6.** The *B. of Genesis.* The twelve books of Vergil's *Æneid.* **8.** *A merchant's books*: his account books. So *cash-b.*, etc.

Phrases. **1.** *B. of God*: God's b., the Bible. *B. of life*, (*the living*): the list of those who shall inherit eternal life (cf. *Phil.* iv. 3: *Rev.* xx. 12). **2.** *By (the) b.*: in set phrase. *In a person's good* (or *bad*) *books*: in favour (or disfavour) with him (see also BLACK BOOK 4). *Without* (†*one's*) *b.*: without authority; also *lit.* from memory. **3.** *To be upon the books*: to have one's name entered in the official list of members, etc.: hence, *to take one's name off the books. To bring to b.*: to cause to show authority; to investigate (a statement, etc.). *To close the books* (of a business): to make no further entries (for a time). *To shut the books*: to suspend business operations. *To speak like a b.*: i.e. with precise information. *To take a leaf out of* (a person's) *b.*: to follow his example.

Comb.: **b.-crab,** = *-scorpion*; **-credit, (-debt),** an amount credited, (debited), to a person's account in a ledger; **-ends,** a pair of (ornamental) props or supports used to keep a row of unshelved books upright; **-holder,** one who or that which holds a b., †*spec.* a theatrical prompter; **-louse,** an insect, *Psocus pulsatorius*, destructive to books; **-mark,** a book-plate; also = **-marker,** anything inserted between the leaves of a b. to mark a place; **-mate,** school-fellow, fellow-student; **-muslin,** a fine kind of muslin folded like a b. when sold in the piece, also *ellipt.* a dress of this; **-oath,** one sworn on the Bible; **-packet,** one which may be sent by b.-post; **-post,** the system under which books and printed matter may be sent through the post-office; **-postage, -rate,** the price charged for carriage by b.-post; **-scorpion,** an insect, *Chelifer cancroides*, resembling a scorpion, found in old books; **-slide,** an expanding stand for books; **-work,** study of text-books; **-wright,** a maker of books.

Book (buk), *v.* [OE. *bōcian*: from the sb.; see prec.] **1.** *trans.* To grant or assign (land) by charter; see BOOK *sb.* 1. *Obs.* exc. *Hist.* **2.** To enter in a book; to record, register ME. Also *fig.* **3.** To enter in a list 1548. **4.** To engage for oneself by payment (a seat or place). Also *absol.* 1826. **b.** To enter (a person's name, etc.) for a seat or place; to issue railway tickets to; *refl.* to take one's ticket 1841. **c.** To enter and pay for the transmission of (goods, etc.) by any conveyance 1829. **5.** *transf.* To engage (a person) as a guest or the like (*colloq.*) 1872.

2. Not eager to b. fresh orders (*mod.*). **4.** Sam Weller booked for them all DICKENS. **5.** I shall b. you for Tuesday (*mod.*).

Bookbinder (bu·kbəindəɹ). ME. One who binds books. So **Boo·kbindery** (*U.S.*), a book-binding establishment; **Bookbinding** *vbl. sb.*

Bookcase (bu·k,kē's). 1742. A case for books; a set of bookshelves shut in by doors.

†**Book-case.** 1552. A law case found on record –1726.

Boo·k-craft. *arch.* OE. Book-learning, literary skill; authorship.

Booker (bu·kəɹ). [OE. *bōcere*; but in mod. use re-coined from BOOK *v.*] †**1.** A writer of books –ME. **2.** A book-keeper 1863.

Boo·kery. 1599. †**1.** Study of books. **2.** A collection of books 1812.

Boo·k-fell. *Obs.* exc. *Hist.* OE. A skin prepared for writing upon; a vellum or parchment manuscript.

Boo·kful, *sb.* 1599. As much as fills a book.

†**Boo·kful,** *a.* Full of book knowledge. POPE.

Bookie (bu·ki). *colloq.* 1885. [See -Y[6].] = BOOKMAKER 3.

Booking (bu·kiŋ), *vbl. sb.* 1643. [f. the vb.] The entering in a book, *esp.* in order to engage a seat or place; also the issuing of tickets, entitling to the same 1884.

Comb.: **b.-clerk,** the clerk who books passengers or goods for conveyance, or who sells tickets at a b.-office; **-office,** one where places are booked for a coach, etc., or goods for transit; also a ticket-office.

Bookish (bu·kiʃ), *a.* 1567. [f. BOOK *sb.* + -ISH.] **1.** Of or belonging to a book or books; literary. **2.** Studious 1570; knowing books only 1593.

2. A b. man, who has no knowledge of the world ADDISON. Hence **Boo·kish-ly** *adv.*, **-ness.**

Book-keeper (bu·k,kīpəɹ). 1555. One who keeps the accounts of a business, public office, etc. So **Boo·k-keeping,** the art of keeping books or accounts.

Bookland. *Obs.* exc. *Hist.* OE. Land taken from the *folcland* or common land, and granted by *bōc* or charter to a private owner; later, all land exc. *folcland.* Hence *Buckland* (place-name).

Book-latin. [OE. *bóc-léden.*] Latin; later, book-language.

Boo·k-lea:rned, *a.* ME. Learned in books or book-knowledge. (Now disparaging.)

Whate'er these booklearn'd blockheads say DRYDEN. Hence **Book-learnedness.** So **Boo·k-lea:rning,** learning derived from books (merely).

Boo·kless, *a.* 1735. Unscholarly (*poet.*); destitute of books 1788.

Booklet (bu·klėt). 1859. A tiny book. So **Boo·kling.**

Boo·k-lore. [An OE. and ME. comb. revived.] Knowledge gained from books.

Book-maker (bu·kmēˡkəɹ). 1515. †**1.** A printer and bookbinder –1711. **2.** One who composes or compiles a book. (Often disparaging.) 1533. **3.** A professional betting-man. Cf. BOOK *sb.* 9. 1862. So **Boo·k-ma:king.**

Bookman (bu·kmæ̆n). 1583. A scholar.

You two are book-men: Can you tell [etc.] SHAKS.

Book-plate (bu·kplēˡt). 1791. A label, usually pasted inside the covers of a book, bearing a device indicating ownership, place, etc.

Boo·k-rea:d, *ppl. a.* 1591. Well-read in books.

Bookseller (bu·kˌse:ləɹ). 1527. A vender of books. So **Boo·kse:lling** *vbl. sb.*; also *attrib.* or *adj.*

Boo·k-ways, boo·kwise, *adv.* 1696. In the form of a book.

Boo·k-wi:se, *a.* 1616. Book-learned.

Book-worm (bu·kˌwɒɹm). 1599. **1.** *lit.* The larva of various beetles, esp. *Anobium hirtum*, destructive to books 1855. **2.** *fig.* One who is always poring over books 1599.

2. Perverted and spoiled by a whoreson b. B. JONS.

Boo·ky, *a. colloq.* 1880. Bookish.

†**Booly.** 1596. [ad. Ir. *buaile*; deriv. of *bo* cow, or ad. L. *bovile.*] A temporary fold used by the Irish who wandered about with their herds in summer; a company of such people and their cattle –1846. Hence †**Booling.** SPENSER.

Boom (būm), *sb.*¹ 1500. [f. BOOM *v.*¹] A loud, deep, resonant sound, as of a cannon, a large bell, etc.: the cry of the bittern.

The dull b. of the disturbed sea RUSKIN.

Boom (būm), *sb.*² 1645. [a. Du. *boom* 'tree, beam, pole'; taken from Du. in senses in which *beam* was not used.] *Naut.* **1.** A long spar run out to extend the foot of a particular sail; as *jib.-b.*, etc. 1662. *pl.* That part of the deck where the spare spars are stowed 1762. †**2.** A pole set up to mark the course of the channel or deep water. (Dicts.) **3.** A bar or barrier consisting of connected spars, pieces of timber, etc., stretched across a river or harbour mouth to obstruct navigation 1645. **4.** A fixed line of floating timber across a river or round an area of water to retain floating logs. (*N.Amer.*) 1702.

3. The sea-works and booms were traced out by Marquis Spinola HOWELL.

Comb.: **b.-iron,** an iron ring fitted on the yard-arm, through which the studding-sail b. slides when rigged out or in; **-jigger,** a tackle for rigging the top-mast studding-sail booms out or in; **-sail,** one which is set to a b. instead of to a yard; **-sheet,** one fastened to a b.; **-spar,** 'a spar of a larger kind' (Smyth).

Boom (būm), *sb.*³ *U.S.* 1879. [prob. a use of BOOM *sb.*¹ and *v.*¹] **1.** A start of commercial activity; a rapid advance in prices; a rush of activity in business or speculation. **2.** The effective launching of anything upon the market, or upon public attention; an impetus given to any enterprise; a vigorously worked movement in favour of a candidate or cause 1879.

2. The Grant 'B.' may be succeeded by the Sherman 'B.' SALA.

Boom (būm), *v.*¹ 1440. [Echoic; cf. Ger. *bummen.*] **1.** *intr.* To hum or buzz, as a bee or beetle; to make a loud deep resonant sound, as a cannon, a large bell, etc.; also the word to express the cry of the bittern; *trans.*, usually with *out* 1837. **2.** *intr.* To rush with violence, as a ship making all the way she can 1617.

1. Unless I get home, Ere the curfew bome BARHAM. **2.** The first of them booming by himself before the wind 1617.

Boom (būm), *v.*² 1627. [f. BOOM *sb.*²] **1.** *Naut. trans.* **a.** *To b. out*: to extend (the front of a sail) with a boom. **b.** *To b. off*: to push off with a pole. Cf. Du. *boomen.* **2.** To furnish (a river, etc.) with a boom to retain floating timber; to collect (logs, etc.) in a boom. (*N. Amer.*) 1879. **3.** Cf. BOOMING *vbl. sb.* 2.

Boom (būm), *v.*³ *U.S.* 1879. [f. BOOM *sb.*³] **1.** *intr.* To go off with a BOOM; to burst into sudden activity; to make rapid (commercial) progress, to advance vigorously. **2.** *trans.* To give a BOOM to; to push, puff, write up. Also *absol.* 1879.

1. Every one says business is booming 1879. **2.** The *World* is booming Mr. Conkling for..Senator 1884.

Boomer¹ (bū·məɹ). 1883. [f. BOOM *v.*³] One who booms an enterprise. *U.S. slang.*

Boo·mer². 1881. Australian name of the male of the largest species of Kangaroo.

Boomerang (bū·məræŋ). 1827. [Native name, N. S. Wales.] An Australian missile weapon: a curved piece of hard wood, with a sharp edge along the convexity of the curve. It can be thrown so as to hit an object in a different direction from that of projection, or so as to return to or behind the starting-point. Also *fig.*

The b. of argument, which one throws in the opposite direction of what he means to hit LOWELL.

Booming (bū·miŋ), *vbl. sb.* 1774. [f. BOOM *v.*¹,²,³ + -ING¹.] **1.** The action of the vb. BOOM¹. **2.** The accumulation and sudden discharge of a quantity of water (in placer mining) 1880. **3.** See BOOM *sb.*³, BOOM *v.*³ 1881. **Boo·mingly** *adv.* with a b. noise.

Boon (būn), *sb.*¹ ME. [a. ON. *bón* = OE. *bén*, ME. BENE, prayer. Prob. influenced in sense-development by the adj. *boon* 'good'.] †**1.** A prayer, petition, request –1623. †**2.** A command couched in the form of a request –1593. **3.** *transf.* The matter prayed for or asked (*arch.*) ME. **4.** A favour, a gift; in 17th c. a gratuity; but now only *fig.* or *arch.* 1460. **5.** A blessing, an advantage, a thing to be thankful for. (The usual current sense.) 1767. **6.** An unpaid service due by a tenant to his lord. Now *dial.* 1634. ¶ **7.** Modern archaists confuse with BOON *a.*

1. The kyng assentede to his bone CHAUCER. **2.** SHAKS. 3 *Hen. VI*, III. ii. 46. **3.** Cousin, you must grant me my b. SCOTT. **7.** For b. or bale 1874. Hence **Boo·nless** *a.*

Boon, *sb.*² ME. [?] The stalk of flax or hemp after the fibre has been removed. See also BUN.

Boon (būn), *a.* ME. [a. OF. *bon, bone*: in general Eng. use 14–17th c.; then dropped, exc. in senses 3 and 4.] †**1.** Good, goodly –1686. †**2.** Fortunate, prosperous: *esp.* in *b. voyage*, prosperous journey, also *fig.* good success. –1657. **3.** Gracious, bounteous, benign; = L. *almus* (*poet.*) 1612. **4.** In *b. companion*, lit. 'good-fellow', also occ. used predicatively: Jolly, convivial 1566.

1. Seint Iulian! lo, bon hostelle CHAUCER. **3.** Flours ..which..Nature b. Powrd forth profuse MILT. *P. L.* IV. 242. **4.** Hight'nd as with Wine, jocund and b. MILT. *P. L.* IX. 793.

Boon, *v. Obs.* or *dial.* ME. [f. BOON *sb.*¹] †**1.** To ask as a boon. †**2.** *intr.* To do boon-work (see BOON *sb.*¹ 6) 1691. **3.** *trans.* To repair (public roads). Now *dial.* 1783.

Boopic (boˌiᵖ·pik), *a. rare.* 1854. [f. Gr. βοῶπις.] Ox-eyed.

Boor (būᵊɹ). 1430. [prob. ad. LG. *būr*, Du. *boer*=OE. *gebūr*, a deriv. of *bur*, f. *bū* to dwell. Cf. EAngl. BOR.] **1.** A husbandman, peasant. *Obs.*, exc. as in 3. **2.** A Dutch or German peasant (Ger. *bauer*) 1581. **b.** A Dutch colonist in Guiana, S. Africa, etc. (In S. Africa now BOER.) 1824. Also *transf.* **3.** A rustic (and therefore coarse); a clown 1598. Also *fig.*

1. A countrie Boore, a goodlie proper swayne 1592. **2.** Germany hath her Boores, like our Yeomen FULLER. **3.** As to manners a mere b. or clown DE FOE. *Comb.* **Boor's Mustard.** [ad. early mod. Ger. *Baurensenfe.*] *Herb.* Name given to *Thlaspi arvense.* Hence **Boo·rish** *a.* (and †quasi-*sb. A. Y. L.* V. i. 54). **Boo·rish-ly** *adv.*, **-ness.**

Boose (būz), *sb. north.* 1440. [f. OE. **bōs.*] A cow- or horse-stall; a crib. var. **Boo·sy.**

Boose, var. of BOOZE.

†**Boost,** *sb.*¹ Also *north.* **bost.** ME. A var. of BOIST, box, pyx –1651.

Boost (būst), *sb.*² *U.S. colloq.* 1858. A lift, a shove up (*mod.*).

Boost (būst), *v. U. S. colloq.* 1848. *trans.* To hoist; to push up from behind. Also *fig.* Hence **Boo·ster** (*Electr.*), a machine for raising voltage.

Boot (būt), *sb.*¹ [Com. Teut.: OE. *bót* fem. :—OTeut. **bôtâ-*, prob. deriv. of *bat-* (Aryan **bhad-*) 'good, useful': see BETTER. Hence BEET *v.*] †**1.** Advantage; profit; avail, use –1693. **2.** The making good or mending of anything; the means of doing so; repair; remedy, relief OE. **3.** Compensation paid for injury or wrong-doing; amends. (Only in OE., and *Hist.*, as OE. *bót*, ME. *bote.*) In comb., as *man-bote*, etc. **4.** Expiation of sin; sin-offering; penance. *Obs.* (exc. *Hist.*).

Phr. *To b.*: to the good, into the bargain; For two books that I had and 6*s.* 6*d.* to b. I had my great book of songs PEPYS. Apply [thy daies] To better b. SPENSER. **2.** Anon he yaf the sike man his boote CHAUCER. *Saint George to b.! Grace to b.!* i.e. to our help. *None other b.*: no alternative.

†**Boot,** *sb.*² 1593. [App. a use of prec., influenced by BOOTY. Cf. BOOT *sb.*¹ 3.] Booty, spoil, *esp.* in phr. *To make b.* SHAKS.

Boot (būt), *sb.*³ [ME. *bote*, a. OF. *bote* (mod.F. *botte*), of unkn. etym.] **1.** A covering for the foot and lower part of the leg, usually of leather. (At first used only by riders.) †**2.** A greave –1609. **3.** An instrument of torture formerly used in Scotland to extort confessions 1513. **4.** Part of a coach; an uncovered space on or by the steps on each side, where attendants sat, facing sideways; later, a low outside compartment in front or behind. Now *Hist.* 1608. **b.** The receptacle for parcels, etc. under the seats of the guard and coachman 1781.

1. Get on thy boots, wee'l ride all night SHAKS. **3.** Shall I draw him on a Scotch pair of boots, Master, and make him tell all VANBRUGH.

Phrases. *The b. is on the other leg*: the case is altered, the responsibility is on the other party. *To have* (*twish*) *one's heart in one's boots*: to be in extreme fear (cf. 'the heart sinks'). †*Over shoes, over boots*: used of reckless persistence in any course. *Boot and saddle* [perversion of Fr. *boute-selle* 'place saddle'; see BOUTE-SELLE], the signal to cavalry for mounting. *Like old boots* (slang): thoroughgoingly.

Comb.: **b.-black,** a shoe-black (chiefly *U. S.*); †**-catcher,** a servant at an inn who pulled off the guests' boots; **-closer,** one who sews together the upper leathers of boots; **-hook,** one for pulling on boots; **-hose, -stocking,** an over-stocking which covers the leg like a jack-boot; **-jack,** a contrivance for pulling off boots; **-last** = *boot-tree*; **-lick** *v.* to toady; *sb.* a toady (*U.S. slang*); **-stretcher, -tree,** a shaped block inserted into a b. to stretch it.

Boot (būt), *v.*¹ [ME. *bōten*, f. *bōt*, BOOT *sb.*¹, replacing *beten* (see BEET).] †**1.** *trans.* To make better –1481. †**2.** To make good, make up –1530. **3.** To profit, avail. (Only in 3rd pers.) ME. **b.** with sense 'it matters' 1752. †**4.** To benefit, enrich. *Ant. & Cl.* II. v. 71.

3. It boots not to look backwards ARNOLD. What boots thy wealth SOUTHEY. **b.** What boots it which prevails 1752.

Boot (būt), *v.*² 1468. [f. BOOT *sb.*³] **1.** *trans.* To put boots on (another or oneself); *intr.* (for *refl.*) to put on one's boots 1597. **2.** *trans.* To torture with the BOOT (*sb.*³ 3) 1580. **3.** *Mil. slang.* To beat, formerly with a jack-boot, now with a waist-belt 1802.

1. Boote, boote, Master Shallow 2 *Hen. IV*, V. iii. 140.

Booted (bū·tėd), *ppl. a.* 1552. [f. prec.] **1.** Having boots on; formerly 'equipped for riding', *esp.* in *booted and spurred.* Also *fig.* **2.** *transf.* Clothed or covered as to the legs 1601.

Bootee (būtī·). [dim. of *boot.*] A high-low boot for ladies; an infant's wool boot.

‖**Boötes** (boˌōᵘ·tīz). 1656. [L., a. Gr. βοώτης.] *Astron.* A constellation, the Wagoner, situated at the tail of the Great Bear.

Booth (būð), *sb.* [ME. *boþe, bōthe*, prob. a. ODa. **bōð*, f. East Norse *bōa* = Icel. *būa* to dwell.] **1.** A temporary dwelling covered with boughs, canvas, or other slight material (*arch.*). **2.** *spec.* A covered stall at a market, fair, etc. See also TOLL-BOOTH. ME. *Comb.* **polling-b.,** a temporary structure for voting purposes at an election.

†**Boot-hale,** *v.* 1598. [f. BOOT *sb.*² booty + HALE *v.*] **1.** *intr.* To carry off booty –1670. **2.** *trans.* To spoil, pillage, plunder –1625.

Bootikin, bootakin (bū·tikin, -ăkin). 1727. [dim. of BOOT *sb.*³ Cf. *mannikin.*] **1.** A soft boot or mitten made of wool and oiled skin, worn as a cure for the gout 1767. **2.** A small kind of boot; a knitted legging with feet, worn by children 1844. 3. = BOOT *sb.*[3] 3. 1727.

†**Boo·ting**, *vbl. sb.*[1] ME. [f. BOOT *v.*[1] + -ING[1].] Relieving, healing, helping; payment to the good; service, avail –1591.

†**Boo·ting**, *vbl. sb.*[2] 1572. [f. BOOT *sb.*[2] or *v.*[2] + -ING[1].] 1. Booty; = BUTIN –1600. 2. Plundering; cf. *freebooting*. HOBBES.

Booting (bū·tiŋ), *vbl. sb.*[3] 1678. [f. BOOT *v.*[3] + -ING[1].] a. Torture with the BOOT (*sb.*[3] 3). b. Punishment by being booted (see BOOT *v.*[2] 3).

Boot-leg. [BOOT *sb.*[3]] The upper part of a tall boot 1634. b. *attrib.* (*U.S.*) with reference to illicit trading in liquor, etc., orig. as conveyed hidden in a boot-leg 1889. Hence **Boo·t-legger, -legging** *vbl. sb.* and *ppl. a.* Boot-leg *v.*

Bootless (bū·tlės), *a.*[1] [OE. *bōtlēas*, f. *bōt*, BOOT *sb.*[1]] †1. Not to be expiated by a 'bote'; see BOOT *sb.*[1] 3. (In OE. law.) †2. Without help or remedy –1659. 3. To no purpose; unprofitable 1559. 4. quasi-*adv.* ME.

3. Bootlesse prayers *Merch. V.* III. iii. 20. Hence **Boo·tless-ly** *adv.*, **-ness.**

Boo·tless, *a.*[2] ME. [f. BOOT *sb.*[3]] Without boots.

Boots (būts). 1623. [pl. of BOOT *sb.*[3], used as sing.] 1. The servant in hotels who cleans the boots 1798. 2. (*slang.*) The youngest officer in a regiment, junior member of a club, etc. 1806. 3. In comb. = 'Fellow'; as *lazy-b.*, etc.

Boo·t-to·pping. 1767. *Naut.* a. The act of cleaning the upper part of a ship's bottom, and covering it with a mixture of tallow, sulphur, etc. b. 'Sheathing a vessel with planking over felt' (Smyth) 1867.

Booty (bū·ti), *sb.* 1474. [ad. ON. *býti* 'exchange', or other word cogn. w. Ger. *beute*, Fr. *butin* (or the latter itself), influenced by *bōt*, *boot*. See BUTIN.] 1. *orig.* Plunder or profit acquired in common and so divisible. a. Spoil of war. b. That taken by thieves 1567. †2. A prize of war, etc. (With *pl.*) –1823. 3. *loosely*, Plunder, spoil; a prize 1580.

3. Phr. *To play b.*: to join with confederates in order to victimize another player; hence, to play or act falsely so as to gain a desired object. Hence: *Booty* = playing b.

†**Boo·ty**, *sb.*[2] 1577. Erron. used for BOOT *sb.*[1]

Booze, boose (būz), *sb. colloq.* = BOUSE *sb.*

Booze, boose (būz), *v.* Var. of BOUSE, perh. dial. Hence **Boo·zer.**

Boozy (bū·zi), *a.* 1529. [f. BOOZE *sb.* + -Y[1].] 1. Affected by drinking. 2. Given up to boozing 1592. Hence **Boo·ziness.**

Bo-peep (bōu·pī·p). 1528. [f. Bo *int.* + PEEP *v.*] A nursery play with a young child, in which the nurse alternately hides, and peeps out unexpectedly, and hides again as suddenly. Also *fig.* and *attrib.*

He playeth b. with the scripture TINDALE.

Bor (bǫɹ), *sb. dial.* 1677. [?:—OE. (*ge*)*būr*; see BOOR.] An East Anglian form of address = Neighbour, gossip, etc.

Bor-, *Chem.*, short for BORON, in comb.; e.g. **Bor-ethyl** $3(C_2H_5)B$, **Bor-methyl** $3(CH_3)B$.

‖**Bora** (bōə·ra). 1864. [Local form of It. *borea*:—L. *Boreas* (Diez).] A severe north wind which blows in the Upper Adriatic.

†‖**Bora·chio.** 1583. [ad. Sp. or It.] 1. A goatskin bag used in Spain for wine, etc. –1775. 2. A drunkard –1729.

Boracic (boræ·sik), *a.* 1801. [f. BORAX + -IC.] *Chem.* Like, pertaining to, or derived from borax. *B. acid* is now called *Boric acid*. Hence **Bo·racite**, native borate of magnesia.

†**Bora·cium.** 1808. [f. BORAX; cf. *sodium*, etc.] *Chem.* Davy's name for BORON, at that time taken for a metal.

Borage (bʊ·rėdʒ). ME. [f. med.L. *borrago*, prob. f. *borra*, *burra* 'rough hair'.] A genus of plants, giving its name to a natural order (*Boraginaceæ*). The common British species (*Borago officinalis*), which has bright blue flowers, and stem and leaves covered with prickly hairs; formerly a cordial, and still used in *cool tankard*, claret cup, etc. Also *attrib.*

Hence—'I B. always bring Courage' SIR W. HOOKER. *Comb.* **b.-wort**, any boraginaceous plant.

Boraginaceous (boræ:dʒinēⁱ·ʃəs), *a.* [f. mod.L. *borago*, *-agin-* + -ACEOUS.] *Bot.* Of or pertaining to the order *Boraginaceæ*; see prec.

Boragineous (bǫrădʒi·nīəs), *a.* [f. as prec.] *Bot.* Of or pertaining to the *Borragineæ*, containing the genus *Borago*; *loosely* = prec.

‖**Bora·sco, -a·sque.** 1686. [Fr. *bourrasque*, ad. It. *burasca*, augmentative of BORA (Diez).] A violent squall of wind.

‖**Borassus** (boræ·sʊ̆s). 1798. [mod.L., ad. Gr. *βόρασσος*.] *Bot.* A genus of palms, with two species, of which *B. flabelliformis* yields palm-wine and palm-sugar.

Borate (bōə·rėⁱt). 1816. [f. BORON + -ATE.] *Chem.* A salt of boric acid.

Borax (bōə·ræks). [ME. *bora·s*, a. OF., prob. ad. (ult.) Pers. *būrah* borax.] 1. A native salt; the acid borate of sodium or biborate of soda ($Na_2B_4O_7$): when pure, a whitish crystal, or white powder, also imported as tincal.

B. beads, beads made of b.. used in blowpipe analysis to distinguish the metallic oxides, and test minerals by the characteristic colours they give in the flame.

†**Bo·rborygm.** 1719. [ad. (ult.) Gr. *βορβορυγμός*.] *Med.* A rumbling in the bowels –1880.

Bord, obs. f. BOARD.

Bordage (bǭ·ɹdėdʒ). ME. [a. OF. = med. L *bordagium*, f. OF. *borde* cot; see BORDAR.] The tenure of a BORDAR; the services due from him. *Hist.*

Bordar (bǭ·ɹdăɹ). 1776. [ad. med.L. *bordarius*, f. *borda* hut, cottage, referred by Diez to Teut. *bord* 'wooden board', etc.] *Feudal Syst.* A villein of the lowest rank, who rendered menial service for a cottage, held at the will of his lord. (In Domesday Book *bordarius*.)

Bordeaux (bǫɹdōu·). 1570. A city in the south of France; hence, the wine of B., claret.

†**Bo·rdel.** ME. [a. OF., med.L. *bordellus*, *-um*, dim. of late L. *borda*; see BORDAR. (Superseded by *brothel*, an entirely different wd.)] 1. A brothel –1850; prostitution ME. only. 2. A good-for-nothing. (Erron. for BROTHEL 1.) CAXTON. Also *attrib.* Hence †**Bo·rdeler**, a keeper or ? frequenter of brothels. var. †**Borde·llo.**

Border (bǭ·ɹdəɹ), *sb.* [ME. *bordure*, a. OF., f. late L. **bordare*, f. *bordus* 'side, edge, border', a. Teut. *bord*. See BORDURE.] 1. A side, edge, brink, or margin; a limit or boundary; the part lying along the boundary or outline. 2. A frontier; *pl.* the marches, the border districts ME. b. The frontier line 1535. 3. A strip of ground forming a fringe to a garden. Also *attrib.* ME. 4. A defined edging, of distinct material, colour, shape, pattern, etc. ME. 5. *fig.* A limit, boundary, verge. (Transferred to time, etc.) 1728.

2. Wolves of war, They kept their b. well SOUTHEY. *Over the b.*: across the frontier line. Phr. *The B.*, *the Borders*: the district adjoining the boundary between England and Scotland. An emphatic B. motto, Thou shalt want ere I want SCOTT. 5. On the borders of eternity HERVEY.

Comb.: **b.-line**, boundary strip of land; *fig.* extreme verge; also *attrib.* verging on the indecent, insanity. **B.-pricker, -rider**, a mounted freebooter living on the B.; **B.-side**, the district about the B.; **B.-warden**, Warden of the Marches; **B.-warrant**, a writ issued on one side of the B. for the apprehension of a person on the other side.

Border (bǭ·ɹdəɹ), *v.* ME. [f. prec.] 1. *trans.* To put a border to. Also *fig.* 2. To form a border to; to bound 1570; †*fig.* to keep within bounds (*Lear* IV. ii. 33). 3. To lie on the borders of, adjoin 1649. 4. *intr.* To lie on the border, be contiguous *on*, *upon* 1535. †5. *trans.* To cut up (a pasty) 1513.

3. Lands bordering the Mediterranean LYELL. 4. Hill tribes, bordering on cultivated countries. Phr. *To b. on* or *upon* (fig.): to resemble closely, verge on; This borders on the common-place 1839.

Borderer (bǭ·ɹdəɹəɹ). 1494. [f. prec. *v.* and *sb.*] 1. One who dwells near a border, *esp.* that of England and Scotland. 2. One who borders *on* or dwells close *to* or *by*; a next neighbour. Formerly said of a country. Also *fig.* 1538.

2. Borderers upon the Roman world SELDEN. Borderers on the savage state HAZLITT.

Bo·rder-la·nd. (Also as one and as two wds.) 1813. A land or district on or near a border; *esp.* that between England and Scotland. Also *fig.*

A neutral strip of borderland GROTE. The b. of old romance LONGF.

†**Bord-land.** ME. *Feudal Syst.* Prob. land held in *bordage tenure* –1664.

†**Bord-lode.** Prob. some service, *e.g.* haulage of timber, due by the BORDAR.

†**Bo·rdman.** [Found only in L. form, *bordmannus*, etc., a synonym of *bordarius*, see BORDAR.] A bordar, a cottier.

†**Bordrage**, var. BODRAGE, hostile incursion.

Bordure (bǭ·ɹdiŭɹ). 1460. [Earlier f. BORDER, q. v.] 1. *Her.* A bearing that goes all round and parallel to the boundary of a shield, always a fifth part of the field in breadth. 2. = BORDER. (An occas. var.) 1664.

Bore (bōəɹ), *sb.*[1] ME. [Partly f. BORE *v.*[1] In sense 4:—OE. *bor* 'borer':—OTeut. **boro-z*; see BORE *v.*[1]] 1. That which is bored; a hole made by boring; an aperture (*arch.*) 2. *spec.* The cylindrical perforation of a tube, gun, etc. Also attrib., as in *smooth-b.*, etc. 1572. b. Hence, the diameter of a tube; the calibre of a gun; also *fig.* and *transf.* 1583. 3. *transf.* The tubular outlet of a geyser 1863. †4. An instrument for boring 1677.

Bore (bōəɹ), *sb.*[2] 1766. [?] †1. The malady of *ennui*; a fit of ennui or sulks; a dull time. 2. A thing which bores; an annoyance 1778. 3. A tiresome or uncongenial person 1812.

1. Your last letter..without that d—d French *b.* 1766. 2. Reproof's a b. 1778. 3. He says the country girls are bores THACKERAY.

Bore (bōəɹ), *sb.*[3] ME. [In sense 1, app. a. ON. *bára* wave.] †1. ? Billow (*rare*). 2. A tide-wave of unusual height, caused either by the meeting of two tides, or by the rushing of the tide up a narrowing estuary. Cf. EAGRE.

The Bristol Channel is very subject to the B. LYELL.

Bore (bōəɹ), *v.*[1] [Com. Teut.: OE. *borian*:—OTeut. **borōn*, f. **boro-z*, whence OE. *bor*, an auger; f. Aryan root meaning to pierce, etc., whence L. *forare*, Gr. *φάρος*, etc.] 1. *trans.* To pierce, make a hole in or through; in mod. use *esp.* to pierce as with an auger. Also with *through.* 2. *trans.* To hollow out evenly (a cylinder, gun, etc.) 1753. 3. *absol.* and *intr.* To make a hole (mod. use limited as in 1). In *Mining*, to sink a bore-hole, as *to b. for coal*, etc. ME. b. To advance as by boring; also *fig.* 1697. c. *trans.* and *intr.* Of a horse: To thrust the head straight forward 1731. 4. *trans.* To make (a hole, tunnel, etc.) by boring (mod. use as in 1, 3) 1523. †5. To gull; ? = BOURD *v.*[1] 2. –1622.

3. b. They take their Flight..boring to the West DRYDEN.

Bore (bōəɹ), *v.*[2] 1768. [app. f. BORE *sb.*[2]] *trans.* To weary by tedious conversation or by failure to interest.

A man..has no unlimited privilege of boring one DE QUINCEY.

Bore, pa. t. and obs. pa. pple. of BEAR *v.*[1]

Boreal (bōə·rĭăl), *a.* 1470. [ad. L. *Borealis*; see BOREAS.] 1. Northern; of or pertaining to the north, or to the north wind. 2. Belonging to the boreal province of the Mollusca 1854.

1. *B. signs*: the six signs of the Zodiac from *Aries* to *Virgo*. *B. dawn* (rare): the *Aurora Borealis.*

Borea·lis. Short for AURORA BOREALIS. BURNS.

Boreas (bōə·rĭæs). ME. [a. L., a. Gr. *Βορέας*.] The north wind; the god of the north wind. Now only in *Mythol.*, and as a personification. Hence **Bo·rean** *a.*

Borecole (bōə·ɹkōul). 1712. [prob. ad. Du. *boerenkool* 'peasant's cabbage'.] A loose and open-headed kind of cabbage, also called Kale.

Boredom (bōə·ɹdəm). 1852. [f. BORE *sb.*[2]] 1. = BOREISM. 1864. 2. The state of being bored; ennui 1852. 3. Bores as a class 1883.

†**Bo·ree.** 1676. [ad. F. *bourrée* (see Littré).] A kind of dance –1730.

Boreism (bōə·riz'm). Also **borism.** 1833. [f. BORE *sb.*[2] + -ISM.] The behaviour of bores; the practice of being a bore.

Borel, var. of BORREL, BUREL.

Borer (bōə·rəɹ). 1483. [f. BORE *v.*[1] + -ER[1].] 1. One who bores; *esp.* a horse that bores 1872. b. A name given to the Myxine or Hag-fish; also to the *Teredo* or shipworm, and to various insects that bore through wood, etc. 1789. 2. An instrument for boring 1572.

Boric (bōə·rik), *a.* 1869. [f. BORON + -IC.] *Chem.* Of or pertaining to boron; containing boron in comb.; as *B. acid*, formerly called *boracic acid* (H_3BO_3).

Boride (bō°·rəid). 1863. [f. as prec. + -IDE.] *Chem.* A primary compound of boron with a metallic element.

Boring (bō°·riŋ), *vbl. sb.*[1] 1440. [f. BORE *v.*[1] + -ING[1].] The action of the vb.; also *concr.* a hole made by boring.

Comb.: **b.-bar,** the suspended bar which carries the bit for boring cannon; **-gauge,** one for limiting the action of the boring tool to the required depth.

Boring (bō°·riŋ), *vbl. sb.*[2] 1868. The action of BORE *v.*[2] Hence **Bo·ringly** *adv.*

†**Bo·ring,** *vbl. sb.*[3] [f. BOREE.] A step in dancing. SHERIDAN.

‖**Bo·rith.** ME. [a. late L. *borith*, a. Heb.; in A.V. 'sope'.] A plant yielding an alkali for cleansing.

Born (bǭɹn), *pple.* and *a.* [In mod. use *to be born* is virtually an intr. vb. See BEAR *v.*] **A.** Senses of *to be born.* **1.** To be brought forth as offspring. (See BEAR *v.*) **2.** *fig.* **a.** Of things: To come into existence (chiefly *poet.* and *rhet.*). **b.** in *Theol.* of persons, *To be b. of God*: to become a child of God; *to be b. again*: to become or be regenerate. ME. **3.** To be ... by the conditions of one's birth, as *to be b. a poet, an Englishman, lucky*, etc. OE. **4.** Of qualities, etc., ***To be born in, with***: to be implanted at birth 1710.

B. Pa. pple. used attrib. **1.** Said of persons: **a.** generally = that (ever) was b. 1550; **b.** qualified or qualifying, as *a b. orator, b. free, eldest-b., Danish-b., gently-b., free-b.*, etc. ME. **2.** Of qualities, etc.: Innate, inherited 1742.

1. Goodliest man of men since b. MILT. *P. L.* IV. 324. **b.** Pet son (her last-b.?) of the Scarlet Woman CARLYLE. Phr. *(One's) b. days*: one's lifetime. *colloq.*

Borne (bō°ɹn), *ppl. a.* [See BEAR *v.*] Carried, sustained, endured, etc. Also used *attrib.*

Borne, obs. f. BOURN.

Borneo (bǭ·ɹni,o). 1876. An island in the Indian Archipelago. Also *attrib.* Hence **Borneene** (bǭ·ɹni,īn), **Borneol** (bǭ·ɹni,ǫl), organic compounds chiefly obtained from the B. camphor tree (*Dryobalanops camphora*); **Bornesite** (bǭ·ɹnīsəit), a volatile substance obtained from *B. caoutchouc.*

Boro- (bō°·ro). 1869. *Chem.* Comb. f. BORON:

borofluo·ride, a compound of fluoride of boron with a metallic fluoride; **borotu·ngstate,** a salt formed by the combination of boric and tungstic acids with the same base; **borogly·ceride,** a compound of boric acid with glycerine, used as an antiseptic; also in *Min.*, **boroca·lcite,** native borate of calcium.

Boron (bō°·rǫn). 1812. [f. BOR(-AX) + (CARB-)ON.] One of the elementary bodies; a non-metallic solid, not fusible at known temperatures. It is obtained as a greenish brown powder (*amorphous b.*); and as crystals (*adamantine b.*). Symbol B.

Borough (bʊ·ro°, bʊ·rǒ). [Com. Teut.: OE. *burg, burh*:—OTeut. **burg-s*. App. f. root of OTeut. **berg-an* 'to shelter'; see BERGH *v.* In early mod. Eng. *burrough*, subseq. *borough* in England and Ireland; the Sc. form is BURGH. The mod. *Bury, -bury* in place-names is from the dat. sing. of OE. *burg.*] †**1.** A fortress, castle, or citadel –ME. †**b.** A court, a manor-house –ME. †**2.** A fortified town; a town possessing municipal organization; any inhabited place larger than a village. (The three notions were orig. co-extensive.) –1483. **3.** A town possessing a municipal corporation and special privileges conferred by royal charter. Also a town which sends representatives to parliament. (Less dignified than a CITY.) ME. See also BURGH. †**4.** A property held by BURGAGE, and formerly qualifying for the parliamentary vote. Cf. BOROUGH-HOLDER. 1715. †**5.** The portion of a city lying outside the wall. Cf. F. *bourg.* –1523. See also BOURG, BURG.

3. Edward VI created fourteen boroughs HALLAM. *The B.*: esp. that of Southwark.

Phrases. *To own a b., to buy a b.*: to possess or to buy the power of controlling the election of a member of parliament for a b. *Close b., pocket b.*, a b. owned by some person. *Rotten b.*: one which had so decayed as no longer to have a real constituency.

Comb., etc. †**a.** Obs. law terms used *Hist.*: **burghbote** [OE. *burh-bōt*], a tax for the repair of fortresses; **burgh-breche** [OE. *burh-bryce*], close-breaking, burglary; **burgh-mote, borough-moot** [OE. *burhgemōt*], the judicial assembly of a b. †**b. borough-folk** [OE. *burh-folc*], the people of a town; **burhwere,** *pl.* **-weren** [OE. *burhwaru, -ware, -waran*], the people of a town, the townsmen.

Borough, obs. f. BURROW.

Borough-English (bʊ·rǒ,i·ŋgliʃ). ME. [f. Anglo-Fr. *tenure en Burgh Engloys*, tenure in (an) English borough.] A custom in parts of England, by which the youngest son inherits the lands and tenements.

Borough-holder (bʊ·rǒ,hōu:ldəɹ). 1712. In Yorkshire: A person who holds property by burgage tenure; see BOROUGH 4. Also explained as = BORSHOLDER.

†**Borough-man.** [OE. *burhman*; see BOROUGH.] A townsman, citizen, burgess. **b.** In Yorkshire: = BOROUGH-HOLDER.

Borough-master (bʊ·rǒmā:stəɹ). 1494. †**1.** A Dutch or Flemish burgomaster; used also transf. **2.** The owner of a BOROUGH (3). BENTHAM.

Boroughmonger (bʊ·rǒmʊ:ŋgəɹ). 1794. One who trades in parliamentary seats for boroughs. (Freq. in discussions on electoral reform up to 1832.) Hence **Bo·roughmonger** *v. rare*; **Bo·roughmongering** *vbl. sb.* and *ppl. a.*; **Bo·roughmongery,** the arts and practices of a b.

Borough-reeve (bʊ·rǒrīv). OE. **a.** A governor of a town or city; substantially = PORTREEVE. *Hist.* **b.** The chief municipal officer in certain unincorporated English towns, before the Municipal Corporations Act, 1835.

Bo·rough-town. *arch.* [Cf. OE. *burhtūn* enclosure surrounding a castle (as in *Burton*).] A town which is a borough. Still in occ. use in Ireland.

Borrachio, var. of BORACHIO.

Borrel, borel (bǫ·rĕl), *a. arch.* ME. [? attrib. use of *borel* BUREL *sb.*] **1.** Belonging to the laity (*arch.*). **2.** Unlearned, rude; rough (*arch.*) 1513.

2. A coarse, ignorant, b. man like me SCOTT.

Bo·rrow, *sb. Obs.* exc. *Hist.* [OE. *borg, borh*, f. root of OTeut. **berg-an* to protect; see BERGH *v.*] **1.** A pledge; a guarantee, bail; suretyship; ransom. Still in *Sc. Law.* **2.** Of persons: A surety; bail, deliverer from prison. –1819. **3.** (f. BORROW *v.*[1]) A borrowing. *Wint. T.* I. ii. 39.

2. Retain as borrows my two priests SCOTT. *Comb.*: (in sense 1) **b.-breach** (OE. *borh-bryce*), breach of covenant; **b.-roll,** a mortgage-roll.

Borrow (bǫ·ro°), *v.*[1] [OE. *borgian*, f. *borg, borh*; see prec.] **1.** *trans.* **a.** To take (a thing) on security given for its safe return; **b.** To take (a thing) on credit on the understanding of returning it or an equivalent; *hence*, to obtain the temporary use of. Const. *of*, occ. *from*, †*at.* **c.** *Arith.* In *Subtraction*, To transfer to the minuend mentally the equivalent of a unit of the next higher denomination, paying back for this at the next step in the process 1594. **2.** *fig.* To render oneself indebted for; to make temporary use of. Const. *from, of*, †*at.* ME. (See also LOAN-WORD.) †**3.** To be surety for; to ransom –1783. †**4.** To give safety to; to rescue; to protect. (Cf. BERGH *v.*) –1522.

1. Let vs borowe money of the kinge vpon vsury COVERDALE 2 *Esdr.* v. 3. **2.** To b. example LATIMER, behauiours from the great SHAKS., Music and Poetry 1763, illustrations 1847. Hence **Bo·rrower.**

Borrow (bǫ·ro°), *v.*[2] 1622. [perh. orig. 'to shelter'; see BURROW.] *Naut.* (*intr.*) To approach closely either to land or wind.

Borrowed (bǫ·ro°d), *ppl. a.* 1440. [f. BORROW *v.*[1]] **1.** Taken on loan. **2.** *transf.* and *fig.* Not one's own; assumed 1571.

Borrowing (bǫ·ro°iŋ), *vbl. sb.* ME. [f. BORROW *v.*[1]] The action of the vb. (senses 1, 2); *concr.*, that which is borrowed.

B. days: the last three days of March (Old Style), said in Scottish folk-lore to have been borrowed by March from April, and supposed to be specially stormy. Called also *borrowed days.* **Bo·rrowingly** *adv.*

Borsholder (bǭ·ɹshōu:ldəɹ). *Hist.* ME. [f. *borges*, gen. case of *borh* BORROW *sb.* + ALDER *sb.*[2]] The chief of a frankpledge; later, a petty constable.

Borstal (bǭ·ɹstăl). 1902. Name of a town in Kent applied orig. to the system adopted there for reforming 'juvenile adult' offenders.

Bort (bǭɹt). 1622. [? a. OF. *bord, bort* bastard.] Coarse diamonds, and small fragments of good diamonds, used as an abrasive.

Borzoi (bǭ·ɹzoi). 1892. [Russ. 'swift'.] The Russian or Siberian wolf-hound.

Boscage, boskage (bǫ·skėdʒ). [ME. *boskage*, a. OF. *boscage* (mod. *bocage*):—late L. *boscaticum*, f. late L. *boscum* wood.] **1.** A mass of growing trees or shrubs; a thicket, grove; sylvan scenery. †**2.** The pictorial representation of wooded landscape; also, of branches, foliage, etc. –1679. †**3.** *Law.* A piece of wood-land (CAXTON); a tax on windfalls (MANWOOD); mast for feeding cattle 1672.

1. The sombre boskage of the wood TENNYSON.

‖**Bosch**[1] (bǫʃ, ‖bos). 1786. [Du.] = BUSH *sb.*[1] *Comb.*: **b.-bok,** a S. Afr. antelope, the Bush-buck; **-man** = BUSHMAN (in Du. *boschjesman*); **-vark,** a species of wild pig in S. Africa.

Bosch[2], **bosh** (bǫʃ). 1879. [In full, *Bosch butter*, i.e. artificial butter made at 's Hertogenbosch or 'Bosch' (Bois-le-duc) in Holland.] An imitation butter; BUTTERINE.

Bosh (bǫʃ), *sb.*[1] 1679. [?] **1.** *pl.* In a blast-furnace, the lower part of the shaft (formerly *four* walls), sloping downwards from the belly to the hearth. **2.** *Mining.* A trough for cooling bloomary tools, hot ingots, etc. 1881.

†**Bosh** (bǫʃ), *sb.*[2] 1726. [Cf. F. *ébauche.*] An outline, rough sketch –1751. Hence †**Bosh** *v.*[1] to cut a dash; to flaunt.

Bosh (bǫʃ), *sb.*[3] *slang* or *colloq.* 1834. [a. Turk.; 'empty, worthless', freq. in Morier's *Ayesha.*] **1.** Stuff; trash; foolish talk or opinions. **2.** *int.* Stuff and nonsense! 1852.

1. This firman is *bosh*—nothing MORIER. Hence Bosh *v.*[2] to spoil; to humbug.

Bosh; see BOSCH[2].

Bosjesman; see BUSHMAN.

Bosk (bǫsk). [ME. *bosk(e*, var. of *busk*, BUSH.] **1.** A bush. Now *dial.* **2.** A thicket of bushes, etc.; a small wood 1814.

Planted with..little bosks and trim hedges (*mod.*).

Bosket, bosquet (bǫ·skėt). 1737. [a. F. *bosquet*, ad. It. *boschetto*, dim. of *bosco.* Cf. BOUQUET.] A plantation in a garden, park, etc., of small trees; a thicket.

Bosky (bǫ·ski), *a.*[1] 1593. [f. BOSK + -Y.] Consisting of or covered with bushes or underwood; bushy. (Also *transf.*)

My boskie acres *Temp.* IV. i. 81. Hence **Bo·skiness.**

Bosky (bǫ·ski), *a.*[2] *dial.* or *slang.* 1730. [? joc. use of prec.] Tipsy.

Bosom (bu·zəm), *sb.* [OE. *bōsm*:—WGer. **bōsm-* (not in EGer.). Remoter etym. unkn.] **A. 1.** The breast of a human being; also *transf.* **b.** The enclosure formed by the breast and the arms. Now only *arch.* ME. **2.** *fig.* (See quots.) OE. **3.** *transf.* That part of the dress which covers the breast; also the space between the breast and its covering, *esp.* as a receptacle for money or letters ME. **4.** A curved recess; a cavity, hollow interior; a sinus. [Cf. L. *sinus.*] **b.** *Mech.* The depression round the eye of a millstone 1813. **5.** The interior, the midst; also *fig.* 1489. **6.** *fig.* The breast considered as the seat of thoughts and feelings; hence 'inward thoughts', 'desire ME. †**7.** Transferred to a person. (Cf. *hand, heart, head*, etc.) –1756.

1. Within my b...My boding heart pants SHAKS. *In Abraham's b.* (fig.): in the abode of the blessed dead. *Wife of one's b.*: orig. a Hebraism, but in Eng. use influenced by sense 6. Hence, *To take to one's b.*: to marry. **2.** The b. of the ground SHAKS., of a river DRYDEN, lake 1816, stormy sea WORDSW. To put money in one's b. BARET. **4.** The b. of a bay 1685, sail 1872. **5.** fig. *In the b. of one's family, of a church*, etc. **6.** *Friend of one's b.*: cf. BOSOM FRIEND. Emptying our bosomes of their counsell swelld *Mids. N.* I. i. 216. You shal haue your bosome on this wretch *Meas. for M.* IV. iii. 139. They come home to Mens Businesse and Bosomes BACON. *Comb.* **b.-staff,** an instrument used in testing the straightness of the faces of millstones (see 4 b).

B. as *adj.* Private, confidential, intimate 1640.

Bosom (bu·zəm), *v.* ME. [f. prec.] †**1.** *intr.* To belly. **2.** *trans.* To put into the bosom 1598. **3.** *trans.* To take to the bosom, embrace. Also *fig.* 1605. **4.** *transf.* and *fig.* To embosom 1632. **5.** *fig.* To hide (a secret) in the bosom; to keep in mind. Also with *up.* 1606.

4. Towers..Bosom'd high in tufted trees MILT. *Alleg.* 78. **5.** Bosome vp my counsell SHAKS.

Bosomed (bu·zəmd), *ppl. a.* 1650. [f. BOSOM *sb.* and *v.*] **a.** Having a bosom, shaped like the bosom; bellied (as a sail). **b.** Enclosed, hidden; confined in the bosom, bated (breath).

Bo·som frie·nd, bosom-friend. 1590. A specially intimate or dear friend. Also †*transf.*

Bo·somy. 1611. [f. BOSOM *sb.*] Full of sheltered hollows.

Boson, obs. f. BOATSWAIN.

Boss (bǫs), *sb.*[1] [ME. *boce, bos,* a. OF. *boce* (mod. *bosse*) = ONF. *boche* BOTCH; perh. conn. w. OHG. *bôz-an* = BEAT *v.* In ME. *boss* and *botch* are partly synonymous.] **1.** A protuberance on the body of an animal or plant; a convex or knob-like process. **2.** *Geol.* Applied to masses of rock protruding through strata of another kind 1598. **3.** A round prominence in hammered or carved work; *e.g.* a raised ornament in bookbinding; one of the metal knobs on each side of the bit of a bridle (F. *bossette*); a metal stud ME. **b.** *spec.* The convex projection in the centre of a shield ME. Also *transf.* and *fig.* **c.** *Archit.* An ornamental projection in a vault at the intersection of the ribs 1823. **d.** *Mech.* The enlarged part of a shaft, on which a wheel is keyed, or at the end, where it is coupled to another. *Shipbuilding.* The projecting part of the stern-post of a screw steamer, which is pierced for the shaft of the propeller to pass through. (Cf. F. *bosse* nave of a wheel.) 1869. **4.** A sort of die used by cutlers 1831. Also *attrib.*

3. In the afternoon I..saw some silver bosses put upon my new Bible PEPYS. **b.** As brood as is the boos of a bokeler CHAUCER. *fig.* Yonder woodland isle, the central b. Of Ocean COWPER.

†Boss, *sb.*[2] 1520. [?] 'A water conduit, running out of a gor-bellied figure' (Bailey): chiefly in 'the B. of Billingsgate' –1657.

Boss, *sb.*[3] 1542. [? a. MDu. *bosse, busse* = Box.] A plasterer's tray, a hod.

Boss (bǫs), *sb.*[4] Now *dial.* 1695. [? corrupt f. BASS *sb.*[2]; but cf. Du. *bos* truss.] A seat of straw; a hassock.

Boss (bǫs), *sb.*[5] 1822. [ad. Du. *baas* master.] *U. S.* A master; a business manager, any one who has a right to give orders. In Eng. = 'swell, top-sawyer'. (*Workmen's slang* or *joc.*) **b.** In U. S. politics, a manager or dictator of a party organization 1882. Also *attrib.* Of persons: Master, chief. Of things: champion. 1860.

attrib. The b. thresher of Ransom county 1884.

Boss (bǫs), *v.*[1] ME. [f. BOSS *sb.*[1]] †**1.** *intr.* To project –1542. **2.** To fashion in relief; to beat or press *out* into a raised ornament, to emboss ME. **3.** To furnish with bosses 1626.

3. Thence to the clasp-makers to have it [my Chaucer] clasped and bossed PEPYS.

Boss (bǫs), *v.*[2] *U.S.* (in Eng. only joc.) 1856. [f. BOSS *sb.*[5]] *trans.* To be the master or manager of; to control, direct.

Bossage (bǫ·sėdʒ). 1704. [a. F., f. *bosse*, BOSS *sb.*[1]] *Archit.* **1.** A stone laid in its place uncut and projecting, to be afterwards carved 1730. **2.** 'Rustic work, which seems to advance before the naked of a building, by reason of indentures or channels left at the joints' (Gwilt). Also *attrib.* 1704.

Bossed (bǫst), *ppl. a.* 1536. [f. BOSS *v.*[1] and *sb.*[1]] **1.** Made to project 1541. **2.** Embossed; also, portrayed in relief 1536. **3.** Furnished with bosses 1586.

3. Turky cushions bost with pearle *Tam. Shr.* II. i. 355.

Bosselated (bǫ·sėlē̍tėd), *ppl. a.* 1873. [f. F. *bosselé*, pple. of *bosseler.*] *Phys.* Formed into small protuberances.

Bosset (bǫ·sėt). 1859. [a. F. *bossette.*] A small protuberance or knob.

Bossism (bǫ·siz'm). *U.S.* 1881. [f. BOSS *sb.*[5]] The system in which political parties are controlled by bosses.

Bossy (bǫ·si), *a.*[1] 1543. [f. BOSS *sb.*[1]] **1.** Swelling in, or like, a boss; projecting in rounded form. **2.** Having bosses or prominences 1812. Hence **Bo·ssiness,** the quality of being b.

Bossy (bǫ·si), *a.*[2] orig. *U.S. colloq.* 1882. [f. BOSS *sb.*[5]] Given to acting like a boss.

‖**Bostangi** (bǫstæ·ndʒi). 1694. [a. Turk.; lit. 'Keeper of the garden'.] A Turkish guard of the palace.

Bo·ston. 1820. [a. F., f. *Boston* in Massachusetts; see Littré.] A game at cards, allied to whist, of which the technical terms refer to the siege of Boston in the American War of Independence.

Bostrychoid, -al (bǫstrikoi·d, -ăl), *a.* 1875. [f. Gr. βόστρυχος.] *Bot.* Having the form or character of a ringlet.

‖**Bostryx** (bǫ·striks). 1880. [a. Gr. βόστρυξ, var. of βόστρυχος.] *Bot.* 'An uniparous helicoid cyme' (Gray).

Boswellian (bǫzwe·liăn), *a.* 1825. [f. *Boswell*, the biographer of Dr. Johnson.] Resembling Boswell as a biographer. Also **Bo·swellism,** the manner of Boswell as a biographer. **Bo·swellize** *v.* to write in Boswell's style.

Bot, bott (bǫt). Usu. in *pl.* 1523. [?] A parasitical worm or maggot; now restricted to the larvæ of flies of the genus *Œstrus*. Prop. the larva of *Œ. equi*, inhabiting the digestive organs of the horse; but applied also to those of *Œ. bovis* and *Œ. ovis*. *The botts* (as sing.): the disease thus caused.

Comb.: **b.-bee, -fly,** an insect of the genus *Œstrus*, whose eggs produce the bots; **-hole,** a hole in a hide made by a b. in escaping.

Bot, bót, OE. form of BOOT *sb.*[1]

Botanic (bŏtæ·nik). 1656. [ad. med.L. *botanicus*, a. Gr., f. βοτάνη plant.] **A.** *adj.* Pertaining to botany. (Now mostly disused, exc. in early names of institutions, etc., as 'The B. Gardens'.) †**B.** *sb.* **1.** A botanist –1676. **2.** Chiefly in *pl.* = BOTANY –1758.

Botanical (bŏtæ·nikăl), *a.* 1658. [f. prec.] Concerned with the study or cultivation of plants; pertaining to botany. Hence **Bota·nically** *adv.*

Botanist (bǫ·tănist). 1682. [a. F. *botaniste.*] One who studies botany.

That diligent b. Bellonius SIR T. BROWNE.

Botanize (bǫ·tănəiz), *v.* 1767. [ad. mod.L. *botanizare*, ad. Gr. βοτανίζειν.] **1.** *intr.* To seek for plants for botanical purposes; to study plants botanically. **2.** *trans.* To explore or examine botanically 1861.

1. To b. in the woods 1775. 2. To b. an island GEIKIE. Hence **Bo·tanizer. Bo·tanizing** *vbl. sb.* and *ppl. a.*

Botano-, repr. Gr. βοτανο-, comb. f. βοτάνη plant. Hence in 17th c. many compounds, formed after those in ASTRO-. **†Botano·loger,** a botanist. **†Botano·logy,** botany. **Bo·tanomancy,** divination by plants.

Botany (bǫ·tăni). 1696. [f. BOTANIC; cf. *astronomy* and *astronomic.*] **1.** The science which treats of plants. **2.** Short for 'Botany Bay'. Usu. *attrib.*, as *B. wool*, now used of all Australian wool; *B. yarn*, yarn made of this.

Botany Bay. 1812. [So named by Captain Cook on account of the great variety of plants found there.] Name of a place in N. S. Wales, formerly a convict settlement; hence = 'transportation'; also *fig.*

Botargo (botā·ɪgo). Pl. **-oes, -os.** 1598. [a. It. (now *buttagra*), ad. Coptic *outarakhon*, f. Coptic *ou-* indef. art. + Gr. ταρίχιον a pickle.] A relish made of the roe of the mullet or tunny.

Drinking great draughts of claret, and eating b., and bread and butter PEPYS.

Botch (bǫtʃ), *sb.*[1] [ME. *boche, bocche* = OF. *boce* (now *bosse*), com. Rom.:—med.L. *bocia, -um*; see BOSS *sb.*[1]] †**1.** = BOSS *sb.*[1] 1. –1519. **2.** A boil, ulcer, or pimple. Now *dial.* ME. **3.** An eruptive plague, as 'the b. of Egypt' (*arch.*) ME.

Botch (bǫtʃ), *sb.*[2] 1605. [f. BOTCH *v.* Cf. prec.] **1.** A botched place or part. Also *fig.* **2.** A bungled piece of work 1648. Also *fig.*

1. To leaue no Rubs nor Botches in the Worke *Macb.* III. i. 133. *fig.* Every Epithet is..a B., which does not add to the thought DENNIS.

Botch (bǫtʃ), *v.* [ME. *bocche-n.* Perh. echoic; cf. 'patch'. See BODGE.] **1.** To patch, mend. Now only: To repair clumsily. Often with *up*. Also *absol.* **2.** To spoil by clumsy work; to bungle 1530. **3.** *fig.* To put or stitch together clumsily; to construct or compose in a bungling manner. Often with *up, together.* 1561.

1. I labour and b...and produce at last a base caricature SCOTT. 2. To b. a block of marble HAWTHORNE. Hence **Bo·tchedly** *adv.*

Botcher[1] (bǫ·tʃəɪ). ME. [f. prec. vb.] **1.** A mender, or patcher; *esp.* a cobbler, or a tailor who does repairs ME. **2.** A clumsy maker up *of*; a bungler 1440.

1. Though but a b., which is something less than a tailor COWPER. Hence **†Bo·tcherly** *adj., adv.* **Bo·tchery,** a botcher's work.

Bo·tcher[2]. 1801. A young salmon, a grilse.

†Bo·tchy, *a.*[1] ME. [f. BOTCH *sb.*[1] + -Y[1].] Pertaining to, or of the nature of, a botch; covered with botches, as *a b. core* –1768.

Botchy (bǫ·tʃi), *a.*[2] [f. BOTCH *sb.*[2] + -Y[1].] Full of bungling work. Hence **Bo·tchily** *adv.*

Bote, ME. form of BOOT *sb.*[1], still in occas. use in legal senses of OE. *bót*: Repair; estover; compensation; expiation.

‖**Bo·terol.** [ad. F. *bouterolle* the tip of a scabbard, etc.] *Her.* Some kind of charge borne on a shield.

Both (bōᵘþ), *a., pron., adv., conj.* [ME. *bāþe, bōþe*, gen. *bāþre, boþer*, ad. ON. *báðar* m., *-ir* f. = (O)HG. *beide*, rel. to OE. *bégen, bá* BO *a.* The suffix is believed to represent the def. article.] **A.** *adj.* **1.** The one and the other; = 'the two, and not merely one of them'. Const.: **a.** *absol.* (occas. †*the b.*). **b.** in *apposition* with a pl. sb. or pronoun: *Both* is placed after the vb. *be* (occas. also after *become, seem*, etc.) and after an auxiliary vb. ME. **c.** in *attrib.* relation to a pl sb. (or two sbs. or pronouns, or a sb. and pron., coupled by *and*): *Both* precedes the sb., or defining wd. (if any), but for emphasis, liveliness, etc. may follow the sb. ME. **d.** in *attrib.* relation to a pl. pronoun: *Both* follows the pron. (but *both which* still occurs; *both of* is the mod. constr.) ME. **e.** with *of*: *Both of* is now used before pronouns instead of *both* (see d) 1590. **2.** = 'the two', as in *between both* (arch.) 1443.

1. **a.** B. were Tories MACAULAY. **b.** We are b. men of the world DICKENS. They have b. gone (*mod.*). **c.** Laughter holding both his sides MILT. Fare you well, Gentlemen b. SHAKS. **d.** They b. speak of death 1816. In b. which [epistles] I stir vp your pure minds 2 *Peter* iii. 1. **e.** You b. of you remember me SHAKS. 2. The argument was supported, for some time, between b. GOLDSM.

B. *adv.* (*conj.*) **1.** Preceding two (or more) homogeneous wds. or phrases, coupled by *and*, *both* adds emphasis by an implied contrast. Thus *B... and* is nearly = *not only.. but.* (As *b... and* = L. *et.. et*, *b.* is often classed as a conj.; but cf. EVEN.) OE. **2.** In the case of two sbs., subjects of the same pl. vb., *b.* may follow, instead of preceding (as in 1). In this case *b.* is often = *too*, or *also.* ME.

1. B. now and evermore *Bk. Com. Prayer.* B. man and bird and beast COLERIDGE. 2. I have seen your brother and your sister b. (*mod.*).

Comb.: **†b.-hands,** a factotum (cf. *one's right hand*).

Bother (bǫ·ðəɪ), *v. colloq.* 1718. [app. Anglo-Irish.] †**1.** To bewilder with noise –1853. **2.** *trans.* To pester, annoy, worry. Also *refl.* 1745. **b.** In the imperative as a mild imprecation 1850. **3.** *intr.* and *absol.* To give trouble to others or to oneself; to make a fuss 1774.

3. Make money; and don't b. about the universe CARLYLE. Hence **Bo·thersome** *a.*, troublesome.

Bother (bǫ·ðəɪ), *sb.* 1803. [f. prec. vb.] †**1.** ? Blarney, humbug, palaver –1822. **2.** Petty trouble, worry; fuss 1823.

2. We had a little b. with him at first M. SCOTT.

Botheration (bǫðərē̍·ʃən). *colloq.* 1801. [f. prec.] The act of bothering; petty vexation; often used as an exclam.

The pipe that allayeth b. G. MEREDITH.

Bothrenchyma (bǫþre·ŋkimă). 1835. [f. Gr. βόθρος pit + ἔγχυμα infusion; cf. PARENCHYMA.] *Bot.* Pitted tissue.

Bothy, Bothie (bǫ·þi). *Sc.* 1771. [? Cf. BOOTH.] **1.** A hut or cottage; *spec.* a one-roomed building in which unmarried farm-labourers (or masons, quarrymen, etc.) lodge together. Also *attrib.*

Botling (bǫ·tliŋ). 1613. [Cf. Du. *bot* stumpy.] The chub or chevin (*Cyprinus cephalus*).

Botoné, -ée, -y (bǫ·tone, -i). 1572. [a. OF., mod. *boutonné.*] *Her.* Ornamented with three bud-like projections resembling a trefoil leaf.

Bo-tree (bōᵘ·trī). 1861. [f. Singhalese *bo*, corruption of Pāli *bodhi* the bo-tree, more fully *bodhi-taru* 'perfect knowledge tree', under which Gautama attained enlightenment and became 'the Buddha'.] The *ficus religiosa* or pīpal tree, allied to the Banyan.

Botrycymose (bǫtri,səimōᵘ·s), *a.* 1880. [f. Gr. βότρυς + CYMOSE.] *Bot.* Racemes cymosely aggregated. GRAY.

Botrylle (bǫtri·l). *rare.* 1835. [ad. mod.L. *botryllus* (oftener used), as if ad. Gr. dim. of βότρυς.] *Zool.* A genus of tunicate molluscs, giving its name to the family *Botryllidæ*. Hence **Botry·llian** *a.*

Botryoid, -al (bǫ·tri,oid, -ăl), *a.* 1747. [ad. Gr. βοτρυοειδής; see -OID, and -AL.] Resembling a cluster of grapes.

Botryolite (bǫ tri,ǫləit). 1850. [f. Gr. βότρυς + λίθος; see -LITE.] *Min.* A radiated spheroidal variety of datholite.

Botryose (bǫ·tri,ōᵘ·s), *a.* 1880. [f. as prec. + -OSE.] *Bot.* Bearing flowers in clusters, which develop successively from the base upward.

Bottine (bǫ·tīn). 1513. [a. F., dim of *botte*.] **1.** A buskin, partly covering the leg. **2.** A half-boot, worn by ladies and children 1866.

†**Bo·ttle**, *sb.*[1] [OE. *botl*:—OTeut. **boþlo-*, from *bu-*, *bo-* to dwell. Cf. BOLD *sb.*[1]] A dwelling.

[In place-names, as *Harbottle*, etc.]

Bottle (bǫ·t'l), *sb.*[2] ME. [a. OF. *bouteille*, com. Rom. = late L. *buticula*, dim. of *butis*, *buttis* BUTT.] **1.** A vessel with a narrow neck for holding liquids; orig. of leather. **b.** A bottleful. Cf. GLASS. Often *attrib.* 1687. Also *fig.* **2.** *transf.* The practice of drinking 1709.

1. Ye were wonte to drynke Of a lether bottell SKELTON. *A five-b. man*: one who drinks five bottles of wine at a sitting. *To bring up on the b.*: to rear an infant by means of a feeding-b. **2.** *Over a b.*: see OVER.

Comb.: **b.-boy**, an apothecary's boy; **-chart**, a chart of ocean surface currents compiled from data obtained by means of bottles thrown from ships and subseq. picked up at a distance; †**-coaster**, a stand on which decanters were passed round the table; **-fish**, the *Saccopharynx ampullaceus*, a fish which can inflate its body so as to resemble a leathern b.; **-glass**, the coarse kind of which common bottles are made; also *attrib.*; **-gourd**, a flask-shaped gourd (*Lagenaria vulgaris*); **-green** *a.*, of the colour of b.-glass; as *sb.* this colour; **-heath**, *Erica tetralix*; **-imp**, one supposed to inhabit a b.; **-jack**, one for roasting, shaped like a b.; **-neck**, a narrow outlet for traffic; **-nest** (= *bottle-tit*); **-ore**, bladder-wrack (*Fucus vesiculosus*); †**slider**, **-slide** (= *bottle-coaster*); **-tit**, **-tom**, the Long-tailed Tit (*Parus caudatus*), from the shape of its nest; **-washer**, one who or that which washes bottles; also (*joc.*) a factotum. Hence **Bo·ttleful**, as much as a b. will hold.

Bottle (bǫ·t'l), *sb.*[3] ME. [a. OF. *botel*, dim. of **bot* = *botte* a bundle.] A bundle of hay or straw.

To look for a needle in a b. of hay: see NEEDLE *sb.*

Bottle (bǫ·t'l), *sb.*[4] 1573. [corruption of *boþel* BUDDLE; also special use of BOTTLE *sb.*[1]] Pop. name of plants, as BLUE-BOTTLE; **White B.**, **Yellow B.**, *Chrysanthemum segetum* (= BUDDLE), etc.

Bottle (bǫ·t'l), *v.* 1622. [f. BOTTLE *sb.*[2]] **1.** To put into a bottle for the purpose of storing. Often with *up*. 1641. **2.** *fig.* To store up as in bottles; to keep under restraint (wrath, etc.); to shut *up*, *in*, *down*, *out*.

1. *To b. off*: to transfer (liquors) from the cask into bottle. **2.** Twenty years of wrath bottled up 1853.

Bottle-brush. 1713. [f. BOTTLE *sb.*[2]] **1.** A brush for cleaning bottles, with bristles diverging on all sides. **2.** *Bot.* Pop. name of the Horse-tail and Mare's-tail 1851.

Bottled (bǫ·t'ld), *ppl. a.* 1594. [f. BOTTLE *sb.*[2] and *v.*] †**1.** Like a bottle, swollen -1769. **2.** Kept in or as in a bottle 1660.

Bottle-head. 1654. [f. as prec.] **1.** var. of BEETLE-HEAD (see BEETLE *sb.*[1]); a stupid fellow (*arch.*). **2.** The Bottle-nosed Whale (so-called) 1819.

Bottle-holder (bǫ·t'l,hōᵘ:ldəɹ). 1753. [f. as prec.] One who holds a bottle; *spec.* one who waits on a pugilist at a prize-fight; *fig.* a second, a supporter.

Bottle-nose (bǫ·t'lnōᵘ:z). 1635. [f. as prec.] **1.** A nose resembling a bottle, a swollen nose. (Usu. written as two wds.) **2.** The Bottle-nosed Whale: a name given to various Dolphins, *esp.* the genus *Hyperoödon* 1668. †**3.** The Puffin (*dial.*) 1678. Hence **Bo·ttle-nosed** *a.* having a bottle nose.

Bo·ttler. ME. [f. BOTTLE *sb.*[2] and *v.* + -ER.] †**1.** A bottle-maker. ME. only. **2.** One who bottles liquor (*mod.*).

Bottom (bǫ·təm). [OE. *botm*, repr. WGer. **boþm-*; cf. Gr. πυθμήν, also Skr. *budhná*, L. *fundus* (for **fud-nus*):—Aryan **bhudhno-*.] **1.** The lowest part of anything, considered as a material thing; the under surface; the base. Applied *spec.* to the keel of a ship, the circular end of a cask, etc. **b.** The sitting part of a man, the posteriors (*colloq.*) 1794. **2.** The ground or bed under the water of a lake, sea, or river OE. †**3.** A deep place; an abyss -1759. **4.** Low-lying land, a valley; an alluvial hollow ME. **5.** The lowest point or locality, the foot (see quots.) ME. **6.** *transf.* The farthest point, or inmost part of a recess, bay, or the like 1603. **7.** *Bottom (of a ship)*: generally, as in 1; *spec.* the part of the hull which is below the wales; also, the hull; *hence*, a ship, boat, etc. 1522. Also *fig.* †**8.** Dregs, sediment -1703. †**9.** That on which anything is built or rests; the foundation -1674. Also *fig.* **10.** The fundamental character, essence, reality 1577. †**11.** A pecuniary basis; capital, resources; *hence*, financial stability -1787. **12.** Staying power 1774. †**13.** A clew on which to wind thread; also a skein or ball of thread. Also *fig.* -1754.

1. Every tub (vat) must stand on its own b. *Provb.* **2.** Phr. *To go to the b.*, *to touch b.*, *to have no b.* (Often *fig.*) **3.** In the Carpathian b. DRYDEN. **5.** The b. of a hill KINGSLEY, the heart 1549, a page, a list, a class, a table, etc. (*mod.*). **7.** Goods imported in foreign bottoms 1883. **9.** *To stand on one's own b.*: to be independent. **10.** *At (the) b.*: in reality. *To be at the b. of*: to be the real author or source of. **12.** [He] died all game and b. BYRON.

Comb.: **b.-heat**, that supplied to plants through the soil; **-ice**, that which forms on the b. of a river or sea; **-lift**, the deepest lift of a mining-pump, or the lowest pump; **-moraine**, débris dropped from icebergs on the b. of the sea; **-up**, **-upwards**, *adv.* Hence **Bo·ttomless** *a.*, without a b. (*b. pit*, hell); baseless; inexhaustible.

Bottom (bǫ·təm), *v.* 1544. [f. prec.] **1.** *trans.* To put a bottom to. †**2.** *fig.* To find a foundation for; to serve as a bottom for; to establish firmly -1685; *intr.* (for *refl.*) to rest as upon a foundation (*lit.* and *fig.*) -1790. †**3.** To wind (as a skein) -1612. **4.** *trans.* To reach the bottom of, to empty. Also *intr.* 1808. Also *fig.*

2. *To b. upon*: to base, found, ground upon; also *refl.* **4.** *fig.* To b. an enquiry SMILES. Hence **Bo·ttomer**, one who puts a bottom to anything; a draught in which the cup is emptied.

Bottomed (bǫ·təmd), *ppl. a.* 1559. [f. BOTTOM *sb.* and *v.* + -ED.] **1.** Having a bottom; usu. in comb., as *full-b.* **2.** Founded, based, grounded; mostly *fig.* 1645.

Bo·ttommost, *a. superl.* 1861. [f. BOTTOM *sb.* as *adj.*] Lowest.

Bottomry (bǫ·təmri). 1622. [f. BOTTOM *sb.* 7.] A species of contract of the nature of a mortgage, whereby the owner or the master of a ship borrows money at a stipulated interest or premium to enable him to carry on or complete a voyage, and pledges the ship as security for repayment. If the ship is lost, the lender loses his money. Also *attrib.* as *b.-bond*, etc. Hence **Bo·ttomry** *v.* to pledge (a ship) as security for money lent.

Botulism (bǫ·tiuliz'm). 1887. [f. L. *botulus* sausage, after G.] Poisoning caused by eating decomposed foods, esp. preserved meats, and due to *Bacillus botulinus*.

†**Bouche**, *sb.*[1] 1440. [a. F.] **1.** Rations granted by a king or noble to his household, his attendants on a military expedition, etc. Only in phr. *to have b. of (in) court*. -1662. **2.** Mouth; *esp.* in *ball*, *bullet in (en) b.* -1650.

†**Bouch(e**, *sb.*[2] ME. [var. of BOTCH *sb.*[1]] A hump, swelling -1538.

Bouche (buʃ), *sb.*[3] 1862. [prob. f. BOUCHE *v.*] A metal plug which is drilled to form the vent of a cannon. var. **Bush** (*sb.*[2]).

Bouche, *v.* 1781. [prob. a. F. *boucher*.] To insert the BOUCHE (*sb.*[3]) into (a cannon).

‖**Bouchées** (bu·ʃē), *sb. pl.* [a. F., f. *bouche*.] *Cookery.* Small baked confections, patties.

†**Boucher.** 1450. [app. corrupt f. *bowger*, f. *bowge*, BOUGE 'bag'; but cf. BOWSER.] A treasurer, cashier, bursar -1583.

Boud. Now *dial.* 1440. [?] A weevil; an insect or worm which breeds in malt, etc.

Boud, = behoved; see BUS *v.*

‖**Bou·derie.** *rare.* [F.] Pouting. THACKERAY.

‖**Boudoir** (bu·dwar). 1781. [a. F., lit. 'a place to sulk in'.] A room, where a lady may retire to be alone, or to receive her intimate friends. Occas. used of a man's 'den'. Hence **Boudoire·sque** *a.* of the kind proper to a b.

†**Bou·ffage.** [a. OF.] A satisfying meal. SIR T. BROWNE.

‖**Bouffe** (buf). [a. F., ad. It. *buffa* jest.] Short for *Opéra b.*; see OPERA.

‖**Bougainvillæa** (būgᵉnvili·ă), commonly -vi·liă). Also **-ea**, **-ia.** 1866. [f. *Bougainville*, French navigator 1729-1811.] A genus of tropical plants of the order *Nyctaginaceæ*, having flowers almost concealed by large leafy bracts.

Bouge, *sb.*[1] *Obs.* or *dial.* ME. [a. OF.:—L. *bulga* a leathern bag, also the womb; of Gaulish origin.] †**1.** = BULGE *sb.* 1. -1600. †**2.** = BULGE *sb.* 2. -1483. **3.** = BILGE 2. 1741. **4.** A cowrie (*rare*) 1875. var. **Bowge.**

†**Bouge**, *sb.*[2] 1461. Corrupt f. BOUCHE *sb.*[1] Also, provisions. B. JONS.

†**Bouge**, *v.* ME. [f. BOUGE *sb.*[1]] **1.** = BILGE *v.* 1. -1600. **2.** = BILGE *v.* 2. 1577. **3.** = BULGE *v.* 3. -1851.

Bouget (bū·dʒĕt). 1592. [Early spelling of BUDGET.] *Her.* A representation of an ancient water vessel.

Bough (bau), *sb.* [Com. Teut.: OE. *bóg*, *bóh*:—OTeut. **bōgu-z*:—Aryan **bhāghu-s*, Skr. *bāhu-s* arm, Gr. πῆχυς (πā-). Not related to the vb. stem. **beug-* to BOW.] †**1.** The shoulder of an animal -ME. **2.** A limb, leg. *Sc.* 1550. **3.** A limb of a tree. (Only in Eng.) OE. **4.** *transf.* A gallows; cf. *tree* 1590.

4. *Legal Provb.* 'The father to the b., the son to the plough': meaning that in Kent, in Gavelkind, attainder for felony does not deprive a man's children of the succession to his property. Hence †**Bough** *v.* to strip of boughs; to send out boughs. **Boughed** *ppl. a.* having boughs, as *dark-b.*; stripped of boughs.

Bough-pot (bau·pǫt). *arch.* 1583 [f. BOUGH *sb.*; cf. BEAU-POT.] A pot, etc. for holding boughs for ornament; a flower-pot; also, in 19th c., a bouquet.

'We have made her a bow-pot.' 'Say a bouquet.. 'tis more genteel.' THACKERAY.

†**Bought**, *sb.*[1] 1460. [prob. f. BOW *v.*, after *byght*, etc.] †**1.** A bend or curve, *esp.* in the animal body. Cf. BIGHT 1, 3. -1675. †**2.** A loop, a fold, a turn or involution -1648. var. **Bout.**

Bought, bught (bauχt, bʊχt), *sb.*[2] 1513. [?] A sheep-fold; *spec.* a pen for ewes at milking-time.

†**Bought**, *v.*[1] 1521. [f. BOUGHT *sb.*[1]] *trans.* and *intr.* To bend, wind, fold; to link -1832.

Bought, bucht, *v.*[2] *Sc.* 1724. [f. BOUGHT *sb.*[2]] **1.** To pen or fold (sheep). **2.** *gen.* To fence in.

Bought (bǭt). 1599. [pa. pple. of BUY, q. v.] var. **Bou·ghten**, used chiefly *dial.*, and in U.S. of purchased as opp. to home-made things.

‖**Bougie** (bu·ʒi). 1754. [a. F., f. *Bougie* (Arab. *Bijiyah*), a town in Algeria which traded in wax.] **1.** A wax-candle, a wax-light 1755. **2.** *Surg.* A thin flexible instrument made of waxed linen, indiarubber, etc., for exploring, dilating, etc., the passages of the body.

‖**Bouillabaisse** (bu·lyabęs). 1863. [Fr., ad. Prov.] Fish stewed in water or white wine.

Bouilli (bu·lyi). 1664. [a. F., pa. pple. of *bouillir*.] Boiled or stewed meat, *esp.* beef.

‖**Bouillon** (bu·lyoṅ). 1656. [Fr.] **1.** Broth, soup. **2.** A saline bath, in which wool is steeped previous to dyeing 1791. **3.** An excrescence of flesh in the foot of a horse.

Bouk. Now *Sc.* and *dial.* [OE. *búc* belly :—OTeut. **būko-z*.] †**1.** The belly -1486. **2.** The trunk of the body; hence, the body ME. **3.** = BULK. *Sc.* and *dial.* 1697.

Boul, bool. Now *Sc.* and *n. dial.* 1513. [perh. a. MDu. *boghel*, f. stem of OTeut. **beu-*

gan to bend.] 1. Anything bent into a curve; a curvature 1513. 2. A curved handle 1560.

Boulangerite (bula·ndʒərəit). 1868. [f. *Boulanger*, French mineralogist.] *Min.* A native sulphide of antimony and lead.

Boulder, bowlder (bōu·ldəɹ), *sb.* 1617. [Short f. BOULDER-STONE.] 1. A rounded water-worn stone, larger than a pebble; a cobble. 2. *Geol.* A large weather-worn mass of stone, frequently carried by natural forces to a distance from the parent rock; an erratic block 1813. 3. *transf.* A lump or mass of some material. Also *attrib.* = 'big, lumpy'. 1861.

1. The Bastille..its ashlars and boulders tumbling down continuously CARLYLE. 3. Boulders of native copper DANA.

Comb.: **b.-clay**, a clayey deposit of the ice-age, containing boulders; **-drift, -formation**, a formation consisting of mud, clay, etc., containing boulders; **-head**, a kind of sea-wall; **-period**, the Glacial Period, in which b.-formations were being produced.

Boulder-stone (bōu·ldəɹstōun). ME. [ME. *bulderston*. Cf. Sw. dial. *bullersten* rumbling stone, f. Sw. *buller* noise, *bullra* to roar.] = BOULDER *sb.* 1, and (later) 2.

Bouldery (bōu·ldəri), *a.* 1859. [f. BOULDER *sb.*[1] + -Y[1].] Marked by the presence of boulders.

†**Boule**[1]. 1449. [app. a var. of BOLL, BOWL.] A measure of lead ore -1670.

Boule[2] (bul). Correct form of BUHL.

‖**Boulevard** (bulǝvar, bulvar). *rarely* **-vart.** 1772. [a. F.; app. corrupted from a Teut. wd. = Ger. *bollwerk* BULWARK.] A broad street or promenade, planted with rows of trees, as *esp.* in Paris. (Orig. the F. word meant the horizontal portion of a rampart; hence the promenade laid out on a demolished fortification.) Hence ‖**Boulevardier** (bulvardye), one who frequents a b.

‖**Bouleversement** (bulvɐrsmañ, bulvǝ̄·ɹsměnt). 1814. [F., f. *bouleverser* to turn as a ball.] A turning upside down, a violent upsetting.

Boulimy, var. of BULIMY.

†**Boultel.** 1460. [a. OF. *buletel (now *bluteau*), f. *buleter* (now *bluter*) to BOLT (*v.*[1])] A kind of cloth for sifting; a sieve (= BOLTER[1] 2); hence, degree of fineness -1660.

Boultell, var. of BOLTEL.

Boulter (bōu·ltəɹ). 1602. [?] A long fishing-line with many hooks. var. **Bulter.**

Boun (baun), *v.* ME. [f. *boun*, older f. BOUND *ppl. a.*[1] Revived by Sir W. Scott.] 1. *trans.* To make or get ready. 2. *intr.* To set out, go ME.

Bounce (bauns), *sb.*[1] 1523. [See BOUNCE *v.*] 1. A sounding knock 1529. †2. The burst of noise produced by an explosion; the explosion itself -1766. 3. A leap, a bound 1523. 4. (from 2.) A boastful lie; swagger 1714.

2. He speakes plaine Cannon fire, and smoake, and b. SHAKS. 4. The whole story is a b. DE QUINCEY.

Bounce (bauns), *sb.*[2] 1709. The Dogfish (*Scyllium Canicula*).

Bounce (bauns), *v.* [ME. *bunsen*; cf. Du. *bons* a thump, *bonzen* (LG. *bunsen*) to thwack; all echoic.] †1. *trans.* and *intr.* To thump, knock loudly -1801. †2. *intr.* To make a noise of explosion, go 'bang' -1719. 3. *intr.* To talk big, bluster; to swagger 1626. 4. *trans.* To talk big at; to bully. *colloq.* To blow up, scold. 1626. 5. *intr.* To bound like a ball; to throw oneself about 1519. 6. To throw oneself, burst, unceremoniously *into, out of* 1679. 7. *trans.* To discharge from employment. *U.S.* [?] 1884.

3. *To b. out* (*with*): to blurt out roundly. Let him b. at his customers if he dares JOHNSON. 4. To b. opponents out of territory 1883. 5. I saw the porpus, how he bounced and tumbled SHAKS. 6. The innkeeper's wife bounced into the room 1883.

Bounce (bauns), *int.* and *adv.* 1523. [Cf. Ger. *bums.*] A. *int.* a. Imitating the sound of a gun. b. Expressing sudden violent movement.

Bownce would hee say SHAKS.

B. *adv.* With a BOUNCE (senses 1, 2, 3) 1604.

Bownce goes the guns DEKKER.

Bouncer (bau·nsəɹ). 1762. [f. BOUNCE *v.* + -ER[1].] 1. One who bounces (sense 3 of the vb.). 2. A bully, a swaggering liar 1833. 3. A large specimen of its kind; a thumping lie 1805.

3. She was a b. (*colloq.*).

Bouncing (bau·nsiŋ), *ppl. a.* 1579. [f. as prec. + -ING[2].] That bounces. Often also (like 'whopping', etc.) used with the sense of 'big', *esp.* 'big rather than elegant'.

A b. head of, I believe, Cleopatra H. WALPOLE. *Comb.* **B.-Bet**, the Soap-wort (*Saponaria officinalis*). Hence **Bou·ncingly** *adv.*

Bound (baund), *sb.*[1] ME. [a. OF. *bodne*, also *bunde, bonde*, in med.L. *bodena*:—earlier *butina* = meta, limes. See Littré *bonde* and *borne*, and cf. BOURNE.] †1. A landmark. ME. only. 2. The boundary line of a territory, etc.; *gen.* a limit or boundary ME. 3. *pl.* The territory near a boundary; a border-land; also land within certain limits, a district ME. Also *sing.* 1 *Hen. IV.* V. iv. 90. b. In *Tin-mining.* The area taken in by a miner 1696. 4. *fig.* A limit to things immaterial, e. g. duration, feeling, etc. ME. Also in *comb.* = BOUNDARY.

2. The utmost bounds of the West 1839. *To beat the bounds*: see BEAT *v.* 4. Thou hast apoynted him [man] his boundes, he can not go beyond them COVERDALE *Job* xiv. 5.

Bound (baund), *sb.*[2] 1553. [f. BOUND *v.*[2]; but cf. F. *bond.*] An elastic spring upward or onward. (*Leap* is used only of animals.)

To take before the b.: to be beforehand with.

Bound (baund), *ppl. a.*[1] ME. [a. ON. *búinn*, pa. pple. of *búa* to get ready, in ME. *boun*; for the added *d* cf. the vulgar *gownd, drownd*, etc.] †1. Ready, prepared. Of persons: Dressed. -1853. 2. Prepared or purposing to go, starting, directing one's course, destined ME. 3. With inf., = about (to), going (to). Only *dial.*

1. Bowne on hor best wise in hor bright wedis ME. Also *Haml.* III. iii. 41. 2. B. on we know not what errand HERSCHELL. Phr. *Homeward b., outward b.*

Bound (baund), *ppl. a.*[2] ME. [pa. pple. of BIND *v.*; shortened from BOUNDEN.] 1. Made fast by a tie, confined; bandaged; also *fig.* 1552. †2. Kept fast in bonds or in prison -1611. 3. Constipated 1530. 4. Tied in the same bundle; intimately connected; also *fig.* 1611. 5. Of books: Provided with a binding. Const. *in.* 1708. 6. Under obligations (of duty, contract, etc.) 1470. b. With inf.: Compelled; under necessity (*esp.* logical or moral); fated, certain; also in *U.S.* determined (*sc.* to go, etc.) ME.

1. A synnar bund with the band of syn 1552. 4. *B. up in* or *with*: (*fig.*) having common interests *with*, 'wrapped *up*' *in*, dependent upon; His life is bound vp in the lads life *Gen.* xliv. 30. 6. Whoever owned land, was bound to military service FROUDE. b. The best horse is b. to win (*mod.*).

Bound (baund), *v.*[1] ME. [f. BOUND *sb.*[1]] †1. *trans.* To limit; to confine within bounds; to mark (*out*) the bounds of -1762. Also *fig.* ME. 2. *trans.* To form the boundary of 1601; †to enclose, contain -1606.

1. He shall..b. his Reign With earth's wide bounds MILT. *P. L.* xii. 370. Views bounded by narrow ideas of expediency 1850. 2. He crossed the little river Rubicon, which bounded his province FROUDE. *To b. on* (intr.): to abut upon, adjoin.

Bound (baund), *v.*[2] 1593. [ad. F. *bondir*, perh. f. L. *bombitare* to hum. (Cf. *All's Well* II. iii. 314.)] †1. To recoil, rebound -1633. 2. *intr.* To spring upwards, leap; to advance with leaps. Also *fig.* 1592. †3. *trans.* To make (a horse) leap -1599.

2. He leaps, he neighs, he bounds *Ven. & Adon.* 265. Like a roe I bounded o'er the mountains WORDSW.

Bound, *v.*[3] *rare.* Var. of BOUN *v.* SPENSER.

Boundary (bau·ndări). 1626. [f. BOUND *sb.*[1] + -ARY[1] B. 2.] That which serves to indicate the limits of anything; the limit itself. b. In cricket, etc., the limits of a match enclosure 1889; a hit to this 1896.

The simple Ideas we receive from Sensation and Reflection are the Boundaries of our Thoughts LOCKE. *Comb.*: **b.-line**, an established line marking the limits of a town, state, etc. 1705; **b.-rider** (Australia), one who rides round the fences of a station and repairs them when broken.

Bounded (bau·ndĕd), *ppl. a.* 1600. [f. BOUND *v.*[1] + -ED.] That has bounds or limits; that has its limits marked. b. *fig.* Limited, circumscribed 1709. †Also, improp. for BOUND, BOUNDEN -1819.

b. The b. level of our mind POPE. Hence **Bou·ndedness**, the quality of being b.; limited range.

Bounden (bau·ndĕn), *ppl. a.* ME. [The fuller form of BOUND *ppl. a.*[2]] †1. = BOUND, in literal senses -1856. 2. Made fast in bonds or in prison (*arch.*) ME. Also *fig.* 3. Under obligation (legal or moral); compelled (*arch.*) ME. 4. Obliged, beholden, indebted (*to*). The usual modern sense. 1530. 5. *esp.* in *b. duty* (occas. found as *bound and duty*) 1530.

2. Her b. thrall SPENSER. 4. I am much b. to your Maiesty *John* III. iii. 29. 5. Our b. duty and seruice *Bk. Com. Prayer.*

Bounder (bau·ndəɹ), *sb.*[1] 1505. [f. BOUND *v.*[1] + -ER[1]; but see sense 3.] 1. One who sets or marks out bounds (*lit.* and *fig.*) 1570. †2. One who occupies a bound of tin-ore ground -1708. 3. A boundary; a landmark; prob. a corruption of BOUNDURE [cf. *border*], taken as *bounder* 'that which bounds'. Now *dial.* 1505.

3. They..builded it for a b. and a testimony GRINDAL. Hence †**Bou·nder** *v.* to bound.

Bounder, *sb.*[2] *slang.* 1890. [f. BOUND *sb.*[1] or *v.*[2]] A would-be stylish person kept at or beyond the bounds of society, or found irrepressible by it.

†**Bou·nding**, *vbl. sb.*[1] 1543. [f. BOUND *v.*[1] + -ING[1].] 1. The action of the vb. Also with *out.* -1614. 2. Abuttal; boundary -1750. 3. *fig.* A limiting or confining -1658.

Bounding (bau·ndiŋ), *vbl. sb.*[2] 1617. [f. BOUND *v.*[2] + -ING[1].] A leaping or springing.

Boundless (bau·ndlĕs), *a.* 1592. [f. BOUND *sb.*[1] + -LESS.] Without limits; unbounded.

My bounty is as boundlesse as the Sea *Rom. & Jul.* II. ii. 133. Hence **Bou·ndless-ly** *adv.*, **-ness.**

Bou·ndly, *a.* ? Finite: opp. to *boundless.* Or ? Bounden. KEATS.

†**Bou·ndure.** 1634. [f. BOUND *sb.*[1] Cf. *closure.*] A bounding, limitation; limit -1654.

Bounteous (bau·ntĭəs), *a.* [ME. *bontyvous, bountevous*, f. OF. *bontif*, f. *bonté*; see BOUNTY.] 1. Full of goodness; in mod. use, always: Full of goodness to others, beneficent; munificent ME. 2. Of things: Proceeding from bounty; liberal, ample, abundant 1542.

1. Colleges on b. Kings depend DRYDEN. 2. A b. crop DRYDEN. Hence **Bou·nteous-ly** *adv.*, **-ness.**

Bountiful (bau·ntifŭl), *a.* 1508. [f. BOUNTY + -FUL.] 1. Of persons: Full of bounty; graciously liberal, generous. 2. Of things: Characterized by bounty, abundantly yielding; also, ample, plenteous 1538.

1. *Lady B.*, a character in Farquhar's *Beaux' Stratagem*; hence, the great lady in a neighbourhood. 2. That's a b. answere that fits all questions *All's W.* II. ii. 15. Hence **Bou·ntiful-ly** *adv.*, **-ness.**

Bou·ntihead. *arch.* 1596. [f. BOUNTY + HEAD.] Bounteousness.

Bounty (bau·nti). ME. [a. OF. *bontet*:—L. *bonitatem.*] †1. Goodness in general, worth, virtue; in *pl.* virtues; also high estate -1623. †b. Valour -1530. †2. Of things: Good quality, excellence -1592. †3. Kindness; an act of kindness (occas. *ironical*) -1651. 4. Goodness shown in giving, munificence ME. b. An act of generosity; a gift, gratuity ME. 5. *esp.* A gift bestowed by the sovereign, or by the state, as a gratuity given to recruits on enlistment, money paid to merchants for the encouragement of any branch of industry, etc. 1719. b. *transf.* and *fig.* A premium or reward 1868.

4. Bountie and largesse is befallyng for kynges UDALL. The b. of Providence JOHNSON. 5. *Queen Anne's B.*: a provision made in the reign of Queen Anne 'for the Augmentation of the Maintenance of the Poor Clergy'. The Parliamentary b. upon the exportation of corn ADAM SMITH.

Comb.: **b.-fed**; **-jumper**, *U.S.* a recruit who enlisted for the b., and soon deserted to enlist again.

Bouquet (bukē·, bu·ke). 1716. [a. F., orig. 'little wood'. Cf. BUSKET.] 1. A bunch of flowers, a nosegay; also *fig.* 2. The perfume exhaled from wine 1846. 3. *transf.* a. A bunch of flavouring herbs. b. A large flight of rockets. c. The flight of pheasants breaking cover from the central point at which the beaters meet; this central spot itself. 1846.

2. The 'b.' is something different from the odour of wine 1865. Hence **Bouque·ted** *a. rare*, furnished with a b. or bouquets.

‖**Bouquetin** (bukətæñ, bū·kĕtin). 1783. [F., app. for *bouc-estain*, Ger. *stein-bock.*] The ibex.

Bour, obs. f. BOOR and BOWER.

†**Bou·rage.** *rare.* [app. erron. f. Fr. *bourg.*] The Borgo in Rome. LD. BERNERS.

Bourbon (burbǫ·ñ), *sb.* 1768. [f. *Bourbon l'Archambault*, France.] 1. A member of the family which long held the thrones of France and Naples, and still holds that of Spain; also *fig.* and *attrib.* **2.** *transf. U.S.* A nickname for 'a Democrat behind the age and unteachable'. 1884. **3.** The former name of the island of Réunion; whence **B. Palm,** a name of the genus *Latania.*

1. Muleteers are typical Bourbons, They learn nothing and they forget nothing TRISTRAM. Hence **Bou·rbonism,** adhesion to the B. dynasty, or to the B. party in U.S. politics; **Bou·rbonist,** a supporter of the B. dynasty.

†**Bourd,** *sb.* [ME. *bourde*, a. OF., Pr. *borda* 'lie, cheating', of unkn. origin.] A jest; jesting -1606. In a bad sense: Mockery -1602. So †**Bourd** *v.* to say things in jest or mockery; †*trans.* to mock. †**Bou·rder,** a mocker.

†**Bourdis.** [ME. *bordis, bourdis*, a. OF. *bordis*, earlier *behordis*, mod.F. *béhourdis*, f. OF. *behourt* lance; see Littré.] Tilting -1450.

†**Bou·rdon** [1], **burdoun.** ME. [a. Fr., med. L. *burdonem, burdo* mule (hence 'pilgrim's staff') Diez.] **1.** A pilgrim's staff -1652. **2.** A stout staff; occ. a spear or spear-shaft -1550.

Bourdon [2], **burdoun** (bū°ɹdǫn). ME. [a. F., = med.L. *burdo* drone, perh. echoic.] †**1.** The low undersong or accompaniment to a melody. [See BURDEN.] -1596. **2.** A bass stop in an organ, usu. of 16 ft. tone; also the drone of a bagpipe 1861.

‖**Bourg** (bur, bū°ɹg). 1450. [F. :—late L. *burgus*, ad. WGer. *burg*; see BOROUGH.] A town or village under the shadow of a castle (*Hist.*); a continental town.

‖**Bourgade** (burgaˑd). 1601. [Fr., f. *bourg*; see prec.] A village or straggling unwalled town. (In 17th c. used as English.)

Dispersed into pettie villages and burgades HOLLAND.

‖**Bourgeois** (burʒwā), *sb.*[1] and *a.* 1564. [F. :—late L. *burgensis*, f. *burgus*; see BOURG.] **A.** *sb. orig.* A (French) citizen or freeman of a burgh, as distinguished from a peasant and a gentleman; *now* a member of the mercantile or shop-keeping middle class of any country 1674.

B. *adj.* **1.** Of, belonging to, or characteristic of the French middle classes; also in *comb.* 1564.

A regular b. physiognomy THACKERAY. Hence ‖**Bourgeoisie** (burʒwazī), the body of freemen of a French town; the French (or other) middle class.

Bourgeois (bɒɹdʒoiˑs), *sb.*[2] 1824. [? f. *Bourgeois*, French type-founder.] A size of type between Long Primer and Brevier, as in:

Bourgeois type.

Bourlaw, var. of BYRLAW, whence **bourlawmen.** *Sc.*

Bourn, bourne (bō°ɹn), *sb.*[1] ME. [south. Eng var. of BURN. Orig. pronounced like *burn.*] A small stream, a brook.

Sundry smal brookes or boornes LAMBARDE.

Bourne, bourn (bō°ɹn), *sb.*[2] 1523. [Early mod. Eng. *borne*, a. F., app. = OF. *bodne, bone, boune* (see BOUND *sb.*[1]). The mod. use is due to Shakspere.] †**1.** A boundary (between fields, etc.) -1790. **2.** A bound, a limit (*arch.*) 1606. **3.** The point aimed at; destination, goal. (Somewhat *poet.*; often *fig.*) 1602. ¶**3.** *incorrectly* for: Domain. KEATS.

1. One that fixes No borne 'twixt his and mine *Wint. T.* I. ii. 134. **3.** The vndiscouered Countrey, from whose Borne No Traueller returnes *Haml.* III. i. 79. [More probably *Borne* means here the 'frontier or pale' of a country.] Hence **Bourn** *v. rare*, to set a limit or bounds to. **Bou·rneless, bournless** *a. rare*, boundless.

Bournonite (bū°ɹnǫnəit). 1805. [f. Count *Bournon*, its discoverer.] *Min.* Antimonial sulphide of lead and copper; a brittle opaque mineral with metallic lustre.

Bournous, obs. f. BURNOUS.

Bourock (bū·rək). *Sc.* 1807. [? dim. of *boor* BOWER; see -OCK.] A little cot; a small heap of stones.

‖**Bourse** (burs, bū°ɹs). 1845. [a. F., lit. 'purse'; cf. BURSE.] An exchange, or place of meeting for merchants; the money-market (of a foreign town). Used *esp.* of the Paris Stock-Exchange.

Bourtree (bū°ɹtrī). Now *Sc.* and *n. dial.* 1450. [?] The Elder-tree (*Sambucus nigra*).

Bouse, bowse (būz, bauz), *v.*[1] [ME. *bousen*, app. a. MDu. *būsen* = Ger. *bausen*; see BOOZE.] **1** *intr.* = BOOZE *v.* Also *trans.* †**2.** *Falconry.* Of a hawk: To drink much -1682. Hence **Bou·ser.**

Bouse, bowse (baus), *v.*[2] 1593. [?] *trans.* To haul with tackle. Also *absol.*

Bouse, bowse (būz, bauz), *sb.*[1] ME. [conn. w. BOUSE *v.*] **1.** *colloq.* Drink, liquor. **2.** A carouse 1786.

Bouse (baus, būs), *sb.*[2] 1653. Lead ore in its rough state.

‖**Boustrophedon** (baustrǫfīˑdǫn, bū-), *adv.* and *a.* (*sb.*) 1783. [Gr., f. βου-στρόφος ox-turning.] (Written) alternately from right to left and from left to right, like the course of the plough; as in some ancient inscriptions. Hence **Boustrophedo·nic** *a.*

Bousy (būˑzi, bauˑzi), *a.*[1] 1529. Var. of BOOZY.

Bout (baut), *sb.* 1541. [App. specialized f. BOUGHT *sb.*[1] 'bending', perh. influenced by BOUT *adv.*[2]] †**1.** A circuit; a roundabout way -1655. **b.** The going and returning of the plough: also *attrib.* 1601. **2.** A round at any kind of exercise, a turn of work 1575. **3.** A round at fighting; a contest 1591. **b.** Used of a fit of drinking 1670. **c.** A turn of illness (*dial.*).

2. *This, that b.*: i.e. occasion, turn, time. **3.** A b. at cudgels 1726, at altercation FIELDING. **c.** A severe b. of influenza (*mod.*).

†**Bout,** *adv.*[1] and *prep.*[1] [ME. *boute, bouten*, early ME. *būte(n* :—OE. *būtan* (*būta, būte*) adv., prep., conj.: orig. *be-ūtan* 'without', L. *extra*; f. *bi* 'BY, with' + *ūtan* orig. 'from without', later 'without', f. *ūt*, OUT. See BUT.] **A.** *adv.* Outside; out -ME. **B.** *prep.* **1.** Outside of -ME. **2.** Without, not having: *esp.* in *bouten ende.* (Still in Sc. in form *bot*, BUT, q. v.) -1500. Also *absol.* -1674. **3.** Except, more than -ME.

Bout (baut), *adv.*[2] and *prep.*[2] [ME. *bute(n*, aphet. f. *abute(n*, as *'bout* of ABOUT.] **A.** *prep.* In senses of ABOUT. (Not in lit. prose.) **B.** *adv.* In *'bout ship* = put about the ship, alter her course 1830.

†**Bouta·de, bouta·do.** 1614. [mod.F. *boutade*, f. *bouter*; see -ADO.] A sally, a sudden outburst or outbreak -1704.

†**Boutefeu.** 1598. [a. F., f. *bouter* + *feu.* Common in 17th c.] An incendiary, a firebrand; also *attrib.* -1754.

A great Boutifieu & firebrand in the Church WOOD.

†**Bou·te-selle.** *rare.* 1628. [a. F., f. *bouter* + *selle.*] A trumpet-call; = *Boot and saddle*; see BOOT *sb.*[3] -1658.

‖**Bouts-rimés** (bū-rīmeˑ), *sb. pl.* 1711. [F.] Rimed endings, given to a versifier to make verses to them in the order given.

Bovate (bōuˑveit). 1688. [ad. med.L. *bovata*, f. *bos.*] An ox-gang, or as much land as one ox could plough in a year; varying from 10 to 18 acres.

Bove, *adv.* and *prep.* [ME. *bove(n* :—OE. *bufen*, f. *bi-* BY, beside + *ufan*, OTeut. **ufana* above, f. *uf* up.] †**1.** (In OE. and early ME.) Early f. ABOVE. **2.** In mod. Eng. *'bove, bove*, shortening of ABOVE, in verse 1591.

Bovey (bɒˑvi). 1760. [Name of a parish near Exeter.] *B. coal*: a lignite or brown-coal of Miocene age, found at Bovey and elsewhere.

Bo·vid, *a.* [f. L. *bos, bovis.*] Of or pertaining to the ox family, or *Bovidæ* of Zoologists, a family of Ruminants, having simply rounded horns, and no lachrymal sinuses.

Bo·viform, *a.* [f. as prec.] Ox-shaped. CUDWORTH.

Bovine (bōuˑvəin), *a.* 1817. [ad. L. *bovinus*, f. *bos, bov-.*] Belonging to, or characteristic of, the ox tribe. Also *ellipt.* = b. animal. **2.** *fig.* Sluggish; stupid; cf. *bucolic* 1855.

2. Where b. rustics used to doze O. W. HOLMES.

Bow (bōu), *sb.*[1] [Com. Teut.: OE. *boga* :—OTeut. **bugon-*, f. stem *bug-* of *beugan* to bend.] **1.** *gen.* A thing bent or curved; a bend, a bent line ME. **2.** *spec.* A rainbow. (Mostly contextual or poet.) OE. **3.** An arch (of masonry). Now *dial.* OE. **4.** A weapon for shooting arrows, etc., consisting of a strip of elastic wood, steel, etc., with a string stretched between its two ends, by means of which the arrow is impelled ME. **b.** *transf.* A bowman (in *pl.*) 1511. †**5.** A yoke for oxen -1721. **b.** *pl.* = SADDLE-BOW. **6.** *Mus.* A rod of elastic wood with a number of horsehairs stretched from end to end; used for playing on stringed instruments. (It was formerly curved, like an archer's bow.) 1580. †**7. a.** The iris of the eye 1611. **b.** The eye-brow 1729. †**8.** An arc of a circle -1674. †**9.** A sort of quadrant formerly used to take altitudes at sea -1706. **10.** An instrument for drawing curves, *esp.* of large radius. (Dicts.) **11.** A ring or hoop of metal, etc. forming a handle. Cf. BAIL *sb.*[2] 1611. **12.** *Archit.* The part of any building which projects from a straight wall 1723. †**13.** A bow's length, as a measure; chiefly in *fig.* phrases -1649. **14. a.** A single-looped knot. **b.** A double-looped knot into which ribbons, etc. are tied (the usual sense). **c.** A necktie, etc. tied up in such a knot. Hence *b.-knot*, 1671. Also *attrib.*

2. A dewie Cloud, and in the Cloud a B. MILT. *P. L.* xi. 865. **3.** After the scole of Stratford atte Bowe CHAUCER. **4.** The b. of Ulysses, which none but its master could bend 1830. **b.** There was among these a thirtie bowes with a bagpipe HOLINSHED. **7.** The Bows her Eyes above 1729.

Phrases. (*f.* sense 4) *To have two (many, etc.) strings to one's b.*: to have two (or many) resources or alternatives. *To draw the long b.*: to exaggerate, lie.

Comb.: **b.-arm,** the arm that holds the b. (in archery or in violin-playing); **-bender,** ? a b.-bearer; **-bent,** bent like a b. MILT.; **-boy,** a boy with a b. (*esp.* Cupid); **-brace** = BRACER[2]; **-drill,** a drill turned by means of a b. and string; **-fin,** a fish (*Amia calva*); **-houghed** *a.* having crooked hips; **-instrument,** one played with a b.; **-knot** (see sense 14); **-pen, -pencil,** a b.-compass with a pen or pencil; **-pin,** a key to fasten the b. of an ox-yoke; **-saw,** one with a narrow blade stretched in a strong frame; **-wood,** the wood of the Osage Orange (*Maclura aurantiaca*).

Bow (bau), *sb.*[2] 1656. [f. BOW *v.*[1] 9.] An inclination of the body or head in salutation, and in token of respect, reverence, submission, etc.; an obeisance.

To make one's b.: to retire, leave the stage.

Bow (bau), *sb.*[3] 1626. [In origin the same word as BOUGH, q. v., but adopted later from LG., Du., or Da.] *Naut.* **1.** The rounded fore-end of a ship or boat. Also in *pl.* 'bows', i. e. the 'shoulders' of a boat. **2.** *transf.* The rower nearest to the bow (*colloq.*) 1830.

1. Phr. *On the b.*: within 45° of the point right ahead. *Comb.*: **b.-chase, -chaser,** a cannon in the b. of a ship, to fire upon any object ahead of her; **-fast,** a hawser at the b. to secure a vessel to a wharf (see FAST); **-grace, -grease,** a junk-fender placed round the bows and sides to prevent injury from floating ice, timber, etc.; (also called BONGRACE); **-oar,** the oar nearest the b.; *transf.* = 2 above; **-pieces,** the ordnance in the bows.

Bow (bau), *v.*[1] Pa. t. and pple. **bowed** (baud). [OE. *būgan* :—OTeut. stem **beug-*, f. root *bug-*, app. = Skr. *bhuj-* to bow, bend, L. *fugere*, Gr. φεύγειν. See also BEY *v.*] **I.** Intrans. uses. (Occas. trans. by ellipsis.) **1.** To assume a bent shape, bend. Now *dial.* †**2.** To turn aside, off, or away; to retreat -1580. †**b.** To bend one's course, go. (Occas. = flee.) -ME. †**3.** To curve -1756. †**4.** To lower the head and body, *esp.* in condescension (*arch.*) ME. **5.** To bend the neck under a yoke; *hence*, to become a subject; to submit OE. **6.** To bend the body, knee, or head, in token of reverence, respect, or submission; to make obeisance. (Also with *down.*) OE. **7.** To incline the body or head (*to*) in salutation, polite assent, acknowledgement, etc. 1651. **b.** *trans.* To express by bowing 1606.

1. Like an Asse, whose backe with Ingots bowes *Meas. for M.* III. i. 26. **4.** She bow'd upon her hands.. She bow'd down And wept in secret TENNYSON. **5.** To b. to the inevitable (*mod.*). **6.** Shall I b. to the stock of a tree HOOKER. **7.** He bowed to Homer, and sat down by him *Tatler*, No. 81 ¶4. **b.** To b. one's assent (*mod.*). *To b. in* or *out*: to usher *in* or *out* with a b. or bows; so *to b. up* or *down* (stairs, etc.).

II. Causative. **1.** *trans.* To cause to bend; to inflect, curve, crook (*arch.* and *dial.*) ME. Also *fig.*, esp. in *To b. the knee*: i. e. to bend it in adoration or reverence ME. †**2.** To incline, turn, direct; *fig.* to influence -1705. **3.** To bend (anything) downwards; to lower (often *fig.*) ME. **4.** To cause to stoop, to crush (as a load does) 1671.

2. *To b. the ear, the eye*: to turn with attention, bending the head downwards; B. downe thine eare, O Lord, heare me *Ps.* lxxxvi. 1. **4.** With sickness and disease thou bow'st them down MILT. *Sams.* 698. Hence †**Bow·able** *a.*; *fig.* complaisant.

Bow (bōu), *v.*[2] 1838. [f. BOW *sb.*[1] 6.] *trans.* and *intr.* To use the bow (on a violin, etc.).

Bow-backed (bōuˑbækt), *a.* 1470. **a.** (f. BOWE *ppl. a.*) Crook-backed. **b.** (f. BOW *sb.*[1]) Having the back arched, as an angry cat.

Bow-bearer (bōu·bēᵊ·rəɪ). 1538. [f. Bow *sb.*[1]] **1.** One who carries a bow 1600. **2.** An under-officer in a forest, who looked after trespasses affecting vert and venison.

Bow-bell, -bells. 1600. The bells of Bow Church, *i.e.* St. Mary-le-Bow, in Cheapside, London. Cf. ARCH. Hence 'within the sound of Bow-bells' = 'within the City bounds'; this church being nearly in the centre of the City. Also *attrib.*

Bow-compass (bōu·kʋ·mpăs),**-compasses** (-ėz). 1796. [f. Bow *sb.*[1]] A pair of compasses with the legs jointed so that the points can be bent inwards; any compasses made for drawing small circles. (Usu. called *bows.*)

Bowdlerize (bau·dlərəiz), *v.* 1838. [f. Dr. T. *Bowdler*, who in 1818 published an expurgated edition of Shakspere.] To expurgate (a book, etc.) by omitting or altering words or passages considered indelicate; to castrate.

†**Bow·-draught.** ME. [Cf. *to draw a bow.*] A bowshot -1716.

Bow·-dye. 1659. [f. *Bow* near Stratford in Essex.] A scarlet dye; also as *adj.* Hence Bow-dye *v.*; **Bow-dyer.**

†**Bowe,** *ppl.a.* [OE. *bogen*, f. *bugan*, to Bow.] Bent, crooked -1500.

Bowel (bau·ėl), *sb.* [ME. *buel, bouel*, a. OF. *boel, buel, bouel*:—late L. *botellus*, dim. of *botulus* a sausage.] **1.** An intestine. Now only in *Med.* †**b.** Any internal organ of the body -1782. **2.** *pl.* The intestines ME. **b.** The inside of the body; also *fig.* Cf. *womb*, etc. (rarely *sing.*) 1532. **3.** *transf.* (Taken as the seat of the tender emotions, hence) Pity, feeling, heart. Chiefly *pl.* (*arch.*) Cf. HEART, BREAST. ME. **4.** The interior of anything 1548. †**5.** Offspring. [Cf. L. *viscera.*] -1682.

1. b. These two bowels, especially the liuer 1620. 2. The bowelles ben cominly called the guttes TREVISA. 3. Bloody Bonner..full (as one said) of guts, and empty of bowels FULLER. So *bowels of compassion, pity*, etc. 4. The bowels of the earth 1593. 5. Thine owne bowels which do call thee, sire *Meas. for M.* III. i. 29. Hence **Bow·elless** *a.* without bowels; unfeeling.

Bowel (bau·ėl), *v.* ME. [f. prec.] To disembowel.

Bowelled (bau·ėld), *ppl. a.* 1589. [f. BOWEL *sb.* and *v.*] **a.** Disembowelled. **b.** Having bowels or recesses.

Bower (bauᵊɪ, bau·əɪ), *sb.*[1] [OE. *būr* dwelling, etc.:—OTeut. **būro(m*:—Aryan *bhūrom*, f. *bhu*, in Teut. *bū-* to dwell. Hence NEIGHBOUR and BOOR.] **1.** A dwelling. In early use *lit.* A cottage; later *poet.* for 'abode'. **b.** A fancy rustic cottage (*mod.*). **2.** An inner apartment, opp. to *hall*; *hence*, a bed-room (*arch.* and *poet.*) OE. **b.** *esp.* A boudoir. Now only *poet.* OE. **3.** A shady recess, arbour 1523. **4.** A structure raised by the bower-bird 1869.

1. The Apartments of Rosamond's B. ADDISON. The bowr of earthly blisse MILT. 2. Merily masking both in bowre and hall SPENSER. b. Love-lorn swain in lady's b. SCOTT. Hence **Bo·wery** *a.* b.-like; leafy.

Bower (bōu·əɪ), *sb.*[2] 1440. [f. Bow *sb.*[1] and *v.*[2]] †**1.** A maker of bows -1733. **2.** One who plays with a bow on a stringed instrument 1668.

Bower (bau·əɪ), *sb.*[3] 1580. [f. Bow *v.*[1]] **1.** One who bows; (see Bow *v.*[1]) 1630. †**2.** That which causes to bend; *esp.* a muscle -1611.

Bower (bau·əɪ), *sb.*[4] 1652. [f. Bow *sb.*[3]; cf. *three-decker*, etc.] The name of two anchors, the *best-b.*, and *small-b.*, carried at the bows of a vessel; also the cable attached to either. Called also *b.-anchor, b.-cable.* Also *fig.*

†**Bow·er,** *sb.*[5] 1430. [a. Du. *bouwer*] = BOOR 1. -1563.

†**Bow·er,** *sb.*[6], **bow·ess.** *rare.* 1460. [f. BOUGH *sb.*] *Falconry.* A young hawk, when it first leaves the nest and clambers on the boughs -1706.

Bower (bau·əɪ), *sb.*[7] 1871. [a. Ger. *bauer* peasant, also 'knave at cards'.] In Euchre the name of the two highest cards—the knave of trumps, and the knave of the same colour, called *right* and *left b.* respectively.

Bower (bauᵊɪ, bau·əɪ), *v.* 1592. [f. BOWER *sb.*[1]] **1.** To embower; to enclose (*lit.* and *fig.*). †**2.** *intr.* To lodge. SPENSER. Hence **Bow·ered** *ppl. a.* embowered; furnished with bowers.

Bower-bird (bauᵊɪ,bɔ̄ɪd). 1847. The name given to several Australian birds of the Starling family, which build bowers or runs, adorning them with feathers, bones, shells, etc., and using them not as nests, but as places of resort.

†**Bowery** (bau·əri), *sb. U.S.* 1809. [ad. Du. *bouwerij.*] A farm; a plantation. Hence 'the Bowery' in New York City. -1876.

Bowess; see BOWER *sb.*6

Bowet (bau·ėt, *Sc.* bū·ĕt). 1440. [? f. med. L. *boeta*, whence F. *boîte* box, case.] A small lantern.

McFarlane's buat [i.e. the moon] SCOTT.

Bowge, var. of BOUGE, bag, wallet; also obs. f. BOUGE, BULGE *v.*

Bow-hand (bōu·hænd). 1588. [f. Bow *sb.*[1]] The hand which holds the bow, i. e. in *Archery*, the left hand, in *Violin-playing*, the right. †(*Wide*)*on the bow-hand*: wide of the mark, out.

Bowie[1] (bau·i, bō·wi). *Sc.* 1538. [? dim. of *bowe* = BOLL or BOWL.] A shallow tub; a wooden milk-bowl.

Bow·ie[2]. Short for BOWIE-KNIFE.

Bowie-knife (bōu·i,nəif). 1842. [f. Colonel *Bowie.*] A large long-bladed knife, curved and double-edged near the point, carried as a weapon in the wilder parts of the United States.

Bowing (bau·iŋ), *vbl. sb.*[1] ME. [f. Bow *v.*[1] + -ING[1].] **1.** The action of the verb; †*concr.* a curved or bent part; a joint -1681. **2.** The action of inclining the body or head in salutation, etc.; also *attrib.*, as in *b. acquaintance* 1616.

Bowing (bōu·iŋ), *vbl. sb.*[2] 1838. [f. Bow *v.*[2]] **1. a.** The playing of (a violin, etc.) with a bow; the method of handling the bow. **b.** The particular manner in which a phrase or passage is to be executed, and the signs by which such a manner is usually marked. **2.** *Hat-making.* The process of distributing the fibres for felting by means of the bow 1842.

Bowl (bōul), *sb.*[1] [Com. Teut.: OE. *bolla*, f. root **bŭl-* to swell. The normal mod. sp. would be BOLL; *bowl* is due to the ME. pronunc. of *-ōll* as *-owl.*] **1.** A vessel to hold liquids. Usually hemispherical or nearly so. **b.** *esp.* as a drinking vessel; whence *the b.*, conviviality OE. Also *fig.* and *transf.* **2.** *transf.* A bowlful 1530. **3.** The more or less bowl-shaped part of anything; *e.g.* of a cup or flagon, tobacco-pipe, spoon, etc. ME. †**4.** *Naut.* A round space at the head of the mast for the men to stand in -1800.

1. Bryngeth eek with yow a bolle or a panne ful of water CHAUCER. *Comb.* **b.-barrow,** a prehistoric mound of the shape of an inverted b.

Bowl (bōul), *sb.*[2] [ME. *boule*, a. F.:—L. *bulla* 'bubble', hence. 'ball'. In *Sc.*, as in Fr., pronounced (bul), and often written *bool*; in Eng. dial. (baul).] **1.** A sphere, globe, ball. *Obs.* in lit. Eng. -1670. **2.** *spec.* **a.** in the game of *bowls* (3): A body of hard wood, made slightly oblate on one side and prolate on the other, so as to run with a BIAS (q. v.). Also applied to those of wood, used in skittles, nine-pins, etc. ME. Also *fig.* **b.** *Sc.* A marble 1826. **3.** *pl.* A game played with bowls: **a.** on a bowling-green; †**b.** in a bowling-alley 1495. **4.** The roller or anti-friction wheel in a knitting-machine on which the carriage traverses.

1. The six Boules of his [the Medici] Arms 1670. 2. Which set a Bias vpon the Bowle, of their owne Petty Ends BACON. 3. The captains and commanders were ..at bowls upon the Hoe at Plymouth OLDYS. *Comb.* †**b.-alley,** a skittle-alley.

Bowl (bōul), *v.* 1440. [f. BOWL *sb.*[2]] **1.** *intr.* To play at bowls; to roll a bowl, etc. along the ground. **2.** *trans.* To cause to roll 1580. **b.** To carry on wheels, i. e. in a carriage, etc. 1819. **3.** *intr.* To move by revolution; to move on wheels (esp. *to b. along*); also *transf.* of a ship. 1759. **4.** *intr.* To deliver the ball at cricket (orig. by trundling along the ground) 1755. **5.** *trans.* in various constructions. **a.** To b. *the ball.* **b.** To b. *a batsman* (*out*): to get him out by bowling the bails off. **c.** To b. *the wicket* (*down*). 1746. Hence *fig.* (*colloq.* or *slang*).

1. Sir, challenge her to boule SHAKS. 2. Children bowling their hoops (*mod.*). 3. The carriage bowls along COWPER. We bowled through..Overton 1872.

Bowlder, var. of BOULDER *sb.*[1]

Bow-legged (bōu·legd), *a.* 1552. [f. *bow-legs.*] Having outwardly bent legs. (In HULOET = *knock-kneed.*)

Bowler[1] (bōu·ləɪ). 1500. [f. BOWL *v.*+-ER[1].] **1.** One who plays at bowls. **2.** The player who bowls at cricket 1755.

Bowler[2] (bōu·ləɪ). [f. BOWL *sb.*[1] or *v.*[2] + -ER[1].] †**1.** A deep drinker. **2.** The workman who shapes the bowl of a spoon (*mod.*).

Bowler[3]. 1861. [f. surname of a London hat-manufacturer.] A hard low-crowned stiff felt hat. Cf. BILLYCOCK.

Bow·less, *a.* Without a bow (in various senses).

Bowline (bōu·lin). ME. [In all Teut. langs. conn. w. the ship's Bow, but found in Eng. before *bow*, and differently pronounced. The alleged ON. *bóglína* is suspect.] **I. 1.** A rope passing from about the middle of the perpendicular edge on the weather side of the square sails (to which it is fastened by subdivisions called 'bridles') to the larboard or starboard bow, for the purpose of keeping the edge of the sail steady when sailing on a wind. **2.** Short for *b.-knot* 1823.

On a b.: said of a ship when close-hauled, so as to sail close to the wind. *Comb.*: **b.-bridle** (see 1); **-knot,** a knot used in fastening the b.-bridles to the cringles.

II. In *Ship-building.* A longitudinal curve representing the ship's fore-body cut in a vertical section.

Bowling (bōu·liŋ), *vbl. sb.* 1535. [f. BOWL *v.* + -ING[1].] **1.** Playing at bowls; the action of rolling a ball, etc. **2.** *Cricket.* The action of delivering the ball 1755.

Comb.: **b.-alley,** an alley for playing at bowls or skittles; **-crease,** the line from behind which the bowler delivers the ball in cricket; **-green,** a smooth level green for playing bowls upon.

Bowman[1] (bōu·măn). ME. [f. Bow *sb.*[1]] One who shoots with a bow; *esp.* a fighting man armed with a bow.

Bowman's root: a name of: *Gillenia trifoliata, Euphorbia corollata*, and *Isnardia alternifolia.*

Bowman[2] (bau·măn). 1829. [f. Bow *sb.*[3]] *Naut.* = Bow *sb.*[3] 2.

Bowne, obs. f. BOUN.

Bow-net (bōu·,net). OE. [f. Bow *sb.*[1]] **1.** A trap for lobsters, etc., viz. a cylinder of wicker-work closed at one end and having a narrow funnel-shaped entrance at the other; also called, a bow-weel. **2.** A net attached to a bow of wood, etc., used by fowlers 1875.

Bowse, bowsie, var. of BOUSE, BOUSY.

†**Bow·ser.** 1534. [? corruption of AF. *bourser*, OF. *boursier*, f. *bourse.*] A treasurer, bursar. Hence **Bow·sery,** a bursary. -1631.

Bowshot (bōu·ʃǫt). ME. [f. Bow *sb.*[1]] The length an arrow can be shot from a bow.

Bowsprit (bōu·sprit). [f. as BOWLINE (q.v.) + OE. *spréot* pole (ME. *spret, spreet*), or its LG. or Du. equivalent. See SPRIT. Prob. of LG. or Du. origin.] **1.** A large spar or boom running out from the stem of a vessel, to which (and the jib-boom and flying jib-boom) the fore-mast stays are fastened. †**2.** *fig.* The human nose (*joc.*) -1691.

†**Bow·ssen,** *v.* 1602. [ad. Cornish *beuzi* 'to immerge, drown'.] To immerse in a holy well.

†**Bowstaff.** Pl. **bowstaves.** ME. [f. Bow *sb.*[1] 4.] A stick to be made into a bow -1720.

Bow-street (bōu·strīt). 1812. A street in London near Covent Garden in which the principal metropolitan police-court is situated: hence **Bow-street officer, -runner,** etc., a police officer.

Bow-string, bowstring (bōu·striŋ). 1486. [f. Bow *sb.*[1]] **1.** The string of a bow; also *fig.* **2.** As used in Turkey for strangling offenders 1603.

Comb.: **b.-bridge,** a bridge consisting of an arch and horizontal tie, to resist the horizontal thrust; hence **-girder; b. hemp,** plants of the genus *Sanseviera*, N.O. *Liliaceæ*, of the fibres of which bow-strings are made. Hence **Bow·string** *v.* to strangle with a bow-string. **Bow·stringer.**

Bowtel(l, var. of BOLTEL.

Bow-window (bōu·wi·ndou). 1753. [f. Bow *sb.*[1]] **1.** A Bay-window segmentally curved on plan. (Erron. taken as generic, *e.g.* in 'square bow windows'.) **2.** *slang.* A big belly. Hence **Bow·-wi·ndowed** *ppl. a.* (in both senses).

Bow-wow, *int.* and *sb.* 1576. [Echoic.] **1.** (bau·wau·) An imitation of the barking of a dog.

2. as *sb.* Also *fig.* 1832. b. *attrib.* (bau·wau), as in *bow-wow theory*, the theory that human speech originated in imitation of animal sounds 1864. Also quasi-*adj.* Dog-like, barking, snarling 1838. 3. *transf.* A dog (*joc.*). COWPER. Hence **Bow-wow·** *v.* to bark; *fig.* to growl.

Bowyer (bōu·iəɹ). ME. [f. BOW *sb.* + -YER; cf. *lawyer.*] 1. One who makes, or trades in, bows. 2. A bowman 1440.

Box (bǫks), *sb.*[1] [OE., ad. L. *buxus*, Gr. πύξος.] *Bot.* 1. A genus (*Buxus*) of small evergreen trees or shrubs of the N.O. *Euphorbiaceæ*; specially *B. sempervirens*, the Common or Evergreen Box-tree. A dwarfed variety (*Dwarf* or *Ground Box*) is used for the edgings of flower-beds. OE. 2. BOX-WOOD. ME. Also *attrib.*

1. The wood of boxe is yelowe and pale TURNER.
Comb.: **b.-berry**, the fruit (and plant) of the winter-green of America (*Gaultheria procumbens*); **-elder, -alder**, a N. Amer. tree, the Ash-leaved Maple (*Acer negundo*); **-holly**, Butcher's broom (*Ruscus aculeatus*); **-thorn**, shrubs of the genus *Lycium*, esp. *L. barbarum.*

Box (bǫks), *sb.*[2] [OE.; either a use of prec., or ad. L. *buxum* or L. *pyxis* (*puxis*, med. L. *buxis*) box.] I. 1. A case or receptacle usually having a lid. Also *fig.* 2. *esp.* A money-box ME. b. *transf.* The money contained in such a box; a fund for a special purpose ME. 3. = CHRISTMAS-BOX 1593. 4. A box under the driver's seat on a coach; hence, the driver's seat 1625. 5. A box and its contents; hence, a measure of quantity ME.

1. Take this boxe of oile in thine hand 2 *Kings* ix. 1. *fig.* Thou damnable b. of enuy thou *Tr. & Cr.* v. i. 29. 4. Our coachmen so drunk, that they both fell off their boxes EVELYN.

II. A compartment partitioned off. 1. A seated compartment in a theatre. In *pl.* a part of the auditorium, 1609. b. *transf.* The occupants of the boxes; *esp.* the ladies 1700. 2. A compartment in the public room of a coffee-house, etc. 1712. 3. = JURY-BOX, WITNESS-BOX 1822. 4. A stall for a horse, etc., in a stable, or a railway truck. Also *horse-b.* 1846.

1. b. The boxes and the pit Are sovereign judges of this sort of wit DRYDEN. 4. *Loose b.*: one in which the animal is free to move about.

III. A box-like shelter, as a sentry's b. 1714. 2. A small country-house; *e.g.* a *shooting-b.* 1714.

IV. Technical. 1. The case in which the needle of a compass is placed 1613. 2. A metal cylinder in the nave of a cart or carriage wheel, which surrounds the axle. b. A journal-box, a bearing. (Cf. BUSH *sb.*[2]) 1711. 3. The piston of a pump; the case containing the valve 1626. 4. *Printing.* One of the cells into which a type-case is divided 1696.

Phrase. *To be in the* (†*a*) *wrong b.*: to be in a wrong position, out of the right place. (The allusion is lost.)
Comb.: **b.-barrow**, one with upright sides and front; **-beam, an** iron beam with a double web; **-chronometer, a** marine chronometer with gimbal arrangements like a ship's compass; **-cloth**, a thick close-woven cloth for riding garments, etc.; **-coat**, a heavy over-coat for driving; **-coupling**, an iron collar used to connect two shafts, etc.; **-crab**, one of the genus *Calappa*, which when at rest resembles a b.; **-drain**, one of quadrangular section; **-fish**, the trunk-fish, *Ostracion*; **-girder**, an iron girder resembling a b., the sides being fastened together by angle-irons; **-iron**, a smoothing iron with a cavity to contain a heater; also *attrib.*; **-keeper**, an attendant at the boxes in a theatre; **-metal**, a metallic alloy of copper and tin, or of zinc, tin, lead, and antimony for bearings; **-office**, an office in a theatre, etc. for booking seats (orig. for hiring a box); **-pleat**, a double pleat in cloth; so **-pleated** *ppl. a.*, **-pleating** *vbl. sb.*; **-slater** (*Zool.*), the genus *Idothea* of Isopods; **-sleigh**, one with a b.-like body; **-tortoise, -turtle**, one of the genus *Pyxis*, which by means of a moveable door or lid can shut itself up in a sort of b.; *joc.* a reticent person; **-wallah** (*Anglo-Ind.*), a native itinerant pedlar in India. Hence **Bo·x-ful** *a.*

Box (bǫks), *sb.*[3] [ME.; perh. echoic.] †1. A blow. Now only as in 2. -1727. 2. *spec.* A slap or cuff on the ear or side of the head 1440.

A B. oth' Ear for a Prologue, you know D'URFEY.

Box (bǫks), *v.*[1] 1477. [f. BOX *sb.*[2]] 1. To furnish or fit with a box 1481. †2. To cup (cf. BOIST *v.*) -1543. 3. To put into, or as into, a box; often with *up, in* 1586. 4. To lodge a document in a Law Court (*mod.*). 5. To fit compactly as in a box; *techn.* to fit with a scarf joint 1794. 6. To make a cavity in the trunk of (a tree) for the sap to collect 1720. 7. *slang.* To overturn in his box (*e.g.* a watchman) 1851.

Box (bǫks), *v.*[2] *Naut.* [ad. Sp. *bojar.*] *To b. the compass*: to repeat the names of the 32 points of the compass in order and backwards; *fig.* to go completely round. *To b. about*: to sail up and down, often changing the direction.

Box (bǫks), *v.*[3] 1519. [f. BOX *sb.*[3]] 1. *trans.* orig. To beat, thrash; *later*, to cuff; *now* usu., to strike (the cheek, ear, etc.) with the hand. 2. *intr.* To fight with fists; now mostly of practice with boxing-gloves 1567. 3. *trans.* To fight (another) with fists 1694.

1. I've a good mind to b. your ears 1876. 2. To leap, to b., to wrestle, and to run COWPER.

Box-calf. 1904. [f. the name of Joseph *Box*, London bootmaker.] Chrome-tanned calf-skin having a grain of rectangularly crossed lines.

Boxen (bǫ·ksĕn), *a. arch.* 1566. [f. BOX *sb.*[1]] 1. Of or pertaining to the box-tree or box-trees 1578. 2. Made of or resembling box-wood 1566.

1. B. Groves DRYDEN. 2. A B. Haut-Boy PHILIPS.

Boxer[1] (bǫ·ksəɹ). 1871. [f. BOX *v.*[1] + -ER[1].] One who puts things up in boxes.

Bo·xer[2]. 1848. [f. BOX *v.*[2] + -ER[1].] One who boxes; a pugilist.

With cap.: A member of a Chinese nationalist secret society (*i ho chuan* 'righteous-harmony-boxers') 1900.

Box-haul (bǫ·ks,hǭl), *v.* 1769. [f. BOX *v.*[2]] To veer a ship round on her heel.

Boxia·na. Notes about boxing MOORE.

Boxing (bǫ·ksiŋ), *vbl. sb.*[1] 1519. [f. BOX *v.*[1] and *sb.*[2] + -ING[1].] I. From the vb. 1. The putting into, or providing with, a box 1607. b. *Law.* The lodgement of pleadings in court (*mod.*). †2. Cupping. Hence *b.-glass*: a cupping-glass. -1610. 3. *Naut.* = BOX-HAULING 1769. II. From the sb. 1. A structure of boxes 1845. 2. *Shipbuilding.* A scarf joint 1850. 3. The cases, one on each side of a window, into which the shutters fold 1823.

Boxing (bǫ·ksiŋ), *vbl. sb.*[2] 1711. [f. BOX *v.*[2] + -ING[1].] The action of fighting with fists.

Bo·xing-day. 1849. The first week-day after Christmas-day, observed as a holiday, on which Christmas-boxes are given.

Bo·x-tree. [OE. *boxtrēow.*] = BOX *sb.*[1] 1.

Bo·xwood. 1652. [f. BOX *sb.*[1]] 1. The wood of the box-tree; much used by turners, wood-engravers, and makers of mathematical instruments. 2. The tree or shrub itself 1768.

American B., *Cornus florida*, having heavy close-grained wood; **Jamaica B.**, *Tecoma pentaphylla.*

Boy (boi), *sb.* [The early variants point to an orig. OF. form with *-ui-* such as **abuié* fettered person (L. *boiæ* fetters).] †1. A servant, esp. one in a humble position ME. -1601. b. *spec.* in *boot-b., link-b., post-b., pot-b.* c. A native personal servant 1609. †2. A male person of the lower orders. †3. Used, like *fellow*, as a vague term of abuse for a male person, and to an inferior. 4. A male child. late ME. 5. a. A male of any age or condition, esp. unmarried (*dial.*) 1730. 6. Used familiarly as a form of address, esp. with *my, old, dear* 1601. 7. A member of a fraternity or group 1590.

1. The very boyes will learn to talk and swear WALTON. 2. b. Our Irish boys 18.. So *Cornish, Western boys.* 5. To sea, boys, and let her goe hang *Temp.* II. ii. 56.

Phrases, etc. *The old b.*: the devil. *Yellow boys*: guineas. **Boy-bishop**, the boy elected by his fellows to play the part of bishop from St. Nicholas' Day to Innocents' Day. **Boy scout**: see SCOUT *sb.*[2] Hence **Boy·ism**, the nature of a b.; a puerility.

Boy (boi), *v.* 1568. [f. the sb.] To play the boy; to call (one) 'boy'; to represent (a woman's part) on the stage (*Ant. & Cl.* v. ii. 220); to furnish with boys. (Nonce-usages.)

‖**Boyar, boyard** (bo͡yā·r, boi·ăɹd). 1591. [a. Russ. *boyárin*, pl. *boyáre* 'grandee'; prob. f. OSlav. root *bol-* great.] A privileged order of Russian aristocracy, next in rank to a *Knyaz* or 'prince', abolished by Peter the Great. Erron. applied in Eng. newspapers to Russian landed proprietors. (The Eng. *boyar* app. represents the pl.; *boyard* is an erroneous Fr. spelling.) Hence **Boy·ardism.**

‖**Boyau** (boi·o). 1847. [F.:—OF. *boel*; see BOWEL.] *Fortif.* A branch of a trench; a zig-zag; a trench in rear of a battery, forming a communication with the magazine; a small gallery of a mine.

Boycott (boi·kǫt), *v.* 1880. [f. Capt. *Boycott*, the original victim of the treatment.] *trans.* To combine in refusing to hold relations of any kind with (a neighbour), on account of political or other differences, so as either to punish him, or coerce him into abandoning his position. The word was first used to describe the action instituted by the Irish Land League towards those who incurred its hostility. Also *transf.* and *fig.* Hence **Boy·co·tter, Boy·co·tting** *vbl. sb.*, **Boy·co·ttism**; also **Boy·cott** *sb.* = *Boycotting*; (U.S.) an application of boycotting. (Now also written without capitals.)

Boydekyn(ne, obs. f. BODKIN.

Boyer (boi·əɹ). 1618. [a. Du. *boeijer* a smack.] A sloop of Flemish construction, with a raised work at each end.

Boyhood (boi·hud). 1745. [f. BOY *sb.*[1] + HOOD.] a. The state of being a boy; the time of life during which one is a boy; also *fig.* the early period. b. Boys collectively. c. Boyish feeling.

Look at him, in his b., ..and in his manhood SWIFT.

Boyish (boi·iʃ), *a.* 1548. [f. BOY *sb.*[1] + -ISH.] 1. Of or pertaining to boys or boyhood. 2. Boylike; puerile 1579.

1. My b. daies *Oth.* I. iii. 132. 2. B. vanities MACAULAY. Hence **Boy·ish·ly** *adv.*, **-ness.**

Boy's love. 1863. Southernwood, *Artemisia Abrotanum*, also called *Lad's love.*

‖**Boyuna** (bo͡yū·nă). [Tupi *boi-una.*] A harmless snake of Ceylon. GOLDSM.

‖**Boza, bosa** (bōu·ză). 1656. [Turk.] An Egyptian drink, made of millet-seed fermented and certain astringents; also an inebriating preparation of darnel-meal, hemp-seed, and water. vars. **Booza, bouza, boosa.**

Brab (bræb). 1698. [? corruption of Pg. *brava* wild, in *palmeira brava* the Pg. name.] The Palmyra palm (*Borassus flabelliformis*).

Brabant (brăbæ·nt). 1840. [f. the name of the Duchy.] A name applied (in error) to a base Flemish coin of the 13th c.

Brabble (bræ·b'l), *v. Obs.* or *arch.* exc. *dial.* 1500. [Cf. BRAWL, BABBLE. ? A corruption of L. *parabolare*, to harangue.] 1. *intr.* To dispute obstinately; to cavil. 2. To quarrel about trifles; *esp.* to squabble 1530. Hence **Bra·bblement**, †cavilling; contentious uproar (*dial.*). **Bra·bbler.** (Both *arch.*)

Bra·bble, *sb.* 1566. [f. prec.] †1. A quibble -1674. †2. A frivolous action at law -1677. 3. A paltry or noisy quarrel 1566; †a brawl, or petty war -1622. 4. Discordant babble 1861.

3. To make a Nationall Warre of a Surplice B. MILT.

Braccate (bræ·ke^i^t), *a.* 1847. [ad. L. *brac(c)atus*, f. *brac(c)æ* trousers.] *Ornith.* Having the legs fully covered with feathers.

‖**Braccio** (bra·ttʃo). Pl. **braccia.** 1760. [It., lit. 'an arm'.] An It. measure of length; = 2 ft.

†**Brace**, *sb.*[1] ME. [a. F. *bras*:—L. *brac(c)hium.*] An arm, esp. an arm of the sea, etc. -1530.

B. of St. George = med.L. *brachium Sancti Georgii*: the Bosporus or the Hellespont.

Brace (brēⁱs), *sb.*[2] ME. [Orig. a. OF. *brace, brache, brase*:—L. *brac(c)hia*; partly f. BRACE *v.*[1]] I. Sense 'pair of arms'. †1. Armour for the arms. (At first 'a pair of brace'.) -1611. †b. A state of defence. *Oth.* I. iii. 24. †2. A measure of length, orig. repr. the length of the extended arms -1710. 3. A carpenter's tool, having a crank handle, and a pad to hold a bit for boring 1567.

II. That which clasps, connects, or fastens. Cf. BRACE *v.*[1] 3. 1. A clasp, buckle, clamp, or the like 1440. 2. One of a pair of straps of webbing, used to support the trousers 1816. 3. A leathern thong which slides up and down the cord of a drum, and regulates the tension of the skins 1596; *transf.* tension -1697. 4. One of the straps by which the body of a carriage is suspended from the springs 1720. 5. *Naut.* One of the metal straps secured with bolts and screws to the stern-post and bottom planks of a ship 1850. 6. A bandage securing a decoy-bird 1768. 7. A sign } used in writing or printing, chiefly to unite together two or more lines, words, staves of music, etc. In *pl.* (occas. but erron.) = square brackets [ ]. 1656.

2. It broke, and .. Carried away both stays and braces. (A pun on BRACE *sb.*[3]) 1816. 3. The laxness

of the tympanum when it has lost its b. or tension HOLDER.

III. Two things taken together; a pair, a couple. Often = *two*. Used *orig.* of dogs; later, generally, *esp.* of game. ME.

B. of howndys 1440. A b. of Deere 1570, of Partridges 1741, pistols 1832, twins TENNYSON, of vulgar demagogues (*mod.*).

IV. That which makes rigid or steady; see BRACE *v.*[1] 6. **1.** A band of metal used for support, *e.g.* in mounting bells 1730. **2.** *Building* and *Mech.* A timber or scantling used in a roof, etc., to stiffen the assemblage of pieces composing it; a piece of timber or iron used to strengthen the framework of a vessel, bridge, pier, etc. 1530.

V. *Mining.* The mouth of a shaft 1881.

Brace (brēⁱs), *sb.*[3] 1626. [a. F. *bras* (*de vergue*), assim. to prec.] *Naut.* A rope attached to the yard of a vessel for the purpose of trimming the sail. Also *attrib.*

Brace (brēⁱs), *v.*[1] ME. [ad. OF. *bracier*, f. *brace* the two arms; see also BRACE *sb.*[2]] †**1.** To embrace –1570. **2.** To encompass; also, *causally*, to make to surround 1513. **3.** To clasp, gird ME. **4.** To make tense; to stretch 1440. **5.** To string up (nerves, etc.), give tone to. Also with *up*. 1736. Also *fig.* **6.** To render firm or steady by binding tightly 1785. **b.** To fix, render firm 1849. Also *fig.* **7.** To couple together 1826.

2. Bigge Bulles of Basan b. hem about SPENSER. **3.** To b. armor on BRYANT. **4.** Their gluttony.. Brac'd like a drum her oily skin SWIFT. **5.** They gave you toils, but toils your sinews b. SHENSTONE. *To b. one's heart, energies*, etc.: to summon up resolution for a task. Hence **Braced** *ppl. a.* in various senses; *Her.* interlaced; var. *brased.*

†**Brace**, *v.*[2] 1447. [Cf. BRACE *v.*[1] (*esp.* sense 5).] To bluster; to assume a defiant attitude; chiefly in *to face and b.* –1563.

Brace (brēⁱs), *v.*[3] 1669. [f. BRACE *v.*[3]] To move or turn (a sail) by means of braces.

Phrases. *To b. about*: to turn the yards round for the contrary tack; *to b. by*, to b. (the yards) in contrary directions on the different masts; *to b. in*, to lay (the yards) less obliquely athwartships; *b. round* = *brace about*; *to b. to*, to ease the lee- and draw in (the weather-braces); *to b. up*, to put (the yards) into a more oblique position. Also *absol.* in these uses.

Bracelet (brēⁱ·slėt). ME. [a. OF., dim. of *bracel*:—L. *bra(c)chiale.*] **1.** An ornamental ring or band worn on the arm or wrist. †**2.** Any ornament of similar shape –1684. **3.** A handcuff 1816. **4.** A piece of armour covering the arm 1580. **5.** *Her.* = BARRULET.

2. About Christian's neck the Shepherds put a B. BUNYAN.

Bracer[1] (brēⁱ·səɹ). 1579. [f. BRACE *v.*[1] + -ER[1].] That which clamps, binds, etc.; a cincture, bandage, brace. **2.** That which braces; *hence* †a tonic (common in 18th c.) 1740.

Bracer[2]. ME. [a. OF. *brasseüre* (L. type **bracchiatura*), infl. by Fr. *brassard.*] The portion of a suit of armour covering the arm. Also a guard for the wrist in archery, etc.

†**Bracery.** 1540. *Eng. Law.* Embracery.

Braces; see BRACE *sb.*[2]

Brach (bræt∫). *arch.* [ME. *braches* pl., prob. a. OF. *brachès*, *brachez*, dim. of *brac*, a. OHG. *bracco.*] A kind of hound which hunts by scent; in later Eng. use, always fem. *fig.* A term of abuse. Cf. BITCH. B. JONS.

Brachelytrous (brǣke·litrəs), *a.* 1847. [f. mod.L. *brachelytra* (f. Gr. βραχύς + ἔλυτρον). *Brachyelytrous* would be more correct.] Pertaining to the *Brachelytra*, a division of beetles with short wing-sheaths.

Brachet (bræ·t∫ėt). *arch.* ME. [a. F. *brachet*, dim. of *brac*; see BRACH.] **1.** = BRACH. **2.** = BRATCHET.

Brachial (bræ·kiăl, brēⁱ·kiăl), *a.* 1578. [ad. L. *brachialis.*] **1.** Belonging to the arm; chiefly in *Phys.*, as in *b. vein, artery, nerve*, etc. Rare exc. techn. Also as quasi-*sb.* **2.** Of the nature of, or resembling, an arm 1835.

2. The mouth, surrounded by four b. appendages 1836.

Brachiate (bræ·kiˌeⁱt, brēⁱ·kiˌėt), *a.* 1835. [ad. L. *brachiatus.*] *lit.* Having arms; in *Bot.* having branches in pairs running out nearly at right angles with the stem and crossing each other alternately.

Brachiferous (brǣki·fĕrəs), *a.* 1877. [mod. f. L. *brachium.*] *Zool.* Arm-bearing. So **Brachi·gerous** *a.*

Brachio-cephalic (bræːkiˌoˌsifæ·lik), *a* 1836. [ad. mod.L. *brachiocephalicus*, f. Gr. βραχίων + κεφαλή.] *Anat.* Pertaining to both arm and head: used chiefly of blood-vessels.

Brachiopod (bræ·kiˌopǫd). Pl. **-pods**, also **-poda.** 1836. [ad. mod.L. *brachiopoda*, sb. pl. f. Gr. βραχίων + πούς, ποδ-.] *Zool.* A bivalve mollusc, having, on each side of the mouth, a long spiral arm, used in procuring food. Also *attrib.* Hence **Brachio·podist**, one versed in the study of brachiopods; **Brachio·podous** *a.*

Brachisto-, comb. f. Gr. βράχιστος, superl. of βραχύς short, hence:

‖**Brachi·sto-ce·phali**, men or races with the shortest skull; **-ce·phaly**, the quality of having the shortest type of skull; **-chrone** [Gr. χρόνος], the curve in which a body descending to a given point under the action of gravity will reach it in the shortest time.

‖**Brachium** (brēⁱ·kiŏm, bræ·kiŏm). 1731. [L.] *Biol.* In Mammalia, the upper arm from the shoulder to the elbow.

Brachman, obs. f. BRAHMIN.

Brachy-, comb. f. Gr. βραχύς short, hence: bra·chy-catale·ctic *a.*, *Pros.* wanting one foot or two syllables; **-ceral**, **-cerous** (sĕr) [Gr. κέρας] *a.*, *Ent.* having short horns or antennæ; **-dia·gonal** *a.*, *Cryst.* pertaining to the shorter lateral axis of a rectangular prism; also as *sb.*; **-dome**, *Cryst.* a prism whose face is parallel to the brachydiagonal axis; **-elytrous**, see BRACHELYTROUS; **-me·tropy**, near- or short-sightedness; **-pi·nacoid**, **-koid** [Gr. πίναξ] *a.*, *Cryst.* pertaining to either of the two planes which in the Orthorhombic system are parallel to the vertical and brachydiagonal axes respectively; **-pleu·ral** [Gr. πλευρά] *a.*, having short ribs; **-pterous** [Gr. πτερόν] *a.*, short-winged, as some diving-birds; **-typous** [Gr. τύπος] *a.*, *Min.* of a short form.

Brachycephalic (bræːkiˌsifæ·lik), *a.* Also **-kephalic.** 1849. [f. BRACHY- + Gr. κεφαλή.] *lit.* Short-headed: used in *Ethnology* of skulls in breadth at least four-fifths of the length; opp. to DOLICHOCEPHALIC. var. **Brachyce·phalous.**

Skulls with a cephalic index of 0·8, or more, are B. HUXLEY. So **Brachycephales**, **-cephali** [mod.L.], men with b. skulls. **Brachyce·phalism, Brachyce·phaly**, the condition of being b.

Brachygraphy (brǣki·grăfi). 1590. [a. F. *brachygraphie*, f. Gr. βραχύς + -γραφία.] = STENOGRAPHY. Also *attrib. Obs.* exc. as a name of old systems. Also *fig.*

Brachylogy (brǣki·lŏdʒi). 1623. [ad. Gr. βραχυλογία.] Laconism; *concr.* a condensed expression.

Brachyurous, -ourous (brǣkiˌūᵊ·rəs), *a.* 1828. [f. mod.L. *brachyura* (f. Gr. βραχύς + οὐρά).] *Zool.* Pertaining to the *Brachyura*, a tribe of Decapod Crustacea, characterized by the non-development of the abdomen or tail, including the crab, etc. So **Brachyu·ral, -ou·ral** *a.*, **Brachyu·ran, -ou·ran** *a* and *sb.*

Bracing (brēⁱ·siŋ), *vbl. sb.* 1536. [f. BRACE *v.*[1] + -ING[1].] **1.** The action of the vb. **2.** An appliance for tying, fastening, supporting, or strengthening (*lit.* and *fig.*) 1849.

Bracing, *ppl. a.* 1750. [f. BRACE *v.*[2] + -ING[2].] That braces, girds, etc. Now chiefly of the air or climate; formerly of tonics.

Brack (bræk), *sb.*[1] [Two formations; see below.] **I.** ME., f. ON. *brak*, f. OTeut. *brekan* to break; cf. L. *fragor*. †**1.** Noise, outcry. –1513. **II.** mod., f. BREAK *v.* †**1.** A breach, rupture –1669; *fig.* a quarrel –1608. **2.** A flaw in cloth 1552. †**3.** A fragment –1674. †**4.** Fault in mining 1747.

†**Brack**, *sb.*[2] *rare.* 1530. [Cf. connexion of *rupes* and *rumpere.*] A cliff, crag, or rock.

Brack, *sb.*[3] 1734. [f. Ger. *bracken* to sort goods.] The system of official sorting in vogue at Baltic ports.

†**Brack**, *sb.*[4] 1482. = BRACKEN[1] –1675.

Brack, *a.* and *sb.*[5] 1513. [prob. a. Du. *brak* brackish.] **A.** *adj.* Salt, brackish. ? *Obs.* †**B.** *sb.* Salt water, brine; the sea. DRAYTON.

Brack (bræk), *v.* 1858. [ad. Ger. *bracken*; see BRACK *sb.*[3]] To sort (goods, produce, etc.) (at the Baltic ports). Hence **Bra·cker**, a government sorter.

Bracken[1] (bræ·k'n). [ME. (north.) *braken*, repr. ON. **brakni*, whence Sw. *bräken* fern.] A fern; *spec. Pteris aquilina*, the 'Brake'. In southern writers often collective. Also *attrib.*

The commune Ferne or brake, which the northerne men cal a bracon TURNER. *Comb.* **b.-clock**, the Rose-beetle (*Phyllopertha horticola*).

†**Bra·cken**[2]. 1652. [ad. Gael. and Ir. *breacan*, f. *breac* chequered.] A tartan plaid –1828.

Bracket (bræ·kėt). 1580. [Orig. *bragget*, ad. Sp. *bragueta*, dim. of *braga*:—L. *braca*, sing. of *bracæ* breeches; the form *bracket* is a corruption. For the Eng. sense-development see N.E.D.] **1.** In *Building*, a piece of stone, wood, or metal projecting from a wall, and having a flat upper surface which serves to support a statue, the spring of an arch, a beam, shelf, etc.; usu. decorated, and sometimes merely a decoration. See CORBEL and CONSOLE. **b.** A small (ornamental) shelf for the wall of a room 1635. **2.** In *Carpentry, Shipbuilding*, etc.: A support consisting of two pieces of wood or metal joined at an angle. Also *attrib.* 1627. **3.** One of the two cheeks of a gun-carriage 1753. **4.** A (decorative) metal pipe projecting from the wall of a room, to support and supply the gas lamps or burners 1876. **5.** One of two marks [ ] or ( ), and in *Math.* also { }, used for enclosing a word or words, a portion of a formula, or the like, so as to separate it from the context. Occas. used (improp.) of the 'vinculum' and the 'brace' (cf. BRACKET *v.*); hence *brackets* (fig.), 'the position of being bracketed equal'. 1750.

1. The angel b. of an oriel window TURNER. **5.** [ ] Brackets or Crochets 1750. On a shorter course Regnard may earn brackets (*mod.*). *Comb.*: **b.-burner, -light,** = sense 4; **-crab,** a windlass attached to a wall or post; **-shelf.**

Bra·cket, *v.* 1861. [f. prec.] **1.** To provide with brackets; to enclose within brackets 1870. **2.** To connect by means of a brace; hence to mention together as equal, or as having something in common.

Bra·cketing, *vbl. sb.* 1823. [f. prec. + -ING[1].] **1.** The action of the vb. 1869. **2.** *Archit.* A skeleton, consisting of wooden ribs nailed to the ceiling, joists, and battening, to support a cornice, cove, or other moulding.

Brackish (bræ·ki∫), *a.* 1538. [f. BRACK *a.* + -ISH[1].] **1.** Of a somewhat salt taste; partly fresh, partly salt. **2.** *fig.* and *transf.* **a.** Spoilt by mixture. **b.** Nauseous. **c.** Nautical. 1611.

1. The southern wind with b. breath MARLOWE. **2.** The [English] language.. b. with the mixture of vulgar Irish SPEED. Hence **Bra·ckishness.**

Bra·ckmard. *Obs.* exc. *Hist.* 1653. [a. F. *braquemart.*] = CUTLASS.

†**Bra·cky**, *a.*[1] 1593. = BRACKISH –1603.

Bra·cky, *a.*[2] 1618. [f. *brack*, var. of BRAKE *sb.*[1] and [2].] **a.** Abounding in bracken. **b.** Of the nature of a thicket.

Bract (brækt). 1770. [ad. L. *bractea* (also used) a thin leaf of metal.] **1.** *Bot.* A small modified leaf, or scale, growing below the calyx of a plant, or upon the peduncle of a flower. Also *attrib.* **2.** A similar appendage found among Hydrozoa 1878. Hence **Bra·cteal** *a.* pertaining to, or like, bracts. **Bra·cted** *ppl. a.* furnished with bracts. **Bra·cteiform** *a.* b.-shaped. **Bra·cteolate, bracte·olate** *a.* furnished with bracteoles. **Bra·cteole**, a small b. **Bracteo·se** *a.* full of, or with conspicuous, bracts. **Bra·ctlet**, a minute or secondary b.

Bracteate (bræ·ktiˌėt). 1845. [ad. L. *bracteatus*; see BRACT.] **A.** *adj.* **1.** *Bot.* Having or bearing bracts. **2.** Formed of metal beaten thin; applied to coins, medals, etc. **B.** *sb.* A bracteate coin or medal; also *attrib.* 1845.

Brad (bræd). ME. [var. of BROD.] **1.** A thin flattish nail of the same thickness throughout, but tapering in width, having a small lip on one edge, instead of a head. **2.** *pl.* Halfpence; money (*slang*) 1812. Hence **Brad** *v.* to fasten with brads.

Bradawl (bræ·dǫl). 1823. [app. f. BRAD *sb.* + AWL.] A small boring tool, a sprig-bit.

Bradoon, obs. f. BRIDOON.

†**Bradypepsy** (bræ·dipe:psi), **-pe·psia.** 1598. [ad. Gr., f. βραδύς + πέψις.] Slowness of digestion -1710.

Bradypod, -pus (bræ·dipǫd, -pǒs). 1833. [ad. Gr., f. βραδύς + πούς.] One of the family of edentate mammals represented by the Sloth. Hence **Brady·podal** *a.*

Brae (brē, *dial.* brē, brīᵊ, brī). Now *Sc.* and *n. dial.* ME. [a. ON. *brá* = OE. *bræ̂w, bréaw* eyelid :—OTeut. **brǣwâ*; cf. BROW and BREE.] **1.** The steep bank bounding a river valley. **2.** A steep, a slope, a hill-side. (= *hill* in Ludgate Hill.) ME. vars. (*dial.*) **brea, breea.**

Brag (bræg), *sb.* ME. [Origin unkn. The related Fr. wds. are later than the Eng. wds. See Diez, Wedgwood, Skeat.] †**1.** The bray of a trumpet 1513. **2.** Arrogant or boastful language; boasting ME. †**3.** Show; pompous demeanour -1632. **4.** *concr.* That which is boasted of 1538. **5.** A braggart 1671. **6.** A game at cards, essentially = 'poker' 1734. Also *fig.* with a reference to sense 2.

2. Cesars Thrasonicall bragge of I came, saw, and ouercame SHAKS. **4.** Beauty is nature's b. MILT.

†**Brag** (bræg), *a.* and quasi-*adv.* ME. [See BRAG *sb.*[1]] **1.** Brisk, mettlesome, valiant -1610. **2.** Boastful (*of*) -1655. **3.** as quasi-*adv.* Boastfully -1579.

Brag (bræg), *v.* ME. [See BRAG *sb.*[1]] †**1.** *intr.* Of a trumpet: To sound loudly; also, to make a loud sound (with a trumpet); *trans.* to sound (a trumpet). ME. only. **2.** *intr.* and *refl.* To talk boastfully, boast oneself. Const. *of, about.* ME. **3.** *trans.* **a.** To challenge; also, to bully. Now *dial.* 1551. **b.** To overawe by boasting (*mod.*). **4.** To vaunt, lay boastful claim to 1588. **5.** To boast. With *subord. cl.* 1563.

2. If I see a Man boast and b. himself, I cannot but deem him a Proud Man 1543. **4.** He brags his seruice *Cymb.* v. iii. 93. Hence **Bra·gger. Bra·ggery,** bragging; †rabble (*rare*).

Braggadocio (brægădōu·ʃio), *sb.* (and *a.*) 1590. [f. BRAG, after It. augmentatives in *-occhio, -occio*; see SPENSER *F. Q.* II. iii.] **1.** An empty idle boaster; a swaggerer 1594. **2.** Empty vaunting 1734. Also *attrib.*

1. He..had much of the sycophant, alternating with b. CARLYLE. **2.** Half blunder, half b. SOUTHEY. Hence †**Braggado·cian** *a.* of the nature of a b.; *sb.* = BRAGGADOCIO.

Braggart (bræ·gărt). 1577. [a. 16th c. F. *bragard*, f. *braguer.*] **A.** *sb.* A vain bragger. **B.** *adj.* Vainly boastful 1613. Hence **Bra·ggartism,** the practice of a b. **Bra·ggartly** *adv.*

Bragget (bræ·gėt). ME. [a. Welsh *bragawd* :—OCelt. **brăcāta*, f. Pliny's *bracem*, a kind of grain.] A drink made of honey and ale fermented together; latterly of sugar and spice and ale. *attrib.* in *Braggot Sunday.*

Bra·gless, *a.* [f. BRAG *sb.*[1] + -LESS.] Without brag. *Tr. & Cr.* v. ix. 5.

†**Bra·gly,** *adv.* 1759. [f. BRAG *a.* + -LY [2].] Briskly -1717.

Brahm, Brahma (brām, brā·mă). 1785. [ad. Skr., *Brahmā* masc., *Brahma* neut., nom. of *Brahman.*] **a.** The supreme God of post-Vedic Hindu mythology. **b.** In the later pantheistic systems, the Divine reality, of which all else is only a manifestation. Hence **Bra·hmahood,** the state of Brahma; absorption into the divine essence.

Brahma, shortened f. BRAHMAPOOTRA.

Brahman, etc.; see BRAHMIN, etc.

Brahmapootra (brāmăpū·tră). 1851. A variety of domestic fowl, brought from Lakhimpur on the River Brahmaputra, in 1846; now abbrev. *Brahma.*

Brahmic (brā·mik), *a.* 1582. [f. Skr. *brahma*, comb. f. BRAHMAN + -IC.] Pertaining to the Indian society called Brahmo Somāj, or to the older Brahma Sabhā.

Brahmin, Brahman (brā·min, -măn). 1481. [ad. Skr. *brahmana*, f. *brahman* praise, worship; *Brahmin* is general in pop. use; latterly writers have used the more correct *Brahman.* (Usu. w. capital B.)] A member of the highest or priestly caste among the Hindus. Also *fig.*

Other peple whiche ben callyd..bragman whiche ben fayrer than they to fore named CAXTON.

Comb.: **B.-beads,** the corrugated seeds of *Elæocarpus*, used by the Brahmins and others as necklaces; **-ox,** a humped variety of the ox. Hence **Brahminee·**, a female b. **Brahmi·nic, -al, -ma·nic, -al,** *a.* **Brahmi·nicide, -ma·nicide,** one who has killed, or the act of killing, a B. **Brah·minism, -manism,** the principles and practice of Brahmins.

Brahminee (brā·minī), *a.* Also **Brahminy.** 1811. [f. BRAHMIN; cf. *Bengalee*, etc.] Pertaining to the Brahmin caste; appropriated to the Brahmins. *B. bull* = Brahmin ox; *B. duck*, the *Casarca rutila*; *B. fig-tree*, the Banyan; *B. kite*, the *Haliastur Indicus.*

Brahmism (brā·miz'm). 1813. [f. BRAHM.] †**a.** The religion of Brahma. **b.** The tenets of the Indian society called Brahma Sabhā, or of the more recent Brahmo Somāj. In the last sense also **Brahmoism.**

Braid (brēɪd), *sb.* [Partly :—OE. *brægd-* = ON. *bragð* :—OTeut. *bragdo-m*, f. str. vb. **bregdan*, *bragd* (see BRAID *v.*[1]), and partly aphet. f. OE. *gebregd.*] †**1.** A sudden movement (*lit.* and *fig.*); a start; a strain -1626. Also †*fig.* †**2.** *transf.* A moment -1657. †**3.** An adroit turn; a trick -1570. **4.** Anything plaited or interwoven; *esp.* A plait of human hair 1530. **5.** A woven fabric of silken, woollen, cotton, gold, or silver thread in the form of a band, used for trimming or binding dress 1706.

5. A chain of gold ye sall not lack Nor b. to bind your hair SCOTT.

†**Braid,** *a. rare.* [?] ? Deceitful. *All's Well* IV. ii. 73.

Braid (brēɪd), *v.*[1] [Com. Teut.: OE. *bregdan* :—OTeut. **bregdan* 'to pull quickly hither and thither, to move suddenly to and fro'.] †**1.** *trans.* To make a sudden movement with (the hand, foot, etc.); to brandish; to deal (a blow); to draw (a sword, etc.); to jerk, snatch, wrench, fling, etc. with a sudden effort -1505. †**2.** *intr.* To start, as out of a sleep, etc.; to break forth abruptly into speech, or crying -1603. †**3.** *intr.* To change suddenly or abruptly -ME. **4.** To twist in and out, interweave, plait; to embroider; to make by plaiting. (Now *poet.* or *dial.*, exc. as used of the hair in the sense 'to arrange in braids'.) OE. Also *transf.* **5.** [f. BRAID *sb.* 5.] To bind (the hair) with a ribbon or the like 1793. **6. a.** To trim with braid. **b.** To outline (a design for point-lace work) by means of braid. **c.** To manufacture braid. 1848.

2. ffor verray wo out of his wit he breyde CHAUCER. **5.** To pull the thorn thy brow to b. SCOTT. Hence **Brai·ding** *vbl. sb.* braids collectively; braided work.

†**Braid,** *v.*[2] ME. ? Aphet. f. UPBRAID -1608.

Braid, obs. and Sc. f. BROAD.

Braider (brēɪ·dəɪ). 1866. [f. BRAID *v.*[1]] One who or that which makes or applies braids.

Braidism (brēɪ·diz'm). 1882. *Med.* Applied to a process of inducing sleep or trance, orig. called MESMERISM, to which Dr. James Braid, who first scientifically applied and explained it in 1842, gave the name HYPNOTISM, q.v.

Brail (brēɪl), *sb.* 1450. [a. OF., earlier *braiel* :—L. *bracale*, f. *bracæ* breeches.] **1.** *pl.* Small ropes fastened to the edges of sails to truss them up before furling. **2.** A girdle for confining a hawk's wing 1828. **3.** *pl.* The feathers about a hawk's rump 1486.

Brail (brēɪl), *v.* 1625. [f. BRAIL *sb.*] *trans.* **1.** To haul *up* (sails) by means of brails. **2.** To confine (a hawk's wings) with a brail 1643.

Braille (brēɪl). 1871. [f. the name of Louis *Braille*, French inventor, 1834.] A system of embossed printing or writing for the blind, in which the characters are represented by tangible points or dots.

Brain (brēɪn), *sb.* [OE. *bræg(e)n* :—OTeut. type **bragno(m)*, perh. conn. w. Gr. βρεχμός forehead.] **1.** The convoluted mass of nervous substance contained in the skull of man and other vertebrates. Formerly restricted to the anterior portion (L. *cerebrum*), as opp. to the posterior portion (L. *cerebellum*); but now used of the entire organ, and extended to the analogous organs of invertebrates. When mere cerebral substance is meant, the pl. is used. **2.** Taken as the seat of sensation, the organ of thought, memory, or imagination. (Usually pl., exc. in dignified language.) ME. **3.** *fig.* Intellectual power, intellect, sense, thought, imagination. (Often pl.) ME.

1. Betwene the brayne and Cerebellum 1578. Ile haue my braines tane out and butter'd *Merry W.* III. v. 7. Phr. *To dash, knock out, blow out* (*any*) *one's brains.* **2.** Was that plan the conception of any one b. STUBBS. **3.** The uncommon gift of brains CHURCHILL.

Phrases. **a.** (sense 2) *To beat, busy, cudgel, drag, puzzle one's brains*: to exert oneself in thinking or contriving. *To have* anything *on the b.*: to be crazy about. *To turn one's b.*: to render giddy, hence *fig.* to render vain or imprudent. **b.** (sense 3) *To suck* (or *pick*) *a person's brains*: to elicit and appropriate the results of his thought.

Comb.: **b.-box, -case, -pan,** the skull; **-cell,** one of the cells forming the tissue of the b.; **-coral,** coral resembling in form the convolutions of the b.; **-fag,** brain weariness; **-fever,** a term for inflammation of the brain, and fevers with brain complications; **-stone** = *brain-coral*; **-tunic,** a membrane enveloping the b.; **-wave,** *colloq.*, a sudden inspiration or bright thought; **-worm,** a worm infesting the b.; *fig.* a wriggling disputant MILT.

Hence **Brai·nish** *a. arch.* passionate, headstrong. **Brai·nless** *a.* devoid of b.; that has had the b. removed; †insane; irrational; wanting intelligence or self-control. **Brai·nless-ly** *adv.*, **-ness.** †**Brai·nlet,** the cerebellum. **Brai·ny** *a.* having brains; acute, clever.

Brain (brēɪn), *v.* ME. [f. the sb.] **1.** *trans.* To dash (any one's) brains out; to kill by dashing out the brains. Also *fig.* SHAKS. †**2.** To conceive in the brain. *Cymb.* V. iv. 147. **3.** To furnish with a brain 1882.

1. Most cruelly murder'd, by being brain'd like an Ox WOOD. Hence **Brained** *a.*, as *addle-brained.*

Brainsick (brēɪ·nsik), *a.* 1483. [f. BRAIN *sb.*] **1.** Diseased in the brain or mind; addle-headed, mad, frantic. **2.** Proceeding from a diseased mind 1571. Hence **Brainsick-ly** *adv.*, **-ness.**

Braird (brēᵊrd), *sb. Sc.* 1450. [= BRERD.] The first shoots of grass, corn, etc. Hence **Braird** *v.* to sprout.

Braise (brēɪz), *v.* 1797. [a. F. *braiser*, f. *braise* hot charcoal.] To cook *à la braise*; i.e. to stew in a tightly-closed pan (prop. with hot charcoal above and below). Hence **Braise** *sb.* braised meat. **Brai·ser** [partly ad. F. *braisière*]. var. **Braize.**

Brake (brēɪk), *sb.*[1] [ME., perh. south. form of north. *bracken*, taken for a pl.; cf. *chick, chicken.*] Fern, bracken.

Brake (brēɪk), *sb.*[2] 1440. [conn. w. MLG. *brake*, occas. used in the same sense.] A clump of bushes, brushwood, or briers; a thicket. Also *attrib.*

So thick entwin'd, As one continu'd b., the undergrowth Of shrubs MILT. *P. L.* iv. 175.

Brake (brēɪk), *sb.*[3] ME. [= MLG. *brake*, or ODu. *braeke*, f. Du. *breken* to BREAK.] **1.** A toothed instrument for braking flax or hemp 1450. **2.** A baker's kneading-machine 1440. **3.** A heavy harrow for crushing clods; a *b.-harrow* 1785. **4.** An instrument for peeling the bark from willows 1824.

Brake (brēɪk), *sb.*[4] ME. [perh. a. OF. *brac*, oblique case of *bras.*] A lever or handle for working a machine; *e.g.* †the winch of a cross-bow (whence, a crossbow, etc.), the handle of a pump, part of an apparatus for boring coal. *Comb.* **b.-pump,** a pump worked by a b.

†**Brake,** *sb.*[5] 1430. [prob. a. ODu. *braeke* (see BRAKE *sb.*[3]).] A bridle or curb -1753.

Brake, *sb.*[6] 1529. [?] †**1.** A cage; a trap; *fig.* a difficulty -1640. **2.** A framework intended to hold anything steady, *e.g.* a horse's foot while being shod 1609. **3.** An instrument of torture. *Hist.* 1530. †**4.** A turner's lathe -1609.

2. *To set one's face in a b.*: to assume an immovable expression of countenance.

Brake, break (brēɪk), *sb.*[7] 1772. [prob. a use of BRAKE *sb.*[4] or [5].] An apparatus for retarding or arresting the motion of any mechanism, as a vehicle, engine, etc.; *esp.* a device including a block or shoe, a lever, or band applied to the rim of a wheel, etc., or a shoe or ratchet applied to the track or roadway.

Comb.: **b.-compartment, -van,** the compartment or the carriage which contains the b. apparatus; **-wheel,** the wheel by which the brakes are worked. Hence **Brakeless** *a.*

Brake, *v.*[1] ME. [f. BRAKE *sb.*[3]] **1.** To beat and crush flax, hemp, etc. **2.** To break (clods) with a harrow 1800. **3.** To knead (dough) 1832.

†**Brake,** *v.*[2] 1530. [f. BRAKE *sb.*[6] 3.] To torture on the rack.

Brake, *v.*[3] 1857. [f. BRAKE *sb.*[4]] *intr.* To attend to a winding engine.

Brake, *v.*[4] 1868. [f. BRAKE *sb.*[7]] To apply a brake to; also *transf.*

†**Brake,** *v.*[5] ME. [allied to BREAK (cf. Ger. *sich brechen*).] *trans.* and *intr.* To spue, vomit –1768.

Brake (brēⁱk), arch. pa. t. of BREAK.

Brakesman (brēⁱ·ksmæ̆n). 1851. [f. BRAKE *sb.*[4] and [7].] **1.** *Coal-mining.* A man who attends to the winding-machine. **2.** The man in charge of the brake-apparatus of a railway-train; in U. S. (*brakeman*) the guard.

Braky (brēⁱ·ki), *a.* 1636. [f. BRAKE *sb.*[1] or [2] + -Y.] Overgrown with brushwood or fern.

Bramah (prop. bræ·mă, often brā·mă). 1836. [f. Joseph *Bramah* (1749–1814).] Attrib. use of proper name, = 'invented by Bramah'; as *B.-key, -lock, -pen*; **Bramah's press,** a hydraulic press of enormous power.

Bramantip. *Logic.* A mnemonic word, repr. the first mood of the fourth syllogistic figure, in which two universal affirmative premisses yield a particular affirmative conclusion.

Bramble (bræ·mb'l). [OE. *brembel, bræmbel*, later form (with euphonic *b*) of *bremel, bræmel*:—OTeut. type **brǣmilo-z*, dim. of the word represented in OE. *brōm* BROOM. See BROOM.] A rough prickly shrub; *spec.* the blackberry bush (*Rubus fruticosus*) OE.

Their defenceless Limbs the brambles tear DRYDEN.

Comb.: **b.-berry,** the fruit of the b.; a blackberry; **-brand,** a fungus (*Aregma rubi*) which appears on the b.; **-flower,** the blossom of a b.; also the Dog-rose (*Rosa canina*); **-rose,** the white trailing dog-rose. Hence **Bra·mbled** *ppl. a.* covered with brambles. **Bra·mbly** *a.*

Brambling (bræ·mbliŋ). 1570. [= Ger. *brämling*, prob. f. WGer. **brāma* BRAMBLE.] The Mountain Finch (*Fringilla montifringilla*).

†**Brame.** [?ad. It. *brama*.] Longing. SPENSER.

Bran[1] (bræn). ME. [a. OF. *bren, bran.* The Celtic wds. quoted as the source are from Fr. and Eng.] **1.** The husk of wheat, barley, oats, etc., separated from the flour after grinding; *techn.*, the coarsest portion of this. Also *fig.* and *transf.* 1577. †**2.** Scurf in the hair –1580.

1. In stide of flour yet wol I yeue hem bren CHAUCER.

†**Bran**[2]. 1610. [prob. special use of prec.; cf. L. *ejusdem farinæ*.] Sort, class, quality –1672.

Bran (bræn), *v.* [f. BRAN *sb.*[1]] *trans.* To clear maddered goods by boiling in bran-water.

Brancard (bræ·ŋkăɹd). 1592. [a. F., f. *branche*.] A horse-litter.

Branch (brɑnʃ), *sb.* ME. [a. F. *branche*:—late L. *branca* paw of an animal.] **1.** A portion or limb of a tree or other plant growing out of the stem or trunk, or out of one of the boughs. (A *branch* is smaller than a bough and larger than a shoot or spray.) **2.** *transf.* Anything analogous to a limb of a tree, in relation to the trunk ME. **3.** *fig.* **a.** One of the portions into which a family or race is divided according to the differing lines of descent from a common ancestor; hence a division, a group ME. **b.** A child, descendant; cf. *scion*. Now only *joc.* 1535. **4.** *fig.* A consequence of a principle; an effect of a cause 1526. **5.** *fig.* A division; a subdivision; a department 1509. **6.** *fig.* A component portion of an organization or system 1696. **7.** *fig.* A local and subordinate office of business 1817. **8.** The certificate of competency given by the Trinity House to pilots 1865. **9.** *attrib.* Having the character of a branch, as *b.-line* (of railway), *b. bank, -office*, etc.

1. As the sprai cometh out of the braunche, the braunche out of the bouȝ PECOCK. 2. A b. of Mount Atlas 1603, of the aorta 1831, of the Great Northern (*mod.*). 3. a. Minyans..a b. of the Greek nation THIRLWALL. 5. Fidelity..a b. of naturall Justice HOBBES. A b. of the prerogative CLARENDON, of Trade STEELE, learning SWIFT, revenue HUME, of a statute 1542, of discourse 1783, of a will 1818. 6. *B. of the legislature*, one of the houses or chambers into which the legislative body is divided.

Phr. *To destroy* (*anything*) *root and b.*: to destroy both the thing itself and all its effects; orig. suggested by the wording (derived from *Mal.* iv. 1) of the London Petition of Dec. 11, 1640, for the total abolition of episcopal government. Hence *Root-and-b. petition, bill, party*; also gen. *root and b. policy*, a radical and destructive policy.

Comb.: **b.-building** *a.*, building in branches; **-chuck** (*Mech.*), a chuck having four branches, and furnished with screws; **-coal,** anthracite (*local*); **-pilot,** one who holds a Trinity House certificate; **b. wines** (Pg. *vinos de ramo*), wines made for home consumption; **-work,** ornamental figured patterns. Hence **Bra·nchery,** branches in the mass. **Bra·nchless** *a.* **Bra·nchlet,** a little branch; in *Bot.* a smaller b. growing from a larger one.

Branch, *v.* ME. [f. prec. sb.: cf. F. *brancher*.] **I.** *intr.* **1.** To put forth branches; occas. with *forth, out.* Also *transf.* and *fig.* **2.** To spring out, as a branch or branches; to strike off in a new path; now chiefly with *out, off*, occas. *away* ME.

1. What subject does not b. out to infinity BURKE. 2. The Foss Way..branched off from the Eastern gate FREEMAN.

II. *trans.* **1.** To divide (anything) into branches 1700. Also *fig.* **2.** To embroider with work representing flowers or branches 1596.

2. A dress All branch'd and flower'd with gold TENNYSON.

Branched (brɑnʃt), *ppl. a.* ME. [f. BRANCH *sb.* and *v.*] **1.** Provided with branches (*lit.* and *fig.*). Often in *comb.* **2.** Adorned with a figured pattern. Cf. BRANCH *v.* II. 2. 1509.

Brancher[1] (brɑ·nʃəɹ). 1610. [f. BRANCH *v.* + -ER[1].] That which puts forth branches.

Brancher[2]. ME. [a. AF. **brancher* = F. *branchier*.] A young hawk, etc., when it first leaves the nest and takes to the branches.

‖**Branchiæ, branchia** (bræ·ŋkiˌī, bræ·ŋkiă), *sb. pl.* ME. [L., ad. Gr. βράγχια.] The organs of respiration in fishes, etc.; gills. Hence **Bra·nchial** *a.* pertaining to, of the nature of, or resembling gills. **Bra·nchiate, -ated** *a.* having gills. **Branchi·ferous** *a.* bearing gills. **Bra·nchiform** *a.* like gills.

Branching (brɑ·nʃiŋ), *vbl. sb.* 1578. [f. BRANCH *v.* + -ING[1].] The action of the vb.; *concr.* a collection of branches. Also *fig.*

Bra·nching, *ppl. a.* ME. [f. as prec. + -ING[2].] **1.** That branches. **2.** Spreading, ramifying, diverging; also, rambling 1720. **3.** Antlered 1667.

Branchio- (bræ·ŋkiˌo), also erron. **brancho-,** comb. f. Gr. βράγχια gills:

branchio-a·nal *a.*, pertaining to the branchiæ and anus; **-ca·rdiac** *a.*, belonging to the gills and heart; **-ga·steropod,** *pl.* **-poda, -pods,** a gasteropod which breathes air through water; also, any gasteropod; **-pa·llial** *a.*, pertaining to the gills and mantle of molluscs; **-pari·etal** *a.*, pertaining to the gills and wall of the atrium (of molluscs).

Branchiopod (bræ·ŋkiˌǒpǫd). Pl. **-opods, -opoda** (-ǫ·pŏdă). 1826. [f. BRANCHIO- + Gr. πούς, ποδ-.] *lit.* 'Gill-footed', — one of the Crustacean order distinguished by having the gills upon the feet. Also *attrib.* Hence **Branchio·podous** *a.*

Branchiostegal (bræŋkiˌǫ·stĭgăl), *a.* 1749. [f. BRANCHIOSTEGE + -AL.] **1.** Pertaining to the membrane which protects a gill chamber; covering the gills. **2.** quasi-*sb.* for *b. ray* 1849.

Branchiostegan (bræŋkiˌǫ·stĭgăn). 1847. [f. mod.L. *branchiostegi* (cf. next) + -AN.] A member of the *Branchiostegi*, an old order of fishes having free gills covered by a membrane.

Branchiostege (bræ·ŋkiˌostīdʒ), *a.* 1748. [a. F., f. BRANCHIO- + Gr. στέγειν.] Covering the gills. Hence **Branchio·stegite,** the membrane covering the gills; **Branchio·stegous** *a.* = BRANCHIOSTEGAL.

Branchiostomous (bræŋkiˌǫ·stŏməs), *a.* 1881. [f. BRANCHIO- + Gr. -στομος + -OUS.] Having the gills in connexion with the mouth.

Branchireme (bræ·ŋkirīm). 1835. [f. L. *branchiæ* + *remus*.] An organ in branchiopods both for respiration and for locomotion.

Branchy (brɑ·nʃi), *a.* ME. [f. BRANCH *sb.*] Bearing branches; full of, or consisting of branches. Also *transf.* Hence **Bra·nchiness.**

Brand (brænd), *sb.* [Com. Teut.: OE. *brand, brǫnd*:—OTeut. **brando-z*, f. *bran-* pret. stem of **brinnan* to BURN.] †**1.** Burning –ME. **2.** A piece of wood that is or has been burning on the hearth; *poet.* a torch, a linstock; also *fig.* and *transf.* OE. **3.** The mark made by burning with a hot iron 1552; hence **b.** *fig.* a mark (usu. of infamy) 1597; **c.** a trade-mark 1827. **4.** A branding-iron 1828. **5.** (*transf.* from 3 c.) A class of goods 1854. **6.** A kind of blight in plants; called also BURN (cf. Ger. *brand*) 1639. **7.** †The blade of a sword, etc. –ME.; hence, a sword. [Perh. from its flashing in the light.] OE.

2. The brands of one of their fires were still smoking W. IRVING. *A b. from the burning* (see *Zech.* iii. 2): a person delivered from imminent danger. *God's b.*: the lightning. *Phœbus' b.*: the burning rays of the sun. (With a blending of sense 7.) 3. The b. of error HOOKER. 7. Th' Eastern side..Of Paradise..Wav'd over by that flaming B. MILT. *P. L.* xii. 643.

Brand (brænd), *v.* ME. [f. prec.] **1.** *trans.* To burn with a hot iron, whether for marking or cauterizing; also *fig.* **2.** To mark indelibly, as a proof of ownership, a sign of quality, etc.; to impress (a device, etc.) by way of brand 1587. **b.** *fig.* To impress indelibly on one's memory 1602. **3.** *fig.* To stamp with infamy 1625.

2. Thou wouldest that God should at leastwise brond him with the broade arrow GOLDING. 3. They..intended by some Vote to B. him, and make him odious CLARENDON.

Bra·nded, *ppl. a. Obs.* exc. *dial.* 1561. [north. var. of *brended*, BRINDED.] Brindled.

Bran-deer. Adaptation of Ger. *brandhirsch*, a stag with dark-brown breast. GOLDSM.

†**Bra·ndenburgh.** 1676. [f. *Brandenburg* in Prussia.] A morning gown –1691.

†**Bra·ndenburgs.** 1753. [See prec.] *pl.* The ornamental facings to the breast of an officer's coat –1691.

Bra·nder, *sb.*[1] 1860. [f. BRAND *v.* + -ER.] One who brands.

Bra·nder, *sb.*[2] Now *Sc.* and *n. dial.* 1450. [var. of BRAND-IRON.] A gridiron. Hence **Bra·nder** *v.* to cook on the b., grill. Prob. also, 'To arrange cross-bars in the form of a gridiron'; whence **Bra·ndering** *vbl. sb.* the covering (of joists) with battens for plastering.

Brand-goose; see BRANT *sb.*

Brandied (bræ·ndid), *ppl. a.* 1833. [f. BRANDY *v.*] Mixed, treated, or fortified with brandy.

Bra·ndi·ron. *Obs.* exc. *dial.* ME. [f. BRAND + IRON.] **1.** A gridiron; used also of andirons, a stand for a kettle, a trivet. See BRANDER *sb.*[2] **2.** In Spenser and Quarles: A sword.

Bra·ndise. Now *dial.* [OE. *brand-īsen*.] Perh. = BRANDIRON.

Brandish (bræ·ndiʃ), *v.* ME. [a. F. *brandiss-, brandir*, f. Teut. BRAND, a sword.] **1.** To wave about (a sword, etc.) by way of threat or display, or in preparation for action. Also *fig.* **b.** To flourish about (the limbs, the head, etc.) (*arch.*) ME. Also *absol.* **2.** *intr.* (for *refl.*) = to be brandished 1649. †**3.** *trans.* To dart forth (rays of light); *occ.*, to irradiate –1656. †**b.** *intr.* To glitter, gleam.

1. I shall b. my sword before them *Ezek.* xxxii. 10. *fig.* Lawes which they so impotently b. against others MILT. Hence **Bra·ndish** *sb.* an act of brandishing. **Bra·ndisher.**

†**Bra·ndle,** *v.* 1606. [ad. F. *branler*; the *d* is inserted.] To shake. Also *intr.* –1655.

Brandling (bræ·ndliŋ). 1651. [f. BRAND *sb.* + -LING; from the colour or markings.] **1.** A red worm, used as bait by anglers. **2.** *dial.* A salmon parr 1730.

Brand-mark (bræ·nd-māɹk). 1655. The mark left by a branding-iron: also *fig.*

Brand-new, bran- (bræ·nd-, bræ·nˌniū·), *a.* 1570. [f. BRAND *sb.*; cf. Shakspere's *fire-new*. Now usu. *bran-*.] Quite new, perfectly new.

†**Bra·ndon.** *rare.* 1649. [a. F.] A torch (*lit.* and *fig.*).

Brandreth (bræ·ndrėþ). ME. [a. ON. *brandreið* a grate, f. *brandr* burning + *reið* vehicle.] **1.** A gridiron; an iron tripod or trivet. Now *dial.* **2.** A framework of wood, as a stand for a cask, or for a hay-rick; a substructure of piles to support a house; a rail round a well 1483.

Brandy (bræ·ndi), *sb.* 1657. [orig. *brandwine, brandewine*, a. Du. *brandewijn* 'burnt' (i. e. distilled) wine. In the full form taken latterly as = *brandy* + *wine*.] Prop. an ardent spirit distilled from wine or grapes; but also a name for other similar spirits.

Comb.: **b.-ball,** a kind of sweet; †**-cherry** = cherry brandy; so **-peach,** etc.; **-snap,** wafer-like gingerbread.

Brandy-bottle (bræ·ndi-bǫ·t'l), *sb.* 1676. **1.** A bottle (for) containing brandy; also *fig.* **2.** *Bot.* The Yellow Water-lily (*Nuphar luteum*) 1846.

Brandy-pawnee (bræ·ndi,pǭ·ni). 1816. [f. BRANDY + Hind. *pānī* water; a camp wd.] Brandy-and-water.

Bra·ngle, *sb. Obs.* exc. *dial.* 1600. [f. BRANGLE *v.*[2]] A brawl, wrangle.

Bra·ngle, *v. Obs.* or *arch.* 1553. [perh. var. of BRANLE *v.*, modified by WRANGLE, etc.] *intr.* To wrangle. Hence **Bra·nglement. †Bra·ngler.**

Brank, *sb.*[1] *dial.* 1577. [?] Buckwheat.

†Brank (bræŋk), *v.*[1] *Sc.* 1574. [app. f. *brank*, sing. of BRANKS.] To bridle, restrain; to put in the branks. Also *fig.* -1664.

†Brank, *v.*[2] *Sc.* and *dial.* ME. [?] **1.** *intr.* Of horses: To prance -1513. **2.** Of persons: To strut; to prank 1550.

†Brank(e. [a. OF. *branc.*] A sword. CAXTON.

Branks (bræŋks). Rare sing. **brank**; also as sing. *a branks.* 1595. [?] **1.** A scold's bridle; an instrument of punishment, consisting of an iron framework for the head, having a sharp metal gag which restrained the tongue. **2.** A sort of wooden muzzle, used as a bridle 1657. **3.** The mumps 1794.

Brank-ursine (bræŋk,ɒ̄·ɹsin). 1551. [ad. med. L. *branca ursina*, lit. 'bear's claw'.] Bear's breech, Acanthus. Erron. used of the Cow-parsnip (*Heracleum Sphondylium.*)

†Bra·nle, *sb.* 1581. [a. F.] **1.** Wavering, ?confusion. **2.** One of several dances of French origin; the music for it -1820.

†Bra·nle, *v. rare.* [a. F. *branler.*] To agitate, toss about. JER. TAYLOR.

Bran-new; see BRAND-NEW.

Branny (bræ·ni), *a.* 1533. [f. BRAN *sb.*[1]] Consisting of, abounding in, or resembling bran.

†Bra·nsle. 1596. [a. F., var. of *branle.*] = BRANLE *sb.* 1, 2. -1829.

Brant (brænt), *sb.* (Also BRENT, q.v.) 1544. [?] The smallest species of wild goose (*Bernicla brenta*). Formerly confounded with the Barnacle-goose. Also **Brant-goose.**

Brant (brænt). [OE. *brant*, *brǫnt* 'high, steep'. Still n. dial.: in Sc. BRENT, q. v.] **A.** *adj.* **1.** Lofty, steep, sheer. **†2.** Of the forehead: Unwrinkled -1483. **†B.** *adv.* Straight, straight up; steeply -1544.

†Bra·ntcorn. 1578. [cf. BRAND *sb.* 6.] Smut (*Uredo segetum*) -1646.

Brant-fox (bræ·nt,fǫks). 1864. [ad. Ger. *brand-fuchs*, ? from the colour.] A variety of fox, having much black in its fur. (Dicts.)

†Bra·ntle. [var. of BRANDLE.] = BRANLE *sb.* 2. PEPYS.

Bra·nular, *a. rare.* [A spurious formation from BRAIN.] Pertaining to or affecting the brain. I. TAYLOR.

Braquemard; see BRACKMARD.

Brasen, obs. f. BRAZEN.

‖**Bra·sero.** 1652. [Sp.] = BRAZIER[2].

Brash (bræʃ), *sb.*[1] Chiefly *dial.* 1573. [perh. echoic.] **†1.** An attack; a bout. *Sc.* and *n. dial.* -1724. **2.** A slight attack of sickness; *esp.* one arising from a disorder of the alimentary canal. Hence *teething-b.*, *weaning-b.* 1785. **3.** An eruption of fluid; as *water-b.*, pyrosis; a sudden dash of rain 1811.

Brash, *sb.*[2] 1722. [perh. corrupt f. F. *brèche*; cf. It. *breccia.*] A mass of fragments, as of rubble, crushed ice, hedge-clippings, etc.

Brash (bræʃ), *a.*[1] Now *U.S.* [perh. echoic.] Fragile, brittle: used chiefly of timber.

Brash, *a.*[2] *dial.* 1824. [? conn. w. prec.] Rash, impetuous.

†Brash, *v.* 1565. [Cf. BRASH *sb.*[1], also BRUSH *v.*[2]] To assault; to breach. Also *fig.* -1638.

Brashy (bræ·ʃi), *a.*[1] [f. BRASH *sb.*[2] + -Y[1].] Broken, crumbly, fragmentary.

Bra·shy, *a.*[2] *Sc.* 1805. [f. BRASH *sb.*[1] 3.] Showery.

Brasier(e, obs. f. BRAZIER.

Brasil, -sile, -sill, obs. ff. BRAZIL.

Brasque (brask). 1871. [a. F.; conn. w. *braser* to solder (Littré).] 'A lining for crucibles and furnaces; generally, a compound of clay, etc. with charcoal dust' (Raymond).

Brass (bras), *sb.* [OE. *bræs*: not found elsewhere.] **1.** *Hist.*: Any alloy of copper with tin or zinc (and occas. other base metals). **b.** In mod. use: A yellow-coloured alloy of copper and zinc, usu. containing about one part in three of zinc. (BRONZE, the Italian word for brass, is now used to distinguish the ancient alloy of copper and tin.) **c.** A type of hardness, imperishableness, insensibility, etc. ME. **†d.** *transf.* Copper -1617. **e.** Iron pyrites in coal. Cf. BRAZIL[2]. **f.** in *Organ-building*: A composition of lead and tin. **2.** Elliptically: **a.** A sepulchral tablet of brass 1613. **b.** A bearing for a shaft 1731. **c.** Musical instruments of brass ME. **3.** Money. **†a.** Copper or bronze coin -1775. **b.** Money in general (*slang* or *dial.*) 1597. **4.** *fig.* Effrontery, impudence, unblushingness 1642.

1. c. Mens euill manners liue in Brasse, their Vertues We write in Water SHAKS. 4. His face is of brasse, which may be said either ever or never to blush FULLER.

Comb.: **b. band,** one with wind instruments of b.; **b. farthing,** emphatic = *farthing*; **b.-foil, -latten,** Dutch leaf made by beating out b. very thin; **b. plate,** a plate of b., bearing an inscription; also, a monumental b. (2 a); **b. rule,** a strip of b., type-high, used to separate lines or columns of type; **-smith; -work, -worker.**

Brass (bras), *v.* 1859. [f. prec.: cf. *to tin.*] To coat with brass 1865; *fig.* to cover with effrontery.

Brassage (bræ·sėdʒ). 1806. [a. F., f. *brasser.*] A mint-charge to cover the cost of coining money.

Brassard (bră̄sā·ɹd). Also **brassart.** 1830. [a. F., f. *bras*; see -ARD.] **1.** Armour for the upper arm. *Hist.* **2.** A badge worn on the arm 1870.

Bra·ssate. 1863. *Chem.* A salt of brassic acid.

Brasse (bræs). 1847. [Cf. BRASSEM.] A kind of perch.

Brassed (brast), *ppl. a.* ME. [f. BRASS + -ED.] Made of, or overlaid with brass.

Brass(e)y (bræ·si). 1888. [var. of BRASSY.] *Golf.* A brass-shod club.

‖**Brassica** (bræ·sikă). 1832. [L.; = cabbage.] *Bot.* A genus of cruciferous plants, containing the cabbage, the turnip, rape, etc. Hence **Bra·ssic** *a.*

‖**Brassière** (bræ·siēɹ). 1912. [Fr.] A woman's underbodice worn to support the breasts.

Brassy (bra·si), *a.* 1583. [f. BRASS *sb.* + -Y[1].] **1.** Of or covered with brass. **2.** Of the nature or appearance of brass 1789. **3.** *fig.* **a.** Hard as brass 1596; **b.** unblushing 1576; **c.** debased yet pretentious 1586; **d.** strident and artificial in tone 1865.

3. b. A b. impudence 1690. c. A b. age TENNYSON. d. That hard, b., overstretched style M. ARNOLD. Hence **Bra·ssiness.**

Brast, *v.*, north. f. BURST.

Brat (bræt), *sb.*[1] Now *dial.* [OE. *bratt*, prob. a. OIr. *brat* (masc., 'cloth, plaid, cloak'.] **1. †a.** (in OE.) A cloak. **b.** in *midl.*, *w.*, and *n. dial.* A pinafore or apron. **c.** A rag. **2.** A jacket for a sheep's back 1862. **†3.** Rubbish 1656. **4.** *Sc.* The skin which forms on porridge, rice pudding, etc. 1795.

Brat (bræt), *sb.*[2] 1505. [? same wd. as prec.] A child (usu. implying insignificance). *fig.* Offspring, product.

I should be glad to hear how the little b. doth CROMWELL. Hence **Bra·tling,** a little b. **Bra·ttery,** a nursery. (*contemptuous.*)

Brat, *sb.*[3] 1759. [var. of BRET.] The turbot.

Brat, *sb.*[4] 1856. [Cf. BRAT[1] 3.] *Mining.* A thin bed of coal mixed with pyrites or carbonate of lime.

Bratchet (bræ·tʃėt). 1600. [App. same wd. as BRACHET.] **1.** = BRACHET. **2.** A little brat. (*contemptuous* or *playful.*)

‖**Brattach** (bra·tăχ). 1828. [Gael. *bratach*, f. *brat* cloth.] An ensign or banner.

Brattice (bræ·tis), *sb.* ME. [More correctly *brettis*; prob.:—Ger. *brett* board, with Rom. suffix *-esca*; thus 'boarding'.] **1.** A temporary breastwork, parapet, or gallery of wood, for use during a siege. (*Hist.*) **2.** (dial. also *brattish*): A partition, generally of deal 1851. **3.** In form *brattish*: A shelf; also a seat with a high back (*n. dial.*).

Comb. **b.-cloth** (sense 2): stout tarred cloth used in mines instead of wooden bratticing.

Brattice, *v.* 1862. [f. prec.] In *To b. up*: to line the sides of a shaft, etc., with planking.

Bratticing (bræ·tisiŋ). 1866. [f. BRATTICE *v.* (or *sb.*) + -ING[1].] **1.** Brattice-work in a coal-pit 1866. **2.** *Archit.* See BRATTISHING.

Brattishing (bræ·tiʃiŋ). 1593. Var. of BRATTICING, used in *Archit.*: A cresting of open carved work on the top of a shrine. Also *dial.* in other senses.

Braunite (brau·nəit). 1839. [f. Mr. *Braun* of Gotha.] *Min.* An anhydrous oxide of manganese, a brittle dark brownish-black mineral occurring both crystallized and massive.

†Brava·de. 1579. [a. F., ad. It. *bravata*; see BRAVE.] = BRAVADO -1833.

†Brava·de, *v. arch.* 1634. [f. prec.] **1.** *intr.* To assume a bold and defiant look -1667. **2.** *trans.* To defy 1676.

Bravado (brăvē̄·do, -ā·do), *sb. pl.* **-oes,** or **-os.** 1599. [ad. Sp. *bravada* and F. *bravade*; see -ADO[2].] **1.** Boastful or threatening behaviour; ostentatious display of courage or boldness. (Now usu. in sing., without *a*: occas. with *a* or in *pl.*) **†2.** A swaggering fellow. Cf. BRAVO. -1825.

1. A sort of b.—an air of affected unconcern JANE AUSTEN. 2. The Hectors & bravadoes of the House PEPYS. Hence **Brava·doism** (*rare*).

Brave (brēⁱv), *a.*, *sb.*, *int.* 1485. [a. F., ad. It. *bravo* gallant, fine. Ulterior etym. unkn.] **A.** *adj.* **1.** Courageous, intrepid, stout-hearted (as a good quality). absol. *The brave* (now only pl.) 1697. **2.** Finely-dressed; = Sc. BRAW; splendid, showy, handsome. (Now app. a literary revival.) 1568. **3.** *loosely*, Capital, fine (*arch.*) (Cf. BRAW *a.*) 1577. **4.** quasi-*adv.* = BRAVELY. (Now *poet.*) 1596.

1. High hopes of living to be b. men, and worthy Patriots MILT. None but the b. deserves the fair DRYDEN. The b. of other lands TENNYSON. 2. The lilies which are braver than Solomon 1593. 3. O that's a braue man, hee writes braue verses, speakes braue words *A. Y. L.* III. iv. 43. Braue punishments *Much Ado* v. iv. 130. Hence **Bra·ve·ly** *adv.*, **-ness.**

B. *sb.* [in sense 1, directly from F. *brave.*] **1.** A brave man, a warrior: since 1800 *esp.* a warrior among the N. American Indians 1601. **b.** A bully; a hired assassin (*arch.*) 1598. **2.** A bravado (*arch.*) 1590.

1. A Blackfoot b. CATLIN. 2. Life's braves should somehow be made good BROWNING.

C. *interj.* [Cf. BRAVO.] Capital! Bravo! Now *dial.* 1593.

Brave (brēⁱv), *v.* 1546. [a. F. *braver*, f. *brave.*] **I.** *trans.* To treat with bravado; to challenge, defy. **2.** To meet or face with bravery; to encounter, defy. (The ordinary current sense.) 1776. **†3.** To make brave 1593. **†4.** To make splendid, adorn -1625. **†5.** To boast -1652.

1. Ossa and Pelion that so b. the sky HEYWOOD. 2. To b. danger 1832, severe weather 1876. 4. Thou [the tailor] hast brau'd manie men SHAKS.

II. *intr.* (and const. *to b. it*). **†1.** To boast, vaunt. *To b. it*: to act the bravo. -1817. **†2.** To dress splendidly -1632. Hence **Bra·vingly** *adv.*

Bravery (brēⁱ·vĕri). 1548. [prob. a. F. *braverie* the action of braving.] **†1.** The action of braving or acting the bravo; daring, defiance; bravado -1814. **2.** Daring, courage, fortitude (as a good quality). (The ordinary current sense.) 1581. **3.** Display, show; splendour 1570. *concr.* Fine clothes; = Sc. BRAWS. 1563. **†b.** A fine thing; an adornment -1657. **†4.** Mere show -1681. **†5.** A gallant, a beau; also *collect*, grandees, chivalry -1670.

1. Ere long thou shalt lament These braveries MILT. *Sams.* 1243. 2. Lancelot, the flower of b. TENNYSON. 3. The brauerie of this world..likened is, to flowre of grasse TUSSER.

Bravissimo; see BRAVO *sb.*[2]

Bravo (brā·vo), *sb.*[1] Pl. **-oes** (**-os**). 1597. [a. It. Long naturalized, whence the pronunc. (brēⁱvo) in some Dicts.] **1.** A daring villain, a hired soldier or assassin; a reckless desperado. **†2.** = BRAVADO (*rare*) -1713.

1. I have been three Nights together dogged by Bravoes STEELE.

Bravo (brā·vo), *int.* and *sb.*[2] 1761. [a. It. *bravo*, superl. *bravissimo* (also used).] Capital! Well done! Hence, as *sb.* A cheer.

‖**Bravura** (bravū·rǎ). 1788. [It.: = bravery, spirit.] 1. Display of daring or defiance; brilliancy of execution; attempt at brilliant performance 1813. 2. A passage or piece of music requiring elaborate execution, written to task the artist's powers. Also *transf.* 1788.

2. A short b. of John Paul Richter..I call it a b., as being intentionally a passage of display and elaborate execution DE QUINCEY. 3. attrib., as *b. player, singer, singing, song.*

Braw (brǭ). *Sc.* 1563. [Sc. f. BRAVE; cf. *ca'* = *calve*, etc.] A. *adj.* 1. = BRAVE *a.* 2. 1724. 2. = BRAVE 3. 1565. B. *sb. pl.* = BRAVERY 3; fine clothes 1724.

Brawl (brǭl), *sb.*[1] 1460. [f. BRAWL *v.*] 1. A noisy turbulent quarrel, a row. †2. Clamour –1611.

†**Brawl**, *sb.*[2] 1521. [cf. BRANLE *v.*] 1. A particular pace or movement in dancing –1531. 2. A kind of French dance; the music for it –1842.

2. Will you win your loue with a French braule *L. L. L.* III. i. 9.

†**Brawl**, *sb.*[3] 1725. A blue and white striped cloth made in India –1788.

Brawl (brǭl), *v.* [Late ME. Origin unkn.] 1. *intr.* To wrangle, to squabble. (At first, perh. simply 'to contend'.) †*trans.* To scold, revile –1649. 2. *intr.* To raise a clamour ME. *trans.* To utter clamorously 1563. 3. *intr.* Of a stream: To make a noise of conflict in its rapid course over stones, etc. 1600.

1. Gyue thou place to hym that brawleth or chideth CAXTON. 2. *To b. in Church*, to indulge in any speaking other than as prescribed in the Prayer Book. 3. Shallowest brooks b. the most SPURGEON. Hence **Braw·ler**. **Braw·lingly** *adv.*

Brawn (brǭn), *sb.* ME. [a. OF. *braon, braoun*, fleshy part, *esp.* of the hind leg; = Pr. *bradon*; ad. W.Ger. *brâdo*, f. *brâdan* to roast (see BREDE *v.*[1]). The spec. sense 'boar's flesh' is Eng. only.] 1. Fleshy part, muscle, *esp.* of the arm, leg, and thumb. Also *transf.* and *fig.* †2. The muscle or flesh of animals as food –1656. 3. *spec.* The flesh of the boar; *esp.* (in recent use) collared, boiled, and pickled or potted. [Cf. *bacon*, a deriv. of *back*.] ME. 4. *transf.* A boar (or swine) as fattened for the table (*dial.*). Cf. BACON. ME. 5. Hardened or thickened skin; also *fig.* L. *callum.* 1578.

1. Hise lymes grete, hise brawnes harde and stronge CHAUCER. 3. Is a man therefore bound..at noon to B., or Beefe MILT. *Comb.* **b.-fallen** *a.* shrunken in flesh.

Brawn (brǭn), *v.* 1571. [f. prec.] 1. To make or become hard; also *fig.* 2. *trans.* To fatten (a boar) 1655. †3. *intr.* To grow fat. (Of a boar.) 1580.

Brawned (brǭnd), *ppl. a.* 1505. [f. BRAWN.] 1. Muscular, brawny. 2. Hardened, callous: mostly *fig.* 1583. †3. Fattened as a boar –1601.

Brawner (brǭ·nəɹ). 1708. [f. BRAWN *v.* + -ER.] A boar fattened for the table.

Brawniness (brǭ·ninės). 1645. [f. BRAWNY + -NESS.] Muscularity; †insensibility.

Brawny (brǭ·ni), *a.* 1420. [f. BRAWN *sb.*] 1. Characterized by muscle or muscular strength 1599. 2. Callous (*lit.* and †*fig.*). Also in *comb.*

1. A brawney arme 1644. 2. A b. conscience 1638.

Braxy (bræ·ksi), *sb.* and *a.* *Sc.* 1785. [prob. from 'the *bracks*'; cf. *poxy*.] 1. Splenic apoplexy in sheep 1791. 2. as *adj.* Characterized by this disease, as *b.-sheep, mutton*; also *absol.* the flesh of a b. sheep 1785.

Bray (brēⁱ), *sb.* ME. [f. BRAY *v.*[1]] †1. Outcry; a shriek –1596. 2. The cry of some animals, *esp.* the ass 1650. 3. *transf.* Any loud harsh sound 1593.

2. No brayes of asses nor of bulls 1650. 3. The b. of rusty bolts SCOTT, of horns 1884.

Bray (brēⁱ), *v.*[1] [ME. *braie, braye*, a. F. *braire* 'to cry' (now only of the ass), perh. Celtic, f. a stem *brag-*, cogn. w. L. *fragor*.] †1. *intr.* To utter a loud harsh cry –1613. 2. Of animals: formerly the cry of horses, oxen, deer, etc.; now *esp.* of the ass ME. b. *contemptuously* of the human voice 1635. 3. *transf.* Of wind, thunder, etc. (now *esp.* of the trumpet): To make a loud harsh jarring sound ME. 4. *trans.* To utter harshly. Often with *out*. ME.

2. Stags pitifully b. DRYDEN. b. None ever brayed so learnedly 1692.

Bray (brēⁱ), *v.*[2] [ME. *brayen*, a. OF. *breier* (mod. *broyer*).] 1. To beat small; to bruise, pound; usu. in a mortar. Also *fig.* 2. Techn.: †a. To crush flax or hemp with a brake. [F. *broyer le chanvre.*] –1530. b. To pound and scour (woollen cloth) 1879.

1. *fig.* Though thou shuldest b. a foole with a pestell in a morter like otemeell, yet wil not his foolishnesse go from him COVERDALE *Prov.* xxvii. 22. Hence **Bray·ing** *vbl. sb.*[2]

Braye. 1512. [a. F. *braie* = med L. *braca* dike: of unkn. origin.] A military outwork. *False b.* (ad. F. *fausse braie*): an advanced parapet surrounding the main rampart. *Hist.*

Brayer[1] (brēⁱ·əɹ). 1598. [f. BRAY *v.*[1] + -ER[1].] One who brays; *esp.* an ass.

Bray·er[2]. 1688. [f. BRAY *v.*[2] + -ER[1].] *Printing.* A wooden pestle used to rub down and temper the ink.

Bray·er[3]. 1770. [?] Part of a compound lever for raising or depressing the upper grindstone in a corn-mill.

Braze (brēⁱz), *v.*[1] [OE. *brasian*, f. *bræs* BRASS; perh. re-coined in 16th c.] 1. *trans.* To make of, or cover with, brass OE. 2. *fig.* To make hard like brass, harden 1602.

Braze (brēⁱz), *v.*[2] 1581. [?a. F. *braser* to solder, in OF. to burn.] †1. To expose to the action of fire. 2. To solder (with an alloy of brass and zinc) 1677.

Brazen (brēⁱ·z'n), *a.* [OE. *bræsen*, f. *bræs* BRASS.] 1. Made of brass; strong as brass ME. 2. *transf.* and *fig.* Like brass. (Often after Homer's οὐρανὸς χάλκεος, etc.) 1596. 3. *fig.* Hardened in effrontery 1573.

1. A brassin ymage 1552. Inuiron'd with a B. wall SHAKS. 2. The brasen sky SPENSER. 3. B. mendacity 1869. Phr. *Brazen age*: the third mythological age of mankind. Hence **Bra·zen-ly** *adv.*, **-ness**.

Brazen (brēⁱ·z'n), *v.* 1555. [f. the adj.] 1. *trans.* With *out*: to face impudently. So *to b. it out.* 2. *trans.* To make bold or reckless 1884.

1. He would talk saucily, lye, and b. it out 1712.

Brazen-face. 1573. [f. BRAZEN *a.* 3.] 1. As two wds.: An unabashed countenance. 2. As one wd.: A brazen-faced person 1598. Hence **Bra·zen-faced** *a.* unblushing, impudent. **Bra·zen-facedly** *adv.*

Brazier[1] (brēⁱ·ziəɹ, -ʒiəɹ). ME. [?f. BRASS *sb.*] One who works in brass. Hence **Bra·ziery**, brazier's work; also *concr.*

Brazier[2] (brēⁱ·ziəɹ, -ʒiəɹ). 1690. [a. F. *brasier*, f. *braise* hot coals.] A large flat pan or tray for holding burning charcoal, etc.

Brazil[1] (brăzi·l). ME. [?a. Sp. *brasil* or It. *brasile*; of unkn. etym. The country was called from the wood, *terra de brasil*, 'red-dye-wood land'.] 1. Orig., the red wood of an East Indian tree (*Cæsalpinia Sappan*), from which dyers obtain a red colour. Later, the similar wood of a S. American species (*C. echinata*), and also other species, all valuable to the dyer. Now usu. called **Brazil-wood**. Also *attrib.* b. Taken as a type of hardness: hence *as hard as b.* Pronounced (bræ·zil, bræ·z'l). 1635. †2. The dye-stuff and dye yielded by this wood –1669. Also *attrib.* 3. A country of S. America, also called 'the Brazils' 1555. Also *attrib.* and in *comb.* 4. **Brazil-nut**: A triquetrous nut, the seed of *Bertholletia excelsa* (N.O. *Lecythidaceæ*) 1830. Hence **Brazi·lian** *a.* and *sb.*

1. c. Are my bones b., or my flesh of oak QUARLES. 3. The Portuguese nam'd it Brazile, from the red wood of that name W. ROGERS.

Brazil (bræ·zil), *sb.*[2] *dial.* Also (perh. better brassil, brazzle. 1747. [?f. BRASS.] 1. Iron pyrites (*midl. dial.*). 2. Coal containing much pyrites 1853. ¶ *As hard as b.*: occas. referred to this wd.

Braziletto (bræzile·to). 1656. [?ad. Sp. *brasilete* 'Jamaica-wood', dim. of *brasil.*] Species of dyewood, inferior to Brazil-wood, imported from Jamaica (*Cæsalpinia brasiliensis* and *crista*; now referred to the genus *Peltophorum*).

Brazilin (bræ·zilin). 1863. [f. BRAZIL + -IN.] The red colouring-matter of Brazil-wood.

Breach (brītʃ), *sb.* [ME. *breche*, partly repr. OE. *bryce, brice* (:—OTeut. **bruki-z* from **brek-*; see BREAK); partly a. F. *brèche.*] †1. The action of breaking; the fact of being broken; breakage, fracture –1676. 2. The breaking of waves on a coast or over a vessel 1601. 3. The breaking of any legal or moral bond or obligation; violation, infraction ME. †4. An irruption *into*, an infringement *upon* –1751. 5. A breaking of relations (*of* union or continuity) 1625. Also *absol.* 6. A broken or injured spot, place, or part; a disrupted place, gap or fissure; *esp.* a gap in a fortification made by a battery ME. Also *fig.* †7. Surf made by the sea breaking over rocks –1707. †8. A break in a coast; a bay, harbour 1611. †9. An interval; a division marked by intervals –1590. 10. A condition of ruptured relations 1745.

2. *Clear b.*, the waves rolling clean over without breaking. *Clean-b.*, when every object on deck is swept away. 3. Nuptial breaches *Lear* I. ii. 162. Phr. *B. of contract, promise, trust.* 5. B. of friendes BARET. 6. *To stand in the b.* (often *fig.*). 8. Asher continued on the sea shore and abode in his breaches [WYCL. hauens] *Judges* v. 17.

Phrases: (sense 2) **b. of arrestment**, illegal disposal of property which has been attached; **b. of close**, trespass; **b. of (the) peace**, a violation of the public peace by an affray, riot, or other disturbance; **b. of pound**, breaking into a pound without warrant; **b. of prison**, escape of a prisoner from confinement; **b. of privilege**, a violation of the rights of a privileged body; **b. of promise**, *spec.* = b. of promise to marry.

Breach (brītʃ), *v.* 1547. [f. the sb.] 1. *trans.* To make a breach in; to break through. Also *fig.* †2. *intr.* To cause a breach; to separate –1641. 3. *Naut.* Of whales: To leap out of the water 1843.

1. The English had breached the fort JAS. MILL.

Breachy (brī·tʃi), *a.* 1800. [f. BREACH + -Y[1].] 1. Of cattle: Apt to break fences, and get out of enclosures. 2. Having breaches.

Bread (bred), *sb.* [OE. *brēad*, pl. *brēadru* :—OTeut. **braudoz-*, meaning orig. 'piece, L. *frustum*', which before 1200 had displaced *hlāf*, now 'loaf', the original Teut. name for bread. Cf. Lowland Sc. *piece.* (Thus not a deriv. of *bru* to BREW.)] †1. (Only in OE.) Bit, piece, morsel (of food). 2. An article of food prepared by moistening, kneading, and baking meal or flour, usu. with the addition of yeast or leaven OE. †3. (with *pl.*) A loaf, a roll –1643. 4. Taken as a type of ordinary food. (Perh. from the Lord's Prayer.) ME. Also *fig.* 5. Means of subsistence 1719. 6. *attrib.* Of bread; about or for bread, as *b. riots* 1783.

2. Better is halfe a lofe than no b. HEYWOOD. 4. *B. of idleness*: food not worked for; so *B. of affliction*, etc. †*Full of b.*: full-fed. 4. He meant no harm in scribbling..'twas..his b. BYRON.

Phrases. *To break b.*: a. to partake of b. or food; b. (from N. T.) to dispense b., or *fig.* the b. of life; also to administer or join in the Communion. *To know on which side one's b. is buttered*: to know where one's interest lies. *To take the b. out of one's mouth*: to take away his livelihood, to take from a person what he is on the point of enjoying. *B. buttered on both sides*: great good fortune.

Comb.: **b. and butter**, b. spread with butter; the means of living; also *attrib.* boyish, girlish, *esp.* school-girlish; **b. and cheese**, *fig.* for plain fare, living; **black b.**, a coarser dark kind, made of rye, etc.; **-meal**, meal for household or brown b.; occ. = rock-meal (Ger. *berg-mehl*); **-root**, *spec.* a species of Psoralea (*P. esculenta*), and *Camassia esculenta* or Quamash; also the root itself.

Bread (bred), *v.* 1727. [f. BREAD *sb.*] a. *Cookery.* To dress with bread-crumbs. b. To clean by rubbing with bread.

Bread(e, var. of BREDE.

Brea·d-basket. 1552. 1. *lit.* A basket for holding or handing round bread. 2. *slang.* The stomach 1753.

Brea·d-corn. ME. Grain for making bread, *e.g.* rye.

Brea·d-crumb. 1769. a. (Prop. two wds.) A crumb of bread; *esp.* (in *pl.*) crumbs for dressing fish, etc. b. The soft part of bread, as opp. to the crust. Hence **Brea·d-crumb** *v.*, to cover with b.-c.

Breaden (bre·d'n), *a.* 1579. [f. BREAD *sb.*] Made or consisting of bread. †*B. god*: polemical for the consecrated host. var. †**Brea·dy**.

Brea·d-fruit. 1697. The farinaceous fruit of a tree; *esp.* of *Artocarpus incisa* of the South Sea Islands, etc., having a whitish pulp of the consistency of new bread.

Breadless (bre·dlės), *a.* ME. [f. BREAD *sb.* + -LESS.] Without bread; without food. Hence **Brea·dlessness**.

Brea·dness. 1866. [f. BREAD + -NESS.] In

discussions on Transubstantiation: The quality of being bread.

Bread-stitch, var. of *brede-stitch*; see BREDE *sb.*[3]

Bread-stuff (bre·dstɒf). 1793. Material for bread; grain, flour: now usu. in *pl.*

Breadth (bredþ). 1523. [f. *breade*, BREDE, after *length*, etc.] **1.** Measure or distance from side to side; width, extent across. Also *fig.* **2.** A piece (of cloth, etc.) of the full breadth; a width 1584. **3.** Extent, length 1595. **4.** *fig.* Largeness (of mind, sentiment, or view), liberality, catholicity; also, wide display of a quality 1847. **5.** *Art.* A broad effect 1788.

1. *To a hair's b.*: to a nicety *Merry W.* IV. ii. 4. 3. The b. of his great voyage *Per.* IV. i. 37. 4. To attack with a b. of calumny 1852. 5. B., or that quality of execution which makes a whole..predominate over the parts FUSELI. Hence **Brea·dthless** *a.* **Brea·dthways, -wise** *adv.* in direction of the b.

Bread-tree (bre·dtrī). 1786. Occas. name of the Bread-fruit tree; also of *Gardenia edulis, Encephalartos caffer*

Bread-winner (bre·dˌwinəɹ). 1818. **1.** One who supports himself and those dependent upon him by his earnings 1821. **2.** The tool, art, or craft with which any one earns his living 1818.

1. The stay and bread-winner of some widowed mother or sister 1863. 2. 'I'se gang hame,—and then get my bread-winner' [a fiddle] SCOTT.

Break (brēⁱk), *v.* Pa. t. Late ME. **brake,** now *arch.*, gave place to **broke** (brōᵘk) early in 16th c. Pa. ppl. **broken** (brōᵘk'n), and in verse **broke.** [OE. *brecan*:—OTeut. stem *brek-*, corresp. to L. *frag-* (*frango*), Aryan **bhreg-*.] **I. 1.** *trans.* To sever into parts by force, to part by violence. Also *intr.* (for *refl.*) Often with *in pieces, asunder*, etc. **2.** *trans.* and *intr.* To burst ME.; to lay open the surface of 1499; to crack ME.

1. A threefold rope is not easily broken BP. BARLOW. To b. windows STEELE, a battle-axe SCOTT. *intr.* If both [points] breake, your gaskins fall *Twel. N.* I. v. 24.

Spec. uses. To cut up: To b. (up) a deer or fox SCOTT. You can carve, breake up this capon *L.L.L.* IV. i 58. †To wreck: The ships were broken 1 *Kings* xxii. 48. To destroy the completeness of; to divide, part: To b. a bottle 1808, the set (*mod.*). Cf. *To b. bulk.* †To dissolve, disband; also *intr.* In phrases: *To b. bread*: see BREAD. *To b. a lance with*: to enter the lists against. 2. The berry breaks before it staineth SHAKS. I will breake thy pate acrosse *Com. Err.* II. i. 78. *To b. Priscian's head*: to violate the rules of grammar. *intr.* Said of †a bell, and hence of a boy's voice PEPYS.

II. 1. To disable, destroy cohesion, solidity, or firmness; to crush, shatter; to overwhelm, ruin, destroy OE. *intr.* To relax 1530. **2.** To crush in spirit; to tame. Now also *to b. in.* 1474.

1. Phr. *To b. the leg, or arm*: i.e. the bones of the limb. *To b. on the wheel*: to dislocate on a wheel, etc. (a form of torture). *fig. To b. the neck of a journey*: to get through the worst of it. *To b. the (one's) heart*: to overwhelm with sorrow. The frost breaketh (*intr.*) 1530. Thou breakest the proude *Ps.* lxxxviii. Of waves, etc. *trans.* and *intr.* ME. *To b. the bank*: to make the bank, or at a gaming-table the 'banker', stop payment. Also *intr.* (for *refl.*) *Merch. V.* III. i. 120. *intr.* His health was breaking fast TREVELYAN. 2. To b. the spirit of the army MACAULAY. About breaking of my horses to the coach PEPYS.

III. To do violence to, to fail to keep sacred or intact OE.

The laws have been shamefully broken JUNIUS. So, *To b. the Sabbath, the King's peace, an indenture, contract, oath*, etc. *To b. a marriage*: to annul it.

IV. 1. To lay open by breaking; often with *open* OE. **†2.** To enter by force or violence. (Now *To b. into*, q.v.) -1768. **3.** To escape violently or suddenly from ME. **4.** Of light, sound, etc.: To penetrate 1599. **5.** To reveal (†one's mind), disclose (news, etc.); now implying caution and delicacy; to utter 1450. **6.** To open, begin 1588.

1. Hunger broke stone wals *Cor.* I. i. 210. 2. John Wesley broke a house 1745. 3. To b. prison SPENSER, bounds, covert or cover (*mod.*). 4. What beam shall b. my night BYRON. 5. I have some news to b. HOOD. To b. a comparison *Much Ado* II. i. 152, a sigh GOLDSM. 6. Phr. *To b. the balls* (*Billiards*): to make the opening stroke.

V. 1. To rupture union or continuity; to disrupt; to stop for the time ME. **2.** To alter abruptly the direction of (a line); also *intr.* 1616.

1. *fig.* To b. the bonds of modesty 1578, a spell MACAULAY. To b. the enemy's ranks MASSINGER, the enemy's line 1769. *absol.* They broke twice and fled like sheep 1781. *intr.* The clouds are breaking DISRAELI. To b. the thread of these Speculations ADDISON. Phr. *To b. one's fall, journey.* To b. one's sleep SHAKS., silence STERNE, one's fast ME. To b. monotony, sameness, etc. (*mod.*). 2. Phr. *To b. joint*: said of bricks, etc., when the lines of junction are discontinuous. *To b. sheer*: see SHEER. So, *To b. away, off. To b., b. in, b. back*: said of the ball or the bowler at *Cricket.*

VI. 1. To sever by breaking; also *intr.* to cease from relation *with*, quarrel *with* ME. **2.** To cashier (an officer) 1695.

1. Thou shalt breake his yoke from off thy necke *Gen.* xxvii. 40. Phr. *To b. (any one) of a practice* or *habit.* Charles broke with his Parliament 1859. To b. with the past FREEMAN. 2. Three other colonels are broke 1695.

VII. *intr.* **1.** To escape from restraint; to issue forth OE. **2.** To burst out of darkness, begin to shine. Const. *on, upon.* (Cf. IV. 4.) 1535. **3.** To make a forcible entrance *into* a place ME.

1. To b. from the trammels of a notion RUSKIN. Cries..broke from them 1833. Phr. *To b. into arms, rebellion, weeping, a laugh.* To b. from concealment STEELE. 2. Let me goe, for the day breaketh *Gen.* xxxii. 26. So of *morning, daylight*, and by confusion *darkness, clouds.* 3. The Lacedemonians afterwards brake into Attica HOBBES.

Phrases. *To b. bulk*: to begin to unload. *To b. (the) ground* (cf. I. 2): **a.** To plough up for the first time. See also *To b. up.* **b.** Of an army: To begin digging trenches. Also *fig.* *To b. the ice*: to make a beginning. *To b. square* or *squares*: to violate the regular order, do harm. *To b. wind*: to void wind from the stomach or bowels.

Comb.: **To b. away. a.** *trans.* To remove by breaking. Also *intr.* (for *refl.*) **b.** *intr.* To start away with abruptness and force. Also *fig.* **To b. down. a.** *trans.* To demolish, destroy. **b.** To decompose. **c.** To crush in strength, health, courage, etc. **d.** *intr.* (for *refl.*) To fall broken; to prove of no avail. **To b. forth. a.** *intr.* To make a rush forward. **b.** Of flame, war, disease, etc.: To burst out. **c.** To break loose. **d.** To burst into utterance. **To b. in. a.** *trans.* = II. 2. **b.** *intr.* To enter forcibly or abruptly. **c.** To infringe *upon*; to interrupt unexpectedly. **d.** To burst *upon* **To b. off. a.** *trans.* To put an abrupt end to. **b.** *intr.* To leave off abruptly. **c.** *trans.* To sever by breaking. **d.** *intr.* To detach oneself abruptly *from.* **e.** To sever connexion (*with*). **f.** *trans.* To draw off sharply. **†g.** *intr.* To begin. **To b. out. a.** *trans.* To force out by breaking. **b.** *intr.* To burst from restraint, or concealment. Said of persons and things. Cf. *To b. out (in* or *into* boils, etc.); to *b. out, into*, or *in* feeling or action. **To b. through.** [cf. Branch VII. Prop. the analysis is *to b. through-a-fence*, not *to b.-through* a fence.] **a.** *trans.* To penetrate by breaking. **b.** To transgress. Also *absol.* **To b. up. a.** To disintegrate (*trans.* and *intr.*). **b.** *trans.* To open up (ground). **c.** Of frost, †an epidemic: To give way. **d.** To fail physically. **†e.** *trans.* To burst open, open forcibly.

Break-. The verb-stem in *comb.* forming sbs. or adjs.

I. With verb + object. 1. Forming *sbs.*, as **b.-bones,** the Ossifrage or Osprey; **-bulk,** a captain that abstracts part of his cargo; **-wind** *dial.*, a disease of sheep. 2. Forming *adjs.*, as **-ax,** that breaks axes, as in **Break-ax Tree,** *Sloanea Jamaicensis*; **-bone,** bone-breaking, as in **b.-bone fever,** the *dengue*; **-covert,** that breaks covert. II. With the vb. used attrib. = *breaking*; as **b.-piece, -iron.**

Break (brēⁱk), *sb.*[1] ME. [f. prec. vb.] **1.** An act of breaking; fracture. **2.** *Cricket.* A twist of the ball on touching the ground 1866. **3.** *Billiards* and *Croquet.* A consecutive series of successful strokes; the points thus scored 1865. **4.** A broken place, gap, or opening: wider than BREACH ME. **5.** An interruption of continuity 1627. **a.** *spec.* the sudden termination or rise in the decks of some merchant ships 1725; **b.** marks [– – –] used in print or writing to indicate abrupt pauses 1733. **6.** *Mus.* The point of separation between the different registers of a voice 1883. **7.** An irregularity, roughness, knot, etc. 1756. *spec.* in *Archit.* 1685. **8.** A portion of ground broken up for cultivation; a tract distinct in appearance 1674.

1. *B. of day* or *morn*: the first appearance of light. So *B. of June*: the beginning of June. 5. b. In modern wit all printed trash is Set off with num'rous breaks – – – and dashes — SWIFT.

Break, *sb.*[2] Also **brake.** 1831. [? a use of BRAKE *sb.*[5]] **1.** A large carriage-frame with no body, used for breaking in young horses. **2.** A large wagonette 1874.

Breakable (brēⁱ·kăb'l), *a.* 1570. [f. BREAK *v.* + -ABLE.] Capable of being broken.

Breakage (brēⁱ·kėdʒ). 1813. [f. BREAK *v.* + -AGE.] **1.** The action or fact of breaking. **2.** The results of breaking; loss or damage caused by breaking 1848. **3.** A break 1871. **4.** *Naut.* The leaving of empty spaces in stowing the hold 1867.

Breakage[2], var. f. BRAKEAGE.

Brea·k-back, *a.* 1556. [cf. BREAK-NECK.] That breaks the back; crushing.

Break-down (brēⁱ·kdaun, also brēⁱ·k dau·n). 1832. [f. *To break down* (see BREAK *v.*).] **1.** The act of breaking and falling down; a collapse (*lit.* and *fig.*). Also *attrib.*, as in *break-down gang*, etc. **2.** A riotous dance, in the style of the negroes. (U.S.; but freq. in Eng.) 1864.

Breaker[1] (brēⁱ·kəɹ). ME. [f. BREAK *v.* + -ER[1].] **1.** One who breaks, crushes, or destroys; often with defining sb., as HOUSE-BREAKER, etc. 1514. **2.** One who violates a law, oath, convention, etc. ME. **3.** One who subdues, tames, or trains 1552. **4.** That which breaks 1661; *spec.* the name of machines for crushing the stems of flax or hemp, and for performing the first operation in carding cotton, etc. 1817. **5.** A heavy ocean-wave which breaks, esp. in passing over reefs or shallows 1684.

1. A b. of idols CARLYLE. 5. *Breakers ahead!* the pass-word to give warning of broken water in the direction of the course.

Breaker[2] (brēⁱ·kəɹ). 1833. [Corrupt f. Sp. *bareca* or *barrica.*] A small keg.

Breakfast (bre·kfăst). 1463. [f. BREAK *v.* + FAST.] **1.** That with which a person breaks his fast in the morning; the first meal of the day. **2.** Occas.: A meal 1526.

1. That men shoulde go to masse as well after sowper as before brekefast MORE. 2. The wolves will get a b. by my death DRYDEN.

Breakfast (bre·kfăst), *v.* 1679. [f. prec.] **1.** *intr.* To take the first meal of the day. **2.** *trans.* To provide with breakfast 1793.

Breaking (brēⁱ·kiŋ), *vbl. sb.* OF. [f. BREAK *v.* + -ING[1].] **1.** The action of BREAK *v.* **2.** A piece of land newly broken up. (*U.S.*) 1883.

Comb.: **b.-up** = BREAK-UP; **-crop,** the first crop on newly broken ground; **-frame,** a machine for drawing out the slivers in spinning wool.

Break-neck (brēⁱ·kne·k). 1562. [f. BREAK *v.* II. 1 + NECK.] **A.** *adj.* Likely to break the neck; headlong (of speed, etc.); precipitous. **†B.** *sb.* 'A fall in which the neck is broken; a steep place endangering the neck' (J.); *fig.* destruction, ruin -1653.

Brea·k-off, *sb.* **1.** The action of breaking off: *esp.* discontinuance of relations 1860. **2.** The metal work of the stock of a gun into which the breech of the barrel fits 1804.

Breakstone (brēⁱ·kstōᵘn). 1688. [tr. L. *saxifraga.*] Herbalists' name for Saxifrages, and some other plants.

Break-up, *sb.* 1795. [f. *To break up.*] The action or fact of breaking up; disruption, separation into parts, disintegration (*lit.* and *fig.*); *e.g.* decay of animal functions; change from fine weather, or from frost; dispersal or dissolution of a society, system, etc.

Breakwater (brēⁱ·kˌwǭtəɹ). 1721. [f. BREAK *v.* + WATER.] **1.** Anything that breaks the force of the waves at a particular place, *esp.* a mole, pier, or the like, erected to form or protect a harbour 1769. **2.** A groyne or barrier on the beach to retain shingle 1721.

Bream (brīm), *sb.* [ME. *breme*, a. F. *brême*, OF. *bresme*, ad. Teut.; ? f. stem of *brehwan* to glitter. (Not conn. w. BARSE.)] **1.** A fresh-water fish (*Abramis brama*), called also Carp-bream, distinguished by its yellowish colour and its high arched back. Also its genus (*Abramis*, family *Cyprinidæ*). **2.** Used also of some acanthopterygious sea-fishes, of the genus *Pagellus* (family *Sparidæ*), and genus *Labrus* (family *Labridæ*), as the Sea Bream (*P. centrodontus*), Spanish Bream (*P. erythrinus*) 1460.

Bream (brīm), *v.* 1626. [? conn. w. Du. *brem* 'broom, furze'.] To clear (a ship's bottom) of shells, sea-weed, ooze, etc., by singeing it with burning reeds, furze, or fagots. Cf. BROOM *v.*

Breards (brīəɹdz), *sb. pl. Sc.* 1733. [The same as BRAIRD.] The short flax recovered from the first tow by a second hackling.

Breast (brest). [OE. *brēost* = OTeut. type **breusto(m)*:—OTeut. **brust-s*. Only Teut. See Kluge *Beiträge* VIII. 510.] **1.** Each of the two soft protuberances situated on the thorax in females, in which milk is secreted for the nourishment of their young; the mamma; also the mammilla in males. **b.** Hence *fig.* Source of nourishment 1611. **2.** The front of the thorax or chest. (In OE. usu. in pl., for dual.) OE. **b.** The part of a garment or armour covering the breast 1651. **c.** The bosom 1650. †**3.** Occas. = the thorax or chest –1766. **4.** The corresponding part in the lower animals ME. **5.** *fig.* and *transf.* The seat of the affections and emotions; the repository of consciousness; the heart; *hence,* the affections, private thoughts and feelings. (Usu. pl. in OE.) OE. †**6.** *transf.* The place of the lungs; *hence,* breath, voice in singing –1711. †**7.** A broad even front of a moving company –1807. **8.** Used of analogous surfaces or parts of things. †In *military* use, a breastwork. ME. **9.** Techn.: **a.** *Archit.* The part of a wall between a window and the floor; also, the part of a chimney between its flues and the rooms; †the *torus* in a column. **b.** *Mining.* The face of a working; also, that side of the hearth of a shaft-furnace which contains the metal-notch. RAYMOND.

1. Come to my Womans Brests And take my Milke for Gall *Macb.* I. v. 48. Past the b. 1647. Put to the B. STEELE. 2. You must cut this flesh from off his b. *Merch. V.* IV. i. 252. 5. What his Brest forges, that his Tongue must vent *Cor.* III. i. 258. *To make a clean b.*: to make a full disclosure. 6. *Twel. N.* II. iii. 19. 7. *In, of, on (a) b.* = ABREAST. *Obs.* 8. The b. of the battle ME., of Heaven SHAKS., earth 1814, a hill (*mod.*).

Comb.: **b.-backstays** (*Naut.*), long ropes to support the masts against an oblique headwind (cf. BACKSTAY); **-band,** a band passing round the breast; also *spec.* = *breast-rope*; **-collar,** a broad pulling strap passing round the b. of a horse; **-drill,** one against which the workman bears his b. while drilling; **-fast,** a large rope or chain, used to confine a ship's broadside to a wharf, quay, etc.; **-height,** the interior slope of a parapet; **-hooks,** large pieces of compass-timber fixed within and athwart the bows of a ship; **-knees** *sb. pl.*, timbers placed in the forward part of a vessel across the stem to unite the bows on each side; **-knot,** a knot or bow of ribbon, etc. worn on the b.; **-pain,** a disease in horses; **-pang,** the *Angina pectoris*; **-pump,** an instrument for drawing milk from the b. by suction; **-rail** (*Naut.*), the upper rail of the balcony, etc.; **-rope** (*Naut.*), a rope for securing the yard-parrels; a rope for supporting the leadsman while sounding; **-strap** (*Harness*), a strap fixed at one end to the collar and supporting the pole of the vehicle; **-weed,** *Saururus cernuus*; **-wimble,** a gimlet or auger upon which the b. presses in working; **-wood,** young shoots of fruit trees trained on espaliers or against walls. Hence **Brea·stwise** *adv.*

Breast (brest), *v.* 1573. [f. prec.] **1.** To oppose the breast to; to meet in full opposition 1599. †**2.** To defend in front or with a breastwork –1624. **3.** To apply the breast to 1820.

1. *To b. a fence, horse,* etc.: to mount by springing so as to bring the breast over. 3. As swift As bird on wing to b. its eggs again KEATS. Hence **Brea·sted** *ppl. a.* having a breast; *esp.* in comb., as *big-b.*

Breast-beam (bre·stˌbīm). 1790. **1.** *Naut.* One of the beams at the fore-part of the quarter-deck, and after-part of the forecastle 1850. **2.** The horizontal beam in front of a loom 1790. **3.** The front cross-beam of the frame of a locomotive.

Breast-board (bre·stbōᵊɹd). 1649. **1.** The mould-board of a plough. **2.** *Rope-making.* A loaded carriage to which the yarn-ends are attached at the foot of the rope-walk.

Breastbone (bre·stbōᵘn). OE. The bone running down the front of the thorax, and articulated by cartilages with the ribs; the sternum.

Breast-high (bre·stˌhəi). 1580. **A.** *adj.* As high as the breast 1677. **B.** *adv.* **1.** To the height or depth of the breast 1580. **2.** Said in *Hunting* of a strong scent which the hounds can follow at a racing pace with heads erect 1858.

Breasting (bre·stiŋ), *vbl. sb.* 1817. [f. BREAST *sb.* and *v.*] **1.** The action of BREAST *v.* **b.** *concr.* A covering for the breast, breastwork. **2.** *techn.* The curved channel in which a breast-wheel works.

Breast-plate (bre·stplēᵗt). ME. **1.** A piece of armour, or any plate, worn on the breast. **2.** A folded piece of embroidered linen worn on the breast of the Jewish high-priest, and adorned with twelve precious stones, representing the twelve tribes. Cf. *Exod.* xxviii, xxxix. 1581. **3.** Techn.: **a.** *Mech.* A plate in which the butt end of a drill is inserted when the breast is applied in boring. **b.** A strap or straps passing across the breast of a riding-horse. 1667.

Brea·st-plough. 1725. A sort of plough pushed by the breast, used for paring turf. Hence **Brea·st-plough** *v.*

Breastsummer, bressummer (bre·səməɹ). 1611. [f. BREAST + SUMMER *sb.*[2] (a. F. *sommier* beam).] A summer or beam extending horizontally over a large opening, and sustaining the whole superstructure of wall, etc.; *e. g.* the beam over a shop-front, and the like.

Breast-wheel (bre·stˌhwīl). 1759. A water-wheel, in which the water is admitted to the float-board nearly on a level with the axle.

Breastwork (bre·stwɒ̄ɹk). 1642. **1.** *Fortif.* A fieldwork thrown up breast-high for defence; a parapet. Also *fig.* **2.** *Naut.* A sort of balustrade which terminates the quarter-deck and poop at the fore ends 1769.

Breath (breþ). [OE. *brǣþ, brēþ*:—WGer. type **brāþ-*, OTeut. **brǣþoz*:—Aryan **bhrēto-*, f. root **bhrē-*, Teut. **brǣ-* to burn, heat; see BREDE *v.*[1], and BROOD. In the sense of 'the air in the lungs or mouth' it took the place of OE. *ǣðm*, ME. *ēþem*. The vowel was originally long, as in BREATHE *v.*] †**1.** Odour –ME. **2.** An exhalation or vapour from heated objects, etc.; steam, smoke, reek –1667. **b.** (cf. 3.) The air exhaled from anything, or impregnated with its exhalations. Also *fig.* 1625. **c.** A whiff 1873. **3.** The air exhaled from the lungs, orig. as smelt or seen; hence generally, The air received into and expelled from the lungs in the act of respiration. Now the main sense. ME. Also *transf.* **4.** A puff; now usu. *of air* or *of wind*; but orig. used absol. ME. **5.** The faculty of breathing. Hence, spirit, life. ME. **6.** A single respiration 1483. **7.** Power of breathing, free or easy breathing; *esp.* in *out of b.* 1590. **8.** Time for breathing; exercise of the respiratory organs. Also *fig.* 1594. **9.** *transf.* Whisper, utterance, speech; will expressed in words ME. **10.** *Phonology.* Voiceless expiration of air, forming a hiss, whish, puff, etc. Also *attrib.* 1867.

2. Like gentle breaths from rivers pure MILT. b. The B. of Flowers BACON. 3. *To draw b.* DRYDEN. *To spend b.* BERKELEY. So *To waste b.* The b. is not the flute BROWNING. 4. A summer night without a b. SHELLEY. Summers b. SHAKS. So 'b. of morn'. The b. of popular applause 1703. 5. The b. of life WYCLIF, of the nostrils *Gen.* vii. 22. *To catch* or *hold one's b.*: to check suddenly or suspend the act of respiration. 6. Phr. *In* (*with*) *one* or *the same b., at a b.* 7. *To take b.*, to recover free breathing. 9. A b. can make them, as a b. has made GOLDSM. Princes and lords are but the b. of kings BURNS. *Below* or *under one's b.*: in a low voice. *Bated b.*: see BATED *ppl. a.* 10. *B. consonant*, a consonant formed by the breath in the mouth without the action of the vocal cords, as k, t, p, etc.

Breathe (brīð), *v.* [ME. *brethe(n*, f. *breth* BREATH; not formed in OE.] **I.** *intr.* †**1.** To exhale, steam, evaporate –1670. †**2.** To emit odour, to smell –1712. *fig.* To be redolent *of* 1697. **3.** To exhale air from the lungs ME. **b.** To exhale and inhale, to respire. (The ordinary current sense.) ME. **c.** To bring (*to, into* a state) by breathing 1816. **4.** To live, exist ME. Also *fig.* **5.** To take breath (see BREATH 7); *fig.* to pause, take rest 1577. **6.** *transf.* To give forth audible breath: to speak, sing, etc. 1598. **7.** Of air, etc.: To blow softly. (Cf. 3.) 1610.

1. A warmth breathes out of her *Per.* III. ii. 94. 2. All Arabia breathes from yonder box POPE. 3. b. When we b., sleep, move HOOKER. 4. A better fellow does not b. (*mod.*). 6. As I wake, sweet music b. MILT. *Penser.* 151. 7. The low wind hardly breathed for fear TENNYSON.

II. *trans.* **1.** To exhale, to emit by expiration (*out*); *fig.* to send *into*, communicate by breathing ME. *transf.* of things 1647. **2.** To inhale and exhale (air, etc.), to respire; *esp.* to inhale. Also *fig.* 1588. **3.** To give utterance to, in various senses (see quots.) 1535. **4.** *trans.* and *refl.* To let breathe; to give a breathing space to; to recreate 1563. **5.** To excite the respiratory organs of: *hence* †to exercise briskly; to put out of breath, exhaust ME. **6.** To give breath to (a wind instrument); to blow 1721.

1. To b. new life into any one MORLEY. Phr. *To b. one's last*: to expire. 2. Free as the air we b. (*mod.*). 3. I would not b. (= whisper) it to another (*mod.*). Breathing (= uttering with vehemence) vengeance SPENSER. Language breathing (= manifesting) the eloquence of truth S. ROGERS. 4. To b. oneself 1563, horses 1596.

Phrases. *To b. through* (sense I. 4): to animate, inform. *To b. again* (sense I. 5): (*fig.*) to be relieved in mind. *To b. freely*: to be at ease, in one's element. *To b. upon* (fig.): to infect; to tarnish (as if with breath); to taint. *To b. a vein*: to lance it so as to let blood. ? *Obs.*

Hence **Brea·thable** *a.* fit or agreeable to b.

Breathed, *ppl. a.* ME. [f. BREATHE *v.* and BREATH *sb.*] **I.** From the vb. (*now* brīðd, brī·ðĕd). **1.** In (good) wind; *esp.* in *well-b.*, etc. *fig.* †*Lust-b.* (in Shaks.): breathing lust. **2.** Winded, exhausted 1599. **3.** Exhaled, respired; uttered in a breath, whispered 1579.

1. As swift As b. Stags SHAKS. 3. No.. b. spell MILT.

II. From the sb. (*now* breþt). **1.** Having breath; as in *long-b.*: long-winded, or -lived 1555. **2.** *Phonology.* Uttered with breath only; surd; cf. SONANT. 1877.

Breather (brī·ðəɹ). ME. [f. BREATHE *v.*] **1.** He who or that which breathes. **2.** A spell of exercise taken to stimulate the breathing, etc. Also, that which puts out of breath. 1836.

1. Breathers of this world, of scandal SHAKS., of an ampler day TENNYSON.

Breathful (bre·þful), *a.* 1583. [f. BREATH.] Full of breath or air; having life; redolent.

Breathing (brī·ðiŋ), *vbl. sb.* ME. [f. BREATHE *v.* + -ING[1].] **1.** Respiration; a single act of respiration. **b.** A short time 1625. **c.** Wind 1667. **d.** *fig.* Influence 1587. †**2.** Time to breathe, pause –1687. **3.** = BREATHER 2. 1755. **4.** Utterance 1606. **5.** Aspiration (*after*), longing (*for*) 1652. **6.** Of the wind: Gentle blowing 1635. †**7.** Ventilation; a vent, air-hole –1697. **8.** The opening of a vein in order to let blood 1612. **9.** *Gram.* An aspiration, an aspirate: *spec.* (Gr. πνεῦμα, L. *spiritus*), in Gr. grammar, (ʽ) or 'rough breathing', and (ʼ) or 'smooth breathing', indicating respectively the presence or absence of the aspirate. See ASPER *sb.*[1], ASPIRATE.

1. Forsake me not..in my last b. HIERON. 4. Hide not thine eare at my b. *Lament.* iii. 55. 6. There's not a b. of the common wind That will forget thee WORDSW.

Comb.: **b.-fit,** pause, rest; **-hole,** a hole or vent for air; **-part, -place,** a place or opening for b.; a pause; **-pore,** a minute opening for the passage of air, a spiracle; **-space,** room or time to breathe; so **-spell, -time, -while.**

Brea·thing, *ppl. a.* ME. In the senses of the vb. **b.** *fig.* Life-like (cf. Vergil's *spirantia signa, æra*) 1697. Hence **Brea·thingly** *adv.*

Breathless (bre·þlĕs), *a.* ME. [f. BREATH + -LESS.] **1.** Without breath: **a.** Without respiration. **b.** Lifeless 1595. †**c.** *Gram.* Unaspirated 1668. **2.** Breathing with difficulty, panting; exhausted 1450. Also *fig.* **b.** Holding one's breath, as with awe, etc. 1802. **3.** Unstirred by a breath of wind 1815.

2. B. and spent 1709. A nun B. with adoration WORDSW. Hence **Brea·thless-ly** *adv.*, **-ness.**

Breathy (bre·þi), *a.* 1528. [f. as prec. + -Y[1].] **1.** Of, pertaining to, or of the nature of breath. **2.** Of the voice: Having the sound of breathing in it. Hence **Brea·thiness,** b. quality.

Breccia (bre·ttʃă, bre·tʃiă). 1774. [a. It., = 'gravel or rubbish of broken walls', cogn. w. F. *brèche*, adapted from Teut.: cf. OHG. *brecha* breaking, f. *brechan*.] *Geol.* A composite rock consisting of angular fragments of stone, etc., cemented, *e. g.* by lime: occas. opp. to *conglomerate.*

Osseous or *bone b.*: one containing fossil bones. Hence **Bre·cciated,** formed into a b., of the structure of a b.

†**Breck.** ME. [? directly f. *brec-* stem of BREAK *v.*] A breach, blemish.

Bred. Now *dial.* [Com. Teut.: OE. *bred*:—OTeut. **bredo(m*, doublet of **bordo(m* BOARD.] A board; a tablet.

Bred (bred), *ppl. a.* Pa. pple. of BREED *v.*; used chiefly in *comb.*, as *country-, ill-, thorough-b.*

†**Brede,** *sb.*[1] [OE. *brǣde*, f. OTeut. *brǣdan*, BREDE *v.*[1] Cf. Ger. *braten*, Eng. BRAWN, from the same root.] Roast meat. (Cf. SWEET-BREAD.) –1535.

Brede, *sb.*[2] Now *n. dial.* [OE. *brǣdu, -o*:—OTeut. **braidjōn-*, abstr. sb. f. **braido-z*, in OE. *brād* BROAD.] Breadth, width.

Brede (brīd), *sb.*[3] *arch.* 1640. [var. of

BRAID *sb.* Cf. BREDE *v.*[3]] = BRAID *sb.* 4. *Comb.* **b.-stitch.**

1. A curious B. of Needle-work DRYDEN.

†**Brede,** *v.*[1] [Com. Teut.: OE. *brǽdan*, app. a deriv. of the vb. root **brǽ-*, **brê-* (Aryan **bhrē-*) to burn, heat; see BREATH, BROOD.] *trans.* To roast, broil, toast -1509.

Brede, *v.*[2] Now *dial.* [Com. Teut.: OE. *brǽdan*, f. *brád* BROAD.] 1. *trans.* To broaden. 2. *trans.* and *intr.* To spread out ME.

†**Brede,** *v.*[3] ME. To intertwine.

†**Bree** (brī), *sb.*[1] Now *n. dial.* [OE. *brǽw*, *bréaw*:—OTeut. **brǽwâ* f. **brǽhwâ*. Prob. the radical sense is 'blinker, twinkler'.] †1. The eye-lid -ME. 2. The eye-brow ME. †3. An eye-lash -1656.

Bree (brī), *sb.*[2] Now *Sc.* OE. [?] †1. A thick pottage made of meal, etc. -ME. 2. Broth, juice. Also *fig.* ME. †3. *fig.* Water, the sea -ME.

2. *Barley-b.*: malt liquor. *Herring-b.*: herring-brine.

Breech (brītʃ), *sb.* [Com. Teut.: OE. *brēc*, pl. of **brōc* fem.:—OTeut. type **brôk-s* 'clothing for the loins and thighs'.] †1. A garment covering the loins and thighs -1642. b. Now always in pl. **Breeches** (bri·tʃėz), or *a pair of breeches.* (*Breeches* come only just below the knee, but *dial.* (and *joc.*) *breeches* includes *trousers.*) ME. 2. The part covered by this garment; the buttocks. ?OE. Also *transf.* 3. *techn.* a. *Gunnery.* The part of a cannon, or other firearm, behind the bore 1575. b. *Shipbuilding.* The outside angle formed by the knee-timber.

1. b. They sewed figge leaues together, and made themselues breeches BIBLE (Genev.) *Gen.* iii. 7.

Phr. *To wear the breeches* (†*breech*): to be master, said of a wife.

Comb.: (sense 3) **b. action,** the mechanism at the b. of a gun; **-block,** a moveable steel block by which the end of the barrel in certain fire-arms is closed; **-pin, -plug,** a pin or plug closing the b. end of a gun; **-screw,** a cylinder of iron with a screw, which presses the vent piece into its place when the gun is loaded; (sense 2) **breeches-ball,** a ball of composition for cleaning breeches; **Breeches Bible,** the Geneva Bible of 1560, so named on account of the rendering of *Gen.* iii. 7, already occurring in Wyclif; **breeches-buoy,** a life-buoy with suspended canvass support resembling breeches.

Breech (britʃ, brītʃ), *v.* 1468. [f. prec.] 1. To cover or clothe with, or as with, breeches; to put (a boy) into breeches. Also *fig.* †2. To flog -1821. 3. *Naut.* To secure (a cannon) by a breeching 1757.

1. *fig.* Their Daggers Vnmannerly breech'd with gore SHAKS. 2. The bois must be britch[t] 1573.

Breeching (brī·tʃiŋ), *vbl. sb.* 1515. [f. BREECH *v.* and *sb.* + -ING[1].] 1. The action of the vb. (sense 1). †2. A flogging -1613. Also *attrib.* 3. A leather strap passing round the breech of a shaft-horse, and enabling him to push backwards. Also *attrib.* 1515. 4. Coarse wool on the buttocks of sheep 1799. 5. *Naut.* A stout rope attached by a thimble to the cascabel of a gun, and securing the gun to the ship's side. Hence *b.-bolt, -loop.* 1627. 6. The parts forming the breech of a gun 1802.

2. Aristarchus' eyes, Whose looks were as a b. to a boy MARLOWE.

Breech-loader (brī·tʃ,lōᵘdəɪ). 1858. A fire-arm which is loaded at the breech. So **Bree·ch-loading** *vbl. sb.* this method of loading (fire-arms). *attrib.* That is loaded at the breech.

Breed (brīd), *sb.* 1553. [f. BREED *v.*] †1. Breeding, birth; extraction -1632. 2. Race, stock; strain; a line of descendants perpetuating particular hereditary qualities. (Abstract and concrete.) 1553. b. *gen.* A species, a set 1588. †3. Offspring; *esp.* a litter, etc. Now BROOD. Also *fig.* -1802.

2. Rammes of the b. of Bashan *Deut.* xxxii. 14. Too good for such a b. 1843. b. The b. of wits so wondered at *L. L. L.* v. ii. 266. 3. A breede of barraine mettall *Merch. V.* I. iii. 135.

Breed (brīd), *v.* Pa. t. and pple. **bred.** [OE. *brēdan* (:—*brōdan*):—OTeut. type **brôdjan*, f. *brôdâ-* 'warmth, BROOD'. With *brood, breed* cf. *food, feed,* etc.] I. *trans.* (and *absol.*) 1. Of a female parent: To cherish (brood) in the womb or egg; to hatch from the egg; to produce (offspring). 2. *absol.* To be pregnant. (Now chiefly *dial.*) 1629. 3. *absol.* Of animal species: To have offspring; to propagate their species ME. Also *fig.* 4. *trans.* Said of countries, etc. (without reference to parental action) ME. 5. To give rise to, engender, develop, produce, be the source of ME. †6. with *compl.* To make (to do something) -1625. 7. To take charge of or promote the engendering of (animals); to raise (cattle) ME. Also *absol.* 8. To train up physically or mentally 1523.

1. Neither thou in begetting him, nor his mother in breeding him GOLDING. 3. *fig.* Shee speakes, and 'tis such sence That my Sence breeds with it *Meas. for M.* II. ii. 142. 4. Waters that b. Trouts WALTON. Dirt breeds fever KINGSLEY. *To b. bad blood*: see BLOOD. 5. Shee is young, wise, faire..And these b. honour *All's Well* II. iii. 140. 8. To b. a bullock to the plough DRYDEN. Bred in All Souls in Oxford FULLER, to the Church SOUTHEY, a smith FRANKLIN.

II. *intr.* (for *refl.*) 1. To come into being, as a continued process; hence, to be engendered or produced ME. †b. To grow, as animal structures, etc. -1688. 2. *fig.* To originate, make their appearance ME.

Phrases. *Born and bred*, or *bred and born*: here *bred* has usu. sense I. 7, though formerly sense I. 1. †*To b. out*: to degenerate *Timon* I. i. 259. *To b. in and in*: to b. always with near relatives. *Comb.* †**Bree·d-bate,** one who breeds bate, or strife.

Breeder (brī·dəɪ). 1531. [f. prec. vb. + -ER[1].] 1. That which, or one who, produces, breeds, or †brings up.

Breeding (brī·diŋ), *vbl. sb.* ME. [f. as prec. + -ING[1].] 1. Bringing to the birth; hatching; production of young. Hence (vulgarly), †extraction -1606. 2. *fig.* Origination, production, development 1549. 3. The bringing up of the young; formerly in sense of 'education' 1577. 4. The results of training as shown in manners and behaviour; usu. = 'good manners' 1596. Also *attrib.*

4. Men of parts and b. BERKELEY.

†**Bree·dling.** [f. as prec.] One born and bred in a place. PEPYS. [Taken by Macaulay for a proper name.]

Breek (brīk). ME. N.Eng. and Sc. var. of BREECH *sb.* Now only in pl. **breeks** = trousers. Hence **Bree·kless** *a.*

Breeze (brīz), *sb.*[1] [OE. *briosa, breosa* masc. Not conn. w. BRIMSE.] 1. A gad-fly; *esp.* of the genera *Œstrus* (BOT-FLY) and *Tabanus* (*arch.* or *dial.*). Also *fig.* †2. Used vaguely of other insects -1483. So **b.-fly.**

Breeze (brīz), *sb.*[2] 1565. [In 16th c. *brize, brieze*, app. ad. OSp. *briza*. Prob. orig. a var. of *bisa, bise* 'north-east wind'. The sense 3 is Eng. only.] †1. *orig.* A north or north-east wind -1706. †2. The cool wind that blows from the sea by day on tropical coasts -1839. b. By extension, the counter-current that blows from the land by night 1700. 3. A gentle or light wind: a current of air lighter than a *wind*. In naut. use = wind in general. 1626. 4. *fig. colloq.* a. A disturbance, row 1785. b. A breath of news, whisper 1879. Also in *comb.*

2. b. From land a gentle b. arose by night DRYDEN. 4. a. The cessation would create a b. in the Konkan WELLINGTON. Hence **Bree·zeless** *a.*

Breeze (brīz), *sb.*[3] 1726. [prob. a. F. *braise*, OF. *brese*.] Small cinders and cinder-dust, used in burning bricks, etc.; small coke and coke-dust.

Breeze, *v. rare.* 1682. [f. BREEZE *sb.*[2]] *intr.* To blow gently, as a breeze.

Phr. *To b. up* (Naut.): (of a wind) to freshen; also *impers.* Of a noise: To rise on the breeze.

Breezy (brī·zi), *a.* 1718. [f. BREEZE *sb.*[2] + -Y[1].] 1. Exposed to breezes. 2. Attended by breezes, windy; *fig.* fresh; airy 1753.

1. The b. shore POPE, elms WORDSW. 2. B. verse LOWELL. Hence **Bree·zily** *adv.*, **Bree·ziness.**

‖**Bregma** (bre·gmă). Pl. **bre·gmata.** 1578. [Gr.] The region of the skull where the frontal and the two parietal bones join; the sinciput. Hence **Bregma·tic** *a.*

Brehon (brī·hǫn). Now *Hist.* 1581. [ad. Ir. *breitheamh*, f. *breth* judgement.] An ancient Irish judge.

B. law, the code of law which prevailed in Ireland before its occupation by the English.

Breithauptite (brəi·t,hauptəit). [f. *Breithaupt*, mineralogist.] Antimonial nickel, a native alloy of these two metals (NiSb) found in the Harz Mountains.

‖**Bre kekekeˑx.** 1607. a. Gr. βρεκεκεκέξ, echoic of the croaking of frogs.

‖**Breloque** (brəloˑk). 1856. [F.] A small ornament fastened to a watch-chain.

†**Bre·mber.** OE. Var. of BRAMBLE -ME.

Breme (brīm), *a.* Still *dial.* [In Branch I, OE. *brēme, brēme,* (*brȳme*), celebrated. In Branch II, ?] I. †1. Celebrated (only in OE.); *hence*, fine, famous -ME. †2. Brilliant; clear, loud, distinct -1617. II. †1. Fierce, wroth -1818. 2. Of the sea, etc.: Raging, rough; usu. echoed from Spenser. In n. dial. *brim.* ME.

Bren(e, obs. f. BRAN, BURN.

Brended, obs. f. BURNT.

†**Bre·ndice.** *rare.* [a. It. *brindesi, brindisi* 'a health to one'; acc. to Diez perverted from Ger. *bring dir's.*] A bumper. DRYDEN.

Bre·nnage. [f. OF. *bren* BRAN.] *Old Law.* A payment in, or in lieu of, bran, made by tenants to feed their lord's hounds.

Brent, *a.* Phonetic var. of BRANT, q. v.

Brent, *sb.* Also **Brent-goose.** = BRANT, q.v.

Brepho-, comb. f. Gr. βρέφος babe; only in nonce-wds., as **Brepho·latry,** baby-worship, etc.

Brerd. Now *dial.* OE. [See BRAIRD and BROD.] The topmost surface or edge; brim. Hence †**Bre·rd-full** *a.* brim-full.

Brere (brīᵊɪ). Orig. f. BRIER (*dial.* and *poet.*).

Bressomer, bressumer, var. of BREAST-SUMMER.

Brest, obs. f. BREAST, BURST.

Bret, *sb.* 1460. [?] †1. = BIRT. 2. = BRIT.

Bre·tessé, bretessee, bretessy. 1572. [a. F. *bretessé* bratticed.] *Her.* Having embattlements on each side.

†**Bre·t-full,** *a.* ME. [var. of BRERDFULL.] Brim-full -1616.

Brethren (bre·ðrėn), special pl. of BROTHER.

Brethrenism. The principles and system of the (*Plymouth*) *Brethren.*

Brett. Short f. BRITZKA, a four-wheeled carriage.

Brettice, brettis, common var. of BRATTICE.

Bretwalda (bretwǭ·ldă). [OE., = 'ruler of the Bretts'.] *Hist.* A title given in the O.E. Chronicle to King Egbert, and (retrospectively) to seven earlier Old English kings, and occas. assumed by later ones: = 'lord of the Britons', or 'of Britain'. (See Freeman *N. C.* I.)

Breu-, see BREV-, BREW-.

Breve (brīv), *sb.* ME. [var. of *bref, brefe,* BRIEF *sb.*] 1. A letter of authority; *spec.* a pope's letter; = BRIEF *sb.* 1, 2. 2. *Music.* A note of the value of two semibreves, now written white and either oblong or oval, with one or two strokes on each side; rarely used in mod. music 1460. †3. *Gram.* A short syllable -1751. 4. *Print.* The mark ˘ placed over a vowel to signify that it is short. 5. [Fr. *brève.*] The Ant-thrush, so named from its short tail.

1. The pope had sent two breves to Garnet 1862.

†**Breve,** *v.* [ME. *breven*, app. a. ON. *brēfa* to write, ad. med.L. *breviare*, f. *breve.*] 1. *trans.* (and *absol.*) To set down in writing -1560. 2. To recount, tell -1448. Hence †**Bre·vement,** brievement, the action of the vb.; *concr.* an entry.

Brevet (bre·vėt), *sb.* ME. [a. F., dim. of *bref*; see BRIEF.] †1. An authoritative message in writing; *esp.* a Papal Indulgence -1754. 2. An official document granting certain privileges; *spec.* in the Army, one conferring nominal rank on an officer, but giving no right to extra pay 1689. Also *transf.* and *fig.* Also *attrib.*

2. The Duke de Chartres..holds this Employment by a b. only 1721. Hence **Bre·vetcy,** b. rank. (Dicts.)

Brevet (bre·vėt), *v.* 1839. [f. prec.] To raise to a certain rank by brevet; also *fig.* Hence **Bre·veted** *ppl. a.*

Brevi- (bre·vi-), comb. f. of L. *brevis* 'short'. **Breviped** [L. *pes, ped-*] *a.*, having short feet (or legs); *sb.* [sc. *bird*]; **-pen** [L. *penna*] *sb.*, a short-winged bird; **-pennate** *a.*, short-winged; **-rostrate** [L. *rostrum*] *a.*, having a short beak.

Breviary (brī·viări). 1547. [ad. L. *breviarium.*] 1. A brief statement, epitome. ?*Obs.* 2. *R. C. Ch.* The book containing the 'Divine Office' for each day, which those who are in orders are bound to recite 1611. Also *fig.*

†**Bre·viate,** *a.* 1509. [ad. L. *breviatus.*] Abbreviated; short -1656.

Breviate (brī·vi*ē*t), *sb.* 1581. [f. prec. adj. used subst.] **1.** A brief statement; a summary, compendium. Also *fig.* †**2.** A brief missive; a note –1748. †**3.** A lawyer's brief –1734.
1. A B. of all Luthers doctrine 1581. 3. As well-fee'd Lawyer on his B. BUTLER *Hud.* II. ii. 612.

†**Bre·viate,** *v.* 1526. [f. as prec.] **1.** To abbreviate –1637. **2.** To abridge; *spec.* to abstract for counsel's instruction –1679. Hence †**Bre·viature,** an abbreviation.

Brevier (brĭvīə·ɹ). 1598. [a. OF. *brevier*:— L. *breviarium*; app. because used in printing breviaries. Cf. *Canon*, etc.] The name of the type in size between Bourgeois and Minion, as in Brevier Type.

Breviloquence (brĭvi·lŏkwĕns). *rare.* 1656. [ad. L. *breviloquentia.*] Brevity of speech; laconism. So **Brevi·loquent** *a.* laconic.

‖**Brevi manu.** 1808. [L.] *Law.* Summarily.

Bre·vit, *v.* Now *dial.* 1600. [? f. BREVET *sb.*, with the sense of 'take by brevet'.] To forage; to beat about for game.

Brevity (bre·vĭti). 1509. [prob. a. AF. *brevete* :—L. *brevitatem.*] **1.** Shortness, esp. as used of time 1542. **2.** The being short in speech or writing; terseness 1509. **3.** Shortness in other relations (*rare* and *forced*) 1597.
2. Since Breuitie is the Soule of Wit..I will be breefe *Haml.* II. ii. 90. 3. 2 *Hen. IV*, II. ii. 135.

Brew (brū), *v.* [Com. Teut.: OE. *brēowan*, perh. f. OTeut. vb.-root **brū*. Cf. BROTH, etc.] **1.** *trans.* Properly: To make (ale, etc.) by infusion, boiling, and fermentation. Also *fig.* **b.** To convert (barley, malt, etc.) into a fermented liquor ME. Also *absol.* †**2.** To mix (liquors) –1641. **3.** *transf.* To make by mixing, as punch; or by infusion, as tea 1626. **4.** To concoct, contrive, cause ME. **5.** *intr.* To be in process of mixing, concocting, etc. ME.
1. She brewes good Ale *Two Gent.* III. i. 304. b. O Willie brew'd a peck o' maut BURNS. 4. To b. bale ME., bitternesse LANGL., some notable matter GOLDING, a storm FALCONER, plagues SOUTHEY.
Comb.: **b.-house,** a brewery.

Brew, *sb.* 1510. [f. the vb.] The action of brewing; the beverage, etc. brewed.

Brewage (brū·ėdʒ). 1542. [f. BREW *v.* + -AGE; prob. conn. in origin w. F. *breuvage* BEVERAGE.] **1.** A concocted beverage; a decoction; something that has been *brewed.* Also *fig.* **2.** The process of brewing 1776. **3.** A boiling (*e.g.* of salt) 1550.
1. Malmsey, or some well spic't bruage MILT.

Brewer (brū·əɹ). ME. [f. as prec. + -ER [1].] **1.** One who brews; *spec.* one whose trade is to make malt liquors. **2.** A concocter *of* 1563.

Brewery (brū·əri). 1658. [f. BREWER; see -ERY.] **1.** A place or establishment for brewing; formerly called a BREWHOUSE. †**2.** The process or trade of brewing –1796.

Brewing (brū·iŋ), *vbl. sb.* 1467. [f. BREW *v.* + -ING [1].] **1.** The action, process, or occupation described under BREW (various senses). *fig.* Concoction 1545. **2.** The quantity brewed at once 1626. **3.** *Naut.* A collection of black clouds betokening a storm. Also *attrib.*
1. Great brewyng, small drinke 1562. I have an *Edinburgh* article in b. ALFORD.

Brewis (brū·ĭs). [ME. *browes, brouwys,* etc. a. OF. *brouetz, brouet* 'soup made with broth of meat'. Cf. BROSE.] **1.** Broth (*dial.*). **2.** Bread soaked in broth or dripping ME.
1. Mountains of beef, and oceans of b. SCOTT. 2. Drops o' fat on Owdham breawis 1857.

Brewster (brū·stəɹ). ME. [f. BREW *v.* + -STER; cf. *baxter.*] **1.** *orig.* A woman that brews. **2.** A brewer. *N. Eng.* and *Sc.* ME.
B. Sessions, sessions for the issue of licences to trade in alcoholic liquors.

Brewsterite (brū·stĕrəit). 1843. [f. Sir David *Brewster.*] A zeolitic mineral, belonging to the hydrous silicates, white in colour, and of uneven fracture.

Briar, etc.; see **BRIER,** etc.

Briareus (brəi,ēə·riŏs, brəi·ăriŭs). 1606. Proper name of a hundred-handed giant of Gr. mythology; often used connotatively.
A gowtie B., many hands and no vse *Tr. & Cr.* I. ii. 30. Hence **Briarean** (-rĭān, -ēə·riăn), of or relating to B.; hundred-handed. Also quasi-*sb.*

Bribable, bribeable (brəi·băb'l). 1829. [f. BRIBE *v.* + -ABLE; see also -BLE.] **A.** *adj.* Capable of being bribed. **B.** *sb.* [sc. *person.*] 1867. Hence **Bribabi·lity, bribe-,** venality.

Bribe (brəib), *sb.* ME. [? f. OF. *bribe* 'piece of bread', *esp.* 'a piece given to a beggar'. For the sense-development cf. *briber.*] †**1.** A thing stolen; robbery; plunder –1509. **2.** 'A reward given to pervert the judgment or corrupt the conduct' (J.) 1535. †**3.** (*perh.*) Rascally behaviour 1560. Also in *comb.*, as *b.-broker.*
2. His sonnes..tooke bribes, and peruerted iudgement 1 *Sam.* viii. 3. His rise hath been his giving of large bribes PEPYS.

Bribe (brəib), *v.* ME. [Cf. the sb.] †**1.** *trans.* To take dishonestly; to extort. Also †*absol.* **2.** To influence corruptly, by a consideration, the action of 1528. Also *absol.* **3.** To purchase by bribery 1718. **4.** *fig.* To gain over by some influence 1595.
2. To b. a trustee..is..to suborn him to be guilty of a breach or an abuse of trust BENTHAM. He fawned, bullied, and bribed indefatigably MACAULAY.

Bri·beless, *a.* 1608. [f. BRIBE + -LESS.] Free from bribes; incorruptible.

Briber (brəi·bəɹ). ME. [a. AF. *bribour* = OF. *bribeor*, later *bribeur*; see BRIBE *sb.*] †**1.** A strolling vagrant –1600. †**b.** Hence: Scoundrel, wretch –1550. †**2.** A thief; a taker of black-mail; an extortioner –1587. †**3.** An official who exacts or accepts bribes –1611. **4.** One who offers or gives a bribe 1583. †**5.** A thing that bribes. *Timon* III. v. 61.

Bribery (brəi·bəri). ME. [a. OF. *briberie.*] †**1.** Theft, robbery –1567. †**2.** Extortion –1589. **3.** The exaction or taking of a bribe (*arch.*) 1549. **4.** The offer or acceptance of bribes; *spec.* the application of such means to gain votes at an election 1570.
1. He knew of bribryes mo Than possible is to telle in yeres two CHAUCER. *Comb.* **b.-oath,** an oath administrable to a voter at a parliamentary election, declaring that he has not received a bribe for his vote.

‖**Bric-à-brac** (bri·kăbræ·k). Also as one wd. 1840. [F.; see Littré.] Old curiosities, knick-knacks, antiquarian odds and ends, such as furniture, plate, china, etc. Also *attrib.*, and quasi-*adj.* (*joc.*)

Brick (brik), *sb.* 1416. [prob. a. F. *brique*, conn. w. Teut. *brekan* to break, in the sense (ult.) of 'piece of baked clay'.] **1.** A substance formed of clay, kneaded, moulded, and hardened by baking with fire, or sun-dried; used in building. **2.** A block of this substance, of a definite size and shape; usually rectangular (†pl. *brick*) 1525. **b.** A similar block or slab of sand and lime, concrete, etc. 1875. **3.** *transf.* Any brick-shaped block, *e.g.* a b. of tea, of bread, etc. 1827. **4.** *fig.* (*colloq.*) A good fellow 1840. **5.** as *adj.* **a.** Of brick. **b.** Brick-shaped. 1440.
2. Goe to, let vs make bricke, and burne them thorowly *Gen.* xi. 3. 4. Robert was no end of a b. (*mod.*).
Phrases. *Like bricks, like a b.*: vigorously, with good will. *To drop a b.*: to commit an indiscretion (*slang*).
Comb.: **b.-box,** a box of wooden bricks for a child to build with; **-bread, -loaf** (see 3); **-burner,** one who attends to a b.-kiln; **-nog, -nogging,** a method of building in which a timber framework is filled in with brickwork; **-press,** a machine for consolidating the moulded clay; **-setter,** = BRICKLAYER; **-tea,** tea leaves pressed into the shape of a small b.; **-trimmer,** an arch of brickwork for receiving the hearth of a fire-place; **-yard,** a place where bricks are made.

Brick (brik), *v.* 1648. [f. the sb.] Mostly in comb. with advbs. **1.** To line, face, or pave with brick; to imitate brickwork on a plaster surface 1825. **2.** *intr.* To work with (load, make, etc.) bricks 1884.
To b. up: to close up with brickwork. *To b. over*: to cover with brick.

Brickbat (bri·kbæt). 1563. [See BRICK *sb.* and BAT *sb.*[2]] A piece (prop. less than one half) of a brick; a typical missile.
She sent a b. after him FOXE.

Brick-dust (bri·kdɒst). 1664. **1.** Powdered brick. **2.** A tint as of brick-dust 1807. Also *attrib.*

Brick-earth (bri·k,ɜ·ɪþ). 1667. Clay suitable for making bricks; in *Geol.* an earth lying below the surface soil in the London basin.

Bri·ck-field. 1801. A field in which bricks are made.

Brick-kiln (bri·k-kil). 1481 A kiln or furnace for burning bricks.

Bricklayer (bri·kleⁱ:əɹ). 1485. One who lays the bricks in building.
Bricklayer's itch: a cutaneous disease produced on the hands of bricklayers through contact with lime. So **Bri·cklaying,** the craft of building with brick.

Brickle (bri·k'l), *a.* Now *dial.* 1460. [Doublet of ME. *bruchel*, f. (ult.) OTeut. *brekan* (OE. *brecan*) to break.] **1.** Liable to break; brittle. Also *fig.* Hence †**Bri·ckleness.**

Bri·ckmaker. 1465. One whose trade is to make bricks. So **Bri·ckmaking.**

†**Bri·ckwall,** *sb.* 1580. = BRICOLE *sb.* 2. [corrupted by pop. etym.] So †**Bri·ckwall** *v.* to cause to rebound.

Bri·ckwork, brick work. 1580. **1.** Builders' work in brick. **2.** Bricklaying 1677. **3.** *pl.* A place where bricks are made 1703.

Bri·cky, *a.* 1596. [f. BRICK *sb.*] **a.** Made or built of brick. **b.** Full of or abounding in bricks. **c.** Brick-red. Hence **Bri·ckiness.**

Bricole (bri·kəl, brikōᵘ·l). 1525. [a. F.:— late L. *briccola.* See Littré.] **1.** An ancient military engine for throwing stones or bolts. **2.** In *Tennis*: The rebound of a ball from the wall of a tennis court, a side-stroke against the wall; also *fig.* an indirect unexpected stroke or action. Similarly in *Billiards.* Cf. BRICK-WALL. 1598. **3.** Harness worn by men in drawing guns, where horses cannot be used. Hence †**Bri·cole** *v.* to cause to rebound.

Brid, var. of BIRD, BRED, BURD.

Bridal (brəi·dăl), *sb.* (*a.*) [OE. *brȳd-ealo,* lit. 'wedding-ale'. The form BRIDE-ALE is still a historical term.] **1.** A wedding feast; a wedding. Now chiefly *poet.* **2.** Used attrib., after adjs. in *-al*, as *nuptial*, etc. 1440. **b.** Also as adj.: = Of or pertaining to a bride, worn by a bride; bride-like 1748.
1. The bridalis of Crist and of the Chirche WYCLIF *Song of Sol.* 2. The b. day SPENSER, chamber SHAKS., bed 1714. Hence **Bri·dalty,** wedding (*rare*).

Bride (brəid), *sb.*[1] [Com. Teut.: OE. *brȳd* :—OTeut. **brūđi-z*, perh. f. the vb.-root *brū-* 'to cook, etc.' In Gothic the only sense found is 'daughter-in-law'. Not known exc. in Teut.] **1.** A woman about to be married or very recently married. Also *fig.* †**2.** A bridegroom –1598.
1. Ripe to be a B. *Rom. & Jul.* I. ii. 11. *fig.* I will shew thee the B., the Lambes wife *Rev.* xxi. 9.
In combination. **Bride-** had orig. the force of 'bridal, wedding'; the sense 'bride' is modern. Hence: **b.-bed** (*arch.*); †**-belt,** the zone worn by a virgin; **-bowl** = BRIDE-CUP; **-cake**; **-chamber,** the room in which a wedding is celebrated; **-couple,** a newly-wedded pair; **-door,** the door of the BRIDEHOUSE; **-knot,** a wedding favour; †**-leader,** = the later BRIDEMAN; †**-mother,** one who acts the part of mother at a wedding; **-price,** money paid for a bride; †**-squire** = BRIDEMAN; **-stake,** a pole set up to dance round at a wedding; **-weed,** a bride's dress or veil; **-wort,** Meadow-sweet.

Bride (brəid), *sb.*[2] ME. [a. F., f. Teut.; see BRIDLE.] †**1.** A bridle, rein. Also *fig.* ME. only. **2.** The network which connects the patterns in lace; also, a bonnet-string 1869.

†**Bride** (brəid), *v.* 1530. [f. BRIDE *sb.*[1]] **1.** *intr.* To act the bride. (Also with *it.*) –1652. **2.** *trans.* To wed –1658.

Bride-ale, bridale (brəi·d,ēⁱ:l). OE. [The analytical form of BRIDAL *sb.*] An ale-drinking at a wedding.

Bri·de-cup. *arch.* 1554. [f. *bride-* = wedding: see BRIDE *sb.*[1]] **a.** A bowl handed round at a wedding. **b.** A spiced cup prepared at night for the bride-couple. Also *fig.*

Bridegroom (brəi·dgrūm). [OE. *brȳdguma.* f. *brȳd* BRIDE + *guma* 'man' (poetic):—OTeut. **gumon-*, cogn. w. L. *homin-*. In 16th c. replaced by *bridegrome*, f. *grome* GROOM, 'lad'.] A man about to be, or just, married. Also *fig.*
He that hath the bryde is the brydegrome *John* iii. 29. *fig.* For me the Heavenly B. waits TENNYSON.

Bri·dehouse. Now *dial.* 1550. [f. as BRIDE-CUP.] The house where a wedding is held.

Bri·de-lace. Now *Hist.* 1575. [f. as prec.] **1.** A piece of lace used to bind up the sprigs of rosemary formerly worn at weddings –1663. **2.** *pl.* The striped ribbon-grass, or Lady's Garters.

†**Bri·delope.** OE. [perh. ad. ON. *brúđhlaup.*] The oldest Teut. name for wedding: *lit.* 'the bridal run', in conducting the bride to her new home. ? Only in OE.

Bri·deman. Now *dial.* 1613. [f. as BRIDE-CUP, or f. BRIDE *sb.*[1] 2.] †1. = BRIDEGROOM. 2. Now = BRIDESMAN. (Formerly called also *brideleader*, because he led the bride to the bridegroom.) 1663.

Bridesmaid (brəi·dzmēⁱd). 1552. [orig. *bridemaid*, f. *bride-* (see BRIDE *sb.*[1]); the *s* is 19th c.] A young unmarried woman or girl attending the bride at a wedding.

Bridesman (brəi·dzmǣn). 1808. [Altered from the earlier BRIDEMAN, q.v.] = BEST MAN, GROOMSMAN.

Bridewell (brəi·dwĕl). 1552. [From *Bride Well*, i. e. (*St.*) *Bride's Well* in London, near which stood a royal lodging, given by Edward VI for a hospital, and converted later into a house of correction.] A house of correction for prisoners; a gaol, prison. Also *fig.* and *attrib.*

Bridge (bridʒ), *sb.*[1] [Com. Teut.: OE. *brycg* :—OTeut. **brugjâ-*. Northern dialects have *brig* from Scand.] 1. A structure forming or carrying a road over a river, a ravine, etc., or affording passage between two points at a height above the ground. (For the different kinds, as *chain-b.*, etc., see the first element of the compound.) 2. a. A gangway for boats. b. A landing-stage, jetty, or pier. Now *dial.* ME. 3. A narrow ridge of rock, sand, or shingle, across the bottom of a channel 1812. 4. *Naut.* A raised platform, extending from side to side of a ship, for the officer in command. 5. *Phys.* The upper bony part of the nose. Also the curved central part of a pair of spectacles, etc. 1450. 6. *Mus.* a. In a violin, etc.: A thin upright piece of wood over which the strings are stretched, and which transmits their vibrations to the body of the instrument 1607. b. The ridge on a piano sound-board. c. The transition from the first to the second subject in sonata form; called also *b. passage.* 7. In various specific and technical uses: *esp.* a. In a furnace or boiler: A low vertical partition which retains the fuel in its place, and deflects the flame, etc. 1838. b. *Electric b.*: a contrivance for measuring electrical resistance 1881.

1. Phr. *B. of boats*: a roadway supported by boats moored abreast across a body of water. *A gold* or *silver b.*: an easy and attractive way of escape.

Comb.: **b.-board**, a board into which the ends of the steps of wooden stairs are fastened (Gwilt); **†-bote**, a tax for the repair of bridges; **-deck** (see 4); **-head**, a fortification covering the end of a b. nearest the enemy = F. *tête de pont*; **-islet**, a portion of land which becomes insular at high water; **-man** = BRIDGE-MASTER; **-money** = *bridge-bote*; **-rail**, a rail having the form of a reversed U; **-stone**, a flag spanning a gutter, etc.; **-train**, a company of Military Engineers equipped with material and appliances for b.-building; **-tree**, a splinter-bar; also, the beam which supports the spindle of the runner in a grain mill; **-way**, the way formed by a b.; also, the water-way beneath it.

Bridge, *sb.*[2] 1886. [Etym. unc.] A game resembling dummy whist, in which in each deal the dealer's partner is dummy, his hand being exposed and played by the dealer.

Auction b., a variety in which the right to name trumps, etc. goes to the player who undertakes to make the highest score. *Contract b.*, a form of this.

Bridge (bridʒ), *v.*[1] [OE. *brycgian*, f. *brycg*, BRIDGE *sb.*] 1. To make a bridge over; to span with a means of passage. b. To span as with a bridge 1872. Also *fig.* 2. To form (a way) by means of a bridge 1667.

1. An arch of ice..bridging a fissure KANE. 2. Xerxes..Over Hellespont Bridging his way MILT.

†Bridge, *v.*[2] ME. [aphet. f. *abregge*, a. F. *abréger*.] To abridge. Also *absol.* -1526.

Bri·dge-house. ME. A house connected with a bridge; *spec.* the house with its officers, etc., formerly connected with the care and repair of London Bridge.

Bri·dgemaster. 1502. An officer having control of a bridge; formerly, in some boroughs, a member of the corporation; a *bridgeman*.

Bridgetin (bri·dʒĕtin). 1533. [f. *St. Bridget*, in L. *Brigidia*.] One of a religious order founded by St. Bridget in the 14th century.

Bridgeward (bri·dʒ,wǭ·ɹd), *sb.* OE. 1. The warden or wardship of a bridge. 2. The main ward of a key.

†Bri·dgewater. 1552. A woollen cloth formerly made at Bridgewater -1607.

Bridging (bri·dʒiŋ), *vbl. sb.* 1839. [f. BRIDGE *v.*[1] or *sb.*[1] + -ING[1].] 1. The action of BRIDGE *v.*[1] 2. Bridges viewed as work 1884. b. *Carpentry.* A bridging piece. (*mod.*).

Comb.: **b.-floor**, a floor having bridging joists; **-joist**, a joist of a flooring resting upon the binding-joists below, and supporting the boarding above; **-piece**, a piece placed between two opposite beams to prevent their nearer approach.

Bridle (brəi·d'l), *sb.* [OE. *brīdel* for earlier **brigdel*, from root of *bregd-an* to pull (see BRAID); cf. *hand-le*, *sadd-le*, etc.] 1. The head-gear, consisting of a head-stall, bit, and rein, by which a horse, etc. is controlled and guided. Also *fig.* 2. *fig.* A restraint, curb, check ME. 3. = BRANKS 1. 1623. 4. The gesture of bridling (see BRIDLE *v.* 3) 1748. 5. Anything resembling a bridle in form or use: *esp.* a. *Naut.* A mooring-cable or 'fast' 1626. b. *Fire-arms.* The plate inside a gunlock, which holds the sear and tumbler in position 1844.

1. *fig.* Giving the b. to a desperate man NORTH. 2. A brydel of lawe..& also a brydell of the drede of God 1530.

Comb.: **b.-arm** (cf. *bridle-hand*); **-bridge** (cf. *bridle-path*); **-cable**, a cable attached to the middle of a ground cable; **-gate**, one leading into a b.-path; **-hand**, the left hand, which holds the b. in riding; **-path**, **-road**, **-way**, a path fit for the passage of a horse, but not of vehicles; **-port**, a port in a ship's bow through which bridles (see 5 a) may be run or chase-guns fired; **-rein**, a rein attached to the bit.

Bridle (brəi·d'l), *v.* [OE. *brīdlian*, f. as prec.] 1. To put a bridle on (a horse); to furnish with a bridle ME. 2. *fig.* To curb, check, hold *in* OE. 3. *trans.* and *intr.* To throw up the head and draw in the chin (as a horse does when reined in), expressing pride, vanity, or resentment. Now usu. *To b. up.* 1460.

1. To be taught to saddle and b. 1833. 2. Rise.. And b. in thy headlong wave MILT. *Comus* 887. Forts ..to b. Rochelle HUME. 3. Everybody bridled up at this remark DICKENS. Hence **Bri·dler**, one who bridles; †a bridle-maker.

Bridoon (bridū·n). 1753. [a. F. *bridon*.] The snaffle and rein of a military bridle, which acts with or independently of the bit.

Brief (brīf), *sb.* [ME. *bref*, a. OF.:—L. *breve*, adj. neut. Not found in OE.] †1. A writing issued by official or legal authority; a royal mandate; a writ, a summons. (tr. L. *breve* in legal senses.) -1641. 2. A letter of the pope, less ample and solemn than a *bull*, and differing from it in form. More fully called *apostolical* or *papal b.* 1460. 3. A letter patent issued by the sovereign as Head of the Church, licensing a collection in the churches throughout England for a specified object; a *Church B.* or *King's Letter. Obs.* in practice. 1588. †4. A letter, dispatch, note -1652. †5. An abridgement, epitome -1691. Also *fig.* †6. A list; an invoice, memorandum -1849. 7. *Law.* A summary of facts and points of law, drawn up for counsel in charge of a case 1631. †8. *Mus.* = BREVE *sb.* 2. -1658.

3. Briefes for a gathering towards the erecting of a colledge 1588. 6. *Mids. N.* V. i. 42. 7. *To hold a b.*: to be retained as counsel *for*. *To take a b.*: to accept the conduct of a case. Hence **Brie·fless** *a.* holding no briefs, unemployed. **Brie·flessness.**

Brief (brīf). [ME. *bref*, a. OF.:—L. *brevem*.] A. *adj.* 1. Of short duration. 2. Concise ME. b. Curt in manner (*rare*). SCOTT. 3. Short, curtailed, limited in space. (Less usual.) 1668. Also †*fig.* ¶4. Rife; as an epidemic disease (*dial.*) (Of obscure origin.) 1595.

1. Out, out, breefe Candle *Macb.* V. v. 23. †*To be b.*, i.e. expeditious *Tr. & Cr.* IV. v. 237. 2. Breefe Chronicles *Haml.* II. ii. 548. *To be b.*: to speak concisely. 3. *fig. Cymb.* V. v. 165.

B. quasi-*sb.* a. *In b.*: in few words. With ellipsis of 'to speak': To sum up. ME. †b. *The b.*, used *absol.* like *the short* -1601. C. quasi-*adv.* a. Shortly, quickly; in few words 1557. b. In brief 1600.

Hence **Brie·fly** *adv.* shortly, in few words; †within a short time. **Brie·fness**, †celerity (*Lear* II. i. 20); brevity.

†Brief, *v.*[1] 1601. [f. prec.] To shorten, abridge -1655.

Brief (brīf), *v.*[2] 1837. [f. BRIEF *sb.*, sense 7.] 1. To reduce to the form of a counsel's brief. 2. To put (instructions) into the form of a brief *to* a barrister. Also *fig.* 1864. 3. To give a brief to (a barrister); to retain 1862.

Brier, briar (brəi·əɹ, brəi·aɹ), **brere** (brī·əɹ), *sb.* [OE.: of unkn. origin. The form *brere* represents the OE. and ME. word. The 16th c. var. *brier* is not accounted for; cf. ME. *frere*, *frier*, FRIAR.] 1. Any prickly, thorny bush or shrub; now usu. a wild rose bush. 2. Brier-bushes collectively ME. 3. A twig, or †thorn of a brier ME. 4. *fig.* (*pl.*) Vexations 1509.

1. Sweet is the Rose, but growes upon a brere SPENSER.

Comb.: **Sweet B.**, a species of wild Rose (*R. rubiginosa*) with fragrant leaves; **Austrian B.**, *R. lutea*; **Green B.**, *Smilax rotundifolia*; **Sensitive B.**, the genus *Schronkia*. **B.-rose**, **-tree**, the Dog-rose. Hence **Bri·ered**, **bri·ared** *ppl. a.* entangled in or covered with briers. Also *fig.* **Bri·ery**, **bri·ary** *a.* full of or consisting of briers; *fig.* vexing.

Brier, briar (brəi·əɹ), *sb.*[2] 1868. [orig. **bruyer**, a. F. *bruyère* heath, erron. identified w. prec.] The White Heath (*Erica arborea*), the root of which is used for making tobacco-pipes; also a pipe of this wood. So **B.-root**, **-wood.**

Brieve (brīv). 1609. [var. of BRIEF *sb.*] *Sc. Law.* A writ or precept issued from Chancery in the Sovereign's name, directing trial to be made of certain points specified.

Brig (brig). 1720. [Abbrev. of BRIGANTINE. Cf. *cab*, *mob*, etc.] a. = BRIGANTINE. b. A vessel with two masts square-rigged like a ship's fore- and main-masts, but carrying also on her main-mast a lower fore-and-aft sail with a gaff and boom. (The changes in rig have accompanied the shortened name only.) 1769. c. A hermaphrodite brig = BRIGANTINE 3. *Comb.* **b.-schooner**, a hermaphrodite b., or brigantine.

Brig, north. f. BRIDGE.

Brigade (brigēⁱ·d), *sb.* 1637. [a. F., ad. It. *brigata*, f. *brigare*, f. late L. *briga*, strife, contention. Milton accented *bri·gad*.] †1. A crew of people -1650. 2. *gen.* A large division of troops 1649. b. *spec.* A subdivision of an army, formerly two regiments or squadrons; but now of variable composition. In the British Army, at present used only of the Horse and Field Artillery. 3. A band of persons more or less organized; e. g. a *fire-b.*, etc. 1806.

2. a. Thither..A numerous Brigad hasten'd MILT. *P. L.* I. 675. *Comb.* **b.-major**, a staff officer attached to a brigade, who assists the brigadier in command.

Brigade (brigēⁱ·d), *v.* 1805. [f. prec.] 1. *trans.* To form into a brigade or brigades. 2. *loosely*, To form (people) as if into a brigade; to combine 1859.

Brigadier (brigădī·əɹ). 1678. [ad. F., f. *brigade*; see -IER.] 1. **B.-General**: A military officer in command of a brigade; the rank was abolished after the war of 1914–18, being superseded by *colonel-commandant*, which was replaced by *b.* in 1928. †2. *B-wig*: a full wig tied back in two curls -1818.

Brigand (bri·gănd). [ME. a. OF., = Pr. *bregan* irregular soldier; prob. ad. It. *brigante*, f. *brigare*; see BRIGUE *v.* and BRIGADE.] †1. A light-armed, irregular foot-soldier -1795. 2. One who lives by pillage and robbery: a bandit; *esp.* a member of one of the gangs infesting districts of Italy, Spain, Turkey, etc. ME. Also *attrib.* Hence **Bri·gandish** *a.* **Bri·gandishly** *adv.* **Bri·gandism.**

Brigandage (bri·găndėdʒ). 1600. [a. F., f. *brigand*; see prec.] 1. The practice of brigands; highway-robbery, freebooting, pillage. 2. Brigands collectively 1875.

1. The b. of the Free Companies SCOTT.

†Bri·gander. ME. [?f. BRIGAND. Not in F.] 1. = BRIGANDINE 1. -1611. 2. A soldier wearing a brigander 1525.

Brigandine, brigantine (bri·găndīn, -tīn). [Late ME., a. OF.; = armour for a BRIGAND (sense 1).] Body armour composed of iron rings or plates, sewed upon, and covered with, canvas, linen, or leather; at first worn in two halves; loosely = 'coat of mail, corslet' 1456. Also *attrib.*

Put on the brigandines *Jer.* xlvi. 4. MILT. *Sams.* 1120.

Brigantine[1] (bri·găntīn). 1525. [16th c. *brigandyn*, a. F. *brigandin* (now *brigantin*), ad. It. *brigantino*, perh. 'skirmishing vessel'; cf. BRIGADE and BRIGAND.] 1. *orig.* A small vessel equipped both for sailing and rowing, employed for purposes of piracy, espionage, landing, etc. Only *Hist.* 2. Applied (loosely) to other similar vessels. Still *poet.* and *rhet.* 1552. 3. A two-masted vessel, with a brig's foremast, square-rigged, and a schooner's mainmast, fore-and-aft-rigged 1695.

Brigantine [2], var. of BRIGANDINE.

Bright (brəit). Comp. BRIGHTER, -EST. [Com. Teut.: OE. *beorht*:—*berht*:—OTeut. **berhto-z*:—a stem **berh*:—Aryan *bhrag-*, whence L. *flagrare, flamma.*] **A.** *adj.* (The opposite to *dull.*) 1. Shining; emitting, reflecting, or pervaded by much light. **b.** *fig.* Lit up with happiness, gladness, or hope 1751. †2. Clear to the mind -1741. 3. Of persons: 'Resplendent with charms' (J.); fair (*arch.*) ME. 4. Of vivid colour ME. 5. Of sounds: Clear, shrill ME. 6. Illustrious, splendid. (L. *clarus*). OE. 7. Lively, brilliant, vivacious; opp. to *dull* 1605. 8. Quick-witted, clever; keen. (Used chiefly of one's inferiors or children.) 1741.

1. A b. starre SHAKS., swerde ME., evening POPE, transparent Æther STEELE. 3. Angels are b. still, though the brightest fell *Macb.* IV. iii. 22. 4. The brightest Bay DRYDEN. Strange b. birds HEMANS. 6. The wisest, brightest, meanest of mankind POPE. 7. B. and Iouiall SHAKS. B. thoughts O. W. HOLMES. 8. A b. specimen! (Ironical.) (*mod.*). A b. look-out R. DANA. Hence **Bri·ghtly** *adv.*

B. *sb.* Brightness, light. *arch.* (*poet.*) ME. Dark with excessive b. MILT. *P. L.* III. 380.

Bright (brəit), *adv.* OE. [f. BRIGHT *a.* + *-e* advb., lost c 1400.] 1. = Brightly. 2. *Comb.*, as *b.-burning*, etc. 1588.

†**Bright**, *v.* [OE. *beorhtian*, f. *beorht* bright.] 1. *intr.* To shine bright -ME. 2. *trans.* To make bright -1686.

Brighten (brəi·t'n), *v.* [ME. *brightn-en* = OE. *beorhtnian*. Later perh. new-formed on *bright.*] 1. *trans.* To make bright 1583. Also *fig.* 2. *intr.* To become bright; to shine ME. Also *fig.* (see BRIGHT *a.*).

1. To b. up the skies DRYDEN. Joy Bright'ns his crest MILT. *P. L.* IX. 634. 2. The boy's eyes.. Brighten'd BYRON.

Brightness (brəi·tnės). [OE. *beorhtnes*, *brehtnis.*] The quality of being bright (see BRIGHT *a.*).

Bright's Disease. [f. Dr. R. *Bright* (1827).] *Med.* 'A generic term including several forms of acute and chronic disease of the kidney usually associated with albumen in the urine'; granular degeneration of the kidneys.

Bri·ghtsome, *a. arch.* 1558. [Cf. *gladsome*, etc.] Partaking of brightness, bright-looking. (Vaguer than *bright.*)

†**Bri·gous**, *a.* ME. [a. AF. **brigous* = OF. *brigeus*, cf. BRIGUE.] Of or pertaining to strife; contentious -1519. var. †**Bri·gose.**

‖**Brigue** (brīg), *sb.* ME. [a. F. = med.L. *briga*. Of unkn. origin. See BRIGAND, etc.] †1. Strife, contention -1678. ‖2. Intrigue, faction. [From mod.F.] *Obs.* (exc. casually). 1701.

†**Brigue** (brīg), *v.* ME. [f. prec., or a. F. *briguer*. But with sense 1 cf. BRIKE.] †1. To ensnare, beguile. ME. only. 2. *intr.* To intrigue; to canvass -1808.

†**Brike.** ME. only. [a. ONF. *brique*, var. of *briche, brice*, trap.] A trap, a snare; a dilemma.

Brill (bril), *sb.* 1481. [Origin and form (*brill, prill*, or *perl*) unkn.] A flat-fish (*Rhombus vulgaris*), allied to the Turbot.

‖**Brillante** (brilla·nte), *a.* [It.] *Mus.* Gay, showy, and sparkling in style.

Brilliance (bri·lyăns). 1755. [f. BRILLIANT. Not in Fr.] Intense or sparkling brightness, radiance, or splendour. Also *fig.*

The b. of a lamp HOWELLS, B. of mind H. ROGERS.

Brilliancy (bri·lyănsi). 1747. [See prec.] The quality of being brilliant; shining quality. She is full of b. MISS MITFORD. The comparative b. of two colours (*mod.*).

Brilliant (bri·lyănt), *a.* (*sb.*) 1681. [a. F. *brillant*, f. *briller* to shine, f. L. type **berillare*, f. late L. *berillus*, L. *beryllus* BERYL.] Brightly shining, glittering, sparkling, lustrous. Also *fig.* of qualities, actions, and persons.

fig. A man of solid though not b. parts MACAULAY. A b. circle of noblemen and gentlemen MACAULAY. Hence **Bri·lliant-ly** *adv.*, **-ness.**

†**B.** as *sb.* = BRILLIANCY -1694.

Bri·lliant, *sb.* 1690. [a. F. *brillant* adj. used subst.] 1. A diamond of the finest cut and brilliancy. Also *attrib.* and in *comb.*

(The *brilliant* differs from the *rose* in having horizontal faces on its upper and under sides, called the *table* and the *collet* respectively, which are surrounded and united by facets. The French brilliant consists of two truncated pyramids placed base to base.)

†2. A kind of silken fabric 1719. 3. A firework 1875. 4. The smallest type used in Eng. printing, being a size less than 'diamond'. (Cf. *pearl, ruby*, etc.)

Brilliant type.

Bri·lliant, *v. rare.* 1752. [f. BRILLIANT *a.*] To cut as a brilliant.

†**Brim**, *sb.*[1] [OE. *brim* surf, (*poet.*) the sea; see BRIM *v.*[1]] The sea; also 'flood', water -1596.

Brim (brim), *sb.*[2] [ME. *brimme*, of unkn. etym.] †1. *orig.* The border, margin, edge, or brink, as of the sea or of any piece of water -1597; also, of other things (*arch.* or *dial.*) 1525. Also †*fig.* 2. Now *esp.* The edge, margin, or lip of a cup, bowl, basin, or the like 1562. 3. The upper edge or surface of water (*arch.* or *poet.*) 1552. 4. The marginal rim of a hat 1592.

1. Let thy love hang at thy hearts bottome, not at the tongues brimme LYLY. 2. A molten Sea of ten cubites, from b. to b. 2 *Chron.* iv. 2. 3. The feet of the Priestes..were dipped in the brimme of the water *Josh.* iii. 15. Hence **Brim-full, brimful** (prop. pronounced (bri·m,fu·ll); erron. (bri·mful), after *mindful*, etc.), full to the brim; on the point of overflowing. **Brimfully** *adv.* (*rare*). **Bri·mless** *a.*

Brim (brim), *v.*[1] ME. [f. OE. *bremman* to roar, rage, f. OTeut. *brem-*, cogn. w. L. *fremere.*] 1. *intr.* Of swine: To be in heat, rut, copulate. 2. *trans.* Said of a boar 1552.

Brim (brim), *v.*[2] 1611. [f. BRIM *sb.*[2]] 1. To fill to the brim. Also *absol.* Also *fig.* and *transf.* 2. *intr.* To be or become brim-full 1818. †3. To provide with a brim 1623.

1. Arrange the board and b. the glass TENNYSON.

‖**Brimborion, -um.** 1653. [Fr.; formerly *bre-, briborion*; a perversion of *breviarium* (Littré).] A thing without use or value; trash, nonsense.

Brimmed (brimd, bri·mėd), *ppl. a.* 1606. [f. BRIM *v.*[2] and *sb.*[2]] 1. Filled to the brim; brim-full 1624. 2. Having a brim, as a hat, etc. Chiefly in *comb.*, as *broad-b.*, etc. 1606.

Brimmer (bri·məɹ), *sb.* 1652. [f. BRIM *v.*[2] + -ER[1].] 1. That which fills to the brim. 2. A brimming goblet 1663. †3. A hat with a brim -1670.

2. Boy! Fill a B., Nay fuller yet COWLEY.

Bri·mming, *ppl. a.* 1667. [f. BRIM *v.*[2] + -ING[2].] 1. That rises to the brim of its vessel, basin, or bed. Also *fig.* 2. Of a vessel: Full to overflowing 1697. Also *advb.*

1. The b. stream MILT. 2. A b. pail DRYDEN. Hence **Bri·mmingly** *adv.*

Brimse. Now *dial.* 1579. [prob. ad. ON. *brims*, f. *brem-* to roar.] A gadfly; = BREEZE *sb.*[1]

Brimstone (bri·mstən). ME. [app. f. *bern-* or *brinn-*, stems of *bernen, brinnen* to BURN + STONE.] 1. Formerly the common vernacular name for SULPHUR. Now used chiefly when referring to its inflammable character, and to the use in *Gen.* xix. 24 and *Rev.* xix. 20. Also *fig.* 2. A virago, spitfire. Cf. BRIM *sb.*[3] 1751. 3. *B. Butterfly*: a butterfly with wings of a sulphur colour, *Gonepteryx Rhamni* 1827.

Comb.: **b. match**, one having its end dipped in b.; **b. moth**, one of sulphur colour, *Rumia cratægata*; **b.-wort**, Sulphur-wort, *Peucedanum palustre* (and *officinale*). Hence **Bri·mstony** *a.*

Brinded (bri·ndėd), *a. arch.* ME. [? f. **brend-en*:—*brand* 'burning, brand'.] Of a tawny or brownish colour, marked with bars of a different hue; *gen.* streaked, spotted; brindled. The b. Cat SHAKS., lioness SHELLEY.

Brindle (bri·nd'l). 1676. [Deduced from *brindled.*] **A.** *adj.* = BRINDED, BRINDLED. **B.** *sb.* **a.** Brindled colour. **b.** A brindled dog.

Brindled (bri·nd'ld), *a.* 1678. [var. of BRINDED, perh. after *kindled*, etc.] 'Streaked, tabby, marked with streaks' (J.).

Brine (brəin), *sb.* [OE. *brýne, brine.* History unkn.] 1. Water saturated, or strongly impregnated, with salt; salt water. 2. The water of the sea; the sea. (Usu. *poet.*) 1598. 3. = Briny tears (*poet.*) 1592.

2. On the level b. Sleek Panope with all her sisters played MILT. *Lycidas.* 3. I should be well seasoned, for mine eyes lye in b. DEKKER.

Comb.: **b.-gauge**, a salinometer; **-pan**, a shallow iron vessel in which b. is evaporated; **-pump**, a pump used to remove b. from a steamer's boilers; **-seeth**, a salt boilery; **-shrimp, -worm**, *Cancer Salinus* (Linn.), a small shrimp or worm which peoples reservoirs of b.; **-smeller**, one who prospects for beds of salt; **-valve**, a valve in a boiler which is opened to allow the escape of b.

Brine (brəin), *v.* 1552. [f. BRINE *sb.*] To treat with brine.

To b. Fields 1677, wheat 1722, hides 1883.

Bring (briŋ), *v.* Pa. t. and pple. **brought** (brǭt). [Com. Teut.: OE. *bringan, brengean* (pa. t. *brōhte*, pple. *brōht*).] 1. To cause to come along with oneself; to fetch. In sense the causal of *come.* 2. To escort (a person) on his way. Now *dial.* 1450. 3. *fig.* To cause one to have; to procure 1450. †4. To deduce, infer -1713. 5. To prefer or lay (a charge, etc.); to set on foot (an action at law); to adduce (a statement, etc.) OE. 6. †a. = *Bring forth* -1795. b. = *Bring in* 1535. 7. *fig.* To cause to come *from, into, out of, to*, etc., or *to be* or *do* something; to cause to become (see quots.) ME. 8. To cause to come (to a certain course of action, etc.); to induce, persuade 1611. 9. *Naut.* To cause to come or go into a certain position or direction, as *to the wind* (see WIND).

1. To b. Trophies home DRYDEN, ships to land 1565. What brings him here (*mod.*). Phr. *To b. an answer, word, tidings.* 2. *Gen.* xviii. 16. 3. *fig.* Those lines ..brought tears into the Duchess's eyes THACKERAY. The loss that brought us pain TENNYSON. 5. To b. an action BLACKSTONE. *To b. home*: see HOME. 6. b. So much money as [a thing] will b. BUTLER *Hud.* II. i. 466. 7. To b. into hatred HOOKER, into difficulties BUTLER, in question 1818; to b. [a man] to himself (= to his senses) CHAUCER. So *to b. to an end, head, issue, to bearings, to nought, shame, to remembrance, to bed* (see BED); *to b. to bear, boil, to pass.*

Combined with adverbs. **B. about. a.** To cause to happen, effect. **b.** To turn round; *fig.* to convert. **c.** = *bring round.* **B. down. a.** To cause to fall to the ground; to kill or wound (a flying bird, etc.). **b.** To cause (punishments, etc.) to alight *on, upon.* **c.** *fig.* To humble. **d.** To lower (price); to simplify. **e.** To continue (information, etc.) to a later date (cf. *Bring up*). **f.** *To bring down the house*, etc.: to evoke applause which suggests the downfall of the building. **B. forth. a.** To give birth to, bear, yield. †**b.** To utter; advance *Isa.* xli. 21. †**c.** To bring to public view. *Macb.* III. iv. 125. **B. forward.** *Book-keeping.* To carry on a sum from the bottom of one folio to the top of another. **B. in. a.** To introduce (customs, etc.). **b.** To bring (money) into the purse or pocket. **c.** To introduce (a bill, etc.). **d.** To introduce (into consideration); to adduce. **e.** Of a jury: *colloq.* to find (guilty, etc.). **B. off. a.** To bring away from; *esp.* by boat from a ship, wreck, the shore 1656. **b.** To rescue, acquit (*arch.*). **B. on.** †**a.** To conduct; to advance the growth of. **b.** To cause (illness, etc.). **c.** To introduce (a subject, etc.). **d.** *techn.* To join, weld together. **B. out. a.** To utter. **b.** To bring into prominence; to develop. **c.** To introduce (a young lady, a company, a loan, etc.). **d.** To produce (a play, etc.); to publish (a book). **B. over.** To cause to come to one's own side or party. **B. round.** To restore from a fainting-fit or an attack of illness. **B. through.** *spec.* To treat successfully through the stages of an illness. **B. to. a.** *Naut.* To tie, bend. **b.** To cause to come to a standstill. Also *intr.* (for *refl.* or *absol.*). †**c.** To cause to acquiesce. **d.** To restore to consciousness or to health. **B. under.** To subdue. **B. up. a.** To raise, rear, build up; to raise to a point or amount, etc. **b.** To rear; to educate. **c.** To bring before a tribunal or for examination. **d.** *Naut.* To bring to anchor, or to a standstill. Also *intr.*, whence 'to stop, pull up'. **e.** To bring under notice or consideration (*esp.* a by-gone matter). **f.** To vomit (*colloq.*). **g.** *B. up the rear* (*arrear*): see REAR.

Bringer (bri·ŋəɹ). ME. [f. prec. + -ER[1].] One who or that which brings (see BRING *v.*).

The first b. of vnwelcome newes 2 *Hen. IV*, I. i. 100.

Brinish (brəi·niʃ), *a.* 1580. [f. BRINE *sb.* + -ISH[1].] 1. Of the nature of brine; saltish; of or pertaining to the sea 1588. 2. *fig.* Bitter 1580.

‖**Brinjal, -jaul** (bri·ndʒǭl). 1611. [Anglo-Ind. ad. Pg. *bringella*, ad. (ult.) Skr. *vātingana*. See N.E.D.] The fruit of the Egg-plant (*Solanum Melongena*).

‖**Brinjarry** (brindʒā·ri). *Anglo-Ind.* 1793. [corruption of Urdū *banjārā*, deriv. of *vanij* trade.] A travelling grain and salt merchant of the Deccan.

Brink (briŋk). [ME. *brink* (*brenk*), cogn. w. ON. *brekka* (:—*brinkā*) 'slope, hill-side, hill'. Not in OE.] 1. The edge, margin, or border of a steep place, *e.g.* a precipice, chasm, grave. (The specific current sense.) 2. The edge of the land bordering a piece of water: formerly = 'bank, shore, brim'; now *esp.* when this is steep ME. 3. = BRIM 4. Now *dial.* ME. 4. *gen.* A margin, border, edge (*arch.*) ME. 5. *fig.* The very verge of some state, time, event, or action (see quots.) ME.

1. A ryall cite vpon the brinke of twede CAXTON. 5. The b. of eternity BARROW, of destruction DE FOE, ruin SWIFT, absurdity JOHNSON.

Briny (brəi·ni), *a.*[1] 1608. [f. BRINE *sb.* + -Y [1].] Of or pertaining to brine or to the sea; saturated with salt.

The b. Flood 1697. B. marshes 1799.

Briny, *a.*[2] (?*sb.*) 1602. [OE. *bryne*, and BURNING *sb.* 3.] Phosphorescent, ? phosphorescence.

‖**Brio** (brī·o). 1855. [It.] Liveliness, go.

Brionine, Briony, vars. of BRYONIN(E), BRYONY.

‖**Briquette, briquet** (brike·t, bri·kėt). 1883. [Fr. *briquette*, dim. of *brique*.] 1. A block of artificial stone. 2. A brick-shaped block of artificial coal 1884.

Brisk (brisk), *a.* 1592. [? Welsh *brysg*, or F. *brusque*.] 1. Sharp or smart in regard to movement (in a praiseworthy sense). 2. In allied senses, chiefly unfavourable, and mostly obs. (See quots.) 1601. †3. Spruce –1603. 4. Of liquors: Effervescent. Of the air: Fresh, keen 1597.

1. Young b. fellows DE FOE. A b. cannonade 1855, traffic 1833, gale 1759, fire 1837. 2. Briske and giddy-paced times *Twel. N.* II. iv. 6. A b. (= 'sharp') letter 1700. Hence **Bri·skish** *a.* **Bri·skly** *adv.* **Bri·skness.** †**Bri·sky** *a. Mids. N.* III. i. 97.

Brisk (brisk), *v.* 1592. [f. prec.] 1. To make brisk. Now with *up*. 1628. Also *intr.* (for *refl.*) †2. *trans.* To smarten *up* –1710. Also *intr.* (for *refl.*)

1. I like a cup to briske the spirits FELTHAM. *To b. up* (intr.): to come up briskly. *To b. about* (intr.): to move about briskly.

Brisket (bri·skėt). 1450. [Cf. OF. *bruschet*, *brischet*.] The breast of an animal, the part covering the breast-bone, esp. as a joint.

Brisling (bri·sliŋ). 1902. A small Norw. fish of the herring family resembling a sardine.

Bristle (bri·s'l), *sb.* [ME. *brustel*:—OE. *byrst*; see BIRSE.] 1. *prop.* One of the stiff hairs that grow on the back of the hog and wild boar. 2. *gen.* Any short, stiff, pointed or prickly hair ME. 3. In plants: A seta 1731.

Comb.: **b.-fern**, *Trichomanes radicans*; **-grass**, the genus *Setaria*; **-moss**, the genus *Orthotrichum*.

Bristle (bri·s'l), *v.*[1] 1480. [f. prec. sb. See BRUSTLE *v.*] I. *intr.* 1. Of hair, quills, etc.: To be, become, or stand, stiff and bristly. 2. Of animals: To raise the bristles, as a sign of anger or excitement. b. Of persons: To show fight. Also with *up*. 1549. 3. To be or become bristly. Also *fig.* 1606.

2. Don't b. up like a hedgehog 1861. 3. France.. bristles with bayonets 1837. To b. with difficulties (*mod.*).

II. *trans.* 1. To erect stiffly (hair, etc.) like bristles: chiefly in anger. Also with *up*. 1595. Also *fig.* 2. To furnish with bristles 1678.

1. Now.. Doth dogged warre b. his angry crest *John* IV. iii. 149.

Bri·stle, *v.*[2] Now *dial.* 1483. [?] To make or become crisp with heat.

Bristletail (bri·s'ltēl). 1706. A wingless insect (*Machilis maritima*) having bristly caudal appendages.

Bristly (bri·sli), *a.* 1591. [f. BRISTLE *sb.* + -Y [1].] 1. Set with bristles or short stiff hairs; setose. Also *fig.* 2. Of the nature of or like bristles 1592. Hence **Bri·stliness.**

Bristol (bri·stəl). [1. A city of England upon the Lower Avon, giving its name to various products.] 2. Short for 'Bristol-stone'; see 3. 1618. 3. *attrib.*, as **B.-board**, a kind of paste-board with a smooth surface; **-brick**, a brick of siliceous material, used for cleaning cutlery; **-diamond, -gem, -stone**, transparent rock-crystal found in the Clifton limestone near Bristol; also *attrib.*; **-fashion** (*Naut.*), in good order; **B. milk**, rich sherry.

Brisure (brizü·r, bri·ʒiŭr). 1623. [a. F.] 1. *Her.* A difference. 2. *Fortif.* A break in the general direction of a rampart or parapet 1706.

Brit, Britt (brit), *sb.*[1] 1602. Local name of the young of the Herring and Sprat; also the spawn of these. Also *transf.*

Brit, Brett, *sb.*[2] [OE. *Bret* (pl. *Brettas*) a Briton, pointing to an OCelt. stem **Britt-os*. Hence *Brettisc, Bryttisc*, BRITISH.] A. A Briton: the ordinary name in the OE. Chronicle; now *Hist.* B. *adj.* British.

Britain (bri·t'n), *sb.* [ME. *Bretayne, -eyne*, a. OF. *Bretaigne*:—L. *Brittannia* or *Brittānia*. The OE. name was *Breoton, Bryten, Breten*; also *Breoton-lond*, etc.] The proper name of the whole island containing England, Wales, and Scotland, with their dependencies; more fully called Great Britain; now also used for the British empire as a whole.

Britain, after the OE. period, was for long used only as a historical term; but in 1604 James I was proclaimed 'King of Great Britain'; and this name was adopted for the United Kingdom at the Union in 1707. *North B.* for Scotland is still occ. in (postal) use. *Greater B.* = 'Great B. and the colonies' dates from 1868.

†2. The duchy of Brittany or Bretagne in France; also called Little Britain –1622.

†**Britain,** *a.* and *sb.* 1547. [ad. L. *Brit(t)annus, Brittānus*. Cf. Gr. Βρεττανοί; see next.] A. *sb.* 1. An ancient Briton –1702. 2. A Breton –1618. B. *adj.* 1. Ancient British –1641. 2. British, in the mod. sense. **B. Crown**, a gold coin struck by James I, orig. = 5*s.*, subseq. 5*s.* 6*d.* 3. Breton 1645. vars. †**Bri·tainer, Bri·taner.**

Britannia (britæ·niă). OE. [L., anciently *Brittannia, Brittānia*, f. *Brittanni* or *Brittāni* = Gr. Βρεττανοί, perh. adopted from the Greeks of Massilia.] The Latin name of Britain; a name for Britain personified as a female; the figure on coins, etc., emblematic of Britain. Also *attrib.*

Comb. **B.-metal**, an alloy of tin and regulus of antimony, resembling silver.

Britannic (britæ·nik), *a.* 1641. [ad. L. *Britannicus*.] Of Britain, British. Used in *His* or *Her B. Majesty*. Hence **Brita·nnically** *adv.* in British fashion; in reference to Great Britain.

†**Brita·nnic,** *sb.* 1567. [a. L. *britannica* (*herba*).] *Herb.* The Water-dock (*Rumex hydrolapathum*) –1601.

†**Bri·tany.** 1579. [ad. L. *Britannia*.] 1. Britain, Great Britain –1662. 2. The French province of Bretagne: 'Little Britany', commonly spelt Brittany.

Brite, *v.* Now *dial.* 1669. [Cf. ON. *brjóta*, corresp. to OE. *brēotan*.] *intr.* Of grain, etc.: To become over-ripe and shatter.

Briticism (bri·tisiz'm). 1883. [f. a possible *Britic*, after *Gallicism*, etc.] A phrase or idiom characteristic of the English of Great Britain. vars. **Bri·tishism, Bri·tticism.**

British (bri·tiʃ), *a.* (*sb.*) [OE. *Brettisc*, etc., f. *Bret*; see BRIT.] 1. Of or pertaining to the ancient Britons. †b. Welsh 1662. 2. Of or belonging to Great Britain or its inhabitants; see BRITAIN. Now chiefly used in political or imperial connexion. ME. †3. Breton 1602. 4. *ellipt.* as *sb. pl.* British people, soldiers, etc. 1641.

1. A road acknowledged to be B. 1870. 2. A stony B. stare TENNYSON. *Comb.*: **B. crown**, a gold coin of the reign of Charles I; **B. Empire** (see EMPIRE *sb.* 5) 1604; **B. gum**, a commercial name of dextrin.

Britisher (bri·tiʃəɹ). 1829. [f. BRITISH + -ER; cf. *foreign-er*.] A British subject (as dist. from an American citizen). (App. of U. S. origin, but disclaimed by U. S. writers.)

Briton (bri·t'n, -ən), *sb.* (*a.*) [ME. *Breton*, a. F.:—L. *Brittōnem*, nom. *Britto*. The mod. *Briton* is assimilated to the erron. L. form *Brito*, pl. *Britōnes*, found in MSS. The OE. name was *Brettas, Bryttas*; see BRIT.] A. *sb.* A native of Britain: a. One of the ancient Britons. †b. A Welshman. c. Since the Union: A native of Great Britain, or of the British empire. *North B.*: a Scotchman. 2. A Breton. var. †**Bri·toner.**

1. Britons, hold your own TENNYSON. Hence **Bri·toness** (*rare*).

†B. *adj.* = British –1605.

Brittle (bri·t'l), *a.* [ME. *britul, britil, bretil* :—OE. **brytel*, f. (ult.) OTeut. *brut-*, **breutan*, OE. *brēotan* to break. Cf. BRICKLE.] Liable to break; fragile; †friable ME. †b. Perishable, mortal –1777. Also *fig.*

1. The ice being b., cracks and snaps HUXLEY. *fig.* A second Eve.. As beauteous, not as b. as the first DRYDEN. *Comb.* **b.-star**, a name for species of starfish of the genus *Ophiocoma*. Hence **Bri·ttlely** *adv.* *rare.* ? *Obs.* **Bri·ttleness.**

Britzka, britzska (bri·tskă, Pol. bri·tʃka). 1832. [a. Polish *bryczka* (*cz* = tʃ), dim. of *bryka* goods-wagon.] An open carriage with calash top, and space for reclining when used for a journey. vars. **Britschka, britzschka, britska.**

Broach (brōᵘtʃ), *sb.* [ME. *broche*, a. F.:—late L. **brocca* spike, akin to *brocchus* adj. in *brocchi dentes* projecting teeth. The same wd. as BROOCH.] 1. Any pointed rod of wood or iron. Still *dial.* 2. *esp.* A spit ME. †3. ? A taper: occas. explained as a spike on which to stick a candle –1504. 4. A piece of tough pliant wood, pointed at each end, used by thatchers ME. 5. A church spire; now, a spire which does not rise from within parapets 1501. 6. *Venery.* 'A start of the head of a young stag' 1575. 7. A general name for tapered boring-bits for enlarging or smoothing holes, sometimes used for burnishing, as in watchmaking; a similar tool used in dentistry; an instrument for broaching casks. Also, the pin in a lock which enters the barrel of the key. 1753. 8. A narrow pointed chisel used by masons. 9. (f. the vb.) A perforation 1519.

Phr. †*A b., on b.*: with a perforation or tap; esp. *to set a (on) b.*: to tap and set running; also *fig.* (Now ABROACH.)

Broach, *a.* *rare.* 1721. [sb. used attrib.] Like a broach or spit; in *Archit.* broach-shaped.

Broach (brōᵘtʃ), *v.*[1] ME. [f. BROACH *sb.*: cf. F. *brocher*. Cf. BROKER.] †1. *trans.* To pierce, thrust through –1631. †2. *spec.* To spur –1530. Also †*absol.* †3. To spit (meat) for roasting –1623. †b. *gen.* To spit –1704. 4. To pierce, as a cask, etc., so as to draw the liquor; to tap ME. Also *transf.* and *fig.* 5. To give publicity to; to give out; to begin conversation or discussion about, introduce. (The chief current sense.) 1579. 6. *techn.* To chisel stone with a BROACH (sense 8) 1544.

3. b. Bringing Rebellion broached on his sword SHAKS. 4. We broached a vessel of ale PEPYS. Blood was ready to be broach'd BUTLER *Hud.* I. ii. 489. 5. To broch a newe and straunge doctrine TOMSON.

Broach (brōᵘtʃ), *v.*[2] 1705. [perh. a use of BROACH *v.*[1], in sense of 'turn'.] *Naut.* 1. *intr.* in *To b. to* (said of the ship): to veer suddenly so as to turn the side to windward, or to meet the sea. 2. *trans.* To cause (the ship) to veer to windward 1762.

Broacher (brōᵘ·tʃəɹ). 1587. [f. BROACH *v.* + -ER [1].] 1. One who BROACHES. †2. A spit –1725.

1. A b. of more newes then hogsheads EARLE. 2. On five sharp broachers rank'd the roast they turn'd DRYDEN.

Broad (brǭd), *a.* (*sb.*) [Com. Teut.: OE. *brád* :—OTeut. **braido-z*; see BREADTH, BREDE.] 1. Extended in the direction measured from side to side; wide. Opp. to *narrow*. †b. *B. gold, money*; see BROAD-PIECE. 2. Less definitely: Of great extent, wide, ample, spacious OE. 3. Wide open; fully expanded OE. b. *esp.* Of day, daylight, etc. ME. 4. Plain, obvious; emphatic, explicit ME. b. Most apparent; main. (Opp. to 'minute'.) 1860. 5. Of language (or the speaker): a. Plainspoken (often in a bad sense); unreserved 1588. †b. Vulgar –1589. c. Loose, indecent 1580. 6. Of pronunciation: Perhaps orig.: With wider or lower vowel-sounds; but commonly used of any strongly-marked dialectal or vulgar pronunciation, *e.g.* 'B. Yorkshire', 'B. Cockney'. *B. Scotch*: the Lowland Scotch. 7. Unrestrained 1602. †8. Widely diffused *Macb.* III. iv. 23. 9. Having a wide range; inclusive, general 1871. 10. Characterized by breadth of opinion or sentiment; catholic, tolerant. (Cf. BROAD CHURCH.) 1832. 11. *Art.* Characterized by artistic breadth. Cf. BREADTH 5. 1862.

1. The braid..way of deadly syn 1552. 2. The hole brode worlde 1526. In ample space under the broadest shade MILT. 3. The worldes b. eye DEKKER. B. day light 1579, sunshine LOCKE, noon-day SHELLEY. 4. A b. hint BENTLEY. b. The b. facts 1860, outlines HUXLEY. 5. c. Without any b. speeches or uncomly jests NORTH. 7. Prankes..too b. to beare with *Haml.* III. iv. 2. B. mirth JOWETT.

Phrase. *It's as b. as it's long* (or *as long as it's b.*): it comes to the same thing either way. Hence **Broa·dish** *a.* **Broa·dness**, breadth; coarseness. **Broa·dway, -ways, -wise** *adv.* laterally.

B. *sb.* [mostly ellipt.] †1. Breadth: only in *in, on, o, a brode*; now replaced by ABROAD *adv.* -1456. 2. The broad part (of the back, etc.) 1741. †3. = BROAD-PIECE -1763. 4. In East Anglia, a piece of fresh water formed by the broadening out of a river 1787.

C. *adv.* [in OE. a distinct word *bráde*, ME. *brode*.] 1. In a broad way; widely, fully; far OE. 2. Outspokenly, unreservedly ME. 3. With a broad pronunciation 1532.

1. *B. awake, b. waking*: fully awake. 2. †*To laugh b.*: to laugh without restraint, grossly.

Comb.: b. bean (see BEAN 1); -bill, a name of birds having broad bills, *esp.* the Shoveller and Spoonbill; -blown *a.*, full-blown; -eyed *a.*, having large eyes, with eyes wide open; -glass, window-glass; -leaf (*Bot.*), a tree (*Terminalia latifolia*) found in Jamaica; -seed (*Bot.*), the genus *Ulospermum*.

Broad-arrow, -head; see ARROW.

Broa·d-axe. ME. An axe with a broad head, used for hewing timber (*U.S.*), formerly in war.

Broa·d-brim. *colloq.* 1797. a. A hat with a broad brim. b. A Quaker, as one who wears such a hat. **Broa·d-brimmed** *a.* 1688.

Broadcast (brǭ·dkast). 1767. [f. BROAD *adv.* and CAST *pa. pple.*] A. *adj.* Of seed, etc.: Scattered over the whole surface. Of sowing: Performed by this method. Also *fig.* B. *adv.* Only in *To sow, scatter, throw*, etc. *b.* (*lit.* and *fig.*) 1814. C. *sb.* 1. Broadcast sowing 1796. 2. Broadcasting by wireless telegraphy 1922.

Broa·dcast, *v.* 1813. [f. as prec. + CAST *v.*] 1. *trans.* To scatter (seed, etc.) broadcast. Also *fig.* 2. To disseminate (audible matter) from a wireless transmitting station 1921.

Broad Church. 1853. [See BROAD *a.* 10.] Designating members of the Church of England who take its formularies and doctrines in a broad sense, and allow wide limits to orthodoxy.

It [another party in the Church of England] is called by different names; Moderate, Catholic, or Broad Church, by its friends; Latitudinarian or Indifferent by its enemies. Its distinctive character is the desire of comprehension. Its watchwords are Charity and Toleration. W. J. CONYBEARE. Hence **Broad-Churchism, Broad-Churchman.**

Broadcloth, broad cloth (brǭ·dklǭþ). 1420. [In *Act 1 Rich. III*, viii, an. 1482, 'broad cloths', two yards within the lists, are distinguished from 'streits', one yard wide.] Fine, plain-wove, dressed, double-width, black cloth, used chiefly for men's garments. (The term now implies quality rather than width. But cloths of less than 54 inches wide are not doubled.) Also *attrib.*

Broaden (brǭ·d'n), *v.* 1726. [f. BROAD *a.* + -EN [1].] 1. *intr.* To become broad or broader 1727. 2. *trans.* To make broad or broader; to widen, dilate 1726.

1. Low walks the sun, and broadens by degrees THOMSON. 2. With broaden'd nostrils..The..heifer snuffs the..gale 1726.

Broad-faced (brǭ·dfēist), *a.* 1607. 1. Having a broad face. †2. *fig.* Undisguised, as *b. treason* -1678.

Broad gauge. 1864. The wider distance at which the rails are laid on some railways. (The ordinary gauge is 4ft. 8 1/2 in.) Often *attrib.* Hence **Broa·d-gauged** *a.*

Broa·d-leaved, *a.* Also **-leafed.** 1552. Having broad leaves; in *Bot.* = L. *latifolius.*

Broadly (brǭ·dli), *adv.* 1580. In a broad manner (see BROAD *a.*).

Broad pendant, pennant; see PENDANT.

†**Broad-piece.** 1678. The 20 shilling-piece ('Jacobus' and 'Carolus'), so called as being broader and thinner than the guinea.

Broad seal, *sb.* 1536. The Great Seal of England. Also *transf.* Also as *v. trans.* B. JONS.

Broadsheet (brǭ·dʃīt). 1705. A large sheet of paper printed on one side only; = BROADSIDE *sb.* 3.

Broadside (brǭ·dsəid), *sb.* 1591. [Formerly two wds.] 1. *Naut.* The side of a ship above the water between the bow and the quarter. Also *attrib.* and *transf.* 2. The whole array, or the simultaneous discharge, of the artillery on one side of a ship of war 1597. 3. = BROADSHEET 1575.

1. *B. on, b. to*, (†*a b.*) (Naut.): with the side of the vessel turned fully to the object considered; transversely. 2. Feare wee broad-sides? No, let the Fiend giue fire 2 *Hen. IV*, II. iv. 196.

Broa·dside, *adv.* 1870. With the side turned full (*to* a point, etc.).

Broa·dsider. *nonce-wd.* One who collects (printed) broadsides. BURTON.

Broadsword (brǭ·dsōəɹd). 1565. 'A cutting sword with a broad blade' (J.). Also *attrib.* b. *transf.* (*pl.*) Men armed with broadswords 1855.

Broa·dway. 1613. [Now usu. two wds.] A wide open road, as opp. to a narrow lane or byway. As a compound, now used as the proper name of a street, as in New York, Hammersmith, etc. b. *attrib.* Applied by Dryden to divines of the English Church who were for widening its basis 1687.

Brob (brǫb). 1874. [prob. related to N. dial. '*brob* to prick with a bodkin' (Grose).] 'A peculiar spike, driven alongside the end of an abutting timber, to prevent its slipping.' RAYMOND.

Brobdingnag (brǫ·bdiŋnæ:g). Also erron. brobdignag. 1727. Swift's name in *Gulliver's Travels* for an imaginary country where everything was on a gigantic scale. Hence *attrib.*: Of, or pertaining to, that country; immense; gigantic. Hence **Brobdingna·gian** *a.* = BROBDINGNAG; *sb.* an inhabitant of B., a giant; erron. vars. **-digna·gian, -naggian.**

Brocade (brokē^i·d). 1563. [Earlier *brocado*, a. Sp., Pg., lit. 'bossed stuff', f. Sp. *broca* (It. *brocca*) a boss = Eng. BROACH.] 1. A textile fabric woven with raised figures, orig. in gold or silver; in later use, any kind of stuff flowered with a raised pattern; also a cloth of gold and silver made in India. Also *fig.* Also *attrib.*

1. Stiff in Brocard, and pinch'd in stays PRIOR. Hence **Broca·de** *v.* to work with a raised pattern. **Broca·ded** *a.* worked or woven like b.; ornamented with b.; dressed in b.

Brocage, var. of BROKAGE.

Brocard [1] (brōu·kāɹd). 1624. [a. F., akin to med. L. *brocarda, brocardicorum opus*, a name given to the 'sentences' of Burchard or Brocard, bishop of Worms in the 11th c.] *Law.* An elementary principle or maxim. Also *gen.* ‖2. Biting speech. [Fr.] 1837.

1. *Dolus latet in generalibus* is a b. of the civilians 1862.

Brocard [2], obs. f. BROCADE.

‖**Brocatelle** (brǫkăte·l). 1669. [F., ad. It. *broccatello*, dim. of *broccato* = Sp. *brocado* (see BROCADE).] 1. An imitation of brocade, usually of silk or wool, for upholstery, etc., now also for dresses. Also *attrib.* 2. = next 1756.

‖**Brocatello** (brǫkate·lo). Also **-tella, -telli.** 1752. [It. *broccatello di Siena*, which is coloured like brocade.] A kind of variegated marble, clouded and veined white, grey, yellow and red, yellow usually prevailing.

Broccoli, brocoli (brǫ·kŏli). 1699. [a. It. *broccoli*, pl. of *broccolo*, dim. of *brocco* stalk (see BROACH).] A cultivated form of the cabbage (*Brassica oleracea botrytis asparagoides*): in its origin a more robust variety of the cauliflower.

Broch, brogh, brough. 1654. [n.e. Scottish, a. ON. *borg* (= OE. *burh*; see BOROUGH, BURGH).] *Archæol.* A prehistoric structure, peculiar to the Orkney and Shetland Isles, and adjacent mainland of Scotland, being a sort of round tower, having an outer and an inner wall of dry stone, the interstitial space containing little chambers for human habitation, while the open centre might be used for cattle.

Brochantite (brǫ·ʃăntəit). 1865. [f. *Brochant* de Villiers, a French mineralogist.] *Min.* A hydrous sulphate, occurring in thin, rectangular, green crystals.

†**Broche,** *v.* 1480. Obs. spelling of BROACH *v.* = F. *brocher* to stitch, brocade -1834. Hence **Broched** *ppl. a.* brocaded, embroidered.

‖**Brochure** (broʃü·r). 1765. [F., f. *brocher* to stitch.] A short printed work, of a few leaves stitched together; a pamphlet.

Brock (brǫk), *sb.* [1] [OE. *broc*, from Celtic:—OCelt. **broccos*, ? cogn. w. Gr. φορκός grey.] 1. A badger, usually qualified as *stinking*. 2. A stinking or dirty fellow; a 'skunk' 1600. Also *attrib.*

Brock, *sb.* [2] ? *Obs.* 1515. = BROCKET.

†**Brock,** *v. rare.* ME. [Cf. OHG. *brochôn*, mod. *brocken* to break into bits, in Swiss 'to use coarse words'.] *app.* To give mouth, speak querulously. CHAUCER.

Brocket (brǫ·kėt). ME. [ad. F. *brocart, broquart*, f. *broque, broche* BROACH; cf. BROCARD [2].] 1. A stag in its second year with its first horns (see BROACH 6). 2. A genus of deer of Brazil, having short prongs for horns 1837.

†**Bro·ckish,** *a. rare.* 1546. [f. BROCK *sb.*[1] 2 + -ISH.] Like a brock; beastly, dirty -1553.

Brod (brǫd), *sb.* Now *dial.* [ME., app. a. ON. *broddr* = OE. *brord* spike. Mainly *Sc.* Cf. PROD.] †1. A sprout. ME. only. 2. A goad, prick ME. 3. A prick from a goad 1549. 4. A round-headed nail made by blacksmiths. Hence **Brod** *v.* †to sprout; to goad, prod, prick (*n. dial.*).

†**Bro·dekin, brodkin.** 1481. [a. F. *brodequin*, related to Flem. *broseken* buskin; see BUSKIN.] A half-boot; a buskin -1725.

Bro·derer. ME. Earlier form of BROIDERER, retained as the name of one of the London City Companies.

Brog (brǫg), *sb. dial.* 1781. [?] 1. A pricking or boring instrument; a bradawl (*Sc.*); also, an awl 1808. 2. A prick with a bradawl, etc. 1808. 3. A short stick, *esp.* one to stick in the ground 1781.

Brog (brǫg), *v. dial.* 1678. [f. prec.] 1. To prick, prod; to push an awl *through* 1774. 2. To insert brogs into (see BROG *sb.* 3) 1875. 3. To BROGGLE for eels, to sniggle (*dial.*) 1678.

‖**Brogan** (brōu·găn). 1846. [Ir., dim. of *brōg* shoe.] A coarse stout sort of shoe.

†**Bro·gger.** 1460. [corrupt f. BROKER. Cf. *brogge* BROGUE *sb.*[1]] An agent; a jobber, *esp.* a corrupt jobber of offices; a BROKER -1720.

Broggers of Corn and Forestallers of Markets 1641.

Broggle (brǫ·g'l), *v. n. dial.* 1653. [freq. f. BROG *v.*] To fish for eels with a brog; to sniggle.

†**Brogue** (brōᵘg), *sb.*[1] Now *Sc.* [?] An escheat; a cheat -1791.

Brogue (brōᵘg), *sb.*[2] 1586. [a. Ir. and Gael. *brōg*:—OIr. *brōce* shoe, app.:—OCelt. *bracca*; see BREECH.] 1. A rude shoe, of untanned hide, worn in the wilder parts of Ireland and the Scotch Highlands. b. (In full *b. shoe.*) A strong shoe, esp. for country and sports wear 1906. †2. *pl.* Hose, trousers -1845. 3. *Fishing brogues*, waterproof leggings with feet 1880.

Brogue (brōᵘg), *sb.*[3] 1705. [? same wd. as prec.] A strongly-marked dialectal pronunciation or accent; now esp. that of the English speech of Ireland.

Charles Morgan. having much of the Irish B. in his Speech 1705. Hence **Brogue** *v.* to utter with a b.

†**Broid,** *v.* ME. [var. of BRAID *v.*; cf. BROIDEN.] To plait, interweave -1624.

Broiden, *ppl. a.* ME. [A pa. pple. of BRAID *v.* (cf. ABRAID, *abroiden*), and thus a (? normal) doublet of *browden.*] Interwoven, braided. (More usu.) *fig.* Skilfully contrived.

Broider (broi·dəɹ), *v. arch.* 1450. [Later form of *broudre, brouder* (15th c.), *browder* (16th c.), taken as = F. *broder, brouder*; the *oi* is due to association with BROID *v.*] To work in needlework upon cloth; to embroider. (Usu. in pa. pple.) Also *transf.* and *fig.*

Theyr noble actes..Freshly were browdred in these clothes royall 1513. The Hyacinth with rich inlay Broiderd the ground MILT. *P. L.* IV. 702. Hence **Broi·derer. Broi·dery,** embroidery.

Broil (broil), *sb.*[1] 1525. [app. f. BROIL *v.*[2]] A confused disturbance, tumult, or turmoil; a quarrel. Also in *comb.*

Prosper this Realme, keepe it from Ciuill Broyles SHAKS.

Broil, *sb.*[2] 1583. [f. BROIL *v.*[1]] 1. A great heat; a very hot state. 2. Broiled meat 1822.

Broil (broil), *v.*[1] ME. [Earlier *bruyle*, ad. OF. *bruillir* to broil, burn (*intr.*).] †1. *trans.* To burn -1568. 2. *spec.* To cook (meat) by placing it on the fire, or on a gridiron over it; to grill ME. 3. To scorch; to make very hot 1634. 4. *intr.* To be subjected to great heat, to be very hot 1613; also *fig.* 1561.

2. He cowde roste, sethe, broille, and frie CHAUCER. 3. I was..half broiled in the sun 1718.

Broil, *v.*[2] ME. [a. F. *brouiller*. Ult. deriv. uncertain.] †1. To mix confusedly -1631. †2.

To involve in confusion or disorder; to set by the ears, embroil -1642. **3.** *intr.* To be or to engage in a BROIL 1567.

Broiler[1] (broi·lǝɹ). 1671. [f. BROIL *v.*[1] + -ER[1].] **1.** One who or that which broils; also said of a very hot day (cf. *scorcher*). **2.** *spec.* A chicken for broiling 1886.

Broiler[2]. 1660. [f. BROIL *v.*[2] + -ER[1].] One who stirs up or engages in broils.

Broi·ling, *vbl. sb.* 1440. [f. BROIL *v.*[1] + -ING[1].] Exposing to scorching heat; *spec.* grilling. Hence **Broi·lingly** *adv.*

†**Bro·kage, brocage.** ME. [See BROKER.] = BROKERAGE. *esp.* **a.** The corrupt jobbing of offices; the bribe unlawfully paid for any office. **b.** Trafficking in match-making, etc. **c.** 'The trade of dealing in old things' (J.). -1755.

Broke, var. BROKEN, surviving in predic. use of sense 7. 1851.

Broke (brōuk), *v.* 1496. [f. BROKER.] †**1** *intr.* To bargain -1625. †**2.** *trans.* To retail 1599. **3.** *intr.* To act as broker 1652.

Broken (brōu·k'n), *ppl. a.* ME. Used esp. in the following senses of BREAK *v.* **1.** Separated forcibly into parts; in fragments; in pieces. **2.** Rent, ruptured, burst ME. **3.** Of organic structures: **a.** Having the bone fractured; **b.** having the surface ruptured ME. **4.** Shattered, as *b. water, a b. wave* 1793. **5.** Crushed or exhausted by labour, etc.; enfeebled 1490. **6.** Crushed in feelings by misfortune, remorse, etc.; humbled, contrite 1535. **7.** Reduced or shattered in worldly estate; bankrupt 1593. **8.** Reduced to obedience, tamed, trained. Often with *in.* 1805. **9.** Violated, transgressed, not kept intact 1605. **10.** Having the ranks broken; routed 1810. **11.** Having continuity or uniformity interrupted 1599. **12.** Fragmentary, disconnected, disjointed, in patches; *esp.* **a.** of sound, voice, etc.: Uttered disjointedly, interrupted 1530; **b.** of language: With the syntax incomplete 1599. **13.** Produced by breaking, severed ME. **14.** Of colours: Reduced in tone by the addition of other colours 1882. †**15.** Of music: Arranged for different instruments, 'part' (music); concerted 1599.

1. Three b. oars DE FOE. *B. bread, meat,* etc.: fragments left after a meal, etc.; extended to drink, as *b. ale,* etc. **2.** Old and b. apparell 1641. **3.** B. limbs SHAKS., Shins ADDISON. **6.** A b. and a contrite hert COVERDALE *Ps.* **7.** The Kings growne bankrupt like a b. man *Rich. II,* II. i. 257. **B. man.** *Sc. Law and Hist.* One under sentence of outlawry, or living the life of an outlaw. **B. clan,** one having no chief able to find security for their good behaviour. **11.** B. sleep ADDISON. **12.** The fruits of b. hours QUARLES. **a.** Her voice..b. with sobs 1853. **b.** Breake thy minde to me in b. English *Hen. V,* v. ii. 265. **13.** *B. number:* a fraction. A b. tale BYRON.

Comb.: **b.-bellied, -bodied** (*dial.*), affected with hernia, ruptured; **-kneed** (*Farriery*), having the knees damaged by stumbling, etc.; also *fig.* Hence **Bro·ken-ly** *adv.*, **-ness.**

Broken-backed (brōu·k'n,bæ·kt), *a.* ME. **1.** Having a broken back; formerly, hunch-backed. Also *transf.* and *fig.* **2.** *Naut.* The state of a ship so loosened in her frame as to droop at both ends 1769.

Broken-hearted (brōu·k'n,hā·ɹtėd), *a.* 1526. Having the spirits crushed by grief or despair.

Broken-hearted widows MACAULAY. Hence **Broken-hea·rted-ly** *adv.*, **-ness.**

Broken wind, broken-wind. 1838. *Farriery.* An incurable disease of horses, caused by the rupture of the air-cells, which disables them from bearing fatigue. Hence **Broken-wi·nded** *a.* affected with broken wind. Also *fig.*

Broker (brōu·kǝɹ). ME. *brocor, -our, brokour,* a. AngloF. *brocour* = ONF. *brokeor* (:—L. type **broccatorem*), agent noun of the ONF. vb. *brokier* (:—L. *broccare*) to 'broach' or 'tap' a cask. See BROACH. The *broker* was lit. a tapster who retailed wine, and hence, any retail dealer, a second-hand dealer, middleman, agent, etc. See N.E.D.] †**1.** A retailer; *contemptuously,* Pedlar, monger -1730. **2.** A dealer in second-hand furniture and apparel; a pawnbroker 1583. **3.** One employed as a middleman to transact business or negotiate bargains; often specialized, as *bill-, cotton-, pawn-, ship-, wool-b.* Formerly also = 'jobber, agent, factor, commission-agent'. ME. †**4.** A go-between in love affairs; a hired match-maker; a pimp, bawd; a pander -1694. **5.** A middleman generally; an interpreter, messenger, commissioner 1530. **6.** A person licensed to sell or appraise household furniture distrained for rent 1818.

1. But B. of anothers wit MARSTON. **2.** A Houndsditch man, sir. One of the deuils neere kinsmen, a b. B. JONS. **4.** *Two Gent.* I. ii. 41. **5.** Two false knaues neede no b. HEYWOOD.

Brokerage (brōu·kǝrėdʒ). 1466. [f. prec. + -AGE.] **1.** The business or action of a broker. **2.** The commission paid to a broker on the business done by him 1622.

†**Bro·kerly.** 1592. [f. as prec. + -LY[1, 2].] **A.** *adj.* Like a broker; huckstering -1611. **B.** *adv.* By the agency of a broker 1593.

†**Bro·kery.** 1583. [f. as prec. + -Y; see -ERY.] **1.** = BROKERAGE **1.** -1641. **2.** A broker's wares; anything second-hand or stale -1634. **3.** Rascally dealing -1654.

Broking (brōu·kiŋ), *vbl. sb.* 1569. [f. BROKE *v.*] **1.** The broker's trade. †**2.** Lending of money upon pawns; fraudulent dealing -1619.

Brolly (brǫ·li). 1874. Colloq. altered f. UMBRELLA.

Brom-; see BROMO-.

†‖**Bro·ma**[1]. 1555. [Sp.] A ship-worm.

‖**Broma**[2] (brōu·mă). 1811. [a. Gr.] **1.** *Med.* Any food that is masticated. **2.** A preparation of chocolate (so called from *theobroma,* the name of the Cacao plant) 1858.

Bromal (brōu·măl). 1875. [f. BROM-INE + AL-COHOL.] A compound analogous to chloral, produced by the action of bromine on alcohol.

Bromate (brōu·meɪt). 1836. [f. BROM-IC + -ATE[4].] A salt of bromic acid.

Bromatology (brōumătǫ·lŏdʒi). 1811. [f. Gr. βρῶμα, βρωματο- + -λογία.] **1.** A discourse on food. **2.** The science of food.

Brome[1] (brōum). 1827. [a. F., f. Gr. βρῶμος stink.] *Chem.* The French name of BROMINE, formerly used in English.

Brome[2] (brōum). 1759. [ad. *Bromus,* Bot. name of the genus, a. Gr. βρόμος (also βρῶμος) oats.] *Bot.* A genus of oat-like grasses (*Bromus*). Also **B.-grass.**

Bromeliaceous (bromī·liǝɪ·ʃǝs), *a.* 1882. *Bot.* Pertaining to the natural order *Bromeliaceæ,* which includes the Pine-apple.

Bromic (brōu·mik), *a.* 1828. [f. BROM-INE.] *Chem.* Containing bromine in combination.

bromic acid ($HBrO_3$), the acid which forms bromates; **b. silver** = BROMYRITE.

Bromide (brōu·mǝid). 1836. [f. BROM-INE + -IDE.] **1.** *Chem.* A primary compound of bromine with an element or organic radical. **2.** (orig. *U.S. slang.*) A commonplace bore, trite remark, conventionalism 1906.

‖**Bromidrosis** (brōu:midrōu·sis). 1866. [f. Gr. βρῶμος + ἱδρώς.] *Med.* A disorder of the sweat glands attended by offensive perspiration.

Bro·minated, *a.* 1875. [f. BROMINE + -ATE[3] 7.] Charged or compounded with bromine.

Bromine (brōu·min, -mǝin). 1827. [f. F. *brome* (f. Gr. βρῶμος stink) + -INE; after F. *iode,* Eng. *iodine,* etc.] *Chem.* A non-metallic element discovered by Balard in 1826; a reddish-black heavy liquid, with a strong irritating smell, and highly poisonous. Symbol Br. Also *attrib.*

Bromism (brōu·miz'm). 1867. [f. BROM-INE + -ISM.] *Med.* The condition produced by misuse of bromine or a bromide.

Bro·mite. 1850. *Min.* = BROMYRITE.

Bromize, -ise (brōu·mǝiz), *v.* 1853. [f. BROM-INE + -IZE.] To treat, compound, impregnate, or infuse with bromine; in *Photogr.,* to prepare (a plate) with bromine or a bromide.

Bromlite (brǫ·mlǝit). 1835. [f. *Bromley* Hill in Cumberland.] *Min.* = ALSTONITE.

Bromo- (brōu·mo), bef. a vowel **brom-.** *Chem.* Comb. f. BROMINE, as in:

bro:mace·tic acid, a compound of bromine and acetic acid ($C_2H_3BrO_2$), forming salts called **broma·cetates; broma·rgyrite** = BROMYRITE; **bromhy·drin,** a class of compounds 'produced by the action of tribromide or pentabromide of phosphorus on glycerin' (Watts); **bro·moform,** a compound analogous to chloroform ($CHBr_3$).

†**Bro·muret.** 1878. [f. BROM-INE + -URET.] *Chem.* The earlier name for a BROMIDE.

Bromyrite (brōu·mirǝit). 1854. [f. BROM-INE; after *argyrite.*] *Min.* The native bromide of silver, an isometric yellow, amber, or green splendent mineral; also called *Bromargyrite, bromic silver.*

‖**Bronchia** (brǫ·ŋkiă), *sb. pl.* 1674. [L., a. Gr. βρόγχια (neut. pl.). Formerly occas. treated as sing., with pl. *bronchiæ.*] The branches of the bronchi within the lungs. Hence **Bro·nchial, Bro·nchic** *a.* pertaining to the bronchi or bronchia. **Bro·nchially** *adv.*

Bronchio- (brǫ·ŋki,o), bef. a vowel **bronchi-.** *Med.* Comb. f. BRONCHIA, as in:

bronchia·rctia [L. *ar(c)tus*], contraction of the bronchial tubes; **bro:nchie·ctasis** [Gr. ἔκτασις], dilatation of the bronchial tubes; **bronchio·cri·sis** [Gr. κρίσις], paroxysmal attacks resembling hooping cough occurring in tabes; **-pneumo·nia,** inflammation of the lungs, beginning in the bronchial membrane; **-pu·lmonary** *a.,* pertaining to the bronchi and lungs.

Bronchiole (brǫ·ŋki,ōul). 1866. [ad. mod. L. **bronchiola,* dim. of *bronchia.*] A minute bronchial tube.

‖**Bronchitis** (brǫŋkǝi·tis). 1814. [f. *bronchi, bronchia* + -ITIS (= Gr. -ῖτις), q.v.] *Med.* Inflammation of the bronchial mucous membrane. Hence **Bronchi·tic** *a.*

Broncho- (brǫ·ŋko), bef. a vowel **bronch-.** *Med.* Comb. f. BRONCHUS, as in:

bro·nchadene [Gr. ἀδήν], one of the bronchial glands; **broncha·rctia** [L. *ar(c)tus*], contraction of a bronchus; **broncho·pneumo·nia** = *bronchio-pneumonia* (see BRONCHIO-); **-lith,** a calcareous deposit in a bronchial gland; **-rrhœ·a,** a kind of chronic bronchitis, etc.

Bronchocele (brǫ·ŋkŏsīl). 1657. [ad. Gr., f. βρόγχος + κήλη.] *Med.* A swelling of the thyroid gland; goitre.

Bronchophony (brǫŋkǫ·fŏni). 1834. [ad. F. *bronchophonie,* f. Gr. βρόγχος + -φωνία.] *Med.* The sound of the voice heard in the bronchi by means of the stethoscope; *esp.* the increased vocal resonance heard in certain diseased conditions of the lungs. Hence **Bronchopho·nic** *a.* var. **Broncho·phonism.**

Bronchotome (brǫ·ŋkŏtōum). 1837. [f. Gr. βρόγχος + -τομος.] *Surg.* A knife, or a pair of scissors, used for bronchotomy.

Bronchotomy (brǫŋkǫ·tŏmi). 1706. [f. Gr. βρόγχος + -τομία.] *Surg.* The operation of making an incision in the wind-pipe; a generic term, including *thyrotomy, laryngotomy,* and *tracheotomy.* Hence **Broncho·tomist,** one who performs b.; (*joc.*) a cut-throat.

‖**Bronchus** (brǫ·ŋkǝs). Pl. **-chi** (*improp.* **-chæ**). 1706. [mod.L., a. Gr. βρόγχος.] *Phys.* Each of the two main branches of the trachea.

‖**Bronco** (brǫ·ŋko). 1883. [Sp., = 'rough, rude'.] An untamed or half-tamed horse, or a cross between the horse and a mustang. (*Western U.S.*)

†**Bro·nstrops.** 1617. [See BAWDSTROT.] A bawd -1661.

‖**Bronte·on.** 1849. [a. Gr. βροντεῖον.] In the Greek theatre, a number of brazen vessels with stones in them placed under the floor, to imitate thunder.

Brontology (brǫntǫ·lŏdʒi). 1731. [f. Gr. βροντή thunder + -λογία.] That part of meteorology which treats of thunder.

‖**Brontosaurus** (brǫntosǭ·rǝs). [mod.L. (1879); cf. next.] A huge dinosaurian reptile.

Brontothere (brǫ·ntoþīǝɹ). 1877. [f. Gr. βροντή + θηρίον.] *Palæont.* An extinct genus of ungulate mammals, having affinities to the elephant and also to the tapir.

Bronze (brǫnz), *sb.* 1721. [a. F., ad. It. *bronzo;* of unkn. origin.] **1.** A brown-coloured alloy of copper and tin, sometimes also containing a little zinc and lead. Formerly included under the term BRASS, q. v. 1739. **2.** (with *pl.*) A work of art, as a statue, etc., executed in bronze 1721. †**3.** *fig.* Unblushingness. (Cf. *brass.*) -1823. **4.** (More fully *b. powder*): A metallic powder (usu. brass, copper, or tin) used in painting, printing, etc. 1753. **5.** A colour like that of bronze 1817. **6.** *attrib.* Made of bronze 1839; bronze-coloured 1828.

1. *Aluminium b.*: see ALUMINIUM. *Phosphor-b.*: an alloy of b. or copper with a little phosphorus added, which increases its tenacity. 2. How little gives thee joy or pain; A print, a b., a flower, a root PRIOR. 3. Imbrown'd with native b., lo! Henley stands POPE. 6. The b. coinage (*mod.*).

Comb.: **b. age** = *bronze period*; **b. man** (*Archæol.*), a man living in the b. period; **b. period** (*Archæol.*), the prehistoric period (preceded by the Stone, and succeeded by the Iron Period) during which weapons, etc. were made of b.; **b. powder** = sense 4; **b. wing**, a Pigeon (*Phaps chalcoptera*) found in Australasia. Hence **Bro·nzy** *a.* tinged with b. colour.

Bronze (brǫnz), *v.* 1645. [a. F. *bronzer.*] 1. *trans.* To give a bronze-like appearance to, by any mechanical or chemical process. 2. *fig.* To render unfeeling or shameless; to harden, steel 1726. 3. To make bronze-coloured 1792. 4. *intr.* To become like bronze 1880.

3. The..veteran..bronz'd by many a summer sun ROGERS.

Bronzed (brǫnzd), *ppl. a.* 1748. [f. prec.] In senses of the vb. 1–3.

Bronzed Skin, *supra-renal melasma* or Addison's disease.

Bro·nzite. 1816. [f. BRONZE *sb.* + -ITE.] *Min.* A bronze-coloured variety of diallage.

Broo. *Sc.* 1440. [Sc. pron. *brö, brü*: ? a. OF. *bro, breu,* broth.] = BREE *sb.*[2] 2.

Brooch (brōutʃ). [ME. *broche*; the same wd. as BROACH. Occas. pronounced (brūtʃ).] 1. An ornamental fastening, consisting of a safety pin, with the clasping part variously fastened and enriched. Now mainly a (female) ornament. †2. Formerly, a necklace, a bracelet, a trinket, etc. -1676. Also †*fig.*

2. *fig.* He is the B. indeed, And Iemme of all our Nation *Haml.* IV. vii. 94. Hence **Brooch** *v. rare*, to adorn as with a b.

Brood (brūd), *sb.* [OE. *brōd*, from Teut. vb.-root *bro-* to warm, to heat.] 1. Progeny, offspring, young; *esp.* of animals that lay eggs. b. Family. (Now usu. *contemptuous.*) ME. c. *fig.* Of things inanimate 1597. 2. The cherishing of the fœtus in the egg or the womb; hatching, breeding (*arch.*) ME. †b. Hence: Parentage, extraction. SPENSER. c. *attrib.* = 'breeding'; as in *b. class*, etc. Often hyphened. 1526. 3. A race, a kind. Now *contemptuous*; = 'swarm, crew, crowd'. 1581. 4. *spec.* The spat of oysters in its second year 1862. 5. *Min.* The heavier kinds of waste ore (*Cornwall*).

1. The Serpents B. DRYDEN. A B. of Ducks ADDISON, of silk-worms 1760. b. A b. of daughters GEO. ELIOT. c. The b. of Folly without father bred MILT. *Penser.* 96. 3. A b. of petty despots FREEMAN. *Comb.* **b.-hen**, a breeding-hen; also, †the Pleiades.

Brood (brūd), *v.* ME. [f. prec.] I. *trans.* (mostly *arch.* or *poet.*) 1. To sit on eggs so as to hatch them. 2. To cherish (young brood) under the wings, as a hen does; often *fig.* 1571. 3. *fig.* To hatch (products or projects) 1613. 4. To cherish in the mind, to nurse (wrath, etc.). Now usu. *to b. on* or *over.* 1571.

3. Hell, and not the heavens, brooded that design FULLER. 4. To b. hope JOHNSON.

II. *intrans.* 1. To sit as a hen on eggs; to sit or hover with outspread wings 1588. 2. *fig.* To sit *on*, or hang close *over*; to hover over. Said esp. of *night, silence, mist, storm-clouds*, and the like. 1697. 3. To meditate moodily *on* or *over*; to dwell closely upon in the mind 1751. b. To brood (*esp.* in a morbid way) 1826. 4. *transf.* a. To breed (interest) 1678. b. To lie as a cherished nestling, etc. 1679.

1. Birds sit brooding in the snow *L. L. L.* V. ii. 933. Also MILT. *P. L.* I. 21. 2. Perpetual Night.. In silence brooding on th' unhappy ground DRYDEN. 3. To b. On dark revenge SCOTT. 4. b. The Injury ..had long been brooding in his mind DRYDEN.

Broo·dy, *a.* 1513. [f. BROOD *sb.* + -Y[1].] 1. Apt or inclined to breed. Now *dial.* 2. Of a hen: Inclined to sit 1523. Hence **Broo·diness.**

Brook (bruk), *sb.* [OE. *brōc*, WGer. **brōka-*, ?f. *brekan* to BREAK; cf. *spring.*] A small stream; *orig.* a torrent. Also *transf.*

These rivers are fed by numberless brooks MORSE. *Comb.* **B. ouzel** or **B. runner,** the Water-rail. Also in many plant-names.

Brook (bruk), *v.* [OE. *brūcan*, a Com. Teut. vb.:—OTeut. stem **bruk-* 'to make use of, enjoy':—Aryan **bhrug-*, whence L. *frui, fructus.*] 1. *trans.* To enjoy the use of, profit by; to possess, hold. *Obs.* exc. *Sc.* and *arch.* †2. To make use of (food); later, to digest, to bear on the stomach -1598. Also *fig.* 3. To put up with [cf. 2]. Now chiefly in neg. constructions. 1530.

1. †*To b. a name* (*well*): to act consistently with it, do it credit. 3. Heav'n.. Brooks not the works of violence and war MILT. *P. L.* VI. 274.

Brookite (bru·kəit). 1879. [f. H. J. *Brooke*, mineralogist.] *Min.* Native titanic anhydride; Jurinite.

Brooklet (bru·klėt). 1813. [f. BROOK *sb.* + -LET.] A little brook. So †**Broo·ket.**

Brooklime (bru·kˌləim). [Worn down from ME. *brok-lemok*, f. *brōc* BROOK + *lemok*:—OE. *hleomoc* name of the plant.] A species of Speedwell (*Veronica Beccabunga*); also Lesser Brooklime (*V. Anagallis*).

Brool (brūl). 1837. [app. ad. Ger. *brüll* roar.] A low deep humming sound; a murmur. Also *fig.*

List to the b. of that royal forest-voice CARLYLE.

Broom (brūm), *sb.* [OE. *brōm* (from WGer. **brǣma-*), pointing to OTeut. **brǣmo-z*: cogn. with BRAMBLE.] 1. A shrub, *Sarothamnus* or *Cytisus Scoparius* (N.O. *Leguminosæ*), bearing yellow papilionaceous flowers. Also the genus to which this belongs, and the allied genus *Genista*, including the White Broom, and Giant or Irish Broom, etc. 2. Any one of various other plants used for sweeping, or fancied to be akin to the broom proper; as BUTCHER'S BROOM, SPANISH BROOM, q.v. 3. Any implement for sweeping, a besom: orig. one made of twigs of broom, heather, etc., fixed to a handle. Cf. BESOM *sb.*[1] 2. ME. Also *fig.* and *transf.*

Comb.: **b.-bush**, *Parthenium Hysterophorus*; **-cod**, the seed-vessel of the b.; **-cypress**, *Kochia scoparia*; **-grass**, *Andropogon scoparius*; **-heath**, *Erica tetralix*; **-sedge**, a species of coarse grass; **-squires**, squatters in the New Forest, and elsewhere, who live by tying heath into brooms; **-tail** (of a horse), a long bushy tail; **-weed**, a tropical American plant (*Corchorus siliquosus*), from the leaves of which a drink is prepared.

Broom (brūm), *v.* 1627. [f. prec. sb.] 1. *trans.* To sweep with a broom 1838. 2. To BREAM a ship (Dicts.) 1627.

Broo·m corn. 1817. [f. (in U.S.) BROOM + (Indian) CORN.] The U.S. name of the Common Millet, *Sorghum vulgare*, of which the panicles are made into brooms, etc.; also the *Sorghum saccharatum* of the East.

Broomrape (brū·mrēˈp). 1578. [tr. med.L. *Rapum genistæ* broom tuber.] A large genus of parasitic herbs (*Orobanche*), which attach themselves to the roots of broom and other plants, having a leafless fleshy stem furnished with pointed scales. First applied to *O. major.*

Broomstaff (brū·mstɑf). *arch.* Also **-stave.** *rare.* Pl. **-staffs, -staves.** 1613. The staff or handle of a broom, a broomstick.

Broomstick (brū·mstik). 1683. Same as BROOMSTAFF.

To marry over the b.: to go through a *quasi*-marriage ceremony, in which the parties jump over a b.; = *to jump the besom.*

Broomy (brū·mi), *a.* 1649. [f. BROOM *sb.* + -Y[1].] 1. Covered with broom. †2. Of or pertaining to a broom or besom. SWIFT. 3. Broom-like (*rare*) 1807.

1. The b. banks of Nith BURNS.

Broose. *Sc.* 1786. [Sc. pron. *brōz, brūz*: of unkn. origin.] A race by the young men present at country weddings in the north, the course being from the bride's former home to the bridegroom's house. (A survival from primitive marriage-customs. Cf. BRIDELOPE.)

Brose (brōuz). 1657. [mod. Sc. f. earlier *browes*, BROWIS, OFr. *broez*. Often treated as pl.] A dish made by pouring boiling water (or milk) on oatmeal (or oat-cake) seasoned with salt and butter.

Pease b.: a similar dish of pease-meal. *Athole b.*: a mixture of whiskey and honey.

†**Bro·tel, brotle,** *a.* [ME. *brotil, brutil*, f. *broten*, pa. pple. of *breotan* to BREAK.] Brittle; mortal -1529. Also *fig.* Hence †**Bro·telness.**

Broth (brǫþ), *sb.* [Com. Teut.: OE. *broþ*, f. (ult.) OTeut. vb.-root *brū*; see BREW.] A decoction; *esp.* that in which meat is boiled; also a thin soup made from this and vegetables, as Scotch 'broth'. Also *fig.* and *transf.*

I am sure..you love B. better than Soup STEELE. Phr. *A b. of a boy*: the essence of what a boy should be.

Brothel (brǫ·þ'l), *sb.* [ME. *broþel*, f. OE. *broðen* ruined. The *brothel* was orig. a person; see sense 3.] †1. A worthless abandoned fellow -1594. †2. A prostitute -1606. 3. Short for *brothel's house, b.-house*; superseding BORDEL: A house of ill-fame 1593. Also *attrib.*

2. A company of concubins and brothels 1606. 3. Keep thy foote out of Brothels *Lear* III. iv. 99. *Comb.* **b.-house** = sense 3. Hence †**Bro·theller**, a whoremonger. †**Bro·thelling**, whoring. †**Bro·thelry**, harlotry; also, a place of prostitutes.

Brother (brʊ·ðəɹ), *sb.* Pl. **brothers, brethren** (breð·rėn). [Com. Teut. and Com. Aryan: OE. *brōðor*:—OTeut. **brōþar*:—OAryan **bhrā·ter, -tor, -tr*, whence also Skr. *bhrātr*, Gr. φράτηρ, L. *frater*, etc. In the 17th c. *brothers* became the ordinary pl.; *brethren* is now eccles. or professional.] 1. A male being related to others (male or female) as the child of the same parents or parent. In the latter case, he is more properly called a *half-b.*, or *b. of the half blood.* b. A kinsman, as uncle, nephew, cousin. (A Hebraism.) ME. c. One who is as a brother 1795. 2. One of the same clan, city, father-land; fellow-man, fellow-creature OE. 3. A fellow-christian; a co-religionist generally. (Pl. *brethren.*) OE. 4. A fellow-member of a guild, corporation, or order; hence, one of the same profession, trade, society, or order. (Pl. *brethren.*) ME. b. Vaguely: One in the same case or position; a comrade, fellow. (Pl. usu. *brothers.*) ME. 5. *esp.* A fellow-member of a religious order (cf. *frater, frère, friar*) 1500. 6. *fig.* Of things ME. 7. *attrib.* Bef. other sbs. (often hyphened) = *fellow-*. *Brother-man*: a man and brother. 1503. Also of things 1822.

1. His borne broder ME. b. *Gen.* xiii. 8. c. My friend, the b. of my love, My Arthur TENNYSON. 2. Adams sonnes are my brethren *Much Ado* II. i. 67. 3. The soul of our dear b. here departed *Bk. Com. Prayer. The Brethren*: in N. T. the members of the early Christian churches. Also adopted by some modern sects who reject orders in the church, e.g. the 'Brethren', or 'Plymouth Brethren'. 4. b. Your B. Kings SHAKS. A b. to dragons, and a companion to owles *Job* xxx. 29. 6. That April morn, Of this the very b. WORDSW.

Comb.: **B.-consanguinean,** one born of the same father; **-uterine,** one born of the same mother.

Bro·ther, *v.* 1573. [f. prec.] 1. To make a brother of; to admit to brotherhood; to address as brother. 2. To be a brother to 1600.

Brother-german (brʊ·ðəɹˌdʒə·ɹmăn). Pl. **brothers-german** (†**brethren-**). ME. [f. BROTHER *sb.* + GERMAN *a.*[1] 2] A brother through both parents. (In early times used also as = 'brother-uterine'.)

Brotherhood (brʊ·ðəɹhud), also †**brotherhead.** [Not in OE.: prob. f. BROTHERRED, assim. to the *-hede* class through *brothered*(*e*.] 1. The relation of a brother, or of brothers mutually. Also in spiritual sense. ME. 2. Brotherliness, friendly alliance ME. †3. The rank of a 'brother' in a corporation. *Tr. & Cr.* I. iii. 104. 4. An association of brothers; a fraternity or guild; also the brethren collectively ME. Also *fig.* of things 1728. 5. Community of feeling uniting man and man 1784.

1 The b. of blood was not to wear out PUSEY. 4. There is a b. of you, but I will breake it 1555. *fig.* A b. of lofty elms WORDSW. 5. The common b. of man D'ISRAELI.

Brother-in-law (brʊ·ðəɹinlǭ:). ME. [App. 'in law' = *in Canon Law*; *esp.* with reference to intermarriage.] *prop.* The brother of one's husband or wife; the husband of one's sister. Occas., the husband of one's wife's (or husband's) sister.

Brotherly (brʊ·ðəɹli), *a.* [Cf. OE. *brōðorlīc.*] Of or pertaining to a brother; also, characteristic of a brother, kind, affectionate. Hence **Bro·therliness. Bro·therly** *adv.*

†**Bro·therred.** [OE. f. *brōðor* + *-rǣden* condition; see -RED.] = BROTHERHOOD, q.v. -1542.

Brothership (-ʃip). [OE. f. as prec. + -SHIP.] a. Brotherly fellowship. b. A fraternity or guild-brotherhood (*mod.*).

Bro·therwort. ME. Wild Thyme.

Brough. Now *Sc.* and *north.* 1496. [app. a. ON. *borg*, in sense of 'wall, enclosure'.] A luminous ring round a shining body; a halo.

Brougham (brūm, brū·əm, brōu·əm). 1851. [f. Lord *Brougham.*] A one-horse closed carriage, with two or four wheels, for two or four persons.

Brought (brǭt). Pa. pple. of BRING *v.*

Brow (brau), *sb.*[1] [OE. *brū*:—OTeut. **brū-s* (= Skr. *bhru-s*, Gr. ὀφρύ-s).] †1. The eye-lash, L. *cilium*. Only in OE. †2. The eye-lid, L. *palpebra*. Usu. *pl.* –1500. 3. 'The arch of hair over the eye' (J.). Usu. *pl.* Now EYE-BROW. ME. 4. *pl.* The prominences of the forehead above the eyes. Now poet. = next sense. 1588. 5. The forehead. (L. *frons*.) 1535. Also *fig.* b. *esp.* as the seat of the facial expressions of joy, sorrow, resolution, etc. (*poet.*) 1593. 6. The projecting edge of a cliff or hill, standing over a steep. (From sense 3; though now occ. assoc. w. sense 5.) ME. 7. *Coal-mining.* A gallery in a coal-mine running across the face of the coal.

3. *To knit, bend one's brows*: to frown. The charm of married brows TENNYSON. 4. Did not they Put on my Browes this wreath of Victorie *Jul. C.* v. iii. 82. 5. Men of more b. then brain FULLER. Thy calm clear b., Wherein is glass'd serenity of soul BYRON.

Comb.: **b.-ague**, strictly supra-orbital neuralgia of malarious origin (now = *Megrim*); **-antler**, the lowest tine of a stag's horn; **-point** = *brow-antler*; **-post** (*Archit.*), a cross-beam; **-snag, -tine** = *brow-antler*; **-stone** (cf. *brow-post*). Hence **Browed** *a.* having a b. or brows; chiefly in *comb.*, as *dark-browed*. †**Bro·wless** *a.* unabashed.

Brow (brau), *sb.*[2] 1867. [app. a. Da. *bru*, ON. *brú* bridge.] *Naut.* Old name for a ship's gangway.

Brow, *v. rare.* 1634. [f. BROW *sb.*[1]] To form a brow to, be on the brow of.

1. The hilly crofts That b. this bottom glade MILT.

Browbeat (brau·bīt), *v.* Pa. t. **browbeat,** Pa. pple. **browbeaten.** 1581. [f. BROW *sb.*[1] + BEAT *v.*] To bear down with stern, arrogant, or insolent looks or words; to bully. Also *fig.*

He browbeat the informers against us FIELDING. Hence **Brow·beater.**

†**Browd,** *v.* ME. [a. OF. *brouder, broder* to stitch.] 1. *trans.* To broider, embroider –1503. 2. To braid. CHAUCER.

†**Brow·et.** ME. [a. F. *brouet, broet*, dim. of OF. *breu*, earlier *bro*, late L. **brodum*, ad. OHG *brod* BROTH.] Soup or broth of the juice of boiled meat, thickened –1500.

Brow·is. Now *dial.* [ME. *broys, browes*, a. OF. *broez, brouetz*, nom. of *braet, brouet*, BROWET.] †1. = BREWIS. –1658. 2. A kind of BROSE; as the *browis* of the Sheffield Cutlers' Feast 1839.

Brown (braun), *a.* [Com. Teut.: OE. *brūn* :—OTeut. **brūn-o-z* :—Aryan type **bhrū-no'-s*, root **bhru-*; cf. BEAVER.] 1. Dusky, dark. (Now only poet.) b. *fig.* Gloomy, serious. See BROWN STUDY. 2. Name of a composite colour produced by a mixture of red, yellow, and black ME. 3. Of persons: Having the skin of a brown or dusky colour; dark-complexioned; tanned OE. †4. Of steel, etc.: Burnished. [Cf. F. *brunir*.] –1802.

1. Umbrage broad, And b. as Evening MILT. *P. L.* ix. 1088. 2. *B. ant, bear, owl*; *b. willow*; *b. hæmatite*, etc. 3. The b. Indian GOLDSM. Phr. *To do b.*: 'to do thoroughly', suggested by roasting; to cheat. *slang.*

Comb.: **b. coal,** lignite, etc.; **b. gannet, b. gull,** the Booby (*Sula fusca*); **b. gum,** the inspissated juice of *Eucalyptus resinifera*; **-heart,** a species of tree in Guiana; **-hen,** the female of the Black Grouse (*Tetrao tetrix*); **-holland** (see HOLLAND); **b. jolly,** corrupt. f. BRINJAL; **b. rust,** a disease of wheat caused by a parasitic fungus (*Trichobasis rubigo vera*); **-spar** (Min.), a variety of dolomite; also used of ankerite, magnesite, chalybite, etc.; **b. stout,** a superior kind of porter; **b. sugar,** unrefined or partially refined sugar; **-thrasher,** the (American) Ferruginous Thrush, called also the Brown Thrush (*Turdus rufus*); **b. ware,** a common kind of pottery. Hence **Brow·nish** *a.* **Brow·nness.**

Brown, *sb.* ME. [The adj. used absol.] 1. Brown colour 1607. b. A pigment of a brown colour, as *Vandyke b.* 1549. 2. Ellipt. (see quots.) ME. b. *slang.* A copper coin 1812.

1. The browns and greens of the heather BLACK. 2. The b. [of roast meat] BURTON. March b. [fly] KINGSLEY.

Brown (braun), *v.* ME. [f. BROWN *a.*] 1. *intr.* To become brown. 2. *trans.* To make brown; to roast brown; to give (by a chemical process) a dull brown lustre to gun-barrels, etc. 1570.

Brown Bess. 1785. Familiar name given in the British Army to the old flint-lock musket, which had a brown walnut stock.

Brown bill, brown-bill. 1589. [See BILL *sb.*[1] 2.] A kind of halberd painted brown, once used by foot-soldiers and watchmen.

Brown Bills levied in the City Made Bills to pass the Grand Committee BUTLER *Hud.*

Brown bread. 1489. Any bread of a darker colour than white bread. Now *spec.* applied in England to bread made of unboulted flour, or whole meal. Also *attrib.*

Brown George. 1688. 1. †A loaf of coarse brown bread. b. A hard coarse biscuit. †2. A kind of wig –1840. 3. A brown earthenware vessel. Cf. BLACK JACK. 1861.

Brownian (brau·niăn), *a.* 1871. [f. Dr. Robert *Brown*, who first described the movement.] *B. movement*: the irregular oscillatory movement of microscopic particles suspended in a limpid fluid.

Brownie (brau·ni). 1513. [dim. of BROWN; = 'a wee brown man'.] 1. A benevolent goblin, supposed to haunt old houses, *esp.* farmhouses, in Scotland, and occ. to do household work while the family slept. 2. A junior member of the Girl Guides 1916.

Brow·ning, *sb.* 1905. An automatic pistol invented by J. M. *Browning* of Utah, U.S.A.

Browning (brau·niŋ), *vbl. sb.* 1769. [f. BROWN *v.* + -ING[1].] 1. The process of making or becoming brown 1791. 2. *Cookery.* A preparation for colouring gravy, etc. brown.

Brow·nism. 1617. [f. the surname *Brown*.] 1. The system of church-government advocated *c* 1581 by the Puritan Robert Brown, and adopted by the Independents. 2. *Med.* The BRUNONIAN system. So **Brow·nist.**

Brown study. 1532. [orig. f. BROWN in sense of 'gloomy'.] A state of mental abstraction or musing: now *esp.* an idle reverie.

Brownwort (brau·nwɒ̆ɹt). ? *Obs.* OE. *Herb.* The Water Betony (*Scrophularia aquatica*), and perh. other species of *Scrophularia.*

Brow·ny, *a. rare.* 1582. [f. BROWN *a.* + -Y.] Inclining to brown.

†**Brow·sage.** 1610. [f. BROWSE *v.*] 1. The browsing of cattle; *concr.* that on which they browse –1688. 2. The right of browsing 1611.

Browse (brauz), *sb.*[1] 1523. [app. a. 16th c. F. *broust* (OF. *brost*, mod. *brout*) 'bud, young shoot'.] 1. Young shoots and twigs of shrubs, trees, etc., used as fodder for cattle. 2. That which is or can be browsed 1552. 3. The action of browsing 1810. Hence **B.-wood.**

1. Their gotes upon the brouzes fedd SPENSER. 2. Th' unworthy browze Of buffaloes DRYDEN.

Browse, *sb.*[2] 1875. *Min.* A variety of slag.

Browse, browze (brauz), *v.* 1523. [f. BROWSE *sb.*[1], or f. 16th c. F. *brouster*, now *brouter*.] 1. *intr.* and *absol.* To feed *on* the leaves and shoots of trees and bushes: said of goats, deer, cattle. (Also carelessly used for *graze*.) 1542. Also *fig.* and *transf.* 2. *trans.* To crop and eat (leaves, twigs, etc.) 1523. 3. *causal.* To feed (cattle) *on* (twigs, etc.) 1550.

1. Cattell forsaking the .. pastures to broose vpon leaues and boughes T. TAYLOR. 2. Trees .. perpetually browsed down by the cattle DARWIN. Hence **Brow·ser,** ? one who feeds the deer in winter time; an animal which browses.

Browsing (brau·ziŋ), *vbl. sb.* 1580. [f. prec. + -ING[1].] The action of the vb.; also *concr.* shoots and leaves; browsing-ground.

‖ **Bruchus** (brū·kɒ̆s). ME. [L., a. Gr. βροῦχος, 'a wingless locust'.] 1. = BRUKE. 2. A genus of rhyncophorous beetles, the larvæ of which are destructive to pease, etc. Hence **Bru·chian,** one of the genus *B.*

Brucine (brū·səin). 1823. [From *Brucea antidysenterica*.] *Chem.* A poisonous vegetable alkaloid existing in false Angostura bark, and in Nux Vomica. var. ‖**Bru·cia.**

Brucite (brū·səit). 1868. [f. A. *Bruce*, an American mineralogist; see -ITE.] *Min.* A native hydrate of magnesia.

Bru·ckle, *v.* Now *dial.* 1648. [prob. a frequentative of Sc. *bruik*.] To begrime.

†**Bruges.** 1517. Name of a city of Flanders, used *attrib.* in *B. satin*, and occas. elliptically.

Bruin (brū·in). 1481. [a. MDu. *bruin* BROWN, name of the bear in *Reynard the Fox*.] Applied, as a proper name, to the Brown Bear. (But now often used without capital B.)

Bruise (brūz), *sb.* 1441. [f. the vb.] †1. A breaking; a breach –1530. 2. An injury to the body by a blunt or heavy instrument, causing discoloration but not laceration of the skin; a contusion 1541. b. Of a plant, fruit, etc. 1678.

One arm'd with metal, th' other with wood, This fit for b., and that for blood BUTLER *Hud.*

Bruise (brūz), *v.* [OE. *brȳsan* to crush, coalescing later with OF. *brisier, bruser*, to break, smash, shatter. See N.E.D.] 1. *trans.* 'To crush by any weight' (J.). But now: To injure by a blow which discolours the skin but does not lacerate it, and breaks no bones; to contuse. Also *transf.* †2. [f. Fr.] To break (*in pieces, down*), to smash –1611. 3. *fig.* (to senses 1, 2, 4) ME. 4. To beat small, crush, bray, grind down ME.

1. It shal b. thy head, and thou shalt b. his heele *Gen.* iii. 15. 2. As yron brusseth and breaketh all thinges COVERDALE *Dan.* ii. 40. 3. An Iron Rod to b. and breake Thy disobedience MILT. *P. L.* v. 884. 4. Pot-herbs .. bruis'd with Vervain DRYDEN.

Hence **Bruised** *ppl. a.*; of blood: extravasated.

Bruiser (brū·zəɹ). 1586. [f. BRUISE *v.* + -ER[1].] 1. One who bruises or crushes. 2. A prize-fighter 1744. 3. *Hunting slang.* One who rides recklessly 1830. 4. A concave tool used in grinding lenses or specula 1777.

2. Bear-garden bruisers H. WALPOLE.

†**Brui·sewort.** OE. *Herb.* A plant supposed to heal bruises, *esp.* the Common Daisy –1830.

Bruit (brūt), *sb.* 1450. [a. F., ppl. sb. from *bruire* to roar, ? f. late L. *brugitus* (Littré), or L. *rugitus* (Diez).] 1. Noise, din, clamour (*arch.*). 2. Report noised abroad, rumour (*arch.*) 1494. †3. Renown –1609. ‖4. *Med.* Any sound heard in auscultation; e.g. *bruit de souffle*. [Fr.]

1. The b. of arms MERIVALE. 2. An uncertain b. from Barbadoes of some disorder there EVELYN.

Bruit (brūt), *v.* 1525. [f. the sb.] 1. *trans.* To noise, report, rumour. Often with *abroad, about*. 1528. Also *intr.* KEATS. 2. *trans.* To speak of, make famous 1553.

1. I finde thou art no lesse then Fame hath bruited 1 *Hen. VI*, II. iii. 68.

Bruke. Now *dial.* ME. [ad. L. *brucus, bruchus*; see BRUCHUS.] 1. A locust without wings; ? the larva of the locust. 2. A field-cricket (*north.*) 1847.

Brum. 1881. Contr. of BRUMMAGEM; *attrib.* 'counterfeit, not genuine'

‖**Brumaire** (brümę̄·r). 1803. [F.; f. *brume* fog; see BRUME.] The second month (Oct. 22 to Nov. 20) in the calendar of the French Republic, introduced in 1793.

Brumal (brū·măl), *a.* 1513. [ad. L. *brumalis*, f. *bruma*, contr. of **brevima*, shortest (day), winter.] Belonging to winter; wintry.

The brumall Solstice SIR T. BROWNE.

Brume (brūm). 1808. [a. F.:—L. *bruma*; see prec.] Fog, mist, vapour.

The drifting b. LONGF.

Brummagem (brɒ·mĕdʒĕm). 1681. **A.** *sb.* 1. A local vulgar form of *Birmingham*. Hence (contemptuously) An article made at Birmingham: *spec.* a. A counterfeit coin; b. a spur. 1834. 2. *Eng. Hist.* = 'Birmingham (i.e. counterfeit) Protestant'. See BIRMINGHAM, ANTI-BIRMINGHAM. 1681.

B. *attrib.* or *adj.* 1. Made at Birmingham. b. With allusion to counterfeit groats, plate, etc.: Counterfeit, sham; cheap and showy 1637. 2. *Hist.* Of or pertaining to the 'Birminghams' of 1680; see A 2. 1681.

1a. I coined heroes as fast as Brumingham groats T. BROWN. B. jewellery 1861.

Brumous (brū·məs), *a.* 1850. [ad. F. *brumeux*.] Foggy, wintry.

†**Brunel, -elle.** 1597. The plant Self-heal.

Brunette (brune·t, brüne·t). 1712. [a. F., fem. dim. of *brun*.] **A.** *sb.* A girl or woman of a dark complexion 1713. **B.** *adj.* Of dark complexion, brown-haired; nut-brown. Also *absol.* the colour.

†**Bru·nion.** 1706. [a. F. *brugnon*.] A nectarine. (Dicts.)

Brunonian (brunōᵘ·niăn), *a.* 1799. [f. *Bruno*, Latinized f. the name *Brown*.] Applied to a system of medicine founded by Dr. John Brown (1735–1788), according to which all diseases arise either from deficiency or excess of excitement, and must be treated with stimulants or sedatives. **b.** *sb.* One who holds this.

Brunswick (brʋ·nzwik). 1480. [LG. *Brunswik, -wyk.*] **1.** The name of a town and province of Germany. **†2.** Hence the name of a textile fabric 1480.

B. black, a black varnish made of turpentine and asphalt or lamp-black; **B. green**, a green pigment consisting of oxychloride of copper.

Brunt (brʋnt), *sb.* ME. [? echoic; cf. DUNT.] **†1.** A sharp blow –1485. **†2.** An onset, violent attack. (Often with *bear*, etc.) –1821. **3.** Shock; violence (of an attack) 1573. **4.** The chief stress; crisis. (Formerly *chief b.*) [Perh. influenced by *burnt* (in Sc. *brunt*).] 1769. **†5.** A sudden effort, or outburst –1670.

3. The first b. of the enemy's attack WELLINGTON. The b. of their argument JOWETT. 4. The b. of the danger seems past CARLYLE.

Brunt (brʋnt), *v. rare.* 1440. [f. BRUNT *sb.*] **†1.** *intr.* To make an assault or attack –1690. **2.** *trans.* To bear the brunt of (*rare*) 1859.

Brunt, obs. and dial. pa. t. and pple. of BURN *v.*

Brush (brʋʃ), *sb.*[1] [ME. *brusche*, a. OF. *brosse* brushwood (whence mod.F. *broussailles*). Diez takes the late L. type as **brustia*, and refers it to OHG. *bursta* bristle; cf. BRUSH *sb.*[2]] **1.** Loppings of trees or hedges; cut brushwood (now in U.S.). **b.** A fagot of such brushwood ME. **2.** The small growing trees or shrubs of a wood; a thicket of small trees or underwood. (*Esp.* in U.S., Canada, and Australia.) 1440. **†3.** Stubble –1790.

Comb.: **b.-kangaroo**, a species inhabiting the Australian b.; **-turkey**, an Australian bird (*Talegalla Lathami*).

Brush (brʋʃ), *sb.*[2] [ME. *brusshe*, a. OF. *brosse* brush. Perh. identical with prec.] **1.** A utensil consisting of a piece of wood or other material, set with small tufts or bunches of bristles, hair, etc., for sweeping or scrubbing dust and dirt from a surface; and generally any utensil for brushing or sweeping. (*Brushes* are of many shapes and materials. They are named according to their use, as *clothes-, hat-, hair-brush*, etc.) **b.** The painter's art or skill 1687. **2.** Any brush-like bunch or tuft; *spec.* the tail of the fox 1581. **3.** *Entom.* A brush-like organ on the legs of bees, etc. 1828. **4.** *Electr.* A brush-like discharge of sparks. **b.** A piece of metal terminating in metallic wires, or strips of carbon or copper, used for securing good metallic connexion between two portions of an electrical instrument 1789. **5.** *Optics.* Bright or dark figures accompanying certain phenomena observed in polarized light, which suggest the idea of brushes 1817. **6.** (f. BRUSH *v.*[2]) An application of a brush 1822. **7.** A graze, *esp.* on a horse's leg 1710. **8.** *attrib.* Brush-like 1675.

1. b. Bretheren of the b. STERNE. 2. The squirrel, flippant..whisks his b. COWPER. 6. He..gives his beaver a b. SCOTT.

Comb.: **b.-grass**, *Andropogon Gryllus*; **-ore, -iron-ore**, an iron ore found in the Forest of Dean; **-wheel**, (*a*) a wheel which turns another by means of bristles, cloth, leather, etc., fixed on their circumferences; (*b*) a circular revolving b. used for polishing, etc. Hence **Bru·shless** *a.*

Brush (brʋʃ), *sb.*[3] ME. [? f. BRUSH *v.*[1]] **1.** A forcible rush, a hostile encounter; now *esp.* a short but smart encounter. Hence *At a* (*the first*) *b.* Also *fig.* **2.** ? A slight attack of illness. (Cf. BRASH.) SWIFT.

1. A smart b. with the Spaniards KINGSLEY.

Brush (brʋʃ), *v.*[1] ME. [? ad. F. *brosser*; or perh. echoic; cf. *rush*, etc.] **†1.** *intr.* To rush with force or speed, usu. into collision –1650. **†2.** To force with a rush –1470. **3.** To burst away with a rush, decamp 1690. **4.** *intr.* (cf. BRUSH *v.*[2]) To move briskly *by, through, against* anything, grazing it or sweeping it aside in passing 1674.

3. He brush'd apace On to the abbey BYRON. 4. A pretty young thing..brushing by me ADDISON.

Brush (brʋʃ), *v.*[2] 1460. [f. BRUSH *sb.*[2], or ad. F. *brosser.*] **1.** *trans.* To pass a brush briskly across (a surface) so as to remove dirt or dust, or to smooth the surface. **2.** To rub softly as with a brush in passing; to graze lightly or quickly 1647. Also *intr.* **3.** To remove (dust, etc.) with a brush, to sweep (away). Also *transf.* and *fig.* To sweep away as with a brush. 1631. **4.** To injure by grazing 1691.

1. A brushes his hat a mornings *Much Ado* III. ii. 41. *To b. up*: to brighten up by brushing; also *fig.* to revive one's acquaintance with anything. *To b.* (*a thing*) *over*: to paint lightly; also *fig.* 3. It is..time to b. this nonsense away 1884. Hence **Bru·sher**, one who brushes or uses a b.; also *techn.* in various trades. **Bru·shing** *vbl. sb.*; whence **brushing-machine**, a name of machines acting as brushes for smoothing, dressing flax, etc.

Brushite (brʋ·ʃəit). 1880. [f. Prof. *Brush* of Yale, U.S.; see -ITE.] *Min.* A hydrous phosphate of lime.

Brushwood (brʋ·ʃwud). 1613. [f. BRUSH *sb.*[1]] **1.** Cut or broken twigs or branches 1637. Also *fig.* **2.** Small growing trees or shrubs; thicket, underwood 1732.

Brushy (brʋ·ʃi), *a.*[1] 1719. [f. BRUSH *sb.*[1] + -Y[1].] Covered with brush.

Bru·shy, *a.*[2] 1673. [f. BRUSH *sb.*[2] + -Y[1].] Brush-like; bushy, shaggy.

†Brusk, *a.* 1486. *Her.* The colour *tawny* or *orange* –1688.

Brusk(e, obs. f. BRUSQUE.

Brusque (brʋsk, brūsk), *a.* 1601. [a. F., ad. It. *brusco* sour, tart, grim-looking (Littré). Ult. history unkn. In 17th c. usu. *brusk.*] **†1.** Tart. (= It. *brusco.*) **2.** Somewhat rough or rude in manner; blunt, offhand 1651.

2. He was brusk, ungracious, scowling, and silent D'ISRAELI. Hence **Bru·sque-ly** *adv.*, **-ness.**

Brusque, *v.* 1826. [f. prec.] To treat brusquely or in an off-handed way.

To b. it: to assume a brusque manner.

‖Brusquerie (brüskəri). 1752. [Fr.] Bluntness, abruptness of manner.

Erring, if at all, ever on the side of b. RUSKIN.

Brussels (brʋ·sĕlz). Name of the capital of Belgium: hence, **1.** Short for 'Brussels carpet' 1845. **2.** *attrib.*, as **B. carpet**, a carpet having a back of stout linen thread and an upper surface of wool; **B. lace**, a costly kind of pillow-lace made in B.; **B. sprout** (usu. *pl.*), the bud-bearing Cabbage (*Brassica oleracea gemmifera*), producing buds like small cabbages in the axils of its leaves 1748.

†Bru·stle, *v.*[1] [ME. *brustlien*. Prob. echoic.] *intr.* To crackle, rustle –1755.

†Bru·stle, *v.*[2] 1648. [var. of BRISTLE *v.*] **1.** *intr.* To bristle as hair. **2.** To bristle *up*, raise the mane 1656. **3.** *esp.* Of birds: To raise the feathers; hence *fig.* To show off, bluster –1800.

†Bru·sure. ME. [a. OF. *briseure*, mod. *brisure*, f. *briser.*] **1.** Bruising or crushing; a bruise –1494. **2.** Breaking, breach; ruin –1506.

‖Brut (brūt). 1450. [= M.Welsh *brut*, mod. W. *brud* 'chronicle', a transf. use of *Brut* = *Brutus*, as in the *Brut* of Layamon.] A British chronicle from the mythical Brutus downward.

†Brut, *v.* 1577. [perh. a. F. *brouter.*] **1.** To browse –1699. **2.** *trans. dial.* To break *off* (young shoots).

Brutal (brū·tăl), *a.* 1450. [f. L. *brut-us* (see BRUTE) + -AL.] **1.** Of or belonging to the brutes, as opp. to man; of the nature of a brute; animal (*arch.*). **2.** Pertaining to or resembling the brutes: **a.** in irrationality 1510; **b.** in sensuality 1534; **c.** in coarseness 1709. **3.** Inhuman; coarsely cruel, savage 1641.

2. a. A sort of b. Courage DE FOE. b. The slaves of b. appetite SMOLLETT. c. [Tyrconnel's] b. manners MACAULAY. 3. The cruel and b. abominations of slavery MORLEY. Hence **Bru·talism**, b. state. **Bru·tally** *adv.*

Brutality (brutæ·lĭti). 1549. [f. prec. + -ITY.] **1.** The condition of the brutes 1711. **2.** The quality of being brutal (see BRUTAL 2) 1549. **3.** Inhumanity; an inhuman action 1633.

1. From b. to reason and speech 1863. 3. The Brutallity of the Turkish Troops 1693.

Brutalize brū·tălәiz), *v.* 1704. [f. as prec. + -IZE.] **1.** To live or become like a brute 1716. **2.** *trans.* To render brutal or inhuman 1704. **3.** To treat brutally 1879.

1. If possible we b. more and more H. WALPOLE. Hence **Bru·taliza·tion.**

Brute (brūt), *a.* and *sb.*[1] 1460. [a. F. *brut, brute*:—L. *brutus* heavy, irrational.] **A.** *adj.* (Often *sb.* used *attrib.*) **1.** Of animals: Wanting in reason, as *b. beasts*, = the 'lower animals'. **2.** Of human beings and their attributes: Brute-like, brutish; stupid; unreasoning; sensual 1535. **b.** Rude, wanting in sensibility 1555. **3.** Of things: Irrational, unconscious, senseless; merely material; *esp.* in *b. matter, force* 1540.

2. A b. conjugality MILT. b. This b. Libel MILT. 3. A tendency to prevail over b. force BUTLER. Hence **Bru·te-ly** *adv.*, **-ness.**

B. *sb.* **1.** One of the lower animals as distinguished from man 1611. **b.** The animal nature in man 1784. **2.** A man resembling a brute in want of intelligence, cruelty, coarseness, etc. Now (*colloq.*) often merely a term of reprobation. 1670.

1. My Image not imparted to the B. MILT. *P. L.* VIII. 441. b. Exalt the b. and sink the man BURNS. 2. The b. of a cigar required relighting GEO. ELIOT. Hence **Bru·tehood.**

†Brute, *sb.*[2] 1513. [In sense 1, a var. of *Brett* or *Britt*, influenced by the *Brutus* myth; in 2, = *Brut, Brutus.*] **1.** A Briton, a Welshman –1586. **2.** The legendary Trojan Brutus, first king of Britain. **b.** A Brutus, a hero of British, Welsh, or Arthurian story. **c.** Hence, generally, a hero, 'brave', 'worthy'. –1599.

Brutify (brū·tifәi), *v.* 1668. [f. L. *bruti-* (comb. form).] To make or become brute-like; to brutalize.

Hopeless slavery effectually brutifies the intellect MILL. Hence **Bru·tifica·tion.**

Brutish (brū·tiʃ), *a.* 1494. [f. BRUTE + -ISH.] **1.** Of or pertaining to the brutes 1534. **2.** = BRUTAL 2. 1555. **†3.** Rude, rough; savage –1773. **†4.** = BRUTE *a.* 3. Of thunder: Striking blindly. [after L. *brutum fulmen.*] –1640.

1. Wandring Gods disguis'd in b. forms Rather then human MILT. *P. L.* I. 481. 2. Slowe and brutysshe wyttes 1555. B. Lusts and Appetites STEELE. Hence **Bru·tish-ly** *adv.*, **-ness.**

Brutism (brū·tiz'm). 1687. The behaviour or condition of a brute.

Brutus (brū·tʋs). 1851. In full *Brutus wig.* A rough-cropped head was so called by the French, after Brutus.

Bry-, in obs. words; see BRI-.

Bryology (brәi,ǫ·lŏdʒi). 1863. [f. Gr. βρύον + -λογία.] That branch of botany which treats of mosses. Also, the mosses (collectively) of any country or place. Hence **Bryolo·gical** *a.*, **-ly** *adv.* **Bryo·logist.**

†Bry·on. 1579. [a. F., a. Gr. βρύον.] A kind of moss –1601.

Bryo·nia. L. form of BRYONY.

Bryonin (brәi·ŏnin). 1836. [f. next.] The bitter principle of the root of *Bryonia dioica.*

Bryony (brәi·ŏni). OE. [ad. L. *bryonia* (Pliny), a. Gr. βρυωνία.] **1.** *prop.* Name of the plant-genus Bryonia (N.O. *Cucurbitaceæ*); and *spec.* the common wild species (*B. dioica*), occas. called Red, or White B. **2.** **Black B.**: Lady's Seal, *Tamus communis* (N.O. *Dioscoreaceæ*) 1626. **3.** **Bastard B.**: *Cissus sicyoides.*

Comb. **b.-vine** = sense 1.

‖Bryozoa (brәiŏzōu·ă), *sb. pl.*; sing. **-zoon** (-zōu·ǫn). 1847. [mod.L. (Ehrenberg, 1831), f. Gr. βρυόν moss-like plant + ζῷα (cf. ZOO-), so called from the appearance of some species.] *Zool.* A phylum of small colonial aquatic animals forming tuft-like or moss-like aggregate masses, each individual having a distinct alimentary canal. Hence **Bryozo·an** *a.*, *sb.*

Brys-, Bryt-, in obs. forms; see BRI-.

Brython (bri·þǫn). 1884. [a. Welsh :—OCelt. *Britton-* BRITON. Prof. Rhŷs's term, correlative to *Goidel* applied to the Scoto-Irish Celts.] A Briton of Wales, Cornwall, or ancient Cumbria. Hence **Brytho·nic** *a.*

Buat, var. of BOWET, *Sc.*, a lantern.

Bub (bʋb), *sb.*[1] 1671. [? echoic.] **1.** Drink, *esp.* strong beer (*slang*). **2.** A mixture of meal and yeast with warm wort and water, used to promote fermentation 1880.

Bub, *sb.*[2] Contr. of BUBBY, in both senses.

†Bub, *v.*[1] *rare.* 1563. [Cf. BUBBLE.] To throw up in bubbles.

†Bub, *v.*[2] *rare.* 1719. [? short for BUBBLE.] ? To bribe, or ? to cheat.

Bubal, -ale (biū·băl). 1461. [ad. L. *bubalus* (ad. Gr. βούβαλος); cf. BUFFALO.] Used to render L. *bubalus*: **a.** (early) with uncertain meaning (antelope or buffalo). **b.** (mod. *Zool.*) A species of antelope (*Antilope bubalus*).

Bubble (bʋ·b'l), *sb.* 1481. [orig. f. the verb: cf. BURBLE *sb.* found *c* 1350.] **1.** A thin vesicle of water or other liquid, filled with air or gas. Often = *soap-bubble.* Also a quantity of air or gas occluded within a liquid; *spec.* the air left in the spirit-level. Occ. a cavity produced by occluded air in a solid that has cooled from fusion. †2. *transf.* A hollow globe or bead of glass produced by blowing -1667. 3. *fig.* Anything fragile, unsubstantial, or worthless; *esp.* a delusive commercial or financial scheme, as the *South Sea B.* 1599. Also *attrib.*, as *b. company*, etc. 1635. 4. The process of bubbling; the sound made by bubbling; a state of agitation 1839. †5. One who is bubbled; a gull -1807.

1. The Earth hath bubbles, as the Water ha's *Macb.* I. iii. 79. 3. The b. Reputation *A. Y. L.* II. vii. 152. 4. *A b. of a sea* (Naut.). *Comb.* **b.-shell**, a sort of mollusc.

Bubble (bʊ·b'l), *v.* ME. [var. of BURBLE *v.* Prob. echoic.] 1. *intr.* To form bubbles (as boiling water, etc.); to rise in bubbles; to emit the sounds due to bubbles forming and bursting. Also *fig.* 2. *intr.* To make a sound as of bubbles in boiling or running water. Also *trans.* (*rare.*) 1602. 3. *trans.* To delude with bubbles (sense 3); to cheat, humbug. Now *rare.* 1675.

1. Water, bubbling from this fountain P. FLETCHER. Phr. *To b. over, up* (with fun, etc.): *fig.* from the bubbling of a pot on the fire. 2. At mine ears Bubbled the nightingale TENNYSON.

Bu·bble-and-squea·k. 1785. [From the sounds made in cooking the dish.] Meat and cabbage fried up together.

†**Bu·bble-bow, -boy.** 1727. [app. f. BUBBLE *v.* 3 + BEAU, as if 'Beau-befooler'.] A lady's tweezer-case -1807.

Bubbler (bʊ·blər). 1720. [f. BUBBLE *v.*] †1. A swindler -1728. 2. A fish of the Ohio river, so called from the noise it makes.

Bubbly (bʊ·bli), *a.* 1599. [f. BUBBLE *sb.*] Full of bubbles. (In *Sc.* = blubbering.)

Bu·bbly-jock. *Sc.* 1814. [f. prec. + *Jock* = JACK. Cf. *gobbler.*] A turkey-cock.

Bu·bby[1]. Now *dial.* 1686. [Cf. dial. Ger. *bübbi* teat.] A woman's breast.

Bubby[2]. 1848. [? corrupt. f. *brother*; or = Ger. *bube.*] A little boy. (*U. S., colloq.*)

Bubo (biū·bo). Pl. **buboes.** ME. [a. late L., ad. Gr. βουβών the groin.] An inflamed swelling in glandular parts of the body, *esp.* the groin or arm-pits. Also *attrib.* Hence **Bu·boed** *ppl. a.* affected with buboes. **Bubo·nic** *a.* attended with the appearance of buboes.

Bubonocele (biubǫ·nǒsīl). 1615. [a. Gr., f. βουβών + κήλη.] Inguinal hernia.

†**Bu·bukle.** Confusion of BUBO and CARBUNCLE. *Hen. V*, III. vi. 108.

Buccal (bʊ·kăl), *a.* 1831. [as if ad. L. **buccalis*, f. *bucca.*] Of or pertaining to the cheek.

‖**Bucca·n, buca·n, bouca·n**, *sb.* 1611. Also **bocan.** [a. F. *boucan*, repr. a Tupi or Brazilian word.] 1. A wooden framework on which meat was roasted or smoked over a fire. (*S. Amer.*) 2. (in form *bocan*) = BARBECUE *sb.* 5. 1857. 3. Boucaned meat. [prop. Fr.] 1860. Hence **Bu·ccan** *v.* to roast or smoke (meat) upon a b.

Buccaneer, -ier (bʊkănīə·ɹ), *sb.* 1661. [a. F. *boucanier*, orig. 'one who hunts wild oxen' (Littré), f. *boucan*; see prec.] †1. *orig.* One who dries and smokes flesh on a *boucan.* The name was first given to the French hunters of St. Domingo. -1761. 2. (From the subsequent habits of these.) One of the piratical rovers who infested the Spanish coasts in America 1690. 3. A filibuster 1846. Hence **Buccanee·rish** *a.*

Buccaneer (bʊkănīə·ɹ), *v.* 1795. [f. prec.] a. = To buccan. b. To act as a buccaneer.

Buccinal (bʊ·ksinăl), *a.* 1846. [f. L. *buccina* + -AL.] Shaped or sounding like a trumpet.

Buccinator (bʊ·ksineɪtəɹ). 1671. [a. L., f. *buccinare.* So called because employed in blowing.] *Anat.* A flat thin muscle which forms the wall of the cheek. So **Bu·ccinatory** *a.* pertaining to a trumpeter or trumpeting.

‖**Buccinum** (bʊ·ksinǒm). 1601. [L.] *Zool.* The genus of gasteropod Molluscs represented by the Whelk. Hence **Bu·ccinoid** *a.* b.-like.

‖**Bucellas** (biuse·lăs). 1836. [Name of a village near Lisbon.] A Portuguese white wine.

Bucentaur (biuse·ntǭɹ, biu·sentǭɹ). 1612. [ad. It. *bucentoro* (also used), ? ad. Gr. *βουκένταυρος, f. Gr. βοῦς + κένταυρος, the figure-head of the vessel representing a creature half man, half ox.] *Hist.* The state barge in which on Ascension Day the Doge of Venice went to wed the Adriatic by dropping a ring into it. Also, a large ship 1623.

Bucephalus (biuse·fălǒs). 1799. [ad. Gr., f. βοῦς + κεφαλή.] The name of Alexander the Great's charger; (*joc.*) any riding-horse.

‖**Buchu** (bʊ·ku, bu·ku). 1731. Native Cape name of the plant formerly called *Diosma crenata*; now assigned to species of *Barosma.*

Buck (bʊk), *sb.*[1] [OE. *buc* male deer:— OTeut. **bukko-z*; and OE. *bucca* he-goat (:— OTeut. **bukkon-*); not dist. in form after 11th c.] 1. The male of: a. †the goat -1551; b. the deer, *esp.* the fallow-deer OE.; c. the reindeer, the chamois, the hare, the rabbit, and in S. Africa (after Du. *bok*) any animal of the antelope kind 1674. 2. *transf.* a. A dashing fellow; a dandy 1725. b. A man: used of S. Amer. Indians. *B. nigger*: a negro man. (*U. S.*)

1. a. *To blow the buck's horn* (Chaucer): to have his labour for his pains. b. The b. is called..the fifth year *a b. of the first head*; and the sixth, *a great b.* 2. a. I remember you a b. of bucks when that coat first came out to Calcutta THACKERAY.

†**Buck**, *sb.*[2] 1577. 1. = BUCK-WHEAT -1807. 2. = BUCK-MAST; beech-mast -1727.

Buck, *sb.*[3] *arch.* and *dial.* 1530. [f. BUCK *v.*[1]] †1. ? A washing tub, a vat in which to steep clothes in lye. 2. Lye in which linen, yarn, etc. is steeped in buck-washing or bleaching 1560. 3. A quantity of clothes, etc. put through the process of bucking; a 'wash' 1532.

Buck (bʊk), *sb.*[4] 1851. A basket used to catch eels. Also *attrib.*

Buck, *sb.*[5] 1691. [? i. q. BOUK, OE. *búc* belly, body, etc.] The body of a cart. (*dial.*)

Buck, *sb.*[6] *U.S.* 1860. [a. Du. *zaag-boc*, or shortly *bock.*] A frame on which wood is cross-cut; a saw-buck.

Comb. **b.-saw**, a heavy frame-saw used with a b.

Buck, *v.*[1] Now *dial.* [ME. *bouken, bowken*, with Teut. and Rom. cognates.] 1. To steep or boil in an alkaline lye in buck-washing, or bleaching. 2. To drench, soak 1494.

Buck (bʊk), *v.*[2] 1530. [f. BUCK *sb.*[1]] To copulate with; said of male rabbits, etc.

Buck (bʊk), *v.*[3] 1859. [f. BUCK *sb.*[1]] To leap vertically from the ground, drawing the feet together like a deer, and arching the back. Also trans. *To b. off.* Cf. BUCK-JUMP.

Buck (bʊk), *v.*[4] *U.S.* 1865. *trans.* [? f. BUCK *sb.*[6]] *trans.* To lay across a log.

Buck (bʊk), *v.*[5] 1683. [Cf. Du. *boken, boocken.*] To break ore small with a bucker.

Buck, *v.*[6] *dial.* or *colloq.* 1854. [f. BUCK *sb.*[1] 2.] In *b. up*: To dress up; to make haste; to make or become vigorous or cheerful; *esp.* in *imper.* Buck up!

Buck-bean (bʊ·kbīn). 1578. [App. tr. Flemish *bocks boonen* 'goat's beans'. (A later (? rationalized) name is *bog-bean.*)] *Herb.* A water plant (*Menyanthes trifoliata*) common in bogs in Britain; it bears racemes of pinkish white flowers.

Buckeen (bʊkī·n). *Anglo-Irish.* 1793. [dim. of BUCK *sb.*[1]; cf. *squireen.*] A young man belonging to the inferior gentry of Ireland, or a cadet of the poorer aristocracy, having no profession, and aping the habits of the wealthy.

Bu·cker[1]. 1884. [f. BUCK *v.*[3]] A horse that bucks.

Bu·cker[2]. 1653. [f. BUCK *v.*[5]] *Mining.* A hammer for bucking ore.

Bucket (bʊ·kėt), *sb.*[1] ME. [app. a. OF. *buket* washing-tub, etc.; cf. OE. *búc* a pail.] 1. 'The vessel in which water is drawn out of a well'. b. 'The vessel in which water is carried, particularly to quench a fire'. (J.)

Buckets are now chiefly of wood, and vary in shape. In England and U. S. they are round pails with arched handles; in Scotland, four-sided vessels for carrying salt, coal, etc.

2. The piston of a lift-pump 1634. 3. One of the compartments on the circumference of a water-wheel, which retain the water while they descend; one of the metal cups on the endless band of a grain-elevator, etc. 1759. 4. *transf.* A leathern socket or rest for a whip, or for a carbine or lance 1833.

1. Like a deepe Well, That owes two Buckets, filling one another *Rich. II*, IV. i. 185. *To kick the b.*: see BUCKET[2].

Comb.: **b.-engine**, a machine having buckets attached to an endless chain running over sprocket-wheels, so as to utilize the power of a small stream of water with a good fall; **-lift**, a set of iron pipes attached to a lift-pump; **-pump**, a lift-pump; **-well**; **-wheel**, a contrivance for raising water, consisting of buckets fixed round a wheel, or attached to a rope passing round a wheel, which fill at the bottom and empty themselves at the top.

Bu·cket, *sb.*[2] 1570. [Perh. a. OF. *buquet* 'balance'.] A beam or yoke on which anything may be hung, as, in Norfolk, a pig by its heels. Hence (?) *To kick the b.*: (*slang*) to die.

Bucket (bʊ·kėt), *v.* 1621. [f. BUCKET *sb.*[1]] 1. *trans.* To lift (water) in buckets. Also *fig.* 1649. 2. To pour buckets of water over 1621. 3. *slang.* To swindle 1812. 4. To ride (a horse) hard; to pump (take it out of him by bucketfuls) 1856. 5. *Rowing. intr.* To hurry the forward swing of the body; also *trans.* 1869.

5. A..tendency to b. the recovery (*mod.*).

Buc·ket-shop. *U.S.* 1882. [? f. BUCKET *sb.*[1]] An unauthorized office used orig. for smaller gambling transactions in grain, and subseq. extended to offices for other descriptions of gambling and betting on the stocks, etc.

Bu·ckety. *Sc.* Paste used by weavers in dressing their webs.

Buck-eye. 1789. [f. BUCK *sb.*[1] + EYE.] *Bot.* 1. The American Horse-chestnut (*Æsculus glabra*). 2. *U. S. colloq.* A native of Ohio, the 'Buckeye State'.

1. Called buck-eye .. from the hilum of the fruit having the appearance of a stag's eye MRS. LOUDON.

Buck-eyed, *a.* 1847. *Farriery.* Having bad or speckled eyes; said of horses.

Buck-horn (bʊ·khǭrn). Also **Buck's horn.** 1447. [f. BUCK *sb.*[1]] †1. The horn of a buck. b. The horn of a goat used for blowing a blast. -1548. 2. The material of a buck's horn; also *attrib.* horny 1613. 3. From its hardness: Dried whiting or other fish 1602.

Buck-hound (bʊ·khaund). 1530. [f. as prec.] A smaller variety of staghound. *Master of the Buckhounds*, an officer of the Royal Household.

Buckie (bʊ·ki). *Sc.* 1596. [?] 1. The whorled shell of any mollusc; *e. g.* a whelk. Cf. L. *buccinum.* 2. (? f. BUCK *sb.*[1]) A perverse or refractory person 1719.

Bucking (bʊ·kiŋ), *vbl. sb.*[1] 1483. [f. BUCK *v.*[1] + -ING[1].] Steeping or boiling yarn, clothes, etc. in a lye, in the old process of bleaching, or in buck-washing; the quantity so treated.

Comb.: **b.-keir**, a large wooden vat used in b.; **-washing**, the annual purification of family linen by means of buck.

Bu·cking, *vbl. sb.*[2] 1875. [f. BUCK *v.*[5]] *Mining.* The bruising of ore with a bucker.

Buckish (bʊ·kiʃ), *a.* 1515. [f. BUCK *sb.*[1] + -ISH[1].] 1. Like or characteristic of a he-goat; lascivious; ill-smelling. 2. Foppish 1806.

Bu·ck-jump. 1878. [f. BUCK *sb.*[1]] A leap like that of a buck. *esp.* A jump of a horse that bucks (see BUCK *v.*[3]). Of American or Australian origin. Hence **Bu·ck-jump** *v.* = BUCK *v.*[3]; also **Buck-jumper.**

Buckle (bʊ·k'l), *sb.* ME. [a. F. *boucle*:—L. *buccula* (dim. of *bucca*), 'cheek-strap of a helmet', 'boss of a shield'.] 1. A rim of metal, with a hinged tongue carrying one or more spikes, for securing a belt, strap, etc., which passes through the rim, and is pierced by the spike or spikes. Often defined, as *shoe-b.*, etc. †2. The drop of an ear-ring. (Fr. *boucle d'oreille.*) 1674. †3. The state of hair when crisped and curled -1789.

Comb.: **b.-covering**, a certain step in dancing; so, *to cover the b.*; **-plates**, plates of iron buckled or bent concave; **-wig**, see BUCKLE *v.* 5.

Buckle (bʊ·k'l), *v.* ME. [f. prec. sb.; but cf. F. *boucler.*] 1. *trans.* To fasten with a buckle. 2. *trans.* To equip, prepare (for battle, etc.). Chiefly *refl.*, and now only *fig.* 1570. Also *intr.* (for *refl.*). 3. *trans.* To join closely; *intr.* (for *refl.*) to close; to grapple, engage. Now *dial.* 1535. 4. *trans.* To unite in marriage (*joc.* or *dial.*) Cf. *splice.* 1724. Also *intr.* †5. To fasten in curl -1796. 6. *trans.* To warp,

crumple, bend out of its plane. Now chiefly techn.: To bend a bar or surface (under longitudinal pressure) into a double curve. 1525. *intr.* To bend under pressure 1597. Also †*fig.*
1. Nailynge the speres, and helmes bokelynge CHAUCER. *To b. in* (fig.): to enclose. *A. Y. L.* III. ii. 140. 2. *To b. to*: to apply oneself vigorously. 4. Dr. R. who buckles beggars for a tester and a dram of Geneva SCOTT. 6. Reason doth b. and bowe the mind unto the nature of things BACON. To b. a saw 1854.
Comb.: †b.-beggar (*Sc.*), a hedge-priest.

Bu·ckler, *sb.*[1] 1650. [f. prec.] One who or that which buckles.

Buckler (bɒ·klə̆ɪ), *sb.*[2] ME. [a. OF. *boucler*, *bucler* (mod. *bouclier*), repr. L. **buccularius*, f. *buccula*; see BUCKLE *sb.*] 1. A small round shield; in England 'used not so much for a shield as for a warder to catch the blow of an adversary' (Fairholt). Also (erron.) Any kind of shield. Also *attrib.* 2. *fig.* Protection, protector ME. 3. Techn.: a. *Naut.* A wooden shutter placed against the inside of a hawse-hole to prevent the water from coming in. A *Blind B.* has no aperture; a *Riding B.*, used at anchor, has a hole in the middle for the passage of a cable. 1832. b. *Anat.*, *Zool.*, etc. Applied to the hard protective covering of parts of the body of the armadillo, the ganoid fishes, and some crustacea; *spec.* the anterior segment of the shell of the trilobites 1828.
1. A swerd and a bocler baar he by his side CHAUCER. 2. A b. of impenetrable indifference C. BRONTË.
Comb.: b.-fern, the genus *Aspidium*; -head, the fossil fish *Cephalaspis*; -mustard, *Biscutella auriculata*; -thorn, *Rhamnus Paliurus aculeatus*. Hence **Bu·cklered** *ppl. a.* furnished with bucklers.

Buckler (bɒ·klə̆ɪ), *v.* 1590. [f. prec.] 1. *trans.* To act as a buckler to; to shield, defend. †2. To ward or catch (blows) 3 *Hen. VI*, I. iv. 50.
1. 'Tis not the king can b. Gaveston MARLOWE.

†Bu·ck-mast. 1425. [:—OE. **bóc-mæst.*] Beech-mast –1607.

†Buck·one. 1625. [ad. It. *boccone*, f. *bocca.*] A mouthful –1659.

‖Buckra (bɒ·krā). 1794. [In negro patois of Surinam, *bakra*, master. In lang. of Calabar coast, 'demon, powerful and superior being'.] A white man (in negro talk).

Buckram (bɒ·krăm), *sb.* ME. [? ad. It. *bucherame.* Etym. unkn.] †1. A kind of fine linen or cotton fabric –1553. 2. A kind of coarse linen or cloth stiffened with gum or paste ME. †b. A lawyer's bag –1622. 3. *fig.* Stiffness; a starched manner 1682. 4. *attrib.* and quasi-*adj.* Of, or like, buckram 1537; *fig.* stuck up; that has a false appearance of strength 1589.
2. Foure Rogues in Buckrom let driue at me SHAKS. 3. A fine..unaffected lad, no pride or b. CORNWALLIS. 4. A wondrous b. style,—the best he [Johnson] could get CARLYLE.

Buckram (bɒ·krăm), *v.* 1783. [f. prec.] *trans.* To pad or stiffen with buckram; to give to anything a starched pomposity or a false appearance of strength.
Written by Walpole, and buckram'd by Mason 1784.

†Bu·ckra·ms. 1578. [? f. BUCK *sb.*[1] + *rams.*] A name for Ramsons or Wild Garlic –1783.

†Buck·s-beard. 1551. [tr. Gr. τραγοπώγων.] Goats-beard; Salsify.

Buck's-horn. 1450. a. *Senebiera Coronopus*, Swine's Cress. b. The Virginia Sumach (*Rhus typhina*). Also **Buck's horn Plantain, Buck's horn Weld.** So called from the appearance of their leaves or branches.

Buck's-horn, var. of BUCK-HORN.

Buck-shot (bɒ·k,ʃɒt). 1447. [f. BUCK *sb.*[1]] †1. The distance at which a buck may be shot (*rare*). 2. A kind of shot, larger than *swan-shot*, used in shooting deer and large game. Also *attrib.* 1776.
Comb. b.-rule, a political nickname for government (of Ireland) upheld by a constabulary with loaded rifles.

Buckskin (bɒ·kskin). 1433. [f. BUCK *sb.*[1]] 1. The skin of a buck. 2. Leather made from buckskin; also from sheepskin 1804. Also *attrib.* 3. Breeches (and perh. gloves) made of buckskin 1481. †4. A nickname of the American troops during the Revolutionary war; hence, a native American –1823.

Bu·ck-stall. 1503. [f. BUCK *sb.*[1]] A net for catching deer. (*Hist.*)

Buckthorn (bɒ·kþǭɹn). 1578. [f. as prec.] The shrub *Rhamnus catharticus*; its berries yield sap-green, and are a strong cathartic.

Bu·ck-tooth. 1753. [f. as prec.] A large projecting tooth. Also *attrib.*

†Bu·ck-wa·shing. 1598. [f. BUCK *sb.*[3]] The process of washing very dirty linen, by boiling it in an alkaline lye (BUCK *sb.*[3]), and afterwards beating and rinsing it in clear water –1879. So **Buck-washer;** also dial. **buck-wash.**

Buckwheat (bɒ·k,hwīt). 1548. [Cf. BUCK-MAST.] 1. A species of Polygonum (*P. Fagopyrum*). The seed is in Europe used as food for horses, cattle, and poultry; in N. America its meal is made into buckwheat cakes. Also *attrib.* 2. Applied also to *P. Convolvulus*, and to *P. tartaricum* 1548.

Bucolic (biuko·lik). 1531. [ad. L. *bucolicus*, a. Gr., f. βουκόλος.] A. *adj.* 1. Of or pertaining to herdsmen or shepherds; pastoral 1613. 2. Rural, rustic, countrified. (Partly *joc.*) 1846. var. **Buco·lical,** whence **Buco·lically** *adv.*
1. Mingling b. details and sentimental effusions SYD. SMITH.
B. *sb.* [cf. L. *Bucolica*, Gr. βουκολικά.] 1. *pl.* Pastoral poems: rarely in *sing.* 1531. 2. = Bucolic poet 1774. 3. A rustic (*joc.*) 1862. 4. *pl.* Agricultural pursuits (*rare*) 1865.
1. [Virgil's] bucolikes ELYOT.

Bucra·ne. Also **bucra·nium.** 1854. [F. *bucrane*, and L. ad. Gr. βουκράνιον, f. βοῦς + κρανίον.] *Archit.* A sculptured ornament representing an ox-skull.

Bud (bɒd), *sb.* [Late ME. *budde*, *bodde*, of unkn. etym.] *Bot.* A little projection found at the axil of a leaf, forming the rudiment of a branch, cluster of leaves, or blossom. Hence, applied to a flower (or leaf) at any stage of growth until fully opened. b. *Zool.* A similar growth in animals of low organization, which develops into a new individual 1836. Also *transf.* and *fig.*
So longe it is called the budde of a rose, as it is not a perfyte rose *Pilgr. Perf.* (W. de W. 1531). *fig.* Now will Canker-sorrow eat my b. [Arthur] *John* III. iv. 82.
Phr. *In b.* (said of plants): budding. *In the b.*: not yet developed. *To nip* or *crush in the b.*: *fig.* to repress or destroy (a project, etc.) in its beginnings.
Comb.: b.-germ (*Zool.*) = b.; -rudiment, the cell in the embryo, from which the b. is developed.

Bud (bɒd), *v.*[1] ME. [f. BUD *sb.*] I. *intr.* a. To put forth buds. b. with *out*: To come or push out, as a bud. 2. *fig.* To begin to grow; to develop 1566. 3. *trans.* To put forth as buds; to produce by gemination; also *fig.* 1591. 4. To cause to bud; also *fig.* 1604. 5. *Gardening.* To ingraft by inserting a bud of a shrub or tree under the bark of another stock. Also *absol.* 1663.
1. The rose is budding fain SCOTT. 2. Many vices b. out of this one H. SMITH. Budding honours SHAKS. Hence **Bu·dder** KEATS. **Bu·dding** *vbl. sb.* and *ppl. a.* that buds; in b.; also *fig.*

Bud, *v. Sc.* = must; see BUS *v.*

Buddha (bu·dă, bu·d,ha). 1681. [a. Skr., pa. pple. of *budh* to awake, know, perceive.] The title given by the adherents of BUDDHISM to the founder of their faith, Sâkyamuni, Gautama, or Siddârtha, who flourished in Northern India in the 5th century B.C. Sâkyamuni is regarded as only the latest of a series of Buddhas, which is to be continued indefinitely.
Hence **Bu·ddhahood,** the condition of a B.; **Bu·ddhaship,** the office of a B.; **Bu·ddhism,** the religious system founded by B.; **Bu·ddhist** *sb.*, a follower of B.; *adj.* relating to Buddhism (vars. **Bu·ddhic, -i·stic, -al** *a.*); †**Bu·ddhite** *sb.* and *a.*

Bu·ddle, boo·dle, *sb.*[1] ME. [?] The Corn-marigold.

Buddle (bɒ·d'l), *sb.*[2] 1531. [?] *Mining.* A shallow inclined vat in which ore is washed.

Buddle (bɒ·d'l), *v.* 1693. [f. prec.] To wash (ore) by means of a buddle.

Buddleia (bɒdlī·ă, bɒ·dlĭă). 1885. [mod.L., f. the name of Adam *Buddle* (died 1715): see -IA [1].] Any plant of the genus of shrubs of this name, bearing clusters of yellow or violet flowers.

Bu·ddy, *a. rare.* 1598. Full of buds; like a bud.

Bude (biūd). 1807. [f. *Bude* in Cornwall.] **B.-burner,** a gas-burner invented at Bude by Sir G. Gurney, consisting of two or three concentric argand rings. **B.-light,** a light obtained by directing a stream of oxy-hydrogen gas on a quantity of pounded egg-shells.

Bude = *behoved*: see BUS *v.*

Budge (bɒdʒ), *sb.*[1] ME. [? f. OF. *bouchet*, *bochet* a kid. But usu. identified with BUDGE *sb.*[2], BOUGE *sb.*[1]] A kind of fur, consisting of lamb's skin with the wool dressed outwards. *Comb.* **b.-bachelor,** one of a company in gowns trimmed with b., who took part in the procession on Lord Mayor's Day (see BACHELOR 2). For *b.-doctor*, see BUDGE *a.*

†Budge, *sb.*[2] 1606. Later sp. of BOUGE *sb.*[1] A leather bag. Cf. BUDGET.

†Budge, *sb.*[3] *slang.* 1673. A sneaking thief –1751.

†Budge, *a.* 1634. [? attrib. use of BUDGE *sb.*[1] Thus *budge doctor* would be originally one who wore budge fur.] 1. Solemn in demeanour, pompous, formal –1781. 2. *dial.* Brisk –1800.
Those b. doctors of the Stoic fur MILT. *Comus* 707.

Budge (bɒdʒ), *v.* 1590. [a. F. *bouger*; acc. to Diez, prob.:—late L. **bullicare*, frequent. of *bullire* to boil.] 1. With neg.: *intr.* To stir; to move from one's place. 2. *trans.* To stir 1598.
1. Not a soul will b. to give him place GOLDSM. 2. Three men..could not b. it 1883. Hence **Bu·dger.**

Bu·dge-ba·rrel. 1627. [f. BUDGE *sb.*[2] = BOUGE *sb.*[1] + BARREL *sb.*] A small powder-barrel, having a leather cover with a long neck drawing together like the mouth of a bag.

Budgerigar (bɒ:dʒĕrigā·ɪ). 1847. [Native Austral. = good cockatoo.] The Australian grass parakeet.

Budgerow (bɒ·dʒərōu). *Anglo-Ind.* 1727. [a. Hindī *bajrā.*] A lumbering keelless barge, formerly much used on the Ganges.

Budget (bɒ·dʒĕt). 1432. [ad. F. *bougette*, dim. of *bouge*; see BOUGE *sb.*[1]] 1. A pouch, bag, wallet, usu. of leather. Now *dial.* 2. *spec.* †a. A leather or skin bottle –1786. b. A boot in a carriage, for carrying luggage. ? *Obs.* 1794. c. A leathern socket for the butt of a cavalry carbine. Cf. BUCKET *sb.*[1] 4. 1816. 3. *transf.* The contents of a bag or wallet; a bundle, a collection or stock 1597. b. A title for a journal (*i. e.* a b. of news, etc.): e. g. *Pall Mall B.* 4. A statement of the probable revenue and expenditure for the ensuing year, with financial proposals founded thereon, annually submitted by the Chancellor of the Exchequer for the approval of the House of Commons. Sometimes put for the condition of the national finances as thus disclosed; also for the financial measures proposed. Hence, any analogous statement, estimate, or proposals 1733. †5. *Her.* = BOUGET 1766. 6. (See MUM-BUDGET, a phr. enjoining silence.) *Merry W.* V. ii. 7.
1. Staff, b., bottle, scrip he wore SCOTT. 3. A B. of Paradoxes DE MORGAN (*title*). 4. The time was now come for *opening the b.*, when it was incumbent on him to state the finances, debts, and calls of government H. WALPOLE. *Comb.*: b.-bar, a bar of timber on which rests the boot of a carriage; -gut, the cæcum. Hence **Bu·dgetary** *a.* pertaining to a b. **Budgetee·r,** one who makes up a b. (in sense 3 or 4). **Bu·dgeter,** one who carries a wallet; †a charlatan; a strolling player.

Bu·dget, *v.* 1618. [f. prec.] *trans.* †a. To put in a wallet; to store *up.* b. *To b. for*: to provide for in the b.

†Bu·dgy, *a. rare.* 1598. [f. BUDGE *sb.*[1]] Of or like lamb's fur.

Bu·dlet. [f. BUD *sb.*[1]] A secondary bud springing from another bud. DARWIN.

Budmash, var. of BADMASH, 'bad character.'

Buff, *sb.*[1] *Obs.* exc. in BLIND-MAN'S-BUFF. ME. [perh. a. OF. *bufe*, *buffe*, a blow; cf. BUFFET *sb.*[1]] A blow, stroke, buffet.
Phr. **To stand buff:** to stand firm, not to flinch.

Buff (bɒf), *sb.*[2] 1552. [app. ad. F. *buffle*; cf. BUFFLE.] †1. A buffalo, or other large species of wild ox –1706. †2. (More fully *buff-leather*): *prop.* Leather made of buffalo-hide; but usu. a very stout kind of leather made of ox-hide, dressed with oil, having a fuzzy surface, and a dull whitish-yellow colour –1756. b. Military attire; a military coat made of buff; = BUFF-COAT. Also the dress of sergeants and catch-poles. 1590. 3. *colloq.* (somewhat *arch.*) The bare skin. *In b.*: naked. 1654. 4. = *buff-stick* or *-wheel*; see *Comb.* 1831. 5. Buff colour;

a dull light yellow. *Blue and b.*, formerly the Whig colours. 1788. 6. *The Buffs*: a name given, from the colour of their facings, to the old 3rd regiment of the line (now the East Kent Regiment) 1806. 7. *Pathol.* = BUFFY COAT. 1739.

2. b. In b. and bandoleer for King Charles SCOTT.

Comb.: **b.-jerkin**, a military jerkin of b.-leather; **-stick, -wheel**, a stick or wheel, covered with b.-leather or other soft material, for polishing metal.

†Buff, *sb.*³ *colloq.* 1708. [cf. BUFFER.] Fellow, 'buffer' –1764.

Buff (bɒf), *a.* 1695. [f. BUFF *sb.*² 2.] 1. Of or like buff-leather. 2. Of the colour of buff-leather; a light brownish yellow 1762. See also BUFF *sb.*² 5, 6.

2. The dress..of a Cavalier..b. with blue ribbands H. WALPOLE.

Buff, *v.*¹ Now *dial.* ME. [prob. echoic; cf. PUFF *v.*] 1. *intr.* **a.** To stutter. **b.** To explode into a laugh, or the like. 2. *trans.* To cause to burst out by sudden force. B. JONS. 3. *intr.* To act and sound as a soft inflated body does when struck 1550. 4. *intr.* and *trans.* To strike a soft inflated body (with this effect) 1600.

Buff, *v.*² 1885. [f. BUFF *sb.*²] **a.** To polish with a buff. **b.** To impart the surface usual in buff leather for belts, etc.

Buffalo (bɒ·fălo). Pl. **buffaloes.** 1588. [a. It. *buffalo*, or (prob.) Pg. *búfalo* :—vulgar L. **bufalus*, a. Gr. βούβαλος, an antelope, also a wild ox.] 1. The name of: *esp.* **a.** *Bos bubalus*, originally a native of India. It is tamed in India, Italy, and elsewhere. 1588. **b.** *B. caffer*, the Cape Buffalo of S. Africa 1699. **c.** *pop.* The American BISON 1789. 2. A fresh-water fish resembling the Sucker 1789. 3. = *buffalo-robe*; see *Comb.* (*colloq. U.S.* and *Canada*) 1856. 4. Short for *b.-horn*: used by cutlers.

Comb.: **b.-bag** (cf. *buffalo-robe*); **-berry**, the edible scarlet fruit of *Shepherdia argentea*, found on the Upper Missouri; **-bird**, an insessorial bird (*Textor erythrorhynchus*) which accompanies herds of buffaloes in S. Africa; **-chips**, *pl.*, the dried dung of the American bison, used as fuel; **-clover**, a species of clover (*Trifolium pennsylvanicum*) found in the prairies; **-fish** = sense 2; **-grass**, a grass (*Sesleria dactyloides*) found in the prairies; **-nut**, a N. American shrub (*Pyrularia oleifera*), or its fruit; **-robe**, a cloak or rug made of the skin of the American bison dressed with the hair on.

Buff coat, bu·ff-coat. 1633. [see BUFF *sb.*²] 1. A stout coat of buff leather, *esp.* one worn by soldiers. Also *fig.* 2. One who wears a buff coat; a soldier 1670. 3. = BUFFY COAT.

Buffed (bɒft), *a.* 1640. [f. BUFF *sb.*²] **a.** Clad in buff. **b.** Coated or covered with buff, having a buffy coat.

†Bu·ffer¹. ME. [f. BUFF *v.*¹] A stammerer.

Buffer² (bɒ·fəɹ). 1835. [app. f. BUFF *v.*¹ 3.] *Mech.* A mechanical apparatus for deadening the force of a concussion, as fixed at the front and back of railway carriages, etc. Extended also to contrivances which sustain without deadening the concussion. (Formerly called *buffing apparatus*.) Also *fig.* and *attrib.*

Comb.: **b.-state**, a neutral state lying between two others and serving to render less possible hostilities between them.

Bu·ffer³. 1854. [f. BUFF *v.*¹ 3.] **a.** One who buffs knives, plate, etc. **b.** = BUFF *sb.*² 4. **c.** A machine for polishing daguerreotype plates.

Bu·ffer⁴. *slang.* 1749. [?] 1. A dog. **b.** *transf.* A pistol; = BARKER 4. 1812. 2. *Sc.* and *dial.* A foolish fellow. 3. A fellow: usu. slightly contemptuous 1749.

1. Here be a pair of b-s will bite as well as bark SCOTT.

Buffet (bɒ·fĕt), *sb.*¹ ME. [app. a. OF., dim of *buffe* BUFF *sb.*¹] A blow; *esp.* one given with the hand. †*Pl.* Fisticuffs (*rare*). Also *transf.* and *fig.* (Cf. BLOW, STROKE.)

The vile Blowes and Buffets of the World SHAKS.

Buffet (bɒ·fĕt), *sb.*² ME. [?] 1. A low stool; a footstool. Now *Sc.* and *n. dial.* var. **Bu·ffet-stool.** 2. A hassock (*dial.*) 1877.

Buffet (bɒ·fĕt), *sb.*³ 1718. [a. mod.F. *buffet*, of unkn. etym. Sense 3 is recent.] 1. A sideboard or side-table for china, plate, etc. 2. A cupboard in a recess for china and glasses 1720. ‖3. (*büfe.*) A refreshment bar 1869. var. **Beaufet.**

Buffet (bɒ·fĕt), *v.* Pa. t. and pple. **-eted.** ME. [f. BUFFET *sb.*¹] 1. To beat, strike, *esp.* with the hand; to cuff, knock about. **b.** To beat back, contend with (waves, etc.) 1601. Also *fig.* 2. *intr.* To deal blows, fight, struggle 1599. Also *fig.* 3. *trans.* To drive, force, or produce, by buffeting 1734. 4. *trans.* To muffle (bells). [? A distinct wd.] 1753.

1. Bang'd and buffeted into Reason BENTLEY. 2. To b. resolutely with hardships W. IRVING. 3. To b. one's way to riches and fame 1865. Hence **Bu·ffeter** (*rare*), one that buffets.

†Bu·ffin. 1572. A coarse cloth in use for gowns in Elizabeth's time; a gown of this. Also *attrib.* –1632.

†Bu·ffle, *sb.* 1511. [a. F. *buffle*:—vulgar L. **bufalus*; see BUFFALO. Cf. also BUFF *sb.*²] 1. = BUFFALO 1 a, b. –1738. Also *attrib.* 2. = BUFFLEHEAD. [After F. *buffle.*] –1710.

Bu·ffle, *v.* 1610. [? Echoic; conn. w. some sense of BUFF; or ? misprint for *bustle*. '*Buffle* to puzzle' in Dicts. is a bogus wd., founded on this misprint.]

Bu·fflehead. 1659. [f. BUFFLE.] A fool, blockhead.

Buffle-headed (bɒ·f'lhe:dĕd), *a.* 1654. [f. prec.] †1. Having a head like a buffalo's –1713. 2. *transf.* and *fig.* **a.** Large-headed. **b.** Foolish.

2. So fell this buffle-headed gyant 1654.

‖**Buffo** (bu·ffo). 1764. [ad. It. *buffo* adj.: see BUFFOON.] **A.** *sb.* A comic actor, a singer in a comic opera. **B.** as *adj.* Comic, burlesque.

Buffoon (bǒfū·n), *sb.* 1549. [a. F., a. It. *buffone*, f. *buffa* a jest, conn. w. *buffare* to puff. In 17th c. (*bu·ffoon*).] †1. A pantomime dance. *Sc.* (*rare*). 2. 'A man whose profession is to make sport by low jests and antick postures' (J.); a clown; a jester, fool (*arch.*) 1585. 3. *transf.* A low jester; a wag, a joker (implying contempt or disgust) 1598. Also *attrib.*

3. Age was authoritie Against a b., and a man had, then..reverence payd unto his yeares B. JONS. Hence **Buffoo·nish, †Buffoo·nly** *a.*; **†Bu·ffoonize, Bu·ffonize** *v.*

Buffoon (bǒfū·n), *v. arch.* 1638. [f. prec.] 1. *trans.* To turn into ridicule; to burlesque. 2. *intr.* To play the buffoon 1672.

Buffoonery (bǒfū·nəri). 1621. [f. BUFFOON *sb.* + -ERY.] The practice of a buffoon; low jesting or ridicule, farce.

Flatterie and Buffonrie swayed all in the Roman Senate 1621.

Buffy (bɒ·fi). 1782. [f. BUFF *sb.*² and *a.* + -Y¹.] 1. Of a colour approaching to buff 1842. 2. *Phys.* Applied to blood having a buff or BUFFY COAT 1782.

Buffy Coat. 1800. *Phys.* A layer of a light buff colour forming the upper part of the clot of coagulated blood under certain conditions.

†Bu·fo. [a. L., lit. 'a toad'.] The black tincture of the alchemists. B. JONS.

Bu·fonite. 1766. [f. L. *bufo.*] = TOADSTONE, q. v.

Bug (bɒg), *sb.*¹ [ME. *bugge*, ? f. Welsh *bwg* a ghost. Surviving only in BUGBEAR. Cf. BOGY, BUGABOO.] An (imaginary) object of terror; a bugbear, bogy; a scarecrow. **b.** A self-important person 1771. *Big bug* (orig. U.S.): a person of great importance 1827.

Warwicke was a Bugge that feared vs all SHAKS.

Bug (bɒg), *sb.*² 1622. [Etym. unkn.] 1. A name given vaguely to various insects, *esp.* beetles, etc., also to grubs, larvæ of insects, etc. Now chiefly *dial.* and *U. S.*; *esp.* with defining wd., as *harvest b.*, etc. 1642. 2. *spec.* The *Cimex lectularius*, more fully *bed-* or *house-b.*, a blood-sucking hemipterous insect. Also, any Hemipteran or Heteropteran. 1622.

1. The b. which breeds the butterfly SHAFTESB. 2. As safe as a b. in a rug 1798. *Comb.* **b.-bane, -wort,** *Cimicifuga fœtida* and allied plants, used to drive away bugs; **-hunter** *slang*, an entomologist.

Bugaboo (bɒ·găbū:). 1740. [? f. BUG + BOO int.] A bogy; a bugbear.

No b. tales POE.

Bugbear (bɒ·gbēᵊɹ). 1580. [App. f. BUG *sb.*¹ + BEAR *sb.*¹] †1. A sort of hobgoblin (? in the shape of a bear) supposed to devour naughty children; hence, generally, any imaginary being invoked by nurses to frighten children –1842. 2. *transf.* An object of (needless) dread; an imaginary terror 1580. Also *attrib.*

1. Meare bugge-beares to scare boyes NASHE. 2. All that thinke originall sinne a bugbeare ROGERS. Hence **†Bu·gbear** *v.* to frighten with bugbears.

Bugger (bɒ·gəɹ). ME. [a. F. *bougre*:—L. *Bulgarus* Bulgarian, heretic, usurer.] 1. A heretic: used esp. of the Albigenses. (*Hist.*) 2. One who commits buggery; a sodomite. In decent use only as a legal term. 1555. **b.** A coarse term of abuse; also, in Eng. dial. and in U.S., = 'chap', 'customer', etc. Hence **Bu·gger** *v.* to commit buggery with. Also *absol.*

Buggery (bɒ·gəri). ME. [f. as prec.] †**a.** Abominable heresy. **b.** Sodomy. Now only as a technical term in criminal law.

†Bu·ggess. 1699. [a. *Bugis*, name given to the dominant race among the Malays.] A name formerly used in the Indian Archipelago for a native soldier in European service –1811.

Buggy (bɒ·gi), *sb.* 1773. [Of unkn. origin; connexion with BOGIE is possible.] A light one-horse (or two-horse) vehicle for one or two persons. The American buggy has four wheels; the English (or Indian) buggy two; in India there is a hood.

I asked for a two-horse b. and driver B. TAYLOR. *Comb.*: **b.-boat**, a boat made so that wheels can be fastened to it, for use on land; **-cultivator, -plough,** a plough having a seat for the ploughman to ride on.

Bu·ggy, *a.* 1714. [f. BUG *sb.*²] Infested with bugs.

Bugle (biū·g'l), *sb.*¹ ME. [a. OF.:—L. *buculus*, dim. of *bos, bovis.*] 1. †**a.** = BUFFALO 1 a. **b.** A young bull (*dial.*). 2. *Mus.* Short for BUGLE-HORN. **a.** A hunting-horn, made originally of the horn of a bugle or wild ox. **b.** A military instrument of brass or copper, resembling the trumpet, but smaller; used as the signal-horn for the infantry. ME.

1. The B. ..is lyke to an oxe and is a fyers beest TREVISA. 2. b. Comb. *b.-blast, -call, -clang, -man.*

Bugle (biū·g'l), *sb.*² ME. [a. F.:—late L. *bugula.*] The Eng. name of plants of the genus *Ajuga*, esp. *A. reptans.* (Occas. confounded with *Buglossa.*)

Bugle (biū·g'l), *sb.*³ 1579. [?] A tube-shaped glass bead, usually black, used to ornament wearing apparel. Also *attrib.*

Adam and Eve in B.-work..upon Canvas STEELE.

Bu·gle, *v.* 1862. [f. BUGLE *sb.*¹ 2.] **a.** *intr.* To sound a bugle. **b.** *trans.* To give forth (a sound) as a bugle; also (*nonce-use*) to summ n by bugle.

Bu·gle-ho·rn. ME. [f. BUGLE *sb.*¹] The horn of a bugle or wild ox, used †**a.** as a drinking vessel –1519. **b.** as a musical instrument, whence = BUGLE *sb.*¹ 2.

b. Two squyers blewe..with ij grete bugles hornes CAXTON.

Bugler (biū·gləɹ). 1840. [f. as prec. + -ER¹.] One who plays on a bugle; *spec.* a soldier who sounds orders on a bugle.

Bu·gle-weed. 1860. *Bot.* An American plant, *Lycopus Virginicus*, occas. used as a remedy for spitting of blood.

Bugloss (biū·glǫs). 1533. [a. F. *buglosse*:—L. *buglossa*, ad. Gr. βούγλωσσος, f. βοῦς + γλῶσσα.] *Bot.* A name of several boraginaceous plants, *esp.* the *Small, Corn*, or *Field B.* (*Lycopsis arvensis*); Viper's B. (*Echium vulgare*), and other species of *Echium*; also of *Helminthia echioides*, Prickly Ox-tongue. *Comb.* **B. Cowslip.**

†Bug-word, bug's-word. 1562. [f. BUG *sb.*¹] A word meant to frighten. Usu. in *pl.* Swaggering or threatening language. –1734.

A Rebellion; O no, that's a bug word NORTH.

Buhl (būl). Also **Boule**, q.v. 1823. [Germanized f. *Boule*, a French wood-carver in the reign of Louis XIV.] Brass, tortoise-shell, etc., worked into ornamental patterns for inlaying; work inlaid with buhl. Also *attrib.*

Build (bild), *v.* Pa. t. and pple. **built,** *poet.* and *arch.* **builded.** [ME. *bulden, bylden, bilden* :—OE. **byldan* to build, f. *bold* a dwelling. The normal mod. sp. would be *bild.*] 1. *trans. Orig.* To construct for a dwelling. *Hence*, To erect, construct, whence, To construct by fitting together of separate parts. 2. *absol.* To erect a building or buildings. Of birds, etc.: To construct nests, etc. ME. 3. *transf.* To construct as by building 1598. 4. *fig.* To construct, frame, raise, by gradual means. Often with *up.* 1440. 5. *lit.* and *fig.* To work up *into.* Also with *up.* ME. 6. *fig.* **a.** *trans.* To found (hope, etc.) *on* a basis 1528. **b.** *absol.* To found one's confidence, establish an argument, etc. *on*; to rely confidently *on* (*obs.* or *arch.*) 1573.

1. Roome was not bylt on one day 1562. *To b. a fire*: to pile the fuel. *To b. a railroad* (only in U.S.), *a gun, a nest*. 2. Our ayerie buildeth in the Cedars top *Rich. III*, I. iii. 264. *Phr. To b. up*: to obstruct (a doorway, etc.) by building. *To b. in*: to enclose by buildings. 3. Built as it were to make a good Boxer BENTLEY. A crystal built up from particles of silica TYNDALL. 4. *To b. up* (the Church, an individual) = to EDIFY. To b. the lofty rhyme MILT., an everlasting name TENNYSON. 6. He that builds upon the people builds upon the sand 1674.

Build (bild), *sb.* ME. [f. prec.; cf. BUILT *sb.*] †1. A building. ME. only. 2. Building; style of construction, make (*lit.* and *fig.*) 1667.

2. The b. of ships PEPYS. A patriot of the old Roman b. 1833.

Builder (bi·ldəɹ). ME. [f. as prec. + -ER [1].] One who builds. Also *fig.* (As the name of a trade, *builder* now = the master artisan, who is instructed by the architect, and employs the manual labourers.)

The builders .. of Babel on the Plain MILT.

Building (bi·ldiŋ), *vbl. sb.* ME. [f. as prec. + -ING [1].] 1. The action of the vb. BUILD (*lit.* and *fig.*) †b. Build (*e.g.* of a ship). 2. That which is built; a structure, edifice ME.

2. By much slouthfulnesse the b. decayeth *Eccles.* x. 18. *Comb.*: **b.-lease**, a lease of land for building upon; **-society**, one in which the members contribute to a fund for lending money to any member who wishes to build (or purchase) a house; **-term**, the duration of a *building-lease*.

†Built, *sb.* 1615. [f. BUILD *v.*; cf. *gilt*, f. *gild.*] Style of construction, build –1794.

Buirdly (bü·rdli), *a. Sc.* ME. [prob. var. of Sc. *buirly* BURLY.] Large and well-made; stalwart; stately; sturdy, stout.

Bukk-; see BUCK-.

‖**Bukshi, bukshee** (bɒ·kʃī). 1615. [a. Pers. *bakhshī* paymaster; cf. BAKSHEESH.] The Paymaster-General of the army in native Indian states; in the Anglo-Indian army a *Paymaster*.

Bulb (bɒlb), *sb.* 1568. [ad. L., a. Gr. βολβός.] †1. An onion –1712. 2. *Bot.* The underground spheroidal portion of the stem of an onion, lily, or the like. b. A bulbil 1845. 3. A bulb-like dilatation, *e.g.* of a hair, a glass tube, etc. 1715. 4. The glass bulb-shaped container of the incandescent filament used for producing electric light in a glow lamp 1882.

1. Bulbs are in reality underground stems in the state of buds CARPENTER. Hence **Bulbed** *a.* b.-shaped, having a b. **Bulbi·ferous** *a.* producing bulbs. **Bu·lbiform** *a.* b.-shaped.

Bulb (bɒlb), *v.* 1681. [f. prec.] *intr.* To swell into a bulb-like form; to form a bulb-shaped root.

Bulbar (bɒ·lbăɹ), *a.* 1878. [f. BULB *sb.* + -AR [1].] Of or pertaining to a bulb; *esp.* to the bulb of the spinal cord.

Bulbil (bɒ·lbil). Also **bulbel.** 1831. [ad. mod.L. *bulbillus*, dim. of *bulbus.*] a. A small bulb formed at the side of an old one. b. A small solid or scaly bud, which detaches itself from the stem, becoming an independent plant. So **Bu·lblet** (in sense b).

†Bu·lbine. 1548. [L. *bulbine*, Gr. βολβίνη.] A bulbous plant mentioned by Pliny; *Gagea lutea* (Turner) –1611.

Bu·lbo-, comb. f. L. *bulbus*.

Bulbous (bɒ·lbəs), *a.* 1578. [f. L. *bulbus*, cf. F. *bulbeux.*] 1. Of, pertaining to, or of the nature of, a bulb. 2. Having bulb-like roots 1578. 3. Bulb-shaped; swollen 1783.

3. A bottle belly and a b. nose SOUTHEY. vars. **Bulba·ceous, Bulbo·se.**

Bulbul (bu·lbul). 1784. [a. (through Pers.) Arab. *bulbul.*] 1. A species of the genus *Pycnonotus*, belonging to the Thrush family; sometimes called the nightingale of the East. 2. *transf.* A sweet singer; also *attrib.* 1848.

1. The fighting B. ..said to be enamoured of the rose 1797.

Bulbule (bɒ·lbiul). 1836. [ad. L. *bulbulus*, dim. of *bulbus.*] A little bulb.

†Bulchin. ME. [var. of BULKIN.] A bull-calf –1727. Used also as a term of contempt, or endearment –1638.

Bulge (bɒldʒ), *sb.* [ME. *bulge*, a. OF. *boulge* (also *bouge*), or ad. L. *bulga* bag.] †1. A wallet or bag, *esp.* one made of hide; = BOUGE *sb.*[1] 1. –1623. 2. A bulging 1741. 3. = mod. BILGE. 1622. Hence **Bu·lgy** *a.* swollen. **Bu·lginess.**

Bulge (bɒldʒ), *v.* 1563. [f. prec.] †1. = BILGE *v.* 1. –1821. †2. *refl.* and *intr.* Of a ship: To strike (*on* or *against*) so as to damage the bilge –1807. 3. *intr.* To form a protuberance, to swell out 1677. 4. *trans.* To make protuberant 1865.

2. It bulged on a rock, and the waves rushed in fast COLERIDGE. 4. A purse bulged with Austrian florin notes 1866.

‖**Buli·mia,** mod.L. f. BULIMY, q.v. Hence **Buli·mic** *a.* indicating b.; voracious; **Buli·mious** *a.* having a voracious appetite.

‖**Bulimus** (biuləi·mɒ̆s). Pl. **bulimi.** 1830. [mod.L., a. Gr. βούλῑμος, perh. taken as adj. with sense 'bulimious'.] A genus of terrestrial gasteropods. Hence **Buli·miform** *a.*

Bulimy (biū·limi). ME. [ad. Gr. βουλιμία, f. βου- (comb. f. βοῦς) + λιμός. Now usu. as L., **bulimia.**] *Med.* 'A morbid hunger, chiefly occurring in idiots and maniacs .. the so-called canine hunger'. Also *fig.*

Bulk (bɒlk), *sb.*[1] 1440. [Cf. ON. **bulki*, Icel. *búlki* 'heap, cargo'. Cf. BOUK.] †1. A heap –1725. b. The cargo of a ship; a cargo as a whole; the whole lot (of a commodity) 1575. †2. The belly; the trunk, the body –1718. b. A huge frame (cf. 4); also *fig.* 1587. †3. *transf.* The hold of a ship; cf. Ger. *bauch* –1678. 4. Magnitude in three dimensions; volume, *esp.* great volume 1449. 5. A mass. Often *esp.* a large mass 1641. 6. Greater part, or number; the main body 1711.

1. b. *To break b.* (see BREAK *v.*). *In b.* (of fish, etc.): lying loose in heaps, without package. *To load* (a ship) *in b.*: to put the cargo in loose, *e.g.* wheat, salt, etc. *To sell in b.*: to sell the cargo as it is in the hold; to sell in large quantities. 2. His B. too weighty for his Thighs is grown DRYDEN. b. The b. of Ajax POPE. 4. They [gold and silver] possess great value in small b. MCCULLOCH. 6. The b. of a people ADDISON.

Bulk (bɒlk), *sb.*[2] 1586. [Cf. ON. *bálk-r*, *bǫlk-r* beam (= BALK).] A framework projecting from the front of a shop; a stall. SHAKS.

Bulk (bɒlk), *v.* 1540. [f. BULK *sb.*[1]] 1. *intr.* To be of bulk; to present an appearance of size (*lit.* and *fig.*) 1672. 2. *trans.* To pile in heaps, as fish for salting. Cf. BULK *sb.*[1] 1. 1822. 3. *Comm.* To ascertain the bulk of 1883.

1. To b. large in the world's eye CARLYLE. Phr. *To b.* (*up*): to swell up. 2. To b. pilchards 1822. 3. Indian teas are 'bulked' by Her Majesty's Customs 1883. Hence **Bulked** *ppl. a.* having bulk.

Bulker (bɒ·lkəɹ). 1857. [f. BULK *v.* 3 + -ER [1].] One who ascertains the bulk of goods. Cf. BULK *v.* 3.

Bulkhead (bɒ·lkhed). 1626. [App. f. BULK *sb.*[2]] 1. One of the upright partitions serving to form the cabins in a ship or to divide the hold into water-tight compartments. Also *transf.* 2. *Mining.* A tight partition in a mine, for protection against water, fire, gas. 3. The roof of a projecting stall; the stall itself. Cf. BULK *sb.*[2] 1722.

1. *Collision b.*: the foremost b. in a vessel. Hence **Bu·lkhea·ded** *ppl. a.* furnished with bulkheads.

†Bu·lkin. 1583. [app. f. BULL *sb.*[1]] a. A bull-calf. b. Used as a term of endearment. –1616.

Bulky (bɒ·lki), *a.* 1687. [f. BULK *sb.*[1] + -Y [1].] Of large bulk, voluminous; occupying (too) much space.

Too b. for the post JOHNSON. Hence **Bu·lkily** *adv.* **Bu·lkiness.**

Bull (bul), *sb.*[1] [ME. *bole* (*bool*(*e*), app. a. ON. *bole, boli*. Possibly an OE. **bulla*, whence ME. *bule, bulle*, and the mod. *bull*. Prob. from the vb.-stem in *büllen, bullen* to roar; see BELL *v.*[4]] 1. The male of any bovine animal; also of the buffalo, etc. 2. The male of other large animals, as the elephant, alligator, whale, etc. 1615. 3. *Astron.* The constellation and sign Taurus 1509. 4. *Stock-Exchange* [see BEAR *sb.*[1]]. One who endeavours by speculative purchases, or otherwise, to raise the price of stocks. *Bull* was orig. a speculative purchase for a rise. 1714. Also *attrib.* 5. *attrib.* a. Male ME. b. Of or pertaining to a bull, bull-like 1814.

1. Bulls aim their horns, and Asses lift their heels POPE. *Bulls of brass, brazen bulls*, as those that guarded the golden fleece, and Phalaris' bull (proverbial as an engine of torture). 5. a. A b. elk 1863, whale 1880. b. A b. neck 1830.

Phrases. *A b. in a china shop*: a symbol of one who produces reckless destruction. *To take the b. by the horns*: to meet a difficulty with courage.

Comb.: **b.-bat**, the American Goatsucker (*Caprimulgus Americanus*); **-boat**, a boat made of hides stretched on a frame; **-comber**, a dung-beetle (*Typhœus vulgaris*); **-feast**, a b.-baiting (Eng.); a b.-fight (Sp.); **-foot** (*Bot.*), Colt's-foot (*Tussilago*); **-hoof** (Bot.), *Murucuja ocellata*; **b.-of-the-bog**, the bittern, from its booming cry; **-poll**, the Turfy Hair-grass (*Aira cæspitosa*); **-pup**, a young bull-dog; **-ring**, the arena for a b.-fight (Sp.); the place where bulls were baited (Eng.); the ring to which a b. was fastened; **-roarer**, a flat slip of wood fastened by one end to a thong for whirling it round, a 'whizzer'; **-rope** (*Naut.*), a hawser let through a block on the bowsprit end to the buoy, to keep the buoy clear of the stem; **†-seg** (*dial.*), **-stag**, a bull gelded when past his prime; **-toad**, ? = -FROG; **-whacker** (Amer.), a bullock-driver in the Western states. b. *Comb.* with gen. *bull's*: **bull's-nose** (*Archit.*), 'the external or other angle of a polygon, or of any two lines meeting at an obtuse angle' (Gwilt); **bull's pizzle**, the penis of the bull. formerly used as an instrument of flagellation.

Bull (bul), *sb.*[2] ME. [ad. L. *bulla.*] 1. A seal attached to a document; *esp.* the leaden seal attached to the Pope's edicts. 2. A papal or episcopal edict or mandate ME. 3. Applied to a non-ecclesiastical edict 1696.

2. Indulgences, Dispenses, Pardons, Bulls, The sport of Winds MILT. *P. L.* III. 492. **Bullantic** *a.* (*rare*), of, pertaining to, or used in papal bulls.

†Bull, *sb.*[3] *rare.* 1561. [a. F. *bulle*:—L. *bulla.*] A bubble.

Bull (bul), *sb.*[4] 1630. [? Cf. OF. *boul, boule, bole* deceit; mod. Icel. *bull* 'nonsense'; also ME. *bull, bul* 'falsehood'.] †1. A ludicrous jest (cf. BULL *v.*[3]) –1695. 2. A self-contradictory proposition; in mod. use, an expression involving a ludicrous inconsistency unperceived by the speaker. The epithet *Irish* is a late addition. [Not conn. w. the Pope's *bulls*, or 'one Obadiah Bull'.]

2. Dumbe Speaker! that's a B. BROME.

Bull (bul), *sb.*[5] 1523. [?] One of the main bars of a harrow. Also *attrib.*

Bull. Short for JOHN BULL, BULL'S-EYE (7).

Bull-. 1450. [usu. = BULL *sb.*[1]; but cf. BOLL *sb.*[1]] Comb. f. as in:

bull-brier, an American brier, from the root of which the Indians make bread; **-oak**, an oak within which bulls take shelter; **-plum**, a sloe (*Prunus spinosa*), cf. however BULLACE; **-sedge**, the reed-mace; **-weed**, *Centaurea nigra*; **-wort**, *Ammi majus*, or Bishop-weed.

Bull (bul), *v.*[1] ME. [f. BULL *sb.*[1]] †1. a. *trans.* Of a bull: To gender with (the cow). b. Of the cow: To take, or desire, the bull. 2. *Stock-Exchange.* To try to raise the price of (stocks, etc.) 1842.

†Bull, *v.*[2] 1563. [f. BULL *sb.*[2]] To insert in a Papal bull; to affix the Papal seal to –1670.

†Bull, *v.*[3] 1532. To make a fool of, to mock; to cheat (*out of*) –1674.

‖**Bulla** (bu·lă, bɒ·lă). Pl. **bullæ.** 1847. [L.] 1. *Pathol.* A vesicle containing watery humour and causing an elevation of the skin 1876. b. *Phys.* The tympanic element of the temporal bone, when, as in the dog, it has a bubble-like appearance 1872. 2. *Zool.* A genus of deep-water molluscs, with thin and fragile shells 1847.

Bullace (bu·lės). ME. [Cf. OF. *beloce* (13th c., Littré).] 1. A wild plum (*Prunus insititia*) larger than the sloe. 2. The tree bearing the plum 1616; var. **B.-tree.**

1. Boollesse, black and white TUSSER.

Bullary (bu·lări). Also **-ery.** 1674. [ad. med.L. *bullarium* (also used), f. *bulla.*] A collection of papal bulls.

Bullate (bu·lėᶦt, bɒ·lėᶦt), *a.* 1819. [ad. L. *bullatus.*] 1. *Bot.* Having blisters; inflated: said of leaves, in which the surface rises above the veins. 2. *Phys.* Having *bullæ* or puffy excrescences on the surface 1872.

Bu·llated, *ppl. a.* 1698. [f. as prec.] †1. *Rom. Ant.* Furnished with a *bulla* worn round the neck. 2. = BULLATE. 1707.

Bull-bait (bu·l,bēᶦt). ? *Obs.* 1656. = BULL-BAITING.

Bu·ll-baiter. 1802. One who baits bulls.

Bu·ll-baiting, *vbl. sb.* 1580. The action of baiting bulls with dogs. (Cf. BULL-DOG.)

†**Bu·ll-beggar.** 1584. [?] A bogy; a scarecrow; a bugbear -1851.
Beggers will needes be somewaies bulbeggers 1588.

Bull-bitch. 1681. The female of the bull-dog.

Bull-dog. (Also 6 **bold-dogge.**) Often as one word, *esp.* in *transf.* uses. 1500. [f. BULL *sb.*[1]] 1. A dog with large bull-head, short muzzle, strong muscular body of medium height, and short smooth hair, formerly much used for bull-baiting. Also *transf.* of persons. Also *attrib.* 2. †A sheriff's officer; one of the Proctor's attendants at Oxford and Cambridge (*colloq.*) 1698. 3. *transf.* Applied joc. to firearms; in mod. use, a kind of revolver. Cf. BARKER. Also *attrib.* 1700. 4. a. A gad-fly (Amer.). b. An ant (Australian) 1865. 5. In *Iron-works*. A refractory material used as furnace-lining, got by calcining mill-cinder.
1. The courage of bull-dogs and game-cocks seems peculiar to England HUME. 3. He whips out his Stiletto and I whips out my bull-dog FARQUHAR.

Bull-dose, -doze (bu·l,dōuz). *U.S.* 1876. [According to U.S. newspapers, f. BULL *sb.*[1] + DOSE.] A. *sb.* ? A severe dose (of flogging). B. *vb.* a. ? To flog severely. b. To coerce by violence. Hence **Bull-dozer**, one who bull-dozes; also, a large pistol.

†**Bu·lled,** *ppl. a.*[1] ME. [f. BULL *sb.*[2] or *v.*[2]] Having a seal attached -1610.

†**Bulled,** *ppl. a.*[2] ? = *bolled*, pa. pple. of BOLL *v.*[1] B. JONS.

Buller (bu·lər), *sb. Sc.* 1513. [Cf. Sw. *buller* noise. Influenced by *boil.*] A roaring noise (of waves, etc.); the boiling of an eddy or torrent. Also *fig.* Cf. *The Buller(s of Buchan.* Hence **Bu·ller** *v. Sc.* to bellow.

Bullescence (bule·sĕns). 1880. [as if ad. L. **bullescentia.*] *Bot.* The condition of being BULLATE 1.

Bullet (bu·lĕt), *sb.*[1] 1557. [a. F. *boulette, boullette*, dim. of *boule* ball.] 1. A small round ball. (Now *transf.* from 3.) 1578. 2. A cannon-ball (of metal or stone). Now *Hist.* 1557. 3. A ball of lead, etc., used in firearms of small calibre; now often conical. Formerly also collective (cf. BALL *sb.*[1]). 1579. Also *fig.* 4. †a. The missile from a sling; also *attrib.* b. The angler's plumb. 1587.
1. Upon the braunches [of the burdock] there groweth small bullets or rounde balles LYTE. 3. *fig.* Paper bullets of the braine *Much Ado* II. iii. 249.
Phr. *Every b. has its billet* (see BILLET *sb.*[1]). *Comb.* **b.-shell**, a shell used with small-arms. Hence **Bu·lleted** *ppl. a.* bullet-shaped; furnished with bullets.

†**Bu·llet,** *sb.*[2] *rare.* 1612. 1. = BILLET *sb.*[1] 2. 2. [ad. It. *bulletta.*] A slip of paper on which the voter wrote the name of the candidate he supported. Cf. BULLETIN. 1615.

Bullet-head. 1690. [f. BULLET *sb.*[1]] a. A head round like a bullet. b. A person with such a head; in U.S. *fig.* a 'pig-headed' person. Hence **Bu·llet-hea·ded, -hea·dedness.**
He aint No more'n a tough old bullethead LOWELL.

Bulletin (bu·lĕtin). 1651. [ad. It. *bullettino, bollettino*, dim. of *bulletta* = BULLET *sb.*[2], and (senses 2, 3) a. F. *bulletin.*] †1. A short note or memorandum. b. A warrant or appointment to an office -1673. 2. A short report of public news, issued by authority; *esp.* a report sent from the seat of war by a commander for publication at home 1791. 3. An official statement as to the health of an invalid 1765.
2. 'False as a b.' became a proverb in Napoleon's time CARLYLE. Hence **Bu·lletin** *v.* (*trans.*) to make known by b.

Bullet Tree, var. *Bully Tree* (BULLY *sb.*[3]).

Bu·ll-fight. 1753. A sport practised esp. in Spain, in which a bull is engaged by horsemen (*picadores*) armed with lances, and by men on foot (*chulos*) having darts and cloaks, and is finally dispatched by a swordsman (*espada*). Hence **Bu·ll-fi:ghter.**

Bullfinch [1] (bu·lfinʃ). Also **bulfinch.** 1570. [f. BULL *sb.*[1] + FINCH.] One of a genus of birds (*Pyrrhula*), allied to the Grosbeaks, having handsome plumage and a short, hard, rounded beak. Also in *comb.*

Bullfinch [2] (bu·lfinʃ). 1832. [? corrupt f. *bull-fence.*] A quickset hedge with a ditch on one side, too high and strong to be cleared. Hence **Bu·llfinch** *v. intr.* to leap a horse through such a hedge. var. **Bullfincher.**

Bu·llfist. 1611. The puff-ball.

Bu·ll-fro:g. 1738. [f. BULL *sb.*[1]] A large American frog (*Rana pipiens*), which has a voice not unlike a bull's.

Bu·llhea:d. 1450. 1. A small fish with a large head; the *Miller's Thumb.* 2. A tadpole. Still *dial.* 1611. †3. A mass of curled or frizzled hair worn over the forehead; also called *bull tour* -1688. 4. A blockhead 1624.

Bullheaded (bu·lhe·dĕd), *a.* 1818. Broad-headed; *fig.* blindly impetuous, blockheaded. Hence **Bu·llhea·dedness.**

Bu·llimong. ME. [?] 1. A mixture of grain (as oats, pease, and vetches) sown together, for feeding cattle. Cf. DREDGE, MESLIN, and L. *farrago.* Also *attrib.* †2. = BUCKWHEAT -1706.

Bullion [1] (bu·liən). ME. [? a. F. *bouillon*; but the senses are purely Eng.] 1. ? Melting-house or mint; but in 16th c. 'place of exchange'. 2. Gold or silver in the lump; also applied to coined or manufactured gold or silver considered as raw metal 1451. Also *fig.* b. Solid gold or silver (as opp. to imitations). Often *fig.* Also *attrib.* 1596. †3. Impure gold or silver; -1820. 4. Any metal in the lump 1590.
2. The B. of neighbour Kingdoms brought to receive a Stamp from the Mint of England CLARENDON. All silver money should be taken only as b. SWIFT. 3. *fig.* The drossie B. of the Peoples sinnes MILT. Hence †**Bu·llioner**, a dealer in b. **Bu·llionist**, one who advocates a metallic currency.

†**Bu·llion** [2]. 1463. [app. a. F. *boulon*, f. *boule* ball; assim. to prec.] A knob or boss of metal; a convex ornament on a book, girdle, harness, or ring -1707. Also *attrib.*

Bullion [3] (bu·liən). 1594. [prob. a. F. *bouillon.*] †1. More fully *b.-hose*; Trunk-hose, puffed out at the upper part, in several folds -1632. 2. A fringe made of twists of gold or silver thread; also, a twist of such fringe. Also *attrib.* [Now occas. assoc. w. BULLION [1].] 1662.
2. All in a blaze of scarlet and b. and steel THACKERAY.

Bullish (bu·liʃ), *a.*[1] 1566. [f. BULL *sb.*[1] + -ISH[1].] 1. Of or pertaining to, resembling or having the nature of, a bull. 2. *Stock-Exchange*, etc. Tending to or aiming at a rise in the price of stocks or merchandise 1882.
2. B. about cotton 1884. Hence **Bu·llishly** *adv.*

†**Bullish,** *a.*[2] *rare.* 1641. [f. BULL *sb.*[4] + -ISH[1].] Having the nature of a bull (BULL [4]) -1660.

†**Bulli·tion.** 1620. [as if ad. L. *bullitionem.*] Bubbling or boiling -1791.

Bullock (bu·lək), *sb.* [OE. *bulluc*; cf. *ballock*, etc. (The form *balluca* is spurious.)] 1. Orig. a young bull, or bull calf; now always, a castrated bull, an ox. 2. *Loosely*, A bovine beast generally. Now *dial.* 1535.
2. 'Yes, she's a purty cow..one of these days she'll make a nice b.' *Sussex dial.*
Comb. a. **Bullock's Eye**, the common Houseleek; **Bullock's Heart**, the fruit of *Anona reticulata*; **Bullock's Lungwort**, the Great Mullein. b. **b.-puncher** (*Austral.*), a bullock-driver.

Bu·llock, *v.* Now *dial.* 1716. = BULLY *v.*

Bu·ll's-eye. 1825. The eye of a bull (cf. F. *œil de bœuf*); hence 1. A boss of glass, or the central protuberance formed in making a sheet of blown glass 1832. 2. *Naut.* A thick disk of glass inserted in the side or deck of a ship, etc., to light the interior 1825. 3. A lens, hemispherical or plano-convex 1839. 4. A glass of similar shape inserted in the side of a lantern; the lantern itself; also *attrib.* 1851. 5. *Naut.* A small pulley in the form of a ring, having a rope round the outer edge, and a hole in the middle for another to slide in 1769. 6. *Archit.* A small circular opening or window 1865. 7. The centre of a target; also, a shot which hits it; also *fig.* 1833. 8. A circular ornament of gold lace 1879. 9. A globular sweetmeat 1825. 10. A little dark cloud, reddish in the middle, common about the Cape of Good Hope, supposed to portend a storm; hence, the storm itself 1849. 11. *slang.* A crown-piece 1690.
4. Policemen, with their Bull's-eyes MAYHEW.

Bu·ll-te:rrier. 1848. A dog of a cross between a bull-dog and a terrier.

Bu·ll-trou:t. 1653. [f. BULL *sb.*[1]] A large fish of the Salmon tribe (*Salmo eriox*).

Bully (bu·li), *sb.*[1] 1538. [perh. ad. Du. *boel* 'lover (of either sex)', also 'brother'. Cf. Ger. *buhle.* Perh. now assoc. w. BULL *sb.*[1]] 1. Sweetheart, darling: orig. used of either sex. Later, of men only. Often as a sort of title, as in Shaks., 'b. Bottom', etc. Now *arch.* Also *attrib.*, as in *b.-boy* 1609. 2. *dial.* Brother, companion, mate 1825. 3. A blustering gallant; a swash-buckler; now *esp.* a person (or animal) who makes himself or herself a terror to the weak or defenceless. b. A hired ruffian (*arch.*) 1730. 4. *spec.* One who protects and lives on prostitutes 1706.
1. From heartstring I loue the louely B. SHAKS. 3. Where London's column, pointing at the skies Like a tall b., lifts the head, and lyes POPE. 4. The b. and the bawd, who fatten on their misery 1750.

Bully (bu·li), *sb.*[2] 1865. 1. *Eton football.* A scrimmage. 2. *Hockey.* Putting the ball in play; hence as *v. trans.* and *intr.* 1886.

Bu·lly, *sb.*[3] Also **bullet.** 1657. [?] *attrib.* in *B. Bay, B.-berry Tree, B. Tree*, genera of the order *Sapotaceæ*, also a species of *Mimusops.*

Bully (bu·li), *sb.*[4] 1800 (*bouillie beef*). [ad. F. *bouilli* boiled.] In full, *b. beef*: tinned beef, esp. as used in the British army.

Bully (bu·li), *a.* 1681. [f. BULLY *sb.*[1]] 1. Of persons: Worthy, jolly, admirable. 2. *U.S.* and *Colonies.* First-rate, crack 1855. b. as an exclam., *esp.* in 'B. for you!' = bravo! 1864. 3. Like or characteristic of a bully 1727.
2. The cook will give you a b. dinner 1855. 3. A b. imposition of sheer physical ascendancy G. MEREDITH.

Bully (bu·li), *v.* 1710. [f. BULLY *sb.*[1]] 1. *trans.* To act the bully towards; to intimidate, overawe. 2. To drive by bullying; with *away, into, out of, to* 1723. 3. *intr.* and *absol.* To bluster, use violent threats; to swagger 1744.
1. To b. the servant 1802. 2. To b. away customers DE FOE.

Bullyrag (bu·liræg), *v. dial.* and *colloq.* Also **ba·llyrag.** 1807. [?] †a. To intimidate. b. To abuse.
b. Irish tenantry..ballyragging their member 1879.

†**Bully-rock, bully-rook.** 1598. [? f. BULLY *sb.*[1] + ROOK.] = BULLY *sb.*[1] 1, 3. -1827.
What saies my Bully Rooke *Merry W.* I. iii. 2.

Bulrush (bu·lrʌʃ). 1440. [f. *bull* in some sense + RUSH.] A book-name for *Scirpus lacustris*; but pop. applied to *Typha latifolia*, the 'Cat's Tail', and in the Bible to the Papyrus of Egypt. Also *fig.* with reference to its fragility.
She tooke for him an arke of bul-rushes *Ex.* ii. 3. *fig.* We leane on the b. of our oune merits 1646.

Bulse (bʌls). *arch.* 1708. [ad. Pg. *bolsa*:—med.L. *bursa.* Cf. BURSE.] A package of diamonds or gold-dust.

Bultell(e, var. of BOULTEL, *Obs.*

Bulwark (bu·lwə̆ɹk), *sb.* ME. [Cf. Du., MHG. *bolwerk*, mod.G. *bollwerk*, Sw. *bolverk*, *lit.* 'log-work' or 'bole-work'. See also BOULEVARD.] 1. A substantial defensive work of earth, etc.; a rampart, a fortification. Now *arch.* or *poet.* b. A breakwater, mole, sea-wall, etc. Also *fig.* 1555. 2. *transf.* and *fig.* A powerful defence or defender 1577. 3. The raised woodwork running along the sides of a vessel above the level of the deck. Usu. *pl.* 1804.
2. To destroy their Fleete: which..are their Walls and Bulwarks CLARENDON.

Bulwark (bu·lwə̆ɹk), *v.* 1450. [f. prec.] 1. *trans.* To furnish with bulwarks. *intr.* To throw up bulwarks (*lit.* and *fig.*). 2. *trans.* To serve as a bulwark to 1610.
2. Friends bulwarked him about BROWNING.

Bum (bʌm), *sb.*[1] ME. [? Cf. BUMP *sb.*, etc. Perh. echoic. Not a contr. of 'bottom'.] The posteriors. Also *transf.* 2. *colloq.* Short for BUMBAILIFF; (like F. *cul* for *pousse-cul*) 1691.

†**Bum,** *sb.*[2] and *int.* 1552. [Imitative.] A child's word for drink -1598.

Bum, *v.*[1] Now *dial.* 1450. [Var. of BOOM *v.*[1]] *intr.* To hum loudly.
I..'eerd un a bummin' awaäy loike a buzzard-clock TENNYSON.

†**Bum,** *v.*[2] 1579. [? f. BUM *sb.*[1]] *trans.* (or *absol.*) To strike, beat, thump -1622.

Bum, *v.*[3] 1833. To act as a bumboat woman.

Bum-; see BOM-.

Bumaloe, Bumaree; see BUMM-.

Bumbailiff (bʌ·mbē¹·lif). 1601. [app. f.

ö (Ger. Köln). ö̇ (Fr. peu). ü (Ger. Müller). ü̇ (Fr. dune). ɐ̄ (curl). ē (ēᵊ) (there). ẹ̄ (ēⁱ) (rein). ẹ̄ (Fr. faire). ɜ (fir, fern, earth).

BUM *sb.*[1] + BAILIFF; cf. F. *pousse-cul.*] 'A bailiff of the meanest kind; one that is employed in arrests' (J.).

A confounded pettifogging bum-bailiff THACKERAY.

†**Bumbard, -art.** 1505. [f. BUM *bumb*, *v.*[2] + -ARD.] A bumble-bee, a drone; also *fig.* -1614.

Bu·mbarge. 1839. [?after and = BUMBOAT.]

Bumbaste, *v.* Now *dial.* 1571. [app. f. BUM *sb.*[1] + BASTE *v.*[3]] To beat on the posteriors; hence, to beat soundly.

Bumbaze (bɒmbē·z), *v.* Chiefly *Sc.* 1725. [Cf. Du. *bazen* to stupefy. App. an intensive.] To confound, bamboozle.

Bumbelo, bu·mbolo. 1854. [a. It. *bombola.*] A glass flask for subliming camphor.

Bu·mble, *sb.*[1] Now *dial.* 1597. [f. BUMBLE *v.*[1]] A bumble-bee. Also, a bittern (*local*).

Bu·mble, *sb.*[2] Now *dial.* 1648. [Cf. JUMBLE, FUMBLE, etc.] 1. A jumble. 2. A blunderer; an idler 1786. ¶3. Associated with this is the name of the beadle in Dickens's *Oliver Twist* (see BUMBLEDOM) 1856.

†**Bumble,** *v.*[1] ME. [f. BOOM *v.*[1], BUM *v.*[1]] 1. *intr.* To boom; to buzz -1868. 2. *trans.* To blame -1781.

1. As a Bitore bombleth in the Myre CHAUCER.

Bu·mble, *v.*[2] Now *Sc.* 1532. [See BUMBLE *sb.*[2]] *intr.* To blunder. *trans.* To do in a bungling manner.

Bumble-bee (bɒ·mb'lbī). 1530. [f. stem of BUMBLE *v.*[1]] A large bee of the genus *Bombus*; a humble-bee.

Bumbledom (bɒ·mb'ldəm). 1856. [f. *Bumble*, name of the beadle in Dickens's *Oliver Twist.*] Stupid officiousness and pomposity; beadledom in its glory.

Bumble-puppy (bɒ·mb'lpɒpi). 1801. [?] a. Nine-holes. b. Whist played unscientifically. Cf. BUMBLE *v.*[2]

Bu·mbo. 1748. [Cf. It. *bombo* a child's word for drink.] A drink composed of rum, sugar, water, and nutmeg, or the like.

Bumboat (bɒ·mbōut). 1671. [app. f. BUM *sb.*[1]] †1. A scavenger's boat, employed to remove filth from ships lying in the Thames -1685. 2. A boat carrying provisions, vegetables, etc., to ships. (Orig. the 'dirt-boats' did this.) 1769. Also *attrib.*, as *b. man, woman*, etc.

Bumkin, bumpkin (bɒ·mkin). 1632. [f. BOOM *sb.*[2] Now usu. *bumpkin.*] *Naut.* 'A short boom projecting from each bow of a ship, to extend the lower edge of the foresail to windward.' Also applied to similar booms.

‖**Bummalo.** 1673. A small fish (*Harpodon nehereus*) found off Southern Asia.

Bummaree (bɒmărī·). 1786. [?] A middleman in the fish trade at Billingsgate.

Bu·mmer. *U.S. slang.* 1865. [cf. Ger. *bummler.*] An idler, loafer. So **Bu·mmerish** *a.*

†**Bu·mmery.** 1663. [a. Du. *bommerye.*] = BOTTOMRY -1836.

Bump (bɒmp), *sb.*[1] 1592. [f. BUMP *v.*[1] Echoic. Cf. THUMP.] 1. A heavyish blow, rather dull in sound; a sudden collision 1611. 2. *Boating.* The impact of the stem of a boat against the stern or side of another 1861. 3. A protuberance such as is caused by a knock; an irregular prominence 1592. 4. *transf.* One of the prominences on the cranium associated by phrenologists with special faculties or propensities; also, the faculties, etc. (*colloq.*) 1815. 5. A variation of air pressure causing irregularity in an aeroplane's motion 1914.

Bump, *sb.*[2] 1528. [f. BUMP *v.*[2]] The cry of the bittern.

Bump, *sb.*[3] [?] a. A kind of matting. b. Cotton threads loosely twisted together, used for candle-wicks, also woven into sheets.

Bump, *v.*[1] 1566. [Echoic.] 1. *trans.* To strike heavily, knock, thump 1611. 2. *intr.* To strike with a violent jolt; to move with a bump or bumps 1843. b. *intr. Cricket.* Of a ball: To rise abruptly on pitching. Also *trans.* of a bowler 1888. 3. *trans. Boat-racing.* To overtake and impinge on. Also *absol.* = 'make a bump'; see BUMP *sb.*[1] 2. 1826. †4. To rise in protuberances, to be convex -1603. 5. *advb.* With a bump, with sudden collision 1806.

1. We bumped ashore a hundred Kegs SCOTT. 2. She bumped several times..losing her false keel 1860.

Bump, *v.*[2] 1646. [Echoic; cf. BOOM *v.*] To utter the cry of the bittern.

Bumper (bɒ·mpəɹ), *sb.*[1] 1676. [perh. f. BUMP *sb.*[1] and *v.*[1]] 1. A cup or glass filled to the brim, *esp.* for a toast. Also *attrib.* 2. *slang.* Anything unusually large. (Cf. *thumper*, etc.) Also *attrib.* 1859. 3. *Theatr. slang.* A crowded house 1839. 4. In *Whist*, etc. Winning two games before the adversaries have scored 1876. 5. The buffer of a railway carriage (*U.S.*) 1839.

1. Full bumpers crown our blisses 1676. 2. A b. rubbee crop 1885.

Bumper, *sb.*[2] 1866. [f. BUMP *v.*[2] and *sb.*[2]] In comb. *bog-b.* = BITTERN.

Bu·mper, *v.* 1696. [f. BUMPER *sb.*[1]] a. To fill to the brim. b. To toast in a bumper. c. *intr.* To drink bumpers.

Bumpkin (bɒ·mpkin). 1570. [? a. Du. *boomken* 'little tree', or f. BUM *sb.*[1]] 1. An awkward country fellow, a lout. 2. ? A kind of dance 1823. Hence **Bu·mpkinet**, a little b. **Bu·mpkinish, Bu·mpkinly** *adjs.* **Bu·mpkinship** (*joc.*).

Bumptious (bɒ·mpʃəs), *a.* 1803. [? f. BUMP *sb.*[1] or *v.*[1], after *fractious* or the like.] Offensively self-conceited; self-assertive (*colloq.* and *undignified*). Hence **Bu·mptious-ly** *adv.*, **-ness**.

Bumpy (bɒ·mpi), *a.* 1865. [f. BUMP *sb.*[1] or *v.*[1] + -Y[1].] Full of bumps; of a road, etc., jolty; causing bumps.

A b. wicket 1884. Hence **Bu·mpiness.**

Bun (bɒn), *sb.*[1] Now *dial.* [OE. *bune*, origin unkn.] The stalky part of flax or hemp.

Bun (bɒn), *sb.*[2] ME. [?] 1. In England, a sweet cake (usu. round and not large); in Scotland, the richest currant bread.

Bun, *sb.*[3] 1587. [?] a. The squirrel. b. The rabbit (*dial.*). c. A term of endearment.

Bunch (bɒnʃ), *sb.* ME. [Prob. echoic; cf. *hunch.*] †1. A protuberance; a hump; a goitre; a tumour -1826. In *pl.* A disease of horses -1775. 2. A collection or cluster of things of the same kind, as grapes, flowers, keys; also a portion of a dress gathered in folds 1570. 3. *fig.* A collection 1622.

1. A camell of Arabia hathe two bonches in the backe TREVISA. 3. She's the best of the b. (*mod.*). *Comb.* **b.-grass**, *Festuca scabrella* of N. America.

Bunch (bɒnʃ), *v.* ME. [f. BUNCH *sb.*] †1. *intr.* To bulge (*out*); to form bunches -1807. 2. *trans.* To make into a bunch; to gather (a dress) into folds; to group (animals) (*U.S.*) 1881.

Bunched (bɒnʃt), *ppl. a.* 1519. [f. BUNCH *sb.* and *v.*] †Having or forming a protuberance; covered with swellings; humped; bulging.

Bunchy (bɒ·nʃi), *a.* ME. [f. BUNCH *sb.* + -Y[1].] 1. Bulging; full of protuberances; humped. 2. Like a bunch; having bunches 1824.

2. Bowers Trellised with b. vine TENNYSON. Hence **Bu·nchiness.**

Bunco: see BUNKO.

Buncombe, bunkum (bɒ·ŋkəm). 1850. [f. *Buncombe*, name of a county in N. Carolina, U.S., the member for which, on one occasion, insisted on speaking because Buncombe expected it, and he was *bound to make a speech for Buncombe.*] 1. *in U. S. use*: a. In phrases, such as, *to talk* or *speak for* or *to Buncombe*, *a bid for buncombe* (i. e. the favour of the electors), and the like 1857. b. Political speaking or action not from conviction; political clap-trap 1850. 2. 'Tall talk'; humbug 1862. Also *attrib.*

1. a. The bill was another bid for b. *N. York Her.* 1859. b. Conventions, rights of independence, caucuses, agitation, and whatever else may be implied by the American expression 'bunkum' 1850. 2. A b. proclamation 1863. Hence **Buncomize** *v.* to talk b.

‖**Bund** (bɒnd). *Anglo-Ind.* 1813. [Of Pers. origin.] In India: Any artificial embankment, a dam, dyke, causeway. In Anglo-Chinese ports, *esp.* the embanked quay along the shore.

‖**Bunder** (bɒ·ndəɹ). *Anglo-Ind.* 1673. [Of Pers. origin.] 'A landing-place or quay; a seaport; a harbour; (sometimes a custom-house)' (Col. Yule). *Comb.* **b.-boat**, a boat in use on the Bombay coast for communicating with ships at anchor, etc.

Bundle (bɒ·nd'l), *sb.* ME. [f. (ult.) **bund-*, pa. pple. stem of OTeut. **bindan* to BIND. Perh. adopted from Du. or LG.] †1. A bandage (*rare*). ME. only. 2. A collection of things fastened together; a package, parcel ME. 3. *fig.* A collection, lot; often contemptuous 1535.

1. A b. of papers 1636, of sweet herbs MRS. GLASSE, linen 1802, glass plates BREWSTER. 3. A b. of calumnies SIR T. BROWNE.

Comb. **b. pillar**, 'a column consisting of a number of small pillars around its circumference' (Gwilt).

Bu·ndle, *v.* 1628. [f. prec.] 1. *trans.* To tie in, or make *up* into, a bundle 1649. †2. *fig.* To gather (*up, together*) into a mass -1690. 3. *intr.* To pack up one's effects for a journey; hence, to go with all one's incumbrances. Also, of several: To go 'all in a b.' (cf. 4) 1787. 4. *trans.* To put or send *away, in, off, out*, etc., hurriedly and unceremoniously. Cf. 'pack off'. 1823. 5. *intr.* To sleep in one's clothes on the same bed or couch *with* (as once was customary with persons of opposite sexes, in Wales and New England) 1781.

4. When he and his are all bundled off to Hades DE QUINCEY. 5. The custom of bundling..among Celtic peoples 1878.

‖**Bundook** (bɒ·nduk). *India.* 1886. [Hind., a. Pers. (cf. BONDUC), ad. Gr. Ποντικόν (sc. κάρυον hazel nut) PONTIC *a.*[1]] A musket.

Bung (bɒŋ). *sb.*[1] ME. [Cf. MDu. *bonghe* in same sense.] 1. A stopper; *spec.* a large cork stopper for the mouth of a cask. 2. *transf.* The bung-hole. (Still *dial.*) 1571. 3. *Naut.* The master's assistant who superintends the serving of the grog 1863.

Comb.: **b.-hole**, the hole in a cask, which is closed with the b.; **-stave**, that in which is the b.-hole.

†**Bung,** *sb.*[2] *Thieves' Cant.* 1567. [?] a. A purse. b. A pick-pocket. *Comb.* **b.-nipper**, a pick-pocket.

You Cut-purse Rascall, you filthy B. SHAKS.

Bung (bɒŋ), *v.* 1589. [f. BUNG *sb.*[1]] *trans.* 1. To stop with a bung 1616. 2. *transf.* and *fig.* To close. Now chiefly in pugilistic slang. 1589. 3. To shut *up*, enclose, as in a bunged cask 1592.

Bungalow (bɒ·ŋgălōu). 1676. [ad. Hind. *banglā* 'belonging to Bengal'.] A one-storied house, lightly built, with a tiled or thatched roof, orig. in the East. Hence **Bu·ngaloid** *a.*, having the appearance or style of a b.; also as *sb.*

Bungle (bɒ·ŋg'l), *v.* 1530. [App. echoic; cf. BUMBLE, BRANGLE, etc.] 1. *trans.* To make or do in a clumsy manner. Now, usually, To spoil by unskilful workmanship. 2. *intr.* To work or act unskilfully or clumsily 1549. Hence **Bu·ngler. Bu·nglingly** *adv.*

Bu·ngle, *sb.* 1656. [f. prec.] A clumsy or unskilful piece of work; a botch, muddle.

Bunion (bɒ·nyən). 1718. [prob. conn. w. BUNNY[1].] An inflamed swelling on the foot, *esp.* of the bursa mucosa at the inside of the ball of the great toe.

Bunjara, -jarree, var. BRINJARRY.

Bunk (bɒŋk), *sb.*[1] 1815. [? conn. w. BANK; cf. BUNKER.] A box or recess serving for a bed; a sleeping-berth. 2. A piece of wood placed on a lumberman's sled to support the ends of heavy pieces of timber (*U.S.*).

Bunk, *sb.*[2] 1914. Abbrev. BUNCOMBE, BUNKUM.

Bunk, *v.*[1] 1861. [f. BUNK *sb.*[1]] To sleep in a bunk; *hence*, to camp out. Also, *To b. it* (*colloq.*, chiefly U.S.).

Bunk, *v.*[2] *colloq.* and *slang.* 1877. To be off. Also as sb. *To do a b.*, to make an escape.

Bunker (bɒ·ŋkəɹ). 1758. [?] 1. A seat or bench (*Sc.*). 2. An earthen seat or bank in the fields (*dial.*) 1805. 3. A receptacle for coal on board ship 1839. 4. *Golf.* A sandy hollow or other obstruction on the links 1824; also as passive vb., to be hit, etc. into a b.; also *fig.*

Bunko, bunco (bɒ·ŋko), *sb.* *U.S. slang.* 1876. Also **banco.** [Cf. Sp. *banco* bank, *banca* a card-game.] Swindling by card-sharping, etc. *Comb.* **b.-steerer**, a swindler. Hence **Bu·nko** *v.*

Bunkum, etc.; see BUNCOMBE, etc.

†**Bu·nny**[1]. ME. [perh. a. OF. *bugne* a swelling caused by a blow; cf. BUNION.] A swelling as on the joints of animals -1784.

Bu·nny[2]. 1606. [f. BUN *sb.*[3] + -Y[6].] A pet name for a rabbit.

Comb. **B.-hug**, an eccentric rag-time dance. **B. Mouth**, the Common Snapdragon.

Bunny[3] (bɒ·ni). *dial.* 1873. A small ravine

opening through the cliff line to the sea. Also any small drain, culvert, etc. (*Hampshire.*)

Bunsen (bu·nsĕn, bʊ·nsĕn). 1879. [Name of Prof. *Bunsen* of Heidelberg, used attrib.] **Bunsen('s) burner, lamp,** a gas-burner, in which air is burnt with gas. **Bunsen('s) battery,** a voltaic battery in which the elements are carbon and zinc, and in which nitric and sulphuric acids, or solution of bichromate of potash and sulphuric acid, are employed. **B. cell,** one of the cells of a B. battery.

Bunsenite (bu·nsĕnəit). 1868. [f. BUNSEN + -ITE.] *Min.* A native protoxide of nickel.

Bunt (bʊnt), *sb.*[1] 1582. [?] **1.** The bagging part of a fishing-net; the funnel of an eel-trap 1602. **2.** *Naut.* The middle part of a sail. **b.** The middle part of a yard: the *Slings.* 1582. *Comb. B. fair* (Naut.): before the wind.

Bunt (bʊnt), *sb.*[2] 1601. [?] *Bot.* **1.** The Puffball (*Lycoperdon bovista*). Now *dial.* **2.** A parasitic fungoid, *Tilletia caries*, or Smutball; also the disease caused by it 1797. Hence **Bu·nted** *ppl. a.* infected with b.

Bunt, *v.*[1] 1611. [f. BUNT *sb.*[1]] *Naut.* **1.** To haul up the middle part of (a sail) in furling. **2.** *intr.* Of a sail: To belly 1681.

Bunt, *v.*[2] Chiefly *dial.* 1825. [cf. BUTT *v.*] *trans.* and *intr.* To knock, push, butt.

Bu·nter. Now *dial.* 1707. [?] A woman who picks up rags about the street; hence, any low vulgar woman.

‖**Bunter**[2] (bu·ntər). 1874. *Geol.* Short for *bunter Sandstein*, i.e. 'mottled sandstone', German name for the New Red Sandstone.

Bunting (bʊ·ntiŋ), *sb.*[1] ME. [?] **1.** Name of a group of insessorial birds, the *Emberizinæ*, a sub-family of *Fringillidæ* allied to the larks. **2.** The grey shrimp (*Crangon vulgaris*) 1836. **3.** A term of endearment; cf. Sc. *buntin*, short and thick, plump 1665.

1. I tooke this Larke for a b. *All's Well* II. v. 7. 3. Bye, baby b. *Nursery rime.*

Bu·nting, *sb.*[2] 1742. [? conn. w. Ger. *bunt.*] An open-made worsted stuff, used for making flags; also, a flag, flags.

Up goes her b. MARRYAT.

Bunting (bʊ·ntiŋ), *ppl. a.* 1584. [f. BUNT *v.*[1]] **1.** Of a sail: Bellying 1702. **2.** Swelling, plump; filled out 1584.

Bunting crow (bʊ·ntiŋ krōᵘ). 1802. [Du. *bonte-kraai*, f. *bont* parti-coloured + *kraai* crow.] The Hooded Crow (*Corvus cornix*).

Buntline (bʊ·ntləi·n). 1627. [f. BUNT *sb.*[1]] *Naut.* A rope fastened to the foot-rope of a sail, and passing in front of the canvas, so as to prevent it from bellying when being furled.

Buoy (boi), *sb.* 1466. [? f. OF. *boye* :—L. *boia* fetter (cf. BOY *sb.*[2]); the buoy being fettered to a spot.] **1.** A floating object fastened in a particular place to point out the position of things under the water (as anchors, shoals, rocks), or the course for ships; or to float a cable in a rocky anchorage (= *cable-, mooring-b.*). *Bell-b.*, a b. fitted with a bell, to ring with the movement of the water. **b.** That which buoys up a person in the water (= *life-b.*) **2.** *fig.* That which marks out a course, indicates danger, or keeps one afloat 1603. **3.** *attrib.*, as *b.-rope*, etc. 1562.

Buoy (boi), *v.* 1596. [In senses 1–3? cf. Sp. *boyar* to float (f. *boya* BUOY *sb.*); in sense 4 from the sb.] †**1.** *intr.* To rise to, or float on, the surface of a liquid; to rise, swell (as the sea) –1674. Also †*fig.* **2.** *trans.* To keep from sinking (in a fluid); *transf.* to keep up. (Usu. with *up.*) 1651. **b.** To raise to the surface of a liquid; to bring afloat (*e.g.* a sunken ship) 1616. **3.** *fig.* To keep up, support. (Usu. with *up.*) 1645. **b.** To raise (the spirits, etc.) (Usu. with *up.*) 1652. **4.** To furnish or mark with a buoy or buoys; to mark as with a buoy 1596.

1. *Lear* III. vii. 60. 2. To b. up a lump of lead BURKE. b. I will descend to thee, And b. thee up BEAUM & FL. 3. b. Hearts sunk down are not to be boyed up FULLER. 4. The captain sounded and buoyed the bar COOK.

Buoyage (boi·ėdʒ). 1858. [f. BUOY *v.* and *sb.* + -AGE.] The providing of (or with) buoys.

Buoyancy (boi·ănsi). 1713. [f. BUOYANT; see -ANCY.] **1.** Power of floating; tendency to float. Power of supporting a floating body (*rare*). *Hydrost.* Loss of weight due to immersion in liquid; the vertical upward pressure of a liquid on a floating body, which is equal to the weight of displaced liquid. **2.** *fig.* Elasticity of spirit 1819. **3.** Tendency to rise in prices, national revenue, etc. 1883.

2. The reckless b. of young blood 1819. var. **Buoy·ance** (*poet.* or *rhet.*).

Buoyant (boi·ănt), *a.* 1578. [? ad. Sp. *boyante*, or OF. *bouyant.*] **1.** Having the power of floating, tendency to float; floating; lightly elastic. Also *fig.* **2.** Having the power of buoying up (BUOY *v.* 2) 1692. Also *fig.*

2. The water under me was b. DRYDEN. *fig.* A man of b. and animated valour 1770. **Buoy·antly** *adv.*

‖**Buprestis** (biuprė·stis). ME. [L., a. Gr. βούπρηστις, lit. 'ox-burner'.] **1.** An insect of the ancients, harmful to cattle. **2.** *Zool.* A genus of tropical beetles, brilliant in colouring. Hence the family *Buprestidæ*, occas. called **Bupre·stidans.** 1835.

Bur, burr (bɔ̄ɪ), *sb.* ME. [app. = Da. *borre* bur, burdock. The spelling *bur* is now usual. See also BURR.] **1.** Any rough or prickly seed-vessel or flower-head of a plant: *esp.* the flower-head of the Burdock (*Arctium lappa*); the husk of the chestnut. **b.** The female catkin of the hop before fertilization. [? A different wd.; cf. 4.] 1846. **2.** Any plant which produces burs 1480. **3.** *fig.* Any (thing or person) which clings like a bur 1590. **4.** A knob or knot in a tree; also, one of the buds of the farcy. [But cf. F. *bourre* vine-bud, *bourrelet* 'round swelling on a tree'.] 1725. **5.** The rounded knob forming the base of a deer's horn. [Cf. BURL.] 1575. **6.** *dial.* The drag-chain and shoe for fastening up a carriage-wheel when going down-hill 1863.

1. I am a kind of Burre, I shal sticke *Meas. for M.* I. iii. 189. 2. Bur and brake and briar TENNYSON. 3. Hang off thou cat, thou bur *Mids. N.* III. ii. 260.

Phr. *Bur in the throat*: anything that appears to stick in the throat; 'a lump in the throat'.

Comb.: **b.-flag** = *bur-reed*; **-knot** = sense 4; **-marigold,** the genus *Bidens*; **-oak,** *Quercus macrocarpa* of N. America; **-reed,** the genus *Sparganum*; **-thistle,** *Carduus lanceolatus*; **-weed,** *Xanthium strumarium.*

Bur, *v.* [f. prec.] To remove burs from (wool). Hence **Bu·rring** *vbl. sb.*, also *attrib.*

Burberry (bɔ̄·ɪbəri). 1903. Trade name of cloth and clothing made by Burberrys Ltd.

Bu·rble, *sb.*[1] ME. [f. BURBLE *v.*[1]] †**1.** A bubble, bubbling –1547. †**2.** A pimple, boil –1622. **3.** A murmurous flow of words 1896.

Burble, *sb.*[2] *Sc. dial.* 1812. [See BURBLE *v.*[2]] 'Trouble, perplexity, disorder' (Jam.).

Bu·rble, *v.*[1] ME. [Echoic.] †**1.** To bubble; to flow in or with (a sound of) bubbles –1577. **2.** To speak, or say (something), murmurously 1891.

Bu·rble, *v.*[2] *Sc. dial.* To perplex, muddle.

Burbot (bɔ̄·ɪbət). 1475. [a. F. *bourbotte* (Littré).] A fresh-water fish (*Lota vulgaris*) of the family *Gadidæ*; also called *Eel-pout* or *Coney-fish.*

Burd. [ME. *burde*, perh. :—OE. **byrde* embroideress, rel. to *borde* embroidery.] A poetic word for 'woman, lady', later = 'young lady, maiden'. *Obs.* exc. in ballads.

Burd, obs. and Sc. f. BIRD, BOARD.

†**Burd-alone,** *a. Sc.* 1572. [? f. BURD = BIRD; cf. *Ps.* cii. 7.] As a solitary person; all alone –1870.

†**Burda·sh.** 1713. [? same as BARDASH (as occas. also spelt).] ? A kind of cravat, or a sash for the waist, worn by men in the time of Queen Anne and George I –1730.

Burden, burthen (bɔ̄·ɪd'n, bɔ̄·ɪð'n). [OE. *byrðen* str. fem., f. (ult.) stem *bur-* of **ber-an* to BEAR. For the forms cf. *murder, murther*, etc. *Burthen* is still often retained for 'capacity of a ship', and also poet. or rhet.] **1.** That which is borne; load. Also *fig.* **2.** A load, as a measure of quantity. Now only the carrying capacity of a ship, stated as so many tons. ME. †**3.** A child, borne in the womb –1667. †**4.** What is borne by the soil; crop –1669. **5.** The bearing of loads, as in *beast of b.*, *ship of b.* (= merchant-ship) ME. **6.** Used in the Eng. Bible as tr. Heb. *massā* 'lifting up (of the voice), oracle' (Gesenius); generally taken in Eng. to mean 'a heavy lot or fate' ME. †**7.** The bass, or undersong; cf. BOURDON[2] 1. –1833. **8.** The refrain or chorus of a song 1598. **9.** *fig.* The leading idea 1649.

1. Oh! by Thine own sad burthen, borne So meekly KEBLE. *fig.* A greeuous burthen was thy Birth to me *Rich. III*, IV. iv. 167. The b. of any fixed money payment FAWCETT. *B. of proof*, etc.: (*onus probandi* in Rom. Law) the obligation to prove a controversial assertion, falling upon the person who makes it. 2. Vessels of from fifteen to thirty tons burthen WELLINGTON. 3. Let wiues with childe Pray that their burthens may not fall this day *John* III. i. 90. 6. The burden of Babylon, which Isaiah the sonne of Amoz did see *Isa.* xiii. 1. 7. *A. Y. L.* III. ii. 261. 9. Mercy and justice..is the burden of the whole Prophetic Teaching STANLEY. Hence **Bu·rdenless** *a.* †**Bu·rdenous, bu·rth-** *a.* burdensome (*lit.* and *fig.*). **Bu·rdensome, bu·rth-** *a.* of the nature of a b. **Bu·rd-, bu·rthensome·ly,** *adv.*, **-ness.**

Burden, burthen (bɔ̄·ɪd'n, -ð'n), *v.* 1541. [f. prec.] **1.** To lay a burden on (*lit.* and *fig.*). †**2.** To charge (a person) *with* (an accusation); to lay as a charge *upon* –1779.

1. Let vs not burthen our remembrances, with A heauinesse that's gon *Temp.* V. i. 199. 2. This is false he burthens me withall *Com. Err.* V. i. 209. Hence **Bu·rdener.**

Burdened, burthened (bɔ̄·ɪd'nd, bɔ̄·ɪð-), *ppl. a.* 1594. [f. BURDEN *sb.* and *v.* + -ED.] †Imposed as a burden; heavily loaded, oppressed.

May thy Cows their burden'd Bags distend DRYDEN.

Burdock (bɔ̄·ɪdǫk). 1597. [f. BUR *sb.*] A coarse weedy plant (*Arctium Lappa*, etc.) bearing burs, and large leaves like those of the dock. **b.** Occas. applied to *Xanthium strumarium.* Also *attrib.*

†**Burdon.** ME. [a. L. *burdonem.*] A mule between a horse and she-ass; a hinny –1607.

Bureau (biu̇ˌrōᵘ, biūᵊrōᵘ); pl. **-x, -s.** 1720. [a. F.; see BUREL.] **1.** A writing-desk with drawers for papers, etc. 1742. **2.** An office, *esp.* for the transaction of public business; a department of public administration. (In this sense often pronounced büro.) 1720.

2. They have made London a shop, a law-court, a record office, a scientific b. EMERSON.

Bureaucracy (biurǭᵘ·krăsi, ǫ·krăsi). 1848. [a. F. *bureaucratie.*] **a.** Government by bureaux; usually officialism. **b.** Government officials collectively.

The Continental nuisance called 'Bureaucracy' CARLYLE. So **Bu·reaucrat,** a member of a b.; one who endeavours to concentrate power in his bureau; occas. = *bureaucratist.* **Bureaucra·tic** *a.* of or pertaining to b. **Bureaucra·tically** *adv.* **Bureau·cratism,** a bureaucratic system. **Bureau·cratist,** a supporter of bureaucrats and b.

Burel. *Obs.* exc. *Hist.* ME. [a. OF. *burel* (now *bureau*), dim. of *bure* 'coarse (? brown) woollen cloth, baize', ? from (ult.) L. *burrus*, taken as ad. Gr. πυρρός red.] A coarse (? brown) woollen cloth (cf. BAIZE); frieze; a garment of this; (plain) clothing.

I wol renne out, my borel for to shewe CHAUCER.

Burette (biure·t). 1483. [a. F., dim. of *buire* vase for liquors.] **1.** A little cruet for oil or vinegar. **2.** A graduated glass tube for measuring small quantities of liquid 1836.

‖**Burg** (būᵊɪg, bɔ̄ɪg). 1753. [ad. late L. *burgus*, ad. OTeut. **burgs* BOROUGH.] **1.** A fortress (BOROUGH 1) or a walled town (BOROUGH 2) of early or mediæval times. **2.** *U.S. colloq.* (bɔ̄ɪg) A town, city 1846.

Burgage (bɔ̄·ɪgėdʒ). ME. [ad. med.L. *burgagium*, f. *burgus* (see prec.).] *Law.* **1.** A tenure whereby lands or tenements in cities and towns were held of the lord, for a certain yearly rent 1502. **2.** A freehold property in a borough; also, a house, etc., held by burgage tenure –1827. Also *attrib.*

Bu·rgall. (*U.S.*) 1860. A fish (*Ctenolabrus ceruleus*).

‖**Burgau** (bürgǭ). 1753. [Fr.] 'The name of several univalve nacreous shells' (Littré).

‖**Burgaudine.** 1753. [Fr.; 'the Academy has *burgandine*' (Littré).] Mother of pearl made from the burgau shell.

†**Burge,** *v.* ME. Short f. BURGEON *v.* –1523.

Burgee (bɔ̄ɪdʒī·). 1848. [?] **1.** A small tapered flag or pennant, three-cornered (or swallow-tailed), used by cutters, yachts, etc. **2.** A size of small coal 1867.

Burgeon (bɔ̄·ɪdʒən), *sb.* [ME. *borioun, bu-*

rioun, -jon, a. OF. bor-, burjon, of unkn. etym.] 1. A swelling bud, a young shoot. Recently revived in poetry. b. Zool. A bud of a zoophyte. Also fig. †2. transf. A pimple 1597.

1. Bounteous with..b. of birth SWINBURNE.

Burgeon (bɔ̈·ɹdʒən), v. ME. [f. prec. Cf. F. bourgeonner.] 1. intr. To bud or sprout; to begin to grow. Also transf. and fig. 2. trans. To shoot out, put forth as buds. Also transf. and fig. ME.

1. fig. The Prelatism of Episcopacy..began then to b. MILT. 2. It shal buriown to thee thornes and brembles WYCLIF Gen. iii. 18.

Burger, -ship; see BURGHER, -SHIP.

Burgess (bɔ̈·ɹdʒės), sb. [ME. burgeis, a. OF. :—late L. burgensis; see BOURGEOIS.] 1. An inhabitant of a borough; strictly, one possessing full municipal rights; a citizen. b. spec. The member of parliament for a borough, corporate town, or University. Used in Virginia, etc. to denote a member of the legislative body called the 'House of Burgesses'. Now techn. and Hist. 1472. 2. spec. A magistrate or member of the governing body of a town. Now Hist. ME. Also attrib.

1. He logyd in a notable burgesse howse LD. BERNERS. b. One of the burgesses for the University 1702. 2. fig. The wild burgesses of the forrest SIDNEY.

Burgess-ship (bɔ̈·ɹdʒės,ʃip). 1467. [See -SHIP.] 1. The status and privileges of a burgess; the freedom of a borough. Also fig. †2. ? The position of burgess for a borough –1695.

Burgh (bɒ·rə). Sc. ME. [Var. of BOROUGH; obs. in ordinary Eng. use since 17th c.] Orig. = BOROUGH; now used only of a Sc. town possessing a charter. Also attrib.

B. and land: town and country. Sc. Till each fair b., numerically free Shall choose its members by the Rule of Three CANNING. Hence **Bu·rghal** a. of or pertaining to a b.

†Bu·rghal-pe·nny. ME. only. Eng. Law. ? A municipal tax of some kind.

Burgh-english, obs. f. BOROUGH-ENGLISH.

Burgher (bɔ̈·ɹgəɹ), sb. 1568. [a. mod. Ger. or Du. burger citizen of a burg or fortified town; assim. to Eng. burgh BOROUGH.] 1. An inhabitant of a burgh, borough, or corporate town; a citizen. Chiefly used of foreign towns. Now arch. Also attrib. 2. A member of that section of the Scottish Secession Church, which upheld the lawfulness of the burgess oath; also attrib. See ANTIBURGHER. 1766.

1. A b. of Antwerp..in a broad Flemish hat 1824.

Burgheristh. Erron. spelling of burh-riht 'borough-right' in Domesday.

Bu·rgherma·ster. rare. = BURGOMASTER.

Burghership (bɔ̈·ɹgəɹʃip). 1568. [f. BURGHER.] The rights and privileges of a burgher.

Burghmaster, erron. f. bergh-, BARMASTER. (Dicts.)

Burglar (bɔ̈·ɹglәɹ). 1541. [ad. Anglo-Lat. burglator (13th c.), burgulator (16th c.), var. of burgator (13th c.), perh. f. burgh- in burghbreche, native Eng. for burglary.] One who is guilty of burglary. var. †**Bu·rglarer.** Hence **Bu·rglar** v. †**Bu·rglarly** adv.

Burglarious (bɔ̈ɹglēᵊ·riəs), a. 1769. [f. BURGLARY. Cf. felonious.] 1. Of or pertaining to burglary; addicted to burglary; involving the guilt of burglary. 2. Burglar-like 1859.

1. The larcenous and b. world SYD. SMITH. Hence **Burgla·riously** adv.

Bu·rglarize, v. U.S. 1871. [f. BURGLAR.] To rob burglariously.

Burglary[1] (bɔ̈·ɹglări). 1532. [AF. burglarie, Anglo-Lat. burgaria, burgeria (13th c.), burglaria (16th c.). The intrusive l is not explained.] The crime of breaking by night into a house with felonious intent. Also with a and pl. Also fig.

Neither can b. be committed in a tent or booth erected in a market or fair BLACKSTONE.

†Bu·rglary[2]. 1533. [as if ad. L. burglarius.] = BURGLAR –1651.

Burgle (bɔ̈·ɹg'l), v. colloq. or joc. 1872. [f. BURGLAR.] intr. To follow the occupation of a burglar; trans. to break feloniously into the house of; to rob or steal burglariously.

A gentleman of the burgling persuasion DICKENS.

Burgomaster (bɔ̈·ɹgomāːstəɹ). 1592. [ad. Du burgemeester, after Eng. MASTER; see also BURGHER-, BOROUGHMASTER.] 1. The chief magistrate (= Eng. mayor) of a Dutch or Flemish town. Used loosely for any member of the governing body of a foreign municipality. Also = BOROUGH-MASTER, q. v. 2. A species of gull (Larus glaucus) 1678.

1. The only daughter of a burgo-master of Leyden JOHNSON.

Burgonet (bɔ̈·ɹgŏnet). Hist. 1563. [ad. OF. bourguignotte, app. f. Bourgogne.] a. A steel cap, worn esp. by pikemen. b. A kind of helmet with a visor. Also fig. Ant. & Cl. I. v. 24.

Burgoo (bɔ̈ɹgū·). 1704. [Arabic.] A thick oatmeal porridge as used by seamen; loblolly.

Burgrave, burggrave (bɔ̈·ɹgrēⁱv). 1550. [ad. Ger. burggraf, f. burg + graf.] The governor of a town or castle; later, a noble ruling by hereditary right a town or castle, with the adjacent domain. Hence **Burgra·viate,** the rank or office of b.

†Burgu·llian. [?] A braggadocio. B. JONS.

Burgundian (bɒɹgɒ·ndiăn). 1578. [f. Burgundy (L. Burgundia, F. Bourgogne).] A. adj. Belonging to Burgundy (any sense). B. sb. 1. An inhabitant of Burgundy. †2. (In form Burgonian) A kind of ship –1627.

Burgundy (bɔ̈·ɹgɒ̆ndi). 1672. [ad. med.L. Burgundia, Fr. Bourgogne. (Swift rimed it with Sunday.)] 1. A kingdom, and later a duchy of the Western Empire, subseq. giving its name to a province of France 1697. 2. ellipt. Wine made in Burgundy 1672. 3. attrib. 1672.

2. At the Rose on Sunday, I'll treat you with b. SWIFT. Comb. **B. Pitch.** [Obtained near Neufchâtel, once Burgundian territory.] The resinous juice of the Spruce-fir (Abies excelsa).

Burh, OE. f. BOROUGH, BURGH, q.v.

Buriable (be·ri,ăb'l), a. 1598. [f. BURY v.] Capable of being buried (lit. and fig.).

Burial (be·riăl). [ME. buryel, biriel, erron. formed as a sing. of byriels, BURIELS, q. v.; assoc. later with sbs. in -al from Fr., e. g. espousal-s.] †1. A burying-place –1612. 2. The act of burying; interment 1453. Also transf. and fig. b. pl. Formerly in computations, etc. of mortality: = Deaths 1687. 3. The depositing of anything under earth or water, or enclosing it in some other substance 1626.

1. fig. Merch. V. I. i. 29. 2. b. A register of births, burials, and marriages BURKE.

Comb.: **b.-aisle,** an aisle in a religious building used for interments, also fig.; **-board,** a body appointed by public authority to regulate burials; **-hill, -mound,** a mound erected over a grave, a barrow; **-service,** a religious service accompanying a b.; the part of a liturgy used at a funeral; esp. that used in the Ch. of England; **-society,** an insurance society for providing money for the expenses of b.

Burial-ground. 1803. A piece of ground set apart as devoted to the regular interment of the dead; a burying-ground.

That..phrase, which calls The burial-ground God's acre LONGF.

Burial-place. 1633. A place of burial.

†Bu·riels. [OE. byrgels, f. burg- ablaut-stem of bergan BERGH to protect + suffix -isli-. See also BURY v. and BURIAL.] 1. A burying-place; a tomb –1483. 2. An interment. ME. only.

Burin (biūᵊ·rin). 1662. [a. F., perh. f. OHG. bora boring-tool.] 1. A graver; the tool used by an engraver on copper; also attrib. b. The style of using the graver 1824. 2. A triangular tool used by marble-workers.

1. b. A fine specimen of Longan's bold b. DIBDIN. Hence **Bu·rinist,** an engraver.

Burke (bɔ̈ɹk), v. 1829. [f. Burke, a criminal executed at Edinburgh in 1829.] 1. To kill secretly by suffocation or strangulation, or in order to sell the victim's body for dissection, as Burke did. 2. fig. To smother, hush up 1840.

1. As soon as the executioner proceeded to his duty, the cries of 'B. him, B. him—give him no rope'..were vociferated Times 2 Feb. 1829. Hence **Bu·rker.** **Bu·rkism.**

Burl (bɔ̈ɹl), sb. ME. [a. OF. bourle tuft of wool; cf. BURR.] 1. A knot or lump in wool or cloth. †2. transf. A pimple –1651. †3. The bud of a red deer's horn. (Cf. BUR sb. 5.) 1611. 4. A knot in wood (U. S.) 1886.

Burl (bɔ̈ɹl), v. 1483. [f. prec.] 1. To dress (cloth), esp. by removing knots and lumps. 2. To pick out (a lock or flock of wool) 1650. †3. To remove burls from the face. HERRICK. Hence **Bu·rler.**

†Burlace, burlake, burlet, corrupt ff. Bourdelais, a variety of grape, cultivated in 17th c.

Burlap (bɔ̈·ɹlæp). 1695. [?] Orig. perh. a sort of holland; now a coarse canvas made of jute and hemp, used for bagging; also, a finer material for curtains.

Burlesque (bɒɹle·sk). 1656. [a. F., ad. It. burlesco, f. burla ridicule.] A. adj. †1. Droll in look, manner, or speech –1848. 2. Of the nature of derisive imitation; ironically bombastic, mock-heroic or mock-pathetic 1700.

1. Graham speaks of Fuller as..b. in his manners H. WALPOLE. 2. B. pictures 1712, authors 1714.

B. sb. 1. That species of composition which excites laughter by caricature of serious works, or by ludicrous treatment of their subjects; a literary or dramatic work of this kind. Also attrib. 1667. 2. Grotesque caricature; concr. an action or performance which casts ridicule on that which it imitates, or is itself a ridiculous attempt at something serious; a mockery 1753.

1. Witty burlesques of the noblest performances TUCKER. B. has been driving pantomime off the stage 1869. 2. A b. upon public worship WESLEY.

Burlesque (bɒɹle·sk), v. 1676. [f. prec.] To turn into ridicule by grotesque parody. Also intr.

Cervantes has burlesqued the old romances 1804.

Burlesquer (bɒɹle·skəɹ). 1657. [f. BURLESQUE v. and sb. + -ER[1].] a. One who burlesques. b. One who acts in burlesques.

†Burle·tta. 1748. [a. It., dim. of burla fun.] A musical farce –1879.

Burly (bɔ̈·ɹli), a. [ME. borlich, north. burli. See N. E. D.] A. adj. †1. Stately, dignified –1664. †b. poet. Of things: Goodly, noble –1873. 2. Stout, sturdy, corpulent ME. †b. Of a garment, or wool: Thick –1805. 3. Big; domineering, bluff (arch.) 1592. B. adv. Sturdily, stoutly ME.

3. Wrote against by som b. standard Divine MILT. Hence **Bu·rlily** adv. **Bu·rliness.** †**Bu·rly** v. to make b. QUARLES.

Burn (bɔ̈ɹn), sb.[1] [Com. Teut.: OE. burna wk. masc., burne wk. fem., burn str. fem., metathetic forms, repr. OTeut. types *brunnon-, *brunno-z.] 1. In OE.: A spring, fountain; a stream or river. In later use: A brook. Now chiefly north.

1. Well watered by a beck or b. 1839.

Burn (bɔ̈ɹn), sb.[2] 1563. [f. BURN v.[1]] 1. The act or effect of burning; esp. a burnt place on the body 1594. 2. A mark made by burning, a brand 1563. Also attrib.

Burn (bɔ̈ɹn), v.[1] Pa. t. and pple. **burned, burnt.** [repr. (1) OE. brinnan, by metathesis *birnan, bernan, beornan 'ardere'; and (2) OE. bærnan (for brennan) 'urere'; both forms ran together in ME. The form burned is arch., and more formal; it occurs usually as pa. t., or in comb. with have.] I. Intrans. 1. To be in the state of activity characteristic of fire; to be in combustion. Also fig. 2. Of matter: To be on fire; to be enveloped in flames OE. Also fig. ¶Phys. Occas. for: To undergo oxidation, as in burning, with evolution of heat 1885. 3. gen. To become or be violently hot. b. In games: of a person getting very near to a hidden object sought. (Cf. WARM.) Hence fig. To approach near to the truth. [Cf. Fr. 'nous brûlons'.] 1821. 4. Of candles, lamps, etc.: To be in process of combustion so as to give light; hence, to flame, give light, shine. Also transf. of the sun, stars, etc. OE. b. Of other objects: To appear as if on fire ME. 5. To suffer the effects of combustion; to be reduced to ashes, a cinder, etc., by fire; to be scorched, charred, etc. Often said of food which is overdone. ME. 6. To suffer death by fire. Now usu. to be burnt. 1600.

1. Sometime a fire [Ile be]..and burne Mids. N. III. i. 113. fig. Let not thine anger burne against thy seruant Gen. xliv. 18. 2. A place that burns with Fire and Brimstone BUNYAN. 4. How ill this taper burns Jul. C. IV. iii. 275. b. The Barge she sat in, like a burnisht Throne, Burnt on the water Ant. & Cl. II. ii. 197. 5. The Capon burnes Com. Err. I. ii. 44. 6. They should all burne for their vilde heresie 1604.

II. Trans. 1. Of fire: To destroy, consume (any object). Of persons: To cause to be destroyed or consumed by fire. Also absol. OE.

b. *spec.* To make a burnt-offering of (incense, a victim) *to* a deity. Also *absol.* ME. **2.** To put to death by fire, *esp.* as a judicial punishment ME. **3.** To consume for warming or lighting; to keep (a candle, etc.) alight 1712. ¶*Phys.* Occas. for: To consume by oxidation with evolution of heat. **4.** *fig.* To inflame with desire, etc. ME. **5.** Of any heating agency: To produce the effects of combustion upon. (Not used for melting or softening.) Of persons: To expose to the action of fire so as to produce the effects of combustion; *esp.* to treat with fire for a specific purpose, as wood, clay, the soil, etc. 1519. **b.** Hence, To produce (charcoal, bricks, etc.) by burning ME. **c.** *transf.* To produce on (anything) an aspect as of burning. Sometimes said of cold, and of certain manures or crops. ME. **6.** To wound or to cause pain to by the contact of fire, etc.: said both of the fire, and of the person who applies it. Often *refl.* Also *absol.* ME. **b.** To cauterize; to brand 1483. **c.** To wound or cause local pain to, as by fire; *e.g.* by vitriol, a blister, etc., occas. by intense cold. Also *absol.* 1509. †**d.** To infect with sores; *esp.* with venereal disease –1590.

1. They were for burning the body outright SOUTHEY. b. The priest..burns the offering with his holy hands POPE. 2. He was brent for an hereticke 1635. 5 b. These [earthen vessels] I burnt in the fire DE FOE. 6. Whan thou shalt go in fyr, thou shalt not be brent WYCLIF *Isa.* xliii. 2. c. The parching air Burns frore, and cold performs th' effect of Fire MILT. *P. L.* II. 595. d. Light wenches will burne, come not neere her *Com. Err.* IV. iii. 58.

Phrases. a. (sense I. 2) *To b.* (*itself*) *out, to be burnt out*: to burn until extinguished by lack of fuel. So *To b. down, low. To b. up*: to get fairly alight. Also, *to b. red, blue, bright*, etc. b. (sense I. 3) fig. *The money*, etc. *burns in one's pocket, burns a hole in one's pocket*, etc., meaning the owner is eager to get rid of it. c. *To b. into* (of fire, a caustic, etc.): to eat its way into. Usu. *fig.*: to make an indelible impression upon (a person's mind). d. (sense II. 1) fig. *To b. one's boats*: to cut oneself off from all possibility of retreat. e. (sense II. 3) fig. *To b. daylight*, to b. candles in the daytime, also to waste or consume the daylight. *To b. the* (or *one's*) *candle at both ends*: see CANDLE. f. (sense II. 5) †*poet.* Of cattle: *To b.* (the ground) *bare*: to crop it close DRYDEN. fig. *To b. the planks*: to remain long sitting. *To b.* (metals) *together*: to join them by melting their edges, etc. g. (sense II. 6) fig. *To b. one's* (*own*) *fingers*: to sustain damage through meddling with something. h. *To b. out of house and home*: to drive (a person) out of a place by burning his dwelling. *To b. in*: *fig.* to make indelible *in* a person's mind. Also, to render indelible (the painting upon pottery, etc.) by burning. *To b. the water*: to spear salmon by torchlight.

Burn-. The vb. or vb.-stem in comb. forming sbs. or adjs.

1. With vb. + obj., as **b.-the-wind, burnewin,** *Sc.*, a blacksmith. 2. With the vb. used *attrib.* = *burning*, as **b.-fire** (*dial.*), perversion of BONFIRE; **-iron,** a brandishing-iron; **-weed** = THORN-APPLE.

†**Burn,** *v.*[2] ME. [a. OF. *burnir*, var. of *brunir*, f. *brun* BROWN.] = BURNISH *v.*[1]

Burnable (bɔ̄·ɹnăb'l), *a.* 1611. [f. BURN *v.*[1] + -ABLE.] Capable of being burnt by fire.

Bu·rn-beat, *v.* Also **-bait.** 1669. [f. BURN *v.*[1] + BEAT *sb.*[3] or *v.*[2]; pa. pple. *burnbeat.*] To pare off and burn rough turf in order to improve the ground.

Burner (bɔ̄·ɹnəɹ). ME. [f. BURN *v.*[1] + -ER[1].] **1.** One who burns with fire. **2.** One who prepares or produces by burning, as *charcoal-b.* 1463. **3.** That part of a lamp, gaslight, etc., from which the flame comes; often defined, as *Argand, Bunsen*, etc. *b.* 1790.

1. Brenneris of houses and cornes WYCLIF.

†**Bu·rnet,** *a.* and *sb.*[1] ME. [a. OF. *burnete, brunette*, dim. of *brun.*] **A.** *adj.* Dark brown. **B.** *sb.* A superior wool-dyed cloth, orig. of dark brown colour ME.

Burnet (bɔ̄·ɹnėt), *sb.*[2] ME. [f. prec. from the colour of its flowers.] Any plant belonging to the genera *Sanguisorba* and *Poterium* (N.O. *Rosaceæ*), as the Great or Common Burnet, the Lesser or Salad Burnet, etc. Also, the Burnet Saxifrage, *Pimpinella Saxifraga*, resembling these in foliage.

The freckled Cowslip, B., and greene Clouer SHAKS. *Comb.*: **b.-fly, -moth** (*Anthrocera* or *Zygæna filipendulæ*), a greenish black moth with crimson spots on its wings; **-rose,** the Scotch rose (*Rosa spinosissima*); **b. saxifrage** (see above).

Bu·rnettize, *v.* 1867. [f. Sir W. *Burnett*, who patented the process.] To steep canvas, cordage, etc., in a solution of chloride of zinc.

Bu·rnie. *Sc.* 1724. Dim. of BURN *sb.*[1]

Burning (bɔ̄·ɹniŋ), *vbl. sb.* ME. [f. BURN *v.*[1]] The action of the vb. BURN. **I.** *intr.* **1.** See BURN *v.*[1] I. 1, 2, 3 b. †**2.** Heat from disease, or a serpent's bite; the disease itself; *esp.* St. Anthony's fire, and venereal disease –1753. **II.** *trans.* See BURN *v.*[1] II. 1, 2, 5, 6 b.

Burning (bɔ̄·ɹniŋ), *ppl. a.* [f. as prec.] That burns in various senses.

Phrases, fig. *B. shame, disgrace*, etc., now perh. 'flagrant, conspicuous'; but often there is a hint of branding, torturing as an inward fire, causing the cheeks to glow, etc. *B. matter, question* (cf. F. *question brûlante*, Ger. *brennende Frage*): one that excites hot discussion or feeling. *B. scent*: very warm scent; *b. chase*: hot, uninterrupted.

Burning Bush. a. 'The bush that burned and was not consumed' (*Exod.* iii), the ensign of the Presbyterian churches of Scotland, assumed in memory of the persecution of the 17th c. **b.** A name of various shrubs or plants, as the Artillery plant, *Pilea Serpylliflora*, the *Dictamnus Fraxinella*, and (U. S.) the *Euonymus atropurpureus* and *E. Americanus.*

Burning-glass (bɔ̄·ɹniŋ-glɑs). 1570. A lens or concave mirror, by the use of which the sun's rays may be concentrated on an object.

Burnish (bɔ̄·ɹniʃ), *sb. rare.* 1647. [f. BURNISH *v.*[1]] Burnishing; a burnishing; *spec.* anything laid over a surface to burnish it.

Burnish (bɔ̄·ɹniʃ), *v.*[1] ME. [f. OF. *burniss-* stem of *burnir*, var. of *brunir*; see BURN *v.*[2]] **1.** To make shining by friction; to furbish; to polish by rubbing with a hard and smooth tool. Also *fig.* **2.** *transf.* To make bright and glossy ME. **3.** Of a stag: To rub the dead skin from his horns [so Fr. *brunir*] 1616. **4.** *intr.* To become bright and glossy; to shine, gleam. Also *fig.* 1624.

1. *fig.* Hye walles & noble, all bournysshed and polysshed with charite 1526. 2. Fruit burnisht with Golden Rind MILT. *P. L.* IV. 249. 4. I've seen a snake..B., and make a gaudy show SWIFT.

Bu·rnish, *v.*[2] Now *dial.* ME. [?] Of the human frame: To grow plump, or stout; to increase in breadth. Also *transf.*

[London] will be found to B. round about, to every point of the compasse FULLER.

Burnisher (bɔ̄·ɹniʃəɹ). 1450. [f. BURNISH *v.*[1] + -ER[1].] He who or that which burnishes; *esp.* a tool, which differs in material and shape according to the purpose and trade.

‖**Burnous, burnouse** (bɔɹnū·s, -nū·z). 1695. [a. F., a. Arab. *burnus.* Occas. treated in Eng. as a pl.] A cloak with a hood, as worn by Arabs and Moors; also, by women.

The burnous..is his [the Arab's] garment by day and by night KINGLAKE.

Burnt, burned (bɔ̄ɹnt, bɔ̄ɹnd), *ppl. a.* ME. [f. BURN *v.*[1] q. v.] In various senses of the verb.

Phrases, etc. **Burnt iron** (*Mining*): iron which has been exposed to oxidation until all its carbon is gone. *Burnt taste*, etc.: a taste, etc., as of something burnt. *The burnt child dreads the fire. Comb.* **burnt-ear,** a disease in corn, in which the ear is blackened, owing to the growth of *Uredo segetum.*

Burnt o·ffering, burnt-o·ffering. ME. A sacrifice offered to a deity by burning; *esp.* Jewish animal sacrifice. So **Burnt sacrifice.**

Burr, bur (bɔ̄ɹ), *sb.*[1] ME. [?] **1.** *gen.* A circle. †**2.** A broad iron ring on a tilting spear just behind the place for the hand –1610. **3.** A washer placed on the small end of a rivet before the end is swaged down 1627. **4.** (see BURR-PUMP.) **5.** A circle of light round the moon (or a star); in mod. use, a nebulous disk of light enfolding it 1631.

5. A burre about the moone is..a presage of a tempest 1631.

Burr, bur (bɔ̄ɹ), *sb.*[2] 1573. [?] A sweetbread.

†**Burr, bur,** *sb.*[3] 1573. [?] The external meatus of the ear. (Dr. Johnson's guess 'the lobe or lap of the ear' was unlucky.) –1688.

Burr, bur (bɔ̄ɹ), *sb.*[4] 1611. [app. the same as BUR *sb.*, but usu. spelt *burr.*] **1.** A rough ridge or edge left on metal or other substance after cutting, punching, etc. **2.** Techn. **a.** short for *b.-chisel, -drill, -saw*; see *Comb.* **b.** A tool used in making screws. 1833.

1. Burr..is caused by the tearing up of the copper by the needle or burin 1876.

Comb. **b.-chisel,** a three-edged chisel for clearing the corners of mortises; **-drill,** a dentist's drill with a serrated or file-cut knob; **-gauge,** a plate with holes of graduated sizes, for determining the sizes of b.-drills; **-saw,** a small circular saw used in turning.

Burr, bur (bɔ̄ɹ), *sb.*[5] Also **buhr.** 1721. [perh. as prec.] **1.** Siliceous rock suitable for millstones. **b.** A whetstone. **2.** A siliceous boss in calcareous, or other softer, formations; a harder part in any freestone 1839. **3.** A clinker 1823. Also *attrib.*

Burr (bɔ̄ɹ, bɒrr), *sb.*[6] 1760. [app. echoic; prob. assoc. with BUR *sb.*] **1.** A rough sounding of the letter *r*; *spec.* the rough uvular trill (= French *r grasseyé*), found *esp.* in Northumberland. (The Scotch *r* is a lingual trill.) **b.** Hence, *loosely*, a rough or dialectal utterance 1849. **2.** [= BIRR 3.] Whirr 1818.

1. Along the line of the Cheviots, the Scotch *r* has driven the *burr* a few miles back J. A. H. MURRAY. b. Betrayed by his Galilæan b. FARRAR. 2. The b. of working wheels and cranks 1860.

‖**Burr, bur,** *sb.*[7] 1813. [Hind.] The Banyan-tree (*Ficus indica*); also *attrib.*

Burr, *v.* 1798. [f. BURR *sb.*[6]] *intr.* To pronounce a strong uvular *r*, as is done in Northumberland. Also, *loosely*, to speak with a rough articulation; to utter the syllable *burr* or the like. **2.** To pronounce (*r*) with a burr (or, *loosely*, with a trill) 1868. **3.** *intr.* To make a whirring noise (*mod.*).

Burras-pipe. ? *Obs.* 1676. [f. *burras*, obs. f. BORAX.] A copper box with a spout, having teeth like a saw; used orig. by goldsmiths; occas. also used by surgeons for the application of corrosives by inspersion.

†**Burratine.** [ad. It. *burattino.*] A puppet. B. JONS.

†**Burree·.** 1719. [a. F. *beurré* (lit. 'buttered').] A pear, called also the Butter Pear, from its soft, delicious, melting pulp.

Burrel, app. misprint for BURREE. (Dicts.)

†**Burrel-fly.** 1678. [?] The gadfly.

Burrel-shot. 1706. Case-shot. (Dicts.)

‖**Burro** (bu·ro). [Sp.] A donkey. SOUTHEY.

Burrock (bɒ·rɒ̆k). 1701. [ad. mod.L. *burrochium*, ad. OF. *burroiche*; see Littré. (Orig. a Dict. wd.)] A small wear or dam in a river where weels are laid for the taking of fish.

Burrow (bɒ·ro[u]), *sb.*[1] ME. [? deriv. of **burg-*, ablaut-stem of OTeut. **bergan* to shelter. See also BERRY *sb.*[3]] **1.** A hole or excavation made in the ground for a dwelling-place by rabbits, foxes, etc. †**b.** A burrowing –1662. **2.** *transf.* and *fig.* A small hole-like dwelling-place, or place of retreat; a hole 1650.

1. Foxis han dichis, or borowis WYCLIF *Matt.* viii. 20. 2. The chief advantage of London is, that a man is always so near his b. BOSWELL *Johnson.*

Bu·rrow, *sb.*[2] *dial.* or *techn.* [repr. (esp. in Cornwall) of OE. *beorg* hill; see BARROW *sb.*[1] and BERRY *sb.*[2]] A heap or mound; earlier, a hillock; now, *esp.* a heap of mine refuse, or of burnt sods. See BEAT *sb.*[3]

Bu·rrow, *sb.*[3] *dial.* 1577. [:—OE. *beorg*, ME. *bergh.*] Shelter.

Enclosed burrowes where their legions accustomed.. to winter 1577.

†**Bu·rrow,** *sb.*[4] 1634. Var. of BOROUGH, BURGH –1650.

†**Bu·rrow,** *sb.*[5] 1499. Var. of BURR *sb.*[1], BROUGH –1656.

Burrow (bɒ·ro[u]), *v.* 1602. [f. BURROW *sb.*[1]] **1.** *intr.* To make a burrow, *esp.* as a hiding- or dwelling-place 1771. **b.** *fig.* To lodge as in a burrow, hide oneself 1614. **c.** *fig.* To bore under the surface 1804. **2.** *refl.* with *pass. pple.* To hide away in, or as in, a burrow 1602. **3.** *trans.* To excavate 1831.

1. b. To b. in mean lodgings MARRYAT. c. Each local body has..to b. its own way GLADSTONE. Hence **Bu·rrower. Burrowing owl,** an American owl (*Noctua cunicularia*) dwelling in burrows.

Burrow-duck. 1678. [f. BURROW *sb.*[1] The bird makes its nest in burrows.] The Sheldrake or Bergander, *Anas tadorna.*

Burrows-town (bɒ·rəstaun). *Sc.* ME. = BOROUGH-TOWN. (Cf. *Borrowston-ness* or *Bo'ness*). Also *attrib.*

Bu·rr-pump, bu·r-pump. 1627. [f. BUR

or BURR *sb.*[1]] *Naut.* A bilge-pump with the piston so made as not to require a valve.

Burr-stone (bɒ̄·ɹ₁stōᵘn). Also **buhr-, burrh-, bur-.** 1690. [f. BURR *sb.*[5]] A siliceous rock of coarse cellular texture, used for mill-stones; a piece of this rock.

Bu·rry, *a.* 1450. [f. BUR *sb.* + -Y[1].] **a.** Full of burs. **b.** Rough, prickly.

‖**Bursa** (bɒ̄·ɹsă). Pl. **bursæ.** 1803. [med.L., a. Gr. βύρσα.] **1.** *Phys.* (more fully *b. mucosa*): A synovial sac interposed between muscles, tendons, or skin, and bony prominences, to lessen friction. **2.** In Germany: A house inhabited by students, under the supervision of a Graduate in Arts 1852. Hence **Bu·rsal** *a.* of or pertaining to a b.; also, fiscal. **Bursa·logy** (better, **Burso·logy**), the doctrine of the *bursæ mucosæ*.

Bursar (bɒ̄·ɹsăɹ). [ad. med.L. *bursarius*, f. BURSA; cf. F. *boursier*.] **1.** A treasurer, *esp.* of a college 1587. **2.** In Scotland: A student who holds a bursary, an exhibitioner 1567. **Bursa·rial** *a.* belonging to a b. or a bursary. **Bu·rsarship,** the office of a b.; also = BURSARY 3.

Bursary (bɒ̄·ɹsări). 1538. [ad. med.L. *bursarius, bursaria*; see prec.] †**1.** ? = BURSAR 1. **2.** A treasury; the bursar's room in a college, etc. 1585. **3.** In Scotland, an exhibition at a school or university 1733; in England, a scholarship enabling a pupil at an elementary school to proceed to a secondary school.

‖**Bursch** (burʃ). Pl. **burschen.** 1830. [Ger. :—MHG. *burse*, a. L. *bursa* = BURSA 2.] A student in a German university.

Burse (bɒ̄ɹs). 1553. [a. F. *bourse* :—med.L. *bursa*, a. Gr. βύρσα hide.] **1.** A purse 1570. †**2.** A purse-like sac. HOLLAND. †**3.** A meeting-place of merchants for transaction of business; an Exchange. [So called at Bruges, where the name arose, from the sign of a purse, or three purses, on the front of the house where the merchants met.] -1732. †**b.** *The B.*: (*spec.*) the Royal Exchange, built by Sir Thomas Gresham in 1566, which contained shops. -1720. †**4.** *Sc.* A fund or foundation to provide bursaries -1753. **5.** = BURSARY 3.

3. b. She says, she went to the b. for patterns 1611. Hence **Bu·rsiform** *a.* purse-shaped.

Bursitis (bɒɹsəi·tis). [See -ITIS.] *Med.* Inflammation of a bursa.

Burst (bɒ̄ɹst), *v.* Pa. t. and pple. **burst.** [Com. Teut. str. vb.: OE. *berstan* :—OTeut. **brestan*, ? from **brek-st-an*, deriv. (intensive) of *brek-an* to BREAK[2]. The form *burst*, superseding *brast* (for all the parts), began to prevail about the end of the 16th c. For other forms see N.E.D.] **I.** *intr.* †**1.** To break suddenly, snap, crack -1803. **2.** To break suddenly when in a state of tension or expansion, to fly asunder or in pieces. Also *fig.*; now often colloq. with *up*. ME. **3.** *hyperbolically*, To be exuberantly full. Also with *out*. 1563. **b.** Of persons: To be unable to contain oneself. Const. *with*; also with *inf.* 1633. Also †*fig.* of the heart ME. **4.** Of a door. Now usu. *to b. open*: to fly open suddenly 1596.

2. Thus drinke we..tyll we b. 1562. And now a bubble b., and now a World POPE. **3.** Thy presses shall b. out with new wine *Prov.* iii. 10. **b.** Ready to b. with..indignation STEELE.

II. *intr. fig.* (With advb. extension.) To break forth into sudden action, activity, or manifestation of an inward force or feeling. Usu. with *out, forth*.

She burst out in tears ADDISON. So *To b. into tears, out laughing, into song speech*, etc.

III. *trans.* (causative). Not in OE. **1.** To break, snap, shatter suddenly. *Obs.* in general sense. ME. **2.** To disrupt, shatter in pieces ME.; to rupture 1712. **3.** To cause (the body) to swell till it bursts; often *refl.* 1530. **4.** *hyperbolically*, To fill to overflowing 1697.

2. Yᵉ new wyne barsteth yᵉ vessels and runneth out COVERDALE *Luke* v. 37. To b. one's sides ARBUTHNOT. Phr. *To b. a blood-vessel*: to cause its rupture by exertion, etc., or simply to suffer the rupture of a vessel.

IV. *intr.* (These uses express more strongly than those of BREAK, branch VII, the notion of sudden violence.) **1.** To issue forth suddenly and copiously by breaking an enclosure or the like. Usu. with an *adv.* ME. Also *transf.* and *fig.* **2.** To rush violently and suddenly *over* ME. **3.** To force a passage impetuously *through* ME. **4.** To break forcibly *into*, come suddenly and impetuously *into*; also with adv. *in*. So *to b. up* (from below). 1563.

1. Blude brist out at voundis vyde BARBOUR. *transf.* The teeres brast out of hir eyghen tuo CHAUCER. *fig.* Defections in Ireland..in the end brast out into open rebellion 1603. **3.** Times when a thankful heart bursts through all forms of prayer NEWMAN. **4.** The first that ever burst Into that silent sea COLERIDGE.

Hence **Burst** *ppl.a.*; also **brast** (*arch.*). **Bu·rsted** *ppl. a.* (now *dial.*). **Bu·rsten** *ppl. a.* (occ. used attrib.). **Bu·rsting charge,** the charge of powder required for bursting a shell or case-shot.

Burst (bɒ̄ɹst), *sb.* [repr. OE. *byrst* (*berst*). Re-formed in 16th c.] †**1.** Damage, harm; loss -ME. **2.** An act of bursting; the result of this act 1611. **3.** A sudden and violent issuing forth 1610. **b.** A sudden opening on the view 1798. **4.** An explosion, outbreak, breaking forth 1649. **5.** A great and sudden manifestation of activity; a spurt 1862. **b.** *Horsemanship*. A hard run 1810. **6.** *colloq.* A 'spree'. Also a big feed. 1881.

2. When beech-buds were near the b. G. MEREDITH. **3.** A b. of flame (*mod.*). A hollow b. of bellowing Like Buls *Temp.* II. i. 311. **b.** A fine b. of country JANE AUSTEN. **4.** Premature bursts [of shrapnel] 1870. A b. of ill humour THIRLWALL. **5.** The b. of creative activity in our literature M. ARNOLD.

†**Burst-cow.** 1646. [f. BURST *v.*] = *burn-cow*, BUPRESTIS, q. v. -1706.

Burster (bɒ̄·ɹstəɹ). 1611. [f. as prec. + -ER[1].] **1.** He who, or that which, bursts. **2.** In *Australia*: A violent southerly gale 1879.

Burthen, etc.; see BURDEN.

Burton (bɒ̄·ɹt'n). Also **barton.** 1704. A small tackle consisting of two or three blocks or pulleys used to set up or tighten rigging, or to shift heavy bodies.

†**Bu·ry,** *sb.* OE. [Orig. dative of *burh*; see BOROUGH.] A manor-house, or large farm. It survives in many local names. -1656.

Bury (be·ri), *v.* [OE. *byrgan* wk. v. :—WGer. **burgjan*, app. f. *burg-* ablaut-stem of OTeut. **berg-an* str. v. to protect; see BERGH.] **1.** To deposit in the ground, in a tomb; to inter. Hence to commit to the sea, with funeral rites. Also *absol.* Also *fig.* **2.** To put under ground; *esp.* in sign of final abandonment or abrogation 1535. **b.** *fig.* To consign to oblivion 1593. **c.** To consign to a position of obscurity, or inaction; often *refl.* and *pass.* 1711. **3.** *gen.* To cover up with earth or other material ME. **b.** Of things: To cover over out of sight 1737. **4.** To plunge deep *in*, so as to hide 1601. Also *fig.* **5.** *pass.* To be profoundly absorbed *in* ME.

1. Let us b. the Great Duke TENNYSON. *To have buried* (one's relatives) = to have lost them by death. *fig.* He would b. you under a mountain of words JOWETT. **2.** *To b. the hatchet*: to put away strife, as the Red Indians b. a tomahawk on the conclusion of peace. **b.** Giue me a bowl of wine, In this I b. all vnkindnesse Cassius *Jul. C.* IV. iii. 159. **c.** Buried in the country JOHNSON. **3.** I..buried 3000 pieces of gold LANE. **4.** B. your steel in the bosoms of Gath BYRON. Hence **Bu·ried** *ppl. a.* **Bu·rier,** one who buries; †a grave-digger. **Bu·rying** *vbl. sb.* the action of the vb.; *concr.* a funeral (*Obs.* or *dial.*); *ppl. a.* as in **b. beetle, -sylph,** a clavicorn beetle, which excavates the ground beneath dead moles, mice, etc., so as to b. them as a nidus for its larvæ.

Bu·rying-ground. 1711. BURIAL-GROUND.

Bu·rying-place. ME. A place of burial, a tomb; now. usu. = prec.

Bus, 'bus (bɒs), *sb.* Occ. **buss.** 1832. Abbrev. of OMNIBUS; also *colloq.* an aeroplane, motor car. Hence **Bus** *v.* in *to b. it*: To go by b.

Bus, *v.* (*3rd sing.*) *n. dial. Pa. t.* **bud**(e. ME. [Contr. f. *behoves, behoved*, chiefly used impers.] †**1.** (It) behoves -1500. **2.** *mod. Sc. Pa. t.* also as *pres.* with subject: Must, ought.

Busby (bɒ·zbi). 1764. [?] †**1.** A large bushy wig -1882. **2.** A tall fur cap, with or without a plume, having a bag hanging out of the top, on the right side; worn by hussars, artillerymen, and engineers; hence, one who wears a busby. Also *b.-bag*.

Buscarl. *Hist.* 1678. Modernized f. 11th c. *butsecarl*, a. ON. *buzukarl* 'seaman, sailor, mariner'. Cf. BUSS *sb.*[1]

Bush (buʃ), *sb.*[1] [ME. *busk*, a. ON. *busk-r*, ad. Rom. *bosco* or late L. *boscum, boscus*, of unkn. origin. Cf. BOSCAGE, BOSK. *Busk* still occurs in n. dial.] **1.** A shrub, *esp.* one with close branches arising from or near the ground; a small clump of shrubs. **2.** In n. dialects extended to *heather, nettles, ferns, rushes*, etc. 1529. †**3.** *collectively*. A thicket; bushy ground. (Now only as in 8.) -1639. †**4.** = AM-BUSH, q. v. -1655. **5.** A branch or bunch of ivy (perh. as sacred to Bacchus) hung up as a vintner's sign; *hence*, the sign-board of a tavern 1532. Hence, a tavern 1625. †**6.** *transf.* Anything resembling a bush -1648. †**7.** A bushy tail, *esp.* of a fox. See BRUSH *sb.*[2] -1610. **8.** (Prob. ad. Du. *bosch*.) Woodland; applied to the uncleared or untilled districts in the British Colonies, even though not wooded; and hence to the *country* as opp. to the *towns* 1780. Hence, *to take to the b.* 1837.

1. The undergrowth Of shrubs and tangling bushes MILT. *P. L.* IV. 176. **2.** Driven..to tak the heather-b. for a bield SCOTT. **4.** *Beggar's-b.*: see BEGGAR. **5.** Good wine needs no b. *A. Y. L.* Epil. **6.** Trymme my busshe, barber PALSGR. **8.** The black man loves the b. CARLYLE. Cheaper in Toronto than away in the b. GEIKIE.

Phr. *To beat* (*go*, etc.) *about the b.*: to go indirectly towards an object.

Comb.: **b. antelope,** ?=*bush-buck*; **b. basil,** *Ocymum minimum*; **-bean** (*U.S.*), the Kidney-bean (*Phaseolus vulgaris*); **-buck,** a small African antelope; **-cat,** the Serval; **-creepers,** tropical birds belonging to the family of the Warblers; **-draining,** the draining of land by trenches filled with brushwood; **-goat** = *bush-buck*; **-hog,** a wild pig of S. Africa, the *boschvaark*; **-hook,** a bill-hook (*U.S.*); **-lawyer,** the New Zealand bramble (*Rubus australis*); **-master,** a venomous S. American snake; **-road,** a road through the B.; **-shrike,** Eng. name of the *Thamnophilinæ*; **-syrup,** a syrup obtained from the flowers of *Protea mellifera* in Cape Colony; **-track** = *bush-road*; †**-tree,** the Box; **b. vetch,** *Vicia sepium*; **-wood,** underwood. Hence **Bu·shless** *a.*

Bush (buʃ), *sb.*[2] 1566. [app. a. MDu. *busse* BOX, bush of a wheel.] The metal lining of the axle-hole of a wheel; hence, the case in which the journal of a shaft revolves. Cf. BOX *sb.*[2] **b.** A cylindrical metal lining of an orifice; a perforated plug, cylinder, or disk. *Comb.* **b.-metal,** an alloy of copper and tin used for journals.

Bush (buʃ), *v.*[1] ME. [f. BUSH *sb.*[1]] †**1.** *trans.* To set in a bush, to place in ambush; *intr.* (for *refl.*) to hide in a bush, lie in ambush. (Cf. BUSH *sb.*[1] 4.) -1623. **2.** To protect or support with bushes. Also *absol.* 1647. **3.** To bush-harrow (ground, etc.) 1787. **4.** *intr.* To grow thick like a bush 1562. Also *transf.*

2. As for netting by night, b. your fields closely 1860. **4.** So thick the Roses bushing round About her glowd MILT. *P. L.* IX. 426.

Bush, *v.*[2] Now *dial.* ME. [?] *intr.* To butt; to push.

Bush (buʃ), *v.*[3] 1566. [f. BUSH *sb.*[2]] To furnish with a bush; to line (an orifice) with metal.

†**Bush,** *v.*[4] 1659. [a. F. *boucher*; see Littré.] To stop an opening -1693.

Bushel (bu·ʃĕl), *sb.*[1] [ME. *boyschel*, a. OF. *boissiel* (mod. *boisseau*), dim. of *boiste* box (Diez).] **1.** A measure of capacity containing 4 pecks or 8 gallons. The *imperial bushel*, used in Gt. Britain, contains 2218·19 cubic inches; the *Winchester bushel*, still used in U. S. and Canada, 2150·4 cubic inches. **b.** *loosely*. A large quantity or number ME. **2.** A vessel used as a bushel measure ME. Also *fig.* (with ref. to Matt. v. 15). 1557.

1. b. Bushels of girls 1873. **2.** Feet..as broad as a b. TOPSELL. *fig.* Trouth vnder bushell is faine to crepe 1557. Hence **Bu·shelful.**

Bushel, *sb.*[2] ME. [cf. BUSH *sb.*[2]] The bush of a wheel. ? *Obs.*

Bushel (bu·ʃĕl), *v. rare.* 1650. [f. BUSHEL *sb.*[1]] To hide under a bushel. Also *fig.*

Bush-fighter (bu·ʃfəi:təɹ). 1760. One accustomed to fight in the bush. So **Bu·sh-fi:ghting** *vbl. sb.* fighting in the bush. Also *fig.*

Bu·sh-hammer. *U.S.* 1884. [prob. ad. Ger. *boss-hammer*, f. *bossen* to beat.] A mason's large breaking hammer, often having square ends cut into pyramidal points.

Bush-harrow (bu·ʃhæ:rou), *sb.* 1770. A heavy frame with bars in which bushes are interwoven underneath, used for harrowing grass land or bushing in seed. Hence **Bu·sh-ha:rrow** *v.* to use the bush-harrow upon.

Bushman (bu·ʃmăn). 1785. [f. BUSH *sb.*[1] 8, app. after Du. *boschjesman*, as used in S. Africa.] **1.** A tribe of aborigines near the Cape of Good

Hope. 2. A dweller or traveller in the Australian bush 1852.

1. Stunted representatives of humanity.. under the name of Bushmen 1845. Hence **Bu·shmanship**, bush-farming.

Bushment (bu·ʃmĕnt). ME. [In senses 1–3, aphet. f. ABUSHMENT, AMBUSHMENT, q.v. In sense 4, cf. BUSH *sb.*[1]] 1. =AMBUSHMENT 1 (*arch.*). †2. =AMBUSHMENT 2. –1550. †3. =AMBUSHMENT 3.–1549. 4. A mass of bushes (? *Obs.*) 1586.

Bush-ranger (bu·ʃrēⁱndʒəɹ). 1817. [f. BUSH [1] 9+RANGER.] An escaped convict living in the bush, and subsisting by robbery with violence. So **Bu·sh-ra·nging** *vbl. sb.* the practice of the b.; var. -**ra·ngering.**

Bush-rope (bu·ʃrōᵘp). 1814. [f. as prec.] A name of species of *Cissus* or Wild Vine.

Bushwhacker (bu·ʃhwæ·kəɹ). *U.S.* 1809. [f. BUSH *sb.*[1]+WHACKER.] *lit.* One who beats bushes; hence 1. A backwoodsman, a bush-ranger. 2. In the American Civil War, irregular combatants who took to the woods, and were variously regarded as patriot guerrillas, or as banditti 1862. 3. An implement used to cut away brushwood 1858.

3. A graduate of the plough..and the b. EMERSON. Hence **Bu·shwhack** *v.* to act as a b. **Bu·shwha·cking** *vbl. sb.* making one's way through bushes; *esp.* the pulling of a boat by means of the bushes along the margin of a stream; bush-fighting.

Bushy (bu·ʃi), *a.* ME. [f. BUSH *sb.*[1]+-Y.] 1. Abounding in bushes; overgrown with bush. 2. Growing thick like a bush 1611. †3. Dwelling among the bushes (*rare*). T. HOWELL.

2. Each odorous bushie shrub MILT. *P. L.* IV. 696. 3. The bushie birdes among T. HOWELL. Hence **Bu·shily** *adv.* **Bu·shiness.**

Busied (bi·zid), *ppl. a.* 1611. [f. BUSY *v.*+-ED.] Attentively occupied, engaged. (The attrib. use is rare.)

The b. monk was tempted but with one Devil 1669.

Busily (bi·zili), *adv.* ME. [f. BUSY *a.*+-LY[2].] In a BUSY manner.

He shoulde haue resysted..more besyly 1508. Byrdes besely syngynge 1513.

Business (bi·znĕs). [OE. (North.) *bisignis*, f. BUSY *a.*, or stem of BUSY *v.* Shortened to a disyllable, since it ceased to be a noun of state.] †1. The state of being busily engaged in anything; diligence –1713. †2. Activity, briskness –1674. †3. Mischievous or impertinent activity –1580. †4. Earnestness, importunity –1543. †5. Anxiety; uneasiness. (The earliest sense.) –1577. †6. Care, attention –1540. †7. Trouble; ado –1693. †8. Diligent labour –1509. 9. That about which one is busy; function, occupation ME. b. That with which one is concerned at the time; often *spec.* the errand on which one comes 1596. 10. Stated occupation, profession, or trade 1477. †b. Active life. See also *Man of b.* –1779. 11. *gen.* Occupation; *esp.* serious occupation, work. Also with *a* and *pl.* ME. 12. A piece of work, a job. (The pl. is now unusual.) 1557. b. *ellipt.* A difficult matter 1843. 13. A matter that concerns a particular person or thing; const. *of*, or *gen. case.* 1525. b. Concern 1759. c. *colloq.* A matter with which one has the right to meddle. Also, justifying motive or right of interference, 'anything to do' (*with*). Const. usu. *with*, or infin. 1690. †14. A subject of consideration or discussion; the subject of a book, etc. –1699. 15. *vaguely*, An affair, concern, matter. (Now often indicating contempt or impatience, *esp.* when preceded by a sb. used attrib.) 1605. 16. Dealings, intercourse (*with*). (*arch.*) 17. *Theat.* Action as opp. to dialogue 1671. 18. *spec.* (from 13 and 19): Trade, commercial transactions or engagements 1727. 19. A commercial enterprise as a going concern (*mod.*). Also in *comb.*

2. The businesse of his [a dog's] taile 1616. 6. Haue thou bisynesse [*curam habe*] of a good name WYCLIF *Ecclus.* xli. 15. 7. Ful mychell besynesse had he or þat he myght his lady wynne CHAUCER. 9. Because a Thing is every Body's B., it is no Body's B. STEELE. b. I asked him his b. (*mod.*). 10. They make Fooling their B. and their Livelihood 1694. 11. The b. of the day is done SOUTHEY. Trade..one of the great businesses of life DE FOE. The b. of a butcher 1878. 12. A b. of moment BIBLE *Pref.* 13. b. My b. is with man JOHNSON. c. That is no b. of ours KINGSLEY. 15. This boat b. SOUTHEY. 18. To do a stroke of b. BURTON, a brisk b. 1884.

Phrases. a. (sense 11) *To mean b.*: to be in earnest (*colloq.*). *On b.*: with an errand or purpose relating to b. *A person's b.*: work to be done on his behalf. b. (sense 13) *To mind one's own b.*: to refrain from meddling with what does not concern one. Now *colloq.* *To go about one's b.*: to go away. So *To send about one's b.*: to send packing. c. *Man of b.* †1. One engaged in public affairs. 2. One engaged in mercantile transactions. 3. A man skilled in business. 4. An attorney. Hence **Bu·siness-like** *a.*

Busk (bɒsk), *sb.* 1592. [a. F. *busc*, ? a doublet of F. *bois* (Scheler); or ? cogn. w. It. *busto* (Littré).] A strip of wood, whalebone, steel, etc., passed down the front of a corset, to stiffen and support it. Applied dial. to the whole corset.

Her bodie pent with buske WARNER.

Busk, *v.*[1] Now *Sc.* and *n. dial.* ME. [Taken as a. ON. *búa-sk*, refl. of *búa* to prepare; cf. *bask.*] 1. *intr.* (and *refl.*) To prepare oneself; *spec.* to dress. 2. To set out; to hie, hurry ME. 3. *trans.* To prepare; to set in order, fit out. Still in *Sc.* ME. 4. To dress. Still in *Sc.* ME. Also *fig.*

3. Time to b. thy body-clothes SCOTT. 4. Hedges, busk'd in bravery CAMPBELL.

Busk, *v.*[2] 1665. [app. a. obs. F. *busquer*, ad. It. *buscare*, 'to filch, to prowl'; ? orig. 'to beat a wood', f. *bosco* wood.] *Naut.* 1. *intr.* Of a ship: To beat about; to tack. b. To cruise as a pirate. [Perh. the orig. sense.] 1867. 2. *fig.* To go about seeking *for*, to seek *after* 1734.

Busk, *v.*[3] 1567. [? as prec.] *intr.* Of fowls: To shift about restlessly or uneasily.

†**Bu·sket.** *rare.* 1579. [f. *busk*, var. of BUSH *sb.*[1], or ad. F. *bosquet.*] 1. Little bushes of hawthorn. 2. =BOSKET 1803.

Buskin (bɒ·skin). 1503. [perh. ad. OF. *bouzequin*, rel. to Sp. *borcegut.*] 1. A covering for the foot or leg reaching to the calf, or to the knee; a half-boot. 2. *spec.* The high thick-soled boot (*cothurnus*) worn in Athenian tragedy; often opp. to the 'sock' (*soccus*) or low shoe worn in comedy 1570. b. Hence *fig.* and *transf.* The tragic vein; tragedy 1579. Also *attrib.*

1. The royal privilege of red shoes or buskins GIBBON. 2. He..knew all niceties of the sock and b. BYRON. Hence **Bu·skined** *ppl. a.* shod with buskins; concerned with or belonging to tragedy; elevated.

†**Bu·skle**, *v.* 1535. A freq. of BUSK –1642.

Busky (bɒ·ski), *a.* 1570. [f. *busk*, var. of BUSH *sb.*[1]+-Y.] Bosky, bushy.

Yon b. hill 1 *Hen. IV*, v. i. 2.

Buss (bɒs), *sb.*[1] ME. [In sense 1, prob. from OF. *busse*, of unkn. etym.] 1. A vessel of burden. (*Hist.*) 2. *spec.* A two- or three-masted vessel of various sizes, used esp. in the Dutch herring-fishery 1471. Also *attrib.*

Buss (bɒs), *sb.*[2] *arch.* and *dial.* 1570. [etym. obscure.] A kiss; kissing.

Buss (bɒs), *v. arch.* and *dial.* 1571. [Conn. w. prec.] 1. *trans.* To kiss. Also *fig.* and *absol.*

We busse our wantons, but our wives we kisse HERRICK.

‖**Bussu.** 1858. [S. American.] A palm (*Manicaria saccifera*), the spathes of which supply a coarse strong cloth. Hence *b. palm, cloth.*

Bust (bɒst), *sb.*[1] 1653. [a. F. *buste*, ad. It. *busto*, primarily 'trunk of the body', of unkn. origin.] 1. A piece of sculpture representing the head, shoulders, and breast of a person. Cf. BUSTO. 1691. 2. The upper front part of the human body; the bosom (*esp.* of a woman) 1727. Also †*transf.* Also *attrib.*

1. Three stone busts of Hermes THIRLWALL. Storied urn or animated b. GRAY.

Bust, *sb.*[2]; see BUSTE.

Bust (bɒst). 1860. Dial. or vulgar pronunc. of BURST *sb.* and *v.*; often *joc.*, *esp.* in U.S. *spec.* 'a frolic, a spree' (Bartlett); cf. BURST *sb.* 6.

Bustard (bɒ·stăɹd). 1460. [In form perh. a fusion of OF. *bistarde* and *oustarde*, both from L. *avis tarda.* The application of the epithet is not understood, as the bird is swift on foot, and capable of speed on the wing.] 1. A genus of birds (*Otis*) showing affinities both to the *Cursores* and *Grallatores.* The Great B. (*Otis tarda*) is the largest European bird. 2. Applied in America to the Canada Goose, *Bernicla Canadensis.* 3. Local var. BUZZARD, a large moth 1886.

1. The b...Forced hard against the wind a thick unwieldy flight WORDSW.

†**Bust(e.** ME. var. of BOIST *sb.* –1566.

Buster (bɒ·stəɹ). 1839. 1. Vulgar f. BURSTER. Hence 2. *slang.* (*U.S.*) a. Something that takes one's breath away. b. A roistering blade. c. A frolic; a spree. 1850.

†**Bu·stian.** 1463. [?] A foreign cotton fabric –1725.

Bustle (bɒ·s'l), *sb.*[1] 1622. [f. BUSTLE *v.*[1]] 1. Activity with excitement, noise, and commotion; stir, ado 1634. Also *transf.* 2. The commotion of conflict; *concr.* a conflict, scuffle (*arch.*) 1622. 3. *Thieves' cant.* Money 1812.

1. He..could be very busy without b. BYRON. 2. Divers were killed in the b. LUTTRELL.

Bu·stle, *sb.*[2] 1788. [Perh. a use of prec.] A pad, or wire framework, worn beneath the skirt of a woman's dress, to expand it behind; a dress-improver.

A waist like a wasp, a magnificent b., and petticoats ..puffed out round the bottom MISS MITFORD.

Bustle (bɒ·s'l), *v.* [ME. *bustelen* is perh. echoic. The mod. vb. (*c* 1560) may be a var. of BUSKLE.] †1. *intr.* ? =BLUSTER *v.* 1 (*rare*). ME. only. 2. *intr.* To be fussily or noisily active 1580. †3. *intr.* To struggle, scuffle, contend –1712. 4. *trans.* and *refl.* To bestir, rouse: also with *up.* Now *rare.* 1579. 5. *trans.* (and *refl.*) To cause to move precipitately; to hurry in a fussy manner 1563.

2. We b. and God works KINGSLEY. 5. To b. (people) out of the house KINGSLEY. Hence **Bu·stler**, one who displays fussy activity. **Bu·stlingly** *adv.*

†**Bu·sto.** Pl. -**os** (-**oes**, -**o's**). 1662. = BUST *sb.*[1] 1. –1863.

†**Bu·sy**, *sb.* [OE. *bisgu, bysgu*, f. *bisig* BUSY.] Occupation; state of being occupied –ME.

Busy (bi·zi), *a.* [OE. *bisig*, later *bysig.* The form *busi* (with *ü*=OE. *y*) is not found (exc. in Layamon) bef. the 15th c.] 1. Occupied with constant attention; actively engaged. (Rare in attrib. use.). 2. Said of things; *fig.* of passions, etc. OE. 3. Constantly occupied or in motion ME. 4. In bad sense: Active in what does not concern one; prying; meddlesome, officious; restless. Cf. BUSYBODY. ME. †5. Solicitous, anxious; careful –1483. 6. Active 1548. †7. Elaborate; 'curious' –1615. 8. Full of stir 1697. 9. That indicates business 1632.

1. B. as a moth over some rotten archive LAMB. 2. For many days rumour was b. KINGLAKE. 3. Curiosity, the busiest passion of the idle SCOTT. 4. A b. and inquisitorial tyranny COLERIDGE. 8. The b. world of men MORLEY. 9. The b. hum of men MILT. *Alleg.* 118. Also as *sb.* (*slang*) a detective 1904.

Busy (bi·zi), *v.* [OE. *bisgian, bysgian*, f. *bisig* BUSY *a.*] 1. *trans.* To make, or keep busy. b. *refl.* (The usual construction.) OE. †2. To trouble the body (only in OE.) or mind; to afflict, worry OE. 3. *intr.* (? for *refl.*) To occupy oneself, take trouble (now *rare*) ME.

1. Thou..busiest all thy wits about it 1587. b. B. thee for good or ill BROWNING.

Busybody (bi·zibǫ·di). 1526. [f. BUSY *a.* 4+ BODY.] An officious person; one who meddles in other people's affairs.

Vaine pratling busie bodies 1570.

Busyness (bi·zinĕs). *rare.* 1868. [f. BUSY *a.*+-NESS.] =BUSINESS I.

But (bɒt), *prep.*, *conj.*, *adv.* [The OE. adv. and prep. *bé-utan, bútan, búta* 'on the outside', in ME. *bouten, boute* BOUT, as adv. and prep., phonetically weakened to *būten, būte, but*, as a conjunction. The prep. and the conj. are not distinctly separable. (See Latham, *Eng. Lang.* ed. 1850, p. 483.) In colloq. use *me, us*, etc. are more common after *but* than *I, we*, etc. and equally correct.]

A. *prep.* 1. Outside of. (OE. and mod.Sc.) 2. Leaving out, barring, with the exception of, except, save. Clearly a prep. in OE.

B. *adv.* 1. Without, outside 1450. b. as *adj.* Outer 1619. c. as *sb.* The outer room of a two-roomed house 1724. 2. In sense: Only.

1. Gae b., and wait (*mod. Sc.*). b. The b. end of a house 1619. c. A cosy b., and a canty ben RAMSAY.

C. *conj.* 1. In a simple sentence; introducing a word or a phrase (rarely a clause): Without, with the exception of, except, save OE. b. *elliptically*: Any but, aught but, anything else than, other than, otherwise than. (Often after *ever, never.*) 1523. 2. In a complex sentence; introducing the subordinate clause. a. With general sense 'except that'; the full expression being *but that*, often reduced to *but* OE. **b.** With general sense 'if not' OE. **c.** With general sense 'that not', L. *quin.* After negative and questioning constructions. ME. **3.** In a compound sentence, connecting the two coordinate members; or introducing an independent sentence connected in sense, though not in form, with the preceding. **a.** On the contrary. = Ger. *sondern.* OE. **b.** Nevertheless, yet, however. = Ger. *aber.* 1535. **c.** After *not only*, *not merely* ME. **d.** However, on the other hand, moreover, yet. = Ger. *aber*, L. *autem.* ME.

1. I am one among a thousand; all of them wrong b. I. [Colloq. also, 'b. me.'] J. H. NEWMAN. Last b. one in the class (*mod.*). Phr. *B. now* = just now, only this moment. b. I should sinne To thinke b. Noblie of my Grandmother *Temp.* I. ii. 18. It can't b. be obvious to them ADDISON. 2. a. Nothing would serve him, b. he must imitate Alexander 1701. Phr. *B. that* = Except for the fact that. (Formerly with *that* occas. omitted.) ME. b. Beshrew me b. I loue her heartily *Merch. V.* II. vi. 52. It is odds b. you lose STEELE. c. Thinke not b. it dooeth brenne my heart LD. BERNERS. It can not be b. offences wyl come CRANMER *Luke* xvii. 1. Heauen defend, b. still I should stand so 1 *Hen. IV*, IV. iii. 38. Who doubted b. (more logically *that*) the catastrophe was over CARLYLE. Never doubt b. I'll go 1879. 3. a. He left not Faction, b. of That was left DRYDEN. b. Her face speaks a Vestal, b. her heart a Messalina STEELE. c. They not only tell lies, b. bad lies JOWETT. d. B. Iesus gave him no answer *John* xix. 9. 'Get money; honestly, if you can: b. get money!' *Mod.*

D. quasi-*sb.* [The adv. used *ellipt.*] See B. 1 c. **E.** quasi-*adj.* [The adv. used *attrib.*] See B. 1 b.

Phrases, etc. *B. and*: see AND. Now *Sc. B. for* = except for: see B. (sense 1). †*But for*: but because; see FOR. *But that*: see B. (sense 2). *But what* for *but that* is now *dial.* and *colloq.*

But, *sb.* 1571. The conj. *but*, used as a name for itself; *hence*, a verbal objection presented.

'Nay, but me no buts' SCOTT. Hence **But** *v.* (*arch.*) to say or use 'but'.

Butch, *v.* Now *dial.* 1785. [erron. back-formation from BUTCHER.] †*trans.* To cut up. *intr.* To follow the trade of a butcher.

Butcher (bu·tʃəɹ), *sb.* [ME. *bocher, boucher*, Anglo-Fr. f. OF. *bochier, bouchier* (mod. *boucher*), f. OF., Pr. *boc* BUCK *sb.*1 Thus *lit.* 'dealer in goat's flesh'; cf. It. *beccaio*, f. *becco.*] **1.** One whose trade it is to slaughter large tame animals for food; one who kills such animals and sells their flesh; now, occas., a tradesman who deals in meat. **b.** *fig.* A 'man of blood'; a brutal murderer 1529. †**2.** An executioner; also *attrib.* -1494. **3.** An artificial fly used by anglers for salmon 1867.

1. Itm payd to the Bochsar for a greyt serlyn xvj*d.* 1525. *fig.* To be b. of an innocent childe SHAKS.

Comb.: **b.-fly**, ? a kind of blow-fly; **butcher's bill**, a sarcastic term for the list of killed in a battle (occas. for the money cost of a war). Hence **Bu·tcherly** *a.* and *adv.*

Butcher (bu·tʃəɹ), *v.* 1562. [f. prec.] **1.** To slaughter in the manner of a butcher (*lit.* and *fig.*). **2.** To inflict torture upon 1642.

1. He, their sire, Butcher'd to make a Roman holiday BYRON. The text is not butchered by misprinting 1850. Hence **Bu·tcherer**, one who butchers.

Bu·tcher-bi·rd. 1668. [f. BUTCHER *sb.*] A name of species of shrike (*Laniadæ*); *Lanius excubitor, L. tertius, L. cinereus*, etc.

†**Bu·tcher-row.** 1581. [Cf. *Saddlers' Row*, etc.] A shambles, meat-market -1702.

Bu·tcher's broo·m. 1562. [Used by butchers for sweeping their shops.] Common name of *Ruscus aculeatus* (N.O. *Liliaceæ*, tribe *Asparageæ*), also called Knee Holly.

Bu·tcher's mea·t, bu·tcher-mea·t. 1632. Meat sold by butchers, as opp. to poultry, etc.

Butchery (bu·tʃəri), *sb.* ME. [a. F. *boucherie*; see BUTCHER *sb.*] **1.** A slaughter-house, shambles; a butcher's shop or stall; also *attrib.* (Now chiefly applied to those in public establishments.) Also *fig.* **2.** The trade of a butcher. Now only *attrib.*, as in *b. business.* 1449. †**3.** Butchers collectively -1525. **4.** Cruel and wanton slaughter. Also *fig.* 1561.

1. This house is but a butcherie: Abhorre it SHAKS. 4. Warres and Butcheries in France 1602.

†**Butin.** 1474. [a. F.; cf. ON. *býti* 'barter' (Littré). Cf. BOOTY.] Spoil, or prey, taken in common; booty -1646.

Butler (bʌ·tləɹ). ME. [a. AF. *butuiller* = OF. *bouteillier*:—med.L. *buticularius*, f. *buticula* BOTTLE *sb.*1] **1.** A servant who has charge of the wine-cellar and dispenses the liquor. Formerly also, one who hands round wine. Now usu. the head-servant of a household, who keeps the plate, etc. Also *fig.* **2.** An officer who originally had charge of the wine for the royal table; hence the title of an official of high rank only nominally connected with the supply of wine, etc. (Cf. MARSHALL, etc.) ME.

2. Sir Nicholas Burdel, Chiefe B. of Normandie, was slaine at Pontoise 1587. Hence **Bu·tlership.**

Butlerage (bʌ·tləɹėdʒ). 1491. [f. as prec. + -AGE.] **1.** A duty on imported wine paid to the king's butler; *prisage.* Now *Hist.* **2.** The office, dignity, or department, of a butler 1615.

Butlery (bʌ·tləri). [ME. *boteleryе*, a. F. *bouteillerie*; now prob. f. BUTLER.] A butler's pantry; a buttery.

Butment (bʌ·tmĕnt). 1624. [f. BUTT *sb.*2 + -MENT.] **1.** *Archit.* = ABUTMENT 3. **2.** An outstanding mass (of rock, etc.) 1865. **3.** A piece of ground abutting on a larger piece 1677.

1. *B. cheeks*: the two solid sides of a mortise.

Butt (bʌt), *sb.*1 ME. [cogn. w. Sw. *butta* turbot. See HALIBUT.] A name of various flat fish, as sole, fluke, plaice, turbot, etc.

Butt (bʌt), *sb.*2 ME. [com. Rom., late L. *butta, buttis* cask, wine-skin, of unkn. origin.] **1.** A cask for wine, ale, etc., holding from 108 to 140 gallons. Later, a measure of capacity = 2 hogsheads, *i. e.* usually in ale measure 108 gallons, in wine measure 126 gallons. **2.** A cask, barrel 1626.

1. Hastely drouned in a Butte of Malmesey MORE. 2. A water-butt 1823.

Butt (bʌt), *sb.*3 ? ME. [? Cf. ON. *butt-r* 'short'; Da., LG. *but*, Du. *bot*, thickset, stumpy; Sp., Pg. *boto* blunt. Also ON. *bút-r* 'log of wood' = sense 2, and 'catkin or bud' = sense 4. Fr. *bout* (OF. *bot, but*) does not mean 'thick end'.] **1.** The thicker end of anything, *e. g.* of a tool or weapon, a whip-handle, fishing-rod, gun, etc. 1470. **2.** The trunk of a tree, *esp.* the part just above the root 1601. **3.** A buttock. *dial.* and *colloq.* in *U. S.* 1450. **4.** The base of a leaf-stalk; the tip of a branch; also *Sc.* a catkin 1807. **5.** *Iron-work.* One of the blocks out of which iron anvils are formed 1831.

¶ See also BUTT *sb.*7, BUTT *sb.*11

Butt (bʌt), *sb.*4 ME. [a. F. *but* goal, perh. infl. in sense 1 by ABUT and BUT *v.*2] †**1.** A terminal point; a boundary mark, *esp.* in *butts and bounds*; a goal; often *fig.* (see BUTT *v.*2, quot.) -1726. **2.** A mark for archery practice; prop. an erection on which the target is set up. Hence a mound in front of which the targets are placed for artillery or rifle practice. ME. Also *transf.* and *fig.* †**3.** The length of the shooting-range -1696. **4.** An aim, object 1594. **5.** An object at which ridicule, scorn, or abuse is aimed; *absol.* a person habitually made the object of jokes 1616.

1. Heere is my journies end, heere is my b. *Oth.* v. ii. 267. 2. The arrow sticks in the B. unto which the marke is fastned REYNOLDS. 5. The b. and byword of liberalism GLADSTONE. *Comb.* †**b.-bolt**, a strong unbarbed arrow.

Butt (bʌt), *sb.*5 Now *dial.* 1693. [? a. F. *butte.* Cf. also BUTTE.] A hillock, mound.

Butt, *sb.*6 1450. [? = F. *bout*; or same as prec.] **1.** A ridge between two furrows of a ploughed field. **2.** Such a ridge when cut short by the irregular shape of the field. (? The orig. sense.) 1523. **3.** *dial.* A small piece of land disjoined from the adjacent lands 1699.

Butt (bʌt), *sb.*7 1627. [? a sense of BUTT *sb.*3] **1.** *Naut.* More fully **b.-end, -head**: The end of a plank or plate in a vessel's side which joins on to the end of the next; the plane of juncture, etc. **2.** *Coal-min.* 'A surface [of coal] exposed at right angles to the face' (Raymond).

Phrases, etc. *B. and b.*: with the b. ends together, but not overlaying each other. **B.-strap**, a strip of metal riveted over the joining of two plates in an iron ship. *Comb.*: **b.-hinge** (also *butt*), a hinge composed of two plates the edges of which meet without overlapping; **-joint**, in *Carpentry* (= *butting*-joint).

†**Butt**, *sb.*8 1598. [? f. BUTT *v.*1 4.] A promontory, as *The Butt of Lewis.*

Butt (bʌt), *sb.*9 1647. [f. BUTTE *v.*1] A push or thrust with the head or horns; also, a thrust in fencing (*rare*).

†**Butt**, *sb.*10 1598. [? a. F. *botte* bundle.] **1.** ? A bundle, pack -1705. **2.** *dial.* A hassock. Hence **b.-woman**, a pew-opener.

Butt (bʌt), *sb.*11 1661. [? a use of BUTT *sb.*3 1, or 3.] The thicker or hinder part of a hide or skin, as *calf-butts*, etc. the thick leather made from this; sole-leather. (Cf. BEND *sb.*2 3.)

Butt (bʌt), *sb.*12 *dial.* 1796. A short and rudely made cart.

Butt (bʌt), *v.*1 ME. [a. OF. *boter, buter* (mod. *bouter*); infl. in senses 3 and 4 by BUTT *v.*2] **1.** *intr.* To strike, thrust, shove (usu. with the head or horns); also *fig.* **2.** *trans.* To strike, *esp.* with the head or horns; to drive or push *away*, *out*, etc. thus 1590. **3.** To come or strike dead against 1875. **4.** *intr.* To run out, jut 1523. ¶**5.** With assoc. of BUTT *sb.*4 To aim (*trans.* and *intr.*) 1593. **6.** Used advb., *esp.* with the adv. *full*: Point-blank, violently ME.

1. *To butt in* (orig. *U.S.*), to intrude, meddle. 2. The beast with many horns butts me away *Cor.* IV. i. 2.

Butt (bʌt), *v.*2 1523. [Partly f. BUTT *sb.*4 1; partly aphet. f. ABUT.] †**1.** To fix or mark (*out*) the limits of lengthwise; to terminate; to limit, bound. Chiefly in the *passive.* -1727. †**2.** *intr.* = ABUT *v.* 2, 3. Also *fig.* -1798. †**3.** *To b. on, upon*: (of a line) to end in (a point); (of a road) to issue into. (Cf. F. *abouter à.*) Also *fig.* -1678. **4.** *intr.* chiefly *techn.*: To come with one end flat *against*, *on* 1670. **5.** *trans.* To place end *against* a surface; to join end to end 1785. ¶ See also BUTT *v.*1 3, 4.

1. Butting it at thends and bounding it at the sides WEST.

Butte (? bŭt, bʌt). *U.S.* 1838. [a. F. *butte*; cf. BUTT *sb.*5] In Western U.S.: An isolated hill or peak rising abruptly. var. **Bute.**

Butt-end (bʌ·t e·nd). 1580. [f. BUTT *sb.*3] **1.** = BUTT *sb.*3 (and now more used). **b.** *fig.* The fag end 1594. †**2.** = BUTT *sb.*3 2. -1760. **3.** *Naut.* = BUTT *sb.*7

Butter (bʌ·təɹ), *sb.*1 [OE. *butere* (in comb. *buttor-*); ad. L. *butyrum*, ad. Gr. βούτυρον, perh. of barbarous origin.] **1.** The fatty substance obtained from cream by churning. *fig.* Unctuous flattery. (Cf. BUTTER *v.*) *colloq.* 1823. **2.** *transf.* Any substance resembling butter in appearance or consistence, as **b. of almonds** = ALMOND-*b.*; **b. of cacao**, a substance obtained from the seeds of the cacao; so **b. of mace, shea b.** (see SHEA), and other *vegetable butters* 1440. **b.** *esp.* in *Chem.*, an old name of several anhydrous chlorides, as **b. of antimony, arsenic, bismuth, tin, zinc** 1641.

1. A grosse fat man.—As fat as B. SHAKS.

Phrases. (*To look*) *as if b. would not melt in one's mouth*: said contemptuously of persons of very demure appearance. *Clarified* or *run b.*: butter melted and potted for culinary use.

Comb.: †**b.-ale** = *buttered ale* (see ALE); **b. and eggs**, pop. name for flowers of two shades of yellow, *esp.* Toadflax (*Linaria vulgaris*), and varieties of *Narcissus*; **b.-back**, a kind of wild duck (*U.S.*); **-bird**, the Bobolink (*U. S.*); **-boat**, a vessel for serving melted b. in; also *fig.*; **-factor**, a tradesman who buys b. from farmers to sell wholesale; **-fish**, the (slimy) Spotted Gunnel; **-flip**, the Avocet (*local*); **-man**, one who makes or sells b.; also *Naut.* a schooner with a certain rig; **-scotch**, a kind of toffee, made of sugar and b.; **-tree**, name of *Bassia butyracea* and *B. Parkii*; **-weed**, a name for *Erigeron canadensis* and *Senecio lobatus*; **-weight**, formerly 18 or more ounces to the pound; *fig.* 'good measure' (*obs.*); **-worker**, a contrivance for pressing the butter-milk out of b.

Butter (bʌ·təɹ), *sb.*2 1611. [f. BUTT *v.*1 + -ER 1.] An animal that butts.

Bu·tter, *sb.*3 1874. [f. BUTT *sb.*3] A machine for sawing off the ends of legs or boards, to render them square.

Butter (bʌ·təɹ), *v.* 1496. [f. BUTTER *sb.*1] **1.** To spread with butter. Also, To cook or dish up with butter. **2.** *fig.* To flatter lavishly 1816. †**3.** *slang.* 'To increase the stakes every throw or every game' (J.) -1719.

1. Fine words, says our homely old proverb, b. no parsnips LOWELL. *To b. one's bread on both sides*: to be wasteful.

Bu·tter-box. 1600. **1.** A box for holding butter 1756. †**2.** Nickname for a Dutchman -1811.

Butter-bump, bitter-. 1671. [f. *butter*, *bitter*, early ff. BITTERN + BUMP *v.*2] The Bittern (*local*).

Butterbur (bʊ·təɹbɒ̄ɹ). 1548. A plant, *Petasites vulgaris*, with large soft leaves, used for wrapping butter in.

Bu·ttercup. orig. *pl.* 1777. A name of species of Ranunculus bearing yellow cup-shaped flowers, esp. *R. bulbosus*, *R. acris*, and *R. repens*. Called also *butterflower*, *gold-cup*, or *king-cup*.

Bu·tter-fi·ngered, *a.* 1615. That takes hold as if with fingers greased with butter; apt to let things fall or slip. Also *fig.* (*colloq.*) **Bu·tter-fi·ngers,** a butter-fingered person; *esp.* one who fails to hold a catch at cricket.

Butterfly (bʊ·təɹfləi). [OE. *buttor-flēoge*. The reason of the name is unkn.] 1. Any diurnal lepidopterous insect, having knobbed antennæ, and carrying its wings erect when at rest. 2. *fig.* A vain, gaudily attired person; a giddy trifler 1605. 3. The guide for the reins on the front of a hansom cab (*mod.*). Also *attrib.*

1. Swich talkyng is nat worth a boterflye CHAUCER. 2. Wee'l..laugh At gilded Butterflies *Lear* V. iii. 13.

Comb.: **b.-block,** *Naut.*, a small block consisting of two wings containing rollers for a chain to pass over; **-cock** = *butterfly-valve*; **-fish,** the Ocellated Blenny; **-flower,** the genus *Schizanthus*; **b. nut** (*Mech.*) = *thumb-nut*; **b. orchis,** *Habenaria chlorantha* and *H. bifolia*; **b. plant,** the name of two Orchids, *Oncidium papilio* and *Phalænopsis amabilis*; **b. screw** (*Mech.*), a thumb-screw; **-shaped** *a.*, *Bot.* = PAPILIONACEOUS; **-shell,** name of the genus *Voluta* of testaceous molluscs; **-valve,** a kind of double clack-valve, resembling, when open, a butterfly's wings; **-weed,** a name of American plants, esp. *Asclepias tuberosa*.

Butterine (bʊ·tĕrīn). 1874. [f. BUTTER *sb.*[1] + -INE.] An imitation butter made from oleomargarine churned up with milk; now called *Margarine*. (See *Act* 50 *and* 51 *Vict.* xxix.)

Butteris (bʊ·tĕris). 1573. [?] A farrier's tool for paring a horse's hoofs.

Buttermilk (bʊ·təɹmilk). 1528. The acidulous milk which remains after the butter has been churned out. Also *fig.* and *attrib.*

Butter-nut (bʊ·təɹ,nʊt). 1753. 1. The large oily nut of the *Juglans cinerea* or White Walnut Tree of N. America. Also, the tree itself. 2. Name of the genus *Caryocar* of S. America (esp. *C. nuciferum*) and its fruit 1845. 3. *attrib.* Of a brownish-grey colour, like the butternut (sense 1) 1861. **b.** Hence *absol.* 1863.

3. b. A 'Butternut' is..one, in fact, who wears the uniform..of the Southern Army 1863.

Butter-print (bʊ·təɹ,print). 1616. 1. A stamp for marking butter-pats; an impression from this 1632. †2. *fig.* A child (*slang*) –1709.

Butterwort (bʊ·təɹwɒ̄ɹt). 1597. A plant with yellowish-green fleshy leaves (*Pinguicula vulgaris*) common on boggy ground; also the Eng. name of the genus *Pinguicula*.

Buttery (bʊ·tĕri), *sb.* ME. [app. a. OF. *boterie* = *bouteillerie* :—late L. *botaria*, f. *bota*, var. of *butta* cask, bottle; see BUTT *sb.*[2]] A store-room for liquor; also, for provisions generally. **b.** In the colleges at Oxford and Cambridge: The place where ale and bread, butter, etc., are kept 1569.

Comb.: **b.-bar,** a ledge on the top of the b.-hatch; **-book** (at the Universities), the book in which are entered the names and buttery accounts of the members of a college; **-hatch,** the half-door over which the buttery provisions are served.

Buttery (bʊ·tĕri), *a.* ME. [f. BUTTER *sb.*[1]] 1. Of the nature of or containing butter. 2. Like butter in consistence 1719. 3. Smeared with butter 1796. 4. *fig.* Given to fulsome flattery (cf. the *sb.*) 1842. Also in *comb.* Hence **Bu·tteriness.**

Bu·tting, *vbl. sb.*[1] 1602. The action of BUTT *v.*[1]

†**Bu·tting,** *vbl. sb.*[2] 1552. [f. BUTT *v.*[2] or *sb.*[7]] 1. Bounding, boundary, limit; also *fig.* –1750. 2. The making of butt-joints 1850.

1. Nature has its buttings and boundings DE FOE.

Bu·tting, *vbl. sb.*[3] 1553. [f. BUT *v.*] The making use of 'buts'.

Butting-joint. 1837. [See BUTT *v.*[2]] *Carp.* A joint formed by the surfaces of two pieces of wood whereof one is perpendicular to the fibres, and the other in their direction, or making an oblique angle with them.

Buttock (bʊ·tək), *sb.* ME. [app. f. BUTT *sb.*[3] + -OCK.] 1. One of the two protuberances of the rump. Usu. in *pl.* the rump, posteriors. 2. *Naut.* 'The breadth of the ship astern from the tuck upwards' (Smyth) 1627. 3. [f. BUTTOCK *v.*] A manœuvre in wrestling 1688.

1. A Barbers chaire that fits all buttockes *All's Well* II. ii. 17. Hence **Bu·ttocked** *a.*, having buttocks; defined as *broad-*, *great-*, etc.

Bu·ttock, *v.* 1617. [f. prec.] †1. In horse-racing: To overtake (a horse). 2. In wrestling: To throw by a manœuvre in which the buttock is used 1883.

Button (bʊ·t'n), *sb.* ME. [a. OF. *boton* (mod. *bouton*), com. Rom. :—late L. **buttōnem*, app. conn. w. late L. **bottare*, whence OF. *boter*, F. *bouter*; prob. (ult.) Teut.] 1. *gen.* A small knob or stud attached to any object for use or ornament; *esp.* A knob or stud of metal, bone, etc., sewn by a shank or neck to articles of dress, usually for the purpose of fastening one part of the dress to another by passing through a *b.-hole*, but often for ornament: also *transf.* 2. A bud, or other part of a plant of similar shape, *esp.* a young mushroom 1513. 3. *transf.* from 1. Used of a knob, handle, catch; the disk of an electric bell. *spec.* An oblong piece of wood or metal, turning on a screw fixed through its centre, used to fasten doors, etc. 1607. 4. Any small rounded body; *spec.* **a.** (*Chem.*) a globule of metal remaining in the crucible after fusion 1801; **b.** a knob fixed on the point of a fencing foil 1649.

1. Pray you vndo this B. *Lear* V. iii. 309. Phr. *Boy in buttons*: a page. A b. therefore for all worldely differences COVERDALE.

Phr. *To take by the b.*: to BUTTONHOLE.

Comb. **a.** (chiefly in *pl.*) *bachelor's*, *beggar's buttons*, see BACHELOR, BEGGAR; used also in comb. of other plants having button-like flowers or seed-vessels. **b.** **b.-ball,** *Platanus occidentalis* (= *button-wood*); **-blank,** a disk of metal, etc., to be formed into a b.; **-boy,** a page; **-bush,** a North American shrub (*Cephalanthus occidentalis*) having globular flower-heads; **-fish,** the sea-urchin (*Echinus*); **-hook; -mould,** a disk of wood, etc., to be covered with cloth to form a b.; **-mushroom** (see sense 2); **-tree,** the genus *Conocarpus*; **-weed,** the genera *Spermacoce* and *Diodia* of tropical *Cinchonaceæ*; also the Knapweed; **-wood,** *Platanus occidentalis* (U.S.); also = *button-bush*; also = *button-tree*. Hence **Bu·ttonless** *a.* **Bu·ttony** *a.*

Button (bʊ·t'n), *v.* ME. [f. prec.] 1. To furnish or adorn with a button, or buttons. 2. To fasten with buttons. Often with *up*. ME. **b.** To fasten the clothes of (a person) with buttons. Usu. *refl.*; also *absol.* 1662. Also *fig.* 3. *intr.* (for *refl.*) To be capable of being fastened (*up*) with buttons 1777.

2. Jack had got Euclid buttoned up inside his jacket 1864. *fig.* As it were, buttoned up, body and soul W. IRVING.

Buttoned (bʊ·t'nd), *ppl. a.* 1534. [f. BUTTON *sb.* and *v.* + -ED.] 1. Having buttons, adorned with buttons, as *silver-*, *eight-b.*, etc. **b.** Wearing buttons 1813. 2. Fastened with buttons. Also with *up*. 1826.

Bu·tton-hold, *v.* 1834. [f. *button-holder*.] To take hold of (a person) by a button, and detain him in conversation against his will.

Bu·tton-ho·lder. 1806. 1. One who button-holds. 2. A case for holding buttons 1870.

Button-hole (bʊ·t'nhōᵘl), *sb.* 1561. 1. The hole through which a button passes. Also *transf.* 2. *colloq.* Short for *button-hole flower*, *bouquet* 1879. Also *attrib.* Hence **Bu·tton-hole** *v.* to sew button-holes; also = BUTTON-HOLD (superseding it). **Bu·tton-ho·ler,** one who makes button-holes; one who button-holes; *colloq.* a button-hole flower.

Bu·ttons. 1848. [*pl.* used as sing.] 1. A boy in buttons, a page (*colloq.*) 2. A name for the tansy and other plants; see BUTTON *sb.*

Buttress (bʊ·très), *sb.* ME. [? a. OF. *bouterez*, nom. sing. (or ? pl.) of *bouteret*, 'flying-buttress', f. *bouter* to push.] 1. A structure of wood, stone, or brick built against a wall to strengthen or support it. Also *fig.* 2. *loosely*, A prop; a pier or abutment 1609. 3. A projecting portion of a hill or mountain 1682.

1. A long dead wall, unbroken by porch or b. FREEMAN.

Bu·ttress, *v.* ME. [f. prec.] To furnish, sustain, or strengthen with a buttress. Also *fig.* Occas. with *up*.

To b. it [the ministry] up with the Grenvilles BURKE.

Butty (bʊ·ti). *dial.* 1802. [? corrupt f. BOOTY *a.*] 1. A confederate, mate. 2. *Mining.* A middleman, who contracts to raise coal or ore at so much per ton. Also in *comb.* 1845.

Butyl (biū·til). 1868. [f. BUT-YRIC + -YL.] *Chem.* 1. The monatomic alcohol radical of the tetra-carbon series, C_4H_9; called also *Valyl*, *Tetryl*, and *Quartyl*. 2. *attrib.* Of butyl, butylic, tetrylic; *esp.* in **b. alcohol,** $C_4H_{10}O$. Hence **Butyla·ctic,** in *Butylactic acid*: the monobasic acid $C_4H_8O_3$, derived from Butyl glycol. **Bu·tylene,** the diatomic hydrocarbon or olefine of the b. series, C_4H_8, also called *Butrene* and *Tetrene*. **Butyle·nic** *a.* **Buty·lic** *a.*

Butyr-, a formative of the names of chemical compounds of the butyric series, and of some minerals. (Cf. BUTYRO-.)

Bu·tyrate, a salt of butyric acid. **Bu·tyrin,** an oily liquid analogous to the acetins, obtained by the action of butyric acid on glycerin. **Bu·tyrone,** the ketone of the butyric series, also called diapropyl ketone $CO.(C_3H_7)_2$.

Butyraceous (biūtirēⁱ·ʃəs), *a.* 1668. [f. L. *butyrum*.] 1. Of the nature of butter. Also *fig.* 2. Producing or containing butter 1863.

Butyric (biuti·rik), *a.* 1826. [f. as prec.] *Chem.* Of or pertaining to butter, *esp.* in reference to its chemical construction and formation. Hence:

B. acid, the monatomic, monobasic, fatty acid of the BUTYL series, $C_4H_8O_2$, of which there are two modifications, *normal b.* and *isobutyric* acid; the former occurring in butter, cod-liver oil, etc., is a colourless viscous liquid, with a smell suggestive of both vinegar and rancid butter. Hence **Buty·rically** *adv.*

Bu·tyro-, comb. f. L. *butyrum*. Cf. BUTYR-.

Bu·tyrous, *a.* 1669. [f. L. *butyrum* + -OUS.] Butyraceous.

Buxeous (bʊ·ksīəs), *a.* 1731. [f. L. *buxeus*.] Of or pertaining to box or the box-tree. (Dicts.)

Bu·xerry. Now *Hist.* 1757. [? Hind. *baksāri* 'native of Buxar' (Yule).] A matchlock-man.

Buxine (bʊ·ksəin). 1836. [f. L. *buxus* + -INE.] A vegetable alkaloid from the box-tree.

Buxom (bʊ·ksɒ̆m), *a.* [Early ME. *buhsum*, *ibucsum*, f. stem of *būgan* BOW *v.*[1]] †1. Tractable (*to*); meek; gracious, obliging, kindly; prone (with *inf.*). †2. Flexible; unresisting (*poet.*) –1700. 3. Blithe, bright, lively, gay (*arch.*) 1590. 4. Full of health, vigour, and good temper; plump and comely, 'jolly'. (Chiefly of women.) 1589.

1. I shall be buxome and obedient to justyces FITZHERB. 2. Wing silently the b. air MILT. *P. L.* II. 842. 3. A Souldier..of buxome valour *Hen. V*, III. vi. 28. 4. A b. dame about thirty SCOTT. Hence †**Bu·xomly,** *adv.*, **-ness.**

Buy (bəi), *v.* [OE. *bycg(e)an*, *bohte*, *geboht*; of unkn. origin. Not found exc. in Teut.] 1. To get possession of by giving an equivalent, usu. in money; to obtain by paying a price; to purchase. (Correl. to *sell*.) Also *absol.* **b.** Of things: To be an equivalent price for; to be the means of purchasing 1599. 2. *fig.* To obtain in exchange for something else, or by making some sacrifice ME. †3. ABY *v.* 2; cf. BYE *v.* Often with *dear*. –1615. 4. To redeem, ransom. *Obs.* exc. in *Theol.*, and now usu. repl. by *redeem*. ME. 5. To engage by money or otherwise *to* or *to do*; to hire (*arch.*) 1652.

1. To b. some little Cornish borough 1714. *To b. into*: to b. a commission in; to purchase stock in, shares in. **b.** Can the world buie such a jewell *Much Ado* I. i. 183. 5. Nor is [he] with Pray'rs, or Bribes, or Flatt'ry bought DRYDEN.

Phrases and Combs. **B. in:** to collect a stock of by purchase (often opp. to *sell out*); also *absol.*; to b. back for the owner, *e.g.* at an auction when the bids are too low; to b. a commission, stock, shares. **B. off:** to get rid of, to induce (a person) to forgo a claim, opposition, etc. by a money payment. **B. out:** †to ransom; to purchase a person's estate, or interest in any concern, and so to turn (him) out of it; to get rid of (any liability) by a money payment. **Buy over:** to gain over by a payment. **B. up:** to purchase with a view of controlling the supply (a stock, or the *whole* of any commodity). *To be bought and sold*: often *fig.*, usu. To be betrayed for a bribe (*arch.*). Hence **Buy·er.**

Buz, var. of BUZZ in various senses.

Buzz (bʊz), *sb.*[1] 1605. [f. BUZZ *v.*[1]] 1. A sibilant hum, as that of bees, flies, or other insects 1645. 2. *transf.* The confused sound made by many people talking or busily occupied;

hence, stir, ferment 1627. 3. *fig.* †a. A whim, fad; (cf. BEE[1] 5). b. A busy rumour. 1605.
2. I found the whole..Room in a Buz of Politics ADDISON. *Comb.* b.-saw, a circular saw. *U.S.*

Buzz, *sb.*[2] 1612. [perh. echoic.] 1. A bur. 2. A downy land-beetle (*Rhizostrogus solstitialis*) used as bait 1760. Also quasi-*adv.*

Buzz, *sb.*[3] Only *attrib.* 1798. [? related to prec.; or short f. BUSBY.] Epithet of a large bushy wig. Also in comb. *buzz-wig*, one wearing such a wig; a bigwig. Also *transf.*

Buzz (bvz), *v.*[1] ME. [Echoic.] 1. *intr.* To make a humming sibilant sound like that of bees, etc.; to fly *out, in*, etc. with such a sound. 2. *fig.* To flutter, hover (*about, over*) like a buzzing insect 1650. 3. To mutter, murmur busily. (Usu. contemptuous.) (*arch.*) 1555. b. To make the hum produced by many people talking 1832. 4. *trans.* To tell in a low murmur, to whisper busily (*arch.*) 1583. 5. To spread as a rumour, with whispering or busy talk 1616. 6. To utter with, or express by, buzzing 1763.
1. Waspes that buz about his Nose *Hen. VIII*, III. ii. 55. 2. Boys and wenches buzzing about the cake-shops like flies SWIFT. 5. A bruit constantly buzzed FULLER. Hence **Bu·zzingly** *adv.*

Buzz, *v.*[2] 1785. To finish to the last drop in the bottle.
Get some more port..whilst I b. this bottle THACKERAY. var. **Buzza.**

†**Buzz**, *int.* 1602. a. An exclam. of impatience. b. = 'hey, presto', etc. –1830.

Buzzard[1] (bv·zăɹd). ME. [a. OF. *basart*, usu. taken as derived from L. *buteonem.*] 1. A bird of the genus *Buteo*, esp. *B. vulgaris.* Applied also, with defining words, to others of the *Falconidæ*: as **Bald B.**, the Osprey; **Honey B.**, *Pernis apivorus*; **Moor B.**, *Circus æruginosus.* (The buzzard was a useless kind of hawk; hence sense 2.) 2. *fig.* A worthless, stupid, or ignorant person. Often with *blind.* Now *dial.* ME. 3. *attrib.* Senseless 1592.
1. An Historian and a Libeller are as different as Hawk and B. NORTH. 3. A b. idol MILT. Hence **Buzzardet**, a hawk like a b., but with longer legs.

Bu·zzard, *sb.*[2] *dial.* 1825. [f. BUZZ *v.*[1]] 1. A name for moths, cockchafers, etc., that fly by night. 2. = BUZZER[1] 3. 1878.
Comb. b.-clock, a cockchafer.

Buzzer (bv·zəɹ). 1602. [f. BUZZ *v.*[1] + -ER[1].] 1. An insect that buzzes. Also *fig.* 1606. †2. One who whispers tales. *Haml.* IV. v. 90. 3. An apparatus for making a loud buzzing noise as a signal; cf. *hooter* 1870.

By, *sb.*[1] [north. OE. *bý*, prob. a. ON. *bœ-r, by-r* habitation, f. *búa* to dwell. Retained in place-names, as *Whitby*, etc.] A place of habitation; a village or town.

By, *sb.*[2]; see after BY *prep.* and *adv.*

By (bəi), *prep., adv.* (*a., sb.*) [OE. *bí* (*bíg*) accented; *bi, be* unaccented:—OTeut. **bi*, ?cogn. w. L. *am-bi-*, Gr. ἀμφί 'about'. (Cf. OTeut. *bo-*, L. *am-bo-*, Gr. ἀμ-φο- both.) Orig. an advb. particle of place.] A. *prep.* I. Of position in space. a. At the side or edge of; near, close to, beside. b. In forms of swearing or adjuration. In Teut. = 'in presence of', 'in touch of', but in ME. use possibly a tr. of F. *par*, of instrumentality OE. c. By the side of; *hence*, in addition to, beside ME. d. In the region or general direction of, towards OE.; *spec.* as in 'North by East', etc., *i. e.* one point towards the east of N., etc. 1682. e. On (vaguely). *Obs.* exc. in *by land*, etc. ME. 2. Of motion. a. Alongside of, along, down over, up, over OE. b. Through; also expanded into *by way of* ME. c. Near to: chiefly in *to come by* (see COME *v.*) ME. d. On alongside of, past ME. e. At, to, or within the distance of ME. f. Expressing the amount of an excess or increase, inferiority or diminution ME. 3. Of time. a. In the course of, at, in, on. Now only in *by day* (L. *interdiu*), and *by night* (L. *noctu*) ME. b. During, for. (Now *for.*) 1460. c. On or before, not later than; †within. Cf. BETIMES. ME. 4. (*fig.* from 1 a.) a. After; with vbs. of *naming*, etc. OE. b. According to, in conformity with OE. c. According to; as *by retail, by the yard, by the day*, etc. OE. d. Indicating succession of groups, quantities, or individuals of the same class, as *two by two, by files, man by man*, etc. ME. e. About, concerning, with respect to, in regard to, as concerns OE. 5. (*fig.* from 2 a.) Indicating the medium, means, instrumentality, or agency OE. 6. Of circumstance, condition, manner, cause, reason. a. The circumstances of an action often pass into the notion of aid or *means*, e. g. in 'to read by candle-light' OE. b. The sense of 'means' often passes into that of 'attendant circumstances', and so into the senses of 'manner', 'cause', 'reason' ME. c. In *Book-keeping*, placed before Credit entries, the person or account being made creditor *by* the amount entered 1695.
1. Com sit me bye 1485. *Bromley-by-Bow.* You'll stand by me upon Occasion CIBBER. b. Neither shalt thou sweare by thy head *Matt.* v. 36. So ellipt. *By our Lady.* c. If we don't get the horse by the bargain DE FOE. d. *By the head* (Naut.): deeper in the water forward than abaft. So *by the stern. By the board*: see BOARD *sb.* 12. 2. a. Moving by the river side 1816. *By the way*: *lit.* in passing along; *fig.* incidentally; *ellipt.*, omitting 'it may be remarked', or the like. b. He that cometh not in by the dore *John* x. 1. e. A miss by a mile 1880. f. He is too moral by half SHERIDAN. 3. c. Ready at the door of the hotel by nine STERNE. 4. b. And tell what rules he did it by BUTLER *Hud.* I. i. 86. So *by book, by heart, by rote*; *by your leave, by consent*, etc. e. Will doe as did the Foxe by the Kidde SPENSER. I know nothing by myself [R.V. against] 1 *Cor.* iv. 4. 5. I did give her a pull by the nose, and some ill words PEPYS. *To set by the ears*: to set quarrelling. To live by food *A. Y. L.* II. vii. 14, by poetry CHURCH. Send check by bearer 1833. So *by the hands of.* So in *To have children by, be pregnant by.* The walls of it were built by Diocletian. Pipes and alcoholic liquors are superseded by matrimony *Punch.* 6. b. He began by banishing 700 families THIRLWALL. So in *By way of*: see WAY. Phr. *By that*: therefore; Warwickes brother, and by that our foe SHAKS.

B. *adv.* [In OE. the adv. may be treated either as prefix to a vb., or as a prep. following its object.] 1. Of position: Near, close at hand, in another's presence or vicinity. See BY- in comb. ME. 2. Aside, out of the way; out of use or consideration ME. 3. Of motion: Past a certain point, beyond. Also transf. of time. ME. †4. In addition, besides, also –1804.
1. Methinks you sit by very tamely BERKELEY. *Stand by!* (Naut.) = be ready. *Full and by* (Naut.): sailing close-hauled to the wind. 2. Stand by, or I shall gaul you *John* IV. iii. 95. To lay something by for a rainy day 1807. *To lie (lay) by* (Naut.): = mod. *lie to.* 3. They marched by in pairs B. JONS.

By, bye, *a.* OE. [Attrib. use of prec. *by-* in adv. (The spelling *bye* is now preferred in this use.)] 1. *gen.* The opposite of *main.* Also *fig.* See BY- in *comb.*, and BY-PATH, etc. 2. *fig.* a. Away from the main purpose, incidental, casual; b. of secondary importance; c. secret, underhand. See BY-MATTER, BY-WORD, etc. OE.
1. The mule preferred the high road to the bye one SOUTHEY. 2. By and idle talke Brome. A bye effect PALEY, consideration 1842.

By[2], **bye**, *sb.* 1567. [Ellipt. use of prec. adj.] †A secondary course or matter; a side issue; usually opp. to *main* –1824. See also BYE.
1. Neither was the main let fall, nor time lost, upon the by NORTH. Phr. **By the by**: by a side way, on a side issue; incidentally. *Obs.* or *arch.* Also quasi-*adj.*: Off the main track, of secondary importance 1615. Also used ellipt., with the omission of 'it may be remarked', or the like 1708.

By- in composition.
A. A ME. var. of the prefix BI-, BE-, as *bycause*, etc.
B. **By-** (occ. **bye-**): the prep., adv., or adj. in comb.
I. Compounds in which *by-* is a prep., as **by-rote** *a.*
II. Compounds in which *by-* has an advb. force: a. with senses 'beside, past'; as *by-stroller, by-flown*, etc. b. with sense '*aside*, SIDE-'; as *by-glance, -thought*, **by-wipe** (= *side-stroke*), etc.
III. 1. Combs. in which *by* has an adjectival force: a. with senses 'at one side', 'out-of-the-way', 'subsidiary'; as in *by-chamber, -window*, etc. b. in the sense 'Running alongside-and-apart', 'devious', 'unfrequented', as *by-alley, -route, -wash*, etc. c. in sense 'SIDE-', as *by-issue*, etc. d. *hence*, 'covert', 'underhand', as *by-aim, -payment*, etc. 2. Incidental, casual, as *by-election, -production* (= Gr. πάρεργον). 3. Opp. to MAIN, as *by-feature, -form* (of a word). 4. Counterfeit, as †**by-fruit**, a gall or the like, †**by-gold**, tinsel.

-by (bi), *suffix*, forming 1. names of places (north.) from BY *sb.*[1], as in *Grimsby*, etc. 2. personal appellations, derisive or playful, as *idlesby, wigsby*, etc. Perh. formed after personal surnames derived from place-names, as *Littleby*, etc.

By and by (bəi· ənd bəi·, bəi· ən bəi·), *advb. phr.* (and *sb.*) ME. [See BY *prep.* 4 d.] †1. Of a succession of things: One by one, one after another, in order –1485. †2. On and on, continuously –1620. 3. Straightway, at once –1690. 4. [Cf. *presently*, and F. *bientôt.*] Before long, soon. (The current sense.) 1526. †5. Therefore; = L. *continuo* –1631. 6. *sb.* a. Procrastination; b. Time coming 1591.
4. To haue slayne the Prophetes before, and byanby Christ OLDE.

Byard (bəi·ăɹd). 1847. *Mining.* A leather strap crossing the breast, used by the men who drag wagons in coal-mines. (Dicts.)

By·bidder. 1880. [See BY- III. 1 c.] A person at an auction who bids with the object of raising the prices (*dial.*).

By-blow (bəi·blōu). 1594. 1. A side-blow or side-stroke (*lit.* and *fig.*). 2. One who comes into being by a side stroke; a bastard. Also *fig.* 1595. †3. A blow that misses its aim –1684.
1. Now and then a by-blow from the Pulpit MILT. 3. Now also with their by-blows, they did split the very Stones in pieces BUNYAN.

†**By·boat.** 1698. [f. BY-.] ? An extra boat. Used esp. of the Newfoundland fishery –1796.

†**By·-chop.** [See BY-, BY-SLIP.] A bastard. B. JONS.

†**Bycoket.** 1464. [a. OF. *bicoquet* casque, dim. of F. *bicoque* = It. *bicocca*; app. f. *bi-* + *cocca* as in *cocca del capo* 'crown of the head'.] A kind of cap or head-dress (peaked before and behind). ¶ Through a series of blunders *a bicocket*, misprinted *abococket*, was turned into ABACOT, in which form it appears in mod. dictionaries.

By·-corner; see BY- III. 1 a.

Bye (bəi). 1603. [Var. of BY *prep.* used subst.] 1. a. *Cricket.* A run scored for a ball which passes the batsman, and is missed by the wicket-keeper and long-stop 1746. b. in *Tennis, Boxing*, etc.: The position of an individual who is left without a competitor when the rest have been drawn in pairs 1883. c. in *Lacrosse*, etc.: A goal, a starting line 1841. d. A by-match or event 1884. 2. The name of a plot against the government of James I. (Distinguished from the *Main* plot.) 1603.

†**Bye, by**, *v.* ME. [aphet. f. ABY, ABYE *v.*] 1. = ABY *v.* 2, BUY *v.* 3. –1599. 2. *absol.* = ABY *v.* 4. ME. only. 3. *intr.* = ABY *v.* 5. –1594.

Bye-bye[1] (bəi·bəiː). 1636. A sound used to lull a child to sleep; *hence*, 'sleep' or 'bed'.

Bye-bye[2] (bəi·bəi·). 1709. Colloq. var. of GOOD-BYE.

By·-end; see BY- III. 1 c, d.

†**By-fellow.** 1856. [See BY- III. 3.] A fellow of a college not on the foundation.

Bygoing (bəi·gōuiŋ), *vbl. sb.* 1637. [f. BY- II. a.] The action of passing by; *esp.* in *In the b.*: in passing.

Bygone, by-gone (bəi·gǫn). ME. [f. BY- II. a.] A. *ppl. a.* 1. That has gone by; that has happened in past time; former. †b. = AGO. Swift. 2. Deceased. Also *transf.* 1513.
B. *sb.* 1. *pl.* Things (*esp.* offences) that are past 1568. b. Arrears 1663. 2. The past (*rare*) 1872.
1. B. shall be b.; the new Era shall begin CARLYLE.

†**By·land.** 1577. A peninsula –1630.

Bylander, obs. f. BILANDER.

By-lane (bəi·lēⁱn). 1587. [f. BY- III. 1 b.] A side lane; *also*, a side passage in a mine.

By-law, bye-law (bəi·lǭ). ME. [In sense 1 a doublet of BYRLAW. In sense 3 used as if f. BY *adv.* + LAW, after *by-path*, etc.; and sense 2 is now used and understood thus.] †1. Var. of BYRLAW. b. Often used spec. of ordinances made by common consent in a Court-leet or Court-baron 1607. 2. A law or ordinance dealing with matters of local or internal regulation, made by a local authority, or by a corporation or association ME. 3. A secondary, subordinate, or accessory law 1541.
2. There was likewise a law to restrain the by-laws, or ordinances of corporations BACON. By lawes wch the..Schollers..have made *Sel. Records, Oxford.* 3. In detail, or what may be called the by-laws of each art SIR J. REYNOLDS. Hence **Bylaw-man** = BYRLAW-MAN.

†By·live, by·lif(e. [OE. *bigleofa.*] That which one lives by; living, sustenance -ME.

By-matter (bəi·mæ:təɹ). 1552. [f. By- III. 1 c, 3.] A side incident; a trivial matter.

Dissenters and Scruplers in by-matters 1674.

Byname, by-name (bəi·nēⁱm), *sb.* ME. [f. By- III. 3.] 1. A name other than the main one; *esp.* a surname; a sobriquet. 2. A nickname 1580.

1. Lions-heart, is..the by-name of K. Richard 1631. 2. Mr. Welbore Ellis..the butt of Junius, under the by-name of Grildrig EARL STANHOPE. Hence **By·name** *v.* to surname, to nickname.

By-pass (bəi·pɑs). 1848. [By- B. III. 1 b, PASS *sb.*[1]] 1. A secondary pipe to allow the free passage of gas, etc.; *esp.* the small tube and pilot light which remains alight when a gas-jet is turned off. 2. A road diverging from and re-entering a main road, esp. for the relief of congestion 1922. Also as vb.

Bypast, by-past (bəi·pɑst), *ppl. a.* ME. [By- II. a.] Gone by, elapsed; former.

Bypath, by-path (bəi·pɑþ). ME. [f. By- III. 1 b.] A side path; a private or unfrequented path. Also *fig.* (Formerly in a bad sense.)

fig. By-pathes, and indirect crook'd wayes SHAKS.

By-play (bəi·plēⁱ). 1812. [f. By- III. 1 c.] Action carried on aside, and often in dumb-show, during the main action. Also *transf.*

By-product (bəi prǫ·dɒkt). 1857. [f. By- III. 2, 3.] A secondary product; a substance obtained in the course of a specific process, but not its primary object.

Byre (bəiəɹ). [OE. *býre*; perh. deriv. (ult.) of *bū-* to dwell; see BOWER.] A cow-house.

He had beeves in the b. BARHAM.

†By·-respect; see By- III. 1 c, d.

Byrla·dy, *int.*; still *dial.* 1570. Contr. of *by our Lady.*

†Byrla·kin. 1528. Contr. of *By our Ladykin* -1625.

By·rlaw. *arch.* or *dial.* ME. [app. a. ON. **býjar-lǫg*, f. *býjar* gen. case of *bý-r* (= By *sb.*), var. of *bœr* village, town, farm + *lǫg* (pl. of *lag*) law; cf. By-LAW.] 1. The local custom or law of a township, manor, or rural district, whereby disputes as to boundaries, trespass of cattle, etc., were settled without going into the law courts. 2. *transf.* A district having its own byrlaw court, or local law 1850. Hence in Yorkshire place-names, as *Brampton Bierlow*, etc.

By·rlawman. ME. [f. prec.] An officer appointed at a Court-leet for duties connected with the framing and execution of byrlaws. Also called **Bierlaw-grayves** (see GREAVE).

By·rnie. Now *Hist.* ME. [Sc. var. of ME. *brynie.*] A coat of mail.

By·-road. 1673. [f. By- III. 1 b.] A road which is not a main road; a little frequented road.

Byronic (bəirǫ·nik), *a.* 1823. [Cf. *Miltonic.*] 1. Characteristic of, or after the manner of, Byron or his poetry. Also *absol.* 2. quasi-*sb. pl.* (after *philippics.*) Declamation or invective in the style of Byron 1850.

1. A B. youth in a turn-down collar 1856. B. mock heroics FROUDE. So **By·ronism**, the characteristics of Byron or his poetry; imitation of Byron.

By·-room; see By- III. 1 a.

‖**Byrsa** (bɔ̄·ɹsă). 1811. [L., a. Gr.] *Med.* A leather skin, to spread plasters upon.

†By·-slip. 1612. [f. By- II. b.] 1. A trivial fault. 2. *transf.* A bastard 1670.

†By·-speech; see By- II, III. 1 c.

†By·-spel, bi·spel. [ME. *bispell*, OE. *bí·spell*, f. *bi* + SPELL story.] 1. A parable. 2. A proverb -1656.

†Byss, *sb.* ME. [a. OF. *bysse*, ad. L. *byssus*; see BYSSUS.] = BYSSUS 1; Fine linen -1648.

Byssa·ceous, *a.* 1835. [f. BYSSUS; see -ACEOUS.] *Bot.* Composed of fine entangled threads.

Byssi·ferous, *a.* 1835. [f. as prec. + -(I)FEROUS.] *Zool.* Furnished with a byssus.

Byssine (bi·sin), *a.* ME. [ad. L. *byssinus*, a. Gr.] 1. Made of byssus 1656. 2. quasi-*sb.* [L. *byssinum.*] = BYSS *sb.*

By·ssoid, *a.* 1857. [f. as prec.] *Bot.* Like a byssus, byssaceous.

Byssolite (bi·sǒləit). 1847. [f. Gr. βύσσος + -LITE.] = ASBESTOID.

Byssus (bi·sǒs). ME. [a. L., a. Gr. βύσσος, ad. Heb. *būts*, translated in Bible of 1611 'fine linen', f. root *būts* to be white, to surpass in whiteness.] 1. An exceedingly fine and valuable textile fibre and fabric known to the ancients; it denoted properly a kind of flax, but was used also of cotton, silk, etc. †2. A name for filamentous fungoid growths, which are now more accurately classified -1838. 3. *Zool.* The tuft of fine silky filaments by which molluscs of the genus *Pinna* and various mussels attach themselves to the surface of rocks; it is secreted by the *byssus-gland* in the foot 1836. 4. *Bot.* The thread-like stipe of some fungi 1866. †5. ASBESTOS.

1. The fayrest of al [flexe] growyth in Egypte; for therof is Bissus made ryght fayre and whyte as snowe TREVISA.

Bystander (bəi·stæ:ndəɹ). 1619. [f. By- II. a.] One who is standing by; a spectator.

Such an act, either in Executioner or b., is in no way justifiable DONNE.

By·-street; see By- III. 1 b.

By-term (bəi·təɹm). 1579 [f. By- III. 3, 4.] †1. A nickname. 2. In Univ. of Cambridge: A term which is not the main one for entering or for taking degrees 1883.

By·-thing; see By- III. 2, 3.

By·-time; see By- III. 2.

By·-turning; see By- III. 1 b.

By·-view. ? *Obs.* 1731. [f. By- II. b, III. 1 c, d.] a. A side glance or glimpse. b. An unavowed or self-interested aim.

No by views of his own shall mislead him ATTERBURY.

By·-walk; see By- III. 1 b.

Byward (bəi·wǭɹd), *sb.* 1840. [f. By- III. 1, 3.] A ward or guard which is not the main one; as in the *B. Tower* of the Tower of London.

By-way (bəi·wēⁱ). ME. [f. By- III. 1 b.] A way other than the highway; a secluded, private, or unfrequented way. Also *transf.* or *fig.*; often depreciatively.

The by-ways and short-cuts to wealth D. JERROLD.

By-west; see BY *prep.*

By-wipe; see By- II. b.

By-word (bəi·wɒ̄ɹd). OE. [f. BY *a.* 2.] 1. A proverbial saying. 2. A person or thing that becomes proverbial, as an object of scorn or contempt 1535. b. A byname 1598. †3. A trick of speech, pet phrase -1710. †4. A hint; a word beside the matter in hand -1658.

1. Is it not a by word, like will to like LYLY. 2. Israel shall be a prouerbe, and a by-word among all people 1 *Kings* ix. 7.

By-work (bəi·wɒ̄ɹk). 1587. [f. By- III. 1 d, e, 2, 3.] 1. Work done in by-times; = Gr. πάρεργον; also, work done with ulterior motives. 2. An accessory work. ? *Obs.* 1587.

Byzantian (bizæ·nʃiăn), *a.* and *sb.* 1619. [f. L. *Byzantius.*] = next.

Byzantine (bizæ·ntəin, bi·zæntəin). 1599. [ad. L. *Byzantinus*, f. *Byzantium*; see BEZANT. The second pronunc. is freq. with classical scholars.] A. *adj.* Belonging to Byzantium or Constantinople. b. *spec.* Pertaining to the style of art, *esp.* of architecture, developed in the Eastern division of the Roman Empire. The Byzantine architecture makes special use of the round arch, cross, circle, dome, and rich mosaic work. 1848. c. Pertaining to the (style of music of the) Eastern Church.

B. historians: those who lived in the Eastern Empire from the 6th to the 15th c.

B. *sb.* 1. An inhabitant of Byzantium 1656. 2. = BEZANT 1. 1599. †3. = BEZANT 2. 1605.

2. A Bizantin, which is..six pence sterling HAKLUYT. So also **Byza·ntine·sque** *a.* in the B. style of art; **Byza·ntinism**, the style and methods of art developed in the B. empire; **Byza·ntinize** *v. trans.* to make B.

C

C (sī), the third letter of the Roman alphaphet, was orig. identical with the Greek *Gamma*, Γ, and Semitic *Gimel*, whence its form. In earlier Latin, it functioned both as (g) and (k); but subseq. it stood for the (k) sound only. When the Roman alphabet was introduced into Britain, C had only the sound (k). The present value of C is the result of developments which took place both in Britain and on the continent during the time covered by the OE. and ME. periods. (See N.E.D.)

In mod. English, C has (1) the 'hard' sound (k) bef. *a, o, u*, bef. a cons. (exc. *h*), and when final; (2) bef. *e, i, y* it has the soft sound (s). In all words from OE. and OF., final *c* is avoided: the (k) sound being written *k*, or *ck*, as in *beak, book*, etc. Final *c* however is written in mod. words from Latin, Greek, or other langs., and (of late) in the ending *-ic*, as in *sac, epic, critic*, etc. But where this *c* is followed in inflexion by *e* or *i*, it is changed to *ck*, as in *physicking, pic-nicker*, etc. When the (s) sound is final, it must be written *-ce*, as in *trace, ice*, etc., and this final *e* is retained in composition bef. *a, o, u*, as in *trace-able*, etc. (3) *Ci* (rarely *ce*) preceding another vowel has frequently the sound of (ʃ), *esp.* in the endings *-cious, -cial, -cion*, as *atrocious*, etc. This sound (which is also taken by *t* in the same position) is comparatively modern.

In foreign words, *c* occas. retains the foreign pronunciation, as in It. *cicerone* (tʃitʃerō·ne).

C springs: see CEE (springs): **C clef**: see CLEF[1].

II. Used to denote serial order with the value of 'third', as quire C. *spec.* a. in *Music*: The key-note of the 'natural' major scale. Also, the scale which has that note for its tonic. b. In *abstract reasoning, law*, etc.: Any third person or thing. **C 3**: the lowest grade of physical fitness for military service; hence *fig.*

III. Abbreviations. 1. C, now rarely c. = L. *centum* a hundred; so CC = 200, CCCC or CD = 400; formerly written ii.c., etc. Also, formerly = cwt. 2. *Mus.* 'As a sign of time C stands for common time, 4 crotchets in a bar; and ₵ for allabreve time, with 2 or 4 minims in a bar' (Grove). C = Counter-tenor, or Contralto; C.F. = *canto fermo*. 3. C. = various proper names, as Charles; C. = Cardinal (*obs.*); C (*Chem.*) Carbon; C (*Electricity*) current; C. = Centigrade (thermometer); c. chapter; c. century; c. (*Cricket*) caught; c. (bef. a date) = L. *circa* about; C.A. Chartered Accountant (*Sc.*); C.B. Companion of the Bath; C.E. Civil Engineer; C.S. Civil Service; C. of E. (sī·əvˌī·) Church of England.

Ca', mod. Sc. f. CALL *sb.* and *v.*, call, drive.

‖**Caaba** (kā·ăbă). 1734. [Arab., 'square (or cubical) house'.] The sacred edifice at Mecca, which contains the 'black stone', and is the 'Holy of Holies' of Islam.

This is the C., which is usually called, by way of eminence, *the House* SALE. var. **Kaaba.**

Caam (kām). 1792. The HEDDLES of a loom.

‖**Cab** (kæb), *sb.*[1] Also **kab.** 1535. [Heb. *qab*, hollow vessel.] A Heb. dry measure; about $2^5/_6$ imperial pints.

†Cab, *sb.*[2] 1650. Abbrev. of *cavalier* (or Sp. *caballero*).

Cab (kæb), *sb.*[3] 1827. 1. Abbrev. of CABRIOLET, but applied more widely; a public carriage with two or four wheels, drawn by one horse, and seating two or four persons. 2. The covered part of a locomotive, which shelters the drivers 1864.

1. Cabs—or cabriolets..—were not known to us until 1820 *Daily News. Comb.*: **c.-rank**, a row of cabs on a stand; **-stand**, a place where cabs are authorized to stand while waiting for hire.

Cab (kæb), *sb.*[4] *slang.* 1876. [short for CABBAGE *sb.*[2]] A crib used by a pupil in getting up his lessons.

Cab (kæb), *v.*[1] *colloq.* 1858. [f. CAB *sb.*[3]] *intr.* (also *to c. it*): To go in a cab.

Cab, *v.*[2] *slang.* [? short for CABBAGE.] To pilfer; to crib.

‖**Cabaan, caban** (kăbā·n). 1693. [a. Arab. and Pers.] A white cloth worn by Arabs over their shoulders.

Cabal (kăbæ·l), *sb.* 1616. [a. F. *cabale*, ad. med.L. *cab(b)ala* CABBALA, q. v. In 17th c. *ca·bal.*] †1. = CABBALA 1. -1663. †2. = CABBALA 2. -1763. 3. A private intrigue of a sinister character formed by a small body of persons 1646. b. = Caballing 1734. 4. A secret meeting, *esp.* of intriguers or of a faction (*arch.*) 1649. 5. A small body of persons engaged in private machination or intrigue; a junto 1660. 6. Applied in the reign of Charles II to a small committee of the Privy Council, which was the precursor of the modern *cabinet* 1665. b. in *Hist.* applied *spec.* to the five ministers of Charles II, viz. Clifford, Arlington, Buckingham, Ashley, and Lauderdale, who signed the Treaty of Alliance with France in 1672; the initials of their names made up the word *cabal* 1673. Also *attrib.*

3. The c. against Washington BANCROFT. b. Centres of c. BURKE. 5. A c. of artists 1859. 6. It being read before the King, Duke, and the Caball PEPYS.

Cabal (kăbæ·l), *v.* 1680. [? f. prec.] 1. *intr.* To combine (*together*) for some private end. (Usu. in a bad sense.) 2. *intr.* To intrigue privately (*against*) 1680. 3. *refl.* To bring *oneself* by caballing. BURKE.

2. Time has been given to c., to sow dissensions, etc. 1789. Hence †**Cabalist, Caba·ller**, one who cabals.

Cabala, var. of CABBALA; also = CABAL (*rare*).

Cabalic, -al, -ism, etc.; see CABBAL-.

†**Ca·ball.** 1450. [ad. L. *caballus.*] A horse -1650.

‖**Caballero** (ka:balʸē·ro). 1877. [Sp.:—L. *caballarius*, f. *caballus.*] A (Spanish) gentleman.

Caballine (ka·bǎləin), *a.* ME. [ad. L. *caballinus.*] Of or belonging to horses; equine.

C. fountain = L. *fons caballinus*, the fountain Hippocrene, fabled to have been produced by a stroke of the foot of Pegasus the winged horse of the Muses; hence = 'fountain of inspiration'.

Caban, cabane, earliest ff. CABIN. Used occ. for local colouring (French or Canadian).

‖**Cabana** (kăbā·nă). The name of a cigar.

‖**Cabaret** (kæ·bărėˡ). 1655. [Fr.; etym. dub.] 1. A drinking-shop. 2. A restaurant where singing and dancing are provided during a meal; also, the entertainment itself (= *c. show*) 1915.

1. Sung two or three years ago in cabarets DRYDEN.

Cabbage (kæ·bėdʒ), *sb.*[1] [ME. *caboche*, a. F. *caboche* head (in the Channel Islands 'cabbage') = It. *capocchia*, f. *capo* :—L. *caput.* The actual Fr. name is *choux cabus.*] 1. A plane-leaved cultivated variety of *Brassica oleracea.* Orig. the 'cabbage' was the 'head' formed by the unexpanded leaves of *B. oleracea*; now the name includes the whole species or genus, whether hearting or not, as in *Savoy C., Wild C.*, etc. 2. Used with epithets of other plants: **Chinese C.**, *Brassica chinensis*; **Dog's C.**, *Thelygonum Cynocrambe*, a succulent herb of the Mediterranean; **Kerguelen's Land C.**, *Pringlea antiscorbutica*; **Meadow** or **Skunk C.**, *Symplocarpus fœtidus*; **St. Patrick's C.** = LONDON PRIDE; **Sea C.** = SEA KALE; **Sea-Otter's C.**, *Nereocystis.* 3. The terminal bud of palm trees. See CABBAGE-TREE. 1638. †4. The burr whence spring the horns of a deer -1611.

1. Take cabaches and cut hom on foure..and let hit boyle 1440.

Comb.: **c. bark**, the narcotic and anthelmintic bark of the **c.-bark tree** or CABBAGE-TREE, *Andira inermis* (N.O. *Leguminosæ*); **c. beetle** = *cabbage flea*; **c. butterfly**, the Large White Butterfly of English gardens and fields, *Pieris Brassicæ*, occ. also the small White (*P. Rapæ*); **-cole** = sense 1; **-flea**, a minute leaping beetle, *Haltica consobrina*, the larvæ of which destroy c. plants; **-fly**, a two-winged fly (*Anthomyia Brassicæ*), the grubs of which destroy the roots of c.; **-head**, see sense 1; *fig.* a brainless fellow; **-lettuce**, a lettuce forming a c.-like head; **-moth**, one of the Noctuina (*Mamestra Brassicæ*), the caterpillar of which infests the c.; **-palm**, *Areca oleracea*, a native of the West Indies, etc.; see CABBAGE-TREE; **-plant**, a young seedling of the c.; **-rose**, a double red rose, with large round compact flower (*Rosa centifolia*); **-wood**, (*a.*) the wood of the cabbage-tree, (*b.*) *Eriodendron anfractuosum*, a tree related to *Bombax*; **-worm**, any larva which devours c. Hence **Ca·bbagy** *a. rare.*

Cabbage (kæ·bėdʒ), *sb.*[2] 1663. [? corrupt f. *carbage*, used by Herrick; see GARBAGE.] 1. Shreds (or large pieces) of cloth appropriated by tailors in cutting out clothes. †2. *slang.* A tailor -1725. 3. *Schoolboy slang.* A crib; = CAB *sb.*[4]

Ca·bbage, *v.*[1] 1528. [f. CABBAGE *sb.*[1]] †1. *intr.* To grow to a head, as the horns of a deer. b. To form a head, as a cabbage 1601. 2. *trans.* See CABOCHE *v.* 1530.

Ca·bbage, *v.*[2] 1712. [See CABBAGE *sb.*[2]] To appropriate surreptitiously, as a tailor does shreds. b. *Schoolboy slang.* To crib 1837.

Your taylor..cabages whole yards of cloath 1712.

Ca·bbage-tree. 1725. [f. CABBAGE *sb.*[1] 1, 2.] 1. Any palm tree, whose terminal bud is eaten like the head of a cabbage; *esp.* **a.** The West Indian tree, *Areca* or *Oreodoxa oleracea*, also called *Cabbage-palm* and *Palmetto Royal.* **b.** *Chamærops Palmetto* of the Southern U. S. **c.** *Euterpe oleracea* of Brazil. **d.** *Livistona inermis* of N. Australia. **e.** *Corypha australis* of Australia. 2. Other plants and trees, as the Cabbage-bark Tree, *Andira inermis* of the West Indies; *Cordyline indivisa* of New Zealand. **Bastard** or **Black C. T.**, *Andira inermis* (see above);—of St. Helena: *Melanodendron integrifolium*;—of S. America: the leguminous genus *Geoffroya.* **Canary Island C. T.**, *Cacolia kleinia nervifolia*, a composite plant. **Small Umbelled C. T.**, *Commidendron spurium.*

‖**Cabbala** (kæ·bălă). 1521. [a. med.L., ad. Heb. *qabbālāh* 'tradition'.] 1. The oral tradition handed down from Moses to the Rabbis of the Mishnah and the Talmud. b. Later, the pretended tradition of the mystical interpretation of the Old Testament. 2. *gen.* †a. An unwritten tradition -1692. b. Mystery, esoteric doctrine or art 1665.

1. Cabala..is derived fro man to man by mouth only and not by wrytynge FISHER. 2. b. Doctors in the cabala of political science BURKE. Hence, **Cabba·lic** *a.* of or pertaining to the C. var. **Cabala.**

Cabbalism (kæ·băliz'm). 1590. [f. prec.] 1. The system or manner of the Jewish Cabbala 1614. 2. Occult doctrine; mystery 1590. 3. ? (Cf. CABAL, CABALIST.) 1847.

3. I do not know that there is more Cabalism in the Anglican, than in other Churches EMERSON. var. **Cabalism.**

Cabbalist (kæ·bălist). 1533. [ad. med.L. *cabbalista.*] 1. One versed in the Jewish Cabbala. 2. One skilled in mystic arts or learning 1592.

2. Cupid is a casuist, A mystic and a cabalist EMERSON. var. **Cabalist.**

Cabbalistic, -al (kæbăli·stik, -ăl), *a.* Also cabal-. 1624. [f. prec.] Of, pertaining to, or like the Cabbala or cabbalists; having a mystic sense; occult.

Certain..cabalistic signs upon the skull TYLOR. Hence **Cabbali·stically** *adv.*

†**Ca·bbalize**, *v.* Also **cabal-.** 1660. [ad. med.L. *cabbalizare.*] *intr.* To use the manner of the cabbalists; to speak mystically.

Ca·bber. *colloq.* [f. CAB *sb.*[3]] A cab-horse.

Ca·bbing, *vbl. sb.* 1870. [f. CAB *v.*] Cab-driving, cab-letting. Also *attrib.*

Cabble (kæ·b'l), *v.* 1849. *Iron-smelting.* To break up flat pieces of partially finished iron for fagotting. Hence **Ca·bbler.**

Ca·bby. *colloq.* 1859. [f. CAB *sb.*[3]] A cab-driver.

Caber (kēˡ·bəɹ). 1513. [a. Gael. *cabar* pole, spar, rafter.] A pole or spar, usually consisting of the stem of a young pine or fir-tree, used in scaffolding, etc.; and *esp.* in the Highland exercise of *throwing* or *tossing the caber.*

Ca·bful. 1856. [f. CAB *sb.*[3] + -FUL.] As much or as many as a cab will hold.

Cabiai (ka·biˌai). 1774. [Fr., a. Galibi.] The Capybara (*Hydrochœrus Capybara*).

‖**Cabilliau, cabeliau** (ka·bilʸō, kā·bėlyau). 1696. [a. F. *cabillaud, cabliau*, Du. *kabeljauw.*] Cod-fish; also, a dish of cod mashed.

Cabin (kæ·bin). [ME. *cabane*, a. F., :—late L. *capanna*, in Isidore 'tugurium parva casa est; hoc rustici capanna vocant'.] †1. A booth, hut, (soldier's) tent, or other temporary shelter -1649. 2. A permanent mud or turf-built hovel, or the like ME. *rhet.* = 'poor dwelling' 1598. †3. A cell -1616. †b. A small room -1620. †4. A natural cave; a wild beast's den -1794. 5. A compartment in a vessel for eating or sleeping in; an apartment in a ship for officers or passengers ME. Also, †a berth -1769. †6. A litter -1631. †7. A (political) CABINET -1676.

1. Make me a willow Cabine at your gate *Twel. N.* I. v. 287. 2. A mud c. here and there 1832. Uncle Tom's Cabin (*title*). 5. Keepe your Cabines..you do assist the storme SHAKS. *Comb.* **c.-boy**, a boy who waits on the officers and passengers on board.

Cabin (kæ·bin), *v.* 1586. [f. the sb.] 1. *intr.* To dwell, lodge, in, or as in, a cabin (senses 1–4). 2. *trans.* To lodge, shelter, as in a cabin 1602. 3. *trans.* To shut up within narrow bounds. (Mostly after Shaks.) 1605.

1. And sucke the Goate, And cabbin in a Caue *Tit. A.* IV. ii. 179. 3. Now I am cabin'd, crib'd, confin'd, bound in *Macb.* III. iv. 24.

Cabined (kæ·bind), *ppl. a.* 1592. [f. CABIN *sb.* and *v.* + -ED.] Made like a cabin; furnished with a cabin; confined in narrow space; *fig.* confined in action, thought, etc.

Cabinet (kæ·binėt). 1549. [Eng. dim. of CABIN; influenced in senses 3–6 by F. *cabinet*, ad. It. *gabinetto* 'closet, press, chest of drawers'.] I. (Cf. BOWER 1–3.) †1. A little cabin, hut, soldier's tent; a rustic cottage; a lodging, tabernacle; a den of a beast -1640. †2. A summer-house or bower -1737. 3. A small chamber, a private room, a boudoir (*arch.*) 1565. †4. A museum, picture-gallery, etc. -1796. 5. A case for the safe custody of jewels, letters, documents, etc.; and thus, a piece of furniture, often ornamental, fitted with drawers, shelves, etc., for the preservation and display of specimens 1550. †6. *fig.* A secret receptacle, treasure-chamber; *arcanum*, etc. -1667. ¶ Short for *Cabinet photograph.*

3. Cabinets shalt thou make in the arke *Gen.* vi. 14. 5. The best jewel in the best c. DONNE.

II. In politics. 1. (cf. 3) The private room in which the chief ministers of a country meet; the council-chamber. Now = 'political consultation and action'. 1607. b. Those who meet in the cabinet. (Formerly called the *Cabinet Council*, as opp. to the *Privy Council.*) 1644. †c. A meeting of this body. Now called a 'Cabinet council', or 'meeting of the Cabinet'. -1805. 2. **Cabinet Council**: a. the earlier name of *the Cabinet*; see II. 1 b. 1625. b. *now*, A meeting of the Cabinet 1679. 3. **Cabinet Counsellor**, a private counsellor; a member of the Cabinet 1611.

1. a. Equally great in the c. as in the field WELLINGTON. b. The members of the President's C. BANCROFT.

III. *Attrib.*, etc. 1. Of the cabinet; private, secret 1607. 2. Fitted for a private chamber, or worthy to be kept in a cabinet. Occ. technical, as in *c. edition, c. organ, c. photograph, c. piano*, etc. 1696. 3. Fit for cabinet-making, as *c. woods* 1849. 4. Of or pertaining to the political cabinet, as *c. minister*, etc.

1. His private C. devotions CLARENDON. 2. It is quite a c. picture MISS MITFORD. *Comb.* **c.-sized** *a.* of fit size for placing in a c.; (a photograph) of the size larger than a carte-de-visite.

Ca·binet, *v.* 1642. [f. prec.] To enclose in or as in a cabinet.

Ca·binet-ma:ker. 1681. 1. One whose business it is to make cabinets (sense I. 5), and fine joiner's work. 2. *casual.* One who constructs a political cabinet 1884.

Cable (kēˡ·b'l), *sb.* [ME. *cable, cabel, kable*, identical with Du. and Ger. *kabel*; cf. F. *câble*, It. *cappio* noose:—late L. *capulum, caplum* a halter for cattle.] 1. A strong thick rope, orig. of hemp or other fibre, now also of strands of iron wire. Also *fig.* 2. *spec.* (*Naut.*) The thick rope to which a ship's anchor is fastened; hence, anything used for the same purpose, as a chain of iron links (*chain cable*) ME. Also *fig.* b. = *a cable's length*, 'about 100 fathoms; in marine charts 607·56 feet' (Smyth). 3. *Telegraphy.* A rope-like line used for submarine telegraphs, containing a core of insulated conducting wires encased in an outer sheathing of strong wire strands. Also b. a bundle of insulated wires, passing through a pipe laid underground. 1854. c. A CABLEGRAM 1883. 4. *Arch.*, etc. (also *cable-moulding*): A convex moulding made in the form of a rope 1859.

1. A threfolde c. is not lightly broken *Eccles.* iv. 12. 2. The c. broke, the holding-Anchor lost SHAKS. 3. Reported by c. to have put into St. Thomas 1880.

Comb.: **c.-bends**, 'two small ropes for lashing the end of a hempen c. to its own part, in order to secure the clinch by which it is fastened to the anchor-ring' (Smyth); **-buoy**, a cask employed to buoy up the c.; **-laid** *a.*, composed of three main strands, each composed of three smaller strands; **-rope** = sense 1; also c.-laid rope; **-stock**, the capstan; **-tier**, the place in a hold, or between decks, where the cables are coiled away; **-tools**, the apparatus used in drilling deep holes, such as artesian wells, etc.

Cable (kēˡ·b'l), *v.* 1500. [f. the sb.] 1. To furnish with a cable or cables; to fasten with or as with a cable, to tie *up.* 2. *Arch.* To furnish (a column) with cable-mouldings (see CABLE *sb.* 4) 1766. 3. *trans.* and *intr.* To transmit (a message, etc.), or communicate by submarine telegraph 1871.

1. Here I am cabled up above their shot SHIRLEY. 3. The exciting news cabled from Ireland 1880.

Cablegram (kē¹·b'lgræm). 1868. [A hybrid; f. CABLE *sb.* + -GRAM, after TELEGRAM.] A message sent by submarine telegraphic cable.

Cablet (kē¹·blĕt). 1575. [f. CABLE *sb.* + -ET.] A small cable or cable-laid rope less than 10 inches in circumference.

†**Ca·blish.** 1594. [prob. a. Anglo-Fr. **cablis* = F. *chablis*. See Littré *chablis*.] Strictly, windfalls, but explained in 16th c. as = brushwood –1852.

Cabman (kæ·bmæ̆n). 1835. [f. CAB *sb.*³] The driver of a public cab.

Cabob (kăbǫ·b). Also **kabob.** 1690. [Arab. *kabāb*, in same sense.] 1. An oriental dish of meat roasted in small pieces on skewers; in India = roast meat in general. (Now in *pl.*) 1698. 2. A leg of mutton stuffed with white herrings and sweet herbs 1690. Hence **Cabo·b** *v.* to cook thus.

‖**Caboceer** (kæbosī³·ɹ). 1836. [ad. Pg. *cabociero*, f. *cabo* head.] The headman (of a W. Afr. village or tribe).

†**Cabo·che,** *v.* ME. [f. F. *cabocher*, f. *caboche* = It. *capocchia* augm. and pejorative of *capo* head. Cf. CABBAGE *v.*¹] To cut off the head of (a deer) close behind the horns.

Caboched, caboshed, cabossed (kăbǫ ʃt, kăbǫ·st), *ppl. a.* 1572. [f. prec.] *Her.* Borne (as the head of a stag, bull, etc.) full-faced, and cut off close behind the ears; trunked.

‖**Cabochon** (kaboʃoṅ·). 1578. [Fr.: augm. of *caboche*.] A precious stone, as a garnet, etc., when merely polished, without being cut into facets or shaped. Chiefly *attrib.*

Caboodle (kăbū·d'l). orig. *U.S.* 1848. [?; cf. BOODLE.] *The whole c.*, the whole lot.

Caboose (kăbū·s). 1769. [Perh. orig. LG.] 1. The cook-room of merchantmen on deck. b. A cooking-oven or fire-place on land 1859. 2. *U.S.* A van or car on a freight train used by workmen or the men in charge 1881.

‖**Cabot** (kabo, kæ·bət). 1611. [f. Romanic *cabo*, *capo* head.] †1. The Miller's Thumb. 2. In the Channel Islands, a half-bushel 1835.

Cabotage (kæ·bŏtėdʒ). 1831. [a. F. *cabotage*, f. *caboter* to coast.] Coasting; coast-pilotage; the coast carrying trade by sea.

‖**Cabré** (kabre), *a.* [F., f. *cabrer*.] *Her.* Said of a horse: Capering, rearing on the hind legs.

‖**Ca·brie, ca·brit.** 1807. [f. Sp. *cabrito*, dim. of *cabra* goat.] The Pronghorn Antelope.

†**Ca·briole.** 1785. [In 1, a. F. *cabriole*.] 1. A capriole, a caper (of a horse) 1814. 2. A kind of small arm-chair 1785. 3. = CABRIOLET –1801.

Cabriolet (ka·bri,olē¹·). 1823. [a. F., f. *cabriole*, so called from its motion.] A two-wheeled one-horse chaise with a large hood.

Caburn (kæ·bəɹn). 1626. [? conn. w. CABLE.] *Naut.* (*pl.*) 'Spun rope-yarn lines, for worming a cable, seizing, winding tacks', etc. (Smyth).

‖**Cacafue·go.** 1625. [f. L. *cacare*, Sp., Pg. *cagar* + Sp. *fuego*, fire.] A spit-fire, braggart.

Ca' canny (ka,kæ·ni). 1896. [See CALL *v.* III. 3, CANNY *a.* 9.] A policy of 'going slow' at one's work for an employer.

Cacao (kăkē¹·o, kăkā·o). 1555. [Sp., ad. Mexican *caca-uatl* 'caca-tree'. See COCOA.] 1. The seed of *Theobroma Cacao*, N.O. *Byttneriaceæ*, from which cocoa and chocolate are prepared. †2. = COCOA –1662. 3. The Cacao-tree 1756. *Comb.* **c.-butter**, a fatty matter obtained from the cacao-nut, used for making pomades, candles, etc.

Caccagogue (kæ·kagǫg). [f. Gr. κάκκη + -αγωγος.] *Med.* An ointment made of alum and honey, and used to promote stool.

†**Cace·mphaton.** *rare.* 1622. [Gr.] An ill-sounding expression.

Cachalot (kæ·ʃălǫt, kæ·ʃălo). 1747. [a. F., app. meaning 'toothed'.] A genus of whales, belonging to the family *Catodontidæ*, having teeth in the lower jaw.

Cache (kaʃ), *sb.* 1595. [a. F.] 1. A hiding-place; *esp.* a hole or mound made by explorers to hide stores. 2. The stores so hidden 1830. Hence **Cache** *v.* to store (provisions) underground; said also of animals.

Cachectic, -al (kăke·ktik, -ăl), *a.* 1634. [ad. (ult.) Gr. καχεκτικός, + -AL¹. Cf. CACHEXY.] Of or pertaining to cachexy.

†**Cachespell, -pule.** *Sc.* 1526. [app. f. MFlem. *caetse* (= Fr. *chasse*, Eng. CHASE + *speel*.] 1. The game of tennis; also *attrib.* –1818. 2. A tennis-court –1597.

‖**Cachet** (kaʃe). 1639. [Fr.; in 18th c. treated as Eng.] 1. A seal. 2. *fig.* Stamp, mark 1840. 3. *Med.* = CAPSULE 5.

1. *Letter of c.* (F. *lettre de cachet*): a letter under the private seal of the French king, containing an order, often of exile or imprisonment.

Cachexy (kăke·ksi). 1541. [ad. mod.L. *cachexia*, ad. Gr. καχεξία, f. κακός + ἕξις.] a. A depraved condition of the body, in which nutrition is everywhere defective. b. A depraved habit of mind or feeling 1652. Also *fig.*

Cachinnate (kæ·kinē¹t), *v.* 1824. [f. L. *cachinnare*.] *intr.* To laugh loudly or immoderately.

Cachinnation (kækinē¹·ʃən). 1623. [ad. L. *cachinnationem*.] Loud or immoderate laughter.

The hideous grimaces which attended this unusual c. SCOTT. So **Ca·chinnator. Ca·chinnato·ry** *a.* of, pertaining to, or connected with c.

Cacholong (kæ·tʃŏlǫŋ). 1791. ['*Kaschtschilon* = 'beautiful stone' of Kalmucks and Tartars' (Dana).] *Min.* A variety of the opal.

‖**Cachou** (kăʃū·). 1708. [Fr.] 1. = CATECHU. 2. A sweetmeat, made of cashew-nut, etc., used by smokers to sweeten the breath.

‖**Cachucha** (kătʃū·tʃă). Erron. **cachuca.** 1840. [Sp.] A lively Spanish dance.

‖**Cacique** (kăsī·k). 1555. [a. Sp. or F. *cacique* = Haytian wd. for 'lord, chief'.] A native chief or prince of the aborigines in the West Indies, etc. Hence **Caci·queship.**

Cack (kæk), *v.* Now *dial.* ME. [app. ad. L. *cacare*.] 1. *intr.* To void excrement. 2. To void as excrement 1485. So **Cack** *sb.*

†**Cackerel** (kæ·kərĕl). 1583. [app. f. (ult.) Pr. *cagar*:—L. *cacare* (see prec.).] 1. A small fish of the Mediterranean: esp. *Smaris gagarella* (Cuv.), and perh. other small sea-breams –1790. 2. Dysentery 1659.

Cackle (kæ·k'l), *sb.* ME. [f. the vb. stem.] 1. A cackler. Now *dial.* 2. Cackling; as of a hen, etc. 1674. 3. *fig.* Silly chatter 1676. b. A chuckle 1856.

2. The silver goose.. by her c., sav'd the state DRYDEN.

Cackle (kæ·k'l), *v.*¹ [Early ME. *cakelen*; echoic.] 1. *intr.* To make a noise as a hen, *esp.* after laying an egg; also as a goose, or other fowl. 2. *fig.* Said of persons: a. To chatter. b. To talk fussily about a petty achievement. c. To chuckle, to giggle. 1530. 3. *trans.* To utter with cackling ME.

1. Some persons are like hens that after laying must be cackling SECKER. 2. Howe these women cackyll nowe they have dyned PALSGR. 3. To c. satisfaction HOWELLS. Hence **Ca·ckler,** *fig.* a blabber.

Ca·ckle, *v.*² 1748. *Naut.* 'To cover a cable spirally with 3-inch old rope to protect it from chafe in the hawse hole' (Smyth).

Caco-, repr. Gr. κακο-, comb. f. κακός bad, evil, used freely in medical terminology to form names of bad states of bodily organs, most of which, however, are not English in form, e. g. *cacogala·ctia* (a condition in which the milk is bad), *cacothymia* (disordered state of mind), etc. **caco-chy·lous** [Gr. κακόχυλος] *a.*, *Path.* characterized by bad chyle; **-chy·lia,** depraved chylification; **-chymy** [Gr. κακοχυμία], unhealthy state of the fluids of the body; whence **-chy·mic** *a.*, ill-humoured; *sb.* [sc. person]; also **-chy·mical; -de·mon, -dæ·mon,** an evil spirit; *Med.* †nightmare; *Astrol.* the (baleful) Twelfth House in a figure of the Heavens; **-doxy** (*rare*), wrong opinion or doctrine; hence **-do·xical** *a.*; **-epy** [Gr. κακοέπεια], bad pronunciation (opp. to *orthoepy*); hence **-epi·stic** *a.*; **-ga·stric** *a.*, having a deranged stomach (*nonce-wd.*); **-genesis** [Gr. γένεσις], morbid or depraved formation; a monstrosity; **-graphy** [Gr. -γραφία], bad writing; incorrect spelling; a bad system of spelling; hence **-grapher, -gra·phic-, -al** *a.*; **-logy** [Gr. -λογία], †evil report; bad choice of words; bad pronunciation; **-magician,** an evil magician or sorcerer; **-pla·stic** [f. Gr. κακόπλαστος after *plastic*] *a.*, *Phys.* imperfectly organized, as morbid deposits; **-rhy·thmic, -rrhythmic** [f. Gr. κακόρρυθμος after *rhythmic*] *a.*, in bad rhythm; **-trophy** [f. Gr. κακοτροφία], imperfect or disordered nutrition; **-type** [cf. CALOTYPE], an imperfect description in print.

Cacodorous (kækōᵘ·dŏrəs), *a. rare.* 1863. [A hybrid; f. Gr. κακο- + ODOROUS.] Ill-smelling.

Cacodyl (kæ·kodil). 1850. [f. Gr. κακώδης stinking + -YL matter.] *Chem.* An organic compound of arsenic and methyl, $As(CH_3)_2$ = Kd, also called *Arsendimethyl*, a colourless liquid, of disgusting odour, which takes fire on exposure to the air. Hence **Cacody·lic** *a.* of cacodyl, as in *Cacodylic acid*, KdO_2H.

‖**Cacoethes** (kæko,ī·þēs, -ī·þiz). 1563. [L., a. Gr. κακόηθες, adj. neut. used subst. (The Gr. (and L.) pl. was *cacoēthē*.)] a. An evil habit. b. A malignant disease. c. An itch for doing something, as in the *insanabile scribendi cacoethes* (incurable itch of writing) of Juvenal. Hence †**Cacoe·thic** *a.* malignant (as a disease).

‖**Cacolet** (kakolę, -let). 1878. [dial. F., applied in the Pyrenees to a mule chair for crossing the mountains.] A military litter in the form either of arm-chairs attached to the pack-saddle of a mule, or of a bed laid along its back.

†**Ca·colike, -leek.** 1582. Perverted f. CATHOLIC, as if conn. w. κακός bad –1626.

Cacoon (kăkū·n). 1854. [? African.] The bean of a tropical climbing shrub, *Entada scandens* (N.O. *Leguminosæ*), used for making into snuff-boxes, scent-bottles, spoons, etc.

Cacophonous (kækǫ·fŏnəs), *a.* 1797. [f. Gr. κακόφωνος.] Ill-sounding. var. **Caco·pho·nic, -al.** Hence **Caco·phonously** *adv.*; var. **Cacopho·nically.**

Cacophony (kækǫ·fŏni). 1656. [a. F. *cacophonie*, ad. Gr. κακοφωνία, f. κακόφωνος.] 1. The quality of having an ill sound; the use of harsh-sounding words and phrases. (Opp. to *euphony*.) 2. *Mus.* A discordant combination of sounds. Also *fig.* Moral discord. 1789. †3. *Med.* A harsh or discordant state of the voice.

1. Avoid c., and make your periods as harmonious as you can LD. CHESTERF.

Cacoto·pia. *nonce-wd.* A place where all is evil; opp. by Bentham to *Utopia* 'nowhere', taken as **Eutopia* 'a place where all is well'.

Cacoxenite (kækǫ·ksėnəit). [f. Gr. κακο- + ξένος; so called as being injurious when present in iron ore.] *Min.* A native phosphate of iron, containing also water, peroxide of iron, and phosphoric acid, occurring in radiated tufts.

†**Caco-zea·l.** 1579. [after Gr. κακοζηλία.] 1. (Also *cacozelon, cacozelia*): Perverse affectation or imitation, as a fault of style –1644. 2. Perverted zeal 1608.

Cacozyme (kæ·kozəim). [f. Gr. κακο- + ζύμη.] *Med.* A particle of matter conceived as the active agent in producing infectious disease, either by fermentation or by propagation.

Cactus (kæ·ktŏs). 1607. [a. L., a. Gr. κάκτος.] †1. In ancient Nat. Hist.: The Cardoon. 2. A genus of succulent plants with thick fleshy stems, and clusters of spines. Now subdivided into about 20 genera, as *Cereus, Echinocactus, Opuntia*, etc., constituting the N.O. *Cactaceæ*.

†**Cad**¹. 1657. [?] A familiar spirit.

Cad² (kæd). 1790. [app., short f. CADEE, CADDIE, CADET. Sense 5 is prob. an application of sense 4.] †1. An unbooked passenger whose fare the driver of a coach appropriated. 2. An assistant or confederate of a lower grade 1835. †3. An omnibus conductor –1848. 4. = Sc. CADDIE, sense 2. At Oxford formerly applied contemptuously to townsmen generally. 1831. 5. *colloq.* An ill-bred vulgar fellow. Now usu., a person (rarely a female) who is lacking in the finer instincts or feelings 1838.

Cad³. Chiefly *dial.* 1651. Var. of CADDIS²; called more fully **cod-bait, c.-bait, -bit, -bote, -worm.**

Cadastral (kăda·străl), *a.* 1858. [a. mod.F.] Of, pertaining to, or according to a CADASTRE.

C. survey: a. *strictly*, a survey of lands for the purposes of a cadastre; b. *loosely*, a survey on a scale showing accurately the extent and measurement of every field and plot of land; *e.g.* on the scale of 1:2500 or 25:344 inches to a mile. So *c. map, plan*, etc.

‖**Cadastre** (kădα·stəɹ). 1804. [ad. F. *cadastre*, ad. mod. Prov. *cadastro*, ad. It. *catast(r)o* (cf. G, *cat-, kataster*), ad. late Gr. *κατάστιχον* register, prop. *κατὰ στίχον* line by line. (The alleged late L. *capitastrum*, cited in Poste's *Gaii Inst.* (1871) 145, as the basis of cadastre, is a figment.)] **a.** A register of property to serve as a basis of taxation. **b.** (in mod. Fr. use) A public register of the quantity, value, and ownership of the real property of a country.

Cadaver (kădēⁱ·vəɹ). 1500. [a. L., perh. f. *cadere*. So F. *cadavre*.] A dead body, *esp.* of man; a corpse. (Now mostly techn.) **b.** A skeleton. SIR T. BROWNE.

Cadaveric (kædăve·rik, kădæ·vĕrik), *a.* 1835. [f. prec. + -IC (Gr. suffix).] **1.** Of, pertaining to, or characteristic of, dead bodies. (More techn. than *cadaverous*.) **2.** Caused by contact with a dead body 1871.

1. C. rigidity 1865, alkaloids 1880. 2. C. warts 1883.

Cada·verine. 1877. [f. as prec. + -INE.] *Chem.* One of the cadaveric alkaloids or Ptomaines.

Cada·verize, *v.* 1651. [f. as prec.] To make cadaverous. Hence **Cada·verizable** *a.* capable of being converted into lifeless matter.

Cadaverous (kădæ·vĕrəs), *a.* 1627. [ad. F. *cadavéreux*, ad. L. *cadaverosus*.] Of or belonging to a corpse; corpse-like; *esp.* of corpse-like pallor.

Some c. smell DERHAM. John Milton..pale, but not c. ELLWOOD. Hence **Cada·verous·ly** *adv.*, **-ness.**

†**Caddesse, cadesse.** 1565. = CADDOW, a jackdaw –1688.

Caddie, cadie (kæ·di). *Sc.* 1634. [ad. F. *cadet*; see CADET and CADEE.] †**1.** = CADEE, CADET 2, q. v. Also *attrib.* **2.** A lad or man who waits about on the look-out for odd jobs 1730. **b.** *Golf.* A boy (or man) who carries the clubs, etc. 1857. **3.** Lad (*familiar*) 1786.

Caddis[1], caddice (kæ·dis). ME. [Two wds.: 1 (sense 1) OF. *cadaz, cadas*; cf. Irish *cadas* = *cadan* cotton; 2 F. *cadis*.] †**1.** Cotton wool, floss silk, or the like, used in padding –1769. †**2.** Worsted yarn, crewel –1721. Also *attrib.*; also short for *caddis ribbon.* †**3.** A kind of (worsted or ? silk) stuff –1553. **b.** A coarse cheap serge. [Mod.F. *cadis.*] –1862.

Caddis[2], caddice (kæ·dis). 1622. [? dim. of CAD[3].] The larva of species of *Phryganea*, which lives in water, and forms for itself a cylindrical case of hollow stems, small stones, etc.; used as a bait by anglers 1651.

Comb.: **c.-bait, -worm** = prec.; **-fly,** a Phryganea, as the May-fly. Hence **Ca·ddised** *ppl. a.* furnished with a c.

Caddish (kæ·diʃ), *a. colloq.* 1868. [f. CAD[2] 5 + -ISH.] Of the nature of a cad; opp. to gentlemanly. Hence **Ca·ddish-ly** *adv.*, **-ness.**

Caddle, *sb. dial.* 1825. **1.** Disorder, confusion, disturbance. **2.** Bother 1865. Hence **Caddle** *v.* to trouble, disturb.

Ca·ddow[1]. Now *dial.* 1440. [perh. f. *ca, ka* jackdaw (Sc. KAE) + DAW.] A jackdaw.

Ca·ddow[2]. Now *dial.* 1579. [Cf. CADDIS[1] 3 b.] A rough woollen covering.

Caddy[1] (kæ·di). 1792. [corrupt f. CATTY, Malay *kati* a weight equal to $1^1/_3$ lb.] **1.** A small box for holding tea; usu. *tea-caddy.* **2.** *U. S.* A can with a lid, for water, etc. 1883.

Ca·ddy[2]. 1781. [? f. CAD[1].] A ghost, bugbear.

Caddy, var. of CADDIE. Also as vb. 1908.

Cade (kēⁱd), *sb.[1]* ME. [a. F., ad. L. *cadus.*] **1.** A cask or barrel. †**2.** *spec.* A barrel of herrings, holding six great hundreds, *i. e.* 720; afterwards 500. –1866.

Cade (kēⁱd), *sb.[2]* (*a.*) 1450. [?] **1.** as *adj.* Of the young of animals: Cast by the mother and brought up by hand, as a pet 1475. **2.** as *sb.* A pet lamb or foal 1450; a spoiled child (*dial.*) 1877. **3.** Of fruit: Fallen, cast (*rare*) 1876.

1. It's ill bringing up a c. lamb GEO. ELIOT. Hence **Ca·dish** *a.* tame.

†**Cade,** *sb.[3]* Var. of KED, a sheep-louse.

Cade (kēⁱd), *sb.[4]* 1575. [a. F. *cade.*] A species of Juniper, *Juniperus oxycedrus*, yielding *Oil of Cade*, used in veterinary surgery.

Cade, *v.[1]* ? *Obs.* 1599. [f. CADE *sb.[1]*] To put into a cade.

Cade, *v.[2]* 1879. [f. CADE *sb.[2]*] 'To breed up in softness' (J.).

‖**Cadeau** (kado). 1845. [Fr.] A gift.

†**Cadee.** 1689. Early form of CADET, CADDIE: A (gentleman) *cadet* in the army –1789.

Cadence (kēⁱ·dĕns), *sb.* ME. [a. F., ad. It. *cadenza*, on L. type *cadentia* sb., f. *cadere*. In form a doublet of CHANCE.] **I.** In verse and music. **1.** 'The flow of verses or periods' (J.); rhythm, rhythmical construction, measure. **b.** The beat of music, dancing, marching, etc. 1605. **2.** 'The fall of the voice' (J.). 1589. **b.** Occ., the modulation of the voice; accent 1709. **3.** The rising and (*esp.*) falling of a storm, the sea, etc. 1667. **4.** *Mus.* The close of a musical movement or phrase. Also occ. = CADENZA. 1597. **b.** A trill or other closing embellishment. **5.** *Horsemanship.* An equal proportion in all the motions of a horse 1833. **6.** *transf.* Applied to colours 1868.

1. The..golden c. of poesie *L.L.L.* IV. ii. 126. **b.** The occasional boom of the kettle-drum, to mark the c. SCOTT. **2.** A low voice, with a..sweet c. at the end of it STERNE. **3.** Blustring winds..now with hoarse c. lull Seafaring men orewatcht MILT. *P.L.* II. 287.

II. In the L. sense. †**1.** Falling; mode of falling –1667. †**2.** Chance 1601.

1. Now was the Sun in Western c. low MILT. *P.L.* X. 92. Hence **Ca·dence** *v.* (*rare*) to compose metrically. **Ca·denced** *ppl. a.* rhythmical, measured.

Cadency (kēⁱ·dĕnsi). 1627. [ad. L. **cadentia*. Not distinguished from *cadence*, exc. in sense 3.] †**1.** = CADENCE II. 2. 1647. **2.** = CADENCE I. 1. 1627. **3.** Descent of a younger branch from the main line of a family; the state of a cadet 1753.

3. *Mark of c.* (Her.): a variation in the same coat of arms intended to show the descent of a younger branch from the main stock.

Cadent (kēⁱ·dĕnt), *a.* 1586. [ad. L. *cadentem.*] **1.** Falling 1605. **2.** *Astrol.* Of a planet: Going down, as *c. houses* in a figure of the heavens 1586. **3.** Having cadence 1613. **4.** *Geol.* Applied to a division of the palæozoic strata of the Alleghanies, corresponding to the lower middle Devonian.

1. With c. Teares fret Channels in her cheekes SHAKS.

‖**Cadenza** (kăde·ntsă). 1836. [It.; see CADENCE.] *Mus.* A flourish given to a solo voice or instrument at the close, or between two divisions, of a movement. (Occ. called *cadence.*) **b.** A brilliant solo passage towards the close of the first or last movement of a concerto, in which the main themes are further developed.

Ca·der, cadar. Now *dial.* ME. [prob. a Welsh *cader* chair.] †**1.** A cradle. ME. only. **2.** A light frame of wood put over a scythe 1679. **3.** (Cf. F. *cadre* frame.) A small frame of wood, on which a fisherman keeps his line (*dial.*).

Cadet (kăde·t). 1610. [a. F., a. Pr. *capdet* :—Rom. **capitello*, dim. of L. *caput*; hence, inferior head of a family.] **1.** A younger son or brother. **b.** A younger branch of a family, or a member of it 1690. **c.** The youngest son 1646. **2.** A gentleman who entered the army without a commission, to learn the profession and find a career for himself. **b.** A junior in the East India Company's service. See also CADEE, CADDIE. 1651. **3.** A student in a naval or military college 1775. **b.** A schoolboy receiving military training, esp. to qualify for the O.T.C. Also *attrib.*, as **c. corps.**

3. Watch Sandhurst too, its debts and its Cadets HOOD. Hence **Cade·tship,** the status of a c.; the commission given to a c.; var. **Cade·tcy.**

Cadew (kæ·diu). 1668. Var. of CADDIS[2].

Cadge (kædʒ), *sb.[1]* 1615. [App. a var. of CAGE perh. influenced by CADGE *v.*] **1.** *Falconry.* A round frame of wood on which hawks are carried for sale. **2.** A pannier.

Cadge, *sb.[2] vulgar.* 1812. [f. CADGE *v.*] The action of cadging.

Cadge (kædʒ), *v.* ME. [? conn. w. CATCH; cf. *grutch, grudge*, etc.] **I.** †**1.** *trans.* ? To tie –1627. †**2.** To bind the edge of a garment 1530. **II.** †**3.** To carry about (*dial.*) 1607. **4.** To stuff the belly (*dial.*) 1695. **5.** *intr.* To go about as a cadger or pedlar; to go about begging 1812. *trans.* To get by begging 1848.

Cadger (kæ·dʒəɹ). 1450. [f. prec. + -ER[1].] **1.** A carrier; *esp.* one who travels between town and country with butter, eggs, etc., and shop-wares. **2.** A hawker, a street-seller 1840. **b.** One who gets his living by begging or questionable means 1851. **3.** *Falconry.* A man who carries hawks. (Cf. OF. *cagier.*) 1834.

1. The King's errand lying in the cadger's gate SCOTT.

Ca·dgy, *a. Sc.* and *n. dial.* 1724. [?] **1.** Wanton; amorous. **2.** Cheerful; glad 1725. Hence **Ca·dgily** *adv.* **Ca·dginess.**

‖**Cadi** (kā·di, kēⁱ·di). 1590. [a. Arab. *qādī* judge.] A civil judge among the Turks, Arabs, etc.; usu. the judge of a town or village. Hence **Ca·diship,** the office of a c.

Cadie, var. of CADDIE.

‖**Cadilesker** (kādile·skəɹ). 1686. [f. CADI + Turk. *leskar* army.] A chief judge in the Turkish empire, whose jurisdiction originally extended to soldiers.

‖**Cadjan** (kα·dʒăn). *Anglo-Ind.* 1698. [ad. Malay *kājāng.*] **1.** Coco-palm leaves matted, used for thatch. **2.** A strip of fan-palm leaf prepared for writing on; a document written on such a strip 1707. Also *attrib.*

Ca·dlock, var. of CHARLOCK.

Cadmean (kædmī·ăn), *a.* Also **Cadmian, -mæan.** 1603. [ad. L. *Cadmeus*, a. Gr. *Καδμεῖος*, f. *Κάδμος*.] Pertaining to Cadmus, the fabulous founder of Thebes in Bœotia, and introducer of the alphabet into Greece.

Cadmean victory (Gr. *Καδμεία νίκη*), a victory involving the victor's ruin; usu. associated with Thebes or the Thebans.

†**Ca·dmia.** 1657. [a. L. *cadmĭa*, a. Gr. *καδμεία* or *καδμία γῆ*.] *Chem.* 'The ancient name of calamine' (Ure); also, a sublimate consisting of oxide of zinc; an ore of cobalt –1837.

Cadmium (kæ·dmiŏm). 1822. [f. CADMIA calamine; cf. *sodium*, etc.] *Chem.* A bluish-white metal, occurring sparsely in zinc ores. Symbol Cd. **C. yellow,** an intense yellow pigment, consisting of cadmium sulphide.

†**Cadou·k.** *Sc.* Also **caduac.** 1637. [app. a. F. *caduc.*] A casualty, a windfall.

‖**Cadre** (kadr). 1830. [F. *cadre* frame. ad. It. *quadro* :—L. *quadrum.*] **1.** A frame, framework; scheme. **2.** *Mil.* **a.** The permanent establishment forming the framework of a regiment 1851. **b.** The complement of officers of a regiment; the list of such officers 1864.

Caduac, perversion of CADOUK.

Caducary (kădiū·kări), *a.* 1768. [ad. L. *caducarius* relating to *bona caduca.*] Subject to, relating to, or by way of escheat or lapse.

‖**Caduceus** (kădiū·siŏs). Pl. **caducei** (-sɪ,əi). 1591. [L., ad. Dor. Gr. *καρύκειον* a herald's wand, f. *κῆρυξ*.] A herald's wand. *spec.* The wand carried by Mercury, the messenger of the gods; usually represented with two serpents twined round it. (The proper sense in Eng.)

He tooke *Caduceus* his snakie wand, With which the damned ghosts he gouerneth SPENSER. var. †**Ca·duce.** Hence **Cadu·cean** *a.* pertaining to a c.

Cadu·ciary, var. of CADUCARY, after *fiduciary*.

Caducibranchiate (kădiū:sibræ·ŋki,eⁱt), *a.* 1835. [f. L. *caducus* + *branchiæ*, whence mod. L. *Caducibranchia*, the Batrachians.] *Zool.* Of Amphibians: Losing their gills before reaching maturity (like the frog). Also as *sb.*

Caducity (kădiū·sĭti). 1769. [ad. F. *caducité.*] **1.** Tendency to fall; transitoriness, frailty 1793. **2.** *esp.* Senility 1769. **3.** *Roman Law.* Lapse of a testamentary gift. **4.** *Zool.* and *Bot.* Quality of being caducous 1881.

1. The..c. of language, in virtue of which every effusion of the human spirit is lodged in a body of death M. PATTISON. **2.** This melancholick proof of my c. CHESTERF.

Caducous (kădiū·kəs), *a.* 1808. [f. L. *caducus*, f. *cadere* + -OUS.] **1.** *Zool.* and *Bot.* Used of organs or parts that fall off naturally when they have served their purpose; as leaves, the placenta, etc. **2.** = CADUKE 2. **3.** *Roman Law.* Applied to testamentary gifts which lapsed from the donee 1880. var. †**Cadu·ce.**

†**Cadu·ke,** *a.* ME. [ad. F. *caduc*, f. as prec.] **1.** Liable to fall. **2.** Transitory, perishable –1688; var. †**Cadu·cal.** **3.** Infirm –1541. **4.** Epileptic. ME. only.

2. Euery thynge in this world is c. FISHER.

Cady, var. of CADI, CADDIE.

Cæ-; see also CE-.

Cæcal (sī·kăl), *a.* 1826. [f. CÆCUM + -AL.] *Phys.* Pertaining to, or like, the cæcum; having a blind end.

‖**Cæ·cias.** ? *Obs.* 1653. [L.; a. Gr. καικίας.] The north-east wind personified.

Cæcilian (sĭsi·liăn). [f. L. *cæcilia* a kind of lizard.] One of the *Cæciliadæ*, a family of Amphibia, having the form of serpents; their eyes are very small.

Cæcity, var. of CECITY, blindness.

‖**Cæcum** (sī·kŏm). Occas. **cecum**; *pl.* **cæca.** 1721. [L.; for *intestinum cæcum.*] *Phys.* 1. The blind gut; the first part of the large intestine, which is prolonged into a cul-de-sac. 2. With pl. *cæca*: Any tube with one end closed, as the *pyloric cæca* in fishes 1753. Hence **Cæ·ciform** *a.* **Cæci·tis**, inflammation of the c.

Cænozoic, var. of CAINOZOIC.

Caen-stone. A lightish-yellow building-stone found near Caen in Normandy.

Cæsar (sī·zăɹ). ME. [The earliest L. wd. adopted in Teut. See also KAISER, and CZAR.] 1. The cognomen of the Roman dictator Caius Julius Cæsar, used as a title of the emperors down to Hadrian (A.D. 138), and subseq. as a title of the heir-presumptive. In mod. use often applied to all the emperors. b. The emperor of the Holy Roman Empire; the German KAISER 1674. 2. *fig.* or *transf.* An autocrat, emperor 1593. b. *contextually*, The temporal monarch; the civil power. (See *Matt.* xxii. 21.) 1601. Also *attrib.*

1. Before whom Cæsars as well as Pontiffs were to quail FREEMAN. 2. Lead thine own captivity captive, and be C. within thyself SIR T. BROWNE. Hence **Cæ·sardom**, the dominion or dignity of the Cæsars. †**Cæsa·reate**, **Cæ·sarship**, the imperial dignity.

Cæsarean, Cæsarian (sĭzē·riăn). 1528. [ad. L. *Cæsarianus*; also f. *Cæsareus.*] **A.** *adj.* Of or pertaining to Cæsar or the Cæsars 1659. **C. birth, operation, section** (in *Obstet. Surg.*): the delivery of a child by cutting through the walls of the abdomen, as was done with Julius Cæsar.

B. *sb.* An adherent of Cæsar, of the Emperor (against the Pope), or of an imperial system.

Cæsarism (sī·zăriz'm). 1857. [f. CÆSAR.] The system of absolute government founded by Cæsar 1857. b. = ERASTIANISM 1876.

Monarchical absolutism, or what I..call modern C. 1857. So **Cæ·sarist**, an imperialist; **Cæ·sarize**, *v. intr.* to play the Cæsar; *trans.* to make like Cæsar or Cæsar's.

Cæsious (sī·ziəs), *a.* 1835. [f. L. *cæsius.*] Bluish or greyish green. (Chiefly *Bot.*)

Cæsium (sī·ziŏm). 1861. [f. L. *cæsium*, adj. neut.] *Chem.* A silvery white metal; named from two blue lines in its spectrum. Symbol Cs.

Cæspitose, cesp- (se·spitōᵘs), *a.* 1830. [ad. mod.L. *cæspitosus*, f. *cæspitem.*] *Bot.* Growing in thick tufts or clumps; turfy.

Cæsura (siziū°·ră, *sis-*). 1556. [a. L. *cæsura* cutting, metrical pause, f. *cæs-* ppl. stem of *cædere.*] 1. In Gr. and L. prosody: The division of a metrical foot between two words, *esp.* near the middle of the line 1727. b. The lengthening of the last syllable of a word by arsis which sometimes occurs in the cæsura 1678. 2. In Eng. prosody: A pause about the middle of a metrical line 1556. 3. *transf.* A formal stop; an interruption 1596.

Cæsu·ral, Cæsu·ric *a.* of or pertaining to a c.

‖**Café** (kæ·fe). 1816. [Fr., coffee, coffee-house.] 1. A coffee-house, a restaurant; now, a certain class of restaurant. 2. Coffee, in **c. au lait** (kæ·fe₁olēⁱ·), coffee with an equal quantity of hot milk; also, the colour of this 1818; **c. noir** (nwār), lit. black coffee, i.e coffee without milk 1863.

†**Caffa.** 1531. 1. A rich silk cloth much used in the 16th c. –1641. 2. A kind of painted cotton cloth made in India –1810.

Caffeic (kæfī·ik), *a.* 1853. [ad. F. *caféique*, assim. to mod.L. *coffea.*] *Chem.* Of or pertaining to coffee; *esp.* in **c. acid** ($C_9H_8O_4$), a substance found in brilliant yellow prisms. So **Ca·ffeidine**, an uncrystallizable base ($C_7H_{12}N_4O$), produced by the action of alkalis on caffeine. **Caffeta·nnate**, a salt of **Caffeta·nnic acid**, an astringent acid found in coffee berries, etc.

Caffeine (kæ·fi₁əin). 1830. [ad. F. *caféine*, f. *café*; see prec.] *Chem.* A vegetable alkaloid crystallizing in white silky needles, found in the leaves and seeds of the coffee and tea plants, the leaves of guarana, maté, etc.

Caffia·ceous, prop. **Coffeaceous**, *a. rare.* 1865. *Bot.* Allied to the genus *Coffea*, of which *C. arabica* is the coffee shrub.

Caffre (kæ·fəɹ). 1599. See also KAFFIR. [ad. Arab. *kafir* infidel, impious wretch, f. *kafara* to conceal, deny.] ‖1. Infidel; a word applied by the Arabs to all non-Mohammedans 1680. 2. *spec.* One of a South African race of blacks belonging to the Bântu family, and living in *Caffraria.* Also the name of their language, and used *attrib.* 1599. 3. A native of Kafiristan in Asia; see KAFIR.

Comb.: **C.-bread**, a S. Afr. cycadaceous tree with edible pith; **-corn**, Indian millet, *Sorghum vulgare.*

‖**Cafila** (kā·filă). 1594. [Arab. *qāfilah* caravan.] A caravan.

‖**Caftan** (kaftā·n, kæ·ftăn). 1591. [Turk. and Pers.] An oriental garment consisting of a long under-tunic tied at the waist with a girdle.

Wily Jews with their high caps and caftans WILLIS.

†**Cag** (kæg), *sb.*[1] 1452. [Same as ON. *kaggi*, Sw. *kagge.* Now corrupted to KEG; cf. the Cockney *keb.*] 1. A keg –1797. 2. A small fishing vessel. (Du. *kaag.*) –1667.

Cag, *sb.*[2] Now *dial.* 1604. A stiff point.

Cag, *v. dial.* 1504. To offend, insult.

Cage (kēⁱdʒ), *sb.* ME. [a. F. *cage*:—late L. **cavja*:—L. *cavea*, f. *cavus.*]

I. 1. A box or place of confinement for birds or other animals, made wholly or partly of wire, or bars of metal or wood, so as to admit air and light. Also *fig.* †2. A lock-up –1850. 3. Anything like a cage ME.

1. Stone walls do not a prison make Nor iron bars a c. LOVELACE. [The soul's] c. of flesh DANIEL. 2. *2 Hen. VI*, IV. ii. 56.

II. Technical.

1. *Mining.* a. An enclosed platform for hoisting in a vertical shaft 1851. b. The drum on which the rope is wound 1854. 2. A confining framework; *esp.* a. *Carpentry.* A framework of timber, enclosing another work within it, as the c. of a windmill. b. One confining the motion of a ball valve. c. A strainer over the mouth of a pipe, etc. d. A cup with a glass bottom and cover, to hold a drop of water for microscopic examination. 3. An iron framework, to contain burning combustibles, used to mark an intricate channel, etc. 1837. 4. *Falconry.* A frame to carry hawks upon. See CADGE *sb.*[1] 1828.

Hence **Ca·geless** *a.* **Ca·geling**, a bird kept in a c. *Comb.* **c.-work**, open work like the bars of a c.; †*Naut.* the upper works of a ship.

Cage (kēⁱdʒ), *v.* 1577. [f. prec.] **a.** To confine in or as in a cage. **b.** To fit as a cage in a mine-shaft 1860.

Caged vp like linnets 1625. Hence **Caged** *ppl. a.* confined in or as in a cage; †closed like a cage, as *caged cloister* SHAKS.

Ca·ggy, *a.* 1848. [f. next.] 1. Unwholesome. 2. Ill-natured (*dial.*) 1855.

Cagmag (kæ·gmæg), *sb.* (*a.*) *dial.* 1771. [?] 1. A tough old goose. b. Unwholesome meat; offal. 2. *adj.* Decaying, refuse 1859.

‖**Cagot** (kago). 1844. [Fr., perh. containing *-goth* (cf. *bigot*); see Littré.] Name of an outcast race in southern France; occ. = 'pariah'.

‖**Cagui** (kā·gi). 1753. [Brazilian.] The fox-tailed monkey.

‖**Cahier** (ka·*ie*). 1849. [F., in OF. *quaier*; see QUIRE.] A book of loose sheets tacked together; whence, reports of proceedings, etc. (Hardly in Eng. use.)

Cahoot (kăhū·t). *U.S.* [prob. a. F. *cahute* cabin.] A company, or partnership. Hence **Cahoo·t** *v.* to act in partnership.

Caic, caïk(e, -jee; see CAIQUE, -JEE.

‖**Caid.** Same as ALCAYDE.

‖**Cailleach** (ka·lʸăχ). In Scott **cailliach.** 1814. [Gael.] An old (Highland) woman, a crone.

Caimacam, var. of KAIMAKAM.

Caiman, var. of CAYMAN.

Cain, kain (kēⁱn). *Sc.* and *Ir.* ME. [a. Celt. *cáin* 'law', 'rent, tribute, fine'.] 1. A rent paid in kind. Also *attrib.* and *fig.* 2. (Ireland) A penalty for an offence 1518.

Cain[2] (kēⁱn). ME. The proper name of the first murderer (*Gen.* iv), used allusively. *To raise C.* (U.S.): to make a disturbance.

Comb. †**C.-coloured**, red or reddish-yellow, the reputed colour of the hair of C. Hence **Cai·nian** = *Cainite.* **Cai·nish** *a.* of the temper of C. **Cai·nism**, the heresy of the Cainites. **Cai·nite**, (*a.*) one of a 2nd c. sect who treated C. and other wicked Scriptural characters as saints; (*b.*) a descendant of C.; also *fig.* **Caini·tic** *a.* pertaining to C. or the Cainites.

Ca'ing-whale (kā·iŋ₁hwēⁱl). *Sc.* 1865. [*Ca'ing* (*calling*; see CALL) = driving like a herd.] The round-headed porpoise, which frequents the shores of Orkney, Iceland, etc.

Cainozoic (kainozōᵘ·ik, kēⁱno-), *a.* Also **kainozoic, cænozoic.** 1854. [f. Gr. καινός + ζῷον. Analogy demands *cænozoic.*] *Geol.* Of or pertaining to the third great geological period (also called TERTIARY), or to the remains or formations characteristic of it.

Caiper-caillie; see CAPER-.

Caique (ka₁ī·k). 1625. [a. F., ad. Turk. *kaik.*] 1. A light skiff propelled by one or more rowers, used on the Bosporus. 2. A Levantine sailing-vessel 1666.

1. Glanced many a light c. along the foam BYRON. Hence **Cai·quejee, cai·kjee**, rower of a c.

Cair, *v.* [ME. *kayre*, a. ON. *keyra* to drive, etc.] †1. *intr.* To go, make one's way (*poet.*) –1470. †2. *trans.* To bring. ME. only. 3. *trans.* and *intr.* To stir about. (*mod. Sc.*)

Caird (kēᵊɹd). *Sc.* 1663. [a. Gael. *ceard*; cogn. w. L. *cerdo*, Gr. κερδώ.] A travelling tinker; a gipsy. Hence **Cai·rdman** *sb.*

Cairn (kēᵊɹn). 1535. [mod. Sc. f. *carn*, a. Gael. *carn* heap of stones. ? = Gaulish *karn-on* neut. 'horn'.] 1. A pyramid of rough stones raised: a. as a memorial or a sepulchral monument. b. as a boundary mark, a landmark on a mountain top, etc., or an indication of a cache 1770. c. A mere pile of stones 1699. 2. The smallest breed of British terrier 1910.

a. *To add a stone to any one's c.*: to do all possible honour to his memory after death. Hence **Cairned** *a.* furnished with a c.

Cairngorm, -gorum (kēᵊ·ɹngōᵊ·ɹm, -gōᵊ·rəm). 1794. [f. the mountain in Scotland (Gael. *Carngorm*, i. e. blue cairn).] (More fully *C. stone*:) A yellow or wine-coloured variety of rock-crystal; much used for ornamenting articles of Highland wear.

Caisson (kēⁱ·sən). Also **caissoon.** 1704. [a. F., f. *caisse.*] 1. *Mil.* a. A chest containing explosives, to be buried and fired as a mine. b. A chest containing ammunition; a wagon for conveying ammunition. Also *fig.* 1704. 2. *Hydraul.* a. A large water-tight chest used in laying foundations of bridges, etc. in deep water 1753. b. A vessel in the form of a boat used as a floodgate in docks 1854. c. A machine for raising sunken ships; = CAMEL, q. v. 1811. 3. *Arch.* 'A sunken panel in ceilings, vaults, and cupolas' (Gwilt).

Comb., etc.: **c. disease**, a disease produced by the sudden variations of atmospheric pressure experienced by men who work in caissons; **-gate** = sense 2 b.

Caitiff (kēⁱ·tif). ME. [a. ONF. *caitif*, *caitive*:—L. *captivum.*] **A.** *sb.* †1. Orig.: A captive, a prisoner –1603. †2. One in a piteous case –1678. 3. A base, mean, despicable wretch; a villain. Cf. *wretch.* ME.

2. Alas poore Caitiffe *Oth.* IV. i. 109. 3. The wickedst caitiffe on the ground *Meas. for M.* V. i. 53. Hence †**Caitive** *v.* to make captive.

B. *adj.* †1. Captive. ME. only. †2. Wretched –1583. 3. Vile, mean; worthless, miserable ME.

1. He..ledde caitifte caytif WYCLIF. 3. Caitiue iudas ME. Hence †**Cai·tifly, -ively** *adv.* †**Cai·tifness, -iveness.**

†**Cai·tifty, -ivetie.** ME. only. [a. OF. *caitivetet*:—L. *captivitatem.*] Captivity; wretchedness; vileness.

‖**Cajan** (kēⁱ·dʒăn, kā·dʒan). 1693. [a. Malay *kāchang.*] A genus of plants, *Cajanus* (N.O. *Leguminosæ*), and esp. *C. Indicus*, cultivated for the seeds or pulse, an article of food, called in India *Dhal*, *Dhol*, in Jamaica *Pigeon-peas.*

Cajaput, cajeput, vars. of CAJUPUT.

Cajole (kădʒōᵘ·l), *v.* 1645. [a. F. *cajoler*, of uncertain origin.] 1. *trans.* To get one's way with, by delusive flattery, specious promises, or the like. Const. *into*, *from*, *out of.* 2. *intr.* or *absol.* To use cajolery 1665.

1. Abused and cajoled, as they call it, by falsities

and court-impudence MILT. Hence **Cajo·lement.** **Cajo·ler.** **Cajo·lingly** *adv.*

Cajolery (kădʒōu·ləri). 1649. [a. F. *cajolerie*, f. *cajoler*.] The action or practice of cajoling; persuasion by false arts.

Those infamous cajolleries EVELYN.

‖**Cajuput** (kæ·dʒəpŏt). 1832. [(Ult.) a. Malay *kayu-putih*, i.e. *kayu* wood + *puteh* white.] **1.** *C. tree*: one or more species of *Melaleuca* (N.O. *Myrtaceæ*), esp. *M. minor* (*Cajuputi*) 1876. **2.** *C. oil*: the oil obtained from these trees 1832. **3.** Also, *Oreodaphne californica* (N.O. *Lauraceæ*). Hence **Cajuputene, Cajputene,** *Chem.* '$C_{10}H_{16}$, the hydrocarbon of which oil of c. is the hydrate' (*Syd. Soc. Lex.*).

Cake (kēɪk), *sb.* [ME. *kake, cake*, prob. a. ON. *kaka* fem., rel. to G. *kuche*.] **1.** With pl.: **a.** *orig.* A smallish flattened sort of bread, regularly shaped, and usually turned in baking. **b.** *esp.* in Scotland, *spec.* A thin hard-baked brittle species of oaten-bread 1572. **c.** In England, a sweetened composition of flour and other ingredients, as eggs, milk, dried fruits, nuts, flavourings, etc., often having its surface partly or wholly iced. **2.** As a substance 1579. **3.** Applied to other preparations; e.g. a *fish-cake, potato-cake*, etc. **4.** A flattened mass of any solidified or compressed substance, as soap, coagulated blood, tobacco, etc. 1528. Also *fig.* **5.** *dial.* and *slang.* A stupid fool 1785.

1. b. *Land of cakes*, Scotland. **4.** To create what may be called a c. of custom BAGEHOT.

Phr. *To take the c.*; to rank first; to beat all. †*One's c. is dough*: one's project has failed of success. *Tam. Shr.* I. i. 110. *Cakes and ale*, good things.

Comb.: **c.-bread**, bread made in cakes, or of the quality of c.; **-house**, †one where cakes are sold; one where cakes (sense 4) are stored; **-meal**, 'linseed meal obtained by grinding the cake after the expression of the oil'; **-urchin**, an echinoderm of a discoid shape. Hence **Ca·ky** *a.* like, or of the nature of a c.; weak-minded (*dial.*).

Cake (kēɪk), *v.* 1607. [f. prec.] **1.** *trans.* To form into a cake or flattish compact mass: also *fig.* (Chiefly *pass.*) **2.** *intr.* (for *refl.*) To form (itself) into a cake. Const. *together.* 1615.

2. The stiff clays..in dry weather..c. SIR H. DAVY.

Cal (kæl). 1875. Cornish name of WOLFRAM.

‖**Calaba** (kæ·lăbă). 1753. [S. Amer.] A tropical evergreen tree (*Calophyllum Calaba*), yielding a lamp-oil, and **Calaba-balsam.**

Calabar, var. of CALABER.

Calabar-bean (kælăbā·ɪ bīn). 1876. [f. *Calabar*, on the Gulf of Guinea.] The seed of *Physostigmum venenosum*, called also the Ordeal-bean, used as a test of witchcraft. Hence **Calabarine,** an alkaloid found in this bean.

Calabash (kæ·lăbæʃ). 1596. [a. F. *calebasse*, ad. Sp. *calabaça*, perh. ad. (ult.) Pers. *kharbuz* 'melon'.] **1.** The name of various gourds or pumpkins 1658. **2.** The fruit of the Calabash Tree of America. Also = *Calabash-tree.* 1596. **3.** The hollow shell of 1 or 2, used as a water-bottle, kettle, or other utensil 1657. Also *transf.* **4.** *U. S.* The head (*joc.*).

Comb., etc.: **c. gourd,** the bottle-gourd (*Lagenaria vulgaris*) = sense 1; **-tree,** a tropical American tree (*Crescentia Cujete*), bearing the fruit called Calabash (sense 2); also, the Baobab tree.

Calaber, calabar (kæ·lăbəɪ). ME. [app. f. F. *Calabre*, Calabria.] **1.** The fur of some kind of squirrel; now, commercially, of the grey or Siberian squirrel: also *attrib.* †**2.** The animal itself –1626.

Calaboose (kælăbū·z). *U.S.* 1837. [Negro Fr., ad. Sp. *calabozo*.] A common prison (*local*).

‖**Calade** (kala·d, kălēɪ·d). 1731. [a. F., ad. It. *calata*, f. *calare*:—L. *chalare*, ad. Gr. χαλᾶν to let down.] The slope of a manège ground, down which a horse is ridden at speed, to supple his haunches. (Dicts.)

‖**Caladium** (kălēɪ·diŏm). 1845. [ad. Malay *kélády*; see N.E.D.] *Bot.* A genus of plants of the Arum family having starchy corms.

Calamanco (kælămæ·ŋko). 1592. [Of unkn. origin.] **1.** A glossy woollen stuff of Flanders, twilled and chequered in the warp, so that the checks are seen on one side only. Also *attrib.* **b.** *ellipt.* [sc. *garments.*] 1859. **2.** *transf.* Used of wood and plaster buildings 1792.

Calamander (kælămæ·ndəɪ). 1804. [? Du.; corruption of *Coromandel.*] An extremely hard cabinet wood of Ceylon and India, the product of *Diospyros quæsita* (N.O. *Ebenaceæ*), specifically akin to ebony.

Calamary (kæ·lămări). 1567. [f. L. *calamarius* pertaining to a calamus or pen.] The general name for Cephalopods or Cuttle-fish of the family *Teuthiaæ*, esp. of the genus *Loligo*, having a long narrow body flanked by two triangular fins, and with the internal shell a horny flexible pen: *e.g.* the Common C., Squid, or Pen-fish.

‖**Calambac** (kæ·lămbæk). 1594. [? Malay.] Aloes-wood or Eagle-wood. (See AGALLOCH.) var. ‖**Calambou·r.** [Fr.]

Calami·ferous, *a.* 1753. [f. CALAMUS.] †Culmiferous; bearing reeds, reedy. So **Ca·lamiform** *a.* of the shape of a reed.

‖**Calamina·ris,** *a.* and *sb.* 1577. [L.: *sc. lapis.*] Earlier f. CALAMINE. var. †**Calami·nary, -ar.**

Calamine (kæ·lăməin). 1601. [a. F., ad. med.L. *calamina*, app. corrupted from L. *cadmia*, Gr. καδμεία, καδμία.] *Min.* An ore of zinc: orig. applied to both the carbonate $ZnCO_3$, and the hydrous silicate Zn_2SiO_4, H_2O, but chiefly, in France and England, to the former. The silicate is distinguished as *Siliceous* or *Electric C.* (See also N.E.D.) Also *attrib.*

Calamint (kæ·lămint). [ME. *calament*, a. F., ad. L. *calaminthe*, a. Gr. καλαμίνθη, καλάμινθος, f. (in pop. etym.) καλός + μίνθη, μίνθος mint.] *Bot.* A genus of aromatic herbs, *Calamintha* (N.O. *Labiatæ*), including *C. officinalis, C. Nepeta, C. sylvatica*, etc.

†**Calami·strate,** *v. rare.* [f. L. *calamistratus*, f. *calamistrum* curling-iron; cf. F. *calamistrer.*] *trans.* To curl or frizzle (the hair). BURTON. Hence **Ca:lamistra·tion.**

Calamite (kæ·lăməit). 1837. [ad. mod.L. *calamites* generic name, f. L. *calamus.*] **1.** *Palæont.* A fossil plant of the Coal Measures, perh. allied to the *Equisetaceæ* or Mare's-tails, but having a woody stem. **2.** *Min.* A variety of tremolite, occurring in reed-like crystals 1882.

Calamitous (kălæ·mitəs), *a.* 1545. [ad. F. *calamiteux, -eus*, ad. L. *calamitosus*, contr. of *calamitatosus.*] **1.** Fraught with or causing calamity; full of affliction or misery. **2.** Involved in calamity or distress –1752.

1. That c. error of the Jewes, misapprehending the Prophesies of their Messias SIR T. BROWNE. Hence **Cala·mitous-ly** *adv.*, **-ness** (*rare*).

Calamity (kălæ·miti). 1490. [a. F. *calamité*, f. L. *calamitatem*; ? from **calamis*, whence *incolumis.*] **1.** The condition of grievous affliction or adversity; deep distress arising from some adverse circumstance or event. **2.** A grievous disaster or misfortune 1552.

1. Thou art wedded to calamitie *Rom. & Jul.* III. iii. 3. **3.** The bearing well of all calamities MILT.

‖**Calamus** (kæ·lămŏs). ME. [a. L., Gr. κάλαμος.] †**1.** A reed, a cane: vaguely used by early writers –1712. **2.** **Sweet C.,** *C. aromaticus*: **a.** an eastern aromatic plant (*Ex.* xxx. 23), taken by some to be the Sweet-scented Lemon Grass of Malabar; **b.** the native Sweet Flag (*Acorus Calamus*) ME. **3.** A genus of palms comprising many species, the stems of which form canes or rattans 1836. **4.** A fistular stem without an articulation. var. †**Ca·lamy.**

†**Cala·nder, -re.** 1599. [a. F. *calandre*, ad. med.L. *calandra*, Gr. κάλανδρος.] A species of lark, *Alauda Calandra* –1803.

‖**Calando** (kala·ndo). [It., = 'slackening'.] *Mus.* A direction: Diminishing in tone and rate.

Calash (kălæ·ʃ), *sb.* Also **caleche, calèche.** 1666. [a. F. *calèche*, of Slav. origin, f. (ult.) *kolo* wheel.] **1.** A light carriage with low wheels, having a removable folding hood. In Canada a two-wheeled, one-seated vehicle, with a seat for the driver on the splashboard. **2.** The folding hood of various vehicles, *e.g.* a carriage, a perambulator, etc. 1856. **3.** A woman's hood, supported with hoops, and projecting beyond the face. Formerly much worn. 1774. Also *attrib.*

1. The Canadians.. were riding about in caleches 1866. **3.** That lady in her clogs and c. THACKERAY.

Calastic, *a.*, for *chalastick*, ad. Gr. χαλαστικός. BURTON.

‖**Calathi·dium.** [mod.L.; dim. f. L. *calathus.*] *Bot.* The flower-head of Compositæ.

‖**Calathus** (kæ·lăþŏs). Pl. **-i.** 1753. [L.; a. Gr. κάλαθος vase-shaped basket.] **1.** An ancient basket (in sculpture, etc.). **2.** = CALATHIDIUM. Hence **Ca·lathiform** *a.*

Calavance (kæ·lăvæns). ? *Obs.* 1620. [Orig. *garvance, caravance*, a. Sp. *garbanzo* chick-pea.] A name for certain varieties of pulse, as *Dolichos barbadensis*, etc.

Salt fish and calavances MARRYAT.

Cala·verite. 1868. [f. *Calaveras* in California + -ITE.] *Min.* A bronze-yellow massive tellurid of gold, or of gold and silver.

Calc- (kælk). 1875. [a. Ger. *kalk* lime, a. L. *calcem* (*calx*).] *Min.* and *Geol.* Lime: used *attrib.* or in *comb.* = 'lime-, calcareous', as in C.-SINTER, -SPAR, -TUFF.

‖**Calcaire** (kalkē·r). 1833. [F. (ad. L. *calcarius*); sb. in *Geol.* 'limestone'.] In *calcaire grossier*, and *c. silicieux* (coarse and siliceous limestone), the French names of two strata of the Paris basin, used by geologists generally.

Calca·neal, Calca·nean, *a.* 1847. [f. L. *calcaneum* + -AL, -AN.] *Phys.* Of or belonging to the heel-bone. Hence **Calca·neo-,** comb. form.

‖**Calcaneum** (kælkēɪ·niŏm). 1751. [L. (*os*) *calcaneum*, f. *calcem.*] The bone of the heel.

Calcar[1] (kæ·lkāɪ). 1662. [ad. It. *calcara*; cf. L. *calcaria* lime-kiln.] **1.** In *Glass-making*: 'A small furnace, in which the first calcination is made of sand and potash, for the formation of a frit' (Ure). **2.** *Metall.* An annealing oven.

‖**Calcar**[2] (kæ·lkāɪ). 1836. [L. *calcar* spur.] *Bot.* A hollow spur from the base of a petal. Hence **Ca·lcarate** *a.* spurred.

Calcareo- (kælkē·ri,o). 1799. Comb. f. CALCAREOUS, 'containing lime', used **a.** with adjs., as *c.-argillaceous* (composed of clay with a mixture of lime, etc.); **b.** with sbs., as *c.-barite*, a white barite from Strontian containing 6 °/ₒ of lime.

Calcareous, -ious (kælkē·riəs), *a.* 1677. [f. L. *calcarius* + -OUS. The sp. in *-eous* is erron.] Of the nature of (carbonate of) lime; composed of or containing lime or limestone.

C. spar = CALC-SPAR; *c. tufa* = CALC-TUFF. Hence **Calca·reous-ly** *adv.*, **-ness.**

Calcariferous (kælkări·fĕrəs), *a.* 1853. [prop. f. L. *calcar* + -(I)FEROUS; in 2 as if f. *calc-*.] **1.** Bearing spurs. **2.** *catachr.* for *calciferous.* So **Calca·riform** *a.* shaped like a spur; having a calcareous, rhomboidal appearance.

Ca·lcarine, *a.* 1871. [f. L. *carcar.*] Spur-like.

†**Ca·lcate,** *v. rare.* 1623. [f. L. *calcat-*, *calcare.*] To stamp under the heel. Hence **Calca·tion** (*rare*).

‖**Calcave·lla, Calcave·llos.** 1816. [f. *Carcavelhos* (kārkăve·lyos) in Portugal.] A sweet white wine brought from Lisbon.

†**Ca·lceate,** *v.* 1656. [f. L. *calceare.*] To shoe, or put on shoes. Hence **Ca·lceated** *ppl. a.*; var. †**Ca·lceate** *a.* (*rare*).

Calcedon, calcedony, etc.; see CHAL-.

Calceiform (kæ·lsi,ifŏɪm), *a.* 1860. [f. L. *calceus* + -(I)FORM.] *Bot.* Calceolate.

Calceolaria (kæ·lsi,olē·riă, kælsiŏ-). 1846. [f. L. *calceolus*, dim. of *calceus* + *-aria.*] *Bot.* 'Slipper-flower' or 'slipper-wort'; a genus of *Scrophulariaceæ*, having a flower which suggests its name. Native to S. America.

Calceolate (kæ·lsĭŏlēɪt), *a.* 1864. [f. as prec.] *Bot.* Shaped like a slipper. Hence **Ca·lceolately** *adv.*

Calces, pl. of CALX.

†**Calce·scence.** [f. L. *calc-*.] Replaced by CALORESCENCE.

Calci-, comb. f. of L. *calx* lime. Hence: **calci·ferous** *a.*, yielding or containing (carbonate of) lime; **-fic** *a.*, forming lime; belonging to calcification; **-fica·tion,** conversion into lime; the hardening of a structure, tissue, etc. by the deposit of salts of lime, as in the formation of teeth, and in petrifaction; *concr.* the product of calcifying; **-genous** *a.*, *Chem.* producing a calx, as some metals; **-gerous** *a.*, containing lime; **-mine,** a white or coloured wash for walls; hence **-mine** *v.* to whitewash; **-miner.**

Calcic (kæ·lsik), *a.* 1871. [f. CALCIUM + -IC.] Of or containing calcium.

Calciform (kæ·lsifǭɹm), *a.* 1782. [f. L. *calc(i)-* lime; in 3 f. L. *calx.*] †1. Of metals: Oxidized –1812. 2. Pebble-shaped 1881. 3. Having a heel-like projection 1881.

Calcify (kæ·lsifəi), *v.* 1836. [f. L. *calc(i)-*, as if from **calcificare.*] 1. To convert into lime; to harden by the deposit of lime 1854. 2. *intr.* To become calcified; see prec. 1859.

†**Ca·lcinate.** 1610. [ad. med.L. *calcinatum.*] *adj.* Calcined. *sb.* [sc. *form* or *product.*] So †**Ca·lcinate** *v.* = CALCINE.

Calcination (kælsinēⁱ·ʃən). ME. [f. med. L. *calcinare*; see CALCINE.] 1. The action or process of calcining. †b. Oxidation –1822. 2. *gen.* A burning to ashes 1616. 3. A calcined condition or (*concr.*) product –1712.

Calcinatory (kælsi·nătəri, kæ·lsi-). 1611. [f. med.L. *calcinat-*; see prec. and -ORY.] *adj.* Serving for calcination. *sb.* [sc. *vessel.*] (Dicts.)

Calcine (kælsəi·n), *v.* ME. [ad. med.L. *calcinare*, a term of the alchemists.] 1. To reduce by fire to a calx, powder, or friable substance. b. To desiccate (air, etc.) by heat 1880. c. *fig.* To purify by consuming the grosser part 1634. 2. *gen.* To burn to ashes 1641. Also *fig.* 3. *intr.* To suffer calcination 1704.

1. Calcining the cities of Sodom and Gomorrah FARRAR. Hence **Calci·nable** *a.* **Calci·ner**, one who, or that which, calcines; *spec.* a kiln for roasting ore. var. †**Ca·lcinize.**

Calcio- (kæ·lsio-), comb. f. CALCIUM, used in names of minerals.

Calcite (kæ·lsəit). 1849. [f. L. *calcem* + -ITE.] *Min.* The native crystallized rhombohedral anhydrous carbonate of lime (calcium carbonate), which exists in a variety of forms: calc-spar, calcareous spar. Also *attrib.*

Ca·lcitrant, *a. rare.* (*pedantic.*) 1866. [ad. L. *calcitrantem.*] Kicking; that kicks at any restriction.

Calcitrate (kæ·lsitrēⁱt), *v.* 1623. [f. L. *calcitrat-, calcitrare*, f. *calcem.*] *trans.* and *intr.* To kick. Hence **Calcitra·tion** (*lit.* and *fig.*).

Calcium (kæ·lsiŏm). 1808. [f. L. *calx, calc(i)-.*] *Chem.* 1. A chemical element, one of the metals of the alkaline earths, being the basis of lime; a greyish-white metal, ductile and malleable, widely diffused, but found in nature only in composition. Symbol Ca. 2. *attrib.* = CALCIC 1864.

Calco- (kæ·lko), comb. f. L. *calcem* [formed after Gr. words].

Calcography, improper sp. of CHALC-.

Calc-sinter (kæ·lkˌsi·ntəɹ). 1823. [ad. Ger. *kalk-sinter*, f. *kalk* + *sinter* slag.] *Min.* A hard crystalline deposit from springs which hold carbonate of lime in solution.

Calc-spar (kæ·lkˌspā·ɹ). 1822. [See CALC-.] *Min.* Calcareous spar.

Calc-tuff (kæ·lkˌtʊ·f). 1822. [See CALC-.] *Min.* A porous deposit of carbonate of lime, formed by the waters of calcareous springs.

Calculable (kæ·lkiŭlăb'l), *a.* 1734. [f. L. *calculare.* So mod.F.] Capable of being calculated. Of a person: Such that his action in given circumstances can be reckoned upon and estimated 1865.

The least consistent, reliable, and c. of public men 1865. Hence **Ca·lculabi·lity.**

Calcular (kæ·lkiŭlăɹ), *a.* 1831. [?f. CALCULUS + -AR [1].] Of or pertaining to a calculus.

†**Ca·lculary,** *sb.* 1674. [f. as next.] A 'congeries of little stony knots' in a pear –1753.

Calculary (kæ·lkiŭlări), *a.* 1660. [ad. L. *calcularius*, f. *calculus* stone.] *Med.* Of or pertaining to a calculus; gravelly.

Calculate (kæ·lkiŭleⁱt), *v.* 1570. [f. L. *calculat-, calculare*, f. *calculus* (see CALCULUS).] 1. *trans.* To compute mathematically, reckon. *absol.* To perform calculations, to form an estimate 1601. 2. *ellipt.* To ascertain beforehand the time or circumstances of (an event, etc.) by astrology or mathematics 1593. †3. To reckon in 1643. 4. To think out (*arch.*) 1654. 5. To arrange, adjust, adapt, or fit *for* a purpose. Const. *for*, or *inf.* with *to*; now only in *pass.* 1639. Hence, in *pa. pple.* = 'suited'. 6. *intr.* To count *upon* or *on* 1807. 7. *U. S. colloq.* To think, opine, suppose, 'reckon'; to intend, purpose 1830.

1. Why Old men, Fooles, and Children c. *Jul. C.* I. iii. 65. 2. To c. a lunar eclipse DE QUINCEY. 5. The coach was calculated to carry six regular passengers SCOTT. 6. To c. on a quiet Sunday 1873. var. †**Ca·lcule** *v.*

Calculated (kæ·lkiŭlēⁱtĕd), *pa. pple.* and *ppl. a.* 1722. [f. prec.] 1. Reckoned, estimated, thought out 1863. 2. Fitted, suited, apt; proper or likely *to* 1722.

1. To speak with a c. caution GEO. ELIOT. 2. Disguises not c. to deceive MANSEL.

Calculating (kæ·lkiŭlēⁱtiŋ). 1710. [f. as prec.] *vbl. sb.* The action of the vb. CALCULATE: chiefly *attrib. ppl. a.* That calculates (*esp.* advantage) shrewdly or selfishly 1809.

He was c. and mercenary MAR. EDGEWORTH. Hence **Ca·lcula·tingly** *adv.*

Calculation (kælkiŭlēⁱ·ʃən). ME. [a. F., ad. L. *calculationem.*] 1. The action of reckoning; computation. 2. *concr.* The form in which reckoning is made; its result 1646. 3. Estimate of probability; forecast 1847.

1. All arithmetic and c. have to do with number JOWETT. 2. If the first c. is wrong, we make a second JANE AUSTEN. 3. His. .attack was never the inspiration of courage, but the result of c. EMERSON. vars. †**Ca·lculate,** †**Ca·lcule** *sbs.*

Calculative (kæ·lkiŭlētiv), *a.* 1766. [f. CALCULATE *v.*; see -ATIVE.] Of or pertaining to calculation; given to calculating.

Extraordinary c. powers 1840.

Calculator (kæ·lkiŭlēⁱtəɹ). ME. [a. L., f. as prec.] 1. One who calculates; a reckoner. 2. A set of tables to facilitate calculations; a calculating machine 1784.

1. Nature hates calculators EMERSON. var. †**Ca·lculer.**

Ca·lculatory, *a.* ? *Obs.* 1611. [f. CALCULATE *v.*] Of or pertaining to calculation.

Calculifrage (kæ·lkiŭlifrēⁱdʒ). [a. F. *calculifrage* adj. 'that breaks calculi'.] *Med.* An instrument for breaking down calculi. Hence **Ca·lculi·fragous** *a.* (medicines) fitted for breaking or reducing calculi.

Ca·lculist. 1829. [f. CALCULUS + -IST.] A mathematician.

Calculous (kæ·lkiŭləs), *a.* 1605. [ad. L. *calculosus.*] 1. *Med.* Of or pertaining to a calculus or the stone; diseased with the stone; calculary. †2. Stony (as the calculary of a pear) 1671. var. †**Calculo·se.**

Calculus (kæ·lkiŭlŏs). Pl. **-i, -uses.** 1684. [L., dim. of *calx* stone.] 1. *Med.* 'A stone. A generic term for concretions occurring accidentally in the animal body' (*Syd. Soc. Lex.*). Specialized as *renal, vesical*, etc. †2. Computation –1817. 3. *Math.* A method of calculation, as the DIFFERENTIAL, INTEGRAL Calculus, etc. The differential calculus is often spoken of as 'the calculus'. 1672.

3. Science. .with all its calculuses, differential, integral, and of variations CARLYLE.

‖**Caldarium** (kældēᵊ·riŏm). 1753. [L.] A (Roman) hot bath or bath-room.

‖**Caldera** (kɑldēᵊ·ră). 1865. [a. Sp.:—L. *caldaria*, pl. of prec.] *Geol.* A deep cauldron-like cavity on the summit of an extinct volcano.

Caldron, var. of CAULDRON.

‖**Calean, callean, calleoon.** 1739. [Pers. *qaliyān.*] A water-pipe for smoking; the Persian hubble-bubble.

Caleche, calèche; see CALASH.

Caledonian (kælĭdōᵘ·niăn). 1656. [f. *Caledonia*, Roman name of part of northern Britain, in mod. poetry, etc., applied to Scotland, or the Scottish Highlands.] *adj.* Of ancient Caledonia; of Scotland. *sb.* A native of ancient Caledonia; *joc.* = Scotchman 1768.

Caledonite (kæ·lĭdŏnəiːt). 1863. [f. as prec. + -ITE.] Cupreous sulpho-carbonate of lead, found at Leadhills in Lanarkshire and elsewhere.

Calefacient (kælĭfēⁱ·ʃiĕnt). 1661. [ad. L. *calefacientem*, f. *calere* + *facere.*] *adj.* Producing warmth. *sb. Med.* [sc. *agent.*] 1661.

Calefaction (kælĭfæ·kʃən). Now *rare.* 1547. [ad. L. *calefactionem*; see prec.] 1. Making warm (*lit.* and *fig.*); heating. 2. Heated condition 1634.

Calefactor (kæ·lĭfæktəɹ). 1605. [f. L. *calefacere.*] †1. He who, or that which, warms. 2. A small kind of stove 1831.

Calefa·ctory (kælĭfæ·ktəri). 1536. [ad. L. *calefactorius*, and med.L. *calefactorium.*] A. *adj.* Adapted for or tending to warming 1711. var. **Calefa·ctive** (now *rare*). B. *sb.* 1. The room in a monastery where the inmates warmed themselves 1681. 2. A warming-pan; the ball of precious metal containing hot water, on which the priest warmed his hands when administering the eucharist in cold weather; the *pome* 1536 †3. = CALEFACIENT *sb.* 1657.

†**Ca·lefy,** *v.* 1526. [ad. med.L. *caleficare*, f. *calere.*] 1. To warm, heat –1657. 2. *intr.* To become warm –1658.

‖**Calembour** (kalaṅbur, kɑlĕmbūᵊr). 1830. [Fr.] A pun.

Calendal (kăle·ndăl), *a.* 1839. [f. L. *calendæ* + -AL.] Of or pertaining to the Calends.

Calendar (kæ·lĕndăɹ), *sb.* ME. [a. AF. *calender*:—L. *calendarium* account-book, f. *calendæ* calends, the day on which accounts were due.] 1. The system according to which the beginning and length of years, and the subdivision of the year, is fixed; as the Babylonian, Jewish, Roman, or Arabic calendar. 2. A table showing the months, days of the week, and dates of a given year; often also giving other data connected with individual days. Often specialized, as *Gardener's C., Racing C.*, etc. Also a series of more detailed tables; an almanac. ME. †3. *fig.* A guide, directory; a model –1602. 4. A list or register. (Now *fig.*) ME. b. *esp.* A list of prisoners for trial at the assizes 1764. c. *spec.* A list of documents arranged chronologically with a short summary of their contents 1467. †5. *fig.* A record –1718.

1. *Julian C.*, that introduced by Julius Cæsar B.C. 46, in which the ordinary year has 365 days, and every fourth year is a leap year of 366 days, the months having the names, order, and length still retained. *Gregorian C.*, the modification of the preceding with reference to astronomical data and the natural course of the seasons, introduced by Pope Gregory XIII in A.D. 1582, and adopted in Great Britain in 1752. See STYLE. 3. He is the card or c. of gentry *Haml.* v. ii. 114. 4. c. C. of State Papers (*title*) 1856. 5. The Kalender of my past endeuours *All's Well* I. iii. 4.

Comb., etc.: **c.-clock**, one which indicates the days of the week or month; **c. month**, one of the twelve months into which the year is divided according to the c.; also the space of time from any date (*e.g.* the 17th) of any month to the corresponding date (the 17th) of the next, as opp. to a lunar month of 4 weeks.

Hence **Calenda·rial, Calenda·rian** *adjs.* (*rare*) of or pertaining to a c. †**Ca·lendarist** (*rare*). †**Ca·lendary** *sb.* = CALENDAR *sb.*; as *adj.* = *Calendarian.* **Cale·ndric, -al** *a.* (*rare*) of the nature of a c.

Calendar (kæ·lĕndăɹ), *v.* 1487. [f. prec.] 1. To register in a calendar or list. 2. *spec.* To arrange, analyse, and index (documents) 1859. Hence **Ca·lendarer.**

Calender (kæ·lĕndəɹ), *sb.*[1] 1513. [a. F. *calandre*:—med.L. *calendra*, L. *cylindrus*, a. Gr. κύλινδρος.] †1. = CALENDERER –1782. 2. A machine in which cloth, paper, etc., is pressed under rollers for the purpose of smoothing or glazing; also for watering or giving a wavy appearance, etc. 1688. Also *attrib.*

1. The c. Will lend his horse to go COWPER.

Ca·lender, *sb.*[2] 1634. [ad. Pers. *qalandar.*] One of an order of mendicant dervishes in Turkey and Persia.

Ca·lender, *v.* 1513. [a. F. *calandrer*; see CALENDER *sb.*[1]] To pass through a calender for the purpose of smoothing, glazing, etc. Hence **Cale·nderer**, one whose business it is to c. cloth, etc. **Ca·lendry**, a place where calendering is done.

Calends, kalends (kæ·lĕndz), *sb. pl.* OE. [ad. L. *kalendæ, -as* sb. pl. f. root *kal-, cal-* of L. *calare*, Gr. καλεῖν.] 1. The first day of any month in the Roman calendar. (In use till 17th c.) ME. †2. In OE. A month; *also*, season. †3. *fig.* Prelude. (Also in *sing.*) –1618. 4. A calendar, record 1470.

3. What is age, but the Calends of death RALEIGH. Phr. *On* (*at*) *the Greek Calends* (L. *ad Græcas kalendas*): joc. for, Never; the Greeks had none.

‖**Cale·ndula.** 1871. [dim. of *calendæ*, perh. 'little weather-glass'.] *Bot.* 1. Generic name of the Common Marigold, and its congeners. 2. *Pharm.* A tincture of the flowers used as a hæmostatic. Also *attrib.*

Calendulin (kăle·ndiŭlin). [f. prec.] *Chem.*

A mucilaginous substance obtained from the common marigold.

Calenture (kæ·lĕntiuəɹ). 1593. [a. F., ad. Sp. *calentura* fever, f. *calentar*, f. L. *calentem.*] A disease incident to sailors within the tropics, characterized by delirium in which, it is said, they fancy the sea to be green fields and desire to leap into it. **2.** *fig.* and *transf.* Fever; burning passion, glow 1596.

2. Knowledge kindles Calentures in some DONNE.

†**Ca·lenture,** *v. rare.* 1649. [f. prec. sb.] To infect with the calenture; *fig.* to fire 1678. *intr.* To become hot or inflamed. DANIEL.

Thirst of empire calentur'd his breast MARVELL.

†**Ca·lepin.** 1568. [a. F., ad. It. *calepino*, from Ambrosio *Calepino*, of Calepio in Italy, who wrote *the* Latin Dictionary of the 16th c.] A dictionary; *fig.* one's notebook –1662.

Calescent (kăle·sĕnt), *a. rare.* 1804. [ad. L. *calescentem.*] Growing warm, glowing with heat. Hence **Cale·scence,** increasing warmth or heat.

Calf [1] (kāf). Pl. (and occ. genit. sing., *esp.* in comb.), calves. [Com. Teut.: OWS. *cealf* :—OTeut. **kalboz, -iz* neut.] **1.** The young (under one year old) of any bovine animal, *esp.* of the domestic cow OE. **b.** *transf.* A dolt; occ. a meek harmless person 1553. **2.** *ellipt.* Leather made from the skin of a calf; *calf-leather* 1727. **3.** The young of other animals; as deer, the elephant, the whale, etc. ME. **4.** *transf.* A small island lying near a larger one; as in 'The Calf of Man' 1833. **5.** An iceberg detached from a coast glacier; a fragment of ice detached from an iceberg 1818.

1. b. Some silly doting brainless calfe DRAYTON. *Essex calf*: a native of Essex.

Comb.: **c.-kill,** a heath-plant (*Kalmia latifolia*); cf. 'lambkill'; **-knee,** knock-knee; **-lick** (*dial.*), a cowlick, a feather; **-love; calves'-snout, calf's-,** ANTIRRHINUM or Snapdragon. Hence **Ca·lfhood. Ca·lfish** *a.* like a c.; raw, untrained. **Ca·lfling.**

Calf [2] (kāf). ME. [app. a. ON. *kálfi.*] The fleshy hinder part of the shank of the leg. Also *transf.*, of a stocking 1659.

fful longe were his legges and ful lene ylyk a staf ther was no c. ysene CHAUCER. Hence **Ca·lfless** *a.*

†**Ca·lfret.** 1600. [ad. F. *calfreter*, ? f. (ult.) Arab. *qalafa* to caulk a ship with palm-tree fibre, etc.] To stop up the seams of (a ship); to caulk –1653.

Calf's-foot, calves-foot. 1450. **1.** *lit.* The foot of a calf; hence *calves-foot jelly* 1620. **2.** *Herb.* The Cuckoo-pint (*Arum maculatum*); see ARUM. [So F. *pied-de-veau.*]

Calf-skin. Also **calf's-, calves-, calve-.** 1590. The skin of a calf; a kind of leather made from this. Occ. = *vellum.*

Cali-, erron. f. *calli-*, from Gr. κάλλος beauty; confused with *calo-* from Gr. καλός.

Caliban (kæ·libæn). 1610. [App. a var. of CANNIBAL, or ? a form of *Carib.*] 'A saluage and deformed slaue' in Shakspere's *Tempest*; whence, a man of degraded bestial nature. Hence **Ca·libanism.**

Calibogus (kæliboᵘ·gəs). *U.S.* 1785. A mixture of rum and spruce beer.

Calibrate (kæ·libreᵉit), *v.* 1864. [f. CALIBRE + -ATE [3].] To determine the calibre of, as of a thermometer tube; to graduate a gauge of any kind with allowance for its irregularities. Hence **Calibra·tion,** the action of calibrating.

Calibre, caliber (kæ·libəɹ: occas. kălī·bɹ), *sb.* 1567. [a. F. *calibre* (*qualibre* in Cotgr.) of unkn. origin; ? f. Arab. *qālib* mould; or ? f. L. *quā librā* of what weight (Mahn). See CALLIPER, and CALIVER.] **1.** †**a.** The diameter of a bullet, cannon-ball, etc. **b.** *Hence,* The internal diameter or bore of a gun. (Hence, derivatively, phrases like 'guns of heavy calibre'.) 1588. **c.** *transf.* The diameter of any body of circular section; also, of a tube or hollow cylinder 1727. **2.** *fig.* †**a.** Degree, quality, rank. [The earliest cited sense: prob. from Fr.] **b.** Degree of personal capacity; weight of character. In wider sense: Stamp, degree of merit or importance. 1567. **3.** *pl. calibers.* = CALLIPERS.

1. c. The caliber of these empty tubes REID, of arteries TODD. 2. Sir Henry Vane, or others of such c. DRUMM. OF HAWTH. The c. of this young man's understanding SCOTT.

Comb., etc.: **c.-rule,** an instrument for determining the c. of a ball from its weight, or vice versa; so **-scale; -compasses, -square**: see CALLIPER. Hence †**Ca·libre, -ber,** *v.* to determine the c. of; to measure with callipers. **Ca·libred** *a.* of or having c.: *esp.* in *comb.*

Ca·liburn, -burno. ME. The name of King Arthur's sword. See EXCALIBUR.

Calic(e, early f. CHALICE.

Caliciform (kæ·lisifǭɹm), *a.* 1849. [ad. mod. L. *caliciformis*, f. L. *calicem.*] Cup-shaped. var. (*erron.*) **Calyciform.** So **Cali·cinated** *ppl. a.*

Calicle (kæ·lik'l). 1848. [ad. L. *caliculus*, dim. of *calix.*] *Biol.* A small cup-like prominence, as in corals. var. (*erron.*) **Calycle.**

Calico (kæ·liko), *sb.* (*a.*) 1540. [In 16–17th c. also *calicut*, from the name of the Indian city (sense 1).] **1.** The name of a city on the coast of Malabar; used *attrib.* in *Calicut-cloth, Calico-cloth.* **2.** Hence: **a.** *orig.* Cotton cloth imported from the East 1578. **b.** Now, in England, Plain white unprinted cotton cloth. **c.** in U.S., Printed cotton cloth, coarser than muslin 1841. **3.** *adj.* Of calico.

Comb.: **c.-printer,** one whose trade is c.-printing; **-printing,** the art or trade of producing a pattern on c. by printing in colours, or other process.

Calicular (kăli·kiŭlăr), *a.* 1658. [f. L. *caliculus*, dim. of *calix.*] †**1.** ? = *calicular* (see CALYCLE). **2.** *Biol.* Of or pertaining to a calicle 1849. Hence **Cali·cularly** *adv.*

Caliculate (kăli·kiŭlĕt), *a.* 1846. [f. as prec.] Having calicles. var. **Cali·culated.**

Calid (kæ·lid), *a. arch.* 1599. [ad. L. *calidus.*] Warm, tepid; hot. Hence †**Cali·dity.** (Chiefly *techn.* in *Med.*)

Caliduct (kæ·lidʊkt). 1651. [f. L. *calidus*, or *calor* + *ductus*, after AQUEDUCT.] A pipe for the conveyance of heat. Cf. F. *caliduc.*

Calif, var. of CALIPH.

†**Ca·ligate,** *a.* 1562. [ad. L. *caligatus*, f. *caliga.*] Wearing *caligæ* or military boots; *esp.* in *knight c.* –1656.

†**Caliga·tion.** 1615. [ad. L. *caligationem.*] *Med.* Dimness or mistiness of sight –1657.

Caliginous (kăli·dʒinəs), *a.* 1548. [ad. L. *caliginosus.*] Misty, dim, murky; obscure, dark; also *fig.* Now *arch.*

The cave C. COWPER. Hence **Caligino·sity** (*arch.*). †**Cali·ginousness.**

‖**Caligo** (kăləi·go). 1801. [L.] Dimness of sight.

Caligrapher, -meter, etc.; see CALLI-.

Cali·gulism. *nonce-wd.* A mad extravagance worthy of Caligula, the third Roman Emperor. H. WALPOLE.

‖**Calin.** 1752. [Fr.] The tin of Siam and Malacca, an alloy, of which the Chinese make tea-caddies, etc.

Calipash (kæ·lipæʃ). 1689. [Perh. ad. W. Indian; cf. Sp. *carapacho*, CARAPACE.] †**a.** The upper shell or carapace of the turtle. **b.** That part next the upper shell, containing a dull green gelatinous substance.

Calipee (kæ·lipī). 1657. [Perh. as prec.] †**a.** The lower shell or plastron of the turtle. **b.** That part next the lower shell, containing a light yellowish gelatinous substance.

Caliper, -compasses; see CALLIPER.

Calipe·va, calli-. 1833. A mullet of the W. Indies, *Mugil liza.*

Caliph, calif (kæ·lif, kēᵉ·lif). [ME. *califfe, caliphe*, etc., a. F., ad. (ult.) Arab. *khalīfah* successor. *Khalīf* is the form now in favour. The pronunciation with long *ā* is bad.] The Mohammedan title for the chief civil and religious ruler, as successor of Mohammed.

Caliphate (kæ·lifeᵉit). Also **-at.** 1614. [f. prec. + -ATE.] **1.** The rank, dignity, office, or term of office, of a caliph 1734; var. **Ca·liphship** (*rare*). **2.** The dominion of a caliph 1614.

Calippic; see CALLIPPIC.

‖**Calisaya** (kælisēᵉ·ă). 1837. [? native S. Amer.] In *C. bark*: the best sort of Peruvian Bark, obtained from *Cinchona calisaya.*

Caliver (kæ·livəɹ, kălī·vəɹ). Now *Hist.* 1568. [App. the same as CALIBRE.] A light kind of harquebus (orig. of a certain calibre), fired without a rest. †**b.** A soldier armed with a caliver –1591.

‖**Calix** (kæ·liks). Pl. **ca·lices.** 1708. [L. (see CHALICE). Confused by mod. scientific writers with Græco-Lat. *calyx*, and written CALYX.] A cup; a cup-like cavity or organ; *e.g.* the body of a Vorticella.

Calixtin, -ine (kali·kstin). 1710. *Eccl. Hist.* **1.** [in F. *Calixtin*, f. L. *calix* cup.] One of a section of the Hussites, who claimed the cup as well as the bread for the laity; a Utraquist. **2.** An adherent of George Calixtus (1586–1656), a Lutheran divine and professor, of conciliatory views; a syncretist 1727.

Calk (kǭk), *sb.* 1587. [app. f. (ult.) L. *calcem, calcaneum*, or *calcar.*] **1.** = CALKIN. **2.** *U. S.* A piece of iron projecting from the heel of a boot, which prevents slipping 1805.

†**Calk,** *v.* [1] ME. [app. shortened from CALCULE.] To calculate; *esp.* astrologically. Also *intr.* or *absol.* –1646.

Calk (kǭk), *v.* [2] 1624. [f. CALK *sb.*] To provide (a shoe) with a calk; to rough-shoe. Hence **Ca·lking** *vbl. sb.*; also *attrib.*, as in **calking-anvil,** an anvil for forming calks; **-tongs,** for sharpening these.

Calk (kǭk, kælk), *v.* [3] 1662. [a. F. *calquer*, ad. It. *calcare*:—L. *calcare.* Cf. CAUK. Not conn. w. CHALK.] To copy (a design) by rubbing the back with colouring matter, and drawing a blunt point along the outlines so as to trace them in colour on a surface placed beneath.

Calk, var. of CAULK; obs. f. CAUK *v.*

†**Ca·lker** [1]. 1535. [f. CALK *v.* [1] + -ER [1].] An astrologer; a magician –1662.

Calker [2] (kǭ·kəɹ). *Sc.* 1794. [f. CALK *v.* [2] + -ER [1].] = CALKIN.

Calker [3], var. of CAULKER.

Calkin (kǭ·kin, kæ·lkin). 1445. [Earlier *kakun*, Du. *kalkoen*, MDu. *calcoen* 'ungula', f. L. *calx.*] **1.** The turned-down ends of a horse-shoe; also a turned edge under the front. **2.** The irons nailed on the heels and soles of shoes or clogs to make them last 1832.

Call (kǭl), *v.* [Com. Teut.:—OTeut. **kallǒjan*, cogn. w. *gol-* in Slav. *gǒlos* voice, sound.]

I. **intr.* **1.** To utter one's voice loudly and distinctly; to shout, cry: often with *out.* Const. *to, after.* OE. Also *fig.* **2.** To make or pay a call. Const. *at, in, on*; also *absol.* (Orig. to call aloud *at a door*; the notion of making a communication to one who answers the door is still essential.) 1593. ** *trans.* **3.** To utter, or read over, in a loud voice; to proclaim. Often with *out.* Also *absol.* ME. **4.** To summon by a call; *hence* to cite; to bid (any one) come; †to invite. Also *absol.* ME. Also *fig.* **5.** To convoke, summon ME. **6.** To nominate by a call ME.; to invite (*esp.* to the pastorate of a church) 1560. **7.** To call upon (a person) *to do.* Said *esp.* of the call of God or duty. 1580.

1. Do you hear, my aunt calls DRYDEN. The throstle calls TENNYSON. *fig.* Deepe calleth unto deepe *Ps.* xlii. 7. *spec.* (*Cards.*) *To call*: to make a demand (for a card, for a show of hands, etc.). 2. [Go, knock and c. *Merry W.* IV. v. 9.] To c. at the Alehouses *Much Ado* III. iii. 44. 3. 'Adsum'!..the word we used at school when names were called THACKERAY. To c. the odds 1855, a halt (*mod.*). 4. Not called to the feast LATIMER. To c. a coach TICKELL, *fig.* to penance MILT. C. me early TENNYSON. † = 'call on' *Twel. N.* III. ii. 56. = 'call for', as *to c. a case* (mod.). *To c. a bond*: to give notice that the amount of the bond will be paid. 6. Paul, called to be an Apostle 1 *Cor.* i. 1. 7. Called to preach the Gospel WESLEY.

II. To name. **1.** To give as name or title to; to speak of as ME. **2.** To call names. Now *dial.* 1633.

1. God called the light; Day *Gen.* i. 5. The woman whom I was taught to c. mother DE FOE.

III. To drive. *Sc.* **1.** To urge forward (an animal or a vehicle); to turn, drive ME. Also *fig.* **2.** To drive (a nail); to fasten by hammering; to forge 1513. **3.** *absol.* and *intr.* (for *refl.*) To drive. Also *fig.*

1. Some ca' the pleugh BURNS. A puir ca-the-shuttle-body [*i. e.* weaver] SCOTT. 3. *To ca' canny*, to drive gently and carefully.

Phrases. *To c. attention to*: to invite notice to; to point out. *To c. cousins*: to claim cousinship or kinship with. *To c. names*: to apply opprobrious terms to. *To c. in question*: to summon for trial or examination; to impeach; to cast doubt upon; †to examine; so †*To c. in doubt. To c. into being*: to give life to, make. *To c. into play*: to bring into action. *To c. to account*: to summon (one) to render an account, or to answer for conduct; *hence*, to reprove. *To c. to the bar*: see BAR *sb.* [1] *To c. to (one's) feet, legs*: to bid one stand up; *spec.* in order to speak, sing, etc. *To c. to memory*, etc.: to recollect, recall; also with *back*. *To c. to witness*, etc.: to appeal to (one) to bear witness, etc.

With prepositions. **C. for. a.** To ask loudly or authoritatively for; *fig.* to require. **b.** To go to or stop at a place and ask *for*. **c.** *Cards. To c. for trumps*: to signal to one's partner to play out trumps. Also *absol.* **To c. on or upon. a.** To call to; to address in a loud voice; to apostrophize the absent. **b.** To invoke, or supplicate (God, etc.). **c.** To appeal to *for*, or *to do*; to make a demand upon. †**d.** To demand (money due). **e.** To pay a short visit to.

With adverbs. **C. back. a.** [sense I. 4]. To recall (*lit.* and *fig.*); to bring back (a thing). **b.** To retract. **C. down. a.** To invoke from above, bring down. †**b.** To decry. **C. forth. a.** *lit.* To cause to come forward. **b.** *fig.* To cause to appear; to summon up (courage). **C. in. a.** To withdraw from the outside, from free action, from circulation. **b.** To summon for assistance or consultation. **c.** To require the payment or repayment of. **C. off.** [See I. 4.] To summon away; *fig.* to divert (the attention). **C. on.** Of hands: To challenge. **C. out. a.** To summon forth; *fig.* to evoke. **b.** To challenge to fight (*esp.* a duel). **C. over.** To read aloud (a list of names, *e.g.* in school); hence **C.-over** *sb.* **C. up. a.** To summon from below (*e.g.* from Hades). **b.** To bring into the mind. **c.** To summon before an authority, *spec.* to perform national service; hence **C.-up** *sb.* **d.** To recall.

Call (kǭl), *sb.* ME. [f. prec. vb.] **1.** A loud vocal utterance; a shout, a cry. **2.** The cry of an animal, *esp.* of a bird 1684. **3.** A cry used to attract birds, etc. 1530; a whistle, etc. imitating the note of birds 1654; †a decoy-bird (*lit.* and *fig.*) *John* III. iv. 174. **4.** *Hunting.* A strain blown on the horn to encourage the hounds 1674. **5.** The act of calling at a place on the way 1783; a short formal visit 1862. **6.** Summons, invitation, bidding. Also *fig.* ME. **b.** *Amer. Land Law.* A matter of description, in a survey or grant, calling for a corresponding object, etc. on the land 1864. **7.** Demand, requisition, claim ME. **8.** A requirement of duty, a need, occasion, right 1674. **9.** A spiritual prompting 1650. †**10.** Vocation –1780. **11.** *Comm.* **a.** A demand for the payment of money; *esp.* a notice to a shareholder to pay up a portion of capital subscribed. Also *attrib.* 1709. **b.** On the Stock Exchange: An option of claiming stock at a certain time at a fixed price 1860. **12.** *Sc.* (now *ca'*, *caw.*) Driving. Applied to: Forced respiration; a place where cattle are driven; a pass between hills. 1765.

1. *spec.* A roll-call: A c. of the House [of Commons] 1723. **2.** The parrot's c. TENNYSON. **5.** The baker's punctual c. COWPER. *To make, pay, receive a c.* (mod.). **6.** Tapsters answering every c. SHAKS. A c. before the curtain (*mod.*). At the c. of Trumpet MILT. *P. L.* VII. 295. *concr.* A silver c. which hung around her neck SCOTT. See also BUGLE-*c.*, TRUMPET-*c.* **7** The c. .. for cheap reprints 1832. **8.** I don't know what c. she had to blush so THACKERAY. **9.** We came by a c. of God to serve him here *Ministers New Eng.* in Ellis. **11. a.** A c. of fifteen per cent. ADAM SMITH.

Phrases. **a.** with preps., as *At c.*: ready to answer a c.; immediately available. *Within c.*: within reach of a summons; hence, *within c. of (a place)*: near to (it). **b.** *To have the c.*: to be in chief demand: in *Long Whist*, to be entitled to call honours. **c.** *C. to the bar*: admission to the status of BARRISTER, q. v.

Comb.: **c.-bell**, a bell for summoning attendance; *spec.* one giving the alarm at a fire-station; **-bird**, a bird for attracting others by its note; **-boy**, a youth employed **a.** (in a theatre) to call the actors when required on the stage, **b.** (on a steamer) to transmit the captain's orders to the engineer, **c.** (in a hotel) to answer the bells; **-day**, in the Inns of Court, the day in each term on which students are called to the bar; **-duck**, a decoy-duck; **-loan**, a loan to be repaid at c.; so **-money**; **-night**, see *call-day*; **-note**, the note used by a bird, etc., in calling to its mate.

‖**Calla** (kæ·lă). 1866. *Bot.* **1.** A genus of floating marsh plants (N.O. *Orontiaceæ*). **2.** A name erroneously given to the White Arum, Ethiopian or Trumpet Lily, *Richardia æthiopica* (N.O. *Araceæ*), a native of the Cape.

Calla-; see CALA-.

Callæsthe·tic, -ics. [f. Gr. κάλλος + αἰσθητικός.] Whewell's proposed name for ÆSTHETICS.

Callant (kɑ·lănt). *Sc.* and *n. dial.* 1716. [ad. Du. *kalant* chap, customer, a. north.F. *caland* = F. *chaland* customer (literally).] A boy of any age.

Callat, Calle, obs. ff. CALLET, CAUL.

Caller (kǭ·ləɪ), *sb.* 1450. [f. CALL *v.* + -ER [1].] **1.** One who or that which calls, in various senses of the vb.; *esp.* **2.** One who pays a short or complimentary visit. (The chief sense.) 1786.

Caller (kɑ·ləɪ), *a.* *Sc.* and *n. dial.* ME. [prob. Sc. form of CALVER, q.v. Cf. *siller*, *silver*, etc.] **1.** Fresh (as opp. to what is beginning to corrupt); said *esp.* of fish. **2.** Of air, water, etc.: Fresh and cool; well-aired 1513.

1. The..fish-wife..shouting 'C. herrings' 1862.

Ca·llet, *sb.* Now *dial.* 1500. [?] **1.** A lewd woman, trull. **2.** ? = 'scold' 1528. Also *attrib.* Hence **Ca·llet** *v.* to scold. **Ca·llety** *a.* ill-tongued.

Calli-, Gr. καλλι-, comb. f. κάλλος beauty. See also CALI-.

†**Ca·llid,** *a. rare.* [ad. L. *callidus*.] Crafty, cunning.

Callidity (kăli·dĭti). Now *rare.* 1524. [ad. L. *calliditatem*.] Craftiness, cunning.

Calligraph (kæ·ligrɑf), *sb.*[1] *arch.* Also cali-. 1853. [a. F. *calligraphe*, ad. med.L. *calligraphus*, ad. Gr. καλλιγράφος, f. καλλι- (see CALLI-) + -γραφος.] One who writes beautifully; *spec.* a professional transcriber of manuscripts; vars. **Calli·grapher, -ist.**

Ca·lligraph, *sb.*[2] 1878. [f. as prec., after *autograph*, etc.] A beautiful specimen of writing. Hence **Ca·lligraph** *v.* to write beautifully or ornamentally. **Calligra·phic, -al** *a.* of or pertaining to calligraphers or calligraphy. **Calligra·phically** *adv.*

Calligraphy (kĕli·grăfi), 1613. [ad. (ult.) Gr. καλλιγραφία, f. as prec.] **1.** Beautiful writing; elegant penmanship. **2.** Penmanship generally 1645.

Calling (kǭ·liŋ), *vbl. sb.* ME. [f. CALL *v.* + -ING [1].] **I.** The action of the vb. CALL.

The c. of partridges 1693, of Parliament 1848, of simples GALE, of names 1687.

II. Summons, vocation. **1.** A divine call; the inward conviction of such a call 1534. †**2.** Station in life. [Founded on 1 *Cor.* vii. 20.] –1691. **3.** Hence, Ordinary occupation, business 1551. *concr.* A body of persons following a profession or trade 1660. Also *attrib.*

1. The conscious warrant of some high c. MILT. A ..pastor..diligent in his c. STUBBES. [The sense here includes the *vocatio* or calling of the Bishop, etc., and the professional 'calling'.] **2.** In the same callinge, wherin he was called 1 *Cor.* vii. 20. [The mod. sense adds sense 1.] **3.** A ferry-man by my c. T. BROWN.

Ca·lling, *ppl. a.* 1634. [f. as prec.] That calls. **b.** *spec.* in names of animals: **C. crab,** a genus of Land-crabs (*Gelasimus*), having one very long claw, which the animal extends, as if beckoning; **C. hare,** a rodent genus (*Lagomys*), having a peculiar call.

Calliope (kăləi·ŏpi). *U.S.* 1863. [Gr. Καλλιόπη (beautiful-voiced).] An instrument consisting of a series of steam-whistles, played by a key-board like that of an organ.

Callipash, Callipee; see CALIPASH, -PEE.

Calliper, caliper (kæ·lipəɪ). 1588. [App. the same as CALIBRE, but from the beginning spelt differently.] **1.** Orig. used attrib. *c. compasses*; afterwards usu. in pl. (*pair of*) *callipers*: A kind of compasses with bowed legs for measuring the diameter of convex bodies; often with a scale attached; also a similar instrument with straight legs and points turned outwards for measuring the bore of tubes, etc. **2.** *transf.* The clip for holding the load in a crane 1769. Hence **Ca·lliper** *v.* to measure with or use callipers.

Callippic (kăli·pik), *a.* 1696. [f. Gr. Κάλλιππος + -IC.] Of or pertaining to Callippus, a Greek astronomer (*c* 350 B.C.).

C. cycle or *period*: a cycle proposed by C. as an improvement on the Metonic cycle, consisting of 4 of the latter or 76 years, at the end of which, by omitting one day, he thought that the full and new moon would be brought round to the same day and hour.

Callipygian (kælipi·dʒiăn), *a.* 1800. [f. Gr. καλλίπυγος adj. f. καλλι- CALLI- + πυγή: the name of a statue of Venus.] Of, pertaining to, or having shapely or finely developed buttocks.

Callis-sand. Now *dial.* 1594. [f. *Callis*, 16th c. form of *Calais*.] A fine white sand, used for blotting ink, scouring, etc.

Callisthenic (kælisþe·nik), *a.* Also **cali-.** 1847. [f. Gr. καλλι- CALLI- + σθένος.] Pertaining to callisthenics. So **Callisthe·nical** *a.* addicted to callisthenics (*rare*).

Callisthe·nics, *sb. pl.* 1847. [f. prec.; cf. *gymnastics*.] Gymnastic exercises suitable for girls; training calculated to develop the figure and to promote graceful movement. **Callisthe·nium,** a place for the practice of c.

‖**Callithrix, -trix** (kæ·liþriks). 1607. [L.] A genus of small Brazilian monkeys.

‖**Callitriche** (kăli·trikĭ). 1836. [mod.L., f. Gr. καλλίτριχος.] *Bot.* Water Star-wort.

Calloo (kălū·). Also **calaw, callow.** 1792. A species of Arctic duck, *Anas* (*Fuligula, Harelda*) *glacialis*, named from its call.

Callose (kælōᵘ·s), *a.* 1864. [ad. L. *callosus*; see CALLOUS.] *Bot.* Having callosities.

Callosity (kălǫ·sĭti). 1578. [a. F. *callosité*:—L. *callositatem*; see CALLOUS.] **1.** The condition of being callous; abnormal hardness and thickness of the skin, etc. **2.** *concr.* A callus; a thickened and hardened part of the skin, caused by friction, etc. Also applied to natural thickenings, *e.g.* on the legs of a horse, etc. 1601. **3.** *fig.* = CALLOUSNESS 2. 1658.

Callot(e, -ott(e, obs. ff. CALOTTE.

Callous (kæ·ləs), *a.* 1578. [ad. L. *callosus*, f. *callum* (*callus*) hardened skin.] **1.** (Chiefly *Phys.* and *Zool.*) Hardened, indurated; as parts of the skin by friction. Also *Bot.*, of plants. **2.** *fig.* Hardened, unfeeling, insensible 1679.

1. C. and hollow ulcers TIMME. C. hands CONGREVE. **2.** C. to impressions of religion BUTLER, to ridicule ARNOLD. Hence **Ca·llously** *adv.*

Ca·llous, *v.* 1834. [f. prec.] To make callous (*lit.* and *fig.*) Only in **Ca·lloused.**

Callousness (kæ·ləsnės). 1660. [f. as prec.] **1.** = CALLOSITY 1, 2. **2.** *fig.* A hardened state of mind or conscience; insensibility 1692.

Callow (kæ·lᵒᵘ). [OE. *calu*:—WGer. *kalwo-*; ? ad. L. *calvus*.] **A.** *adj.* †**1.** Bald –ME. **2.** Without feathers; downy 1603. **3.** *fig.* Raw, unfledged 1580. **4.** Of land: **a.** Bare; **b.** (*Ireland*) Low-lying 1677.

2. Yoong c. birds which are not yet fethered HOLLAND. **3.** Young and c. orators H. WALPOLE.

B. *sb.* †**1.** A bald-pate –ME. †**2.** A callow nestling; also *fig.* –1670. **3.** The stratum of vegetable soil lying above the subsoil; the top bed of a quarry (*dial.*) 1863. **4.** (*Ireland*) A low-lying damp meadow 1862. Hence **Ca·llowness. Ca·llowy** *a.*

‖**Ca·llum.** ME. [L.] = CALLUS –1646.

Callus (kæ·lŏs). Also (*erron.*) **callous.** Pl. **calluses.** 1563. [a. L.] **1.** = CALLOSITY 2. **2.** *Path.* The bony material thrown out around and between the two ends of a fractured bone in healing 1678. **3.** *Bot.* A hard formation in or on plants 1870. **4.** *fig.* A callous state of feeling, etc. 1692.

Calm (kām), *sb.*[1] [ME. *calme*, a. F., ad. It. or Sp. *calma*; ? f. late L. *cauma*, a. Gr. καῦμα burning heat (Diez).] Stillness, tranquillity, serenity; freedom from agitation or disturbance. Also *fig.* and *attrib.*

There was a great calme *Matt.* viii. 26. = 'want of wind (usu. in *pl.*): Chained in tropic calms J. WILSON. *fig.* The c. of despotism CALHOUN. A good man's c. WORDSW.

Calm, *sb.*[2] Now *Sc.* 1535. **1.** A mould in which metal objects are cast. **2.** The heddles of a loom. See CAAM.

Calm (kām), *a.* ME. [a. F. *calme*, f. the sb.] Free from agitation or disturbance; still, tranquil, serene; not stormy. Also *transf.* and *fig.*

So shall the sea be calme *Jonah* i. 12. It fell stark C. 1711. C. satisfaction BUTLER, manners and conversation 1641. The calmest life MILT. *P. L.* VI. 461. Hence **Ca·lmly** *adv.* **Ca·lmy** *a. poet. arch.* (rarely *fig.*).

Calm (kām), *v.* ME. [f. prec., or perh. a. F. *calmer*.] **1.** *intr.* Of the sea or wind: To become calm. *Obs.* exc. w. *down*. Also *fig.* **2.** *trans.* To make calm; to quiet, appease, pacify (*lit.* and *fig.*) 1559. †**3.** To becalm –1753.

1. It..raineth, thundereth, and calmeth 1598. **2.** She calm'd herself SOUTHEY. **3.** *Oth.* I. i. 30. Hence **Ca·lmant** *sb. Med.* = *calmative* sb. **Ca·lmative** *a.* sedative; *sb.* a sedative agent: also *fig.* **Ca·lmer.**

Calmness (kā·mnės). 1516. [f. CALM *a.*] The state or quality of being calm; stillness, tranquillity, quietness. Also *transf.* and *fig.*

The sea was returned to its..settled c. DE FOE. C. of speech HOOKER.

Calo-, Gr. καλο-, comb. f. καλός beautiful; occ. interchanging with CALLI-.

Ca·logram. 1868. [f. Gr. κάλως cable.] A suggested substitute for CABLEGRAM.

Calomel (kæ·lǒmĕl). 1676. [In F. *calomel*, *calomélas*, f. Gr. καλός + μέλας (Littré). The history of the name is wanting.] Chiefly *Med.* Mercurous chloride, or protochloride of mercury (Hg_2Cl_2); much used as a purgative; also found native as *horn-quicksilver*.

She dosed them with c. and jalap KINGSLEY.

†**Calor, -our.** 1599. [L. *calor.*] Heat, warmth –1656.

Calorescence (kælǒre·sĕns). 1865. [f. L. *calor*; suggested by *calcescence*, etc. (Incorrect in form, and not expressing the fact.)] *Physics.* Tyndall's name for the change of non-luminous heat-rays into rays of higher refrangibility so as to become luminous. See also CALCESCENCE.

Caloric (kălǫ·rik). 1792. [a. F. *calorique*, f. L. *calorem.*] *Physics.* Lavoisier's name for a supposed elastic fluid, to which the phenomena of heat were formerly attributed. (Now abandoned.) **2.** = 'heat'; also *fig.* 1794. *Comb.* **c.-engine**, Ericsson's improved hot-air-engine. Hence **Calo·rically** *adv.* as heat.

Caloricity (kælǒri·sĭti). 1836. [f. CALORIC + -ITY.] *Biol.* The faculty in living beings of developing heat so as to maintain a fairly uniform temperature.

Caloriduct (kălǫ·ridvkt). 1864. [f. L. *calorem*, after *aqueduct.*] A tube or channel for conducting heat.

Calorie (kæ·lǒri). Also **calory.** 1870. [a. F., arbitrarily f. L. *calor.*] *Physics.* (More fully *great* or *major calorie.*) The amount of heat required to raise the temperature of 1 kilogramme (or, in later use, 1 gramme, *lesser calorie*) of water one degree centigrade.

Calorifacient (kălǫ:rifē¹·ʃiĕnt), *a.* 1854. [as if f. L. **calorifacientem.*] *Phys.* Heat-producing. var. **Calo·rifi:ant.**

Calorific (kælǒri·fik), *a.* 1682. [a. F. *calorifique* :—L. *calorificus.*] *Physics.* **1.** Producing heat. **2.** *loosely.* Of or pertaining to heat. var. †**Calori·fical.** Hence **Calori·fically** *adv.* by means of heat.

Calorification (kălǫ:rifikē¹·ʃən). 1836. [a. F., f. L. type **calorificare.*] *Phys.* The production of heat, *esp.* in living animal bodies.

Calorify (kălǫ·rifəi), *v.* 1841. [repr. L. type **calorificare.*] To make hot. Hence **Calo·rifier**, an air-heater.

Calorimeter (kælǒri·mĭtəɹ). 1794. [f. L. *calorem* + -METER.] An instrument for measuring actual quantities of heat, or the specific heat of bodies. Hence **Calo:rime·tric, -al** *a.* of or pertaining to calorimetry; also, loosely, thermometric. **Calori·metry,** the measurement of heat.

Calorimotor (kălǫ:rimōᵘ·tǒɹ). 1832. [f. L. *calorem* + *motor.*] A voltaic arrangement consisting of one or more pairs of very large plates, producing considerable heat effects.

Calorist (kæ·lǒrist). *rare.* 1864. [f. CALORIC + -IST.] One who held heat or caloric to be a material substance.

Calotte (kălǫ·t). ? 1632. [a. F., dim. of *cale* caul.] **1.** A plain skull-cap; *esp.* that worn by Roman Catholic ecclesiastics, etc.; †the coif of a serjeant-at-law. **2.** A cap-like crest on a bird's head 1874. ‖**3.** Any thing having the form of a small cap; the cap of a sword-hilt, of a pistol, etc. (Chiefly Fr. uses.) 1886. ‖**4.** *Arch.* A concavity in the shape of a cup, serving to connect the proportions of a chapel, etc. 1727.

Calotype (kæ·lǒtəip), *sb.* 1841. [f. Gr. καλός + τύπος.] *Photogr.* The process of producing photographs by the action of light upon silver iodide; also called *Talbotype*, after Fox Talbot its inventor. Hence **Ca·lotype** *v.* to represent by the c. process. **Caloty·pic** *a.*, **Ca·loty:pist.**

‖**Caloyer** (kæ·lǫyəɹ). 1615. [a. F., ad. It. *caloiero*, ad. late Gr. καλόγηρος, f. καλός+γηρο-, -γηρος in comb. old, aged.] A Greek monk, *esp.* of the order of St. Basil.

How name ye yon lone C. BYRON.

‖**Calpac, calpack** (kæ·lpæk). 1813. [Turki *qālpāq.*] A felt cap, worn by Turkis, Tartars, etc.; an oriental cap generally. var. **Ka·lpack.**

Calque, var. of CALK *v.*

‖**Caltha** (kæ·lþă). 1599. [L.] *Bot.* The Marsh Marigold; also its genus.

Caltrop (kæ·ltrǫp), **Caltrap.** [ME. *calke-*, *kalketrappe*; OE. *coltetræppe*, *calcatrippe*; prob. f. (ult.) L. type **calcatrappa*, or **calcitrappa*, app. f. *calcem* (influenced by *calcāre*) + *trappa* trap. *Gall-trap* is due to pop. etym.] †**1.** A trap, gin, or snare for the feet –1850. **2.** *Mil.* An iron ball armed with four sharp prongs, placed so that when thrown on the ground it has always one projecting upwards: Used to impede cavalry, etc. 1519. Also *fig.* **3.** *Herb.* Now usu. *Caltrops*: A name for various plants that entangle the feet, or suggest the military instrument; as the Star-thistle (*Centaurea Calcitrapa*); **Land Caltrops** (*Tribulus terrestris*); **Water Caltrops** (*Potamogeton densus* and *P. crispus*), which entangle swimmers; also for the seed of *Trapa natans.*

Calumba (kălʊ·mbă). 1811. [f. *Colombo* in Ceylon, because supposed wrongly to come from thence.] *Med.* The root of *Jateorhiza palmata* (N.O. *Menospermaceæ*), indigenous to the forests of Mozambique, used as a mild tonic and stomachic. Hence **Calu·mbin, Calu·mbic acid,** bitter substances found in Calumba root.

Calumet (kæ·liŭmĕt). 1717. [a. F. *calumet* (Norman f. *chalumet*), a parallel form to *chalumeau*, in OF. *chalemel* :—L. *calamellus*, dim. of *calamus* reed.] A tobacco-pipe with a bowl of clay, and a long reed stem carved and ornamented with feathers. Used among the Amer. Indians as a symbol of peace.

The French desired to smoak the c. of peace 1754.

Calumniate (kălʊ·mni,ē¹t), *v.* 1554. [f. L. *calumniat-*, *calumniari.*] *trans.* To asperse with calumny; to charge falsely and maliciously with something criminal or disreputable; to slander. *intr.* (*absol.*) To utter calumnies 1606.

We must not c. even the Inquisition WHEWELL. Hence **Calu:mnia·tion,** the action of calumniating; a calumny. **Calu·mniator. Calu·mniato:ry** *a.* calumnious. var. †**Ca·lumnize** (*trans.*).

Calumnious (kălʊ·mniəs), *a.* 1490. [ad. L. *calumniosus*, f. *calumnia*; see CALUMNY.] Of the nature of a calumny or a calumniator; slanderous, defamatory.

A foule mouth'd and c. knaue *All's Well* I. iii. 61. A c. fable 1855. Hence **Calu·mnious-ly** *adv.*, **-ness.**

Calumny (kæ·ləmni). 1564. [ad. L. *calumnia* and F. *calomnie.*] **1.** False and malicious misrepresentation, to the injury of another; libellous detraction, slander. **2.** A slanderous report 1611.

1. The Shrug, the Hum, or Ha (these Petty-brands That Calumnie doth vse) SHAKS. **2.** To invent calumnies..requires neither labour nor courage JOHNSON.

‖**Calva·ria, calva·rium.** ME. [L. *calvaria*, f. *calvus* bare, *calva* the scalp.] *Anat.* The part of the skull above the orbits, temples, ears, and occipital protuberance. **Calva·rial** *a.*

Calvary (kæ·lvări). ME. [a. L. *calvaria*, used as tr. Aram. *gogolpā* 'the skull', in Gr. transliteration γολγοθά, name of the mount of the Crucifixion.] **1.** Proper name of the place where Christ was crucified. (In OE. *Headpanstow.*) Also used generically. **2.** [F. *calvaire*] in *R.C.Ch.* **a.** A life-size representation of the Crucifixion, on a raised ground in the open air; **b.** A series of representations, in a church or chapel, of the scenes of the Passion 1727.

C. cross, cross C., in *Her.*, a cross mounted on a pyramid of three steps.

Calve (kāv), *v.*[1] [OE. *cealfian*, f. *cealf* CALF *sb.*[1]] **1.** *intr.* To give birth to a calf. Cf. CALF *sb.*[1] I, 3. **2.** *trans.* To bring forth ME. **3.** Of a glacier, etc.: To throw off a mass of ice 1837.

2. The cow..caluede not a deed calf WYCLIF *Job* xxi. 10. **3.** The icebergs 'calved' as they went along 1882. Hence **Ca·lven** [after *shaken*, etc.] *ppl. a.* that has calved. **Ca·lver,** a cow that calves.

Calved (kāvd), *ppl. a.* 1593. [f. *calve(s* (see CALF[2]) + -ED.] Having calves.

†**Calver,** *a.* ME. [? Perh. earlier f. Sc. CALLER (cf. *silver*, *siller*).] An epithet of salmon or other fish. ? 'Fresh' (E. Müller); or 'dressed while alive'. –1865.

Ca·lver, *v.* 1651. ? *Obs.* [app. f. prec.] **1.** To treat or cook as a calver fish; to CRIMP; or, according to others, to cut into slices while fresh, or alive, and pickle. **2.** *intr.* Of fish: To behave when cooked as a calver fish.

Calvinian (kælvi·niăn). 1566. [f. pr. n. Calvin, L. *Calvinus.*] *adj.* Of, belonging to, or following the doctrine of, Calvin. †*sb.* = CALVINIST –1691.

Calvinism (kæ·lviniz'm). 1570. [f. as prec.] The doctrines of John Calvin (1509–1564), *esp.* his theological doctrines on grace, in which Calvinism is opp. to ARMINIANISM. **b.** Adherence to these doctrines.

The 'five points of Calvinism' are: (1) Particular election. (2) Particular redemption. (3) Moral inability in a fallen state. (4) Irresistible grace. (5) Final perseverance.

Calvinist (kæ·lvinist). 1579. [f. as prec.] An adherent of Calvinism.

Calvini·stic, *a.* 1820. [f. prec.] Of or belonging to Calvinism, following the doctrines of Calvin. Hence **Calvini·stic-al** *a.*, **-ly** *adv.*

Ca·lvinize, *v.* 1659. [See -IZE.] *intr.* To follow Calvin, to teach Calvinism. *trans.* To imbue with Calvinism.

Calvish (kā·viʃ), *a.* 1570. [f. CALF[1] + -ISH.] Resembling a calf; doltish, stupid.

Calvity (kæ·lvĭti). *rare.* 1623. [ad. L. *calvities.*] Baldness.

Calx (kælks). Pl. **calces,** †**calxes.** 1460. [L. *calx* lime.] **1.** The powder or friable substance produced by calcining a mineral or metal; formerly taken as the essential substance of the crude mineral. †**2.** Occ. = quick-lime –1834. **3.** *Eton slang.* The goal-line (at foot-ball) 1864.

Calybite. [f. Gr. καλύβη.] One of the early saints who passed their lives in huts.

‖**Calycanthus** (kælikæ·nþǒs). 1864. [mod. L., f. Gr. κάλυκ- CALYX + ἄνθος.] *Bot.* A North American genus of shrubs; esp. *Calycanthus floridus* or Carolina Allspice.

Calycifloral (kæ:lisi,flōᵊ·răl, kăli·si-), *a.* 1872. [f. L. *calycem* (*calyx*) + *florem* + -AL.] *Bot.* Having the stamens and petals inserted in the calyx. So **Calyciflo·rate, Calyciflo·rous** *adjs.*, in same sense.

Calyciform (kæ·lisifǭɹm, kali·si-), *a.* 1831. [f. as prec. + -FORM.] *Bot.* Having the form of a calyx. Also erron. sp. of CALICIFORM cup-shaped.

Calycine (kæ·lisəin, -in), *a.* 1816. [f. as prec. + -INE.] Of or belonging to the calyx; resembling a calyx. Hence **Caly·cinal, Caly·cinar,** in same sense.

Calycle (kæ·lik'l). 1731. [ad. L. **calyculus** (also used), dim. of *calyx.*] *Bot.* **1.** A row of bracts round the base of the calyx, resembling a smaller outer calyx. **2.** Erron. f. CALICLE 1794. Hence **Caly·cular** *a.* relating to or composing a c. **Caly·culate** *a.* having a c. †**Caly·culated,** (having fruit) enclosed in a c. var. **Ca·lycule.**

†**Calyon.** ME. only. [?] Flint or pebble stone.

‖**Calyptra** (kăli·ptră). 1753. [mod.L. a. Gr. καλύπτρα covering, veil.] *Bot.* A hood or cover; *spec.* the hood of the sporecase in mosses. Hence **Caly·ptrate** *a.* having a c.; hooded, operculate. **Caly·ptriform** *a.* calyptra-shaped. **Caly·ptrogen,** the outer zone of the meristem of the youngest part of plants.

Calyx (kæ·liks, kē¹·liks). Pl. **calyces** (kæ·lisīz), rarely **calyxes.** 1693. [L., a. Gr. κάλυξ (from root of καλύπτειν). Often confused with CALIX, q. v.] **1.** *Bot.* The whorl of leaves (sepals), usually green, forming the outer covering of a flower while in the bud. Also *transf.* **2.** *Phys.* and *Biol.* Variant sp. of CALIX 1831.

1. The c. is nothing but the swaddling clothes of the flower RUSKIN.

†**Calzoo·ns,** *sb. pl.* 1615. [From Fr., Sp., Pg., or It. :—late L. *calciones*, augment. f. *L. *calcea*, f. *calceus* shoe.] Drawers, hose, trousers –1677.

Cam (kæm), *sb.*[1] Also **camb, camm.** 1777. [prob. a. Du. *kam*, the same word as Eng. COMB; whence Fr. *came* 'cog, tooth', etc.] A projecting part of a wheel or other revolving piece of machinery, adapted to impart an alternating or variable motion to another piece, by sliding or rolling contact. Much used where a uniform revolving motion is employed to actuate any kind of non-uniform, alternating, elliptical, or rectilineal movement.

Cam, *sb.*[2] *n. dial.* 1788. [= Sc. *kame, kaim*, a. ON. *kamb-r* COMB, crest, etc. The same word originally as prec. and COMB.] A ridge; a mound of earth; the bank on which a hedge is planted or the like.

Cam, *a.* and *adv.* Now *dial.* Also †**kamme.** 1579. [prob. a. Welsh *cam*, repr. an OCelt. **cambo-s* crooked.] *adj.* Crooked, twisted. Hence *mod. dial.* Perverse. 1600. *adv.* Awry, askew (also *fig.*). Cf. KIM KAM. 1579.

‖**Camaieu** (kamayö̆). 1596. [F.; see CAMEO.] 1. = CAMEO. 2. A method of painting in monochrome 1727.

Camail. Now *Hist.* 1670. [a. F.; f. *cap* head + *mail* MAIL (Diez).] 1. A piece of chain-mail attached to the head-piece, and protecting the neck and shoulders 1826. 2. A hood worn by the R. C. clergy; also, a blue or purple ornament worn by a bishop over his rochet 1670. Hence **Camailed** *a.* having a c.

Cama·ldolite. Also **Camaldulite, -dulian, -dule, -dolensian.** 1727. A member of the religious order founded by S. Romuald at Camaldoli in the 11th c.

Camara[1] (kæ·mără). 1880. [a. Gr. καμάρα (see CAMERA).] *Bot.* a. One of the cells of a fruit. b. A carpel.

‖**Camara**[2] (kæ·mără). 1866. [Native name in Guiana.] The hard durable timber of *Dipteryx odorata* (N.O. *Leguminosæ*).

‖**Camaraderie** (kamara·dərī). 1840. [Fr., f. *camarade* COMRADE.] Comradeship; loyalty to, or partiality for, one's comrades; *esprit de corps*.

‖**Camarilla** (kæmări·lă, Sp. -ī·lʸa). 1839. [Sp., dim. of *camara* CHAMBER.] 1. A small chamber 1860. 2. A private cabinet of counsellors; a cabal, clique.

†‖**Ca·marine.** 1576. [f. *Camarina* (Καμάρινα) in Sicily.] A fetid swamp. Also *fig.* –1681.

‖**Camas, camash, cammas,** var. ff. QUAMASH (*Camassia esculenta*), a liliaceous plant whose bulbs are eaten by the N. Amer. Indians.

Camber (kæ·mbəɹ), *sb.* Also GAMBER. 1618. [a. F. *cambre*, f. *cambrer*; see next.] 1. The condition of being slightly arched or convex above. *concr.* A flattened arch. 2. A camber-beam 1677. 3. 'The part of a dock-yard where cambering is performed and timber kept' (Smyth) 1885.

Comb.: **c.-beam,** a beam cut arching in the middle; **-slip,** a piece of board made convex on one or both edges, used as a rule.

Camber (kæ·mbəɹ), *v.* 1627. [app. a. F. *cambrer*, repr. of L. *camerare*, f. *camera* vault.] 1. *intr.* To be or become slightly arched or curved so that the centre is higher than the ends. 2. *trans.* To bend (a beam, etc.) upwards in the middle; to arch slightly 1852.

Ca·mberwell Beau·ty. 1847. [from *Camberwell*, London.] A species of butterfly, *Vanessa Antiopa*.

Cambial (kæ·mbiăl), *a.* 1864. [ad. late L. *cambialis*, f. *cambium*; see CAMBIUM.] 1. Relating to exchange in commerce. 2. *Bot.* Pertaining to cambium 1881.

Cambiform (kæ·mbifǭɹm), *a.* 1882. [f. CAMBIUM + -FORM.] *Bot.* Of the form of, or like cambium.

‖**Ca·mbio.** 1645. [It.:—L. *cambium.*] 1. A bill of exchange. 2. A place of exchange.

Ca·mbism. *rare.* 1837. [See next.] The theory and practice of exchanges.

Cambist (kæ·mbist). 1809. [a. F. *cambiste*; see CAMBIUM.] 1. One skilled in the science of exchanges; one who deals in bills of exchange. 2. *transf.* As title of a manual of foreign exchanges 1811. Hence **Ca·mbistry.** (Dicts.)

Cambium (kæ·mbiŏ̆m). 1643. [a. late L. *cambium.*] †1. Exchange, barter. b. A place of exchange. (Dicts.) †2. One of the four humours formerly supposed to nourish the body –1800. 3. *Bot.* A viscid substance lying immediately under the bark of exogens, in which the annual growth of the wood and bark takes place 1671. Also *attrib.*

Camblet, var. of CAMLET.

Camboge, obs. f. GAMBOGE.

Camboose, var. of CABOOSE.

Cambrel (kæ·mbrĕl). Cf. CHAMBREL, GAMBREL. 1450. [? conn. w. CAMBER, F. *cambrer*; cf. CAMBER *sb.* 2.] 1. A bent piece of wood or iron used by butchers to hang carcasses on. 2. The bend of the upper part of a horse's hind leg; the hock. Now *dial.* 1610. Also *attrib.*

‖**Cambresine** (kæmbrĕzī·n). Also **cambrasine.** 1750. [F.] 'A species of fine linen made at Cambray' (Littré); also an eastern fabric.

Cambrian (kæ·mbriăn), *a.* (*sb.*) 1656. [f. *Cambria*, var. of *Cumbria* till differentiated; latinized deriv. of *Cymry* Welshmen.] 1. Pertaining to Wales, Welsh; *sb.* a Welshman. 2. *Geol.* A system of Palæozoic rocks lying below the Silurian, in Wales and Cumberland 1836.

Cambric (kēɪ·mbrik). 1530. [f. *Kameryk*, Flemish name of *Cambray*:—L. *Camaracum.*] A kind of fine white linen, orig. made at Cambray in Flanders. (Also an imitation made of hard-spun cotton yarn.) b. As the material of handkerchiefs 1886. Also *attrib.*

I would your Cambrick were sensible as your finger *Cor.* I. iii. 95.

Cambric, var. of CAMMOCK.

Came (kēɪm). 1688. [app. i.q. CALM[2], q.v.] A small grooved bar of lead used for framing the glass in latticed windows: chiefly in *pl.*

Came (kēɪm), pa. t. of COME *v.*; Sc. f. COMB.

Camel (kæ·mĕl). [Late OE., ad. L. *camelus*, a. Gr. κάμηλος, adopted from Semitic.] 1. A large hornless ruminant quadruped, having a humped back, long neck, and cushioned feet; not found wild, but domesticated in Western Asia and Northern Africa, where it is the chief beast of burden. There are two species, the Arabian or one-humped (including the dromedary), and the Bactrian or two-humped. Also *fig.* 2. *techn.* A machine for adding buoyancy to vessels, and thus enabling them to cross bars, shoals, etc.; also for raising sunken ships, removing rocks, etc. It consists generally of two or more water-tight chests provided with plugs and pumps. 1716.

Well, therefore, has the C... been termed 'the Ship of the Desert' 1847. *fig.* A Drayman, a Porter, a very Camell *Tr. & Cr.* I. ii. 271.

Comb.: **c.-bird,** the Ostrich; **-engine** = sense 2; **-gut,** the dried gut of a c. used to furnish strings for musical instruments; **-insect,** a name for members of the genus *Mantis*, from their elongated thorax; **-kneed** *a.*, callous-kneed, like a camel; **-locust** = *camel-insect*; **camel('s)-thorn,** a leguminous plant (*Alhagi camelorum*); **-tree,** *Acacia giraffæ*. Hence **Ca·melcade,** a train of people on camels. **Ca·meldom,** the region of camels. (*nonce-wds.*) **Camelee·r,** a c.-driver; a cuirassier mounted on a c. **Ca·meline** *a.* belonging to a c., or to camels. **Ca·melish** *a.* obstinate as a c.; **Ca·melishness. Ca·melry,** troops mounted on camels; a place where camels are laden and unladen.

Cameleon, obs. f. CHAMELEON.

Camel-hair; see CAMEL'S-HAIR.

Cameline (kæ·mĕlin, kæ·mlin), *sb.*[1] ME. [a. OF. *camelin*, ad. med.L. *camelinum* adj. neut.] *orig.* A kind of stuff supposed to be made of camel's hair; cf. CAMLET. Also, a garment of this 1599.

Cameline (kæ·mĕləin), *sb.*[2] ME. [a. F.] A genus of cruciferous plants; esp. *Camelina sativa*. Also *attrib.* 1578.

†**Camelion.** ME. [In 14th c. taken as *camel* + *lion*.] A camelopard –1535.

Camellia (kăme·liă, kămī·liă). 1753. [After *Kamel* (latinized *Camellus*), a Jesuit who botanized Luzon.] A genus of evergreen shrubs belonging to the tea family (*Ternströmiaceæ*), chiefly natives of China and Japan. Also *attrib.*

Camelopard (kæ·mĕlo͡,pā:ɹd, kăme·lŏ̆paɹd). ME. [ad. L. *camelopardus, -pardalis*, a. Gr., f. κάμηλος + πάρδαλις. Confused with *leopard* in med.L., Fr., and Eng., whence *ca·mel-leo·pard.*] 1. The GIRAFFE; an African ruminant quadruped with long legs, very long neck, and skin spotted like that of the panther. 2. *Astr.* A constellation situated between Ursa Major and Cassiopeia 1836.

Camelopa·rdel. 1830. [f. prec.] *Her.* An animal, figured as a camelopard with the horns of an ibex.

Camelot, obs. f. CAMLET.

Camel's-hair. Also **camel-hair.** ME. 1. The hair of the camel. (But cf. next.). 2. The long hairs from the tail of a squirrel, used to make artist's pencils. Also *attrib.* 1771.

Camel-yarn. 1670. [In Da. *kameelgarn*: app. from a mistaken notion; cf. CAMLET and MOHAIR.] Yarn made from the wool of the Angora-goat, mohair yarn.

Camenes. *Logic.* A mnemonic word, repr. the second mood of the fourth syllogistic figure, in which the major premiss is a universal affirmative, the minor premiss and the conclusion universal negatives.

Cameo (kæ·mi͡o). 1561. [a. It. *camëo, camméo*, med.L. *cammæus*: of unkn. deriv.] A precious stone, as the onyx, agate, sardonyx, etc., having two layers of different colours, in the upper of which a figure is carved in relief, while the lower serves as ground. Also, shells similarly carved. Also *attrib.*

Camera (kæ·mĕră). 1708. [a. L. *camera* (*camara*) vault, arched chamber, = Gr. καμάρα. In late L. in sense 'chamber'; see CHAMBER.] ‖1. In L. sense: An arched or vaulted roof or chamber. Prob. not in Eng. use. b. A judge's chamber; hence *in camerâ*, opp. to 'in open court'. ‖2. [It. or Sp.] A chamber; a council or legislative chamber; a department of the papal curia 1712. 3. *Optics.* Short for *camera obscura* 1727. b. *esp.* That form used in photography 1840.

Ca·mera obscu·ra [L.; lit. 'dark chamber'.] *Optics.* A darkened chamber or box, into which light is admitted through a double convex lens, forming an image of external objects on paper, glass, etc., placed at the focus of the lens. Also *lit.* Dark room. **Ca·mera lu·cida** [L.; lit. 'light chamber'.] *Optics.* An instrument by which the rays of light from an object are reflected by a prism, and produce an image on paper placed beneath the instrument, which can be traced with a pencil.

Ca·meral, *a.* 1762. [a. Ger. *kameral*, ad. med.L. *cameralis*, f. *camera*.] Of or pertaining to the *camera* or chamber; relating to the management of the state property (in Germany). Hence **Ca:merali·stic** *a.*, **Ca:merali·stics** *sb. pl.*

†**Ca·merate,** *v.* 1623. [f. L. *camerat-, camerare*.] *trans.* To vault, to arch. Hence **Ca·merated** *ppl. a.*, (*Arch.*) arched, vaulted; (*Zool.*) divided into chambers, as some shells; var. **Ca·merate** *a.* **Camera·tion,** (*Arch.*) vaulting, arching; (*Zool.*) division into chambers.

Camerine; see CAMARINE.

Cameronian (kæmĕrōᵘ·niăn). 1690. [f. the name *Cameron*.] *adj.* Pertaining to Richard Cameron, his tenets, or his followers.

Cameronian Regiment: the old 26th Regiment of Foot (now the 1st Battalion of the Scottish Rifles), formed originally of Presbyterians who rallied to the cause of William III.

sb. A follower of Richard Cameron, a Scottish Covenanter and field preacher, who rejected the indulgence granted to nonconforming ministers and formally renounced allegiance to Charles II. His followers became the 'Reformed Presbyterian Church of Scotland'.

†**Camery.** 1572. A disease of horses; the *frounce* –1727.

Camestres. *Logic.* A mnemonic word, repr. the second mood of the second syllogistic figure, in which the major premiss is a universal affirmative, the minor premiss and the conclusion universal negatives.

†**Ca·mis, camus.** [In Spenser, prob. ad. Sp. or Pg. *camisa*:—late L. *camisia, camisa* (see CHEMISE).] A light loose dress of silk or linen.

Ca:misa·do. *Obs.* or *arch.* 1548. [ad. Sp. *camiçada, camisada*, f. *camisa* shirt.] *Mil.* 1. A night attack; orig. one in which the attackers wore shirts over their armour as a means of mutual recognition. Also *fig.* 2. (*erron.*) The shirt thus worn 1618. var. **Camisa·de.**

By night I wil the cammassado give GASCOIGNE.

†**Camisard, camisar.** 1703. [a. F., f. Pg. *camisa* shirt.] 'Name given to the Calvinist insurgents of the Cevennes, during the persecution which followed the revocation of the edict of Nantes' (Littré). Also *attrib.* –1883.

‖**Camise, camiss** (kămī·s). In Byron **camese.** 1812. [Arab. *qamīç*, under-tunic; perh. ad. L. *camisia, camisa*; see CHEMISE.] The shirt worn by Arabs and other Mohammedans.

Camisole (kæ·misōᵘl). 1816. [a. F., ad. Sp. *camisola*, dim. of *camisa*; see CHEMISE.] 1. Formerly applied to jackets of various kinds. 2. A woman's underbodice 1895. Hence in attrib. form *cami-* in comb., as *cami-knickers* (1915).

Ca·mister. *Thieves' cant.* 1851. [f. CAMIS surplice.] A clergyman.

Camlet (kæ·mlėt), *sb.* ME. [Fr. *camelot*; associated with *camel*, but prob. a. Arab. *khamlat*, f. *khaml* pile or nap.] A name orig. for a costly eastern fabric, subseq. for substitutes, made of various combinations of wool, silk, hair, and latterly cotton or linen. Also, a garment of camlet. Also *fig.* and *attrib.*

Stuffs made from the hair of [the Angora goat] .. known among us by the name of *camlet* GOLDSM. Hence **Ca·mlet** *v.* to mark as (watered) c. **Camletee·n, -ine,** an imitation c. **Ca·mleting,** stuff of c.

Cammas, var. of QUAMASH; see CAMAS.

Cammed (kæmd), *a.* Now *dial.* ME. [app. f. CAM *a.*; cf. *wicked*.] †**1.** = CAMOIS –1440. **2.** Crooked, perverse 1746.

Cammock[1] (kæ·mək). [OE. *cammoc*, of unkn. origin.] **1.** The plant *Ononis spinosa* (N.O. *Leguminosæ*), also called *Rest-harrow*. **2.** Used dial. of other yellow flowers, as St. John's Wort, Ragweed, etc. 1878.

Cammock[2], **cambock** (kæ·mək). Now *Sc.* [ME. *kambok*, ad. late L. *cambuca*, f. *cambo*-CAM.] **1.** A crooked staff; *esp.* a hockey-stick, or the like; hence, the game in which it is used. **2.** A crooked piece of wood 1450.

†**Ca·mois, camus,** *a.* (*sb.*) ME. [a. F. *camus*, *-use*. See Diez and Littré.] **1.** Of the nose: Low and concave. Of persons: Pug-nosed. –1877. Also *fig.* **2.** quasi-*sb.* A person or animal with a camois nose –1751. Hence †**Ca·moised** *a.* having a c. nose. †**Ca·moisly,** ca·mously *adv.* concavely.

Camomile, cham- (kæ·mŏməil). ME. [a. F. *camomille*, ad. L. *chamomilla*, altered f. *chamæmelon*, a. Gr., f. χαμαί + μῆλον; so called from the apple-like scent of its blossoms. The sp. *cha-* is chiefly in pharmacy, after L.] **1.** A Composite plant, *Anthemis nobilis*, a creeping herb, with downy leaves, and flowers white in the ray and yellow in the disk. The flowers are used in Medicine for their bitter and tonic properties. **b.** A name for the genus *Anthemis*, and pop. applied to allied plants, esp. *Matricaria Chamomilla* (Wild C.); *Blue* or *Purple C.*, the Sea Starwort, etc.

‖**Camorra** (kămǫ·ră). 1865. [It.] **1.** A kind of smock-frock or blouse 1869. **2.** A secret society of lawless malcontents in the Neapolitan district. Hence **Camo·rrism,** lawlessness, anarchy. **Ca·morrist,** a member of a c.

‖**Camouflage** (kæ·muflāʒ), *sb.* 1917. [Fr., f. *camoufiet*, etym. dub.] The disguising of any object used in war, by means of paint, smoke-screens, etc., in such a way as to conceal it from the enemy; the disguise used in this way. Also *fig.* Hence **Ca·mouflage** *v.*

Camp, *sb.*[1] Now *dial.* [OE. *camp*, *cǫmp*, prob. ad. (ult.) L. *campus*.] †**1.** Martial contest, battle, war –ME. **2. Camp-ball:** An ancient form of football played by large sides 1600.

Camp (kæmp), *sb.*[2] 1528. [a. F. *camp* (16th c.):—L. *campus*. ME. had only CHAMP.] **1.** The place where a body of troops is lodged in tents or other temporary shelter, with or without intrenchments. (In mod. use, the collection of tents, equipments, etc. is the chief notion.) Also, a permanent station for the training of troops in campaigning duties generally. **2.** A body of troops on a campaign. (Earlier *the host.*) 1584. Also *fig.* **3.** The scene of military service; the military life 1725. **4.** *transf.* The temporary quarters of nomads, sportsmen, lumbermen, field-preachers, etc.; an encampment 1560. **5.** A camping out 1865. **6.** The whole body of persons encamped together 1750.

1. The Youth of Rome.. pitch their sudden C. before the Foe DRYDEN. **2.** To follow the c. 1706. *Flying c.*, *c. volant*: a body of horse and foot that keeps the field. **3.** Love rules the court, the c., the grove SCOTT. *Comb.*: **c.-bed, -bedstead,** one for use in field-service; hence, *spec.* a compact folding bedstead; **-chair,** a form of folding chair; **-fever,** any epidemic fever occurring in camps, chiefly typhus; **-fire,** a fire lit in an encampment; hence a military social gathering; **-follower,** one, not a soldier, who hangs on to an army; **-furniture; -seat, -stool,** a light portable folding stool. Hence **Ca·mpish** *a.* savouring of the c. **Ca·mpless** *a.* **Ca·mpward(s** *adv.*

Camp, *sb.*[3] *dial.* 1713. [?] A conical heap of potatoes or turnips, in the open air, covered with straw and earth, for winter storage; a *bury*, *pie*, or *pit*.

Camp, *v.*[1] Now *dial.* [OE. *campian*, *cǫmpian*, f. *camp* fight.] **1.** To contend; *esp.* at camp-ball. **2.** To scold 1606.

Camp (kæmp), *v.*[2] 1543. [a. F. *camper*; see CAMP *sb.*[2]] **1.** *intr.* To live in a camp or a tent; to encamp; *famil.* to lodge. Often with *out*. **2.** *trans.* To place in camp; to lodge 1549.

1. There Israel camped before the mount *Ex.* xix. 2. The messenger .. camping at night in the snow THACKERAY. **2.** *Ant. & Cl.* IV. viii. 33.

‖**Campagna, campagnia** (kampā·nʸa). 1641. [It. :—L. *campania*.] †**1.** = CHAMPAIGN (*rare*) –1717. †**2.** A (military) CAMPAIGN (*rare*) –1663. **3.** Now only as proper name 'the Campagna' in Italy; see CAMPANIA.

‖**Campagnol** (kampănʸǫl). 1835. [Fr.; f. *campagne*.] The Short-tailed Field-mouse.

Campaign (kămpē·n). 1628. [a. F. *campagne*, ad. It. *campagna*; see CAMPANIA.] **I.** †**1.** = CHAMPAIGN 1, 3. –1765. **2.** *Mil. orig.* The time for which an army kept the field, without entering into quarters; *now*, A continuous series of military operations, constituting the whole, or a distinct part, of a war 1656. **3.** *Ironworks.* The period during which a furnace is in continuous operation 1871. **4.** *fig.* Any course of action analogous to a military campaign 1770.

4. A reading c. DICKENS, an electoral c. (*mod.*).

II. *attrib.* **a.** Belonging to the open country 1628. **b.** Of, belonging to, or used on, a military campaign 1677.

b. A c.-coat 1677. Hence **Campai·gn** *v.* to serve in, or go on, a c.

Campaigner (kămpē·nəɹ). 1771. [f. CAMPAIGN *v.*] One who serves in a campaign; *esp.* one who has served in many campaigns; also *fig.*

†**Ca·mpal,** *a.* 1598. [a. Sp.] Pertaining to the field –1611.

‖**Campana** (kămpā·nă). 1613. [late L.] **I.** A church bell 1706. **2.** ? The pasque flower. DRAYTON. **3.** *Arch.* The body of the Corinthian capital; also = GUTTA 1823. Hence **Ca·mpanal** *a.* (*Bot.*) including the *Campanulaceæ* and their allies.

Campane (kămpēⁱ·n). 1662. [a. F.:–L. *campana*.] *Her.* A bell. Hence **Campa·ned** *ppl. a.* furnished with bells.

‖**Campanero** (kæmpănēᵊ·ro). 1825. [a. Sp.; 'bell-man'.] The Bell-bird of S. America.

†**Campa·nia.** 1601. [? ad. It. *campagna*, spelt phonetically.] **1.** = CHAMPAIGN –1698. **2.** = CAMPAIGN *sb.* 2. –1698.

Campaniform (kămpæ·nifǭɹm), *a.* 1757. [f. late L. *campana*; see -FORM.] *Bot.* Bell-shaped.

‖**Campanile.** 1640. [It., f. as prec. *Pl.* in It. *-i*, in Eng. usu. *-es*. Usu. pronounced as It. (kampanī·le), but also as Fr. (kampănī·l), and as Eng. (kæ·mpănil, -əil).] A bell-tower; *esp.* a lofty detached bell-tower; a steeple.

The great C. at Christ-church Oxford H. WALPOLE. Hence **Campani·liform** *a.* shaped like a c.

Campanist (kæ·mpănist). 1872. [ad. med. L. *campanista*.] One versed in bells.

Campanology (kæmpănǫ·lŏdʒi). 1847. [ad. mod.L. *campanologia*.] The subject of bells; the science and art of bell-founding, bell-ringing, etc. Hence **Campano·loger, -logist.**

Campanula (kămpæ·niŭlă). 1664. [mod. L., dim. of *campana*.] *Bot.* A bell-flower; a genus of plants, giving its name to the N.O. *Campanulaceæ*. Hence **Campanula·ceous** *a.* belonging to the N.O. *Campanulaceæ*. **Campa·nular** *a.* bell-shaped. ‖**Campa·nula·ria,** (*Zool.*) a genus of hydroid Zoophytes having the polype-cells bell-shaped and supported on long footstalks.

Campanulate (kæmpæ·niŭlėt), *a.* 1668. [ad. mod.L. *campanulatus*, f. *campanula*.] *Bot.* and *Zool.* Bell-shaped. var. **Campa·nulated, Campa·nulous.**

Campeachy wood. 1652. [From *Campeachy* on the coast of Yucatan.] = LOGWOOD.

‖**Campement** (kãnpəmaṅ). 1821. [Fr.] A detachment whose duty is to mark out the ground for a camp in advance of the army.

Camper (kæ·mpəɹ). 1631. [f. CAMP *sb.*[2], *v.*[2] + -ER.] †**1.** A military man; a camp-follower –1691. **2.** One who goes into camp; one who lodges in a tent 1856. Also *camper out.*

Campestral (kămpe·străl), *a. rare.* 1750. [f. L. *campester*, *campestris* + -AL.] Pertaining to fields or open country; growing in the fields. var. †**Campe·strial.**

†**Camp-fight.** 1605. [tr. med.L. *pugna campi.*] In law writers (from 17th c.) the trial of a cause by duel.

Camph-, abbrev. of CAMPHOR, taken as a stem on which to form names of related substances, as **Ca·mphene,** generic name for the hydrocarbons isomeric or polymeric with oil of turpentine ($C_{10}H_{16}$); = TEREBENE. **Ca·mphine** (-əin), an illuminating oil procured by distillation from oil of turpentine. **Ca·mphogen** = CYMENE, $C_{10}H_{14}$; also, loosely, *camphene* or *camphine*. **Ca·mphol** = BORNEOL. **Campho·lic acid,** $C_{10}H_{18}O_2$. **Ca·mphyl,** the radical of Camphol, $C_{10}H_{17}$; whence **Camphy·lic** *a.*

Camphor (kæ·mfəɹ, -ǒɹ). ME. [a. F. *camfre*, *camphre* = med.L. *camphora*, a. Arab. *kafūr*, in Skr. *karpūram*. Till *c* 1800 usu. *camphire*.] **1.** A whitish translucent crystalline volatile substance ($C_{10}H_{16}O$), belonging to the vegetable oils, distilled from *Camphora officinarum* (*Laurus Camphora*), and purified by sublimation. It has a bitter aromatic taste and a characteristic smell. †**2.** A tree or plant which yields camphor; esp. *Camphora officinarum* and *Dryobalanops Camphora* –1684. Also *attrib.*

2. Here also grew Camphire, with Spiknard, and Saffron BUNYAN. Hence **Ca·mphor** *v.* to camphorate (*rare*). **Camphora·ceous, Ca·mphorous, Ca·mphory** *adjs.* of the nature of c. **Campho·ric** *a.* (*Chem.*) of or pertaining to c.; containing c. in chemical combination.

Camphorate (kæ·mfŏrėt), *sb.* 1794. [See next.] *Chem.* A salt of camphoric acid.

Camphorate (kæ·mfŏrēⁱt), *v.* 1641. [f. med. L. *camphorat-us.*] To impregnate or treat with camphor.

†**Ca·mping,** *vbl. sb.*[1] ME. [f. CAMP *v.*[1]] **1.** Fighting in CAMP-FIGHT 1481. **2.** Fighting –1587. **3.** Football playing. Also *attrib.* –1567.

Ca·mping, *vbl. sb.*[2] 1572. [f. CAMP *v.*[2] + -ING[1].] The action of CAMP *v.*[2] Also *attrib.*

†**Ca·mpion**[1]. [ME. *campiun*, a. ONF.:—late L. *campio*, a combatant in the campus. A doublet of CHAMPION. Cf. KEMP *sb.*] **1.** One who fights in single combat –1536. **2.** A champion –1651.

Campion[2] (kæ·mpiən). 1576. [? same as prec.; or ? f. L. *campus*, or Fr. *compagnon.*] *Herb.* The name of certain plants, species of the genus *Lychnis*, including Rose Campion, *L.* (now *Agrostemma*) *coronaria*, etc. Extended, with a qualification, to allied species, as **Bladder C.,** *Silene inflata*, etc.

Cample (kæ·mp'l), *v.* Now *dial.* 1621. [app. f. CAMP *v.*[1]] *intr.* To answer in anger; to wrangle.

Ca·mp-mee·ting. 1809. *U.S.* A religious (usu. Methodist) meeting held in the open air, and often lasting for some days, during which those who attend encamp on the spot.

Campoo (kæmpū·). *Anglo-Ind.* 1803. [ad. Pg. *campo.*] A camp; also, †a brigade under European commanders in the Mahratta service.

Camp-shedding, -sheeting. 1819. = next.

Ca·mp-shot. 1691. [?] A facing of piles and boarding along the bank of a river, or at the side of an embankment.

‖**Campus** (kæ·mpŏs). *U.S.* 1774. [L. *campus* field, plain, level space.] The grounds of a college or university.

Campylospermous (kæ·mpilo,spɔ̄·ɹməs), *a.* 1880. [f. Gr. καμπύλος bent + σπέρμα + -OUS.] *Bot.* Said of carpels, *e.g.* those of some Umbelliferæ, in which the contained seed produces a longitudinal furrow on the ventral face.

Campylotropous (kæmpilǫ·trŏpəs), *a.* 1835. [f. as prec. + Gr. -τροπος, f. τρέπειν + -OUS.] *Bot.* Said of the ovule of phanerogamous plants when its nucleus is curved upon itself. var. **Campy·lo·tropal.**

Camstone (kæ·mstōᵘn). *Sc.* 1791. **a.** A compact, prob. whitish, limestone. **b.** A bluish-white clay used to whiten hearths, etc.

Camus, var. of CAMIS and CAMOIS.

Cam-wood (kæ·mwud). 1698. [? ad. Afr. *Kambi.*] = BARWOOD.

Can (kæn), *sb.* [Com. Teut.: OE. *canne* :—WGer. *kanna* :—OTeut. type **kannôn-*.] 1. A vessel for holding liquids; now of tin or other metal, usually cylindrical in form, with a handle over the top. **b.** A chimney-pot 1833. **2.** *Sc.* A measure 1809. **3.** A vessel of tinned iron, in which fruit, fish, etc. are sealed up air-tight for preservation (chiefly in U. S.) 1874.

There weren set sixe stonun cannes WYCLIF *John* ii. 6. Hence **Ca·nful.**

Can (kæn), *v.*[1] *irreg.* Pa. Ind. **could.** [A Teut. *preterite-present* vb.: OE. *cunnan*, pres. Ind. *can* (*cǫn*), pa. *cúðe* (:—*cunðe*). The original meaning of the present was 'I have learned', *whence*, 'I know'; the original present stem being **kin-n-* or **ken-n-*, pre-Teut. **gen-n-*.]

I. †1. To know –1649. **2.** *intr.* To have knowledge *of* (*arch.*) ME.

1. He coulde it by hart 1541. She could the Bible in the holy tongue B. JONS. 2. The king couthe of venery 1420.

II. With inf., as auxiliary of predication. **1.** To know how (*to do* anything) OE. **2.** To be able; to have the power or capacity. (The current sense.) ME. **3.** Expressing possibility: *can you* . . ? = is it possible for you to . . ? 1542. **4.** *ellipt.* 1440.

1. Well couth he tune his pipe SPENSER. 2. The Egyptians could not drink of the water *Ex.* vii. 21. Such language can do no good (*mod.*). 3. And can you blame them STUBBES. Thy way thou canst not miss MILT. *P. L.* III. 735. 4. I could no more, I was really exhausted 1807. *Cannot but*: see BUT. See also CON.

†**Can**, *v.*[2] (*pa. tense.*) ME. and early mod. Eng. used for GAN, pa. t. of *ginnan* to begin; see GIN *v.* Replaced by *did.*

Can, *v.*[3] 1871. [f. CAN *sb.*[1]] To put in a can or cans; to 'tin', as fruit, beef, etc. Hence **Ca·nner.**

Canaan (kē¹·năn). 1637. [ad. Heb.] The ancient proper name of Western Palestine; *fig.* the land of promise, heaven, etc.

Canaanite (kē¹·nănəit), *sb.*[1] ME. [f. prec.] 1. A native of Canaan. *fig.* 'No true Israelite'. 2. (prop. **Cananæan**): One of a Jewish sect fanatically opposed to the Romans; *hence*, a zealot.

2. Simon the Canaanite *Matt.* x. 4. [*R.V.* Cananæan.] Hence **Canaani·tic, Canaani·tish** *adjs.* belonging to Canaan; of or like a C. Also *fig.*

Ca·naanite, *sb.*[2] 1844. *Min.* A variety of pyroxene found near Canaan, Ct., U.S.

Canada[1] (kæ·nădă). The name of a British dominion in N. America, used attrib. in names of plants, animals, products, etc.

C. balsam, a pale balsam derived from *Abies balsamea*, and *A. canadensis*, used in medicine, etc.; **C. rice**, *Hydropyrum esculentum*; **C. turpentine** = *Canada balsam.*

‖**Cañada**[2] (kănʸā·dă). 1850. [a. Sp., f. *caño* gutter.] In Western U.S.: A narrow valley or glen; a small cañon.

Canadian (kănē¹·diăn). 1805. [f. CANADA[1] + -IAN.] *adj.* Of or belonging to Canada or its people. *sb.* A native or inhabitant of Canada.

†‖**Cana·glia.** 1605. [a. It.] = next –1734.

‖**Canaille** (kana·ʸy, -ē¹·l). 1676. [a. F., ad. It. *canaglia*, f. *cane*, L. *canis*, *lit.* 'pack of dogs'. In 17–18th c. app. naturalized.] The vile populace; the rabble, the mob.

Let the Canaile wait as they should do 1676.

Canakin, var. of CANIKIN.

Canal (kănæ·l), *sb.* 1449. [a. F. *canal*, earlier F. *chenal*, refash. after L. *canalem*. Cf. CHANNEL.] †1. A pipe for conveying liquid; also a tube or tubular cavity –1698. **2.** *Phys.* A duct, as the *alimentary canal*, the *semicircular canals* of the ear, etc. (The second current sense.) 1626. †**3.** A CHANNEL; *esp.* a strait –1829. †**4.** A long and narrow piece of water ornamenting a garden or park –1827. **5.** An artificial watercourse uniting rivers, lakes, or seas, for purposes of inland navigation, irrigation, or conveyance of water-power. (The chief mod. sense.) 1673. Also †*fig.* **6.** *Arch.* A groove, fluting, CHANNEL 1727. **7.** *Zool.* The groove in the shells of certain molluscs, for the protrusion of the siphon 1835.

4. Having a Boat on the C. in St. James's Park 1725. *Comb.*: **c.-built** *a.*, of a build adapted to use on a c.

Cana·l, *v. rare.* 1870. [f. prec.] To make a canal through; to furnish with canals.

Canal-bone, -coal, vars. of CANNEL-BONE, -COAL.

Canalicular (kænăli·kiŭlăɹ), *a.* 1878. [ad. mod.L. *canalicularis.*] *Nat. Hist.* Of, pertaining to, or resembling a canaliculus; minutely tubular.

Canali·culate, *a.* 1828. [ad. mod.L. *canaliculatus.*] *Nat. Hist.* Having a longitudinal groove; minutely channelled. var. **Canali·culated** *ppl. a.*

Ca·nalicula·tion. 1880. [See prec.] A canaliculate formation; a minute grooving.

‖**Canaliculus** (kænăli·kiŭlŏs). Pl. **-li.** 1563. [a. L., dim. of *canalis.*] †1. *Arch.* = CANAL 6. 2. *Phys.* A small duct, as in bone-structure, etc. 1854. var. **Cana·licule.**

Canaliferous (kænăli·fĕrəs), *a.* 1835. [f. mod.L. *canalifer.*] *Nat. Hist.* Having a canal: said of shells of molluscs.

Canalize (kæ·năləiz), *v.* 1855. [a. F. *canaliser.*] *trans.* **a.** To cut a canal through; to furnish with canals. **b.** To convert (a river) into a canal. Also in *Phys.* and *Pathol.*

This system of canalising Egypt PUSEY. Hence **Ca·naliza·tion.**

‖**Canard** (kanar, kănā·ɹd). 1850. [Fr.; lit. 'duck'. See Littré.] An extravagant or absurd story circulated as a hoax; a false report.

Canary (kănē°·ri), *sb.* 1592. [a. F. *Canarie*, ad. Sp. *Canaria*, in L. *Canaria insula* 'Isle of Dogs', so called from its large dogs (*canarius*, f. *canis* Pliny).] The name of an island (*Gran Canaria*), and of the group Canary Isles. Hence 1. A lively Spanish dance, now antiquated. †2. = *Canary wine*, a light sweet wine from the Canaries –1848. 3. = CANARY-BIRD. Occ. *fig.* 1655. ¶4. A malapropism for *quandary. Merry W.* II. ii. 61.

1. A medicine That's able . . to make you dance Canari *All's Well* II. i. 77. 2. Thou lack'st a cup of Canarie *Twel. N.* I. iii. 85.

Comb.: **c.-creeper**, a garden name for *Tropæolum aduncum* (wrongly called *T. canariense*); **-finch** = CANARY-BIRD; **-grass**, *Phalaris canariensis*, which yields canary-seed; **-seed**, the seed of c.-grass, used as food for canaries; **-stone**, a yellow variety of carnelian; **-wood**, the light orange-coloured wood of *Persea indica* and *P. canariensis*, obtained from Brazil.

Cana·ry, *a.* 1854. [prec. used attrib.] Canary-coloured, bright yellow.

†**Cana·ry,** *v.* 1588. [f. CANARY *sb.* I.] To dance the canary. *L. L. L.* III. i. 12.

Canary-bird. 1576. [See CANARY *sb.*] 1. An insessorial singing bird, a kind of finch (*Fringilla* or *Carduelis canaria*, family *Fringillidæ*), originally brought from the Canary Islands. The wild bird is green. 2. *Thieves' slang.* A jail bird 1673.

Canaster (kănæ·stəɹ). 1827. [a. Sp. *canastra* :—L. **canastrum*, a. Gr. Cf. CANISTER.] 1. A rush basket used to pack tobacco in. 2. A kind of tobacco made of the dried leaves coarsely broken, formerly imported in rush baskets 1827.

‖**Canaut** (kănǭ·t). *Anglo-Ind.* 1625. [Urdu.] The side-wall of a tent; a canvas enclosure.

Ca·n-buoy. 1626. [f. CAN *sb.*[1] + BUOY *sb.*] *Naut.* A large cone-shaped buoy, usu. painted of a definite colour for purposes of recognition.

‖**Cancan** (kãnkan, kæ·nˌkæn). 1848. [F. (16th c. in Littré); of unkn. etym.] A kind of dance performed at the public balls of Paris, with extravagant and indecorous gestures.

Cancel (kæ·nsĕl), *sb.* 1596. [(1) ad. L. *cancelli* (see CANCELLI); (2) f. the vb.] †I. *pl.* Prison bars, bounds, confines. Chiefly *fig.* –1667. II. 1. The act of cancelling 1884. 2. *Print.* The suppression and reprinting of a page or leaf. Hence *concr.* **a.** a page so cancelled; **b.** the new page substituted. 1806.

Cancel (kæ·nsĕl), *v.* 1440. [a. F. *canceller* :—L. *cancellare*, f. *cancellus*, *cancelli* crossbars, lattice. Cf. CHANCEL.] 1. To deface or obliterate (writing), properly by drawing lines across it lattice-wise; to cross out. Of deeds, etc.: To annul by so marking, †cutting or †tearing up. 2. *fig.* To render void 1494. 3. *gen.* To obliterate; to put an end to 1530. 4. *Arithm.* To strike out (a figure) by drawing a line through it; *esp.* in removing a common factor or equivalents of opposite signs; also *absol.* 1542. Hence *fig.* To neutralize 1633. 5. *Print.* To suppress (a page, etc.) after it has been set up or printed off 1738. †6. To enclose with lattice-work or rails –1650.

1. A deed may be avoided by delivering it up to be cancelled; that is to have lines drawn over it, in the form of lattice-work or *cancelli* BLACKSTONE. 2. Shake hands for ever, Cancell all our Vowes DRAYTON. 3. Canceld from Heav'n and sacred memorie MILT. *P. L.* VI. 379. To c. one's fortunes SHAKS., anxieties BYRON. 4. *fig.* With publick zeal to c. private crimes DRYDEN. 6. Cancelling, and railing it with posts FULLER. Hence **Ca·ncellable, cancelable** *a.* **Ca·nceller.**

Cancelee·r, *sb.* 1599. [a. ONF. *canceler*, mod.F. *chanceler* to swerve.] *Hawking.* The action of a hawk in canceleering; see next. Also *fig.*

Cancelee·r, cancelie·r, *v.* 1633. [f. prec.] Of a hawk: To turn (once or twice) upon the wing, in order to recover herself before striking. *fig.* To digress.

The partridge sprung, He makes his stoop, but, wanting breath, is forced To cancelier MASSINGER.

Cancellarian (kænsĕlē°·riăn), *a. rare.* 1846. [f. L. *cancellarius.*] Of, or of the nature of, a chancellor. So **Cancella·riate** (*rare*), chancellorship.

Cancellate (kæ·nsĕlĕt), *a.* 1661. [ad. L. *cancellatus, cancellare.*] Marked with cross lines like lattice-work; reticulated.

Cancellated (kæ·nsĕleⁱtĕd), *ppl. a.* 1681. [f. prec.] 1. = prec. 2. *spec.* Having CANCELLI, as the spongy portion of bones 1836.

Cancellation (kænsĕlē¹·ʃən). 1535. [ad. L. *cancellationem*; see CANCEL *v.*] 1. The action of the vb. CANCEL. 2. *etymologically.* The action of marking with cross lines lattice-wise. (*nonce-use.*) 1843.

1. C. of a will POSTE, of indebtedness 1878. var. **Ca·ncelment.**

‖**Cancelli** (kænse·ləi), *sb. pl.* 1642. [L., dim. of *cancer*, pl. *cancri* crossing bars, grating.] 1. Bars of lattice-work; *spec.* the latticed screen between the choir and body of the church; hence, the CHANCEL. (? In Eng. use.) 2. *Phys.* The lattice-work of the spongy portion of bones, consisting of thin plates and bars interlacing with each other 1802. ¶Improperly applied to the interstices between these plates and bars 1845. Hence **Ca·ncellous** *a.* (*Phys.*) having an open porous structure as of network.

Cancer (kæ·nsəɹ), *sb.* ME. [L. *cancer* (*cancrum*) crab, also gangrene. OE. *cancer, cancor*, helped by Norman Fr. *cancre*, gave ME. CANKER. The L. form was re-introduced later for techn. use.] 1. A crab. (Now *Zool.*) 1562. **b.** *Med.* An eight-tailed bandage 1753. 2. *Astron.* **a.** The Zodiacal constellation lying between Gemini and Leo. **b.** The fourth of the twelve signs of the Zodiac (♋), beginning at the summer solstitial point, which the sun enters on the 21st of June ME. 3. *Pathol.* A malignant growth or tumour, that tends to spread and to reproduce itself; it corrodes the part concerned, and generally ends in death. See also CANKER. 1601. Also *fig.* †4. A plant: perh. *cancer-wort* –1609.

2. *Tropic of C.*: the northern Tropic, forming a tangent to the ecliptic at the first point of C. 3. C. is decidedly a hereditary disease ROBERTS. *fig.* Sloth is a C., eating up . . Time KEN. *Comb.* (in sense 3) **c.-root**, *Conopholis* (*Orobanche*) *americana* and *Epiphegus virginiana*; **-wort**, *Linaria spuria* and *L. Elatine*; also the genus *Veronica.*

Cancer (kæ·nsəɹ), *v.* 1774. [f. prec.] To eat into as a cancer. Hence **Ca·ncered** *ppl. a.* affected with cancer.

Cancerate (kæ·nsĕreⁱt), *v.* 1688. [f. L. *canceratus.*] To become cancerous, to grow into a cancer. Hence **Cancera·tion.** (Dicts.)

Cancerin (kæ·nsĕrin). An artificial guano from Newfoundland.

Ca·ncerite, ca·ncrite. 1848. *Palæont.* A fossil crab.

Cancerous (kæ·nsĕrəs), *a.* 1563. [f. CANCER *sb.* + -OUS.] Of the nature of, or affected with, cancer. Also *fig.*

C. tumours 1872. C. close arts H. VAUGHAN. Hence **Ca·ncerously** *adv.* **Ca·ncerousness.**

Cancriform (kæ·ŋkrifǭɹm), *a.* 1826. [f. L. *cancr-* (*cancer*) + -FORM.] 1. Crab-shaped. 2. *Pathol.* Looking like cancer.

Cancrine (kæ·ŋkrəin), *a.* 1755. [f. L. type **cancrinus*, f. *cancer*.] Having the qualities of a crab; crab-like. Applied to (Latin) verse: Palindromic.

Cancrinite (kæ·ŋkrinəit). 1844. [f. *Cancrin*, a Russian statesman.] *Min.* A massive mineral found in the Urals, a silico-carbonate of aluminium and sodium.

Cancroid (kæ·ŋkroid, -o,id). 1826. [f. L. *cancer, cancr-*.] **A.** *adj.* 1. Like the crab in structure. 2. *Pathol.* Resembling cancer 1859. Also **-ide.** **B.** *sb.* 1. A crustacean of the crab family 1852. 2. A disease resembling cancer 1851. Also **-ide.**

Cand (kænd). 1880. Fluor spar (*local*).

Candareen (kændărī·n). 1615. [Malay *kandūri*.] A Chinese money of account, = 10 cash. As a weight, about 6 grains Troy.

‖**Candelabrum** (kændĭlē·brŏm). *Pl.* **-bra.** Also in mod. use **candelabra**, *pl.* **-as.** 1815. [L., f. *candela*.] 1. *Antiq.* A (usu. ornamental) candlestick. b. A lamp-stand 1834. 2. An ornamental branched candlestick; a chandelier.

Candent (kæ·ndĕnt), *a. arch.* 1577. [ad. L. *candentem*.] At a white heat; glowing with heat. Also *fig.* (*rare.*)

Lord of the c. lightenings COWPER.

Candescent (kănde·sĕnt), *a. rare.* 1824. [ad. L. *candescentem*.] Glowing with, or as with, heat. Hence **Cande·scence. Cande·scently** *adv.*

Candid (kæ·ndid), *a.* 1630. [ad. L. *candidus*, or F. *candide*.] 1. †White -1805; *fig.* †fortunate -1715; clear 1647. 2. Free from bias; impartial (*Obs.* or *arch.*) 1635. †3. Free from malice; favourably disposed, kindly -1800. 4. Frank, ingenuous, sincere in what one says 1675.

1. The stones came c. forth, the hue of innocence DRYDEN. This c. and joyful day Bentley. His c. stile COWLEY, fame BROWNING. 2. A c. state of suspense CHATHAM. 3. Laugh where we must, be c. where we can POPE. 4. Let us be c., and speak out our mind GOLDSM. Also *ironically*: Save, save, oh! save me from the C. Friend CANNING. Hence **Ca·ndid·ly** *adv.*, **-ness.**

Candidacy (kæ·ndidăsi). 1864. [f. CANDIDATE.] The position or status of a candidate; CANDIDATESHIP, CANDIDATURE.

Candidate (kæ·ndidĕit), *sb.* 1613. [ad. L. *candidatus* adj., clothed in white, sb. a candidate (because candidates for office wore a white toga), f. *candidus*.] 1. One who offers himself or is put forward by others as aspiring to be elected or appointed to an office, privilege, or position of honour. Const. *for*; †occ. *of*. 2. *fig.* and *transf.* Aspirant, seeker for 1647; one thought likely or worthy to gain a post, etc. 1766. 3. *Hist.* One of the *cohors candidatorum* (so called from their white dress) who served as the body-guard of the Roman Emperors after A. D. 237. -1751.

1. A c. for Holy Orders 1704, for a degree 1804. 2. A c. for Tyburn GOLDSM.

Candidateship (kæ·ndidăt,ʃip). 1775. = CANDIDACY.

Candidature (kæ·ndidătiŭɹ). 1851. [a. F.] Standing as a candidate, candidateship.

Candied (kæ·ndid), *ppl. a.* 1600. [f. CANDY *v.* + -ED[1].] 1. Preserved or encrusted with sugar 1616. *transf.* and *fig.* Covered as with crystallized sugar, as hoar-frost 1600. 2. Crystallized, congealed 1641. 3. *fig.* 'Sugared', glozing 1602.

1. C. ginger VENNER. The winter's candy'd thorn SHENSTONE. 3. The C. tongue *Haml.* III. ii. 65.

†**Candify**, *sb.* 1727. [? f. CANDY.] *Herb.* Fuller's Herb or Soapwort.

Candite (kæ·ndəit), *sb.* 1844. [f. *Candy* in Ceylon.] *Min.* A variety of Spinel, dark green or brown to black, also called Ceylonite.

Candle (kæ·nd'l), *sb.* [OE. *candel, cǫndel* fem., ad. L. *candela*, f. *candere*.] 1. A (usually cylindrical) body of wax, tallow, spermaceti, or the like, formed round a wick of cotton or flax, or formerly of the pith of a rush, and used to give artificial light. †2. *fig.* (See quots.) -1634. Also *transf.*

1. This C. burnes not cleere *Hen. VIII*, III. ii. 96. There was for euery Saint his c. COTGR. 10,500 cubic feet of 25-candle (= *candle power*) gas to the ton URE. 2. Nights candles are burnt out *Rom. & Jul.* III. v. 9. The c. of letters DANIEL. Out, out, breefe C. *Macb.* V. v. 23. *Medicated c.*: a candle containing some drug for diffusion by burning.

Phrases. 1. *Candle, book, and bell*: see BELL *sb.*[1] 2. *Not able* or *fit to hold a c. to*: not fit even to hold a subordinate position to, not to be compared with. *To hold a c. to the devil*: *orig.* to treat as a saint, and placate with a c.; *now*, to assist an evil person, be active in evil. 3. *To sell by inch of c.*, etc.: to sell by auction in which bids are received only so long as a small piece of c. burns. Also *fig.* and *transf.* 4. *The game*, etc. *is not worth the c.*: the enterprise does not justify the labour or expenditure. 5. *To burn* or *light the c. at both ends*: to be excessively wasteful or extravagant.

Comb.: **c.-bomb**, a small glass bubble filled with water, which, if placed in the flame of a c., explodes; **-fish**, an oily Amer. sea-fish of the salmon-family, used when dried as a c.; †**-fly**, a moth; **-lamp**; †**-mine** (*fig.*), a mine of fat or candle-material; **-nut**, the fruit of the Candleberry tree; **-power**, the illuminating power of a standard spermaceti candle; †**-rush**, the common rush, formerly used for rush-lights; **-shrift**, penance done with candles; **-wick.**

Candle-beam. *Hist.* ME. 1. A rood-beam 1463. 2. ? A hanging beam to hold candles.

Candleberry (kæ·nd'lberi). 1753. A name for the fruit and plants of: (*a*) *Myrica cerifera*, whose berries yield bayberry tallow. (*b*) *Aleurites triloba*, which produces the candle-nut of commerce 1866.

Candle-end (kæ·nd'l e·nd). 1547. 1. The end-piece of a burnt-down candle. 2. *fig.* A trifle, fragment, scrap. Usu. *pl.* 1626.

Ca·ndle-ho:lder. *rare.* One who lights those who work by night; a candle-bearer. *Rom. & Jul.* I. iv. 38.

Candlelight (kæ·nd'l,ləit). [OE. *candel leoht*.] 1. The light given by candles; artificial light. 2. The time during, or at, which candles are lighted; dusk, nightfall 1663.

1. To study by Candle-light ADDISON. He frequently painted candle-lights (= candle-light effects) H. WALPOLE. 2. The lords satt till after c. LUTTRELL.

Ca·ndle-li:ghter. One who, or that which, lights candles; an acolyte; a spill.

Candlemas (kæ·nd'lmăs). [OE. *candelmæsse*, f. *candel* + *mæsse* MASS.] 1. The feast of the purification of the Virgin Mary (or presentation of Christ in the Temple) celebrated with many candles. 2. The date of this, Feb. 2. A Sc. quarter-day. OE. Also *attrib.*

†**Ca·ndle-rent.** 1611. Rent from house-property (which constantly deteriorates) -1655.

Ca·ndle-snuff. 1552. The burnt wick of a candle. Hence **Ca·ndle-snu:ffer, he who, or** that which, snuffs candles.

Candlestick (kæ·nd'l,stik). [OE. *candelsticca*, the stalk or shaft of a candelabrum.] A support for a candle; formerly including chandeliers, etc. Also *fig.* (See *Rev.* i. 20.)

Set up one.. branching c. of lights BACON.

Ca·ndle-tree. 1691. 1. = Candleberry Myrtle. Hence *Candle-tree oil.* 2. *Parmentiera cerifera* (N.O. *Crescentiaceæ*); from the appearance of its fruit 1866.

Ca·ndle-wa:ster. One who wastes candles by late study or dissipation. *Much Ado* V. i. 18.

Ca·ndle-wood. 1712. 1. Resinous wood 1753. 2. Trees which yield such wood, as Californian C., *Fouquiera splendens*, etc.

Can-dock (kæ·ndǫk). 1661. [f. CAN *sb.*[1] + DOCK *sb.*[1]] The Yellow Water-lily. Also, the White Water-lily.

Candour (kæ·ndəɹ). 1610. [17th c. *candor*, a. L., f. *cand-* root of *candere*. Cf. F. *candeur*.] †1. Brilliant whiteness -1692. †2. Purity, innocence -1704. 3. Freedom from bias, impartiality (*Obs.* or *arch.*) 1637. †4. Freedom from malice, kindliness -1802. 5. Freedom from reserve in speech; frankness, ingenuousness 1769.

3. Writing thyselfe, or judging others writ, I know not which th' hast most, candor or wit B. JONS. 4. Sincere, but without c. 1751. 5. Openness and c. 1876.

Ca·ndroy. 1858. A machine used in preparing cotton cloths for printing.

Candy (kæ·ndi), *sb.*[1] 1769. [a. F. *candi* in *sucre candi*; a. Arab., orig. Pers. *qand* sugar; cf. Skr. *khaṇḍa* 'piece', f. *khaṇḍ* to break.] (More fully SUGAR-CANDY.) Crystallized sugar, made by boiling, and slow evaporation; also any confection made of or with this. (In U. S. including toffy, and the like.)

Comb.: **c.-man**, an itinerant seller of c.; in the north of England, a bum-bailiff (see N.E.D.); **-pull** (*U.S.*), a party of young people at which toffy is made; **-sugar** = SUGAR-CANDY.

†**Ca·ndy**, *sb.*[2] 1597. Obs. f. Candia (formerly Crete): used in CANDYTUFT.

‖**Ca·ndy**, *sb.*[3] 1618. [Mahr. *Khaṇḍī*.] A weight used in India, averaging 500 pounds.

Candy (kæ·ndi), *v.* 1533. [f. CANDY *sb.*[1], after F. *candir*, f. *candi* taken as pa. pple.] 1. To preserve by boiling with sugar; to encrust with sugar. Also *fig.* 2. To form into crystals, congeal in a crystalline form 1598. 3. *transf.* To cover with crystalline substance, as hoar-frost, etc. 1607. 4. *intr.* To crystallize or congeal, to become encrusted with sugar 1657.

1. Gynger.. candyd with Sugar ELYOT. *fig.* To c. over studies with pleasure FULLER. 2. To c. [a dropping show'r] SYLVESTER, Sea-salt water 1713, molasses 1880. 3. Hoary frosts had candy'd all the plaines W. BROWNE. 4. Preserves c. by long keeping (*mod.*).

Candytuft (kæ·ndi,tɒft). 1664. [f. CANDY *sb.*[2] + TUFT.] A plant, *Iberis umbellata*, orig. from Candia; by extension, the genus *Iberis* (N.O. *Cruciferæ*).

Cane (kēⁱn), *sb.*[1] [ME. *canne, cane*, a. OF. :—L. *canna*, a. Gr. κάννα, κάννη, perh. from Semitic.] 1. The hollow jointed ligneous stem of various reeds or grasses, as Bamboo and Sugar cane; the solid stem of the genus *Calamus* (the Rattan), or some other palms; the stem of the Raspberry and its congeners. b. = SUGAR-CANE (hence *c.-sugar*) 1781. †2. A dart or lance made of a cane -1700. 3. A length of a cane stem, used as a walking-stick, or as a rod for beating. Hence, any slender walking-stick. 1590. †4. A pipe or tube -1720. 5. Used of a rod of sealing-wax, sulphur, or glass (solid) 1681.

1. Ther growe in many places [of ynde] canes.. ful of sugre CAXTON. Ribs of split c. (without *pl.*) *mod.* 2. Some flying Parthian's darted C. SEDLEY. 3. Sending the boy down into the cellar.. I followed him with a c., and did there beat him PEPYS.

Comb.: **c.-brake**, (*a.*) a thicket of canes; (*b.*) a genus of grasses, *Arundinaria*; **-gun**, a gun made in the form of a walking-stick; **-harvester**; **-juice**; **-killer**, a plant (*Alectra brasiliensis*); **-mill**, a mill for crushing (sugar) cane; **-press**; **-stripper**, a knife for stripping and topping the sugar-cane; **-trash**, the refuse of sugar-canes.

Cane, *sb.*[2] 1612. [Obs. f. KHAN[2].] An eastern inn -1743.

Cane, *sb.*[3] *local.* A weasel. G. WHITE.

Cane, *sb.*[4], var. of CAIN, payment in kind.

Cane, *sb.*[5], obs. f. KHAN[1], an eastern lord.

Cane (kēⁱn), *v.*[1] 1667. [f. CANE *sb.*[1]] 1. To beat with a cane. 2. To drive (a lesson) *into* with the cane (*mod.*). 3. To fit (a chair, etc.) with cane; to furnish with a cane 1885.

2. I had a little Greek caned into me 1866.

Cane, *v.*[2] *dial.* 1483. To form a head, as ale becoming 'mothery'.

†**Ca·nel, canell(e.** [ME. *canele*, a. OF. :— med.L. *canella*, dim. of *canna*.] Cinnamon, perh. including Cassia bark -1721.

‖**Canella** (kăne·lă). 1693. [med.L.; see prec.] †1. = CANEL. 2. *Bot.* A genus of plants (N.O. *Canellaceæ*); esp. *C. alba*, or Wild Cinnamon. Also, the inner bark of *C. alba*, or *white cinnamon*; used in medicine, and as a condiment.

Cane·phorus. Also **ca·nephor, cane·phora.** 1849. [a. L., Gr. κανηφόρος adj. (f. κάνεον + -φορος), also as sb.] In ancient Greece, one of the maidens who carried on their heads baskets containing the sacred things used at the feasts of Demeter, Bacchus, and Athena; hence, *Arch.* applied to figures of young persons, of either sex, bearing baskets on their heads.

Canescence (kăne·sĕns). *rare.* 1855. [f. as next.] Dull whiteness.

Canescent (kăne·sĕnt), *a.* 1847. [ad. L. *canescentem, canescere*, f. *canus*.] Rather hoary; greyish or dull white.

‖**Canette** (kăne·t). 1881. [F. dim. of *cane*, *canne* CAN.] A little (earthenware) can or pot.

Caneva, -as. Obs. f. CANVAS. Also, a woollen fabric made to resemble canvas (*mod.*).

Cangenet. [? Error.] = CANZONET. Shaks.

‖**Cangia** (ka·ndʒă). 1715. [cf. It. *cangia*.] A light boat used on the Nile.

Ca·ngica-wood. 1875. A light yellow-brown Brazilian wood, used for cabinet-work.

‖**Cangue, cang** (kæŋ). 1727. [In F. *cangue*, ad. Pg. *cango*, conn. w. *canga* yoke.] A broad heavy wooden frame or board worn round the neck like a kind of portable pillory as a punishment in China. Hence **Cangue** *v.*

Can-hook. 1626. [? f. CAN *sb.*¹ + HOOK *sb.*] A short rope or chain with a flat hook at each end, used for slinging a cask.

Ca·nicide. 1852. [f. L. **canicida.*] A dog-killer.

Canicular (kăni·kiʊ̆lăɹ), *a.* (*sb.*) ME. [ad. L. *canicularis*, f. *canicula*, dim. of *canis.*]

A. *adj.* 1. *Canicular days*: the DOG-DAYS, q. v. 2. Of or pertaining to the dog-days 1577. 3. *C. year*: the ancient Egyptian year, computed from one heliacal rising of Sirius to the next 1660. 4. *joc.* Pertaining to a dog 1592.

2. The sun..Afflicts me with c. aspect GREENE.

B. *sb.* †1. The dog-star; *pl.* the dog-days –1727. 2. *joc.* (*pl.*) Doggrel verses 1872.

Canicule (kæ·nikiʊl). *rare.* 1719. [a. F., ad. L. *canicula.*] The dog-days.

Canine (kănəi·n, kæ·nəin), *a.* (*sb.*) 1607. [ad. L. *caninus*, f. *canis.*] A. *adj.* 1. Of, belonging to, or characteristic of, a dog; having the nature or qualities of a dog 1623; of appetite, hunger, etc.: Voracious 1613. 2. *Canine tooth*: one of the four strong pointed teeth situated between the incisors and the molars; a cuspidate tooth 1607.

1. The c. race 1870. *C. appetite, hunger*: BULIMY. *C. madness*: hydrophobia. *C. fossa*: (*Anat.*) a depression in the upper jaw-bone behind the c. prominence. *C. prominence* or *ridge*: a ridge on the upper jaw-bone caused by the fang of the c. tooth.

B. *sb.* = Canine tooth (see A. 2). Also *joc.* = 'dog'. var. †**Cani·nal.** Hence **Cani·niform** *a.* shaped like a c. tooth. **Cani·nity,** canine trait; dog nature; sympathy with dogs.

Ca·nion, ca·nnion, canon. 1583. [In form *canion*, a. Sp. *cañon* tube, augm. of *caña.*] *pl.* Ornamental rolls, laid like sausages round the ends of the legs of breeches. Now *Hist.*

Canister (kæ·nistəɹ). 1697. [ad. L. *canistrum*, ad. Gr. *κάναστρον*, f. *κάννα* reed.] 1. A case or box for holding tea, coffee, shot, etc. 1711. 2. A basket for bread, flowers, etc. [tr. L. or Gr.] 1697. 3. = *canister-shot* 1801.

2. Full Canisters of fragrant Lillies POTTER. *Comb.* **c.-shot,** small bullets packed in cases fitting the bore of a gun. **Ca·nister** *v.* to put in a c.; to fasten a c. to.

Cank (kæŋk), *v. dial.* 1741. [Echoic.] To cackle as geese; to chatter.

Canker (kæ·ŋkəɹ), *sb.* OE. [a. ONF. *cancre* :—L. *cancrum* crab, also gangrene. See CHANCRE.] 1. An eating, spreading sore or ulcer; a gangrene. Used as = CANCER till *c* 1700. Now *spec.* A gangrenous affection of the mouth, with fetid sloughing ulcers; *canker of the mouth*, or *water c.* b. *Farriery.* A disease of a horse's foot, with a fetid discharge from the frog. 2. Rust. Now *dial.* 1533. 3. A disease of plants, *esp.* fruit trees, attended by decay of the bark and tissues 1555. 4. A canker-worm ME. 5. The dog-rose (*Rosa canina*). Now *local.* 1582. 6. *fig.* Anything that frets, corrodes, corrupts, or consumes slowly and secretly 1564.

1. No cankar fretteth flesh so sore 1559. 4. Cankers in the muske rose buds SHAKS. 5. 1 *Hen. IV*, I. iii. 176. 6. Enuie which is the c. of Honour BACON.

Comb.: **c.-berry,** the fruit of the dog-rose; also the plant *Solanum bahamense*; **-bloom,** the blossom of the dog-rose; **-blossom,** a canker (sense 4); also *fig.*; **-rash,** a form of scarlet fever in which the throat is ulcerated; **-rose,** (*a.*) the Dog-rose; (*b.*) the wild poppy (*Papaver Rhæas*).

Canker (kæ·ŋkəɹ), *v.* ME. [f. prec.] 1. To infect or consume with canker; †to corrode. 2. *fig.* To infect, corrupt; to consume like a canker ME. 3. *intr.* To become cankered; †to rust; to fester (*dial.*). Also *fig.* 1519.

2. No lapse of moons can c. Love TENNYSON. 3. So his minde cankers *Temp.* IV. i. 192. Silvering will sully and c. more than gilding BACON.

Cankered (kæ·ŋkəɹd), *ppl. a.* ME. [f. prec.] 1. In the senses of the vb. CANKER. 2. *fig.* Malignant, envious; spiteful; ill-tempered. (Frequent in 16th c.) 1513.

1. C. sores 1720, gold *Jas.* v. 3, Tulips EVELYN, waters 1679, heresy 1555. 2. A wicked will.. A cankred Grandams will *John* II. i. 194. Hence **Ca·nkered·ly** *adv.*, **-ness.**

Ca·nkerfret, *sb. dial.* 1618. †1. Corrosion by rust. 2. Copperas. 3. A blister in the mouth.

†**Ca·nkerfret,** *a.* ME. [f. FRET *pa. pple.*] Eaten away with gangrene; corroded with rust.

†**Ca·nkerfret,** *v.* 1642. *trans.* To eat with canker. *intr.* To become cankered; to rust.

Cankerous (kæ·ŋkərəs), *a.* 1543. [f. CANKER *sb.*, after It.] 1. Of the nature of a CANKER. 2. Corroding, infectious 1691. Also *fig.*

2. C. fetters MRS. BROWNING. *fig.* A c. regret 1881.

Cankerworm (kæ·ŋkəɹwɒ̄ɹm). 1530. [CANKER *sb.* 4.] A caterpillar that destroys buds and leaves. *spec.* (in U. S.) The larva of the *Geometra brumata* or winter moth. Also *fig.*

That which the locust hath left, hath the cankerworme eaten *Joel* i. 4. *fig.* Lies.. are cankerworms, and spoil all causes FROUDE.

Cankery (kæ·ŋkəri). ME. [f. CANKER *sb.* + -Y¹.] †1. Gangrenous. ME. only. 2. Affected with canker 1669. 3. *fig.* Crabbed. *Sc.* 1786.

Cann, *v. Naut.* See CON.

‖**Canna** (kæ·nă), *sb.* 1664. [L.] *Bot.* A genus of tropical plants (N.O. *Marantaceæ*), with showy flowers and ornamental foliage.

Canna, Sc. form of *cannot.*

Cannabic (kănæ·bik), *a.* 1731. [f. Gr. *κάνναβις.*] Of the nature of hemp. **Ca·nnabene** (*Chem.*), a volatile, colourless, strong-smelling liquid obtained from Indian hemp. **Ca·nnabin** (*Chem.*), the poisonous resin of the extract of Indian hemp. **Ca·nnabine** *a.* of or pertaining to hemp. ‖**Cannabis indica,** Indian hemp; the dried flowering tops of the female plants of *Cannabis sativa.*

Cannach (kɑ·năχ). *Sc.* Also **canna.** 1803. [a. Gael.] The Cotton-grass.

†**Cannel, canel** (kæ·nĕl), *sb.*¹ [ME. *canel, kanel*, a. ONF. *canel* :—L. *canalem* pipe, channel, etc. See CHANNEL and CANAL.] †1. (*canel*) The bed of a stream. Now CHANNEL. ME. only. †2. (*canel, cannel*) A gutter. Now KENNEL *sb.*², q.v. –1756. †3. (*canel*) A pipe; a tap for a cask –1629. †4. The neck. = KENNEL *sb.*³ ME. only.

Cannel (kæ·nĕl), *sb.*² 1538. [Of northern origin. ? = Sc. *can'le, cannle*, and thus = 'candle-coal'.] A bituminous coal, which burns with a bright flame, and is rich in volatile matter: it can be cut and polished like jet. Also called *cannel coal*, and often (since 1700) written *candle-coal.*

†**Ca·nnel-bone.** ME. [See CANNEL *sb.*¹ 4.] The neck-bone; the clavicle; ? the ilium of an animal –1664.

†**Ca·nnellate, -elate,** *a.* 1673. [After It. *cannellato.*] *Arch.* Channelled, fluted –1676.

Cannelure (kæ·nĕliŭɹ). 1755. [a. F.] A groove, fluting. Hence **Ca·nnelured** *a.*

Cannery (kæ·nĕri). 1879. [f. CAN *v.*³] A factory where meat, fruit, etc. are canned.

Ca·nnet. [a. F. *canette*, dim. of *cane.*] *Her.* A duck, borne as a charge, without feet or bill.

Cannibal (kæ·nibăl). 1553. [In 16th c. pl. *Canibales*, a. Sp., a form of *Carib* or *Caribes*, a nation of the W. Indies who were *anthropophagi. Caribe* signifies 'brave and daring' (Oviedo). Not conn. w. L. *canis.* Cf. CALIBAN = *carib-an.*] 1. A man (*esp.* a savage) that eats human flesh; a man-eater. Also *fig.* 2. An animal that devours its own species 1796. 3. *attrib.* Pertaining to a cannibal, cannibal-like; bloodthirsty 1596.

1. The Canibals that each others eate *Oth.* I. iii. 143. 3. He.. swarmeth in vile Canniball words NASHE. Hence **Cannibale·an** (*rare*), **Canniba·lic** *adjs.* of, pertaining to, or characteristic of, a c. **Ca·nnibalish** *a.* savouring of cannibalism. **Cannibali·stic** *a.* addicted to or pertaining to cannibalism. **Cannibali·stically** *adv.* **Ca·nnibally** *adv.* after the manner of a c.; also *fig. Cor.* IV. v. 200.

Cannibalism (kæ·nibăliz'm). 1796. [f. prec.] The practice of eating one's kind. *fig.* Bloodthirsty barbarity.

The political c. of the mob D'ISRAELI. var. **Cannibality** (*rare*).

Cannie; see CANNY.

Cannikin, canikin (kæ·nĭkin). 1570. [dim. f. CAN *sb.*¹] A small can or drinking vessel.

Cannily (kæ·nĭli), *adv. Sc.* (and *n. dial.*) 1636. [f. CANNY *a.*] In a CANNY manner.

Canniness (kæ·ninĕs). *Sc.* 1662. [f. as prec.] Sagacity, cautiousness; gentleness.

Canning (kæ·niŋ), *vbl. sb.* 1872. [f. CAN *v.*³] The preserving of meat, fish, etc. by sealing up in cans; tinning. Also *attrib.*

Cannon (kæ·nən), *sb.*¹ 1525. [In 16th c. also *canon*, a. F. = It. *cannone*, lit. 'great tube', augm. f. *canna* CANE, reed, tube, etc.] †1. A tube –1616. 2. A piece of ordnance; a gun of a size which requires it to be mounted for firing 1525. (The leading current sense.) Also *collect.*, and as *pl.* 3. *Mech.* A hollow cylindrical piece capable of revolving independently on a shaft. 4. A smooth round bit. Also *cannon-bit.* 1596. 5. The part of a bell by which it is hung; the *ear* 1872. 6. *Billiards.* A stroke in which the player's ball hits two balls in succession; a *carrom* 1839. Also *transf.*

2. Then a Soldier..Seeking the bubble Reputation Euen in the Canons mouth *A. Y. L.* II. vii. 153.

Comb.: †**c.-basket,** a gabion; **-bone,** the single bones between the knee or hough and fetlock (of a horse, etc.); **-clock,** a c. with a burning-glass so fixed as to fire the priming at noon; **-fodder** [tr. G. *kanonenfutter*; cf. 'food for powder' 1 *Hen. IV*, IV. ii. 72], men regarded as material to be consumed in war; **-lock,** a contrivance for exploding the charge of a c.; **-pinion,** the perforated pinion which carries the minute hand of a watch, and drives the minute wheel; **-royal,** an 8½-inch gun, firing 66 lb. shot. Hence **Ca·nnoned** *a.* furnished with cannon. **Ca·nnonry,** cannonading; artillery.

Ca·nnon, *sb.*² 1800. [Cf. CANION.] A sausage-like curl, properly horizontal.

Ca·nnon, *v.* 1691. [f. the sb.] 1. To cannonade. 2. *Billiards.* To make a CANNON (sense 6). Of the ball: To strike and rebound 1844. 3. *trans.* To come into rebounding collision with 1864. Also *intr.*

Cannonade (kænŏnē¹·d), *sb.* 1655. [f. as prec.] A continued discharge of cannon; an attack with cannon. Also *fig.*

Cannona·de, *v.* 1670. [f. prec.] 1. To batter with cannon; to discharge cannon against. 2. To discharge cannon continuously 1702.

Ca·nnonarchy. 1841. [cf. *anarchy*, etc.] Government by cannon.

Ca·nnon-ba·ll. 1663. [See BALL *sb.*¹] A ball, usu. of iron, to be thrown from a cannon. (Also *collect.* and as *pl.*)

Cannon-ball fruit, the globular woody fruit of a S. American tree, *Couroupita guianensis* (N. O. *Lecythidaceæ*) or **Cannon-ball Tree.**

Cannonee·r. 1562. [a. F. *canonnier.*] An artilleryman who lays and fires cannon.

Ca·nnon-proof. 1601. [See PROOF.] *sb.* Impenetrability to cannon-shot; cannon-proof armament. *adj.* Proof against cannon 1632.

Ca·nnon-shot. 1580. [See SHOT *sb.*] 1. The discharge of a cannon 1606. 2. Shot from or for a cannon 1591. 3. The range of a cannon 1580.

Cannot (kæ·nɒ̆t), the usual mod. way of writing *can not.*

‖**Cannula** (kæ·niʊ̆lă). 1684. [a. L., dim. of *canna.*] *Surg.* A tubular instrument introduced into a cavity or tumour in order to allow fluid to escape. Hence **Ca·nnular** *a.* tubular.

Ca·nnulate, -ated, *a.* Also (*erron.*) **canu-.** 1684. [f. prec.] Tubular; channelled or grooved.

Canny (kæ·ni), *a. Sc.* (and *north.*) 1637. [App. f. CAN *v.* 'to know how'.] 1. Sagacious, prudent; cautious. *Sc.* (*arch.*) *esp.* Cautious in worldly matters. (Perh. from Scott's use.) 1816. †2. Wily –1794. 3. Skilful, 'cunning' (in the old sense) 1768. †4. Supernaturally wise. *Sc.* –1816. 5. Safe to meddle with. Cf. UNCANNY. *Sc.* 1718. 6. Frugal. *Sc.* (*arch.*) 1725. 7. Careful or cautious in motion or action; *hence*, quiet, gentle. (The usual sense in mod. Sc.) 1785. 8. Snug. *Sc.* 1758. 9. Seemly, comely; good, satisfactory. In N. Lancs. 'of good size'. Not a Sc. sense. 1802. Also *advb.*, as in *to ca' canny*; see CA'CANNY.

3. *C. wife*: 'wise woman', midwife (Fr. *sage-femme*); hence *c. moment*: moment of childbirth.

Canoe (kănū·), *sb.* 1555. [In 16th c. *canoa*, a. Sp., a. Haytian, as found by Columbus.] 1. A boat in use among uncivilized nations, hollowed out of a tree-trunk, or otherwise rudely constructed, and usually propelled by paddles. 2. In civilized use: A small light boat or skiff propelled by paddling 1799.

1. The Boate of one tree called the Canoa RALEIGH. 2. A thousand miles in the Rob Roy Canoe (*title*) 1865. 'Paddle your own c.' *Pop. Song.*

Comb.: **c. birch,** *Betula papyracea*; **c. wood,** the wood of the Tulip tree. Hence **Canoe·ist,** one who paddles a c.

Canoe (kănū·), *v.* 1842. [f. prec.] To paddle a canoe; to move as in a canoe.

Canon[1] (kæ·nən). [OE., a. L., a. Gr. κανών rule.] **1.** A rule, law, or decree of the Church; *esp.* a rule laid down by an eccl. Council. **2.** *gen.* A law, rule, edict; a general rule or axiom of any subject, as canons of descent, etc. 1588; a standard of judgement 1601. †**3.** *Math.* A general rule, formula, table –1798. **4.** The list of books of the Bible accepted by the Christian Church as genuine and inspired. Also *transf.* ME. **5.** The portion of the Mass included between the Preface and the *Pater*, and containing the words of consecration ME. **6.** *Mus.* A species of composition in which the different parts take up the same subject one after another in strict imitation 1597. **7.** 'A Prestation, Pension, or Customary payment upon some religious Account.' From *Rom. Law.* 1633. **b.** A quit-rent 1643. **8.** A chief epoch or era, serving to date from 1833. **9.** A book of the rules of a monastic order 1727. **b.** The list of saints canonized by the Church 1727. **10.** *Print.* A size of type-body equal to 4-line Pica; so called perhaps as being that used for printing the canon of the Mass 1683. **11.** = CANNON *sb.*[1] 5. 1688. Also *attrib.*

1. *The canon* = *Canon law. Canon law* (formerly *law canon*: cf. F. *droit canon*): ecclesiastical law, as laid down in decrees of the Pope and statutes of councils. Selfe-loue..the most inhibited sinne in the Cannon *All's Well* I. i. 158. 2. Or that the Euerlasting had not fixt His Cannon 'gainst Selfe-slaughter *Haml.* I. ii. 132. The canons of pathology 1806, of taste 1874, of criticism 1879. 6. Cf. ROUND *sb.*[1] IV. 1 a, b. **Ca·non** *v. Mus.* to treat in c. fashion 1894.

Canon[2] (kæ·nən). [In OE. *canonic*, ad. L. *canonicus* used subst., f. *canon* rule.] **1.** *Eccl. Hist.* A clergyman living with others in a clergy-house (*claustrum*), or (later) within the precinct of a cathedral, etc., and ordering his life according to the canons of the church ME. **2.** A member of an ecclesiastical chapter 1561.

Those who renounced private property were known as *Augustinian* (*Austin*) or *regular*, the others were *secular* canons. *Minor* or *Petty Canon*: a clergyman taking duty in a cathedral, but not a member of the chapter. *Honorary Canon*: a titular member of the chapter, non-residentiary and unpaid.

Cañon (kæ·nʸən, kæ·nyən). 1850. [a. Sp. *cañon* tube, etc. (augm. of *caña* :–L. *canna*); thus the same word as Eng. *cannon* and *canion*.] A deep gorge or ravine with steep sides, at the bottom of which a river flows. var. **Canyon.**

Canoness (kæ·nŏnės). 1682. [f. CANON *sb.*[2] + -ESS; cf. F. *chanoinesse*.] **1.** *Eccl. Hist.* One of a community of women living under a rule, but not under a perpetual vow; hence, a woman holding a prebend or canonry. **2.** *joc.* The wife of a canon (*mod.*).

Canonic (kănǫ·nik). [in OE. as *sb.* = CANON[2]. Perh. a. F. *canonique*.] *adj.* = CANONICAL 1, 2, 3, 4, 6. **B.** *sb.* **1.** = CANON *sb.*[2] OE. **2.** A system of dialectic; = the Epicurean τὸ κανονικόν 1655.

Canonical (kănǫ·nikăl), *a.* (and *sb.*) 1483. [f. med.L. *canonicalis*, f. *canonicus*.] **1.** Prescribed by, or having reference to, canon law 1570. **2.** Of or belonging to the canon of Scripture, or any other sacred canon 1568. **3.** *gen.* Authoritative; orthodox; standard 1553. **4.** *Math.* Furnishing, or according to, a formula (see CANON[1] 3) 1738. **5.** *Mus.* In canon form 1609. **6.** Of or belonging to an eccl. chapter, or to a canon (see CANON[2]) 1579. **7.** *sb. pl.* Canonical robes 1748.

1. *C. hours*: (*a.*) stated times of the day appointed by the canons for prayers, etc.; (*b.*) the hours (from 8 a.m. to 3 p.m.) within which marriage can be legally performed in a parish church in England; also *transf. C. obedience*: the obedience to be rendered by inferior clergy to the bishop, and others, according to the canons. 2. *C. epistles*: *esp.* the seven catholic epistles of James, Peter, John, and Jude. 3. Wisedome vnder a ragged coate is seldome canonicall 1603. Hence **Cano·nical-ly** *adv.*, **-ness.**

Canonicate (kănǫ·nikět). 1652. [a. med.L. *canonicatus*.] The office of a canon; a canonry.

Canonicity (kænŏni·siti). 1797. [f. L. type **canonicitas*.] Canonicalness, *esp.* the fact of being within the Canon of Scripture.

Canonist (kæ·nŏnist). 1542. [a. F. *canoniste*.] One skilled in canon law. Hence **Canoni·stic, -al** *a.*

Ca:noniza·tion. ME. [ad. L. *canonizationem*.] The action of canonizing; *esp.* formal admission into the calendar of saints. Also *fig.*

He sent hym to heauen by his canonyzacyon BALE.

Canonize (kæ·nŏnəiz), *v.* ME. [ad. med.L. *canonizare*.] **1.** *trans.* To place formally in the canon of saints. Also *fig.* †**2.** To consecrate. ME. only. †**3.** To deify –1794. **4.** To admit into the Canon of Scripture. Also *transf.* ME. **5.** To sanction by the authority of the Church ME.

1. *fig.* But women are as it were canonised here TOMSON. 4. They canonized the Books of the Maccabees 1657. 5. Canonized doctrines 1635.

Canonry (kæ·nənri). 1482. [f. CANON[2], in L. *canonia*.] The benefice of a canon; the status or office of a canon.

His Canonry of X[t] Church HEARNE.

Canoodle (kănū·d'l), *v. slang.* (orig. *U.S.*) 1859. [Obscure.] *intr.* To indulge in caresses and fondling endearments. Hence **Canoo·dler, -ling.**

Two canoodlers tied up in knots 1903.

Canopic (kănōᵘ·pik), *a.* 1878. [ad.L. *Canopicus*, f. *Canopus*.] Of or pertaining to Canopus, a town of ancient Egypt.

Canopic vase: a vase used in Egypt, chiefly for holding the entrails of embalmed bodies.

‖**Canopus** (kănōᵘ·pɒs). 1555. [L., a. Gr.] **1.** The bright star α in the southern constellation Argo. **2.** = Canopic vase 1836.

1. We..lit Lamps which out-burn'd C. TENNYSON.

Canopy (kæ·nŏpi), *sb.* ME. [In 15th c. *canape*, a. F. *canapé* = med.L. *canopeum*, cl. L. *conopeum*, a. Gr. κωνωπεῖον a bed with mosquito curtains, f. κώνωψ gnat.] **1.** A covering suspended over a throne, couch, bed, etc., or held over a person, the Host, etc., in a procession. **2.** *transf.* and *gen.* A covering, an overhanging shade or shelter: used *esp.* of the firmament 1602. Also *fig.* **3.** *Arch.* A roof-like ornamental projection, over a niche, door, window, tomb, etc. 1682.

2. Their shadowes seeme A C. most fatall, vnder which Our Army lies *Jul. C.* v. i. 88. A c. of trees POPE, of perpetual clouds MAURY. Where dwel'st thou? Vnder the C. *Cor.* IV. v. 41. Hence **Ca·nopied** *ppl. a.* covered with, or as with, a c.

Canopy (kæ·nŏpi), *v.* 1600. [f. prec.] To cover with, or as with, a canopy.

Trees..from heat did canopie the herd SHAKS.

Canorous (kănōᵊ·rəs), *a.* 1646. [f. L. *canorus*.] Singing, melodious, musical; ringing.

A..c. peal of laughter DE QUINCEY. Hence **Cano·rous-ly** *adv.*, **-ness.**

†**Canstick.** Short f. CANDLESTICK. SHAKS.

Cant (kænt), *sb.*[1] ME. [? a. OF. *cant* or LG. *kant*; cf. It. *canto* edge, and L. *canthus* corner of the eye, also tire of a wheel.] **I.** sb. senses. †**1.** ? Edge (ME. only); a corner, angle, niche –1688. **2.** One of the side pieces in the head of a cask 1611. **3.** The oblique line or surface which cuts off the corner of a square or cube; an oblique, inclined, or slanting face 1840. **4.** A squared log. *U.S.* 1877. **5.** *Naut.* A piece of wood laid upon the deck of a vessel to support the bulkheads, etc. 1794.

II. f. CANT *v.* **1.** A toss, pitch, or throw, which overturns, etc. 1736. **2.** A sudden movement which tilts up or turns over 1806. **3.** A slope; a deflexion from the perpendicular or horizontal 1847. **4.** *Whale fishing.* A cut made in a whale between the neck and the fins for the cant purchase 1867.

1. I gave him a c. 1736.

Comb.: **c.-block,** one of the large purchase blocks used by whalers to cant the whales round in flensing; †**-ceiling,** a ceiling which slants to meet the wall, as in attics; **-dog,** a hand-spike with a hook; in *U.S.* = *cant-hook*; **-hook,** a lever with an iron catch near the end for canting over timber; **-moulding,** one with a bevelled surface or surfaces; **-purchase,** a purchase formed by a block suspended from the mainmast head, and another block made fast to the c. cut in a whale; **-spar,** a hand-mast pole; **-timbers,** timbers at the two ends of a ship which rise obliquely from the keel.

Cant (kænt), *sb.*[2] Now *dial.* 1541. [cf. CANT *v.*[1] and CANTLE.] A portion; a share; a parcel; a division.

Cant (kænt), *sb.*[3] 1501. [App. repr. L. *cantus* (Pr. *cant*, Fr. *chant*).] **I.** Sporadic uses, f. L. *cantus.* †**1.** Singing –1708. †**2.** Intonation –1763. **II. 1.** A whining manner of speaking 1640. **2.** The secret or peculiar language or jargon of a class, †sect, or subject. (*Depreciative* or *contemptuous.*) 1684. Also *attrib.* **3.** A set form of words repeated mechanically; *esp.* a stock phrase temporarily in fashion 1681. Also *attrib.* **4.** Affected or unreal phraseology; *esp.* language (or action) implying goodness or piety which does not exist 1709. Also *attrib.* **5.** A person who uses this language 1725.

2. The c. of particular Trades and Employments ADDISON. 3. Measures, and not men, is the common c. of affected moderation JUNIUS. 4. My dear friend, clear your mind of c. JOHNSON. Religious phraseology passes into c. ROBERTSON.

Cant (kænt), *sb.*[4] 1705. [Goes with CANT *v.*[4] Perh. aphet. f. **encant*, a. OF. *encant*, mod.F. *encan* in same sense. Cf. L. *incantare.*] Sale by auction. Chiefly *Irish.*

Cant (kænt), *a. Sc.* and *n. dial.* ME. [Perh. f. CANT *sb.*[1] 'edge'.] Bold, brisk, lusty, hale.

†**Cant,** *v.*[1] ME. [?] To divide –1533.

Cant (kænt), *v.*[2] 1542. [f. CANT *sb.*[1]] **I.** *trans.* **1.** To give a cant edge to; to bevel. **2.** To slope, tilt up 1711; to turn *over* completely 1850. **3.** To throw off by tilting up 1658. **4.** To pitch; to toss, to throw with a sudden jerk 1685.

1. To c. off corners SMEATON. 2. To c. a barge 1792. 3. To c. ballast HOOD. 4. A sudden yaw..which canted me overboard 1791.

II. *intr.* **1.** To tilt, turn over; often with *over* 1702. **2.** To lie aslant, slope 1794. **3.** *Naut.* To swing round from a position 1784.

3. In canting the ship got stern way 1784.

Cant (kænt), *v.*[3] 1567. [See CANT *sb.*[3]] **1.** *intr.* To whine like a beggar; to beg. **2.** *intr.* To use the cant of thieves, etc. 1609; to talk (*dial.*) 1567. Also *trans.* †**3.** To use the current stock phrases –1716. **4.** To affect the cant of a school, party, or subject 1728; *esp.* to affect religious or pietistic cant 1678. Also *trans.* †**5.** *trans.* and *intr.* To sing –1768.

1. [He] bad me c. and whine in some other place JOHNSON. 4. Don't c. in defence of savages JOHNSON. To set up King Jesus: a phrase much canted 1641.

Cant (kænt), *v.*[4] 1720. [cf. CANT *sb.*[4]] To dispose of by auction. Chiefly *Irish.*

Can't (kānt), colloq. contr. of *cannot.*

Ca·ntab. 1750. Colloq. abbrev. of CANTABRIGIAN.

Cantabank (kæ·ntăbænk). *rare.* 1834. [ad. It. *cantambanco*, f. *cantare* + *banco*.] A singer on a platform; hence, *contemptuously*, a common ballad-singer.

‖**Cantabile** (kantā·bile). 1730. [It.] *Mus.* **A.** *adj.* In a smooth flowing style, suited for singing. **B.** *sb.* Cantabile style; a piece of music in this style 1744.

Cantabrigian (kæntăbri·dʒiăn), *a.* and *sb.* 1645. [f. *Cantabrigia*, L. form of *Cambridge.*] Of or belonging to Cambridge; a member of the University of Cambridge.

Cantaloup (kæ·ntalup). Chiefly *U.S.* 1839. [a. F., ad. It. *Cantalupo*, a former country seat of the Pope near Rome, where, on its introduction from Armenia, it was first grown.] A small round ribbed variety of musk-melon. vars. **Cantalupe, -leup,** etc.

Cantankerous (kæntæ·ŋkərəs), *a. colloq.* 1772. [? f. ME. CONTECK contention, whence **contakerous*, subseq. influenced by *cankerous*, *rancorous*, etc.] Ill-conditioned and quarrelsome, perverse, cross-grained.

Canta·nkerous -ly *adv.*, **-ness.**

Cantar (kæ·ntāɹ). 1730. [f. It., Sp. *cantaro*, *cantara* :–L. *cantharus.*] A measure of capacity used in countries bordering on the Mediterranean, varying from 74³/₄ lb. in Rome to 502³/₄ lb. in Syria.

‖**Cantata** (kantā·tă). 1724. [It., f. *cantare.*] Orig., a narrative in verse set to recitative, or recitative and air, for a single voice, with accompaniment; now a choral work, either sacred, resembling a short oratorio, or secular, as a lyric drama set to music but not intended to be acted.

‖**Cantate** (kæntē·ti, kæntā·te). *c* 1550. [a. L. *cantate* sing ye, the first word of the psalm.] The ninety-eighth psalm (ninety-seventh in the Vulgate) used as a canticle.

Canta·tion. *rare.* 1623. [ad. L. *cantationem.*] †Singing; incantation.

‖**Canta·tor.** *rare.* 1866. [L.] A (male) singer.

‖**Cantatrice** (It. kantatrī·tʃe, Fr. kañtatrīs). 1866. [a. It. and Fr., fem. of *cantator.*] A female professional singer.

Canted (kæ·ntėd), *ppl. a.* 1649. [f. CANT *sb.*[1] and *v.*[2]] In various senses of CANT *v.*[2]; tilted up; sloping in surface; etc.

Canteen (kæntī·n). 1737. [a. F. *cantine*, ad. It. *cantina* cellar, of doubtful origin.] *Mil.* 1. A sutler's shop in a camp, etc., where provisions and liquors are sold to soldiers. Now under regimental control. 1744. b. A refreshment-counter, etc., at entertainments and in institutions 1886. ‖2. A small case for carrying bottles. [Fr.] 1737. 3. A chest fitted with cooking and table utensils, and other articles, used by officers, etc. 1817. b. A chest or case of domestic plate or cutlery 1895. 4. A small tin or vessel for water or liquor, carried by soldiers on the march, travellers, etc. 1744.

Cantel, var. of CANTLE.

Canter (kæ·ntəɹ), *sb.*[1] 1609. [f. CANT *v.*[3] + -ER [1].] 1. One who uses the cant of thieves, etc.; a rogue, vagabond (*arch.*). 2. A talker of professional or religious cant 1652.

Ca·nter, *sb.*[2] 1755. [f. CANTER *v.*[2] + -ER [1].] A Canterbury gallop; an easy gallop. Also *fig.*
Hermitage *won in a c.* (*i.e.* without needing to gallop at the finish) 1874.

Canter (kæ·ntəɹ), *v.*[2] 1706. [abbrev. of CANTERBURY *v.*] 1. *intr.* Of horse and rider: To move in a moderate gallop. Also *transf.* 2. *trans.* To make (a horse) go at a canter, to ride at a canter 1856. Hence **Ca·nterer.**

Canterbury (kæ·ntəɹbĕri, -bəri), *sb.* ME. [A city of England long famous as the see of the Archbishop and Primate of all England. The shrine of Thomas à Becket (St. Thomas of Canterbury) was at one time an object of pilgrimage. See CHAUCER *Prol.* 16.]
A. *attrib.* Of or pertaining to *Canterbury*, to the *Canterbury pilgrims*, or to the tales told on the way, as *C. tale* or *story*, later taken as a long tedious story.
C. pace, rack, rate, trot, gallop, etc., the pace, etc., of the mounted pilgrims. A verie old womans fable or Cantorburie tale TURBERV.
B. *sb.* †1. A hand-gallop; a CANTER –1729. 2. A stand with light partitions to hold music, etc. 1849. Hence †**Ca·nterbury** *v.* to canter.

Canterbury Bell(s. 1578. [See BELL *sb.*[1]; app. assoc. with the bells worn on their horses by the pilgrims.] A flowering plant of the genus *Campanula*; orig. a name of *C. Trachelium*, erron. transferred to *C. Medium*, and, loosely, to other species.

Cantharic (kĕnþæ·rik), *a.* 1871. [f. CANTHAR-IDES + -IC.] In *Cantharic acid*, a substance of the same composition as cantharidin.
So **Cantha·ridal** *a. Med.*, pertaining to, made with, or caused by cantharides. **Cantha·ridate** *sb.* a salt of cantharidic acid; *v.* to treat with cantharides. **Canthari·dian, -i·dean,** of the nature of, or composed of, cantharides. **Canthari·dic** *a.* of the nature of cantharides, as in *Cantharidic acid.* **Cantha·ridin,** the vesicating principle of cantharides. **Cantha·ridism,** the poisonous action of cantharides. **Cantha·ridize** *v.* to treat with cantharides (*esp.* as an aphrodisiac); also *fig.*

‖**Cantharides** (kĕnþæ·ridīz), *sb. pl.* ME. [L., pl. of *cantharis*, a. Gr.] 1. (sing. *Cantharis* in *Entom.*) A genus of coleopterous insects of the family Trachelidæ; the officinal species (*C. vesicatoria* or Spanish Fly) has golden-green elytra. 2. The pharmacopœial name of the dried beetle *C. vesicatoria.* Used externally as a vesicant; internally as a diuretic, and †an aphrodisiac.

‖**Canthus** (kæ·nþŏs). 1646. [L., a. Gr. κανθός.] *Phys.* The outer or inner corner of the eye, where the lids meet. Hence, from comb. f. *canth(o-*, **Canthopla·stic** *a.* of or pertaining to **Ca·nthoplasty,** the operation of enlarging the palpebral aperture.

†**Ca·ntic(k,** *sb.* 1483. [a. F. *cantique.*] A song –1669.

Canticle (kæ·ntik'l). ME. [ad. L. *canticulum*, dim. of *canticum.*] 1. A (little) song; a hymn; *spec.* one of the hymns (mostly from the Scriptures) used in the public services of the Church, as the *Benedicite.* Also *transf.* 2. *pl.* The Song of Solomon 1526. †3. A canto –1647.
1. The sweetest C. is, Nunc dimittis BACON.

‖**Cantile·na.** 1789. [It. or L.] The plain-song in old church music; the melody in any composition. Also, a ballad.

Cantilever (kæ·ntĭlīvəɹ). 1667. [? f. CANT *sb.*[1] (in some sense) + LEVER.] 1. *Arch.* A projecting bracket which supports a balcony, a cornice, or the like; also *attrib.* 2. *Bridge-building.* A projecting arm of great length, two of which, stretching out from adjacent piers, are united by a girder which completes the span; also *attrib.* 1850.

Cantillate (kæ·ntilĕⁱt), *v.* 1864. [f. L. *cantillat-, cantillare.*] To chant; to recite with musical tones. Hence **Cantilla·tion,** musical recitation.

Canting (kæ·ntiŋ), *vbl. sb.*[1] 1769. The action of CANT *v.*[2] Also as *ppl. a.*[1]

Ca·nting, *vbl. sb.*[2] 1567. [f. CANT *v.*[3]] 1. The practice of using thieves' cant; the jargon of thieves, beggars, etc. 2. The use of the jargon of a class or subject; gibberish 1625. 3. Hypocritical talk 1659.
1. Peddelars Frenche or C. 1567. 3. *Canting coat*, the Geneva gown DRYDEN.

Ca·nting, *vbl. sb.*[3] *n. dial.* 1651. [f. CANT *v.*[4]] Sale by auction.

Ca·nting, *ppl. a.*[2] 1625. [f. CANT *v.*[3]] 1. In the senses of CANT *v.*[3] 2. *Her. Canting arms*: = *allusive arms* (see ALLUSIVE). So *c. heraldry, herald, coat.* Hence **Ca·ntingly** *adv.* **Ca·ntingness.**

‖**Cantinier.** 1721. [Fr.] A canteen-keeper. (Also *cantinière* fem.)

†**Ca·ntion.** 1579. [ad. L. *cantionem.*] A song –1660; an incantation –1678.

Cantle (kæ·nt'l), *sb.* ME. [a. ONF. *cantel*, med.L. *cantellus*, dim. of *cant, cantus* corner.] †1. A corner –1605; a slice –1627. 2. A segment; a cut of bread, cheese, etc. ME. 3. A portion (viewed apart) ME. 4. The hind-bow of a saddle 1592. 5. The crown of the head. *Sc.* 1822.
2. The huge c. which it used to seem to cut out of the holiday LAMB. 5. My c. will stand a clour wad bring a stot down SCOTT. Hence **Cantle-wise** *adv.* by cantles. **Ca·ntlet,** a small c.

†**Ca·ntle,** *v.*[1] 1548. [f. prec.] 1. To cut into portions –1693. 2. To piece together –1568.

†**Ca·ntling.** *rare.* 1616. [app. f. CANT, CANTLE; but cf. SCANTLING.] 1. A small cantle 1674. 2. A support under a cask 1616.

Canto (kæ·ntŏ). Pl. **-os.** 1590. [a. It.] †1. A song, ballad –1710. 2. One of the divisions of a long poem; so much as the minstrel might sing at one 'fit' 1590. ‖3. *Mus.* The upper part or melody in a composition; anciently the tenor, now the soprano.

‖**Canto fermo** (kaˑnto fe·rmo). 1789. [It.] 'The simple unadorned melody of the ancient hymns and chants of the church' (Grove); plainsong; hence, any simple subject of like character to which counterpoint is added.

Canton (kæ·ntŏn, kĕntǫ·n), *sb.*[1] 1534. [a. OF. = It. *cantone*, augm. of *canto* corner; see CANT *sb.*[1]] †1. A corner, an angle –1653. 2. *Her.* A square division less than a quarter, occupying the upper (usually dexter) corner of a shield 1572. †3. A quarter; a piece –1686. 4. A subdivision of a country 1601; a portion of space 1643. 5. *spec.* a. One of the sovereign states of the Swiss confederation 1611. b. In France, a division of an arrondissement 1611.
2. The King gave us [the Royal Society] the arms of England to be borne in a c. in our arms EVELYN. 3. Hee quarters out his life into foure cantons, eating, drinking, sleeping, and riding 1631. 4. This little C., I mean this System of our Sun LOCKE. Hence **Ca·ntŏnăl** *a.* of, pertaining to, or of the nature of, a c. **Ca·ntonalism,** a cantonal system. **Cantoner,** the inhabitant of a c.

†**Ca·nton,** *sb.*[2] 1594. Var. of CANTO 1, 2.
Write loyall Cantons of contemned loue SHAKS.

Canton (kæ·ntŏn, kĕntǫ·n), *v.* Also †**cantoo·n.** 1598. [f. CANTON *sb.*[1], and repr. F. *cantonner* to quarter.] 1. To divide or subdivide. 2. To divide *from* or cut *out* of a whole (*arch.*) 1653. 3. To quarter (soldiers). (*Pronounced* kĕntǫ·n *and* kĕntū·n.) 1700. Also *fig.* 4. *intr.* (for *refl.*) To take up cantonments or quarters 1697. 5. *Her.* To furnish (a shield or cross) with a canton or cantons; to place in a canton 1688.
2. They c. out to themselves a little Goshen in the intellectual world LOCKE. 4. Orders to c. 1707.

Cantoned (see the vb.), *ppl. a.* 1611. [f. CANTON *sb.* and *v.*] 1. Formed into cantons. 2. Quartered in cantonments 1790. 3. *Arch.* Having angles decorated with columns, pilasters, or other similar projections 1727. 4. *Her.* See CANTON *v.* 5.

†**Ca·ntonize,** *v.* 1606. [f. CANTON *sb.*[1]] 1. To divide –1807. 2. *intr.* To form an independent community –1809. 3. To canton (troops); to locate –1674.

Cantonment (kĕntǫ·nmĕnt, -tū·nment). Also †cantoonment. 1756. [a. F. *cantonnement*; see CANTON *v.*] 1. The cantoning of troops 1757. 2. The place of lodging assigned to a section of a force when cantoned out; also (often in *pl.*) a place or places of more permanent encampment for troops, *e.g.* while in winter quarters; in India, a permanent military station 1756. 3. *transf.* Quarters 1837.

‖**Cantor** (kæ·ntǫɹ, -əɹ). 1538. [L.] †1. A singer –1656. 2. A precentor 1538. 3. A soloist who sings liturgical music in church or synagogue. Hence **Canto·rial, ca·ntoral** *a.*, pertaining to a c.; used of the north side of a choir, where the precentor sits. **Ca·ntorship.**

‖**Cantoris** (kæntōᵊ·ris). 1724. [L., gen. of CANTOR.] *C. side, stall*, opposite to DECANI.

Ca·ntred. *Hist.* ME. [ad. W. *cantref*, assim. to *hundred.*] A district containing a hundred townships. **Ca·ntref, -ev** 1606.

Cantrip (kæ·ntrip). *Sc.* Also **-raip.** 1719. [?] A spell of necromancy; a witch's trick. Also *joc.* a playful or extravagant act.

‖**Cantus firmus.** [med.L.] = Canto fermo.

Canty (kæ·nti), *a.* *Sc.* and *n. dial.* 1724. [f. CANT *a.*] Cheerful, lively, gladsome.
A cantie quean 1775, day BURNS. Hence **Ca·ntily** *adv.* **Ca·ntiness.**

Canuck (kănʊ·k). 1855. *U.S.* A (French) Canadian; a Canadian horse.

Canvas, canvass (kæ·nvăs), *sb.* [ME. *canevas*, a. ONF. = It. *canavaccio*:—late L. **cannabaceus*, f. *cannabis* hemp. The sp. *canvas*, pl. *canvases*, is better etymologically, and more used; see also CANVASS.] 1. A coarse unbleached cloth made of hemp or flax, used for sails, tents, etc. 2. A covering over the ends of a racing boat 1880. 3. *spec.* Sail-cloth; *hence*, sails collectively 1609. 4. *spec.* A piece of canvas primed for painting 1705; an oil-painting; also paintings collectively 1764. Also *fig.* 5. A clear unbleached cloth woven in regular meshes, used for working tapestry with the needle 1611. Also *attrib.* or *adj.*
1. *Under c.*: in a tent or tents. 3. *Under c.*: with sails spread. Obliged to reduce our c. SIR J. ROSS. 4. To fill up a c. JUNIUS. The c. glow'd GOLDSM. *Comb.* **c.-length** (in sense 2), about 15 ft.

Canvas (kæ·nvăs), *v.* Also **-ss.** 1556. [f. prec.; see also CANVASS *v.*] †1. *Hawking.* To entangle in a net; also *transf.* and *fig.* –1653. 2. To cover, line, or furnish with canvas 1556.
2. To c. over a door DICKENS.

†**Canvasa·do, -za·do.** 1581. [Cf. CANVASS *v.*] 1. A sudden attack –1599. 2. = CAMISADO –1617. 3. ? A stroke in fencing: a countercheck –1605.

Canvas-back. 1605. [f. CANVAS *sb.*] 1. A back of a garment made of canvas; also *fig.* 2. A North American duck (*Fuligula valisneriana*), so named from the colour of the back feathers 1813.
2. The canvass-back duck stands alone 1832.

Canvass, canvas (kæ·nvăs), *v.* 1508. [f. CANVAS *sb.*, in its former spelling *canvass.* The development of sense 6 is not accounted for.] †1. *lit.* To toss in a canvas sheet, etc. –1611. †2. *transf.* To knock about; to beat, batter –1643. †3. *fig.* To buffet in writing; to criticize destructively –1618. 4. *fig.* To discuss (a subject, etc.); to criticize, scrutinize fully 1530. Also *intr.* 1631. †5. ? To bargain with 1688. 6. *intr.* To solicit, as support, votes, orders, contributions, etc. 1555. 7. †To sue for (a thing) –1774; to solicit (persons, a district) for votes, custom, orders, etc.; *esp.* to solicit the support of a constituency, by interviewing each elector; to ascertain thus the number of one's supporters 1812.
1. 1 *Hen. VI*, I. iii. 36. 4. To c. the character of

witnesses 1798. 6. This crime of canvassing or soliciting for Church-Preferment AYLIFFE. 7. His inability to canvas the Livery in person 1812. Hence **Ca·nvasser** (in all senses); *U.S.* a scrutineer.

Canvass (kæ·nvăs), *sb.* 1608. [f. prec. vb.] †1. A shaking up 1611. †2. A sudden attack –1627. †3. Repulse (*e.g.* at an election, etc.) –1626. †4. Full discussion –1687. 5. The action of personally soliciting votes before an election, and ascertaining the amount of one's support 1691. 6. A solicitation of support, custom, etc. 1790.

5. Their success on the c. quite astonished them 1788.

Cany (kēⁱ·ni), *a.* 1667. [f. CANE *sb.* + -Y.] Of cane; 'full of canes' (J.); cane-like.

Canyon. Also **kanyon.** = CAÑON.

‖**Canzona** (kantsō·na). 1880. [It.; f. next.] 1. = CANZONE. 2. *Mus.* The setting to music of the words of a canzone; an instrumental piece in the style of a madrigal; †app. = sonata.

‖**Canzone** (kantsō·ne). 1590. [It.:—L. *cantionem*, f. *cant-*, *canere.*] In *It.* or *Prov. Lit.*: A song, resembling the madrigal but less strict in style. var. **Ca·nzon** (freq. in 17th c.).

Canzonet (kænzone·t). 1593. [ad. It. *canzonetta*, dim. of prec.] A little or short song; a vocal solo in more than one movement; now usually, a light airy song.

Caoutchin (kau·tʃin). 1863. [f. CAOUTCHOUC + -IN.] *Chem.* A hydrocarbon, $C_{10}H_{16}$, contained in the oils produced by distillation of caoutchouc and gutta-percha.

Caoutchouc (kau·tʃuk, kū·-). 1775. [a. F., ad. Carib *cahuchu.*] 1. India-rubber, or Gum Elastic; the milky resinous juice of certain tropical trees, chiefly the Brazilian *Siphonia elastica* (N.O. *Euphorbiaceæ*), which coagulates on exposure to the air, and becomes elastic, and is waterproof. Also *attrib.* See VULCANITE.

Mineral C. = ELATERITE.

Caoutchoucin (kau·tʃusin). 1863. [f. prec. + -IN.] *Chem.* A thin volatile oily liquid, obtained from caoutchouc by dry distillation.

Cap (kæp), *sb.*¹ [OE. *cæppe*, a. late L. *cappa* 'cap'. Isidore, *a.* 636, has 'cappa . . quia capitis ornamentum est'. The deriv. of *capa* from *capere* 'quia quasi totum capiat hominem', cited as from Isidore, is from Papias *c* 1053, and is due to pop. etym.]

I. A covering for the head. 1. A hood. 2. A head-dress for women, now of muslin, or the like, and ordinarily worn indoors. Cf. MOB-CAP. ME. 3. A head-dress of cloth, or the like, for men and boys; distinguished from a hat by not having a brim; applied also to many official, professional, and special head-dresses ME. 4. In names of plants; see FRIAR'S CAP, etc. 5. Short for CAP-PAPER 1630.

2. Gentlewomen weare such caps as these SHAKS. 3. He toke of his c. and saluted the duke LD. BERNERS. Spec. uses: = a cardinal's biretta: The Pope expects more windfalls, before he will give any Caps 1666; = *cap of fence*: a helmet 1530; = the raising of the cap in salutation: They shall have cappe and knee, and many gaye good morrowes in this lyfe 1581; *fig.* = top: *Timon* IV. iii. 363.

II. Things of similar shape, position, or use. 1. A cap-like covering; a top stratum or layer; a cap-like top ME. 2. A cap-shaped part forming the top or covering the top or end ME. 3. A cover or case 1688. 4. = *Gun cap, Percussion cap* 1826. 5. A part laid horizontally or flat along the top of various structures 1677. 6. *Arch.* The uppermost part of any assemblage of principal parts 1870. 7. *Naut.* A collar of wood, used to hold two masts together 1626.

1. The pileus, or c. of [a Fungus] 1762. The c. of a man's knee STERNE. Caps of semi-conglomerate corn-stone MURCHISON. A c. on the crest of the Æggischorn TYNDALL. 2. The c. of a thimble 1693, of a receiver 1783. Toe-caps of boots 1870. The c. of a magnetic needle 1794, of the lens of a camera 1879. 3. The c. of a gun = APRON 1704. A *breast-* or *nipple-c.* 1688. The c. of a watch 1884. 5. A C. or Head over the Door 1688. 7. *To lower the Flag*, is to pull it down upon the C. 1692.

Phrases. *C. of maintenance*: (*a*) see MAINTENANCE; (*b*) A cap borne before the sovereign of England at the coronation, also before some mayors. *C. of liberty* or *Phrygian bonnet*: the conical cap given in Roman times to slaves on emancipation, used as a republican symbol. *C. and bells*: the insignia of the jester: cf. FOOL'S CAP. *To put on one's thinking c.*: to take time for thinking over. *The c. fits*: what is said suits or is felt to suit. *To set one's c. at* (colloq.): said of a woman who sets herself to gain the affections of a man.

Comb.: **c.-money** (also †*cap*), money collected for the huntsman at the death of the fox; **-sheaf**, the top sheaf of a shock or stook, also *fig.*; **-square**, one of the broad pieces of iron locked over the trunnions of a gun with an iron pin. **Capped, capt** *ppl. a.*

Cap (kæp, kap), *sb.*² *Sc.* 1724. [? a form of *cop* (cf. *tap, top*, etc.):—OE. *copp* cup, vessel.] 1. A wooden bowl used as a drinking vessel. 2. A measure of quantity: = COP, q.v. 1879.

Cap (kæp), *v.*¹ 1483. [f. CAP *sb.*¹] I. *trans.* To put a cap on. 2. To cover as with a cap or capping, to cover at the end 1602. 3. To form a cap to; to crown; to lie on the top of 1808. 4. To overtop, outdo, beat; also *dial.* to pass the comprehension of 1736. 5. *intr.* To take off the cap in token of respect. Const. *to.* 1555. Also *trans.* (*to* omitted) 1593.

1. To c. the head VENNER. I had capped the nipples BAKER. 2. To c. stone-dikes 1853. *To c. a rope*: to cover the end with tarred canvas 1794. 3. Basalts.. capping the hills LYELL. 5. And c. the fool whose merit is his Place CHURCHILL.

Phrases. *To c. the climax, to c. all*: see sense 4. *To c. an anecdote, proverb, quotation*, etc.: to follow it up with another; to quote alternately in contest. *To c. verses*: to reply to one quoted with another, that begins with the final or initial letter of the first or otherwise corresponds with it.

Cap, *v.*² 1589. [a. OF. *caper* to seize. But cf. CAPIAS.] †1. To arrest –1611. 2. To appropriate by violence (*Mod. Sc.*).

‖**Capa** (kā·pă). 1787. [Sp.; see CAPE.] A Spanish cape.

Capability (kēⁱpăbi·lĭti). 1587. [f. CAPABLE. Not found in Fr.] 1. The quality of being CAPABLE in various senses. 2. (usually *pl.*) An undeveloped faculty or property; a condition capable of being turned to use 1778.

2. ['Capability Brown'] got his nickname from his habit of saying that grounds which he was asked to lay out had *capabilities* G. B. HILL.

Capable (kēⁱ·păb'l), *a.* 1561. [a. F., ad. late L. *capabilem*, irreg. f. L. *capere*, perh. influenced by *capax.*] †1. Able to take in; having room for –1775. Also *fig.* †2. *absol.* Roomy –1650; comprehensive *Oth.* III. iii. 459. 3. Open to; susceptible. Const. *of*, also *absol.* 1590. 4. Having capacity, power, or fitness for. Const. *of*, and †*inf.* 1597. 5. *absol.* Having general capacity; qualified, gifted, able 1606. †6. Having a legal capacity or qualification. Const. *of*, also *absol.* –1818.

1. C. of a bushel of wheate 1601. *fig.* Not c. her eare Of what was high MILT. *P. L.* VIII. 51. 3. C. of good seed 1612, of wounds SHAKS., of moral improvement BUTLER, of explanation 1794. 4. C. of better things BP. WATSON, of every wickedness FREEMAN. 5. A c. witness BLACKIE. 6. *Lear* II. i. 87. Hence **Ca·pableness. Ca·pably** *adv.*

†**Capa·cify.** *rare.* = CAPACITATE. Barrow.

Capacious (kăpēⁱ·ʃəs). 1614. [f. L. *capaci-* (*capax*) + -OUS.] †1. Able to take in or hold –1779. 2. Able to hold much; roomy, spacious 1634. 3. Qualified for the reception *of* (*arch.*); †of capacity *to do* 1677.

Hence **Capa·ciously** *adv.* **Capa·ciousness.**

Capacitance (kăpæ·sităns). 1916. [f. CAPACITY + -ANCE.] *Electr.* Electrostatic capacity.

Capacitate (kăpæ·sitēⁱt), *v.* 1657. [f. CAPACITY + -ATE.] To endow with capacity *for* or *to do*; to fit; to qualify in law.

Hence **Capacita·tion.**

Capacity (kăpæ·sĭti). 1480. [15th c. *capacyte*, a. F. *capacité*, ad. L. *capacitatem*, f. *capax.*] †1. Ability to take in or hold –1702. Also *fig.* 2. Hence, Content: †area; volume 1571. †3. A containing space, area, or volume; *esp.* a hollow space –1756. Also *fig.* 4. Mental receiving power; ability to take in impressions, ideas, knowledge 1485. 5. Active power of mind; talent 1485. 6. *gen.* The power, ability, or faculty for anything in particular. Const. *of, for*, or *inf.* 1647. 7. Capability, possibility 1659. 8. Position, condition, character, relation 1649. 9. *Law.* Legal qualification 1480.

1. *Ant. & Cl.* IV. viii. 32. *fig.* A large c. of happiness DE QUINCEY. *C. for heat, moisture*, etc.: the power of absorbing heat, etc. b. The power of an apparatus to store static electricity; also, any apparatus which gives additional capacity 1903. 2. *Measure of c.*: the measure applied to the content of a vessel, and to liquids, grain, etc. which take the shape of that which holds them. 5. A person of diligence and c. STEELE. 6. A c. for self-protection BUCKLE. 7. A c. for infinite division DAUBENY. †*In, into*, or *out of a c.*: i.e. a position which enables or renders capable. 8. I am.. dead in a natural c... dead in a poetical c... and dead in a civil c. POPE.

attrib. passing into *adj.* That reaches the utmost c., as *c. audience* 1920.

Cap-à-pie (kæpapī·), *adv.* 1523. [OF., = mod.F. *de pied en cap.*] From head to foot: in reference to arming or accoutring.

The rest all in bright harnesse capa pe 1556.

Caparison (kăpæ·risən). 1598. [a. F. *caparasson*, now *caparaçon*, a. Sp. *caparazon*, augm. of med.L. *caparo*, deriv. of *capa* CAPE.] A covering, often ornamented, spread over the saddle or harness of a horse; housings 1602. 2. *transf.* Dress and ornaments 1598.

1. To esteeme .. a horse by his trappinges and c. FULBECKE. 2. *Wint. T.* IV. iii. 27.

Caparison (kăpæ·risən), *v.* 1594. [a. F. *caparassoner*, f. the sb.] To put trappings on; to deck, harness. Also *fig.*

C. my horse. Caparison'd like a man SHAKS.

†**Capa·x.** ME. [a. OF.: cf. CAPACIOUS.] Of capacity; able and ready to take or receive –1556. var. **Capack(e)s.**

†**Ca·p-case.** 1577. [? f. CAP *sb.*¹ or CAPE *sb.*¹] 1. A travelling-case, bag, or wallet –1641. 2. A receptacle; a case (L. *capsa*). Also *fig.* 1597.

Cape (kēⁱp), *sb.*¹ *n. dial.* and *Sc.* ME. [Early form of COPE. Cf. ONF. *cape.*] A cloak with a hood; a cloak; a cope.

Cape (kēⁱp), *sb.*² 1565. [ad. F. *cape* (*cappe*), ad. Sp. or It.] †1. A Spanish cloak (with a hood) –1580. 2. The tippet of a cloak 1596. 3. A short loose sleeveless cloak, fitting round the neck and falling over the shoulders 1758.

Cape (kēⁱp), *sb.*³ ME. [ad. F. *cap*, ad. It. *capo*:—Rom. *capo* for L. *caput.*] 1. A piece of land jutting into the sea; a headland or promontory.

The Cape: any familiar headland; *esp.* the Cape of Good Hope in S. Africa. Hence = *Cape Colony*, and ellipt. *Cape* (*colony*) *wine, wool, funds*, etc.

attrib. **C. elk**, the Eland; **C.-hen**, a small kind of Albatross; **C. jasmine**, *Gardenia florida*; **C. pigeon**, a Petrel; **C. weed**, *Roccella tinctoria* 'a dye lichen, obtained from the Cape de Verde Islands'.

†**Cape**, *sb.*⁴ 1588. [a. OF. *cape* sb. fem., ad. L. *cape* imperat. of *capere.*] *Old Law.* The first word and name of a judicial writ relative to a plea of lands and tenements –1706.

†**Cape**, *sb.*⁵ 1650. [var. of COP.] Top –1812.

†**Cape**, *v.* 1500. [app. f. F. *cap* (see Littré).] *Naut.* To head, keep a course, bear up. Said of sailors and ship. –1867.

Caped (kēⁱpt), *a.* 1550. [f. CAPE *sb.*²] Having a cape; clad in a cape.

Capel¹ (kēⁱ·p'l). 1801. *Min.* A composite stone of quartz, schorl, and hornblende, occurring in the walls of tin and copper lodes.

Capel², var. of †CAPLE, a horse.

Capelet (kæ·pĕlĕt). Also **capellet.** 1731. [a. F., Picard for *chapelet*, from the resemblance.] A wen-like swelling on the heel of a horse's hock, or on the point of the elbow.

Capelin, caplin (kæ·pĕlin, -plin). 1620. [= Fr. *capelan, caplan.*] A small fish resembling a smelt, found on the coast of Newfoundland; used as a bait for cod.

Capeline (kæ·pĕlin). 1470. [a. F., ad. It. *cap(p)ellina*, dim. of *cappella* (see CHAPEL), dim. of *cap(p)a* CAP, CAPE.] †1. A skull-cap of iron worn by archers in the Middle Ages. 2. *Surg.* A bandage which forms a kind of cap for the head, or in amputations 1706. 3. A woollen hood of loose texture, worn by ladies. [Fr.] 1868.

‖**Capella** (kăpe·lă). 1682. [L., she-goat.] A star of the first magnitude in Auriga.

†**Cape·llane.** 1661. [ad. med.L. *capellanus.*] a. A keeper of sacred relics. b. A chaplain.

Capelo·cracy. [f. Gr. κάπηλος + -κρατία rule.] The shop-keeping interest. LYTTON.

†**Ca·pe-me·rchant.** Also **Cap-.** 1581. [App. ad. *cap-* or *capo-* head-.] A supercargo; also the head merchant in a factory. Also *fig.* –1697.

fig. The French .. were the cape-merchants in this adventure [the Crusades] FULLER.

Caper (kēⁱ·pəɹ), *sb.*¹ [ME. *caperis, caperes*, a. L. *capparis*, a. Gr. Treated as a pl.; hence *caper* sing.] 1. A shrub (*Capparis spinosa*) of trailing habit, abundant on walls and rocky places in the South of Europe. **2.** (usu. in *pl.*) The flower-buds of the same, used for pickling 1481. **3.** A scented tea 1864.

1. The erbe caperis shal be scatered WYCLIF *Eccles.* xii. 5. *Comb.* etc.: *Capucine, Capuchin Capers, English Capers*: the seed-vessels of the Nasturtium (see CAPUCINE), or of the Caper Spurge, used for pickling; also the plants. **C.-bush, -plant, -spurge,** names of *Euphorbia Lathyris*; **-tree,** *Busbeckia arborea* of N. S. Wales.

Caper (kēⁱ·pəɹ), *sb.*² 1592. [app. abbrev. of CAPRIOLE *sb.*; cf. *cab* from *cabriolet.*] A frolicsome leap, as of a kid; a frisky movement; *fig.* a freak.

We that are true Louers, runne into strange capers SHAKS. *To cut a c.* or *capers*: to dance or act fantastically *Twel. N.* I. iii. 129.

Ca·per, *sb.*³ 1657. [a. mod. Du. *kaper*, f. *kapen* to take, plunder.] A privateer; the captain of a privateer. Now *Hist.*

Caper (kēⁱ·pəɹ), *v.*¹ 1588. [Cf. CAPER *sb.*²] To dance or leap in a frolicsome manner, to skip for merriment; to prance. Also *fig.*

Dancing and capering like a Kid BOYLE. The Italians..c. with their voices DOULAND.

Capercailye, capercailzie (kæpəɹkēⁱ·lyi, -kēⁱ·lzi). 1536. [Corruption of Gael. *capull coille* great cock of the wood.] The Wood-grouse (*Tetrao urogallus*); the male is also called Mountain Cock or Cock of the Woods. Formerly indigenous in the Highlands.

†**Caperdew·sie, caperdo·chy.** 1600. [Cf. CAPPADOCHIO.] The stocks; prison –1663.

Ca·perer. 1693. [f. CAPER *v.* + -ER ¹.] **1.** One who capers. **2.** A caddis-fly (*Phryganea*); from its flight 1855.

Capernaite (kăpə̄·ɹne,əit). 1549. [f. *Capernaum* in Galilee + -ITE.] An inhabitant of Capernaum; *hence* (see *John* vi. 52) A controversial term for a believer in transubstantiation. Hence **Cape:rnai·tic, -al** *a.* †**Cape·rnize** *v.*

Capernoitie (kæpəɹnoi·ti), *sb. Sc.* 1719. [?] Head, noddle. Hence perh. **Capernoi·ted** *a.* crabbed; slightly muddled with drink.

Ca·pful. 1719. [f. CAP *sb.*] As much as a cap will contain.

A c. of wind (Naut.): a light flaw.

Capharnaism (kăfă·ɹne,iːz'm). 1656. [f. *Capharnaum*, Aram. f. *Capernaum.*] The doctrine of the Capernaites.

‖**Capias** (kæ·piæs). 1467. [L., 'take'.] *Law.* A writ or process commanding the officer to take the body of the person named in it, that is, to arrest him; also called *writ of capias.*

The term includes: *C. ad respondendum*, to enforce attendance at court; *C. ad satisfaciendum*, after judgement, to imprison the defendant, until the plaintiff's claim is satisfied; *C. utlagatum*, to arrest an outlawed person; *C. in Withernam* (see WITHERNAM).

Capibara, var. of CAPYBARA.

Capillaceous (kæpilēⁱ·ʃəs). 1731. [f. L. *capillaceus*, f. *capillus*; see -ACEOUS.] Hair-like, thread-like. Cf. CAPILLARY.

‖**Capillaire** (kæpīlē·ɹ). 1754. [F., ad. L. *capillaris, capillaris herba* the maidenhair.] **a.** A syrup of maidenhair fern. **b.** A syrup flavoured with orange-flower water.

†**Capi·llament.** 1681. [ad. L. *capillamentum* the hair collectively.] **1.** A hair-like fibre, filament, as of a root, or nerve –1785. **2.** *Bot.* A stamen –1751.

Capillarimeter (kăpi·lări·mītəɹ). 1874. [f. L. *capillaris.*] An instrument for measuring the strength of wine, etc. on the principle of capillary attraction.

Capillarity (kæpila·rĭti). 1830. [ad. F. *capillarité*, f. L. *capillaris.*] Capillary quality; *esp.* that of exerting capillary attraction or repulsion. Also, capillary attraction.

Capillary (kăpi·lări, kæ·pilări). 1646. [f. L. *capillaris.*] **A.** *adj.* **1.** Of or pertaining to hair; resembling hair, *esp.* in tenuity 1656. **2.** Having a hair-like bore; as a *c. tube* 1664. **3.** Of, pertaining to, or occurring in, capillaries 1809.

3. *C. Attraction, Repulsion*: see ATTRACTION, REPULSION. var. †**Capi·llar.**

B. *sb.* †**1.** Anything hair-like 1697. **2.** A capillary vessel. Cf. A. 2. *esp.* One of the minute blood-vessels, in which the arterial circulation ends and the venous begins 1667. †**3.** *Bot.* The Maidenhair Fern (*Adiantum capillus Veneris*); also other ferns and allied plants –1751.

†**Capilla·tion.** *rare.* 1646. [ad. L. *capillationem*, f. *capillatus.*] Hairy or hair-like condition; hence *concr.* a capillary –1751.

Capi·lliform. 1835. [f. L. *capillus* + -FORM.] Hair-shaped.

‖**Capilli·tium.** 1866. [L., f. *capillus.*] *Bot.* Entangled filamentary matter in fungals, bearing sporidia.

Capillo·se. 1843. [ad. L. *capillosus.*] *adj.* Full of hair, hairy. *sb.* (*Min.*) = MILLERITE.

Capital (kæ·pităl), *sb.*¹ ME. [repr. L. *capitellum* (dim. of *caput*), but now assim. to the adj. CAPITAL.] **1.** The head or top of a column or pillar. **2.** The cap of a chimney, crucible, etc. 1715. ¶**3.** = CAPITLE. Scott.

1. A c. is only the cornice of a column RUSKIN.

Capital (kæ·pităl), *a.* and *sb.*² ME. [a. F., ad. L. *capitalis* in learned use.]

A. *adj.* **I.** Relating to the head. †**1.** Of or pertaining to the head or top –1688. **2.** Affecting the head or life 1483; punishable by death 1526; †fatal –1701. †**3.** Deadly, mortal –1762. Also *fig.*

1. His [the Serpent's] c. bruise MILT. *P. L.* XII. 383 2. A c. sentence CAXTON, verdict 1868, crime 1526. It was c. to preach even in houses HALLAM. 3. A c. enmyte 1502. *fig.* A c. error PRESCOTT.

II. Standing at the head (*lit.* and *fig.*). †**1.** Of words and letters: Initial –1811. **2.** Chief, head-; important ME.; of ships: 'Of the line' 1688. **3.** In mod. use: First-rate. Often as an exclam. 1762. **4.** Of or pertaining to the original funds of a trader, company, or corporation; principal 1709.

1. *C. letters*: letters of the form and relative size used at the head of a page, or at the beginning of a line or paragraph. 2. To rase Som C. City MILT. *P. L.* II. 924. My c. secret *Sams.* 394. *C. manor*, one held *in capite*, or directly from the King. 4. The C. Stock of the Bank of England 1709.

B. *sb.*² [The adj. used ellipt.] **1.** A capital letter. (Cf. A. II. 1.) 1649. **2.** A capital town or city 1667. **3.** A capital stock or fund. **a.** *Comm.* The trading stock of a company, corporation, or individual on which profits or dividends are calculated. **b.** *Pol. Econ.* Accumulated wealth employed reproductively 1630. Also *fig.* **4.** *Fortif.* An imaginary line bisecting the salient angle of a work 1706.

2. Pandæmonium, the high C. of Satan MILT. *P. L.* I. 756. 3. You began ill.. You set up your trade without a c. BURKE. *Fixed c.*: that which remains in the owner's possession, as machinery, tools, etc. *Circulating, floating c.*: that which is constantly changing hands or form, as goods, money, etc. *To make c. out of* (fig.): to turn to account. *C. levy*, confiscation by the State of a proportion of all property.

Capitalism (kæ·pităliːz'm, kăpi·tăliz'm). 1854. [f. next; see -ISM.] The condition of possessing capital or using it for production; a system of society based on this; dominance of private capitalists.

Capitalist (kæ·pităliːst, kăpi·tălist). 1792. [ad. F. *capitaliste*; see CAPITAL *sb.*², -IST.] One who has capital, esp. one who uses it in business enterprises (on a large scale).

Capitalize (kæ·pităləiːz, kăpi·t-). 1850. [f. CAPITAL *a.* and *sb.*², partly after F.] **1.** *trans.* To write or print in capitals, or with initial capital. **2.** To convert into capital 1868. **3.** To compute or realize the present capital value of 1856.

2. The project of capitalizing incomes 1856. Hence **Ca·pitaliza·tion.**

Capitally (kæ·pităli), *adv.* 1606. [f. CAPITAL *a.* + -LY ².] **1.** In a manner involving loss of life 1619. **2.** Seriously 1606; eminently 1786; admirably 1750.

1. He was c. impeached THIRLWALL.

‖**Capitan** (kapita·n, kæ·pitæ̆n). 1755. [Sp.] Mostly *attrib.*, as in *C.* (or *Captain*) *Pacha*, chief admiral of the Turkish fleet. Hence ‖**Capitana** (sc. *nave*), the admiral's ship.

‖**Capitano** (kapitā·no). 1611. [It.] A captain, headman, or chief.

Capitate (kæ·pite¹t), *a.* 1661. [ad. L. *capitatus*, f. *caput.*] *Nat. Hist.* **1.** Having a distinct head. **2.** *Bot.* Having the inflorescence in a head, as in composite flowers 1686. Also **Ca·pitated** *ppl. a.*

Capitation (kæpitēⁱ·ʃən). 1614. [ad. L. *capitationem.*] **1.** The counting of heads or persons. **2.** The levying of a tax by the head, *i. e.* upon each person; a tax, fee, or payment per head. *Comb.* **c. grant,** a grant of so much per head subject to certain conditions.

‖**Ca·pite** (kæ·pitī). 1616. L., ablat. of *caput*, occurring in *tenere in capite* to hold (of the king) in chief; whence *tenant, tenure in capite*, and *capite* in Law Dicts. as the name of a tenure by which land was held immediately of the king or of the crown.

Capitellate (kăpi·tele¹t), *a.* 1870. [f. next.] Furnished with a CAPITELLUM. Cf. CAPITATE.

‖**Capite·llum.** 1872. [L., dim. of *caput.*] A little head; the rounded eminence on the outer surface of the lower end of the humerus.

†**Ca·pitle.** ME. only. [a. ONF., ad. L. *capitulum*, dim. of *caput.* A var. of CHAPITLE, chapter.] **1.** A chapter of a book. **2.** A summary.

Capitol (kæ·pitǫl). [ME. *capitolie, capitoile*, a. ONF., ad. L. *capitolium*, f. *caput.*] **1.** *lit.* A citadel on the top of a hill. *esp.* The temple of Jupiter Optimus Maximus, on the Saturnian or Tarpeian (subseq. called Capitoline) Hill at Rome; occ. used of the whole Hill. Also *transf.* and *fig.* **2.** *U. S.* The edifice occupied by the congress of the United States. Also, in some states, the state-house. 1843.

1. There the C. thou seest.. On the Tarpeian rock MILT. *P. R.* IV. 47. Hence **Capito·lian, Capi·toline** *a.* of or pertaining to the C.; *Capitoline games*: games in honour of Capitoline Jove.

‖**Capitoul** (kapitūl). 1753. [F.:—late L. *capitolium*, for *capitulum* chapter.] A name given to the municipal magistrates of Toulouse.

Capi·tulant. 1839. [a. F.] One who capitulates.

Capitular (kăpi·tiŭlăɹ). 1611. [ad. med.L. *capitularis* adj., *capitulare* sb., f. *capitulum.*]

A. *adj.* **1.** Of or pertaining to an eccl. chapter. **2.** *Phys.* Of or pertaining to a capitulum (see CAPITULUM 2) 1872. **3.** *Bot.* Growing in small heads, as the Dandelion 1846. Hence †**Capi·tularly** *adv.* as a chapter.

B. *sb.* [The adj. used ellipt.] **1.** A member of a chapter 1726. **2.** = CAPITULARY B. 2. 1660. **3.** ? A law or statute of a chapter; also *fig.* 1667. **4.** ? A heading 1846.

Capitulary (kăpi·tiŭlări). 1650. [ad. med. L. *capitularius, -ium.* Cf. CAPITULAR.] **A.** *adj.* Of or pertaining to a chapter 1774. **B.** *sb.* **1.** A member of an eccl. chapter 1694. **2.** A collection of ordinances, *esp.* those made by the Frankish Kings 1650. **3.** A heading 1824.

2. The capitularies of Charle-Magne 1747.

†**Capi·tulate,** *ppl. a.* 1528. [ad. med.L. *capitulatus, capitulare*, f. *capitulum*, dim. of *caput.*] Reduced to heads; stipulated –1600.

Capitulate (kăpi·tiŭle¹t), *v.* 1580. [f. prec.] †**1.** To draw up in chapters or under heads or articles; to specify –1678. †**2.** *intr.* To draw up articles of agreement; to treat, parley –1816. †**3.** *trans.* To make terms about; to arrange for –1661. **4.** To make terms of surrender, to surrender on stipulated terms. (The ordinary use.) *intr.* and *trans.* 1689.

2. We must not c. with mutiny in any shape WELLINGTON. 4. Want of provisions quickly obliged Trevulci to c. 1769. *fig.* To c. to badges and names EMERSON. Hence **Capi·tulator** (Dicts.).

Capitulation (kapi:tiŭlēⁱ·ʃən). 1535. [a. F., ad. med. L. *capitulationem*; see CAPITULATE.] The action of the vb. CAPITULATE. †**1.** Arranging in chapters or heads 1613. **2.** A statement of heads, summary, enumeration; cf. *recapitulation.* 1579. †**3.** The making of terms –1721; *pl.* terms –1728; a covenant, convention, treaty –1843. **4.** The action of capitulating (sense 4) 1650; the instrument containing the terms of surrender 1793.

2. C. is not description STEVENSON. 3. *Spec. uses.* (*a.*) The conditions sworn to by the former German emperors at their election. (*b.*) The agreements made by the Swiss cantons with foreign powers respecting the Swiss mercenaries. (*c.*) The articles by which the Porte gave immunities and privileges to French subjects, and subseq. to others. 4. The c. of Metz (*mod.*).

Capitulatory (kăpi·tiŭlătəːri), *a.* [f. the vb.] Of or pertaining to CAPITULATION (sense 2).

In their..c. brass monuments LAMB *Elia.*

‖**Capitulum** (kăpi·tiŭlǒm). 1721. [L., dim. of *caput.*] A little head or knob. **1.** *Phys.* A protuberance of bone received into a hollow portion of another bone 1755. **2.** *Bot.* A close head of sessile flowers 1721. **3.** *Zool.* The part of a barnacle borne by and forming a head to the peduncle 1872.

Capivi, var. of COPAIBA.

Caplan, obs. f. CAPELIN.

Ca·ple, capul. Now *dial.* [ME. *capel* = Icel. *kapall* (for *kapal-r*) nag; prob. f. (ult.) L. *caballus*.] A horse: in ME. chiefly *poetical*.

Caplin, capling (kæ·plin, -liŋ). 1688. [f. CAP.] The cap of leather on a flail, through which the thongs pass that connect the swingel and the staff.

Caplin, -ling, var. of CAPELIN.

Capnomancy (kæ·pnomænsi). 1610. [f. Gr. καπνός + μαντεία.] Divination by smoke.

Capnomor (kæ·pnomǫɹ). 1838. [f. as prec. + (?) μόρα, Doric for μοῖρα.] *Chem.* A colourless transparent oil of peculiar smell, one of the constituents of smoke, obtained from wood-tar.

‖**Ca·poc.** 1750. = KAPOK, q.v.

†**Capo·che,** *v. trans. rare.* ? 'To strip off the hood' (J.); or joc. use of CABOCHE *v.* BUTLER *Hud.* II. II. 529.

Capon (kē¹·pən), *sb.* [OE. *capun*, ad. L. *caponem*.] **1.** A castrated cock. †**2.** *transf.* A eunuch -1691. **3.** *joc.* One of various fish; *esp.* a red-herring 1640. †**4.** A billet-doux. Cf. F. *poulet.* *L. L. L.* IV. i. 56.

1. In faire round belly, with good C. lin'd *A. Y. L.* II. vii. 154. *Comb.*: **c.-justice**, a magistrate who is bribed by gifts of c.; **-money**, money in commutation of a payment of capons; †**capon's feather**, the Common Columbine (*Aquilegia vulgaris*); †**capon's tail**, a plant, *Valeriana pyrenaica*. Hence **Ca·pon** *v.* to castrate; so **Ca·ponize.** †**Ca·ponet**, a little c.

Caponier (kæpŏnī·ɹ). 1683. [a. F. *caponnière*, ad. Sp. *caponera*; orig. a capon-cote, f. *capon*.] A covered passage across a ditch, serving to shelter communication with outworks, and affording a flanking fire to the ditch.

‖**Caporal** (kapora·l). 1598. [a. Sp. and F.] †**1.** A corporal. (*Sp.*) **2.** A kind of tobacco. (*Fr.*) 1850.

Capot (kăpǫ·t, †kæ·pət), *sb.*[1] 1651. [a. F.] In *Piquet.* The winning of all the tricks by one player. Hence **Capo·t** *v.* to score a c. against; also *transf.*

‖**Capot** (kapo), *sb.*[2] 1775. [a. F., dim. of *cape.*] = CAPOTE.

Capote (kăpōᵘ·t). 1812. [a. F., a fem. form of prec.] A long shaggy cloak or overcoat with a hood; a long mantle, worn by women.

†**Capou·ch**, var. of CAPUCHE.

Cappadine (kæ·pădin, -dīn). 1678. [? f. F. *capade*, f. *cap* head.] 'A sort of silk flock or waste obtained from the cocoon after the silk has been reeled off.'

†**Cappado·chio.** = CAPERDEWSIE, q.v.

Cappagh (kæ·pă). 1875. A place near Cork in Ireland; whence *Cappagh* or *Cappah brown*, a brown pigment.

Cap-paper (kæ·pˌpē¹:pəɹ). 1577. [f. CAP in different senses.] **1.** A kind of wrapping paper. **2.** A size or kind of writing paper (perh. named from the watermark of a cap) 1854.

Capparid (kæ·părid). [f. L. *capparis* the caper.] *Bot.* A plant, one of the *Capparidaceæ*. **Capparida·ceous** *a.* of the natural order Capparidaceæ (erron. f. *Capparaceæ*), of which the Caper is the type.

Cappe·lenite. 1886. *Min.* A silico-borate of yttrium and barium, from Norway.

Capper (kæ·pəɹ). ME. [f. CAP *sb.* and *v.* + -ER[1].] †**1.** A capmaker -1805. **2.** One who caps (see CAP *v.*) 1587. **3.** *dial.* A person or thing that caps or beats all others; a puzzler 1790.

Cappie (kæ·pi). *Sc.* 1824. [dim. of CAP *sb.*[2]] **1.** A small drinking vessel. **2.** A kind of beer between table-beer and ale.

Capping (kæ·piŋ), *vbl. sb.* 1592. [f. CAP *v.*[1]] **1.** The action of the vb. CAP in various senses. **2.** Cap-making 1662. **3.** That with which anything is capped or overlaid 1713.

Comb. **c.-plane** (*Joinery*), a plane for working the upper surface of the balustrade on a staircase.

Cappy (kæ·pi), *a.* 1865. [f. CAP *sb.* + -Y[1].] Characterized by, or like, a cap.

Hairless and c. age 1865.

Caprate (kæ·preᶦt). 1836. [f. CAPR-IC + -ATE[4].] *Chem.* A salt of capric acid.

†**Ca·preol(e.** 1578. [ad. L. *capreolus*, dim. of *capreus* roe, f. *caper.*] **1.** A variety of roe-buck 1655. **2.** A tendril -1725.

Capreolate (kæ·priŏleᶦt, kăprī·ŏleᶦt), *a.* 1737. [ad. L. **capreolatus*, f. *capreolus*; see prec.] *Bot.* Furnished with tendrils.

Capreoline (kăprī·ŏləin), *a.* 1835. [f. L. *capreolus* + -INE.] *Zool.* Of or belonging to the genus Capreolus of Cervidæ.

Capric (kæ·prik), *a.* 1836. [f. L. *caper, caprum* + -IC.] **1.** Of or belonging to a goat (*nonce-use*) 1881. **2.** *Chem. Capric acid* ($C_{10}H_{20}O_2$), a fatty acid obtained from butter, coco-nut oil, fusel oil, etc.: a colourless crystalline body, having a slight odour of the goat.

‖**Capriccio** (kaprī·ttʃo). 1601. [a. It., app. f. *capro* goat.] **1.** A prank, trick, caper 1665. †**2.** = CAPRICE **1.** -1824. **3.** A thing or work of fancy 1678; *Mus.* a composition more or less free in form and whimsical in style 1696.

‖**Capriccioso** (kaprittʃō·so), *a.* [It., f. prec.] *Mus.* A direction: In a free fantastic style.

Caprice (kăprī·s). 1667. [a. F. *caprice*, It. *capriccio.* Pope rimed the word with *vice.*] **1.** A sudden turn of the mind without apparent motive; a freak, whim, mere fancy. **b.** Capriciousness 1709. Also *transf.* of things. **2.** = CAPRICCIO **3.** 1721.

1. The caprices of woman-kind are not limited by climate or nation SWIFT. **b.** Of less judgment than c. POPE. A c. of language FREEMAN.

Capricious (kapri·ʃəs), *a.* 1594. [ad. F. *capricieux*, ad. It. *capriccioso*; see above.] †**1.** Humorous, fantastic, full of conceits -1710. **2.** Subject to, or characterized by CAPRICE; whimsical 1605. Also *transf.* of things.

1. The most c. Poet honest Ouid *A. Y. L.* III. iii. 8. **2.** Arbitrary and c. JOHNSON. A c. climate HELPS. Hence **Capri·cious-ly** *adv.*, **-ness.**

Capricorn (kæ·prikǭɹn). ME. [ad. L. *capricornus*, f. *caper, caprum* + *cornu*; cf. Gr. αἰγόκερως.] **1.** *Astron.* **a.** The Zodiacal constellation of the He-Goat. **b.** The tenth sign of the Zodiac, beginning at the most southerly point of the ecliptic, which the sun enters about the 21st of December. †**2.** A goat-horned animal; ? a chamois 1646. **3.** *C. beetle*: any beetle of the genus Cerambyx 1700.

1. As deep as Capricorne MILT. *P. L.* x. 677. *Tropic of C.*: the southern Tropic forming a tangent to the ecliptic at the first point of C.

Caprid (kæ·prid), *a.* 1864. [f. mod.L. *capridæ*, f. *caper.*] *Zool.* Of or belonging to the Capridæ or goat tribe.

Caprification (kæ:prifikē¹·ʃən). 1601. [ad. L. *caprificationem*, f. *caprificare*, f. *caprificus* the wild fig-tree.] **1.** A process of ripening figs by means of the puncture of insects produced on the wild fig, or by puncturing them artificially. ¶**2.** Erron. used for: Artificial fertilization 1836.

Caprifoil (kæ·prifoil). 1578. [ad. med.L. *caprifolium*; cf. F. *chèvrefeuille.*] The Honeysuckle or Woodbine; also, Eng. name for plants of the N.O. *Caprifoliaceæ*.

Caprifoliaceous (kæ:prifōᵘliˌē¹·ʃəs), *a.* 1852. [See prec.] *Bot.* Belonging to the N.O. *Caprifoliaceæ*.

Capriform (kæ·prifǭɹm), *a.* 1847. [f. L. *caper, capr(i)* + -FORM.] Goat-shaped.

Caprine (kæ·prəin, -in), *a.* 1607. [ad. L. *caprinus*, f. *caper.*] Of or pertaining to a goat; goat-like.

Capri·nic, *a. Chem.* Older name for CAPRIC.

Capriole (kæ·priˌōᵘl), *sb.* 1594. [a. F. (now *cabriole*).] **1.** A leap or caper, as in dancing. **2.** *Horsemanship.* A high leap made by a horse without advancing, the hind legs being jerked out together at the height of the leap 1605.

1. Caprioles and pirouettes DE QUINCEY. *fig.* Caprioles of fancy HAWTHORNE.

Capriole (kæ·priˌōᵘl), *v.* 1580. [f. prec.] To leap, skip, caper. Also *fig.*

Caproic (kăprōᵘ·ik), *a.* 1839. [f. L. *caper, capr-* (from its smell) + *-oic*, -IC.] *Chem. Caproic acid*: a peculiar acid found in butter, etc., a form of the hexoic acids ($C_6H_{12}O_2$).

From same source **Ca·proate**, a salt of c. acid.

†**Ca·pron.** 1460. [a. F., NF. dial. f. *chaperon* hood.] A hood -1561. *Capron hardy*: an impudent fellow.

Capryl (kæ·pril). [f. CAPR-IC + -YL.] *Chem.* Applied to the radical ($C_8H_{17}O$) of caprylic acid. Hence **Ca·prylate**, a salt of caprylic acid.

Capry·lic, *a.* 1845. [f. as prec.] *Chem. Caprylic acid*: one of the octylic fatty acids.

Caps. Printers' abbrev. of *capitals*.

‖**Capsicum** (kæ·psikǒm). 1725. [mod.L.; ? irreg. f. L. *capsa* case.] **1.** A genus of tropical plants (N.O. *Solanaceæ*), characterized by their hot pungent capsules or seeds 1796.

Guinea Pepper (*C. annuum*), and Spur Pepper (*C. frutescens*) produce the chillies of commerce, whence Cayenne pepper.

2. The fruit of the capsicum 1725. Hence **Ca·psicine**, *Chem.* the active principle of the capsules of c.

Capsize (kæpsəi·z), *sb.* 1807. [f. next.] The act of capsizing; an upset. var. **Capsi·zal.**

Capsize (kæpsəi·z), *v.* 1783. [prob. ad. Sp. *capuzar* to sink (a ship) by the head.] *trans.* To upset, overturn. Also *intr.* (for *refl.*).

To c. a boat BYRON, a stool PEACOCK.

Capstan (kæ·pstăn). ME. [a. F. *cabestan*, or Pr. *cabestan*, earlier *cabestran*:—L. *capistrant-, capistrare*, f. *capistrum* halter, f. *capere.*] **1.** A cylinder or barrel revolving on a vertical axis, the power being applied by movable bars inserted in horizontal sockets made round the top, and pushed by men walking round; used *esp.* on board ship for weighing the anchor, also for hoisting heavy sails, raising weights, etc.

Phrases. *To rig the c.*, to insert the bars; *to pawl the c.*, to drop the pawls or catches into their sockets so as to prevent recoil; *to surge the c.*, to slacken the rope while heaving.

Comb. **c.-swifter**, a rope passed horizontally through notches in the outer ends of the bars, to steady the men, and to give room for more.

Cap-stone (kæ·pstōᵘn). 1665. **1.** A stone which caps or crowns. **2.** *Geol.* A fossil Echinite of the genus Conulus 1677.

1. The c. of a cromlech 1851, of a quarry SMEATON.

Capsular (kæ·psiŭlăɹ), *a.* 1730. [ad. mod. L. *capsularis.*] Of, pertaining to, or of the nature of a capsule. var. †**Ca·psulary** *a.*

†**Ca·psulate**, *a.* 1668. [ad. mod.L. *capsulatus*, f. *capsula.*] *Bot.* Enclosed in, or formed into, a capsule -1803. So †**Ca·psulated.**

Capsule (kæ·psiŭl). 1652. [a. F., ad. L. *capsula* (also used), dim. of *capsa* box.] †**1.** *gen.* A little case -1713. **2.** *Phys.* A membranous integument; a bag or sac 1693. **3.** *Bot.* A dry dehiscent seed-vessel, containing one or more cells 1693. **4.** *Chem.* A shallow saucer, for roasting samples of ores, or for evaporating 1727. **5.** *Med.* A small envelope of gelatine to enclose a dose of medicine 1875. **6.** A metallic cap or cover for a bottle 1858. **7.** A percussion cap; the shell of a metallic cartridge. [Fr.] Hence **Ca·psule** *v.* to furnish or close with a c.

Capsuli-, capsulo-, comb. ff. L. *capsula* CAPSULE; as in

Capsuli·ferous *a.*, bearing capsules. **Ca·psuliform** *a.*, having the form of a capsule. **Capsuli·genous** *a.*, giving origin to capsules. **Ca·psulo-lenti·cular** *a.*, of the capsule of the lens of the eye.

Captain (kæ·ptĕn), *sb.* [ME. *capitain*, a. late OF., ad. late L. *capitanus* adj. and sb., f. *caput, capit-.*] **I. 1.** One who stands at the head of others; a chief or leader. (Now only *fig.* in special senses.) **2.** *esp.* A military leader ME. **3.** A great military leader; an able general; a strategist 1590.

1. Homer, that C. of all poetry 1683. **2.** *Meas. for M.* II. ii. 130. **3.** Foremost C. of his time TENNYSON.

II. The head of a division. **1.** *gen.* An officer holding subordinate command ME. **2.** *spec.* In the army: The officer who commands a company or troop, ranking between the major and the lieutenant 1567. **3.** The officer who commands a man-of-war, ranking, in the British navy, between a rear-admiral or a commodore and a commander. Also, a courtesy title of commanders. 1554. **b.** The chief sailor of a gang having specific duties 1801. **4.** The master or commander of a vessel of any kind 1704. **5.** The superintendent of a mine 1602; the foreman of a workshop 1886; the head boy of a school 1706. **6.** *Cricket*, etc.: The leader of a side, the chief of a club, etc. 1857. **7.** As a term of address (*familiar*). Cf. *governor.* 1607.

3 b. C. of a gun at the Battle of the Nile 1801. 4. The c. of a slaver MORLEY. 7. Come Captaine, We must be neat; not neat, but cleanly, Captaine SHAKS.
III. A name for the Grey Gurnard 1810.

Comb. †c.-pacha: see CAPITAN. Hence **Ca·ptainess**, a female c. **Ca·ptainless** *a.* †**Ca·ptainry**, captaincy; a district under a c.

†**Ca·ptain**, *a.* 1566. [prec. sb. used attrib.] Chief, head- –1635.

Captain (kæ·ptėn), *v.* 1598. [f. the sb.] To act as captain to, head. Also *intr.*

Captaincy (kæ·ptėnsi). 1818. [f. CAPTAIN *sb.*, after *infancy*, etc.] 1. The position or action of a captain. 2. The district under the rule of a captain (e. g. in Brazil). [Sp.] 1821.

Captain Ge·neral, captain-general. 1514. [F. and Sp.] †Chief commander of a force. Also the governor of a Spanish province or colony.

Captain-lieute·nant. 1658. A military officer who commanded a company or troop, with a captain's rank and lieutenant's pay. (The rank is extinct.)

Ca·ptainship. 1465. [f. CAPTAIN *sb.*] 1. The office, position, authority or rank of a captain. 2. *joc.* The dignity or personality of a captain; cf. *lordship* 1611. 3. = CAPTAINCY 2. 1680. 4. 'Skill in the military trade' (J.). 1606.
1. The c. of the Scottish Guards CARTE.

†**Ca·ptate**, *v.* 1628. [f. L. *captat-*, *captare*, freq. of *capere*.] To catch at, seek after –1671.

Captation (kæptē·ʃən). 1523. [a. L. *captationem*; see prec.] An endeavour to get, *esp.* by address or art; the making of *ad captandum* appeals.
Popular captations..in speeches *Eikon Bas.*

Caption (kæ·pʃən). ME. [ad. L. *captionem*, f. *capt-*, *capere*.] 1. Seizure, capture (now *rare*). b. *Law.* Apprehension by judicial process 1609. †2. The action of taking exception; a quibble, sophism. (L. *captio*.) –1734. 3. *Law.* 'That part of a legal instrument, as a commission, indictment, etc., which shows where, when, and by what authority it is taken, found, or executed' (Tomlins) 1670. 4. The heading of a chapter, section, or article (orig. *U.S.*), now esp. on a cinema screen.
2. So vain a C. HEYLIN. 4. Under the c., 'A Budget of Paradoxes' GROSART.

Captious (kæ·pʃəs), *a.* ME. [ad. L. *captiosus* (see CAPTION).] 1. Apt to catch or take one in; fallacious, sophistical 1447. 2. Disposed to find fault; cavilling, carping ME.
1. A c. question, sir COWPER. 2. The world is c. COVERDALE. C. of other mens doinges 1561. Nonce uses: = Capacious *All's Well* I. iii. 208; = Taking 1776. Hence **Ca·ptious-ly** *adv.*, **-ness.**

†**Capti·vance.** *rare.* = CAPTIVITY. Spenser.

Captivate (kæ·ptivēᵗt), *v.* 1526. [f. late L. *captivat-*, *captivare*, f. *captivus*; cf. CAPTIVE *v.*] †1. To make or hold captive –1825. †2. *fig.* To subjugate (the mind, etc.). Const. *to*. –1838. 3. *esp.* 'To overpower with excellence' (J.); to enslave, fascinate, charm 1535.
1. Thy bragging banners.. Shall all be captivated by this hand 1595. 3. Hir bewtye captyuated his mynde *Judith* xvi. 9. Hence **Ca·ptivatingly** *adv.* **Ca·ptivator**, †**-er.**

Captivation (kæptivē·ʃən). 1610. [ad. L. *captivationem*; see prec.] 1. The action of taking or holding captive; being taken or held captive; now only *fig.* 2. A fascination. SCOTT.

Captive (kæ·ptiv). ME. [a. F. *captif*, *-ive*, ad. L. *captivus*, f. *captus*.]
A. *adj.* 1. Taken prisoner, *esp.* in war; kept in confinement or bondage. Also *transf.* 2. *fig.* Captivated, enslaved in will or feeling 1594. 3. Of or belonging to a captive 1590.
1. The captiue Iewes 2 *Macc.* viii. 10. A c. lark, balloon, etc. (*mod.*). 2. Whose words all eares took captiue *All's Well* v. iii. 17. 3. His c. state MILT.
B. *sb.* 1. A person taken prisoner; one taken and held in confinement ME. Also *transf.* 2. *fig.* One captivated or enslaved by beauty, personal influence, etc. 1732.
1. A man of the captiues of Iudah *Dan.* ii. 25.

Captive (kæ·ptiv), *v. arch.* ME. [a. F. *captiver*; see prec.] To take captive (*lit.* and *fig.*). (In MILT. *captī·ve.*)
Their inhabitants slaughtered and captived BURKE.

Captivity (kæpti·viti). ME. [ad. L. *captivitas*, *-atem*; see CAPTIVE.] 1. The condition of a captive; *spec.* that of the Jews at Babylon. 2. *fig.* The subjection of the reason, will, or affections 1538. †3. Captives collectively. (A Hebraism.) 1526.
1. A c. implies a removal of the inhabitants PUSEY. 3. *To lead c. captive*: now often, to lead one's captors into c. (*Eph.* iv. 8); but see also *Judges* v. 12.

Captor (kæ·ptəɹ, -ǫɹ). 1688. [a. L.; see CAPTURE.] One who takes by force a prisoner or a prize. So **Ca·ptress** (*rare*).

Capture (kæ·ptiŭɹ), *sb.* 1541. [a. F., ad. L. *captura*, f. *capt-*, *capere*.] 1. The fact of taking forcibly, or by stratagem, or of being thus taken; *esp.* the seizing as a prize. 2. The prize, prey, or booty so taken 1706.
2. To bring a dubious c. into port 1750.

Ca·pture, *v.* 1795. [f. prec. sb., repl. CAPTIVE *v.*] To make a capture of (*lit.* and *fig.*).
The value of the property so captured WELLINGTON. Hence **Ca·pturable** *a.* **Ca·pturer.**

Capuche (kapū·ʃ, kăpū·tʃ). 1600. [a. F., ad. It. *cappuccio* (in Florio *capuccio*, used by Spenser), augm. of *cappa*; see CAP, CAPE.] The hood of a (Capuchin's) cloak. Hence **Capu·ched** *a.* hooded. †‖**Capuchon**, a hood.

Capuchin (kæ·piŭtʃin, kæpŭʃī·n), *sb.* Also **-ine.** 1599. [a. 16th c. F. (now *capucin*), ad. It. *capuccino*; see prec.] 1. A Franciscan friar of the new rule of 1528. So called from the sharp-pointed capuche, first worn by them in 1525. 2. 'A female garment, consisting of a cloak and hood, made in imitation of the dress of capuchin friars' (J.) 1749.
attrib. **C. monkey**, an American monkey (*Cebus capucinus*) with black hair at the back of the head, looking like a cowl. **C. pigeon**, a sub-variety of the Jacobin pigeon, with a cowl-like arrangement of feathers on the back of the head. **Capuchin's beard**, a variety of endive. **Capuchin capers**; see CAPER *sb.*[1]

†‖**Capucine** (kapüsīn). 1693. [Fr.; fem. of *capucin*; see prec.] 1. The Nasturtium. 2. The dark orange colour of its flowers 1791.

Ca·pulet. = CAPELET.

Caput (kæ·pɒt). 1716. [L.] 1. Occas. *techn.* for 'head' or 'top', *esp.* in *Anat.* †2. Short for CAPUT MORTUUM, q. v. †3. The former ruling body or council of the University of Cambridge –1830.

‖**Ca·put mo·rtuum.** 1641. [L.; = dead head.] †1. A skull 1658. 2. *Chem.* The residuum remaining after distillation or sublimation 1641. 3. *fig.* Worthless residue 1711.

Capybara (kæpibā·rā). Also **capi-.** 1774. [Native name in Brazil.] The largest extant rodent quadruped (*Hydrochœrus Capybara*), nearly allied to the Guinea Pig. Cf. CABIAI.

Car (kāɹ), *sb.* [ME. *carre*, a. ONF. :—late L. *carra*, parallel to *carrus*, a. OCelt. **karros*.] 1. A wheeled vehicle: orig. used generally, but since 16th c. chiefly poetic and grandiose. 2. In U.S.: A name for vehicles (as carriages, trucks, wagons, etc.) designed for travelling on railways 1837. In Gt. Britain applied to those of street tramways. b. = MOTOR CAR 1. 1896. 3. The part of a balloon in which aeronauts sit 1794. †4. The seven stars of the Great Bear, called also the Plough or Wain –1697.
1. Forty carres (*vehicula*) HOLLAND. Phoebus fiery carre SPENSER. The Carr of Night MILT. The towering c., the sable steeds TENNYSON. The c. of Juggernaut 1853. 2. The cars of a railway 1850. The cars on the tramways in London (*mod.*).

Ca·rabid, cara·bidan. 1835. [f. mod.L. pl. *carabidæ*, f. L. *carabus* crab.] *Ent.* One of the *Carabidæ*, a family of large carnivorous beetles.

†**Carabin** (kæ·răbin). 1590. [a. F. *carabin*.] A mounted musketeer; a carabineer –1735.

Carabineer (kæ:răbinīᵊ·ɹ), **carbineer** (kāɹbinīᵊ·ɹ). 1672. [a. F. *carabinier* (also used), f. *carabine*.] A soldier who carries a carbine.

Caraboid, *a.* [f. L. *carabus* (see CARABID) + -OID.] *Ent.* Like or related to the genus *Carabus* of beetles.

Caracal (kæ·răkæl). 1760. [a. F., a. Turk. *qarah-qulak* black ear.] A feline animal (*Felis caracal*) found in Africa and Asia, supposed to be the 'lynx' of the ancients.

‖**Caracara** (kărakā·ra). Also **carcara.** 1838. [From its cry.] Name for S. Amer. birds of the *Polyborinæ*, an aberrant sub-family of *Falconidæ*, with affinities toward the Vultures.

Carack, var. of CARRACK.

Caracol (kæ·răkǫl), **caracole** (-kōᵘl), *sb.* 1614. [a. F., ad. It. *caracollo*, ad. Sp. *caracol* snail, spiral shell, also winding stair.] †1. A spiral shell 1622. 2. *Arch.* A staircase in the form of a helix 1721. 3. A half-turn to the right or left executed by a horseman 1614.

Ca·racol, caracole, *v.* 1656. [a. F. *caracoler*; see prec.] To execute a caracol or caracols; *trans.* to make (a horse) caracol.
The Captain..caracolling majestically THACKERAY. Hence **Ca·racoler, -coller.**

†‖**Caracoli.** 1753. [? Carib.] An alloy of silver, copper, and gold, imitating one formerly used in the Caribee Islands.

‖**Caracore.** 1794. 'A sort of vessel used in the Philippine Isles' (Littré).

†**Caract, carect**, *sb.* [ME. *caracte*, *carect*, a. (ult.) Gr. χαρακτός, -ή, -όν, taken absol. as = *character*.] A mark, CHARACTER –1655.
Characts, titles, formes *Meas. for M.* v. i. 56. Hence †**Caract** *v.* to mark.

Caracul, kara- (kæ·răkŭl). 1894. [Russ.] A kind of astrakhan fur; cloth imitating this.

Carafe (karā·f). 1786. [a. F., a. It. *caraffa*; Arab.] A glass water-bottle for the table, bedroom, etc. Also corrupted to *craft*, *croft*.

Carag(h)een, var. of CARRAGEEN.

‖**Carambola.** 1598. [a. Pg., of doubtful origin.] The East Indian *Averrhoa Carambola* (N.O. *Oxalidaceæ*); also its acid fruit.

Carambole (kæ·rămbōᵘl), *sb.* 1775. [a. F., ad. Sp. *carambola* the red ball at billiards, the stroke, a trick: deriv. unkn.] *Billiards.* The stroke otherwise called a CANNON. Hence **Carambole** *v.* to make a cannon.

Caramel (kæ·rămel), *sb.* 1725. [a. F., ad. Sp. *caramelo*, of unkn. origin.] A black or brown porous substance obtained by heating sugar; burnt sugar. b. A kind of candy or sweet. Also *attrib.*

†‖**Caramoussal, carmousal.** 1587. A Turkish and Moorish ship of burden, noted in the 17th c.

‖**Caranx** (kæ·ræŋks). 1836. [mod. L.] A genus of fishes of the family *Scomberidæ*.

Ca·rap. 1865. [from the native name.] *C. oil*: an oil yielded by the seeds of *Carapa guianensis*.

Carapace (kæ·răpēᵗs). 1836. [a. mod.F., a. Sp. *carapacho*: of unkn. origin.] The upper body-shell of tortoises and of crustaceans. var. **Ca·rapax.**

Carat (kæ·răt). 1552. [a. F., ad. It. *carato*; cf. Sp. *quilate*, earlier *quirate*, a. Arab. *qīrāt* 'weight of 4 grains', ad. Gr. κεράτιον 'little horn, fruit of carob tree', a weight = 1/3 of an obol (Freytag).] †1. The bean of the carob-tree 1601. 2. A measure of weight used for diamonds, etc., originally 3 1/3 grains, now 3 1/5 grains. It is divided into 4 *carat-grains*. Also *attrib.* 1575. 3. A proportional measure of one twenty-fourth used in stating the fineness of gold. Also *attrib.* 1555. †4. (Confused with CHARACT.) Worth, value; estimate –1680.
2. A Diamond of 10 Carats 1667. 3. [Gold of] 22 caracts fine HUTTON. 4. 2 *Hen. IV*, IV. v. 162.

‖**Caratch** (karā·tʃ). 1682. [Arab. *kharāj*.] The tribute levied by the Turks on their Christian subjects.

Caravan (kæ·răvæn, kæravæ·n). 1599. [In 16th c. *carouan*, a. Pers. *kārwān*.] 1. A company of merchants, pilgrims, or others, in the East or northern Africa, travelling together for the sake of security, esp. through the desert. Also *attrib.* 2. A fleet of Turkish or Russian ships, *esp.* of merchant vessels, with their convoy 1605. 3. *transf.* A company in motion. Also *fig.* 1667. 4. A covered carriage or cart (now gen. superseded by VAN *sb.*[4] 7); a house on wheels, as those used by gipsies and showmen 1674.
1. Trauailing by Carauan, that is, Great Droues of laden Camels 1602. 2. A C... sailing in the vast ocean FULLER. Hence **Caravanee·r**, the leader of an (oriental) c.

Caravanserai, -era, -ary (kæravæ·nsĕrai, -ĕrā, -ĕri). 1599. [ult. a. Pers. *kārwān-sarāī*, f. *kārwān* caravan + *sarāī* palace, mansion, inn.] A kind of inn in the East where caravans put up, being a large quadrangular building enclosing a spacious court. Also *transf.* and *fig.*

Caravel (kæ·rǎvel). 1527. [a. F. *caravelle*, ad. It. *caravella* (Sp. *carabela*), prob. dim. of Sp. *caraba*; cf. late L. *carabus*, Gr. *κάραβος*.] *Naut.* 1. A kind of ship: a. The same as CARVEL, q. v.; b. The Portuguese *caravela*, a small ship with lateen sails; c. The Turkish war-frigate, called in Italian *caravella*. 2. The floating mollusc *Ianthina* 1707.

Caraway (kæ·răwe¹). Also †carr-. ME. [From med.L. *carui*, or some allied Rom. form: cf. F., It., Sp. *carvi* (whence Sc. *carvy*), OSp. *alcaravea*, a. Arab. *al-karawiyā*: also Gr. *κάρον*, *κάρεον*.] 1. An umbelliferous plant (*Carum Carui*): its seeds are aromatic and carminative, and yield a volatile oil. †2. The seed of the caraway; also a sweetmeat or confection containing caraway-seeds –1712.

2. A dish of Carrawayes 2 *Hen. IV*, v. iii. 3.

Carb-. *Chem.* Comb. f. CARBON, used before vowels, as in:

Ca·rbanil [ANIL], an amido-derivative of the benzene group, cyanate of phenyl, CO = N—C_6H_5, a mobile liquid with a pungent odour. **Ca·rbazol** [AZO- + -OL], an amido-phenyl, $2C_6H_4$ = NH, occurring in coal-tar oil, and as a by-product of aniline. **Carbazo·tic acid** [AZOTIC], an earlier name of Picric acid; its salts are **Carba·zotates.**

Carbamide (kā·ɹbămәid). 1865. [f. CARB- + AMIDE.] *Chem.* Analytical name of UREA. Also **Carba·mic** [see AMIC] *a.*, as in *Carbamic acid*, CO.NH_2.OH. **Ca·rbamate**, a salt of carbamic acid.

Carbide (kā·ɹbәid). 1865. [f. CARB- + -IDE.] *Chem.* A compound of carbon with an element or a metal; earlier *carburet*. b. = *calcium c.* 1898.

Carbine (kā·ɹbәin), **ca·rabine.** 1605. [In 17th c. *carabine*, a. F.; see CARABIN.] A kind of fire-arm, shorter than the musket, used by mounted soldiers.

Carbinol (kā·ɹbinǫl). [f. CARBON + -OL.] *Chem.* A generic name introduced by Kolbe *c* 1868 for the monatomic alcohols. Simple *Carbinol* is methyl alcohol, COH.H_3.

Carbo-. 1810. *Chem.* Comb. f. CARBON, used before consonants.

Carbo-hydrate (kā:ɹbo,hәi·dre¹t). 1869. [f. CARBO- + HYDRATE.] *Chem.* An organic compound of carbon with oxygen and hydrogen in the proportion to form water. They are divided into *Sugars proper*, *Glucoses*, and *Amyloses*.

Carbolic (kaɹbǫ·lik), *a.* 1865. [f. CARB- + -OL + -IC.] *Chem.* In **Carbolic acid**, a substance also called *Phenol* or *Phenyl alcohol*, C_6H_5.OH, found in the heavy coal oils and elsewhere. Much used as a disinfectant. Hence **Ca·rbolate**, a salt of carbolic acid. **Ca·rbolize** *v.* to impregnate with carbolic acid.

Carbon (kæ·ɹbǫn, -әn). 1789. [ad. F. *carbone*, f. (by Lavoisier) L. *carbo*.] 1. *Chem.* One of the non-metallic elements, occurring uncombined in three allotropic forms—two crystalline (diamond and graphite) and one amorphous (charcoal), and in combination in carbonic acid gas, and nearly all organic compounds (hence called 'the carbon compounds'). Carbon (symbol C) is a tetrad; atomic weight 12. 2. *Electr.* A pencil of fine charcoal. Two of these are placed with their points close to each other, and a current of galvanic electricity transmitted through them renders the carbon points intensely luminous. 1860.

attrib. etc.: **c. printing, process**, a photographic process producing permanent prints, the shades of which are produced by the c. of lamp-black; **C. dioxide**, CO_2, carbonic acid gas; **C. monoxide**, CO, carbonic oxide gas. Hence **Ca·rbonous** *a.*

Carbonaceous (kāɹbǒnē¹·ʃәs), *a.* 1791. [f. L. *carbonem*.] Of the nature of, consisting of, or containing carbon. 2. *Geol.* Coaly 1833.

†**Carbona·do**, *sb.* 1586. [ad. Sp. *carbonada*; see -ADO.] Fish, flesh, or fowl, scored across and broiled upon the coals. Often *transf.* –1687. var. **Carbona·de.**

Carbona·do, *v. arch.* 1596. [f. prec.] 1. To score across and broil or grill 1611. 2. *transf.* To cut, slash, hack 1596.

1. How she long'd to eate .. Toads carbonado'd *Wint. T.* IV. iv. 268. 2. *Lear* II. ii. 41. var. **Carbona·de** *v.*; whence **Carbona·ded** *ppl. a.*

‖**Carbonari** (karbǫnā·ri), *sb. pl.* 1823. [It.; pl. of *carbonaro* charcoal-burner (occ. also used).] The members of a secret political association formed in the kingdom of Naples early in the 19th c., with the design of introducing a republican government. Hence **Carbona·rism.**

Carbonate (kā·ɹbǒnět), *sb.* 1794. [a. F., ad. mod.L. *carbonatum*.] 1. *Chem.* A salt of carbonic acid. 2. *ellipt.* Ore containing a large proportion of carbonate of lead.

Carbonate (kā·ɹbǒne¹t), *v.* 1805. [f. prec.] 1. To CARBONIZE 1831. 2. *Chem.* To form into a carbonate; also, to aerate 1805. Hence **Carbona·tion**, formation of a carbonate; aeration.

Carbonated (kā·ɹbǒne¹tėd), *a.* 1797. [f. mod.L. *carbonatus*; see CARBON.] †Carbonized –1825; †CARBURETTED –1805; chemically combined or impregnated with carbonic acid 1803.

†**Carboned**, *ppl. a.* ? misprint for *carbonaded*. PEPYS.

Carbonic (kaɹbǫ·nik), *a.* 1791. [f. CARBON or L. *carbonem* + -IC.] 1. Of or pertaining to carbon; of or caused by carbonic acid gas. 2. Of coal; of the Carbonari (BYRON). Also *sb.*

C. acid, formerly known as *fixed air*, and now called **Carbon(ic dioxide** or **Carbonic anhydride**, CO_2, the gas which is formed in the ordinary combustion of carbon, disengaged from fermenting liquors, given out in the breathing of animals, and known as the choke-damp or foul air of mines, etc. This is still popularly called *c. acid gas*, but the name *C. acid* is applied in chemistry to the compound CH_2O_3 supposed to be formed when carbon dioxide comes in contact with water, of which the carbonates are the salts. **C. oxide** = *carbon monoxide*, CO.

Carboniferous (kāɹboni·fěrәs), *a.* 1799. [f. L. *carbonem* + -FER + -OUS.] Producing coal.

Applied in *Geol.* to the series of strata with which seams of coal are associated, the *C. System* or *Formation*, lying next above the Devonian, and including the Coal Measures, Millstone Grit, and Mountain Limestone; also to the rocks, fossils, etc., of this formation, and to the *C. Age*, *Era*, or *Period*, during which these strata were deposited, and the vegetation existed that formed the coal-beds.

Carbonify (kaɹbǫ·nifәi), *v.* 1803. [f. L. *carbonem* + -FY.] To CARBONIZE. Hence **Carbo:nifica·tion**, conversion into coal.

Carbonize (kā·ɹbonәiz), *v.* 1806. [f. CARBON + -IZE.] 1. To convert into mere carbon. 2. To CARBURET (*arch.*) 1808. 3. To cover with charcoal, lamp-black, etc. Hence **-iza·tion.**

Ca·rbon pa:per. 1895. Thin paper coated on one side with a preparation of lamp-black, used between two papers to make a duplicate copy of what is written on the upper sheet.

Carbonyl (kā·ɹbŏnil). 1869. [f. CARBON + -YL(E).] *Chem.* The divalent compound radical CO (*carbon monoxide*) considered as a constituent of urea, alloxan, creatin, etc.

Carborundum (kāɹbǒrʊ·ndǒm). 1893. [f. CARBO(N + CO)RUNDUM.] A crystalline compound of carbon and silicon used for polishing and scouring.

Carboxyl (kaɹbǫ·ksil). 1869. [f. CARBON + OX(YGEN) + -YL.] *Chem.* A name given to the monad group —CO.OH, contained in all the fatty acids; thus *Formic acid* is H—CO.OH.

Carboy (kā·ɹboi). 1753. [corrupt f. Pers. *qarābah*, 'a large flagon'.] A large globular bottle, of green or blue glass, covered with basket-work for protection, used chiefly for holding acids and other corrosive liquids.

Carbuncle (kā·ɹbʊŋk'l). [ME. *charbucle*, *-bocle*, a. OF., var. of *charbuncle*:—L. *carbunculus* small coal, carbuncle stone, red tumour, dim. of *carbo*; assim. later to the L. form.] 1. (Formerly **carbuncle-stone**): A name of various precious stones of a red or fiery colour; anciently of sapphires, spinels or rubies, and garnets; in mod. lapidary work of the garnet when cut *en cabochon*. 2. *Her.* A charge or bearing supposed to represent a carbuncle with its rays; = ESCARBUNCLE ME. 3. *Med.* An inflammatory, circumscribed, malignant tumour, caused by inflammation of the skin and cellular membrane. It differs from a boil in having no central core; an anthrax. Also, a red spot or pimple on the nose or face caused by drinking. 1530. Also *attrib.* Hence **Carbu·ncular** *a.* of, pertaining to, resembling, or characterized by carbuncles. **Carbu·nculous** *a.* of, full of, or of the nature of carbuncles.

Carbuncled (kā·ɹbʊŋk'ld), *ppl. a.* 1606. [f. prec.] 1. Adorned with carbuncles. 2. Affected with a carbuncle or carbuncles; spotted, pimpled; red like a carbuncle 1664. Also *transf.*

1. Carbunkled Like holy Phoebus Carre *Ant. & Cl.* IV. viii. 28. 2. C. and Tun-bellied *Tatler* No. 66.

†**Carbu:ncula·tion.** 1673. [ad. L. *carbunculationem*.] The blasting of the buds of trees or plants by excessive heat or cold –1755.

Carburet (kā·ɹbiŭret), *sb.* 1795. [f. CARBON + -URET, q. v.] *Chem.* = CARBIDE, q. v.

Ca·rburet, *v.* 1869. [f. prec.] *trans.* To combine chemically or impregnate with carbon.

Carburetted, -eted (kā·ɹbiŭretėd), *ppl. a.* 1802. [f. prec.] *Chem.* Combined or impregnated with carbon, as in *C. hydrogen*, the fire-damp of miners, and chief constituent of coal-gas.

Ca·rburettor, -etter. 1866. [f. as prec.] 1. An apparatus for passing hydrogen, coal-gas, or atmospheric air through or over a liquid hydrocarbon, so as to add illuminating power. b. The apparatus for mixing air with petrol vapour for combustion in motor engines 1896.

Carburize (kā·ɹbiŭrәiz), *v.* [f. F. *carbure* + -IZE.] *trans.* To combine with carbon or a carbon compound; used *esp.* of the process of imparting carbon to wrought iron in making cement steel; also = CARBURET *v.* Hence **Carburiza·tion.**

‖**Carcajou** (ka·ɹkaʒu). 1774. [N. American Fr.; app. of Indian origin.] 1. The Glutton or Wolverene (*Gulo luscus*). ¶ 2. Applied erron. to the American Badger, and by Charlevoix to the Canadian Lynx 1839.

Carcake (kā·ɹ,ke¹k). *Sc.* 1816. [First part as in CARE-SUNDAY.] A small cake baked with eggs, and eaten on Fastern's Een (Shrove Tuesday) in parts of Scotland.

†**Carcan.** 1534. [a. F., f. Teut.; cf. ON. *kverk*, in *kverka-* throat.] 1. An iron collar used for punishment –1777. 2. = next –1694.

Carcanet (kā·ɹkănet). *arch.* 1530. [dim. of prec.] A collar or necklace, usually of gold or jewelled (*arch.*) Also *transf.* and *fig.*

Carcass, carcase (kā·ɹkăs), *sb.* [Two types: α. ME. *carkoys*, *-cays*, *-keis*, a. Anglo-F. *carcois*, *carcas* = med.L. *carcosium*; β. 16th c. *carcasse*, a. Fr., ad. It. *carcassa*. Ult. deriv. unkn. Both forms are common.] 1. The dead body of man or beast; now used of the human corpse only in contempt. 2. A term of contempt or ridicule for the human body, dead or alive 1586. 3. *fig.* The lifeless shell or husk 1612. 4. *transf.* The skeleton of a vessel or edifice 1596. 5. *Mil.* An iron shell, filled with combustibles, and pierced with holes through which the flame blazes; fired from a mortar or gun to set fire to buildings, ships, etc. (Spelt *carcass*.) 1684.

1. The carkeise of Iezebel 2 *Kings* ix. 37. A c. of meat JEVONS. 2. To pamper his own carcass SOUTH. 3. The mere c. of nobility SHENSTONE. 5. Carcasses, bombs, and red-hot balls 1790. *Comb.* **c.-flooring, -roofing** (*Arch.*), the framework of timber which supports the boarding of the floor or roof (see 4). Hence **Ca·rcassed** *ppl. a.* †dead; having a c.

Ca·rcass, *v.* 1881. [f. prec. sb., sense 4.] *trans.* To put up the carcass of (a building).

Carcel (kā·ɹsěl). 1845. [name of inventor.] *Carcel lamp*, one in which the oil is pumped up to the wick by clockwork. Called also the *French lamp*.

†**Ca·rceral**, *a.* 1563. [ad. L. *carceralis*, f. *carcer*.] Of or belonging to a prison –1696.

Ca·rcerist. *nonce-wd.* [f. L. *carcer*.] One who advocates prisons. SYD. SMITH.

Carcinology (kāɹsinǫ·lǒdʒi). 1852. [f. Gr. *καρκίνος* crab.] *Zool.* That part of zoology which treats of crustaceans. Hence **Ca:rcinolo·gical** *a.*, **Carcino·logist.**

‖**Carcinoma** (kāɹsinōu·mă). Pl. **-mata.** 1721. [L., a. Gr. *καρκίνωμα*; cf. CANCER.] 1. *Med.* The disease CANCER. (By some restricted to indolent tumours, or to the early stages only of cancer.) †2. *Med.* A disease of the cornea –1753. Hence **Carcino·matous** *a.* characterized by, or of the nature of, c.

‖**Carcinosis** (kāɹsinōu·sis). 1866. [mod.L., f. Gr. *καρκίνος* crab, cancer.] *Med.* The production and development of cancer; also = CANCER.

‖**Carcoon** (kāɹkū·n). *Anglo-Ind.* Also **-koon.**

1803. [Mahrattī *kārkūn* clerk, a. Pers., f. *kār* business.] A clerk.

Card (kāɹd), *sb.*^{1} ME. [a. F. *carde* teasel-head, f. (ult.) L. *carduus* thistle.] **1.** An implement for raising a nap on cloth; *esp.* an iron instrument with teeth, or (later) a wire brush. **2.** A similar instrument used to part, comb out, and set in order the fibres of wool, hemp, etc.; now, a wire brush, consisting of a strip of leather or indiarubber, into which short steel wires are inserted ME. *Comb.* **c.-cloth,** the leather or indiarubber backing of a c.

Card (kāɹd), *sb.*^{2} ME. [repr. of F. *carte*, ad. It. *carta*:—L. *charta* (*carta*), ad. Gr. *χάρτης* papyrus leaf.] **1.** One of a pack of small oblong pieces of pasteboard now called more specifically *playing-cards.* (The earliest sense in Fr. and Eng.) †**2.** A map or plan; = CHART *sb.*^{1} –1650. **3.** The circular piece of stiff paper on which the 32 points of the compass are marked 1605. Also *fig.* **4.** *gen.* A flat piece of stiff paper or thin pasteboard, usually rectangular; used to write or draw upon or for other purposes 1610. **5.** *transf.* (*U.S.*) A published note, containing a short statement, request, explanation, or the like 1887. **6.** *Mech.* One of the perforated pasteboards or sheet metal plates in the Jacquard attachments to looms 1831. **7.** *slang* or *colloq.* '*The card*' = 'the correct thing', the TICKET, q. v. 1851.

1. *Playing-cards*: cards used in playing whist and other games. The whist pack consists of 4 suits, each of 13 cards, 10 of which bear respectively 1, 2, 3, etc. (up to 10) pips all of one form, and the remaining 3 have habited figures, 'King', 'Queen', and 'Knave', called COURT (i. e. *coat*) or *picture-cards.* Tell thy cardes, and then tell me what thou hast wonne 1562. *A house of cards* (fig.): any insecure scheme, etc. Phr. *To play cards* or *at cards.* *Sure c.*: an expedient or person sure to bring success. So *knowing, old, queer*, etc. *c.* *To play one's cards well, badly*, etc. *To throw up one's cards*: to abandon a project. *To show one's cards*: to reveal one's plans or strength. *On the cards*: liable to turn up. 2. *Haml.* v. ii. 114. 3. All the Quarters that they know I' th' Ship-mans C. *Macb.* I. iii. 17. Reason the c., but Passion is the gale POPE. *To speak by the c.*: to be exact to a point. *Haml.* v. i. 149. 4. In spec. uses: POST-CARD (in U.S. *postal c.*). So *correspondence-c.* A c. for a party 1876. *Visiting c.*; hence, *To leave a c. on.* *Wedding cards.* *Business c.* Also *birthday, Christmas*, etc. *cards*; *window-c., show-c., pattern-c., sample-c.*

Comb., etc.: **c.-case**; **-catalogue,** one in which each item is entered on a separate c.; so **c. index** (also as vb.); **-sharper** [SHARP *v.* 4, SHARPER 2], one who makes a trade of cheating at cards; so **-sharping**; **c. vote,** a vote in which each (trade union) delegate's vote counts as for his constituents.

†**Card,** *sb.*^{3} 1658. [a. F. *carde*, CHARD.] The central leaf-stalk of the artichoke.

Card (kāɹd), *v.*^{1} ME. [f. CARD *sb.*^{1}] **1.** *trans.* To prepare wool, tow, etc. for spinning by combing out and disentangling with a card. Also with *out*, and *absol.* Also *fig.* and *transf.* †**2.** To stir and mix with cards; to mix –1635. †**3.** To comb or cleanse (of impurities) 1612. **4.** To scratch or tear the flesh with a wool-card or the like, as a method of torture 1556. **5.** *Sc.* 'To scold sharply' (Jamieson).

1. Boþe to karde and to kembe LANGL. 2. You Tom Tapster..carde your beere..halfe smal & halfe strong GREEN. 4. Carded to death 1827.

Card (kāɹd), *v.*^{2} 1548. [f. CARD *sb.*^{2}] †**1.** *intr.* To play at cards; to play one's cards. **2.** *trans.* (*U. S.*) To send a message by post-card to. Cf. WIRE *v.* 1875. **3.** To fix on a card, as patterns 1884.

‖**Cardamine** (kaɹdæ·minī, kā·ɹdăməin). 1753. [mod.L., a. Gr. *καρδαμίνη*, f. *κάρδαμον* cress.] *Bot.* A genus of cruciferous plants, including the Lady-smock or Cuckoo-flower (*C. pratensis*); Meadow-cress.

Cardamom (kā·ɹdămŏm). 1553. [ad. L. *cardamomum*, a. Gr., f. *κάρδαμον* + *ἄμωμον* AMOMUM.] A spice consisting of the seed-capsules of species of *Amomum* and *Elettaria* (N.O. *Zinziberaceæ*), natives of the East Indies and China; used as a stomachic and a condiment. (Occas. the plant itself.) Also *attrib.*

Ca·rdboard. 1858. [f. CARD *sb.*^{2}] Pasteboard of the thickness of card, for cutting cards from, etc. Also *attrib.*

†**Ca·rdecu.** 1605. [a. F. *quart d'écu.*] An old French silver coin, worth ¼ of the gold *écu*, or 2*s.* 1½*d.* –1819.

‖**Cardel.** Also **kardel.** 1694. [ad. Du. *kardeel, quardeel.*]

Carder^1 (kā·ɹdəɹ). 1450. [f. CARD *v.*^{1} + -ER^1.] One who or that which cards wool, etc.

†**Ca·rder**^{2}. 1530. [f. CARD *v.*^{2} + -ER.] A card-player –1712.

‖**Ca·rdia.** 1782. [Gr.; 'heart'.] *Anat.* The upper or cardiac orifice of the stomach, where the œsophagus enters it.

Cardiac (kā·ɹdiæ̆k), *a.* (and *sb.*) 1601. [a. F. *cardiaque*, ad. L. *cardiacus*, a. Gr., f. prec.]

A. *adj.* **1.** Of or pertaining to the heart; var. **Ca·rdial.** **2.** Of medicines: Cordial 1661. **3.** Pertaining to or affected with disease of the heart 1748. **4.** *Anat.* Distinctive epithet of the CARDIA, q. v. 1843. **5.** Heart-shaped (in *cardiac wheel*) 1864.

1. The C. Nerves 1726, arteries 1835. C. action 1883. 3. C. symptoms KANE. var. †**Cardi·acal.**

B. *sb.* †**1.** An affection of the heart; ? = *cardiac passion*, cardialgia, heartburn –1483. **2.** A cordial. Also *fig.* 1746.

†**Cardiacle.** ME. [L. *cardiaca*; cf. *chronicle*, etc.] = *Cardiac passion* –1485.

Cardiagraphy, erron. f. *cardiography.*

Cardialgy (kā·ɹdi,ældʒi). 1655. [ad. mod. L. *cardialgia* (also used), a. Gr., f. *καρδία* + *ἄλγος.*] *Med.* The affection called 'heartburn' (because anciently referred to the heart), consisting of pain and a sensation of heat about the cardiac orifice of the stomach, often accompanying indigestion. Hence **Cardia·lgic** *a.*

Cardigan (kā·ɹdigăn). 1868. [f. the Earl of *Cardigan*, who fought in the Crimean war (1855).] A knitted woollen over-waistcoat, with or without sleeves.

Cardinal (kā·ɹdinăl), *a.* ME. [a. F., ad. L. *cardinalis*, f. *cardo, cardinem* hinge.] **1.** *gen.* On which something else hinges, fundamental; chief, principal. **2.** *Zool.* Pertaining to the hinge of a bivalve shell 1836. **3.** [f. CARDINAL *sb.*] Of the colour of a cardinal's cassock; deep scarlet 1879.

1. The cardinall grace, that on which all other graces move 1639. Four c. Angels 1650. In fig. uses: *C. virtues*: in scholastic philosophy, justice, prudence, temperance, and fortitude, the four chief 'natural' virtues; also used in the general sense (1). *C. numbers* (Arith.): the primitive numbers *one, two, three*, etc. as opp. to the ORDINAL numbers *first, second, third*, etc. *C. points*: **a.** the four intersections of the horizon with the meridian and the prime vertical; the north, south, east, and west points. *C. winds*: the four chief winds which blow from these points. **b.** Of the prime vertical: '*Astrol.* The rising and setting of the sun, the zenith and nadir' (Webster); = *cardines* (see CARDO). *C. veins* (Phys.): the venous trunks which transmit the blood in the early embryo from the vertebral column and the parietes of the trunk to the sinus venosus by means of the ducts of Cuvier. In R. C. Ch. *C. bishop, priest*, etc.: tr. L. *episcopus, presbyter*, etc. *cardinalis*; see CARDINAL *sb.* Hence **Ca·rdinally** *adv.* pre-eminently; *joc.* for *carnally* SHAKS.

Cardinal (kā·ɹdinăl), *sb.* OE. [prec. used absol., after late L. *cardinalis.*] **1.** One of the ecclesiastical princes (six cardinal bishops, fifty cardinal priests, and fourteen cardinal deacons) who constitute the pope's council, or the sacred college, and when the papal chair is vacant elect a pope from among themselves. **2.** A short cloak worn by ladies, orig. of scarlet cloth with a hood 1745. **3.** *slang.* Mulled red wine. **4.** In *pl.* = the adj. with a sb. pl., as cardinal points, winds, etc. ME.

1. b. Title of two of the minor canons of St. Paul's Cathedral, London 1748.

Comb. (in sense 1): **c.-bird, grosbeak,** a N. American singing-bird (*Cardinalis virginianus*) with scarlet plumage; **cardinal's hat,** the red hat worn by a c., taken for his dignity or office; **c. red,** the scarlet of a cardinal's robes. Hence **Ca·rdinalate,** the office or dignity of a c. **Ca·rdinali·sm,** the institution of cardinals. **Ca·rdinali·st,** a partisan of cardinals or of a c. (Now *Hist.*) †**Ca·rdinali·ze** *v.* to raise to the rank of a c.; *joc.* to make scarlet. **Ca·rdinalship,** the state, office, or tenure of a c.

Cardinal-flower. 1698. [From its colour.] *Bot.* The Scarlet Lobelia (*L. cardinalis*).

Cardines, pl. of CARDO.

Carding (kā·ɹdiŋ), *vbl. sb.* 1468. [f. CARD *v.*^{1} + -ING^1.] The action of CARD *v.*^{1}; *concr.* the carded product.

attrib. **c. engine, -machine,** a machine for combing wool or cotton, in which a small cylinder set with cards works in connexion with smaller cylinders and a hollow shell, also set with cards.

Cardio- (kā·ɹdi,o; with disyllabic endings kā·ɹdi,ǫ·), comb. f. Gr. *καρδία* heart:

Ca·rdiograph [Gr. -*γράφος*], an instrument which registers the motions of the heart by tracing a curve on paper, etc. So **Cardio·graphy.** **Cardio·logy** [Gr. -*λογία*], knowledge of, or a treatise on, the heart. **Cardio·meter** [Gr. -*μέτρον*], an instrument for measuring the force of the heart's action; also *fig.*; hence **-me·trical** *a.* **Cardio·metry** [Gr. -*μετρία*], the measurement of the size of the heart by percussion and auscultation. **Cardio·pathy** [Gr. -*παθία*], disease of the heart.

Cardioid (kā·ɹdi,oid). 1753. [ad. Gr. *καρδιοειδής* heart-shaped.] *Math.* A curve something like a heart in shape.

‖**Carditis** (kaɹdəi·tis). 1783. [mod.L., f. Gr. *καρδία* + -ITIS.] *Med.* Inflammation of the muscular substance of the heart.

‖**Cardo** (kā·ɹdo). Pl. **cardines** (kā·ɹdinīz). 1571. [L.] †**1.** *Astrol.* in *pl.* = CARDINAL *points* –1660. †**2.** *fig.* A hinge –1657. **3.** *Conch.* The hinge of a bivalve shell 1755.

Cardoon (kaɹdū·n). 1611. [a. 16th c. F. *cardon*, ad. It. *cardone*, augm. of *cardo* :—L. *cardus, carduus* thistle.] A composite plant (*Cynara Cardunculus*), nearly allied to the Artichoke; cultivated for the fleshy stalks of the inner leaves.

‖**Cardo·phagus.** Pl. **-gi.** [f. Gr. *κάρδος* thistle + -*φαγος.*] A thistle-eater, *i. e.* donkey. THACKERAY.

‖**Carduus** (kā·ɹdiu,ŏs). ME. [L.] Occ. used for *Carduus benedictus*; esp. *attrib.*

Care (kēᵊɹ), *sb.*^{1} [Com. Teut.: OE. *caru, cearu*:—OTeut. **karâ-*. (Not conn. w. L. *cura.*)] †**1.** Mental suffering –1718. **2.** Burdened state of mind arising from fear, doubt, or concern about anything; also in *pl.* anxieties, solicitudes OE. **3.** Serious mental attention; concern; caution, pains OE. *Hence*, Regard arising from desire or inclination *to* or *for* ME. **4.** Charge; oversight with a view to protection, preservation, or guidance ME. **5.** An object or matter of care 1590.

1. When one is passed another c. we have, Thus woe succeeds a woe HERRICK. 2. Fretting C., that kills a Cat 1682. 3. The busy c. of a noble man UDALL. If any c. for what is here Survive in spirits render'd free TENNYSON. 4. The c. of all the churches 2 *Cor.* xi. 28. Nemo, c. of Mr. Krook DICKENS. 5. Cares of state JOWETT. *Comb.* **c.-worn** *a.*

Care, *sb.*^{2} 1849. The Mountain Ash (*local*).

Care (kēᵊɹ), *v.* [Com. Teut.: OE. *carian* :—OTeut. **karôjan*, f. **karâ-* CARE *sb.*] †**1.** To sorrow –1530. **2.** To feel concern or interest OE.; to take care or thought 1593. **3.** In neg. and condit. const.: *Not to care* passes to 'not to mind, be indifferent', and hence 'be disposed *to*'. Const. *for*, etc. 1489. **4.** To have a regard or liking *for*, be inclined *to* 1530.

2. As for the Asses..c. not thou for them for they are founde 1 *Sam.* ix. 20. The Lorde careth for us *Ps.* xxxix. 17. 3. I don't c. what people say (*mod.*). *To c. a pin, a button, a straw, a rap*, etc. I don't c. if I go with you for once 1841. 4. He never cared to give money GOLDSM. People I c. for 1750.

Ca·re-cloth. *Hist.* 1530. [? = *carde-clothe* some fabric used for canopies, etc. PALSG.] A cloth held over (or placed upon) the heads of the bride and bridegroom as they knelt during the marriage-service.

Careen (kărī·n), *sb.* 1591. [a. F. *carène* fem., keel, as in *en carène.*] *Naut.* The position of a ship laid over on one side.

On the c.: turned over on one side for repairing, or by stress of weather, etc.

Careen (kărī·n), *v.* 1600. [? f. the sb., or (through Fr., Sp., or It.) f. L. *carina* keel.] *Naut.* **1.** *trans.* To turn (a ship) over on one side for cleaning, caulking, or repairing; to clean, caulk, etc. Also *absol.* and *fig.* **2.** *trans.* To cause (a ship) to heel over 1833. **3.** *intr.* To incline to one side or lie over when sailing on a wind (said of a ship) 1763. Hence **Caree·nage,** the expense of careening; a careening-place (cf. *anchorage*).

Career (kărīᵊ·ɹ), *sb.* 1534. [a. F. *carrière* :—late L. *carraria* (*via*), f. *carrus* wagon.] †**1.** A race-course; the space within the barrier at a tournament. Also *transf.* –1751. †**2.** Of a horse: A short gallop at full speed. Also a charge, encounter. -1764. Also *fig.* **3.** Hence, A (swift) running, course, as of the sun or a star through the heavens. *abstr.* Full speed, impetus. 1534. Also *fig.* **b.** *Hawking.* A flight of the bird 1727. **4.** A person's course or progress through life (or a distinct portion of life); so of a nation, a party, etc. (Now *esp.*) A profession affording opportunities of advancement. 1803.

2. Mortal combat or carreer with Lance MILT. *P. L.* I. 766. 3. The Sun in his carriere BARROW. *In full c. fig.* The careere of [a man's] humour *Much Ado* II. iii. 250. 4. A diplomatic c. 1803. A public c. 1815.

Career (kărīᵊ·ɹ), *v.* 1594. [See the sb.] †**1.** To take a short gallop; to charge; to turn this way and that in running (said of a horse) -1672. **2.** *transf.* and *fig.* To move at full speed 1647.

1. How we Tilt and C. 1672. **Caree·ringly** *adv.*

Carefree (kēᵊ·ɹfrī), *a.* 1854. Free from care.

Careful (kēᵊ·ɹfŭl), *a.* [OE. *carful, cearful,* f. *caru* care.] †**1.** Full of grief -1599. **2.** Full of care; anxious, concerned (*arch.*) OE. **3.** Full of care *for*, taking good care *of* OE. **4.** Applying care, attention, or pains to what one has to do; painstaking; circumspect OE. †**5.** On one's guard against, wary -1579. **6.** Of things: Fraught with sorrow or anxiety (*arch.*) ME.; done with care 1651.

1. A c. widow 1470. 2. Be not c. therefore for the morrovv (Rhem.) *Matt.* vi. 34. 3. My wife more carefull for the latter-borne *Com. Err.* I. i. 79. 4. A c. and learned antiquary 1845. 5. C. of new acquaintance STEELE. 6. A c. throne FORD, drawing 1883. Hence **Ca·reful-ly** *adv.*, **-ness.**

Careless (kēᵊ·ɹlės), *a.* [OE. *carlēas*; see CARE *sb.*] **1.** Free from care or apprehension. (Now *arch., poet.*, or *nonce-wd.*). **2.** Unconcerned; not solicitous, regardless; having no care *of, about,* †*to* OE. **3.** Not taking due care, negligent, thoughtless; inaccurate 1579. **4.** Of things: †Uncared for; artless, *négligé* (*arch.*); (now *esp.*) done, caused, or said heedlessly. Also as quasi-*adv.*

1. They dwelt carelesse *Judg.* xviii. 7. 2. Yet a Boy C. of books WORDSW. 3. C. writers BERKELEY, eyes WORDSW. 4. A carelesse Trifle *Macb.* I. iv. 11. To frame the c. rhyme BEATTIE. C. work (*mod.*). Hence **Ca·reless-ly** *adv.*, **-ness.**

†**Carene.** *rare.* 1647. [ad. med. L. *carena*, f. *quarantena* (Du Cange). Cf. QUARANTINE.] A forty days' fast; an indulgence from such a fast. ? var. †**Carentane.**

Caress (kăre·s), *sb.* 1647. [a. F. *caresse*, ad. It *carezza* :—late L. **caritia*, f. *carus.*] An action of endearment, a fondling touch, a blandishment. Also *fig.*

Solve high dispute With conjugal Caresses MILT. *P. L.* VIII. 56. *fig.* The caresses of faction HUME.

Caress (kăre·s), *v.* 1658. [a. F. *caresser*; see prec.] To treat affectionately or blandishingly, to touch, stroke, or pat endearingly; to fondle. Also *transf.* and *fig.* *absol.* 1683.

To c. a fawn 1870. *fig.* Its.. echoes c. the ear LOWELL. William was thus busy in half caressing, half coercing, his English subjects FREEMAN. Hence **Care·sser. Care·ssingly** *adv.* **Care·ssive** *a.*

Care·ssant, *a. rare.* 1861. [a. F.] Caressing.

Care Sunday. *Sc.* 1536. [Cf. Ger. *karfreitag*, and *karwoche.* OE. *caru*, CARE, trouble, grief.] The fifth Sunday in Lent.

Caret (kæ·rėt, kēᵊ·rėt). 1710. [L. *caret* (there) is wanting, f. *carere.*] A mark (‸) placed in writing below the line to indicate that something (written above or in the margin) has been omitted in that place.

Ca·re-ta·ker. 1858. [f. CARE *sb.* + TAKER.] One put in charge of any thing or person; *esp.* in Ireland, of an 'evicted farm'.

‖**Carex** (kēᵊ·rėks). Pl. **carices** (-isīz). ME. [L.] *Bot.* A large genus, N.O. *Cyperaceæ*, of grassy-looking plants; a sedge.

Carf. *Obs.* or *dial.* [OE *cyrf* (ME. *kyrf, kerfe*), repr. OTeut. *kurbjô-* from ablaut stem of CARVE *v.*] **1.** Cutting, a cut. †**2.** ? The cut part at the end of a piece of wood -1799.

Carf, obs. pa. t. of CARVE *v.*

Carfax, -fox (kā·ɹfæks, -fǫks). [ME. *carfuks, -fouk*, repr. *carreforc(s, -four* :—L. *quadrifurcus* four-forked.] **1.** A place where four (or more) roads meet. **2.** Hence, the proper name of such a place, *e.g.* at Oxford 1527.

Ca·rfour, carrefour. 1477. [a. F. *carrefour*: cf. prec.] = prec. (Now only as Fr.)

‖**Ca·rga.** 1622. [Sp. *carga*, f. late L. *caricare* to load; see CHARGE, CARGO.] A 'load' as a measure of weight.

†**Ca·rgason, -azon.** 1583. [a. Sp., double augm. of prec.] **1.** A cargo. Also *fig.* -1882. **2.** A bill of lading. [So F. *cargaison.*] 1599.

Cargo¹ (kā·ɹgo). Pl. **cargoes.** 1657. [a. Sp. *cargo*, or *carga*; see CHARGE.] The freight or lading of a ship; a shipload. Also *transf.*

A very rich c. DE FOE. A c. of novels 1806.

†**Ca·rgo²**. 1602. [perh. f. Sp. *cargo, carga.*] **1.** A contemptuous term for a person. B. JONS. **2.** An exclam. -1615.

Ca·rgoose. 1677. [app. f. CARR *sb.²*: cf. *carr swallow.*] The Crested Grebe.

†**Cargued, carged,** *a.* 1580. [?; cf. F. *carguer* to charge.] *Naut.* In *High-cargued* or *-carged*, var. *high-charged*=*high-carved* -1591.

Carib (kæ·rib). In 6 pl. **caribeis, caribes, caribes.** 1555. [a. Sp. *caribe*; see CANNIBAL.] One of the native race which occupied the southern islands of the West Indies at their discovery: in early use often connoting *cannibal*. Hence **Ca·ribal** *a.* (after *cannibal*). **Caribbe·an** *a.* and *sb.* used of certain of the West Indian islands, and of the sea between them and the mainland. var. **Caribee·.**

Caribou, -boo (kæribū·). 1774. [Canadian F.] The North-American Reindeer.

Caricature (kæ·rikătiūᵊ·ɹ), *sb.* 1748. [a. F., ad. It. *caricatura* (formerly used), f. *caricare* to load. The stress is often still on *u*, esp. in the verb.] **1.** In *Art.* Grotesque or ludicrous representation by exaggeration of parts, as in a portrait, etc. Also *transf.* **2.** An exaggerated or debased likeness, or copy, naturally or unintentionally ludicrous 1767. Also *attrib.*

2. A c. of French cookery W. IRVING. The monkey, the c. of our species SMILES.

Caricature (see prec.), *v.* 1749. [f. the sb.] *trans.* To represent in caricature; to make a grotesque likeness of 1762. *transf.* and *fig.* To burlesque 1749

He could draw an ill face or c. a good one LYTTELTON. Hence **Ca·ricatu·rish** *a.* **Ca·ricatu·rist.**

Carices, pl. of CAREX.

Caricous (kæ·rikəs), *a.* [f. L. *carica* a kind of dry fig.] Resembling a fig, as *c. tumour.*

Caries (kēᵊ·ri,īz). 1634. [L.] **a.** *Pathol.* Decay of the bones or teeth. **b.** *Bot.* Decay of vegetable tissue.

‖**Carillon** (ka·rīlʸoṅ, -īlyoṅ). 1803. [Fr.; f. 'med.L. *quadrilionem* a quaternary' (of bells) Littré.] **1.** A set of bells so hung and arranged as to be played upon either by hand or by machinery 1836. **2.** A melody played on the bells 1803. **3.** An instrument imitating a peal of bells 1819. Hence ‖**Carilloneu·r.** [Fr.]

‖**Carina** (kărəi·nă). 1704. [L.] *Zool.* and *Bot.* A name of structures of the form of a keel; *esp.* the two petals forming the base of a papilionaceous corolla; also, the median ridge on the sternum of birds. Hence **Cari·nal** *a.* pertaining to the c.

‖**Carinaria** (kærinēᵊ·riă). 1847. [f. L. *carina.*] *Zool.* A genus of Heteropodous Molluscs, having a delicate shell of glassy translucency which protects the heart and liver.

Carinate (kæ·rinēᵗt), *a.* 1781. [ad. L. *carinatus.*] *Zool.* and *Bot.* Furnished with a CARINA or ridge; keeled.

Carinate (kæ·rineⁱt), *v.* 1698. [f. L. *carinat-, carinare*, f. *carina.*] To furnish with a carina, keel, or central ridge. Hence **Ca·rinated** *ppl. a.* =prec. **Carina·tion,** a keel-like formation.

Cariosity (kæri,ǫ·sĭti). 1638. [ad. mod.L. *cariositatem*, f. *cariosus.*] *Pathol.* A carious condition, or formation.

Carious (kēᵊ·riəs), *a.* 1530. [ad. F. *carieux.*] *Pathol.* Of bones, teeth, etc.: Affected with caries. Also *transf.* Hence **Cariousness.**

†**Ca·rity.** 1530. [ad. L. *caritas.*] Dearness -1656.

Cark (kāɹk), *sb.* *Obs.* or *arch.* ME. [a. AF. *karke, kark*, a north. F. form of *carche, charche*; see next.] †**1.** (?) A load (of 3 or 4 cwt.) -1550. †**2.** Charge, responsibility -1580. **3.** A burden of anxiety; anxious solicitude, labour, or toil. (Usu. w. *care.*) ME. †**4.** Care, pains -1603.

3. He woundeth himselfe with his greedy carke 1639.

Cark (kāɹk), *v.* *Obs.* or *arch.* [ME. *carken* repr. ONF. *carkier* :—late L. *carcare*, contr. f. *carricare* to load.] †**1.** *trans.* To burden; *also*, to charge. ME. only. **2.** To burden *with care*; to harass, trouble (*arch.*) ME. **3.** *intr.* To be anxious, fret oneself; to labour anxiously (*arch.*) ME. †**4.** To take thought -1603.

2. Thee nor carketh care nor slander TENNYSON. 3. A covetous man..carking about his bags BARROW.

Carl, carle (kāɹl), *sb.¹* OE. [a. ON. *karl* man, male, etc.; see also CHURL.] **1.** A man of the common people, particularly a husbandman; †a villain. **2.** Hence, a base fellow, a churl ME. *Sc.* A niggard 1542. **3.** = Fellow. *Sc.* 1550. **4.** The female or seed-bearing hemp plant; also called *Carl hemp.* [f. CARL 'male', by a popular error.] 1523. Also *attrib.*

1. A stout carl for the nones CHAUCER. 2. A crossgrained carle 1882. Hence **Ca·rlish** *a.*; **-ness.**

Carl, *sb.²* *dial.* 1688. [cf. CARL *v.²*] **1.** =CARLING². 1875. **2. Carl Sunday**=Carling or Care Sunday.

Carl, *v.¹* 1602. [? f. CARL *sb.¹*] *intr.* (?) To To behave like a carl; to snarl. Still *dial.*

Carl, *v.²* *dial.* 1611. [? back-formation from CARLING².] To parch (peas); to bristle.

†**Ca·rlin.** Also **carline.** 1705. [a. F., ad. It. *carlino*, f. *Carlo* Charles, *esp.* CARLO I, 1266.] A silver coin current in Naples and Sicily, worth four-pence English, or, later, twopence -1818.

Carline¹, -ing (kā·ɹlin). ME. [a. ON. *kerling*, fem. of *karl.*] A woman, *esp.* an old one; particularly a witch.

Carline² (kā·ɹlin). 1578. [a. F. *carline*, Sp., It., and med.L. *carlina*, said to be for *Carolina*, from Carolus Magnus (Charlemagne), to whom it was revealed as a remedy for pestilence.] A genus of Composite plants, allied to the thistles, whence called Carline Thistle.

Carling¹, carline (kā·ɹliŋ, -lin). 1611. [? Cf. F. *carlingue.*] **1.** *Naut.* One of the pieces of timber about 5 inches square in section, lying fore and aft under the deck of a ship, with their ends let into the beams. **2. Carling-knee**: a piece of timber lying transversely from the ship's side to the hatchway, serving to support the deck between the two 1626.

Carling² (kā·ɹliŋ). 1562. [? f. *care* in CARE-SUNDAY.] Peas parched, or otherwise prepared, for eating on C. or Care Sunday. *Carling Sunday*: =CARE SUNDAY.

Carlism (kā·ɹliz'm). 1830. [a. F. *carlisme*, f. *Carlos* Charles.] Attachment to Don Carlos, second son of Charles IV of Spain, and his heirs; Spanish legitimism. So **Carlist** *sb.* and *a.*

Carlock (kā·ɹlǫk). 1768. [a. Russ. *karlúk* isinglass.] Isinglass from the bladder of the sturgeon, imported from Russia. (Dicts.)

†**Ca·rlot.** [f. CARL *sb.¹*] A churl, peasant. *A. Y. L.* III. v. 108.

Carlovingian (kāɹlovi·ndʒiăn), *a.* 1781. [ad. F. *carlovingien*, for *carlingian.*] Belonging to the dynasty of kings founded by Carl the Great (Charlemagne).

Carlylism (kaɹləi·liz'm). 1841. [f. Thomas *Carlyle.*] The literary manner or teachings of Carlyle; a mannerism of Carlyle. So **Carly·lean** *a.* and *sb.* **Carly·lese,** the style of Carlyle.

‖**Carmagnole** (karmanʸo·l). 1796. [Fr.] **1.** A popular song and dance of the time of the French Revolution 1827. **2.** A nickname for a French soldier of that time; applied by Burns to Satan 1796. **3.** A bombastic report from the French revolutionary army 1860.

2. That curst c., auld Satan BURNS.

Carman¹ (kā·ɹmæ̆n). 1580. [f. CAR *sb.*] A man who drives a car; a carter, carrier.

†**Ca·rman²**. OE. [a. ON. *karmann*, var. of *karlmann.*] A man, an adult male -ME.

Carmelite (kā·ɹmĕləit), *sb.* and *a.* 1500. [a. F. :—L. *Carmelites, -a* inhabitant of Carmel.] **1.** A member of an order of mendicant friars founded on Mount Carmel in the 12th century; a *White Friar.* Also as *adj.* **2.** A fine woollen stuff; perh. = Fr. *carmeline* 'wool of the *vicugna*' (Littré) 1828. vars. †**Carme,** †**Ca·rmelin,** †**Ca·rmelitan.** Hence **Ca·rmeli·tess,** a female C.

†**Ca·rminate,** *v.* 1601. [f. L. *carminat-, carminare*, f. *carmen* a card for wool. Cf. CAR-

MINATIVE.] Of medicines: To expel (wind) from the stomach or bowels -1655.

Carminative (kā·mineitiv). 1655. [f. as prec.] *adj.* Of medicines, etc.: Having the quality of expelling wind; *orig.*, of making 'grosse humors fine and thin' (Florio). *sb.* [sc. *medicine* or *agent.*] 1671.

Carmine (kā·min). 1712. [a. F. or Sp., in med.L. *carminus*, contr. f. *carmesīnus*, f. (ult.) *qirmiz*, KERMES, ALKERMES, the scarlet grain insect.] 1. A beautiful red or crimson pigment obtained from cochineal. *Chem.* = *Carminic acid*. 2. *transf.* As the name of a colour 1799. Also as *adj.* Hence **Carmi·nic** (*Chem.*), in *C. acid*: the colouring matter of cochineal.

†**Carmot.** 1851. *Alch.* The substance of which the philosopher's stone was supposed to consist. (Dicts)

‖**Carnac** (kā·næk). *rare.* 1704. [? Indian.] The driver of an elephant, a mahout.

Carnage (kā·medʒ). 1600. [a. F., ad. It. *carnaggio* :—late L. *carnaticum* flesh-meat.] 1. Carcases collectively; *esp.* of men slain in battle. ? *Obs.* 1667. 2. The slaughter of a great number, *esp.* of men; butchery, massacre 1600. Also personified.

1. The future c. of the fight GAY. 2. Such as delight only in c. and bloudshed HOLLAND. Yea, c. is Thy daughter WORDSW.

†**Carnal,** *sb.* 1528. Perversion of *cardinal* -1598.

Carnal (kā·năl), *a.* ME. [ad. L. *carnalis* fleshly; cf. CHARNEL.] †1. Bodily, corporeal -1847; related 'according to the flesh' -1598. 2. Pertaining to the body; fleshly, sensual; sexual ME. 3. Not spiritual (*arch.*) 1483. †4. Carnivorous; *fig.* bloody SHAKS. Also in *comb.*

1. C. interment SIR T. BROWNE. His c. mother 1509. 2. Blynded with sensualite & carnall pleasure 1526. C. desire MILT. 3. To minister vnto them in carnall things *Rom.* xv. 27. Doubt And c. fear MILT. *P. L.* XI. 212. Hence †**Ca·rnal** *v.* (*rare*) to make c.; *intr.* to have c. intercourse *with*. **Ca·rnalism,** the practice of what is c. (*rare*). †**Ca·rnalist,** a fleshly-minded man; var. †**Ca·rnalite.** **Ca·rnally** *adv.* **Ca·rnalness.**

Carnality (kanæ·liti). ME. [ad. L. *carnalitas.*] 1. Fleshiness. 2. Sensuality; carnal intercourse ME. 3. Unspirituality; *concr.* a carnal thing, etc. 1483.

2. To give up oneself to lewd c. BAXTER. The carnalitie of the lawe UDALL.

Carnalize (kā·năləiz), *v.* 1685. [f. CARNAL *a.*] To make carnal; to rob of spirituality.

Ca·rnallite. 1876. [f. Von *Carnall*, a Prussian.] *Min.* A hydrous chloride of potassium and magnesium, occurring in the salt mines in Prussia and Persia.

†**Carnary** (kā·nări). 1538. [ad. med.L. *carnarium* adj. neut., used subst. In F. *charnier.*] A charnel-house.

Carnassial (kanæ·siăl), *a.* (*sb.*) 1849. [f. F. *carnassier* carnivorous, f. L. **carnaceus*, f. *carnem* + -AL.] *Anat. adj.* Relating to flesh eating: used of certain teeth. *sb.* A carnassial tooth.

†**Carna·tion**[1]. ME. [a. OF.] = Incarnation -1710.

Carnation[2] (kanē·ʃən). 1535. [ad. L. *carnationem*, f. *carnem*; cf. F. *carnation.*]

A. *sb.* 1. †Flesh-colour; a light rosy pink, or occas. crimson. 2. *pl.* 'Flesh tints' in a painting 1704. 3. A variety of cherry 1664.

1. Her complexion of the most delicate c. LYTTON. Hence **Carna·tioned** *a.* †flesh-coloured; reddened.

B. *adj.* [The sb. used attrib.] Flesh-coloured; rose-pink 1565.

Carnation[3] (kanē·ʃən). 1538. [? corruption of *coronation*, or aphet. f. *incarnation.*] *Bot.* Name for the cultivated varieties of the Clove-pink (*Dianthus caryophyllus*).

Carnations, and streak'd Gilly-vors *Wint. T.* IV. iv. 82.

†**Ca·rnel.** ME. only. [a. ONF., var. of *kernel*, in OF. *crenel*; see KERNEL.] Battlement, embrasure. Hence †**Carneled** *a.*

Carnelian (kanī·liăn). 1695. [var. of CORNELIAN, after L. *carnem.*] CORNELIAN; a flesh-coloured, deep red, or reddish-white variety of Chalcedony. var. †**Ca·rneol.**

Carneous (kā·nĭəs), *a.* 1578. [f. L. *carneus* + -OUS.] 1. Consisting of flesh, fleshy. †2. Flesh-coloured, pale red 1679.

Carney, *sb.* ? *Obs.* 1678. [?] A disease in horses in which the mouth becomes furred so that they cannot eat.

‖**Carnifex** (kā·nifeks). Now *Hist.* 1521. [L.; in ancient L. 'executioner', but in med. L. often 'butcher'.] An executioner. Hence **Carnifi·cial** *a.* belonging to an executioner, or to a butcher.

Carnification (kā:nifikē·ʃən). 1734. [f. CARNIFY.] †1. The formation of flesh. 2. The act or process of conversion into flesh 1758.

2. *C. of the lung* 1881. The miracle of c. 1827.

Carnify (kā·nifəi), *v.* 1639. [On type of F. **carnifier*, L. *carnificare*, f. *carnem* + *facere.*] 1. To convert into flesh; (*intr.*) to become like flesh. 1643. †2. To generate flesh -1829.

Carnival (kā·nivăl). 1549. [a. It. *carnevale*, conn. w. med.L. *carnelevarium*, etc., originating in a L. **carnem levare* 'the putting away of flesh (as food)'. The connexion with L. *vale*, as if 'farewell to flesh', is due to pop. etym.] 1. The week (*orig.* the day) before Lent, devoted in Italy and other Roman Catholic countries to revelry and riotous amusement, Shrove-tide; the festivity of this season. 2. *fig.* Any season or course of feasting or riotous revelry 1598.

1. *attrib.* In their Carnoual time (which we call shroftide) 1549. BYRON *Beppo* vi. 2. A c. of intellect without faith LOWELL. Hence **Ca:rnivale·sque** *a.* of the style of the c.

‖**Carnivora** (kani·vŏră), *sb. pl.* 1830. [L. *carnivora* (sc. *animalia*); see CARNIVOROUS.] *Zool.* A large order of flesh-eating Mammalia, including the feline, canine, and ursine families. (For a sing., see CARNIVORE.) Also, occ. applied to other animals, as beetles, etc.

Ca:rnivora·city. Appetite for flesh. POPE.

Carnivore (kā·nivōə). 1854. [a. F.] One of the CARNIVORA. Also, a carnivorous plant.

Carnivorous (kani·vŏrəs), *a.* 1646. [f. L. *carnivorus* (f. *carni-* + *-vorus*) + -OUS.] Feeding on flesh; applied: (*Zool.*) to animals which naturally prey on other animals (*esp.* to the CARNIVORA); (*Bot.*) to plants which absorb animal substances as food; and (*Med.*) to caustics as destructive of flesh.

Carno·se, *a.* 1562. [ad. L. *carnosus.*] = CARNOUS.

Carnosity (kanǫ·sĭti). 1533. [a. F. *carnosité*, f. L. *carnosus*; see -ITY.] †1. Fleshiness; pulpiness; flesh or pulp -1657. 2. A morbid fleshy growth, a caruncle 1559. Also †*fig.*

1. The c. of an olive HOLLAND, of an apple 1657. 2. A c. in the bladder 1618. *fig.* [Consciences] overgrown with a c. SPELMAN.

Carnoso- (kanōu·so), comb. form of L. *carnosus*, = 'carnose and ..'.

Carnous (kā·nəs), *a.* 1577. [ad. L. *carnosus*; see -OUS.] 1. Consisting of or abounding in flesh; fleshy. 2. Of fruits, roots, etc.: Pulpy, fleshy 1601.

1. A fair and c. state of Body SIR T. BROWNE.

Carny, carney (kā·ni), *v. dial.* and *colloq.* 1811. [?] To act in a wheedling or coaxing manner. Also *trans.*

Carob (kæ·rǫ̆b). 1548. [a. F. *carobe*, *carrobe*, a. Arab. (*al*) *kharrūbah* 'bean-pods, carobs'.] The fruit of an evergreen leguminous tree (*Ceratonia siliqua*), Carob-tree, a native of the Levant: a long flat horn-like pod containing numerous hard seeds embedded in pulp. Also called *carob-bean*, *-pod*. Also, the tree 1548.

Supposed to be the husks of *Luke* xv. 16; and the locusts eaten by the Baptist, whence called *Locust-pods* and *St. John's Bread.*

Caro·che, *sb. arch.* 1591. [a. 16th c. F. *carroche*, ad. It. *carroccio*, *-ia*, augm. of *carro* :—L. *carrus*; see CAR.] The 17th c. name of a coach representing the modern carriage for town use. Now *Hist.* Hence †**Caro·che** *v.* to ride or convey in a c. **Caro·ched** *ppl. a.* seated in a c.

Caroigne, obs. f. CARRION.

Carol (kæ·rəl), *sb.* ME. [a. OF. *carole*; ? conn. w. Gr.-L. *chorus*, or L. *corolla*. The Celtic forms are from Eng. and Fr.] 1. A ring-dance with song. Hence 2. A song; now usually one of a joyous strain ME. 3. A song or hymn of joy; *esp.* a Christmas *carol* 1502. †4. A ring, *e.g.* of standing stones -1470. †5. An enclosure or study in a cloister (? hence *c.-window*) -1810.

1. Faire is carole of maide gent ME. 2. The whiles the maydens doe theyr carroll sing SPENSER. The fife-like c. of the lark CAMPBELL. 3. Holly carolles SURREY. MILT. *P. L.* XII. 367.

Carol (kæ·rŏl, -əl), *v.* ME. [a. OF. *caroler*; see prec. The deriv. forms are usually spelt with *ll* (*carolled*, etc.) for no good reason.] †1. *intr.* To dance in a ring and sing -1530. Hence 2. To sing; now usu.: To sing a lively or joyous song ME. 3. *trans.* To sing; to celebrate in song 1575.

2. And c. lowd of love, and loves delight P. FLETCHER. Merrily merrily c. the gales TENNYSON. 3. To carroll out this roundelay GREENE. The shepherds .. C. her goodness loud in rustic lays MILT. *Comus* 849. Hence **Ca·roler, -oller.** †**Ca·rolet,** a little c.

‖**Carolin** (kæ·rǒlin). 1821. [f. L. *Carolus* Charles.] A gold coin formerly current in Bavaria and Würtemberg, and worth about 20*s.* sterling.

Carolina (kærǒləi·nă). 1734. The name (after Charles II) of a N. American colony; hence used in **Carolina Pink,** *Spigelia Marilandica*, also called Indian Pink. Hence **Caroli·nian** *a.* belonging to North or South C.

Ca·roline, *sb.* 1555. [See CAROLIN, CARLIN.] A name of various coins.

Caroline (kæ·rǒləin), *a.* 1652. [f. *Carolus.*] Of or pertaining to Charles; *e.g.* to Charles the Great, or to Charles I and II of England and their period.

Caroli·ngian, *a.* = CARLOVINGIAN.

Caroli·tic, *a. Arch.* Erron. f. COROLLITIC.

Carolus (kæ·rǒlǒs). 1687. [f. *Carolus*, Latinized form of Karl, Charles.] A gold piece struck in the reign of Charles I; worth orig. 20*s.*, later 23*s.*

Carom, carrom (kæ·rəm). 1779. Abbrev. f. CARAMBOLE; now corrupted to CANNON.

Caromel, var. of CARAMEL.

†**Caroo·n, carroo·n, caroo·me.** 1720. [? f. CAR, or F. *carre.*] 'A licence by the Lord Mayor of London to keep a cart' (Wharton) -1832.

†**Caro·sse.** 1598. [a. F. *carosse* (now *carrosse*), ad. It. *carozza*, augm. of *carro.*] A CAROCHE -1657.

‖**Carotee·l, -e·l.** 1704. [? ad. Arab.] A tierce or cask for dried fruit, etc. averaging about 7 cwt.

Carotic (kărǫ·tik), *a.* 1656. [ad. Gr. καρωτικός, f. καροῦν to stupefy.] *Phys.* 1. Having power to stupefy; of the nature of or pertaining to stupor or carus 1684. 2. = CAROTID (*rare*).

1. C. sleep 1881. 2. C. Arteries 1656, blood 1843.

Carotid (kărǫ·tid). 1667. [ad. Gr. καρωτίδες, f. καροῦν to stupefy, because compression of these arteries produces stupor (Galen).]

A. *adj.* Epithet of the two great arteries of the neck, which supply blood to the head. b. Pertaining to or adjoining the carotid arteries 1842. var. †**Caro·tidal, Caroti·dian.**

B. *sb.* A carotid artery 1741.

Carou·ba. A var. of CAROB (tree).

Carousal (kărau·zăl). 1765. [f. CAROUSE *v.*, perh. through *carousel.*] A fit of carousing, a carouse; a drunken revel.

The swains were preparing for a c. STERNE.

†**Carou·se,** *adv.* 1567. [a. Ger. *gar aus* (*trinken*). Cf. ALL OUT.] (*To drink, quaff*, etc.) to the bottom, a full bumper -1667.

Carouse (kărau·z), *sb.* 1559. [The prec. adv. taken for obj. of the vb.] †1. The act or fashion of 'drinking carouse' -1611. †2. A full bumper, a toast -1813. 3. A drinking bout 1690.

2. Quaffe Carowses to our Mistresse health *Tam. Shr.* I. ii. 277. 3. The early feast and late c. POPE

Carouse (kărau·z), *v.* 1567. [f. CAROUSE *adv.*] *intr.* To drink 'all out', drink freely and often; to drink a bumper *to*. Also †*trans.*

Some..garoused of his wine till they were reasonable pleasant RALEIGH. Hence **Carou·ser.**

Carousel (karuze·l). Also **carrousel.** 1650. [a. F. *carrousel*, ad. It. *carosello*, *garosello*, prob. dim. of *carro* chariot.] A tournament in which knights, in companies, variously dressed, engaged in plays, exercises, chariot races, etc. ¶By many erron. identified with *carousal.*

Carp (kāɹp), *sb.* ME. [a. OF. *carpe* :—late L. *carpa*, of unkn. source.] 1. A freshwater fish, *Cyprinus carpio*, the type of the family *Cyprinidæ*; commonly bred in ponds. 2. Applied to other species of the genus, as the Gold and Silver Fish, etc. 1786.

1. The C...a stately, a good, and a very subtle fish WALTON.

Carp (kāɹp), *v.* ME. [? partly a. ON. *karpa* to brag; in later senses f. or affected by L. *carpere.*] †1. To speak (*trans.* and *intr.*) –1605. †2. *intr.* To sing or recite –1802. †3. To prate, chatter –1557. 4. *spec.* To talk querulously, censoriously, or captiously; to find fault, cavil. (The current sense.) 1548. Also with *at.* †5. To take exception to –1678. ¶Assoc. w. CARK.

4. The king..carpeth upon the marriage DIGGES. To c. at a great writer M. ARNOLD. Hence **Ca·rper.**

Carpal (kā·ɹpăl), *a.* 1743. [ad. mod.L. *carpalis*, f. *carpus.*] *Anat.* Of or pertaining to the carpus or wrist. *sb. pl.* = Carpal bones 1855.

Carpel (kā·ɹpĕl). 1835. [f. Gr. καρπός, after mod.L. dim. **carpellum*; cf. F. *carpelle.*] *Bot.* One of the cells of a compound pistil or fruit; or the single cell of a simple pistil or fruit. Hence **Ca·rpellary** *a.* pertaining to, or of the nature of, a c. var. **Ca·rpid.**

Carpent (kā·ɹpĕnt), *v. rare.* 1623. [ad. med. L. *carpentare*; cf. F. *charpenter.*] To make as a carpenter; also *fig.* Hence †**Ca·rpentage,** carpentry.

Carpenter (kā·ɹpĕntəɹ), *sb.* ME. [a. Anglo Fr. *carpenter* (F. *charpentier*):—late L. *carpentarius*, f. *carpentum*; ? conn. (ult.) w. OCelt. **carrom*; see CAR.] 1. 'An artificer in wood' (J.); one who does the framework of houses, ships, etc., as opp. to a joiner, cabinet-maker, etc. 2. = *c.-ant, -bee*, etc. 1883.

1. Is not this the c., the sonne of Mary *Mark* vi. 3. *Comb.*, etc.: **c.-ant,** a species of tree-ant which bores into the trunk of a tree; **-bee,** a genus of solitary bees, *Xylocopa*, the females of which excavate cells in decaying wood in which to deposit their eggs; *carpenter's measure*, tonnage as measured by the cubic foot. Hence **Ca·rpentership,** the art of a c.

Ca·rpenter, *v.* 1815. [f. prec.] To do carpenter's work; to make by carpentry; to put together mechanically.

Carpentry (kā·ɹpĕntri). ME. [a. ONF. *carpenterie* (F. *charpenterie*):—L. *carpentaria* (sc. *fabrica*) carriage-maker's workshop.] 1. The trade or art of cutting, working, and joining timber into structures. 2. Timber-work constructed by the carpenter; *e.g.* the pieces of a roof, floor, centre, etc. 1555. Also *attrib.*

Carpet (kā·ɹpėt), *sb.* [ME. *carpete, carpette*, f. (through F. or med.L.) It. *carpetta* 'a carpet for a table' (Florio). Cf. F. *charpie.*] †1. A thick fabric, commonly of wool, used to cover tables, beds, etc.; a table-cloth –1728. 2. A similar fabric, generally worked in a pattern of divers colours, used to spread on a floor or the ground, or (now usually) to cover a floor or stair. Also the material. ME. 3. *fig.* A covering resembling a carpet in smoothness, softness, or colouring 1593. 4. = *c.-moth* 1856.

1. A C. for the Communion Table 1702. *On the c.*: under consideration. 2. No Persian carpets spread th' imperial way DRYDEN. †*Knight of the c.*: one dubbed in time of peace upon the c., as opp. to one dubbed in the field; also = CARPET-KNIGHT. 3. Vpon the Grassie C. of this Plaine *Rich. II*, III. iii. 50.

Comb., etc. **c.-dance,** an informal dance for which the c. is not taken up; **-moth,** a name for species of Geometer moths, from their variegated colouring; **-snake,** a large Australian snake (*Morelia variegata*); **-sweeper,** a mechanical apparatus for sweeping a carpet. Also CARPET-KNIGHT (q.v.), and the like, in which *carpet* implies haunting the boudoir, dilettantism, etc. Hence **Ca·rpetless** *a.*

Carpet (kā·ɹpėt), *v.* 1626. [f. the sb.] 1. To cover or spread with or as with a carpet. 2. *colloq.* To call into a room to be reprimanded 1840.

1. A fair Chamber..carpeted under Foot BACON. 2. They had done nothing! Why were they carpeted? 1840.

Ca·rpet-ba·g. 1844. A travelling bag, properly one made of carpet. Also *attrib.*

Ca·rpet-bagger. orig. *U.S. slang.* 1868. [f. prec.] A scornful appellation for Northerners who went south after the American Civil War of 1861–5, seeking private gain or political advancement; a political candidate in a locality with which he is unconnected. Hence **-bagging.**

Carpeting (kā·ɹpėtiŋ), *sb.* 1806. [f. CARPET *sb.* or *v.* + -ING[1].] 1. The action of covering (as) with carpet. 2. Material for carpets 1806. Also *transf.*

Ca·rpet-kni·ght. 1576. Orig., perh. = *Knight of the carpet*; but, usually, a contemptuous term for a stay-at-home soldier.

Brave C. Knights in Cupid's fights D'URFEY.

Carpholite (ka·ɹfŏləit). 1844. [Ger. *karpholith*, f. Gr. κάρφος a straw + λίθος.] *Min.* A hydrous silicate of alumina and manganese, occurring in silky fibres of a straw-yellow colour.

Carphology (kaɹfǫ·lŏdʒi). 1851. [ad. Gr. καρφολογία (Galen), f. κάρφος + λέγειν to collect.] *Med.* The movements of delirious patients, as if searching for imaginary objects, or picking the bed-clothes; floccilation.

Carpo-[1], comb. f. Gr. καρπός, CARPUS, wrist.

Carpo-[2], comb. f. Gr. καρπός fruit, as in: **Ca·rpolite, -lithe** [Gr. λίθος], a fossil fruit. **Carpo·logy** [Gr. -λογια], the part of botany which is concerned with the study of fruits; hence **Carpolo·gical** *a.*, **-lo·gically** *adv.*, **-logist. Carpo·phagous** [Gr. -φαγος] *a.*, (*Zool.*) fruit-eating. **Ca·rpophore** [Gr. -φορος], (*Bot.*) a prolongation of the axis of a flower, raising the pistil above the stamens, as in *Geraniaceæ* and *Umbelliferæ*. **Ca·rpophyll** [Gr. φύλλον], (*Bot.*) the modified leaf which by its folding produces a carpel. **Ca·rpospore** [Gr. σπόρος], (*Bot.*) in Thallophytes, the spore formed in a sporocarp or spore-fruit; hence **Carpospo·rous** *a.*, applied to certain Algae.

Carpocra·tian. 1587. A follower of Carpocrates of Alexandria (A. D. 120), who asserted the mortality of Christ's body and the creation of the world by angels.

‖**Carpus** (kā·ɹpŏs). 1679. [mod.L., a. Gr. καρπός.] *Anat.* The part of the skeleton which unites the hand to the fore-arm, consisting in the higher vertebrates of eight small bones. In man it forms the *wrist*; in the horse, the *knee*.

Carr[1] (kāɹ). *dial.* OE. A rock; now *esp.* used of insulated rocks off the Northumbrian and Scottish coasts.

Carr[2], **car** (kāɹ). *local.* ME. [From ON.] 1. A pool; a fen; now usu., wet boggy ground; a meadow recovered from the bog. 2. A fenny copse ME. Also *attrib.*

Carrack, carack (kæ·răk). Now *Hist.* ME. [a. OF. *carraque, caraque*, of unkn. origin.] A large ship of burden, also fitted for warfare, formerly used by the Portuguese in trading with the East Indies; a galleon.

Here a vast Carrack flies, while none pursue DE FOE.

Carrageen, -gheen (kæ·răgīn). 1834. [f. *Carragheen* in Ireland.] A kind of seaweed (*Chrondus crispus*), also called *Irish moss*, of a cartilaginous texture and a purplish colour, becoming yellowish-white when dried. It yields a jelly, used for food and in medicine.

Carrat, Carraway; see CARAT, CARAWAY.

Carrefour; see CARFOUR.

Carrell, obs. f. CAROL.

Carriage (kæ·ridʒ). ME. [a. ONF. *cariage*, f. *carier* (mod. *charrier*) to carry (in a cart, etc.).]

I. 1. The action of carrying; conveyance (*esp.* of merchandise). †2. A toll on transport –1771. †3. An obsolete feudal service. Cf. AVERAGE *sb.*[1] –1835. 4. The cost of carrying 1753. †5. Power or capacity for carrying –1740. 6. Action of carrying out; conduct, administration 1601. 7. The carrying (of a motion) 1879.

1. Mules or horses for c. DE FOE. 5. *L. L. L.* I. ii. 74. 6. C. of affaires 1601, of an Enterprise 1652, a sale, an order (*mod.*).

II. 1. Manner of carrying (one's body, or any part of it, oneself); mien; deportment; behaviour 1590. 2. Habitual conduct. (Referring to *morals.*) 1588. †3. Manner of conducting –1696.

1. A stately c. 1653. A graceful c. of the head DE QUINCEY. *Com. Err.* III. ii. 14. 3. The present c. of matters at Court EVELYN.

III. 1. Something carried; a load 1458. †2. Baggage –1743. †3. Meaning (of words) –1607.

2. Dauid left his cariage in the hand of the keeper of the cariage 1 *Sam.* xvii. 32. †3. *Haml.* I. i. 94.

IV. 1. Means of conveyance; *esp.* a wheeled vehicle 1450. Often in *comb.* 2. *spec.* A wheeled vehicle kept for private use for driving in 1771.

1. A cart, or other cariage 1611. Comb.: *Railway-, travelling-c.* 2. A c. and pair (*mod.*). *Techn. uses*: (*a.*) A wheeled support; *e.g.* a gun-c., the c. of a coach, etc. (*b.*) A mechanical contrivance which moves and carries some part of a machine 1688. (*c.*) *Arch.* A supporting framework, *e.g.* the c. of a staircase 1823.

Comb.: **c.-company,** people who keep private carriages; **c. dog,** a Dalmatian dog; **-drive; -horse,** one that runs in a c.; **-way,** that part of roads, etc., intended for vehicular traffic. Hence **Ca·rriageable** *a.* portable (*rare*); practicable for wheeled carriages **Ca·rriaged** *a.* †having a deportment; furnished with carriages.

Ca·rrick be·nd. 1819. [? f. *carrick*, var. of CARRACK.] *Naut.* A kind of knot for splicing two ropes together.

Ca·rrick bi·tts. 1847. [f. as prec.] *Naut.* The BITTS near the end of the windlass; windlass-bitts.

Carrier (kæ·riəɹ). ME. [f. CARRY *v.* + -ER[1].] 1. One who or that which carries (see CARRY *v.*); a bearer. 2. One whose occupation is to carry loads, a porter 1511. 3. *spec.* One who undertakes for hire the conveyance of goods and parcels. (The familiar current sense.) 1471. 4. = CARRIER-PIGEON 1641. 5. A conduit for water, etc. 1797. 6. A person or animal that carries and disseminates disease-germs 1906.

1. A carier of letters 1580. One of Cupid's Carriers *Merry W.* II. ii. 141. *Techn. uses.* Used of parts of instruments and machines which act as bearers and transmittors; in *Mech.* esp. a piece of iron in a lathe by which what is being turned is carried round in the machine. *Electr.* The wave, or current, or frequency transmitted in electrical communication. 3. By the Cork c. BERKELEY. 'North Western Railway Company, carriers' (*mod.*).

Comb.: **c.-bird,** the pelican, the carrier-pigeon; **-shell, -trochus,** a genus of molluscs, which attach pieces of stone, coral, etc., to their shells.

Ca·rrier-pi·geon. 1647. A breed of pigeons with strong homing instincts, used for carrying letters. Also *fig.*

Carriole (kæ·ri,oul). 1808. [a. F., = med. L. *carriola*, dim. of *carra* CAR.] 1. a. A small open carriage with a seat for one 1834. b. A light covered cart 1860. 2. A sledge used in Canada 1808.

Carrion (kæ·riən), *sb.* (and *a.*) [ME. *caronye, caroine*, a. ONF. *caro·niē*, later *caroine*, f. Rom. type **caronia*, ? irreg. deriv. of *caro* flesh.]

A. *sb.* †1. A dead body –1763. 2. Dead putrefying flesh of man or beast; flesh unfit for food ME. Also *fig.* †3. Used of a living human body, or living person –1661; also of animals (in sense 'vermin'; occ. merely 'worthless beast') –1639.

2. Whan a beast is tourned to careine LYDG. 3. Old feeble Carrions *Jul. C.* II. i. 130. Hence †**Ca·rrionly** *a.* and *adv.*

B. *attrib.* 1. Of, or pertaining to, corrupting flesh 1535. Also *transf.* 2. †Carrion-like; rotten; loathsome 1565.

2. Mounted .. on lean c. Tits that were nothing but skin and bone 1653. *Comb.* **c.-flower,** the genus *Stapelia*, also *Smilax herbacea*, from the scent of their blossoms.

Carrion crow. 1528. A species of Crow (*Corvus Corone*) which feeds on carrion, small animals, poultry, etc.

Carritch, -es (ka·ritʃ, -iz). *Sc.* 1761. [Corruption of CATECHIZE *sb.* F. *catéchèse.*] = CATECHISM.

Carriwi·tchet, carwi·tchet. 1614. [?] A pun, quibble; a hoaxing question.

Wounded with a quibble or a carwitchet at the Mermaid SCOTT.

Carrom, var. of CAROM, CARAMBOLE.

Carronade (kærŏnē·d). 1779. [f. *Carron*, in Scotland, where first cast.] *Mil.* A short piece of ordnance, usually of large calibre, having a chamber for the powder like a mortar: chiefly used on shipboard.

Carron oil. 1884. [From *Carron* ironworks, where much used.] A liniment of linseed oil and lime water in equal parts.

Carrot (kæ·rət). 1533. [a. F. *carotte*:—L. *carota*; ad. Gr. καρωτόν, ? f. κάρα head.] 1. An umbelliferous plant (*Daucus Carota*) having a large tapering root, which in cultivation is bright red, fleshy, and edible 1538; usually the root itself 1533. 2. *pl.* (*joc.*) Red hair, or a name for one who has such hair 1685. Hence **Ca·rroty** *a.* red; Of persons: red-haired.

†**Ca·rrow.** 1577. [?] An Irish itinerant gambler –1829.

Carry (kæ·ri), *v.* ME. [a. ONF. *carier* :— late L. *carricare*, f. *carrus* CAR. Cf. CARK, CHARGE, CARGO.] **I. 1.** *trans.* To convey, orig. by cart, hence in any vehicle, on horseback, etc. Also *absol.* and *fig.* **2.** To bear from one place to another; to go supporting ME. Also *fig.* **3.** To conduct, lead, take with one; to take *to.* Now *arch.* and *dial.* 1513. **4.** To transfer (a number, an entry, etc.) to another column, book, etc. 1745. **5.** To cause to go or come; to conduct, impel 1703. **6.** *fig.* To continue to have with one as one moves on 1777. **7.** To extend or continue (a line, a piece of work) ME.; also *fig.* 1711. **8.** To take as the result of effort, to win: also with *off* 1607. **9.** To take by assault 1601. Also *transf.* and *fig.* **10.** To gain victory for (a measure, one's candidate, etc.) 1619. **11.** To conduct, manage (an affair, etc.). Now *arch.* 1590. **12.** *Falconry.* To fly away with the quarry. [So Fr. *charrier.*] 1615.

1. C. corne *Gen.* xlii. 19. To c. 40*l.* in toys DE FOE, wheat 1801. *fig.* To c. (a person) through Virgil's Æneid CHATHAM. 2. Wel coude she carie a morsel CHAUCER. He shall..carrie them [the lambes] in his bosome *Isa.* xl. 11. *To c. coals* (fig.); see COAL. *To c. a hawk*, i.e. bear it on the fist 1826. To c. a letter 1591. *fig.* [Private judgment] carried into politics BUCKLE. 3. To c. a ship to Lisbon DE FOE, a horse to water 1822, [a person] before a justice 1799. 5. *To c. all before one.* To c. water, sound, etc., as a channel, drain, pipe, etc. 1601. As high as a cross-bow can c. 1869. Where winds can c. POPE. 7. To c. a wall from sea to sea 1878. *fig.* To c. Good-manners to an Excess ADDISON. 8. *To c. it*: to win the contest. So *To c. the day.* 9. To c. a position 1876.

II. 1. To bear, hold up, while marching, running, or moving about; to bear about with one; to bear ME. **2.** To bear (the body, head, etc.) in a certain way 1583. **3.** *refl.* To comport, behave, demean oneself 1593. **†4.** To wield –1651. **5.** *Mil.* To hold a weapon in position for saluting 1796. **6.** To support, sustain the weight or burden of, bear 1626.

1. *To c. weight* (in *Horse-racing*): i.e. such extra weight as equalizes the competitors. To c. a swerd WYCLIF, the Standard 1703, arms JOWETT. More rum than he could c. SMOLLETT. Mrs. Thrale..fancies she carries a boy JOHNSON. To c. a distinction in our thoughts BERKELEY. To c. a grave face 1873, value 1693, weight 1691, authority BUTLER, a sense, as words HOBBES, a consequence 1877. A contract which carries interest BLACKSTONE. 2. To carry one's head high 1723. 3. Carrying themselves rudely 1719. 4. †*To c. a (great) stroke*: to wield great influence. 6. *To c. sail*: said of the ship or those who work it 1631. Arches carried by pillars RUSKIN. To c. a crop 1799, cattle 1884, an inference, etc. (*mod.*).

III. Combined with adverbs, in specialized combinations. (See also the preceding senses and the adverbs.)

Carry about. To drive hither and thither, *Ephes.* iv. 14. **Carry away. a.** *trans.* = *carry off*, a. **b.** To move forcibly from the footing of reason and judgement. **c.** *trans.* To break off; to lose by breakage; and *intr.* Chiefly *Naut.* **d.** *To c. it away*: to gain the day. *Haml.* II. ii. 377. **Carry forward.** To transfer to another column, page, or book, or to the next account. **Carry off. a.** To remove from this life. **b.** To win. **c.** To make passable. **d.** To bear it out. **Carry on. a.** To advance (a proceeding). **b.** To keep up. **c.** To work at, prosecute. **d.** *intr.* (*Naut.*) To move on. **e.** (*colloq.*) To behave or 'go on'. **Carry out. a.** To conduct to conclusion; to carry into practice, etc. **b.** *To c. out one's bat* (in Cricket): to be 'not out' at the close of the innings or the game. **c.** To bear out for burial. **Carry over. a.** To take with one to the other side. **b.** To allow an account to remain open over the day when its settlement is due; also said of the debtors. **Carry through.** To conduct safely through difficulties; to prosecute to the natural end. **Carry up. a.** To continue (building, etc.). **b.** To trace back in time. **†c.** To hold up. **d.** = *Carry over* or *forward* in accounts.

Carry (kæ·ri), *sb.* 1605. [f. prec.] **1.** A vehicle; *spec.* a two-wheeled barrow. *Sc.* and *n. dial.* **2.** The position required by the command to 'carry arms'; cf. CARRY *v.* II. 5. 1833. **3.** Range (of a gun) 1858. **4.** A portage between navigable rivers or channels. *U. S.*, etc. 1860. **5.** The drift of the clouds. *Sc.* 1819.

Carry-all, carryall (kæ·ri,ǭl). *U.S.* 1837. [f. CARRY *v.* + -ALL: altered by pop. etym. from CARRIOLE.] A light carriage for one horse, usually four-wheeled, with room for several persons. Also *transf.*

Carrying (kæ·ri,iŋ), *vbl. sb.* **1.** The action of the vb. CARRY. **2.** *attrib.*, as in *carrying power*, etc.; **c.-place** = CARRY *sb.* 4; **c. trade,** the business of carrying goods, *esp.* by sea.

Carryke, obs. var. of CARRACK.

†Ca·rry-tale. 1577. A tale-bearer –1824.

Carse (kāɹs, Sc. kęrs). *Sc.* ME. [? = *carrs*, pl. of CARR *sb.*²] The stretch of low alluvial land along the banks of some Scottish rivers.

Cart (kāɹt), *sb.* [ME. *cart(e*, f. ON. *kartr* cart. In OE. *cræt.*] **†1.** A carriage of any kind; a chariot, car –1602. **2.** *spec.* A strong springless vehicle with two wheels, used in farming operations, for carrying heavy goods, etc. (see CART *v.* 2); specialized as *baggage-*, *harvest-*, *hay-*, etc. *cart* ME. **3.** A two-wheeled vehicle of lighter make, with springs; a *spring-cart*, *mail cart*, *village cart* 1823.

1. Phoebus C. *Haml.* III. ii. 165. 2. Like thief and parson in a Tyburn-c. DRYDEN.

Phr. *In the c.* (slang), in an awkward or losing position. *To set* or *put the c. before the horse*: to reverse the natural or proper order.

Comb.: **†c.-bote, -boot** (*Feudal Syst.*), an allowance of wood to a tenant for making and repairing carts (see BOOT *sb.*¹); **-head** (cf. *cart's-tail*); **-horse,** a horse used to draw a cart; a horse used for heavy work; **-house,** a shed in which carts are kept; **†a** house on wheels; **-load,** the load which a c. can carry; *fig.* a heap; **-man,** a man who drives a c.; **-road** = *cart-way*; **cart's-tail,** *occ.* **cart-tail,** the hinder part of a c., to which offenders were tied to be whipped through the streets; **-way,** a way passable by carts; **-whip,** a long heavy horse-whip; also as *v.*

Cart (kāɹt), *v.* ME. [f. the sb.] **1.** To carry or convey in a cart; also *fig.* **†2.** *spec.* To carry in a cart through the streets, by way of punishment –1812. **3.** *intr.* or *absol.* To work with or use a cart ME.

2. To see Bawds carted BUTLER *Hud.* II. i. 81.

Ca·rtable, *a.* 1684. [f. CART *sb.* or *v.* + -ABLE.] That can be carted; passable by carts.

Ca·rtage (kā·ɹtėdʒ). ME. [f. as prec. + -AGE.] The process or cost of conveying by cart.

Carte¹ (kāɹt, kart). ME. [a. F. *carte* :—L. *carta, charta.*] **†1.** A chart, plan –1683; a charter –1640. **2.** *Sc.* A playing-card; *pl.* cards 1497. **‖3.** A bill of fare. [mod.Fr.] 1818. **‖4.** = CARTE-DE-VISITE 1861.

Carte² (kāɹt). 1707. [(Also QUART(E): a. F. *quarte*, ad. It. *quarta* fourth.] *Fencing.* One of the eight parries and two usual guards of the small-sword.

‖Carte blanche (kart blāṅʃ). 1707. [Fr.: = blank paper.] **1.** A blank paper given to any one to fill up with his own terms. **2.** Hence *fig.* Full discretionary power 1766. **3.** *Piquet.* A hand without picture-cards 1820.

‖Carte-de-visite (ka·rt,də,vizi·t). Pl. **cartes-de-visite.** 1861. [Fr.; = visiting card.] A small photographic portrait mounted on a card, 3½ by 2½ inches.

Cartel (kā·ɹtĕl), *sb.* 1560. [a. F., ad. It. *cartello*, dim. of *carta.*] **1.** A written challenge; a letter of defiance. **2.** A written agreement as to the exchange or ransom of prisoners; such exchange itself 1692; also = *cartel-ship*, a ship employed in such exchange 1769. **3.** *gen.* A paper or card, with writing or printing 1693.

1. To send a c. of defiance 1560. 2. To establish a c. of exchange WELLINGTON. 3. A c. with some Greek verses H. WALPOLE. Hence **†Ca·rtel** *v. trans.* to serve with a challenge. **Ca·rtelling** *vbl. sb.* making of cartels, exchanging of prisoners.

Carter (kā·ɹtəɹ). ME. [f. CART *sb.*] **†1.** A charioteer –1580. **2.** One who drives a cart ME.; *hence*, a boor 1509. **3.** = **Carter-fish:** the WHIFF 1884. Hence **†Ca·rterly** *a.* and *adv.*

Cartesian (kaɹtī·ziăn, -ʒ̆ăn). 1656. [ad. mod.L. *Cartesianus*, f. *Cartesius*, latinized f. René *Descartes.*] **A.** *adj.* Pertaining to Descartes, his philosophy or mathematical methods. **B.** *sb.* A follower of Descartes 1660.

A. *Cogito*: *Ergo sum*, this famous enthymem of the C. philosophy HALLAM.

Cartesian devil, C. diver: a hollow figure, partly filled with water and partly with air, and made to float in a vessel nearly filled with water, having an air-tight elastic covering. By pressing down the covering, the air inside is compressed, and more water forced through an aperture into the figure, which sinks, to rise again when the pressure is removed. Hence **Carte·sianism,** the philosophy of Descartes.

‖Carthamus (kā·ɹþămɒ̆s). 1548. [mod.L., ad. Arab.] A genus of composite plants; esp. *C. tinctorius* (Safflower or Bastard Saffron), yielding red and yellow dyes. Hence **Cartha·mic** *a.* as in *Carthamic acid* = **Ca·rthamin,** the red colouring matter of safflower.

Carthusian (kaɹþiū·ziăn, -ʒ̆ăn). ME. [ad. L. *Cartusianus*, *Cartusiensis*, from the *Catursiani montes*, or from *Catorissium*, *Chatrousse*, a village in Dauphiné. In F. *chartreux.*] **1.** *adj.* Of or belonging to an austere order of monks founded in Dauphiné, by St. Bruno, in the year 1086. *sb.* A monk of this order. **2.** *adj.* Of the Charterhouse School, founded on the site of a Carthusian monastery in London. *sb.* A scholar of this school. 1860.

Cartilage (kā·ɹtilėdʒ). 1541. [a. F., ad. L. *cartilago* gristle.] A firm elastic tissue, of a translucent colour; gristle; a gristly part, as the *costal cartilages.*

Temporary c. is that which occurs in early life, and subsequently ossifies; *permanent c.*, e.g. the *articular c.* which coats the joints, always retains its character. Hence **Ca·rtilagi·nifica·tion,** the formation of or conversion into c. **Ca·rtilagi·niform** *a.* resembling c. **Cartila·ginoid** *a.* of the form or nature of c.

Cartilaginous (kāɹtilæ·dʒinəs), *a.* 1541. [ad. F. *cartilagineux*; see -OUS.] **1.** Of, or of the nature of, cartilage. **2.** *Bot.* Of the texture of cartilage 1677. var. **†Cartilagi·neous.**

1. *C. fishes*: an order of fishes having a c. skeleton.

Cartographer (kaɹtǫ·grăfəɹ). Also **charto-.** 1863. [f. F. *carte*, or L. *charta*, *carta* + Gr. -γραφος. The *c* spelling is commoner.] One who makes charts or maps.

Cartography (kaɹtǫ·grăfi). Also **charto-.** 1859. [f. as prec. + Gr. -γραφία.] The drawing of charts or maps. Hence **Cartogra·phic, -al** *a.*

Cartomancy (kā·ɹtomæ:nsi). 1871. [f. It. *carta* playing-card + Gr. μαντεία.] Divination by playing-cards.

Carton (kā·ɹtən). 1864. [a. F., papier-mâché; see CARTOON.] **1.** A white disk within the bull's-eye of a target; a shot which hits this. **2.** A light pasteboard or cardboard box or case for holding goods; the material used for this 1891.

Cartoon (kaɹtū·n), *sb.* 1671. [a. It. *cartone*, augm. of *carta* paper.] **1.** A drawing on stout paper as a design for painting, tapestry, mosaic, etc. **2.** A (full-page) illustration in a (comic) paper or periodical 1863.

1. Cartoons and other drawings of Raphael EVELYN. Hence **Cartoo·n** *v.* to design, as a c. (sense 1); to caricature. **Cartoo·nist,** one who draws cartoons.

Cartouche (kaɹtū·ʃ). 1611. [a. F. *cartouche* fem. Also a. F. *cartouche* masc., a. It. *cartoccio*, augm. f. *carta* paper.] **1.** (= Fr. *cartouche* fem.) *Mil.* A roll or case of paper, etc., containing a charge for a firearm; a cartridge. ? *Obs.* **†b.** A case of wood, etc., containing iron balls to be shot from a cannon –1768. **c.** = *cartridge-box.* **2.** (= Fr. *cartouche* masc.) *Arch.* **a.** A corbel, mutule, or modillion; var. **†Cartouse** 1726. **b.** Any ornament in the form of a scroll 1611. **c.** A tablet for an inscription or for ornament, representing a sheet of paper with the ends rolled up; a drawing of this. Often *attrib.* 1776. **d.** *Archæol.* Name for the oval figures in Egyptian hieroglyphics, enclosing royal or divine names or titles 1830. *Comb.* **c.-box** = *cartridge-box.*

Cartridge (kā·ɹtridʒ). 1579. [A corruption of CARTOUCHE.] **1.** *Mil.* The case in which the exact charge of powder for fire-arms is made up; of pasteboard, flannel, metal, etc. Also *transf.* and *fig.* **†2.** *Arch.* = CARTOUCHE 2 a, b, c. –1756.

Comb., etc.: **ball-c.,** a c. containing a bullet; **blank c.,** a c. containing no ball; **c.-bag,** a flannel bag, etc., containing the charge of powder for a cannon; **-belt,** a belt having pockets for cartridges; **-box,** a box for storing or carrying cartridges; **-case,** = *cartridge-box*; also, the paper which contains the powder of a c.; **-paper,** a strong kind of paper, used for making cartridges, and also for rough drawings, etc.

Cartulary (kā·ɹtiŭlări). Also **Chartu-,** q. v. 1541. [ad. med.L. *cart-*, *chartularium*, f. *cart-*, *chartula*, dim. of *carta*, *charta*; see CHART.] 'A place where papers or records are kept' (J.); whence, the records (of a monastery, etc.); or the book containing them; a register. var. **†Ca·rtuary, Cha·rt-.**

†Ca·rtware. 1562. [See WARE.] A team of horses –1577.

Ca·rt-wheel. ME. **1.** The wheel of a cart. **2.** *joc.* Any large coin, as a crown, etc. 1867.

To turn cart-wheels: to execute lateral somersaults, as if the hands and feet were spokes of a wheel.

Cartwright (kā·ɹtˌrəit). ME. [f. CART *sb.* + WRIGHT.] A carpenter who makes carts.

†**Ca·ruage.** *erron.* **carvage.** 1610. [a. ONF. (mod. *charruage*) on L. type **carrucaticum*.] *Old Law.* **1.** Ploughing –1688. **2.** = CARUCAGE.

Carucage, carr- (kæ·riukėdʒ). 1577. [ad. med. L. *car(r)ucagium*, f. med. L. *carruca* plough.] *Feudal Syst.* A tax levied on every carucate of land.

Carucate, carr- (kæ·riukeᵉt). 1577. [ad. med. L. *car(r)ucata*, f. *car(r)uca* plough.] *Feudal Syst.* As much land as could be tilled with one plough (and 8 oxen) in a year; a ploughland. var. †**Carue,** *erron.* **carve.**

Caruncle (kărʊ·ŋk'l). 1615. [ad. 16th c. F. *caruncule*, ad. L. *caruncula* (also used), dim. of *caro*.] **1.** A small fleshy excrescence: applied in Anat. to the lachrymal and urethral caruncles, the wattles of the turkey-cock, etc. **2.** *Bot.* 'An excrescence at or about the hilum of certain seeds' (Gray). Hence **Ca·runcular** *a.* of the nature of or like a c. **Caru·nculate(d** *a.* having a c. or caruncles; var. **Caru·nculous.**

‖**Carus** (kēᵊ·rɒs). 1678. [med.L.; = L. *caros*, a. Gr. κάρος heavy sleep.] *Med.* Extreme insensibility; *esp.* the fourth degree of insensibility, the others being sopor, coma, and lethargy.

Carvage, erron. sp. of CARUAGE.

Carve (kāɹv), *v.* [Com. Teut.: OE. str. vb. *ceorfan, cearf*: OTeut. type **kerfan, karf*; cogn. w. Gr. γράφειν. The strong pa. pple. *carven* is still in use as *arch.*] †**1.** To CUT –1560. **2.** To hew, cut, or sculpture (*out of* stone, *in* ivory, etc.) OE.; to shape by cutting 1535. **3.** To cut or engrave *on* (*in, into*) a surface; to cover with cut figures ME. Also *intr.* or *absol.* **4.** To cut up meat at table ME. Also *trans.* **5.** *fig.* To do or †take at one's pleasure 1602. **6.** To cut up or subdivide 1711.

1. Quen corne is coruen ME. *To c. in two, in* or *to pieces.* To c. a way 1490. Also *fig.* **2.** An angel ..carved in stone TENNYSON. To c. mount Athos into a statue of Alexander BENTLEY. **3.** We carved not a line and we raised not a stone WOLFE. Wrinkles carved his Skin TENNYSON. We c. and paint EMERSON. **4.** A man who .. cannot c. CHESTERF. *To c. a fowl*, etc. **5.** *Haml.* I. iii. 20. **6.** To c. the whole fee in particular estates CRUISE. **To c. out:** (in *Legal lang.*) To cut a smaller estate out of a larger one. Also *transf.* (*Macb.* I. ii. 19), and †*fig.* (*L. L. L.* V. ii. 323). Hence **Carve** *sb.* a stroke of carving. **Carved** *ppl. a.*; also **carven** (*poet.* and *rhet.*).

Carvel (kā·ɹvėl). 1462. [a. OF. *caruelle, kirvelle*; see CARAVEL.] *Naut.* The Eng. form of the name for a small, light, and fast ship, chiefly of Spain and Portugal. (Since 1650 only *Hist.*, and written *caravel.*) †**2. a.** The Paper Nautilus. **b.** The floating mollusc *Ianthina*. **c.** A jelly-fish (*Medusa*).

Comb. **c.-built,** (*Naut.*) having the planks all flush and smooth, instead of clinker-built, i. e. overlapping. So **c.-planked** *a.*

Carvene (kā·ɹvīn). 1876. *Chem.* A hydrocarbon $C_{10}H_{16}$, found in oil of Caraway.

Carver (kā·ɹvəɹ). ME. [f. CARVE *v.* + -ER [1].] **1.** *gen.* One who cuts or carves. **2.** *spec.* One who carves wood, ivory, stone, etc.; a sculptor ME. **3.** One who carves at table ME. **b.** A carving knife (*mod.*).

2. The carver's chissel DODSLEY. **3.** An expert c. (*mod.*). *A pair of carvers*: a carving knife and fork.

Carving (kā·ɹviŋ), *vbl. sb.* ME. [f. as prec. + -ING [1].] **1.** The action of the vb. CARVE. **2.** Carved work; a carved figure or design ME.

2. The c. on the reading-desk SCOTT.

†**Carvist.** 1677. *Falconry.* A hawk in its first year, of proper age to be carried on the fist –1800.

Carvy, Sc. f. CARAWAY.

Caryatid (kæriˌæ·tid). Pl. usu. **-ides**; also **-ids.** 1563. [ad. L. *Caryatid-es*, a. Gr. Καρυάτιδες, pl. of Καρυᾶτις, a priestess of Artemis at Καρύαι in Laconia, also a figure as below.] *Arch.* A female figure used as a column to support an entablature. Also *attrib.*

Caryophyllaceous (kæriofilēᵉ·ʃəs), *a.* 1835. [ad. mod. L. *Caryophyllaceæ*, f. *caryophyllus* the clove-pink.] *Bot.* **a.** Belonging to the order *Caryophyllaceæ*. **b.** Used of a corolla having five petals with long claws, as in the clove-pink. var. **Ca:ryophy·lleous.**

‖**Caryopsis** (kæriǫ·psis). Pl. **-ides** (-idīz). 1830. [mod.L. f. Gr. κάρυον nut + ὄψις.] *Bot.* A small one-seeded dry indehiscent fruit, whose pericarp adheres to the seed throughout so as to form one body with it, as in wheat, barley, etc.

Ca. sa. (kā sā). 1796. Short for *capias ad satisfaciendum* (see CAPIAS).

Casal (kēᵉ·săl), *a.* 1834. [f. CASE + -AL.] Of or belonging to grammatical case.

‖**Casal, casale.** 1506. [It. *casale*, f. *casa*.] A hamlet (in Italy, Malta).

Cascabel (kɑ·skăbel). 1639. [a. Sp. *cascabel* little round bell, child's rattle, rattlesnake.] **1.** *Gunnery.* Formerly the knob at the rear end of a cannon; now all behind the base ring. ‖**2.** A rattlesnake; also its rattle. [Sp.] 1760.

Cascade (kæskēᵉ·d), *sb.* 1641. [a. F., ad. It. *cascata*, f. *cascare* to fall.] A waterfall; usually, a small fall; *esp.* one of a series. Also *transf.* and *fig.*

An artificial c. MRS. PIOZZI. A c. of ice TYNDALL, of lace (*mod.*).

Cascade (kæskēᵉ·d), *v.* 1702. [f. the sb.] To fall or pour in a cascade. Also *transf.* **b.** *vulgar.* To vomit 1805.

‖**Cascara** (kɑ·skăra). 1882. [Sp.] A bark canoe (in Spanish America).

Cascarilla (kæskări·lă). 1686. [a. Sp., dim. of *cascara* bark.] The bark of the plant *Croton eleuteria*, used as a tonic. Also called *c. bark.* Hence **Cascari·llin,** a bitter substance $(C_{12}H_{18}O_4)$ obtained from c. bark.

†**Caschielawis.** *Sc. pl.* 1596. An instrument of torture.

‖**Caschrom** (ka·sχrɒm). 1806. [Gael. *cas* foot, *chrom* crooked.] An instrument of tillage, called also 'foot-plough'.

Case (kēᵉs), *sb.* [1] [ME. *cas, caas*, a. OF. *cas* :—L. *casus*, f. *cas-*, *cadere*.] †**1.** A thing that befalls or happens; an event, occurrence, hap, or chance –1596. †**2.** Chance, hazard, hap –1560. **3.** An instance ME. **4.** *The case*: The actual state of matters; the fact ME. **5.** Condition (*esp.* physical condition), plight ME. **6.** *Law.* **a.** A cause or suit. **b.** A statement of the facts of a matter *sub judice*, for a higher court. **c.** A decided case. **d.** The case as put by one of the parties 1596. **7.** *Med.* **a.** The condition of disease in a patient 1709. **b.** An instance of disease; 'a record of the progress of disease in an individual' (*Syd. Soc. Lex.*) 1732. **c.** *U. S. slang.* A 'cure' 1848. **8.** *Grammar.* [L. *casus* used as tr. Gr. πτῶσις, restricted by the Stoics to nouns, and including the nominative.] **a.** One of the forms of a sb., adj., or pron., which express its relations to some other word, *e. g.* as subject, object, etc. **b.** *loosely*, The relation itself. ME.

1. I you recount a ruefull cace SPENSER. **2.** By caase of fortune CAXTON. **3.** In manye Caasis 1449. **4.** The c. with me is the reverse MACAULAY. *It is not the c.* (mod.). When a lady's in the c. GAY. †*All a c.*: all one. **5.** [They] came home ageyne in werse caas than they wente CAXTON. *In good case*: well off; also, in good physical condition (*arch.*). *In c. to* or *for*: prepared, ready. **6. c.** *A leading c.*: one frequently cited as having settled some point. **d.** 'That is our c., my lord' (*mod.*). †*Action on the c.*: a form of procedure in common law, for remedy in cases not specifically provided for, so called from the words *in consimili casu* in the Statute of Westminster the Second. Called also *trespass on the c.*, or *c.* simply. *C. of conscience* (tr. L. *casus conscientiæ*): a question of conduct concerning which conscience may be in doubt, and requiring CASUISTRY to deal with it. **7. b.** A c. of small-pox 1851.

Phrases. *In case*: †**a.** in fact; **b.** if; **c.** lest; **d.** *In case of*: in the event of. †*If case*: if perchance. *To put* or *set* (*the*) *case*: to suppose. *In any case*: †by any means; at all events, anyhow. So *In no case. Comb.*: †**c.-divinity,** casuistry; **-law,** the law as made by decided cases; †**-putting,** stating of a legal c., the making of hypotheses.

Case (kēᵉs), *sb.* [2] ME. [a. ONF. *casse*, mod. *châsse* (= It. *cassa*) :—L. *capsa*, f. *capere*.] **1.** A thing fitted to contain something else; a box, chest, bag, sheath, etc. **2.** The covering part of anything ME. Also *fig.* **3.** The frame in which a door or window is set; cf. STAIR-CASE. 1663. **4.** The shell or carcass of a building 1677. **5.** A box with its proper contents 1540; hence, A set 1599. **6.** *Printing.* The frame in which the compositor has his types, divided into compartments. (Ordinarily there are two, the *upper case* for capitals, etc., and the *lower case* for the small letters, etc.) 1588. **7.** *Mil.* = *case-shot* 1667.

1. A c. for books WOTTON. *A candle-, card-, cigar-c.* (mod.). **2.** The c. of a watch, of a fire-work, a sausage, a chrysalis, etc. *spec.* In *Book-binding*: The boards and back of a book bound in cloth; also, a cover to hold pamphlets, etc., without binding 1868. *fig.* The c. of that huge Spirit now is cold *Ant. & Cl.* IV. xv. 89. **5.** A c. of arms, glass, etc. A c. of teeth SCOTT. *A c. of pistols*: a brace.

Case, *sb.* [3] Also **case-char.** 1751. One of the family *Salmonidæ*.

†**Case,** *v.* [1] 1647. [f. CASE *sb.* [1]] To put as a supposition; *intr.* = *To put cases* (see CASE *sb.* [1] Phrases).

Case (kēᵉs), *v.* [2] 1575. [f. CASE *sb.* [2]] **1.** *trans.* To enclose in or as in a case; to encase, surround *with*. **2.** To fit with cases 1884. †**3.** To strip of the case; to skin –1803.

1. Bones of seals .. now cased in ice KANE. Men cased in iron 1863. To c. a brick wall with stone GWILT. **3.** *All's Well* III. vi. 111.

Caseation (kēᵉsiˌēᵉ·ʃən). 1866. [f. L. *caseatus*, treated with cheese; see -ATION.] The coagulation of milk; in *Pathol.* a degeneration of morbid products into a cheesy material.

Case-harden (kēᵉ·sˌhā·ɹd'n), *v.* 1677. [f. CASE *sb.* [2] (in locative constr.).] **1.** To harden on the surface, as iron by partial cementation. **2.** *fig.* To harden in constitution or spirit 1713.

2. A case-hardened or weather-beaten tar FALCONER.

Caseic (keˈsīˌik), *a.* 1840. [f. L. *caseus* + -IC.] *Chem.* In *C. acid* = *Lactic acid.*

Casein (kēᵉ·siˌin). *Erron.* **-ine.** 1841. [f. as prec.] *Chem.* A Proteid or Albuminoid, one of the chief constituents of milk; chemically identical with the Legumin (or *vegetable c.*) of the seeds of leguminous plants. It is coagulated by acids, and forms the basis of cheese.

Case-knife (kēᵉ·sˌnəif). 1704. [f. CASE *sb.* [2]] **a.** A knife carried in a case or sheath. **b.** A large table knife.

Casemate (kēᵉ·sˌmēᵉt). 1575. [a. F., app. f. Sp. or It. *casa* + ?.] **1.** *Fortif.* A vaulted chamber built in the thickness of the ramparts of a fortress, with embrasures for the defence of the place; used as a barrack, a battery, or both. **2.** *Arch.* = CASEMENT 1. Hence **Ca·semated** *a.* provided with casemates; strongly fortified.

Casement (kēᵉ·smĕnt, kēᵉ·z-). ME. [? f. CASE *sb.* [2]] **1.** *Arch.* A hollow moulding, such as the *cavetto*. **2.** A frame forming a window or part of a window, opening on hinges attached to the upright side of the frame in which it is fixed. (The usual sense.) 1556. Also *fig.*

2. A c. of the great chamber window *Mids. N.* III. i. 57. *C. cloth*, cotton fabric such as is used for c. curtains. Hence **Ca·semented** *a.*

Caseous (kēᵉ·siəs), *a.* 1661. [f. L. *caseus* cheese.] **1.** Of the nature of cheese, cheesy. **2.** *Pathol.* Cheese-like in appearance 1753.

1. (*joc.*) That c. and wrathful people [the Welsh] SYD. SMITH.

Casern, -e (kăzē·ɹn). 1696. [a. F., ad. Sp. *caserna*, f. *casa*.] One of a series of small (temporary) buildings for soldiers between the ramparts and houses of a fortified town; also a barrack.

Case-shot (kēᵉ·sˌʃǫt). 1625. [f. CASE *sb.* [2]] *Mil.* A collection of small projectiles put up in cases to fire from a cannon; canister-shot. Also, a shrapnel-shell.

Ca·se-weed. 1578. [f. CASE *sb.* [2]] Shepherd's Purse.

Ca·se-worm. 1606. [f. as prec.] A caddis-worm; see CADDIS [2].

Cash (kæʃ), *sb.* [1] 1596. [ad. F. *casse* (mod. *caisse*), or It. *cassa* :—L. *capsa* CASE.] †**1.** A box for money, a cash-box –1734; a sum of money –1752. **2.** Money; in the form of coin, ready money 1596. *Banking* and *Comm.*: Specie; also, more loosely, bank-notes which are at once convertible, as opp. to bills, etc.

1. This bank is properly a general c., where every man lodges his money TEMPLE. **2.** Those who have c., come here to spend 1810. So *Hard c.*, *ready c.*, *c. in hand.* He bets..freely when he is in c. THACKERAY. Also *Out of c.*

Comb., etc.: **c.-book,** in *Book-keeping*, a book in which is entered a record of c. paid and received;

-credit, an overdrawn account; **-payment**, *spec.* the payment of c. for government paper, etc.; **-price**, the price for payment in ready money; **-register** (orig. *U.S.*), a till furnished with an apparatus which visibly records the amounts put into it; **-sale**, a sale for ready money.

Cash (kæʃ), *sb.*² 1598. [ad. (ult.) Tamil *kāsu*, a small coin or weight of money. The earlier Eng. form was *cass.*] One of various coins of low value in the East Indies and China: *esp.* The Chinese *le* and *tsien*, coins made of an alloy of copper and lead, with a square hole in the centre; of these 1000 made a tael or liang.

†**Cash**, *v.*¹ 1564. [var. of CASS *v.*] = CASHIER I. –1829.

Cash (kæʃ), *v.*² 1811. [f. CASH *sb.*²] To give or get the cash for; to convert into cash, as 'to c. a cheque'.

‖**Cashel** (kæ·shĕl). 1845. [= Ir. *caiseal*, prob. ad. L. *castellum.*] *Ir. Antiq.* A circular wall enclosing a group of churches and their appurtenances.

Cashew (kăʃū·). 1703. [ad. F. *acajou*, ad. Brazil. *acajoba.*] *C.-tree*, a large tree (*Anacardium occidentale*) cultivated in tropical countries, bearing a kidney-shaped fruit (*cashew-nut*) placed on the end of a fleshy pear-shaped receptacle (*c. apple*), popularly taken for the fruit. *Comb.* **c.-bird**, *Tanagra zena.*

Cashier (kăʃīə·ɹ), *sb.* 1596. [ad. F. *caissier.*] One who has charge of the cash of a bank or mercantile firm, paying and receiving money, and keeping the cash account. †b. A money-dealer –1687.

Cashier (kăʃīə·ɹ), *v.* 1592. [a. Flem. or Du. *casseren*; cf. Ger. *kassiren*; and see CASS *v.*, CASH *v.*¹] †1. To dismiss from service or fellowship; also generally –1791. 2. To dismiss from a position of command or authority; to depose. Also *transf.* and *fig.* 1599. 3. To discard, get rid of 1603; †to make void –1650. ¶ In *Merry W.* I. i. 184, app. = 'to ease of cash'.

2. *spec.* in the army and navy involving disgrace and disqualification from further government employment in any capacity (cf. DISMISS *v.* 3). *Oth.* II. iii. 381. To c. the King LD. SHEFFIELD. 3. To casheere their Ruffianly Haire PRYNNE. To c. an election 1601. Hence **Cashie·rer. Cashie·rment.**

Cashmere (kæ·ʃmīəɹ, kæʃmīə·ɹ). 1822. [Place-name, used attrib.] a. More fully *C. shawl*: A costly shawl made of fine wool obtained from the Cashmere goat and the wild goat of Tibet. b. The material of which these shawls are made. c. A woollen fabric made in imitation of the true cashmere.

Cashmerette (kæːʃmĭre·t). 1886. [f. prec.] A dress fabric with a soft and glossy surface, made in imitation of cashmere.

Cashou, Cashu, obs. ff. CACHOU.

Ca·sing, *sb. n. dial.* Usu. in pl. 1516. Dried dung of cattle used for fuel.

Casing (kēⁱ·siŋ), *vbl. sb.* 1575. [f. CASE *v.*² + -ING¹.] 1. The action of the vb. 2. *concr.* Something that encases, as the c. of a fly, a building, a well, etc. Also in techn. uses. 1791.

Casino (kăsī·no). 1789. [a. It., dim. of *casa.*] ‖1. A summer-house (in Italy) 1831. 2. A public room used for social meetings; *esp.* a public music or dancing saloon 1789. 3. A game of Cards; see CASSINO.

Cask (kɑsk), *sb.* 1557. [app. a. F. *casque*, ad. Sp. *casco* a head-piece, a head, a sconce, an earthen pot, etc. Sense 1 appears only in Eng.] 1. A wooden vessel of cylindrical form, made of curved staves bound together by hoops, with flat ends; a barrel. Cf. BARREL *sb.* 1. Also *fig.* 2. A cask and its contents; hence as a measure of capacity 1727. †3. = CASKET. b. Case, shell –1727. †4. = CASQUE –1696. Also *attrib.* and in *comb.*

Cask, *v.* 1562. [f. prec.] To put into a cask.

†**Caskanet.** 1607. [Made up of *casket* and *carkanet*, perh. orig. a misprint.] Used by some as = CARCANET, by others as = CASKET –1693.

A c. of Jewells 1621. A c. wᵗʰ red stones in it 1638.

Casket (kɑ·skėt), *sb.*¹ 1467. [Of unkn. etym.: in form a dim. of, but earlier than, CASK.] 1. A small box or chest for jewels, letters, or other things of value, itself often of value and richly ornamented. Also *fig.* b. Occ. the title of a book of selections 1850. 2. A coffin. *U. S.* 1870.

1. A richly carved c. of ivory 1876. *fig.* They found him dead..An empty c. *John* v. i. 40.

Casket, *sb.*², var. of GASKET.

Ca·sket, *v.* 1601. [f. CASKET *sb.*¹] To enclose or put up in a casket.

I have..casketted my treasure *All's Well* II. v. 26.

Casque (kɑsk). 1580. [a. F., ad. Sp. *casco* in same sense.] A piece of armour to cover the head; a helmet. Used loosely of all military head-pieces, and now hist., poet., or foreign. Also *transf.* in *Bot.* and *Zool.*

My good blade carves the casques of men TENNYSON. Hence **Casqued** *ppl. a.* having a c. on.

Casquet (kɑ·skėt, kaske). 1611. [a. F., dim. of *casque.*] A light and open helmet.

†**Cass**, *a.* 1549. [ad. L. *cassus.*] Dismissed, cashiered; null –1651.

Cass, *v.* Still *Sc.* 1460. [a. F. *casser*, f. L. *quassare* to break in pieces, annexing in later times the senses of L. *cassare* to annul.] 1. To make void, annul, quash. *Sc. Law.* †2. To dismiss; disband, cashier –1709.

Cassada, var. of CASSAVA.

‖**Cassareep** (kæ·sărīp). 1832. [Carib.] 'The inspissated juice of the cassava, which is highly antiseptic, and forms the basis of the West Indian pepper-pot' (*Treas. Bot.*).

†**Ca·ssate**, *v.* 1512. [f. L. *cassat-*, *cassare.*] = CASS *v.* –1744.

Cassation (kæsēⁱ·ʃən). ME. [ad. late L. *cassationem*; see CASS *v.* So in F.] The action of making null and void.

Court of C. [Fr. *Cour de cassation*], in France, the supreme court of appeal, having power to quash (*casser*) decisions of the other courts.

Cassava (kăsā·vă). 1555. [In F. *cassave*, Sp. *casabe*, from the Taino lang. of Hayti.] 1. A plant, *Manihot utilissima* (N.O. *Euphorbiaceæ*), called also Manioc, with fleshy tuberous roots, used as food in tropical America.

There are two varieties, Sweet C. (*M. Aipi*), prepared as a vegetable, and Bitter C., containing a virulent but volatile poisonous juice, which is expelled by heat.

2. The nutritious starch obtained from the roots; the bread made from this 1577.

Casse paper, cassie-. 1688. [? F. *papier cassé* broken paper.] The paper of the two outside quires of a ream.

‖**Casserole** (kæsĕrōu·l). 1706. [F., dim. of *casse* an open-mouthed pan.] 1. A kind of stew-pan 1725. 2. The edging of certain dressed dishes.

‖**Cassette** (kase·t). 1793. [Fr., dim. of *casse*, *caisse* (cf. CASE).] 1. A casket. 2. *Photogr.* A small flat box used as a container in transporting a plate or film. 3. *Ceramics.* = SAGGAR 1.

†**Casshe.** Also **Caxes.** 1548. The wild chervil; used vaguely of other plants –1640.

Cassia (kæ·sia). OE. [a. L., a. Gr. κασία, ad. Heb.] 1. An inferior kind of Cinnamon, *esp.* the bark of *Cinnamomum Cassia.* More fully *C.-bark.* 2. The tree, *Cinnamomum Cassia* 1553. 3. *poet.* A fragrant shrub or plant. (Cf. *Ps.* xlv. 8.) 1594. 4. *Bot.* A genus of trees, shrubs, or herbs (N.O. *Leguminosæ*) of many species, the leaflets of several of which are the *Senna leaves* of medicine. The name *Cassia fistula* was given early to one species, the Pudding Pipe tree, a native of India, but cultivated elsewhere, which produces the *cassia pods* containing a pulp used as a laxative. Thence the name has been extended to the genus. ME. b. Any medicinal product obtained from this 1543.

Comb., etc.: **c.-bark**, also called **c. lignea** (see above, 1); **-buds**, the unexpanded buds of several species of Cinnamon, esp. *Cinnamomum aromaticum*, used like cloves; **-oil**, common oil of cinnamon.

Cassi·deous, *a.* 1835. [f. L. *cassidem.*] *Bot.* Helmet-shaped. So **Cassi·diform** *a.*

†**Cassidoine, -done, -dony**¹. ME. [a. OF. *cassidoine*, pop. var. of *calcidoine*, ad. L. *chalcedonius* (*lapis*).] = CHALCEDONY –1753.

Cassidony² (kæ·sidəni). 1578. [? = prec.] *Bot.* 1. The plant *Lavandula Stœchas*, French lavender. 2. *Mountain* or *Golden C.*: the Gnaphalium of books.

Cassie, -y (kæ·si). *dial.* 1693. [= Icel. *kass*, mod. *kassi* a case, creel, etc.] A kind of basket made of straw. (Orkney and Caithness.)

Cassimere (kæ·simiəɹ). 1774. [in F. *casimir*, another form of CASHMERE.] A thin fine twilled woollen cloth used for men's clothes. Cf. KERSEYMERE.

†‖**Cassine.** 1708. [F.; cf. It. *casino.*] *Mil.* A farm-house, where a number of soldiers have posted themselves, to make a stand –1753.

Cassinette (kæsine·t). 1846. [? Suggested by *cassimere.*] A modification of cassimere, with the warp of cotton, and the weft of fine wool, or wool and silk.

Cassinian (kæsi·niăn), *a.* 1726. [f. proper name *Cassini.*] Of or pertaining to G. D. Cassini (1625–1712), or his descendants, French astronomers, or to their researches.

C. oval: = CASSINOID.

Cassino (kăsī·no). Also **casino.** 1792. [var. of CASINO.] A game at cards in which the ten of diamonds (*great cass*) counts two points, and the two of spades (*little cass*) one; eleven points constituting the game.

Cassinoid (kæ·sinoid). [a. F. *cassinoide*; see CASSINIAN.] *Geom.* An oval having two foci, such that the product of the focal radii of any point on the curve is constant: a curve which Cassini wished to substitute for the ellipse, in explaining planetary movements.

Cassioberry (kæ·sio͟,be:ri). 1753. The fruit of *Viburnum lævigatum*, the *C.-bush.*

Cassiope·ian, *a.* 1630. Of Cassiopeia, a northern constellation. (In 1572 a brilliant new star appeared in this constellation, only to disappear again.)

Cassique, obs. f. CACIQUE. Also, the Mocking Bird of Guiana 1825.

Cassiterite (kăsi·tĕrəit). 1858. [f. Gr. κασσίτερος + -ITE.] *Min.* Native stannic dioxide, the most common ore of tin, occurring as tin stone, wood tin, toad's-eye tin, stream tin, etc. **Cassi:terota·ntalite**, a tantalite which contains much stannic acid.

Cassius (kæ·siŏs). Name of a German physician of 17th c.; whence *Purple of C.*, a purple pigment produced by the action of chloride of tin on a solution of chloride of gold.

Cassock (kæ·sək), *sb.* 1550. [a. F. *casaque* long coat (whence probably It. *casacca*, Sp. *casaca*); perh. a back-formation from *casaquin* (taken as a diminutive), f. (ult.) Pers. *kazagand.*] †1. A cloak or long coat worn by some soldiers; also that of a horseman –1699. †2. A long loose coat or gown, orig. worn by both sexes –1628. 3. A close-fitting garment with sleeves, fastened up to the neck and reaching to the heels, worn under surplice, alb, or gown by clerics, choristers, etc., at church services; or as ordinary clerical costume 1663. 4. = clerical office; wearer of a c. 1628.

4. During the war, he laid aside the cassoc ROBERTSON. He had a suspicion of all cassocks THACKERAY. Hence **Ca·ssock** *v.* to dress in a c.

Cassolette (kæsəle·t). 1657. [a. F., double dim. of *casse* pan.] 1. A vessel in which perfumes are burned. 2. A box with a perforated cover to diffuse perfumes 1851.

†**Cassonade.** 1657. [a. F., f. *casson* chest.] Unrefined cane sugar imported in casks –1810.

Cassoon (kăsū·n). 1799. Occ. var. of CAISSON, q. v.

Cassowary (kæ·sŏwĕri). 1611. [a. Malay *kasuārī.*] 1. A genus of large cursorial birds, related to the Ostrich, inhabiting New Guinea, etc. They stand about five feet high; the wings are useless for flight, but are furnished with quills, like spines, which serve for combat or defence. 2. *New Holland C.*: the EMEU. 1842.

‖**Cassumu·nar.** 1693. [app. Eastern.] *Med.* The tuberous root of an East Indian plant; it is warm, bitter, aromatic, and smells like ginger. (Cf. ZEDOARY.) var. **Casumuniar.**

Cast (kɑst), *sb.* ME. [f. the vb.] I. 1. The act of casting or throwing (simply); a throw; the distance thrown. 2. *spec.* A throw of dice 1509. Also *fig.* 3. A throw or stroke of fortune; *hence*, fortune; fate. *Obs.* or *dial.* ME. 4. A throw of a sounding-lead, fishing-line, net, dredge, etc. 1616; *spec.* in *Angling*, that which is so cast 1556; a spot suitable for casting 1823. 5. A throwing of the eye in any direction; a glance, a look, expression. ? *Obs.* ME. 6. A lift in a conveyance. Also *fig.* 1630. **7.** *fig.* 'A stroke, a touch' (J.), specimen, taste 1553.

1. The disputed c. was a drawn one SCOTT. *A measuring c*: one in which the results require measurement. About a stones c. *Luke* xxii. 41. 2. 'Tis no winning c. MILT. *To set, stake upon a c.* 3. Black be their c. 1722. †*At the last c.*, i.e. the last shift. 4. The right to a c. of the net BURTON. A c. suited to the state of the water 1883. 5. With a sad, leaden, downward c. MILT. *Pens.* 43. 7. A c. of one's office 1575, cunning 1589, politics 1676.

II. A throw in wrestling; an overthrow (*arch.*) ME.

III. A throwing; the quantity thrown 1450.

A c. of scatter'd dust DRYDEN. A c. (= a couple) of hawks, etc. 1470. †A c. (=a batch) of bread B. JONS. A c. (=the number in one throw, viz. three or four, a warp) of herrings 1577.

IV. That which is thrown off or out.

A c. (=a second swarm) of bees FULLER. The c. (= what is thrown up from the crop) of a hawk TENNYSON. The c. of an earthworm WHITE.

V. Calculation; *techn.* the addition of the columns of an account 1575.

†**VI.** Device, design; trick -1609.

VII. Form into which a thing is thrown; disposition, arrangement 1579. **2.** *Theat.* The assignment of the parts in a play to the several actors; †the part assigned to any actor; the set of actors collectively 1631.

1. The c. of draperies (in *Painting*) 1784, of a sentence M. ARNOLD. 2. A powerful c. (*mod.*).

VIII. †**1.** Casting or founding 1602. **2.** A model made in a mould; *occ.*, the negative impression taken from the original, a mould 1502. Also *transf.* and *fig.*

1. C. of Brazon Cannon *Haml.* I. i. 73. 2. Books, pictures, castes EVELYN. A c. of my head JOHNSON. *Renal casts*: the urinary tubules found in kidney disease.

IX. A twist or turn, *esp.* to one side; a bearing 1505.

C. of the eye: a slight squint.

X. 1. Dash or shade of colour; tinge, hue; shade 1602. Also *fig.* **2.** A dash 1662.

1. The pale C. of Thought SHAKS. A deeper c. of dejection 1820. 2. A c. of ironical humour SCOTT.

XI. Kind, sort, style, quality, stamp, type 1653.

A sinister c. of countenance MARRYAT. This C. of mind ADDISON. A C. (= bent) towards Devotion 1711. A c. of talk JOHNSON. Heroines of such a c. GIBBON.

XII. *Hunting.* The spreading out of the hounds in search of a lost scent 1830. Also *fig.*

Cast (kast), *v.* Pa. t. and pa. pple. **cast.** [ME. *casten*, a. ON. *kasta* to cast; replacing OE. *weorpan* (see WARP), and now itself replaced in the literal sense by THROW, q. v.] **I. 1.** *trans.* To project with a force of the nature of a jerk; to THROW; to fling, hurl, pitch, toss. Also *fig.* Occ. *absol.* **2.** *refl.* To throw oneself (not colloq.) ME. **3.** To throw forth ME. †**4.** To emit -1742. **5.** To cause to fall *on, over*, etc. ME. †**6.** To toss (the head) -1792.

1. Certayn men.. keste water vpon him CAXTON. †*To c. seed.* Now usu. *fig.* C. thy bread vpon the waters *Eccles.* xi. 1. To c. dice 1565, a vote (*mod.*). *To c. lots*: see LOT. †To c. an arrow WYCLIF. *C. ashore, away*, etc. 2. Low on her knees herself she cast TENNYSON. 3. To c. a net 1526, an angle B. JONS., a flye 1651, an anchor 1798, a lure 1682. *To c. an eye, glance, look*, etc. †*To c. a reflection upon.* 5. *To c. light, a shadow* (*on*). *To c. into the shade.*

II. 1. To throw down, overthrow, defeat 1481. †**2.** To find guilty, convict -1849. †**3.** To condemn. Const. *for* (the penalty) -1816. Also *fig.* and *transf.*

1. The king was cast from the throne 1755. To c. a horse 1577, a sheep 1882. To c. in wrestling *Macb.* II. iii. 46. Now *arch.* Cast in damages 1854. 3. Cast for transportation MACKENZIE.

III. 1. To throw off, out, away ME. **2.** *esp.* To shed, or drop, out of due season 1477. **3.** To vomit. Now only of hawks, etc. (exc. *dial.*) ME. Also *absol.* **4.** To dismiss, reject; *esp.* as disqualified or unfit ME.

1. To c. a shoe SCOTT, a rider SPENSER. Cast not a clout till May be out *Old Maxim.* To c. the skin, as reptiles, caterpillars 1626; so, to c. hair, horns, teeth, leaves (now *arch.*). To c. spawn WALTON, eggs ADDISON, young 1769. To c. a swarm (of bees) 1523. 2. As a figge tree casteth her vntimely figs *Rev.* vi. 13. To c. a calf, a lamb 1523. 3. *To c. the gorge*: to retch. *Temp.* II. i. 251. To c. a sigh CAXTON, a shout POPE. 4. The State.. Cannot with safetie c. him *Oth.* I. i. 150. Horses cast from the cavalry 1817. C. in an examination 1854.

IV. To throw up with a spade or shovel; *hence*, †to clear out (a ditch, etc.) -1614; †to raise (a mound, etc.) -1667.

To c. sods, turf, peat (north.). To c. a rampart MILT.

V. 1. To put with force, decisiveness, or haste. (Now usu. *throw.*) ME. Also *fig.* **2.** To put *into* ME. †**3.** To set *to* (*upon*) some action -1662. **4.** To confer, allot (*arch.*) 1612.

1. Cast thy mantle aboute the *Acts* xii. 8. To c. cares 1751, blame 1842, an imputation 1883, upon a person. 2. To c. into prison ME., into hell JOWETT. 4. To c. an estate upon the heir TOMLINS.

VI. To reckon, calculate (orig. by means of counters) ME.

(*intr.*) †*To c. at accounts.* To c. and balance at a desk TENNYSON. (*trans.*) The books were cast 1805. *To c. accounts*: orig. to sum up accounts; now to perform the operations of arithmetic. To c. the tides 1642. *To c. a horoscope, nativity*, etc. Also *absol.* †*To c. water*: to diagnose by the inspection of (urine). *To c. beyond the moon*: to conjecture wildly. †(trans.) *To c. danger, peril, the worst.*

VII. To resolve in one's mind, deliberate ME.; to contrive ME.; †to design (*to do*) -1808.

They caste..how they myght breng hym out of prison CAXTON. Cast to have the wind on your back WALTON.

VIII. 1. To dispose, arrange ME. **2.** *Theat.* To allot (the parts) *to* the actors; to appoint (actors) *for* the parts 1711.

1. To c. streets in comely fashion BIBLE *Pref.* 8. To c. (facts) under heads 1710, *into* a series of letters H. MILLER. †To c. a drapery (in *Painting*) 1706. 2. Our parts in the other world will be new cast ADDISON. They..cast me for the part 1809.

IX. To form (metal, etc.) *into* a shape, by pouring it when melted into a mould; to found. (Now a frequent literal sense.) ME. Also *fig.*

To c. into candlesticks 1814. A figure cast in soft wax HOGARTH. *fig.* To c. inventions in a new mould 1606.

X. To turn, twist. [Parallel to *warp.*] **1.** Of timber, etc.: To warp 1544. **2.** *Naut.* To veer 1671. Also *trans.* **3.** To turn (the scale or balance) (*arch.*) (Cf. *casting-vote.*) 1597.

1. Oake.. will shrink, cast, drawe a nayle BEST. 2. To c. to port NARES. 3. To c. the balance J. H. NEWMAN.

†**XI.** To cover by casting (mortar, etc.) on. (Cf. ROUGH-CAST.) -1663.

XII. Unplaced senses. †**1.** To tie (a knot) -1825. **2.** *Hunting. intr.* To spread out and search for a lost scent 1704. Also *transf.* and *fig.* (*trans.*) To throw off, put on the scent 1781.

2. Cast forward first.. Cast far and near, cast all around R. EG.-WARBURTON. *fig.* To c. for excuses BROWNING.

Phrases and Combs. **1. To c. loose**: to unfasten with force, set adrift. **To c. anchor, a damper, lots, a spell**: see those words. **2.** (See also simple senses and advbs.) **To c. about: a.** *intr.* to turn about; *Naut.* to change the course; **b.** to go searching this way and that, *orig.* a hunting locution; **c.** to devise means. **To c. aside**: to throw aside from use. **To c. away: a.** to put from one; **b.** to throw away, i.e. in waste or loss; **c.** to wreck; to strand. **To c. back**: to go back over the same course, revert. †**To c. by**: to throw aside from use. **To c. down: a.** to demolish; **b.** to bend and turn downward (the eyes, etc.); **c.** to deject in spirits. **To c. forth: a.** to expel, eject; †**b.** to throw out (branches, etc.). **To c. in**: to throw in (as something extra); in *To c. in one's lot among* or *with*: to become a partner with. **To c. off: a.** to throw off (clothes, etc.); also *fig.*; **b.** *fig.* to put from one, abandon; **c.** to slip (dogs); to let fly (hawks); **d.** *Naut.* to loosen and throw off (a rope, etc.). **e.** to estimate space taken in print by MS. copy. **f.** *Knitting.* to close loops and make selvedge. **To c. out: a.** to expel, make an outcast (*lit.* and *fig.*); **b.** to thrust out of doors, society, etc.; **c.** to vomit; also *transf.* and *absol.*; **d.** *intr.* to quarrel (*Sc.* and *n. dial.*). **To c. up**: †**a.** to vomit; said also of the sea; **b.** to raise suddenly (the eyes, the head); **c.** to throw up (with a shovel); **d.** to rake up and throw in one's teeth (*Sc.* and *n. dial.*); **e.** to add up, calculate; **f.** *intr.* to turn up, appear (*Sc.* and *north.*).

Ca·stable, *sb. rare.* 1821. [f. prec.] The projection of waste metal on cast articles.

Castalia (kæstē¹·liă), **Castalie, -ly** (kæ·stăli). 1591. [L. and Gr., pr. name.] A spring on Mount Parnassus, sacred to the Muses; often used allusively. Hence **Casta·lian** *a.* of Castalia or the Muses.

†**Castane, -anie, -ayne.** ME. [a. ONF. *castanie, castaine* (mod. *châtaigne*):—L. *castanea.*] A chestnut -1567.

Castaneous (kæstē¹·niŏs), *a.* 1688. [f. L. *castaneus.*] Chestnut-coloured. So **Casta·nean.**

Castanet (ka·stănet, -ane·t). 1647. [ad. Sp. *castañeta*, dim. of *castaña* :—L. *castanea.*] A small concave shell of ivory or hard wood, used by the Spaniards, Moors, and others, to produce a rattling sound or rhythmic tapped accompaniment to dancing; a pair of them, fastened to the thumb, are held in the palm of the hand, and struck with the middle finger. Usu. in *pl.*

Castinettas, knackers, of the form of chesnuts used ..by the Spaniards in their dances STAPYLTON.

Castaway (ka·stăwē¹). 1526. [f. CAST *v.*]

A. *adj.* Rejected; reprobate; useless; stranded 1542.

C. bones of the deer, bear, and wild-ox PAGE.

B. *sb.* One who or that which is cast away or rejected; a reprobate 1526; a shipwrecked man 1799. Also *fig.*

Reprobates and castawaies 1563. Wreck and stray and c. SWINBURNE. The castaways of society 1869.

Caste (kast). 1555. [ad. Sp. and Pg. *casta* race, lineage; orig. 'pure (stock or breed)', f. *casta*, fem. of *casto* :—L. *castus* (see CHASTE). Formerly written *cast.*] †**1.** A race, stock, or breed -1774. **2.** *spec.* One of the hereditary classes into which society in India has long been divided. Also *transf.* 1613.

The members of each caste are socially equal, have the same religious rites, and generally follow the same occupation or profession; they have no social intercourse with those of another caste. The original castes were four: 1st, the *Brahmans* or priestly caste; 2nd, the *Kshatriyas* or military caste; 3rd, the *Vaisyas* or merchants; 4th, the *Sudras*, or artisans and labourers. Now almost every variety of occupation has its caste.

3. *fig.* A class who keep themselves socially distinct, or inherit exclusive privileges 1807. **4.** This system among the Hindoos; also the position it confers, as in *To lose*, or *renounce c.* 1811. Also *gen.* and *fig.*

3. That repose Which stamps the c. of Vere de Vere TENNYSON. 4. *fig.* Loss of c. in society 1816.

†**Ca·sted**, *ppl. a.* Earlier f. CAST. SHAKS.

Castellan (ka·stĕlăn). [ME. *castelain*, a. ONF. (mod. *châtelain*) :—L. *castellanus*, f. *castellum*; refash. after L.] The governor or constable of a castle. Hence **Ca·stellany,** the lordship of a castle, or its district.

Castellar (kæ̆ste·lăı), *a.* 1789. [f. L. *castellum* + -AR.] Pertaining to, or of the nature of, a castle.

Castellated (kæ·stĕlē¹tĕd), *ppl. a.* 1679. [f. med.L. *castellatus.*] **1.** Built like a castle; having battlements. Also *transf.* †**2.** 'Enclosed within a building, as a fountain or cistern' -1766. **3.** Dotted with castles 1808. **4.** Lodged in a castle (*rare*) 1837.

1. *transf.* C. mountains H. WALPOLE. 3. The c. Rhine BYRON. So **Ca·stellate** *a.* (*rare*). Hence **Ca·stellate** *v.* to build with battlements.

Castellation (kæstĕlē¹·ʃən). 1818. [ad. med. L. *castellationem.*] The building of castles; the furnishing of a house with battlements; *concr.* a castellated structure; a battlement.

Ca·stellet, -elet. ME. [a. ONF. *castelet*, dim. of *castel.* See also CHATELET.] A small castle. var. †**Ca·stlet.**

Casten, *ppl. a.* By-form of CAST pa. pple. Now *dial.*

Caster (ka·stəı). ME. [f. CAST *v.*] One who casts (see CAST *v.*). **2.** See CASTOR [2].

A c. of accounts 1598, of nativities 1611, of the evil eye 1887. *spec.* A c. in brass 1662, of cannon 1884.

Castigate (kæ·stigē¹t), *v.* 1607. [f. L. *castigat-, castigare* (f. *castus*) + -ATE [3].] **1.** To chastise, correct; to subdue by punishment or discipline; now usu., to punish or rebuke severely. Also †*transf.* **2.** To correct, revise, and emend 1666. Hence **Ca·stigator,** one who castigates. **Ca·stigatory,** *a.* corrective, punitive; †*sb.* an instrument of chastisement.

Castigation (kæstigē¹·ʃən). ME. [ad. L. *castigationem*; see prec.] **1.** †Corrective punishment or discipline -1677; now, severe punishment or rebuke, flagellation 1640. **2.** Correction, emendation 1611.

1. A well-merited c. 1831.

Castile soap (kăstī·l sō^u·p). Formerly castle-soap. 1616. [f. *Castile*, in Spain, where orig. made.] A fine hard soap, white or mottled, made with olive oil and soda.

Casti·lian, *sb.*[1] 1570. [var. of CASTELLAN.] One living in a castle; one of the garrison of a castle. Now *Hist.*

Castilian (kæsti·liăn), *a.* and *sb.*[2] 1526. [In sense 1, ad. Sp. *Castellano* pertaining to Castile

(*Castella*, so called from the forts erected by Alfonso I for its defence).] 1. Of or pertaining to Castile; a native of Castile; the language of that province, *hence*, standard Spanish 1796. 2. A Spanish gold coin worth about 5*s*. *Hist.*

Casting (ka·stiŋ), *vbl. sb.* ME. [f. CAST *v.* + -ING [1].] 1. The action of the vb. 2. *concr.* a. Any product of casting in a mould. b. The earth cast up by worms. c. Vomit; *esp.* what is cast up by hawks and the like.

1. A c. of the skin BACON, of a story M. ARNOLD, of a nativity 1825. *intr.* Reasoning is..c. about LOCKE. C. or warping 1823.

Comb., etc.: **c.-box**, †a dice-box; also, a box used for taking a cast in stereotyping; †**-counters** *pl.*, counters used in calculation; **-bottle**, a vinaigrette.

Casting (ka·stiŋ), *ppl. a.* ME. [f. as prec.] 1. That casts (see CAST *v.*). 2. That turns the scale, deciding, as in *c. voice, vote, weight* 1622.

Cast iron, cast-i·ron. 1664. 1. Iron run in a molten state into moulds where it has cooled and hardened. Also *attrib.* (*commonly hyphened.*) 2. *fig.* Hard, insensible to fatigue; rigid, stern; wanting in pliancy. (*hyphened.*) 1830.

2. A cast-iron Statesman 1830, rule 1876.

Castle (ka·s'l), *sb.* [(1) OE. *castel* neut., ad. L. *castellum* in the Vulgate, rendering κώμη village; (2) *castel* masc., a. ONF. *castel* (mod. F. *château*) :—L. *castellum* fortress, dim. of *castrum*. Cf. CHESTER.] I. From Latin. †1. As tr. L. *castellum* of the Vulgate, village -1564. †2. *pl.* As tr. L. *castra* camp -1483.

II. From French. 1. A large building or set of buildings fortified for defence; a fortress. Retained as a name for large mansions which were formerly feudal castles OE. Also *fig.* (or *allegorical*). 2. *poet.* or *rhet.* for: A large ship 1642. 3. A tower borne on the back of an elephant ME. 4. *Naut.* A tower on the deck of a ship. Cf. FORECASTLE. ME. 5. Applied (in proper names) to ancient earthworks, as *Round C.* near Oxford, etc. 6. *Chess.* A piece, made to represent a castle; a ROOK 1649.

1. A castel al of lime and ston CHAUCER. The mill buys out the c. EMERSON. *The Castle*, in reference to Ireland, means specifically *Dublin Castle*, as the seat of the vice-regal court and administration; hence, in politics, the authority centred there, the officials who administer the government of Ireland. Also *attrib.* Phr. *An (English)man's house is his c.* 2. The floating Castles dance upon the Tide BLACKMORE.

Phrase. **Castle in the air**, visionary project, day-dream, idle fancy. Occ. *castle in Spain* [= F. *château en Espagne*] is found; also *castle* alone.

Comb.: †**c.-bote**, the keeping of a c. in repair, a contribution levied for this purpose; **-soap**, see CASTILE SOAP; **-town**, a town defended by a c.; also (*Sc.*) a collection of houses lying under or near a c. Hence **Ca·stle-like** *a.* and *adv.*

Castle (ka·s'l), *v.* ME. [f. prec.] 1. To enclose in, or as in, a castle 1587. †2. To ornament with battlements. CHAUCER. 3. *Chess.* To move the king laterally towards the castle (rook), which is then moved to the square next to him on the other side 1656.

Ca·stle-bui·lder. 1711. One who builds castles in the air, a day-dreamer, a visionary schemer. So **Ca·stle-bui·lding** *vbl. sb.* and *ppl. a.*

Castled (ka·s'ld), *ppl. a.* 1662. [f. CASTLE + -ED.] 1. Furnished with a castle or castles. 2. Castellated 1789.

1. Norham's c. steep SCOTT. 2. In the c. house.. Which sheltered their childhood M. ARNOLD.

Castle-guard. 1. The guard of a castle. 2. *Feudal Syst.* A kind of knight-service, whereby a tenant was bound, when required, to defend the lord's castle; the tenure of such service 1576. 3. A tax orig. in commutation of this service; also the land chargeable therewith 1576.

†**Ca·stlery, castelry.** 1679. [f. *castel* CASTLE *sb.*] The jurisdiction of a castle; the territory subject to it. var. †**Ca·stleship.**

Ca·stleward. ME. †1. The warden of a castle WYNTOUN. 2. = CASTLE-GUARD 2, 3. 1576.

†**Castling** (ka·stliŋ), *sb.* 1580. [dim. of CAST *ppl. a.* or *sb.*] 1. The offspring of an untimely birth; an abortion -1704. 2. The second (or third) swarm from one hive in the season -1662.

1. C. Foles of Bal'am's Ass BUTLER *Hud.* II. ii. 539.

Ca·stling, *vbl. sb.* See CASTLE *v.*

†**Cast-me-down.** Corrupt f. CASSIDONY.

Ca·st-off, *ppl. a.* and *sb.*[1] 1741. [f. CAST *ppl. a.*] *ppl. a.* Thrown off, discarded: as clothes, a lover, etc. 1746. *sb.* [sc. *person* or *thing.*] (*Cast-offs* is the better pl.)

Cast-off, *sb.*[2] 1881. [f. CAST *sb.*] The twist of a gun-stock.

Castor[1] (ka·stəɹ). 1547. [a. F. and L., a. Gr. κάστωρ beaver.] 1. The beaver. (Now *rare.*) 2. A reddish-brown unctuous substance, having a strong smell and nauseous bitter taste, obtained from two sacs in the inguinal region of the beaver; used in medicine and in perfumery; castoreum 1601. 3. A hat, orig. of beaver's fur; later of rabbit's fur and spelt *caster.* Now *colloq.* or *slang.* Cf. BEAVER. 1640. 4. 'A heavy quality of broadcloth used for overcoats' (Webster).

3. A Beaver [and] a new Caster 1688.

Castor[2] (ka·stəɹ). Also **caster.** 1676. [var. of CASTER, f. CAST *v.*] 1. A small vessel with a perforated top, from which to cast ground pepper, etc.; extended to other vessels used to contain condiments at table, as in 'a set of castors'. 2. A small wheel and swivel attached to furniture, so that it may be turned without lifting; see CAST *v.* X. 1748.

1. *C. sugar*: powdered sugar, so called as being suitable for use in a c.

Ca·stor[3]. 1526. The first star in the constellation Gemini or the Twins, the second being Pollux; the two representing the twin sons of Tyndarus and Leda. 2. CORPOSANT or St. Elmo's fire 1708.

Castor[4] (ka·stəɹ). 1888. [? corruption of CASTANE, or L. *castanea.*] The piece of horn inside the hock of the horse. Cf. CHESTNUT.

Castor[5]. *Min.* See CASTORITE.

‖**Castoreum** (kæstōᵊ·riŏm). ME. [L., f. *castor* beaver.] = CASTOR [1] 2. var. †**Ca·story.**

Casto·rial, *a.* [f. CASTOR [1] 3.] (*joc.*) Pertaining to a hat. LOWELL.

Ca·storin. 1831. [f. CASTOR [1].] *Chem.* A crystalline substance obtained from castoreum.

Ca·storite. 1868. [This mineral and another were at first named *Castor* and *Pollux.*] *Min.* A variety of Petalite.

Castor oil (ka·stəɹ oi·l). 1746. [?] A pale yellow oil obtained from the seeds of *Ricinus communis* or Palma Christi; used as a purgative, and, locally, in lamps. Also *attrib.*

Castral (kæ·străl), *a.* 1844. [f. L. *castra* + -AL.] Belonging to the camp.

Castrametation (kæ:strămĭtē¹·ʃən). 1679. [a. F., f. L. *castra metari.*] The art or science of laying out a camp.

Ca·strate, *a.* (*sb.*) 1639. [ad. L. *castratus*; see next.] *adj.* Castrated. *Obs.* exc. in *Bot.* 1704. †*sb.* [sc. *man.*] -1691.

Castrate (kæ·streɪt), *v.* 1613. [f. L. *castrat-*, *castrare.*] 1. To remove the testicles of; to geld. Also *transf.* and *fig.* 2. To mutilate (a book, etc.) by removing parts of it; *esp.* to remove obscene or objectionable passages from; to expurgate 1627.

2. The following letter, which I have castrated in some places ADDISON. Hence **Castra·tion.**

‖**Castrato** (kastrā·to). Pl. **castrati.** 1763 [It.; pa. pple. of *castrare* used subst.] A male singer castrated in boyhood so as to retain a soprano or alto voice.

Castrensian (kæstre·nsiăn), *a.* 1657. [f. L. *castrensis* + -AN.] Of or pertaining to a camp; camp-. So †**Castre·nsial.**

Casual (kæ·ʒ¹uăl, kæ·ziuăl), *a.* (*sb.*) ME. [a. F. *casuel*, ad. L. *casualis*, f. *casus.*] 1. Subject to or produced by chance; accidental, fortuitous. 2. Coming at uncertain times; not to be calculated on, unsettled 1460. 3. Occurring without design 1667. †4. Liable to happen -1645. †5. Subject to chance or accident -1729. 6. Of persons, etc.: Not to be depended on, uncertain, happy-go-lucky (*colloq.*) 1883. †7. Casuistic (*rare*) -1753. ¶8. = CAUSAL 1578.

1. That which seemeth most c. and subject to fortune RALEIGH. 2. Both the known and c. Revenue CLARENDON. 3. To talk of c. things DE FOE. 6. A c. man 1883. Hence *c.* (= occasional) *labourer, poor, ward*, etc. A c. *ejector* (*Law*) was a fictitious ejector in an action formerly allowed to determine the title to land. Hence **Ca·sual-ly** *adv.*, **-ness** (*rare*).

B. *sb.* †1. A chance. (Chiefly in *pl.*) -1652. 2. [sc. *revenue*] 1825. 3. *colloq.* = c. workman, visitor, pauper, ward, etc. 1860.

Ca·sualism. 1873. [f. prec.] The doctrine that all things exist or happen by chance; a state of things in which chance reigns. So **Ca·sualist,** one who holds the doctrine of c.

†**Casua·lity.** 1540. [a. F. *casualité*; see CASUAL. Now CASUALTY.] 1. Chance; a chance; *esp.* an unfortunate accident -1792. 2. A casual source of income -1649.

Casualty (kæ·ʒ¹uˌălti, kæ·ziuˌălti). ME. [ad. L. *casualitas*, after *royalty*, etc.; formerly CASUALITY.] 1. Chance (as a state of things). ? *Obs.* 2. A chance occurrence, an accident; now generally a fatal or serious accident. b. *Mil.* Used of losses by death, desertion, etc. 1494. †3. Liability to accident -1812. 4. A casual charge or payment 1529. ¶ Erron. for CAUSALITY 1635.

1. Combinations of..genius with happy c. JOHNSON. 2. Casualties of the service 1810, on our coast 1861. *attrib.* in *c. ward*, the ward in a hospital where accidents are treated.

‖**Casuarina** (kæ:siuˌărəi·nă). 1806. [f. mod. L. *casuarius* cassowary, from the likeness of the branches to the feathers of the bird.] *Bot.* A genus of trees, with jointed leafless branches, resembling gigantic horse-tails (*Equiseta*), natives of Australia, etc. The Australian species is known as *Beef-wood*, and Oak.

Casuist (kæ·ziuˌist, kæ·ʒ¹uˌist). 1609. [a. F. *casuiste*, f. L. *casus.*] One who studies and resolves cases of conscience. (Often used in a sinister sense; see CASUISTRY.)

Casuists willing and competent to soothe his conscience with Sophisms MACAULAY. Hence †**Ca·suist** *v.* to play the c. **Ca·suistess,** a female c. **Casui·stic, -al** *a.* pertaining to casuists or casuistry. **Casuis·tically** *adv.*

Casuistry (kæ·ziuˌistri, kæ·ʒ¹u-). 1725. [f. CASUIST. At first contemptuous; cf. *sophistry*, etc.] The science, art, or reasoning of the casuist; that part of Ethics which resolves cases of conscience, applying the general rules of religion and morality to particular instances which disclose special circumstances, or conflicting duties. Often applied to a quibbling or evasive way of dealing with difficult cases of duty; sophistry. 2. A register of (medical) cases 1883.

1. C. destroys, by distinctions and exceptions, all morality BOLINGBROKE.

†**Ca·sule.** [OE. *casul*, ad. L. *casula* (dim. of *casa*).] = CHASUBLE -1824.

†‖**Ca·sus.** 1571. [L.] Each of the segments of the base of a triangle cut off by a perpendicular falling from the vertex.

Cat (kæt), *sb.*[1] [OE. *catt* masc., *catte* fem.; Common European word of unkn. origin.] I. 1. A carnivorous quadruped, *Felis domesticus*, which has long been domesticated. Wild c., *Felis sylvestris*, native and still found in Great Britain, is larger than the domestic cat. Also *fig.* 2. *Zool.* (usu. in *pl.*) A member of the genus *Felis* or *Panthera*, including the lion, tiger, etc. 1607. 3. Used of animals of similar appearance, as *civet-*, *pole-c.*, etc.; also in **flying-c.**, an owl (cf. F. *chat-huant*); **sea-c.**, the Wolf-fish 1553. †4. = CAT-SKIN -1677.

1. The mouse hounter or catte is an onclene beste 1520. *fig.* His mother called me an old c. MARRYAT. 3. *A. Y. L.* III. ii. 70.

II. Transf. 1. A movable pent-house, used in sieges, also called *cat-house* 1489. †Also = CAVALIER (*Fortif.*) -1652. 2. *Naut.* Applied to different parts of the tackle used to raise an anchor out of the water to the deck of the ship, or suspend it outside clear of the bows; chiefly = CAT-HEAD 1626. 3. = CAT-O'-NINE-TAILS 1788. 4. A double tripod with six legs, so placed that it always rests on three legs 1806. 5. A term used in games: *esp.* A piece of wood tapering at each end, used in tip-cat; also, the game itself 1598.

3. This Cat's a cousin-german to the Knout WOLCOTT. Phrases. *To turn c. in pan*: to change sides, from motives of interest, etc. *To see* (*watch*) *which way the c. jumps*: i. e. which direction events are taking. *To let the c. out of the bag*: see BAG. *To grin like a Cheshire c.* (see N. & Q. 1852 V. 402).

Comb., etc.: **c.-block** (*Naut.*), a two- or three-fold block forming part of the c.-tackle; **-fall** (*Naut.*), the rope between the c.-block and the sheaves in the c.-head; **-gold, cat's-gold** (Ger. *katzengold*), a yellowish variety of mica (cf. *cat-silver*); **-ha·mmed,** having hams like those of a c.; **-hook** (*Naut.*), a strong hook on the c.-block; **-house** (see 1 above); **-ice, cat's ice,** thin ice of a milky white appearance in shallow places; **-ladder,** a kind of ladder used on sloping roofs; **-nap,** a short nap while sitting; **-purchase** (*Naut.*)=*cat-tackle*; **-rope** (*Naut.*), a line for hauling the c.-hook about; **-salt,** a kind of common salt, finely granulated, formed out of the bittern or leach brine; **-silver,** mica with a silvery appearance; **-sleep**=*cat-nap*; **-tackle** (*Naut.*), the tackle to raise the anchor to the c.-head.

†**Cat,** *sb.*² Also **catt.** 1699. [Orig. the same wd. as prec.] A strong vessel with a narrow stern, projecting quarters, and a deep waist; formerly used in the coal and timber trade on the north-east coast -1825. ? Hence **c.-boat,** a sailing-boat having the mast placed very forward and rigged with one sail; **c.-rig,** a rig of one fore-and-aft mainsail.

Cat (kæt), *v.* 1769. [f. CAT *sb.*¹] **1.** *Naut.* To raise (the anchor) from the surface of the water to the cat-head. **2.** To flog with the cat-o'-nine-tails 1856. **3.** *slang.* To vomit 1877.

Cata- (kata-), cat-, cath-. [Gr. κατα-, κατ-, καθ-, used in comp.] **a.** Down (locally); **b.** down, away, entirely; **c.** implying disparagement (= *mis-*); **d.** inferior; **e.** down upon; **f.** against and reflected back, *hence*, answering to; **g.** intensive, downright, completely; **h.** *hence*, like Eng. *be-*, making a vb. transitive.

†**Cataba·ptist.** 1561. [ad. Gr. καταβαπτιστής.] One who opposes baptism -1864.

‖**Cataba·sion.** 1753. [Gr.] A place for relics under the altar of a Greek church.

Catabatic (-bæ·tik), *a.* 1881. [ad. Gr. καταβατικός, f. καταβαίνειν.] *Med.* Of a fever: Declining by degrees.

Catacaustic (kætăkǭ·stik), *a.* and *sb.* 1708. [mod. f. Gr. κατα- back + καυστικός CAUSTIC.] *C.* (*curve*): a caustic curve formed by reflection.

‖**Catachresis** (kætăkrī·sis). 1589. [a. L., a. Gr. κατάχρησις, f. καταχρῆσθαι to misuse.] Improper use of words; application of a term to a thing which it does not properly denote; abuse of a trope or metaphor.

Lakes..by the figure c. called seas 1605. Hence **Catachre·stic, -al** *a.* of the nature of c.; **-ly** *adv.*

Catachthonian, -thonic, *a.* 1884. [f. Gr. καταχθόνιος.] Subterranean.

Cataclasm (kæ·tăklæz'm). 1829. [ad. Gr. κατάκλασμα, f. κατα-κλᾶν.] A break or disruption. Hence **Catacla·smic** *a.*

Cataclysm (kæ·tăkliz'm). 1637. [a. F. *cataclysme*, ad. Gr. κατακλυσμός deluge (also *fig.*), f. κατά + κλύζειν.] A great and general flood of water; *esp.* the Flood. (In *Geol.* used vaguely for a sudden convulsion or alteration of physical conditions.) Also *fig.*

fig. That the Indian army surgeons will be swept away in the general c. 1861. Hence **Catacly·smal, Catacly·smic** *adjs.* of, pertaining to, or like a c.

Cataclysmist (kætăkli·zmist). 1887. [f. prec. + -IST.] One who adopts the hypothesis of cataclysms in Geology; a catastrophist. var. **Catacly·smatist** (*rare*).

Catacomb (kæ·tăkōᵘm). OE. [a. F. *catacombe*, ad. It. *catacomba*:—late L. *Catacumbas*, ? the cemetery or the locality.] **1.** A subterranean place for the burial of the dead, consisting of galleries with recesses in their sides for tombs.

a. Used in the 5th c. in connexion with the cemetery under the Basilica of St. Sebastian, on the Appian Way, near Rome. **b.** Applied later (in the pl.) to all the subterranean cemeteries lying around Rome. In the sing. applied to a single crypt or gallery. 1662. **c.** Extended to similar works elsewhere, as in Egypt, etc. 1705.

2. Any subterranean receptacle of dead bodies, as the catacombs of Paris, which are worked-out stone quarries; also *fig.* **3.** *transf.* A compartment with recesses in a wine-cellar 1795.

2. *fig.* A perfect c. for monsters of extinct races DARWIN.

Catacoustics (kætăkau·stiks). 1683. [mod. f. CATA- in sense **f.** + ACOUSTICS. Cf. CATOPTRICS.] The science of reflected sounds.

Catadioptric, -al (kæ:tă,dəi,ǫ·ptrik, -ăl), *a.* 1723. [f. CATA- in CATOPTRIC + DIOPTRIC.] Pertaining to or involving both the reflection and the refraction of light. So **Catadio·ptrics,** the science of c. phenomena.

Catadrome (kæ·tădrōᵘm). 1623. [ad. Gr. κατάδρομος.] †**1.** A course for tilting. (Dicts.) **2.** A machine for lifting or lowering heavy weights 1656.

Catadromous (katæ·drŏməs), *a.* 1881. [f. Gr. κατά down + -δρομος running. Cf. ANADROMOUS.] **1.** *Zool.* Of freshwater fishes: Descending to or towards the sea to spawn; as the Eel. **2.** *Bot.* Of ferns: Having the lowest secondary branches originating on the posterior side of the pinnæ (*mod.*).

†**Ca·tadupe.** 1596. [a. F., ad. L. *catadupa* (pl.), ad. Gr. κατάδουποι (pl.) the cataracts of the Nile, f. κατά down + δοῦπος thud. (But see L. and S.)] A cataract or waterfall, *orig.* those of the Nile -1755.

Catafalque (kæ·tăfælk). 1641. [a. mod. F., ad. It. *catafalco* (also used); of unkn. deriv. See SCAFFOLD.] **1.** A temporary structure of carpentry, representing a tomb or cenotaph, and used in funeral ceremonies. **2.** An open hearse 1855. Also *transf.*

Catagma·tic, *a.* 1657. [a. F. *catagmatique*, f. Gr. κάταγμα, f. καταγνύναι to break.] *Med.* Of or belonging to fractures or their treatment 1684. quasi-*sb.* A medicine of use in healing fractures.

†**Catai·an,** *a.* 1598. Var. of *Cathaian*, a man of Cathay or China; ? a thief, scoundrel, blackguard (*Twel. N.* II. iii. 80) -1649.

Catalan (kæ·tălĕn), *a.* 1480. Of or belonging to Catalonia. As *sb.* A native of Catalonia; the language of Catalonia.

C. forge, a blast-furnace for reducing iron ores, much used in Catalonia and the neighbouring districts.

Catalectic (kætăle·ktik), *a.* 1589. [ad. late L. *catalecticus*, a. Gr. καταληκτικός, f. καταλήγειν to leave off. Cf. F. *catalectique.*] *Pros.* Of a verse: Wanting a syllable in the last foot.

†**Ca·talects,** *sb. pl. rare.* 1610. [ad. L. *catalecta*, a. Gr. *κατάλεκτα, f. καταλέγειν to reckon among. Cf. ANALECTA.] In sense of L., a collection of short poems ascribed to Vergil; also, detached pieces.

Catalepsy (kæ·tălepsi). ME. [ad. med. L. *catalepsia*, f. Gr. κατάληψις.] **1.** *Med.* A disease characterized by a seizure or trance, with suspension of sensation and consciousness. **2.** *Philos.* Comprehension, apprehension 1656. var. (in L. form) **Catalepsis.**

Cataleptic (kætăle·ptik), *a.* 1684. [ad. late L. *catalepticus*, a. Gr., f. καταλαμβάνειν.] **1.** *Med.* Of, pertaining to, or affected by, catalepsy. **2.** *Philos.* Pertaining to apprehension 1847. As *sb.* One affected by catalepsy. Hence (in *Med.*) **Catale·ptiform, Catale·ptoid** *adjs.* resembling catalepsy.

Catallactic (kætălæ·ktik), *a.* 1831. [ad. Gr. καταλλακτικός, f. καταλλάσσειν.] *adj.* Pertaining to exchange 1862. As *sb. pl.* Political Economy as the 'Science of Exchanges'. Hence **Catalla·ctically** *adv.* by way of exchange.

†**Catalogize** (kæ·tălǫdʒəi:z, -gəi:z). 1602. [f. Gr. καταλογίζεσθαι; influenced by CATALOGUE. Cf. *cataloguize.*] **1.** To reckon up. **2.** To insert in a catalogue -1665.

Catalogue (kæ·tălǫg), *sb.* 1460. [a. F., and ad. late L. *catalogus*, a. Gr. κατάλογος, f. καταλέγειν.] **1.** A list, register, or complete enumeration; in this sense now *arch.* Also *fig.* **2.** Now, a list or enumeration systematically arranged in alphabetical or other order, often with the addition of brief particulars 1667.

1. The C. of the Slain ADDISON. **2.** Finished my C. of books PEPYS. Hence **Catalo·gic, -al** *a.* of the nature of, or pertaining to, a c.

Catalogue (kæ·tălǫg), *v.* 1598. [f. prec.] **1.** *trans.* To make a catalogue or list of. **2.** To insert in a catalogue. Also *fig.* 1635.

1. To c. a woman's features, a library (*mod.*). **2.** To c. innocent acts with sins H. WALPOLE. Hence **Ca·talo·guer,** one who catalogues; also **Ca·talo·guist,** var. **Catalogist.** **Ca·talogui·ze** *v.* (*trans.*) to CATALOGUE.

‖**Catalpa** (kătæ·lpă). [Indian of Carolina, where Catesby discovered *C. bignonioides* in 1726.] *Bot.* A genus of trees (N.O. *Bignoniaceæ*), natives of N. America, W. Indies, Japan and China, having large simple leaves, and terminal panicles of trumpet-shaped flowers.

Catalysis (kătæ·lisis). 1655. [a. Gr. κατάλυσις, f. καταλύειν.] †**1.** Dissolution, destruction, ruin (*rare*) -1660. **2.** *Chem.* Berzelius' name for the effect produced in facilitating a chemical reaction, by the presence of a substance, which itself undergoes no permanent change. Also called *contact action.* 1836.

1. This sad c. and declension of piety EVELYN. Hence **Cataly·tic** *a.* of the nature of, or pertaining to, c.; having the power of acting by c. **Cataly·tically** *adv.*

Catamaran (kæ:tămăræ·n, kătæ·mărăn). 1697. [ad. Tamil; 'tied tree or wood'.] **1.** A kind of raft or float, consisting of two or more logs tied together side by side, the middle one being longer than the others; used, *esp.* on the Coromandel coast, for communication with the shore. Also applied to similar craft used in the West Indies, off the coast of S. America, and on the St. Lawrence and its tributaries. Also *attrib.* †**2.** A kind of fire-ship or torpedo -1832. **3.** A cross-grained person, *esp.* a woman. *colloq.* [? Assoc. w. *cat.*] 1833.

2. He experimented with Fulton's 'catamarans'—the prototypes of the modern fish torpedoes—against the Boulogne flotilla ALLARDYCE.

‖**Catamenia** (kætămī·niă), *sb. pl.* 1754. [Gr., neut. pl. of καταμήνιος monthly.] The menstrual discharge. Hence **Catame·nial** *a.*

Catamite (kæ·tăməit). 1593. [ad. L. *Catamitus*, corrupt f. *Ganymedes.*] A boy kept for unnatural purposes.

Catamount (kæ·tămaunt). 1664. [Short f. CATAMOUNTAIN.] †**1.** = CATAMOUNTAIN -1736. **2.** In U. S. the puma or cougar 1794.

Catamountain, cat o' mountain (kætămau·ntĕn, -ǫ,mau·ntĕn). ME. [app. Eng.] **1.** *Orig.*, the leopard or panther; also the Ocelot (*Felis pardalis*), or other Tiger-cat. **2.** *transf.* A wild man from the mountain 1616.

2. *attrib.* Cat-a-Mountaine lookes *Merry W.* II. ii. 27.

†**Catana·dromous,** *a.* 1753. [f. mod. L. *catanadromi*, f. Gr. κατά + ἀνά + -δρομος.] *Zool.* = ANADROMOUS.

Cat and dog, cat-and-dog. 1579. **1.** *attrib.* Full of strife; inharmonious. **2.** A game played with a piece of wood called a **cat** (cf. CAT *sb.*¹) and a club called a dog 1808.

Phr. *To rain cats and dogs*: to rain very heavily.

Catapan (kæ·tăpæn). 1727. [ad. med. L. *catapanus, cate-*; f. Gr. κατεπάνω τῶν ἀξιωμάτων (he who is) placed over the dignities (Littré).] The officer who governed Calabria and Apulia under the Byzantine emperors.

†**Ca·tapasm.** 1657. [ad. Gr. κατάπασμα, f. καταπάσσειν to besprinkle.] *Med.* An old name for any dry medicine in powder which was sprinkled on ulcers.

Catapetalous (kætăpe·tăləs), *a.* 1847. [f. Gr. κατά each to each + πέταλον PETAL.] *Bot.* Having the petals united only by cohesion with united stamens, as in Mallow.

Catapho·nic, *a.* [f. Gr. κατά + φωνή + -IC.] Pertaining to cataphonics (Dicts.).

Cataphonics (kætăfǫ·niks), *sb. pl.* 1683. = CATACOUSTICS.

Cataphract (kæ·tăfrækt). 1581. [ad. L. *cataphractes* (in sense 2 *cataphractus*), a. Gr.; f. καταφράσσειν to clothe in mail.] **1.** An ancient coat of mail. *Hist.* Also *transf.* in *Zool.* **2.** A soldier in full armour 1671. ¶*Catachr.* for CATARACT 1581.

2. Archers and slingers, cataphracts and spears MILT. *Sams.* 1619. Hence **Ca·taphracted** *a., Zool.* covered with a scaly armour. **Cataphra·ctic** *a.* pertaining to or resembling a c.

Cataphrygian (kætăfri·dʒ'ăn), *a.* and *sb.* 1585. *Ch. Hist.* A Montanist; so called because the sect originated in Phrygia.

†**Cataphy·sic, -al,** *a.* 1654. [f. Gr. κατά + φύσις + -IC, + -AL.] Contrary to nature. So **Cataphysics** *sb. pl.* (*nonce-wd.*)

Cataplasm (kæ·tăplæz'm). 1563. [a. F. *cataplasme*, ad. L., a. Gr. κατάπλασμα.] *Med.* A poultice; †a plaster. Also *fig.* Hence **Catapla·smic, -al** *a.* of the nature of a c.

Cataplexy (kæ·tapleksi). 1883. [mod. f. Gr. κατάπληξις, f. καταπλήσσειν.] The hypnotic state in animals when 'shamming dead'. Hence **Catapl·ectic** *a.* of or pertaining to c.

†**Catapuce.** ME. [a. F.] *Herb.* Lesser Spurge -1794.

Catapult (kæ·tăpvlt). 1577. [a. L. *catapulta*, a. Gr. καταπέλτης, prob. f. κατά against

+ πάλλειν to hurl.] **1.** An ancient military engine worked by a lever and ropes for discharging darts, stones, etc. **2.** A boy's shooting contrivance consisting of a forked stick and elastic band 1871. **3.** Applied to mechanical contrivances by which objects are shot out at a great speed. **Catapu·ltic** *a.* **Catapultie·r** [-IER(2)].

Catapult, *v.* 1848. [f. prec.] To hurl as from a catapult; to shoot (at) with a catapult. *intr.* To discharge a catapult.

Cataract (kæ·tărækt), *sb.* ME. [a. F. *cataracte*, ad. L. *cataracta*, a. Gr. καταρ(ρ)άκτης, f. καταράσσειν to dash down, or ? καταρρηγνύναι to break down.] †**1.** *pl.* The 'flood-gates' of heaven (see *Gen.* vii. 11, viii. 2) -1684. Used also of waterspouts; and *transf.* **2.** A waterfall; prop. a large one, falling over a precipice, as opp. to CASCADE 1594. Also *transf.* and *fig.* †**3.** A portcullis. [Early in Gr. but rare in Eng.] -1853. **4.** *Pathol.* An opacity of the crystalline lens of the eye, or of its capsule, or of both, producing impairment of sight, but never complete blindness. [App. a fig. use of 3.] 1547. Also *fig.* **5.** *Mech.* A form of governor for single-acting steam-engines, in which the stroke is regulated by the flow of water through an opening 1832.

1. MILT. *P. L.* xi. 824. 2. *fig.* Cataracts of declamation COWPER. Hence **Ca·taracted** *ppl. a.* having cataracts. †**Catara·ctic** *a.* of the nature of a c. **Catara·ctous** *a.*, *Pathol.* affected with c.

Cataract, *v.* 1796. [f. prec.] *trans.* To pour like a cataract (*nonce-use*). *intr.* To fall in a cataract.

Catarrh (kătā·ɹ). 1533. [a. F. *catarrhe*, ad. L. *catarrhus*, ad. Gr. κατάρρους, f. καταρρεῖν to flow down.] †**1.** The profuse discharge from nose and eyes which generally accompanies a cold, formerly supposed to run down from the brain; a running at the nose -1796. †**2.** Cerebral effusion or hæmorrhage; apoplexy -1708. **3.** Inflammation of a mucous membrane, causing increased flow of mucus, and often attended with sneezing, cough, and fever 1588.

3. *Epidemic c.*, influenza. *Summer c.*, hay-asthma. Hence **Cata·rrhal** *a.* **Cata·rrhous** *a.* ?*Obs.*

Catarrhine, catarhine (kæ·tărəin), *a.* 1862. [f. Gr. κατά + ῥίς, ῥῖνα nose.] *Zool.* A division of the order *Quadrumana*, including apes or monkeys having the nostrils close together, oblique, and directed downwards.

Cataspilite (kătæ·spiləit). 1868. [f. Gr. κατάσπιλος spotted.] *Min.* A hydrous silicate of alumina, with some iron, manganese, etc.

‖**Catasta.** 1650. [a. L. *catasta* scaffold.] *Hist.* **a.** A block on which slaves stood for sale. Also **b.** a bed of torture.

Catastaltic, *a.* 1851. [ad. L. *catastalticus*, a. Gr., f. καταστέλλειν to repress.] *Med.* Restraining, checking: used of astringent and styptic substances.

‖**Catastasis** (kătæ·stăsis). 1656. [Gr.; f. καθιστάναι.] **1.** The third part of the ancient drama, in which the action is heightened for the catastrophe. **2.** *Rhet.* The narrative part of a speech, usu. the exordium, in which is set forth the subject to be discussed (Dicts.). **3.** *Med.* The state or condition of anything; constitution; habit of body (Dicts.).

1. No catastrophe, rather a c. or heightening CARLYLE.

Catasterism (kătæ·stĕriz'm). 1803. [ad. Gr. καταστερισμός a 'placing among the stars', (ult.) f. κατά and ἀστήρ. Cf. ASTERISM.] **a.** *pl.* A treatise attributed to Eratosthenes giving the legends of the different constellations. **b.** A constellation.

Catastrophe (kătæ·strŏfi). 1579. [a. Gr. καταστροφή, f. καταστρέφειν.] **1.** The change which produces the final event of a dramatic piece; the dénouement. **2.** 'A final event; a conclusion generally unhappy' (J.); overthrow, ruin 1601. **3.** An event producing a subversion of the order or system of things 1696. *esp.* in *Geol.* A sudden and violent physical change, such as an upheaval, depression, etc. (See CATACLYSM, CATASTROPHISM.) 1832. **4.** A sudden disaster. (Used very loosely.) 1748.

2. The late war, and its horrid c. MARVELL. Used *joc.* in 2 *Hen. IV*, II. i. 66. Hence **Catastro·phic, -al** *a.* of the nature of, or belonging to, a c.; **-ly** *adv.*

Catastrophism (kătæ·strŏfiz'm). 1869. [f. CATASTROPHE 3 + -ISM.] The theory that certain geological and biological phenomena were caused by catastrophes, or sudden and violent disturbances of nature. So **Cata·strophist,** one who holds this theory.

Catawba (kătǭ·bă). 1857. [f. the river in S. Carolina, U.S. (named from the *Katahba* Indians), where the grape was found.] **a.** An American species of grape (*Vitis Labrusca*). **b.** The light sparkling wine made from this grape.

Catbird (kæ·tbɔ̄ɹd). 1731. [From its cry of alarm.] An American thrush (*Mimus Carolinensis*).

Catcall (kæ·tkǭl), *sb.* 1659. [From the waul of the cat.] **1.** A squeaking instrument, used *esp.* in play-houses to express disapprobation, etc. **2.** The sound, a shrill screaming whistle, made with this or with the voice 1749.

1. I was very much surprised with the great Consort of Cat-calls..a kind of Catterwawling ADDISON. Hence **Ca·tcall** *v.* to sound a c.; *trans.* to assail with catcalls.

Catch (kætʃ), *sb.*[1] ME. [f. the vb.] **1.** The act or fact of catching (see CATCH *v.*) 1580. **2.** The catching of fish; the number caught at one time 1465. †**3.** *Sc.* Tennis -1599. †**4.** A catching question -1693. **5.** Something intended to catch the attention, etc. 1781. †**6.** A glimpse -1796. **7.** *concr.* That by which anything is caught and held 1496. **8.** That which is caught or is worth catching 1596. †**9.** A fragment or scrap of anything caught up; a snatch -1830. **10.** *Mus.* Orig. a ROUND; subseq. a round in which one singer catches at the words of another, producing ludicrous effects 1601.

1. †*To lie (be) at (upon) the c.*, to be on the watch for an opportunity of catching or seizing something: On the c. for a husband JANE AUSTEN. To miss a c. (*Cricket*) 1770. Also *transf.*: H. J. Ford; a safe c. 1884. 5. This is a ha'penny c. 1871. 7. For a katch for my gate *jd.* 1520. 8. The Gentleman had got a great C. of her, as they say DRYDEN. 9. It has been writ by catches, with many intervals LOCKE (J.). We retain a c. of these pretty stories GLANVILL.

†**Catch,** *sb.*[2] [ME. *cache*, ? f. CATCH *sb.*] = KETCH -1693.

Catch, *a.*; see CATCH-.

Catch (kætʃ), *v.* Pa. t. and pple. **caught** (kǭt), though *catched*, *cotched* are still in dial. and vulgar use. [ME. *cachen*, *cacchen*, a. ONF. *cachier*:—late L. **captiare*, f. *captus*, replacing in Rom. *captare*, and in late use = *venari* 'to hunt, chase'. For this sense *chacen* = OF. *chacier*, *chace* was adopted by 1300.]

I. †**1.** To chase. *trans.* and *intr.* -1526.

II. 1. To capture, *esp.* that which tries or would try to escape. (The main sense.) ME. **2.** *fig.* To ensnare; to deceive ME. †**3.** *fig.* To attain -1605. **4.** To overtake (an agent in motion). Now usu. *to c. up.* 1610. *Hence*, To reach in time 1826. **5.** To come upon suddenly or unexpectedly; to surprise (*in*, *at*, or *doing* something) 1610. **6.** To reach with a blow. Said also of the missile, etc. To hit. 1583.

1. To c. a Butterfly *Cor.* I. iii. 6, a Bird 1672. 2. To c. him in his words *Mark* xii. 13. 4. To c. a horse near the winning post (*mod.*). Caught in a shower ADDISON. To c. a train, the post, etc. (*mod.*). 5. Caught napping 1734, in the act DICKENS.

III. 1. To seize and keep hold of ME. Also *fig.* (*Obs.* exc. of fire.) **2.** *intr.* (for *refl.*) To become entangled or fixed 1787.

1. The fire caught many houses CARLYLE. *intr.* The fire hath caught SOUTHEY. *Oth.* III. iii. 90. 2. The bolt would not c. (*mod.*).

IV. To take ME. Also *fig.*

Catching cat-naps as I could KANE.

V. To snatch, *esp.* with *away*, *up*, *at* 1525.

He..hastily caught His bundle..and went his way TENNYSON.

VI. To intercept and lay hold of (anything) in its course 1548.

To c. a ball (in *Cricket*) 1849. Hence *To c. out* or *c.* (*a person*): to put him out by catching the ball from his bat. To c. an opportunity SIR T. BROWNE. *To c. one's breath*: see BREATH. His robe being catched by a bramble 1734.

VII. To get or take a thing passively; *esp.* to take, incur, or contract by exposure, infection, sympathy, or imitation ME.

To c. one's death of cold, a mischief, it (colloq.). To c. the breeze ADDISON. Used also *ellipt.* with reference to fire, frost, the wind. To c. the plague *Twel. N.* I. v. 314. She 'caught the trick of grief, and sighed' MRS. GASKELL.

VIII. To seize by the senses or intellect; to apprehend 1560.

To c. a sound GOLDSM., what a man says HAZLITT, the meaning 1837, an attitude from life 1883.

IX. To arrest the attention, mind, fancy, etc.; to captivate ME.

To c. the fair DRYDEN, the eye *Tr. & Cr.* III. iii. 183. Phrases. *C. me (at it)!* (see II. 5). *To c. it*: to get a thrashing or a scolding (*colloq.*). *To c. the eye of* another: to arrest the glance of the other. *To c. fire*: *fig.* to become inflamed or inspired. *To c. a* CRAB, *a* TARTAR: see these wds.

Comb. (with advs.) **C. away:** to snatch away. **C. on: a.** *intr.* to join on (*colloq.*); **b.** *U.S.* to apprehend; **c.** to 'take' (*colloq.*). **C. up: a.** to carry suddenly aloft; **b.** to lift suddenly; **c.** to adopt quickly; **d.** to interrupt, pull up; **e.** *U.S.* to prepare the horses and mules for the march. *trans.* and *absol.* Hence **Ca·tchable** *a.* that can be caught. **Ca·tcher,** one who or that which catches. **Ca·tching** *ppl. a.* that catches; (*spec.*) infectious; uncertain; (*fig.*) deceptive, catchy; taking. **Ca·tchingness.**

Catch-, in *comb.* and *attrib.* Mainly the vb. in phraseological combination: **a.** with sbs., in sense 'one who or that which catches' (the object), as *c.-all*, etc.; also in sense 'to catch, the catching of (the object)', as *c.-ball*, *-cold*, etc.; **b.** in attrib. relation to a sb., in sense 'that catches or for catching', as **c.-basin,** the receptacle placed beneath the grating of a sewer, etc., to catch the dirt that is washed in; **-drain, -water, -work,** a drain to catch the surface water; **-meadow,** ? a meadow irrigated by c.-drains.

Catchfly (kæ·tʃfləi). 1597. [f. CATCH *v.*] A name orig. for *Silene Armeria*; now for *Lychnis Viscaria* and the various species of *Silene*.

Catchment (kæ·tʃmĕnt). 1847. [f. CATCH *v.* + -MENT.] = CATCHING; appropriated to the catching of the rainfall over a natural drainage area, in *c. basin*, *area*.

Catchpenny (kæ·tʃpeni), *a.* (*sb.*) 1759. [f. CATCH- + PENNY.] **1.** Got up merely to sell. **2.** *sb.* Any catchpenny production.

Catchpole, -poll (kæ·tʃpōᵘl). OE. [a. med. L. *cacepollus*, lit. 'chase-fowl'.] †**1.** A tax-gatherer; a Roman publican -1652. **2.** A sheriff's officer, *esp.* a bum-bailiff ME. Also *attrib.* Hence **Ca·tchpolery, -pollery. Ca·tchpolled** *ppl. a.* arrested by a c.

Ca·tchup, ca·tsup. 1690. = KETCHUP, q.v.

Ca·tchweed. 1776. [f. CATCH *v.*] *Herb.* CLEAVERS, q.v.

Catchword (kæ·tʃwɔ̄ɹd). 1730. [f. CATCH-b.] **1.** *Printing.* The first word of the following page inserted at the right-hand lower corner of each page of a book, below the last line. (Now rarely used.) **2.** A word so placed as to catch the eye; *spec.* the last word in an actor's speech, serving as a guide to the next speaker; a cue 1780. **3.** A word caught up and repeated, *esp.* in connexion with a party 1795.

3. The catchwords of party politics LOWELL.

Catchy (kæ·tʃi), *a. colloq.* 1831. [f. CATCH *v.* + -Y[1].] **1.** Attractive, taking. **2.** That entraps 1885. **3.** Readily caught up 1881. **4.** Spasmodic, fitful 1872.

Cate, usu. in *pl.* **cates** (kēᵢts). 1461. [aphet. f. ACATE: orig. = purchase.] †**1.** *pl.* Provisions bought (as opp. to home-made); later, = victuals, food -1866. Hence **2.** Choice viands; dainties, delicacies 1578. Also *fig.*

2. These curious cates are gracious in mine eye GREENE. *Tam. Shr.* II. i. 190. Taste of every c. HEYWOOD. Hence †**Cate** *v.* to dress (food).

‖**Catechesis** (kætĭkī·sis). 1753. [L., a. Gr. κατήχησις, f. κατηχεῖν to instruct orally, orig. to resound, etc., f. κατά thoroughly + ἠχεῖν to sound, ring.] **1.** Oral instruction given to catechumens; catechizing. **2.** A book for such instruction 1753. var. †**Catechese.**

Catechetic (kætĭke·tik). 1661. [ad. L., a. Gr. κατηχητικός, f. κατηχητής; see prec.] *adj.* Of or pertaining to catechesis; according to the manner of a catechism. See next. *sb.* mostly *pl.* **catechetics.** That part of Christian theology which treats of catechesis.

Catechetical (kætĭke·tikăl), *a.* 1618. [f. as prec. + -AL.] **1.** Of, pertaining to, or connected with catechetics or catechesis 1624. **2.** Of, pertaining to, or in accordance with the catechism of a church 1618. **3.** 'Consisting of questions and answers' (J.) 1691.

3. Socrates introduced a c. Method of Arguing ADDISON. Hence **Cateche·tically** *adv.*

Ca·techin. 1853. *Chem.* A substance obtained from catechu, etc., after the removal of the tannin; a white powder composed of small silky needles.

Catechise (kæ·tĭkiz). Now *dial.* 1552. [app. ad. F. *catéchèse*, confounded with the vb. CATECHIZE, in F. *catéchiser.*] = CATECHESIS, CATECHISM.

Catechism (kæ·tĭkiz'm). 1502. [ad. L. *catechismus*, on Gr. type; see CATECHESIS.] †1. Catechetical instruction; catechesis –1600. 2. A treatise for instruction in the elements of the Christian religion, in the form of question and answer, as the *(Church) C.*, the *Longer* and *Shorter Catechisms*, etc. 1509. Also *transf.* 3. *fig.* A course of question and answer 1596.

1. *A. Y. L.* III. ii. 241. 2. We can never see Christianity from the c. EMERSON. *transf.* The Freethinker's C. 1754. Hence **Catechi·smal** *a.* of the nature of, or pertaining to, a c.

Catechist (kæ·tĭkist). 1563. [ad. L. *catechista*, ad. Gr. κατηχιστής; see above.] A teacher who gives oral instruction according to a catechism, or by question and answer; a native teacher in a mission church. Hence **Catechi·stic, -al** *a.* of or pertaining to a c., or to a catechism; consisting of question and answer. **Catechi·stically** *adv.*

Catechize (kæ·tĭkəiz), *v.* ME. [ad. L. *catechizare*, f. Gr. κατηχίζειν, a factitive form of κατηχεῖν to din in, etc.] 1. To instruct orally; to give systematic oral instruction, *esp.* in the elements of religion, by repeating it until it is learnt by heart, or by question and answer; in the Ch. of England, to teach the catechism. 2. To examine with or as with a catchism 1684. 3. To question or interrogate; *esp.* with a view to reproof or condemnation 1604.

3. Catechising him where he had been SWIFT. Hence **Ca·techizer**, one who catechizes.

Catechu (kæ·tĭʃu, -tʃu). 1683. [app. ad. Malay *kachu* catechu (of acacia). See also CACHOU, CASHOU.] A name given to several astringent substances, containing from 40 to 55 per cent. of tannin, which are obtained from *Acacia Catechu* and other Eastern trees and shrubs. Used in medicine, and in the arts. Called also GAMBIER, *Terra Japonica*, CUTCH, etc. Hence **Catechu·ic** *a.* of or pertaining to c., as in *catechuic acid*=CATECHIN.

Catechumen (kætĭkiū·mĕn). ME. [ad. F. *catéchumène*, ad. L. *catechumenus* (also used), ad. Gr. κατηχούμενος; see CATECHESIS.] A new convert under instruction before baptism. Used in reference to the ancient church and to modern missions. Occ. applied to young Christians generally, *esp.* those preparing for confirmation. Also *transf.* var. †**Catechu·menist.** Hence **Catechu·menate**, condition or position of a c., var. **Catechu·menism**; also, a house for catechumens. **Catechu·menical** *a.* of or pertaining to catechumens. †**Catechu·menize** *v.* to instruct as a c.

Categorem (kæ·tĭgŏre·m, kăte·gŏrem). 1588. [ad. Gr. κατηγόρημα, f. κατηγορεῖν; cf. κατήγορος accuser, etc., f. κατά + ἀγορά.] *Logic.* †PREDICATE; a categorematic word.

Categorematic (kæ·tĭgǫrĭmæ·tik), *a.* 1827. [f. Gr. *κατηγορηματικός; see prec.] Of a word: Capable of being used by itself as a term.

†**Categorema·tical,** *a.* = CATEGORICAL. JER. TAYLOR.

Categoric (kætĭgǫ·rik). ? *Obs.* 1677. [ad. L. *categoricus*, a. Gr.; see CATEGOREM.] *adj.* = CATEGORICAL. *sb.* [sc. *proposition.*]

Categorical (kætĭgǫ·rikăl), *a.* (*sb.*) 1598. [f. as prec. + -AL.] *adj.* 1. *Logic.* Of a proposition: Asserting absolutely; unqualified. *gen.* Direct, explicit, unconditional 1619. 2. *Logic.* Of or belonging to the categories 1817. 3. *sb.* A categorical proposition or syllogism 1619.

1. *C. syllogism*: one consisting of c. propositions. I could never persuade her to be c. MAD. D'ARBLAY. Hence **Catego·ricalness. Catego·rically** *adv.*

Categorist (kæ·tĭgŏrist). *rare.* 1847. [f. next; see -IST.] One who classifies; one who deals with the categories.

Categorize (kæ·tĭgŏrəiz), *v.* 1705. [f. CATEGORY + -IZE.] To place in a category or categories; to classify.

Category (kæ·tĭgŏri). 1588. [ad. L., a. Gr. κατηγορία, abst. sb. f. κατήγορος; see CATEGOREM.] 1. *Logic* and *Metaph.* A term (meaning literally 'predication' or 'assertion') originally used by Aristotle, whose ten categories or predicaments are 'a classification of all the manners in which assertions may be made of the subject' (L. and S.). Kant applied the term to: The pure *a priori* conceptions of the understanding, in which (as forms) the mind envisages matter. 2. A predicament; a class to which a predication applies 1678. b. A class, or division, in a scheme of classification 1660.

2. Any offender who was not in any of the categories of proscription MACAULAY. b. With him there are but two moral categories, riches and poverty HAZLITT.

Catel, obs. f. CATTLE.

Catelectrode (kætĭle·ktrōd). [f. Gr. κατά + ELECTRODE; cf. ANELECTRODE.] The negative pole of a galvanic battery.

‖**Catelectrotonus** (kæ:tĭlectrǫ·tǫ̆nǫ̆s). 1866. [f. κατά + ἤλεκτρον (see ELECTRIC) + τόνος tension; cf. ANELECTROTONUS.] *Phys.* A state of increased irritability produced in a nerve near the negative pole of an electric current which traverses it. Hence **Ca telectroto·nic** *a.*

‖**Catena** (kătī·nă). 1644. [L.] A chain, a connected series. Also *transf.*

A c. of opinions MAURICE, of platitudes 1883.

Catenary (katī·nări). 1788. [ad. L. *catenarius*; see prec.] **A.** *sb. Math.* [mod.L. *catenaria.*] The curve formed by a chain or rope of uniform density hanging freely from two fixed points not in the same vertical line. **B.** *adj. C. curve*=CATENARY. 2. Relating to a catena or series 1855. var. **Catena·rian** *a.* (*sb.*)

Catenate (kæ·tĭneɪt), *v.* 1623. [f. L. *catenat-*, *catenare.*] To form into a catena. *fig.* To chain. Hence **Catena·tion**, a linking into a chain; connected succession.

Catenulate (kătĕ·niŭlĕt), *a.* 1880. [f. L. *catenula*, dim. of *catena.*] *Bot.* Formed of parts united end to end like the links of a chain. *Zool.* Having on the surface a chainlike series of oblong tubercles.

†**Ca·ter,** *sb.*[1] [ME. *catour*, aphet. f. *acatour*, ACATER, q. v.] A CATERER –1621. *transf.* and *fig.* =Purveyor –1665.

Cater (kēɪ·təɹ, kæ·təɹ), *sb.*[2] 1519. [ad. F. *quatre.* See QUATRE.] †1. Four (*rare*) 1553. †2. Four at dice or cards; also *cater-point.* (Dicts.) 3. *pl. Change-ringing.* A name for the changes on nine bells 1872.

Cater (kēɪ·təɹ), *v.*[1] 1600. [f. CATER *sb.*[1]] 1. *intr.* To act as caterer *for.* Also *absol.* and *trans.* 2. *transf.* and *fig.* To provide (requisites, things desired, etc.) *for* 1650. Occas. with *to* (*mod.*).

1. He that .. prouidently caters for the Sparrow *A. Y. L.* II. iii. 44.

Cater (kēɪ·təɹ), *v.*[2] *dial.* 1577. [f. CATER *sb.*[2]] To set rhomboidally; to cut, go, etc. diagonally. So **Ca·ter** *adv. dial.*, diagonally. **Ca·ter-cornered** *a.*

Cateran (kæ·tĕrăn). ME. [Lowland Sc. *catherein*, repr. Gael. *ceathairne* 'peasantry'. Cf. KERN.] 1. *prop.* †Common people of the Highlands in a band. Hence, One of such a band; a Highland reiver. 2. Freebooter (*mod.*).

†**Ca·terbrawl.** 1565. [f. CATER *sb.*[2]] A kind of dance or 'brawl' –1618.

†**Ca·tercap.** 1588. [f. as prec.] The square cap worn by academics. Hence *transf.* A university man –1691.

Cater-cousin (kēɪ·təɹ,kɒ:z'n). 1547. [? f. CATER *sb.*[1] + COUSIN, perh. as = 'catering cousin'; cf. *foster-father*, etc.] A name for persons on terms of cousinship or familiarity with each other, who were not cousins by blood (cf. to CALL *cousins*).

To be cater-cousins: to be good friends.

Caterer (kēɪ·tərəɹ). 1592. [f. CATER *sb.*[1] or *v.*[1]] One who caters. Also *fig.* So **Ca·teress.**

Caterpillar (kæ·təɹpiləɹ). 1440. [? f. OF. *chate* cat + *piller*, *pilour* pillager, either directly or through OF. *chatepelose* 'hairy cat' treated as pl. The corruption *caterpillar* (? after *pillar*) was adopted by Johnson.] 1. The larva of a butterfly or moth; occ. those of other insects, as saw-flies. 2. *fig.* A rapacious person; an extortioner; one who preys upon society 1541. 3. *Herb.* A name for plants of the genus *Scorpiurus* from the shape of their pods 1597. 4. In full *caterpillar tractor*: A tractor with two endless metal belts fitting over two cogged wheels, one on each side of the machine, to enable the tractor to travel over rough ground 1915.

2. The Augustine friers in London..those Caterpillers and blouddy beastes BARNES.

Comb.: **c.-catcher, -eater**, a sub-family of shrikes which feed on caterpillars; **-plant** = sense 3 above.

Caterwaul (kæ·təɹwǭl), *v.* ME. [f. *cater* (rel. to CAT *sb.*[1]) + *waul*, earlier *wrawen* (Caxton), *wraulen*, *wraule*, prob. echoic.] 1. *intr.* To make the noise proper to cats at rutting time. Also *transf.* 2. To be in heat; to behave lasciviously; to woo (*contemptuous*) 1599.

2. Always together, always caterwauling FIELDING. Hence **Ca·terwaul** *sb.* **Ca·terwauler.**

†**Ca·tery.** 1455. [aphet. f. ACATERY; see CATER *sb.*[1]] The office concerned with the catering for the royal household –1779.

Cates; see CATE *sb.*[1]

Cat-fish. 1620. 1. A name given to: a. The *Anarrhicas* or Wolf-fish. b. Species of *Pimelodus*, esp. *P. catus*, the common cat-fish. 2. The cuttle-fish or other cephalopod 1678.

Catgut (kæ·tgɒt). 1599. [So in Du. *kattedarm.* Explanation of *cat* doubtful.] 1. The dried and twisted intestines of sheep, also of the horse and ass; used for strings of musical instruments, etc. 2. A violin; stringed instruments 1709. 3. A coarse cloth of thick cord, formerly used as stiffening 1731. Also *attrib.*

†**Ca·tharan.** 1574. [f. Gr. καθαροί.] One who professes superior purity, as a Novatian, Paulician, etc., also an English Puritan –1657.

Ca·tharist. 1600. [ad. med. L. *Catharistæ* (= Gr. καθαρισταί).] A Paulician, Manichæan, etc.; cf. CATHARAN. Hence **Ca·tharism**, the doctrine of the Catharists.

Catharize (kæ·þărəiz), *v.* 1832. [ad. Gr. καθαρίζειν.] To purify.

Cat-harpings; see HARPINGS.

‖**Catharsis** (kăþā·ɹsis). 1803. [mod. L., a. Gr., f. καθαίρειν.] 1. Purgation. 2. Purification of the emotions by vicarious experience, as through the drama (in ref. to Aristotle's *Poetics* 6) 1904.

Cathartic (kăþā·ɹtik). 1612. [ad. L., a. Gr. καθαρτικός; see prec.] **A.** *adj. Med.* Cleansing (the bowels), purgative. Also *gen.* (and *fig.*). Hence **Catha·rtical-ly** *adv.*, **-ness.** **B.** *sb.* A purgative. More strictly: 'a medicine .. producing the second grade of purgation, of which laxative is the first and drastic the third' (*Syd. Soc. Lex.*) 1651.

Catha·rtin. 1830. [See -IN.] A bitter substance extracted from senna, a purgative.

Cat-head (kæ·t,hed). 1626. 1. *Naut.* A beam projecting at each side of the bows of a ship, for raising the anchor, or carrying it suspended. See also CAT *sb.* 2. *Mining.* A small capstan; also, a broad-bully hammer.

‖**Cathedra** (kăþī·dră, -e·dră, kæ·þĕdră). 1829. [L., a. Gr. καθέδρα chair.] The chair of a bishop in his church; hence, the episcopal see.

Ex cathedrâ L.; 'from the chair', *i.e.* in the manner of one speaking officially, with authority; also *attrib.* = officially uttered.

Cathedral (kăþī·drăl), *a.* ME. [ad. med. L. *cathedralis*; see prec.] 1. Of or pertaining to the bishop's throne or see; *esp.* in *c. church* = CATHEDRAL *sb.* 2. Of or pertaining to the chair of office or authority; *ex cathedrâ* 1603.

2. The c. utterances of Leo XIII. The Schoolmens ..C. Decisions HALES.

Cathedral (kăþī·drăl), *sb.* 1587. [orig. *cathedral church*; see prec.] 1. The principal church of a diocese, containing the bishop's cathedra or throne. 2. *fig.* Chief centre of teaching 1643. Also *attrib.*, as *c. glass, music, walk* (= resembling an aisle in a c.). Hence **Cathe·draled** *a.* like or having a c. **Cathedra·lic** *a.* like a c. †**Cathe·dralist**, a supporter of the c. system; one of the c. clergy.

†**Cathedrated,** *ppl. a.* 1626. Installed in a cathedra –1654.

Cathedra·tic, *a.* 1661. [ad. med. L. *cathedraticus*, f. *cathedra.*] 1. *Law.* Pertaining to the bishop's seat or see, as *c. payment, right,* etc. 2. Pronounced *ex cathedrâ* 18... Also as quasi-*sb.* = *c. payment.*

Catheretic (kæþĕre·tik), *a.* 1634. [ad. Gr. καθαιρετικός, f. καθαιρεῖν.] *Med.* Having power to destroy, reduce, or consume; corrosive. As *sb.* Any mild caustic used to consume superfluous flesh 1887.

Catherine (kæ·þĕrin). Also **Catharine, Kath-.** 1861. [mod.L. *Catharina*, earlier *Katerina*, repr. Gr. Αἰκατερίνα, assim. to καθαρός.] Name of a legendary Saint and Martyr of Alexandria; whence a female Christian name.

C. wheel. 1. The figure of a wheel with spikes projecting from its circumference (in reference to St. Catherine's martyrdom). *esp.* in Her. 2. *Arch.* = *Catherine-wheel window*, a circular window with radiating spokes. 3. A firework which rotates in the manner of a wheel. Also *transf.* and *fig.*

Ca·thern. 1596. [Corrupt f. CATHERINE.] A festival on St. Catherine's day (Nov. 25).

Catheter (kæ·þĭtəɹ). 1601. [a. L., a. Gr. καθετήρ, f. καθιέναι to send or let down.] *Med.* A tubular instrument, more or less curved at the end, for passing into the bladder to draw off urine, etc.; a similar tube for use with other canals (*e. g.* the Eustachian c.). Hence **Ca·theterize** *v.* to employ a c. **Ca·theterism, Ca·theteriza·tion,** the employment of a c.

Cathetometer (kæþĭtǫ·mĭtəɹ). 1864. [f. CATHETUS + METER.] An instrument for measuring vertical distances, *esp.* small differences of level of liquid columns in tubes.

‖**Cathetus** (kæ·þĭtǫ̆s). Also **kath-.** 1571. [a. L., a. Gr. κάθετος (sc. γραμμή), f. καθιέναι to let down.] A straight line falling perpendicularly on another straight line or surface.

Cathodal (kæ·þodăl), *a.* Also **kath-.** 1882. [f. Gr. κάθοδος way down, f. κατά + ὁδός.] *Electr.* Belonging to the cathode.

Cathode (kæ·þōᵘd). Also **kath-.** 1834. [ad. Gr. κάθοδος: see prec.] *Electr.* The path by which an electric current leaves the electrolyte and passes into the negative pole; the point or surface in contact with the negative pole. b. The negative pole. Opp. to *anode*.

Cathodic (kăþǫ·dik), *a.* Also **kath-.** 1852. [f. as prec.] *Phys.* Of nerve force: Efferent.

Cat-hole, *sb.* OE. †1. The den of the wild cat. OE. only. 2. A hole large enough to let a cat through 1625. 3. *Naut.* One of the two holes at the stern of the ship, through which a cable or hawser can be passed 1642.

Catholic (kæ·þǒlik). ME. [a. F. *catholique*, ad. late L. *catholicus*, a. Gr., f. καθόλου (i. e. καθ' ὅλου) on the whole, generally, universally.]

A. *adj.* I. 1. *gen.* Universal 1551. †2. Universally prevalent or applicable –1752; entire –1671. 3. Embracing all 1566.

1. Science is truly c. (*mod.*). 2. Just reasoning is the only C. remedy HUME. In C. Health DRYDEN. 3. A taste so c., so unexcluding LAMB.

C. Epistle: a name for the 'general' epistles of James, Peter, and Jude, and the first of John, as not being addressed to particular churches or persons.

II. In eccl. use. 1. Of or belonging to the church universal, universal Christian 1579. 2. Of or belonging to the church universal as organized on an accepted basis of faith and order; of the true apostolic Church, orthodox 1500. 3. As applied (since the Reformation) to the Church of Rome = ROMAN CATHOLIC, q. v. 4. Recognizing all Christians 1658.

1. *C. Church*: the whole body of Christians, the Church universal. 2. And the Catholike faithe is this: that we worship one God in trinitie [etc.] *Bk. Com. Prayer.* The C. fathers 1593. The Anglo-C. Church HOOK. 3. She [Q. Eliz.] hath abolished the C. religion ALLEN. †*C. seat*: = APOSTOLIC *See*. *C. King*, etc.: a title of the kings of Spain. 4. The Lord Protector is..a man of a c. spirit, desirous of the unity and peace of all the servants of Christ BAXTER. *C.* (*and*) *Apostolic Church*: the Irvingites.

B. *sb.* 1. A member of a church recognized or claiming to be 'Catholic' in sense A. II. 2; *esp.* of the Western or Latin Church ME. 2. *spec.* A member of the Roman Church 1570. †3. = CATHOLICOS –1735.

2. The Catholicks (meaning Popish Romanists) A.V. *Pref.* *German C., Old C.*: names taken by religious parties who separated from the R. C. communion in Germany, the former under Rouge in 1845, the latter after the Vatican Council in 1870–71. *attrib.* in *C. Emancipation*, etc. Hence †**Catho·lical** *a.* = CATHOLIC *a.* I. **Catho·lically** *adv.*

Catho·licate. 1878. [ad. med. L. *catholicatus*.] Jurisdiction of an Armenian *catholicus*.

Catholicism (kăþǫ·lisiz'm, kæ·þǒlisiz'm). 1609. [f. CATHOLIC + -ISM.] 1. The system, faith, and practice of the Catholic Church, or adherence thereto 1656; usu. of the Roman Catholic Church 1613. b. A note or act of a good Catholic 1609. †2. = CATHOLICITY 3. JER. TAYLOR. 3. = CATHOLICITY 1 (*rare*) 1796.

Catholicity (kæþŏli·sĭti). 1830. [f. as prec. + -ITY.] 1. The quality of being catholic in feeling, etc. 1841. 2. Universality 1843. 3. The character of belonging to, or being in accordance with, the Catholic Church 1830. b. *spec.* of the Church of Rome: The doctrine or faith of that Church, catholicism 1847.

1. The lessons of c. and toleration 1882. 3. A sincere ..trust in the C. of the Church of England 1868.

Catholicize (kăþǫ·lisəiz, kæ·þŏlisəiz), *v.* 1611. [f. as prec. + -IZE.] To make, or become, catholic or a Catholic.

Ca·tholicly, *adv.* 1542. [f. as prec. + -LY.] 1. Universally. ? *Obs.* 1631. 2. In a Catholic manner 1542.

†**Ca·tholicness.** 1605. [f. as prec. + -NESS.] Catholic quality, catholicity –1674.

Catho·lico-. Comb. f. CATHOLIC.

Catholicon (kăþǫ·likǫ̆n). 1483. [a. F., a. Gr. καθολικόν adj., neut. sing.] 1. A universal remedy; panacea. Also *fig.* 2. A comprehensive †formula 1647, treatise 1483.

‖**Catholicos** (kăþǫ·likǫ̆s). 1625. [a. Gr.] The Patriarch of Armenia.

Ca'-thro'. *Sc.* [f. *Ca'* drive.] A great disturbance. SCOTT.

Catiline, *a.* 1592. [ad. L. *Catilina.*] A Roman who conspired against his country B. C. 36: taken as a type. Hence **Catilina·rian** *a.*

Cation (kæ·tiǫ̆n). 1834. [a. Gr. κατιόν, f. κατιέναι to go down.] *Electr.* Faraday's name for an ion carrying a positive charge of electricity by virtue of which it is attracted, on electrolysis, to the cathode. Cf. ANION.

Catkin (kæ·tkin). 1578. [f. Du. *katteken*, dim. of *katte* cat.] *Bot.* A unisexual inflorescence, consisting of rows of apetalous flowers ranged in circles along a slender stalk; the whole forming a cylindrical, downy-looking, usu. pendant, spike; an amentum.

Cat-lap (kæ·tlæp). *dial.* or *slang.* 1785. [Cf. *Temp.* II. i. 288.] Stuff fit for a cat to lap; tea or other weak drink.

Ca·t-like, *a.* (*adv.*) 1600. Like a cat, or that of a cat; *esp.* stealthy, noiseless.

Catling (kæ·tliŋ). 1606. [dim. of CAT.] 1. A little cat; a kitten 1630. 2. Catgut; a small-sized lute-string 1606. 3. *Surg.* A double-edged, sharp-pointed, straight knife for amputations 1612. †4. ? Misprint for CATKIN –1704.

Catlinite. 1858. [f. Geo. *Catlin*, the delineator of the American Indians.] *Min.* The sacred pipe-stone of the American Indians, a red clay from the Upper Missouri region.

Catmint (kæ·tmint). ME. [Cf. med.L. *herba catti.*] *Bot.* A labiate plant, *Nepeta Cataria*. Also the Eng. name of the genus. Called in U. S. Cat-nip.

‖**Catoblepas.** ME. [L., Gr. κατώβλεψ, f. κάτω + βλέπειν.] *Zool.* In ancient authors, some African animal, perh. the gnu. Now the name of a genus including the GNU.

Catocathartic (kæ:tokăþā·ɹtik). 1704. [f. Gr. κάτω + καθαρτικός; cf. ANOCATHARTIC.] *adj.* Purgative. *sb.* [sc. *medicine.*]

‖**Catochus** (kæ·tǒkǒs). 1656. [Gr., = κατοχή, f. κατέχειν to hold down.] *Med.* Catalepsy; a similar affection, but with rigidity of the limbs; also, coma-vigil. var. †‖**Catoche.**

Cat o'mountain; see CATAMOUNTAIN.

Catonian (kătōᵘ·niăn). 1534. [ad. L. *Catonianus*, f. *Cato*, *esp.* Cato the Censor, and Cato of Utica.] *adj.* Pertaining to or resembling Cato; severe 1676. *sb.* A follower of Cato. So **Cato·nic** *a.*, **Ca·tonism;** also **Ca·toism.**

Cat-o'-ni·ne-tails, *sb.* 1695. [See CAT.] 1. A whip with nine knotted lashes; an instrument of punishment formerly used in the British army and navy. 2. A bulrush. *U. S.* 1858.

Catoptric (kætǫ·ptrik). 1570. [ad. Gr. κατοπτρικός, f. κάτοπτρον mirror.] *adj.* Relating to a mirror, or to reflection 1774. Hence **Cato·ptrical** *a.*, **-ly** *adv.* B. *sb.* 1. *pl.* **Catoptrics:** That part of Optics which treats of reflection 1570. †2. An instrument for producing effects by reflection –1644.

Catoptromancy (kătǫ·ptrǒmænsi). 1613. [f. Gr. κάτοπτρον + μαντεία] Divination by means of a mirror. Hence **Catoptroma·ntic** *a.*

Cat's-cradle. 1768. [prob. fanciful.] A children's game in which two players alternately take from each other's fingers an interwined cord so as to produce a symmetrical figure.

Cat's-eye. 1555. 1. The eye of a cat; a cat-like eye. 2. A variety of chalcedonic quartz, displaying, when held to the light, a lustre resembling the contracted pupil of a cat's eye 1599. 3. The Germander Speedwell, *Veronica Chamædrys*; also the Forget-me-not, etc. 1817.

3. The glow Of the wild cat's eyes KEATS.

Cat's foot. 1597. 1. The foot of a cat; †used *lit.* in reference to the tale of a monkey using the foot or paw of a cat to rake roasted chestnuts out of the fire 1661. †2. Hence *fig.* = CAT'S-PAW 2. –1699. 3. a. Ground-ivy, *Nepeta Glechoma*. b. Mountain Cudweed, *Antennaria dioica* 1597.

Cat's-head. 1617. 1. 'A kind of apple' (J.). 2. An ornament in Norman architecture 1848. 3. Var. of CAT-HEAD.

†**Ca·tso.** *slang.* 1602. [a. It. *caggo* membrum virile, also exclam.] In 17th c. in the It. senses; also = Rogue, scamp –1708.

Cat's pa·w, ca·t's-paw. 1769. 1. The paw of a cat; also *fig.* 1821. 2. A person used as a tool by another; see CAT'S-FOOT 1785. 3. *Naut.* A slight and local breeze, perceived by ripples on the surface of the sea 1769. 4. *Naut.* A twisting hitch in the bight of a rope, so as to form two bights, to hook a tackle on 1794. Hence **Cat's-pawed** *ppl. a.* (in senses 3, 4).

Cat's tail, ca·t's-tail. Also **cat-tail.** 1450. 1. The tail of a cat; name of a fur for the neck 1550. 2. A name given to plants from the resemblance of parts; *esp.* the Reed-Mace, *Typha latifolia*, from its long cylindrical furry spikes; also the Horse-tail, *Equisetum* 1450. 3. = *Cat's-tail grass*: the genus *Phleum*; esp. *P. pratense*, Timothy grass 1597. 4. A catkin 1611. 5. *Naut.* The inner end of the CAT-HEAD.

Ca·t-stick. 1626. A stick used in tip-cat and trap-ball.

Catsup = CATCHUP and KETCHUP.

†**Ca·tting,** *vbl. sb.* 1681. Caterwauling; going after the opposite sex –1725.

Cattish (kæ·tiʃ), *a.* 1598. Of or like a cat. b. *fig.* Sly and spiteful 1883.

Cattle (kæ·t'l), *sb.* [ME. *catel* (in 16th c. *cattel(l)*, a. ONF. :—late L. *captale*, L. *capitale* head-, principal, CAPITAL, adj. neut., used subst. in the sense of 'property'; cf. mod.Eng. CAPITAL = stock in trade. Under the feudal system applied chiefly to movable property, and in English *esp.* to live stock. Only since 1600 spelt *cattle*. See also CHATTEL.]

†I. (*catel, cattel(l)*. †1. Property; strictly personal property –1495. *fig.* Rubbish. MILT. †2. = CHATTEL, with *collect. pl.* (From law-Latin.) –1720.

1. By loue of worldly catall W. DE WORDE. 2. *Goods and cattell*: see CHATTEL.

II. Live stock. (*Catel, cattel(l, cattle.*) 1. A collective name for the bovine genus, but formerly, and still locally, for live animals held as property, or reared to serve as food, or for their milk, skin, wool, etc. ME. 2. Extended to vermin, insects, etc. 1616; also to men and women (*arch.*) 1579. Also *attrib.*

1. Hors, asse, mule, ox, camell..all þair catell ME. In breeding of Cattell, as Pigs, Hens, and Chickens, and the like 1622. *Neat c., horned c.*: oxen. *Black c.*: 'oxen, bulls, and cows' (J.); prob. at first used only of black Highland cattle. 2. Nelly,..concubines, and cattell of that sort EVELYN. Astrologers, and such like c. H. WALPOLE.

Comb.: c.-gate, a 'walk' or pasture for one's c., beast-gate; -leader, a nose-ring for c.; -lifter, a marauder who steals c.; so *cattle-lifting*; -piece, a painting of c.; -post, -ranche, -range, -run,

-station, a district, tract of country, etc., occupied for the pasturing of c.

Ca·ttle-guard. 1843. A trench on each side of a level crossing, to prevent cattle from straying along the line. (In U.S.)

Ca·ttle-plague. 1866. A highly contagious disease affecting cattle, called also *rinderpest.*

Catty (kæ·ti), *sb.* 1598. [Malay-Javanese; see CADDY.] A weight = 16 taels or $1^1/_3$ lb. avoird., used in China and the Eastern Archipelago.

Ca·tty, *a.* 1886. [-Y [1].] = CATTISH.

†‖**Catur.** 1653. [?] A light rowing vessel formerly used on the coast of Malabar -1686.

Ca·t-witted, *a.* 1673. Small-minded, obstinate, and spiteful.

‖**Caubee·n.** 1831. [? dim. of Ir. *cába* cap.] An Irish hat.

Caucasian (kǭkē·ʃiăn), *a.* 1807. [f. *Caucasus*, name of a mountain-range between the Black Sea and the Caspian.] Of or belonging to the region of the Caucasus; Blumenbach's name for the 'white' race of mankind, which he derived from this region. Hence *sb.* A member of this family; an Indo-European. (Now discarded.)

Caucus (kǭ·kəs). 1763. [? f. Algonkin *cau'-cau-as'u* 'one who advises, urges, encourages' (Dr. J. H. Trumbull).] **1.** In *U. S.* A private or preliminary meeting of members of a political party, to select candidates for office, or to concert measures for furthering party interests; a meeting of wire-pullers. **2.** In England: a committee popularly elected for the purpose of securing concerted political action in a constituency; as a term of abuse, an organization seeking to manage the election and dictate to the constituencies 1878. Also *attrib.*

1. A c. rather than a general gathering MOTLEY. 2. 'Government by Caucus' 1882. Hence **Cau·cus** *v.* to hold a c.; to control by caucuses.

Caudal (kǭ·dăl), *a.* 1661. [f. L. *caudalis.*] *Zool.* Of, belonging to, or of the nature of, a tail; situated in or near the tail. As quasi-*sb.* (= *c. fin, vertebra*, etc.) 1834.

The male..bird, remarkable for his c. plumes DARWIN. Hence **Cau·dally** *adv.*

Caudate (kǭ·dēᵗt), *a.* 1600. [ad. L. *caudatus*, f. *cauda*; see -ATE.] Having a tail; *Zool.* and *Bot.* having an appendage resembling a tail 1830. var. **Cau·dated.**

†**Caudebeck.** 1680. [f. *Caudebec* in Normandy.] A kind of woollen hat.

‖**Caudex** (kǭ·deks). Pl. **caudices** (kǭ·disīz). 1830. [L.] *Bot.* The axis of a plant, consisting of stem and root; *esp.* of palms, ferns, etc.

Caudicle (kǭ·dik'l). 1830. [ad. L. *caudiculus*, dim. of *caudex.*] *Bot.* The small stalk-like appendage to the *pollinia* or pollen-masses of orchids. var. **Caudi·cula.**

Caudiform (kǭ·difǭɹm), *a.* 1839. [f. L. *cauda*; see -FORM.] Tail-shaped.

Caudle (kǭ·d'l), *sb.* ME. [a. ONF. *caudel* :—med.L. *caldellum*, dim. of *cal(i)dum* adj. neut. 'a hot drink'.] A warm drink; thin gruel, mixed with wine or ale, sweetened and spiced, given to sick people; also to their visitors. *Hempen c.*: = hanging. 2 *Hen. VI*, IV. vii. 95.

Caudle (kǭ·d'l), *v.* 1607. [f. prec.] **1.** To administer a caudle to. **2.** To mix, as in a caudle 1790.

1. Cawdled like a Haberdashers Wife 1672.

Cauf, Sc. f. CALF [1], CHAFF; dial. f. CORF.

Caufle, var. of COFFLE.

Caught (kǭt), pa. t. and pple. of CATCH *v.*

Cauk (kǭk), *sb.* ME. [perh. north. f. CHALK.] **1.** = CHALK (*dial.*). †**2.** Lime. **3.** Barytes, or heavy spar; see CAWK.

†**Cauk**, *v.* ME. [a. ONF. *cauquer* :—L. *calcare.*] *intr.* To tread, as birds -1704.

Cauking (kǭ·kiŋ), *vbl. sb.* See CAULK *v.*

Caul (kǭl), *sb.* [1] ME. [a. F. *cale.* See also KELL.] **1.** A netted cap, worn by women; a net for the hair (*Hist.*); the back part of a woman's cap 1740. †**2.** *gen.* A net -1681. †**3.** A spider's web -1631. †**4.** *Anat.* Any investing membrane -1684. **5.** *spec.* **a.** The epiploön or omentum ME. **b.** The amnion or inner membrane enclosing the fœtus before birth; *esp.* this or a portion of it sometimes enveloping the head of the child at birth, regarded as lucky, and supposed to be a preservative against drowning 1547. Also *attrib.*

1. The peculiar net cap, with its high c. and neat little border 1862. 4. *C. of the heart*: app. the pericardium; also *fig.* (*Hosea* xiii. 8). 5. b. Yo' were borne with a caule o' your head B. JONS.

†**Caul**, *sb.* [2] OE. [ad. L. *caulis*; see also COLE, KALE.] **1.** A cabbage -1727. **2.** Stem, stalk. ME. only.

Cauldrife (kǭ·ldrif), *a. Sc.* 1768. [f. *cauld* cold + RIFE, q. v.] Causing, or susceptible to, cold. Also *fig.*

Cauldron, caldron (kǭ·ldrən). [ME. *caud(e)ron*, corresp. to It. *calderone*, augment. of **calderio* :—L. *caldarium* hot-bath. Refash. after L. The sp. *cauldron* now preponderates.] A large kettle or boiler. Also *transf.*

Fire burne and Cauldron bubble *Macb.* IV. i. 11. Vesuvio's horrid cauldrons roar SHENSTONE. Hence **Cau·ldron** *v.* to put in, or as in, a c. (*rare*).

Caulescent (kǭle·sĕnt), *a.* 1794. [f. L. *caulis*, after *arborescent*, etc.] *Bot.* Having an obvious stem.

Caulicle (kǭ·lik'l). 1657. [ad. L. *cauliculus*, dim. of *caulis.*] *Bot.* A little stalk or stem; *spec.* the radicle in an embryo.

Caulicole (kǭ·likoᵘl). 1816. [a. F., (ult.) ad. L. *cauliculus.*] *Arch. pl.* 'The eight lesser branches or stalks in the Corinthian capital springing out from the four greater or principal caules or stalks' (Gwilt).

Caulicule (kǭ·likiul). 1835. [a. F.; see next.] *Bot.* The point of union of the base of the plumule with the radicle and cotyledons.

‖**Cauliculus** (kǭli·kiŭlŏs). 1830. [L.; see CAULICLE.] In *Bot.* = CAULICLE, CAULICULE; in *Archit.* = CAULICOLE.

Cauliflower (kǫ·liflauəɹ), *sb.* 1597. [In 16th c. *cole-florye, colie-florie*, f. F. *chou-flori, -fleuri*, assim. to Eng. COLE. The later forms are assim. to *flower.*] A cultivated variety of the cabbage (*Brassica oleracea botrytis cauliflora*), the young inflorescence of which forms an edible head. Also *attrib.* Hence **Cau·liflower** *v.* ? to powder (a wig) (*rare*).

Cau·liform, *a.* 1847. [f. L. *caulis* + -FORM.] Stem-shaped.

Cauline (kǭ·ləin), *a.* 1756. [ad. mod. L. *caulinus.*] *Bot.* Of or belonging to the stem. var. **Cau·linar, -ary.** (Bad.)

‖**Caulis** (kǭ·lis). Pl. **caules** (kǭ·līz). 1563. [L.] **1.** *Arch.* Each of the four principal stalks in the Corinthian capital. **2.** *Bot.* The stalk or stem of a (herbaceous) plant 1870.

Caulk (kǭk), *sb.* 1833. [? f. CAULK *v.*] *Naut. slang.* A dram.

Caulk, calk (kǭk), *v.* 1500. [In 15th c. *calke, caulke* (= CAUK *v.*), a. OF. *cauquer* :—L. *calcare* to tread, etc. The sp. *calk* is not now in use.] **1.** To stop up the seams of (a ship, etc.) by driving in oakum, or the like, melted pitch being afterwards poured on, to prevent leaking. **2.** To stop up the crevices of (windows, etc.) 1609. **3.** *Naut. slang. trans.* To 'shut up'; *intr.* to sleep 1836.

1. Shyppes calked with towgh 1552. 2. The windores close shut, and calk'd B. JONSON.

Caulker (kǭ·kəɹ). 1495. [f. prec. + -ER [1].] **1.** One who caulks ships. †**2.** ? A caulking-iron -1779. **3.** *slang.* A dram 1808. **4.** *slang.* Anything incredible, etc.; cf. *crammer.*

Caulo- (kǭ·lo), comb. f. Gr. καυλός (or L. *caulis*) stem of a plant, as in **Cauloca·rpic, Cauloca·rpous** *a.* producing flowers and fruit on its stem year after year, as ordinary shrubs.

Caulome (kǭ·lōum). 1875. [f. Gr. καυλός, after *rhizome.*] *Bot.* The leaf-bearing axis of a plant; a stem or branch, or the like. var. **Cau·loma.** Hence **Caulo·mic** *a.*

‖**Cauma** (kǭ·ma). 1811. [L., a. Gr.] *Med.* The burning heat of a fever. Hence **Cauma·tic** *a.* relating to c.

Caunter. *dial.* 1810. [app. a. CANT *sb.* [1] or *v.* [2]] *Mining.* A cross-vein. Also *attrib.*

†**Cau·ponate**, *v.* 1653. [f. L. *caupōnat-, cauponari.*] **1.** To sell liquor or victuals (Dicts.). **2.** To deal like a huckster with -1715. Hence †**Caupona·tion**, petty dealing; adulteration.

†**Cau·ponize**, *v.* 1652. [f. L. *cauponem* (cf. prec.) + -IZE.] **1.** To act as victualler 1765. **2.** To mix and adulterate for gain -1771.

‖**Cau·sa.** ME. The L. word for CAUSE, occas. used in Eng.

Causable (kǭ·zăb'l), *a. rare.* 1646. [f. CAUSE *v.* + -ABLE.] That can be caused.

Causal (kǭ·zăl), *a.* (*sb.*) 1530. [ad. L. *causalis.*] **1.** Of or relating to a cause or causes 1570. **2.** Of the nature of, or acting as, a cause 1642. **3.** Of the nature of cause and effect 1656. **4.** *Gram.* and *Logic.* Expressing a cause 1530.

4. C. propositions are, where two propositions are joined by c. particles WATTS.

B. *sb.* A causal conjunction or particle 1530.

Causality (kǭzæ·liti). 1603. [f. L. *causalis* CAUSAL.] **1.** Causal quality, or agency. **2.** The operation or relation of cause and effect 1642. **3.** *Phren.* The faculty of tracing effects to causes 1874.

1. To ascribe a real C. to free-will HARTLEY. 2. The necessary laws of C. and Time BOWEN.

Causally (kǭ·zăli), *adv.* 1638. [f. CAUSAL + -LY [2].] In the manner of, or as being the cause; by way of cause and effect.

C. guilty of Calamities 1640.

Causation (kǭzē·ʃən). 1646. [ad. L. *causationem*, used in med.L. sense.] The action of causing; the operation of causal energy; the relation of cause and effect.

The c. of a movement STUBBS. Some latent chain of c. W. IRVING. Hence **Causa·tionism**, the theory of universal c. **Causa·tionist**, one who adopts this.

Causative (kǭ·zătiv), *a.* ME. [a. F. *causatif*, ad. L. *causativus*; see CAUSE *v.*] **1.** Effective as a cause; productive *of.* **2.** *Gram.* = CAUSAL 4. As *sb.*, a causative word. 1600.

1. A superhuman c. agency MORLEY. Hence **Cau·satively** *adv.* **Causati·vity**, c. quality.

†‖**Causa·tor.** [med. L.] A causer. SIR T. BROWNE. So †‖**Causa·trix.** ‖**Causa·tum**, the product of causation.

Cause (kǭz), *sb.* ME. [a. F., ad. L. *causa.*] **I.** General. **1.** That which produces an effect. (*Cause* and *effect* are correlative terms.) **2.** A person or other agent who occasions something, with or without intention ME. **3.** That which moves a person to action; ground of action; reason, motive; *esp.* adequate ground of action. ME. **4.** The object of action; purpose, end. (*Obs.* exc. in *Final cause.*) ME.

1. The occasion, not the c., of joy POLLOK. The c. of a phenomenon..the antecedent or concurrence of antecedents, on which it is invariably and unconditionally consequent MILL. 2. Howe much mischiefe such women bee c. of 1540. 3. Just c. of suspicion CUDWORTH. A c. of action 1883. *To show c.*, esp. in Eng. Law, to argue against the confirmation of a 'rule nisi', etc. 4. *Final c.*: the purpose or end of the thing caused. (The other three of Aristotle's *four causes* were the *efficient c.*, the producing agency; the *formal c.*, the form or essence; and the *material c.*, the matter.) *Occasional causes*: see OCCASIONAL. Phr. †*For my* (*his*, etc.) *c.*: for my (his, etc.) sake.

II. Legal, etc. **1.** *Law.* The case of one party in a suit ME. Also *fig.* **2.** *Law.* A matter in litigation; an action, process, suit; = CASE *sb.* [1] 6. ME. Also *fig.* †**3.** A matter of concern -1660. **4.** That side of a question espoused, advocated, and upheld by a person or party 1581. †**5.** Disease -1607.

1. *To plead a c.* 4. The c. of the Poles BURKE. Phr. *To make common c.* (*with*). 5. *All's Well* II. i. 114. Hence **Cau·seful** *a.* having (good) c.; that is a c. *of* (*rare*).

Cause (kǭz), *v.* ME. [ad. med. L. *causare* in sense *efficere.*] **1.** *trans.* To be the cause of; to effect, bring about, produce, induce, make. †**2.** To give excuses [= L. *causari*] SPENSER. Hence **Cau·ser.**

1. A Drench of Wine..the Patient's Death did c. DRYDEN. I will c. the Sunne to go downe at noone *Amos* viii. 9. This caus'd, that many died..in the streets suddenly DE FOE.

Cause, 'cause, *conj.* 1513. *dial.* = BECAUSE.

‖**Cause célèbre** (kōz selę̄br). 1858. [Fr.] A notorious legal case.

Causeless (kǭ·zlės), *a.* ME. [f. CAUSE *sb.* + -LESS.] **1.** Having no antecedent cause. **2.** Without (good) cause; groundless ME.

1. His c. power, the cause of all things known 1712. 2. A c. pain KEN. Hence **Cau·seless·ly** *adv.*, **-ness.**

‖**Causerie** (kōu·zəri, kozri). 1827. [Fr., f. *causer* to talk.] Informal talk; a chatty article.

‖**Causeuse** (kozö·z). 1883. [F., fem. of *causeur.*] A small sofa for two persons.

Causeway (kǭ·zwēᵗ), *sb.* [In 15th c. *caucé-*

wey, f. *caucé* CAUSEY + WAY; largely superseding *causey*.] 1. = CAUSEY 2. 2. = CAUSEY 3. 1611. Also *fig.* Hence **Cau·sewayed** *ppl. a.*, **Cau·sewaying** *vbl. sb.* (Mostly for *causeyed*, *-ing*.)

Causey (kǭ·zeⁱ, kǭ·seⁱ), *sb.* [ME. *caucé*, a. ONF. *caucie* (mod. *chaussée*) :—late L. *calceata*, *calciata*; prob. f. a late L. *calciare* 'to stamp with the heels, to tread'.] †1. A mound, embankment, or dam -1774. 2. A raised way formed on a mound, *esp.* across low wet ground, a bog, marsh, etc. Now CAUSEWAY. ME. 3. Hence, A highway; *esp.* a paved way; the paved part of a way (still *dial.*) ME. (*Sc.*) A small area paved with cobbles 1481.

2. A Stone-Causey thorow a Bogg 1643. 3. The c., called Via Appia HEARNE. Hence **Cau·sey** *v.* to pave with small stones. (Chiefly *Sc.* and *dial.*)

Causidical (kǭzi·dikăl), *a.* 1797. [f. L. *causidicus* pleader + -AL.] Of or pertaining to a pleader of legal causes.

†**Cau·son.** ME. [a. (ult.) Gr. καύσων; see next.] ? Inflammation, ? heartburn -1661.

Caustic (kǭ·stik). 1555. [ad. L. *causticus*, a. Gr., f. καυστός burnt, f. και- (fut. καυσ-) to burn. Cf. F. *caustique*.] **A.** *adj.* 1. Burning, corrosive, destructive of organic tissue. 2. *fig.* Sharp, biting, sarcastic 1771. 3. *Math.* Epithet of a curved surface formed by the ultimate intersection of luminous rays proceeding from a single point and reflected or refracted from a curved surface. A caustic by reflection is called a *catacaustic*, that by refraction a *diacaustic*. So *c. line*, *surface*. 1727.

1. *C. alkali* (*Chem.*): a name of the hydrates of potassium and sodium, called *c. potash* (KHO) and *c. soda* (NaHO) respectively; *c. lime*, quicklime (CaO). 2. His shrewd, c...remarks SCOTT. Hence †**Cau·stical**, *a.*, **-ly** *adv.*; var. **Cau·sticly** (*rare*).

B. *sb.* 1. *Med.* A substance which burns and destroys living tissue when in contact with it 1582. Also *fig.* 2. *Math.* = *C. curve* or *surface*; cf. A. 3.

1. *Common* or *Lunar c.*: nitrate of silver.

Causticity (kǭsti·siti). 1772. [f. prec.] 1. Caustic quality; corrosiveness. 2. *fig.* Of speech or humour 1785.

2. I..endeavoured to repair my c. H. WALPOLE. So **Cau·sticness** (*rare*).

†**Cau·tel**, *sb.* ME. [a. F. *cautèle*, ad. L. *cautela*, f. *caut-*, *cavere*.] 1. A crafty device -1611. 2. Craftiness, trickery -1580. 3. Heedfulness -1664. 4. A precaution; in *Law*, etc. an exception by way of precaution. Hence †**Cau·telous** *a.* full of cautels; crafty; cautious. †**Cau·telously** *adv.* **Cau·telousness.**

Cauter (kǭ·təɹ). 1534. [a. F. *cautère*, ad. L. *cauterium*, a. Gr. καυτήριον.] = CAUTERY 1.

Cau·terant. 1846. A cauterizing substance.

†**Cau·terism.** 1640. [f. after CAUTERIZE.] The application of cautery -1688.

Cauterize (kǭ·tĕrəiz), *v.* Also **-ise.** 1541. [ad. late L. *cauterizare*, f. *cauterium*; see CAUTER.] 1. *Med.* To burn or sear with a hot iron or a caustic. Also *absol.* 2. *fig.* To sear (the conscience, etc.). See 1 Tim. iv. 2. 1586.

1. To c. a wound 1865. *fig.* To c. unsoundness of doctrine LANDOR. Hence **Cau·teriza·tion.**

Cautery (kǭ·tĕri). 1543. [ad. L. *cauterium*; see CAUTER.] 1. A hot iron or the like used for burning or searing organic tissue; also a caustic drug or medicine. The former is called an *actual*, the latter a *potential*, c. 2. The operation of cauterizing, the application of a caustic 1575. Also *fig.* †3. An eschar thus made. [So Gr.] 1651.

Caution (kǭ·ʃən), *sb.* ME. [a. F.:—L. *cautionem*, f. *caut-*, *cavere* to take heed.] 1. Security given for performance of an engagement; bail; a guarantee. Still in Sc. law, and in U.S. †2. A proviso -1667. 3. A caveat, monition 1605. **b.** *slang.* (orig. U. S.) An extraordinary thing or person 1835. 4. The taking of heed; 'provident care, wariness against evil' (J.); cautiousness, circumspectness 1651. †5. (with *pl.*) A precaution -1801.

1. To give c. of his future obedience HOBBES. Hostages, as cautions for.. 1586. On the payment of c. (= caution-money) BP. MONK. 3. For thy good c. thanks *Macb.* IV. i. 73. 4. Godfrey..had learned c. MILMAN. 5. *Macb.* III. vi. 44.

C.-money, money deposited as security for good conduct, *esp.* by a student on entering a college. Hence †**Cau·tionate** *v.* to take precautions; to guard with provisos. **Cau·tioner**, a surety (*Sc. Law*); one who cautions. (Dicts.) **Cau·tionless** *a.* **Cau·tionry** = CAUTION *sb.* 1. (*Sc. Law*.)

Caution (kǭ·ʃən), *v.* 1641. [f. the sb.] †1. *intr.* To give a warning -1678. †2. To guard with a saving clause -1681. 3. To advise or charge to take heed. Usu. with *against* or *to* with *inf.* 1683.

3. To c. any one to be moderate in his food 1845.

Cautionary (kǭ·ʃənări), *a.* 1597. [f. L. **cautionarius*; cf. F. *cautionnaire*.] 1. Of, pertaining to, of the nature of a pledge or security; held as a pledge or security. Now *Hist.* or *Sc.* †2. Cautious -1831. 3. Warning, admonitory 1638. †4. Precautionary -1826. Also as *sb.*

1. C. towns 1597. 3. C. precepts STEELE. Hence †**Cau·tionarily** *adv.*

Cautious (kǭ·ʃəs), *a.* 1640. [as if f. L. **cautiosus*.] Distinguished by caution; heedful, wary, careful, circumspect. Const. †*of*, *how*, *lest*, *to* (formerly in sense *not to*) with *inf.*

C. speed SOUTHEY. A c. policy 1842. Be c. how you trump out *Hoyle' Games*. **Cau·tious-ly** *adv.*, **-ness.**

‖**Cava.** 1809. *Phys.* Short f. *vena cava.*

Cavalcade (kævălkēⁱ·d), *sb.* 1591. [a. F., ad. Pr. *cavalcada*, f. *cavalcar* :—late L. *caballicare*, f. *caballus*.] †1. A march or raid on horseback -1647. 2. A procession on horseback, *esp.* on a festive or solemn occasion. ? *Obs.* 1644. Also *concr.* 3. *transf.* and *fig.* Procession 1670.

2. The c. of the new Pope EVELYN. 3. He made a C. of his Devils..through the Town *Rabelais*. Hence **Cavalca·de** *v.* to ride in a c.

Cavalier (kævălīᵊ·ɹ). 1560. [a. F., ad. It. *cavaliere*, f. *cavallo*. Orig. adopted in the form *cavallero*, *cavaliero*, etc. from Sp.]

A. *sb.* 1. A horseman, *esp.* a horse-soldier; a knight 1600. 2. 'A gay sprightly military man' (J.); *gen.* a courtly gentleman, a gallant 1589. 3. A name (orig. reproachful) for those who fought for Charles I against the Roundheads; a 17th c. Royalist 1641. 4. *Fortif.* 'A work generally raised . . higher than the rest of the works . . to command all the adjacent works and the country round' (Stocqueler) 1560.

C.-servant, or in It. form *cavaliere-servente*: a man who devotes himself wholly to attendance on a lady as her professed slave. Hence **Cavalier** *v.* to play the c.; to escort (a lady). **Cavalie·r-ish** *a.*, **-ism.**

B. *attrib.* or *adj.* †1. Gallant 1641. 2. Offhand in manner, free and easy 1657. **b.** Haughty, disdainful, supercilious 1751. 3. Royalist; see A 3. 1844.

1. Not valiant, and not much c. SUCKLING. 2. This c. tone from an unknown person..did not please me CARLYLE. 3. An old C. family DISRAELI. Hence **Cavalie·rly** *a.* and *adv.*

Cavally (kăvæ·li). 1634. [ad. Sp. and Pg. *cavalla*, It. *cavallo* mackerel.] A name of 17th c. navigators for species of horse-mackerel.

Cavalry (kæ·vălri). 1591. [In 16–17th c. *cavallery*, a. F. *cavalerie*, f. (ult.) L. *caballarius* horseman. (See also CHIVALRY.)] †1. Horsemanship -1670. †2. Knighthood; an order of chivalry -1632. 3. That part of a military force which consists of mounted troops. Opp. to *infantry*. (Usu. w. pl. vb.) 1591. *transf.* Horses, horsemen, etc., collectively 1684. Also *attrib.*

‖**Cavatina** (kɑvătī·nă). 1836. [It.] *Mus.* A short song of simple character, prop. one without a second strain and a repeat; occ. 'a smooth melodious air, forming part of a grand scena or movement' (Grove).

Cave (kēⁱv), *sb.* ME. [a. F.:—L. *cava*, pl. of *cavum* adj. neut., used subst.] 1. A hollow place opening under the ground; a cavern, den, habitation in the earth. †2. *gen.* Any hollow place, a cavity -1626. 3. *Political slang.* The secession of a small body of politicians from their party on some special question; the body so seceding; see ADULLAMITE 1866.

1. *Idols of the Cave* (*idola specus*): see IDOL. 2. So is the Eare a sinuous Caue BACON.

Comb., etc.: **c.-breccia** (*Geol.*), breccia deposited in caves; **-deposit** (*Geol.*); **-dweller**, one of the prehistoric men who dwelt in caves; **-fish**, a (blind) fish inhabiting subterraneous streams or lakes in caves; **-man** = *cave-dweller*. Also in names of extinct animals whose remains are found in caves, as *c.-bear*, etc.

†**Cave**, *a.* 1540. [a. F., ad. L. *cavus*.] Hollow, concave. Of the moon: Waning (L. *luna cava* Plin.). -1677.

Cave (kēⁱv), *v.*[1] 1541. [f. CAVE *sb.*] 1. *trans.* To hollow, hollow out. 2. *intr.* To lodge in a cave 1611.

1. Where the mouldred earth had cav'd the banke 1596. 2. Such as wee Caue heere, hunt heere SHAKS.

Cave (kēⁱv), *v.*[2] 1796. [Usu. *cave in*: perh. f. CALVE *in* (q. v.), but assoc. with CAVE *v.*[1]] 1. *To cave in*: to fall in over a hollow, as earth on the side of a pit or cutting; to fall in in a concave form. Chiefly *colloq.* 2. *fig. colloq.* To yield to pressure; to break down, give way, submit 1837. Hence **Cave-in** *sb.*

Cave (kēⁱv), *v.*[3] ME. Dial. f. CHAVE.

‖**Cave** (kēⁱ·vi), *int.* 1868. [L.] Beware!

Caveat (kēⁱ·viˌæt), *sb.* 1557. [L. *caveat* let him beware.] 1. *Law.* A notice given by some party to the proper officer not to take a certain step until the party has been heard in opposition 1654. 2. *transf.* A warning, admonition, caution 1557. †3. = CAUTION *sb.* 2, 5. -1648. 4. *U. S. Patent Laws.* A description of some invention, designed to be patented, lodged in the office before the patent right is taken out, operating as a bar to other applications respecting the same invention 1879.

1. Phr. *To enter* or *put in a c.*: also *fig.* 2. A caueat, to be ware of to moche confidence RECORDE. She enters a silent c. by a blush FULLER. Hence **Ca·veat** *v.* †to enter a c. against; †to serve with a c.; *Fencing*, to shift one's sword to the other side of one's adversary's sword, to disengage. **Ca·vea·tor.**

Ca·vel, *sb. n. dial.* ME. [= Du. *kavel* lot.] 1. A lot (that is cast). Also *fig.* 2. A division made by lot; an allotment 1652. Hence **Ca·vel** *v.* to cast lots; to allot. (Now *dial.*)

Cavendish (kæ·vĕndiʃ). 1839. [? f. the maker's name.] Tobacco softened and pressed into solid cakes.

Cavern (kæ·vəɹn), *sb.* ME. [a. F. *caverne* cave, ad. L. *caverna*, f. *cavus*.] A hollow place underground; a cave. (More rhet. than *cave*.) Also †*transf.*

transf. The cauerne..of the Eare BACON, of the forehead BUCHAN. Hence **Ca·vern** *v.* to enclose as in a cavern; to hollow out into caverns.

Cavernous (kæ·vəɹnəs), *a.* 1447. [ad. L. *cavernosus*; see CAVERN.] 1. Abounding in caverns. 2. Full of cavities and interstices 1597. 3. Of the nature of or resembling a cavern 1830. 4. Of or pertaining to a cavern 1833.

2. It [cancer] is hard, unequall, and c. or hollow 1597. 3. C. eyes 1865. var. **Cave·rnal** (in sense 4).

Cavernulous (kăvə·miŭləs), *a.* 1757. [f. L. *cavernula*, dim. of *caverna* + -OUS.] Full of minute cavities; porous.

Copper..is c. and weak BLACK. var. **Cave·rnulated** *a.*

Cavesson (kæ·vĕsən). 1598. [a. F. *caveçon*, ad. It. *cavezzone*, augm. of *cavezza* halter; repr. (ult.) L. *capitia*, from *capitium* (Diez).] A kind of nose-band, used to curb unmanageable horses. Earlier *cavezan*, *-zon*.

‖**Cavetto** (kɑve·tto). 1677. [It., dim. of *cavo*, f. L. *cavus*.] *Arch.* A hollowed moulding, whose profile is the quadrant of a circle.

Caviar, caviare (kɑviˌā·ɹ, kɑvˌyā·ɹ, also kɑviˌēᵊ·ɹ). 1591. [Found in Turk. as *khāvyār*; in Ital. in 16th c. as *caviale* (whence Eng. *cavialy*). Of uncertain origin. *Cavia·rie* (Shaks.) and *cavee·r* (Swift) are recognized archaic forms.] The roe of the sturgeon, etc., pressed and salted, and eaten as a relish; *esp.* in the east of Europe.

And for our home-bred British Cheer, Botargo, Catsup, and Caveer SWIFT. *Caviarie to the Generall*: a phrase from *Haml.* II. ii. 457, referring to the circumstance that *caviar* is generally unpalatable to those who have not acquired a taste for it.

Cavicorn (kæ·vikǭɹn). [f. L. *cavus* + *cornu*.] *Zool.* One of a family (*Cavicornia*) of Ruminants having hollow horns.

Cavie (kēⁱ·vi). *Sc.* 1756. [app. (ult.) a late L. **cavia*, for *cavea*, f. *cavus*.] A hen-coop.

Cavil (kæ·vil), *sb.* 1570. [f. the vb.] 1. A captious, quibbling, or frivolous objection. 2. Cavilling 1600. †3. Gibe 1615.

1. That's but a c. SHAKS. 2. Liable to c. 1729.

Cavil (kæ·vil), *v.* 1548. [a. OF. *caviller*, ad. L. *cavillari*, f. *cavilla*, a jeering, etc.] 1. *intr.* 'To raise captious and frivolous objections' (J.); to find fault unfairly or without good reason. Const. *at*, *about*. 2. *trans.* To object to captiously 1581.

1. But in the way of Bargaine..Ile cauill on the ninth part of a hayre SHAKS. Hence Ca·viller.

Cavillation (kævilē·ʃən). ME. [a. F., ad. L. *cavillationem*; see CAVIL *v.*] †In early use, *esp.* The use of legal quibbles, so as to overreach or defraud; hence, chicanery, overreaching sophistry. Subseq. = Cavilling 1540; CAVIL *sb.* 1 (*arch.*) 1532.

†**Ca·villato·ry,** *a. rare.* 1641. [ad. L. *cavillatorius.] Of the nature of cavilling –1643.

†**Ca·villous,** *a.* 1572. [ad. L. *cavillosus*; see CAVIL.] Full of cavils or cavilling; apt to cavil –1851. Hence †**Ca·villous-ly** *adv.*, †**-ness.**

Cavin (kæ·vin). 1708. [a. F.:–OF. *cavain*, f. L. *cavus.*] *Mil.* A hollow way, capacious enough to cover troops, and facilitate their approach to a fortress. (Dicts.)

Cavitary (kæ·vitări), *a.* (*sb.*) 1835. [f. L. *cavitas*; cf. *voluntas, voluntary.*] †1. Having a cavity, as *c. worms.* (Adaptation of Cuvier's term, *vers cavitaires*, used of intestinal worms having a distinct mouth and anus.) Also as *sb.* –1847. 2. Of the nature of, or belonging to, a cavity 1861.

Cavity (kæ·viti). 1541. [a. F. *cavité*, f. L. type *cavitatem, f. *cavus.*] †1. Hollowness (*rare*) 1679. 2. A hollow place; a void space within a solid body 1541. 3. *Naval Arch.* Displacement 1850.

2. The cavities as well of the mouth as of the stomache HOLLAND. Little cavities, or vesicles, in this scoria HUXLEY.

‖**Cavo-rilie·vo.** [It. (kā·vo rīlye·vo) = hollow relief.] A style of relief in which the highest portions of the figures are on a level with the general surface.

Cavort (kăvǭ·ɹt), *v. U.S. vulgar.* 1848. [? corrupt f. *curvet* (Bartlett).] *intr.* To curvet, caper about, frisk.

Cavy (kē·vi), *sb.* 1796. [= CABIAI, q. v. (Perh. through Sp. or Pg.)] A rodent of the genus *Cavia* or family *Cavidæ*, natives of America, as the Guinea-pig or the Capybara.

Caw (kǭ). 1666. [Echoic.] The cry or call of a rook, crow, raven, etc. Also as *int.*

Caw (kǭ), *v.* 1589. *intr.* Of rooks, crows, etc.: To utter their natural cry 1590. Also *transf.* Of persons 1589.

Choughes..(Rising and cawing at the guns report) *Mids. N.* III. ii. 22.

Cawk, *sb.*[1] var. of CAUK, q.v. Hence **Caw·ky** *a.* barytous.

Cawk (kǭk), *sb.*[2] 1856. [Echoic.] The cry of rooks, divers, etc. Hence **Cawk** *v.*

Cawker, var. of CAULKER; also of CALKER[2].

Cawl (kǭl). Now *dial.* [OE. *cawl, ceawl.*] A basket; in Cornwall, a creel.

†**Caxon**[1] (kæ·ksən). 1756. [? f. the surname.] A kind of wig –1834.

‖**Caxon**[2]. ? *Obs.* 1669. [OSp., now *cajon* (kaχo·n), augm. of *caxa*, now *caja* CASE; cf. F. *caisson.*] A chest of ores for refining.

Caxton (kæ·kstən). 1811. [f. the surname.] 1. *ellipt.* A book printed by William Caxton (died 1492). 2. A variety of type, imitating that of Caxton.

Cay (kē, kī). Also KEY[2], q.v. 1707. [ad. Sp. *cayo* shoal, barrier-reef, OF. *cay, caye* sand bank or bar; referred by Diez to Celt. *cae.* See QUAY.] A low insular bank of sand, mud, rock, etc.; a range of low-lying reefs or rocks.

Cayenne (kē,e·n, kai,e·n). 1756. [ad. native name in Tupi (Brazilian); but pop. referred to *Cayenne* in French Guiana.] (Also *Cayenne pepper.*) A very pungent powder obtained from the dried and ground seeds and pods of species of *Capsicum*, esp. *C. annuum* and *C. frutescens*, of S. America; used as a condiment; formerly called Guinea pepper. Also *fig.* Hence **Caye·nned** *ppl. a.* seasoned with c.

Cayleyan (kē·liăn). 1852. [f. Prof. *Cayley* of Cambridge.] *Math.* A certain curve of the third order.

Cayman, caiman (kē·măn). 1577. [app. from Carib (through Sp. or Pg.).] A name applied to some large saurians, *esp.* the S. American ALLIGATOR; and, *loosely*, to all large American saurians, including crocodiles.

†**Cay·nard.** ME. only. [a. F. *cagnard*, f. It. *cagna* bitch.] A sluggard.

Cayuse (ka,yū·s). *U.S. local.* 1882. [Chinook Indian.] An Indian pony.

‖**Ca·zimi.** 1614. *Astrol.* The centre of the sun. *In cazimi*: said of a planet when distant not more than 17 minutes from the sun.

Cazique, var. of CACIQUE.

Ce (sī), name of the letter C. Cf. CEE.

Cease (sīs), *v.* [ME. *cessen*, a. F. *cesser*:– L. *cessare*, freq. of *cedere* to yield.]

I. *intr.* 1. To stop, give over, discontinue, desist. †2. To rest –1660. 3. Of actions, feelings, etc.: To come to or be at an end ME. †4. To fail, become extinct, pass away –1710.

1. To c. from wanderings TENNYSON, to fyght CAXTON. 3. Miracles are ceast SHAKS. 4. The poore shall neuer c. out of the land *Deut.* xv. 11.

II. *trans.* 1. To stop ME. †2. To cause to leave off (*of* an action); to quiet –1585.

1. He, her fears to c., Sent down the meek-eyed Peace MILT. Fond Nature, c. thy strife POPE. The snow never ceased falling TYNDALL. Hence †**Ceased** *ppl. a.* that has come to an end. †**Cea·ser.**

Cease (sīs), *sb.* ME. [a. OF. *ces*, f. *cesser*; see prec.] = *ceasing*, CESSATION. *Obs.* exc. in *Without cease.* (Cf. F. *sans cesse.*) Hence **Cea·seless** *a.* without ceasing. **Cea·selessly** *adv.* **Cea·selessness.**

‖**Cebus** (sī·bǒs). 1863. [mod. L. a. Gr. κῆβος.] A genus of long-tailed monkeys of S. America, including the Sapajous. Hence **Ce·bine** *a.*

Cecity (sī·sĭti). *arch.* 1528. [ad. L. *cæcitas*; cf. F. *cécité.*] Blindness. (Usu. *fig.*)

After life's term, a term of c. M. ARNOLD.

Cecum, var. of CÆCUM, the blind-gut.

Cecutiency (sĭkiū·ʃiĕnsi). [f. L. *cæcutient-*, *cæcutire* to be blind.] A tendency to blindness; partial blindness. SIR T. BROWNE.

Cedar (sī·dəɹ). [OE. *ceder* (ME. *cedre*, a. OF.), ad. L. *cedrus*, a. Gr. κέδρος.] 1. An evergreen conifer, the *Pinus Cedrus* of Linnæus, *Abies Cedrus, Cedrus Libani* of other botanists, called Cedar of Lebanon from its most famous early locality. The wood of this tree ME. 2. Applied to the genus *Cedrus*, or subgenus of *Abies*, including the Mount Atlas or Silvery Cedar and the Deodara or Indian Cedar. Also to various trees more or less resembling the true cedar: including species of *Cedrela, Juniperus, Thuja, Cupressus, Pinus*, etc. 1703. Also *attrib.*

1. The beames of our house are cedars *Song of Solomon* i. 17. *Comb.* **c.-bird**, the American Waxwing, *Ampelis carolinensis*, a species of Chatterer haunting cedar trees. Hence **Ce·dared** *ppl. a.* furnished with cedars (*rare*). **Ce·darn** *a. poet.* of cedar-trees or -wood. †**Ce·dary, Ce·dry** *a.* having the properties of c. **Ce·drine** *a.* of or pertaining to c.

Cede (sīd), *v.* 1633. [ad. L. *cedere.*] †1. *intr.* To give way, yield *to* –1756. 2. *trans.* To give up, grant; to yield, surrender 1754.

2. This copy has been ceded to me as a favor T. JEFFERSON. To c. provinces to the Company WELLINGTON. Hence **Ce·der.** So **Ce·dent,** one who assigns property to another. *Sc. Law.*

Cedilla (sĭdi·lă). 1599. [ad. Sp. *cedilla*, dim. of *ce*, the letter C. Cf. It. *cediglia*, G. *cedille.*] The mark ̧ written under *c* when it precedes *a, o, u*, and has the sound (s). Also var. †**Cerilla** 1591, ad. Sp. *cerilla*; cf. F. †*cérille.*

Cedr-, repr. L. *cedrus* cedar, forming terms of chemistry, etc.:

Ce·drene, a liquid hydrocarbon ($C_{32}H_{21}$) found in the resin of the cedar of Lebanon. **Cedriret,** a product obtained from the tar of beechwood, crystallizing in fine needles.

Cedrat, -ate (sī·drĕt). 1781. [a. F., ad. It. *cedrato*, f. *cedro* (:–L. *citrus*) citron.] A variety of the citron or lemon. var. ‖**Ce·dre.** [Fr.]

‖**Cedrela** (sĭdrī·lă). 1836. [mod. L., a. Sp., dim. of *cedro, cedra* CEDAR.] A genus of large trees, species of which are called *Cedar* or *Bastard Cedar.* Hence **Cedrela·ceous** *a.* (*Bot.*) of or pertaining to the *Cedrelaceæ*, or Cedrela order.

Ce·dron. 1859. A small tree of New Granada (*Simaba Cedron*, N.O. *Simarubaceæ*); also its fruit. Also *attrib.*

‖**Ce·dula.** 1724. [Sp. *cédula* (þe·dula), SCHEDULE, q.v.] A permit or order issued by the Spanish government; also a name of some S. American securities.

Cedule, early f. SCHEDULE.

†**Ce·duous,** *a. rare.* [f. L. *cæduus*; see -UOUS.] Ready for felling. EVELYN.

Cee (sī). 1542. Name of the letter C. Formerly, a term for a certain quantity of beer. Hence **Cee spring, C-spring,** in *Coach-building.*

‖**Ceiba** (sɔi·bă). 1812. [Sp. (þei·ba); perh. W. Indian.] The God-tree, Silk Cotton-tree of the W. Indies, *Eriodendron anfractuosum* (*Bombax Ceiba*). (Miller.)

Ceil (sīl), *sb. poet. rare.* 1840. [f. next.] = CEILING.

Ceil, ciel (sīl), *v.* ME. [conn. with med. L. *cælum*, F. *ciel* canopy, but the deriv. is doubtful. Cf. CELURE.] †1. ?To furnish with a canopy, hangings, or a screen. ME. only. †2. To line (the roof or walls of a room, etc.) with woodwork, plaster, etc.; to wainscot –1615. 3. *esp.* To line the roof of, construct an inner roof for; *usually*, to plaster the roof 1519.

2. The greate house syled he with Pyne tre COVERDALE 2 *Chron.* iii. 5. Hence **Ceiled, cieled** *ppl. a.* †wainscoted; provided with a ceiling; also *fig.*

Ceiling, cieling (sī·liŋ), *vbl. sb.* ME. [f. prec.] 1. The action of the vb. CEIL 1497. †2. *concr.* A screen of tapestry, a curtain –1632. 3. †Panelling; wainscoting –1634; *Naut.* = FOOT-WALING 1633. 4. *esp.* The undercovering of a roof or floor, concealing the timbers; the plaster at the top of a room 1535. b. Maximum height of an aeroplane 1917. Hence **Cei·linged** *ppl. a.*

†**Ceinte.** ME. [a. OF. *ceint, ceinct*:–L. *cinctus.*] A girdle –1530.

‖**Ceintu·re.** *rare.* 1856. [F.:–L. *cinctura.*] = CINCTURE.

Celadon (se·lădǫn). 1768. [a. F. (see Littré).] A pale willow-green colour. Also as *adj.* Hence **Ce·ladonite,** *Min.* green earth of Verona.

Celandine (se·lăndəin). [ME. *celydoine*, a. OF. *celidoine*, (ult.) ad. Gr. χελιδόνιον, f. χελιδών swallow. For the *n* cf. *messenger.*] a. Common or Greater Celandine, *Chelidonium majus* (N.O. *Papaveraceæ*); called by Lyte *swallow-wort.* Its thick yellow juice was supposed to benefit weak sight. b. Small or Lesser Celandine, the Pilewort, *Ranunculus Ficaria* 1578. var. †**Ce·lidony.**

Celarent (sĭlē·rĕnt). 1551. [L.] A mnemonic word designating the second mood of the first syllogistic figure, in which a universal negative major premiss and a universal affirmative minor give a universal negative conclusion.

Ce·lation. 1567. [f. L. *celare*; see -ATION.] Concealment; *esp.* of birth or pregnancy.

Celature (sī·lătiŭɹ). ME. [ad. L. *cælatura*, f. *cælare* to emboss, engrave.] Embossing; *concr.* that which is embossed.

†**Cele,** *sb.* 1708. [mod. L., a. Gr. κήλη.] *Med.* A tumour caused by the protrusion of any soft part –1881.

Celebrant (se·lĭbrănt). 1839. [ad. L. *celebrantem.*] One who celebrates; *esp.* the priest who officiates at the Eucharist.

†**Ce·lebrate,** *ppl a.* 1471. [ad. L. *celebratus*, *celebrare*, f. *celebrem* renowned, etc.] 1. Performed with due rites: solemnly held –1564. 2. Celebrated –1680. 3. Consecrated 1632.

Celebrate (se·lĭbreʼt), *v.* 1534. [f. prec.] 1. To perform publicly and in due form (any religious ceremony); to hold (a church council); to solemnize 1564. Also *absol.* (with the Eucharist as implied obj.) 1534. Also †*transf.* 2. To observe with solemn rites; to honour with ceremonies, festivities, etc. 1560. 3. To make publicly known, proclaim 1597. 4. To extol, publish the fame of 1611.

1. To c. the holy communion 1574, nuptials 1772, (*transf.*) a contract WEST. 2. To c. the Sabbath 1560. 3. Whose name..we c. with due honour HOOKER. 4. Death cannot c. thee *Isa.* xxxviii. 18. Hence **Cele·brative** *a.* pertaining to celebration (*rare*). **Ce·lebrator, †-er,** one who CELEBRATES. var. †**Ce·lebre, -er.** CAXTON.

Celebration (selĭbrē·ʃən). 1529. [ad. L. *celebrationem.*] 1. The action of celebrating. †2. = CELEBRITY –1779.

1. To go to early c. (*mod.*). C. of Easter LINGARD. His memory deserving a particular c. CLARENDON.

Celebrious (sĭle·briəs), *a.* 1555. [f. L. *celebris*; cf. *alacrious.*] †1. Frequented; attended by throngs; festive –1680. 2. Renowned (*arch.* or *dial.*) 1608. var. †**Ce·lebrous** (sense 2).

Celebrity (sǐle·briti). 1600. [ad. L. *celebritatem*, f. *celebrem* famous, thronged.] †1. Solemnity –1631. †2. A solemn ceremony, a celebration –1774. 3. The condition of being much talked about; famousness, notoriety 1600. 4. A person of celebrity 1849.

1. To hold a synod with great c. 1612. 3. They had c., Spinoza has fame M. ARNOLD. 4. One of the celebrities of wealth and fashion EMERSON.

Celeriac (sǐle·riæ̆k). 1743. [Eng. deriv. of CELERY; the *-ac* is obscure.] A turnip-rooted variety of the garden celery.

Celerity (sǐle·rĭti). [ME. *celerite*, a. F. *célérité*, ad. L. *celeritatem*.] 1. Swiftness, speed. Now *esp.* of living beings. 1483. †2. A rate of speed. (Repl. in science by *velocity*.) –1794.

Celery (se·lĕri). 1664. [a. F. *céleri*; (ult.) repr. Gr. σέλινον parsley (see Littré).] An umbelliferous plant (*Apium graveolens*); its blanched stalks are used as a salad and vegetable.

Celeste (sǐle·st). 1880. [mod. a. F. *céleste*.] 1. A colour, sky-blue [Fr. *bleu céleste*] 1881. 2. (= *voix céleste*): A stop on the organ or harmonium. Also, a form of the soft pedal on a piano.

Celestial (sǐle·stiăl). ME. [a. OF. *celestial*, *-el*, f. L. *cælestis*.] **A.** *adj.* 1. Of or pertaining to the material heavens. 2. Of or pertaining to heaven, as the abode of God, angels, spirits, etc. ME. 3. Divine, heavenly ME. Also as quasi-*sb.*

1. The altitude of the sonne or of othre c. bodies CHAUCER. 2. The lorde that is Celestyall FABYAN. 3. C. food NEALE, beauties 1704. Hence **Celes·tia·lity. Cele·stially** *adv.*

The C. Empire: tr. native name for China. So *C. Emperor*; and (*joc.*) *celestial* = Chinese.

B. *sb.* 1. An inhabitant of heaven 1573. 2. A Chinese 1863.

†**Cele·stify**, *v. rare.* 1646. [f. L. *cælestis* + -FY.] To make heavenly –1768.

†**Ce·lestine**, *a.* and *sb.*[1] ME. ? = CELESTIAL *a.* and *sb.* –1509.

Celestine (se·lĕstəin, -tin, sǐle·stin), *sb.*[2] 1530. [ad. L. *Cælestinus*, f. the proper names *Cælestius* and *Cælestinus*.] a. One of a sect named after Cælestius, an associate of Pelagius, in 5th c. b. One of a reformed branch of the Benedictines, founded by Celestine V. in 13th c.

Celestine (se·lĕstin), *sb.*[3] 1798. [? ad. It. *celestino* sky-blue.] *Min.* = CELESTITE. Formerly also a blue alabaster.

Celestite (se·lĕstəit, sǐle·stəit). 1854. [Dana's var. of CELESTINE.] *Min.* Native-sulphate of strontia, $SrO.SO_3$, so called from the sky-blue colour it occ. presents.

Cele·stitude. 1824. [f. L. *cælestis*, after *altitude*, etc.] *joc.* A Celestial (Chinese) dignitary. var. **Cele·stia·lity.** LANDOR.

‖**Celeu·sma.** *rare.* 1680. [late L., a. Gr. κέλευσμα.] A watchword, battle-cry, etc.

Celiac, var. of CŒLIAC.

Celibacy (se·libăsi). 1663. [f. L. *cælibatus*, f. *cælebs*.] The state of living unmarried.

St. Paul's advice for cœlebacy 1663.

Celibatarian (se:libătē°·riăn), *a.* 1839. [f. CELIBATE *sb.*[1]] Characterized by, or characteristic of, celibacy; favouring celibacy. As *sb.* One who lives in or advocates celibacy 1863.

The Queen's c. prejudices 1839.

Celibate (se·libe̊t), *sb.*[1] *arch.* 1614. [ad. F. *célibat*, ad. L. *cælibatus*.] State of celibacy; order of celibates. Hence **Celiba·tic** *a.* **Ce·libatist**, an advocate of celibacy.

Celibate (se·libe̊t), *a.* and *sb.*[2] 1829. [f. L. *cælibem* + -ATE (not on L. analogy).] *adj.* Unmarried, single; bound not to marry. *sb.* [sc *man* or *woman.*] 1869. var. **Ce:libatai·r(e** (*rare*). Hence **Ce·libate** *v.* to compel to celibacy.

Celido·graphy. 1775. [f. Gr. κηλίς spot + -γραφία. In F. *célidographie*.] A description of the spots in the sun or planets. (Dicts.)

Cell (sel). [ME *celle*, a. OF. :—L. *cella*. In late OE. *cell*, pl. *cellas*; perh. ad. L.] I. †1. A store-closet –1583. 2. A monastery or nunnery dependent on some larger house OE. 3. A dwelling consisting of a single chamber, inhabited by a solitary ME. 4. One of a number of small apartments, as in a monastery, a nunnery, a prison, occupied by a single person ME. 5. *Arch.* = CELLA.

2. The house was once a c. to the Abby PENNANT. 3. The c. of an anchorite H. E. MANNING. *poet.* Poore shepheards' cels QUARLES. Hunted stag, in mountain c. SCOTT. Nor dreaming of the narrow c. NEALE. 4. *Condemned c.*: a c. occupied by one who is condemned to death.

II. 1. *gen.* A compartment, *e.g.* of a cabinet, a honeycomb, etc. 1577. 2. *spec.* a. in *Archit.* The space between the ribs of a vaulted roof 1850. b. *Entom.* The space between the nerves of the wings of insects 1881. c. *Electr.* Orig., a compartment of a wooden trough; now, a vessel containing one pair of plates immersed in fluid; or a voltaic apparatus containing one pair of metallic elements. Several *cells* united form a battery 1828.

III. 1. An enclosed space, cavity, or sac, in organized bodies, or (*transf.*) in mineral products ME. 2. *Biol.* The ultimate element in organic structures; a minute portion of protoplasm, enclosed usu. in a membrane 1672.

1. *Cells of the brain*: the imaginary cavities in that organ, supposed to be the seats of particular mental faculties, or pigeon-holes for knowledge. Now only *fig.* ME. The cells of lava DARWIN. 2. Hepatic cells 1845, nerve cells BAIN.

IV. Any hollow receptacle or containing cavity 1704. Also *attrib.* Hence †**Cell** *v.* to shut up, or dwell, in a c. (*rare*).

‖**Cella** (ṣe·lă). 1676. [L.] *Arch.* The body of the temple, as dist. from the portico, etc.

Cellar (se·ləɹ), *sb.* [ME. *celer*, a. Anglo-F. (mod. *cellier*) :—L. *cellarium* set of cells, f. *cella* CELL.] 1. A store-house or store-room, above or below ground, for provisions. *Obs.* exc. in *fish-c.* 2. An underground chamber ME. 3. = *wine-c.*; hence *transf.* a person's stock of wines 1541. †4. A case; *esp.* of bottles. (For SALT-CELLAR cf. SALER.) –1667. Also *attrib.*

3. *Temp.* II. ii. 137. 4. A c. of waters of her own distilling PEPYS. Hence **Ce·llar** *v.* to store up in or as in a c. **Ce·llarer**, the officer in a monastery, etc., who had charge of the c. So **Ce·llaress. Ce·llaring** *sb.* = CELLARAGE 1. **Ce·llerman. Ce·llarous** *a.* (*joc.*) of or pertaining to a c. DICKENS.

Cellarage (se·lərėdʒ). 1512. [f. prec. + -AGE.] 1. Cellar accommodation; cellars 1602. Also *transf.* 2. †A feudal duty upon wine when placed in the cellar; charge for the use of a cellar.

Cellaret (selərē·t). 1806. [f. as prec.] A case of cabinet-work, or a sideboard with compartments, made to hold wine-bottles, etc.

Celled (seld), *ppl. a.* 1650. [f. CELL + -ED.] 1. Furnished with cells; made or arranged in the form of cells. So **Ce·llate** *a.*, **Ce·llated.** 1776. 2. Enclosed in a cell.

Cellepore (se·lǐpōᵊɹ). 1811. [f. *cella* CELL, after MADREPORE.] A genus of *Polyzoa*, consisting of a group of vase-like chambers with a beak on one or both sides. Also *attrib.*

Celliferous (seli·fĕrəs), *a. rare.* [f. *celli*- comb. f. L. *cella* + -FEROUS.] Bearing or producing cells. So **Ce·lliform** *a.* cell-shaped.

'Cello (tʃe·lo). 1881. Short f. VIOLONCELLO. So **'Ce·llist, 'Ce·lloist**, a VIOLONCELLIST.

Celloid (se·loid), *a.* 1849. [f. CELL + -OID.] Cell-like.

Cellular (se·liŭlăɹ), *a.* 1753. [perh. ad. F. *cellulaire*, f. *cellule*, which in F. has replaced *celle*.] 1. Of, pertaining to, or characterized by cells 1823. 2. Containing cells; porous 1816. 3. *Phys.* Consisting of cells. As used of vegetable tissues, opp. to *vascular*. As *sb. pl.* Cellular plants (in L. form *Cellulares*); those without distinct stem or leaves, as Cryptogams 1879.

1. C. discipline LAMB. 2. C. basalt DARWIN. 3. *C. tissue*, †*membrane*, in Animal Physiology, a synonym of *areolar* or *connective tissue*. *C. pathology*: the study of morbid changes in the cells. Hence **Cellula·rity**, c. quality or condition. var. **Ce·llulate, Ce·llulated** *ppl. a.* (in senses 2, 3). **Cellula·tion**, development of cells.

Cellule (se·liul). 1652. [ad. L. *cellula*, dim. of *cella*.] †1. A pigeon-hole –1819. 2. A minute cell, cavity, or pore 1830. Hence **Cellu·lic** *a.* of or pertaining to cellules or cells. **Celluli·ferous** *a.* bearing or producing cellules. **Ce·llulin** (*Chem.*) = CELLULOSE. **Ce·lluloid** *a.*

Cellulitis (seliulǝi·tis). 1861. [f. L. *cellula* + -ITIS.] Inflammation of the cellular tissue.

Cellulo-, comb. f. CELLULE, L. *cellula*, forming adjs., with sense CELLULAR: e.g. *c.-adipose*, (tissue) partly cellular partly adipose.

Celluloid (se·liŭloid), *sb.* 1871. [loosely f. CELLULOSE *sb.*] A substance consisting essentially of soluble cellulose nitrate and camphor.

Cellulose (se·liŭlōus). 1753. [ad. mod.L. *cellulosus*, f. *cellula*.] **A.** *adj.* Consisting of cells; full of minute cavities. var. **Ce·llulous.**

B. *sb.* [a. F.] One of the AMYLOSES. A substance also called *lignin*, which constitutes the essential part of the solid framework of plants, and occurs in the animal body. It is amorphous, tasteless, inodorous, insoluble in water, alcohol, ether, dilute acids, and alkalis. 1835. b. In popular use, designating compounds of cellulose, esp. c. acetate and c. nitrate, solutions of which give the 'cellulose' finish used in varnishing metal, woodwork, etc. 1898.

C...in fine linen and cotton, which are almost entirely composed of it WATTS. Hence **Cellulo·sity**, the condition of being c.; also *concr.*

Celo·tomy. Also **ke-.** 1847. [ad. Gr. κηλοτομία, f. κήλη rupture + -τομία.] *Surg.* The operation for strangulated hernia by cutting down and dividing the stricture. So **Ce·lotome**, the knife used in c.

Ce·lsitude. 1450. [a. F., ad. L. *celsitudo*.] †1. Loftiness –1680. 2. Height. (Now *joc.*) 1678.

Celt[1] (selt). Also **Kelt.** 1607. [a. F. *Celte*, ad. L. *Celta*, sing. of *Celtæ*, in Gr. Κελτοί.] 1. *Hist.* Applied to the ancient peoples of Western Europe; the Gauls and their (continental) kin. 2. A general name for peoples speaking languages akin to those of the ancient Galli, including the Bretons, the Cornish, Welsh, Irish, Manx, and Gaelic. See also CELTIC. 1773.

Celt[2] (selt). 1715. [ad. (reputed) L. *celtes* stone-chisel.] A prehistoric edged implement of bronze or stone (occ. of iron).

Celtic (se·ltik), *a.* Also **Keltic.** 1656. [a. F. *celtique* or ad. L. *celticus*.] 1. *Hist.*, etc. Of or belonging to the ancient Celtae. 2. Epithet of the languages and peoples akin to the ancient Celtic; *esp.* of the great branch of the Aryan family of languages which includes Breton, Welsh, Irish, Manx, Gaelic, Cornish, and the ancient languages which they represent. Also absol. = *Celtic tongue*. 1707. Hence **Ce·ltically** *adv.* **Ce·lticism**, a C. custom or expression; devotion to C. customs. **Ce·lticize** *v.* to render C.; *intr.* to adopt C. fashions, etc.

Celto-, comb. f. CELT[1], as in **Ce·ltophil**, a friend of the Celts and Celtic studies.

†**Ce·lure.** ME. [See CEIL *v.*] A canopy. Also the hangings of a bed, etc. –1553.

Ce·mbalist. *rare.* 1871. [f. It. *cembalo*, prop. cymbal.] *Mus.* One who plays the pianoforte in an orchestra.

Cement (sǐme·nt, †se·mĕnt), *sb.* [ME. *cyment*, a. OF. *ciment* :—L. *cæmentum* (also used as *cementum*), contr. for *cædimentum* cutting, produce of chipping, f. *cædere*; refash. after L.] 1. Any powdered substance that, made plastic with water, is used in a soft and pasty state (which hardens on drying) to bind together bricks, stones, etc. in building, to cover floors, walls, etc., or (with a suitable aggregate) to form concrete. (See HYDRAULIC *c.*, PORTLAND *c.*, ROMAN *c.*) 2. *gen.* Any substance applied to the surface of solid bodies to make them cohere firmly 1562; *fig.* a principle of union (*rare*) 1604. 3. *transf.* a. A cement-like substance used for stopping up small cavities (e.g. in teeth) 1489. b. *Physiol.* The bony tissue forming the outer crust of the fang of the tooth 1849. c. *Metall.* A finely divided metal obtained by precipitation, esp. in *c.-copper*, *-gold*, *-silver* 1874.

1. The name was also formerly, and is still loosely, applied to *mortar*. *In c.* adj. phr. applied to brick-work, etc. built with mortar composed of c. and sand (*c. mortar*). Hence **Ceme·ntal** *a.*

Cement (sǐme·nt), *v.* ME. [f. the sb.] 1. To unite with or as with cement. Also *fig.* 2. To apply cement to 1886. 3. *intr.* (for *refl.*) To cohere firmly by the application of cement; to stick 1677. Also *fig.*

Hence **Ceme·nter. Ceme·nting** *vbl. sb.*

Cementation (sǐmĕntē̆i·ʃən). 1594. [f. prec.] 1. The action or process of cementing; the state thus produced. Also *fig.* 1660. 2. The process by which one solid is made to combine with another at a high temperature so as to change the properties of one of them, without liquefaction taking place 1594. 3. Encasing or lining with cement (*mod.*).

Cementi·tious, *a. rare.* 1828. [ad. L. *cæmentitius*; but in sense from CEMENT.] Of the nature of cement.

Cemetery (se·mĭtĕri). 1460. [ad. L. *cœmeterium*, ad. Gr. κοιμητήριον dormitory.] A place, usually a ground, set apart for the burial of the dead; †a churchyard; any burial-ground. *fig.* It is with libraries as with other cœmeteries SWIFT. Hence **Cemete·rial** *a.* relating to a c.

Cenacle (se·năk'l). ME. [a. F. *cénacle*, ad. L. *cenaculum* (also used), f. *cena.*] A supping room; an upper chamber; *esp.* that in which the Last Supper was held.

Cenanthy (sĭnæ·nþi). 1881. [f. Gr. κενός + ἄνθος.] *Bot.* The absence of stamens and pistils in a flower.

†**Cena·tion.** 1599. [ad. L. *cenationem.*] Dining, supping –1646. So †**Ce·natory** *a.* pertaining to c. (*rare*).

‖**Cendre.** 1805. [F., 'cinder, ash'.] Ash-.

†**Cene.** ME. [a. F. *cène*:—L. *cena.*] The Last Supper; also = *Cene Thursday*, Maundy Thursday –1491.

Cenobite, -itic, cenobium; see CŒ-.

Cenogamy; see CŒ-.

Cenotaph (se·nŏtaf). 1603. [a. F. *cenotaphe*, ad. Gr. κενοτάφιον, f. κενός + τάφος.] An empty tomb; a sepulchral monument erected in honour of a person whose body is elsewhere. *The C.*, erected in Whitehall, London, as a memorial to the British who fell in the war of 1914–18.

Cenozoic, var. sp. of CÆNO-, CAINO-.

†**Cense**, *sb.*[1] ME. Aphetic f. INCENSE –1540.

†**Cense**, *sb.*[2] 1524. [a. OF. *cense* (mod. *cens*) :—L. *census*, f. *censere* to estimate, etc.] 1. = CENSUS 1, 2, 3, –1763. 2. Rating; income –1650.

Cense (sens), *v.*[1] ME. [f. CENSE *sb.*[1]] 1. To perfume with odours from burning incense; to offer incense to. †2. *intr.* To burn or offer incense –1732. var. †**Censer** (*rare*).
1. In the temple..hem to scence bothe clene and pure ME.

†**Cense**, *v.*[2] 1606. [ad. L. *censere.* Cf. CENSE *sb.*[2]] 1. To estimate, reckon –1697. 2. To take a census of. ADDISON.

Censer (se·nsəɹ), *sb.* ME. [a. OF. *censier* (*senser*), short f. *encensier*; in sense 2, f. CENSE *v.*] 1. A vessel in which incense is burnt; a thurible. b. = CASSOLETTE. *Tam. Shr.* IV. iii. 91. 2. One who perfumes with incense 1670.
1. Another aungel..hauynge a golden c. WYCLIF.

Censor (se·nsəɹ), *sb.* 1533. [a. L.; see CENSE *v.*[2]] 1. One of two magistrates in ancient Rome, who drew up the census of the citizens, etc., and had the supervision of public morals. b. *transf.* One who has the supervision of the conduct of a body of people, as in some colleges 1592. 2. *spec.* An official whose duty it is to inspect books, journals, plays, etc., before publication, to secure that they shall contain nothing immoral, heretical, or offensive or injurious to the State 1644. b. One who censors private correspondence (as in time of war) 1914. 3. †A critic; a fault-finder 1599. 4. *Psychoanalysis.* A power within the soul which represses certain elements in the unconscious 1913. [Mistranslation of Freud's *zensur* censorship.]
1. b. Punch is a censor but not censorious 1871. C. of Non-collegiate Students *Oxf. Univ. Cal.* 2. The censors of the press W. IRVING. 3. Eulogists or censors MACAULAY. Hence **Ce·nsor** *v. trans.* to examine (books, plays, news, correspondence) as c. **Ce·nsorship**, the office or function of a c.; official supervision 1591.

Censorial (sensōə·riăl), *a.* 1592. [f. L. *censorius* + -AL.] 1. Of, pertaining to, or characteristic of a censor 1772. †2. Censorious –1596.
1. The c. inspection of the publick eye BURKE. So **Censo·rian.**

Censorious (sensōə·riəs), *a.* 1536. [f. as prec. + -OUS.] 1. Addicted to censure; severely critical; fault-finding. Const. *of*; †*on*, †*upon.* †2. Befitting a censor; grave, severe –1660.
1. To read with a c. eye CAMDEN. 2. His [Bacon's] language..was nobly c. B. JONS. Hence **Censo·rious-ly** *adv.*, **-ness.**

Censual (se·nsiuăl), *a.* 1613. [ad. late L. *censualis*; see CENSUS.] Of or relating to a census, as a *c. roll.*

Censure (se·nsiŭɹ, se·nʃiŭɹ), *sb.* ME. [a. F., ad. L. *censura*, f. *cens-* stem of *censere.*] †1. A judicial (*esp.* ecclesiastical) sentence; a condemnatory judgement –1727. †2. A formal opinion (of an expert, etc.) –1625. 3. *gen.* Judgement; opinion; criticism (*arch.*) 1576. 4. *spec.* An unfavourable opinion, hostile criticism; blaming, finding fault with, or condemning as wrong; expression of condemnation. (The usual sense.) 1603. 5. Censorship 1534. 6. Correction; *esp.* critical recension (*rare*) 1613.
1. He was brought to..the House of Lords to receive his C. MAY. The censures of holy churche 1494. 4. No might nor greatnesse in mortality can c. scape SHAKS. 6. The c. of the Vulgate text HALLAM.

Censure (se·nsiŭɹ, se·nʃiŭɹ), *v.* 1589. [a. F. *censurer.*] †1. To form or give a censure or opinion of; to estimate, criticize, judge –1729. Also †*intr.* with *of* or (occ.) *on*; and †*absol.* †2. To pronounce judicial sentence on; to sentence *to* –1682. 3. To pronounce an adverse judgement on, criticize unfavourably; to find fault with, blame, condemn. (The current sense.) 1596. Also *absol.* †4. To exercise censorship over. BACON.
1. *Jul. C.* III. ii. 16. Content to be censured idle SIR R. CECIL. C. better of me LATHAM. 3. Would not C., or Speake ill of a Man BACON. Hence **Ce·nsurer. Ce·nsureship** = CENSORSHIP.

Census (se·nsŏs), *sb.* 1613. [L. *census.*] 1. The registration of citizens and their property in ancient Rome for taxation 1634. †2. A poll-tax –1864. 3. An official enumeration of the population of a country, etc., with statistics relating to them. Also *attrib.* 1769.
A census of the population has been taken every tenth year since 1801 in Great Britain.

Cent[1] (sent). ME. [a. F., or ad. L. *centum.*] †1. ? A hundred. [a. F. *cent.*] ME. only. 2. *Per cent*: for (in, to) every hundred; used in stating a proportion. [? At first in It. form *per cento*; or due to F. *pour cent.*] 1568. 3. A hundredth. [? Contr. of *centime, centesimum*, or the like.] 1685. Hence, 4. In U. S.: The hundredth part of a dollar; a coin of this value 1782; in France, etc.: A centime 1810.
2. Th' interest of xij. per cent by the yeare GRESHAM. *Three* (etc.) *per cents* = three (etc.) per cent stocks, *i.e.* stocks bearing that rate of interest. C. per c. 1677. Hence **Ce·ntage**, now PER-CENTAGE.

†**Cent**[2]. 1532. 1. An old game at cards, said to have resembled piquet, with 100 as the point that won the game –1636. 2. A counter used in playing Ombre –1878.

Cental (se·ntăl). [L. *centum*, ? after *quintal.*] A weight of one hundred pounds avoirdupois, introduced into the Liverpool corn-market in 1859, and since legalized.

Centaur (se·ntǫɹ). ME. [ad. L. a. Gr. κένταυρος; see Liddell and Scott.] 1. *Mythol.* A fabulous creature, with the head, trunk, and arms of a man, joined to the body and legs of a horse. Also *fig.* 2. One of the southern constellations 1667. †3. A kind of ship 1622. Hence various *nonce-wds.*, as **Ce·ntaurdom**, etc.

Centaury (se·ntǫri, -əri). ME. [ad. med.L. *centaurea, -ia*, for L. *centaureum* or *centaurion*, a. Gr. κενταύρειον, or κενταύριον, f. κένταυρος CENTAUR.] *Bot.* 1. A plant, said to have been discovered by Chiron the centaur; its two species, *Centaurion majus* and *C. minus*, have been identified (prob. correctly) with *Chlora perfoliata* and *Erythræa Centaureum.* 2. In 16th c. *Great C.* was applied to a composite plant or plants; and to the genus containing these Linnæus gave the name *Centaurea.* 'Centaury' has since been extended as a book-name to all the species. 1551.
American C.: a name for *Sabbatia*, a genus of N. American herbs of the Gentian family.

Centenarian (sentĭnēə·riăn). 1846. [f. L. *centenarius.*] A. *adj.* 1. A hundred years old 1849. 2. Of or belonging to a centenary celebration 1864. B. *sb.* A person a hundred years old 1846.

Centenary (se·ntĭnări, also sentī·nări; *erron.* sente·nări). 1598. [ad. L. *centenarius*, f. *centeni.* In F. *centenaire.*] A. *adj.* 1. Of or pertaining to the space of a hundred years 1647. 2. *gen.* Of or belonging to a hundred 1768.
1. C. years returned but seldom FULLER.
B. *sb.* †1. A weight of a hundred pounds –1788. 2. A centennium or century 1607. 3. A centennial anniversary; the celebration of the accomplishment of a centennium 1788.
1. Thirty-four centenaries of gold GIBBON. 2. To complete one's c. (*mod.*). 3. The second c. of Handel's birth 1885.

Centenier (se·ntĕnīəɹ). ME. [a. F.:—L. *centenarius.*] †1. A centurion –1603. 2. A police-officer in Jersey 1862.

Centennial (sente·niăl), *a.* (*sb.*) 1797. [f. (after *biennial*, etc.) L. **centennium*, f. *centum* + *annus.*] 1. Of a hundred years' standing; a hundred years old; completing a hundred years; of or relating to the hundredth anniversary. 2. *sb.* A hundredth anniversary or its celebration; a centenary 1876.
Centennial State (U. S.): appellation of Colorado, admitted as a state in the c. year of the existence of the United States (1876).

Cente·nnium. [f. L. *centum* + *annus*, after *biennium*, etc.] A period of a hundred years.

Center; see CENTRE.

Centering, centreing (se·ntəriŋ), *vbl. sb.* Also **centring.** 1766. [f. *center* CENTRE *v.*; *centering* is the general spelling.] 1. The action of the vb. CENTRE. 2. *spec.* The setting of lenses so that their axes are in the same straight line 1768. 3. *Arch.* The temporary framing, whereon any vaulted work is constructed 1766. Also *attrib.*

Centesimal (sente·simăl), *a.* (*sb.*) 1682. [f. L. *centesimus, centesima* (*pars*), f. *centum.* Cf. *decimal.*] †1. Hundred-fold. 2. Hundredth 1809. 3. *sb.* A hundredth part 1698.
3. The Height..in Inches and Centesimals 1698. Hence **Cente·simally** *adv.* **Cente·simate** *v.* to select every hundredth for punishment. So **Cent·esimation**, execution of every hundredth man.

†**Ce·ntesm.** 1483. [a. OF. *centiesme*, mod. *centième, centime*:—L. *centesimum.*] A hundredth part –1827.

†**Ce·ntgrave.** 1649. [ad. Ger. *centgraf, zentgraf*, f. MHG. *zente*, ad. late L. *centa*, a district of 100 hamlets.] Used as tr. OE. *hundredes ealdor*; also as tr. Ger. *centgraf* –1762.

Centi-, comb. f. L. *centum* hundred, used in the Metric System for the hundredth part of a unit, as *centiare*, $^1/_{100}$ of an are, etc.

Centigrade (se·ntigre'd), *a.* 1812. [a. F., f. L. *centum* + *gradus.*] Having a hundred degrees; usually applied to Celsius's thermometer, in which the space between the freezing and boiling points of water is divided into 100 degrees. (Symbolized by C., as 40° C.)

Centigramme (se·ntigræm, Fr. sañtigram). 1801. [F.; see CENTI- and GRAMME.] A weight = $^1/_{100}$ of a gramme, or ·1543248 of a grain troy. So **Ce·ntilitre** (se·ntilītəɹ, Fr. sañtilitr), a measure of capacity = $^1/_{100}$ of a litre, or ·61028 of a cubic inch.

Centi·loquy. 1588. [ad. L. **centiloquium.*] A work attributed to Ptolemy, consisting of a hundred aphorisms of astrology.

‖**Centime** (sañtī·m). 1801. [Fr.; see CENTESM.] A French coin = $^1/_{100}$ of a franc.

Centimetre (se·ntimītəɹ, Fr. sañtimetr). 1801. [F.; see CENTI- and METRE.] A measure of length = $^1/_{100}$ of a metre, or ·3937 (nearly $^2/_5$) of an inch.

Centinel, obs. f. SENTINEL.

†**Centinody.** 1611. [ad. L. *centinodia* (*herba*), f. *centum* + *nodus.* Cf. F. *centinode.*] *Bot.* The plant Knotgrass (*Polygonum aviculare*).

Centipedal (senti·pĭdăl), *a.* 1879. [f. L. *centum* + *ped-, pes* + -AL.] Of one hundred (metrical) feet.

Centipede (se·ntipĭd). 1601. [ad. L. *centipeda*, f. as prec. Cf. F. *centipède.*] A name for wingless vermiform articulated animals having many feet, constituting the order *Cheilopoda* of the class *Myriapoda.* Those in tropical countries are venomous. Also *transf.* and *fig.* var. **Centiped** (in Dicts.).

Centner (se·ntnəɹ). 1683. [a. Ger., ad. L. *centenarius.*] 1. A measure of weight used in Germany, varying from 100 to 120 English lb. 2. *Metall.* A weight divisible first into a hundred parts, and then into many smaller parts. The centner of the metallurgists is 100 lb., of the assayers 1 dram. 1753.

Cento (se·nto). Pl. (now usu.) **centos.** 1605. [a. L. *cento*, pl. *centones*, garment of patchwork.] †1. A piece of patchwork –1643. 2. 'A composition formed by joining scraps from other authors' (J.) 1605. Also *transf.*

1. His apparel is a c. SHIRLEY. 2. Quilted..out of sherds of diuers Poets, such as Schollers do call a C. CAMDEN. Hence **Ce·ntoism** (also **Ce·ntonism**).

Central (se·ntrăl), *a.* 1647. [ad. L. *centralis*, f. *centrum*; cf. F. *central.*] 1. Of or pertaining to the centre or middle; situated in, proceeding from, containing or constituting the centre. 2. *fig.* Chief, leading, dominant; controlling the branches (opp. to *local*) 1647. 3. *Phys.* Of or pertaining to a nerve-centre; in *Pathol.* used of local affections caused by lesions of the brain or spinal cord, as opp. to local causes 1865.

1. A good c. position (*mod.*). 2. The c. figure of a poem JOWETT. The approbation of the C. Junta WELLINGTON. 3. On C. Paralysis (*title*) 1865.

Phr. *C. force* (*Math.*): a force attracting to or repelling from a centre. *C. fire*: applied *attrib.* to a cap or cartridge having the fulminate in a central position. Hence **Ce·ntralism**, a centralizing system, centralization. **Ce·ntralist**, an upholder of centralization. **Ce·ntrally** *adv.* **Ce·ntralness.**

‖**Centrale** (sentrē̆i·li). 1872. [L.] *Anat.* Short for *os centrale*, a bone of the carpus.

Centrality (sentræ·lĭti). 1647. [f. CENTRAL; in F. *centralité.*] The quality or fact of being central; central nature or position. Also *fig.* *fig.* Clear grasp of ideas, c. of purpose 1862.

Centralization (se·ntrălǝizē̆i·ʃǝn, -izē̆i·ʃǝn). 1801. [f. CENTRALIZE.] 1. The action of centralizing; being centralized; gathering to a centre. 2. *esp.* The concentration of administrative power in a central authority 1801.

2. To combine..local self-government and c. 1863.

Centralize (se·ntrălǝiz), *v.* Also **-ise.** 1800. [perh. ad. F. *centraliser.*] 1. *intr.* To come together at a centre; to concentrate. 2. *trans.* To bring to a centre, make central; *esp.* to concentrate (administrative powers) in a single head or centre 1801.

2. Business always tends to c. itself HELPS. Hence **Ce·ntralizer**, one who centralizes or promotes centralization.

†**Centra·tion.** *rare.* 1647. [ad. med. L. *centratio.*] Centering; placing in the centre –1736.

Centre, center (se·ntǝr), *sb.* and *a.* ME. [a. F. *centre*, ad. L. *centrum.* Spelt *center* in U.S.; usually *centre* in Great Britain.]

I. 1. The middle point of a circle or sphere, equally distant from all points on the circumference. Also *fig.* 2. *ellipt.* The centre of the earth ME.; the earth, as the centre of the universe 1606. 3. The point, pivot, axis, or line round which a body turns or revolves ME. 4. A form of bearing adjustable in the direction of its length and having a conical point entering into a corresponding depression in the end of the revolving object which it supports, as in the lathe 1797. 5. *fig.* (See quots.) 1626. 6. = *nerve-centre* 1847. 7. A leader of the Fenians 1865. 8. The part of a target between the bull's-eye and the outer; also (*ellipt.*) the hitting of this 1887.

2. *Haml.* II. ii. 159. As from the Center thrice to th' utmost pole MILT. *P. L.* I. 74. 3. As a c., firm *P. R.* IV. 534. 5. The Center of Business STEELE. The c. of a world's desire TENNYSON. Centres of nutrition 1872.

II. 1. The middle point or part, the middle or midst of anything. Also *fig.* 1591. 2. The point or position of equilibrium of a body. Also *fig.* ME. 3. *Archit.* A temporary framework upon which an arch or dome is supported while building; also *gen.* 1611. 4. *Politics.* In the French Chamber (which is in the form of an amphitheatre), the deputies of moderate opinions who occupy the central benches in front of the president, between the extreme parties who sit to the right and left. Also used *transf.* of the political opinions so indicated; and of the politics of other countries. 1837.

1. The c. of a deep but narrow bay SCOTT. *C. of a higher curve* (*Geom.*): the point in which two diameters meet. *fig.* The very Center and life of Logicke 1628. 2. If the man is off his c., the eyes show it EMERSON. *C. of gravity*, etc. 3. *Wint. T.* II. i. 102.

Phrases. *C. of an army*: the main body of troops occupying the space between the two wings. *C. of attraction*: the point to which bodies tend by gravity, etc.; also *fig.* *C. of curvature*; see CURVATURE. *C. of a fleet*: the division between the van and the rear, or between the weather and lee divisions. *C. of gravity* orig. = *c. of attraction*; subseq. = *c. of mass*: the point of a body or system of bodies about which all the parts exactly balance each other, and which being supported, the body or system will remain at rest in any position. *C. of gyration*: the point at which if the whole mass of a revolving body were collected, the rotatory motion would remain the same. *C. of inertia*: = *c. of gravity* or *mass*. *C. of mass*: that point in relation to a body or system of bodies so situated that any plane whatever that passes through it divides the body or system into two parts of which the masses are exactly equal. *C. of motion*: the point which remains at rest while all the other parts move round it. *C. of oscillation*: the point of a body suspended by an axis at which, if all the matter were concentrated, the oscillations would be performed in the time actually taken. *C. of percussion*: in a moving body, that point where the percussion is greatest, in which the whole percutient force of the body is supposed to be collected. *C of pressure*: the point at which the whole amount of pressure may be applied with the same effect as when distributed.

Combs. etc.: **c.-bit**, an instrument turning on a projecting c.-point, for boring holes; **-board**, in a sailing-boat, a board or plate that can be lowered through the keel 1849; **-fire** = *central fire* (see CENTRAL); **-piece**, *spec.* a piece of plate or glass for the c. of a table; **-second(s**, a seconds hand on a clock or watch mounted on the centre arbor.

Centre, center (se·ntǝɹ), *v.* 1610. [f. CENTRE *sb.* In 17th and 18th c. spelt *center*, as still in U.S.]

I. *intr.* †1. To rest as on a centre, to repose –1719. 2. To find or have their (its) centre; to be concentrated; 'to be collected to a point' (J.), to gather as round a centre; to be placed as at a centre; to move round as a centre. Often with a mixture of notions. 1691.

2. That bliss which only centres in the mind GOLDSM. The supreme authority centered at last in a single person ROBERTSON.

II. *trans.* 1. To place or fix in the centre; to provide with a centre 1610. †2. To fix *to*, repose *upon*, as a centre –1721. 3. To collect, bring, as to a centre; to concentrate *in*, *on* 1702.

3. In reverie centred GOLDSM. To c. one's hopes in. (Cf. sense 2.) 1844. Hence **Ce·ntred, Ce·ntered** *ppl. a.*

Ce·ntremost, *a. rare.* 1866. [Superl. of CENTRE *sb.*, used *attrib.*] Most central, midmost. Cf. *middlemost.*

Centric (se·ntrik), *a.* 1590. [ad. Gr. κεντρικός, f. κέντρον; see CENTRUM.] 1. That is in or at the centre, central. 2. Of, pertaining to, or characterized by a centre; *spec.* (in *Phys.*) a nerve centre 1712. 3. quasi-*sb.* A circle with the earth in its centre 1667.

1. This c. earth MARLOWE. 2. C. forces MRS. BROWNING, tetanus SIR T. WATSON. So **Ce·ntrical** *a.* Hence **Centrica·lity** (*rare*). **Ce·ntrically** *adv.* **Ce·ntricalness** (*rare*). **Centri·city**, c. quality or position; relation to a centre.

Centrifugal (sentri·fiŭgăl), *a.* 1721. [f. mod.L. *centrifugus* (Newton, f. *centrum* + -*fugus*) + -AL. Cf. CENTRIPETAL.] 1. Flying or tending to fly off from the centre. Also *fig.* 2. *Bot.* a. Of inflorescence, in which the terminal flower opens first and the lateral ones successively after. b. Of an embryo: Having the radicle turned towards the sides of the fruit. 1830. 3. *Phys.* Of nerve fibres: Conveying impulses from a centre (see CENTRE *sb.* I. 6); efferent 1855.

C. force, tendency: the force with which a body moving round a centre tends to fly off from that centre; the tendency of a revolving body to do this. ('Centrifugal force' is really Inertia.) **C. machine**, *gen.* any machine in which c. force is employed; *spec.* a machine for drying yarn, cloth, sugar, etc., these being placed in a rapidly revolving cage, whence the moisture is thrown off by c. force, a *hydro-extractor*. **C. pump**, a rotary pump in which the fluid is driven outward and upward from a centre. Hence **Centri·fugally** *adv.* **Centri·fugence.** EMERSON.

Ce·ntrifuge. 1801. [a. F.] *adj.* = prec. *sb.* A machine for separating cream from milk by rotary motion.

Centring, -ering, -reing, *vbl. sb.* and *ppl. a.* See CENTRE *v.*, and CENTERING.

Centripetal (sentri·pĭtăl), *a.* 1709. [f. mod. L. *centripetus* (Newton) centre-seeking + -AL.] 1. Tending towards the centre; opp. to *centrifugal*. Also *fig.* and *transf.* 2. *Bot.* Tending or developing from without toward the centre 1870. 3. *Biol.* a. Proceeding from the exterior to the interior or centre. b. Of nerves: Conveying an impulse from the periphery to the centre; afferent. 1836.

1. *C. force*: a force which draws or impels a body toward some point as a centre; also called *c. tendency*. 2. *C. inflorescence*: that in which the lowest or outermost flowers blossom first, as in spikes or umbels. Hence **Centri·petally** *adv.*

Centri·petence. 1847. [f. L. *centripetentia; cf. *centrifugence.*] Centripetal motion or action. So **Centri·petency.**

Centrist (se·ntrist). 1872. [a. F. *centriste*, f. *centre.*] A member of the (French) Centre.

Centro- (sentro). Stem of L. *centrum* and Gr. κέντρον, used as a comb. form, with senses 'centre, central, centrally'.

Centrocli·nal *a.* (*Geol.*), applied to strata dipping to a common centre. **Centroli·nead** (*Geom.*), an instrument for drawing lines to inaccessible vanishing points in perspective. **Centroli·neal** *a.*, applied to a series of lines converging to a centre. **Centrosta·ltic** *a.* (*Med.*), applied by Hall to the action of the vis nervosa in the spinal centre.

Centrobaric (sentrobæ·rik), *a.* 1727. [f. CENTRO- + Gr. βάρος.] Of or relating to the centre of gravity, or to the process of finding it.

C. method (*Math.*): a method of determining the area, or the volume, generated by the revolution of a line or surface respectively about a fixed axis, on the principle that the superfices or solid so formed is equal to the product of the generating line or surface and the length of the path of its centre of gravity; sometimes called the *theorem of Pappus.*

Centrode (se·ntrōud). 1878. [f. L. *centrum* + Gr. ὁδός.] *Math.* A locus traced out by the successive positions of an instantaneous centre of pure rotation. (See next.)

Centroid (se·ntroid). 1876. [f. CENTRE + -OID.] *Math.* 1. = CENTRODE. (Now abandoned.) 2. Centre of mass, or of gravity 1882.

Centronote (se·ntronōut). 1836. [a. F., ad. mod.L., f. Gr. κέντρον + νῶτος.] A genus of fishes (*Centronotus*) having a spur-like prickle pointing forwards on the back.

‖**Centrum** (se·ntrŏm). 1854. [L., a. Gr. κέντρον.] The L. wd. for centre, used techn. in *Animal Phys.*: The body of a vertebra.

†**Centry**, *sb.* 1583. [f. CENTRE; the -*y* is obscure.] 1. Centre, midst –1594. 2. The centre or centering of a bridge –1834.

†**Centry**, *a.* 1486. Also **sentry.** [a. F. *centré* centred.] In *Her.*

‖**Centum.** [L.] A hundred; see CENT.

‖**Centu·mvir.** pl. **Centu·mviri.** 1601. [L. *centum* + *viri.*] *Rom. Antiq.* (In *pl.*) A body of judges appointed by the prætor, called for conciseness 'the Hundred Men', but numbering 105, and, later, 180. Hence **Centu·mviral** *a.* of or pertaining to the centumviri. **Centu·mvirate**, the office of the Roman centumviri; the centumviri collectively; a body of 100 men.

Centuple (se·ntiup'l), *a.* 1609. [a. F., ad. L. *centuplus*, in late use for *centuplex*, f. *centum* + -*plic*-, stem of *plicare*. Cf. *quadruple*, etc.] A hundred-fold. Hence **Ce·ntuple** *v.* to multiply a hundred-fold; var. **Centu·plicate** *v.*, whence **Centu·plicate** *a.* and *sb.* hundred-fold; **Centu·plica·tion.**

†**Ce·nture, ce·nter.** 1595. [ad. F. *ceinture.*] A CINCTURE.

Centurial (sentiū̆·riăl), *a.* 1610. [ad. L. *centurialis*, f. *centuria*; see CENTURY.] Of or pertaining to a CENTURY.

C. Assemblys 1656. Legionary or c. tablets 1851. C. associations LOWELL.

†**Centu·riate**, *a.* 1600. [ad. L. *centuriatus*, *centuriare.*] In *c. assemblies*, tr. L. *comitia centuriata*, in which all the Roman people voted by centuries (see CENTURY 2).

†**Centu·riate**, *v. rare.* [f. L. *centuriat-*; see prec.] 'To divide into bands of hundreds' (Bailey 1721).

Centuriator (sentiū̆·riē̆i·tǝɹ). 1660. [a. L., f. as prec.] *pl.* (usu. *Centuriators of Magdeburg*): A number of 16th c. Protestant divines who compiled a Church History in thirteen volumes, each volume embracing a century. Formerly called CENTURISTS.

Centurion (sentiū̆·riǝn). ME. [ad. L. *centurio* (also used), f. *centuria* CENTURY.] The commander of a century in the Roman army. Also *transf.*

†**Centurist.** = CENTURIATOR.

Century (se·ntiŭri). 1533. [a. F. *centurie* or ad. L. *centuria.*] 1. *Rom. Hist.* A division of the Roman army, constituting half a maniple, and prob. consisting orig. of 100 men. *transf.* Any body of 100 men 1612. 2. *Hist.* One of the 193 divisions by which the Roman people voted in the *Comitia centuriata* 1604. **3.** A group of a hundred things; a hundred (*arch.*) 1598. **4.** A period of 100 years; orig. 'a c. of years' 1626. **5.** Each of the successive periods of 100 years, reckoning from a received chronological epoch, *esp.* from the birth of Christ. **6.** *pl.* The Church History of the CENTURIATORS, divided into centuries 1606.

1. *Cor.* I. vii. 3. 3. A c. of prayers *Cymb.* IV. ii. 391, of sonnets BROWNING. To score a c. in an innings 1883. 5. The rebellion in the last c. 1771. *The first c.* (A.D. 1–100 inclusive). *The nineteenth c.* (A.D. 1801–1900). *Comb.*: **c.-plant**, the AGAVE or American Aloe; **-writer** = CENTURIATOR. Hence **Ce·nturied** *a.* centuries old.

Century, obs. var. of SENTRY.

Ceorl (kʸeᵊrl, tʃeᵊrl). OE. = CHURL, q.v.

†**Cepa·ceous, cæ-,** *a.* 1657. [f. L. *cæpa*, *cepa* onion.] Of the nature of an onion.

Cephalalgy (se·fălældʒi). 1547. [ad. L. *cephalalgia* (also used in *Med.*), a. Gr., f. κεφαλή + -αλγία, f. ἄλγος; cf. F. *céphalalgie.*] Headache. Hence **Cephala·lgic** *a.* of, pertaining to, or affected with c.; *sb.* a medicine for c. (Dicts.)

‖**Cephala·nthium.** 1880. [mod.L., f. Gr. κεφαλή + ἄνθος.] *Bot.* = ANTHODIUM.

‖**Cephala·spis.** 1842. [mod.L., f. Gr. κεφαλή + ἀσπίς.] *Palæont.* A genus of fossil ganoid fishes found in the Old Red Sandstone, having a large buckler-shaped plate attached to the head: also called *buckler-heads.*

Cephalate (se·fălĕt). 1862. [f. G. κεφαλή + -ATE². Cf. F. *céphalé.*] A mollusc having a distinct head, or belonging to the Encephalous division (*Cephalata*).

Cephalic (sĭfæ·lik), *a.* (*sb.*) 1599. [a. F. *céphalique*, ad. L., a. Gr. κεφαλικός, f. κεφαλή.] **1.** Of or pertaining to the head; of the nature of a head. **2.** Relieving disorders of the head 1656. As *sb.* A cephalic remedy 1656.

1. *C. index*: a number indicating the ratio of the transverse to the longitudinal diameter of the skull. *C. vein*: the principal vein of the arm, which anciently was opened to relieve disorders of the head. Hence **Cepha·lically** *adv.* in relation to the head.

‖**Cephalitis** (sefălǝi·tis). 1811. [f. Gr. κεφαλή + -ITIS.] *Med.* Inflammation of the brain and its membranes.

Cephalization (se:fălǝizē·ʃǝn). 1864. [f. Gr. κεφαλή: cf. *specialization.*] *Biol.* Dana's term to express the degree to which the head is developed and dominates over the rest of the body. So **Ce·phalized** *a.* having the head developed.

Cephalo- (se·fălo), comb. f. Gr. κεφαλή head, used:

a. in combs., such as **c.-catha·rtic** *a.* purging the head; **-extra·ctor**, an instrument for extracting a fœtus by the head.

b. in derivative formations, as **Ce·phalocele** [see CELE], a tumour in the head. **Cephalo·logy**, a treatise on the head. †**Ce·phaloma:ncy** [Gr. μαντεία], divination by means of a head. **Cephalo·meter** [Gr. μέτρον], an instrument formerly used for measuring the size of the fœtal head during parturition; also *gen.* **Cephalo·phorous** *a.* [Gr. -φορος], epithet of the Cephalates. **Cephalo·pterous** [Gr. πτέρον] *a.*, having a winged or feathered head. **Ce·phalosta:t** [Gr. στατός], a head-rest. **Ce·phaloto:me** [Gr. -τομος adj., cutting], an instrument for cutting the head of the fœtus in embryotomy. **Cephalo·tomy** [Gr. -τομία sb.], the dissection of the head; also, as under *cephalotome.* **Ce·phalotri:be** [Gr. τρίβειν], an instrument used in cephalotripsy. **Ce·phalotri:psy** [Gr. τρῖψις], the operation of crushing the head of the fœtus with a cephalotribe, in cases of difficult delivery.

Cephaloid (se·făloid), *a.* 1847. [a. Gr. κεφαλοειδής.] Shaped like a head.

Cephalopod (se·fălǒpǫd). 1826. [?a. mod. F. *céphalopode*, *-es*, ad. next.] *Zool.* One of the *Cephalopoda.*

‖**Cephalopoda** (sefălǫ·pǒdă), *sb. pl.* *Sing.* **-pod** or **-podan.** 1802. [mod.L., f. Gr. κεφαλή + πούς (ποδ-).] *Zool.* The most highly organized class of *Mollusca*, characterized by a distinct head with arms or tentacles attached to it; comprising Cuttle-fishes, the Nautilus, etc., and many fossil species. Hence **Cephalo·podal, Ce:phalopo·dic, Cephalo·podous** *adjs.* belonging to the *Cephalopoda*; pertaining to a cephalopod; **Cephalo·podan** *a.*; as *sb.* = prec.

Cephalothorax (se·fălǫþō·ræks). 1835. [f. Gr. κεφαλή + THORAX.] *Zool.* The anterior division of the body, consisting of the coalesced head and thorax, in certain *Arachnida* and *Crustacea* (as spiders and crabs). Hence **Ce:phalothora·cic** *a.*

Cephalous (se·fălǝs), *a.* = CEPHALATE.

†**Ce·phen.** 1609. [a. Gr. κηφήν.] A drone-bee –1657.

†**Ce·pous,** *a.* 1657. [f. L. *cepa.*] Like an onion; bulbous.

Ceraceous (sĭrē·ʃǝs), *a.* 1768. [f. L. *cera.*] Of the nature of wax, waxy.

Cerago (sĭrē·go). 1839. [f. L. *cera.*] Bee-bread.

Ceral (sīᵊ·răl), *a.* 1874. **1.** [f. CERE.] Pertaining to the CERE of a bird's bill. **2.** [f. L. *cera.*] Relating to wax 1883.

Ceramic (sĭræ·mik), *a.* (*sb.*) Also **ker-.** 1850. [ad. Gr. κεραμικός, κεραμική (τέχνη), f. κέραμος. Cf. F. *céramique.*] **1.** Of or pertaining to pottery, *esp.* as an art. **2.** As *sb.* in *pl.* The ceramic art. So **Ce·ramist**, a c. artist.

Cerargyrite (sĭrā·ɹdʒirǝit). 1868. [improp. f. Gr. κέρας (κερατ-) + ἄργυρος.] *Min.* Native chloride of silver, horn silver.

Cerasin (se·răsin). 1838. [f. L. *cerasus* + -IN.] *Chem.* The insoluble portion of the gum of the cherry, and other trees.

‖**Cerastes** (sĭræ·stīz). ME. [L., a. Gr. κεράστης, f. κέρας horn.] *Zool.* A genus of venomous serpents found in Africa, etc., having a horny scale above each eye; the horned viper.

C. hornd MILT. *P. L.* x. 525. var. †**Cerast(e.**

Cerate (sīᵊ·rĕt). 1543. [ad. L. *ceratum*, *cerare*, varied with *cerotum*, a. Gr. κηρωτόν, neut. of κηρωτός waxed.] *Med.* A stiff ointment composed of wax, lard or oil, and other ingredients. Hence **Ce·rated** *a.* covered with wax.

Ceratinous (sĭræ·tinǝs), *a.* 1881. [f. Gr. κεράτινος, f. κέρας.] Of horny structure or nature.

†**Ceration.** 1610. [ad. med.L. *cerationem*, f. L. *cerare* to wax.] *Alchem.* The action of covering anything with wax, or of softening a hard substance; also, the fixation of mercury –1751.

‖**Ceratium** (sĭrē·ʃiǒm). 1880. [L. = *siliqua*, a. Gr. κεράτιον carob-bean, dim. of κέρας.] *Bot.* A siliquiform capsule. GRAY.

Cerato- (se·răto), comb. f. Gr. κέρας, κερατ- horn, used chiefly to denote relation to a cornu or horn, or to the cornea.

Cerato-bra·nchial [Gr. βράγχια gills] *a.*, *Anat.* epithet of one of the main portions of permanent branchial cartilage in fishes and Amphibia. **Ceratocele** (-sīl) [Gr. κήλη tumour], *Pathol.* a hernia of the cornea of the eye. **Cerato-hy·al** [see HYOID] *a.*, the part of the hyoid arch in mammals below the styloid process. **Ce·ratoplasty** [Gr. πλάσσειν], *Med.* the artificial restoration of the cornea.

Ceraunics (sĭrǭ·niks), *sb. pl. rare.* [f. Gr. κεραυνός + -ICS; see -IC.] That branch of physics which treats of heat and electricity. (Dicts.)

†**Ceraunite** (sĭrǭ·nǝit). 1814. [ad. Gr. κεραυνίτης (λίθος).] Thunder-stone; used of meteorites, or meteoric iron; also of belemnites, and of flint arrow-heads.

Ceraunoscope (sĭrǭ·nǒskǒup). 1827. [ad. Gr. κεραυνοσκοπεῖον.] A machine used by the ancients in their mysteries to imitate thunder and lightning.

Cerberus (sǭ·ɹbĕrǒs). ME. [L., a. Gr.] *Gr. and L. Mythol.* The watch-dog which guarded the entrance of the infernal regions, represented as having three heads. Used allusively.

1. I must give the C. a sop, I suppose. (Cf. *Æneid* vi. 417.) FOOTE. Hence **Cerbe·rean** *a.* (*improp.* -ian). **Cerbe·ric** *a.*

‖**Cercaria** (sǝrkēᵊ·riă). 1841. [mod.L., f. Gr. κέρκος tail.] *Zool.* A kind of trematode worm in its second larval stage, shaped like a tadpole. Hence **Cerca·rial, -ian, -iform** *adjs.*

‖**Cercopithecus** (sǭ:ɹkopiþī·kǒs). 1572. [L., a. Gr., f. κέρκος + πίθηκος.] *Zool.* A genus of long-tailed African monkeys, having cheek-pouches, and callosities on the buttocks. Hence **Cercopithe·coid** *a.*

Cere (sīᵊɹ), *sb.* 1486. [a. F. *cire*:—L. *cera.*] *Ornith.* The naked wax-like membrane at the base of the beak in certain birds, in which the nostrils are pierced. var. **Sear.**

Cere (sīᵊɹ), *v.* 1465. [a. F. *cirer*:—L. *cerare*, f. *cera.*] †**1.** To cover with wax, to wax –1601. **2. a.** To wrap in a cerecloth. †**b.** To anoint with spices, etc. 1465. †**c.** To seal up (in lead, etc.) 1525. Also *fig.*

Cereal (sīᵊ·riˌăl), *a.* (*sb.*) 1818. [ad. L. *Cerealis* pertaining to Ceres; cf. F. *céréale.*] *adj.* Of or pertaining to corn or edible grain 1818. *sb.* (usu. in *pl.*; also in L. form *cerealia.*) Any grasses which are cultivated for their seed as human food; commonly comprised under the name of *corn* or *grain* 1832.

Cerealin (sīᵊ·riălin). 1861. [f. prec.] *Chem.* A nitrogenous substance found in bran, closely resembling diastase.

‖**Cerebellum** (serĭbe·lǒm). Also †**ce·rebel.** 1565. [L., dim. of *cerebrum.*] *Phys.* The little or hinder brain, situated behind and below the cerebrum, and above the medulla oblongata. Hence **Cerebe·llar, Cerebe·llic** *adjs.* of or pertaining to the c.

Cerebral (se·rĭbrăl), *a.* (*sb.*) 1805. [a. F. *cérébral*, f. L. **cerebralis*, f. *cerebrum.*] **1.** Pertaining or relating to the brain; analogous to a brain 1816. **2.** *Cerebral letters*: name for a class of consonants in Sanskrit, etc., developed from the dentals by retracting the tongue and applying its tip to the palate. Also as *sb.*

1. A c. ganglion (*mod.*). Hence **Ce·rebralism**, the theory that mental operations arise from the action of the brain. **Ce·rebralist**, one who holds this.

Cerebrate (se·rĭbreᵗt), *sb.* 1872. *Chem.* A salt of cerebric acid.

Cerebration (serĭbrē·ʃǝn). 1853. [f. L. *cerebrum.*] Brain-action (*esp.* unconscious). Hence **Ce·rebrate** *v.* to perform by c. (*rare*).

Cerebric (sĕre·brik), *a.* 1839. [f. L. *cerebrum* + -IC.] Pertaining to the brain.

C. acid (*Chem.*), a fatty acid obtained from the brain.

Cerebriform (sĕre·brifǭɹm), *a.* 1834. [f. as prec. + -FORM.] Resembling the brain in form or texture; encephaloid.

Cerebri·fugal, *a.* [f. as prec. + L. *-fugus* + -AL.] Epithet of nerve-fibres which run from the brain to the spinal cord, and convey cerebral impulses outward. So **Cerebri·petal** *a.* epithet of nerve-fibres which run in the opposite direction, and convey sensations to the brain.

Cerebrin (se·rĭbrin). Also **-ine.** 1830. [f. as prec. + -IN.] *Chem.* A name used for several substances obtained from the brain; *esp.* a light white hygroscopic powder, obtained by the action of baryta and heat on brain-tissue.

‖**Cerebritis** (serĭbrǝi·tis). 1866. [f. as prec. + -ITIS.] *Path.* Inflammation of the substance of the brain.

Cerebro- (se·rĭbro), comb. f. L. *cerebrum* brain; used:

a. as in **cerebro-ca·rdiac** *a.*, relating to the brain and heart. **b.** in forming hybrid derivatives, as **Cerebro·logy** [see -LOGY], the science or discussion of brains. **Cerebro·meter** [see -METER], an instrument for recording cerebral pulsations. **Cerebro·pathy** [Gr. -πάθεια], the series of hypochondriacal symptoms accompanying overwork of the brain. **Cerebro·scopy** [Gr. -σκοπια, f. σκοπεῖν], the use of the ophthalmoscope to determine the state of the retina and deduce the condition of the brain.

Cerebroid (se·rĭbroid), *a.* 1854. [f L. *cerebrum.*] Resembling or akin to brain; brainlike.

Cerebro·se, *a. rare.* [ad. L. *cerebrosus.*] 'Brain-sick, mad-brained, wilful, stubborn' (Bailey 1727). Hence †**Cerebro·sity.**

Cerebro-spinal (se:rĭbroˌspǝi·năl), *a.* 1826. [f. CEREBRO- + SPINAL.] Relating to the brain and spinal cord.

Cerebro-spinal axis: the brain and spinal cord as together constituting the central or main part of the *cerebro-spinal system*, the chief of the two great nerve systems of vertebrates. *Cerebro-spinal fluid*: a serous fluid occupying the space between the arachnoid membrane and *pia mater.*

‖**Cerebrum** (se·rĭbrɒ̆m). 1615. [L.] The brain proper; the anterior, and, in the higher vertebrates, largest part of the brain; in man it fills nearly the whole cavity of the skull.

Cerecloth (sīᵊ·ɹklǫþ), *sb.* 1540. [orig. *cered cloth*; see CERED.] Cloth smeared or impregnated with wax or some glutinous matter: used **a.** as a winding-sheet 1553; †**b.** as a plaster in surgery –1818; **c.** as a waterproof material 1540.
b. To bed, & there had a c. laid to my foot PEPYS.
Hence †**Ce·recloth** *v.* to apply a c. to; to wrap in a c.

Cered (sīᵊɹd), *ppl. a.* ME. [f. CERE *v.*] Smeared, anointed, or saturated with wax, *esp.* in *Cered cloth* = CERECLOTH.

Cerement (sīᵊ·ɹmĕnt, also *erron.* se·rĭ-). 1602. [a. F. *cirement*, f. *cirer* to wax Always concr. in Eng.] Usu. in *pl.* Waxed wrappings for the dead; *loosely*, grave-clothes. Rarely in *sing.* = cerecloth; shroud. Also *fig.*
Tell Why thy Canoniz'd bones Hearsed in death Haue burst their cerments *Haml.* I. iv. 48.

Ceremonial (se·rĭmōᵘ·niăl), *a.* and *sb.* ME. [ad. L. *ceremonialis*, f. *cærimonia*. So mod.F. *cérémonial*.]
A. *adj.* **1.** Relating to, or consisting of, ceremonies or rites; ritual; formal. †**2.** Addicted to ceremony or ritual; formal, ceremonious –1653.
1. The ceremoniall rites of marriage *Tam. Shr.* III. ii. 6. C. manners 1851.
B. *sb.* †**1.** A ceremonial commandment or ordinance –1621. **2.** A prescribed system of ceremonies; a ritual. *rarely*, A rite or ceremony. 1672. **3.** = CEREMONY 2, 3. 1749. †**4.** A ceremonial robe; = CEREMONY 4. 1610. **5.** *R.C.Ch.* The order for rites and ceremonies, or a book containing this 1612.
2. The c. prescribed in the Anglican service D'ISRAELI. Hence **Ceremo·nialism**, addiction to external ceremonies in religion; ritualism. **Ceremo·nialist**, a ritualist. **Ceremo·nially** *adv.*

†**Ceremo·niary.** [Cf. *breviary*, etc.] A directory or rule of ceremony. JEWELL.

Ceremonious (serĭmōᵘ·niəs), *a.* 1555. [ad. F. *cérémonieux*, or L. *cærimoniosus*; see CEREMONY.] **1.** Pertaining to, or consisting of ceremonies; = CEREMONIAL. **2.** Full of ceremony; accompanied with rites 1611. **3.** According to customary formalities or punctilios 1593. **4.** Addicted to ceremony; punctilious in observance of formalities 1553.
1. The c. lawe of Moises 1555. **2.** *Wint. T.* III. i. 7. **3.** His..somewhat c. politeness 1863. Hence **Ceremo·nious·ly** *adv.*, **-ness.**

Ceremony (se·rĭməni). [ME. *cerymonye*, prob. a. OF. *cerymonie*, ad. L. *cærimonia*; for which see Lat. Dicts.] **1.** An outward rite or observance, religious or held sacred; the performance of some solemn act according to prescribed form; a solemnity; *disparagingly*, An empty form 1533; *loosely*, A stately formality 1802. **2.** A usage of courtesy, politeness, or civility ME. **3.** (without *a.* or *pl.*) **a.** Performance of (religious) rites, ceremonial observance 1759. **b.** Precise observance of conventional forms of deference or respect 1603. **c.** Pomp, state (*arch.*) 1599. †**4.** *concr.* An external accessory or symbolical attribute of worship, state, or pomp –1709. †**5.** A portent, omen 1601.
1. The ceremonyes of the Masse 1535. Old antiquated Ceremonies 1710. A mere c. THIRLWALL. The c. of dinner 1802. **2.** The c. of waiting for answers MISS BURNEY. **3. a.** A..christian, in substance, not in c. JUNIUS. **b.** *Without c. To stand upon c.* **4.** *Jul. C.* I. i. 70. **5.** *Jul. C.* II. i. 197.
Master of the ceremonies: the person who superintends the ceremonies observed in a place of state or on some public occasion. Hence †**Ce·remony** *v.* to sanctify or treat with c. QUARLES.

Cereous (sīᵊ·rĭ,əs), *a.* 1601. [f. L. *cereus* + -OUS.] Of the nature of wax, waxen, waxy.

Cererite, Cererium; see CERITE, CERIUM.

‖**Cereus** (sīᵊ·rĭ,ɒ̆s). 1730. [L., f. *cera*.] *Bot.* A large genus of cactuses, natives of tropical America; the Torch-thistle.

Cerevi·sial, *a.* [f. L. *cerevisia* beer + -AL.] Of or pertaining to beer. See CERVISIAL.

†**Ce·rfoil.** *rare.* ME. [a. OF., (ult.) ad. Gr. χαιρέφυλλον.] = CHERVIL –1567.

Ceric (sīᵊ·rik), *a.*[1] 1863. [f. CERIUM + -IC.] *Chem.* Of or belonging to cerium; as in *c. salts.*

Ce·ric, *a.*[2] 1838. [f. L. *cera* + -IC.] *Chem.* Chemically related to wax; as in *C. acid*, obtained by treating cerin with nitric acid.

†**Ceri·lla.** 1591. [Sp. var. of *cedilla.*] = CEDILLA –1863.

Cerin (sīᵊ·rin). 1850. [f. L. *cera* + -IN.] *Chem.* **1.** A waxy substance extracted by alcohol or ether from grated cork. †**2.** A name applied to the portion of bees-wax which is readily soluble in alcohol –1865.

Cerine (sīᵊ·rəin). 1814. [f. CERIUM + -INE.] *Min.* A variety of ALLANITE or cerium-epidote.

Cerinthian (sĭri·nþiăn), *a.* 1576. [f. *Cerinthus* + -IAN.] Of or pertaining to the teaching of Cerinthus (*c* A.D. 88), who attempted to unite Christianity with a mixture of Gnosticism and Judaism. As *sb.* A follower of Cerinthus.

Ceriph (se·rif). 1830. [?] One of the fine lines of a letter, *esp.* the fine hair-line at the top or bottom of capitals, as of I.

‖**Cerise** (səri·z), *a.* and *sb.* 1858. [a. F.] A light bright clear red, resembling that of some cherries.

Cerite (sīᵊ·rəit). 1804. [f. as CERIUM + -ITE.] The rare mineral hydrated silicate of Cerium.
C. metals: cerium, didymium, and lanthanum.

Ce·rite[2]. 1811. [a. F. *cérite*, ad. mod.L. *cerithium*, name of the genus.] *Palæont.* A genus of fossil brachiopod molluscs. Also *attrib.*

Cerium (sīᵊ·riɒ̆m). 1804. [Named, along with its source *cerite*, after the planet CERES, discovered in 1801. Klaproth, in 1807, proposed the names *cererium* and *cererite*, to avoid confusion with L. *cera* wax.] *Chem.* A rare metallic element, discovered in the mineral called CERITE; it has the colour and lustre of iron, and takes a high polish, but tarnishes in moist air; it is malleable and ductile, of specific gravity 6·63 to 6·73. Atomic weight 138; symbol Ce. Also *attrib.* = CERIC [1].

†**Cern**, *v.* For CONCERN. *Tam. Shr.* V. i. 77.

Cernuous (sɔ̄·ɹniu,əs), *a.* 1653. [f. L. *cernuus* + -OUS.] Bowing downwards; in *Bot.* drooping, nodding: said of a flower.

Cero-, comb. f. L. *cera* or Gr. κηρός wax; also the first element in many derivatives.

Cerography (sĭrǫ·grăfi). 1593. [ad. Gr. κηρογραφία, f. κηρός + -γραφία.] Writing or painting on wax, as the encaustic painting of the ancients. **b.** Applied also to a method of taking stereotype plates from superposed sheets of engraved wax. So **Ce·rograph**, a writing on wax. **Cerogra·phic, -al** *a.* pertaining to c. **Cero·graphist.**

Cerolite (sīᵊ·rǒləit). Also **ker-**. 1868. [f. Gr. κηρός + λίθος.] *Min.* A hydrous silicate of aluminum, having a waxy lustre and greasy feel.

‖**Ceroma** (sĭrōᵘ·mă). [L., a. Gr. κήρωμα, ointment for wrestlers, anything made of wax.] 'An apartment in the Gymnasium and baths of the ancients, where the bathers and wrestlers were anointed' (Gwilt).

Ceromancy (sīᵊ·rǒmænsi). 1652. [a. F. *céromancie*, med.L. *ceromantia*, f. Gr. κηρός + μαντεία.] Divination by dropping melted wax into water.

Ceromel (sīᵊ·rǒmel). [a. F. *céromel*, f. L. *cera* + *mel.*] A mixture of wax and honey, used as an ointment in hot climates.

Ceroo·n. U.S. var. of SEROON.

Ceroplastic (sīᵊroplæ·stik), *a.* 1801. [a. Gr. κηροπλαστικός, f. κηρός + πλάσσειν.] **1.** Relating to modelling in wax. **2. Ceroplastics** *sb.* the art of modelling in wax; *concr.* waxworks. 1882. So **Ce·roplasty**, modelling in wax.

Cerosin (sīᵊ·rǒsin). 1865. [f. L. *cerosus + -IN.] *Chem.* A wax-like substance obtained by scraping the surface of some kinds of sugar-cane.

Ceroso-. *Chem.* Comb. f. CEROUS *a.*

†**Cerote.** 1562. [ad. L., a. Gr. κηρωτόν.] = CERATE –1669.

Cerotic (sĭrǫ·tik). 1850. [f. Gr. κηρωτόν + -IC.] *Chem.* In *C. acid*, $C_{27}H_{54}O_2$, the essential constituent of cerin (see CERIN 2). Its salts are called **Ce·rotates.** So **Ce·rotene**, an olefine ($C_{27}H_{54}$) obtained by the dry distillation of Chinese wax; **Ce·rotin**, hydrate of ceryl, $C_{27}H_{56}O$; **Ce·rotyl** = CERYL.

Cerous (sīᵊ·rəs), *a.* 1863. [f. CERIUM + -OUS.] *Chem.* Applied to compounds in which cerium combines as a triad, as in *c. salts*, etc.

†**Cerre-tree.** *rare.* 1577. [ad. L. *cerrus.*] The Turkey Oak or the Holm Oak. So †**Ce·rrial**, *a.* ME. [a. OIt. *cereale*, f. *cerro*, L. *cerrus*] of or pertaining to evergreen oak –1500.

‖**Cert** (sɔ̄ɹt). 1889. [Abbrev. of CERTAIN-(TY).] *slang* (orig. *Racing*). A horse that is certain to win; a 'sure thing'.

Certain (sɔ·ɹtĕn, -t'n), *a.*, *sb.*, and *adv.* ME. [a. OF. *certain*, repr. late L. type *certanus, f. *certus*, orig. pa. pple. of *cernere*.]
I. 1. Determined, fixed; not variable. (Occ. put after its sb. in this sense.) **b.** Definite, exact (*arch.*) ME. **2.** Sure, reliable ME.; inevitable ME.; unfailing 1636. **3.** Not to be doubted; established as a truth or fact ME. **4.** Having no doubt; assured; sure (= 'subjectively certain'). Const. *of*, *that* with *cl.* ME. †**5.** Self-determined, resolved; steadfast –1690.
1. Payment of money on a day c. STEPHEN. **2.** To repose upon .. c. experience JOHNSON. The certeine perill he stood in SPENSER *F. Q.* I. i. 24. A c. remedy for a distemper 1754. **3.** A fact as c. as it appears incredible HUME. **4.** *Ant. & Cl.* II. ii. 57. *Morally c.*: so sure that one is justified in acting upon the conviction. **5.** I with thee have fixt my Lot, C. to undergoe like doom MILT. *P. L.* IX. 953.
II. Used to indicate things which the mind particularizes, but which are not further identified in speech: in *sing.* = a particular, in *pl.* = some particular, some definite ME.
Till some c. shot be paid *Two Gent.* II. v. 6. *A c. age.* (Mostly said of women.) *Spec. uses.* **a.** = some at least: He kept up a c. degree of intercourse S. AUSTIN. **b.** = unknown except by name: A c. lord Archibald Hamilton COWPER.
B. quasi-*sb.* or *ellipt.* †**1.** What is certain; certainty –1631. †**2.** A definite quantity or amount (*of*) –1621.
1. *For c.*: as a certainty, assuredly. [= F. *pour certain.*] ME. †*In c.*: in truth, truly –1493. *Of a c.* (arch.), formerly *of c.*: as a matter of certainty, assuredly 1485.
C. *adv.* **1.** Certainly ME. **2.** Emphasizing *sooth*, *true*, *sure*. (Now *dial.*) 1500.
Hence **Ce·rtainly** *adv.* with certainty; fixedly; without doubt; unquestionably. †**Ce·rtainness.**

†**Certain**, *v. rare.* ME. [f. prec.; cf. ASCERTAIN.] To make certain; to certify –1523.

Certainty (sɔ̄·ɹtĕnti). ME. [a. Anglo-Fr. *certeinté*, OF. *certaineté*.] **1.** That which is certain, the fact, the truth. ? *Obs.* **2.** A fact or thing certain or sure (with *pl.*) 1611. †**3.** Surety. ME. only. **4.** The quality of being certain ME. †**5.** A definite number or quantity –1603.
2. Small certainties are the bane of men of talents 1775. **4.** The c. of Geometry 1738. To affirm with c. ADDISON. *Moral c.*; see CERTAIN. *For*, (†*in*, †*at*), *of*, *to* (*a*) *c.*: as a matter of c., beyond doubt, assuredly.

Certes (sɔ̄·ɹtĕz), *adv. arch.* [ME., a. OF. *certes* (= *a certes*) :—L. *a certis from certain (grounds) Littré.] Of a truth, assuredly.
This, certs, I know FULLER. And c. not in vain WORDSW. ? Hence **Certie, certy** (*Sc.*) (taken as sing. of *certes*).

Certi·ficate, *ppl. a.* 1547. [See next.] Certified.

Certificate (səɹti·fikĕt), *sb.* 1472. [ad. med. L. *certificatum*, pa. pple. of *certificare*, used subst.] †**1.** Certification –1661. **2.** A document wherein a fact is formally certified 1489; occ. = *licence* 1549; also *gen.*, a certification 1718. **3.** *Law.* A writing made in one court, by which notice of its proceedings is given to another 1607. Also *attrib.*
2. A c. of health DE FOE, of character 1790, of baptism, SCOTT. The suspension of Captain Stone's c. 1863. **3.** *Trial by c.*: a form of trial in which the testimony of facts as certified by any proper authority decides the point at issue.

Certificate (səɹti·fikeᶦt), *v.* 1768. [f. the sb.] **1.** To attest by a certificate. **2.** To furnish with a certificate 1818.
2. To c. midwives 1870, teachers 1864.

Certification (sɔ̄ɹtifikēᶦ·ʃən). 1440. [a. F., or ad. L. *certificationem*.] The action of certifying or fact of being certified; the form in which this is embodied.
The c. of elementary teachers (*mod.*).

Certificatory (səɹti·fikătəri), *a.* 1520. [ad. med.L. *certificatorius.*] Of the nature of a certificate, as *Letter c.*: a written testimonial.

Certify (sɔ̄·ɹtifəi), *v.* ME. [a. F. *certifier*, ad. med.L. *certificare*, f. *certus.*] **1.** To make (a thing) certain; to guarantee as certain; to give certain information of. 2. To declare or attest by a formal or legal certificate 1461. 3. To make (a person) certain (*of*); to assure; to give (a person) legal or formal attestation (*of*) ME. 4. *intr.* To testify *to*, vouch *for* 1625.

1. To certefye this thinge, sende for the damoysell LD. BERNERS. 2. Cause sertified and allowed by the Captain 1651. 3. These are to Certifye all whom it may concerne 1575. To c. a person that [etc.] TINDALE. 4. To c. to a person's insanity (*mod.*). Hence **Ce·rtifiable** *a.* **Ce·rtifier.**

Certiorari (sɔ̄ːɹʃiˌorēᵊ·rəi). 1523. [L., occurring in the original L. words of the writ, 'we, being desirous for certain reasons, that the said record should by you *be certified* to us'.] *Law.* A writ, issuing from a superior court, upon the complaint of a party that he has not received justice in an inferior court, or cannot have an impartial trial, by which the records are called up for trial in the superior court.

Certiorate (sɔ̄ːɹʃiorēᵊt), *v.* 1637. [f. L. *certiorare.*] To inform authoritatively.

Certitude (sɔ̄·ɹtitiūd). ME. [a. F., f. late L. *certitudinem.*] 1. Subjective certainty. (The prevailing sense.) With *a.* and *pl.* 1611. 2. Objective certainty. ? *Obs.* 1538.

Cerulean (sǐrū·liǎn), *a.* Also **cæ-**. 1667. [f. L. *cæruleus.*] Of the colour of the cloudless sky, blue, azure. Chiefly *poet.* As quasi-*sb.* Cerulean hue 1756; (*joc.*) a blue-stocking 1821.

He spread the pure C. Fields on high BLACKMORE. vars. **Ce·rule** (*poet.*), †**Ceru·leous** *adjs.*

Cerulein (sǐrū·liˌin), **Cerulin** (sīᵊ·rūlin). Also **cæ-**. 1810. [f. as prec. + -IN.] A deep blue substance in many essential oils; azulene.

Ceru·leo-, comb. f. L. *cæruleus.*

†**Ceruli·fic**, *a. rare.* 1701. [f. L. *cærulus.*] 'Having the power to produce a blue colour' (J.).

Cerumen (sǐrū·men). 1741. [a. mod.L., f. L. *cera.*] The yellow wax-like secretion in the external canal of the ear. Hence **Cerumini·ferous** *a.* producing c. **Ceru·minous** *a.* of, of the nature of, or secreting, c., as *c. glands.*

Ceruse (sīᵊ·rus, sǐrū·s). ME. [a. F., or ad. L. *cerussa*, ? f. (ult.) Gr. κηρός wax.] 1. = WHITE LEAD; used as a white paint, or a cosmetic: often vague. 2. = CERUSSITE.

1. Eye-sight..too weak to distinguish c. from natural bloom MACAULAY. Hence †**Ceruse** *v.* to paint (the face) with c.

Cerussite, cerusite (sīᵊ·rɒ̆səit). 1850. [f. L. *cerussa* CERUSE + -ITE.] *Min.* Native carbonate of lead, white lead ore.

Cervantic (sɔ̄ɹvæ·ntik), *a.* 1759. Pertaining to Miguel de *Cervantes* Saavedra (1547–1616), Sp. novelist and dramatist. So **Cerva·ntist.**

Cervantite (səɹvæ·ntəit). 1856. [f. *Cervantes* (in Galicia, Spain).] *Min.* A native tetroxide of antimony (Sb_2O_4), called also *antimony ochre.*

‖**Cervelat** (sęrvəla). 1864. [OF., ad. It. *cervellata* sausage.] A short reed musical instrument, resembling the bassoon in tone. var. **Cervalet.**

Cervical (sɔ̄·ɹvikǎl, sɔ̄ɹvəi·kǎl), *a.* 1681. [f. L. *cervix, -icis*; cf. F. *cervical.*] *Phys.* Of or belonging to the CERVIX. As *sb.* = c. nerve, vertebra, etc.

Ce·rvicide. *rare.* 1864. [ad. med.L. *cervicida.*] The killing of a deer.

Cervico- (səɹvəi·kǝ), comb. f. of L. *cervix, -īcis* neck, as in **cervi:co-bra·chial** *a.* belonging to the neck and arm, etc.

Cervine (sɔ̄·ɹvəin), *a.* 1832. [ad. L. *cervinus*, f. *cervus.* In F. *cervin.*] Of or belonging to deer, or to the family *Cervidæ.* Also as *sb.*

Cervi·sial, *a. joc.* 17... [f. L. *cervisia* beer + -AL.] Of or pertaining to beer.

‖**Cervix** (sɔ̄·ɹviks). 1741. [L.] *Phys.* The neck. Also applied to analogous parts of the womb, the bladder, etc.

Ceryl (sīᵊ·ril). 1873. [f. Gr. κηρός wax + -YL.] *Chem.* The hypothetic radical ($C_{27}H_{55}$) of *Ceryl* or *Cerotyl alcohol* or cerotin, $C_{27}H_{56}O$, a waxy substance obtained from Chinese wax.

Cesar, -ean, etc.; see CÆ-.

Cesare (sī·zǎri). 1588. *Logic.* A mnemonic word representing the first mood of the second syllogistic figure, in which a universal negative major premiss and a universal affirmative minor yield a universal negative conclusion.

Cespititious (sespiti·ʃəs), *a.* 17... [f. L. *cæspiticius* + -OUS.] Made of turf, turfen.

Cespitose (se·spitǒᵘ·s), *a.* Also CÆSPITOSE, q. v. Turfy, growing in tufts or clumps.

Cess (ses), *sb.*[1] Also SESS(E. 1531. [prop. SESS, aphet. f. ASSESS *sb.*] 1. An assessment, tax, or levy. In Eng. use replaced by *rate*, exc. *dial.*; in Ireland still the official term. 2. *Ireland.* The obligation to supply the soldiers and the lord deputy's household with provisions at prices 'assessed'; hence *loosely*, military exactions. Now *Hist.* 1571. †3. Assessment, estimation –1596.

3. The poore Iade is wrung in the withers, out of all cesse SHAKS.

†**Cess**, *sb.*[2] 1689. [var. of CEASE.] 1. Cessation 1703. 2. = CESSER 3. 1869.

Cess (ses), *sb.*[3] *Anglo-Irish.* 1859. [? from CESS[1] 2.] In *bad cess to* = 'evil befall'.

Cess (ses), *v.*[1] 1494. [See CESS *sb.*[1]] †1. = ASSESS *v.* 1. –1764. †2. = ASSESS *v.* 2. –1612. 3. *Ireland.* To impose (soldiers) upon a community, to be supported at a fixed rate. Now *Hist.* 1612. †4. = ASSESS *v.* 3. –1738. †5. = ASSESS *v.* 4. STOW.

†**Cess**, *v.*[2] 1555. [var. of CEASE *v.*] *intr.* To cease to perform a legal duty –1741.

†**Ce·ssant**, *a. rare.* 1648. [ad. L. *cessantem.*] That ceases to act –1746. Hence **Ce·ssantly** *adv.* intermittently.

Cessation (sesē̆i·ʃən). ME. [ad. L. *cessationem*; treated as n. of action from Eng. *cease.*] 1. Ceasing, discontinuance, stoppage. †b. ellipt. = *Cessation of* or *from arms*: armistice, truce –1755. †2. Inactivity –1697.

1. The C. of the Oracles NORTH. 2. The spent Earth may..better'd by C., bear the Grain DRYDEN.

‖**Cessavit** (sesē̆i·vit). 1555. [L., f. *cessare* = CESS *v.*[2]] A writ to recover lands, which lay when a tenant ceased to pay rent, or perform legal duties, for the space of two years.

Cesser (se·səɹ). 1531. [a. F. *cesser.*] 1. *Law.* Ceasing (of a tenant) to pay rent, or perform legal duties, for the space of two years. 2. Cessation, termination 1809. †3. = CESSION 2. –1689.

†**Ce·ssible**, *a. rare.* 1645. [ad. L. **cessibilis*, f. *cessus, cedere.*] Yielding; ready to give way. Hence †**Cessibi·lity**, yieldingness.

‖**Cessio bonorum** (L. 'cession of goods') = CESSION 3 b.

Cession (se·ʃən). ME. [a. F., ad. L. *cessionem.*] †1. The action of giving way or yielding –1693. †2. The vacating of an office either by retirement or death –1738. b. *Eccl. Law.* The vacating of a benefice by taking another without dispensation 1641. 3. The action of ceding to another rights, property, etc.; concession ME. b. *Civil Law.* The voluntary surrender by a debtor of all his effects to his creditors 1622.

3. The c. of Maestricht TEMPLE.

Cessionary (se·ʃənări). 1611. [ad. med.L. *cessionarius*, f. L. *cessio* (*bonorum*).] †1. A bankrupt who makes *cessio bonorum* –1694. 2. An assignee 1754

†**Ce·ssment.** 1540. [var. of SESSMENT, aphet. f. ASSESSMENT.] = ASSESSMENT –1733.

†**Ce·ssor**[1]. Also †**-er.** 1565. [f. CESS *v.*[1] + -ER[1], -OR.] = ASSESSOR, q. v. –1596.

Cessor[2] (se·sǫɹ, -əɹ). 1727. [f. CESS *v.*[2] + -OR.] *Law.* One who cesses; see CESS *v.*[2]

Cesspipe (se·sˌpəip). [f. *cess* in CESSPOOL.] A pipe for carrying off the overflow from cesspools, sinks, or drains. So **Cesspit**, a pit for the reception of night-soil and refuse; a midden.

Cesspool (se·sˌpūl). 1671. [Of uncertain etym.; see N.E.D.] 1. A well made in the bottom of a drain, under a grating, to collect sand or gravel carried by the stream. 2. A well sunk to receive the soil from a water-closet, kitchen sink, etc. Also *fig.* 1782.

2. *fig.* The c. of agio CARLYLE.

Cest(e. 1577. [a. F. *ceste.*] = CESTUS[1].

Cestoid (se·stoid). Also **cestode.** 1836. [f. L. *cestus.* Cf. F. *cestoïde*, and mod.L. *Cestoidea*, given to an order of Entozoa by Zeder in 1808.] A. *adj.* Ribbon-like, as the tape-worm. B. *sb.* A worm of this kind. Also *attrib.* 1837.

†**Ce·ston.** 1583. [= F. *ceston.*] = CESTUS[1].

‖**Cestracion** (sestrēᵊ·siǫn). 1876. [Cf. Gr. κέστρα a kind of fish, also κέστρος sharpness, and ἀκή point.] A kind of shark now peculiar to Australia; the Port Jackson shark. It has sharp teeth in front, and flat pavement-like teeth behind. Hence **Cestra·ciont**, belonging to the C. family of fishes.

Cestrian (se·striǎn), *a.* 1703. [f. *Cester*, OE. form of *Chester.*] Of or pertaining to Chester or to Cheshire.

‖**Cestui** (se·stwi, se·twi). Also **cestuy**, pl. **cestuis.** 1555. [AF., OF. *cestui*:—late L. *ecce istum.*] The person (who), he (who).

Cestui que (*qui*) *trust, cestui que use*, more fully *cestui a que use* (= *al use de qui*) *le trust est créé*: the person for whose benefit anything is given in trust to another. *Cestui* (*a*) *que vie*: he on or for whose life land is held or granted.

‖**Cestus**[1] (se·stɒ̆s). 1577. [L. *cestus*, ad. Gr. κεστός; prop. 'stitched'.] A belt or girdle for the waist; *esp.* that of Aphrodite or Venus. Also *fig.*

‖**Cestus**[2] (se·stɒ̆s). 1734. [a. L. *cæstus*, ? incorrect sp. of *cestus*; see prec.] A covering for the hand made of thongs of bull-hide, loaded with strips of iron and lead. Used by boxers of ancient Rome.

Cesure; see CÆSURA.

Cet-, f. L. *cetus*, Gr. κῆτος whale, comb. f. signifying 'derived from spermaceti'.

Cetane (sī·tēᵊn), the paraffin of the hexdecyl or cetyl series, $C_{16}H_{34}$. **Cetene** (sī·tīn), the olefine of the same series, $C_{16}H_{32}$. **Ce·tic** *a.* of the whale, or of spermaceti. **Cetin** (sī·tin), a white crystalline fatty substance ($C_{32}H_{64}O$), forming the essential part of spermaceti. **Ce·tyl**, the hydrocarbon radical ($C_{16}H_{33}$) assumed to exist in Cetic acid, and the other members of the *Cetyl* or *Cetylic* series, including *Cetyl* or *Cetylic Alcohol*, or *ethal* ($C_{16}H_{33}.OH$). **Cety·lic** *a.* of cetyl, as in *Cetylic Alcohol.*

‖**Cetacea** (sǐtēᵊ·ʃiǎ), *sb. pl.* 1830. [f. L. *cetus*, a. Gr. κῆτος whale.] *Zool.* The order of marine Mammalia containing the whales and their congeners. Hence **Ceta·cean** *a.* of or pertaining to the *C.*; *sb.* [sc. *animal*]. **Ceta·ceous** *a.* belonging to the *C.*; of the whale kind or nature.

Cete[1] (sīt). ME. [a. OF., ad. L. *cete*, pl. neut. a. Gr. κήτη whales.] A whale, a sea-monster.

†**Cete**[2]. 1486. [? ad. L. *cœtus.*] A 'company' of badgers.

Ceteosaur, -us (sī·tiˌosǭɹ, -sǭ·rɒ̆s). 1872. [f. Gr. κῆτος (gen. κήτεος) + σαῦρος lizard.] *Palæont.* A gigantic fossil saurian, found in the oolite and chalk.

Ceterach (se·tĕræk). 1551. [a. med.L. *ceterach, cetrach*; ? Arab. or Celt.] *Bot.* A genus of ferns, including *C. officinarum*, Scale-fern.

Cetology (sǐtǫ·lŏdʒi). *rare.* 1851. [f. Gr. κῆτος + -λογία.] That part of zoology which treats of the whales. Hence **Cetolo·gical** *a.* **Ceto·logist.**

Cetrarin (se·trărin, sǐ-). 1861. [f. mod.L. *cetraria*, generic name of Iceland moss, f. L. *cetra* targe.] *Chem.* A white crystalline substance ($C_{18}H_{16}O_8$) forming the bitter principle of Iceland moss (*Cetraria islandica*). Also called **Cetra·ric acid.**

Ceylonite, ceylanite (sī·lənəit). 1802. [a. F. *ceylanite*, f. *Ceylan*, Fr. form of Ceylon.] *Min.* Iron-Magnesia Spinel from Ceylon.

Ch, a consonantal digraph, has the sound of (tʃ) in all native words; of (k) in words taken from Greek (or Hebrew through Greek); of *sh* (ʃ) in words from modern French; and of (χ) only in Scotch, Welsh, and foreign words. OE. *c*(*e*)-, *c*(*i*)- has regularly become *ch-*; and other CH- words in mod. Eng. are supplied by the Old French words in *ch-* from L. *ca-*. For the history of the digraph see N.E.D.

†**Ch, 'ch**, *pron. dial.* ME. Aphet. f. *ich, utch* = I, occurring before verbal forms beginning with a vowel, *h*, or *w*; as in *cham* (tʃam), (earlier *icham*) I am, *chave, chad*, etc.

‖**Cha.** 1616. [Chinese (Mandarin) *ch'a* tea.] A Chinese name of TEA occas. used in Eng. at its first introduction.

Chabazite, chabasite (kæ·băzəit). Also **chabasie, -zie.** 1804. [f. *χαβάζιε, erron. sp. of Gr. χαλάζιε, voc. of χαλάζιος, f. χάλαζα hail. The name ought to be **Chalazite.**] *Min.* A colourless, or flesh-coloured, mineral occurring in glassy rhombohedral crystals, composed chiefly of silica, alumina and lime.

‖**Chablis** (ʃablī). 1668. [Fr.] A white French wine made at *Chablis* (Yonne), in central France.

Cha·bot. 1610. [a. F., earlier F. *cabot* (see CABOT).] *Her.* The fish called Miller's Thumb.

‖**Chabouk, -buk** (tʃā·buk). 1815. [Pers. and Urdū.] A (Persian) horsewhip. See also CHAWBUCK.

Chace, obs. f. CHASE.

Chack (tʃæk), *v.* 1513. [In sense 1, echoic; cf. *clack.*] **1.** *Sc.* To snap with the teeth; to crush with a snap of the jaws, or by the sudden shutting of a door, window, etc.; to clack. **2.** A sudden toss of a horse's head, to avoid the subjection of the bridle. ? *Obs.*

Chack (tʃæk), *sb. Sc.* 1804. [f. prec.] **1.** The act of chacking (in sense 1). **2.** A snack 1818. **3.** Name of the Wheat-ear (from its note) 1804.

‖**Chacma** (tʃæ·kmă). 1835. A kind of baboon (*Cynocephalus porcarius*) found in S. Africa.

Chaco (ʃæ·ko). Also **chako,** and usu. SHAKO, q. v. 1826. [a. Magyar *csákó.*] A military cap having the form of a truncated cone with a peak in front.

‖**Chaconne** (ʃakǭ·n, tʃækǫ·n). 1685. [Fr., ad. Sp. *chacona,* ad. Basque *chucun* pretty.] An obsolete dance; the music to which it was danced, moderately slow, and usu. in 3–4 time.

Chad, var. of SHAD.

‖**Chætodon** (kī·tǫdǫn). 1750. [f. Gr. χαίτη hair + ὀδούς (ὀδοντ-) tooth.] *Zool.* A Linnæan genus of spiny-finned fishes (modern family *Chætodontidæ*) having bristle-like teeth and bright colours.

Chætophorous (kītǫ·fŏrəs), *a.* 1877. [f. Gr. χαίτη hair, mane.] *Zool.* Bristle-bearing; applied to certain Annelids.

Chætopod (kī·tǫpǫd). 1864. [f. as prec. + πούς (ποδ-).] *Zool.* Belonging to the order *Chætopoda* of Annelids, with bristle-bearing feet.

Chafe (tʃēⁱf), *v.* [ME. *chaufen,* a. OF. *chaufer,* mod. *chauffer* :—late L. **calefare,* contr. f. L. *calefacere,* f. *calere* + *facere.*]

I. *trans.* †**1.** To heat (*lit.* and *fig.*) –1716. **2.** To rub with the hand; *esp.* in order to restore warmth or sensation ME. **3.** To rub so as to abrade; to fret, gall. Also *fig.* ME.

2. He took his arms..and chafed and rubbed them with his hands DE FOE. *absol.* Keep chafing, for she moans BROWNING. 3. All the boats were badly chafed KANE. *fig.* I c. you if I tarrie. Let me go SHAKS.

II. *intr.* †**1.** To become warm or hot –1581. **2.** To rub; to press or strike with friction (*on, upon, against*) 1605. **3.** *fig.* To wax warm; to be angry, to rage; now usu., to display irritation by fretting and fuming 1525.

2. Seamen say, a Rope chafes 1704. If the currents c. upon it MAURY. 3. Let the loser c. COWPER. To c. under an affront PRESCOTT. The great sea chafes PROCTER. Hence **Cha·fant** *a.* (*Her.*) applied to a boar when enraged.

Chafe (tʃēⁱf), *sb.* 1551. [f. the vb.] **1.** Heat; rage, passion, fury; temper (*arch.*). **2.** Rubbing, fretting, friction 1848. **3.** A chafing against restraints 1869.

1. The pope is in a wonderful c. ASCHAM. 2. The c. of the sail NARES.

Chafer¹, **chaffer** (tʃēⁱ·fəɪ, tʃæ·fəɪ). [OE. *cefer, ceafor,* ? f. (ult.) *kaf-* to gnaw (see CHAVEL), or from the stem of CHAFF.] The COCKCHAFER; used also of the ROSE-CHAFER.

Chafer² (tʃēⁱ·fəɪ). ? *Obs.* ME. [f. CHAFE *v.* + -ER¹.] †**1.** A vessel for heating water, var. †**Cha·fern, cha·ffern;** also, a chafing-dish –1825. †**2.** = CHAFE-WAX –1805. **3.** One who chafes or fumes. ? *Obs.* 1625.

Chafery (tʃēⁱ·fəri). 1663. [prob. from **chauferie,* a. F. *chaufferie,* f. *chauffer.*] *Metall.* A forge in which iron is reheated.

†**Cha·fe-wax.** Also **chaff-.** 1607. [f. CHAFE *v.* (sense I. 1).] An officer in Chancery who prepared the wax for sealing documents.

Cha·feweed, †**cha·ffweed.** 1548. [f. CHAFE + WEED.] *Herb.* A name for species of *Gnaphalium* and the allied *Filago.*

Chaff (tʃɑf), *sb.*¹ [OE. *ceaf,* related to OHG. *cheva* husk, and perh. to a Teut. root *kef-* gnaw: cf. CHAVEL, JOWL.] **1.** *collect.* The husks of corn or other grain separated by threshing or winnowing. Also *fig.* and †*transf.* **2.** Cut hay and straw used for feeding cattle OE. **3.** *Bot.* **a.** The bracts of the flower of grasses, *esp.* the inner pair. **b.** The bracts at the base of the florets in Compositæ. 1776 **4.** *transf.* and *fig.* Refuse ME.

1. The light c., before the breezes borne POPE. *fig. Merch. V.* I. i. 117. *An old bird is not caught with c.* Provb. 4. The chaffe and ruine of the times *Merch. V.* II. ix. 48. *Comb.* **c.-cutter,** a machine for cutting hay and straw for fodder.

Chaff (tʃɑf), *sb.*² *colloq.* ? 1648. [? fig. use of prec.; or light use of *chaff* CHAFF *v.*] Banter, ridicule; badinage. (Somewhat vulgar.)

Chaff, *v.*¹ 1552. [f. CHAFF *sb.*¹] **1.** = CHAVE *v.*¹ **2.** To cut (hay, etc.) for fodder 1883.

Chaff (tʃɑf), *v.*² *colloq.* 1827. [See CHAFF *sb.*²] *trans.* To banter, rail at, or rally, in a light manner. Also *absol.* (Considered slangy.)

Palmerston.. pleasantly 'chaffing' militia colonels MCCARTHY. Hence **Cha·ffingly** *adv.*

Chaffer (tʃæ·fəɪ), *sb.*¹ [:—OE. **céapfaru,* f. *céap* bargain + *faru* faring, ME. *chapfare,* in sense 'trading journey'. In mod. use, from the vb.] †**1.** Trade; dealing –1662. **b.** In mod. use: Chaffering, haggling as to price 1851. †**2.** Wares –1693. Also †*fig.* Hence †**Cha·ffery** (*rare*), wares; traffic. **Cha·ffless** *a.* (*rare*).

Chaffer (tʃɑ·fəɪ), *sb.*² *colloq.* 1851. [f. CHAFF *v.*² + -ER¹.] One who chaffs.

Chaffer (tʃæ·fəɪ), *v.*¹ [ME. *chapfari,* f. *chapfare,* CHAFFER *sb.*¹; cf. *to trade,* etc.] †**1.** *intr.* To trade, deal in merchandise –1640. **2.** Now: To bargain, haggle about terms or price 1725. **3.** *transf.* and *fig.* To haggle, bandy words ME. †**4.** *trans.* To buy and sell; to traffic in; to barter –1680. Also †*fig.* ¶**5.** 'To talk much and idly' *Trench.* But qy.

1. (passing into 2) To c. for preferment with his gold DRYDEN. 2. They will c. half a day about a penny W. PALGRAVE. 3. To stand chaffering with Fate CARLYLE. 4. He chaffred Chayres in which Churchmen were set SPENSER. Hence **Cha·fferer.**

Chaffinch (tʃɑ·finʃ). 1440. [f. CHAFF *sb.*¹; cf. late L. *furfurio,* f. *furfur* bran.] A very common British bird, *Fringilla cœlebs,* with pretty plumage and pleasant short song.

Cha·ffron, var. of CHAMFRON.

Chaff-weed (tʃɑ·fˌwīd). 1776. [app. orig. CHAFEWEED.] †**1.** = CHAFEWEED. **2.** *Centunculus* or Bastard Pimpernel.

Chaffy (tʃɑ·fi), *a.* 1552. [f. CHAFF *sb.*¹ + -Y¹.] **1.** Full of or covered with chaff. **2.** Consisting, or of the nature, of chaff; *spec.* in *Bot.* paleaceous 1597. **3.** Resembling chaff 1583. **4.** *fig.* Light, empty, and worthless as chaff 1594.

1. Like..c. grain COLERIDGE. 3. The c. snow. 4. Chaffye thoughtes 1594. A c. lord, Not worth the name of villain *Two Noble K.* III. i. 41.

Chafing (tʃēⁱ·fiŋ), *vbl. sb.* ME. [f. CHAFE *v.* + -ING¹.] The action of the vb.

Comb.: **c.-dish,** a vessel to hold burning fuel, for heating anything placed upon it; a portable grate; **-gear** (*Naut.*), 'the stuff put upon the rigging and spars to prevent their being chafed' (Smyth); **-pan** = *chafing-dish.*

Chaft (tʃɑft). Now *n. dial.* ME. [a. ON. **kjǫft-* jaw.] The jaw, chap; usu. in *pl.*

‖**Chagan** (kagā·n). *Hist.* 1776. [ad. (ult.) Old Turk. *khāqān*; see CHAM and KHAN.] Var. of KHAN; applied to the sovereign of the Avars in the 6th and 7th centuries.

Chagrin (ʃăgrī·n, -gri·n), *sb.* 1656. [a. F. *chagrin* (1) rough skin, SHAGREEN, (2) ill-humour, etc. Sense 2 is a fig. use of sense 1. (See Littré.)] †**1.** A species of skin or leather with a rough surface: now usu. spelt SHAGREEN, q. v. –1842. †**2.** That which frets or worries the mind –1847. **3.** *esp.* Mortification arising from disappointment, thwarting, or failure 1716. In *pl.* Vexations 1744.

2. Hear me, and touch Belinda with c. POPE. 3. The c. of an unfortunate wretch who had not obtained what he wanted LANGHORNE. To have one's own petty chagrins MISS FERRIER.

†**Chagrin,** *a.* 1666. [a. F., f. the sb.] **1.** Troubled –1722. **2.** Chagrined –1711.

Chagrin (ʃagrī·n, -gri·n), *v.* 1733. [a. F. *chagriner,* f. the sb.] *trans.* To worry, vex; *esp.* to mortify 1748.

Chagrined at his disappointment MORSE.

Chain (tʃēⁱn), *sb.* [ME. *chayne, cheyne,* a. OF. *chaeine, chaaine,* etc. :—L. *catena.*] **I. 1.** A connected series of links (usually of metal) passing through each other, or otherwise jointed together, so as to form a strong but flexible ligament or string. **2.** As employed to restrain or fetter; hence a bond or fetter; *esp.* in *pl.*; *abstr.* imprisonment, captivity. Also *fig.* ME. **3.** As a personal ornament; occ. an ensign of office ME. **4.** *fig.* A connected series; a sequence 1651.

1. Gold, iron, cable, draught, watch chains (*mod.*). 2. To dwell In Adamantine Chains and penal Fire MILT. *P. L.* I. 48. *fig.* The c. of habit HAZLITT. 3. The Mayor wearing his c. of office (*mod.*). 4. The c. of Discourse HOBBES, of Thought STEELE, of proofs BENTHAM, of events FREEMAN, of nerve ganglia ROLLESTON, of lakes 1867. The c. (= *mountain-chain*) called Olympus GROTE.

II. Spec. uses.

1. A chain used as a barrier; a boom ME. 2. A chain fixed to a door-post, to secure the door when slightly opened 1839. 3. A measuring line, used in land-surveying, formed of one hundred iron rods called links. (The one now adopted is Gunter's chain, measuring 66 feet or 4 poles, divided into 100 links.) 1610. b. A chain's length = 66 feet or 4 poles 1661. 4. *Arch.* A bar of iron, etc., built into walls to increase cohesion 1764. 5. *Mil.* = CHAIN-SHOT 1804. 6. *Weaving.* The warp 1721. 7. *Naut.* A contrivance, consisting of c.-wale, c.-plates, dead-eyes, etc., used to carry the lower shrouds of a mast outside the ship's side 1627.

III. *attrib.* Of chains; chain-like; of the nature of chain-mail ME.

Combs.: **c.-armour** = *chain-mail*; **-belt,** a c. adapted as a belt for transmitting power; **-boat,** a boat fitted with windlasses, etc., for raising mooring-chains, anchors, etc.; **-bolt,** (*a.*) *Naut.* one of the bolts by which c.-plates are fastened to the ship's side; (*b.*) the knob at the end of a door c. (see II. 2); **-bond** (*Arch.*), a c. or tier of timber built in a brick wall to increase its cohesion (see II. 4); **-cable,** a ship's cable formed of a c.; also *attrib.*; **-coupling,** a secondary coupling, consisting of chains and hooks, between railway carriages or trucks; **-gang,** a gang of convicts chained together while at work, etc.; **-hook,** *Naut.* an iron rod with a hook at one end, for hauling the c.-cables about; **c. letter,** a letter, copies of which are designed to pass from one to another of a series of recipients; **-mail,** mail made of interlaced links or rings; **-moulding,** a moulding imitating chains; **-pier,** a pier supported by chains like a c.-bridge; **-plate** (*Naut.*), one of the iron plates by which the shrouds are secured to the ship's side; **-pulley,** a pulley having depressions in its periphery to fit the links of a chain with which it is worked; **-rule,** a rule of arithmetic, by which is found the relation of equivalence between two numbers for which a c. of intervening equivalents is given; **-saw** (*Surg.*), a vertebrated saw forming a c.; **-timber** = *chain-bond*; **-wale,** *Naut.* = CHANNEL *sb.*²; **-wheel,** (*a*) a wheel used with a c. for the transmission of power; (*b*) a machine which is an inversion of the c.-pump, the descending water pressing upon the plates or buckets and so driving the machinery. Hence **Chai·nless** *a.* (*poet.*). **Chai·nlet,** a little c.

Chain (tʃēⁱn), *v.* ME. [f. the sb.] **1.** *trans.* To bind, fasten, secure, with a chain. Also *transf.* and *fig.* **2.** To fetter or confine with a chain or chains; to put in chains ME. Also *fig.* **3.** To obstruct or close with a chain 1603. †**4.** To surround like a chain 1606. **5.** To measure with a (surveyor's) chain 1610.

1. The rampant Beare chain'd to the ragged staffe *2 Hen. VI,* v. i. 203. *fig. Two Gent.* I. i. 3. 2. *fig.* Horror chained My parting footsteps 1870. 3. To c. or obstruct a street 1674. 4. *Ant. & Cl.* IV. viii. 14.

Chai·n-bri·dge. 1818. A suspension-bridge supported by chains.

Chained (tʃēⁱnd), *ppl. a.* 1552. **1.** From the vb.: In the senses of the vb. 1613. **2.** From the sb.: Fitted, provided, or adorned with a chain or chains 1552. **3.** Of lightning: Having the form of a long zigzag line 1859.

Chai·n-pump. 1618. A machine for raising water by means of an endless chain; most commonly the chain, passing upwards through a tube, raises the water by means of disks or valves which fit the tube.

Chai·n-shot. 1581. Two balls, or half-balls, connected by a chain, chiefly used in naval warfare to destroy masts, rigging, and sails; a discharge of this. Also *fig.*

Chai·n-stitch. 1598. **1.** In needle-work: An ornamental stitch resembling the links of a chain; chain-work. **2.** In a sewing-machine: A stitch produced by looping the upper thread into itself on the under side of the work, or by using a second thread to engage the loop of the upper thread; opp. to the lock-stitch. Also *attrib.* 1867.

Chai·n-work, chain work. 1551. **1.** Ornament resembling chains. **2.** Work consisting of metal links or rings intertwined 1864. **3.** A texture formed by knitting or looping with a single thread, as in hosiery 1833.

Chair (tʃēᵊɹ), *sb.* [ME. *chaere, chaiere*, a. OF. :—L. *catedra, cathedra*, a. Gr.; see CATHEDRA. In Eng. orig. of three syllables, later of two, *cha·-yer*, and finally of one, *chair.*] **1.** A seat for one person; now usu. the movable four-legged seat with a rest for the back. Also *fig.* **2.** A seat of authority, state, or dignity; a throne, bench, judgement-seat, etc. ME. Also *fig.* **3.** The seat of a bishop in his church; hence *fig.* episcopal dignity or authority (*arch.*) 1480. **4.** A pulpit (*arch.*) 1648. **5.** The seat, and hence the office, of a professor 1449, of a mayor 1682, of chairman of a meeting, or of the Speaker of the House of Commons 1647. †**6.** A vehicle for one person; a sedan carried on poles –1836; a light chaise drawn by one horse –1821. **7.** *Railways.* An iron or steel socket with a deep notch, to receive the rail and secure it to the sleeper 1816.

1. *To take a c.*: to be seated. *fig.* The scorner's c. WESLEY. [Thy Father's] drooping Chaire 1 *Hen. VI*, III. ii. 51. 2. At the Soldans c. Defi'd the best of Panim chivalry MILT. *P. L.* I. 764. 3. His first C., namely that of Antioch BREVINT. 5. The C. of Poetry at Oxford M. ARNOLD. *Past, above*, or *below the C.* (of aldermen of the City of London): having served or not served as Lord Mayor. *To take the c.*: to assume the position of chairman. *To put in the c. In the c. To leave or vacate the c. To address, support*, the c. (*i. e.* the chairman). Cries of 'Chair' (*i. e.* appeals to the chairman) DICKENS. 6. She..lik'd three footmen to her c. SWIFT. A one-horse c. 1753. *Comb.* **c.-days**, old age; **c. organ**: see CHOIR ORGAN.

†**Chair**, *sb.*[2] ME. [Var. of CHAR, assim. to prec.] A chariot or car –1814.

Chair (tʃēᵊɹ), *v.* 1552. [f. CHAIR *sb.*[1]] **1.** *trans.* To place in a chair. **b.** To place in a chair or seat, and carry aloft in triumph 1761. **2.** To provide with a chair or chairs 1844.

Chairman (tʃēᵊ·ɹmæn). 1654. **1.** The occupier of a chair of authority; the person chosen to preside over a meeting, a company, a corporate body, etc. **2.** One whose occupation it is to carry persons in chairs, or to wheel a Bath-chair 1682. Hence **Chai·rmanship**, the office of c.; the action of presiding as c. **Chai·r-woman**, a woman who occupies the chair.

Chaise (ʃēⁱz). 1701. [a. mod.F. *chaise*, phonetic var. of *chaire* CHAIR (sense 6). Vulgarly treated as pl., with sing. CHAY, SHAY.] A pleasure or travelling carriage; *esp.* a light open carriage for one or two persons, with a top or calash, orig. drawn by one horse; *loosely*, any pleasure cart or light carriage. Also, = POST-CHAISE, q. v. Hence **Chai·seless** *a.*

‖**Chaise-longue** (ʃēz,loṅg). 1825. [F., 'long chair'.] A kind of sofa with a rest for the back at one end only.

†‖**Chaise-marine** (ʃēz,marī·n). 1739. [F.] ? A kind of chaise, the body of which rests on suspension-straps between cee-springs –1823.

‖**Chal.** 1865. The Gipsy word for 'person, man, fellow', with fem. *chai.*

Chalastic (kălæ·stik), *a.* 1621. [ad. mod. L., a. Gr. χαλαστικός laxative.] *Med.* Having power to remove rigidity or stiffness; relaxing. Also as *sb.*

‖**Chalaza** (kălēⁱ·ză). Pl. **-æ.** 1704. [mod.L., a. Gr. χάλαζα hail.] **1.** *Zool.* Each of the two membranous twisted strings by which the yolk-bag of an egg is kept in position; the tread or treadle. **2.** *Bot.* A spot on the seed where the nucleus joins the integuments 1830. Hence **Chala·zal** *a.* **Chalazi·ferous** *a.* bearing the c. or chalazæ.

‖**Chalazion** (kălēⁱ·ziǫn). Occas. as L. *chalazium.* 1708. [a. Gr., dim. of χάλαζα; see prec.] A small pimple or tubercle; *esp.* a stye.

†**Cha·lcanth, chalca·nthum.** 1678. [a. L. *c(h)alcanthum, -us*, a. Gr. χάλκανθον, f. χαλκός + ἄνθος.] Blue vitriol (sulphate of copper); also, an ink made from it –1718. Hence **Chalca·nthite**, *Min.* native blue vitriol. †**Chalca·nthous** *a.* of the nature of ink or blacking (*rare*).

Chalcedonic (kælsĭdǫ·nik), *a.* 1828. [f. CHALCEDONY.] Of or belonging to chalcedony.

Chalcedony, cal- (kælse·dəni, kæ·lsĭdəni). See also CASSIDOINE, -DONY. ME. [ad. L. *c(h)alcedonius*, used in the Vulgate as tr. Gr. χαλκηδών, in *Rev.* xxi. 19, found nowhere else. The supposed connexion with Chalcedon in Asia Minor is very doubtful.] *Min.* A precious stone; a crypto-crystalline sub-species of quartz (a true quartz, with some disseminated opal-quartz), having the lustre nearly of wax, and being either transparent or translucent. In mod. lapidary work called variously *agate, cornelian, cat's eye, chrysoprase, onyx, sard*, etc., according to colour and structure.

Chalchuite (tʃæ·ltʃu,əit). 1843. [f. the Mexican name *chalchihuitl.*] *Min.* A green variety of turquoise from Mexico.

Chalcidian (kælsi·diăn). [f. mod.L. *chalcidæ* (f. L. *chalcis* = Gr. χαλκίς a kind of lizard.] *Zool.* Of or pertaining to the family of Chalcidæ or Snake Lizards.

‖**Chalci·tes.** [L., ad. Gr. *χαλκῖτις copper-ore.] Green vitriol (sulphate of copper). BACON.

Chalco- (kæ·lko). Occas. **chalko-.** Stem and comb. form of Gr. χαλκός copper, brass, used in the names of minerals, as in **Cha·lcocite**, native sulphide of copper, copper glance; **Cha·lcopy·rite** [+PYRITE], an ore of copper, called yellow or copper pyrites, native sulphide of copper and iron.

Chalcographer (kælkǫ·grăfəɹ). 1662. [f. mod.Gr. χαλκογράφος.] One who engraves on copper. So **Chalcogra·phic, -al** *a.* of, pertaining to, or of the nature of, chalcography. **Chalco·graphist**, = CALCOGRAPHER. **Chalco·graphy**, the art of engraving on copper.

Chaldaic (kældē·ik). 1662. [ad. L. *Chaldaicus.*] *adj.* Of or pertaining to Chaldæa. *sb.* The language of the Chaldeans. So **Chalda·ical** *a.* **Cha·ldaism**, a C. idiom or mode of speech. †**Cha·ldic** *a.* = CHALDEE.

Chaldean (kældī·ăn). 1581. [f. L. *Chaldæus* = Gr. Χαλδαῖος.] *adj.* Of or pertaining to Chaldæa or the Chaldeans; hence, to occult science 1732. *sb.* A native of Chaldæa, *esp.* (as at Babylon) one skilled in occult learning, astrology, etc.; hence *gen.* a soothsayer, astrologer. (So in Gr. and L.) 1581.

Chaldee (kæ·ldī, kældī·). ME. *adj.* = CHALDEAN, CHALDAIC. *sb.* **1.** A native of Chaldæa. **2.** The language of the Chaldeans; also the biblical Syriac or Aramaic.

Chalder[1] (tʃǭ·ldəɹ). *Sc.* ME. [app. a. OF. *chaudiere* :—L. *caldaria*, f. *cal(i)dus*; or ? short f. CHALDRON.] **1.** An obsolete dry measure of capacity; in Scotland 16 bolls or 64 firlots of corn; for lime and coal 32 to 64 imperial bushels. †**2.** In England = CHALDRON, but for coal and lime varying from 32 to 40 bushels –1778.

Chalder[2] (tʃǭ·ldəɹ). *Naut.* A rudder-brace or gudgeon.

†**Chalde·se**, *v.* Also **caldese.** 1664. [? f. *Chaldee* or *Chaldees.*] To cheat, trick, take in –1697.

Chaldron (tʃǭ·ldrən, tʃā·drən). 1555. [var. of CAULDRON; a. OF. *chauderon*, mod. F. *chaudron*, augm. of *chaudère, chaudière*; see CHALDER[1].] †**1.** = CAULDRON –1750. **2.** A dry measure of 4 quarters or 32 bushels; now only used for coals (36 bushels) 1615.

Chaldron, obs. f. CHAWDRON.

‖**Chalet** (ʃale). 1817. [F. *chalet* (not *châlet*) a Swiss word; see Littré. Perh. dim. of *casella*, dim. of *casa* house.] **1.** A herdsman's hut on the Swiss mountains; hence, the small wooden cottage of the Swiss peasant; *gen.* a villa built in the style of a Swiss cottage. **2.** = F. *chalet de nécessité*, a street lavatory, etc. 1882.

1. On the slopes were innumerable châlets TYNDALL.

Chalice (tʃæ·lis). [central OF. *chalice*, ousting (*c* 1350) earlier OE. forms *cęlic, cælic, cælc*, and OF. *caliz, calice* :—L. *calix, calicem* cup.] **1.** A drinking cup or goblet. (Now only in poetic or elevated language.) Also *fig.* **2.** *spec.* The cup used in the celebration of the Eucharist OE. *transf.* A flower-cup 1650. Hence **Cha·liced** *a.* having a cup-like blossom; contained in a cup.

‖**Chalicosis** (kælikōᵘ·sis). [mod. f. Gr. κάλιξ small stone.] *Med.* Disease of the lungs caused by the inhalation of fine siliceous particles.

Chalk (tʃǭk), *sb.* [Common WGer.; OE. *cealc*, a. L. *calcem, calx* lime. See also CAUK *sb.*] †**1.** ? Lime –1572. **2.** An opaque soft white earthy limestone, consisting chemically of carbonate of lime with some impurities OE. **3.** Applied to other earths resembling chalk 1601. *spec.* Applied to preparations used in the form of crayons for drawing. With *pl.* Also *attrib.* drawn with chalk 1481. **4.** A score at an ale-house, etc. (formerly written up with chalk); credit, 'tick' 1529. **5.** A mark, line, or score made with chalk, as in various games 1680.

3. *Fuller's c.*: ? fuller's earth. *Brown c.*: umber. *French c.*: a kind of steatite. *Red c.*: a bed of chalk of a red colour in Norfolk; also, ruddle. Two heads in chalks 1832. *attrib.* A c. head of a dog (*mod.*).

Phrases. (*By*) *a long c.*, also *by long chalks, by chalks* (colloq.): in a great degree, by far (see senses 4, 5). *To walk one's chalks* (slang): to be off.

Comb., etc.: **c.-bed**, a stratum of c.; **-drawing**, one executed in c.; **-flint, -fossil**, etc., one found in c.; **-line**, a line rubbed with c., used for laying down straight lines, as a guide in cutting; **-marl**, an argillaceous stratum just beneath the Lower White C.; **-pit, -quarry**, one from which c. is dug; **-white** *a.*

Chalk (tʃǭk), *v.* 1575. [f. prec. sb.] **1.** To manure (land) with chalk. **2.** To rub, mark, or write with chalk 1592. *fig.* To make white or pale as by rubbing with chalk; to blanch 1633.

2. One chalks down nine figures 1823. †*To c. it*: to run up a score. *fig.* Fear.. chalk'd her face TENNYSON.

Phr. **Chalk out.** *fig.* †**a.** To mark *out*, as with chalk. **b.** To sketch *out*, adumbrate. **c.** *fig.* To trace *out*, as a course to be followed.

Chalk-stone (tʃǭ·k,stōᵘn). ME. †**1.** Lime, limestone. †**2.** ? A piece of chalk –1611. **3.** A chalk-like concretion, chiefly of sodium urate, occurring in the tissues and joints, *esp.* of the hands and feet, in severe gout.

Chalky (tʃǭ·ki), *a.* ME. [f. CHALK *sb.* + -Y[1].] **1.** Consisting of, or abounding in, chalk; resembling chalk 1611. **2.** *Pathol.* Of the nature of chalk, or of a CHALK-STONE (sense 3), or containing chalk-stones 1782.

1. The c. cliffs salute their longing eyes FALCONER. C. white flowers 1882. Hence **Cha·lkiness.**

Challenge (tʃæ·lėndʒ), *sb.* [ME. *calenge, chalange*, a. OF. *ca-, chalenge, -lange*, orig. *-longe* :—L. *calumnia* trickery, false accusation, etc. Cf. *songe* from L. *somnium.* The same word as *calumny.*] †**1.** An accusation, reproach, objection –1692. **2.** The act of calling to account; *esp.* the act of a sentry in demanding the countersign ME.; in *Hunting*, the opening and crying of hounds at finding the scent. **3.** *Law.* An exception taken, against persons or things; *spec.* an objection made to jurymen in a trial. Also, an exception taken to a vote, etc. 1530. **4.** A calling in question; the being called in question 1820. †**5.** A claim –1750. **6.** An invitation to a trial or contest of any kind; a defiance ME. **7.** *spec.* A summons to fight, *esp.* to single combat or duel 1530. Also *attrib.*

3. *Principal challenge*, mostly in civil actions, a cause of exception allowed at once if found true. *Peremptory c.*, in criminal actions, an exception allowed without cause alleged. *C. to the array*, an exception to the whole panel. *C. to the polls*, an exception to particular jurors. *C. to the favour*, an exception on probable circumstances of suspicion, as acquaintance, and the like. 4. To bring her title into c. SCOTT. 6. A c. to scrutiny L. HUNT. 7. Heere's the C., reade it *Twel. N.* III. iv. 157.

Challenge (tʃæ·lėndʒ), *v.* [ME. *kalangen, chalangen*, a. OF. *ca-, chalonger, -langer, -lenger* :—late L. *calumniare*, for *calumniari* to accuse falsely; see prec. Cf. F. *songer* from L. *somniare.*] †**1.** *trans.* To accuse, bring a charge against –1693. Also *absol.* To accuse one of –1485. **2.** To reprehend; to call to account. Now only *dial.* exc. as said of a sentinel (see CHALLENGE *sb.* 2), and in *fig.* uses. ME. **3.** *Law.* To object to (a juryman, evidence, etc.). Also *absol.* ME. **4.** To call in question ME. **5.** To lay claim to, demand as a right, claim *for* (*arch.* or *Obs.*) ME. Also *fig.* **6.** To summon to a contest of any kind; to defy, dare. (Often *to do*, or *to* an *action.*) 1513; to invite (hostile or critical action of any kind) 1614. 7. *spec.* To call upon to answer an imputation by combat 1588. *intr.* or *absol.* ME.

2. On any one approaching his post, he must c. them by the words '*Who comes there?*' *Reg. Instr. Cavalry* 1833. When a hound challenges P. BECKFORD. 4. To c. the wisdom of a measure HUXLEY. 5. A Gentleman that challenges the Title of Honourable BENTLEY. To c. place among the [chief] cities of Europe 1673. To c. the admiration of all ages 1787. 6. I..c. Dagon to the test MILT. *Samson* 1151. To c. controversy 1882. 7. *absol.* They c., and encounter breast to breast DRYDEN. Hence **Cha·llengeable** *a.* open to challenge. **Cha·llengee·**, one who is challenged (*rare*). **Cha·llenger**, one who challenges.

Challis (tʃæ·lis, ‖ʃa·li). 1849. [app. of Eng. origin, perh. f. the proper name.] A fine silk and worsted fabric, very pliable and without gloss, used for ladies' dresses. Also *attrib.*

†**Chalon.** ME. [app. f. *Châlons-sur-Marne* in France.] A blanket for a bed -1616. Hence †**Cha·loner**, a maker of chalons.

‖**Chaloupe** (ʃalu·p). 1699. [F.; prob. ad. Du. *sloep* SLOOP.] A kind of French boat; = SHALLOP.

‖**Chalumeau** (ʃalümō). 1713. [Fr. (ult.) :— L. *calamellus*, dim. of *calamus*.] a. A reed, pipe. b. The lowest register of the clarinet.

Chalybean (kælibī·ăn), *a.* [f. L. *chalybeius*, f. Gr. χαλυβηΐς, f. χάλυψ, χάλυβος, 'sing. of Chalybes', also 'steel'.] Pertaining to the Chalybes, an ancient nation of Asia Minor famous for their skill in working iron. MILT.

Chalybeate (kăli·biĕt), *a.* 1634. [app. ad. mod.L. *chalybeatus*, but the reg. L. form would be *chalybatus*; cf. F. *chalybé*; see prec.] Impregnated or flavoured with iron. As *sb.* A chalybeate medicine or spring 1667. Hence †**Chaly·beate** *v.* to impregnate with iron.

Chalybite (kæ·libəit). 1847. [f. Gr. χάλυβ- steel.] *Min.* = SIDERITE.

Cham (kæm), *sb.* 1553. [a. F. and med.L. *cham*, *chan*, *can*, ad. Turki *khān* KHAN, contr. form of CHAGAN.] An obs. form of KHAN, q. v. Also *transf.* and *fig.*

That great C. of literature, Samuel Johnson SMOLLETT.

Cham, chamm (tʃæm), *v.* Still *dial.* ME. (See CHAMP *v.*] 1. To bite, chew. 2. To pound, mash. *Sc.*

‖**Chama** (kē·mă). 1753. [L., a. Gr. χήμη cockle, f. χα- stem of χαίνειν to gape.] *Zool.* A genus of bivalve molluscs, including *C. gigas*, the largest known.

‖**Chamade** (ʃama·d). 1684. [F., ad. Pg. *chamada*, f. *chamar* :—L. *clamare*.] *Mil.* A signal by beat of drum or sound of trumpet inviting to a parley.

‖**Chamærops** (kămī·rǫps). 1852. [L., a. Gr. χαμαίρωψ, f. χαμαί + ῥώψ shrub, bush.] *Bot.* A northern genus of palms, including *C. humilis*, the smallest of the order, and *C. Fortuni*.

‖**Cha·mbellan.** 1710. The French form of CHAMBERLAIN, used as a foreign title.

Chamber (tʃē·mbəɹ), *sb.* ME. [a. F. *chambre* :—L. *camera*, *camara*, in Gr. καμάρα vault; prob. f. Aryan root *kam-* to curve.] I. A room (in a house). 1. An apartment; a private room; now *esp.* a bedroom. (In colloq. use repl. by *room*.) Also *fig.* 2. *pl.* Sets of rooms occupied by single persons; *esp.* rooms in the Inns of Court by lawyers. b. The room in which a judge sits to transact minor business. 1641. 3. A hall in which a deliberative, legislative, or judicial body meets. b. A judicial or deliberative body; now *esp.* one of the divisions of a legislative body, as 'the popular c.', i. e. the House of Commons ME. 4. The place where the funds of a government, corporation, etc. are (or were) kept; chamberlain's office; treasury. [Cf. med. L. *camera*.] 1632. †5. [= med.L. *camera*, F. *chambre*.] A province, city, etc., directly subject, and yielding revenue to the king; more loosely: Metropolis; ? royal port -1699. 6. The hangings and furniture of a chamber. ? *Obs.* 1612. b. *euphem.* for *chamber-pot*, q. v.

1. They laid her in an vpper c. *Acts* ix. 37. *Presence-*, *audience-c.*: the reception room in a palace. 2. I have chambers in the Temple STEELE. 3. *C. of Commerce*, a board organized to protect the interests of commerce. 5. London..the kings of England's c. HOLLAND.

II. An enclosed space, cavity, etc. 1. An enclosed space in the body of an animal or plant ME. 2. An artificial space, cavity, or room for various purposes 1769. 3. †a. A detached charge piece put into the breech of a gun -1627. †b. A small piece of ordnance without a carriage, standing on its breech, used to fire salutes -1727. c. That part of the bore of a gun in which the charge is placed 1627. d. The cavity in a mine for the reception of the powder.

1. The chambers of the brain ME., of a shell (*mod.*). 2. The c. of a pump (*i.e.* the part in which the piston works) 1769, of a canal lock (*i.e.* the space enclosed between the gates) 1837. 3. b. 2 *Hen. IV*, II. iv. 57.

Phr. **C. of Dais.** *Sc.* Also **c. of deas.** A parlour; also a best bedroom. (Jam.)

Comb.: **c.-concert**, a concert where c.-music is performed; **-counsel**, private counsel *Wint. T.* I. ii. 237; opinion given by a lawyer in private chambers (see I. 2); a lawyer who gives opinions in private, not in court, so **-counsellor**; **-fellow** (*arch.*), one who shares a room or rooms with another; **-lye**, urine, *esp.* as used for washing; **-milliner**, one who carries on business in a private house, not in a shop; **-music**, music specially fitted for performance in a private room or small audience hall; **-orchestra**, **-organ**, a small orchestra or organ; **-pot**, a vessel used in a bedroom for urine and slops (often euphemized as *chamber*); **-practice** (*Law*), practice in chambers and not in court; **-vessel** = *chamber-pot*.

Chamber (tʃē·mbəɹ), *v.* ME. [f. the sb.; cf. F. *chambrer*.] 1. To place in, or as in, a chamber; to shut *up* (*arch.*) 1575. Also †*fig.* 2. To form into a chamber or chambers 1674. 3. To provide (a gun) with a chamber 1708. †4. To lodge in, or as in, a chamber 1611. ¶5. To indulge in lewdness 1607.

1. The best blood chamber'd in his bosome SHAKS. Hence **Cha·mbered** *ppl. a.* in senses of sb. and vb.; †also = cambered (see CAMBER *v.*). **Cha·mbering** *vbl. sb.* †the furnishing of a room; †*concr.* hangings -1480; †sexual indulgence -1613; also *attrib.*: the providing (a gun) with a chamber.

Chamber-deacon, -deakin, -deken, etc. ME. [app. f. CHAMBER + DEACON.] 1. One of the poor clerks, chiefly from Ireland, who frequented the English Universities in the 15th c., and did not belong to any college or hall. Now *Hist.* †2. An attendant who kept the chambers of noblemen and others attending court -1483.

Chamberer (tʃē·mbərəɹ). *arch.* ME. [a. OF. *chamberier* (mod.F. *chambrier*) :—late L. *camerarius*, f. *camera*; also a. F. *chambrière* fem.] †1. A chambermaid -1733. †2. A chamberlain, valet -1640. 3. One who frequents ladies' chambers; a gallant (*arch.*) 1604.

Chamberlain (tʃē·mbəɹlin). ME. [a. OF., a. Ger. **kamarling*, f. *kamara* (a. L. *camara*, *camera*) CHAMBER + LING.] 1. a. A chamber attendant of a lord or king (*arch.*); also = CHAMBERER 1 (*obs. rare*). b. An officer having charge of the private chambers of a sovereign or nobleman. 2. A steward; an officer who receives the rents and revenues of a corporation or public office (see CHAMBER *sb.* I. 4) ME. †3. An attendant at an inn, in charge of the bedchambers -1829.

1. *Lord Great Chamberlain of England*: a hereditary officer, whose duty it is to attend upon and attire the sovereign at his coronation, to furnish Westminster Hall and the Houses of Parliament on state occasions, to attend upon peers and bishops at their doing of homage, etc. *Lord Chamberlain of the Household*: a chief officer, who shares the oversight of all officers of the Royal Household. He appoints the royal tradesmen, etc., has control of the actors at the royal theatres, and is the licenser of plays. Hence **Cha·mberlainship**, the office of c.

Chambermaid (tʃē·mbəɹmēd). 1587. 1. A female servant in a house or inn, who attends to the bedrooms. †2. A lady's maid -1719.

Cha·mber-master. 1851. *Shoemaking.* A shoemaker who works in his own house.

‖**Chambertin** (ʃaṅbęrtęṅ). 1775. [Fr.; place-name.] A wine, a superior kind of Burgundy.

‖**Chambranle** (ʃaṅbrā·nl'). 1704. [Fr.; of unkn. origin.] *Arch.* 'An ornamental bordering on the sides and tops of doors, windows, and fireplaces' (Gwilt).

Chambrel, var. of CAMBREL (sense 2).

Chameleon (kămī·liən). ME. [a. L. *chamæleon* (also used), a. Gr. χαμαιλέων, f. χαμαί on the ground, dwarf + λέων.] 1. A saurian reptile of the genus *Chamæleo*, distinguished by a prehensile tail, long tongue, eyes moving independently, but esp. by their power of changing the colour of the skin, varying through different shades of yellow, red, gray, brown, and dull inky blue. Formerly supposed to live on air (*Haml.* III. ii. 98). Also *fig.* (= variable person.) 1586. 2. One of the southern circumpolar constellations 1835. Also *attrib.*

Comb.: **c. fly**, *Stratiomys chamæleon*; **-like** *a.* and *adv.*

White C. (*Bot.*), *Carlina gummifera*; **Black C.**, *Cardopatium corymbosum*. *Mineral c.*, or *c. mineral* (*Chem.*), manganate of potassium (K_2MnO_4), the solution of which in water changes colour, on exposure to the air, from deep green to deep purple, owing to the formation of the permanganate ($KMnO_4$) Hence **Chame·leo·nic** *a.* given to change. **Chame·leonize** *v.* to change colour like a c. (*rare*).

Chamfer (tʃæ·mfəɹ), *sb.* 1601. [app. ad. F. *chanfrein*, formerly also *chamfrain*.] †1. A small groove, channel, etc. -1708. 2. The surface produced by bevelling off a square edge or corner equally on both sides; if made concave, it is called a *hollow c.* 1842.

Chamfer (tʃæ·mfəɹ), *v.* 1565. [f. OF. *chanfraindre*, perh. = L. *cantum frangere* to break the edge or side.] 1. To channel, flute, furrow. 2. To make a chamfer on; to bevel *away*, *off*; var. †**Cha·mfret** *v.* 1688. Hence **Cha·mfering** *vbl. sb.* (? the earliest word, and directly ad. F. *chamfrein*, *-frin*).

Cha·mfrain, -fron. *arch.* 1465. [a. OF. *chaufrain*, *chanfrain*, of unkn. origin. (Distinct from *chanfrein*, CHAMFER.)] The frontlet of a barded horse.

Chamlet(t, -lot, -lyt, obs. ff. of CAMLET.

Chamois (ʃæ·moi, ʃæ·mi, ‖ʃamwā). 1560. [a. F.; prob. from Swiss Romanic. Cf. OHG. *gamz*, mod.G. *gemse*.] 1. A capriform antelope (*A. rupicapra* or *Rupicapra tragus*), inhabiting the loftiest parts of the Alps, Pyrenees, Taurus, etc. Its agility and keen scent make its chase most difficult. Also *attrib.* 2. A soft leather, orig. prepared from the skin of the chamois, now also from the skins of sheep, goats, deer, etc. More fully *chamois-* (*shamoy-*, *shammy-*) *leather.* See SHAMMY. 1575. *attrib.* as a material 1603. 3. Of the colour of this leather, fawn-coloured (*mod.*). Hence **Chamois** *v.* [F. *chamoiser*] to prepare leather in imitation of c.-leather.

Chamoisite (ʃæ·mwăzəit). 1832. [f. *Chamoison*, in the Valais.] *Min.* A hydrous silicate of iron often occurring in grains.

Chamomile, -mel, vars. of CAMOMILE.

†**Champ**, *sb.*[1] ME. [a. F. *champ* :—L. *campum*; cf. CAMP *sb.*[2]] 1. A field -1816. 2. *Her.* The field of a shield -ME. 3. The ground, as in embroidery, painting, etc. 1573.

1. *Champ clos*, *c. of battle*: the ground enclosed for a judicial duel, or tourney; also, a battle-field.

Champ (tʃæmp), *sb.*[2] 1604. [f. CHAMP *v.*] 1. The action of champing. *dial.* Appetite. 2. *dial.* Anything champed or mashed 1825.

Champ (tʃæmp), *sb.*[3] 1830. [ad. Hindī *champa* = CHAMPAC.] The timber of the Champac tree. Also *champ-wood*.

Champ (tʃæmp), *v.* 1530. [perh. echoic; cf. JAM.] 1. To chew by vigorous and noisy action of the jaws; to munch. Also *fig.* 2. To bite upon (anything hard) 1577. *intr.* and *absol.* 1558. †3. To gnash (the teeth), close the jaws with violence and noise -1791. 4. *Sc.* To crash, mash, pound; to trample underfoot 1788.

1. Champing golden grain the horses stood TENNYSON. 2. To c. the bit GODWIN, a bullet 1655. *absol.* The war-horse..Champs SCOTT.

Champac (tʃæ·mpăk, tʃʊ·mpʊk). 1770. [a. Hind. *champak*.] A species of Magnolia (*Michelia Champaca*), an Indian tree, bearing orange-coloured highly fragrant flowers.

The Champak odours fail SHELLEY.

Champagne (ʃæmpē·n). 1664. [See CHAMPAIGN, CAMPAIGN.] A province of eastern France; hence, a well-known wine, white and red, and still or sparkling, made in this district. Also *attrib.*

French kick-shaws, cellery, and Champain 1688.

Champaign (tʃæ·mpēn; occas., in the 19th c. only, tʃæmpē·n). [ME. *champayne*, *champaigne*, a. OF. *champaigne* :—L. *Campania*, f. *campus*. See also CAMPAIGN.]

A. *sb.* 1. An expanse of level, open country. †2. Unenclosed or common land -1649. †3. The field of military operations -1665. 4. *transf.* and *fig.* 1596.

1. Looking round the c. wide KEATS. (Without *pl.* or *article*): Fair Champain with less rivers interveind MILT. *P. R.* III. 257. (With *the*; without *pl.*): Where the mountains sink down upon the c. SCOTT. 4. Through Heav'ns wide champain MILT. *P. L.* VI. 2.

B. *adj.* (or *sb.* used *attrib.*) 1. Of the nature of a champaign; level and open 1523. 3. Field-; of champaign land 1599.

†**Champain.** 1562. [cf. F. *champagne* field.] *Her.* A broken or deflected line in an ordinary –1708.

‖**Champart** (ʃanpar). 1651. [a. F. *champart*, in ONF. *campart* :—L. *campi pars.*] A form of tenure, in which the landlord receives a fixed share of the produce. Still in use in the Channel Islands.

Champed, *ppl. a.*¹ In senses of CHAMP *v.*

†**Champed,** *ppl. a.*² *Sc.* **champit.** 1501. [? f. CHAMP 'ground'.] Having raised figures; embossed, diapered. (Jam.)

Champer (tʃæ·mpəɹ). 1599. [f. CHAMP *v.* + -ER¹. One who or that which champs, chews, or mashes.

†**Cha·mpertor.** 1500. [a. Anglo-F. *champartour*, f. *champarter* vb., f. CHAMPART.] One guilty of champerty –1668.

Cha·mpertous *a.* Of the nature of champerty.

Champerty (tʃæ·mpəɹti). ME. [Prop. *champarty*: a deriv. of CHAMPART.] †1. Division of lordship –1532. 2. *Law.* The illegal proceeding, whereby a party not naturally concerned in a suit engages to help one of the litigants to prosecute it, on condition that, in the event of success, he is to receive a share of the property in dispute ME.; an act or case of champerty 1450. Also *fig.*

1. Thus may ye seen þat wysdom ne richesse .. Ne may with Venus holde champartie CHAUCER. ¶ Lydgate, followed by others, took this phrase to mean 'to hold contest *against*, resist'.

†**Champian, -ion,** *a.* and *sb.* 1523. A var. of CHAMPAIGN, -PAIN, in all senses and constructions –1751.

Champignon, -pinion (tʃæmpi·niən, ʃæm-). 1578. [a. F. *champignon* :—L. **campinionem*, f. *campus.*] orig. Fungi or mushrooms generally; in 18th c. edible mushrooms, esp. *Agaricus campestris*; subseq. only the Fairy Ring Agaric.

Champine, var. of CHAMPAIGN, etc.

Champion (tʃæ·mpiən), *sb.*¹ [ME. *champiun, -on*, a. OF. :—late L. *campio, -onem* combatant in the *campus*, f. L. *campus*; see CAMP *sb.*¹, ².] 1. A fighting man; a stout fighter. Also *fig.* 2. One who fights on behalf of another, or of any cause ME.; one who fights in 'wager of battle' in his own cause 1593. *fig.* and *transf.* ME. 3. One who has defeated all opponents in any trial of strength or skill, and is open to contend with any new competitor 1825; used *transf.* of animals, plants, etc. (*mod.*). Also *attrib.*

1. A stouter C. neuer handled Sword 1 *Hen. VI*, III. iv. 19. 2. God will raise me up a c. SCOTT. To heauen, the widdowes C. *Rich. II*, I. ii. 43. The c. of vaccination 1806. 3. Five tons of Scotch Champions 1880. *attrib.* C. fighting-cock 1860, lode 1880, pugilist 1887. Hence **Cha·mpioness**, a female c. **Cha·mpionless** *a.*

Champion, *sb.*² and *a.*; see CHAMPIAN.

Champion (tʃæ·mpiən), *v.* 1605. [f. prec. sb.] †1. To challenge to a contest (*rare*) –1821. 2. To fight for; to defend or protect as champion 1820. Also *fig.*

1. *Macb.* III. i. 72. 2. Championed or unchampioned, thou diest by the stake and fagot SCOTT. *fig.* To c. a cause 1844, an idea DICKENS.

Championize (tʃæ·mpiənəiz), *v. rare.* 1598. [See -IZE.] †*intr.* To play the champion –1637; *trans.* to act as champion of 1840.

Championship (tʃæ·mpiənʃip). 1825. [f. CHAMPION.] 1. The position or office of a champion; advocacy, defence 1840. 2. The position of champion in any contest or trial 1825. Also *attrib.*

Chance (tʃɑns), *sb.* [ME. *chea(u)nce*, a. OF. *cheance* :—late L. *cadentia* falling; cf. CADENCE.] 1. The happening of events; the way in which things fall out; fortune; case; a fortuitous circumstance; = ACCIDENT 1 b. 2. (with *pl.*) A fortuitous event or occurrence; often a mischance (*arch.*) ME. †3. (One's) hap, luck, lot –1674. 4. An opportunity ME. 5. A possibility or probability: as distinct from a certainty. *Math.* = PROBABILITY; so also *theory* or *doctrine of chances.* 1778. 6. Absence of design or assignable cause, fortuity; often spoken of as a cause of events; = ACCIDENT 2. 1526.

1. The c. of war Is equal, and the slayer oft is slain BRYANT. It was a c. that happened to vs *Sam.* vi. 9. 2. All the changes and chances of this mortal life *Bk. Com. Prayer.* 3. *Twel. N.* III. iv. 177. 4. A change of climate is his only c. BURKE. 5. The chances are a hundred to one that [etc.] EMERSON.

Phrases. *By chance*: As it falls or fell out; without design. *On the c.*: acting on the possibility (*of* or *that*..); see sense 5. *To take one's c.*: to take what may befall one, to risk it; to seize one's opportunity (see sense 4). *The main c.*: †a. the paramount issue; b. that which is of chief importance; now *esp.* the chance of gain, one's own interests. (A cant phrase; see further under MAIN.) *To stand a (good, fair) c.*: see STAND.

B. *attrib.* or *adj.* That occurs or is by chance; casual, incidental 1676.

C. as *adv.* By chance, haply 1595.

Comb. (cf. B), = by chance, casual, -ly; as *c.-comer*; also **-child**, an illegitimate child; **-wise** *adv.*

Chance (tʃɑns), *v.* ME. [f. prec. sb.] 1. *intr.* To come about by chance. (Often with *it* preceding the vb., and the subject cl. following it (*arch.*).) 2. To happen to come (*on* or *upon*). Somewhat *arch.* 1536. †3. To speed, have luck –1553. 4. *trans.* To risk, take one's chance of (*colloq.*) 1859. ¶ In *How chance* = 'how chances it that', *chance* takes no inflection, and is almost an adv. *Merry W.* V. v. 230.

1. Bare graine, it may c. of wheat 1 *Cor.* xv. 37. 2. Wee chanced on a .. shippe .. bound for Callis 1630. 4. We'll c. it A. R. HOPE.

Chanceable (tʃɑ·nsăb'l), *a. arch.* 1549. [f. prec.] Fortuitous. Hence **Cha·nceableness. Cha·nceably** *adv.*

Chanceful (tʃɑ·nsful), *a.* 1591. [f. CHANCE *sb.*] Dependent on chance (*arch.*) 1594; †risky –1610; eventful 1849. Hence **Cha·ncefully** *adv.*

Chancel (tʃɑ·nsĕl). ME. [a. OF. *chancel* :—late L. *cancellus*, f. L. *cancelli* bars of lattice-work.] The eastern part of a church, appropriated to the use of the officiating clergy, and separated from the other parts by a screen, railing, etc. Also †*transf.* of the temple at Jerusalem, heathen temples, etc. *Comb.* **c.-table**, a communion-table. Hence **Cha·ncelled** *pa. pple.* and *ppl. a.* placed in, or having, a c.

Chancellery, -ory (tʃɑ·nsĕləri). ME. [a. OF. *chancel(l)erie*, f. *chancelier* CHANCELLOR. Contracted to *chancelry*, CHANCERY; also, refash. as †*cha·ncellary.*] 1. The position or dignity of a chancellor. 2. A chancellor's court or office, with its officials 1803. 3. The office of a court secretary or notary 1683. 4. The office attached to an embassy or consulate 1869. 5. The building or room occupied by the chancellor's office 1831.

4. The Chancelleries of the Great Powers 1881.

Chancellor (tʃɑ·nsĕləɹ). [ME. and AFr. *canceler, chanceler*, a. OF. *cancelier, chancelier* :—L. *cancellarius* usher of a law court, who was stationed *ad cancellos* at the *bar* of a basilica or other law court. In late OE. *canceler.* See -OR.]

[In the Eastern Empire this officer had risen to be a secretary or notary, and, later, had judicial functions. Edward the Confessor introduced the office into England, and its importance increased under the Norman Kings. From the Roman Empire the office also passed into the Church.]

I. *gen.* Secretary, official secretary: †a. of the King of England –1500; b. of ancient potentates ME.; c. of great lords SHAKS. Occas. used as repr. Fr. *chancelier*, the chief secretary of an embassy 1788.

II. Mod. uses.

1. *Chancellor of England*, also called *Lord C.*, and *Lord High C.*: orig. the *King's C.*, or official Secretary (see I). He is the highest judicial functionary in England, and ranks after princes of the blood and the archbishop of Canterbury; he is keeper of the Great Seal, is styled 'Keeper of the King's conscience', and is prolocutor of the House of Lords; he presides in the Chancery Division of the Supreme Court; appoints all justices of the peace; is the general guardian of infants, lunatics, and idiots; etc. OE.

2. *C. of the Exchequer*: the highest finance minister of the British government; historically, he is the under-treasurer of the Exchequer ME.

3. *C. of the Duchy of Lancaster*: a minister of the crown, who presides in the Duchy Court of Lancaster, deciding on all matters of equity connected with lands held of the crown in that Duchy 1553.

4. *C. of a chapter*: a. *of a cathedral*: one of the four chief dignitaries in the cathedrals of old foundation. He applies the seal, writes letters, etc. 1578; b. *of an order of Knighthood*: the officer who seals the commissions and mandates of the chapter and assembly of the knights, keeps the register, and delivers their acts under the seal of their order 1577.

5. The titular head of a university. The actual duties are performed in the English Universities by a *Vice-C.*, appointed from the Heads of Colleges. ME.

6. In *Scotland*, the foreman of a jury 1762.

III. In foreign countries.

1. Most of the European countries have or formerly had a chief minister with this title; it was abolished in France at the Revolution; it is retained in Austro-Hungary from the Holy Roman Empire, and is used in the new German Empire, as title of the President of the Federal Council, who has the general conduct of the imperial administration.

2. *U. S.* The title of certain judges of courts of chancery or equity, established by the statutes of separate states.

Hence **Cha·ncellorate, Cha·ncellorship**, the office of c.

Chance-medley (tʃɑ·ns,me·dli). 1494. [a. AF. *chance medlée* (var. of *meslée*) mixed chance; see CHANCE and MEDDLE.] 1. *Law.* Casualty not *purely* accidental, but of a mixed character. Also *fig.* 2. Haphazard action into which chance largely enters. (*Erron.* put for 'pure chance', and for 'a fortuitous medley'.) 1583. Also *attrib.*

1. *Manslaughter by chance-medley* (called later *chance-medley*): homicide by misadventure. 2. Left to the guidance of unreason and chance medley JOWETT.

Chancery (tʃɑ·nsĕri). ME. [A worn-down form of *chancelry, chancelery*, CHANCELLERY.] †1. Chancellorship –1658. 2. The court of the Lord Chancellor of England, the highest court of judicature next to the House of Lords; but, since 1873, a division of the High Court of Justice ME. b. Applied to similar courts elsewhere; in U. S. 'a court of Equity' (Webster) 1555. c. An office in the General Register House, Edinburgh (formerly called *chancellary*), in which is kept a record of writs, crown charters, etc. 1807. Also *fig.* 3. A court of record; archives; also *fig.* 1523. 4. = CHANCELLERY 2. 1561. 5. = CHANCELLERY 5. 1578. 6. *Pugilism.* (From the control of the Court of Chancery, and the certainty of cost and loss to property 'in chancery'.) The position of the head when held under the opponent's left arm to be pommelled; hence *fig.* an awkward predicament. 1832.

2. The heiress is a ward in C. (*mod.*). 6. He'll not 'put his head in chancery', that's clear MARRYAT.

Chancre (ʃæ·nkəɹ). 1605. [a. F. *chancre* :—L. *cancer* crab. Cf. CANCER, CANKER.] A venereal ulcer. Hence **Cha·ncriform** *a.* of the form or nature of a c. **Cha·ncrous** *a.*

Chancroid (ʃæ·ŋkroid), *sb.* 1861. [f. prec. + -OID.] A synonym of *soft chancre.* Also *attrib.*

Chancy (tʃɑ·nsi), *a.* 1513. [f. CHANCE *sb.* + -Y¹.] 1. *Sc.* Lucky. 2. *Sc.* Lucky to meddle with; 'canny' 1774. 3. Uncertain, risky, untrustworthy (*colloq.*) 1860. Hence **Cha·nciness**, casual quality.

Chandelier (ʃændĕlīᵊ·ɹ). 1663. [mod. a. F.; see CHANDLER.] 1. An ornamental branched support to hold a number of lights (originally candles), usu. hung from the ceiling 1736. 2. *Mil.* 'A wooden frame, which was filled with fascines, to form a traverse in sapping' (Stocqueler) 1663. Also *attrib.*

Chandler (tʃɑ·ndləɹ). [ME. *chaundeler, chandeler*, a. AF. *chandeler* :—L. type *candel(l)arius*, f. *candel(l)a* CANDLE.] †1. A candlestick; a chandelier. (Chiefly *north.*) –1733. 2. One who makes or sells candles ME. 3. Hence, A retailer of provisions, groceries, etc.: often contemptuous. In *comb.* = dealer, as in CORN-, SHIP-CHANDLER. 1583.

3. Another steps into the chandler's shop, to purchase a pound of butter SCOTT. Hence **Cha·ndlerly** *a.* c.-like, pertaining to a c. MILT. †**Cha·ndling** *vbl. sb.* the business of a c. (*rare*).

Chandlery (tʃɑ·ndləri). 1601. [f. CHANDLER + -Y; cf. *bakery.*] 1. A place where candles, etc., are kept. 2. The commodities sold by a chandler (also in pl. *chandleries*) 1601.

‖**Chandoo, -du** (tʃændū·). 1847. [Hindī.] A preparation of opium used in China for smoking.

†**Cha·ndry.** 1478. [Contr. f. *chandlery*; cf.

chancery.] 1. = CHANDLERY 1. –1668. 2. = CHANDLERY 2. 1651. 3. Candlemas 1478.

||**Chanfrin** (ʃãnfrẽn). 1730. [a. F. *chanfrein*; cf. CHAMFRON.] The fore-part of a horse's head. (Dicts.)

Change (tʃēⁱndʒ), *sb.* ME. [a. AF. *chaunge*, OF. *change* :—late L. *cambium*, f. *cambire* to CHANGE.] 1. The act or fact of changing (see CHANGE *v.* 1, 2); substitution or succession of one thing in place of another; substitution of other conditions, variety. †2. Exchange, *esp.* of merchandise –1606. 3. A place where merchants meet for the transaction of business, an exchange. (Since 1800, erron. written *'Change*, as if for *Exchange.*) ME. 4. Alteration in the state or quality of anything; variation, mutation ME. 5. That which is or may be substituted for another of the same kind. (In this sense occas. with pl. *change.*) 1592. 6. Money given in exchange for coins, notes, etc., of another kind; hence generally, small money. Hence, the balance returned when anything is paid for by a piece of money greater than its price. 1622. *slang.* Something given or taken in return, as in *take your c. out of that!* (*mod.*). 7. *spec.* in *pl.* †a. *Math.* Permutations –1751. b. *Bell-ringing.* The different orders in which a peal of bells may be rung 1669. 8. *Sc.* An alehouse; =CHANGE-HOUSE 1730.

1. C. of Consuls COWLEY. Our fathers did, for c., to France repair DRYDEN. I waite, till my c. come *Job* xiv. 14. † *To put the c. upon*: to deceive, mislead (a person). 2. *Much Ado* IV. i. 185. 4. C. is the law of organic life 1858. *Lear* I. i. 291. *C. of life*: the period in the life of a woman when menstruation is about to cease. The changes of the Moone *Oth.* III. iii. 178. 5. Thirtie sheetes, and thirtie c. of garments *Judg.* xiv. 12. 6. C. for a guinea SHERIDAN. No c. given (*mod.*). 7. Four bells admit twenty-four changes in ringing HOLDER.

Phr. *To ring the changes* (sense 7): *fig.* to go through all the possible variations of any process, set of words, argument, etc. (Constr. *on, upon*; now usu. contemptuous.) (*b.*) *slang.* To substitute bad money for good. *Comb.* **c.-wheel**, one of a set having varying numbers of cogs of the same pitch, used to connect the main arbor of the lathe with the feed-screw.

Change (tʃēⁱndʒ), *v.* [ME. *changen*, a. OF. *changer*:—late L. *cambiare*; used for cl. L. *cambire*: perh. cogn. w. Gr. καμπ- to bend.] 1. *trans.* To put or take another (or others) instead of; *spec.* to give or procure money of another kind in exchange for. *intr.* To change one's clothes (*colloq.*) 1634. 2. With pl. obj.: To quit one and take another, as *to change carriages* 1670. Also *intr.* or *ellipt.* 3. *trans.* To give and receive reciprocally, interchange. (Now repl. by *exchange*, exc. *dial.*, *arch.*, and *poet.*, and in 'change places', etc.) 4. *intr.* To make an exchange 1567. 5. *trans.* To render different, alter, transmute. Also with *into* or *to.* ME. 6. *intr.* (for *refl.*) To become different, alter. Also with *into* or *to.* ME. Of the moon: (*a*) To pass through her phases. (*b*) To pass through the phase of new moon; occas. of full moon. ME. †*spec.* To change countenance. SHAKS. 7. *intr.* To be shifted or transferred (*rare*; occas. with *about, over,* etc.) ME.

1. To c. one's things 1805, a Rauen for a Doue *Mids. N.* II. ii. 114, a guinea SCOTT, English gold BURNABY. *intr.* After dinner I..washed and changed COLERIDGE. 3. Wilt thou c. Fathers *A.Y.L.* I. iii. 93. I scorn to c. my state †*with kings* (*i.e.* with that of kings) SHAKS. 4. But might I of Jove's nectar sip I would not c. for thine B. JONS. 5. To c. one's purpose PALEY. To c. (or *turn*) milk (*colloq.*). 6. I am the Lord, I c. not *Malachi* iii. 6. And every winter c. to spring TENNYSON.

Phrases. *To c. arms*: (*Mil.*) to shift the rifle from one shoulder to the other. *To c. front*: (orig. *Mil.*) to face in another direction; usu. *fig.* *To c. hands* (see sense 2): to pass from one person's possession to another's. *To c. hand* or *c. a horse*: (*Horsemanship*) to turn the horse's head from right to left or *vice versa.* *To c. one's note* or *tune*: to alter one's manner of speaking, to speak more respectfully (*colloq.*). *To c. sides*: see sense 2. *To chop and c.*: see CHOP *v.*[2]

Changeable (tʃēⁱndʒăb'l), *a.* ME. [a. F., f. *changer* to CHANGE; see -ABLE.] 1. That may change or be changed (by others); subject to change; mutable, variable, inconstant. 2. Showing different colours in different aspects; shot, changing-coloured (*arch.*) 1480. Also as *sb.* [sc. *person* or *thing.*] (*rare.*)

1. C. weather (*mod.*), places of meeting D'ISRAELI. 2. C. sylke 1550. Hence **Changeabi·lity, Cha·ngeableness**, the quality of being c. **Cha·ngeably** *adv.* in a c. or changing manner.

Changeful (tʃēⁱ·ndʒful), *a.* 1606. [f. CHANGE *sb.* + -FUL.] Full of change; variable, inconstant. (Chiefly *poet.*)

The c. year KEBLE. **Cha·ngeful-ly** *adv.*, **-ness.**

Cha·nge-house. *Sc.* 1620. [f. the sbs.] A small inn or alehouse. (Perh. a wayside inn at which horses were changed.)

Changeless (tʃēⁱ·ndʒlės), *a.* 1580. [f. CHANGE *sb.* + -LESS.] Without change, unchanging, immutable.

Changelesse fate HEALEY. **Cha·ngeless-ly** *adv.*, **-ness.**

Changeling (tʃēⁱ·ndʒliŋ), *sb.* (*a.*) 1555. [dim. of CHANGE *sb.*] 1. One given to change; a waverer, turncoat (*arch.*). 2. A person (*esp.* a child) or thing (surreptitiously) put in exchange for another 1561. Also *attrib.* 3. A half-witted person (*arch.*) 1642. †4. *adj.* Variable –1702.

1. That c. the Moon HOWELL. 2. *Haml.* V. ii. 53. Such, men do chaungelings call, so chaung'd by Faeries theft SPENSER. *attrib.* A little c. boy *Mids. N.* II. i. 120. 3. Just like a fool or c. PEPYS.

Cha·ngement. *rare.* 1584. [a. F.] Change.

Changer (tʃēⁱ·ndʒəɹ). [ME. *changeour*, a. OF. *changeor* (mod.F. *changeur*):—late L. **cambiatorem*; also immed. f. CHANGE *v.*] 1. One who or that which changes anything; see CHANGE *v.* 1, 5. †2. A money-changer –1611. 3. An inconstant person (*rare*) 1605.

Chank (tʃæŋk). 1698. [a. Hindī.] A large kind of shell (*Turbinella rapa*) used by the Hindus for offering libations, etc., and for cutting into ornaments. Also *attrib.*

Channel (tʃæ·nĕl), *sb.*[1] [ME. *chanel*, a. OF. :—L. *canalem*; see CANAL.]

I. 1. The hollow bed of running waters; also, the bed of the sea, etc. †2. A stream –1705. 3. A gutter. (Still common locally.) ME. 4. *Geog.* A piece of water, somewhat wider than a strait, connecting two larger pieces, usually seas 1553. *The Channel*: *spec.* the English Channel (Fr. *La Manche*). †5. = CANAL –1683. 6. A tube or tubular passage, usually for liquids or fluids ME.

1. Flye from thy chanell Thames 1563. 3. Overturned in the c. as we were going to the playhouse VANBRUGH.

II. *fig.* from I. 1. Course in which anything moves outward; line of action, thought, etc. 1631. 2. That through which information, news, trade, etc. passes; means, agency 1537.

1. The world went on in the old c. SWIFT. 2. The great Channels of Trade 1719.

III. *transf.* 1. A groove or furrow; *spec.* in *Arch.* a fluting of a column 1682. †2. The neck; the throat. (Cf. CANNEL-BONE.) –1590. 3. *Sc.* Gravel 1743.

Comb.: **c.-bill**, an Australian bird, *Scythrops Novæ Hollandiæ*; †**-bone** = CANNEL-BONE; **-stone**, a stone used in paving gutters.

Cha·nnel, *sb.*[2] 1769. [corrupt f. *chain-wale*; cf. *gunwale* (gɒ·nĕl).] *Naut.* One of the broad thick planks projecting horizontally from the ship's side, nearly abreast of the masts.

Comb.: **c.-plate** = *chain-plate*; **-wale**, one of the strakes worked between the gun-deck and the upper deck ports of large ships.

Channel (tʃæ·nĕl), *v.* 1596. [f. CHANNEL *sb.*[1]] 1. *trans.* To form channels in; to wear or cut into channels; to furrow, groove. 2. To cut out as a channel 1816. 3. To convey through or as through a channel 1648. †4. *intr.* To pass by (or as by) a channel –1664.

1. No more shall trenching Warre channell her fields 1 *Hen. IV*, I. i. 7.

Channelled, -eled (tʃæ·nĕld), *ppl. a.* 1567. [f. CHANNEL *sb.*[1] and *v.*] 1. Having channels or grooves; having a gutter; in *Bot.* =CANALICULATE. 2. Conveyed along a channel; formed with a channel 1796.

Cha·nnelling, -eling, *vbl. sb.* 1580. [f. as prec.] 1. Channelled work; grooving. 2. Making of channels; providing with a gutter 1885.

Cha·nnelly, -ely, *a. Obs.* exc. *Sc.* 1615. [f. CHANNEL *sb.*[1] III. 3.] Gravelly.

Cha·nnelure. = CANNELURE.

||**Chanson** (ʃãnsoñ). [Fr. :—L. *cantionem.*] A song (French, or of France). *Haml.* II. ii. 438.

||**Chansonette** (ʃansone·t). 1813. [Fr.; dim. of prec.] A little song.

The Miller's maid Colette Sung, while he supped, her c. S. ROGERS.

Chant (tʃɑnt), *sb.* Also **chaunt.** 1671. [? a. F. :—L. *cantum*, or immed. f. the vb.] 1. A song, a melody; singing. *poet.* (and in rogues' cant). 2. *Mus.* A short melody or phrase to which the Psalms, Canticles, etc., are sung in public worship 1789; a psalm, etc., so chanted 1856. 3. A measured monotonous song; the musical recitation of words 1815; a distinctive intonation 1848.

1. C. of tuneful birds MILT. *P. R.* II. 290. 3. The low monotonous c. of an Arab party 1882.

The *Anglican c.* (derived from the old Gregorian) is either single or double. A *single c.* is sung to one verse of a psalm, and consists of two strains, of 3 and 4 bars respectively, each beginning with a reciting-note. A *double c.* has twice the length of a single one, and is sung to two verses.

Chant (tʃɑnt), *v.* ME. [a. F. *chanter* :—L. *cantare*, freq. of *canere.*] 1. *intr.* To sing, warble (*arch.* or *poet.*). Also *transf.* 2. *trans.* To utter musically. Chiefly *poet.* 1588. 3. To celebrate in song. *poet.* 1583. 4. *Mus.* To recite musically, intone; to sing to a CHANT (sense 2). *intr.* ME.; *trans.* 1526. 5. *fig.* To talk monotonously 1572. 6. *slang.* (*trans.*) To cry up (a horse) fraudulently 1816.

1. To c. to the sound of the viol *Amos* vi. 5. 2. [The wild swan] chanted a melody loud and sweet TENNYSON. 5. To c. of prerogatives MILT. To c. the praises of the Darwinian system 1885. Hence **Cha·ntable** *a.*

||**Chantage** (ʃãnta·ʒ, tʃɑ·ntėdʒ). 1874. [Fr.] A mode of extorting money by threatening to make scandalous revelations.

||**Chantant** (ʃãntañ, tʃɑ·ntănt), *a.* 1789. [a. F.] Of a singing style, melodious, tuneful.

†||**Chantepleure.** ME. only. [Fr.] Name of a French poem addressed to those who sing in this world and shall weep in the next; hence, a mixture of joy and sorrow.

Chanter (tʃɑ·ntəɹ). [ME. and AF. *chauntour* :—L. *cantatorem.* In sense 1, ? aphet. f. ENCHANTER.] †1. A magician. ME. only. 2. One who chants or sings; a chorister; a precentor ME. 3. The finger-pipe of a bagpipe, on which the melody is played 1631. 4. The Hedge-sparrow (*Accentor modularis*) 1865. 6. One who sells horses fraudulently. Hence **Cha·ntership**, the office of a c.

||**Chanterelle**[1]. 1601. [a. F., It. *cantarella* treble string.] †1. A decoy bird. 2. The highest string of a musical instrument 1878.

Chanterelle[2] (tʃɑ·ntėre·l). 1775. [a. F.: in mod.L. *cantharellus*, dim. of *cantharus.*] The edible fungus *Cantharellus cibarius.*

Chant(e)y. var. ff. of SHANTY[2].

Chanticleer (tʃɑ·ntiklīəɹ). ME. [a. OF. *chantecler* (mod.F. *chanteclair*), name of the Cock in *Reynard the Fox.*] A proper name applied to a cock; but now mostly written without a capital. (Cf. *Bruin*, etc.)

Sche had a cok hight Chaunticlere CHAUCER.

||**Chantier.** 1880. [Canadian Fr.] SHANTY[2].

Chantress (tʃɑ·ntrės). ME. [a. OF. *chanteresse*; see CHANTER and -ESS.] †1. A female magician. ME. only. 2. A female chanter or singer; also of birds, etc. (*arch.* or *poet.*) 1450.

Chantry (tʃɑ·ntri). [ME. *chaunterie*, a. OF. *chanterie*, f. *chanter.*] †1. Chanting (of the mass). ME. only. †2. Incantation –1460. 3. An endowment for the maintenance of priests to sing masses, usually for the soul of the founder. Also, the body of priests so endowed. ME. b. A chapel or altar so endowed ME.

Chaos (kēⁱ·ǫs). ME. [a. L., a. Gr. χάος, f. vb.-stem χα- to yawn, gape.] †1. A gaping void, yawning gulf, chasm, or abyss –1667. 2. The 'formless void' of primordial matter 1531. b. *personified.* 1651. 3. *transf.* and *fig.* A state of utter confusion and disorder 1606; a confused mass 1579. †4. An amorphous lump –1593. †5. ? Element –1753.

1. Betweene us and you there is fixed a great chaos N.T. (*Rhem.*) *Luke* xvi. 26. 2. In the Beginning how the Heav'ns and Earth Rose out of C. MILT. *P. L.* I. 10. 4. 3 *Hen. VI*, III. ii. 161.

Chaotic, -al (keiǫ·tik, -ăl), *a.* 1713. [f. CHAOS + -IC, + -AL.] Of, pertaining to, or resembling chaos; utterly confused or disordered. Hence **Chao·tically** *adv.*

Chap (tʃæp), *sb.*[1] ME. [f. CHAP *v.*[1]] 1. An open fissure or crack; *esp.* a crack in the skin, descending to the flesh. Also *fig.* **2.** A stroke, knock, rap. *Sc.* and *n. dial.* 1785.

Chap (tʃæp), *sb.*[2] 1555. [? f. CHAP, CHOP.] **1.** Either of the two bones (with its covering of flesh, etc.) which form the jaw; in *pl.* the jaws as forming the mouth; used of animals, and colloq. of human beings. **2.** The cheek 1708. **3.** The lower jaw 1846. †**4.** *pl. Mech.* The jaws of a vice, etc. -1831.

1. Open your chaps againe *Temp.* II. ii. 89. 2. She threatned to slap my chaps 1708. *Chaps of the Channel*: see CHOP *sb.* Hence **Cha·pless** *a.* without the lower jaw.

Chap (tʃæp), *sb.*[3] 1577. [Abbrev. f. CHAPMAN.] **1.** A buyer, customer. Still *dial.* **2.** *colloq.* 'Customer', fellow, lad. (Now chiefly of young men.) 1716.

1. Perhaps Mrs. Mead would buy .. but she would be a hard c. WILKES.

Chap (tʃæp), *v.*[1] [ME. *chappen*; cf. later MDu. *cappen*, also CHIP.] †**1.** (with *off*). To chop *off.* ME. only. **2.** To crack or cause to crack in fissures ME. **3.** To strike, to rap at a door. *n. dial.* 1565. **4.** *Sc.* To choose 1720.

2. Chapped with the winters blast LYLY. 3. *To c. hands*: to strike hands in concluding a bargain. Till the hour c. 1652.

Chap, *v.*[2] *dial.* [OE. *cēapian.*] To buy; to buy and sell; to truck. Cf. CHEAP, CHOP.

‖**Chaparejos** (tʃæpărē·hōus). 1861. [Mex. Sp.] Trousers worn by cowboys as a protection against thorny bushes (cf. next). Abbrev. **Chaps.**

‖**Chaparral** (tʃæpăræ·l). *U.S.* 1850. [a. Sp., f. *chaparra, -arro* evergreen oak.] *prop.* A thicket of low evergreen oaks; hence *gen.* Dense tangled brushwood, as in Mexico and Texas.

C. cock: a species of cuckoo (*Geococcyx californianus*) in the west of North America.

Chap-book (tʃæ·pˌbuk). 1824. [f. *chap* in CHAPMAN.] A small pamphlet of popular tales, ballads, tracts, etc., as hawked by chapmen.

Chape (tʃēɪp), *sb.* ME. [a. F. *chape*, f. late L. *capa, cappa* hood, cape, whence Sp. and Pg. *chapa* thin piece of metal for plating anything.] †**1.** A plate of metal with which anything is overlaid. ME. only. **2.** The metal plate of a scabbard; *esp.* that which covers the point ME. (See also N.E.D.) **3.** The tip of a fox's tail 1677. **4.** The part of a buckle by which it is fastened to a strap. [So in F.] 1679. Hence **Cha·peless** *a.* wanting a sheath. SHAKS.

Chape, *v.* ME. [f. prec.] To furnish a scabbard, etc., with a chape. CHAUCER.

‖**Chapeau** (ʃapō). 1523. [F., in OF. *capel, chapel*:—L. *cappellum*, dim. of *cappa* CAP.] A covering for the head. Now chiefly in *Her.*

Chapeau-bras (ʃapō brā): a small three-cornered flat silk hat which could be carried under the arm: worn by gentlemen at court or in full dress in 18th c.

Chapel (tʃæ·pĕl), *sb.* [ME. *chapele*, a. OF. *chapele*:—med.L. *cappella*, dim. of *cappa*, cloak, cape, cope (see CAP). From the *cappella* or cloak of St. Martin, the name was applied to the sanctuary in which this was kept under the care of its *cappellani* or chaplains, and thence generally to a sanctuary, and ult. to a building for worship, not being a church. The earlier name for a church was *Oratorium*, ORATORY.] **1.** *gen.* A place of Christian worship, not being a parish or cathedral church; an oratory. **2.** *spec.* A private place of worship ME. **3.** A place of public worship of the Established Church, subordinate to, or dependent upon, the church of the parish (see quots.) 1491. **4.** Used of places of Christian worship other than those of the established church of the country 1662. (Now 'church' is used for 'chapel' by Roman Catholics, Scotch Episcopalians, and many Nonconformists.) **5.** A chapel service 1662. **6.** *gen.* A lesser temple, fane, or sanctuary, having an altar to a deity ME. **7.** A body of singers attached to a chapel (usu. of a king or prince) ME. **8.** The sacred vessels, etc., used in a church or chapel. Now *Hist.* **9.** A printing-office; an association of the journeymen in a printing-office. Hence *to hold a c.*, to have a meeting of the association. 1688.

2. The c. of the Castle WALPOLE, of New College EVELYN. *Mortuary c.*: an oratory in a mausoleum, burial vault or aisle, etc., having an altar for masses for the soul of the deceased (*chantry c.*). Hence, a compartment of a cathedral, etc. (usu. in the aisle), separately dedicated and having its own altar. *Lady-c.*: see LADY. 3. *C. of ease*: one built for the use of parishioners who live far from the parish church. *Parochial c.*: that of an ancient division of a parish attached to it by custom and repute; now usually called CHURCH. *Free c.*: one founded by the king, and not subject to the jurisdiction of the ordinary. 5. *To keep a c.*: to attend chapel once. So to *miss, lose a c.*

Comb. **c.-master**, occas. tr. of Fr. *maître de chapelle* or Ger. *Kapellmeister*, director of the music of a royal (or other) c. (sense 7). Hence **Cha·pel** *v.*[1] *nonce-wd.* To put (bury, etc.) in a c. **Cha·pel** *v.*[2] *Naut.* To turn a ship round in a light breeze when close-hauled, so as to make her lie as she did before. **Cha·pelwa·rden**, now 'churchwarden'.

†**Cha·pelet**[1]. 1587. [f. prec.] A little CHAPEL -1675.

Chapelet[2] (tʃæ·pĕlĕt). 1753. [a. F. *chapelet* CHAPLET.] **1.** A pair of stirrup leathers, with stirrups, buckled together, and fastened to the pommel of the saddle. **2.** A chain pump with buckets attached to an endless chain passing over two axles. So called in French from its likeness to a rosary. 1874.

†**Cha·pelize,** *v.* To make into a chapel. FULLER.

Cha·pellage. *rare.* = CHAPELRY 2. Scott.

Cha·pellany. ? *Obs. rare.* 1726. [a. F. *chapellenie* benefice of a chaplain.] = CHAPELRY.

Chapelry (tʃæ·pĕlri). 1591. [a. OF. *chapelerie.*] **1.** The district attached to a chapel. **2.** A chapel with its precinct, etc.; a chapel-stead 1817.

Chaperon (ʃæ·pĕrǫ̆n, -ōᵘn). ME. [a. F., dim. of *chape* cape, cope (cf. *moucheron*, f. *mouche*).] **1.** A hood or cap. Now *Hist.* †**2.** A small escutcheon placed (*esp.*) on the forehead of a horse drawing a hearse -1783. **3.** *fig.* A person, *esp.* a married woman, who, for the sake of propriety, accompanies a young unmarried lady in public, as guide and protector 1720. Also *transf.*

1. *C.*, the Hood anciently worn by the Knights of the Garter PHILLIPS. Hence **Cha·peronage**, attendance as c.

Chaperon (ʃæ·pĕrǫ̆n), *v.* 1796. [f. prec.] *trans.* To act as chaperon to; to escort.

I shall be very happy to c. you JANE AUSTEN.

Chap-fallen (tʃæ·pˌfǭlĕn), *a.* Also **chop-.** 1598. [f. CHAP *sb.*[2]] **1.** With the chap or lower jaw hanging down, as an effect of exhaustion, a wound, or *esp.* of death. **2.** *fig.* Dispirited; crest-fallen 1608.

1. Trooping from their mouldy dens The chap-fallen circle spreads TENNYSON.

Chapiter (tʃæ·pitəɹ). ME. [a. F. *chapitre* :—OF. *chapitle*, early ad. L. *capitulum.*] †**1.** *gen.* Earlier sp. of CHAPTER. †**2.** *spec.* A summary -1670. **3.** *Arch.* The capital of a column -1878.

†**Cha·pitle.** ME. only. [See prec.] = CHAPTER 1, 4.

Chaplain (tʃæ·plĕn). OE. [a. OF. *chapelain* :—med.L. *cappellanus*, f. *cappella* CHAPEL, q.v. **1.** *gen.* The priest, clergyman or minister of a CHAPEL; in ME. a chantry priest. **2.** *spec.* A clergyman who conducts religious services in the private chapel of a sovereign, lord, or high official, of a public institution, or in the household of a person of quality, in a legislative chamber, regiment, ship, etc. OE. Used of a nun who officiates in a nunnery ME. Also *transf.* Hence **Cha·plaincy, Cha·plainry** = *chaplainship.* **Cha·plainship**, the office of a c.

Chaplet (tʃæ·plĕt). [ME. *chapelet*, a. OF., dim. of *chape, chapeau*, head-dress, etc.] **1.** A wreath for the head; a circlet, coronal. *Her.* A bearing representing a garland of leaves with four flowers at equal distances 1688. **2.** A string of beads; *esp.* one used for counting prayers, one third of the length of a rosary. Also, the prayers themselves. 1653. Also *transf.* **3.** A moulding of the astragal species 1623. **4.** *Founding.* One of the metal supports of the core of a hollow moulding, e.g. of a cylindrical pipe 1885. **5.** See CHAPELET[2].

1. A c. of precious stones 1450, of flowers GREENE, of Roses STEELE. Hence **Cha·pleted** *a.*

Chapman (tʃæ·pmæ̆n). [OE. *cēapmann*, f. *cēap* barter, dealing + *mann*; see CHEAP *v.*] **1.** A man who buys and sells; a merchant, trader, dealer (*arch.*). **2.** An itinerant dealer; a hawker, pedlar 1592. †**3.** A broker -1659. †**4.** A customer -1807. Hence †**Cha·pmanhood**, **-head** = *chapmanship.* **Cha·pmanship**, the employment of a c.

Cha·p-money. *dial.* 1881. A small sum returned by the vendor to the purchaser on receiving payment.

†**Chapourn.** 1688. *Her.* = next.

Chapournet. 1562. [? corrupt f. F. *chaperonnet.*] *Her.* In a coat of arms, a chief divided by a bow-shaped line, said to represent a hood.

‖**Chappe.** 1825. [a. F. *chape.*] A cape or cloak.

Chapped (tʃæpt), *ppl. a.*[1] 1460. [f. CHAP *v.* and *sb.*[1]] **1.** Fissured; cracked; as the ground in summer, or the hands with frost. *slang.* Thirsty. **2.** Chopped small 1730.

Chapped (tʃæpt), *ppl. a.*[2] 1678. [f. CHAP *sb.*[2]] Having a chap or jaw; chiefly in *comb.*

Chappie, -y (tʃæ·pi). *colloq.* 1821. [f. CHAP *sb.*[3] + -IE, -Y[6].] Little chap or fellow. Orig. *Sc.*

‖**Chappow** (tʃapau·). *Anglo-Ind.* 1860. [a. Pushtoo.] A plundering expedition; a raid.

Chappy (tʃæ·pi), *a.* 1611. [f. CHAP *sb.*[1] + -Y[1].] Full of chaps or clefts.

Chapter (tʃæ·ptəɹ), *sb.* ME. in *Sc.* [syncopated f. CHAPITER, q. v. Cf. also CAPITULUM, CAPITLE, CHAPITLE.] **1.** A main division of a book, or of the Acts of Parliament of a single session. **2.** *fig.* Heading, subject, category. (Usu. preceded by *on, upon.*) (*arch.*) ME. **3.** A short lesson read in some services of the Latin Church 1450. **4.** A general meeting or assembly of the canons of a collegiate or cathedral church, of the members of any monastic or religious order, or of an order of knights. (The name *chapter* was thus transferred to the *meeting* at which a chapter (sense 3) was read, and thence to those who met.) ME. **5.** The members of such an assembly as a body: *esp.* The body of canons of a collegiate or cathedral church, presided over by the dean 1491. **6.** A decretal epistle 1726. †**7.** *Arch.* The capital of a column: cf. CHAPITER 3.

1. Unable to read a c. in the bible JOHNSON. *fig. Twel. N.* I. v. 242. A curious c. in modern history EMERSON. 2. And more particularly on the c. of women CARLYLE.

Phrases. *C. and verse*: (*fig.*) exact authority *for. To the end of the c.*: (*fig.*) throughout. *The c. of accidents*: the unforeseen course of events.

Comb.: **c.-house**, a building attached to a cathedral, etc., where a c. meets; **-lands**, lands belonging to a c. (sense 5).

Chapter (tʃæ·ptəɹ), *v.* 1485. [f. prec.] **1.** To divide into chapters. **2.** To reprove, take to task. [Cf. F. *chapitrer.*] 1693.

1. Langton's chaptering the Bible FULLER.

Chaptrel (tʃæ·ptrĕl). 1677. [dim. of CHAPTER (in sense 7).] *Arch.* An impost.

†**Cha·pwoman.** 1624. [after CHAPMAN.] A female dealer or hawker -1823.

†**Char,** *sb.*[1] See CHARE.

†**Char,** *sb.*[2] ME. [a. F. :—L. *carrus.*] **1.** A chariot; a cart, wagon -1677. **2.** ? A cart-load -1721.

2. *Char of lead*: thirty pigs, each pig containing 70 pounds. [*Charge of lead*, due to Bailey, and copied into mod. Dicts., is non-existent.]

Char (tʃāɹ), *sb.*[3] 1662. [? Celtic; cf. Gael. *ceara* red, *cear* blood.] *Zool.* **1.** A small fish (*Salmo salvelinus*) of the trout kind, found in the lakes of mountainous districts. **2.** The Brook Trout (*Salmo fontinalis*) of U. S.

Char, *sb.*[4] 1879. [f. CHAR *v.*[2]] A charred substance.

Char, *v.*[1] See CHARE.

Char (tʃāɹ), *v.*[2] Pples. **charred, charring.** 1679. [app. f. *char-* in CHARCOAL.] **1.** To reduce by burning to charcoal or carbon; to burn slightly or partially, scorch. **2.** *intr.* To become reduced to charcoal 1727.

Char, *v.*[3] 1846. [? Cf. F. *carrer* :—L. *quadrare* to square.] To hew (stone).

Char-, see CHARE *sb.*[1], and CHARWOMAN.

‖**Chara** (kēᵊ·ră). 1753. [L. name of an unkn. plant.] *Bot.* A genus of aquatic acrogenous plants, type of the N.O. *Characeæ*, which become encrusted with calcareous matter. Hence **Chara·ceous** *a.* **Cha·racin,** (*Chem.*) a camphorous substance found in *Characeæ*, etc.

‖**Char-à-banc** (ʃarabaṅ). 1832. [a. F.] A long and light vehicle with transverse seats looking forward.

Charact (kæ·rækt). *arch.* ME. [a. OF. *characte*; see CARACT.] †1. An engraved or impressed mark; a stamp; a letter, figure, etc. -1603. 2. A cabbalistic sign or emblem 1560.
2. Inscribed with talismans and characts BURTON.

Charact, obs. f. CARAT.

Character (kæ·rĕktəɹ), *sb.* [ME. *caracter(e*, a. F., ad. L., a. Gr. χαρακτήρ instrument for graving, f. χαράττειν to cut furrows in, engrave. Refash. in Eng. in the 16th c.]

I. Literal senses. 1. A distinctive mark; a brand, stamp. Also *fig.* 2. *esp.* A graphic symbol standing for a sound, syllable, or notion, used in writing or printing 1490. 3. *collect.* Writing, printing 1600; handwriting 1603; style of type 1641. 4. = CHARACT 2. 1590. †5. *gen.* A symbol; an expression -1702. 6. A cipher for secret correspondence 1659.
1. *fig.* Stamped with the c. of sublimity 1794. 2. [The] caracters *y* and *v* PALSGR. Runic characters 1851. 3. SHAKS. *Sonn.* lix. Imitation of printed Roman c. LYTTON. 6. I..interpreted my Lord's letter by his c. PEPYS.

II. Fig. senses. 1. A feature, trait, characteristic. Now *esp.* in *Nat. Hist.* 1502. 2. Essential peculiarity; nature; sort 1659. †3. Personal appearance. *Twel. N.* I. ii. 51. 4. Mental or moral constitution 1647. 5. Distinct or distinguished character 1735. 6. Good repute 1712. 7. A detailed report of a person's qualities 1645; *esp.* one given to a servant by an employer 1693. Also †*transf.* of things. 8. Recognized official rank; status; position 1645. 9. A personage 1749. 10. A personality in a novel or a play 1749. 11. *colloq.* An odd or eccentric person 1773. Also *attrib.*
1. Tell me, what one c. of liberty the Americans have BURKE. 2. To give to the war the c. of a crusade MACAULAY. 4. Thorough selfishness formed the basis of Henry's c. 1839. 5. Most Women have no Characters at all POPE. Men of c. WHISTON. 6. Shops of established c. MCCULLOCH. 7. [I] took the rascal upon his word without a c. 1785. 9. Eminent characters have..played the fool FIELDING. 10. The comic c. of Sir Trusty J. WARTON. *In* (or *out of*) *c.*: in (*or* at variance with) the part assumed; hence *gen.* in (*or* out of) harmony. 11. The old man..was a bit of a c. 1832.

Character (kæ·rĕktəɹ), *v.* 1591. [f. prec. In Shaks. and in 17th c. often *chara·cter.*] 1. To engrave; to inscribe. Also *fig.* 2. To represent (*arch.*) 1594. 3. = CHARACTERIZE *v.* 3. 1618. 4. = CHARACTERIZE *v.* 4. 1647. 5. = CHARACTERIZE *v.* 5. 1654.
1. What's in the braine that Inck may c. SHAKS. *Sonn.* cviii. *fig. Haml.* I. iii. 59.

†**Characte·rical**, *a.* 1634. [f. Gr. χαρακτηρικός + -AL.] 1. Of or pertaining to symbolic characters, magical symbols, or charms -1691. 2. Characteristic -1766.

†**Characterism** (kæ·rĕktĕri·z'm). 1614. [ad. L. *characterismus*, Gr. χαρακτηρισμός.] 1. = CHARACTERIZATION -1825. 2. A CHARACTERISTIC -1871.

Characterist (kæ·rĕktĕrist). 1691. [f. CHARACTER *sb.*] †a. One who employs magical symbols. b. One who depicts character.

Characteristic (kæ:rĕktĕri·stik). 1664. [ad. Gr. χαρακτηριστικός.] A. *adj.* That serves to indicate character; distinctive; typical 1665.
The c. letter, and the termination of verbs GIBBON.

B. *sb.* 1. A distinctive mark; a distinguishing peculiarity or quality 1664. 2. *Math.* The whole number in a logarithm 1727.
1. Superstition is..not the c. of this age JUNIUS.

Cha:racteri·stical. *arch.* 1621. [f. as prec. + -AL.] *adj.* = CHARACTERISTIC *a.* *sb.* = CHARACTERISTIC *sb.* 1. 1660. Hence **Cha:racteri·stically** *adv.* in cipher; in a c. manner. **Cha:racteri·s·ticalness.**

Characterization (kæ:rĕktĕrəizē¹·ʃən). 1570. [f. next.] The action or result of characterizing; portrayal in words; creation of fictitious characters.

Characterize (kæ·rĕktĕrəiz), *v.* 1591. [ad. med.L. *characterizare*, ad. Gr. χαρακτηρίζειν, f. χαρακτήρ CHARACTER.] †1. = CHARACTER *v.* 1. -1811. †2. = CHARACTER *v.* 2. -1710. 3. To describe the peculiar qualities of 1626. 4. To be a characteristic of 1744. 5. To impart character to; also *absol.* 1807.
3. I do not choose to use the expression which alone could c. it RUSKIN. 4. The excellent taste which characterises her writings SCOTT. 5. To leave out.. all that characterises OPIE. Hence **Cha·racteri:zer.**

Cha·racterless, *a.* 1606. [f. CHARACTER *sb.* + -LESS.] Without distinctive feature; without individuality; without (testimony to) personal character. Hence **Cha·racterlessness.**

Charactery, rarely **-try** (kæ·rĕktĕri; in Shaks. kăræ·ktĕri). 1588. [f. CHARACTER *sb.*; see -ERY.] 1. Expression of thought by symbols or characters; the characters or symbols collectively 1598; †*spec.* shorthand 1588. †2. Delineation of character 1614.
1. I will construe to thee All the Charractery of my sad browes *Jul. C.* II. i. 308. Nor mark'd with any sign or c. KEATS.

Charade (ʃărā·d). 1776. [a. F.; ? f. Pr. *charrada* chatter (Littré), or Sp. *charrada* speech or action of a clown (Skeat).] A kind of riddle, in which each syllable of a word to be guessed, and sometimes the word itself, is enigmatically described, or acted. Also *attrib.*

Charbocle, obs. f. CARBUNCLE.

‖**Charbon** (ʃarbon). 1753. [Fr.] 1. A small black spot or mark remaining in the cavity of the corner tooth of a horse after the large spot or mark has become obliterated. ? *Obs.* 2. = ANTHRAX 2. 1869.

Charcoal (tʃā·ɹkōul), *sb.* ME. [app. f. *char* (of unkn. origin) + COAL. The suggestion that *char-* = CHARE *v.* or *sb.*[1], as if *turn-coal*, i.e. wood *turned* into *coal*, lacks support.] 1. The black porous residue, consisting (when pure) wholly of carbon, obtained from partly burnt wood, bones, etc. Hence specified as *wood*, *vegetable*, *animal c.* †2. *collect. pl.* in sense of 1. -1719. 3. A charcoal crayon 1688. 4. A charcoal drawing 1884.
1. Sea-coal last longer than Char-coal BACON.
Comb.: **c.-black**, a pigment obtained from c.; **-iron**, iron containing a percentage of carbon; **-point** (*Electr.*) = *carbon-point* (see CARBON). Hence **Cha·rcoal** *v.* to mark with c.; to suffocate with the fumes of c.

†**Chard**[1], **charde.** 1570. [fusion of CARD and CHART.] Card, map, chart -1611.

Chard[2] (tʃāɹd). 1658. Var. of CARD *sb.*[3]

Chare, char (tʃē³ɹ, tʃāɹ), *sb.*[1] [OE. *cerr*:—OTeut. **karriz* or **karziz*; cf. CHARE *v.*[1] In mod. Eng. usually *char*, exc. in sense 2; in U.S. also CHORE.] †1. The returning of a time -ME.; a turn -1680. 2. *esp.* An odd job, *esp.* of household work; in *pl.* the housework of a domestic servant ME. Also in *comb.*, as *char-parson*, etc. 1662.

Chare (tʃē³ɹ), *sb.*[2] ME. [? CHARE turning; cf. Sc. *wynd.*] A narrow lane, or wynd. *local.*

Chare, *sb.*[3], chariot, car; see CHAR *sb.*[2]

†**Chare**, *a.* 1564. = CHARY -1587. Hence †**Cha·rely** *adv.*

Chare, char (tʃē³ɹ, tʃāɹ), *v.* [OE. *çerran*:—*çerre*, CHARE *sb.*[1] Now usually *chare.*] †1. To turn; *esp.* to turn away or aside. *trans.*, *intr.*, and *refl.* -1674. 2. *trans.* To do (a turn of work) (*arch.*) 1570. 3. *intr.* To do odd jobs, *esp.* of housework by the day; hence *colloq.* to do the cleaning work of (a house) 1732.

†**Charet, charette.** ME. [a. OF. *charrette*, dim. of OF. *charre* CAR *sb.*[1] The word used in the Bible of 1611, but changed in later editions to *chariot.*] 1. A wheeled conveyance (for persons or goods) -1654; a war-chariot -1676. Hence †**Cha·reter**, a charioteer.

Charge (tʃāɹdʒ), *sb.* ME. [a. F. *charge*:—Rom. *carga*, late L. *carrica*, f. *carricare*; see CHARGE *v.*, and cf. CARK.]

I. †1. A (material) load, burden, weight -1704. [¶ *Charge of Lead*: see CHAR *sb.*[2] 2.] 2. The quantity of anything, as powder, coal, ore, etc., which any receptacle, piece of mechanism, etc., *e.g.* a fire-arm, gas-retort, furnace, is constructed to bear, take in, or receive at one time 1653. 3. *Her.* A BEARING 1599. 4. *Farriery.* A thick adhesive plaster 1607.

II. 1. *fig.* A load (of trouble, inconvenience, etc.) *Obs.* *concr.* Anything burdensome. ME. †2. *fig.* Importance, moment -1598. 3. Pecuniary burden; cost 1460; the price demanded for services or goods 1848. *pl.* Expenses: in much the same sense as the sing. (*arch.*) 1514. *Comm.* Incidental expenses 1546. 4. A liability to pay money laid upon a person or estate 1570. 5. Commission, trust, responsibility ME. 6. Care, custody, superintendence ME. 7. A thing or person entrusted to the care of any one. *spec.* The people or district committed to the care of a clergyman. 1530. 8. A precept, injunction, mandate, order ME. *spec.* An official instruction or admonition given by a judge to a jury, by a bishop to his clergy, etc. 1690. 9. Accusation 1477. *spec.* The accusation upon which a prisoner is brought up for trial; hence *colloq.*: A prisoner so brought up. 1859.
2. The Letter was..full of c., Of deare import *Rom. & Jul.* v. ii. 18. 3. Thou hast lytle money & much c. MORE. *pl.* At his own charges THACKERAY. 5. Pastors have a dreadfull c., not performed by a formal preachment twice a week MILT. 6. He shall geue his angels c. ouer the COVERDALE *Ps.* xc[i]. 11. Children in c. of a nurse. A nurse in c. of children (*mod.*). So, *Officer, clerk, curate in c.* *To give* (a person) *in c.*: to hand over to the custody of the police. 9. *To lay to one's c.*: to charge one with.

III. An impetuous attack, etc. †1. The position of a weapon ready for action -1650. 2. *Mil.* An impetuous attack or onset; the act of bearing down impetuously upon the adversary. Also said of a bull, an elephant, a player at football, etc. 1568. Also *fig.* 3. *Mil.* A signal for the attack sounded upon a trumpet, etc. 1650.
1. 2 *Hen. IV*, IV. i. 120. 2. The two armies rushed with equal fury to the c. GIBBON. 3. The pipers on both sides blew their c. SCOTT.
Comb.: **bursting c.**: see BURST *v.*; **c.-inspector**, an officer who inspects the charges in a c.-sheet; **-sheet**, the paper kept at a police-station on which are entered all names of persons arrested, with the charge against them, etc. Hence †**Cha·rgeful** *a.* burdensome; responsible. **Cha·rgeless** *a.* free from cost; without a (clerical) c. †**Cha·rgeous** *a.* heavy; burdensome.

Charge (tʃāɹdʒ), *v.* ME. [a. OF. *charger*, -*ier*:—L. *carricare* to load, f. *carrus* car. Cf. CARK, and CARRY.]

I. To cause to bear. †1. *trans.* To load -1854. †2. To place as a load *upon* -1601. 3. To put in or on (a thing) or cause it to receive what it can bear or is adapted to receive ME.; *spec.* to load (a fire-arm) 1541. Also *fig.* 4. *Her.* To place a bearing on 1572. Also *transf.* 5. To fill (any substance) *with* other matter (*e.g.* the air *with* vapour, etc.) Usu. in pa. pple. 1756.
1. A tre, That charged was with fruyt CHAUCER. 3. To c. a rocket 1799, an accumulator (*mod.*), a pipe BROWNING. Canon charged to the mouthes *John* II. i. 382. *fig.* A face charged with memories GEO. ELIOT. *fig.* *L. L. L.* v. ii. 88. 5. Clouds charged with electricity PHILLIPS.

II. To load heavily. †1. To overload -1784. †2. To press hard -1568. †3. *fig.* To burden *with* sin, care, sickness, etc. -1633. †4. To put to expense -1647. 5. To burden, entrust, commission *with*, †*of* ME. Also *refl.* 6. To lay a command or injunction upon; to exhort authoritatively. Const. with *inf.*, or with cl.; also *simply.* ME. Also *absol.* to deliver a charge. Cf. CHARGE *sb.* II. 8. 1618. 7. To censure; to accuse ME. 8. *To c.* (a fault, etc.): see quots. 9. To subject (a person, estate, etc.) to a pecuniary liability. Const. *with*, †*to.* 1626. 10. *To c.* (a sum or price): see quots. 11. *To c.* (a thing sold or offered for sale): see quots.
1. To c. childrens memories with rules LOCKE. 4. Let not the church be charged 1 *Tim.* v. 16. 5. What you haue charg'd me with, that haue I done *Lear* v. iii. 163. 6. On thy life I c. thee, hold *Twel. N.* IV. i. 49. To c. a jury 1618, the clergy of a diocese 1870. 7. To c. me with offence 1559. 8. To impute as a fault: C. the crime, On native sloth DRYDEN. †To impute *to*: It [a poem] is charged to me SWIFT. To state in an indictment: We ought..not to c. what we are unable to prove BURKE. 10. To impose as a liability *on*: Debts .. charged upon the real estate CRUISE. To state as the price due *for*: [The price] she charged for eggs 1787. Also *absol.* 11. To put as a charge *to* or *against*: C. these to (*or* against) me (*mod.*). To rate: He charges coal at 8*d.* a cwt. (*mod.*).

†III. To attach weight or importance to; to regard -1587.

IV. To attack impetuously, etc. 1. To place (a weapon) in position for action; to level 1509. 2. To bear down upon with impetuosity. *Esp.* in military use. Cf. also CHARGE *sb.* III. 2. 1583. Also *intr.* and *absol.*
1. *C. bayonets!*: advance on the enemy with bayonets fixed. 2. The bull charged one of the horses (*mod.*). *absol.* 'C., Chester, c.! On, Stanley, on!' SCOTT. Hence **Charged** *ppl.a.* filled, etc.; now *esp.* = 'Charged with electricity'.

‖**Chargé**, in full **Chargé d'affaires** (ʃa·rʒe dafē·r). 1850. [F.; = (one) in charge of affairs.]

1. A minister who transacts diplomatic business during the temporary absence of the ambassador; also, the representative of a country at a minor foreign court 1876. 2. *gen.* Man or officer in charge (for the time).

Chargeable (tʃā·ɹdʒăb'l), *a.* 1480. [f. CHARGE *v.* + -ABLE.] †1. Of the nature of a charge or burden; responsible; burdensome; costly -1796. 2. Capable of being, or liable to be, charged (see CHARGE *v.*) 1546.

1. A c. office FRITH. C. apparell 1568. 2 *Sam.* xiii. 25. 2. Writing signed by the party c. STEPHEN. C. with guilt JOHNSON, with money 1641, to a Parish ADDISON, upon the Rector 1654, to general average SIR C. BOWEN. Hence **Chargeabi·lity**, the condition of being c. **Cha·rgeableness.** †**Cha·rgeably** *adv.*

†**Cha·rgeant,** *a.* ME. only. [a. F.] Burdensome.

Cha·rgeant, *sb.* 1887. [See prec.] = CHARGEE.

Chargee (tʃāɹdʒī). 1884. [f. CHARGE *v.* or *sb.* + -EE.] The holder of a charge upon property, or of a security over a contract.

Cha·rge-house. †1. A house for the charge of youth *L. L. L.* v. i. 87. 2. A building in which cartridges are charged.

Charger[1] (tʃā·ɹdʒəɹ). [ME. *chargeour*, ? ad. OF. **chargeoir*, f. L. **carricatorium* utensil for loading.] A large plate or flat dish.

Giue me heere Iohn Baptists head in a c. *Matt.* xiv. 8.

Cha·rger[2]. 1483. [f. CHARGE *v.*; cf. F. *chargeur.*] 1. One who or that which charges. 2. One who has a charge on an estate, etc. 1869. 3. A horse ridden by an officer in the field or in action 1762.

3. Furious every c. neighed CAMPBELL.

Charily (tʃē·ᵊrili), *adv.* 1579. [f. CHARY + -LY[2].] In a CHARY manner; carefully; cautiously; sparingly.

Chariness (tʃē·ᵊrinės). 1571. [f. as prec.] 1. The quality of being CHARY. †2. Scrupulous integrity -1794.

2. The charinesse of our honesty *Merry W.* II. i. 102.

Chariot (tʃæ·riət). ME. [a. OF. *chariot*, augm. of *char* CAR. Since 17th c. *chariot* has also replaced CHARET.] 1. A wheeled vehicle; †a cart -1693; a carriage of state ME.; also *fig.*; a car used in ancient warfare 1581. *spec.* A light four-wheeled carriage with only back seats 1661. †2. *fig.* Vehicle -1678.

1. *fig.* Like the sun's c. at mid-day 1883. He burneth the c. in the fire *Ps.* xlvi. 9.

Chariot (tʃæ·riət), *v.* 1627. [f. prec.] To carry or convey in a chariot 1659. Also *absol.*

Bright-charioted Aurora COWPER.

Chariotee (tʃæ:riŏtī·). 1864. [f. as prec.] A light covered pleasure chariot, with four wheels and two seats. (Webster.)

Charioteer (tʃæ:riŏtīᵊ·ɹ), *sb.* ME. [app. f. OF. *charioteur*, and OF. *charetier.*] The driver of a chariot. Hence **Charioteership**, performance as a c.

Charioteer, *v.* 1802. [f. prec.] 1. *intr.* To act as charioteer; to drive. 2. *trans.* To drive (a chariot, a person in a chariot) 1849.

Chariotry (tʃæ·riətri). 1828. [f. as prec + -RY.] The body of soldiers who fought from chariots. Cf. *cavalry*, etc.

Charism (kæ·riz'm). Pl. **-ata** and **-s.** 1641. [f. Gr. χάρισμα, pl. -ατα.] A favour specially vouchsafed by God; a grace, a talent. Hence **Charisma·tic** *a.* of or pertaining to a c.

Charitable (tʃæ·rităb'l), *a.* ME. [a. OF., f. *charité.*] †1. Showing Christian charity or the love of God and man -1641. †2. Tender-hearted; well-disposed -1634. 3. Full of active charity; *esp.* liberal in almsgiving to the poor ME. 4. Connected with an object of charity, *esp.* as defined in statutes; of the nature of a charity 1597. 5. Inclined to judge favourably of men, their actions, etc. 1626.

3. With your charatable almes the poore man to comforte ME. 4. The great statute of c. uses is st. 43 El. c. 4 POWELL. To aid some c. object 1872. 5. A c. construction 1626, hope 1846. Hence **Cha·ritableness**, the quality of being c. **Cha·ritably** *adv.*

†**Cha·ritative,** *a.* 1582. [a. OF. *charitatif.*] Of the nature of charity or a charitable gift -1751.

Charity (tʃæ·riti). OE. [a. OF. *charité*, ad. L. *caritatem.* Cf. CHERTE.] 1. Christian love; *esp.* the Christian love of our fellow men. Often personified. ME. 2. Love, natural affection; spontaneous goodness ME. *pl.* Affections 1667. 3. A disposition to judge hopefully of men and their actions, and to make allowance for their shortcomings 1483; †fairness, equity -1647. 4. Benevolence, *esp.* to the poor; charitableness; alms-giving OE. *pl.* Acts of charity done to the poor 1607. 5. Alms ME. 6. A bequest, foundation, institution, etc., for the benefit of others, *esp.* of the poor or helpless 1697.

1. The charite [A. V. love] of God, that is in Jhesu Crist oure Lord *Rom.* viii. 39. The c. of the Gospel should extend to men of every Religion 1796. *In, out of, c.*: in or out of the Christian state of c. 2. *pl.* MILT. *P. L.* IV. 756. 3. C. bids hope for the best DRYDEN. 4. C., or tenderness for the poor JOHNSON. *pl.* Deferre not Charities till Death BACON. 5. To beg a c. DRYDEN. 6. Christ's Hospital..a..noble, pious and admirable c. EVELYN.

Phrases. *C. begins at home*: used to express the prior claims of ties of family, friendship, etc. (cf. 1 *Tim.* v. 8). *Brother or Sister of C.*: a member of a religious organization devoted to c.

attrib., etc. (see senses 4-6), as *c. land, money*; *c.-boy, -girl*, etc.; **c.-school**, one supported by charitable bequests or gifts, for the education of the poor.

Charivari (ʃɑ:riˌvɑ·ri). 1735. [a. F., of unkn. origin; see Littré.] A serenade of rough music, made with kettles, pans, tea-trays, etc., used in France, in derision of incongruous marriages, etc.; hence a babel of noise.

Chark (tʃāɹk), *sb.*[1] 1708. [app. short. from *chark coal*, due to erron. analysis of CHARCOAL. Cf. CHARK *v.*[2]] Wood or coal charred; charcoal; coke.

‖**Chark** (tʃāɹk), *sb.*[2] 1591. [Russ.] A small (Russian) glass.

Chark, *v.*[1] Now *dial.* [OE. *cearcian*; in ME. also *cherk*, CHIRK.] †1. To creak -ME. 2. To be querulous. *Sc.* 1825.

Chark (tʃāɹk), *v.*[2] 1655. [See CHARK *sb.*[1]] To char; to coke (coals).

Charlatan (ʃā·ɹlătăn, -tæn). 1618. [a. F., ad. It. *ciarlatano* = *ciarlatore*, f. *ciarlare* to babble, act the mountebank. Cf. *quack.*] †1. A mountebank who descants volubly in the street; *esp.* an itinerant vendor of drugs, etc. -1771. 2. An empiric who pretends to wonderful knowledge or secrets, *esp.* in the healing art; an impostor, a quack 1680. Also as *adj.*

2. A c. in religion is sure to like other sorts of charlatans GEO. ELIOT. Hence **Charlata·nic, -al** *a.* **Cha·rlatanish** *a.* **Cha·rlatanism**, the practice of a c.; the being a c. **Cha·rlatanry**, quackery.

Charles's Wain. [OE. *Carles wægn* the wain of Carl (Charlemagne). Orig. the wain of *Arcturus*, verbally assoc. with *Arturus*. Arthur and Charlemagne are associated in legend.] The asterism comprising the seven bright stars in Ursa Major; known also as The Plough.

Charley, Charlie (tʃā·ɹli). *colloq.* 1812. [var. of CHARLES.] 1. A night-watchman. 2. A small triangular beard, as worn by Charles I 1834. 3. A proper name for the fox 1857.

Charlock (tʃā·ɹlǫk). [OE. *cerlic*, *cyrlic* of unkn. etym.] *Bot. Sinapis arvensis* or Field Mustard; also used of other field-weeds.

Joint-podded c.: *Raphanus Raphanistrum.*

Charlotte (ʃā·ɹlət). 1855. [F.] Apple marmalade covered with bread-crumbs. Hence **C. Russe**, custard enclosed in sponge-cake.

Charm (tʃāɹm), *sb.*[1] [ME. *charme*, a. F.:—L. *carmen.*] 1. *orig.* The chanting of a verse having magic power; incantation; hence, a magic spell; a talisman; an amulet, etc. Also *fig.* (cf. *spell.*) 2. *fig.* That which fascinates or attracts, exciting love and admiration. In *pl.*, esp. of female beauty. 1697. b. (without *pl.*) Attractiveness 1830. c. *Charms* (*U.S. slang*): Money. 3. A small trinket worn fastened to a watch-chain or girdle 1865.

1. To..woundes..Somme hadden salues and somme hadden charmes CHAUCER. *fig.* The c. of the Roman name STUBBS. 2. Scornful virgins who their charms survive POPE. 3. A bunch of charms (*mod.*). Hence **Cha·rmless** *a.* **Cha·rmlike** *a.*

Charm (tʃāɹm), *sb.*[2] 1548. [var. of *cherme* CHIRM, ? assoc. w. prec.] 1. A blended noise, as of birds, school-children, etc. †2. Song -1633.

1. [Morn's] rising sweet With c. of earliest Birds MILT. *P. L.* IV. 642.

Charm (tʃāɹm), *v.*[1] ME. [a. F. *charmer*; see CHARM *sb.*[1]] 1. *trans.* To act upon with or as with a charm or magic; to put a spell upon; to bewitch, enchant. 2. To endow with supernatural powers by means of charms; *esp.* to fortify against dangers 1564. 3. *intr.* To work charms, use spells, practise magic ME. 4. To subdue, as if by magic power; to soothe, allay 1540. 5. *fig.* To powerfully attract (the mind, senses, etc.); to fascinate ME. Also *absol.* †6. To conjure, entreat -1734. †7. To tune, play -1609. Also *intr.* (of an instrument).

1. They wanted me to c. or cure him KANE. 2. I, in mine owne woe charm'd, Could not finde death *Cymb.* v. iii. 68. 3. That she shulde not heare the voyce of the charmer, charme he neuer so wysely *Ps.* lvii[i]. 5. 4. Music the fiercest grief can c. POPE. 5. There's something charms me mightily about London SWIFT. Hence **Cha·rmedly** *adv.*

Charm, *v.*[2], dial. var. of CHIRM.

Charmer (tʃā·ɹməɹ). ME. [f. CHARM *v.* + -ER[1].] 1. One who uses magic powers; an enchanter. 2. One who fascinates; usually applied to a woman 1676. †**Cha·rmeress,** a female c.

Cha·rmful, *a.* 1656. Full of spells or charms.

His c. lyre COWLEY. Hence **Cha·rmfulness.**

Charming (tʃā·ɹmiŋ), *vbl. sb.* ME. [f. CHARM *v.*[1] + -ING[1].] 1. The operation or using of charms. 2. Fascination (*obs.*); now, fascinating 1720. Also *attrib.*

2. She has lost none of her power of c. (*mod.*). Hence **Cha·rming-ly** *adv.*, **-ness.**

†**Cha·rneco.** 1593. A kind of wine -1631.

Charnel (tʃā·ɹnĕl), *sb.*[1] (and *a.*). ME. [a. OF. :—late L. *carnale* flesh-house, = *carnarium.*] A cemetery (*obs.*); a charnel house. Also *attrib.*

The commune charnell of the city 1526.

B. *adj.* Of, pertaining to, or fit for a charnel, or the remains there preserved; sepulchral; ghastly 1824.

C. house: a house or vault for the bones of the dead.

†**Charnel** (tʃā·ɹnĕl), *sb.*[2] ME. [a. OF., prob. :—L. *cardinale*, f. *cardo.*] A hinge -1741.

Charon (kēᵊ·rǫn). 1513. [Gr. pr. name.] 1. *Gr.* and *Rom. Mythol.* The ferryman who conveyed the shades across the Styx. 2. Ferryman (*joc.*) 1861.

‖**Charpie** (ʃā·ɹpī, ʃarpī). 1797. [F.; pa. pple. fem. of *charpir* to card; see CARPET.] Old linen unravelled into short ends of thread for surgical dressings.

‖**Charpoy** (tʃā·ɹpoi). *Anglo-Ind.* 1845. [a. Urdū *chārpāī.*] The common Indian bedstead.

‖**Charqui** (tʃā·ɹki). 1760. [Peruv. *echarqui.*] Beef cut into thin slices and dried in the sun and wind; 'jerked' beef (see JERK *v.*[2]).

Charry (tʃā·ri), *a.* 1786. [f. CHAR-COAL.] Of the nature of charcoal.

Chart (tʃāɹt), *sb.* 1571. [a. OF. *charte*:—L. *carta*, *charta.* See also CARD.] 1. A map or chart; *spec.* a map for the use of navigators; a delineation of a portion of the sea, indicating the outline of the coasts, the position of rocks, sandbanks, channels, anchorages, etc. Also *fig.* 1696. 2. A sheet bearing information of any kind arranged in a graphical or tabular form. Also *transf.* and *fig.* 1792. †3. = CARD *sb.*[2]: An ordinary card; a playing-card; the compass-card -1796. †4. A charter; a deed or document of any kind -1775.

1. Our navigation is safer for the c. EMERSON. A magnetic c. (*mod.*). A c. of temperature (*mod.*). A military c. 1580. 2. A barometric c. (*mod.*). Gentone's C. of Inheritance (*title*) 1840. Hence **Cha·rtless** *a.*

Chart (tʃāɹt), *v.* 1842. [f. prec.] To make a chart of; to map. Also *fig.*

‖**Charta** (kā·ɹtă). OE. [L., ad. Gr. χάρτης a leaf of papyrus or paper.] †1. In OE. form *carta*: Paper, letter. 2. A CHARTER; *esp.* in MAGNA CHARTA. Also used *fig.* 1698.

Chartaceous, cart- (kaɹtē·ʃəs), *a.* 1655. [f. L. *c(h)artaceus*, f. *charta.*] Of the nature of paper; papery.

Charter (tʃā·ɹtəɹ), *sb.* [ME. *chartre*, a. OF. :—L. *cartula*, dim. of *carta*, *charta*. Cf. CHAPTER :—L. *capitulum.*] *lit.* A leaf of paper (in OE. called *bóc* BOOK). 1. A written document delivered by the sovereign or legislature: a. granting privileges or recognizing rights; b. creating a borough, university, company, or other corporation 1474. 2. A written evidence, instrument, or contract executed between man and man; *esp.* a conveyance ME. *spec.* A CHARTER-PARTY, q. v. Also the contract thereby made. 1794. 3. Privilege, exemption, publicly conceded right 1565.

1. a. *Great C.*: see MAGNA CHARTA. Charters are donations of the sovereign; and not laws, but exemptions from law HOBBES. b. The renewal of the Company's c. 1844. *People's C.*: the document (published 8 May, 1838) embodying the principles and demands of the Chartists. 3. Ye haue a C. to speake what ye list JEWEL.

Comb.: c.-bond = CHARTER-PARTY; -land, land held by c.; freehold land (in OE. *bócland*). Hence **Cha·rterless** *a.*

Charter (tʃā·ɹtəɹ), *v.* ME. [f. prec.] 1. To establish by charter. 2. To privilege 1542. 3. To hire (a ship) by charter-party. Hence *colloq.* to hire (a vehicle, etc.). 1806.

1. The different Chartered Companies 1800. 2. The Ayre, a charter'd Libertine *Hen. V*, I. i. 48.

Cha·rterer. 1598. [f. CHARTER *sb.* and *v.*] 1. A freeholder; a freeman of a chartered borough. 2. One who charters a ship 1833.

Charterhouse (tʃā·ɹtəɹhaus). 1534. [var. (by pop. etym.) of AF. *chartrouse* = F. *chartreuse*, i. e. *maison chartreuse*.] 1. A Carthusian monastery (*arch.*). 2. Hence: Name of a hospital founded in London, in 1611, upon the site of the Carthusian monastery, which has since become a public school 1655. As *attrib.* Carthusian 1577.

†**Cha·rterism, -ist,** early ff. CHARTISM, -IST.

Charter-party (tʃā·ɹtəɹ,pā·ɹti). [In 16th c. *charte-*, *chartipartie*, a. F. *charte partie*, in med.L. *charta partita* (also *divisa*) a divided charter; an indenture.] †1. *gen.* An INDENTURE, q. v. 2. Now only: The charter or deed made between owners and merchants for hire of a ship, and safe delivery of the cargo 1539.

Cha·rter School. One of the schools established in Ireland by the Charter Society founded in 1733, to provide Protestant education for the Catholic poor.

Chartism (tʃā·ɹtiz'm). [f. L. *charta* CHARTER + -ISM.] *Eng. Hist.* The democratic movement and principles of the Chartists, 1838–48.

Chartist (tʃā·ɹtist). 1838. [f. as prec. + -IST.] One of the body of political reformers (chiefly operatives), whose principles were embodied in the 'People's Charter' (CHARTER *sb.* 1 quots.). Also *attrib.*

Chartographer (kaɹtǫ·grăfəɹ). 1864. = CARTOGRAPHER. So **Chartogra·phic, -al** *a.*, **Charto·graphist, Charto·graphy.**

‖**Chartreuse** (ʃartrö·z). 1866. [Fr.; fem. of *Chartreux*; see next and CHARTERHOUSE.] 1. A liqueur made by the monks of La Grande Chartreuse, near Grenoble, with aromatic herbs and brandy. 2. A colour; pale apple-green 1884.

‖**Chartreux** (ʃa·rtrö). ME. [a. OF., corrupt f. *charteus* :—L. *Carthusius.*] 1. A Carthusian; also *attrib.* 2. The Charterhouse (School) 1779.

Chartulary[1] (ka·ɹtiŭlări). 1571. [ad. med. L. *c(h)artularium*, f. *chartula* CHARTER.] A collection or set of charters; = CARTULARY, q.v.

Cha·rtulary[2]. 1678. [ad. L. *chartularius*; see prec.] A keeper of the archives.

Charwoman (tʃā·ɹwu:măn). 1596. [f. CHARE *sb.*[1] and *v.*[1]] A woman hired by the day to do odd jobs in a house. So **-lady** *joc.* 1895.

Chary (tʃē°·ri), *a.* [OE. *cearig* :—OTeut. **karag-oz*, f. *karā-* sorrow, care. Cf. CAREFUL.] †1. Sorrowful -ME. †2. Dear; cherished -1820. 3. Careful, cautious, shy, frugal, sparing (*of*) 1542. 4. quasi-*adv.* Carefully 1590.

2. Fill the stirrup cup..from a butt yet charier SCOTT. 3. 'Faith, I am very c. of my health COWPER. *Haml.* I. iii. 36.

Charybdis (kări·bdis). 1597. [L.; a. Gr.] A dangerous whirlpool on the coast of Sicily (now Calofaro), opposite the Italian rock Scylla. Used allusively, *esp.* in combination with Scylla, of the danger, in avoiding one peril, of running into its opposite.

Chase, chace (tʃēⁱs), *sb.*[1] [ME. *chace*, a. OF. :—Rom. **captia*, f. **captiare*; see CHASE *v.*] 1. The action of chasing (see CHASE *v.* 1). 2. The right of hunting over a tract of country; also, that of keeping beasts of the chase therein 1460. 3. A tract of unenclosed land reserved for breeding and hunting wild animals ME. 4. That which is hunted ME. 5. Those who hunt 1811. 6. The chase-guns of a ship; the part of the ship where the chase-ports are 1622. 7. *Tennis.* Applied to the second impact on the floor (or in a gallery) of a ball which the opponent has not returned. (See N.E.D.) ME.

1. *The c.*: Ardently fond of the c. LANE. To give c. to (= pursue) a ship 1634. *Stern c.*: a c. in which the chaser follows the chased astern. 3. Their wide enclosed parks, and unenclosed chaces STUBBS. 6. *Stern c.*: the guns in the stern.

attrib. and *Comb.*: c.-gun, a gun removed to the c.-ports ahead or astern; -ports, the ports at the bows or through the stern of the ship.

Chase (tʃēⁱs), *sb.*[2] 1580. [a. F. *châsse* :—L. *capsa* box, case.] 1. The setting of a gem. 2. *Printing.* The quadrangular iron frame in which pages or slips of type are locked up 1612.

Chase (tʃēⁱs), *sb.*[3] 1611. [a. F. *chas* enclosure, etc. :—late L. *capsum* thorax, etc.] *gen.* A groove or furrow. 1. The cavity of a gun barrel; the part of a gun in front of the trunnions 1647. 2. A groove cut in the face of a wall, to receive a pipe, etc.; a trench for drain tiles 1871. 3. *Shipbuilding.* A kind of joint by which the overlapping joint of clinker-built boats passes at the stem and stern into a flush joint as in carvel-built boats.

Chase, chace (tʃēⁱs), *v.*[1] [ME. a. OF. *chacier*, later *chasser* :—late L. **captiare* (freq. of *capere*). Cf. CATCH.] 1. To pursue with a view to catching (see quots.). Also *intr.* (*absol.*) and *fig.* 2. *trans.* To run after in play 1830. 3. *intr.* To run with speed. Still *dial.* ME. 4. To drive precipitately *from*, *out of*, *to*, *into*, etc.; to drive *away*, *forth*, etc. ME.; to put to flight (*arch.*) ME. †5. To drive (cattle, etc.) -1670.

1. To c. the hart TENNYSON, the process-server (*mod.*), a ship SWIFT. *intr.* To c. in the woods LD. BERNERS, with the squadron 1748. *fig.* To c. riches BURNS. 2. Chasing each other merrily TENNYSON. Hence **Cha·seable, Cha·sable** *a.* fit to be hunted.

Chase (tʃēⁱs), *v.*[2] ME. [short. f. ENCHASE.] 1. To adorn (metal, etc.) with work embossed or engraved in relief. 2. To set (a gem, etc.) *in.* Also *fig.* (*rare*) 1859.

Chase, *v.*[3] 1823. [f. CHASE *sb.*[3]] To groove, indent.

Chaser[1] (tʃēⁱ·səɹ). ME. [a. OF. *chaceür*, mod. *chasseur*; see CHASE *v.*[1]] 1. One who chases or hunts. 2. One who or that which pursues ME. 3. *Naut.* A *chase-gun*; see BOW-, STERN-CHASER 1794.

Chaser[2] (tʃēⁱ·səɹ). 1707. [f. CHASE *v.*[2] + -ER.] 1. One who chases or engraves metal. 2. A tool used for cutting the threads of screws 1881.

Chasing (tʃēⁱ·siŋ), *vbl. sb.* 1835. [f. CHASE *v.*[2] + -ING[1].] 1. The act or art of embossing or engraving in relief; also *attrib.* b. *concr.* The figures or design so produced 1862. 2. The cutting of a screw 1881.

Chasm (kæ·z'm). 1596. [ad. L. *chasma* (also used), a. Gr.] 1. A deep yawning rent in the surface of the earth or other cosmical body; later, a fissure or gap 1636. 2. A wide crack, break, void, hiatus. Also *fig.* 1641.

1. Volcanic chasms CARLYLE. 2. Chasms in a rampart SCOTT. The c. of Seven Centuries CARLYLE. The c. Tom's departure has made MACAULAY. Hence **Cha·smal** *a.* **Cha·smed** *ppl. a.* having chasms. **Cha·smy** *a.* abounding with chasms; of the nature of or like a c.

‖**Chasse**[1] (ʃās). 1670. [F. *châsse* :—L. *capsa* CASE.] A case for the relics of a saint.

‖**Chasse**[2] (ʃas). 1800. [Fr.; short for *chasse-café*, f. *chasser* to CHASE, drive away.] A small glass of some liqueur, taken to remove the taste of coffee, etc. So ‖**Chassé** *pa. pple.* treated with a chasse.

‖**Chassé** (ʃase), *sb.* 1867. [Fr.; lit. 'chasing, chase'.] *Dancing.* A gliding step, executed by bringing one foot behind the other while this is at the same time advanced; also, a figured step containing two of these, the direction for which is *chassez croisez.*

‖**Chassé,** *v.* Also **chassez.** 1803. [f. F. *chasser.*] 1. *Dancing.* To execute the step or movement called a *chassé*. 2. *trans.* To dismiss. (*Society slang.*) 1847.

2. He was *chasséd* on the spot THACKERAY.

‖**Chasselas** (ʃasəlā). 1664. [Fr.] A white grape named from *Chasselas*, near Mâcon.

‖**Chasse-marée** (ʃas,marē). 1801. [Fr. = chase-tide.] A coasting-vessel, used on the French side of the Channel.

‖**Chassepot** (ʃa·spǫ). 1869. [f. *Chassepot*, the inventor.] A breech-loading, centre-fire needle-gun adopted for the French army in 1866.

‖**Chasseur** (ʃasö·r). 1796. [Fr.; see CHASE *v.*[1]] 1. A huntsman; a hunter. 2. A soldier equipped and trained for rapid movement 1796. 3. An attendant upon a person of rank and wealth, dressed in a military style 18...

1. Chasseurs..beat its woods OUIDA. 3. A servant in chasseur's livery entered GEO. ELIOT.

‖**Chassis** (ʃa·si). 1664. [F. *châssis* frame, app. f. *chas*, late L. *capsum*, -*us* 'locus inclusus'. See also SASH.] †1. A SASH -1711. 2. The base-frame, on which the carriage of a barbette or casemate gun slides backward and forward 1869. 3. The base-frame of a motor car 1903.

Chaste (tʃēⁱst), *a.* ME. [a. OF., ad. L. *castus, casta.*] 1. Pure from unlawful sexual intercourse; continent, virtuous. Also *transf.* †2. Celibate, single -1596. †3. Morally pure, innocent -1535. Also *fig.* 4. Decent; free from indecency or offensiveness 1621. 5. *fig.* Chastened; restrained from all excess 1774.

1. *transf.* Chast and honest eyes 1565. 2. *Rom. & Jul.* I. i. 223. 3. *fig.* Let me not name it to you, you c. Starres *Oth.* V. ii. 2. 4. C. deportment STERNE. 5. A. c. interpretation of nature REID. C. tastes 1825. A c. and correct writer WARTON.

C. tree: the tree AGNUS CASTUS. Hence **Cha·stely** *adv.* **Cha·steness,** the quality or state of being c.

†**Chaste,** *v.* [ME. *chasten, chastien*, f. OF. *chastier* :—L. *castigare.* Repl. by CHASTEN.] To CHASTEN -1621.

Chastelain (tʃa·stĕlēⁱn). Now *Hist.* ME. [a. OF. :—L. *castellanus.*] = CASTELLAN.

Chasten (tʃēⁱ·s'n), *v.*[1] 1526. [f. CHASTE *v.* + -EN[2].] 1. To correct or discipline by punishment; to chastise. (Usu. of Divine chastisement.) 2. To render pure in character or style; to refine 1715. 3. *fig.* To restrain from excess; to moderate 1856.

1. Whom the Lorde loveth, him he chasteneth *Hebr.* xii. 6. 3. Time and experience have chastened me KANE. Hence **Cha·stenedly** *adv.* (*rare*). **Cha·stener.**

†**Cha·stiment.** ME. [a. OF. *chastiement*; see CASTIGATE.] Chastisement; rebuke -1500.

Chastise (tʃæstəi·z), *v.* ME. [= earlier CHASTE *v.* Of unkn. formation. Orig. stressed *cha·stise.*] †1. To correct (authoritatively) the faults of; to reform -1579. †2. To censure -1699. 3. To punish, with a view to amendment; also simply, to inflict (*esp.* corporal) punishment on ME. 4. = CHASTEN 2 (*arch.*) 1620. 5. = CHASTEN 3 (*arch.*) 1704.

2. He chastises me for saying [etc.] BENTLEY. 3. My father hath chastised you with whippes, but I will c. you with scorpions 1 *Kings* xii. 11. A plan to c. the intruder ELPHINSTONE. 5. With Pity to c. Delight STEELE. Hence **Chasti·ser.**

Chastisement (tʃæ·stizmĕnt). ME. [f. prec. + -MENT.] †1. Discipline, training -1601. 2. Disciplinary punishment; also simply punishment ME. 3. Restraint; refining (*arch.*) 1849.

1. Experyence is a good c. EARL RIVERS. 2. The chasticement..of our peace was vpon him T. NORTON.

Chastity (tʃæ·stĭti). [ME. *chastete, -etie*, a. OF. *chastete*, ad. L. *castitatem* influenced by the adj. *chaste.*] The quality or state of being chaste (see CHASTE *a.* 1–3, 5).

[Una]..the flowre of faith and c. SPENSER *F. Q.* I. iii. 23. The law wych byndyth prestys to chastyte STARKEY. C. of dress SHENSTONE, of Style HALLAM, of Renown STEELE.

Chastize, var. of CHASTISE.

†**Chasty,** *v.* ME. [a. OF. *chastier* (mod. F. *châtier*) :—L. *castigare.*] To correct, amend -1500; to reprove ME. only; to inflict disciplinary punishment on -1549.

Chasuble (tʃæ·siŭb'l). [ME. *chesible*, a. OF., repl. since 1700 by *chasuble*, = med.L. *casubula*, late L. **casipula*, **casupula*, pop. forms used instead of L. *casula*, dim. of *casa*, applied to an outer garment without sleeves, 'quod totum hominem tegat, quasi minor casa' (Isid. XIX. xxi. 17).] 1. An ecclesiastical vestment, a sleeveless mantle covering the body and shoulders, worn over the alb and stole by the celebrant at Mass or the Eucharist. †2. Used also of the Jewish ephod, etc. ME. only. var. †**Chasule.** FULLER.

Chat (tʃæt), *sb.*[1] 1530. [f. CHAT *v.*] †1. Chatter –1768. 2. Familiar and easy talk or conversation 1573. 3. *dial.* Impudence.

2. A c. about old times E. PEACOCK.

Chat (tʃæt), *sb.*[2] 1697. [f. as prec., in reference to their voice.] A name applied to several birds, chiefly *Sylviadæ* or Warblers; as the Furze-c., Stone-c., and Wheat-ear; in N. America, to the Yellow-breasted C. (*Icteria polyglotta*) and Long-tailed C. (*I. longicauda*).

Chat (tʃæt), *sb.*[3] ME. [a. F. *chats* lit. 'cats', barren (downy) flowers of walnut, hazel, willows, etc.; cf. F. *chatons*, Eng. CATKINS.] 1. A name given to the catkin, †inflorescence, or †seed of various plants. *Obs.* or *dial.* 2. A small branch or twig 1670. Also Chat-wood (*dial.*).

Chat, *sb.*[4] *dial.* 1840. A small poor potato.

Chat, *sb.*[5] 1876. *Mining.* Ore with rock adhering to it.

Chat (tʃæt), *v.* ME. [short. f. CHATTER.] 1. †*intr.* To chatter –1617. Also †*trans.* 2. *intr.* To talk in a light and informal manner; to converse familiarly 1556. †*trans.* To talk of –1607.

1. *Tam. Shr.* III. ii. 123. 2. The shepherds on the lawn..Sat simply chatting in a rustic row MILT.

‖**Château** (ʃɑto). Pl. **châteaux.** 1789. [Fr. :—OF. *chastel*; see CASTLE.] A castle; a large mansion or country-house: now used only in reference to the Continent.

The c. of a German nobleman H. WALPOLE.

‖**Chatelain** (ʃātəlěn, ʃɑ·tēlein). 1523. [a. mod.F. *châtelain.*] = CHASTELAIN, CASTELLAN. (*Obs.* as an Eng. title.)

‖**Chatelaine** (ʃɑ·tĕlein). 1851. [a. F.; see prec.] 1. A female castellan; the mistress of a country house 1855. 2. An ornamental appendage worn by ladies at their waist, having short chains attached for keys, scissors, penknife, thimble-case, etc. Also *attrib.*

Cha·telet. Now *Hist.* 1494. [a. OF. *chastelet*, dim. of *chastel* CASTLE.] A little castle; the name of an ancient prison in Paris.

Chatellany (ʃɑ·tĕlăni). 1668. [ad. F. *châtellenie.*] = CASTELLANY.

†**Chateus, -eux.** ME. only. [a. OF., pl. of *chatel.*] = CHATTELS.

†**Chatoyant** (ʃatwayań, ʃătoi·ănt). 1798. [F., pres. pple. of *chatoyer* (on L. type *caticare*).] A. *adj.* Having a changeable, undulating lustre, like that of a cat's eye in the dark –1860. B. *sb.* 1. Chatoyant quality 1798. 2. A chatoyant stone, as the Cat's eye. So ‖**Chatoy·ement,** changing or undulating lustre (*rare*).

‖**Chatta** (tʃæ·tă, tʃā·tă). 1796. [Hindī.] *Anglo-Ind.* An umbrella (in India).

Chattel (tʃæ·t'l). ME. [a. OF. *chatel* :—late L. *captale*, L. *capitale*; see CATTLE.] †1. Property; goods; money ME. only; live stock (*rare*) –1696. 2. With *pl.* A movable possession; any piece of property other than real estate or a freehold. (Usu. in *pl.*) 1549. Also *transf.* and *fig.*

2. *Goods and chattels*: all kinds of personal property. *Chattels personal*: all movable goods, as money, plate, cattle. *Chattels real*: such as concern the realty, as leases, etc. *Comb.* c.-**interest**, an interest in leasehold property. Hence **Cha·ttelism,** the system of holding human beings as chattels.

Chatter (tʃæ·təɹ), *v.* ME. [Echoic; cf. *twitter*, etc. See also CHITTER.] 1. Of birds: To utter short vocal sounds in rapid succession; now applied to sounds approaching those of the human voice. 2. Of human beings: To talk rapidly, incessantly, and with more sound than sense. *intr.* and *trans.* ME. 3. To make a noise by rapidly repeated collisions. Also *causally.* ME.

1. The jay makes answer as the magpie chatters WORDSW. 2. To c. about marriage 1549, like Apes *Temp.* II. ii. 9. 3. My teeth c. BOYLE. The vibration causes the work and the tool to c. upon each other HOLTZAPFEL. Hence **Chattera·tion** (*joc.*), systematic chattering. **Cha·tterbox,** an habitual chatterer. **Cha·tteringly** *adv.*

Chatter (tʃæ·təɹ), *sb.* ME. [f. prec.] 1. The chattering of birds, apes, etc. 2. Incessant trivial talk; prate, tattle 1851.

2. Your words are but idle and empty c. LONGF.

Chatterer (tʃæ·tərəɹ). 1540. [f. as prec. + -ER[1].] 1. One who chatters; a tattler. var. †**Cha·tter.** 2. Any bird of the family *Ampelidæ*; *esp.* the Bohemian C. or Waxwing (*Ampelis garrula*); in N. Amer. the Cedar-bird or C. of Carolina (*A. carolinensis* or *cedrorum*) 1730.

†**Cha·ttery,** *sb.* [Cf. *battery.*] Chatter. MAD. D'ARBLAY.

Cha·ttery, *a.* Given to chatter (*rare*).

‖**Chatty** (tʃɑ·ti), *sb.* 1781. [Hindī *chāṭī.*] *Anglo-Ind.* An East Indian pot for water.

Chatty (tʃæ·ti), *a.* 1762. Given to chat. Hence **Cha·ttiness,** the quality of being c.

Chaucerian (tʃǫsīə·riăn), *a.* (*sb.*) 1660. [f. the pr. name.] 1. Of, pertaining to, or characteristic of Chaucer or his writings. 2. *sb.* A student of Chaucer 1868. So **Chau·cerism,** an expression used by, or imitated from, Chaucer.

Chaud-mellé, mella. ME. [a. OF. *chaude mellee* 'heated affray'; see MÊLÉE. (Erron. identified with *chance medley*.)] *Sc. Law.* A sudden affray arising from the heat of passion; hence, the wounding or killing of a man in such an affray, without premeditation.

‖**Chaudron** (ʃōdroṅ). 1883. [F., 'a cauldron'.] A reddish colour, resembling copper. Also *attrib.*

Chaudron, obs. f. CHALDRON.

Chauffer (tʃǭ·fəɹ). 1833. [var. of CHAFER, perh. influenced by F. *chauffoir.*] A metal basket containing fire, formerly used in lighthouses; a small portable furnace, usually of iron, with air-holes and a grate.

Chauffeur (ʃō·fəɹ, *colloq.* ʃo·vəɹ, Fr. ʃofør). 1899. [a. F. *chauffeur* 'fireman' (see FIREMAN 2). The first motor cars were steam-driven.] A professional driver of a motor car.

Chauldron, obs. f. CHALDRON.

Chaum, *sb.* and *v. dial.* = CHAWM.

‖**Chaumontel** (ʃōmǭntĕl). 1755. [Name of a village in France.] A large variety of pear.

Chaun-, obs. sp. of CHAN-.

Chau·noprockt. [ad. Gr. χαυνόπρωκτος.] A 'wide-breeched' person. BROWNING.

‖**Chaussée** (ʃose). 1817. [Fr. :—L. type *calceata*; see CAUSEY.] A causeway; a high road (in France, Belgium, etc.).

‖**Chausses.** *pl. Hist.* 1484. [a. OF. *chauces*, mod.F. *chausses*, f. L. *calceus*, *calcius*, shoe, half-boot. Formerly naturalized (tʃɑu·sĕz).] Pantaloons or tight coverings for the legs and feet; *esp.* of mail (in OF. *chauces de fer*).

‖**Chaussure** (ʃosü·r). ME. [F. :—L. **calceatura*, f. *calceare.* Formerly naturalized.] Anything worn on the feet; shoes, boots, etc.

‖**Chauvin** (ʃověn). [F.; from Nicolas *Chauvin* of Rochefort, a veteran soldier of the First Republic and Empire, whose demonstrative patriotism was ultimately ridiculed by his comrades.] Popularized as name of a character in Cogniard's vaudeville, *La Cocarde Tricolore*, 1831. Hence,

Chauvinism (ʃōu·viniz'm). 1870. [ad. F. *chauvinisme*, f. *Chauvin*; see prec. and -ISM.] Exaggerated and bellicose patriotism. So **Chau·vinist.** **Chauvini·stic** *a.*

†**Chave,** *v.* ME. [f. CHAFF.] 1. To mix or strew with chaff. ME. only. 2. To separate the chaff from –1726.

Chavel, ME. form of JOWL, q. v. Hence †**Cha·vel** *v.* to wag the jaws, chatter; *trans.* to mumble (food).

Cha·vender. 1475. = CHEVIN, the chub (fish).

†**Chaw, chawe,** *sb.*[1] 1530. [var. of JAW, influenced by *chew.*] *pl.* Jaws –1626. Rarely in *sing.* A jaw –1601.

Chaw, *sb.*[2] (now *vulgar*). 1772. [f. CHAW *v.*] An act of chewing; also, that which is chewed.

Chaw (tʃǭ), *v.* (now *vulgar*). 1530. [A by-form of CHEW (OE. *cēowan*).] 1. To chew; now *esp.* to chew without swallowing; to champ. Also *intr.* †2. *fig.* To mumble (words) –1649; to ruminate upon, brood over 1558. 3. *U.S. slang. To c. up*: to 'do for' 1844.

1. Chawe your meat well 1562. As venemous as a chaw'd bullet 1683. 2. To c. one's malice 1600. Hence **Chaw·er** (*rare*).

Chaw·-bacon. 1822. [f. prec.] A country bumpkin.

†**Chaw·buck,** *sb.* 1698. [a. Pers. and Urdu.] A whip; flogging with a whip –1784. Hence †**Chaw·buck** *v.* to whip.

Chaw·dron. [ME. *chaudoun*, a. OF. *chaudun* (*caldun*) :—L. type *caldunum*, app. from *calidus.* Corrupted later to CHALDRON. (See also CHOWDER.)] †1. A sauce, consisting of chopped entrails, spice, etc. –1615. 2. Entrails, *esp.* as used for food (*arch.*) 1578.

†**Chawn,** *sb.* 1601. [perh. :—CHINE *v.*[1]] A gap, cleft, fissure; a chine –1799. Hence †**Chawn** *v.* to gape or cause to gape open.

Chaw·-stick. 1756. [f. CHAW *v.*] A species of Gouania (*G. domingensis*, N.O. *Rhamnaceæ*), so called in Jamaica because its stems are chewed as a stomachic.

‖**Chay, Choy** (tʃēi, tʃai, tʃoi), **chaya** (tʃai·a). 1598. [ad. Tamil *saya.*] The root of the Indian plant *Oldenlandia umbellata* (N.O. *Cinconaceæ*), which yields a deep red dye.

Chay, vulgar corruption of CHAISE.

†**Che** (tʃə), *pron.* An expanded form of CH, for *ich* I.

†**Cheap,** *sb.* [A com. Teut. sb.: OE. *cēap* barter, etc. :—OTeut. **kaupoz.* The sense 'cattle' is found only in OE.] 1. A bargain; bargaining –ME. 2. Market; a market-place. (Hence in place-names, as *Cheapside*, etc.) –1596. 3. Price –1440. 4. Goods, *esp.* (live) cattle (OE. only).

2. *Good cheap*: a cheap market. (Hence *cheap* alone: Plenty; opp. to *dearth.*) quasi-*adj.* That is a good bargain; cheap. quasi-*adv.* Cheaply.

Cheap (tʃīp). 1509. [Short. from 'good cheap'.]

A. *adj.* 1. Low in price; inexpensive. Opp. to *dear.* Also *transf.* (of the price, the market, etc.) 1598. 2. Well worth the price 1611. 3. *fig.* Costing little labour, trouble, etc. 1603. 4. Hence, Worthless 1571. 5. Lightly esteemed, common 1591.

1. Cheapest, say the prudent, is the dearest labour EMERSON. 2. Goods may be low-priced, and not c. DE FOE. 4. His c. Latin 1872. 5. Making the king c. PEPYS. Phr. *Dirt c.*: as c. as dirt. So *Dog c.* (colloq.). Hence **Chea·p-ish** *a.*, **-ly** *adv.*, **-ness.**

B. *advb.* At a low price, cheaply; easily 1568.

C. *subst.* in *On the c.*: on the cheap scale, cheaply 1888.

Comb.: C. **Jack** or C. **John,** a travelling hawker who offers bargains; c. **trip**: see TRIP; hence **cheap-tripper.**

†**Cheap,** *v.* [A com. Teut. vb.: OE. *cēapian*, f. *cēap* CHEAP *sb.* Now repl. by CHEAPEN.] 1. *orig.* (*intr.*) To barter; to trade –ME. 2. *trans.* To buy –ME.; to offer to buy, price –1614; to offer for sale –1580.

Cheapen (tʃī·p'n), *v.* 1574. [f. CHEAP *a.* or *v.*] 1. To ask the price of, bid for. Also *fig.* (*arch.*). 2. To make cheap, lower the price of 1833. Also *fig.* 3. *intr.* To become cheap (*lit.* and *fig.*) 1805.

1. I cheapened a pig and was asked only eighteen sols WILKES. 2. To c. production MILL. Hence **Chea·pener,** †a bidder, var. †**Chea·per**; one who makes a thing cheap.

†**Chea·ping,** *vbl. sb.* OE. [f. CHEAP *v.*] 1. Bargaining; buying and selling –1580. 2. Market, a market-place. (Hence in place-names, as *Chipping Norton*, etc.) –1587.

Cheare, obs. f. CHAIR, CHEER.

Cheat (tʃīt), *sb.*[1] [In sense 1, ME. *chet(e)*, aphet. f. *achet*, var. of *eschet*, ESCHEAT. Sense 3 is of doubtful origin; senses 4–6 are from the vb.] †1. An ESCHEAT –1649. †2. Booty, spoil –1610. †3. *Thieves' Cant.* 'Thing, article', usually with a descriptive word –1826. 4. †The action of cheating; fraud –1696; a fraud, an imposition 1648. 5. One who or that which cheats 1532. 6. Local name for grasses, which resemble the grain among which they grow.

3. *The c.* (= *nubbing-*, *topping-*, *treyning-c.*): the gallows. 4. Those who live by cheats and quirks 1690. 5. Extortioners and cheats FARRAR. Callinge ..the dice Chetes 1532.

†**Cheat,** *sb.*[2] 1450. [?] Wheaten bread of the second quality; see MANCHET –1655.

Cheat (tʃīt), *v.* 1440. [ME. *chete*; see CHEAT *sb.*] †1. *trans.* To escheat. ME. only. 2. To deprive *of* by deceit 1590; to impose upon 1634. 3. *intr.* To practise deceit 1647. 4. To beguile (weariness, etc.) 1712. †5. To obtain by cheating –1737.

2. The Scaffold of its prey to c. 1821. To c. the eye with blear illusion MILT. 3. To c. in an examination (*mod.*). 4. To c. the time SCOTT. Hence **Chea·table** *a.* that may be cheated. **Cheatee·**, one who is cheated (*colloq.*). **Chea·ter**, †an escheator; one who cheats. (An habitual *cheater* is now called a CHEAT.) **Chea·tery**, the practice of cheating.

Che·bacco. 1837. [app. a. Pg. *xabeco* (ʃabe·ko); cf. next and XEBEC.] *C.-boat*: A kind of vessel employed in the Newfoundland fisheries; called also *pinkstern*.

Chebec, -ck (ʃī·be·k). Now usu. **Xebec.** 1762. [a. F. *chebec*; of unkn. origin.] A small three-masted Mediterranean vessel, a XEBEC.

‖ **Chebule** (kĕbū·l). 1599. [a. F. *chébule*; ?ad. Urdu *Kābulī* of Cabul.] The dried prune-like astringent fruit of *Terminalia Chebula*, imported under the name of myrobalan. Also *attrib.* Hence **Chebu·lic** *a.*

Check (tʃek), *int.* and *sb.*[1] [ME. *chek*, aphet. f. **eschek*, *-chak*, a. OF. *eschec*, *eschac*, med.L. *scaccus*, *scāchus*; ad. (through Arab.) Pers. *shāh* 'king', also the 'King' in chess. Hence the Arab. phrase *shāh māt(a* 'the King is dead'; see CHECKMATE. See also CHESS.]

A. *int.* A call at chess by which an opponent is notified that his King is exposed. Also *fig.*

fig. Therewith Fortune said Checke here CHAUCER.

B. *sb.* 1. *Chess.* The act of threatening the King; the position of the King when he is exposed to the attack of one of the opponent's men ME. Also *fig.* and *transf.* †2. A taunt –1635; a rebuke, censure –1751. 3. A sudden arrest given to the onward course of anything; a rebuff, repulse, reverse 1515. 4. *Hawking.* A false stoop, when a hawk forsakes her quarry for baser game. *Hist.* ME. Also, the baser game itself 1575. 5. A sudden stoppage or pause 1532. †6. A stoppage of wages or a fine; the amount stopped –1708. 7. Restraint upon action or conduct by a controlling power 1579. 8. Any person or thing that checks 1647. 9. Control by which accuracy, etc., is secured 1786. 10. A mark made against an item in an account, list, etc., to show that it has been checked. 11. A counterfoil, token, ticket, or other means to secure accuracy, security from fraud, etc. 1706. 12. A counter used in games at cards. *U.S.* 1870. †13. Short for CHECK-ROLL –1611.

3. A c. to industry MᶜCULLOCH. Our c. in Holland 1799. The hounds ran him without a c. WHYTE-MELVILLE. 4. *To fly at c.* Of dogs: *To run at c.* 5. †*To take c.*: to pull up, take offence. 7. *In c.*: under control. 8. Of the checks to population MALTHUS. 12. *To hand in one's checks*: to die (*colloq.*).

Clerk of the c.: an officer in the royal household keeping the c.-roll and having control of the yeomen of the guard, etc.; †formerly, an officer of control in the dockyards, etc.

Check (tʃek), *sb.*[2] ME. [Cf. CHECK *v.*[2]] 1. *Her.* and *gen.* A pattern of cross lines forming small squares, as in a chess-board. 2. A fabric with such a pattern 1614. Also *attrib.*

Check, *sb.*[3], var. of CHEQUE.

Check (tʃek), *v.*[1] [ME. *chek-en*, aphet. f. *achek-*, **eschek-*, a. OF. *eschequier*, *eschecquer* to play chess; see CHECK *sb.*[1]] I. 1. *Chess.* To give check to an opponent's King (see CHECK *sb.*[1] 1) 1614. Also *fig.* †2. To strike, hit –1608; *intr.* to clash –1632.

2. If it (Loue) checke once with businesse BACON.

II. 1. To stop or retard the motion or course of ME. †2. *intr.* (for *refl.*) To stop short; to stand *at*; to wince (*at*) –1724. *Hawking.* To forsake the quarry and fly at baser game (cf. CHECK *sb.*[1] 4). †3. To stop (a person) from receiving part of his wages; to fine, mulct –1803.

1. *To c. a brace* (Naut.): to ease it off when too stiffly extended. *C. her* (a ship): stop her way. (Adm. Smyth.) 2. That which you c. at is the immortality of the soul JER. TAYLOR. *To c. at the fist* (Hawking): to shy at, recoil from, the fist.

III. †1. To taunt, revile –1592. 2. To rebuke 1514.

2. †*To c. at* (intr.): to aim reproof at.

IV. 1. *fig.* To stop (action, growth, etc.); to repress, restrain 1581. 2. To curb, control; to act as a check on 1630. 3. To control (a statement, account, etc.) by some method of comparison. Also *to c. a person* (in his account, etc.) 1695.

1. If I can checke my erring loue, I will *Two Gent.* II. iv. 213. To c. a laugh JANE AUSTEN. 2. In England, the strong classes c. the weaker EMERSON. 3. *To c. off*: to tick off as found correct. *To c. up*: to examine or count up in detail.

V. *intr.* To draw a cheque (*upon* a person, *for* an amount). *U.S.* 1843.

Hence **Checked** *ppl. a.*[1] stopped in progress; repressed; restrained. **Checker** *sb.*[1] one who checks.

Check (tʃek), *v.*[2] ME. [? Short for *checker*, *chequer*; or aphet. f. **escheck*, a. OF. *eschequié*. So CHECK *sb.*[2]] To mark with a pattern of †squares, or crossing lines. Also *transf.* and †*fig.* Hence **Checked** *ppl. a.*[2] **Che·cker** *sb.*[2] =CHEQUER, q. v.; *spec.* in *pl.* Draughts.

Check-, in *comb.* [from the stem of CHECK *v.*[1]]:

check-book, a book in which items of control are entered (but see also CHEQUE); **-clerk**; **-key**, a latch-key; **-lock**, a small lock for securing a lock, bar, bolt, etc.; **-man**, one who checks fares, tickets, etc.; **-nut**, a nut screwed over another one to keep it from loosening; **-rein**, (*a*) a coupling-rein; (*b*) a strap which prevents a horse from lowering his head; **-strap**, the strap of a helmet, etc., running under the chin; **-taker**; **-till**, a till with a contrivance to check the receipts; **-weigher**, **-weighman**, at collieries, a man acting for the workmen who checks the weight of the coal sent up.

Checker, *v.*; see CHEQUER.

Che·cker-berry. 1823. [Cf. CHEQUER *sb.*[2]] The fruit of *Gaultheria procumbens*; hence the plant itself; the winter-green. ¶ The Partridge-berry, *Michella repens* (Webster).

†**Che·cker-roll, che·quer-roll.** 1461. [f. *checker*, CHEQUER *sb.*[1]] A roll of persons chargeable to the royal exchequer; CHECK-ROLL. *transf.* A roll of persons. –1589.

Che·ckery. ME. [Aphet. f. OF. *eschekeré*; see CHEQUER *v.*] †Checked cloth –1472; chequed pattern (*rare*) 1837.

†**Checklaton,** var. of CICLATON. Spenser.

†**Che·ckle,** *v.* 1627. [= north. KECKLE.] *intr.* To laugh giddily –1684.

Che·ckless, *a. rare.* 1604. [f. CHECK *sb.*[1] + -LESS.] Unchecked.

Checkmate (tʃe·kmē·t), *int.* and *sb.* [ME. *chek mat(e*, ad. (ult.) Arab. *shāh māt(a*; see CHECK *sb.*[1]]

A. *int.* Exclam. at chess by a player on putting the opponent's King into inextricable check, whereby the game is won; orig. meaning '(your) King is dead'. (Now MATE.) Also *transf.*

B. *sb.* 1. This exclam. as a name for itself, and for the conclusive move which it announces. *To give c. to*: to make this move. (Also MATE.) ME. Also *fig.* and *transf.* †2. (*erron.*) An equal in a contest, a match; as if 'a mate that checks' –1651.

1. *fig.* Loue they him called, that gaue me c. SPENSER.

Checkmate (tʃe·kmē·t), *v.* ME. [f. the sb.] 1. *Chess.* To give checkmate to; see the sb. sense 1. (Now to MATE.) 1789. 2. *transf.* To arrest or defeat utterly. Now, often: To defeat the 'game' of, by a counter-move. ME.

2. To c. the ingenuity of the local taxmasters (*mod.*).

†**Check-roll.** 1450. [later var. of CHECKER-ROLL, influenced by CHECK *v.*] 1. =CHECKER-ROLL –1769. 2. A list of servants –1636. 3. *fig.* A muster-roll –1653.

Che·ck-stone. 1587. [? In Sc., *chuckie-stones.*] A small smooth round pebble; a game played with these. Also *fig.* Still *dial.*

Che·ck-string. 1774. A string by which the occupant of a carriage may signal to the driver to stop.

Che·cky, chequee, *a.* 1486. [orig. aphet. f. OF. *eschequié*; see CHECK *v.*[2]] *Her.* and *gen.* Checked, chequered.

Che·ddar. 1666. Name of a village in Somerset. Hence *Cheddar cheese* (or *Cheddar*).

†‖**Chedreux.** 1678. [pr. name.] A kind of peruke –1745.

‖**Chee-chee.** 1781. [Hindī *chhī-chhī* fie! (*lit.* filth).] *Anglo-Ind.* The minced English of half-breeds or Eurasians; the class of half-breeds.

Cheek (tʃīk), *sb.* [OE. *cēce*, *cēace*:—WGer. type **kăkā*. Only Teut.] I. *lit.* †1. The jaw, jaw-bone –ME.; *pl.* (also *sing.*) the fauces –1450. 2. The side of the face below the eye OE. Also *fig.* 3. *colloq.* Insolence in speaking to any one 1840; cool confidence, effrontery 1852.

2. *fig.* Ocean's c. BYRON. 3. *To give c.*: =CHEEK *v.* *To have the c.* (to do anything). *To one's own c.* (vulgar): to oneself. Phr. **C. by jowl**: side by side; in the closest intimacy.

II. Transf. and techn. Mostly in *pl.* 1. *gen.* Side 1555. 2. The side-posts of a door, gate, etc. ME. 3. *Harness.* The ring or other part at each end of the bit 1617. 4. *Mech.*, etc. Those parts of machines, etc., which are arranged in lateral pairs: *e.g.* the side-pieces of a piece of ordnance; the jaws of a vice; in *Founding*, one of the parts of a flask consisting of more than two parts 1650. 5. *Naut.*: a. the projections on each side of a mast on which the trestle-trees rest; b. the outside wooden part of a block, etc.

1. By the cheeks of a red fire STEVENSON. 2. To name sic a word at my door c. SCOTT.

Comb.: **c.-bone**, †the bone of the lower jaw; the bone above the c. forming the lower boundary of the orbits of the eyes; **-pouch**, a pouch-like enlargement of the c., *esp.* in some monkeys; **-tooth**, a molar.

Cheek (tʃīk), *v.* 1538. [f. prec.] I. *trans.* To form a cheek or side to. 2. *colloq.* To address cheekily; to face with effrontery 1840.

Cheeked (tʃīkt), *a.* 1552. Having a cheek or cheeks; in *comb.* as *red-c.*, etc.

Cheeky (tʃī·ki), *a. colloq.* 1859. [f. CHEEK *sb.* I. 3 + -Y[1].] Characterized by cheek. Hence **Chee·kiness** (*colloq.*).

Cheep (tʃīp), *sb.* Chiefly *Sc.* 1774. [f. next.] A faint shrill sound, such as the voice of a young bird or a mouse.

Cheep (tʃīp), *v.* Chiefly *Sc.* 1513. [Echoic.] *intr.* To utter cheeps, like young birds, mice, bats, etc. Also *trans.*

trans. 'Hold hard now', cheeps little Conchy M. SCOTT. Hence **Chee·per**; *esp.* of the chicks of partridge and grouse. **Chee·py** *a.* given to cheeping.

Cheer (tʃīᵊɹ), *sb.* [ME. *chere*, a. OF. *chiere*, *chere*:—late L. *cara* face; of unkn. origin.] †1. The face –1590; the expression of the face; countenance (*arch.*) –1830. 2. Disposition, mood; usu. qualified as 'good', 'glad', etc. ME. 3. Gladness, mirth, gaiety ME. †4. Hospitable reception or entertainment –1666. 5. *concr.* Fare, viands, food ME. 6. Solace; encouragement 1549. 7. A shout of encouragement, welcome, approbation, or congratulation; *esp.* in *pl.* 1720.

1. To dreden the chere of them WYCLIF *Jer.* i. 17. 2. So I piped with merry c. BLAKE. *To be of good c.* *What c.*: 'how are you?' 5. To fede on simple cheare 1567. *The fewer the better c.*, i. e. the more for each to eat. 7. The result was received with cheers and counter-cheers (*mod.*). Hence **Chee·rless** *a.* devoid of c. **Chee·rless-ly** *adv.*, **-ness.**

Cheer (tʃīᵊɹ), *v.* ME. [f. the sb.] †1. *refl.* and *intr.* To assume a disposition or state of mind –1725. 2. To make of good cheer ME.; *refl.* to take heart (mostly in imper.) ME. 3. To make cheerful ME.; also †*intr.* 4. *trans.* †To feast –1697; to solace as food does 1548. 5. To brighten up (the face, etc.) 1611. 6. To encourage, inspirit, animate or incite; now *esp.* by cries or shouts ME. 7. To salute with cheers 1798. Also *intr.*

1. How c. you gentlemen GREENE. 2. So cheard he his fair Spouse MILT. *P. L.* v. 129. 4. The cups, That c. but not inebriate COWPER. 6. He cheer'd the dogs to follow her who fled DRYDEN. 7. The ship was cheer'd COLERIDGE.

Cheer up, to raise the spirits of by cheering words; *intr.* (for *refl.*) to take courage. Hence **Chee·rer**, he who or that which cheers; *Sc.* a cheering cup. **Chee·ringly** *adv.*

Cheered (tʃīᵊɹd), *a.* ME. [f. CHEER *sb.* and *vb.*] 1. Having a (certain) cheer or countenance. 2. *ppl. a.* Made cheerful.

Cheerful (tʃīᵊ·ɹfŭl), *a.* ME. [f. CHEER *sb.* + -FUL.] 1. Full of cheer; of good cheer; blithe, lively and in good spirits. 2. Cheering, animating; bright, enlivening 1460.

1. God loveth a c. giver 2 *Cor.* ix. 7. 2. C. Chambers BACON, colours BURKE. **Chee·rfulize** *v.* to make c. **Chee·rful-ly** *adv.*, **-ness.**

Cheerio (tʃīᵊriō̆ᵘ·), *int.* Also **cheero.** 1910. [f. CHEER(Y) + O *int.*] A parting exclamation of encouragement.

Cheerly (tʃīᵊ·ɹli). 1558. [f. CHEER *sb.* + -LY[1] and [2].] A. *adj.* Cheerful (*arch.*) 1571. B. *adv.* 1. Cheerily (*arch.*) 1558. *spec.* Heartily, with a will. *Temp.* I. i. 6. 2. Cheeringly 1794. Hence †**Chee·rliness.**

Cheer-up, var. CHIRRUP.

Cheery (tʃīᵊ·ri), *a.* 1611. [f. CHEER *sb.*

More colloq. than CHEERFUL.] 1. Abounding in cheerfulness; lively. 2. Such as to cheer; cheering 1720.

1. The Corporal, with c. eye STERNE. 2. A c. bowl GAY. Hence Chee·rily *adv.* Chee·riness.

Cheese (tʃīz), *sb.*[1] [OE. *cēse*, ad. (ult.) L. *caseus*. Cf. Ger. *käse*.] 1. The curd of milk (coagulated by rennet) separated from the whey and pressed into a solid mass; (with *pl.*) a shaped mass of this. 2. *transf.* (in *Cider-making*) A mass of pomace pressed together in the form of a cheese 1796. 3. The fruit of the common Mallow (*Malva silvestris*), of a flattened cheese-like shape 1527.

1. See also GREEN c. 2. b. A conserve of fruit pressed into the consistency of cheese (cf. DAMSON-CHEESE).

Phr. *To make cheeses* [F. *faire des fromages*]: a school-girls' amusement, consisting in turning rapidly round and then suddenly sinking down, so that the petticoats take something of the form of a cheese. Hence occas., a deep curtsying.

Comb.: **c.-cake**, a tart, orig. containing c.; now filled with a mixture of milk-curds, sugar, and butter, or whipped egg and sugar; **-fly**, a small black fly (*Piophila casei*) bred in c.; **-hopper**, the maggot of the c.-fly; also the fly; **-maggot** = *cheese-hopper*; **-mite**, the minute arachnid (*Acarus domesticus*) which infests old c.; **-press**, an apparatus for pressing the curds in cheese-making; **-rennet**, **-running**, *Galium verum*, Lady's Bedstraw, occas. used to coagulate milk; **-vat**, †**-fat**, the mould in which the curds are pressed and the c. shaped.

Cheese (tʃīz), *sb.*[2] *slang.* 1818. [prob. a. Urdū *chīz* 'thing'.] The correct thing.

Cheese, *v.* 1812. *Thieves' slang.* To stop, leave off. *C. it!* = have done! run away!

Chee·selip, -lep[1]. Now *dial.* [OE. *cēse-lyb(b*; f. CHEESE + a word = ON. *lyf* herb, mod. G. dial. *lüpp* rennet.] 1. Rennet, for use in cheese-making. 2. The dried stomach of a calf, etc., similarly used OE.

†**Chee·selip, -lep**[2]. 1530. [?] The common wood-louse; also, the allied Armadillo wood-louse (? *dial.*).

Chee·semonger. 1510. One who deals in cheese.

Chee·se-pa·ring. 1597. [f. CHEESE *sb.*[1]] *sb.* A paring of the rind of cheese. Also *fig.* *vbl. sb.* The paring of cheese. *fig.* Parsimonious saving 1871. *ppl. a.* Parsimonious 1867.

Cheesy (tʃī·zi), *a.* ME. [f. CHEESE *sb.*[1] + -Y[1].] 1. Of or belonging to, abounding in, or resembling, cheese. ¶2. [prob. f. CHEESE *sb.*[2]] Fine, showy 1858. Hence **Chee·siness.**

Cheetah (tʃī·tă). 1781. [a. Hind. *chītā*.] The Hunting Leopard, *Acinomyx jubatus* (*Felis jubata*), used for hunting deer in India.

Cheewink, che- (tʃī,wiŋk). 1796. [From its note; also *towhee*.] A N. Amer. bird (*Pipilo erythrophthalmus*), also called Ground-robin.

‖**Chef** (ʃef). 1842. [F.; = 'head'.] A head cook in the kitchen of a large household.

‖**Chef d'œuvre** (ʃedö·vr). Pl. **chefs-d'œuvre.** 1762. [F.; *lit.* 'chief (piece) of work'.] A masterpiece.

Chego, obs. f. CHIGOE.

Cheil-, cheilo-, repr. Gr. χειλο- lip, used more commonly in the Latinized spelling *chil-*, CHILO-, q. v.

Cheir-, cheiro-, repr. Gr. χειρ(ο, comb. f. χείρ hand; also written *chir-*, CHIRO-, q.v.

Chei·ropod, -ped. 1837. [f. Gr. χειρο- hand + -ποδος footed.] *Zool.* A name applied to mammals possessed of hands, including the Bimana and Quadrumana.

‖**Cheiroptera** (kəirǫ·ptĕrā), *sb. pl.* Occas. **chir-**. 1835. [f. as prec. + -πτερος winged.] *Zool.* An order of Mammalia, having elongated finger-bones supporting a membrane attached to the posterior limbs and the side of the body, and adapted for flight; the Bats. Hence **Cheiro·pteran** *a.* and *sb.* **Cheiro·pterous** *a.*

‖**Cheirotherium** (kəiᵊroþī·riə̆m). 1855. [f. as prec. + θηρίον beast.] *Palæont.* A large extinct four-footed animal, whose footprints resemble a human hand. Hence **Cheirothe·rian** *a.*

Cheka: see **Tcheka.**

‖**Chela**[1] (kī·lă). Pl. **chelæ** (kī·lī). 1646. [ad. Gr. χηλή.] The prehensile claw of crabs and lobsters; also, of scorpions. Hence **Che·late, Cheli·ferous, Che·liform** *adjs.*

‖**Chela**[2] (tʃē·lă). 1883. [Hindī; = 'slave, servant'.] In esoteric Buddhism, a novice. Hence **Che·laship.**

Chele·rythrine. [f. L. *chel(idonium* celandine + Gr. ἐρυθρός.] *Chem.* An alkaloid forming orange-red salts, obtained from *Chelidonium*.

Chelicer, -cere (ke·lisəɹ, -sīᵊɹ). 1835. [a. F. *chélicère*, L. *chelicera* (also used), f. Gr. χηλή (see CHELA[1]) + κέρας.] One of the prehensile claws which arm the proboscis of scorpions and spiders. Hence **Cheli·ceral** *a.*

Chelidonic (kelidǫ·nik), *a.* 1863. [f. L. *chelidonium* CELANDINE or Swallow-wort + -IC.] *Chem.* In *C. acid*, $C_7H_4O_6$, obtained from the juice of the Greater Celandine.

‖**Chelifer** (ke·lifəɹ, kī·li-). 1865. [f. CHELA[1] + L. *-fer* bearing.] *Zool.* A genus of Spiders having the appearance of small tailless scorpions, called also *Book-scorpion*.

Cheloid (kī·loid). 1876. [a. mod.F. *chéloïde*, f. Gr. χηλή.] *Med.* A disease of the skin, having claw-like processes radiating from its extremities. Also *attrib.*

Chelonian (kĭlōᵘ·niăn), *a.* 1826. [f. mod. L. *Chelonia*.] Of or belonging to the order of reptiles called *Chelonia*, distinguished by having the body enclosed in a double shell, and comprising tortoises and turtles. *sb.* [sc. *animal.*]

†**Chelydre.** ME. [a. OF. *chelidre*, f. (ult.) χέλυς + ὕδρος, f. ὕδωρ.] A kind of fetid amphibious serpent -1607.

Chemiatric (kemi,æ·trik), *a.* 1837. [f. Gr. χημία alchemy, chemistry + ἰατρεία.] Relating to a (Paracelsian) theory of medicine, according to which diseases are referred to disturbances of fermentations in the body, and are treated accordingly. As *sb.* One who held this theory.

Chemic (ke·mik). 1576. [a. F. *chimique*; see ALCHEMY.] A. *adj.* 1. Alchemic. †2. = CHEMIATRIC *a.* -1763. 3. Of or belonging to chemistry. (*poet.* for CHEMICAL.) 1634.

1. Chimick Gold DRYDEN. 3. The c. labour of the blood TENNYSON.

B. *sb.* †1. An ALCHEMIST -1673. †2. = CHEMIATRIC *sb.* -1660. †3. A chemist -1651. 4. *Bleaching.* Chloride of lime (*mod.*).

Che·mic, *v.* 1614. [f. prec.] †1. To transmute by or as by alchemy -1720. 2. *Bleaching.* To treat with solution of chloride of lime (*mod.*).

Chemical (ke·mikăl), *a.* 1576. [f. CHEMIC *a.* + -AL.] †1. Alchemical -1747. †2. = CHEMIATRIC, as opp. to 'Galenical' -1782. 3. Relating or belonging to chemistry; obtained by chemistry 1576. 4. Versed in chemistry 1615. 5. as *sb.* (*esp.* in *pl.*) A substance obtained or used in chemical operations 1747.

3. *C. affinity, attraction*, etc.: see AFFINITY, ATTRACTION, etc. The c. composition of plants SIR H. DAVY, of the atmosphere HUXLEY. Che·mically *adv.*

Chemico- (ke·miko), comb. f. CHEMIC *a.*, in sense 'chemically', 'relating to chemistry in connexion with . . .'; as in *c.-agricultural*.

Chemise (ʃĭmī·z). ME. [a. OF., F. *chemise* :—late L. *camisia* shirt, surplice (whence OE. *cemes*).] 1. A body garment: formerly variously used, later *spec.* a woman's undergarment (= SHIFT *sb.* III. 3), now largely superseded (see CAMISOLE). Cf. SHIMMY[1]. 2. *Fortif.* A wall with which a bastion, etc. is lined 1704.

Chemisette (ʃemize·t). 1807. [a. F., dim. of *chemise*.] 1. A bodice, more or less like the upper part of a chemise. 2. An article, usually of lace or muslin, made to fill in the open front of a woman's dress 1844.

Chemism (ke·miz'm). *rare.* 1851. [a. F. *chemisme*, parallel to *chimiste*.] Chemical action, activity, or force.

Chemist (ke·mist, ki·mist). 1562. [a. F. *chimiste*, ad. mod.L. *chimista*, for earlier *al(chimista*.] †1. = ALCHEMIST -1732. †2. = CHEMIATRIC *sb.* -1616. 3. One versed in chemistry; one who makes chemical investigations 1626. 4. One who deals in or retails medicinal drugs 1683. var. (now *rare*) **Chy·mist.** Hence †**Che·mistic (-al)**, *adjs.* (*rare*).

Chemistry (ke·mistri). 1605. [In 17th c. *chymistrie*, f. *chymist* CHEMIST; ?orig. contemptuous.] †1. ALCHEMY -1788. †2. The 'Chemical' or 'Paracelsian' practice of medicine -1711. 3. That branch of science which deals with the several elementary substances, or forms of matter, of which all bodies are composed, the laws that regulate the combination of these elements in the formation of compound bodies, and the phenomena that accompany their exposure to diverse physical conditions. (The reference in early writers and dictionaries is to chemistry as an art only, i. e. *practical* or *applied* c.) 1646. Also *fig.*

3. *Chymistry*, is the Anatomy of natural Bodies by fire BAILEY. *Inorganic c.*: that which deals with inorganic bodies. *Organic c.*: that treating of the substances found only in organic structures. *Agricultural c.*: that bearing upon agriculture. *fig.* The world has a sure c., by which it extracts what is excellent in its children EMERSON.

Chemitype (ke·mitəip). 1851. [f. *chemi-* in CHEMIC, etc. + TYPE.] A stereotype, obtained in relief from an engraved plate by a chemical process; hence *c. process*, **Che·mitypy.**

Chemolysis (kĭmǫ·lisis). *rare.* 1872. [f. *chem-* in CHEMIC + Gr. λύσις; after *electrolysis*.] The decomposition of organic compounds into more simple substances by merely chemical agents. So **Chemoly·tic** *a.* relating to c.

‖**Chemosis** (kĭmōᵘ·sis). 1708. [a. Gr., f. χήμη a cockle-shell.] *Med.* An affection of the conjunctiva of the eye, which causes it to be elevated and projected over the edge of the cornea. Hence **Chemo·sed** *ppl. a.*

‖**Chemosmosis** (kemǫzmōᵘ·sis). [mod.L., f. *chem-* + OSMOSIS.] Chemical action taking place through an intervening membrane (Dicts.).

‖**Chenar** (tʃīnāɹ). 1634. [Pers. *chinar*.] Name of the Oriental Plane-tree.

Chenille (ʃĭnī·l). 1738. [a. F.; *lit.* hairy caterpillar :—L. *canicula*, dim. of *canis*.] Velvety cord, having fibres of silk and wool standing out round a core of thread or wire; used in trimming and bordering dresses, etc.

Chenopod (ke·nopǫd). 1555. [ad. mod L. *chenopodium*, f. Gr. χηνόπους goose-foot.] *Bot.* The plant genus *Chenopodium* or Goose-foot.

Cheque, check (tʃek). 1706. [See CHECK *sb.*[1] 10 and CHECK *v.*[1] IV. 3. *Cheque* is a var. of *check* (also used, *esp.* in U.S.).] †1. The counterfoil of a bank bill, draft, etc. -1782. 2. A draft form having a counterfoil 1717. 3. A written order to a banker directing him to pay money as stated therein 1774. Also *fig.*

3. *Blank c.*: a cheque signed by the drawer but with the amount left blank to be filled up by the donee. *Comb.*: c.-book, *formerly*, a book in which the Bank kept a register of cheques issued; *now*, a book containing cheque forms with their counterfoils.

Chequeen, chequin (tʃĭkī·n). *arch.* 1583. [ad. It. *zecchino* (tsekkī·no), f. *zecca* the mint at Venice.] = SEQUIN, q.v.

Chequer, checker (tse·kəɹ), *sb.*[1] [ME. *cheker*, aphet. f. *escheker*, a. OF. *eschekier* :—late L. *scaccarium* orig. a chess-board. The sp. *chequer* is most used.]

I. †1. A chess-board -1828. †2. The game of chess. ME. only. 3. *pl.* The game of draughts (*dial.* and *U.S.*) 1838. 4. A chess-board as the sign of an inn; a name for a public-house ME.

II. †1. The Court of EXCHEQUER -1691. †2. Treasury (*lit.* and *fig.*) -1692.

III. 1. *pl.* Squares or spots like those of a chess-board 1629. 2. Chequer-work 1779. 3. *Arch.* in *pl.* 'In masonry, stones in the facing of walls which have all their thin joints continued in straight lines, without interruption or breaking joints' (Gwilt).

Che·quer, *sb.*[2] *dial.* 1649. [app. from the appearance of the fruit.] In *pl.* The berries of the Wild Service tree, *Pyrus torminalis.* In *sing.* also the tree.

Chequer, checker (tʃe·kəɹ), *v.* ME. [f. CHEQUER *sb.*] 1. *trans.* To divide or mark like a chess-board in sections (with or without reference to colour) 1486. 2. To diversify with or as with a different colour or shade; to interrupt the uniformity of ME. 3. To arrange chequer-wise 1677. †4. To deposit in an exchequer -1734.

2. *Rom. & Jul.* II. iii. 2. His sleep was checkered with starts and moans DICKENS. The good and ill that c. life COWPER.

†**Chequer-chamber.** 1494. 1. Treasury-room -1611. 2. A court of appellate jurisdiction; = EXCHEQUER-CHAMBER -1714.

Chequered, checkered (tʃe·kəɹd), *ppl. a.*

1486. [f. CHEQUER *sb.* and *v.*] 1. Marked like a chess-board; hence, having a pattern of various crossing colours. 2. Diversified in colour, light and shade, character; full of alternation (*esp.* for the worse) 1656.

1. His chequer'd plaid SCOTT. 2. Dancing in the Chequer'd shade MILT. Weather..chequered, a fair and a rainy day SWIFT.

Che·quer-wise, *adv.* ME. Like a CHEQUER or chess-board. (Orig. *in chequer-wise.*)

Che·quer-work, che·cker-work. 1519. 1. Work chequered in pattern. Also *attrib.* 2. *transf.* and *fig.* Anything chequered with contrasting characters 1618.

1. The checkerworke pavements HOLLAND. 2. Now joy with sorrow, checkerworke T. ADAMS.

Chequin, var. of CHEQUEEN.

†**Chere,** *a.* ME. [a. F. *cher, chère.*] 1. Dear; precious –1450. 2. Careful (*over*). Cf. CHARY. –1496. Hence †**Che·rely** *adv.*

‖**Cherimoya** (tʃerimoi·ă). Also **chiri-, -moyer.** 1736. [ad. Peruv. (Quichua).] 1. A small tree (*Anona Cherimolia*), a native of Peru. 2. The pulpy fruit of this tree 1760.

Cherish (tʃe·riʃ), *v.* [ME. *cheriss, -isch,* a. F. *cheriss-, chérir,* f. *cher.*] †1. *trans.* To hold dear, tenderly care for –1745; to fondle –1814. 2. To foster. Also *transf.* and *fig.* ME. †3. To entertain kindly (a guest) –1738; to cheer –1734. 4. To keep warm; to give ease to (*arch.*) ME. 5. To entertain in the mind, harbour fondly, cling to (a hope, etc.). (The usual current sense.) ME.

2. As a nurse cherisheth her children *Thess.* ii. 7. 3. 1 *Hen. IV,* III. iii. 194. 4. To c. Our Limbs benumm'd MILT. *P. L.* x. 1068. 5. To c. Rebellion SHAKS., fancies MARVELL, errors 1798, resentment 1866. Hence **Che·risher. Che·rishingly** *adv.*

Cherishment (tʃe·riʃmĕnt). 1561. [f. prec. + -MENT.] The process or fact of cherishing; †*concr.* nourishment –1689.

Chermes, obs. f. KERMES.

‖**Cherni·tes.** 1731. [Gr.] An ivory-like marble.

†**Che·rogril, chœ·rogryl.** ME. [ad. L., ad. Gr. χοιρογρύλλιος, f. χοῖρος young pig + γρύλλος pig.] The CONEY of the A. V.

Cheroot (ʃĭrū·t, tʃ-). 1669. [ad. F. *cheroute,* repr. Tamil *shuruṭṭu* roll (of tobacco).] A cigar made in Southern India or Manila. Hence, any cigar truncated at both ends.

Cherry (tʃe·ri), *sb.* (*a.*) [OE. *ciris, cyrs* (known only in comb.). The ME. *chery* is prob. f. ONF. *cherise,* whence perh. an early ME. *cherise, cheris,* subseq. treated as pl. in *-s.* App. ad. (ult.) pop. L. **ceresia,* **ceresea.*] 1. A well-known stone-fruit; the pulpy drupe of certain species of *Prunus* (N.O. *Rosaceæ*). When unqualified it usually means the fruit of the cultivated tree (*Prunus cerasus* or *Cerasus vulgaris*); the common Wild Cherry or Gean, a form of this, is sometimes considered a distinct species (*P. Avium*). 2. Short for **C.-tree** 1626; **C.-wood** 1793. 3. With qualifying words, applied **a.** to many species of the genus *Prunus,* including BIRD C., CHOKE C., GROUND C., etc., q. v.; **Black C.,** a name of the Wild Cherry (*P. Avium*), **American Wild Black C.** (*P. serotina*), etc. **b.** Also to trees resembling the cherry-tree in fruit, wood, etc. See BARBADOES C., WINTER C., etc. Also used *fig.* 4. *Mech.* A spherical bur or reaming-tool 1874. 5. *adj.* Cherry-coloured 1447.

Comb.: **c.-bay** = *cherry-laurel*; **-bird,** the American Wax-wing or Cedar-bird; **-blossom; -bounce** = *cherry-brandy* (*colloq.*); also, brandy and sugar; **-brandy,** brandy in which cherries have been steeped, sweetened with sugar; **-chopper, snipe, -sucker,** the Spotted Fly-catcher; **-laurel,** the common Laurel (*Cerasus Laurocerasus*); **-pepper,** a species of Capsicum (*C. cerasiforme*); **-pit,** a child's game, in which cherry-stones are thrown into a small hole; a c.-stone *U. S. dial.*; **-red** *a.*; **-ripe** *a.*; **-rum,** rum in which cherries have been steeped; **-stone; -tree,** the tree which bears cherries; **-wine,** wine made from cherries, *esp.* MARASCHINO; **-wood,** the wood of the c.-tree; the Wild Guelder-rose (*Viburnum Opulus*).

†**Che·rry,** *v.* To cheer. SPENSER.

Cherry-me·rry, *a. colloq.* 1775. [? f. *cheery* + *merry.*] Merry: *esp.* from conviviality.

Chersonese (kə·ɹsŏnīˑs). 1601. [ad. L., a. Gr. χερσόνησος, f. χέρσος dry land + νῆσος island.] A peninsula; spec. the Thracian peninsula west of the Hellespont. (Now usu. *poet.* or *rhet.*)

Chert (tʃɔ̄ɹt). 1679. [?] A flint-like quartz, occurring in strata; *hornstone.* Also applied to various impure siliceous rocks, including the jaspers. Also *attrib.* Hence **Che·rty** *a.*

†**Che·rte, -tee.** ME. [a. OF. *chierte,* later *cherté*:—L. *caritatem,* f. *carus.* See also CHARITY.] 1. Dearness –1613. 2. Cheerfulness –1505.

Cherub (tʃe·rŏb). Pl. **cherubs, cherubim** (tʃe·rⁱubim). [OE. and ME. *cherubin,* ME. and mod. *cherub*; repr. OTest. Heb. *k'rūb, k'rūbīm.* The form *cherub* was introduced by WYCLIF. The early pl. '*cherubins*' became successively *cherubims, cherubim.*] †1. In early use: (*Cherubin, -yn, -m,* treated as sing. or collect.) †**a.** The seat of the Deity –1568. †**b.** The proper name of an angel; *esp.* of *Uriel* –1537. †**c.** An order of angels –1613. 2. In extant use: **a.** One of the 'living creatures' mentioned in the OTest., and figured in the Jewish Temple. **b.** One of the second order of angels, excelling specially in knowledge; a conventional representation of such a being. (In early Christian art they were app. coloured red. In mod. art, a cherub is represented as a beautiful winged child, or child's head.) ME. 3. *transf. esp.* A beautiful and innocent child (*cherub*) 1705. Also *attrib.*

1. a. That sittest vpon cherubyn WYCLIF *Ps.* lxxix. [lxxx.] 2. ¶ In the *Te Deum,* in 15th c., *cherubin* and *seraphin* may have been taken as singular. They are now taken as plural. 3. *Oth.* IV. ii. 63. The..rosy cherub before him SCOTT. Hence **Cheru·bic, -al** *a.,* **Cherubi·mic, -al** *a.,* †**Cherubi·nical** *a.*

Cherubim, -in, *sb.*; see CHERUB.

Cherup, obs. f. CHIRRUP.

Chervil (tʃɔ̄·ɹvil). [OE. *cærfille, cerfille,* ad. L. *chær(e)phylla,* pl. of *chærephyllum,* a. Gr., perh. f. χαῖρε + φύλλον.] *Bot.* A garden pot-herb (*Anthriscus Cerefolium*), the aromatic leaves of which are used to flavour soups, etc.

†**Che·sboll.** ME. [?] A poppy –1688; = CHIBOL, an onion –1500.

Chese, obs. f. CHEESE, CHOOSE.

Cheselip, -lope, obs. ff. CHEESELIP 1 and 2.

Cheshire (tʃe·ʃəɹ). The name of an English county. Hence **C. cheese** (a well-known kind). Phr. *To grin like a C. cat.* [unexplained.]

Chesil 1, **chisel** (tʃe·zil, tʃi·zĕl). [OE. *cisil, ceosel, cysel*:—OTeut. type **kesulo-,* **kisilo-,* deriv. of **kiso-,* whence Ger. *kies* gravel. Now dial., or in place-names.] Gravel, shingle. (Earlier, also = a siliceous stone, with *pl.*)

Chesil 2, **chissal.** 1664. A small, smooth green variety of Pear.

Cheslep(e, -lip, -lop(e, obs. ff. CHEESELIP.

†**Che·soun,** *sb.* ME. Aphet. f. ACHESOUN, ENCHESOUN, q. v. –1560.

Chess (tʃes), *sb.*1 [ME. *ches, chess,* aphet. f. OF. *esches,* 'chequers, chess,' pl. of *eschec* CHECK *sb.*1] 1. A game of skill, played by two persons, on a board divided into sixty-four squares; each player having a set of sixteen men, viz. king, queen, two bishops, two knights, two castles or rooks, and eight pawns; the object of the game is to place the adversary's king in checkmate. Also *fig.* †2. = The CHESS-MEN –1618. 3. Used as tr. Gr. ἀστράγαλοι, L. *tesseræ,* etc. Hence **Che·ss-board.**

Chess, *sb.*2 Now *dial.* 1460. [?] 1. A tier or layer; a storey; a row. 2. *Mil.* in *pl.* The parallel planks of a pontoon bridge 1803.

Chess, *sb.*3 1736. [?] A kind of grass (*Bromus secalinus*), which grows as a weed among wheat; now chiefly in *U.S.* Cf. *cheat, cheats.*

†**Chess-apple.** 1640. [Cf. CHEQUER *sb.*2] The fruit of the WHITE-BEAM, *Pyrus Aria.*

Chessel. 1721. [app. f. CHEESE + WELL.] A cheese-vat.

Chess-men (tʃe·smen). Rarely in sing. **-man.** 1474. [ME. *chesse-meyne,* containing *meyne* a company, a. OF. *meyné.*] The pieces with which chess is played.

†**Che·ssom,** *a.* 1626. [?] Loose, friable, and free from grit –1675. ¶ Taken erron. by Johnson for a sb.

Che·ss-tree. 1627. [? f. CHASE *sb.*3] A piece of wood bolted perpendicularly on a ship's side, used to confine the clew of the mainsail.

Chest (tʃest), *sb.*1 [OE. *cest, cist, cyst,* app. ad. L. *cista,* a. Gr. κίστη. Cf. KIST, CIST.] 1. A box, a coffer; now mostly a large box of strong construction, used for the safe custody of the contents. (Often including the contents.) Also *fig.* 2. A coffin. Still *dial.* OE. 3. *Comm.* A case in which certain commodities, as tea, sugar, etc. are packed for transport; hence, a measure of quantity 1708. 4. That part of the body enclosed by the ribs and breast-bone; the thorax 1530. Also †*fig.* –1647.

1. *A seaman's c.*; *a carpenter's, surgeon's c.*, *a medicine c.* A pittance from the University C. 1883. 2. He is now..nayled in his c. CHAUCER.

Phr. *C. of drawers*: see DRAWER 2 b. *C. of viols*: a chest containing a set of viols: the set of viols itself; also a party of players so equipped. *Comb.*: **c.-founder, -foundering**: see FOUNDER *sb.*4 2.

†**Chest,** *sb.*2 [OE. *céast,* refash. of *céas,* a. L. *causa* CAUSE.] Strife, contention –1450.

Chest (tʃest), *v.* 1473. [f. CHEST *sb.*1] 1. *trans.* To put into a chest or coffin. 2. To meet or strike with the chest 1843.

1. He dieth and is chested *Gen.* l. (*headnote*).

Chested (tʃe·stĕd), *ppl. a.* 1601. 1. [f. prec.] Enclosed in a chest or coffin. 2. [f. CHEST *sb.*1] Having a chest; chiefly in comb., as *deep-c.,* etc.

†**Chesteine, chesten.** [ME. *chasteine,* a. OF. *chastaigne, -aine*:—L. *castanea,* a. Gr. καστανέα, synonym of καστάνειον (in full καστάνειον κάρυον nut of Καστανaία in Pontus, or Castana in Thessaly. See also CHESTNUT.] A chestnut-tree –1601; a chestnut –1674.

Che·ster. [OE. *ceaster*:—prehist. OE. **cæstra,* a. L. *castra.* Still existing in place-names; also in the forms *-caster, -cester.*] A walled town; orig. one that had been a Roman station in Britain.

Chesterfield (tʃe·staɹfīld). [f. an Earl of *Chesterfield.*] A kind of overcoat 1889, also a kind of large overstuffed sofa 1900. **Chesterfie·ldian** *a.* relating to or characteristic of the fourth Earl (1694–1773), a writer on manners and etiquette.

Chesterlite (tʃe·stəɹləit). 1850. [f. *Chester* Co., Penn., U.S.] *Min.* A variety of orthoclase.

Chestnut, chesnut (tʃe·snɒt). 1519. [f. *chesten,* late form of CHESTEINE + NUT. *Chesnut* was till 1820, *chestnut* is, the current form.] **A.** 1. The edible nut of the chestnut-tree (*Castanea vesca*), said to have been introduced from Asia Minor. Two or more of the nuts are enclosed in a prickly burr. 2. The tree itself; also its wood 1578. 3. Applied to the HORSE-CHESTNUT, or its seed 1832. 4. The hard knob in the skin of the horse at the inner side of the fore-legs 1859. 5. *slang.* A venerable joke or story 1886. **B.** as *adj.* 1. Of the colour of a chestnut; deep reddish brown 1656. 2. Short for *c. horse.* (*colloq.*) 1840.

Chetah, var. of CHEETAH.

†**Chevachee.** ME. [a. OF. *chevauchie*:—Rom. type *cavalcata, cavalcare*:—late L. *caballicare,* f. *caballus.* Cf. CAVALCADE.] An expedition on horseback; a raid, campaign –1592.

Che·vage. Now *Hist.* 1461. [a. F., f. *chef, chief* (*chev-*) head.] Capitation or poll-money.

‖**Cheval** (ʃəva·l). 1609. Fr. for 'horse', used in comb., as in CHEVAL-GLASS, and in the Fr. phrase *à c.* 'on horseback', 'with one foot on each side'; *Mil.* 'in command of two roads or lines of communication'.

‖**Cheval de frise**; usu. pl. **Chevaux de frise** (ʃəvō· də frīˑz). 1688. [Fr.; lit. 'horse of Friesland'; because first employed there.] *Mil.* A large joist, with six sides, traversed with iron-pointed spikes above six feet long, and crossing one another; used to check cavalry charges, and stop breaches. Also *transf.*

The Danes..had planted themselves..behind their Chevaux de Frize 1710.

‖**Chevalet** (ʃəvale). 1810. [Fr., dim. of *cheval.*] A trestle for a bridge.

Cheval-glass (ʃəva·lglɑs). 1855. [f. Fr. *cheval* + GLASS.] A mirror swung on a frame, and large enough to reflect the whole figure.

Chevalier (ʃevălīəˑɹ). [ME., a. AF. *chevaler, chivaler,* mod.F. *chevalier*:—L. type *caballarius,* f. *caballus.* Also pronounced as Fr.

(ʃəvalye).] 1. A horseman; *esp.* a mounted soldier, a knight (*arch.*). 2. A member of certain orders of knighthood, etc. 1728. 3. A chivalrous man; a gallant 1630.

The C. or *C. de St. George*: James Stuart, son of James II, the Old Pretender. *The Young C.*: Charles Edward Stuart, the Young Pretender. *C. of industry* (F. *chevalier d'industrie*) also *C. of fortune*: one who lives by his wits, a sharper.

Chevaline (ʃe·vălin), *a.* 1550. [a. F.] Of or pertaining to horses, horse-. Also *subst.* horse-flesh.

†**Che·vance, chie·vance.** ME. [a. F. Cf. ACHIEVANCE.] 1. Acquisition of wealth; *concr.* estate –1603. 2. Raising of money –1645. 3. Achievement –1600.

†**Cheve, chieve,** *v.* ME. [a. OF. *chever*, f. *chef.*] 1. *intr.* To fare (*well, ill*, etc.) –1674. 2. *intr.* To get (*to* a place). ME. only. 3. To acquire. ME. only. 4. *intr.* To happen. ME. only. 5. To do homage *to*. ME. only. 6. To achieve –1530.

‖**Chevelure** (ʃəvĕlü·r). 1470. [a. F.:—L. *capillatura*, f. *capillatus*, f. *capillus* a hair.] 1. A head of hair; †a wig. 2. *transf.* The luminous appearance surrounding the nucleus of comets; the diffused light round certain nebulous stars. [So in Fr.] 1672.

Cheven, obs. f. CHEVIN.

Cheventayn, -eyn, etc.; see CHEVETAINE.

†**Che·verel.** [ME. *chevrelle*, a. OF., dim. of *chèvre*:—L. *capra*; in mod.F. repl. by *chevrette.*] *lit.* Kid; used in the sense of kid-leather –1609. *fig.* Flexible, elastic –1705. Also *attrib.*

fig. The lawiers have such chauerell consciences STUBBES. Hence †**Che·verelize** *v.* to make capable of stretching, like c.-leather (*rare*).

†**Che·vesaile.** ME. [a. OF. *cheveçaille*, f. OF. *chevece*:—L. *capitia*, pl. of *capitium* opening for the head in a tunic, etc.; cf. CAVESSON.] The collar of a coat, gown, etc.; in the 14th c. often ornamented.

‖**Chevet** (ʃəvę). 1809. [F. *chevet* pillow.] The apsidal termination of the east end of a church.

†**Che·vetaine.** [ME., a. OF.; see CAPTAIN.] = CHIEFTAIN –1586.

‖**Cheville** (ʃĕvī·l). 1883. [a. F.] A word or phrase inserted solely to round off a sentence or complete a verse.

Chevin (tʃe·vin). 1450. [a. F.; of unkn. etym.] The CHUB.

Cheviot (tʃī·viət, tʃe·v-). 1815. [Name of a range of hills in Scotland.] 1. *C. sheep*, in pl. *Cheviots*: a breed of short-wooled sheep, thriving on the C. hills, and valued for their wool. 2. A cloth made from this wool 1883.

†**Che·visance.** ME. [a. OF., f. *chevir*; see CHEVISE *v.*] 1. Achievement; furtherance (ME. only); resource –1650; provision, supply (also *concr.*) –1611; booty –1658. 2. *spec.* Borrowing; a loan; gain (in a bad sense) –1626. 3. The lending of money, goods, etc. for profit; dealing for profit –1602. ¶Confused by Spenser and others with *chevance, chivalry, chevauchee*, etc.: Enterprise; chivalry; prowess, etc.

†**Che·vise,** *v.* [ME. *chevis-*, a. F. *cheviss-*, *chevir* to bring to a head or end, f. *chef.*] 1. *trans.* To achieve; *intr.* to succeed. ME. only. 2. *intr.* (*refl.*) To get on *with* –1491. 3. *refl.* To help, take care of (*oneself*) –1500. 4. To provide, obtain; to borrow –1487.

‖**Chevrette** (ʃəvre·t). 1731. [F.; dim. of *chèvre*, L. *capra.*] †1. A machine for raising guns or mortars into their carriages –1772. 2. A thin goatskin leather for gloves (*mod.*).

Chevron (ʃe·vrən), *sb.*[1] ME. [a. F.:—L. type **caprionem*, f. *caper* goat. Cf. Sp. *cabriol.*] 1. A beam or rafter; *esp.* in *pl.* the couples of the roof which meet at the ridge 1580. 2. *Her.* A charge on the escutcheon, consisting of a bar bent like two meeting rafters, thus, ∧ ME. 3. The same shape used in decorative art, etc. 1608. 4. *esp.* A distinguishing mark on the sleeve of non-commissioned officers, policemen, etc. 1813.

Comb.: **c.-bone**, the V-shaped bone branching from the vertebral column of some animals; **-moulding**, a moulding of a zigzag pattern; **-work**. Also **-wise** (**-ways**) *adv.*, in the manner of a c. Hence †**Che·vron** *v.* to fit with chevrons or chevronwise (*rare*).

†**Che·vron,** *sb.*[2] 1754. [app. an error for CHEVEREL.] A glove.

Chevronel (ʃe·vrŏnel). 1572. [dim. of CHEVRON *sb.*] *Her.* A bent bar on the escutcheon half the breadth of the chevron.

Chevrotain, -in (ʃe·vrotein, -tin). 1774. [a. F., dim. of OF. *chevrot*, dim. of *chèvre.*] The smaller species of Musk Deer, found in S.E. Asia.

Chevy, chivy (tʃe·vi, tʃi·-), *sb.* Also **chivvy.** 1785. [?f. *Chevy chase.*] 1. A hunting cry. 2. A chase 1824.

Chevy Chase: the scene of a Border skirmish; hence, *transf.* a running pursuit; a bustle.

Chevy, chivy (tʃe·vi, tʃi·-), *v.* 1830. [See the sb.] To chase; *intr.* to scamper.

Chew (tʃ[i]ū), *v.* [OE. *cēowan*:—OTeut. **kewwan.*] 1. To crush, bruise, and grind by the action of the molar teeth; *esp.* to masticate (food). 2. *fig.* and *transf.* To examine or plan deliberately; to meditate on ME. 3. *intr.* To perform the action described in sense 1; to bite, champ (*on, upon*) ME. 4. *fig.* To meditate, ruminate *upon, on*, occas. *at* 1580.

Phr. *To c. the cud*: to bring food back into the mouth and c. it over again, as a cow does; *fig.* to ruminate. Hence **Chew·er.** **Chew·ing** *vbl. sb., attrib.* **c.-gum** (*U.S.*), a flavoured preparation of the gum-like substance (*chicle*) obtained from the bully tree and the sapodilla, used as a masticatory.

Chew (tʃ[i]ū), *sb.* ME. [f. prec.] 1. The action of the vb. 2. That which is chewed or for chewing; *spec.* a quid 1725.

†**Chew·et**[1]. ME. [?] A dish of various kinds of meat and fish, minced and seasoned –1688.

†**Chew·et**[2]. *rare.* [a. F. *chouette.*] A chough; applied to a chatterer. 1 *Hen. IV*, v. i. 29.

Chewink, var. of CHEEWINK.

†**Chey·ney.** 1668. [var. of CHINA.] A worsted or woollen stuff –1757.

‖**Chia.** 1601. = CHA, q.v.

Chian (kəi·ăn), *a.* 1631. [f. L. *Chius* adj. (a. Gr.).] Of or pertaining to Chios (now Scio) in the Ægean Sea. *absol.* An inhabitant of Chios; also = *C. wine.*

C. earth (*Chia terra*): an earth obtained from Chios, formerly used as an astringent and a cosmetic.

Chianti (kiæ·nti). 1833. A dry red wine produced in the *Chianti* Mountains, Tuscany.

‖**Chiaroscuro** (kyā:rǫskū·ro). 1686. [It.; f. *chiaro* (:—L. *clarus*) + *oscuro* (:—L. *obscurus*); cf. F. *clair-obscur.*] †1. The style of pictorial art in which only the light and shade are represented; black (or sepia) and white –1830. 2. The disposition of the brighter and darker masses in a picture 1686. Also *transf.* and *fig.* Also *attrib.* var. **Chiaro-oscuro.** Hence **Chiaroscu·rist,** a painter distinguished for his c.

‖**Chiasma** (kəiæ·zmă). Also **chiasm.** 1839. [a. Gr., f. χιάζειν to mark with or like a *chī* (X, χ).] *Anat.* Intercrossing or decussation.

Optic c.: the optic commissure or decussation of the fibres of the optic nerves. Hence **Chia·smal** *a.* of the nature of c.

‖**Chiasmus** (kəiæ·zmŏs). 1871. [mod.L., a. Gr. χιασμός; see prec.] *Gram.* A figure by which the order of words in one clause is inverted in a second clause. Hence **Chia·stic** *a.* marked by c.

Chiastolite (kəiæ·stŏləit). 1800. [f. Gr. χιαστός arranged crosswise (see CHIASMA) + -LITE.] *Min.* A variety of Andalusite, a transverse section of which often exhibits the figure of a cross.

‖**Chiaus** (tʃaus, tʃauʃ). 1599. [Turk. *chāush.*] A Turkish messenger, lictor, or sergeant.

Chibol (tʃi·bəl). Still *dial.* ME. [a. NFr. **chiboule*:—L. *ce-, cæpulla*, f. *cepa, cæpa* onion.] 1. A species of Allium (*A. fistulosum*), known also as Welsh Onion. 2. A spring onion with the green stalk attached 1848.

‖**Chibouk, chibouque** (tʃibu·k). 1813. [a. Turk. The spelling *chibouque* is Fr.] The long pipe smoked by the Turks.

‖**Chic** (ʃīk), *sb. slang.* 1856. [F.; of unkn. origin.] Artistic skill and dexterity; style. As *adj.* [Not so used in F.] Stylish.

‖**Chica** (tʃī·kă). 1830. [Native name.] A red pigment obtained from the *Bignonia Chica*, a native of Guiana and Columbia, used by some tribes for painting the skin.

Chica [2]; see CHICHA.

Chicane (ʃikē[i]·n), *sb.* 1676. [a. F., of unkn. origin.] 1. = CHICANERY 1. 1692. †2. (with *pl.*) An instance of chicanery; a subterfuge, quibble –1752.

1. C. in furs, and Casuistry in lawn POPE. 2. One who takes advantage of such chicanes, is not commonly regarded as an honest man HUME.

Chicane (ʃikē[i]·n), *v.* 1672. [a. F. *chicaner.*] 1. To employ chicanery; to quibble, cavil. 2. *trans.* To quibble over; to overreach by chicanery. 3. *Bridge.* The condition of holding no trumps 1886. Hence **Chica·ner.**

Chicanery. 1613. [a. F. *chicanerie.*] 1. Legal trickery, pettifogging; the use of subterfuge and trickery in debate or action; quibbling, sophistry. 2. (with *pl.*) A dishonest artifice of law; a sophistry, quibble, trick 1688.

1. The c. of the lawyers RICHARDSON. 2. Impatient of such chicaneries BOSW. SMITH.

Chich (tʃitʃ), *sb.* ? *Obs.* [ME. *chiche*, a. OF., :—(ult.) L. *cicer.*] *Bot.* The CHICK-PEA; occas. used of the Lentil (*Ervum Lens*).

‖**Chicha** (tʃī·tʃă). Also *erron.* **chica.** 1760. [Haytian.] A fermented liquor made from maize by the natives of S. America.

Chich(e)ling, obs. f. CHICKLING.

†**Chi·chevache.** ME. [A perversion of Fr. *chicheface*, lit. 'thin face', found only in Eng.] A fabulous cow that fed only on patient wives, and was therefore always lean and hungry.

Chick (tʃik), *sb.*[1] ME. [Short for CHICKEN. Treated as a dim. of CHICKEN; but in s. w. dial., *chick* is sing., *chicken* pl.] 1. A chicken; occas., the young of any bird. 2. *transf.* A child; a term of endearment ME.

‖**Chick, cheek,** *sb.*[2] 1698. [Hindī *chik.*] A screen-blind made of finely split bamboo, laced with twine; used in doorways or windows.

Chick, *sb.*[3] *Sc.* 1791. A tick (of a clock, etc.).

Chick, *v.* Now *dial.* ME. [Echoic; cf. CHIP.] *intr.* To sprout; to crack as a seed does in sprouting; to chap. Also *trans.*

Chickabiddy. 1785. [f. CHICK + BIDDY [2].] A term of endearment to a child.

Chickadee (tʃikădī·). *U. S.* 1854. [From its note.] The Black-cap Titmouse (*Parus atricapillus*) of N. America.

Chickaree (tʃikărī·). *U.S.* 1854. [From its cry.] The larger American Red Squirrel.

Chicken (tʃi·kėn). [OE. *cicen.* Cf. Du. *kicken, kuiken*, MHG. *küchen*; whence Ger. *küchlein.*] 1. The young of the domestic fowl; its flesh. Occas. used as *pl.* or *collect.*; esp. *dial.* 2. *transf.* A child ME. 3. *fig.* One young and inexperienced 1711; one who is CHICKEN-HEARTED 1611.

2. *Macb.* IV. iii. 218. 3. Your hints that Stella is no c. SWIFT. Chikins, to be afraid of every cloud 1633.

Phr. *Mother Cary's* (or *Carey's*) *c.*: a sailors' name for the Stormy Petrel; also (in *pl.*) for falling snow.

Comb.: **c.-breast**, a malformed projection of the breast-bone; hence **-breasted** *a.*; **-cholera**, an infectious disease of chickens; **-heart**, a heart as timorous as a chicken's; a cowardly person; hence **-hearted** *a.*; **-pox**, a mild eruptive disease, which chiefly attacks children; Varicella; **chickenwort**, = CHICKWEED. Hence **Chi·ckenhood.**

Chi·cken-ha·zard. 1845. See HAZARD.

Chi·cken-meat, chicken's meat, chickmeat, [OE. *cicena mete.*] Food for chickens. Hence, a name for various plants, including endive; now *dial.* for CHICKWEED.

Chi·ckling [1]. A tiny chick. (Dicts.)

Chickling [2], **chichling** (tʃi·kliŋ, tʃi·tʃliŋ). 1548. [In 16th c. *cicheling, chicheling*, dim. of *ciche* CHICH, repr. L. *cicercula* as dim. of *cicera.* App. at first a misprint.] *Bot.* The Common cultivated Vetch (*Lathyrus sativus*), grown in England for fodder. Now **Chickling Vetch.**

Chick-pea (tʃi·k pī·). 1548. [Orig. *cich-, chich-pease*, f. *cich* CHICH + PEASE, after Fr. *pois chiche*; altered in 18th c. by some error.] *Bot.* A dwarf species of pea (*Cicer arietinum*), widely used for food. Called earlier *cich*, CHICH.

Chickweed (tʃi·kwīd), occas. **chickenweed.** ME. [f. CHICKEN *sb.* + WEED, as eaten by chickens.] *Bot.* A name applied *esp.* to *Stellaria media* (N.O. *Caryophyllaceæ*), and to many allied or merely similar plants.

Chicory (tʃi·kŏri). 1450. [a. F. *cichorée* (now *chichorée*):—L. *cichorium, cichoreum*, ad.

Gr. κίχορα, κιχόρεια (neut. pl.).] The plant *Cichorium Intybus* (N.O. *Compositæ*); also its root, ground and roasted as an addition to or substitute for coffee.

Chide (tʃəid), *v.* Pa. t. **chid** (tʃid); pa. pple. **chid, chidden** (tʃi·d'n). [OE. *cīdan* wk. vb.: Eng. only.] **1.** *intr.* †**a.** To contend with loud and angry altercation, brawl, wrangle –1693; †**b.** to scold –17..; **c.** to utter rebuke ME. Also *fig.* *Const.* With preps., esp. †*at*, †*with*, (later, *against*). **2.** *trans.* To scold, rebuke, find fault with. (The main mod. use, but now chiefly *lit.* and *arch.*) ME. Also *fig.* and *transf.* **3.** With *adv.*, etc.: To drive, impel, or compel by chiding 1590.

1. c. To..present My true account, lest he, returning, c. MILT. *Sonn.* xiv. *fig.* The silver snarling trumpets 'gan to c. KEATS. 2. Having chidden her for undutifulness JOHNSON. *fig.* The Sea That chides the Bankes of England 1 *Hen. IV*, III. i. 45. 3. He hath chid me hence *Mids. N.* III. ii. 312. Hence **Chi·der**, one who chides; so †**Chi·deress**, †**Chi·dester**, a female chider. **Chi·dingly** *adv.*

Chide, *sb.* ME. [f. prec.] †**1.** Wrangling; an angry rebuke –1666. **2.** *transf.* Brawling (of streams) (*rare*).

2. The c. of streams and hum of bees THOMSON.

Chief (tʃīf), *sb.* [ME. *chef*, *chief*, a. OF.:– Rom. type **capum*:–L. *caput*.]

I. †**1.** *lit.* The head (of the body) (*rare*) –1535. †**2.** The head, top, upper end –1579. **3.** *Her.* The upper third of the field 1440.

3. *In c.*: borne on the upper part of the shield.

II. Transf. and fig. **1.** The head of a body of men, of an organization, state, town, party, office, etc.; foremost authority, leader, ruler ME.; *spec.* the head man of a clan, tribe, etc. 1587. †**2.** The head town or city; the CAPITAL –ME. †**3.** The best part; the height –1607. †**4.** Chief position, excellency –1602. **5.** = *chief-rent* 1601.

1. The c. of the Kitchen THACKERAY, of Glengarry SCOTT. Chiefs out of war, and Statesmen out of place POPE. 3. In the c. of summer 1607. 4. *Haml.* I. iii. 74.

Phr. *In chief.* **a.** *Feudal Law.* [med.L. *in capite.*] Applied to a tenant holding, or tenure held, immediately from the Lord Paramount. Hence extended to tenancy by a perpetual ground-rent. **b.** In the chief place or position. Often in titles, as *Commander-in-C.*, etc. **c.** Chiefly. *Comb.*: **c.-rent**, a rent paid under a tenure in c.; now=quit-rent. Hence **Chie·fdom**, the estate, position, or dominion of a c. **Chie·fery, chie·fry**, (*Ir.*) the office and territory of an Irish c.; the dues belonging to the chief of a clan or district; the analogous payments of rent or tribute. **Chie·fess**, a female (ethnic) c. **Chie·fless** *a.* **Chie·fly** *a.* pertaining to a c. **Chie·fship**, the office and function of c.

Chief (tʃīf), *a.* and quasi-*adv.* ME. [f. prec.] **1.** = HEAD-; as *C. Baron*, *Constable*, *Justice*, *Rabbi*, *Secretary*, etc. **2.** At the head in importance; principal, foremost, greatest ME. **3.** 'Of the first order' (J.); prominent, leading. (In this use, formerly compared *chiefer*, *chiefest*.) ME. †**4.** Best, finest; choice –1660. **5.** *Sc.* Intimate (see *Prov.* xvi. 28) 1530. **6.** *absol.* or *ellipt.* **a.** *pl.* Chief people 1568. **b.** The most; the bulk 1833. **7.** *adv.* Chiefly, principally (*arch.*) 1553. So *chiefest*.

2. His c. intimate HAWTHORNE. My cheif design BOYLE. 3. The cheiffe peeres of the realme 1536. A c. object of the expedition MACAULAY. 4. His c. companion was ever some c. book FULLER. Phr. *Chief good*: used as tr. L. *summum bonum*.

Chiefage, var. of CHEVAGE.

Chiefly (tʃī·fli), *adv.* ME. [f. CHIEF *a.* + -LY[2].] **1.** In particular; pre-eminently; especially; most of all. **2.** Mainly, for the most part ME.

1. Not life, but a good life, is to be c. valued JOWETT. 2. Cæsar's character is c. made up of Good-nature ADDISON.

Chieftain (tʃī·ftėn). [ME. *chef-*, *chieftayne*, var. of CHEVETAINE, partly assim. to *chef* CHIEF.] †**1.** = CHIEF *sb.* II. **1.** –1837. **2.** A captain (*arch.* and *poet.*) ME. **3.** The CHIEF of a clan or tribe 1587. †**4.** One who takes a leading part –1600.

3. Chieftains, which in the Highland acceptation, signifies the head of a particular branch of a tribe, .. Chief, ..the leader and commander of the whole name SCOTT. Hence **Chie·ftaincy** [after *lieutenancy*, etc.], the position of a c.; government by a c. **Chie·ftainess**, a female chief or c. **Chie·ftainry**, the rank, rule, or territory of a c.; a body of chieftains collectively. **Chie·ftainship**, the position of a c.

†**Chie·fty.** 1552. [f. CHIEF.] Headship; chief place or degree –1644.

Chield (tʃīld). *Sc.* 1758. [var. of CHILD.] Fellow, chap.

Chierete, chierte(**e**, obs. ff. CHERTE.

Chieve: see CHEVE.

Chiff-chaff (tʃi·f,tʃaf). 1780. [From its note.] A bird, one of the *Sylviinæ* or Warblers, also called Lesser Pettychaps (*Phylloscopus rufus*).

‖**Chiffon** (ʃifoṅ). 1876. [F.; f. *chiffe* rag.] **1.** *pl.* Ornamental adjuncts to a lady's dress, 'fal-lals'; feminine dress. **2.** (ʃi·fǫn). A diaphanous silky muslin used in dressmaking 1890.

Chiffonier (ʃifonīə·ɹ). Also **-onnier**(**e**, **cheffonier.** 1806. [a. F. *chiffonier*, *-ière* rag gatherer, *transf.* a piece of furniture with drawers for odds and ends.] **1.** A small cupboard with a top forming a sideboard. ‖**2.** A rag-picker; a collector of scraps. [Fr.] 1856.

‖**Chignon** (ʃinʸoṅ). 1783. [a. F. *chignon* nape of the neck; orig. a var. of *chaînon* link, f. *chaîne* chain.] A large coil or hump of hair, worn by women at various times on the back of the head.

These girls .. are all alike—from c. to ankle 1871.

Chigoe (tʃi·go). Also JIGGER. 1691. [West-Indian: F. *chique*, ?from Sp. *chico* small (Littré).] A small species of flea (*Pulex* or *Sarcopsylla penetrans*), found in the West Indies and South America. The female burrows beneath the skin of the human feet (and hands), and causes itching and painful sores.

Chilblain (tʃi·lbleʲn). 1547. [f. CHILL + BLAIN.] An inflammatory swelling produced by exposure to cold, affecting the hands and feet, accompanied with heat, itching, and occasionally ulceration. Hence **Chi·lblained** *a.* affected with chilblains. **Chi·lblainy** *a.*

Child (tʃəild), *sb.* Pl. **children** (tʃi·ldrĕn). [OE. *cild* (pl. *cildru*, *-ra*) :—OTeut. type **kilþo* from root **kilþ-*, whence Goth. *kilþei* womb. Not found elsewhere. The ME. pl. *childre*, *childer* became *childer-en*, *childre-n* in the south, and this is now the standard form.]

I. 1. Fœtus, infant. *spec.* A female infant (*dial.*) 1611. **2.** A boy or girl OE. In the Bible, used, as tr. Heb., of youths entering upon manhood (see *Dan.* i. 17). **3.** *transf.* One who is as a child in character, manners, attainments, and *esp.* in experience or judgement ME. **4.** A pupil at school ME.; a chorister 1510. **5.** A youth of gentle birth: used as a kind of title (*arch.* and now spelt *chylde* or *childe.*) OE. †**6.** A lad in service; a page, etc. –1610.

1. If she beare a maid c. *Lev.* xii. 5. A boy, or a Childe I wonder? *Wint. T.* III. iii. 71. 3. Men are but children of a larger growth DRYDEN. 4. *spec.* Campaspe, played..by..the children of Paules LYLY. 5. Childe Rowland *Lear* III. iv. 187.

II. As correlative to parent. **1.** The offspring, male or female, of human parents ME. Also *fig.* and *transf.* **2.** *pl.* In Biblical and derived uses: Descendants; members of the tribe or clan ME. **3.** Applied (chiefly in *pl.*) to disciples *of* a teacher. (Chiefly Biblical.) ME. **4.** *fig.* Expressing origin, extraction, dependence, attachment, or natural relation to a place, time, circumstance of birth, ruling quality. Orig. a Hebraism. ME.

1. *fig.* Thou c. of the devil *Acts* xiii. 10. Dreames: Which are the children of an idle braine *Rom. & Jul.* I. iv. 97. 2. *Judg.* iv. 6. *C. of God* (Theol.): *i. e.* by creation or by regeneration and adoption. 3. 1 *John* ii. 1. 4. Children of the East *Judg.* vi. 3, of nature WORDSW.; of light ME., yre ME., death 2 *Kings* vi. 32; of fancy MILT.; of the Renascence 1874.

Phrases. **a.** *With c.*: *lit.* pregnant; †*fig.* teeming; eager (*to* do a thing). **b.** *Child's play*: *lit.* childish sport; *fig.* a piece of work easily done, trifle.

Comb.: **c.-crowing**, spasmodic croup; **-rites** *sb. pl.*, the rites connected with the baptism of children.

Hence **Chi·lded** *ppl. a.* provided with a c. or children. †**Chi·lder**, dial. pl. of CHILD, whence †**Chi·lderless. Childie**, dim. of CHILD (*rare*). †**Chi·lding** *vbl. sb.* child-bearing; also *ppl. a.* **Chi·ldless** *a.* **Chi·ldlessness. Chi·ldling** (*rare*). **Chi·ldly** *a.* childish or childlike; also as *adv.* **Chi·ldliness. Chi·ldness**, †childish humour *Wint. T.* I. ii. 170; quality of being a c. **Chi·ldship** (St. Paul's υἱοθεσία), the relation of child to parent; filiation, adoption.

†**Child** (tʃəild), *v.* ME. [f. prec.] **1.** *intr.* To be delivered –1808. **2.** *trans.* To bring forth (a child) –1611. Also *fig.*

1. Within ii dayes they chylded both LATIMER.

Chi·ld-bearing, *vbl. sb.* ME. Parturition; gestation (*rare*).

Childbed (tʃəi·ldbed). ME. [f. CHILD *sb.* + BED *sb.*] **1.** The bed in which a child is born 1594. **2.** The state of a woman in labour ME. **3.** The womb. Now *dial.* 1535. Also *attrib.*

Child-birth (tʃəi·ldbōɹþ). 1549. [f. as prec. + BIRTH.] The bearing or birth of a child.

Childe; see CHILD *sb.* I. 5.

Childermas (tʃi·ldəɹmæs). *arch.* [Repr. an OE. wd., f. *cildra* gen. pl. + *mæsse*.] The festival of the Holy Innocents (the 28th of December), commemorating the slaughter of the children by Herod (*Matt.* ii. 16). Usually *c.-day*, *-tide*.

Childhood (tʃəi·ldhud). [OE. *cildhād*; see -HEAD.] **1.** The state or stage of life of a child; the time during which one is a child; the time from birth to puberty. Also *fig.* **2.** *concr.* This state or age personified 1605. †**3.** Childishness –ME. †**4.** = *childship* –1626. Also *attrib.*

1. *fig.* The C. of our ioy *Rom. & Jul.* III. iii. 95. 2. The well-governed c. of this realm SCOTT. 4. *Lear* II. iv. 181. Phr. *Second c.*: the state of childishness incident to extreme old age.

Childish (tʃəi·ldiʃ), *a.* [OE. *cildisc*; see -ISH [1].] **1.** Of, belonging, or proper to a child or to childhood. **2.** Not befitting mature age; puerile, silly ME.

1. C. trebble *A. Y. L.* II. vii. 162. 2. What cannot be auoided, 'Twere c. weaknesse to lament 3 *Hen. VI*, V. iv. 38. Hence **Chi·ldish-ly** *adv.*, **-ness.**

Childlike, child-like (tʃəi·ldləik), *a.* 1586. [f. CHILD *sb.*] **1.** Belonging to or becoming a child; filial. **2.** Like a child; (of qualities, etc.) like those of a child. (Usu. in a good sense, as opp. to *childish*.) 1738. Also as *adv.*

1. Her child-like dutie *Two Gent.* III. i. 75. 2. The c. heart WESLEY. Hence **Chi·ldlikeness.**

†**Childre, children**, pl. of CHILD.

Childwife, child-wife. †**1.** (tʃəi·ld,wəif), A woman in, or just out of, childbed –1636. **2.** (tʃəi·ld,wəi·f), A wife who is a child. (Always with hyphen.) 1852.

†**Childwite** (tʃəi·ldwəit). ME. [f. OE. *cild* + *wīte* penalty.] *Old Law.* A fine paid to the lord for getting his bondwoman with child –1607.

Chile, chili, vars. of CHILLI.

Chiliad (ki·liăd). 1598. [ad. L. *chilias*, *-ad-*, a. Gr.] **1.** A group of 1,000 (things); a thousand. **2.** A period of 1,000 years 1653; *esp.* the millennium (*Rev.* xx. 1–5) 1702.

2. After some..Centuries, or even Chiliads HARTLEY.

Chiliagon (ki·liăgǫn). 1692. [f. Gr. χίλιοι + γωνία.] A plane figure with a thousand angles.

Chiliahedron (ki·liăhī·drǫn). *rare.* 1690. [f. Gr. χίλιοι + ἕδρα.] A plane figure having a thousand sides.

Chiliarch (ki·li,aɹk). 1656. [ad. L., a. Gr. χιλιάρχης, -ος, f. χίλιοι + ἀρχός.] The commander of a thousand men. So **Chi·liarchy**, †a body of a thousand men; the post of c.

Chiliasm (ki·li,æz'm). 1610. [ad. Gr. χιλιασμός, f. χιλιάς.] The doctrine of the millennium; the opinion that Christ will reign in bodily presence on earth for a thousand years. So **Chi·liast**, an adherent of c. **Chilia·stic**, †**-al** *a.*, **-ally** *adv.*

†**Chili·ndre.** ME. [ad. med.L. *chilindrus*, for L. *cylindrus*, a. Gr.] A portable sun-dial of cylindrical form used in early times –1530.

Chilio-; see KILO-.

Chill (tʃil), *sb.* [OE. *cęle*, *ciẓle* :—OTeut. type *kaliz*, f. *kalan* to be COLD. App. obs. by 1400, but revived since *c* 1600.]

†**I.** In OE. and ME. (*chile*, *chele*, *cheele*.) Replaced by mod. COLD.

II. [f. the vb. or adj.] (*chill.*) **1.** An unnaturally lowered bodily temperature marked by shivering, etc.; the cold fit of an ague; now *esp.* a sudden affection of physical cold, which is often a first stage or symptom of illness 1601. **2.** A coldness of the air, water, etc., which makes one shiver; a cold which has a depressing effect on the body 1788. Also in *pl.* **3.** *fig.* A depressing influence upon the feelings; depressing coldness of manner 1821. **4.** *techn.* An iron mould, or a piece of iron in a sand mould, for making chilled castings; cf. CHILL *v.* 1874.

1. *To catch, give one, a c.* 2. *To take the c. off* (a liquid): to raise it to a temperate heat. The chills of night 1833. 3. A c. Comes o'er my heart BYRON. *To cast* or *throw a c. over.*

Chill (tʃil), *a.* ME. [app. f. prec.] **1.** Cold; now always depressingly or injuriously cold; that chills, or causes to shiver. **2.** Depressingly affected by cold 1608. **3.** *fig.* That tends to repress warmth of feeling, etc. ME.; repressed, deadened, in feeling 1633.

1. A c. easterly wind SCOTT. 2. My veins are c. *Per.* II. i. 77. 3. C. Penury repress'd their noble rage GRAY. Hence **Chi·llish** *a.* (*rare*). **Chi·llness,** c. quality or condition.

Chill (tʃil), *v.* ME. [app. f. as prec.] **I.** *intr.* **1.** To become cold. **2.** To take a chill 1830.

II. *trans.* **1.** To make cold; to affect injuriously with cold ME. **2.** *fig.* To affect as with cold; to check (warmth, etc.); to damp, dispirit 1597. **3.** *techn.* To cool and harden the surface of cast iron by contact with cold iron, or by casting in an iron mould. Also *gen.* 1831. **4.** *Painting.* To deaden (a varnished surface) by cold, etc. 1859. **5.** *colloq.* To take the chill off 1825.

1. Ev'ry Lady's Blood with Fear was chill'd DRYDEN. 2. Nothing chills the heart like..distrust 1849. Hence **Chi·ller. Chi·llingly** *adv.* *Comb.* **c.-room,** a room for chilling meat.

Chilli, chilly (tʃi·li). 1662. [In Sp. *chile, chili,* a. Mexican *chilli.*] The dried pod of species of Capsicum or Red Pepper; also, the shrub which bears chillies.

‖**Chi·llum.** 1781. [Hindī *chilam.*] The part of the hookah containing the tobacco, etc.; *loosely,* the hookah, the act of smoking, the 'fill' of tobacco.

‖**Chillumchee.** 1715. [Hindī *chilamchī.*] A wash-hand basin of brass or tinned copper.

Chilly (tʃi·li), *a.* 1570. [f. CHILL *sb.* + -Y[1].] **1.** That chills; disagreeably cold. **2.** Affected by a chill; sensitive to cold 1611. **3.** *fig.* Adverse to warmth of feeling 1841.

3. *fig.* C. to general theories MORLEY. Hence **Chi·llily** *adv.*; also **Chi·lly. Chi·lliness,** c. state or condition.

Chilognathan (kəilǫ·gnăþăn), *a.*, *sb.* 1835. [f. mod.L. *Chilognatha* sb. pl., name of the order, f. Gr. χεῖλος lip + γνάθος jaw.] *Zool.* Belonging to, or one of, an order of Myriapoda or Centipedes, with segmented bodies and heads furnished with two pairs of maxillæ, of which the second pair are united to form a lower lip. Hence **Chilogna·thiform** *a.*

‖**Chiloma** (kəilōu·mă). [mod.L., a. Gr., f. χεῖλος.] *Zool.* The upper lip of a mammal when tumid and continued without interruption from the nose.

Chilopod (kəi·lǫpǫd). 1837 [f. mod.L. *chilo·poda* sb. pl. (also used), f. Gr. χεῖλος + πούς, ποδ-.] *Zool.* One of the *Chilopoda,* an order of Myriapoda, having segmented bodies, and two anterior pairs of legs converted into foot-jaws. The order contains the Centipedes proper. Hence **Chilo·podan** *a.* and *sb.* **Chilo·podous** *a.* of the nature of the Chilopoda.

Chilostomatous (kəilǫstǫ·mătəs), *a.* 1881. [f. Gr. χεῖλος + στόματ-.] *Zool.* Having the cell-mouth closed with a movable lip.

Chiltern (tʃi·ltəɹn). [In OE. Chron. anno 1009 *Ciltern*: unexplained.] **1.** Proper name of a range of hills which extend from Oxfordshire, across Buckinghamshire, into Bedfordshire and Hertfordshire. **2.** *a.* and *sb.* Applied to a kind of soil, and to districts having this soil 1523.

Chiltern Hundreds: a tract of Crown lands which contain the Chiltern Hills. The *Stewardship of the Chiltern Hundreds* is by a legal figment held to be an office of profit under the Crown, and is conferred on any member of parliament desiring to resign his seat, which by law he cannot do, so long as he is duly qualified. A member who accepts an office of profit under the Crown must vacate his seat, subject to re-election.

Chilver (tʃi·lvəɹ). [OE. *cilfer-, cilfor-lǫmb* ewe-lamb; cf. Swiss *kilber* masc. 'young wether'.] A ewe-lamb: commonly **c.-lamb** (*dial.*)

Chimæra, var. of CHIMERA.

Chimæroid (kəimīə·roid), *a.* 1854. *Zool.* Related to the genus of fishes *Chimæra,* having the tail ending in a thread, the head pointed, and only one spiracle.

Chimbe, var. of CHIME.

Chimbley, dial. var. of CHIMNEY.

Chime (tʃəim), *sb.*[1] ME. [conn. w. L. *cymbalum* CYMBAL; but of obscure history.] †**1.** A cymbal. ME. only. **2.** An apparatus for striking a set of bells so as to make them chime 1463. **3.** Hence, A set of bells, so attuned as to chime when thus struck, or when slightly swung 1562. **4.** The series of musical sounds thus produced 1530. **5.** The rhythm of verse; jingle 1649. **6.** *transf.* and *fig.* A system of which all the parts are in harmony 1630; harmony, accord 1847.

3. Noise Of clocks and chimes TENNYSON. 4. Wee haue heard the Chymes at mid-night 2 *Hen. IV,* III. ii. 228. 5. Now the C. of Poetry is done DRYDEN. 6. Nature's c. MILT.

Chime, chimb (tʃəim), *sb.*[2] [ME. *chimb(e*; cf. alleged OE. '*cimstanas* base of a pillar'. Also Du. *kim,* G. *kimme* edge, etc. In late use often altered to CHINE.] **1.** The rim at the ends of a cask, formed by the ends of the staves. **2.** *Naut.* That part of the water-way which is left the thickest, and above the deck-plank 1833.

Chime (tʃəim), *v.*[1] [ME. *chimbe, chyme*; see CHIME *sb.*[1]] **1.** *intr.* To resound when struck, give forth a musical sound. Also *trans.* (*arch.*) 1613. **2.** *intr.* To produce a musical sound from a bell by striking it ME.; *trans.* to strike (a bell, etc.) so that a musical sound is given forth 1697. **3.** To ring chimes. *intr.* (and *trans.*, with the bells as obj.) 1530. **4.** Said of a set of bells. *trans.* and *intr.* 1562. Also *fig.* **5.** To recite or repeat in cadence or mechanically. *trans.* and *intr.* ME. **6.** To rime or jingle 1667; *fig.* (*intr.*) to harmonize, agree 1690.

2. They..c. their sounding Hammers in a Row DRYDEN. 4. Those great bells Began to c. TENNYSON. *fig.* My guts c. twelve 1693. 5. To c. verse BYRON. 6. The intention and expectation c. or go together AUSTIN. To c. with one's mood DICKENS.

Phr. **Chime in.** To join in harmoniously (in music, conversation, etc.). So *To c. in with*: to be in complete (but subordinate) accord *with*.

Chime (tʃəim), *v.*[2] 1880. [f. CHIME *sb.*[2]] To groove or chamfer cask-staves for the chime.

Chimer[1], **chimere** (tʃi·məɹ, tʃimīə·ɹ). ME. [OF. *chamarre* (mod.F. *simarre*) 'a loose and light gowne' (Cotg.). In med.(Anglo-)L. *chimera, chimæra,* whence perh. the Eng. form.] A loose upper robe; *esp.* that worn by a bishop, to which the lawn sleeves are attached.

Chimer[2] (tʃəi·məɹ). 1611. [f. CHIME *v.*] One who chimes bells.

Chimera, chimæra (kimīə·ră, kəi-). [ME. *chimere* (tʃi·mer), a. F. *chimère,* ad. L. *chimæra,* a. Gr. χίμαιρα she-goat or monster. The earlier form from Fr. is to be preferred.] **1.** *Gr. Myth.* A fire-breathing monster, with a lion's head, a goat's body, and a serpent's tail, killed by Bellerophon. **2.** In *Arch., Painting,* etc. A grotesque monster 1634. **3.** *fig.* A mere wild fancy; an unfounded conception. (The ordinary mod. use.) 1587. Also *attrib.*

2. An excellent Hand at a Chimera ADDISON. 3. Exploded chimera's, the..philosopher's stone, etc. 1712. Hence **Chime·ric, -al** *a.* imaginary, fanciful, visionary; prone to entertain chimeras. **Chime·rically** *adv.* †**Chi·merize** *v.* to indulge in chimeras.

†**Chi·min.** 1613. [a. F. *chemin.*] *Old Law.* A way -1670.

Chi·minage. 1594. [a. OF. *cheminage* right of way.] *Feudal Law.* A toll for liberty of passage through a forest.

Chimney (tʃi·mni). [ME. *chimenee,* etc., a. OF. *cheminée*:—late L. *caminata,* f. L. *caminus* 'furnace, forge, oven'.] **1.** A fireplace or hearth. Now *dial.* †**2.** As tr. Gr. κάμινος furnace -1611. †**3.** A (portable) stove -1616. **4.** The passage or flue by which the smoke from a fire, etc., ascends ME.; the part which rises above the roof ME. **5.** The funnel of a steamboat, etc.; the tube of glass placed over the wick of a lamp 1816. Also *transf.* **6.** A cleft in a vertical cliff by which it may be scaled 1871. **7.** *Mining.* An ore-shoot. Also *attrib.*

1. Stretch'd out all the chimney's length MILT. *L'Alleg.* 111. 2. 2 *Esdras* vi. 4. 4. Our Chimneys were blowne downe *Macb.* II. iii. 60. 5. *transf.* The chemineys of Veseuus CHAUCER.

Comb.: **c.-board,** a board used to close up a fire-place in summer; **-breast,** the projecting part of the wall between the c.-flue and the room; **-corner,** the corner or side of the old-fashioned open fire-place or hearth; hence, the seat of the old, infirm, or idle; also *attrib.*; **-hook,** a hook on which to suspend pots and pans over a fire, etc.; †**-money,** a tax on fire-hearths in England and Wales; †**-man,** the collector of this tax; **-pot,** a cylindrical pipe of earthenware, sheet-metal, etc., fitted on the top of a c.-shaft; hence, *c.-pot hat,* from its shape; **-shaft** = *chimney-stalk*; **-stack,** a group of c.-stalks; **-stalk,** (*a*) the part of a c. which rises from a house-top; (*b*) a tall mill- or factory-c.; **-swallow,** the common swallow, *Hirundo rustica*; **-tax** = *chimney-money*; **-sweep, -sweeper,** one who sweeps chimneys and clears them of soot; **-top,** the part of a c. which rises above the roof, *esp.* its flat upper surface.

Hence **Chi·mney** *v.* (*nonce-wd.*) to furnish with chimneys LAMB. **Chi·mneyless** *a.*

Chi·mney-piece. 1611. [PIECE in the artistic sense.] †**1.** A picture, etc., placed as an ornament over a fire-place -1672. **2.** The ornamental structure over and around the open recess of a fireplace; now often used for the MANTEL-SHELF 1680.

1. The Chimney-peece Chaste Dian, bathing SHAKS.

Chimpanzee (tʃimpæ̆nzī·, tʃimpæ·nzi). 1738. [Native name in Angola, in W. Africa. (Cf. F. *chimpansé, -zé, -zée.*)] A genus of African apes (*Anthropopithecus*), resembling man more closely than any of the anthropoids. *A. Troglodytes* (formerly *T. niger*) was long the only species recognized.

Chin (tʃin), *sb.* [OE. *cin* (prob. fem.):—WGer. *kinni*:—OTeut. **kinnjo*ᵐ- (cf. Gr. γένειον), f. **kinn-* (retained in ON. *kinn* 'cheek, lower jaw', and in Eng. in comb.).] The part of the face below the under-lip formed by the prominent extremity of the lower jaw. Also *fig.*

Phr. *Up to the c.*: reaching to the c.; deeply immersed *in*. *Comb.*: **c.-music** (*U.S.*), talk, chatter; **-mute,** a mute applied to the violin by the action of the c.; **-wag** (*slang*), chat, talk; **-welk,** a disease affecting the c. Hence **Chin** *v.* to bring (a fiddle) up to the c.; to chat, chatter (*U.S.*). **Chi·nless** *a.* without a c.; also *fig.* **Chinned** *a.* having a c.

China[1] (tʃəi·nă), *sb.* and *a.* 1555. [? See *Babylonian & Or. Recd.* I. Nos. 3 and 11.]

I. a. The country so called, in Asia. †**b.** A Chinaman -1634. Also *attrib.*, but now mostly repl. by CHINESE *a.*

Comb.: **C.-aster** (see ASTER); **-crape,** a kind of silk crape; **-grass,** *Bœhmeria* (*Urtica*) *nivea*; also its strong fibre, used in the making of grass-cloth; **-ink** = INDIAN-INK; **-orange,** the sweet orange of commerce, originally brought from China; **-pink,** *Dianthus chinensis*; **-root** (see CHINA[2]); **-rose,** (*a*) the Monthly Rose (*Rosa indica*) and the Red Rose (*R. semperflorens*) with their varieties; (*b*) *Hibiscus Rosa-sinensis* (N.O. *Malvaceæ*), a tree 20 to 30 feet high; **-tree** (*U.S.*) the AZEDARAC; **-ware,** ware from China (see below); **-wax,** a white crystalline wax, the product of *Coccus sinensis*.

II. China Porcelain, China-ware, china. [The Pers. name, widely diffused as *chīnī,* was prob. introduced in the 17th c. into England, whence the former pronunc. tʃē·ni, also tʃi·ni, tʃī·ni, which still survive in the dialects.] A fine, semi-transparent earthenware, brought from China into Europe in the 16th c. by the Portuguese, who named it *porcelain.* (*China-ware* meant orig. 'ware from China'. This, shortened to *China,* became the name also of the material, so that 'china-ware' is now 'ware made of china or porcelain'.) Also *fig.* and *attrib.*

[A] collection of China-ware MRS. PIOZZI. Women, like Cheney, shou'd be kept with care 1685.

Comb.: **C.-clay,** a fine white potter's clay, called also kaolin; also *attrib.*; **-glaze,** a preparation for painting blue fret, composed of glass, lead, and blue calx; †**-metal,** porcelain or majolica; **-ware.**

III. = CHEYNEY, q. v.

China[2] (tʃəi·na). 1582. [From *China* in Asia.] The thick fleshy root-stock of a plant (*Smilax China,* L.) akin to Sarsaparilla; called also *China root.* Hence **C.-ale,** ale flavoured with china root; **-broth,** etc.

China[3] (kəi·na, kī·na). 1866. [var. of *kina* or *quina* (see QUININE), Peruv. for 'bark'.] A name of Cinchona bark. Also, a homœopathic medicine prepared from cinchona. In comb. *chin-* = QUIN-.

Chinaman (tʃəi·nămæ̆n). 1772. **1.** A dealer in porcelain. **2.** A native of China 1854. Hence **Chinaman's hat,** a gastropod shell, also called *Cup-and-Saucer.*

China-mania, chinama·nia. 1875. [See CHINA[1].] A mania for collecting (old) china. Hence **China-ma·niac.**

†**Chin-bone.** OE. The jaw-bone -1592.

‖**Chincapin, chinquapin** (tʃi·nkăpin). 1676. [Corruption of Indian name.] The Dwarf Chestnut (*Castanea pumila*), a native of Virginia, etc., a shrubby tree, from 6 to 20 ft. high, with a small, very sweet nut.

Chinch (tʃintʃ), *sb.*[1] 1625. [a. Sp. *chinche* :—L. *cimicem.*] **1.** The bed- or house-bug. (Now only *U.S.*) **2.** An insect resembling the bed-bug in its disgusting odour, which is very destructive to wheat and other grasses; called also *chinch-*, *chink-bug*. (Webster.)

†**Chinch,** *a.* and *sb.*[2] [ME. *chiche*, a. OF. (and mod.) *chiche* parsimonious. In later F. it became *chinche.*] *adj.* Niggardly. *sb.* A niggard, miser; a wretch –1570.

Chinchilla (tʃintʃi·lă). 1604. [Sp.; app. dim. of *chinche* bug; perh. from its supposed smell.] **1.** A genus of small rodents peculiar to S. America; also, short for *c. fur* 1824. **2.** A cloth with a long nap gathered in little tufts. **3.** A variety of rabbit bred for its fur 1904.

‖**Chin-chin** (tʃin tʃin), *sb.* 1795. [Chinese *ts'ing ts'ing.*] An Anglo-Chinese phrase of salutation. Hence **Chin-chin** *v.* to salute.

Chinchona; see CINCHONA.

Chincough (tʃi·nˌkǫf). Now *dial.* 1519. [For *chink-cough*, from the stem (Saxon) *kink-*, OTeut. *kik-* to chink, kink, gasp. By pop. etym. connected with *chin* and *chine.*] Now called HOOPING-COUGH, q. v.

Chine (tʃəin), *sb.*[1] [OE. *cinu*, *-an*, f. (ult.) root *ki-* to split; cf. CHINE *v.*[1]] †A fissure or crack –1582. *spec.* A deep and narrow ravine cut in soft rock by water, as *Shanklin C.* in the I. of Wight.

Chine (tʃəin), *sb.*[2] ME. [aphet. f. **achine*, for OF. *eschine* (mod.F. *échine*).] **1.** The spine, or backbone; 'the part of the back in which the spine is found' (J.) (*arch.* and *techn.*). †**2.** The back –1775. **3.** *Cookery.* The whole or part of the backbone of an animal, with the adjoining flesh ME. **4.** *transf.* A ridge, crest, arête 1855.

3. A c. or saddle of mutton MRS. GLASSE. Hence **Chined** *a.* having a c.

Chine (tʃəin), *sb.*[3] 1460. = CHIME *sb.*[2], q.v.

†**Chine,** *v.*[1] [OE. *cinan*, *cán*, etc. :—OTeut. *kinan*, f. stem *ki-*; see CHINE *sb.*[1]] To burst asunder; to crack, chink, etc. –1530.

Chine, *v.*[2] 1513. [f. CHINE *sb.*[2]; cf. F. *échiner.*] **1.** To cut along or across the chine; to cut the chine-piece. **2.** To break the back of 1596. **3.** *intr.* and *trans.* To ridge. (In Blackmore only.)

1. And the Pigge you shal c. MARKHAM. You c. the Salmon 1651. 2. Ill c. the villain OTWAY.

†**Chine·nses,** *sb. pl.* 1621. [Cf. L. *Sinenses.*] Chinese –1649.

Chinese (tʃəinī·z). 1577. [f. CHINA; in F. *chinois.*]

A. *adj.* Of or pertaining to China.

C. compliment: a pretended deference to the opinions of others, when one's mind is already made up.

B. *sb.* **1.** A native of China 1606. [pl. †*Chineses* (17th c.), *Chinese*. The sing. *Chinee* is U. S. colloq.] **2.** The Chinese language 1727.

1. Where Chineses drive With Sails and Wind MILT. *P. L.* III. 438. var. †**Chi·nian, -ean** *a.* and *sb.*

Chink (tʃiŋk), *sb.*[1] 1767. [f. CHINK *v.*[1]] A convulsive fit of coughing or laughing.

Chink (tʃiŋk), *sb.*[2] 1535. [? var. of CHINE (*sb.*[1]).] **1.** = CHINE *sb.*[1] Also *fig.* **2.** A long and narrow aperture through an object; a slit, etc. 1552. var. †**Chi·nker.** Hence **Chi·nky** *a.*

Chink (tʃiŋk), *sb.*[3] 1581. [Echoic.] **1.** The short, sharp sound produced by pieces of metal or glass striking one another; any similar sound. †**2.** *pl.* Coins –1611. **3.** *colloq.* Ready cash 1573. **4.** [from its note.] The Chaffinch (*dial.*) 1797.

1. The c. of their money FULLER. 2. *Rom. & Jul.* I. v. 119. 3. A man of c. SWIFT.

Chink, *sb.*[4] 1901. orig. *U.S.* A Chinaman.

Chink (tʃiŋk), *v.*[1] *dial.* Also KINK[1]. [OE. **cincian*; cf. LG. and Du. *kinken* to cough. See also CHINK *sb.*[1]] *intr.* To gasp convulsively for breath in coughing or laughing.

Chink (tʃiŋk), *v.*[2] 1552. [See CHINK *sb.*[2], CHINE *v.*, and CHINSE *v.*] †**1.** *intr.* To open in cracks –1693. †**2.** *trans.* To crack or chap –1656. **3.** To fill (*up*) chinks 1822.

3. The women c. the cracks 1881.

Chink (tʃiŋk), *v.*[3] 1589. [See CHINK *sb.*[3]] **1.** *intr.* To emit a short, sharp, ringing sound, as coins or glasses do in striking each other. **2.** *trans.* To cause (things) to make this sound by striking them together; *esp.* coins 1728. Hence **Chi·nkle** *v.* to c. continuously.

Chink, *v.*[4] *dial.* 1825. [f. Teut. **kink-* to twist, etc.] To give a twist to; to sprain.

†**Chino,** *sb.* Also **Chinao.** 1588. [a. OSp.] **1.** A Chinese –1641. **2. Chino-** in comb., as in *Chino-Japanese*, etc. (*mod.*).

Chinoidine (kinoi·dəin). 1875. [f. CHINA[3].] A resinous substance, contained in the refuse of quinine.

†**Chinois.** 1613. [a. F.] = CHINESE –1684. Hence ‖**Chinoiserie** [mod.F.], Chinese conduct, art, notion, etc.

Chinoline (ki·nŏləin). 1853. [f. CHINA[3] + L. *oleum* + -INE.] A tertiary amine, C_9H_7N (belonging to the series $C_nH_{2n-11}N$), an oily fluid, obtained by the distillation of quinine with potassium hydroxide; and also by the dry distillation of coal.

Chino·logist. = SINOLOGIST, q. v.

Chinook (tʃinū·k). *U. S.* 1840. [Native name of an Indian tribe on the Columbia river, N. America.] A jargon which originated in the intercourse of the Hudson Bay Company's servants with the Indians of Oregon and Columbia, and is used as a means of intercourse between different tribes and with the white man.

C. wind: an ocean wind, warm in winter, cool in summer, which blows on the Pacific slope of the Rocky Mountains.

Chinquapin, var. of CHINCAPIN.

Chinse (tʃins), *v.* 1513. [App. the typical form is *chinch*, dial. var. of CHINK *v.*[2]] **1.** *dial.* = CHINK *v.*[2] 3. **2.** To caulk; now *Naut.* to caulk slightly or temporarily. Hence **Chinsing-iron,** a caulker's tool.

Chintz (tʃints). *pl.* **chintzes.** 1614. [Orig. *chints*, pl. of *chint* (afterwards treated as sing.), a. Hindi *chīnt*; also formerly *chite*, a. Mahrāti *chīt*; both :—Skr. *chitra* variegated. Cf. *baize* for *bays.*] *orig.* The painted calicoes imported from India; *now*, a name for cotton cloths fast-printed with designs of flowers, etc., in a number of colours, and usually glazed. Also *attrib.*

Chiolite (kəi·ŏləit). [Named 1846; f. Gr. χιών snow: a better form would be *chionolite.*] *Min.* A fluoride of aluminium and sodium occurring in the Ilmen mountains.

Chiopin(e, obs. f. CHOPINE.

Chip (tʃip), *sb.*[1] ME. [conn. w. CHIP *v.*[1]] **1.** A small, and *esp.* thin, piece of wood, or other (specified) material, separated by hewing, cutting, or breaking; a thin fragment chopped or broken off. Also *fig.* **2.** *spec. Naut.* A small quadrant-shaped piece of wood at the end of a log-line 1874. **3.** *spec.* A counter used in games of chance; hence, *slang.* a sovereign 1873. **4.** A name for the keys of a spinet (SHAKS. *Sonn.* cxxviii). **5.** Wood (or woody fibre) split into thin strips for making hats and bonnets 1771. **6.** Anything worthless, without flavour, innutritious, or dried up 1639. **7.** A slight fracture caused by chipping; also *dial.* an act of chipping (*mod.*). Also *attrib.* and *Comb.*, as *c.-bonnet*, *-hat* (see 5); also **c.-shot** (*Golf*), a short lofting stroke, played with back-spin.

1. Lyke sawdust or drye chyppes SKELTON. To make Orange Chips MRS. RAFFALD. *fig. C. of the old block*: one that resembles his father; also applied to things. 6. To roast things to a c. A. YOUNG. 7. The cup has a c. on the edge (*mod. colloq.*).

Chip (tʃip), *sb.*[2] 1830. [f. CHIP *v.*[2]] *Wrestling.* **1.** A trip, a trick, a special mode of throwing one's opponent. **2.** A tiff (*dial.*).

Chip (tʃip), *v.*[1] 1461. [prob. in OE. **cippian.* Cf. EFris. *kippen* to cut, and MDu., MLG. *kippen* to chip eggs, to hatch.] †**1.** *To c. bread*: to pare away the crust –1727. **2.** *gen.* To hew or cut with an ax, adze, etc. 1606. **3.** To break off small fragments from wood, stone, etc. (*esp.* from an edge); to shape by so doing. (A kind of dim. of *chop.*) 1859. Also *intr.* (for *refl.*) †**4.** *trans.* To chap –1508. †**5.** *intr.* To break open, burst –1734. **6.** To crack and break (the shell) 1606. **7.** *Australia.* To harrow (ground) 1798.

3. Statues were chipped..into decency GREEN. 5. When..trees did c. [*note*, blossom] COLVIL. 6. Thou isle! .. That saw'st the unfledged eaglet c. his shell BYRON.

Phr. *To c. in* (colloq.): to interpose smartly, cut in. *Comb.* **c.-ax,** a small ax used in chipping. Hence **Chi·pper,** one who or that which chips.

Chip (tʃip), *v.*[2] Chiefly *north.* 1788. [Cf. ON. *kippa* 'to scratch, pull', *refl.* 'to struggle'; also Du. *kippen* to seize.] *trans.* To trip up. *intr.* To trip along; to fall *out.*

Chipmuck, -munk (tʃi·pmɒk, -mɒŋk). Also -minck, -monk, -muk. 1842. [? Indian; or ? an Eng. compound.] A species of ground-squirrel, the Striped Squirrel, Hackee, or Chipping Squirrel, of N. America.

Chippendale (tʃi·pĕndeᶦl), *a.* 1876. [f. T. *Chippendale*, an 18th c. cabinet-maker.] Applied to a style of light and elegant drawing-room furniture; also to a style of book-plates.

Chipper (tʃi·pəɹ), *a.* *U.S.* 1837. [App. = north. *kipper.*] Lively, cheerful; chirpy.

Chipper (tʃi·pəɹ), *v.* *dial.* and *U.S.* 18... [partly a metathesis of *chirrup*; partly echoic.] **1.** *intr.* To twitter; to babble, chatter. **2.** *trans.* To make chipper, cheer *up* (*U. S.*) 1873.

Chipping (tʃi·piŋ), *vbl. sb.* ME. [f. CHIP *v.*[1]] **1.** The action of the verb CHIP 1611. **2.** *concr.* †A paring of the crust of a loaf. (Usu. in *pl.*) –1727. Also *gen.* ME.

Comb.: **c.-bird,** a small species of sparrow (*Zonotrichia socialis*); **-squirrel** = CHIPMUCK.

Chippy (tʃi·pi), *a.* 1729. [f. CHIP *sb.*[1] and *v.*[1] + -Y[1].] **1.** Of, or composed of, chips. **2.** Resembling a chip; as dry as a chip 1866. Hence **Chi·ppiness** (*joc.*).

†**Chira·grical,** *a.* 1644. [f. L. *chiragricus*, f. *chiragra*, a. Gr. + -IC + -AL.] Pertaining to, or having, gout in the hand –1646.

‖**Chirayta** (tʃirai·tă), **chiretta** (tʃire·tă). 1831. [a. Hindi *chirāītā* :—Skr. *kirāta-tikta*, butter plant of the Kirātas, an ancient Indian forest tribe.] A plant, *Ophelia* (or *Agathotes*) *Chirayta*, N.O. *Gentianaceæ*; also the bitter tonic obtained from it.

Chi-rho (kəi rōᵘ). 1868. First two letters of XPICTOC CHRIST, used to symbolize the name.

Chirk (tʃəɹk), *v.* OE. [orig. a var. of CHARK :—OE. *cearcian*, *stridere.*] **1.** *intr.* To make a strident noise; to grate, creak, croak. Now *Sc. dial.* **2.** To chirp; to squeak (*arch.* and *dial.*) ME. **3.** To cheer *up* (*U.S. colloq.*) 1860.

Chirk (tʃəɹk), *a.* *U.S. colloq.* 1828. [? f. prec.] Lively, in good spirits.

Chirl (tʃəɹl), *v.* *Sc.* 1818. [Echoic.] To warble. Hence **Chirl** *sb.*

Chirm (tʃəɹm), *sb. arch.* and *dial.* OE. [conn. w. CHIRM *v.*] **1.** Din, chatter, vocal noise; *esp.* the mingled noise of many birds or voices. †**2.** A flock (of finches) –1688.

Chirm (tʃəɹm), *v. arch.* and *dial.* [OE. *cirman*, to cry out. Cf. Du. *kermen* to mourn.] *intr.* To cry out, roar; now only, to chatter or warble, as birds. Also *trans.*

Chiro-, chir-, = Gr. χειρο-, χείρ hand.

Chiro·gnomy, cheir- [Gr. γνώμη], the art or science of estimating character by the inspection of the hand; hence, **Chiro·gnomist. Chiro·gy·mnast** [Gr. γυμναστής], an apparatus for exercising the fingers for pianoforte playing. **Chiro·logy** [a. F. *chirologie*], †the art of speaking by signs made with the hands or fingers; the study of the hand, whence **Chiro·logist, Chirolo·gical** *a.*, **-ally** *adv.* **Chi·romancy, cheir-** [Gr. μαντεία], divination by the hand, palmistry; hence, **Chi·romancer, Chi·romant, Chiroma·ntic** *a.* and †*sb.*, **Chiroma·ntical** *a.* **Chi·romys, cheir-** [Gr. μῦς], the AYE-AYE of Madagascar. **Chiro·nomy, cheir-** [Gr. -νομος], the art or science of gesticulation in oratory, pantomime, etc.; hence, †**Chiro·nomer, Chirono·mic** *a.*, †**Chironoma·tic** *a.* **Chi·roplast** [Gr. πλάστης], an apparatus for keeping the hands in a correct position in pianoforte playing; hence, **Chi·roplastic** *a.* **Chi·ropod**; see CHEIROPOD. **Chiro·podist** [Gr. πούς, ποδ-], one who treats diseases of the hands and feet; now usu. one who treats corns and bunions; so **Chiropo·dical** *a.* pertaining to chiropody; **Chiro·podism, Chiro·podistry** = *Chiropody*; **Chiropodo·logy,** a treatise on corns, warts, etc.; **Chiro·pody,** the art of treating corns, warts, defective nails, etc., on feet or hands. **Chiro·sophist, cheir-** [Gr. σοφός], †one who practises sleight of hand; =

Chiromancer; so **Chiro·sophy.** **Chiro·tony** [a. Gr. χειροτονία], election by vote (*rare*).

Chirograph (kəi°rograf). 1483. [a. F. *chirographe*, ad. L., a. Gr. χειρόγραφον, -ος. A technical word in later L. (cf. Gaius iii. 134).] **1.** One of various documents formally written, engrossed, or signed. **a.** = CHARTER-PARTY 1. Now *Hist.* 1727. **b.** The indenture of a fine; one of the counterparts of such indenture 1671. **c.** A bond given in one's own handwriting 1483. **d.** A form of Papal expression in writing 1528. **2.** *gen.* Any formal written document; handwriting (*rare*) 1613. Hence **Chiro·graphal** *a.*, **Chiro·graphary** *a.* related to or given in one's own handwriting; **Chiro·graphate,** to set one's hand to; **Chirogra·phic, -al** *a.* of, pertaining to, or in handwriting; **Chiro·graphist** (used by Pope for *chirognomist*).

Chirographer (kəirǫ·grăfəɹ). ME. [Cf. *geographer*, etc.] **1.** *Law.* The officer appointed to engross fines (chirographs), in the Court of Common Pleas. (Abolished in 1833.) **2.** A writing-master; a copying clerk 1755.

Chirography (kəirǫ·grăfi). 1654. [See CHIROGRAPH.] Handwriting; †autograph.

Chiropractic (kəi°roprǣ·ktik). 1908. [f. Gr. χειρο- + πρακτικός: see CHIRO- and PRACTIC *a.*] **a.** *sb.* Manipulation of the joints, esp. of the spine, as a method of curing disease; also, a practitioner of this. **b.** *adj.* That practises or is concerned with this method. Hence **Chiropra·ctor.**

Chirp (tʃɔ̄ɹp), *v.* ME. [Echoic. See also CHIRR.] **1.** *intr.* To utter a short sharp thin sound, as of a bird or insect. Also *trans.* **2.** To make a sound more or less like the chirp of a bird; to cheep, talk cheerfully, CHIRRUP 1575. Hence **Chirp** *sb.* **Chi·rper.** **Chi·rpiness.** **Chi·rpingly** *adv.* **Chi·rpy** *a. colloq.* given to chirping; lively, merry.

Chirr (tʃɔ̄ɹ, tʃɔrr), *v.* 1639. [Echoic.] *intr.* To trill, as a grasshopper. (Expressing a more continuous and monotonous sound than CHIRP.)

Rustles the lizard, and the cushats chirre BROWNING. Hence **Chirr** *sb.* the sound itself.

Chirrup (tʃi·rʊ̆p), *v.* 1579. [f. *chirp* by trilling the *r*, but assoc. w. *cheer*, *cheer up*.] **1.** *intr.* To chirp, *esp.* with a sustained and lively effect. Also *trans.* **2.** To make a sharp thin sound (by suction) with the lips compressed by way of encouragement (to a horse, etc.) 1726. Also *trans.* **3.** To speak in sprightly tones 1775.

1. Whit, whit, whit, . . chirrupt the nightingale TENNYSON. Hence **Chi·rrup** *sb.* **Chi·rruper.** **Chi·rrupy** *a. colloq.* given to c.; lively, cheery.

Chirt (tʃɔ̄ɹt), *v.* Now *Sc.* ME. [A parallel form to CHIRK, CHIRR.] †**1.** *intr.* To chirp. ME. only. **2.** *intr.* To spirt 1513. **3.** *trans.* To squeeze, press out 1805. Hence **Chirt** *sb.*

Chirurgeon (kəirɒ̄·ɹdʒən, tʃi-). *arch.* [In ME. a. OF. *cirurgien*:—Rom. **cirurgiano*, f. *cirurgia*; see CHIRURGY. Cf. SURGEON.] A SURGEON. †**Chiru·rgeonly** *adv.* SHAKS.

Chirurgery (kəirɒ̄·ɹdʒĕri). *arch.* [In ME. a. OF. *cirurgerie*, altered, after the Renascence, to *chir-*.] = SURGERY.

†**Chiru·rgy.** *rare.* [In ME. *cirurgie*, *sir-*, a. OF.:—Rom. type *cirurgia*, repr. L. *chirurgia* (*cir-*), a. Gr. χειρουργία, f. χειρουργός (sc. ἰατρός). Altered, after the Renascence, to *chir-*. Formerly the *ch* was soft.] = Surgery, CHIRURGERY. Hence **Chiru·rgic, -al** *a.* (*arch.*).

Chisel (tʃi·zĕl), *sb.*[1] ME. [a. ONF.:—late L. type *cisellum*, dim. f. **cisum* = *cæsum*, f. *cædere*; see SCISSORS.] A cutting tool of iron or steel with the cutting face transverse to the axis, and more or less bevelled on one or both sides; used for cutting wood, metal, stone, bone, etc., and worked by pressure or by the blows of a mallet or hammer. Also *attrib.*

What fine Chizzell Could euer yet cut breath SHAKS.

Chisel, chissel (tʃi·z'l, tʃi·s'l), *sb.*[2] 1607. [The same wd. as CHESIL.] Bran; occas. 'whole meal'.

Chisel (tʃi·zĕl), *v.* 1509. [f. CHISEL *sb.*[1] Cf. F. *ciseler.*] **1.** To cut, grave, pare, shape, etc. with a chisel. Often with *out*. Also *transf.* and *fig.* **2.** *colloq.* To cheat 1808. Hence **Chi·selled, -eled** *ppl. a.* shaped with or like a chisel; also *fig.* **Chi·seller, -eler.**

Chiselly (tʃi·z'li), *a.* and *adv.* *dial.* 1649. [f. CHESIL, CHISEL *sb.*[2]] Gravelly; grittily.

Chit (tʃit), *sb.*[1] ME. [Cf. *kitten*, *kitling*; also Cheshire dial. *chit* 'puss'. See also CHIT *sb.*[3]] †**1.** The young of a beast; whelp; kitten –1713. **2.** A (very young) child (cf. *kid*); *contemptuous*, a girl or young woman 1624.

2. A little c. of a miller's daughter of eighteen DICKENS.

†**Chit,** *sb.*[2] 1533. [f. CHICH, corrupted to *chits*, and taken as plural.] **1.** = CHICH –1610. **2.** A freckle or wart –1755.

Chit (tʃit), *sb.*[3] Now *dial.* 1601. [?f. ME. CHITHE, OE. *cīð*; unexplained.] A shoot, sprout.

†**Chit,** *sb.*[4] 1610. [From its feeble note.] A bird; the Titlark –1668.

Chit (tʃit), *sb.*[5] *Anglo-Ind.* 1785. Short for CHITTY.

Chit, *sb.*[6] A small cooper's cleaving tool.

Chit (tʃit), *v.* Now *dial.* 1601. [conn. w. CHIT *sb.*[3]] To sprout.

Chit-chat (tʃi·t,tʃæt). 1710. [f. CHAT *sb.*[1] by reduplication.] **1.** Light familiar chat. **2.** Matter of current gossip 1710. Also *attrib.*

†**Chithe.** [OE. *cīð*, f. (ult.) root *ki-* to split; see CHINE *sb.*[1], *v.*[1]] A tiny shoot or sprout; a mote –ME.

Chitin (kəi·tin). Also **-ine.** 1836. [a. F. *chitine*, f. Gr. χιτών. A better form would be *chitonin.*] *Zool.* and *Chem.* The organic substance which forms the elytra and integuments of insects and the carapaces of crustacea. Hence **Chi·tinize** *v.* to convert into c. **Chi·tiniza·tion.** **Chi·tinous** *a.* like, or consisting of, c.

Chitling (tʃi·tliŋ). Also **chitlin.** 1848. [See CHITTERLING.] **1.** = CHITTERLING (*dial.* and *U.S.*) 1886. **2.** *fig.* (in *pl.*) Rags, tatters (*U.S.*).

‖**Chiton** (kəi·tǫn). 1816. [a. Gr. χιτών.] ‖**1.** The Greek tunic 1850. **2.** A genus of Molluscs having a shell composed of eight plates overlapping each other.

Chitter (tʃi·təɹ), *v.* ME. [A parallel form to CHATTER; cf. *jabber*, *jibber*, etc.] **1.** Of birds: To utter a series of sharp thin sounds (?*dial.*). **2.** To shiver or chatter with cold (*dial.* and *Sc.*) 1526. Hence **Chi·tter** *sb.* twitter.

Chitterling (tʃi·təɹliŋ). Mostly in *pl.* ME. [?] **1.** The smaller intestines of the pig, etc., *esp.* as fried for food. Also *fig.* †**2.** The frill down the breast of a shirt; also *gen.* (The mesentery is called by Butchers the 'frill'.) –1849. **3.** [as dim. of CHIT *sb.*[1]] A little chit 1675.

Chitty, *sb.* *Anglo-Ind.* 1698. [a. Hindī.] A letter or note; also, a certificate or pass.

†**Chitty,** *a.*[1] *rare.* 1552. [f. CHIT *sb.*[2] + -Y[1].] Freckled or warty –1729.

Chitty, *a.*[2] 1616. [assoc. w. CHIT *sb.*[1]] Pinched in face; baby-like, puny.

†**Chitty-face.** 1601. [? orig. F. *chicheface* (see CHICHEVACHE).] **1.** A term of reproach: pinched-face; later, baby-face –1725. Hence **Chitty-faced** *a.* (*dial.*)

Chiule. *Hist.* [OE. *ciol*, *céol*:—WGer. *kiul*; see KEEL.] An old English or Norse war-ship.

Chivachee, -ie, obs. var. of CHEVACHEE.

Chivalresque (ʃivălre·sk), *a.* Also **chev-.** 1800. [See CHEVALIER and -ESQUE.] Wearing the garb, manners, or spirit of chivalry.

Chivalric (ʃivæ·lrik, ʃi·vălrik, tʃ-), *a.* 1797. [f. CHIVALRY; cf. *geometric*, etc. (The poets sanction *chiva·lric.*)] Chivalrous.

Some extant spirit of c. kind CAMPBELL.

Chivalrous (ʃi·vălrəs, tʃi·v-), *a.* [ME., a. OF. *chevalerous* (not in mod.F.), f. *chevalier* CHEVALIER. Obs. bef. 1600, but subseq. revived.] †**1.** Like a (mediæval) knight or man-at-arms; *esp.* doughty –1596. **2.** Of or pertaining to the Age of CHIVALRY, or to its knights 1774. **3.** Of, belonging to, or characteristic of, the ideal knight; gallant, courteous, magnanimous. Occas. = 'quixotic'. 1818.

1. In brave poursuitt of chevalrous emprize SPENSER *F. Q.* I. ix. 1. Hence **Chi·valrous·ly** *adv.*, **-ness.**

Chivalry (ʃi·vălri, tʃi·-). [ME., a. OF. *chevalerie*:—L. *caballarius*, CAVALIER. (Hence also CAVALRY.) The proper historical pronunc. is with tʃ-; but ʃ- is more usual, after mod.Fr.] **1.** *collect.* Knights or horsemen equipped for battle; *esp.* the mediæval 'men-at-arms'; more widely, gallant gentlemen. **2.** The position and character of a knight, knighthood ME. †**3.** A knightly feat –1823. **4.** The knightly system of feudal times with its religious, moral, and social code and practices 1765. **5.** The character of the ideal knight; disinterested bravery, honour, and courtesy 1790. **6.** *Old Law.* Tenure by knight's service (abolished in 1662). Now *Hist.* 1574. ¶ **7.** *improp.* Team of horses. WORSLEY.

1. Busiris and his Memphian Chivalrie MILT. *P. L.* I. 307. Belgium's . . Beauty and her C. BYRON. 2. *Rich. II*, II. i. 54. Orders of C. BACON. The feats of Chivaldry BOLTON. 4. The age of c. is gone BURKE. *Flower of C.*: fairest type of knighthood; pick of a force of armed knights.

†*Court of C.* (*curia militaris*): a court formerly held before the Lord High Constable and the Earl Marshal of England, having cognizance of matters relating to deeds of arms done out of the realm.

Chive[1] (tʃəiv), also **cive** (səiv). ME. [In form *cive*, a. F. *cive*:—L. *cepa*, *cæpa* onion.] **1.** A cultivated species of *Allium* (*A. Schœnoprasum*). Its leaves are used in soups and stews. **2.** A small bulb or bulbil; *esp.* one of the cloves of a bulb of garlic 1551. Also *attrib.*

†**Chive**[2]. (Mostly in *pl.*) 1530. [app. orig. *chithe*, partly affected by CHIVE *sb.*[1]] **1.** *Bot.* The filament of the stamen, or the stamen as a whole –1807. **2.** = CHITHE 1610. **3.** One of the lamellæ of an agaric 1721.

Chive[3] (tʃiv). *Thieves' Cant.* 1673. A knife. Hence **Chive** *v.* to 'knife'.

Chivy, var. of CHEVY *sb.* and *v.*

Chlamydate (klæ·midēᶦt), *a.* [f. Gr. χλαμύδ- (χλαμύς).] *Zool.* Having a mantle; applied to certain molluscs.

Chlamydeous (klămi·diəs), *a.* [f. mod.L. *chlamydeæ*, f. as prec. + -OUS.] *Bot.* Having one or more floral envelopes.

Chlamydophore (klæ·midofō°ɹ). Also **chla·myphore.** 1836. [ad. mod.L. *chlamydophorus* (erron. *chlamyphorus*); see CHLAMYDATE.] A South American edentate mammal allied to the Armadillo, having the upper surface covered with a cuirass of leathery plates.

‖**Chlamys** (klæ·mis). 1748. [a. Gr.] **1.** *Gr. Antiq.* A short mantle worn by men in ancient Greece. **2.** *Bot.* The floral envelope.

‖**Chloasma** (klo,æ·zmă). *Pl.* **-mata.** 1876. [f. Gr. χλοάζειν to become green.] *Med.* An affection of the skin, characterized by yellowish-brown or blackish patches. *pl.* These patches.

Chlor-[1], comb. f. Gr. χλωρός green, used bef. a vowel; cf. CHLORO-[1].

Chlor-[2]. *Chem.* Comb. f. *chlorine* (*chloric*, *chloride*, and *chlorous*) used (chiefly bef. a vowel) in forming names of chlorine compounds: *e.g.* **a.** **Chlorace·tic,** name of acids derived from Acetic acid, by substitution of 1, 2, or 3 atoms of chlorine for hydrogen. Similarly *chlo·ramide*, *chlora·nil*, *-anila·mic*, etc. **b.** Also **Chlora·lum,** a disinfecting agent, consisting of aluminium chloride and sulphide with some impurities; **Chlorau·rate;** see CHLORO-AURATE in CHLORO-[2]; **Chlorhy·drate,** a salt of **Chlorhy·dric** acid = Hydrochloric acid (HCl); **Chlorhy·drin,** a chlorhydric ether of glycerin, analogous to bromhydrin; **Chlorio·dic,** combining chlorine and iodine. **c.** *Min.* **Chloralu·minite,** 'a hydrous chloride of aluminium' (Dana); **Chlora·patite,** a variety of APATITE, containing chlorine.

Chloral (klō°răl). [mod. f. CHLOR(INE) + AL(COHOL), after *ethal.*] *Chem.* A thin colourless oily liquid with a pungent odour, obtained by the action of chlorine upon alcohol; = *trichloraldehyde* ($CCl_3.CHO$). Pop. and comm. = *chloral hydrate* ($CCl_3.CH.2OH$), a white crystalline substance resulting from the combination of water and chloral, and much used as a hypnotic and anæsthetic. Hence **Chlo·ralism** (*Med.*), a morbid condition produced by the long-continued use of chloral hydrate; **Chlo·ralize** *v.* to bring under the influence of c.

Chloranthus (kloræ·nþəs), *a.* 1871. [f. CHLOR-[1] + Gr. ἄνθος.] *Bot.* Having green flowers. Hence **Chlora·nthy,** a condition in which the coloured floral organs of a plant return to leaves.

Chlorate (klōᵊ·rē̆t). 1823. [f. CHLOR-IC.] *Chem.* A salt of chloric acid, e. g. *c. of potash.*

Chloric (klōᵊ·rik), *a.* 1810. [f. CHLOR-INE + -IC; cf. F. *chlorique.*] *Chem.* Of or pertaining to chlorine; containing chlorine in smaller proportion, relatively to oxygen, than *chlorous* compounds; as in *chloric acid,* HO_3Cl.

Chloric ether, = *ethyl chloride,* C_2H_5Cl; in *Med.* occas. applied to a solution of chloroform in alcohol.

Chloridate (klōᵊ·ridēⁱt), *v.* [f. next.] *Photography.* To treat with a chloride; *e.g.* to treat (a plate) with chloride of silver, so as to render it sensitive.

Chloride (klōᵊ·rid, -əid). Rarely **chlorid.** 1812. [f. CHLOR-INE + -IDE.] **1.** *Chem.* A simple compound of chlorine with a metal or an organic radical. **2.** Applied to various bleaching and disinfecting compounds, such as 'c. of lime', 'c. of potash', 'c. of soda', which are not simple chlorides 1826. **3.** A name for ores containing c. of silver. *U.S.* Hence **Chlo·ridize** *v.* = CHLORIDATE; *Mining,* to convert into c.

Chlorimeter, -try; see CHLOROMETER, -TRY.

Chlorinate (klōᵊ·rineⁱt), *v.* (Chiefly in *pass.*) 1865. [f. CHLORINE + -ATE³.] To act upon or impregnate with chlorine.

Chlorination (klōᵊrinēⁱ·ʃən). 1854. [f. as prec.] *Chem.* Treatment with chlorine; *Mining,* the process of extracting gold and silver from certain ores by means of chlorine.

Chlorine (klōᵊ·rin, -əin), *sb.* 1810. [Named by Davy from its colour; f. Gr. χλωρός. In F. *chlore,* Ger. *chlor.*] *Chem.* One of the non-metallic elements; a yellowish-green heavy gas, having a peculiar irritating smell, and very active chemical properties. It is a powerful bleaching and disinfecting agent. Symbol Cl; atomic weight 35·5. As *attrib.* = *chloric, chlorous, of chlorine.* Hence **Chlorini·ferous** *a.* **Chlo·rinize** *v.* to treat with c. **Chlo·rinous** *a.*

Chlo·rine, *a. rare.* 1849. [f. as prec.] Light-green.

Chlorite¹ (klōᵊ·rəit). 1794. [ad. Gr. χλωρῖτις, f. χλωρός; see -ITE.] *Min.* A name applied to certain green hydrous silicates of magnesia and alumina occurring in ancient rock-formations; orig. specific, but now a vague popular term. Also *attrib.* as in **c. schist, slate,** a green slaty rock, consisting largely of c. in foliated plates. Hence **Chlori·tic** *a.*, **Chloritous** (klorəi·təs) *a.* consisting of, or containing, c.

Chlo·rite². 1853. [f. CHLOR-INE + -ITE.] *Chem.* A salt of chlorous acid; *e.g.* c. of silver.

Chloritoid (klōᵊ·ritoid). 1837. [f. CHLORITE¹ + -OID.] *Min.* A foliated hydrous silicate of alumina and iron, varying in colour from greenish-black to grey; *chlorite spar.*

Chloro-¹ (klōᵊ·ro), bef. a vowel usually CHLOR-. [a. Gr. χλωρο-, comb. f. χλωρός green, pale-green.] Hence:

Chlorocru·orin [+ CRUORIN], a green substance supposed to be the cause of the green colour in some species of Sabella; **Chloro·melan, -ite** [Gr. χλωρομέλαν-], *Min.* CRONSTEDTITE; **Chlorophæ·ite** [Gr. φαιός brown], *Min.* a hydrated silicate of iron, of a dark green colour, changing on exposure to brown or black; **Chlo·rophane** [Gr. -φανης, -φανος showing], *Min.* a variety of fluor spar showing a green phosphorescence when heated; **Chlo·rophyte** [Gr. φυτόν], *Bot.* any plant having a successive evolution and green parts or expansions.

Chloro-². *Chem.* Comb. f. *chlorine, chloride, chloric, chlorous,* used chiefly bef. a consonant; see CHLOR-². Hence: **a. Chlorobe·nzene,** formed from benzene by the substitution of one or more chlorine atoms for hydrogen atoms; and the like. **b. Chloro-aurate,** a compound of chloride of gold with a basic chloride or a hydrochlorate; **chlorobromide,** a compound containing chlorine and bromine in union with a metal or organic radical, as 'c. of silver'; **chlorocarbonic acid,** a synonym of Carbonyl chloride or Phosgene gas ($COCl_2$); **chlorocyanic acid,** early name of **cyanogen chloride,** CNCl; **chloropi·crin,** a colourless oily liquid formed by distilling picric acid with chloride of lime; **chloropla·tinate,** a compound of tetrachloride of platinum; so **chloropla·tinous** *a.*; and the like.

Chlorodyne (klōᵊ·rŏdəin). 1863. [f. *chloroform* + *anodyne.* (But the elements are Gr. χλωρός green + ὀδύνη pain.)] A popular anodyne composed of chloroform, morphia, Indian hemp, prussic acid, etc.

Chloroform (klōᵊ·rŏfǭɹm), *sb.* [a. F. *chloroforme* (1834), f. CHLORO-² + FORM(YL, as being a chloride of *formyl* (in its obs. sense CH = methenyl.] A thin colourless liquid, Cl_3CH, having an ethereal odour and a sweetish taste, the vapour of which when inhaled produces insensibility; hence used as an anæsthetic in surgical and obstetrical operations. Hence **Chlo·roformic** *a.* relating to c. **Chlo·roformist,** one who administers c. **Chlo·roformi·ze** *v.* = CHLOROFORM *v.*; whence **Chlo·roformiza·tion,** the occurrence or the induction of anæsthesia due to c.

Chloroform (klōᵊ·rŏfǭɹm), *v.* 1848. [f. prec. sb.] To administer or apply chloroform to. Also *transf.* and *fig.*

Chloroid (klōᵊ·roid), *a.* [f. CHLOR-INE.] *Chem.* and *Electr.* Akin to or resembling chlorine.

Chlorometer (klorǫ·mĭtəɹ). Also **chlori-.** 1826. [f. CHLORO-, comb. f. CHLORINE.] An instrument for measuring the bleaching power, etc., of chlorine in chlorinated lime, soda, potash. Hence **Chlorome·tric** *a.*; **Chloro·metry** (also *chlori-*).

Chloropal (klorōᵘ·păl). 1826. [f. CHLOR-¹ + OPAL.] *Min.* A greenish opal-like hydrated silicate of iron.

Chlorophyll (klōᵊ·rŏfil). (Also **-phyl(e, -phylle.**) 1819. [a. F. *chlorophylle,* f. Gr. χλωρός + φύλλον.] *Bot.* and *Chem.* The colouring matter of the leaves, etc., of plants; found usually in the cells as minute granules. It occurs also in various green water-animalcules, e. g. *Hydra viridis.* Hence **Chlorophy·llous** *a.* characterized by, or of the nature of c.

Chlorosis (klorōᵘ·sis). 1681. [f. Gr. χλωρός; lit. 'a making green'.] **1.** *Path.* Green sickness; a disease of young women, marked by anæmia, irregularity of the menses, and a pale or greenish complexion. **2.** *Bot.* A disease of plants, in which the green parts lose their colour, or parts normally of another colour turn green 1807. Hence **Chloro·tic** *a.* affected with c.

Chlorous (klōᵊ·rəs), *a.* 1845. [f. CHLORINE + -OUS.] *Chem.* and *Electr.* **1.** Abounding in chlorine; *spec.* containing chlorine in greater proportion relatively to oxygen than chloric compounds, as in **c. acid,** $HClO_2$, the salts of which are *chlorites.* **2.** Of the quality of chlorine: applied to elements or radicals which unite with hydrogen to form an acid, and are relatively electro-negative 1881.

Choak, obs. f. CHOKE *sb.* and *v.*

Choanite (kōᵘ·ănəit). 1846. [f. Gr. χοάνη funnel.] *Palæont.* A fossil Zoophyte, characterized by a funnel-shaped skeleton.

Choanoid (kōᵘ·ănoid), *a.* 1839. [f. as prec.] *Phys.* Funnel-shaped; applied to one of the muscles of the eye in many vertebrata.

‖**Chobdar** (tʃōᵘ·bdāɹ). 1701. [Pers. and Urdū.] *Anglo-Ind.* In India, an usher bearing a staff, who attends on persons of consequence.

Chock (tʃǫk), *sb.* Also **choak** and CHUCK, q. v. 1674. [Cf. ONF. **chuque, choque, chouque* = OF. *çuche, zuche, çouche, souche* 'log or block of wood'. In Eng. influenced by CHOKE.] **1.** A log, *esp.* for burning. **2.** *Turning.* = CHUCK. Also *attrib.* 1703. **3.** A block of wood (usually wedge-shaped), or stone, used to stop a cask, wheel, etc. from moving, or to add weight and steadiness to a machine 1769.

Chock (tʃǫk), *v.*¹ 1662. [f. prec. sb.] †**1.** *intr. To c. in*: to wedge in -1786. **2.** *trans.* To fit or make fast with a chock or chocks; to wedge (a wheel, cask, etc.); also with *up* 1854.

Chock, *v.*², obs. f. SHOCK.

Chock, *adv.* Also **choke.** 1799. [f. CHOCK *sb.* and *v.*; but influenced by CHOCK-FULL.] As close or tight as can be. Also with adverbs, as *c.-aft, -home,* etc. **b. Chock-a-block** (*Naut.*), said of two blocks run close together in a tackle; *transf.* crammed (*with*), chock-full (*of*) 1840.

Chock-full, choke- (tʃǫ·kful, tʃōᵘ·kful), *a.* ME. [?f. CHOKE *v.*; or CHEEK (ME. *cheke,* CHOKE *sb.*²); or ME. CHOK, *chokke*? to ram in. *Choke-full* is a conjecture.] Filled so as to leave no vacant space; cram-full.

Chocolate (tʃǫ·kŏlĕt), *sb.* (*a.*). 1604. [a. F. *chocolat,* Sp. *chocolate,* ad. Mexican *chocolatl,* not conn. w. Mexican *cacauatl* 'cacao'.] **1.** A beverage made from the seeds of the cacao-tree; now, that made by dissolving chocolate cake in boiling water or milk. **2.** A paste or cake composed of the seeds of the cacao-fruit roasted and ground, sweetened and flavoured with vanilla, etc. 1659. **b.** *esp.* (in full *eating c.*) A sweet-meat made with this in the form of cakes, bars, etc. †**3.** *erron.* The cacao-tree or its fruit -1794. **4.** Chocolate colour 1776; as *adj.* 1771.

Comb.: **c.-house,** a house for the supply of c., as a beverage; **-nut,** the cacao-fruit or its seed (not a *nut*); **-tree,** the cacao-tree, *Theobroma Cacao.*

Choctaw (tʃǫ·ktǭ). 1892. [Name of a tribe of N. Amer. Indians.] *Skating.* A step from either edge on one foot to the opposite edge on the other foot, in an opposite direction.

‖**Chœnix** (kī·niks). 1603. [L., a. Gr. χοῖνιξ.] A dry measure, = 1 quart or 1½ pints imperial.

Chogset (tʃǫ·gset). *U.S.* 1848. [Indian name.] A small salt-water fish; the Burgall.

Choice (tʃois), *sb.* [ME. *chois, choys,* a. OF. *chois,* f. *choisir*:—Rom. **causire,* ad. Ger. *kausjan,* deriv. of *kiusan* to try, see, CHOOSE.] **1.** The act of choosing; preferential determination between things proposed; selection, election. **2.** The power, right, or faculty of choosing; option ME. **3.** That which is chosen or to be chosen, the preferable part of anything, the pick, flower, *élite* 1494. Also *concr.* **4.** Scope or field for choice 1586; a well-chosen supply 1591. †**5.** Care in choosing, judgement, discrimination -1765. †**6.** Estimation 1601. **7.** An ALTERNATIVE 1794. Also *attrib.*

1. Grace to gyde my choyce MORE. *To take one's c.*: to choose what one will have. *For c.*: by preference. **2.** *To have one's c. Hobson's c.*: the option of taking the thing offered or nothing. See *Spect.* 1712 No. 509. **3.** The flower and c. of many Provinces MILT. *P. R.* III. 313. For me, the Wilds and Desarts are my C. DRYDEN. **4.** Faith..there's small choise in rotten apples *Tam. Shr.* I. i. 138. Repleate with c. of all delights *1 Hen. VI,* V. v. 16. **5.** Collected with Iudgement, and C. BACON. **6.** *All's Well* III. vii. 26. Hence **Choi·ceful** *a.* fickle in choosing; offering choices. **Choi·celess** *a.* (*rare*).

Choice (tʃois), *a.* ME. [?ME. *chīs* adj. 'nice', assoc. w. prec. sb.] **1.** Worthy of being chosen, select, of special excellence. **2.** Well-chosen 1588. †**3.** Nice in choosing -1656. Hence **Choi·ce·ly** *adv.*, **-ness.**

Choil. 1888. *Cutlery.* The indentation in a pocket-knife where the edge of the blade adjoins the 'tang' or thick part by which it is hafted. Hence **Choil** *v.* to make this; **Choi·ler,** an instrument for making it.

Choir, quire (kwəiᵊɹ), *sb.* [ME. *quer, quere,* a. OF. *cuer* (mod. *chœur*):—L. *chorus,* a. Gr. χορός; cf. CHORUS. The spoken word is still *quire*; the sp. *choir* is app. after Gr.-L. *chorus* or F. *chœur.*] **1.** The organized body of singers in cathedral or church service. **2.** That part of a church appropriated to the singers; the chancel ME. **3.** *gen.* A company of singers; a choral society or institution 1553. **b.** A chorus or subdivision of a chorus. **4.** = CHORUS *sb.* 1. 1656. **5.** *gen.* An organized company or collection ME. **6.** *Mus.* A group of instruments of the same class in an orchestra, or of players on them: cf. BAND *sb.*³ 4. **b.** = CHOIR ORGAN.

Comb.: **c.-boy,** a boy who sings in a c.; so **-man; -master,** an instructor of a c.; **-office,** a service appointed to be recited in choir (the canonical hours, Anglican matins and evensong); *attrib.* or as *adj.* belonging to that class in a religious order which is bound to recitation of the choir offices (contrasted with *lay*), as *c. brother, monk, nun, sister.*

Choir, quire (kwəiᵊɹ), *v. poet.* 1596. [f. prec. sb.] To sing, as a choir, *trans.* and *intr.*

Choired (kwəiᵊɹd, kwəiᵊ·rĕd), *ppl. a. rare.* 1796. [f. CHOIR *sb.* or *v.*] Assembled in a choir.

Choir organ. 1776. Also **chair organ** 1606-1796. [The original name was *chair* (*chayre*) *organ,* which has been taken by some to refer to the fact that in cathedrals it often formed the back of the organist's seat; others allege that *chair* is a blunder for *choir.*] One of the aggregated organs which go to make up a large organ, having stops of a light and soft character and used principally for accompaniments.

Choise, *v.* Now *Sc.* 1505. = To CHOOSE.

†**Chok, chokke**, *v.* ME. only. [? a. F. *choquer*; see SHOCK *v.*] ? To thrust, push, or drive with force.

Choke (tʃōᵘk), *sb.*[1] 1562. [f. CHOKE *v.*] **1.** What chokes. **2.** The action and noise of choking 1839. †**3.** A dead-lock -1729. **4.** A constriction; *e.g.* in the case of a rocket, etc. Cf. CHOKE-BORE. 1786. **5.** The mass of immature florets in the centre of an artichoke head. Cf. ARTI-CHOKE, pop. taken as 'choke in the heart'. 1736. Hence **Cho·kage**, a choked up state.

Choke, *sb.*[2] Now *dial.* ME. [? var. of CHEEK; but cf. mod.Sc. *chowk.*] The chops.

Choke (tʃōᵘk), *v.* Pa. t. and pple. **choked.** [ME. *choke, cheke*, ? aphet. f. *achoke*; or conn. w. CHEEK.] **1.** To stop the aperture of the throat so as to prevent breathing; to suffocate completely or partially. **2.** *intr.* (for *refl.*) To suffer suffocation ME. Also *transf.* **3.** *transf.* To smother, stifle 1526; also *fig.*; †to silence in argument -1649. Also *intr.* (for *refl.*) **4.** To close or greatly narrow (a tube, etc.) 1635; to block up a channel; to congest 1612. Also *intr.* (for *refl.*) **5.** To fill chock-full (*lit.* and *fig.*) 1712. **6.** To stop the movement of by clogging, etc. 1712. **7.** To fit *in* tightly, jam *in* 1747.

1. Choked with bones FULLER, dust BUNYAN, Spleen and Rage SWIFT, smoke JOHNSON, contending emotions LYTTON. **2.** I must say—or c. in silence BROWNING. **3.** To c. the *breath, tongue, utterance*, etc. Field choked with briars 1874. All pitty choak'd *Jul. C.* III. i. 269. *Macb.* I. ii. 9. **4.** To c. a rocket 1635, the neck of a bottle BOYLE, the avenues of the capital MACAULAY. **5.** Party-lies..the press is chok'd with them ADDISON. Hence **Cho·kingly** *adv.*

Choke-, in *comb.* [the stem of the vb.] **1.** = 'choking, that chokes': as **c.-coil**, a coil of low resistance inserted in an alternating-current circuit to impede or modify the current; **-damp**, the carbonic acid gas which accumulates in the lower parts of coal-mines, wells, etc.; after an explosion it rises and contributes to constitute the *after-damp*; **-strap**, a strap which connects the collar with the belly-band and keeps the collar in place when a horse backs; *esp.* with fruit- and plant-names, as **c.-apple**, the Crab-apple; **-berry**, the astringent fruit of *Pyrus arbutifolia*; **-cherry**, *U.S.*, two N. Amer. species of cherries with astringent properties; also the trees, *Prunus borealis* and *P. hyemalis*; **-pear**, name for harsh and unpalatable varieties of the pear, used for perry; *fig.* a difficulty, something hard to 'swallow'; **-weed**, species of Broomrape, *Orobanche Rapum.* **2.** = 'what chokes': as **c.-dog**, a name for hard Dorset cheese, etc.

Choke-bore (tʃōᵘ·kˌbōᵊɹ). 1875. The bore of a fowling-piece which narrows towards the muzzle and thus keeps the shot together. Also a fowling-piece with such a bore. So **Choke-bored** *ppl. a.*

Choke-full, *a.*; see CHOCK-FULL.

Choker (tʃōᵘ·kəɹ). 1552. [f. CHOKE *v.* + -ER.] **1.** One who or that which chokes. **2.** *slang.* A large neckerchief worn high round the throat; as a *white c.*, worn *esp.* by clergymen 1848. Hence **Cho·kered** *ppl. a.* attired in a c.

Chokidar (tʃōᵘ·kidāɹ). *Anglo-Ind.* 1696. [Urdū.] A watchman, in India.

Choky (tʃōᵘki), *sb. Anglo-Ind.* 1608. [Hindī *chaukī* shed.] **1.** A custom or toll station, in India; a station for horses, etc.; a police-station. **2.** A lock-up (in India) 1866. (Similarly in Eng. *slang*, by assoc. w. *choke.*)

Choky (tʃōᵘ·ki), *a.* Now *colloq.* 1579. [f. CHOKE *v.* + -Y[1].] **1.** Apt to choke; harsh, dry, and gritty. Of fruit, and *transf.* **2.** Having tendency to choking 1857.

2. To feel rather chokey HUGHES.

Chol-, var. of CHOLE-, Gr. χολή bile, used bef. a vowel: **Cholæ·mia** (also *cholehæ·mia*), bile in the blood, as in jaundice; hence **Cholæ·mic** *a.* **Cho·late**, a salt of cholic acid.

Cholagogue (kǫ·lagǫg). 1671. [a. F., f. (ult.) Gr. χολή + ἀγωγός.] *Med.* A medicine that carries off bile.

Chole- (kǫlĭ), repr. Gr. χολή gall, bile; **Cho·leate**, a salt of choleic acid. **Chole·ic** *a.* = taurocholic (acid). **Cho·lelith**, a gall-stone.

Cholecyst (kǫ·lĭsist). *rare.* 1881. [ad. mod. L. *colecystis*, f. Gr. χολή + κύστις.] The gall-bladder. Hence **Cholecysti·tis**, ulceration of the c.; **Cholecyste·ctomy** [Gr. ἐκτομία], cutting out of the c.; **Cholecysto·tomy** [Gr. τομία], the opening of the c. in order to remove gall-stones.

Choledoch (kǫ·lĭdǫk), *a.* 1681. [a. F. *cholédoque*, f. mod.L. *choledochus* :—Gr. χοληδόχος.] *Med.* Containing or receiving bile; as *c. duct, canal.* As *sb.* The c. duct.

†**Choledo·graphy, choledo·logy.** Barbarous forms of CHOLOGRAPHY, CHOLOLOGY.

Choler (kǫ·ləɹ), *sb.* [ME. *colre*, and *colere, coler*, a. OF. *colre* and *colère*, ad. L. *cholera*, a. Gr. χολέρα = CHOLERA **2.** App. f. χολή bile, in which sense alone it survived in Romanic. Refash. after L. in 16th c.] **1.** Bile; formerly as one of the four humours, supposed to cause irascibility of temper. **2.** Anger, heat of temper, wrath; irascibility. Cf. *bile.* 1530.

1. I conseille yow..That bothe of Colere and of Malencolye Ye purge yow CHAUCER. **2.** Hollis, in c., pulled him by the Nose CLARENDON.

C. adust, also **Black c.** = *black bile*, ATRABILE, q.v. Hence †**Cho·lerous** *a.*

Cholera (kǫ·lĕră). ME. [a. L. :—Gr. χολέρα, name of a disorder = sense **2.** Taken into Eng. as var. of CHOLER, q. v.] †**1.** = CHOLER **1.** -1561. **2.** A disorder, attended with bilious diarrhœa, vomiting, stomach-ache, and cramps. (Called also *C. morbus, C. nostras, Summer C.*, etc.) It is rarely fatal to adults. 1601. **3.** A malignant disease (not bilious), endemic in India and occas. epidemic elsewhere. It is characterized by violent vomiting, purging with watery rice-coloured evacuations, severe cramps, and collapse, death often occurring in a few hours. (Called also *Asiatic, Epidemic, Malignant*, etc., *C.*, and vulgarly *C. morbus.*) 1819.

Comb.: **Chicken C.**: an infectious disease of chickens; so called from its prevalence during a c. epidemic, but not akin to CHOLERA 2, 3; **c.-fungus**, a name for certain fungi, etc., occurring in the dejections of those suffering from malignant c.; **-typhoid**, the secondary fever of malignant c. Hence **Cholera·ic** *a.* **Cholera·iza·tion**, the artificial communication of c. to the lower animals. **Cho·lerifo·rm** *a.* **Cho·leroid** *a.*

Choleric (kǫ·lĕrik), *a.* ME. [a. F. *cholérique*, ad. L. *cholericus* :—Gr. χολερικός; see CHOLERA.] **1.** Having CHOLER as the predominant humour; bilious Now *Hist.* †**2.** Subject to or causing biliousness -1634. **3.** Irascible, passionate 1583. **4.** In a passion, angry 1590. **5.** Choleraic 1834.

1. The Reue was a sclendre colerik man CHAUCER. **4.** A chollericke word *Meas. for M.* II. ii. 130. So †**Chole·rical.** Hence †**Cho·leric-ly** *adv.*, †**-ness.**

Cholerine (kǫ·lĕrəin, -īn). 1847. [a. F., dim. of *choléra.*] **1.** British or Summer Cholera. **2.** A mild diarrhœa; the early stage of cholera 1850. **3.** The zymotic cause of malignant cholera 1852.

Cholesterin (kǫ̆le·stĕrin). 1827. [f. Gr. χολή + στερεός + -IN.] *Chem.* A tasteless, inodorous, fatty-looking substance ($C_{26}H_{44}O$), found in most animal liquids and solids, and in the fruit and seed of many plants. In a crystallized form it is the chief constituent of gall-stones. (Now superseded by **Chole·sterol.**) Hence **Cholester·ric** *a.* pertaining to or produced from c.

Choliamb (kōᵘ·liæmb). 1844. [ad. L., a. Gr. χωλίαμβος, f. χωλός lame + ἴαμβος.] *Pros.* An iambic verse with a spondee or trochee instead of an iambus in the last (sixth) foot. Hence **Cholia·mbic** *a.* and *sb.* (in *pl.*). **Cholia·mbist.**

Cholic (kǫ·lik), *a.* 1846. [ad. Gr. χολικός, f. χολή.] Of or pertaining to bile.

C. acid, an acid ($C_{24}H_{40}O_5$), which is produced from the nitrogenized acids of bile during its putrefaction. Formerly a name for *Glycocholic acid.*

Choline (kǫ·ləin). 1869. [f. Gr. χολή + -INE.] *Chem.* An organic base, identical with or akin to neurine. Hence **Choli·nic** *a.*

Cholo-, Gr. χολο-, comb. f. χολή bile: **Cho·lochrome** [Gr. χρῶμα], general name for the colouring matters of bile, including **Cholophæ·in**, the brown pigment, etc. **Cholo·graphy**, a treatise on the bile. **Cho·lolith**, a gall-stone. **Cholo·logy**, the part of physiology and pathology which deals with the bile.

Cho·loid, *a.* [f. Gr. χολή.] Resembling bile.

Choltry, var. of CHOULTRY.

‖**Cho·lum.** 1858. [Tamil.] A grass, the Indian Millet, grown for food in India.

Chomp, var. (*U.S.* and *dial.*) of CHAMP *v.*

Chondre. *rare.* 1882. [ad. Gr. χόνδρος grit. In Ger. *chondrum.*] One of the small rounded grains which occur in some stony meteorites.

Chondrify (kǫ·ndrifəi), *v.* 1872. [f. Gr. χόνδρος cartilage + -FY.] To turn into cartilage. Hence **Chondrifica·tion.**

Cho·ndrigen = CHONDRO-.

Chondri·genous, *a.* 1882. Furnishing cartilage.

Chondrin (kǫ·ndrin). (Formerly **-ine.**) 1838. [f. Gr. χόνδρος.] *Chem.* A substance resembling gelatin, obtained from the cellular cartilages by boiling them in water.

Cho·ndrite. [f. mod.L. *chondrus*, a genus of sea-weeds (a. Gr. χόνδρος) + -ITE.] *Palæont.* A fossil marine plant of the chalk and other formations.

‖**Chondritis** (kǫndrəi·tis). 1836. [mod.L., f. Gr. χόνδρος.] *Med.* Inflammation of cartilage.

Chondro- (kǫ·ndro), comb. f. Gr. χόνδρος, a grain, cartilage: **Cho·ndrogen** = Chondrin, or 'the tissues which yield chondrin'. **Chondroge·nesis**, the development of cartilage. **Chondro·logy** [Gr. -λογία], a discourse or treatise on cartilages. **Chondro·meter** [Gr. μέτρον], a steelyard for weighing grain. **Cho·ndropterygian**, *sb.* a member of the order *Chondropterygii*, fishes having a cartilaginous endo-skeleton, as the shark, ray, and sturgeon; *adj.* = **Cho·ndroptery·gious** *a.*, belonging to the *Chondropterygii.* **Chondro·stean** *a.*, belonging to the *Chondrostea*, a sub-order of ganoid fishes, in which the vertebral column consists of a simple soft *chorda*; *sb.*, a member of this sub-order. **Chondro·tomy** [Gr. -τομία], dissection or cutting of cartilage.

Chondrodite (kǫ·ndrŏdəit). 1822. [f. Gr. χονδρώδης (f. χόνδρος) + -ITE.] *Min.* A yellowish or brownish-red silicate of magnesium containing a little fluorine. It often occurs in imbedded grains.

Chondroid (kǫ·ndroid), *a.* 1847. [f. Gr. χόνδρος + -OID.] Resembling cartilage.

‖**Chondrosis** (kǫndrōᵘ·sis). [f. as prec.] *Phys.* The formation of cartilage.

Chonicrite (kǫ·nikrəit). Also **-krite.** 1834. [f. Gr. χωνεία fusion + κριτός separated.] *Min.* A native fusible silicate of aluminium and magnesium.

Choose (tʃūz), *v.* Pa. t. **chose** (tʃōᵘz), pa. pple. **chosen** (tʃōᵘ·z'n). [OE. *céos-an*, str. vb. Prob. ME. *chōse* represented OE. *cēose*, for *céose*, and regularly passed into *choose.* The type *chuse* was earlier than *choose*, and was the prevailing form in 17–18th c. See also N.E.D.] **1.** To take by preference out of all that are available; to select. Also with *infinitive obj.* ME. **2.** To will, to wish; to desire to have (*vulgar*) 1619. **3.** *intr.* or *absol.* To exercise choice ME. †**4.** To gather at pleasure -ME. †**5.** To pick out by sight -ME.

1. Chuse thee what armes thou likest SIDNEY. To c. a man Pope *2 Hen. VI*, I. iii. 65. Some chose to go by the worlde 1526. **2.** To c. to remain concealed GOLDSM. The landlady returned to know if we did not c. a more genteel apartment GOLDSM. **3.** Here doe I c., and thriue I as I may *Merch. V.* II. vii. 60. *Cannot c.*: = have no alternative. (*Obs.* exc. with *but.*) He cannot c. but hear COLERIDGE. Phr. *To pick and c.*: to select with careful scrutiny. Hence **Choo·seable, choosable** *a.* (*rare*). **Choo·ser**, one who chooses. **Choo·singly** *adv.* by choice.

†**Choose**, *sb.* ME. [var. of CHOICE treated as vbl. sb. from CHOOSE.] The act, power, right, or privilege of choosing -1620.

Chop (tʃǫp), *sb.*[1] ME. [f. CHOP *v.*[1]] **1.** An act of chopping; a cutting blow. **2.** A piece chopped off; a slice (*esp.* of mutton or pork), a cutlet. Also *fig.* 1461. †**3.** A fissure, cleft, crack; a CHAP in the skin -1767. **4.** A short broken motion (of waves) 1858.

Phr. †*At the first c.*: at the first stroke (F. *du premier coup*); immediately (F. *tout à coup*).

Chop (tʃǫp), *sb.*[2] 1505. [var. of CHAP *sb.*[2]] **1.** A jaw; usu. *pl.* jaws; sides of the face. **2.**

pl. The jaws as forming the mouth, fauces, parts about the mouth. (Usu. contemptuous or humorous.) 1589. **3.** *transf.* The entrance of an abyss, cannon, valley, channel, etc. 1636.

3. Cruising in the chops of the Channel 1748.

Chop (tʃǫp), *sb.*³ 1670. [f. CHOP *v.*²] An exchange, barter.

C. and change: a change; cf. CHOP *v.*²

Chop, *sb.*⁴ 1653. [f. CHOP *v.*³] A snap with the jaws.

Chop (tʃǫp), *sb.*⁵ 1614. [ad. Hindī *chhāp* stamp, brand.] **1.** In *India, China.* A seal; an official impress or stamp. **2.** A licence or permit duly authenticated 1699. **3.** *China trade.* A trade-mark; hence, a brand of goods. Also *attrib.* 1828.

3. *First* (*second*) *c.*: first (or other) rank, quality, etc.; also *attrib.*: A sort of second-c. dandies THACKERAY.

Comb.: **c.-boat,** a licensed lighter for transporting goods; **-house,** a custom-house where transit duties are levied.

Chop (tʃǫp), *v.*¹ ME. [A form of CHAP *v.*¹] **1.** To cut with a quick and heavy blow, *e.g.* with an ax or cleaver; to cut into pieces; to mince. Often with *up.* Also *fig.* **2.** *intr.* To aim a hacking or hewing blow *at* ME. †**3.** To thrust, to go or come, with suddenness or force (*esp.* with *in, into*) –1816. **4.** = CHAP *v.*¹ 2. –1759. Also *trans.* †**5.** = CHAP *v.*¹ 3. *Sc.* –1657.

1. They breake their bones, and c. them in pieces *Micah* iii. 3. *fig.* She was nervous..and chopped her words 1882. 3. You c. in the word *offer* SIR E. DERING. [They] c. in with their nimble tongues DE FOE. *To c. to an anchor* (Naut.): to come to an anchor hastily.

Chop (tʃǫp), *v.*² [Appears bef. 1400 in *choppe-church.* Perh. a var. of CHAP. Not conn. w. Flemish *kōpen, koopen,* or the like.] **1.** To barter. *trans.* and †*intr.* Also *fig.* 1485. **2.** *intr.* To change; esp. *Naut.* Of the wind: To veer or shift its direction suddenly 1642. Also *transf.* and *fig.* **3.** To bandy words 1525. Also †*intr.*

1. To c. horses in Smithfield SHADWELL. **To c. and change**: to buy and sell (*trans.* and *intr.*); to make frequent changes; to make different. 2. The wind..soon chopped about FIELDING. 3. *To c. logic.* (Also referred *erron.* to CHOP *v.*¹ 1, as if 'to mince'.) 1525. *intr.* Let not the Counsell at the Barre, c. with the Iudge..after the Iudge hath Declared his Sentence BACON.

Chop (tʃǫp), *v.*³ 1581. [app. f. CHOP *sb.*²] †**1.** To take into the jaws and eat; to snap *up* –1701. Also †*fig.* †**2.** *intr.* To snap, to bite *at* –1694. **3.** *Hunting.* To seize (prey) before it is fairly away from cover 1624.

†**Chop-cherry.** 1561. [f. prec.] A game; = BOB-CHERRY –1684.

†**Cho·p-church.** ME. [See CHOP *v.*²] A trafficker in ecclesiastical benefices –1695.

Cho·p-fa·llen, *a.* 1602. [f. CHOP *sb.*²] = CHAP-FALLEN.

Chop-house. 1690. [f. CHOP *sb.*¹ 2.] An eating-house where mutton-chops and the like are supplied.

Chopin (tʃǫ·pin), *sb.* ME. [? a. F. *chopine* = half a pint; f. *chope,* mod. Ger. *schoppen.*] A liquid measure containing, in France, half an Old French *pinte,* in Scotland a Scotch half-pint = about an English quart. Also *attrib.* Hence †**Chopin** *v.* to tipple.

Chopine, chopin (tʃǫpī·n, tʃǫ·pin), *sb. arch.* 1577. [app. orig. Sp. *chapin,* f. *chapa* plate of metal, etc.] A kind of shoe raised above the ground by means of a cork sole or the like. Spelt *c* 1600 *cioppino,* pl. *cioppini,* as if Italian.

Neerer Heauen.. by the altitude of a Choppine *Haml.* II. ii. 445.

†**Cho·p-lo·gic.** 1533. [f. CHOP *v.*² 3.] **1.** Disputatious argument –1688. **2.** One who chops logic; a sophistical arguer –1592. So †**Chop-loge.** Hence **Chop-logical** *a.*

Chopper¹ (tʃǫ·pəɹ). 1552. [f. CHOP *v.*¹ + -ER¹.] **1.** One who chops. **2.** An instrument for chopping; *spec.* a butcher's cleaver 1818.

Chopper². 1581. [f. CHOP *v.*² + -ER¹.] One who barters; *esp.* a trafficker in ecclesiastical benefices.

Chopper³ (tʃǫ·pəɹ). *Anglo-Ind.* 1780. [a. Hindī *chhappar.*] A thatched roof. Also *attrib.* Hence **Choppered** *a.* thatched.

Chopping (tʃǫ·piŋ), *a.* 1566. [f. CHOP *v.*¹] Big and vigorous; strapping.

Choppy (tʃǫ·pi), *a.*¹ 1605. [f. CHOP *sb.*¹ + -Y¹.] **1.** = CHAPPY *a.*¹ **2.** Of the sea: Breaking in short abrupt waves 1867.

Choppy, *a.*² 1865. [f. CHOP *v.*²] Given to change like the wind; unstable, as 'c. markets'.

Chop-stick (tʃǫ·pstik). 1699. [= 'quick sticks'.] *pl.* The two small sticks of bone, wood, etc., held between the thumb and fingers of one hand by the Chinese in place of a fork.

Chop-suey (tʃǫ·psū·i). 1904. [Chinese, 'mixed bits'.] A Chinese dish, consisting of meat, rice, etc. fried in sesame oil.

Choragic (koræ·dʒik, -ē·dʒik), *a.* 1763. [f. CHORAGUS.] Pertaining to a choragus.

The c. monument of Lysicrates 1820.

‖**Choragium.** 1682. [L.] Dancing-ground.

‖**Choragus** (korē·gǒs). Also **choregus.** Pl. -agi, -egi. 1626. [L., a. Gr. χορηγός, f. χορός + ἄγειν.] **1.** *Gr. Antiq.* The leader of a CHORUS; *spec.* at Athens, one who defrayed the cost of bringing out a chorus 1820. **2.** The title of a functionary in the University of Oxford, originally appointed to superintend the practice of music 1626. Also *transf.* and *fig.*

Choral (kōᵊ·răl), *a.* 1587. [ad. F. *choral.*] Of or belonging to, sung by a choir or in chorus; containing a chorus or choruses.

C. service: a church service in which the canticles, anthem, etc., are sung by the choir; in a *full c. service* the versicles, responses, etc., are also chanted. *Vicar c.*: a cathedral officer whose duty it is to sing that part of the music of the services which can be performed by laymen or men in minor orders. **Cho·ralist,** one who sings in a chorus. **Cho·rally** *adv.*

Choral, chorale (korā·l). 1841. [a. G. *chora·l,* in *choral-gesang.*] *Mus.* A metrical hymn set to a simple devotional tune, and usually sung in unison; as Luther's '*Ein' feste Burg*'.

Chord (kǭɪd), *sb.*¹ 1570. [Refash. of CORD, after L. *chorda.*] **1.** A string or small rope. Now CORD. 1645. **2.** *spec.* A string of a musical instrument. (Now only *poet.*) 1667. Also *fig.* of the emotions, feelings, etc. 1784. **3.** *Phys.* Applied to structures in an animal body resembling strings 1541. **4.** The straight line joining the extremities of an arc 1570.

3. *Vocal, spermatic, spinal,* etc. *c.* (see VOCAL, etc.).

Chord (kǭɪd), *sb.*² ? 1475. [Orig. *cord,* aphet. f. ACCORD *sb.,* q.v.; confused with prec.] †**1.** = ACCORD *sb.* 4. –1636. †**2.** *Mus.* A CONCORD. *pl.* The notes added to a bass to make up a 'chord' in the mod. sense (see 3) –1753. **3.** *Mus.* A combination, rarely of two, usually of three or more, simultaneous notes 1752. Also *transf.* of colours 1856.

3. *Common* (also *perfect*) *c.*: the combination of any note with its third (major or minor), perfect fifth, and octave. The c. of C inverted BURNEY.

Chord, *v.*¹ *rare.* [perh. a survival of CORD *v.*²] *intr.* To form a cord (with); to harmonize; to sound together in harmony. **b.** *trans.* To cause to accord or harmonize.

Chord, *v.*²; var. CORD *v.*¹

Chordal (kǭ·ɪdăl), *a.* 1619. [f. CHORD *sb.*¹ and ² + -AL.] Relating to, consisting, or of the nature, of a chord or chords. So **Cho·rded** *a.* having chords; combined in chords, in harmony.

Chordee (kǭ·ɪdī). 1708. [ad. F. *cordée* in *chaudepisse cordée.*] *Path.* A painful inflammatory downward curving of the penis.

†**Chore, chor** (kōᵊɪ), *sb.*¹ OE. [ad. L. *chorus* (see CHORUS).] = CHOIR (exc. in sense 1) –1680.

Chore (tʃōᵊɪ), *sb.*² *dial.* and *U.S.* 1746. [var. of *char,* CHARE *sb.*¹] = CHARE *sb.*¹ 2. Hence **Chore** *v.* (*intr.*) to do chores.

‖**Chorea** (korī·ă). 1686. [Short for L. *chorea Sancti Viti*; L. *chorea,* a. Gr. χορεία, f. χορός; see CHORUS.] *Path.* St. Vitus's dance; a convulsive disorder, characterized by irregular involuntary contractions of the muscles; also affecting horses. Hence **Chore·al, Chore·ic** *adjs.* pertaining to or affected with c.

Choree (korī·). 1586. [ad. L. *choreus,* a. Gr. χορεῖος *a.* pertaining to a dance.] *Pros.* The foot more commonly called TROCHEE, q. v. Hence **Chore·ic** *a.* characterized by trochees.

Choregy (korī·dʒi, kǫ·rědʒi). 1847. [ad. Gr. χορηγία; see CHORAGUS.] *Gr. Antiq.* The function of a choragus in ancient Athens.

Choreic; see CHOREA and CHOREE.

Choreograph (kǫ·riŏgraf). 1876. [f. Gr. χορεία + -γραφος. In mod.F. *chorégraphe.*] A designer or arranger of a ballet. So **Choreo·grapher.** **Cho·reogra·phic** *a.* pertaining to (ballet-) dancing. **Choreo·graphy,** †the written notation of dancing; the choreographer's art.

†**Chorepiscope.** *rare.* 1660. [ad. late L. *chorepiscopus* (the form now used), a. Gr., f. χώρα or χῶρος + ἐπίσκοπος.] A country or suffragan bishop of the early church –1844. Hence **Chorepi·scopal** *a.* belonging to a c.

Chori- (kōᵊri), bef. a vowel **choris-** (kōᵊris), a. Gr. χῶρι, χωρίς asunder, apart: as in **Chori·pe·talous** *a.,* having separate petals, etc.

Choriamb (kōᵊ·riæmb, kǫ·r-). 1844. [ad. L. *choriambus* (also used), a. Gr., f. χορεῖος CHOREE + ἴαμβος IAMB.] *Pros.* A foot composed of a choree followed by an iamb (—◡◡—). Hence **Choria·mbic** *a.* consisting of or containing choriambs; also as *sb.* [sc. *verse, foot.*]

Choric (kǫ·rik, kōᵊ·rik), *a.* 1819. [ad. L. *choricus,* a. Gr., f. χορός; see CHORUS.] Of, pertaining to, or in the style of, a chorus. Hence **Chorics** *sb. pl.* (*nonce-wd.*; cf. *heroics,* etc.) the verses of a chorus. So **Cho·rical** *a.* (*rare*).

‖**Chorion** (kōᵊ·riǫn). 1545. [a. Gr. χόριον.] **1.** *Anat.* The outermost membrane enveloping the fœtus before birth. **2.** *Bot.* The pulpy substance of the nucleus of the seed 1816. **3.** *Anat.* The *cutis vera* or true skin; = CORIUM 1831. Hence **Cho·rial** *a.* of or pertaining to the c.

Chorisis (kōᵊ·risis). 1835. [a. Gr., f. χωρίζειν.] *Bot.* The splitting of an organ into parts, each of which is a perfect organ. So **Cho·rism, Choriza·tion.** **Cho·ristate** *a.* formed by c.

Chorist (kǫ·rist, kōᵊ·rist). 1538. [a. F. *choriste.*] †**1.** A member of a choir –1766. **2.** *Gr. Antiq.* A member of the chorus 1762. **3.** One who sings in a chorus 1835.

Chorister (kǫ·ristəɹ). [ME. *querestre, -istre,* ad. med.L. *chorista,* after *cuer, quer,* CHOIR.] **1.** A member of a choir; *spec.* a choir-boy. †**2.** A singer. –1640. †**3.** *Gr. Antiq.* A member of the chorus 1603. Hence **Cho·ristership.**

Chori·stic, -al, *a. rare.* 1660. [f. as prec. + -IC, + -AL.] Choric, choral.

‖**Chorizontes** (kōᵊrizǫ·ntīz), *sb. pl.* 1887. [a. Gr. χωρίζοντες, χωρίζειν.] A name for those grammarians who ascribed the Iliad and Odyssey to different authors. So **Chorizo·ntal, -ic,** *adjs.*; **Chorizo·ntist.**

Chorograph (kōᵊ·rograf). 1839. [f. Gr. χώρα or χῶρος + -γραφος.] An instrument to determine the position of a station, given the angles made by it to three points in the same plane whose positions are known.

Chorography¹ (korǫ·grăfi). 1559. [ad. L., a. Gr. χωρογραφία, f. as prec. + -γραφια.] The art of describing, or of delineating on a map, particular regions or districts; opp. to *geography,* and *topography.* Also *concr.* and *transf.*

transf. I have..beheld..the C. of their provinces SIR T. BROWNE. Hence **Choro·grapher.** **Chorogra·phic, -al** *a.* **Chorogra·phically** *adv.*

Chorography² (korǫ·grăfi). ? *Obs.* 1710. [f. Gr. χορός + -γραφια.] Dance notation.

Choroid (kōᵊ·roid), *a.* (*sb.*) 1741. [ad. Gr. χοροειδής, corrupt for χοριοειδής, f. χόριον (see CHORION) + εἶδος.] *Anat.* Applied to structures resembling the chorion in form and vascularity; as the *c. coat* (or *tunic*) of the eye-ball, and the *c. plexus,* a plexus of blood-vessels connected by a thin membrane derived from the *pia mater,* in each lateral ventricle of the brain, etc. Also as *sb.* [sc. *coat.*] Hence **Choroi·dal** *a.* **Choroi·dean** *a.* **Choroidi·tis,** *Path.* inflammation of the c. coat.

Chorology (korǫ·lŏdʒi). 1879. [f. Gr. χώρα, χῶρος + -λογια.] The scientific study of the geographical extent or limits of anything.

Its *Distribution* or *C.* HUXLEY. Hence **Choro·lo·gical** *a.*

Chorometry (korǫ·mĕtri). 1823. [f. Gr. χωρομετρία.] The art of surveying a country.

Chortle (tʃǭ·ɪt'l), *v. intr.* 1872. A word coined by the author of *Through the Looking-Glass*; app. a fusion of *chuckle* and *snort.*

Chorus (kōᵊ·rǒs), *sb.* Pl. **choruses.** 1561.

[a. L., a. Gr. χορός. Cf. CHOIR.] 1. *Gr. Antiq.* An organized band of singers and dancers in the religious festivals, etc.; also, their song. (In the Attic tragedy, the chorus gave expression, between the acts, to the moral and religious sentiments evoked by the action of the play.) b. In English drama, reduced by Shakspere and others to a single personage, who speaks the prologue, and explains or comments on the course of events 1561. Also *fig.* 2. An organized band of singers, a choir; *spec.* those who sing the choral parts in an opera, oratorio, etc. 1656. 3. The simultaneous utterance of song by many; anything sung by many at once 1711. Also *transf.* of speech, laughter, the cry of hounds, etc. 1735. 4. *Mus.* A vocal composition, written in any number of parts, each part being sung by a number of voices 1744. 5. The burden of a song, which the audience join the performer in singing 1599. Also *transf.*

1. b. Y'are as good as a C., my Lord *Haml.* III. ii. 255. 3. One c. let all Being raise POPE. *transf.* A c. of loud laughter 1862.

Chorus (kōᵊ·rŏs), *v.* Pa. t. and pple. **chorused** (-ŏst). 1703. [f. prec. sb.] 1. To sing or speak in chorus. *trans.* and *intr.* 1748. 2. *trans.* To furnish with a chorus. Also *fig.* 1703.

‖**Chose** (ʃoz), *sb.* ME. [a. F. :—L. *causa.*] 1. *Law.* A thing, chattel, piece of property 1670. †2. Thing (as a vague general term). ME. only.

1. *C. in action*, is a thing incorporeal and onely a right, as an annuity,..—and generally all Causes of Suit for any Debt or Duty, Trespass or Wrong BLOUNT. Choses in possession (movables) POSTE. 2. CHAUCER *Wife's Prol.* 447.

Chose, pa. t. and †pple. of CHOOSE *v.*

Chosen (tʃōᵘ·z'n), *ppl. a.* ME. [See CHOOSE *v.*] 1. Selected, picked out. 2. *Theol.* Chosen of God; *absol.* (mostly *pl.*) elect ME.

1. A c. array R. ELLIS. 2. The c. people ADDISON. He..inspireth Light, into the Face of his C. BACON.

‖**Chouan** (ʃu,ān), *sb.*[1] 1794. [F.; ? f. Jean *Chouan.*] A name given to irregular bands who maintained in the west of France a partisan war against the Republic and the first Empire, after 1793; hence, a partisan of the Bourbons. Also *attrib.* Hence **Chouanize** *v.* to play the C.

†‖**Chouan**, *sb.*[2] 1712. [F.] The seed of *Anabasis tamariscifolia* –1819.

Chough (tʃɒf). [ME. *choȝe*, etc.; OE. had only *cīo, céo, ciae, chyae* (? for *cyhae*). Cogn. w. MDu. *cauwe*, Du. *kauw*, app. from a WGer. type **kāwa.*] 1. A bird of the crow family; applied to any of the smaller chattering species. 2. Now, the Red-legged Crow (*Fregillus Graculus*), which frequents the sea-cliffs in many parts of Britain, *esp.* in Cornwall; the *Cornish Chough* 1566.

2. The Crowes and Choughes, that wing the midway ayre *Lear* IV. vi. 13.

Choule, obs. f. JOWL.

‖**Choultry** (tʃau·ltri). Also **choltry.** *Anglo-Ind.* 1698. [Corruption of Telugu *chāwadi.*] 1. A caravanserai. 2. The colonnade of a temple 1772.

Chouse (tʃaus), *sb.* 1610. [Usu. identified w. CHIAUS; but ? as to the meaning. Gifford's note is suspect.] †1. = CHIAUS, q. v. –1639. †2. A cheat, a swindler –1658. †3. A dupe, tool –1755. 4. *slang.* [f. the vb.] A swindle, sham, 'sell' 1708.

Chouse (tʃaus), *v. colloq.* 1659. [f. prec. sb.] To dupe, cheat, trick; to defraud *of* or *out of.*

[He] only wants to c. you MISS BURNEY. Hence **Chou·ser.**

‖**Chout** (tʃaut). 1674. [Mahrātī *chauth* 'a fourth part'.] The black-mail of one-fourth of the revenue formerly exacted by the Mahrattas. Also similar exactions.

Chow (tʃau). 1889. Short for next, 3.

‖**Chow-chow** (tʃau·tʃau). 1845. [?] 1. *sb.* A medley; *e.g.* mixed pickles 1850. 2. *adj.* Miscellaneous, mixed, assorted; of water, 'broken'. *Chow-chow chop*: the last lighter containing the sundry small packages to fill up a ship. 3. A domestic dog of a Chinese breed 1886.

Chowder (tʃau·dəɪ), *sb.* 1762. [f. Fr. *chaudière* pot. See *N. & Q.* 4 Ser. VII. 85.] 1. A dish made of fresh fish (*esp.* cod) or clams, stewed with slices of pork or bacon, onions, and biscuit. 2. *C. beer*: 'a liquor made by boiling the black spruce in water and mixing molasses with the decoction' (Webster). Hence **Chow·der** *v.* to make a c.

‖**Chowry** (tʃau·ri). 1777. [a. Hindī *chaunrī.*] A whisk or fly-flapper (prop. the bushy tail of the Tibetan Yak).

Choy, var. of CHAY.

Chrematist (krī·mătist). *rare.* 1845. [ad. Gr. χρηματιστής; see next.] One who studies the science of wealth; a political economist.

Chrematistic (krīmăti·stik). 1752. [ad. Gr. χρηματιστικός, f. χρηματίζειν, f. χρῆμα, χρήματ-.] 1. *adj.* Of, pertaining to, or engaged in the acquisition of wealth. 2. *sb.* usually **Chrematistics**, the science of the wealth of nations; political economy, or a branch thereof. [Gr. ἡ χρηματιστική.]

Chreotechnics (krīote·kniks). *rare.* [f. Gr. χρεία + τέχνη.] The useful arts, *esp.* agriculture, manufactures, and commerce.

Chrestomathy (krestǫ·măþi). 1832. [ad. Gr. χρηστομάθεια, f. χρηστός useful + -μαθεια learning. Cf. F. *chrestomathie.*] A collection of choice passages, *esp.* one intended to be used in the acquirement of a language.

C. of the Pushtu or Afghan Language 1847. Hence **Chrestoma·thic** *a.* teaching useful matters.

Chrism (kriz'm). [OE. *crisma*, ad. L. *chrisma*, a. Gr. χρῖσμα; whence also Rom. *cresma*, OF. *cresme* (= *crême*). Refash. in 16th c., after L. See also CREAM *sb.*[1]] 1. Oil mingled with balm, consecrated for use as an unguent in the administration of certain sacraments; an unguent 1833. Also *fig.* 2. A sacramental anointing; unction ME.; *spec.* Confirmation 1597. Also *transf.* and *fig.* 3. = CHRISOM OE. Also *attrib.* Hence †**Chrismed** *ppl. a.* anointed with c. **Chri·smal** *a.* of or pertaining to c.

†**Chrisma·tion.** 1537. [ad. med.L. *chrismationem.*] Application of the chrism; sacramental unction –1753.

C., or consigning with ointment, was us'd in baptism JER. TAYLOR.

Chrismatory (kri·zmătəri). 1450. [ad. med. L. *chrismatorium*; see CHRISM.] 1. The vessel containing the chrism. 2. Sacramental anointing; unction 1563.

Chrisom (kri·səm). ME. [orig. a disyllabic pronunc. of CHRISM.] 1. (In full *c.-cloth, -robe*, etc.): A white robe, put on a child at baptism as a token of innocence. If the child died within a month from baptism, it was used as a shroud. 2. (In full *c.-child, -babe*, etc.): orig. A child in its chrisom-cloth; an innocent babe. (In obituaries, etc., applied to a child that died during the first month, or ? that died unbaptized.) ME. Also *gen.* Infant, innocent 1596. Also *attrib.* var. †**Chriso·mer** (in sense 2).

Christ (krəist). [OE. *crist*, ad. L. *Christus*, a. Gr. χριστός, sb. use of χριστός anointed, tr. of Hebr. *māschīaχ*, MESSIAH, 'anointed,' more fully *m'shīaχ yahweh* the Lord's anointed. Spelt with *ch-* since 1500.] 1. The Messiah or 'Lord's Anointed'. (In the Geneva and 1611 versions of the N.T. often preceded by *the.*) 2. The title given to Jesus of Nazareth, as fulfilling Messianic prophecy; treated as a proper name OE. Also *fig.* †3. In versions of the O.T. = 'a king by divine right' (see ANOINTED) –1609. ¶ Exc. CHRISTEN *v.*, the derivs. of *Christ* are now always written with a capital.

1. If thou be the Christe, tel vs plainly BIBLE (Genev.) *John* x. 24.

Comb. **Christ's thorn**, a name given to several shrubs, fabled to have formed Christ's crown of thorns.

Christ-cross, criss-cross (kri·s,krǫs). ME. [lit. *Christ's cross*; treated in sense 2 as a reduplication of *cross.*] 1. †The figure of a cross (✠) in front of the alphabet in horn-books, etc. –1659; hence, the alphabet (now *dial.*) 1553. Also *fig.* 2. The mark of a cross 1607.

1. *fig.* Christ's cross is the chriss-cross of all our happiness QUARLES.

Christ-cross-row, criss-cross-row (kri·s,krǫs,rōᵘ). 1563. [f. prec.] 1. The alphabet; so called from the figure of a cross prefixed to it in horn-books. Also CROSS-ROW, q. v. (*arch.* and *dial.*) †2. *fig.* The whole series –1652.

Christdom (kri·stdəm). *rare.* 1463. Short for CHRISTENDOM, the Christian domain. (*Obs.*).

Christed, *pa. pple.* 1641. Made one with Christ. (A 'Familist' wd.)

†**Christen**, *a.* (*sb.*) [OE. *cristen* :—WGer. *cristin*, ad. L. *christianus.* Refash. with *ch-* in 16th c., and subseq. assim. to L., as CHRISTIAN.] 1. = CHRISTIAN –1640. 2. *absol.* A Christian (with pl. *-s* after 1500) –1530. Hence †**Chri·stenly** *adv.* †**Chri·stenman, cri·.** †**Chri·stenmas** = CHRISTMAS.

Christen (kri·s'n), *v.* [OE. *cristnian*, f. prec., lit. to make Christian.] 1. To christianize (*arch.*). 2. To administer baptism to ME. Also *absol.* 3. To give a name to at baptism; usu. *pass.* 1450; †to stand sponsor to at baptism –1667. Also *transf.* 4. *gen.* To name; call by the name of (*colloq.*) 1642.

3. *transf.* To c. bells 1533, ships CLARENDON. 4. Chambermaids c. this worm a deathwatch SWIFT.

Christendom (kri·s'ndəm). [OE. *cristendóm*, f. *cristen* (CHRISTEN *a.*); see -DOM.] †1. = CHRISTIANITY 3. –1681. †2. = CHRISTIANITY 2. –1649. 3. Christians collectively; the church ME.; the Christian domain ME. †4. Baptism; christening –1680.

3. The creed of C. LIDDON. The king of Kirsendom MIDDLETON. 4. A world Of pretty fond adoptious christendomes *All's Well* I. i. 188.

†**Christenhead, -hood.** *rare.* 1449. [f. CHRISTEN *a.*; see -HOOD, -HEAD.] Christianity; christening; a Christian domain –1762.

Christhood (krəi·st,hud). ME. [f. CHRIST.] Messiahship.

Christian (kri·styăn). 1526. [ad. L. *christianus*; see CHRISTEN *a.*]

A. *adj.* 1. Believing, or professing, the religion of Christ 1553. 2. Pertaining to Christ or Christianity 1553. 3. Following the precepts and example of Christ; Christ-like 1597. 4. Of or belonging to a Christian or Christians 1596. 5. Human; civilized, decent, respectable (*colloq.* or *slang*) 1577.

1. The Rulers of this C. land KEBLE. *Most C.*: a title of the kings of France. 2. To be buried in C. buriall *Haml.* v. i. 2. *Court C.*: an ecclesiastical court. Now *Hist.* 3. The mutual exercise of C. Charity HOOKER. 4. *Merch. V.* IV. i. 310.

Phrases. *C. name*: the name given at christening; the personal name, as opp. to the family name or *surname. C. era*: the era reckoned from the accepted date of the birth of Christ. Hence †**Chri·stian** *v.* to christen. **Chri·stian-ly** *adv.*, **-ness** (*rare*).

B. *sb.* 1. One who believes or professes the religion of Christ 1526. 2. One who follows the precepts and example of Christ 1529. 3. A human being; a decent, respectable, or presentable person (*colloq.*) 1591. 4. Used as a sectarian name, as in 'Bible Christians', etc. 1818. †5. A variety of pear or plum –1655.

1. So that the disciples were at Antioche first named CHRISTIANS N.T. (Rhem.) *Acts* xi. 26. †*Even C.*: fellow-C. 3. A fitter food for a horse than a C. FIELDING. Hence †**Chri·stiandom** = CHRISTENDOM. **Chri·stianlike** *a.* and *adv.* **Chri·stianly** *a.*

Christianism (kri·styăniz'm). 1576. [a. F. *christianisme.*] 1. The Christian religious system. (*Obs.* exc. as an *-ism.*) 2. Christianity of a sort or form (*disparaging*) 1674.

Christianity (kristi,æ·nĭti). ME. [repr. (orig. through OF. *crestienté*) L. *christianitatem*, f. *christianus* CHRISTIAN; see CHRISTEN *a.*] †1. The whole body of Christians, CHRISTENDOM –1650. 2. The Christian faith; the system of doctrines and precepts taught by Christ ME. 3. State or fact of being a Christian; Christian spirit or character ME. †4. *Eccl.* Ecclesiastical jurisdiction –1878.

1. To Walys fledde the Cristyanytee Of olde Britons, dwellynge in this Ile CHAUCER. 4. *Dean of C.*, orig. = Rural Dean.

Christianize (kri·styănəiz), *v.* 1593. [f. CHRISTIAN *a.*; cf. med.L. *christianizare.*] 1. To make Christian, convert to Christianity. 2. To give a Christian character or form to 1693. 3. *intr.* To adopt Christianity 1598.

1. He was Christianized and baptiz'd I. MATHER. Hence **Chri·stianiza·tion** (in senses 1, 2). **Chri·stiani·zer.**

Christia·no-, comb. f. L. *Christianus* CHRISTIAN, as in *C.-Platonical a.*; **†-ma·stic**, a scourge of Christians.

Christian Science. 1866. A theory, founded on principles formulated by Mrs. Eddy of U.S.A., according to which disease, etc., is an error of the mind and may be cured without medical treatment by mental effect of patient's Christian faith. So **C. Scientist.**

Christless (krəi·stlės), *a.* 1652. Without Christ; unchristian. Hence **Christlessness.**

Christ-like (krəi·stləik), *a.* 1680. [Cf. OE. *cristlic.*] Like Christ or that of Christ. Hence **Christlikeness.** So **Chri·stly** *a.*

Christmas (kri·smăs), *sb.* [Late OE. *Cristes mæsse*, the mass of Christ.] **1.** The festival of the nativity of Christ, kept on the 25th of December; Christmas-time. **2.** *dial. and nursery lang.* Holly, etc., used for decorations at Christmas 1825. Also *attrib.*

1. Christmasse cometh but once a yeare CAMDEN *Proverbs. Comb.*: **C.-box,** †a box, in which gratuities were collected at Christmas, by apprentices, etc., and afterwards shared; a present or gratuity given at Christmas; **-day,** the 25th of December; **-eve,** the evening before Christmas-day; **-flower,** (*a*) the Christmas Rose, *Helleborus niger*; (*b*) the Winter Aconite, *Eranthis hyemalis*; **-tide,** the season of Christmas; **-tree,** a small (fir-) tree, set up in a room, illuminated, decorated, and hung with Christmas presents; borrowed from Germany. Hence **Chri·stmas(s)y** *a. colloq.* characteristic of C.

Christmas (kri·smăs), *v. colloq.* 1594. [f. prec.] To adorn with Christmas decorations; *intr.* to celebrate Christmas.

Christo- (kri·sto), comb. f. Gr. Χριστός or L. *Christus* CHRIST, as in **C.-centric** *a.* having Christ as its centre, etc.

Christology (kristǫ·lŏdʒi). 1673. [f. Gr. Χριστός + -λογια.] That part of theology which relates to Christ; a doctrine or theory concerning Christ. Hence **Christolo·gical** *a.* **Christo·logist,** one who treats of C.; one who holds a theory about Christ.

Christo·phany. 1846. [f. as prec. + -φανια or -φανεια.] An appearance of Christ.

Christopher (kri·stŏfəı). ME. [ad. (ult.) Gr. Χριστοφόρος Christ-bearing.] †**1.** A figure of St. Christopher -1488. †**2.** A bearer 1563. **3.** *Herb C.*: the Bane-berry (*Actæa spicata*); also formerly *Osmunda regalis* 1578.

†**Christ-tide.** 1589. Christmas -1656.

Christward. 1645. Towards Christ.

Christy minstrel. 1873. One of a troupe of minstrels imitating negroes, such as that originated by George *Christy* of New York.

Chromascope (krōᵘ·măˌskoᵘp). [irreg. f. Gr. χρῶμα + -σκοπος.] *Optics.* Lüdicke's instrument for showing the optical effects of colour.

Chromate (krōᵘ·mėt). 1819. [f. CHROMIUM + -ATE [4].] *Chem.* A salt of chromic acid.

Chromatic (kroᵘmæ·tik), *a.* (and *sb.*) 1603. [ad. Gr. χρωματικός, f. χρῶμα.] **A.** *adj.* **1.** Of or belonging to colour or colours; consisting of or produced by colour 1841. **2.** Highly coloured 1864. **3.** *Mus.* Pertaining to or including notes which do not belong to the diatonic scale 1603. **b.** Of, pertaining to, or giving all tones of the c. scale. **c.** *transf.* of persons 1711.

1. C. memory, or the memory of colours 1869. *C. aberration*: see ABERRATION. *C. printing*: printing from blocks or types inked with various colours. 3. *C. scale*: a scale which proceeds by semitones. Hence †**Chroma·tical** *a.*, **-ally** *adv.*

B. quasi-*sb.* †**1.** The art of colouring -1761. **2.** *Chromatics.* The science of colour 1790. **3.** *pl.* Chromatic notes, harmonies, etc. 1708. **4.** = ACCIDENTAL B. b.

Chromatin (krōᵘ·mătin). 1882. [f. Gr. χρῶμα, χρώματ- + -IN.] *Biol.* Tissue which can be stained by immersion in colouring matter.

Chromatism (krōᵘ·mătiz'm). ? *Obs.* 1721. [ad. Gr. χρωματισμός.] **1.** Natural colouring. **2.** *Optics.* Chromatic aberration 1854. **3.** = CHROMISM.

Chromato- (krōᵘ·măto), bef. a vowel **chromat-,** comb. f. Gr. χρῶμα colour:

Chromato·genous *a.*, *Path.* generating colour. **Chromato·graphy** [+ -GRAPHY], description of colours. **Chromato·logy** [+ -LOGY], the science of colours. **Chromato·meter** [+ -METER], a measure or scale of colours. **Chro·matophore,** also **-phor** [+ Gr. -φορος], *Phys.* a pigment-cell, possessing contractile processes, contained in the skin of Cephalopoda, and other animals; hence **Chromato·phorous** *a.* **Chromato·scopy,** the examination of the colour of bodies. **Chro·matosphere** [+ SPHERE] = CHROMOSPHERE.

Chromatrope (krōᵘ·mătroᵘp). 1860. [irreg. f. Gr. χρῶμα + -τροπος.] A magic-lantern slide consisting of two superposed circular glasses, brilliantly coloured, one of which rotates in front of the other.

Chromatype; see CHROMOTYPE.

Chrome (krōᵘm). 1800. [a. F., f. Gr. χρῶμα; so named from the brilliant colour of its compounds.] *Chem.* **1.** The metal CHROMIUM. **2.** The yellow pigment and colour obtained from chromate of lead; as *orange, lemon, c.*

attrib. and *Comb.*: **c. alum,** a double sulphate of chromium and an alkali-metal, isomorphous with common alum; **c. green,** (*a*) the sesquioxide of chromium (Cr_2O_3), used as a pigment; (*b*) a pigment made by mixing chrome yellow with Prussian blue; **c. orange, c. red,** pigments prepared from the dibasic chromate of lead ($2PbO, CrO_3$); **c. yellow,** the neutral chromate of lead ($PbCrO_4$), used as a pigment; also *attrib.*

Chromic (krōᵘ·mik), *a.* 1800. [f. prec. + -IC.] *Chem.* Of or belonging to chromium; containing chromium in chemical combination. Applied to compounds in which chromium combines as a triad, as *c. acid* or *c. anhydride*, CrO_3, etc.

Chro·mism. [mod. f. Gr. χρῶμα + -ISM.] *Bot.* Abnormal excess of coloration in plants.

Chromite (krōᵘ·məit). 1840. [f. CHROME + -ITE.] *Chem.* A compound of sesquioxide of chromium (Cr_2O_3) with the protoxide of another metal. Hence *Min.* Name for **chrome iron ore,** consisting chiefly of chromic oxide (Cr_2O_3) and ferrous oxide (FeO).

Chromium (krōᵘ·miŏm). 1807. [Latinized f. Fr. *chrome.*] *Chem.* A metallic element, symbol Cr, not found free, discovered by Vauquelin in 1797. It is remarkable for the brilliant colours of its compounds.

Chromo- (krōᵘ·mo).

1. *Chem.* Comb. f. CHROMIUM, as in *c.-carbon.* **2.** Short for CHROMATO-, q. v. Hence,

Chro·moblast [Gr. βλαστός], a variety of connective tissue corpuscles containing a black pigment. **Chro·mogen** [+ -GEN], (*a*) a supposed vegetable colouring matter which is acted upon by acids and alkalis in producing red, yellow, or green tints; (*b*) the compound which requires only the presence of a salt-forming group to convert it into a dye-stuff. Hence **Chromoge·nic** *a.* **Chro·mograph** [+ -GRAPH], an apparatus for multiplying copies of written matter; hence, **Chro·mograph** *v.* **Chromo·meter** [+ -METER], an instrument for determining by means of colour the presence of minerals in ores. **Chro·mophane** [Gr. -φανής], the colouring matters present in the inner segments of the cones of the retina where they are held in solution by a fat. **Chro·mophore** [Gr. -φορος], the body whose presence, in conjunction with a salt-forming group, determines the possession of tinctorial power (cf. *Chromogen*). **Chromophoto·graphy,** the production of photographs in colour. **Chromopho·tolithograph,** a photolithograph produced in colours. **Chro·mophyll** [Gr. φύλλον], the colouring principles of plants other than chlorophyll. **Chro·moxylo·graphy,** printing in colours from wooden blocks.

Chromo (krōᵘ·mo). *colloq.* 1868. Short for CHROMOLITHOGRAPH. Also in comb.

Chromoli·thograph, *sb.* 1860. [f. CHROMO- 2.] A picture printed in colours from stone. Also *attrib.* So **Chromoli·thograph** *v.* to print thus. **Chromolitho·grapher. Chromolithogra·phic** *a.* **Chro·molitho·graphy.**

Chromosome (krōᵘ·mŏsōᵘm). 1890. [ad. G. *chromosom* (Waldeyer, 1888), f. CHROMO- 2 + Gr. σῶμα body.] *Biol.* Each of the rods or threads into which the chromatin of the cell-nucleus is transformed previous to the mitotic division of the cell.

Chromosphere (krōᵘ·mŏˌsfiəı). 1868. [f. CHROMO- 2 + SPHERE. Cf. σπερμο- for σπερματο-.] *Astron.* The red gaseous envelope round the sun, outside the photosphere. Hence **Chromosphe·ric** *a.*

Chromotype (krōᵘ·mŏtəip). Also **chroma-.** 1843. [f. CHROMO- 1.] *Photogr.* A process for obtaining photographs by means of paper sensitized by a salt of chromium; a picture thus produced. Also *attrib.* Hence **Chro·motypo·graphy, -typy,** printing in colours.

Chromous (krōᵘ·məs), *a.* 1840. [f. CHROME.] *Chem.* Of or pertaining to chromium; applied to compounds in which it combines as a dyad.

†**Chromule.** 1835. [f. Gr. χρῶμα + ὕλη.] = *chromophyll* (see CHROMO- 2) -1870.

Chronal (krōᵘ·năl), *a. rare.* [mod. f. Gr. χρόνος + -AL.] Of or relating to time.

Chronic, -al (krǫ·nik, -ăl), *a.* 1601. [a. F. *chronique*, ad. L., a. Gr. χρονικός, f. χρόνος; see -IC, and -AL [1].] †**1.** Of or relating to time; chronological 1605. **2.** [= Gr. χρόνιος.] Lasting a long time, lingering, inveterate; opp. to *acute* 1601. *transf.* Constant; also, bad 1860.

2. C. pains, which surely kill, though slow H. VAUGHAN. A c. invalid 1842. *transf.* C. doubts; the weather is c. (*mod.*). Hence **Chro·nically** *adv.* **Chroni·city,** c. quality or condition (of disease).

Chronicle (krǫ·nik'l), *sb.* [ME. *cronikle, -ykle*, a. AF. *cronicle* = OF. *cronique*, see CHRONIQUE. Spelt with *ch-* since the Renascence.] **1.** A detailed and continuous register of events in order of time. Also *fig.* **2.** spec. *Chronicles*: name of two historical books of the O.T. 1535. **3.** *gen.* A record, narrative ME.

1. Broþer Ranulf. .compiled and made þis present cronicle TREVISA. *fig. Tr. & Cr.* IV. v. 202.

Chronicle (krǫ·nik'l), *v.* ME. [f. prec.] To enter or record in a chronicle; *gen.* to put on record, register.

To..c. small Beere *Oth.* II. i. 161. Hence **Chro·nicler,** a writer of a chronicle, a recorder of events.

†**Chro·nique.** ME. [a. OF. *cronique*, ad. med.L. *cronica, chronica*, from L. *chronica* pl. 'matters of time', a. Gr., f. χρόνος.] A CHRONICLE -1671.

†‖**Chrono·crator.** 1647. [Gr.] *Astrol.* A ruler of time -1862.

Chronogram (krǫ·nŏgræm). 1621. [f. Gr. χρόνος + γράμμα. Cf. F. *chronogramme.*] A phrase, sentence, or inscription, in which certain letters (distinguished from the rest) express by their numerical values a date or epoch.

Thus a pamphlet published in 1666, when an engagement between the English and Dutch navies was expected, had in place of the imprint of the year this sentence: 'LorD haVe MerCIe Vpon Vs.' The sum of the numerical values of the capital letters is 1666. (See *Athenæum*, No. 2868.) Hence **Chro·nogramma·tic, -al** *a.*, **-ally** *adv.* **Chronogra·mmatist,** a maker of chronograms.

Chronograph (krǫ·nŏgrɑf). 1662. [f. Gr. χρονογράφος.] †**1.** = CHRONOGRAM. **2.** An instrument, *esp.* a watch or clock, for recording time with exactness 1868. Also *attrib.* Hence **Chronogra·phic, -al** *a.* (in both senses). **Chronogra·phically** *adv.*

Chronographer (krǫnǫ·grăfəı). 1548. [f. as prec. + -ER.] A writer of chronography, a chronicler, chronologist.

Chronography (krǫnǫ·grăfi). Also †**crono-.** 1548. [f. Gr. χρονογραφία, f. as prec.] The chronological arrangement of past events; †chronology.

Chronologer (krǫnǫ·lŏdʒəı). 1572. [f. CHRONOLOGY + -ER [1].] One who studies chronology; a chronologist.

Chronology (krǫnǫ·lŏdʒi). 1593. [ad. mod. L. *chronologia*, f. Gr. χρόνος + -λογία.] **1.** The science of computing time or periods of time, and of assigning events to their true dates. **2.** A chronological table, list, or treatise 1614.

1. If C. had not contradicted it, it would have been concluded, that he had been an Auditour of Pythagoras himself CUDWORTH. Hence **Chronolo·gic, -al** *a.* of, belonging to, or in accordance with c.; arranged in order of time; relating to or dealing with c. **Chronolo·gically** *adv.* **Chrono·logist,** a CHRONOLOGER. **Chrono·logize** *v.* †to chronicle; to apply c. to, to arrange chronologically.

†**Chronoma·stix.** *rare.* 1628. [f. Gr. χρόνος + μάστιξ.] A scourge of the time.

Chronometer (krǫnǫ·mĭtəı, krǫ-). 1735. [f. Gr. χρόνος + μέτρον.] **1.** An instrument for measuring time; spec. applied to time-keepers having a special escapement and a compensation balance, used for determining longitude at sea, and for other exact observation. Also *fig.* †**2.** *Mus.* A METRONOME 1837.

Phr. *To rate a c.*: to compare its daily loss or gain with the true time. *Comb.* **c.-escapement,** one in which the movement of the balance is opposed by the wheels at only one point in a complete oscillation.

Chronometry (krǫnǫ·mĕtri). [mod. f. Gr.

χρόνος; see -METRY.] The art or science of accurately measuring time; measurement of time. Hence **Chronome·tric, -al** *a.* of or pertaining to c.; relating to the measurement of time. **Chronome·trically** *adv.*

Chronopher (krǫ·nŏfəɹ). 1867. [f. Gr. χρόνος + -φορος.] An apparatus for the distribution of electric time-signals.

Chronoscope (krǫ·noˌskōup). 1704. [f. Gr. χρόνος + -σκοπος.] An instrument for observing and measuring very short intervals of time; *esp.* one invented by Wheatstone, used chiefly in determining the velocity of projectiles. Hence **Chronosco·pic** *a.* So **Chrono·scopy**, observation and exact estimation of time.

Chrys- (kris), comb. f., bef. a vowel, of Gr. χρυσός gold; properly denoting compounds of a golden-yellow colour: as

Chrysa·niline, a brilliant golden-yellow dye ($C_{20}H_{17}N_3$), obtained as a secondary product in the manufacture of rosaniline. **Chrysa·robin**, the medullary matter of the stem and branches of *Andira Araroba* dried and powdered, Goa Powder. **Chry·sene**, a crystalline hydrocarbon ($C_{18}H_{12}$), of the Anthracene group, obtained in bright yellow glistening scales, etc., etc.

Chrysalid (kri·sălid). 1777. [f. L. *chrysal(l)id-*, Gr. χρυσαλλιδ-, stem of χρυσαλλίς CHRYSALIS.] 1. = CHRYSALIS. Also *fig.* 2. *attrib.* Of or pertaining to a chrysalis (*lit.* and *fig.*) 1802.

Chrysalis (kri·sălis). Pl. **chrysalides** (krisæ·lidīz) or **chrysalises** (kri·sălisėz); also *chrysalids*; cf. *orchids.*] 1658. [a. L. *chrysal(l)is*, a. Gr. χρυσαλλίς 'the gold-coloured sheath of butterflies', f. χρυσός.] The state into which the larva of most insects passes before becoming an imago. In this state it is wrapped in a hard sheath. Also *fig.* Also *attrib.* Hence **Chry·saline** *a.* [irreg. as if f. *chrysal-*] of, or of the nature of, a c. So **Chry·salize** *v. nonce-wd.* **Chry·saloid** *a.* c.-like.

Chrysanthemum (krisæ·nþĭmŏm). 1578. [a. L., a. Gr. χρυσάνθεμον, f. χρυσός + ἄνθεμον.] 1. The Corn Marigold (now *C. segetum*), a composite plant with brilliant yellow flowers: hence the name of the genus, having species with flowers of many colours, *e.g.* the Ox-eye Daisy. 2. *Hort.* Usually applied to a number of cultivated late-blooming species of this genus, esp. *C. sinense* 1798. Also *attrib.*

Chryselephantine (krisˌelĭfæ·ntin), *a.* 1827. [ad. Gr. χρυσελεφάντινος, f. χρυσός + ἐλέφας, ἐλέφαντ-.] Of gold and ivory: applied to statues overlaid with gold and ivory, such as the Olympian Zeus, etc. Also *fig.*

Chryso- (kriso), bef. a vowel CHRYS-, comb. f. Gr. χρυσός gold.

1. **Chry·sobull**, a golden bull or *bulla aurea.* **Chry·sochlore** [Gr. χλωρός green], the Cape Mole, whose fur has a gold-green lustre. **Chryso·cracy** [after *aristocracy*], plutocracy. **Chryso·graphy** [Gr. χρυσογραφία], writing in letters of gold. So **Chry·sograph** *v.* **Chryso·logy** [Gr. -λογια], the science of gold or wealth. **Chryso·philist, -philite** [Gr. χρυσόφιλος], a lover of gold. **Chrysopoe·tic** [Gr. ποιητικός] *a.*, gold-making; also quasi-*sb.* in *pl.* †**Chry·sosperm** [Gr. σπέρμα], *Alch.* a substance that is the 'seed of gold'. **Chry·sotype** [see -TYPE], *Photogr.* a process in which chloride of gold is used to develop the negative; a picture thus produced.

2. *esp.* in *Chem.* and *Min.* **Chry·sogen** [see -GEN], an orange-coloured hydrocarbon contained in crude anthracene. **Chry·sophan(e** [Gr. *φαν-, φαίνειν], *Chem.* a name for an orange-red bitter substance contained in the alcoholic extract of rhubarb; also for *chrysophanic acid.* **Chry·sophane**, *Min.* = CLINTONITE. **Chry·sophyll** [Gr. φύλλον], the yellow colouring matter of plants. **Chry·sotile** [Gr. τίλος fibre], a fibrous variety of serpentine.

Chrysoberyl (kri·soberil). 1661. [ad. L. *chrysoberyllus*, f. Gr. χρυσός + βήρυλλος BERYL.] *Min.* †1. A variety of beryl, with a tinge of yellow. 2. A yellowish green gem, in composition an aluminate of glucinum. A variety is cymophane or *c. cat's-eye.*

Chrysocolla (krisokǫ·lă). 1600. [ad. L. *chrysocolla*, a. Gr. χρυσόκολλα.] 1. A name meaning 'gold-solder', anciently given to borax, malachite, or other minerals. Now *Hist.* var. †**Chry·socoll.** 2. *Min.* A hydrous silicate of copper, green, with a shining lustre 1794.

Chrysoidine (krisō·idəin, -oi·dəin). 1878. [f. Gr. χρυσοειδής.] *Chem.* A colouring base ($C_{12}H_{12}N_4$), intermediate between aniline yellow and phenylene brown. The chrysoidine of commerce is the hydrochloride.

Chrysolite (kri·sŏləit). [ME. *crisolite*, a. OF., f. (ult.) Gr. χρυσός + λίθος. Refash. after L.] A name formerly given to various gems of a green colour, such as zircon, tourmaline, topaz, and apatite. Now restricted to a yellow variety of olivine, a species which includes the green mineral peridot as another of its varieties. It is a silicate of magnesia and iron found in lava. Also *attrib.*

One entyre and perfect C. *Oth.* v. ii. 144.

Chrysoprase (kri·sŏpreⁱz). In *Rev.* xxi. 20 **chrysoprasus** (krisǫ·prăsŏs). [ME. *crisopace* = *chrysopassus*. In the form *chrysoprasus*, f. (ult.) Gr. χρυσός gold + πράσον leek.] 1. The ancient name of a golden-green precious stone, perh. a variety of the beryl. 2. *Min.* An apple-green variety of chalcedony ME.; also, its colour 1835.

1. Crisopassus is..hyd in lyghte and seen in derknesse TREVISA.

Chrysosto·mic, *a. rare.* 1816. [f. Gr. χρυσόστομος.] Golden-mouthed, an epithet applied to orators.

Chthonian (kþōu·niăn), *a.* 1850. [f. Gr. χθόνιος, f. χθών.] Dwelling in or beneath the earth. So **Chthonic** *a.*

Chub (tʃɒb). 1496. [Late ME. *chubbe*, of unkn. origin.] 1. A river fish (*Cyprinus* or *Leuciscus cephalus*) of the Carp family (*Cyprinidæ*), also called the Chevin. In U. S., the Black Bass (*Perca huro*); also the Blackfish (*Tautoga americana*). †*transf.* A dolt -1745. 2. *dial.* A wood-log 1796. 3. *attrib.* C.-like 1681. Hence †**Chubbed** *a.* = CHUBBY 1, 2; of or belonging to a dolt. †**Chu·bbish** *a.*

Chubb (tʃɒb). 1833. [Inventor's name.] Short for *Chubb-lock*: a patent lock with tumblers, that cannot be picked.

Chubby (tʃɒ·bi), *a.* 1611. [f. CHUB + -Y.] †1. Short and thick like a chub. 2. Round-faced; plump 1722. Also *transf.*

2. A sow and her c. pigs 1859. **Chu·bbiness.**

Chuck (tʃɒk), *sb.*[1] ME. [Echoic.] A species of cluck; *e.g.* that of a hen calling chickens.

Chuck (tʃɒk), *sb.*[2] 1588. [? corrupted from *chick, chicken.*] 1. A term of endearment. 2. Chick, chicken, fowl. *n. dial.* Also *fig.* 1675.

1. Vse lenitie sweet C. *Hen. V*, III. ii. 26.

Chuck (tʃɒk), *sb.*[3] 1611. [? f. F. *choc* (see SHOCK); cf. CHUCK *v.*[2]] 1. A slight tap under the chin. 2. A toss, a jerk 1843; a throw. *colloq.* 3. Short for *chuck-farthing* 1711. 4. *Sc.* A small rounded quartz pebble used in the game of 'chuckie-stanes'; hence *chucks* a name of this game. Also *chuckstone.* 1822.

1. There's a double c. at a double chin HOOD.

Chuck (tʃɒk), *sb.*[4] 1674. [app. a var. of CHOCK.] 1. A CHOCK; a CHUNK. Chiefly *dial.* 2. A cut of beef extending from the horns to the ribs, including the shoulder-piece (*dial.*) 1881. 3. A boat-chock 1789. 4. *Turning.* A contrivance for fixing the material to be turned to the mandril of the lathe. Formerly CHOCK. 1703.

Chuck, *v.*[1] ME. [Echoic; cf. CHUCK *sb.*[1]] 1. *intr.* To make a clucking noise like a fowl. †2. *intr.* To chuckle -1599.

Chuck, *v.*[2] 1583. [In 16th c. *chock*; cf. F. *choquer*; prob. mainly echoic.] 1. To give a gentle blow under the chin. 2. To throw with the hand with little action of the arm; to toss; prob. at first said of tossing light things only; by workmen used for *throw* in all senses 1593. 3. *intr.* To play chuck-farthing 1735.

2. They'll..c. us into the sea 1825.

Comb.: **c.-farthing**, a game in which coins were pitched at a mark, and then chucked at a hole; **-half-penny**, = *chuck-farthing*; **-hole**, (*a*) = *chuck-farthing*; (*b*) 'a deep hole in a waggon-rut' (Webster).

Chuck, *v.*[3] 1869. [f. CHUCK *sb.*[4]] To fix on the lathe by means of a CHUCK, q. v.

Chuck, *adv.* 1751. = CHOCK; with direct impact.

Chucker (tʃɒ·kəɹ). 1760. [f. CHUCK *v.*[2] + -ER.[1]] 1. A small pebble. (Cf. CHECKER.) 2. One who chucks or throws 1884.

Chucker-out (*vulgar colloq.*), a bully who ejects fleeced victims from a gambling-hell, tavern, or brothel; a rough hired to expel opponents from a political or other meeting.

Chuckie. *Sc.* 1793. [dim. of CHUCK[3], sense 4.] Quartz pebble: also *c. stone* or *stane.* *C.-stanes*: = *Chucks.*

Chuckie; see CHUCKY.

Chuckle (tʃɒ·k'l), *v.* 1598. [Echoic; cf. CHUCK *v.*[1]] †1. *intr.* To laugh vehemently or convulsively -1823. 2. To laugh in a suppressed manner; to make or show inarticulate signs of exultation 1803. 3. To cluck as a hen 1700.

Chuckle (tʃɒ·k'l), *sb.*[1] 1754. [f. CHUCKLE *v.*[1]] 1. An act or state of chuckling (see CHUCKLE *v.* 1, 2). 2. The call of some birds to their young; the cackle of a hen 1773.

Chuckle (tʃɒ·k'l), *a.* and *sb.*[2] 1721. [? conn. w. CHUCK *sb.*[4]] *adj.* Big and clumsy, blockish: used *esp.* of the head. *sb.* A big hulking fellow, a chuckle-head 1731. Hence **c.-head**, a blockhead; a stupid lout; **-headed** *a.*; **-headedness.**

‖**Chuckler** (tʃɒ·kləɹ). 1759. [Corruption of Tamil *shakkili.*] One of a very low caste in Southern India, the members of which are tanners or cobblers; *colloq.* a native shoemaker.

Chuck-will's-widow. 1828. [from its cry.] *U.S.* A species of Goat-sucker (*Caprimulgus carolinensis*).

Chucky (tʃɒ·ki). Also *Sc.* **chuckie.** 1727. [dim. of CHUCK *sb.*[2]] 1. Little or dear chuck. 2. A chicken; a fowl 1789.

‖**Chuddar** (tʃɒ·dăɹ). *Anglo-Ind.* 1614. [Hindī *chadar.*] A large sheet worn as a shawl by women in northern India.

Chuet, obs. var. of CHEWET.

Chufa (tʃū·fă). *U.S.* 1860. The Earth Almond (*Cyperus esculentus*), a plant producing small tubers about the size of a bean. (In F. *souchet comestible.*)

Chuff (tʃɒf), *sb.*[1] ME. [?] A rustic, boor, clown, churl.

A Rich Penurious C. 1668. Hence **Chu·ffy** *a.*[1] **Chu·ffily** *adv.* **Chu·ffiness.**

†**Chuff**, *sb.*[2] 1530. [?] A cheek swollen with fat -1611. Hence **Chu·ffy** *a.*[2]

Chuff (tʃɒf), *a.*[1] Now *dial.* 1609. [See prec.] 1. Puffed out with fat; chubby. 2. Pleased, happy 1860.

Chuff, *a.*[2] Now *dial.* 1832. [See CHUFF *sb.*[1]] Churlish; gruff, morose.

Chukker (tʃɒ·kəɹ). 1900. Also **chucker.** [Hind. *chak(k)ar* = Skr. *cakra* WHEEL.] *Polo.* Each of the 'periods' of play.

Chum (tʃɒm), *sb.* Now *colloq.* 1684. [? abbrev. of *chamber-mate*, or the like.] One who shares apartments with another or others; also, an associate, an intimate friend. In colloq. use with school-boys, students, criminals, etc. Hence **Chu·mmy** *a.* **Chu·mship.**

Chum (tʃɒm), *v. colloq.* 1730. [f. prec.] 1. To share chambers, to live together. 2. *trans.* To put as a chum 1837.

2. You'll be chummed on somebody DICKENS. Hence **Chu·mmage**, the system of chumming one person on another; also, garnish, footing.

Chu·mmy, *sb.*[1] *low colloq.* 1836. [f. *chumley* = CHIMNEY.] A chimney-sweeper's boy.

Chummy, *sb.*[2] *colloq.* 1864. Dim. of CHUM.

Chump (tʃɒmp). 1703. [Cf. CHUNK, *chop*, *lump*, etc.] 1. A short thick lump of wood; an end-piece. 2. The blunt end of anything; also *c.-end.* 3. *fig.* A block, blockhead 1883.

2. *Off his c.* (joc.): off his head. *Comb.* **c.-chop**, a chop from the c.-end of a loin of mutton.

‖**Chunam** (tʃunā·m). 1687. [Tamil *chunnam* lime.] Cement or plaster made of shell-lime and sea-sand. Used in India. Also *attrib.* Hence **Chuna·m** *v.* to cover with c.

Chunk (tʃɒŋk). *colloq.* and *dial.* 1691. [app. modified f. CHUCK *sb.*[4]] A thick solid lump cut off anything. Also *fig.* Hence **Chu·nky** *a.*

‖**Chupatty** (tʃŏpɑ·ti). *Anglo-Ind.* 1810. [Hindī *chapātī.*] A small cake of unleavened bread, of coarse wheaten meal, flattened, and baked on a griddle.

‖**Chuprassy** (tʃǒprɑ·si). 1828. [Hindī *chaprási*.] A wearer of an official badge; an attendant, messenger, or henchman.

Church (tʃɒ̄ɹtʃ), *sb.* [OE. *cirice*, *circe*, ME. *chereche*. *chiriche*, *chirche*, whence *churche*, *cherche*, etc. App. common WGer. :—Gr. κυριακόν (sc. δῶμα, or the like), = 'house of the Lord'. See further in N.E.D.]

I. 1. A building for public Christian worship. (Cf. CHAPEL, ORATORY.) **2.** Applied to public places of worship of any religion, as Mohammedan mosques, etc.

II. 1. The Christian community collectively. (More fully the *C. Universal* or *Catholic*.) OE. **2.** A particular organized Christian society, separated by peculiarities of doctrine, worship, or organization, or confined to limits territorial or historical OE. **3.** The ecclesiastical organization of Christianity, or of a great Christian society; *esp.* The clergy, etc., of this society as a corporation having continuous existence, and as an estate of the realm. (In this sense opp. to 'State'.) OE.

1. *C. militant*: the C. on earth as warring against the powers of evil. *C. triumphant*: the portion of the church which has overcome the world and entered into glory. 2. *C. of England*, *English or Anglican C.*: the English branch of the Western Church, which at the Reformation asserted the supremacy of the Sovereign over all persons and in all causes in his dominions. *Established C.*: the Church as by law established in any country, as the state-recognized form of religion. So *State C.* 3. *Holy C.*: the Church Catholic, as divinely instituted and guided; also, in early times = the clergy. *High*, *Low*, *Broad C.*: see these words.

III. A congregation of Christians locally organized ME.

IV. 1. a. Used as tr. of L. *ecclesia*, Gr. ἐκκλησία, of the Vulgate and the LXX, in its pre-Christian sense 'congregation'. **b.** Later, a retrospective application of the Christian sense to the Israelites, and the 'Old Testament saints'. **2.** Applied to various societies, religious and other (*e.g.* the *C. of Humanity*, the Comtists) 1528.

1. a. Why have you brought forth the C. of our Lord into the wildernesse BIBLE (Douay) *Numb.* xx. 4. Also *Acts* vii. 38. b. History of the Jewish C. (*title*) STANLEY.

V. *attrib.* 'Church' is used (often hyphened) with the function of an adjective, signifying 'of the church, of a church, of churches, ecclesiastical', and in England *spec.* 'of the Church of England'.

Comb.: **c.-†ale**, a periodic festive gathering held in connexion with a c.; **-bell**; **-book**, one belonging to, or used in, connexion with, a c.; **-flag**, a flag hoisted on board a ship during divine service; **-folk**, people at c.; adherents of the established c., as opp. to 'chapel-folk'; **-goer**, one who regularly goes to c.; so **-going** *vbl. sb.* and *a.*; **†-hawe**, **-hay**, a churchyard; **-house**, one belonging to a or the c., or used for c. purposes; **-land**, land belonging to a or the c.; **-lease**, a lease of c. property; **-living**, a living in an established c.; *esp.* in the C. of England; **-me·mber**, a member of the or a c.; so **-me·mbership**; **-mode**, a mode in mediæval c.-music; **-office**, an office in the c.: the form prescribed for the conduct of a c.-service; **-officer**; **-owl**, the BARN-OWL; **-rate**, a rate levied on parishioners for the maintenance of the c. and its services; **†-reeve**, a churchwarden; **-service**, the public worship of a c.; *pop.* a service-book; *esp.* the Book of Common Prayer, with the lessons, psalms, etc., added; **†-soken**, the territory of a c.; inhabitants of this district; **-text**, the Old English or Black-letter; **-way**, the public way leading to a c.; **-woman**; **-work**, work at the edifice of a c. (= work that proceeds slowly); work for, or in connexion with, a c.; so **-worker**.

Hence **Chu·rchdom**, ecclesiastical status; the system of a c. **Churchia·nity** [after *Christianity*], devotion to the C. rather than to Christianity. **Chu·rchiness**. **Chu·rchish** *a.* (*rare*) = CHURCHY. **Chu·rchism**, ecclesiasticism; c.-partisanship; often short for *English Churchism*. **Chu·rchless** *a.* not having or belonging to a c.; not blessed by the c. **Chu·rchlet**, a little c. **Chu·rchlike** *a.* like a c.; befitting a c. **Chu·rchly** *a.* ecclesiastical. **†Churchship**, the being a c. **Chu·rchward** *a.* and *adv.*, **-wards** *adv.* **Chu·rch-wise** *a.* and *adv.*

Church (tʃɒ̄ɹtʃ), *v.* ME. [f. prec. sb.] To bring, take, or conduct to church, in order to receive its rites or ministrations. Said *esp.* of a woman after childbirth, when thanks are publicly offered for her safe delivery.

†Church-chopper. 1631. [See CHOP *v.*[2]] A trafficker in ecclesiastical benefices –1656.

Church-door. OE. The outer door of a church, where marriages, etc., were ordained to be performed.

Housbondes at chirche dore she hadde fyue CHAUCER.

†Church-gang. ME. only. Going to church; churching of a woman after childbirth.

Church-garth. *dial.* 1570. [See GARTH.] A churchyard.

Church-government. 1594. The government of the affairs of a church; the form of polity, as Episcopal, Presbyterian, etc., upon which a church is organized. So **Church-governor.**

Churchman (tʃɒ̄·ɹtʃmǣn). ME. **1.** 'An ecclesiastic; a clergyman' (J.). **†2.** A churchwarden –1598. **3.** A member of the Anglican or other established church 1677. Hence **Chu·rch-manly** *a.* **Chu·rchmanship**, the position, quality, or action of a c.

†Church-papist. 1601. In 17th c., a Roman Catholic who conformed outwardly to the Church of England –1682.

Church-scot, -shot. [f. OE. *ciric-* + *sceat*.] lit. = *Church-tribute*: in OE. times a custom of corn collected on St. Martin's day; extended to other similar contributions.

Church-ward, *sb.* Now *Hist.* (= OE. *ciricweard*). The custodian of a church (building).

Churchwarden (tʃɒ̄·ɹtʃwǭ:ɹd'n). 1494. [See WARDEN.] **1.** One of the lay officers (usually two) elected annually to assist the incumbent of a parish or district church, to manage various parochial offices, and generally to act as the lay representative of the parish in matters of church-organization. **2.** *colloq.* A clay pipe with a very long stem 1863. Hence **Chu·rchwa·rdenship.**

Churchy (tʃɒ̄·ɹtʃi), *a. colloq.* 1864. Strongly smacking of the Church; obtrusive in conformity to the Church.

Churchyard (tʃɒ̄·ɹtʃyaɹd). ME. [See YARD *sb.*[1]] **1.** The enclosure in which a church stands; a burial-ground. **†2.** The precincts of a church (*rare*) –1577. Also *attrib.*

1. Like Graues i'th holy C. *Cor.* III. iii. 51. 2. In Powles churche yarde 1577.

Churl (tʃɒ̄ɹl). [OE. *ceorl*:—WGer. *kerl*; see CARL.] **1.** A man; *esp.* as correlative to 'wife'. (In ME. mixed with other senses.) **2.** In OE. times: A man; a member of the lowest rank of freemen. Now *Hist.* **†3.** A serf –1607. **4.** A rustic, boor ME. **5.** A rude low-bred fellow ME. **6.** *spec.* A niggard; a miser 1535.

2. The Saxons. .made three degrees of freemen; to wit—an earl, a thane, and a c. RISDON. Gentleman or C. SHELTON. 6. The c. [shall be no more] said to be bountiful *Isa.* xxxii. 5. Hence **†Chu·rldom**, the state of being a c. **Chu·rlhood**, †the quality of a c.; the order of the churls.

Churlish (tʃɒ̄·ɹliʃ), *a.* [OE. *cierlisc* or *ceorlisc*, f. *ceorl* + *-isc*, -ISH.] **1.** Of or relating to a churl; pertaining to churls (*arch.*). **2.** Brutal, surly, ungracious ME. Also *transf.* and *fig.* **3.** Sordid, niggardly, grudging 1566. **4.** Difficult to work, intractable 1577. Also *fig.*

1. C. birth FREEMAN. 2. The reply C. *A. Y. L.* v. iv. 98. C. Blasts CUDWORTH. 3. Thy c. courtesy.. Reserve SCOTT. 4. C. ground 1577, metal FULLER. Hence **Chu·rlish·ly** *adv.*, **-ness**. **Chu·rly** *a.* (*rare*).

Churn (tʃɒ̄ɹn), *sb.* *N. dial.* KIRN, q. v. [OE. *cyrin* str. fem. for *cirn, *ciern, com. Teut.] **1.** A vessel or machine for making butter, in which cream or milk is shaken, beaten, or broken, so as to separate the oily globules from the serous parts. Used also of vessels or instruments resembling this, as a pump, a milk-can, etc. **2.** [from the vb.] Churning (of water, etc.) 1882. Also *attrib.*

Churn (tʃɒ̄ɹn), *v.* ME. [f. prec. sb.] **1.** To agitate *milk* or *cream* in a churn so as to make butter; to produce *butter* thus. Also *intr.* **2.** To agitate, stir, and intermix; to produce (froth, etc.) thus 1697. Also *intr.*

2. Winds churn'd white the waves CAMPBELL. Hence **Chu·rning** *vbl. sb.* the quantity of butter produced at a churning. **Chu·rner.**

Comb.: **c.-milk**, butter-milk; **-owl**, the Night-Jar (*dial.*); **-staff**, a staff for agitating the milk in the c.

Churr (tʃɒ̄ɹ), *v.* 1555. [Echoic.] To make a deep trilled or whirring sound, as some birds. Hence **Churr** *sb.* this sound; also, any bird which makes this sound, *esp.* the Partridge (*local*).

‖**Chu·rrus.** 1860. [Hindī *charas*.] The resinous exudation of the hemp-plant (*Cannabis Indica*), used in India as an intoxicant.

Chu·rr-worm. 1668. [from the sound it makes; see CHURR.] The Mole-cricket. *local.*

Chuse, var. of CHOOSE *v.*, q. v.

Chusite (tʃiū·zəit). 1811. [perh. f. Gr. χύσις.] *Min.* A variety of Olivine.

Chut (tʃɒt), *int.* 1825. [Cf. TUT.] An exclam. of impatience.

Chute (ʃūt). Also **shute.** 1847. [f. F. *chute* and Eng. SHOOT.] **1.** A fall of water; a steep channel by which water descends in force. **2.** A sloping channel or passage for the conveyance of water, or things floating on water, to a lower level 1878. **3.** A steep channel or enclosed passage down which ore, coal, grain, or the like is shot. In England, usually *shoot.* 1881. **4.** A steep slope or cutting 1847.

Chutney, chutnee (tʃɒ·tni). 1813. [Hindī *chatni*.] A relish compounded of sweet fruits with acid flavouring from lemons, etc. and sour herbs, and hot seasoning from chillies and spices.

†Chyazic (kəiæ·zik), *a.* 1819. [f. *c-arbon*, *hy-drogen*, and *az-ote* + -IC.] *Chem.* Now called *Prussic* (*Acid*).

Chylaqueous (kəilē¹·kwiₗəs), *a.* 1859. [f. CHYLE + -AQUEOUS.] Of the nature of chyle mixed with water.

C. fluid: a transparent colourless fluid circulating in some invertebrata.

Chyle (kəil). 1541. [a. F.:—L. *chylus* (also used), a. Gr. χυλός juice, f. stem χυ- (χεv-, χε-); cf. CHYME.] The white milky fluid formed by the action of the pancreatic juice and the bile on the chyme, and contained in the *lacteals*. Also *attrib.* Hence **Chyla·ceous** *a.* (*rare*). **Chy·loid** *a.* (*rare*).

Chyli·ferous, *a.* 1669. [f. L. *chylus* + *-fer* + -OUS.] Bearing or containing chyle.

Chylific (kəili·fik), *a.* 1836. [f. L. type **chylificus*.] Chyle-producing. So **Chylifa·cient** *a.* (*rare*). **Chylifa·ctive** *a.* (*rare*). **Chylifa·ctory** *a.*

Chylify (kəi·lifi), *v.* 1663. [mod. f. on L. type *chylificare*; see CHYLE.] To turn into or produce chyle. Hence **Chy:lifica·tion**, **†Chylifa·ction**, chyle-making.

Chylo- (kəilo), comb. f. Gr. χυλός CHYLE, as in *c.-serous*, etc.

Chylopoietic, -poetic (kəi:lopoie·tik, -poₗe·tik), *a.* 1735. [ad. mod.L. *chylopoieticus*, a. Gr., f. χυλός + ποιεῖν.] Of or relating to the formation of chyle; chyle-producing.

Chylous (kəi·ləs), *a.* 1666. [f. L. type *chylosus*.] Of, pertaining to, like, or full of chyle.

‖**Chyluria** (kəilūᵊ·riă). 1860. [mod.L., f. Gr. χυλός + οὖρον.] *Path.* The disorder of chylous urine.

Chym-; see CHIM-.

Chyme (kəim). 1607. [ad. L. *chymus*:—Gr. χυμός juice, f. stem χυ- (χεv-, χε-). See Liddell & Scott.] **1.** The semi-fluid pulpy acid matter into which food is converted in the stomach by the action of the gastric secretion. From the stomach it passes into the small intestine, where it is converted into chyle. **2.** The sap of plants. Hence **Chymi·ferous** *a.* **Chy:mifica·tion.** **Chy·mify** *v.* to turn into c. **Chy·mous** *a.*

Chymic, Chymist, etc.; see CHEMIC, etc.

Chymo- (kəi·mo), bef. a vowel CHYM-, comb. f. L. *chymus* CHYME, as in **Chy·mosin** = pepsin, etc.

Chyometer (kəiǫ·mǐtəɹ). 1880. [f. Gr. χυ-stem of χέειν + μέτρον.] An instrument, consisting of a tube with a graduated piston-rod moving in it, used for measuring liquids.

Ci-. In words beginning with CI- and *cy-*, which (exc. CINDER) are all non-Teutonic, *c* has normally the sound of *s*.

†Ci·baries, *sb. pl.* 1599. [ad. L. *cibaria*.] Things used for food, victuals –1657.

Cibarious (sibēᵊ·riəs), *a. rare.* 1656. [f. L. *cibarius*.] Relating to or useful for food.

†Ciba·tion. 1471. [ad. L. *cibationem*.] **1.** *Alchem.* Name of a process, 'feeding the matter' –1662. **2.** *gen.* Taking food 1651.

Cibol, ciboule (si·bǒl). 1632. [a. F. *ciboule*; in *Sc.* SYBOW.] Var. of CHIBOL.

‖**Ciborium** (sibō°·riǒm). 1651. [med.L., a. Gr. κιβώριον (*a*) the cup-shaped seed-vessel of the Egyptian water-lily; (*b*) a drinking-cup made of this.] 1. *Arch.* A canopy raised over the high altar 1787. 2. A receptacle for the reservation of the Eucharist.

Cicada (sikē̆·dă). ME. [L.] A homopterous insect with large transparent wings, living on trees or shrubs. The male makes a shrill chirping sound.

‖**Cicala** (sikā·lă). 1821. [a. Ital. :– L. *cicada*.] = CICADA.

The shrill cicalas, people of the pine BYRON.

Cicatrice (si·kătris). ME. [a. F., ad. L. *cicatricem*.] The scar of a healed wound; a scar-like mark. Also *transf.* Hence **Cicatri·cial** *a.* of, pertaining to, or of the nature of, a c.

Cicatricula (sikătri·kiŭlă). Also **Cicatricle** (sikæ·trik'l), **Cicatricule** (sikæ·trikiŭl). 1664. [a. L., dim. of *cicatrix*.] 1. *Biol.* A round white spot on the surface of the yolk-bag of a bird's egg, consisting of the germinal vesicle. 2. *Bot.* Applied to the hilum of grains, etc. 1828. 3. *Med.* A small scar 1783. Hence **Cicatri·cular** *a.*

Cicatrisive (sikătrəi·siv), *a.* 1730. [irreg. f. CICATRIZE, *-ise* vb.] Tending to promote the formation of a cicatrice. (Dicts.)

‖**Cicatrix** (sikē̆·triks, si·kătriks). 1641. *Pl.* -**trices** (trəi·sīz). [a. L. The word in scientific use.] 1. *Pathol.* The scar or seam of a healed wound, sore, or ulcer. Also *fig.* 2. *Bot.* The scar left by the fall of a leaf, etc.; the hilum of seeds 1826.

Cicatrizant (sikătrəi·zănt). 1661. [ad. mod. L. *cicatrizantem*.] *adj.* That heals by forming a cicatrice. *sb.* [sc. *medicine*, or *application*.]

Cicatrize (si·kătrəiz), *v.* 1563. [ad. mod.L. *cicatrizare*, ad. L. *cicatricare*.] 1. To heal by inducing a cicatrice; to skin over. Also *intr.* 2. To mark with scars. Also *fig.* 1708. Hence **Ci:catriza·tion**, the formation of a cicatrice. **Ci·catrizer**, one who or that which cicatrizes.

Cicely (si·sĭli, səi·sli). 1597. [? ad. L. *seselis*, Gr. σέσελις, σέσελι SESELI.] A popular name of several umbelliferous plants, almost co-extensive with CHERVIL; as Sweet C. (*Myrrhis odorata*), etc.

†‖**Cicer** (si·səɹ). ME. [L.] A chick-pea –1764.

‖**Cicerone** (tʃitʃerō·ne, sisĕrōᵘ·nĭ). *Pl.* -**o·ni**, rarely -**o·nes**. 1726. [It. (:—L. *Ciceronem*), the Roman orator, Cicero. Of unkn. history.] A guide who shows the antiquities or curiosities of a place to strangers. Also *transf.*

An army of virtuosi, medalists, ciceroni POPE. Hence **Cicero·ne** (tʃitʃerō·n, sisĕrōᵘ·n) *v.* to act as c. to.

Ciceronian (sisĕrōᵘ·niăn). 1581. [ad. L. *Ciceronianus*.] *adj.* Pertaining to, or after the manner of, Cicero 1661. *sb.* An admirer or imitator of Cicero's style.

The superstitious avoidance of new or post-Augustan words which the Ciceronians affected M. PATTISON. Hence **Cicero·nianism**, imitation of Cicero in Latin style and diction; *concr.* a Ciceronian expression.

†‖**Cichar.** [Heb. *kikka·r*.] A talent. HOOKER.

Cichoraceous (sikŏrē̆·ʃəs), *a.* 1729. [f. mod. L. *cichoraceæ*, f. *Cichorium* CHICORY.] *Bot.* Of or belonging to the sub-order *Cichoraceæ*, comprising Chicory, Dandelion, etc.

Cich-pea, obs. f. CHICK-PEA.

‖**Cicisbeo** (tʃitʃizbē·o). *Pl.* -**bei**, also -**beos**. 1718. [It.] 1. In Italy: The recognized gallant or *cavalier servente* of a married woman. 2. A knot of ribbon fastened to a sword-hilt, walking-stick, etc. 1771. Hence **Cicisbe·ism** (tʃitʃisbī·iz'm), the practice of a c.

†**Ciclatoun.** ME. [a. OF. *ciclaton*, *-un*, etc., f. (ult.) Pers. *sakarlāt*, whence SCARLET.] Cloth of gold or other rich material, much esteemed in the Middle Ages –1400.

†**Cicone, ciconie.** ME. [ad. L. *ciconia*.] A stork –1549.

†**Ci·curate,** *v.* 1606. [f. L. *cicurat-*, *cicurare*.] To tame; to render mild –1710. var. †**Cicure** *v.* (*rare*). Hence †**Cicura·tion.**

‖**Cicuta** (sikiū·tă). ME. [L.] A genus of poisonous umbelliferous plants, including the Water Hemlock, *C. virosa*. Formerly a name of the Common Hemlock. Hence **Cicutene, Cicutine, Cicutoxin**, chemical principles or compounds obtained from *C.*

‖**Cid** (sid, Sp. þīd). 1687. [Sp., a. Arab. *sayyid* lord.] A title given in Spanish literature to Ruy Diaz, Count of Bivar, a champion of Christianity against the Moors in the 11th century; and to the epic celebrating his exploits.

‖**Ci·daris.** 1658. [L.] The royal tiara of the ancient Persians.

-**cide** (səid), *suffix.* 1. a. F. *-cide*, L. *-cida*, f. *cædere*, in comp. *-cidere*, to cut, kill, as in *homicide, lapicide, regicide*, etc. 2. a. F. *-cide*, L. *-cidium*, cutting, killing, of same deriv. as 1. The two imply each other, as in 'the homicide is he who commits homicide', etc.

Cider (səi·dəɹ). [ME. *sidre*, *siþer*, etc., a. OF. *sidre* (now *cidre*); prob. repr. late L. *sicera*, Gr. σίκερα, used by the LXX, etc. as tr. Heb. *shēkār* 'strong drink'; cf. *ladre* from *Lazarus*. See also SICER.] A beverage made from the juice of apples expressed and fermented. Formerly including drinks made from other fruits.

Comb.: **c.-brandy**, a brandy distilled from c.; **-cellar**, a cellar in which c. is stored; name of a drinking-shop in Maiden-lane, London; **-mill**, a mill in which apples are crushed for making c.; **-press**, a press in which the juice of the crushed apples is expressed. Hence **Ci·derish** *a.* (*rare*). **Ci·derist**, one who makes or affects c. **Ci·dery** *a.* (*rare*).

Ciderkin (səi·dəɹkin). 1676. [dim. of CIDER.] A kind of weak cider made by watering the cider-pressings and subjecting them to a second pressure; *water-cider.*

‖**Ci-devant** (sidəvaṅ), *a.* 1790. [Fr.; = heretofore.] Former, late; that was formerly.

A *ci-devant* friend of mine BURNS.

Cierge (sīᵊ·ɹdʒ, or as Fr. sięrʒ). ME. [a. OF. *cerge, cirge, cierge* :—L. *cereus, cerius*, f. *cera* wax. Now arch. as Eng.] A wax candle, *esp.* as used in religious ceremonies.

‖**Ciga·la, ciga·le.** = CICADA, CICALA.

Cigar, segar (sigā·ɹ). 1735. [ad. Sp. *cigarro*; not of W. Indian origin.] A compact roll of tobacco-leaves for smoking. Hence **Cigare·sque** *a.* having a c. (or cigars) as a prominent feature (*joc.*). **Ciga·rless** *a.*

Cigarette (sigăre·t). 1842. [ad. F.; see -ETTE.] A roll of finely-cut tobacco in a cylindrical case, usu. of thin paper, open at both ends. Earlier **Cigar(r)i·to** (Sp.-Amer.) 1838.

‖**Cilia** (si·liă), *sb. pl.* Sing. *cilium* (rare). 1715. [L. *cilia*, pl. of *cilium*.] 1. The eyelids, the outer edges of the eyelids; the eye-lashes 1838. 2. Delicate hairs resembling eye-lashes, *e.g.* on the margins of leaves, the wings of some insects, etc. 1794. 3. *Phys.* Minute hair-like appendages found on the tissues of most animals, and in some vegetable organisms. They are in incessant vibratile movement, and in some of the lower animal forms that live in water serve as organs of locomotion 1835. Hence **Ci·liiform, -liform** *a.* **Ci·liolate** *a. Bot.* fringed with minute c.

Ciliary (si·liări). Also †**ci·liar.** 1691. [f. L. type **ciliarius*; see prec.] 1. Of or pertaining to the eyelids or eye-lashes. 2. Pertaining to or caused by, CILIA (sense 3) 1835.

1. *C. muscle* or *circle*: unstriped muscular fibres situated beneath the sclero-corneal junction behind the iris and around the margin of the lens. *C. processes*: the plaits into which the anterior part of the choroid membrane is gathered around the crystalline lens. 2. *C. motion*: the vibratile motion of the cilia, also locomotion by means of this.

Ciliate (si·liět), *a.* 1794. [f. L. type **ciliatus*; see CILIA.] 1. Fringed or surrounded with cilia. 2. Furnished with vibratile cilia (see CILIA 3) 1868. var. **Ci·liated** *a.* Hence **Cilia·tion**, ciliated condition.

Cilice (si·lis). [OE. *cilic*, ad. L. *cilicium* :— Gr. Κιλίκιον, f. Κιλικία Cilicia. In mod. Eng., a. F.] Hair-cloth; a rough garment of this.

Monks..with their shaven crowns, hair-cilices, and vows of poverty CARLYLE. Hence **Cili·cious** *a.*

Cilicism (si·lisiz'm). 1848. [f. *Cilicia*, in Asia Minor.] A form of speech characteristic of Cilicia.

Ciliograde (si·liogrĕid). 1835. [ad. mod.L. *ciliogradus*, f. *cilium* + *-gradus*.] *adj.* Moving by means of vibratile cilia. *sb.* One of the *Ciliograda*, a tribe of Acalephans which swim by means of cilia 1835.

Cilio-spi·nal, *a.* 1881. In *C. centre*, the direct centre in the spinal chord, where the nerve-fibres that cause contraction, etc., of the pupil of the eye take their origin.

Cill, var. of SILL, still occas. used.

‖**Cillosis** (silōᵘ·sis). 1811. [irreg. f. L. *cillere* to move, after Gr.] A spasmodic trembling of the eyelids.

Cima, var. of CYMA.

†‖**Cimelia**, *sb. pl. rare.* 1664. [med.L., a. Gr. κειμήλια.] Treasures laid up in store –1736. So †**Cime·liarch**, treasurer; store-house.

Cimeter, -itar, -iter, obs. ff. SCIMITAR.

‖**Cimex** (səi·meks). Pl. **cimices.** 1585. [a. L.] A bed-bug. Now only as the name of the genus. Hence **Cimi·cic** *a. Chem.*, in *Cimicic Acid*: a yellow crystallizable acid, of rancid odour, obtained from the liquid secreted by a bug. vars. **Cimise, cimisse.**

Cimmerian (simīᵊ·riăn), *a.* 1598. [f. L. *Cimmerius* (Gr. Κιμμέριος).] Of or belonging to the Cimmerii, a people fabled by the ancients to live in perpetual darkness. Hence, an epithet of dense darkness.

In dark C. desert MILT. *L'Allegro* 10.

Cimnel, obs. f. SIMNEL.

Cimolite (si·moləit). 1801. [f. L. *Cimolia* (also used), Gr. Κιμωλία (γῆ), a soft earth found in Cimolus, now Argentiera.] *Min.* A soft hydrous silicate of alumina, allied to fuller's earth.

Cinch (sintʃ, sinʃ), *sb. U.S.* 1872. [ad. Sp. *cincha* cingle.] 1. The saddle-girth used in Mexico, etc., usually made of separate twisted strands of horse-hair. 2. *fig.* A firm hold; a certain thing, dead certainty. *U.S.* 1888. **Cinch** *v.* to girth tightly; *fig.* to 'put the screw on'.

Cinchona (siŋkōᵘ·nă). Also **chinchona.** 1742. [Named by Linnæus after the Countess of *Chinchon*, who, when vice-queen of Peru, was cured of a fever by Peruvian bark, and afterwards brought a supply of it into Spain.] 1. A genus of evergreen trees or shrubs growing in the tropical valleys of the Andes, and now extensively cultivated in India and Java for the sake of the bark. 2. The bark of species of Cinchona, Peruvian bark; also the drug prepared from it 1800. Also *attrib.*

Comb.: **c.-bark**, the bark of species of c., of value as a tonic and febrifuge. Called also *Jesuit's bark*, *Peruvian bark*, *Quinquina*.

Hence **Cinchona·ceous** *a.* belonging to the natural order of *Cinchonaceæ* of which C. is the typical genus. **Cincho·nal** *a. Bot.* related to the *Cinchonaceæ*. **Cincho·nia**, *Chem.* = *Cinchonine*. **Cincho·nic** *a.* of or pertaining to c., as in *Cinchonic Acid*, $C_{11}H_{14}O_9$. **Cincho·nicine, Cincho·nidine**, two of the cinchona bases, isomeric with cinchonine. **Ci·nchonine**, *Chem.* an organic alkaloid, $C_{20}H_{24}N_2O$, with febrifuge qualities, commonly associated with quinine, in various cinchona barks. **Ci·nchonism**, the condition produced by the excessive use of quinine. **Ci·nchonize** *v.* to act upon with quinine.

Cinct (siŋkt), *ppl. a. rare.* ME. [ad. L. *cinctus*.] Girt, encircled. (Cf. *compact*.)

Cincture (si·ŋktiŭɹ), *sb.* 1587. [ad. L. *cinctura*.] 1. A girding, encompassing, or encircling; enclosure, girdle. 2. *concr.* That which encircles or encompasses 1667; in *Arch.* 'the ring, list, or fillet at the top or bottom of a column which divides the shaft from the capital and base' (Gwilt) 1696.

2. Her dress A vest with woollen c. tied WORDSW.

Cincture (si·ŋktiŭɹ), *v.* 1791. [f. prec.] To gird; to encompass, surround.

Cinder (si·ndəɹ), *sb.* [Erron. sp. of *sinder*, OE. *sinder* (*synder*) scoria, slag; cf. ON. *sindr*, etc. Not conn. etymologically w. F. *cendre*, L. *cinerem* ashes.] 1. Scoria, slag. (Usu. in *sing.*) Now *techn.* 2. The residue of a combustible substance, *esp.* coal, after it has ceased to flame, and so also, after it has ceased to burn 1530. b. *pl.* Vaguely used for: Residue of combustion, ashes. Also *fig.* ME. 3. *slang.* Brandy, whisky, etc., taken in tea, or other drink 1873.

1. Smith's cinders 1646. The volcano ejected cinders GOLDSM. 2. A red-hot c. (*mod.*). Sifting cinders STEELE. b. *Tit. A.* II. iv. 37.

Comb.: **c.-bed**, a stratum of cinders; in *Geol.* a stratum in the Middle Purbeck series, consisting chiefly of oyster-shells; **-notch**, the hole through which cinder is tapped from a furnace; **-path**, a running-path laid with cinders.

Hence **Ci·nderous** *a.* (*rare*). **Ci·ndery** *a.* of the nature of a c.; full of cinders.

Cinder (si·ndəɹ), *v.* ME. [f. prec.] To reduce to cinders. Also *fig.*

Cinderella (sindərelă). Name of the heroine of a familiar fairy-story; *allus.* a drudge; a despised partner, etc. Also short for *c. dance*, a dance stopping at midnight.

Cine- (si·nĭ), abbrev. of next in comb. 1897.

Cinema (si·nĭmă). 1910. [ad. F. *cinéma*, abbrev. of *cinématographe*, f. Gr. κίνημα movement: see -GRAPH.] Short for **Cinematograph** (sinĭmæ·tŏgraf) 1896. A device by which a series of instantaneous photographs of moving objects is projected on a screen so as to produce the effect of a single motion scene; also, short for *cinema hall, theatre*. So **Ci:nemato·grapher**, one who takes **Ci:nematogra·phic** pictures, or practises **Cinemato·graphy** 1897.

Cinenchym(a (sine·ŋkim(ă). 1835. [f. Gr. κινεῖν + ἔγχυμα.] *Bot.* Laticiferous tissue.

‖**Cineraria** (sinĕrē·riă). Pl. **-as.** 1597. [mod. L., fem. of L. *cinerarius*, f. *ciner- cinis* ash. So named from the ash-coloured down on the leaves.] *Bot.* A genus of composite plants, natives of S. Africa, with bright-coloured flowers.

‖**Cinerarium** (sinĕrē·riŏm). 1880. [L.; cf. next.] A place for depositing the ashes of the dead after cremation.

Cinerary (si·nĕrări), *a.* 1750. [ad. L. *cinerarius*.] Of or pertaining to ashes.

C. urn, vase: a sepulchral urn used in ancient times to preserve the ashes of the dead after cremation.

Cinereous (sinīº·rĭəs), *a.* 1661. [f. L. *cinereus* + -OUS.] Of the nature of ashes; ash-coloured, as *c. crow.*

Cineritious (sinĕri·ʃəs), *a.* 1686. [f. L. *cineritius* + -OUS.] **1.** Ash-coloured, ashen-gray, as the 'gray or c. matter' of the brain. **2.** Of the nature of ashes or cinders 1732.

Cingalese (siŋgălī·z). 1613. [f. Skr. *Sinhalam* Ceylon.] *adj.* Of Ceylon. *sb.* A native of Ceylon; the language of Ceylon.

Cingle (siŋ·g'l). ME. [a. OF. *cengle*:—L. *cingulum*.] A girdle; a girth, a belt. Hence †**Cingling** *vbl. sb.* (*rare*).

‖**Cingulum** (si·ŋgiulŏm). 1847. L.; ='girdle, belt', occas. used techn. for **a.** The girdle of a priest's alb. **b.** A surgical cincture; also, the waist. **c.** A band surrounding the base of the crown of the tooth. **d.** The *clitellum* of earthworms.

†‖**Ciniphes**, *sb. pl.* 1571. [repr. Gr. σκνῖφες of the LXX.] The insects which constituted the third plague of Egypt (*Exod.* viii. 17); ? gnats, lice, fleas -1662.

Cinnabar (si·năbaɹ). ME. [ad. L. *cinnabaris* (also used), Gr. κιννάβαρι, a wd. of oriental origin; cf. Pers. *zanjifrah*.] **1.** The red or crystalline form of mercuric sulphide (Hg″S). Originally applied to native cinnabar, a rhombohedral mineral, the most important ore of mercury 1599. **2.** The same used as a pigment; VERMILION ME. †**3.** DRAGON'S-BLOOD, q. v. -1607. **4.** *attrib.* Vermilion-coloured 1807.

1. *Hepatic c.*: a variety of native c. of a liver-brown colour. Hence **Cinnaba·ric**, **Ci·nnabarine** *adjs.* consisting of, containing, or pertaining to, c.

Ci·nnamate. [f. L. *cinnamum* + -ATE.] A salt of cinnamic acid. So **Cinna·mein** = benzyl-cinnamate $C_9H_7O_2.C_7H_7$. **Ci·nnamene**, an aromatic hydro-carbon C_8H_8, or C_6H_5—C_2H_3; also called **Cinnamol** and *Styrol*. **Cinna·mic** *a.* of or pertaining to cinnamon, as in *Cinnamic acid* $C_9H_8O_2$, or C_6H_5—$C_3H_2O.OH$. **Ci·nnamyl**, the aromatic monatomic radical, C_9H_7O', of cinnamic acid, etc.

Cinnamo·mic, *a.* 1837. [f. L. *cinnamomum* (see next) + -IC.] Of cinnamon; in *Chem.* = *Cinnamic*. var. **Cinnamo·nic** *a.*

Cinnamon (si·nămən). ME. [a. F. *cinnamome*, ad. L. *cinnamomum*, a. Gr. κιννάμωμον; cf. also a later Gr. κίνναμον, whence L. *cinnamon, cinnamum*. The Gr. = Heb. *quinnāmōn*, cinnamon.] **1.** The inner bark of an E. Indian tree (*Cinnamomum zeylanicum*, N.O. *Lauraceæ*), dried in the sun, and used as a spice. It is yellowish-brown in colour, brittle, fragrant, and aromatic, and acts as a carminative and restorative. **2.** The tree itself ME. **3.** *attrib.* Cinnamon-coloured.

1. White C.: the inner bark of *Canella alba*; see CANELLA. **2. Wild C.**, *Canella alba* and *Myrcia acris*. *Comb.*: **c.-oil**, or *oil of c.*, a sweet aromatic yellow oil obtained from c.-bark, cassia-bark, etc., consisting chiefly of cinnamic aldehyde; **-stone**, a name for brown and yellow varieties of garnet.

†**Cinquanter.** 1611. [app. f. F. *cinquante*.] A man of fifty; an old stager -1675.

Cinque, cinq (siŋk). ME. [a. OF. *cink, cinc*, mod. *cinq*:—L. *quinque*.] **1.** The number five, as marked on dice; a throw which turns up five. **2.** *pl. Change-ringing.* A name for the changes on eleven bells 1872. Hence †**Ci·nquangle, cinkangle**, a pentagon; **cinquangled** *a.*

Comb. **c.-spotted** *a.* having five spots *Cymb.* II. ii. 38.

‖**Cinquecento** (tʃiŋkwe,tʃe·nto). 1760. [It. = five hundred.] The 16th century (15—), and that style of art which arose in Italy about 1500. Also *attrib.* Hence **Cinquece·ntist**, an artist or writer of that period.

Cinquefoil, cinqfoil (si·ŋkfoil). ME. [f. OF. type **cinkfoil*, mod. *quintefeuille*, repr. L. *quinquefolium*.] **1.** The plant *Potentilla reptans* (N.O. *Rosaceæ*), with compound leaves each of five leaflets. Also used of other species, and of the genus. 1545. **2.** An ornamental design resembling the leaf of cinquefoil; in *Arch.* an ornament used in the Pointed style, inscribed in an arch or in a circular ring ME. As *adj.* = **Ci·nquefoiled** *a.* furnished with cinquefoils, cinquefoil-shaped.

1. *Marsh c.*: = *Comarum palustre*.

†**Cinquepace** (si·ŋkəpēⁱs). 1570. [= F. *cinq* + *pas*.] A lively dance, identified with the *galliard*; 'the steps were regulated by the number five' (Nares) -1647.

Cinque Ports. [In 13th c. *sink pors*, repr. OF. *cink porz*, L. *quinque portus*.] A group of English sea-ports (orig. five, viz. Hastings, Sandwich, Dover, Romney, Hithe, and later also Rye and Winchelsea with the privileges of ports), which in ancient times furnished the chief part of the navy, and in return had many important privileges and franchises. **b.** = 'Barons of the Cinque Ports' SHAKS. Also *attrib.*

Cintre (si·ntəɹ). *rare.* ME. [a. F. *cintre*, ? f. *cincturare* (Diez).] *Arch.* The centre or centering of a bridge or arch.

‖**Cion** (səi·ən). 1811. [Gr. κίων.] **a.** The uvula. **b.** The septum between the nostrils. Hence **Cio·notome**, an instrument for excision of the uvula. **Ciono·tomy.**

Cion, obs. f. SCION.

Cipher, cypher (səi·fəɹ). ME. [a. OF. *cyfre, cyffre* (mod. *chiffre*), med.L. *cifra, ciphra*, f. Arab. *çifr* 'zero' or 'nought', f. *çafara* to be empty.] **1.** An arithmetical symbol (0) of no value by itself, but which when placed after a figure or figures in whole numbers increases their value tenfold. **2.** *fig.* He who or that which fills a place but is of no importance, a nonentity 1579. **3.** A figure or number 1530. †**4.** *gen.* A symbolic character -1614. **5.** A secret manner of writing by any of various methods intelligible only to those possessing the key. Also anything written in cipher, and the key to such a system. 1528. Also *fig.* **6.** An intertexture of letters, *esp.* the initials of a name; a literal device, monogram 1631. **7.** The continuous sounding of any note upon an organ, owing to the imperfect closing of the valve 1779. Also *attrib.*

1. You are..like cyphers, which supply a place but signifie nothing 1593. **2.** The Raja was a cypher: the Dewan usurped the whole power H. H. WILSON. **5.** Cypher letter .. which I cannot decypher, for Colonel Stewart took the cypher with him GORDON. *Comb.* **c.-key**, the key to writings in c.

Cipher (səi·fəɹ), *v.* 1530. [f. prec. sb.] **1.** *intr.* To use the Arabic numerals in the processes of arithmetic; to work the elementary rules of arithmetic; to think *out* (*U. S. colloq.*) 1837. **2.** To express by (occult) characters 1563. †**3.** *gen.* To express, delineate. Const. *forth, out.* -1640. †**4.** To decipher SHAKS. †**5.** To express by a monogram, etc. -1688. **6.** *intr.* Of an organ: To sound any note continuously without pressure on the corresponding key 1779. **7.** *Naval Arch.* To bevel *away* 1674.

1. To read, write, and c. M. PATTISON. **2.** His notes he cyphered with greeke characters 1630. **3.** To c. me how fondlie I did dote SHAKS. Hence **Ci·pherable** *a.* **Ci·phered** *ppl. a.* (senses 2, 7). **Ci·pherer.**

Cipolin (si·pŏlin). Occas. **cipollino** (tʃipolli·no). 1798. [a. F., ad. It. *cipollino*, dim. of *cipolla* onion; so called from its foliated structure like the coats of an onion.] An Italian marble interfoliated with veins of talc, mica, quartz, etc., showing alternations of (*esp.* white and green) colourings.

‖**Cippus** (si·pŏs). 1621. [L.] **1.** [as in late L.] The stocks. **2.** *Arch.* A small low column, sometimes without a base or capital, and usually bearing an inscription, used by the ancients as a landmark, a sepulchral monument, etc. 1708.

Circ, var. of CIRQUE.

Circa (sɔ̄·ɹkă), L. *prep.* and *adv.* Around, round about, about, as *circa* 1400 (*c* 1400), *circa-continental* adj., etc.

‖**Circar** (sɔ̄·ɹkāɹ). 1782. [Corrupt f. Pers. *sarkār* 'administrator, province'.] A province or division of Hindustan under the Moguls. See also SIRKAR.

‖**Circa·ssian.** 1853. [A gentile name, from Circassia.] A thin worsted fabric.

Circe (sɔ̄·ɹsĭ). ME. [L.; Gr. Κίρκη.] **1.** *Mythol.* The name of an enchantress who dwelt in the island of Æa, and transformed all who drank of her cup into swine; often used allusively. **2.** *Astr.* One of the asteroids 1855.

1. *Com. Err.* v. i. 270. Hence **Circe·an** *a.*

Circensian (səɹse·nsiăn), *a.* 1598. [f. L. *circensis* (*ludi circenses*, the games in the Circus Maximus at Rome).] Of, pertaining to, or celebrated in the Roman Circus (see CIRCUS). var. †**Circe·nsial.** SIR T. BROWNE.

Circinal (sɔ̄·ɹsinăl), *a.* *rare.* [mod. f. L. *circinus*, a. Gr. κίρκινος a circle + -AL.] *Bot.* = CIRCINATE.

Circinate (sɔ̄·ɹsinĕt), *a.* 1830. [a. L. *circinat-us*, *circinare* to make round, f. *circinus*.] *Bot.* Rounded, made circular; spec. of that mode of vernation in which the leaf is rolled up on its axis from the apex to the base, as in ferns.

Circination (sɔ̄ɹsinē·ʃən). 1592. [a. L. *circinationem*.] †**1.** *gen.* A circling or turning round -1681. Also †*concr.* **2.** *Bot.* Circinate vernation 1857.

1. *concr.* The circinations and sphærical rounds of Onyons SIR T. BROWNE.

‖**Circinus** (sɔ̄·ɹsinŏs). 1837. [L.] *Astr.* The Compasses, a southern constellation.

Circle (sɔ̄·ɹk'l), *sb.* [In OE. *circul*, a. L. *circulus*; in ME. *cercle*, a. F. :—L. *circulus*, dim. of *circus*. Refash. after L.]

I. A figure or appearance. **1.** A perfectly round plane figure. In *Geom.* a plane figure bounded by a single line, called the circumference, which is everywhere equidistant from a point within it called the centre. Also, the circumference alone. Often used vaguely. ME. **2.** *Astr.* (See quots.) OE. **3.** *formerly*, The sphere or heaven in which a heavenly body was supposed to revolve; *now*, The orbit of a planet or other body ME. **4.** The orb of a heavenly body (?) 1667. **5.** A luminous ring in the sky, a halo OE.

1. *To square the c.*: see SQUARE. Fairie circles 1596. Love..in the c. of his arms Enwound us both TENNYSON. **2.** *C. of altitude*: a small c. parallel to the horizon, having its pole in the zenith; an almacantar. *C. of curvature*: see CURVATURE. *C. of declination*: a great c. passing through the poles of the celestial equator. *C. of latitude*: a great c. perpendicular to the plane of the ecliptic; also used = *parallel of latitude*. *C. of longitude*: a small c. parallel to the ecliptic. *C. of perpetual apparition*: that c. around the elevated celestial pole at any place, within which the stars never set. *C. of perpetual occultation*: that c. around the depressed pole, within which the stars never rise. *C. of position*: see POSITION. *Diurnal c.*: the c. described by a heavenly body in its apparent diurnal rotation round the earth. *Great c.* (*of a sphere*): a c. on the surface of a sphere, whose plane passes through the centre; if not through the centre, the c. is a *small c.* *Horary circles*: the lines marking the hours on a sun-dial. *Vertical c.*: a great c. perpendicular to the horizon. **3.** Hee thought the Sunne, would soner have fallen from his c. 1568.

II. 1. Any material object that is circular, as a ring, crown, coronet ME.; one of the tiers of seats in a theatre 1623. **2.** *Archæol.* A series of stones set up in a ring, as at Stonehenge, etc. 1772. **3.** *Astr.* An instrument of observation, the graduated limb of which consists of an entire circle, as *mural, reflecting, repeating, transit c.* (see MURAL, etc.).

1. *Dress c.*: the lowest gallery in a theatre; *upper* or *family c.*: that above.

III. Transf. and fig. **1.** The circuit or compass

of a place ME. 2. A cycle, period; 'any series ending as it begins, and perpetually repeated' (J.) ME. 3. A completed series of parts forming a system 1531. 4. *Logic*. A fallacious mode of reasoning, wherein a premiss is used to prove a conclusion, and the conclusion is used to prove the premiss. Hence *to reason* or *argue in a c.* 1646. 5. A group of persons surrounding a centre of interest 1714. 6. A set or coterie; a class or division of society 1646. 7. A territorial division; *esp.* in Germany under the Holy Roman Empire 1675. 8. The area over which anything exerts influence 1664.

1. Within the cercle of the Cité ME. 2. The Wheele is come full c. *Lear* v. iii. 174. 3. Orr's C. of Sciences (*title*) 1854. 5. A c. of lookers on JOWETT. 6. Political, social, and literary circles 1885. 8. Within the c. of possibilities POWER.

Phr. †*To give the lie in c.*: i.e. circuitously, indirectly B. JONS.

Circle (sɔ̄·ɹk'l), *v.* ME. [f. the sb.; or a. F. *cercler*.] 1. = ENCIRCLE 1. (Now *poet.*) 2. To move round 1583. 3. *intr.* To move in a circle (*round, about*, etc.) ME. 4. *intr.* To stand or extend in a circle (*rare*) 1613.

1. Th' Imperiall mettall, circling now thy head SHAKS. 2. Other planets c. other suns POPE. 3. While the bowl circles POPE. Hence **Ci·rcled** *ppl. a.* surrounded with, or as with, a circle; marked with a circle or circles; circular. **Ci·rcler**, one who encircles; one who or that which moves in a circle; cyclic poet (as tr. L. *scriptor cyclicus*) B. JONS.

Circlet (sɔ̄·ɹklėt). 1481. [a. F. *cerclet*, dim. of *cercle*.] 1. A small CIRCLE (in various senses) 1528. 2. A ring or band (*e. g.* of gold or jewels) worn as an ornament, *esp.* on the head 1481. Also *gen.* †3. A round piece of wood, etc., put under a dish at table –1878.

1. Sure pledge of day, that crownst the smiling Morn With thy bright C. MILT. 2. A plain c. of gold was the substitute for the crown STUBBS.

Ci·rcle-wise, *adv.* 1542. [See -WISE.] In the form of a circle.

Circocele, var. of CIRSOCELE.

†**Ci·rcue**, *v.* 1450. [ad. F. *circuir*, ad. L. *circuire*; see next.] To go or travel round –1494.

Circuit (sɔ̄·ɹkit). ME. [a. F., ad. L. *circuitus*, f. *circu(m)ire*.] 1. The line described in going round any area; the distance round; the circumference. †*concr.* = CIRCLET. Shaks. 2. The space enclosed by a containing line; area, extent 1483. Also *fig.* 3. The action of going or moving round or about; a roundabout course; *fig.* revolution, round ME. 4. *spec.* The journey of judges (and others) through various places in succession, for the purpose of holding courts, etc. 1494; *concr.* those making the circuit; now *esp.* the barristers 1714. 5. The district through which the judge makes his circuit 1574. 6. A district of Methodist churches supplied by a series of itinerant preachers 1766. 7. *Electr.* The course traversed by an electric current between the two poles of a battery; the path of a voltaic current 1800. †8. Roundabout process or mode of speech or of reasoning –1836; *Law* = CIRCUITY –1751. 9. *Path.* The period of a disease.

1. Java..is nyghe 2000 Myle in circuyt MAUNDEV. 2. A great c. of ground in a very good soyle EARL ESSEX. 3. I devoted many hours..to the c. of Paris GIBBON. *fig.* The daies cercuit 1601. *To make a c.*: to make a detour. 8. To avoid c. of speech BACON.

Comb.: **c.-breaker**, an instrument which at regular intervals interrupts an electric current; **-court**, in Scotland, a court held periodically in the principal towns; in U.S. (*a*) Federal Courts intermediate in authority between the District Courts and the Supreme Court; (*b*) various State Courts. Hence **Circuitee·r**, a judge or barrister on c.; *gen.* one who makes a c.; var. **Ci·rcuiter**. †**Circuitee·r** *v.* to go on c.

Circuit (sɔ̄·ɹkit), *v.* 1549. [f. prec. sb.] 1. To go or travel round. 2. *intr.* To go or move in a circuit 1611.

1. The Phenicians circuited the greatest part of the habitable world GALE.

Circuition (sɔɹkiṳ̆,i·ʃən). *arch.* 1533. [ad. L. *circuitionem*; see CIRCUIT.] A going round or about; *fig.* circumlocution.

‖**Circuitor** (sɔɹkiū̆·itɔɹ). 1811. [L.] One who goes his rounds, a travelling inspector, etc.

Circuitous (sɔɹkiū̆·itəs), *a.* 1664. [ad. late L. *circuitosus*, f. *circuitus* CIRCUIT.] Of the nature of a circuit, roundabout, indirect. Hence **Circu·itous-ly** *adv.*, **-ness**.

Circuity (sɔɹkiū̆·iti). 1542. [a. OF. *circuité*, f. L. *circuitus*; cf. *vacuité*, etc.] †1. Ambit –1580. 2. Circuitous quality or process 1626.

2. *C. of action* (Law): an action rightfully brought, but unnecessarily roundabout.

Circulable (sɔ̄·ɹkiŭlăb'l), *a.* 1793. [See CIRCULATE.] That can be circulated.

Circular (sɔ̄·ɹkiŭlăɹ). [ME. *circuler*, a. AF. = OF. *circulier*, var. of *cerclier*:—L. *circularis*, f. *circulus*. Refash. after L.]

A. *adj.* 1. Of the form of a circle; round in superficies ME. †2. *transf.* Perfect, full –1659. 3. Moving in or passing over a circle, as *c. tour* 1450. Also *fig.* 4. Of the nature of arguing in a circle 1646. 5. Circuitous 1617. †6. = CYCLIC (*rare*). J. DENNIS. 7. Affecting or relating to a number of persons 1659. 8. Of or pertaining to the circle or its properties 1599.

2. In this, sister, Your wisdom is not c. MASSINGER. 4. To praise the Work from the Vertue of the Worker, is a c. proof HOBBES. 7. *C. letter*, 'a letter addressed in identical terms to several persons'. *C. note* (*a*) = *Circular letter*; (*b*) a letter of credit addressed by a banker to several other bankers, in favour of a person named therein. 8. *C. arc, cubic*, etc. *C. line*, (*a*) one of such straight lines as are divided by means of an arc of a circle, as Sines, Tangents, etc.; (*b*) the imaginary straight line joining the centre of any circle to either of the two circular points, and forming a tangent to the circle. *C. points*, the two imaginary points at infinity through which all circles pass, also called *focoids*. *C. instruments*, instruments for measuring angles, graduated round the whole circumference of a circle, *i. e.* 360°. *C. number*, a number whose powers terminate in the same digit as the number itself. *C. sailing* (Naut.): navigation by the arc of a great circle (see CIRCLE *sb.*).

Hence **Ci·rcularism**, a theory that space is c. **Ci·rcularly** *adv.* **Ci·rcularness.** var. †**Ci·rculary** *a.*

B. *sb.* †1. A circular figure or space (*rare*) –1815. 2. Short for *circular letter* or *circular note*: now *esp.* a business notice, reproduced in large numbers for circulation 1818.

Circularity (sɔ̄ɹkiŭlæ·rĭti). 1582. [f. prec. + -ITY.] Circular quality, form, or position.

Circularize (sɔ̄·ɹkiŭlărəiz), *v.* 1799. [f. CIRCULAR + -IZE.] 1. To make circular. 2. To send circulars to 1848.

Circulate (sɔ̄·ɹkiŭlėɪt), *v.* 1471. [f. L. *circulat-, circulare, circulari*, f. *circulus*.] †1. *Old Chem.* To subject to continuous distillation in a circulatory (see CIRCULATORY *sb.*) –1696. 2. *intr.* To move round, revolve; now round a circuit, circuitous course, system of pipes, etc. 1672. Also †*trans.* 3. *intr.* To pass from place to place, from hand to hand, or from mouth to mouth; to pass into the hands of readers, as a newspaper 1664. 4. *trans.* To put into circulation 1777. 5. *Math.* Of decimal fractions: To recur in periods of several figures 1768.

2. Blood is blood which circulates EMERSON. 3. Air EVELYN, money, trade LOCKE, circulates. 4. To c. a report SHERIDAN, the Bible 1815, the loving cup 1884. **Circulating library**, a library of which the books circulate among subscribers 1742.

Circulation (sɔɹkiŭlē·ʃən). 1535. [a. F., or ad. L. *circulationem*.] †1. Movement in a circle, or in a course or round which returns into itself –1795. †2. A continuous repetition of a series of actions, events, etc.; a round –1731; alternation –1647. †3. *Old Chem.* Continuous distillation in a CIRCULATORY –1641. 4. The circuit of the blood from the heart through the arteries and veins, and back to the heart; often called 'the c.' Hence, of sap through the vessels of plants 1656. 5. Transmission or passage from hand to hand, or from person to person; dissemination, publication 1684; the extent to which a newspaper, etc., is circulated 1847. †6. A statement circulated BURKE. 7. *concr.* A circulating medium, a currency 1790.

1. The waters of the earth are in a state of constant c. HUXLEY. 4. Stoppage of the C. ARBUTHNOT. 5. The free c. of information McCULLOCH. A limited c. DE QUINCEY. 7. A paper c. BURKE.

Circulative (sɔ̄·ɹkiŭlėɪtiv), *a.* 1635. [See -IVE.] Circulating; producing circulation.

Circulator (sɔ̄·ɹkiŭlėɪtəɹ). 1607. [a. L.] He who or that which circulates; *spec.* †a travelling mountebank –1659; †a traveller –1734; a scandal-monger, etc. 1792; a circulating decimal. Hence †**Circulato·rious** *a.* (*rare*).

†**Ci·rculatory**, *sb.* 1559. [ad. med.L. *circulatorium*.] An alembic or retort having the neck or necks bent back so as to re-enter the lower part of the retort, a 'pelican'; used in the old chemical process of distillation –1751.

Circulatory (sɔ̄·ɹkiŭlătəri), *a.* 1605. [ad. L. *circulatorius*.] 1. Of the nature of, or pertaining to, CIRCULATION (senses 3, 4). †2. Of or pertaining to a mountebank –1774. †3. *C. letter*: = Circular letter –1735.

†**Ci·rcule**, *v.* By-form of CIRCULATE, CIRCLE.

Circulet, obs. f. CIRCLET.

‖**Circulus** (sɔ̄·ɹkiŭlŏs). L. for 'circle, ring'; name for various instruments in Surgery, etc.; also, a tool for cutting circular portions of glass, also for cutting off the necks of glass-ware.

Circum- (sɔ̄ɹkŏm). 1. A Latin adv. and prep. meaning 'around, round about', much used in composition with vbs., and the sbs. and adjs. formed from them, such as:

†**Circumcu·rsation** [f. L. *circumcursare*], running round or about; rambling. **Circumdenuda·tion**, *Geol.* denudation all around. †**Circu·mflant** [L. *circumflantem*] *a.*, blowing around. †**Circumfu·lgent** [L. *circumfulgentem*] *a.*, shining around. **Circumu·ndulate** *v.*, to flow round in undulations; so **Ci·rcumundula·tion**. †**Circumve·ct** [f. L. *circumvehere*] *v.*, to carry about; so †**Circumve·ction**.

2. A rarer use, after L., in which *circum* (= around, surrounding) prepositionally governs a sb. implied in the second part of the compound, gives *circumpolar, circumlittoral*, etc.

†**Circuma·ction**. 1578. [ad. L. *circumactionem*.] Communication of circular motion –1667.

Circumadja·cent, *a.* 1762. [CIRCUM- 1.] Lying immediately around.

†**Circuma·gitate**, *v.* 1655. [f. CIRCUM- 1.] *trans.* To move round or about –1667. So †**Circumagita·tion**.

Circuma·mbages. *rare*. 1650. [f. CIRCUM- 1.] Roundabout methods or modes of speech.

Circumambient (sɔɹkŏm,æ·mbiĕnt), *a.* 1641. [f. CIRCUM- + AMBIENT.] Going or extending round; encompassing, environing, as *c. gloom, air*, etc. Also *fig.* and *absol.* Hence **Circuma·mbience**, the act or fact of going round or surrounding. **Circuma·mbiency** = prec.; also, c. quality or condition; environment.

Circumambulate (sɔɹkŏm,æ·mbiŭlėɪt), *v.* 1656. [f. L. *circumambulare*.] To walk round about. Also *intr. fig.* To beat about the bush. 1837. Hence **Ci·rcumambula·tion**. **Circuma·mbulator**.

Circumbendibus (sɔɹkŏmbe·ndibŏs). 1681. [Joc. f. CIRCUM + BEND, as a L. ablative pl.] A roundabout process or method; a twist; circumlocution.

Circumcellion (sɔɹkŏmse·liən). 1564. [ad. L. *circumcelliones*, f. *circum* + *cella*.] 1. *pl. Eccl. Hist.* Donatist fanatics in Africa in the 4th c., who used to rove from house to house. b. Vagabond monks. †2. *transf.* A vagrant –1631.

Circumcise (sɔ̄·ɹkŏmsəiz), *v.* ME. [ad. OF. *circonciser, -cisier*:—L. *circumcidere* to cut round.] 1. To cut off the foreskin or prepuce of (males), or the internal labia of (females). *fig.* To purify spiritually ME. †2. To cut round –1672; *fig.* to cut short; to cut off –1672. var. †**Circumcide** *v.* Hence **Ci·rcumcised** *ppl. a.* (Allusively used for 'Jewish' or 'Mohammedan'.) **Ci·rcumciser**.

Circumcision (sɔɹkŏmsi·ʒən). ME. [a. OF. *circumcisiun* (mod. *circoncision*), ad. L. *circumcisionem*.] 1. The action of circumcising; practised as a religious rite by Jews and Mohammedans; also as a surgical operation. *fig.* Spiritual purification. 2. *transf.* The circumcised people, the Jews; *fig.* 'the Israel of God' ME. 3. *Eccl.* The festival of the Circumcision of Christ, observed on the 1st of January ME. †4. Cutting round –1761.

Circumclu·de, *v. rare*. 1677. [ad. L. *circumcludere*.] To shut in on all sides. So **Circumclu·sion**.

†**Ci·rcumdate**, *v.* 1578. [f. L. *circumdare*.] To surround –1657.

Circumduce (sɔɹkŏmdiū̆·s), *v.* 1578. [ad. L. *circumducere*.] †1. To carry or move round (an axis) –1657. 2. *Sc. Law.* To declare (the term) elapsed for leading a proof 1609.

Circumduct (sɔ̄ɹkɒ̆mdɒ̆·kt), *v.* 1599. [f. L. *circumduct-*; see prec.] 1. = CIRCUMDUCE 1. 2. *Law.* To cancel, annul 1726.

Circumduction (sɔ̄ɹkɒ̆mdɒ̆·kʃən). 1578. [ad. L. *circumductionem.*] 1. A leading round or about 1602. 2. *Phys.* The rotatory movement by which a limb is made to describe a cone having its apex at the joint 1578. 3. *Law.* Annulling; cancellation 1609.

†**Circumfe·r,** *v.* 1605. [ad. L. *circumferre.*] To carry or bear round –1648.

Circumference (sɔɹkɒ̆·mfĕrĕns), *sb.* ME. [ad. L. *circumferentia* (as tr. Gr. περιφέρεια).] 1. The line that forms the encompassing boundary, *esp.* of anything rounded in form; *spec.* in *Geom.* periphery. †2. The surface of anything circular or rounded –1794; the whole circle 1667. 3. *gen.* Compass, bound 1598. 4. Environment (*rare*) 1643. †5. A circuit –1700. Also *fig.*

2. MILT. *P. L.* I. 286. Hence **Circu·mference** *v.* to form the c. of (*rare*). So †**Circu·mferent** *a.* forming the c. of; travelling around. **Circu·mfere·ntial** *a.* of, pertaining to, or of the nature of the c.; †circuitous, indirect. **Circu·mfere·ntially** *adv.*

Circumferentor (sɔɹkɒ̆·mfĕrentəɹ). 1610. [f. *Circumferent*; see prec.] 1. *Surveying.* An instrument consisting of a flat brass bar with sights at the ends and a circular brass box in the middle, containing a magnetic needle, which plays over a graduated circle; the whole being supported on a tripod. (Now mostly superseded by a THEODOLITE.) 2. An instrument for measuring the circumference of a wheel; a tire-circle 1874.

Circumflect (sɔ̄ɹkɒ̆mfle·kt), *v.* 1643. [ad. L. *circumflectere.*] 1. *Gram.* To mark with a circumflex accent. 2. To bend round (Dicts.).

Circumflex (sɔ̄·ɹkɒ̆mfleks), *a.* and *sb.* 1577. [ad. L. *circumflexus*; see prec.; as applied to the accent, used as tr. Gr. περισπώμενος 'drawn around', in reference to its shape. The sb. partly repr. L. *circumflexus* sb.]

A. *adj.* 1. *Gram.* An accent-mark ^, ⌒, or ~, placed, originally in Greek, over long vowels having a particular accent (see ACCENT 1); and in Latin, etc. indicating a contraction, or a particular variety of long vowel. Occas. applied to the tone, quantity, or quality thus indicated. 2. Bent or bending round; †circuitous 1707. 3. *Anat.* Applied to structures of curved form, or which bend round others; as the *c. arteries* of the arm, thigh, and knee; the *c. nerve* of the arm; the *c. muscle* of the palate 1831.

B. *sb.* 1. *Gram.* A circumflex accent (sign); see A. 1. †2. Bending round, winding, curve –1773. 3. A curved line, (or {, bracketing two or more lines of writing. ? *Obs.* 1801.

Circumflex, *v.* 1565. [f. L. *circumflex-*, *circumflectere*; but in 2 from prec.] 1. *trans.* To bend or wind round 1644. Also †*intr.* 2. *trans.* To write or pronounce with a circumflex 1565. Hence **Circumfle·xion, -fle·ction.**

Circumfluence (sɔɹkɒ̆·mfluĕns). *rare.* 1881. [as if ad. L. **circumfluentia.*] A flowing round.

Circumfluent (sɔɹkɒ̆·mfluĕnt). 1577. [ad. L. *circumfluentem.*] Flowing round; ambient as a fluid.

Whose bounds the deep c. waves embrace POPE.

Circumfluous (sɔɹkɒ̆·mfluəs), *a.* 1615. [ad. L. *circumfluus* + -OUS.] 1. = CIRCUMFLUENT 1638. 2. Flowed round, surrounded by water.

Circumforaneous (sɔ̄ːɹkɒ̆mforēⁱ·niəs), *a.* Now *rare.* 1650. [f. L. *circumforaneus* (f. *circum* + *forum*) + -OUS.] Strolling from market to market; vagrant; quack.

The c. Emperick 1654. vars. †**Circumfora·neal,** †**-nean** *adjs.*

Circumfuse (sɔ̄ɹkɒ̆mfiū·z), *v.* 1596. [f. L. *circumfus-*, *circumfundere.*] 1. To pour or spread (a fluid) *around* or *about* (anything) 1648. 2. To surround *with* or *in*; to bathe.

2. A face, all circumfused with light B. JONS. Hence **Circumfu·sion.**

Circumfu·sile, *a. rare.* [f. as prec.] Poured or spread around. POPE.

Ci·rcumgesta·tion. ? *Obs.* 1564. [f. L. *circumgestare.*] A carrying about (ceremonially or in procession).

C. of the Eucharist to be adored JER. TAYLOR.

Circumgyrate (sɔ̄ɹkɒ̆mdʒəi·reⁱt), *v.* 1647. [f. CIRCUM + L. *gyrat-*, *gyrare.*] 1. *trans.* To cause to turn or wheel round. ? *Obs.* 2. *intr.* To turn or roll round; to travel round 1683. Hence **Ci·rcumgyra·tion,** the act of turning, rolling, or wheeling round; also *fig.* **Circumgy·ratory** *a.* marked by circumgyration. var. †**Circumgy·re** *v.*

Circumincession (sɔ̄·ɹkɒ̆m,inse·ʃən). 1644. [ad. med.L. *circumincessionem*, lit. 'going round'. Often altered to *circuminsession* 'an insitting reciprocally', the sense in which the term is used.] *Theol.* The reciprocal existence of the persons of the Trinity in one another.

Circumjacence (sɔ̄ɹkɒ̆mdʒēⁱ·sĕns). 1884. [See CIRCUMJACENT.] The fact or condition of being circumjacent.

Circumjacency (sɔ̄ɹkɒ̆mdʒēⁱ·sĕnsi). 1748. [See next.] The quality of being circumjacent; *concr.* (in *pl.*) circumjacent parts.

Circumjacent (sɔ̄ɹkɒ̆mdʒēⁱ·sĕnt), *a.* 1490. [ad. L. *circumjacentem*, *circumjacere.*] Lying around, adjacent on all sides.

Circumjovial (sɔ̄ɹkɒ̆mdʒōᵘ·viăl), *a.* (*sb.*) 1696. [f. CIRCUM- 2 + *Jovem*; cf. *jovial.*] *Astr.* Revolving round Jupiter. †*sb.* A satellite of Jupiter.

Circumli·ttoral, *a.* [f. CIRCUM- 2; cf. *littoral.*] Bordering the shore.

Circumlocution (sɔ̄·ɹkɒ̆mlokiū·ʃən). 1510. [ad. L. *circumlocutionem.*] Roundabout speaking; the use of several words instead of one, or many instead of few; a roundabout expression.

Circumloquution..as when we say: The Prince of Peripateticks, for Aristotle 1595. *C. Office*: a satirical name applied, by Dickens, to Government Offices, on account of the multiplication of formality in which they excel. Hence **Circumlocu·tional, -ary, -ory** *adjs.* pertaining to, given to, or marked by c.

Circum-meri·dian, *a.* 1852. [CIRCUM- 2.] *Astr.* Situated about or near the meridian.

Circummure (sɔ̄ɹkɒ̆mmiūᵊ·ɹ), *v.* 1603. [f. CIRCUM- + L. *murare.*] To wall round.

Circumna·vigable, *a.* 1691. [f. as next; see -ABLE.] That can be circumnavigated.

Circumnavigate (sɔ̄ɹkɒ̆mnæ·vigeⁱt), *v.* 1634. [f. L. *circumnavigare.*] To sail round.

With a design of circum-navigating the island COOK. Hence **Ci·rcumnaviga·tion. Circumna·vigator. Circumna·vigatory** *a.*

Circumnutate (sɔ̄ɹkɒ̆mniū·teⁱt), *v.* 1880. [CIRCUM- 1 + NUTATE.] *Bot.* To move in CIRCUMNUTATION.

Circumnutation (sɔ̄·ɹkɒ̆mniutēⁱ·ʃən). 1880. [f. as prec.] *Bot.* A movement of growing plants, in which the growing part (*e. g.* the apex of a stem) describes a sort of circular spiral path. So **Circumnu·tatory** *a.*

Circumo·ral, *a.* 1847. [f. CIRCUM- 2 + L. *os, or-.*] *Phys.* Situated round the mouth.

†**Circumple·ct,** *v.* 1578. [ad. L. *circumplectere.*] To clasp around. Also †**Circumple·x** *v.*, †**Circumple·xion.** –1660.

Circumpolar (sɔ̄ɹkɒ̆mpōᵘ·lăɹ), *a.* 1686. [f. CIRCUM- 2 + L. *polus*; cf. *polar.*] Round or about the pole; in *Astr.* applied to stars which describe the whole of their diurnal circles above the horizon.

Circumpose (sɔ̄ɹkɒ̆mpōᵘ·z), *v.* ? *Obs.* 1578. [repr. L. *circumponere*, after *compose*, etc.] To place around; †to place within any encircling space; to pot (a plant). So **Ci·rcumposi·tion.**

†‖**Circumqua·que.** 1556. [L.] A CIRCUMBENDIBUS, q. v. –1591.

Circumrotation (sɔ̄·ɹkɒ̆mrotēⁱ·ʃən). 1610. [f. L. *circumrotare.*] 1. Turning round as a wheel; revolution on an axis; a complete rotation 1656. †2. A changing about in rotation –1767. So **Circumro·tatory** *a.*

†**Circumsatu·rnian,** *a.* (*sb.*) 1664. [f. CIRCUM- + SATURN.] *Astr.* Round Saturn; a satellite of Saturn –1714.

Circumsciss (sɔ̄·ɹkɒ̆msis), *a.* 1870. [ad. L. *circumscissus*, *circumscindere.*] *Bot.* Opening by circumscissile dehiscence.

Circumscissile (sɔ̄ɹkɒ̆msi·sil), *a.* 1835. [f. as prec.] *Bot.* Dehiscing or opening by a transverse circular line, said of the seed-vessel (*pyxidium*).

Circumscribe (sɔ̄ɹkɒ̆mskrəi·b), *v.* 1529. [ad. L. *circumscribere.*] 1. To draw a line round; to encompass, bound; to encircle 1578. 2. To mark out the limits of; to confine (usually *fig.*); *esp.* to hem in, restrain, abridge 1529. 3. *Geom.* To describe (a figure) about another figure so as to touch it at certain points without cutting; also with the figure as subject of the verb 1570. †4. To write or inscribe around (*esp.* a coin, etc., *with* an inscription, or an inscription *on* or *about* a coin, etc.) –1692.

1. I was alone, circumscribed by the ocean DE FOE. 2. Therefore must his choyce be circumscrib'd *Haml.* I. iii. 22. Hence **Circumscri·bable** *a.* that may be circumscribed; var. †**Circumscri·ptible. Circumscri·ber,** one who or that which circumscribes; *esp.* one who signs a round robin. **Ci·rcumscript** *a.* circumscribed. (Now *rare.*) **Ci·rcumscri·ptly** *adv.* (*rare*).

Circumscription (sɔ̄ɹkɒ̆mskri·pʃən). 1531. [ad. L. *circumscriptionem*, f. as prec.] 1. The action of circumscribing or fact of being circumscribed; limitation, restriction; the having defined limits 1604. 2. *concr.* Boundary, outline, periphery 1578. 3. A material surrounding 1578. 4. A circumscribed space or place 1831. 5. *fig.* Definition 1531. 6. *Geom.* The act of circumscribing one figure about another (see CIRCUMSCRIBE 3) 1570. 7. An inscription around something, *e. g.* a coin, etc. 1569.

1. *Oth.* I. ii. 27. 4. The diocese or ecclesiastical c. MORLEY. 5. Drunkennesse..hath its c. 1654.

Circumscriptive (sɔ̄ɹkɒ̆mskri·ptiv), *a.* 1565. [f. L. *circumscript-*, *-scribere.*] Pertaining to, or having the attribute of, limitation in space. Hence **Circumscri·ptively** *adv.* with limitation in space. ? *Obs.*

†**Circumscrive,** *v.* = CIRCUMSCRIBE.

Circumsession (sɔ̄ɹkɒ̆mse·ʃən). ? *Obs. rare.* 1652. [ad. L. *circumcessionem.*] 1. Besetting. 2. *Theol.* Erron. for CIRCUMINCESSION.

Circumso·lar, *a.* 1846. [f. CIRCUM- 2 + L. *sol.*] Revolving round, or situated about, the sun.

Circumspect (sɔ̄·ɹkɒ̆mspekt), *a.* ME. [ad. L. *circumspectus*, *-spicere.*] 1. Marked by circumspection, well-considered, cautious. 2. Attentive to all circumstances that may affect action or decision, cautious 1430.

1. C. Remedy 1562. 2. High-reaching Buckingham growes c. *Rich. III*, IV. ii. 31. Hence **Circumspe·ction,** vigilant and cautious observation of circumstances or events; circumspect action or conduct; caution, circumspectness. So **Circumspe·ctive** *a.* scanning on all sides; given to circumspection. **Circumspe·ctively, Ci·rcumspectly** *advs.* **Ci·rcumspectness,** the quality of being c.

Circumstance (sɔ̄·ɹkɒ̆mstăns), *sb.* ME. [a. OF. *circum-*, *circonstance*, ad. L. *circumstantia*, f. *circumstantem.* Orig. a sb. of action or condition, not taking *a* or *pl.*]

I. †1. That which stands around or surrounds; surroundings –1562. 2. *pl.* The adjuncts of an action or fact; in *sing.* any one of these ME. 3. The state of (*esp.* pecuniary) affairs surrounding and affecting an agent ME. (Mere situation is expressed by '*in* the circumstances', action takes place '*under* the circumstances'.)

2. Neither in time, manner, or other c. *Meas. for M.* IV. ii. 109. 3. The web of c. 1887. Easy in their circumstances ADDISON.

II. Words or ado made *about* anything; circumlocution; ceremony ME.

Pompe and C. of glorious warre *Oth.* III. iii. 354.

III. 1. That which is non-essential, accessary, or subordinate; a detail, a particular ME. 2. An incident; a matter or fact 1586.

1. Tell us the sum, the c. defer MILT. *Sams.* 1557.

Circumstance (sɔ̄·ɹkɒ̆mstăns), *v.* ME. [f. prec.] †1. To condition –1736. 2. To place in particular circumstances or relations. Chiefly in pa. pple. 1644. †3. To supply with attendant circumstances –1774.

3. The Poet took the matters of Fact as they came down to him, and circumstanced them after his own manner ADDISON. Hence **Ci·rcumstanced** *ppl. a.* placed in certain circumstances or relations; †subject to circumstances *Oth.* III. iv. 201; circumstantiated.

†**Ci·rcumstant.** 1494. [ad. L. *circumstantem.*] *adj.* Standing around, circumjacent –1666; incidental –1656. *sb. pl.* Bystanders –1675.

The c. cold ayre 1545, causes 1656.

Circumstantial (sɔ̄ɹkɒ̆mstæ·nʃăl). 1600. [f. L. *circumstantia* + -AL.] A. *adj.* 1. Of, relating to, or dependent on circumstances; *esp.* adventitious, accidental 1608. 2. Full of circumstances, details, or minutiæ, particular 1611.

1. *C. evidence*: indirect evidence founded on cir-

cumstances which limit the number of admissible hypotheses. *The lie c.* (Shaks.); a contradiction given indirectly by circumstances. The c. part and pomp of life POPE. C. prosperity COLERIDGE. **2.** C. detail H. WALPOLE.

B. *sb.* (*pl.*) Circumstantial matters; particulars; non-essentials 1647.

Ye fools and blind! to fix your whole attention on the circumstantials of religion WESLEY.

Hence **Ci·rcumstantia·lity**, c. quality, particularity; a detail. **Circumsta·ntially** *adv.* in a c. manner; incidentally; in every particular, minutely. †**Circumsta·ntialness**, circumstantiality.

Circumstantiate (sɔ̄ɹkʊ̆mstæ·nʃieᶦt), *v.* 1638. [f. L. type **circumstantiare.*] †**1.** 'To place in particular circumstances' (J.), to define or limit by imposed conditions –1711. **2.** To set forth, or support, with circumstances 1658.

1. A Committee to consider how that title [Lord Protector] may be bounded, limited, and circumstantiated 1657. **2.** To c. false historical records DE QUINCEY. Hence **Circumstantia·tion**, circumstantiating. **Circumsta·ntiator.**

†**Circumterra·neous**, *a.* 1678. [f. CIRCUM- 2 + L. *terra.*] Situated, dwelling, etc., round the earth, as *c. demons.* So †**Circumterre·strial** *a.*

Circumvallate (sɔ̄ɹkʊ̆mvæ·lėt), *a.* 1661. [ad. L. *circumvallatus*; see next.] Surrounded as with a rampart or trench.

Circumvallate (sɔ̄ɹkʊ̆mvæ·leᶦt), *v.* 1823. [f. L. *circumvallare*, f. CIRCUM- + *vallum.*] To surround with or as with a rampart or trench.

Five circumvallating walls were not uncommon 1884.

Circumvallation (sɔ̄ːɹkʊ̆mvæ̆lēᶦ·ʃən). 1641. [f. prec.] **1.** The making of a rampart, etc. round a place. **2.** A rampart or entrenchment constructed round any place by way of investment or defence 1645. Also *transf.* and *fig.*

1. At night we rode about the lines of c. EVELYN.

Circumvent (sɔ̄ɹkʊ̆mve·nt), *v.* 1553. [f. L. *circumvent-*, *-venire.*] **1.** To surround by hostile stratagem. **2.** To encompass with evils, or malice; to try to entrap in conduct or speech 1581. **3.** To get the better of by craft or fraud; to overreach 1564. Also *absol.* **4.** To encompass (*literally*) 1824. **5.** To go round 1840.

3. Should Man..Fall circumvented thus by fraud MILT. *P. L.* III. 152. Hence **Circumve·ntor, -er,** one who circumvents; also = CIRCUMFERENTOR. var. **Circumve·ne.** (Chiefly *Sc.*)

Circumvention (sɔ̄ɹkʊ̆mve·nʃən). 1534. [ad. L. *circumventionem*; see prec.] The action of circumventing; overreaching. ¶ *ellipt.* = the *means of* circumvention *Cor.* I. ii. 16.

The..circumuention of the false wilye diuel MORE.

†**Circumve·st**, *v.* 1599. [ad. L. *circumvestire.*] To enwrap as with a garment –1657.

†**Circumvoisin**, *a.* 1548. [a. F. *circonvoisin.*] Neighbouring on all sides –1641.

Circu·mvolant, *a.* 1623. [ad. L. *circumvolantem.*] Flying around. So **Circumvola·tion.**

Circumvolute (sɔɹkʊ̆·mvolᶦūt), *v.* 1599. [f. L. *circumvolut-*, *-volvere.*] **1.** *trans.* To roll round. Also *fig.* **2.** To enwrap by twisting or winding something round 1599.

Circumvolution (sɔ̄ːɹkʊ̆mvolᶦū·ʃən). 1447. [f. as prec.] **1.** Rolling round an axis or centre; revolution; a revolution. Also *fig.* **2.** The rolling of a thing round something else; a fold or turn 1599. **3.** A winding or moving in a sinuous course; *concr.* a sinuosity 1633. Also *fig.*

1. To behold the c. of the stars HEALEY. **3.** Neither time nor temper for sentimental circumvolutions DISRAELI. The circumuolutions..in the brayne 1578.

Circumvolve (sɔ̄ɹkʊ̆mvǫ·lv), *v.* Now *rare.* 1599. [ad. L. *circumvolvere* (trans.).] **1.** *trans.* To turn, move, or roll round 1647; to move round in a circular path (*rare*) 1610. Also *intr.* †**2.** To wind, fold, or twist round –1704. Also *fig.*

Circus (sɔ̄·ɹkʊ̆s). 1546. [L., a. Gr. κίρκος, κρίκος.] **1.** *Rom. Antiq.* A large building, generally oblong or oval, surrounded with rising tiers of seats, for the exhibition of public spectacles, races, and the like. **2.** *Mod.* A circular arena surrounded by tiers of seats, for the exhibition of equestrian, acrobatic, and other performances. Also, the troupe of performers and their equipage. 1791. **3.** A natural amphitheatre; a rounded hollow or plain encircled by heights 1836. †**4.** A circle or ring –1748. **5.** *vaguely.* Compass (*rare*) 1817. **6.** A circular range of houses. Often in proper names as *Oxford C.*, etc. 1771. Also *attrib.*

5. The narrow c. of my dungeon wall BYRON.

‖**Cire perdue** (sīr pęrdü). 1876. [Fr. 'lost wax'.] A method of casting bronze in which the wax covering the model is melted out.

Cirl (sɔ̄ɹl), in **Cirl bunting.** 1783. [It. *cirlo*, prob. f. *zirlare* to whistle as a thrush.] A species of Bunting, *Emberiza Cirlus.*

Cirque (sɔ̄ɹk). 1601. [a. F.] = CIRCUS 1–4.

The grassy c. SHENSTONE. A dismal c. Of Druid stones, upon a forlorn moor KEATS. *Comb.* **c.-couchant**, lying coiled up in circles KEATS.

Cirrated (si·reᶦtėd), *a. rare.* 1854. [f. L. *cirratus* (f. *cirrus*) + -ED.] Fringed with cirri.

Cirrh-, bad spelling of *cirr-*, in CIRRUS and its derivs., as if a. (non-existent) Gr. κιρρός = *cirrhus*; for other words see below.

Cirrhopod (si·ropǫd). 1843. [ad. mod.F. *cirrhopode*, mod.L. pl. *Cirrhopoda* (see CIRRH-).] *Zool.* = CIRRIPED.

Cirrhosis (sirōᵘ·sis). Occas. **cirrho·se.** 1839. [mod.L., f. Gr. κιρρός orange-tawny, referring to the presence of *yellowish* granules; cf. F. *cirrhose.*] *Path.* A disease of the liver, consisting in chronic interstitial hepatitis, with atrophy of the cells and increase of connective tissue. Subseq. extended to similar conditions of the kidneys, lungs, etc. Hence **Cirrho·sed**, **Cirrho·tic** *adjs.* affected with c.

Cirriferous (siri·fĕrəs), *a.* Erron. **cirrh-.** 1819. [f. L. *cirrus* + *ferus* + -OUS.] Cirrus-bearing.

Cirriform (si·rifǭɹm), *a.* 1815. [f. as prec.] *Meteor.* and *Zool.* Cirrus-shaped.

Cirrigerous (siri·dʒĕrəs), *a.* 1736. [f. as prec.] Bearing cirri.

Cirrigrade (si·rigreᶦd), *a.* 1837. [ad. mod. L. *cirrigradus*, f. as prec. + *-gradus* going.] *Zool.* Moving by means of cirri.

Cirriped, -pede (si·riped, -pīd). Erron. **cirrhi-.** 1828. [a. mod.F. *cirripède*, f. mod.L. pl. *cirripeda*, *-pedia* (also used), f. *cirrus* + *pes*, *ped-*. See CIRRHOPOD.] *Zool.* A member of the *Cirripedia* or *Cirripeda*, a class of marine animals of the sub-kingdom Annulosa, closely related to the Crustacea; including the barnacles and acorn-shells. The legs can be protruded like a curled lock of hair from between the valves of the shell; hence the name.

Cirro- (si·ro), comb. f. CIRRUS, as in:

Ci·rrostome *a.*, having the mouth cirrose or bearded; also *subst.* **Cirro-cu·mulus**, *Meteor.* a form of cloud combining the shapes of the cirrus and cumulus, and consisting mainly of a series of roundish and fleecy cloudlets in contact; hence **-cumular, -cumulated, -cumulative, -cumulous** *adjs.* **Cirro-stra·tus**, a form of cloud combining the shapes of the cirrus and stratus, consisting of horizontal or inclined sheets attenuated upwards into light cirri; hence **-strative, -stratous** *adjs.*

Cirrose (sirōᵘ·s), *a.* Erron. **cirrh-.** 1814. [f. L. *cirrus.*] **1.** *Bot.* and *Zool.* Bearing a cirrus or cirri 1819. **2.** *Meteor.* Of the nature of cirrus-clouds.

Cirrous (si·rəs), *a.* Erron. **cirrh-.** 1658. [f. as prec.] **1.** *Bot.* and *Zool.* Of the nature of a cirrus or cirri; bearing cirri. **2.** Of or pertaining to cirrus-clouds 1815.

‖**Cirrus** (si·rʊ̆s). Erron. **cirrh-.** 1708. [L.] ‖**1.** *lit.* A curl-like tuft, fringe, or filament. **2.** *Bot.* A tendril 1708. **3.** *Zool.* A filamentary process or appendage, as the beard of some fishes, the feet of *Cirripedes*, etc. 1753. **4.** *Meteor.* A form of cloud, generally at a high elevation, presenting the appearance of diverging filaments or wisps, often resembling a curl or lock of hair or wool 1803. Also *attrib.*

Comb. **c.-bag**, 'the sheath containing the cirrus of trematode and other worms'.

Cirrus, ? misprint of CERUSE *sb.* BACON.

Cirsocele (sɔ̄·ɹsosīl). Erron. **circo-.** 1708. [ad. Gr., f. κιρσός enlargement of a vein + κήλη tumour.] *Path.* A varicose enlargement of the spermatic vein.

Cirsoid (sɔ̄·ɹsoid), *a.* 1860. [ad. Gr. κιρσοειδής; see prec.] *Path.* Varix-like, varicose.

Cirsotome (sɔ̄·ɹsotoᵘm). [f. Gr. κιρσός + -τομός, f. τέμνειν.] *Surg.* An instrument used for extirpating varix. So **Cirso·tomy.**

Cis-, prefix, repr. L. *cis* prep. 'on this side of'; opp. to *trans* or *ultra*, across, beyond; also used in comb. as in *cis-alpinus*, etc.

In mod. use, either as ad.L., as **Cis-alpine**, on this (the Roman) side of the Alps, *i. e.* south; **Cis-padane**, on this side the Po, etc., or formed on the adjs. belonging to modern names, as **Cis-atlantic**; **Cis-leithan**, on this side the Leitha which separates Austria and Hungary, etc. Also *transf.* to *time* = Since, as *cis-Elizabethan*, etc.

‖**Cisco** (si·sko). *U.S.* 1848. A fish of the herring kind which abounds in Lake Ontario.

Cismontane (sismǫ·ntēᶦn), *a.* 1792. [ad. L. *cismontanus.*] On this side of the mountains, *esp.* of the Alps: opp. to *ultramontane*; spec. of the Gallican Church movement. Also *sb. pl.*

Cissoid (si·soid). 1656. [ad. Gr. κισσοειδής ivy-like. The cusp of the c. resembles the re-entrant angles of an ivy-leaf.] *Math.* A curve of the second order invented by Diocles. Hence **Cissoi·dal** *a.* pertaining to a c.

Cissy (si·si). 1915. Variant of SISSY.

Cist (sist). Erron. **cyst.** 1804. [ad. L. *cista*, a. Gr. κίστη. In sense 1 from Welsh *cist*; see KISTVAEN.] **1.** *Archæol.* A sepulchral chest or chamber excavated in rock, etc.; *esp.* a stone-coffin formed of slabs placed on edge, and covered on the top by one or more horizontal slabs. **2.** *Gr. Antiq.* A small receptacle for sacred utensils carried in procession on the occasion of mystic festivals 1847. Hence **Ci·sted** *a.* containing a c. or cists. **Ci·stula**, a little c.

Cist, obs. f. CYST bladder, confused w. prec.

Cistaceous (sistēᶦ·ʃəs), *a.* [f. mod.L. *Cistaceæ*, f. CISTUS.] *Bot.* Of or pertaining to the genus *Cistus* or Rock Rose and its congeners, of the N.O. *Cistaceæ.* Hence **Ci·stal** *a.*

Cistercian (sistɔ̄·ɹʃian), *a.* 1602. [ad. L. type **Cistercianus*, f. *Cistertium*, now *Cîteaux*, the site of an abbey near Dijon.] Of or belonging to the monastic order founded at Cîteaux in 1098 by Robert, abbot of Molesme. It was an offshoot of the Benedictines. As *sb.* A monk of this order 1616.

Cistern (si·stəɹn). ME. [a. OF. *cisterne* :— L. *cisterna*, deriv. of *cista* box, basket, etc.; cf. *caverna.*] **1.** An artificial reservoir for water, or other liquid; *esp.* a water-tight tank. **2.** A natural reservoir or depression containing water, *e.g.* a pond 1606. **3.** Applied to a cavity, or vessel in an organism 1615. Also *fig.* and *attrib.*

1. Broken cisternes *Jer.* ii. 13. A copper c. for the table PEPYS *Diary* 7 Sept. 1667. A c. of punch 1815. **2.** Lakes..are real reservoirs, or cisterns of water 1796. Hence **Ci·stern** *v.* to enclose in, or fit with, a c.

Cistus (si·stʊ̆s). 1551. [mod.L., a. Gr. κίστος, κίσθος, prob. f. cistus.] *Bot.* A genus of shrubs (N.O. *Cistaceæ*) known as Rock Rose and Gum Cistus. *Ladanum* or *Labdanum* is obtained from several species, esp. *C. creticus* and *C. ladaniferus.*

Cistvaen; see KISTVAEN.

Cit (sit). *arch.* 1644. Short for *citizen*; usually applied, more or less contemptuously, to a townsman or to a shopkeeper.

The cits of London and the boors of Middlesex JOHNSON.

Ci·table, *a.* 1820. [f. CITE *v.*] That can be cited.

Citadel (si·tădĕl). 1586. [a. F. *citadelle*, ad. It. *cittadella*, dim. of *città*, *cittade* :—L. *civitatem.* Lit. little city.] **1.** The fortress commanding a city, which it serves both to protect and to dominate. (Used as tr. Gr. ἀκρόπολις and L. *arx.*) **2.** *gen.* A stronghold 1796. Also *transf.* and *fig.* **3.** The heavily plated erection containing the guns in an ironclad (*mod.*).

2. *fig.* Within these citadels of superstition SCOTT.

†**Cital** (səi·tăl). *rare.* 1596. [f. CITE *v.*] **1.** *Law.* Citation, summons 1760. **2.** *fig.* 'Impeachment' (Johnson); 'mention' (Schmidt). See 1 *Hen. IV*, v. ii. 62.

Citation (səitēᶦ·ʃən). ME. [a. F., ad. L. *citationem.*] **1.** *Law.* A citing to a court of justice, a summons; the form of summons, or the document containing it. †**2.** Recital (*rare*) 1666. **3.** The action of citing any words or written passage, quotation; in *Law*, a reference to cases or authorities 1651. **4.** *concr.* A quotation 1548.

1. Ecclesiastical causes commence by *c.* of the defendant COX.

Citatory (səi·tătəri), *a.* 1611. [ad. L. *citatorius*; see next.] Having the faculty of citing; concerned with citation; *esp.* in *Letters c.* vars. **Ci·tative** *a.* (*rare*), †**Citato·rial** *a.*

Cite (səit), *v.* 1483. [a. F. *citer*, ad. L. *citare*, freq. of *ciere* to set in motion, call.] 1. To summon officially to appear in court of (usu. eccles.) law. Also *fig.* 2. *gen.* To summon; arouse 1534. 3. To quote (a passage, book, or author) 1535. 4. To adduce by way of example, proof, precedent, etc. 1663. 5. To call to mind; mention; refer to *as*; †evidence 1588.

1. Fee but the Sumner, and he shall not c. thee 1616. 2. In a storm cited by the finger of God he died DE QUINCEY. 3. The diuell can c. Scripture for his purpose *Merch. V.* I. iii. 99. 5. We cited vp a thousand heauy times *Rich. III*, I. iv. 14. *All's Well* I. iii. 216. Hence **Citee·**, one who is cited (Dicts.). **Ci·ter.**

Citess. 1685. [f. CIT.] 1. A female cit. †2. A citizeness. (Used in U.S. as tr. F. *citoyenne.*)

‖**Cithara** (si·þără). 1789. [L., a. Gr. κιθάρα; cf. *cithern*, *guitar*, *zither*, etc.] *Mus.* An ancient instrument of triangular shape with from seven to eleven strings; a sort of lyre. Hence **Ci·tharist**, a player on the c. **Citharœ·dic** *a.* pertaining to a citharist or c. (*rare*).

Cither (si·þəɹ). 1606. [ad. L. *cithara.*] An anglicized form of CITHARA, applied also to the CITHERN, ZITHER, etc.

Cithern, cittern (si·þəɹn, si·təɹn). *arch.* 1566. [app. f. L. *cithara*, perh. after *gittern*, F. *guiterne.*] *Mus.* A sort of guitar, strung with wire, and played with a plectrum. (The ZITHER is the Tyrolese form of this.)

Comb. †**cittern-head**, a term of contempt, referring to the grotesquely carved head of a c. SHAKS.

Citicism; see CITYCISM.

Citied (si·tid), *a.* 1612. [f. CITY.] Made into or like a city; occupied by a city or cities. Kinsfolk on the c. earth KEATS.

Citigrade (si·tigreid), *a.* 1845. [f. L. *citus* + *gradus*; cf. F. *citigrade.*] *lit.* Moving swiftly; applied to a tribe of spiders, *Citigrada*, and *subst.* one of these.

Citizen (si·tizĕn). [ME. *citesein*, etc., a. Anglo-Fr. *citeseyn*, *-zein*, etc., altered form of OF. *citeain*, etc., later *citeyen*, *citoyen* :—L. type **civitatanum*, f. *civitatem.* The *z* is unexplained.] 1. An inhabitant of a city or (often) of a town; *esp.* a freeman of a city; a townsman 1514; a civilian 1607. 2. A member of a state, an enfranchised inhabitant of a country, as opp. to an alien; in U.S. a person, native or naturalized, who has the privilege of voting for public offices, and is entitled to protection in the exercise of private rights ME. 3. *transf.* Inhabitant, denizen ME. 4. *adj.* City-bred (*nonce-use*) *Cymb.* IV. ii. 8. Also *attrib.*, as *c.-king.*

1. I am a man..of Tarsus..a citeseyn or burgeys, of a citee not unknown WYCLIF *Acts* xxi. 39. Both citizens and peasants S. AUSTIN. 2. *Citizen of the World*: one who is at home, and claims his rights, everywhere. Hence **Ci·tizen** *v.* to address as 'citizen'. **Ci·tizeness**, a female c. **Ci·tizenhood**, the state of being a c.; the body of citizens. **Ci·tizenish** *a.* of the nature of or relating to citizens. **Ci·tizenism**, the principle of citizenship; CIVISM. **Ci·tizenize** *v.* †to make citizen-like; to make a c. **Ci·tizenry**, citizens collectively; *a citizenry*, a body of citizens. **Ci·tizenship**, the position or status of a c.

Citole. Now *Hist.* ME. [a. OF., app. a deriv. of L. *cithara*, with dim. ending. Orig. *ci·tole*, now *cito·le* after OF. or It.] *Mus.* A stringed instrument of 13–15th c.; perh. a special form of the *cithara*. Hence †**Citoler.**

Citr-, citro-, f. L. *citrus* citron, used as comb. f. *citric* and its derivs.; as **Citraco·nic** [see ACONIC] *a.*, in *Citraconic acid*, $C_5H_6O_4$, obtained in a crystalline form in the distillation of citric acid. Its salts are **Citraconates.**

Citra- (sitră), *prefix* [L. *citra* adv. and prep., on this side (of), prop. abl. fem. of *citer* adj., 'hither'], as in **Citramo·ntane** *a.* = CISMONTANE.

Citrate (si·treit). 1794. [f. CITRIC + -ATE[4].] *Chem.* A salt of citric acid.

Citrean (si·triăn), *a.* 1616. [f. L. *citreus* + -AN.] 1. Made of citrus-wood (CITRUS 2). †2. Citron-coloured 1656.

Citric (si·trik), *a.* 1800. [f. L. *citrus* + -IC.] *Chem.* Derived from the citron; as in *C. acid*: a colourless inodorous acid, $C_6H_8O_7$, of a very sharp taste, found in the juice of oranges, lemons, limes, citrons, etc.

Ci·tril. 1688. [app. shortened f. It. *citrinella*, dim. of *citrina* citrine-coloured (bird).] In **c.-finch**: *Fringilla citrinella.*

†**Citrination** (sitrinēⁱ·ʃən). ME. [ad. med.L. *citrinationem.*] *Alch.* The turning of a substance yellow, looked upon as indicating the state of perfection or complete digestion –1645.

Citrine (si·trin). ME. [a. F. *citrin*, f. L. type **citrinus*, f. *citrus.*] **A.** *adj.* Greenish-yellow; lemon-coloured; var. **Ci·trinous.** **B.** *sb.* 1. Citrine colour (*mod.*). 2. *Min.* A glassy wine-yellow variety of quartz; *false topaz* 1748.

C. ointment: the ointment of nitrate of mercury.

Citron (si·trən). 1530. [a. F., ad. It. *citrone*, augm. of L. type **citrum*; cf. L. *citrus*, *citreum* (*malum*), Gr. κίτρον.] 1. An ovate acid juicy tree-fruit, larger, less acid, and thicker in the rind than the lemon. Formerly the name included the LEMON, and perhaps the LIME. 2. The tree *Citrus Mĕdica*, which bears this fruit 1530. 3. = CITRINE B. I. 1610. †4. = CITRUS 2. Also *attrib.* –1740. †5. = *Citron-water* –1735. Also *attrib.*

5. Now drinking c. with his Grace and Chartres POPE. *Comb.* †**c.-water**, a drink made from brandy flavoured with c.- or lemon-peel.

†**Citronize**, *v.* *Alch.* To become of a citron colour. B. JONS.

†**Citrul.** ME. [a. F. *citrouille*, med.L. *citrullus*, dim. from L. *citrus*; from the colour.] The Water-Melon; also the Pumpkin –1755.

‖**Citrus** (si·trŏs). 1865. [L.; cf. Gr. κίτρον, etc.] *Bot.* 1. The name now used for the genus which includes the citron, lemon, lime, orange, shaddock, and their varieties 1882. 2. Roman name of an African tree, prob. *Callitris quadrivalvis*, the fragrant wood of which was prized for making furniture.

Cittern; see CITHERN.

City (si·ti). [ME. *cite*, a. OF. *cité*, earlier *citet* :—L. *civitatem*, sb. of state f. *civis*; hence in L. primarily 'citizenship', and only later = *urbs.*] †1. *orig.* A town or other inhabited place –1611. 2. *spec.* A title ranking above that of 'town'. **a.** used vaguely ME. **b.** in Great Britain and Ireland: Associated with episcopal seats, and ancient royal burghs, and in recent times conferred by royal authority on important boroughs, as Birmingham, etc. ME. **c.** in *U.S.*: 'A town or collective body of inhabitants incorporated and governed by a mayor and aldermen' (Webster); also, in the newer States, used loosely 1843. Also *transf.* and *fig.* 3. The community of the inhabitants of a city ME. 4. *The City*: short for *the City of London*, that part of London situated within the ancient boundaries 1556; *esp.* the business part, or the business community, in the neighbourhood of the Exchange and Bank of England 1751. 5. As tr. Gr. πόλις, L. *civitas*, a self-governing city or state 1540. 6. *attrib.* Of or pertaining to a city or the City. (Often hyphened.) ME.

1. A citie called Nain *Luke* vii. 11. 2. **b.** My Lord Coke's Observation, that every C. is, or was, a Bishop's See, is not very exact FORTESCUE-ALAND. *Holy C.*, Jerusalem. *Eternal C.*, *C. of the Seven Hills*, Rome. 5. SHAKS. *Cor.* III. i. 199.

Comb.: **C.-article**, the summary of financial and commercial news in a newspaper; **C. Company**: see COMPANY; **C.-editor**, the editor of the C.-article, etc.; **c.-father**, a civic ruler; **-ward**: see WARD.

Hence **Ci·tycism**, c. manners, etc.; **Ci·tyful**, as many as a c. will contain; **Ci·tyish** *a.* smacking of the c.; **Ci·tyless** *a.* without a c. or cities; †that is no c. (*nonce-use*); **Ci·tyward(s** *adv.*

Cive (səiv). Now CHIVE, q.v.

Civet (si·vĕt), *sb.*[1] 1532. [a. F. *civette*, f. (ult.) the Arab. name *zabād*, *zubād*. See also ZIBET.] 1. A genus of carnivorous quadrupeds, yielding the secretion called by the same name. Spec., the central African species, *Viverra civetta*; called also *Civet Cat*. The allied Asiatic species *V. zibetha* is often called ZIBET. The Javanese species is the Rasse. 1532. 2. A yellowish or brownish unctuous substance, having a strong musky smell, obtained from glands in the anal pouch of the Civet. It is used in perfumery 1553. Also *attrib.*

†**Civet**, *sb.*[2] 1531. = CIVE or CHIVE –1712.

†**Civet**, *sb.*[3] 1708. [OF. *civé*, conn. w. *cive* CHIVE (Littré).] A way of dressing chickens, hares, etc., first frying them brown, and then stewing them in broth –1727.

Civet, *v.* 1601. [f. CIVET *sb.*[1]] To perfume with civet.

Civet-cat. 1607. = CIVET 1. (Also, a person perfumed with civet.)

Civic (si·vik), *a.* 1542. [a. L. *civicus*, f. *civis*; cf. F. *civique.*] Of or pertaining to citizens; to a city 1656, or to citizenship 1789.

C. crown [L. *corona civica*]: a garland of oak-leaves and acorns, bestowed upon one that saved the life of a fellow-citizen in war. *C. oath* [F. *serment civique*]: an oath of allegiance to the new order of things, demanded from citizens in the French Revolution. So †**Ci·vical** *a.*, whence **Ci·vically** *adv.* **Civics**, *pl.* used *subst.*, the theory of the rights and duties of citizenship.

Civicism (si·visiz'm). 1874. [f. prec. + -ISM.] Civic system; the principle that all citizens have equal rights and duties.

Civil (si·vil), *a.* ME. [a. F., ad. L. *civilis* (f. *civis*).] 1. Of or belonging to citizens; †of the nature of a citizen 1592. 2. Of or pertaining to the community of citizens 1494. †3. Civic –1713. 4. Of, pertaining to, or befitting a citizen 1526. †5. Orderly, well-governed –1685. 6. Civilized 1553. †7. Educated; refined –1716. †8. Sober, decent, grave –1691. †9. Humane, gentle –1684. 10. Polite; in recent use, 'decently polite', 'not (actually) rude' 1606. Also *transf.* 11. Pertaining to the *ordinary* life and affairs of a citizen; as distinguished from *military*, *ecclesiastical*, etc. 1592. 12. *Law.* Pertaining to the *private* rights and remedies of a citizen; as distinguished from *criminal*, *political*, etc. 1611. 13. *Legal* as distinguished from *natural* 1656. 14. Of divisions of time: Legally recognized 1601. 15. Of or according to the Roman CIVIL LAW. See also CIVIL LIST, CIVIL SERVICE, *Civil Servant* (see CIVIL SERVICE), *Civil Engineer* (see ENGINEER).

1. Where c. blood makes c. hands unclean *Rom. & Jul.* Prol. 2. C. dominion HOOKER, war 1550. 4. Slaves have no c. liberty LANE. C. knowledge H. WALPOLE. 5. Ciuill streets SHAKS. 7. C. and well bred men LOCKE. 10. 'Well, he was c., which is something' (*mod.*). 11. *C. righteousness*: goodness as a citizen, but not as a saint. 13. *C. death* (*i.e.* in all that respects legal rights or standing).

†**B.** as *sb.* 1. = CIVILIAN 1. ME. only. 2. *pl.* Civil matters; τὰ πολιτικά –1717.

†**C.** as *adv.* = CIVILLY –1767.

Civilian (sivi·liăn). ME. [a. OF. *civilien*, as in *droit civilien*, f. *civil*, L. *civilis.*] 1. One who studies or has studied the Civil Law. †2. *Theol.* One who followed after civil righteousness (see CIVIL 11, quot.) –1645. 3. A non-military man or official 1766. Also *attrib.*

1. Both the Canonists and the Civilians BAXTER. 3. Civilians and Indian officers returning from sick furlough 1829.

Civilisation, -ise; see CIVILIZATION, -IZE.

†**Civilist.** 1549. = CIVILIAN 1, 2. –1725.

Civility (sivi·lĭti). ME. [a. OF. *civilité*, ad. L. *civilitatem.*]

I. Obs. senses, connected with citizenship, etc. †1. Citizenship –1568. †2. A civil capacity. LATIMER. †3. Polity –1670. †4. Social order –1611. †5. Good citizenship –1758. †6. Secular quality –1649. †7. Civil righteousness; see CIVIL 11, quot. –1640.

4. To inbreed and cherish in a great people the seeds of vertu, and publick civility MILTON.

II. Senses connected with civilization. 1. The state of being civilized (*arch.*) 1549. 2. Polite or liberal education (*arch.*) 1533. 3. Behaviour proper to the intercourse of civilized people; politeness; an act of politeness 1561. †4. Seemliness; see CIVIL 8. –1672.

1. The progress of arts and c. JOHNSON. 2. Bring c. and learning into France WARTON. 3. The common forms of c. MACAULAY. †*C.-money*: money given in consideration or anticipation of good offices.

Civilizable (si·viləizăb'l), *a.* 1840. [See -ABLE.] Capable of being civilized.

Civiliza·de. *nonce-wd.* [Cf. *Crusade*, etc.] A crusade on behalf of civilization. MILL.

Civilization (sivilizēⁱ·ʃən, -əizēⁱ·ʃən). Also **-isation.** 1704. [f. CIVILIZE + -ATION.] †1. *Law.* The assimilation of the Common Law to the Civil Law –1812. 2. The action or process of civilizing or of being civilized 1775. 3. (More usually) Civilized condition or state 1772. Also *transf.*

3. The more advanced the c., the less powerful is the individual HELPS. Hence Ci·viliza·tional *a.*

Civilize (si·viləiz), *v.* 1601. [f. F. *civilizer* (Cotgr.) now *civiliser*; f. (ult.) L. *civilis* CIVIL + *-izare*, Eng. -IZE, q. v.] To make CIVIL; to bring out of a state of barbarism, to instruct in the arts of life; to enlighten and refine. Also *transf.* †2. To make proper in a civil community (*rare*) 1643. 3. *intr.* To become civilized or elevated 1868.

1. To c. the rude unpolish'd world ADDISON. 2. With an ignominious note of civilizing Adultery MILT. Hence **Civilizee·**, a person civilized. **Ci·vilizer.**

Civil law, †right. ME. [L. *jus civile.*] The law of Roman citizens; thence, the Roman law as a whole. (See LAW.) Also, the law of any city or state regulating the private rights and duties of the inhabitants.

Civil List. 1712. *orig.* A list of the charges for the civil administration of the state; the establishment supported by the moneys voted on this list (*obs.*); *now,* the amount voted by parliament for the household and personal expenses of the monarch, and for the *Civil List pensions, i. e.* pensions granted by the royal bounty.

Civilly (si·vili), *adv.* 1552. [f. CIVIL *a.*] In a civil manner (see CIVIL 4, 6, 7, 8, 11, 15). **Ci·vilness,** civility (*rare*).

Civil Service. 1785. *orig.* That part of the service of the East India Company carried on by the covenanted servants who did not belong to the Army or Navy (cf. SERVICE); *now,* all the non-warlike departments of the public administrative service of the state. Also the body of servants of the state employed in this service. **Civil Servant,** a member of the Civil Service.

Civism (si·viz'm). 1791. [a. F. *civisme,* f. L. *civis.*] Principles of good citizenship. (A term of the French Revolution.) Also *fig.*

†Civy, civey. ME. [a. F. *civé.*] A broth or sauce for a hare. (Cf. CIVET[3].) –1460.

Cizar, -zer, obs. ff. SCISSOR, SIZAR.

Cize, obs. f. SIZE.

Clabber (klæ·bəɪ). 1634. [a. Irish *clabar.*] 1. *dial.* Mud 1824. 2. = BONNY-CLABBER, q.v. Hence **Clabber** *v. intr.* to curdle, as milk.

Clachan (kla·χăn). *Sc.* and *north-Ir.* ME. [Gael., app. f. *clach* stone.] A small village in the Highlands of Scotland.

The c. yill had made me canty BURNS.

Clack (klæk), *sb.* ME. [conn. w. CLACK *v.*[1]; cf. Fr. *claque.*] 1. A sudden, sharp, dry sound as of two flat pieces of wood striking each other 1598. 2. Anything which makes this noise, as †the clapper of a mill, a clack-valve, a rattle to scare away birds, etc. ME. 3. Clatter of human tongues; senseless or continuous chatter ME. 4. *contemptuously,* The tongue. (Cf. 2.) 1598.

1. The great wheel's measured c. MORRIS. 3. Whose chief intent is to vaunt his spiritual c. SOUTH.

Comb.: **c.-box,** the box or chamber containing the c.-valve of a pump; **-dish,** a wooden dish with a lid clacked by beggars to attract notice; **-door,** an opening into the c.-box; **-valve,** a form of valve in pumps, hinged at one side, which is raised by the upward motion of the fluid, and falls back with a c.

Clack (klæk), *v.*[1] [ME. *clacken*; app. echoic. Cf. F. *claquer*; also CLAP, CRACK.] A. 1. *intr.* To chatter, prate, talk loquaciously; *trans.* to blab 1590. 2. To cluck, or cackle, as a hen 1712. 3. *intr.* To make a sound intermediate between a clap and a crack as one flat piece of wood does in striking another 1530; *trans.* to cause to make such a sound 1542.

1. 'Tis not euer true, that what the hart thinketh the tongue clacketh GREENE. 3. He clackt his whip HOBBES. Hence **Cla·cker, †Cla·cket,** that which clacks; the clapper of a mill, etc.

†B. Used advb.: At once, pat, 'slick' 1734.

†Clack, *v.*[2] ME. [orig. Flemish *klacken.*] *trans.* To remove the dirty clots, etc., from (a fleece of wool) –1726.

Clad (klæd), *ppl. a.* [ME. *clad(d,* f. OE. *claðod, -ed*; see CLOTHE *v.* Also *yclad* with prefix *y-*, revived by the archaists.] Covered with or as with clothing; arrayed, decked.

Clad, *v. arch.* 1579. [app. f. prec.] To CLOTHE. Also *transf.* and *fig.*

†Clade. ME. [ad. L. *clades.*] A disaster, plague –1604.

Clado- (klædo, klǣdo), bef. a vowel **clad-**, comb. f. Gr. κλάδος young shoot or branch, as in **Clada·nthous** *a.*, bearing the fructification on short lateral branchlets, as some Mosses; so **Cladoca·rpous** *a.*; **Cla·dophyll,** also **-phyllon,** pl. -a, a branch assuming the form of foliage.

‖**Cladodium** (klădōu·diŏm). Also **cla·dode.** 1870. [f. late Gr. κλαδώδης (f. κλάδος).] *Bot.* An axis flattened and more or less leaf-like.

Claes (klēz). 1549. *Sc.* and *n. dial.* form of CLOTHES.

Clag, *sb. n. dial.* 1641. [f. the vb.] 1. The process or product of clagging. 2. An encumbrance. *Sc.* 1697. Hence **Cla·ggy** *a.* adhesive.

Clag (klæg), *v. n. dial.* 1470. [Cf. OE. *clæg,* CLAY; perh. influenced by *clog.*] 1. *trans.* To bedaub, to clot *with* anything sticky; to clog by so doing 1526. 2. *intr.* To stick tenaciously; also *transf.* 1563. 3. *dial.* = CLACK *v.*[2] 1863. Hence **Cla·ggum,** treacle-toffy.

Claik (klēk), *sb. Sc.* 1455. [f. CLAIK *v.*] 1. The call of geese, etc. 1549. 2. The Barnacle-goose (prob. from its call).

Claik, *v. Sc.* 1513. [prob. :—ON. *klaka* to chatter; cf. CLACK *v.*] *intr.* To cry as geese, etc.; to chatter.

Claim (klēⁱm), *sb.* ME. [a. OF. *claime* (*clame*), f. *clamer* to CLAIM.] 1. A demand for something as due; an assertion of a right to something. (Const. as in 2.) 2. Right of claiming; right or title (*to* something or *to* with *inf. phrase*; also *on, upon* a person, etc.) ME. 3. That which is claimed; *spec.* in *U.S.* and *Australia,* a piece of land allotted and taken, *esp.* for mining purposes 1863. †4. A call, shout. SPENSER *F. Q.* IV. x. 11.

1. *To lay c. to*: to claim. 2. A c. to kindness JOHNSON, to call itself owner PENNANT. Hence **Clai·mless** *a.* (*rare*).

Claim (klēⁱm), *v.* ME. [a. OF. *claime-*, stem of *clamer* (*claimer*) :—L. *clamare.*] 1. To demand as one's own or one's due; to seek or ask for on the ground of right. 2. To assert and demand recognition of (an alleged right, title, or the like); to assert as one's own ME. In *U.S., loosely,* To assert. 3. Of things: To call for; to be entitled to 1606. †4. To proclaim (with *complement*) –1596. 5. *intr.* To put forward a claim. (Later, app. an absolute use of 1 or 2.) ME.

1. To c. Precedence MILT. *P. L.* II. 32, to be exempt ME., that his word should be law MERIVALE. 2. That claymethe gentyle for to be CHAUCER. 4. †*To claim quit,* also *to quit claim* (a person or thing); to proclaim quit or released. 5. Say from what scepter'd ancestry ye claim POPE. Hence **Clai·mable** *a.* **Clai·mance,** the action of claiming. **Clai·mant,** one who makes or enters a claim; one who has a claim *upon* anything. **Clai·mer,** a claimant.

Clairaudience (kleᵊrǭ·diĕns). 1864. [f. F. *clair* + AUDIENCE, after CLAIRVOYANCE.] The faculty of mentally perceiving sounds beyond the range of hearing, alleged to be induced under certain mesmeric conditions. So **Clairaudient** *a.* and *sb.*

Clair-obscure. 1717. = CHIAROSCURO, q.v.

‖**Clairschach** (klā·ɪʃăχ). 1490. [Ir. and Gael. *clairseach.*] The old Celtic harp strung with wire. Hence ‖**Clai·rschacher,** a player on the c.

Clairvoyance (kleᵊrvoi·ăns, or as F. klęrvoyāns). 1847. [Fr.] 1. The faculty of mentally perceiving objects at a distance or concealed from sight, attributed to certain persons, or to persons under certain mesmeric conditions. 2. Keenness of mental perception, insight 1861. So **Clairvoy·ant(e** *a.* and *sb.* (in both senses). **Clairvoy·antly** *adv.*

Clake, clakke, obs. ff. CLAIK, CLACK *v.*

Clam (klæm), *sb.*[1] [OE. *clam(m, clǫm(m*; prob. from an OTeut. **klam-*, **klamm-*, or **klamb-*, to squeeze together. See also CLEM *v.*] †1. Anything that holds tight; bond, chain; *pl.* bondage. (In OE.) 2. An instrument for clasping rigidly or holding fast; a clamp, vice, pair of pincers, etc.; also, a lining for the jaws of a vice ME. †3. *pl.* Clutches, claws –1574.

Clam (klæm), *sb.*[2] 1500. [Orig. *clam-shell*: app. from prec.] 1. A name applied to various bivalve shell-fish; *esp.* a. in Scotland, to the genus *Pecten*; b. to the Giant C. or Clamp (*Tridacna gigas*) of the East Indies; c. in U.S., to the Hard or Round C. (*Venus mercenaria*), and the Soft or Long C. (*Mya arenaria*): whence *c.-bake* and *c.-chowder.* Also applied to fresh-water mussels. 2. *U.S.* A term of contempt; one who is 'as close as a c.' 1871. 3. *U.S. slang.* The mouth 1825.

Comb.: **c.-bake,** a baking, Indian-fashion, upon hot stones, of a mass of clams, a favourite feature of seaside picnics in U.S.; hence, the picnic party; **-chowder,** one made with clams.

Clam (klæm), *sb.*[3] 1554. [? a back-formation from CLAMMY.] †1. A soft mass. (Cf. CLOAM.) 2. Clamminess 1694.

Clam (klæm), *sb.*[4] 1702. [perh. echoic, with more notion of crash than *clang.*] The crash of two or more bells of a peal rung together.

Clam (klæm), *a.*[1] Now *dial.* ME. [Cf. CLAM *v.*[1]] Sticky; cold and damp; clammy.

Clam, *a.*[2] 1829. [? L. *clam.*] *Sc.* Base, mean; a school term. ? *Obs.*

Clam (klæm), *v.*[1] Now *dial.* ME. [var. of *cleme,* OE. *clǣman*; see CLEAM *v.*] 1. To smear, or spread unctuous matter *on*; to daub *with.* 2. To bedaub (a thing) so that it sticks 1598. 3. To clog or choke up 1527. 4. *intr.* To be moist and sticky; to stick, adhere 1610.

Clam (klæm), *v.*[2] 1674. [See CLAM *sb.*[4]] 1. Of bells: To crash together (*trans.* and *intr.*) 1702. 2. *fig.* To silence 1674.

Clamant (klǣ·mănt, klæ·m-), *a.* 1639. [ad. L. *clamantem.*] 1. *lit.* Clamorous. 2. *fig.* Crying, urgent 1723.

1. C. for food 1806. 2. C. abuses 1858. Hence **Cla·mantly** *adv.*

†Clama·tion. 1502. [ad. L. *clamationem.*] A crying out, invocation. SIR T. BROWNE.

Clamber (klæ·mbəɪ), *v.* ME. [app. f. CLIMB *v.* (pa. t., ME. *clamb, clam*). Cf. Ger. *sich klammern* to hook oneself on.] *intr.* To climb by catching hold with hands and feet; to climb with difficulty. Also *trans.* Of plants: To climb by means of tendrils, etc. 1601. Also *transf.* and *fig.*

The Kitchen Malkin..Clambring the Walls to eye him *Cor.* II. i. 225. The narrow street that clamber'd toward the mill TENNYSON. Hence **Cla·mber** *sb.* an act of clambering. **Cla·mberer,** he who or that which clambers; *esp.* a climbing plant.

Clamjamphrie (klæmdʒæ·mfri). *Sc.* and *n. dial.* 1816. [?] Trumpery; spoken rubbish, 'rot'; rabble, canaille.

Clammy (klæ·mi), *a.* ME. [? f. CLAM *a.*[1] and *v.*[1] + -Y.] 1. Soft, moist, and sticky; viscous, adhesive. †2. *fig.* Sluggish 1613.

The c. water [of the Dead Sea] FULLER. C. fogs 1697, sweat 1703, hands 1626. Hence **Cla·mmily** *adv.* **Cla·mminess.** **†Cla·mmish** *a.* somewhat c.

Clamor, var. of CLAMOUR.

Clamorous (klæ·mŏrəs), *a.* 1526. [= med. L. *clamorosus,* and obs. F. *clamoreux,* f. L. *clamorem* CLAMOUR.] 1. Of the nature of clamour; uttered with, or accompanied by, shouting; noisy. 2. Vociferous; loudly urgent. Said of persons and other agents; also *transf.* of places where they are. 1540. Also *fig.*

1. The c. nonsense of the hour EMERSON. 2. C. War-pipes SCOTT, river-banks CORY. *fig.* C. debts ARBUTHNOT. Hence **Cla·morous-ly** *adv.*, **-ness.**

Clamour, -or (klæ·məɪ), *sb.* ME. [a. OF. *clamor, -ur, -our* :—L. *clamorem.*] 1. Loud shouting or outcry, vociferation: commonly implying a mingling of voices. Also with *a,* and *pl.* ME. 2. *fig.* General vehement expression of feeling, *esp.* of discontent, or disapprobation; popular outcry ME. 3. Any loud noise, as of beasts, birds, a storm, etc. 1593.

2. The c. for war continued D'ISRAELI. Hence **Cla·mourist** (*rare*), one who belongs to a party of c. **Cla·moursome** *a.* (*n. dial.*)

Clamour, -or (klæ·məɪ), *v.* ME. [f. prec. sb.] 1. *intr.* To make a clamour; to raise an outcry, make a noise or din of speech. 2. *intr.* To raise an outcry *for*; to demand importunately *to do* a thing 1651. 3. *trans.* †To disturb with clamour, din –1671; also with *out of, into, down,* etc. 4. To utter clamorously 1856.

1. The obscure Bird clamor'd the liue-long Night *Macb.* II. iii. 65. 2. Men were eagerly clamouring to go home FREEMAN. 3. Clamouring thir God with praise, Who had made thir dreadful enemy thir thrall MILT. *Sams.* 1621. 4. Hungry crows.. Clamoured their piteous prayer incessantly LONGF. Hence **Cla·mourer.**

Cla·mour, -or, *v.*[2] Also **clamber.** 1611. [f. CLAM *v.*[2], or conn. w. prec.] **1.** *Bell-ringing.* To repeat the strokes more quickly, when they are at the height, in order to cease them 1747. **2.** To silence 1611.

2. Clamor your tongues, and not a word more *Wint. T.* IV. iii. 250.

Clamp (klæmp), *sb.*[1] ME. [? a. Du. *klamp* 'clamp, cleat', from a WGer. stem *klamp-, by-form of *klamb-; see CLAM *sb.*[1]] **1.** A brace, clasp, or band, usually of rigid material, used for strengthening or fastening things together: *e.g.* a piece of wood inserted into another to prevent warping, etc. Also *fig.* **2.** A name of appliances with opposite parts which may be brought together, so as to seize, hold, compress, or pinch anything: *e.g.* with *Joiners*, an appliance for holding articles together while being formed; a check for a vice, etc. 1688. **3.** *Naut.* One of the thick planks in a ship's side below the shelf-piece which support the ends of the deck-beams 1626. Also *attrib.*

Comb.: **c.-nail**, a large-headed nail for fastening iron clamps; **-plate** (*Ship-building*), an iron plate serving to unite two bodies.

Clamp, *sb.*[2] 1624. [Cf. prec.] **†1.** *U.S.* Earlier name of CLAMS. **2.** Usu. *C.-shell*: the large bivalve shell of the molluscs *Chama* and *Tridacna* (Family *Chamaceæ*) 1835.

Clamp (klæmp), *sb.*[3] 1596. [? a. Du. *klamp* 'heap'.] A heap or pile of bricks for burning, of earth to cover potatoes, etc., of ore for roasting, of coal for coking, etc.

Clamp, *sb.*[4] Chiefly *dial.* 1879. [ECHOIC.] A heavy, solid tread, or stamp with the feet.

Clamp (klæmp), *v.*[1] 1677. [f. CLAMP *sb.*[1]] *trans.* To make fast with a clamp or clamps. Hence **Cla·mper**, that which clamps; clams, pincers, an ice-creeper, etc.

Clamp, *v.*[2] 1834. [f. CLAMP *sb.*[3]] To pile *up* (bricks, earth, etc.) in a heap; to store (potatoes, etc.) in a clamp. Hence **Cla·mper** *v.*[1] to botch, patch up.

Clamp, *v.*[3] Chiefly *dial.* 1808. [Cf. CLAMP *sb.*[4]] To tread or stamp heavily; to clump. So **Cla·mper** *v.*[2]

Clan (klæn), *sb.* ME. [a. Gael. *clann*, OIr. *cland, clann*, app. a. L. *planta* sprout, etc. Goidelic substituted *k* for *p*.] **1.** A number of persons claiming descent from a common ancestor, and associated together; a tribe. **2.** *contemptuously*, A collection of people having common attributes; a fraternity, party, set, lot 1536. in *comb.* Also *transf.* and *fig.* Also *attrib.*

1. 'The Gathering of the Clans' (*mod.*). Another c. of the Arabs MAUNDRELL. **2.** The whole c. of the enlightened among us BURKE. A c. o' roosty craws STEVENSON. Hence **Clan** *v.* (*rare*) to combine as members of a c. **Cla·nless** *a.* (*rare*).

†Cla·ncular, *a.* 1621. [f. L. *clancularius*, f. *clanculum* adv., dim. of *clam* in secret.] Secret; clandestine -1735. So **†Cla·nculary.** Hence **†Cla·ncularly** *adv.*

Clandestine (klænde·stin), *a.* 1566. [ad. L. *clandestinus*, f. *clam.*] Secret, concealed; usually in a bad sense; underhand, surreptitious.

A certain c. Hostility cover'd over with the name of Peace MILT. Hence **Clande·stinely** *adv.* **Clandesti·nity,** secrecy; usually in bad sense.

Clang (klæŋ), *sb.* 1596. [app. f. CLANG *v.* Cf. L. *clangor*, prob. cogn. w. Gr. κλάζειν, κλαγγή. The echoic nature of the word has also influenced its use.] **1.** A loud resonant ringing sound; orig., as in L., that of a trumpet; now that of metal when struck. Also *fig.* (Cf. Ger. *klang* 'sound') 1660. **2.** The loud harsh scream of certain birds. (As in L. and Gr.) 1667. **3.** *Acoust.* = Ger. *klang*: A composite musical sound 1867.

1. Trumpetts clangue *Tam. Shr.* I. ii. 207. *fig.* A c. of turgid extravagances MERIVALE. **2.** Their [cranes'] loud c. SOMERVILLE. So **†Clange.** CHAPMAN.

Clang (klæŋ), *v.* 1576. [app. ad. L. *clangere*; see CLANG *sb.*] **1.** *intr.* To emit a CLANG. **2.** *trans.* To strike together with clanging sound 1720. **3.** *intr.* Of some birds: To utter their loud harsh cry 1832.

1. Armes clatter and c. FLORIO. **2.** They [eagles] wheel on high, And c. their wings POPE.

Clangor, -our (klæ·ŋgəɹ, klæ·ŋəɹ), *sb.* 1593. [ad. L. *clangor.* Usually spelt with *-or*, exc. by Johnson, till end of 18th c.] Loud resonant ringing sound; a CLANG. Occas. with *a*, and *pl.* Hence **Cla·ngor, -our** *v. intr.* to clang. **Cla·ngorous** *a.* full of c.; so **†Cla·ngous** *a.* (*rare*) SIR T. BROWNE. **Cla·ngorously** *adv.*

Clanjamfray, -phrey; see CLAMJAMPHRIE.

Clank (klæŋk), *sb.* 1656. [? a. Du. *klank* clinking noise; or echoic.] A sharp abrupt sound, as of *e.g.* links of a heavy chain struck together; differing from *clang* in ending abruptly like a *clink*.

The c. of machinery 1845. Hence **Cla·nkless** *a.* (*rare*).

Clank (klæŋk), *v.* 1614. [See CLANK *sb.*] **1.** *intr.* To make, or move with, a clanking sound. **2.** *trans.* To cause to emit, or to utter with, a clanking sound 1743.

1. The old dinner-bell will clang, or rather c., in a few minutes SCOTT.

Clannish (klæ·niʃ), *a.* 1776. [f. CLAN *sb.*] Of or pertaining to a clan; having the sympathies, prejudices, etc. of a clan; attached to one's own clan. Hence **Cla·nnish-ly** *adv.*, **-ness.**

Clanship (klæ·nʃip). 1772. [f. CLAN *sb.* + -SHIP.] **1.** The system of clans; union of persons in, or as in, a clan. **2.** Clannishness 1809.

Clansman (klæ·nzmæ̆n). 1810. [f. *clan's* + MAN.] A man belonging to a clan.

Clap (klæp), *sb.*[1] [ME. *clappe, cleppe*; ? f. OTeut. *klappo-; echoic.] **1.** An abrupt explosive noise, as of two hard flat surfaces struck on one another. **2.** = CLACK. Now *dial.* ME. **3.** The noise made by striking the hands together; the act of so doing; applause 1599. **4.** A sounding blow; in *Sc. esp.* a pat ME. **†5.** A sudden stroke (*lit.* and *fig.*). (Cf. AFTER-CLAP.) -1768. **6.** *Falconry.* The lower mandible of a hawk 1486. **†7.** A poster -1735. **8.** = CLAPPER *sb.*[1] (in various senses) ME. **9.** *Farriery.* A disease of horses. ? *Obs.* 1684.

1. A terrible c. of thunder HAKLUYT. **3.** Applause.. with c. of hands, and thump of sticks HAWTHORNE. **5.** *In a c.*: at once. (Cf. Fr. *coup.*) **7.** Plaster'd posts, with claps in capitals POPE.

Comb.: **c.-bill** = sense 7; **-bread, -cake**, oatmeal cake, beaten thin, and baked hard; **-dish** = *clack-dish*; **-net**, a net used by fowlers, entomologists, etc., which can be suddenly closed by pulling a string.

Clap (klæp), *sb.*[2] Now *vulgar.* 1587. [?] Gonorrhœa. Also with *a*, and *pl.*

Clap (klæp), *v.*[1] [ME. *clappen*, OE. type *clappian, perh. f. (ult.) OTeut. *klappo- CLAP *sb.*[1]] **1.** *intr.* To make the noise described under CLAP *sb.*[1] (Now *dial.*) 1509. **†2.** = CLACK *v.*[1] **1.** -1562. **3.** *intr.* To make this noise by †rapping, shutting (*to*), etc. ME. **4.** *trans.* To strike the palms of *the hands* together with noise ME.; also *ellipt.* to clap the hands at 1555; *intr.* (without 'hands') to applaud by clapping hands 1613. **5.** *trans.* To strike with sounding blows (*arch.*) ME. **†6.** To strike (hands) reciprocally, in token of a bargain -1614. **7.** Of a bird: To flap (the wings) ME. **8.** To slap with the palm of the hand, in token of approval; in *n. dial.* to pat 1530. **9.** To put, place, set, or stick, with promptness and effect 1559; *esp.* to put *in* prison. Also simply *to clap up.* 1515. **10.** *fig.* To impose as with authority *upon, on*, etc. 1609. **†11.** To stick *together*, put *up*, hastily -1711. **†12.** *intr.* (for *refl.*): To throw oneself, strike *in* -1750. Also *†fig.* to strike *into* SHAKS. Also *absol.* (colloq.).

1. Doors creak and windows c. R. BLAIR. **3.** [Sche] clapt the wyndow to CHAUCER. **4.** Clappyn hondys togedyr for ioy ME. **6.** And so c. hands, and a bargaine *Hen. V*, v. ii. 133. Cf. *Wint. T.* I. ii. 104. **9.** C. on more sailes *Merry W.* II. ii. 142. The uncivil Lord..clapt irons on my heels 1605. To c. spurs to a horse 1710. *To c. eyes on* (colloq.). Let them be clapt vp close SHAKS. **10.** To c. a writ upon his back 1690. **11.** Was euer match clapt vp so sodainly *Tam. Shr.* II. i. 327. **12.** *Meas. for M.* IV. iii. 43.

Clap (klæp), *v.*[2] Now *vulgar.* 1658. [f. CLAP *sb.*[2]] To infect with clap.

Clapboard (klæ·pˌbōəɹd, klæ·boɹd), *sb.* 1520. [A form of CLAPHOLT, with *board* for LG. *holt.*] **1.** A small size of split oak, for barrel-staves, and wainscoting. **2.** In *U.S.* A board, thinner at one edge, used to weather-board the sides or roofs of houses 1641. **†3.** Used without *a* or *pl.* -1745. Hence **Cla·pboard** *v.* to cover or line with clapboards (*U.S.*).

Clape (klēp). 1860. [? f. CLEPE *v.*] A bird; the FLICKER.

†Clapholt. 1477. [a. LG. *klappholt*, f. stem of *klappen* to CLAP + *holt* wood.] = CLAPBOARD *sb.* 3. -1721.

Cla·pmatch. 1743. [app. a. Du. *klapmuts* sailor's cap; so called from the cartilaginous hood which covers its eyes.] A kind of seal.

Clapped, clapt, pa. pple. of CLAP *v.*

Clapped, *ppl. a.* [f. CLAP *sb.*[1] 9.] *Farriery.* Affected with clap. STERNE.

Clapper (klæ·pəɹ), *sb.*[1] ME. [f. CLAP *v.*[1] + -ER.] **1.** That which claps or makes a noise, as the CLACK of a mill, the tongue of a bell, etc.; also *fig.* the human tongue. **2.** One who claps; a claquer 1824.

†Cla·pper, *sb.*[2] ME. [a. F. *clapier*; in med. L. *claperius, -um, -a*, 'rabbit-hole', previously 'heap of stones'.] A rabbit-burrow -1725.

Clapper (klæ·pəɹ), *v.* 1872. [f. CLAPPER *sb.*[1]] **1.** To sound (a bell) by pulling the clapper. **2.** *intr.* To make a noise like a clapper 1884.

Clapperclaw (klæ·pəɹklǭ), *v. arch.* 1590. [app. f. CLAPPER *sb.* + CLAW *v.*] **1.** *trans.* To claw with the open hand and nails; to drub. **2.** *fig.* To revile 1692. Hence **Cla·pperclawer.**

Clapperdudgeon. *arch.* 1567. [app. f. CLAPPER *sb.* + DUDGEON hilt of a dagger.] *Cant.* A beggar born; also, as a term of insult.

Claps(e, obs. and dial. f. CLASP.

Claptrap (klæ·pˌtræp). 1727. [f. CLAP *sb.*[1] 3 + TRAP *sb.*] **1.** A trick, device, or language designed to catch applause. (Also without *a* or *pl.*) Also *attrib.* **†2.** A contrivance for making a clapping noise in theatres, etc. -1866. Hence **Cla·ptrappy** *a.* (*nonce-wd.*)

‖Claque (klɑk). 1864. [F.; f. *claquer* to clap.] A band of hired applauders in a theatre; also *transf.* of political followers.

Claquer (klæ·kəɹ), **‖claqueur** (klakör). 1837. [a. F. *claqueur*, f. as prec.] A hired applauder.

Clarabella (klārabe·lă). Also **clari-.** 1840. [f. L. *clarus, -a*, + *bellus, -a.*] An organ-stop of a powerful fluty tone, invented by Bishop.

Clare. 1818. A nun of the order of St. Clare.

Clarence (klæ·rĕns). 1837. [f. the Duke of *Clarence*, afterwards William IV.] A close four-wheeled carriage with seats for four inside; also *attrib.*

Clarenceux, -cieux (klæ·rĕnsiū). ME. [f. *Clarence*, L. *Clarencia*, an English dukedom named from Clare in Suffolk.] The second King-of-Arms in England, who officiates south of the river Trent.

Clarendon (klæ·rĕndən). 1848. *Printing.* A thick-faced condensed type, in capital and small letters, made in many sizes.

Clare-obscure, = CLAIR-OBSCURE.

†Claret, *sb.*[1] ME. [ad. med.L. *claretum*, f. OF. *claré, claret*, CLARY.] = CLARY *sb.*[1] -1559.

Claret (klæ·rĕt), *sb.*[2] ME. [a. OF. *claret*, in *vin claret* (mod.F. *clairet*), dim. of *clair* 'clear, light, bright'.] **1.** *orig.* A name of yellowish or light red wines, as distinguished from 'red' and 'white' wines; used, about 1600, for red wines generally. Now applied to the red wines imported from Bordeaux. Also as *†adj.* **2.** *slang.* Blood 1604. **3.** The colour of claret 1648; also as *adj.* claret-coloured 1547. Hence **Claretee·r,** a drinker of c. **Cla·rety** *a.*

Claribella, var. of CLARABELLA.

Cla·richord. *Hist.* 1502. [A perversion of CLAVICHORD, assoc. w. L. *clarus.*] = CLAVICHORD, q.v. So **†Claricy·mbal** = CLAVICYMBAL.

Clarification (klæ·rifikēi·ʃən). 1612. [a. F., ad. L. *clarificationem*; see CLARIFY.] **1.** The action or process of clarifying, *esp.* liquids. **†2.** Glorifying; transfiguration -1683.

2. Elevation and c. of his veri mortal Bodie 1683.

Clarify (klæ·rifəi), *v.* ME. [a. OF. *clarifier*, ad. late L. *clarificare*, f. *clarus.*] **†1.** *trans.* To CLEAR, in various senses -1696. Also *intr.* (for *refl.*). Also *fig.* **†2.** *fig.* To make illustrious; to glorify -1649. **3.** To make pure, or clean (*physically*, also *morally*); to free from all impurities, defecate ME. Also *fig.*

1. To c. the day LYDG., the sight 1525, the voice 1585; (*fig.*) to c. a subject 1841. **2.** Fadir, clarifie thi name WYCLIF *John* xii. 27. **3.** To c. butter 1769, the atmosphere 1879; (*fig.*) to c. the intellect 1851, the popular creed LECKY. Hence Cla·rifier, one who or that which clarifies; *spec.* a vessel used in clarifying sugar.

†**Cla·rigate**, *v. rare.* 1601. [f. L. *clarigare*, f. *clarus*; cf. *fumigate*, etc.] To make through heralds a solemn demand for redress, prior to declaration of war. Hence †**Clariga·tion** (*rare*).

†**Cla·rine.** ME. By-form of CLARION –1620.

Clarinet (klæ·rinet, -ne·t). 1796. [a. F. *clarinette*, dim. of *clarine*.] A wooden single-reed instrument, having a cylindrical tube with bell-shaped orifice, and played by means of holes and keys. Hence **Clarine·ttist**.

‖**Clarino** (klărī·no). [It.] = CLARION 1, 3.

Clarion (klæ·riən), *sb.* ME. [a. OF. *claron, cleron, clairon*; in med.L. *clarionem, claronem*, f. *clarus*; cf. CLARINE.] **1.** A shrill-sounding trumpet with a narrow tube. (Now chiefly *poet.* or *Hist.*) **2.** *poet.* The sound of a trumpet, or any similar rousing sound 1667. **3.** An organ-stop of like quality of tone 1670. **4.** *attrib.* Of or pertaining to, or sounding like, a clarion ME.

1. The warlike sound Of..Clarions MILT. *P. L.* I. 532. 2. The cock's shrill c. GRAY. 4. The c. couplets of Pope F. HARRISON. Hence **Cla·rion** *v.* (*rare*) to blow the c.; also *trans.* †**Cla·rioner**, †**Cla·rionist.**

Clarionet (klæ·riŏnet, -e·t). 1784. = CLARINET. Also *fig.*

†‖**Clari·ssimo.** 1605. [It. superl. of *claro*:— L. *clarissimus*.] A Venetian grandee –1630.

†**Cla·ritude.** 1560. [ad. L. *claritudo*.] Clearness, brightness; a thing of brightness –1670.

Clarity (klæ·rĭti). ME. [Orig. ME. *clarté*, a. OF.:—L. *claritatem*. Recently revived.] †**1.** Brightness –1698. †**2.** Glory –1675. **3.** Clearness: in various senses 1616.

3. C. of understanding SIR T. BROWNE, of style FULLER, heaven BROWNING, a gem R. ELLIS.

Clarkia (klā·ɹkiă). 1864. [mod.L., f. name of W. *Clarke*, U.S. explorer.] A plant of the genus of this name, consisting of annuals bearing white, rose, lake, and purple flowers.

†**Claro obscuro.** 1706. = CHIAROSCURO.

Clarre, -y, obs. ff. CLARY.

Clart (klāɹt), *sb. Sc.* and *n. dial.* 1808. [?] Sticky or claggy dirt; (with *pl.*), a daub of sticky dirt. Hence **Cla·rty** *a.* dirty, sticky.

Clart (klāɹt), *v. trans.* 1681. [?] To smear or daub with or †as with dirt 1808.

†**Cla·ry**, *sb.*[1] [ME. *claré*, a. OF.:—L. type *claratum* that which is clarified.] A liquor consisting of a mixture of wine, clarified honey, pepper, ginger, etc. Occas. *c. wine.* –1700.

Clary (klēᵊ·ri), *sb.*[2] [In OE. *slarie, slarege*; in 16th c. *claré, clarie*, repr. med.L. *sclarea*, of unkn. origin. Resolved by apothecaries into *clair-ye, clear-eye*.] A labiate plant, *Salvia sclarea*; also other plants, app. as considered good for the eyes, *e.g.* Celandine, and species of Fennel. Also *attrib.*

Comb. c.-water, cordial made from c. flowers.

†**Cla·ry**, *v.* 1440. [app. f. CLARION.] To clarion –1587.

Clash (klæʃ), *sb.* 1513. [app. echoic; cf. *clap, dash*, etc.] **1.** A loud but broken sound resulting from collision. **2.** Collision, conflict; *esp.* of arguments or opinions 1646. **3.** Chatter; the country talk; an item of gossip (usu. malicious). *Sc.* and *n. dial.* 1685.

1. The c. of hail SHELLEY, of Swords STEELE, cymbals MACAULAY, rain COLERIDGE. 2. The c. of arguments and jar of words COWPER.

Clash (klæʃ), *v.* 1500. [See prec. sb.] **1.** *intr.* To make the sound described under CLASH *sb.* 1; also *trans.* with object of result 1667. **2.** *trans.* To strike (things) together with this noise 1686. **3.** *intr.* To come into violent collision, or conflict (*with, against*) 1618; also *fig.* to conflict; to be incompatible; to disagree (*with*). (The chief current use.) 1646. **4.** To strike in conflict (*trans.* and *intr.*) 1650. **5.** = *dash*. Often with *down*. *Sc.* 1805. **6.** To slam (a door, etc.). Now *dial.* 1637. **7.** *intr.* To talk maliciously; to gossip. *Sc.* 1697.

1. Arms on Armour clashing bray'd Horrible discord MILT. *P. L.* VI. 209. 3. His Lordship's statement.. may seem to c. with Lord Eldon's J. POWELL. Hence **Cla·sher. Cla·shingly** *adv.*

‖**Clashy, -ee**, *sb. Anglo-Ind.* 1785. [ad. Urdu.] A tent-pitcher; a native sailor.

Clasp (klɑsp), *sb.* ME. [Also *clapse*. Origin unkn.] **1.** A fastening, generally of metal, consisting of two interlocking parts; used for holding together parts or ends of anything, *e.g.* parts of garments, the ends of a belt, the covers of a book, etc. Also *fig.* **2.** The act of surrounding or comprehending and holding; embrace (*lit.* and *fig.*) 1604. **3.** A military decoration; a bar of silver bearing the name of a battle, etc., fixed transversely upon the ribbon by which a medal is suspended 1813.

Comb.: c.-hook, a pair of hooks, etc., with overlapping jaws; -knife, a large knife the blade of which folds or shuts into the handle; -nail, a nail with a flat head to clasp the wood.

Clasp (klɑsp), *v.* ME. [f. prec. sb.; perh. infl. later by CLIP *v.* and *grasp*.] **1.** *trans.* To fasten with or as with a clasp. Also with †*to*, †*together*. **2.** To furnish with a clasp 1460. **3.** To take hold of by means of encircling parts; *loosely* and *poet.* to surround, enfold ME.; to embrace (*lit.* and *fig.*) 1549. **4.** To hold with close pressure of the curved hand 1583. †**5.** *intr.* To lay hold by clasping –1730. **6.** *causal.* To bend or fold tightly *round* or *over* 1798.

3. Thy suppliant I beg, and c. thy knees MILT. *P. L.* x. 918. 4. We'll c. hands *Per.* II. iv. 57. Hence **Clasped** *ppl. a.* held by or in a clasp; also [f. *sb.*], having a clasp or clasps.

Clasper (klɑ·spəɹ). 1551. [f. prec. + -ER.] **1.** One who or that which clasps: *Bot.* a tendril 1577; *Zool.* (in *pl.*) appendages of the male of certain fishes and insects, serving to hold the female 1839. **2.** One who makes clasps 1885.

1. The claperes of the fyshe called polypus TURNER.

Class (klɑs), *sb.* 1656. [In 17th c. *classe*, a. F., ad. L. *classis*; see CLASSIS.] **1.** *Rom. Hist.* Each of the six orders into which Servius Tullius divided the Roman people for purposes of taxation **2.** A division of society according to status 1772; rank (*esp.* high rank), caste 1845. **3.** A division of scholars or students receiving the same instruction or ranked together as of the same standing 1656. **4.** A division of candidates according to merit. Also *attrib.*; and *ellipt.* a class degree 1807. **5.** A division of things according to grade or quality, as *high* or *low, first, second*, etc. 1694. **6.** *gen.* A number of individuals (persons or things) possessing common attributes, and grouped together under a general or 'class' name; a kind, sort, division. (Now the leading sense.) 1664. **b.** *Nat. Hist.* A group intermediate between a *Kingdom* and an *order* 1753. **7.** In the Methodist societies: A subdivision of a congregation or society, meeting under a class-leader for religious purposes 1742. Also *attrib.*

2. Higher (Upper), Middle, Lower Classes (*mod.*). 4. *To take a c. at Oxford*: to take an honours degree.

Comb.: c.-list, a list of the members of a c. (sense 3); also *spec.* a list of names of candidates arranged in classes according to merit, as a result of examination; -man, one whose name appears in a class-list; -name, a general name.

Class (klɑs), *v.* 1705. [f. prec. sb.] †**1.** To CLASSIFY –1794. **2.** To place in a class, or class-list 1776. **3.** *intr.* (for *refl.*) To rank; to be classed 1748.

2. You c. injustice with wisdom and virtue JOWETT. Tom was not classed at all THACKERAY. Hence **Cla·ssable** *a.*; also (badly) **Cla·ssible. Cla·sser.**

Classic (klæ·sik). 1613. [ad. F. *classique*, or L. *classicus* of *the* (*i.e.* the highest) class, f. *classis*. Infl. later by the sense of 'Used in the classes of schools, etc.']

A. *adj.* **1.** Of the first rank or authority; standard, leading. **2.** Of the standard Greek and Latin writers; belonging to the literature or art of Greek and Roman antiquity 1628. **3.** Belonging to Greek and Latin antiquity 1701. **4.** = CLASSICAL 6. 1744. **5.** *transf.* Of literary or historical note 1787. **6.** *joc.* Recognized, standard 1648. †**7.** = CLASSICAL 7. –1648.

1. But in Latin we have none of c. authority extant MILT. 2. The Classick Authors STEELE, Renaissance SIR G. SCOTT. 3. In c. lands COLERIDGE. 4. A c. purity of design (*mod.*). 5. C. ground BURNS. 6. *C. races*: the Two Thousand, One Thousand, Derby, Oaks, and St. Leger.

B. *sb.* **1.** A writer, or work, of the first rank and of acknowledged excellence; *esp.* (as originally used) in Greek or Latin literature; in *pl.* the general body of Greek and Latin literature 1711. **2.** A classical scholar 1805. **3.** One who adheres to classical rules and models. (Opp. to *romantic*.) 1885. **4.** Short for *c. style, art*, etc. (see A. 4) 1864.

1. The study of the classics GODWIN. Dante was the c. of his country D'ISRAELI. 2. A fine c., and a youth of promise LAMB.

Classical (klæ·sikăl), *a.* 1599. [f. L. *classicus* (see prec.) + -AL.] **1.** = CLASSIC *a.* 1. **2.** = CLASSIC *a.* 2. 1607. **3.** Learned in the classics CLASSIC *sb.* 1) 1711. **4.** Relating to the classics (CLASSIC *sb.* 1) 1839. **5.** = CLASSIC *a.* 5. 1820. **6.** Of literature: Conforming to the rules or models of Greek and Latin antiquity; hence *transf.* of art; opp. to *romantic* 1820. **7.** *Hist.* Of or pertaining to a classis in a Presbyterian Church (see CLASSIS 3) 1586. †**8.** Class-. –1819.

6. The problem is to present new and profound ideas in a perfectly sound and c. style M. ARNOLD. 7. C., provincial, and national synods MACAULAY. Hence **Cla·ssicalism** = CLASSICISM. **Cla·ssicalist. Classica·lity**, c. quality or character; c. scholarship; an instance of c. learning, etc. **Cla·ssicalize** *v.* = CLASSICIZE. **Cla·ssically** *adv.*

Classicism (klæ·sisiz'm). 1837. [f. CLASSIC + -ISM.] **1.** The principles of classic literature or art; adherence to classical style. **2.** A classical (*i.e.* Latin or Greek) idiom or form 1873.

Classicist (klæ·sisist). 1839. [f. as prec + -IST.] An upholder of classic style or form; also, one who advocates the teaching of the Greek and Latin classics in schools.

Classicize (klæ·sisəiz), *v.* 1854. [f. as prec. + -IZE.] To make classic; *intr.* to affect classic style or form.

Classico-, comb. f. L. *classicus* CLASSIC.

Classifiable (klæ·sifəiăb'l), *a.* 1846. [f. CLASSIFY + -ABLE.] Capable of being classified.

Classific (klæsi·fik), *a. rare.* 1809. [f. L. *classis* CLASS + *-ficus*.] That constitutes a class or classes; pertaining to classification.

Classification (klæ:sifikēⁱ·ʃən). 1790. [f. as CLASSIFY.] **1.** The action of classifying. **2.** The result of classifying; a systematic distribution or arrangement, in a class or classes 1794. Hence **Cla:ssifica·tional** *a.* of or pertaining to c.

Classificatory (klæ·sifikēⁱ:təri), *a.* 1837. [f. L. **classificare*; see -ORY.] Tending, or relating, to classification, as the *c. sciences*.

Classify (klæ·sifəi), *v.* 1799. [as if ad. L. **classificare*; see -FY.] To arrange or distribute in classes according to a method or system. Hence **Cla·ssifier**, one who classifies.

‖**Classis** (klæ·sis). Pl. **classes.** 1593. [a. L. *classis* CLASS.] **1.** = CLASS *sb.* 1. 1601. †**2.** A division according to rank; a CLASS –1714. **3.** *Eccl.* In certain churches: an inferior judicatory consisting of the elders or pastors of the parishes or churches of a district; a presbytery 1593; the district thus united 1653. †**4.** In a library: The compartment formed by the bookshelves in the adjacent sides of two stalls, together with those under the window between them –1710.

Cla·ssmate, -mate. 1862. A fellow student in the same class.

Classy (klɑ·si), *a. slang* or *colloq.* 1891. [f. CLASS *sb.* + -Y [1].] Superior, high-class.

Clastic (klæ·stik), *a.* 1875. [f. Gr. type *κλαστικός, f. κλαστός, f. κλάειν.] **1.** *Geol.* Consisting of broken pieces of older rocks 1877. **2.** *Anat.* (Of a model) Composed of separable pieces; pertaining to such a model 1875.

Clathrate (klæ·þreⁱt), *a.* [ad. L. *clathratus*, *clathrare*, f. *clathri* (pl.) lattice (Gr. κλῆθρα bars).] *Bot.* Resembling lattice-work; cancellate. So **Cla·throid** *a.*

Clatter (klæ·təɹ), *sb.* 1460. [In 15th c. *clater*; echoic. Cf. Du. *klater* a rattle.] **1.** A rattling noise made by the rapidly repeated collision of sonorous bodies that do not ring 1578. **2.** Noisy talk; gabble 1460; in *mod. Sc.*, gossip, tittle-tattle 1596.

1. The c. of the hoes among the pebbles KINGSLEY. 2. Hold stille thi clattur 1460. Such a c. of tongues in empty heads LONGF. Hence **Cla·ttery** *a.* (*colloq.*).

Clatter (klæ·təɹ), *v.* [OE. *clatrian*; echoic. Cf. Du. *klateren* to rattle.] **1.** *intr.* To make the noise described under CLATTER *sb.*; to rattle. Said of the instruments or the agent. Also with *along, down, over*, etc. **2.** *trans.* To cause to rattle 1537. **3.** *intr.* To chatter, babble; in *mod. Sc.*, to tattle ME. †**4.** To utter in a chattering way; prate about –1735. Also *advb.*

1. They fall a-clattering with..drums and kettles DE FOE. 2. The servants c. the plates and glasses

TUCKER. 3. The Load-starre of Reformation as some men c. MILT. Hence Cla·tterer.

Claucht; see CLAUGHT.

Claude Lorraine glass. Also **Claude-glass.** 1789. [Named from *Claude* (of) *Lorraine* (1600–1682).] A somewhat convex dark or coloured hand-mirror, used to reduce the proportions of a landscape.

†**Clau·dicant,** *a.* 1624. [ad. L. *claudicantem.*] Lame, halting (*lit.* and *fig.*) –1708. So †**Claudica·tion** the action of limping.

Claught, pa. t. of CLEEK *v.*, to snatch, clutch. Also as *sb.* and *v. Sc.* 1800.

Clause (klǭz). ME. [a. OF., ad. med.L. *clausa*, in sense of L. *clausula*; f. L. *claudere, clausum.*] 1. A short sentence; a single passage of a discourse or writing; a distinct member of a sentence, *esp.* in *Gram.* one containing a subject and predicate. 2. A particular and separate article, stipulation, or proviso, in any formal or legal document ME. †3. Close; *esp.* the close of a sentence –1724.

2. The passing of a statute of twenty clauses STUBBS. *Penal C., Saving C.* 3. The sweet falling of the clauses BACON. *Comb.* **C.-rolls,** = CLOSE ROLLS.

†**Clau·ster, -re.** [OE. *clauster*, a. L. *claustrum*, f. *claus-, claud-* to shut. Cf. CLOISTER.] A cloister, cell, or monastery –1726.

Claustral (klǭ·străl), *a.* ME. [ad. late L. *claustralis*; see CLOISTER.] 1. Pertaining to a cloister. 2. Cloister-like 1862.

Claustrophobia (klǭstrŏfōᵘ·biă). 1879. [mod.L., f. *claustrum* CLOISTER + -PHOBIA.] *Path.* A morbid dread of confined places.

†**Clau·sure.** ME. [ad. L. *clausura*; cf. *closure.*] The action of closing or enclosing –1670; closed condition –1815; that which encloses –1669.

Claut (klǭt), *sb. Sc.* and *n. dial.* 1697. [? conn. w. *claw* or *claught.*] A handful, a rakeful, a scraping. So **Claut** *v.* to scratch, claw, rake, scrape out, etc.

Clavate (klē¹·veⁱt), *a.* 1661. [ad. L. *clavatus, clavare*, f. *clavus* nail. In sense 2 as f. L. *clava* club.] †1. Knobbed. 2. *Zool.* and *Bot.* Club-shaped; thickened towards the apex like a club 1813. So **Cla·vated** *a.*

Clave, pa. t. of CLEAVE *v.*

‖**Clavecin** (klæ·vĭsin). 1819. [F., ad. med.L. *clavicymbalum*; see CLAVICYMBAL.] The French name of the Harpsichord. Hence **Cla·vecinist,** a player on the c.

Clavel (klæ·vĕl). Now *dial.* 1602. [a. OF. :—L. **clavellus*, dim. of *clavus* nail.] The lintel over a fire-place. Also in *comb.*, as **c.-piece,** mantelpiece. var. **Clavy.**

†**Cla·vellated,** *a.* 1660. [f. med.L. *clavellatus*, OF. *clavelée*, in *cendre clavelée*, mod.F. *cendre gravelée.*] In *Clavellated Ashes*: Potash obtained from the dried and calcined lees of wine, for the use of dyers –1735.

Claver (klē¹·vəɪ), *sb. Sc.* and *n. dial.* 1689. [?] Idle garrulous talk; a piece of idle gossip. Ane Knox deaving us a' wi' his clavers? 1689.

Claver (klæ·vəɪ), *v.*[1] Now *dial.* ME. [Cf. Da. *klavre*, and mod.Du. *klaveren*, in same sense.] To climb, clamber.

Claver (klē¹·vəɪ), *v.*[2] *Sc.* and *n. dial.* 1605. [?] To talk idly; to gossip, prate.

Clavichord (klæ·vikǭɪd). Now *Hist.* 1483. [ad. 15th c. L. *clavichordium*, f. *clavis* + *chorda.* See also CLARICHORD.] A musical instrument with strings and keys, in its developed form resembling a square pianoforte.

Clavicle (klæ·vik'l). 1615. [ad. L. *clavicula*, dim. of *clavis* key: in med.L. 'collar-bone'.] 1. *Anat.* The collar-bone, which extends from the breast-bone to the shoulder-blade, forming part of the pectoral arch. In birds the two clavicles are united into the furculum or merry-thought. †2. *Bot.* A tendril –1750. †3. *Conch.* The head of a spiral shell –1774.

Clavicorn (klæ·vikǭɪn). [ad. mod.L. *clavicornis*, f. *clava* + *cornu.*] *Ent.* Club-horned: applied to the *Clavicornes*, a subsection of pentamerous beetles having club-shaped antennæ.

Clavicular (klævi·kiŭlăɪ), *a.* 1824. [f. L. *clavicula* + -AR.] Of or pertaining to the CLAVICLE. Hence **Clavi·cularly** *adv.*

Clavicymbal (klævisi·mbăl). Now *Hist.* 1492. [ad. med.L. *clavicymbalum*, f. *clavis* key + *cymbalum* CYMBAL. See also CLARICYMBAL, CLAVECIN.] An old name of the Harpsichord.

‖**Clavicytherium** (klævisiþīᵊ·riŏm). [Better *clavicitherium*, f. L. *clavis* + CITHER.] An early musical instrument; in effect, an upright spinet. var. **Clavici·thern.** BROWNING.

‖**Cla·vier.** 1708. [F. *clavier*, orig. a key-bearer (on L. type *claviarius*, f. *clavis* key). Cf. G. *klavier.*] 1. The keyboard or set of keys of a musical instrument. 2. (klăvīᵊ·r). A German name of all keyboard instruments with strings; now *esp.* the pianoforte. 3. A dummy keyboard for practice.

Claviform (klæ·vifǭɪm), *a.* 1817. [f. L. *clava* club + -FORM.] Club-shaped.

†**Claviger** (klæ·vidʒəɪ). 1606. [a. L.] One who carries a key or a club –1712. So **Clavi·gerous** *a.* (Dicts.)

‖**Clavis** (klē¹·vis). 1649. [L.] A key.

‖**Clavus** (klē¹·vŏs). [L. *clavus* nail.] 1. = CORN *sb.*[2] 2. The disease ERGOTISM.

Claw (klǭ), *sb.* [OE. *clawu*, obl. cases *clawe*, pointing to a type **klawâ*. See also CLEE.] 1. The sharp horny nail arming the feet of birds and some beasts; also *transf.*; *loosely*, the foot thus armed OE. †2. A hoof, or one of the parts of a (cloven) hoof –1661. 3. *fig.* ME. 4. *transf.* Any contrivance resembling a claw OE. 5. *Bot.* The narrow sharpened base of the petal, in some flowers, by which it is attached 1794.

3. *In one's claws*: in one's possession or power. 4. The C. of a Hammer 1677.

attrib. and *Comb.*: **c.-hammer,** a hammer with a c. for extracting nails; **-hammer coat** (*colloq.*), a tail coat for evening dress; **†-poll,** a toady (cf. *claw-back*).

Hence **Clawed** *a.* having claws. **Claw·less** *a.*

Claw (klǭ), *v.* Pa. t. and pple. **clawed.** [OE. *clawian*, deriv. of *clawu* CLAW.] 1. *trans.* To scratch or tear with or as with claws. 2. To seize, grip, clutch, or pull with claws 1557; *intr.* to grasp or clutch (*at*, etc.); to scratch *at* ME. 3. *trans.* To scratch gently, so as to relieve itching or to soothe ME. Also †*fig.* 4. Hence: To flatter, cajole, fawn upon. Now *dial.* ME. Also †*intr.* 5. *Naut.* (*intr.*) To beat to windward from a lee-shore. Also *to c. off* or *from* (the shore). 1642. †6. To strike as with claws; to beat. Now *dial.* 1584.

2. But Age..hath clawed me in his clutch *Haml.* v. i. 80. 3. If eny wight wold c. us on the galle CHAUCER.

Phrases. †*To c. the back of* (see sense 3); hence †**Claw·-back,** a toady. *C. me and I'll c. thee* (see sense 4). †*To c. away, off*: to rate soundly, scold; †to get rid of.

Clay (klē¹), *sb.* [Com. Teut.: OE. *clǣg*:—OTeut. **klaijâ-*, verbal root *kli-* (*klei-, klai-*), to stick, cleave + suffix *-ja*. See CLEAM, CLAM.] 1. A stiff viscous earth, consisting mainly of aluminium silicate, and derived mostly from the decomposition of felspathic rocks. It is found in beds or other deposits at various depths, and forms with water a tenacious paste which may be moulded into any shape, and hardens when dried. †2. Used *transf.* of *bitumen*, etc. –1584. 3. Used loosely for: Earth, moist earth, mire, mud ME. 4. Earth as the material of the human body (cf. Gen. ii. 7); hence, the human body; the material part of man ME. 5. Short for *clay-pipe* (colloq.) 1863. 6. *attrib.* Of or made of clay 1523.

1. *Boulder, Kimmeridge, London, Oxford, Purbeck C.*, etc. *Brick, fire, plastic, porcelain, potter's c.*; *pipe-c.*, etc. 2. The toughe cleye of Babilon called Bitumen EDEN. C. and C., differs in dignity *Cymb.* IV. ii. 4. *To moisten* or *wet one's c.* (joc.): to drink.

Comb.: **c.-band,** a thin stratum of c.; hence *c. band ironstone*, a variety of Chalybite; **-brained** *a.*, dull, clod-pated; **-cold,** as cold as c.: usually of a dead body; **c. iron-ore, c. ironstone,** any iron-ore containing much c., *esp.* argillaceous hæmatite; **-mill,** a mill for mixing and tempering c.; **-pipe,** a tobacco-pipe made of baked c. (pipe-c.); **-pit,** a pit from which c. is dug; **-puddle** (see PUDDLE); **-slate,** an argillaceous sedimentary rock, of bluish or greenish colour, having a cleavage which crosses the original stratification at all angles; **-stone,** *Min.* a felspathic rock which emits an odour of damp c. when breathed upon.

Hence **Cla·yen** *a.* (*arch.*) of c.; clay-. **Clay·ey** *a.* full of c.; of the nature of c.; soiled with c.; c.-like; also *fig.* of 'mortal clay'. **Clay·ish** *a.* ? *Obs.*

Clay (klē¹), *v.* 1523. [f. prec. sb.] 1. To cover, or dress, with clay. 2. To treat (sugar) with clay in refining 1703.

Claye (klē¹). 1708. [a. F. *claie*, in 14th c. *claye*:—late L. *cleta* (cf. *seta*; *seie, soie*).] A hurdle.

Claymore (klē¹·mōᵊɪ). 1772. *Hist.* [ad. Gael. *claidheamh* (klai·ăv) *mòr* 'great sword'.] The two-edged (rarely *two-handed*) broadsword of the ancient Scottish Highlanders. Also *ellipt.* a man armed with this.

Cleach, cleech (klītʃ), *v.* Now *dial.* [ME. *cleche*, f. OE. **clǣc(e)an*, **clǣhte.*] 1. To clutch (*trans.* and *intr.*) 2. To lift (water, etc.) in the hollow of the hand, or with a shallow vessel.

Clead, cleed, *v.* [ME. (north.) *cleþe*, pa. t. *cledde*, pa. pple. *cled*; f. OTeut. type **klaiþjan*, f. *klaiþo-* cloth.] = CLOTHE *v.* Hence **Clea·ding** *vbl. sb.* clothing (*Sc.* and *n. Eng.*); *Mech.* a casing (as of felt or wood), to prevent radiation of heat, etc.

Cleam, cleme, *v.* Now *dial.* [OE. *clǣman*:—OTeut. **klaimjan*, f. **klaimo-*, in OE. *clam* 'cloam'. Cf. CLAM.] To smear, bedaub, plaster; to cause to stick.

Clean (klīn), *a.* [Com. Teut.: OE. *clǣne*:—preh. **clâni*:—WGer. **klaini*. The original sense was 'clear, pure'.] †1. Clear; undimmed –1708. 2. Pure; free from foreign matter OE. 3. Free from dirt or filth. Now the ordinary sense. OE. 4. Free from spiritual or moral pollution. Const. †*of, from.* OE. 5. Free from ceremonial or sanitary defilement OE. 6. Clean in habit 1568. 7. Of style or language: Free from faults, correct, pure (*arch.*) ME. 8. Proper; well-built, shapely; clever, smart, dexterous ME. 9. Clear of obstructions, inequalities, or unevennesses ME. 10. With nouns of action, etc.: Entire, complete, perfect, sheer. (Cf. *To sweep clean.*) ME. Also in *comb.*; see after the adv.

1. All of Diamond perfect pure and cleene SPENSER *F. Q.* I. vii. 33. 2. C. water ME., coal 1872, land (*mod.*). 3. Cleane linnen *Mids. N.* IV. ii. 41. A c. ship DE FOE. A c. copy (*mod.*). *C. Bill of Health* (fig.): see BILL *sb.*[3] *To make a c. breast* (fig.): see BREAST. 4. Create in mee a cleane heart, O God *Ps.* li. 10. 7. A clene and elegant stile ELYOT. 8. The hocks and legs.. 'clean' 1836. A .. c. field *Cricket Annual.* 9. C. coast, harbour SMYTH, oak 1884. A c. wound 1807. 10. To make cleane work COTGR. Hence **Clea·nish** *a.* pretty c.

Clean (klīn), *adv.* [OE. *clǣne, clēne*, f. the adj.; orig. *clâne*.] 1. In a clean manner (see CLEAN *a.* 1, 2, 8, 10). 2. Without anything omitted or left; wholly, quite, absolutely OE.

1. The room must be c. swept (*mod.*). 2. C. off his head 1883. C. dismay'd SPENSER, bowled (*mod.*).

Clean-, *adj.* and *adv.* in *comb.*

1. With pples., as *c.-built, -complexioned, -going*, etc. 2. **c.-cut,** sharply defined; **-fingered,** with nimble fingers; scrupulous, honest; **-handed,** having clean hands, free from wrong-doing; **-limbed,** shapely of limb; **-timbered,** well-built, clean-limbed.

Clean (klīn), *v.* 1450. [In 15th c. *clene*, f. the adj.; in current use more literal than *to cleanse.*] To make CLEAN (see CLEAN *a.*). Also *absol.* and *intr.* 1708.

To c. shoes 1714, a portrait TYNDALL, a ship's bottom DAMPIER, fish LANE, land 1886.

Phrases. *To c. out*: to c. by emptying; *transf.* to exhaust, leave bare. Also *fig.* *slang.* To rook. Hence **Clea·nable** *a.* **Clea·ner,** one who or that which cleans.

Clean, *sb.* 1872. An act of cleaning: chiefly in comb., as *a clean up, out*, etc. *spec.* (in *U.S. Mining*) *clean-up*: the collecting of all the product of a given period or operation.

Cleanly (kle·nli), *a.* [OE. *clǣnlîc*, f. *clǣne* CLEAN + *lîc* body.] †1. Morally or spiritually clean –1683. †2. Clean: as clothes, etc. –1590. 3. Habitually clean; habitually kept clean 1500. 4. Conducing to cleanness 1611. †5. Neat; dexterous, elegant –1712.

1. A man of c. behaviour 1683. 3. Some plain but c. country maid DRYDEN. An honest c. Alehouse WALTON. 4. A c. diet BURTON. Hence **Clea·nlily** *adv.* **Clea·nliness,** c. quality or state.

Cleanly (klī·nli), *adv.* [OE. *clǣnlîc.*] In a clean manner (see CLEAN *a.*); †completely –1655; †ably, adroitly –1642.

Ile purge..and liue c. *1 Hen. IV*, v. iv. 169.

Cleanness (klī·nₙnĕs). [OE. *clǣnnes.*] The quality or state of being CLEAN (*lit.* and *fig.*). †*C. of teeth*: scarcity of food. (*Amos* iv. 6.)

Cleansable (kle·nzăb'l), *a.* 1483. [f. CLEANSE *v.*] That can be cleansed.

Cleanse (klenz), *v.* [OE. *clǣnsian, clensian* :—WGer. *klainisōn, f. *klaini*, OE. *clǣne.* The sp. follows *clean.*] **1.** To make clean; to purify, to free from dirt, infection, guilt, pollution, a charge, etc. Also *absol.* In the literal senses now usually *clean.* **2.** To clear, to rid *of, from* ME. **3.** To purge; also *absol.* OE.

1. You cannot c. your heart with tears TRENCH. What God hath cleansed, that call not thou common *Acts* x. 15. Hence **Clea·nser.**

Clear (klīᵊɹ), *a., adv.*, and *sb.* [ME. *cler, a.* OF. :—L. *clarum.* Partly infl. by CLEAN.]

A. *adj.* **I. 1.** Of light: †*orig.* Brightly shining –1667; *now*, pure, unclouded. Of a fire: Without flame or smoke. 1611. **2.** Fully light, bright, serene (*arch.*); free from cloud, mists, and haze; *fig.* serene ME. **3.** Transparent, translucent ME. **4.** Shining; lustrous ME.; †of women: Beauteous –1578. †**5.** *fig.* Illustrious. [So L. *clarus.*] –1605.

1. Cleare as the sun *Song Sol.* vi. 10. 2. Almost cleere dawn *Meas. for M.* IV. ii. 226. A c. frosty evening (*mod.*). *fig.* His brow grew c. LYTTON.

II. 1. Clearly seen, distinct 1835. **2.** Easy to understand, perspicuous ME. **3.** Distinct, free from confusion ME. **4.** Evident, plain ME. **5.** Of the eyes, etc.: Having keen perception 1576. **6.** That discerns without confusion of ideas ME. **7.** Of persons: Subjectively free from doubt; certain, positive, determined 1604.

2. The words are cleare and plaine 1615. To make oneself c. JOWETT. 3. C. notions of law and government MACAULAY. 4. Quoth Hudibras, The case is c. BUTLER. 6. C. thinkers always have a c. style BUCKLE. 7. I am not c. on the point HT. MARTINEAU.

III. Of sound: Ringing, pure and well-defined; distinctly audible ME.

IV. 1. *fig.* from I. 3: Pure, unsophisticated ME. **2.** Unspotted; innocent ME.

1. Fame is the spur that the c. spirit doth raise *Lycidas* 70. 2. Duncane..hath bin So cleere in his great Office *Macb.* I. vii. 18.

V. 1. Unencumbered; net 1500. **2.** Unqualified; absolute, complete; sheer 1529. **3.** Free from contact; quite free; quit, rid 1658. **4.** Unobstructed; unoccupied; open 1568. **5.** Emptied of contents, load, or cargo 1607. **6.** Free from legal or other complications 1635. **7.** *U.S. slang.* Unadulterated, pure, real 1837.

1. A c. thousand a year for doing..nothing COBBETT. 2. Three feet c. 3. Let me be cleere of thee *Twel. N.* IV. i. 4. 4. Seeing the coast cleere GREENE. 6. I was now a c. man DE FOE.

B. *adv.* [Partly the adj. used predicatively; partly after native Eng. advs., *esp.* CLEAN *adv.*] **1.** Brightly ME. †**2.** = CLEARLY –1782. †**3.** = CLEAN *adv.* 2. –1690.

C. *sb.* **I.** Ellipt. †**1.** A fair lady. (in ME.) †**2.** Brightness, clearness –1611. **3.** Clear space 1715.

2. Thy cleere with cloudy darkes is scar'd LODGE. 3. *In the c.*: in interior measurement.

II. Verbal sb. f. CLEAR *v.* A clearing of the sky, weather, etc. 1694.

Comb.: **c.-cut** *a.* sharply chiselled, sharply defined; **-eyed** *a.* having clear eyes (*lit.* and *fig.*); **-headed,** having, or characteristic of, a clear head; **-hea·dedness; -si·ghted** *a.* having clear sight; **-ness.**

Hence **Clea·rish** *a.* **Clea·rly** *adv.* **Clea·rness.**

Clear (klīᵊɹ), *v.* ME. [f. CLEAR *a.*] **1.** To make or become CLEAR or bright. Also with *up.* **2.** To make pure from stain; to purify, clarify; to prove innocent; to acquit ME. **3.** To make (a person) clear as to a matter ME.; to elucidate ME.; †to prove –1770. **4.** To make clear of things or persons that obstruct or cumber a space 1530. **5.** Hence, *gen.* To free or rid *of.* Now a leading sense. 1535. **6.** To remove, so as to leave the place or way clear. Also with *away, off, out.* 1672. **7.** *intr.* To depart, so as to leave the place clear. Also with *off, out.* 1832. **8.** To make or become clear of contents or burden; to exhaust 1699. **9.** To get (a thing or oneself) clear *of* or *from* 1599; to pass clear of, get clear through or away from 1634; to leap clear over, pass over 1791. **10.** To settle, discharge a *debt, bill*, etc. Also with *off.* 1596. †*intr.* To settle *with* –1796. **11.** To set free from debt, etc. 1704. Also *absol.* **12.** To free (a ship or cargo) by satisfying the customs, harbour dues, etc. 1703; also *absol.*; *hence*, to leave a port under such conditions 1807. **13.** To make in clear profit 1719. **14.** To pass through the Clearing-House (*mod.*).

1. *To c. the air*: *orig.* to free from mists, etc.; *now*, from sultry conditions which precede a storm. To c. the sight SHAKS., the brain DISRAELI, the Voice DE FOE. 2. How! would'st thou c. rebellion ADDISON. To c. oneself of an imputation LOCKE. 3. To c. one's meaning (*mod.*). The evidence of time doth c. this assertion BACON. 4. Police to c. the way SALA. To c. the coasts 1530, the decks 1870, a ship for action 1889, land (for cultivation) 1705. 5. To c. the house of people 1860, cotton †*from* dirt URE. 6. To c. a wreck 1823. 8. *To c. a ship*: to discharge it of its cargo. 9. With one brave bound the copse he cleared SCOTT. 11. To c. an encumbered estate W. PENN. 12. The steamer..cleared at Christiania..bound for New York 1889.

With adverbs: **To c. out: a.** To 'clean out' of cash. **b.** To clear on leaving port. **To c. up:** To make or become clear, orderly, or perspicuous.

Hence **Clea·rage,** the action of clearing; †a clearing. **Clea·rer,** one who or that which CLEARS; also used *techn.*

Clearance (klīᵊ·răns). 1563. [f. CLEAR *v.* + -ANCE.] **1.** The action of clearing, or making clear. **2.** *Comm.* The clearing of a ship at the Custom-House. Cf. CLEAR *v.* 12. 1731. **3.** A clear space. *spec.* In the steam-engine: the distance between the cylinder-cover and the piston when at the end of its stroke. 1788. **4.** A CLEARING (sense 2) 1839. **5.** A certificate that a ship has been cleared on leaving port 1727. **6.** Clear or net profit (*rare*) 1864.

1. The c. of a property from encumbrances 1884, of a storm FROUDE. The Highland clearances 1883.

Clear-cole (klīᵊ·ɹkoul). 1823. [ad. F. *claire colle.*] A preparation of size mixed with whiting or white-lead used as a first coating in house-painting; a coating of size in gilding.

Clearing (klīᵊ·riŋ), *vbl. sb.* ME. [f. CLEAR *v.*] **1.** The action of the vb. CLEAR, in various senses. **2.** A piece of land cleared for cultivation 1823. †**3.** *Comm.* = CLEARANCE 2. –1769. **4.** The passing of cheques, bills, etc., through a clearing-house 1883. Also *attrib.*

1. Upon his said Justification, and C. 1604. 2. A tiny c. pared from the edge of the wood LOWELL.

Clearing House, clearing-house. 1832. An institution in London established by the bankers for the adjustment of their mutual claims for cheques and bills, by exchanging them and settling the balances. Extended to similar institutions, as the *Railway Clearing House*, etc. Also *attrib.*

Clear-obscure. [After F. *clair-obscur.*] 1778. = CHIAROSCURO.

Clear-starch, *v.* 1709. To stiffen and dress linen with clear or colourless starch.

Clear-story, var. of CLERESTORY.

Cleat (klīt), *sb.* [OE. *clēat*; cf. Du. *kloot* ball, Ger. *kloss* CLOT, clod, lump. The primary sense was 'firm lump'.] **1.** A wedge ME. **2.** *Naut.* Orig. a small wedge of wood bolted on its side to a spar, etc., to stop anything from slipping (*stop-c.*), afford a footing (*step-c.*), or serve as a point of attachment or resistance ME. Extended to pieces of wood (or iron) of various shapes, bolted on to parts of a ship for various purposes, as a *belaying c.*, a *launching c.*, etc. 1769. **3.** A wedge-shaped or other piece fastened on, or left projecting, for any purpose; *e.g.* as a handle 1611.

Cleat (klīt), *v.* 1794. [f. prec. sb.] To fasten to, or with, a cleat; to strengthen with thin plates of metal (*dial.*).

Cleavable (klī·văb'l), *a.* 1846. [f. CLEAVE *v.*¹ + ABLE.] That can be cloven, cleft, or split.

Cleavage (klī·vėdʒ). 1816. [f. as prec. + -AGE.] **1.** The action or faculty of cleaving or splitting asunder; the state of being cleft; division (*lit.* and *fig.*) 1867. **2.** *spec.* (*Min.*) Arrangement in laminæ which can be split asunder, and along the planes of which the substance naturally splits; the property of splitting along such planes 1830. **3.** (*Geol.*) *Slaty c.*: the fissile structure in clay slate and similar rocks, whereby these split into the thin laminæ or slates used in roofing, etc. This structure is quite distinct from, and in origin posterior to, the stratification and jointing. 1839. (with *pl.*) The plane in which a crystal or rock may be split 1817.

Cleave, *sb. Ir.* 1586. [ad. Ir. *cliabh.*] A basket.

Cleave (klīv), *v.*¹ Pa. t. **clove, clave, cleaved, cleft;** Pa. pple. **cloven, clove, cleaved, cleft.** [Com. Teut.: OE. *clēofan, clēofan* :—OTeut. type *kleuƀ-, *klauƀ—kluƀum, kluƀano-*, = pre-Teut. *gleubh-, in Gr. γλυφ- 'to cut with a knife', and perh. L. *glub-* 'to flay'.] **1.** *trans.* To part or divide by a cutting blow; to hew asunder; to split; to pierce and penetrate 1558. **2.** To separate or sever by dividing or splitting ME. **3.** *intr.* (for *refl.*) To split or fall asunder ME. **4.** *intr.* To cleave one's way 1655.

1. Abraham..claue the wood for the burnt offering *Gen.* xxii. 3. To cleaue a heart in twaine *Meas. for M.* III. i. 63. To c. the flood MILT. *P. R.* III. 433. 3. The ground claue asunder *Numb.* xvi. 31.

Cleave (klīv), *v.*² Pa. t. **cleaved, clave;** Pa. pple. **cleaved.** [OE. *clifan* str. vb., and *clifian, cleofian* wk. vb. :—OTeut. *klīƀan, perh. f. root *kli-* to stick. The form *clave* is perpetuated by the influence of the Bible of 1611.] **1.** To stick fast or adhere, as by a glutinous surface, *to.* Also *fig.* **2.** In wider sense: To cling or hold fast *to*; to attach oneself *to* ME. **3.** To adhere or cling *to* (a person, party, principle, etc.); to remain attached *to* ME. †**4.** To remain steadfast –1594.

1. Their tongue cleaued to the roof of their mouth *Job* xxix. 10. *fig.* A..phrase cleaving as it were to the memory PALEY. 3. He schal clyue to his wyf WYCLIF *Ephes.* v. 31. The mercenary soldiers..clave to King Henry FREEMAN.

Cleavelandite (klī·vlăndəit). 1823. [f. *Cleaveland* the mineralogist.] *Min.* A variety of albite from Chesterfield, Mass.

Cleaver (klī·vəɹ). 1483. [f. CLEAVE *v.*¹] One who or that which cleaves; *spec.* a butcher's chopper for cutting up carcasses.

Cleavers (klī·vəɹz), **cli-** (kli-). [In OE. *clife*, f. root of *clifian* to adhere; app. confused later with *clive* CLEAVE.] *Bot.* The climbing plant *Galium Aparine* or Goose-grass, which adheres by its hooked prickles to clothes, etc.

‖**Cleché, -ée** (kle·tʃi, ‖kleʃe), *a.* 1688. [F., f. L. type *clavicatus 'key-holed', f. *clavis.*] *Her.* **a.** Voided or hollowed throughout, as a cross showing only a narrow border. **b.** Of a cross: Having the extremities shaped like the handle of an ancient key.

Cleck (klek), *v.* Chiefly *Sc.* ME. [a. ON. *klekja* to hatch.] *trans.* Of birds: To hatch. Also *transf.* and *fig.* Hence **Cle·cking** *vbl. sb.* hatching.

Cledge (kledʒ). 1723. [prob. conn. w. CLAG.] In Kent, etc., clay or clayey soil; in Bedfordshire, the upper of the two beds of Fuller's Earth. Hence **Cle·dgy** *a.* clayey; sticky.

Clee. Now *dial.* OE. [var. of CLAW, repr. OE. *clēa* (*cleo*). See CLAW.] = CLAW *sb.* 1, 2.

Cleek (klīk), *sb.* Chiefly *Sc.* ME. [Cf. CLEEK *v.*, and CLICK.] **1.** A large hook or crook for catching hold of something. **2.** *Golf.* An iron-headed club with a straight narrow face and a long shaft 1829.

Cleek (klīk), *v. n. dial.* Pa. t. **claucht, claught.** ME. [= CLEACH, ME. *clechen.*] **1.** *trans.* To seize with the clutch or hand; to clutch firmly, suddenly, or eagerly. **2.** To snatch ME. **3.** To lay hold of with a cleek 1857.

Clef¹ (klef). 1579. [a. F. :—L. *clavem* key.] *Mus.* A character placed on a particular line of a stave, to indicate the name and pitch of the notes standing on that line, and hence of the other notes. Occas. loosely = *stave.* Also *fig.*

There are three clefs in use, the C, tenor, or alto clef, the G or treble clef, and the F or bass clef, which denote respectively the middle C on a piano, the G above, and the F below. They are written respectively as here shown. In modern music the C clef is called the soprano, alto, or tenor clef, as it is placed upon the first, third, or fourth line of the stave.

†**Clef**². *rare.* 1494. [app. Anglo-Fr. *clef, ad. L. *clavus* pin.] The pin of a weighing beam –1568.

Cleft, clift, *sb.* [ME. *clyft, clift* (app. OE. *clyft) :—OTeut. *kluftiz, f. *kluƀ-, kleuƀ-, clēof-* to cleave. *Cleft* is assim. to *cleft*, pa. pple. of CLEAVE. In 16–18th c. confounded with CLIFF.] **1.** A space or division made by cleaving; a split, fissure, crack, crevice. **2.** *spec.* **a.** The parting of the thighs, the fork. Now *dial.* ME. **b.** A crack of the skin; a disease of the feet of horses 1576. **3.** Split wood, *esp.* for fuel. Now *dial.* ME.

Comb. **c.-graft** *v.* to graft in a c. or slit made for the purpose.

Cleft (kleft), *ppl. a.* ME. [f. CLEAVE *v.*[1]; cf. CLOVEN.] Split asunder; partly split; bifurcate. Also *fig.*

C. palate: a malformation in which a longitudinal gap exists in the middle or on either side of the roof of the mouth. *A c. stick*: a position in which advance and retreat are alike impossible, a fix. *C. foot, hoof*: = *cloven foot*, etc.

Cleft, pa. t. and pple. of CLEAVE *v.*[1]; occas. of CLEAVE *v.*[2]

Cleg (kleg). Now *Sc.* and *dial.* 1449. [a. ON. *kleggi*, mod. Norw. *klegg*.] A gadfly, horse-fly, or breeze.

Cleido-mastoid (kləidoˌmæ·stoid), *a.* [f. Gr. κλείς, κλειδ- + MASTOID.] *Anat.* Pertaining to the clavicle and mastoid process.

Cleistogamic (kləistogæ·mik), *a.* 1877. [f. Gr. κλειστός closed + γάμος + -IC; cf. *phanerogamic.*] *Bot.* Applied to certain small inconspicuous permanently closed flowers, adapted for self-fertilization, occurring in various plants on the same individuals as the normal flowers, which in such cases are either cross-fertilized or barren. So **Cleisto·gamous** *a.* **Cleisto·gamy,** the occurrence of cleistogamous flowers.

Cleithral (kləi·þrăl), *a.* 1850. [f. Gr. κλεῖθρον, f. κλείειν to close + -AL.] *Gr. Arch.* Of a temple: Covered in: opp. to HYPÆTHRAL.

Clem (klem), **clam** (klæm), *v. dial.* 1540. [app. f. (ult.) Com. Teut. *klammjan, f. *klamm-*, OE. *clamm, clǫmm* sb. fetter, cramp, etc.; see CLAM *sb.*[1]] *trans.* To pinch; to waste with hunger, starve. Also *intr.*

Clematis (kle·mătis). 1551. [a. L., a. Gr. κληματίς, prob. periwinkle, f. κλῆμα vine-branch. Erron. *clemā·tis.*] *Bot.* A genus of twining shrubs (N.O. *Ranunculaceæ*), having flowers with a showy calyx and no corolla, and seed-vessels adorned with long feathery appendages. The only British species is *C. Vitalba*, also called Virgin's Bower, Traveller's Joy, and Old Man's Beard. †**2.** The Periwinkle –1607.

†**Cle·mence.** = next.

Clemency (kle·mĕnsi). 1553. [ad. L. *clementia.*] **1.** Mildness or gentleness of temper in the exercise of authority or power; mercy, leniency. **2.** Mildness of weather or climate 1667.

1. A prince..famous for his c. FULLER. C... is the standing policy of constitutional governments HALLAM.

Clement (kle·mĕnt), *a.* 1483. [ad. L. *clementem.*] **1.** Mild and humane in the exercise of power or authority; merciful, lenient, kindly. **2.** Of weather, etc.: Mild; opp. to *inclement* (*rare*) 1622. Hence **Cle·mently** *adv.* var. †**Cleme·ntious, -ly.**

Clementine (kle·mĕntəin), *a.* ME. [ad. L. *clementinus*, f. *Clemens*, the adj. used as a pr. name.] Of or pertaining to Clement: *esp.* to Clement of Rome and writings ascribed to him; also, to Pope Clement V and his Constitutions. Also as *sb.* (in both applications).

Clench (klenʃ), *sb.* 1598. [f. CLENCH *v.*] **1.** = CLINCH *sb.* q. v. **2.** The action of clenching (the fists, etc.); *fig.* conclusive confirmation, etc. Formerly also CLINCH. 1779.

Clench (klenʃ), *v.* [ME. *clenchen* :—OE. *clęnc(e)an* :—OTeut. type *klankjan to make to cling together, to rivet. See CLINCH *v.*] **1.** = CLINCH. **2.** To set firmly together, close tightly (the fingers, fist, teeth). Formerly also CLINCH. 1747. Also *fig.*

Clenched (klenʃt, *poet.* kle·nʃĕd), *ppl. a.* ME. [f. prec.] Firmly fastened, tightly closed.

Clencher (kle·nʃəɹ). 1559. [f. as prec.] He who or that which clenches; a conclusive statement, argument, etc. (more commonly *clincher*).

Clencher-built: see CLINKER *sb.*[3]

†**Clepe,** *v.* [OE. *clipian*, repr. an OTeut. type *klipōjan. Cf. CLAP *v.*] **1.** *intr.* To cry, call –1563. **2.** *trans.* To call (a person) –1567; to address –1513. **3.** To call by the name of, call, name. Still used as *arch.*, esp. in the pa. pple. *ycleped, yclept* (ikle·pt). OE. **4.** *ellipt.* To speak of. CHAUCER. Hence †**Clepe** *sb.* a call (*rare*).

‖**Clepsydra** (kle·psidră). Pl. **-as,** and **-æ.** 1646. [L., a. Gr. κλεψύδρα, f. κλεψ- (κλέπτειν) + ὕδωρ.] A water-clock used by the ancients to measure time by the discharge of water.

Cleptomania, var. of KLEPTOMANIA.

Clerestory (klīə·ɹstōəri). ME. [f. *clere* CLEAR + STORY. (*Clere* must here have meant 'light, lighted'; see CLEAR *a.*)] The upper part of the nave, choir, and transepts of any large church, containing a series of windows, clear of the roofs of the aisles, admitting light to the central parts of the building. Also *transf.*

attrib. Clerestory window: a window having no cross piece to divide the light.

†**Cle·rete.** [ME. *clertė, cleertė*, var. of *clartė*, a. OF. :—L. *claritatem.* Cf. CLARITY.] Clearness, brightness, lustre; glory, renown –1520.

Clergess. *Hist.* ME. [a. OF.: fem. of *clerc.*] A female scholar; a member of a female religious order.

†**Cle·rgion.** Also **-eon.** ME. [a. OF. *clerjon*, mod. *clergeon*, dim. of *clerc.*] A young clerk or chorister; also *fig.* –1540.

Clergy (klə̄·ɹdʒi). ME. [a. OF. *clergie, clargie*, lit. 'clerkship', f. *clerc* :—L. *clericus* CLERK. In 1–3, the proper word was L. *clericatus*, OF. *clergié*, F. *clergé* masc.] †**1.** The clerical office –1561. **2.** *concr.* The clerical order; the body of men set apart by ordination for religious service in the Christian church; opp. to *laity*. (Orig. a term of the Catholic church.) ME. †*transf.* of the priestly order in non-Christian religions –1727. **3.** As tr. Gr. κλῆρος, and of κλήρων in 1 *Pet.* v. 3 ME. **4.** Clerkly skill; learning (mod.F. *clergie*). *Obs.* exc. in provb. ME. **5.** Old Law. *Benefit of* (*his*) *clergy*, also simply (*his*) *clergy*: orig. the privilege allowed to clergymen of exemption from trial by a secular court; modified and extended later to every one who could read. (Thus 'benefit of the clerical office' became = 'benefit of scholarship'.) Abolished in 1827. Cf. NECK-VERSE. ME. Also *attrib.*

2. The c. and laity BLACKSTONE. A married c. WHATELEY. **4.** An Ounce of Mother-Wit is worth a Pound of C., or Book-learning 1690. **5.** By the Laws of this Realm the Benefit of C. is not allowed to Women convicted of Felony 1623. Hence **Cle·rgiable** *a.* admitting benefit of c. †**Cle·rgial** *a.* clerkly.

Clergyman (klə̄·ɹdʒimæ̆n). 1577. A man of the clerical order; an ordained minister of the Christian church. (In England, commonly meaning a minister of the Church of England.) †*transf.* (see CLERGY 2) –1693. So **Cle·rgywoman,** †a nun; †a priestess; a clergyman's wife, etc. (*joc.*)

Cleric (kle·rik). 1621. [ad. late L. *clericus*, prop. 'of or belonging to the *clerus*'; a. Gr. κληρικός, in Christian use 'of or belonging to the sacerdotal order', f. κλῆρος lot, heritage. See Bp. Lightfoot *Philippians* (1868) 245–6.] **A.** *adj.* Of or pertaining to the clergy, CLERICAL. **B.** *sb.* A clergyman. Often used instead of CLERK (sense 1), as less ambiguous. 1621.

Clerical (kle·rikăl), *a.* (*sb.*) 1592. [f. L. *clericalis*, f. *clericus*; see prec.] **1.** Of, pertaining to, or characteristic of, the clergy or a clergyman. **2.** Of or pertaining to a CLERK or penman, of clerks 1798. **3.** *sb.* A cleric 1837.

1. C. garb LYTTON. **2.** A c. error GURWOOD. Hence **Cle·ricalism,** c. principles; c. rule; c. partisanship. **Clerica·lity,** a c. trait; c. quality or condition. **Cle·rically** *adv.*

Cle·ricate. [ad. L. *clericatus.*] Clerical office. BROWNING.

Clericity (klĭri·sĭti). [mod. f. L. type **clericitas.*] Clerical quality or status.

Clerico- (kle·riko), comb. f. L. *clericus*, = clerically-, clerical and . . ., as in *c.-liberal*, etc.

Clerisy (kle·rĭsi). 1818. [app. after Ger. *clerisei*, in late L. *clericia.*] **1.** Learned men as a body, scholars. **2.** = CLERICITY 1858.

1. A learned body, or c., as such COLERIDGE.

Clerk (klāɹk, klə̄ɹk), *sb.* [OE. had *cleric, clerec, clerc*, immed. from Latin; see CLERIC, and cf. OF. *clerc.* The ordinary sense is now penman. In U.S., and, of late, occas. in London, the pronunc. is klə̄ɹk.] **1.** A churchman, clergyman, or ecclesiastic. (Now often repl. by CLERIC.) **2.** Before the Reformation, *esp.* a member of the five 'minor orders', as distinct from 'holy orders'. Hence, applied to laymen who perform such of these offices as survive. 1549. **3.** A man (or woman) of book learning, one able to read and write; a scholar. (Now *arch.*) ME. †**4.** In early times, *Clerks* (in sense 1, identical with 3) transacted all business involving writing –1555. **5.** Hence, in current use: **a.** An officer who has charge of the records, correspondence, etc., and conducts the business, of any department, court, corporation, or society 1526. **b.** A subordinate employed to make written entries, keep accounts, etc. 1512.

1. The placing of one c. in two churches HOOKER. **2.** *The Parish C.*, the lay officer of a parish church who assists the clergyman by leading the people in responses, assisting at marriages, baptisms, etc. *Bible C.*, a scholar who reads the lessons in some college chapels. **3.** That noble poete and grete clerke vyrgyle CAXTON. **5. a.** *C. to the School-board, Town-c.*, etc. **b.** A telegraph c. (*mod.*).

Hence **Clerk** *v.* (*colloq.*) to act as c. **Cle·rkage,** clerk's work. **Cle·rkdom,** the status or function of a c.; clerks collectively. **Cle·rkhood,** the status of a clergyman (*arch.*), or of an office c. **Cle·rkish** *a.* **Cle·rkless** *a.* **Clerk-like** *a.* and *adv.* **Cle·rkling,** a young or petty c. **Cle·rkship,** the position or function of a c.; book-learning.

Clerkly (klā·ɹkli), *a.* 1528. [f. CLERK *sb.*] **1.** Clerical 1565. **2.** Book-learned (*arch.*) 1528. **3.** Skilled in penmanship 1808. **4.** Of or belonging to an office clerk 1845. So **Cle·rkly** *adv.* Hence **Cle·rkliness,** c. quality.

Clero- (klīə·ro), comb. f. L. *clerus*, Gr. κλῆρος, in the sense of 'clergy', as †**Clerola·ical** *a.*, composed of clergy and laity.

Cle·romancy. ? *Obs.* 1620. [f. Gr. κλῆρος lot + -MANCY.] Divination by lots.

Clerstory, obs. f. CLERESTORY.

Cleruch (klīə·rŏk, -ŭk). 1847. [ad. Gr. κληροῦχος, f. κλῆρος + ἔχειν.] *Gr. Antiq.* At Athens, a citizen who received an allotment of land in a foreign state, but retained his rights as a citizen at home. Hence **Cleruchy** (klīə·rŭki) [Gr. κληρουχία], allotment of land among cleruchs; a body of cleruchs.

‖**Cle·rum.** 1655. [Short for *concio ad clerum.*] A Latin sermon preached on certain occasions at the English Universities.

Cletch, *sb. dial.* Also **clatch.** 1691. [f. CLECK *v.*; cf. *bake, batch*, etc. Cf. CLUTCH.] A hatching (of chickens); *contempt.* a family.

Cleuch, cleugh (kliuχ, klūχ). *Sc.* ME. [Sc. form of CLOUGH, q. v.] **1.** A ravine with steep sides, usually that of a stream or torrent. (Freq. in place-names, as *Buccleuch*, etc.) **2.** The precipitous side of a gorge 1533.

Cleve, cleeve (klīv). Now *local.* [ME. *cleof, cleove*, var. of *clif* CLIFF, founded on OE. *cleofu, cleofum.* (Occas. erron. *cleave*, as if conn. w. *cleave* to split.) Freq. in local names, as *Clevedon, Cleveland*, etc.] **1.** = CLIFF (*dial.*). †**2.** The shore of the sea. ME. only. **3.** = Sc. *brae* ME.

Clever (kle·vəɹ), *a.* Also **cliver, cleaver.** ME. [? related to ME. *clivers* 'claws', in the sense of 'nimble of claws, sharp to seize'. At first a local and colloquial word.] **1.** Nimble-handed; adroit, dexterous in the use of the limbs, etc. **2.** Possessing skill or talent; dexterous; adroit. (The current sense.) 1716. Of things: Done with adroitness or skill, ingenious 1704. **3.** Nimble, active (*dial.*) 1694. **4.** Clean-limbed, well-made; handsome. Now *dial.* and in *U.S.* 1674. **5.** Handy 1715; 'nice'; convenient; agreeable, amiable 1738. Also as quasi-*adv.* (*dial.*).

1. The old mare is as c. as a cat (*mod. colloq.*). **2.** C. drawings MAD. D'ARBLAY. **4.** The girl was a tight c. wench as any was ARBUTHNOT (J.). **5.** A c. boat STEVENSON. Then come, put the jorum about, And let us be merry and c. GOLDSM. Hence **Cle·verish** *a.* somewhat c. **Cle·verly** *adv.* in a c. manner (in all senses); *dial.* and *U.S.* completely; quite, 'clean'. **Cle·verness,** the quality of being c.

Clevis (kle·vis). 1592. [? an OE. *clyfes* :—**kluƀisi*, f. weak stem of *kleuƀ-, clēof* to CLEAVE. Occas. treated as pl. with sing. *clevy, clevvy.*] A U-shaped piece of iron, with a pin or bolt passing through holes in the two ends, for bolting on to the end of a beam or the like so as to form a loop to which tackle may be attached.

Clew (kliū), *sb.* See also CLUE. [OE. *cliwen, cleowen*, etc. = MLG. *kluwen*, Du. *kluwen* (all neut.). ME. *clywe, clewe*, prob. by loss of the OE. final *-n.*] †**1.** A globular body; a ball –1796. **2.** *esp.* A ball of thread or yarn. (The regular term in Sc. and n. Eng.) OE. Also *fig.*

3. Hence, that which guides or threads a way through a maze, perplexity, difficulty, intricate investigation, etc. ME.; hence, an indication to follow, a key. See CLUE. 1724. 4. A thread or cord (in a series) 1700; the series of cords by which a hammock is suspended 1834. 5. *Naut.* A lower corner of a square sail, or the aftmost corner of a fore-and-aft sail.

2. *fig.* You haue wound a goodly clewe *All's Well* I. iii. 188. 3. With clews like these they tread the maze of state CRABBE. The c. to the great puzzle FREEMAN. *Comb.*: **c.-bottom**, a reel to wind a c. on; **-garnet, clue-garnet**, *Naut.* a tackle to clew up the courses or lower square-sails in furling; **-line, clue-line,** a tackle connecting the c. of a sail to the upper yard or the mast; occas. = *c.-garnets.*

Clew, clue (klū), *v.* ME. [f. prec.] 1. *trans.* To coil *up* into a ball. 2. To point *out* as by a clew 1625. 3. To track as by a clew 1663. 4. *Naut. To c. up*: to draw the clews (of sails) up to the yard in preparation for furling. *To c. down*: to let down (sails) by the clews in unfurling them. Also *absol.*

2. A woman might..clew me out the way to happinesse BEAUM. & FL.

‖**Cliché** (kliʃe). 1832. [Fr., pa. pple. of *clicher*, var. of *cliquer* to click; see Littré.] A stereotype block; a cast or 'dab'; *esp.* a metal stereotype of a wood-engraving used to print from. b. *fig.* A stereotyped expression, a commonplace phrase 1892.

Click (klik), *sb.*[1] 1611. [See CLICK *v.*[1]] 1. A slight, sharp, hard, non-ringing sound of concussion, thinner than a *clack*, such as is made by the cocking of a gun, etc. 2. *Mech.* A piece of mechanism which makes this noise; *e.g.* the catch or detent which falls into the notches of a ratchet-wheel; the catch for a lock or bolt, a latch, etc. 3. A defect in a horse's action, causing the toe of the hind hoof to strike the shoe in front 1886. 4. *Zool.* A name for beetles of the family *Elateridæ*, from the clicking sound with which they spring upward when they have fallen on their backs. Also *c.-beetle.* 1848. 5. A class of articulations occurring in certain languages of S. Africa, consisting of sharp non-vocal sounds formed by suction, with the sudden withdrawal of the tongue from the part of the mouth with which it is in contact. Also CLUCK. 1857. *Comb.* **c.-beetle** (see sense 4). Hence **Cli·cky** *a.* full of clicks (sense 5). **Click-clack** *sb.* and *v.*, also **Click-click,** expressions for recurring or successive sounds of the c. type, also for chattering.

Click, *sb.*[2] 1872. [var. of CLEEK; also CLICK *v.*[2] used as *sb.*] 1. = CLEEK 1883. 2. A jerk with a cleek or hook 1886. 3. *Wrestling.* A trick, whereby the adversary's foot is sharply knocked off the ground 1872.

Click (klik), *v.*[1] 1581. [Echoic; cf. Du. *klikken*; also OF. *cliquer.*] 1. *intr.* To make the sound described under CLICK *sb.*[1] 1. 1611. 2. *trans.* To strike with this noise; to cause to make such a noise 1581.

1. The solemn death-watch click'd GAY. 2. They.. clicked their glasses together MARRYAT. Merry milk-maids c. the latch TENNYSON.

Click (klik), *v.*[2] Chiefly *dial.* 1674. [var. of CLEEK.] = CLEEK. Also with *up.*

Cli·cker. 1690. [f. CLICK *v.*[1] or [2].] 1. *slang.* A shop-keeper's tout. 2. A foreman shoemaker who cuts out the leather and gives out work. (App. the orig. sense.) 1690. 3. *Printing.* The foreman of a companionship of compositors who distributes the copy, etc. 1808.

Clicket (kli·kėt), *sb.* Now *dial.* ME. [a. OF. *cliquet.*] 1. The latch of a door or gate. Still *dial.* †2. A latch-key –1579. †3. A contrivance for making a clicking sound; as a clapper, bones, etc. –1737. *Comb.* **c.-gate,** a gate with a latch. Hence **Cli·cket** *v.* to chatter; of a fox, to be in heat.

Cliency (kləi·ĕnsi). *rare.* 1660. [ad. late L. *clientia.*] The state of being a client.

Client (kləi·ĕnt). ME. [ad. L. *cliens, clientem,* earlier *cluens,* from *cluere* to listen; ? 'one who is at the call of' his patron.] 1. *Rom. Antiq.* A plebeian under the protection of a patrician, in this relation called a patron (*patronus*). 2. *gen.* One who is under the protection or patronage of another, a dependant ME. 3. *spec.* One who employs the services of a legal adviser; he whose cause an advocate pleads ME.; also *transf.* a customer 1608.

2. We are very Curious to observe the Behaviour of great Men and their Clients STEELE. 3. Good Counsellors lacke no Clients *Meas. for M.* I. ii. 109. Hence **Cli·entage,** a body of clients; the relation of c. to patron. **Clie·ntal** *a. rare,* of or pertaining to a c. or clients. †**Cli·ented** *ppl. a.* furnished with clients. **Cliente·lage,** = *Clientage.* **Cli·entless** *a.* **Cli·entry,** the relation of clients; a body of clients. **Cli·entship,** state or relation of a c.: cf. *patronage.*

Clientele (kləiĕntī·l, -te·l). Also **-el, -elle,** and in Fr. form **clientèle.** 1563. [ad. L. *clientela*; see CLIENT. *Obs.* in 17th c., but re-adopted from Fr. *c* 1860, in sense 3.] †1. The relation or status of a client; clientship –1654; patronage –1692. 2. A body of clients or dependants; a body of adherents; a following 1563. 3. The whole professional connexion of a lawyer, physician, etc.; a body of supporters or customers generally 1865.

Cliff (klif). [OE. *clif* neut., pl. *clifu,* orig. *cleofu* :—OTeut. **kliƀom.* In 15th c. confused with *clift,* CLEFT; see CLIFT.] 1. A high steep face of rock; *esp.* (now) a steep face of rock on the seashore. †2. Hence, Shore, coast, strand –1600. 3. = CLEVE 3. ME. 4. The strata of rock lying above or between coal seams 1676.

1. There the Eagle and the Stork On Cliffs and Cedar tops thir Eyries build MILT. *P. L.* VII. 424. Hence **Cliffed** *ppl. a.* having cliffs. **Cli·ffy** *a.* having cliffs, precipitous, craggy.

Clift, *sb.*[1] Now usually CLEFT, q. v. Hence **Cli·fted** *a.*

Clift (klift), *sb.*[2] = CLIFF, q. v. Hence **Cli·fty** *a.*

†**Climacter.** 1609. [a. Gr. κλιμακτήρ, f. κλῖμαξ ladder.] A CLIMACTERIC year or epoch –1656.

Climacteric (kləimæktẹ·rik, -æ·ktĕrik). 1601. [ad. L. *climactericus,* a. Gr. κλιμακτηρικός, f. κλιμακτήρ CLIMACTER. English orthoepists prefer *climacte·ric.*]

A. *adj.* 1. Pertaining to or constituting a climacter or critical period in human life; *transf.* critical, fatal. 2. = CLIMACTIC 1791.

1. *C. year* = *climacteric,* also = *grand climacteric*: see B. *C. disease*: an unexplained disease of advanced life, characterized by loss of strength, sleeplessness, etc.

B. *sb.* 1. A critical stage in human life; a period supposed to be specially liable to change in health or fortune. Some held all the years denoted by multiples of 7 (7, 14, 21, etc.), others only the odd multiples of 7 (7, 21, 35, etc.) to be climacterics; some included the multiples of 9. 1634. 2. *transf.* A critical point or period 1630.

1. *Grand* (†*great*) *c.* (occas. *the c.*): the 63rd year of life (63 = 7 × 9), supposed to be specially critical. (According to some, also the 81st year.) 2. At her advanced age, every day is a c. POPE. var. **Climacte·rical** *a.* and *sb.*

†**Clima·ctery.** 1654. [a. F. *climacterie*; see prec.] 1. = CLIMACTERIC B. 1. 1658. 2. Progress by successive steps –1734.

Climactic (kləimæ·ktik), *a.* 1872. [f. CLIMAX, but not on Greek analogies.] Pertaining to or forming a climax or ascending series. Hence **Clima·ctically** *adv.*

Climatal (kləi·mătăl), *a.* 1830. [f. CLIMATE.] Of or pertaining to climate.

†**Climata·rchic,** *a. rare.* 1794. [f. Gr. κλιμάταρχος.] Presiding over a climate.

Climate (kləi·mĕt), *sb.* ME. [a. F. *climat,* ad. late L., a. Gr. κλίμα, κλιματ-, f. κλι- root of κλίνειν to slope. Adopted in late L. in sense of 'clime'.] †1. A belt of the earth's surface contained between two given parallels of latitude –1796. †b. *vaguely*: A region of the earth, a clime –1794. 2. A region considered with reference to its atmospheric conditions, or to its weather 1601. 3. Condition (of a region or country) in relation to prevailing atmospheric phenomena, as temperature, humidity, etc., *esp.* as these affect animal or vegetable life 1611. †4. = CLIMACTER –1586.

1. There are 24 climates between the equator and each of the polar circles MORSE. 3. The Clymat's delicate, the Ayre most sweet *Wint. T.* III. i. 1. Hence †**Cli·mate** *v.* to sojourn in a particular c. **Clima·tic, -al** *a.* relating to c. **Clima·tically** *adv.* **Cli·matize** *v. rare* = ACCLIMATIZE.

Climato·graphy. 1864. [f. source of CLIMATE + -γραφία.] The description of a climate or climates (Dicts.).

Climatology (kləimătǫ·lŏdʒi). 1843. [f. Gr. κλίμα, κλιματ- + -λογία.] That branch of science which deals with climate, and investigates climatic conditions. (Occas. used for the conditions themselves as a subject of science.) Hence **Cli:matolo·gic, -al** *a.,* **-ally** *adv.* **Climato·logist.**

†**Cli·mature.** 1604. [app. f. L. *climat-,* F. *climat,* after *temperature,* etc.] 1. ? A region *Haml.* I. i. 126. 2. Meteorological condition resulting from latitude; = CLIMATE 3. –1806.

Climax (kləi·mæks), *sb.* 1589. [a. L., a. Gr. κλῖμαξ ladder.] 1. *Rhet.* A figure in which a number of propositions or ideas are set forth in a series in which each rises above the preceding in force; gradation. †2. *gen.* An ascending series –1793. 3. [A misuse of the term.] The last term of a rhetorical climax 1856; also *gen.* the highest point, culmination, acme 1789.

2. The top of the c. of their wickedness BURKE. 3. Jerusalem is the c. of the long ascent STANLEY. Hence **Cli·max** *v. prop.* to ascend, or arrange, in a c.; *pop.* to come, or bring to, a culmination.

Climb (kləim), *v. Pa. t.* and *pple.* **climbed** (kləimd); *arch.* **clomb** (klōum). [OE. *climban* :—WGer. **klimban.* Believed to be a nasalized form of OTeut. **kliƀan* (see CLEAVE *v.*[2]). The *b* is lost in pronunciation.] 1. *intr.* To raise oneself by grasping or clinging, or by the aid of hands and feet; to ascend a steep place. Often with *up.* 2. *trans.* To ascend by hands and feet; to mount, scale ME.; to attain (a point) by climbing 1580. 3. To mount slowly upwards. *trans.* and *intr.* ME. 4. Of plants: To creep up by the aid of tendrils or by twining. *trans.* and *intr.* 1796. 5. *transf.* To rise, force its way upward. *trans.* and *intr.* Also *fig.* OE.

1. *To c. down*: *fig.* to retreat from a position taken up. 2. They shall clime the wall like men of warre *Joel* ii. 7. I must climbe her window *Two Gent.* II. iv. 181. 3. Where entrance up from Eden easiest climbes MILT. *P. L.* XI. 119. The slow moon climbs TENNYSON. 5. Let the labouring Barke climbe hills of Seas *Oth.* II. i. 189. *fig.* To clym to kyngs astate ME. Hence **Climb** *sb.* the act of climbing; an ascent. **Cli·mbable** *a.* that can be climbed. **Cli·mber,** one who or that which climbs; *spec.* (*Bot.*) a plant which climbs; (*Ornith.*) in *pl.* an order of birds (L. *Scansores*), which climb. **Cli·mbing** *vbl. sb.* and *ppl. a.*; whence **climbing-perch,** a fish (*Anabas scandens*): see ANABAS.

Clime (kləim). Now chiefly *poet.* 1542. [ad. L., a. Gr. κλίμα; see CLIMATE.] †1. = CLIMATE 1. –1697. 2. = CLIMATE 1 b. 1542. *fig.* = Region, realm 1667. 3. = CLIMATE 3. Also *fig.* = Atmosphere. *poet.* 1598.

2. Every man of every c. BLAKE. *fig.* The Climes of bliss MILT. *P. L.* XI. 708.

‖**Clinamen** (kləinē·men). 1704. [L.] An inclination, bias.

‖**Clina·ndrium.** 1864. [mod.L., f. Gr. κλίνη couch + ἀνδρ- male, taken for 'stamen'.] *Bot.* The cavity at the apex of the gynostemium in Orchids, in which the anther is embedded.

‖**Clina·nthium, clina·nthus.** 1881. [mod. L., f. as prec. + ἄνθος.] *Bot.* The receptacle or torus of a Composite flower.

Clinch (klinʃ), *sb.* 1627. [var. of CLENCH *sb.*; cf. CLINCH *v.*] 1. A fastening in which the end of a nail or bolt is beaten back or flattened after passing through anything; the clinched point of a nail; a clinched nail or bolt. Occas. CLENCH. 1659. 2. *Naut.* 'A method of fastening large ropes by a half-hitch, with the end stopped back to its own part by seizings' (Adm. Smyth): that part of a rope which is clinched 1627. 3. A thing which clutches, grips, or fixes fast 1822. 4. A clinching or riveting together 1855. 5. A word-play, a pun 1630. 6. *U.S.* A struggle at close grips 1860. b. *Boxing.* Grappling at close quarters 1899.

4. Give my conviction a c. BROWNING. *Comb.* **c.-work,** lap-jointed work.

Clinch (klinʃ), *v.* 1570. [Later var. of CLENCH *v.*; prob. by assimilation to CLINK.] 1. *trans.* To fix (a nail or bolt) securely, *esp.* by beating back or flattening the end which has been driven through anything; to make fast thus. Also *absol.* Occas. CLENCH. †2. To close tightly (the hand or fist). Now always

CLENCH. -1802. Also †*intr.* (for *refl.*). 3. *trans. Naut.* To make fast the end of a rope in the way described under CLINCH *sb.* 2. 1769. 4. *intr.* To fix oneself *on* 1793. 5. *trans.* To make firm and sure (an argument, bargain, etc.); to drive home; to make conclusive, confirm, establish. Also CLENCH. 1716. †6. To secure (*rare*). (Cf. *nail.*) 1803. †7. To make clinches or puns -1688. 8. *Boxing*, etc. (Cf. CLINCH *sb.* 6) 1860.

5. The council of Trent..clincheth the business SOUTH. Hence **Cli·ncher**, one who or that which clinches; *esp.* a conclusive statement, argument, etc.; †a *clinker-built* vessel; see CLINKER.

†Clinchpoop, clenchpoop. 1568. A term of contempt; = lout -1589.

†Cline, *v.* ME. [a. OF. *cliner.*] To bow, incline -1538.

Cling (kliŋ), *v. Pa. t.* and *pple.* **clung** (klɒŋ). [OE. *clingan, clang, clungen.* The original sense was 'to stick fast'. Cf. CLENCH, CLINK *v.*[2]] †1. *intr.* To adhere together in a stiff mass -1577. 2. To become 'drawn', to shrink up, wither. Now *dial.* OE. 3. *trans.* To cause to adhere, stick *together* (*dial.*) 1627; to cause to shrink or draw together 1540. 4. *intr.* To adhere, stick *to* ME. 5. *intr.* To adhere, attach oneself firmly *to*. (Now the leading sense.) ME. Also *transf.* 6. *fig.* To cleave *to* 1583. †7. To cause to cling, make fast. (Perh. a by-form of CLINCH or CLINK.) -1774.

3. Vpon the next Tree shalt thou hang aliue Till Famine c. thee *Macb.* v. v. 40. 4. His Armes clung to his Ribs MILT. *P. L.* x. 512. 5. The broken ice clung to the rocks KANE. My maids clung round me JOHNSON. *transf.* Some heavy clouds..clung to the mountains TYNDALL. 6. To c. to a doctrine MACAULAY. 7. I clung my legs as close to his sides as I could SWIFT. Hence **Cling** *sb.* the act of clinging; adhesion; *spec.* a disease of cattle, which makes them hidebound. **Cli·nger. Cli·ngy** *a.* sticky, tenacious.

Cli·ngstone, *a.* and *sb.* 1840. A variety of the peach in which the flesh clings to the stone.

Clinic (kli·nik), *sb.*[1] and *a.* 1626. [ad. L., a. Gr. κλινικός, f. κλίνη bed.] A. *sb.* 1. One who is confined to bed by sickness or infirmity. 2. *Ch. Hist.* One who deferred baptism until the death-bed 1666. B. *adj.* 1. Of or pertaining to the sick-bed 1626. 2. = CLINICAL 1. 1751.

1. *C. baptism*: private baptism administered on the sick bed.

Clinic, *sb.*[2], **clinique.** 1843. [= F. *clinique*, ad. Gr. κλινική the clinic art.] 1. The teaching of medicine or surgery at the bedside of a sick person. 2. a. A private hospital, etc., to which patients are recommended by individual doctors. b. An institution attached to a hospital, etc., at which patients receive treatment free of cost or at reduced fees 1892.

Clinical (kli·nikăl), *a.* 1780. [f. as CLINIC[1] + -AL.] 1. *Med.* Of or pertaining to the sick-bed, *spec.* to that of indoor hospital patients. 2. *Eccl.* Administered on the sick-bed 1844.

1. *C. lecture*, a lecture at the bedside of the patient upon his case. *C. medicine, surgery*, medicine or surgery as taught at the bedside, *esp.* in hospital practice. Hence **Cli·nically** *adv.* **Clini·cian**, a c. investigator.

Clink (kliŋk), *sb.*[1] ME. [Cf. Du. *klink.* See CLINK *v.*[1]] 1. A sharp abrupt ringing sound, clearer and thinner than a *clank*, as of glasses struck together. 2. Mere assonance of rime 1716. 3. *dial.* A smart sharp blow 1722. 4. *colloq. Sc.* COIN; = CHINK 1729.

1. The clinke and fall of Swords *Oth.* II. iii. 234.

Clink, *sb.*[2] 1515. [? f. CLINK *v.*[2]] The name of a prison in Southwark; also (*esp.* in Devon and Cornwall) a small prison-cell; a lock-up.

Clink (kliŋk), *v.*[1] [ME. *clinken*; echoic. Cf. Du. *klinken*, LG. *klingen*, etc. See CLANK.] 1. *intr.* To make the sound described under CLINK *sb.*[1] 1. 2. To cause to sound in this way ME. 3. *intr.* To rime 1729. Also *trans.* 4. *intr.* To move with a clinking sound 1818.

1. As the fool thinketh, so the bell clinketh 1684. 2. And let me the Cannakin clinke, clinke *Oth.* II. iii. 71.

Clink (kliŋk), *v.*[2] *n. Eng.* and *Sc.* ME. [Northern form; = CLINCH, CLENCH.] *trans.* To clench, rivet.

Clinkant, obs. f. CLINQUANT.

Clink-clank. 1790. A succession or alternation of clinking sounds; *fig.* a senseless jingle of words

Clinker (kli·ŋkəɹ), *sb.*[1] 1641. [ad. Du. *klinckaerd*, in mod.Du. *klinker*, f. *klinken* to ring.] 1. A very hard brick of a pale colour, made in Holland, and used for paving. 2. A brick whose surface has been vitrified by intense heat; a mass of bricks fused by excessive heat, and adhering together 1659. 3. A hard mass formed by the fusion of the earthy impurities of coal, limestone, iron ore, or the like, in a furnace or forge; a mass of slag 1769. 4. A mass of hardened volcanic lava 1850. 5. A scale of oxide of iron formed in forging.

Cli·nker, *sb.*[2] 1690. [f. CLINK *v.*[1]] He who or that which clinks; *spec.* in *pl.* fetters (*slang*).

Cli·nker, *sb.*[3] 1656. [f. CLINK *v.*[2]] He who or that which clinches (*lit.* and *fig.*). *Comb.* c.-built *a.*: applied to ships and boats, the external planks of which overlap each other below, and are fastened with clinched copper nails; cf. CLINCHER.

Cli·nkstone. 1811. [After Ger. *klingstein*: so called from its clinking when struck.] *Min.* A compact greyish-blue felspathic rock, of lower specific gravity than grey basalt.

Clino- (kləi·no). Comb. f. Gr. stem κλιν- in the sense of 'sloping, inclining'; used in connexion with the monoclinic system of crystals, characterized by one plane of symmetry.

Clinoba·sic *a.* = *clinorhombic.* **Clinodia·gonal** *sb.*, the inclined axis in the monoclinic system of crystals; *adj.* pertaining to, or in the line of, this axis. **Clinopi·nacoid** [Gr. πίναξ, πίνακος a board], one of the three principal planes in the monoclinic system, running parallel to the vertical and inclined axes. **Clinorho·mbic, -rho·mboid** *adjs.*, crystallizing in an oblique form, monoclinic.

Clinographic (kləinogræ·fik), *a.* [f. CLINO- + Gr. γραφικός.] Pertaining to that mode of projection in drawing, in which the rays are assumed to fall obliquely on the plane of projection (Dicts.).

Clinoid (kləi·noid), *a.* 1741. [f. Gr. κλίνη bed; see -OID.] *Anat.* Resembling a bed: applied to the four apophyses of the sphenoid bone.

Clinometer (kləinǫ·mītəɹ). 1811. [f. CLINO- + μέτρον.] A measurer of slopes and elevations; *esp.* an instrument for measuring the dip of mineral strata, or the slope of cuttings, embankments, etc.; also for taking altitudes. Hence **Clinome·tric, -al** *a.* pertaining to or determined by the c.; *Min.* pertaining to the measurement of oblique crystalline forms. **Clino·metry** (Dicts.).

Clinquant (kli·ŋkănt). 1591. [a. F., f. †*clinquer*, a. Du. *klinken* to ring.] *adj.* Glittering with real or mock gold or silver; tinselled, 'dressed in spangles' (J.). Also *fig.* *sb.* Tinsel, Dutch gold. Also *fig.* 1691.

Clint (klint), *sb.* Chiefly *Sc.* ME. [a. Da. and Sw. *klint*:—OSwed. *klinter* rock.] A hard or flinty rock. Hence **Cli·nty** *a.* consisting of or characterized by clints.

Clio (kləi·o). 1835. [Gr. Κλειώ (f. κλείειν to celebrate), the Muse of epic poetry and history; also a sea-nymph.] 1. *Zool.* A genus of pteropods found in the Arctic seas. 2. *Astron.* The 84th asteroid 1867.

Clip (klip), *v.*[1] [OE. *clyppan*:—OTeut. type **kluppjan.*] 1. *trans.* To clasp with the arms, embrace, hug (*arch.* and *dial.*). Also *fig.* Also *absol.* and *intr.* 2. *trans.* To surround closely, encompass, hug. Also with *about, in.* OE. 3. To grip tightly OE.

1. He kisseth hire and clippeth hire ful ofte CHAUCER. 2. Yon fair sea that clips thy shores COWPER.

Clip (klip), *v.*[2] [ME. *clippen*, prob. a. ON. *klippa* in this sense; perh. also echoic.] 1. To cut with scissors or shears. Also with *away, off, out, from.* 2. *fig.* To cut short 1588. Also *absol.* and *intr.* 3. *intr.* To move the wings rapidly (*arch.*) 1613. 4. *intr.* (*colloq.*) To move or run rapidly. Cf. *cut.* 1833.

1. I'll c. his wings MARLOWE. To c. the heads of the peasant-girls 1859, sheep WYCLIF, coin GRAFTON. 2. To c. the Queen's English 1755. 3. Some falcon.. flies at check and clips it down the wind DRYDEN. Hence Clipped, clipt *ppl. a.*

Clip (klip), *sb.*[1] 1470. [f. CLIP *v.*[1]] †1. An embrace -1683. 2. That which clips or clasps, *e.g.* in *Carriages*, the embracing-strap which connects the spring and axle; in *Farriery*, a projecting flange on the upper surface of the toe of a horseshoe, which clasps the front of the hoof; a spring-holder for letters, etc. 1470. Also *transf.* and *fig.* 3. *attrib.* That has, or acts as, a clip 1861.

Clip (klip), *sb.*[2] 1681. [f. CLIP *v.*[2]] 1. *pl.* Shears. 2. That which is clipped; a clipping (*esp.* a season's clipping of wool) 1825. 3. An act of clipping or shearing 1825. 4. A smart blow, stroke, or cut 1830. Also *attrib.*

Clipper (kli·pəɹ). ME. [f. as prec. + -ER.] 1. One who clips; *spec.* one who clips coin. Also *fig.* 2. That which clips; *e.g.* a pruning-hook, and in *pl.* scissors, etc. 1578. 3. One who or that which moves swiftly, or scuds along (cf. CLIP *v.*[2] 4); *e.g.* a vessel with sharp forward-raking bows and masts raking aft 1830. 4. *slang.* Anything first-rate of its kind 1848

1. Fals money makers and clepars of money ARNOLDE. 4. Wasn't Reynolds a c. THACKERAY. *Comb.* c.-built *a.*

Clipping (kli·piŋ), *vbl. sb.* ME. [f. CLIP *v.*[2] + ING[1].] 1. The action of cutting with (or as with) shears or scissors. 2. That which is clipped off, a cutting, paring, shaving, shred, etc. 1461.

1. The Jews.. were also accused of c. of money 1460. 2. Clippings from popular writers 1866.

Clipping (kli·piŋ), *ppl. a.* 1635. [f. CLIP *v.*[2] + ING[2].] 1. That cuts with shears; that flies or moves fast. 2. *slang.* First-rate 1861.

†Clips(e, *sb.* and *v.* ME. Aphetic f. ECLIPSE *sb.* and *v.* -1612.

Clique (klīk). 1711. [a. F., f. *cliquer* to click, clack, clap; orig. the same as *claque* (Littré).] A small and exclusive party or set, a narrow coterie or circle: a term of reproach or contempt. Hence **Clique** *v. colloq.* to combine in, or act as, a c. **Cli·quish** *a.* savouring of a c. or cliques. **Cli·quishness. Cli·quism, cliqueism**, the spirit, principles, and methods of a c.; party exclusiveness. **Cli·quy, -ey** *a.* of the nature of, or characterized by, cliques.

Clish-ma-claver (kliʃmăklǣ·vəɹ), *sb.* *Sc.* 1728. [partly echoic.] Gossip, foolish talk. Also as vb.

Clitch (klitʃ), *v.* Now *dial.* [OE. *clycc(e)an*; see CLUTCH.] †1. *trans.* To crook or bend; to close (the hand), clench (the fist) -1574. 2. To grasp tightly ME. 3. To make fast; in mod. dial. to stick (things) *to* or together ME.

Clite (kləit). 1597. [Cf. *clete*, CLOTE.] 1. The burdock. ? *Obs.* 2. The Cleavers or Goose-grass 1847.

‖**Clitellum** (kləite·lǒm). 1839. [mod.L., f. L. *clitellæ* a pack-saddle.] *Zool.* The raised band encircling the body of earth-worms towards the middle.

‖**Clitoris** (kləi·tǫris). 1615. [a. Gr. κλειτορίς, ? f. κλείειν to shut.] *Phys.* A homologue of the male penis, present in the females of many of the higher vertebrata.

†Cli·ver, *sb.* OE. [app. f. *clif-, cliƀ-, clifan*, to cleave, climb.] A claw, talon -ME.

Clivers, var. of CLEAVERS, q. v.

‖**Cloaca** (klo₍ē·kă). Pl. **-æ.** 1656. [L., f. *cluere* to purge.] 1. An underground conduit for drainage, a sewer; a privy. Also *fig.* and *transf.* 2. *Phys.* The common excrementory cavity at the end of the intestinal canal in birds, reptiles, most fishes, and the monotremate animals 1834. Hence **Cloa·cal** *a.*

Cloak (klōᵘk), *sb.* ME. [a. OF. *cloke*:—med.L. *cloca, clocca* cape, the same word as *cloke, cloche* bell, so called from its shape. See CLOCK.] 1. A loose outer garment worn by both sexes over their other clothes. †2. A clerical gown; *esp.* the Geneva gown -1727. 3. *fig.* That which covers over and conceals; a pretext, pretence, outward show 1526.

1. My Russett ryding clok SIR R. BOYLE. 3. I haue nights cloake to hide me from their eyes *Rom. & Jul.* II. ii. 75. *Comb.* †c.-**bag**, a bag in which to carry a c. or other clothes; a valise; also *fig.* Hence **Cloa·kless** *a.* without a c.

Cloak (klōᵘk), *v.* 1509. [f. prec.] 1. To cover with or wrap in a cloak 1514. 2. *fig.* †To cover, protect -1590; to cover over, conceal, disguise 1509.

2. To cloke her guile with sorrow SPENSER *F. Q.* II. i. 21. Hence **Cloaked** *ppl. a.* (*lit.* and *fig.*); †**Cloa·k-**

edly *adv.* apparently; disguisedly. **Cloa·king** *vbl. sb.* concealment; material for cloaks.

Cloa·k-room. 1852. A room in which cloaks, coats, hats, etc., may be left; also, an office at railway-stations, etc., where luggage is temporarily taken charge of.

Cloam (klōᵘm), *sb.* Now *s. w. dial.* [OE. *clām* :—WGer. **klaim*, f. *klī-* to daub (root of CLAY).] In OE. Mud, clay. Hence, now: Earthenware, clay. Also *attrib.*

Clobber (klǫ·bəɹ), *sb.* [?] A black paste used by cobblers to fill up and conceal cracks in leather. DICKENS.

‖**Cloche.** 1882. [Fr.] **1.** = BELL-*glass*. **2.** = BELL *sb.*¹ 5. **3.** A close-fitting bell-shaped hat for women 1907.

Clocher (klōᵘ·ʃəɹ), *sb.* ME. [a. F. *clocher, clochier*, f. (ult.) *cloc(c)a, cloque, cloche* a bell.] A bell-tower; a belfry.

Clock, *sb.*¹ [ME. *clok(ke, clocke*, either a. MDu. *clocke*, or a. ONF. *cloke, cloque* = Central Fr. *cloche* 'bell', f. late L. *cloc(c)a*. Perh. of Celtic origin, and echoic. The Romanic word for 'bell' is *campana*.] †**1.** A bell. *Later*, the gong of a striking watch. –1664. **2.** An instrument for the measurement of time; properly, one which strikes. The mechanism consists of a train of wheels set in motion by weights or a spring, actuating and regulated by a pendulum or balance-wheel; the passage of hours, minutes, etc., is indicated by hands on a dial-plate. ME. Also *transf.* and *fig.* †**3.** The hour as struck by the clock *Cymb.* III. iv. 44. **4.** A watch. *Obs.* exc. in mod. slang. 1559. **5.** The pappus of the dandelion, etc. 1847.

2. Like damag'd clocks, whose hand and bell dissent YOUNG. *O'clock* is short for *of the clock*; other variants were †*of clock*, †*a clock* (see A *prep.*²).

Phr. *To know (find) what o'clock it is*: to know (discover) the real state of things.

Comb.: **c.-face**, the dial-plate of a c., *techn.* the time shown by it; **-like** *a.* regular, monotonous; **-quarters**, the bells in a large c. on which the quarter-hours are struck; **-tower**, one built for a large c.; **-watch**, one that strikes; **-wise**, in the direction in which the hands of a clock move.

Clock (klǫk), *sb.*² 1530. [?] An ornamental pattern in silk worked on the side of a stocking. Hence **Clocked** *a.* embroidered with clocks.

Clock (klǫk), *sb.*³ 1550. [?] A name for any kind of beetle; esp. *Geotrupes stercorarius*.

Clock, *v.*¹ 1872. [f. CLOCK *sb.*¹] **1.** *trans.* To time by a clock or stop watch 1883. **b.** with *in, off, on, out*: To register one's entry or exit by means of an automatic clock 1924. **2.** = CLAPPER *v.* 1.

Clock (klǫk), *v.*² Now *Sc.* and *n. dial.* [OE. *cloccian*; echoic. Cf. CLUCK.] **1.** *intr.* and †*trans.* To cluck. **2.** *intr.* and *trans.* To sit on eggs. (The current use in n. dial.) 1721. Hence **Clo·cker,** a sitting hen.

Clock-work (klǫ·kwɒɹk). 1662. The mechanism of a clock, or mechanism similar to that of a clock; *esp.* with reference to its automatic action, or its unvarying regularity. Also *fig.* **2.** *attrib.* Of or like clock-work 1764.

Clod (klǫd), *sb.* [ME. var. of CLOT; now differentiated, as shown in *clod of earth*, and *clot of blood*.] †**1.** = CLOT –1758. **2.** A mass or lump *of* any solid matter, *e.g.* earth, loam, etc. (Formerly CLOT.) ME. **3.** Without *pl.* The soil or dust of the ground in its lumpy character. (Often *depreciatory*.) 1573. **4.** *fig.* That which is of 'clay', or 'of the earth, earthy', as the body of man, etc. 1595. **5.** *fig.* A clod-pate; a clodhopper 1605. **6.** The coarse part of the neck of an ox, nearest the shoulder 1601. **7.** *Coal-Mining.* Soft shale or slate 1867.

1. Clods of bloud FAIRFAX, of a slimy substance CAREW (J.). 2. Two massie clods of Iron and Bras MILT. *P.L.* XI. 565. The crumbling Clods DRYDEN. 5. This fleamy clodd of an Antagonist MILT. Hence **Clo·ddish** *a.* somewhat c.-like; boorishly stolid, awkward. **Clo·ddishness.**

Clod (klǫd), *v.* ME. [f. CLOD *sb.*; cf. CLOT *v.*] †**1.** *trans.* To free (land) from clods –1743. **2.** To form or turn into clods or (formerly) clots. *trans.* and *intr.* 1530. **3.** *trans.* To pelt with clods 1755. **4.** *gen.* To heave or throw heavily. *n. dial.* 1815.

Hence **Clo·dded** *ppl. a.* stuck together in clods; also formerly = Clotted.

†**Clo·dder,** *v.* 1499. = CLOTTER *v.* –1876.

Cloddy (klǫ·di), *a.* 1545. [CLOD *sb.* + -Y¹.] †Clotted –1658; characterized by, or full of, clods 1545; clod-like 1712. Hence **Clo·ddiness.**

Clo·d-hopper. 1690. [? after *grass-hopper*.] One who walks over ploughed land; a ploughman; hence, a clumsy awkward boor. So **Clo·d-hopping** *a.* following the plough; boorish.

Clo·d-pate. 1636. [See PATE.] A thick-head. Hence **Clo·d-pated** *a.*

Clo·d-poll, clod-pole. 1601. [See POLL.] = CLOD-PATE.

Clof, cloff. *Sc.* and *n. dial.* 1538. [f. weak grade of *kleuƀ-* to CLEAVE.] A cleft, fissure.

Cloff (klǫf). Also *erron.* **clough.** 1502. [?] *Commerce.* An allowance (now of 2 lbs. in 3 cwt.), given with certain commodities, to make the weight hold good when they are sold by retail.

Clog (klǫg), *sb.* ME. [?] **1.** A thick piece of wood; a block, clump. Still in *Sc.* **2.** A block of wood, or the like, attached to a man or beast, to impede motion 1450. **3.** *fig.* Anything that impedes; an impediment, encumbrance, hindrance 1526. †**4.** The cone of the fir tree –1727. **5.** A wooden-soled shoe, or overshoe, worn to protect the feet from wet and dirt ME. †**6.** A kind of calendar notched upon a square block of wood, etc. –1843.

1. *Yule c.*: a Christmas log. 2. With a clogge upon myn hele 1461. 5. I remember at the play-house, they used to call on Mrs. Oldfield's chair, Mrs. Barry's clogs, and Mrs. Bracegirdle's pattens H. WALPOLE. *Comb.*: **c.-almanac** = sense 6; **-dance,** a dance performed in clogs, or wooden-soled shoes; hence, **-dancer.** Hence **Clo·ggy** *a.* knotty, lumpy; apt to clog; full of clogging matter. **Clo·gginess.**

Clog (klǫg), *v.* ME. [f. the sb.; cf. CLAG *v.*] **1.** To fasten a clog or block of wood to; to fetter by this means. **2.** *fig.* To load so as to encumber; to hamper, impede 1583. **3.** To encumber by adhesion 1526. **4.** To fill up so as to impede action or function; to choke *up*, obstruct 1586. †**5.** *fig.* To cloy –1704. **6.** *intr.* (for *refl.*) To become obstructed, to stick (*lit.* and *fig.*) 1633. **7.** To put wooden soles on (shoes, etc.) 1640.

1. Chained, locked, and clogged, to staie his running awaie 1587. 2. Fingers clogged with rings 1583. Clogging it [an Estate] with Legacies COWPER. To c. enterprise 1876. 3. *Twel. N.* III. ii. 66. 4. When the Eustachian tube is clogged up with mucus DUFTON. 6. Move it sometimes..that the seeds c. not together EVELYN. Hence **Clo·gger,** one who makes clogs, or wooden soles for shoes.

‖**Cloison** (kloi·z'n, klwazoṅ). 1693. [Fr. :— L. type **clausionem*, f. *clausus*; cf. POISON.] A partition, division.

‖**Cloisonné** (klwazone), *a.* (*sb.*) 1863. [Fr. f. prec.] Divided into compartments: applied to enamels. Also = *cloisonné enamel*.

In cloisonné enamels the compartments are made with thin plates set on edge upon a foundation plaque, and into these the variously coloured enamels are put in the state of powder, and then melted in the furnace. In *champlevé*, i.e. field-raised, enamel the compartments are excavated in the substance of the foundation plaque itself.

Cloister (kloi·stəɹ), *sb.* [ME. *cloistre*, a. OF. :—L. *claustrum*, f. *claud-, claus-*.] **1.** An enclosed place, enclosure (*arch.*). **2.** A place of religious seclusion; a monastery or nunnery ME. Also *fig.* **3.** A covered walk or arcade connected with a monastery, college, or other building, serving sometimes as a place of exercise or study; often running round the open court of a quadrangle ME.

2. Fitter for a Cloyster than a Crowne DANIEL. *The c.*: monastic life. 3. To walk the studious cloister's pale MILT. *Pens.* 156. *Comb.*: **c.-garth,** the open court enclosed by a c.; **-wise** *adv.* Hence **Cloi·steral,** var. of CLOISTRAL. **Cloi·sterer,** one who dwells in a c.; whence †**Cloi·stress,** a nun. **Cloi·sterless** *a.* **Cloi·sterly** *a.* proper to, or of the nature of, a c.

Cloister (kloi·stəɹ), *v.* 1581. [f. the sb.] **1.** To shut *up* in a CLOISTER (sense 2) 1591. **2.** To shut up in any seclusion 1581. **3.** *fig.* To confine, restrain 1627. **4.** To furnish with a CLOISTER (sense 3) 1625.

1. High thee to France, And Cloyster thee in some Religious House *Rich. II*, v. i. 23. 4. Where, cloister'd round, the garden lay SCOTT.

Cloistral (kloi·străl), *a.* 1605. [f. as prec. + -AL.] Pertaining to, or dwelling in, a cloister; cloister-like.

A C. Exercise DANIEL. C. glades 1844.

Cloke, var. of CLOAK.

Clomp, *v.*, dial. f. CLAMP or CLUMP.

Clong, obs. f. CLUNG.

Clonic (klǫ·nik), *a.* 1849. [f. Gr. κλόνος violent confused motion + -IC.] *Path.* Of spasms in which violent muscular convulsions take place; opp. to *tonic*. So ‖**Clonus** (klōᵘ·nɒ̆s) [mod.L., a. Gr.], a series of muscular contractions in which the individual contractions are visible 1899.

Cloop (klūp), *sb.* 1848. [Echoic.] The sound made by drawing a cork from a bottle, or any similar sound.

He can imitate any .. c. of a cork wrenched from a bottle THACKERAY. So **Cloop** *v.* to make this sound.

Cloot (klut, *Sc.* klüt). *Sc.* and *n. dial.* 1725. [prob. a. ON. *kló* CLAW.] **1.** The hoof, or one of its divisions, in the ox, sheep, swine, etc. **2.** pl. *Cloots*: the Devil 1787. Hence **Cloo·tie,** dim. of CLOOT (in both senses).

Close (klōᵘs). ME. [a. F. *clos* :—L. *clausum*. The final *e* is merely graphic.]

A. *adj.* **I. 1.** *gen.* Closed, shut. Of vowel-sounds: Pronounced with lips partly closed, or with contraction of the oral cavity. Opp. to *open*. 1760. **2.** Enclosed or shut in; confined, narrow. Const. *in, from*. 1489. **3.** Strictly confined; also applied to the confinement ME. **4.** Shut up from observation; hidden; secluded ME. **5.** Of the atmosphere or weather: Confined, stifling, without free circulation; opp. to *fresh* 1591. **6.** Practising secrecy; reserved, uncommunicative; not open ME. **7.** Close-fisted 1654. **8.** Not open to public access or competition 1812. **9.** Of a season: Closed for the purposes of sport 1814. †**10.** Strict, severe –1770.

1. A c. mouth catcheth no flies 1712. A c. carriage (*mod.*). 2. To c. prison *Two Gent.* III. i. 235. C. alleys SCOTT. A c. landscape 1845. 3. Kept c. in a Castell GRAFTON. In c. arrest WELLINGTON. 4. My hid and c. sins 1554. In a c. Parloure 1581. *To keep c., lie c.*, etc. 5. Keepe them [silkworms] not in roomes too hot and c. 1599. C. and sultry weather ANSON. 6. For secrecie, No Lady closer 1 *Hen. IV*, II. iii. 113. 7. A c., griping fellow SWIFT. 8. *C. borough*: see BOROUGH. 10. Devowt and clos conversation 1464. *C. mourning*: deep mourning.

II. Of proximity. The primary notion is that of having intervening space or spaces *closed* up. **1.** Having the component parts near together; dense or compact in consistency or arrangement, *e.g.* of *thickets*, close-planted; *fig.* of *reasoning*, concise 1500. **2.** In immediate proximity, very near 1489; hence, with nouns of condition, e.g. *close order*, or of action, as *close fight*, etc. 1625. Also *fig.* **3.** Close-fitting 1488. **4.** Closely attached, intimate, confidential 1577. **5.** Of attention, etc.: Strict, minute, searching 1662. **6.** Said of a contest in which the two sides are very nearly equal 1855.

1. The water made itself way through the pores of that very c. metal LOCKE. *fig.* A c. reasoner COLERIDGE. 2. But in c. fight a champion grim SCOTT. In c. proximity 1886. C. shaving as the cause of collisions at sea ADM. COLOMB. *fig.* A c. translation 1718. Naut. *Close to (by, on, upon) a wind*. 3. Her simple c. cap SCOTT. 4. A c. Intimacy STEELE, alliance 1815, friendship MACAULAY. 5. Under a c. cross-questioning 1857. 6. Vehement debates and c. divisions MACAULAY.

B. *adv.* (For the adverbial use of the adj. *closely* is now preferred.) **1.** As near as can be, very near ME. †**2.** Secretly, covertly –1650. **3.** Tightly 1596. **4.** = CLOSELY 1642.

1. Where all the guests sit c. G. HERBERT. 3. C. plastered HARINGTON. 4. It is good to follow the light c. FULLER.

Comb.: †**c.-guard,** a guard in fence; **-harbour,** one enclosed by breakwaters or excavated in the shore; **-rolls,** the rolls in which c.-writs, etc., are recorded; **-up,** part of a cinema film taken at short range in order to magnify detail; also *fig.*; **-writs,** writs closed and sealed under the great seal.

Close (klōᵘs), *sb.*¹ ME. [a. F. *clos* :—L. *clausum*; see the adj.] **1.** *gen.* An enclosed place. **2.** An enclosure about or beside a building; *e.g.* †a quadrangle –1646; a farm-yard ME.; the precinct of a cathedral ME. **3.** An entry or passage. Now, in Scotland, *esp.* one leading from the street to dwelling-houses, etc., at the back, or to a common stair. †**4.** An enclosing line, circuit –1645.

1. †*In c.*: in a closed place; shut up. *Breaking one's c.* (law L. *clausum fregere*): i.e. the visible or invisible boundary which encloses the land of every owner or occupier. 2. Alle the hennes in the clos

CHAUCER. Closes surrounded by the venerable abodes of deans and canons MACAULAY.

Close (klōᵘz), *sb.*² ME. [f. CLOSE *v.*] **1.** The act of closing; conclusion, end. **2.** *Mus.* The conclusion of a musical phrase, theme, or movement; a CADENCE 1597. **3.** A closing or uniting together; union, junction 1591. **4.** A closing in fight; a grapple 1596. †**5.** The closing in (of night, etc.). DRYDEN.

1. When he shall come to his last c. [death] BP. HALL. 2. The air..prolongs each heavenly c. MILT. 3. The holy c. of lippes *Twel. N.* v. i. 161. 4. In eager c. With Death B. CORNWALL.

Close (klōᵘz), *v.* [ME. *closen*, a. F. *clos-* stem of *clore* :—L. *claudere.*] **I. 1.** *trans.* To stop up (an opening); to shut, cover in. (*Close* is more general than *shut*, and hence is more used when the notion is that of the resulting state.) **2.** *intr.* (for *refl.*) To shut itself, become shut ME. **3.** *trans.* To ENCLOSE, confine, shut up *in*, *within*. *Obs.* or *arch.* ME. Also *fig.* **4.** To fill up; to bound, shut in 1697. **5.** To cover from a blow or aim, or from sight ME.

1. To c. a dore LD. BERNERS, weary lips GRAY. Sleep .. clos'd mine eyes MILT. *P. L.* VIII. 459. 2. The grave had closed over all he loved (*mod.*). 3. *fig.* I clung to all the present for the promise that it closed TENNYSON. 4. Lebanon closes the Land of Promise on the north STANLEY.

II. 1. To bring to a close; to finish, complete ME. **2.** *intr.* To come to an end 1821.

1. To c. one's days ME., a bargain DICKENS. *To c. an account*: see ACCOUNT *sb.* 2. The sweet summer closes TENNYSON.

III. †**1.** To bring close together so as to leave no gap; to conjoin, unite, bind together, etc. –1655. Also *techn.* (see quots.). **2.** *intr.* To come close together; to join, coalesce, meet in a common centre 1551. **3.** *intr.* To draw near, approach close; also with *about*, *on*, *round*, *upon* 1523. *trans.*, chiefly *Naut.* 1673. **4.** To come to grips; to grapple *with* 1590. **5.** To come to terms (*with* a person) 1603; *to close with* an offer, etc.: to accede to, accept 1645; *to close upon*, to agree upon 1698.

1. To c. files 1649, ranks 1796. *Shoemaking. To c. a shoe*: to join together the uppers. *Electr. To c. a circuit*: to unite its parts so as to make it complete. 2. Many Lynes c. in the Dials centre *Hen. V*, I. ii. 210. 3. The men closed round him (*mod.*). *To c. the wind*: to come near to it, to luff. 4. Achilles closes with his hated foe POPE. 5. C. with him, giue him Gold *Wint. T.* IV. iv. 830.

Clo·se-bodied, *a.* 1677. **1.** Of a coat, etc.: Fitting closely. **2.** Of close grain 1726.

Closed (klōᵘzd). 1481. [CLOSE *v.*, -ED¹.] Shut up; †enclosed; limited to certain persons, etc. *C. shop*, an establishment in which only trade-union members are employed 1923.

†**Clo·se-fights,** *pl.* 1602. *Naut.* Barriers of wood fitted with loopholes, stretching across a vessel in several places; used as a place of retreat when a ship is boarded.

Clo·se-fi·sted, *a.* 1608. That keeps the hand tightly shut; usu. *fig.* loath to give, niggardly, penurious. Opp. to *open-handed*.

Clo·se-grained, *a.* 1754. Having the structural elements fine and closely arranged; of close texture.

Clo·se-ha·nded, *a.* 1585. **1.** = CLOSE-FISTED (*arch.*). **2.** Hand-to-hand.

Clo·se-hauled, *ppl. a.* 1769. [See HAUL.] *Naut.* With the sail-tacks hauled close, for sailing as near the wind as possible.

Closely (klōᵘ·sli), *adv.* 1552. [f. CLOSE *a.* + -LY².] **1.** In a CLOSE manner; usually opp. to *openly*. †**2.** Secretly, covertly, privately –1643.

1. C. confined (*mod.*). Hair c. cut PAYN. Molecules c. packed TYNDALL. C. connected with the Sanskrit BORROW. To look at a case c. LINDLEY. 2. We have c. sent for Hamlet hither *Haml.* III. i. 29.

Closeness (klōᵘ·snės). 1450. [f. as prec.] CLOSE quality or condition.

Small diffrens betweene cloosnes and consealyng 1562. Almost stifled by the c. of the room SWIFT. C. of texture 1692. C. of an imitation H. D. TRAILL. An Affectation of C. and Covetousness ADDISON.

Close quarters, *pl.* 1753. **1.** *Naut.* = earlier CLOSE-FIGHTS. **2.** *fig.* Immediate contact with the foe 1809.

†**Clo·ser**¹. ME. [a. Anglo-Fr. *closere* :—late L. *clausaria*, f. *clausus*.] **1.** An enclosed place; a closet –1530. **2.** That which encloses. [App. = CLOSURE in this sense.] –1605.

Closer² (klōᵘ·zəɪ). 1611. [f. CLOSE *v.*] **1.** One who or that which closes (in various senses); *spec.* the workman that closes the uppers of boots. **2.** *Building.* A small stone or brick, used to end a wall, or course of brickwork 1703.

Close-reef (klōᵘ·s,rīf), *v.* 1758. [See REEF.] To take in all the reefs of (a sail or ship); *orig.* in pa. pple. **Clo·se-reefed.**

Close-stool (klōᵘ·s,stūl). ME. A chamber utensil enclosed in a stool or box. Also *attrib.*

Closet (klǫ·zėt), *sb.* ME. [a. OF., dim. of *clos* :—L. *clausum*; see CLOSE *sb.*¹] **1.** A room for retirement; a private room; in later use always a small room. Also *transf.* and *fig.* **2.** The private apartment of a monarch or potentate. Now *Hist.* ME. **3.** A cabinet 1601; a side-room or recess for storing utensils, provisions, etc. **4.** Short for 'Water-closet' 1662. **5.** *attrib.* 1612.

1. When thou prayest, enter into thy c. *Matt.* vi. 6. A play for the c. W. A. WRIGHT. †*C. of the heart*: the pericardium; also *fig.* 3. I haue lock'd the Letter in my Closset *Lear* III. iii. 12. 5. †*C.-sins*: secret sins.

Closet (klǫ·zėt), *v.* 1595. [f. prec. sb.] To shut up in a closet, as for private conference, or secret treaty; also *fig.*

Our Constitution was overthrown .. by closetting and corrupting Members of Parliament 1690. *fig.* Oh why doth Neptune c. vp my deere 1595.

†**Closh,** *sb.*¹ 1477. [a. Flem. and Du. *klos* bowl (for playing).] A game, supposed by Cowell to be ninepins, prohibited by many statutes in 15–16th c. –1861.

Closh, *sb.*² 1572. Swollen neck, a distemper in cattle –1727. *erron.* = FOUNDER 1726.

Closure (klōᵘ·ʒiŭr). ME. [a. OF. :—L. *clausura*, f. *claus-*, *claudere.*] †**1.** That which encloses, shuts in, or confines –1871. †**2.** An enclosed place –1609. †**3.** The act of enclosing, etc.; being enclosed; enclosure –1711. **4.** The act of shutting 1600; closed condition 1845. †**5.** An agreeing upon terms; agreement, union –1668. †**6.** That by which anything is fastened; a fastening –1744; *spec.* = CLOSER² 2. 1703. **7.** A bringing to a conclusion; end 1588. **8.** *spec.* The closing of a debate in a legislative assembly by vote of the house or by other authority. See also CLOTURE, the French term, occasionally used at first. 1882.

1. Within the guiltie C. of thy Walls *Rich. III*, III. iii. 11. 4. Before Augustus's second c. thereof [i. e. of the temple of Janus] HOLLAND. 5. So much do I desire a c. with you CROMWELL. 6. Without a seal, wafer, or any c. whatever POPE. Hence **Clo·sure** *v.* to apply the c. to (a debate or speaker).

Clot (klǫt), *sb.* [OE. *clott*, *clot*, app. f. WGer. *klott-* :—OTeut. **klutto-*, f. same root as Du. *klos* block, log, and CLEAT, Ger. *kloss* lump, etc. See also CLOD.] **1.** A mass, lump, rounded mass; *esp.* a semi-solid lump formed of coagulated liquid. **2.** A = CLOD 1. Still *dial.* ME. **3.** *fig.* A dull fellow. B. JONS.

1. Clots of gold STOW, of bloud 1676. The white of an egg, with spirit of wine, doth bake the egg into clots, as if it began to poch BACON (J.). *The c.*: that part of blood which turns solid, and separates from the *serum* or permanently liquid part.

Clot (klǫt), *v.* 1500. [f. prec.] **1.** *trans.* To free (lands) from clods; *absol.* to crush clods. Still *dial.* Cf. CLOD *v.* **2.** *intr.* To form into clots, lumps, etc. 1530. **3.** Of fluids: To coagulate, run into clots 1591. **4.** *trans.* To cause to cohere in clots; to cover with clots 1697.

†**Clot-bird.** 1544. [f. CLOT clod.] The wheat-ear (*Saxicola œnanthe*): so named as frequenting fallow-land. *local.* –1753.

Clot-bur (klǫ·t,bɒɪ). 1548. [f. CLOTE *sb.* + BUR; cf. *bonfire*.] The Burdock.

Clote (klōᵘt). [OE. *clāte* :—OTeut. type **klaitôn-*: prob. conn. w. *glei-* to stick (see CLAY).] The Burdock; also its prickly burs. Also applied to Clivers, the Bur-weed, the Yellow Water Lily, etc. OE.

Cloth (klǫþ), *sb.* Pl. CLOTHES in the sense 'garments'; in other senses **cloths** (klǫþs, klǭðz). [OE. *clāþ*, with WGer. cognates.]

I. With *a* in *sing.* Pl. *cloths*, †*clothes*. **1.** A piece of woven or felted stuff, suitable for wrapping, spreading over, etc.; as, a TABLE-CLOTH; †a sail; a breadth of canvas in a sail; a CANVAS for painting on; etc. †**2.** A length of woven fabric; a piece –1721.

1. Having a c. round the waist LANE.

II. Without *a* in *sing.* A fabric woven, felted, or otherwise formed, of filaments, as of wool, hair, silk, the fibres of hemp, flax, cotton, asbestos, spun glass, wire. When used simply, usually a woollen fabric suitable for wearing apparel; also, more specifically, a *plain-wove* woollen fabric; as BROAD-CLOTH. ME.

C. of gold: a c. woven wholly or partly of threads of gold. *American c.*: an enamelled leather-like c. *To cut the coat according to the c.* (see CUT *v.*).

III. [See CLOTHES.] †**1.** *collect.* Clothing (no *pl.*) –1816. †**2.** A (single) garment –ME. †**3.** The distinctive dress worn by members of any calling or profession –1823. **4.** Hence: One's profession; *esp.* the clerical profession. Cf. COAT *sb.* 5. 1634.

1. Gentle folks .. hae .. meat and claith SCOTT. 3. Unworthy of the king's c. 1740. 4. *The c.*: the clergy; the office of a clergyman.

Comb.: **c.-measure**, the lineal measure used for c., in which the yard is divided into quarters and nails (sixteenths); **-paper**, a coarse paper used to lay between the folds in pressing and finishing woollen cloths; **-shearer**, one who shears off the superfluous nap on woollen clothing after teaseling; **-wo·rker**, a manufacturer of woollen c.; **-yard**, the yard by which c. was measured: chiefly in *Cloth-yard shaft*. Hence **Clo·th(e)less, clothesless,** *a.*

†**Cloth** (klǫþ), *v.* 1599. [f. prec.] To make into cloth –1641. See also CLOTHE.

Clothe (klōᵘð), *v.* Pa. t. and pple. **clothed** (klōᵘðd), **clad** (klæd). [Two types: *a.* OE. *clāðian*; whence ME. *clathe* (n. dial.), *clothe*. *β.* OE. *clǣðan*, whence ME. *cladde*, *clad*. Both f. (ult.) **klaiþom* a CLOTH.] **1.** *trans.* To cover or provide with clothing; to dress. Const. *with*, *in*. **2.** *intr.* (for *refl.*) To clothe oneself or be clothed ME. **3.** *trans.* †To put on (ME. only); to cover as with clothing ME. **4.** To cover with a cloth or cloths; *Naut.* to rig ME. **5.** *transf.* To cover as or as with clothing ME. **6.** *fig.* To cover, invest, or endow, as with a garment. Const. *with*, *in*. ME.

1. Drousinesse shall cloath a man with ragges *Prov.* xxiii. 21. 2. Care no more to cloath and eate *Cymb.* IV. ii. 266. 3. In mighty armes he was yclad anon SPENSER *F. Q.* I. ii. 11. 5. Winter when 'tis clad with snow COWLEY. Will .. blossoms c. the hawthorn spray SCOTT. 6. Hast thou clothed his necke with thunder *Job* xxxix. 19. So shall I cloath me in a forc'd content *Oth.* III. iv. 120. Thoughts .. in sighs thus clad MILT. *P. R.* II. 65.

Clothes (klōᵘðz, *colloq.* klōᵘz), *sb. pl.* [:— OE. *clāðas*, ME. *clothes*. See CLOTH.] **1.** Covering for the person; wearing apparel; dress, raiment, vesture. **b.** *spec.* Garments washed or to be washed ME. **2.** = BED-CLOTHES ME.

1. Freend, hou entridist thou hidir withut bride clothis WYCLIF *Matt.* xxii. 12. To wear fine cloaths FIELDING. Send the c. to the wash (*mod.*). 2. So a bad me lay more C. on his feet *Hen. V*, II. iii. 24.

Comb.: **c.-brush**; **-horse**, a wooden frame on which c. are hung out to dry; **-line, -rope**, a cord or wire on which to hang out washed c. to dry; **-moth**, a small moth, of the genus *Tinea*, the larva of which is destructive to c.; **-peg, -pin**, a forked peg used to fasten c. on a c.-line; **-press**, a receptacle for c.

Clothier (klōᵘ·ðiəɪ). ME. [orig. *clother*; see -IER.] A maker of woollen cloth; one who sells cloth and men's clothes; a fuller and dresser of cloth (*U.S.*); etc.

Clothing (klōᵘ·ðiŋ), *vbl. sb.* ME. [f. CLOTHE *v.* + -ING¹.] **1.** The action of CLOTHE *v.*; also *fig.* **2.** Clothes collectively, apparel, dress ME.; †livery, a Livery Company –1610. Also *fig.* **3.** A covering or casing of cloth, or the like; *Mech.* = CLEADING 1789; *Naut.* sails 1798. †**4.** Clothmaking –1662. Also *attrib.*

2. The Scribes, which loue to goe in long c. *Mark* xii. 38. *fig.* Words are the Cloathing of our Thoughts SWIFT. 4. C. is plied in this city FULLER.

Clo·th-maker. ME. A maker of woollen cloth.

Clot-poll, -pole. 1606. = CLOD-POLL.

Clotted (klǫ·tėd), *ppl. a.* 1605. [f. CLOT *v.*] **1.** Gathered into clots, or clods. **2.** Stuck together in or with clots; covered with clots 1725.

1. **Clotted cream**: = CLOUTED-cream. Wash off The c. blood MASSINGER. 2. The c. scourge 1804.

†**Clo·tter,** *v.* ME. [f. CLOT *v.*; cf. *stutter*, etc.] To run together in clots, to coagulate. *trans.* and *intr.* Also *fig.* –1700.

The gore congealed was clottered in his hair DRYDEN. Hence †**Clo·ttered** *ppl. a.* = CLOTTED.

Clotty (klǫ·ti), *a.* 1523. [f. CLOT *sb.* + -Y¹.] Full of clots, inclined to clot; †CLODDY.

‖**Cloture** (klōtür). 1871. [F. :—OF. *closture* :— L. *claustura*, var. of *clausura*, infl. by *claustrum*.] = CLOSURE 8. Hence **Cloture** *v. trans.* and *intr.* (*colloq.*)

Clo·tweed. *rare.* 1804. [f. CLOTE *sb.*] The Bur-weed.

‖**Clou** (klū). 1883. [Fr., = nail, peg.] The point of greatest interest, the chief attraction.

Cloud (klaud), *sb.* [OE. *clúd*, on OTeut. type **klûdoz*, f. same root as CLOD, in sense of 'mass formed by agglomeration, cumulus'.] †1. A mass of rock, a hill –ME. †2. = CLOD 2, 3. –1460. 3. A visible mass of condensed watery vapour floating at various heights in the upper air ME. *rhet.* in *pl.* The heavens ME. 4. *transf.* A cloud-like mass of smoke or dust floating in the air ME. 5. An appearance of dimness in a clear liquid or transparent body 1533; a patch of indeterminate outline on a surface of another colour 1606. 6. A cloud-like body of insects, birds, etc.; hence, a multitude, a crowd ME. 7. A loose-knitted woollen scarf worn by ladies 1877. 8. *transf.* and *fig.* Anything that obscures or conceals 1509. 9. *fig.* Anything that darkens or overshadows with gloom, trouble, suspicion; a state of gloom, etc.; a darkening of the countenance ME.

3. Euery C. engenders not a Storme 3 *Hen. VI*, v. iii 10. She is aduan'st Aboue the Cloudes, as high as Heauen it selfe *Rom. & Jul.* IV. v. 74. *Magellanic Clouds*: the two large nebulæ near the south pole of the heavens so named. 4. A thicke c. of incense went vp *Ezek.* viii. 11. *To blow a c.*: to smoke tobacco (*slang*). 5. A plain iron gray Nag, with a c. in his face 1675. 6. So greet a c. of witnessis WYCLIF *Heb.* xii. 1. A c. of gnattes SPENSER, Locusts MILT., arrows GIBBON. 8. To go abroad under c. of night 1752. *In the clouds*: obscure; fanciful; above the range of common understanding. 9. A c. of ignorance 1572, suspicion MERIVALE. *Under a c.*: in trouble or difficulties; out of favour; with a slur on one's character.

Comb.: **c.-assembler,** he who collects the clouds (tr. Gr. νεφεληγερέτα, epithet of Zeus in Homer); **-built** *a.* built of clouds; *fig.* built in the clouds; **-burst** [Ger. *Wolkenbruch*] (*U.S.*), a violent storm of rain, a waterspout; **-capt, -capped** *a.* having clouds about its summit; **-compeller,** = *cloud-assembler*; also *joc.* a smoker; **-drift,** a body of clouds drifting through the air; **-rack,** a collection of broken clouds drifting across the sky; **-ring,** *spec.* the cloudy zone of calms and variable winds at some distance on each side of the equator; **-wards** *adv.*; **-world,** = CLOUDLAND

Hence **Clou·dage.** *rare.* [see -AGE.] **Clou·dless** *a.* unclouded; **Clou·dlessly** *adv.*; **Clou·dlessness. Clou·dlet,** a little c. **Clou·dscape** [after *landscape*], a scene composed of clouds (*rare*).

Cloud (klaud), *v.* 1513. [f. prec. sb.]

I. *trans.* To cover or darken with clouds; *fig.* to overshadow; to darken with trouble 1583. 2. *transf.* and *fig.* To render obscure; to dim, darken 1513. †3. To veil –1711. 4. To cast a slur upon, asperse, sully 1611. 5. To diversify with patches of undefined outline 1710.

1. The moon being clouded presently is miss'd SHAKS. Your dislikes.. Doth c. my ioyes with danger, and with sorrow 3 *Hen. VI*, IV. i. 74. 2. Our moral judgement may.. be clouded 1856. 4. To heare My Soueraigne Mistresse clouded so *Wint. T.* I. ii. 280.

II. *intr.* 1. To become cloudy or dim; to become overcast with clouds. Const. *over, up.* 1562. 2. *fig.* To become gloomy 1588.

2. Worthies away, the Scene begins to c. SHAKS.

Cloudland (klau·dlænd). 1817. *poet.* and *rhet.* 1. The region of clouds; a 'cloudscape'. 2. *fig.* A region of fancy, myth, or unreality 1847.

Cloudy (klau·di), *a.* OE. [f. CLOUD *sb.* + -Y.] †1. Rocky; hilly –ME. 2. Of cloud; of or pertaining to the clouds ME. 3. Characterized by, or full of, clouds ME. 4. Not clear; having cloud-like markings 1587. 5. *fig.* Darkened by ignorance, etc.; dim, obscure, indistinct ME. 6. Darkened by misfortune, grief, anger, forebodings, etc.; gloomy, sullen, frowning ME.

2. He spake unto them in the c. pillar *Ps.* xcix. 7. The cloudie region 1635. 3. The c. north DRYDEN. 4. C. Ale 1679. 5. The c. knowledge of mankinde SIDNEY. 6. The Scithians.. have all c. foreheads 1650. Hence **Clou·dily** *adv.* **Clou·diness.**

Clough (klʋf, klau). [Repr. OE. **clóh*, *clóges*, prob. = OHG. *klâh* (Sievers).] 1. A ravine or valley with steep sides ME. †2. *Occas.* = 'cliff' –ME.

Clough, erron. sp. of CLOFF, CLOW.

Clour (klūᵊɹ), *sb. Sc.* and *n. dial.* 1508. [?] A bump (on the head); a knock such as would raise a bump; a dint. Hence **Clour** *v.* to raise a lump on (the head), etc.

Clout (klaut), *sb.*[1] *arch.* and *dial.* [OE. *clút*, ? f. an OTeut. **klûtoz*, pre-Teut. type **gludo'-s* from same root as CLOT, CLEAT, in the sense of 'lump, piece of stuff'.] 1. A piece of cloth, leather, metal, etc.; a patch. 2. A plate of iron; *esp.* one fixed on an axletree, to prevent wear. [Cf. CLEAT.] Now *dial.* OE. 3. *spec.* A rag; a cloth (*esp.* one put to mean uses) ME. †4. *spec.* in *pl.* Swaddling clothes –1826. †5. *Archery.* The mark shot at; *ellipt.* a shot that hits the mark –1820. 6. A heavy blow, *esp.* with the hand. Cf. CLOD *sb.* Now *dial.* ME.

1. Cloutes and patches pieced one by one 1563. 3. Driven, like turkeys to market with a stick and a red c. STERNE. Till May be out Ne'er cast a c. *Provb.* 5. Though the c. we do not always hit B. JONS. *Comb.* **c.-nail,** a flat-headed nail, used for fastening a c. on an axle, studding boots, etc.

Clout, *sb.*[2] Now *dial.* [ME. *clute*, ? f. (ult.) OTeut. **klûton-*; same root as prec.] 1. Clot of earth, clod. †2. Clouted cream –1648.

Clout (klaut), *v.* Now *arch.* or *dial.* ME. [f. CLOUT *sb.*[1]] 1. *trans.* To mend with a CLOUT; to patch. Also *fig.* †2. To put *in*, *on*, or *to* by way of a patch. Also *absol.* To add patches –1581. 3. To protect with an iron plate; also, to stud shoes with clout-nails ME. †4. *fig.* To patch clumsily or botch *up* –1602. 5. To cover with, or as with, a cloth (*arch.*) 1579. 6. To cuff heavily. Now *dial.* ME.

1. *fig.* He clowteth the old broken holes with patches of papistry BALE. 5. He.. showed a leg clouted up 1709. 6. The late Queen of Spain took off one of her chapines, and clowted Olivarez about the noddle with it HOWELL. Hence **Clou·ted** *ppl. a.*[1] **Clou·ter,** a cobbler or patcher; a botcher. †**Clou·terly** *a.* and *adv.*

Clou·ted, *ppl. a.*[2] 1542. [f. CLOUT *sb.*[2]] Said of cream obtained by scalding, which makes it thick or clotted.

†**Clou·t-shoe.** Now (*arch.*) **Clouted shoe.** 1463. [? pa. pple. of CLOUT *v.* + SHOE.] 1. A shoe studded with large-headed nails. (Or ? a patched shoe.) †2. One who wears clouted shoes; a boor. (Cf. *Colin Clout.*) –1704.

1. The dull swain.. with his clouted shoon MILT. [Cf. 'clowted brogues' *Cymb.* IV. ii. 214.]

Clove (klōᵘv), *sb.*[1] [OE. *clufu* :—OTeut. **klubâ-, klobâ-*; f. weak-grade stem of **kleuf-*, CLEAVE.] 1. One of the small bulbs which make up the compound bulb of garlic, shallot, etc. 2. A natural segment of a fruit 1634. Hence †**Cloved** *ppl. a.* divided into cloves.

Clove (klōᵘv), *sb.*[2] [ME. *clow(e*, a. F. *clou*, in full *clou de girofle*, 'girofle nail' (see CLOVE-GILLYFLOWER), *clou* being added to *girofle* from the resemblance of a single bud with its stalk to a nail, *clou*, L. *clavus*.] 1. The dried flower-bud of *Caryophyllus aromaticus*, much used as a pungent aromatic spice. (Usu. in *pl.*) 2. The tree, *Caryophyllus aromaticus*, orig. a native of the Moluccas 1594. 3. Short for *clove-pink*, or *clove-gillyflower* 1746. 4. *Cloves.* A cordial flavoured with this spice 1852.

Comb.: **c.-bark,** the bark of *Cinnamomum Culilawan*, which has a flavour of cloves; **-pink,** a c.-scented species of *Dianthus*: see CLOVE-GILLYFLOWER.

Clove, *sb.*[3] ME. [Repr. Anglo-L. *clavus*, Anglo-Fr. *clou.*] A weight formerly used for wool and cheese, equal to 7 or 8 lbs. avoirdupois.

Clove, *sb.*[4] *U. S.* 1779. [a. Du. *klove*, also *kloof*, split, cleft.] A rocky cleft; a gap, ravine: used chiefly in place-names; as, *C. of Kaaterskill, Stony C.*

Clove (klōᵘv), *v.* 1863. [f. CLOVE *sb.*[2]] To spice with cloves; to stick (an onion, etc.) with cloves.

Clove, *pa. pple.* 1561. Short f. CLOVEN, still occas. in verse. Hence **c.-hitch,** a hitch round a spar, etc., formed by passing the rope twice round in such a way that both ends pass under the centre of the loop in front; **-hook,** an iron clasp in two overlapping parts, used for bending chain-sheets to clews of sails, etc.

Clove, pa. t. of CLEAVE *v.*

Clove-gillyflower (klōᵘv dʒi·liflauᵊɹ). ME. [a. F. *clou de girofle* (*girofre, gilofre*); see CLOVE[2]. Fr. *girofle* (*girofre, gilofre*) repr. Rom. *garofilo, garofilo*, late L. **carophilum*, a. Gr. καρυόφυλλον the clove, f. κάρυον nut + φύλλον leaf. In Eng. the Anglo-Fr. *gilofre* has passed through *gillofer, gilloflower*, to *gillyflower* (and *July-flower*). See also GILLYFLOWER.] †1. The spice CLOVE *sb.*[2] 1. –1486. 2. A clove-scented species of Pink (*Dianthus Caryophyllus*), whence the carnation, etc. 1535.

Cloven (klōᵘ·v'n), *ppl. a.* ME. [pa. pple. of CLEAVE *v.*] Divided lengthwise; split.

C. hoof or *foot*, the divided hoof of ruminant quadrupeds; ascribed in pagan mythology to the god Pan, and thence to the Devil, and often used allusively as the indication of Satan, or Satanic agency. Hence **c.-hoofed, -foo·ted** *adjs.*

Clover (klōᵘ·vəɹ). [OE. *clabre, cláfre*, app. :—OTeut. type *klaibrôn-*; cf. OHG. *chlêo, -wes* (MHG. *klê -wes*, mod.G. *klee*) masc. 'clover.' The usual ME. form was *claver*.] The common name of the species of Trefoil (*Trifolium*, N.O. *Leguminosæ*), esp. *T. repens* and *T. pratense*, both cultivated largely for fodder. Applied also locally to many plants with similar characters.

Phr. *To live* (or *be*) *in c.*: to live luxuriously, as cattle do in a field of c.

Comb.: **c.-hay worm,** the larva of a moth, *Asopia costalis*, very destructive to clover-hay in N. America; **-weevil,** a small weevil, *Apion apricans*, which feeds on the seeds of c. Hence **Clo·very** *a.* (*rare*).

Clo·ver, *v.* 1649. [f. the sb.] To sow or lay down with clover. So **Clo·vered** *ppl. a.* sown or covered with clover.

†**Clover-grass.** = CLOVER.

Clow (klau), *sb.* ME. [A false singular f. *clowes, clowis*, in ME. *clowse, clowze*, OE. *clúse*, a. late L. *clusa*, var. of *clausa*, a closed place or way. In the 18th c. erron. spelt *clough*, by engineers, etc.] 1. A dam for water. ? *Obs.* 2. A sluice 1483.

Clow(e)-gilofre, etc., earlier f. CLOVE-GILLYFLOWER.

Clown (klaun), *sb.* 1563. [prob. of Low German origin.] 1. A countryman, or peasant; a boor. 2. *transf.* An ignorant, uncouth, ill-bred man 1583. 3. A fool or jester; in mod. use, one of the characters in a pantomime, a circus, etc. 1600. Also *attrib.*

1. The c., the child of nature, without guile COWPER. A clod-pated C. 1753. 2. By blood a king, at heart a c. TENNYSON. 3. The clowne shall make those laugh whose lungs are tickle a' th' sere *Haml.* II. ii. 336. Hence †**Clow·nage,** behaviour or function of a c. **Clow·nery,** clownishness, performance of a c.

Clown (klaun), *v. rare.* 1579. [f. the sb.] To perform as a (stage-)clown. *To c. it*: to play the clown.

Clownish (klau·niʃ), *a.* 1570. [f. CLOWN *sb.* + -ISH.] 1. Of, belonging, or proper to a CLOWN. 2. Clown-like, rude, boorish; ignorant; clumsy; coarse 1581.

1. In c. apparell 1581. 2. C. or uncivill fashions 1586. Hence **Clow·nish·ly** *adv.*, **-ness.**

Clownship (klau·nʃip). 1606. [See -SHIP.] The condition or estate of a clown or clowns; also as a mock title.

Cloy (kloi), *v.*[1] ME. [Aphet. f. *acloy* ACLOY.] †1. To nail (ME. only). †2. To pierce with or as with a nail –1726. †3. To spike (a gun) –1768. †4. To stop up, block (a passage, etc.); to crowd or fill *up* –1636. †5. *fig.* To clog (movement, etc.); to weigh down –1665. 6. To fill to loathing; to surfeit. *lit.* and *fig.* Also *absol.* 1530.

2. He never shod horse but he cloyed him BACON. [A wild boar] with his cruell tusk him deadly cloyd SPENSER *F. Q.* III. vi. 48. 4. To c. a harbour by sinking ships laden with stones SPEED. 6. Who can .. c. the hungry edge of appetite By bare imagination of a Feast *Rich. II*, I. iii. 296. *fig.* Often preaching cloyeth the people UDALL. †**Cloy·ment,** satiety (*rare*). **Cloy·some** *a. rare*, of cloying quality.

†**Cloy,** *v.*[2] *rare.* ? 'To claw' (Steevens); 'to strike the beak together' (Johnson). *Cymb.* V. iv. 118.

Cloy·less, *a.* 1606. That does not CLOY (sense 6).

†**Cloyne, cloine,** *v.* 1538. [cf. OF. *cluigner*, var. of *cligner*.] 1. *intr.* To cheat, deceive –1569. 2. *trans.* To take furtively or fraudulently; to grab –1566.

Club (klʋb), *sb.* [ME. *clubbe, clobbe*, prob. ad. ON. *clubba*, var. of *klumba*; f. same root as CLUMP, q. v. Cf. *club-foot(ed.*]

I. 1. A heavy staff for use as a weapon, thin at one end for the hand, and thicker at the other; also = *Indian clubs.* 2. A stick or bat used in various games of ball, as golf, hockey, etc. 1450. 3. The butt-end of a gun 1724. 4. Any club-shaped organ, structure, etc. 1707.

1. The geaunte bare a clubbe CAXTON. †*Clubs are trump*: physical force is to rule the day; a punning allusion to II. 4. A nose which had a red c. to it MARRYAT. A c., otherwise a very thick pigtail 1850.

II. In cards. *pl.* The suit of cards distinguished by the representation of a trefoil leaf in black; in *sing.* a card of this suit.

[A tr. of Sp. *basto*, or It. *bastone* (see BASTO, BASTON), the 'club' figured on Spanish cards. The English figure is the French *trèfle*, trefoil.]

III. A combination. [See the vb. The course of development is uncertain.] †1. Combination into one mass; aggregate –1674. †2. A combination of contributions to make up a total sum; one share of this –1792. †3. A social meeting the expenses of which are jointly defrayed –1801. †4. A clique; a secret society –1730. 5. An association of persons meeting periodically (under certain regulations), at some house of entertainment, for social intercourse, etc. 1670. 6. An association of persons interested in the promotion of some object; as *Alpine, Yacht C.*, etc.; *Benefit, Goose C.*, etc. 1755. 7. An association of persons formed mainly for social purposes, and having buildings for the exclusive use of the members, and always open to them as a place of resort, or, in some cases, of temporary residence 1776; the buildings occupied by such a society 1837. Also *attrib.*

2. We dined merry: but my c. and the rest come to 7/6*d.*, which was too much PEPYS. 3. This Tavern, where they held their C. DE FOE. 4. The Jacobite clubb LUTTRELL. 5. In my absence they had erected a C. and made me one SWIFT. 7. They sent for me at my c. 1883.

Comb.: **c.-house**, the house occupied by a c.; **-land** (*colloq.*), the vicinity of St. James's, in London; **-money**, subscription to a benefit c. or provident society; **-root**, a disease of turnips, etc., anbury; **-wood**, CASUARINA. Hence **Clu·bbable, clubable** *a.* fit to be a member of a c. **Clu·bbish** *a.* clownish (*dial.*); addicted to clubs. **Clu·bless** *a.*

Club (klɒb), *v.* 1593. [f. CLUB *sb.* I.] 1. To beat with or as with a club. 2. To gather into a club-like mass 1625; hence, to gather together 1641. 3. *intr.* To combine together 1649. 4. To combine, or contribute, to a common end 1632. 5. To combine, or contribute, to make up a total sum 1655. 6. *Mil.* To throw into a confused mass 1806. 7. *Naut.* To drift down a current with an anchor out (Dicts.).

1. *To c. a musket*: to use it as a club. 2. Hair clubbed, atop, Chinese fashion FORREST. To c. quotations MILT. 4. They clubbed their small means together CARLYLE. 5. To find out a ninepence to c. with me for the coach PEPYS. 6. To c. the battalion WINDHAM. Hence **Clu·bbing** *vbl. sb., spec.* a disease in cabbages, etc.

Clubbed (klɒbd), *ppl. a.* ME. 1. [f. the sb. + -ED.] Shaped like a club; thick-set. 2. [f. the vb.] Used as a club 1724; thrown into a confused mass, as a *c. battalion* 1823.

Clubber (klɒ·bəɹ). 1633. [f. CLUB *v.* or *sb.* + -ER.] 1. One who clubs or belongs to a club. 2. One who wields a club 1887.

Clubbism (klɒ·biz'm). 1837. [f. CLUB *sb.* + -ISM.] The club system.

To passionate Constitutionalism..C. will..seem the root of all evil CARLYLE. So **Clu·bbist**, a member or supporter of the political clubs of the French Revolution, or of their principles, a member of a club.

†**Club-fist.** 1575. A large clenched fist; hence, a rough, brutal fellow –1589. So **Club-fisted** *a.*

Clu·b-foot. 1538. 1. A name for various distortions, generally congenital, which give the foot a lumpy, club-like appearance. 2. A foot of a stunted, lumpy appearance 1683. Also *attrib.* Hence **Clu·b-foo·ted** *a.*

Club-haul (klɒ·b,hǭl), *v.* 1794. *Naut.* To tack a ship by letting the lee-anchor down as soon as the wind is out of the sails, by which her head is brought to wind; when she then pays off, the cable is cut, and the sails are trimmed to the other tack: a last resort in very perilous positions.

Club-law. 1612. The use of the club, or physical force, as contrasted with argument; law of the physically stronger.

Argumenta ad baculum, vulgarly termed club-law 1829.

Club-man (klɒ·bmæn). 1597. 1. A man armed with a club. 2. A member of a club 1851.

Club-moss (klɒ·b,mǫs). 1597. [tr. L. *Muscus clavatus*.] A name properly applied to *Lycopodium clavatum* from the club-like shape of its upright fertile spikes of spore-cases; thence extended to other, and occas. to all, *Lycopodiaceæ*.

Clu·b-ri·ser. 1645. *Eng. Hist.* = CLUBMAN 1.

Clu·b-rush. 1677. Any plant of the genus *Scirpus* (N.O. *Cyperaceæ*).

Club-shaped (klɒ·b,ʃēpt), *a.* 1770. Thickening towards one extremity which is blunt and rounded; in *Zool.* and *Bot.* = CLAVATE.

Clu·bster. 1727. [See -STER.] = CLUBMAN.

Cluck (klɒk), *sb.* 1703. [Echoic; cf. CLUCK *v.*] 1. *interj.* An imitation of the abrupt hollow guttural sound made by a hen desiring to sit or calling her chickens 1829. 2. A name for this, or any similar sound, *e.g.* the S. African click (see CLICK *sb.*[1] 5) 1703.

Cluck (klɒk), *v.* 1481. [Echoic; cf. CLOCK *v.*[2] (OE. *cloccian*).] 1. *intr.* To make the sound described under CLUCK *sb.*, or any similar sound 1611. †2. *trans.* To call (chickens) as a hen does. Also *fig.* –1687.

2. *fig.* That he may c. sinners to himself 1658.

Clu·dder, *v.*, a var. of CLODDER, q. v.

Clue (klū, kliū). 1596. A later sp. of CLEW, q. v. Used in all senses, but *esp.* in the *fig.*

A c. of yarn 1834. And treads the maze of life without a c. POMFRET. A c. to the identity of one C. BRONTË. Research which has..joined the broken c. of history from contemporaneous monuments BIRCH. Hence **Clue·less** *a.* *Comb.* **c.-line**: see CLEW-LINE.

†**Clum,** *sb.* (*interj.*) ME. [?] 1. Silence, quiet (ME. only). 2. ?A note of silence; cf. *mum!* –1616.

Clumber (klɒ·mbəɹ). 1865. [f. *Clumber*, a seat of the Duke of Newcastle.] Name of a breed of spaniels.

Clump (klɒmp), *sb.* 1586. [= LG. *klump*, MLG. *klumpe*. Cf. OE. *clympre* CLUMPER. In ON. *klump-* appears as *klumb-*, whence *klumba*, *klubba*, CLUB.] 1. A compact (shapeless) mass, a heap, a lump 1690. 2. A cluster; a tuft; a patch 1586. 3. *Clumps*: a parlour game of questions and answers 1883. 4. A thick extra sole on a shoe 1879. 5. *Mining.* = CLUNCH 1865. ¶ *Erron.* used for CLAMP 1825.

2. A c. of Scots Fir Trees 1759. New clumps of young plants VINES. *Comb.* **c.-boot, -shoe**, one with a c.-sole, or thick double sole for rough wear. Hence **Clu·mpish** *a.* heavy and clumsy. **Clu·mpy** *a.* clump-like; clumpish.

Clump (klɒmp), *v.* 1665. [Partly f. CLUMP *sb.*; also echoic.] 1. To tread heavily and clumsily. 2. *trans.* To put together into a clump; to plant in a clump 1824. 3. To add an extra thick sole; to clog. Hence **Clumped** *ppl. a.* †clubbed, as in *clumped foot*; furnished with clumps of trees, or with clump-soles.

Clumper, *sb.* Now *dial.* [OE. *clympre*; see CLUMP *sb.*] = CLUMP *sb.* 1.

†**Clumper,** *v.* 1562. [f. prec.] To form into lumps or masses –1647.

Vapours..Clumper'd in balls of clouds H. MORE.

Clumps, a game; see CLUMP *sb.* 3.

Clumse, *a.* (*sb.*) Now *dial.* 1611. [prob. of Norse origin; cf. CLUMSE *v.*] Benumbed with cold; hence, stupid; unhandy, lazy; in mod. dial., also, surly.

†**Clumse,** *v.* [ME. *clumsen*; perh. of Norse origin. Cf. mod. Norw. *klumsa*, intensive of *kluma*, to make motionless, etc. The stem *klum-* is in ablaut relation to *klam-* in CLAM and CLEM.] 1. To be or become numb with cold (ME. only). 2. *trans.* To stupefy (ME. only). Hence †**Clumsed, clumst** *ppl. a.*

Clumsy (klɒ·msi), *a.* 1597. [App. f. CLUMSE *v.* + -Y. Not in Shaks.] †1. Benumbed with cold –1602. 2. Acting or moving as if benumbed; heavy and awkward; ungainly, unhandy 1597. 3. *fig.* Ill-contrived, awkward 1681. 4. Rudely constructed; inelegant, unwieldy 1763.

1. Clumsie winter MARSTON. 2. Clumsie fingers RAY. A c., aukward, and unhandy people SWIFT. 3. In c. verse, unlick'd, unpointed DRYDEN. C. apologies SWIFT. 4. The boots..are a trifle c. (*mod.*). Hence **Clu·msily** *adv.* **Clu·msiness,** c. quality.

Clunch, *a.* Now *dial.* 1776. [prob. f. LG. *klunt*, Du. *klont* 'lump, clod, clown'.] Lumpy; stiff; thickset, 'chunky' in figure.

She is fat, and c., and heavy, and ugly MAD. D'ARBLAY.

Clunch (klɒnʃ), *sb.* 1602. [prob. sb. use of prec. But cf. *bump, bunch*, etc.] 1. A lump (*dial.*). 2. A lumpish fellow, a lout. Now *dial.* 1602. 3. Any of various stiff clays 1679. 4. A soft limestone forming one of the beds of the lower chalk 1823.

Clunch, *v. rare.* 1628. By-form of CLENCH. Hence †**Clunchfist**, a clenched fist (*lit.* and *fig.*); a miser.

Clung (klɒŋ), *ppl. a. arch.* and *dial.* ME. [f. CLING *v.*] Drawn together, shrunk; of soil: Clinging, stiff.

Clung, pa. t. and pple. of CLING *v.*, q. v.

†**Clung,** *v.* 1601. By-form of CLING *v.* –1715.

Cluniac (klū·niæk). 1631. [ad. med.L. *Cluniacus*, f. *Cluny*.] *adj.* Belonging to the monastery of Cluny, near Mâcon in France. *sb.* A monk of Cluny. So **Cluniace·nsian, Clunist.**

Clupeoid (klū·pi,oid). 1880. [f. L. *clupea* a kind of small river-fish, taken as the generic name of the herring, etc. + -OID.] A fish belonging to the herring family (*Clupeidæ*).

Cluster (klɒ·stəɹ), *sb.* Also **gluster** (*Spenser*). [OE. *clyster*, occas. *cluster* = NGer. *kluster*, app. from same root as *clot, clout, cleat*; see CLOT.] 1. A collection of things of the same kind, growing closely together; a bunch. †2. A rounded mass; a clot –1548. 3. A number of persons, animals, or things close together; a group, swarm, crowd ME. Also *fig.*

1. The glusters of ripe grapes SPENSER. A c. of nuttis 1483, egges EDEN, flowers GRAY. 3. As bees.. all in a c. PURCHAS. Clusters of islets SIR J. ROSS, stars 1854. *fig.* Ideas..in clusters TUCKER. *Comb.* **c.-candlestick**, a branched candlestick. Hence **Clu·stery** *a.* (Dicts.)

Cluster (klɒ·stəɹ), *v.* ME. [f. prec. sb.] 1. *trans.* To gather or group in clusters; to cover with clusters ME. 2. *intr.* To congregate in a cluster 1541; to grow or be situated in a cluster or clusters 1590.

1. Not less..would..The foxglove c. dappled bells TENNYSON. Ylion was..clustrit with towres ME. 2. Woes c.; rare are solitary woes YOUNG. [Curls] clustered round her head WORDSW. Hence **Clu·stered** *ppl. a., spec.* in *clustered pillar*, etc.: 'several slender pillars or shafts attached to each other so as to form one' (Gwilt). **Clu·steringly** *adv.*

†**Clusterfist.** 1611. [f. CLUSTER in sense of lump; cf. *clunchfist*.] A clumsy- or close-fisted fellow; a lout, a niggard –1675.

Clutch (klɒtʃ), *sb.*[1] [ME. *cloke*, Sc. *cluke*. *Clutch* is app. assim. to CLUTCH *v.*, q. v.] 1. The claw of a beast or bird of prey, or of a fiend: mostly in *pl.*; also *contempt.* the human hand. 2. The hand, or in *pl.* 'hands in a sense of rapacity and cruelty' (J.). Now usu. *grasp.* 1526. 3. Tight grip or grasp; clutching 1784. 4. An act of grasping *at* 1831. 5. *Mech.* A coupling for throwing the working parts into or out of action at will 1814. 6. *Mech.* A contrivance with two hooked arms for clutching bodies to be lifted by a crane, etc. 1874.

2. But Age .. hath caught me in his c. *Haml.* v. i. 80. The Clutches of the Hangman STEELE. 3. The c. of poverty COWPER. 4. An expiring c. at popularity CARLYLE. *Comb.* **c.-fist,** a miser· also as *adj.*

Clutch, *sb.*[2] 1721. A var. of CLETCH.

Clutch (klɒtʃ), *v.*[1] [ME. *clucche(n*, app. a var. of *clicche*, CLITCH. The ME. *cloke* took the form, and reacted on the meaning, of *clutch*, so that '*to clutch*' is now mainly 'to grasp with *clokes* or claws'.] †1. = CLITCH 1, 2. –1703. 2. *trans.* To seize with claws or clutches; to seize eagerly ME. Also *absol.* 3. To hold tightly in the closed hand 1602. Also *fig.* 4. *intr.* To make a clutch *at* 1831.

1. Not that I haue the power to c. my hand, When his faire Angels would salute my palme SHAKS. 2. I clutched up the cat HELPS. 3. Is this a Dagger, which I see before me? Come, let me c. thee SHAKS. *fig.* To c. the globe in one intellectual grasp COLLIER. 4. How we c. at shadows CARLYLE.

Clutch, *v.*[2] [f. CLUTCH *sb.*[2]] To hatch (chickens). GOLDSM.

Clutter (klɒ·təɹ), *sb.* 1580. [Cf. with sense 1 CLOTTER; with others *cluster* and *clatter*.] †1. A clotted mass –1611. 2. A confused collection 1666; crowded confusion, litter (*dial.* and *U.S.*) 1694. 3. Bustle, stir (*arch.*) 1649; hubbub (*arch.*) 1656; mingled rattle (*arch.*) 1655.

2. A c. of Citations 1666. He saw what a C. there was with huge, over-grown Pots R. L'ESTRANGE. 3. I heard such a c. of small shot VANBRUGH.

Clu·tter, *v.* 1556. [See the sb.] †1. *intr.* To clot. Also *trans.* –1676. 2. To crowd together in heaps 1556. 3. To run in bustling disorder or with a confused noise; to make a clatter 1602. 4. To crowd *with* a litter of things 1674. 5. To utter words confusedly 1654. Hence **Clu·tterment**, confused bustle, crowd.

Cly, *sb.* *Thieves' cant.* 1690. [prob. from same root as CLAW.] Money; also, a pocket. So **Cly** *v.* to take; *esp.* to steal.

Clydesdale (kləi·dzdeᵻl). 1831. A breed of heavy draught horses orig. from the Clyde valley, Scotland.

Clypea·ster. 1836. [f. L. *clypeus* (= *clipeus*) + Gr. ἀστήρ.] *Zool.* A genus of echinoid Echinoderms, allied to the common sea-urchin, but having mouth and vent both below. Hence **Clypea·stroid** *a.* and *sb.*

Clypeate (kli·pi,eᵻt), *a.* 1711. [f. as prec.] Shaped like a round shield. So **Cly·peiform** *a.*

Clypeo-, comb. f. CLYPEUS, as in *c.-frontal* (*Entom.*), common to the clypeus and front.

Clypeole (kli·piōᵘl). 1882. [ad. L. *clypeolum*, dim. of *clypeum.*] A little shield; 'term applied to the lamina on the inner surface of which the sporangia are attached in Equisetum'. Hence **Cly·peolar** *a.* formed like a c. **Cly·peolate** *a.* furnished with clypeoles.

‖**Clypeus** (kli·piŏs). 1834. [a. L., prop. *clipeus.*] *Entom.* The broad shield-shaped part of the head of some insects. Hence **Cly·peal** *a.* of or pertaining to the c.

Clysmian (kli·zmiăn), *a. rare.* 1882. [f. as next + -IAN.] Epithet of soils produced by transport and mechanical deposit, of which water has been the agent.

Clysmic (kli·zmik), *a.* 1847. [f. Gr. κλυσμός + -IC.] Washing, cleansing.

Clyster (kli·stəɹ), *sb.* ME. [a. L. *clyster*, Gr. κλυστήρ, f. κλύζειν to wash out, drench.] 1. A medicine injected into the rectum; an injection, enema; *occas.*, a suppository. †2. The pipe or syringe used in injection 1527. Hence **Cly·ster** *v.* to treat with clysters. †**Cly·sterize** *v.* to inject as a c. *Comb.* c.-pipe = CLYSTER 2.

Cn-, in OE. and early ME. See KN-.

Cnemial (knī·miăl), *a.* 1871. [f. Gr. κνήμη + -(I)AL.] Relating to the tibia.

‖**Cnida** (knəi·dă). Pl. **cnidæ.** 1876. [mod. L., a. Gr. κνίδη nettle.] *Zool.* The nettle cell of the *Cœlenterata* (jelly-fish, etc.), in which their sting resides: usually called *nematocyst.* Hence **Cni·doblast** [Gr. βλαστός], the cell in which a nematocyst is developed. **Cni·docil** [L. *cilium*], the external irritable ciliary process of cnidoblasts. **Cnidophore** [Gr. -φορος], a process bearing a battery of cnidoblasts.

Co. 1759. 1. (kōᵘ). An abbrev. of COMPANY; used *esp.* for: The partners of a firm whose names do not appear in the style or title. 2. A written abbrev. of *county* 1886.

Co-, *prefix*, repr. L. *com-*, *con-*, *co-*, in the sense of 'together', 'in company', 'in common', 'joint, -ly', 'equal, -ly', 'reciprocally', 'mutually'. It combines with verbs, adjs., adverbs, and sbs. 2. *Math.* (short for *complement*). Used in the sense '... of the complement', or 'complement of ...'; see COSINE, CO-LATITUDE, etc.

†**Coacervate** (as next, or kōᵘ,ăsə·ɹvēt), *a.* 1626. [ad. L. *coacervatus*; see next.] Heaped together; gathered into one place –1677.

Coacervate (ko,æ·səɹveᵻt), *v.* ? *Obs.* 1623. [ad. L. *coacervat-*, *coacervare.*] To heap together; accumulate; also *fig.* Hence **Coacerva·tion**, the action of heaping together, or fact of being heaped together; a mass heaped together.

Coach (kōᵘtʃ), *sb.* 1556. [In 16th c. *coche*, a. Fr. Cf. Sp. and Pg. *coche*, It. *cocchio*; Ger. *kutsche*, etc. All are from Magyar *kocsi* (pronounced kotʃi), 'ungaricum currum [quem] kotczi vulgo vocant'. *Kocsi* is in form an adj., meaning 'of Kocs (kotʃ)', a place between Raab and Buda.] 1. A large kind of carriage: in 16th and 17th centuries, usually a state carriage; now, usually, a large close carriage with four wheels, with seats inside, and several outside, used for public conveyance of passengers (see STAGE COACH). Applied by railway employés to a railway carriage: in U.S. *esp.* a sleeping-car 1866. 2. *Naut.* An apartment near the stern of a man of war, usually occupied by the captain 1660. 3. *Univ. colloq.* A private tutor who 'coaches' a pupil 1848; also, *transf.*, one who trains others for an athletic contest 1885.

1. The roiall Dame..for her coche doth call SPENSER *F.Q.* I. iv. 16. 2. The Commanders all came on board, and the council sat in the c. PEPYS. 3. Kitcat, a Trinity c., has a party at Drumnadrochet CLOUGH.

Comb.: c.-dog, a spotted Dalmatian dog, kept to run in attendance on a carriage; †fellow, a horse yoked in the same carriage with another; *joc.* a companion, mate; -horse; -house, an out-house for a c., etc.; -office, a booking-office for a stage-coach; -wagon, tr. Ger. *kutsch-wagen*, coach.

Coach, *v.* 1612. [f. sb.] †1. To convey in or provide with a coach. 2. *intr.* To ride or drive in a coach (*colloq.*) 1630. 3. *Univ. colloq.* To prepare *for* an examination, or *in* special subjects; also, to train for an athletic contest 1849; *gen.* to prime with information. *intr.* To read with a coach 1849.

2. To c. it thro' the town 1797. 3. *intr.* Do you mean to c. this term (*mod.*).

Coa·ch-box. 1651. [f. COACH *sb.* + BOX *sb.*[2], in the sense of 'seated compartment'.] The seat occupied by the driver of a coach.

Coachee, coachy (kōᵘ·tʃi). 1790. [Cf. *cabby*, etc.] A coachman (*colloq.*). So **Coa·cher**, a coach-horse.

Coachful (kōᵘ·tʃful). 1654. As many as will fill a coach.

Coachman (kōᵘ·tʃmæn). 1579. 1. The man who drives a coach. 2. *Angling.* A kind of artificial fly 1839. Hence **Coa·chmanship**, skill in driving a coach.

Coa·ch-whip. 1736. 1. A whip used in driving a coach 1833. 2. *fig.* A long thin strip; *pl.* shreds 1781. 3. *Naut.* 'The pendant' (Adm. Smyth).

Coa·ch-whip snake: a snake so called from its resemblance to the lash of a coach-whip.

†**Coact**, *ppl. a.* ME. [ad. L. *coactus.*] Compelled, forced –1635.

Coact (ko,æ·kt), *v.* ME. [f. L. *coact-*, *coagere*, *cogere.*] †1. *trans.* To compel, force –1651. †2. To restrain (*rare*) –1529. †3. To contract; to concentrate –1657. 4. *intr.* To act together (*rare*) 1606.

4. If I tell how these two did c. SHAKS. Hence **Coa·ction**, coercion (now *rare*); action in concert.

Coactive (ko,æ·ktiv), *a.* 1596. [See prec. and -IVE.] 1. Of the nature of force or compulsion. (Qualifying *power* or the like. Now *rare.*) 1605. †b. In passive sense: Compulsory –1661. 2. Acting or taking place together 1611.

1. A c., or coercitive jurisdiction JER. TAYLOR. C. obedience USSHER. 2. With what's vnreall thou c. art *Wint. T.* I. ii. 141. Hence **Coa·ctively** *adv.* by way of compulsion. †**Coactivity**, activity in concert; c. quality.

Co-adaptation (ko,ædæptē·ʃən). 1803. [See CO-.] Mutual adaptation.

Coadjacent (kōᵘ,ădʒē·sĕnt). 1842. [See CO-.] *adj.* Adjacent to each other, mutually contiguous. *sb.* Any object or idea so related to another. Hence **Co-adja·cence, -ency.**

Co-adjust (kōᵘ,ădʒɒ·st), *v.* 1864. [See CO-.] To adjust mutually. Hence **Coadjustment.**

Coadjutant (kōᵘ,ădʒiū·tănt, ko,æ·dʒutănt). 1708. [See COADJUTOR.] *adj.* Helping another or others; co-operating. *sb.* One who helps another or others 1728. So †**Coadju·te** *v.*; whence †**Coadju·ting** *ppl. a.* †**Coadju·tive** *a.*

Coadjutor (ko,ădʒiū·təɹ). ME. [a. OF. *coadjuteur*, ad. L. *coadjutor*, *-orem*, f. CO- + *adjutor*, f. *adjuvare.* No L. **coadjuvare* or **coadjutare* is found; mod. words pointing to these are suggested by *coadjutor.*] 1. One who works with and helps another; an assistant. 2. *spec. Eccl.* One appointed to assist a bishop or other ecclesiastic. Cf. SUFFRAGAN. 1549.

1. Euery one a c. to the worke of all the other 1619. Hence **Coadju·torship**, the office of a c.; helping co-operation. **Coadju·tress**, †**Coa·djutrice**, **Co-adju·trix**, a female c. var. **Coa·djutator** (*rare*).

Coadjuvant (ko,æ·dʒuvănt). 1625. [See COADJUTOR.] *adj.* Assisting, helpful. ? *Obs.* *sb.* *Med.* An ingredient that assists the main agent 1864. **Coa·djuvancy**, c. quality or action.

Coadnate, *a.* 1866. [See CO-.] *Bot.* = CONNATE.

Coadunate (ko,æ·diunēt), *a.* 1839. [ad. L. *coadunatus*, *coadunare.*] *Phys.* and *Bot.* Joined together; congenitally united. var. **Coa·dunated.**

Coadunation (ko,æ:diunē·ʃən). 1558. [ad. L. *coadunationem*; see prec.] The action of joining or state of being joined together in one.

A..c. of body, soul, and spirit CDL. MANNING. So †**Coadunition.**

Co-adve·nture, *v.* 1642. [See CO-.] To venture together (with). So **Coadve·nture** *sb.* a joint adventure; **Co-adve·nturer.**

Coæ-; see COE-.

†**Co-afforest**, *v.* [See CO-.] To afforest as an addition to an existing forest. HOWELL.

Co-agency (ko,ē·dʒĕnsi). 1611. [See CO-.] Joint or combined agency. So **Co-a·gent.**

†**Coagitate**, *v.* 1545. [ad. late L. *coagitat-*, *coagitare.*] To shake or mix together –1741.

Coagment (ko,ægme·nt), *v.* ? *Obs.* 1603. [ad. L. *coagmentare*, f. *coagmentum*, f. *co-agere*, *cogere.* Only found as pa. pple.] To cement or join together. var. †**Coa·gmentate** *v.*

†**Coagmenta·tion.** 1578. [ad. L. *coagmentationem*; see prec.] 1. The action of joining, or state of being joined, together; junction, concretion –1674. 2. A mass formed by this action –1684.

Coagulable (ko,æ·giŭlăb'l), *a.* 1652. [f. L. *coagulare.*] That can be coagulated; capable of coagulation. Hence **Coa:gulabi·lity**, c. quality; capacity of coagulating. So **Coagulant**, a coagulating agent, as rennet.

Coagulate (ko,æ·giŭlēt), *ppl. a.* ME. [ad. L. *coagulatus*; see prec.] 1. *v.* as *adj.* Coagulated; congealed. ? *Obs.* †2. as *ppl. a.* Concreted; combined in a mass –1610.

Coagulate (ko,æ·giŭleᵻt), *v.* 1549. [f. prec.] 1. *trans.* To convert (certain fluids) into a soft solid mass, as by chemical action, heat, etc.; to curdle, clot, congeal 1611. 2. To form into a mass. *lit.* and *fig.* ? *Obs.* 1610. 3. *intr.* To become converted into a soft solid mass 1606; †to solidify by evaporation –1713.

1. Albumen .. is coagulated by heat, alcohol, etc. R. KNOX. 2. Venus..was..coagulated of that foam HOWELL. 3. The blood..began to c. in the Vein 1667. Hence **Coa·gulative** *a.* having the property of producing or undergoing coagulation. **Coa·gulator**, that which coagulates. **Coa·gulatory** *a.* productive of coagulation (*rare*).

Coagulation (ko,ægiŭlē·ʃən). 1477. [a. F., f. as prec.] 1. The action or process of coagulating; clotting, curdling, setting; *concr.* a coagulated mass 1683. †2. Solidification by evaporation –1718. 3. The forming or uniting into a mass; concretion, cohesion 1610. Also *fig.* *concr.* A concreted mass 1664.

1. A c., like that of whites of egges SIR T. BROWNE. The c. of the blood ABERNETHY. 3. The casuall c. of atomes HEALEY.

†**Coa·gule**, *v.* ME. [a. F. *coaguler.*] Earlier f. COAGULATE –1549.

Coa·guline. 1868. A kind of cement.

‖**Coagulum** (ko,æ·giŭlŏm). Pl. **coagula.** 1658. [L., f. CO- + *agere.*] †1. A substance that coagulates a liquid –1713. 2. A mass of coagulated matter, a clot of blood 1658; that part of the blood which clots 1800. Also *fig.*

‖**Coaita** (ko·aitā·). 1774. [Tupi; = Red-faced Spider-monkey.] *Zool.* The Red-faced Spider-monkey (*Ateles paniscus*) found in tropical S. America. Also other species of *Ateles.*

Coak (kōᵘk), *sb.* 1794. [? repr. ONF. **coque* = Fr. *coche*, It. *cocca* notch; cf. COCK *v.*, also CAUKING.] 1. A tabular projection left on the face of a scarfed timber, to fit into a recess in the face of another which is to be joined to it, so as to prevent slipping. ? *Obs.* †2. A pin of hard wood, a dowel, used for the same purpose as in sense 1. –1874. 3. The bush of a block or sheave in which the pin revolves. Also called *cock*; see COCK *sb.*[1] 1862.

Coak (kouk), *v.* 1794. [Cf. prec., and COCK *v.*] To join by the aid of coaks. Also *intr.*

Coak, obs. f. COKE.

Coal (kōᵘl), *sb.* [OE. *col* neut. corresp. to OHG. *chol* n., *cholo* m., MDu. *cole* f., etc.; ON. *kol* neut.] 1. A piece of carbon glowing without a flame. (Now *arch.*) Also *fig.* †2. A piece of burnt wood, etc., that is still capable of combustion without flame -1611; cinder, ashes -1665. Also *fig.* †3. = CHARCOAL. Used in *pl.*, or as a *collect. sing.* -1799. Also *attrib.* 4. A mineral, solid, hard, opaque, black or blackish, found in seams in the earth, and largely used as fuel; it consists of carbonized vegetable matter. (According to the degree of carbonization it is *anthracite* or *glance* coal, *black* or *bituminous* coal, or *brown* coal or *lignite.*) In the ordinary sense, used without qualification, as *collect. sing.*, and (of coal in pieces for burning) in *pl.* ME. Used also with defining words, as *sea*, BROWN, CANNEL C., etc.

1. Þair hertes sal bryn with-in als a cole HAMPOLE. *Coals of fire*; *hot, live, quick coal(s.* 2. Phr. *Black as a c.* (now usu. assoc. with sense 4). Starres, Starres, And all eyes else, dead coales *Wint. T.* v. i. 68. *fig.* Affection is a coale that must be coold SHAKS.

Phrases. *To heap*, etc., *coals of fire on the head* (see Rom. xii. 20): to produce remorse by requiting evil with good. *To haul, call*, etc., *over the coals*: to reprimand, call to task; orig. in reference to the treatment of heretics. *To carry coals to Newcastle*: to do what is absurdly superfluous.

Comb.: **c.-bearing** *a.* (*Geol.*), carboniferous; **-bed** (*Geol.*), a stratum of c.; **-black**, as black as a c., dead black; **-box**; **-breaker**, *techn.* a building containing the machinery for breaking, sizing, and cleaning c.; **-factor**, an agent between coal-owners and customers; **-field**, a series of strata containing c.; the tract of country occupied by them; **-flap**, a flap (on the pavement) covering the entrance to a c.-cellar; **-goose**, the cormorant (*local*); **-heaver**, a labourer employed in carrying c.; **-master**, a c.-owner; **-oil**, an early name of petroleum; **-owner**, the owner of a colliery; **-plant**, a plant of the c.-measures; **-seam**, =*coal-bed*; **-yard**. Hence **Coa·lery**; now COLLIERY.

Coal (kōul), *v.* 1602. [f. the sb.] 1. To convert into charcoal; to char. †2. To write with charcoal. CAMDEN. 3. To supply (a steamship, etc.) with coal for fuel 1864. 4. *intr.* To take in a supply of coal 1858.

1. Buying the wood..fetching the same when it is coaled CAREW. Hence **Coa·ler**, one who or that which coals steam-vessels.

Coalesce (kōuˌăle·s), *v.* 1541. [ad. L. *coalescere*, f. *co-* + *alescere* to grow up.] †1. To cause to grow together, to unite -1790. 2. *intr.* To grow or come together, so as to form one body or association 1656.

2. Carpels which have coalesced to form the ovary VINES. When two Vowels .. c. in one Syllable 1668. The Conquerors and Conquered coalesced into one and the same people MILT. Never to c. with Pitt MACAULAY.

Coalescence (kōuˌăle·sĕns). 1541. [f. L. *coalescere*; see -ENCE.] 1. The process or action of the vb. COALESCE; coalesced condition or group. 2. *Biol.* The growing together of separate parts 1541. So †**Coale·scency**.

Coalescent (kōuˌăle·sĕnt), *a.* (*sb.*) 1655. [ad. L. *coalescentem.*] 1. That coalesces; coalescing; growing together or combining. 2. *sb.* One who or that which coalesces.

Coa·l-fish. 1603. [From the dusky pigment which tinges its skin.] A fish (*Merlangus* or *Pollachius carbonarius* or *Gadus virens*), allied to the Cod. (In U.S. called *pollock.*)

Coa·l-gas. 1809. The mixture of gases produced by the destructive distillation of coal, consisting mainly of carburetted hydrogen; when purified, it is the common lighting gas.

Coa·l-house. 1555. A covered-in place for storage of coal.

Bishop Bonner used his coal-house as a place of confinement during the Marian persecution (1553-8); hence many contemporary and historical allusions.

Coalier, obs. f. COLLIER.

Coalise, -ize (kōu·ăləiz), *v.* 1794. [a. F. *coaliser*, f. *coalition.*] To enter into, or form, a coalition. Hence **Co·aliser.**

†**Co·alite**, *v.* 1735. [f. L. *coalit-*, *coalescere.*] *intr.* and *trans.* To form into a coalition; to unite -1791.

Let the friends of liberty .. c. BOLINGBROKE. Time has .. blended and coalited the conquered with the conquerors BURKE. So **Co·alite** *a.* grown together.

Coalition (kōuˌăli·ʃən). 1612. [ad. L. *coalitionem*; see prec. Orig. = *coalescence.*] †1. Coalescence -1767. 2. Combination 1620. 3. *esp.* in *politics*: A temporary alliance of distinct parties for a limited purpose 1645. Also *attrib.*

1. The C. of several Corpuscles into one visible body BOYLE. 2. [A] c. of vowels WHEWELL, of interests JOHNSON. 3. I am sick of coalitions, royal, military or ministerial LD. AUCKLAND. Hence **Coali·tioner**, one who forms or joins a c.; so **Coali·tionist.**

Co-ally·. 1828. [See Co-.] A joint ally. So **Co-allie·d** *ppl. a.*

Coa·l-man. 1582. A man who has to do with coal; also, a coal-ship or collier (*nonce-use*).

Coa·l-measure. 1665. 1. A measure for measuring coal. 2. †A stratum of coal. In *pl.* (*Geol.*) The whole of the series of rocks formed by the seams of coal and the intervening strata of clay, sandstone, etc., in a coal-field, constituting the upper division of the carboniferous formation. Also *attrib.* [The different seams of a coal-field have long been named by their measure or thickness.]

Coa·l-meter. 1648. One who measures or weighs coal; formerly an official of the corporation of London.

Coalmouse, colemouse (kō·lmaus). [ME. *colmose* :—OE. *colmāse*, f. *col* coal + *māse*; see MOSE (corrupted later to *mouse*).] A bird, *Parus ater*; also called *Coal* (or *Cole*) *Titmouse.*

Coa·l-pit. OE. 1. A place where charcoal is made. Still in *U.S.* 2. A pit where coal is dug 1447.

Coa·l-sack. 1632. 1. A sack to carry coal in. 2. A name given to black patches in the Milky Way; *esp.* to one near the Southern Cross.

Coa·l-scuttle. 1825. A coal-scoop. Hence *Coal-scuttle bonnet*: a woman's bonnet resembling an inverted coal-scuttle, usually projecting much beyond the face.

†**Coal-stone.** 1728. 'A sort of cannel-coal' (J.).

Coal-tar. 1785. A thick, black, viscid liquid, a product of the destructive distillation of bituminous coal. It is a compound of many substances, chiefly hydrocarbons; and is the source of paraffin, naphtha, benzene, creosote, the aniline or *coal-tar colours*, etc.

Coa·l-tit, coal-ti·tmouse. 1777. = COALMOUSE, q. v.

Coa·l-whipper. 1836. One who raises coal out of a ship's hold by means of a pulley.

Coa·l-works. 1665. A place where coal is worked; a colliery. (Cf. *ironworks.*) So **Coa·l-working**, in same sense.

Coaly (kōu·li), *a.* 1565. [f. COAL *sb.* + -Y.] Abounding in coal; covered with coal or coal-dust; carbonaceous; coal-black.

Coaming (kōu·miŋ). 1611. [?] In *pl.*: The raised borders about the edge of the hatches and scuttles of a ship, which prevent water on deck from running below. (*Erron.* identified with *combings.*)

Co-appea·r, *v. rare.* 1635. [See Co-.] To appear together or in conjunction. So **Co-appearance**, †**Co-appari·tion.**

Coapt (koˌæ·pt), *v.* 1570. [ad. late L. *coaptare*; see Co-.] To fit together 1655; †to make fit -1586.

Coaptation (kōuˌæptēi·ʃən). 1561. [ad. L. *coaptationem*; see prec.] Adaptation or adjustment of things, parts, etc., to each other, *e. g.* of the ends of a fractured bone.

Co-aration (kōuˌărēi·ʃən). 1883. [See Co-.] Co-operative tillage. SEEBOHM.

‖**Coarb** (kōu·aɹb). 1656. [a. Ir. *comharba.*] *Celt. Ch.* Successor in an ecclesiastical office, abbot, vicar; an order of old Irish monks.

†**Coa·rct**, *v.* ME. [ad. L. *coar(c)tare*, f. Co- + *artare*, f. *artus* confined. See ART *v.*[1]] 1. *trans.* To press or draw together -1604. 2. To restrict the action of (a person) -1819. 3. To confine within narrow limits; also *fig.* -1628.

Coarctate (koˌā·ɹkteit), *a.* ME. [ad. L. *coarctatus*; see prec.] Pressed close together, contracted, confined; in *Entom.* applied to a pupa enclosed in a smooth horny case, which conceals its form.

†**Coa·rctate**, *v.* 1620. [See prec. and -ATE [3].] = COARCT -1669.

Coarctation (kōuˌaɹktēi·ʃən). 1545. [ad. L. *coar(c)tationem*; see prec.] 1. The action of compressing tightly; compressed state. 2. Confinement or restriction as to limits 1605.

1. A c. and straitness of the Urinary Duct 1684.

Coarse (kōəɹs), *a.* ME. [Spelt identically with the sb. COURSE down to the 18th c. Hence, perh. an adj. use of *course*, with the sense 'ordinary', as in *of course.*] †1. Ordinary, common; of inferior quality or value -1695. 2. Wanting in delicacy of texture, granulation, or structure; consisting of comparatively large parts or particles. Opp. to *fine.* 1582. 3. Rough, harsh, or rude 1607. 4. Wanting in refinement or delicacy, rough; rude, vulgar 1680; indecent 1711.

1. Too [two] cors bordcloþes ME. Now I feele Of what course Mettle ye are molded *Hen. VIII*, III. ii. 239. 2. Course black canvas 1796. C. shingle TYNDALL, lips KINGSLEY, complexions 1883. 3. C. fare 1607, travelling DE FOE, weather BADHAM, quality of tone STAINER. 4. Appetites too c. to taste OTWAY. A c. age MILMAN, joke DORAN. *Comb.* **c.-fibred**, **-grained** *a.*, having c. fibres, or texture; also *fig.* having a c. nature. Hence **Coa·rsely** *adv.* **Coa·rsen** *v.* to make or become c. **Coa·rseness**, c. quality. **Coa·rsish** *a.* somewhat c.

Coarti·culate, *v.* 1578. [See Co-.] *Anat.* To unite to form a joint.

Coarticula·tion. ? *Obs.* 1615. [ad. mod.L. *coarticulatio*, tr. Gr. συνάρθρωσις.] Jointing together of two bones.

Co-asse·ssor. 1644. [See Co-.] A joint assessor.

Co-assi·st, Co-assu·me; see Co-.

Coast (kōust), *sb.* [ME. *coste*, a. OF. :—L. *costa* rib, flank, or side. The spelling *coast* is rare bef. 1600.] †1. The side of any body -1818; *transf.* the side (of anything) -1704. 2. The side of the land next the sea, the seashore ME. †3. The border of a country; borderland. (Chiefly *pl.*) -1618. †4. A tract or region -1667. †5. SIDE, quarter, part -1513. 6. [repr. F. *côte* hill-side.] A slope down which one slides on a sled; the act of so sliding down. (*U.S.* etc.) 1775. 7. Hence, A run down-hill on a bicycle, etc. without pedalling 1886.

1. Take a c. of lamb, and parboil 1676. 2. Capernaum, which is vpon the Sea c. *Matt.* iv. 13. *The coast*: a term applied to specific littoral districts, as the Coromandel c. *The c. is clear*: *i.e.* of enemies who would dispute an attempt to land or embark; hence, 'the danger is over, the enemies have marched off' (J.). See CLEAR *a.* V. 4. 3. Judah tooke Gaza with the c. therof *Judg.* i. 18. 4. The costes of the firmament CHAUCER.

Comb.: **c.-cocket**, a certificate for the carriage of goods by water along the c.; **-guard**, a body of men employed originally to prevent smuggling, but now, under the Admiralty, a general c.-police; hence **-guard-man** (also *coastguardsman*); **-line** [LINE *sb.*[2] II. 7], the contour of a coast 1860; **-rat**, the Sand-mole of S. Africa, a species of *Bathyergus*; **-waiter**, a custom-house officer who superintends the landing and shipping of goods coastwise; **-ward(s** *a.* and *adv.*; **-ways**, **-wise** *adv.* by way of, or along, the c.; **-wise** *a.* carried along the c.

Hence **Coa·stal** *a.* pertaining to the c. 1883.

Coast (kōust), *v.* [ME. *costey-en*, *-ay-en*, occ. *costi-en*, a. OF. *costeier*, rarer *costier* (mod. *côtoyer*) :—Rom. type *costicare*, f. *costa*; see prec. Assim., in form, to COAST *sb.*] †1. *trans.* To keep by the side of; *esp.* to march on the flank of -1670; *intr.* -1548. †2. *trans.* To go or move by the side of; to skirt -1742; *intr.* with *by*, *along*, etc. -1837. 3. To proceed by the coast of (*arch.*) ME. 4. *intr.* To sail *by* or *along* the coast; to sail from port to port of the same country 1555. †5. To explore, scour -1633; *intr.* with *about*, *through*, etc. -1643. †6. To border upon, adjoin, bound -1630; *intr.* with *on*, *upon*, etc. -1652. Also *fig.* †7. To accost (see ACCOST *v.*) -1713. †8. *trans.* To place with reference to the points of the compass -1715. 9. in *U.S.* To slide down a slope in a sled. Hence, to run down-hill on a bicycle, etc. without pedalling 1859.

2. [He] coasted aloofe lyke a Hawke that lykethe not her praye GRAFTON. 3. To c. the lake WORDSW. To c. it along the lake COOK. 4. C. along the shore in sight of land DRYDEN. 5. To c. the seas HALL, the country MASSINGER. 7. 3 *Hen. VI*, I. i. 268.

Coa·sted, *ppl. a.* ME. [f. COAST + -ED.] Situated beside, or on the coast of -1611.

Coaster (kōu·stəɹ). 1574. [f. COAST *v.* + -ER.] 1. One who or that which sails along the coast; a coasting-vessel, its master, or its pilot. 2. One who dwells by the sea-coast 1612. 3. A low round stand for a decanter 1887. 4. *U.S.* One engaged in the sport of coasting; also, a sledge for coasting 1881.

Coasting (kōu·stiŋ), *vbl. sb.* 1606. [f. COAST *v.* and *sb.*] 1. Sailing along a coast or trading between the ports of a country 1679. **2.** The configuration of the coast; delineation of a coast-line 1621. **3.** *U.S.* The sport of sliding on a sled down hill, or shooting down hill on a bicycle, etc. 1855. Also *attrib.* and in *comb.*, as *c.-trade, -vessel*, etc.

Coat (kōut), *sb.* [ME. *cote*, a. OF. (mod. *cotte* petticoat), repr. med.L. *cotta*, of doubtful origin.] **1.** An outer garment, *esp.* one worn by men; usually of cloth, with sleeves. **2.** A petticoat. Usu. in pl. = *petticoats.* Now *dial.* ME. **3.** Used as tr. L. *tunica*, Gr. χιτών, Heb. *k'thōneth, kuttōneth* ME. **4.** *Her.* = COAT OF ARMS ME. †**5.** Garb as indicating profession (*e.g.* clerical); hence, profession, class, sort, party. Common in 17th c. (Cf. CLOTH.) –1774. **6.** *transf.* A natural covering or integument, as of an animal, an organ of an animal body, a plant, etc. (see quots.) ME. **7.** *Naut.* A piece of tarred canvas nailed round the mast, bowsprit, or pumps, where they enter the deck, to keep the water out 1626. **8.** A layer of any substance covering a surface; a coating 1663. **9.** *fig.* Anything that covers, invests, or conceals 1611. †**10.** = COAT-CARD –1630. †**11.** = COAT-MONEY –1712. Also *attrib.*

1. *C. of mail*: a linen or leathern jacket quilted with rings or plates of steel (see MAIL). Ther was kut mony a kote ME. Ladies' Long Cloth Coats 1889. **2.** A child in coats LOCKE (J.). **3.** A c. of many colours *Gen.* xxxvii. 3. **4.** They may giue the dozen white Luces in their Coate *Merry W.* I. i. 17. *fig.* She was sought by spirits of ritchest cote SHAKS. **5.** I know no man of his c. who would fall in so well with you BURKE. **6.** A Hawk of the first c. 1681. A mule's c. FORD. The *arachnoid c.* of the brain. The *choroid c.* of the eye. The Coats of the Bean 1671, of an Onion CHEYNE. **8.** A c. of rich mould SWIFT. **9.** A c. of darkness 1771.

Phrases. *To cut the c. according to the cloth*: see CLOTH *sb.* †*To turn one's c.*: to desert one's party (cf. TURNCOAT). *To wear the king's c.*: to serve as a soldier. *Comb.* **c.-link**, a pair of buttons joined by a short link, or a button with a loop, for holding together the lappets of a c.

Coat (kōut), *v.* ME. [f. prec. sb.] **1.** To provide with a coat; to clothe. **2.** To cover with a coating or coatings of any substance; also predicated of the substance 1753.

2. To c. electrical jars with leaf tin FRANKLIN. Layers of ice..coating a white centra. mass HUXLEY.

Coat-armour (kōut,ā·ɹməɹ). ME. [See COAT and ARMOUR.] †**1.** = COAT OF ARMS 1. –1639. †**2.** = COAT OF ARMS 2. –1625. **3.** (without *pl.*) Blazonry, arms 1486. Hence †**Coat-armoured** *a.*

†**Coat-card.** 1563. A playing card bearing a coated figure (king, queen, or knave); now corrupted into COURT-CARD –1690.

Coated (kōu·tėd), *ppl. a.* 1563. [f. COAT *sb.* and *v.*] **1.** Furnished with or having a coat or coats. Often in *comb.* **2.** Covered with a coating of some substance 1766.

Coatee (kōutī·). 1775. [f. COAT *sb.*] A close-fitting coat with short tails.

Coati (ko,ā·ti). 1676. [a. Tupi, f. *cua* cincture + *tim* nose.] An American plantigrade carnivorous mammal of the genus *Nasua* (family *Ursidæ*), resembling the Racoon, with a remarkably elongated flexible snout. Also called **Coati-mondi.** [f. Braz. *mondi* solitary.]

Coating (kōu·tiŋ), *vbl. sb.* 1770. [f. COAT *v.* and *sb.*] **1.** = COAT *sb.* 8. **2.** Clothing of the nature of a coat 1798. **3.** [f. the sb.] Material for coats. (Cf. *shirting*, etc.) 1802.

1. A thin..c. of vegetation STANLEY.

Coatless (kōu·tlės), *a.* 1586. [f. COAT *sb.*] **1.** Without a coat of arms. **2.** Without a coat (garment) 1850.

Coa·t-money. 1557. *Hist.* Money to provide a coat for each man furnished for military service.

The new Taxe of Coate and Conduct Mony, with undue meanes used to inforce the payment of it 1640.

Coat of arms. 1489. [tr. Fr. *cotte d'armes.*] *Her.* **1.** *Hist.* A coat or vest embroidered with heraldic arms; a tabard. **2.** The distinctive bearings of a gentleman (*armiger*) originally borne on a 'coat of arms'; a shield, escutcheon 1562. Also *fig.* †**3.** = *Coat of mail* –1844.

Co-atte·st, *v.* 1650. [See Co-.] *trans.* To attest together or in conjunction (*with*). So **Co-attesta·tion, Co-attesta·tor.**

Coax (kōuks), *v.* 1589. [f. COKES *sb.* Orig. 'to make a *cokes* of'; cf. *to fool*, etc.] †**1.** *trans.* To befool –1806. †**2.** To make a pet of; to fondle –1831. **3.** To persuade by caresses, flattery, etc.; to wheedle 1663. **4.** *intr.* To employ coaxing 1706.

3. It was Seneca's principle..to c., rather than drive, his pupil into virtue MERIVALE. Hence **Coax** (*colloq.*), **Coa·xer**, one who coaxes. **Coa·xingly** *adv.*

Coaxal (ko,æ·ksăl), *a.* 1879. *Math.* = COAXIAL.

†**Coaxation** (kōu,æksē·ʃən). 1642. [f. L. *coaxare* (f. Gr. κοάξ) + -ATION.] The croaking of frogs –1696.

Coaxial (ko,æ·ksiăl), *a.* 1881. [f. Co- + AXIS + -AL.] *Math.* Having a common axis. Hence **Coa·xially** *adv.*

Cob (kǫb), *sb.*[1] ME. [?] **I.** With the notion 'big' or 'stout'. **1.** A great man, big man, leading man; †a wealthy man, a miser –1681. **2.** A male swan; also *cob-swan* 1570. †**3.** A fish, the Miller's Thumb –1804. **4.** A short-legged, stout variety of horse 1818.

1. The rich cobs of this worlde UDALL.

II. With the notion 'rounded', 'rounded mass' or 'lump'. **1.** Applied to: COB-NUTS 1589; the stone of a fruit 1825; a testicle (*dial.*) 1818. **2.** A small stack of hay (*dial.*) 1616; a chignon (*colloq.*) 1865; a small heap or lump *of* (anything), as coal, bread, etc. (*dial.*) 1606.

III. With the notion 'head', 'top'. †**1.** The head of a (red) herring. (The sense 'young herring' is prob. a mistake for this.) –1632. **2.** The seeding head of wheat, clover, etc. (*dial.*) 1847. **3.** The rachis on which the grains of maize grow 1702.

1. Lord high regent of rashers of the coles and red herring cobs NASHE.

Comb. **c.-coal,** also *cobbles*, large pit-coals; **-loaf,** a small loaf made with a round head.

Cob (kǫb), *sb.*[2] 1602. [?] Clay (marl or chalk) mixed with gravel and straw, used for building walls, etc.

The poor Cottager contenteth himself with C. for his Wals CAREW.

Cob, cobb (kǫb), *sb.*[3] 1580. [= EFris. *kobbe*, NewFris. *kub*, Du. *kobbe, kob*, etc. Etym. unkn.] A species of Gull, *esp.* the Greater Black-backed Gull (*Larus marinus*); also called *Sea-cob*(*b.*

†**Cob,** *sb.*[4] *rare.* 1657. [prob. from COBWEB, ME. *coppe-web.*] A spider.

Cob (kǫb), *sb.*[5] 1672. [See COB *sb.*[1] I.] A name formerly given in Ireland to the Spanish dollar or 'piece of eight'. *Comb.* **c.-money** (*U.S.*): old silver coins found at Fort Edward.

Cob, cobb (kǫb), *sb.*[6] *dial.* 1691. A wicker basket to carry on the arm.

Cob, cobb (kǫb), *sb.*[7] *local.* 1605. A mole or pier (? as constructed of cobble-stones).

Cob, cobb, *sb.*[8] 1828. [f. COB *v.*[1]] A blow.

Cob (kǫb), *v.*[1] ME. [perh. echoic.] †**1.** *intr.* To give blows. ME. only. **2.** To crush (ore) 1778. **3.** To strike; esp. *Naut.* To strike on the buttocks with a flat instrument 1769. **4.** To thresh or beat out (seed). Also *intr.* of the seed. 1796. **5.** To throw (*dial.*) 1867.

Cob, *v.*[2] *dial.* Also **cop.** 1847. [f. COB *sb.*[1]] *trans.* To top, excel, beat.

Cobalt (kōu·bǫlt). 1728. [a. Ger. *kobalt*, app. the same word as *kobold*, etc., goblin of the mines; the ore having been so called by the miners as (then reputed) worthless, and mischievous.] **1.** A metal of a greyish colour inclining to red, brittle, slightly magnetic; in many respects resembling nickel; not found native, but extracted from various ores. Symbol Co. **2.** The blue pigment, also called **c.-blue,** prepared from this mineral. Also the colour of this. 1835. In this sense also as *adj.*

Comb.: in names of colours or pigments prepared from salts of c., as *cobalt-blue* (see sense 2), *green, ultramarine, yellow*; also **c.-bloom,** = ERYTHRITE; †**-crust,** the earthy variety of *cobalt-bloom*; **-glance** [Ger. *Kobalt-glanz*], = COBALTITE; **-vitriol,** = a native sulphate of c., also called *Bieberite.*

Hence **Coba·ltic** *a.* of, pertaining to, or of the nature of, c.; applied to the tri-compounds of the metal, as *Cobaltic oxide*, Co_2O_3. **Cobalti·ferous** *a.* containing or yielding c. **Coba·ltous** *a.* of the nature of c.; applied to the di-compounds of the metal, as *Cobaltous oxide*, CoO.

Coba·lti-. *Chem.* Comb. f. COBALT used in the names of tri-compounds, as in *c.-cyanide* of copper, etc.

Cobaltite (kōu·bǫltəit). 1868. [f. COBALT + -ITE.] *Min.* Native sulpharsenide of cobalt, of silver-white colour, with metallic lustre, also called *cobalt-glance*, and †*cobaltine.*

Coba·lto-. *Chem.* Comb. f. COBALT used in the names of di-compounds, as *c.-cyanide* of potassium, etc.

†**Co·bbing,** *a.* 1599. [f. COB *sb.*[1] I.] Playing the cob –1608.

Of them all c. countrey chuffes which make their bellies and their bagges theyr gods are called riche cobbes NASHE.

Cobble (kǫ·b'l), *sb.*[1] 1475. [app. related to COB *sb.*[1]] **1.** A water-worn rounded stone, *esp.* of the size suitable for paving. Also *transf.* **2.** *pl.* Coal of the size of small cobble stones 1815.

1. Their slings held cobles round FAIRFAX.

Cobble, *sb.*[2] 1859. [f. COBBLE *v.*[1]] A clumsy mending.

Cobble, *sb.*[3], var. of COBLE.

Cobble (kǫ·b'l), *v.*[1] 1496. [Goes with *cobbler* sb.; etym. unkn.] **1.** *trans.* To mend (*esp.* shoes); to mend roughly or clumsily; to patch. Also with *up.* Also *absol.* **2.** To put together roughly or clumsily. Also *intr.* or *absol.* 1589.

1. Men..c. up old houses PETTY. **2.** To coble verse as well as shoes LLOYD.

Co·bble, *v.*[2] 1691. [f. COBBLE *sb.*[1]] To pave with cobbles.

Cobbler (kǫ·bləɹ). ME. [See COBBLE *v.*[1]] **1.** One who mends shoes. **2.** A botcher 1594. **3.** *colloq.* 'A drink made of wine, sugar, lemon, and pounded ice, and imbibed through a straw'.

2. *Jul. C.* I. i. 11. *Comb.*: **c.-fish,** a W. Indian fish, *Blepharis crinitus*, having long rays likened to a cobbler's strings; **cobbler's punch,** a warm drink of ale with spirit, sugar, and spice added.

Cobble-stone. 1475. = COBBLE *sb.*[1] 1.

Cobby (kǫ·bi), *a.* 1691. [f. COB *sb.*[1]] **1.** Stout, hearty (*dial.*). **2.** Headstrong 1785. **3.** Of the nature of or like a cob (horse) 1871.

Cobdenism (kǫ·bdəniz'm). 1887. [f. name Richard *Cobden* (1804–1865).] A policy advocating free trade, peace, and international co-operation. So **Co·bdenite.**

Cob-iron. Now *dial.* 1485. [app. f. COB *sb.*[1] II. 2 + IRON, referring to knobs at the ends.] *pl.* The irons which supported the spit. Also explained as = ANDIRON.

Co-bi·shop. *rare.* 1726. A coadjutor bishop.

Coble (kōu·b'l). OE. [In ONorthumbrian *cuopl.* ? Celt., containing the root *ceu-, cau-* hollow; cf. Welsh *ceubal, ceubol* ferry-boat, skiff, etc.] **1.** *Sc.* A short flat-bottomed rowing-boat for crossing rivers, etc. **2.** A sea fishing-boat with a flat bottom, square stern, lug-sail, and rudder extending 4 or 5 feet below the bottom; used chiefly on the NE. coast of England 1493. Also *attrib.*

Cob-nut (kǫ·b,nʊt). ME. [orig. *cobill nut*; cf. COBBLE *sb.*[1], COB *sb.*[1]] **1.** A large short ovate nut, borne by a cultivated variety of the hazel; also the tree. Also *transf.* **2.** A game played by children with nuts ME.

Cobra (kōu·bră, kǫ·bră). 1817. Short for next. Also *attrib.*

‖**Cobra de capello** (kōu·bră *di* kăpe·lo). 1668. [Pg.; = 'snake with hood'. Pg. *cobra* :—L. *colubra*; *capello*, F. *chapeau.*] The Hooded or Spectacle snake (*Naja tripudians*), a venomous serpent found in India, having the power of dilating the head and neck when irritated, so as to produce the resemblance of a hood.

Co-bro·ther. 1589. Brother in the same craft; = F. *confrère.*

Cob-swan; see COB *sb.*[1] I. 2.

Coburg (kōu·bɒɹg). 1882. [f. *Coburg* in Germany.] A thin fabric of worsted and cotton or worsted and silk for women's dresses.

Cobweb (kǫ·b,web). [ME. *coppeweb*, f. *coppe* spider (see COP[3]) + WEB. Cf. COB *sb.*[4]] **1.** The fine network spun by a spider to catch its prey; also, the substance. **b.** A single thread spun by a spider 1837. †**2.** Threads similar to the spider's –1626. **3.** *fig.* See quots. **4.** Short for *Cobweb bird*, the Spotted Flycatcher, which uses spiders' webs in constructing its nest 1712. Also *attrib.*

1. b. The immoveable c., or zero of the scale [of the

c. micrometer] 1837. 3. The sophist's rope of c. BEATTIE. The dust and cobwebbes of that vnciuil age SIDNEY. The cobwebs of petty inquisitiveness JOHNSON. C. Laws MILT.

Comb.: †c. lawn, a very fine transparent lawn; **c. micrometer**, one with c. threads instead of wires; **c. bird**; see sense 4.

Hence **Co·bwebbed** *ppl. a.* covered or hung with, or (*Bot.*) as with, cobwebs. **Co·bwe·bbery**, the spinning of cobwebs; a texture of cobwebs. **Co·bwebby** *a.* cobwebbed; resembling cobwebs.

Coca (kōu·kă). 1616. [a. Sp., a. Peruv. *cuca.*] The name in Bolivia of *Erythroxylon Coca*; hence, applied to its dried leaves, which are chewed, with powdered lime, to appease hunger, and stimulate the nervous system. Also *attrib.*

Cocaigne; see COCKAIGNE.

Cocaine (kokēⁱ·n; prop. kōu·ke,əin). 1874. [f. COCA + -INE.] An alkaloid obtained from the leaves, etc., of the coca plant, valuable as a local anæsthetic.

Cocao, obs. f. CACAO.

Cocarde; see COCKADE.

Coccagee (kǫ·kăgī). 1727. [ad. mod.Ir. *cac a' gheidh* goose-dung, from its colour.] A cider apple formerly in repute; also, the cider made from it.

Cocceian (kǫksī·iăn), *a.* 1685. [f. the pr. name.] Of, or pertaining to the opinion of, John Cocceius of Leyden, who taught that the Old Testament history was a foreshadowing of the history of Christ and his church.

‖**Coccidium** (kǫksi·diŏm). 1867. [mod.L., as if f. dim. of Gr. κοκκίς, -ιδ-, dim. of κόκκος grain, berry.] *Bot.* A spherical or hemispherical conceptacle found in the rhodospermous algæ.

†**Cocci·ferous**, *a.* 1727. [f. L. *coccum.*] Berry-bearing –1755. So †**Cocci·gerous** *a.*

Coccin (kǫ·ksin). 1836. [f. mod.L. *coccus* COCCUS + -IN.] *Chem.* A nitrogenous principle obtained from the cochineal and other insects.

†**Cocci·neous**, *a.* 1654. [f. L. *coccineus* + -OUS.] Scarlet –1693.

‖**Cocco.** Also **cocoa, coco,** pl. **cocoes.** 1756. The tuber of an Araceous plant, *Colocasia esculenta* or taro-plant, cultivated as an article of food in the W. Indies.

Coccolite (kǫ·kŏləit). 1801. [f. Gr. κόκκος + -LITE.] *Min.* A granular variety of pyroxene of green or greenish colour.

Coccolith (kǫ·kŏlip). 1868. [f. Gr. κόκκος + λίθος.] *Biol.* Huxley's name for minute round or oval disk-like organic bodies found in deep-sea dredging, etc. Now believed to be of algal nature.

Coccosphere (kǫ·ko,sfiəɹ). 1868. [f. as prec. + Gr. σφαῖρα.] *Biol.* A spheroidal aggregation of coccoliths.

Cocco·steid. 1862. *Palæont.* A member of the family *Coccosteidæ* of ganoid fishes, which includes the fossil genus *Coccosteus* [f. Gr. κόκκος + ὀστέον], so called from the berry-like tubercles with which the plates were studded.

Coccule (kǫ·kiul). 1835. [ad. mod.L. *cocculum.*] *Bot.* A small berry or coccus. Hence **Cocculi·ferous** *a.* c.-bearing.

‖**Co·cculus i·ndicus.** 1591. [mod.L.] The dried berry of *Anamirta* (formerly *Menispermium*) *Cocculus*, a climbing plant found in Malabar and Ceylon. It is a violent poison.

‖**Coccus** (kǫ·kŏs). 1763. [mod.L., a. Gr. κόκκος; see ALKERMES.] 1. The genus of Homopterous insects which includes the Cochineal (*C. cacti*), the Kermes (*C. ilicis*), the Lac insect (*C. Lucca*), and others. 2. One of the carpels of a dry fruit, which burst from the common axis 1800.

Coccy- (kǫ·ksi). Short for *coccygo-*, comb. f. COCCYX.

Coccygeal (kǫksi·dʒiăl), *a.* 1836. [f. med. L. *coccygeus* + -AL.] Pertaining to the coccyx. So **Coccy·gean** *a.*

Coccygo- [Gr. κόκκυγο-], bef. a vowel coccyg-, comb. f. COCCYX.

Coccyx (kǫ·ksiks). 1615. [L., a. Gr. κόκκυξ, -υγ- cuckoo, also the *os coccygis*, so called in man as resembling the bill of the cuckoo.] *Anat.* The small triangular bone appended to the sacrum, and terminating the spinal column in man, formed by the coalescence of four rudimental vertebræ; also, an analogous part in other animals.

Cochin-china (kǫ·tʃin tʃəi·nă). 1853. Name of a country in the Eastern Peninsula; hence, short for *Cochin-China fowl*, a breed of poultry from Cochin-China.

Cochineal (kǫ·tʃinīl). 1586. [a. F. *cochenille*, ad. Sp. *cochinilla* or It. *cocciniglia*, f. (ult.) L. *coccum* scarlet, grain, orig. 'berry'.] 1. A dye-stuff consisting of the dried bodies of the insect *Coccus cacti*, found on several species of cactus in Mexico and elsewhere. It is used for making carmine, and as a scarlet dye. 2. The colour of this dye, scarlet 1632. 3. The cochineal-insect (*Coccus cacti*) 1697. 4. *C. Fig*: the cactus-plant, *Opuntia* (*Nopalea*) *cochinillifera*, on which the cochineal-insect feeds 1697.

‖**Cochlea** (kǫ·kli,ă). 1538. [a. L. *coclea, cochlea*, ad. Gr. κοχλίας snail, screw, etc.] †1. A spiral staircase; a screw; the water-screw of Archimedes –1679. 2. *Phys.* The spiral cavity of the internal ear 1688. 3. *Conch.* A snail-shell 1846. Hence **Co·chlean, Co·chlear** *adjs.* pertaining to a c.

‖**Cochleare** (kǫkli,ēᵊ·rī). 1708. [L. *coc(h)lear* or *coc(h)leare* a spoon.] *Med.* A spoon or spoonful (in prescriptions).

Cochleariform (kǫkli,ēᵊ·rifǫɹm), *a.* 1836. [See prec.] Spoon-shaped.

†**Co·chleary**, *a.* 1646. [See above.] Resembling a snail-shell, spiral, winding –1664. So **Co·chleate(d** *a.* in same senses.

Co·chlite. 1698. [f. mod.L. *cochlites*, f. Gr. κόχλος + -ITE.] *Palæont.* A fossil spiral shell.

Co·cin, co·cinin (Watts). 1865. [f. COCO + -IN.] *Chem.* A fat (glyceride of Cocinic acid, a fatty acid obtained from coco-nut oil).

Cock (kǫk), *sb.*[1] [OE. *cocc, coc, kok*; cf. F. *coq*. Prob. echoic.]

I. 1. The male of the common domestic fowl, *Gallus domesticus* OE.; also of various other birds ME. b. Short for WOODCOCK 1530. 2. = Crow of cock; also as an imitation of the cluck of the bird CHAUCER. 3. A weather-cock 1605.

1. *Fighting c.*: one bred and trained for cock-fighting. 2. We were carowsing till the Second C. *Macb.* II. iii. 27. 3. You Cataracts, and Hyrricano's spout, Till you haue drench'd our Steeples, drown the Cockes *Lear* III. ii. 3.

II. 1. One who arouses slumberers: applied to ministers of religion 1614. 2. Leader, head, chief man; formerly, also, victor 1542. 3. *colloq.* One who fights with pluck. Hence, a vulgar term of appreciation. 1639.

2. At cuffs I was always the c. of the school SWIFT. *C. of the walk*: see WALK. 3. The Doctor being a shy c. SMOLLETT.

IV. Techn. 1. A spout with an appliance for controlling the flow of liquids through it; a tap 1481. 2. In fire-arms, a lever, or spring hammer, part of the mechanism for discharging the piece. (So called from its original shape.) 1566. 3. The pointer of a balance 1611; the gnomon of a sundial 1613. 4. A bracket attached to the plate of a watch or clock to support the outer end of the pivot of a wheel or pendulum 1678. 5. = COAK 3. 1627. 6. The mark at which curlers aim 1787. 7. = PENIS (*vulgar*) 1730.

2. *At c., at (on) full c.*: with the c. drawn full back. *At (on) half-c.*: with the c. lifted to the first catch, at which position the trigger does not act.

Cock (kǫk), *sb.*[2] ME. [= dial. Ger. *kocke*, Norw. *kok* heap, *esp.* of dung, also lump; cf. ON. *kökkr*, etc.] A conical heap of produce or material; *esp.* of hay (rarely corn) in the field.

†**Cock**, *sb.*[3] ME. [var. of COG *sb.*[1], but only in sense of the Fr. dim. *coquet.*] Now always COCK-BOAT –1631.

Cock (kǫk), *sb.*[4] 1711. [f. COCK *v.*[1]] 1. An upward or significant turn 1717. 2. An upward turn of the brim of a hat; the turned-up part 1711.

1. With a knowing c. of his eye to his next neighbour SCOTT. 2. The wind being high, he let down the cocks of his hat BOSWELL.

Cock, *sb.*[5] [f. COCK *v.*[2]] A cocked position of the hammer of a pistol or gun.

†**Cock**, *sb.*[6] ME. Perversion of the word GOD, used in oaths and exclams., as *by cock and pie, cock's body*, etc.

[**Cock**, *sb.*[7] 'The notch of an arrow' (J.). Prob. an etymological figment. See N.E.D.]

Cock (kǫk), *v.*[1] ME. [From the name of the fowl. But, with sense 1, cf. Ir. *cog-aim* 'I war', stem in OIr. *coc-*.] †1. *intr.* To fight –1600. †2. To strut, brag, crow *over* –1713. 3. To stick stiffly *up* or *out* 1600; *intr.* to stick conspicuously up 1629. 4. To turn up the brim of (a hat) 1663. *intr.* 1672. 5. *intr.* To train or use fighting cocks 1546. 6. To shoot woodcocks 1696.

3. *To c. the ears*: to prick up the ears in attention, said humorously of persons. *To c. the nose*: to turn it up in contempt. *To c. the eye*: to turn the eye with a knowing look; to wink. *To c. the hat*: to stick it jauntily on one side of the head. 4. Mrs. Stewart.., with her hat cocked and a red plume PEPYS.

Cock, *v.*[2] 1598. [f. COCK *sb.*[1]] †1. To place (a match) in the cock of an old matchlock gun. –1648. 2. To draw the cock back 1649.

2. Cock'd—fired—and miss'd his man BYRON.

Cock, *v.*[3] Also **cauk, caulk, calk**, and recently cog. 1663. [Cf. COAK.] 1. To secure crossing beams by means of a dove-tail, a mortice and tenon, or the like. 2. See COAK *v.*

Cock, *v.*[4] ME. [f. COCK *sb.*[2]] To put up in cocks.

†**Cock**, *v.*[5] ? Short f. COCKER *v.* TUSSER.

Cock, *v.*[6] *dial.* To rough-shoe; = CALK *v.*[2]

Cockabondy (kǫkəbǫ·ndi). 1852. [W. *coch a bon ddhu* 'red with black stem'.] An angler's artificial fly.

Cockade (kǫkēⁱ·d). Also †**cockard.** 1709. [a. F. *cocarde*, in 16th c. *coquarde*, deriv. of *coq*; so called from the cock's comb (Littré). But first found in Rabelais, in the phrase *bonnet à la coquarde*, any cap 'worne proudly, or peartly on th' one side' (Cotgr.).] A ribbon, knot of ribbons, rosette, etc., worn in the hat as a badge of office or party, or as part of a livery dress.

He's ta'en the field wi' his white c. *Jacobite Song.* Hence **Cocka·ded** *ppl. a.* wearing a c.

Cockadoodledoo·. 1573. The crow of a cock.

Cock-a-hoop. ME. [Of obscure origin.] †1 Phr. *To set (the) cock on (the) hoop*: app. to turn on the tap and drink without stint –1658. 2. as *pred. adj.* In a state of elation; crowing with exultation 1663. Also *attrib.* Exultant 1837.

Cockaigne, Cockayne (kǫkēⁱ·n). [ME. *cokaygne*, a. OF. *coquaigne, cokaigne*, mod.F. *cocagne*, 'lubberland'.] 1. An imaginary country, the abode of luxury and idleness. 2. *joc.* London, as the country of Cockneys 1824.

Cockal (kǫ·kăl, kǫ·k,ǫl). ? *Obs.* 1562. [orig. *cock all*; ?] 1. The knuckle-bone or astragalus. 2. A game played with knuckle-bones; 'dibs'. Also, as tr. L. *ludus talaris*. 1586.

1. A little transverce bone; Which boyes and bruckel'd children call (Playing for points and pins) cockall HERRICK.

Cock-a-leekie, var. of COCKY-LEEKY.

Cockalo·rum. *colloq.* 1715. [An arbitrary deriv. of COCK.] 1. Applied to a person: = Little cock, bantam: self-important little man. 2. Crowing 1884.

Hey (hay, high) c.: an exclam.; also a boys' game in which some make a chain of backs and others jump astride them.

Cock-and-bull. 1621. [Cf. F. *coq-à-l'âne.*] 1. *lit.* 1660. 2. *A story of a cock and a bull*: a long, rambling, idle story 1621. 3. *A cock and bull story*: an idle, concocted, incredible story; a canard 1796.

†**Cock-and-pie.** 1550. [f. COCK *sb.*[6] and PIE, the ordinal of the R.C.Ch.] Used in an asseveration –1854.

Cockatiel, -eel (kǫkătī·l). 1880. [ad. Du. *kaketielje*, Du. or ad. Pg. dim.] The Cockatoo Parrakeet, or Crested Grass Parrakeet of S. Australia (*Calopsitta* or *Nymphicus Novæ-Hollandiæ*).

Cockatoo (kǫkătū·). 1634. [ad. Malay *kakatúa*, through Du. *kaketoe*; app. infl. by *cock.*] The name of numerous birds of the parrot kind, *esp.* the genus *Cacatua*, inhabiting Australia and the E. Indian Islands, distinguished by a crest on the head, which can be raised or depressed at pleasure. 2. *Australia.* (*colloq.*) A small farmer 1864.

Cockatrice (kǫ·kătrəis, -tris). [ME. *cocatris, -ice*, a. OF. *cocatris*, corresp. to Pr. *calcatriz*, repr. L. **calcatrix* 'tracker', app. tr. Gr. ἰχνεύμων ichneumon. For the sense-history see N.E.D.] 1. A serpent, identified with the BASILISK, fabled to kill by its glance, and to be hatched from a cock's egg. (Used in Bible versions as tr. L. *basiliscus, regulus.*) †*Occas.* confounded with the CROCODILE -1583. In *Her.* figured with head, wings, and feet of a cock, terminating in a serpent with a barbed tail 1563. 2. *fig.* applied to persons 1500. †3. A whore -1747.

1. He shal put his hande in to the Cockatryce denne COVERDALE *Isa.* xi. 8. The death-darting eye of C. *Rom. & Jul.* III. ii. 47. 2. This little C. of a King that was able to destroy those that did not espie him first BACON.

Co·ck-bill, *sb.* 1648. *Naut.* In *a-cock-bill.* See A-COCK-BILL Hence **Co·ck-bill** *v.* to place a-cock-bill.

Cock-boat (kǫ·kbōut). ME. [f. COCK *sb.*[3] + BOAT.] A small ship's boat, *esp.* one towed behind a vessel going up or down river.

But a c. compared with the Warrior 1861.

†Cock-brain. 1567. One having the brain of a cock; a light-headed, foolish person. Cf. *bird-witted.* -1675. Hence **Co·ck-brained** *a.* foolish and light-headed, silly.

Cockchafer (kǫ·kˌtʃēⁱ:fəɹ). 1712. [f. *Cock* + CHAFER beetle.] A coleopterous insect or beetle (*Melolontha vulgaris*); it comes forth from the chrysalis late in May (hence called Maybug), and flies with a whirring sound.

Co·ck-crow. ME. = COCK-CROWING.

Co·ck-crowing. ME. The crowing of a cock; the time when cocks crow, early dawn.

Cocked (kǫkt), *ppl. a.* 1647. [f. COCK *v.*[1]] Set erect; having a pronounced upward turn.

Cocked hat. 1. A (three-cornered) hat with the brim permanently turned up. Now, a triangular hat (without cocks) pointed before and behind and rising to a point at the crown. 1673. 2. A game like nine-pins, played with three pins, set up in a triangular position. *U. S.* Phr. *To knock into a cocked hat* to damage beyond recognition.

Co·cker, *sb.*[1] Now *dial.* [A common WGer. sb.: OE. *cocer* QUIVER.] †1. A case for arrows -ME. 2. A casing for the leg; a high laced boot, or a kind of legging ME.

Cocker (kǫ·kəɹ), *sb.*[2] ME. [f. COCK *v.*[1]] †1. A fighter -1460. 2. A patron of cock-fighting; one who breeds and trains game-cocks 1689. 3. A breed of spaniels trained to start woodcocks, etc. 1823.

Cocker, *sb.*[3], **coker.** ME. [app. f. COCK *v.*[4]] Orig., one who puts hay in cocks, a hay-worker; later, a harvest-labourer.

Cocker (kǫ·kəɹ), *sb.*[4] 1825. [Name of an arithmetician (d. 1675).] *According to C.*: in accordance with strict rule or reckoning.

Cocker (kǫ·kəɹ), *v.* 1440. [Cf. COCKLE *v.*[2]] *trans.* To pamper; to treat with excessive tenderness or care. Also with *up.* Also *fig.*

C. thy childe, and hee shall make thee afraid *Ecclus.* xxx. 9. *fig.* To c. up an evil 1861.

Cockerel (kǫ·kĕrĕl). ME. [app. a dim. of COCK *sb.*[1] Cf. *mongrel, pickerel* (small pike), etc.] A young cock (*arch.* or *dial.*). Also *fig.* of a young man 1571.

†Cockerno·ny. *Sc.* 1718. [?] The gathering up of a young woman's hair in a snood -1833.

Cocket (kǫ·kėt), *sb.*[1] ME. [?] 1. *Hist.* A seal belonging to the King's Custom House. 2. A sealed document delivered to merchants as a certificate that their merchandise has been duly entered and has paid duty. (Now disused.) ME. 3. The customs duty 1483.

Co·cket, *sb.*[2] ME. [?] A second quality of bread; also, a loaf of this. Now *Hist.*

Co·cket, *a.* Now *dial.* 1537. [perh. a. F. *coquet, coquette,* infl. later by *cocky.*] 'Stuck up'; pert; brisk; in *mod. dial.* merry.

Co·cket, *v.*[1] ME. [f. COCKET *sb.*[1]] *trans.* To furnish with a cocket.

Co·cket, *v.*[2] 1583. [Cf. COCK *v.*[3]] *Arch.* To mortise, joint.

Cock-eye. *colloq.* 1825. [app. f. COCK *v.*[1]] A squinting eye. Hence **Co·ck-eyed** *a.*, squinting, cross-eyed; *transf.* and *fig.* crooked, askew.

Cock-fight (kǫ·kˌfəit). 1494. A match or fight between cocks. Also *transf.*

Co·ckfighter. 1721. = COCKER *sb.*[2] 2.

Co·ck-fighting. 1450. The sport of making cocks fight each other; made illegal by Act 12 & 13 Vict. c. 92.

To beat c.: to surpass everything (*colloq.*).

Cock-horse (kǫ·kˌhǭ·ɹs). 1540. 1. Anything a child rides astride upon, a hobby-horse, any one's knee, etc. *transf. A-cock-horse, on* (*a*) *cock-horse*: mounted; astride. 1564. †2. *fig.* An exalted position. Usu. with *on, a-.* -1829. 3. *fig.* A high horse; a stallion 1599. Also as *adv.*, in senses of 1, 2.

1. 'Ride a cock-horse To Banbury Cross' *Nursery Rime.* Riding a cock-horse on a star COMBE. 2. A slave, whom vilany hath set a cock-horse 1658.

Cockie-leekie, var. of COCKY-LEEKY.

Co·cking, *vbl. sb.* ME. [f. COCK *v.*[1]] †1. Fighting, strife -1542. 2. = COCK-FIGHTING 1546; a cock-fight 1630. 3. The shooting of woodcocks 1696. *Comb.* **c.-dog, -spaniel,** one of a breed used in hunting woodcocks, etc.

Cockish (kǫ·kiʃ), *a.* 1546. [f. COCK *sb.*[1] + -ISH.] 1. Cocklike (*joc.*) 1577. 2. Strutting, self-assertive, cocky 1546. 3. Lecherous. Now *dial.* 1570. Hence **Co·ckish-ly** *adv.*, **-ness.**

Cock-laird. *Sc.* 1721. A small landholder; a yeoman.

Cockle (kǫ·k'l), *sb.*[1] [OE. *coccul, coccel*; in no other Teut. lang.] 1. The name of a plant, *Lychnis* (or *Agrostemma*) *Githago,* which grows in cornfields. Also called *Corn Cockle.* 2. Used as tr. *zizania* (Matt. xiii), or L. *lolium.* (The plant thus named was the grass *Lolium temulentum* or Darnel, not cockle.) OE. Also *fig.*

fig. The C. of Rebellion, Insolence, Sedition SHAKS.

Cockle (kǫ·k'l), *sb.*[2] [ME. *cokille,* a. F. *coquille*:—L. type **coquilia,* by-form of *conchylia* pl., a. Gr., dim. of κογχύλη = κόγχη (whence L. *concha*) mussel or (perh.) cockle.] 1. The English name of bivalve molluscs of the genus *Cardium,* esp. *C. edule,* much used for food. (Formerly applied more vaguely.) 2. = COCKLE-SHELL 1507. 3. *Cockles of the heart*: explained (1) by the likeness of a heart to a cockleshell; (2) by the zool. name for the cockle, *Cardium* (Latham). Also *attrib.* *Comb.*: **c.-hat,** a hat with a c. or scallop-shell in it, worn by pilgrims; **-stairs,** winding stairs. Hence **Co·ckled** *a.* furnished with a shell. **Co·ckler,** one who gathers cockles.

Cockle, *sb.*[3] 1522. [Goes with COCKLE *v.*[1]] A pucker, or bulge on what ought to be a flat surface, as cloth, paper, etc.

Cockle, *sb.*[4] 1688. [? ad. 16th c. Du. *kakel,* ad. Ger. *kachel* stove-tile, etc.] 1. The fire-chamber of a hop or malt kiln. Also called **c. oast.** 2. A kind of heating stove, also called **c. stove.** Sometimes used of 'the fireplace of an air stove' or of 'the dome of a heating furnace'. 1774.

†Cockle, *sb.*[5] 1761. A miner's name for Black Tourmaline -1788.

†Cockle, *a.* 1708. [? attrib. use of COCKLE *sb.*[1]] Whimsical. Hence *c.-brained, -headed.*

Cockle (kǫ·k'l), *v.*[1] 1552. [Cf. F. *coquiller* to form *coquilles,* i. e. blisters on the crust of bread.] 1. *intr.* To go into rucks, to pucker, as cloth, paper, etc. 2. *trans.* To cause to pucker, to wrinkle, crease 1691. 3. *intr.* To rise into short tumbling waves.

†Cockle, *v.*[2] 1570. [See COCKER *v.*] = COCKER *v.* -1579.

Cockle-shell (kǫ·k'lˌʃel). ME. [See COCKLE *sb.*[2]] 1. The shell of the cockle; usu. one of its valves. Formerly applied more widely. 2. A small frail boat 1829.

1. Wearers of the C., the emblems of a pilgrimage to Compostella BLADES.

†Cockloche. ? *slang.* 1611. [?] A silly coxcomb -1863.

Cock-loft. 1589. [Cf. Sc. *hen-loft.* But *cock* may be fig. or transf. *Cockle-loft* also occurs.] A small upper loft, usually reached by a ladder; 'the room over the garret' (J.).

Co·ck-master. 1610. One who rears game-cocks.

†Co·ck-match. 1680. A cock-fighting match -1814.

Co·ck-nest. 1859. A nest built by a male-bird, to roost in.

Cockney (kǫ·kni), *sb.* (*a.*) [ME. *coken-ey, -ay,* app. = *coken* of cocks + *ey, ay* (OE. *æg*) egg.] A. *sb.* †1. An egg; or perh. one of the small or malformed eggs called popularly 'cocks' eggs', in Ger. *hahneneier* -1600. †2. 'A child that sucketh long'; a cockered child; hence, a milksop -1783. †3. *contempt.* A townsman -1826. 4. *spec.* One born in the city of London. (Always contemptuous or bantering.) 1600.

1. I haue no salt Bacon, Ne no Cokeneyes, bi Crist, Colopus to maken LANGL. [Egs, as we say cockanegs FLORIO.] 2. Brought up with great cockering, as Cockneys bee 1598. 4. I scorne..To let a Bow-bell C. put me downe 1600.

B. *adj.* (*sb.* used *attrib.*) 1. Cockered; squeamish 1573. 2. Pertaining to or marking the London Cockney 1632.

Hence **Co·ckneydom,** the domain of cockneys; cockneys collectively. **Co·ckneyfy, -ify** *v.* to render or become c. **Co·ckneyish** *a.* savouring of the c. **Co·ckneyism,** c. quality; a c. characteristic (*e.g.* in idiom or pronunciation). **Co·ckneyize** *v.* to make c.; to play the c., use cockneyisms.

†Cockney, *v.* 1583. [f. COCKNEY *sb.* (sense 2).] To cocker -1625.

Cock-paddle. Also **-paidle.** *Sc.* 1672. [?] The Common Lump-fish, *Cyclopterus lumpus.*

†Co·ck-pe·nny. 1524. A customary payment at Shrovetide, formerly made to the schoolmaster in certain schools in the north of England. (Originally applied to defray the expense of cock-fighting.) -1870.

Cockpit (kǫ·kpit). 1587. 1. A pit or enclosed area constructed for cock-fighting. †b. Applied to a theatre; and to the PIT of a theatre -1635. Also *fig.* 2. *Naut.* The after part of the orlop deck of a man-of-war; in action appropriated to the wounded 1706.

1. A Circle dug in the Earth, like a C. DE FOE. †*The Cockpit*: (*a*) name of a theatre in London, in 17th c., on the site of a c. (*b*) The block of buildings on the site of the C. at Whitehall, London, used as government offices; hence = 'the Treasury', 'the Privy Council'. *fig.* Belgium..the C. of Europe 1858.

Cockroach (kǫ·krōutʃ). 1624. [app. ad. Sp. *cucaracha*; assim. to *cock* and app. to *roach.*] The name of orthopterous insects of the genus *Blatta,* esp. *B. orientalis,* commonly called *black-beetle,* infesting kitchens in large numbers.

†Co·ck-road, rood. 1648. = COCKSHOOT -1751.

Cocks. Also *Fighting cocks.* 1847. *dial.* The Ribwort Plantain.

Cock's-comb, cockscomb (kǫ·kskōum). Also, in fig. senses, COXCOMB, q. v. ME. 1. The comb of a cock. 2. A jester's cap, resembling a cock's-comb 1562. †3. *joc.* The head -1654. †4. A conceited fool. Now COXCOMB. -1706. 5. A name given to plants; *esp.* the Yellow Rattle (*Rhinanthus Crista-galli*), *Celosia cristata,* and in the W. Indies *Erythrina Crista-galli.* 6. A kind of oyster having both valves plaited 1776. Also *attrib.*

Co·ck's-foot, cocksfoot. 1697. A grass, *Dactylis glomerata.*

Cock's-head, cockshead. ME. Applied to some kinds of Trefoil; *esp.* a species of Sainfoin, *Onobrychis Caput-galli*: also common Red Clover. Also Plantain, Knapweed, etc. (*local*).

†Co·ckshoot. 1530. [f. COCK *sb.*[1] I. 1 b + SHOOT.] A broad glade in a wood, through which woodcocks might dart or shoot, so as to be caught by nets stretched across the opening -1691. Hence in local names, as *Cockshott Wood, Farm,* etc. ¶ The statement that the net itself was the *cockshoot,* and the spelling *cock-shut,* are dictionary blunders.

Cock-shut (kǫ·kˌʃʋt). Now *dial.* 1594. [f. COCK *sb.*[1] + SHUT: perh. the time when poultry are shut up.] 1. *attrib.* in *c. light, time,* etc.: twilight. 2. *sb.* Twilight 1598.

Cock-shy (kǫ·kˌʃəi·). *colloq.* 1836. [f. COCK *sb.*[1] + SHY.] 1. Applied to cock-throwing and the like 1851. 2. A shy at an object set up for the purpose, as a form of amusement. Also *transf.* and *attrib.* 1836. 3. The object at which the shy is made. Also *transf.* 1836. 4. A pitch where sticks may be thrown at coco-nuts for payment 1879.

3. What a fine c. he would make 1836.

Co·ckspur. 1591. 1. The spur of a cock. 2. A kind of Caddis-worm 1653. 3. Short for *c. burner, thorn* 1808. *Comb.*: **c.-burner,** a gas-burner with three holes;

c. hawthorn, c. thorn, *Cratægus Crus-galli*, a native of N. America.

Cock-sure (kǫk₁ʃūᵊɹ), *a.* 1520. [? As sure as the action of a COCK or tap.] †1. Absolutely safe or certain -1742. 2. Feeling perfectly certain. Const. *of, about.* 1672. 3. Dogmatically self-confident 1755. Also as **adv.**

1. To make the Event cock sure NORTH. 2. 'Are you sure?' said his mother. 'Cock sure!' said Andy S. LOVER. 3. A conceited and c. style DARWIN. *adv.* We steale as in a Castle, c. 1 *Hen. IV*, II. i. 94.

Cockswain, earlier f. COXSWAIN.

Cocksy, coxy (kǫ·ksi), *a.* 1825. [Cf. *tricksy*, etc.] Impudent, bumptious, cocky. Hence **Co·xiness.**

Cocktail (kǫ·ktēⁱl). Also **cock-tail.** 1808. [*lit.* 'a tail like that of a cock', or 'a tail that cocks up'.] 1. A cocktailed horse (see COCK-TAILED 1); any horse of racing qualities, but not thorough-bred. *transf.* of persons 1854. Also as *adj.* 2. (more fully *C. Beetle*): A brachelytrous beetle which cocks up its tail when irritated; the Devil's Coach-horse 1880. 3. A drink made of spirit, bitters, some sugar, etc. Chiefly *U.S.* 1809. Also as *adj.*

1. *transf.* Such a .. coxcomb as that, such a c. THACKERAY.

Co·ck-tailed, *a.* 1769. 1. Of horses: Having the tail docked. 2. Having the tail (or hinder part) cocked up 1798.

Co·ck-up, cockup. 1693. [f. *cock up*; see COCK *v.*¹] 1. A distinct turn up at the end 1826. 2. A hat or cap cocked up in front 1693. 3. A freshwater fish of India (*Lates calcarifer*) 1845. 4. As *adj.* 1832.

Cockweed (kǫ·kwīd). Now *dial.* 1585. †1. ? A species of *Lepidium* -1783. 2. = Corn Cockle.

Co·cky, *sb.* 1687. Dim. of COCK *sb.*¹ (Formerly a term of endearment.)

Cocky (kǫ·ki), *a.* 1768. [f. COCK *sb.*¹ + -Y¹.] Arrogantly pert (*colloq.*).

Cocky-leeky (kǫki₁lī·ki). *Sc.* 1771. Soup made of a cock boiled with leeks.

Cockyolly (kǫki₁ǫ·li). 1837. In *c. bird*: = 'dear little bird'; cf. *Dicky-bird.*

Coco, cocoa (kōᵘ·ko). 1555. [a. Pg. and Sp. *coco* 'grinning face'; the name referring to the face-like appearance of the base of the shell. The spelling *Cocoa* was originated (app. by accident) in Dr. Johnson's Dictionary. See next.] †1. = COCO-NUT below -1740. 2. The palm-tree *Cocos nucifera*, which produces the coconut 1555. Also *attrib. Comb.*: **Coco-nut, cocoa-nut, coker-nut. a.** The nut or seed of the coco-palm. **b.** = *Coco-nut palm.* **c.** In pugilistic slang: The human head. **Double Coco-nut,** in Fr. *coco-de-mer, coco-des-Maldives*: the immense woody nut of a gigantic palm, *Lodoicea sechellarum*, found native only on two small islands of the Seychelles group.

Cocoa (kōᵘ·ko). 1707. [A corruption of Sp. CACAO, ad. *cacaua-tl*, the Mexican name of the cacao-seed. The word was orig. of 3 syllables.] †1. The seed of *Theobroma Cacao*: more correctly called CACAO -1790. 2. The Cacao-tree. (*rare* and *improper.*) 1876. 3. A powder made from the seeds; also, a beverage made from this powder, or from the prepared seeds. (The ordinary sense.) 1788.

Comb.: **c.-nib,** the cotyledon of the cacao seed; **†-nut,** a name for the cacao seed; now disused.

Cocoon (kokū·n). 1699. [a. F. *cocon*, app. a deriv. of *coque* shell.] The case of silky threads, in which the silkworm is enclosed in the chrysalis state; hence, analogous structures formed by any insects; also the silken case spun by spiders to receive their eggs. Also *fig.* and *attrib.* Hence **Cocoo·nery** (*U.S.*), a room for rearing silkworms and obtaining cocoons.

Coco-plum. 1676. The fruit of a W. Indian tree, *Chrysobalanus Icaco*; also the tree.

†Coct, *v.* 1605. [f. L. *coct-, coquere.*] *trans.* To boil -1624; to digest 1662; to bake (earthenware) -1678.

Coctile (kǫ·ktil, -təil), *a.* 1678. [ad. L. *coctilis*, f. as prec.] Made by baking; formed of baked bricks.

Coction (kǫ·kʃən). Now *rare.* 1572. [ad. L. *coctionem*; see above.] 1. Boiling; cooking 1605. †2. The action of heat in preparing any substance -1766. †3. *Old Med.* The ripening of morbific matter before elimination from the body -1738. 4. *Phys.* Digestion. ? *Obs.* 1667.

Cocus (kōᵘ·kǫs). 1794. The wood of *Brya Ebenus*, a W. Indian tree, used by turners. Also *c.-wood.*

Cod (kǫd), *sb.*¹ [OE. *cod(d*:—OTeut. **kuddoz.*] 1. A bag. 2. A husk; a pod; cf. PEASCOD. Now *dial.* OE. 3. The scrotum; improp. in *pl.* testicles. (Not in polite use.) ME. †4. A cocoon. (Cf. 2.) -1802.

1. The bag or c. [of a net] to enclose the fish 1750.

Cod (kǫd), *sb.*² *North.* ME. [a. ODa. *kodde*, ON. *koddi*, pillow; from same root as prec.] 1. A pillow, cushion. *Sc.* and *n. dial.* 2. One of the bearings of an axle ME.

Cod (kǫd), *sb.*³ ME. [Origin unkn. Not conn. w. Gr. γάδος (mod. Zool. L. *gadus*).] 1. A well-known sea-fish, *Gadus morrhua*, which inhabits the Atlantic and its connected seas. Sometimes extended (with qualifications, drawn from their habitats, colour, food, etc.) to other members of the *Gadidæ* or Cod-tribe. (Pl. now rare: *cod* being used instead.) More fully **cod-fish.** 2. Applied to other fishes which take the economic place of the true cod in other regions; *esp.* to the *Bastard, Blue, Buffalo, Cultus, Green cod* of the Pacific coast 1880. See also ROCK COD.

Comb.: **c.-bank,** a submarine bank (BANK¹) on which c. are caught; **-fishery,** fishing for c., *esp.* as a branch of industry; **-line,** a line used in fishing for c.; **-oil** = COD-LIVER OIL.

Cod, *sb.*⁴ *slang.* 1690. [?] A fool, (old) fellow, CODGER.

†Cod (kǫd), *v.*¹ 1532. [f. COD *sb.*¹] 1. *intr.* To produce pods -1710. 2. *trans.* To gather the pods of (peas) -1730. 3. *intr.* with *out.* To shake out. Hence **Co·dder** (in sense 2) (*dial.*).

Cod, *v.*² 1861. [f. COD *sb.*³] To fish for cod.

Cod, *v.*³ *slang.* or *dial.* 1873. [? f. COD *sb.*⁴, 'fool'.] *trans.* To hoax, 'stuff', fool.

‖**Coda** (kō·da, kōᵘ·dă). 1753. [It.:—L. *cauda* tail.] *Mus.* A passage added after the natural completion of a movement, so as to form a more definite and satisfactory conclusion.

Cod-bait. 1626. = CAD-BAIT (see CAD³).

†Co·dding, *a.* [? f. COD *sb.*¹ 3.] ? Lecherous. *Tit. A.* V. i. 99.

Coddle (kǫ·d'l), *v.*¹ 1598. [?] To boil gently, parboil, stew (*esp.* fruit). Also *fig.*

We'll go.. said my father, whilst dinner is coddling STERNE. *fig.* Hee is tane from Grammar-schoole halfe codled OVERBURY.

Coddle (kǫ·d'l), *v.*² 1815. [? var. of CAUDLE *v.*] To treat as an invalid; to nurse overmuch, cocker. Often with *up.*

Let womankind alone for coddling each other SCOTT. Hence **Coddle** *sb. colloq.* one who coddles himself or is coddled.

Coddle, *v.*³, dial. f. CUDDLE.

Coddy-moddy. *dial.* 1676. The Black-headed Gull.

Code (kōᵘd), *sb.* ME. [a. F., f. L. *codex, codicem*; see CODEX.] 1. *Rom. Law.* One of the systematic collections of statutes made by the later emperors; *spec.* the *code of Justinian.* Hence, 2. A digest of the laws of a country, or of those relating to any subject 1735. 3. *transf.* A system of rules or regulations on any subject 1809. 4. A system of signals 1808; (*Telegr.*) a system of words arbitrarily used for other words or phrases, to secure brevity and secrecy; also *attrib.* 1880. †5. A collection of writings forming a book, or volume -1794.

3. In the legislative as in the religious c. COLERIDGE. 4. A c. of signals for the army WELLINGTON. *attrib.* C. telegrams 1880.

Code (kōᵘd), *v. rare.* 1815. [f. CODE *sb.*] To enter in a code.

Co-defe·ndant. 1640. [See CO-.] Joint defendant.

Codeine (kōᵘ·dī₁əin). 1838. [f. Gr. κώδεια head, poppy-head.] *Chem.* A white crystalline alkaloid ($C_{18}H_{21}NO_3$) contained in opium, and used as a hypnotic; called also *codeia.*

‖**Codetta** (kode·tta). 1869. [It., dim. of CODA.] *Mus.* A short coda.

Codex (kōᵘ·deks). Pl. **codices** (kōᵘ·disīz). 1581. [a. L. *codex*, earlier *caudex*, trunk of a tree, etc.] †1. = CODE *sb.* 1-3. -1753. 2. A manuscript volume: *e.g.* the *Codex Sinaiticus, Vaticanus*, etc. of the Scriptures 1845. 3. *Med.* 'A collection of receipts for the preparation of drugs'. Hence **Co·dical** *a.* (Webst.)

Cod-fish; see COD *sb.*³

Codger (kǫ·dʒəɹ). *dial.* and *colloq.* 1756. [? dial. var. of CADGER.] 1. *dial.* A mean or miserly (old) fellow; *occas.* a pedlar or tramp 1796. 2. *low colloq.* A term applied irreverently to an elderly man, with a whimsical implication 1756; more generally = Fellow, chap 1839.

2. A gouty old c. of an alderman W. IRVING.

Codicil (kǫ·disil). 1422. [ad. L. *codicillus* (chiefly in pl.), dim. of *codex* CODEX.] 1. *Law.* A supplement to a will. 2. *transf.* and *fig.* Supplement, appendix 1784.

2. A [bitter] c. to a most severe Winter H. WALPOLE. Hence **Codici·llary** *a.* of the nature of, or belonging to, a c.

Codify (kōᵘ·difəi, kǫ·d-), *v.* 1800. [prob. after F. *codifier.*] 1. To reduce (laws) to a code. 2. *gen.* To systematize 1873. Hence **Co:difica·tion,** reduction to a code; systematization. **Co·difier,** one who codifies.

Codilla (kodi·lă). 1785. [app. dim. of It. *coda*:—L. *cauda* tail.] The coarse tow of flax or hemp.

Codille (ko·dil). 1712. [F., ad. Sp. *codillo* knee, angle, etc., dim. of *codo* elbow.] A term used at ombre when the game is lost by the player who challenges to win it.

†Codi·niac. 1539. [a. F. *codignac* in same sense.] Quince-marmalade, quiddany -1668.

Codist (kōᵘ·dist). *rare.* 1853. [f. CODE, app. after *jurist.*] One learned in legal codes.

Codling¹ (kǫ·dliŋ). ME. [f. COD *sb.*³ + -LING.] 1. A young or small cod. 2. *U.S.* Applied to fishes and the genus *Phycis*, allied to the cod.

Codling², **-lin** (kǫ·dliŋ, -lin). late ME. [Early *querdling* is identical with the surname *Querdling* = *cœur-de-lion* lionheart.] 1. A variety of apple, elongated and tapering towards the eye. (Formerly, a hard kind of apple, not suitable to be eaten raw; hence, any half-grown apple.) **b.** A tree bearing codlings 1657. †2. *fig.* A raw youth -1663.

1. As.. a C. when tis almost an Apple *Twel. N.* I. v. 167. *Hot codlings*: roasted apples (formerly sold hot in London streets). *Comb.* **c.-moth,** a species of moth (*Carpocapsa pomonella*), the larva of which feeds on the apple.

Co·dling³. 1874. A balk sawed into lengths for staves.

Co·d-liver oi·l. 1783. Oil expressed from the liver of the cod-fish, much used in medicine.

†Cod-piece. 1460. [f. COD *sb.*¹ 3.] A bagged appendage to the front of the breeches; often conspicuous -1761. Also *fig.* and *attrib.*

†Cods, cod's. 1569. A perversion of *God's*, in oaths, etc. -1689.

Coe, *sb. local.* Also Sc. **cow.** 1653. [= Du. *kouw*:—WGer. type **kauja*, a. L. *cavea.*] *Mining.* A little hut built over a mine-shaft.

Cœcal, cœcum, etc.; see CÆCAL, etc.

Co-ed (koᵘe·d). *U.S. colloq.* [See next.] A female co-educational student.

Co-educa·tion. 1874. [See CO-: of U.S. origin.] Education of the two sexes together in school, etc. **Co-e·ducate** *v.*, **-educa·tional** *a.*

Co-effe·ct. 1768. A joint effect.

Co-e·fficacy. *rare.* Joint efficacy. BROWNE.

Coefficient (kōᵘ₁ĕfi·ʃent). 1665. [See CO-. In senses A and B 1 often with a hyphen.]

A. *adj.* Co-operating to produce a result.

B. *sb.* 1. A coefficient cause 1708. So **†Co-effi·ciency** (*rare*). 2. *Math.* A number or quantity placed (usually) before and multiplying another quantity known or unknown; thus in $4x^2 + 2ax$, 4 is the c. of x^2, 2 of ax, and $2a$ of x. 1708. 3. *Physics.* A multiplier that measures some property of a particular substance, for which it is constant, while differing for different substances; e.g. *c. of friction, expansion*, etc. 1829.

Differential c.: the quantity which measures the rate of change of a function of any variable with respect to that variable.

Coehorn, cohorn (kōᵘ·hǫɹn). 1705. [f. Baron *Coehorn*, the Dutch military engineer.] *Mil.* A small mortar for throwing grenades. In full *c. mortar.* Also *attrib.*

Cœlacanth (sīˑlăkænþ). 1864. [ad. mod.L. *Cœlacanthus*, name of the typical genus, f. Gr. κοῖλος + ἄκανθα.] *adj.* Having a hollow spine; said of an extinct family of fishes. *sb.* A fish of the genus *Cœlacanthus* or the family *Cœlacanthidæ*. Hence **Cœlacaˑnthid**, one of this family. **Cœlacaˑnthine** *a.* pertaining to Cœlacanths. **Cœlacaˑnthoid, Cœlacaˑnthous** *adjs.*

Cœlelminth (sīˑlelminþ). 1836. [f. Gr. κοῖλος + ἑλμινθ-.] *Zool.* One of the *Cœlelmintha*, a cavitary intestinal worm.

‖**Cœlenterata** (sīlentĕrēˑtă), *sb. pl.* Also **cœlentera**. 1872. [mod.L., f. Gr. κοῖλος + ἔντερον.] *Zool.* **1.** The group of the Animal Kingdom comprising *Ctenophora, Actinozoa*, and *Hydrozoa*, distinguished by having a digestive cavity with which a peripheral system of canals frequently communicates, with prehensile organs round the mouth, and nearly all provided with nematocysts. **2.** In later classifications the lower subdivision of the Metazoa, having an intestinal canal but no cœlome. It includes also the *Porifera* or Sponges. So **Cœlenterate**, belonging to, or one of, the *Cœlenterata*.

Cœlestial, etc.; see CEL-.

Cœliac, †-al (sīˑliæk, -ăl), *a.* 1662. [ad. L. *cœliacus*, a. Gr. κοιλιακός, f. κοιλία belly.] Of or belonging to the cavity of the abdomen.

C. artery or *axis*, a short thick branch issuing from the aorta just below the diaphragm. †*C. passion* or *flux*, a kind of chronic flux of the intestines. *C. canal*, in crinoids, one which runs into the arms from the cœloma.

Cœlio- (sīˑlio), bef. a vowel **cœli-**, comb. f. Gr. κοιλία belly.

Cœlo-[1] (sīˑlo), bef. a vowel **cœl-**, comb. f. Gr. κοῖλος hollow:

Cœˑlodont [Gr. ὀδούς, ὀδοντ-], *a.* hollow-toothed (epithet of certain lizard-like reptiles). **Cœlospeˑrmous** [Gr. σπέρμα], *a.* hollow-seeded; having the seed excavated on the flat side, as in coriander; etc.

Cœlo-[2], prop. **cælo-**, comb. f. L. *cælum* heavens.

Cœloma; see CŒLOME.

‖**Cœlomata** (sīlōuˑmătă), *sb. pl.* 1877. [mod. L., f. Gr. κοίλωματ- hollow, cavity; see CŒLOME.] *Zool.* A name for the higher division of Enterozoa (= *Metazoa*); see CŒLENTERATA 2. It comprises all the more highly developed animals, together with *Vermes*. Hence **Cœlomate** *a.* having a cœlome; belonging to the *Cœlomata*; *sb.* [sc. *animal*.] So **Cœloˑmatous** *a.*

Cœlome, cœlom (sīˑlōum, -ǫm). Also in L. form **cœloˑma**. 1878. [ad. Gr. κοίλωμα, f. κοῖλος.] *Zool.* The body-cavity of a cœlomate animal. Hence **Cœlomic** *a.* pertaining to, or of the nature of, a c.

Coemption (koˌeˑmpʃən). ME. [ad. L. *coemptionem*.] **1.** The buying up of the whole supply of any commodity. **2.** *Rom. Law.* A form of civil marriage consisting in a mutual fictitious sale of the two parties 1677. Hence **Coeˑmptive** *a.* of the nature of c.

‖**Cœnæsthesis** (sīnesþīˑsis). 1837. [f. Gr. κοινός + αἴσθησις.] *Psychol.* The general sense of existence arising from the sum of bodily impressions; the vital sense.

Cœnenchym (sīneˑŋkim). Also in L. form **cœneˑnchyma**. 1875. [f. Gr. κοινός + ἔγχυμα.] *Zool.* **a.** The calcareous frame-work by which corallites are united into one corallum. **b.** The cœnosarc of a compound Anthozoan.

Cœno- (sīˑno), bef. a vowel **cœn-**, comb. f. Gr. κοινός common:

‖**Cœnœˑcium** [Gr. οἶκος], *Zool.* the common dermal system of a colony of Polyzoa. **Cœnoˑgamy** [Gr. -γαμια, γάμος], community of husbands or wives. **Cœˑnosarc** [Gr. σάρξ, σαρκ-], *Zool.* the common living basis or flesh which unites the individuals of a compound zoophyte. ‖**Cœnoˑsteum** [Gr. ὀστέον], *Zool.* the common calcareous skeleton of the Hydrocorallina, a division of the Hydrozoa.

Cœnobite, cenobite (sīˑnobəit, seˑnobəit). 1638. [ad. late L. *cœnobita*, f. *cœnobium*; see below. (Eng. usage prefers *cœ-*.)] A member of a religious order living in a community; opp. to an *anchoret*. Hence **Cœnobiˑtic, -al, cen-**, *a.* pertaining to a c.; relating to, or of the nature of, a monastic community. **Cœˑnobitiˑsm, ceˑn-**, the practice or system of cœnobites.

‖**Cœnobium, cen-** (sīnōuˑbiŏm). Pl. **cœnobia**. 1817. [late L., a. Gr. κοινόβιον, f. κοινός + βίος.] **1.** = CŒNOBY. **2.** *Bot.* **a.** The multilocular fruit of *Labiatæ*, etc. 1866. **b.** A structure formed by the union of a number of cells, as in certain Algæ 1882. **3.** *Zool.* A cluster of 'colonial' Protozoa 1888.

Cœnoby, cen- (sīˑnobi, seˑn-). 1475. [See above.] A conventual establishment.

Cœnure (sīˑniuɹ). 1847. [ad. mod.L. *cœnurus* (more commonly used), f. Gr. κοινός + οὐρά.] *Zool.* The many-headed bladder-worm; the hydatid which produces staggers in sheep; it is the cystic stage of *Tænia cœnurus*, one of the tapeworms of the dog.

Coequal (koˌīˑkwǫl), *a.* 1460. [See Co-. Cf. L. *coæqualis*, and F. *coégal*.] **1.** Equal *with* (†*to, unto*) one another or others in rank, power, etc. **2.** Co-extensive *with* 1853. As *sb.* One who is the equal of another 1577.

1. If once he come to be a Cardinall, Hee'l make his cap coequall with the Crowne 1 *Hen. VI*, v. i. 33. Hence †**Coeˑqual** *v.* to be or become c. with; to make equal with. **Coequaˑlity**, c. state or condition. **Coeˑqually** *adv.*

†**Co-equate, Coequaˑted**, *ppl. a.* 1592. [ad. L. *coæquatus*.] Made equal with something else. In *c. anomaly*, the true anomaly of a planet; see ANOMALY. -1769.

Coerce (koˌǝˑɹs), *v.* 1475. [ad. L. *coercere*, f. *co-* + *arcere* to shut up, keep off, etc.] **1.** To constrain or restrain by force, or by authority resting on force. Also *absol.* 1659. †**2.** To subject to restraint in the matter of (*rare*) 1780. **3.** To effect by compulsion. (*U. S.*) 1850.

1. The Punishments .. sufficient to c. this profligate sort of Men AYLIFFE. **2.** The debtor is ordered .. to be coerced his liberty until he makes payment BURKE. **3.** To c. obedience WEBSTER. Hence **Coeˑrcer**. **Coeˑrcible** *a.* that can be coerced.

Coercion (koˌǝˑɹʃən). 1495. [a. OF. *cohercion, cohertion* (mod. *coercion*), ad. L. *coer(c)tionem*, in med. spelling *coercionem*, a by-form of *coercitionem*, f. *coercit-, coercere*.] **1.** The action of coercing; constraint, restraint, compulsion. **2.** Government by force; the employment of force to suppress political disaffection and disorder. Also *attrib.* 1798. **3.** Physical pressure; compression 1830. †**4.** Coercitive power or jurisdiction -1700. Also *fig.*

1. The moral c. of public opinion MILL. C. of outrage HALLAM. **2.** The cant which brands as 'coercion' that which is the duty of every Government DK. ARGYLL. Hence **Coeˑrcionist**, one who supports government by c., *esp.* in Ireland.

Coercive (koˌǝˑɹsiv), *a.* 1600. [irreg. f. COERCE, after *aspersive*, etc.] Of the nature of coercion; coercing. Also as quasi-*sb.*

In painful dungeons and c. chains POPE.

C. force: the hypothetical force in a magnetic substance which resists magnetization or demagnetization 1839.

var. **Coeˑrcitive** *a.* (and *sb.*). ? *Obs.* Hence **Coeˑrcively** *adv.* **Coeˑrciveness**, c. quality.

Coessential (kōuˌeseˑnʃăl), *a.* 1471. [Co-.] **1.** United in being. **2.** One in essence 1587.

2. Wee blesse and magnifie that Coessentiall Spirit eternally proceeding from both HOOKER. Hence **Coesseˑntiaˑlity**, c. quality or nature. (*Theol.*)

Co-estaˑblishment. 1791. [See Co-.] Joint or concurrent establishment.

Co-estaˑte. 1756. [See Co-.] An estate or state possessing co-ordinate authority or rank with another.

†**Coetaˑnean.** 1616. [f. as next.] *adj.* = next -1641. *sb.* A contemporary, a coeval; var. †**Coˑetan(e** (*rare*) -1694.

Coetaneous (kōuˌitēˑniəs), *a.* Also **coæt-**. 1608. [f. late L. *coætaneus* (f. *co-* + *ætat-* + *aneus* adj. suffix) + -OUS.] = COEVAL *a.* in all senses. Hence **Coetaˑneousˑly** *adv.*

Coeternal (kōuˌitǝˑɹnăl), *a.* ME. [See Co-.] Equally eternal. Also as *sb.*

Hail holy light, ofspring of Heav'n first-born, Or of th' Eternal C. beam MILT. *P. L.* III. 2.

var. †**Coeteˑrn(e** *a.* Hence **Coeteˑrnally** *adv.*

Coeternity (kōuˌitǝˑɹniti). 1587. [See Co-.] Coeternal existence or quality; eternal existence with another; equal eternity.

Aristotle's tenet of the c. of matter MILMAN.

Coeval (koˌīˑvăl), *a.* and *sb.* 1605. [f. L. *coævus*.]

A. *adj.* Const. *with*, †*to*. **1.** Of contemporaneous origin 1622. **2.** Equally old 1700. **3.** Existing at the same time 1704. **4.** Of coincident duration 1742.

1. Ideas in the Understanding are c. with Sensation LOCKE. **4.** Were men to live c. with the sun YOUNG. vars. †**Coeˑve**, †**Coeˑvous**. Hence **Coevaˑlity**, var. †**Coeˑvity**, c. quality. **Coeˑvally** *adv.*

B. *sb.* **1.** One of the same age or standing 1656. **2.** A person (or thing) belonging to the same period 1605.

1. He is forlorn among his coevals; his juniors cannot be his friends LAMB.

Co-executor (kōuˌekseˑkiŭtəɹ, -ǒɹ). ME. [See Co-.] A joint executor. So **Co-exeˑcutrix**, a joint executrix.

Co-exist (kōuˌegziˑst), *v.* 1677. [See Co-.] To exist at the same time, in the same place, etc., *with* another.

They [Generations of Mankind] never c., but are successive HALE. No real greatness can c. with deceit COLERIDGE. Hence **Coexiˑsting** *ppl. a.* existing together.

Coexistence (kōuˌegziˑstĕns). 1646. [See Co-.] Existence together or in conjunction.

In the relation to each other .. of succession and not of c. 1822. var. †**Coexiˑstency**.

Coexistent (kōuˌegziˑstĕnt). 1662. [See Co-.] *adj.* Existing together or in conjunction. *sb.* That which coexists with something else 1846.

Coexteˑnd, *v.* 1617. [See Co-.] To make or be coextensive.

The manhood is not coextended with the Godhead 1656. So **Coexteˑnsion**, coincidence in extension.

Coextensive (kōuˌeksteˑnsiv), *a.* 1771. [See Co-.] Extending over the same space or time; coinciding in limits; in *Logic*, having the same logical extension. Also as *sb.*

C. to dominion is jurisdiction BENTHAM. So **Coexteˑnsiveˑly** *adv.*, **-ness**.

Co-feoffee (kōuˌfefīˑ). 1458. [See Co-.] A joint feoffee.

Coffee (kǫˑfi). 1598. [ad. Arab. *qahwah*, in Turkish pronounced *kahveh*.] **1.** A drink made by infusion or decoction from the seeds of a shrub (see sense 3) roasted and ground or (in the East) pounded. **b.** A repast or course including or consisting of coffee. **2.** The berries (collectively), either whole or ground 1626. **3.** The shrub from which coffee is obtained; a species of *Coffea*, chiefly *C. arabica*, a native of Abyssinia and Africa, but now widely cultivated throughout the tropics. It bears fragrant white flowers, succeeded by red fleshy berries, each containing two seeds (*coffee-beans*). 1623.

1. There came in my time [i. e. 1636] to the College, one Nathaniel Conopios, out of Greece .. He was the first I ever saw drink c. EVELYN. *Black c.*: c. without milk.

Comb.: **c.-berry**, the fruit of the c.-plant, also, loosely, the seed; **-bug**, an insect (*Lecania coffeæ*) of the family *Coccidæ*, destructive to c.-plants; **-grounds** *sb. pl.*, the granular sediment remaining in coffee after infusion; †**-man**, a man keeping a c.-house; **-pot**, a pot in which c. is made or served; **-rat**, an insular variety of *Mus hirsutus*, found in Southern India; **-wit**, a wit who frequents c.-houses.

Coˑffee-house. 1615. A house of entertainment where coffee and other refreshments are provided. (Much frequented in 17th and 18th c. for the purpose of political and literary conversation, circulation of news, etc.) Also *attrib.*

The leaders of the legislative clubs and coffee-houses BURKE.

Coˑffee-room. 1712. A public room where coffee and similar refreshments are served; now, generally, the public dining-room in a hotel.

Coffer (kǫˑfəɹ), *sb.* [ME. *cofre, coffre*, etc., a. OF. :—L. *cophinum, cophinus*, a. Gr. κόφινος basket. Cf. L. *ordinem*, F. *ordre*, etc.] **1.** A box, chest: *esp.* a strong box in which money or valuables are kept. In *pl.*: often = Treasury, funds ME. †**2.** An ark -1711. †**3.** A coffin -1555. **4.** *Arch.* A sunk panel in a ceiling or soffit, of ornamental character 1664. **b.** A space within a wall, etc., filled up with concrete or rubble 1715. †**5.** *Fortif.* A trench dug athwart a dry moat, and furnished with a parapet and embrasures, for purposes of defence. **6.** *Hydraulics.* A caisson or COFFER-DAM, q. v.; 'the lock for a barge' 1822.

1. He gooth vn to his cofre And broghte gold

CHAUCER. The coffers of the government had long been empty H. MARTINEAU. 3. My body to be buryed in a cofer of tree 1488. *Comb.* **c.-fish,** a trunk-fish, a species of *Ostracion.*

Coffer (kǫ·fəɹ), *v.* ME. [f. the sb.; cf. F. *coffrer.*] 1. To enclose in, or as in, a coffer; to treasure *up* (*arch.*). 2. *Arch.* To adorn with coffers (see COFFER *sb.* 4). 3. *Mining.* 'To secure a shaft from leaking by ramming in clay behind the masonry or timbering' 1881.

Coffer-dam. 1736. [f. COFFER + DAM.] A water-tight enclosure, usually made of piles with clay packed between them, from which the water is pumped to obtain a dry foundation for bridges, piers, etc.

Cofferer (kǫ·fərəɹ). Now *Hist.* ME. [a. OF. *coffrier*, f. *coffre* COFFER.] 1. A treasurer; *spec.* one of the treasurers of the royal household 1538. †2. One who makes coffers -1515.

†**Co·ffer-work.** 1708. [f. COFFER *sb.* 4 b.] *Arch.* Masonry having coffers fitted with rubble, etc. Formerly also, building in concrete. -1742.

Coffin (kǫ·fin), *sb.* [ME. *cofin, coffyn*, etc., a. OF. *cofin, coffin*, ad. L., a. Gr. κόφινος basket.] †1. A basket -1552. †2. A chest, case, casket, box -1677. 3. *spec.* The box in which a corpse is enclosed for burial. (The current sense.) 1525. Applied (*Naut.*) to an unseaworthy vessel (*colloq.*) 1833. †4. *Cookery.* The crust of a pie -1750; a pie-dish -1662. 5. A paper case; *spec.* a cornet for groceries, etc. 1577. 6. *Farriery.* The whole of a horse's hoof below the coronet 1607. 7. *Printing.* The carriage of a printing machine 1659. 8. A case in which articles are baked or fired in a furnace; = F. *cassette* 1679. 9. *Mining.* An old open working (*Cornwall*); also, the mode of open working by casting up ore, etc., from platform to platform 1778.

2. A c. for a book 1677. 3. His coffers from the c. could not save SWIFT. 4. Of the paste a coffen I will reare *Tit. A.* v. ii. 189.

Comb.: **c.-bone,** a small spongy bone in a horse's hoof, being the last phalangeal bone of the foot; **-joint,** the joint at the top of a horse's hoof; **-plate.** Hence **Co·ffinless** *a.*

Coffin (kǫ·fin), *v.* 1564. [f. the sb.] To enclose in, or as in, a coffin (see COFFIN *sb.* 3, 4).

Wouldst thou have laugh'd had I come coffin'd home *Cor.* II. i. 167. C. them alive In some kind clasping prison B. JONS.

Coffle (kǫ·f'l). 1799. [ad. Arab. *qāfilah*; see CAFILA.] A train of slaves or beasts driven along together.

Coffret (kǫ·frėt), **cofferet** (kǫ·fėrėt). 1485. [a. F., dim. of *coffre.*] A small coffer.

Cog, *sb.*[1] Now *Hist.* [ME. *cogge, kogge*; prob. f. OF. *cogue*, also *coque*, with dim. *coquet* cock-boat.] 1. An early form of ship; broadly built, with roundish prow and stern. 2. Also app. = COCK *sb.*[3], COCK-BOAT ME.

Cog (kǫg), *sb.*[2] [ME. *kogge*, cogn. w. Sw. *kugge*, Norw. *kug, kugger*, in same sense.] 1. One of a series of teeth, etc., on the circumference of a wheel, etc., which, by catching similar projections on another wheel, etc., transmit or receive motion. 2. Short for: †a. The series of cogs round a wheel; b. a cog-wheel 1712. 3. *Mining.* A block used in building up a support for the roof of a mine 1881.

Cog, *sb.*[3] 1856. [See COG *v.*[2]] *Carpentry.* A tenon on the end of a beam, which is received into a corresponding mortice on the surface of another beam or support; in a scarf-joint, etc.

†**Cog,** *sb.*[4] 1532. [f. COG *v.*[3]] 1. The act of cogging at dice; a way of doing this -1658. 2. A deception, trick -1630.

Cog (kǫg), *v.*[1] 1499. [f. COG *sb.*[2]] 1. To furnish (a wheel, etc.) with cogs. 2. To steady anything with a wedge. *n. dial.* 1635.

Cog, *v.*[2] 1823. [app. var. of COCK *v.*[3]] To connect timbers by means of a cog; cf. COCK *v.*[3]

Cog (kǫg), *v.*[3] 1532. [?] 1. *intr.* (*Dicing.*) To practise certain tricks in throwing dice. 2. *trans.* *To c. a die* or *the dice*: fraudulently to control their fall 1565. †3. *intr.* To cheat -1683. 4. To jest, quibble (*arch.*) 1588. †5. To fawn, wheedle -1728. †6. *gen.* To produce cunningly and fraudulently -1651.

3. Out-facing .. boyes, That lye, and c., and flout *Much Ado* v. i. 95. 5. *Merry W.* III. iii. 76. 6. Every Cobler can cogge a Syllogisme FRAUNCE.

Cogency (kōu·dʒĕnsi). 1690. [f. COGENT.] †1. Compulsion 1702. 2. The quality of being cogent; *esp.* power of compelling assent 1690. *concr.* (with *pl.*) A convincing argument 1851.

2. The c. of distress JOHNSON, of Axioms LOCKE. var. Co·gence (*rare*).

Cogenial, cogenite; see CONGENIAL, etc.

Cogent (kōu·dʒĕnt). 1659. [a. F., ad. L. *cogentem, cogere.*] 1. Constraining; powerful, forcible 1718. 2. *esp.* Having power to compel assent; convincing 1659.

1. To insist in c. terms KINGLAKE. 2. Undeniable c. demonstrations LOCKE. The testimony of a number is more c. than the testimony of two or three NEWMAN. Hence **Co·gently** *adv.* in a c. manner.

Cogged (kǫgd), *ppl. a.*[1] 1825. [f. COG *sb.*[2] or *v.*[1]] Furnished with cogs; having cog-wheels.

C.-wheel breathing, rhythm (*Med.*): a jerky respiratory sound in chest-affections, as of a cogged wheel in motion.

Cogged (kǫgd), *ppl. a.*[2] 1589. [f. COG *v.*[3] + -ED.] 1. Corruptly influenced 1781. †2. Feigned in order to cheat -1656. ¶ 3. Of dice: Loaded. (A misuse.) 1806.

Cogger (kǫ·gəɹ). 1576. [f. as prec. + -ER.] A sharper; a false flatterer. So †**Co·ggery,** trickery; *concr.* a trick.

Coggle (kǫ·g'l), *sb.*[1] Now *dial.* ME. [perh. echoic.] A rounded water-worn stone; *esp.* a cobble. Hence **Co·ggly** *a.* shaky, unsteady when stepped on.

†**Coggle,** *sb.*[2] 1695. [app. an error.] A small boat.

Cogie, coggie (kō·gi). *Sc.* 1750. [f. COGUE.] A small wooden bowl or its contents.

Cogitable (kǫ·dʒităb'l), *a.* 1688. [ad. L. *cogitabilis.*] That can be thought or conceived; thinkable, conceivable. Also as *sb.*

Something not perceivable by sense, but only c. GROTE. Hence **Cogitabi·lity,** c. quality (*rare*).

Cogitabund (kǫ·dʒităbʊnd), *a.* 1649. [ad. L. *cogitabundus*, f. *cogitare.*] Meditative, deep in thought.

Co·gitant, *a. rare.* 1681. [ad. L. *cogitantem.*] Thinking.

Cogitate (kǫ·dʒiteit), *v.* 1563. [f. L. *cogitat-*, *cogitare* (app. contr. for *co-agitare*).] 1. *intr.* To think; to exercise the thinking faculties 1631. 2. *trans.* with object. Hence: To devise, plan 1563.

1. For he that calleth a thing into his mind, whether by impression or recordation, cogitateth and considereth, and he that employeth the faculty of his phansie also cogitateth, and he that reasoneth. tr. BACON. 2. To c. objects a priori, tr. KANT. To c. mischief (*mod.*).

Cogitation (kǫdʒitēi·ʃən). ME. [a. OF. *cogitaciun*, ad. L. *cogitationem.*] 1. The action or faculty of thinking. 2. (with *pl.*) A thought or reflection ME.; a design 1538.

1. What by c., wee find to be the cause of anything' HOBBES. 2. The cogitations and purposes of your adversaries FLEMING.

Cogitative (kǫ·dʒiteitiv), *a.* 1490. [a. F. *cogitatif, -ive.*] 1. Having the faculty of thought; thinking. 2. Given to cogitation 1651.

1. The cogitatiue or knowing soule 1594. Hence **Co·gitati·vity,** c. capacity (*rare*).

†**Co·gmen.** *rare.* ME. only. Men to whom the cloth called *cogware* was sold.

Cognac (ko·nyak). 1594. [F., place-name.] 1. *C. wine*: wine produced at Cognac. 2. A French brandy distilled from Cognac wine; any French brandy 1687.

Cognate (kǫ·gneit). 1645. [ad. L. *cognatus*, f. *co-* + *gnatus.*] A. *adj.* 1. Descended from a common ancestor; of the same family, coming from the same stock or root 1827. 2. *gen.* Akin in origin; allied in nature, and hence, akin in quality; having affinity. (Const. *with*, rarely *to.*) 1645.

1. C. tribes 1827. A c. language G. HIGGINS, word GLADSTONE. *C. accusative*: one of kindred sense or derivation; *spec.* one that may adverbially follow an intr. vb., as in 'to die the death'. 2. Geometry and the c. sciences JOWETT.

B. *sb.* 1. *Rom. Law.* One related by blood to another; a kinsman; *pl.* those descended from the same ancestor, whether through males or females. Hence, *Sc. Law.* A relative on the mother's side. 1754. 2. A cognate word, term, or thing 1865.

Hence **Cogna·teness,** c. quality. **Cogna·tic** *a.* pertaining to or reckoned through cognates.

Cognation (kǫgnēi·ʃən). ME. [ad. L. *cognationem*; see COGNATE.] 1. Relationship by descent from a common ancestor. In *Sc. Law*, Relationship through females only. 1751. †2. *collect.* Kindred, relations -1542. 3. *Philol.* Relationship by descent from a common source or a common root 1741. 4. Affinity, connexion, relation, likeness. (Now *rare* or *Obs.*) 1555.

1. The c. [of the Phenicians] with the Jews GALE. 3. The difference between c. and derivation 1862.

Cognition (kǫgni·ʃən). 1447. [ad. L. *cognitionem*, f. *cognit-*, *cognoscere*; see COGNOSCE.] 1. †The action or faculty of knowing; knowledge, consciousness -1796; a product of such an action 1819. 2. *Law.* = COGNIZANCE 3. (Chiefly *Sc.*) 1523. †3. Recognition. EVELYN.

1. I will not be my selfe, nor haue c. Of what I feele *Tr. & Cr.* v. ii. 63. Hence **Cogni·tional** *a.*

Cognitive (kǫ·gnitiv), *a.* 1586. [f. L. *cognit-*, see above, -IVE.] Of or pertaining to cognition; having the attribute of cognizing, as *c. powers.*

Cognizable, -isable (kǫ·gnizăb'l, kǫ·ni-), *a.* 1678. [f. COGNIZE + -ABLE. In sense 1, often (kǫgnəi·zăb'l).] 1. Capable of being known, perceived, or apprehended; perceptible; recognizable. 2. Capable of being, or liable to be, judicially tried; within the jurisdiction of a court of law, etc. 1681.

2. *Cognizable offence* (Anglo-Ind. Law): any offence for which a police-officer may arrest without warrant. Hence **Co·gnizabi·lity,** c. quality (*rare*). **Co·gnizably** *adv.* in a c. manner.

Cognizance, -sance (kǫ·gnizăns, kǫ·ni-). ME. [a. OF. *conis(s)ance, conus(s)ance*, var. of *conois(s)ance*, f. *conoissant, conoistre.* In legal use (kǫ·nizăns) is still usual.] 1. †Knowledge -1651; †recognition SPENSER; *esp.* knowledge as attained by observation or information; perception, notice, observation 1642. 2. *Law.* a. The hearing and trying of a cause. b. The right of dealing with any matter judicially; jurisdiction. Also *fig.* 1523. 3. Acknowledgement; admission of a fact alleged; *esp.* acknowledgement of a FINE. b. A plea in replevin that defendant holds the goods in the right of another as his bailiff. Cf. AVOWRY. 1570. 4. A device by which a person, company, etc., is distinguished, as a crest, etc.; a badge; *spec.* in *Her.* a device borne for distinction by all the retainers of a noble house. Also *fig.* ME.

1. The tree of cognizance of Good and Evill HOBBES. SPENSER *F. Q.* II. i. 31. Phrases. *To have c. of*; *to come* (*fall, be, lie*) *under, within, beyond, out of the c.*; *to take c. of.* 4. In the chief three mullets stood, The cognizance of Douglas Blood SCOTT. If generous honesty, valour, and plain dealing, be the c. of thy family SIR T. BROWNE.

Cognizant, -isant (kǫ·gnizănt, kǫ·ni-), *a.* 1820. [prob. f. COGNIZANCE, COGNIZE.] Having cognizance (see COGNIZANCE 1, 2); aware (*of*); *Philos.* that cognizes 1837.

Cognize, -ise (kǫgnəi·z), *v.* 1658. [After *cognizance*, etc., and *recognize.*] †1. *Law* (*absol.*) To take cognizance. 2. *trans.* To take cognizance of, notice, observe 1821. 3. *Philos.* To make (anything) an object of cognition 1836.

3. They first know—they first cognise, the things and persons presented to them SIR W. HAMILTON.

Cognizee, -isee (kǫgnizī·, kǫni-). 1531. [Correl. to COGNIZOR.] *Old Law.* The party in whose favour a fine of land was levied.

Cognizor, -isor (kǫ·gnizǭɹ, kǫ·ni-). 1531. [f. (ult.) *conois(s-*, *conoistre* to know; see CONNOISSEUR.] *Old Law.* The party who levies a fine of land.

‖**Cognomen** (kǫgnōu·men). 1809. [L.] 1. The third or family name of a Roman citizen, as Caius Julius *Cæsar*; also, an agnomen 1879. Hence, 2. A nickname 1811. 3. An (English) surname 1809. 4. *loosely.* Name, appellation. [So in L.] 1852. Hence **Cogno·minal** *a.* having the same c., of or pertaining to a c.; †*sb.* namesake. **Cogno·minally** *adv.*

Cognominate (kǫgnǫ·mineit), *v.* 1609. [f. L. *cognominat-*, *cognominare.*] To give a surname or nickname to; to name. Hence **Cognomina·tion,** the action of cognominating; *concr.* = COGNOMEN.

Cognosce (kǫgnǫ·s), *v.* Chiefly *Sc. Law.* 1583. [ad. L. *cognoscere.*] 1. *intr.* To make inquiry; to take cognizance of a cause, etc. 2. *trans.* To take judicial cognizance of; to investigate, try 1607. 3. Judicially to examine and pronounce to be of a certain status; *esp.*

(*ellipt.*) to pronounce to be an idiot or lunatic 1670. 4. = COGNIZE 1874.

3. 'If he gangs daft, we'll hae him cognosced' SCOTT. Hence **Cogno·scence**, = COGNIZANCE 1. **Cogno·scent** *a.* (*rare*), cognitive; cognizant. **Cognoscibi·lity**, knowableness. **Cogno·scible** *a.* capable of being known; *sb.* that which can be known. **Cogno·scitive** *a.* [non-etymological var. of COGNITIVE], apprehensive; **Cogno·scitively** *adv.*

‖**Cognoscente** (konʸoʃe·nte). Pl. **-ti** (-tī). 1778. [It.:—L. *cognoscentem.*] One who knows a subject thoroughly; a connoisseur.

‖**Cognovit** (kǫgnōᵘ·vit). 1762. [In full '*cognovit actionem*'.] *Law.* An acknowledgement by a defendant that the plaintiff's cause is just; whereupon judgement is entered without trial.

Co-gua·rdian. 1643. [Co-.] Joint guardian.

Cogue, cog (kōᵘg, *Sc.* kōg, kǫg). Chiefly *Sc.* 1568. [?] 1. (*Sc.*) A wooden pail. 2. A small cup, of wood; also †a cogueful 1690. Hence **Cogueful, cogful**, as much as a c. will hold.

†**Co·gware.** ME. A coarse cloth, resembling frieze, made of the poorest wool –1483.

Cog-wheel. ME. [See COG *sb.*²] A wheel with cogs or teeth; a gear-wheel.

Cog-wood. 1725. [f. COG *sb.*²] A timber-tree of Jamaica, *Laurus Chloroxylon.*

Cohabit (kohæ·bit), *v.* 1530. [a. F. *cohabiter*, ad. L. *cohabitare*; see HABIT.] 1. To dwell or live together (*with*) (*arch.*) 1601; *fig.* of things 1653. 2. To live together as husband and wife: often used *spec.* of persons not legally married 1530.

1. They were not able to c. with that Holy Thing [the Ark] SOUTH. *fig.* Peace, and patience, and a calm content did c. in the cheerful heart of Sir Henry Wotton WALTON. So **Coha·bitancy**, the state or fact of being a cohabitant (*rare*). **Coha·bitant**, one who dwells together with another or others. **Coha·biter** (*rare*) = *Cohabitant.*

Cohabitation (kohæbitēⁱ·ʃən). 1450. [a. F., ad. late L. *cohabitationem*; see COHABIT.] 1. Dwelling or living together; community of life (*arch.*) (or hyphened). Also *transf.* and *fig.* 2. Living together as husband and wife 1548.

2. For..holding correspondence and c. with one not his wife LUTTRELL.

Coheir (ko,ēᵊ·ɹ). 1532. [f. CO- + HEIR.] One who participates in an inheritance; a joint heir. Also *fig.* (See *Romans* viii. 17.)

Wint. T. II. i. 148. **Cohei·rship.** So **Cohei·ress.**

Cohere (kohīᵊ·ɹ), *v.* Also †**cohære.** 1598. [ad. L. *cohærere*, f. *co-* + *hærere* to stick.] 1. *intr.* To cleave or stick together; said of parts, and of the mass 1616; *transf.* of non-material things, etc. 1603. 2. To unite or remain united in action 1651. 3. To be congruous or consistent 1598; †to agree –1634.

1. The grains simply c. RUTLEY. The hard mass became fluid. It still cohered KINGLAKE. The moral principles by which society coheres LECKY. 3. *Twel. N.* v. i. 259. Hence **Cohe·rer**, *spec.* a detector of electric waves consisting of a glass cylinder containing metal filings which cohere when struck by a wave. **Cohe·ring** *ppl. a.*; in *Bot.* united externally to each other, as anthers, etc.

Coherence (kohīᵊ·rěns). Also †**cohærence.** 1580. [a. F. *cohérence*, ad. L. *cohærentia*; see COHERENT.] 1. *lit.* The action or fact of sticking together; cohesion 1613. Also *transf.* and *fig.* 2. Logical connexion; congruity, consistency 1588; †agreement –1680. 3. Harmonious connexion of the several parts of a discourse, system, etc., so that the whole hangs together 1623. †4. Context –1737.

1. *transf.* They have not enough of c. among themselves, nor of estimation with the publick BURKE. 3. The c. in dreams 1856. So **Cohe·rency**, the quality of being coherent.

Coherent (kohīᵊ·rěnt), *a.* (*sb.*) 1555. [a. F. *cohérent*, ad. L. *cohærentem.*] 1. That sticks or clings firmly together. Const. *to, with.* Said of parts and of the mass. 1578. Also *transf.* †2. Accordant logically or in sense; congruent –1601. 3. Of thought, speech, etc.: Of which all the parts are consistent, and hang together 1580. Also said of persons 1724. †4. *sb.* One who or that which coheres –1657.

1. *transf.* C. with this is a Third property of..love BARROW. 2. *All's Well* III. vii. 39. 3. Good C. Sense CUDWORTH. A c. story BURNET, thinker WATTS. Hence **Cohe·rently** *adv.*

Cohe·ritor. 1550. [See CO-.] = CO-HEIR.

†**Cohe·rt**, *v.* 1475. [? f. L. *coert-*, a form of the stem of *coercere.*] = COERCE –1543.

Cohesion (kohī·ʒən). Also †**cohæsion.** 1678. [a. F. *cohésion*, f. *cohæs-, cohærere.*] 1. The action or condition of cohering; *spec.* the force with which the molecules of a body cleave together; cf. ATTRACTION *of Cohesion.* 2. *Bot.* The superficial union of like organs 1835. 3. *transf.* Of non-material union 1690.

1. Water..loosens the c. of a steep bank GEIKIE. 3. Ideas that have no natural c. LOCKE.

Cohesive (kohī·siv), *a.* 1727. [f. L. *cohæs-*; see prec.] Having the property of cohering; characterized by cohesion.

Tracts of c. soil 1799. A soft c. mass SIR H. DAVY. To show how little c. force the league possessed S. AUSTIN. Hence **Cohe·sive-ly** *adv.*, **-ness.**

Cohibit (kohi·bit), *v.* Now *rare.* 1544. [f. L. *cohibit-, cohibere*, f. *co(m)-* + *habere*; cf. *adhibit*, etc.] To restrain, check; to restrict. So **Cohibi·tion**, restriction; stoppage.

†‖**Cohob.** [? root of next, or contr. of *cohobation.*] *Med.* A Paracelsian term meaning repetition.

Cohobate (kōᵘ·hobeⁱt), *v.* 1641. [See prec.] *Old Chem.* To subject to repeated distillation, by pouring a liquid back again and again upon the matter from which it has been distilled. Hence †**Cohoba·tion**, this operation.

Cohorn; see COEHORN.

Cohort (kōᵘ·hǫɹt), *sb.* 1489. [a. F. *cohorte*, ad. L. *cohortem* (*cohors*), f. *co-* + *hort-*, found also in *hortus*; see GARDEN. Hence also F. *court*, Eng. COURT.] 1. *Rom. Antiq.* A body of from 300 to 600 infantry; the tenth part of a legion. 2. *transf.* A band of warriors 1500. 3. *fig.* A company, band 1719. 4. *Zool.* and *Bot.* A large group superior to a natural order; in *Bot.* = ALLIANCE 1845.

2. The C. bright Of watchfull Cherubim MILT. *P. L.* XI. 127. 3. The c. of the Fathers Who kept the Faith below NEALE.

Cohortation (kōᵘhǫɹtēⁱ·ʃən). *arch.* 1642. [ad. L. *cohortationem.*] Exhortation. So **Coho·rtative** *a.* (*sb.*) pertaining to c.: in *Heb. Grammar*, the future paragogic.

Cohosh (kohǫ·ʃ). 1796. [The Indian name.] Name of N. American plants which have been used medicinally. **Black c.**, *Cimicifuga racemosa.* **Blue c.**, *Caulophyllum thalictroides.* **Red c.**, *Actæa spicata.* **White c.**, *Actæa alba.*

Cohow, cahow, cohoo (kəhū·). 1615. [From its cry.] A bird of the Bermudas, a species of Shearwater, now nearly exterminated.

‖**Cohune** (kohū·n). 1805. A species of palm (*Attalea Cohune*) found in Honduras.

Coif (koif), *sb.* [ME. *coyfe*, a. OF. *coife*, *coiffe*:—late L. **cuffia*, supposed to represent an OHG. **kupphja*, deriv. of OHG. *chuppha*, MHG. *kupfe* cap.] 1. A close-fitting cap covering the top, back, and sides of the head, worn by both sexes. †2. An ecclesiastical head-dress –1574. 3. A white cap formerly worn by lawyers; *esp.* that worn by a serjeant-at-law as part of his official dress ME. Hence, The position or order of serjeant-at-law 1522. 4. The skull-cap of a helmet. Now *Hist.* ME. 5. The calyptra of mosses 1882.

1. The c.—the apron—the blue-checked gown, were all those of old Ailie SCOTT. 3. A linnen Coife..an ornament which onely Sergeants at Law doe weare HOOKER. A Brother of the C. ADDISON.

Coif (koif), *v.* Pa. t. and pple. **coifed.** 1530. [orig. ad. OF. *coifer, coiffer*; but latterly from COIF; cf. *to cap*, etc.] 1. To cover with, or as with, a coif; to invest with the serjeant's coif. 2. To dress (the hair). Cf. *coiffure.* 1862.

1. There be in these times that are coif'd with such Opinions, that to shew Scripture to be Reason, is to make it lose weight with them J. HARRINGTON.

‖**Coiffeur, -euse** (kwa-). 1858. [Fr.: see prec.]. A male, female hairdresser.

‖**Coiffure** (kwafüˑr). 1631. [f. as prec.] A fashion of dressing the hair; head-dress.

Coign (koin), *sb.* Also **coigne.** 1605. [archaic form of COIN, QUOIN, q.v.] 1. A projecting corner. 2. *Occas.* a. A corner-stone 1843. b. A wedge (in *Printing*, etc.) 1755.

Coign of vantage: a position affording facility for observation or action. *Macb.* I. vi. 7.

Coigne, coigny (*Irish Hist.*); see COYNYE.

†**Coil**, *v.*¹ ME. [a. OF. *coillir*, now *cueillir* :—L. *colligere.*] = CULL *v.*¹ –1800.

†**Coil**, *v.*² Also **coyle.** 1530. [?] To beat, thrash –1590.

Coil (koil), *v.*³ 1611. [? f. as COIL *v.*¹] 1. To lay up (a cable, etc.) in concentric rings. Const. with *up.* 2. To enwrap within coils 1616. 3. To twist in or into a circular, spiral, or winding shape; to wind round. Also *refl.* 1664. 4. *intr.* (for *refl.*) To throw oneself into a spiral or winding form; often with *round* 1798. 5. To move in a spiral or winding course 1816.

3. Quoil'd in Dust like Snake or Adder 1711. 4. Convolvuluses That coil'd around the stems TENNYSON.

Coil (koil), *sb.*¹ *arch.* or *dial.* 1567. [? orig. slang; cf. *pother, row*, etc. Said, without evidence, to be Gael.] 1. Noisy disturbance, row. 2. Clutter, rattle 1582. 3. Fuss, ado; a 'business' 1593.

3. *To keep a c.*: to make or keep up a disturbance. *Mortal c.*: the bustle of this mortal life SHAKS.

Coil (koil), *sb.*² 1627. [Goes with COIL *v.*³, q.v.] 1. *orig.* (*Naut.*) A length of cable, rope, etc., when coiled; hence, the whole quantity coiled. 2. A series of concentric rings in which a body has been disposed 1661. 3. A single complete turn of any coiled body 1805. 4. An arrangement of a wire, sheet metal, etc., in windings 1826. 5. In gun-making: A bar of wrought iron coiled and welded into a tube 1859.

2. A Snake..lying round in a C. 1723. High-looped coils on the top of the head 1888. 4. The induction-c...a primary c. of thick wire and few convolutions SPOTTISWOODE. Coils of hot-water pipes 1869.

Coil (koil), *sb.*³ *n.* and *midl.* 1800. [Cf. COIL *v.*¹] A cock of hay.

Coillen, -on, obs. ff. CULLION.

Coin (koin), *sb.* ME. [a. F. *coin* wedge, corner, die:—L. *cuneum* (*-us*). See also QUOIN, COIGN.] 1. A corner-stone; also, a wedge-shaped stone of an arch. Now usu. QUOIN. †2. *gen.* A corner, angle –1658. †3. A wedge –1779. †4. A die (? wedge-shaped), for stamping money; the device stamped upon money –1682. 5. A piece of metal of definite weight and value, stamped with an officially authorized device; a piece of money ME. 6. (without *pl.*) Coined money; specie, money ME. Also *fig.*

1. *Cor.* v. iv. 1. 5. A coyne that bears the figure of an Angell *Merch. V.* II. vii. 56. 6. A faire tongue with a foule heart is false quoyne 1569. To pay a slanderer in his own c. 1713. *Comb.* **c.-balance**, a delicate balance for weighing gold coins.

Coin (koin), *v.*¹ ME. [a. OF. *coignier, cungner*, f. *coin* COIN.] 1. To make (money) by stamping metal. Also *transf.* and *fig.* 2. To make (metal) into money by stamping pieces of definite weight and value with authorized marks ME. *intr.* (for *refl.*) 1700. Also *fig.* 3. *fig.* (from 1.) To make, devise, produce; *esp.* in a bad sense 1561.

1. The kynge caused, in siluer, the halfe-peny to be coygned FABYAN. *To c. money* (mod. colloq.): to gain it rapidly and with ease. 2. Tin was coined by Charles II, in 1684 CRUMP. 3. Let them coyne his Nose 1 *Hen. IV*, III. iii. 90. To c. a smile GREENE, a lie 1780, a word DRYDEN. Hence **Coi·nable** *a.* that may be coined (*lit.* and *fig.*). **Coi·ner**, one who coins (*esp.* false) money; *fig.* a fabricator.

Coin (koin), *v.*² 1488. [f. as prec. Now usually COIGN.] To furnish with quoins, wedges, or corner-stones.

Coinage (koi·nėdʒ). ME. [a. OF. *coignaige.*] 1. The action or process of coining money. 2. *concr.* Coins collectively; a system of coins in use; the currency 1467. 3. *fig.* The formation or fabrication of something new or specious 1693. 4. *concr.* That which is formed or fabricated. (Often disparaging.) 1602.

2. The bronze c. (*mod.*). 3. The right of c. of Political Lyes SWIFT. Words of modern c. FREEMAN. 4. This is the very coynage of your Braine SHAKS.

Coincide (kōᵘ,insəi·d), *v.* 1715. [a. F. *coïncider*, ad. med.L. *coincidere* (also used in 17th c.), f. *co-* + *incidere.*] 1. *intr.* To occupy the same portion of space (as *e.g.* the superposed triangles in Euclid I. 8); to be identical in position and area. 2. To occur at the same time; to occupy the same space of time 1809. 3. To be identical; to agree exactly *with* 1722. 4. To concur (in opinion, etc.) 1734.

1. If the equator and eclиptick had coincided CHEYNE. 2. The chief feast of the year..coincides with the Festival of the vintage STANLEY. 3. His interest happily coincided with his duty FREEMAN. 4. To c. in a doctrine LYELL. Hence **Co,inci·der** (*rare*).

Coincidence (ko,i·nsidĕns). 1605. [a. F.; see COINCIDENT and -ENCE.] 1. The fact or condition of being coincident 1626. Also *fig.* and *transf.* (with *pl.*) A case of coincidence 1837. 2. Occurrence or existence at the same time 1650. 3. Exact correspondence in substance, nature, character, etc. 1605. (with *pl.*) An instance of this 1661. 4. Concurrence (in opinion or sentiment) 1795. †5. Blending 1645.

1. The c. of planes CHEYNE, points 1870. 2. There might be a casuall c. of this feast and his presence at Jerusalem FULLER. A 'strange c.' BYRON. 3. Evidence arising from various coincidences BUTLER. So †**Co,i·ncidency**, c. quality or state.

Coincident (ko,i·nsidĕnt), *a.* 1563. [a. F. *coïncident*, ad. med.L. **coincidentem*; see COINCIDE.] Occupying the same place 1656; exactly contemporaneous 1598; in exact agreement, wholly consonant *with* 1563. Also as †*sb.*

Duty and interest are perfectly c. BUTLER. Hence **Co,incide·ntal** *a.*; -ly *adv.* **Co,i·ncidently** *adv.*

†**Co,i·ndicate**, *v.* 1623. [f. CO- + INDICATE.] To indicate conjointly; *spec.* in *Med.* to furnish coindicant symptoms. So †**Co,i·ndicant** *a.* (*sb.*).

Co,indica·tion. 1623. [f. CO- + INDICATION.] Conjoint or concurrent indication; a concurrent sign.

Co-i·nfinite, *a.* 1654. [See CO-.] Equally infinite with another or others; conjointly infinite.

†**Co-inha·bit**, *v.* 1624. [See CO-.] *intr.* To dwell together. So **Co-inhabitant**; †**Co-inhabitor.**

Co-inhere (kōu,inhīᵊ·ɹ), *v.* 1836. [See CO-.] *intr.* To inhere together. So **Co-inhe·rence.**

Co-inhe·ritor. 1526. [See CO-.] A joint heir. So **Co-inhe·ritance.**

†**Co,i·nquinate**, *v.* 1528. [ad. L. *coinquinat-*, *coinquinare.*] To soil all over, pollute, defile (*lit.* and *fig.*) –1652. So †**Co,inquina·tion.**

Coinstantaneous (ko,instăntē·niəs), *a.* 1768. [See CO-.] Occurring or existing at the same instant. var. †**Co,instanta·nean.**

Cointense (ko,inte·ns), *a.* 1855. [See CO-.] Conjoined or equal in intensity. Hence **Cointe·nsion.**

Coir (koiᵊɹ). 1582. [ad. Malayālam *kāyar* cord.] The prepared fibre of the husk of the coco-nut, used for making ropes, cordage, matting, etc. Orig. the cordage made of this fibre. Also *attrib.*

Coistrel. ? *Obs.* 1577. [var. of CUSTREL, q. v.] 1. A groom or servant in charge of the horses of a knight. 2. A term of reproach or contempt: Knave, base fellow, low varlet 1581.

Coit, coite, obs. ff. QUOIT.

Coition (ko,i·ʃən). 1541. [ad. L. *coitionem*, f. *coit-*, *coire.*] †1. Going or coming together; conjunction –1761. 2. Sexual conjunction, copulation 1615. Also *transf.* and *fig.* vars. †**Co·it**, ‖**Co·itus** (in sense 2).

†**Cojoin**, obs. var. of CONJOIN *v.*

Cojuror. 1735. [See CO-.] One who takes an oath along with, or in confirmation of, another.

Coke (kōuk), *sb.* 1669. [? = COLK *sb.* (also spelt *coke*), a core.] Mineral coal deprived by dry distillation of its volatile constituents.

Coke (kōuk), *v.* 1804. [f. prec. sb.] To convert into coke. Also *intr.* (for *refl.*).

Coker, obs. f. COCO.

†**Cokes.** 1567. [? related to *cockenay* COCKNEY.] A silly fellow, ninny, simpleton –1690.

Cokewold, Cokil(le, obs. ff. CUCKOLD, COCKLE.

‖**Col** (kol). 1853. [Fr. :–L. *collum* neck.] A depression in the summit-line of a mountain chain, generally forming a pass.

Col-, form of the prefix COM- bef. *l.* See COM-.

Cola (kōu·lă). 1795. [*Kola*, etc., in Negro langs. of W. Africa.] A genus of trees, N.O. *Sterculiaceæ*, natives of western tropical Africa; esp. *C. acuminata.*

Comb. **c.-nut, -seed**, the seed, brownish and bitter, of *C. acuminata*, largely used for chewing.

Cola, pl. of COLON.

Co-la·bourer. 1859. [See CO-.] Fellow-labourer.

†**Co·lament.** [f. L. *colare* to strain.] Product of straining. SIR T. BROWNE.

Colander, cullender (kɒ·lĕndəɹ). 1450. [= med.L. *colatorium*, f. *colare* to strain. The form of the Eng. word is not explained.] A vessel, usually of metal, closely perforated at the bottom with small holes, and used as a drainer in cookery. Also *transf.* and *fig.* 2. A similar vessel used in the casting of shot 1875. Hence as *vb.*, to strain, to perforate with holes.

†**Co·laphize**, *v.* 1450. [f. (ult.) Gr. κόλαφος.] To buffet –1656.

Cola·tion. 1612. [f. L. *colare* to strain.] The action of passing through a strainer. ? *Obs.*

Co-la·titude. 1790. [See CO-.] *Astron.* The complement of the latitude, *i. e.* the difference between it and 90 degrees.

Co·lature. ? *Obs.* 1548. [ad. late L. *colatura*, f. *colare* to strain.] 1. Colation 1657. 2. The product of straining 1601. 3. A strainer (also called *colatory*) 1548.

†**Colbertine.** Also **-een.** 1685. [f. *Colbert*, French proper name.] 'A kind of open lace with a square ground' –1851.

[She] Scarce knows what difference is between Rich Flanders lace and Colberteen SWIFT.

Colchicine (kǫ·lkisəin), also **Colchicia** (kǫlki·ʃia). 1853. [f. COLCHICUM + -INE.] *Chem.* An organic alkaloid, $C_{17}H_{19}NO_5$, found in all parts of the *Colchicum autumnale.*

‖**Colchicum** (kǫ·lkikɒ̆m, *vulg.* kǫ·ltʃikɒ̆m). 1597. [L., a. Gr. κολχικόν meadow-saffron, neut. of κολχικός of Colchis. The name has reference to the poisonous arts of Medea.] 1. *Bot.* A genus of liliaceous plants, the best-known species of which is *C. autumnale*, the Meadow-saffron. 2. A medicine containing the active principle of this plant, used in gout and rheumatic affections 1791.

Colcothar (kǫ·lkoþəɹ). 1605. [ad. Arab. *qolqotār.*] A brownish red peroxide of iron obtained from iron sulphate. Called also *rouge*, and *Crocus Martis.*

Cold (kōuld), *a.* [OE. Anglian *cald* (WSax. *ceald*) :–OTeut. **kaldo·-z*, from OTeut. vb.-stem *kal-* to be cold, cogn. w. L. *gel-* in *gelu.* See also CHILL, COOL, etc.] I. *lit.* 1. Of a temperature sensibly lower than that of the living human body. Comp. *colder, coldest.* 2. Of a relatively low temperature; not heated ME. 3. Feeling cold. (Usu. in predicate.) 1570. 4. Of soil: Slow to absorb heat ME.

1. I'th c. wind *All's Well* I. i. 115. A thrust of c. iron SMOLLETT. I would Thy toung were coold J. HEYWOOD. 2. *C. bath, bathing*: a bath in unheated water. C. chicken 1883. 3. When I am c., he heates me with beating *Com. Err.* IV. iv. 33. 4. Clay soils are c. 1877.

II. *fig.* †1. In ME. physiology applied (with *hot, dry, moist*) to the 'complexion' of things –1732; the opposite of pungent –1614. 2. Void of warmth, or intensity of feeling; indifferent, apathetic ME.; †free from passion, cool 1794; cold-blooded 1849. 3. Not cordial or friendly 1557. 4. Gloomy, dispiriting ME. 5. Felt as cold, chilling ME. 6. Without power to move; stale 1705. 7. *Hunting.* Of scent: Not strong, faint; weak 1592. 8. *Painting.* Applied to blue and grey, and tints akin to these 1706.

2. The c. charities of man to man CRABBE. A c. forgery PALEY. C. chastity SHAKS. The too c. calculation of our powers RUSKIN. 3. A c. welcome 1703. C. looks 1833. 4. A c. misgiving and a killing dread COWPER. 5. C. comfort J. H. NEWMAN. 6. The jest grows c....when it comes on in a second scene ADDISON. 7. At a c. sent *Twel. N.* II. v. 134.

Comb.: **c. abscess** [F. *abscès froid*], an abscess formed without the first three of the Celsian symptoms of inflammation (pain, redness, heat, and swelling); **c. bed** *Gardening*, opp. to HOT-BED; so *c. frame*; **c. blast**, air forced into a furnace unheated; **c. chisel**, a strong chisel of iron or steel highly tempered, so as to cut cold iron; **c. feet** *slang*, fear, funk; **c. war**, a state of hostility consisting in threats, obstruction, propaganda, etc., without physical violence; **c. without** (*colloq.*), spirits and cold water without sugar. Hence **Co·ldly** *adv.* **Co·ldness.**

Cold (kōuld), *sb.* [OE. *cald, ceald* neut., the adj. used subst.] 1. The opposite or the absence of heat; coldness. (Usually spoken of as a positive agent.) ME. 2. The sensation produced by loss of heat from the body, or by exposure to a lower temperature ME. Also *fig.* 3. An indisposition of the body caused by exposure to cold; *esp.* catarrh ME.

1. Heat and C. are Natures two hands, whereby she chiefly worketh BACON. 15 *degrees of c.* = 15 degrees below the freezing-point of water (32° Fahr.). Phr. *To be left out in the c.*, i.e. neglected. 3. I haue taken colde... This wounde on your heed hath caught ouermoche colde MALORY.

†**Cold**, *v.* [OE. **caldian, cealdian*, f. *cald, ceald*, COLD *a.*] To make or become cold; also *fig.* –1598.

Cold blood. 1608. [See COLD *a.* II. 1.] In *in c. blood*: Without excitement; with cool deliberation.

A resolution framed in c. blood SIR F. VERE. Killing in c. blood ADDISON.

Cold-blooded, *a.* 1595. [f. prec. + -ED.] 1. Having the blood (physically) cold, or not warmer than the external air or water: said *esp.* of fishes and reptiles 1602. 2. Without excitement or sensibility, callous; deliberately cruel 1595.

2. Cold-blooded malice MACAULAY, crime 1882.

Cold-finch. 1676. *Ornith.* The Pied Fly-catcher.

Co·ld-hea·rted, *a.* 1606. [f. *cold heart* + -ED[2].] Wanting in sensibility or natural affection; unkind. Hence **Cold-hea·rtedness.**

Co·ld-short, *a.* 1601. [Cf. Sw. *kallskör*; the second element *skör*, brittle, pronounced ʃör, gave (ult.) the Eng. *-short*, as in *short-bread.* Cf. RED-SHORT.] Of iron: Brittle when cold.

Cold shoulder. 1816. Used *fig.*, chiefly in *to show the cold shoulder*, 'to appear cold and reserved'. Hence **Cold-shoulder** *v.* to treat with coldness or contemptuous neglect.

Cole[1] (kōul). Now *rare.* [OE. *cāwel*, ME. *col, cole*, f. L. *caulis.*] 1. A name for various species of *Brassica*; now *esp.* Rape (*B. Napus*); also applied to Sea-kale. †2. Pottage; = KALE or *kail* –1674.

†**Cole**[2]. ME [?] 1. ? Jugglery –1564. 2. A sharper (at dice) 1532.

Cole[3] (kōul). *Cant.* 1673. [? slang use of *cole* = COAL.] Money.

To post the c.: to pay down the money.

Cole·ctomy. 1882. [f. Gr. κόλον + ἐκτομή.] *Surg.* Excision of part of the colon.

Cole-goose; see *coal-goose*, s.v. COAL.

Colemanite (kōu·lmănəit). 1884. [f. W. T. *Coleman.*] *Min.* A hydrous borate of calcium, found in California.

Colemouse, var. of COALMOUSE.

Coleopter (kǫli,ǫ·ptəɹ). 1860. [See next.] One of the Coleoptera.

Coleoptera (kǫli,ǫ·ptĕră), *sb. pl.* In sing. coleopteron (*rare*); see also prec. 1763. [mod. L., a. Gr. κολεόπτερος (f. κολεός sheath + πτερόν wing) + -OUS.] *Zool.* An order of insects having the anterior pair of wings converted into elytra or hard sheaths which cover the other pair when not in use; the Beetles. (See BEETLE *sb.*[2]) Formerly, the elytra of beetles. 1826. Hence **Coleo·pteral, Coleo·pterous** *adjs.* belonging or relating to the C. **Coleo·pteran** *sb.* one of the C. **Coleo·pterist**, one who studies the C. **Coleo·pteroid** *a.* like the C. var. **Coleo·ptra.**

‖**Coleorhiza** (kǫ·liorəi·ză). 1866. [f. Gr. κολεός sheath + ῥίζα root.] *Bot.* The root-sheath in the embryo of grasses, etc.

†**Cole-prophet.** Also, later, **cold(e prophet.** 1532. [App. f. COLE *sb.*[2] *Cold* is due to pop. etym.] A wizard, diviner, necromancer, fortune-teller –1614.

Colera, obs. f. CHOLERA (in sense *choler*).

Cole-rake, colrake. ME. [? f. *col, cole*, COAL + RAKE.] An instrument for raking ashes, etc., out of an oven or furnace.

Coleseed (kōu·lsīd). 1670. [f. COLE *sb.*[1] + SEED; see also COLZA.] The seed of *Brassica campestris* or *Napus*, var. *oleifera*; also the plant.

Cole-slaw (kōu·l,slǭ). *U.S.* 1862. [a. Du. *koolsla* = *kool-salade*, f. *kool* cabbage + *salade.*] Sliced cabbage dressed as a salad.

Co-lessee, co-lessor; see CO-.

Cole-staff, var. of COWL-STAFF.

†**Co·let.** ME. [Short f. ACOLYTE.] = ACOLYTE –1765.

Cole-tit, var. of COAL-TIT.

‖**Coleus** (kōu·liɒ̆s). 1885. [mod.L., f. Gr. κολεός sheath, so called from the union of the filaments.] *Bot.* A genus of Labiate plants, allied to the Mints.

Colewort (kōu·lwɒɹt). *arch.* ME. [See COLE *sb.*[1]] 1. Orig., any plant of the cabbage kind, genus *Brassica.* 2. Later, *esp.* kale, greens, etc., which do not heart, or cabbage-plants before they heart 1683.

Coleworts twice sodden: stale news.

†**Co·lfox, colefox.** ME. only. [f. *col* COAL + FOX = *coal-fox*, as in *cole-tit*, etc.] The BRANT-FOX, a variety with much black in its fur.

†**Colia·nder.** [OE. *cellendre*, ME. *coliaundre*, repr. pop. L. *coliandrum*=L. *coriandrum.*] = CORIANDER, q. v. -1614.

‖**Colibri** (kǫ·libri). 1740. [orig. Carib.] A kind of humming-bird.

Colic (kǫ·lik). ME. [a. F. *colique*, ad. L., a. Gr. κολικός, pertaining to the κόλον (or κῶλον). First found as a sb. repr. med. L. *colica* (*passio*).]

A. *sb.* A name for severe paroxysmal griping pains in the belly, due to affections of the bowel or other parts; also for the affections themselves.

The colike..ingendreth in a gutte named colon 1528. *Comb.* **c.-root,** a name for *Aletris farinosa, Dioscorea villosa*, and *Liatris squarrosa.*

B. *adj.* 1. Of or pertaining to the colon, as in *c. arteries* 1615. 2. Affecting the colon; of, or of the nature of, colic; in *c. passion*=COLIC A., *c. pains*, etc. 1586. Hence **Co·lical** *a.* of, pertaining to, or of the nature of, c.; subject to c. **Co·licky** *a.* colical; tending to produce c.

Colies (kōu·liz), *sb. pl.* 1847. [f. mod.L. *colius*, ad. Gr. κολιός a kind of woodpecker.] *Ornith.* The *Colidæ*, a family of African birds.

Colin (kǫ·lin). 1678. [Erron. form of Mex. *çolin.*] The American quail; also called *bob-white.*

Coliseum, var. of COLOSSEUM.

‖**Colitis** (kǫlai·tis). 1860. [mod.L., f. COLON.] *Med.* Inflammation of the colon.

Colk. Now *dial.* ME. [?] The core of an apple, etc., of a horn, heart of wood, or the like.

†**Coll,** *v.*[1] ME. [? a. F. *coler* = *accoler*, f. *col* :—L. *collum* neck.] To embrace, hug.

Coll, *v.*[2] Now *Sc.* 1483. [?] To poll, cut off the hair of, clip, cut close.

Collaborate (kǫlæ·bŏreit), *v.* 1871. [f. L. *collaborare.*] To co-operate; *esp.* in literary, artistic, or scientific work. Hence **Colla:bora·tion. Colla·borator,** one who works in conjunction with another or others.

‖**Collaborateur** (kolaboratör). 1801. [Fr.; see prec.] = *Collaborator.*

Collagen (kǫ·lădʒen). 1865. [ad. F. *collagène*, f. Gr. κόλλα glue + *-gène* = -GEN 'producing'.] *Biol.* That constituent of connective tissue which yields gelatin on boiling. Hence **Collage·nic, Colla·genous** *adjs.* of the nature of, or containing c.

Collapse (kǫlæ·ps), *sb.* 1801. [ad. medical L. *collapsus*; see next.] 1. The action of collapsing (see COLLAPSE *v.*). Originally a term of physiology. 1833. 2. *Med.* The sudden loss of vital properties and consequent general or local prostration under exhaustion or disease 1808. 3. Failure, break-down (of an institution, enterprise, etc.) 1856.

Collapse (kǫlæ·ps), *v.* 1732. [f. L. *collaps-*, *collabi*, f. *col-* + *labi*, *laps-* to fall. The ppl. adj. *collapsed* is found in 1609.] 1. *intr.* To fall together, as the sides of a body, or the body itself, by external pressure or withdrawal of the contents; to break down, fall in; to shrink together suddenly, contract. 2. *transf.* and *fig.* To break down, come to nothing, fail; to lose force suddenly 1801.

1. The sides of the canals c. ARBUTHNOT. The air suddenly collapsed to a fraction of its original dimensions TYNDALL. The extensive warehouse..collapsed 1888. 2. The present agitation would c. 1887. Hence **Colla·psed** *ppl. a.*; †*spec.* lapsed, fallen (used in 17th c. of 'perverts' to the Church of Rome). **Colla·psible, -able** *a.* capable of collapsing; made to fold together. †**Colla·psion,** the action of collapsing (*lit.* and *fig.*); a collapsed condition.

Collar (kǫ·lăɹ), *sb.* [ME. *coler*, a. AF. *coler* = OF. *colier* (mod. *collier*) :—L. *collare*, f. *collum* neck.]

I. 1. Something worn or placed about the neck; now *esp.* the band of linen, muslin, lace, etc. worn as a finish to the upper part of the ordinary dress of men and women. 2. *spec.* The ornamental chain which forms part of the insignia of orders of knighthood 1488. 3. A leather-covered roll fitted round the neck of a draught animal, forming that part of the harness through which the power of drawing is directly exerted; in *breast collar*, applied to parts of the breast harness serving the same purpose ME.

1. The coler of his haubrek 1450. Collars of golde HULOET, of Pearl 1642. A grehownd colere 1475. Yeomen of the c. 1530. 2. A c. of the garter 1577. *Collar of SS., S's*, or *Esses*: a chain consisting of a series of S's; originally a badge of the House of Lancaster. 3. A tedious and stiff pull against the c. (*mod.*). Phr. †*To slip* (*the*) *c.*: to escape. *Out of* (or *in*) *c.*: out of (or in) regular employment.

II. Transf. and techn. 1. An encompassing or restraining band or strap 1507. 2. *Mech.* A ring, circle, flange, or perforated disk, surrounding a rod, shaft, pipe, etc., for restraining lateral motion; forming a steam-, or water-tight joint, and the like; a short piece of pipe serving as a connexion between two pipes, etc. 1703. b. *Coining.* A metal ring, which prevents the blank from spreading when stamped 1826. 3. *Naut.* a. 'A rope formed into a wreath, with a dead-eye seized in the bight, to which the stay is confined at the lower part'. b. 'An eye in the end or bight of a shroud or stay to go over the mast-head' (Smyth). 1626. 4. *Mining.* The timbering round a shaft's mouth 1849. 5. *Arch.* a. = COLLARINO 1727. b. Short for *collar-beam* 1856. 6. *Zool.* A band of a distinct colour or texture round the neck of an animal 1664. In Molluscs: A thickened muscular and glandular border of the mantle 1847. 7. *Bot.* a. 'The ring upon the stipe of an agaric'. b. 'The point of junction between the radicle and the plumule'. 1866. 8. †a. The neck-piece (of brawn). b. A piece of meat, a fish, etc., tied up in a roll. 1610.

Comb: **c.-beam,** a horizontal beam connecting a pair of rafters, which prevents them from sagging; **-day,** a day on which Knights wear the c. of their Order, when taking part in any court ceremony; **-gall,** a wound produced (on a horse) by the rubbing of the c.; **-like** *a.*; **-proud** *a.* (*dial.*) restive when in harness; **-work,** work in which a horse strains hard against the c.; severe work.

Hence **Co·llarless** *a.* without a c.

Collar (kǫ·lăɹ), *v.* 1555. [f. prec. sb.] 1. To put a collar on; to surround as with a collar 1601. 2. To seize by the collar; loosely: To capture 1613. 3. *slang.* To appropriate, master 1700. 4. *Cookery.* To roll up (meat, etc.) and tie it with a string; also, to cut up and press into a roll 1670.

Co·llar-bone. 15.. *Anat.* The CLAVICLE.

Collard (kǫ·lăɹd). *dial.* and *U.S.* 1755. [corrupt f. *col'ort*, *colewort.*] A variety of cabbage which does not heart; = COLEWORT 2.

Collared (kǫ·lăɹd), *ppl. a.* ME. [f. COLLAR *sb.* and *v.*] 1. Wearing a collar (round the neck); in *Her.* 1681. 2. Furnished or fitted with or as with a collar 1650. 3. See COLLAR *v.* 4. 1681.

1. The c. knights MRS. BROWNING. 2. A coat c. with velvet 1823. The c. turtle-dove 1865. 3. *C. pork, head*, etc.

Collarette, -et (kǫlăre·t). 1690. [ad. F. *collerette* (also used), dim. of *collier* COLLAR.] A small collar; a collar of linen, lace, etc.

‖**Collarino** (kǫlărī·no). 1688. [It., dim. of *collare* COLLAR.] *Arch.* 1. The astragal of a column. 2. The neck of a column 1715.

Collate (kǫlēi·t), *v.* 1558. [f. L. *collat-*, *conferre* to CONFER.] 1. To put or bring together 1678. 2. To compare 1612; *esp.* to compare critically (a copy of a text) *with* other copies or *with* the original, in order to correct and emend it 1658. 3. *Printing* and *Bookbinding.* To examine the sheets of a printed book, so as to verify their number and order 1770. †4. To bestow *on*, *upon*; to give *to* -1717. 5. *Eccles.* †To confer (a benefice) *on* -1670; to institute (a cleric) *to* a benefice (now said of an ordinary who has the benefice in his own gift) 1647. *absol.* To appoint to a benefice 1606.

2. I collated such copies as I could procure JOHNSON. 5. *absol.* If the Bishop does not c. in half a year more, it [the Living] lapses to the Archbishop 1708. Hence **Colla·table** *a.* that may be collated. **Colla·ted** *ppl. a.* compared; conferred.

Collateral (kǫlæ·tĕrăl). ME. [ad. med.L. *collateralis*, f. L. *col-* + *later-*, *latus*; cf. *lateral.*]

A. *adj.* 1. Situated or running side by side, parallel 1450. Const. *to* 1833. 2. *fig.* Attendant, concomitant ME.; †co-ordinate -1656; corresponding 1653. 3. Lying aside from the main subject, action, issue, etc.; side-; subordinate, indirect ME. Const. *to* 1614. 4. Descended from the same stock, but in a different line; pertaining to those so descended. Opp. to *lineal.* ME. Also *transf.* and *fig.* 5. *Law.* (See quots.)

1. From his radiant seat he rose Of high c. glory MILT. *P. L.* x. 86. *C. circulation* (Phys.): 'circulation carried on through lateral or secondary channels after stoppage or obstruction in the main vessels' (*Syd. Soc. Lex.*). 2. We mistake..a c. effect for a cause HUME. 4. *C. ancestor*: a brother or sister of a lineal ancestor. 5. *C. assurance*, assurance made over and above the principal deed; *c. security*, any property or right of action, given as additional to the obligation of a contract or the like; so *c. bond, surety. C. issue*, where a criminal convict pleads any matter allowed by law, in bar of execution, as pregnancy, etc.

B. *sb.* †1. A colleague, an assessor -1726. †2. An equal in rank -1660. 3. An accompanying circumstance (*rare*) 1635. 4. A collateral kinsman 1691. 5. Anything given as collateral security 1887. Hence **Colla:tera·lity** (*rare*), c. quality or position. **Colla·terally** *adv.* in a c. manner or position (*lit.* and *fig.*).

Collation (kǫlēi·ʃən), *sb.* ME. [a. OF., ad. L. *collationem*; see COLLATE.]

I. †1. A bringing together or collection, *esp.* of money; a contribution -1725. b. *Roman* and *Scotch Law.* The bringing together of the possessions of several persons, in order to an equal division of the whole; hotch-pot; L. *collatio bonorum* 1828. 2. Comparison ME. 3. *esp.* Textual or critical comparison of documents, manuscripts, or editions 1532; also, the recorded result of such comparison 1699. 4. *Printing*, etc. The action of collating the sheets or quires of a book or MS. 1834.

1. '*C. of seals* (in ancient Deeds), when one Seal was set on the Back of another, upon the same Ribbon or Label' KERSEY.

II. †1. A (private or informal) conference -1666; a discourse; a treatise -1655. 2. The title of Cassian's *Collationes Patrum* ME. 3. The reading from the *Collationes* instituted by St. Benedict in his monasteries before compline ME. 4. The light repast taken after this reading. 5. Hence, A light repast (often 'a cold collation') 1525.

5. Come to the Hope about one and there .. had a collacion of anchovies, gammon, etc. PEPYS.

III. †1. Conferring or bestowal -1775. 2. *Eccles.* a. The bestowal *of* a benefice upon a clergyman. b. (more usually) The appointment of a clergyman to a benefice; now *techn.* Institution by the ordinary to a living which is in his own gift. ME. c. Right of institution 1480.

1. The indiscriminate c. of degrees JOHNSON.

Hence †**Colla·tion** *v.* to COLLATE; to partake of, or entertain with, a c. †**Colla·tioner,** a collator; one who partakes of a c.

Collatitious (kǫlăti·ʃəs), *a.* 1656. [f. L. *collaticius* raised by contribution (*collatio*) + -OUS.] Characterized by collation; done by way of general contribution -1670.

Collative (kǫlēi·tiv), *a.* 1617. [ad. L. *collativus* (see COLLATE).] †1. = COLLATITIOUS -1813. 2. That confers or can confer. Const. *of.* 1644. 3. *Eccl.* Where the ordinary (being himself the patron) collates 1725.

Collator (kǫlēi·təɹ). ME. [a. L. (see COLLATE).] †1. One who collects (*rare*) -1430. 2. One who collates texts, documents, the sheets of a book, etc. 1601. 3. One who bestows 1627. 4. *Eccl.* One who collates to a benefice 1612.

†**Collaud** (kǫlǭ·d), *v.* 1512. [ad. L. *collaudare.*] To praise highly, extol -1670. Hence **Collauda·tion** (*arch.*).

Colleague (kǫ·līg), *sb.* 1533. [a. F. *collègue*, ad. L. *collega*, f. *col-* + *legere* to choose.] One who is associated with another (or others) in office, or special employment. (Not applied to partners in trade or manufacture.) Also *fig.*

fig. Mercie collegue with Justice MILT. *P. L.* x. 59. Hence **Co·lleagueship,** position or relation of a c.

Colleague (kǫlī·g), *v.* 1534. [ad. OF. *colliguer*, *colleguer*, ad. L. *colligare*: spelt in Eng. after LEAGUE. (Not related etymologically to prec.)] *intr.* and †*trans.* To join in alliance; also (*intr.*), to conspire, cabal. Hence †**Collea·guer,** one who colleagues (*rare*).

Collect (kǫ·lekt), *sb.* ME. [a. F. *collecte*, ad. L. *collecta* sb., a gathering together, f. *collectus*, *colligere*.] †1. Collection -1681. †2. Assembly, *esp.* for worship -1728. 3. *Liturg.* A short prayer usu. concerned with one topic; *spec.* the prayer appointed to be used for a particular day (*c. of the day*) or season at the choir-offices and at the Eucharist (before the Epistle).

3. I learnt the collects and the catechism MRS. BROWNING.

Colle·ct, *ppl. a.* ME. [ad. L. *collectus.*] = COLLECTED as *pa. pple.* (obs.) or *adj.* (arch.).

Collect (kǫle·kt), *v.* 1573. [a. OF. *collecter*, f. *collecte* sb., infl. by prec.] 1. To gather together into one place or group; to gather in (money, debts, etc.) 1643; to make a collection of (specimens, curiosities, etc.) 1643. 2. *intr.* (for *refl.*) To assemble, accumulate 1794. 3. *trans.* To regain control over (one's thoughts, feelings, or energies); to summon up (courage, etc.) 1602. 4. To form a conclusion, draw an inference. Now usually *gather*. 1581.

1. To c. materials for a work RUSKIN. In Collecting of Customs PETTY. To c. Editions DIBDIN. 2. A force was collecting at Bridport MACAULAY. 3. Affrighted much, I did in time c. my selfe *Wint. T.* III. iii. 8. 4. What the Judges collected to be the intention of the testator CRUISE. Hence **Colle·ctable** *a.* that may be collected.

‖**Collectanea** (kǫlektē¹·niă), *sb. pl.* 1791. [L., neut. pl. of *collectaneus*.] Passages, remarks, etc., collected from various sources; (as *collect. sing.*) a miscellany.

Collected (kǫle·ktėd), *ppl. a.* 1610. [f. COLLECT *v.*] 1. *lit.* Gathered together 1670. 2. *fig.* Composed, self-possessed. Opp. to *distracted*. 1610. Hence **Colle·cted-ly** *adv.*, **-ness**.

Collection (kǫle·kʃən). ME. [a. OF., ad. L. *collectionem*.] 1. The action of collecting or gathering together. 2. *spec.* The action of collecting money for a religious or charitable purpose, or to defray expenses; also *concr.* the money so collected 1535. b. The gathering in of money due, as taxes, etc. 1659. 3. *concr.* A group of things collected or gathered together; *e. g.* of literary materials 1460; of specimens, works of art, etc. 1651; of waters 1697. †4. An abstract, summary -1703. †5. The action of inferring; an inference -1705. 6. A collectorate 1786. 7. *pl.* A college examination held at the end of each term in Oxford, Durham, and elsewhere 1799.

1. C. of himself B. JONS. Collections and Deliveries *P. O. Notice*. 2. Collections for the poore STUBBES. 3. A c. of proverbs TRENCH, of plants EVELYN, of floating vapours HERVEY.

Collective (kǫle·ktiv), *a.* 1520. [ad. L. *collectivus*, f. *collectus*.] 1. Formed by collection; constituting a collection; aggregate, collected. (Opp. to *individual*, and to *distributive*: so in sense 2.) 1600. 2. Of, pertaining to, or derived from, a number of individuals taken or acting together 1650. 3. Denoting (in the singular) a collection of individuals; as a *collective noun*, *idea*, *notion*, etc. †4. That deduces or infers; inferential -1646. †5. Having the attribute of collecting (*rare*) 1742. As *sb.* (*ellipt.*) A collective noun, body, or whole.

1. A c. edition of his works 1819. *C. fruit* (*Bot.*): fruit formed by the aggregation of several flowers, as the mulberry, etc. 2. *C. note*: in diplomacy, an official note signed by the representatives of several governments. 3. C. ideas of substances, as a Troop, Army 1727. 4. Controulable .. by criticall and c. reason SIR T. BROWNE. Hence **Colle·ctively** *adv.* in a c. manner or capacity; in a body, in the aggregate. **Colle·ctiveness**, c. quality (*rare*).

Collectivism (kǫle·ktiviz'm). 1880. [f. prec.; cf. F. *collectivisme*.] The theory that land and the means of production should be owned by the community for the benefit of the people as a whole. So **Colle·ctivist**, one who adheres to c.; also *attrib.*

Collectivity (kǫlekti·vĭti). 1862. [f. as prec.] 1. Collective state or quality; *concr.* the aggregate. 2. Collective ownership 1872. 3. The State 1881.

Collector (kǫle·ktəɹ). [ME., a. AF. *co(l)lectour*, ad. late or med.L. *collectorem*, f. *colligere* to COLLECT.] 1. One who or that which collects or gathers together; *spec.* one who collects specimens, works of art, curiosities, etc.; also, a compiler (now *rare*) 1582. 2. One who collects money; an officer who receives money due, as taxes, customs, etc. ME. 3. In India, the chief administrative official of a district, whose special duty is the collection of revenue 1772.

1. Conductors or electric collectors of copper and lead FARADAY. A c. of butterflies GOLDSM., proverbs D'ISRAELI. 2. A c. of poor rates 1885. 3. Such a magnificent person was the C. of Boggleywallah THACKERAY. Hence **Colle·ctorate** (*Anglo-Ind.*), the district under the jurisdiction of a c. **Colle·ctorship**, the office of a c.; in India = *collectorate*; the practice of a c. of curiosities. **Colle·ctress** (*rare*).

‖**Colleen** (kǫlī·n, kǫ·līn). *Anglo-Ir.* 1828. [Ir. *cailin* girl. (*Cailin bán*, anglicized *colleen bawn* = white girl.)] A girl.

Collegatary (kǫle·gătări). 1590. [ad. L. *collegatarius*, f. *col-* + *legatarius* LEGATARY.] A co-legatee.

College (kǫ·lėdʒ), *sb.* ME. [a. OF. *collège*, ad. L. *collegium*, f. *collega* COLLEAGUE.] 1. An organized society of persons performing certain common functions and possessing special rights and privileges. 2. *loosely.* Company, collective body, assemblage ME.; *occas.* repr. Ger. *collegium* 'reunion, club' 1703. 3. A community of clergy living together on a foundation for religious service, etc. Now chiefly *Hist.* ME. 4. A society of scholars incorporated within, or in connexion with, a University, or otherwise formed for purposes of study and instruction ME. 5. The building or set of buildings occupied by such society ME. Also *transf.* 6. A course of lectures at a foreign university; a distinct course of study leading to a degree (*U.S.*) 1700. 7. A charitable foundation of the collegiate type, as *Chelsea College* 1694. 8. *slang.* A prison. (*fig.* from 7.) 1690. Also *attrib.* (chiefly in sense 4).

1. *Apostolic c.*: the body of Christ's Apostles (or their descendants). *Sacred c.*: the 70 cardinals. I would the Colledge of the Cardinalls Would chuse him Pope 2 *Hen. VI*, I. iii. 64. The Colledge of physitians BROME. *C. of Justice*: in Scotland, the supreme civil courts. 2. Thick as the c. of the bees in May DRYDEN. 3. A Colledge of a hundred priests MORE. 4. New C.; Winchester C.; Gresham C.; Harvard C.; Owens C.; Royal Naval C.; Cheltenham C. 5. The quere of Wynchestre C. at Oxenford 1448. *Comb.* **c.-living**, a benefice in the gift of a c.

Colleger (kǫ·lėdʒəɹ). 1560. [f. prec. + -ER.] †A member of the same college; *spec.* one of the 70 boys on the foundation of Eton College.

Collegial (kǫlī·dʒiăl), *a.* 1530. [ad. L. *collegialis*, f. *collegium*.] 1. Of the nature of, or constituted as, a college. 2. Of or belonging to a COLLEGE (senses 1, 4) 1603.

1. *C. church*: = collegiate church. Hence **Colle·gialism**, the theory that the (or a) church is a voluntary association (*collegium*), and stands in no other relation to the civil magistrate than any other voluntary association. **Collegia·lity**, colleagueship. **Colle·gially** *adv.* in a c. manner or capacity.

Collegian (kǫlī·dʒiăn). 1462. [prob. ad. med.L. *collegianus*; cf. *oppidanus*.] A member or inmate of a college; also *spec.* a 'colleger' 1462; (*slang*) an inmate of a prison 1837. As *adj.* = COLLEGIAL. So **Colle·gianer**. *Obs.* exc. *Sc.*

Collegiate (kǫlī·dʒiĕt). 1514. [ad. L. *collegiatus* member of a college.]

A. *adj.* 1. Of the nature of, or constituted as, a college 1581. 2. Of or belonging to a college 1564. 3. Corporate; combined 1625.

1. *C. church*: (*a*) one which is endowed for a chapter, but has no bishop's see; (*b*) in Scotland, one served by joint pastors; (*c*) in U.S. 'one united with others under the joint pastorate of several ministers'. 2. A c. life did not suit me DE FOE. 3. Mutuall Ayds and C. endeavours 1665.

B. *sb.* †1. = COLLEGIAN -1818. †2. *slang.* An inmate of an asylum, prison, or the like -1734. †3. A colleague -1696.

Hence **Colle·giate** *v.* to constitute as a college or c. church. **Colle·giately** *adv.* in a c. manner.

Collenchyma (kǫle·ŋkimă). 1835. [f. Gr. κόλλα glue + ἔγχυμα infusion.] *Bot.* †1. The cellular substance in which pollen is generated -1866. 2. Tissue of cells with walls thickened at the angles, as in the leaf-stalks and young stems of many Dicotyledons. Hence **Collenchy·matous** *a.* belonging to or of the nature of c.

Collery (kǫ·ləri). *Anglo-Ind.* 1763. [ad. Tamil *kallar* thieves.] The name of a non-Aryan race inhabiting part of India east of Madura; hence **C.-horn** (corrupted into *cholera-horn*); **C.-stick**, a boomerang used by the Colleries.

Collet (kǫ·lėt), *sb.*[1] 1528. [a. F., dim. of *col*:—L. *collum*.] †1. The neckband of a garment; a necklet -1644. 2. An encompassing ring or band; as, a ring, collar, or flange on a rod or spindle, a circular metal lining to a hole, a ferrule or socket, etc. Also *attrib.* 1530. 3. *Jewelry.* The circle or flange in a ring in which the stone is set 1528. Also *fig.* Hence **Co·llet** *v.* to set in, or provide with, a c.

Collet (kǫ·lėt), *sb.*[2] 1675. [Earlier f. CULET[2], q. v.; cf. prec., sense 3.] The horizontal base of a diamond when cut as a brilliant.

‖**Colleter** (kǫlī·təɹ). 1875. [a. Gr. *κολλητήρ, f. κολλᾶν to glue.] *Bot.* One of the glandular hairs found on leaf-buds, etc., which secrete the blastocolla or bud-glue.

‖**Colleterium** (kǫlĭtīə·riŭm). 1864. [See prec.] *Zool.* An organ in certain insects, secreting a substance for cementing the ova together. Hence **Collete·rial** *a.* of the nature of, or pertaining to, a c.

Colletic (kǫle·tik). ? *Obs.* 1715. [ad. Gr. κολλητικός, f. κολλᾶν to glue.] *adj.* Agglutinant. *sb.* An agglutinant.

Colley; see COLLIE.

Collide (kǫləi·d), *v.* 1621. [ad. L. *collidere*, f. *col-* + *lædere*.] 1. To bring into collision, strike or dash together. Now *rare* or *Obs.* 2. *intr.* To come into collision, strike or dash together; *fig.* to clash, conflict 1700.

2. The flints .. thus toss'd in air, c. DRYDEN. The attraction urges them [atoms]. They c., they recoil TYNDALL. *fig.* Colliding passions LECKY.

Collidine (kǫ·lidəin). 1855. [f. Gr. κόλλα + εἶδος + -INE.] *Chem.* An alkaloid, $C_8H_{11}N$, found among the products of the dry distillation of animal substances and of coal. It is a colourless, oily, aromatic liquid.

Collie, Colly (kǫ·li), *sb.* 1651. [? = *coaly* 'the colour being originally black'; cf. COLLY *a.*] A Scotch sheep-dog with long hair, pointed nose, and bushy tail. Often *c. dog.*

Collier (kǫ·liəɹ). [ME. *colier*, *colyer*, etc., f. *col* COAL.] †1. A maker of wood charcoal -1608. †2. One who carries coal (orig. charcoal) for sale -1719. 3. A coal-miner 1594. 4. *transf.* A ship engaged in the carriage of coal. Also *attrib.* 1625. b. One of its crew 1727.

Colliery (kǫ·liəri). 1635. [f. prec.] 1. A place where coal is worked; a coal-mine. †2. The coal trade 1673. †3. The ships, or a ship, employed in the coal trade -1763. Also *attrib.*

Collieshangie (kǫliˌʃæ·ŋi). *Sc.* 1745. [?] Noisy quarrel; confused fight.

Colliflower, obs. f. CAULIFLOWER.

†**Colligance.** 1541. [a. OF., f. L. *colligare*.] Attachment together, connexion -1708. †**Colligate** *a.* bound together, attached (*lit.* and *fig.*).

Colligate (kǫ·ligeⁱt), *v.* 1545. [f. L. *colligat-*, *colligare* (f. *col-*, *com-* + *ligare*).] †1. To bind together, connect -1773. Also *fig.* 2. *Logic.* To connect together (isolated facts) by a general notion or hypothesis 1856.

1. Conbyndyng, colligatyng, or knittyng together the muskles RAYNOLD. 2. The phenomena which we are attempting to c. MILL.

Colligation (kǫligē¹·ʃən). 1502. [ad. L. *colligationem*; see prec.] 1. †Material binding together -1646; *fig.* conjunction 1651. 2. *Logic.* The binding together of a number of isolated facts by a general notion or hypothesis 1837.

2. The c. of facts WHEWELL. The c. of social phenomena MAINE.

Colligible (kǫ·lidʒib'l), *a.* ? *Obs.* 1650. [f. L. *colligere*; see -BLE.] That may be collected.

Collimate (kǫ·limeⁱt), *v.* 1623. [f. '*collimare*', a false reading of L. *collineare* to bring together into a straight line.] *trans.* To adjust the line of sight of (a telescope); to place (two lenses, etc.) so that their optical axes are in the same line. Also, to make parallel, as a lens, the rays of light passing through it.

Collimation (kǫlimē¹·ʃən). 1686. [f. prec. Better *collineation*.] The adjustment of the line of sight of a telescope, etc. Also *attrib.*

Line of c.: the line of sight or optical axis. *Error of c.*: the amount by which the line of sight deviates from its position of accurate adjustment.

Collimator (kǫ·limē¹təɹ). 1825. [f. as prec.] 1. A small fixed telescope with cross-wires at its focus, used for adjusting the line of collimation of another instrument. 2. The tube with a slit and lens (or the lens itself) used in the spectroscope to collect the light and throw it upon the prism in parallel rays 1865.

Collin (kǫ·lin). 1882. [f. Gr. κόλλα + -IN.] Gelatin of absolute purity. Hence **Colli·nic** *a.* (*Chem.*), as in *C. acid*, $C_6H_4O_2$, an Aromatic acid, obtained from gelatin, etc.

†**Colline,** *sb.* 1630. [a. F., ad. L. *collina* (sc. *terra*), f. *collis*.] A small hill -1697.

A..wooded, and watered park, full of fine collines and ponds EVELYN.

Collinear (kǫli·niăı), *a.* 1863. [See COL-.] *Geom.* Lying in the same straight line. Hence **Colli·nea·rity,** the quality or fact of being c. **Colli·nearly** *adv.* in the same line.

Collineate (kǫli·nie¹t), *v.* 1631. [f. L. *collineat-*, *collineare*; see COLLIMATE.] †1. *intr.* To meet together or converge, as lines, to a point; also *fig.* -1651. 2. = COLLIMATE, q. v. Hence **Collinea·tion,** the act of aiming anything in a straight line towards an object; also, = COLLIMATION.

Collingual (kǫli·ŋgwăl), *a. rare.* 1847. [See COL-.] Agreement together in language.

†**Colli·quable,** *a. rare.* 1666. [f. L. *colliquare* (see COLLIQUATE).] Capable of being liquified or dissolved -1677.

†**Colli·quament.** *rare.* 1656. [f. as prec.] Something melted or of a liquid consistence; hence, applied by Harvey to the earliest embryo -1657.

†**Co·lliquate,** *v.* 1603. [f. *colliquat-*, *colliquare*, f. *col-* + *liquare* to melt.] 1. *trans.* To fuse together -1680. 2. To reduce to a liquid consistence -1684. 3. *intr.* To melt 1646.

1. When Ashes and Sand are Colliquated into Glass BOYLE. 3. Ice..will c. in water SIR T. BROWNE.

†**Colliquation** (kǫlikwē¹·ʃən). 1601. [a. F.; cf. prec.] 1. The action or process of melting together -1681. 2. Melting, fusion. Also *fig.* -1744. 3. *spec.* in *Old Phys.* and *Path.* **a.** The melting down of solid parts, as in an abscess; the excessive fluidification of the humours, *esp.* the blood -1710. **b.** The wasting away of the solid parts of the body; consumption -1756.

1. When Sand and Ashes are well melted together.. there is generated by the c. that sort of Concretion we call Glasse BOYLE.

Colliquative (kǫli·kwătiv), *a.* 1666. [a. F., f. L. *colliquat-*; see prec.] *Med.* Having the power or effect of liquefying; as, *c. diarrhœa.*

†**Colli·quefa·ction.** *rare.* 1612. [f. L. *colliquefact-*, *colliquefacere*.] Melting together -1626.

Incorporation of metals by simple c. BACON.

Collision (kǫli·ʒən). ME. [ad. L. *collisionem*; see COLLIDE.] 1. The action of colliding; violent encounter of a moving body with another; now *esp.* of railway trains or ships. 2. *fig.* Clashing, hostile encounter 1662; coming into contact (without opposition) 1664. Also *attrib.*

1. C. of carriages on the..railway 1835. The c. of harsh consonants GRAY. 2. The c. of contrary false principles WARBURTON. Constant c. with good company CHESTERF. *Lett.* So **Collisive** (kǫlai·siv) *a.* pertaining or tending to c. (*rare*).

Collocal (kǫlōu·kăl), *a. rare.* 1813. [See COL-.] Of, belonging to, or occupying the same place with another.

†**Co·llocate,** *ppl. a.* 1529. [ad. L. *collocatus*, *collocare*, f. *col-* (*con-*) + *locare*, f. *locus*.] Set, placed; *fig.* laid out -1626.

Collocate (kǫ·lŏke¹t), *v.* 1513. [f. L. *collocat-*; see prec.] To arrange; to set in a place or position.

To marshall and c. in order his battailes MORE. Original Sin (somewhat oddly collocated in the list) G. S. FABER. Hence **Co·llocative** *a.* of the nature of, or relating to, collocation.

Collocation (kǫlokē¹·ʃən). 1605. [ad. L. *collocationem*; see prec.] The action of setting in a place or position; disposition or arrangement with, or in relation to, others; the state of being so placed.

All languages use greater freedom of c. in poetry than in prose EARLE. Hence **Colloca·tional** *a.* of or belonging to c. (*rare*).

Collocution (kǫlokiū·ʃən). *rare.* 1460. [ad. L. *collocutionem*, f. *colloqui*.] Talking together, colloquy. So **Collocutor** (kǫ·lŏkiŭtəı, kǫlǫ·kiŭtəı), one who takes part in a dialogue or conversation. **Collo·cutory** *a.* of the nature of dialogue (*rare*).

Collodio- (kǫlōu·dio), comb. f. COLLODION, as in c.-type, a photograph obtained by the collodion process; also, the process itself.

Collodion (kǫlōu·diən). Also **collodium.** 1851. [f. Gr. κολλώδης glue-like, f. κόλλα.] A solution of gun-cotton in ether, forming a colourless gummy liquid, which dries rapidly; used in photography for covering plates with a thin film, and in surgery for coating wounds, burns, etc. Also *attrib.*, as *c. process* (in photography), etc. Hence **Collo·dionize** *v.* to treat with c.

Collogue (kǫlōu·g), *v.* 1602. [?] †1. *intr.* To gloze; to deal flatteringly or deceitfully *with* -1719. †2. *intr.* To feign agreement or belief -1649. †3. *trans.* To influence by blandishment -1755. 4. *intr.* To have a private understanding *with*; to intrigue, conspire. Now *dial.* 1646. 5. To confabulate (*colloq.* or *joc.*) 1811.

4. To bring this to effect, it was necessary for him to c. with England EARL MONM. 5. They wagged their old heads sadly when they collogued in clubs THACKERAY. Hence **Collo·guer,** a glozer, intriguer.

Co·lloid. 1847. [f. Gr. κόλλα; see -OID.]

A. *adj.* 1. Of the nature or appearance of glue. 2. *Chem.* Applied to a state of aggregation in which substances exist; opp. to *crystalloid.* So called because gelatin may be taken as the type of the class. 1861. 3. *Min.* One of the forms in which minerals occur; distinguished from *crystalline, vitreous*, and *amorphous* 1879.

1. *C. degeneration*: transformation of tissue into a homogeneous or slightly granular glue-like substance, as in *c. cancer.*

B. *sb.* 1. *Path.* The jelly-like substance formed in colloid degeneration 1849. 2. *Chem.* A substance in which the particles vary from molecular size to that of coarse suspensions (see A. 2) 1860.

So **Colloi·dal** *a.* in the same senses; see -AL *suffix*¹. Hence **Colloida·lity.**

Collop¹ (kǫ·ləp). ME. [Of obscure deriv.; cf. Sw. *kollops*, mod. *kalops*. The first element is prob. COAL *sb.*] 1. †An egg fried on bacon -1530; later, called *collops and eggs* by itself 1542. 2. A slice of meat ME.; *locally*, meat cut into small pieces 1648. †3. *transf.* A piece of flesh -1666. 4. A thick fold of fat on the body. Now *Sc.* and *dial.* 1560. 5. *fig.* A slice; a cantle 1580.

2. *Scotch collops*: now, a steak with onions. 3. To say this Boy were like me..Most dear'st, my C. *Wint. T.* I. ii. 137. Hence **Co·lloped** *ppl. a.* having thick folds of fat.

‖**Collop**². *Anglo-Ir.* 1672. = Ir. *colpa*, 'A full-grown cow or horse'. Hence, a cow's grass for a year, or its equivalent.

Colloque, *sb. Obs.* (exc. as Fr.) 1482. [a. F., ad. L. *colloquium*.] †1. A place for conversation (in a monastery). †2. A conference -1677. ‖3. = COLLOQUY 3. 1846. So **Collo·que** *v.* to hold colloquy.

Colloquial (kǫlōu·kwi,ăl), *a.* 1751. [f. L. *colloquium* COLLOQUY.] 1. Of or pertaining to colloquy; conversational. 2. *spec.* Of words, phrases, etc.: Belonging to common speech or ordinary conversation. (The usual sense.) 1752.

1. His..c. judgments DE QUINCEY. 2. To clear it [our language] from c. barbarisms JOHNSON. The c. language of real life GREEN. Hence **Collo·quialism,** c. quality or style; a c. expression. **Collo·quialist,** a (good) talker; one who uses colloquialisms. **Collo quia·lity,** = *Colloquialism.* **Collo·quially** *adv.*

Colloquist (kǫ·lŏkwist). 1792. [f. as prec.] One who takes part in a conversation; an interlocutor.

‖**Colloquium** (kǫlōu·kwi,ŏm). 1609. [L.] †1. A colloquy -1765. 2. An assembly for discussion; a conference, council. (Not in ordinary Eng. use.) 1844.

Colloquize (kǫ·lŏkwəiz), *v.* 1823. [f. as prec.] *intr.* To engage in colloquy.

Colloquy (kǫ·lŏkwi), *sb.* 1581. [ad. L. *colloquium*.] 1. A talking together; a dialogue; converse. †2. A meeting for conference -1679. 3. *Eccl.* = CLASSIS, PRESBYTERY 1672.

1. Frantick men that boasted of..colloquies with God 1660. Shunning..All further c. BYRON. Hence **Co·lloquy** *v.* to hold c.

Collotype (kǫ·lŏtəip). 1883. [f. Gr. κόλλα glue + -TYPE.] A thin sheet of gelatin, the sensitized surface of which has been etched by the action of the actinic rays, so that it can be printed from; also the print, and the process. Hence *c. plate, process, printing*, etc.

Collow (kǫ·lōu, -ŏ), *v.* Now *dial.* [ME. *colwen*, perh. :—OE. **colgian*, f. **colig* coaly, f. *col* COAL. See also COLLY *v.* and *a.*] To blacken, smut, begrime. ? Hence **Co·llow** *sb.* (now *dial.*), soot; smut; coal-dust.

Colluctation (kǫlɒktē¹·ʃən). *arch.* 1611. [ad. L. *colluctationem*, f. *colluctari*.] A wrestling or struggling together; conflict, opposition.

Colluctations between the flesh and the Spirit DONNE. vars. †**Collu·ctance** (*rare*), †**Collu·ctancy** (*rare*).

Collude (kǫl¹ū·d), *v.* 1525. [ad. L. *colludere*, f. *col-* + *ludere* to play.] 1. *intr.* To act in secret concert *with*; to play into one another's hands; to conspire; to play false; to act in play merely. †2. *trans.* To stir up by collusion -1834. †3. To elude by trickery -1679.

1. The French sought to weaken the King by colluding with his factious Enemies NORTH. Hence **Collu·der,** one who colludes.

Collusion (kǫl¹ū·ʒən). ME. [a. F., ad. L. *collusionem*; see prec.] 1. Secret agreement or understanding for purposes of trickery or fraud; underhand scheming or working with another; deceit, fraud, trickery. 2. *spec.* in *Law.* See quot. 1509. †3. A trick, or ambiguity, in words or reasoning -1659.

1. Yf he can by sume collucione Do his neyghtboure wronge CHAUCER. But for the c. of the false Templars and Hospitallers with the infidels FULLER. 2. *C.* is a deceitful agreement or contract between two or more persons, for the one to bring an action against the other, to some evil purpose, as to defraud a third person of his right TOMLINS.

Collusive (kǫl¹ū·siv), *a.* 1671. [f. L. *collusus*, *colludere* to COLLUDE + -IVE.] 1. Characterized by collusion; fraudulently concerted or devised 1678. 2. Given to collusion 1671.

1. C. ambiguity MARVELL. A c. treaty with the enemy 1747. 2. C. ministers of justice 1671. Hence **Collu·sively** *adv.* in a c. manner.

†**Collu·sory,** *a.* 1706. [ad. late L. *collusorius*.] Collusive -1755. Hence †**Collu·sorily** *adv.*

†**Collu·tion.** 1601. [ad. late L. *collutionem*, f. *colluere*.] A wash or rinse for the mouth; a lotion -1684.

‖**Colluvies** (kǫl¹ū·vi,īz). 1647. [L., f. *colluere*.] 1. Chiefly *Med.* A collection of foul matter; *spec.* foul discharge from an ulcer 1651. 2. Conflux (of waters, etc.) 1665. 3. Medley, rabble 1647. Hence **Collu·vial** *a.* of or pertaining to a c.; sink-like (*rare*).

Colly (kǫ·li). Now *dial.* 1708. [f. COLLY *a.*] 1. Soot; smut. 2. The Blackbird 1805.

Co·lly, *a.* Now *dial.* 1609. [16th c. *colie* COALY.] Dirtied with coal-dust or soot; grimy; coal-black.

Colly (kǫ·li), *v.*¹ *arch.* and *dial.* 1590. [App. a var. of COLLOW *v.*, q. v.] To blacken with coal-dust or soot; to begrime, blacken. Also *fig.*

An old hag Collied with chimney-smutch COWPER. Briefe as the lightning in the collied night SHAKS.

†**Co·lly,** *v.*² ME. [a. OF. *coleier*, f. *col*, *cou*; cf. *manier*.] To move the neck; to turn the head from side to side: said of birds -1783.

†**Co·llybist.** ME. [ad. L. *collybista*, ad. Gr. κολλυβιστής, f. κόλλυβος small coin.] A money-changer, usurer; miser -1615.

Collyridian (kǫliri·diăn). 1565. [f. (ult.) Gr. κολλυρίς, -ίδα cake.] One of a sect of heretics in the 4th and 5th c. who worshipped the Virgin Mary and offered cakes to her as 'Queen of Heaven' (cf. Jer. vii. 18). Also as *adj.*

Collyrite (kǫ·lirəit). 1826. [f. Gr. κολλύριον eye-salve, also 'Samian earth'; see -ITE.] *Min.* A hydrous silicate of alumina, a white clay-like mineral, with a greasy feel.

‖**Collyrium** (kǫli·riŏm). Pl. **collyria** (kǫli·riă). ME. [L., a. Gr. κολλύριον poultice, eye-salve.] 1. An eye-salve or eye-wash 1624. 2. A suppository 1748. vars. †**Collyre,** †**Collyrie.**

Collywobbles (kǫ·liwǫb'lz). 1841. *colloq.* [f. COLIC, WOBBLE.] Pain or looseness in the bowels.

Colmar (kǫ·lmăı). 1727. [A town in Alsace.] 1. A kind of pear 1741. 2. A kind of fan of Queen Anne's time.

‖**Colobium** (kolōu·biŏm). 1603. [a. Gr. κολόβιον, f. κολοβός curtailed.] A half-sleeved or sleeveless tunic worn by the early clergy, by monks, and by kings at their coronation. In later eccles. use repl. by the DALMATIC.

‖**Coloboma** (kǫlǫbōu·mă). 1843. [mod.L., a. Gr., f. κολοβός curtailed.] *Path.* A malformation or mutilation of an organ; *spec.* a defect in the iris of the eye, due to imperfect closure of the choroidal fissure.

‖**Colocolo, -la** (kǫlokōu·lŏ, -lă). 1880. Native name for the wild cat of S. America (*Felix colocolo*).

Colocynth (kǫ·lŏsinþ). 1565. [ad. L. *colocynthis* (also used, with pl. *-ides*, and var. *-ida*), a. Gr. κολοκυνθίς. See also COLOQUINTIDA.] The Bitter-apple (*Citrullus Colocynthis*), a plant of the Gourd family, the fruit of which contains a light spongy and extremely bitter pulp, furnishing a purgative drug. Also the fruit, and the drug. Also *attrib.* Hence **Colocy·nthin** (*Chem.*), the bitter principle of c., a resin-like substance, readily soluble in alcohol.

Cologne (kǫlōu·n). ME. [In F. *Cologne*, Ger. *Köln* :—L. *Colonia Agrippina.*] Name of a German city on the Rhine: used *attrib.* to designate things obtained from the city or district, as *C. brand, sword*, etc.

C. earth (umber, brown), a brown pigment obtained or prepared from lignite, orig. from a bed near C. **C. water** = EAU DE COLOGNE, a perfumed spirit, manufactured at C. since 1709; in U.S. often called simply *Cologne.*

Cololite (kǫ·lŏlait). 1837. [f. Gr. κόλον COLON[1] + λίθος.] *Geol.* An intestine-like mass or impression found in the oolitic rocks of Solenhofen, and regarded as worm-casts.

Colombier, etc.; see COLUM-.

Colombo, obs. f. CALUMBA.

Colon[1] (kōu·lǫn). ME. [a. L., a. Gr. κόλον.] *Anat.* The greater portion of the large intestine, extending from the cæcum to the rectum. †Formerly, *pop.*, the belly or guts.

Colon[2] (kōu·lǫn). 1589. [a. L., a. Gr. κῶλον limb.] ‖1. In *Gr. Rhetoric* and *Poetry*, a member of a sentence or rhythmical period; hence in *Palæography*, a clause or group of clauses written as a line, or taken as a standard of measure in ancient MSS. or texts. *pl.* **cola.** 2. A punctuation-mark [:] usually indicating a discontinuity of grammatical construction less than that marked by a period. *pl.* **colons.**

Co·lon[3]. *rare.* 1606. [ad. L. *colonus.*] A husbandman.

Colonel (kɒ̄·ɹnĕl). 1548. [In 16th c. *coronel*, a. F. *coronnel*, ad. It. *colonnello*, f. *colonna* COLUMN. *Colonel* (c 1580) was orig. trisyllabic, but later was reduced in pronunciation to *col'nel.* In 1780 (kɒ̄·ɹnel) occurs, founded on the earlier and popular *coronel.*] The superior officer of a regiment. He ranks above the *Lieutenant-Colonel*, and below the general officer, who is attached to no one regiment. Hence **Colonel** *v.* to make a c. of; *intr.* to play the c. **Colonelcy** (kɒ̄·ɹnĕlsi), the post, rank, or commission of c. **C. commandant**: see BRIGADIER.

†**Co·loner.** 1600. [f. F. *colon* or L. *colonus* + -ER.] = COLONIST –1610.

Colonial (kǫlōu·niăl), *a.* (*sb.*) 1796. [f. L. *colonia* + -AL.] 1. Of, belonging to, or relating to a colony, or (*spec.*) the British colonies; in American history, of or belonging to the United States while they were still colonies. 2. *Biol.* Forming a colony (see COLONY) 1885. 3. *sb.* An inhabitant of a colony; a colonist 1865.

1. C. Councils BURKE, articles McCULLOCH, mints JEVONS. Hence **Colo·nialism**, a c. practice, idiom, or manner; the c. system. **Colo·nially** *adv.* in a c. manner; in relation to the colonies.

†**Colo·nical**, *a.* [f. L. *colonicus* + -AL.] Of or pertaining to husbandmen or tillage. SPELMAN.

Colonist (kǫ·lŏnist). 1701. [f. COLONIZE; see -IST.] 1. One who settles in a new country; an inhabitant of a colony. 2. *transf.* Of animals and plants 1878.

Colonitis (kǫlŏnai·tis). 1834. [Better COLITIS; f. COLON[1] + -ITIS.] *Med.* Inflammation of the colon.

Colonization (kǫ:lŏnaizē·ʃǝn). 1770. [f. COLONIZE.] The action of colonizing or fact of being colonized; establishment of a colony or colonies.

Our growth by c. and by conquest BURKE. Hence **Coloniza·tionist**, an advocate of c.; *spec.* in *U.S. Hist.* an advocate of the c. of Africa by negroes from America.

Colonize (kǫ·lŏnəiz), *v.* 1622. [f. L. *colonus*, and Eng. COLONY + -IZE; cf. F. *coloniser.*] 1. To settle (a country) with colonists; to plant or establish a colony in. 2. To establish in a colony 1816. 3. *intr.* To form or establish a colony or settlement; to settle. Also *transf.* of animals and plants. 1817.

1. They that would thus c. the stars with Inhabitants HOWELL. Hence **Co·lonizable** *a.* that can be colonized. **Co·lonizer.**

Colonnade (kǫlŏnē·d). 1718. [a. F., f. *colonne*; see -ADE.] 1. *Arch.* A series of columns placed at regular intervals, and supporting an entablature. 2. *transf.* of trees, etc. 1784.

2. A length of C...These chestnuts rang'd in corresponding lines COWPER. Hence **Colonna·ded** *a.* having a c.

Colonne·tte. 1872. [a. F., dim. of *colonne.*] A small column.

Colony (kǫ·lŏni). [ME. *colonie*, ad. L. *colonia*, f. *colonus*; cf. OF. *colonie.*]

I. After Roman use. †1. A farm, estate in the country –1656. 2. Applied to a Roman *colonia, i.e.* a settlement of Roman citizens in a hostile or newly conquered country ME. 3. Applied to a Greek ἀποικία, *i.e.* a settlement of 'people from home' as an independent self-governed πόλις or state 1580.

II. In mod. use. 1. A settlement in a new country; a body of settlers, forming a community politically connected with their parent state; the community so formed, as long as the connexion lasts 1548; the territory thus peopled 1612. 2. *transf.* A number of people of one nationality residing in a foreign city or country; the quarter thus occupied 1711. 3. *transf.* and *fig.* of animals, etc. 1658. 4. *Biol.* An aggregate of individual animals or plants, forming a physiologically connected structure, as the coral-polyps, etc. 1872. Also *attrib.*

1. The British colonies are divided into three classes: CROWN colonies; colonies with representative governments, in which the crown partly controls the legislature and has the right of veto on local legislation; colonies with responsible governments, the crown having only the right of veto.

Coloph-, Colophon-, short for COLOPHONY, used as stems for names of related substances, as **Co·lophene** ($C_{20}H_{32}$), an oily colourless liquid obtained by distilling oil of turpentine with strong sulphuric acid.

Colophon (kǫ·lŏfǫn). 1621. [a. late L., a. Gr. κολοφών summit.] †1. Finishing stroke –1635. 2. *spec.* The inscription or device formerly placed at the end of a book, etc., and containing the title, the printer's name, date and place of printing, etc. 1774.

When the c., or final description, fell into disuse.. since the titlepage had become the principal direct means of identifying the book DE MORGAN.

Colophonite (kǫ·lŏfǫnəit). 1808. [f. COLOPHONY + -ITE.] *Min.* A brown or reddish variety of garnet, resembling colophony.

Colophony (kǫ·lŏfouni, kǫlǫ·fŏni). ME. [ad. L. *colophonia* for *Colophonia resina* resin of Colophon (a town of Lydia).] Rosin.

Coloquintida (kǫlŏkwi·ntidă). ME. [a. med.L. *coloquintida*, f. **coloquinthid-*, *colocynthid-*, stem of *colocynthis*: *qu-* repr. the *k* sound of Gr. κολοκυνθίδ-.] The COLOCYNTH. Also *fig.*

Color, -ed, -ing, etc.; see COLOUR, etc.

Colorado (kǫlŏrā·dǫ). One of the States of the American Union, named after its great river [Sp. *Rio Colorado* 'coloured river']. Hence **Colorado (Potato) Beetle**, a yellow beetle (*Doryphora decemlineata*), first observed (c 1824) near the Upper Missouri. Its larva, the *potato-bug*, is destructive to the potato.

Coloradoite (kǫlŏrā·dǫ,əit). 1876. *Min.* A native telluride of mercury, found in Colorado.

Colorant (kǫ·lŏ-, kɒ·lərănt). *rare.* 1884. [a. F., f. *colorer.*] A colouring matter, pigment.

†**Co·lorate**, *a.* 1678. [ad. L. *coloratus.*] Coloured –1691.

Coloration, colouration (kǫlŏrē·ʃən, kɒlə-). 1612. [a. F.] The action or mode of colouring; coloured condition; colouring.

‖**Coloratura** (kolorat*ū*·ra). 1876. [It., f. L. *colorat-*, *colorare* to COLOUR: see -URE. Cf. next.] *Mus.* Florid ornaments in vocal music, such as runs, trills, etc. **b.** Music characterized by this style, or the ability to sing it; also, a singer of c. parts. Also *attrib.* or as *adj.*

Colorature (kǫ·lŏ-, kɒ·lərătiuɹ). 1753. [ad. It.: see prec.] = prec.

Colorific (kǫlŏ-, kɒlǝri·fik), *a.* 1676. [ad. F. *colorifique*; see -FIC.] Producing colour or colours; *loosely*, pertaining to colour. Also *fig.*

Colorimeter (kǫlŏ-, kɒləri·mĭtəɹ). 1863. [f. L. *colorem* + -METER.] An instrument for measuring intensity of colour. Hence **Colorime·tric, -al** *a.* **Colori·metry.**

Colorize, colour- (kɒ·lərəiz), *v. rare.* 1611. [f. L. *color* or Eng. COLOUR + -IZE.] *trans.* To colour. Hence **Co:loriza·tion, co·lour-.**

Coloss, -osse (kǫlǫ·s). *arch.* 1561. [a. F. *colosse* :—L. *colossus.*] = COLOSSUS.

Colossal (kəlǫ·săl), *a.* 1712. [f. COLOSSUS + -AL; cf. F. *colossal.*] Like a colossus, of vast size, gigantic, huge.

Hence **Colo·ssally** *adv.* var. **Colosse·an** (*arch.*).

‖**Colosseum, coliseum** (kǫlǫsī·ɒ̆m, kǫli-). 1708. [a. L. *colosseum*; orig. neut. of adj. *colosseus* gigantic, f. COLOSSUS, q.v.] The amphitheatre of Vespasian at Rome. Also *transf.*

While stands the Coliseum, Rome shall stand BYRON. var. †**Colossee, colisee.**

Colossus (kǫlǫ·sɒ̆s). Pl. **-i, -uses.** ME. [a. L., a. Gr. κολοσσός gigantic statue, orig. applied by Herodotus to those of Egypt.] 1. A statue of very large dimensions; *esp.* the bronze statue of Apollo at Rhodes, reputed to have stood astride the entrance to the harbour. 2. *transf.* and *fig.* Anything gigantic 1794.

He doth bestride the narrow world Like a C. SHAKS. 2. Laud stood the c. of his own cast D'ISRAELI. The C. of the North [Russia] 1831. var. †**Colo·sso.**

‖**Colostrum** (kǫlǫ·strɒ̆m). 1577. [L. (also *colostra* fem. sing., and neut. pl.)] *Med.* The first milk secreted by a mammal after parturition; the 'beestings' or 'green milk'. Hence **Colostra·tion**, an indisposition of new-born children attributed to the c.

Colotomy (kolǫ·tŏmi). 1867. [f. Gr. κόλον COLON[1] + -τομια.] *Surg.* The operation of opening the colon.

Colour, color (kɒ·ləɹ), *sb.* [ME. *colur, colour, color*, a. OF. *color, colur*, later *colour, coulour, couleur* :—L. *colorem*. *Color* has been used occasionally in Eng. from 15th c., and is now the prevalent spelling in U.S.]

I. 1. The quality in virtue of which objects present different appearances to the eye, in respect of the kind of light reflected from their surfaces. 2. A particular hue or tint; often spec. one distinct from the prevailing tone, as in *Bot.* any hue save green ME. **b.** *spec.* The hue of the darker varieties of mankind 1796. 3. Complexion, hue; freshness of hue ME. 4. *spec.* in *Art.* Colouring 1661. Also *fig.*

1. Would you say that whiteness is c. or a c. JOWETT. 2. *Accidental colours, Complementary c.*: see these words. *Fundamental, Primary*, or *Simple colours*: formerly, the seven colours of the spectrum; now, red, green, and violet (or, with painters, red, yellow, and blue). *Secondary colours*: colours resulting from the mixture of primary colours. Al colours of the Rainebow 1577. **b.** She is a woman of c. STEVENSON. 3. The duke a lytell chaunged c. LD. BERNERS. 4. *Dead c.*: the first laying-in of a portrait. The dead c. of my wife is good above what I expected PEPYS.

II. 1. (in *pl.*) A coloured device, badge, or dress ME. Also *fig.* 2. (usu. in *pl.*) A flag, ensign, or standard of a regiment or a ship 1590. Also *fig.* 3. A colouring matter, pigment, paint 1580. 4. *pl.* Coloured dresses 1716. 5. *Mining.* 'A particle of metallic gold'. RAYMOND.

1. The servants..wore the colours of the Prince's household SCOTT. To come out in one's true colours DICKENS. 2. Sound Trumpets, let our bloody Colours waue SHAKS. A soldier..deserting his colours MACAULAY. *A pair of colours*: an ensign's commission (*arch.*). To hang out false colours STEELE.

III. Fig. 1. Outward appearance, show, aspect, semblance *of* (something) ME. 2. A show of reason ME.; †*occas.*, excuse –1724. 3. *esp.* in *Law.* An apparent or *prima facie* right, as in *C. of title.* Also *spec.* in Pleading, 'a probable but really false plea, the design of which was to draw the decision of the case from the jury to the judges'. 1531. 4. *pl.* Rhetorical modes or figures; ornaments of style or diction ME.

5. *Mus.* Timbre. Also, variety of expression (cf. next). 1597. 6. (an extension of III. 1). General complexion or tone; kind 1600.

1. A Table of Coulers, or appearances of good and euill BACON. 2. No man should have even a c. to assert that I received a compensation BURKE. Phrases. *Under c. of*; *without c.*; *to give c.*; †*to take c. with*, i.e. to side ostensibly with. 4. I lerned neuere Rethorik.. Colours ne knowe I none CHAUCER. 6. Boyes and women are for the most part, cattle of this c. *A. Y. L.* III. ii. 435. Words of an opposite c. 1822.

Comb.: **c.-blind,** *a.* blind to certain colours, unable to discriminate between colours; also *fig.* of racial colour, etc.; hence, **-blindness**; **†-de-roy,** orig. purple, later, bright tawny; **-man,** one who deals in colours; **-serjeant, -sergeant,** an army serjeant who performs the duty of attending the regimental colours on ceremonial occasions.

Colour, color (kʌ·ləɹ), *v.* [ME. *coloure(n*, etc., a. OF. *coulourer, colorer* :—L. *colorare*, f. *color.*] 1. *trans.* To give colour to; to paint, stain, dye. Also with *over.* Also *fig.* 2. To represent in fair colours; to gloss, cloak, disguise, excuse; to render specious or plausible. Const. *out, over.* ME. b. To misrepresent ME. †3. To lend one's name to; represent as one's own -1726. 4. To imbue with its own character 1835. 5. *intr.* To become coloured 1667. 6. *spec.* To blush. Also with *up.* 1721.

1. Color hit with safroune ME. 2. Whych thyng, though it be colowryd *per Jus Regale*, yet it is Tyrannye FORTESCUE. b. To suppress and c. evidence DICKENS. 5. This meerschaum won't c. (*mod.*). 6. The poor woman coloured 1787. Hence **Co·lourer, co·lorer.**

Colourable, color- (kʌ·lərăb'l), *a.* ME. [a. OF. *colorable.*] †1. Possessed of colour -1705. 2. *fig.* Having an appearance of truth or right; specious, plausible ME.; pretended ME.; deceptive, as ship's papers, etc. 1750.

2. C. error 1581, grounds of complaint DE QUINCEY. The conveyance was c. and collusive DALLAS. Hence **†Co·lourableness, co·lor-,** c. state or quality. **Co·lourably, co·lor-,** *adv.* in a c. manner.

Co·lour-box. 1858. 1. A paint-box. 2. *Calico printing.* The box which supplies calico to the printing rollers 1858. 3. An instrument for compounding the colours of the spectrum in any given proportion 1870.

Coloured, colored (kʌ·ləɹd), *ppl. a.* ME. [f. COLOUR *v.* or *sb.* + -ED.] 1. Having a colour or colours. (Strictly, exclusive of black and white; also, exclusive of the prevailing hue, *e.g.* in *Bot.* of green.) Also *fig.* of style, etc. 1855. 2. Of the complexion, as *fresh-c.*, etc.; *spec.* having a skin other than white 1611; of or belonging to the negro race 1866. †3. Made to look well; specious -1576; glossed over -1557; pretended -1610.

1. *C. vision*: see VISION. White or c. shirts (*mod.*). 2. The.. Negro women, or the c. women as they are called here 1760. C. suffrage 1878. 3. A false fained and c. frende GRAFTON.

Colouring, coloring (kʌ·ləriŋ), *vbl. sb.* ME. [f. COLOUR *v.* + -ING[1].] 1. The action of the vb. COLOUR; esp. *fig.* the giving of a specious appearance to what is bad 1549. 2. The effect of the application of colour, the style in which anything is coloured 1707; pervading character 1769. 3. Colouring matter 1460.

1. Let them leaue their colouryng and cal them by their Christian name Brybes LATIMER.

Colourist, colorist (kʌ·lərist). 1686. [? a. OF. *coloriste.*] A painter skilful in colouring; a master of colour. Also *fig.* of writers.

Colourless, colorless (kʌ·ləɹlės), *a.* ME. [f. COLOUR *sb.* + -LESS.] 1. *gen.* Without colour. 2. Without distinctive character, vividness, or picturesqueness 1861; neutral 1868.

1. A c. and transparent body HUXLEY. A c. face TENNYSON, landscape 1878. 2. A c. religion MAX MÜLLER. C. words (*mod.*). Hence **Co·lourlessly** *adv.* **Co·lourlessness, color-,** c. quality or state.

Coloury, colory (kʌ·ləri), *a.* 1853. [f. as prec. + -Y[1].] *Comm.* Having a colour characteristic of good quality, as hops, coffee beans, etc.

Colp. Irish; see COLLOP[2].

‖**Colportage** (kǫlportaˑʒ, kǫ·lpǫɹtėdʒ). 1846. [Fr., f. *colporter*, app. f. *col* neck + *porter*; see -AGE.] The work of a colporteur.

‖**Colporteur** (kǫlpǫrtör, kǫ·lpǫɹtəɹ). 1796. [Fr., f. as prec.] A hawker of books, newspapers, etc., *esp.* (in Eng. use) one employed by a religious society.

Colstaff, var. of COWL-STAFF.

Colt (kōult), *sb.*[1] [OE. *colt* young ass, young camel; of obscure origin. Cf. Sw. dial. *kult* pig, hardy boy.] 1. The young of the horse, or of animals of the horse kind; also, in Scripture, of the camel. Cf. FOAL. 2. *fig.* A young or inexperienced person ME.; *spec.* in *Cricket*, a professional cricketer during his first season (*mod.*). 3. *Legal slang.* The barrister that attended on a serjeant-at-law at his induction 1765. 4. *Naut.* A piece of rope used as an instrument of chastisement 1769.

Comb.: **Colt's tooth**: *lit.* one of the first set of teeth of a horse (or ass); *fig.* youthful desires; inclination to wantonness; **c.-drift,** the drift of colts or ponies on Dartmoor (see DRIFT). Hence **Co·lthood,** quality of being a c.

Colt (kōult), *sb.*[2] 1852. A type of repeating pistol invented by Samuel Colt (d. 1862).

Colt (kōult), *v.* 1580. [f. COLT *sb.*[1]] †1. *intr.* To frisk or run wild as a colt (usually implying wantonness) (*rare*) -1746. †2. *trans.* To befool, take in -1618. †3. (See quot.) 4. To beat with a colt (see COLT *sb.*[1] 4) 1732.

3. She hath bin colted by him *Cymb.* II. iv. 133. Hence **Co·lting** *vbl. sb.* (sense 4).

Colter, var. of COULTER.

Coltish (kōu·ltiʃ), *a.* ME. [f. COLT *sb.*[1] + -ISH.] Of, pertaining to, or like a colt or colts; frisky, †salacious.

He was al coltissch, ful of ragerye CHAUCER. Hence **Co·ltish-ly** *adv.*, **-ness.**

Colt-pixie. 1542. [See PIXIE.] A mischievous sprite, in the form of a ragged colt.

Coltsfoot (kōu·ltsfut). ME. [From the shape of the leaves.] A name of *Tussilago Farfara* (N.O. *Compositæ*); its leaves used for smoking as a cure for asthma; an infusion of the leaves.

Colt's tail. 1735. 1. A cloud with a ragged edge, portending rain. (Cf. *mare's tail.*) 2. The Canadian Flea-bane, *Erigeron canadensis.*

‖**Coluber** (kǫ·liŭbəɹ). 1763. [L.] *Zool.* A genus of harmless snakes. (The name was formerly not limited to harmless snakes.)

Colubriform (kǒliŭ·brifǭɹm), *a.* 1847. [See prec. and -FORM.] Having the form of a coluber; applied to certain venomous snakes.

Colubrine (kǫ·liŭbrəin), *a.* (*sb.*) 1528. [ad. L. *colubrinus.*] 1. Of or belonging to a snake. 2. *Zool.* Of the nature of the Coluber or snake: applied to serpents 1844. 3. *sb.* A colubrine snake.

Columba; see CALUMBA.

Columbaceous (kǫlʌmbēi·ʃəs), *a.* 1693. [f. L. *columba.*] Of the nature of a dove or a pigeon; pertaining to the sub-order Columbacei.

‖**Columbarium** (kǫlʌmbēə·riǒm). Pl. **-ia.** 1846. [L.] 1. A pigeon-house, dove-cote; a pigeon-hole 1881. 2. *Rom. Antiq.* A subterranean sepulchre with niches in its walls for cinerary urns; one of these niches.

Columbary (kǫ·lʌmbări). 1549. [See prec.] A pigeon-house or dove-cote.

Columbate (kǒlʌ·mbĕⁱt). 1816. [f. COLUMBIUM.] *Chem.* A salt of columbic acid.

Columbiad (kǒlʌ·mbi,æd). 1798. [See next.] 1. An epic of America. 2. A kind of heavy cast-iron cannon formerly used in the U.S. army 1844.

Columbian (kǒlʌ·mbiăn), *a.* 1828. [f. mod. L. *Columbia*, poet. name for America (f. Columbus).] Of or belonging to America or (*esp.*) the United States.

Columbic (kǒlʌ·mbik), *a.*[1] 1807. [f. COLUMBIUM + -IC.] *Chem.* Of or pertaining to columbium.

C. acid: the same as *niobic acid*; see NIOBIC.

Colu·mbic, *a.*[2], var. of *calumbic*; see CALUMBA.

Columbier (kǒlʌ·mbiəɹ). 1875. [a. F. *colombier.*] A size of paper measuring about $34^1/_2$ inches by 24.

Columbi·ferous, *a.* 1828. [f. COLUMBIUM + -FEROUS.] Yielding or containing columbium.

Columbin (kǒlʌ·mbin). 1882. [Transf. use of F. *colombin.*] *Elect.* An insulating material (now made of a mixture of calcium and barium sulphates) used for connecting the sockets of the Jablochkoff candle.

Columbin(e, var. of *calumbin*; see CALUMBA.

Columbine (kǫ·lʌmbəin), *a.* and *sb.*[1] [ME., a. F. *colombin*, ad. L. *columbinus*, f. *columba* dove.] Of, belonging to, or of the nature of, a dove or pigeon 1656; dove-like, as *c. simplicity* ME.; dove-coloured ME. quasi-*sb.* Short for *columbine colour* 1606.

Columbine (kǫ·lʌmbəin), *sb.*[2] ME. [a. F. *colombine.*] The English name for plants of the genus *Aquilegia*, esp. *A. vulgaris*; †also, a name for *Verbena officinalis* -1597. Also *attrib.*

Columbine (kǫ·lʌmbəin), *sb.*[3] 1727. [ad. It. *Colombina*, fem. proper name, f. *colombino* dove-like.] The mistress of Harlequin in Pantomime or Harlequinade.

Columbite (kǒlʌ·mbəit). 1805. [f. COLUMBIUM.] *Min.* The native ore of columbium, a black columbate of iron and manganese; niobite.

Columbium (kǒlʌ·mbiǒm). 1801. [f. *Columbia* poet. name for America.] *Chem.* A metallic element, occurring in columbite and other minerals. Discovered in a specimen of columbite brought from Massachusetts. Symbol Cb. Now called *niobium.*

Columbo, var. of CALUMBA.

Columel (kǫ·liŭmel). 1610. [ad. L. *columella.*] A small column. Also *transf.* and *attrib.*

‖**Columella** (kǫliume·lă). 1585. [L., dim. of *columna.*] 1. *Anat.* Applied to the uvula, the axis of the cochlea of the ear (*c. cochleæ*), and other analogous structures. 2. *Conch.* The axis of a spiral shell 1755. 3. *Bot.* a. 'The long axis round which the parts of a (dehiscent) fruit are united'. b. The axis of the spore-case of an urn-moss. c. The axis over which the spore-cases of such ferns as *Trichomanes* are arranged. 4. *Zool.* a. A part of the pterygoid bone in the skull of lizards (*c. cranii*). b. A delicate bone in the middle ear of birds, reptiles, and amphibians (*c. auris*). c. The central axis of the visceral chamber of many corals. 1848. Hence **Colume·llar** *a.* of or belonging to a c. **Colume·lliform** *a.* shaped like a little pillar.

Column (kǫ·lǒm), *sb.* ME. [orig. a. OF. *colompne, colombe* :—L. *columna* (*columpna*), a collateral form of *columen, culmen*, f. root *cel-* (*-cellere*).] 1. *Arch.* A cylindrical or slightly tapering body of considerably greater length than diameter, erected vertically as a support for some part of a building; *spec.* in the classic orders, a round pillar, with base, shaft, and capital supporting the entablature. Sometimes standing alone as a monument: *e.g.* Trajan's Column at Rome. 1481. b. Anything of columnar shape or appearance, as *a c. of water, air, mercury, smoke, the spinal c.*, etc. 1673. c. *fig.* Support or prop. (Cf. *pillar.*) 1619. 2. A narrow division of a page, etc., formed by vertical lines or separating spaces; also, letterpress, letters, or figures arranged vertically. In *pl.* said *esp.* of the vertical divisions in a newspaper, etc. ME. 3. *Bot.* The upright structure formed by the coalescence of the filaments, as in the mallow, or by the union of the stamens with the style, as in orchids 1807. 4. *Mil.* A formation of troops narrow laterally and deep from front to rear 1677. 5. *Naut.* A body or division of ships 1805.

1. Where the shatter'd columns lie, Showing Carthage once had been SCOTT. *Comb.* **c.-rule** (*Printing*), a thin piece of brass used to separate columns of type.

‖**Columna** (kǒlʌ·mnă). Pl. **-æ.** 1758. [L.] A column or pillar; a name given to many parts of the body.

Columnar (kǒlʌ·mnăɹ), *a.* 1728. [ad. late L. *columnaris*, f. *columna.*] 1. Of the nature or form of a column (or columns). Also *fig.* 2. Written or printed in columns 1846. 3. Characterized by, or raised on, columns 1849. vars. **Colu·mnal, Columna·rian** (*rare*), **†Colu·mnary.**

Columned (kǫ·lǒmd), *ppl. a.* 1791. [f. COLUMN.] 1. Furnished with columns. (Chiefly *poet.*) 2. Columnar 1871. 3. Divided into columns 1821.

1. Ilion's c. citadel TENNYSON. vars. (in sense 1) **Co·lumnated, Colu·mniated** *ppl. adjs.*

Columnia·tion. 1592. [app. after *intercolumniation*, f. L. *intercolumnium.* Better *Columnation.*] 1. *Arch.* 'The employment of columns in a design' (Gwilt). 2. Division (of a page) into columns. LAMB.

Columni·ferous, *a.* 1730. [f. L. *columnifer.*]

Bearing a column or columns. In *Bot.* cf. COLUMN 3. So **Colu·mniform** *a.* column-shaped.

Colure (kolᶦūᵊ·ɹ, kōᵘ·liuɹ). ME. [ad. L. *colurus*, Gr. κόλουρος (f. κόλος docked + οὐρά tail), as sb. pl. (αἱ) κόλουροι (sc. γραμμαί) the colures, so called because their lower part is always cut off from view (*i. e.* in Greece, etc.).] *Astron.* Each of two great circles which intersect each other at right angles at the poles, and divide the equinoctial and the ecliptic into four equal parts. One passes through the equinoctial, the other through the solstitial, points of the ecliptic.

From Pole to Pole, traversing each C. MILT. *P. L.* IX. 66.

‖**Colutea** (kolᶦū·tīᵢă). 1664. [L., ad. Gr. κολουτέα.] *Bot.* Bladder-senna.

Coly, see COLIES.

Colza (kǫ·lză). Also **colsa.** 1712. [a. F. *colza*, earlier *colzat*, a. LGer. *kôlsât*, Du. *koolzaad* COLE-SEED.] The French name of COLE-SEED. **C.-oil**: the oil expressed from the seeds, much used for burning in lamps.

Com-, *prefix*, the archaic form of cl. L. *cum*, meaning, 'together, together with, in combination or union', also 'altogether, completely', and hence *intensive*. The form *com-* is used before *b, p, m*, and before a few words beginning with vowels; the *m* was assimilated before *r, l*, and in later times *n*; dropped before vowels generally, *h* and *gn-*; before all other consonants *com-* became CON-, q. v. See also CO-.

Coma[1] (kōᵘ·mă). 1646. [a. Gr. κῶμα (κωματ-); cf. κοιμάειν.] *Pathol.* A state of unnatural, heavy, prolonged sleep, with complete unconsciousness and slow, stertorous breathing, frequently ending in death.

Coma vigil: a state in which a typhus fever patient lies with wide open eyes, totally unconscious, but muttering in delirium.

Coma[2] (kōᵘ·mă). Pl. **-mæ** (-mī). 1669. [a. L., a. Gr. κόμη.] **1.** *Bot.* **a.** A tuft of silky hairs at the end of some seeds. **b.** A tuft of bracts occurring beyond the inflorescence. **c.** The arrangement of branches forming the head of a tree. **2.** *Astron.* The nebulous envelope round the nucleus of a comet 1765. **Co·mal** *a.*

Co-ma·rt. See 1605 (Q°.) SHAKS. *Haml.* I. i. 93. The Folios have 'cou'nant'.

Co-ma·rtyr, comma·rtyr. 1555. [a. L. (see COM-).] A fellow-martyr.

‖**Comarum** (kǫ·mărǒm). 1778. [Bot.L., a. Gr. κόμαρον.] *Bot.* A Linnæan genus of *Rosaceæ*, including the Purple Marsh Cinquefoil.

Co-mate (kōᵘᵢmēᶦt: the stress varies). 1576. [See CO-.] Companion, fellow, mate.

†**Co·mate,** *a.* 1600. [ad. L. *comatus.*] Hairy.

Comatose (kōᵘ·mătōᵘs), *a.* 1755. [f. as COMA[1] + -OSE.] **1.** Affected with coma; of the nature of coma 1761; drowsy, lethargic 1828. var. †**Co·matous.**

‖**Comatula** (komæ·tiulă). Pl. **-læ** (-lī). 1851. [L. fem. of *comatulus*, dim. of *comatus.*] *Zool.* A genus of free-swimming Crinoid Echinoderms, of a radiate shape with (usually) ten cirrous arms; the feather-star. So **Coma·tulid**, any of the *Comatulidæ*, the family containing the c.

Comb (kōᵘm), *sb.*[1] [Com. Teut.: OE. *cǫmb, camb*:—OTeut. **kamboz*, pre-Teut. **gombhos*; cf. Gr. γόμφος, Skr. *gambhas* tooth.] **1.** A strip of wood, bone, horn, metal, etc., with teeth; used for disentangling, cleaning, and arranging the hair, or keeping it in place. Also *fig.* **2.** An instrument composed of a series of such strips, used for currying horses; a CURRY-COMB ME. **3.** *transf.* Anything resembling a comb in function, structure, or appearance; as (*a*) a toothed instrument used in dressing wool or flax; (*b*) a tool with teeth, used for cutting the thread of a screw or work in the lathe; (*c*) a toothed instrument used in graining or marbling; (*d*) the notched scale of a wire-micrometer; (*e*) *Electr.* a comb-like row of brass points for collecting the electricity from the plate of an electrical machine. **4.** Any natural formation resembling a comb; *esp.* a. *Zool.* (*pl.*) the pair of abdominal appendages in Scorpions 1834; **b.** the red fleshy crest or caruncle on the head of the domestic fowl (cf. COCK'S-COMB) OE. **5.** Anything resembling a cock's comb in position or appearance (= crest); as, the crest of a helmet OE., of a wave 1886, the projection on the top of the cock of a gun-lock 1867, and the like. **6.** The flat cake or plate consisting of a double series of hexagonal cells of wax made by bees; a honeycomb [Eng. only] ME.

4. b. *To cut the c. of*: to take down, humiliate. All the Counts in Cumberland shall not cut my c. SCOTT. **6.** Wordis wel set togidere is a coomb of hony WYCLIF *Prov.* xvi. 24. Hence **Co·mbwise** *adv.* **Co·mby** *a.* having combs or a comb-like structure.

Comb (kŭm), *sb.*[2], var. of COOMB[1], a measure.

Comb (kūm), *sb.*[3], var. of COOMB[2], a valley.

Comb (kōᵘm), *v.* ME. [f. COMB *sb.*[1]] **1.** *trans.* To clean, disentangle, or arrange with a comb. **2.** To dress with a comb 1577; *transf.* to scrape or rake as with a comb 1654. **3.** *intr.* Of waves: To roll over and break with a foamy crest 1807. orig. *U.S.* **4.** *trans.* To search (as with a tooth-comb) 1904; to clean *out* 1916.

1. Combe downe his haire 2 *Hen. VI*, III. iii. 15. **2.** They don't..c. wool in the Monasteries DE FOE. Voters to be combed off by a Radical GEO. ELIOT. **3.** The waves combed over the vessel W. C. RUSSELL.

Comba·ron. ME. [Fr.] *Hist.* A fellow-baron (of the Cinque Ports).

Combat (kǫ·mbæt, kɒ·mbæt), *sb.* 1567. [a. F., f. *combattre.*] **1.** An encounter or fight between two persons (parties, animals, etc.). Hence, *single combat.* 1622. **2.** *gen.* A fight between opposing forces; usually on a smaller scale than a *battle* 1583. Also *fig.*

1. *Trial by c.*: = BATTLE 2. Where Champions bold ..Defi'd the best of Panim chivalry To mortal c. MILT. *P. L.* I. 766. **2.** *fig.* The combate of wits HOBBES.

Combat (kǫ·mbæt, kɒ·mbæt), *v.* 1564. [ad. F. *combattre*, a Com. Rom. vb.:—late L. **combattere.* Cf. ABATE, DEBATE.] **1.** *intr.* To fight or do battle (orig. *esp.* in single combat). Const. *with, against.* Also *fig.* **2.** *trans.* To fight with, engage, oppose in battle 1590. Also *fig.* (Now most usual.)

1. I will not c. in my shirt *L. L. L.* v. ii. 711. *fig.* His face still combating with teares and smiles *Rich. II*, v. ii. 32. **2.** He hath no more Antagonists to combate 1652. *fig.* To c. reasons MILT *Sams.* 864, truth WOLLASTON, prejudice BURKE. Hence **Co·mbatable** *a.* capable of being combated (*rare*). **Co·mbater** (*rare*). **Co·mbative** *a.* given to c., pugnacious. **Co·mbatively** *adv.* **Co·mbativeness,** propensity to fight. (Orig. a Phrenological term.)

Combatant (kǫ·m-, kɒ·mbătănt). 1489. [a. OF. (mod.F. *combatt-*).] **A.** *adj.* Fighting, ready to fight 1632. **b.** *Her.* Rampant with the fore-paws raised as if in fight; said of two lions, etc. rampant and facing each other (*affronté*). (Freq. spelt *combattant.*) 1500.

B. *sb.* One who combats, a fighter; in early use *esp.* one who fought in single combat 1489. Also *fig.*

So frownd the mighty Combatants MILT. *P. L.* II. 719.

Co·mb-brush. 1611. **1.** 'A brush to clean combs'. †**2.** A lady's maid -1749.

Combe, var. of COOMB[2]; obs. f. COOMB[1].

Comber[1] (kōᵘ·məɹ). 1646. [f. COMB *v.* + -ER.] **1.** One who or that which combs; *spec.* one who combs wool. **2.** A combing wave; see COMB *v.* 3, and cf. *beach-comber* 1840.

Comber[2] (kǫ·mbəɹ). 1769. A fish: *Serranus cabrilla*; also, short for *Comber Wrasse.*

Combinable (kǒmbəi·năb'l), *a.* 1749. [f. COMBINE *v.* + -ABLE.] Capable of combining or of being combined. Hence **Combi·nableness.**

Combinant (kǫ·mbinănt). 1628. [ad. late L. *combinantem.*] †**1.** A confederate. **2.** *Math.* (See quot.)

2. An invariant of a system of quantics of the same degree is called a c. if it is unaltered (except by a constant multiplier) not only when the variables are lineally transformed, but also when for any of the quantics is substituted a linear function of the quantics SALMON. Hence **Co·mbinantive** *a.* pertaining to, or of the nature of, a c.

Combinate (kǫ·mbinēᶦt), *a. rare.* 1583. [ad. late L. *combinatus.*] Combined. In *Meas. for M.* III. i. 231 taken as 'Betrothed, promised, settled by contract' (J.).

Combination (kǫmbinēᶦ·ʃən). 1532. [a. OF. (mod.F. *combinaison*), ad. late L. *combinationem.*] **1.** The action of combining two or more separate things 1613. **2.** Combined state or condition; conjunction 1597. **3.** *concr.* A group of things combined into a whole 1532. **4.** The association of persons for a common object; usually in a bad sense 1593; *concr.* an association thus formed 1571. **5.** *Math.* (*pl.*) The different groups of a definite number which can be made of any number of given individuals without regard to the order of arrangement 1673. **6.** *Chem.* Chemical union, in which substances combine to form new compounds; *concr.* a compound so formed 1766. **7.** Short for *c.-room* 1749. **8.** *pl.* = *c.-garment* 1884. **9.** A motor-cycle with side-car attached 1914.

1. Combinations of letters CUDWORTH, of ideas LOCKE. **2.** The same images in the same c. JOHNSON. **4.** Either by c. or by any other sort of violence 1776. A solemne C. shall be made Of our deere soules SHAKS.

Comb.: **c. garment**, an under-garment consisting of combined chemise or undershirt and drawers, worn mostly by women; **c. laws**, laws directed against combinations of masters or workmen, repealed in 1824; **c. pedal** = COMPOSITION *pedal*; **c. -room** (**-chamber**), in the University of Cambridge (England) = COMMON-ROOM. Hence **Combina·tional** *a.* of or pertaining to c.

Co·mbinator. *rare.* 1611. = COMBINER.

Combinative (kǫ·mbinēᶦtiv), *a.* 1855. [f. L. *combinat-*, *combinare* + -IVE.] **1.** Having the faculty of combination. **2.** Of, pertaining to, or of the nature of combination; cumulative 1867. var. **Combina·tory.** So **Co·mbinato·rial** *a.* of or relating to (mathematical) combinations.

†**Combi·nd,** *v.* 1477. [Fusion of *combine* and *bind.*] *trans.* and *intr.* = COMBINE -1605.

Combine (kǒmbəi·n), *v.* ME. [ad. late L. *combinare*, f. *com-* + *bini* two together.] **1.** *trans.* To couple or join together; to join in action, condition, or feeling; to conjoin, associate, ally. **2.** To cause to unite or coalesce into one body or substance; *esp.* in *Chem.* 1799. **3.** To unite (distinct qualities) 1827. **4.** *intr.* To come together into one body, coalesce; *esp.* in *Chem.* Cf. COMBINATION 6. 1712. **5.** To unite together for a common purpose; to form a union, *spec.* for some economic, social, or political purpose; to form a combination 1605. Also *fig.* of things. ¶ **6.** In *Meas. for M.* IV. iii. 149, perh. = To bind.

1. To c. a sinew cut asunder 1599. God..C. your hearts in one, your Realmes in one *Hen. V*, v. ii. 388. Phr. *To c. efforts, forces*, etc. **3.** Combining French clearness with old English depth CARLYLE. **5.** When bad men c., good men must associate BURKE. Hence †**Combi·nement,** combination. **Combi·ner,** one who or that which combines.

Combine (kǫ·mbəin, kǒmbəi·n), *sb.* 1610. [f. prec.] †A conspiracy. **b.** *U.S. colloq.* A combination of persons for commercial, political, or fraudulent ends 1887.

Combined (kǒmbəi·nd), *ppl. a.* ME. United; confederated; performed by agents acting in combination; produced by combination. Hence **Combi·nedly** *adv.* **Combi·nedness.**

Combing (kōᵘ·miŋ), *vbl. sb.* 1575. [f. COMB *v.* + -ING[1].] **1.** The action of COMB *v.* **2.** *concr.* (usu. *pl.*) The produce of combing; hairs combed off; borders, etc. made of these 1656.

2. The baldnesse, thinnesse, and..deformity of their haire, is usually supplyed by borders and combings 1656. *Comb.* **c.-machine,** one for combing wool.

Combing (kōᵘ·miŋ), *ppl. a.* 1857. [f. as prec.] That combs; *esp.* of a wave (see COMB *v.* 3).

Combing, var. of COAMING.

Combless (kōᵘ·mlės), *a.* 1596. Without a comb (in various senses; see COMB *sb.*[1]).

Combre, obs. f. CUMBER.

Combretaceous (kǫmbrĭtēᶦ·ʃəs), *a.* 1864. [f. bot.L. *Combretaceæ*, f. *Combretum* (prob. a kind of rush).] *Bot.* Of or belonging to the N.O. *Combretaceæ*, of which the typical genus *Combretum* consists of trailing or climbing tropical shrubs.

†**Combu·re,** *v.* 1570. [ad. OF. *comburir*, ad. L. *comburere*, f. *com-* + ?*burere* (whence *bustum*).] To burn up. Also *intr.* (for *refl.*) -1613. So **Combu·rence,** comburent quality or action (*rare*). **Combu·rent** *a.* and *sb.* †burning, causing combustion (*rare*).

Comburgess (kǫmbɒ̄·ɹdʒės). 1517. [after med.L. *comburgensis.*] *Hist.* **1.** A fellow-burgess, fellow-citizen or freeman of a borough. †**2.** One of the municipal magistrates formerly chosen by and from among their fellow-burgesses in certain English boroughs -1835.

Combust (kǒmbɒ·st), *a.* ME. [a. OF., ad. L. *combustus*; see COMBURE.] †**1.** Burnt; *spec.*

calcined -1678; adust -1607. **2.** *Astrol.* Of the planets: Burnt up (as it were) by the sun in or near conjunction; (app.) extinguished by the sun's light ME.

2. Planets that are oft Combust..untill the opposite motion of their orbs bring them..where they may be seen MILT. Hence **Combu·st** *v.* to burn up; to calcine. (Now joc. or affected.)

Combustible (kǫ̆mbʊ·stib'l), *a.* (*sb.*) 1529. [a. F., f. late L. *combustibilis*; see COMBURE.] **1.** Capable of being consumed by fire, fit for burning, burnable. **2.** *fig.* Easily kindled to violence or passion; excitable; inflammable 1647. **3.** *sb.* [sc. substance or matter.] Also *fig.* 1688.

1. Stubble, and such like c. matter GOLDSM. 2. The commons, aware of what c. materials the army was composed HUME. *sb.* Tar and other combustibles 1748. Hence **Combustibi·lity, Combu·stibleness,** c. quality.

Combustion (kǫmbʊ·stiən, -tʃən). 1477. [a. OF., ad. late L. *combustionem*; see COMBURE.] **1.** The action or process of burning 1600; †a conflagration -1664. Also *fig.* and *transf.* **2.** The development of light and heat, chemical combination 1477. **b.** In the obs. sense of 'combination of a body with oxygen', applied to processes of oxidation unaccompanied by evolution of light, as *internal c.*, etc. 1800. †**3.** *Path.* A burn; also, inflammation -1656. †**4.** *Astrol.* Obscuration by proximity to the sun. See COMBUST *a.* 2. -1743.

1. The c. of incense 1867. *Spontaneous c.*: see SPONTANEOUS. In spiritual invisible c. [mounts up] one authority after another CARLYLE. The inn-yard was in a sort of c. SCOTT. Hence †**Combu·stious** *a.* burning; combustible; tumultuous. So **Combu·stive** *a.* having the quality of causing c.

Come (kʊm), *v.* Pa. t. **came** (kē^i^m); pa. pple. **come** (kʊm). [A com. Teut. str. vb.: OE. *cuman* :—OTeut. *kuman* :—Aryan *g^w^m-*, cf. Skr. and Zend. *gam*, Gr. βαίνω (:—*βάνjω :—*gwmjo-), etc. The perfect tenses were originally formed with *be*; now, *be* expresses the resulting state, *have* the action.] *gen.* An elementary intrans. vb. of motion expressing movement towards the speaker or a point where he mentally places himself, towards the person spoken to, or towards the person spoken of; opp. to *go*.

I. 1. To move towards; *esp.* to reach by moving towards; hence, To arrive. Const. with *infin.*, with *to*, *vbl. sb.* with *a*, *and*, pple. in *-ing*, *advb. accus.* **2.** To move or be brought hitherward or *to* a particular position. Const. as in 1. ME. **3.** To extend, reach, to or towards ME.

1. Here comyn our enmyes CAXTON. 2. The winde came Easterly 1633. The..arrows came thick among them DE FOE. The horse..came on his head 1804. 3. Does the railway c. near the town (*mod.*). Phr. *To c. to an end, a point*, etc.

II. 1. To fall to one ME. **2.** To happen *to*, befall OE. **3.** To flow, be derived, descend *from*, *of* ME. **4.** To enter *into* 1513. **5.** To come into existence, appear ME.

1. The Papacy came to Alexander the Third 1674. 2. All things c. alike to all *Eccl.* ix. 2. A knock came to his door 1849. Phr. *To c. into one's head, to one's knowledge.* 3. Come of gentle kin C. BRONTË. Some Mischief will c. of it BUTLER *Hud.* I. i. 758. 4. To c. into fashion 1825, existence 1850, contact 1850, play 1850. 5. To churn milk till butter c. 1641

III. 1. To arrive at in due order ME.; to be present in due course ME. **2.** To reach, attain *to*, as an end 1475. **3.** To come about; to arrive, take place ME. **4.** To be brought, attain *to* ME. **5.** To become, get to be ME.; to turn out to be 1862.

1. We now c. to the reign of Queen Mary 1781. The time must c. 1833. 2. To c. to an understanding FIELDING, to abusive words SCOTT, to blows MACAULAY. 3. How commeth this 1548. For March, There come Violets BACON. 4. His Sonnes c. to honour *Job* xiv. 21. He comes to his full Growth in a Year 1758. 5. To 'come untied' DICKENS. Law comes rather expensive (*mod.*).

†**IV.** To become, belong *to*, befit. [L. *convenire.*] -1670.

V. Quasi-*trans.* uses. **1.** To act, to perform one's part (*colloq.*) 1812; to play (a dodge or trick), *esp.* with *over* (*colloq.*) 1785; to act the part of (*slang* or *colloq.*) 1837. **2.** To attain to, reach, achieve (*dial.* and *colloq.*) 1888. **3.** *To come* or *be coming* (now *rising*) *six*, etc.: to be in one's sixth year 1675.

1. To c. it strong 1825. To c. the religious dodge THACKERAY. To c. the bully over 1850. 2. To c. a cropper: see CROPPER. 3. She is in Fole, and cometh six 1682.

VI. Spec. uses of parts of the verb.

1. *To come*, the dative infinitive, is used: **a.** *attrib.* (after sb.) = That is to come ME.; **b.** *absol.* The future 1597. **2.** *Come*, the imperative, is used: **a.** as an invitation to action, usu. along with the speaker OE.; **b.** as a call or appeal. implying impatience, remonstrance, or mild protest ME. **3.** *Come*, the present conj., is used: **a.** with a future date following as subject, as in 'come Easter', *i.e.* let Easter come (*arch.* and *dial.*) ME.; **b.** with an interval of time (week, month, etc.) following and qualifying a date, as in 'at Midsummer come a year'. Now *dial.* ME. **4.** *Coming*, pres. pple., used of age: see V. 3. **b.** = 'I am coming', 'directly!' 1701.

VII. With prepositions.

1. The preposition naturally following *come* is *to*; instead of which, however, any other may follow, in which the notion *to* is contained or involved, as *into*, *unto*, *towards*, *against*, *on*, *upon*, *about*, *around*, *beside*, *near*, *above*, *beneath*, *before*, *behind*, *over*, *under* the point of direction; *before* a person, a tribunal, etc. Relations of other kinds may also be considered, e. g. *from* the point left, *across*, *along*, *through*, *by*, *over*, *under*, *up*, *down* a route followed or things passed, *with* a companion, etc., *by*, *in* a conveyance, *for* a thing wanted, *after* a person or thing followed or sought.

2. In specialized senses. **To c. across —.** To meet, meet with; to fall in with by chance. **To c. at —** (= L. *accedere*). †**a.** To come so as to be present *at*. †**b.** To touch or know carnally. **c.** To get at, reach (with effort), obtain. **d.** To make for, attack. **To c. by —.** To come near, to get at; hence, to obtain. **To c. into —. a.** See II. 3. †**b.** To accede to. **c.** To come into possession of. **To c. of —. a.** See II. 3. **b.** = Become of. **To c. on —.** = *Come upon* (see below). **To c. over —. a.** See above. †**b.** To surpass. **c.** To take possession of (*fig.*). So *Come over with* (Shaks.). **d.** To befall. **e.** To get the better of. **To c. round —.** = *Come over* e. **To c. to —. a.** See above. **b.** To succeed in due course to. **c.** To amount to. **d.** To cost. **e.** *fig.* To mean. **f.** To turn in the end to. **g.** *Come to oneself*, etc.: To recover consciousness; to come to one's right mind. **To c. under —. a.** To rank, fall, be classed under. **b.** To be subjected to. **To c. unto —. a.** See above. †**b.** = *Come to.* **To c. upon —. a.** See above. **b.** To attack, invade. **c.** To make a demand or claim upon. **d.** To become a burden on. **e.** To meet with as it were by chance. **To c. within —** see WITHIN.

VIII. With adverbs in specialized senses.

To c. about. a. = *Come round* b, c, d. **b.** To come to pass. †**c.** To fulfil itself *Rom. & Jul.* I. iii. 45. **To c. abroad.** To come forth from house or seclusion; to appear (*arch.*). **To c. again.** To return. **To c. along.** To move onward (toward or with the speaker). **To c. away. a.** To come on one's way; see AWAY. **b.** To come from the place; see AWAY. **c.** To detach itself; see AWAY. **d.** To grow apace. **To c. back.** To return (hither), in space or time. **To c. by.** To come near; to pass. **To c. down. a.** To descend; see DOWN *adv.* **b.** To extend downward. **c.** To fall. **d.** To be lowered. **e.** *To come down upon —*: to descend with authority, severity, hostility, or suddenness upon. **f.** *To come down* (*with*) —: to bring or put down (*esp.* money) (*colloq.*) **To c. in. a.** To enter hither, *esp.* into a house, room, land, etc. †**b.** (in *Script.*) *To come in unto*: to have carnal intercourse with. **c.** To move or advance inwards; to arrive. †**d.** *Fencing.* To get within the opponent's guard. †**e.** To submit. **f.** To be successful in a candidature; to come into power. **g.** Of things: To be brought or given in. **h.** To begin to be in season, use, or fashion; to be opportune. **i.** To take its place. **j.** To begin, as a time or season. **k.** *To come in for*: to receive incidentally. **l.** *To come in upon, on*: to enter one's mind. **To c. near.** To approach in place, order, qualities, etc.; see NEAR. So *come nigh.* **To c. off. a.** To come away from *e.g.* a ship, a coast, etc. **b.** To become detached. **c.** To retire or extricate oneself from any engagement; as *to c. off second best*, etc. †**d.** Of things: To turn out. **e.** To take place. †**f.** To pay. **To c. on. a.** To advance hitherward. **b.** To advance in growth or development. **c.** To supervene: said of bad weather, fits of illness, etc. **d.** To come in course to be dealt with. **e.** To come upon the scene of action. **f.** *Come on!* used *esp.* as a challenge or call of defiance. **To c. out. a.** *lit.* i. e. out of a place, a house, etc. **b.** *esp.* 'out into the field', *i. e.* to fight. **c.** To leave one's employment, *e.g.* on strike. **d.** To emerge from a contest, competition, etc. **e.** To appear, as the sun, etc. **f.** To protrude. **g.** To come into public view; to become public; to be played, as a card. **h.** To result. **i.** To develop; as flowers, diseases, etc. **j.** To become evident. **k.** To be published. **l.** To show or declare oneself. **m.** To make a *début.* **n.** To make a formal entry into society. **To c. out of. a.** *lit.* To issue from. **b.** To escape. **c.** To extend out of (a place); to project or grow out of. **To c. out with.** To bring out; to utter, give vent to. **To c. over. a.** *lit.* To come, passing over; to cross. **b.** To change sides, hitherward. **To c. round. a.** To come by a circuitous route; to come in an informal way. **b.** To come with the revolution of time or events. **c.** To veer round, as the wind, to a more favourable quarter; to turn favourably in opinion. **d.** To return to a normal state or to a better mood; to recover from a swoon, etc. **To c. to. a.** = OE. *tō-cuman* to arrive; L. *advenire*. **b.** *Naut.* To come to a standstill; also, to come close to the wind. **c.** To come round to accord, or a pleasant mood. Now *dial.* **d.** To recover (from a swoon, etc.). **To c. up. a.** *lit.* To ascend; to come to a place viewed as higher, or as a centre, *e.g.* the capital or a university. **b.** To come close forward (*to*). **c.** To come right forward from the rear; esp. *to c. up with*, to overtake. **d.** To spring up, as a plant. **e.** To originate, come into use. **f.** To turn up; to arise in the mind. **g.** To amount *to*; to equal. **h.** *Naut.* To come to a direction. **i.** To slacken (a rope, cable, etc.), as in *C. up Capstan*, i. e. 'slack the Cable which you heave by'. **j.** In the imperative, a call to a horse. **k.** *Marry c. up!* see MARRY.

Phrases. **C. and go. a.** To come to a place and depart again; to pass to and fro. **b.** To be first present and then absent; to approach and recede; to arrive and pass, as time, etc. *C. your ways*: see WAY.

For other phrases, as *c.* AMISS, HOME, SHORT, of AGE, to ANCHOR, to BLOWS, to CLOSE QUARTERS, to GRIEF, to HAND, to HEEL, to LIFE, to LIGHT, to NATURE, to the FRONT, to the POINT, to TERMS, to TIME, to an UNDERSTANDING, up to the MARK, to the SCRATCH, etc., see under these words.

Come (kʊm), *sb.* [OE. *cyme* :—OTeut. type **kumiz*, f. *kuman* to come.] Approach, arrival, coming. (*Obs.* exc. in comp., as *income*, etc.) *C. and go*: passage to and fro. Also *attrib.*

Come-at-able (kʊm,æ·tăb'l), *a.* *colloq.* 1687. [f. phr. *to come at* (see COME *v.*).] That may be come at or reached; accessible.

Co·me-back. **1.** An act of retaliation; a retort (*U.S.*) 1889. **2.** A return 1922.

Co·me-by-chance. *colloq.* 1760. One who or that which comes by chance; a bastard.

Comedian (kǒmī·diăn). 1581. [ad. F. *comédien*, a. (ult.) Gr. κωμῳδία COMEDY.] **1.** A player in comedies; *occas.*, an actor 1601. Also *fig.* **2.** A writer of comedies 1581. Also *attrib.*

1. Are you a C. SHAKS. var. †**Come·diant.**

‖**Comédienne** (komedie·n). [Fr., fem. of *comédien.*] A comedy actress.

Comedietta (kǒmīdi,e·tă). 1836. [a. It., dim. of *comedia.*] A short or slight comedy.

‖**Comedo** (kǫ·mīdo). Pl. **-ones, -os, -ons.** 1866. [L., a glutton, f. *comedere.*] 'A small worm-like yellowish black-tipped pasty mass which can in some persons be made, by pressure, to exude from hair follicles. They are found on the cheeks, forehead, and nose'. Also, the skin disorder in which these are found.

Come-dow·n, *sb.* 1563. [f. phr. *to come down*; see COME *v.*] A downfall; a notable reverse 1840.

Comedy (kǫ·mĭdi). ME. [a. F. *comédie*, ad. L. *comœdia*, a. Gr. κωμῳδία, f. (ult.) either κῶμος revel or κώμη village + ἀείδειν (cf. ODE).] **1.** A light and amusing stage-play, with a happy conclusion to its plot. Applied also, formerly, to narrative poems, mystery plays, and interludes, with a happy ending. **2.** That branch of the drama which adopts a humorous or familiar style, and depicts laughable characters and incidents. (Occas. *personified.*) ME. *fig.* of incidents, etc. in real life 1570. Also *attrib.*

1. Mr. William Shakespeares Comedies, Histories, & Tragedies (*title*) 1623. 2. Persons, such as c. would choose, When she would show an image of the times, And sport with human follies, not with crimes B. JONS. *fig.* The great human c. MORLEY.

Comeliness (kʊ·mlinės). ME. [f. COMELY *a.*] The quality of being COMELY.

Hee hath no forme nor comelinesse *Isa.* liii. 2. Things.. which a Man cannot, with any Face or Comelines, say or doe Himselfe BACON.

Comeling (kʊ·mliŋ). *arch.* and *dial.* [OE. **cumeling*, f. *cuman* to come.] An immigrant, not a permanent resident; also †a novice.

These new comelings began to molest the homelings 1577.

Comely (kʊ·mli), *a.* [OE. *cȳmlīc*, f. *cȳme* fine :—WGer. *kūmi-* + *līc*; see LIKE, -LY [1].] **1.** Fair, pretty, beautiful, nice. (As used of persons, it implies a homelier style of beauty, which pleases without exciting admiration.) **2.** Pleasing to the moral sense or æsthetic taste; becoming, proper, decorous ME.

1. Comly apparell 1535. Civil-suited Morn..Cherchef't in a comly Cloud MILT. *Pens.* 1632. No comlyar creatur of goddes creacyon 1485. Rather c. than beautiful GAY. 2. Prayse is c. for the vpright *Ps.* xxxiii. 1. Marching home In c. order POPE. Hence **Co·melily** *adv.* ? *Obs.* †**Co·mely** *adv.*

Come-o·ff, *sb.* 1634. [f. phr. *to come off*; see COME *v.*] 1. A finish-up, a conclusion. 2. An evasion, excuse for non-performance 1849.

Comer (kv·mǝɹ). ME. [f. COME *v.* + -ER[1].] 1. One who comes; a visitor, an arrival. Often qualified, as *first c.*, NEW-COMER, etc. †2. Of a plant: A grower. BACON.

1. *All comers*: everybody or anybody that comes.

‖**Comes.** 1683. [L., f. *com-* + *ire.*] **a.** *Eccl. Antiq.* A book containing the epistles and gospels read at mass. **b.** *Mus.* The answer to the first subject (*dux*) in a fugue.

†**Comessation.** ME. [a. OF. *comessacion*, ad. L. *comessationem*, f. *comessari*, better *comissari.*] 1. Feasting, 'riotous eating' -1642. 2. Eating together -1686.

Comestible (kǫme·stib'l). 1483. [a. F., f. (ult.) L. *com-* + *edere.*] †*adj.* Fit to eat, edible -1683 *sb.* Anything to eat; *pl.* eatables. (Usually *joc.*) 1837.

1. All the metes of therthe that ben c. CAXTON. So †**Come·stion**, eating; also *fig.* of fire.

Comet (kǫ·mėt). [In late OE. *cometa*, a. L. (also *cometes*), a. Gr. κομήτης (sc. ἀστήρ) long-haired star.] 1. A celestial body moving about the sun in an elongated elliptical, or a parabolic orbit, and consisting (when near the sun) of a star-like nucleus surrounded with misty light, and a train of light or 'tail'. Also *fig.* †2. A card-game -1742. 3. = *Cometes*, a genus of Humming-birds with long tails 1862.

1. *fig.* The grave of him who blazed The c. of a season BYRON. *Comb.*: **c.-finder, -seeker,** a telescope of low power and large field, used in searching for comets; **-wine**, wine made in a c.-year, reputed to have superior flavour; **-year,** one in which a notable c. has appeared.

Hence **Cometa·rium,** a contrivance for illustrating motion in an eccentric orbit. **Co·metary** *a.* pertaining to a c. or comets; c.-like. **Come·tic, -al,** *a.* cometary; *fig.* blazing, portentous, erratic. **Cometo·grapher,** one who describes comets. **Cometo·graphy,** that part of astronomy which treats of comets. **Cometo·logy.** (Dicts.)

Comfit (kv·mfit), *sb.* [ME. *comfyt*, a. OF. *confit, confite*:—L. *confectum, confecta* pa. pple. (used sb.), f. *conficere* (f. *com-* + *facere*). Cf. CONFECT.] A sweetmeat made of some fruit, root, etc., preserved with sugar; a sugar-plum. Hence †**Co·mfit** *v.* to preserve, to pickle; *esp.* to make into a c.

Comfiture (kv·mfitiŭɹ). ? *Obs.* ME. [a. F. *confiture*; see prec. and cf. CONFECTURE.] †1. A preparation of drugs. CHAUCER. 2. A preserve, confection 1558.

Comfort (kv·mfǝɹt), *v.* ME. [a. OF. *cun-, conforter*:—L. *confortare*, f. *con-* intensive + *fortis*. The change to *com-* is Eng.] †1. To strengthen; to encourage; to support; to invigorate -1674. †2. To aid, abet, countenance. (Formerly common in legal use.) -1726. †3. To cheer -1612; to relieve -1798. 4. To soothe in grief or trouble; to console. (The current sense.) ME. *pass.*, also †*intr.* (for *refl.*) To take comfort ME. 5. To make comfortable (*mod.*).

1. Wynges, to c. the bataylles, if nede requyred LD. BERNERS. To c. the memory LYTE, the braine 1637, the stomach 1671. 2. Guilty of comforting and assisting the Rebels AYLIFFE. 3. A mynstral . . alle peuple to comfortye LANGL. To c. the poor 1529. 4. To c. the afflicted state of Christians 1641. *intr.* Liue a little, c. a little, cheere thy selfe a little *A.Y.L.* II. vi. 5. 5. A comforting beverage (*mod.*).

Comfort (kv·mfǝɹt), *sb.* ME. [a. OF. *cun-, confort*; see prec.] †1. Strengthening; encouragement; aid, support, countenance. (*Obs.* exc. in legal phr. *aid and c.*) -1769. †*concr.* A support -1577. †2. Pleasure, delight -1568; relief or aid in want, etc. -1647. 3. Consolation, solace ME.; the production of content and restfulness (*mod.*); a source or means of comfort ME.; a comforting fact or reflection 1553. 4. The condition or quality of being COMFORTABLE 1814. 5. A thing that ministers to enjoyment and content. (Usu. *pl.*; opp. to *necessaries*, and *luxuries.*) 1659. 6. A quilted coverlet 1863. †7. As an interjection; = Take comfort. SHAKS.

1. That we may receiue the fruites of the yearth to our comforte *Bk. Com. Prayer.* *concr.* Oure confort and Defender 1455. 3. None else there is gives c. to my griefe DRAYTON. When other helpers fail and comforts flee 1847. Nobody . . can lose a penny by me—that is one c. SCOTT. 4. In peace and c. WORDSW. 5. *Creature comforts*: food, etc. So *home comforts.* 7. *Wint. T.* IV. iv. 848. Hence **Co·mfortful** *a.* full of c. **Co·mfortless** *a.*, **-ly** *adv.*, **-ness.**

Comfortable (kv·mfǝɹtăb'l), *a.* (*sb.*) ME. [a. Anglo-F. *confortable*, f. *conforter* to COMFORT. (Mod.F. *confortable* is from Eng.)]

A. *adj.* **I.** 1. Strengthening or supporting (*arch.*) ME.; †helpful -1725. †2. Affording pleasure or delight -1748; satisfactory; tolerable (*colloq.*) -1728. 3. Consolatory: of persons (*obs.*) or things (*arch.*) ME. 4. Affording or fitted to give tranquil enjoyment and content. (This and II. 2 are the current senses.) 1769. Also *absol.*

1. The c. expectation of Immortality BERKELEY. This c. cordial 1744. 2. The c. Sense of his [God's] Presence HARTLEY. His [the boy's] Skull seems to be of a c. thickness 1728. 3. For heauens sake speake c. words SHAKS. 4. In c. circumstances (*mod.*).

II. With pass. or neut. sense. †1. In a state of consolation; cheerful -1755. 2. Free from pain and trouble; at ease 1770; *colloq.* of persons, placidly self-satisfied 1856.

1. His c. temper forsook him *Timon* III. iv. 71. 2. Let it freeze without, we are c. within SCOTT. A motherly c. woman 1878.

B. *sb.* †1. That which gives comfort; *pl.* comforts -1675. 2. **a.** A worsted covering for the wrist. **b.** A COMFORTER for the neck. **c.** (*U.S.*) = COMFORT *sb.* 6. 1835.

Hence **Co·mfortableness,** the state of being c. **Co·mfortably** *adv.* in a c. manner.

†**Comforta·tion.** Also **con-.** ME. [a. OF. *confortacion.*] Comforting; delight -1485; strengthening -1626.

†**Comfortative,** *a.* and *sb.* [ME. *confortatif*, a. F.; see COMFORT *v.*] *adj.* Having the quality of comforting -1683. *sb.* A cordial. Also *fig.* -1742. var. †**Co·mfortive.**

Comforter (kv·mfǝɹtǝɹ). ME. [a. Anglo-F. *confortour*:—OF. *conforteor*; see COMFORT *v.*] 1. One who or that which comforts or consoles. In *Theol.* the Holy Spirit. †2. A small kind of spaniel -1790. †3. One who aids, countenances, or abets. (Chiefly legal.) -1570. 4. A long woollen scarf worn round the throat 1833. **b.** = COMFORT *sb.* 6. (*U.S.*) 5. A baby's dummy teat 1898.

1. The doctor is the best of comforters FIELDING. WYCLIF *John* xiv. 16. See also JOB *sb.*[3]

Co·mfortress. *rare.* ME. [a. OF. *conforteresse*, fem. of *conforteère.*] A female comforter.

Comfrey (kv·mfri, kǫ·m-). ME. [a. OF. *confirie, confire, confière*; ? corruption of L. *conferva*. Called also *consolida* ('quia habet vim consolidandi').] The Eng. name of *Symphytum officinale* (N.O. *Boraginaceæ*), a tall plant, with rough leaves; formerly esteemed as a vulnerary. Also applied to other plants.

Comfy (kv·mfi), *a.* 1829. *colloq.* (orig. infantile or feminine). = COMFORTABLE.

Comic (kǫ·mik). 1576. [ad. L., a. Gr. κωμικός, prob. f. κῶμος; cf. COMEDY.]

A. *adj.* 1. Of, proper, or belonging to comedy, as dist. from tragedy. 2. Burlesque, funny 1839. 3. = COMICAL 4. 1751.

1. C. opera is the opera of comedy, not 'comic' in the vulgar English sense HULLAH.

B. *sb.* †1. = COMEDIAN 1, 2. -1738. 2. *colloq.* = *c. paper* 1889. 3. quasi-*sb.* *The c.*: that which is c. 1842.

Comical (kǫ·mikăl), *a.* 1557. [f. as prec.] †1. = COMIC 1. -1725. †2. Trivial, low; opp. to *tragical*, or *elevated* -1687. †3. Like the ending of a comedy; fortunate. (Opp. to *tragical.*) -1677. 4. Mirth-provoking, humorous; ludicrous, laughable. (The ordinary sense.) 1685. 5. Queer (*colloq.* and *dial.*) 1793.

1. One Plautus, a comicall poet 1577. 3. But Comicall was the end of Job FULLER. 4. But the dog [S. Foote] was so very c., that I was obliged to . . laugh it out JOHNSON. Hence **Comica·lity,** c. or comic quality. **Co·mical-ly** *adv.*, **-ness.**

‖**Comices,** *sb. pl. rare.* 1533. [Fr., ad. L. *comitia* (cf. *notice*, etc.).] = COMITIA 1.

Comico- (kǫ·miko), comb. f. L. *comicus*, Gr. κωμικός.

Co·micry. *rare.* 1850. [f. COMIC + -RY.] Comic action or practice.

Coming (kv·miŋ), *vbl. sb.* ME. [f. COME *v.* -ING[1].] 1. The action of the vb. COME: drawing near; arrival, advent. †2. Access -1715. Coming in. **a.** Entrance, commencement, etc. 1586. †**b.** A means of entrance -1719. **c.** *pl.* Revenues, receipts; income 1599.

Co·ming, *ppl. a.* 1460. [f. as prec. + -ING[2].] 1. Approaching in space or time. 2. Inclined to make or meet advances; forward 1600.

1. The comming morne *Mids. N.* v. i. 372. Indications of a c. storm MACAULAY. 2. Sometimes c., sometimes coy SEDLEY.

Comintern (kǫ·mintǝɹn). 1925. [Russ.] The *Com*munist *Intern*ational party of the U.S.S.R.

Comitadji (kǫmitæ·dʒi). 1903. [Balkan, f. F. *comité.*] A band of irregular soldiers.

‖**Comitatus** (kǫmitē·tǫs). 1875. [L., f. *comes, comitem.*] 1. A body of *comites*; a retinue of warriors or nobles attached to the person of a king or chieftain. 2. An (English) county, as in *posse comitatus*, q.v.

‖**Comitia** (kǫmi·ʃiă), *sb. pl.* 1625. [L., f. *com-* + *-itium*; cf. *exitium*, etc.] 1. *Rom. Antiq.* An assembly of the Roman people for electing magistrates and passing laws. Formerly COMICES. 2. An assembly (*rare*) 1625. 3. A name formerly given to the Encænia at Oxford 1714.

Comitial (kǫmi·ʃiăl), *a.* 1533. [ad. L. *comitialis.*] Of or pertaining to the Roman comitia, or to some modern assemblies.

Comity (kǫ·miti). 1543. [ad. L. *comitatem*, f. *comis.*] Courtesy, civility, urbanity; kindly and considerate behaviour towards others, as *c. of manner*, etc.

Comity of nations: **a.** The courteous and friendly understanding by which each nation respects the laws and usages of every other, so far as may be without prejudice to its own rights and interests. **b.** *erron.* The company of nations mutually practising this.

Comma (kǫ·mă). Pl. **commas** (formerly -aes); as L. or Gr. commata (kǫ·mătă). 1586. [a. L., Gr. κόμμα, f. κοπ-, κόπτειν to strike, cut.] 1. In *Gr. Rhet.* and *Pros.*: A group of words less than a colon (q.v.). Hence †A short member of a period. 2. A punctuation-mark [now ,] used to separate the smallest members of a sentence. (Often erron. said to be the mark of a short pause.) 1589. *fig.* = Break, pause 1602. 3. *Mus.* A minute interval or difference of pitch 1597. 4. One of the quotation-marks now called *inverted* commas 1705.

C. (*butterfly*): a butterfly (*Grapta Comma album*) with a white c.-shaped mark on the underside of the wing. *C.* (*bacillus*): a bacillus of curved shape, said to be present in cholera.

Command (kǫmɑ·nd), *v.* [ME. *coma(u)nden*, a. OF. *cumander, comander*, f. (ult.) L. *com-* intensive + *mandare*. Cf. COMMEND.] 1. To order, enjoin, bid with authority or influence. (For const. see quots.). Also *fig.* of things. *absol.* ME. 2. To order to come or go *to, from, into, upon, away, here, home*, etc. ME. *fig.* To cause to come 1611. †3. To demand with authority; occas. with *of* or *from* -1786. 4. *trans.* To have authority over; to be master of; to sway, rule ME. Also *fig.* *absol.* To have the command 1601. 5. To have at one's call or disposal 1561. 6. To exact, compel (respect, etc.) 1591. 7. To dominate; to control; *spec.* said of the artillery of a fortified eminence 1603; to overlook 1697. †8. = COMMEND -1530.

1. C. mee any seruice to the worlds end *Much Ado* II. i. 271. The Scriptures we are commanded to search A.V. *Transl. Pref.* If you can c. these Elements to silence *Temp.* I. i. 23. Iacob had made an end of commanding his sonnes *Gen.* xlix. 33. The rule of life which religion commands FROUDE. He . . commanded Paul to be brought *Acts* xxv. 6. *absol.* Man to c., and woman to obey TENNYSON. 2. To c. them off DE FOE. *fig.* I will c. my blessing vpon you *Lev.* xxv. 21. 3. *Cymb.* I. v. 9. 4. The haughty Dane commands the narrow Seas MARLOWE. *absol.* Born to c. 1799. To c. his old soldiers 1848. To c. oneself 1706. 5. 'Tis not in mortals to c. success ADDISON. It is not every day I can c. that sum BURKE. C. me while I liue *Two Gent.* III. i. 23. Phr. *Yours to c.* 6. She . . must . . c. your sympathy 1802. 7. The vantage ground of Truth: a hill not to be commanded BACON. A Window commanding a very lovely view RUSKIN. Phr. *To c. a suit of cards* (mod.). 8. Phr. *To c. to God.*

Command (kǫmɑ·nd), *sb.* 1552. [prob. f. prec.] 1. The act of commanding; bidding 1591. 2. A COMMANDMENT 1552. 3. The faculty of commanding; rule, control, sway. Also *fig.* 1593. 4. Power of control; mastery; possession with full power to use 1642. 5. Coercion 1692. 6. The power of dominating surrounding country 1628; range of vision 1697.

7. A position in which one commands; *e.g.* a naval commander's post. 8. The body of troops or district under a commander 1592.

1. Doeth the Eagle mount vp at thy commaund *Job* xxxix. 27. 3. High c. Spake in his eye BYRON. [To] have the c. of a ship PEPYS. 4. Phr. *C. of language, words*, etc. *At c.*: ready to receive or obey orders; available to use, spend, etc. 6. His c. of the passes of the Alps FREEMAN. 7. District Commands (Home) Aldershot 1886. 8. Colonel Dodge ordered the c. to halt 1841. The city of Paris is to be divided into four commands 1871.

Comb.: **c.-in-chief**, supreme military c.; **-night**, the night on which something is performed by (royal) c.

Comma·ndable, *a.* 1646. [f. COMMAND *v.* + -ABLE.] Capable of being commanded.

Commandant (kǫmǎndǎ·nt), *sb.* 1687. [a. Fr., orig. pr. pple. = 'commanding'.] A commanding officer: irrespective of rank. Applied often as a foreign title, as *the c. from Seville.* Hence **Commanda·ntship.**

†**Comma·ndatory**, *a.* 1659. [f. late L. *commandat-, commandare.*] Mandatory -1670.

‖**Commandee·r**, *v.* 1881. [ad. S. Afr. *kommande·ren*, f. F. *commander.*] To command for (or as for) military service. Also *fig.* and *gen.*

Commander (kǫma·ndəɹ). ME. [a. OF. *comandere* :—L. type *commandator*; see COMMAND *v.*] 1. One who commands, or has the disposal *of*; one who exercises authority, a leader. 2. *spec.* The officer in command of a military force 1598. b. In the *Navy*: An officer who ranks next above a first lieutenant 1450. 3. The administrator of a COMMANDERY, a COMMENDATORY 1611. 4. Hence, a member of a higher class in certain Orders of Knighthood 1846. 5. A large wooden mallet or beetle 1573. †6. *Surg.* = AMBE -1783.

1. King and C. of our Common-weale *Tit. A.* I. ii. 247. *C. of the Faithful* (cf. ADMIRAL): a title of the caliphs, first assumed (*c* 640) by Omar I. 2. **Commander-in-chief.** The supreme commander of all the military land forces of a State. b. In U.S. vested in the President. c. In the *Navy*: The senior officer in any port or station holding command over all other vessels within assigned limits. Hence **Comma·ndership**, the office or position of c.

Commandery, -dry (kǫma·ndəri, -a·ndri). 1534. [orig. a. F. *commanderie*, med.L. *commendaria* (f. *commenda*), benefice given *in commendam*, *i.e.* into charge or trust. Assoc. later with *commander.*] †1. A benefice held *in commendam* -1807. 2. *esp.* in *Hist.* An estate or a manor belonging to an Order of Knights, and placed under the charge of one of them (with title of *commendator*, COMMANDER 3) 1534. b. *Occas.* applied to the buildings 1712. 3. The rank of a Commander in an order of Knighthood 1611. †4. The office of a commander -1630. †5. A district under a commander -1813.

2 b. The C. here..is a fine old House of Timber, in the Form of a Court DE FOE.

Commanding (kǫma·ndiŋ), *ppl. a.* 1483. [f. COMMAND *v.*] 1. *gen.* Possessing or exercising command, ruling, controlling. 2. Indicating or expressing command 1591. 3. Dominating by height or position; having a wide outlook 1634.

1. C. ship 1758, officer 1796. 2. The majesty of c. beauty MASSINGER. 3. A high and c. turret 1634. C. views in literature EMERSON. Hence **Comma·ndingly** *adv.*, **-ness** (*rare*).

‖**Commandite** (komǎndī·t). 1844. [F., f. *commander* in sense to entrust.] 'A company to which persons advance capital without assuming the functions of partner, or incurring any responsibility' (Littré).

Commandment (kǫma·ndmĕnt). ME. [a. OF. *com-, commandement*, f. late L. *commandare.* Orig. 4 syllables, and spelt *com-, commandement*, etc.] 1. An authoritative order or injunction; a precept (*arch.*). 2. *esp.* A divine command ME. *spec.* (*pl.*) The *Ten Commandments* of the Mosaic Decalogue ME. Also used allusively 1577. 3. slang. *The ten commandments*: the ten finger-nails (*esp.* of a woman) 1540. †4. The action or fact of commanding; bidding -1676. †5. Authority, control; military command -1641. †6. *Old Law.* 'The offence of inducing another to transgress the law' -1641.

1. To the contrary I haue expresse c. *Wint. T.* II. ii. 8. 2. A newe commaundement geve I vnto you TINDALE *John* xiii. 34. 2 *Hen. VI*, I. iii. 145. 5. Haue I commandement on the pulse of life *John* IV. ii. 92.

‖**Commando** (kǫma·ndo). *S. Afr.* 1834. [a. Pg. = 'party commanded', f. *command-ar.*] A party called out for military purposes; a (quasi-military) expedition (*esp.* of the Boers) against the natives.

Commandress (kǫma·ndrĕs). 1592. A female commander. Also *fig.*

Commandrie, -ry, vars. of COMMANDERY.

†**Commark.** *rare.* 1612. [ad. Sp. *comarca*, f. L. *com-* + *marca* MARCH.] Border-country -1654.

Commata, L. and Gr. pl. of COMMA.

†**Commate·rial**, *a.* [See COM-.] Identical in material. BACON.

Commatic (kǫmæ·tik), *a. rare.* 1844. [See COMMA.] Consisting of short clauses or lyric measures. So **Co·mmatism**, c. character.

Commea·surable, *a.* = COMMENSURABLE.

Commeasure (kǫme·ʒiūɹ), *v.* 1614. [See COM-.] To equal in measure or extent.

Until..the full-grown will, Circled thro' all experiences..C. perfect freedom TENNYSON.

Commeate (kǫ·mi,eˡt), *v.* ? *Obs.* 1655. [f. L. *commeat-, commeare.*] *intr.* To pass to and fro, penetrate in all directions.

‖**Comme il faut** (kǫm il fōᵘ), *adj. phr.* 1756. [Fr., 'as it is necessary'.] As it should be, proper.

Commemorate (kǫme·mŏreˡt), *v.* 1599. [f. (ult.) L. *com-* + *memorare.*] 1. *trans.* †a. To make mention of or rehearse. b. To mention as worthy of remembrance; to celebrate in speech or writing. 2. To call to remembrance by some solemnity or celebration 1638. 3. Of things: To be a memorial of 1766.

1. The..Tempter did c. unto her..the Prohibition 1693. 2. We are called upon to c. a revolution..happy in its consequences ATTERBURY. 3. Dates, which c. events D'ISRAELI. Hence **Comme·morative** *a.* having the attribute of commemorating; also as *sb.* **Comme·morator** (*rare*), one who commemorates. **Comme·morato·ry** *a.* (*rare*), commemorative.

Commemoration (kǫme:mŏrēˡ·ʃən). ME. [ad. L. *commemorationem.*] 1. †a. Recital, mention -1631. b. Eulogistic mention 1823. 2. A calling to remembrance by some solemnity or celebration ME. b. A service, or a prayer, in memory of a saint or of a sacred event ME. c. At Oxford, an annual celebration in memory of the Founders and Benefactors 1750.

1. b. Yet there were several [names] worth c. BYRON. 2. To celebrate the c. of the most glorious death of thy Son *Bk. Com. Prayer.* The c. of the Martyrdom of King Charles Ist 1779.

Commence (kǫme·ns), *v.* [ME. *comence*, a. OF. *cumencer, comencer* :—late L. type **cominitiare*, f. *com-* intensive + *initiare*; see INITIATE. The double *m* is not justified. Formerly more formal than *begin*; now often an affected substitute.] 1. *trans.* To begin, enter upon. 2. *intr.* with *infin.* To begin *to do* ME. 3. *intr.* To make a start ME.; to begin to be; to start as (*arch.*) 1642. 4. [tr. med.L. *incipere.*] To take a full degree *in* any faculty at a university ME. Also *transf.* and *fig.*

1. Commencing with the Sun his Toil 1696. Phr. *To c. an action, a suit, proceedings*, etc. 2. And comenced to loue hir anonright ME. 3. Here the anthem doth c. SHAKS. The time..when pig is to c. bacon SOUTHEY. 4. He..that hath comensid in art WYCLIF. This is mi year to commens master of art G. HARVEY. Hence **Comme·nceable** *a.* that can commence (sense 4) or be commenced. **Comme·ncer**, one who commences. (*Obs.* in sense 4 of the verb.)

Commencement (kǫme·nsmĕnt). Earlier com-. ME. [a. OF. *co(m)mencement*; see COMMENCE.] 1. The action or process of commencing; beginning; time of beginning. 2. The action of taking a full degree; *esp.* at Cambridge, Dublin, etc., the great ceremony when these are conferred ME. Also *transf.* and *fig.*

1. The Origin and Commencement of this greefe *Haml.* III. i. 185.

Commend (kǫme·nd), *v.* ME. [ad. L. *commendare*, f. *com-* intensive + *mandare*; see MANDATE. Repl. *command(e* in this sense.] 1. To give in trust or charge; to commit. 2. To present as worthy of acceptance or regard; to direct attention to, as worthy of notice; to RECOMMEND ME. 3. *gen.* To praise ME. Also *absol.* †4. To set off; to adorn or grace -1644. 5. To recommend to kindly remembrance (now *arch.*) 1463. 6. *Eccl.* To bestow *in commendam.* Also *absol.* 1616. 7. *Hist.* To place under the protection of a feudal lord 1867.

1. To her white hand see thou do c. This seal'd-vp counsaile *L. L. L.* III. i. 169. I comende you my wyfe ..& my children CAXTON. 2. Harts-ease..is commended for a rupture COGAN. I c. vnto you Phebe our sister *Rom.* xvi. 1. 3. C. it, or come and mend it 1634. 4. What..more commendeth a woman than constancie LYLY. Phr. *C. me (us) to*: = 'give me by choice'. Orig. of a person. Hence **Comme·nder.** †**Comme·ndment.**

†**Comme·nd**, *sb.* 1470. [a. F. *commende* (in sense 1), and from prec.] 1. *Eccl.* = COMMENDAM 1. *Sc.* -1513. 2. Commendation -1608. 3. A greeting, remembrance -1645.

2. Speak in his just c. *Per.* II. ii. 49. 3. Tell her I send to her my kind commends *Rich. II*, III. i. 38.

Commendable (kǫme·ndăb'l), *a.* ME. [a. OF., ad. L. *commendabilis*; see prec. and -ABLE.] 1. Proper to be commended, laudable. †2. Commendatory 1576. Hence **Comme·ndableness. Comme·ndably** *adv.*

‖**Commendado·r.** 1580. [Sp. *comendador.*] A commander.

Commendam (kǫme·ndæm). 1563. [acc. sing. of med.L. *commenda*, in phr. *dare in commendam*, to give (*sc.* a benefice) in charge or trust.] 1. In the phrase *in commendam*: used of the tenure of a benefice 'commended' or given in charge to a clerk or layman to hold with enjoyment of the revenues until an incumbent was provided or for life. (Abolished in England in 1836.) Also *transf.* 1658. 2. As English *sb.* (with *pl.*) The tenure of a benefice held as above 1563; the benefice or office so held 1607.

Comme·ndatary. 1539. [f. L. *commendat-*; see COMMENDATE.] 1. *adj.* = COMMENDATORY 2. 2. *sb.* a. *Eccl.* A commendator. b. *gen.* A commissioner.

Commendation (kǫmĕndēˡ·ʃən). ME. [a. OF., ad. L. *commendationem.*] 1. The action of COMMENDING; †giving in charge 1583; approval, recommendation ME. 2. (gen. in *pl.*) Remembrances sent to those at a distance; respects, greetings (*arch.*) 1529. †3. A thing that recommends -1697. 4. *Liturg.* (gen. in *pl.*) An office commending the souls of the dead to God ME. 5. *Feudal Law.* The cession by a freeman of himself and his lands to the protection of a feudal lord 1818. 6. *Eccl.* The giving of benefices *in commendam* 1883.

1. You haue deseru'd High c. *A. Y. L.* I. ii. 275. This letter of owre c. EDEN. 2. Aftyr my moste herty commendacions WOLSEY. 3. Good-nature is the most godlike c. of a man DRYDEN.

Commendator (kǫ·mĕndēˡtəɹ). 1561. [a. late L., f. *commendare.*] 1. One who holds a benefice *in commendam* 1561. †2. The president of a COMMANDERY -1688. 3. = COMMENDADOR 1583.

Commendatory (kǫme·ndătəri). 1555. [ad. late L. *commendatorius.*]

A. *adj.* 1. Having the attribute of commending or recommending. 2. Holding a benefice *in commendam* 1682. 3. Pertaining to feudal commendation 1867.

1. *C. letters* 1555. *C. prayer*: one commending a dying person to God's mercy. 2. C. abbots BURKE.

B. *sb.* †1. A commendatory fact or word -1716. †2. A knight-commander -1762. †3. One who holds a benefice *in commendam* -1726. †4. = COMMANDERY -1762.

1. A sufficient evidence and c. of his own piety MILT.

†‖**Comme·ndum.** = COMMENDAM 2.

Commensal (kǫme·nsăl). ME. [a. F., f. (ult.) L. *com-* + *mensa.*]

A. *adj.* 1. Eating at the same table. 2. *Biol.* Applied to animals or plants which live as tenants of others and share their food (dist. from *parasitic*) 1877.

B. *sb.* 1. A messmate 1460. 2. *Biol.* A commensal animal or plant 1872. Hence **Comme·nsalism**, a c. condition. **Commensa·lity**, c. state. So †**Commensa·tion**, eating at the same table. SIR T. BROWNE.

Commensurable (kǫme·nsiŭrăb'l, -ʃŭr-), *a.* (*sb.*) 1557. [ad. L. *commensurabilis*, f. (ult.) *com-* + *mens-, metiri* to measure.] 1. Having, or reducible to, a common measure; measurable by the same standard. 2. Proportionable in measure, etc.; proportionate *to* 1645. †3. Measurable (*by* something) -1660. Also as *sb.*

1. Mind is not c. with Space DOVE. Hence **Comme·nsurabi·lity**, c. quality. **Comme·nsurableness**, c. quality or state. **Comme·nsurably** *adv.*

Commensurate (kǫme·nsiŭrĕt, -ʃŭr-), *a.* 1641. [ad. L. *commensuratus*; see prec.] **1.** Having the same measure; coextensive. Const. *with*, †*to*. **2.** Of corresponding extent or degree; proportionate, adequate. Const. *to*, *with*. 1649. †**3.** Corresponding in nature (*with*, *to*) –1678. **4.** = COMMENSURABLE 1 (*rare*) 1690.

1. Matter and gravity are always c. BENTLEY. 2. You know how it can act when its power is c. to its will BURKE. Hence **Comme·nsurate-ly** *adv.*, **-ness.**

†**Commensurate** (kǫme·nsiŭreᶦt, -ʃŭr-), *v.* 1643. [f. prec.] **1.** *intr.* To agree or square *with* (*rare*). **2.** *trans.* To make commensurate, to proportion –1711. **3.** To reduce to a measure or standard; to define the extent of –1660.

Commensuration (kǫme:nsiŭrēᶦ·ʃən, -ʃŭr-). Now *rare.* 1526. [a. F., ad. L. *commensurationem.*] **1.** The measuring of things against each other. †**2.** Measurement –1682. **3.** The action of proportioning, or fact of being proportioned; proportion 1626.

3. A c. or proportion between the Body moved, and the force BACON.

Comment (kǫ·ment), *sb.* ME. [a. OF., ad. L. *commentum*, f. L. *commentus*, *comminisci* (root *com-men-*) to invent.] †**1.** An exposition; a commentary –1877. **2.** A remark or note in explanation or criticism of a literary passage; an annotation 1509. Also *collect.* and *fig.* 1589. **3.** The action of commenting; criticism 1847.

1. This tretys .. this lytil coment 1475. 2. Some Comments clear not, but increase the doubt CLEVELAND. *fig.* Some adopted the c., others stuck to the text BURKE.

Comment (kǫ·ment, kǫme·nt), *v.* 1450. [ad. med.L. *commentare* to devise, and immed. f. COMMENT *sb.*] †**1.** *trans.* To devise, invent (*esp.* in a bad sense) –1596. **2.** *trans.* To furnish with comments; to annotate (*arch.*) 1599. **3.** *intr.* To write explanatory or critical notes (*on*, *upon*) 1611. **4.** To make (unfavourable) comments (*on*, *upon*) 1591. †**5.** To ponder –1602.

1. SPENSER *F. Q.* VII. vii. 53. 2. To c. an author JOHNSON. 4. Not an eye that sees you, but is a Physician to c. on your Malady *Two Gent.* II. i. 42. 5. *Rich. III*, IV. iii. 51.

Co·mmentaried, *ppl. a. rare.* [f. COMMENTARY *sb.* or *v.*] Chronicled; annotated. G. DANIEL.

Commentary (kǫ·mĕntări). 1531. [ad. L. *commentarium*, orig. adj. neut., f. *commentum*; see COMMENT.] †**1.** A note-book (*rare*) –1538. **2.** A memoir; in *pl.* memoirs, historical records (less formal than a *history*). (Chiefly *Hist.*) 1538. **3.** A treatise consisting of a series of comments on a text 1538; also *transf.* and *fig.*

2. Cesars Commentaries 1547. 3. The commentaryes of Auicen and Aueroyes BALE. 3. *fig.* A just Pronunciation is a good C. 1748.

Commentate (kǫ·mĕnteᶦt), *v. rare.* 1794. [app. f. COMMENTATOR.] **1.** *trans.* = COMMENT *v.* 2. **2.** *intr.* = COMMENT *v.* 3–5. 1859.

Commentation (kǫmĕntēᶦ·ʃən). 1579. [ad. L. *commentationem*; for sense cf. *comment*, *commentary*, etc.] †**1.** A comment; a commentary –1712. †**2.** Invention, concoction –1734. **3.** The making of comments 1833.

2. By subtile commentations, and wild inferences NORTH.

Co·mmentator. 1641. [a. L.; see prec.] **1.** The writer of a COMMENTARY (sense 3). **2.** An eyewitness whose description of a ceremony, sporting event, etc., is broadcast by wireless.

1. Cornelius à Lapide, a.. great Commentatour upon holy Scripture 1641. Hence **Commentato·rial** *a.* pertaining to a c. or commentators. **Co·mmentatorship,** the office or performance of a c.

Commenter, -or (kǫ·mentəɹ, kǫme·ntəɹ). ME. [f. COMMENT *v.* + -ER, -OR.] One who comments. (*Obs.* in spec. sense.)

†**Commentitious** (kǫmenti·ʃəs), *a.* 1614. [f. L. *commenticius* (*-titius*), f. *comment-*; see COMMENT.] Feigned, fictitious, lying –1849.

Commerce (kǫ·məɹs), *sb.* 1537. [a. F., ad. L. *commercium*, f. *com-* + *merx*, *merci-* merchandise. Orig. stressed on second syllable.] **1.** Exchange between men of the products of nature and art; buying and selling together; exchange of merchandise, *esp.* on a large scale between different countries or districts 1587. **2.** Intercourse in the affairs of life; dealings 1537. **3.** Intercourse of the sexes; *esp.* in a bad sense 1624. †**4.** Interchange (*esp.* of letters, ideas, etc.) –1741. †**5.** Communication –1757. **6.** *Cards.* A game in which barter is the chief feature 1732.

1. There c. plenty brings from foreign coasts GAY. *Chamber of Commerce*: see CHAMBER *sb.* 2. He is now in some c. with my Ladie *Twel. N.* III. iv. 191. For.. c. to be had between God and us HOOKER. †*Of good c.*: pleasant to meet.

Commerce (kǫmə̄·ɹs), *v.* 1587. [f. prec. sb.; cf. L. *commerciari.*] †**1.** *intr.* To trade, traffic –1660. **2.** To hold intercourse or communication, associate *with* (*arch.*) 1596.

1. To c. and exchange with one another 1660. 2. With.. looks commercing with the skies MILT. *Pens.* 39. Hence †**Comme·rcer,** a trader; a person that one has to do with.

Commercial (kǫmə̄·ɹʃăl), *a.* (*sb.*) 1687. [f. L. *commercium* + -AL.] **1.** Engaged in commerce; trading. **2.** Of or relating to commerce or trade 1744. **3.** Such as passes current in the transactions of commerce 1752. **4.** Viewed as a matter of profit and loss 1882. **5.** *sb.* = *Commercial traveller* 1855.

1. A rich c. city BURKE. 2. The c. History of.. Japan 1744. C. Laws 1765. C. freedom MᶜCULLOCH. A c. crisis MILL. 3. C. morality 1879. The c. acid is generally not quite pure 1865. 4. A c. success 1882. Phrases. *C. letter*, *note*: sizes of writing paper in U.S. *C. traveller*: an agent for a manufacturer, etc., who travels over a district, soliciting orders.

Hence **Comme·rcialism,** the c. spirit and practice. **Comme·rcialist,** one engaged in commerce; an adherent of commercialism. **Comme:rcia·lity,** c. quality or nature. **Comme·rcialize** *v.* to make a matter of trade; to subject to commercialism. **Comme·rcially** *adv.*

†**Commigra·tion.** 1627. [ad. L. *commigrationem.*] Migration; *esp.* on a large scale –1755.

†**Commi·litant.** 1577. [f. L. *commilitantem.*] A fellow-soldier –1728. So †‖**Commilito.**

Comminate (kǫ·mineᶦt), *v.* 1611. [f. L. *comminat-*, *comminari.*] *trans.* To anathematize. Also *intr.* Hence **Co·mminative** *a.* conveying a commination (*rare*). **Co·mminator.** **Co·mminatory** *a.* denunciatory.

Commination (kǫminēᶦ·ʃən). 1460. [a. F., f. (ult.) *com-* intensive + *minari.*] **1.** Denunciation of punishment or vengeance; *loosely*, denunciation (*mod.*). **2.** *Liturgy.* A recital of Divine threatenings against sinners; part of an office appointed to be read in the Church of England on Ash-Wednesday and at other times. Also, the whole office. 1552. Also *attrib.*

1. The terrible comminacion and threate.. in the Apocalyps vnto the byshoppe of Ephesy MORE. Their orthodox c. of all taxation 1865.

Commingle (kǫmi·ŋg'l), *v.* 1626. [See COM-.] To mingle or mix together; to blend.

Comminute (kǫ·miniŭt), *v.* 1626. [f. L. *comminut-*, *comminuere*, f. (ult.) *com-* + root of *minus.*] **1.** *trans.* To reduce to minute particles; to pulverize, triturate. **2.** *transf.* To divide minutely or into small portions 1667.

1. To c. hard bones 1880. 2. To c. Bloud 1667, patronage SIR H. TAYLOR. Hence **Co·mminuted** *ppl. a.* reduced to minute particles; *Surg.* broken into several pieces, as in *c. fracture.*

Comminution (kǫminiŭ·ʃən). 1578. [f. L. type *comminutionem.*] **1.** Reduction into small fragments; pulverization, trituration. *Surg.* Cf. *Comminuted.* 1820. **2.** *transf.* 1751.

2. This natural and necessary c. of our lives JOHNSON.

†**Commis.** 1573. [a. F.] A deputy, delegate, clerk –1779.

†**Commi·se,** *v.* Earlier f. COMMIT *v.*

Commiserable (kǫmi·zĕrăb'l), *a.* 1609. [f. L. *commiserari.*] Deserving commiseration.

Commiserate (kǫmi·zĕreᶦt), *v.* 1606. [f. L. *commiserat-*, *commiserari*, f. (ult.) *com-* + *miser.*] **1.** *trans.* To feel or express pity for; to compassionate. **2.** To condole with 1655.

1. This great victory.. did move the Britains more to c. than to fear MAULE. 2. The aptitude.. to c. and comfort 1767. Hence **Commi·seratingly** *adv.* †**Commi·serator,** one who commiserates.

Commiseration (kǫmi:zĕrēᶦ·ʃən). 1585. [ad. L. *commiserationem*; see prec.] The action of commiserating; sorrow for the affliction or distress of another; pity, compassion.

Let no man help him, nor take c. vpon his infants 1604.

Commissar (kǫmisā·ɹ). 1918. [Russ.] The head of a government department of the U.S.S.R. So **Commissa·riat** 1918.

Commissarial (kǫmisēᵊ·riăl), *a.* 1702. [f. med.L. *commissarius* + -AL.] Of or pertaining to a commissary.

Commissariat (kǫmisēᵊ·riăt). Also **-ot.** 1609. [a. F., and f. COMMISSARY.] **1.** *Sc. Law.* A commissary court; the office, jurisdiction, or district of a commissary. **2.** *Mil.* That department charged with the duty of providing food and supplies for the army 1779. **3.** *transf.* 1812. **4.** Food-supply 1861. Also *attrib.*

3. There is no c. for supplying London SOUTHEY.

Commissary (kǫ·misări). ME. [ad. med.L. *commissarius*, f. *commissus* committed, entrusted.] **1.** One to whom a special duty or charge is committed by a superior power; a commissioner; a delegate. **2.** *Eccl.* An officer exercising jurisdiction as the representative of the bishop in parts of his diocese ME. **3.** *Eng. Univ.* †**a.** At Oxford, the Vice-Chancellor. **b.** At Cambridge, an assistant or assessor to the vice-chancellor in his court 1797. **4.** *Mil.* An officer or official who has charge of the supply of food, stores, and transport; †also, formerly, one who inspected musters 1489. **5.** A superior officer of police (in France) 1855.

1. *fig.* Great Destiny, the C. of God DONNE. 4. The Commissaries for victuall 1623. Commissaries of the Musters 1633.

Phrases. **C. court. a.** The court of a bishop's c. **b.** *Sc. Law.* A sheriff or county court which appoints and confirms executors of deceased persons leaving personal property in Scotland. **C. general.** A chief or head c.; *spec.* (*Mil.*) the chief of a commissariat service. Hence **Co·mmissaryship,** the office of a c.

Commission (kǫmi·ʃən), *sb.* ME. [a. F., ad. L. *commissionem*; see COMMIT.] **1.** Authoritative charge to act in a prescribed manner. **2.** Authority committed to any one 1480; *spec.* that of an officer in the army or navy 1672. **3.** An instrument conferring such authority ME.; *spec.* the warrant by which an officer in the army or navy is appointed to the rank and command he holds 1643. **4.** An office conferred by such a warrant 1708. **5.** The condition of being authoritatively entrusted or given in charge 1573. **6.** A body of persons charged with some specified function 1494. **7.** The entrusting *of* (authority, etc., *to*) 1883. **8.** A charge or matter entrusted to any one to perform 1570. **9.** Authority given to act as agent for another in business 1622. **10.** A *pro rata* remuneration for work done as agent 1725. **11.** The committing (of crime, etc.) 1597.

1. I have it in c., to comfort the feeble minded BUNYAN. 2. Act within your C. SELDEN. *spec.* Cowards must lay their bought Commissions down 1705. *C. of the peace*: the authority given under the Great Seal empowering certain persons to act as Justices of the Peace. 3. Whil'st our C. from Rome is read *Hen. VIII*, II. iv. 1. My c. [as lieutenant] had been made out MARRYAT. Phrases (combining senses 2 and 3, and sometimes 6): *C. of array* (see ARRAY); †*c. of bankruptcy*, a c. issued by the Lord Chancellor, appointing commissioners to administer a bankrupt's estate on behalf of the creditors; *c. of lunacy*, a c. issued to investigate whether a person is a lunatic or not. 5. *In commission.* Of an office: Placed by warrant in the charge of a body of persons, instead of the ordinary constitutional administrator. Of a ship of war: Manned, armed, and ready for sea; said also of the officer in command. So *Out of c.* 6. The Parnell C. (*mod.*). 8. If I can execute any little c. for you DICKENS. 9. Sold by c. from the makers DE FOE. 11. Sinnes of omission and c. HOWSON.

Comb.: **c.-agent, -merchant,** an agent, etc., who transacts business for others on the principle of percentage; so *c.-business*; **-broker,** an agent for the sale or purchase of commissions in the army or navy.

Commission (kǫmi·ʃən), *v.* 1661. [f. prec. sb.] **1.** *trans.* To furnish with a commission or legal warrant. **2.** To empower; to entrust with an office or duty 1683. **3.** To send on a mission 1697. **4.** To give a commission or order to or for 1790.

1. Commissioned to ride the circuit FULLER, for the 'Adamant' of fifty guns BENTINCK. The new ships we c. BURKE. 3. A chosen band He first commissions to the Latian land, In threat'ning embassy DRYDEN. var. †**Commi·ssionate** (in senses 1–3).

Commissionaire (komi:sionēᵊ·ɹ). 1765. [a. F.] ‖**1.** One entrusted with small commissions; a messenger or light porter. **2.** *spec.* One of the *Corps of Commissionaires*, an association of pensioned soldiers, started in London in 1859, organized to act as porters, messengers, etc.

Commissional (kǫmi·ʃənăl), *a.* 1540. [f. COMMISSION *sb.* + -AL.] Of or pertaining to a commission.

†**Commi·ssionary,** *a.* 1600. [f. as prec.] Appointed by warrant; delegated -1649.

Our judges..are either ordinary or c. HOOKER.

Commissioner (kǒmi·ʃənəɹ). 1448. [f. COMMISSION *sb.* + -ER [1].] 1. One appointed by commission to carry out some specified work; a delegate; a member of a commission. b. A member of a permanently constituted government board 1532. c. The representative of the supreme authority in a district, governmental department, etc. 1535. 2. A book-maker (*slang*) 1860. 3. Occas. = COMMISSIONAIRE (*mod.*).

1. One of the.. commysioners to make inquisicion of these thre pointes 1557. b. Charity Commissioners for England and Wales 1886. c. Special C. in Bechuanaland 1884.

Lord High C.: the representative of the Crown at the annual General Assembly of the Church of Scotland. Hence **Commi·ssionership.**

Commissive (kǒmi·siv), *a.* 1816. [f. *commis-, committere* to COMMIT; see -IVE.] Characterized by commission. **Commi·ssively** *adv.*

Commissure (kǫ·misiŭɹ). ME. [ad. L. *commissura*, f. *commiss-, committere*; see COMMIT.] 1. A joining together; the place where two bodies touch or unite; a joining, juncture, seam. 2. The line of junction or angles of the two lips, eyelids, etc. 1755. 3. Various bands of nerve-substance, which connect parts of the brain, the two sides of the spinal cord, etc. 1809. 4. *Bot.* The line of the cohering faces of two carpels, moss-cells, etc. 1830. Hence **Commissu·ral** *a.* of, pertaining to, or of the nature of a c.

†**Commi·stion.** ME. = COMMIXTION, COMMIXTURE -1667.

Commit (kǒmi·t), *v.* [ME. *committe*, ad. L. *committere* to put together, to put for safety, f. *com-* + *mittere*. Cf. COMMISE.] 1. To give in charge or trust, entrust, consign *to*. 2. *spec.* To consign officially to custody or confinement 1467. 3. To refer or entrust (a bill) to committee 1621. †4. To charge with a duty or office -1549. 5. To perpetrate or perform (in a bad sense); as, a crime, a folly, etc. 1490. Also †*absol.* -1660. 6. To put together 1545; to engage (parties) as opponents, to match (*with*) 1612; to embroil 1855. 7. To involve, compromise 1770; to pledge by implication *to* 1839.

1. Committe alle thy causes to god EARL RIVERS. Phr. *To c. to writing* (*to paper*, etc.), †*history, memory, the earth, the flames*, etc. 2. Commytted to prison for felony 1467. Committed for cheating at play FIELDING. 5. *absol.* C. not with any mans sworne Spouse *Lear* III. iv. 83. (*joc.*) 'Committing' puns DISRAELI. 6. I apprehend everything from his committing the army with Buonaparte EARL BATHURST. *fig.* Committing short and long [quantities] MILT. 7. Without committing the honor of your sovereign JUNIUS. Committed to the slave trade cause W. E. FORSTER. To c. oneself to an evil line of conduct J. H. NEWMAN. Hence **Commi·ttable, -ible** *a.* that may be committed. **Commi·tter.**

Commitment (kǒmi·tmĕnt). 1611. [f. COMMIT *v.* + -MENT.] 1. The action of entrusting, giving in charge, or commending 1677. 2. The action of committing to custody, or the state of being so committed 1621; a warrant or order for imprisonment 1755. 3. *Legisl.* The action of referring or entrusting (a bill, etc.) to a committee 1640. †4. = COMMISSION II. -1738. †5. Hostile engagement (*rare*) -1793. 6. Committing oneself or being committed (*to*) 1793; an engagement 1864.

2. This dubious interval between the c. and trial BLACKSTONE. 3. Deferring the motion till the day of the c. H. WALPOLE. 6. The commitments of this country are too great DISRAELI.

Committal (kǒmi·tăl). 1625. [f. as prec. + -AL.] The action of committing; COMMITMENT.

Committee (see below). 1495. [Subst. use of late AFr. *committe, committee* pa. pple., repl. F. *commis*, f. *commettre* to COMMIT. Orig. pronounced (kǒmitī·), as still in branch I; *now* (kǒmi·ti).]

I. 1. A person to whom some charge, trust, or function is committed. *Obs.* exc. in *Court of Committees* (of Guy's Hospital). 2. *Law.* A person to whom the charge of a lunatic or idiot is committed 1765.

1. To the .. Four and Twenty Committees of the Honorable the East-India Company 1681. 2. She was the c. of the lunatic 1884.

II. *Now* (kǒmi·ti). A body of persons appointed or elected for some special business or function. (Each member was originally called *a committee* in sense I. 1.) 1621. Also, †a meeting of such a body -1742. Also *attrib.*

C. of the whole House: the whole of the members sitting as a Committee to consider the details of a measure which has been committed, or for kindred purposes, as in the *C. of Ways and Means*, etc. *Standing C.*: a permanent committee to deal with all matters within a particular sphere, during the existence of the body appointing them. Hence **Committee·ship**, the office or function of a c. (now in sense I. 2).

Committor (kǒmi·tǭɹ). [f. COMMIT *v.* + -OR.] *Law.* A judge (usu. the Lord Chancellor) who commits a lunatic or idiot to the custody of a *committee* (see COMMITTEE I. 2).

Commix (kǒmi·ks), *v.* ME. [f. L. *commixtus*, first adopted as *commixt* pa. pple., whence *commix*. See s.v. MIX.] To mix or mingle together; to blend. Now *arch.* or *poet.* Also *intr.*

Profit must with honour be commix'd 1596. *intr.* These elements..c. together daily 1519. Hence **Commi·xed, -mi·xt** *ppl. a.* var. †**Commi·xt** *v.* (*rare*).

Commi·xtion, -xion. ME. = COMMIXTURE (now only in sense 5).

Commixture (kǒmi·kstiŭɹ). 1588. [ad. L. *commixtura*, f. *commixt-, commiscere.*] 1. The action of mixing or mingling together 1592. 2. The condition or product resulting from this; a mixture, a compound 1593. †3. Complexion 1588. †4. Sexual union 1682. 5. The putting of a small piece of the host into the chalice, typifying the reunion of body and soul at the resurrection 1850.

1. By a c. of good and euil Actes BACON. 2. Demetrius was a C. of vertues, and vices CORNWALLYES. 3. *L.L.L.* v. i. 296.

Commodate (kǫ·mǒdĕ̄t). 1727. [ad. L. *commodatum*, pa. pple. neut. used sb.; cf. F. *commodat.*] *Rom. Law.* A free loan, for use, of anything not perishable.

†**Commo·de,** *a.* 1637. [a. F., ad. L. *commodus.*] 1. Convenient, suitable -1740. 2. Accommodating; usu. in a bad sense -1760. Hence †**Commo·dely** *adv.*

Commode (kǒmōu·d), *sb.* 1688. [a. F., adj. used sb.; see prec.] 1. A tall head-dress formerly worn by women, consisting of a wire frame-work variously covered with silk or lace. †2. A procuress -1753. 3. A piece of furniture with drawers and shelves; a chest of drawers; a chiffonier 1786. 4. An article of furniture enclosing a chamber utensil; a close-stool 1851.

1. Wir'd Comode .. Cock'd Three Stories high D'URFEY.

†**Commo·derate,** *a. rare.* 1647. [f. (ult.) L. *com-* + *moderare.*] Brought into due measure; commensurate *to.* So †**Commodera·tion.**

Commodious (kǒmōu·diəs), *a.* ME. [ad. F. *commodieux, -euse*, med.L. *commodiosus*, irreg. f. L. *commodum.*] †1. Profitable, of use -1751. 2. Convenient (*arch.*) 1549; †opportune -1750. †Of persons: Accommodating. SHAKS. 3. Convenient for accommodation, shelter, etc. (*arch.*) 1568; *absol.* roomy, spacious (the current sense) 1553. †4. Of *life, living*: Endowed with conveniences -1663.

1. Nothing..c..., except fyshe BOORDE. 2. A work c. in form DIBDIN. A c. drab *Tr. & Cr.* v. ii. 197. 3. C. to winter in *Acts* xxvii. 12. C. dwellings BEWICK. Hence **Commo·dious-ly** *adv.*, **-ness.**

Commodity (kǒmǫ·dĭti). ME. [a. F. *commodité*, ad. L. *commoditatem*; see COMMODE *a.*] †1. The quality of being commodious; commodiousness -1682. 2. Convenience (*arch.*) 1488; †expediency -1788; †advantage, profit, (selfish) interest -1836. †3. Opportunity, occasion -1632. 4. *concr.* A thing of use or advantage to mankind; *spec.* in *Comm.* a kind of thing produced for use or sale; in *pl.* goods, merchandise, produce ME. Also *fig.* and *transf.* †6. A parcel. SHAKS.

2. Doubled in two..For more c. of carriage BROWNING. *John* II. i. 573. 4. Cattle, Corne, and all Commodities will thrive AUSTEN. Some offer me Commodities to buy SHAKS. *Staple c.*: leading article of trade. 6. Now Ioue in his next c. of hayre, send thee a beard *Twel. N.* III. i. 50. (See also D'Israeli *Cur. Lit., Usury*, and cf. *Meas. for M.* IV. iii. 5.)

Commodore (kǫ·mǎdōəɹ). 1694. [In 17th c. *commandore*, ?ad. Du. *kommandeur* (see COMMANDER).] 1. *Naval.* An officer in command, ranking above captain and below rear-admiral. (In the British Navy, a temporary rank, given to senior officers in command of detached squadrons.) 1695. 2. A courtesy-title given to: a. the senior captain when ships of war are cruising in company; b. the senior captain in a fleet of merchantmen; c. a captain of pilots; d. the president of a yacht-club. 3. The commodore's ship 1694; also, the leading vessel in a fleet of merchantmen 1769.

†**Commoi·gne.** ME. [a. OF. *commoine.*] Brother-monk -1670.

†**Commoli·tion.** *rare.* [f. L. *commolit-, commolere.*] Grinding together. SIR T. BROWNE.

Common (kǫ·mən), *a.* [Early ME. *co(m)mun*, a. OF. *comun* :—L. *communis*; ?f. *com-* + *-munis* (:—*moinis*) bound; or ??f. *com-* + *unus*, in early L. *oinos* one.]

I. 1. 'Belonging equally to more than one' (J.); belonging to all mankind alike. 2. Joint, united ME. 3. General ME. 4. Of or belonging to the community, or to a corporation; public ME. 5. Free to be used by every one; public ME. 6. Generally known 1568. †7. [L. *communis.*] Generally accessible -1609.

1. A C. enemy MILT. *Sams.* 1416. Longing the c. light again to share DRYDEN. 2. This was the comyn voys of every man CHAUCER. *To make c. cause* (*with*). 3. C. notions ABP. THOMSON. 4. *C. crier*, public or town crier. *C. seal*, the official seal of a corporation. So *C. Council, Hall, Serjeant, C. hangman.* The cok, commune astrologer CHAUCER. *C. right*: the right of every citizen. 5. A theeuish liuing on the c. rode *A. Y. L.* II. iii. 33. *C. woman, prostitute. C. alehouse, lodging-house*, etc. 6. *C. bruit, fame*, etc. *C. scold, nuisance*, etc.

II. 1. In general use; ordinary, prevalent, frequent ME. 2. Undistinguished; ordinary ME. 3. Belonging to the commonalty. (Occas. *contemptuous.*) ME. 4. Familiar, not specific ME. 5. Of inferior quality or value, mean ME.; vulgar, as persons 1866. 6. Not ceremonially clean. (In N.T.: = Hellenistic Gr. κοινός.) ME.

1. The word is not c. among us 1586. 2. The c. Run of Mankind ADDISON. C. manners SWIFT, honesty JOWETT. Dayes, whether c. or sacred BP. HALL. 3. The c. herd JOWETT. *C. soldier*: one without rank or distinction. 4. C. fire..as well as electrical fire FRANKLIN. 5. He is but the commonest clay BYRON. She has rather a c. look (*mod.*). 6. *Acts* x. 14.

III. Technical uses.

1. *Math.* Said of a number or quantity which belongs equally to two or more quantities; as in *c. divisor, measure, multiple*, etc. 1594. 2. *Gram. & Logic.* Applicable to each individual of a class or group, as *c. noun, name, term*, etc. b. In L. and Gr., etc.: Of either gender. In mod. Eng. Grammar: Applicable to individuals of either sex, as *parent*, etc. c. *Pros.* Of syllables: Optionally short or long. (Marked thus: ⏑ or ⏑̄). d. *Anat.* Said of the trunk from which two or more arteries, veins, or nerves are given off, as the *c. carotid arteries.*

Phrases (*mostly from* I.):

C. assurances: legal evidences of the translation of property. *C. bench*: see BENCH *sb. C. field, land*: = COMMON *sb. C. jury*: see JURY. *C. metre*: an iambic stanza of 4 lines containing 8 and 6 syllables alternately. *C. recovery*: see RECOVERY. *C. school* (U.S.): one publicly maintained for primary education.

†B. quasi-*adv.* = COMMONLY -1784.

Common (kǫ·mən), *sb.* ME. [Partly repr. F. *commune* = med.L. *communa, communia* (see COMMUNE *sb.*[1]); partly L. *commune*, or the Eng. adj. as sb.] †1. The community or commonalty; *occas.*, the commonwealth. (L. *commune*, Gr. τὸ κοινόν.) -1646. †2. The common people. Often = the COMMONS, q.v. -1663. 3. A common land or estate; the undivided land held in joint-occupation by a community. Now often applied to unenclosed or waste land. 1479. Also *fig.* 4. *Law.* (Also *right of c., c. right.*) The profit which a man has in the land or waters of another; as *c. of* PASTURE, PISCARY, TURBARY, ESTOVERS (see these words); = COMMONAGE, COMMONTY ME. 5. *Eccl.* [L. *commune*, F. *commun.*] A service common to a class of festivals. (Opp. to *proper.*) ME.

2. The c. is deuided into marchauntes and manuaries 1581. Touching the Weale a' th' C. *Cor.* I. i. 154. 3. They enclose oure commens 1550.

Phrases. **The c.** (quasi-*sb.*): (*a*) that which is ordinary; (*b*) the vulgar tongue *A. Y. L.* v. i. 54. **In c.**, †in general; ordinarily; in joint use or possession; holding by several titles, but by unity of possession, as *tenants in c.*, etc.; in communion; in participation. **In the c. of** (*Sc.*): in the debt of.

†**Common** (kǫ·mən), *v.* [ME. *comunen, comonen*, a. OF. *comuner*, f. *comun* COMMON. Cf. COMMUNE.] I. 1. *trans.* To communicate -1548. 2. *intr.* To participate, share *with, in*

–1602. 3. To have intercourse –1555. II. (cf. COMMUNE.) 1. *intr.* To confer, converse –1596. 2. *trans.* To confer about; talk of –1607. 3. To administer the Communion to; *refl.* and *pass.* to communicate –1508. III. (f. COMMON, (-s,) *sb.* or *adj.*) 1. *intr.* To exercise a right of common –1697. 2. To eat at a common table –1766.

Commonable (kǫ·mənăb'l), *a.* 1620. [f. COMMON *v.* III. 1.] 1. That may be pastured on common lands. 2. That is or may be held in common; pertaining to commoning 1649.

1. C. beasts are either beasts of the plough, or such as manure the ground BLACKSTONE. 2. C. land AUSTIN, rights ROGERS.

Commonage (kǫ·mənėdʒ). 1610. [f. COMMON *sb.* (or *v.*) + -AGE.] 1. The practice of commoning; right of common (usu. 'of pasture'); the condition of land held in common 1808; *concr.* common land, a common 1771. 2. The estate of the commons 1649.

1. Open fields.. shackled with the rights of c. A. YOUNG. 2. The whole baronetage, peerage, c. of England THACKERAY.

Commonalty (kǫ·mənălti). ME. [a. OF. *comunalté, -auté*, f. L. **communalitatem*.] †1. A community, commonwealth –1631; a self-governing community –1660. 2. A body corporate 1425. 3. The common people, as dist. from 'the upper classes'; the commons ME. †4. The Commons as an estate of the realm –1648. 5. *transf.* The general body 1594.

2. The Maire and cominaltie of the Citie of New Sarum SIR R. ELYOT. 3. Plebs in englishe, is called the comunaltee ELYOT. 5. The c. of mankind GALT. var. **Commona·lity.**

†Commo:nefa·ction. 1619. [f. L. *commonefacere*.] An admonition –1679.

Commoner, compar. of COMMON *a.*

Commoner (kǫ·mənəɹ), *sb.* ME. [f. COMMON *sb.* and *v.*] †1. A burgess –1643. 2. One of the common people. (Now used of all below the rank of a *peer*.) ME. 3. A member of the House of Commons. Now *rare.* 1648. †4. One who shares in anything –1661. 5. At Oxford: An undergraduate who is not on the foundation of a college, but pays for his commons (called at Cambridge a *pensioner*) 1613. 6. One who enjoys a right of common 1540. Also *fig.* †7. A common harlot –1695.

2. He dyned at a knyghtes bridale, and woulde not eate at the bridale of a communer ELYOT. 6. *fig.* The Birds, great Nature's happy Commoners ROWE.

Co·mmonish, *a. rare.* 1792. [f. COMMON *a.* + -ISH.] Rather common.

Commonition (kǫmǫni·ʃən). *rare.* 1730. [ad. L. *commonitionem*.] Admonition; a formal reminder. So **†Commo·nitive** *a.* serving as a c. **†Commo·nitory** *a.* serving to admonish; *sb.* a commonitory writing.

Common law. ME. [cf. L. *jus commune.*] †1. The general law of a community, as opp. to local or personal customs –1551. 2. The unwritten law of England, administered by the King's courts, based on ancient and universal usage, and embodied in commentaries and reported cases. (Opp. to *statute law.*) ME. b. The law administered by the King's ordinary judges. (Opp. to *equity, eccl.* and *admiralty* law, etc.) 1848. Also *attrib.* Hence **Common lawyer**, one versed in, or practising, this.

Commonly (kǫ·mənli), *adv.* ME. [f. COMMON *a.*; see -LY[2].] †1. Generally, universally –1656. †2. Unitedly –1563. †3. Familiarly –1590. †4. Publicly –1611. 5. Usually, ordinarily ME. 6. Meanly, cheaply (*mod.*).

3. SPENSER *F. Q.* I. x. 56. 5. In this Land the shining Ones c. walked BUNYAN. Hardly c. civil 1706.

Commonness (kǫ·mən,nės). 1530. [f. COMMON *a.*] 1. The state or quality of being common or usual. 2. Meanness; want of distinction. (Less offensive than *vulgarity*.) 1872.

1. Communion is a c. .. between God and a man 1657. C. of use 1876.

Co·mmonplace. 1549. [tr. L. *locus communis* = Gr. κοινὸς τόπος a general topic.]

A. *sb.* **As two words.* †1. A passage of general application –1581. 2. A notable passage, entered, for use, in a COMMONPLACE-BOOK 1561. †3. A commonplace-book –1749. **As one word.* 4. A statement generally accepted; a stock theme; a platitude 1560. 5. Anything common and trite 1802; *collect.* 1732. 6. Commonplace quality 1842.

2. Whatever in my small Reading occurs, concerning this our Fellow-Creature [Ass], I do never fail to set it down by way of Common Place SWIFT. 4. The paradoxes of one age often become the commonplaces of the next JOWETT. 6. The c. of his [Addison's] ideas M. ARNOLD.

Comb. **c.-book**, a book in which one records passages to be remembered or referred to.

B. *adj.* [attrib. use of A.; now written as one word.] Of the nature of a commonplace; trite, trivial, hackneyed 1609.

A Common-Place Talker STEELE. C. virtues MORLEY. *The c.*: that which is c., commonplaceness.

Hence **Co:mmonpla·ceness**, c. quality. **Co·mmonpla:cer**, †a c. book; a person who keeps one.

Co·mmonplace, *v.* 1656. [f. prec.] 1. *trans.* To arrange under general heads; to enter in a commonplace-book. 2. *intr.* To cite, repeat, or utter commonplaces 1609.

Common Pleas. ME. [repr. Anglo-Fr. *communs pletz*, pl. of *plait* :—L. *placitum*; see PLEA.] Civil actions at law brought by one subject against another. (Opp. to *pleas of the crown*; see Blackstone *Comm.* III. 40.) Used chiefly as a contr. of *Court of Common Pleas*, now merged in the King's Bench Division of the High Court of Justice.

Common prayer. 1526. Prayer in which worshippers publicly unite; *esp.* the liturgy of the Church of England, set forth in the *Book of Common Prayer* of Edward VI. Also, = *Common Prayer Book* 1712.

Co·mmon-room. 1670. At Oxford, the college-room to which the fellows and others retire after dinner. Also *transf.* Hence, the members of this room, as a body.

Commons (kǫ·mənz), *sb. pl.* ME. [Pl. of COMMON *sb.*]

I. 1. The commonalty; the lower order, as dist. from those of noble or knightly or gentle rank. 2. The third estate in the English (or other similar) constitution. (In early use excluding the clergy.) Hence, the representatives of the third estate in Parliament; the Lower House. ME.

1. Rude Comouns MANDEV. Your Highnes pore commons 1546. 2. The commons included the whole people, not lords 1817. An assembly called the house of commons..to represent the wisdom of the whole nation SWIFT.

II. 1. Provisions for a community or company in common; the common expense of such provisions; also the share due to each member ME. b. Used as *sing.* A common table; cf. *Doctors' Commons. spec.* At Oxford, a definite portion of victuals supplied from the college buttery or kitchen, at a fixed price. 1641. 2. Rations; daily fare 1540.

1. A C. of Bread and Water DRYDEN. 2. *Short c.*: scant fare.

Common sense, -sense. 1535. [repr. Gr. κοινὴ αἴσθησις, L. *sensus communis*.] †1. An internal sense which was regarded as the common bond or centre of the five senses 1543. 2. Ordinary, normal, or average understanding. (Without this a man is foolish or insane.) 1535. b. Good sound practical sense; general sagacity 1726. c. A thing approved by common sense 1803. 3. The general sense of mankind, or of a community 1596. 4. *Philos.* The faculty of primary truths 1758. Also *attrib.* (hyphened).

2. Common sense will not teach us metaphysics any more than mathematics JOWETT. b. Rich in saving common-sense. c. Is this common sense MACKINTOSH. 4. *Philosophy of Common Sense*: the theory which accepts as the criterion of truth the primary cognitions of mankind. Hence **Common-se·nsible** *a.* possessing, or marked by, common sense; **-bly** *adv.*

Commonty (kǫ·mənti). ME. [a. OF. *comuneté* (*comm-*) :—L. *communitatem*.] †1. The commonalty –1600. †2. A community –1523. 3. Commonage. *Sc.* 1540. 4. Land held in common; 'a common'. *Sc.* 1600. ¶5. *joc.* for *comedy. Tam. Shr.* Induct. ii. 140.

Common weal, commonweal (kǫ·mənwīl). *arch.* ME. [COMMON *a.* + WEAL, q. v.] 1. (Prop. two wds.) Common well-being 1469. 2. = COMMONWEALTH 2.

Commonwealth (kǫ·mənwelþ). 1470. [See COMMON *a.* and WEALTH.] 1. Public welfare; general good. *Obs.* in ordinary use. 2. The body politic; a state, *esp.* viewed as a body in which the whole people have a voice or an interest 1513. 3. A republic 1618. 4. The republican government in England between 1649 and 1660. 5. *transf.* and *fig.* 1551.

3. Better things were done..under a C. than under a King PEPYS. b. Since 1891 the title of the federated states of Australia. 5. The Common-wealth of Learning 1664, of nations BURKE. Hence **Co·mmonwealth's-man**, †one devoted to the c.; an adherent of the English C. (*Hist.*); †*gen.* a republican.

Commorancy (kǫ·mŏrănsi). 1586. [f. COMMORANT; see -ANCY.] *Law.* Abiding; sojourning; tarrying. var. **†Co·mmorance.**

Commorant (kǫ·mŏrănt). 1556. [ad. L. *commorantem*.] *adj.* Abiding, dwelling, resident. *sb.* A dweller, sojourner, resident 1670. So **†Commora·tion.**

Commorient (kǫmōᵊ·riĕnt), *a.* 1646. [ad. L. *commorientem*.] Dying together or simultaneously. Also as *sb.*

†Commo·rse. [f. *commors-, commordere*, after *remorse*.] Compassion. DANIEL.

‖**Commot** (kʋ·mət). 1495. [a. Welsh *cymwd*.] *Welsh Hist.* A division subordinate to a *cantred*; occas., a seigniory or manor.

Commote (kǫmōᵘ·t), *v. rare.* 1852. [f. L. *commot-*; see COMMOVE.] To put into commotion, disturb.

Commotion (kǫmōᵘ·ʃən). 1471. [a. OF. *com(m)ocion*, ad. L. *commotionem*; see COMMOVE.] †1. *lit.* Continuous or recurring motion –1650. 2. Physical disturbance, more or less violent 1592. 3. Bustle, stir 1616. 4. Public disturbance; tumult, sedition 1471. †5. Mental perturbation; agitation –1768.

2. The billows' c. SOUTHEY. 4. The open c. of your people FULLER. The punishment of the Leaders..in a C. HOBBES. 5. Achilles in c. rages *Tr. & Cr.* II. iii. 185. Hence **†Commo·tioner**, one who excites or takes part in a c.

Commove (kǫmū·v), *v.* Chiefly in pa. pple. ME. [a. F. *commouvoir*.] 1. *trans.* (*lit.*) To move violently, set in commotion; to disturb. 2. To move in mind or feeling; to excite ME.

1. From its depths commoved, Infuriate ocean raves SOUTHEY.

Communal (kǫ·miunăl), *a.* 1811. [a. F., f. L. *communa* COMMUNE.] 1. Of or belonging to a COMMUNE; of or pertaining to the Paris Commune 1871. 2. Of or pertaining to a (or the) community 1843; esp., in India, of any of the racial or religious communities. Hence **Co·mmunalism**, a theory of government which advocates the widest extension of local autonomy for each locally definable community. **Co·mmunalist**, a supporter of a communal system. **Co:mmunali·stic** *a.* of or pertaining to this theory. **Co:mmunaliza·tion**, the rendering of anything (*e.g.* land, gas, etc.) c. **Commu·nalize** *v.* to render c. **Co·mmunally** *adv.*

Communard (kǫ·miunaɹd). 1874. [f. COMMUNE + -ARD depreciatory.] An adherent of the Commune of Paris of 1871. Also *attrib.*

Commune (kǫ·miūn), *sb.*[1] 1792. [a. F. (med.L. *communa*) :—late L. *communia*, adj. neut. pl. as sb. fem. (cf. *bible*).] 1. *Hist.* As tr. med.L. *communa*, etc.: a. the commonalty; b. a municipal corporation; c. a community 1818. 2. In France, a small territorial division governed by a maire and municipal council 1792; any similar division elsewhere 1832.

2. The average of France is nearly fifteen communes to a canton 1837. *The C.* (*of Paris*): (*a*) a body which usurped the government of Paris, and played a leading part during the Reign of Terror, till suppressed in 1794; (*b*) the government on communalistic principles established in Paris in 1871; (*c*) the principles and practices embodied in the latter.

Commune (kǫ·miūn), *sb.*[2] 1814. [f. COMMUNE *v.*; cf. *converse*.] The action of communing (see COMMUNE *v.*).

Commune (kǫmiū·n, kǫ·miūn), *v.* [ME. *comune*, a. OF. *comuner* to make common. Cf. COMMON *v.*]

†I. Var. of COMMON *v.* I. 1–3. –1827.

II. Current senses, now always *commune*. †1. *intr.* To talk together, converse; to confer –1611. 2. *intr.* To hold intimate (mental or spiritual) intercourse (*with*). (Now only literary, devotional, and poetic.) 1671. 3. *intr.* To receive the Holy Communion, to communicate. (Common in U. S.) 1550.

1. *Acts* xxiv. 26. 2. As thus he communed with his soul apart POPE.

Communicable (kǫmiū·nikăb'l), *a.* ME.

[prob. a. F.] †1. Communicating -1677. 2. That may be communicated or imparted 1534. †3. Suitable for communication (*rare*) -1643. 4. Affable 1534.

2. Lost bliss, to thee no more c. MILT. *P. R.* I. 419. 4. Be..c. with your inferiours LD. BERNERS. Hence **Commu·nicabi·lity, Commu·nicableness,** the quality or faculty of being c. **Commu·nicably** *adv.* in the way of communication.

Communicant (kǒmiū·nikănt). 1552. [f. L. *communicantem.*]

A. *sb.* 1. One who partakes of the Holy Communion. 2. One who, or that which, communicates, in various senses 1597.

1. There are..1500 Communicants in that Parish HALE. 2. An anonymous c. 1881.

B. *adj.* (*rare.*) 1. Having a part in common 1557. 2. Furnishing communication 1703. 3. Being a communicant (see A. 1) 1834.

1. Two c. or overlapping Genera BOWEN.

Communicate (kǒmiū·nikeᶦt), *v.* 1526. [f. L. *communicat-*, *communicare*, f. *communis.*] 1. *trans.* To give to another as a partaker; to impart, confer, transmit. Const. *to.* 1538. 2. *spec.* To impart (information, etc.); to inform a person of. Const. *to*, †*with*, or *absol.* 1529. 3. To give, bestow. ? *Obs.* 1582. 4. To share in; to use, or enjoy, in common *with*; to share *with* (*arch.*) 1526. †5. *intr.* To participate, share -1709. 6. To partake of the Holy Communion 1549; †*trans.* -1709. 7. To administer the Communion to 1539. 8. *intr.* To hold intercourse or converse; to make a communication. Const. *with.* 1598. †*intr.* -1781. 9. To open into each other; to have communication or continuity of passage 1731.

1. To receive or c. pleasure JOHNSON. To c. the pestilence to 1769. 2. To c. a secreate to 1555, information (*mod.*). 4. Thousands that c. our loss B. JONS. 5. Ye did c. with my affliction *Philipp.* iv. 14. 6. Every one who was baptized communicated daily WESLEY. 7. Whether children ought to be communicated 1616. 8. No means of communicating with others but by signs TYLOR. 9. A system of such canals, which all c. with one another ARBUTHNOT. A dressing-room to c. with the bedroom (*mod.*).

Communication (kǒmiūnikēᶦ·ʃən). ME. [a. OF. *co(m)municacion*, ad. L. *communicationem*; see prec.] 1. The action of communicating. Now rare of material things. 2. *spec.* The imparting, conveying, or exchange of ideas, knowledge, etc. (whether by speech, writing, or signs) 1690. 3. *concr.* That which is communicated, as a letter, or its contents 1490. †4. Interchange of speech -1605. 5. Converse, intercourse 1580. 6. Access or means of access between two or more persons or places; passage 1684. †7. Common participation -1771. 8. The Holy Communion; its observance (*rare*) 1610. 9. *Rhet.* A figure, in which a speaker assumes his hearer as a partner in his sentiments, and says We, instead of I or Ye 1553.

1. C. of commodities 1623, of a disease 1806, of motion (*mod.*). 2. To make Words serviceable to the end of C. LOCKE. 4. Euil communications corrupt good manners 1 *Cor.* xv. 33. 6. Two vessels at different temperatures in c. with each other B. STEWART. Lee's communications through South-Western Virginia 1864.

Communicative (kǒmiū·nikēᶦtiv), *a.* ME. [f. L. *communicat-*; see above and -IVE.] 1. That has the quality or habit of communicating; ready to communicate information, etc.; open, talkative 1654. †2. Communicable -1742. 3. Of or pertaining to communication 1670.

1. That no less C. then Judicious Antiquary FULLER. 2. C. Distempers RICHARDSON. 3. A c. or social principle 1710. Hence **Commu·nicative·ly** *adv.*, **-ness.**

Communicator (kǒmiū·nikēᶦtəɹ). 1662. [a. L.] One who or that which communicates. **Commu·nicatory** *a.* tending to the communication or imparting of anything, as †*C. letters* (*Eccl. Hist.*).

Communion (kǒmiū·niən, -yən). ME. [a. F., or ad. L. *communionem.*] 1. Sharing or holding in common; participation; community. 2. Fellowship 1553; spiritual intercourse 1600; communing (*poet.*) 1800; †common action -1796. 3. The fellowship between members or branches of the same church ME. 4. An organic union of persons united by common religious faith and rites 1565. 5. Community of functions 1538. 6. Intercourse 1614. 7. Participation in the sacrament of the Lord's Supper; also, the sacrament itself, the Eucharist ME. †b. = *C. Service* (cf. SERVICE¹ III. 4, 5) -1575.

1. Having no c. of nature with other things GROTE. 2. What c. hath light with darknesse 2 *Cor.* vi. 14. A close c. with Nature FORD. 3. The c. of saints, their c. not with one another merely, but [etc.] TRENCH. (Note. The phrase *c. of saints* has been used also in sense 4.) 4. Some of the Romish C. 1642. 5. To dissever the soul from the c. of the body JOWETT. 7. Phrases. *C. in one kind, in both kinds, half c.*, etc.: terms of the dispute whether the laity should receive one or both elements in the c. *Close* or *strict, free* or *open c.*: among Baptists, a division as to admitting to the Lord's Table persons not baptized by immersion. Hence **Commu·nionist,** (*a*) †a communicant; an adherent of a communion 1644; †(*b*) a communist 1827.

Communion table. 1566. [COMMUNION 7.] The table used in celebrating the Communion of the Lord's Supper. See under ALTAR.

‖**Communiqué** (kǒmiū·nikē, ‖komünike). 1852. [Fr., pa. pple. *communiquer* to communicate, used subst.] An official intimation or report.

Communism (kǫ·miuniz'm). 1843. [f. L. *communis* or F. *commun* + -ISM.] 1. A theory of society according to which all property should be vested in the community and labour organized for the common benefit. 2. Any practice which carries out this theory; also *transf.* 1857.

2. In these curious creatures c. prevails to its fullest extent, one for all and all for one J. G. WOOD.

Communist (kǫ·miunist). 1841. [f. as prec. + -IST. Cf. F. *communiste.*] An adherent of the theory of communism.

attrib. The C. doctrine of not paying a man in proportion to his work W. E. FORSTER. Hence **Communi·stic** *a.* (in both senses).

Communitarian (kǒmiūnitēᵊ·riăn). 1841. [Cf. *unitarian*, etc.] A member of a community practising communistic theories. So **Communito·rium,** the home of such a community.

Community (kǒmiū·niti). ME. [a. OF. *com(m)uneté, com(m)unité*:—L. *communitatem.*]

I. 1. The quality of appertaining to all in common; common ownership, liability, etc. 1561. 2. Common character; agreement, identity 1587. 3. Social intercourse; communion 1570. 4. Society, the social state 1652. †5. Commonness -1646.

1. Anabaptists, that hold c. of goods USSHER. 2. The points of c. in their nature WORDSW. 3. Men have a certain c. with God in this world 1570. 4. [Marriage] is the foundation of c. STEELE. 5. 1 *Hen. IV*, III. ii. 77.

II. †1. The commonalty -1700. 2. A body of people organized into a political, municipal, or social unity ME. 3. *spec.* A body of persons living together, and practising community of goods 1727. 4. *transf.* and *fig.* 1746.

2. Those little communities .. [called] Neighbourhoods 1711. The Jewish c. 1888. *The c.*: the people of a country (or district); the public. 3. The Abbot and C. of St. Mary's SCOTT. The Mormon c. 1890. 4. Creatures that in communities exist WORDSW.

Commutable (kǒmiū·tăb'l), *a.* 1649. [ad. L. *commutabilis*; see COMMUTE and -BLE.] That may be commuted or exchanged.

Offences not c. by fine 1880. Hence **Commu·tabi·lity,** the quality of being c.

Commutation (kǫmiutēᶦ·ʃən). 1496. [a. F. *commutacion*, ad. L. *commutationem*; see COMMUTE.] 1. The action or process of changing or altering; change, mutation. ? *Obs.* 1509. †2. Exchange, barter -1744. 3. Substitution, interchange 1597. 4. *spec.* a. The substitution of one kind of payment for another; also *fig.* 1597. b. *Law.* The substitution of a lesser punishment for a greater. (See COMMUTE *v.*) 1824. c. *concr.* The price paid by way of commutation 1707. 5. *Electr.* The altering of the course of an electric current. (See COMMUTATOR.) 1876. 6. *Angle of c.*: (*Astron.*) the distance between the sun's true place seen from the earth, and the place of a planet reduced to the ecliptic 1751.

1. Such a scene of revolution and c. SYD. SMITH. 2. The use of money..is that of saving the c. of more bulky commodities ARBUTHNOT. 4. The c. of Penance 1640. A c. of his own sentence from death to the galleys W. IRVING. The C. of Tithes SYD. SMITH.

Comb.: **C. Act,** an act for the c. of tithes in England, passed in 1836; **-ticket** (*U.S.*), a ticket issued by a railway company, etc., entitling the holder to travel, etc., during its currency at a reduced rate; a season-ticket.

Commutative (kǒmiū·tĕtiv, kǫ·miutēᶦtiv), *a.* 1531. [ad. med.L. *commutativus*, f. L. *commut-*; see COMMUTE and -IVE.] †1. Pertaining to exchange -1631. 2. Relating to or involving substitution or interchange 1836.

1. C. Justice, is .. a Performance of Covenant HOBBES. 2. Every..crime had its c. fine MILMAN. Hence **Commutatively** *adv.* in a c. manner. var. **Commu·tato·rial** (in sense 1).

Commutator (kǫ·miutēᶦtəɹ). 1839. [f. L. *commutare.*] He who or that which commutes; *Electr.* a contrivance for altering the course of an electric current.

Commute (kǒmiū·t), *v.* 1633. [f. L. *commutare*, f. *com-* + *mutare*; cf. *transmute.*] 1. *trans.* To change (*for* or *into*); to exchange; to interchange 1667. 2. To change an obligation, etc., into something lighter or more agreeable. Const. *for, into*, occ. *with.* 1633. 3. To change (a punishment, or a sentence) *for* (*to, into*) a lighter one, or a fine 1642. 4. To change (one kind of payment) *into* or *for* another 1795. *absol. spec.* (*U.S.*) To purchase and use a commutation-ticket. 5. *intr.* To make up, compound *for*; to serve as a substitute *for* 1645.

1. May..exchange and c... Moneys currant of England, into Moneys of..Ireland 1633. 2. To c. a penance 1633, one Duty for another 1723. 3. To c. whipping into money FULLER, punishments for fines LD. BROUGHAM. 4. To c. average receipts into a fixed charge MILL. To c. an annuity into a capital sum LD. SELBORNE. 5. Perhaps the shame and misery of this life may c. for hell 1663. Hence **Commu·ter,** one who commutes; one who holds a commutation-ticket (*U.S.*).

Commutual (kǒmiū·tiuăl), *a.* 1602. [See CO-, COM-.] Mutual, reciprocal. (Chiefly *poet.*)

Since..Hymen did our hands Vnite comutuall *Haml.* III. ii. 170.

Comose (kōᵘmōᵘ·s), *a.* 1793. [ad. L. *comosus*; see COMA².] Furnished with a COMA; of seeds: Downy or hairy. var. **Co·mous.**

Compact (kǫ·mpækt), *sb.*¹ 1590. [Cf. OF. *compact*, ad. L. *compactum, compacisci*; see PACT. In Shaks. usu. (kǒmpæ·kt).] A covenant or contract between two or more. Used without *a* in phrases, as *by c.*, etc. †b. In a bad sense: Plot, conspiracy -1652.

Family c., social c.: see FAMILY, SOCIAL.

†**Compact,** *sb.*² 1601. [subst. use of COMPACT *ppl. a.*¹] A structure; a composition; build; compaction -1817.

Compact (kǒmpæ·kt), *ppl. a.*¹ ME. [ad. L. *compactus, compingere*, f. *com-* + *pangere.*]

I. *pa. pple. arch.* 1. Compacted, firmly put together. 2. Composed *of* 1531.

1. A farre greater Empire..and better c. 1636. 2. If he c. of jarres, grow Musicall *A. Y. L.* II. vii. 5.

II. *adj.* 1. Closely packed or knit together; dense, firm ME.; not scattered or diffuse 1642. 2. *transf.* and *fig.* 1576.

1. The c. tissue [of bones] 1831. Paris is c.; [her] strength is collected and condensed within a narrow compass BURKE. 2. A man..c., instant, selfish, prudent EMERSON. In verse well-disciplined, complete, c. COWPER. Hence **Compa·ct-ly** *adv.*, **-ness.**

†**Compa·ct,** *ppl. a.*² 1597. [ad. L. *compactus, compacisci.*] Joined in compact. *Meas. for M.* V. i. 242.

Compact (kǒmpæ·kt), *v.*¹ 1530. [f. COMPACT *a.*] 1. *trans.* To join or knit (things) firmly and tightly together, or *to* each other; to consolidate; to condense, solidify 1633. Also *transf.* and *fig.* 2. To make up or compose 1570. Also *fig.*

1. The Ligaments, that should c. and keep them [Limbs] in their Functions 1709. Now the bright sun compacts the precious stone BLACKMORE. 2. Who out of nothing all things did c. 1652. Hence **Compa·cted-ly** *adv.* (*rare*), **-ness. Compa·cter, -or.**

†**Compa·ct,** *v.*² 1535. [app. a. OF. *compacter* 'faire un pacte', f. *compactum* COMPACT *sb.*¹] 1. *intr.* To make a compact -1690. 2. To plan by compact 1667.

1. Slaves could never have a right to c. or consent LOCKE.

†**Compa·ctile,** *a. rare.* [ad. L. *compactilis.*] Made up by being joined or put together. SIR T. BROWNE.

Compaction¹ (kǒmpæ·kʃən). ME. [a. OF., ad. L. *compactionem*; see COMPACT *v.*¹] The action or process of making or becoming compact; the state of being so compacted.

†**Compa·ction**². 1528. [a. OF., f. L. *compact-, compacisci.*] The making of an agreement; an agreement made -1539.

†Compa·cture. 1590. [ad. L. *compactura*; see COMPACT *v* [1]] Manner of putting closely together; compact structure –1641.
With comely compasse and c. strong SPENSER.

Compages (kǫmpē·dʒīz). 1638. [a. L., f. *com-*+*pag-*, *pangere*; cf. COMPACT *ppl. a.*[1]] 1. A whole formed by the compaction of parts; a complex structure. Also *fig.* and *transf.* 2. Solid structure, consistency (as a quality) 1660.
1. The structure and c. of the human frame 1819. *fig.* The whole c., or fabrick of the Christian faith WATERLAND. var. **†Compage** (cf. *jointage*, etc.).

Compaginate (kǫmpæ·dʒineⁱt), *v.* 1648. [f. late L. *compaginat-*, *compaginare*, f. *compago* = *compages*; see COMPAGES.] To join firmly together; to connect, unite (*lit.* and *fig.*).
The side-pieces which .. c. the whole frame 1648. So **Compa·gina·tion.**

†Companable, *a.* ME. [a. OF. *cum-*, *compagnable*, f. *compagnier* to COMPANY.] Sociable, companionable –1611.

†Co·mpanage. ME. [a. OF. :—late L. *companaticum*, f. *com-* + *panis.*] Anything eaten with bread as a relish, *e.g.* butter, cheese, meat, etc. –1679.

†Compa·niable, *a.* ME. Var. of COMPANABLE –1822.

Companion (kǫmpæ·nyən), *sb.*[1] ME. [a. OF. *compaignon*, *-pagnon* :—late L. *companionem*, f. *com-*+*panis.*] 1. One who associates with or accompanies another; a mate, a fellow. †2. An associate in some specific or legal relation; a colleague, partner, etc. –1769. 3. *fig.* of things 1577. 4. As a term of contempt. Cf. 'fellow'. –1764. 5. A knight, formerly of any, now of the lowest, grade in certain orders 1568. 6. A person employed to live with another in need of society. (Now usu. of women.) 1766. 7. A thing which matches another 1762. Also *attrib.* and quasi-*adj.*
1. Companions in sin QUARLES. *Boon c.*: see BOON *a.* 2. Thyne owne companyon and married wife COVERDALE *Malachi* ii. 14. 3. With no c. but a pocket compass 1882. 4. 2 *Hen. IV*, II. iv. 132. 5. *C. of the Bath* (C.B.). Hence **Compa·nionage,** companionship (*rare*); the body of (Knight) Companions. **Compa·nionhood** = COMPANIONSHIP. **Compa·nionless** *a.* without a c.

Companion (kǫmpæ·nyən), *sb.*[2] 1762. [Cf. Du. *kompanje* 'quarter-deck', f. (ult.) It. *compagna* (in *camera della compagna* galley storeroom) = COMPANAGE, *companaticum* provisions. In Du. and Eng. applied to other structures erected on deck.] A skylight or window-frame to admit light to a lower deck or cabin; a wooden hood over the entrance of the master's cabin in small ships. *Occas.* = *c.-ladder*, *-way.*
Comb.: **c.-hatch, -head,** a wooden covering over the staircase to a cabin; **-ladder,** a ladder leading from the deck to a cabin; also, the ladder by which officers ascend to, and descend from, the quarter-deck; **-way,** the staircase or porch of the ladder-way to the cabin.

Companion (kǫmpæ·nyən), *v.* 1606. [f. prec. *sb.*[1]] †1. *trans.* To make companion or fellow –1803. 2. To go or be with as a companion 1622. 3. *intr.* To keep company 1845.
1. *Ant. & Cl.* I. ii. 30. 2. His statue..still companions the winged lion on the opposing pillar of the piazzetta RUSKIN.

Compa·nionable, *a.* 1627. [f. COMPANION *v.* or *sb.*] 1. Fitted for companionship; sociable. 2. Fitted to match (*rare*) 1823.
A C. life FELTHAM, wit CLARENDON. Hence **Compa·nionableness. Compa·nionably** *adv.*

Companionate (kǫmpæ·nyəneⁱt), *a.* 1927. [f. COMPANION *sb.*[1] + -ATE[2].] *C. marriage*, marriage with legalized birth-control and provision for divorce by mutual consent.

Compa·nioned, *ppl. a.* 1820. [f. COMPANION *sb.*[1] and *v.* + -ED.] Having, or accompanied by, a companion or companions.

Companionship (kǫmpæ·nyənʃip). 1548. [f. COMPANION *sb.*[1] + -SHIP.] 1. The relation of being a companion; association of persons as companions; fellowship. (Also said of things.) 2. A body of companions; *spec.* in *Printing*, a company of compositors working together under a clicker 1824. 3. The dignity of a Companion in an order of knighthood 1870.

Company (kɒ·mpăni), *sb.* ME. [a. OF. *cum-*, *compaignie*, *-pagnie*, *-pegnie*, f. stem *compagn-*; see COMPANION.] 1. Companionship, fellowship, society; †also *transf.* of things. †2. Sexual connexion –1616. 3. A number of individuals assembled or associated together ME. 4. *collect.* Persons casually or temporarily brought into association. More loosely, 'People such as prevent privacy'. ME. b. The person or persons with whom one habitually associates 1601. Also *fig.* 5. A gathering of people for social intercourse; a circle; †an assembly 1653; society (*arch.*) 1576. 6. A body of persons combined or incorporated for some common object; *esp.* to carry on some commercial or industrial undertaking ME. b. The partner or partners in a firm whose names are not included in the style or title; generally written Co., COMP. 7. *Mil.* A body of soldiers ME.; *spec.* a subdivision of an infantry regiment commanded by a captain 1590. 8. *Naut.* (in full *ship's c.*) 'The whole crew of any ship, including her officers, men, and boys' 1610.
1. My sone .. be wele ware of womans companye 1440. *For c.*: for company's sake. *To keep c.* (*with*): to associate *with*; *esp.* (*vulgar* and *dial.*) to court. 3. A compagnie Of sondry folk CHAUCER. A c. of horses *Song Sol.* i. 9. 4. C. coming in, they made off LUTTRELL. b. Phr. *To know a man by his c.* 5. Another of the c. that shall be nameless WALTON. To let them see C. FORDYCE. 6. Companies or guilds 1839. A c. of players DENNIS (J.). *Joint Stock C.*: see JOINT STOCK. *Chartered C.*: see CHARTERED. *John C.*: see JOHN.

Company (kɒ·mpăni), *v.* ME. [a. OF. *compaignier*; see COMPANION.] 1. *trans.* To accompany; to keep company with (*arch.*). †2. To associate in companionship –1590. 3. *intr.* To keep company, consort ME.; †to cohabit (*with*) –1680. Also *absol.* †4. *intr.* 'To be a gay companion' (J.). SPENSER.
1. Best companied when most I am alone DRUMM. OF HAWTH. 2. To c. my heart with sad laments MARLOWE.

Comparable (kǫ·mpărăb'l), *a.* ME. [a. F., ad. L. *comparabilis.*] 1. Able to be compared (*with*). 2. Worthy of comparison; to be compared (*to*) 1483.
2. None c. to hyr in wytte and wysdom CAXTON. **Co·mparableness. Co·mparably** *adv.*

†Co·mparate. 1650. [ad. L. *comparatus.*] *adj.* Of comparison, comparative –1668. *sb. Logic.* A thing compared with another –1680. So **†Compara·tion,** COMPARISON.

Comparative (kǫmpæ·rătiv). ME. [ad. L. *comparativus.*]
A. *adj.* 1. Of or pertaining to comparison 1602; *spec.* involving comparison as a method, as *c. anatomy, philology*, etc. 1675. 2. *Gram.* Expressing a higher degree of the quality or attribute denoted by the simple adjective or adverb, as *tru-er, more often.* Cf COMPARISON, POSITIVE. ME. 3. Estimated by comparison 1597; relative 1774. †4. Comparable –1819.
1. An Act of Choice or Preference is a c. Act EDWARDS. The C. method of investigation MAINE. 3. The c. claims of pleasure and wisdom JOWETT. A matter of c. indifference JEVONS.
B. *sb.* 1. *Gram.* The comparative degree (see A. 2); an adjective or adverb in the comparative degree 1530. †2. A compeer, rival –1611. †3. ? One ready to make comparisons –1823.
1. *Older* and *oldest* are the ordinary comparatives now in use MORRIS. 2. Gerrard ever was His full c. BEAUM. & FL. 3. The push Of euery Beardlesse vaine Comparatiue 1 *Hen. IV*, III. ii. 67.
Hence **Compa·ratively** *adv.* by way of comparison; somewhat, rather. **Compa·rativist,** one who employs the c. method.

Comparator (kǫ·mpăreⁱtəɹ). 1883. [f. L. *comparare.*] An instrument for comparing, *e.g.* the lengths of nearly equal bars.

†Compa·rcioner. ME. [a. OF. *comparçonnier*, f. (ult.) L. *com-* + *partitionem.*] = COPARCENER –1537.

Compare (kǫmpēᵊ·ɹ), *sb.*[1] 1536. †1. An equal, rival, COMPEER –1617. 2. *Without c.*: = 'without compeer'. (Referred later to COMPARE *v.*; see next.) 1621. Hence **†Compa·reless,** peerless, incomparable.

Compare (kǫmpēᵊ·ɹ), *sb.*[2] 1589. [f. COMPARE *v.*[1]; see prec.] Comparison. Chiefly in *beyond* (*past*) *c.*
Wit beyond c. 1621. Nor are its churches anything considerable in c. to Oxford EVELYN.

Compare (kǫmpēᵊ·ɹ), *v.*[1] ME. [a. OF. *comperer* :—L. *comparare*, f. *com-*+*par.*] 1. *trans.* To represent as similar; to liken. Const. *to.* 2. To mark the similarities and differences of; to bring together for the purpose of noting these. Const. *with, to*; *together.* 1509. 3. *Gram.* To form the comparative and superlative degrees of (an adjective or adverb) 1612. 4. *intr.* (for *refl.*) To be compared; to bear comparison; to vie *with*, rival 1450.
1. All the things thou canst desire, are not to be compared vnto her *Prov.* iii. 15. He compares it to a Sloe, in shape and taste DAMPIER. 2. To c. Great things with small MILT. *P. L.* II. 921. *To c. notes* (often *fig.*): to exchange views, confer, discuss. 3. Words of one syllable are usually compared by *er* and *est* W. WARD. Some adverbs are compared, thus; 'Soon, sooner, soonest' .. Those ending in *ly* .. by *more* and *most* L. MURRAY. 4. Art, stryving to compayre With Nature SPENSER *F. Q.* II. v. 29. Hence **Compa·rer. Compa·ringly** *adv.*

†Compare, *v.*[2] *rare.* 1532. [ad. L. *comparare*, f. *com-*+*parare.*] 1. *trans.* To get, acquire –1590. 2. ? To allege 1536.
1. To fill his bags, and richesse to c. SPENSER.

Comparison (kǫmpæ·risən), *sb.* ME. [a. OF. *comparaison* :—L. *comparationem*, f. *comparare.* Cf. *orison*, etc.] 1. The action, or an act, of comparing or likening. 2. Capacity of being compared; comparable condition or character. (Always with negative expressed or implied.) ME. 3. 'A simile in writing or speaking; an illustration by similitude' (J.) ME. 4. The action, or an act, of noting similarities and differences; see COMPARE *v.*[1] 2. ME. 5. *Gram.* The action of comparing an adj. or adv. 1530.
1. The c. of philosophy to a yelping she-dog JOWETT. 2. A Pallace without c. to any other 1662. Phr. *Without c., out of all c., beyond all c.* 3. Comparisons may sometimes illustrate, but prove nothing JUNIUS. A man.. Full of comparisons, and wounding floutes *L. L. L.* v. ii. 854. 4. The Words Great and Little..do import a C. to something else 1640. The Sculptor's art is limited in c. of others SIR J. REYNOLDS. A sterre in clerenes [is] nothinge in comparyson to the sonne WYCLIF. In c. with other things 1646. Penrith .. seems here, by c., like a metropolis SOUTHEY. 5. *Degrees of c.*: the positive, comparative, and superlative degrees of an adjective or adverb.

†Compa·rison, *v.* ME. [f. prec. sb.] 1. = COMPARE *v.*[1] 1, 2. –1626. ¶ 2. In Wyclif as tr. L. *comparare.*

Compart (kǫmpā·ɹt), *v.* 1575. [ad. OF. *compartir* or L. *compartiri.*] †1. To divide –1605. 2. To partition into smaller parts 1785.
2. The interior was comparted by willow screens 1876.

Compartition (kǫmpaɹti·ʃən). 1624. [f. L. *compartiri.*] The action of comparting; one of the parts so marked out and divided.
Save in their Temples..which needed no Compartitions WOTTON.

Compartment (kǫmpā·ɹtmĕnt). 1564. [a. F., f. as prec.] 1. A division separated by partitions; a part partitioned off; *e.g.* one of the divisions of a railway-carriage, a large ship, etc. †2. The proper disposition and distribution of the parts of any design –1736.
1. The ceiling was divided into thirty-nine compartments 1873. *Comb.* **c.-bulkhead,** one of the partitions which divide the hold of a ship into watertight compartments.

†Compa·rtner. 1563. A CO-PARTNER –1701.

Compass (kɒ·mpăs), *sb.*[1] (*a.* and *adv.*) ME. [a. F. *compas*, f. L. type **compassus*, f. *com-* together + ? *passus* step. Or ? from the vb.] 1. †Measure, proper proportion –1612; due limits (now *dial.*) 1579. †2. Artifice, ingenuity; craft, cunning –1597; an artifice –1559. 3. An instrument for taking measurements and describing circles, consisting (in its simplest form) of two straight and equal legs connected at one end by a movable joint. Now usu. in *pl.*; also *pair of compasses.* ME. †4. A circumference, a circle –1655; anything circular in shape –1681, †5. A circular arc, sweep, curve –1697. 6. A circumference, boundary, enclosing line or limit ME.; circuit, girth 1526. 7. Circumscribed area; space, area, extent ME. Also *transf.* and *fig.* 8. *fig.* Bounds, limits; range, reach, scope 1555. 9. *Mus.* The full range of tones which a voice or instrument can produce 1597. 10. Circuit, round; a roundabout course or journey (*arch.*) ME.; a circuit of time 1601. 11. An instrument for determining the magnetic meridian or one's direction with respect to it, consisting of a magnetized needle turning on a pivot; used *esp.* at sea (the *Mariner's* or *Seaman's c.*) 1515. Also *fig.*
1. Phr. *By c.*, with measure and order, regularly.

Within or *out of c.* 2. Things that proceede from our owne care, and compasse BACON. Fetches and.. far compasses to bring things to their purposes LATIMER. 3. Bow-COMPASSES, *beam-, calliper-, hair-compasses*, etc.: see these words. 5. The shaft..flyeth a round compace ASCHAM *Toxoph.* 6. To touch the c. of a wide subject RUSKIN. The Duke's chase, thirty miles in c. SHORTHOUSE. 7. Of the tryne compas lord and gyde CHAUCER. In the C. of a Crown piece 1710, (*fig.*) of one verse 1734. 8. Within the compasse of mans Wit *Oth.* III. iv. 21, of our belief FULLER. 9. *Haml.* III. ii. 383. 10. They wenten in compas, Daunsinge aboute this flour CHAUCER. Where I did begin, there shall I end: My life is run his compasse *Jul. C.* v. iii. 25. Phr. *To cast, fetch, go, set, take a c.* 11. *C. box*: see BOX *sb.*[2] *C. card*: see CARD *sb.*[2] *Points of the c.*: see POINT. *To box the c.*: see BOX *v.*[1] *Azimuth c.*: see AZIMUTH. (*Note.* The *dip, surveying, variation compasses*, etc. are varieties of the Mariner's compass specially constructed for particular purposes.) *fig.* Profit is the Compasse by which Factious men steer their course 1649.

B. *adj.* Round, circular, curved. (Still techn.) 1523.

A c. ring, set round with little diamonds CHESTERF.

C. *adv.* [Cf. *in c.*] †1. In compass -1587. †2. In a circular arc, curvedly -1655. †b. Archery. *To shoot c.*: to shoot high, so as to allow for the curve of the projectile -1611.

Comb.: (sense 11) *c.-bowl, -needle*, etc.; †**c.-dial**, a portable sun-dial adjustable by an attached c.-needle; **-flower, -plant**, a N.Amer. composite (*Silphium laciniatum*) with large much-divided leaves, of which the lower 'are said to present their faces uniformly north and south' (Asa Gray); **-saw**, a saw with a narrow blade for cutting out curves of moderate size; **-timber**, curved timber, *esp.* as used for ship-building; **-window**, a semicircular bay-window.

†**Co·mpass**, *sb.*[2] 1573. Corrupt f. COMPOST -1700.

Compass (kv·mpăs), *v.*[1] ME. [a. F. *compasser* to measure:—L. type **compassare*.] †1. To design (a work of art). ME. only. 2. To contrive, devise, machinate (a purpose). Usually in a bad sense. ME. 3. To pass or move round; to make the circuit of ME. Also *absol.* 4. To close round, as a multitude; to surround, with friendly or hostile intent; to hem in; occas. *spec.* 'to besiege, block' (J.) ME. Also *fig.* 5. To encircle, environ, lie round and enclose. Also with *round, about, in.* ME. 6. To surround *with* ME. 7. To grasp with the mind 1576. 8. To accomplish 1549; to attain 1591. †9. To circumvent -1642. 10. To curve or be curved 1542.

2. To compasse or imagine the imprisonment of the King 1681. 3. The Bisquayn Ship..wherein Magellan compassed the World H. COGAN. 4. Myne enemies.. compassed me rounde aboute COVERDALE *Ps.* xxvi[i]. 6. *fig.* All the blessings Of a glad father, c. thee about *Temp.* v. i. 180. 5. Like the Sea they c. all the land POPE. 8. That were hard to compasse *Twel. N.* I. ii. 45. To compasse such a bondlesse happinesse *Per.* I. i. 24. 10. *Merry W.* III. v. 112. Hence **Co·mpassable** *a.* attainable. **Co·mpassed** *ppl. a.* †contrived; encircled; circumscribed; †curved, †circular, †arched. **Co·mpasser.**

†**Co·mpass**, *v.*[2] 1557. [See COMPASS *sb.*[2]] To COMPOST -1632.

Compassion (kŏmpæ·ʃən), *sb.* ME. [a. F., ad. late L. *compassionem*, f. *compati* (*compass-*).] †1. Suffering together with another; fellow-feeling, sympathy -1625. 2. Pity that inclines one to spare or to succour. ME. †3. Grief -1590.

2. Every claim to c. that can arise from misery and distress JUNIUS. Phr. *To have* (†*take*) *c.* (*upon*, †*of*).

Compa·ssion, *v. rare.* 1588. [prob. ad. F. *compassioner.*] To have compassion on, to pity. *Tit. A.* IV. i. 124. Hence **Compa·ssionable** *a.* †pitiful; pitiable (*rare*).

Compassionate (kŏmpæ·ʃənĕt), *a.* 1587. [Latinized ad. F. *compassionné.*] 1. Affected with, or expressing compassion; pitiful, sympathetic. †2. Fitted to excite compassion; pitiable, piteous -1767.

1. It is a fault..to bee too c. of an Heretique DONNE. Hence **Compa·ssionate·ly** *adv.*, **-ness.**

Compassionate (kŏmpæ·ʃəneit), *v.* 1598. [f. prec.] To regard or treat with compassion; to commiserate (a person, or his distress, etc.).

Men..naturally c. all..whom they see in distress BUTLER.

Compassive (kŏmpæ·siv), *a.* 1612. [f. L. *compass-, compati.*] Compassionate, pitiful.

Co·mpassless, *a.* 1864. [f. COMPASS.] Without a compass.

†**Co·mpassment.** ME. [a. OF., f. *compasser.*] Compassing; contrivance, machination -1593.

Compaternity (kŏmpătə·rnĭti). ME. [ad. med.L. *compaternitatem*, f. *compater* godfather.] The relationship existing between godparents mutually, or between them and the actual parents of a child.

Compatibility (kŏmpæ:tĭbi·lĭti). 1611. [See next.] The quality of being compatible; mutual tolerance, consistency, congruity.

The c. of such properties in one thing BARROW.

Compatible (kŏmpæ·tĭb'l), *a.* 1490. [a. F., f. L. *compati* (see COMPASSION).] †1. Sympathetic -1618. 2. Mutually tolerant; capable of existing together in the same subject; accordant, consistent, congruous. Const. *with.*

2. Wedlocke and priesthod be not repugnant but c. of their nature MORE. Heat is c. with Moisture 1688. Hence **Compa·tibleness. Compa·tibly** *adv.*

†**Compa·tient**, *a.* ME. [a. OF., ad. L. *compatientem.*] Suffering along with, sympathetic, compassionate -1646. So †**Compa·tience.**

Compatriot (kŏmpēi·triət, -pæ·t-). 1611. [a. F. *compatriote*, ad. L. *compatriota*, f. *com-* + *patriota* countryman.] A fellow-countryman. *attrib.* and *adj.* Of the same country 1744.

They..are ready to think a c. braver..and more deserving than any foreigner TUCKER. And Wolfe's great name c. with his own COWPER. Hence **Compatrio·tic** *a.* of or pertaining to compatriots; belonging to the same country. **Compa·triotism**, the position of being compatriots; c. feeling or sympathy.

Compear (kŏmpīə·ɹ), *v. Sc.* 1450. [a. F. *comparoir*:—L. *comparere.* Cf. APPEAR.] †1. To appear -1661. 2. *Sc. Law.* To appear in a court, either in person or by counsel 1450. So **Compea·rance.**

Compeer (kŏmpīə·ɹ), *sb.* [ME. *comper*, a. OF., f. *com-* + *per* (*peer*), mod. *pair*:—L. *parem.* See PEER, PAIR.] 1. One of equal rank or standing; an equal, peer. 2. A companion, comrade, fellow ME. Also *transf.* and *fig.*

1. Brian Boroimhe..a c. of King Alfred and of Washington 1886. 2. He axed lodgynge..for hym and his Comperys FABYAN. Dryden and several of his compeers MACAULAY. Hence †**Compee·r** *v. rare*, to equal, rival, be the c. of.

Compel (kŏmpe·l), *v.* ME. [a. OF. *compeller* and *compellir*, ad. L. *compellere*, f. *com-* + *pellere.*] 1. *trans.* To urge irresistibly, to constrain, oblige, force. 2. †To take or get by force, to extort -1601; to constrain (an action); to bring about by force, or moral necessity; to command 1671. 3. To force to come, go, or proceed; to force. Also (as in L.): To gather into a company by force. Cf. *cloud-compeller.* (Now *rare* and *poet.*) 1447. 4. To force by pressure, compress. *Obs.* exc. *fig.* 1657. †5. To overpower, constrain (*rare*) 1697.

1. C. them to come in *Luke* xiv. 23. C. the idle into occupation RUSKIN. 2. We give expresse charge, that..there be nothing compell'd from the Villages *Hen. V*, III. vi. 116. He compell'd the Devil's assent FLAVEL. 3. Compelling here and there the Stragglers to the Flock SWIFT. †5. Easy sleep their weary limbs compell'd DRYDEN. Hence **Compe·llable** *a.* that may be compelled. (Const. *to do, to*, or *absol.*) (Chiefly in legal use.) **Compe·llent, -ant** *a.* compelling. **Compe·ller**, one who compels or constrains; one who drives.

Compellation (kŏmpĕlēi·ʃən). Now *arch.* 1603. [ad. L. *compellationem*, f. *compellare.*] 1. Addressing or calling upon any one; an address (*arch.*). 2. Addressing by a name or title; style of address; an appellation 1637.

1. His c., Incline thine eare, hearken unto me 1642. 2. The..c. of him by his Christian name 1691. The name and c. of little Flocke 1643. Abraham..agreed with her..to go by the C. of his sister 1654.

Compellative (kŏmpe·lătiv). *rare.* 1656. [f. *compellat-*, *compellare* + -IVE.] A word used as a name, title, or appellation.

Compend (kŏ·mpĕnd). 1596. [ad. L. *compendium.*] = COMPENDIUM.

The C. of Aldrich SIR W. HAMILTON.

†**Compe·ndiary.** 1589. [ad. L. *compendiarium* adj. neut. used subst.] *sb.* A compendium -1631. *adj.* Compendious, expeditious, brief -1815.

†**Compe·ndiate**, *v.* 1614. [f. L. *compendiat-*, *compendiare.*] *trans.* To sum up concisely -1639.

Compendious (kŏmpe·ndiəs), *a.* ME. [a. Anglo-Fr., ad. L. *compendiosus*; see below and -OUS.] 1. Containing the substance within small compass, concise, summary. †2. Of a way, method, etc.: That saves time or space, expeditious, direct; summary -1774.

1. Man..an extract or c. image of the world BACON. 2. A way not so safe as c., when the tyde is out CAREW. Hence **Compe·ndious·ly** *adv.*, **-ness.**

Compendium (kŏmpe·ndiŏm). Pl. **-ums, -a.** 1581. [a. L., f. *compendere* to weigh together.] †1. A short cut. 2. An abridgement of a larger work or treatise, giving the sense and substance, within smaller compass; an epitome, a summary, a brief 1589. 3. *transf.* and *fig.* An embodiment in miniature; an abstract 1602. †4. Economy -1812.

2. Compendiums of mathematics and natural philosophy 1793.

Compenetrate (kŏmpe·nĭtreit), *v.* 1686. [See COM-.] To penetrate in every part, pervade. Hence **Compenetra·tion.**

Compensate (kŏ·mpĕnseit, kŏmpe·nseit), *v.* 1646. [f. L. *compensat-*, *compensare*, f. *com-* + *pensare*, freq. of *pendere.*] 1. *trans.* To counterbalance, make up for, make amends for 1656. Also *absol.* 2. *intr.* To be an equivalent, to make up *for* 1648. 3. *trans.* To make equal return to, to recompense or remunerate (a person) *for* 1814. 4. *Mech.* To provide with mechanical compensation; to make up for (the variations of a pendulum). *trans.* and *intr.* 1819.

1. To c. their neglect H. MORE. Compensating good with good 1672. To c. to us..what we have lost BURKE. 2. Skill might c. for defective numbers FROUDE. 3. To c. yourself for your rent and services CRUISE. Hence **Compensatingly** *adv.*

Compensation (kŏmpĕnsēi·ʃən). ME. [ad. L. *compensationem*; see prec.] 1. The action of compensating, or condition of being compensated; counterbalance, requital, recompense. b. *Mech.* The balance or neutralization of opposing forces 1789. 2. Recompense, remuneration, amends 1610. b. Recompense *for* loss or damage 1804. c. *Civil Law.* (See quot.) 1848.

1. The Spartan idea of human life was one of strict c... you must fight for the state if it is to keep you MOZLEY. 2. The c. which the borrower pays to the lender ADAM SMITH. c. *Compensation*..a sort of right by set-off, whereby a person who has been sued for a debt demands that the debt may be compensated with what is owing to him by the creditor WHARTON.

Comb. **c.-balance, -pendulum**, in a chronometer, a balance-wheel or a pendulum having arrangements which neutralize the effect of the expansion or contraction of the metal under variations of temperature. Hence **Compensa·tional** *a.* of or relating to c. **Compe·nsative** *a.* = *Compensatory.*

Compensator (kŏ·mpĕnseitəɹ). 1837. [f. L. *compensare.*] One who or that which compensates; *spec.* a contrivance for producing mechanical compensation, as the *magnetic c.* Hence **Compe·nsatory** *a.* compensating.

†**Compe·nse**, *v.* ME. [a. OF. *compenser*:—L. *compensare.*] = COMPENSATE *v.* 1, 2. -1825.

‖**Compère** (koṅpēɹ, kŏ·mpēəɹ). 1928. [Fr.] The organizer or general director of a musical or vaudeville entertainment. So **Co·mpère** *v.*

†**Compert.** 1534. [ad. L. *compertum.*] A thing found out by judicial inquiry -1539.

Compesce (kŏmpe·s), *v. arch.* ME. [ad. L. *compescere.*] To restrain, repress, curb.

†**Compester**, *v.* 1628. [See COMPOST.] To manure -1696.

†**Compete**, *v.*[1] *rare.* 1541. [a. F. *compéter*, ad. L. *competere* to fall together, etc.] To be suitable, applicable, or competent.

Compete (kŏmpī·t), *v.*[2] 1620. [repr. L. *competere*, f. *com-* together + *petere* to seek, etc. Cf. *competitor.*] 1. *intr.* To enter into or be put in rivalry *with.* 2. To strive *with* another, *for*, or *in doing*, something 1795.

1. The sages of antiquity will not dare to c. with the inspired authors 1800. 2. And man competes with man, like foe with foe CAMPBELL.

Competence (kŏ·mpĭtĕns). 1594. [a. F. *compétence*, f. L. *competent-*, *competere*; see COMPETE *v.*[1] and [2].] †1. Rivalry. †2. A sufficiency *of* -1740. 3. = COMPETENCY 3. 1632. 4. Sufficiency of qualification, capacity 1790; *esp.* (*Law*), legal capacity 1708; adequacy 1851.

2. A c. of land freely allotted MASSINGER. 3. A c. is vital to content YOUNG. Robbed of c., And her obsequious shadow, peace of mind WORDSW. 4. To make men act zealously is not in the c. of law BURKE.

Competency (kŏ·mpĭtĕnsi), 1594. [ad. L. *competentia*; see -ENCY.] †1. Rivalry -1638. †2. = COMPETENCE 2. -1734. 3. A sufficiency, without superfluity, of the means of life 1598; the condition of having a sufficient income 1596. 4. = COMPETENCE 4. 1597.

2. A c. of discretion and foresight CLARENDON. 3. To retire upon a c. SMILES. 4. References as to character and c. C. BRONTË.

Competent (kǫ·mpĭtĕnt), *a.* ME. [a. F. *compétent*, and ad. L. *competentem*; see COMPETE *v.*[1]] †1. *gen.* Suitable, fit, proper –1791. 2. Answering the requirements of the case (*arch.*) ME.; sufficient in amount, quality, or degree ME. 3. Properly qualified 1647. 4. *Law.* Legally qualified or sufficient 1483. 5. Of things, etc.: Belonging *to*; within one's rights; legitimate 1614.

2. A c. annuite for lyff ME., liuing TUSSER. A c. while before Christmas EVELYN. A c. reason 1597. 3. A matter..allowed by all c. Judges BENTLEY. 4. Any competente courte 1536. C. witnesses BLACKSTONE. 5. Though it is c. for Parliament to legislate for the colonies STEPHEN. Hence **Co·mpetently** *adv.*

Co·mpetent, *sb.* Pl. also **-entes.** 1655. [ad. L. *competens.*] *Eccl. Hist.* A candidate for baptism.

†**Competible**, *a.* 1586. [app. f. L. *competere* to be suitable, to correspond + -IBLE.] Appropriate, suitable, befitting; competent –1660. Also with *to, with.*

Competition (kǫmpĭti·ʃən). 1605. [ad. L. *competitionem*; see COMPETE.] 1. 'The action of endeavouring to gain what another endeavours to gain at the same time' (J.); the striving of two or more for the same object; rivalry 1608; in *Commerce*, rivalry in the market 1793. Const. *for*, †*to*. 2. (with *a* and *pl.*) A contest for the acquisition of something; a match; a trial of ability 1618.

1. The place will be filled by open c. (*mod.*). From c. among traders [comes] reduction of prices BENTHAM. C. to the crown there is none nor can be BACON (J.). The Priest-hood, which ever hath been in some c. with Empire BACON. 2. For the next lot there was a keen c. (*mod.*). *Comb.* **c.-wallah** [Urdū *-wālā* = L. *-arius*, Eng. *-er*] = *Competitioner*; applied in 1856 to members of the I. C. S., then first admitted on the competitive system. Hence **Competi·tioner**, a competitor; one who enters a service, etc., by c.

Competitive (kǫ̆mpe·titiv), *a.* 1829. [f. L. *competit-*, *competere* (see COMPETE *v.*[2]) + -IVE.] Of, pertaining to, or characterized by competition; as a *c. examination.*

Competitor (kǫ̆mpe·titəɹ). 1534. [a. F. *compétiteur*; see COMPETE *v.*[2]] 1. One who competes; one who seeks an object which others also seek; a rival. †2. An associate –1681.

1. They..cannot brooke Competitors in loue *Tit. A.* II. i. 77. 2. *Two Gent.* II. vi. 35. Hence **Compe·titorship**, the office or action of a c. **Compe·titory** *a.* belonging to competitors or competition; competitive. So **Compe·titress, †-trice, †-trix,** a female c.

Compilation (kǫmpilēɪ·ʃən). ME. [a. F., ad. L. *compilationem*, f. *compilare* to COMPILE.] 1. The action of compiling; see COMPILE *v.* 2. *concr.* That which is compiled; a literary work or the like formed by compilation ME. †3. Accumulation –1728.

2. That all compilations are useless I do not assert JOHNSON. So **Co·mpilator**, a compiler. **Compi·latory** *a.* belonging to a compiler or a c.

Compile (kǫ̆mpəi·l), *v.* ME. [a. F. *compiler*, (commonly taken as):—L. *compilare* to plunder. The history is obscure.]

I. 1. To collect and put together (materials), so as to form a treatise. 2. To construct (a written or printed work) out of materials collected from various sources ME. †3. To compose (*e.g.* a sonnet) –1598.

1. Compiling notes to the Iliad from Eustathius L. STEPHEN. 2. To c. a Dictionary 1748. 3. *L. L. L.* IV. iii. 134.

II. †1. To heap together, pile up –1812. †2. To construct by putting together materials –1682. 3. *Cricket slang.* To 'pile up' (a large number of runs) 1884.

3. New South Wales 'compiled'..412. 1884. Hence †**Compi·lement**, compilation; *concr.* that which is compiled. **Compi·ler**, one who compiles, †composes, or †builds.

†**Compi·nge**, *v.* [ad. L. *compingere.*] To compress. BURTON.

Compital (kǫ·mpităl), *a.* 1656. [ad. L. *compitalis*, f. *compitum* place where roads cross.] *Rom. Antiq.* Of or pertaining to the cross-ways, as a *c. shrine*; also to the *compitalia*, an annual festival in honour of the Lares. Also as *sb.*

Complacence (kǫ̆mplēɪ·sĕns). Now *rare.* ME. [ad. med.L. *complacentia* = F. *complaisance*, f. L. *complacere.*] 1. Self-satisfaction. †2. Pleasure, delight, satisfaction –1754; *concr.* An object of pleasure and satisfaction 1667. †3. Disposition to please; complaisance –1749.

1. This c. is vayn glorye CAXTON. 2. A Man unable to take C. in wicked Persons or Things EDWARDS. *concr.* O Thou My sole c. MILT. *P. L.* III. 276. 3. All people were so full of c. BUTLER.

Complacency (kǫ̆mplēɪ·sĕnsi). 1643. [f. as prec. + -ENCY.] 1. The fact or state of being pleased with a thing or person; tranquil satisfaction. 2. *spec.* Self-satisfaction 1650. 3. Pleasure, delight (*arch.*) 1652. †4. Contented acquiescence –1709. 5. = COMPLACENCE 3. 1651.

1. He regards the enemies of pleasure with c. JOWETT. 2. The c. of such women BULWER. 5. The c. of a few courtiers FROUDE. Hence †**Complace·ntial** *a.* complaisant; **-ly** *adv.*

Complacent (kǫ̆mplēɪ·sĕnt), *a.* 1660. [ad. L. *complacentem*; see above.] †1. Pleasant –1772. 2. *spec.* Self-satisfied 1767. 3. Obliging in manner, complaisant 1790.

1. In the c. moneth of May 1660. 2. With c. smile 1767. 3. The..c. flattery of Leicester SCOTT. Hence **Compla·cently** *adv.*

Complain (kǫ̆mplēɪ·n), *v.* [ME. *compleigne*, f. F. *complaign-*, *complaindre* :—late L. *complangere.*] †1. *trans.* To bewail, lament –1700. Also †*refl.* †2. *intr.* To give expression to sorrow; to make moan, lament –1647. 3. *intr.* To suffer, be ailing. (Now *dial.*) 1607. 4. *intr.* To express discontent; to murmur, grumble ME. With *of.* (Now the leading use.) 1584. 5. *intr.* (orig. *refl.*) To make a formal complaint *to* or *before*; to bring a charge 1449. 6. *transf.* and *fig.* To emit a mournful sound 1697; to groan or creak, as a mast 1722.

1. To complayne the dethe of the king LD. BERNERS. 3. *To c. of*: to let it be known that one is suffering from (any pain, etc.). 4. The Heat they c. of cannot be in the Weather ADDISON. Others..c. that Fate Free Vertue should enthrall to Force or Chance MILT. *P. L.* II. 550. 5. Domitius Corbulo..complained before the Lords of the Senate..that[etc.] 1598. Hence **Complai·n** *sb.* complaining (*Obs.* exc. *poet.*). **Complai·nable** *a.* to be complained of. **Complai·ner**, one who complains; in *Law*=COMPLAINANT. **Complai·ning-ly** *adv.*; **-ness.**

Complainant (kǫ̆mplēɪ·nănt). 1495. [a. F. *complaignant*, *complaindre*; see COMPLAIN *v.* and -ANT.] 1. *Law.* One who enters a legal complaint; a plaintiff or prosecutor. 2. *gen.* One who complains 1525. Also as †*adj.*

1. The same compleynaunt, nor provyng the mater of his seid bill to be true 1495. 2. No want of complaint, nor of complainants CARLYLE.

Complaint (kǫ̆mplēɪ·nt). [ME., a. F. *complainte*; see COMPLAIN.] 1. The action of complaining; grieving. 2. An expression of grief; a plaint ME. 3. Utterance of grievance ME.; a statement of injustice suffered ME. 4. *Law.* A statement of injury or grievance laid before a court (prop. a Court of Equity) for purposes of prosecution and redress; an accusation or charge; in *U.S.* the plaintiff's case in a civil action ME. 5. The subject of complaint 1745. 6. *spec.* A bodily ailment or disorder (*esp.* of chronic nature) 1705.

1. For whom was maked moch compleynt CHAUCER. 2. Compleynte of Pité CHAUCER (*title*). 3. Tho was compleinte on every side GOWER. 5. The poverty of the clergy of England hath been the c. of all who wish well to the church SWIFT. 6. This..was mistaken for a bowel c. 1809. Hence †**Complai·ntful** *a.* full of c.

Complaisance (kǫ·mpleza:ns, kǫ:mpleza·ns). 1651. [a. F.; see COMPLACENCE.] The action or habit of making oneself agreeable; desire and care to please; deference to the wishes of others; obligingness, courtesy, politeness; (with *pl.*) an act of complaisance.

Compleasance; that is to say, That every man strive to accommodate himselfe to the rest HOBBES. For c., and breeding sake I'll do it SHADWELL. How the complaisances we use..shame us now EMERSON. var. †**Co·mplaisancy** (*rare*).

Complaisant (kǫ·mpleza:nt, kǫ:mpleza·nt), *a.* 1647. [a. F., pr. pple. of *complaire* :—L. *complacere.*] Disposed to please; obliging, courteous; accommodating.

That's very c... Mr. Bayes, to be of another Man's Opinion, before he knows what it is VILLIERS *Rehearsal.* The French..are c., cordial, and well-bred SMILES. Hence **Complaisantly** *adv.*

†**Co·mplanate**, *v.* 1643. [f. L. *complanat-*, *complanare.*] To make plane, to flatten –1713. So **Co·mplanate** *a.* made plane, lying in one plane, flattened. **Complana·tion**, making plane or level, flattening out.

Complect (kǫ̆mple·kt), *v.* 1523. [ad. L. *complecti*, in late L. *complectere.*] †1. To embrace (*lit.* and *fig.*) –1657. 2. To connect together; to interweave. Hence **Comple·cted** *ppl. a.*[1]

Comple·cted, *ppl. a.*[2] *U.S. dial.* or *colloq.* [app. f. COMPLEXION.] = COMPLEXIONED.

Complement (kǫ·mplĭmĕnt), *sb.* ME. [ad. L. *complementum*, f. *complere* to fill up. In II latterly supplanted by COMPLIMENT.]

I. †1. The action of fulfilling or completing –1721. †2. Completeness, fullness –1677. *Her.* Fullness (of the moon) 1610. 3. That which completes or makes perfect; the completion, consummation ME. 4. The quantity or amount that completes or fills; complete set; totality 1589. 5. That which, when added, completes a whole; each of two parts which mutually complete each other. (See quots.) 1827.

3. Love is the c. of the law and the supplement of the Gospel TRAPP. 4. Matter sufficient to make a full periode or c. of sence PUTTENHAM. Brains that want their c. of wits WOLCOTT. *The c. of a ship*: the full number required to man it. 5. *Math. Arithmetical c.*: the sum which, added to a given number, makes up unity, ten, or the next higher multiple of ten. *Complements of a parallelogram*: the two lesser parallelograms not on the diagonal, made by drawing lines parallel to the sides of a given parallelogram, through the same point in its diagonal. *C. of an arc or angle*: the amount which, added to the arc or angle, makes up 90 degrees. *Mus. C. of an interval*: the interval wanting to make up a complete octave.

II. †1. A completing accessory –1692. †2. A personal accomplishment or quality –1636. †3. A ceremony, a formality –1646.

Complement (kǫmplĭme·nt), *v.* 1612. [f. prec.] 1. To make complete or perfect; to form the complement to 1641. †2. = COMPLIMENT *v.* 1, 2, 4. Hence **Compleme·nter, -or,** one who, or that which, complements; †formerly = COMPLIMENTER.

Complemental (kǫmplĭme·ntăl), *a.* 1602. [f. COMPLEMENT *sb.* + -AL.] 1. Of the nature of a complement; complementary (*to*). †2. Accessory –1655; ceremonious –1695; accomplished –1636. †3. = COMPLIMENTAL 2. –1703.

1. *C. air*: the air, 100 cubic inches, which can be added after an ordinary inspiration [230 cubic inches]. *C. male* (in *Zool.*): Darwin's name for a minute rudimentary male parasitic on the hermaphrodite in certain cirripeds, etc. Hence **Compleme·ntally** *adv.*

Complementary (kǫmplĭme·ntări). 1599. [f. COMPLEMENT *sb.* + -ARY.]

A. *adj.* 1. Forming a complement, completing 1836. †2. Ceremonious –1657.

1. *C. angles*: two angles which together make up a right angle. *C. colours*: colours which, when mixed, produce white light.

B. *sb.* †1. A master of accomplishments. B. JONS. 2. Short for 'c. colour' 1865.

Complete (kǫ̆mplī·t), *a.* ME. [ad. L. *completus*, *complere.* About 1600 often *co·mplete.*] 1. Having all its parts or elements; entire, full. 2. Whole; finished, ended, concluded ME. 3. Entire 1645. 4. Without defect ME. 5. Consummate. ? *Obs.* 1526. 6. quasi-*adv.* = COMPLETELY.

1. Shoulders broad for c. armour fit MARLOWE. C. intelligence JOHNSON. 2. The space of v yeres c. FABYAN. 3. C. inability to obtain drink KANE. C. combustion 1854. 5. The Compleat Angler WALTON. Phr. *C. flower*: †(*a*) one which possesses stamens and pistils; (*b*) one which also possesses the floral envelopes. Hence **Comple·te-ly** *adv.*, **-ness.**

Complete (kǫmplī·t), *v.* 1530. [f. the adj.] 1. *trans.* To bring to an end, finish. 2. To make whole or entire 1726. 3. To make perfect 1667. 4. To accomplish (a vow, etc.) (*rare*) 1680.

1. To c. a work 1751. 2. To c. the sense MASON. 3. That fair femal Troop..completed to the taste Of lustful appetence MILT. *P. L.* XI. 618. Hence †**Comple·tement**. **Comple·ter.** **Comple·tive** *a.* completing.

Completion (kǫ̆mplī·ʃən). 1657. [ad. L. *completionem.*] The action of making complete; the condition of being completed; accomplishment (of a wish, etc.).

They may tend to the c. of the business CROMWELL. The apparent completions of prophecy BUTLER.

Completory (kǫ̆mplī·tŏri). 1450. [ad. eccl. L. *completorius*, f. *complet-*; see above.] *adj.* Having the function of completing 1659. *sb.* 1. A completory thing 1659. 2. = COMPLINE 1450.

adj. C. of ancient..predictions BARROW.

Complex (kǫ·mpleks), *sb.* 1652. [ad. L. *complexus* (cf. next).] A complex whole. **b.** Jung's term for a group of ideas associated with a particular subject; hence, pop., a mental tendency or obsession, as *inferiority c.* 1910.

Government, taken in the whole c. of it, cannot.. provide against all Emergencies 1695.

Complex (kǫ·mpleks), *a.* 1652. [ad. L. *complexus*, pa. pple. of *complectere*; cf. *complicated*.] **1.** Comprehending various parts connected together; composite, compound. **2.** *esp.* Consisting of parts involved in various degrees of subordination; involved, intricate 1715.

1. Ideas thus made up of several simple ones put together I call C.; such as are Beauty, Gratitude, a Man, an Army LOCKE. *C. fraction* in *Arith.*: one that has a fraction for its numerator, or denominator, or both. (Cf. COMPOUND.) *C. number* in *Math.*: a number of which part is real and part imaginary. Hence **Co·mplexly** *adv.* †collectively; in a c. manner. **Co·mplexness.**

Complex (kǫmple·ks), *v. rare.* 1470. [f. L. *complex-*, *complectere*.] †**1.** To attach. **2.** To combine into a complex whole; to complicate 1658. Hence †**Complexed, complext** *ppl. a.* **Comple·xedness.** ? *Obs.*

Complexion (kǫmple·kʃən), *sb.* ME. [a. F., ad. L. *complexionem*, f. as prec.]

I. From Rom. and med.L. **1.** The combination of qualities (*cold* or *hot*, and *moist* or *dry*), or of 'humours', in a certain proportion; 'temperament'. *Obs.* exc. *Hist.* †**b.** Also = 'humour', or 'collection of humours' –1689. †**2.** Bodily or mental habit; nature –1856. **3.** The colour and texture of the skin, *esp.* of the face; *orig.* as showing the 'temperament'. (Now the ordinary sense.) 1580. †**b.** Face. *Oth.* IV. ii. 62. **4.** *transf.* and *fig.* 1589.

2. Mee thinkes it is very soultry, and hot for my C. *Haml.* v. ii. 102. A very amorous c. HUME. **3.** Mislike me not for my c. *Merch. V.* II. i. 1. **4.** The c. of the Skie *Rich. II*, III. ii. 194, of the times FULLER.

II. From old L. senses. †**1.** Embrace (*rare*) 1493. †**2.** Complication, combination –1725. Also quasi-*concr.* †**3.** = COMPLEX *sb.* 1. –1741.

Hence **Comple·xional** *a.* †of or pertaining to the (physical or mental) constitution; pertaining to the c. (of the skin). **Comple·xionally** *adv.* †**Comple·xionary** *a.* pertaining to the c. **Comple·xionless** *a.* pale, colourless.

Complexion (kǫmple·kʃən), *v.* ME. [f. prec. sb.] †**1.** To constitute by combination of various elements –1658. **2.** To give a colour or tinge to 1612.

Complexioned (kǫmple·kʃənd), *ppl. a.* ME. [f. prec. sb. and v.] †**1.** Having a (specified) temperament –1795. **2.** Having a (specified) colour and texture of skin 1615. Also *transf.*

1. A wel complexyoned body LYDG., Soul NORRIS. **2.** The people..are all fair-c. LANG.

Complexity (kǫmple·ksĭti). 1721. [f. L. *complexus* + -ITY.] **1.** The quality or condition of being complex; intricacy. **2.** quasi-*concr.* A complicated condition; a complication 1794.

1. C. of organisation DARWIN. **2.** The..many-corridor'd complexities Of Arthur's palace TENNYSON.

†**Comple·xive**, *a.* 1654. [a. L. *complexivus*.] Comprehensive –1672.

‖**Complexus** (kǫmple·ksŏs). 1871. [f. L. *com-* + *plexus*.] An interwoven structure; a complex, 'tissue'.

Compliable (kǫmplai·ăb'l), *a.* 1635. [f. COMPLY *v.* + -ABLE.] **1.** Apt or inclined to comply; compliant. ? *Obs.* †**2.** Reconcilable –1746.

1. The uniting of another c. mind MILT. **2.** The Jews..had made their religion c. and accommodated to their passions JORTIN.

Compliance (kǫmplai·ăns). 1641. [f. COMPLY *v.* + -ANCE.] †**1.** Complaisance –1732; accord –1722. **2.** The acting in accordance *with* a desire, condition, etc.; an acceding *to*; practical assent. Often *absol.*; also in bad sense. 1647.

1. All her words and actions mixed with love And sweet c. MILT. *P. L.* VIII. 603. **2.** All politics necessitates questionable compliances W. PHILLIPS. In c. with your wishes 1866. var. **Compli·ancy.**

Compliant (kǫmplai·ănt), *a.* 1642. [f. COMPLY *v.*] **1.** Complying, disposed to comply; complaisant. †**2.** Pliant –1793. Also as *sb. Obs.*

1. C. with the royal will GREEN. Hence **Compli·antly** *adv.*

Complicacy (kǫ·mplikăsi). 1827. [f. L. *complicatus*.] **1.** Complicated quality. **2.** A complicated structure, matter or condition 1849.

2. Difficulties, complicacies, very many CARLYLE.

Complicate (kǫ·mplikĕt), *ppl. a.* 1626. [ad. L. *complicatus*; see next.] **1.** Interwoven (*arch.*). **2.** Compound, complex (*arch.*) 1638; intricate 1672. **3.** *Bot.* = CONDUPLICATE 1866. Hence †**Co·mplicate·ly** *adv.*; †**-ness.**

Complicate (kǫ·mplikeit), *v.* 1621. [f. L. *complicat-*, *complicare*, f. *com-* + *plicare*.] †**1.** To fold, wrap, or twist together –1691. †**2.** To combine intimately –1691. **3.** To mix up *with* in an involved way 1673. †**4.** To compound –1707. **5.** To make complex or intricate 1832.

3. A disease complicated with other diseases ARBUTHNOT. **4.** Ideas..complicated of various simple Ideas LOCKE. Hence **Co·mplicated·ly** *adv.*, **-ness.**

Complication (kǫmplikēi·ʃən). 1611. [ad. L. *complicationem*, f. as prec.] †**1.** The action of folding together; the condition of being folded together –1691. †**2.** Combination, conjunction –1699. **3.** An involved condition or structure 1666. **4.** Complicated condition, structure, or nature; involved relation 1793; quasi-*concr.* a complicated mass or structure 1647.

3. That c. of probabilities by which the Christian history is attested PALEY. **4.** Amid tumult and c. J. H. NEWMAN. The coexistence of a dislocation with a fracture, is a serious c. HOLMES.

†**Co·mplicative**, *a.* (*sb.*) [See COMPLICATE *v.* and -IVE.] **1.** Tending to complicate. **2.** *sb.* 1654.

Complice (kǫ·mplis). 1475. [a. F., ad. L. *complex*, *-plicem*.] †**1.** *gen.* An associate –1734. **2.** *spec.* An associate in crime (*arch.*). Now ACCOMPLICE. 1581.

1. 2 *Hen. IV*, I. i. 163. **2.** To quell these Traitors and their compleases 1594.

Complicity (kǫmpli·sĭti). 1656. [f. L. *complex*, *-plicem*; see -TY.] **1.** The being an accomplice. **2.** = COMPLEXITY 1847.

1. The charge..of c. in the designs of his patron HALLAM.

Complier (kǫmplai·əɹ). 1612. [f. COMPLY *v.* + -ER [1].] †**1.** An accomplice –1649. **2.** One who complies *with* (any humour, fashion, etc.); †*spec.* a conformist in politics or religion 1644.

2. In the changes of religion he was a c. STRYPE.

Compliment (kǫ·mplimĕnt), *sb.* 1654. [a. F., 16th c. ad. It. *complimento*. A doublet of COMPLEMENT; cf. also COMPLY.] **1.** A ceremonial act or expression as a tribute of courtesy, 'usually understood to mean less than it declares' (J.); now, *esp.* a neatly-turned remark addressed to any one, implying praise; complimentary language. **2.** usually in *pl.* Formal respects 1733. **3.** A complimentary gift (*arch.* or *dial.*) 1722. Also *fig.*

1. C.—a thing often paid by people who pay nothing else HOR. SMITH. In a style of c. POPE. **2.** Make my compliments to your mamma CHESTERF. Hence **Complime·ntal** *a.* †formal; of the nature of a c.; †given to paying compliments. **-ally** *adv.*

Compliment (kǫ·mpliment), *v.* 1663. [a. F. *complimenter*, f. *compliment*; see prec.] **1.** *intr.* To employ formal courtesy in act or expression. **2.** *trans.* To address with formal expressions of civility, etc.; to pay a compliment to; to flatter with delicate praise 1735. Also *fig.* **3.** To congratulate formally (*up*)*on* 1717. **4.** *spec.* To present *with* as a mark of courtesy 1717.

1. Believe me, I never c. JANE AUSTEN. **3.** To c. a boy on his progress 1884.

Complimentary (kǫmplime·ntări), *a.* 1716. [f. prec. + -ARY.] Expressive of, conveying, or of the nature of a compliment.

Compline, complin (kǫ·mplin). [ME. *cumplie*, a. OF. :—L. *completa* (sc. *hora*). The forms *compelin* (13th c.), *complin*, are obscure. The final *e* is modern and unhistorical.] In Catholic ritual: The last service of the day, completing the services of the canonical hours; also, the hour of that service. Also *attrib.*

At complyn hyt was y-bore To the beryynge, That noble corps of Jhesu Cryst SHOREHAM.

†**Co·mplish**, *v.* [ME. *complyssen*, a. OF. *compliss-*, *complir*, repr. L. *complere*; see COMPLETE.] **1.** To fill up 1450. **2.** To fulfil –1596. Hence †**Co·mplishment.**

Complot (kǫ·mplǫt), *sb.* Now *rare.* 1577. [a. F.; of uncertain origin. In Shaks., etc., also stressed *complo·t*.] A covert design planned in concert; a conspiracy, a PLOT.

To lay a c. to betray thy Foes *Tit. A.* v. ii. 147.

Complot (kǫmplǫ·t), *v.* Now *rare.* 1579. [a. F. *comploter*; see prec.] **1.** *intr.* To combine in a plot. **2.** *trans.* To combine in plotting (some act, usually criminal) 1593.

2. To plot, contriue, or c. any ill *Rich. II*, I. iii. 189. Hence †**Complo·tment**, conspiracy; secret plan. **Complo·tter**, a conspirator.

Complutensian (kǫmplute·nsiăn), *a.* 1660. [f. L. *Complutensis*.] Of or belonging to *Complutum*, a town in Spain, now *Alcalá de Henares*, as the *C. Polyglot*, published at Alcalá.

‖**Compluvium** (kǫmplū·viŏm). 1832. [L.] *Rom. Antiq.* A square opening in the roof of the atrium, through which fell the rain-water collected from the roof.

Comply (kǫmplai·), *v.*[1] 1602. [repr. L. *complere* to COMPLETE; cf. SUPPLY. Influenced by PLY.] †**1.** *trans.* To fulfil (*rare*) –1634. †**2.** To observe the formalities of civility (*with* any one) –1639. †**3.** To be complaisant *with*, *to*, in conduct or action –1683. **4.** To accede, or consent to 1650. Also *absol.* †**5.** To accord *with* or *together* –1655. †**6.** *trans.* To conform *to* –1683. †**7.** To ally oneself *with* –1651. †**8.** Of a thing: To fit. Const. *with* (*to*). –1704.

3. Willing to flatter and c. with the rich ETHEREDGE. †*To c. with* (intr.): to accommodate oneself to (circumstances, etc.); to conform to (opinions, customs, etc.); also *absol.* **4.** How reddy we are to c. with his desire 1650. He that complies against his will Is of his own opinion still BUTLER *Hud.* III. iii. 547. **6.** To my sad tears c. these notes of yours DRUMM. OF HAWTH. **8.** To make the Jewish Year c. with the Solar Year HEARNE.

†**Comply·**, *v.*[2] *rare.* 1611. [app. f. L. *complicare*.] **1.** *trans.* To compose by intertexture. **2.** To enfold. HERRICK.

Compo (kǫ·mpo). 1823. [Short for *composition*, *composite*.] **1.** Stucco, cement. Also *attrib.* **2.** A metallic or other composition 1879. **3.** A composition paid by a debtor. **4.** *attrib.* = COMPOSITE 1878.

†**Compo·ne**, *v.* ME. [ad. L. *componere*.] **1.** *trans.* To compose –1848. **2.** *intr.* To compound –1645.

Compo·né, compony, *a.* 1572. [a. OF. *componné*, also *couponné*, ? f. L. *componere*, or OF. *coupon*.] *Her.* Composed of a row of squares of two alternate tinctures. var. †**Compo·ned** *ppl. a.*

Component (kǫmpōu·nĕnt). 1645. [ad. L. *componentem*.] *adj.* Composing, making up, constituent 1664. *sb.* A constituent part or element.

adj. Thy c. dust SOUTHEY. Hence **Compo·nency**, composition (*rare*).

Comport (kǫmpōə·ɹt), *v.* 1565. [ad. L. *comportare* and F. *comporter*.] †**1.** *trans.* To bear –1818. **2.** *refl.* To conduct or behave oneself; to behave 1616. Also †*intr.* (for *refl.*) –1734. †**3.** *lit.* To collect (*rare*) –1660.

1. *To c. with* (intr.): to bear with. **2.** He comported himself with extraordinary courage WOODHEAD. *To c. with* (intr.): to accord with; to befit.

Phr. †*To c. the pike*: to carry it grasped near the middle and pressed to the right side of the body, with the point raised. Hence †**Compo·rtable** *a.* †**Compo·rtance**, bearing, behaviour; accordance. †**Comporta·tion**, collecting; a collection.

†**Comport** (kǫmpōə·ɹt), *sb.*[1] 1635. [f. as prec.] **1.** The action or position of comporting a pike –1690. **2.** Comportment –1700.

2. I..mark'd their rude c. DRYDEN.

Co·mport, *sb.*[2] 1771. [app. abbrev. of *comportier* (1764), var. of COMPOTIER, infl. by COMPOTE.] A dessert dish raised upon a stem.

Comportment (kǫmpōə·ɹtmĕnt). Now *rare.* 1599. [a. F. *comportement*.] Personal bearing, carriage; behaviour.

Ceremoniall in his outward c. SANDYS.

†**Compo·sal.** 1630. [f. COMPOSE + -AL.] The action of composing –1700.

Co·mposant, comozant, corrupt ff. CORPOSANT, q. v.

Compose (kǫmpōu·z), *v.* 1481. [a. F. *composer*, f. *com-* + *poser* :—Rom. *posare* = late L. *pausare*; see POSE, REPOSE. The sense is that of L. *-ponere*, but there is no connexion in origin. See COMPONE.]

I. †**1.** *trans.* To make by putting together parts or elements; to make up, frame, fashion, produce –1788. **2.** To constitute 1665; *pass.* 1541. **3.** *spec.* To make or produce in literary form, to write as author (poetry, essays, or the like) 1483. Also *absol.* **4.** *Mus.* To invent and put into proper form 1597; to set to music 1691.

Also *absol.* **5.** *Print.* To set up (type); to set up (an article, etc.) in type 1637. Also *absol.* **6.** To put together so as to make a whole; *spec.* in artistic use 1655; *intr.* (for *refl.*) to admit of artistic grouping 1828.

1. So well compos'd a man D'URFEY. 2. He is compos'd and fram'd of treacherie *Much Ado* v. i. 257. 3 To c. a philosophical poem WORDSW. Easier to criticize than to c. PARR. 6. Symmetry without proportion is not composition. To c. is to arrange unequal things RUSKIN.

II. *trans.* To settle, adjust, arrange 1563. Also *absol.*

To c. a difference HUME, the country FROUDE.

III. 1. *trans.* To adjust to any attitude, to 'make up' 1606; †to dispose, to order –1674. **2.** To arrange, adjust; to lay out (a dead body) 1677. **3.** To make calm or tranquil 1607.

1. To c. oneself to write 1716, to sleep 1709. 2. To c. one's countenance THACKERAY. 3. To c. this midnight noise PRIOR. For Heaven's sake, Amanda, c. yourself MRS. OLIPHANT. Hence **Compo·sed** *ppl. a.* †made up of parts; †elaborately put together; made calm or tranquil; calm and self-possessed (opp. to *excited*); *Her.* = COMPONÉ. **Compo·sedly** *adv.* **Compo·sedness,** c. state or quality.

Composer (kǫmpōᵘ·zəɹ). 1561. [f. COMPOSE *v.* + -ER [1].] **1.** One who or that which composes (see COMPOSE *v.*). **2.** One who composes music. (The usual sense, when used without defining words.) 1597.

1. Composers of green Arbours 1693, of Tragedies HOLLAND. A Printer's C. 1708. Composers of the soul HAMMOND. 2. The well studied chords of some choice c. MILTON.

Composing (kǫmpōᵘ·ziŋ), *vbl. sb.* 1574. [f. COMPOSE *v.*] The action of the verb COMPOSE.

Comb. (in sense I. 5 of the verb): **c.-frame,** the frame at which a compositor stands; **-rule,** a brass or steel rule against which the type is set in a c.-stick, a setting-rule; **-stand** = *composing-frame*; **-stick,** an instrument, now of metal, of adjustable width, in which the type is set before being put on a galley.

Composite (kǫ·mpǒzit, †kǒmpǫ·zit), *a.* and *sb.* 1500. [ad. L. *compositus, componere.*] **1.** Made up of various parts or elements; compound 1678. **2.** *Arch.* The name of the fifth of the classical orders, being 'composed of the Ionic grafted upon the Corinthian'. At first *Composita* (sc. *columna*). 1563. **3.** *Bot.* Belonging to the N.O. *Compositæ,* in which the head is made up of many florets sessile on a common receptacle, and surrounded by a common involucre of bracts; as the daisy, etc. Also *sb.* A plant of this order. 1832. **4.** In various techn. uses (see quots.) 1845.

1. We cannot decompose what is not already c. SIR W. HAMILTON. *C. number* (Math.): one which is the product of two or more factors, greater than unity. 2. *C. arch*: 'the pointed or lancet arch' (Gwilt). 4. *A c. vessel*: one built of both wood and iron. *C. carriage*: a railway carriage with compartments of different classes. *C. candle*: one made of stearic acid and the stearin of coco-nut oil. *C. sailing* (*Naut.*): a combination of great-circle and parallel sailing.

B. *sb.* †**1.** A component part (*rare*) 1657. **2.** A compound 1656. **3.** *Gram.* A compound word or term (*rare*) 1708.

Hence **Co·mposite·ly** *adv.*, **-ness.**

Composition (kǫmpǒzi·ʃən). ME. [a. F., ad. L. *compositionem*; see COMPONE and COMPOSE.]

I. 1. The action of combining; the fact of being combined; combination (of parts or elements of a whole). **2.** The forming (*of* anything) by combination of parts, etc.; formation, construction 1555. **3.** Orderly arrangement; ordering (*arch.*) 1598. **4.** Specifically:

a. = SYNTHESIS 1570. **b.** Combination of factors, ratios, forces, or elements, so as to produce a compound resultant 1557. **c.** *Gram.* The combination of two (or more) words to form one compound word 1530. **d.** The art of constructing sentences and of writing prose or verse 1553. **e.** The practice or art of literary production 1577. **f.** The action or art of disposing the parts of a work of art, so as to form a harmonious whole 1695. **g.** The action or art of composing music 1597. **h.** *Printing.* The setting up of type; the composing of matter for printing 1832. **i.** The settling of a debt, liability, etc., by some mutual arrangement; compounding 1557.

1. The C. of Atomes in Bodies GREW. 2. The c. of a pudding GOLDSM. 4. a. As in Mathematicks, so in Natural Philosophy, the investigation..by the method of analysis, ought ever to precede the method of c. NEWTON. *Fallacy of c.* (Logic): the fallacy of arguing that what is true of each of several things is true of all taken together. b. *C. of forces*: the uniting of two or more forces into one, which shall have the same effect. d. All candidates must pass in Latin prose c. (*mod.*). e. [Dryden's] haste of c. JOHNSON. i. To come to C., and lose one half of the Debt to save the rest 1707.

II. 1. The manner in which a thing is composed; constitution, make, with reference to ingredients ME. **2.** The state or quality of being composite 1541. **3.** Mental or †bodily constitution 1593. **4.** Artistic manner, style 1532. †**5.** Consistency. *Oth.* I. iii. 1.

1. The c. of white light BREWSTER. 3. *Rich. II,* II. i. 73. Whatever there is of the man of business in my c. LAMB. 4 The c. of a speech STANHOPE, of a natural landscape POE.

III. The product. **1.** *quasi-concr.* A combination, aggregate, mixture *of* 1551. **2.** *concr.* A substance formed by combination of various ingredients (in techn. uses often shortened to COMPO) 1555. **3.** A literary, artistic, or other intellectual production 1601. **4.** An agreement (*arch.*); a contract, a treaty (*arch.*); a compromise ME. **5.** A compounding for some claim or liability; *spec.* an agreement by which a creditor accepts part of a debt, in satisfaction, from an insolvent debtor 1570; the sum paid 1581. Also *attrib.*

1. Every soil is a c. of different earths 1765. 3. Aldhelm's Latin compositions 1774. Handel's compositions BURNEY. 5. The Irish admitted the c. or fine for murder HALLAM.

Comb.: **c.-cloth,** a waterproof material made from long flax, used for trunk-covers, etc.; **-deed,** a deed for effecting a composition (see III. 5) between a debtor and creditors; **-face** (*Crystallogr.*) = *composition-plane*; **-metal,** a kind of brass composed of copper, zinc, etc., used for the sheathing of ships; **c. pedal,** an organ pedal which acts on a number of stops at once; **-plane** (*Crystallogr.*), the common plane or base between the two parts of a twin crystal.

Compositive (kǒmpǫ·zǐtiv), *a.* 1601. [ad. L. *compositivus.*] †**1.** Of composite nature or character –1687. **2.** Synthetic 1652.

Compositor (kǒmpǫ·zitəɹ). ME. [a. AF. *compositour,* ad. L. *compositorem*; see COMPONE, COMPOSE.] †**1.** One who composes –1533. **2.** *Printing.* A type-setter 1569. Hence **Compositorial** *a.* of or pertaining to composers or compositors.

Compo·sitous, *a. rare.* 1859. [f. Bot. L. *Compositæ.*] = COMPOSITE *a.* 3.

‖**Compos mentis** (kǫ·mpǫs me·ntis), *adj. phr.* 1679. [L.] Having control of one's mind, in one's right mind. Also simply *compos.*

Compo·ssible, *a.* 1638. [See COM-.] Possible in coexistence with something else.

Compost (kǫ·mpǒst), *sb.*[1] ME. [a. OF. :— L. *compositum, compostum.*] **1.** A composition, combination, compound 1640. †**2.** *Cookery.* = COMPOTE –1601. **3.** A prepared manure or mould 1587. Also *fig.* Also *attrib.*

3. *fig.* Martyrs ashes are the best c. to manure the church FULLER.

†**Co·mpost,** *sb.*[2] 1535. [a. OF., corrupt f. *compot*:—late L. *computus.*] = COMPUTUS; *esp.* a calendar –1656.

Compost (kǫ·mpǒst), *v.* 1499. [a. OF. *composter* to manure.] **1.** To treat with compost, to manure. **2.** To make into compost 1829.

Composture (kǒmpǫ·stiŭɹ). Now *dial.* 1607. [a. F., ad. L. *compos(i)tura.* Cf. *posture, imposture.*] **1.** Composition, composure 1614. **2.** Compost, manure 1607.

Composure (kǒmpōᵘ·ʒ'ŭɹ). 1599. [From *compose*; after *enclosure,* etc.] †**1.** = COMPOSITION, in nearly all senses. **2.** Composed condition of mind, feelings, etc.; calmness 1667.

2. To whom the Virgin Majestie of Eve..With sweet austeer c. thus reply'd MILT. *P. L.* IX. 272.

Compotation (kǫmpotē'·ʃən). 1593. [ad. L. *compotationem.*] A drinking together, drinking-bout, symposium. So **Co·mpotator,** a fellow-drinker. **Compo·tatory** *a.*

Compote (kǫ·mpoᵘt). 1693. [a. F.; see COMPOSITE, COMPOST.] **1.** Fruit preserved in syrup. **b.** A dish of fruit salad or (mixed) stewed fruit 1863. ‖**2.** A manner of preparing pigeons 1769.

‖**Compotier** (kǫmpǒtiᵊ·ɹ, ‖ koṅpotye). 1755. [a. Fr., f. COMPOTE.] = COMPORT *sb.*[2]

Compound (kǒmpau·nd), *v.* [ME. *compounen, -pownen,* ad. OF. *compon(d)re*:—L. *componere*; see COMPONE, and EXPOUND.]

I. †**1.** *trans.* To put together; to apply –1660. **2.** To combine, mix (elements, etc.) ME. Also †*intr.* (for *refl.*). **3.** To make up by the combination of elements ME. **4.** To compose; to form ME.; †to constitute, as elements –1691.

2. Thus saugh I fals and sothe compouned CHAUCER. SHAKS. *Sonn.* lxxi. 3. I..did c. for her A certaine stuffe *Cymb.* V. v. 254. 4. To c. a riddle JOWETT, an army of great strength RALEIGH.

II. †**1.** *trans.* To settle (disturbance, strife, etc.) –1757. **2.** To compromise (a matter) 1659. **3.** To settle or discharge a debt, or other liability, by an agreement for the payment of a sum of money, or the like 1665. †**4.** *intr.* To agree, make terms (*with, for*) ME. **5.** To come to terms by mutual concession 1528; to come to terms and pay *for*; to compromise; to pay 1555. **6.** To settle with creditors and pay a percentage in discharge of their full claims 1654. **7.** To accept a composition in lieu of one's full claims, etc. 1611; hence, to accept terms of settlement in lieu of prosecution 1576.

1. To c. a quarrell *Tam. Shr.* I. ii. 28. 2. To c. a suit CRUISE. 3. Pitkin..has compounded his debts for 8*s.* 6*d.* in the pound LUTTRELL. *To c. a felony*: to forbear prosecution for a consideration. So *To c. an information.* 5. C., and share the prize QUARLES. Their purses c. for their follies SIR T. BROWNE. C. for Sins they are inclin'd to By damning those they have no mind to BUTLER *Hud.* I. i. 215. 6. He failed ..compounded, and went to America FRANKLIN.

Hence **Compou·ndable** *a.* capable of being combined or commuted for money. **Compou·nder,** one who compounds, in the various senses of the vb.; *Hist.* One of those who wished for a restoration of James II on conditions. **Co·mpoundness.**

Compound (kǫ·mpaund), *a.* ME. [Orig. pa. pple. of *compoune, compone* (see COMPOUND *v.*).] Made up by the combination of elements or parts; composite ME.; combined, collective 1711.

The Gryphons, those c. animals 1798.

Phrases. **a.** *Surg.* and *Med.* in *c. fracture,* usually fracture of a bone, with a coexisting skin wound with which it communicates. **b.** *Arith.* and *Alg.* (*a*) Made up by combination of several elements, as in *c. fraction,* a fraction of a fraction; *c. number,* a composite number; *c. quantity* (in *Alg.*), a quantity consisting of more than one term; (in *Arith.*) a quantity expressed in terms of various denominations, as pounds, shillings, and pence; *c. ratio,* the ratio formed by multiplying together the antecedents, and also the consequents, of two or more ratios. (*b*) Dealing with numbers of various denominations, as in *c. addition, subtraction, multiplication, division.* (*c*) Proceeding by other than simple process, as *c. interest, proportion.* **c.** *Archit. C. order*: COMPOSITE order. **d.** *Zool.* and *Bot.* Consisting of a combination of individual organisms, as *c. animal, zoophyte, coral,* etc., or of simple parts, as *c. eye, stomach, flower, fruit, leaf, umbel,* etc. **e.** *Mech.* and *Physics,* as in *c. engine,* a condensing engine in which the mechanical action of the steam is begun in one cylinder and ended in a larger cylinder; *c. microscope,* one in which not less than two lenses are employed; *c. motion,* that which is produced by two or more forces, acting in different directions, on the same body, at the same time; *c. screw.* **f.** *Mus.* in *c. interval,* one exceeding an octave; *c. time,* time or rhythm, usu. in multiples of three, in which each bar is made up of more than one bar of simple time. **g.** *C. householder*: a householder whose rates are included in his rent, and paid by the landlord.

Compound (kǫ·mpaund), *sb.*[1] 1530. [The adj. used subst.] **1.** *quasi-concr.* A combination *of* elements 1621. **2.** *concr.* A compound substance 1611, word 1530, thing 1890. †**3.** A thing made up –1773. **4.** Compounding 1671.

1. A c. of Two very different Liquors ADDISON. 2. These most poysonous Compounds (i.e. compounded drugs) *Cymb.* I. v. 9.

Compound (kǫ·mpaund), *sb.*[2] *Anglo-Ind.* 1679. [prob. f. Malay *kampong* enclosure.] The enclosure within which a residence or factory (of Europeans) stands, in the East; also, any similar enclosure round native houses.

Comprador (kǫmprădōᵊ·ɹ). 1615. [a. Pg. :— late L. *comparatorem,* f. *comparare* to provide, purchase.] **1.** Formerly, a native house-steward. *Obs.* in India. **2.** Now, in China, a native servant, employed as head of the native staff, and as agent, by European houses.

Comprecation (kǫmpriˈkē'·ʃən). 1635. [ad. L. *comprecationem.*] A praying together, joint supplication.

Comprehend (kǫmpriˈhe·nd), *v.* ME. [ad. L. *comprehendere,* f. *com-* + *prehendere.*] †**1.** To lay hold of –1650; †to overtake, or attain to; †to accomplish –1607. **2.** To grasp with the mind, take in ME. **3.** To apprehend with the senses, *esp.* sight. [L. *comprehendere visu.*] ME. †**4.** To embrace or describe summarily

-1612. 5. To take in, include, comprise, contain ME. Also *transf.* and *fig.*

2. To c. is to know a thing as well as that thing can be known DONNE. 4. All precepts concernyng kinges, are in effect comprehended, in those two Remembrances BACON. 5. In this boke I cannot comprehende..yᵉ sege of Rone 1530. A single term to c. both divisions of the..period LYELL. As able to c. the sea in a cockle-shell 1662. *fig.* As muche ioye as herte may comprehende CHAUCER. Vnder lesse then three lines, can no figure be comprehended 1570. The Air, comprehending the Earth STURMY. Hence **Comprehe·nder** (*rare*). **Comprehe·ndible** *a. rare*, comprehensible. **Comprehe·ndingly** *adv.*

Comprehensible (kǫmpri̇he·nsĭb'l), *a.* 1529. [ad. L. *comprehensibilem*; see COMPREHEND and -ABLE.] 1. That may be comprised or contained. 2. That may be grasped: †palpable -1579; intelligible 1598.

1. He is not comprehensyble nor circumscribed no where MORE. 2. C. to the meanest capacity 1815. Hence **Comprehensibi·lity**, quality of being c. So **Comprehe·nsibleness. Comprehe·nsibly** *adv.*

Comprehension (kǫmpri̇he·nʃən). 1541. [ad. L. *comprehensionem*. Cf. F. *compréhension*.] 1. The action of comprehending, comprising, or including; the fact of being so comprehended or comprised; *spec.* in *Rhet.* (see quots.). 2. The faculty of comprehending; comprehensiveness 1614. †3. A summation *of* any matter -1684. 4. *Logic.* The sum of the attributes comprehended in a concept 1725. 5. The action, condition, or faculty of comprehending with the mind; understanding 15... †6. Physical grasping -1768.

1. In the Old Testament there is a close c. of the New, in the New an open discovery of the Old HOOKER. *Comprehension*, a..figure, whereby the name of a whole is put for a part; or that of a part for a whole CHAMBERS *Cycl.* An Act of C...for admitting of all persuasions in religion to the public observation of their particular worship PEPYS. 5. The c. which she hath of God HOOKER. A..constitution, beyond our c. BUTLER. Hence †**Comprehe·nsional** *a. rare*, comprehensive.

Comprehensive (kǫmpri̇he·nsiv), *a.* 1614. [ad. L. *comprehensivus*, f. *comprehens-*, *comprehendere*; see COMPREHEND. Cf. F. *compréhensif*, *-ive*.] 1. *gen.* Characterized by comprehension; comprising much; of large content or scope; *occas.*, compendious. 2. Characterized by mental comprehension 1628. 3. *Logic.* Intensive 1725.

1. His Aim is more C. STANLEY. 2. C. knowledge 1641. He [Chaucer] must have been a man of a most wonderful c. nature DRYDEN. Hence **Comprehe·nsive-ly** *adv.*, **-ness.**

†**Comprehe·nsor.** 1653. [See prec.] One who has attained to full comprehension. (In 17th c. Divinity, with reference to *Philipp.* iii. 12-13.)

Thou art yet a traveller, they [Saints] comprehensors BP. HALL.

†**Compre·nd**, *v.* ME. = COMPREHEND -1594.

†**Compre·sbyter.** 1600. [See COM-.] A fellow-presbyter -1650.

Compress (kǫ̆mpre·s), *v.* ME. [a. OF. *compresser*, ad. L. *compressare*, freq. of *comprimere*. Usually treated as repr. *compress-*, *comprimere*.] 1. To press together, to squeeze; *Surg.* to close by compression. 2. To squeeze together, so as to make more firm and solid ME.; to reduce in volume by, or as by, pressure; to condense, concentrate 1677. †3. *fig.* To keep under restraint -1847. †4. To embrace sexually -1725.

1. To c. an artery MARRYAT. 2. To c. a sponge 1789, air HALE, water TYNDALL, thoughts BURKE. To collect and c. feeble rays of light 1851. Hence **Compre·ssingly** *adv.*

Compress (kǫ·mpres), *sb.* 1599. [a. F. *compresse*, ad. L. *compressa*, from *compressus*; see prec.] 1. *Surg.* A soft pad of linen lint, etc., used with a bandage, to maintain due pressure on any part. In hydropathic use, a piece of cloth, wetted with water, and tightly covered with an impervious bandage, applied to the body for the relief of inflammation. 2. A machine for pressing cotton-bales, etc. 1874.

Compressed (kǫ̆mpre·st), *ppl. a.* ME. [f. COMPRESS *v.*] 1. Pressed together closely, so as to occupy small space; pressed into a smaller volume; condensed; also *fig.* 2. Having the two opposite sides nearly plane or flat 1668.

Compressed air engine: an engine operated by compressed air, as an elastic substitute for steam. Hence **Compre·ssedly** *adv.*

Compressibility (kǫ̆mpresĭbi·lĭti). 1691. [f. next; cf. F. *compressibilité*.] The quality of being compressible; *esp.* in *Physics*, the quality in virtue of which the volume of a gas, etc., may be diminished without decrease of its mass.

Compressible (kǫ̆mpre·sĭb'l), *a.* 1691. [f. COMPRESS *v.* (referred to L. *compress-us*) + -IBLE.] That may be compressed; capable of compression; applied to a feverish pulse, which seems to vanish under pressure.

Compression (kǫ̆mpre·ʃən). ME. [a. F., ad. L. *compressionem*; see COMPRESS *v.*] 1. The action of compressing; also *fig.* 2. A state of being compressed; also *fig.* 1603. 3. *Surg.* Short for 'compression of the brain' 1847.

2. C. of thought JOHNSON, of heart FARRAR. Hence **Compre·ssional** *a.*

Compressive (kǫ̆mpre·siv), *a.* 1572. [f. L. *compress-*, *comprimere*. So F. *compressif*, *-ive*.] Having the attribute of compressing; tending to compress. Hence **Compre·ssively** *adv.*

Compressor (kǫ̆mpre·səɹ). 1839. [a. L.] One who or that which compresses. *Spec.* a. *Anat.* A muscle which compresses a part. b. *Surg.* An instrument for compressing a nerve, artery, duct, or other part; also a tourniquet. c. An instrument for compressing objects in microscopical investigations; called also *compressorium*. d. *Naut.* An iron lever for checking or stopping the chain-cable as it runs out. e. *Gun.* A mechanism for pressing a gun-carriage to its platform during the recoil. f. A machine for compressing air; an *air-compressor*.

Compressure (kǫ̆mpre·ʃiŭɹ, -əɹ). 1644. [f. L. *compress-*, *comprimere*.] Compressing; pressure together; †repression.

†**Compriest.** A fellow-priest. MILT.

†**Comprint**, *v. rare.* 1634. [See COM-.] To share in printing; as the Universities of Oxford and Cambridge shared with the King's Printer and the Company of Stationers the right to print privileged books -1684.

¶ The meaning 'to print surreptitiously another's copy' and **Comprint** *sb.* are mod. dict. figments.

Comprisal (kǫ̆mprəi·zăl). ? *Obs.* 1643. [f. COMPRISE *v.* + -AL.] The action of comprising; a compendium.

Comprise (kǫ̆mprəi·z), *v.* Also 7-9 **comprize.** ME. [f. F. *comprendre* (pa. pple. *compris*) :—L. *comprendere*, contr. from *comprehendere*; cf. *apprise*, *surprise*.] †1. To lay hold on, seize; *Sc.* to 'attach' -1637. †2. To take in (mentally), comprehend -1680. 3. To include, embrace; to comprehend compendiously ME. 4. To contain, consist of 1481; to extend to, cover 1541. †5. To put together (a treatise) -1628. †6. To constitute (*rare*) -1794.

3. Behold a Nation in a Man comprised DRYDEN. 4. The house comprises box-room, nine bed-rooms, etc. (*Mod. Advt.*). Hence **Compri·sable** *a.*

†**Co·mprobate**, *v.* 1531. [f. L. *comprobat-*, *comprobare*, f. *com-* intensive + *probare*.] *trans.* To prove, confirm; to approve -1660. So †**Co·mprobate** *pa. pple.* †**Comproba·tion.**

†**Comprodu·ce**, *v. rare.* 1630. [See COM-.] *trans.* To produce together (*with*) -1674. So †**Comprodu·ction**, production in combination, joint product.

Compromise (kǫ·mprŏməiz), *sb.* ME. [a. F. *compromis*, ad. L. *compromissum*, *compromittere*; see COMPROMIT.] †1. A joint promise or agreement made by contending parties to abide by the decision of an arbiter. ME. only. 2. Arbitration 1479. 3. Arrangement of a dispute by concessions on both sides; partial surrender of one's position, for the sake of coming to terms; the terms offered by either side 1516. 4. *fig.* Adjustment for practical purposes of rival courses of action, systems, theories, etc., by the surrender of a part of each 1711; anything that results from or embodies such an arrangement 1797. 5. A putting in peril, exposure to risk or suspicion; see COMPROMISE *v.* 4. 1603.

3. War'd he hath not, But basely yeelded vpon comprimize, That which his Ancestors atchieu'd with blowes *Rich. II*, II. i. 253. 4. Logic admits of no c.; the essence of politics is c. MACAULAY. All virtue is a c. between opposite motives and inducements GODWIN.

Compromise (kǫ·mprŏmaiz), *v.* 1596. [f. the sb.; in some uses replacing COMPROMIT.] †1. To adjust or settle (differences, etc.) between parties. Also *fig.* -1798. 2. Of the parties: To settle by mutual concession 1679. 3. *intr.* To come to terms by mutual concession 1656. 4. To expose (oneself, one's own or another's reputation, credit, etc.) to risk or danger, to imperil; to involve in a hazardous course, to commit (oneself) 1696.

1. †*To be compromised*: to be agreed by compromise (*Merch. V.* I. iii 79). 2. With much difficulty, the dispute was compromised MACAULAY. 3. To induce him to c. on those terms RICHARDSON. 4. It behov'd him not to C. his Honour and his Reputation 1696. Hence **Co·mpromiser**, †one who acts as arbiter; one who compromises or advocates compromise. **Co·mpromisingly** *adv.*

†**Compromi·ssion.** ME. [ad. med.L. *compromissionem*.] 1. Submission to an arbitrator for decision -1524. 2. Election by compromise, *i. e.* by agreement of the electing body to entrust the election to one or more of its members. *Hist.* ME. 3. A compromising -1624.

Compromit (kǫmprǫ̆·m·it), *v.* ME. [ad. L. *compromittere*. The ppl. stem *compromiss-* gave COMPROMISE.] †1. *refl.* (and *pass.*) To bind themselves mutually (see COMPROMISE *sb.* 2) -1565. †2. *trans.* To refer to arbitration -1606. Also *fig.* †3. To settle by arbitration -1693. Also *fig.* †4. To delegate to another or others one's right of voting in an election -1573. 5. *U.S.* (*Obsolescent.*) = COMPROMISE *v.* 4. 1787.

Comprovi·ncial, *a.* 1590. [See COM-.] Of or belonging to the same province. As *sb.* A bishop of the same province 1642.

‖**Compsognathus** (kǫmpsǫ·gnăþŏs). 1878. [mod.L., f. Gr. κομψός elegant + γνάθος.] *Palæont.* A genus of reptiles, remarkable for their bird-like affinities. Hence **Compso·gnathous** *a.*; **Compso·gnathid** *a.* and *sb.* (a member) of the family *Compsognathidæ* (order *Deinosauria*) to which these creatures belonged.

†**Compt**, *a.* ME. [ad. L. *comptus*, *comere*.] Dressed, as to the hair; *more gen.*, trim, spruce, polished. Also *transf.* -1693. Hence †**Co·mptly** *adv.* †**Co·mptness.**

Compt, Comptable, etc.; see COUNT, etc.

Compter (kau·ntəɹ). ME. Old spelling of COUNTER *sb.*, formerly used in all senses, and from 17th c. as: The name of certain city prisons for debtors, etc., in London, Exeter, etc.

‖**Comptoir** (kǫ̃ntwar). 1722. [Fr.] A commercial agency or factory (in a foreign country).

Comptonite (kǫ·mptənəit). 1822. [f. Earl *Compton*, who brought it from Vesuvius.] *Min.* = THOMSONITE.

Comptrol, etc.; see CONTROL, etc.

Comptroller (kǫ̆ntrōᵘ·ləɹ). An erroneous spelling of CONTROLLER, introduced *c* 1500; still retained in certain official designations. Hence **Comptrollership.**

Compulsative (kǫ̆mpɒ·lsătiv), *a.* [f. L. *compulsat-*, *compulsare*, freq. of *compellere*; see COMPEL and -IVE.] Of the nature of compulsion, compulsory. *Haml.* I. i. 103. Hence **Compu·lsatively** *adv.*

†**Compulsatory** (kǫ̆mpɒ·lsătəri), *a.* 1603. [f. as prec. + -ORY.] Of the nature of or subject to compulsion; compulsory -1827. Hence **Compu·lsatorily** *adv.*

Compulse (kǫ̆mpɒ·ls), *v.* ? *Obs.* ME. [See prec.] †1. *trans.* To compel, force -1632. 2. To force to move. (Cf. *repulse.*) CARLYLE.

Compulsion (kǫ̆mpɒ·lʃən). 1462. [a. F., ad. L. *compulsionem*.] The action, or an act, of compelling, or the condition of being compelled; constraint, obligation, coercion.

Wherefore was there such c. us'd..about conforming to a Liturgy MILT. The tribute..would not be forthcoming except on c. LEWIN.

Compulsitor (kǫ̆mpɒ·lsitəɹ). 1816. [app. corrupt f. *compulsator*.] *Sc. Law.* A compulsatory instrument, act, or proceeding.

Compulsive (kǫ̆mpɒ·lsiv), *a.* 1602. [f. L. *compuls-*, *compellere*. Cf. F. *compulsif*, *-ive*.] 1. = COMPULSORY *a.* 2. †2. = COMPULSORY *a.* 1. -1836.

1. The power of the magistrate is c. 1873. 2. Freed ..from all c. tributes and taxes MILT. Hence **Compu·lsively** *adv.*

Compulsory (kǫ̆mpɒ·lsəri). 1516. [f. L. type **compulsorius*; see -ORY.]

A. *adj.* **1.** Produced by or acting under compulsion; forced 1581. **2.** Coercive 1631.
1. Of compulsary single life 1581. **2.** C. process for obtaining witnesses 1789.
B. *sb.* A compulsory agency or means; a legal mandate compelling obedience 1516.
Hence **Compu·lsorily** *adv.* **Compu·lsoriness.**

†Compu·nct, *ppl. a.* ME. [ad. L. *compunctus, compungere.*] Affected with compunction. (Usually construed as a pple.) -1659. var. **†Compu·ncted.**

Compunction (kǫ̆mpʊ·ŋkʃən). ME. [a. OF., ad. L. *compunctionem* (in Christian writers) sting of conscience, f. *compungere.*] **1.** Pricking or stinging of the conscience or heart; uneasiness of mind consequent on wrong-doing; remorse, contrition. **2.** In mod. use: A slight or passing regret for wrong-doing, or a feeling of regret for some slight offence (sometimes including pity for the person wronged) 1712. **†3.** In physical sense: The action of pricking -1656.
1. A remorse, and c. for former sins DONNE. **2.** They quitted it [the Reformed Communion] without c. BUCKLE. Hence **Compu·nctionless** *a.*

Compunctious (kǫ̆mpʊ·ŋkʃəs), *a.* 1605. [f. stem of *compunction* + -OUS; cf. *factious.*] **1.** Of the nature of compunction. **2.** Having compunction 1816.
1. Stop vp th' accesse, and passage to Remorse, That no c. visitings of Nature Shake my fell purpose *Macb.* I. v. 46. Hence **Compu·nctiously** *adv.* So **†Compu·nctive** *a. rare*, tending to compunction.

†Compu·pil. A fellow-pupil. WALTON.

Compurgation (kǫmpɒ̄ɹgē¹·ʃən). 1658. [ad. L. *compurgationem*, f. *compurgare* to purify completely; but cf. next.] **1.** The action of clearing a man from a charge by the oaths of a number of others; also, generally, vindication; evidence to this effect. **2.** *esp.* The Old English mode of trial and purgation by means of the *consacramentales*; known to the Common Law as WAGER OF LAW. See COMPURGATOR 1. 1658.
1. [He] was priviledged..from suspicion of Incontinency and needed no c. HACKET.

Compurgator (kǫ·mpɒɹgē¹təɹ, kǫ̆mpɒ̄·ɹgātəɹ). 1533. [a. med.L.; app. f. L. *com-* together + *purgator* purger.] **1.** A witness to character who swore along with the person accused, in order to the acquittal of the latter. (Originally a term of the Canon Law; applied by modern historians to the 'oath-helpers' (in Ger. *Eideshülfe*) of the Old English mode of trial and purgation, and sometimes used by modern legal writers with reference to WAGER OF LAW.) **2.** *gen.* One who vouches for, or clears from any charge. Also *fig.* 1613.
1. The compurgators of our oldest law were not a jury in the modern sense, but they were one of the elements out of which the jury rose FREEMAN. **2.** He calleth God to be his c. SANDERSON. Hence **Compurgato·rial** *a.* of or pertaining to compurgators; so **Compu·rgatory** *a.*

Compu·rsion. [joc. f. COM-, PURSE *v.*] A pursing together. STERNE.

Computable (kǫ̆mpiū·tăb'l, kǫ·mpiutăb'l), *a.* 1646. [ad. L. *computabilis.*] Capable of being computed.

†Co·mputate, *v.* 1602. *trans.* = COMPUTE -1619.

Computation (kǫmpiutē¹·ʃən). ME. [ad. L. *computationem*; cf. F. *computation.*] **1.** The action or process of computing; a method of reckoning. **2.** A computed result 1713. **†3.** Ratiocination -1656.
1. The Gregorian C...being eleven days before the Julian STEELE. Hence **Computa·tional** *a. rare*, of or pertaining to c. So **Compu·tative, co·mp·** *a.* given to c. **†Co·mputator,** a calculator.

Compute (kǫ̆mpiū·t), *sb.* Now *rare.* ME. [a. F. *comput* COMPUTUS (in sense 1), and f. the vb.] **†1.** (*co·mpute*) = COMPUTUS 2. -1533. **2.** Computation; now chiefly in *beyond c.* 1588. **†3.** Judgement -1682.

Compute (kǫ̆mpiū·t), *v.* 1631. [a. F. *computer*, ad. L. *computare.*] **1.** *trans.* To determine by calculation; to reckon, count; to take account of 1647. **2.** *intr.* To make computation 1634.
1. The radii of curvature for these lenses, as computed by Mr. Herschel BREWSTER. What's done we partly may c., But know not what's resisted BURNS. **2.** To c. by weight 1872. Hence **Compu·ter,** one who computes; *spec.* one employed to make calculations in an observatory, etc. **Co·mputist,** one skilled in the computus or calendar; †an accountant; a computer.

‖Computus (kǫ·mpiutŏs). *Hist.* Also **compotus.** [late L., f. *computare.* In F. *comput*, OF. *compot, compost.*] **1.** A reckoning; an account 1848. **2.** A set of mediæval tables for astronomical and calendarial calculations 1832.

Comrade (kǫ·mrĕd). 1591. [Orig. *camerade*, a. F. (See next.) The disyllabic *comra·de* occurs in Shaks. and Milton. Walker and others have also (kʊ·mrē¹d).] *orig.* One who shares the same room, tent, etc., a 'chum'; *esp.* a fellow-soldier (also *Comrade-in-arms*); hence *gen.* an associate in friendship, occupation, fortunes, etc., mate. Also *transf.* and *fig.*
His comrade's face each warrior saw SCOTT. To be a C. with the Wolfe and Owle *Lear* II. iv. 213. Hence **Co·mrade** *v.* to associate *with*, as a c.; **Co·mradely** *a.* like a c. **Co·mradery** (*rare*), **Co·mradeship,** the position of being a c., camaraderie.

†Comra·do. 1598. [a. Sp. *camarada*, 'a chamberful, a company that belongs to one chamber, tent, or cabin'; applied to a single person, and in this sense occas. altered to *camerado*. The *o* in *comrado, comrade*, etc. prob. = the Sp. *a.*] = COMRADE -1636.

Co·mrogue. *arch.* 1621. A fellow-rogue.

‖Comte (kōnt). 1611. [Fr.] A French title: COUNT.

Comtian (kǫ·mtiăn, ko·ntiăn). Also **Comtean.** 1855. [f. Auguste *Comte* (d. 1857), a French philosopher, the founder of POSITIVISM.] *adj.* Of or originating with Comte. *sb.* A Comtist. So **Co·mtism,** positivism. **Co·mtist,** a positivist; also *attrib.* or as *adj.*

‖Comus (kōᵘ·mŏs). 1634. [L., a. Gr. κῶμος.] A revel; revelry personified as a deity.

Con (kǫn), *v.*[1] [Mainly repr. ME. *cunn-* or *conn-* from OE. *cunn-* (= kun); but in part ME. *con*, from OE. *cǫn*, for *can* (= kǫn). See further under CAN *v.*[1]]
†I. 1. To know: repl. by CAN *v.* -1674. **2.** To know how; hence, to be able; repl. by CAN *v.* -1489.
II. 1. To get to know; to study or learn; hence, to pore over, commit to memory; to inspect, examine ME. **2.** *To cun* or *con thank(s* (OE. *þanc cunnan*): to acknowledge one's gratitude; to thank OE. So **†***To (cun) con gree* or *malgre*: to express one's satisfaction or displeasure [F. *savoir gré*].
1. An Oration which..Lysander should have conned without book NORTH. Conning old topics like a parrot SWIFT.

Con, conne, cun (kʊn, kǫn), *v.*[2] 1626. [app. weakened f. COND. But cf. CON *v.*[1]] *trans.* To direct the steering of (a ship). Also *absol.* and *fig.*

Con, conn (kʊn, kǫn), *sb.*[1] 1825. [f. CON *v.*[2]] The action or post of conning a ship, steerage.

Con (kǫn), *sb.*[2] 1620. [Cf. F. *cogner.*] A rap with the knuckles, a knock.

Con (kǫn), *sb.*[3] *n. dial.* 1600. A squirrel.

Con (kǫn), *adv.* (*sb.*) 1470. Short for L. *contra* 'against', in PRO and CON (q. v.) 'for and against'. As *sb.* A reason, argument, or arguer against, *esp.* in *pros and cons.*

‖Con, *prep.* It.:—L. *cum* with, as in CON AMORE, q. v., *con affetto, con brio*, etc.

Con-, *prefix*, of L. origin. The form assumed by L. *com-* bef. all consonants exc. *h, r*, and (in later times) *l*. For meaning see COM-.

†Co·nable, *a.* ME. Short for COVENABLE, q.v.

Conacre (kǫ·nē¹kəɹ), *sb.* Also **corn-acre.** 1824. [corrupt f. *corn-acre.*] The letting by a tenant, for the season, of small portions of land ready prepared for a crop (*Ireland*). Hence **Co·nacre** *v.* to sublet in c. **Co·nacrer,** one who uses a piece of land on this system.

Conama·rin. [f. L. *conium* hemlock + *amarus.*] A bitter principle said to exist in *Conium maculatum.*

‖Con amore (kǫnămōᵊ·ri). 1826. [It.; = '*with love*'.] With love, zeal, or delight. Also as quasi-*adj.*

Conario- (konēᵊ·riǫ). 1881. Comb. f. CONARIUM, -AL, as in *c.-hypophy·sial canal*, a passage connecting the infundibulum with the pineal gland; so *c.-h. tract.*

‖Conarium (konēᵊ·riŏm). 1656. [mod.L., a. Gr. κωνάριον, dim. of κῶνος pine-cone.] The pineal gland of the brain.

Conation (konē¹·ʃən). 1615. [ad. L. *conationem.*] **†1.** Endeavour. **2.** *Philos.* The faculty of volition and desire; also (with *a* and *pl.*) the product of this faculty 1836. So **Co·native** *a.* pertaining to, or of the nature of, c.

‖Conatus (konē¹·tŏs). 1665. [L., f. *conari* to endeavour.] **1.** An effort, endeavour 1722. **2.** *transf.* A force, impulse, or tendency simulating a human effort; a nisus.
2. What blind c. of nature should produce it in birds PALEY.

Conaxial (kǫnæ·ksiăl), *a.* = COAXIAL.

Concamerate (kǫnkæ·mĕrē¹t), *v.* 1611. [ad. L. *concamerat-, concamerare* to vault; see CAMERA.] **1.** To vault or arch. ? *Obs.* **2.** To divide into chambers or cells 1746.
2. The nautilus..is a concamerated shell 1754. Hence **Concamera·tion,** vaulting, vaulted roof, etc.; division into chambers or cells; a chambered formation; one of the chambers of a series.

†Concarnation (kǫnkaɹnē¹·ʃən). *rare.* 1638. [ad. L. *concarnationem.*] Union of flesh with flesh, or of a bone with another bone by means of muscles -1685.

Concatenate (kǫnkæ·tĭnē¹t), *v.* 1598. [f. L. *concatenat-, concatenare*, f. *con-* + *catenare*; see CHAIN.] To chain together (*obs.*); to connect like the links of a chain, to link together. *fig.*
The world concatenated together vnder a Crowne Imperiall MALYNES. So **Conca·tenate** *ppl. a.* Hence **Conca·tenator,** one who concatenates.

Concatenation (kǫnkætĭnē¹·ʃən). 1603. [ad. L. *concatenationem.*] **1.** Union by linking together; concatenated condition. **2.** *esp.* Union in a series or chain 1614. **3.** quasi-*concr.* A concatenated series or system, an unbroken sequence, a chain 1622.
2. The necessary c. of ideas which should reproduce the c. of objects LEWES. **3.** This vile c. of straight lines RUSKIN.

Concate·rvate, *ppl. a.* 1882. [ad. L. *concatervatus.*] Heaped up together.

Concaule·scence. *rare.* 1882. [See CON-.] *Bot.* The coalescence of separate axes, *e g* of the leaf-stalk and stem.

Concause (kǫ·nkǭz). 1619. [ad. med.L. *concausa.*] A co-operating cause. Hence **Conca·usal** *a.* (and *sb.*).

Concave (kǫ·nkē¹v), *sb.* 1541. [a. OF., from *concave* adj.; cf. L. *concava* hollows. Also stressed *conca·ve* by poets.] **1.** †A hollow -1814; a concave part of a machine 1874. **2.** A concave surface 1552; *spec.* the vault of heaven 1635. **†3.** A concave lens, speculum, etc. -1797.
2. On high within the c., as are the..starres SWAN.

Concave (kǫ·nkē¹v), *a.* 1571. [a. F., ad. L. *concavus*; see CAVE.] **†1.** Hollow -1659. **2.** Having the outline or surface curved like the interior of a circle or sphere; the reverse of convex; incurvated 1571.
1. As concaue as..a Worme-eaten nut *A. Y. L.* III. iv. 26. **2.** The c. mirror is the staple instrument of the magician's cabinet BREWSTER. Hence **Co·ncavely** *adv.*, **-ness.** var. **†Co·ncavous.**

Concave (kǫ·nkē¹v), *v.* 1652. [f. prec.; cf. L. *concavare.*] *trans.* To make concave; †to vault. Hence **†Concava·tion** (Dicts.).

Concavity (kǫ̆nkæ·vĭti). 1483. [a. F. *concavité*, ad. L. *concavitas.*] **1.** The condition of being concave 1578. **2.** A concave surface or side 1483. **3.** A hollow; a cavity 1513.

Concavo- (kǫ̆nkē¹·vo), in comb. = Concavely, concave and —, as in **C.-co·ncave,** concave on both sides; **C.-co·nvex,** concave on one side and convex on the other, and thinnest in the centre.

Conceal (kǫ̆nsī·l), *v.* ME. [a. OF. *conceler* :—L. *concelare*, f. *con-* together, completely + *celare.*] **1.** *trans.* To keep from the knowledge or observation of others. **2.** *trans.* To put or keep out of sight or notice, to hide 1595.
1. Thy praise hee..Conceales not from us MILT. *P. L.* IX. 751. To dissemble or concele that Fidelity ..they ow'd CLARENDON. **2.** The Army, that lies conceal'd for him in Knightsbridge 1671. Hence **Concea·lable** *a.* (*rare*). **Concea·led·ly** *adv.*, **-ness.**

Concealer (kǫ̆nsī·ləɹ). 1514. [a. Anglo-F. *concelour*, f. *conceler*; cf. CONCEAL.] **a.** One who conceals. **†b.** *Law.* In 17th c., applied to persons who sought by surreptitious means to disturb possessors of 'concealed land', *i. e.* land privily held from the king without a proper title. See CONCEALMENT 1 b.

Concealment (kǫnsī·lměnt). ME. [a. OF. *concelement*, f. as prec.] **1.** The concealing (of any information). In *Law*, The intentional suppression of truth or fact known, to the injury or prejudice of another. **b.** *esp.* The holding of land against the king's rights, without a proper title 1623. **2.** *gen.* The action of concealing 1600. †**3.** A secret, a mystery –1622. **4.** The condition of being concealed 1605; the capacity of concealing; in *pl.* conditions that conceal 1728.

2. Let c. like a worme i'th budde Feede on her damaske cheeke SHAKS. **4.** Some dear cause Will in c. wrap me up a while SHAKS. The clefted tree Offers its kind c. to a few (birds) THOMSON.

Concede (kǫnsī·d), *v.* 1632. [ad. L. *concedere*; see CEDE.] **1.** *trans.* To admit, allow, grant (a proposition, claim, etc.); *occas.*, To allow formally for the sake of argument 1646. **2.** To grant, yield, or surrender (*e.g.* a right, a privilege 1632. **3.** *intr.* or *absol.* To make a concession 1780.

1. Conceding, for a moment, that there is any analogy between a bee and a man DICKENS. **3.** When..I wished you to c. to America, at a time when she prayed concession at our feet BURKE. Hence †**Conce·dence.** RICHARDSON. **Conce·der.**

Conceit (kǫnsī·t), *sb.* ME. [f. *conceive*; after *deceive, deceit*, etc.] †**1.** That which is conceived in the mind, a conception, notion, idea, thought; device –1823. †**2.** The faculty or action of conceiving; conception; apprehension –1805. †**3.** Personal opinion or judgement, usually 'in a neutral sense' (J.) –1759. **4.** Favourable opinion, esteem. Now *dial.*, exc. in *out of c. with.* 1462. **5.** Short for SELF-CONCEIT 1605. **6.** A fanciful notion; a whim 1530; fancy 1578. **7.** A fanciful, ingenious, or witty notion or expression; an affectation of thought or style; = CONCETTO 1513; a trick 1520; sentiment 1589; wit 1597. †**8.** *concr.* A fancy article –1823. †**9.** A (morbid) seizure of the body or mind; see CONCEIVE *v.* –1622.

1. Fluent in language to express their conceits FULLER. A glimmering c. of some such thing LAMB. **2.** A Gentleman of good c. *A. Y. L.* v. ii 48. Wise in C., in Act a very sot DRAYTON. **3.** That good selfe-conceit and opinion of his owne HOLLAND. **4.** To be out of c. with our lot in life NEWMAN. **5.** It takes the c. out of a man FORD. **6.** In c. build castles in the sky GREENE. **7.** How..our toung may be framed to pretie conceiptes 1581. Some to c. alone their taste confine POPE. 2 *Hen. IV*, II. iv. 263. **9.** The Conceipt of the stone..hath..so stopped my urine FLORIO. Hence †**Concei·tful** *a.* witty; imaginative. **Concei·tless** *a.* **Concei·ty** *a.* (*Sc.*) abounding in conceits, or in self-conceit.

Conceit (kǫnsī·t), *v.* 1557. [f. CONCEIT *sb.*] †**1.** To form a conception of; to conceive –1602. †*intr.* To conceive –1828. **2.** To imagine 1600. **3.** *trans.* To inspire with a fancy 1587. Also *refl.* **4.** To take a fancy to. Now *dial.* 1589. †**5.** To conceive as a design –1638.

1. *Jul. C.* I. iii. 162. *intr.* One that so imperfectly conceits *Oth.* III. iii. 149. **2.** I did c. a most delicious feast G. HERBERT. **3.** *refl.* We..c. ourselves that we contemplate absolute existence SIR W. HAMILTON.

Conceited (kǫnsī·těd), *ppl. a.* 1542. [f. CONCEIT *sb.* and *v.*]

I. †**1.** Having a conceit (of such a kind); ingenious; witty –1681. **2.** Having an opinion, opinioned. Now *dial.* 1587. †Possessed with a good opinion *of* –1734. **3.** Vain. Orig. *self-c.* (The principal existing sense.) 1608. Also with *of* 1618. **4.** Full of notions, fastidious. Now *dial.* 1609.

3. The c. are rarely shy DARWIN. The less a man knows, the more c. he is of his proficiency NEWMAN.

II. From the *vb.* **1.** Conceived (*arch.*) 1598; †imagined; imaginary –1703. **2.** †Ingeniously devised 1594; 'fancy' 1615.

2. A conceyted chayre to sleep in with the legs stretcht out EVELYN. Hence **Concei·tedly** *adv.* in a c. manner. **Concei·tedness,** †cleverness; †imagination; self-conceit.

Conceivable (kǫnsī·văb'l), *a.* 1646. [f. CONCEIVE *v.*] That can be imagined, or thought of; *occas.*, = just credible. Also as *sb.* [sc. *thing.*]

A particle..minuter than all..c. dimension PALEY. Hence **Conceivabi·lity,** c. quality or condition. **Concei·vableness. Concei·vably** *adv.*

Conceive (kǫnsī·v), *v.* ME. [a. OF. *conceveir, -oir*:—L. *concipere.* The primary notion was app. 'to take in and hold'; cf. CATCH.] **1.** *trans.* To receive (seed) in the womb; to become pregnant with (young); *pass.* to be created in the womb. **2.** *intr.* To become pregnant ME. †**3.** *pass.* To become or be pregnant –1646. †**4.** *transf.* To take on (any state: e.g. *fire, moisture,* etc.) –1756. **5.** To take or admit into the mind; to become affected with ME. **6.** To form in the mind, devise ME. **7.** To form or have a conception of ME. Also *absol.* or *intr.* **8.** To grasp with the mind; to apprehend; cf. CATCH *v.* ME. **9.** To be of opinion; to fancy; also used as a modest way of expressing one's opinion ME. †**10.** (after L.) To take in, comprise –1571. †**11.** To institute (an action at law). [L. *concipere actionem.*] –1574. **12.** To formulate. [Cf. L. *concipere aliquid verbis.*] 1560.

1. Through faith also Sara her selfe receiued strength to conceiue seede *Heb.* xi. 11. **2.** And the flockes conceiued before the rods *Gen.* xxx. 38. **4.** To c. a siknesse GOWER. **5.** To c. prejudices SHERLOCK, a dislike 1802, a good opinion HOBBES. **6.** He first conceives, then perfects his design COWPER. **7.** I cold not conceve wherefore the same was spooken THYNNE. *To c. of* a better course 1623. **8.** I conceyve youre entent ME. I doe now conceave you SPENSER. **12.** To c. an answer in the tone of insult GIBBON. Hence **Concei·vement** (*rare*), conception. **Concei·ver.**

Concelebrate (kǫnse·lĭbrēⁱt), *v.* 1572. [ad. L. *concelebrat-, concelebrare.* Cf. F. *concélébrer.*] †**1.** *trans.* To celebrate together –1610. **2.** *R. C. Ch.* Said of newly ordained priests: To celebrate mass along *with* the ordaining bishop. Hence **Concelebra·tion.**

Concent (kǫnse·nt), *sb.* Also 6–7 (confused with) consent. 1585. [ad. L. *concentus*, f. *concinere*, f. *con-* + *canere* (*cantus*).] **1.** Harmony (of sounds); concord of voices or parts. Also with *a* and *pl.* ? *Obs.* 1589. **2.** *transf.* and *fig.* Harmony; accord 1588.

2. So their affections, set in keys alike, In true c. meet, as their humours strike DRAYTON. Hence †**Conce·nt** *v* to make to accord.

Concenter; see CONCENTRE.

Concentrate (kǫ·nsĕntrēⁱt, kǫnse·ntrēⁱt), *v.* 1640. [f. L. type **concentrat-*; see CONCENTRE.] **1.** *trans.* To bring to or towards a common centre, or focus; to collect as at a centre 1646. Also *fig.* **2.** *Chem.* To increase the strength of (a solution) by contraction of its volume 1689. **3.** *Mining.* To separate metal or ore from the gangue 1872. **4.** To bring the parts of into closer union; to condense 1758. Also *intr.* and *absol.* (usually for *refl.*) 1640. *Mil.* of troops: To collect in one quarter 1813.

1. The different rays concentrated by the lens BREWSTER. To c. attention 1879. **2.** To c. spirit of vinegar 1731. **4.** The obstinacy of my whole sex.. was concentrated in me C. BRONTË. *intr.* The news ..obliged him to c. on the Elbe 1813. Hence **Conce·ntrate** *a.* concentrated; *sb.* the product of concentration.

Concentration (kǫnsĕntrēⁱ·ʃən). 1634. [f. prec. vb. Cf. F. *concentration.*] **1.** The action of concentrating; the state of being concentrated. Also *fig.* **2.** *Chem.* The strengthening of a solution by contraction of its volume (*e.g.* by evaporation); the condition thus produced 1790. **3.** *Mining.* The removal by mechanical means of the less valuable parts of ore 1873. **4.** Condensation 1865.

1. The c. of your force in one position WELLINGTON. The power of intellectual c. 1846. **4.** My affected c. of language RUSKIN. *C. camp*, a camp where non-combatants of a district are accommodated.

Concentrative (kǫnse·ntrătiv), *a.* 1822. [f. CONCENTRATE *v.* + -IVE.] Concentrating; characterized by concentration.

Your nature is c., rather than diffuse 1881. Hence **Conce·ntrativeness,** c. quality. (Orig. *Phrenol.*)

Concentrator (kǫ·nsĕntrēⁱtəɹ). 1853. [f. as prec.] One who or that which concentrates. **1.** An apparatus for concentrating solutions, etc. 1853. **2.** *Fire-arms.* A ring of hard paper or wire fitted inside the cartridge case, to keep the shot together after discharge 1875. **3.** An apparatus for the mechanical concentration of ores 1873.

Concentre, -center (kǫnse·ntəɹ), *v.* 1591. [a. F. *concentrer* 'to joyne in one centre' Cotgr.; L. type **concentrare*, f. *con-* + *centrum.*] **1.** *trans.* To bring or direct to a common centre 1633; *occas.*, to attract to itself as a centre 1795. Also *fig.* **2.** To pack closely as round a centre; *hence*, to increase the vigour or intensity of 1598. **3.** *intr.* (for *refl.*) To move towards, or meet in, a common centre (*lit.* and *fig.*) 1630. †**4.** To agree, coincide –1755.

1. *fig.* To c. the mind on one sole object BURKE. **3.** This jealousy of control from without concentred in the subject of taxation BANCROFT.

Concentric, -al (kǫnse·ntrik, -ăl), *a.* (and *sb.*) ME. [ad. med.L. *concentricus* (f. *con-* + *centrum*) + -IC, + -AL; cf. *centric, eccentric.*] *adj.* Having a common centre. *sb.* A concentric circle, etc. 1551.

Mil. C. fire: firing concentrated on one point. Hence **Conce·ntrically** *adv.* **Concentri·city.**

†**Conce·ntricate,** *v.* 1641. = CONCENTRATE –1787.

Conce·ntual, *a. rare.* 1785. [f. L. *concentus.*] Harmonious, accordant.

‖**Conce·ntus.** 1609. [L.: in med.L. applied to that part of the choral service of the Church in which the whole choir joined.] A singing or sounding together in accord; harmony.

Concept (kǫ·nsept), *sb.* 1556. [ad. L. *conceptum*, f. *concipere*; *occas.*, a refash. of CONCEIT, after L.] †**1.** = CONCEIT, in various senses –1591. **2.** *Logic* and *Philos.* The product of the faculty of conception; an idea of a class of objects, a general notion 1663.

2. Concepts are merely the results, rendered permanent by language, of a previous process of comparison SIR W. HAMILTON.

Conceptacle (kǫnse·ptăk'l). 1611. [ad. L. *conceptaculum* (also used), f. *concept-, concipere.*] †**1.** A receptacle –1855. **2.** †**a.** *Anat.* Any cavity of the body –1668. †**b.** *Bot.* = FOLLICLE 1823. **c.** *Biol.* A cavity-like organ containing the reproductive cells in some plants and animals of low organization 1835. Hence **Concepta·cular** *a.* of or pertaining to conceptacles.

†**Conce·ptible,** *a.* 1650. [cf. mod.F. *conceptible*, (prob.) med.L. *conceptibilis.*] = CONCEIVABLE –1695. Hence †**Conceptibi·lity,** c. quality. CUDWORTH.

Conception (kǫnse·pʃən). ME. [a. F., ad. L. *conceptionem*; see CONCEIVE.] **1.** The action of conceiving, or fact of being conceived, in the womb. Also *fig.* and †*transf.* **2.** *concr.* That which is conceived; embryo, †child ME. **3.** The action or faculty of conceiving in the mind; apprehension, imagination ME. **4.** *Philos.* **a.** In a general sense = prec.; †**b.** reproductive imagination (STEWART); **c.** the action or faculty of forming a CONCEPT 1830. **5.** That which is conceived in the mind; an idea, notion 1526; †a mere fancy (SHAKS.). **6.** *Philos.* **a.** In a general sense = 5. 1640. **b.** A general notion, a CONCEPT 1785. **7.** Origination in the mind 1822; an original idea; a design, plan 1606. †**8.** A conceit. DRYDEN.

1. *fig.* Ioy had the like c. in our eies, And at that instant, like a babe sprung up *Timon* I. ii. 115. **3.** Lovely beyond c. TYNDALL. *In my c.*: to my apprehension. **4. a.** All evidence is c., and all c. is imagination, and proceedeth from sense HOBBES. **5.** I can give you no c. of my welcome here DICKENS. **6. a.** The mind..can never attain a full and adequate c. of infinity HUME. **b.** The object of a c. is universal, of a perception, individual CAIRD. **7.** I haue a young c. in my braine *Tr. & Cr.* I. iii. 312. Hence **Conce·ptional** *a.* pertaining to, or of the nature of, a c. †**Conce·ptionalist,** erron. f. *Conceptualist.* So **Conce·ptionist.** †**Conce·ptious,** apt to conceive.

Conceptive (kǫnse·ptiv), *a.* 1640. [ad. L. *conceptivus*, f. *concept-*; see above and -IVE.] Having the faculty or attribute of conceiving. (Rare in the physical sense.)

Conceptual (kǫnse·ptiuăl), *a.* 1834. [ad. med.L. *conceptualis*, f. *conceptus*; cf. F. *conceptuel.*] Of, pertaining to, or relating to, mental conceptions or concepts.

Conceptualism (kǫnse·ptiuăliz'm). 1837. [mod. f. prec. + -ISM.] **1.** The scholastic doctrine that universals exist as mental concepts (only): opp. to Realism and Nominalism. **2.** The psychological doctrine that the mind is capable of forming an idea (*i. e.* mental image) corresponding to the general term 1837. So **Conce·ptualist,** an adherent of C. Also *attrib.*

Concern (kǫnsɔ̄·ɹn), *v.* 1450. [ad. F. *concerner*, ad. L. *concernere*, f. *con-* + *cernere* to sift, separate, discern, regard.] †**1.** To distinguish, perceive –1589. **2.** *trans.* To have relation or reference to 1526. **3.** To affect; to involve 1586. 4. To be of importance to 1603. Also †*absol.* or *intr.* †5. To engage the attention of -1749. †6. To cause to have a part *in*; to engage -1679. 7. In the imperative = 'Confound!' *dial.* 1877. 8. Passive, *To be concerned.*

This occurs in senses 5, 6, which are obsolete in the active; in other senses it is more used than the active.

2. Prudence concerns the present time EMERSON. *As concerns* (= *as it concerns*): with regard to. 3. Such things as..concerne the honour of the Scotish nation THYNNE. 4. *Meas. for M.* I. i. 78. *Two Gent.* II. ii. 77. 5. Which to deny, concernes more than auailes *Wint. T.* III. ii. 87. 6. *To c. oneself*: to interest oneself *with, in, about, to do a thing.* 8. I..am Concerned to see the time goe away and nothing done 1693. (Cf. sense 5.) To be concern'd in a Patent BENTLEY, riot 1802. (Cf. sense 6.)

Concern (kǫnsɔ̄·ɹn), *sb.* 1589. [f. prec. vb.; cf. *regard, respect.*]

I. †1. Regard; concernment -1694. 2. (Usu. in *pl.*) A business or practical relation 1699. 3. Interest, share *in* 1720. 4. Solicitous regard, anxiety 1697.

2. *To have no c.* (formerly *concerns*) *with*: to have nothing to do with. 3. How many gentlemen.. took a c. in the..undertaking of 1745 SCOTT. 4. Without c. he hears..Of..distant war DRYDEN.

II. 1. A matter that relates to some person or thing 1707. *pl.* Affairs 1675. 2. A matter that affects or touches one 1700. †3. *pl.* Belongings 1693. 4. A business; a firm 1681. 5. *familiarly.* Any contrivance or object; usu. depreciatory 1834.

1. †*General* or *public c.*: the commonwealth. Of.. every-day concerns SOUTHEY. 2. It is no c. of mine (*mod.*). 4. The bank..became a flourishing c. CRUMP. 5. A tin c., like a chimney-cowl S. LOVER.

†**Conce·rnancy.** *rare.* ? = CONCERNMENT. *Haml.* V. ii. 128 (Qq.).

Concerned (kǫnsɔ̄·ɹnd), *ppl. a.* 1656. [f. CONCERN *v.*] 1. Interested, involved; troubled, anxious; showing concern. 2. U.S. *slang.* Confounded. 3. *adv.* 1848.

Phr. *C. with* (*in*) *drink*: the worse for liquor; also simply *concerned.* Now *low* or *dial.* Hence **Conce·rned-ly** *adv.*, **-ness.**

†**Conce·rning,** *vbl. sb.* 1594. [f. as prec. + -ING[1].] The taking of concern; concernment; a concern -1642.

Conce·rning, *ppl. a.* 1649. [f. as prec. + -ING[2].] That is of concern; important (*arch.*).

So c. a truth MORE. Soul-c. doctrines 1869. Hence †**Conce·rningly** *adv.* in a c. manner. **Conce·rningness,** importance; bearing.

Concerning (kǫnsɔ̄·ɹniŋ), *prep.* 1535. [f. prec.; cf. *regarding, touching.*] 1. Regarding, touching, in reference or relation to; about. †2. = 'As to'. (Now usually *as concerns.*) -1656.

1. I spake it not to you c. bread *Matt.* xvi. 11.

Concernment (kǫnsɔ̄·ɹnmĕnt). 1610. [f. CONCERN *v.* + -MENT.] †1. A matter concerning any person or thing -1654. 2. An interest (*arch.*) 1627. 3. An affair, business, concern 1621. 4. Relation. Commonly after *of.* 1622. 5. Importance 1642. †6. Interest -1691. 7. Interference, participation 1647. 8. Solicitude, anxiety, etc. 1652.

2. The concernments of the poor FULLER. 3. Our civil concernments WATTS. 4. Matters of private c. LD. BROUGHAM. 5. Matter of vital c. MORLEY. 8. A sensible c. at what had passed 1693.

Concert (kǫ·nsəɹt), *sb.* 1665. [a. F., ad. It. *concerto*, f. *concertare* to CONCERT. See CONSORT.] 1. Agreement in a plan, or design; union formed by such agreement; accordance, harmony. †2. Accordance of voices or instruments -1770. Also *transf.* and *fig.* †3. A choir -1743. 4. A musical performance in which several performers take part 1689.

1. By c. and agreement DE FOE. To work in c. TYNDALL. 2. A rare c. of four Trumpets Marine 1674. 4. Going..to Martini's c. at Milan STERNE. *Dutch c.*, 'where each performer plays a different tune'. *Slang Dict. Comb.* **c.-pitch,** 'a pitch slightly higher than the ordinary pitch, used at concerts for brilliancy and effect' (Grove); also *fig.*

Concert (kǫnsɔ̄·ɹt). *v.* 1598. [ad. F. *concerter*, ad. It. *concertare* to proportion together; of obscure origin.] †1. *trans.* To bring to unity -1696. 2. To arrange by mutual agreement 1694; to plan 1712; *intr.* to form plans (? *Obs.*) 1707. †3. [L. *concertare.*] To dispute 1689.

2. To c. an insurrection THIRLWALL. I must now c. matters about y[t] Affair HEARNE. *intr.* We concerted on the most proper methods NELSON. Hence **Conce·rted** *ppl. a.* agreed upon; planned, contrived; done in concert; *Mus.* arranged in parts for several voices or instruments. **Conce·rter.**

‖**Concertante** (kontʃerta·nte), *sb.* and *a.* 1730. [It. ppl. a. f. *concertare.*] *Mus.* A piece of music for orchestra in which there were parts for solo instruments; also, a composition for several solo instruments without orchestra. Now usu. *attrib.*

†**Concerta·tion.** 1509. [ad. L. *concertationem.*] Contention; disputation -1677.

Concertina (kǫnsəɹtī·nă). 1837. [f. CONCERT + -INA.] A portable musical instrument, consisting of a pair of bellows, usually polygonal in form, with a set of keys at each end, which on being pressed admit wind to free metallic reeds. Hence **Concerti·nist.**

‖**Concertino** (kontʃertī·no). 1880. [It. dim. of *concerto.*] *Mus.* 1. A shorter concerto. 2. The group of solo instruments in a concerto.

†**Conce·rtion.** YOUNG *Nt. Th.* ix. 1422. Some edd. have *consertion.* App. irreg. f. *concert* vb. = 'contrivance'.

‖**Concerto** (kontʃe·rto, kǫnsɔ̄·ɹto). 1730. [It.] *Mus.* A composition for one, or sometimes more, solo instruments accompanied by orchestra; now usually in three movements. (Formerly applied to various compositions for a number of instruments.)

Concessible (kǫnse·sib'l), *a.* 1767. [f. L. *concess-*; see CONCESSION and -IBLE.] That can be conceded.

Concession (kǫnse·ʃən). 1611. [ad. L. *concessionem*, f. *concess-*, *concedere* to CONCEDE.] 1. The action of conceding (anything asked or required) 1647; a grant 1611. 2. Admission of a point claimed in argument 1628. 3. A grant by government of a right or privilege, or of land 1656; land so allotted 1846.

1. The c. of these charters was in a parliamentary way HALE. 2. The atheists of the age have been described as triumphing in my concessions PRIESTLEY. 3. The execution of the [Suez] canal..A Frenchman has obtained the c. 1856. In Canada..Between the concessions there are roads, called c. roads 1846. So ‖**Concessionaire, -onnaire,** a person who has obtained a c. Hence **Conce·ssionary** *a.* pertaining to, or of the nature of, c.; *sb.* = *Concessionaire.* **Conce·ssionist,** one who advocates c.

Concessive (kǫnse·siv), *a.* (and *sb.*) 1711. [ad. L. *concessivus*; see above.] 1. Of the nature of or tending to concession 1876. 2. *Gram.* Expressive of concession. 3. *sb. Gram.* A concessive particle, clause, etc. 1765. Hence **Conce·ssive-ly** *adv.*, **-ness.**

Concessor (kǫnse·səɹ). *rare.* 1660. [f. L. *concess-*; see above.] One who concedes. Hence †**Conce·ssory** *a. rare* = CONCESSIVE 1.

‖**Concetto** (kontʃe·tto). Pl. **-tti.** 1737. [It. :—L. *conceptum.*] = CONCEIT *sb.* 7. Hence **Conce·ttism,** use of *concetti* in literature.

Conch (kǫŋk). 1520. [ad. L. *concha*, a. Gr. κόγχη mussel, shell-like cavity, etc.] 1. A shell-fish; orig. a bivalve; later, a large gastropod, esp. *Strombus gigas.* 2. The shell of a mollusc 1774. 3. Such a shell used as an instrument of call. *esp.* That used by Tritons as a trumpet. 1764. 4. A Roman vessel [L. *concha*], used for oil, salt, etc. Also *fig.* 1839. 5. *Archit.* The domed roof of a semicircular apse; also, the apse 1849. 6. *Anat.* The external ear; = CONCHA 4. 1836. 7. (Also *conk.*) A nickname for the lower class of inhabitants of the Bahamas, the Florida Keys, etc., from their use of conchs as food. Hence **Co·nched** *ppl. a.* having a c.

‖**Concha** (kǫ·ŋkă). Also (in sense 2) **conca.** 1613. [L.; see prec.] †1. *Zool.* = CONCH 1, 2. -1776. 2. *Archit.* = CONCH 5; also, a coved ceiling 1613. 3. = CONCH 4. 4. *Anat.* The central concavity of the external ear; *occas.*, the whole external ear 1683. Hence **Co·nchate** *a.* = *Conched.* **Conchi·fera** *sb. pl.*, *Zool.* a division of Molluscs: the *Lamellibranchiata* or ordinary bivalves, as the Oyster, etc.; *sing.* **Co·nchifer,** one of these. **Conchi·ferous** *a.* shell-bearing; *occas.*, bivalve; *Geol.* containing shells.

Co·nchinine. [transp. of *cinchonine.*] *Chem.* = QUINIDINE.

Conchiolin (kǫŋkəi·ŏlin). 1870. [L. *concha* + *-ol-* dim. + -IN.] *Chem.* The organic constituent of the shells of molluscs.

†**Conchite** (kǫ·ŋkəit). 1677. [ad. Gr. κογχίτης (λίθος).] A stone resembling a shell, a fossil shell -1758. Hence **Conchi·tic** *a.*, *Geol.* abounding in (fossil) shells.

Conchoid (kǫ·ŋkoid). 1797. [ad. Gr. κογχοειδής mussel-like: in mod.F. *conchoïde.*] *sb. Geom.* A plane curve of the fourth order invented by Nicomedes 1798. As *adj.* = CONCHOIDAL.

Conchoidal (kǫŋkoi·dăl), *a.* 1666. [f. as prec.] 1. *Geom.* Pertaining to, or resembling, a conchoid. 2. *Min.*, etc. Applied to a fracture presenting smooth shell-like convexities and concavities 1802.

Conchologist (kǫŋkǫ·lŏdʒist). 1784. [f. CONCHOLOGY + -IST.] A student of conchology; a collector of shells; a carrier-shell mollusc.

Conchology (kǫŋkǫ·lŏdʒi). 1776. [f. Gr. κογχο-, comb. f. Gr. κόγχη; see -LOGY.] The science or study of shells and shell-fish. Hence **Concholo·gical** *a.* of or relating to c. **Concholo·gically** *adv.*

Conchometer (kǫŋkǫ·mītəɹ). 1828. [f. as prec.] An instrument for measuring shells and the angles of their spires. So **Concho·metry.**

Conchospi·ral. 1864. [f. Gr. κογχο- (see CONCHOLOGY) + -SPIRAL.] A kind of spiral curve exemplified in shells.

Conchy (kǫ·nʃi). *War slang.* 1917. abbrev. of '*consci*entious objector' (to military service).

†**Conchyle.** 1610. [ad. L. *conchylium*; see next; and cf. COCKLE.] A shell-fish; a conch -1706. Hence †**Conchyla·ceous** *a.* shelly 1799.

‖**Conchy·lia,** *sb. pl.* 1619. [L. pl. of *conchylium*, a. Gr. κογχύλιον, dim. of κογχύλη = κόγχη; see CONCH.] Shell-fish, *Conchifera.* Hence **Conchylia·ceous** *a.* of the nature of molluscous shells; shelly. **Conchy·liated** *a.* embodied in or derived from shells. **Conchyli·ferous** *a.* conchiferous. **Conchylio·logist, -o·logy** = CONCHOLOGIST, -OLOGY. **Conchylio·meter, -o·metry** = CONCHOMETER, etc. **Conchyliomo·rphite,** the fossil impression of a shell. **Conchy·lious** *a.* of or belonging to the CONCHYLIA.

†**Conciator.** [ad. It. *conciatore* mender.] A workman who assorts and allots the proportion of salt required in glass-making. (Never in Eng. use.)

‖**Concierge** (końsyęrʒ). 1646. [F.: deriv. unkn.] 1. The custodian of a house, castle, prison, etc. Now *Hist.* 2. In France, etc.: The person who has charge of the entrance of a building; a janitor, porter. Hence ‖**Concie·rgerie,** the office, lodge, or residence of a c.; also, name of a prison belonging to the Palace of Justice in Paris.

†**Conci·le,** *v.* ME. [ad. L. *conciliare*; see CONCILIATE.] To reconcile; to conciliate -1744. Hence †**Conci·liable** *a.*

†**Conci·liable,** *sb.* 1521. [ad. L. *conciliabulum*, f. *concilium.*] A small or secret assembly; a conventicle -1642. var. **Conci·liabule.** (Also in mod.F.)

Conciliar (kǫnsi·liăɹ), *a.* 1677. [f. L. *concilium* + -AR.] Of or pertaining to a council. var. †**Conciliary.**

Conciliate (kǫnsi·li‚eit), *v.* 1545. [f. L. *conciliat-*, *conciliare*, f. *concilium* COUNCIL.] †1. *trans.* To procure as an addition -1794. 2. To gain (goodwill, etc.) by acts which induce friendly feeling. Const. *to, for.* 1545. 3. To reconcile, make accordant 1573. †4. *intr.* To make friends *with* -1775. 5. To soothe, placate. Also *absol.* 1782.

2. The arts which c. popularity MACAULAY. 3. To c. the qualities of a soldier with those of a philosopher GIBBON. Hence **Conci·liative** *a.* conciliatory. **Conci·liator.** **Conci·liatoriness.** **Conci·liatory** *a.* tending, or calculated, to c.

Conciliation (kǫnsi·li‚ē·ʃən). 1543. [ad. L. *conciliationem.*] The action of conciliating, or state of being conciliated.

A policy of studied c. FROUDE. The c. of human libertie with Divine predetermination of the wil GALE. *Court of c.*: a court for composing disputes by offering to the parties a voluntary settlement.

‖**Conci·lium.** 1834. The Latin equiv. of COUNCIL; occas. used in techn. language.

Concinnate (kǫnsi·nēt), *ppl. a. rare.* 1548. [ad. L. *concinnatus*; see next.] †1. As *pa. pple.* Made fit -1613. 2. *adj.* Of language: Of studied beauty 1548.

ö (Ger. Köln). ǒ (Fr. peu). ü (Ger. Müller). ü (Fr. dune). ɒ (curl). ē (ēə) (there). ē (ēi) (rein). ę (Fr. faire). ɔ̄ (fir, fern, earth).

Concinnate (kǫnsi·neᵉit), *v.* Now *rare.* 1601. [f. L. *concinnat-*, *concinnare*, f. *concinnus* neatly put together.] To put together fitly; to set right; to trim, adjust. So †**Conci·nne** *a.*

Concinnity (kǫnsi·nĭti). 1531. [ad. L. *concinnitas*; see -ITY.] **1.** Skilful fitting together of parts; harmony; a harmony. **2.** Studied elegance of style 1577.

2. The graceful c. of Livy 1881.

Concinnous (kǫnsi·nəs), *a.* 1654. [f. L. *concinnus* + -OUS.] **1.** Fitly put together, harmonious (*rare*) 1662. **2.** Characterized by studied elegance of style 1831.

2. That most c... of professors, Mr. Heyne DE QUINCEY.

†**Co·ncion.** 1533. [ad. L. *contionem*, abbrev. of *co(n)ventionem* CONVENTION. Cf. OF. *concion, -tion.*] **1.** An assembly -1587. **2.** An oration before an assembly; a public speech -1644. Hence †**Co·ncional** *a.*; var. †**Co·ncionary.** †**Co·ncionate** *v.* to deliver an oration; to preach. †**Co·nciona:tor,** a preacher. †**Co·nciona:tory** *a.* belonging to a concionator.

Conci·pient, *a. rare.* 1812. [ad. L. *concipientem.*] That conceives, conceiving.

Concise (kǫnsəi·s), *a.* 1590. [ad. L. *concisus*, *concidere* to cut up, f. *con-* + *cædere.* Cf. F. *concis.*] Brief and comprehensive in statement; not diffuse: used of speech or writing; also of persons. Also *transf.*

The c. style, which expresseth not enough, but leaves somewhat to be understood B. JONS. No wonder he was c. JANE AUSTEN. *transf.* His c. repast COWPER. Hence **Conci·se-ly** *adv.*, **-ness.**

†**Concise** (kǫnsəi·z), *v. rare.* 1659. [ad. L. *concis-*; see prec.] To cut off, mutilate -1660.

Concision (kǫnsi·ʒən). ME. [ad. L. *concisionem.*] **1.** A cutting to pieces or cutting away. **2.** In *Phil.* iii. 2, as tr. Gr. κατατομή 'cutting up', applied to the Judaizing Christians 1557; hence, †a schism -1716. **3.** = CONCISENESS 1774.

1. Peplis in the valley of concisioun or sleaynge to gydre WYCLIF *Joel* iii. 14.

†**Conci·te,** *v. rare.* 1554. [a. OF. *conciter*, ad. L. *concitare.*] To stir up, excite -1642. So †**Concita·tion.**

†**Conci·tizen.** ME. [See CON-.] Fellow-citizen -1604.

Concla·mant, *a. rare.* 1890. [ad. L. *conclamant-*, *conclamare.*] Calling out together.

Conclamation (kǫnklămē·ʃən). 1627. [ad. L. *conclamationem*; see prec.] A loud calling out of many together.

Before his funerall c. MAY. Applauses and conclamations HOWELL.

Conclave (kǫ·nklēv). ME. [a. F. :—L. *conclave*, f. *con-* + *clavis* key.] †**1.** A private room, closet -1753. Also *fig.* **2.** *spec.* The place in which the Cardinals meet in private for the election of a Pope ME. **3.** The assembly of cardinals met for this purpose 1625; *loosely*, the body of cardinals 1613. Also *attrib.* **4.** Any close assembly 1568.

2. He..takes care to have the C. built with Timber 1691. 3. Allotting it to the Conclaue of Cardinals HEYLIN. 4. The three..who composed the secret c. or cabinet MOTLEY. Hence **Co·nclavist,** †one of the cardinals in c.; one who attends on a cardinal in c.

Conclude (kǫnklū·d), *v.* ME. [ad. L. *concludere*, f. *con-* + *claudere.*]

I. 1. To shut up, enclose, include (*arch.*). †**2.** To comprehend, comprise -1828; to restrict -1679. †**3.** To shut up *from*; to estop -1705. **b.** To shut up *to*; to bind (still in legal use) ME. †**4.** To overcome in argument; to confute; to convince -1704.

1. *fig.* God hath concluded them all in vnbeliefe *Rom.* xi. 32. 2. Schortly to concluden al his wo CHAUCER. 3. b. In settling the value of a copyhold fine the tenant is not concluded by the amount of rent..reserved on the premises 1883.

II. 1. To bring to an end; to finish ME. **2.** *absol.* To end, finish, close (*with* or *by*) 1514. **3.** *intr.* To come to an end; to close 1592.

1. This concluded the proceedings (*mod.*). 2. And to c., The Victorie fell on vs *Macb.* I. ii. 57. 3. Her heavy anthem still concludes in woe SHAKS.

III. 1. To come to a conclusion, infer, deduce ME. †**2.** *trans.* To lead to the conclusion; to prove -1797. †**3.** *intr.* To be conclusive -1714.

1. Therefore wee c., that a man is justified by faith *Rom.* iii. 28. 3. Thy reason in this case concludeth not 1526.

IV. 1. *trans.* To bring to a decision; to settle 1523. **2.** To decide (*to do* a thing), determine, resolve ME. †**3.** *intr.* To come to a decision *of, on, upon* -1796; to come to terms *with* -1680. †**4.** *trans.* To decide upon -1603.

1. To c. a truce GRAFTON, peace SHAKS. 2. It was concluded to bring him to trial HALLAM. 3. To c. on another maner of peace LD. BERNERS.

Hence †**Conclu·dence, -dency,** concludent quality. †**Conclu·dent** *a.* conclusive, convincing. †**Conclu·dently** *adv.* **Conclu·der.** **Conclu·dingly** *adv.*

†**Conclu·sible,** *a.* 1654. [f. L. *conclus-* + -IBLE.] That may be concluded or inferred.

Conclusion (kǫnklū·ʒən). ME. [a. F., ad. L. *conclusionem.*] **1.** The end, close, finish, wind up (*e.g.* of a speech). **2.** An issue, outcome ME. **3.** *Logic.* A judgement arrived at by reasoning; an inference, deduction, induction ME.; *spec.* the third proposition of a syllogism, deduced from the two premisses 1474; the action of inferring (*rare*) 1532. †**4.** A proposition, dogma -1687; a problem -1663; an experiment -1670. †**5.** Purpose, end. ME. only. **6.** Final determination; final agreement ME. **7.** The concluding (*of* a peace, etc.) 1568. **8.** *Law.* A binding act; an estoppel 1531. **9.** *Sc. Law.* The concluding clause of a Summons 1826.

1. To drawe to a conclusyoun Of thys long tale 1447. The c. is a clarkely gatherynge of the matter spoken before 1553. 2. What will be the c. of all this 1635. Phr. *Inc.*: †at last; to conclude; also (formerly) in short. 3. The sober conclusions of science TYNDALL. He granted him both the major and the minor; but denied him the c. ADDISON. Your Wife Octauia, with her modest eyes, and still C. *Ant. & Cl.* IV. xv. 28. 4. Certayn..conclusions towchyng women CAXTON. She hath persu'de Conclusions infinite Of easie wayes to dye *Ant. & Cl.* v. ii. 358. Phr. *To try conclusions*: to experiment; *transf.* to engage in a trial of skill, etc. (Now assoc. with sense 2, as if = 'to try the issue.') 6. He has come to the c. not to prosecute (*mod.*). 7. By the c. of treaties SEELEY.

Conclusive (kǫnklū·siv), *a.* 1590. [ad. late L. *conclusivus*; see CONCLUDE and -IVE.] †**1.** Summing up. **2.** Occurring at or forming the end; final. (Now *rare.*) 1612. **3.** That closes the question; decisive 1649. †**4.** *Law.* Binding 1649.

2. A c. revolt from Rome FROUDE. 3. Whether these Arguments be c. or no LOCKE. Hence †**Conclu·sive·ly** *adv.*, **-ness.** var. **Conclu·sory.**

‖**Conclusum** (kǫnklū·sǒm). 1798. [L. pa. pple. of *concludere.*] *Diplomacy.* A *résumé* of the demands of a government; dist. from an *ultimatum*, as being open to discussion.

Concoct (kǫnkǫ·kt), *v.* 1533. [f. L. *concoct-*, *concoquere*, f. *con-* + *coquere.*] †**1.** *trans.* To make ready, or mature, by heat (*lit.* and *fig.*) -1673. †*intr.* (for *refl.*) -1830. †**2.** To digest -1825. Also †*fig.* †**3.** To digest in the mind, ruminate on -1654; to brook -1679. †**4.** To secrete -1741. **5.** To make up by mixing a variety of ingredients 1675. **6.** To make up, plan by concert; to make up (a story, project, etc.) 1792.

5. The most potent ale, concocted with spices and a little white sugar SCOTT. 6. A fraud which he had either concocted or condoned BLACK. Hence †**Conco·ct** *pa. pple.* and *ppl. a.* **Conco·cter, -or.**

Concoction (kǫnkǫ·kʃən). 1531. [ad. L. *concoctionem.*] †**1.** Digestion (of food) -1788. Also †*fig.* †**2.** Ripening, maturation -1706. **3.** The act of concocting or preparing from a variety of ingredients; a broth, drink, etc., so concocted 1851. **4.** The making up (of a story, plot, or scheme) to suit a purpose 1823; a statement fictitiously made up 1885.

4. His affidavit was a c. from beginning to end 1885.

Concoctive (kǫnkǫ·ktiv), *a.* 1578. [See CONCOCT and -IVE.] Of or pertaining to concoction; digestive.

Concolorous (kǫnkɒ·lŏrəs), *a.* 1840. [f. L. *concolor* (f. *con-* + *color*) + -OUS.] *Nat. Hist.* Of uniform colour. vars. **Conco·lorate,** †**Co·ncolour.**

Concomitance (kǫnkǫ·mităns). 1535. [ad. med.L. *concomitantia*, f. *concomitantem*; see CONCOMITANT and -ANCE.] **1.** The fact of being concomitant; subsistence together; quasi-*concr.* an instance of this 1652. **2.** *Theol.* The coexistence of the body and blood of Christ in each of the eucharistic elements (*esp.* in the bread) 1535. **3.** *Math.* Exact correspondence of functional transformation between two sets of variables. var. **Conco·mitancy.**

Concomitant (kǫnkǫ·mitănt). 1607. [ad. L. *concomitantem*, *concomitari.*]

A. *adj.* Going together, accompanying, concurrent, attending. Const. *with.*

Either c., assisting, or sole causes.. of melancholy BURTON. Hence **Conco·mitantly** *adv.*

B. *sb.* **1.** An attendant state, quality, circumstance, or thing 1621. †**2.** A companion -1794. **3.** *Math.* Sylvester's name for 'all functions whose relations to the quantic are unaltered by linear transformation' 1853.

1. Death is not so terrible in it selfe, as the concomitants of it BURTON.

†**Conco·mitate,** *v.* 1604. [f. L. *concomitat-*; see above.] To go with, accompany -1666. Hence †**Concomita·tion.**

Concord (kǫ·nkǫɹd, kǫ·ŋkǫɹd), *sb.* ME. [a. F. *concorde* :—L. *concordia*, f. *concors* adj., f. *con-* + *cor, cord-.*] **1.** Agreement between persons. **2.** A state of peace and amity between nations; a treaty establishing such relations ME. **3.** *Law.* An agreement made in court respecting the conveyance of a fine of lands 1531. **4.** Agreement or harmony between things ME. **5.** *Mus.* A combination of notes which is in itself satisfactory to the ear; opp. to *discord* 1589. **6.** *Gram.* Agreement between words in case, number, gender, and person 1530.

1. Devil with Devil damn'd Firm C. holds MILT. *P. L.* II. 497. 2. Abiding by the c. of Salamanca PRESCOTT. 4. C. of sweet sounds *Merch. V.* v. i. 84. If Nature's c. broke MILT. *P. L.* vi. 311. Hence **Concordal** *a.* of or relating to c. (in *Gram.*).

Concord (kǫnkǫ·ɹd), *v.* Now *rare.* ME. [a. F. *concorder*; see prec.] **1.** *intr.* To agree. †**2.** *trans.* To arrange by agreement -1670; to bring into concord -1670. Hence †**Conco·rdable** *a.* †**Conco·rdably** *adv.*

Concordance (kǫnkǫ·ɹdăns), *sb.* ME. [a. F. :—late L. *concordantia*, f. *concordantem*; see CONCORDANT and -ANCE.] **1.** Agreement, harmony 1450. †**2.** *Gram.* = CONCORD *sb.* 6. 1570. **3.** †A citation of parallel passages in a book, *esp.* in the Bible -1714. **b.** An alphabetical arrangement of the principal words contained in a book (*orig.* in the Bible), with citations of the passages in which they occur. Orig. in *pl.*, each group of parallel passages being properly a *concordantia.* ME.

1. Contrasts, and yet concordances CARLYLE. 3. With a true Concordaunce in the margent COVERDALE. I had not a Bible or C. at hand BOYLE. Hence **Conco·rdance** *v.* to make a c. to. **Conco·rdancer.** **Concorda·ntial** *a.* of or pertaining to a c.

†**Conco·rdancy.** 1586. [See prec. and -ANCY.] Agreement -1793.

Concordant (kǫnkǫ·ɹdănt), *a.* 1477. [a. F. :—L. *concordantem*, *concordare*; see CONCORD *v.*] Agreeing; harmonious; consistent; correspondent.

The c. Voice of all the curious Judges 1691. On four c. lines E. DARWIN. Hence **Conco·rdantly** *adv.*

Concordat (kǫnkǫ·ɹdæt). 1616. [a. F., ad. L. *concordatum.*] An agreement, a compact; now, an agreement between church and state, *esp.* between the Roman See and a secular government relative to matters that concern both.

The Agreement settled between Pope Leo X. and Francis I. by an Instrument called the C. 1688.

‖**Concorda·tum.** 1625. [L. pa. pple. of *concordare.*] In *Irish Hist.*, An order in Council relative to the disposal of money set apart for particular purposes of state; a payment under such an order; *loosely*, the *c.-fund*, whence such payments were made.

Concorporate (kǫnkǫ·ɹpŏreᵉit), *v.* 1552. [f. L. *concorporat-*, *concorporare.*] To unite or coalesce into one body or mass. So **Conco·rporate** *a.* united into one body or mass. †**Concorpora·tion.**

Concourse (kǫ·nkoᵊɹs, kǫ·ŋ-). ME. [a. OF. :—L. *concursum*; see CONCUR. In Milton *concou·rse.*] **1.** A running, flowing together, or meeting; †hostile encounter -1667. **2.** An assemblage of people or things; a crowd, throng ME. †**3.** The place of meeting of lines, surfaces, or bodies -1811. †**4.** Concurrence in action, co-operation -1837. †**5.** Course (of time) -1657.

1. Riga, a citty of great c. 1601. The coalition of the good frame of the Universe was not the product of chance, or fortuitous c. of particles of matter HALE. 2. The whole admiring c. gazed on him COWPER. Under some c. of shades MILT. *P. R.* IV. 404. 4. Gods c. working this or that 1617.

Concreate (kǫnkriˌē·t), *v.* Now *rare.* 1625. [See CON-.] *trans.* To create together.

To create a Soul, is to c. the qualities..of it MORE. So †**Concreate** *a.* coeval in creation.

†**Concre·dit,** *v.* 1593. [f. L. *concredit-, concredere*; cf. CREDIT *v.*] **1.** To entrust -1689. **2.** To accredit 1659.

Concremation (kǫnkrĭmē̆·ʃən). *rare.* 1730. [ad. L. *concremationem.*] **1.** Cremation together. **2.** Consumption by fire 1860.

Co·ncrement. 1656. [ad. L. *concrementum*, f. *concre-, concrescere.*] A growing together; growth by assimilation; a concretion.

Concrescence (kǫ̆nkre·sĕns). 1610. [ad. L. *concrescentia*, f. *concrescentem*, f. *con-* + *crescere.*] †**1.** Growth by assimilation 1614. **b.** *Biol.* Growing together of cells, organs, etc.; the coalescence of two individual organisms of low type in generation 1878. **2.** A concretion. ?*Obs.* 1610. So **Concre·scible** *a.* capable of solidifying; capable of growing together. †**Concre·ssion,** erron. f. CONCRETION.

Concrete (kǫnkrīt). 1471. [ad. L. *concretus*, f. *concrescere*; see prec. Orig. stressed *concre·te*, now usually *co·ncrete*]

A. *adj.* †**1.** Grown together -1650. **2.** Made up *of* various elements; composite, compound. ?*Obs.* 1536. **3.** Formed by union or cohesion of particles into a mass; solid (as opp. to *fluid*) 1533. **4.** *Logic* and *Gram.* Applied to a quality viewed *concreted* or adherent to a substance, viz. the adjective; thus *white* (paper, etc.) is the concrete quality, as dist. from *whiteness*, the abstract quality 1528. **5.** Hence, *gen.* Embodied in matter, actual practice, or a particular example. Opp. to *abstract.* (The ordinary current sense) 1656. **6.** Made of concrete.

3. Even to the c. bloud That makes the liver CHAPMAN. 4. The reader should carefully observe that adjectives are c., not abstract JEVONS. 5. It is with man in the c... you are to be concerned BURKE. Hence **Concrete·ly** *adv.*, **-ness.**

B. *sb.* **1.** quasi-*sb.* *A c., the c.*; see A. 4, 5. 1528. **2.** *gen.* A concreted mass; a concrete substance. Also *fig.* (*Obs.* in *lit.* sense, exc. as in next.) 1656. **3.** *spec.* A composition of stone chippings, sand, gravel, pebbles, etc. formed into a mass with cement (or lime); used for building under water, for foundations, pavements, etc. Often *attrib.* 1834.

2. That..c. of truth and error..the Roman Catholic Church 1831.

Concrete (kǫ̆nkrī·t), *v.* 1635. [f. CONCRETE *a.*] **1.** *trans.* To form by cohesion or coalescence of particles, to form into a mass; †to combine (attributes, etc.) -1829. **2.** *intr.* To run into a mass, form a concretion 1677. **3.** To render concrete (*rare*) 1654. **4.** *co·ncrete.* [f. the *sb.* 3.] To treat with concrete; *intr.* to use concrete in building 1875.

1. Sensations combined, blended, or (if one may so speak) concreted together BERKELEY. 3. Without being concreted into an earthly deed HAWTHORNE. Hence **Concre·ter, -or,** one who or that which concretes.

Concretion (kǫ̆nkrī·ʃən). 1541. [ad. L. *concretionem*; see CONCRETE.] **1.** The action or process of concreting; concrescence, coalescence 1603. **2.** Congelation or coagulation of a liquid 1612. †**3.** Union with something material or actual -1741. **4.** quasi-*concr.* A concrete mass *of* 1626. Also *fig.* **5.** *concr.* A solid mass formed by aggregation and cohesion of particles; a lump, nodule, clot; *esp.* (*Path.*) a calculus; (*Geol.*) a mass formed by aggregation of solid particles, usually round a nucleus 1646.

3. The soul..because of her c. with this mortal body 1652. 4. Salt is a C. of Sea Water 1697. 5. He cut a stony C. out of the Liver 1702. Hence **Concre·tional** *a.* of or pertaining to concretions. **Concre·tionary** *a.* (*Geol.*) of the nature of a c.; consisting of, containing, or characterized by, concretions.

Concretism (kǫ·nkrītiz'm). *rare.* 1865. [f. CONCRETE *a.* + -ISM.] The practice of regarding what is abstract as concrete.

Concretive (kǫ̆nkrī·tiv), *a. rare.* 1646. [f. L. *concret-* (see CONCRETE *v.*) + -IVE.] †**1.** Apt to produce concretions. SIR T. BROWNE. †**2.** = CONCRETE *a.* 5. 1656. **3.** Mentally constructive. Hence **Concre·tively** *adv.*

†**Concrew·,** *v.* [f. F. *concroître* :- L. *concrescere*; cf. ACCRUE.] *intr.* To grow into a mass. SPENSER *F. Q.* IV. vii. 40.

Concubinage (kǫ̆nkiū·binédʒ). ME. [a. F., f. *concubin.*] The cohabiting of a man and a woman who are not legally married; the practice of having a concubine; the state of being a concubine. **b.** *Rom. Law.* 'A kind of inferior marriage of which the issue were natural children, not bastards' (Milman). vars. †**Concu·binacy, Concu·binate.**

Concubinary (kǫ̆nkiū·binări). 1563. [ad. med.L. *concubinarius.*] *adj.* Relating to concubinage; living in, or sprung from, concubinage *sb.* One who lives in concubinage 15... var. **Concubina·rian** *a.*

Concubine (kǫ·ŋkiubəin), *sb.* ME. [a. F. *concubin, concubine* :—L. *concubinus, concubina*, f. *con-* + *cubare.*] **1.** A woman who cohabits with a man without being his wife; a kept mistress. Among polygamous peoples: A 'secondary wife', having a legal status inferior to that of a wife. †**2.** A male paramour -1540.

Co·ncubine, *v. rare.* 1596. [f. prec.] †**1.** To take as a concubine. **2.** To furnish with a concubine or concubines 1800.

†**Concu·lcate,** *v.* 1555. [f. L. *conculcat-, conculcare.*] To tread under foot -1708. Also *fig.* Hence †**Conculca·tion.**

†**Concu·mbency.** [f. L. *concumbere.*] A lying together. JER. TAYLOR.

Concupiscence (kǫ̆nkiū·pisĕns). ME. [ad. L. *concupiscentia*, f. *concupiscere*, inceptive of *concupere*, f. *con-* intensive + *cupere.*] **1.** Vehement desire; in *Theol.* use, desire for the 'things of the world'. **2.** *esp.* Libidinous desire, sexual appetite, lust ME.

1. Such is the fire of c., raging within, that..no houses or fields content these PUSEY. var. †**Concu·piscency** (*rare*). So **Concu·piscent** *a.* eagerly desirous; lustful; **-ly** *adv.* Hence †**Concupisce·ntial** *a.* relating to, or of the nature of, c. So †**Concupisce·ntious** *a.*

Concupiscible (kǫ̆nkiū·pisib'l), *a.* ME. [a. F., ad. L. *concupiscibilis.*] †**1.** Vehemently to be desired -1762. **2.** Vehemently desirous; of the nature of concupiscence ME.

2. The irascible or the c. principle is ever insurgent against reason NEWMAN.

†**Co·ncupy.** ? Abbrev. of *concubine*; or ? = *concupiscence. Tr. & Cr.* V. ii. 177.

Concur (kǫ̆nkʊ̄·ɹ), *v.* 1470. [ad. L. *concurrere.*] **1.** *intr.* To run together; to meet; to converge and meet, as lines, etc.; to coincide. *Eccl.* Of two feasts: To fall on two consecutive days, so that the second vespers of the one coincide with the first of the other 1883. **2.** To combine in action, to co-operate 1549. **3.** To agree in opinion (*with*) 1590. †**4.** To agree in quality, character, etc. -1788. **5.** *Law.* Of rights, etc.: To cover the same ground; hence, to conflict 1613.

1. Anon, they fierce encountring both concur'd, With griesly looks 1587. The..humours do concurre together unto the offended part 1643. Right and victory do not always c. SELDEN. 2. All things concurre to give it a perfection G. HERBERT. 3. For the censure I doe concurre with Mr Chancellor 1631. 4. It was now twilight concurring with the disorder of his mind H. WALPOLE. Hence **Concu·rringly** *adv.*

Concurbit, obs. f. CUCURBIT. CHAUCER.

Concurrence (kǫ̆nkʊ·rĕns). 1525. [ad. med. L. *concurrentia*, or ? f. *concurrent.*] **1.** A running together in time or place; meeting, combination. *Eccl.* (see CONCUR *v.* 1) 1863. **2.** Co-operation of agents or causes 1525. **3.** Agreement; assent, consent 1669. ‖**4.** Competition. (Now a Gallicism.) 1603. **5.** Joint right or authority 1809.

1. A c. of three strong tides BRERETON. A c. of all nations LITHGOW. The c. of the optic axes BERKELEY. Our Behaviour in every C. of Affairs ADDISON. 2. Their mutual C. in doing good ADDISON. 4. To reduce, by increased c., the wages of the remainder LECKY. var. **Concu·rrency.**

Concurrent (kǫ̆nkʊ·rĕnt). 1495. [ad. L. *concurrentem.*]

A. *adj.* **1.** Running together in space; going on side by side; existing or arising together; conjoint, associated. **2.** *Geom.* Meeting in or tending to the same point. **3.** Acting in conjunction; co-operating 1532. **4.** Agreeing; expressing concurrence 1542. **5.** *Law.* Covering the same ground (hence = conflicting, as titles); co-ordinate 1531.

1. The c. existence of two distinct systems of jurisprudence WILLIAMS. 4. A c. consent of all Histories R. COKE. 5. The chancery has a c. jurisdiction with them BLACKSTONE. **Concu·rrent-ly** *adv.*, **-ness.**

B. *sb.* **1.** A concurrent circumstance, a contributory cause 1667. **2.** A competitor. Now *rare* (exc. as a Gallicism). 1581. †**3.** A contemporary person or thing -1668. **4.** 'One of the supernumerary days of the year over fifty-two complete weeks;—so called because they concur with the solar cycle, the course of which they follow' (Webster).

1. Each of these three concurrents must be considered as a partial cause, for, abstract one, and the effect is not produced SIR W. HAMILTON.

Concu·rsion. ? *Obs.* 1533. [ad. L. *concursionem.*] Rushing together; concourse.

Concuss (kǫ̆nkʊ·s), *v.* 1597. [f. L. *concuss-, concutere*; f. *con-* + *quatere.*] **1.** *trans.* To shake violently. Chiefly *fig.* **2.** To injure by concussion 1689. **3.** To force by threats (*into, to do*); also *absol.* 1839. Hence †**Concussa·tion,** violent shaking.

Concussion (kǫ̆nkʊ·ʃən). 1490. [ad. L. *concussionem*; see prec.] **1.** The action of violently shaking; particularly, the shock of impact. Also *transf.* and *fig.* **2.** *Surg.* Injury caused to the brain, spine, etc., by the shock of a heavy blow, fall, etc. 1541. **3.** Extortion by threats or violence. Orig. in *Rom. Law.* 1597.

1. A c. of the Heavens HOBBES. 3. C., rapine, pillories, Their catalogue of accusations fill DANIEL. *Comb.* **c.-fuse,** a fuse (in a shell) ignited by c. or impact. Hence †**Concu·ssionary,** one who practises c. (sense 3). So **Concu·ssive** *a.* of the nature of or pertaining to c. **Concu·tient** *a.* meeting with c. THACKERAY.

Concyclic (kǫ̆nsi·klik), *a.* 1871. [See CON-.] *Geom.* **a.** Lying (as a series of points) on the circumference of one circle. **b.** Of two or more conicoids: Giving circular sections when cut by the same system of parallel planes. Also *absol.*

Cond, cund (kʊnd, kǫnd), *v.* ? *Obs.* ME. [app. f. *condie* CONDUE.] = CON *v.*[2]

Condemn (kǫ̆nde·m), *v.* ME. [a. OF. *condem(p)ner, condamner*, ad. L. *condem(p)nare.*] **1.** To pronounce an adverse judgement on; to censure, blame. **2.** To give judicial sentence against; to convict. Opp. to *acquit, absolve.* ME. **3.** To pronounce guilty *of* 1535. **4.** *fig.* To doom 1653. **5.** To adjudge or pronounce forfeited, as a prize of war, etc. 1705. **6.** To adjudge or pronounce to be unfit for use or consumption 1745. **7.** Of a door or window: To close or block up 1565.

1. A fault in reasoning which Aristotle condemns REID. Their looks c. them (*mod.*). 2. The Iudges..shall justifie the righteous, and condemne the wicked *Deut.* xxv. 1. Condemned in as much as they are worth 1642, to do penance in the streets of London GREEN. 3. Condempned of highe treason 1535. 4. Condemn'd in bus'ness or in arts to drudge POPE. Hence **Conde·mnable** *a.*; **-bly** *adv.* **Conde·mned** *ppl. a.* in the senses of the vb.; *spec.* appropriated to condemned persons, or things rejected. **Conde·mner.** **Conde·mningly** *adv.*

Condemnation (kǫndemnē̆·ʃən). ME. [ad. L. *condemnationem.*] **1.** The action of condemning; judicial conviction; expression of disapprobation. **2.** The fact or condition of being condemned 1557. **3.** The ground or reason for condemning 1534. **4.** A sentence of forfeiture. Cf. CONDEMN 5. 1885.

1. A manifest c. of the Innocent HOBBES. His illiberal c. of a medicine 1803. 2. To whom belongs But c., ignominy and shame MILT. *P. R.* III. 136. 3. Speake, or thy silence on the instant, is Thy c. and thy death *Cymb.* III. v. 98.

Condemnatory (kǫnde·mnătəri), *a.* 1563. [f. L. *condemnat-, condemnare* to CONDEMN + -ORY.] Having the character of condemning; expressing condemnation.

After their c. sentence SPEED.

Condensable (kǫnde·nsăb'l), *a.* Also *erron.* **-ible.** 1644. [f. L. *condensare* to CONDENSE; see -BLE.] That may be condensed, as *c. vapour.* Hence **Condensabi·lity.**

Condensate (kǫ̆nde·nsēᶦt), *v.* Now *rare* or *Obs.* 1555. [f. ppl. stem of L. *condensare.*] To condense (*trans.* and *intr.*). So †**Conde·nsate** *ppl. a.* **Conde·nsate** *sb.* a product of condensation. Hence **Conde·nsator** (*rare*), a condenser.

Condensation (kǫndensē̆·ʃən). 1603. [ad. L. *condensationem.*] **1.** The action of making or becoming more dense. **2.** *spec.* The conversion of a substance from the state of gas or vapour to the liquid, or (rarely) to the solid, condition 1614. **3.** Condensed condition 1626;

a condensed mass *of* anything 1665. 4. *fig.* Compression of thought into few words 1794.

1. The c. of air in the receiver LARDNER. C. (of light) by means of a lens 1832. 2. The c. of milk into a viscous mass (*mod.*). 4. A want of arrangement and c. in his memoirs LYELL.

†**Condense,** *a.* 1610. [ad. L. *condensus.*] Dense, condensed -1794.

Condense (kǫ̆nde·ns), *v.* 1477. [ad. F. *condenser*, ad. L. *condensare*, f. *condensus.*] 1. To make dense, increase the density of; to reduce in volume; to compress, thicken, concentrate. 2. To reduce from the form of gas or vapour to the liquid or (rarely) the solid condition 1662. Also *intr.* 3. *transf.* and *fig* To bring together closely or in small compass; to concentrate 1803. 4. *intr.* (for *refl.*) To become dense; to become reduced in volume 1704.

1. Sweet Honey some c. DRYDEN. A lens..to collect and c. [the light] on the object 1787. To c. electricity 1870. 2. The air was condensed into clouds 1662. 3. Pope had the art of condensing a thought SHENSTONE. Hence **Conde·nsedness.** **Conde·nsedly** *adv.* **Conde·nsing** *vbl. sb.* and *ppl. a.* (=' for condensing ').

Condenser (kǫ̆nde·nsəɹ). 1686. [f. CONDENSE *v.* Cf. F. *condenseur.*]

I. One who or that which condenses.

Mountain ranges .. serve as condensers for the aqueous vapour HAUGHTON. The c. of Bolingbroke LOWELL.

II. Specific and technical senses:

1. A vessel or apparatus in which vapour is reduced to the liquid (or solid) form; *esp.* **a.** *Steam Engine.* A chamber in which the steam is condensed into water on leaving the cylinder, either by injection of cold water, or by exposure to a chilled surface (*surface c.*) 1769. **b.** *Gas-works.* An apparatus in which the tar, ammonia, etc. mixed with the heated gas are condensed and separated by cooling 1809. **c.** The worm of a still 1874. 2. *Pneumatics.* An apparatus for compressing air; a pneumatic force-pump 1727. 3. *Electr.* An apparatus for accumulating or increasing the intensity of an electric charge 1782. 4. *Optics.* A lens or system of lenses by which light is concentrated on one point or object 1798.

Condensible; see CONDENSABLE.

Condensity (kǫ̆nde·nsĭti). 1611. [ad. F. *condensité*, f. L. *condensus*; cf. *density.*] †1. Density -1814. 2. Pithiness 1885.

†**Co·nder.** 1603. [f. COND *v.*] 1. One who conds or cons a ship -1751. 2. A man stationed on a height overlooking the sea to direct fishing-boats after a shoal of herrings or pilchards; a balker -1867.

Condescend (kǫndĭse·nd), *v.* ME. [ad. F. *condescendre*, ad. L. *condescendere*, f *con-* + *descendere* to DESCEND.] †1. *lit.* To descend -1686. 2. *fig.* To stoop, so far as a particular action is concerned, from one's position of dignity or pride; to deign ME. 3. To be condescending in one's relations with others 1611. †4. To make concessions; to agree -1774. 5. †To come definitely *to* (a point in narration) -1528; to particularize 1549.

2. The Cavaliers condescended to take a lesson in the art of taxation from the Roundheads MACAULAY. 3. Like a true lout, he does not see that they have condescended to him 1863. 4. He was resolved to c. no further to the whims of a person GODWIN. To which desire he condescended WHISTON. 5. We are not going to c. upon particulars 1888. Hence †**Condescended** *ppl. a.* agreed. **Condesce·ndence,** condescension; compliance, concession; *Sc.* a specification of particulars. So †**Condesce·ndency.** **Condesce·ndent,** one who condescends. **Condesce·nder** (*rare*).

Condesce·nding, *ppl. a.* 1654. [f. prec.] 1. That condescends; characterized by condescension. Now usually, Patronizing 1707. †2. Consenting 1654. 3. *Sc.* Going into details 1755. Hence **Condesce·ndingly** *adv.*

Condescension (kǫndĭse·nʃən). 1642. [ad. late L. *condescensionem*; see CONDESCEND.] The action, habit, or quality of condescending. 1. Affability to one's inferiors 1647. †2. The action of stooping to things unworthy -1797. 3. Complaisance 1650. †4. Concession -1720.

1. Familiarity .. in Superiors [is] C. STEELE. 2. Every vice, every c. was imputed to the Duke H. WALPOLE. 3. In..c. to the custom of their Country BENTLEY. So †**Condesce·nsive** *a.* characterized by or given to c. †**Condesce·nt,** condescension; act of condescending.

Condiction (kǫ̆ndi·kʃən). 1818. [ad. L. *condictionem.*] *Rom. Law.* A formal claim of restitution; reclaim of undue payment. So **Condicti·tious** *a.* pertaining to a c.

Condign (kǫ̆ndəi·n), *a.* ME. [a. F. *condigne*, ad. L. *condignus* wholly worthy.] †1. Equal in worth or dignity (*to*) -1854. †2. Worthy, deserving -1632. †3. Worthily deserved, merited; adequate -1683. **b.** Since 1700 usually = ' merited by crimes '.

2. As most condigne to beare the principalite 1513. 3. Euery man shall receaue condigne rewarde or punyshement EDEN. **b.** Brought to c. punishment as a traitor MACAULAY. **Condi·gn·ly** *adv.*, **-ness.**

Condignity (kǫ̆ndi·gnĭti). 1554. [ad. med. L. *condignitas*; see prec.] †1. Worthiness, merit -1668. *spec.* in *Scholastic Theol.* That worthiness of eternal life which a man may possess through good works performed while in a state of grace 1554. †2. Desert -1654.

Condiment (kǫ·ndimĕnt), *sb.* ME. [a. F., ad. L. *condimentum*, f. *condire*; see CONDITE *a.*] Anything of pronounced flavour used as a relish, or to stimulate the appetite.

As for Raddish, and Tarragon..they are for Condiments BACON. Hence †**Condiment** *v. rare*, to season or flavour with a c. **Condime·ntal** *a.* of or belonging to a c.; spicy.

Condisciple (kǫndisəi·p'l). 1554. [See CON-.] A fellow-disciple; a schoolfellow or fellow-student.

†**Condite,** *sb.* 1610. [ad. F. *condit*, or L. *conditum*, neut. of *conditus*; see next.] A preserve or pickle; an electuary -1657.

†**Condi·te,** *a.* ME. [ad. L. *conditus*, pa. pple. of *condire* to season, pickle, etc.] Preserved, pickled; seasoned -1639.

†**Condi·te,** *v.* ME. [f. ppl. stem of L. *condire*; see above.] 1. *trans.* To preserve; to pickle -1725 2. To embalm. Also *fig.* -1659. 3. To season. Also *fig.* -1679.

Condition (kǫ̆ndi·ʃən), *sb.* [ME. *condicion*, a. OF., ad. L. *condicionem* (later *condit-*); app. conn. w. *condicere.*]

I. 1. Something demanded or required as a prerequisite to the granting or performance of something else; a provision, a stipulation. 2. *Law.* In a legal instrument, a provision on which its legal force or effect is made to depend 1588. †3. Covenant, contract, treaty -1718. 4. Something that must exist or be present if something else is to be or take place; a prerequisite ME. †5. A restriction or qualification -1841. 6. A clause expressing a condition in sense 4; called in Logic the *antecedent*, in Grammar the *protasis*, of a conditional proposition 1864.

1. Wilt thou enjoy the good, Then cavil the conditions MILT. C. (= *on c. that*) I had gone bare-foote to India SHAKS. 2. *Conditions of sale*: the provisions under which sale by auction takes place. 3. *Merch. V.* I. iii. 149. 4. The air I breathe, is the c. of my life, not its cause COLERIDGE.

II. 1. Mode or state of being ME. 2. State in regard to wealth; circumstances; hence, social position, estate, rank ME. †3. Mental disposition; character; temper -1611; †*pl.* personal qualities -1830. †4. Nature, character -1586. †5. A characteristic, attribute (of men or things) -1712.

1. His fall'n C. MILT. *P. L.* III. 181. Out of C. to keep the field 1719. *To change one's c.*: to get married (*arch.*). 2. I am, in my c. A Prince *Temp.* III. i. 59. All sorts and conditions of men *Bk. Com. Prayer.* Dress'd like a Woman of C. STEELE. 3. Ye have knavysche condycyouns SHELTON. 5. Heere is the Cate-log of her Conditions *Two Gent.* III. i. 273. Hence †**Condi·tionly** *adv.* = *Conditionally.*

Condi·tion, *v.* 1494. [a. OF. *condicionner*; f. *condition-* CONDITION *sb.*] 1. *intr.* To treat about conditions; to make conditions, bargain *with.* 2. *trans.* To stipulate for; to make the condition 1549; to agree by stipulation *to do* something 1624. 3. To make conditional *on*, *upon* 1530. 4. To govern as a condition 1619. 5. *Metaph.* To subject to the qualifying conditions of finite existence or cognition. Also *transf.* 1829. 6. To charge (a bond) with clauses or conditions 1675. 7. *Comm.* To test the condition or state and quality of goods; *esp.* the amount of moisture in silk 1858. 8. *U.S. Colleges.* To admit under conditions; *i. e.* to admit (a student) to a class conditionally on his passing within a given time in any subject in which he failed at his entrance examination.

1. Dishonouring .. to c. or make any tearmes with such Rascalls SPENSER. 2. We c. with him to obey him 1629. 4. Limits we did not set C. all we do M. ARNOLD. 5. The natural human tendency to c. God by time KINGSLEY. 6. Recognizances..to be Conditioned in the Form hereunder expressed 1675.

Conditional (kǫ̆ndi·ʃənăl). [ME. *condicionel*, a. OF., ad. L. *condicionalem*; see CONDITION *sb.*]

A. *adj.* 1. *gen.* Subject to, depending on, or limited by, one or more conditions; not absolute; made or granted on certain terms ME. 2. *Logic* and *Gram.* Expressing a condition 1530.

1. A Possessor of a Bill may protest against a limited and c. Acceptance SCARLETT 2. *C. judgement* or *proposition*: one consisting of two categorical clauses, the former of which, expressing a condition, is called the *antecedent* (in Grammar *protasis*), the latter, stating the conclusion, is called the *consequent* (*apodosis*). *C. syllogism*: one having a c. proposition for its major premiss.

B. *sb.* (the adj. used ellipt.) A conditional word, clause, conjunction, mood, proposition, or syllogism 1533.

Disjunctives may be turned into Conditionals ATWATER. Hence **Conditiona·lity,** c. quality. **Condi·tionally** *adv.* in a c. manner; †on condition (that).

Conditionate (kǫ̆ndi·ʃənĕt), *a.* 1533. [ad. med.L. *conditionatus*, *conditionare*; cf. F. *conditionné.*] Conditioned; limited by conditions; formerly said of limited monarchs. Hence **Condi·tionately** *adv.* As *sb.* A thing conditioned; a contingency 1678.

Conditionate (kǫ̆ndi·ʃəneit), *v.* 1533. [ad. med.L. *conditionare.*] †1. To stipulate (*trans.* and *intr.*) -1642. 2. *trans.* To limit as a condition; to be, or act as, a condition of 1646.

Conditioned (kǫ̆ndi·ʃənd), *ppl. a.* 1450. [f. CONDITION *sb.* and *v.*] 1. (from the *sb.*) Having a (specified) disposition or temperament; in a (specified) condition or state 1548; circumstanced, situated 1831. 2. (from the *vb.*) Subjected to conditions or limitations 1841. †3. Used *absol.* = Provided, on the condition -1641.

1. An ill-c. woman 1860, planet HELPS. 2. The ultimate purpose of all c. existence 1849. *The c.* (*Metaph.*): That which is subject to the conditions of finite existence and cognition; opp. to the *unconditioned, absolute*, or *infinite* 1829.

†**Co·nditory.** 1705. [ad. L. *conditorium.*] A repository; *spec.* for the dead.

Condivi·sion. 1837. [See CON-.] One of two or more co-existing logical divisions.

†**Condo·g,** *v.* 1592. [? joc. for *concur* (*cur* = dog).] *intr.* To concur -1678.

Condolatory (kǫ̆ndōu·lătəri), *a.* 1730. [f. CONDOLE *v.*: not on L. analogies.] Expressive of or intending condolence.

Condole (kǫ̆ndōu·l), *v.* 1460. [ad. L. *condolere.*] 1. *intr.* †To sorrow greatly -1650; to grieve or express sympathy *with* 1603. Also *absol.* †2. *trans.* To grieve over, lament -1788; to grieve with (a sufferer) -1827. Also †*refl.*

1. I contented myself to sit by him, and c. with him in Silence STEELE. 2. A person..whose sufferings I c. RICHARDSON. Let vs c. the Knight SHAKS. Hence **Condo·lement,** condolence; †lamentation. **Condo·ler.** **Condo·lingly** *adv.*

Condolence (kǫ̆ndōu·lĕns). 1603. [f. L. *condolere.*] †1. Sympathetic grief -1721. 2. Outward (*esp.* formal) expression of sympathy with the grief of others 1619.

2. Compliments of C. H. WALPOLE. The condolences of his numerous friends JEFFREY. vars †**Condoleance, Condolance** (in sense 2); †**-ency.**

Condolent (kǫ̆ndōu·lĕnt), *a.* 1460. [ad. L. *condolentem.*] †1. Sorrowing greatly -1490. 2. Sorrowing for another; expressing sympathetic grief 1598.

‖**Condominium** (kǫndomi·niǒm). 1714. [mod.L.: see CON-, DOMINIUM.] Joint control of a state's affairs vested in others.

Condonation (kǫndonē̆·ʃən). 1625. [ad.L. *condonationem*, f. *condonare* to CONDONE.] The pardoning or remission (now *esp.* by implication) of an offence or fault. **b.** *Law.* The action of a husband or wife in the forgiving, or implying forgiveness, of matrimonial infidelity 1788.

Mrs. Brander's easy c. of the sins of one who was 'so pleasant in society' 1885.

Condone (kǫ̆ndōu·n), *v.* 1857. [ad. L. *condonare*; see DONATION, PARDON.] 1. *trans.* To forgive or overlook (an offence); *esp.* to forgive tacitly by not allowing the offence to make any difference in one's relations with the offender. **2.** Of actions, facts: To cause the condonation of 1871.

1. To c. the adultery LD. ST. LEONARDS, his cowardice DE QUINCEY. 2. That fact alone would c. many shortcomings 1871. Hence **Condo·ner.**

Condor (kǫ·ndǫɹ). 1604. [a. Sp., ad. Peruvian *cuntur.*] **1.** A very large S. American bird of the vulture kind (*Sarcorhamphus gryphus*), inhabiting chiefly the high regions of the Andes. **b.** *California Condor*: the great vulture of California (*Cathartes californianus*). **2.** A S. American gold coin.

‖**Condottiere** (kǫndǫttyę̄·re). Also (erron.) -ero. *Pl.* condottieri (-rī). 1794. [It., f. *condotto* conduct.] A professional military captain, who raised a troop, and sold his service to states or princes at war. The system prevailed over Europe from the 14th to the 16th c.

Conduce (kǫ̆ndiū·s), *v.* 1475. [ad. L. *conducere*, f. *con-* + *ducere* to lead, draw. Cf. COND, CONDUCT.] †**1.** *trans.* To lead, conduct, bring (*lit.* and *fig.*). Const. *to.* –1658. †**2.** To bring about –1529. **3.** *intr.* *To c. to*: to lead or tend towards (a result); to contribute to, make for. (The current sense.) 1586.

1. To c. hither the most lovely and vertuous princesse 1651. 3. How circumstances c. severally to the production of effects HOBBES. Virtues which c. to success in life MACAULAY. Hence †**Condu·ceful** *a.* conducive. †**Condu·cement**, the action of conducing, or conducing *to*; tendency. †**Condu·cent** *a.* that conduces; serviceable. †**Condu·cible** *a.* conducive; advantageous; *sb.* a conducible or conducive thing. †**Conducibi·lity.** †**Condu·cibleness. Condu·cingly** *adv.*

Conducive (kǫ̆ndiū·siv), *a.* 1646. [f. CONDUCE *v.* after *conduct, conductive*, etc.] **1.** Conducing or tending to (a specified end); fitted to promote or subserve. Const. *to, towards.* †**2.** Advantageous (*rare*) 1710.

1. Early rising is c. to health 1803. Hence **Condu·civeness.**

Conduct (kǫ·ndǒkt), *sb.*[1] ME. [f. L. *conductus*, *conducere* to CONDUCT, CONDUCE.]

I. 1. The action of conducting; guidance, leading (*lit.* and *fig.*) 1534. **2.** Provision for guidance or conveyance; an escort, a convoy; a pass. *Obs.* exc. in SAFE-CONDUCT. ME. †**3.** A conductor, guide (*lit.* and *fig.*) –1684. †**4.** = CONDUCT-MONEY –1721.

1. By c. of some star SPENSER. Under the c. of chance JOHNSON. 2. I desire of you A C. ouer Land, to Milford-Hauen *Cymb.* III. v. 8.

II. 1. Leadership, command 1470. **2.** Direction, management; handling 1475. †**3.** Skill in managing affairs; discretion –1815. **4.** Manner of conducting oneself or one's life; behaviour. (Now the leading sense.) 1673. (with *a*) †**A** proceeding; a course of conduct (*rare*) 1706.

1. The c. of the arrere-guard HOLLAND, of the vessel 1812. 2. Conduycte of a mater PALSG. The nice c. of a clouded cane POPE. The c. of the background SIR J. REYNOLDS. 3. Thus c. won the prize when courage fail'd DRYDEN. Owing to the Prudence and C. of the Lord Mayor DE FOE. 4. I trusted to profession, when I ought to have attended to c. BURKE.

III. The leading (of water) by a channel 1847; †a CONDUIT, q. v.

Conduct, *pa. pple.*, *a.*, and *sb.*[2] ME. [ad. L. *conductus* hired.] †**A.** *pa. pple.* and *ppl. a.* **1.** Hired –1526. **2.** Conducted –1620. **B.** *sb.* †**1.** A hired workman –1647. **2.** †A salaried priest –1830. **b.** An Eton College chaplain.

B. 2. Standing over against a c. to be catechised H. WALPOLE.

Conduct (kǫ̆ndv·kt), *v.* ME. [f. as CONDUCT *sb.*] **1.** To lead, guide; to escort. Also *fig.* and *absol.* **2.** To lead, command 1450; to direct (an orchestra, a meeting, etc.) 1791; to manage 1632. **3.** *refl.* To comport or behave oneself (in a specified way) 1706. **4.** To convey; (*Physics*) to transmit, serve as a channel or vehicle for ME. †**5.** = CONDUCE –1685.

1. They that conducted Paul, brought him vnto Athens *Acts* xvii. 15. 2. Hasten his Musters, and conduct his powres *Lear* IV. ii. 16. Conducting the correspondence and accounts HT. MARTINEAU. 3. The army never .. conducted itself better WELLINGTON. 4. They conducted water across hills and vallies 1808.

Conductance (kǫ̆ndv·ktăns). 1885. [f. CONDUCT *v.* + -ANCE.] *Electr.* Conducting power.

Conductible (kǫ̆ndv·ktĭb'l), *a.* 1847. [f. L. *conduct-* ppl. stem + -BLE.] Capable of conducting (heat, etc.) or being conducted. Hence **Conductibi·lity**, capacity for conducting (heat, etc.); capacity of being conducted (*rare*).

Conduction (kǫ̆ndv·kʃən). 1538. [ad. L. *conductionem.*] †**1.** = CONDUCT *sb.*[1] I. 1. –1653. †**2.** = CONDUCT *sb.*[1] II. 1–3. –1644. **3.** The conducting of (liquid through a channel or pipe) 1612. **4.** *Physics.* The transmission of heat, etc. from particle to particle of a substance. (The chief current sense.) 1814. **5.** Hiring. *Obs.* exc. in *Rom. Law.* 1538.

4. We know of no other mode of employing a nerve thread than in C. BAIN.

Conducti·tious, *a.* 1607. [f. L. *conduct-*, *conducere* to 'hire'; see -ITIOUS.] Hired; open to hire.

Conductive (kǫ̆ndv·ktiv), *a.* 1528. [f. L. *conduct-* ppl. stem + -IVE.] †**1.** Having the property of conducting or leading –1654. **2.** *Physics.* Conducting, or pertaining to the conduction of, some form of energy (as heat, etc.) 1840.

2. Bodies are c.; and their property is conductivity WHEWELL. Hence **Conducti·vity**, c. quality; var. **Conducti·lity** (*rare*). **Condu·ctively** *adv.* by means of conduction.

Co·nduct-money. 1512. [See CONDUCT *sb.*[1]] **1.** *Hist.* Money paid for the travelling expenses of soldiers; also, an impost exacted under this head by Charles I. **2.** Money paid for the travelling expenses of seamen for the navy 1702, or of witnesses in a trial 1864.

Conductor (kǫ̆ndv·ktəɹ). 1450. [f. L. *conductorem*, f. *conducere* to CONDUCT.] **1.** One who leads, guides, or escorts; a leader, guide (*lit.* and *fig.*) 1481. **2.** †A commander –1649; a director (esp. *Mus.* of an orchestra or chorus) 1784; a manager 1634. **3.** The official who has charge of the passengers, collects fares, etc., on an omnibus, tram-car, or (in U.S.) railroad train (= F. *conducteur*) 1837. **4.** One who hires. [Only as Latin.] 1652. **5.** Anything that conducts, leads, or guides; a channel 1796. †**6.** *Surg.* An instrument formerly used in lithotomy to guide the course of the forceps; a gorget –1847. **7.** *Physics.* A substance having the property of conducting heat, electricity, etc.; *spec.* the name of a certain part of a frictional electric machine, for collecting the electricity, the *prime c.*; also short for *lightning-c.* 1770.

1. Pray do you go along with us, I will be your C. BUNYAN. A principal C. for the Artillery for draught Horses and Ammunition 1661. Hence **Condu·ctorship**, the office or function of a c. **Condu·ctress.**

†**Condue·, condye·,** *v.* (ME. only.) [ad. OF. *conduire.*] To conduct, guide.

Conduit (kv·ndit, kǫ·ndit). ME. [OF. *conduit*, med.L. *conductus*, pronounced as the ME. form *condit* or *cundit.*] **1.** An artificial channel or pipe for conveying water, etc.; an aqueduct, a canal. Also *transf.* and *fig.* **b.** *Electr.* A tube or trough for protecting electric wires; also *attrib.*, as *c. system* 1884. **2.** A fountain (*arch.*) ME. **3.** *Archit.* A walled passage underground for secret communication 1875.

1. As water, whanne the conduyte broken ys CHAUCER. The pores and conduites of the skinne LYTE. *fig.* Language being the great C., whereby Men convey .. Knowledge, from one to another LOCKE. 2. The conduits round the garden sing ROSSETTI. *Comb.* **c.-pipe**, a c. of tubular form; also *fig.*

Conduplicate (kǫ̆ndiū·plikět), *a.* 1777. [ad. L. *conduplicatus*, *conduplicare.*] *Bot.* Doubled or folded together: said of leaves folded down lengthwise along the middle. var. **Condu·plicated.** (Dicts.) So **Conduplica·tion**, a doubling, a repetition 1619.

Condurrite (kǫndv·rəit). 1827. [f. *Condurrow.*] *Min.* A soft black arsenical ore of copper, found in the Condurrow mine, Cornwall.

Condyle (kǫ·ndil). Also **condyl.** 1634. [prob. a. F. *condyle*, ad. L. *condylus*, a. Gr. κόνδυλος a knuckle.] **1.** *Anat.* A rounded process at the end of a bone serving to form an articulation with another bone. **2.** Applied to the rounded ends of the tibia, and similar parts in arthropoda. Hence **Co·ndylar** *a.* pertaining to a c. **Co·ndyloid** *a.* resembling a c.; pertaining to a c.

‖**Condyloma** (kǫndilōu·mă). In 7 **-ome.** Pl. -omata. 1656. [a. L., a. Gr. κονδύλωμα, f. κόνδυλος; see CONDYLE.] *Pathol.* A conical or discoidal prominence of the skin, sometimes syphilitic, occurring near the external openings of the mucous passages, in the larynx, or elsewhere. Hence **Condylo·matous** *a.* of the nature of a c.

Condylopod (kǫndi·lǒpǫd). 1855. [f. mod. L. *condylopus* (= Gr. κονδυλόπους knob-footed).] *Zool.* One of the *Condylopoda*, now called ARTHROPODA. var. **Co·ndylope.**

‖**Condylura** (kǫndiliū°·ra). 1837. [mod.L., f. Gr. κόνδυλος (see CONDYLE) + οὐρά.] *Zool.* Generic name of the Star-nosed Mole of N. America; so called from the knotty appearance of the tail in dried specimens.

Cone (kōun), *sb.* 1562. [ad. L. *conus*, a. Gr. κῶνος pine-cone, etc.] **1.** A solid figure or body, of which the base is a circle, and the summit a point, and every point in the intervening space is in a straight line between the vertex and the circumference of the base 1570. (Called a *right circular c.* when the vertex is on the perpendicular to the centre of the base; an *oblique c.*, when it lies without it. **b.** In *mod. Geom.*, a solid generated by a straight line which always passes through a fixed point called the vertex, and describes any fixed curve (not necessarily a circle) 1865. **c.** A conical mass *of* any substance 1577. **2.** Any cone-shaped object; *esp.* a volcanic peak, formed by the accumulation of scoriæ round the crater 1830. **3.** *Bot.* The fruit of pines and firs; a dry scaly multiple fruit, formed by hard persistent imbricated scales covering naked seeds; a strobile 1562. **4.** *Conchol.* A marine shell of the genus *Conus*, or family *Conidæ*, of Gastropods 1770. **5.** *Meteorol.* A cone-shaped vessel, hoisted as a foul-weather-signal 1875. **6.** *Phys.* One of the minute cone-shaped bodies which form, with the rods, the bacillary layer of the retina 1867. **7.** Any conical apex or point; *e. g.* the apex of a helmet, †of the heart 1603. Also †*transf.*

C. of rays (in *Optics*): a pencil of rays of light diverging from an illuminating point and falling upon a surface. *C. of shade* (in *Astr.*): the conical shadow projected into space by a planet on the side turned from the sun. [Cf. L. *coni umbræ.*] MILT. *P. L.* iv. 776.

Comb.: **c.-bit**, a conical boring-bit; **-flower**, the genus *Rudbeckia*; **-gear**, a method of transmitting motion, by means of two cones rolling together; **c.-in-c.**, a peculiar geological structure, suggesting a number of cones packed one inside another; **-pulley**, a pulley shaped like a truncated c.; **-seat**, a piece of iron forming a seat for the c. or vent-plug in fire-arms; **-shell**, = CONE 4; **-wheel**, a wheel shaped like a truncated c, for transmitting a variable motion to another wheel. Hence **Cone** *v.* to shape like a c. or segment of a c.; *intr.* to bear cones.

Coneine; see CONIINE.

Conenchyma (kǫune·ŋkimă). 1866. [f. Gr. κῶνος + ἔγχυμα.] *Bot.* The tissue of the hairs of plants consisting of conical cells.

‖**Conepatl** (kōu·nīpat'l). 1774. [Mexican: lit. 'little fox'.] An American skunk (genus *Conepatus*, J. E. Gray, 1837).

Conessine (kǫne·səin). [f. *Conessi.*] A bitter base from the bark of *Wrightia antidysenterica* (*Conessi cortex*). Also called *Wrightine.*

Coney, var. of CONY, q. v.

Confab (kǫ̆nfæ·b), *sb.* 1701. [Colloq. abbrev. of CONFABULATION.] A talk together; familiar talk. So **Confa·b** *v.*

Confabulate (kǫ̆nfæ·biŭleit), *v.* 1613. [f. ppl. stem of L. *confabulari*; see FABLE.] *intr.* To talk familiarly together, converse, chat.

I shall not ask Jean Jacques Rousseau If birds c. or no COWPER. Hence **Confabula·tion**, familiar talk; a chat. **Confa·bulator. Confa·bulatory** *a.*

Confarreation (kǫ̆nfærĭ,ē¹·ʃən). 1598. [ad. L. *confarreationem*, f. *confarreare* to unite in marriage by the offering of bread, f. (ult.) *con-* + *far, farris.*] *Rom. Antiq.* The most solemn form of marriage among the Romans, in which an offering of bread was made in the presence of the Pontifex Maximus and ten witnesses.

Confa·ted, *ppl. a.* 1768. [See CON-.] Fated together with (something else).

Confect (kǫ·nfekt), *sb.* 1587. [ad. med.L. *confectum, confecta*, subst. uses of the pa. pple. of *conficere*; see COMFIT.] A comfit.

Cacao .. roasted, and made into Confects H. STUBBE.

Confect (kǫ̆nfe·kt), *v.* 1545. [f. L. *confect-*, *conficere*, f. *con-* + *facere.*] *trans.* †**1.** To put together; to compound –1651. **2.** To make into a confection. ?*Obs.* 1558. †**3.** To prepare (food) for digestion –1605. **4.** To make. [after F. *confectionner.*] 1677.

1. The Phisitions prescription confected by the Apothecary 1580. 4. Patchwork quilts, confected by

fingers of three or four years 1880. So †**Confe·ct** *ppl. a.* confected.

Confection (kǫ̆nfe·kʃən), *sb.* ME. [a. F., ad. L. *confectionem*; see prec.] **1.** Making by mixture of ingredients; mixing, compounding 1477. **2.** A preparation of drugs; a conserve, an electuary ME.; a preparation of fruits, spices, sugar, or the like ME. ‖ **3.** *Dress-making.* The French word for any ready-made article of attire; *esp.* for mantles, cloaks, wraps, etc. 1885.

1. Pots of jam of her c. THACKERAY. 2. Confections are medicinal substances beaten up with sugar into a pasty mass 1875. Delicat confections of spiceries STUBBES. Hence **Confe·ction** *v.* to make into a c.

Confectionary (kǫ̆nfe·kʃənări). 1599. [f. prec. + -ARY.]

A. *adj.* Of the nature of a confection; pertaining to confections or confectioners' work 1669.

The biscuit or c. plum COWPER. C. doings 1824.

B. *sb.* †**1.** A confectioner –1641. **2.** A place where confections are kept or prepared 1616. **3.** A sweetmeat 1599. **4.** *erron.* for CONFECTIONERY 1743.

1. And he will take your daughters to be confectionaries, and to be cookes 1 *Sam.* viii. 13.

Confectioner (kǫ̆nfe·kʃənəɹ). 1591. [f. CONFECTION *v.* + -ER [1].] †**1.** A compounder of medicines, poisons, etc. –1651. **2.** One who makes or sells confections 1591.

Confectionery (kǫ̆nfe·kʃənəri). 1769. [f. prec. + -Y. Often confused with CONFECTIONARY.] **1.** Things made or sold by a confectioner; a collective name for sweetmeats and confections. **2.** The art and business of a confectioner 1872. **3.** A confectioner's shop (*mod.*).

†**Co·nfectory,** *a.* 1648. [ad. L. *confectorius.*] Pertaining to the making of confections.

†**Confe·cture.** ME. [ad. med.L. *confectura.*] = CONFECTION, CONFITURE –1693.

†**Confe·der,** *v.* ME. [a. F. *confédérer*, ad. L. *confœderare.*] The earlier equiv. of CONFEDERATE *v.* –1596.

Confederacy (kǫ̆nfe·dĕrăsi). ME. [f. stem of L. *confœderatio.*] **1.** A union by league or contract between persons, bodies of men, or states, for mutual support or joint action; an alliance, compact. **b.** *Law* (and thence *gen.*): A league for an unlawful or evil purpose; a conspiracy ME. **2.** Condition or fact of being confederate; alliance; conspiracy 1594. **3.** quasi-*concr.* A body of confederates; now *esp.* a union of states, a confederation 1681.

1. A general c. against the Ottoman power 1769. 2. In a perpetual state of c. and rebellion 1828. 3. The stile of this c. shall be 'The United States of America' *U.S. Senate Manual* 1777. The literary world is made up of little confederacies W. IRVING. *Southern C.*: the Confederate States of America.

Confederal (kǫ̆nfe·dĕrăl), *a.* 1866. [after *federal*; see CON-.] Pertaining to a confederation; *spec.* in *U.S. Hist.* pertaining to the organization of the United States under the Articles of Confederation of 1781. Hence **Confe·deralist,** a member of a confederation.

Confederate (kǫ̆nfe·dĕrĕt), *a.* and *sb.* ME. [ad. L. *confœderatus*, pa. ppl. of *confœderare* (trans.); see FEDERATE.]

A. *adj.* **1.** United in a confederacy; leagued, allied, confederated. Also *fig.* **2.** Of or belonging to the Confederate States of America 1861.

1. Syria is c. with Ephraim *Isa.* vii. 2. My heart is not c. with my hand *Rich. II*, v. iii. 53. 2. The C. flag 1861, army 1863.

Phr. *C. States* (*of America*), abbreviated *C.S.A.*: the name assumed by the eleven southern states which seceded from the American Union in 1860–61, and formed a confederacy of their own, which was finally overthrown in 1865.

B. *sb.* **1.** A person or state in league with another or others for mutual support or joint action; an ally 1548. **2.** *Law* (and thence *gen.*): An accomplice 1495. **3.** *U.S. Hist.* One belonging to or on the side of the Confederate States in the War of Secession, 1861–65.

1. The confederates of Cambray MACAULAY. 2. Betrayers of their country, confederates with Wood SWIFT.

Confederate (kǫ̆nfe·dĕrᵉit), *v.* 1531. [perh. f. CONFEDERATE *a.*] To unite in a league. *trans.* and *intr.* (for *refl.*)

To c. others in their design BURKE. The wits easily confederated against him JOHNSON.

Confederation (kǫ̆nfedĕrēⁱ·ʃən). ME. [a. F., ad. L. *confœderationem* (Jerome).] **1.** The action of confederating, or condition of being confederated; a league, an alliance (now only between states); †conspiracy. **2.** A number of states (or formerly of persons) united by a league (now usually on a more permanent basis than in the case of *confederacy*) 1622.

1. Articles of C. and perpetual union between he States of New Hampshire, Massachusetts Bay, Rhode Island, etc. 1777 (*title*). [A] scheme for the c. of the colonies 1885. *Articles of c.*: provisions (in clauses) in accordance with which parties confederate.

Confederative (kǫ̆nfe·derĕtiv), *a.* 1819. [f. L. *confœderat-*; see CONFEDERATE.] Of or relating to confederates or confederating.

Confederator (kǫ̆nfe·dĕrēⁱtəɹ). ? *Obs.* 1536. [f. L. *confœderare.*] A confederate, conspirator.

Confer (kǫ̆nfə̄·ɹ), *v.* 1528. [ad. L. *conferre*, f. *con-* together, and intensive + *ferre.* Cf. COLLATE.] †**1.** *trans.* To bring together, collect –1618. †**2.** To contribute. Const. *to.* –1677. Also †*absol.* **3.** To grant, bestow 1570. †**4.** To bring into comparison, compare, collate. Also *absol.* –1753. †**5.** *intr.* To conform (*with, to*) –1641. **6.** *intr.* To converse, talk together; to take counsel, consult 1545. †**7.** *trans.* To consult about –1689.

2. It confers somewhat to the need, convenience, or comfort of those..creatures BARROW. 3. The stile and title..which the king is pleased to c. BLACKSTONE. The joy of heart which perfect health confers TYNDALL. 4. C. future and times past with present BURTON. 6. They sit conferring by the Parler fire *Tam. Shr.* v. ii. 102. Hence **Conferee·**, one who is conferred with (*U.S.*); one on whom something is conferred. **Confe·rment,** the action of conferring; †something conferred. **Confe·rrable** *a.* that may be conferred. **Confe·rrer.**

Conference (kǫ·nfĕrĕns), *sb.* 1538. [a. F. *conférence*; see CONFER. Cf. COLLATION.] †**1.** Collection; adding up –1651. †**2.** Comparison, *esp.* of texts; collation –1663. **3.** The action of conferring or taking counsel, now always on a serious matter; formerly: Conversation 1555. †**4.** Communication –1651. **5.** A formal meeting for consultation or discussion 1586. **6.** The annual assembly of ministers, etc., of the Wesleyan Methodist Connexion, constituting its central governing body; also the name of other religious bodies. (With capital C.) 1744.

3. Reading maketh a full man, c. a readye man, and writing an exacte man BACON. Moments of serious c. JANE AUSTEN. 5. A message came..from the Lords for present C. upon four bills sent up to them MARVELL. 6. 'C. has forbid the women preaching' GEO. ELIOT. Hence **Co·nference** *v. rare*, to hold c. **Conferе·ntial** *a.* of or relating to c., or to a c.

Conferruminate (kǫnferū̆·minĕt), *a.* 1855. [ad. L. *conferruminatus*; see FERRUMINATE.] *Bot.* Of cotyledons: Consolidated into one body by the coalescence of the contiguous faces. var. **Conferru·mina·ted** *ppl. a.*

‖**Conferva** (kǫ̆nfə̄·ɹvă). Pl. **-væ** (-vi). 1757. [L., perh. comfrey.] *Bot.* A genus of plants consisting of certain fresh-water Green Algæ (*Chlorophyllæ*), composed of unbranched many-celled filaments, and reproduced by zoospores. Formerly of more heterogeneous application. Hence **Conferva·ceous** *a.* of the nature of or allied to the genus *C.*; belonging to the N.O. *Confervaceæ*, comprising that genus and its allies. **Confe·rval** *a.* and *sb.* = *confervoid.* **Confe·rvite,** a fossil plant, allied to C., found chiefly in the chalk. **Confe·rvoid** *a.* of the nature of or resembling a *C.*; *sb.* an alga of the genus *C.* or of any allied genus.

Confess (kǫ̆nfe·s), *v.* ME. [a. OF. *confesser* :—late L. *confessare* = **confessari*, freq. of *confiteri*, ppl. stem *confess-*, f. *con-* + *fateri, fass-*, prob. conn. w. *fari* to speak, utter.]

I. *gen.* **1.** *trans.* To declare or disclose (something previously kept secret as being prejudicial to oneself); to acknowledge, own, or admit (a crime, charge, fault, or the like). Also *absol.* **b.** Often introducing a statement of private feeling or opinion 1450. **2.** To acknowledge for oneself (an assertion or claim, that might be challenged) 1450. **3.** To avow formally *that*, *esp.* as an article of faith 1509. **4.** To declare belief in (a person or thing) as having a certain character or certain claims 1526. **5.** *fig.* To manifest, prove, attest (*poet.*) 1646.

1. And both confess'd..thir faults, and pardon beg'd MILT. *P. L.* x. 1100. b. The hazard I confesse is great 1632. 2. You c. that parliaments are fallible JUNIUS. 4. Al they that do confesse thy holy name *Bk. Com. Prayer.* 5. The voice divine confess'd the warlike maid POPE.

Phr. *C. to* (a thing): To plead guilty to (a charge), own to (a fault); to admit; also, short for *c. to have* (or *having*), as in *to c. to* [*having*] *a dread.*

II. *specifically.* **1.** *Law. intr.* To admit the truth of what is charged; *trans.* to admit as proved or legally valid 1586. **2.** *Eccl.* To acknowledge sins orally as a religious duty (*spec.* to a priest), with repentance and desire of absolution ME. **3.** *trans.* Of the priest: To hear the confession of, to shrive. Also *absol.* ME. *pass.* Of the penitent: To be shriven ME.

1. Phr. *To c. and avoid*: to admit a charge, but show it to be invalid in law. 2. C. yourselves to Almighty God with full purpose of amendment of life *Bk. Com. Prayer.* 3. I haue confes'd her, and I know her vertue *Meas. for M.* v. 533.

Hence **Confe·ssant,** one who confesses, *esp.* to a priest. **Confe·ssed** *ppl. a.* acknowledged as true; admitted; made manifest; shriven. **Confe·ssedly** *adv.* admittedly; avowedly. **Confessee·**, one who is confessed; one to whom confession is made (*rare*). **Confe·sser,** one who confesses or makes confession.

†**Confe·ssary.** 1618. [ad. med.L. *confessarius* (also used).] **1.** A casuist who deals with confession –1649. **2.** A father confessor 1656. **3.** A confessant.

Confession (kǫ̆nfe·ʃən). ME. [a. F., ad. L. *confessionem*; see CONFESS.] **1.** A making known or acknowledging of one's fault, wrong, crime, weakness, etc. 1602. **b.** *Law.* Acknowledgement before the proper authority of the truth of a statement or charge 1574. **2.** The acknowledging of sin or sinfulness ME.; *spec.* the confessing of sins to a priest; more fully, *sacramental* or *auricular c.* ME. **3.** Acknowledgement of a statement, claim, etc.; admission ME. **4.** The acknowledging (of a person or thing) as having a certain character or certain claims ME. **5.** The matter confessed ME. **6.** A formulary containing a general acknowledgement of sinfulness 1535. **7.** (More fully *C. of Faith.*) A formulary in which a church or body of Christians sets forth the religious doctrines which it considers essential; a creed 1536. **8.** A tomb in which a martyr or confessor is buried; the structure erected over it; the crypt, shrine, etc., in which the relics are placed 1670.

1. When we would bring him on to some C. Of his true state *Haml.* III. i. 9. b. *C. and avoidance*: admission to the truth of an adverse allegation, with the allegation of matter tending to avoid its legal effect. 2. Public c. they thought necessary by way of discipline HOOKER. 4. *Haml.* IV. vii. 96. 5. His c. is taken *All's Well* IV. iii. 130. 6. A General C. for every sinner 1535.

Hence **Confe·ssionary** *a.* of or pertaining to c. **Confe·ssionary** *sb.* a confessional; also = CONFESSION 8. **Confe·ssionist,** an adherent of a religious c., *spec.* a Lutheran; a confessionalist. **Confe·ssionless** *a.* having no C. of Faith.

Confe·ssional, *sb.* 1727. [a. F.] A stall or box in which a priest hears confessions.

Confessional (kǫ̆nfe·ʃənăl), *a.* 1817. [f. CONFESSION + AL.] **1.** Of the nature of or pertaining to confession. **2.** Of or pertaining to Confessions of Faith or Creeds 1882. Hence **Confe·ssionalism,** the principle of formulating a Confession of Faith; adherence to a formulated theological system. **Confe·ssionalist,** one who makes confession.

Confessor (kǫ̆nfe·səɹ). ME. [a. L. (and F.), f. L. *confiteri* to CONFESS. Formerly stressed *co·nfessor.*] **1.** *gen.* One who makes confession of anything. **2.** *Eccl.* One who avows and adheres to his faith under persecution and torture, but does not suffer martyrdom. (The earliest sense in English.) ME. **3.** (Often kǫ·nfĕsǫɹ) A priest who hears confessions, prescribes penance, and grants absolution ME.

2. Alle the seyntes of that cuntre [Ireland] be confessores, and noo martir tr. *Higden* (Rolls). *The C.*: = King Edward the C. (d. 1066), canonized in 1611. Hence **Confe·ssoress. Confe·ssorship.**

Confest, etc., var. CONFESSED, etc.

‖**Confetti** (kǫ̆nfe·ti), *sb. pl.* 1860. [It., pl. of *confetto* COMFIT.] Bonbons, or imitations of these, thrown during carnival in Italy; in Eng., *esp.* little disks of coloured paper thrown at weddings, etc.

†**Confi·cient.** *rare.* 1614. [ad. L. *conficient-em.*] An officiating priest –1638.

Confidant (kǫ·nfidæ̆nt). 1714. [Littré has F. *confident* only. The Eng. *-ant* may represent the pronunciation of the F. *-ent, -ente.*] 'A person trusted with private affairs, commonly with affairs of love' (J.). Now used more widely.

He was accustomed to make her his c. in his ecclesiastical proceedings J. H. NEWMAN. So **Co·nfida·nte,** a female c. (perh. formed before the masc.)

Confide (kǫ̆nfəi·d), *v.* 1455. [ad. L. *confidere,* f. *con-* intensive + *fidere.*] **1.** *intr.* To trust or have faith; to put trust, repose confidence *in,* †*on,* †*to.* Also *absol.* **2.** *trans.* To impart in confidence (*to* a person) 1735; to entrust (an object, task, etc.) *to* a person with reliance on his fidelity or competence 1861.

1. Such a person..'as they could c. in' (an expression that grew from that time to be much used) CLARENDON. Judge before Friendship, then c. till Death YOUNG. 2. The execution of the plan was confided to Aranda BUCKLE. Hence **Confi·der. Confi·ding-ly** *adv.*, **-ness.**

Confidence (kǫ·nfidĕns). ME. [ad. L. *confidentia,* f. *confidentem*; see CONFIDENT. Cf. F *confidence.*] **1.** The mental attitude of trusting in or relying on; firm trust, reliance, faith. Const. *in* (†*to, on, upon*). **2.** Assurance; assured expectation 1555. **3.** Assurance arising from reliance (on oneself, circumstances, etc.) 1526. **4.** Excess of assurance, hardihood, presumption, impudence 1594. **5.** That which gives confidence 1535. **6.** Confidential intimacy 1592. **7.** A confidential communication 1748. †**8.** Trustworthiness, as a personal quality –1800. †**9.** *Law.* = TRUST –1848.

1. C...in foraigne ayde 1649. 2. A vain c. of his own abilities 1790. In c. thereof, the Duke left him 1654. 3. Your wisedome is consum'd in c.: Do not go forth to day *Jul. C.* II. ii. 49. 5. For the Lord shalbe thy c. *Prov.* iii. 26. 6. Speaking in c., for I should not like to have my words repeated JOWETT. 7. He will.. be well informed.. by the confidences made him CHESTERF. 8. A person of c. 1777.

Phr. *C. trick* (*game,* etc.): a method of swindling, in which the victim hands over valuables as a token of c. in the sharper. *C. man*: one who practises this trick. So **Co·nfidency** (*rare*).

Confident (kǫ·nfidĕnt). 1588. [ad. L. *confidentem*; and partly a. F. *confident, -ente.*]

A. *adj.* †**1.** Trustful, confiding –1666. **2.** Having confidence; feeling certain, fully assured, sure 1601. **3.** Full of assurance, self-reliant, bold; having no fear of failure 1576. **4.** Overbold; forward, presumptuous, impudent. *Obsolescent.* 1597. **5.** Positive; dogmatical 1611. †**6.** Trusty –1714. **7.** Confidential 1608.

1. Rome, be as iust and gracious vnto me, As I am c. and kinde to thee *Tit. A.* I. i. 61. 2. Reasons they had to be c. of victory THIRLWALL. C. in thy defence WESLEY. 3. His forces strong, his Souldiers c. *John* II. i. 61. 4. A c. slut FIELDING. 5. Your c. and positive way of talking BERKELEY. 6. C. newes 1619. 7. A. c. servant of my masters 1623. Hence **Co·nfidently** *adv.*

B. *sb.* **1.** A trusty adherent; a confidential friend 1619. **2.** *spec.* = CONFIDANT 1647.

Confidential (kǫnfide·nʃăl), *a.* 1759. [f. L. *confidentia* CONFIDENCE + -AL.] **1.** Of the nature of confidence; spoken or written in confidence 1773. **2.** Betokening private intimacy 1759. **3.** Enjoying another's confidence; entrusted with secrets 1805.

1. *C. communication*: one made between parties who stand in a c. relation to each other, and therefore privileged in law. 2. Talking the c. language of friendship in the public theatre BURKE. Hence **Confidentia·lity,** c. quality. **Confide·ntial-ly** *adv.*, **-ness.**

Configurate (kǫ̆nfi·giŭrēɪt), *v.* Now *rare.* 1566. [f. ppl. stem of L. *configurare*; see CONFIGURE *v.*] **1.** *trans.* To frame; to give a configuration to. Also *fig.* †**2.** (?) *intr.* ? To show congruity of structure 1650.

2. Where pyramids to pyramids relate, And the whole fabric doth c. JORDAN. So **Confi·gurative** *a.* of or pertaining to configuration. **Confi·gurature,** shape of countenance.

Configuration (kǫ̆nfigiŭrēɪ·ʃən). 1559. [ad. L. *configurationem*; see CONFIGURE.] **1.** Arrangement of parts in a form or figure; the form resulting from such arrangement; conformation; outline, contour (of geographical features, etc.) 1646. **2.** *Astron.* Relative position, apparent or actual, of celestial bodies; *esp.* the planetary 'aspects', recognized in Judicial Astrology 1559. †**3.** An image. HALE.

1. The remarkable c. of the Atlantic sea-bed HUXLEY. 2. The Disease is found out..from the Configurations of the Planets SALMON.

Configure (kǫ̆nfi·giŭɹ), *v.* Now *rare.* ME. [ad. L. *configurare*; see FIGURE *v.* Cf. F. *configurer.*] **1.** *trans.* To fashion according to a model. **2.** To put together in a form or figure 1652. Also *fig.*

Confinable (kǫ̆nfəi·năb'l), *a.* 1610. [f. CONFINE *v.* + ABLE.] To be confined, capable of confinement.

Vertue..not c. to any limits BP. HALL.

†**Confine,** *a.* 1579. [a. F. *confin, -fine* :—L. *confinis.*] Neighbouring, adjacent –1653.

†**Confine,** *sb.* Always *pl.* **confines.** 1531. [ad. L. *confinis.*] *pl.* Neighbours –1598.

Confine (kǫ·nfəin), *sb.*[2] Mostly in *pl.* **confines.** ME. [a. F. pl. *confins,* in L. *confinia* bounds.] **1.** *pl.* Boundaries, borders 1548; †region –1670. Rarely in *sing.* Also *fig.* **2.** (kǫ̆nfəi·n). Confinement; limitation (*poet.*) 1597; †a place of confinement –1650.

1. Thextreme confines of Egypt EDEN. Heere in these confines slily haue I lurk'd SHAKS. *fig.* The.. confines between Virtue and Vice BENTLEY. 2. Think on the dungeon's grim c. BURNS. Th' extrauagant, and erring Spirit, hyes To his c. *Haml.* I. i. 155. Hence **Confi·neless** *a.* unlimited. *Macb.* IV. iii. 55.

Confine (kǫ̆nfəi·n), *v.* 1523. [a. F. *confiner,* ad. It. *confinare,* f. *confino, confine* :—L. *confinis.* Cf. med.L. *confinare.*] **1.** *intr.* To have a common boundary *with*; to border *on,* be adjacent *to.* Now *rare.* †**2.** *trans.* To border on, bound –1694. †**3.** To relegate *to* certain limits; to banish –1653; to shut up, imprison 1602; to fasten, keep in place 1595. **4.** To keep indoors, or in bed. Usually in passive. Const. *to.* 1634. **5.** *fig.* To limit, restrict 1597. **6.** To constipate; to BIND 1870.

1. The princes which c. uppon that sea 1577. 3. And for the day confin'd to fast in Fiers *Haml.* I. v. 11. Now let not Natures hand Keepe the wilde Flood confin'd 2 *Hen. IV,* I. i. 154. 4. To be confined by gout BERKELEY. Phr. *To be confined*: to be in childbed; to be delivered *of.* 5. Cabin'd, crib'd, confin'd, bound in, To sawcy doubts, and feares *Macb.* III. iv. 24. Hence **Confi·ned-ly** *adv.*, **-ness.**

Confinement (kǫ̆nfəi·nmĕnt). 1646. [a. F., f. *confiner.*] **1.** The action of confining; being confined; imprisonment. **2.** Restriction, limitation 1678. **3.** *spec.* The being in childbed; delivery, accouchment. (The ordinary term in colloq. use.) 1774.

1. The c. of his body within four walls JUNIUS. 2. C. to spare diet BENTHAM.

†**Co·nfiner**[1]. 1599. [f. CONFINE *sb.* or *v.* + -ER[1].] **1.** One who dwells on the confines; a borderer, neighbour –1682. **2.** One living within the confines; an inhabitant 1611.

2. Happie confiners you of other landes DANIEL.

Confi·ner[2]. *rare.* 1654. [f. CONFINE *v.* + -ER[1].] One who or that which confines.

Confinity (kǫ̆nfi·nĭti). ? *Obs.* 1544. [a. F., f. *confin*; see -ITY.] Neighbourhood, contiguity.

Confirm (kǫ̆nfə̄·ɹm), *v.* [ME. *confermen,* a. OF. *confermer* :—L. *confirmare,* f. *con-* + *firmare,* f. *firmus.* In 14–16th c. confused with CONFORM.] **1.** *trans.* To make firm or more firm, to add strength to, establish firmly. **2.** To make valid by formal authoritative assent; to ratify, sanction ME. **3.** *Eccl.* To administer CONFIRMATION to; formerly 'to bishop' ME. **4.** To strengthen (in an opinion, action, or purpose) 1485. **5.** To corroborate; to verify, put beyond doubt ME. †**6.** To affirm *that* –1668. †**7.** To assure, convince –1771.

1. His alliance will confirme our peace 1 *Hen. VI,* V. v. 42. Confirme the feeble knees *Isa.* xxxv. 3. 2. The charters were confirmed by *inspeximus* on the 12th [Oct. 1297] STUBBS. He was confirmed bishop of Couentrie HOLINSHED. Confirme the Crowne to me and to mine Heires 3 *Hen. VI,* I. i. 172. 3. He ordeyned that a chylde sholde be confyrmed as soone as it myght, namely after it was crystened CAXTON. 4. When Mackbeth is confirming himself in the horrid purpose JOHNSON. 5. The News..has not yet been confirmed ADDISON. Hence **Confi·rmable** *a.* that may be confirmed. †**Confi·rmance,** confirmation. **Confi·rmative** *a.* having the property of confirming; **-ly** *adv.* †**Confirmator,** one who or that which confirms. **Confi·rmatory** *a.* corroborative; †*Eccl.* relating to confirmation. **Confirmee·.** *Law.* One to whom a confirmation is made. *Eccl.* One who is confirmed. **Confi·rmer,** one who or that which confirms. †**Confi·rmment,** confirmation. **Confi·rmor** (*Law*), a party who confirms a voidable estate, etc.

Confirmation (kǫnfəɹmēɪ·ʃən). ME. [a. OF., ad. L. *confirmationem*; see CONFIRM.] **1.** The action of making firm or sure; strengthening, settling, establishing 1480. **2.** The action of confirming or ratifying ME. **3.** The action of corroborating, or verifying; verification, proof ME.; a confirmatory statement or circumstance 1553. **4.** *Law.* See quots. Also as in 2. 1495. **5.** *Eccl.* A rite administered to baptized persons in various Christian churches; formerly called 'bishoping'. (It is held to convey special grace which strengthens the recipient for the practice of the Christian faith.) ME.

1. C. of our faith SANDYS, of a title FREEMAN. 2. *C. of the Charters*: *spec.* the c. of Magna Charta and the Charter of the Forests by Edward I in 1297. C. of the Speaker 1886. 3. *Oth.* III. iii. 323. 4. A C. is a conueyance of an estate or right in esse, whereby a voidable estate is made sure and vnauoidable, or whereby a particular estate is encreased COKE *on Litt.*

Confirmed (kǫ̆nfə̄·ɹmd), *ppl. a.* ME. [f. CONFIRM *v.*] **1.** In the senses of the vb. **2.** *spec.* Of a disease: Firmly established in the system; inveterate, chronic; as a *c. cancer* ME. **3.** Firmly established in the habit, etc., expressed by the appellative, as a *c. invalid* 1826.

Confiscate (see the vb.), *ppl. a.* 1533. [ad. L. *confiscatus, confiscare.*] **1.** Appropriated to the use of the state, adjudged forfeited. **2.** Deprived of property as forfeited 1618.

1. And let it be c. all *Cymb.* V. v. 323.

Confiscate (kǫ·nfiskēɪt, -fi·skēɪt), *v.* 1533. [f. L. *confiscat-, confiscare,* through Fr. Till 1835 stressed *confi·scate.*] **1.** *trans.* To appropriate (private property) to the public treasury by way of penalty. †**2.** To deprive of property as forfeited to the state –1662. **3.** *loosely.* To seize as if by authority 1819.

2. The forenamed Lords..were condemned and confiscate RALEIGH. 3. The cargoes he confiscated BYRON. So **Confi·scable** *a.* liable to confiscation. **Confisca·table** *a.* **Co·nfiscator,** one who confiscates. **Confi·scatory** *a.* of the nature of, or tending to, confiscation; robbing under legal authority (*colloq.*).

Confiscation (kǫnfiskēɪ·ʃən). 1543. [ad. L. *confiscationem*; see prec.] **1.** The action of confiscating. **2.** Robbery under legal authority 1832.

1. The C. of the Abbey lands FROUDE. Ruined by fines and confiscations GIBBON.

Confit, -fite, obs. f. COMFIT *sb.* and *v.*

Confitent (kǫ·nfitĕnt). 1606. [ad. L. *confitentem.*] One who confesses; a penitent.

‖**Confiteor** (kǫ̆nfi·tiˌǭɹ). ME. [L., initial word of the formula.] A form of prayer or confession of sins, used in the Latin Church at the beginning of the mass, and elsewhere.

‖**Confiture.** Obs. f. COMFITURE; also the mod.F. form (koṅfitü·r), occas. used for 'Confection'.

Cates and confitures DISRAELI.

Confix (kǫ̆nfi·ks), *v.* 1603. [See CON-.] To fix firmly, fasten. *Meas. for M.* V. i. 232. So **Confi·xative** *a.* (*rare*). †**Confi·xure,** firm fixing.

Conflagrate (kǫ·nflăgrēɪt), *v.* 1657. [f. ppl. stem of *conflagrare*; see FLAGRANT, FLAME.] **1.** *intr.* To catch fire. Also *fig.* **2.** *trans.* To set ablaze; to burn up. Also *fig.* 1835. So **Confla·grant** *a.* in conflagration.

Conflagration (kǫnflăgrēɪ·ʃən). 1555. [ad. L. *conflagrationem*; see prec.] †**1.** The burning up *of* (anything) –1825. **2.** A great and destructive fire; the burning of a town, a forest, or the like 1656. Also *fig.* and †*transf.*

2. The Burning of London..that dreadful C. 1680. So **Co·nflagrative** *a.* productive of c. **Co·nflagrator,** an incendiary. **Confla·gratory** *a.* inflammatory.

Conflate (kǫ·nflēɪt), *ppl. a.* 1541. [ad. L. *conflatus*; see next.] †**1.** Blown together; composed of various elements –1638. **2.** *spec.* Formed by fusion of two readings 1881.

Conflate (kǫ̆nflēɪ·t), *v.* 1610. [f. L. *conflat-, conflare,* f. *con-* + *flare*; see FLATE.] **1.** *trans.* To blow or fuse together; to bring together; to compose; produce, bring about. Now *rare.* **2.** To combine two readings into a composite reading. (In *passive.*) 1885.

1. The States-General, created and conflated by the passionate effort of the whole Nation CARLYLE.

Conflation (kǫ̆nflēɪ·ʃən). 1626. [ad. L. *conflationem*; see prec.] **1.** The action of blowing or fusing together. Also *concr.* the result of this action. **2.** The fusion of two readings into a composite reading. Also *concr.* the reading thus formed. 1881.

Conflict (kǫ·nflikt), *sb.* ME. [ad. L. *conflictus*, f. ppl. stem of *confligere*. Cf. OF. *conflit*.] 1. An encounter with arms; a fight; *esp.* a prolonged struggle. Also *transf.* and *fig.* 2. Dashing together of physical bodies 1555.

1. Fourty thousand were slaine in the c. 2 *Macc.* v. 14. *fig.* With c. of contending hopes and fears COWPER. 2. The conflicts of the ice-masses in their rotation KANE.

Conflict (kǫnfli·kt), *v.* ME. [f. L. *conflict-*; see prec.] 1. *intr.* To fight, contend, do battle. Also *transf.* and *fig.* 2. *fig.* Of interests, etc.: To come into collision, to clash; to be incompatible. (Now the chief sense.) 1647.

1. These two with Hector and his host Conflicted COWPER. *transf.* A horrible thundering of fire and water conflicting together BACON. 2. The perplexities of conscience..in which duties appear to c. with each other T. H. GREEN. Hence **Confli·ction**, the action of conflicting; conflicting condition. **Confli·ctive** *a. rare*, of conflicting nature.

†**Conflo·w**, *v.* 1606. [See CON-.] To flow together, as rivers, crowds, etc. –1627.

Confluence (kǫ·nfluěns). ME. [ad. (late) L. *confluentia*; see CONFLUENT.] 1. A flowing together; the junction and union of two or more streams, etc. 1538. Also *fig.* and *transf.* 2. The place where two or more rivers, etc., unite 1538. 3. A combined flood 1615. 4. A flocking together; concourse ME. 5. A numerous concourse or collection ME.

1. An island, formed by the c. of two rivers STEUART. 2. Built upon the c. of the rivers JEPHSON. 5. You see this c., this great flood of visitors *Timon* I. i. 42. A c. of associations STANLEY.

Confluent (kǫ·nfluěnt), *a.* 1611. [ad. L. *confluentem*, *confluere*, f. *con-* + *fluere*; cf. FLUENT.] 1. Flowing or running together; uniting so as to form one 1612. Also *fig.* 2. Flowing together in a body 1718. Also *fig.* 3. Meeting or running into each other, so as to form one mass or surface; as the vesicles in smallpox, spots, markings, etc. 1722. †4. Affluent *in*. CHAPMAN.

1. C. floods DRAYTON, roads DE QUINCEY, valleys GEIKIE, leaves CRABB, bones OWEN. 3. The c. variety of Small-pox CARPENTER.

Confluent (kǫ·nfluěnt), *sb.* 1600. [See prec.] †1. A confluence of rivers; the place where they unite. Rarely in *pl.* –1611. 2. A stream which unites and flows with another; *occas.* but *loosely*, used for *affluent* 1850.

Conflux (kǫ·nflɒks). 1606. [f. L. *conflux-*, *confluere*.] 1. Flowing together; flowing into a common body. 2. = CONFLUENCE 2. 1712. 3. = CONFLUENCE 4. 1614. 4. = CONFLUENCE 5. 1654.

1. As knots by the c. of meeting sap, Infect the sound Pine *Tr. & Cr.* I. iii. 7. 4. Such a c. of misery JOHNSON. So †**Confluxibi·lity**, tendency to flow together. †**Conflu·xible** *a.* †**Conflu·xion**, the action of flowing together.

Confocal (kǫnfōu·kal), *a.* 1867. [See CON-.] *Geom.* Having the same focus or foci, as *c. hyperbolas*.

Conform (kǫnfǭ·ɹm), *a.* ? *Obs.* ME. [a. F. *conforme*, ad. L. *conformis*.] 1. = CONFORMABLE 1, 2. †2. Conforming religiously, conformist –1711.

1. Made conforme to the Image of the same God MARBECK. C. to usage 1805. †**Confo·rmly** *adv.*

Conform (kǫnfǭ·ɹm), *v.* ME. [a. F. *conformer*, ad. L. *conformare*. In 14–16th c. confused with *confirm*, and prob. so pronounced (?dial.).] 1. *trans.* To form according to some model; to make like. 2. To bring into harmony or conformity; to adapt. Also *refl.* = 3. ME. 3. *intr.* (for *refl.*) To act conformably or in conformity *to* ME.; *spec.* to comply with the usages of the Church of England 1619. 4. Of things: To follow in form or nature 1699.

1. In all thynge to conforme my wyll to thy blessed wyll 1526. 3. To c. to the ways of the world LAW. When any dissenter conforms LOCKE. 4. The path.. conforms to the water DODSLEY. Hence **Confo·rmance**, the action of conforming. †**Confo·rmant** *a.* conforming. SIR T. BROWNE. **Confo·rmate** *a. rare*, conformed. **Confo·rmer.**

Conformability (kǫnfǭɹmăbi·lĭti). 1864. [f. next + -ITY.] The quality or condition of being conformable; *spec.* in *Geol.*, the relation of strata, one of which rests on the other and lies parallel to it.

Conformable (kǫnfǭ·ɹmăb'l), *a.* 1511. [f. CONFORM *v.* + -ABLE: perh. after *agree-able*; cf. also *comfortable*, etc.] 1. According in form or character *to*; like. Const. *to*. 2. Corresponding so as to fit; consistent, harmonious; fitting 1555. 3. Disposed or wont to conform; tractable; compliant *to* 1525; *spec.* conforming to the usages of the Church of England 1597. 4. *Geol.* Having the same direction or plane of stratification: said of strata in contact 1813. Also as quasi-*adv.* Conformably *to* 1588.

1. True holinesse is c. to the first pattern of holinesse 1646. 2. What is c., or disagreeable to Reason, in the actions of common life HOBBES. To make matters somewhat c. for the old Knight SCOTT. 3. In the meantime be humble and c. OTWAY. Hence **Confo·rmableness. Confo·rmably** *adv.* in a c. manner; in conformity with; agreeably; compliantly; *Geol.* in c. order.

Conformation (kǫnfǫɹmēⁱ·ʃən). 1511. [ad. L. *conformationem*.] 1. The action of conforming or bringing into conformity (*to*). 2. The forming or fashioning of a thing in all its parts 1615. 3. Form depending upon arrangement of parts; structure, organization 1646.

1. I shall speak..Of C. ..Be not conform'd to this World COLET. 2. Male children..haue their c. the thirtieth day CROOKE. 3. Government wants amendment in its c. BURKE.

Conformist (kǫnfǭ·ɹmist). 1634. [f. CONFORM *v.* + -IST.] One who conforms *to* any usage or practice; *spec.* in *Eng. Hist.* to the usages of the Church of England; opp. to *dissenter, non-conformist*. Also *attrib.*

Several pliant conformists with all changes HALLAM. vars. †**Confo·rmitan**, †**Confo·rmitant.**

Conformity (kǫnfǭ·ɹmĭti). ME. [a. F. *conformité*, f. L. type **conformitatem*, f. *conformis*; see CONFORM. *Confirmity* also occurs.] 1. Correspondence in form or manner; agreement in character; likeness; congruity. 2. Action in accordance with some standard; compliance, acquiescence 1494. 3. *spec.* Conformity in worship; in *Eng. Hist.* compliance with the usages of the Church of England 1622.

1. The C. of these Moons with our Moon 1665. With strict c. to nature JOHNSON. The c. between the testimony and the facts JAS. MILL. 2. Their C. to the Roman Religion BRAMHALL. 3. The Act for universal C. MARVELL.

Confort, earlier f. COMFORT *v.* and *sb.*, found also in all the ME. derivatives.

Confound (kǫnfau·nd), *v.* ME. [a. OF. *confondre*, *confundre* :—L. *confundere*, f. *con-* + *fundere* to pour. Cf. CONFUSE *v.*] 1. *trans.* To overthrow, defeat, or bring to nought; †to waste –1701. 2. In curses or imprecations = 'to bring to perdition'. Since 1700 considered a milder curse. ME. 3. To discomfit, abash, put to shame. (Usu. in *pass.*) Chiefly Scriptural. ME. 4. To throw into confusion or disorder; to perplex ME. 5. To mix up so that the elements become difficult to distinguish; to CONFUSE 1538. 6. To mix up in idea, fail to distinguish 1581.

1. Lest He in wrath c. me SOUTHEY. C. their politicks CAREY. He did c. the best part of an hour 1 *Hen. IV*, I. iii. 100. 2. Mahounde confounde the LD. BERNERS. C. her impudence J. PAYN. 3. Silent, and in face Confounded long they sate, as struck'n mute MILT. *P. L.* IX. 1064. 4. Pale and dumb he stood, like one confounded 1682. Confusion worse confounded MILT. 5. *Rich. II*, IV. i. 141. 6. To c. Puritanism with Presbyterianism GREEN.

Hence **Confou·ndable** *a.* (*rare*). **Confou·nded** *ppl. a.* discomfited, abashed; confused, etc.: used as a mild curse (sense 2); also as *adv.* **Confou·nded-ly** *adv.*, -**ness. Confou·nder.**

†**Confra·ct**, *a.* [ad. L. *confractus*.] Completely broken, crushed. H. MORE.

†**Confra·ction.** 1541. [ad. L. *confractionem*; see prec.] Breaking into small fragments; smashing, smash; crushing –1646.

†**Confrago·se**, *a.* [ad. L. *confragosus*.] Rough with breaks; broken. EVELYN.

Confraternity (kǫnfrătǝ̄·ɹnĭti). 1475. [ad. med.L. *confraternitas*.] 1. A brotherhood; an association of men united for some purpose, or in some profession. var. †‖**Confrai·ry.** 2. Brotherly union or communion 1680.

1. The Lord Maior with his c. of Aldermen 1654. A c. of monks 1882.

Confrere (kǭnfrɛ̄r, kǫnfrēᵊ·ɹ). ME. [a. F., med.L. *confrater*. Now written *confrère*.] 1. A fellow-member of a fraternity, a colleague in office –1688. vars. †‖**Confra·ter**, †**Confrier.** ‖2. A fellow-member of a learned profession, scientific body, etc. [From mod.F.] 1753.

†**Confrication** (kǫnfrikēⁱ·ʃən). ME. [ad. L. *confricationem*.] Rubbing together, friction –1798. var. †**Confri·ction.**

Confront (kǫnfrɒ·nt), *v.* 1568. [a. F. *confronter*, med.L. *confrontari*, f. L. *con-* + *frontem*. Cf. AFFRONT.] †1. *intr.* To border *upon*, *against* –1614. 2. *trans.* To stand or meet facing; to face, *esp.* in hostility or defiance; to present a bold front to (*lit.* and *fig.*) 1568. 3. *trans.* To bring together face to face; to bring face to face *with* 1627. 4. To set face to face or side by side *with* for purposes of comparison, etc. 1613.

2. We foure indeed confronted were with foure In Russia habit *L. L. L.* V. ii. 367. He spoke, and then confronts the bull DRYDEN. To c. an accuser JAS. MILL. 3. To c. a man with his accusers MACAULAY. 4. The old order of things..when confronted with the new JOWETT. Hence †**Confro·nt** *sb.* frontier (*rare*); the act or position of facing; an affront. **Confronta·tion**, the action of confronting. **Confro·nter. Confro·ntment**, opposition; confronting.

‖**Confronté** (kǫnfrɒ·nte). 1823. [F.] *Her.* 'Facing one another, or full-faced'.

Confucian (kǫnfiū·ʃian). 1837. [f. name *Confucius*, Latinized f. the Chinese *K'ung Fû tsze*, = 'K'ung the Master (or Philosopher)'.] A. *adj.* Of or relating to the Chinese philosopher Confucius, or his teaching, or followers. B. *sb.* A follower of Confucius. Hence **Confu·cianism**, the doctrines or system of Confucius and his followers; **Confu·cianist**, an adherent of Confucianism; also *attrib.*

†**Confuse**, *a.* [ME. *confus*, *-use* :—L. *confusus*, *confundere* to CONFOUND.] = CONFUSED –1737. Hence †**Confu·sely** *adv.*

Confuse (kǫnfiū·z), *v.* [Inferred from *confused*, ad. F. *confus* or L. *confusus*.] [†1. *trans.* = CONFOUND 1. Only *passive*. –ME.] 2. To discomfit in mind or feelings; to abash; to bewilder. Till 19th c. only *passive*. ME. 3. To throw into disorder or confusion. Till 19th c only *passive*. 1635. [4. = CONFOUND 5. Only *passive*. 1550.] 5. To mix up in the mind, fail to distinguish 1862. Also *intr.* (*rare*).

2. Or has the shock .. Confused me TENNYSON. 3. He has done more to c. and mystify the subject than to clear it up 1861. 4. A thick nose, confused on either side with the projecting cheek 1819. 5. We in reality c. wealth with money RUSKIN. Hence **Confusabi·lity** (*rare*). **Confu·singly** *adv.*

Confused (kǫnfiū·zd), *ppl. a.* ME. [f. CONFUSE *v.* + -ED [1].]

I. As *pa. pple.* this dates back to 14th c.

II. as *adj.* 1. Amazed, bewildered, disconcerted, etc. 2. Disordered, disorderly 1576. †3. Blended, mixed (*rare*) –1677. 4. Obscure, indistinct 1611. Hence **Confu·sed-ly** *adv.*, -**ness.**

Confusion (kǫnfiū·ʒən). ME. [a. OF. :—L. *confusionem*.] 1. Discomfiture, ruin. ? *Obs.* 2. Mental discomfiture ME. 3. Embarrassment, perplexity 1596. 4. The action of throwing into disorder ME. 5. A disordered condition 1530. 6. Tumult; civil commotion 1555. 7. Mixture in which the distinction of the elements is lost ME. 8. The quality of being confused 1729. 9. Failure to distinguish 1771.

1. Ruin seize thee, ruthless King! C. on thy banners wait GRAY. 3. You amaze me. How shall I conceal my c. GOLDSM. 4. The c. of tongues BACON. 5. The enemy..fled in the utmost c. WELLINGTON. 6. The late unhappy confusions *Bk. Com. Prayer*. 7. In the case of *c. of goods*, where those of two persons are so intermixed that the several portions can no longer be distinguished BLACKSTONE. 8. C. in writing BUTLER. Hence **Confu·sional** *a.* characterized by (mental) c.

†**Confu·sive**, *a.* 1611. [f. L. *confus-*, *confundere* + -IVE.] That tends to confuse –1790. Hence †**Confu·sively** *adv.*

Confutation (kǫnfiutēⁱ·ʃən). 1526. [ad. L. *confutationem*.] The action of confuting; disproof; the complete argument in which anything is confuted.

Confutations were published GIBBON.

Confute (kǫnfiū·t), *v.* 1529. [ad. L. *confutare*, f. *con-* intensive + *-futa-*, prob. from same root as *fundere* (*fud-*) to pour out, overthrow.] 1. *trans.* To prove (a person) to be wrong; to convict of error by argument or proof 1533. Also *transf.* 2. To prove (an argument or opinion) to be false, invalid, or defective; to refute 1529. 3. To render futile 1589.

1. If you want to win a man's heart, allow him to c. you DISRAELI. *transf.* Goliath..shall be confuted with a pebble 1614. 2. Macaulay himself..presently confutes his own thesis M. ARNOLD. Hence **Confu·table** *a.* that can be confuted. So †**Confu·tant,** one who confutes. MILTON. **Confu·tative** *a.* tending to confutation. **Co·nfutator,** a confuter. †**Confu·te** *sb.* confutation. So **Confu·tement.** MILTON. **Confu·ter,** one that confutes.

‖**Congé;** see CONGEE.

‖**Congé.** 1703. [a. F., same word as CONGEE.] *Arch.* APOPHYGE.

†**Congeable,** *a.* 1574. [a. F. *congéable.*] Permissible, allowable -1654.

Congeal (kǫndʒī·l), *v.* [ME. *congelen,* a. OF. *congeler,* ad. L. *congelare.*]

I. *trans.* 1. To convert, by cold, from a fluid or soft to a solid state; to freeze. †2. To solidify as by freezing -1678. 3. To curdle, clot, coagulate ME. Also *fig.*

1. Whan ayre is congelyd it makyth snowe and hayle TREVISA. 2 Salt, congealed by the sun 1727. 3. Too much sadnesse hath congeal'd your blood *Tam. Shr.* Induct. ii. 134.

II. *intr.* 1. To become solid and stiff by or as by freezing; to freeze, †to crystallize, †petrify ME. 2. To coagulate, clot, or curdle ME Also *fig.*

1. Wine of it owne nature will not congeale and freeze HOLLAND. 2 My blood congeals MARLOWE. *fig.* Least zeale now melted.. Coole and congeale againe to what it was *John* II. i. 479.

Hence **Congea·lable** *a.*; -**ness.** **Congea·led** (also †*co·ngeal'd*) *ppl. a.* **Congea·ler.** **Congea·lment,** the act of congealing and of being congealed; *concr.* a congealed mass.

Congee, ‖**congé** (kǫ·ndʒi, kǫ̃nʒe), *sb.* [ME. *congye, congie, -eye,* a. OF. *cungied, -et, conget* :—L. *commeatus* passage, leave to pass, furlough. In 15–17th c. naturalized; now usually as French.] †1. Authoritative leave to depart; passport -1789. †2. Ceremonious dismissal and leave-taking -1830. 3. A bow; orig at taking one's leave (*arch.*) 1586 4. Dismissal without ceremony. [From mod F, and often *joc.*] 1847. 5. Permission (for any act) 1475.

2. Phr. †*To take congee*: to take leave (to go). Also †*to give c.*: to bid farewell. 3. With coniayes all salute him DRAYTON. 4. Should she pay off old Briggs, and give her her *congé* THACKERAY.

Congé d'élire [AF. *conge de eslire*]: royal permission to a monastic body or cathedral chapter, to fill up a vacant see or abbacy by election.

Congee, *sb.* and *v. Anglo-Ind.*; see CONJEE.

Congee, congé, *v. arch.* ME. [a. OF. *congeer, congier,* f. *congié* sb.] †1. *trans.* To dismiss -1577. †2. To license -1532. 3. *intr.* To pay one's respects at leaving 1601. 4. To bow in courtesy or obeisance. Also *fig.* 1606.

Congelation (kǫndʒĭlē·ʃən). ME. [a. F., or ad. L. *congelationem.*] 1. The action of congealing or freezing; the process or state of being congealed 1536; *concr.* a frozen mass 1686. 2. *gen.* Conversion from a fluid to a solid state ME.; *concr.* a concretion, crystallization, petrifaction 1605. Also *transf.* and *fig.*

1. The solid obtained by the c. of water is termed ice HUXLEY. *concr.* A Multitude of Congelations in Jellies of various Colours ADDISON. So †**Co·ngelative** *a.* having the quality of congealing.

Congener (kǫ·ndʒĭnəɹ). 1730. [a. L., f. *con-* + *gener-* (*genus*) kind.] A member of the same kind or class (rarely 'of the same genus') with another, or nearly allied to another in character.

This sort of fruit hath been by many people grafted upon the Lawrel, to which it is a c. MILLER. Hence †**Conge·neracy,** community or affinity of origin, kind, or nature. **Conge·nerate** *v.* to beget together; to class as a c. (*rare*). **Conge·nerate** *a.* (*rare*). **Congene·ric, -al** *a.* of the same genus, kind, or race; allied in nature or origin.

Congenerous (kǫndʒe·nĕrəs), *a.* 1646. [f. as CONGENER.] Of the same kind, akin in nature or character; congeneric.

C. muscles (Phys.): muscles which concur in the same action. Hence **Conge·nerousness.** var. †**Conge·nious** *a.*

Congenial (kǫndʒī·niăl), *a.* 1625. [f. L. *con-* + *genialis*; see GENIAL, GENIUS.] 1. Partaking of the same disposition, or temperament; kindred, sympathetic. Const. *with* (occ. *to*). 2. Suited to one's temperament or disposition 1770. Also *transf.* †3. CONGENITAL -1775; native -1774; congenerous -1804.

1. A soul c. to his [Chaucer's] DRYDEN. C. tastes FREEMAN. 2. To me more dear, c. to my heart GOLDSM. *transf.* C. to the liberal Arts SHAFTESB. Hence **Congenia·lity,** the quality of being c.; affinity of genius or disposition; agreeableness to one's nature. **Conge·nialize** *v.* to make c.; *intr.* to be or become c. *with* (*rare*). **Conge·nially** *adv.*

Congenital (kǫndʒe·nităl), *a.* 1796. [f. L. *congenitus* (see CONGENITE).] Existing or dating from one's birth, born with one.

C. hernia S. COOPER, differences of character KINGSLEY. Hence **Conge·nitally** *adv* from birth.

†**Conge·nite,** *a.* 1610. [ad. L. *congenitus,* f. *con-* + *genitus.*] Born or produced along with, connate, congenital; natural. Of ideas, etc.: Innate. Const. *to, with.* -1716.

Sinful habits..congenit with our natures SOUTH.

†**Co·ngeon, co·njon.** ME. [prob. of Fr. origin:—late L. *cambio, cambionem,* a CHANGELING.] A dwarf -1768; a half-wit; also as a term of contempt, abuse, or dislike (ME. only).

Conger[1] (kǫ·ŋgəɹ). ME. [a. OF. *congre* :— L. *congrum* (conger), ad. Gr. γόγγρος.] A species of eel living in salt water and attaining a length of from six to ten feet; the sea-eel

Conger[2] (kǫ·ŋgəɹ). 1700. [?] A Society of Booksellers, who sold or printed books for their common advantage. Now *Hist.*

Conger-eel (kǫ·ŋgəɹ,ī·l). 1602. [f. CONGER[1].] 1. = CONGER[1]. 2. In U.S. applied also to other species of eel.

Congeries (kǫndʒīᵊri,īz). 1619. [a. L.; see CONGEST.] A collection of things merely heaped together; a mass, heap.

†**Congest,** *sb. rare.* 1630. [ad. L. *congestus*; see next.] A collected mass -1657.

Congest (kǫndʒe·st), *v.* 1538. [f. L. *congest-, congerere* to carry together, heap up, etc.] †1. *trans.* To gather together; to heap up, to mass -1758 Also *refl.* and *intr.* 2. *trans.* To affect with congestion 1758.

1. He had congested and amassed together such infinite monies 1619. So **Conge·stive** *a.* of the nature of, relating to, or produced by, congestion.

Congested (kǫndʒe·stĕd), *ppl. a.* 1578. [f. prec.] †1. Heaped together -1651. 2. *Med.* Overcharged with an unnatural accumulation of blood; affected with congestion 1758; hence, *transf.* Overcrowded 1862. 3. *Bot.* 'Crowded very closely' 1866.

2. The c. state of the goods traffic 1891.

Congestion (kǫndʒe·styən). 1593. [a. F., ad L. *congestionem.*] †1. The action of heaping together in a mass; accumulation -1671; †*concr.* a heap -1834. †2. *Med.* The accumulation of blood or morbid matter in any part of the body -1811. 3. *transf.* and *fig.* Overcrowded condition 1868.

1. The c. of dead bodies one upon another EVELYN. 2. C. of the lungs 1875. 3. That local c. of the population 1887.

Congiary (kǫ·ndʒiări). 1601. [ad. L. *congiarium.*] *Rom. Antiq.* A gift distributed among the people or the soldiers, orig. something measured in a congius, *e.g.* corn or wine.

‖**Congius** (kǫ·ndʒiŏs). Pl. **-ii.** ME. [L.] 1. *Rom. Antiq.* A measure for liquids, containing about 7 pints. 2. *Pharm.* A gallon, often shortened to the letter C.

†**Congla·ciate,** *v.* 1646. [f. ppl. stem of L. *conglaciare* to freeze up.] 1. *trans.* To make into or like ice -1686. 2. *intr.* To become ice -1808. So †**Conglacia·tion.**

Conglobate (kǫ·nglŏbeᵗt), *v.* 1635. [f. ppl. stem of L. *conglobare*; see next.] To gather or form into a ball or globe, or a rounded mass. *trans.* and *intr.* (for *refl.*)

Not conglobated into one bodie as the stars are SWAN. Hence **Congloba·tion.**

Conglobate (kǫ·nglŏbeᵗt), *a.* 1649. [ad. L. *conglobatus, conglobare,* f. *con-* + *globare* to make into a ball, f. *globus.*] Formed or gathered into a ball, rounded, globular.

The kidnies are c. HOME. Lymphatic glands, named also c. glands QUAIN. Hence **Co·nglobately** *adv.* in a rounded form or manner.

Conglobe (kǫnglōᵘ·b), *v.* 1535. [a. F. *conglober,* ad. L. *conglobare* to CONGLOBATE.] = CONGLOBATE *v.*

Conglo·bulate, *v. rare.* [f. L. *con-* + *globulus* + -ATE[2].] *intr.* To collect into a rounded or compact mass. JOHNSON.

Conglomerate (kǫnglǫ·mĕrĕt). 1572. [ad. L. *conglomeratus*; see next.]

A. *adj.* 1. Gathered together into a more or less rounded mass, or consisting of parts so gathered; clustered. Also *fig.* 2. *Geol.* Composed of the fragments of pre-existing rocks cemented together 1813.

1. The Beams of Light, when they are multiplied and c. BACON. *C. glands,* a synonym of Acinous glands *Syd. Soc. Lex.* C. tumours 1870.

B. *sb.* The adj. used *absol.* 1. *Geol.* (= *c. rock.*) A composite rock of rounded and waterworn fragments of previously existing rocks, united by some kind of cement; often called *pudding-stone.* (Cf. BRECCIA.) 1818. Also *transf.* 2. *fig.* A mixture of various elements, clustered together without assimilation 1837.

1. Shell c. is largely burnt for lime 1880. 2. That immense c. of useful and useless knowledge 1864.

Hence **Conglo merа·tic** *a.* of the nature or character of c. (*sb.* 1); var. **Conglomeri·tic.**

Conglomerate (kǫnglǫ·mĕreᵗt), *v.* 1596. [f. the ppl. stem of L. *conglomerare,* f. *con-* + *glomerare,* f. *glomer-* (*glomus*) ball.] To form into a ball or (more or less) rounded mass, or (*transf*) into a compact body (*trans.* and *intr.*). Also *fig.*

Conglomeration (kǫnglǫmĕrē·ʃən). 1626. [ad. L. *conglomerationem*; see prec.] 1. The action of conglomerating, or condition of being conglomerated. 2. quasi-*concr.* †A coil or ball; a cluster, coherent mass 1659.

Conglutin (kǫnglᵢū·tin). 1879. [See CON-.] *Chem.* The legumin of almonds and lupins.

†**Conglu·tinant,** *a.* 1828. [repr. L. *conglutinantem*; see next.] Gluing, uniting; healing. As *sb* A medicine that heals wounds. (Dicts.)

Conglu·tinate, *ppl. a.* 1531. [ad. L. *conglutinatus*; see next.] †1. Conglutinated -1610. 2. *Bot.* Cohering as if glued together 1866.

Conglutinate (kǫnglᵢū·tineᵗt), *v.* Now *rare.* 1546 [f. L. *conglutinat-, conglutinare,* f. *con-* + *glutinare,* f. *gluten, glutin-* glue.] 1. *trans.* To glue together, to cause to cohere. †2. *Med.* To unite (wounded parts or broken bones); to heal -1797. Also *fig.* 3. *intr.* To cohere (*lit.* and *fig.*) 1625

1. This medicine..conglutinates ruptured vessels 1797. Hence **Conglu tina·tion,** the action of conglutinating, or condition of being conglutinated. **Conglu·tinative** *a.* having the property of conglutinating or (*Med*) uniting wounded parts. **Conglu·tinator** (*rare*), an agent that conglutinates. var. †**Conglu·tine** (*rare*).

Congo (kǫ·ŋgo). The name of a country on the west coast of Africa, south of the Equator. Hence, 1. A negro from Congo 1886 2. **C. monkey,** a black S. Amer. monkey, a species of the Howler, *Mycetes palliatus*; **C. snake,** a name of one or two blue-black amphibians, species of *Amphiuma* (U.S.).

Congou (kǫ·ŋgu, kǫ·ŋgō). Also **congo.** 1725. [ad. Chinese *kung-fu* work, *kung-fu-ch'a* app. tea on which work is expended.] A kind of black tea imported from China.

Congratulate (kǫngræ·tiŭleᵗt), *v.* 1548. [f. L. *congratulat-, congratulari,* f *con-* + *gratulari.*] †1. *intr.* To rejoice along *with* another. Const. *with* the person, *for, on* the thing. -1824. †2. *trans.* To express sympathetic joy on the occasion of; to express pleasure at -1819; †to celebrate *with* (some act) -1661. †3. To rejoice at -1741. 4. To compliment upon any happy event; to felicitate 1548. Const. *on, upon,* †*for,* or with *cl.* Also *absol.* †5. To salute -1611.

1. I c. with you, for losing your great acquaintance SWIFT. 2. The obsequious assembly congratulated their own and the public felicity GIBBON. 4. The king in person..Comforts the sick, congratulates the sound DRYDEN. A stranger's purpose in these lays Is to c. and not to praise COWPER. 5. *L. L. L.* v. i. 93. So **Congra·tulable** *a.* calling for congratulation. **Congra·tulant** *a.* that congratulates; *sb.* a congratulator. Hence **Congra·tulatingly** *adv.* **Congra·tulator.** **Congra·tulatory** *a.* conveying congratulations; inclined to c.

Congratulation (kǫngræ:tiŭlē·ʃən). 1591. [ad. L. *congratulationem*; see above.] 1. The action of congratulating; felicitation; (with *pl.*) an expression of such pleasure 1632. †3. Rejoicing on one's own behalf -1623.

1. I thank you for your kind congratulations on my marriage 1781.

†**Congree,** *v.* [? f. CON- + GREE, aphet. f. *agree.* But the Quarto has CONGRUE, q. v.] *intr.* To accord. *Hen. V,* I. ii. 182 (Fo.).

†**Congree·t,** *v.* [See CON-.] *intr.* To greet mutually *Hen. V,* v. ii. 31.

Congreganist (kǫŋgre·gǎnist), *a.* 1861. [a. F. *congréganiste*, as *sb.* a member of a congregation of laymen directed by ecclesiastics, as *adj.* in *école c.*, opp. to *école laïque.*] Of French schools: Conducted by the Brethren of the Christian Schools, or by Sisters of various religious orders.

Co·ngregate, *ppl. a.* ME. [ad. L. *congregatus, congregare*, f. *con-* + *gregare*, f. *gregem* (*grex*) flock; see GREGARIOUS.] **1.** Congregated. **2.** Collective 1890.

Congregate (kǫ·ŋgrĭgeⁱt), *v.* ME. [f. ppl. stem of *congregare*; see prec.] **1.** *trans.* To collect or gather together into a mass or crowd; to assemble. **2.** *refl.* and *intr.* To flock or assemble together; to meet in a large body 1538.

1. These waters were afterwards congregated and called the sea RALEIGH. Bells..to c. the People EVELYN. 2. Euen there where Merchants most doe c. *Merch. V*, I. iii. 50. Hence **Co·ngregated** *ppl. a.* in the senses of the vb.; (*Bot.*) aggregated; †organized on a Congregational basis. **Co·ngregative** *a.* tending to c.; **-ness.** **Co·ngregator,** one who congregates or assembles.

Congregation (kǫŋgrĭgēⁱ·ʃən). ME. [a. F. *congrégation*, ad. L. *congregationem*; see CONGREGATE.] **1.** The action of congregating or collecting in one body or mass. **2.** A gathering, assemblage, or company ME. **3.** *Acad.* A general assembly of the members of a University, or of such of them as possess certain qualifications 1532. **4.** In the O.T.: The collective body, or an actual assembly, of the Israelites in the wilderness: so *c. of the Lord*, etc. Hence, in certain phrases = whole body. ME. **†5.** Used by Tindale as tr. ἐκκλησία in the N.T., and by the 16th c. Reformers instead of CHURCH 1526. **6.** A body of persons assembled for religious worship. (The most common modern use.) 1526. **b.** The body of persons who belong to a particular place of worship 1597. **7.** *Sc. Hist.* The party of Protestant Reformers during the reign of Mary 1557. **8.** *R.C.Ch.* A community or order bound together by a common rule, without (solemn) vows. **b.** A group of monasteries of some great order, united by closer ties of doctrine and discipline 1885. **c.** Any of the permanent committees of the Roman College of Cardinals; *spec.* the Congregation *de propaganda fide* 1670.

2. A squadron of men is..a c. of souldiers orderly ranged and set BARRET. A foule and pestilent c. of vapours *Haml.* II. ii. 315. The anger of that terrible C. [the Long Parliament] CLARENDON. 4. It is a sinne offering for the C. *Lev.* iv. 21. The c. of hypocrites *Job* xv. 34. 7. *Lords of the C.*: the nobles and other chief men who subscribed the National Covenant. Hence **†Congrega·tioner,** a member of the association of Reformers formed in 1557 (see CONGREGATION 7); a Congregationalist. **Congrega·tionist,** †a Congregationalist; also = CONGREGANIST. **Congrega·tionless** *a.* having no c.

Congregational (kǫŋgrĭgēⁱ·ʃənǎl), *a.* 1639. [f. prec. + -AL.] **1.** Of or pertaining to a congregation; performed by a congregation. **2.** Of or pertaining to CONGREGATIONALISM; Independent 1642.

1. We heard..fine c. singing 1860. 2. *Congregational* is a word used of such Christians as hold every congregation to be a separate and independent church JOHNSON. Hence **Congrega·tionally** *adv.*

Congregationalism (kǫŋgrĭgēⁱ·ʃənǎliz'm). 1716. [f. prec. + -ISM.] **1.** A form of church polity in which all legislative, disciplinary, and judicial functions are vested in the local Congregation of believers. Also called Independency. **2.** The congregational practice within the pale of a church territorially organized 1882. So **Congrega·tionalist,** an adherent of the Congregational church polity; a member of a Congregational church; an Independent. **Congrega·tionalize** *v.* to make congregational.

Congress (kǫ·ŋgres), *sb.* 1528. [ad. L. *congressus*, f. *congress-*, *congredi.*] **1.** The coming together (of persons); a meeting, interview. **†2.** A coming together, meeting (of things) -1759. **†3.** An encounter -1727. **4.** Sexual union 1589. **5.** Social intercourse, converse 1628. **6.** An assembly or conference for the discussion or settlement of some question; *spec.* (in politics) a formal meeting of envoys, deputies, or plenipotentiaries representing sovereign states, or of sovereigns themselves, for the settlement of international affairs. Also a periodical meeting or series of meetings of some association or society, or of specialists. 1678. **7.** The national legislative body of the United States of America (as a permanent institution, and as a body elected for two years; also the session of this body) 1775. **8.** The corresponding body in the republics of South and Central America 1837.

2. A fortuitous C. of Atoms WOODWARD. 3. In divers hazardous congresses and battels 1646. 5. *Bird of c.*: a gregarious bird; The crane..is also a bird of c. 1766. 6. Deputies..had been sent to Vienna during the C. 1847. An architectural c. BERESF. HOPE. The haunters of Social Science Congresses M. ARNOLD. 7. 'The *C. of the United States* (commonly referred to simply as 'Congress'), which met for the first time on 4 March 1789, was preceded by the *C. of the Confederation*, representing the several states under the Articles of Confederation, from 1781 to 1789, and this again by the three so-called *Continental Congresses* of the revolting colonies, which met in 1774, 1775, and 1776 respectively. But these last were properly congresses in sense 6.' N.E.D. The *Indian National Congress* (usu. abbrev. *Congress*), founded in 1885 by A. O. Hume for the fusion of all elements and strengthening of union with England, became dominated in 1920 by Mahatma Gandhi and subsequently worked for the independence of India.

Comb.: **C. boot,** a high boot with elastic sides; **C. water,** a mineral water from Congress Springs, Saratoga, N.Y.

Congressional (kǫ̆ngre·ʃənǎl), *a.* 1691. [f. L. *congressionem* + -AL.] Of or pertaining to a congress; *esp.* to a legislative Congress, as of the United States, etc. Hence **Congre·ssionalist,** a supporter of a congress; a member of a c. party. So **Congre·ssionist.** **Co·ngressist** (*rare*).

Co·ngressman. 1834. A member of Congress (in U.S.).

Congreve (kǫ·ŋgrīv). 1809. [f. Sir W. *Congreve*, the inventor of both.] **1.** Also *C. rocket*: A kind of rocket for use in war, invented in 1808. **2.** Also *C. match*: A kind of friction match.

Congrid (kǫ·ŋgrid). [f. mod.L. *Congridæ*, f. *congrus* CONGER.] *Zool.* A fish belonging to the family *Congridæ*, or allied to the CONGER.

Congroid (kǫ·ŋgroid). [f. L. *congrus.*] *adj.* Allied to the conger and its family. *sb.* A fish allied to the conger.

†Congrue·, *a.* ME. [a. F. *congru*, *-grue*, ad. L. *congruus*, f. stem of *congruere.*] **1.** Fitting, suitable -1587. **2.** Grammatically correct -1569. Hence **†Congrue·ly, -gru·ly** *adv.* congruously. So **Congrue** *v. rare*, to agree, accord.

Congruence (kǫ·ŋgruˌĕns). ME. [ad. L. *congruentia*; see CONGRUENT.] **1.** The fact or condition of according or agreeing; correspondence. Const. *with*. 1533. **2.** = CONGRUITY 2, 3, †4, 5. **3.** *Theory of Numbers.* The relation between two numbers which being divided by a third number, called the *modulus*, give the same remainder; also an expression exhibiting two congruous quantities in the form of an equation; thus $A \equiv B$ (mod. *P*). 1889.

Congruency (kǫ·ŋgruˌĕnsi). 1494. [f. as prec.] **1.** = CONGRUENCE 1. **2.** *Geom.* A system of lines in which the parameters have a two-fold relation, such as a system of lines each of which twice touches a given surface 1864.

Congruent (kǫ·ŋgruˌĕnt), *a.* ME. [ad. L. *congruentem.*] **1.** = CONGRUOUS 1, 2. Hence **Co·ngruently** *adv.*

Congruism (kǫ·ŋgruiz'm). 1885. [= F. *congruisme*, f. L. *congruus.*] *Theol.* The doctrine which derives the efficacy of grace from its adaptation to the character and circumstances of the person called. So **Co·ngruist,** one who holds the doctrine of C. **Congrui·stic** *a.*

Congruity (kǫ̆ngrū·ĭti). ME. [ad. L. *congruitatem*, f. *congruus.*] **1.** The quality of being congruous; agreement in character or qualities; accordance, harmony. Const. *with*, occas. *to*. **2.** Self-accordance 1827. **3.** Accordance with the requirements of the case; fitness, propriety 1530. **†4.** *Gram* Agreement or concord; hence, grammatical correctness -1736. **5.** *Theol.* **a.** (*Doctrine of Merit.*) With the Schoolmen, its being 'congruous' that God should confer the 'first grace' in response to the performance of good works by man. Opp. to CONDIGNITY. 1553. **b.** (*Doctrine of Grace.*) The suitability of divine grace to the character and circumstances of the person called, to which some theologians attribute its efficacy (see CONGRUISM) 1650. **†6.** *Geom.* Coincidence; exact agreement in superposition -1755.

1. There is, at least, moral c. between the outward goodness and the inner life TYNDALL. These..congruities [of poesy] with man's nature and pleasure BACON. 5. **a.** Neither do thei [workes done before the grace of Christe]..deserue Grace of congruitie *Articles of Relig.* xii.

Congruous (kǫ·ŋgruˌəs), *a.* 1599. [f. L. *congruus* (see CONGRUE *a.* + -OUS).] **1.** Agreeing or corresponding in character or qualities; accordant, suitable, in harmony. Now usu. *with*. **2.** Having CONGRUITY (senses 2, 3, †4, 5, †6) 1631, or CONGRUENCE (sense 3) 1859.

1. All the parts of his bodie were in good proportion, and c. as a man could wish 1599. Hence **Co·ngruous-ly** *adv.*, **-ness.**

†Congu·stable, *a.* [See CON-.] Having a like taste. HOWELL.

Conhydrine (kǫ̆nhəi·drəin). 1863. [f. CON(INE) + HYDR(ATE) + -INE.] *Chem.* An alkaloid existing, together with conine, in the flowers and seeds of *Conium maculatum*, and crystallizing in iridescent laminæ; also **Conhy·dria.**

Conia (kōᵘ·niǎ). 1842. [f. L. *conium* hemlock.] = CONINE.

Conic (kǫ·nik). 1570. [ad. Gr. κωνικός, f. κῶνος cone. Cf. F. *conique.*]

A. *adj.* **1.** Having the form of a cone; cone-shaped, CONICAL 1614. **2.** Of or pertaining to a cone 1570.

1. A succession of c. hills WOODWARD. 2. *C. section*: a figure formed by the section of a right circular cone by a plane; a plane curve of the second degree. The section is an ELLIPSE, HYPERBOLA, or PARABOLA, as the inclination of the cutting plane to the axis is greater or less than that of the edge of the cone, or parallel to the edge. Hence **Coni·city.**

B. *sb.* **1.** pl. *Conics*: that branch of Geometry which treats of the cone and the figures formed by plane sections of it. (Now regarded as the *pl.* of 2.) 1571. **2.** A conic section 1879.

Conical (kǫ·nikǎl), *a.* 1570. [f. as prec. + -AL.] **1.** Shaped like a cone. **2.** Of, pertaining, or relating to a cone 1570.

1. Taproots are..C., when tapering regularly..as in carrots GRAY. 2. *C point*: a singular point on a surface at which the tangent lines form a cone. Hence **Co·nical-ly** *adv.*, **-ness.**

Conichalcite (kǫnikæ·lsəit). 1850. [f. Gr. κονία in sense 'powdered lime' + χαλκός.] *Min.* A green hydrous phosphate and arseniate of lime and copper.

Conico- (kǫ·niko), bef. a vowel occas. **conic-** [Gr. κωνικο-], comb. f. CONIC *a.*: = Conically-, with a tendency to being conical; as **C.-cylindrical,** nearly cylindrical, but slightly tapered like a cone; **C.-hemispherical,** nearly hemispherical, but with a tendency towards the conical; *c.-elongate*, etc.

Conicoid (kǫ·nikoid). 1863. [f. CONIC, after *ellipsoid*, etc.] *Geom.* A surface of which every plane section is a conic (see CONIC B. 2); a surface of the second degree.

‖**Conicopoly** (kǫnikǫ·pǒləi). *Anglo-Ind.* 1680. [Corrupt f. Tamil *Caṇakka-pi'llai* account-man.] A native clerk or writer in the Madras Presidency.

‖**Conidium** (kǫni·diǒm). Pl. **-dia.** 1870. [As if repr. dim. of Gr. κόνις dust.] *Bot.* A unicellular asexual reproductive body occurring in certain fungi. Hence **Coni·dial** *a.* of, or pertaining to, of the nature of or relating to, a c. or conidia. **Conidii·ferous** *a.* [L. *-fer*], **Conidio·phorous** *a.* [Gr. -φορος], bearing conidia. **Coni·dioid** *a.* like a c. **Coni·diophore,** a stalk or branch of the mycelium bearing conidia.

Conifer (kōᵘ·nifəɹ). 1851. [ad. L., f. *conus* + *-fer*. So F. *conifère*. *Coniferæ* is often used as pl.] *Bot.* A plant belonging to the *Coniferæ*, an order of gymnospermous exogens, comprising trees (mostly evergreen) bearing cones.

Coniferin (kǫni·fĕrin). 1867. [f. as prec. + -IN.] *Chem.* 'A glucoside occurring in the cambium of coniferous woods' (Watts).

Coniferous (kǫni·fĕrəs), *a.* 1664. [f. L. *conifer* (see above) + -OUS.] *Bot.* Bearing cones; belonging to the *Coniferæ* (see CONIFER); pertaining to or consisting of conifers.

Coniform (kōᵘ·nifǫɹm), *a.* 1790. [f. L. *conus*; see -FORM.] Cone-shaped.

Conine, coniine (kōᵘ·nəin, kōᵘ·niˌəin). 1831.

[f. L. *conium*, Gr. κώνειον hemlock + -IN.] *Chem.* An alkaloid ($C_8H_{15}N$) which forms the poisonous principle of hemlock (*Conium maculatum*); it is an oily liquid, with a suffocating odour, and violently poisonous. Also *conia, conicine.*

‖**Coniomycetes** (kǫ·niǫ͵məisī·tīz), *sb. pl.* 1866. [mod.L., f. Gr. κονία, κόνις + μύκης (pl. μύκητες) mushroom.] *Bot.* A group of fungi, so named from their dusty spores. The division is no longer retained. Hence **Coniomycetous** *a.*

Coniospermous (kǫniǫspə·ɹməs), *a.* 1874. [f. as prec. + Gr. σπέρμα seed.] *Bot.* Of fungi: Having spores resembling dust.

Coniroster (kōunirǫ·stəɹ). 1842. [ad. F. *conirostre*, ad. mod.L. *conirostris*, f. *conus* + ROSTRUM beak, bill.] *Zool.* A member of the *Conirostres*, a group of insessorial birds having a conical bill. So **Coniro·stral** *a.* conical-billed.

Conisance, -sante, etc., obs. ff. COGNIZANCE, etc.

Conite (kō͡u·nəit). 1808. [?f. Gr. κόνις, κονία.] *Min.* A magnesian variety of DOLOMITE; in colour ash-gray or greenish gray.

‖**Conium** (kōunəi·ǒm). 1862. [ad. L., a. Gr. κώνειον hemlock.] **a.** *Bot.* The umbelliferous genus to which the common Hemlock belongs. **b.** *Med.* The hemlock or its extract as a drug.

†**Conject** (kǒndʒe·kt), *v.* ME. [ad. L. *conjectare*, freq. of *conjicere*, f. *con-* together + *jacere* to throw.] To conjecture -1734; to plot, plan -1552; to throw (*rare*) -1657. Hence †**Conje·ctor.**

Conjecturable (kǒndʒe·ktiŭrăb'l), *a.* 1656. [f. CONJECTURE + -ABLE.] That may be conjectured. Hence **Conje·cturably** *adv.*

Conjectural (kǒndʒe·ktiŭrăl), *a.* 1553. [ad. L. *conjecturalis.*] **1.** Of the nature of, depending on, or involving conjecture. **2.** Given to making conjectures 1642.

1. I doubt it is too Conjecturall to venture upon BACON. C. criticism JOHNSON, solutions PALEY, emendations 1883. 2. Her touching, foolish lines We mused on with c. fantasy MRS. BROWNING. Hence †**Conjectura·list** (*rare*), one who deals in guesses. †**Conjectura·lity** (*rare*), c. quality; *pl.* c. matters or statements. SIR T. BROWNE. **Conje·cturally** *adv.*

Conjecture (kǒndʒe·ktiŭɹ, -tʃəɹ), *sb.* ME. [ad. L. *conjectura*, f. *conject-*, *conjicere* to throw together.] †**1.** Divining; a prognostication -1697. †**2.** Supposition -1599. **3.** The action or habit of guessing or surmising 1535. **4.** (with *a* and *pl.*) An opinion offered on insufficient presumptive evidence; an unverified supposition 1527. †**5.** A contrivance; a plot -1494.

1. To cast Ominous c. on the whole success MILT. *P. L.* II. 123. 2. *Hen. V*, IV. Prol. 1. 3. But this is only c. BOYLE. 4. Dreams, Conjectures, fancies, built on nothing firm MILT. *P. R.* IV. 292.

Conjecture (kǒndʒe·ktiŭɹ), *v.* ME. [f. F. *conjecturer.*] †**1.** *trans.* and *intr.* To divine, prognosticate -1652. †**2.** *trans.* To infer from probabilities -1618. **3.** To form an opinion or supposition on grounds admittedly insufficient; to guess, surmise 1530. **4.** *intr.* To form a conjecture, guess. Const. *of* (arch.), †*at.* 1587.

3. As I c., it wyll be founde PALSGR. 4. As a mother Conjectures of the features of her child Ere it is born TENNYSON. Hence **Conje·cturer**, one who †divines or conjectures.

Conjee, congee (kǫ·ndʒi). *Anglo-Ind.* 1698. [ad. Tamil *kañji*: of doubtful origin.] The water in which rice has been boiled. *Comb.* **c.-house**: a military 'lock-up'; so called because the inmates are fed on c.

Conjobble (kǒndʒǫ·b'l), *v.* 1694. [? conn. w JOB *sb.* and *v.*, or *jabber.*] 'To concert, to settle, to discuss: a low cant word' (J.). Still in colloq. use

Conjoin (kǒndʒoi·n), *v.* [ME. *conjoignen*, a. F. *conjoign-*, stem of *conjoindre*:—L. *conjungere.* Cf. CONJOINT, CONJUNCT.] **1.** *trans.* To join together; to connect, unite. **2.** To combine, ally ME. **3.** *intr.* To become joined together; to unite 1578.

1. The knowledge of God and of ourselves, are things conjoyned 1561. Any inward impediment why you should not be conioyned *Much Ado* IV. i. 13. 2. Whome a like punishment conioyned, a farre vnlike cause disioyned 1588. Hence **Conjoi·ned** *ppl. a.* joined together; allied; in *Her.* connected together, as two or more charges. **Conjoi·nedly** *adv.* **Conjoi·ner**, one who or that which conjoins.

Conjoint (kǒndʒoi·nt), *a.* ME. [a. F.:—L. *conjunctus.*] †**1.** As pa. pple. of CONJOIN *v.* -1694. **2.** as *adj.* United, combined, conjoined, as *c. causes* 1725.

C. degrees (Mus.): two notes which immediately follow each other in the order of the scale. Hence **Conjoi·ntly** *adv.*

Conjubilant (kǒndʒū·bilănt), *a. rare.* 1851. [ad. L. *conjubilantem.*] Jubilant together.

Conjugable (kǫ·ndʒŭgăb'l), *a. nonce-wd.* 1890. [f. L. *conjugare.*] That can be conjugated.

Conjugacy (kǫ·ndʒŭgăsi). 1659. [f. CONJUGATE *a.*; see -ACY.] †**1.** Married state (*rare*). **2.** Conjugate relation 1881.

Conjugal (kǫ·ndʒŭgăl), *a.* 1545. [ad. L. *conjugalis*, f. *conjugem* (nom. *conju(n)x*), f. *con-* + *jug-* root of *jungere.*] Of or pertaining to marriage or to husband and wife in their relation to each other, matrimonial.

To countenance the c. state of her clergy STRYPE. Phr. *C. rights*: the privilege which husband and wife have of each other's society, comfort, and affection. Hence **Conjuga·lity**, c. state or condition. **Co·njugally** *adv.*

Conjugate (kǫ·ndʒŭgeɪt), *v.* 1530. [f. L. *conjugat-*, *conjugare*, f. *con-* + *jugare*, f. *jugum.*] **1.** *trans.* To yoke together, to couple; to unite (*rare*) 1570. **2.** *Gram.* To inflect (a verb) in its various forms of voice, mood, tense, number, and person 1530. **3.** *intr.* To unite sexually; *Biol.* to unite in CONJUGATION 1790.

Conjugate (kǫ·ndʒŭgět). 1471. [ad. L. *conjugatus*; see prec.]

A. *adj.* **1.** Joined together, *esp.* in a pair, coupled; connected. **2.** *Gram.* Said of words directly derived from the same root or stem, and therefore usually of kindred meaning. [L. *conjugata verba.*] **3.** *Chem.* Of compounds, etc.: Formed by the direct union of two bodies, with elimination of water 1882. **4.** *Bot.* Said of leaves which grow in pairs 1794. **5.** *Path.* *C. deviation*: the forced and persistent turning of both eyes to one side while their relation to each other remains unaltered 1882. **6.** *Math.* and *Physics.* Joined in a reciprocal relation, as two points, lines, quantities, or things which are interchangeable with respect to the properties of each 1680.

(Math.) *C. axes* or *diameters* (of a conic): two axes, etc., such that each is parallel to the tangent at the extremity of the other. *C. axis* (or *diameter*) of an ellipse or hyperbola: that which is c. to the transverse axis, the minor axis. *C. hyperbolas*: those which have the same axes and asymptotes, but the principal axis of each is the second axis of the other. *C. point* (of a curve): an acnode. (Optics.) *C. mirrors*: two parabolic mirrors so placed face to face that rays of heat or light emanating from the focus of either are reflected in parallel lines to the second, and thence to its focus. var. **Co·njugated** *ppl. a.*

B. *sb.* **1.** One of a group of conjugate words (see CONJUGATE *a.* 2) 1586. †**2.** Anything connected in idea with another -1663. **3.** *Chem.* Short for *c. compound, acid,* or *radical.* **4.** *Math.* Short for *c. axis, diameter, point,* etc. 1726.

1. The word *utility*, and its conjugates, do not express our judgments in cases of moral conduct WHEWELL.

Conjugation (kǒndʒŭgē͡ɪ·ʃən). 1528. [ad. L. *conjugationem*; see CONJUGATE.] **1.** The action of joining together or combining; the being joined together; conjunction, union, combination 1605. †**2.** Relation; the relation of conjugate words -1656. **3.** *Gram.* **a.** A scheme of all the inflexional forms belonging to a verb; a division of verbs according to differences of inflexion 1528. **b.** The inflexion of a verb 1530. **c.** In the Semitic langs., the simple and each of the derivative forms which express a modification of meaning corresponding to the distinction of voice, etc., in Aryan languages 1593. †**4.** *Phys.* Each pair of the cerebral nerves -1713. **5.** *Biol.* The union or fusion of two (apparently) similar cells for reproduction, occurring in plants and animals of low organization 1843.

1. The doctrine of C. of men in Society BACON. The elements and their conjugations 1626. Hence **Conjuga·tional** *a.* of or pertaining to c.; *Phys.* Situated at the junction of two bones; **-ly** *adv.* So **Co·njugative** *a.* tending to c.

Conjuga·to-, comb. f. L. *conjugatus* CONJUGATE, in sense 'conjugately, conjugate and —'.

Conjugial (kǒndʒiū·dʒiăl), *a.* 1790. [ad. rare L. *conjugialis*, f. *conjugium*, f. *conjugem*; see CONJUGAL.] Used by Swedenborg instead of CONJUGAL.

Conjunct (kǒndʒɒ·ŋkt), *a.* (*sb.*) ME. [ad. L. *conjunctus*: a doublet of CONJOINT.] **A.** *adj.* Joined together, conjoined, united, combined in conjunction. **B.** *sb.* A person or thing conjoined or associated with another 1667.

Mus. C. degrees: see CONJOINT.

Conjunction (kǒndʒɒ·ŋkʃən). ME. [a. OF., ad. L *conjunctionem*; see CONJOIN.] **1.** The action of conjoining; the fact or condition of being conjoined; union, connexion, combination. †**2.** *spec.* Sexual union -1794. **3.** *Astrol.* and *Astron.* An apparent proximity of two planets or other heavenly bodies; the position of these when they are in the same longitude or right ascension ME. **4.** *Gram.* One of the Parts of Speech; an uninflected word used to connect words, clauses, or sentences ME.

1. We will vnite the White Rose, and the Red. Smile Heauen vpon this faire C. *Rich. III*, V. v. 20. The c. of so many and so great calamities 1684. 3. The technical phrase 'conjunction' does not necessarily imply any very close proximity 1889. 4. Conjunctions show the relation of one *thought* to another. Hence conjunctions for the most part join one sentence to another MASON. Hence **Conju·nctional** *a.* pertaining or relating to c. or to a c.; **-ly** *adv.*

‖**Conjunctiva** (kǫndʒɒŋktəi·vă). 1543. [mod. L.; short for *membrana c.*; see CONJUNCTIVE.] *Anat.* The mucous membrane which lines the inner surface of the eyelids and is reflected over the front of the eye-ball, thus conjoining this with the lids. Hence **Conjuncti·val** *a.* of or pertaining to the c.

Conjunctive (kǒndʒɒ·ŋktiv). 1581. [ad. L. *conjunctivus*; see CONJUNCT.]

A. *adj.* **1.** Serving to conjoin or unite; connective. **2.** = CONJUNCT 1602. **3.** *Gram.* Connective; uniting the sense as well as the construction, as a *c. conjunction* 1667; which can be used only in conjunction with another verb, as the *c. mood* 1730. **4.** *Logic.* Conditional 1848. Hence **Conju·nctive-ly** *adv.*, **-ness.**

B. *sb.* **1.** *Gram.* A conjunction; a copulative conjunction; the conjunctive mood 1589. **2.** *Logic.* A conjunctive proposition or syllogism 1848. **3.** *Math.* A syzygetic function of a given set of functions 1853.

Conjunctivitis (kǒndʒɒŋktivəi·tis). 1835. [f. CONJUNCTIVA + -ITIS.] *Path.* Inflammation of the conjunctiva.

Conjunctly (kǒndʒɒ·ŋktli), *adv.* 1514. [f. CONJUNCT *a.* + -LY[2].] In conjunction, in combination, conjointly, unitedly, together.

Conjuncture (kǒndʒɒ·ŋktiŭɹ). 1605. [app. a. F. *conjoncture*; see CONJUNCT and -URE.] †**1.** The action of joining together; the fact or state of being joined together; a joining, conjunction, combination -1736. **2.** *spec.* A meeting of circumstances or events; a juncture, crisis. (The only current sense.) 1605.

1. By the c. of philosophy and divinity HOBBES. 2. In certain conjunctures, ignorance and folly..may have their advantages BUTLER. In this c. of tyme 1624, of affairs STERNE.

Conjuration (kǫndʒurē͡ɪ·ʃən). ME. [a. OF., ad. L. *conjurationem*; see CONJURISON, the earlier type.] †**1.** A swearing together; a making of a league by a common oath; a conspiracy -1771. **2.** A solemn charging or calling upon by appeal to something sacred or binding; solemn entreaty, adjuration (*arch.*) 1450. **3.** The effecting of something supernatural by a spell or by the invocation of a sacred name ME. **4.** A magic spell, incantation, charm ME. **5.** *transf.* Conjuring 1734.

1. The coniuracion, that Catilina inuented agaynste his countreye 1533. 2. We charge you in the name of God take heed..Vnder this Coniuration, speake my Lord SHAKS. 3. A..generall abuse of Scripture is the turning of Consecration into C. HOBBES.

Conjurator (kǫ·ndʒureɪtəɹ). 1549. [a. AF. *conjuratour*, ad. L. *conjuratorem*; see CONJURE.] One joined with others by an oath; a fellow-conspirator.

Conjure (kɒ·ndʒəɹ and kǒndʒūə·ɹ), *v.* ME. [a. OF. *conjurer*:—L. *conjurare*, f. *con-* + *jurare.* (The pronunciation kɒ·ndʒəɹ now suggests the art of the conjurer.)] †**1.** *intr.* To swear together; to conspire -1656. **2.** *trans.* To call upon, constrain by oath, or by appealing to some sacred person or thing; to adjure -1797. Also *intr.* or *absol.* 3. To appeal solemnly or earnestly to; to implore 1450. †4. *trans.* To affect by invocation or incantation; to charm, bewitch -1834. 5. To affect, effect, bring *out*, convey *away*, by or as by magic or the arts of the conjurer 1535.

1. Art thou hee Who..Drew after him the third part of Heav'ns Sons Conjur'd against the highest MILT. *P. L.* II. 693. 2. I c. the in the name of the fader, sone and holy goste that thow haue no power me to be-gyle 1450. The fiend himself they c. from his den G. FLETCHER. 3. He conjured them to act like men S. TURNER. 5. Christ took bread and left it bread: the priest taketh bread and conjureth it away GRINDAL. The very sight of the narrow old streets conjures up the scene MRS. OLIPHANT. Hence **Co·njured** *ppl. a.* †sworn as a member of a conspiracy; †exorcised. †**Conjurement**, the exorcising of spirits by invocation; adjuration, solemn appeal.

Conjurer, conjuror (see senses). ME. [f. CONJURE *v.*] 1. (kʊ·ndʒərəɪ). One who practises conjuration, a magician; a juggler 1727. Also *fig.* and *transf.* 2. (kǫndʒūə·rəɪ). One who is bound with others by a solemn oath; one who solemnly entreats. (Dicts.)

1. *No c.*: one who is far from clever. A man, without being a c., might guess BERKELEY. So **Co·njuress**, a female c., a sorceress.

†**Conju·rison.** ME. [a. OF. *conjureison, -ison*:—L. *conjurationem*; see CONJURE.] = CONJURATION 1, 3, 4. -1483.

Conk (kǫŋk). *slang.* 1812. [? fig. from CONCH.] The nose. Hence **Co·nky**, nosey.

Conkers (kǫ·ŋkəɪz), *sb. pl.* 1877. [dial. *conker* snail-shell.] A boys' game, orig. played with snail-shells, now with horse-chestnuts through which a string is threaded, the object being to break that held by the opponent.

†**Conna·scency.** 1646. [f. L. *connascentem*; see -ENCY.] a. A being born together; a monstrous birth in which two individuals are united. b. A growing together. -1676. So **Connascence** (J.). **Conna·scent** *a. rare*, born together; produced at the same time.

Connate (kǫ·nēɪt), *a.* 1641. [ad. L. *connatus*, *connasci*, f. *con-* + *nasci.*] 1. Born with a person; inborn, innate, congenital. (Usu. of ideas, etc.) 1652. var. †**Conna·tive.** 2. Born together, as qualities, etc. 1819. 3. Akin or agreeing in nature; allied; congenial 1641. 4. *Bot.* and *Zool.* Congenitally united; used, *e. g.*, of leaves united at the base; of elytra (in insects), bones (in vertebrates), etc. 1794.

C.-perfoliate (in *Bot.*): used of opposite leaves united at the base so as apparently to form a single broad leaf through which the stem passes, as in *Chlora perfoliata*.

Connation (kǫnēɪ·ʃən). 1846. [f. L. *connatus* CONNATE.] †1. Union by birth. 2. Connate condition; see CONNATE 4. 1854.

Connatural (kǫnæ·tiūrăl), *a.* 1592. [ad. med.L. *connaturalis.*] 1. Belonging to or inherent by nature or from birth; congenital, innate, natural. 2. Of the same or like nature, allied, cognate, congenerous 1601. †3. Congenial -1687. Also as *sb.* [sc. *person, thing.*]

1. Vice is congenit or connaturall to beasts H. MORE. Hence **Conna·tura·lity**, c. quality; likeness or agreement of nature. **Conna·turalize** *v.* to make c. (senses 2, 3). **Conna·tural·ly** *adv.*, **-ness.**

Connature (kǫnēɪ·tiŭɪ). 1872. [See CON-.] Likeness or sameness of kind or nature; connaturality.

C.; or to speak .. more comprehensibly .. sameness in kind H. SPENCER.

Connect (kǫne·kt), *v.* 1537. [ad. L. *connectere*, f. *con-* + *nectere.* Cf. CONNEX.] 1. *trans.* To join, fasten, or link together. Const. *to, with.* Also *fig.* 2. To associate in occurrence, action, or idea 1709. 3. To unite (a person) *with* others. Chiefly *pass.* and *refl.* 1750. 4. *intr.* (for *refl.*) To become united or joined; to join on 1744. Also *fig.*

1. He fills, he bounds, connects, and equals all POPE. The connexion of each intermediate idea with those it connects LOCKE. 3. People connected with the Court MRS. CARLYLE. 4. I connected much more with him than I am apt to do with new acquaintances H. WALPOLE. Hence **Conne·cted** *ppl. a.*; **-ly** *adv.*; **-ness.** **Conne·ctible** *a.* that can be connected.

Connecter, -or (kǫne·ktəɪ). 1795. [f. CONNECT *v.* The L. form is *connexor*, not *connector.*] 1. One who, or that which, connects 1815. 2. *spec.* a. A small tube of india-rubber, etc., for connecting other tubes. b. *Electr.* A device for holding two parts of a conductor in contact. c. A railway-coupling.

Conne·cting, *ppl. a.* 1690. [f. CONNECT *v.* + -ING[2].] That connects, joining.

Phr. *C. link*: *fig.* that which connects or links one thing or member of a series with another; *techn.* a link with a movable section, used to connect two links of a broken chain. **C. rod.** *gen.* A rod serving to connect a crank with any other part of a machine. †b. The outside coupling rod which connects together the wheels of some locomotive engines.

Connection; see CONNEXION.

Connective (kǫne·ktiv). 1655. [f. CONNECT *v.*; not on L. analogies; see CONNEXIVE.]

A. *adj.* Serving or tending to connect.

C. tissue (in *Phys.*): one of the tissues of the animal body, which serves to connect and support the various organs, and to form the framework in which their proper cells are sustained; it consists of fibres and corpuscles imbedded in a structureless substance. Also called *areolar* or *cellular tissue.* (Some physiologists make it include cartilaginous and osseous tissues.)

B. *sb.* [the adj. used ellipt.] 1. *Gram.* A connective word or particle 1751. 2. *Bot.* The portion of the filament which connects the lobes of the anther. 3. *Phys.* = *Connective tissue* 1883.

Hence **Connecti·val** *a.* of or belonging to the c. **Conne·ctively** *adv.*

Connector; see CONNECTER.

Conner[1] (kʊ·nəɪ, kǫ·nəɪ). *arch.* [OE. *cunnere*, f. *cunnian*, ME. CUN to prove, try.] One who tries, tests, or examines; an inspector.

Conner[2] (kǫ·nəɪ). 1809. [f. CON *v.*[1] + -ER[1].] One who cons.

Conner[3] (kǫ·nəɪ, kʊ·nəɪ). = CONDER (sense 2).

Conner[4], var. of CUNNER, name of a fish.

Connex, *sb.* 1490. [a. F. *connexe*, ad. L. *connexus*, f. ppl. stem of *connectere.*] †1. A bond or tie (*rare*). †2. A connected incident -1676. †3. A connex proposition -1660. 4. *Math.* The aggregate of an infinite number of points and an infinite number of lines represented by an equation which is simultaneously homogeneous in point- and line-coordinates 1874.

†**Connex,** *a.* 1589. [ad. L. *connexus*; see CONNECT.] 1. Connected -1680. 2. *Logic.* = CONNEXIVE 1. -1699.

†**Conne·x,** *v.* 1541. [a. F. *connexer*: repl. by CONNECT, q. v.] To CONNECT -1699.

Connexion, connection (kǫne·kʃən). 1609. [ad. L. *connexionem*, f. *connectere* to CONNECT. The etymological spelling *connexion* is most used in England.] 1. The action of connecting; the condition of being connected. 2. Relation between things one of which is bound up with, or involved in, another 1613. 3. Anything that connects 1712. 4. A personal or practical relation; a having to do *with.* Often with *pl.* 1768. 5. Relationship by family ties, as marriage, etc. 1773; a person who is connected with others by ties of any kind; *esp.* a relative by marriage, etc. 1777. 6. A body, or circle of persons connected together, or with whom one is connected by political, religious, or commercial ties. Hence, as used by Wesleyans, etc. = 'denomination'. 1753. 7. The meeting of one means of communication by another at an appointed time and place 1862. 8. The phr. *in c. with* occurs in most of the senses 1768.

1. The c. of Church and State BRYCE. Martin took the sentence out of its c. PORSON. 2. Knowledge and Wisdom..Have ofttimes no c. COWPER. 4. A criminal c. BOSWELL. My c. with glaciers TYNDALL. 5. He was, by hereditary c., a Cavalier MACAULAY. 6. The Dissenting c. 7. Phr. *To run in c., to make connections*, etc. Hence **Conne·xional** *a.*, also **Conne·ctional**, pertaining to, or of the nature of, c.; of or pertaining to the Methodist C. **Conne·xionalism**, the system of the Methodist C. in theory and practice.

Connexity (kǫne·ksiti). 1603. [a. F. *connexité*, f. *connexe*, L. *co(n)nexus* CONNEX *a.*] Connectedness.

†**Conne·xive,** *a.* 1584. [ad. L. *co(n)nexivus*; see CONNEX *v.*] 1. Conditional, hypothetical -1725. 2. Conjunctive -1776. 3. Connective, as *c. tissue* 1776. Hence †**Conne·xively** *adv.*

‖**Connexi·vum.** 1882. [L.] *Entom.* The expanded border of the sides of the abdominal segments in hemipterous insects (bugs).

†**Conne·xure.** 1615. [f. L. *co(n)nex-.*] = CONNEXION -1669.

Co·nning, *vbl. sb.*[1] ME. [f. CON *v.*[1]] 1. Obs. f. CUNNING, q. v. 2. Studying or learning, *esp.* by repetition; poring over ME.

Conning, *vbl. sb.*[2], directing the helm. Hence **Conning-tower**, the pilot-house of a war-ship.

Connivance, -ancy; see CONNIVENCE, -ENCY.

Connive (kǫnəi·v), *v.* 1602. [ad. L. *connivere*, f. *con-* + **nivere* not found, but app. conn. w. *nicere, nictare* to wink; cf. F. *conniver.*] 1. *intr.* To shut one's eyes to a thing that one dislikes but cannot help, to pretend ignorance. Const. *at* (*arch.*). 2. To wink *at*, be secretly privy. (The ordinary sense.) 1632. †3. To remain dormant (*rare*). (So in L.) -1671. †4. *trans.* To wink at, tacitly permit, pass over -1643. †5. *intr.* To wink. ADDISON. 6. *Nat. Hist.* To be CONNIVENT, q. v. (*rare*) 1830.

2. To c. at abuses while pretending to remove them MACAULAY. To c. at knaves and tolerate fools CHESTERF. 3. MILT. *Sams.* 465. 4. Divorces were not conniv'd only, but with open eye allow'd of old MILT. 5. To teach them how..to c. with either Eye ADDISON. Hence **Conni·ver**, one who connives.

Connivence, -ance (kǫnəi·vĕns). 1596. [ad. L. *co(n)niventia*; see CONNIVE. The prevalent spelling *connivance* is not justified by derivation.] 1. The action of conniving; the action of winking at, overlooking, or ignoring; tacit sanction; encouragement by forbearing to condemn 1611. †2. *lit.* Winking -1614. 3. *Nat. Hist* The fact of being CONNIVENT, q. v. 1830. var. **Conni·vency** (*arch.*).

Connivent (kǫnəi·vĕnt), *a.* 1642. [ad. L. *co(n)niventem.*] †1. Conniving; disposed to connive at -1648. †2. Dormant. MILT. 3. *Nat. Hist.* Gradually convergent; approaching at the extremity: of the anthers, etc., in flowers, and the wings in certain insects 1757.

3. *C. valves* (*valvulæ conniventes*): circular folds in the mucous membrane of the small intestine

Connixation. [f. L. *nix* snow, after *conflagration.*] H. WALPOLE.

‖**Connoissa·nce.** 1730. [F., now *connaiss-.*] See quot.

Being in search of a proper term for this science, Mr. Prior proposed to name it *connoissance*; but that word has not obtained possession as *connoisseur* has H. WALPOLE.

‖**Connoisseur** (konesö̆r, kǫnisiūə·ɪ). 1714. [F., now *connaisseur* :—OF. *conoiseor* :—L. *cognoscitorem*; see COGNOSCE.] †1. One who knows -1734. 2. *spec.* A critical judge of art, *esp.* of one of the fine arts; also, a judge in other matters of taste (*e.g.* of wines, etc.) 1714.

1. No ordinary c. in the sciences NORTH. 2. Painters and connoisseurs are the only competent judges HOGARTH. Hence **Connoisseu·rship.**

†**Connotate,** *v.* 1596. [f. L. *connotat-*, *connotare*; see CONNOTE.] = CONNOTE 1, 2. -1697.

Connotation (kǫnotēɪ·ʃən). 1532. [ad. med-L. *connotationem.*] 1. The signifying in addition; inclusion of something in the meaning of a word besides what it primarily denotes; implication. 2. *Logic.* The attribute or attributes connoted by a term; *loosely*: Meaning 1662.

Connotative (kǫnōu·tătiv), *a.* 1614. [ad. med.L. *connotativus*; see CONNOTE.] Having the quality of connoting; pertaining to connotation.

C. term: according to J. S. Mill, one which denotes a subject and connotes its attributes. Hence **Conno·tatively** *adv.*

Connote (kǫnōu·t), *v.* ME. [ad. med.L. *connotare*, f. L. *con-* + *notare* to mark, to NOTE.] 1. *trans.* To signify secondarily or in addition; to include or imply along with the primary meaning 1664. 2. Of things or facts: To imply or involve 1655. †3. To have a meaning only when conjoined -1805. 4. *Logic.* With J. S. Mill: To imply attributes, while denoting a subject 1829; hence, loosely: To imply 1865.

1. Good..over and above the bare Being of a Thing, Connotes also a certain sutableness or agreeableness of it to some other thing SOUTH. 2. But 'punishment always connotes guilt' WESLEY.

Connubial (kǫniū·biăl), *a.* 1656. [ad. L. *co(n)nubialis*, f. *connubium*, f. *con-* + *nubere*; see NUPTIAL.] 1. Of or pertaining to marriage or the married state; nuptial, matrimonial. **2.** *transf.* Married, wedded; also *fig.* 1808.

1. The Rites Mysterious of c. Love MILT. *P. L.* iv. 743. 2. C. vines 1808. Hence **Connubia·lity,** c. state or condition; the practice or right of marrying; (with *pl.*) any action characteristic of the married state. **Connu·bialize** *v. intr.* (*joc.*) to marry. **Connu·bially** *adv.*

Connu·merate, *v. rare.* 1678. [f. L. *connumerat-, connumerare.*] *trans.* To reckon or count together. Hence **Connumera·tion.**

Co·nnusable, -ance, -ant, -or, obs. ff. COGNIZABLE, etc.

Conny, n. Eng. dial. f. CANNY.

Conocarp (kōᵘ·nokāɹp). 1866. [= mod.L. *conocarpium*, f. Gr. κῶνος + καρπός.] A fruit consisting of carpels arranged upon a conical centre, as the strawberry. So **Conoca·rpous** *a.* having conical fruit.

Conocuneus (kōᵘno,kiū·ni,ŭs). 1662. [f. L. *conus* + *cuneus.*] *Geom.* A figure with a circular base like a cone, but having instead of an apex a ridge or edge like a wedge.

Conodont (kōᵘ·nodǫnt). 1859. [f. Gr. κῶνος + ὀδοντ-.] *Palæont.* A small conical tooth-like body, at first supposed to be a tooth of a cyclostomous fish; now considered to be the remains of some invertebrate animal.

Conoid (kōᵘ·noid). 1664. [ad. Gr. κωνοειδής, κωνοειδές.]

A. *adj.* Approaching a cone in shape 1668.

B. *sb.* **1.** *Geom.* **a.** A solid generated by the revolution of a conic section about its axis; a conicoid of revolution (*esp.* a paraboloid or hyperboloid). This is the κωνοειδές of Archimedes. 1664. **b.** A surface generated by a straight line which continues parallel to a given plane, and passes through a fixed straight line and a fixed curve 1862. **2.** *gen.* Any body of a shape more or less approaching a cone 1793. **3.** *Anat.* The pineal gland; called also *conoid body* 1828. So **Conoi·dal** *a.* pertaining to, or of the form of, a c.; approaching in shape to a c. **Conoi·do-,** comb. f. of CONOID.

Co-nominee; see CO- *prefix.*

Conormal (kǫnǭ·ɹmăl), *a.* [See Co-.] *Math.* Having common normals.

‖**Conoscente** (kǫnoʃe·nte). Pl. **-ti** (-tī). 1766. [It.] = COGNOSCENTE, q. v.

†**Conquassate,** *v. rare.* 1656. [f. L. *conquassare.*] To shake violently -1666. So **Conqua·ssant** *a.* shaking severely. †**Conquassa·tion.**

Conquer (kǫ·ŋkəɹ), *v.* [ME. *cuncwear-i, conquer-e(n,* a. OF. *conquerre*:—L.**conquærere,* f. *con-* expressing completion + *quærere* to seek.] †**1.** *trans.* To acquire, get possession of (by effort); to win, gain, attain to -1552. **2.** To acquire by fighting, win in war; to subjugate ME. Also *fig.* **3.** To overcome (an adversary), vanquish, subdue ME. **4.** *transf.* and *fig.* To get the better of; to master, overcome 1654. **5.** *absol.* and *intr.* To be the conqueror, make conquests, be victorious ME.

2. By conquering this new world MILT. *P. L.* iv. 391. For to conquere a name in armes CAXTON. *fig.* C. his daily bread by the threats of his dragoman KINGLAKE. 3. If we be conquered, let men c. vs, And not these bastard Britaines *Rich. III*, v. iii. 332. 4. The ruling Passion conquers Reason still POPE. 5. Hee went foorth conquering, and to conquere *Rev.* vi. 2. Hence **Co·nquerable** *a.* capable of being conquered, or overcome. **Co·nquerableness. Co·nqueress,** a female conqueror. **Co·nqueringly** *adv.* **Co·nquerless** *a.* (*poet.*) invincible. †**Co·nquerous** *a.* victorious.

Conqueror (kǫ·ŋkərəɹ). ME. [a. AF. *conquerour*, OF. *conquereor*; see CONQUER.] One who gains possession of a country, etc., by force of arms; one who conquers, subdues, or overcomes. Also *transf.* and *fig.* **b.** *colloq.* = Conquering game (*mod.*).

1. Both tugging to be victors, brest to brest: Yet neither C., nor Conquered 3 *Hen. VI*, II. v. 12.

The C.: in *Eng. Hist.* surname of William I.

Conquest (kǫ·ŋkwest), *sb.* ME. [repr. (1) OF. *conquest* (now *conquêt*) m.; (2) OF. *conqueste* (now *conquête*) fem.; see CONQUER.] **1.** The action of gaining by force of arms; subjugation of a country, etc. [OF. *conqueste.*] Also *transf.* and *fig.* **2.** The action of overcoming; gaining of victory. Also *fig.* ME. **3.** That which is acquired by force of arms: formerly including booty. [OF. *conquest.*] ME. Also *transf.* and *fig.* **4.** *Sc. Law.* **a.** The personal acquisition of real property otherwise than by inheritance. **b.** Real estate so acquired, as opp. to *heritage*. ME.

1. C....is the Acquiring of the Right of Soveraignty by Victory HOBBES. 3 *Hen. VI*, v. ii. 10. 3. Wherefore reioyce? What C. brings he home *Jul. C.* I. i. 37. *transf.* To resign Conquests is a Task as difficult in a Beauty as an Hero STEELE.

Phr. *The C.* or *Norman C.*: the acquisition of the Crown of England by William, Duke of Normandy, in 1066. So †**Conquest** *v.* to gain; to conquer; to vanquish. †**Conquest** *pa. pple.* gained (*Sc.*); conquered; vanquished. †**Conquestor** = CONQUEROR.

†**Conquisi·tion.** *rare.* [ad. late L. *conquisitionem.*] A getting together, procuring with care. BP. HALL.

‖**Conquistador** (kǫŋki·stadǭ·ɹ). 1830. [Sp.] = CONQUEROR.

†**Conrey.** ME. only. [a. OF. *conrei*; see ARRAY, and CORRODY.] **1.** Equipment. **2.** A company equipped for fight.

†**Consacre,** *v.* 1491. [a. F. *consacrer.*] To consecrate, dedicate -1618.

Consanguineous (kǫnsæŋgwi·nĭəs), *a.* 1601. [f. L. *consanguineus* + -OUS.] **1.** Of the same blood, related by blood, akin; of or pertaining to those so related. **2.** *Rom. Law.* Related as children of the same father: opp. to *uterine*; pertaining to those so related 1861. vars. **Consa·nguine, Consangui·nean.** Hence **Consangui·neously** *adv.*

Consanguinity (kǫnsæŋgwi·nĭti). ME. [a. F. *consanguinité*, ad. L. *consanguinitatem.*] **1.** Relationship by descent from a common ancestor; blood-relationship. (Opp. to *affinity*, *i. e.* relationship by marriage.) Also *transf.* and *fig.* †**2.** *collect.* Blood-relations (*rare*) -1705.

1. He inhibited the marriage as within the fourth degree of c. MILMAN.

†**Consa·rcinate,** *v.* 1610. [f. ppl. stem of L. *consarcinare.*] *trans.* To patch together -1656. Hence **Consarcina·tion.** ? *Obs.*

Conscience (kǫ·nʃĕns). ME. [a. F., ad. L. *conscientia* privity of knowledge (with another), knowledge within oneself, f. *conscient-, conscire,* f. *con-* + *scire.* The earlier term was INWIT.] †**1.** Inward knowledge or consciousness; internal conviction -1745. †**2.** Inmost thought; mind, heart -1611. **3.** The internal recognition of the moral quality of one's motives and actions; the faculty or principle which pronounces upon the moral quality of one's actions or motives, approving the right and condemning the wrong ME. †**4.** Conscientious observance *of*, or regard *to* -1671. **5.** Conscientiousness (*arch.*) ME. †**6.** Tenderness of feeling. ME. only. †**7.** Scruple; also compunction -1608. **8.** *Mech.* = BREASTPLATE 1874.

1. Without sense of good or c. of evil DE FOE. 2. By my troth, I will speake my c. of the King *Hen. V*, IV. i. 123. 3. And I will place within them as a guide My Umpire C. MILT. *P. L.* III. 195. I feele not This Deity in my bosome: Twentie consciences That stand twixt me and Millaine, candied be they, And melt, ere they mollest *Temp.* II. i. 278. 5. I cannot with c. take it *Wint. T.* IV. iv. 660.

Phrases. *Upon, in (one's) c.*: by one's sense of right, truly. Also as a mere exclam. (*Sc.*). *In (all) c.*: in reason or fairness (*colloq.*). *A matter of c.*: a matter in which c. is concerned; hence *to make (a thing) a matter of c.*: to deal with it conscientiously. *To make (a) c.* (obs. or arch.): to make it a matter of c., to have scruples about.

Comb.: **c. clause,** a clause in an act or law to ensure respect for the consciences of those affected, *spec.* one relating to religious teaching in public schools; **c. money,** money sent to relieve the c., *esp.* in connexion with previous evasions of the income-tax; **c.-wise** *adv.* in relation to the c.

Hence **Co·nscienced** *ppl. a.* having a c. (of such a kind). **Co·nscienceless** *a.*; **-ly** *adv.*; **-ness.**

Conscient (kǫ·nʃĭĕnt), *a.* (*sb.*) Now *rare.* 1605. [ad. L. *conscientem.*] Conscious. As *sb.* A conscious being 1768.

Conscientious (kǫnʃi,e·nʃəs), *a.* 1611. [ad. F. *conscientieux*, med.L. *conscientiosus*, f. *conscientia*; see -OUS.] **1.** Obedient to conscience; habitually governed by a sense of duty; scrupulous. **2.** Of or pertaining to conscience; done according to conscience; scrupulous 1631. †**3.** Conscious (*of*) -1656.

1. A c. tradesman DE FOE. 2. To live in the c. practice of all that is good BUTLER. Hence **Conscie·ntiously** *adv.* **Conscie·ntiousness,** the quality of being c.; loyalty to conscience.

Conscionable (kǫ·nʃənăb'l), *a.* Now app. *Obs.* 1549. [f. *conscion*, taken illiterately as a singular of *conscience*; cf. *fashionable.*] **1.** Having a (good) conscience; conscientious -1708. **2.** Showing regard for, or conformable to, conscience; conscientious -1702.

2. Truly a very fair and c. Reckoning MARVELL. Hence **Co·nscionableness.** ? *Obs.* **Co·nscionably** *adv.* ? *Obs.*

Conscious (kǫ·nʃəs), *a.* 1601. [f. L. *conscius* knowing something with others, knowing in oneself + -OUS.] †**1.** Knowing together with another -1664. **2.** *fig.* Chiefly *poet.* 1601. **3.** Inwardly sensible or aware 1620; †having guilty knowledge (*of*); also *absol.* -1827. **4.** Having internal perception or consciousness; also *absol.* 1690. **5.** Characterized by the presence of consciousness 1725. **6.** Aware of what one is doing or intending to do 1860. **7.** = SELF-CONSCIOUS 1728. **8.** *transf.* Of things: **a.** Known to oneself, felt. **b.** Aware of itself. 1667.

2. The c. air SOUTHEY. 3. If they say, That a man is always c. to himself of thinking LOCKE. 4. Who, c. of the occasion, feared the event DRYDEN. Thought is c. of itself 1863. 5. Man, as a c. being MOZLEY. And when at last he was c. LYTTON. 6. Pope was.. a c. and deliberate artist L. STEPHEN. 7. The c. simper POPE. 8. b. Knowledge is c. power HAZLITT. Hence **Co·nsciously** *adv.*

Consciousness (kǫ·nʃəsnės). 1632. [f. prec. + -NESS.] †**1.** Mutual knowledge (*rare*) 1681. **2.** Knowledge as to which one has the testimony within oneself; *esp.* of one's own innocence, etc. 1632. **3.** The state or fact of being conscious *of* 1746. **4.** *Philos.* The state or faculty of being conscious, as a concomitant of all thought, feeling, and volition 1678; (with *a* and *pl.*) state of consciousness 1805. **5.** The totality of the impressions, thoughts, and feelings, which make up a person's conscious being. Also limited by a qualifying epithet to a special field. In *pl.* = Conscious personalities. 1690.

2. Happy in the c. of a well-spent life JOWETT. 4. C. is the perception of what passes in a Man's own mind LOCKE. Consciousnesses not to be subdued WORDSW. 5. The commencement of a moral c. MARY HOWITT. Matters of so-called universal c. 1837.

Phr. *Double c.*: a condition showing in some measure two independent trains of thought and two independent mental capabilities in the same individual.

Conscribe (kǫ̆nskrəi·b), *v.* 1548. [ad. L. *conscribere.*] †**1.** *trans.* To enroll; to enlist -1660. †**2.** To circumscribe -1704. **3.** To enlist by CONSCRIPTION, q. v. 1820. Also *transf.*

Conscript (kǫ·nskript). 1533. [ad. L. *conscriptus*; see prec.]

A. *adj.* **1.** Enrolled or elected a senator. **2.** Enrolled or formed by conscription, as a soldier, or an army 1823.

C. fathers [L. *patres conscripti*, orig. *patres et conscripti*]: a collective title of the Roman senators; also applied allusively to members of the administrative council of a nation, municipality, etc.; rarely in *sing.*

B. *sb.* [F. *conscrit.*] One compulsorily enlisted for military (or naval) service 1800.

Conscript (kǫ̆nskri·pt), *v.* 1813. [f. CONSCRIPT *a.*] *trans.* To compel to military service by conscription.

Conscription (kǫ̆nskri·pʃən). ME. [ad. L. *conscriptionem*; see CONSCRIBE.] †**1.** Writing down together -1483. †**2.** Enrolment or enlistment (of soldiers) -1656. **3.** *spec.* The compulsory enlistment of men for military (or naval) service 1800; the conscripts collectively 1823.

3. The C. of 1813 has furnished 160,000 men 1813. Hence **Conscri·ptional** *a.*

Consecrate (kǫ·nsĭkrėt), *ppl. a.* ME. [ad. L. *consecratus.*] = CONSECRATED.

Consecrate (kǫ·nsĭkreit), *v.* ME. [f. prec.] **1.** *trans.* To set apart as sacred to the Deity; to dedicate solemnly to some sacred or religious purpose; to make sacred or holy. Const. *to*, *unto*. Also *fig.* **2.** *transf.* To devote or dedicate *to* some purpose 1555. **3.** To make an object of veneration; to hallow, sanctify; to sanction [= mod.F. *consacrer*] 1693. †**4.** To devote or doom. [A Latinism.] -1652. †**5.** To apotheosize. [A Latinism.] -1736.

1. To c. churches or chapels COKE, bread and wine *Bk. Com. Prayer*, a king TREVISA. 2. To c. one's life to letters PRESCOTT. 3. Writers, whose reputation consecrates their opinions LINGARD.

Hence **Co·nsecrated** *ppl. a.* dedicated to a sacred

purpose; hallowed; set apart with religious forms for public worship, or the burial of the dead, and having the status this gives; *fig.* sanctioned by usage. **Co·nsecrator. Co·nsecra·tory** *a.* that consecrates.

Consecration (kǫnsǐkrēⁱ·ʃən). ME. [ad. L. *consecrationem*, f. *consecrare* to CONSECRATE.] **1.** The action of consecrating (see CONSECRATE *v.*). **2.** *Rom. Antiq.* Apotheosis; also *transf.* 1490. **3.** Dedication or devotion to some purpose or pursuit; also, appropriation to a special purpose 1781. **4.** Sanction by law, custom, or usage. [mod.F.] 1861.

1. The c. of a church 1570, of the bread and wine PEARSON, of a bishop MORE.

Consectary (kǫnse·ktări). 1588. [ad. L. *consectarius*, f. *consectari*, freq. of *consequi*; see CONSECUTE.]

†**A.** *adj.* Following logically; consequent –1650.

B. *sb.* A consequence; a deduction, conclusion, corollary. (Common in 17th c.) 1588.

To mind fundamentals more than consectaries BERKELEY.

†**Co·nsecute,** *v. rare.* 1536. [f. L. *consecut-*, *consequi.*] To follow with success, overtake, attain –1589.

Consecution (kǫnsǐkiū·ʃən). 1532. [ad. L. *consecutionem*; see prec.] **1.** Logical sequence; inference; a train of reasoning. **2.** Succession, sequence 1651.

†*Month of c.* in *Astr.*: a lunar or synodic month, a lunation.

Consecutive (kǫnse·kiŭtiv), *a.* 1611. [a. F., on L. type **consecutivus*; see CONSECUTE and -IVE.] **1.** Following continuously; following each its predecessor in uninterrupted succession. **2.** Characterized by logical sequence 1755. †**3.** Following as a consequence or effect; consequent (*to*) –1705. **4.** *Gram.* Expressing consequence or result 1871. **5.** *Mus* Applied to the immediate succession of intervals of the same kind (*esp.* fifths and octaves) occurring between two voices or parts in harmony 1819. (As *sb.* in *pl.* = C. fifths or octaves.) **6.** *Magnetism. C. points*; see CONSEQUENT *a.*

1. The actions of a Man c. to volition LOCKE. 2. The ground of a c. reasoning SIR W. HAMILTON. Hence **Conse·cutive-ly** *adv.*, **-ness.**

Consenescence (kǫnsǐne·sĕns). 1692. [f. L. *consenescere*; see -ENCE.] The growing old together; general decay.

†**Con-sense.** [See CON-.] Joint-sense (= consciousness). CUDWORTH.

Consension (kǫnse·nʃən). *rare.* 1563. [ad. L *consensionem.*] Agreement.

Consensual (kǫnse·nsiuăl, -ʃuăl), *a.* 1754. [f. L. *consensus* + -AL.] **1.** Relating to or involving consent. **2.** Happening as if by consent, caused by sympathetic action independently of the will, as the *c. actions in man* 1800.

1. *C. contract* (in *Rom. Law*): a contract which requires only consent of the parties to make it obligatory: so *c. obligation.* Hence **Conse·nsually** *adv.*

‖**Consensus** (kǫnse·nsŏs). 1854. [a. L., f. *consens-*, *consentire.*] **1.** *Phys.* General concord of different organs of the body in effecting a given purpose; sympathy. Also *transf.* **2.** Agreement in opinion. Also *transf.* 1861

2. The c. of the Protestant missionaries 1861. *C. of opinion, authority, testimony*, etc. (*mod.*).

Consent (kǫnse·nt), *v.* ME. [a. OF. *cun-, consentir*:—L. *consentire*, f. *con-* + *sentire.*] **1.** *intr.* To agree together, or *with*, †*to*, †*unto* (*arch.*). †**2.** To act or be affected in sympathy –1756. **3.** Voluntarily to accede to or acquiesce in a proposal, request, etc.; to agree, comply, yield. Const. *to*, *to do*, or *that.* ME. †**4.** *trans.* To allow, agree to, consent to –1588.

1. All your Writers do c., that ipse is hee *A. Y. L.* v. i. 48. 3. He wold haue consentyd to the deth of Huon LD. BERNERS. And whispering 'I will ne'er c.'—consented BYRON. †*To be consented*: to be agreed; to be a consenting party (*to*). 4. Interpreters.. will not c. it to be a true story MILT. Hence **Conse·nter. Conse·nting-ly** *adv.*, **-ness. Conse·ntive** *a.* = CONSENTIENT.

Consent (kǫnse·nt), *sb.* Also 4–6 **concent(e.** [ME. *consente*, a. OF.; see prec.] **1.** Voluntary agreement to or acquiescence in what another proposes or desires; compliance, concurrence, permission. **2.** Agreement as to a course of action; concert ME. **3.** Agreement of opinion, consensus (*arch.*) 1529. **4.** Agreement in feeling, sympathy; accord (*arch.*) ME. †**5.** *Phys.* Sympathy between one organ or part of the body and another. Cf. CONSENSUS 1. –1797. †**6.** Feeling, opinion –1599.

1. The C. of a Subject to Soveraign Power HOBBES. Silence gives c. RAY. *Age of c.*: the age fixed by law at which a person's c. to certain acts (*e.g.* marriage, sexual intercourse) is valid in law. 2. Phr. *With one c.*, *by common c.* 3. The general c. of Antiquity HOOKER. 4. Such is the World's great harmony, that springs From Order, Union, full C. of things POPE. 6. 1 *Hen. VI*, I. ii. 44.

Consentable (kǫnse·ntăb'l), *a.* 1853. [a. OF., f. *consentir.*] In the law of Pennsylvania: Agreed upon by consent of parties, as a *c. line* of boundary.

Consentaneous (kǫnsentēⁱ·niəs), *a.* 1625. [f. L. *consentaneus* (f. *consentire*) + -OUS.] **1.** Agreeing, accordant; suited. **2.** Done by common consent, unanimous, concurrent 1774.

1. Inducements..c. to our own feelings MILL. So **Consentane·ity,** c. quality. Hence **Consenta·neous-ly** *adv.*, **-ness.**

Consentant (kǫnse·ntănt), *a.* ME. [a. F., f. *consentir.*] Consenting.

Consentience (kǫnse·nʃiĕns). 1877. [f. next.] **1.** Consentient quality or condition; agreement of opinion 1879. **2.** The sensuous equivalent, in unconscious, involuntary, or reflex action, of consciousness in conscious action.

Consentient (kǫnse·nʃiĕnt), *a.* 1622. [ad. L. *consentientem*, *consentire* to CONSENT.] **1.** United in opinion; concurrent; having or exhibiting consentience (sense 2). **2.** Accordant in opinion, or consenting, *to* 1661.

1. The c. acknowledgment of mankind PEARSON. With great and c. labour RAMSAY. Hence **Conse·ntiently** *adv.*

†**Conse·ntment.** ME. [a. OF. *consentement.*] The action of consenting, consent –1660.

Consequence (kǫ·nsǐkwĕns), *sb.* ME. [a. F. *conséquence*, ad. L. *consequentia*, f. *consequentem.*] **1.** A thing or circumstance which follows as an effect or result from something preceding **2.** The action, or condition, of so following; the relation of a result to its cause or antecedent 1656. **3.** A logical result or inference ME.; logical sequence 1571. **4.** Importance, moment, weight. (Originating in the phr. *of c.*: *i. e.* having results, and therefore important.) 1593. **5.** Importance in rank and position 1602. **6.** *Astr.* Motion from west to east; also a position more to the east 1683.

1. Death is the c. of Adam's sin BURNET. 2. Such fatal c. unites us three MILT. *P. L.* x. 364. 3. Phr. *In, of, by c.*: as a result or inference; consequently. 4. As often as we do anything of note or c. A. V. *Transl. Pref.* 5. A person of some c. SWIFT. No form of property gives its owners so much c. as land FROUDE. Hence †**Co·nsequence** *v.* to draw inferences. MILT.

†**Co·nsequency.** 1548. [ad. L. *consequentia.*] = CONSEQUENCE 1–3. –1718.

Consequent (kǫ·nsǐkwĕnt), *sb.* ME. [a. F. *conséquent*, ad. L. *consequens, -ent-*, pr. pple. used subst.] †**1.** = CONSEQUENCE 1. –1756. **2.** †**a.** *Logic.* = CONSEQUENCE 3. –1838. **b.** The second part of a conditional proposition 1628. **3.** Anything which follows something else; *Math.* the second of two numbers, etc., in a ratio; the second and fourth in a compound ratio 1570. †**4.** A person who follows –1654.

2. The Antecedent is false. Therefore the C. falls of course WESLEY. 3. Justification [is] a c. of believing, no effect issuing out of the virtue and merit of faith 1627.

Consequent (kǫ·nsǐkwĕnt), *a.* 1475. [a. F. *conséquent*, ad. L. *consequentem*, f. *consequi.*] **1.** Following as an effect or result 1509. **2.** Following as a logical conclusion 1638. †**3.** Following in time or order (contrasted with *antecedent*) –1742. **4.** Logically consistent 1849. Also quasi-*adv.*

1. The very rapid increase of Trade, and the c. influx of Wealth 1800. 4. To be c., they should have shewn that, etc. LEWES.

C. points (in Magnetism): successive points in the length of a magnetized bar, at which the direction of the magnetization is reversed. Also called *consecutive points.* Hence **Co·nsequently** *adv.* †subsequently; †in sequence; by consequence; consistently.

Consequential (kǫnsǐkwe·nʃăl), *a.* 1626. [f. L. *consequentia* CONSEQUENCE.] **1.** Following, *esp.* as an effect, immediate or eventual, or as a logical inference. **2.** = CONSEQUENT *a.* 4. 1659. †**3.** Of consequence, important –1821. **4.** Having social consequence 1833. **b.** Self-important 1758. **5.** *sb. pl.* Consequential matters 1734.

1. Wars and their c. burdens 1829. *C. damages* 'losses or injuries which follow an act, but are not direct and immediate upon it' (Wharton). These are c. to our former conclusions LD. PRESTON. 4. b. Pampered and c. freedmen FARRAR. Hence **Conseque·ntia·lity,** logical consistency; air of importance. **Conseque·ntially** *adv.* †subsequently; †as a consequence; indirectly; with logical consistency; in a c. manner. **Conseque·ntialness** (*rare*).

Consertion; see CONCERTION.

Conservable (kǫ̆nsō·ɹvăb'l), *a.* 1623. [ad. L. *conservabilis.*] Capable of being conserved; preservable.

†**Conse·rvacy.** 1558. [a. AF. *conservacie* = L. *conservatio.*] Repl by CONSERVANCY –1758.

Conservancy (kǫ̆nsō·ɹvănsi). 1755. [f. L. *conservant-*, *conservare*; see -ANCY.] **a.** A commission or court to regulate the fisheries, navigation, etc., of a port or river. **b.** The official preservation of trees, forests 1859. Also *gen.*

†**Conse·rvant,** *a.* 1588. [ad. L. *conservantem.*] That conserves, preserving, as in *c. cause* (med. L. *causa conservans*) –1679. So **Co·nservate** *v.* to CONSERVE, preserve (*rare*).

Conservation (kǫnsəɹvēⁱ·ʃən). ME. [ad. L. *conservationem*] **1.** The action of conserving; preservation from destructive influences, decay, or waste; preservation in being, health, etc. **2.** Official charge and care of rivers, sewers, forests, etc.; conservancy 1490. **3.** The preserving of fruit or the like 1873.

1. Matter .. cannot subsist without the divine c. BERKELEY. C. of order 1538, of existing territorial limits 1864.

Phrases. *Psychol. Faculty of c.*: the power of retaining knowledge, as dist. from reminiscence, the power of recalling it. *Nat. Phil. C. of energy* or *force*: the doctrine that 'the total energy of any body or system of bodies is a quantity which can neither be increased nor diminished by any mutual action of those bodies, though it may be transformed into any one of the forms of which energy is susceptible'; and that the universe is such a system. So *c. of mass*, etc. *Astron. C. of areas*: the describing of equal areas in equal times by the radius vector of a planet moving in its orbit. Hence **Conserva·tional** *a.*

Conservatism (kǫ̆nsō·ɹvătiz'm). 1835. [f. CONSERVATIVE + -ISM.] The doctrine and practice of Conservatives; = Toryism. Hence, generally, conservative principles in politics, theology, criticism, etc.

Conse·rvatist. *rare.* 1867. [See -IST.] *sb.* One who would preserve (institutions, etc.) unchanged. *adj.* = CONSERVATIVE.

Conservative (kǫ̆nsō·ɹvătiv). ME. [a. F., f. L. *conservat-*, *conservare* to CONSERVE.]

A. *adj.* **1.** Characterized by a tendency to preserve or keep intact and unchanged; preservative. **2.** Designation of the English political party, the characteristic principle of which is the maintenance of existing institutions, political and ecclesiastical. (*With capital C.*) 1830. **b.** [from the *sb.*] Of, belonging to, or characteristic of Conservatives, or the Conservative party 1831. **3.** Applied to a similar spirit in general politics, theology, business, etc. 1845. **b.** orig. *U.S.* Of an estimate, etc.: Moderate, cautious, purposely low 1900.

1. The c. virtues of lock and key W. IRVING. *C. faculty* (Psychol.): the faculty of CONSERVATION, q.v. *C. system* (Physics): a system of bodies in which the doctrine of the Conservation of Energy is exemplified. 3. The c. side of the Conqueror's policy FREEMAN. Hence **Conse·rvatively** *adv.* So **Conse·rvatize** *v.* to make or become c. (*rare*).

B. *sb.* [The adj. used absol.] **1.** A preserving agent or principle; a preservative ME. **2.** *Eng. Politics.* A member of the Conservative party, a Tory; in early use, a supporter of Sir Robert Peel 1831. **b.** In general politics, religion, criticism, etc. 1843.

1. Education, as a corrective and c. SOUTHEY. 2. b. Bull is a born c. CARLYLE.

‖**Conservatoire** (koǹsęrvatwā·r). 1771. [F. = It. *-orio*, L. (and Ger.) *-orium*; see CONSERVATORY *sb.*] A public establishment for special instruction in music and declamation.

Conservator (kǫ·nsəɹvēⁱtəɹ). ME. [a. AF. *conservatour* = F. *-ateur*, ad. L. *conservatorem.* Also accented *conserva·tor* (J.), and earlier *conse·rvător.*] **1.** One who preserves from injury; a preserver, guardian, keeper, custodian. **2.** In various titles official or descriptive ME.

1. The infinite C. of the World DERHAM. The c. of a museum 1835. 2. *Conservators of the Peace* (*Custodes Pacis*): applied in a general sense, to the Sovereign, Lord Chancellor, the Justices of the King's Bench, etc. *Conservators of a river*: see CONSERVANCY a. So †**Conse·rvatrice, -a·trix**, a female c. Hence **Conserva·torship.**

Conservatory (kǫ̆nsɜ̄·ɹvătəri), *sb.* 1563. [repr. L. type **conservatorium*, and F. *conservatoire.*] †1. That which preserves, a preservative -1660. 2. A place where things are preserved; *esp.* a greenhouse for tender flowers or plants 1664. †3. A hospital for the rearing of foundlings and orphans -1693. 4. A school or academy of music; a CONSERVATOIRE, q.v. (Freq. in U.S.) 1842.

The Italian *conservatorios* originated in hospitals for foundlings (see prec. sense), in which a musical education was given.

Conservatory (kǫ̆nsɜ̄·ɹvătəri), *a.* 1576. [f. L. *conservator*; see -ORY.] 1. Adapted to conserve. 2. = CONSERVATIVE 1822. 3. Of or pertaining to conservators 1881.

Conserve (kǫ̆nsɜ̄·ɹv), *sb.* ME. [a. F. = med. L. *conserva*, f. *conservare*; see next.] †1. A preservative -1590. †2. A greenhouse. EVELYN. †3. A store -1651. 4. A medicinal or confectionary preparation of some part of a plant, preserved with sugar. *pl.* Preserves. 1530.

1. A conserue against such lawlesse concupiscence GREENE. 2. *Tam. Shr.* Induct. ii. 3.

Conserve (kǫ̆nsɜ̄·ɹv), *v.* ME. [a. F. *conserver* :—L. *conservare.*] 1. To keep in safety, or from harm, decay, or loss; now usually, to preserve in its existing state from destruction or change. †2. To preserve in being; to keep alive -1698. †3. To make into a conserve; to preserve in sugar, etc. -1773.

1. One ancient lancet window has been carefully conserved 1861. Hence **Conse·rver.**

Consider (kǫ̆nsi·dəɹ), *v.* ME. [a. F. *considérer*, ad. L. *considerare*, f. *con-* + a radical, according to Festus, derived from *sidus, sider-*. ? A term of Astrology.] 1. To view attentively, to survey, examine, inspect (*arch.*). 2. *intr.* To look attentively ME. 3. *trans.* To contemplate mentally; to think over, meditate on, give heed to, take note of. Also with *of* (*arch.*) ME. 4. *intr.* To think deliberately, bethink oneself, reflect 1460. †5. *trans.* To judge of -1539. 6. To take into practical consideration; to regard, make allowance for ME. †7. To recognize in a practical way; to requite, recompense; see CONSIDERATION -1698. 8. To hold in consideration; to esteem, respect 1692. 9. To look upon (*as*), take for 1533; with *obj. clause*: To think, suppose 1830.

1. She considreth a field and byeth it *Prov.* xxxi. 16. 3. Is man no more then this? C. him well *Lear* III. iv. 107. Thou must consyder thy seruantes be men as thou arte CAXTON. 4. 'Twere to c. to curiously to c. so *Haml.* v. i. 227. The matter's weighty, pray c. twice POPE. 6. Blessed is he that considereth the poor *Ps.* xli. 1. 7. *Meas. for M.* I. ii. 114. 8. A pamphlet..which was..enough considered to be both seriously and ludicrously answered JOHNSON. 9. He considers wealth of little importance 1784. I c. him to have acted disgracefully (*mod.*).

Hence **Consi·dered** *pa. pple.*; also used *absol.* = 'being taken into account'. **Consi·derer. Consi·dering** *vbl. sb.* and *ppl. a.*; also as *prep.* = 'taking into account'; *ellipt.* considering everything: used *advb.* (*colloq.*). **Consi·deringly** *adv.* thoughtfully; in a considering manner, tone, or attitude.

Considerable (kǫ̆nsi·dərăb'l), *a.* (and *sb.*) 1449. [ad. med.L. *considerabilis*, f. *considerare.*] †1. That may be considered or viewed (*rare*) -1668. †2. That should be considered, taken into account, or noted; notable -1707. 3. Worthy of consideration or regard, important; of consequence 1619. 4. Worthy of consideration by reason of magnitude; pretty large; a good deal of. (The usual current sense.) 1651. 5. As *adv.* = CONSIDERABLY. Now *dial.* 1657. †6. *sb.* A thing to be considered. Chiefly *pl.*; cf. *valuables*, etc. -1677.

3. The town is still a very c. place YEATS. Some of the most c. citizens were banished HALLAM. 4. A very c. part of the people HOBBES. A c. sum of money MAR. EDGEWORTH.

Hence **Consi·derabi·lity**, the quality of being c. **Consi·derableness**, importance. **Consi·derably** *adv.* †in a way or to a degree that ought to be noticed; much, a good deal.

†**Consi·derance.** ME. [a. OF., ad. L. *considerantia*; see prec.] The action of considering; reflection -1597.

Considerate (kǫ̆nsi·dərĕt), *a.* 1572. [ad. L. *consideratus.*] 1. Marked by consideration; well-considered, deliberate. 2. Of persons, etc.: Having or showing consideration; thoughtful, deliberate, prudent. *Obsolescent.* 1581. †3. Having regard, regardful *of* -1667. 4. Thoughtful for others. Now the chief sense. 1700.

1. The national courage..c. and determined EMERSON. 2. C. and careful parentes MULCASTER. 4. Was I more c. of you and your comfort JANE AUSTEN. Hence **Consi·derate·ly** *adv.*, **-ness.**

Consideration (kǫ̆nsi:dərē¹·ʃən). ME. [a. F. *considération*, ad. L. *considerationem*; see CONSIDER.] †1. The action of looking at; beholding, contemplation -1651. 2. The keeping of a subject before the mind; attentive thought, reflection, meditation ME.; (with *pl.*) a reflection 1489. 3. The action of taking into account; the being taken into account; regard 1548. 4. The taking into account of anything as a reason or motive; a fact or circumstance taken, or to be taken, into account 1460. 5. Something given in payment; a reward, remuneration; a compensation 1607. 6. *Law.* Anything regarded as recompense or equivalent for what one does or undertakes for another's benefit; *esp.*, in the law of contracts, 'the thing given or done by the promisee in exchange for the promise' (Langdell 1880 § 45) 1530. 7. Regard for the circumstances, feelings, etc. of another ME. 8. Estimation; regard among men; consequence 1598.

2. C. like an Angell came, And whipt th' offending Adam out of him SHAKS. Phr. *To take into c.*, *under c.* 3. Wherefore, in c. of the premisses, be it enacted [etc.] 1540. 4. Induced to adopt this course by considerations of state policy SMILES. 5. They hoped that I would giue them some c. to be carryed in a chaire to the toppe CORYAT. 6. C. is the materiall cause of a contract, without the which no contract can binde the partie *Termes de la Ley* 77. 8. A man of the first c. 1859. There is nothing in this World that is of any C. in comparison with Eternity LOCKE.

†**Consi·derative**, *a.* 1449. [a. F. *considératif*, *-ive.*] = CONSIDERATE 1, 2, 4. -1825.

†**Consi·derator.** 1658. [a. L.] One who considers -1695.

Consign (kǫ̆nsəi·n), *v.* ME. [repr. F. *consigner*, ad. L. *consignare*, f. *con-* + *signare* to mark, sign, seal.]

I. †1. *trans.* To mark with the sign of the cross; *spec.* to confirm; with *to, unto*: To dedicate thus 1533. †2. To attest, confirm, ratify -1849. †3. To seal, sign, subscribe 1623. †4. *intr.* To set one's seal, subscribe, agree *to* -1611.

4. All Louers young, all Louers must Consigne to thee, and come to dust *Cymb.* IV. ii. 275.

II. To hand over formally. 1. To make over as a possession, to deliver formally or commit, *to* a state, fate, etc. 1632. 2. To hand over to another for custody 1528. 3. To deposit (money) 1633. 4. *Comm.* To deliver or transmit (goods) for sale or custody: usually implying their transit by ship, railway, etc. 1653.

1. When this vital breath Ceasing, consigns me o'er to rest and death PRIOR. To c. anything to a use DRYDEN, to writing ADDISON. 2. Consigning our horses to the care of our grooms LYTTON. 3. To c. money in a public bank 1861. 4. A ship..laden with goods and consigned to Robert Morris 1866. Hence **Consi·gnable** *a.* that can be consigned. **Consi·gnatary**, a consignee. ? *Obs.* **Consignee·**, a person to whom goods are consigned. **Consi·gner.**

Consignation (kǫnsignē¹·ʃən). 1537. [ad. L. *consignationem*; see CONSIGN.] †1. The action of marking with the sign of the cross -1642. Also *fig.* †2. Sealing; confirmation; attestation -1849. †3. A consigning *to* a state or condition -1684. †4. Formal delivery -1678. 5. The action of formally paying over money, as into a bank, etc. 1588. 6. = CONSIGNMENT 3. 1755.

6. *To the c. of*: = addressed to as consignee.

Consignatory, var. of COSIGNATORY.

‖**Consigne** (kǫnsiⁿʸ). 1864. [F.] Order given to a sentinel; watchword; countersign.

‖**Consigné** (kǫnsinʸe). [Fr.] A person commanded to keep his quarters, or to stay within certain bounds. (Dicts.)

Consignificant (kǫnsigni·fikănt), *a. rare.* 1612. [See CON-.] Conjointly significant; having a meaning in combination. So **Co·nsigni·ficative** *a.* (*rare*).

Consigni·ficate. [ad. med.L. *consignificatum.*] That which is consignified.

Consignification (kǫ̆nsi·gnifikē¹·ʃən). *rare.* 1701. [ad. med.L. *consignificationem*, f. *consignificare.*] Joint signification; connotation; conjoint signification.

Consignify (kǫ̆nsi·gnifəi), *v. rare.* 1646. [f. med.L. *consignificare.*] To signify conjointly; to signify when combined with something.

The cypher, which has no value of itself, and only serves..to connote and c. HORNE TOOKE.

Consignment (kǫ̆nsəi·nmĕnt). 1563. [f. CONSIGN *v.* + -MENT.] 1. Sealing or dedicating with a sign. 2. Delivering over; committal; allotment 1668. 3. The consigning of goods or a cargo, *esp.* to an agent for sale or disposal 1709. 4. *concr.* A quantity of goods consigned to an agent or factor 1722.

4. A large c. of pearls entrusted to the captain 1877.

Consignor (kǫnsəinǭ·ɹ). 1789. [f. as prec. + -OR.] One who dispatches goods to another; opp. to *consignee*. More techn. than *consigner*.

†**Consi·liary**, *a.* 1642. [ad. L. *consiliarius*, f. *consilium.*] Of, pertaining to, or of the nature of, counsel; giving counsel -1662.

Consilient (kǫ̆nsi·liĕnt), *a.* 1867. [ad. L. type *consilient-*, f. *con-* + *salire.*] 'Jumping together', concurrent, accordant. Hence **Consi·lience**, the fact of 'jumping together'; coincidence, concurrence: said of inductions.

Consimilar (kǫ̆nsi·milăɹ), *a.* Now *rare.* 1548. [f. L. *consimilis* after SIMILAR.] †1. = CONSIMILE -1651. 2. Entirely similar, like 1645. Hence **Consimila·rity** (*rare*).

†**Consi·milate**, *v.* 1731. [f. L. *consimilat-*, *consimilare.*] To make or become like -1756.

†**Consi·mile**, *a.* ME. [ad. L. *consimilis.*] Like throughout, homogeneous, as animal tissues, etc. -1577. So †**Consimi·litude**, †**Consimi·lity**, similarity, mutual likeness.

Consist (kǫ̆nsi·st), *v.* 1542. [ad. L. *consistere*, f. *con-* + *sistere* to cause to stand, etc.] 1. *intr.* To have a settled existence, subsist, hold together, exist, be (*arch.*) 1551. †2. To exist together as compatible facts, to co-exist -1814; to be possible and so compatible *with* -1846. 3. To be consistent; to be congruous; to harmonize (*with*) 1638.

1. And by him all things c. *Col.* i. 17. 2. Fayeth can not consiste with an euell conscience 1548. Health consists with temperance alone POPE. 3. To c. and hang together BERKELEY.

With preps. †**C. on** or **upon**: to stand on, rest upon; to insist *upon* 2 *Hen. IV*, IV. i. 187. So †**C. by. C. in**: to have its being in; to be comprised or contained in; to be constituted of (now the usual sense); to be composed of (*arch.*). So †**C. by. C. of**: to be made up or composed of. (*Of* was here orig. = *from, out of.*)

Consistence (kǫ̆nsi·stĕns). 1598. [app. a. F., now *consistance*, f. L. *consistent-*, *consistere*; see CONSIST.] †1. Standing or remaining still, quiescence; state of rest -1751. †2. A settled condition -1702. 3. Material coherence and permanence of form; solidity enough to retain its form 1626; †*concr.* matter dense enough to cohere (*poet.*) -1774. 4. The degree of firmness with which the particles of a substance cohere; degree of density. (Usu. of more or less viscous liquids.) 1626. Also *fig.* †5. Combination -1702. †6. Coexistence as compatible facts 1659. 7. = CONSISTENCY 4, 5. 1670.

3. Putrefaction; which ever dissolveth the C. of the Body BACON. *fig.* Reports..begin to acquire c. 1884. 4. A due C. of the Blood is very necessary for Health ARBUTHNOT.

Consistency (kǫ̆nsi·stĕnsi). 1594. [f. L. *consistentem*; see CONSISTENT.] †1. = CONSISTENCE 2. -1705. 2. = CONSISTENCE 3. 1594. 3. = CONSISTENCE 4. 1661. 4. The quality, state, or fact of being consistent; agreement (*with* something, *of* things, etc.) 1658. 5. The quality of being self-consistent; see CONSISTENT 7. 1787.

4. The c. of the two records PALEY. 5. C. of behaviour ADDISON. The doubtful virtue of c. MAINE.

Consistent (kǫ̆nsi·stĕnt). 1574. [ad. L. *consistentem*; see CONSIST.]

A. *adj.* †1. Standing still or firm; not moving or giving way -1664. †2. Settled, persistent; durable -1684. †3. Consisting *in* or *of*, composed *of* -1671. 4. Holding together as a coherent material body. (Now *rare.*) 1647. †5.

Existing together or simultaneously *with* (*rare*) –1733. 6. Agreeing or according in substance or form; congruous, compatible. (This and 7 are the current senses.) 1646. †b. Used *advb.* = Consistently –1842. 7. Of persons or conduct: Marked by consistency; constantly adhering to the same principles of thought or action 1732.

2. †*C. age*: the age when growth has ceased and decay has not begun. 4. A black c. peat-earth 1799. 6. An habite .. not c. with the words of our Saviour SIR T. BROWNE. A solid, regular, and c. Structure LEONI. 7. C. in our follies and our sins POPE.

†B. *sb. Eccl. Hist.* One of the fourth class of penitents (*consistentes*) in the Eastern Church, who took their station with the faithful, but were not admitted to communion.

Hence **Consi·stently** *adv.* in a c. manner.

†Consi·stible, *a.* Also **-able.** 1642. [f. CONSIST; see -BLE.] That may consist (*with* something); compatible –1660.

Consistorial (kǫnsistōᵊ·riăl), *a.* 1450. [ad. med.L. *consistorialis*, f. *consistorium*.] 1. Of or pertaining to a consistory. 2. Of or pertaining to church government by consistories; Genevan, presbyterian 1561.

1. The c. court of the archdeaconry of Wells 1805. 2. The c. or presbyterian form of polity 1889. var. **†Consisto·rian** *a.*

Consistory (kǫ·nsistəri, kǫnsi·stəri). ME. [a. ONF. *consistorie*, ad. L. *consistorium*, f. *consistere*; see CONSIST.]

I. †1. A place where councillors meet, a council-chamber –1756. 2. A meeting of councillors, a council. *Obs.* exc. *Hist.* or *poet.* ME. Also †*fig.* †3. A tribunal –1685. †4. A court, as in *heavenly c.* –1641.

2. In mid air To council summons all his mighty peers..A gloomy c. MILT. *P. R.* I. 40. 3. This false Iuge..As he was wont sat in his Consistorie And yaf his doomes CHAUCER.

II. Eccl. senses. 1. The senate in which the Pope, presiding over the Cardinals, deliberates upon the affairs of the church. Also, a meeting of this body. ME. 2. The diocesan court, held by the chancellor of the diocese ME. Also *fig.* 3. In the Lutheran Church, a board of clerical officers, usually appointed by the sovereign, to supervise ecclesiastical affairs 1698. 4. In the Reformed, Genevan, or Presbyterian polity, a court of presbyters; corresponding, in Holland, etc., to the kirk-session in Scotland; in France, to a presbytery 1593. Also *attrib.*

1. His Holiness said that he would deliberate upon the appeal with the c. FROUDE.

†Consi·tion. *rare.* 1656. [ad. L. *consitionem*.] A sowing –1692.

Conso·ciate. 1471. [ad. L. *consociatus*; see next.] *adj.* Associated together. In early use as *pa. pple.* = CONSOCIATED. *sb.* A partner, confederate 1579.

Consociate (kǫnsōᵘ·ʃiₗeᶦt), *v.* 1566. [f. L. *consociat-*, *consociare*, f. *con-* + *sociare*, f. *socius*.] 1. *trans.* To bring into association, companionship, partnership; to conjoin in action, etc. 2. *intr.* To enter into association; *spec.* in New England, to join in a consociation of churches 1638. 3. To keep company *with* 1656.

1. Colly consociateth its waters with Axe RISDON. 2. They c...to fight against his annoynted TRAPP.

Consociation (kǫnsōᵘ·ʃiₗēᶦ·ʃən, -siₗēᶦ·ʃən). 1593. [ad. L. *consociationem*; see prec.] 1. The action or fact of associating together; combination 1593. 2. Fellowship, companionship 1609. †3. An alliance or confederation –1685. 4. *Eccl.* A confederation of Christian churches or religious societies. In U.S. a body of the nature of a permanent Council, elected from and representing the Congregational churches of a district, and possessing a certain tacitly conceded ecclesiastical authority. 1644.

1. The c. of tribes for plunder or defence 1804. 2. She glorifieth her nobilitie, having c. with God BIBLE (Douay) *Wisd.* viii. 3. Hence **Consocia·tional** *a.* **Consocia·tionism,** the c. of churches.

Consol (kǫnsǫ·l). Pl. **consols.** 1770. In *pl.* Short for *Consolidated Annuities*, i.e. the government securities of Great Britain; see CONSOLIDATED. (The sing. is used only *attrib.* and in *comb.*)

†Consolate (kǫ·nsŏlĕt), *ppl. a.* 1475. [ad. L. *consolatus*.] 1. Consoled, comforted –1818. 2. *loosely.* Consolatory 1748.

†Consolate (kǫ·nsŏleᶦt), *v.* 1475. [f. L. *consolat-*, *consolari*.] = CONSOLE –1773.

Consolation (kǫnsŏlēᶦ·ʃən). ME. [a. F., ad. L. *consolationem*.] 1. The action of consoling; the state of being consoled; alleviation of sorrow or mental distress. 2. (with *pl.*) An act or instance of consolation; a person or thing that affords consolation ME.

1. Some source of c. from above MILT. *Sams.* 664. Pericles in the funeral oration is silent on the consolations of immortality JOWETT. Phr. *C. race, match*, etc.: one open only to those who have been defeated in the preceding 'events'. So *c. stakes.*

†Consola·tor. 1540. [a. L.] Consoler.

Consolatory (kǫnsǫ·lătəri). ME. [ad. L. *consolatorius*, f. *consolator*.] *adj.* Tending to console; bringing consolation. †*sb.* 'A speech or writing containing topicks of comfort' (J) –1671. Hence **Conso·latorily** *adv.*

Consolatrix (kǫnsŏlēᶦ·triks). *rare.* 1632. [a. (med.)L.] A female consoler.

Console (kǫ·nsōᵘl), *sb.* Also **consol.** 1706. [a. F. *console*: ?abbrev. from *consolider* (Littré).] 1. *Arch.* A variety of the bracket or corbel; 'an ornament in any material which projects about half its height or less, for the purpose of carrying anything'. 2. Short for *c.-table* (see below) 1840. 3. The desk from which an organ is played, containing keyboards, stop action, etc. 1881.

1. The drawing-room, in which, on consoles, are the twelve Caesars BP. POCOCKE. *Comb.* **c.-table,** a table supported by a fixed bracket against a wall; also, a movable side-table supported by consoles.

Console (kǫnsōᵘ·l), *v.* 1693. [a. F. *consoler*, ad. L. *consolare*, collateral f. *consolari*, f. *con-* + *solari*. Repl. CONSOLATE.] *trans.* To comfort in distress or depression; to alleviate the sorrow of; 'to free from the sense of misery' (J.).

What, thou think'st men speak in courtly chambers Words by which the wretched are consoled M. ARNOLD. Earth can c., Heaven can torment no more SHELLEY.

Hence **Conso·lable** *a.* that can be consoled. **Conso·ler,** one who consoles; repl. CONSOLATOR.

†Conso·lidant. 1661. [a. F., prop. pr. pple. of *consolider*.] *adj.* That consolidates. Of medicines. Tending to unite or heal (wounds, fractures, etc.) 1755. *sb.* A c. medicine. (Now only in Dicts.)

Consolidate (kǫnsǫ·lidĕt), *ppl. a.* 1531. [ad. L. *consolidatus*; see next.] = CONSOLIDATED.

Consolidate (kǫnsǫ·lideᶦt), *v.* 1511. [f. L. *consolidat-*, *consolidare*, f. *con-* + *solidare*, f. *solidus*.] 1. *trans.* To make solid; to form into a compact mass; to solidify 1653. 2. To make firm or strong; to strengthen (now chiefly power, etc.) 1540. 3. To combine compactly into one mass, body, or connected whole 1511. †4. *spec.* To cause (the parts of a wound or fracture) to unite and so to heal –1788. Also *absol.* 5. *intr.* (for *refl.*) To become solid or firm; to combine or unite solidly or compactly 1626.

2. To c. an empire THIRLWALL, the social order MORLEY. 3. To c. two Churches PRIDEAUX, the Scottish Acts BURTON, the customs duties MᶜCULLOCH. 5. Hurts and ulcers of the head..dryness maketh them more apt to c. BACON. Hence **Conso·lidative** *a.* serving to c. **Conso·lidator,** one who or that which consolidates.

Consolidated (kǫnsǫ·lideᶦtĕd), *ppl. a.* 1753. [f. prec. vb.] Made solid, firm, or compact; combined, unified: said *esp.* of sources of revenue, funds, debts, etc.

C. Annuities: the Government securities of Great Britain, which were consolidated in 1751 (25 George II, c. 27) into a single stock bearing interest at 3 per cent. (Now reduced to 2½.) See also CONSOL(S. *C. Fund*: the united product of various branches of the revenue of Great Britain and Ireland, whence the interest of the national debt, the grants to the Royal Family, the Civil List, etc., are paid.

Consolidation (kǫnsǫlidēᶦ·ʃən). ME. [ad. L. *consolidationem*; see CONSOLIDATE *v.* Cf. F. *consolidation*.] 1. The action of consolidating; solidification 1603. Also *fig.* 2. Combination into a compact mass, single body, or coherent whole; combination, unification 1677. 3. *Bot.* = ADNATION 1851.

1. Formed..by the c. of fibrin CARPENTER. *fig.* The c. of our Union 1787. 2. The first germs of social c. and growth MORLEY. The 'Companies' Clauses C. Act' 1846. The c. of the customs duties MᶜCULLOCH. *C. of actions*: the merging of two or more actions at law by a court or judge to save expense and delay. Hence **Consolida·tionist,** one who advocates c.

Consols, *sb. pl.*; see CONSOL.

‖**Consommé** (koṅsome). 1824. [F., f. *consommer*, ad. L. *consummare* to CONSUMMATE, complete.] A strong broth or soup made from meat; now *esp.* clear soup.

Consonance (kǫ·nsŏnăns). ME. [a. 14th c. F. (now *consonnance*), ad. L. *consonantia*; see CONSONANT.] 1. = ASSONANCE 1. 1589. 2. Pleasing combination of sounds 1594. 3. *Mus.* The sounding together of two notes in harmony; the quality or fact of being CONSONANT. (Opp. to DISSONANCE.) 1694. b. A consonant 'interval', a concord 1624. 4. *fig.* Agreement, harmony, concord ME.

2. Winds and Waters flow'd in C. THOMSON. 4. The c. and agreement they have either with reputation or dignity 1592. Phr. *In c. with.* var. **Co·nsonancy** (in senses 1, 2, 4).

Consonant (kǫ·nsŏnănt), *a.* 1483. [a. 14th c. F. (now *consonnant*), ad. L *consonantem*, *consonare*, f. *con-* + *sonare* to SOUND.] 1. In agreement, accordance, or harmony; accordant (*to*); consistent (*with*) 1489. †b. *advb.* –1744. †2. Consistent –1744. 3. Of sounds or music: Harmonious 1515; *Mus.* concordant, constituting a consonance 1609. 4. Of words: Agreeing in sound 1645. †5. Of the nature of a consonant (*rare*) 1751.

1. With one c. heart and voice *Homilies* II. The opinion is c. to law COKE. C. with the doctrine of St. Paul 1857. 3. An euphonious melody and consonent cadence K. WHITE. 4. The four c. rhymes required in each [Spenserian] stanza PALGRAVE. Hence **Co·nsonantly** *adv.* Const. *to*, *with.*

Consonant (kǫ·nsŏnănt), *sb.* ME. [a. 13–14th c. F., ad. L. *consonantem*, sb. use (sc. *consonans littera*) of pr. pple.; see prec.] 1. An alphabetic or phonetic element other than a vowel; an elementary sound of speech which in the formation of a syllable is combined with a vowel. Applied both to sounds and letters.

Elementary sounds have been classed, according to the degree in which they may function as vowels, as (1) vowels, (2) semi-vowels (Eng. y and w), (3) liquids (l, lʸ, r), (4) nasals (m, n, nʸ, ŋ), (5) fricatives or spirants, *voice* (v, ð, z, ʒ, γ), and *breath* (f, þ, s, ʃ, χ), (6) mutes or stops, *voice* (b, d, g), and *breath* (p, t, k). Only class 6 have the consonantal function exclusively, *p, t, k,* being the most typical consonants. Consonants may also be classed, according to the part of the mouth where they are formed, into labials (p, b, f, v, m, w), dentals, palatals, gutturals, and other minor groups.

†2. *Mus.* = CONSONANCE 3 b. –1712. Also *attrib.* Hence **Consona·ntal** *a.* of the nature of a c.; characterized by consonants; var. **Consona·ntic** (*rare*). **Co·nsonanti·sm,** use of consonants; a consonant formation. **Co·nsonantize** *v.* to turn (a vowel) into a c. (e. g. *u* into *w*).

Co·nsonate, *v. rare.* 1882. [f. L. *consonat-*, *consonare*.] *intr.* To sound in sympathy.

Consonous (kǫ·nsŏnəs), *a. rare.* 1654. [a. L. *consonus* + -OUS.] 1. Harmonious. †2. = CONSONANT *a.* 1. 1660.

†Co·nsopite, *v.* (erron. in Dicts. **consopiate.**) 1647. [f. L. *consopit-*, *consopire*.] *trans.* To lay or lull to sleep; to compose; to stupefy. (Usu. *fig.*) –1685. So **†Co·nsopite** *ppl. a.* laid to sleep. **†Consopi·tion** (erron. *consopiation*), a laying or lulling to sleep.

Consort (kǫ·nsǭɪt), *sb.*[1] ME. [a. F., ad. L. *consors*, *-ortem*, f. *con-* + *sors*, *sortem* lot.] †1. A partner, companion; a colleague –1755. Also *fig.* 2. A ship sailing in company with another 1602. 3. A husband or wife, a spouse 1634. Also, of animals 1796.

1. To seeke good consorts and companions GREENE. 2. Our c., the Rescue KANE. 3. The Queen, whether regnant or c. STEPHEN. *Prince-c.*: the title of Prince Albert, husband of Queen Victoria.

†Consort (kǫ·nsǭɪt), *sb.*[2] 1584. [n. of action f. CONSORT *v.*, and in II. erron. f. F. *concert*, It. *concerto*. Till 1612 accented by the poets *conso·rt.*]

I. 1. A fellowship, partnership, company –1702. 2. Accord; agreement –1793.

1. Wilt thou be of our c.? Say I, and be the captaine of vs all *Two Gent.* IV. i. 64. Five or six boates in a c. 1591. Experiments in C. BACON. 2. To act in c. with me 1793.

II. CONCERT of music. 1. The accord of instruments or voices –1711. Also *fig.* 2. A company of musicians making music together –1704. 3. = CONCERT 4. –1774. Also *attrib.*

1. Visit by night your Ladies chamber-window With some sweet C. *Two Gent.* III. ii. 84. 2. Lord

place me in thy c.; give one strain To my poore reed G. HERBERT.

Consort (kǫ̆nsǭ·ɹt), *v.* 1588. [Of obscure origin. Cf. CONSORT *sb.*[1], *sb.*[2], and SORT Not found in French.] †1. *trans.* To accompany; to escort, attend –1622. †2. To be a consort to –1618. 3. To sort together. Const. *with.* 1588. †4. *refl.* To associate *oneself* (*with*) –1692. 5. *intr.* To associate 1588. 6. To accord. Const. *to, with.* 1599. †7. To play, sing, or sound together –1734.

1. Sweet health..c. your grace *L. L. L.* II. i. 178. 3. C. me quickly with the dead 1596. 4. When he begins to c. himself with men, and thinks himself one LOCKE. 5. Men c. in camp and town EMERSON. To c. with Lutherans MACAULAY. 6. It did not c. with his idea MILL.

Hence †**Conso·rtable** *a.* capable of consorting together or of being consorted. **Conso·rter.** So †**Conso·rtion**, intercourse; alliance. †**Conso·rtment**, association as partners.

Consortism (kǫ·nsǭɹtiz'm). 1880. [f. CONSORT *sb.*[1] + -ISM.] *Biol.* The association during life of two organisms, each of which is dependent on the other for its existence or well-being. Cf. SYMBIOSIS.

‖**Consortium** (kǫ̆nsǭ·ɹʃiǒm). 1881. [L., f. *consors.*] Partnership, association. So **Conso·rtial** *a.* pertaining to a c.

Consortship (kǫ·nsǭɹt,ʃip). Now *rare.* 1592. [f. CONSORT *sb.*[1] + -SHIP.] The state or position of a consort; association, partnership.

†**Consoude**, now **Consound** (kǫ̆nsau·nd), *sb.* OE. [a. OF. *consolde, consoulde, consoude* :—L. *consolida*, so called app. f. L. *consolidare*; cf. COMFREY. *Consound* is a corruption.] *Herb.* A herb to which healing virtues were attributed; probably the comfrey (*Symphytum officinale*) –1807. So †**Consoude, consou·nd** *v.* = CONSOLIDATE *v.* 4.

Consound; see CONSOUDE.

Conspe·cies. 1837. [See CON-.] In *pl.* Fellow species of a genus. Hence **Conspeci·fic** *a.* specifically identical.

†**Conspe·ction.** *rare.* 1611. [ad. L. *conspectionem.*] The action of beholding –1654.

†**Conspectu·ity.** [app. joc. f. L. *conspectus.*] Faculty of sight, vision. *Cor.* II. i. 70.

‖**Conspectus** (kǫ̆nspe·ktǒs). 1836. [a. L.] 1. A comprehensive survey. 2. More usually *concr.* A synopsis, digest 1838.

1. To get at a c. of the general current of affairs rather than to study minutely a single period 1879.

Consperse (kǫ̆nspə̄·ɹs), *a.* [ad. L. *conspersus.*] Sprinkled; *spec.* in *Entom.* thickly strewn with minute punctures or dots. So †**Conspe·rsion**, the action of sprinkling; *concr.* dough, paste. [Cf. Vulg. 1 Cor. v. 7.]

Conspicuity (kǫnspikiū·ĭti). Now *rare.* 1601. [f. CONSPICUOUS.] = CONSPICUOUSNESS.

Conspicuous (kǫ̆nspi·kiu,əs), *a.* 1545. [f. L. *conspicuus.*] 1. Clearly visible, obvious or striking to the eye. 2. Obvious to the mental eye, plainly evident; striking; hence, eminent, remarkable, noteworthy 1613.

1. A Rock Of Alablaster, pil'd up to the Clouds, C. farr MILT. *P. L.* IV. 545. 2. Frankfurt—a city c. for its loyalty to the imperial house S. AUSTIN. Phr. *C. by its absence.* (Cf. Tac. *Ann.* iii. 76.) Hence **Conspi·cuous-ly** *adv.*, **-ness.**

Conspiracy (kǫ̆nspi·răsi). ME. [f. L. *conspiratio* CONSPIRATION; see -ACY.] 1. The action of conspiring. 2. (with *a* and *pl.*) A combination of persons for an evil or unlawful purpose; an agreement between two or more to do something criminal, illegal, or reprehensible; a plot ME.; †a body of conspirators –1600. 3. *fig.* Union or combination for one end or purpose (*arch.*) 1538.

1. Combin'd In bold c. against Heav'ns King MILT. *P. L.* II. 751. 2. In all conspiracies there must be great secrecy CLARENDON. 3. So is the c. of her several graces, held best together to make one perfect figure of beauty SIDNEY.

Conspirant (kǫ̆nspəi^ə·rănt). *rare.* 1603. [a. F., f. *conspirer.*] *adj.* Conspiring. *sb.* A conspirator.

Conspiration (kǫnspirē^i·ʃən). *Obs.* exc. *fig.* ME. [a. F.] = CONSPIRACY.

Conspirator (kǫ̆nspi·rătəɹ). [ME. *conspiratour*, ad. L. *conspiratorem.*] One engaged in a conspiracy; one who conspires with others to commit treason. Hence **Conspi rato·rial** *a.* pertaining to or characteristic of conspirators or conspiracy. **Conspi·ratress**, †**-trice**, a female c.

Conspire (kǫ̆nspəi^ə·ɹ), *v.* ME. [a. F. *conspirer*, ad. L. *conspirare* lit. 'to breathe together'.] 1. *intr.* To combine privily to do something criminal, illegal, or reprehensible (*esp.* to commit treason or murder, excite sedition, etc.); to plot. 2. *trans.* To plot, devise, contrive ME. 3. *intr.* To combine in action or aim; to concur, co-operate as by intention 1575. †4. To agree –1737. †5. *trans.* To unite in producing –1669.

1. They conspired against him, to slay him *Gen.* xxxvii. 18. 2. The Countree waxed wery of hym, & conspyrid his deth FABYAN. 3. Therefore must your labour c. with my inventions 1657. Hence **Conspi·rer, Conspi·ringly** *adv.*

†**Conspissate**, *v.* 1647. [f. L. *conspissat-* ppl. stem, f. *con-* + *spissare.*] *trans.* To thicken, condense –1681. Hence †**Conspissa·tion.**

†**Conspurcate**, *v.* 1600. [f. L. *conspurcat-* ppl. stem, f. *con-* + *spurcare*, f. *spurcus* unclean.] *trans.* To defile, pollute (*lit.* and *fig.*) –1669. Hence †**Conspurca·tion.**

Constable (kʊ·nstăb'l, kǫ·n-). [ME., a. OF. *cunestable, conestable*, repr. late L. *comes stabuli* count of the stable, marshal. Cf. the sense-development of *marshal.*] 1. *gen.* The chief officer of the household, court, administration, or military forces of a ruler. 2. The governor or warden of a royal fortress or castle. (Still in Eng. use.) ME. 3. A military officer ME. 4. An officer of the peace 1597.

1. *C. of France*: the principal officer of the household of the early French kings, who ultimately rose to be commander-in-chief of the army in the absence of the monarch. He was the supreme judge of questions of chivalry. (Abolished in 1627.) *C. of England, Lord High C.*: one of the chief functionaries in the English royal household, with duties and powers similar to those of the same officer in France. The office was forfeited in 1521; since which time the title has been granted only for particular occasions, *esp.* the sovereign's coronation. 4. *High C.*: an officer of a hundred or other like district, appointed to act as conservator of the peace within his district, and to perform various other duties. (Abolished in 1869.) *Petty* or *Parish C.*: a conservator of the peace, etc., within a parish or township. (Now incorporated in the County Police system.) *Chief C.*: the officer at the head of the police force of a county or equivalent district. *Special C.*: a person sworn in to act as c. on special occasions.

Phr. *To outrun the c.*: to go at too great a pace, to go too far; to spend more money than one has; to get into debt; also *to overrun the c.*

Hence †**Constablery**, the office of, or district under, a c. **Co·nstableship**, the office of c. **Co·nstablewick**, †the office of a c. (in the earlier sense); the district of a (petty) c. So **Co·nstabless**, a female c.; the wife of a c.; also a foreign title.

Constabulary (kǫ̆nstæ·biŭlări), *sb.* 1587. [ad. med.L. *constabularia*, f. *constabulus*; see -ARY.] †1. Constableship –1747. 2. A constablewick 1631. 3. The organized body of constables of a country or specified district 1837.

Constabulary (kǫ̆nstæ·biŭlări), *a.* 1824. [ad. med.L. *constabularius*; see prec.] 1. Of or pertaining to petty constables or to police officers. 2. Of the nature or function of constables 1856. var. **Consta·bulatory.**

Constancy (kǫ·nstănsi). 1526. [ad. L. *constantia.*] 1. The state or quality of being unmoved in mind; steadfastness, firmness, fortitude. 2. Steadfastness of attachment to a person or cause; fidelity 1548. 3. The quality of being invariable; uniformity, unchangingness, regularity 1600. 4. (with *a*) A permanency 1710. †5. = CONSISTENCE –1794.

1. C...wherby man or woman holdeth hole, and is not broken by impacyency 1526. 2. A fellow of plaine and vncoyned Constancie *Hen. V*, v. ii. 161. 3. The polar wind blows with equal c. in both the frigid zones 1794. var. †**Constance** (in senses 1, 2).

Constant (kǫ·nstănt), *a.* (*sb.*) ME. [a. F., ad. L. *constans, constantem, constare*, f. *con-* + *stare.*]

A. *adj.* 1. Standing firm in mind; steadfast, resolute. 2. Steadfast in attachment to a cause or person; faithful, true (*to*) ME. †3. Certain –1667. 4. Of things: Invariable, fixed, unchanging, uniform 1549. 5. *Math.* and *Physics.* Remaining the same in quantity or amount under uniform conditions. Opp. to *variable.* 1753. 6. Of actions, conditions, etc.: Continuing without intermission; continually recurring 1653; also *transf.* of a person 1639. †7. Steady (physically) –1741. †8. Consistent 1580.

1. The c. sufferings of ancient martyrs BP. HALL. 2. To one thing c. neuer *Much Ado* II. iii. 67. Tho' fortune change, his c. spouse remains POPE. 3. †*It is c.* = L. *constat.* 4. Time keeps his c. pace FELTHAM. †*C. age*: see CONSISTENT. 6. By c. vigils worn SHENSTONE. A c. reader of St. Paul's Epistles MILT. 7. *Temp.* II. ii. 119.

B. *sb.* *Math.* and *Physics.* A quantity which does not vary throughout an investigation: opp. to *variable.* Also *fig.* 1832.

The proportion between the circumference and diameter of a circle is a determinate c. 1837.

Hence **Co·nstant-ly** *adv.*, **-ness.**

Constantinian (kǫnstănti·niăn), *a.* 1641. Of or belonging to the Roman Emperor Constantine the Great, or his period (A. D. 306–337).

Constantinopolitan (kǫ̆nstæ:ntinǫ,pǫ·lităn), *a.* 1568. [ad. L. *Constantinopolitanus.*] Of or pertaining to Constantinople (Gr. Κωνσταντίνου πόλις), or to the Eastern Empire or Church; Byzantine.

‖**Constat** (kǫ·nstæt). 1570. [L., = 'it is certain'; see CONSTANT.] †1. *Law.* A certificate stating what appears (*constat*) upon record in the Court of Exchequer touching any matter. Also an exemplification of the enrolment of letters-patent under the Great Seal. –1670. †2. *fig.* Certifying evidence –1661.

Constate (kǫ̆nstē^i·t), *v. rare.* 1773. [a. F. *constater*, prob. f. L. *constat-*, ppl. stem of *constare.*] To establish, ascertain, state.

Constellate (kǫ·nstĕlĕt, kǫ̆nste·lĕt), *ppl. a.* 1649. [ad. L. *constellatus* starred.] = Constellated (see CONSTELLATE *v.* 2).

Constellate (kǫ·nstĕle^it, kǫ̆nste·le^it), *v.* 1621. [f. L. *constellat-*; see prec.] †1. *trans. Astrol.* a. To fashion under a particular constellation. b. To cast the horoscope of. c. *pass.* To be predestined (*to*) by one's 'stars'. –1829. 2. To form into, or set in, a constellation. Often *transf.* 1643. 3. To stud 1691. 4. *intr.* To cluster together, as stars in a constellation 1647.

2. To them that know how to C. those lights BOYLE. 4. Flowers, that c. on earth MRS. BROWNING.

Constellation (kǫnstĕlē^i·ʃən). ME. [a. F., or ad. L. *constellationem.*] †1. *Astrol.* The position of 'stars' (*i. e.* planets) in regard to one another; *esp.* their position at the time of a man's birth; disposition as influenced by one's 'stars' –1651. 2. A number of fixed stars grouped together within the outline of an imaginary figure traced on the face of the sky 1551. Also *transf.* and *fig.*

1. Some men holde opinion That it is constellacion Which causeth al that a man dothe GOWER. 2. The c. which the Greeks called the Argo, was a representation of the sacred ship of Osiris SULLIVAN. A c. of fair ladies BOYLE.

Constellatory (kǫ̆nste·lătəri), *a. rare.* 1652. [See CONSTELLATE and -ORY.] †1. Pertaining to constellations (sense 1) –1801. 2. Relating to, or of the nature of, a group of 'stars' 1823.

Consternate (kǫ·nstəɹne^it), *v.* 1651. [f. L. *consternat-, consternare*, collateral form to *consternere.*] To fill with amazement and terror.

Consternation (kǫnstəɹnē^i·ʃən). 1611. [a. F., or ad. L. *consternationem*; see prec.] Amazement and terror such as to prostrate one's faculties; dismay.

It is a question of c., a question that should strike him that should answer it dumb DONNE.

†**Co·nstipate**, *ppl. a.* 1542. [ad. L. *constipatus*, f. *con-* + *stipare* to press, stuff.] = Constipated –1733.

Constipate (kǫ·nstipe^it), *v.* 1533. [f. L. *constipat-* ppl. stem; see prec. Cf. COSTIVE.] †1. *trans.* To crowd, pack, or press closely together; to condense, thicken (liquids) –1709. †2. *Med.* To bind together (the tissues); to close (the pores or vessels) –1763. 3. *spec.* To confine the bowels; to render costive 1533.

1. Vapours..constipated and condensed into clouds 1709.

Constipation (kǫnstipē^i·ʃən). ME. [a. F., or ad. L. *constipationem.*] †1. The action of pressing closely together; the state of being so compressed; condensation –1713. †2. *Med.* Contraction or constriction of organic tissues, the veins, etc. –1660. 3. *spec.* A state of the bowels in which the evacuations are obstructed or stopped; costiveness 1549.

1. A pretty close C. and mutual Contact of its Particles BENTLEY.

Constituency (kǫ̆nsti·tiuˌĕnsi). 1831. [f. CONSTITUENT; cf. *regency*, etc.] A body of constituents, the body of voters who elect a representative member of a public body; in looser use, the whole body of residents in a place so represented, the place itself. Also *transf.* = CLIENTELE 3.

Constituent (kǫ̆nsti·tiuˌĕnt). 1622. [ad. L. *constituentem, constituere* to CONSTITUTE.]

A. *adj.* †1. That constitutes a thing what it is -1833. 2. That jointly constitute or compose; component 1660. 3. That constitutes, appoints, or elects a representative 1769. 4. Having the power to frame or alter a (political) constitution, as in *c. assembly, power* 1801.

2. The c. parts of water PALEY. 3. A question of right arises between the c. and the representative body JUNIUS. Hence **Consti·tuently** *adv.* as regards c. parts.

B. *sb.* 1. One who constitutes another his agent or representative 1622. 2. *spec.* One of those who elect another as their representative; an elector, loosely, any inhabitant of the place so represented 1714; † = CONSTITUENCY -1797. †3. One who constitutes or frames 1677. 4. A constituent element or part 1756.

1. The factor is answerable personally to his c. DALLAS. 2. Twenty-four Members whose constituents are upwards of 200,000 in number BRIGHT. 4. What is the special and necessary c. of royalty MAURICE.

Constitute (kǫ·nstitiūt), *v.* 1477. [f. L. *constitut-* ppl. stem, f. *con-* intensive + *statuere* to set up, place; see STATUTE.] †1. *trans.* To set, place -1728. 2. To set up, ordain, appoint 1477. 3. To set up 1549; to give legal form to 1638. 4. To frame, form; to make up, compose 1646. 5. To set up as 1534. 6. (with simple *obj.*) To make (a thing) what it is 1848.

2. Where one Man .. is constituted Representative of the whole number HOBBES. Laws..constituted by lawful authority PRIDEAUX. 3. To c. a tribunal MACAULAY, the House G. LOCKHART. 4. Many .. whose Livers are weakely constituted SIR T. BROWNE. The things which c. wealth HT. MARTINEAU. 5. He had constituted himself her companion BLACK. Hence **Co·nstituter, -or,** one who or that which constitutes.

†**Co·nstitute,** *ppl. a.* (*sb.*) 1483. [ad. L. *constitutus*; see prec.] 1. Constituted; see the verb -1808. 2. *sb.* An ordinance -1610.

Constitution (kǫnstitiū·ʃən). ME. [a. F., ad. L. *constitutionem.*] 1. The action of constituting; see the verb 1582. †2. The action of decreeing or ordaining -1661. 3. A decree, ordinance, law, regulation; *spec.* in *Rom. Law*, an enactment made by the emperor. Also *fig.* (Now *Hist.*) ME. 4. The way in which anything is constituted or made up; make, frame, composition 1601. 5. *spec.* a. Physical nature or character of the body in regard to healthiness, strength, vitality, etc. 1553. b. Nature, character, or condition of mind; disposition, temperament 1589. 6. The mode in which a state is constituted or organized 1610. 7. The system or body of fundamental principles according to which a nation, state, or body politic is constituted and governed 1735. Also *attrib.*

1. Before c. of Soveraign Power all men had right to all things HOBBES. 3. *Apostolical Constitutions* (in *Eccl. Hist.*): a collection of ecclesiastical regulations, ascribed to the apostles, but known to be of much later date. The Constitutions of Clarendon .. forbad the ordination of villains FREEMAN. 4. C. of Nature BUTLER, of society HT. MARTINEAU, the world EMERSON, the solar spectrum BREWSTER. 5. a. His c. was far from robust PRESCOTT. b. His failings.. flowed from his c., not his will MIDDLETON. 6. The original c. of England was highly aristocratical HALLAM. 7. The Twelve eldest are sent solemnly to fetch the C. itself, the printed Book of the Law CARLYLE. By the English c. we understand a few great traditional principles of government, any fundamental breach of which would involve either tyranny or anarchy 1864. Hence **Constitu·tioned** *a.* having (such and such) a c.

Constitutional (kǫnstitiū·ʃənăl), *a.* (*sb.*) 1682. [f. prec. + -AL.]

A. *adj.* 1. Of, belonging to, or inherent in a person's constitution. 2. Beneficial to the (bodily) constitution 1750. 3. Forming an essential part or element; essential 1750. 4. In harmony with, authorized by, or supporting, the political constitution 1765. Of a sovereign: Ruling according to a constitution 1801. 5. Of, pertaining to, or dealing with the political constitution 1841.

1. Pope's c. irritability L. STEPHEN. 2. C. walks 1860. 3. The difference .. between things .. c. and arbitrary WARBURTON. 4. A c. proceeding 1846. A c. king 1801, government 1841. 5. C. History of England STUBBS (*title*).

B. *sb.* 1. A walk taken for the benefit of one's health (*colloq.*) 1829. 2. = CONSTITUTIONALIST 2. 1793.

1. He taketh a c. of forty minutes every day 1836. Hence **Constitu·tionalize** *v.* to make c.; to take a c.

Constitutionalism (kǫnstitiū·ʃənăliz'm). 1832. [f. prec. + -ISM.] 1. A constitutional system of government. 2. Adherence to constitutional principles 1871.

Constitu·tionalist. 1766. [f. as prec. + -IST.] 1. One who studies or writes on the (political) constitution. 2. An adherent of constitutional principles, or of a particular constitution. In England, about 1870-80, = CONSERVATIVE. 1793. var. **Constitu·tionist** (*rare*).

Constitutionality (kǫnstitiū·ʃənæ·lĭti). 1801. [f. as prec. + -ITY.] The quality of being in accordance with the constitution; constitutional character.

The c. of the execution by electricity 1890.

Constitutionally (kǫnstitiū·ʃənăli), *adv.* 1742. [f. CONSTITUTIONAL + -LY².] 1. In constitution or composition 1767. 2. As to the (bodily) constitution 1796. 3. By virtue of one's constitution; naturally 1742. 4. In accordance with the (political) constitution 1756.

3. All you English are c. sullen FOOTE. 4. His wish seems to have been to govern c. MACAULAY.

Constitutive (kǫ·nstitiūtiv), *a.* 1592. [f. L. *constitut-* ppl. stem; see CONSTITUTE and -IVE.] 1. Having the power of constituting; constructive. 2. That makes a thing what it is; essential 1610. 3. That goes to make up; constituent, component 1640. 4. With *of*: That constitutes 1658.

1. These ideas, if not c. principles to extend our knowledge beyond the bounds of experience, are regulative principles to arrange experience J. H. STIRLING. 2. The c. essences of all individual created beings CUDWORTH. 3. The c. parts of the drama are six HARRIS. Hence **Co·nstitutive-ly** *adv.*, **-ness.**

Constrain (kǫ̆nstrēɪ·n), *v.* ME. [ad. OF. *constreindre, -aindre* :—L. *constringere*, f. *con-* + *stringere* to draw tight.] 1. *trans.* To force, compel, oblige; also *absol.*; in *Dynamics*, to restrict the motion of (a body or particle) to a certain course 1834. †2. To force out; 'to produce in opposition to nature' (J.) -1725. †3. To take by force; to violate -1699. †4. To straiten; to oppress, afflict -1859. †5. To compress into small compass; to contract (*rare*) ME. 6. To confine forcibly, keep in bonds, imprison ME. Also *fig.* †7. = CONSTRINGE, CONSTRICT -1697.

1. Constreynyd to lerne the Latyn tong 1538. String constrained by pulley 1856. To c. assent WATTS. 2. To c. a smile POPE. 3. *Tit. A.* v. ii. 178. 6. How the strait stays the slender waste c. GAY (J.). 7. When Winter Frosts c. the Field with Cold DRYDEN. Hence **Constrai·nable** *a.* (*rare*). **Constrai·ned** *ppl. a.* forced; not natural; embarrassed; cramped. **Constrai·ned-ly** *adv.*, **-ness.** **Constrai·ner** (*rare*). **Constrai·ningly** *adv.*

†**Constrai·nt,** *ppl. a.* ME. [a. OF. (pa. pple. of *constreindre*):—popular L. type **constrinctus* for *constrictus.*] = Constrained.

Constraint (kǫ̆nstrēɪ·nt), *sb.* ME. [a. OF. *constreinte*, fem. sb., f. prec.] 1. Coercion, compulsion 1534. 2. Confinement; restriction of liberty 1590. †3. Oppression, affliction -1579. 4. Compulsion put upon the expression of feelings or the behaviour: always implying unnaturalness or embarrassment 1706. 5. *Dynamics.* See CONSTRAIN *v.* 1. 1856.

1. Not from c. but choice ROBERTSON. 2. Let the captain talk of boisterous war; The prisoner of immured dark c. 1596. 4. You see I write to you without any sort of c. or method, as things come into my head 1706. Hence †**Constrai·ntive** *a.* having tendency to constrain (*rare*).

Constrict (kǫ̆nstri·kt), *v.* 1732. [f. L. *constrict-, constringere*. Cf. CONSTRAIN, CONSTRINGE.] 1. *trans.* To draw together as by tightening an encircling string; to make small or narrow (an orifice, etc.); to contract, compress 1759. 2. To cause to contract or shrink 1732.

1. The neck should not be constricted by a tight collar 1871. 2. Such things as c. the Fibres ARBUTHNOT. Hence **Constri·cted** *ppl. a.* drawn together by constriction; *Nat. Hist.* narrowed at some part, as if by constriction. **Constri·ctive** *a.* that tends to c.

Constriction (kǫ̆nstri·kʃən). ME. [ad. L. *constrictionem*; see CONSTRINGE, CONSTRICT, CONSTRAIN.] 1. Drawing together as by an encircling pressure; the condition of being so drawn together; compression, contraction. 2. *concr.* A constricted part 1826. 3. Something which constricts 1650.

1. The c. of the pores..of the body VENNER. 2. A c. of the vast channel narrows it to a mile PARKMAN.

Constrictor (kǫ̆nstri·ktəɪ). 1735. [a. L.; see CONSTRINGE.] 1. *Anat.* A muscle which draws together a part. 2. *Surg.* An instrument for producing constriction; a compressor 1882. 3. A large snake which crushes its prey; a BOA-CONSTRICTOR 1845.

Constringe (kǫ̆nstri·ndʒ), *v.* 1604. [ad. L. *constringere.* Cf. CONSTRICT.] 1. *trans.* = CONSTRICT 1. ? *Obs.* 1606. 2. *Phys.* = CONSTRICT 2. 1604. 3. *intr.* To become close or dense. BROWNING.

1. The neck [of the Bladder] is constringed with a muscle BURTON. 2. Constringing such [parts] as are dilated POTT.

Constringent (kǫ̆nstri·ndʒĕnt). 1603. [ad. L. *constringentem.*] Causing constriction. Hence **Constri·ngency,** c. quality.

Construable (kǫ̆nstrū·ăb'l), *a.* 1657. [f. CONSTRUE *v.* + -ABLE.] That may be construed.

Construct (kǫ̆nstrʊ·kt), *ppl. a. arch.* ME. [ad. L. *constructus.*] 1. *pa. pple.* Constructed. 2. *adj.* in *C. state, state c.*, in *Heb. Gram.*: the form of the substantive used when standing before another having an attributive (or genitive) relation to it.

Construct (kǫ̆nstrʊ·kt), *v.* 1610. [f. L. *construct-, construere* to pile up. Cf. CONSTRUE.] 1. *trans.* To make or form by fitting the parts together; to frame, build, erect 1663. Also *absol.* 2. *Gram.* To combine in grammatical construction. (Used chiefly of the manner.) 1864. †3. To CONSTRUE. *Sc.* -1676.

1. To c. a ship 1794, road 1863, system JOHNSON. Hence **Constru·cted** *ppl. a.* (Usu. qualified, as *well-c.*) **Constru·cter, -or,** one who constructs or designs the construction of (*esp.* of ships for the navy).

Construction (kǫ̆nstrʊ·kʃən). ME. [ad. L. *constructionem*; see prec.]

I. 1. The action of framing, devising, or forming, by the putting together of parts; erection, building; the art or science of constructing. 2. The manner in which a thing is constructed or formed; structure 1707; constructive faculty 1826. 3. A thing constructed 1796.

1. [The] Director of Naval C. 1891. *Arch of c.*: an arch built in the body of a wall or other structure to relieve the part below it. *C. of equations*: the method of reducing a known equation into lines and figures, whereby its truth may be demonstrated geometrically. 2. The bad c. of the hospitals 1799.

II. 1. *Gram.* The action of syntactically arranging words in a sentence: syntactical connexion 1530; in *Heb. Gram.*, the relation of a sb. in the construct state 1762. †2. The action of construing; translation -1643. 3. The construing, explaining, or interpreting of a text, statement, action, words, etc.; sense 1483.

1. That stands in c. with all tenses 1640. 3. C. of the tenor of a letter WELLINGTON.

Comb. **c.-way, -railway,** a temporary railway for use in the c. of a permanent railway, canal, or the like. Hence **Constru·ctional** *a.* of or pertaining to c. **Constru·ctionally** *adv.*

Constru·ctionism. 1924. [f. prec. + -ISM.] Artistic expression by means of mechanical structures.

Constructionist (kǫ̆nstrʊ·kʃənist). 1844. [f. as prec. + -IST.] 1. One who practises or advocates construction. 2. With *strict, loose*, etc.: One who puts a strict, loose, or other construction upon a law, etc. (Used chiefly in reference to the Constitution of the United States.) 3. One who follows the principles of constructionism 1924.

Constructive (kǫ̆nstrʊ·ktiv), *a.* 1680. [ad. med.L. *constructivus*, f. *construct-* ppl. stem; see -IVE.] 1. Having the quality of constructing 1841. 2. Of or pertaining to construction 1817. 3. Resulting from a certain interpretation; not directly expressed, but inferred 1680.

1. A clear-headed c. theologian J. H. NEWMAN. 2. C. and Engineering Staff 1899. Design should be

based upon c. exigencies 1874. 3. Phr. *C. blasphemy, notice, possession, treason, trust*, etc. *C. total loss* (in Marine Insurance): the assumption of the loss of a ship or cargo as total under certain circumstances, as when arrival or recovery seems highly improbable, etc. Hence **Constru·ctive·ly** *adv.*, **-ness.**

Constru·ctivism. 1924. [f. prec. + -ISM.] = CONSTRUCTIONISM. Hence **Constru·ctivist** *a.*

†**Constru·cture.** 1620. [f. L. stem *construct-* + -URE, after *structure.*] Construction –1840.

Construe (kǫ·nstru, kǫ̆nstrū·), *v.* [ME. *construen*, ad. L. *construere.* Formerly spelt and pronounced *conster.*] †1. *trans.* To CONSTRUCT –1605. 2. *Gram.* To combine (words, or parts of speech) grammatically 1530. 3. *Gram.* To analyse the grammatical construction of a sentence, adding, if necessary, a word for word translation; hence loosely, to translate a passage orally ME. Also *intr.* (for *pass.*) 4. *trans.* To give the sense or meaning of; to take in a specified way ME. 5. *transf.* To interpret, put a construction on (actions, things, or persons) 1465. 6. To deduce; to infer 1450. Also *absol.*

2. The verb *hearken* is construed with *to, unto* (mod.). 3. He cannot c. a Greek author MACAULAY. 4. One crabbed question more to c. or *vulgo* conster BROWNING. Authority is of very little use in construing an unskilfully drawn will 1885. 5. To c. silence as an affront 1833. Hence **Co·nstrue** *sb.* an act of construing; a verbal translation. **Construer. Construing** *vbl. sb.*

†**Co·nstuprate,** *v.* 1550. [f. L. *constuprare.*] To violate, ravish. Hence †**Constupra·tion.**

Consubsi·st, *v. intr.* To subsist together. TUCKER.

Consubstantial (kǫnsɒbstæ·nʃăl), *a.* 1483. [ad. L. *consubstantialis*, f. L. *con-* + *substantia*; repr. Gr. ὁμοούσιος, f. ὁμός + οὐσία.] Of one and the same substance or essence; the same in substance. Also as quasi-*sb.*

The sone..is consubstançial, that is to saye, he is of one nature and substaunce with the father 1526. Hence **Consubsta·ntialism,** the doctrine of consubstantiation. **Consubsta·ntialist,** one who believes in the consubstantiality of the three Persons of the Godhead; one who holds the doctrine of consubstantiation. **Consubsta·ntially** *adv.*

Consubsta ntia·lity. 1526. [ad. L. *consubstantialitas* (Cassiodorus); repr. Gr. τὸ ὁμοούσιον, ὁμοουσιότης.] Identity of substance, *esp.* of the three Persons of the Trinity.

Our Lord's C. and Coeternity with the Father J. H. NEWMAN.

Consubstantiate (kǫnsɒbstæ·nʃi,eᶦt), *v.* 1597. [f. ppl. stem of med.L. *consubstantiare*; see CONSUBSTANTIAL.] 1. *trans.* To unite in one common substance. Also *intr.* †2. To believe in consubstantiation –1715.

1. It [Gold] is not easily consubstantiated with us 1651. 2. The consubstantiating Church and Priest Refuse communion to the Calvinist DRYDEN. So **Consubsta·ntiate** *ppl. a.* made one in substance.

Consubstantiation (kǫ·nsɒbstæ:nʃi,ēᶦ·ʃən). 1597. [ad. 16th c. L. *consubstantiationem.* Formed after *transubstantiation.*] 1. The doctrine of the real substantial presence of the body and blood of Christ together with the bread and wine in the Eucharist, as dist. from *transubstantiation.* (A term used controversially to designate the Lutheran view, but not accepted by Lutherans.) †2. A rendering consubstantial –1774. Hence **Consubstantia·tionist,** one who holds the doctrine of c.

†**Consue·te,** *a.* ME. [ad. L. *consuetus.*] Accustomed –1656.

Consuetude (kǫ·nswĭtiud). ME. [a. OF., ad. L. *consuetudo*, short for *consuetitudo*, f. *consuetus.* Cf. CUSTOM.] 1. Custom, usage, habit. (Chiefly *Sc.*) 2. Familiarity; social intercourse. [So in L.] 1803.

1. The lawis and consuetudes of the burgh 1575. Hence **Consuetu·dinal** *a.* and *sb.* = next.

Consuetudinary (kǫnswĭtiū·dinări). 1494. [ad. L. *consuetudinarius* (see prec.).] *adj.* Customary 1590. *sb.* A manual of customs or usages, local or particular to some body. Cf. ORDINARY.

Consul (kǫ·nsɒ̆l), *sb.* ME. [a. L. *consul* (in sense 1); in the later senses conn. w. L. *consulere.*] 1. The title of the two annually elected magistrates who exercised conjointly supreme authority in the Roman Republic. 2. Hence, a title for the three chief magistrates of the French Republic, from 1799 to 1804. 3. Used by mediæval Latin writers as = *comes*, count, earl. *Obs.* exc. *Hist.* 1494. †4. A member of a council –1753. †5. English appellation of various foreign officials and magistrates, *e.g.* the *savii* of Venice –1757. 6. Hence: An agent commissioned by a sovereign state to reside in a foreign town or port, to protect the interests of its subjects there, and to watch over its commercial rights and privileges. So *C.-general, Vice-C.* (The ordinary current sense.) 1599. Also *transf.*

2. The late discussion with the First Consul 1802. 3. The Sherife was deputy of the Consull or Earle COKE *On Litt.* 5. Many of the Consuls, rais'd and met, Are at the Dukes already *Oth.* I. ii. 43. The consuls of the district waited on her to offer her a guard 1787. Hence **Co·nsulage,** consular charge or dues. **Co·nsuless,** the wife of a c. **Co·nsulship,** the office, or term of office, of a c.

Consular (kǫ·nsiŭlăɹ), *a.* (*sb.*) ME. [ad. L. *consularis.*] 1. Of, pertaining to, or of the nature of a consul 1533. var. **Co·nsulary.** 2. *sb.* A man of consular rank.

Consulate (kǫ·nsiŭlĕt, -sɒ̆lĕt). ME. [ad. L. *consulatus*; so F. *consulat.*] 1. Consular government; the office, dignity, or position of the consuls. 2. The consular government in France, and its period (1799–1804). 3. The office or establishment of a consul 1702.

Consult (kǫ̆nsɒ·lt), *v.* 1540. [ad. L. *consultare*, freq. of *consulere, consultum*, related to *consul* and *consilium* COUNSEL.] 1. *intr.* To take counsel together, deliberate, confer 1565. †2. *trans.* To confer about, deliberate upon, consider –1703. †3. To take counsel to bring about; to plan, devise, contrive –1658. 4. To provide for by consultation; to have an eye to. [L. *consulere alicui.*] 1658. 5. To ask advice of, seek counsel from; to have recourse to for instruction or professional advice 1635; *spec.* to refer to (a book or author) 1635.

1. Come Gentlemen, Let vs c. vpon to morrowes Businesse *Rich. III*, v. iii. 45. Phr. *C. with*: to take counsel *with* (a person, a book, etc.). 2. Many things were then consulted for the future CLARENDON. 3. Thou hast consulted shame to thy house *Hab.* ii. 10. 4. Every man.. Consulted soberly his private good DRYDEN. 5. To c. a practitioner 1878, the writings of learned men BERKELEY. *fig.* To c. one's pillow: see PILLOW. Hence **Co·nsultee·**, a person consulted. **Consu·lter, -or,** one who consults.

Consult (kǫ̆nsɒ·lt, kǫ·nsɒlt), *sb. Obs.* exc. *Hist.* 1533. [a. F. *consulte* = med.L. *consulta.* In sense 3 repr. L. *consultum.*] 1. The action of consulting; consultation 1560. 2. A meeting for consultation; in 17th c. often *spec.* a cabal 1634. 3. *Rom. Hist.* A decree of the senate. [L. *senatus consultum.*] 1533.

1. Seen In close c. POPE. Their consults produced resolutions of violence CARTE. 2. At a c. of the Jesuits in London SCOTT.

‖**Consulta** (konsu·ltă). 1768. [It. and Sp.; cf. prec.] A meeting of council (It., Sp., or Pg.); the minutes of such a meeting.

Consultant (kǫ̆nsɒ·ltănt). 1697. [ad. L. *consultantem.*] 1. One who consults (an oracle). 2. A consulting physician, engineer, etc. 1878.

Consultary, obs. f. CONSULTORY.

Consultation (kǫnsɒltēᶦ·ʃən). ME. [a. F., or ad. L. *consultationem.*] 1. The action of consulting or taking counsel together; deliberation, conference 1548. 2. A conference in which the parties, *e.g.* lawyers or medical practitioners, consult and deliberate 1425. 3. The action of consulting (a book) 1751. 4. *Law.* A writ by which a cause having been removed by prohibition out of the ecclesiastical court to another, is returned thither again 1548.

1. If bishops did often use..the help of mutual c. HOOKER.

Consultative (kǫnsɒ·ltătiv), *a.* 1583. [f. L. *consult-* ppl. stem.] Of or pertaining to consultation; deliberative, advisory.

To have a consultatiue..voice onely STUBBES.

Consultatory (kǫ̆nsɒ·ltătəri), *a.* 1600. [ad. L. *consultatorius.*] Pertaining to or serving for consultation (*e.g.* of an oracle, etc.); consultative.

Consu·lting, *ppl. a.* 1796. [See -ING [2].] That consults or asks advice.

C. physician, engineer, etc.: one who makes a business of giving professional advice. [F. *médecin consultant*; from obs. sense of *consulter* to give (professional) counsel.]

†**Consu·ltive,** *a.* 1616. [f. L. *consult-*, ppl. stem.] Having the function of counselling or consulting; consultative –1823; deliberate. JER. TAYLOR. Hence †**Consu·ltively** *adv.* (= L. *consulto*).

†**Consu·lto.** 1659. [ad. Sp. and Pg. *consulta.*] = CONSULTA –1670.

Consultory (kǫ̆nsɒ·ltəri), *a.* ? *Obs.* 1616. [f. L. type **consultorius.*] Relating to consultation (*e.g.* of an oracle, etc.); advisory.

Consumable (kǫ̆nsiū·măb'l), *a.* 1641. [f. CONSUME *v.*] Capable of being consumed by fire, etc.; suited for consumption as food, etc. As *sb. pl.* Articles of consumption 1802.

†**Consuma·tion.** 1551. [a. OF. *consumacion*, var. of *consummation, -sommation.*] 1. Destruction –1632. 2. The disease CONSUMPTION 1551.

Consume (kǫ̆nsiū·m), *v.*[1] ME. [ad. L. *consumere*, f. *con-* + *sumere.*] 1. *trans.* To make away with, destroy, as by fire, evaporation, †decomposition, †disease, or the like. Also *fig.* 2. To waste, squander 1460. 3. To use up 1527; *esp.* to eat up, drink up 1587. 4. To take up, spend, waste (time) 1533. 5. *intr.* To waste away 1526; to burn away 1591.

1. To c. the remains in the forum MERIVALE. As the cloud is consumed *Job* vii. 9. The rest were consumed either by Poverty or Diseases MANLEY. *pass.* to be 'eaten up' *with* (envy, etc.). 2. Caste her a-way & c. her goodes 1530. 4. To c. the best years of one's life in custody HALLAM. 5. Their beauty shall c. in the graue *Ps.* xlix. 14.

Hence **Consu·med** *ppl. a.* used up; †wasted with disease; † = 'confounded', as a term of dislike. **Consu·medly** *adv.* excessively, hugely. (App. at first = *confoundedly.*) **Consu·ming·ly** *adv.*, **-ness.**

†**Consu·me,** *v.*[2] 1483. [a. F. *consumer*, var. of *consummer, -sommer*, ad. L. *consummare.*] *trans.* To accomplish, complete –1541.

Consumer (kǫ̆nsiū·məɹ). 1535. [f. CONSUME *v.*[1] + -ER.] He who or that which consumes; in *Pol. Econ.* opposed to *producer.*

Every man is a c., and ought to be a producer EMERSON.

Consummate (kǫ̆nsɒ·mĕt, kǫ·nsɒmĕt), *a.* ME. [ad. L. *consummatus*; see next.] †1. as *pa. pple.* Completed, perfected –1832; of marriage: Consummated –1765. 2. *adj.* Complete, perfect 1527; supremely qualified 1643; supreme; utmost 1526.

2. Last the bright c. floure MILT. *P. L.* v. 481. The c. hypocrite MACAULAY. C. happiness WORDSW. Hence **Consummately** *adv.*

Consummate (kǫ·nsɒ̆meᶦt, kǫ̆nsɒ·meᶦt), *v.* 1530. [f. prec., or L. *consummat-*, ppl. stem of *consummare*, f. *con-* + *summa, summus.*] 1. *trans.* To bring to completion; to accomplish, fulfil, complete, finish. 2. To complete *marriage* by sexual intercourse 1540. Also *absol.* †3. To make perfect –1678. Also *intr.* (for *refl.*)

1. God also consummated the Universe in six days RAY. Hence **Co·nsummative, consu·mmative** *a.* tending to c.; completory, final. **Co·nsummator.**

Consummation (kǫnsɒ̆mēᶦ·ʃən). ME. [a. OF. *consommation* (*-somation, -sumation*), ad. L. *consummationem*; see prec.] 1. The action of consummating (see CONSUMMATE *v.* 1, 2). 2. Completion, conclusion, as an event or condition; end, death 1475. 3. The action of perfecting; perfection, acme 1526.

1. Between the beginning and c. or finishing of it 1665. She would have the wedding before c. FARQUHAR. 2. 'Tis a c. Deuoutly to be wish'd *Haml.* III. i. 63. Quiet consumation haue, And renowned be thy graue *Cymb.* IV. ii. 280. The general c. of all things PRIESTLEY.

†**Consu·mpt,** *ppl. a.* ME. only. [ad. L. *consumptus.*] Consumed; as *pple.* and *adj.*

Consumption (kǫnsɒ·mᵖʃən). ME. [ad. L. *consumptionem*; see CONSUME. In F. ousted by *consommation.*] 1. The action or fact of consuming by use, waste, etc. (see CONSUME *v.*). 2. Decay, wasting away, or wearing out; waste 1513. 3. Wasting of the body by disease; a wasting disease; now applied *spec.* to pulmonary consumption ME. Also *fig.* 4. *Pol. Econ.* The destructive employment of industrial products; the amount of them consumed 1662.

1. Till the c. of the world FOXE. The c. of heat in mechanical work TYNDALL. 2. The C. of a Man's Estate 1691. 4. Increased price will cause a diminished c. BABBAGE. This immense home c. MᶜCULLOCH. Hence †**Consu·mptioner,** consumer. †**Consu·mptionish,** phthisical.

Consumptive (kǫ̆nsɒ·mᵖtiv). 1647. [f. L. *consumpt-* ppl. stem.]

A. *adj.* **1.** Having a tendency to consume; destructive 1664. †**2.** Characterized by being consumed –1664. **3.** Affected by wasting disease; sickly, reduced 1655. **4.** *spec.* Relating or belonging to, or affected by, phthisis 1660. **5.** *Comm.* Of or for consumption of produce 1864.

1. Too c. of time EVELYN. 2. C. offerings to Saints JER. TAYLOR. 4. A c. Cough WESLEY, patient 1757. 5. Phr. *A c. demand*: a demand for purposes of c., not a *speculative* demand.

B. *sb.* [the adj. used ellipt.] †**1.** A consumptive or corrosive agent –1758. **2.** A consumptive person 1666.

Hence **Consu·mptive·ly** *adv.*, **-ness.**

†**Co·nsy.** ME. only. [? F. *concis*, L. *concisus.*] *Cookery.* An ancient mode of cooking capons cut into small pieces, stewed, seasoned, and coloured with saffron.

Contabescent (kǫntăbe·sĕnt), *a.* 1868. [ad. L. *contabescentem* pr. pple.] Wasting away, atrophied; in *Bot.* characterized by suppression of pollen in the anthers of flowers. Hence **Contabe·scence.**

Contact (kǫ·ntækt). 1626. [ad. L. *contactus*, *contingere* to touch (each other).] **1.** The state or condition of touching. Also *transf.* and *fig.* **2.** *Math.* The meeting of two curves (or surfaces) at a point so as to have a common tangent (or tangent plane) at that point 1660. **3.** *Geol.* 'The plane between two adjacent bodies of dissimilar rock' (Raymond) 1881.

1. Phr. *To make* or *break c.*: to complete or interrupt an electric circuit. *To come in c. with*: to meet, come across. *Comb.*: **c.-level**, an instrument in which a form of spirit-level is used to determine minute differences of length; **-mine**, a mine which explodes by c. Hence **Co·ntact** *v.* to bring or come into, or be in, c. (*rare, techn.*). **Conta·ctual** *a.* of or relating to c. (*rare*).

Conta·ctile, *a. rare.* 1882. [f. *contact-* ppl. stem.] Relating to contact and the sensation of contact.

†**Conta·ction.** 1612. [f. as prec.] The action of touching –1682.

‖**Contadino** (kontadī·no). It. pl. **-ini.** 1835. [It.; f. *contado*:—L. *comitatus*; see COUNTY.] An Italian peasant. Hence ‖**Contadi·na** fem.; pl. **-ine.**

Contagion (kǫ̆ntē¹·dʒən). ME. [a. F., or ad L. *contagionem* a touching.] **1.** The communication of disease from body to body by contact direct or mediate 1535; contagious influence 1596. **2.** A plague or pestilence ME. **3.** = CONTAGIUM 1603; *concr.* a poison that infects the blood. *poet.* 1602. **4.** *fig.* Contagious influence ME.; moral corruption 1533.

1. The Jewish Nation..to avoid c. or pollution, in time of pestilence, burnt the bodies of their friends SIR T. BROWNE. To dare the vile c. of the night *Jul. C.* II. i. 265. 2. That terrible c. known as the Black Death 1856. 3. *concr.* Ile touch my point With this c. [a poisonous ointment] *Haml.* III. ii. 408. 4. The c. of fanaticism GIBBON, of example FROUDE. A few eminent men .. were exempt from the general c. MACAULAY. Hence **Conta·gioned** *ppl. a.* affected by c. **Conta·gionist,** one who believes that certain diseases, as the plague, etc., are contagious.

Contagious (kǫ̆ntē¹·dʒəs), *a.* ME. [a. OF. *contagieus*, ad. (late) L. *contagiosus*; see prec.] **1.** Of the nature of or characterized by contagion. Also *fig.* **2.** Of diseases: Communicable by contact ME. **3.** Tainted with and communicating contagion 1586. **4.** *fig.* Apt to be communicated from one to another 1660. †**5.** Apt to breed or infect with disease –1792. †**6.** Pernicious, noxious –1653.

1. The c. vices of the court SOUTHEY. 2. The Contagious Diseases (Animals) Act, 1878. *Times.* 3. The absorption of..bile, milk, c. matters 1813. 4. I see this Folly is c. SHADWELL. 5. Noisom and c. Vapours RAY. 6. C. weather HAKLUYT. A c. broode of Scismatickes WEEVER. Hence **Conta·gious-ly** *adv.*, **-ness.**

‖**Contagium** (kǫ̆ntē¹·dʒiǒm). Pl. **-ia.** 1654. [L., = *contagio*; see CONTAGION.] †**1.** = CONTAGION. **2.** *spec.* The supposed substance by which a contagious disease is transmitted 1870.

Contain (kǫ̆ntē¹·n), *v.* [ME. *conteine(n, contene*, a. OF. *contenir*:—L. *continere*, f. *con-* + *tenere.*] **1.** *trans.* To HOLD. **2.** To comprise; to have in it ME. **3.** †To measure –1703; to be equal to ME. †**4.** To take up, occupy –1736. **5.** To enclose. *Obs.* exc. *pass.* ME. †**6.** To hold together –1579. †**7.** To keep under control, restrain, restrict, confine; to retain –1831. Also *refl.* **8.** *refl.* or *intr.* To restrain oneself; †*spec.* to be continent, keep oneself in chastity ME.

1. This pot contayneth eyght quartes PALSGR. 2. And Grandsires Grandsons the long List contains DRYDEN. The rock..contains a good deal of iron TYNDALL. 3. A pound avoirdupois contains 7000 grains (*mod.*). 5. That part conteined betweene the French Seas POWEL. 8. But if they cannot conteine, let them marry 1 *Cor.* vii. 9. Hence **Contai·nable** *a.* that can be contained. **Contai·ner.** **Contai·nment** (*rare*), the action or fact of containing; holding; restraint; CONTENEMENT.

Contaminate (kǫ̆ntæ·minĕt), *ppl. a. arch.* 1552. [ad. L. *contaminatus*; see next.] Contaminated, defiled.

Contaminate (kǫ̆ntæ·minē¹t), *v.* 1526. [f. L. *contaminat-*, *contaminare*, f. *contamen* (for *contagmen*), f. *con-* + *tag-* stem of *tangere.*] *trans.* To render impure by contact or mixture; to corrupt, defile, pollute, sully, taint, infect.

Shall we now C. our fingers with base bribes *Jul. C.* IV. iii. 24. Air that is contaminated by respiration SULLIVAN. Hence **Conta:mina·tion**, the action of contaminating or state of being contaminated; that which contaminates. **Conta·minative** *a.* causing contamination. **Conta·minator.** So †**Conta·minous** *a.* infectious.

Contango (kǫ̆ntæ·ŋgo). 1853. [App. a fortuitous formation from *continue.*] *Stock Exchange.* The percentage which the buyer of stock pays to the seller to postpone transfer to the next settling-day; opp. to BACKWARDATION. **Conta·ngo** *v.*, to pay c. on (stocks or shares).

†**Co·nteck,** *sb.* [ME. *contek*, a. AF.] Strife or debate at law; discord; contumely –1618.

Contek with bloody knyf, and scharp manace CHAUCER. So †**Conte·ck** *v.* to contend. †**Contecker,** one who contends.

†**Conte·ction.** [f. L. *contect-* ppl. stem.] Covering up. SIR T. BROWNE.

Contemn (kǫ̆nte·m), *v.* 1450. [a. OF. *contemner*, ad. L. *contem(p)nere*, f. *con-* + *temnere.* Now chiefly a literary wd.] *trans.* To treat as of small value, view with contempt; to slight, scorn, disdain, despise.

I haue done pennance for contemning Loue *Two Gent.* II. iv. 129. Mr. Cooper contemned my lords' order, and would not obey it MRS. HUTCHINSON. Hence **Conte·mner, -or.** **Conte·mningly** *adv.*

Conte·mper, *v.* ? *Obs.* 1579. [ad. L. *contemperare* to temper by mixing.] **1.** To mingle together. **2.** To moderate, qualify 1605. **3.** To adjust (*to*) by tempering 1600.

3. He contempereth his phrases to our capacitie 1600. Hence †**Conte·mperament**, the action of contempering or condition of being contempered.

†**Conte·mperate,** *v.* 1605. [f. L. *contemperat-* ppl. stem; see prec.] **1.** *trans.* To blend together 1655. **2.** = CONTEMPER 2. –1766. **3.** = CONTEMPER 3. –1713.

2. To c. the acrimony of the blood FULLER. Hence †**Contempera·tion**, a blending together; blended condition; the action of tempering or moderating; adjustment; compromise.

Conte·mperature. Now *rare.* 1567. [f. L. *contemperare*; cf. *temperature.*] A blending together; the product of such blending; harmonious mixture.

Whether colour be a quality emergent from the different c. of the elements SOUTH.

‖**Contempla·men.** *rare.* 1678. [mod.L., f. *contemplari*; cf. *certamen*, etc.] An object of contemplation.

Contemplant (kǫ̆nte·mplănt), *a.* 1794. [ad. L. *contemplantem.*] That contemplates.

Contemplate (kǫ·ntĕmplē¹t, kǫ̆nte·mplē¹t), *v.* 1592. [f. L. *contemplat-* ppl. stem; see CONTEMPLE.] **1.** *trans.* To look at with continued attention, gaze upon, observe, BEHOLD 1605. **2.** To view mentally; to meditate upon, ponder, study 1594. **3.** To consider in a certain aspect, regard 1799. **4.** To have in view; to expect, take into account as a contingency 1792; to purpose 1816. **5.** *intr.* To be occupied in contemplation; to meditate, muse 1592.

1. The day whereon God did rest and c. his own works BACON. 2. C. all this work of Time TENNYSON. 3. To c. a bill with satisfaction 1844. 4. Their opinions, however, c. the employment of force 1807. 5. So many Houres, must I C. 3 *Hen. VI*, II. v. 33. Hence **Contemplatingly** *adv.*

Contemplation (kǫntĕmplē¹·ʃən). ME. [a. OF., ad. L. *contemplationem*; see prec.] **1.** The action of beholding 1480. **2.** The action of mentally viewing; attentive consideration, study; meditation ME. **3.** *spec.* Religious musing ME. **4.** *ellipt.* Matter for contemplation 1725. **5.** The action of taking into account; consideration, regard; view 1673. **6.** Prospect, expectation; intention 1659.

2. The sundrie c. of my trauells *A. Y. L.* IV. i. 18. 3. In contemplacion and prayer CAXTON. 5. At the c. of our prayers 1536. In c. of law 1819. 6. *In c.*: in view (as a contingency, or an end).

Conte·mplatist. *Obsolesc.* 1669. [f. L. *contemplat-* (see above).] One given to contemplation.

Contemplative (kǫ̆nte·mplătiv). ME. [a. OF. *contemplatif, -ive*, ad. L. *contemplativus.*]

A. *adj.* **1.** Given to contemplation; meditative; †speculative. **2.** Characterized by, or tending to, contemplation ME. **3.** Opp. to *active* ME.

1. This Letter wil make a contemplatiue Ideot of him *Twel. N.* II. v. 23. 2. Fix'd and c. their looks, Still turning over Nature's books DENHAM. 3. Wrangling..whether the contemplatiue, or the actiue life doe excell SIDNEY. Phr. *C. of*: contemplating. Hence **Conte·mplative·ly** *adv.*, **-ness.**

B. *sb.* A person devoted to religious meditation; one who leads the contemplative life ME.

Contemplator (kǫ·ntĕmplē¹təɹ). 1607. [a. L.] One who contemplates.

†**Conte·mple,** *v.* 1502. [a. F. *contempler*, ad. L. *contemplare* (orig. *-ari*), f. *con-* + *templum* an open place for observation marked out by the augur; see TEMPLE.] To CONTEMPLATE –1605.

Contemporaneity (kǫ̆nte:mpŏrănī·ĭti). Also *erron.* **cot-.** 1772. = *Contemporaneousness.*

Contemporaneous (kǫ̆nte:mpŏrē¹·niəs), *a.* Also *erron.* **cot-.** 1656. [f. L. *contemporaneus.*] **1.** Existing or occurring at the same time. **2.** Of the same historical or geological period 1833.

1. Strictly c. testimony J. H. NEWMAN. 2. Tumuli of the stone period believed to be c. with the mounds LYELL. vars. †**Conte·mporane,** †**Contempora·nean.** Hence **Contempora·neous·ly** *adv.*, **-ness.**

Contemporary (kǫ̆nte·mpŏrări). Also **cot-** ('a downright barbarism' Bentley). 1631. [f. L. *con-* + *temporarius* of or belonging to time.]

A. *adj.* **1.** Living, existing, or occurring together in time 1655. **2.** Equal in age, coeval 1667. **3.** Occurring at the same moment of time, or during the same period; contemporaneous, simultaneous 1656.

1. Writers c. with the events they write of M. PATTISON. 2. A neighbouring Wood born with himself he sees, And loves his old c. trees COWLEY.

B. *sb.* One who lives at the same time with another or others 1646. Also *transf.* of journals, etc.

Contemporize (kǫ̆nte·mpŏrəiz), *v.* 1646. [f. as L. *contemporare.*] To synchronize or cause to synchronize. So †**Conte·mporate** *v.* to synchronize.

Contempt (kǫ̆nte·mᵖt), *sb.* ME. [ad. L. *contemptus*, f. *contempt-*, *contemnere.* Cf. OF. *contemps, contempt.*] **1.** The action of contemning or despising; the mental attitude in which a thing is considered as of little account, or as vile and worthless. **2.** The condition of being contemned or despised; dishonour, disgrace 1450. †**3.** = Object of contempt –1832. **4.** *Law.* Disobedience or open disrespect to the authority or lawful commands of the sovereign, the privileges of the Houses of Parliament or other legislative body; and *esp.* action of any kind that interferes with the proper administration of justice by the various courts of law; in this connexion called *C. of Court* 1621.

1. An outward c. of what the public esteemeth sacred BERKELEY. All the contempts they could cast at him were their shame not his MRS. HUTCHINSON. 2. He would like to bring military glory into c. JOWETT. 4. Phr. *In c.*: in the position of having committed c., and not having purged himself. Hence †**Conte·mpt** *v.* to contemn. †**Conte·mptful** *a.* contemptuous, contemptible.

Contemptible (kǫ̆nte·mᵖtib'l), *a.* ME. [ad. (post-cl.) L. *contemptibilis* (see above).] **1.** To be despised; worthy only of contempt; despicable. **2.** Exhibiting contempt; full of contempt. *Obs.* in educated use. 1594.

1. So small and c. an animal [the Flea] 1664. 2. 'Tis very possible hee'l scorne it, for the man .. hath a c. spirit *Much Ado* II. iii. 187. Hence **Conte·mptibi·lity**, the quality or fact of being c. **Conte·mptibleness.** **Conte·mptibly** *adv.*

Contemptuous (kǫ̆nte·mᵖtiuəs), *a.* 1529. [f. L. *contemptus* + -OUS.] **1.** Showing contempt; disdainful, scornful, insolent 1595. †2. Contemptible -1796.

1. Satan with c. brow MILT. *P. L.* IV. 885. An air of c. indifference GEO. ELIOT. 2. C. base-borne Callot as she is 2 *Hen. VI*, I. iii. 86. Hence Conte·mptuous-ly *adv.*, -ness.

Contend (kǫnte·nd), *v.* Pa. t. **contended**; †**content.** 1514. [ad. L. *contendere*, f. *con-* + *tendere*; see TEND *v.*] †1. *intr.* To strive earnestly; to endeavour, to struggle. 2. To strive in opposition; to engage in conflict or strife; to fight 1529. Also *transf.* and *fig.* 3. To strive in argument or debate; to dispute keenly; to argue 1530. 4. To compete, vie 1589. †5. *trans.* To contest, dispute (an object) -1697. ¶ 6. To urge one's course 1600.

1. I have contended to bring in honest men 1659. 2. In Ambitious strength, I did C. against thy Valour *Cor.* IV. v. 119. A cause for which they are ready to c. to their life's end JOWETT. *transf.* Mad as the Seas, and winde, when both c. Which is the Mightier *Haml.* IV. i. 7. 3. Chymistry, about which name we do not c. 1671. This plasticity [of ice] has been contended for by M. Agassiz TYNDALL. 5. When Carthage shall c. the world with Rome DRYDEN. Hence †**Conte·ndent**, one who contends. **Conte·nder**, one who contends or is given to contention. **Conte·ndress** (*rare*), a female contender; one who urges her way (Chapman).

†**Conte·nement.** 1502. [a. OF., med.L. *contenementum*, f. *contenir* to CONTAIN.] As tr. *contenementum* in Magna Carta: ? Holding, freehold; or ? Property necessary to the freeman's position -1818.

Content (kǫnte·nt, kǫ·ntent), *sb.*[1] 1481. [repr. L. *contentum*, plural *contenta*. Not found in mod. Rom. langs. Many now use *co·ntent*, but *conte·nt* is historical.] 1. Now only in *pl.* (with *of* or possessive): That which is contained (in a vessel or the like, a writing, a book, etc.). †2. Tenor, purport (of a document) -1667. 3. That which is contained in a conception; the substance or matter (of cognition, of art, etc.): opp. to the *form* 1845. 4. Containing power (of a vessel, etc.); capacity 1491. 5. Extent, area (now *rare*) 1570; volume (now the usual sense) 1612.

1. The contents of a Letter *A. Y. L.* IV. iii. 21, of the kiln 1832. *Table of contents*: a summary of the matters contained in a book, in the order in which they occur. Also simply *contents* (†*content*). 3. The inner c. or meaning of words WHITNEY. 4. Fifteen hundred strong ships of great C. BACON. 5. The area or c. of the Rectangle BORROW. The solid c. and height of any Tree 1612.

Content (kǫnte·nt), *sb.*[2] 1579. [f. CONTENT *v.* or *a.* Cf. It. *contento.*] 1. Satisfaction, pleasure; a contented condition. †2. Acceptance of conditions or circumstances, acquiescence -1752. †3. A satisfaction; *pl.* pleasures, delights -1716.

1. In Concord and C. the Commons live, By no Divisions rent DRYDEN. I wish your Ladiship all hearts c. *Merch. V.* III. iv. 42. 2. Phr. *To take upon c.*: to accept without examination. The sense they humbly take upon c. POPE. Hence **Conte·ntful** (now *rare*), full of c. †**Conte·ntless** *a.* unsatisfied.

Content (kǫnte·nt), *a.* (*sb.*) ME. [a. F. :—L. *contentus*, pa. pple. of *continere* to CONTAIN.] 1. Having one's desires bounded by what one has; desiring nothing more, or nothing different; satisfied, contented. 2. Pleased, gratified (= F. *content*); now only in *well c.* (*arch.*) ME. †3. Consenting, willing, ready -1709. b. *ellipt.* as an exclam.: = I am content -1820. c. In the House of Lords *C.* and *Not C.* = AYE and NO in the House of Commons. Hence as *sb.* in *pl.* Those who vote 'Content' 17...

1. I haue learned in whatsoeuer state I am, therewith to bee c. *Phil.* iv. 11. *Be c.* (Shaks.): be satisfied in mind. 3. c. The House then divided on the second reading..C. 84, Not C. 23.

Content (kǫnte·nt), *v.* ME. [a. F. *contenter* = med.L. *contentare*, f. *content* adj.] 1. *trans.* 'To satisfy so as to stop complaint' (J.); to be enough for; †to please, gratify 1477. Also *refl.* and †*intr.* 2. *refl.* To be satisfied *with*; to limit one's action 1538. †3. To satisfy, pay in full; to remunerate ME.

1. Pylate willinge to c. the people, loused Barrabas TINDALE *Mark* xv. 15. *Two Gent.* III. i. 93. 2. [He] contents himself with reporting the results of other scholars MAX MÜLLER. 3. To c. a dette 1433, the workeman for his paynes USSHER. Hence **Conte·ntable** *a.* satisfactory; able to be contented. **Conte·nted** *ppl. a.* satisfied; willing to put up *with* something; †willing (*to do* something). **Conte·nted-ly** *adv.*, -ness. †**Conte·ntive** *a.* fitted to c.

Contenta·tion. 1494. [ad. med.L. *contentationem*, f. *contentare.*] †The action of satisfying; †the fact of being satisfied; satisfied condition (*arch.*).

Contention (kǫnte·nʃən). ME. [a. F., ad. L. *contentionem.*] 1. The action of straining or striving earnestly; effort, endeavour (*arch.*) 1580. 2. Strife, dispute, verbal controversy ME. 3. Competition 1576; †the matter in competition 1712. 4. That which is contended for in argument; the point or thesis which a person strives to make good 1635. ¶ †5. = CONTENTATION -1579.

2. A great matter in contencion & debate betwene them MORE. *Bone of c.*: see BONE. The lot causeth contentions to cease *Prov.* xviii. 18. 3. A kinde c., and emulation of aymiable Vertue 1633. 4. This then is your c.—that [etc.] BLACK.

Hence **Conte·ntional** *a.* of the nature or character of c. †**Conte·ntioner**, one given to c.

Contentious (kǫnte·nʃəs), *a.* ME. [ad. F. *contentieux* :—L. *contentiosus*; see prec. and -OUS.] 1. Given to contention; prone to strife or dispute; quarrelsome 1533. Also *transf.* 2. Characterized by or involving contention ME. 3. *Law.* Of or pertaining to differences between contending parties 1483.

1. To dwell.. with a c. and angry woman *Prov.* xxi. 19. *transf.* This c. storme *Lear* III. iv. 6. 2. Forbearing to raise c. issues GLADSTONE. 3. Phr. *C. jurisdiction*: right of jurisdiction in causes between contending parties. **Conte·ntious-ly** *adv.*, -ness.

Contentment (kǫnte·ntmĕnt). 1474. [a. F. *contentement*, f. *contenter* to CONTENT. In Eng. chiefly a noun of quality, as if = *contentedness.*] 1. The action of satisfying; the process of being satisfied; satisfaction (*arch.*). 2. The fact, condition, or quality of being contented; contentedness. (The usual mod. sense.) 1597. †3. Pleasure, gratification -1795; a pleasure -1692.

1. The guests took their leave.. to the c. of mine host SCOTT. 2. Godlinesse with c. is great gaine 1 *Tim.* vi. 6. 3. As for reading, I am past that c. LADY RUSSELL.

Contents; see CONTENT *sb.*[1]

†**Co·ntenu, co·ntinue.** 1477. [a. F. *contenu*, *-ue* sb., f. pa. pple. of *contenir.*] = CONTENT *sb.*[1] 2

Conte·rminable, *a. rare.* [f. L. *conterminare* + -BLE.] Liable to end together. WOTTON.

Conterminal (kǫntə·ɹminăl), *a.* 1802. [ad. med.L. *conterminalis*; see CONTERMINOUS.] 1. = CONTERMINOUS 1. 2. *Entom.* Attached end to end.

Conterminant (kǫntə·ɹminănt), *a.* 1640. [ad. L. *conterminantem*; see CONTERMINATE.] †1. = CONTERMINOUS 1. 2. Terminating together (in time). LAMB.

Conterminate (kǫntə·ɹminĕt), *a.* 1578. [ad. L. *conterminatus.*] = CONTERMINOUS.

†**Conte·rminate**, *v.* 1637. [f. L. *conterminat-*, *conterminare.*] To end together -1709. Hence †**Contermina·tion**.

Conterminous (kǫntə·ɹminəs), *a.* 1631. [f. L. *conterminus* + -OUS.] 1. Having a common boundary, bordering upon. 2. Meeting at their ends 1734. 3. Exactly coextensive 1817.

1. The side of Germany c. to France LECKY.

†**Conterra·neous**, *a.* 1644. [f. L. *conterraneus* + -OUS.] Of or belonging to the same country -1711. var. †**Conterra·nean.**

†**Contessera·tion.** 1620. [ad. L. *contesserationem* (Tertullian).] 1. Contraction of friendship by means of the divided tessera, etc. 2. [L. *tessera* a chequer.] A mosaic 1671.

2. So unusual a c. of elegancies B. OLEY.

†**Contest**, *sb.*[1] 1551. [repr. med.L. **contestis.*] A joint witness -1602.

Contest (kǫ·ntest), *sb.*[2] 1643. [app. f. CONTEST *v.*] 1. Strife in argument, keen controversy, debate. 2. Struggle for victory, for an object, etc.; conflict, strife, contention 1647. 3. Amicable conflict; competition 1647.

1. Between Nose and Eyes a strange c. arose COWPER. 2. The assistance they could not hope to receive from Athens in their c. with the enemy THIRLWALL. 3. Musical contests JOWETT.

Contest (kǫnte·st), *v.* 1579. [a. F. *contester* = It. *contestare* 'to strive, debate'. The orig. source is L. *contestari* to take or call to witness, whence *contestari litem*, to introduce an action by calling witnesses, to bring an action.]

I. †1 *trans.* To swear to (a fact or statement) -1613. †2. To attest (*rare*) -1649. †3. To call to witness, adjure, charge, etc. -1621; *intr.* to bear witness -1609.

II. [f. L. *contestari litem.*] 1. *intr.* To contend (*with* or *against*) in argument; to dispute keenly 1603. 2. *trans.* To argue (a point, etc.); to dispute, controvert, call in question 1633. 3. *intr.* To contend (generally) 1618. 4. *trans.* To fight for; to dispute with arms 1626. 5. *intr.* To contend in rivalry, vie (*with*) 1607. 6. *trans.* To contend for in emulation 1725.

1. Inexplicable Thy Justice seems; yet to say truth, too late I thus c. MILT. *P. L.* x. 756. 2. To c. the right of the pope S. AUSTIN. 3. For Forms of Government let Fools c. POPE. 4. To c. the crown GREEN. 5. Of man, who dares in pomp with Jove c. POPE. 6. To c. a race 1832.

Hence **Conte·stable** *a.* that may be contested. **Conte·ster.**

Contestant (kǫnte·stănt). 1665. [a. F., f. *contester*; cf. *combatant.* Common during Civil War in U.S., and since.] One who takes part in a contest.

†**Contestate**, *v. rare.* 1575. [f. L. *contestat-* ppl. stem.] = CONTEST *v.* -1656.

Contestation (kǫntestē·ʃən). 1548. [ad. L. *contestationem*; see CONTEST *v.*] †1. The action of calling or taking to witness, adjuration -1703. †2. Solemn asseveration -1642. 3. Disputation or controversy; contention, conflict, emulation (now *Sc.*) 1580. 4. The contesting (of a point, claim, etc.) 1638; a contention 1880.

3. Weary with the contestations of certain Pleaders NORTH. Fire and water cannot meet without a hissing c. T. ADAMS. A c. of honour and preferment HOBBES. 4. Phr. *In c.*: in dispute.

†**Conte·x**, *v.* 1542. [ad. L. *contexere.*] To weave or knit together -1684. var. †**Conte·xt** *v.* Hence †**Conte·xt** *ppl. a.* woven or knit together; var. †**Conte·xted.**

Context (kǫ·ntĕkst), *sb.* ME. [ad. L. *contextus*, *contexere.*] †1. Construction of speech -1645. †2. *concr.* A continuous text or composition -1641. †3. The connexion of the parts of a discourse -1641. 4. *concr.* The parts which immediately precede or follow any particular passage or text and determine its meaning 1568. Also *transf.* and *fig.*

4. To this I answer plainly according to all the light that the contexts afford in this matter SHARP. Hence **Conte·xtual** *a.* of or belonging to the c.; depending only on the c. **Conte·xtually** *adv.*

Contexture (kǫnte·kstiŭɹ). Now *rare.* 1603. [a. F., f. *context-* ppl. stem; cf. L. *textura* TEXTURE.] 1. The action of weaving together; the being woven together; texture 1649. Also *transf.* and *fig.* 2. A mass *of* things interwoven together 1603; a fabric 1603. 3. The weaving together of words, sentences, etc. in connected composition; the structure of a literary composition; a connected passage 1603. 4. = CONTEXT 4. 1608.

1. The profitable C. of the Silk-worm 1691. *transf.* He was not of any delicate c.; his limbs rather sturdy than dainty WOTTON (J.). 2. The most ingenious c. of truth and lies CHESTERF. Hence **Conte·xtural** *a.* **Conte·xture** *v.* to weave (*rare*).

Conticent (kǫ·ntisĕnt), *a. rare.* 1859. [ad. L. *conticentem*, f. *con-* + *tacere.*] Keeping silence, silent.

The servants have left the room; the guests sit c. THACKERAY.

†**Contignate**, *v. rare.* [f. ppl. stem of *contignare*, f. *con-* + *tignum.*] *trans.* To join together with beams. HOWELL.

Contignation (kǫntignē·ʃən). *arch.* 1592. [ad. L. *contignationem*; see prec.] 1. The joining together of beams or boards; jointing together 1630. 2. Any conjoined structure 1634. 3. *spec.* A floor, story, or stage 1592.

1. *fig.* Linked by a c. into the edifice of France BURKE.

†**Conti·guate**, *a.* ME. [ad. med.L. *contiguatus* = *contiguus.*] Contiguous *to*; in contact *with* -1632.

Contiguity (kǫntigiū·ĭti). 1641. [ad. F. *contiguïté*, f. *contigu*, L. *contiguus.*] 1. The condition of being in contact; proximity. Also *fig.* †2. A continuous mass 1784.

1. Communicating expansion to all bodies in c. with it W. GROVE. C. in time or place HUME. 2. Some boundless c. of shade COWPER.

Contiguous (kǫnti·giu̦əs), *a.* 1611. [f. L. *contiguus*, f. *contig-* ppl. stem (= *con-* + *tag-*).] **1.** Touching, in contact; adjoining. †**2.** Continuous –1725. **3.** *loosely.* Neighbouring 1710.
1. An heiress whose land lies c. to mine JOHNSON. Two c. Moments of Time HARTLEY. *C. angles* (Math.): = adjacent angles. var. †**Conti·gual.** Hence **Conti·guous-ly** *adv.*, **-ness.**

Continence (kǫ·ntinĕns). ME. [a. F., or ad. L. *continentia*: a doublet of COUNTENANCE.] **1.** Self-restraint. **2.** *spec.* Self-restraint in the matter of sexual appetite, in the sense either of due moderation or (more frequently) of entire abstinence ME. **3.** Continuity 1726.
1. He knows when to leave off, a c. which is practised by few writers DRYDEN. **2.** Chastity is either abstinence or c.: abstinence is that of virgins or widows; c. of married persons JER. TAYLOR. var. (in senses 1, 2) **Co·ntinency.** (Now *rare.*)

Continent (kǫ·ntinĕnt), *a.* ME. [a. OF., ad. L. *continentem*; see CONTAIN.] **1.** Self-restraining, *esp.* in relation to bodily passions, appetites, or indulgences; temperate. **2.** *spec.* Self-restraining in the matter of sexual indulgence; chaste ME. †**3.** Restrictive –1605. **4.** Containing; capacious (*rare*) 1580. †**5.** Continuous in space 1470. **6.** Continuous in duration; not intermittent. (*Old Med.*) 1605.
1. Of such c. moderation was he in coveting 1635. **2.** The chore or quyer signefieth the continente. And the body signefyeth thordre of them that ben maryed CAXTON. **3.** *Macb.* IV. iii. 64. **5.** The mayne and c. land of the whole worlde GRAFTON. **6.** A C. Fever CULLEN. Hence **Co·ntinently** *adv.* chastely, temperately; †continuously.

Continent (kǫ·ntinĕnt), *sb.* 1494. [ad. L. *continentem*; see prec. and CONTAIN.] **1.** That which contains; also *fig.* Now *rare.* 1541. †**2.** Containing capacity–1666. †**3.** Land; the earth –1677. **4.** *esp.* Mainland. *Obs.* exc. as in 5. 1576. **5.** One of the main continuous bodies of land on the earth's surface, as Europe, Asia, Africa, America, North and South, and ? Australia, and the supposed Antarctic C. 1614. Also *transf.* and *fig.* †**6.** *Amer. Hist.* The colonies or states collectively (during the War of Independence) –1784. **7.** *Eccl. Hist.* = ENCRATITE 1702.
1. Heart, once be stronger then thy C., Cracke thy fraile Case *Ant. & Cl.* IV. xiv. 40. **3.** *2 Hen. IV*, III. i. 47. **4.** It is not known whether that country be an island or the c. DE FOE. Phr. *The C.*: the mainland of Europe, as dist. from the British Isles.

Continental (kǫntine·ntăl). 1760. [f. prec.]
A. *adj.* **1.** Belonging to, or characteristic of, a continent 1818. **2.** *spec.* Of, on, or belonging to 'the Continent', *i.e.* the mainland of Europe 1760. **3.** *Amer. Hist.* Of or belonging to the colonies or States collectively (during and immediately after the War of Independence), as in *C. Congress* (see CONGRESS) 1775.
1. At the north it [the climate] was c., and consequently dry PETERMANN. **2.** The c. tour LYTTON. *The C. System* (Hist.): the plan of Napoleon Bonaparte for cutting off Great Britain from all connexion with the continent of Europe; instituted by the Berlin Decree of 19th Nov., 1806, which declared the British Islands in a state of blockade. **3.** The C. debt MORSE. C. money H. PHILLIPS.
B. *sb.* **1.** An inhabitant of a continent; *spec.* of the continent of Europe 1828. **2.** *Amer. Hist.* **a.** A soldier of the C. army in the War of Independence 1847. **b.** A currency note issued by the C. Congress; whence the phrase *Not worth a c.* 1872.

Contine·ntalist. 1834. [f. prec. + -IST.] **1.** = CONTINENTAL *sb.* 1. **2.** *Amer. Hist.* An advocate of the federation of the States after the War of Independence.

Contingency (kǫnti·ndʒĕnsi). 1561. [f. L. *contingent-* CONTINGENT; see -ENCY.] †**1.** Touching, contact –1677. **2.** Connexion, affinity of nature 1612. **3.** The quality or condition of being contingent 1561. **4.** A chance occurrence; a juncture 1616. **5.** An event conceived as of possible occurrence in the future 1626. **6.** A thing or condition of things contingent upon an uncertain event 1818. **7.** A thing incident to something else 1626.
3. The c. of human actions BP. WATSON. **4.** Drawing from the starres the euents of future contingencies 1620. **5.** A future estate of freehold, to arise either upon a c., or at a period certain CRUISE. **7.** All the ..contingencies of marriage, number of children, etc. COBBETT. So **Conti·ngence** (in senses 1–4).

Contingent (kǫnti·ndʒĕnt). ME. [a. F., or ad. L. *contingentem*, *contingere*, f. *con-* + *tangere*.]
A. *adj.* †**1.** In contact; tangential –1703. **2.** Liable to happen or not ME. **3.** Happening or coming by chance; fortuitous 1613. †**4.** Not determined by necessity; free –1796. †**5.** Subject to accidents –1745. **6.** *Metaph.* True only under existing conditions 1588; that exists in dependence on something else 1785; non-essential 1628. **7.** Dependent *on* or *upon* something prior 1613. **8.** *Law.* Dependent on a probability; conditional; not absolute 1710.
2. If Death were only c., and not certain 1684. C. expenses 1747. **3.** By various local and c. events 1799. **4.** If human actions are not C., what think you of the morality of actions BP. WATSON. **5.** The c. nature of trade DE FOE. **6.** *C. matter* (in Logic): the subject-matter of a proposition which is not necessarily or universally true. **7.** Things..altogether c. and dependent of mans will SALKELD. Hence **Continge·ntial** *a.* of c. nature, non-essential (*rare*). **Conti·ngently** *adv.* in a c. manner.
B. *sb.* **1.** An accident 1548. **2.** A thing that may or may not happen 1623. **3.** 'The proportion that falls to any one on a division' (J.); a quota, *esp.* of troops 1727. Also *transf.* and *fig.*
2. It [Humane providence] cannot ascertain future Contingents SIR E. DIGBY. **3.** The Nizam's C. as this force was denominated WELLINGTON.

Continual (kǫnti·niuăl), *a.* ME. [a. OF. *continuel*, f. L. *continuus*; see -AL.] **1.** Always going on, incessant, perpetual; regularly recurring (*arch.*) 1500. †**2.** *transf.* Of persons and things: Continually existing or acting; constant, perpetual –1864. †**3.** Of diseases: Chronic, not intermittent –1751. †**4.** Continuous; forming a continuous series –1753.
1. One almost c. eruption PHILLIPS. Continuall victory maketh leaders insolent 1630. **2.** Yore contynwel servaunt and bedeman 1462. **4.** *C. proportion* (Math.): = CONTINUED proportion. Hence **Conti·nually** *adv.* always; very frequently; continuously. **Conti·nualness** the quality of being c. (*rare*).

Continuance (kǫnti·niu̦ăns). ME. [a. OF., f. *continuer* (pr. pple. *continuant*); see -ANCE.] **1.** Keeping up, going on with, maintaining, or prolonging (an action, process, state, etc.). **2.** *Law.* The adjournment of a suit or trial till a future date or for a period ME. **3.** Perseverance, persistence (said of agents) (*arch.*) ME.; the going on (of an action), the lasting (of a state) 1530. (The most usual current sense.) **4.** Stay ME. **5.** Course or length of time (*Obs.* or *arch.*) ME. †**6.** Lasting quality –1664; antiquity –1699; continuity (*lit.* and *fig.*) –1756. **7.** *concr.* = CONTINUATION 1552. Also *attrib.*
1. His own preservation, or the c. of his species ADDISON. **3.** By patient c. in well doing *Rom.* ii. 7. The c. of disorder HOBBES, a quarrel FROUDE. **4.** Cloy'd With long c. in a setled place SHAKS.

†‖**Continua·ndo.** 1607. [L., = 'by continuing'.] *Law.* In an indictment for trespass: A continuance or repetition of the act alleged. Hence *transf.* –1734.

Continuant (kǫnti·niu̦ănt). 1610. [a. F.]
A. *adj.* †**1.** Continuing, persisting in time; remaining in force –1660. **2.** Capable of a continuous sound, as some consonants.
B. *sb.* **1.** A consonant of which the sound can be prolonged, as f, v, s, etc. 1861. **2.** *Math.* In *Theory of Equations*, 'A determinant in which all the constituents vanish except those in the principal diagonal and two bordering minor diagonals'. SALMON.

†**Conti·nuate,** *ppl. a.* 1471. [ad. L. *continuatus* pa. pple.] **1.** *pa. pple.* CONTINUED. **2.** *adj.* Continued without break or interstices –1656. **3.** Long-continued, chronic –1635.
3. An vntyreable and c. goodness *Timon* I. i. 11.

†**Conti·nuate,** *v.* 1578. [f. L. *continuat-* ppl. stem.] To make continuous in space or time –1834.

Continuation (kǫnti·niu̦ē¹·ʃən). ME. [a. F., ad. L. *continuationem.*] †**1.** The action of continuing; perseverance –1483. †**2.** Continuity in space –1726. **3.** Continuous existence or operation 1469. **4.** The causing of anything to continue 1586. **5.** *Math.* In Fluxions: = integration by parts –1786. **6.** *Stock Exchange.* The carrying over of an account till next settling-day; see CONTANGO 1813. **7.** *concr.* That by which anything is continued 1580. **8.** *pl.* Gaiters continuous with 'shorts'. Hence, in *mod. slang*, trousers, as a c. of the waistcoat 1825.
3. The c. of weakness T. BROWN. **4.** A decree made for the c. of the league KNOLLES. **7.** Where it is crossed by the c. of Mount Imaus ELPHINSTONE.

Continuative (kǫnti·niu̦ĕtiv). 1530. [ad. L. *continuativus*, f. *continuat-* ppl. stem.]
A. *adj.* **1.** Serving to continue or impart continuity 1684. **2.** Expressing continuance.
B. *sb.* (the adj. used *absol.*) Anything that serves to continue or impart continuity; *spec.* †**a.** a conjunction that introduces a subordinate clause –1751; †**b.** a proposition expressing continuance, as *Rome remains to this day* 1725.

Continuator (kǫnti·niu̦ē¹tər). 1646. [f. L. *continuare*; see -OR; cf. F. *continuateur.*] **1.** One who continues. **2.** One who continues work (*esp.* a book) begun by another 1656.

Continue (kǫnti·niu), *v.* ME. [a. F. *continuer*, ad. L. *continuare*, f. *continuus.* Frequently confused with ME. *contene* = *contain.*]
I. *trans.* **1.** To carry on, keep up, persist in (an action, usage, etc.). **2.** To cause to last or endure; to prolong (something external to the agent) ME.; to keep on, retain (in a place, condition, etc.) 1460. †**3.** To attach *to* –1646. **4.** To take up (a narrative, etc.); to carry on in space, succession, or development ME. **5.** *Law* and *Stock Exch.* To adjourn, put off 1469.
1. To c. a resolve SHAKS., a metaphor FIELDING, struggle 1874. **2.** A good Way to c. their Memories SIR T. BROWNE. To c. him at School WALTON. **4.** To c. the Story (with Sir John in it) *2 Hen. IV*, Epil. To c. lines MOXON.
II. *intr.* **1.** To remain in existence or in its present condition; to last, endure ME. **2.** To remain (*in* a place) ME.; to remain (in a specified state or capacity) 1503. **3.** To persevere; to keep on. (Now rare of persons.) ME **4.** To proceed in one's discourse; to resume 1711.
1. But now thy kingdom shall not c. *1 Sam.* xiii. 14. **2.** They continued there not many days *John* ii. 12. To c. unhappy (*mod.*). **3.** The breeze continued LADY BRASSEY. Phr. *To c. doing* or *to do.* **4.** Lord Erskine continues thus: 'If' [etc.] 1885.
†**III.** = CONTAIN –1572.
Such blasfemyes ben foundun & contynnued in þes sectis WYCLIF.
Hence **Conti·nuable** *a.* **Conti·nuingly** *adv.*

Continued (kǫnti·niud), *ppl. a.* ME. [f. prec. + -ED.] **1.** Carried on without cessation; continual. **2.** Carried on in space, time, or series; continuous 1607.
1. Cold Weather, and continu'd Rain DRYDEN. Phr. *C. fever*: see CONTINUAL *a.* 3. **2.** *C. proportionals*: a series of quantities such that the ratio is the same between every two adjacent terms. Such quantities are in *C. proportion. C. fraction*: a fraction whose denominator is an integer *plus* a fraction, which latter fraction has a similar denominator, and so on. †*Continued bass* = BASSO *continuo.*

Continuer (kǫnti·niu̦ər). 1548. [f. as prec. + -ER [1].] **1.** = CONTINUATOR 2. **2.** One who continues, in various senses.
2. I would my horse had the speed of your tongue, and so good a c. *Much Ado* I. i. 143.

Continuity (kǫntiniū·iti). 1543. [a. F. *continuité*, ad. L. *continuitatem.*] **1.** The state of being continuous; uninterrupted connexion or succession; coherence, unbrokenness. **2.** Uninterrupted duration (*rare*) 1646. **3.** quasi-*concr.* A continuous or connected whole 1601.
1. The c. of the frontier WELLINGTON. C. of attention W. GROVE. **2.** Their stedfast c. of gaze 1840.
Phrases. *Law* or *principle of c.*: the principle that all change, sequence, or series in nature is continuous, and does not go *per saltum*. *Solution of c.*: the fact or condition of being or becoming discontinuous; fracture, rupture, breakage, break. Orig. used of wounds, etc. in an animal body.

‖**Continuo** (kǫnti·niu̦o). *Mus.* 1876. [It.] = BASSO *continuo.*

Continuous (kǫnti·niu̦əs), *a.* 1642. [f. L. *continuus* (f. *continere* 'to hang together', etc.) + -OUS.] **1.** Characterized by continuity; extending in space without a break; having its parts in immediate connexion; connected, unbroken 1673. **2.** Uninterrupted in time, sequence, or essence; going on without interruption 1751.
1. In most cases the area inhabited by a species is c. DARWIN. Anciently c. with Malacca RAY. **2.** The power of..c. thought is very rare JOWETT. Phrases. *C. brake*: a c. series of carriage brakes controlled from one point in a train. *C. consonant*: = CONTINUANT *sb.* 1. *C. function* (Math.): one that varies continuously. *C. stem* (Bot.), one without articulations. *C. voyage*: one which is regarded, in spite of stoppages, as a single voyage in ref. to the object with which it was undertaken 1806. Hence **Conti·nuous-ly** *adv.*, **-ness.**

‖**Continuum** (kǫnti·niu,ʊ̆m). Pl. **-a** (-ă). 1650. [L.] A continuous thing, quantity, or substance; a continuous series of elements passing into each other.

To these animals [the wolf and dog] the external world seems a c. of scents LEWES.

Co·nt-line. 1848. [? for CANT-*line* (see CANT *sb.*[1]).] **1.** The spiral intervals between the strands on the outside of a rope. **2.** 'The space between the bilges of two casks stowed side by side'. SMYTH.

Conto (kǫ·nto). 1601. [Pg. :—L. *computus*; see COUNT *sb.*] In Pg., a million; hence, short for a million reis, worth about £220.

Contorniate (kǫntǭ·mi,ĕt). 1692. [f. It. *contorno* contour.] *adj.* Of a medal or coin: Having a deep furrow round the disk, within the edge. var. **Conto·rniated.** *sb.* A medal (or coin) so furrowed: applied to certain brass pieces of Nero and other Roman Emperors.

‖**Contorno** (kontǭ·rno). 1758. [It.; see prec.] Contour, outline of a statue, etc.

Contorsion, obs. f. CONTORTION.

Contort (kǫntǭ·ɹt), *v.* 1622. [f. L. *contort-*, *contorquere*, f. *con-* + *torquere* to twist.] *trans.* To twist, twist together; to draw awry; to distort greatly by twisting. Also *fig.*

The features are violently contorted BAIN. *fig.* Contorted from their established signification 1836.

Contorted (kǫntǭ·ɹtėd), *ppl. a.* 1622. [f. prec.] **1.** Twisted, twisted together; twisted awry or out of shape. **2.** *Bot.* Of petals: Overlapping at one margin and overlapped at the other 1760.

1. I'll..hang thee In a c. chain of icicles MASSINGER.

Contortion (kǫntǭ·ɹʃən). 1611. [ad. L. *contortionem*; see CONTORT *v.*] **1.** The action of contorting; the fact of being contorted; distortion by twisting. **2.** A contorted condition, state, or form 1664.

1. We strive .. to alter ourselves by ridiculous contorsions of body MRS. CHAPONE. 2. The curious contortions of the rocks BLACK. Hence **Conto·rtionist,** one who professes and practises c.

Contortive (kǫntǭ·ɹtiv), *a.* 1859. [f. L. *contort-*, *contorquere*.] Characterized by contortion.

Contortuplicate (kǫntǭtiŭ·plikĕt), *a.* 1816. [ad. L. *contortuplicatus*, f. *contortus* + *plicatus*.] *Bot.* Twisted back upon itself.

Contour (kǫ·ntūᵊɹ, kǫntūᵊ·ɹ), *sb.* 1662. [a. F., f. *contourner* (cf. TURN); see also CONTORNO.] **1.** The outline of any figure; *spec.* the line separating the differently coloured parts of a design. **2.** *gen.* 1769.

1. The whole c of her form..resembled that of Minerva SCOTT. 2. The undulating line indicates the general c. of the surface of the country HUXLEY.

Comb.: **c.-feathers, -hairs,** those which form the surface and c. of an animal. **C. line,** a line representing the horizontal c. of the earth's surface at a given elevation. The c. line of a mountain at a given height represents the edge of a horizontal plane cutting the mountain at that height.

Contour (kǫntūᵊ·ɹ), *v.* 1871. [f. prec.] **1.** *trans.* To mark with contour lines. **2.** To carry (a road, etc.) round the contour of a hill

‖**Contourné** (koṅtu·rne), *a.* 1727. [Fr.] *Her.* Turned about, *i. e.* towards the sinister or left.

‖**Contra** (kǫ·ntră), *adv., prep.* (*sb.*) ME. [L.; orig the ablative case fem. of **cont(e)r-*, a comparative form of *com, con* prep For the sense cf. OE. *wið, wiðer*, as in *wiðer-sæcgan* = *contradicere*.]

A. *prep.* Against. Chiefly in *pro and contra* (now *con*) 'for and against' (the motion, etc.) 1450.

B. *adv.* On or to the contrary, contrariwise ME.

C. *sb.* The contrary or opposite; in *Book-keeping*, the opposite (*esp.* the credit) side of an account. Also *transf.* 1648.

Contra-, *prefix.* The L. adv. and prep. *contra* (see prec.), signifying 'against, in opposition to, opposite, in the opposite direction', used in comb. in many English words derived from or formed after L. or It. In the names of musical instruments and of organ-stops it denotes a pitch of an octave below; as in CONTRABASS; **Contrafagotto,** the double bassoon; etc.

Contraband (kǫ·ntrăbænd). 1529. [ad. Sp. *contrabando* smuggling, a. It. *contrabando* (now *-trabb-*), f. *contra* + *bando* proclamation, statute :—late L. *bandum, bannum*; see BANDON, BAN.]

A. *sb.* **1.** Illegal or prohibited traffic. **2.** Anything prohibited to be imported or exported; smuggled goods 1599. **3.** (In full *C. of war.*) Anything (*esp.* arms, stores, etc. available for hostile purposes) forbidden to be supplied by neutrals to belligerents in time of war 1753. **4.** *U.S.* During the Civil War: A negro slave, *esp.* a fugitive or captured slave 1862; from a decision of Gen. Butler in 1861 that such slaves were contraband of war 1862.

1. This folly has thrown open folding-doors to c. BURKE. Hence **Co·ntraband** *v.* to smuggle; †to declare c. **Co·ntrabandism,** smuggling. **Co·ntrabandist,** a smuggler; var. ‖**Co·ntrabandi·sta.**

B. *adj.* Prohibited by law, proclamation, or treaty, to be imported or exported 1656.

Plate..is not counterband in its metallic capacity H. WALPOLE. *fig.* A c. preacher SOUTHEY.

Contrabass (kǫ·ntrăbēˢs). Now *rare.* 1598. [ad. It. contrabasso, F. contrebasse (also used); see CONTRA- + BASS *sb.*[5]] **1.** *Mus.* The DOUBLE-BASS, used to add the lower octave to the bass in the orchestra. **2.** Applied to other instruments taking a similar part; chiefly *attrib.*, as *c. posaune* a kind of trombone, *c. tuba*, the bombardon.

Contraception (kǫntrăse·pʃən). 1910. [irreg. f. CONTRA- + *-ception* in CONCEPTION.] Prevention of uterine conception. So **Contrace·ptive** *a.* and *sb.* pertaining to a (means of) procuring this 1897.

Earlier names were *anticonception, -ive, contraceptics.*

Contract (kǫ·ntrækt), *sb.*[1] ME. [a. OF., now *contrat*, ad. L. *contractus*, f. *contract-*; see below.] **1.** A mutual agreement between two or more parties that something shall be done or forborne by one or both; also, 'a writing in which the terms of a bargain are included' (J.). **2.** *Law.* An agreement enforceable by law ME. Also used *gen.* **3.** *spec.* of marriage; also, †betrothal ME. †**4.** Mutual attraction –1654. **5.** *attrib.*, as *c. work*, etc. 1665.

1. *C. bridge*: see BRIDGE *sb.*[2] 3. [Time] trots hard with a yong maid, between the c. of her marriage, and the day it is solemnizd *A.Y.L.* III. ii. 332.

Contract (kǫntræ·kt), *ppl. a.* (and *sb.*[2]). ME. [a. OF., ad. L. *contractus*.] = CONTRACTED. *sb.* A contracted form or word 1669.

Contract (kǫntræ·kt), *v.* 1530. [f. L. *contract-*, *contrahere*, f. *con-* + *trahere* to draw. The ppl. adj. *contract* was much earlier in use.] **1.** *trans.* To agree upon, establish by agreement, to undertake mutually, or enter upon. Now *rare*, exc. as in 3. 1548. **2.** *intr.* To enter into an agreement or contract 1530. **3.** *spec.* as to marriage. *trans.* To constitute by contract 1530; to betroth or engage 1536; *intr.* 1660. **4.** *trans.* To enter into, incur, become involved in, acquire 1553. †**5.** To draw or bring together, collect, concentrate –1782. **6.** To draw the parts of together; to cause to shrink; to knit (the brow) 1602. **7.** To reduce to smaller compass as by drawing together; to narrow, shorten 1626. Also *fig. intr.* (for *refl.*) 1641.

1. We haue contracted an inviolable amitie, peace and league with the aforesaid queene HAKLUYT. 2. To c. for a loan MCCULLOCH. 3. Of unsound mind and incapable of contracting marriage 1885. We were contracted before my father's death SHERIDAN. 4. Phr. *To c. friendship, acquaintance*, etc. To c. the displeasure of the world PEPYS, Colds 1691, guilt MOZLEY, a habit CHESTERF., a debt 1719. 6. Aches c., and sterue your supple ioynts *Timon* I. i. 257. 7. You c. your eye, when you would see sharply BACON. *fig.* To c. his expence PEPYS, a vowel 1884.

Hence **Contra·ctable** *a.* liable to be contracted or acquired. **Contra·ctant,** a contracting party (*rare*). **Contra·ctible** *a.* contractile. **Contractabi·lity, -ibi·lity. Contra·ctive** *a.* having the property of contracting; tending to produce contraction.

†**Contracta·tion.** 1555. [a. F., f. *contracter.*] Mutual dealing, exchange –1725.

Contracted (kǫntræ·ktėd), *ppl. a.* 1548. [f. CONTRACT *v.* + -ED[1].] **1.** Established by agreement. ? *Obs.* 1589. †**2.** Betrothed –1624. **3.** Acquired 1640. **4.** Narrowed, shortened, shrunken, etc. 1603; *fig* concise 1595; restricted 1710.

1. Our old c. amitie GREENE. 2. 1 *Hen. IV*, IV. ii. 17. 3. A self-contracted wretchedness GLANVILL. 4. Narrow c. vallies 1786. *fig.* In his Style..he is C. and Fluent HEARNE. Petty c. ideas LD. BROUGHAM. Hence **Contra·cted-ly** *adv*, **-ness.**

Contractile (kǫntræ·ktil, -təil), *a.* 1706. [a. F., f. L. *contract-* ppl. stem; cf. *ductile.*] **1.** Having the property of contracting. **2.** Of, pertaining to, or of the nature of contraction; producing contraction 1725.

1. The substance of the heart is c. HUXLEY. 2. The c. action takes place in every direction TODD. Hence **Contracti·lity,** c. quality.

Contraction (kǫntræ·kʃən). 1582. [a. F., ad. L. *contractionem.*] **1.** The action of contracting or establishing by contract; *spec.* the action of contracting marriage; †also, betrothal 1598. **2.** The action of contracting (a debt, disease, habit, etc.) 1683. **3.** The action of contracting (*trans.* and *intr.*), or state of being contracted; shrinking, shortening, narrowing. (The most usual sense.) 1589. Also *fig.* **4.** Abbreviation; condensation (*arch.*) 1655. **5.** *Gram.* etc. The action of shortening (a word, etc.) by omitting or combining some elements, or by reducing two vowels or syllables into one 1706. **6.** *concr.* A contracted form of a word, etc. 1755.

1. *Haml.* III. iv. 46. 2. Anterior to the c. of the.. debt EARL SELBORNE. 3. A c. of the heart 1594. The c. of Liquors by Cold 1665. C. of the brow SMOLLETT, of certain muscles 1876. *fig.* The c. of credit MILL. Free from any narrowness or c. MISS BURNEY. Hence **Contra·ctional** *a.* relating to or produced by c. **Contra·ctionist,** one who advocates c. of the currency; opp. to *expansionist.*

†**Contra·ctly,** *adv.* 1570. [f. CONTRACT *ppl. a.* + -LY [2].] By contraction –1675.

Contractor (kǫntræ·ktəɹ). Also 6–7 **-er.** 1548. **1.** One who contracts; a contracting party. *Obs.* exc. as in 2. **2.** *spec.* One who contracts to furnish supplies, or to perform any work or service at a certain price or rate; one who undertakes work by contract 1724. **3.** One who or that which contracts, narrows, or shortens; used *esp.* of certain muscles 1682.

Contractual (kǫntræ·ktiuăl), *a.* 1861. [f. L. *contractus* CONTRACT + -AL.] Of the nature of, pertaining or relating to, a contract, as *c. obligations.*

Contracture (kǫntræ·ktiŭɹ). 1658. [a. F., or ad. L. *contractura.*] *Path.* A condition of persistent contraction and rigidity in the muscles or the joints. Hence **Contra·ctured** *ppl. a.* affected by c.

Co·ntra-dance, -danse, corrupt ff. COUNTRY-DANCE; see CONTRE-DANSE.

Contradict (kǫntrădi·kt), *v.* 1570. [f. L. *contradict-*, *contradicere*, in cl.L. *contra dicere.* Cf. F. *contredire.*] †**1.** *trans.* To speak against; to oppose in speech; to forbid; to oppose –1754. †*intr.* 1616. **2.** *trans.* To affirm the contrary of; to declare untrue or erroneous; to deny 1582. Also *absol.* **3.** *transf.* To be contrary to; to go counter to, go against 1600.

1. Stand in his face to c. his claime *John* II. i. 280. 2. The statement has been officially contradicted (*mod.*). Deare Duff, I prythee c. thy selfe, And say, it is not so *Macb.* II. iii. 94. 3. Their liues..c. their doctrine PRYNNE.

Hence **Contradi·ctable** *a.* †**Contradi·cter, -or.**

Contradiction (kǫntrădi·kʃən). ME. [a. F., ad L. *contradictionem.*] **1.** The action of contradicting or opposing; gainsaying. **2.** Declaring to be untrue or erroneous; affirming the contrary; denial 1526. **3.** A statement that contradicts another 1724. **4.** A state of opposition in things compared; variance; (logical) inconsistency 1576. **5.** A statement or phrase containing contradictory propositions or terms 1795. **6.** A contradictory act, fact, or condition 1614. **7.** A person made up of contradictory qualities 1735.

1. Those who pursue their own Way out of a Sourness and Spirit of C. STEELE. 2. Without c. I haue heard that *Ant. & Cl.* II. vii. 40. 3. It contains an official c. of the rumour (*mod.*). 4. The manifest c. between these two accounts PRIESTLEY. Phr. *The principle* (or *law*) *of c.*: the axiom that 'a thing cannot be and not be at the same time' or 'that nothing can have at the same time and at the same place contradictory and inconsistent qualities'. 5. Both parts of a c. cannot possibly be true HOBBES. A virtuous tyrant is a c. in terms JOWETT. 7. Woman's at best a c. still POPE. Hence **Contradi·ctional** *a.* contradictory (*rare*). **Contradi·ctious** *a.* †contradictory, contrary; self-contradictory (*arch.*); given to c.; disputatious. **Contradi·ctious-ly** *adv.*, **-ness.**

Contradictive (kǫntrădi·ktiv), *a.* 1627. [f. L. *contradict-* ppl. stem + -IVE.] **1.** Of contradictory quality or tendency. †**2.** Contradictious –1673. Hence **Contradi·ctively** *adv.*

Contradictory (kǫntrădi·ktəri). ME. [ad. L. *contradictorius*; cf. F. *contradictoire.*]

A. *adj.* 1. *Logic* and *gen.* Having the quality of contradicting; denying that a thing stated is completely true 1605; that contradict each other; mutually inconsistent 1534; inconsistent in itself 1868. 2. Of opposite character; diametrically opposed, contrary 1736. 3. Contradictious 1891.

1. *C. opposition* (in Logic): the opposition between two *C. propositions*, i.e. such as differ both in quantity and quality (e.g. *All A is B*: *Some A is not B*); of which one must be true and the other false. *C. terms*: such as 'A and not-A'.

B. *sb.* 1. A contradictory proposition, assertion, or principle; *spec.* in *Logic*; see A. 1. ME. 2. The opposite, the contrary 1840.

1. You shall never be good logician, that would set together two contradictories: for that, the schoolmen say, God cannot do CRANMER.

Hence **Contradi·ctorily** *adv.* in a way that contradicts; *Log.* with c. opposition. **Contradi·ctoriness.** var. †**Co·ntradicto·rious.**

Contradistinct (kǫ·ntrădisti·ŋkt), *a.* 1621. [See CONTRA-.] Contradistinguished; distinct and in contrast.

Contradistinction (kǫ:ntrădisti·ŋkʃən). 1647. [See CONTRA-.] The action of contradistinguishing; distinction by contrast or opposition.

An *actual* possession by the bankrupt, in c. to a *constructive* possession 1789.

Contradistinctive (kǫ:ntrădisti·ŋktiv), *a.* 1641. [See CONTRA-.] Serving to contradistinguish; marking contradistinction (*rare*). Also as *sb.*

Contradistinguish (kǫ:ntrădisti·ŋgwiʃ), *v.* 1622. [See CONTRA-.] *trans.* To distinguish by contrasting.

The development which contradistinguishes the Hellene from the barbarian M. ARNOLD.

Contrafago·tto; see CONTRA-.

†**Contrafi·ssure.** 1676. [See CONTRA-.] *Surg.* A fracture of the skull produced on the contrary side to that which received the blow -1783.

Contrafocal (kǫntrăfōᵘ·kăl), *a.* 1866. [See CONTRA-.] *Math.* Of two conics, etc.: Having the sums of the squares of two corresponding axes equal: opp. to CONFOCAL conics.

Contragre·dient, *a.* 1853. [f. L. *contra-* + *-gredient.*] *Math.* Of two systems of variables: Such that when one undergoes linear substitution, the other undergoes linear substitution simultaneously, but of a contrary kind. So **Contragre·dience,** the quality of being c.

Contrahent (kǫ·ntrăhĕnt). 1524. [ad. L. *contrahentem.*] *adj.* Contracting. *sb.* A contracting party.

Contra-indicant (kǫ:ntră,i·ndikănt). 1623. [See CONTRA-. Cf. next.] *Med.* A symptom which makes against a particular diagnosis, and indicates contrary or other treatment.

Contra-indicate (kǫ ntră,i·ndikeᶦt), *v.* 1666. [See CONTRA-.] *Med. trans.* To give indications contrary to; said *esp.* of symptoms which make against a particular treatment or remedy.

Other urgent or contraindicating symptoms must be observed HARVEY.

Co·ntra-indica·tion. 1623. [See CONTRA-.] *Med.* An indication which makes against a particular treatment.

Contrala·teral, *a.* 1882. [See CONTRA-.] *Med.* That is on the opposite side.

Contra-lode (in *Mining*); see COUNTER-LODE.

Contralto (kǫ̆ntra·ltǫ). Pl. **-ti, -tos.** 1730. [It.; 'a counter treble in musicke' (Florio).] *Mus.* **a.** The part sung by the highest male or the lowest female voice; **b.** a voice of this compass; **c.** a singer having a contralto voice. (Now usually restricted to the female voice.) Also *attrib.* or *adj.*

Contramure, obs. var. of COUNTERMURE *v.*

Contranatural (kǫ·ntră,næ·tiŭrăl), *a.* 1633. [See CONTRA-.] Contrary to what is natural; opposed to nature.

Contraplex (kǫ·ntrăpleks), *a.* 1879. [Cf. *simplex*, etc.] *Telegr.* Having two currents passing in opposite directions at the same time.

Contrapo·se, *v.* 1617. [f. L. *contraponere*; see COMPOSE.] 1. To set in opposition, or over against each other. 2. *Logic.* To convert by contraposition.

Contraposition (kǫ:ntrăpŏzi·ʃən). 1551. [ad. L. *contrapositionem* (Boethius).] 1. A placing over against; antithesis, opposition 1581. 2. *Logic.* A mode of conversion in which from a given proposition we infer another having the contradictory of the original predicate for its subject; thus 'All S is P' becomes 'No not-P is S'. (Also called Conversion by Negation.)

Contrapositive (kǫ:ntrăpǫ·zitiv). 1870. [f. L. *contraposit-* ppl. stem.] *adj.* Of, belonging to, or produced by contraposition. *sb.* Anything characterized by contraposition 1870.

Co·ntraprove·ctant. [See CONTRA-.] *Math.* A covariant regarded as generated by operating on any covariant with a contraprovector. So **Co:ntraprove·ctor,** the operator obtained by replacing the facients by symbols of partial differentiation in any contravariant. CAYLEY.

Contraption (kǫ̆ntræ·pʃən). 1834. *colloq.* [etym. dub.] A device, contrivance.

Contrapuntal (kǫntrăpʊ·ntăl), *a.* 1845. [f. It. *contrapunto*, f. *contra* + *punto* point; see COUNTERPOINT.] Of, pertaining to, or of the nature of counterpoint; according to the rules of counterpoint. Hence **Contrapu·ntally** *adv.* **Contrapu·ntist,** one skilled in counterpoint.

Co:ntra-rela·ted, *ppl. a.* 1866. [See CONTRA-.] *Dynamics.* Having as their kinematical exponents contrafocal ellipsoids.

Co:ntra-remo·nstrant. 1618. [See CONTRA-.] One who remonstrates in answer or opposition to a remonstrance. Also *attrib.* So **Co:ntra-remo·nstrance.**

Contrariant (kǫ̆ntrē·riănt), *pple., a.* and *sb.* ME. [a. OF., ad. med.L. *contrariantem*, *contrariare*, f. L. *contrarius.*] †*pple.* Opposing. *adj.* 1. Opposed, contrary *to* 1530; †contrary -1649. 2. Mutually antagonistic 1560. *sb.* One who or that which is opposed in purpose or nature 1657. Hence **Contra·riantly** *adv.*

Contrariety (kǫntrărəi·ėti). ME. [a. OF. *contrarieté*, ad. late L. *contrarietatem.*] 1. The state or quality of being contrary; opposition, repugnance, disagreement; inconsistency; (with *a* and *pl.*) an instance of this. 2. Opposition to one's purpose or advantage; hence (with *a* and *pl.*) an adversity, mishap, disadvantage ME. 3. *Logic.* Contrary opposition 1553.

1. That in the words of our Saviour there can be no c. MILT. He will be here, and yet he is not here: How can these contrarieties agree 1 *Hen. VI*, II. iii. 59. 2. To shelter them from C. of Seasons 1620.

Contrarily, *adv.* 1485; = CONTRARIWISE. So **Contrariness** late ME.

Contrarious (kǫ̆ntrēᵊ·riəs), *a.* Now *rare.* ME. [a. OF. *contrarious*, ad. med.L. *contrariosus.*] 1. †Contrary or repugnant -1656; opposed ME.; perverse ME. 2. Adverse, untoward; vexatious ME. Hence **-ly** *adv.*, **-ness.**

Contrariwise, *adv.* ME. [f. CONTRARY *a.* Pronunciation kǫ·ntrări,wəi:z (the most frequent); also kǫntræ·riwəiz, and kǫntrēᵊ·riwəiz.] 1. On the other hand, on the contrary. 2. In the opposite way, order, or direction; *vice versâ* 1570.

1. Heaven is compared to an hill..Hell c. to a Pit 1605. 2. It hath seldome or neuer been seene, that the farre Southern People have inuaded the Northern, but c. BACON.

Co:ntra-rota·tion. 1729. [See CONTRA-.] Rotation in the opposite direction.

Contrary (kǫ·ntrări). ME. [a. early F. *contra·rie*, ad. L. *contrarius*, f. *contra*; cf. *adversary.* Originally stressed *contra·ry*, which is still *dial.*]

A. *adj.* 1. Opposed in nature or tendency; mutually opposed; †different -1696. 2. The opposite, the other (of two things) ME. 3. Of persons and actions: †Hostile -1662; contrarious. (Only in popular use, and pronounced *contrā·ry.*) 1850. †4. Of things: Prejudicial, untoward -1737. 5. Opposite in position or direction ME. 6. *Logic.* See quots.

1. Other .. helde contrarye oppynyon CAXTON. C. diseases should have c. remedies HOOKER. 2. All ignorant of her c. sex SPENSER. 3. Mary, Mary, quite c. *Nursery Rime.* 4. Wayes..either crosse or c. BP. HALL. 6. *C. propositions*: those most opposed to each other in quality, each denying every possible case of the other, as *All A is B*: *No A is B*. *C. terms*: those furthest apart within the same class, as *black* and *white.* *C. opposition*: that of c. propositions or terms. var. †**Co·ntrair.** [f. OF. *contraire.*]

B. *sb.* [the adj. used *absol.*] †1. Opposite position or side *Wint. T.* I. ii. 372. 2. An object, fact, or quality that is the very opposite of another; often in *pl.* ME. †3. Hostility; an act of hostility -1565. †4. A denial -1555. †5. An adversary, enemy -1622. 6. *Logic.* A contrary term or proposition; see A. 6. 1655.

2. For good and wikkednesse ben tuo contraries CHAUCER. Phr. *By contraries*: by direct contrast; also, just in the opposite way. *The c.*: the exact opposite or reverse. *On the c.*: on the other hand, in contradistinction; by no means, far from it. *To the c.*: to the opposite effect.

C. *adv.* 1. Contrarily, contrariwise (*to*) 1463. 2. Adversely 1497. 3. On the contrary (*arch.*) 1549. 4. In an opposite way; in *Her.* = COUNTER 1596.

2. What storme is this that blowes so contrarie? *Rom. & Jul.* III. ii. 64.

Contrary, *v.* Now *dial.* ME. [a. F. *contrarier*, ad. late L. *contrariare.*] 1. *trans.* To oppose, thwart; to contradict; to do what is contrary to 1581. 2. *intr.* To act, speak, or write in opposition ME.

1. The winds contrarying his course 1649.

Contrast (kǫ̆ntra·st), *v.* 1489. [a. OF. *contraster*:—late L. *contrastare*, f. L. *contra* + *stare.* Reintroduced from F. *c* 1700 as a term of Art.] †I. To resist, *trans.* and *intr.* -1688.

II. 1. *trans. Fine Arts.* To put in contrast differences of form, colour, etc., so as to heighten the total effect 1695. 2. *gen.* To set (objects) in opposition in order to bring out their differences, and compare their superiorities or defects. (Usu. of mental comparison only.) 1799. 3. Of things: To set off (each other) by contrast 1695; to form a contrast to 1767. 4. *intr.* To form a contrast; to exhibit a difference on comparison (*with*) 1715. (Also *pass.* of 3 in same sense.)

1. Contrasted by contrary motions, the most noble parts foremost in sight DRYDEN. 3. The figures of the groups..must c. each other by their several positions DRYDEN. Hence **Contra·stive** *a.* forming a contrast; standing in contrast (*to*).

Contrast (kǫ·ntrast), *sb.* 1597. [a. F. *contraste* (masc.), ad. It. *contrasto*, f. *contrastare*; see prec.] †1. Contention, strife -1670. 2. *Fine Arts.* The juxtaposition of forms, colours, etc., so as to heighten the effect of corresponding parts and of the whole 1711. 3. Comparison of objects of like kind whereby the difference of their qualities is brought out; an instance of this 1731. 4. A person or thing of most opposite qualities 1764.

2. C. increases the splendour of beauty, but it disturbs its influence RUSKIN. 3. A lucky parallel or a striking c. JOHNSON. 4. What a c. from such an intention was the event MAD. D'ARBLAY. var. †**Contra·sto** (in sense 1).

Contrastimulant (kǫ:ntră,sti·miŭlănt). 1831. [ad. It. *contrastimolante.*] *Med.* A medicine that acts in opposition to a stimulant, or that reduces the force of the vital actions.

Contrate (kǫ·ntrĕᶦt), *a.* 1450. [f. L. type **contratus*, f. *contra*; cf. med. L. *contrata* COUNTRY.] †1. ? Opposed. 2. *C. wheel*: a wheel having teeth set at right angles to its plane, as in certain watches 1696.

†**Contratenor** (kǫntrăte·nəɹ). 1552. [ad. It. *contratenore*; see CONTRA-.] *Mus.* = COUNTERTENOR -1782.

Contravallation (kǫ:ntrăvælē̆ᶦ·ʃən). 1678. [ad. F. *contrevallation*, f. L. *contra-* + *vallationem.*] *Mil.* A chain of redoubts and breastworks, constructed by besiegers, to protect their camp against sorties of the garrison.

Contravariant (kǫntrăvēᵊ·riănt). 1853. [See CONTRA-.] *Math.* 'A function which stands in the same relation to the primitive function from which it is derived as any of its linear transforms to an inversely derived transform of its primitive' (Sylvester).

Contravene (kǫntrăvī·n), *v.* 1567. [ad. F. *contrevenir* :—L. *contravenire* (Augustine).] 1. *trans.* To go counter to; to transgress (a law, etc.); to come in conflict with. 2. To oppose in argument; to contradict, dispute, deny 1722.

1. Either to conform to the tenour of the article, or to c. it BURKE. To..warn them against acts which c. this duty 1793. 2. Conclusions so firmly based that we may not c. them HUXLEY. Hence **Contrave·ner.**

Contravention (kǫntrăve·nʃən). 1579. [a. F., f. (ult.) L. *contravenire.*] The action of contravening; violation, transgression.

C. of the church catechism DICKENS, of the chronological order STANLEY.

Contrave·rsion. *rare.* [f. L. *contraversus.*] A turning in the opposite direction. CONGREVE.

Contrayerva (kǫntrăyə̄·ɹvä). 1656. [Sp.; = 'counter-herb', *i. e.* one used as an antidote, f. CONTRA- + *yerva* (now *yerba*) HERB.] The root-stock of species of *Dorstenia* (*D. Contrayerva* and *D. braziliensis*, N. O. *Urticaceæ*) native to tropical America, used as a stimulant and tonic, and formerly against snake-bites.

Contre-, *prefix.* F. *contre* :—L. *contra* has regularly given in Eng. COUNTER, q. v. Frequent in heraldic terms, as *c.-barré*, etc.; = COUNTER-BARRY, etc., q. v.

‖**Contrecoup** (koṅtrəku). 1830. [F., f. *contre* + *coup.*] 1. 'A repulse in the pursuit of any object' (Jamieson). 2. *Surg.* The effect of a blow, as an injury, fracture, produced exactly opposite, or away from, the part actually struck.

Contrectation (kǫntrektē̆·ʃən). 1602. [ad. L. *contrectationem.*] Handling, touching.

Contre-dance, ‖-danse, contra-dance. 1803. [after F. *contre-danse*, It. *contraddanza*, and Sp. *contradanza*, corruptions of Eng. COUNTRY-*dance*, by the perversion of *country* into *contre-*, *contra-*. See N.E.D.] A country-dance; esp. a French country-dance.

Contrefort; see COUNTER-.

‖**Contretemps** (kōṅtr'taṅ). 1684. [F. *contre-temps* bad or false time, etc.] †1. *Fencing.* A pass or thrust made at a wrong or inopportune moment –1725. 2. An inopportune occurrence; an unexpected mishap or hitch 1802.

2. Grieved..by a cruel c. MAR. EDGEWORTH.

Contributable (kǫ̆ntri·biutăb'l), *a.* 1611. [f. CONTRIBUTE + -ABLE.] 1. Liable to contribute. [So F. *contribuable.*] 2. Payable as contribution 1824.

†**Contributary** (kǫ̆ntri·biutări), *a.* (and *sb.*) ME. [f. as prec. + -ARY. Now CONTRIBUTORY.] Contributing; tributary –1801. *sb.* One who contributes; one who pays tribute –1599.

Contribute (kǫ̆ntri·biut), *v.* 1530. [f. L. *contribut-* ppl. stem, f. *con-* + *tribuere.* (Formerly stressed *co·ntribute*, which is still *dial.*)] †1. *trans.* To levy tribute upon (*rare*) 1559. †2. *intr.* To pay tribute (*to*). MARLOWE. 3. To give or pay jointly with others; to furnish to a common fund or purpose 1530; *intr.* or *absol.* to give or make contribution 1610. 4. *transf.* and *fig.* To give or furnish along with others to a collective stock 1653. *intr.* or *absol.* 1864. 5. *fig.* To lend (agency or assistance) to a common result or purpose. *trans.* and (more usually) *intr.* 1605.

3. Every hand is open to c. something JOHNSON. *intr.* A fund was raised..to which all parties..contributed SMILES. 4. Essays, contributed to the Edinburgh Review MACAULAY. 5. *intr.* He contributed greatly to improve the national music W. IRVING. Hence **Contri·butive** *a.* that has the quality or power of contributing; fitted to c. (*to*).

Contribution (kǫntribiū·ʃən). ME. [a. F., ad. L. *contributionem*; see prec.] 1. The action of contributing (see CONTRIBUTE *v.*) 1582. 2. A sum or thing contributed; now, *esp.* An imposition levied upon a district for the support of an army in the field ME. *transf.* and *fig.* 1648. 3. *Law.* The payment by each of the parties interested of his share in any common loss or liability 1641. Also *attrib.*

1. To make a certaine c. for the poore sainctes that are in Hierusalem *Rom.* xv. 26. Phr. *To lay under c.*: to force to contribute. 2. The smallest c. thankfully received (*mod.*). *transf.* A letter..apparently ..a c. from a fresh hand 1882. Hence **Contribu·tional** *a.* of or pertaining to a c.

Contributor (kǫ̆ntri·biutəɹ). 1530. [a. AF. *contributour* (mod.F. *-eur*), f. L. *contribut-*; see CONTRIBUTE.] 1. One that contributes; *spec.* one who contributes literary articles to a journal, magazine, etc. †2. One who pays tribute –1630.

Contributory (kǫ̆ntri·biutəri). 1467. [f. L. *contribut-* ppl. stem (see CONTRIBUTE) + -ORY.]

A. *adj.* 1. That contributes; †tributary –1601. 2. Of the nature of contribution 1836.

1. C. allies GROTE. C. to our own destruction CLARENDON. *C. negligence*: negligence on the part of a person injured, which has conduced to the injury.

B. *sb.* 1. One who, or that which, contributes 1467. 2. *Eng. Law.* One who is bound, on the winding up of a joint stock company, to contribute toward the payment of its debts.

†**Contri·st**, *v.* 1490. [ad. F. *contrister* :—L. *contristare.*] *trans.* To make sad –1818. var. †**Contri·state**; whence †**Contrista·tion.**

Contrite (kǫ·ntrəit), *a.* (and *sb.*) ME. [a. F. *contrit*, ad. L. *contritus*, pa. pple. of *conterere*, f. *con-* + *terere.* Originally stressed *contri·te.*] †1. *lit.* Bruised, crushed (*rare*) –1755. 2. *fig.* Crushed or broken in spirit by a sense of sin; reduced to contrition ME.

1. A c. reed JER. TAYLOR. 2. A broken and a c. heart, O God, thou wilt not despise *Ps.* li. 17. In very c. and earnest words 1868. So †**Contri·ted** *ppl. a.* Hence **Co·ntrite·ly** *adv.*, **-ness** (*rare*).

Contrition (kǫ̆ntri·ʃən). ME. [a. OF. *contriciun*, now *contrition*, ad. L. *contritionem*, f. *conterere*; see prec.] †1. *lit.* The action of rubbing together; grinding, pounding, or bruising (so as to pulverize) –1684. 2. *fig.* The condition of being bruised in heart; affliction of mind for some fault or injury done; *spec.* penitence for sin. Cf. ATTRITION. ME.

1. Triturable, and reduceable to powder, by c. SIR T. BROWNE. 2. In the tyme of thy repentaunce and contrycyon 1530.

Contriturate (kǫ̆ntri·tiŭrĕ't), *v. rare.* 1822. [f. CON- + TRITURATE.] To triturate thoroughly, pulverize.

Contrivance (kǫ̆ntrəi·văns). 1627. [f. CONTRIVE *v.*[1] + -ANCE.] 1. The action of contriving; inventing, plotting, or planning 1646. 2. Adaptation of means to an end; design 1695. 3. The faculty of contriving; inventive capacity 1659. †4. The way in which a thing has been contrived –1834. 5. Something contrived for a purpose; a plan, an artifice 1627; a mechanical device 1667. Also *fig.*

1. The preparations..yet are..in c. and agitation MAY. 2. Proofs of C. in the Structure of the Globe WOODWARD. 5. The grand Scheme and C. for our Redemption EDWARDS. *fig.* The contrivances by which Orchids are fertilized DARWIN. vars. †**Contri·val.** **Contri·vancy** (in sense 3).

Contrive (kǫ̆ntrəi·v), *v.*[1] ME. [a. OF. *controver* = It. *controvare*, f. *con-* + *trovare* :—L. *turbare* to disturb, etc. The phonetic change to *contrive* is unexplained.] 1. *trans.* To invent, devise, excogitate with ingenuity and cleverness. †2. *intr.* To form devices; to plot, conspire –1641. 3. *trans.* To devise, design ME. †4. To find out –1600. †5. To concoct, fabricate. [Cf. F. *controuver.*] –1468. 6. To bring to pass 1530. †7. To bring by ingenuity or skill *into* a place, position, or form –1701.

1. I will..sodainely contriue the meanes of meeting betweene him, and my daughter *Haml.* II. ii. 216. 2. The Fates with Traitors do c. SHAKS. 3. To c. a tubular bridge 1856. 6. Prophecies when once they get abroad..C. their own fulfilment SHELLEY.

Hence **Contri·vable** *a.* that can be contrived. †**Contri·vement**, = CONTRIVANCE 1, 4, 5. **Contri·ver.**

†**Contri·ve**, *v.*[2] ME. [app. irreg. f. L. *contrivi*, pret. of *conterere.*] *trans.* To wear down; to pass (time) –1596. *Tam. Shr.* I. ii. 276.

Control (kǫ̆ntrōu·l), *sb.* 1590. [prob. f. CONTROL *v.*] 1. The fact of controlling, or of checking and directing action; domination, command, sway. 2. Restraint, check 1594. 3. A method or means of restraint; a check 1752. 4. A person who acts as a check; a controller 1786.

1. Quenching my familiar smile with an austere regard of controll *Twel. N.* II. v. 74. 2. Speak what thou know'st, and speak without controul POPE. 3. The..checks and controuls provided by the constitution HUME. *C.-experiment*: a test experiment devised to check the inferences deduced from an experiment, by application of the Method of Difference. 4. b. The apparatus for controlling an aeroplane or motor vehicle 1908. c. A section of the road over which speed is controlled, or where contesting machines are allowed time to stop for overhauling, etc. 1900.

Control (kǫ̆ntrōu·l), *v.* 1475. [a. F. *contrôler*, earlier *contreroller*, f. F. *contrerolle* (now *contrôle*), corresp. to med.L. *contrarotulus*, f. *contra* against, counter + *rotulus* ROLL. Still occas. spelt *controul.*] 1. *trans.* To check or verify, and hence to regulate (payments, etc.): *orig.* by comparison with a duplicate register. Also *transf.* †2. Hence: To call to account, reprove (a person) –1692; to reprehend, object to (a thing) –1738. 3. To exercise restraint or direction upon the free action of; to dominate, command 1495. Also *refl.* 4. †To overpower –1755; in *Law*, to overrule 1724.

1. To controlle the receytes & all the yssues of the Thesaurers office 1475. *transf.* To c. statements 1878. 3. But (oh vaine boast) Who can controll his Fate *Oth.* V. ii. 265. Hence **Contro·llable** *a.*

Controller (kǫ̆ntrōu·ləɹ). ME. [a. AF. *contrerollour*, f. OF. *contreroller*; see CONTROL. The first syllable of the reduced form *countrollour*, mistaken for *count*, etymologically *compt*, gave *comptroller*, a form affected by official scribes, and still retained in connexion with various offices.] 1. One who keeps a counter-roll so as to check a treasurer or person in charge of accounts. †2. A censorious critic –1614. 3. One who or that which controls; *Naut.* an apparatus for regulating or checking the motion of a chain-cable as it runs towards the hawse-holes 1867.

1. Comptroller of the houshold SWIFT, of the Navy SIR J. ROSS. 3. It makes the great controwler of the world, a bare spectator PRYNNE. **C.-general**: an officer entrusted with the supreme control. Hence **Contro·llership**, the office of c.

Controlment (kǫ̆ntrōu·lmĕnt). *arch.* 1494. [f. CONTROL *v.* + -MENT.] †1. The controlling of accounts –1565. 2. = CONTROL *sb.* 1. 1494. 3. = CONTROL *sb.* 2. 1525. †4. Censure –1646.

3. Heere haue we war for war, & bloud for bloud, Controlement for controlement *John* I. i. 20.

†**Controve·rsal**, *a.* 1612. [f. L. *controversus* (see CONTROVERSE) + -AL.] 1. Turned or looking in opposite directions 1644. 2. = CONTROVERSIAL –1697.

1. The Temple of Janus with his two c. faces MILTON.

†**Co·ntroverse**, *sb.* 15.. [a. F., ad. L. *controversia.*] = CONTROVERSY –1636.

The c. of beauties soveraine grace SPENSER.

†**Co·ntroverse**, *v.* 1601. [f. CONTROVERSED *ppl. a.* = F. *controversé.*] 1. *trans.* To discuss, debate –1755. 2. *intr.* To dispute *with* 1699.

†**Co·ntroversed**, *ppl. a.* 1575. [ad. L. *controversus*; earlier than the verb. See CONTROVERT.] Made the subject of controversy; controverted –1663. So †**Co·ntroverser**, **-or.**

Controversial (kǫntrŏvə̄·ɹʃăl), *a.* 1583. [ad. L. *controversialis*; see CONTROVERSY and -AL.] 1. Subject to controversy; questionable; disputed. 2. Of, pertaining to, or of the nature of controversy; polemical 1659. 3. Disputatious 1659.

1. As c. a point as the authorship of Junius J. WILSON. 2. Polemical or c. divinity BP. BULL. 3. The c. pen CRABBE. var. †**Controve·rsary, -ory.** Hence **Controve·rsialist**, one who is skilful in controversy; a disputant. **Controve·rsially** *adv.*

Controversion (kǫntrŏvə̄·ɹʃən). 1677. [ad. med.L. *controversionem.*] †1. A controversy –1762. 2. The action of controverting 1762. 3. = CONTRAVERSION, q. v. 1684.

Controversy (kǫ·ntrŏvəɹsi), *sb.* ME. [ad. L. *controversia*, f. *controversus*, f. *contro* (= *contra*) + *versus.*] 1. Dispute, contention (*esp.* when carried on in writing); contention as to rights, claims, and the like, or on a matter of opinion. 2. (with *a* and *pl.*) A dispute, contention; *esp.* a discussion of contrary opinions 1573.

1. He..made hym a Iudge in causes of controuersie EDEN. Tossed..with their unballasted wits in fathomless and unquiet deeps of c. MILTON. Phr. *Without, beyond c.* [L. *sine controversia*]: without or beyond question or doubt. 2. The great c. respecting the 'Origin of Evil' H. ROGERS. Hence †**Co·ntroversy** *v.* = CONTROVERSE *v.*

Controvert (kǫ·ntrŏvə̄ɹt, kǫntrŏvə̄·ɹt), *v.* 1609. [f. L. type **controvertere*, after L. *controversus*, and *convert*, *pervert*, etc.] †1. *trans.* To dispute or contest (a title, etc.) –1682. 2. To make the subject of controversy; to dispute about 1612. 3. To oppose in argument; to dispute, deny 1613. 4. *intr.* To engage in a controversy 1616.

2. Why melancholy men are witty..is a problem much controverted BURTON. 3. The existence hereof men do not c. SIR T. BROWNE.

Hence **Controverted** *ppl. a.* subjected to controversy. **Controverter**, one who controverts. **Controve·rtible** *a.* capable of being controverted; disputable. **Controvertist**, a controversialist.

†**Contru·de**, *v.* 1609. [ad. L. *contrudere.*] *trans.* To thrust or crowd together –1651. Hence †**Contru·sion** (*rare*).

Contubernal (kǫntiū·bəɹnăl). 1842. [ad. L. *contubernalis.*] *sb.* One who occupies the same tent. *adj.* Of or relating to occupation of the same tent 1873. So †**Contube·rnial** *a.* sharing the same tent. CHAUCER.

Contumacious (kǫntiumē[i]·ʃəs), *a.* 1600. [f. L. *contumaci-*; see CONTUMAX.] **1.** Exhibiting contumacy; stubbornly perverse, insubordinate, rebellious 1603. **2.** *Law.* Wilfully disobedient to the summons or order of a court 1600.

1. To reduce the c. monks to obedience 1772. Hence **Contuma·cious·ly** *adv.*, **-ness.**

Contumacy (kǫ·ntiŭmăsi). ME. [ad. L. *contumacia*, f. *contumax.*] **1.** Perverse and obstinate resistance of authority. †**2.** Of diseases, etc.: Reluctance to yield to treatment -1661. **3.** *Law.* Wilful disobedience to the summons or order of a court ME.

1. Such acts Of contumacie will provoke the highest MILT. *P. L.* x. 1027. var. **Contuma·city** (*rare*).

†**Co·ntumax,** *a.* ME. [a. L., f. *con-* + *tum-*, conn. w. *tumere*, or ? *temnere.*] = CONTUMACIOUS -1587.

Contumelious (kǫntiumī·liəs), *a.* 1483. [a. OF. *contumélieus*, ad. L. *contumeliosus*; see -OUS.] **1.** Exhibiting CONTUMELY; despiteful; superciliously insolent 1548. †**2.** Reproachful, disgraceful -1663.

1. With scoffes and scornes, and c. taunts SHAKS. Curving a c. lip TENNYSON. 2. In so base and c. a condition COWLEY. Hence **Contume·lious-ly** *adv.*, **-ness.**

Contumely (kǫ·ntiumĭli). ME. [a. OF. *contumelie*, ad. L. *contumelia*; prob. cogn. w. CONTUMAX.] **1.** Insolent reproach or abuse; insulting or contemptuous language or treatment; despite; scornful rudeness; now *esp.* such as tends to dishonour or humiliate. (Also with *a* and *pl.*) **2.** Disgrace, reproach 1555.

1. The Oppressors wrong, the poore mans C. *Haml.* III. i. 71. 2. It..casteth a kind of c. upon the author of it PEARSON.

Contund (kǫntɒ·nd), *v. rare.* 1599. [ad. L. *contundere.*] †**1.** *trans.* To pound, beat small -1656. **2.** To affect with contusions; to pound (adversaries). *joc.* or *affected.* 1654.

†**Contu·ne,** *v.* Var. of CONTINUE.

†**Conturba·tion.** 1470. [ad. L. *conturbationem.*] Disturbance (physical or mental) -1816

Contuse (kǫntiū·z), *v.* 1541. [f. L. *contus-* ppl. stem; see CONTUND.] **1.** *trans.* To injure as by a blow without breaking the skin; to bruise. †**2.** To pound, beat small, bray -1626.

2. Roots, Barks, and Seeds, contused together 1626.

Contusion (kǫntiū·ʒən). ME. [a. F., ad. L. *contusionem*; see prec.] **1.** The action of bruising, or condition of being bruised. Also *transf.* **2.** An injury, as from a blow with a blunt instrument or heavy body, which does not break the skin; a bruise 1593. †**3.** Beating small, pounding, or braying -1764.

2. That Winter Lyon who in rage forgets Aged contusions 2 *Hen. VI*, v. iii. 3. So **Contu·sive** *a.* bruising; of or belonging to a c.

Conundrum (kǒnɒ·ndrǒm). 1596. [Origin lost.] †**1.** ? Crotchet-monger. NASHE. †**2.** A whim, crotchet, maggot -1719. †**3.** A pun or word-play depending on similarity of sound in words of different meaning -1794. **4.** A riddle the answer to which involves a pun; also, any puzzling question, problem, or statement 1790. **5.** A 'what-d'ye-call-it' (*rare*). SCOTT.

2. (Tipsy man says) I begin To have strange conundrums in my head MASSINGER. 4. 'You speak in conundrums,' said Morley; 'I wish I could guess them' DISRAELI.

†**Co·nusable, -ance, -ant,** etc.; see COGNIZABLE, etc.

Convalesce (kǫnvăle·s), *v.* 1483. [ad. L. *convalescere*, f. *con-* + *valescere*, inceptive of *valere.* Only in Caxton and Sc. writers till 19th c.] **1.** *intr.* To recover from sickness, get better. **2.** *Rom. Law.* To become valid 1875.

1. That illness when one does not c. at all THACKERAY. Hence **Convale·scence,** gradual recovery of health after illness. So **Convale·scency** (*rare*). **Convale·scent** *a.* recovering health after illness; *sb.* one who is recovering from sickness; *attrib.* of or for convalescents. **Convale·scently** *adv.*

Convallamarin (kǫnvælämē·rin). 1863. [f. L. *convallium* (in *Lilium Convallium*) + *amarus* + -IN.] *Chem.* A bitter glucoside, $C_{23}H_{44}O_{12}$, obtained from the Lily of the Valley (*Convallaria Majalis*). So **Convalla·rin,** an acrid purgative glucoside, $C_{34}H_{62}O_{11}$, obtained from the Lily of the Valley.

†**Convally.** Adopted form of *Convallium* in L. *Lilium Convallium* (*Vulgate*, Cantic. ii. 1), used by herbalists. vars. **Conval, convaile.**

Convection (kǫnve·kʃən). 1623. [ad. L. *convectionem.*] *Physics.* The action of carrying; conveyance; *spec.* the transportation of heat or electricity by the movement of a heated or electrified substance, as in the ascension of heated air or water. Also *attrib.*

The passage of electricity from one place to another by the motion of charged particles is called Electrical C. or Convective Discharge MAXWELL.

Convective (kǫnve·ktiv), *a.* 1859. [f. L. *convect-*, ppl. stem of *convehere.*] **1.** Having the property of conveying. **2.** Of the nature of or relating to convection 1862.

1. The c. force of a stream of water 1862. Hence **Conve·ctively** *adv.*

†**Conve·ll,** *v.* 1536. [ad. L. *convellere.* Cf. CONVULSE.] **1.** *lit.* To tear, wrench -1694. **2.** *fig.* To overthrow completely -1724. So **Conve·llent** *a.* wrenching, pulling up.

†**Convenable** (kǫ·nvĭnăb'l), *a.*[1] ME. [a. F., f. stem of *convenir* (:—L. *convenire* to CONVENE).] **1.** Suitable, meet -1815. **2.** Consistent -1579. **3.** Convenient -1641.

1. A conuenable marriage J. STUBBES. 2. With his word his work is c. SPENSER. Hence †**Co·nvenably** *adv.*

Convenable (kǫnvī·năb'l), *a.*[2] 1755. [f. CONVENE *v.*] Capable of being convened.

‖**Convenance** (koṅvənãṅs). 1483. [a. F., f. *convenir.* Earlier COVENANCE (OF. *covenance*).] †**1.** A convention, covenant (*rare*). †**2.** Concurrence (*rare*) -1677. ‖**3.** Conventional usage; in *pl.* the conventionalities 1847.

3. Her utter ignorance of London *convenances* and proprieties 1881.

Convene (kǫnvī·n), *v.* ME. [a. F. *convenir* :—L. *convenire* to come together, etc.]

I. 1. *intr.* To come together; to meet, *esp.* for a common purpose; *transf.* of things: To occur together 1541; †to unite -1738. **2.** *trans.* To cause to come together; to convoke 1596. **3.** To summon before a tribunal ME.

1. The two princes convened..in the suburbs of Calais BACON. If the rays c. before the retina 1738. 2. The Senate was convened by the tribunes FROUDE. 3. Knapwell was convened before the Archbishop HOOK.

II. †**1.** *intr.* Of persons: To agree -1652. †**2.** To be suitable or fitting -1627. **3.** *intr.* To harmonize 1855.

3. Articles which the marriage-mongers cannot make to c. at all, tempers..tastes, etc. THACKERAY.

Convener (kǫnvī·nəɹ). 1572. [f. prec. + -ER[1].] **1.** One who assembles with others -1641. **2.** One who convokes (a meeting, etc.); *spec.* one appointed to summon the meetings of a committee, etc. (*Sc.*) 1680.

Convenience (kǫnvī·niĕns), *sb.* ME. [ad. L. *convenientia*, f. *convenientem* CONVENIENT.] †**1.** Agreement, accordance -1652. †**2.** Accordance of nature; fitness -1756. **3.** The quality of being convenient, generally; suitability, commodiousness 1601. **4.** The quality of being personally convenient; ease in use or action; material advantage; commodity, comfort 1703. **5.** (with *a* and *pl.*) That which is convenient 1606; *pl.* convenient material arrangements or appliances. (Rarely in *sing.*) 1672.

3. The great c. and pleasure of navigation H. MORE. 4. Phr. *At one's c.*, *to await one's c.*, *marriage of c.*, etc. A building for the c. of the drinkers 1756. 5. Riches..with divers other conveniences 1647. That he may buy Books the next c. HEARNE. A c. to spit in SMOLLETT. To make a c. of one (*mod.*). All the conveniences of a palace LADY M. W. MONTAGU.

Hence **Conve·nience** *v.* to accommodate. var. **Conve·niency** (now little used).

Convenient (kǫnvī·niĕnt), *a.* ME. [ad. L. *convenientem.*] †**1.** Agreeing (in opinion) 1485. †**2.** Accordant, congruous (*to*) -1654. †**3.** In keeping with; befitting, becoming (*to* or *for*); proportionate (*to*) -1677. †**4.** Suitable, appropriate (*to* or *for*) -1790. †**5.** Morally becoming; proper -1727. **6.** Personally suitable; favourable to one's comfort or ease; commodious. (The current sense.) 1477. **7.** *colloq.* and *dial.* Handy 1848.

2. Equitable and c. to reason 1654. 4. *Prov.* xxx. 8. 5. Neither filthinesse, nor foolish talking, nor iesting, which are not conuenient *Eph.* v. 4. 6. And so by conveniente jorneys came to the towne of Edenborough HALL. 7. Heretics used to be brought thither c. for burning hard by THACKERAY. Hence **Conve·niently** *adv.*, †**-ness,** c. quality.

Convent (kǫ·nvĕnt), *sb.* [ME., a. AF. *covent, cuvent, couvent* = OF. *convent*, mod.F. *couvent* :—L. *conventum*, f. *convenire* to CONVENE. The ME. form remains in *Covent Garden.*] †**1.** A gathering; a meeting -1661. †**2.** A company; *spec.* that of the twelve apostles -1548. **3.** A religious association; a body of monks, friars, or nuns forming one local community ME. **4.** The buildings occupied by such a community. (The restriction of the word to a convent of women is not historical.) 1528. Also *attrib.*

1. In the c. of other witches GAULE. 3. Saynt Audry, than abbesse, toke her holy couent And mette the sayd kynge BRADSHAW. 4. Out of his c. of gray stone..Walked the Monk Felix LONGF. Hence **Conve·ntical** *a.* conventual (*rare*).

Convent (kǫnve·nt), *v.* Now *Hist.* 1514. [f. L. *convent-* ppl. stem; cf. *prevent.*] **1.** = CONVENE *v.* I. 1-3. -1718. †**2.** ? To covenant to give 1587. ¶**3.** ? = CONVENE *v.* II. 2.

3. When that is knowne, and golden time conuents A solemne Combination shall be made Of our deere soules *Twel. N.* v. i. 391.

Conventicle (kǫnve·ntik'l). ME. [ad. L. *conventiculum*, dim. of *conventus* in form, but in cl.L. not in sense.] †**1.** An assembly -1650. **2.** A meeting (*esp.* a religious meeting), of a private, clandestine, or illegal kind, as of Nonconformists or Dissenters in England, or of Covenanters in Scotland during the reigns of Charles II and James II. 1438. †**3.** *contempt.* A 'hole-and-corner' meeting -1682. **4.** A place of meeting 1596; *esp.* a nonconformist or dissenting meeting-house. (Now *rhet.* or *contempt.*) 1550. †**5.** A small convent -1603.

1. He [the Mayor] called a Conuenticle of his Brethren GREENE. 2. My selfe had notice of your Conuenticles, And all to make away my guiltlesse Life 2 *Hen. VI*, III. i. 166. When some Men seeke Christ, in the Conuenticles of Heretikes BACON. A c. of gloomy sullen Saints DRYDEN.

Comb. **C. Acts,** the acts 16 Chas. II, c. 4 and 22 Chas. II, c. 1 'to prevent and suppress seditious Conventicles'.

Hence **Conve·nticle** *v.*, *intr.* to meet in a c.; to hold or frequent conventicles. **Conventiclee·r, Conve·nticler,** a frequenter of conventicles; a schismatic.

Convention (kǫnve·nʃən). ME. [a. F., or ad. L. *conventionem.*]

I. †**1.** The action of coming together -1782. Also †*fig.* of things. **2.** The action of summoning an assembly 1647. †**3.** The action of summoning before a tribunal -1726. **4.** An assembly of persons for some common object; *esp.* a formal assembly, ecclesiastical, political, or social 1552. **5.** *Eng. Hist.* An assembly of the Houses of Parliament, without the summons of the Sovereign; as that of 1660, which restored Charles II, and that of 1688, which declared the throne abdicated by James II. Hence *c. parliament.* 1660.

1. In this place of c. of merchants from all parts of the world EVELYN. 2. The c. of the parliament CLARENDON. 4. If that suffice not, they may call a new c. of estates HOBBES. 5. In 1689, the C. declared itself a Parliament GREEN.

II. 1. An agreement or covenant between parties ME. **2.** *spec.* **a.** In *Diplomacy*: An agreement between sovereigns or states: formerly = TREATY; now an agreement less formal than a treaty 1603. **b.** *Mil.* An agreement made between the commanders of armies in time of war 1780. **3.** General agreement or consent, as embodied in any accepted usage, standard, etc.; in a bad sense: Conventionalism 1778. **4.** A conventionalism 1790.

1. Fraudulent conventions oblige not BP. HALL. 2. a. An International C. respecting the Liquor traffic in the North Sea 1888. b. The conventions for suspending hostilities agreed upon by me with Marshals Soult and Suchet WELLINGTON. 3. This Gorgon of C. and Fashion EMERSON.

Comb. **c.-coin, -dollar,** coins struck according to monetary conventions between different German states.

Conventional (kǫnve·nʃənăl), *a.* 1583. [ad. L. *conventionalis*, f. *convention-* CONVENTION.] **1.** Of, pertaining to, or of the nature of a convention or assembly 1812. **2.** Relating to, of the nature of, or settled by a convention or compact. In *Law*: Founded on contract (opp. to *legal* or *judicial*). 1583. 3. Relating to convention or general agreement; established by social convention; arbitrarily or artificially determined 1761. 4. Characterized by convention; not natural, original, or spontaneous; in *Art*, consisting in, or resulting from, an artificial treatment of natural objects; following traditions 1851.

3. In matters merely c., examples are more powerful than principles GIBBON. 4. The c. phraseology with which English preaching had been so long encumbered STANLEY. Specimens of c. or imaginary foliage SIR G. SCOTT. Phr. *The c.*: that which is c. Hence **Conve·ntionally** *adv.*

Conventionalism (kǫ̈nve·nʃənăliz'm). 1837. [f. prec. + -ISM.] 1. Adherence to or regard for that which is conventional (in conduct, thought, or art). 2. (with *a* and *pl.*) Anything that is merely conventional; a conventional principle, idea, usage, or practice.

1. The incubus of c. HT. MARTINEAU.

Conventionalist (kǫ̈nve·nʃənălist). 1801. [f. as prec. + -IST.] 1. A member or supporter of a Convention. 2. One who follows conventional usage 1846.

Conventionality (kǫ̈nvenʃənæ·liti). 1834. [f. as prec. + -ITY.] 1. The quality or state of being conventional; conventional character or style; obedience to mere convention 1842. 2. A conventional thing or practice.

Conventionalize (kǫ̈nve·nʃənăləiz), *v.* 1854. [f. as prec. + -IZE.] *trans.* To make conventional; to bring under conventional rules; in *Art*, to treat conventionally, represent in a conventional manner. Hence **Conve:ntionaliza·tion.**

Conventionary (kǫ̈nve·nʃənări), *a.* and *sb.* 1602. [ad. med.L. *conventionarius*.] 1. Applied to tenants and tenure on terms originally fixed by convention (see CONVENTION II. 1) as distinguished from custom. 2. *sb.* A c. tenant or tenure 1828.

Conventionist (kǫ̈nve·nʃənist). 1768. [See -IST.] 1. A member of a convention 1823. †2. One who enters into a contract. STERNE.

Conventual (kǫ̈nve·ntiuăl), *a.* and *sb.* ME. [ad. L. *conventualis*, f. *conventus* CONVENT.]

A. *adj.* Of or belonging to a religious convent; characteristic of a convent.

In c. garb PRESCOTT. The c. discipline of prose LOWELL. Hence **Conve·ntually** *adv.*

B. *sb.* 1. A member of a convent 1611. 2. A member of that branch of the Franciscan order which lives in large convents and follows a mitigated rule; dist. from the Observants 1533.

Converge (kǫ̈nvə̄·ɹdʒ), *v.* 1691. [ad. late L. *convergere*, f. *con-* + *vergere*.] 1. *intr.* To tend to meet in a point; to approach nearer together. The opposite of *diverge*. Also *fig.* 2. *Math.* To approximate in the sum of its terms toward a definite limit 1796. 3. *trans.* To cause to come together 1768.

1. The sides of the Ship c. into an Angle 1691. *fig.* Every circumstance converges to the same effect on the mind HALLAM. 3. Power of converging the optic axes 1863.

Convergence (kǫ̈nvə̄·ɹdʒĕns). 1713. [f. CONVERGENT.] 1. The action or fact of converging; movement toward or terminating in the same point. Also *fig.* and *transf.* 2. *Math.* Of convergent series or fractions 1858.

1. In the metropolis of commerce the point of c. was the Exchange MACAULAY. *fig.* C. of effort LEWES.

Conve·rgency. 1709. [f. as prec.] 1. Convergent quality. 2. = CONVERGENCE 1791.

Convergent (kǫ̈nvə̄·ɹdʒĕnt), *a.* 1727. [ad. L. *convergentem*; see CONVERGE.] 1. Inclining towards each other, or towards a common point of meeting; tending to meet in a point or focus. Also *fig.* and *transf.* 2. *Math.* = CONVERGING 2. 1816.

1. Rays [of light] may be either divergent, parallel, or c. TYNDALL. A c. attack 1862.

Conve·rginerved, *a.* [irreg. f. *convergenti-*, comb. f. L. *convergentem*.] *Bot.* 'When the ribs of a leaf describe a curve and meet at the point' (*Treas. Bot.* 1866).

Converging (kǫ̈nvə̄·ɹdʒiŋ), *ppl. a.* 1727. [f. CONVERGE *v.*] 1. = CONVERGENT 1. 1776. 2. *Math.* Applied to an infinite series of terms, the sum of which, beginning with the first, continually approximates towards a definite limit as more and more are taken 1727. 3. Causing convergence 1833.

3. The gathering or c. power of any glass. Hence **Conve·rgingly** *adv.*

Conversable (kǫ̈nvə̄·ɹsăb'l), *a.* (erron. -ible.) 1598. [a. F., ad. med.L. *conversabilis*, f. *conversari*. In 17th c. *co·nversable*.] 1. That may be conversed with (see CONVERSE *v.*); pleasant in conversation; disposed to converse. 2. Of or pertaining to social converse 1631.

2. The evening was quiet and c. Hence **Conve·rsableness,** c. quality. **Conve·rsably** *adv.*

Conversance (kǫ·nvəɹsăns). 1609. [f. CONVERSANT; see ANCE.] The state or quality of being conversant. So **Co·nversancy.**

Conversant (kǫ·nvəɹsănt). ME. [a. OF.:—L. *conversantem*, *conversari*. Orig. *conversa·nt*.]

A. *adj.* (usu. predicative). †1. Dwelling habitually or frequently *in* a place. 2. Having familiar intercourse *with*, †*in*, †*among*, †*about* ME. 3. Occupied *in*, †*about*, †*upon*; having to do *with* ME. 4. Versed *in*; familiar *with* 1573. †5. Frequently occurring; familiar –1651.

2. C. with women STEELE, with Heaven COWPER. Conuersant in princes courtes BARET. 3. C. in studies BACON, with man or men's affairs MILT., about language WHATELY. 4. C. in the Scriptures BACON, with questions of finance LECKY.

†B. *sb.* One who is intimate with another –1680.

Conversation (kǫnvəɹsē·ʃən). ME. [a. OF.; see CONVERSE *v.*] †1. The action of living or having one's being *in* or *among*. Also *fig.* –1705. †2. The action of consorting with others; living together; commerce, society, intimacy –1770. 3. Sexual intimacy 1511. †4. *fig.* Occupation *with* things; intimacy with a matter –1721. †5. Circle of acquaintance, society –1712. 6. Behaviour, manner of life (*arch.*) ME. 7. Interchange of thought and words; familiar discourse or talk 1580; a talk 1694. †8. An 'At Home' –1787. 9. (In full *c. piece*): A kind of *genre* painting representing a group of figures. H. WALPOLE. ¶10. = CONVERSION ME.

1. For our conuersation is in heauen *Phil.* iii. 20. 3. *Criminal c.* (abbrev. to *crim. con.*): adultery. 4. Out of..much c. in books 1626. C. with Antiquity 1702. 6. To him that ordereth his conuersation aright *Ps.* l. 23. 7. To lead the c. JOHNSON. 8. Lady Pomfret has a charming c. once a week H. WALPOLE.

Hence **Conversa·tional** *a.* ready to converse; addicted to c.; of, belonging to, or proper to c. **Conversa·tionalist, Conversa·tionist,** one who excels in c. **Conversa·tionally** *adv.* †**Conversa·tioned** *ppl. a.* behaved. BEAUM. & FL.

Conversative (kǫ̈nvə̄·ɹsătiv), *a. rare.* 1631. [f. L. *conversat-* ppl. stem; see CONVERSE and -IVE.] †Sociable; talkative.

‖**Conversazione** (kǫ·nvəɹsætsiōu·ni). Pl. -oni (-ōu·ni), now usu. -ones. 1740. [a. It.] ‖1. In Italy, an evening assembly for conversation, and recreation. †2. In England, an 'At Home'. Cf. CONVERSATION 8. –1823. 3. A *soirée* or other assembly of an intellectual character, in connexion with literature, art, or science 1792.

1. A *c.*, a sort of assembly at the principal people's houses, full of I cannot tell what GRAY.

Converse (kǫ̈nvə̄·ɹs), *v.* ME. [a. F. *converser* = late L. *conversare* :—L. *conversari*; middle voice of rare *conversare*, freq. of *convertere*. The sense 'talk with' is recent in Fr. and Eng.] †1. *intr.* To move about, live *in* (*on*, *upon*), *among* (*with*) –1727. †2. To consort, keep company; to be familiar *with* –1819. 3. To be engaged *in*; to have to do *with*; to be conversant *with*. *Obs.* exc. as *fig.* 1586. †4. To interchange ideas *with*, by speech or writing or otherwise –1771. 5. *spec.* 'To convey the thoughts reciprocally in talk' (J.); to talk *with*. The ordinary current sense. 1615.

1. Cetaceous Fishes which c. chiefly in the northern Sea RAY. 2. MILT. *P. L.* II. 184. They may lawfully c. together as man and wife 1656. 3. A man..who has conversed, not only with books, but with lawyers and merchants..statesmen and princes MACAULAY. 4. Like ships at sea, they must c. by signals DE FOE. 5. You are cheerful, and love to c. upon death SOUTHEY. Hence **Conve·rser.**

Converse (kǫ·nvəɹs), *sb.*[1] 1604. [f. prec.; orig. stressed like the vb.] 1. = CONVERSATION 2, 3. *Obs.* exc. in certain expressions now referred to 3. 1610. †2. = CONVERSATION 4. –1727. 3. = CONVERSATION 7. Now *poet.* or *rhet.* 1604. 4. Spiritual or mental communion 1668. †5. Manner of life –1702.

1. C. with the world will do more for you DISRAELI. 3. Sweet is thy c. to each Social ear POPE. 4. With Nature here high c. hold SHENSTONE.

†**Converse,** *a.*[1] and *sb.*[2] ME. [a. F. *convers*, ad. L. *conversus* (also used).] *adj.* Converted in mind or feeling. ME. only. *sb.* A lay member of a convent –1691.

Converse (kǫ·nvəɹs), *a.*[2] and *sb.*[3] 1570. [ad. L. *conversus*; see CONVERT *v.*]

A. *adj.* Turned round; opposite or contrary in direction or action 1794.

The c. arts of destruction and defence BURTON. Hence **Conve·rsely** *adv.*

B. *sb.* 1. *gen.* A form of words derived from another by the transposition of two antithetical members; a thing or action which is the exact opposite of another 1786. 2. *Math.* (One proposition is the c. of another, when the datum and conclusion of the one are respectively taken as the conclusion and datum of the other.) 1570. 3. *Logic.* A converted proposition: formerly applied to the CONVERTEND, but now usually to that which results from conversion 1827.

1. What we gain in power is lost in time; and the c. EMERSON. 2. The 8 proposition being the conuerse of the fourth BILLINGSLEY. 3. The absolute quantity of the C. must be exactly equal to that of the Convertend SIR W. HAMILTON.

Conversible (kǫ̈nvə̄·ɹsib'l), *a.* 1660. [ad. late L. *conversibilis*, f. *convers-* ppl. stem; see CONVERT *v.* and -BLE.] Capable of being converted or transposed. ¶ See also CONVERSABLE.

Conversion (kǫ̈nvə̄·ɹʃən). ME. [a. F., ad. L. *conversionem*, f. *convertere*; see CONVERT *v.*]

I. †1. The action of converting; rotation –1726; turning –1712; returning –1682. 2. Transposition, inversion; *spec.* in *Logic*, the transposition of the subject and predicate of a proposition to form a new proposition 1551. 3. *Math.* The substitution of the difference of antecedent and consequent for the consequent in each of the ratios forming a proportion. ? *Obs.* 1570. 4. *Law.* The action of (wrongfully) converting something to one's own use 1615.

1. The c. of the needle to the north SIR T. BROWNE. 4. There may be a trover and no c., if he keep and lay up the goods, for the Owner COKE.

II. 1. The action of converting, or fact of being converted, to a religion, a belief, or opinion; *spec.* to Christianity ME. 2. *Theol.* The turning of sinners to God; a spiritual change from sinfulness to a religious life ME. 3. Change of form or properties, condition, or function 1549. Hence in many techn. uses in *Manuf.* †4. *Mil.* A change of front to a flank –1863.

1. The conuersion of the gentyles EDEN. 2. See how God wrought for my conuersion GREENE. 3. Not by conuersion of the Godhead into flesh *Bk. Com. Prayer.* The c. of a muzzle-loader 1874.

III. †1. Translation; a translation, version –1653. 2. *Math.* Change of a number or quantity into another denomination 1557. 3. Substitution of or exchange for something else 1607. b. *spec.* in *Law.* The operation of converting property (see CONVERT III. 2) 1788.

3. The c. of the four per cents into three and a half per cents was facilitated 1826. b. The usual trusts for sale and c. (*mod.*).

Conversive (kǫ̈nvə̄·ɹsiv), *a.* 1607. [a. F. *conversif*, f. *convers-* ppl. stem; see CONVERT *v.* and -IVE.] 1. Having the power or function of conversion 1655. 2. Convertible 1864. Hence †**Conversively** *adv.* conversely.

Convert (kǫ̈nvə̄·ɹt), *v.* ME. [a. OF. *convertir*:—pop. L. **convertire*, for cl. L. *convertere*, f. *con-* + *vertere*.]

I. †1. *trans.* To turn about, direct. *refl.* = To turn (*intr.*) –1738. Also †*fig.* †2. *trans.* To turn back –1633. 3. †To invert, transpose –1551. b. *Logic.* To transpose the terms of (a proposition) by CONVERSION 1638. †4. *fig.* To reverse the course of; *pa. pple.* = opposite, contrary –1703. 5. To turn or apply *to* (another use), to divert; *spec.* in *Law*, wrongfully to appropriate and apply *to* (one's own use). (Cf. CONVERSION I. 4.) 1480.

1. Priests..who usually in their Sacrifices..C. themselves unto the East SIR T. BROWNE. 5. Receiuours of his reuenues..conuerted the same to their owne singuler profit 1542.

II. †1. *trans.* To turn in mind, feeling, or conduct –1577; *intr.* to turn *from* a course of conduct, etc. –1600. 2. *trans.* To cause to turn to a religion, belief, or opinion; *spec.* to bring to Christianity ME. Also †*intr.* 3. *Theol.* To cause to turn from a sinful to a religious life ME. Also †*intr.* 4. To turn *into* something different; to transform; to change in character or function; also †*intr.* ME.

1. Blessid be Love, that can thus folk c. CHAUCER. *intr.* When thou from youth conuertest SHAKS. *Sonn.* xi. 2. Þar was conuerted thusand fiue ME. 3. Rather that he should be conuerted and liue *Bk. Com. Prayer.* 4. That still lessens The sorrow, and converts it nigh to joy MILT. *Sams.* 1564. To c. the Enfield rifle into a breech-loader 1874. In Rugby football, to kick a goal from (a try) 1896.

III. 1. To change by substituting an equivalent; †*spec.* to translate -1651. 2. *Law.* To change the quality of property, as from real to personal, joint to separate, or *vice versâ* 1793.

1. To c. goods into money SMILES.

Convert (kǫ·nvəɹt). 1561. [?abbrev. for *converted*; influenced by CONVERSE *sb.*²]

†**A.** *adj.* 1. Brought over to a religious faith. 2. *C. brother, sister*: = CONVERSE *sb.*² -1693.

B. *sb.* A person brought over to any religious faith, or (*transf.*) to any opinion, party, etc. 1561.

Convertend (kǫnvəɹte·nd). 1837. [ad. L. *convertendus.*] *Logic.* The proposition as it stands before conversion; opp. to *converse.*

Converter (kǫ̆nvə̄·ɹtəɹ). Also *erron.* **-tor.** 1533. [f. CONVERT *v.* + -ER¹.] 1. One who makes converts 1570. 2. One who converts (see CONVERT *v.*) 1533. 3. That which converts: in *Steel Manuf.*, a retort, made of iron and lined with some refractory material (usually *ganister*), in which pig-iron is converted into steel by the Bessemer process; see BESSEMER.

Convertible (kǫ̆nvə̄·ɹtib'l), *a.* (*sb.*) ME. [a. F., ad. late L. *convertibilis*; see CONVERT *v.*] 1. That may be converted; interchangeable. 2. Capable of being turned to a particular use or purpose 1818. 3. Capable of being turned *into* something else; capable of being changed in form, condition, or qualities 1533. 4. Capable of being converted by exchange into property of another kind 1834. 5. As *sb. pl.* = C. things or terms 1615.

1. [Those who] put prelacy and popery together as terms c. SWIFT. 3. A rogue alive to the ludicrous is still c. EMERSON. Heat is c. into electricity HUXLEY. 4. By rendering paper money c. into metallic currency HT. MARTINEAU. Hence **Conve·rtibi·lity,** c. quality. **Conve·rtibly** *adv.*

Convertite (kǫ·nvəɹtəit). *arch.* 1565. [f. CONVERT *v.* or *sb.* Revived in 19th c.] A (professed) convert to religion; *spec.* a reformed Magdalen. Also *transf.*

Convex (kǫ·nveks). 1571. [ad. L. *convexus* (= *convectus*, pa. pple. of *convehere.* By Milton, and occas. since, stressed *conve·x.*]

A. *adj.* Having a curvature that bulges towards the point of observation; the reverse of *concave.*

The convexe or out-bowed side of a vessell BP. HALL. The light is made by a c. glass or lens to converge to one point or focus N. ARNOTT.

B. *sb.* [the adj. used *ellipt.*] †1. A convex body or surface -1796. 2. A convex glass or lens 1705.

1. In circuit to the uttermost c. Of this great round MILT. *P. L.*

Hence **Convex** *v. rare,* to make c.; *intr.* to bow or bend convexly. **Convexed** *ppl. a.* made in a c. form. †**Conve·xedly, Co·nvexly** *advs.* in a c. form or manner. **Convexness,** c. quality.

Convexity (kǫ̆nve·ksiti). 1600. [ad. L. *convexitas*, f. *convexus*; cf. F. *convexité.*] 1. The condition of being convex; outward bulging 1605. 2. A convex curve, surface, side, or part.

1. The finiteness or c. of heaven BACON.

Convexo- (kǫ̆nve·kso). In comb. = Convexly, convex and —, as in **c.-concave,** convex on one side and concave on the other; of the form of a meniscus; **c.-convex,** convex on both sides; **c.-plane,** convex on one side and flat on the other = *plano-c.*

Convey (kǫ̆nvēⁱ·), *v.* ME. [a. OF. *con-, cunveier*, now *convoyer*, f. L. *con-* + OF. *veie, voie* :—L. *via* way. Cf. CONVOY.] †1. *trans.* To CONVOY, escort -1710. †2. To lead, conduct; also *fig.* -1713. 3. To transport, carry, take from one place to another ME. †4. To take *away*, remove, *esp.* clandestinely -1697; hence, *euphem.* to steal -1753. †*refl.* -1697. 5. To lead or conduct as a channel or medium 1601. 6. †To transmit, or cause to pass -1741; *esp.* to communicate, impart (an idea, benefit, etc.) ME.; hence, to express in words 1576. 7. To transfer, as property, to another; now only in *Law*, to transfer by deed or legal process; also *absol.* 1495. †8. To bring down, derive -1606. †9. To conduct (an affair); to manage with privacy or craft -1661.

3. Luggage conveyed by these coaches will be charged for (*mod.*). 4. *Merry W.* I. iii. 31. Iesus had conueyed himself away *John* v. 13. 5. Thro' reeden Pipes c. the Golden Flood DRYDEN. To c. the impressions of sound 1854. 6. To c. a lesson 1766, Thoughts to one another SOUTH. 7. The cost of conveying a small estate 1863. 9. *Lear* I. ii. 109.

Hence †**Convey** *sb.* conveyance; a CONVOY. **Convey·able** *a.* that may be conveyed. **Convey·al,** the act of conveying, conveyance.

Conveyance (kǫ̆nvēⁱ·ăns). 1503. [f. prec.] †1. Convoying -1604. 2. The action of conveying, or transporting; carriage 1520. 3. Furtive carrying off; stealing 1526. 4. The communicating (*of* a thing *to* any one) 1662. 5. Transmission, transference 1646. 6. *Law.* The transference of (*esp.* real) property from one person to another by deed or writing 1523; the instrument of transfer 1576. 7. The conveying of anything by a channel or medium 1577. †8. The conveying of meaning by words; hence, style -1775. †9. Management; *esp.* skilful, or cunning, management -1704; an artifice -1641. 10. A conducting way, passage, etc. 1542. 11. A means of transport from place to place 1598. †12. *fig.* A 'vehicle' (of thought, etc.) -1841.

1. *Oth.* I. iii. 286. 2. Arrangements for the c. of money 1870. 3. The simile..is stolen from Cowley, however little worth the trouble of c. JOHNSON. 6. Covenous and fraudulent..conveyaunces..as well of landes..as of goodes and catals 1571. *Haml.* v. i. 119. 7. C. by Condit or pumpe 1577. 9. A pretty slip-skin c. MILT. 10. *Cor.* v. i. 54. 11. The steam-packet is a beastly c. DISRAELI.

Conveyancer (kǫ̆nvēⁱ·ănsəɹ). 1623. [f. prec.; see -ER¹ 1.] One who or that which conveys; *esp.* a lawyer who practises conveyancing.

Conveyancing (kǫ̆nvēⁱ·ănsiŋ), *vbl. sb.* 1676. [f. as prec. + -ING¹.] †1. Deceitful contrivance -1690. 2. The drawing of deeds and other instruments for the transference of property from one person to another; the branch of the law which deals with titles and their transference 1714.

Conveyer (kǫ̆nvēⁱ·əɹ). 1513. [f. CONVEY *v.* + -ER.] 1. One that conveys, carries, or transmits. †2. A light-fingered thief. *Rich. II*, IV. i. 317. 3. One who transfers property 1647. 4. That which conveys, or transmits; *spec.* any mechanical contrivance for conveying grain in a mill, timber in a saw-mill, etc. 1880. var. **Convey·or** (in senses 3, 4).

†**Convi·ciate,** *v.* 1604. [f. ppl. stem of L. *conviciari*, f. *convicium.*] *trans.* To revile, slander, rail at -1646. So †**Convi·ciatory,** †**Convi·cious** *adjs.* railing; reproachful.

†**Convici·nity.** *nonce-wd.* [See CON-.] Vicinity to each other. WARTON.

Convict (kǫ̆nvi·kt), *ppl. a.* ME. [ad. L. *convictus* pa. pple.; see CONVINCE.] *pa. pple.* and *adj.* 1. Proved or pronounced guilty. 2. Overcome ME.

C. of having four Wives at one and the same time COTTON.

Convict (kǫ·nvikt), *sb.* 1530. [f. prec.] 1. One judicially convicted of a criminal offence (*arch.*). 2. *spec.* A criminal serving a sentence of penal servitude 1786. Also *attrib.*

2. Escape of a c. from Dartmoor (*mod.*).

Convict (kǫ̆nvi·kt), *v.* ME. [f. L. *convict-* ppl. stem; see CONVINCE. Cf. CONVICT *ppl. a.*] 1. *trans.* To prove to be guilty, or in the wrong; *esp.* by judicial procedure. Also *absol.* 1841. †2. To demonstrate or prove -1656. 3. To bring conviction home to (a person) 1526. 4. To disprove, refute (*arch.*) 1594. †5. To overcome -1607.

1. No englishman should be conuicted except by English Judges POWEL. Convicted of want of sensibility MORLEY. 3. They..being conuicted by their owne conscience, went out one by one *John* viii. 9. 4. Which conceit being already convicted, not only by Scaliger, etc. SIR T. BROWNE. 5. *John* III. iv. 2. Hence **Convi·ctable, -ible** *a.* (*rare*).

Conviction (kǫ̆nvi·kʃən). 1491. [ad. L. *convictionem*; see CONVINCE.] 1. Legal proof or declaration of guilt; the fact or condition of being convicted. †2. Demonstration, proof -1647. †3. Confutation -1661. †4. Detection and exposure -1724. 5. The act of convincing 1664. 6. The condition of being convinced; settled persuasion 1699. 7. A settled persuasion 1841. 8. *Theol.* The fact or condition of being convicted or convinced of sin 1675.

1. Summary convictions, without the intervention of a jury W. BELL. 4. Further reproof and c. of the Roman errors JER. TAYLOR. 5. The C. of those who are either of a contrary opinion..or who are in doubt WHATELY. 6. A painful c. of his defects JOHNSON. Phr. *To carry c.* 8. My soul was at that very time groaning under deep convictions 1821.

Convictism (kǫ·nvikti'zm). 1864. [f. CONVICT *sb.* + -ISM.] The system of penal settlements for convicts. **b.** The convict class or body.

b. The invasion of c. from Swan River 1868.

Convictive (kǫ̆nvi·ktiv), *a.* 1612. [f. L. *convict-* ppl. stem (see CONVINCE) + -IVE.] Having power to produce conviction.

The c. answer of Christ BP. HALL. Hence **Convi·ctive·ly** *adv.*, **-ness.**

Convictor (kǫ̆nvi·ktəɹ, -ǭɹ). 1647. [a. L., f. *convivere.*] A table companion; a commoner.

Convince (kǫ̆nvi·ns), *v.* 1530. [ad. L. *convincere*, f. *con-* + *vincere.*]

I. †1. To overcome, vanquish. Also *absol.* -1633. †2. To overcome in argument; to confute -1708. 3. To bring to acknowledge the truth *of*; to satisfy by argument or evidence. In *pass.*, To be brought to a full conviction. (= CONVICT 3.) 1632.

1. *Macb.* I. vii. 64. 2. There was none of you that conuinced Iob, or that answered his words *Job* xxxii. 12. 3. I am convinced..and have nothing more to object JOWETT. To c. of a mistake 1797, of sin 1648.

II. †1. = CONVICT *v.* 1. -1776. †2. = CONVICT 2. -1730. †3. = CONVICT 4. -1625.

1. Which of you conuinceth mee of sin *John* viii. 46. 2. This may be easily convinced as false SALKELD. 3. God neuer wrought Miracle to conuince Atheisme, because his Ordinary Works conuince it BACON. Hence **Convi·nced** *ppl. a.* brought to a state of conviction. **Convi·ncement,** conviction. **Convi·ncer** (*rare*). **Convi·ncing·ly** *adv.*, **-ness,** c. quality. †**Convi·ncive** *a.* having the power of convincing (*rare*).

Convincible (kǫ̆nvi·nsib'l), *a.* 1643. [ad. L. *convincibilis* (Isidore).] 1. Capable of being †convicted or convinced. †2. Of convincing power 1647.

†**Convi·val.** 1615. [ad. L. *convivalis*, f. *conviva.*] *adj.* = CONVIVIAL -1755. *sb.* A guest 1615.

‖**Convive** (kōṅvīv, kǫ·nvəiv), *sb.* 1648. [a. F., ad. L. *conviva.*] One who feasts with others; a fellow-banqueter. Hence †**Co·nvive** *v.* to feast together (*rare*).

Convivial (kǫ̆nvi·viăl), *a.* 1668. [ad. L. *convivialis*, f. *convivium*; cf. CONVIVAL.] 1. Of or belonging to a feast or banquet; festive. 2. Fond of feasting and good company, jovial 1784.

1. Which feasts c. meetings we did name DENHAM. 2. The plump c. parson COWPER. Hence **Convi·vialist,** a person of c. habits. **Convi·vially** *adv.*

Conviviality (kǫ̆nvi:vi,æ·līti). 1791. [f. as prec.] Convivial quality; the enjoyment of festive society, festivity; convivial spirit.

His [Pope's] disqualifications for the coarsest forms of c. L. STEPHEN.

Co·nvocate, *ppl. a.* 1532. [ad. L. *convocatus*; see next.] *pa. pple.* and *adj.* Convocated (*arch.* and *poet.*).

Convocate (kǫ·nvokeⁱt), *v.* 1540. [f. L. *convocat-* ppl. stem; see CONVOKE.] *trans.* To call or summon together (*arch.*).

Convocation (kǫnvokēⁱ·ʃən). ME. [ad. L. *convocationem.*] 1. The action of calling together or assembling by summons. 2. An assembly of persons thus convoked ME. 3. *Eng. Ch.* A provincial synod, constituted by statute and called together to deliberate on ecclesiastical matters ME. 4. At Oxford: The great legislative assembly of the University, consisting of all qualified members of the degree of M.A.; a meeting of this body 1577.

1. The c. of the Army 1678. 2. And in the first day there shalbe an holy conuocation *Ex.* xii. 16. 3. They [the Thirty-nine Articles] were made at three several Convocations SELDEN. *Comb.* **C.-house,** the place where a c. meets; the assembly itself. Hence **Convoca·tional** *a.* of, belonging to, or of the nature of, a c. **Convoca·tionist,** a supporter of C.

Convoke (kǫ̆nvōᵘ·k), *v.* 1598. [ad. F. *con-*

voquer, ad. L. *convocare.*] *trans.* To call together; to bring together by summons. Also *fig.*
For five years afterwards the Queen did not c. Parliament HALLAM.

Convolute (kǫ·nvŏliūt), *a.* 1794. [ad. L. *convolutus* pa. pple.; see CONVOLVE.] **1.** *Bot.* Coiled laterally upon itself, as a leaf in the bud. **2.** *gen.* Rolled or folded together; having convolutions 1874. Also as *sb.* So **Co·nvolute** *v. rare*, to coil up; *intr.* to wind about. **Co·nvoluted** *ppl. a.* coiled, twisted, or sinuous; exhibiting convolutions.

Convolution (kǫnvŏliū·ʃən). 1545. [f. L. *convolut-* ppl. stem; see CONVOLVE.] **1.** The action of coiling, twisting, or winding together; the condition of being convoluted 1597. **2.** A fold, twist, turn, winding, sinuosity (of anything rolled or coiled up) 1545. **3.** *Anat.* Each of the sinuous folds of the cerebrum 1615.
1. Toss'd wide around, O'er the calm sky, in c. swift THOMSON.

Convolve (kǫnvǫ·lv), *v.* 1599. [ad. L. *convolvere*, f. *con-* + *volvere.*] †**1.** *trans.* To enclose in folds –1794. **2.** To roll together, coil, twist 1650. **3.** *intr.* To revolve together 1808.
2. Then Satan first knew pain, And writh'd him to and fro convolved MILT. *P. L.* VI. 329.

Convolvulaceous (kǫnvǫlviulē·ʃəs). 1847. [f. mod.L. *Convolvulaceæ.*] *Bot.* Of or belonging to the natural order *Convolvulaceæ*, of which *Convolvulus* is the typical genus.

Convo·lvulin. 1850. [f. CONVOLVULUS + -IN.] *Chem.* A glucoside, $C_{31}H_{50}O_{16}$, obtained from the rhizome of *Convolvulus Schiedanus*, the officinal jalap-root.
Hence **Convolvuli·nic** acid, also called **Convo·lvulic**, $C_{31}H_{54}O_{18}$, a product of the action of fixed alkalis upon c.

Convolvulus (kǫnvǫ·lviulŏs). Pl. **-luses**, rarely **-li.** 1551. [a. L., f. *convolvere.*] *Bot.* A large genus of plants, having slender twining stems and trumpet-shaped flowers, including the English BINDWEEDS.
The lustre of the long convolvuluses That coil'd around the stately stems TENNYSON.

Convoy (kǫnvoi·), *v. trans.* ME. [a. F. *convoyer* = It. *conviare*; see CONVEY.] **1.** To escort. **2.** To escort with, or as, an armed force, either by sea or land, for protection 1559. †**3.** To convey, carry (*lit.* and *fig.*) –1703. †**4.** To manage. *Sc.* –1662.
1. To c. Miss Bellenden home SCOTT. **2.** The squadron..which convoyed the homeward trade in the next autumn J. K. LAUGHTON. Hence †**Convoy·ance**, artful management; conveyance. **Convoy·er**, one that convoys; a guide; a convoy-ship.

Convoy (kǫ·nvoi), *sb.* 1500. [a. F. *convoi*, f. *convoyer*; see prec.] †**1.** Conduct (of oneself or of affairs). *Sc.* –1599. **2.** The act of escorting, for honour, guidance, or protection 1557. **3.** An escort 1523. **4.** A protecting escort; *esp.* ships of war 1596. †**5.** A guide –1726. **6.** A thing that conducts, a channel, way, etc.; *spec.* a clog or brake for conducting a vehicle down an incline 1764. **7.** An individual or company under escort; a supply of ammunition or provisions, or a fleet of merchant ships, under escort 1577. Also *attrib.*
2. Your C. makes the dangerous Way secure DRYDEN. **3.** Heavie funerals and convoies of the dead HOLLAND. **4.** And with a c. send him safe away DRYDEN. **7.** A c. of bread 1710, of mules laden with merchandise 1827, of Merchant-ships 1743.

Convulse (kǫnvʊ·ls), *v.* 1643. [f. L. *convuls-* ppl. stem of *convellere*, f. *con-* + *vellere* to pluck, pull, tear.] **1.** *trans.* To shake violently; to agitate or disturb. **2.** *Path.* To affect with violent involuntary contractions of the muscles, so as to agitate the limbs or the whole body; to throw into convulsions. (Chiefly in *pass.*) 1681. **3.** *intr.* To become convulsed 1684.
1. To..be convulst and tremble at the name of death SIR T. BROWNE. **2.** Convulsing them with irresistible laughter JOHNSON. Hence **Convulse** *sb.* convulsion (*rare*). **Convu·lsingly** *adv.*

Convulsion (kǫnvʊ·lʃən). 1585. [ad. L. *convulsionem*; see prec.] †**1.** The action of wrenching, or condition of being wrenched –1825. Also †*fig.* **2.** *Path.* †**a.** Cramp; tetanus –1772. **b.** (usually *pl.*) An affection marked by irregular contractions or spasms of the muscles, alternating with relaxation 1650. **3.** Violent social, political, or physical disturbance 1643.
1. These two massy pillars With horrible c. to and fro He tugged, he shook MILT. *Sams.* 1649. **3.** A c. of the whole kingdom 1769. Earthquakes, volcanos, and convulsions SULLIVAN. Hence **Convu·lsional** *a.* of, pertaining to, or of the nature of c. (*rare*).

Convulsionary (kǫnvʊ·lʃənări). 1741. [f. prec.]
A. *adj.* Pertaining to, affected with, or marked by convulsion (*lit.* and *fig.*) 1798. **b.** Pertaining to the Convulsionaries 1814.
C. struggles SCOTT. **b.** The C. delusion 1874.
B. *sb.* One of a number of Jansenist fanatics in France in the 18th century, who fell into convulsions, etc., at the tomb of François de Pâris at St.-Médard 1741.

Convu·lsionist. 1865. [f. CONVULSION + -IST.] **1.** = CONVULSIONARY B. **2.** *Geol.* = CATASTROPHIST 1880.

Convulsive (kǫnvʊ·lsiv), *a.* 1615. [f. L. *convuls-* ppl. stem.] **1.** Of the nature of, or characterized by convulsion. Also *fig.* **2.** Affected with convulsion (*lit.* and *fig.*) 1686. **3.** Productive of convulsion 1700.
1. *fig.* C. and perilous reforms 1835. **3.** Nothing so ..c. to society, as the strain to keep things fixed STANLEY. Hence **Convu·lsive-ly** *adv.*, **-ness.**

Cony, coney (kōu·ni, kʊ·ni), *sb.* Pl. **conies** (coneys). [ME. *cunin*, a. OF. *con(n)in* = *conil* :—L. *cuniculus* rabbit.] **1.** A rabbit. Still used in the Statutes, and in *Heraldry*. **2.** The fur of the rabbit. Now *dial.* ME. **3.** In O.T. as tr. Heb. *shāphān*, a small pachyderm (*Hyrax Syriacus*) ME. **4.** Applied locally to the Cape Hyrax or Das, the Pica or Calling Hare (*Lagomys princeps*), etc. 1555. †**5.** A dupe –1736. †**6.** Some kind of shell-fish; ? a cone 1782. **b.** The Nigger-fish (*Epinephelus punctatus*) of the West Indies.
3. The conies are but a feeble folk, yet they make their houses in the rocks *Prov.* xxx. 26.
Comb.: †**c.-catch**, *v.* to dupe, gull; †**-catcher**; †**-catching** *vbl. sb.* and *ppl. a.*; **-fish**, the Burbot; **-garth**, a rabbit-warren; **-wool**, the fur of the rabbit.

†**Co·nyger, co·nynger.** [ME. *conynger(e*, a. OF. *coninière* = *conilière* :—L. type *cunicularia* neut. pl.] A rabbit-warren –1701.

Conylene (kǫ·nilīn). 1876. [f. CONIA + -YL + -ENE.] *Chem.* A liquid non-poisonous hydrocarbon, C_8H_{14}, having a pungent odour.

‖**Conyza** (konəi·ză). ME. [L., a. Gr. κόνυζα.] *Bot.* A genus of strong-smelling Composite plants, formerly including the Flea-banes.

Coo (kū), *v.* 1670. [Echoic.] **1.** *intr.* To make the soft murmuring note characteristic of doves and pigeons. Also *transf.* **2.** To converse caressingly or amorously; usu. in phr. *to bill and coo* 1816. **3.** To utter by cooing 1798; to send *to rest*, etc. by cooing 1814.
1. So, two kind turtles sit alone, and c. DRYDEN. *transf.* He [the Baby] coos like a pigeon-house EMERSON. Hence **Coo** *sb.* a note of or as of doves or pigeons. **Coo·er**, one that coos.

Co-o·bligant. 1818. [See CO-.] One under joint-obligation. So **Co-o·bligor**, one who binds himself together with others.

Co-occupant; see CO-.

Cooee, cooey (kū·ī, kū·i), *sb.* 1790. The call (kūūūū,ī· !) used as a signal by the Australian aborigines, and adopted by the colonists in the bush. Hence **Coo·ee, coo·ey** *v. intr.* to utter this cry.

Cook (kuk), *sb.* [OE. *cōc*, ad. L. *coquus*, late L. *cocus.*] One whose occupation is the preparation of food for the table; see COOK *v.* Orig. always masculine.
Comb.: **c.-book**, a cookery-book (U.S.); **-fish**, **-wrasse**, the male of a species of Wrasse (*Labrus mixtus*); **-house**, *Naut.* a ship's galley; **-maid**, a maid who cooks, or assists the c.; **-room**, a kitchen, or ship's galley; **-shop** (*orig.* **cook's shop**), an eating-house.

Cook (kuk), *v.*[1] ME. [f. the sb.] **1.** *intr.* To act as cook. (Now taken as *absol.* use of 2.) **2.** *trans.* To prepare (food); to make fit for eating by application of heat, as by boiling, baking, roasting, broiling, etc. 1611. *intr.* (for *refl.*) 1857. **3.** *fig.* Also with *up* 1588. **b.** To concoct 1624. **c.** To manipulate, tamper with (*colloq.*) 1636. **4.** To 'do for' (*slang*) 1851.
2. I will tel you..how to c. him WALTON. *intr.* These pears do not c. well (*mod.*). **3. b.** We cooked up a bill for that purpose CHESTERF. **c.** Some falsified printed accounts, artfully cooked up SMOLLETT. **4. b.** Phr. *To c. any one's goose*: to 'do for'; to ruin or kill (*slang*). Hence **Coo·kable** *a.* and *sb.*

†**Cook**, *v.*[2] 1599. [Echoic.] To utter the note of the cuckoo –1724.

Cooker (ku·kəɹ). 1884. [f. COOK *v.*[1] + -ER[1].] **1.** A stove for cooking; a vessel in which food is cooked. **2.** A fruit, etc., that cooks well 1887.

Cookery (ku·kəri). ME. [f. COOK *sb.* or *v.*[1] + -ERY 2.] **1.** The art or practice of cooking. †**2.** A product of the cook's art. NORTH. †**3.** A place for cooking; a kitchen, etc. –1837. *Comb.* **c.-book**, a book of receipts, etc., in c.

Cookie (ku·ki). *Sc.* and *U.S.* 1730. [prob. a. Du. *koekje* (kū·kyĕ), dim. of *koek* cake.] In Scotland, a baker's plain bun; in U.S., a small flat cake, with, or (locally) without, sweetening.

Cooking-range: cf. RANGE *sb.*[1] III. 1.

Coo·kish, *a. rare.* 1611. [-ISH[1].] Like a cook.

Cool (kūl), *a.* [OE. *cōl* :—OTeut. **kōluz*, f. *kal-* = L. *gel-* cold; see COLD.] **1.** Moderately cold; neither warm nor disagreeably cold; producing or maintaining coolness; cooling. Also *fig.* **2.** *transf.* Applied to analogous sensations; or to anything which produces them 1647. †**3.** *fig.* Chilled; chilling –ME. **4.** Not affected by passion or emotion; unexcited; deliberate; calm OE. **5.** Deficient in ardour, interest, or zeal; wanting in cordiality 1593. **6.** Calmly audacious or impudent in making a proposal or demand; said of persons and their actions 1825. **7.** *colloq.* Applied to a large sum of money, to give emphasis to the amount 1728.
1. Vnder the coole shade of a Siccamore *L. L. L.* v. ii. 89. A c. dress (*mod.*). *fig.* Coole patience *Haml.* III. iv. 124. **2.** A c. taste 1800, scent 1647, colour (*mod.*). **4.** Coole reason *Mids. N.* v. i. 6. A c. and steady fire 1798. Phr. *In c. blood.* **5.** A c. friend BLACKIE, reception 1706. **6.** Such a request was a trifle c. BLACK. **7.** He had lost a c. hundred FIELDING.
Comb.: **c.-headed** *a.*, having a c. head; not easily excited in mind; hence **-hea·dedness**; **c. tankard**, a cooling drink, made of wine, water, lemon-juice, spices, and borage.

Cool (kūl), *sb.*[1] ME. [f. COOL *a.*] **1.** That which is cool; the cool part, place, time, thing, etc. †**2.** A cool breeze –1573. **3.** Coolness; also *fig.* ME.
1. In the coole of the daye *Gen.* iii. 8. **3.** MILT. *P. L.* IX. 1109.

Cool (kūl), *sb.*[2] 1858. [var. of COWL *sb.*[2]] *Comm.* A tub of butter, usually of 28 lb.

Cool (kūl), *v.* [OE. *cōlian* :—OTeut. **kōlōjan* to be cold or cool, f. *kōluz*; see COLD *a.*] **1.** *intr.* To become cool or less hot. **2.** *fig.* To lose the heat of excitement or passion; to become less zealous or ardent OE. †**b.** Of things: To lose opportuneness. SHAKS. **3.** *trans.* To make cool; to cause to become less hot ME. Also *absol.* **4.** *fig.* To make less ardent or zealous ME.; to deprive (a thing) of its opportuneness 1716.
1. No fear lest Dinner coole MILT. *P. L.* v. 396. **2.** Thou hast describ'd A hot friend cooling *Jul. C.* IV. ii. 19. **b.** Aduantage, which doth euer coole Ith' absence of the needer *Cor.* IV. i. 43. **3.** To be throwne into the Thames, and coold..like a Horse-shoo *Merry W.* III. v. 122. **4.** Which cools the resolutions of the zealousest Prince 1670.
Phr. *To c. one's heels* (†*hoofs*): *i. e.* by rest, after walking; hence, *ironically*, to be kept standing or waiting.

Cooler (kū·ləɹ). 1575. [f. COOL *v.* + -ER.] **1.** Anything that cools or makes cool. **2.** A vessel in which anything is cooled; *esp.* one used for cooling the wort in brewing 1616. **3.** *U.S.* (*Thieves' slang.*) A prison 1884.

†**Cooley.** *rare.* = CULLIS[1]. MRS. GLASSE.

Coolie, cooly (kū·li). 1598. †**1.** A var. of *kulī* or *kolī*, an aboriginal tribe of Guzerat –1885. **2.** A native hired labourer or burden-carrier in India and China and elsewhere 1638. Also *attrib.*, as *c. labour*. Hence **Coo·lieism**, the c. system, the importation of coolies as labourers.

Cooling (kū·liŋ), *vbl. sb.* ME. [f. COOL *v.* + -ING[1].] The action of the vb. COOL.
Comb.: **c.-cup**, a cup for cooling liquids, into which is plunged another containing a heat-absorbing substance, as a solution of ammonium nitrate; **-floor**, a large shallow tank in which wort is cooled.

Cooling-card. *arch.* [CARD *sb.*[2] 1.] Something that dashes one's expectations.

Coolish (kū·liʃ), *a.* 1759. Somewhat cool.

Coolly (kū·lˌli), *adv.* 1580. [f. COOL *a.* + -LY[2].] **1.** With coolness; without heat (*lit.* and *fig.*). 2. Indifferently; without enthusiasm 1626. 3. With calm assurance 1844.

2. To receive a proposition c. MACAULAY.

Coolness (kū·lnės). OE. [f. as prec.] 1. *lit.* The condition of being or feeling cool. 2. *fig.* Freedom from excitement 1651. 3. Want of fervour; absence of friendly warmth 1674. 4. Calm assurance 1751.

3. They parted with such c. towards each other, as if they scarce hoped to meet again CLARENDON (J.).

Coolth (kūlþ). Now chiefly *joc. colloq.* 1547. [f. COOL *a.*, after *warmth.*] Coolness.

†**Coo·ly**, *a. rare.* 1594. [f. COOL *sb.* + -Y[1].] Cool –1710.

Coom (kūm), *sb.* 1587. [In senses 1–2 app. var. of CULM. ? Two words.] 1. Soot. Now *Sc.* 2. Coal dust or refuse 1611. †3. The grease and dust from axles or bearings –1786. 4. Saw-dust, etc. (*dial.*) 1811.

Coomb[1], **comb** (kūm). *dial.* OE. [? f. an OTeut. type **kumbo-*, **kummo-*, by-form **kumpo-*, with general sense of hollowed-out receptacle.] †1. (OE. cumb.) A vessel, cup. †2. A brewing vat –1688. 3. A dry measure, equal to four bushels ME.

Coomb[2], **combe, comb** (kūm). [OE. *cumb* masc. 'small valley, hollow', prob. of British origin; cf. Welsh *cwm* (kum), *-cwm, -gwm.* But cf. prec.] A deep hollow or valley; *esp.* one on the flank of a hill (*local*) 1674.

Coon (kūn). 1839. [U.S. abbrev. of RACOON.] 1. The RACOON (*Procyon lotor*). 2. a. One of the old U.S. Whigs, who had the coon as an emblem 1848. b. A sly, knowing fellow 1860.

Phrases. (*U.S. slang.*) *A gone c.*: a person or thing that is in a hopeless case. *A coon's age*: emphatic for 'a long time'.

Coontah, coontie (kuntă, -ti). 1852. The name in U.S. of a species of cycad (*Zamia integrifolia*), found in the West Indies, Florida, etc.; also of the arrowroot yielded by it.

Coop (kūp), *sb.*[1] [ME. *cupe, coupe* basket; with Ger. cognates, doubtfully considered to be a. L. *cupa* cask. See KIPE.] †1. (ME. *cupe, coupe*, pl. *-en.*) A basket. 2. A cage or pen of basket-work or the like for confining poultry, etc. ME. Also *transf.* and *fig.* 3. A wicker-work basket used in catching fish; a KIPE 1469.

2. *fig.* Sunnebright honour pend in shamefull coupe SPENSER.

Coop, *sb.*[2], var. of COUP, a dung-cart.

Coop (kūp), *sb.*[3] 1825. [?] A small heap, as of manure.

Coop (kūp), *v.*[1] 1563. [f. COOP *sb.*[1]] *trans.* To put or confine in a coop; hence, to confine within a small space; also *c. up, in* 1563.

What! c. whole armies in our walls again POPE. They imagine that their souls are cooped and cabined in BURKE.

†**Coop**, *v.*[2] *rare.* 17... = COOPER *v.*[1]

Shaken tubs..be new cooped HOLLAND.

Co-op (ko,ǫ·p). 1873. Colloq. abbrev. of CO-OPERATIVE 2; often ellipt. for *c. store.*

Coopee, obs. f. COUPEE.

Cooper (kū·pəɪ), *sb.* ME. [app. of LG. origin, f. (ult.) *cupa* cask; see COOP. (Not a deriv. of *coop*, which app. has never meant 'cask'.)] 1. A craftsman who makes and repairs wooden vessels formed of staves and hoops, as casks, buckets, tubs. 2. One engaged in the trade of sampling and bottling wine; a wine-cooper 1502. 3. ? A six- (or twelve-) bottle basket, used in wine-cellars 1817. 4. A drink composed half of stout and half of porter. (So called in London.) 1871.

3. Give me a roaring fire and a six bottle c. of claret T. L. PEACOCK.

Cooper (kū·pəɪ), *v.* 1746. [f. COOPER *sb.*[1]] 1. To make or repair (casks, etc.). 2. To put or stow in casks 1746. 3. *intr.* To work as a cooper (Dicts.). 4. To 'do for' (*slang*) 1851.

1. Coopered with brass hoops weather-tight 1834. Hence **Coopering** *vbl. sb.* the occupation of a cooper.

Cooperage (kū·pəredʒ). 1714. [f. COOPER *sb.*[1] + -AGE.] 1. A cooper's workshop. 2. Cooper's work 1740. 3. Money payable for cooper's work 1755.

Co-operant (ko,ǫ·pěrănt), *a.* 1598. [ad. L. *cooperantem*; see next.] Working together or to the same end. Also as *sb.*

C. factors of human progress A. M. FAIRBAIRN. Hence **Co-o·perancy**, c. condition; †co-operation.

Co-operate (ko,ǫ·pěreit), *v.* 1604. [f. L. *cooperat-* ppl. stem, f. *co(m)-* (see CO-) + *operari* to work.] 1. *intr.* To work together, act in conjunction (*with* another person or thing, *to* an end, or *in* a work). 2. *intr.* To practise economic co-operation 1830.

1. Man..cooperateth with man unto repentance USSHER. All things c. for the best QUARLES.

Co-operate (ko,ǫ·pěrět), *a.* 1868. [ad. L. *cooperatus*; cf. *corporate.*] Caused to co-operate; brought into co-operation.

Co-operation (ko,ǫ,pěrēi·ʃən). ME. [ad. L. *cooperationem*; see CO-OPERATE.] 1. The action of co-operating; joint operation. 2. *Pol. Econ.* The combination of a number of persons, or of a community, for purposes of economic production or distribution. (As orig. used by Owen, the name contemplated communism.)

1. Not Holpen by the C. of Angels or Spirits BACON. 2. The essential characteristic of c. is a union of capital and labour FAWCETT. Hence **Co-opera·tionist**, one who practises or advocates c.

Co-operative (ko,ǫ·pěrătiv), *a.* (*sb.*) 1603. [f. L. *cooperat-* ppl. stem; after *operative.*] 1. Working together or with others to the same end; pertaining to co-operation. 2. *Pol. Econ.* Pertaining to industrial co-operation 1821. 3. *sb.* A co-operationist; a member of a co-operative society 1829.

1. Four great principles..mutually c. MILMAN. 2. *C. society*: a union of persons for the production or distribution of goods, in which the profits are shared by all the contributing members. *C. store*: a store or shop belonging to a c. society, where goods are sold at a moderate price, the profits, if any, being distributed among the members and customers.

Co-operator (ko,ǫ·pěreitəɪ). 1600. [a. L. (Vulgate).] 1. One who co-operates with another or others. 2. A member of a co-operative society 1863.

1. They are..Co-operatours with God BARROW.

Cooper's-wood. 1866. An Australian name for the wood of Red Ash (*Alphitonia excelsa*), and Victorian Hazel (*Pomaderris apetala*).

Coopery (kū·pəri). 1558. [f. COOPER *sb.* + -Y[3]; see -ERY.] Cooper's work; a cooper's workshop; cooper's ware. Also *attrib.*

Basket, C., and Turnery Wares 1695.

Co-opt (ko,ǫ·pt), *v.* 1651. [ad. L. *cooptare.*] *trans.* To elect into a body by the votes of its existing members.

These eight co-opted two more STUBBS.

Co-optate (ko,ǫ·pteit), *v. arch.* 1623. [f. L. *cooptat-* ppl. stem; see prec.] Now = CO-OPT; formerly, less definitely = To choose or elect to an office, into a body, etc.

Co-optation (ko,ǫptēi·ʃən). 1533. [ad. L. *cooptationem*; see CO-OPT.] Election into a body by the votes of its existing members; formerly, Election, choice, adoption.

The first election and c. of a friend HOWELL. var. **Co-o·ption.**

Co-ordain (ko,ǫɪdēi·n), *v. rare.* 1679. [See Co-.] *trans.* To ordain together. So **Co-ordai·ner.**

Co-o·rder, *v. rare.* 1678. [See Co-.] To arrange co-ordinately.

Co-o·rdinal, *a.* 1875. [See Co-.] *Geom.* Having (so many) co-ordinates. CAYLEY.

Co-ordinate (ko,ǭ·ɪdinět). 1641. [f. L. *co-* + *ordinatus*; cf. *subordinate.* In some senses = Co- + ORDINATE.]

A. *adj.* 1. Of the same order; equal in rank (*with*); opp. to *subordinate.* In *Gram.* used *esp.* of the clauses of a compound sentence. 2. Involving co-ordination 1769.

1. All these Churches are but C., not among themselves Subordinate 1641. 2. So complex and c. a movement 1876. Hence **Co-o·rdinately** *adv.*

B. *sb.* 1. One who or that which is co-ordinate; an equal; a co-ordinate element 1850. 2. *Math.* Each of a system of two or more magnitudes used to define the position of a point, line, or plane, by reference to a fixed system of lines, points, etc. (Usually in *pl.*) 1823. Also *attrib.*

In the original system of *Cartesian co-ordinates*, the co-ordinates of a point (in a plane) are its distances from two fixed intersecting straight lines (the *axes of co-ordinates*), the distance from each axis being measured in a direction parallel to the other axis. The co-ordinates are *rectangular* when the axes are at right angles; otherwise *oblique*.

Hence applied to other systems; as *Polar co-ordinates*, co-ordinates defining a point (in a plane) by reference to a fixed line (*initial line* or *axis*) and a fixed point (*origin* or *pole*) in that line; the co-ordinates of any point being the length of the straight line (*radius vector*) drawn to it from the pole, and the angle which this line makes with the axis.

Both systems have been applied by an extension to points *in space.*

Co-ordinate (ko,ǭ·ɪdineit), *v.* 1655. [prob. f. Co- + L. *ordinare*; cf. *subordinate.*] 1. *trans.* To make co-ordinate; to place in the same order, rank, or division. 2. To place (things) in proper position relatively to each other and to the system of which they form parts 1847. 3. *intr.* (for *refl.*) To act in combined order for the production of a particular result 1863.

1. These two..are not opposed, but co-ordinated 1665. 2. An omnipresent humanity co-ordinates all his [Shakspere's] faculties EMERSON. So **Co-o·rdinative** *a.* †co-ordinate; having the function of co-ordinating. **Co-o·rdinator.**

Co-ordination (ko,ǭɪdinēi·ʃən). 1605. [f. CO-ORDINATE *v.*] 1. The action of co-ordinating; the condition of being co-ordinated or co-ordinate; co-ordinate relation. 2. Harmonious combination of agents or functions towards the production of a result; said *esp.* in *Phys.* of the combined action of a number of muscles in the production of certain complex movements 1855.

1. What consent and c. there is in the leaves and parts of flowers SIR T. BROWNE. 2. In each of these acts, the c. of a large number of muscular movements is required CARPENTER.

Co-o·rganize, Co-ori·ginal, etc.; see Co-.

Co-ortho·gonal, *a.* *Geom.* [See Co-.] = next.

Co-orthotomic (ko,ǭɪþǭtǫ·mik), *a.* 1884. [See Co-.] *Geom.* Cutting one another at right angles at each point of intersection, as circles.

Co-ossify (ko,ǫ·sifəi), *v.* 1877. [See Co-.] To unite into one bone (*trans.* and *intr.*). Hence **Co-o·ssifica·tion.**

Coot (kūt). [ME. *cote, coote*, corresp. to Du. *koet*, of unkn. history. Not conn. w. Welsh *cwt* short.] 1. A name originally given vaguely to various swimming or diving birds; often to the Guillemot (*Uria troile*). 2. Later, the Bald Coot (*Fulica atra*, fam. *Rallidæ*), a web-footed bird, having the bill extended so as to form a broad white plate on the forehead (whence the epithet *bald*); in U.S., *F. Americana* 1440. 3. Locally applied to the Water-rail and Water-hen 1547. 4. *fig.* A silly person, simpleton (*colloq.*) 1848.

2. The Brain-bald C. DRAYTON. Phr. *As bald* (*bare, black*) *as a c.*; *as stupid as a c.*

Cooter (kū·təɪ). 1884. A Southern U.S. name of two tortoises, the Carolina Box-turtle (*Cistudo carolina*), and the 'Florida Cooter' (*Chrysemys concinna*), family *Testudinidæ*.

Cooth (kūþ). 1793. The Coal-fish. (*Orkney & Shetland.*)

Coo·tie, *sb.* *Sc.* A small wooden bowl or basin. BURNS.

Coo·tie, cooty, *a.* *Sc.* Having feathered legs. BURNS.

Co-ow·ner. 1858. [See Co-.] A joint owner.

†**Cop**, *sb.*[1] OE. [Cf. MLG. and Du. *kop*, MHG. *kopf* beaker; also It. *coppa*, F. *coupe.*] A drinking-vessel, a cup –1520. *Comb.*: **c.-ambry**, a closet for cups, etc.; **-house**, a house or room for cups, etc.

Cop (kǫp), *sb.*[2] [OE. *cop, copp* top; cf. prec.] 1. The top of anything; *esp.* of a hill –1599; a crest on the head of a bird –1787. †2. A round piece of wood within the top of a beehive 1609. 3. *Spinning.* The conical ball of thread wound upon a spindle or tube in a spinning machine 1795. 4. ? A heap, mound (*dial.*) 1666. 5. A hedge-bank (*dial.*) 1600. 6. The central ridge of a butt of ploughed land (*dial.*) 1859.

1. Upon the c. right of his nose he hade A werte, and theron stood a tuft of heres CHAUCER.

Comb.: **c.-bone**, the knee-cap (*dial.*); **-spinner**, a machine combining the advantages of the throstle and the mule; **-tube** (see sense 3); **-waste**, the waste cotton from the cops; **-yarn**, cotton yarn in cops.

†**Cop** (kǫp), *sb.*[3] ME. only. [OE. *-coppa* masc., prob. f. same stem as prec.; see ATTERCAP, and COBWEB, ME. *coppeweb.*] A spider.

Cop, *sb.*[4] *slang.* 1859. [Cf. COP *v.*[2]] A policeman.

Cop (kǫp), *v.*[1] Now *dial.* 1552. [f. COP *sb.*[2]]

1. *trans.* To pile up in a heap or mound. 2. To put up unbound hay or corn in cops 1581.

Cop (kǫp), *v.*[2] *n. dial.* and *slang.* 1704. [?] *trans.* To capture, catch.

Copaiba, -aiva (kopai·bă, -ē·bă, -ai·vă). 1712. [a. Sp. and Pg., ad. Braz. *cupauba.*] A balsam of aromatic odour and acrid taste, obtained from S. American plants of the genus *Copaifera*; used in medicine and the arts. Also *attrib.* Hence **Copai·vic** *a.* of or pertaining to c.

Copal (kōu·păl). 1577. [a. Sp., ad. Mexican *copalli* incense.] A hard translucent odoriferous resin obtained from various tropical trees, and from which a fine transparent varnish is prepared. b. *Fossil c.*: = COPALITE. Also *attrib.* Hence **Co·paline** (*Min.*) = COPALITE.

‖**Copalche, -chi** (kopæ·ltʃi). 1866. [Mexican native name.] A shrub of Mexico, *Croton pseudo-China* or *niveus*, N.O. *Euphorbiaceæ*, yielding the *C.-bark*, used as a febrifuge; also a Brazilian tree, *Strychnos pseudo-China.*

Copalite (kōu·pălait). 1868. [f. COPAL + -ITE.] *Min.* Dana's name for the fossil *Highgate resin*, found in the blue clay of Highgate Hill.

Co·palm. 1858. In *c. balsam*, a yellowish balsam, exuding from the Sweet Gum-tree of N. America.

Coparcenary, -ery (kou͵pā·ɹsĭnĕri), *sb.* 1503. [f. CO- + PARCENARY. The sp. in -ERY is preferable.] *Law.* 1. Joint share in an inheritance; joint heirship. 2. Co-partnership; joint ownership. Also *fig.* 1593. Hence **Copa·rcenary** *a.* of or pertaining to coparceners. var. **Co·pa·rceny.**

Coparcener (kou͵pā·ɹsĭnəɹ). 1503. [f. Co- + PARCENER.] *Law.* One who shares equally with others in inheritance of the estate of a common ancestor.

†**Copa·rt,** *v.* 1613. [f. CO- + PART *v.*] *trans.* and *intr.* To share -1670.

Copartiment, copartment, obs. vars. of COMPARTMENT.

Copartner (kou͵pā·ɹtnəɹ). 1503. [See Co-.] One who shares or takes part with others in any business, office, enterprise, or common interest. (Formerly = COPARCENER.) Also *transf.* of things.

You that have been copartners in our wars HEYWOOD. Hence **Copa·rtnership,** the relation of copartners; a company of copartners. var. **Copa·rtnery.** †**Copa·rtning** *ppl. a.* being or acting as copartners. MILT.

†**Copataine.** *rare.* App. = COPINTANK, q. v. *Tam. Shr.* V. i. 69.

Co-patriot, var. of COMPATRIOT.

Cope (kōup), *sb.*[1] [In 12th c. *cāpe*, ME. *cōpe*, repr. an OE. **cāpe* wk. fem., a. med.L. *cāpa* cope; see CAP.] 1. †A long cloak or cape -1745; *spec.* a cape or tippet of ermine worn by doctors of divinity on special occasions at Cambridge 1798. 2. *Eccl.* A vestment resembling a long cloak made of a semicircular piece of cloth, worn by ecclesiastics in processions, at Vespers, etc. ME. 3. *fig.* Anything resembling a cloak, canopy, or vault ME. ¶ In later use, vaguely used for (*a*) vertex; (*b*) firmament, expanse 1603. 4. *Founding.* The outer portion or case of a mould 1856. 5. The COPING of a wall, etc. 1847.

2. After them came..Friers in their rich Coapes singing, carrying many Pictures and Lights PURCHAS. 3. Undyr the c. of heven that is above CHAUCER. The cheapest country under the c. *Per.* IV. vi. 132. Larks in heaven's c. sing TENNYSON.

†**Cope,** *sb.*[2] 1525. [perh. a. F. *coup.*] The shock of combat; encounter. Also *fig.* -1773.

Cope, *sb.*[3] Now *dial.* 1520. [f. COPE *v.*[3]] †1. A bargain -1590. 2. *Derbyshire Mines.* A duty paid by the miner for permission to raise lead-ore 1631.

Phr. †*God's c.*: a very large sum.

Cope (kōup), *v.*[1] ME. [f. COPE *sb.*[1]] 1. *trans.* To furnish with a cope. 2. *Archit.* To cover with, as, or as with, a COPING 1842. 3. To cover as with a vault 1704. 4. *intr.* To slope downwards or hang *over* like a coping 1601. Hence **Coped** *ppl. a.* (in senses 1, 4).

Cope (kōup), *v.*[2] ME. [a. F. *couper* to strike (now to cut), f. OF. *colp, cop, coup*; see COUP.] †1. *intr.* To strike; to come to blows, encounter, engage. (Often with *with.*) -1725. 2. To be or prove oneself a match for, contend successfully with 1583. Also *fig.* 3. To have to do with (*arch.*) 1593. †4. *trans.* To meet, come into contact (hostile or friendly) with -1603. †5. To match (a thing) *with* (an equivalent). *Merch. V.* IV. i. 412.

1. Swear to stand neutral, while we c. in fight POPE. He wolde nevyr c. whithe no man 1467. 2. Not a matche to coape with Achilles STANYHURST. To c. with evil 1850. 3. *Haml.* III. ii. 60. 4. They all straine curt'sie who shall c. him first SHAKS.

Cope (kōup), *v.*[3] Now *dial.* ME. [Of LG. origin; cf. Du. *koopen*, LG. *kôpen* to buy, etc. See CHEAP *v.*, the native Eng. form.] †1. *trans.* To buy -1599. 2. To exchange, barter 1570. †3. *intr.* To make an exchange, bargain -1614. 4. *Derbyshire Mines.* 'To agree to get ore at a fixed sum per *dish* or measure.' J. MAWE.

2. I've seen scores of nets coped away for brandy MATHER *Nor'ard of Dogger* iii. 37.

Cope (kōup), *v.*[4] 1575. [app. a. F. *coper, couper.* Cf. COPE *v.*[2]] *Falconry.* To cut, pare the beak or talons of a hawk.

Cope, *v.*[5] *dial.* 1601. [?] To tie or sew up the mouth of (a ferret); also *fig.*

Your lips coaped like a ferret DEKKER.

Copeck (kōu·pek). 1698. [ad. Russ. *kopeika*, dim. of *kopyé* lance.] A Russian copper coin, the $^1/_{100}$ part of a rouble, now worth from $^1/_4$ to $^1/_3$ of a penny English.

Co·peman, †**copesman.** *arch.* 1566. [orig. *copesman*, f. COPE *sb.*[3] (in possess. *cope's*) + MAN.] A chapman, dealer.

He would have sold his part of Paradise For ready money, had he met a copeman B. JONS.

†**Co·pemate, copesmate.** 1565. [orig. *copemate*, f. COPE *v.*[2] + MATE; assim. later to *copesman* or the like.] 1. A person with whom one copes; an adversary -1645. 2. A partner or colleague; an associate. Also *fig.* -1686. 3. = FELLOW, in the vague sense -1744.

2. *fig.* Mis-shapen Time, copesmate of ugly Night SHAKS.

Copepod (kōu·pĭpǫd). 1836. [f. Gr. κώπη handle, oar-handle, oar + -ποδ- footed.] *Zool.* A. *adj.* Belonging to the order *Copepoda* of minute entomostracous Crustaceans, having four or five pairs of oar-like feet. B. *sb.* A member of this order. Hence **Cope·podan, Cope·podous** *adjs.*

Coper[1] (kōu·pəɹ). 1609. [f. COPE *v.*[3] + -ER[1].] One who copes (see COPE *v.*[3]); *spec.* (= *horse-c.*) a horse-dealer.

Coper[2], **cooper** (kōu·pəɹ). 1881. [a. Fl. and Du. *kooper*, f. *koopen* to buy, deal, trade.] A vessel fitted out to supply spirits, etc., usually in exchange for fish, to the deep-sea fishers in the North Sea; a floating grog-shop. Hence **Co·pering, coopering** *vbl. sb.*

Copernican (kopə̄·ɹnikăn). 1667. [f. *Copernicus*, L. form of *Koppernik*, name of an astronomer, a native of Thorn in Prussian Poland (1473-1543).] *adj.* Of or pertaining to Copernicus. *sb.* One who holds the C. theory 1677.

C. system, theory: the astronomical system or theory propounded by Copernicus (and still held) that the planets move in orbits round the sun as a centre, and not round the earth. Hence **Cope·rnicanism.**

Copesman, -mate; see COPEMAN, -MATE.

Cope-stone (kōu·pstōun). 1567. [f. COPE *sb.*[1] + STONE; infl. in sense by COP top, or perh. by *cap.*] The top stone of a building; usu. *fig.*

‖**Cophosis** (kofōu·sis). 1657. [mod.L., a. Gr. κώφωσις, f. κωφός.] Total deafness.

Cophouse; see COP *sb.*[1]

‖**Copia** (kōu·piă). 1713. [L.; = plenty.] Plenty, a plentiful supply; now chiefly in the L. phrase *c. verborum*, a copious vocabulary.

Copiable (kǫ·pi͵ăb'l), *a. rare.* 1755. [f. COPY *v.* + ABLE.] Capable of being copied.

Copiapite (kōu·piăpəit). 1850. [f. *Copiapo* in Chili + -ITE.] *Min.* A yellow translucent hydrous silicate of iron; *yellow copperas* or *misy.*

Copier (kǫ·pi͵əɹ). 1597. [f. COPY *v.* + -ER[1].] One who copies or makes a copy; a transcriber; an imitator.

Coping (kōu·piŋ), *sb.* 1601. [f. COPE *v.*[1] sense 2 + -ING[1].] 1. *Archit.* The uppermost course of masonry or brickwork in a wall, usually of a sloping form to throw off rain. 2. An overhanging shelf to protect wall-fruit 1881. *Comb.* **c.-stone,** one of the stones forming the c. of a wall.

†**Copintank, copentank, coptank.** 1508. [Prob. conn. with *cop, copped, copple*, but *tank* is unexplained. Cf. COPATAINE.] A sugar-loaf hat -1603.

With a high coptank Hat on his head, narrow in the top, as the Kings of the Medes..do use to wear them NORTH.

Copious (kōu·piəs), *a.* ME. [ad. L. *copiosus*, f. *copia.*] †1. Furnished plentifully with anything -1838. 2. Abounding in matter 1500, †language -1672, or words 1549. 3. Existing in abundance; plentiful. *Obs.* or *arch.* with names of material substances. ME. 4. *adv.* Copiously 1791.

1. C. sources of knowledge PRESCOTT. 2. This c. subject 1716. She will waxe c. and chop logicke MORE. A c. language HOBBES. 3. A c. display of flowers 1845. Hence **Co·pious-ly** *adv.*, **-ness.**

†**Co·pist.** 1682. [a. F. *copiste.*] Early f. COPYIST- 1779.

Coplanar (kōuplē·năɹ), *a.* 1862. [f. CO- + L. *planaris*; see PLANE.] *Math.* Situated or acting in the same plane.

Coplanation, erron. f. COMPLANATION.

Copolar (kōupōu·lăɹ), *a.* 1852. [See Co-.] *Math.* Having the same pole.

Copo·poda, var. of *Copepoda*; see COPEPOD.

‖**Copopsia** (kopǫ·psiă). [mod.L., f. Gr. κόπος + ὄψις.] *Path.* Fatigue of sight.

†**Copo·rtion.** [See Co-.] A joint portion. SPENSER.

Copped (kǫ·pėd, kǫpt), *ppl. a.* OE. [f. COP *sb.*[2]] †1. Polled. (OE. only.) 2. 'Rising to a top or head' (J.); peaked ME. 3. Crested. Now *dial.* ME. Also *fig.*

Copper (kǫ·pəɹ), *sb.*[1] [OE. and ME. *coper*, ad. pop.L. *cuprum*, or a var. **coprum.* The cl.L. name was *Cyprium æs, Cyprium*, i.e. Cyprian metal, so called in Italy from *Cyprus*, Gr. Κύπρος, whence Κύπριος *Cyprius.*] 1. A well-known metal of a peculiar red colour; it is malleable, ductile, and very tenacious, and is found native and in many ores. Chemically it is a dyad: symbol Cu. Used, with qualification, in the names of various compounds and ores of the metal. 2. Copper money; a copper (or bronze) coin 1712. 3. A vessel made of copper; in *pl.*, *esp.* the large cooking vessels on board ship 1667. 4. A COPPER-PLATE, q. v. 1668. 5. A copper implement like a cotton reel hollow and open at the ends; used in annealing 1828. 6. The copper sheathing of a vessel (*rare*) 1836. 7. *attrib.* Made of copper; pertaining to copper; worthless; copper-coloured 1597.

2. He has 'no more c.' about him HONE. 7. A c. Kettell 1624, mine 1776, crowne SHAKS. A hot and c. sky COLERIDGE.

Phr. *Hot coppers*: a mouth and throat parched through excessive drinking.

Comb.: a. **c.-beech** (see BEECH 1); **-belly,** the c.-bellied Snake (*Coluber erythrogaster*); **-bo·ttomed** *a.*, having the bottom sheathed with c.; **-ca·ptain,** a sham captain; **-co·loured** *a.*; **-faced** *a.*, 'brazen-faced'; of printing-type, faced with c.; **-fastened** *a.* (of a ship), fastened with c. bolts to prevent corrosion; **-finch,** the Chaffinch (*local*); **-head,** the head of a c. or boiler; see also COPPERHEAD; **-nose,** a red nose caused by disease, intemperance, etc.; **-powder,** a precipitate of metallic c. used for bronzing; **-work, works,** a place where c. is worked or manufactured; **-zinc,** *attrib.*, of c. and zinc.

b. In the names of chemical compounds and of minerals: **c.-blende,** a sulpharsenite of c., TENNANTITE; **-emerald** = *emerald c.*, DIOPTASE; **-glance,** native cuprous sulphide, CHALCOCITE; **-nickel** [G. *kupfer-nickel*] = NICCOLITE; etc.

Hence **Co·pperish** *a.* somewhat coppery (*rare*). **Co·ppery** *a.* resembling or containing c.

Copper (kǫ·pəɹ), *sb.*[2] *slang.* 1859. [app. f. COP *v.*[2]] A policeman.

Copper (kǫ·pəɹ), *v.* 1530. [f. COPPER *sb.*[1]] *trans.* To cover with copper; to sheathe the bottom and sides of a ship with copper.

A cast-iron statue coppered by electricity 1862. Hence **Co·pperer** (*rare*). **Co·ppering** *sb.* the copper sheathing of a ship's bottom.

Copperas (kǫ·pərăs). ME. [In 15th c. *coperose*; cf. med.L. *cuperosa, cuprosa*, prob. short for **aqua cuprosa* = Ger. *kupferwasser.*] 1. A name given from early times to the sulphates of copper, iron, and zinc (distinguished as *blue, green,* and *white* copperas respectively);

in Eng. use, now exclusively to *green* copperas or ferrous sulphate ($FeSO_4$), also called *green vitriol*, used in dyeing, tanning, and making ink. **2.** *Min.* Applied generically to a group comprising the ordinary vitriols 1868. Also *attrib.* *Comb.* †**c.-stone**, iron pyrites or Marcasite. Hence †**Coppero·se** *a.* of or belonging to c. or vitriol.

Copperhead (kǫ·pəɹhed). 1823. [prob. attrib. = *copperhead snake.*] **1.** A venomous N. American snake (*Trigonocephalus contortrix*); so called from the coppery red colour of the top of its head. (It strikes without warning, and has thus become a type of unexpected hostility.) **2.** *U.S.* A nickname, during the Civil War, for a northern sympathizer with the Secessionists 1862. Also *attrib.*

Co·pper-pla·te, co·pperplate. 1663. **1.** *gen.* (Better as two words.) A plate of copper; also *collect.* 1665. **2.** *spec.* A polished plate of copper on which a design is engraved or etched 1668. **3.** An impression from such a plate 1663. **4.** *collect.* Copperplate engraving or printing 1817. **5.** *attrib.* (Better as one word.) 1824. Hence **Co·pperplate** *v.* to engrave on and print from a c.

Co·pper-smith. ME. **1.** An artificer in copper. **2.** In India, the Crimson-breasted Barbet (*Xantholæma Indica*).

1. Alexander the coppersmyth did me moche evyll TINDALE 2 *Tim.* iv. 14.

†**Co·pper-worm.** 1755. **1.** The ship-worm, *Teredo navalis.* **2.** A clothes-moth. **3.** 'A worm breeding in one's hand' (J.).

Coppice (kǫ·pis), *sb.* 1538. [a. OF. *copeïz, couppeiz, colpeïz* :—late L. type **colpaticium* 'having the quality of being cut', f. *colpat-, colpare* :—(ult.) L. *colaphus*, a. Gr. κόλαφος blow. Cf. COPSE.] A small wood or thicket of underwood grown for the purpose of periodical cutting; underwood. *Comb.* **c.-wood** (see COPSEWOOD). vars. **Copy, coppy** [f. Fr. *copys* pl.]. Hence **Co·ppice** *v.* = COPSE *v.* 1. **Co·ppiced** *ppl. a.* cut down periodically; furnished with a c. or coppices.

Co·pping, *vbl. sb.* 1793. [f. COP *sb.*[2] + -ING[1].] The formation of cops of thread. Used *attrib.*, as *c.-beam*, etc.

†**Co·pple.** 15.. [dim. of COP *sb.*[2]] **1.** A crest on a bird's head –1600. **2.** A little summit or eminence; = F. *coupeau* 1600.

2. It is a low Cape, and vpon it is a c. not very high HAKLUYT. Hence †**Co·ppled** *ppl. a.* crested; rising conically to a point.

Co·pple-crown. Now *dial.* 1634. [See prec.] A tuft of feathers on a fowl's head; a crest.

Like the Copple-crowne The Lapwing has RANDOLPH. Hence †**Co·pple-crowned** *ppl. a.* crested, peaked.

†**Copple-stone.** 1728. [Cf. COPPLING *ppl. a.* 3.] A COBBLE-STONE.

†**Co·ppling, copling,** *ppl. a.* 1667. [Related to COPPLE *sb.* 2.] **1.** Swelling upwards towards a summit –1745. **2.** Of the sea: Tumbling 1667. **3.** Of stones, etc.: Unsteady, toppling 1825.

Copps, obs. f. COPSE.

Coppy, obs. f. COPPICE.

‖**Copra** (kǫ·pra). 1584. [a. Pg., app. ad. Malayālam *koppara*, in Hindī *khoprā* coco-nut.] The dried kernel of the coco-nut, from which coco-nut oil is expressed.

Co-pre·sence. 1817. [See CO-.] Presence together; the state or fact of being co-present. So **Co-pre·sent** *a.* present together.

Copro-, bef. a vowel **copr-,** comb. f. Gr. κόπρος dung: hence,

Copræ·mia [Gr. αἷμα], blood-poisoning from the fæces in cases of costiveness. **Copre·mesis** [Gr. ἔμεσις], stercoraceous vomiting. **Co·prolite** [Gr. λίθος], a stony roundish fossil, supposed to be the petrified excrement of an animal. Hence **Coproli·tic** *a.* **Co·prolith,** a ball formed of hardened fæces in the bowels; also = *coprolite.* Hence **Copro-, koproli·thic** *a.* **Copro·logy** [cf. Gr. κοπρολόγος], a gathering of ordure; also *fig.* **Copro·phagan,** a dung-eating beetle. **Copro·phagist,** a dung-eater. **Copro·phagous** *a.*, dung-eating. **Copro·philous** *a.*, fond of dung; feeding or growing upon dung. **Copro·stasis** [Gr. στάσις a stopping], constipation.

Cop-rose, copper-rose. 1776. [? conn. w. F. *couperose* copperas, or copper-nose.] A local name of the Red Corn Poppy (*Papaver Rhœas*).

Cops, copse (kǫps). [OE. *cops, cosp* = OS. *cosp.*] †**1.** A shackle for any part of the body –ME. **2.** A hasp for a door or gate ME. **3.** = CLEVIS 1797.

Copse (kǫps), *sb.* 1578. [Syncopated f. *copys, coppis*, COPPICE.] = COPPICE. Also as *pl.*, whence an erron. sing. *cop.* Also *transf.* and *fig.*

The willows and the hazel copses green MILT. *Lycidas* 42. *fig.* So to cares cops I came G. HERBERT. Hence **Copse** *v.* to make a c. of; to clothe with a c. **Co·psy** *a.* planted with copses.

Co·psewood, co·ppice-wood. 1543. **1.** A COPSE. ? *Obs.* **2.** The underwood of a copse 1809. Also *attrib.*

Copsole, copsil. Now *dial.* 1562. [f. COPS *sb.* + ?] = COPS *sb.* 3.

Copt (kǫpt). 1615. [ad. Arab. *quft, qift* 'the Copts', with relative adj. *qufṭī, qifṭī* Coptic, most prob. ad. Coptic *gyptios*, repr. Gr. Αἰγύπτιος Egyptian.] A native Egyptian Christian, belonging to the Jacobite sect of Monophysites. Hence **Co·ptic** *a.* of or pertaining to the Copts; *sb.* the language of the Copts. So †**Co·ptite.**

Coptine (kǫ·ptəin). 1879. *Chem.* A colourless alkaloid found in *Coptis trifolia*, a ranunculaceous plant of N. America.

Copula (kǫ·piulă). 1650. [a. L., f. *co(m)-* + *apere* to fasten.] **1.** *Logic* and *Gram.* That part of a proposition which connects the subject and predicate; the present tense of the verb *to be* (with or without a negative). **2.** *gen.* A connexion 1656. **3.** *Anat.* A part (*e.g.* a bone, cartilage, or ligament) connecting other parts 1681. **4.** = COUPLER 2a. 1852. **b.** *Mus.* A short transition passage 1880. **5.** Sexual union. [A term of Roman Law.] 1864. Hence **Co·pular** *a.* pertaining to or of the nature of a c.

†**Co·pulate,** *a.* (*sb.*) ME. [ad. L. *copulatus*; see next.] **1.** Coupled; conjoined –1645. **2.** Copulative; as *sb.* A copulative word –1672.

Copulate (kǫ·piuleᶦt), *v.* 1632. [f. L. *copulat-, copulare*, f. *copula*; see above.] †**1.** *trans.* To couple, conjoin –1822. †**2.** *intr.* To become conjoined or united 1645. **3.** *intr.* To unite in sexual congress 1632.

Copulation (kǫpiulēᶦ·ʃən). ME. [a. F. *copulation*, ad. L. *copulationem*; see prec. and -ATION.] †**1.** The action of coupling or condition of being coupled; connexion, union –1752. **2.** The union of the sexes in the act of copulating 1483.

1. Wit..is the unexpected c. of ideas JOHNSON.

Copulative (kǫ·piulătiv, -eᶦtiv). ME. [a. F. *copulatif, -ive*, ad. L. *copulativus*, f. *copulat-* ppl. stem; see above.]

A. *adj.* **1.** Serving to couple or connect. †**2.** Connective –1676. **3.** *Zool.* and *Anat.* Relating to or serving for copulation 1841.

1. These c. particles, *and, again* GOUGE. The c. judgment ('*S* is both *p* and *q* and *r*') 1884. Hence **Co·pulatively** *adv.*

B. *sb.* **1.** *Gram.* A copulative conjunction or particle 1530. †**2.** *pl.* (*joc.*) Persons about to be coupled in marriage. *A. Y. L.* v. iv. 58.

Copulatory (kǫ·piulătəri), *a.* 1839. [f. L. *copulator*; see -ORY.] *Zool.* Pertaining to or serving for copulation, as *c. organs.*

Copy (kǫ·pi), *sb.* (*a.*) ME. [a. F. *copie* = Pr. *copia*, ad. L. *copia* plenty; in med.L. 'transcript'.]

A. †**1.** Plenty, abundance, a copious quantity –1656. **2.** A transcript, reproduction, or imitation of an original, as a writing, a picture, or other work of art ME. Also *fig.* **3.** *Eng. Law.* The transcript of the manorial court-roll (see COPYHOLD) 1463; a COPYHOLD 1626. Also *fig.* **4.** An individual example of a manuscript or print 1538. **5.** That from which a copy is made ME.; †*fig.* pattern, example –1775. **6.** *Printing.* Manuscript (or printed) matter prepared for printing 1485; †property in 'copy' –1781. **7.** Name of a size of paper 1712.

1. To excel in..copie of words 1586. 2. Never buy a c. of a picture RUSKIN. *fig.* Pompey, the Clown, is a c. from the life MRS. C. CLARKE. 3. *fig. Macb.* III. ii. 38. 4. Being printed from a foul c. 1689. Copies of the fourth..Vol. of Leland HEARNE. The acting c. of a play DICKENS. 5. Conferring the translation with the Coppie 1586. Why the Scholar writeth not like his C. BAXTER. *fig. All's Well* I. ii. 46. 6. When he carried his copie to the Presse NASHE. Steele..sold the c. for fifty guineas JOHNSON.

Phr. *A c. of verses*: a short composition in verse: now chiefly applied to a school or college exercise.

B. †*adj.* = COPYHOLD 3. –1639.

Comb.: **c.-book,** a book containing copies of documents, accounts, etc. (now *U.S.*); a book containing lines of writing for pupils to imitate; also an exercise book; **-holder,** a proof-reader's assistant who reads the copy aloud to the proof-reader; †**-money,** money paid to an author for his c. or copyright.

Copy (kǫ·pi), *v.* ME. [a. F. *copier*, ad. med.L. *copiare* to transcribe, f. *copia* 'transcript'; see COPY *sb.*] **1.** *trans.* To make a copy of (a writing, a picture, or other work of art); to transcribe; to reproduce or represent in a picture, etc. **2.** *fig.* To imitate, reproduce, follow 1647. **3.** *absol.* or *intr.* 1680.

1. I like the worke well..I would haue it coppied *Oth.* III. iv. 190. [He] has copied it out in full 1881. 2. A wish to c. what he must admire COWPER. 3. No painter who is worth a straw will ever c. RUSKIN.

Copyhold (kǫ·pihoᵘld). 1483. [f. COPY *sb.* 3 + HOLD *sb.*[1] II. 1; cf. *freehold.*] **1.** Tenure of lands being parcel of a manor, 'at the will of the lord according to the custom of the manor', by copy of the manorial court-roll. Also *fig.* **2.** An estate thus held; a copyhold estate 1529. **3.** *attrib.* or *adj.* Held by, relating to, or of the nature of, copyhold 1511.

1. *C.*, a base tenure founded upon immemorial custom and usage..No c. estate can..be created at the present day WHARTON. Hence **Copyholder,** one who holds an estate in c.

Copying (kǫ·pi,iŋ), *vbl. sb.* 1580. The action of the verb COPY, q. v.

attrib. and *Comb.*, *esp.* of appliances for copying writing by some transfer process, as *c.-book, -ink, -paper, -pencil, -press*; also **c.-ribbon,** a ribbon used in a type-writing machine, when a duplicate copy is taken; **-telegraph,** a telegraphic apparatus by which a written message placed in the transmitter is reproduced in the receiver on the passage of the current.

Copyism (kǫ·pi,iz'm). 1814. [f. COPY *sb.* or *v.* + -ISM.] The practice of copying; an instance of this. (Usu. contemptuous.)

Copyist (kǫ·pi,ist). 1699. [Earlier COPIST; f. COPY *v.*] One who copies; *esp.* one who transcribes documents.

Copyright (kǫ·pirəit). 1767. [f. COPY *sb.* 6 + RIGHT *sb.*] **1.** The exclusive right given by law for a certain term of years to an author, composer, etc. (or his assignee) to print, publish, and sell copies of his original work. **2.** *attrib.* or *adj.* Protected by copyright 1881.

1. We have international copyrights JEVONS. Hence **Co·pyright** *v. trans.* to secure c. for.

‖**Coque** (kǫk), *sb.* 1821. [a. F. *coque* shell.] †**1.** *Bot.* A COCCUS. **2.** *Millinery.* A small loop of ribbon, used in trimming.

‖**Coquelicot** (ko·kliko). 1795. [Fr.; the name of the Red Poppy.] The colour of the common Red Poppy, a brilliant orange-red. Also *attrib.*

†**Coqueluche.** 1611. [a. F., f. L. *cucullus* cowl, applied orig. to a kind of *grippe*, for which patients wore a *coqueluche*.] In 16th c. an epidemic catarrh; later, hooping-cough –1749.

Coquet (kǫke·t). 1696. [a. F., orig. sb., dim. of *coq* cock; as adj. 'forward, wanton, gallant'; cf. COCK *v.*[1], also COCKISH *a.*, COCKY *a.*, and COCKET *a.* The sb. was formerly masc. and fem.; later the fem. became *coquette*, and the masc. obsolete.]

A. *adj.* †**1.** = COCKY. †**2.** Amorously forward –1711. **3.** Coquettish 1697.

3. Not far from Paris I observed two very c. sphinxes H. WALPOLE.

†**B.** *sb.* **1.** A male flirt –1732. **2.** Earlier f. COQUETTE, q. v.

Coquet, coquette (koke·t), *v.* 1701. [a. F. *coqueter*, f. *coquet*; see prec. The sp. *coquette* is modern.] **1.** *intr.* 'To act the lover' (J.); to practise coquetry, to flirt *with.* (Now only of a woman.) †**2.** *trans.* 'To treat with an appearance of amorous tenderness' (J.); to flirt with –1773. **3.** *intr.* To dally, trifle, or toy *with* 1780.

2. He caught me one morning coquetting his wife SWIFT. 3. He coquetted with peace to retain a county member 1796.

Coquetoon (kǫkətūn). 1846. [Native name.] A small W. African antelope (*Cephalophus rufilatus*, Gray).

Coquetry (kōᵘ·kėtri). 1656. [a. F. *coquetterie*, f. *coqueter.*] **1.** Attractive pertness in women; the use of arts intended to excite admiration or love, merely for the gratification of vanity; a coquettish act. **2.** *fig.* and *transf.* 1770.

1. Coquettry is one of the main ingredients in the natural composition of a woman VANBRUGH.

Coquette (kokeˑt), *sb.* 1611. [a. F., fem. of *coquet*; see COQUET *a.* and *sb.*] **1.** A woman who uses arts to gain the admiration and affection of men without any intention of responding to the feelings aroused; a flirt. Also *transf.* and *fig.* **2.** A genus of crested humming-birds. [F. *coquet* masc.] 1866. **3.** *attrib.* = COQUET *a.* 3. 1743.

1. Cocquet..also a wanton Girl that speaks fair to several Lovers at once PHILLIPS. Hence **Coqueˑttish** *a.* like a c.; of or characterized by coquetry; **-ly** *adv.*

‖**Coquilla** (kokīˑlʸă). 1851. [app. Sp. or Pg., dim. of *coca* shell; cf. F. *coquille.*] In *C.-nut*, the nut of the Brazilian palm-tree, *Attalea funifera*, the shell of which is much used by turners.

Coquimbite (kokiˑmbəit). 1844. [f. *Coquimbo*, Chili.] *Min.* A native ferric sulphate, found chiefly in parts of S. America; native White Copperas.

Coquimbo owl; see OWL.

‖**Coquina** (kokīˑna). 1883. [Sp., deriv. of OSp. *coca* :—L. **cocca*, by-form of *concha* mussel, shell.] A soft whitish rock made up of fragments of marine shells united by a calcareous cement; found in the West Indies and Florida, where it is used as a building material.

‖**Coquito** (kokīˑto). 1866. [Sp.; dim. of *coco* coco-nut.] A Chilian palm-tree, *Jubæa spectabilis*, from the sap of which palm-honey is obtained.

‖**Cor**¹ (kǭi). ME. [Heb. *kōr* lit. 'round vessel'.] A Hebrew measure of capacity, called earlier a *homer*.

‖**Cor**². 1870. [F., = horn.] In **c. anglais** (kōr aṅglę), lit. 'English horn': the tenor oboe; also, an organ stop of similar tone.

Cor-¹, assim. f. COM-, CON- *prefix*, bef. *r*. For the sense see COM-.

Cor-², **coro-** (**core-**). Gr. κόρη girl, doll, pupil of the eye (cf. BABY), taken as the basis of mod. surgical terms relating to the pupil. Hence **Coreˑctomy, Coroˑtomy** (**core-**), excision and incision of the pupil, **Coˑroplasty** (**core-**), an operation for forming an artificial pupil; etc.

Coracine (kǫˑrăsəin). 1624. [ad. L. *coracinus*, a. Gr., f. κόραξ raven: so called from its black colour.] A Nile fish, resembling a perch.

Coracle (kǫˑrăk'l). 1547. [a. Welsh *corwgl*, ?dim. of *corwg* = Ir. *curach* boat.] A small boat made of wickerwork covered with some water-tight material, used by the ancient Britons, and still by fishermen in Wales and Ireland.

Coraco- (kǫˑrăko-), now used in *Anat.* as comb. f. CORACOID, in sense 'relating to the coracoid process and ——', as **c.-acromial**, connecting the coracoid and the acromial, as the *c.-acromial ligament*; **-clavicular**; **-costal** = COSTO-CORACOID; **-humeral**; etc.

Coracoid (kǫˑrăkoid). 1741. [ad. medical L. *coracoides*, a. Gr. κορακοειδής raven-like, f. κόραξ.]

A. *adj.* **1.** Beaked like a crow. Applied to a process of bone (*c. process*), extending in man from the scapula toward the sternum; also to the bone (*c. bone*) homologous with this process, which, in birds and reptiles, extends from the scapula to the sternum, and forms the distal or ventral element of the scapular arch. **2.** Pertaining to, or connected with, the coracoid process 1836.

B. *sb.* = *C. process* or *bone*; see A. 1.

Coracomoˑrphic, *a.* [f. mod.L. *Coracomorphæ* (f. Gr. κορακο- + -μορφος, f. -μορφή).] *Zool.* Of or belonging to the group *Coracomorphæ* or birds of the crow form, nearly corresp. to PASSERINE.

‖**Coracosteon** (kǫrăkǫˑstiˌǫn). 1882. [mod. L., f. as prec. + -ὀστέον.] *Zool.* An additional symmetrical osseous centre formed in the sternum in certain birds. Hence **Coracoˑsteal** *a.*

Corage, obs. f. COURAGE.

Co-raˑdicate, *a.* 1882. [See Co-.] In *Etym.*: Having the same root.

‖**Coraggio** (koraˑdʒo), *int.* 1601. [It.] Courage! as a hortatory exclam.

Corah (kōᵊˑră), *a.* 1833. [Urdū *kōrā* new, unbleached.] Plain, undyed: as *sb.* 'an Indian pattern silk handkerchief' (Simmonds).

Coral (kǫˑrăl), *sb.* ME. [a. OF., later *corail* :—L. *corallum*, *coralium*, a. Gr. κοράλλιον red coral.] **1.** A hard calcareous substance consisting of the continuous skeleton secreted by many tribes of marine cœlenterate polyps for their support and habitation. Found, according to the species, in single specimens growing plant-like on the sea-bottom, or in accumulations (*coral-islands, -reefs*). **a.** Historically the name belongs to the *Red Coral*, an arborescent species, found in the Red Sea and Mediterranean. *Pink c.*: a variety of this. **b.** Afterwards extended to other kinds, as **White c., Black c.** (*Antipathes*), **Blue c.** (*Heliospora*), **Yellow c.**, etc.; and more recently, with reference to the appearance of the aggregate skeleton, to **Brain c.** (*Meandrina*), **Cup c.** (family *Cyathophyllidæ*), **Mushroom c.** (*Fungia*), **Organ-pipe c.** (*Tubipora*), **Star c.** (*Astroides*), etc. See also MADREPORE, MILLEPORE. 1600. **2.** (with *a* and *pl.*) = CORALLUM 1579; also, a piece of (red) coral 1607. **3.** A toy of polished coral, given to teething infants 1613. **4.** *fig.* ME. **5.** *transf.* The roe of the lobster: so called from its colour when boiled 1768. **6.** *attrib.* Formed or made of coral; of the colour of red coral 1452.

3. Art thou not breeding teeth..I'll..get a c. for thee BEAUM. & FL. 4. Where she stood, Blood's liquid c. sprang her feet beneath DRUMM. OF HAWTH. 6. C. clasps and amber studs MARLOWE. India's c. strand HEBER. Corral lips SHAKS.

Comb.: **c.-berry**, an American shrub (*Symphoricarpus vulgaris*), having the berries deep red; **-fish**, a name for fishes of the families *Chætodontidæ* and *Pomacentridæ* which frequent c.-reefs; **-insect**, erron. name for a c.-polyp; **-mud**, mud formed by decomposed c.; **-polyp**, one of the individual animals of a c. polypidom; **-rag**, *Geol.* the upper member of the Middle Oolite series; **-root**, book-name of the orchideous plant *Corallorhiza*; **-sand** (cf. *coral-mud*); **-zoophyte** = *coral-polyp*. See also C.-PLANT, etc. Hence **Coˑral** *v. rare*, to make red like c. **Coralˑlaˑceous** *a.* of the nature of c. (*rare*). **Coˑralled** *a.* furnished or covered with c. **Coraˑllian** *a. arch.* = CORALLINE *a.* **Coralliˑferous** *a.* c.-bearing. **Coraˑlliform** *a.* having the form of c. **Coralliˑgenous** *a.* c.-producing.

Corallin (kǫˑrălin). 1873. [ad. L. *corallinus*; see -IN.] *Chem.* A red colouring matter, called also *Pæonin*, obtained by treating phenol with sulphuric and oxalic acids. *Yellow c.* (=*Aurin*), a yellowish red dye, obtained by heating carbolic acid with the same substances; so called because it can be converted into the *red c.*

Coralline (kǫˑrăləin), *sb.*¹ 1543. [ad. It. *corallina*, dim. of *corallo* CORAL.] A name given to organisms thought to be of the nature of coral, but of more minute size, etc.; as the calcareous sea-weeds, esp. *Corallina officinalis*, the Polyzoa or Bryozoa, etc.

C. zone: the third of the zones of the sea-depths, being that in which Polyzoa abound.

Coralline (kǫˑrălin, -əin), *a.* and *sb.*² 1633. [ad. L. *corallinus*, f. *corallum* CORAL.]

A. *adj.* **1.** Of the colour of red coral. **2.** Of the nature of coral 1660. **3.** Coral-like 1860.

B. *sb.* (improper uses.) **1.** A coral zoophyte 1860. **2.** = CORAL (the calcareous substance) 1779.

Corallite (kǫˑrăləit). 1815. [f. L. *corallum* + -ITE.] **1.** A fossil coral. **2.** The coral skeleton of an individual polyp 1861. **3.** Corallitic or coralline marble 1883. So **Coralliˑtic** *a.* of the nature of coral.

Coralloid (kǫˑrăloid). 1604. [f. L. *corallum* + -OID.] *adj.* Resembling or akin to coral. *sb.* Any coralloid organism 1748. So **Coralloiˑdal** *a.*

‖**Corallum** (koræˑlǒm). 1846. [L.] A coral; the calcareous skeleton of a coral polypidom; also the horny tubular envelope of any zoophyte, whether colonial or simple.

Coral-plant. 1774. †**1.** A coral of plant-like form. **2.** The plant *Jatropha multifida* (N.O. *Euphorbiaceæ*) 1813.

Coral reef. 1745. A reef formed by the growth and deposit of coral. The reef-building corals are chiefly madrepores of the genera *Meandrina*, *Caryophyllia*, and *Astroides*.

Coˑral-snake. 1760. A local name for various snakes marked with red zones; *esp.* the species of the genus *Elaps* found in southern U.S. and Central America.

Coral-tree. 1635. †**1.** The red or other branched coral –1698. **2.** The popular name of the trees of the genus *Erythrina* 1756.

Coˑral-wood. 1693. A hard red cabinet-wood from Central and S. America.

Coˑralwort. 1597. [See WORT.] Name of the plant *Dentaria bulbifera*, in allusion to its curiously toothed white rhizomes.

‖**Coram** (kōᵊˑræm). 1607. A Latin preposition meaning 'before, in the presence of', used in *c. judice* before a judge, *c. populo* in public, etc.

Phr. *To bring under c.*, *call to* or *in c.*: to call to account, bring to book.

Coran, var. KORAN.

Cor anglais. *Mus.* See ‖COR ².

Coranoch, etc. var. CORONACH.

Coranto¹ (koraˑnto). Now *Hist.* 1564. [f. (ult.) F. *courante* lit. 'running (dance)'; assim. to It. and Sp. words in *-o*.] = COURANTE 1, 2. Also *attrib.*

Laolta's high and swift Carranto's *Hen. V*, III. v. 33.

†**Coraˑnto**². 1621. [var. of COURANT; see prec.] = COURANT *sb.*² –1635.

‖**Corban** (kǫˑɪbæ̆n). ME. [Heb. = offering.] **1.** *Heb. Antiq.* An offering given to God, *esp.* in performance of a vow. †**2.** The treasury of the temple at Jerusalem, where money offerings of this sort were placed; also *transf.* Church treasury –1610.

†**Corbe.** *rare.* Shortened f. CORBEL. Spenser.

‖**Corbeau** (korbō). 1833. [F. = raven.] A trade name for a dark green colour verging on black.

Corbed, var. of †COURBED, bent, curved.

Corbeil, ‖**corbeille.** 1706. [ad. F. *corbeille* (korbęˑlʸ) :—L. *corbicula*, dim. of *corbis* basket.] †**1.** *Fortif.* A basket filled with earth and placed on a parapet to cover the defending soldiers **2.** *Archit.* Carved work in the form of a basket. (Occas. erron. corbel.) 1734. ‖**3.** As Fr., used for an elegant fruit or flower basket 1800.

Corbel (kǭˑɪbĕl), *sb.* ME. [a. OF. *corbel*, now *corbeau* :—late L. *corvellum* (nom. *-us*), dim. of *corvus* raven. In some Eng. Dicts. erron. identified with prec.] †**1.** A raven. (ME. only.) **2.** *Archit.* A projection jutting out from the face of a wall to support a superincumbent weight. (The word was associated with grotesque ornamentation by Sir W. Scott; a corbel is not technically ornamental.) ME. **b.** A short timber laid upon a bearer to give a better bearing upon the wall or pier; a *c.-block* 1703.

2. The corbels were carved grotesque and grim SCOTT. *Comb.*: **c.-piece** = CORBEL; **-step**, a conjectural substitute for *Corbie-step*; **-table**, a projecting course resting on a series of corbels. Hence **Coˑrbel** *v.* to support or (*intr.*) project on or as on corbels. **Coˑrbelled** *ppl. a.* furnished with corbels; fashioned as a c. **Coˑrbelling** *sb.* work consisting of corbels; also *attrib.*

†**Corbet.** [a. F. *corbet*:—Rom. type **corvetto*, dim. of *corvus* raven.] = CORBEL *sb.* 2. CHAUCER.

‖**Corbicula** (kǫɪbiˑkiulă). Also erron. **corbiculum.** 1816. [L., dim. of *corbis* basket.] *Entom.* A part of the hinder leg of a bee adapted to carry pollen; cf. BASKET. Hence **Corbiˑculate** *a.* having *corbiculæ*.

Corbie (kǭˑɪbi). *Sc.* 1450. [f. OF. *corb.*] A raven; also, the carrion-crow, called also **c.-crow.**

Comb.: **c.-gable**, a gable having c.-steps; **c.-steps**, projections in the form of steps on the sloping sides of a gable. var. †**Corbin.**

‖**Corbula** (kǭˑɪbiulă). 1861. [L., dim. of *corbis.*] *Zool.* **1.** A receptacle in which groups of gonangia are enclosed, in some of the Cœlenterata. **2.** (*With capital C.*) A genus of bivalve molluscs living in mud or sand, related to the clam. var. **Coˑrbule.**

Coˑrcass. 1796. [Corrupt. of Ir. *corcach* marsh.] Name of the salt marshes along the banks of the Shannon and Fergus.

‖**Corchorus** (kǭˑɪkŏrŭs). 1759. [a. Gr. κόρχορος name of a plant.] *Bot.* **1.** A genus of *Tiliaceæ*, including some species which yield jute. **2.** A name of *Kerria japonica* (N.O. *Rosaceæ, Spiræidæ*), of which the double-flowered variety is often trained as a wall plant for its yellow blossoms.

Corcle (kǭ·ɹk'l), **corcule** (kǭ·ɹkiul). 1810. [ad. L. *corculum*, dim. of *cor* heart.] *Bot.* The embryo in the seed of a plant.

Cord (kǭɹd), *sb.* ME. [a. F. *corde* :—L. *chorda*, ad. Gr. χορδή gut. Cf. CHORD.] **1.** A string, or (small) rope, composed of several strands twisted together. Also *transf.* **2.** A structure in the animal body resembling a cord; as the *spermatic, spinal*, and *umbilical c.*, the *vocal cords*, etc. (Cf. NERVE.) ME. †**3.** *Mus.* = CHORD, q. v. –1830. †**4.** *Math.* = CHORD 1551. **5.** *Farriery.* (Usu. *pl.*) String-halt. ?*Obs.* 1523. **6.** A raised cord-like rib on cloth; corduroy; in *pl.* corduroy breeches 1776. **7.** A measure of wood, stone, or rock (?originally measured with a cord); a pile of wood, usu. 8 feet by 4, and 4 high 1616. **8.** *fig.* Chiefly with reference to the binding power of a cord ME.

8. The wicked shall be held fast in the cords of his own sin HOOKER. The cords of discipline STEVENSON.

Comb.: **c.-drill**, a drill worked by a c. twisted round it and pulled backwards and forwards; **-wood**, wood stacked in cords; wood for fuel cut in lengths (usually) of 4 feet.

Cord (kǭɹd), *v.*[1] ME. [f. CORD *sb.*[1]] **1.** *trans.* To furnish with a cord. **2.** To bind or fasten with a cord or cords 1610. **3.** To stack (wood) in cords 1762.

†**Cord**, *v.*[2] ME. [Aphet. f. ACCORD *v.*] = ACCORD *v.* in most senses –1535.

Cordage (kǭ·ɹdėdʒ). 1490. [app. a. F., f. *corde* CORD.] Cords collectively; *esp.* the ropes in the rigging of a ship. Also *transf.* and *fig.*

Wee'l give our hair for C., and our finest Linnen for Sails 1643. *fig.* The c. of his life CARLYLE.

†**Cordal.** 1688. [a. OF. :—L. type *chordale* sing., f. *chorda* CORD.] *Her.* The string of the mantle or robe of estate –1828.

Cordate (kǭ·ɹdeit), *a.* 1651. [ad. L. *cordatus* wise; in sense 3, ad. mod.L. *cordatus* (Linnæus), after *ovatus* egg-shaped.] †**1.** Wise, prudent –1734. †**2.** Cordial (*rare*) –1671. **3.** Heart-shaped, as *c. leaves* 1769. Hence **Co·rdately** *adv.*

‖**Cordax** (kǭ·ɹdæks). 1531. [Gr.] A dissolute dance of the Old Greek Comedy.

Co·rded, *ppl. a.* ME. [f. CORD[1].] **1.** Bound with cords; *Her.* bound or wound about with cords 1486. **2.** Made of or furnished with cords ME. **3.** Having lines or stripes like cords 1760. **4.** Piled in cords (see CORD *sb.*[1] 7) 1847.

2. A Corded-ladder SHAKS. 3. C. stuffs 1760. The hand..was lean, c., and knuckly STEVENSON.

Cordelier (kǭɹdėlīə·ɹ). ME. [a. F., f. *cordele* (now *cordelle*), dim. of *corde.*] **1.** A Franciscan friar of the strict rule: so called from the knotted cord they wear round the waist. **2.** *pl.* One of the political clubs of the French Revolution (*club des Cordeliers*), which met in an old convent of the Cordeliers 1837.

Cordeliere. 1725. [a. F. *cordelière*, the cord of the Franciscans, f. prec.; see Littré.] *Her.* A knotted cord, put round armorial bearings in token of devotion to St. Francis of Assisi.

Cordelle (kǭ·ɹdĕl), *sb.* 1823. [a. F., dim. of *corde.*] †**1.** A twisted cord. HALLIWELL. **2.** *Canada* and *U.S.* A towing line or rope. Hence **Co·rdelle** *v.* to tow (a boat) with a c.

Corder (kǭ·ɹdəɹ). ME. [f. CORD *v.*[1] + -ER[1].] One who or that which cords or fastens with a cord; *spec.* an appliance in a sewing-machine for stitching a piping-cord, or the like, between the folds of a fabric.

Cordial (kǭ·ɹdiăl). ME. [ad. med.L. *cordialis*, f. L. *cor, cord-*.]

A. *adj.* †**1.** Of or belonging to the heart –1646. **2.** Stimulating, comforting, or invigorating the heart; reviving, cheering 1471. Also *fig.* **3.** Hearty; heartfelt; sincere, genuine, warm 1477.

1. *C. spirits* (in Mediæval Physiology) = VITAL *spirits*, for 'the Vital Spirit resides in the heart, etc.' 2. This c. julep here..With spirits of balm and fragrant syrups mixed MILT. *Comus* 672. 3. He was a stout and valiant gentleman, a c. protestant FULLER. Hence **Co·rdial-ly** *adv.*, **-ness.**

B. *sb.* A medicine, food, or beverage which invigorates the heart and stimulates the circulation. *Comm.* Aromatized and sweetened spirit, used as a beverage. Also *transf.* and *fig.* ME.

For gold in Phisik is a c., Therfore he louede gold in special CHAUCER.

Cordiality (kǭɹdiæ·lĭti). 1611. [f. prec. + -ITY.] †**1.** The quality of relating to the heart. SIR T. BROWNE. **2.** Heartiness; warmth 1611.

2. Margaret of Parma hated the Cardinal with great c. MOTLEY. His c. towards progress MORLEY.

Cordialize (kǭ·ɹdiălaiz), *v.* 1774. [f. as prec. + -IZE.] **1.** *trans.* To make into a cordial. **2.** To make cordial 1817. **3.** *intr.* To become cordial; to fraternize (*with*). Chiefly *Sc.* 1834.

Cordierite (kǭ·ɹdiərait). 1814. [f. *Cordier*, a French geologist.] *Min.* = IOLITE.

Cordiform (kǭ·ɹdifǭɹm), *a.* 1828. [f. L. *cor, cordi-* + -FORM.] Heart-shaped, as *c. tendon*, the central tendon of the diaphragm.

‖**Cordillera** (kǭrdilyē·ră). 1704. [Sp. = mountain-chain, f. *cordilla*, dim. of *cuerda* :—L. *chorda.*] A mountain-chain or ridge, one of a series of parallel ridges; in *pl.* applied originally by the Spaniards to the parallel chains of the Andes in S. America.

Cordinar, -er, obs. f. CORDWAINER.

Cording (kǭ·ɹdiŋ), *vbl. sb.* 1571. [f. CORD *v.*[1]] **1.** Hanging 1619. **b.** *Weaving.* The connexion of the treadles of a loom with the leaves of heddles by cords, so as to produce the pattern required 1822. **2.** Cordage; corded work 1571.

Cordite (kǭ·ɹdəit). 1889. [f. CORD + -ITE.] A smokeless explosive, so called from its cord-like appearance.

Cordon (kǭ·ɹdən, -ǭn), *sb.* 1578. [a. F., augment. and dim. of *corde* CORD.] **1.** *Fortif.* A course of stones forming the coping of the escarp 1598. **2.** *Archit.* A string-course, or projecting band of stone, usually flat, on the face of a wall 1706. **3.** *Mil.* A line of men placed at detached intervals, to prevent passage to or from the guarded area; a chain of military posts 1758; *transf.* and *fig.* 1792. Also *attrib.* **4.** A guarded line between affected and unaffected districts, to prevent intercommunication and spread of a disease or pestilence; a *sanitary c.* 1826. **5.** An ornamental cord or braid forming a part of costume, or used as a heraldic bearing. Also, the cord worn by Franciscans. 1578. ‖**6.** A ribbon, usually worn scarfwise, as part of the insignia of a knightly order. [As Fr. (kordoṅ) or a Gallicism.] 1727. **7.** *Hort.* A fruit-tree made by pruning to grow as a single stem 1878.

6. *Grand c.*: that distinguishing the highest grade of a knightly order. *Blue c.* (F. *cordon bleu*): the sky-blue ribbon worn by the Knights-grand-cross of the Holy Ghost. Also applied to the wearers, and by extension to other persons of distinction; *cordon bleu*, jocularly or familiarly, a first-class cook.

‖**Cordonnet.** 1858. [F. (kordonẹ), dim. of *cordon.*] A loosely spun thick silk thread or weak cord, made from waste silk, and used for fringes, outlines of lacework, etc.

Cordovan (kǭ·ɹdŏvæn). 1591. [a. Sp. *cordován* (now *cordobán*); *cordováno* adj., of *Cordova*. Cf. CORDWAIN.]

A. *adj.* Of or pertaining to Cordova; made of leather of Cordova.

B. *sb.* **1.** One who belongs to Cordova 1599. **2.** = CORDWAIN 1625. †**3.** A skin of this leather –1750.

Corduroy (kǭɹdərɔi·), *sb.* 1787. [App. Eng., repr. a supposed Fr. **corde du roi*; or ? f. the Eng. surname *Corderoy*.] **1.** A kind of coarse thick-ribbed cotton stuff 1795. **2.** *pl.* Corduroy trousers (*colloq.*). **3.** A corduroy road (see 4) 1836. **4.** *attrib.* Made of corduroy 1795; ribbed like corduroy 1865; in *U.S.* applied to a road made of logs laid together transversely across a swamp or miry ground 1830.

4. Picking our way along the swampy c. road H. MARTINEAU. Hence **Corduroy·** *v.* to form a c. road; to cross (a swamp) by such a road.

Cordwain (kǭ·ɹdwe[i]n). *arch.* [ME. *corduan(e, cordewan(e*, a. OF., prop. adj. 'of Cordova', f. Sp. *Cordova* :—L. *Corduba* a town of Spain, where this leather was made.] Spanish leather, made of goat-skins tanned and dressed, or, later, of split horse-hides; = CORDOVAN. Much used for shoes, etc., by the wealthy during the Middle Ages.

His schoon of cordewane CHAUCER. Hence **Co·rdwainer** (*arch.*), a worker in c.; a shoemaker. (Still used as the name of the trade-gild of shoemakers.) **Co·rdwainery**, shoemaker's work.

†**Cordyl.** 1607. [ad. Gr. κορδύλος water-newt.] A book-name of the water-newt; now applied to a genus of lizards (*Cordylus*).

‖**Cordyline** (kǭɹdiləi·nɨ). 1866. [f. Gr. κορδύλη club.] *Bot.* A liliaceous genus of trees, sometimes called palm-lilies.

Core (kōᵊɹ), *sb.*[1] ME. [?] **1.** The dry horny capsule embedded in the centre of the pulp and containing the seeds of the apple, pear, quince, etc. Also †*fig.* **2.** An unburnt part in the centre of a coal, piece of limestone, etc. ME. **3.** The hard centre of a boil; also †*fig.* 1532; a disease in sheep, caused by worms in the liver 1750. **4.** *transf.* A central portion that is cut out; *e.g.* of rock 1649; or left: *e.g.* of a hay-rick, and in *Archæol.* of a flint nodule, from which flint knives have been chipped 1800. **5.** *transf.* A central part of different character from that which surrounds it: chiefly technical 1784. **6.** *Hydraul. Engineering.* A wall impervious to water, placed in a dike of porous material 1884. **7.** *Founding.* An internal mould filling the space intended to be left hollow in a hollow casting 1727. **8.** *Electr.* The central cord of insulated conducting wires in a cable 1892. **9.** The inner-most part or heart of anything, as of a superficial area 1556. **10.** Used for 'heart' 1611.

1. *fig.* The coare of Adams apple is still in their throat DONNE. 3. *fig.* The Canker, or Coar, of the late Rebellion NORTH. 9. In the C. of the Square, she raised a Tower RALEIGH. A solid c. of heat TENNYSON, of fact B. GOULD. 10. In my hearts C.: I, in my Heart of heart *Haml.* III. ii. 78.

Comb.: **c.-barrel** (*Gunnery*), a long cylindrical iron tube through which cold water is run, used in casting guns to cool them from the inside; **-box**, a box in which a c. is made in founding; **-print**, a projecting piece on a pattern to form a recess in the mould, into which the end of the c. is inserted.

Core (kōᵊɹ), *sb.*[2] 1622. [app. for F. *corps*; see CORPS.] **1.** A body of people, a company. (Chiefly *Sc.*) **2.** A gang of miners working together in one shift 1778. **3.** A turn of work in a (Cornish) mine; a shift 1778.

1. In a C. of People, whose affections he suspected BACON.

Core (kōᵊɹ), *v.* 1597. [f. CORE *sb.*[1]] **1.** *trans.* To take out the core of; also with *out.* **2.** To enclose in the centre, enshrine 1816. **3.** *Founding.* To mould with a core 1865.

1. He's like a corn upon my great toe..he must be cored out MARSTON.

Core, var. of COR, Hebrew measure.

Core-, in surgical terms relating to the pupil of the eye; see COR-[2].

Co-regent (kōᵘ,rī·dʒĕnt). 1799. [See CO-.] A joint regent or ruler.

Co-rela·tion. 1839. [See CO-.] Joint or mutual relation; CORRELATION.

Coreless (kōᵊ·ɹlės), *a.* 1813. [f. CORE *sb.*[1]] Without a core; hollow; heartless.

Co-religionist (kōᵘ,rĭli·dʒənist). 1842. [See CO-.] An adherent of the same religion.

Corella (kŏrelă). 1885. The parakeet *Calopsitta Novæ-Hollandiæ*, also called *Cockateel.*

‖**Coreopsis** (kǭri,ǫ·psis). 1753. [mod.L., f. Gr. κόρις bug + ὄψις appearance, in reference to the bug-like shape of the seed.] *Bot.* An American genus of *Compositæ*, several species of which are cultivated for their flowers with yellow or parti-coloured rays.

Corer (koᵊ·rəɹ). 1796. [f. CORE *v.* + -ER[1].] An instrument for coring fruit.

Co-respondent (kōᵘrĭspǫ·ndĕnt). 1857. *Law.* In a divorce suit, a man charged with the adultery and proceeded against together with the respondent or wife.

Corf (kǭɹf). Pl. **corves** (kǭɹvz). 1483. [Cf. LG. *korf*, perh. a. L. *corbis* basket. Webster's *Corb* is unknown in England.] †**1.** A basket –1543. **2.** *Mining.* A large basket formerly used in carrying or hoisting ore or coal 1653; *transf.* the wooden or iron tub which has replaced the basket 1831. **3.** *Fishing.* A basket, or a box with holes in it, in which fish, etc., are kept alive in the water 1825.

Coriaceous (kǭri,ēⁱ·ʃəs, kōᵊri-), *a.* 1674. [f. L. *coriaceus*, f. *corium*; see -ACEOUS.] **1.** Resembling leather in texture, appearance, etc.; leathery. **2.** Made of leather (*affected*) 1824.

Coriander (kǭri,æ·ndəɹ). ME. [a. F. *coriandre*, ad. L. *coriandrum*, ad. Gr. κορίαννον (app. a foreign word). Cf. CORIANDER.] An annual plant, *Coriandrum sativum*, N.O. *Umbelliferæ*, the fruit of which is carminative and aromatic. Also *attrib.*

Corindon (kǫri·ndǫn). 1802. [F.] *Min.* An early name of CORUNDUM, q.v.

Corinth (kǫ·rinþ). ME. [F. *Corinthe*, Gr. Κόρινθος.] **1.** A city of ancient Greece celebrated for its artistic elegance, luxury, and licentiousness. †**2.** *pl.* Corinthians -1642. **3.** = CURRANT, q.v.

†**Corinthiac** (kǒri·nþiæk), *a. rare.* 1677. [ad. Gr. Κορινθιακός.] = next.

Corinthian (kǒri·nþiǎn), *a.* (*sb.*) 1577. [f. L. *Corinthius* + -AN.]

A. *adj.* **1.** Of or pertaining to Corinth. **b.** *Archit.* The lightest and most ornate of the three Grecian orders, having a bell-shaped capital adorned with rows of acanthus-leaves giving rise to graceful volutes and helices 1656. **c.** *C. brass* (*bronze*) [L. *Corinthium æs*]: an alloy of gold, silver, and copper, produced at Corinth. Also *fig.* (from the *fig.* sense of BRASS) shamelessness. Hence also *Corinthian* = 'brazen'. 1594. **2.** After the style of Corinthian art 1860. **3.** Profligate; in 19th c. use: Given to elegant dissipation 1642. **4.** (*U.S.*) *Yachting.* Amateur 1885.

2. The C. grace of Gertrude's manners EMERSON. 3. The sage and rheumatic old prelatess, with all her young C. laity MILTON.

B. *sb.* **1.** A native or inhabitant of Corinth 1526. **2.** †**a.** A wealthy man; a gay, licentious man; a brazen-faced fellow -1879. **b.** A man about town 1819. **c.** A wealthy amateur of sport; *esp.* in *U.S.* an amateur yachtsman 1823. Hence **Cori·nthianism. Cori·nthiane·sque** *a.* approximating to the C. style. **Cori·nthianize** *v. intr.* to live licentiously; to imitate the C. order of architecture.

‖**Corium** (kōə·riǒm). 1826. [L.] **1.** *Phys.* The true skin under the epidermis 1836. **2.** *Entom.* The horny basal portion of the wing of a heteropterous insect 1826. **3.** *Antiq.* A leathern body-armour formed of overlapping flaps 1834.

Co-rival (kōᵘ,rəi·văl). 1678. [mod. f. *corival*, an old var. of CORRIVAL; see Co-.] A joint rival with others. Also as *adj.* Hence **Co-ri·valry. Co-ri·valship. Co-ri·val** *v.* var. of CORRIVAL *v.*

Cork (kǭɹk), *sb.*[1] 1463. [Cf. Sp. *corcha*, *corche*, repr. L. *corticem* bark.] **1.** The bark or periderm of the cork-oak 1570. **2.** Anything made of cork; *e.g.* †a slipper; †a sole or heel for a shoe; a float for an angler, or a swimmer; *esp.* a stopper for a bottle, cask, etc. 1463. **3.** The cork-tree or cork-oak (*Quercus Suber*) 1601. **4.** *Bot.* A protective tissue in the higher plants, forming the inner division of the *bark*. It consists of closely-packed air-containing cells, nearly impervious to air and water 1875. **5.** *transf.* 1671. **6.** *attrib.* Of cork 1716.

1. *Virgin c.*: the outer casing of the bark formed during the first year's growth. 5. *Fossil c.*, *mountain-c.*, *rock-c.*: names of a very light asbestos.

Comb.: **c.-fossil** = *fossil-c.*; **-jacket**, a jacket made partly of, or lined with c., to support a person in the water; **-oak**, the tree (*Quercus Suber*) from which c. is obtained; **-tree** = *cork-oak*; **-wing**, a fish, *Crenilabrus melas* or *cornubicus*.

Cork (kǭɹk), *sb.*[2] 1483. [app. a contr. of *corkir*, a. Gael. *corcur*, ad. L. *purpur.*] = CUDBEAR.

Cork, *sb.*[3], **Corlk**, erron. spellings of CAUK.

Cork (kǭɹk), *v.*[1] 1580. [f. CORK *sb.*[1]] **1.** To furnish with a cork (as a †cork heel, a float, etc.). **2.** To stop (a bottle, etc.) with, or as with, a cork; and so to shut *up* (the contents); also *transf.* 1650. **3.** To blacken with burnt cork 1836.

Cork, *v.*[2], erron. f. CAULK *v.*

Corkage (kǭ·ɹkėdʒ). 1838. [f. CORK *sb.*[1] or *v.*[1] + -AGE.] The corking or uncorking of bottles; hence (= *c.-money*) a charge made by hotel-keepers, waiters, etc., for every bottle of wine, etc., uncorked and served, orig. when not supplied by them.

Corked (kǭɹkt), *ppl. a.* 1519. [f. CORK *v.*[1] and *sb.*[1]] †**1.** Furnished with a cork sole or heel -1615. **2.** Stopped with a cork; also *fig.* 1836. **3.** Blackened with burnt cork 1836. **4.** Of wine: Tasting of the cork 1830.

Corker (kǭ·ɹkəɹ). 1723. [f. CORK *sb.*[1] + -ER[1].] †**1.** ?A cork-cutter. **2.** *slang.* Something that closes a discussion; a 'settler'. Hence, something astonishing, *e.g.* a monstrous lie. 1837.

†**Corking-pin.** 1690. [App. corrupt f. *cawking*, CALKIN.] 'A pin of the largest size' (J.). -1840.

Corkscrew (kǭ·ɹkskrū), *sb.* 1720. [f. CORK *sb.*[1] + SCREW.] **1.** An instrument for drawing corks from bottles, consisting of a steel screw or helix with a sharp point and a transverse handle. **2.** *attrib.* Resembling a corkscrew; spirally twisted, as *c. curls*, a *c. staircase* 1830.

Corkscrew (kǭ·ɹkskrū), *v. colloq.* 1837. [f. prec.] **1.** To move or cause to move in a spiral course. **2.** To draw *out* as with a corkscrew 1852.

1. Mr. Bantam corkscrewed his way through the crowd DICKENS.

Corkwood (kǭ·ɹkwud). 1756. [f. CORK *sb.*[1] + WOOD.] A name given to several light and porous woods, and the trees yielding them; *e.g.* in the W. Indies, to *Anona palustris*, *Ochroma Lagopus*, etc.; in N. S. Wales to *Duboisia myoporoides*.

Corky (kǭ·ɹki), *a.* 1601. [f. CORK *sb.*[1] + -Y.] **1.** Like cork in nature or character 1756. †**2.** *fig.* Dry and stiff, withered -1605. **3.** *fig.* Light, frivolous; buoyant, lively; hence, restive (*colloq.*) 1601. **4.** = CORKED 4. (Dicts.)

2. Binde fast his c. armes *Lear* III. vii. 29. Hence **Co·rkiness**, c. quality.

†**Corm**[1], **corme.** 1578. [a. F. *corme*, app. :—L. *cornum* (see CORNEL).] **1.** The service-tree, *Pyrus domestica*; also its fruit, the sorb -1658. **2.** The cornel-tree 1676.

Corm[2] (kǭɹm). 1830. [a. Gr. κορμός, the trunk of a tree with the boughs lopped off, f. κείρειν (κερ-, κορ-).] *Bot.* A bulb-like subterraneous stem of a monocotyledonous plant; also called *solid bulb*.

Cormo-, comb. f. Gr. κορμός trunk of a tree, stem: as in

Cormo·geny [Gr. -γένεια descent], that branch of ontogeny which deals with the germ-history of races or social aggregates. **Cormo·phyly** [Gr. φυλή, φῦλον], that branch of phylogeny which deals with the tribal history of races.

Cormogen (kǭ·ɹmǒdʒen). 1846. [f. Gr. κορμός + -γενής; cf. *acrogen*.] = CORMOPHYTE. So **Cormo·genous** *a.* belonging to or like a c.; also, corm-bearing.

Cormophyte (kǭ·ɹmofəit). 1852. [f. Gr. κορμός + φυτόν.] *Bot.* Endlicher's name (*Cormophyta*) for one of his two primary divisions of the Vegetable Kingdom, comprising all plants that have a proper stem or axis of growth. Hence **Cormophy·tic** *a.* of the nature of a c.

Cormorant (kǭ·ɹmǒrănt). ME. [ad. F. *cormoran*; app. f. an OF. *corp-marin :—L. *corvus marinus* sea-raven; see -ANT[3].] **1.** A large and voracious sea-bird (*Phalacrocorax carbo*), about 3 feet in length, and black in colour, widely diffused over the northern hemisphere. Also the name of the genus. **2.** *fig.* An insatiably greedy person or thing 1531. **3.** *attrib.* 1568.

2. Light vanity, insatiate c. *Rich. II*, II. i. 38. 3. The C. belly *Cor.* I. i. 125.

‖**Cormus.** 1800. [mod.L.; see CORM.] **1.** = CORM, q.v. **2.** Haeckel's name for the common stock of a plant or 'colonial' animal, bearing a number of individuals which originate by gemmation.

Corn (kǭɹn), *sb.*[1] [Com. Teut. :—OTeut. *korno-, f. earlier *kurnóm grain, corn :—Aryan type *gr̥nóm; from the vb. stem *ger-* (*gor-*, *gr-*), in Skr. *jr* to wear down; whence also L. *granum*. A *corn* or *grain* is thus a 'worn-down particle'.] **1.** *gen.* A small hard particle, a grain, as of sand, salt, gunpowder. OE. and *mod. dial.* **2.** *spec.* The small hard seed or fruit of a plant; now usually with qualification, as *barley-*, *pepper-c.*, etc. OE. **3.** *spec.* The seed of the cereal or farinaceous plants; grain. (Locally, the word is understood to denote the leading crop of the district; hence in England 'corn' is = *wheat*, in Scotland = *oats*; in U.S., as short for *Indian corn*, it is = *maize*.) OE. **4.** Applied to the cereal plants while growing, or while still containing the grain OE. †**b.** A corn-stalk (*rare*) -1590. **5.** *attrib.* ME.

2. Each [coffee] berry contains two corns 1876. 3. An ancient churl.. Went sweating underneath a sack of c. TENNYSON. 4. Her Foes shake like a Field of beaten Corne *Hen. VIII*, v. v. 32. **b.** Playing on pipes of Corne *Mids. N.* II. i. 67.

Comb.: **c.-ball** (*U.S.*), a sweetmeat made of popped c. or maize; **-beef**, corned beef; **-beetle**, a very small beetle, *Cucujus testaceus*, the larva of which often ravages stores of grain; **-bells**, a species of fungus, *Cyathus vernicosus*, found in England in corn-fields, etc.; **-bind**, the wild Convolvulus; also Running Buckwheat, *Polygonum Convolvulus*; **-cockle**, the common Cockle, *Lychnis Githago*; **-crib**, a crib for corn; **-cutter**; **-fly**, any of the genera *Chloris* and *Oscinis* which do great injury to growing crops; **-fritter** (*U.S.*), a fritter made of batter mixed with grated green Indian c.; **-land**; **-ma·rigold**, *Chrysanthemum segetum*; **-meal**, meal made of grain; in Scotl., oatmeal; in U.S., meal of maize; **-mill**; **-mint**, a species of Calamint, *C. Acinos*; also, the Field-mint, *Mentha arvensis*; **-moth**, a species of moth, *Tinea granella*, the larva of which is destructive to c.; **-oyster** (*U.S.*), a c.-fritter with a taste as of oysters; **-parsley**, a kind of wild parsley, *Petroselinum segetum*, found in cornfields; **-popper** (*U.S.*), a wire pan or covered tray used in popping Indian c.; **-popping** (*U.S.*), the making of popped Indian c. by roasting it till it splits and the white flour swells out; a social gathering for doing this; †**-powder**, gunpowder that has been granulated; †**-rate** = -RENT; **-rose**, the Corn Poppy; also, the Cockle; **-shuck**, *U.S.* = C.-HUSK; **-thrips**, a small insect, *Thrips cerealium*, which deposits its eggs on wheat, oats, grasses, etc.; †**-tree** = CORNEL-TREE; †**-violet**, *Campanula Speculum*; **-worm**, the larva of the Corn-moth or other insect, destructive to c.

Corn (kǭɹn), *sb.*[2] ME. [a. OF. *corn*, later *cor* :—L. *cornu*.] A horny induration of the cuticle, with a hard centre, caused by undue pressure, chiefly on the toes and feet. Cf. AGNAIL.

Phr. *To tread on any one's corns*: to wound his susceptibilities.

Corn (kǭɹn), *v.* 1560. [f. CORN *sb.*[1]] **1.** *trans.* To form into grains, as gunpowder. †**2.** *intr.* To become granular -1679. **3.** *trans.* To sprinkle with salt in grains; to season, pickle, or preserve with salt 1565. **4.** To give (a horse) a feed of oats. *Sc.* 1753. **5.** = KERN *v.* 1632. **6.** *trans.* To crop (land) with corn 1649.

3. The beef was woundily corned RICHARDSON. 4. To c. a horse before a journey SCOTT.

Cornaceous (kǭɹnē¹·ʃəs), *a.* [f. mod.L. *Cornaceæ*.] *Bot.* Belonging to the Order *Cornaceæ*, of which the genus *Cornus*, Cornel, is the type.

Cornage (kǭ·ɹnėdʒ). [a. OF., f. *corn*, *corne* horn: in med.L. *cornagium*.] A feudal service, being a form of rent fixed by the number of horned cattle; horngeld. ¶An erroneous explanation given first by Littleton, as an 'it is said', makes cornage 'to wind a horn when the Scots or other enemies entered the land'.

Cornbrash (kǭ·ɹn,bræʃ). 1815. [f. CORN *sb.*[1] + BRASH *sb.*[2]] *Geol.* The coarse brashy calcareous sandstone which forms the upper division of the Lower Oolite in parts of England.

Corn-cob (kǭ·ɹn,kǫb). *U.S.* 1817. [See COB *sb.*[1]] The receptacle to which the grains are attached in the ear of maize. Also *attrib.*

Corn-crake (kǭ·ɹn,krēᶦk). 1455. [See CRAKE.] A bird, also called Landrail, *Crex pratensis*, which lives concealed among standing corn, etc. It has a harsh grating note.

Cornea (kǭ·ɹni,ă). 1527. [L., short for med. L. *cornea tela* horny tissue, later *c. tunica* horny coating, f. L. *corneus* CORNEOUS.] *Anat.* The horny transparent convexo-concave portion of the anterior covering of the eye-ball. Hence **Co·rneal** *a.*

Corned (kǭɹnd), *a.*[1] 1577. [f. CORN *sb.*[1] and *v.* + -ED.] **1.** Granulated. **2.** Of meat: Cured with salt 1621. **3.** Bearing seeds or grains 1800. **4.** *slang.* Intoxicated [cf. CORNY *a.*[1]] 1785.

†**Corned**, *a.*[2] 1529. [f. F. *corné*, with -ED for -*é*.] Horned, peaked, pointed -1841.

Co·rneine. Also **-ean, -een.** 1839. [f. L. *corneus* + -INE.] *Min.* = APHANITE.

‖**Corneitis** (kǭɹni,əi·tis). 1854. [f. CORNEA + -ITIS.] *Path.* Inflammation of the cornea.

†**Cornel**[1]. ME. var. of CARNEL, KERNEL = battlement -1602.

Cornel[2]. Now *dial.* ME. [a. OF. *cornal*

:—late L. *cornale* corner, f. L. *cornu*.] Corner, angle (of a house, etc.).

Cornel [3] (kǭ·ɹnĕl). 1551. [f. (ult.) F. *cornouille*, referred by Diez to a pop. L. **cornuculum* (in pl. *-a*), dim. of L. *cornum* 'cornel-cherry'.] 1. English name of the botanical genus *Cornus*, formerly distinguished into *C. mas*, and *C. femina*. *C. mas* was the *Cornel-tree* or Cornelian Cherry-tree; *C. femina* the *Cornel-bush*, *Wild* or *Common Cornel*, or Dogwood (*C. sanguinea*). b. The fruit of the Cornel Tree 1601. 2. *attrib.* Of cornel-wood 1671.

Comb.: c.-tree, the Cornelian cherry-tree; **-berry**, **-fruit**: = 1 b; **-wood**, the wood of *Cornus mascula*, of which anciently javelins, arrows, etc. were made.

Cornelian [1] (kǫɹnī·liăn). ME. [Refash. f. ME. *corneline*, a. 15th c. F. (now *cornaline*); prob. from its likeness in colour to the Cornelberry. CARNELIAN is a perversion, after L. *carnem* flesh.] A variety of chalcedony, a semi-transparent quartz, of a deep dull red, flesh, or reddish white colour; used for seals, etc. var. †**Co·rneole.**

Cornelian [2] (kǫɹnī·liăn). 1625. [f. CORNEL [3]; cf. prec.] †1. The fruit of the cornel-tree; also the tree -1664. 2. **C. cherry** = 1; †**c. tree**, cornel-tree -1796.

†**Cornemuse.** ME. [a. F., f. Rom. *corna*, F. *corne* horn + *musa* pipe.] A horn-pipe; an early form of bagpipe -1882.

Co·rneo-. 1. Comb. f. L. *corneus*, meaning 'with a horny admixture', as in **c.-calca·reous**; **c.-sili·cious**. 2. Comb. f. CORNEA, as in **c.-iritis**, inflammation of the eye affecting both cornea and iris; **c.-sclero·tic**, pertaining to the cornea and sclerotic coat.

Corneous (kǭ·ɹnĭəs), *a.* 1646. [f. L. *corneus* (f. *cornu* + -OUS.] Horny, horn-like, as *c. membrane*, etc. (Now only techn.)

Corner (kǭ·ɹnəɹ), *sb.* [ME. *corner*, a. AF. = OF. *cornier*, f. (ult.) L. *cornu* horn.] 1. *gen.* The meeting-place of converging sides or edges, forming an angular projection. Also *fig.* 2. A salient angle ME. 3. The space included between sides and edges at their meeting-place ME. 4. *transf.* An out-of-the-way, secluded place, that escapes notice ME. Also *fig.* 5. An end of the earth; a region; †a direction or quarter 1535. 6. *Bookbinding.* A triangular tool used in gold or blind tooling. 7. *Association Football* and *Hockey* (= *c.-kick*, *-hit*), a free kick or hit from the corner of the field obtained by the opposite side when a player sends the ball over his own goal-line 1887. †b. *Whist.* A point in a rubber -1824. 8. *Comm.* A speculative operation in which a combination buy up the whole, or the whole available supply, of any stock or commodity, so as to compel speculative sellers to buy of the corner-men at their own price 1857. 9. *attrib.* 1535.

1. The..hed of the c. WYCLIF *Ps.* cxvii[i]. 22. 2. Now is shee without, now in the streetes, and lieth in waite at euery c. *Prov.* vii. 12. 3. In a c. of the halle CHAUCER. Phr. *To drive into a c.*: to drive into straits. 4. For this thing was not done in a c. *Acts* xxvi. 26. Phr. *Hole and c.*: see HOLE. 5. Sits the winde in that c. *Much Ado* II. iii. 103.

Comb.: †**c.-cap**, a cap with four (or three) corners, worn by divines, etc.; also *fig.*; †**-cree·per**, *fig.* one whose proceedings are underhand and stealthy; **-kick** (see sense 7); **-tooth**, one of the four outer incisors in the jaw of a horse, which shoot in its fifth year.

Corner (kǭ·ɹnəɹ), *v.* ME. [f. the sb.] 1. *trans.* To furnish with corners. (Chiefly in *pa. pple.*) 2. To place in a corner ME. 3. To drive into a corner; to force into an awkward or desperate position; to bring to bay. Also *fig.* (*colloq.*) 1841. 4. *Comm.* To operate against by means of a CORNER (sense 8); to bring under the control of a corner. (Of *U.S.* origin.) 1857. 5. *intr.* To abut *on* at a corner; to meet at an angle (*U.S.*) 1863.

3. A rat will fight a man if cornered 1884. *fig.* Morally cornered YATES. 4. Those gentlemen who attempt to 'corner' cotton 1883.

Cornered (kǭ·ɹnəɹd), *ppl. a.* ME. [f. CORNER *sb.* + -ED [2].] 1. Having a corner or corners. 2. See CORNER *v.* 2, 3.

†*C. cap*: = CORNER-CAP.

Co·rner-man. 1873. 1. The end man of a row of negro minstrels. 2. A rough who lounges about street corners 1885. 3. *Comm.* One who makes a CORNER (sense 8). 1881.

Co·rner-stone. ME. 1. One of the stones forming the quoin or salient angle of a wall. Also *fig.* †2. The coving of a fire-place 1703.

1. See you yond Coin a' th' Capitol, yond corner stone *Cor.* v. iv. 2. *fig.* Why should we make an ambiguous word the c. of moral philosophy JOWETT.

Co·rnerwise, *adv.* 1474. [See -WISE.] So as to form a corner; diagonally.

Cornet (kǭ·ɹnĕt), *sb.*[1] ME. [a. OF. = It. *cornetto*, dim. of Rom. *corno* :—L. *cornu*.] 1. A wind-instrument: †a. In early times a horn. b. Now a brass instrument, with valves or pistons for producing notes additional to the natural harmonics; also called *cornet à piston*, and CORNOPEAN. c. The name given to several organ-stops 1660. 2. A piece of paper rolled in a conical form and twisted at the apex, used by grocers, etc. 1530. b. A small funnel-shaped pastry, usu. filled with cream; also, an ice-cream cone. †3. A farrier's instrument for blood-letting -1721. 4. *Metall.* In gold assaying: The small flat coil into which the gold-and-silver alloy is rolled after cupelling, before being boiled in nitric acid to free it from silver; the small coil of purified gold finally remaining. Also *cornette*. 1800. 5. *Dressmaking.* The cuff of a sleeve opening like the large end of a trumpet.

1. *Cornet à piston, à pistons*: = 1 b; also the player. *Comb.* **c.-stop** = 1 c. Hence †**Co·rneter**, one who plays the c. **Co·rnetist**, a solo c.-player.

Cornet (kǭ·ɹnĕt), *sb.*[2] Also *erron.* **coronet**(t. [a. F. *cornette*, dim. of *corne* :—Rom. *corna* f. sing., horn :—L. *cornua* n. pl.] 1. A kind of head-dress formerly worn by ladies. 2. A scarf anciently worn by Doctors of Physic or Law 1658. †3. The standard of a troop of cavalry -1838. †4. A troop of cavalry, so called from carrying such a standard -1838. 5. The fifth commissioned officer in a troop of cavalry, who carried the colours. (Not now in use.) 1579.

4. A certaine Captaine over a c. of horse-men HOLLAND. 5. I had notice that Cornet Joyce..had seized on the King's person LD. FAIRFAX. Hence **Co·rnetcy**, the position or rank of a c.

Cornette, var. of CORNET.

Corneule (kǭ·ɹnĭ,ŭl). 1839. [a. F. *cornéule*, dim. of *cornée*.] The outer transparent covering of the compound eyes of arthropods.

Co·rnfactor. 1699. A dealer in grain.

Co·rn-flag. 1578. [See FLAG.] A plant of the genus *Gladiolus*, N.O. *Iridaceæ*.

Co·rn-flour. 1851. Meal of ground Indian corn; also of rice or other grain.

Co·rn-flower. 1578. Any of various plants growing amongst corn; *esp.* the common Blue-bottle (*Centaurea Cyanus*), or the common Wild Poppy.

Co·rn-husk. *U.S.* 1808. The husk of coarse leaves enclosing the ear of Indian corn. So **Co·rn-husker**, one who or that which husks Indian corn. **Co·rn-husking.**

Cornic (kǭ·ɹnik), *a.* 1838. [f. L. *cornus* (see CORNEL) + -IC.] *Chem.* In *C. acid*, a synonym of CORNIN, q. v.

Cornice (kǭ·ɹnis), *sb.* Also **cornish**, etc. 1563. [ad. (ult.) It. *cornice*, in form identical with *cornice* :—L. *cornix*, *-icem* crow. The derivations from L. *corona* and Gr. κορωνίς lack evidence.] 1. *Arch.* A horizontal moulded projection which crowns a building or some part of a building; *spec.* the uppermost member of an entablature. 2. An ornamental moulding running round the wall of a room, etc.; a picture-moulding, or the like; also, the ornamental projection within which curtains are hung 1670. ||3. Applied to a path or road along the edge of a precipice. (Not an Eng. sense.) 1823.

Comb. **c.-ring**, the ring or moulding on a cannon next behind the muzzle-ring; = ASTRAGAL.

Hence **Co·rniced** *ppl. a.* having a c. †**Co·rnicement**, **Co·rnicing**, work consisting of a c. or cornices.

Cornicle (kǭ·ɹnik'l). 1646. [ad. L. *corniculum*, dim. of *cornu*.] A little horn (*obs.*); a small horn-like process, as the horns of a snail, etc. Hence **Corni·culate** *a.* horned; having horn-like projections.

†**Corni·culer.** ME. [ad. L. *cornicularius*.] An assistant officer -1447.

Corniferous (kǫɹni·fĕrəs), *a.* 1650. [f. L. *cornifer*.] †1. Producing or having horns. 2. *Geol.* Producing or containing hornstone 1873.

Cornify (kǭ·ɹnifəi), *v.* 1611. [f. L. *cornu* + -FY.] †1. *trans.* To fit with horns; to cuckold. 2. *Phys.* and *Zool.* To turn into horn or horny substance 1859. Hence **Cornifica·tion.**

Corni·gerous, *a.* 1646. [f. L. *corniger* + -OUS.] Bearing horns; producing horn.

Cornin (kǭ·ɹnin). 1831. [f. L. *cornus* (see CORNEL) + -IN.] *Chem.* A bitter crystalline substance obtained from the root of *Cornus florida*; also called *cornic acid*.

Corning (kǭ·ɹniŋ), *vbl. sb.* 1560. [f. CORN *v.* + -ING [1].] 1. Granulation. 2. Pickling with salt 1655.

Comb. **c.-house**, the part of a powder-mill where the granulating is done.

Cornish (kǭ·ɹniʃ), *a.*[2] (*sb.*) 1547. [f. first element in *Cornwall* (OE. *Cornwealas* = Corn-Welsh) + -ISH. *Corn* is prob. Celtic *corn*, *cornu* 'horn', headland.] 1. Of or belonging to Cornwall; applied *esp.* to the people and language; hence **Cornishman.** 2. *sb.* The ancient language of Cornwall, a member of the Brythonic branch of the Celtic languages 1547.

C. chough (see CHOUGH); **C. boiler**, the cylindrical flue-boiler invented by Smeaton; **C. engine**, a form of single-acting condensing steam-engine, used for pumping up water, first used in Cornwall; **C. pump**, a pump worked by a C. engine.

Co·rn-law, Corn Law. 1766. A law regulating the trade in corn, *esp.* its import and export. In England used spec. of the laws restricting the importation of cereals which were repealed in 1846. (In this application usually spelt with capitals.)

†**Co·rn-master.** 1580. One who has corn to sell -1667.

Cornmuse, var. of CORNEMUSE.

||**Corno** (korno). Pl. **corni.** 1818. [It. :—L. *cornu*.] A HORN, *esp.* the French horn. *C. inglese* = COR ANGLAIS; *c. di bassetto*, the basset-horn; also name of an organ-stop.

Cornopean (kǫɹnōu·piăn). 1837. *Mus.* 1. A name for the *cornet à piston*; see CORNET *sb.*[1] 2. An 8 ft. reed-stop on an organ 1840.

Co·rn-rent. 1809. A rent paid in corn, or one determined each year by the price of corn.

Co·rn-sa·lad. 1597. A plant, *Valeriana olitoria*, or Lamb's-Lettuce, found wild in corn-fields; used for salad.

Co·rn-snake. 1676. A large harmless snake, *Coluber guttatus*, common in the southern U.S.

Co·rn-stalk. 1816. 1. A stalk of (in *U.S.* Indian) corn. 2. *fig.* A tall lithe person; hence, a nickname, *esp.* for persons of European descent born in N. S. Wales 1865.

Cornstone (kǭ·ɹnstōun). 1822. [f. CORN *sb.*[1]] *Geol.* An earthy concretionary limestone bed found in the Old Red Sandstone formation in parts of Britain. Also *attrib.*

||**Cornu** (kǭ·ɹniu). Pl. **cornua.** 1691. [L.] A horn: applied in *Anat.* to processes likened to a horn, as the *cornua uteri*, into which the Fallopian tubes open, etc. Hence **Co·rnual** *a.* of or pertaining to cornua.

Cornucopia (kǭɹniu,kōu·piă). Also **-copiæ.** 1592. [A late L. form of *cornu copiæ*; the symbol of fruitfulness and plenty.] 1. The horn of plenty; in art, a goat's horn overflowing with flowers, fruit, and corn; also, an ornamental receptacle of similar shape. 2. *fig.* An overflowing store 1611.

2. Her common-place book..Of scandal..a c. SWIFT. Hence **Cornuco·pian** *a.* pertaining to a c.; overflowingly abundant.

†**Cornu·te.** 1605. [ad. L. *cornutus*, f. *cornu*.] 1. A retort for distilling -1736. 2. A forked pennon 1625. 3. One who is 'horned'; a cuckold -1707. 4. *Logic.* A 'horned' argument, dilemma; the sophism 'Cornutus' -1739.

4. To take for an example of this fallacy, the κεράτινος or Cornutus :—it is asked ;—Have you cast your horns? [etc.] HAMILTON. So **Cornu·te** *v.* to cuckold (*arch.*). **Cornu·ted** *ppl. a.* horned; horn-shaped; cuckolded. †||**Cornu·to**, a cuckold. †**Cornu·tor.**

Cornutus; see CORNUTE *sb.* 4.

Corny (kǭ·ɹni), *a.*[1] 1580. [f. CORN *sb.*[1] + -Y [1].] 1. Of or pertaining to corn. 2. Of ale: ?Tasting strong of the malt. Now *dial.* ME. 3. Producing corn; abounding in grains of corn 1580. 4. Tipsy; = CORNED (*dial.*) 1825.

1. Up stood the cornie Reed MILT. *P. L.* VII. 321.

2. A draughte of c. ale CHAUCER. 3. That rich c. country CARLYLE. The c. chaff 1826.

†Co·rny, *a.*[2] *rare.* 15... [Cf. L. *corneus.*] Hard as horn, horny –1755.

Corny (kǫ·ɹni), *a.*[3] 1707. [f. CORN *sb.*[2]] Having corns on the feet; pertaining to corns.

Coro-; see COR-[2].

Corody, etc.; see CORRODY, etc.

Corolla (korǫ·lă). Pl. **corollas.** 1671. [a. L., dim. of *corona.*] †1. A little crown, coronet. 2. *Bot.* The whorl of leaves (petals) forming the inner envelope of the flower; usually 'coloured' (*i.e.* not green). Cf. CALYX. 1753. Also in *comb.* var. **†Co·rol.** Hence **Corolla·ceous** *a.* of the nature of a c. So **Coro·llar** *a.* **Co·rollate** *a.* having or resembling a c. So **Co·rollated** *a.* **Corolli·ferous** *a.* corollate. **Coro·lline** *a.* pertaining to the c. **Coro·llist,** one who classifies plants according to their corollas (*rare*). **Coro·llule** = COROLLET.

Corollary (korǫ·lări, kǫ·rǫ̆lări). ME. [ad. L. *corollarium* money paid for a garland, gratuity, corollary, f. *corolla*; see prec.] 1. In *Geom.*, etc. A proposition appended to another which has been demonstrated, and following obviously from it; hence *gen.* an immediate inference, deduction, consequence. 2. *transf.* A practical consequence, result 1674. †3. An appendix; a finishing or crowning part –1717. †4. Something additional; a surplus; a supernumerary –1681.

1. This is but a c. from what goes before WOLLASTON. 2. The art of Writing, of which Printing is a..c. CARLYLE. 4. Now come my Ariell, bring a Corolary, Rather then want a Spirit *Temp.* IV. i. 57.

Corollary, *a. rare.* 1449. [ad. L. *corollarius*; see prec.] 1. Of the nature of a corollary. 2. *Bot.* Corolline 1882.

†Coro·llet. 1794. [f. COROLLA + -ET.] *Bot.* The floret in an aggregate flower –1823.

Corollifloral (korǫ·liflōᵊ·răl), *a.* 1845. [f. mod.L. *Corolliflorœ* (f. *corolla* + *flos, flor-*) + -AL.] *Bot.* Of or belonging to the *Corolliflorœ*, a subclass of dicotyledonous plants having calyx and corolla, the petals being united and the stamens usually attached to the corolla. (See De Candolle.) So **Corolliflo·rous.**

Corollitic (kǫrǫli·tik), *a.* 1819. [ad. F. *corollitique*, f. L. *corolla* (Littré).] *Arch.* Of columns: Having foliated shafts. vars. **Carolitic, -ytic.**

‖**Corona** (korōᵘ·nă). Pl. **-næ** (-nī), rarely **-as.** 1563. [L.] 1. A small circle or disc of light (usually prismatic) appearing round the sun or moon. Also applied to other similar phenomena. 2. *Astron.* The halo of radiating white light seen around the disc of the moon in a total eclipse of the sun; now known to belong to the sun 1851. 3. A circular chandelier suspended from the roof of a church; more fully *corona lucis* 1825. 4. *Arch.* A member of the cornice, above the bed-moulding and below the cymatium, usually of considerable projection; also called *drip* or *larmier* 1563. 5. *Anat.*, etc. Applied to parts resembling or likened to a crown; also to the upper portion of any part, as of a tooth; cf. CROWN 1712. 6. *Bot.* a. A crown-like appendage on the inner side of the corolla in some flowers, as the daffodil and lychnis. b. The *medullary sheath* in the stems of Dicotyledons and Gymnosperms. c. The crown of the root. 1753. 7. (*Astron.*) *C. australis*, *C. borealis*: the Southern and Northern Crown, consisting of elliptical rings of stars.

Coronach (kǫ·rănaχ). *Sc.* and *Ir.* 1500. [a. Ir. *coranach*, Gael. *corranach*, f. *comh-* together + *rànach* outcry.] †1. *gen.* A shouting of many –1680. 2. *spec.* A funeral song or dirge in the Highlands of Scotland and in Ireland 1530.

2. Eachan Macrimmon is playing a c. as it were for a chief W. C. SMITH.

Coronal (kǫ·rǫ̆năl), *sb.* ME. [app. ad. AF. **coronal*, f. *coroune*. In 4 prob. ad. L. *coronalis.*] 1. A circlet for the head; a coronet. Also *transf.* and *fig.* 2. A wreath for the head; a garland 1579. Also *transf.* †3. The head of a tilting lance, ending in three or four short spreading points. (Often *cronall, cronel, curnall.*) –1470. †4. *Anat.* The frontal bone; cf. next –1758.

1. On hir head a coronall all of greet pearles HOLINSHED. 2. Of rosemary a simple c. T. MARTIN. Hence **Co·ronalled** *a.* adorned with a coronet.

Coronal (korōᵘ·năl, kǫ·rǫ̆năl), *a.* 1543. [a. F., or ad. L. *coronalis*, f. *corona.*] †1. Pertaining to a crown, or to coronation –1813. 2. *Anat.*, etc. a. *C. suture*: the suture separating the frontal bone from the parietal bones. So *c. region* (of the forehead), etc. *C. bone*: the frontal bone. 1543. b. Of or pertaining to the crown of the head 1828. c. Pertaining to the corona (see CORONA) 1846. 3. *Bot.* Pertaining or similar to a corona (see CORONA) 1870.

1. The Law and his C. Oath requires his undeniable assent to what Laws the Parlament agree upon MILTON. 2. c. So abundant is the c. light..during totality 1871. Hence **†Coronally** *adv.* in the manner of a crown or coronet.

Coronary (kǫ·rǫ̆nări), *a.* 1610. [ad. L. *coronarius*, f. *corona.*] †1. Of the nature of or resembling a crown; pertaining to or forming a crown –1659. †2. Suitable for garlands or wreaths –1682. 3. *Anat.* Encircling like a crown, as the *c. arteries* and *veins* of the heart, etc. 1679. 4. *absol.* as *sb.* = CORONET 4. 1847.

1. *C. gold* [tr. L. *coronarium aurum*]: 'a present of gold collected in the provinces for a victorious general; orig. expended for a golden crown' (Lewis and Short).

†Co·ronate, *pa. pple.* 1470. [ad. L. *coronatus.*] Crowned –1513.

Coronate (kǫ·rǫ̆nĕt, -eɪt), *a.* 1846. [f. as prec.; see CORONA.] *Bot.* and *Zool.* = CORONATED.

Coronate (kǫ·rǫ̆neɪt), *v. rare.* 1623. [f. as prec.] To crown. (See also next.)

Coronated (kǫ·rǫ̆neɪtėd), *ppl. a.* 1676. [f. as prec.] †1. Of flowers: Arranged in a whorl. 2. *Bot.* and *Zool.* Furnished with a corona; *spec.* in *Conchol.* of spiral shells which have their whorls surmounted by a row of tubercles 1698. †3. = CORONETED 1767.

Coronation (kǫrǫ̆nē̆ɪ·ʃən). ME. [a. OF. *coronacion, -ation*; see CORONATE *v.*] 1. The action of crowning; the ceremony of investing with a crown as an emblem of royal dignity. Also *transf.* 2. *fig.* Crowning of a work; completion 1582. 3. *attrib.* 1587.

3. *C. oath*, that taken by a sovereign at his c.

†Corone. Early f. CROWN, obs. by 1500.

Coronel(l, obs. f. COLONEL, CORONAL.

Coroner (kǫ·rǫ̆nəɹ). ME. [a. AF. *coruner*, *corouner*, f. *corune*, *coroune* CROWN, the original title being *custos placitorum coronæ* guardian of the pleas of the crown. The ending is = F. *-ier*, L. *-arius*, but was early confused with that of verbal agents in *-er*, whence L. *coronator* (in *Magna Carta*).] An officer of a county, district, or municipality (formerly also of the royal household), originally charged with maintaining the private property of the crown; in mod. times his chief function is to hold inquest on the bodies of those supposed to have died by violence or accident.

Coroner's inquest: the investigation as to the cause of death held by the *Coroner's Court*, consisting of the c. and twelve jurymen summoned for the inquest. Hence **Co·ronership,** the office of a c.

Coronet (kǫ·rǫ̆nėt), *sb.* 1494. [a. OF. *coronete, -ette*, dim. of *corone*, later *couronne*, CROWN. Refash. as CROWNET, q. v.] 1. A small or inferior crown; *spec.* a crown denoting a dignity inferior to that of the sovereign. 2. A fillet or wreath for the head; *esp.* a decorative plate or band of metal, or the like, worn by women round the brow, as part of a head-dress 1590. 3. = CORONA 6a. 1657. 4. *Farriery.* The lowest part of the pastern of a horse 1696. 5. = CORONAL *sb.* 3. 1731.

1. I sawe Marke Antony offer him a Crowne, yet 'twas not a Crowne neyther, 'twas one of these Coronets *Jul. C.* I. ii. 239. 2. And on her brow..A c. of pearls S. ROGERS.

Hence **Co·ronet** *v.* to confer a c. upon; to adorn as with a c. (*rare*). **Co·roneted, -etted** *ppl. a.* **Coronetty, -ee** *a. Her.* ornamented on the upper side c.-wise.

Coro·niform, *a. rare.* 1776. [f. L. *corona*; see -FORM.] Crown-shaped.

‖**Coronis** (korōᵘ·nis). 1670. [L., a. Gr. κορωνίς curved stroke or flourish at the end of a book or chapter, hence *fig.*] †1. The end. 2. *Greek Gram.* A sign ('), placed over a vowel as a mark of contraction or crasis; *e.g.* κἀγαθός for καὶ ἀγαθός 1833.

Coronium (korōᵘ·niǝm). 1890. [f. CORONA 2.] An element supposed to exist in a gaseous state in the sun's corona. (Cf. HELIUM.)

†Co·ronize, *v.* 1592. [f. L. *corona.*] To crown, adorn with a coronet or coronal –1623.

Coro·nograph. 1885. [f. *corono-*, comb. f. CORONA + -GRAPH, Gr. -γραφος.] *Astron.* An instrument for photographing the sun's corona in full sunlight. Hence **Coronographic** *a.*

Coronoid (kǫ·rǫ̆noid, korōᵘ·noˌid), *a.* 1741. [f. Gr. κορώνη crow; see -OID.] Applied to processes that are curved like a crow's beak, and to parts in connexion with these; as the *c. process* of the lower jaw, and that of the ulna, and the *c. fossa* of the humerus.

Coronule (korōᵘ·niul). 1806. [ad. L. *coronula* (also used), dim. of *corona.*] 1. *Bot.* A small crown or coronet surmounting a seed, etc. 2. *Zool.* A kind of barnacle of the genus *Coronula* of Cirripeds; parasitic on Cetacea.

Coroplasty, Corotomy; see COR-[2].

Corosif, obs. f. CORROSIVE.

Coroun(e, corowne, obs. ff. CROWN.

‖**Corozo** (korōᵘ·so). 1760. [Native name.] A South American tree, *Phytelephas macrocarpa*, allied to the palms; the hardened albumen of its seed (the *C.-nut* or *ivory-nut*) furnishes the substance called vegetable ivory.

Corp, Sc. and n. Eng. dial. f. CORPSE.

Corporal (kǭ·ɹpŏrăl), *a.* ME. [a. OF., later *corporel*, ad. L. *corporalem*, f. *corpus.*] 1. Of or belonging to the body; bodily. †2. Of the nature of matter; corporeal, physical –1726. †3. Large of body –1630. †4. Solid –1667.

1. The c. or bodelye sight CAXTON. Corporall liberty HOBBES. 2. What seem'd corporall Melted, as breath into the Wind *Macb.* I. iii. 81. 3. A sufficient corporall Burgher 1630. Phrases. *C. oath* [med. L. *corporale juramentum*; cf. BODILY *Oath*]: an oath ratified by corporally touching a sacred object, *esp.* the gospels, but sometimes the host, or relics; dist. from a verbal oath. (The view that the attributive 'corporal' refers to the host is not historically tenable.) *C. punishment*: punishment inflicted on the body (as opp. to a fine, etc.). Now usually confined to flogging. *C. works of mercy*: works of mercy to the bodies of men, as, to feed the hungry, etc. Hence **Co·rporally** *adv.*

Corporal (kǭ·ɹpŏrăl), *sb.*[1] OE. [ad. med.L. *corporalis* (*palla*), *corporale* (*pallium*).] *Eccl.* †1. An ancient eucharistic vestment –1660. 2. A linen cloth upon which the consecrated elements are placed during celebration, and with which they are subseq. covered. Called also *c.-cloth.* ME.

Corporal (kǭ·ɹpŏrăl), *sb.*[2] 1579. [a. 16th c. F. *corporal*, var. of *capporal*, *caporal* (Littré), ad. It. *caporale*. Prob. f. It. *corpo*, L. *corpor-* body (*i.e.* of troops), subseq. affected by *capo.*] 1. A non-commissioned military officer ranking under a sergeant. 2. *Naut.* Formerly, a petty officer on board ship, who taught the sailors the use of small-arms; now, a superior petty officer, who attends solely to police matters under the master-at-arms 1626.

1. *Corporal's guard*: a small armed detachment under a c. Hence *fig.* a small body of supporters. †*C. of the field*: in the 16th and 17th c. a kind of aide-de-camp to the sergeant-major. Hence **Co·rporalship,** †a body of soldiers under a c.; the office of a c.

Corporality (kǭɹpŏræ·lĭti). ME. [ad. late L. *corporalitas.*] 1. The quality of being corporal (see CORPORAL *a.* 2); materiality. 2. Embodied existence or condition 1642. †3. Corporate organization of a society, town, etc.; a CORPORATION –1603. 4. *pl.* Corporal matters. Cf. *temporalities.* 1748.

Corporas (kǭ·ɹpŏrăs). [ME. *corporaus*, a. OF. (earlier *corporals*), nom. sing. of *corporal.*] = CORPORAL *sb.*[1] 2.

Corporate (kǭ·ɹpŏrĕt), *ppl. a.* ME. [ad. L. *corporatus*, f. *corporare.*]

A. as *pa. pple.* 1. United into one body (*arch.*). †2. Embodied 1555.

B. *adj.* †1. Corpulent –1533. †2. Pertaining to the body –1613. †3. Embodied; material –1865. 4. Forming a body politic, or corporation 1512. Also *transf.* 5. Of or belonging to a body politic, or corporation, or to a body of persons 1607.

4. *C. body, body c.*: see BODY *sb.* *C. town*: a town possessing municipal rights, and acting by means of a corporation. 5. *C. name*: the name by which a corporation engages in legal acts. Hence **Co·rpo-**

rately *adv.* †as regards the body; in a c. capacity. **Co·rporateness.**

Corporate (kǭ·ɹpŏreɪt), *v. arch.* 1531. [f. L. *corporat-* ppl. stem.] †1. *trans.* To incorporate –1631. 2. To combine in one body 1545. 3. *intr.* To unite in one body (*rare*) 1647.

Corporation (kǭɹpŏrēɪ·ʃən). ME. [ad. L. *corporationem* (Tertullian).] †1. The action of incorporating, the condition of being incorporated –1542. 2. A body of persons 1534. 3. *Law.* A body corporate legally authorized to act as a single individual; an artificial person created by royal charter, prescription, or legislative act, and having the capacity of perpetual succession 1611. 4. A trade-guild, a city 'company'. (Now only legal or formal.) 1530. 5. The body; the abdomen. *colloq.* and *vulgar.* 1753. Also *attrib.*

3. *C. aggregate*: one comprising many individuals, as the mayor and burgesses of a town, etc. *C. sole*: one consisting of only one person and his successors, as a king, bishop, etc. *Municipal c.*: the mayor, aldermen, and councillors of a borough or incorporated town or city.

Corporative (kǭ·ɹpŏrătiv), *a.* 1833. [ad. L. *corporativus.*] = CORPORATE *a.* 5.

Corporator (kǭ·ɹpŏreɪtəɹ). 1784. [f. L. *corporare* to embody.] A member of a (municipal) corporation.

†**Corporature.** 1555. [ad. L. *corporatura*, f. as prec.] 1. Physique –1696. 2. = CORPORALITY 1. 1647.

Corporeal (kǭɹpōə·riăl), *a.* (*sb.*) 1610. [f. L. *corporeus* (f. *corpus, corpor-*) + -AL.] 1. Of the nature of the animal body as opp. to the spirit; physical; bodily; mortal. 2. Material 1619. 3. *Law.* Tangible; consisting of material objects; *esp.* in *C. hereditament* 1670. †4. In sense of CORPORAL –1831.

1. To couple a spiritual grace with matters of c. repast FULLER. 2. Are genera and species c. or incorporeal REID.

B. *sb. pl.* Things material; things pertaining to the human body (*rare*).

Hence †**Corpo·realism,** materialism. †**Corpo·realist,** a materialist. **Corporea·lity,** the quality or state of being c.; materiality. **Corpo·really** *adv.* in or as to the body; bodily. **Corpo·realness,** c. quality or state (*rare*).

Corpo·realize, *v.* 1797. [See -IZE.] To render corporeal; to materialize. Hence **Corporealization.**

Corporeity (kǭɹpŏrī·ĭti). 1621. [ad. med.L. *corporeitas*, f. *corporeus*; see CORPOREAL and -ITY. Cf. F. *corporéité.*] 1. The quality of being, or having, a material body; *concr.* bodily substance. †2. Carnality –1681. 3. Material nature or state. †Occas. = Density. 1664.

1. The notion of a Spirit, or substance void of c. HALE. 3. His [Newton's] views of colours were entirely independent of his belief in the c. of light 1880.

†**Corpo·rify,** *v.* 1644. [f. L. *corpor-* body; see -FY.] 1. To cause to assume a material form –1707. 2. To incorporate –1707. Hence †**Corpo:rifica·tion.** So †**Co·rporize** *v.*

Corposant (kǭ·ɹpŏzænt). 1561. [ad. Pg. *corpo santo.*] The ball of light sometimes seen about the masts or yard-arms of a ship during a storm; St. Elmo's fire.

Corps (kōəɹ). Pl. **corps** (kōəɹz). ME. [See CORPSE.] †1. Earlier var. of CORPSE, q. v. 2. *Mil.* A division of an army, forming a tactical unit; a body of troops regularly organized; a body of men assigned to a special service 1711. Also *fig.* 3. *gen.* A body of persons associated in a common organization, or acting under a common direction 1730.

1. ‖*Corps d'armée* (Fr.): a main division of an army in the field, an army-corps. 3. The whole dramatic c. CARLYLE. ‖*Corps diplomatique* (Fr.): the diplomatic c. or body accredited to a particular Court or Capital. ‖*Corps de ballet* (Fr.): the company of dancers in a ballet.

‖**Corps de garde.** 1587. [F.; often corrupted to *Court o' guard*, COURT OF GUARD.] 1. The small body of soldiers stationed on guard or as sentinels. 2. A guard-room or guard-house 1587.

Corpse (kǭɹps, kǭɹs), *sb.* [ME. *corps*, orig. a var. of ME. *cors* (see CORSE), a. OF. *cors*:— L. *corpus.* In Eng., at first, as in Fr., the *p* was mute. The final *e* (perh. taken from the mod. pl. *corpses*) now differentiates the word from CORPS.] †1. (rarely *corpse.*) The body of a man or animal; a (living) body; a person –1707. 2. *esp.* The dead body of a man (or formerly any animal) ME. †3. (rarely *corpse.*) Collective whole or mass; BODY (of law, science, etc.) *Corps of Law* = *Corpus juris.* –1651. 4. (*corps*, rarely *corpse.*) The endowment of an office, †civil or ecclesiastical; *esp.* of a prebend. (med.L. *corpus prebendæ.*) 1580.

2. Then make a Ring about the Corpes of Cæsar *Jul. C.* III. ii. 162. On the same day his Corps (pl. = 'remains') were buried at Westminster FULLER. 4. Other portions of the estates..became the corpses of various prebends FREEMAN.

Comb.: **c.-gate** (*dial.* **-yat, -yett,** etc.) = LICH-GATE; **-light** = CORPSE-CANDLE 2.

Corpse (kǭɹps), *v. slang.* 1874. [f. prec. sb.] 1. To kill (*vulgar*) 1884. 2. *Actors' slang.* To confuse or put out (an actor), or spoil (a piece of acting), by some blunder.

Co·rpse-can:dle. 1694. [f. as prec.] †1. 'A thick candle formerly used at lake-wakes' (Halliwell). 2. A lambent flame seen in a churchyard, and believed to portend a funeral 1694.

Corpulence (kǭ·ɹpiŭlĕns), **Corpulency** (kǭ·ɹpiŭlĕnsi). 1477. [a. F., ad. L. *corpulentia.*] †1. Habit of body; size –1491. 2. Bulk of body; obesity 1581. †3. Material quality or substance; density (*rare*) –1691.

3. The heaviness and c. of the water RAY.

Corpulent (kǭ·ɹpiŭlĕnt), *a.* ME. [a. F., ad. L. *corpulentus*, f. *corpus.*] †1. Solid, dense, gross –1650. 2. Fleshy, fat ME. †3. Corporeal; material –1643.

2. A goodly portly man yfaith, and a c. 1 *Hen. IV*, II. iv. 464.

‖**Corpus** (kǭ·ɹpɒs). Pl. **corpora** (kǭ·ɹpŏră). ME. [L.] 1. The body of a man or animal. (Now joc. or grotesque.) 2. *Phys.* A structure of a special character or function in the animal body, as *c. callosum*, the transverse commissure connecting the cerebral hemispheres; so also *corpora quadrigemina, striata*, etc. of the brain; *c. spongiosum* and *corpora cavernosa* of the penis, etc. 3. A complete collection of writings or the like 1727. 4. The body or material substance of anything; principal, as opp. to interest or income 1844.

Phrases. *C. delicti*: 'the sum or aggregate of the ingredients which make a given fact a breach of a given law' (Austin). *C. juris*: a body of law. †*By c. bones*: ? a confusion of *c. Domini* and *Goddes bones.*

‖**Corpus Christi** (kǭ·ɹpɒs kri·stəi, -ti). ME. [L.; = Christ's body.] *R.C.Ch.* The feast of the Blessed Sacrament or Body of Christ, observed on the Thursday after Trinity Sunday.

Corpuscle (kǭ·ɹpɒs'l, kǭɹpɒ·s'l). 1660. [ad. L. *corpusculum*, dim. of *corpus.*] 1. A minute body or particle of matter. Occas. = *atom*, or *molecule.* 2. *Phys.* Any minute body (usu. of microscopic size), forming a distinct part of the organism; *esp.* (*pl.*) minute rounded or discoidal bodies, constituting a large part of the blood in vertebrates 1741. 3. *Bot.* = CORPUSCULUM 1 b.

2. Such corpuscles of protoplasm as are provided with a nucleus are called cells BELL.

Corpuscular (kǭɹpɒ·skiŭlăɹ), *a.* 1667. [f. L. *corpusculum*; see prec. and -AR.] 1. Pertaining to, of the nature of, or consisting of, corpuscles 1671. 2. Concerned with atoms; atomic; *esp.* in *C. philosophy, theory* 1667.

2. *C. theory* of light = EMISSION theory: see CORPUSCULE. Hence **Corpu:scula·rian** *a.* = CORPUSCULAR 1; *sb.* an adherent of the c. or atomic philosophy, or of the c. theory of light.

Corpuscule (kǭɹpɒ·skiul). 1816. [a. F., ad. L. *corpusculum.*] = CORPUSCLE.

According to the former [theory], light consists in 'Corpuscules', or excessively minute material particles darted out in all directions from the luminous body HERSCHEL.

Corpusculous (kǭɹpɒ·skiŭləs), *a.* 1871. [f. L. *corpusculum* + -OUS.] Characterized by the presence of corpuscles.

‖**Corpu·sculum.** Pl. **-ula.** 1650. [L.; dim. of *corpus.*] 1. = CORPUSCLE 1. b. *Bot.* The central cells of the archegonia of Gymnosperms 1844. †2. A small body of men –1659.

†**Corra·de,** *v.* 1619. [ad. L. *corradere*, f. *cor-* = *com-* + *radere.*] 1. *trans.* To scrape together (*lit.* and *fig.*) –1659. 2. To scrape, wear down by scraping 1646. Hence †**Corra·sion.**

Corradial (kǭrēɪ·diăl), *a. rare.* 1825. [See COR-¹.] Radiating to or from the same centre.

Corradiate (kǭrēɪ·dieɪt), *v. rare.* [See COR-¹.] *intr.* To radiate together; to unite their rays. So **Corradia·tion** (*rare*).

Corral (koræ·l), *sb.* 1582. [Sp.; = an enclosed place.] a. An enclosure for horses, cattle, etc.; a fold; a stockade. Cf. KRAAL. Also *transf.* b. An enclosure formed of wagons in an encampment, for defence against attack 1847. c. An enclosure for capturing wild animals 1845.

Corral (koræ·l), *v.* Chiefly *U.S.* 1847. [f. prec.] 1. *trans.* To form (wagons) into a corral 1851. 2. To shut up in, or as in, a corral 1847. 3. *U.S. slang.* To lay hold of, 'collar' 1868.

2. Here they coralled us [prisoners] to the number of seven or eight thousand 1890.

Corrasive; see CORROSIVE.

Correal (kǭrī·ăl), *a.* 1875. [f. L. *correus*, f. *cor-, con-* + *reus* one under obligation.] *Rom. Law.* Under joint obligation. So **Correa·lity,** c. quality or state.

Correct (kǭre·kt), *v. Pa. pple.* **corrected,** also, 5–8 **correct.** ME. [f. L. *correct-, corrigere*, f. *cor-* = *com-* + *regere.*] 1. *trans.* To set right, amend. Occas., loosely, to point out or mark the errors or faults in. Also *absol.* 2. To set right, rectify (an error or fault) ME. 3. To set right, amend (a person); to admonish or rebuke, or to point out the errors or faults of, in order to amendment ME. 4. To punish for faults of character or conduct (prop., in order to amendment); to chastise ME. 5. To bring or reduce to order 1594. 6. To counteract or neutralize; to remove or prevent the ill effect of 1578. 7. *Math.* To bring (a result) into accordance with certain standard conditions 1774. 8. *Optics.* To eliminate the aberration of a lens, etc. 1831.

1. To c. a drawing D'ISRAELI, proof-sheets MORLEY. 3. If I speak incorrectly you can c. me LAMB. 4. Vagrants..are oftener corrected than amended FULLER. To c. an abuse JUNIUS. 5. His pruning-hook corrects the vines POPE. 6. The heart..corrects the folly of the head FROUDE. Hence **Corre·ctable** *a.* (*rare*). †**Corre·ctedly,** correctly.

Correct (kǭre·kt), *pa. pple.* and *a.* 1460. [ad. L. *correctus*; see CORRECT *v.*]

†A. *pa. pple.* Corrected; punished, amended –1712.

B. *adj.* 1. In accordance with an acknowledged standard, *esp.* of style, or of behaviour; proper 1676. 2. In accordance with fact, truth, or reason; right 1705. 3. Of persons: Adhering exactly to a standard 1734.

1. The c. thing FORD. 2. Always use the most c. editions 1711. Mr. Hunt is..quite c. in saying [etc.] MACAULAY. *C. card*: see CARD *sb.*² 3. C. with spirit, eloquent with ease POPE. Hence **Corre·ct-ly** *adv.*, **-ness.**

Correction (kǭre·kʃən). ME. [a. F., ad. L. *correctionem.*] 1. The action of correcting or setting right; amendment. Hence, loosely, pointing out or marking of errors. 2. (with *a* and *pl.*) An act or instance of emendation 1528. †3. Reprehension, rebuke, reproof –1814. 4. The correcting by disciplinary punishment; chastisement; flogging (*arch.*) ME. 5. The counteracting of the ill effect of 1477. 6. *Math.* and *Phys.* The addition or subtraction of some quantity to or from a result, to bring it into accordance with certain standard conditions; the quantity so added or subtracted 1743. 7. *Optics.* The counteraction of the aberration in a lens, etc. 1856. †8. Correctness 1759.

1. The c. of the calendar WHEWELL. *C. of the press*: i. e. of printers' errors. *Under c.*: subject to c.; an expression of deference. 3. All Scripture..is profitable..for c. 2 *Tim.* iii. 16. 4. Their ordinary c. is to beate them with cudgels CAPT. SMITH. *House of c.*: a building for the detention and punishment of offenders; a bridewell. Hence **Corre·ctional** *a.* of or pertaining to c.; corrective. †**Corre·ctioner,** one who administers c. SHAKS.

Correctitude (kǭre·ktitiŭd). 1893. [f. CORRECT, after *rectitude.*] Correctness of conduct.

Corrective (kǭre·ktiv). 1531. [a. F. *correctif, -ive*, f. L. *correct-* ppl. stem + -IVE.]

A. *adj.* Having the property of correcting, counteracting something hurtful, or restoring to a healthy condition 1533.

The penalty..is..c., not penal 1853. *C. justice*, a tr. of Aristotle's διορθωτικὸν δίκαιον (see COMMUTATIVE); used by Hooker in sense 'punitive'.

B. *sb.* [The adj. used *ellipt.*] 1. That which is corrective or counteractive. Also *fig.* 1610. 2. Something that tends to set right what is wrong, to counteract an evil, etc. 1734. 3. Something that acts so as to correct what is erroneous 1677.

1. We take..some varieties of fruit as a c. HOLLAND. 2. Patriotism is a c. of superstition BUCKLE. 3. A c. of error JOWETT.

Hence Corre·ctive·ly *adv.*, -ness.

Corrector (kǫre·ktəɹ). ME. [ad. (ult.) L. *correctorem.*] 1. One who or that which corrects. 2. An official title = director, controller ME.

1. The c. of the press, or *reader* URE. To giue them [children] maisters, or correcters NORTH. The ..proper c. of opium..is vineger TIMME. So **Corre·ctress, †-trice, †-trix,** a female c.

Correctory (kǫre·ktŏri). ? *Obs.* 1607. [f. prec.; see -ORY.] *adj.* Of the nature of a corrector or correction 1620. †*sb.* A corrective -1620.

‖**Corregido·r.** 1594. [Sp. *corregidor* (koreɣidō·r); cf. CORRECTOR.] The chief magistrate of a Spanish town.

Correlate (kǫ·rĭleit), *sb.* 1643. [f. COR- + L. *relatum.*] Either of the terms of a relation, viewed in reference to the other 1644.

Correlate (kǫ·rĭlĕt), *a. rare.* 1842. [f. COR- + L. *relatus*, pa. pple. of *referre.*] Mutually related; involving correlation.

Correlate (kǫrĭlē¹·t), *v.* 1742. [f. COR- + RELATE.] 1. *intr.* To have a mutual relation; to be correlative (*with* or *to* another). 2. *trans.* To place in or bring into correlation 1849. 3. *pass.* To have correlation (*with*, occ. *to*) 1862.

1. Ethical obligation correlates..with ethical right GROTE. 2. To c. interglacial beds J. GEIKIE. Hence **Correla·table** *a.*

Correlation (kǫrĭlē¹·ʃən). 1561. [See COR-.] 1. The condition of being correlated; mutual relation of two or more things (implying intimate or necessary connexion). 2. *Biol.* Mutual relation of association between different structures, characteristics, etc. in an animal or plant 1859. 3. *Geom.* The reciprocal relation between propositions, figures, etc. derivable from each other by interchanging the words *point* and *plane*, or *point* and *line*; cf. CORRELATIVE *a.* 2. 4. The action of correlating 1879.

1. How in animall natures, even colours hold correspondencies, and mutual correlations SIR T. BROWNE.

Phr. *C. of forces* (in *Physics*): the mutual relation that exists between the various forms of force or energy, by virtue of which any one form is convertible into an equivalent amount of any other. (Cf. *conservation of energy*, s. v. CONSERVATION.)

Correlative (kǫre·lătiv). 1530. [f. L. *cor-* = *com-* + *relativus*; cf. F. *correlatif, -ive.*]

A. *adj.* 1. Having, or involving, a reciprocal relation. Const. *with*, rarely *to*. 1690. 2. *Geom.* Said of propositions, figures, etc. reciprocally related so that to a *point* in either corresponds (in solid geometry) a *plane*, or (in plane geometry) a *straight line* in the other 1881.

1. Father and son, husband and wife, and other such c. terms LOCKE. Hence **Corre·lative·ly** *adv.*, -ness. **Correlati·vity.**

B. *sb.* Each of two things correlative to one another 1545.

The words used..are what are called correlatives, one implies the other J. H. NEWMAN.

Correligionist, = CO-RELIGIONIST.

Correption (kǫre·pʃən). ME. [ad. L. *correptionem*, f. *corripere.*] †1. Reproof -1737. †2. A seizure. (Cf. RAPTURE.) -1664. 3. *Gram.* Shortening in pronunciation 1873.

1. Of charitable correpcion or reproving WYCLIF. 3. Liable to c. of its accented syllable EARLE.

Correspond (kǫrĭspǫ·nd), *v.* 1529. [a. med. L. *correspondere*; cf. F. *correspondre.*] 1. *intr.* To answer to something else in the way of fitness; to agree *with*; be conformable *to*; be congruous or in harmony *with*. 2. To answer *to* in character or function; to be similar *to* (rarely *with*) 1645. †3. To respond -1826. 4. To hold communication or intercourse (*with*). *Obs.* exc. as in 5. 1605. 5. *esp.* To communicate (*with* another) by interchange of letters 1645. †6. *trans.* To answer to -1675.

1. Our nature corresponds to our external condition BUTLER. 2. A richsdach, an assembly that corresponds to our parliament HOWELL. The silver penny..was supposed to c. with a pennyweight JEVONS. 5. Locke and Newton had corresponded on the prophecies of Daniel as early as 1691 BREWSTER.

Correspondence (kǫrĭspǫ·ndĕns). ME. [ad. med.L. **correspondentia*; cf. F. *correspondance.*] 1. The action or fact of corresponding; congruity, agreement. 2. Similarity, analogy 1605. †3. Concordant response -1680. †4. Relation between persons or communities. (Common in 17th c.) -1835. 5. Intercourse, communication. *Obs.* exc. as in 6. 1603. Also *fig.* 6. Communication by letters 1644; the letters sent and received; also, letters contributed to a newspaper 1771.

1. The c. of actions to the nature of the agent BUTLER. 4. Our ill c. with the French Protestants MARVELL. 6. Letter for letter is the law of all c. COWPER. The c. of Pope and Swift EMERSON. var. **Correspo·ndency** (*esp.* in senses 1, 2). Now *arch.*

Correspondent (kǫrĭspǫ·ndĕnt). ME. [f. med.L. *correspondentem.* In F. *correspondant.*]

A. *adj.* [Now more freq. CORRESPONDING.] 1. Answering to or agreeing with something else or with each other; congruous *with*; conformable, analogous *to*. †2. Responsive; submissive -1647. †3. Answerable -1658. Hence **Correspo·ndently** *adv.*

B. *sb.* 1. A correlative 1650. †2. A confederate, accomplice -1771. 3. A person who has regular business relations with another (*esp.* in a distant place) 1674. 4. One who communicates with another by letters. (The ordinary mod. use.) 1630. b. One who contributes letters to a journal; *spec.* one employed by a journal to supply it with news from some particular place 1711.

3. I..had gotten..a c. in London, with whom I traded DE FOE. 4. The lady was a voluminous c. 1872. So **Corresponde·ntial** *a.* pertaining to correspondence, or to a c.

Corresponding (kǫrĭspǫ·ndiŋ), *ppl. a.* 1579. [f. CORRESPOND *v.* + -ING².] 1. That corresponds or answers to another; correspondent. 2. That corresponds by letters 1760.

1. His reserve..was met by a c. caution GREEN. 2. *C. member* of a society: one residing at a distance, who corresponds with it by letters, but has no deliberative voice in its affairs. Hence **Correspo·ndingly** *adv.*

Correspo·nsive, *a.* Now *arch.* 1606. [f. med. L. *correspons-* ppl. stem; cf. *responsive.*] Corresponding, answering. *Tr. & Cr.* Prol. 18.

Corridor (kǫ·ridǭɹ). 1620. [a. F., ad. It. *corridore* (also *corridoio*) *lit.* 'running-place', f. *correre* to run.] †1. A passage or covered way between two places -1814. †2. *Fortif.* The covered way that surrounds the fortifications of a place -1706. 3. An outside gallery or passage round the quadrangle or court of a building 1644. 4. A main passage in a large building, upon which many apartments open 1814. b. A strip of a State's territory running through that of another, and giving access to the sea, etc. 1919. *Comb.* c.-train 1892.

Corrie (kǫ·ri). *Sc.* Also **correi.** 1795. [a. Gael. *coire* (pronounced ko·re) cauldron; hence, circular hollow.] A circular hollow on a mountain side, where the deer often lie.

†**Corrige,** *v.* ME. [a. F. *corriger*, ad. L. *corrigere.*] To correct -1490. So ‖**Corrige·ndum** (usu. in *pl.* -da), something to be corrected.

†**Co·rrigent,** *a.* 1860. [ad. L. *corrigentem.*] Corrective. Also as *sb.* -1882.

Corrigible (kǫ·ridʒĭb'l), *a.* 1483. [a. F., ad. L. **corrigibilis.*] 1. Capable of being corrected. 2. Capable of reformation 1673. 3. Submissive to correction 1583. †4. Deserving chastisement -1649. †5. Corrective -1604.

2. The other abuses will be easily c. O'CONNELL. 3. Bending downe His c. necke *Ant. & Cl.* IV. xiv. 74. 5. *Oth.* I. iii. 329. Hence **Co·rrigibi·lity, Co·rrigibleness, Co·rrigibly** *adv.*

Corrival (kǫrəi·văl), *sb.* and *a. arch.* 1579. [ad. rare L. *corrivalis.* Cf. CO-RIVAL.] 1. One of several rivals. †2. A compeer, partner -1596. 3. *adj.* Rival 1646. Hence †**Corri·val** *v.* to rival; *intr.* to vie *with*. †**Corriva·lity,** †**Corri·valry,** competition. †**Corri·valship,** the position of a c.

†**Co·rrivate,** *v. rare.* 1621. [f. L. *corrivat-*, *corrivare* to draw together into one stream.] To cause to run together into one. (Misused by Burton.) Hence †**Corriva·tion,** the confluence of streams.

†**Corri·ve,** *v.* 1586. [? f. CORRIVAL.] = CORRIVAL *v.* -1608.

Corroborant (kǫrǫ·bŏrănt), *a.* and *sb.* 1626. [a. F., or ad. L. *corroborantem*; see CORROBORATE *v.*] 1. *adj.* Strengthening, invigorating. 2. *sb.* A strengthening agent; a tonic 1727. 3. A corroboratory fact 1805.

2. The best corroborants which we know, are the Peruvian bark and wine 1789.

Corroborate (kǫrǫ·bŏrĕt), *ppl. a. arch.* [ad. L. *corroboratus.*] Strengthened, confirmed.

There is noe trusting to the force of Nature..except it be c. by Custome BACON.

Corroborate (kǫrǫ·bŏreit), *v.* 1530. [f. L. *corroborat-* ppl. stem (f. *cor-* intensive + *roborare*); see -ATE³.] 1. To strengthen, make strong 1533. 2. To support, confirm 1530. †3. To concur in testimony (*rare*) -1784.

1. Nothing that I know corroborates the stomach so much as tar-water BERKELEY. To c. their Faith HEARNE. 2. To c. a conveyance CRUISE. This observation corroborates those of Professor Forbes TYNDALL. var. †**Corro·bore** (*rare*). Hence **Corro·borator,** one who or that which corroborates. **Corro·boratory** *a.* corroborative.

Corroboration (kǫrǫ:bŏrē¹·ʃən). 1529. [a. F., or ad. L. **corroborationem.*] †1. Strengthening -1816. 2. Confirmation 1552. 3. That which corroborates 1542.

3. It has thus much of c. from history, that [etc.] FREEMAN.

Corroborative (kǫrǫ·bŏrătiv). 1583. [a. F. *corroboratif, -ive*; see CORROBORATE *v.* and -IVE.] 1. *adj.* Having the quality of corroborating. †2. *sb.* A strengthening agent or measure; in *Med.* = CORROBORANT -1805.

Corroboree (kǫrǫ·bəri). 1793. [Native name.] The native dance of the Australian aborigines; it is either festive or warlike.

Corrode (kǫrō^u·d), *v.* ME. [ad. L. *corrodere.*] †1. *trans.* To eat into; to eat or gnaw away -1747. 2. *transf.* To wear away or destroy gradually, as if by eating or gnawing away the texture ME. Also *fig.* 3. *absol.* and *intr.* (in prec. senses) 1610. 4. *intr.* (for *refl.*) To become corroded. (*lit.* and *fig.*) 1820.

1. No moth can c. their texture HERVEY. 2. *Dürer* ..the first who corroded his plates with *aqua-fortis* URE. 3. Gold and silver do not rust, c., or decay ROGERS. Hence **Corro·der,** one who or that which corrodes. **Corro·dible** *a.*

Corrodent (kǫrō^u·dĕnt). ? *Obs.* 1599. [ad. L. *corrodentem.*] *adj.* Corroding, corrosive. *sb.* [sc. *agent.*] 1614.

Corrodiary (kǫrō^u·diări). 1638. [ad. med.L. *corrodiarius*; see CORRODY.] The recipient of a corrody; a prebendary. var. **Corro·dier.**

Corrody, corody (kǫ·rŏdi). ME. [ad. med. L. *corrodium*, also *-radium*, vars. of *corredium*, earlier *conredium*; see CONREY. The primary sense was 'outfit'; hence, 'provision'.] Provision for maintenance, aliment; pension.

Corrosible (kǫrō^u·zĭb'l), *a.* 1721. [f. L. *corros-* ppl. stem; see CORRODE.] = CORRODIBLE. Hence **Corro:sibi·lity.**

Corrosion (kǫrō^u·ʒən). ME. [a. OF., or ad. L. *corrosionem.*] 1. The action or process of corroding; the fact or condition of being corroded. Also *fig.* 2. *concr.* A product of corrosion, as rust (*rare*) 1779.

1. C. of the stomach 1882. *fig.* Peevishness..wears out happiness by slow c. JOHNSON.

Corrosive (kǫrō^u·siv, †kǫ·rŏsiv). ME. [a. F. *corrosif*, OF. *corosif, -ive.* The vowel of the second syllable, which was obscure, was variously represented by *e, i, a*, and at length lost; whence CORSIVE.]

A. *adj.* 1. Having the quality of eating away, consuming, or destroying. 2. *fig.* a. Destructive 1581. b. Fretting, wearing 1600.

1. The corrosiue aire of London EVELYN. C. fires MILT. *P. L.* II. 401, Ulcers SALMON. 2. b. A pensive and c. desire that we had done otherwise HOOKER. Hence **Corro·sive·ly** *adv.*, -ness.

B. *sb.* A substance that corrodes, an acid, drug, remedy, etc. Also †*fig.*

fig. In things past cure, care is a corasiue GREENE.

C. sublimate: mercuric chloride or bichloride of mercury ($HgCl_2$), a white crystalline substance which acts as an acrid poison.

Corrugant (kǫ·rᵘugănt), *a.* 1706. [ad. L. *corrugantem.*] Corrugating, wrinkling.

Corrugate (kǫ·rᵘugĕt), *ppl. a.* 1742. [ad. L. *corrugatus*; see next.] 1. Wrinkled; contracted into folds or wrinkles. Also *fig.* 2. *Med.* and *Zool.* Having a wrinkled appearance; marked with parallel ridges and furrows 1826.

Corrugate (kǫ·rᵘugeit), *v.* 1620. [f. L. *corrugat-*, *corrugare*, f. *cor-* (*com-*) intensive +

rugare, f. *ruga*.] *trans.* To wrinkle (the skin), contract into wrinkles; hence *gen.* to draw, contract, or bend into parallel folds or ridges. *intr.* (for *refl.*) = To become corrugated 1753.
It [the muscle] corrugates the skin of the nose transversely TODD. Hence **Co·rrugated** *ppl. a.* wrinkled, marked as with wrinkles; bent into regular curved folds or grooves, as *c. iron.* **Co·rrugative** *a.* characterized by corrugation (*rare*).

Corrugation (kǫrŭgēⁱ·ʃən). 1528. [ad. L. type **corrugationem*.] 1. The act of corrugating or state of being corrugated. 2. That which is corrugated; a wrinkle, fold, etc. 1829.
2. A succession of mountain chains folded in broad corrugations C. KING.

Corrugator (kǫ·rŭgēⁱtəɹ). 1782. [a. mod. L.] 1. Anything which causes corrugation (*rare*) 1782. 2. *Anat.* Each of the two small muscles which contract the brows 1839.

Corru·gent, *a.* 1727. Erron. f. CORRUGANT; in *c. muscle* = CORRUGATOR 2.

†**Corru·mp**, *v.* ME. [a. OF. *corompre* :—L. *corrumpere*, f. *cor-* intensive + *rumpere*.] 1. *trans.* To bring to naught –1489. 2. To corrupt –1532. 3. *intr.* To become corrupt –1470. Hence †**Corru·mpable** *a.* = CORRUPTIBLE.

Corrupt (kǒrʊ·pt), *ppl. a.* ME. [ad. L. *corruptus*. By Chaucer often stressed *co·rrupt*.] †**A.** as *pa. pple.* Corrupted –1600.
B. as *adj.* 1. Changed from the naturally sound condition; putrid, rotten or rotting; infected or defiled (*arch.*). †2. Adulterated; debased, as money –1683. 3. Debased in character; depraved; perverted ME. 4. Influenced by bribery or the like; venal ME. 5. Of language, texts, etc.: Destroyed in purity, debased; vitiated by errors or alterations ME.
1. A c. and stagnant air GOOCH. No title can be deduced through the c. blood of the father BENTHAM. 3. A c. form of Christianity 1877. 4. The general laws against c. practices at elections H. COX. 5. The emendation of c. passages THEOBALD. Hence **Corru·pt·ly** *adv.*, **-ness.**

Corrupt (kǒrʊ·pt), *v.* ME. [app. f. CORRUPT *ppl. a.* (cf. *to content*); but subseq. referred to L. *corrupt-* ppl. stem, superseding CORRUMP *v.*] 1. *trans.* To turn from a sound into an unsound impure condition; to make rotten; to putrefy (*arch.*). Also *fig.* 2. To infect, taint 1548; †to adulterate –1697. 3. To render morally unsound; to pervert (a good quality); to debase, defile ME. 4. To induce to act dishonestly or unfaithfully; to make venal; to bribe 1548. 5. To debase, destroy the purity of (a language, etc.); to vitiate (a text, etc.) by errors or alterations 1630. 6. To spoil (anything) in quality 1526. 7. *intr.* To become corrupt or putrid; to putrefy, rot, decay ME.
1. The infectious air, that corrupted the blood of strangers LITHGOW. *fig.* The attainder of the father only corrupts the lineal blood CRUISE. 3. That their virgynite shulde be corrupted PALSGR. 4. By corruptyng with money diverse Burgesses of the towne HALL. 5. The Hereticks corrupted the New Testament HEARNE. 7. Gold never corrupteth by rust FULKE. Hence **Corru·pted·ly** *adv.*, **-ness.** **Corru·pter**, **-or**, one who or that which corrupts. **Corru·ptful** *a.* fraught with corruption. **Corru·ptless** *a.* **Corru·ptress**, a female corrupter; also *fig.*

Corruptible (kǒrʊ·ptĭb'l), *a.* ME. [ad. L. *corruptibilis*.] 1. Liable to corruption; perishable, mortal. (Chiefly Scriptural.) †2. Corrupt –1620. 3. Capable of moral corruption; venal 1677.
1. This c. must put on incorruption 1 *Cor.* xv. 53. 3. The House of Commons..was itself c. H. COX. Hence **Corru:ptibi·lity.** **Corru·ptibleness.** **Corru·ptibly** *adv.*

Corruption (kǒrʊ·pʃən). ME. [a. F., ad. L. *corruptionem*. Adopted from theol. Latin.] †1. The destruction or spoiling of anything, *esp.* by disintegration or decomposition; putrefaction –1718. †2. Infection, infected condition; also *fig.* contagion, taint –1598. 3. *concr.* Decomposed or putrid matter; pus. *Obs.* exc. *dial.* 1526. Also *fig.* 4. A making or becoming morally corrupt; the fact or condition of being corrupt; moral deterioration; depravity ME. 5. Evil nature, 'the old Adam'; temper. Now *colloq.* 1799. 6. Perversion of integrity by bribery or favour; the use or existence of corrupt practices ME. 7. The perversion of anything from an original state of purity ME.
1. If you provide against the causes of Putrefaction, matter maketh not that haste to c., that is conceived BACON. 2. *Law. C. of blood*: the effect of an attainder, by which the blood of the person attainted was held to have become tainted or 'corrupted' by his crime, so that he could no longer hold land, nor leave it to heirs, nor could his descendants inherit from him. 3. *fig.* That foule Sinne gathering head, Shall breake into C. 2 *Hen. IV*, III. i. 77. 4. The general C. of Manners in Servants STEELE. 6. Simoniacal c. HOOKER. 7. The c. then of Monarchy is call'd Tyranny J. HARRINGTON. The continual C. of our English Tongue SWIFT. Hence **Corru·ptionist**, a supporter or practiser of c., *esp.* in public affairs.

†**Corru·ptious**, *a.* 1540. [f. as prec.; see -OUS.] Characterized by corruption –1604.

Corruptive (kǒrʊ·ptiv), *a.* 1593. [ad. L. *corruptivus*; see -IVE.] †1. Liable to corruption –1691. 2. That tends to corrupt 1609.
1. Some c. quality for so speedy a dissolution of the meat RAY. Hence **Corru·ptively** *adv.*

‖**Co·rsac, corsak.** 1838. [Turkī.] *Zool.* The Tartar fox.

Corsage (kǭ·ɹsėdʒ, or, more freq. as Fr. korsā·ʒ). 1481. [a. OF., f. *cors* body.] †1. Size and shape of body –1658. †2. The bust –1600. 3. The body of a woman's dress; a bodice 1857.

†**Corsaint.** ME. [a. OF. *cors* (mod. *corps*) *saint*.] The body of a saint; a sainted person, (departed) saint –1500.

Corsair (kǭ·ɹsēəɹ). 1549. [a. F. *corsaire*, med.L. *cursarius*, f. med.L. *cursus*, *cursa* hostile excursion, plunder (L. *cursus* a run).] 1. A privateer; chiefly applied to the authorized cruisers of Barbary. In English often = *pirate*. 2. A pirate-ship sanctioned by the country to which it belongs 1632. Also *attrib.*
2. Tuscan corsairs covered the Western Mediterranean RAWLINSON.

Corse (kǭɹs), *sb.* [ME. *cors*, a. OF. :—L. *corpus*; see also CORPSE.] †1. = CORPSE 1. –1586. 2. = CORPSE 2. ME. †3. *transf.* Of things: The main bulk –1506. †4. A ribbon, serving as a ground for ornamentation, and used as a girdle, garter, etc. –1573. †5. *Archit.* (*cors*) A square shaft or slender pier supporting a terminal 1478.
1. Hire semly cors for to embrace LYDG. 2. The sencelesse c. appointed for the graue SPENSER *F. Q.* I. xi. 48. *Comb.* †**c.-present**, a mortuary.

Corse, course, *v.* Now *dial.* ME. [? identical with COSS *v.*; cf. SKORSE.] To exchange; to barter; to deal in (horses). Hence †**Corser, courser,** a jobber; *esp.* a horse-couper.

Corselet, var. of CORSLET.

Corset (kǭ·ɹsėt). ME. [a. F., dim. of OF. *cors* body.] 1. A close-fitting outer body-garment worn by women, and formerly also by men. 2. A closely-fitting inner bodice stiffened with whalebone, etc., and fastened by lacing; worn chiefly by women to give shape and support to the figure; stays 1795. Also *attrib.*
1. Her senesshal..in a rich c. of grene LD. BERNERS. Hence **Co·rseted** *ppl. a.* enclosed in a c.

Co·rsie, *sb.* and *a.* Now *dial.* 1450. [Reduced from *corĕsive*, CORROSIVE.] 1. *sb.* = CORROSIVE *sb.*; *fig.* a grievance. 2. *adj.* Corrosive 1598. Hence †**Co·rsie** *v. rare*, to treat with a c.; *fig.* to vex. var. †**Corsive** *a.* and *sb.*

Corslet, corselet (kǭ·ɹslėt), *sb.* 1500. [a. F. *corselet*, double dim. of *cors* body.] 1. A piece of defensive armour covering the body 1563; †a soldier armed with a corslet –1709. 2. A (tight-fitting) garment covering the body as dist. from the limbs 1500. 3. The thorax of an insect 1753.
1. Surely a c. is no canonicall coat for me FULLER. Hence **Co·rslet** *v.* to encircle with, or as with, a c. (*rare*). †**Corsletee·r**, a soldier armed with a c.

Corsned (kǭ·ɹsned). Now *Hist.* [OE. *corsnǽd*, f. *cor* choice + *snǽd* bit, piece, f. *snīdan* to cut.] In OE. law, the morsel of trial, a piece of bread consecrated by exorcism (*panis conjuratus*) which an accused person was required to swallow as a trial of his guilt or innocence.

†**Corsy**, *a.* ME. [ad. F. *corsé*, f. *cors* body.] Corpulent –1607.

‖**Cortège** (kǫɹtē·ʒ). 1679. [a. F., ad. It. *corteggio*, deriv. of *corte* COURT.] A train of attendants, a procession.

‖**Cortes** (ko·ɹtes). 1668. [Sp. and Pg. pl. of *corte* COURT.] The two chambers, constituting the legislative assembly of Spain and Portugal.

‖**Cortex** (kǭ·ɹteks). Pl. **cortices** (kǭ·ɹtisīz). 1660. [L.] †1. *fig.* The outer shell or husk –1665. †2. *Med.* The bark of various trees; *absol.* Peruvian bark –1803. 3. Applied to various external structures in a plant, animal body, or organ. *spec.* **a.** *Anat.* The outer gray matter of the brain. **b.** *Bot.* The bark.

Cortian (kǭ·ɹtiăn), *a.* 1872. [f. *Corti*, an Italian anatomist + -AN.] *Anat.* In *C. fibres, membranes*, etc., parts of the internal ear.

Cortical (kǭ·ɹtikăl), *a.* 1671. [ad. mod.L. *corticalis*, f. *cortex*.] 1. Belonging to the cortex or external part of a plant or animal body, or organ. (Opp. to *medullary*.) †2. *fig.* External, superficial –1856.
1. The Nerves arise from the medullary, not the c. Part HARTLEY. 2. The C. or literal sense H. MORE.

Corticate (kǭ·ɹtikĕt), *a.* 1846. [ad. L. *corticatus*.] Having bark; made of the nature of bark. So **Co·rticated** *ppl. a.*

Cortici·ferous, *a. rare.* 1828. [f. L. *corticem* + -FER + -OUS.] Bearing bark or a cortex. So **Corti·ciform** *a.* bark-like (*rare*).

Corticin (kǭ·ɹtisin). 1863. [f. as prec. + -IN.] *Chem.* An amorphous yellowish substance, found in the bark of the aspen.

Corticine (kǭ·ɹtisin). 1880. [f. as prec. + -INE.] Name of a floor-covering made of ground cork with India rubber or the like.

Corticolous (kǫɹti·kŏləs), *a.* 1856. [f. L. *corticem* + *-cola* inhabitant + -OUS. (Better *corticicolous*.)] *Bot.* Growing or living in the bark of trees. var. **Co·rticole.**

Corticose (kǭ·ɹtikōᵘ·s), *a. rare.* 1730. [ad. L. *corticosus*.] Abounding in bark; barky. var. **Co·rticous** (*rare*).

‖**Cortile** (kortī·le). 1841. [It., deriv. of *corte* COURT.] (In Italy.) An enclosed area or court-yard within or attached to a building: usu. roofless; occ. used as a court of entrance.

Corundum (korʊ·ndəm). 1728. [a. Tamil *kurundam* 'ruby'. Cf. also CORINDON.] 1. A crystallized mineral belonging to the same species as the sapphire and ruby, but more or less opaque; called also *Adamantine Spar*. 2. *Min.* A mineral species, comprising the transparent sapphire (including the ruby, the oriental amethyst, emerald, and topaz), the opaque adamantine spar (= prec. sense), and the granular emery. It consists of crystallized alumina (Al_2O_3) variously coloured. Also *attrib.*, as in *c. tool*, etc.

Coruscant (korʊ·skănt), *a.* 1485. [ad. L. *coruscantem*; see CORUSCATE.] Coruscating. Also *fig.*

Coruscate (kǫ·rŏskeⁱt), *v.* 1705. [f. ppl. stem of L. *coruscare*.] *intr.* To give forth intermittent flashes of light; to sparkle, glitter.

Coruscation (kǫrŏskēⁱ·ʃən). 1490. [ad. L. *coruscationem*.] The action of coruscating; usually: A vibratory or quivering flash of light, or a series of such flashes. Also *fig.*
The coruscations of the Aurora borealis E. DARWIN. *fig.* Coruscations of epigrammatic wit TODHUNTER.

Corve, var. CORF; obs. pa. t. and pple. of CARVE.

†**Corved**, *ppl. a.* 1641. [app. identical with MDu. *korfharinck*.] In *c. herring* (corruptly *corred, cored*): ? Brought ashore in baskets, as dist. from barrelled.

‖**Corvée** (korve·). ME. [F. :—(ult.) late L. *corrogata* : *corrogata opera* requisitioned work: f. L. *corrogare*, f. *cor-* + *rogare*.] *Feudal Law.* A day's work of unpaid labour due by a vassal to his feudal lord; the whole forced labour thus exacted; in France, extended to the statute labour upon the public roads exacted before 1776.

Corven, obs. pa. t. (pl.) and pa. pple. of CARVE.

Corvette (kǫɹve·t). 1636. [a. F., ad. Pg. *corveta*, Sp. *corbeta*; cf. L. *corbita* (*navis*) a slow-sailing ship of burden, f. *corbis* basket. (A basket was hoisted as a signal by the Egyptian grain-ships.)] A flush-decked war-vessel, ship-, bark-, or brig-rigged, having one tier of guns; now, a small naval escort vessel.

Corvetto; see CURVET.

Corvine (kǭ·ɹvəin), *a.* 1656. [ad. L. *corvinus*, f. *corvus*.] Of or pertaining to a raven or crow; of the crow kind.

Corvorant, perverted f. CORMORANT, q.v.

Corybant (kǫ·ribænt). Pl. **Corybants,** or, in L. form, **Corybantes** (kǫribæ·ntīz). ME. [a. F. *Corybante*, ad. L. *Corybantem*, a. Gr. Κορύβαντα.] A priest of the Phrygian worship of Cybele, which was performed with noisy and extravagant dances.

Those mad Corybants, who dance and glow On Dindymus high tops DRUMM. OF HAWTH.

Hence **Coryba·ntian** *a.* of or pertaining to the Corybantes or their worship. **Coryba·ntiasm,** *Path.*, a sort of frenzy, in which the patient has fantastic visions. †**Coryba·ntiate** *v.* to act like a C. **Coryba·ntic, Coryba·ntine** *a.*, Corybantian.

Corydaline (kǫ·ridăləin). 1838. [f. *Corydalis.*] *Chem.* An alkaloid existing in the root of *Corydalis tuberosa* and some allied plants.

Corydon (kǫ·ridǭn). 1581. [L., Gr. Κορύδων proper name, applied to a shepherd; cf. Verg. Ecl. ii. 56.] A generic proper name in pastoral poetry for a rustic.

Where C. and Thyrsis met, Are at their savoury dinner set..Which the neat-handed Phillis dresses MILT. *L'Allegro* 83.

†**Co·rylet.** *rare.* 1610. [ad. L. *coryletum.*] A hazel copse.

Corymb (kǫ·rimb). 1706. [a. F. *corymbe*, ad. L. *corymbus* (also used), a. Gr. κόρυμβος head, cluster.] **1.** *Bot.* A species of inflorescence; a raceme in which the flowers form a flat or slightly convex head. Before Linnæus, applied to the discoidal head of a composite flower. ¶ **2.** A cluster of ivy-berries or grapes. (Not an Eng. sense.) 1706.

1. Sea Aster..The flower-heads are in a compact c. MRS. LANKESTER. Hence **Co·rymbed** *ppl. a.* fashioned as a c. †**Cory·mbiate** *a.* set with clusters of ivy-berries. **Corymbi·ferous** *a.* bearing corymbs; *spec.* belonging to the *Corymbiferæ*, a sub-order of Composite plants. **Cory·mbiform** *a.* of the form of a c. **Corymbo·se** *a.* growing in corymbs; like a c. **Corymbo·sely** *adv.* in corymbs.

Corynid (kǫ·rinid). 1870. [f. mod.L. *Corynidæ*, f. *Coryne*, generic name of a Hydromedusa, a. Gr. κορύνη club.] *Zool.* A member of the family *Corynidæ*, of the order *Hydroidea* of Cœlenterates. So **Cory·niform** *a.* having the form of a c.

Corynite (kǫ·rinəit). 1868. [f. Gr. κορύνη club.] *Min.* A native sulph-arsen-antimonide of nickel.

‖**Coryphæus** (kǫrifī·ŏs). 1633. [L.; a. Gr. κορυφαῖος, in the Attic Drama 'leader of the chorus'; f. Gr. κορυφή head.] **1.** The leader of a chorus 1678. **2.** *fig.* The leader of a party, sect, school, etc. 1633.

2. Strauss, the c. of modern scepticism 1871.

‖**Coryphée** (korifē·). 1866. [F.; ad. L. *coryphæus.*] A leader of the corps de ballet.

Corystoid (kori·stoid), *a.* 1852. [f. *Corystes*, a. Gr. κορυστής helmeted soldier, f. κόρυς helmet.] *Zool.* Allied to the genus of crabs *Corystes*, or the family *Corystidæ*.

‖**Coryza** (korəi·ză). 1634. [L.; ad. Gr. κόρυζα.] *Path.* The running at the nose which accompanies a cold in the head; catarrh.

Cos (kǫs). 1699. [Gr. Κῶς, an island in the Ægean (now Stanchio).] In full *C. lettuce*: a variety of lettuce introduced from Cos.

Cos, abbrev. of COSINE.

Co·salite. 1868. [f. *Cosala* in Mexico.] *Min.* A native sulphide of lead and bismuth.

‖**Cosaque** (kosa·k). 1858. [App. f. Fr. *Cosaque* Cossack; prob. with reference to their irregular firing.] A cracker bon-bon.

Coscinomancy (kǫ·sinomænsi). 1603. [f. (ult.) Gr. κοσκινόμαντις, f. κόσκινον sieve.] Divination by the turning of a sieve (held on a pair of shears, etc.).

Cosecant (kōusī·kănt). 1706. [See Co-. F. *cosécante.*] *Trig.* The secant of the complement of a given angle. (Abbrev. *cosec*)

Coseismal (kōusəi·zmăl), *a.* 1851. [See Co-.] Relating to the points of simultaneous arrival of an earthquake wave on the earth's surface; in *c. line, curve, zone*, etc. As *sb.* = *c. line, curve.* So **Cosei·smic** *a.* (in same sense).

Cosen, -age, -er, obs. ff. COUSIN, COZEN, etc.

Co-sentient (kouse·nʃiěnt), *a.* 1801. [See Co-.] Jointly sentient. So **Co-se·ntiency.**

Cosey; see COSY.

Cosh (kǫʃ), *a. Sc.* and *dial.* 1774. [?] Quiet; snug; trim.

Cosher (kǫ·ʃəɹ), *v.*[1] *Ireland.* 1634. [repr. Ir. *coisir* feast.] *intr.* To feast; to live at free quarters upon dependants or kinsmen. Hence **Co·sherer,** one who coshers. **Co·shering** *vbl. sb.* †feasting; *spec.* = the custom of COSHERY.

Cosher (kǫ·ʃəɹ), *v.*[2] 1861. *trans.* To pamper; to cocker *up*.

Co·sher, *v.*[3] *colloq.* 1833. *intr.* To chat familiarly.

Cosher, *a.* (in Jewish use); see KOSHER.

Coshery (kǫ·ʃəri). *Ireland.* 1583. [f. Ir. *coisir* (kōʃər) feast, feasting.] Feasting; *spec.* entertainment for themselves and their followers exacted by Irish chiefs from their dependants.

C...is somewhat analogous to the royal prerogative of purveyance HALLAM.

Cosier, a cobbler; see COZIER.

Co-signatory (kōusi·gnătəri). 1865. [See Co-.] *adj.* Signing jointly with others 1891. *sb.* A joint signatory.

Cosignificative, -ficator; see CONSIG-.

Cosily (kōu·zili), *adv.* Also **cozily,** etc. 1721. [f. COSY *a.*] In a cosy manner; snugly and comfortably.

Cosin, -age, obs. ff. COUSIN, COZEN, -AGE.

Cosine (kōu·səin). 1635. [See Co-.] *Trig.* The sine of the complement of a given angle. Abbrev. *cos* (no period).

Cosiness (kōu·zinės). Also **cozi-.** 1834. [f. COSY *a.*] The quality or state of being cosy.

†**Co·sins.** [f. the maker's name.] A kind of stays. POPE.

Cosmete (kǫ·zmīt). [ad. Gr. κοσμητής, f. κοσμεῖν to order.] A state officer in charge of the ephebi at Athens.

Cosmetic (kǫzme·tik). 1605. [ad. Gr. κοσμητικός, f. κοσμεῖν to arrange, adorn.]

A. *adj.* Having power to beautify (*esp.* the complexion); also, relating to cosmetics 1650. var. **Cosme·tical.**

B. *sb.* **1.** A preparation for beautifying the hair, skin, or complexion 1650. **2.** The art of adorning or beautifying the body. Also *pl.* [= Gr. ἡ κοσμητική.] 1605. **3.** One who practises the cosmetic art. *nonce-use.* 1713.

Cosmic (kǫ·zmik), *a.* 1649. [ad. Gr. κοσμικός, f. κόσμος.] †**1.** Of this world. **2.** Of or belonging to the universe considered as an ordered system or totality 1846; relating to the cosmos 1874. **3.** Belonging to the material universe as distinguished from the earth; extra-terrestrial 1871; characteristic of the vast scale of the universe and its changes 1874. **4.** Orderly; not *chaotic* (*rare*) 1858.

2. The great c. law of gravitation WHITNEY. *C. philosophy*: = COSMISM. **3.** C. dust CARPENTER. *C. rays*, any of a class of rays having peculiar properties, still largely unascertained, which pass (or are believed to pass) through space, chiefly outside the earth's atmosphere.

Cosmical (kǫ·zmikăl), *a.* 1583. [f. as prec. + -AL.] †**1.** Relating to the world, *i.e.* the earth -1819. **2.** = COSMIC 2. 1685. **3.** = COSMIC 3. 1842. **4.** *Astron.* Coincident with the rising of the sun; said of the rising or setting of a star 1594. Hence **Co·smically** *adv.* (*esp.* in sense 4).

Cosmism (kǫ·zmiz'm). 1861. [f. COSMOS + -ISM.] The theory which explains the cosmos as a self-existent, self-acting whole, according to the methods of positive science. So **Co·smist,** a believer in c.; a Secularist.

Cosmo-, bef. a vowel **cosm-,** comb. f. Gr. κόσμος COSMOS: hence,

Co·smocrat, lord or ruler of the world (*rare*); so **Cosmocra·tic** *a.*; **Cosmo·crator** = *Cosmocrat*; **Co·smogene·tic** *a.* of or pertaining to cosmogeny; **Cosmo·geny,** origin or evolution of the universe; **Co·smolabe,** an ancient instrument resembling the astrolabe; **Cosmo·latry,** worship of the world; †**Cosmo·metry,** measurement of the universe; **Cosmopla·stic** *a.* †maintaining an inanimate plastic nature to be the highest principle of the universe; moulding the universe; **Cosmora·ma,** a peep-show containing views of all parts of the world; also *transf.* and *fig.*; **Cosmora·mic** *a.*; **Cosmo·sophy,** knowledge or science of the cosmos; **Co·smosphere,** a hollow glass globe representing the celestial sphere, having within it a terrestrial globe, for showing the position of the earth, at any given time, with respect to the fixed stars; **Cosmothe·ism** (*rare*), the doctrine that identifies God with the cosmos; pantheism; **Cosmothe·tic, -al** *a.* that posits an external world, as *C. Idealism.*

‖**Cosmognosis** (kǫzmognōu·sis). [f. COSMO- + Gr. γνῶσις.] 'The instinct which teaches animals the right time for migration, and the fitting place to which to go' (*Syd. Soc. Lex.*).

Cosmogony (kǫzmǫ·gŏni). 1696. [ad. Gr. κοσμογονία, f. κόσμος + -γονια. In F. *cosmogonie.*] **1.** The generation of the existing universe 1776. **2.** A theory, system, or account of the generation of the universe.

2. The vast and imaginative cosmogonies of the East MILMAN. Hence **Cosmo·gonal, Cosmogo·nic, -al** *adjs.* of or pertaining to c. **Cosmo·gonist,** one who studies c.; †one who holds that the world was created.

Cosmographer (kǫzmǫ·grăfəɹ). 1527. [f. Gr. κοσμογράφος, f. κόσμος + -γράφος.] One skilled in cosmography. Formerly often = *geographer.*

Cosmography (kǫzmǫ·grăfi). ME. [ad. Gr. κοσμογραφία description of the world. Cf. F. *cosmographie.*] **1.** The science which describes and maps the general features of the universe (both the heavens and the earth). Formerly often = *geography.* 1519. **2.** A description or representation of the universe or of the earth in its general features ME.

2. The Body [of Man]..being..a little C. or Map of the Universe SOUTH. Hence **Co·smogra·phic, -al** *a.* of or relating to c. **Cosmogra·phically** *adv.* **Cosmo·graphist** (*rare*), cosmographer.

Cosmoline (kǫ·zmǒlin). 1876. [f. as COSMETIC + -OL + -INE.] 'A name of purified solid paraffin' (*Syd. Soc. Lex.*).

Cosmology (kǫzmǫ·lŏdʒi). 1656. [f. Gr. κόσμος + -λογια.] The theory of the universe as an ordered whole, and of the general laws which govern it. Also, a particular system of the universe and its laws. **b.** *Philos.* That part of metaphysics which deals with the idea of the world as a totality of all phenomena in space and time 1753.

b. Metaphysics..are subdivided [by Wolff] into Ontology, C., Psychology, Natural Theology J. H. STIRLING. Hence **Cosmolo·gic, -al** *a.* of or pertaining to c. **Cosmolo·gically** *adv.* **Cosmo·logist,** one who studies or discourses on c.

Cosmopo·licy. = *Cosmopolitism.* SHELLEY.

Cosmopolitan (kǫzmopǫ·lităn). 1645. [f. COSMOPOLITE.]

A. *adj.* **1.** Belonging to all parts of the world; not restricted to any one country or its inhabitants 1848. **2.** Free from national limitations or attachments 1844. **3.** *Nat. Hist.* Found in all or many countries 1860.

1. Capital is becoming more and more c. MILL. **2.** [A] c. indifference to constitutions and religions MACAULAY.

B. *sb.* = COSMOPOLITE 1645.

He was no c. He was an Englishman of the English 1868. Hence **Cosmopo·litanism,** c. character.

Cosmopolite (kǫzmǫ·pǒləit). 1614. [ad. Gr. κοσμοπολίτης citizen of the world. Cf. F. *cosmopolite.*] **1.** A citizen of the world; one who has no national attachments or prejudices. (Often contrasted with *patriot.*) 1618. **2.** *transf.* At home in all parts of the world, as a plant, etc. 1832. †**3.** A man of this world -1657. **4.** *attrib.* and *adj.* = COSMOPOLITAN *a.*

1. You..have merged the patriot in the c. MEDWIN. **4.** C. doctrines 1862. Hence **Cosmopo·litic** *a.* cosmopolitan; *sb.* (*pl.*) world-politics. **Cosmopoli·tical** *a.* belonging to universal polity. **Cosmo·politism,** cosmopolitanism.

‖**Cosmos**[1] (kǫ·zmǫs). 1650. [a. Gr.] **1.** The world or universe as an ordered system. **2.** Order, harmony; a harmonious system 1858. **3.** A plant of the American genus *Cosmos*, characterized by showy flowers.

1. As the greater World is called Cosmus from the beauty thereof 1650.

†**Cosmos**[2]. 1598. Early f. KOUMISS -1630.

Co-so·vereign. 1793. [See Co-.] A joint sovereign.

†**Coss,** *sb.*[1] Also **cosse.** 1570. [a. obs F. *cosse*, ad. It. *cosa*, tr. of Arab. *shai* 'thing' = the unknown quantity (or *x*) of an equation, etc.] In *Rule of C.* = Algebra -1796.

‖**Coss, cos** (kǫs), *sb.*[2] *Anglo-Ind.* (*Pl.* same as *sing.*) 1616. [a. Hindī *kōs* :—Skr. *kroça* a call, calling distance, etc.] A measure of length in India, varying from 2½ miles or more down to about 1¼.

Coss, *v.* Chiefly *Sc.* 1470. [Of unkn. deriv. See SCORSE *v.*] *trans.* To barter, exchange.

Cossack (kǫ·sæk). 1598. [ad. F. *Cosaque* or G. *Kosak*, ad. Russ. *Kazák*, ad. Turkī *quzaq* vagabond, nomad.] Name of a group of peoples of the southern U.S.S.R. noted as horsemen from early times, when they had the task of guarding the frontiers of south-east Europe and adjoining parts of Asia.

C. and Russian Reel'd from the sabre-stroke TENNYSON.

Cosset (kǫ·sėt), *sb.* 1579. [? same as OE. *cot-sǣta* cot-sitter, cottar (Skeat).] A lamb (colt, etc.) brought up by hand; hence, a pet of any kind; a spoilt child. Also *attrib.* Hence **Co·sset** *v.* to fondle, pet, pamper; also *absol.*

†**Co·ssic, -al,** *a.* 1557. [ad. It. *cossico*; see COSS *sb.*[1]] Pertaining to algebra –1839.

‖**Cossid** (kǫ·sid). *Anglo-Ind.* 1682. [a. Arab. *qāçid* courier.] A running messenger.

Cossyrite (kǫ·sirəit). 1882. [f. *Cossyra*, now the island of Pantellaria.] *Min.* A silicate of iron found in lava.

†**Cost,** *sb.*[1] OE. [ONorthumb., a. ON. *kostr* :—OTeut. **kus-tuz*, f. wk. grade *kus-* of *keus-*, *kaus-*, to taste, prove; cf. L. *gustus, gustare*, Gr. γεύ(σ)ειν, to taste. See also CUST.] **1.** Way, manner; available course. *Needes c.*: in the way of necessity, necessarily. Hence prob. the mod. *at any cost.* –1449. **2.** A quality, habit; nature, character. Often in *pl.* –1440.

Cost (kǭst), *sb.*[2] ME. [a. OF. *cost, coust* (now *coût*); see COST *v.*] **1.** That which must be given in order to acquire, produce, or effect something; the price paid for a thing. **2.** *Law.* (*pl.*) The expenses of any legal transaction; *esp.* those allowed by law or by the court against the losing party ME. **3.** *transf.* Expenditure of time, labour, etc. ME. †**4.** A costly thing (*rare*) –1600. Also *attrib.*

1. Which of you, intending to build a tower, sitteth not down first, and counteth the c. *Luke* xiv. 28. *Prime c.*: the first cost of production, before distribution. **2.** Thus much for judgments; to which costs are a necessary appendage BLACKSTONE. **3.** After so much c. Of time and blood HOBBES. **4.** SHAKS. *Sonn.* lxiv.

Phrases. *At the c. of* (*something*): at the expense of sacrificing it. So *at little c.*, *at any c.*, etc. *To any one's c.*: to his loss or detriment. *Comb.* **c.-book** (*Mining*), a book containing an abstract of all costs incurred in working a mine, and all returns from sales, etc. Also *attrib.*

†**Cost,** *sb.*[3] [OE., ad. L. *costum* (*costos*), a. Gr. κόστος = Arab. *qust.*] The herb also called ALECOST or COSTMARY –1598.

Cost (kǫst), *sb.*[4] 1572. [a. OF. *coste* (mod. *côte*) rib :—L. *costa.*] *Her.* = COTISE.

Cost (kǭst), *v.* ME. [a. OF. *coster, couster* (mod. *coûter*) :—L. *constare*, f. *con-* together + *stare* to stand. The verb is really intrans., with an adverbial object of the amount or price. Cf. the Latin *Hoc constitit mihi tribus assibus*, 'this stood (to) me in three *asses*'.] **1.** To be acquired or acquirable at (so much); to be of the price of, be bought or maintained for, necessitate the expenditure of (so much, *much, little*, etc.). **b.** With personal object (indirect): To 'stand (a person) in' (so much) ME. **2.** *fig.* ME. †**3.** Of persons: To be at charges; quasi-*trans.* to spend –1490. **4.** *Comm.* To estimate the cost of production of an article, etc. 1884.

1. [He] thereby knows what everything costs at first hand DE FOE. **b.** His Breeches cost him but a Crowne *Oth.* II. iii. 93. **2.** I am for you, though it cost mee ten nights watchings *Much Ado* II. i. 387. Phr. *To c.* (*one*) *dear*(*dearly*): to entail great loss upon.

‖**Costa** (kǫ·stă). Pl. **costæ** (kǫ·stī). 1866. The L. word for rib, applied in Nat. Hist. and Phys. to various rib-like parts, also (after F. *coste, côte*) to the edges of certain parts.

†**Co·stage.** ME. [a. AF. = OF. *coustage*, f. *coster, couster* to COST.] Expense, cost –1670.

Costal (kǫ·stăl), *a.* (*sb.*) 1634. [a. F., ad. med.L. *costalis*, f. *costa*; see above.] **1.** *Phys.* Pertaining to or connected with the ribs, as *c. respiration.* **2.** *Nat. Hist.* Pertaining to, or like, a COSTA, q.v. 1839. **3.** *sb.* Short for *c. vein, muscle, plate*, etc. 1828. Hence **Co·stally** *adv.* in a c. manner, position, or direction.

Costard (kǫ·stăɹd). ME. [? f. OF. and AF. *coste* rib, meaning a *ribbed* apple.] **1.** A kind of apple of large size. **2.** Applied derisively to the head (*arch.*) 1530.

2. Ice try whither your C., or my Ballow be the harder *Lear* IV. vi. 247.

Costard-monger, obs. f. COSTERMONGER.

Costate (kǫ·stĕ't), *a.* 1819. [ad. L. *costatus*, f. *costa* rib.] *Nat. Hist.* Having a rib or ribs; see COSTA. var. **Co·stated.**

Costean, costeen (kǫstī·n), *v.* 1778. [f. Cornish *cothas* dropped + *stean* tin.] *Cornish Mining.* To sink pits down to the rock in order to ascertain the direction of a lode. Usually **Costea·ning** *vbl. sb.* Hence **c.-pit.**

Coste·llate, *a. rare.* 1864. [dim. of COSTATE.] Finely ribbed.

†**Co·ster**[1]. ME. [a. AF. *coster* = OF. *costier* side, f. *coste.*] A hanging for a bed, the walls of a room, etc. –1482.

Coster[2] (kǫ·stəɹ). *colloq.* 1851. Short for next. Also *attrib.*

Costermonger (kǫ·stəɹmʋŋgəɹ). 1514. [f. COSTARD + MONGER.] *orig.* An apple-seller. Now, in London, a man who sells fruit, vegetables, fish, etc. in the street from a barrow. Also used as a term of abuse. *2 Hen. IV*, I. ii. 119.

Costiferous (kǫsti·fĕrəs), *a.* 1878. [f. L. *costa.*] *Anat.* Bearing ribs. So **Co·stiform** *a.* having the form of a rib or COSTA.

†**Costious,** *a.* ME. [a. AF. *coustous* = OF. *cousteus*, now *coûteux*, f. *cost* COST *sb.*[2]] Costly, expensive –1564.

Costive (kǫ·stiv), *a.* ME. [app. a. OF. *costivé* :—L. *constipatus.*] **1.** Suffering from hardness and retention of the fæces; constipated. **2.** *fig.* Slow or reluctant in action; †reticent; niggardly 1594. †**3.** Hard and impervious 1707.

2. Somewhat caustiue of beliefe Toward your stone B. JONSON. **3.** Clay in dry seasons is c. MORTIMER. Hence **Co·stively** *adv.* **Co·stiveness,** the state or condition of being c. (*lit.* and *fig.*).

Costless (kǭ·stlės), *a.* 1509. [f. COST *sb.*[2]] Without cost.

†**Co·stlew,** *a.* ME. [f. COST *v.* or *sb.*[2] + -LEWE.] Costly, expensive; extravagant –1502.

Ther is also c. furrynge in hir gownes CHAUCER.

Costly (kǭ·stli), *a.* ME. [f. COST *sb.*[2] + -LY[1].] **1.** That costs much; sumptuous; expensive, dear. **2.** Lavish in expenditure (*arch.*) 1632.

1. Rare, exotic, and c. shrubs EVELYN. His wars are c. and chargeable HOOKER. **2.** To curse the C. Sex DRYDEN. Hence **Co·stliness,** c. quality.

Costmary (kǫ·stmēᵊri). ME. [f. COST *sb.*[3] + (St.) *Mary.*] An aromatic perennial plant, *Chrysanthemum Balsamita*, N.O. *Compositæ*, cultivated in English gardens; formerly used in medicine and to give a flavour to ale; see ALECOST.

Costo- (kǫ·sto), taken as comb. f. *costa* a rib, mostly in sense 'pertaining to, or connecting, the ribs and . .', as in **c.-abdominal, -central, -chondral** [Gr. χόνδρος], pertaining to the ribs and their cartilages. Also **Co·stotome** [Gr. -τομος], an instrument for cutting through the ribs or costal cartilages in dissection.

Costrel (kǫ·strĕl). Now *dial.* ME. [a. OF. *costerel* = *costeret*; in form dims. of *costier* 'that is by the side'.] A large bottle with an ear or ears by which it could be suspended from the waist; a 'pilgrim's bottle'; also a wooden keg similarly used.

And therwithalle a c. taketh he And seyde 'Hereof a draught, or two, or three' CHAUCER. var. †**Costret.**

Costume (kǫstiū·m, kǫ·stium), *sb.* 1715. [a. F., a. It. *costume* :—L. *consuetudinem* CUSTOM.] **1.** In historical art: The costume and fashion proper to the time and locality in which a scene is laid (*obs.*). Also *transf.* **2.** The mode of personal attire and dress belonging to a nation, class, or period 1802. **3.** Dress considered with regard to its fashion or style; garb 1818. Also *fig.* **4.** (with *a* and *pl.*) A complete set of outer garments; a woman's gown, as the chief piece of her costume 1839.

1. I was extremely delighted with the poetical beauty of some parts [of the Lay of the Last Minstrel] . . The c., too, is admirable SIR J. MACKINTOSH. **2.** The clergy had no canonical c. KENDALL. **3.** A Court c. BEACONSFIELD. Hence **Costu·me** *v.* to provide with a c.; to arrange the get-up of a theatrical piece. **Costu·mer,** a dealer in costumes. **Costu·mery** arrangement of costumes; costumes in the mass (*rare*). **Costu·mic** *a. nonce-wd.*, of or pertaining to c.; in c.

Costumier (kǫstiū·miəɹ). 1831. [a. F., f. *costumer* to COSTUME.] A dealer in costumes; *esp.* one who sells or lets out on hire costumes and properties for actors, etc.

Co-subordinate, -suffer, etc.; see CO- *pref.*

†**Co-supreme.** 1599. [See CO-.] One who is supreme jointly with another; a joint over-ruler –1619.

Cosy, cosey, cozy (kōᵘ·zi). 1709. [orig. Sc. : deriv. unkn.]

A. *adj.* Snug; comfortable; sheltered and thus warm; sheltering.

B. *sb.* **1.** A quilted covering for a tea-pot, etc., to retain the heat 1863. **2.** A cosy seat; *spec.* a canopied seat for two. [F. *causeuse.*]

Cot (kǫt), *sb.*[1] [OE. *cot* neut. (pl. *cotu*) :—OTeut. type **kutom*. See also COTE.] **1.** A small house, a cottage; now chiefly *poet.*, and connoting humbleness, rather than the rudeness of *hut.* **2.** A small erection for shelter or protection; a COTE. Also in comb., as *bell-, sheep-c.* 1450. **3.** A case or sheath; a finger-stall; the covering of a drawing-roller in a spinning frame, etc. Now *dial.* or *techn.* 1617.

1. A few humble fishermen's cots 1849.

Comb.: **c.-house, co·te-house,** a small cottage; a shed, outhouse, etc.; **-town,** a hamlet of c.-houses. Hence **Co·tted** *a.* having cots.

Cot (kǫt), *sb.*[2] *dial.* [ME. and AF. *cot*; ? same as med.L. *cottum, cotum* 'stuffed mattress' = ONF. *coute, coete*, OF. *coilte, coite*, mod.F. *couette* quilt.] **1.** Wool matted together in the fleece. **2.** A tangle 1851.

Cot (kǫt), *sb.*[3] *Irish.* 1537. [Ir. and Gael.] A small roughly-made boat; a 'dug-out'.

Cot (kǫt), *sb.*[4] Also 7–9 **cott.** 1634. [ad. Hindī *khāt* bedstead, couch, hammock.] **1.** *Anglo-Ind.* A light bedstead. **2.** *Naut.* A sort of swinging bed on board ship, made of canvas, stretched by a frame, and suspended from the beams 1769. **3.** A small bed for a child; prop. a swing-cot 1818; hence, a bed in a children's hospital 1884. Also *attrib.*

Cot, abbrev. of COTANGENT.

Cotabulate, var. of CONTABULATE.

Cotangent (koᵘtæ·ndʒĕnt), *sb.* (*a.*) 1635. [See CO-.] *Trig.* The tangent of the complement of a given angle. (Abbrev. *cot*) So **Cotange·ntial** *a.* having the same tangent.

Cotarnine (kotā·ɹnəin). 1857. [a. F., f. *narcotine* by transposition.] *Chem.* A non-volatile organic base, $C_{12}H_{13}NO_3 + H_2O$, obtained by the action of oxidizing agents on narcotine.

Cote (kōᵘt), *sb.*[1] [OE. *cote* fem.; cf. COT *sb.*[1]] **1.** A cot or cottage. Now *dial.* **2.** A shed, stall, or the like, for shelter or storage; *spec.* a sheep-cote. (Now chiefly in comb., as in *dove-, bell-c.*, etc.) ME.

2. Stalles for all maner of beasts, and cotes for flocks 2 *Chron.* xxxii. 28.

Cote (kōᵘt), *sb.*[2] 1575. [f. COTE *v.*[1]] *Coursing.* The action of COTE *v.*[1]

Cote (kōᵘt), *v.*[1] ? *Obs.* 1555. [? doublet of COAST, mod.F. *côtoyer*; cf. COAST *v.*] **1.** *trans.* (*Coursing.*) Of one of two dogs running together: To pass by (its fellow) so as to turn the hare, etc. **2.** *transf.*, etc. To pass by, outstrip 1566.

2. Wee coated them on the way *Haml.* II. ii. 330.

Cote (kōᵘt), *v.*[2] 1630. [f. COTE *sb.*[1]] To put in a cote.

Cote, *v.*[3] ME. Obs. f. QUOTE, q.v.

Cotemporanean, etc.; see CONT-.

Co-te·nant. 1822. [See CO-.] A joint tenant. Hence **Co-te·nancy.**

Coterell (kǫ·tĕrĕl). ME. [a. OF. *coterel*, dim. of OF. *cotier*, the occupant of a *cota* or cot. Cf. COTERIE.] *Feudal Antiq.* A cottar; also, *erron.*, a cot.

Coterie (kōᵘ·tĕri). 1738. [a. F., orig. 'a certain number of peasants united to hold land from a lord'.] †**1.** A club –1774. **2.** A circle of persons associated together and distinguished from 'outsiders'; a set; a clique 1738; a meeting of such a circle 1805.

2. The Holland House c. 1828. Catiline, Clodius, and some of that c. DE QUINCEY.

Cotesian (kotī·ziăn, -ʒ̄lăn), *a.* 1753. Pertaining to Roger Cotes or his mathematical discoveries.

Cotham (kǫ·tăm), name of a village near Bristol, designating a dendritic argillaceous limestone 1822.

Cothe, coath (kōᵘð), *sb.* Now *dial.* [OE. *coðu, coðe* disease, pestilence.] †1. Sickness; an attack of illness –1460. 2. Now a disease of sheep, etc.; cf. COE 1784. Hence **Cothe** *v. dial.*, to give (sheep) the 'coe' or rot; *intr.* to faint.

Cothurn (kōᵘ·þɹn, koþɹ̄·ɹn). 1606. = next.

‖**Cothurnus** (koþɹ̄·ɹnɒs). 1727. [L., ad. Gr. κόθορνος.] A thick-soled boot reaching to the middle of the leg, worn anciently by tragic actors; a buskin; *fig.* tragedy, a tragic style.

fig. She too wears the mask and the c., and speaks to measure THACKERAY. Hence **Cothu·rnal** *a.* of or pertaining to the c.; of tragedy, tragic. **Cothu·rnate** *a.* shod with the c.; tragic. So †**Cothurnated, Cothurned** *ppl. a.*

†**Coti·cular**, *a. rare.* 1799. [f. L. *coticula*, dim. of *cos, cotem* + -AR.] Of the nature of a whetstone.

Co-tidal (kōᵘtəi·dăl), *a.* 1833. [See CO-.] Of or pertaining to the coincidence in time of tidal phenomena, *esp.* that of high water.

C. line, a line on a map connecting at those places at which high water occurs at the same hour.

Cotillion, ‖**cotillon** (koti·lyən, kotīˡyoṅ). 1766. [ad. F. *cotillon* petticoat, dim. of *cotte* coat; see Littré.] 1. The name of several dances, chiefly of French origin, consisting of a variety of steps and figures. (In Eng. usage now only as Fr.; but in U.S. a generic name for quadrilles.) 2. A piece of music arranged for the dance 1828. 3. A woollen material in black and white for ladies' skirts 1858.

Cotinga (koti·ŋgă). 1783. [F.; orig. native name in S. America.] A S. Amer. bird, or family of passerine birds, of brilliant plumage. **Coti·ngine** *a.* pertaining or related to the c.

Cotise (kǫ·tis), *sb.* Also **cottise.** 1572. [a. F., of unkn. origin.] *Her.* An ordinary, in breadth the fourth part of a bend, usually one of two; cf. COST *sb.*⁴ Hence **Co·tise** *v.* to border (a bend, etc.) on both sides with cotises, barrulets, etc.

Co·tland. Also **coth-.** *Hist.* OE. [f. COT *sb.*¹] The land (about 5 acres) held with his cot by the Old English cottar.

Co·tman. *Hist.* OE. [f. as prec.] The tenant of a cot.

Co·to. 1879. In *C.-bark*, an officinal bark, obtained from Bolivia. Hence **Co·toin** (*Chem.*), a substance, in yellowish white crystals, obtained from c.-bark.

Cotoneaster (kotōᵘniˌæ·stəɹ). 1753. [Bot. L. f. *cotonea* quince.] A genus of small trees or trailing shrubs, N.O. *Rosaceæ*, inhabiting northern Europe and the Himalayas.

†**Cotquean** (kǫ·tkwīn). 1547. [f. COT *sb.*¹ + QUEAN.] 1. The housewife of a cot; hence, a vulgar beldam, scold (cf. *huzzy* from *housewife*) –1633. 2. A man that acts the housewife, and meddles with women's matters –1825.

1. Scold like a cot-quean; that's your profession FORD. 2. I cannot abide these aperne husbands; such cotqueanes DEKKER. Hence **Cotquea·nity.** B. JONSON.

Co-trustee, etc.; see CO-.

Co·tset. *Hist.* [OE. *cot-sǣta*, lit. 'occupant of a cot', f. COT *sb.*¹ + *-sǣta* sitter.] In *OE. Law*: A villein who held a cot with an attached plot of land by service of labour. (See COTTAR.) var. †**Cotsetla**, †**cotsetle.**

Cotswold (kǫ·tswōld). 1537. [f.? + WOLD.] Name of a range of hills in Gloucestershire, England, noted for their sheep-pastures, and for a breed of long-woolled sheep named after them. Hence *C. lion*, (*joc.*) a sheep.

‖**Cotta** (kǫ·tă). 1848. [med.L.; see COAT.] *Eccl.* A surplice.

‖**Cottabus** (kǫ·tăbɒs). 1823. [L., a Gr. κότταβος.] *Gr. Antiq.* An amusement in vogue at drinking parties in ancient Greece, consisting in throwing the wine left in a cup into some vessel, so as to strike it in a particular manner.

Cottage (kǫ·tédʒ). ME. [app. a. AF. **cotage*, f. *cota* COTE¹, COT¹.] 1. A small or humble dwelling-house. Also *transf.* and *fig.* (obs.). †2. A small erection for shelter; a cot, hut, shed, etc. –1796. 3. A small country or suburban residence 1765; in U.S. *spec.* a summer residence (often large and sumptuous) at a watering-place 1882.

1. A poure wydwe..Was whilom dwellyng in a narwe cotage CHAUCER. (*fig.*) *Clay* or *earthen c.*: the body. Phr.: **c. allotment** (see ALLOTMENT); **c. farming**, spade husbandry; **c. hospital**, a small hospital, in a c., or the like; also, a hospital arranged on the principle of having several detached cottages. Hence **Co·ttaged** *ppl. a.* furnished with cottages. †**Co·ttagely** *a.* proper to a c.; humble, mean, poor.

Cottager (kǫ·tédʒəɹ). 1550. [f. COTTAGE + -ER¹.] One who lives in a cottage; used *esp.* of agricultural labourers.

The yeomanry, or middle people, of a condition between gentlemen and cottagers BACON.

Cottar, cotter (kǫ·təɹ). 1552. [ad. med.L. *cotarius*, f. *cota* cot (prob. repr. OE. *cotsǣta*); later, f. COT *sb.*¹] 1. = COTSET, q. v. 2. *Sc.* A peasant who occupies a cottage belonging to a farm as a sort of out-servant 1552. 3. *Irish.* = COTTIER 2. 1791. Also *attrib.*

1. The cottar, the bordar, and the labourer were bound to aid in the work of the home-farm GREEN.

Cotted (kǫ·téd), *ppl. a.* 1793. [f. COT *sb.*² and *v.*²] Matted, tangled; said *esp.* of a fleece.

Cotter, *sb.*¹; see COTTAR.

Cotter (kǫ·təɹ), *sb.*² 1649. [See COTTEREL *sb.*] A pin, key, wedge, or bolt which fits into a hole and fastens something in its place. Hence **Co·tter** *v. trans.* to fasten with a c.

Cotterel (kǫ·tərĕl), *sb. dial.* 1570. [? primitive or dim. of COTTER *sb.*²] 1. = COTTER *sb.*² Chiefly *north.* 2. A trammel, crane, or bar, to hang a pot over a fire. *s.dial.* 1674. 3. A washer 1869. Hence **Co·tterel** *v. dial.* to cotter.

Cottier (kǫ·tiəɹ). ME. [a. F. *cotier, cottier* = med.L. *cotarius*, f. *cota* cot.] 1. A peasant who lives in a cottage; *orig.* a COTSET, q. v. 2. *spec.* In Ireland, a peasant renting a small holding under the system of *c.-tenure*, under which the land is let annually in small plots directly to labourers, the rent being fixed by public competition 1832.

1. They had cottiers, day labourers established in cottages, on their estate MAR. EDGEWORTH. Hence **Co·ttierism**, the system of cottier-tenure.

Cottise, -ize; see COTIZE.

Cottoid (kǫ·toid), *a.* (*sb.*) 1854. [f. mod.L. *Cottus* name of a genus of fishes + -OID.] *Zool.* Belonging to a family of fishes of which the type is *Cottus*, a genus related to the 'Miller's thumb'. As *sb.* A fish of this family.

Cotton (kǫ·t'n), *sb.*¹ [ME. *coton*, a. F., a. (ult.) Arab. *qutn, qutun.* See also ACTON.] 1. The white fibrous substance which clothes the seeds of the cotton plant (*Gossypium*); used for making cloth and thread, etc. 2. The cotton plant; the genus *Gossypium.* Also, cotton plants collectively. ME. 3. Thread spun from cotton yarn; in full *c. thread* 1848. 4. Any fabric made of cotton; in *pl.* cotton fabrics, also cotton garments ME. 5. *transf.* A cotton-like down growing on other plants 1551. 6. *attrib.* (without hyphen.) Made of cotton 1552.

Comb.: **corkwood c.**, the silky down of *Ochroma Lagopus* (cf. SILK-COTTON); **c.-bagging**, a coarse wrapping material used for baling cotton-wool; **-cake**, compressed c.-seed freed from the oil, used for feeding cattle; **-chopper**, a machine for cleaning c. by scutching, blowing, etc.; **c. famine**, the failure of the supply of c. to English mills during the American Civil War; **c. flannel**, a strong c. fabric with a long plush nap, also called *c. plush* and *Canton flannel*; **c. gin**, a machine for freeing cotton-wool from the seeds; **c.-grass**, a general name for the species *Eriophorum*; **-mill**, a factory where cotton is spun or woven by steam or water power; **-opener**, a machine for loosening and blowing c. after its transport in compressed bales; **-picker**, one who or that which picks c. from the bolls of the plant; a machine for cleaning c.; **c. plush** = *cotton flannel* (above); **c. powder**, an explosive made from gun-c.; **c.-press**, a machine (or warehouse) for pressing c. into bales; **c. print**, c. cloth printed with a design in colours; **c.-rat**, a rodent (*Sigmodon hispidus*) common in southern U. S.; **-rose**, the plant-genus *Filago*; **-seed, c. seed**, the seed of the c. plant; also *attrib.*; **-spinner**, a c.-manufacturer or worker; **-stainer**, a heteropterous insect, *Dysdercus suturellus*, which gives a reddish stain to c.; **-tail**, the common rabbit of the U.S., *Lepus sylvaticus*, which has a white fluffy tail; **-thistle**, a tall species of thistle, *Onopordum Acanthium*, entirely covered with white cottony down; **-tree, c. tree**, (*a*) a name of species of *Bombax* and *Eriodendron*; (*b*) a name for *Viburnum Lantana* and *Populus nigra*; also = COTTONWOOD; **c. velvet**, a c. fabric made with a pile like velvet; **c. waste**, refuse yarn from c.-mills, used for cleaning machinery, etc.; **-wool, c. wool**, raw c., as gathered from the bolls of the plant; **-worm**, the larva of an insect (*Aletia xylina*) very destructive to the c. crops of America; **c. yarn**, c. prepared for weaving into fabrics; **mineral c.**, a wool-like metallic fibre, made by sending a jet of steam through a stream of liquid slag; †**philosophic c.**, an old name for flowers of zinc.

Hence †**Co·ttonary** *a.* cottony (Sir T. Browne). †**Co·ttoned** *ppl. a.* having a nap, friezed. **Cottonee·**, a Turkish fabric of c. and silk satinet. **Cottonee·r** (*rare*), a c.-manufacturer or worker. **Co·ttonize** *v.* to reduce (flax, hemp, etc.) to a short c.-like staple. †**Co·ttonous** *a.* cottony. **Co·ttony** *a.* downy; nappy; like, or of the nature of, c.

†**Cotton**, *sb.*² 1503. [? same as prec., conn. w. the sense 'down, nap'.] A woollen fabric of the nature of frieze, formerly manufactured in Lancashire, Westmorland, and Wales (*Manchester, Kendal*, and *Welsh c.*) –1840.

Cotton (kǫ·t'n), *v.* 1488. [f. the sb. Cf. F. *cotonner.*]

I. *lit.* †1. *trans.* To form a down or nap on; to frieze –1598. 2. *intr.* Of cloth, etc.: To rise with a nap. ? *Obs.* 1608. 3. *trans.* To furnish, clothe, stop *up*, with cotton 1661.

II. *fig.* (*intr.*) 1. To prosper, 'get on' well. Now *dial.* 1560. 2. To 'get on' together 1567. 3. To fraternize. Const. *together, with.* 1648. 4. To take *to*; to become drawn *to* 1805.

2. John a Nokes and John a Style and I cannot c. 1605. 3. I love to see 'em hug and cotten together, like Down upon a Thistle CONGREVE. Phr. *C. up*: to make up to. 4. 'I don't object to Short,' she says, 'but I c. to Codlin' DICKENS. Hence **Co·ttoner**, one who puts a nap on cloth.

Cottonade (kǫt'nē̆ᵢd). Also **cotonnade.** 1858. [a. F. *cotonnade.*] A name for various coarse cotton fabrics; cotton check. Also *attrib.*

Cotton lord, cotton-lord. 1823. A magnate of the cotton trade.

Cottonocracy (kǫt'nǫ·krăsi). *colloq.* 1845. [Cf. *aristocracy.*] Cotton lords as a class.

Cottonopolis (kǫt'nǫ·pŏlis). 1886. [Cf. *metropolis.*] 'Cotton City'; *i.e.* Manchester.

Cotton plant, cotton-plant. 1751. A plant that yields cotton; a plant of the genus *Gossypium* or of an allied genus.

Co·ttonweed. 1562. A name for the species of *Gnaphalium* and the allied genera.

Co·ttonwood, co·tton-wood. 1823. The name of several species of poplar (*Populus*) in U.S.; so called from the cotton-like covering of the seeds.

Cotunnite (kotɒ·nəit). 1834. [f. Dr. *Cotugna* of Naples; see -ITE.] *Min.* Native lead chloride found in white acicular crystals in the crater of Vesuvius.

Cotwal, var. of KOTWAL, an Indian police-officer.

‖**Cotyle** (kǫ·tilī). 1707. [Gr. κοτύλη (in L. form *cotyla*).] 1. *Gr. Antiq.* A deep cup, taken as a measure of capacity. (Not in Eng. use.) 2. *Anat.*, etc. A cup-like cavity or organ; *spec.* the ACETABULUM 1882. Hence **Co·tyliform** *a.* cup-shaped. **Cotyli·gerous** *a.* bearing cotyles or cup-like organs.

Cotyledon (kǫtilī·dən). 1545. [a. L., a. Gr. κοτυληδών (f. κοτύλη; see prec.).] 1. *Phys.* One of the separate patches of villi on the fœtal chorion of Ruminants. 2. *Bot.* A genus of plants of the N.O. *Crassulaceæ*; the British species is *C. Umbilicus*, Navelwort or Pennywort 1601. 3. *Bot.* The primary leaf in the embryo of Phanerogams; the seed-leaf 1776. Hence **Cotyle·donal** *a.* (*rare*). **Cotyle·donary** *a.*, *Bot.* of the nature of a c.; *Phys.* characterized by the presence of cotyledons (sense 1). **Cotyle·donoid**, *Bot.* a name for the germinating threads of mosses. **Cotyle·donous** *a.* characterized by the presence of cotyledons.

Cotyloid (kǫ·tiloid), *a.* 1760. [See COTYLE and -OID.] *Anat.* Shaped like a cup: applied *esp.* to the socket of the hip-joint (*c. cavity*); also to the coxal cavity in insects.

Cotylophorous (kǫtilǫ·fŏrəs), *a.* [f. Gr. κοτύλη + -φόρος.] *Zool.* Having a cotyledonary placenta; belonging to the *Cotylophora* or typical Ruminants of Huxley's classification.

Couch (kautʃ), *sb.*[1] ME. [a. F. *couche*, f. *coucher*; see COUCH *v.*[1]] 1. A frame, with what is spread over it, on which to lie down; a bed. Now, in lit. use, vaguely, that on which one sleeps. Also *transf.* and *fig.* 2. The lair or den of a wild beast ME. 3. A lounge for reclining or sitting on 1450. 4. A layer (*esp.* of paint), a stratum, bed 1661. 5. *Malting.* A layer of grain laid on the floor to germinate; also the floor 1615. 6. *Paper Manuf.* A board covered with felt or flannel on which the sheets of pulp are placed to be pressed 1886.

1. I bad men schulde me myn couche make CHAUCER. *fig.* A c. whereupon to rest a searching and restless spirit BACON. 2. A dog-otter..rushed from his c. among the roots MEDWIN. *Comb.* **c.-bed, -bedstead,** a c. used as a bed.

Couch (kautʃ, kūtʃ), *sb.*[2] 1578. [var. of QUITCH :—OE. *cwice.*] A species of grass, *Triticum repens*, with long creeping root-stalks; usu. **c.-grass.** Also applied to other creeping grasses. Hence **Cou·chy** *a.* full of c.-grass.

Couch (kautʃ), *v.* ME. [a. F. *coucher* = It. *colcare* :—L. *collocare*, f. *com-* intensive + *locare* to place.]

I. *trans.* 1. To cause to lie down, to lay down; to put to bed; also *refl.* *Obs.* exc. in *pa. pple.* = Laid on, or as on, a couch. Also *fig.* †2. To cause to lie close; in *pa. pple.* prostrated, cowering -1725. †3. To lay (things); to set, bed, overlay, etc. -1794. †4. To lay, overlay, inlay, spread, set *with* (*of*). Chiefly in *pa. pple.* -1611. b. To embroider with gold thread or the like laid flat. Also *absol.* ME. 5. *Malting.* To spread (grain) on a floor to germinate 1562. 6. *Paper Manuf.* To lay (a sheet of pulp) upon a felt to be pressed 1751. 7. To lower (a spear, etc.) to the position of attack; to level as a gun 1470. 8. To lay down, lower, depress (a part of the body, etc.) 1611. 9. *Surg.* To remove (a cataract) by depressing the opaque crystalline lens with a needle, until it lies below the axis of vision. Also *to c. the eye* or *a person.* 1601. †10. To place in a lodging; *pass.* to be lodged or located -1690. †11. To hide, conceal -1814. †12. To collocate, comprise -1729. 13. To put together (words, etc.); to put into words 1529; to express in an obscure or veiled way 1563. Also †*transf.*

1. Thou look'st sunk-eyed; go c. thy head MARSTON. The Hind..Then couched her self securely by his side DRYDEN. 3. I c. it..with all..humilitie at her Majesties..feete 1589. 4. b. A cloth of Tars, Cowched of perlys whyte CHAUCER. 7. A brauer Souldier neuer couched Launce 1 *Hen. VI*, III. ii. 134. 8. Some six or eight thorns, some erect, others couched 1753. 11. C. thee midway on the wold SCOTT. 13. The words wherein the question..is couched HOBBES.

II. *intr.* (Now chiefly of beasts.) 1. To lie; *esp.* to lie at rest or in sleep ME. 2. To crouch, cower; †to stoop under a burden; †to bow in obeisance; *fig.* to submit, succumb ME. Also †*transf.* of plants, etc. 3. To lie in ambush, to lurk 1583. 4. Of leaves, etc.: To lie in a heap for decomposition, etc. 1770.

1. The deep that coucheth beneath *Deut.* xxxiii. 13. 2. An aged Squire..That seemd to c. under his shield SPENSER. 3. Bertram couches in the brake and fern, Hiding his face SCOTT.

Hence **Cou·ching** *vbl. sb.* the action of the *vb.*; (*Embroidery*) couched work; also *attrib.*

Couchancy (kau·tʃănsi). 1695. [f. COUCHANT; see -ANCY.] *Law.* The fact of being *couchant*; see next. var. **Cou·chance.**

Couchant (kau·tʃănt), *a.* 1496. [a. F. *couchant*, pr. pple. of *coucher* to lie, COUCH.] 1. Lying down; couching; *esp.* of an animal. 2. *Her.* Of an animal: 'Lying on his belly, but with his head lifted up' 1766. †3. Bending down, crouching (*rare*) -1706. †4. Lurking (*lit.* and *fig.*) -1720.

1. *C. and levant*: lying down and rising up; said of cattle in permanent occupation of pasture. 2. His crest was covered with a c. Hownd SPENSER.

‖**Couché** (kuʃe), *a.* 1727. [Fr.; pa. pple. of *coucher.*] Of a shield: Suspended by the sinister corner so as to hang slanting. Of a chevron: Borne sideways.

‖**Couchee** (kuʃe). Rarely **coucher.** 1676. [a. F. *couché*, var. of *coucher* (subst. use of *coucher* inf.).] An evening reception.

Royal Drawing-rooms, Levees, Couchees CARLYLE.

Coucher[1] (kau·tʃəɹ). ME. [app. a. AF. **couchour* = F. *coucheur*; see COUCH *v.*] 1. One lying down; in *Sc.* a poltroon. 2. One who couches or crouches. BROWNING. †3. A large book, *e.g.* a breviary such as lay permanently on a desk or table -1559. †4. A resident factor in a foreign place -1706.

Comb. †**c.-book**, a large cartulary.

Cou·cher[2]. 1751. [F. *coucheur* (etymol. = prec.) and *couchart.*] *Paper Manuf.* One who or that which couches pulp to be pressed.

Couéism (kū·eᵢiz'm). 1922. [f. name of Émile *Coué*, French psychologist.] Systematic auto-suggestion, usu. of a sanguine kind.

Cougar (kū·găr). Also **couguar** (kū·gwaɪ). 1774. [a. F., repr. (ult.) Guarani *guaçu ara* or *guazu ara.*] A large feline quadruped (*Felis concolor*); also called *puma*, *catamount*, *red tiger*, *American lion*, etc.

Cough (kǫf), *sb.* ME. [f. COUGH *v.*; cf. *laugh.*] 1. A diseased condition of the respiratory organs manifesting itself in fits of coughing. (Till 1600 usually called *the cough*; *a cough* is a specific attack.) 2. A single act of coughing; a violent expulsion of air from the lungs with the characteristic noise 1742.

Cough (kǫf), *v.* [ME. *coȝ-*, *cowh-en*; akin to MDu. *cuchen*, mod.Du. and LG. *kuchen* to cough; of echoic origin.] 1. *intr.* To expel air from the lungs with a violent effort and characteristic noise; usually in order to remove something from the air-passages. 2. *trans.* To express by coughing 1450.

Phr. *To c. out, up*: to eject by coughing; †*fig.* to disclose. *To c. down*: to put down or silence a speaker by coughing. Hence **Cou·gher.**

Could (kud), pa. t. of CAN *v.*, q.v.

Coulée (kule, kū·lī). Also (*U.S.*) **-ee, -ie, coolie, -ey.** 1807. [a. F. *coulée*, f. *couler* to flow.] 1. *Geol.* A stream of lava, whether molten or solidified; a lava-flow 1839. 2. In Western U.S. and Canada: A deep ravine or gulch scooped out by heavy floods, but dry in summer.

‖**Couleur** (kulǒr). 1783. The Fr. for COLOUR. Hence *c. de rose* rose-colour; used in Eng., a. as *adj.* 'rose-coloured', 'roseate'; b. as *adv.* 'in a (too) rosy light'.

‖**Coulisse** (kulī·s). 1819. [F., subst. use of fem. of *coulis*, f. *colare* in Romanic to flow.] 1. A groove in which a sluice-gate or the like slides up and down 1864. 2. One of the side scenes of the stage in a theatre; also the space between them, the wings.

‖**Couloir** (kulwar). 1855. [F. *couloir* colander, etc. :—late L. *colatorium*, f. *colare.*] A steep gorge or gully on a mountain side.

Up this c. we proposed to try the ascent TYNDALL.

Coulomb (kulǫ·m). 1881. [After the French physicist, C. A. de *Coulomb* (1736–1806).] The unit of electrical quantity; the quantity of electricity conveyed in one second by a current of one ampère. (Previously called *Weber.*)

Comb. **c.-meter**, a metre for measuring electricity in coulombs.

Coulter, colter (kōᵘ·ltəɹ). [OE. *culter*, a. L. *culter*. The sp. *colter* is preferred in U.S.] The iron blade fixed in front of the share in a plough; it cuts the soil vertically. Also *attrib.*

Cou·lterneb. 1678. [f. COULTER + NEB.] A local name for the Puffin, so called from the shape of its bill.

Coumarin (kū·mărin). 1830. [a. F. *coumarine*, f. *coumarou* = *cumarú*, native name in Guiana of the Tonka bean.] *Chem.* A crystalline substance ($C_2H_6O_2$), found in the seeds of the *cumarú*, *coumarou*, or Tonka bean; also in melilot, woodruff, etc. Hence **Cou·maric** *a.*, in *c. acid*, an acid ($C_9H_8O_3$) obtained from coumarin; **Cou·marate**, a salt of coumaric acid.

Council (kau·nsĭl), *sb.* OE. [repr. OF. *cuncile*, ONF. *concilie* = L. *concilium* (f. *con-* together + *cal-* to call). In English, confused with *conseil*, later *counsel*, till the 16th c.]

I. f. L. *concilium.* †1. *gen.* An assembly called together for any purpose. (ME. only.) 2. *spec.* An assembly of ecclesiastics (with or without laymen) convened to regulate doctrine or discipline in the church, or, earlier, to settle points in dispute between the ecclesiastical and civil powers, and variously qualified according to its sphere, as *œcumenical*, *general*, *national*, *patriarchal*, *primatial*, *provincial*, *diocesan* (this = synod). 3. In the N.T., used as tr. Gr. συνέδριον, Vulg. *concilium* ME.

2. All synods and councils since the Apostles' times, whether general or particular, may err, and many have erred *Westm. Confess. Faith.*

II. f. L. *consilium*, F. *conseil.* An assembly or meeting for consultation or advice, as a *family c.*, a *c. of physicians* ME.

Great C. (in *Eng. Hist.*): occas. applied to a *Witenagemót*; more often to the assemblies under the Norman kings of tenants-in-chief and great ecclesiastics, out of which the House of Lords originated. *Cabinet C.*: see CABINET. *C. of War*: a. an assembly of officers called to consult with the general or commanding officer, usually in an emergency; b. a permanent advisory committee on military affairs. *Common C.*: the administrative body of a corporate town or city. (In England, retained as a title only in the case of London.)

III. A body of counsellors (or councillors). 1. A body of men chosen or designated as permanent advisers on matters of state ME. 2. A deliberative and administrative committee, associated with the president (or directors) of a society or institution 1682.

Comb.: **c.-board**, the table at which the councillors sit; hence, the councillors in session; **-book**, the book in which the acts of a c. are registered; the register of privy-councillors; **-chamber, -hall, -room**, an apartment appropriated to c.-meetings; **-fire**, a fire kindled by North American Indians when in c.; **-general**, a general or common c.; **-house**, (*a*) a house in which a c. meets; in Scotland, a town-hall; (*b*) a house erected under the authority of a town or district council; **-table** = *council-board*; †the Privy Council.

†**Cou·ncilist.** [f. prec.] One versed in the subject of COUNCILS (sense I. 2). MILTON.

†**Cou·ncillary,** *a.* 1651. [f. as prec.] CONSILIARY. Hobbes.

Councillor (kau·nsĭləɹ). ME. [var. of earlier *counsellor*, by assimilation to *council.*] An official member of a council. Hence **Cou·ncillorship**, the office of a c.

†**Co-u·ne,** *v. rare.* 1627. [f. L. *co-* + *unare.*] *trans.* To unite, combine -1677.

Co-uni·te, *v.* 1548. [See CO-.] To unite together (*trans.* and *intr.*). So †**Co-uni·te** *pa. pple.* = co-united.

Counsel (kau·nsĕl), *sb.* [ME. *con-*, *counseil*, etc., a. OF. *con-*, *cunseil* :—L. *consilium*, f. *con-* + **sal-* a root prob. cogn. w. Skr. *sar-* to go. See also COUNCIL.] 1. Interchange of opinions; consultation, deliberation. 2. Advice, direction, as the result of deliberation ME. 3. The faculty of counselling; judgement; prudence; sagacity. (*arch.*) ME. 4. That in which deliberation results; resolution, purpose; plan ME. †5. A secret purpose or opinion -1652; a secret; a confidence -1613. †6. A body of advisers. Now COUNCIL. -1549; a counsellor -1654. 7. A body of legal advisers, engaged in the conduct of a cause. (Usually a collective pl.; formerly treated as collective sing.) ME. b. as *sing.*: A single legal adviser 1709.

1. Who is this that darkneth counsell by words without knowledge *Job* xxxviii. 2. 2. Taak no conseil of a fool CHAUCER. *C. of perfection* (see *Matt.* xix. 21). *Evangelical counsels* (Theol.): the obligations of poverty, chastity, and obedience to a religious superior. 3. *Job* xii. 13. 4. Hii..were alle at conseyl to worry Engelond R. GLOUC. 5. †*In c.*: in private, in confidence. *To keep* (†*hold*) *c.*: to observe secrecy (*arch.* and *dial.*). *To keep one's* (*own*) *c.*: to be reticent about one's intentions, etc. 7. The second of our three C. was the best PEPYS. *King's* (*Queen's*) *C.*: barristers appointed (on the nomination of the lord-chancellor) c. to the crown; also a member of this body. (*Abbrev.* K.C., Q.C.)

Hence †**Cou·nselful** *a.* **Cou·nselless** *a.*

Counsel (kau·nsĕl), *v.* [ME. *conseillen*, a. F. *conseiller* :—late L. *consiliare*, for cl. *consiliari*, f. *consilium*; see prec.] 1. To give or offer counsel or advice to; to advise. Also *absol.* 2. To recommend (a plan, suggestion, etc.) ME. †3. To consult -1547. Also †*refl.* to consider; also = next. (ME. only.) †4. *intr.* To take counsel with others; to deliberate -1795.

1. Pray be counsail'd *Cor.* III. ii. 28. Consail me fader, how to liue ME. 2. Thus Belial..Counsel'd ignoble ease MILT. *P. L.* II. 227. 4. Wives must c. with husbands LATIMER. Hence **Cou·nsellable, -elable** *a.* willing to be counselled; to be recom-

mended. **Cou·nselled, -eled** *ppl. a.* determined; recommended. **Cou·nselling, -eling** *vbl. sb.* giving or taking of counsel.

Counsellor, -elor (kau·nsĕləɹ). [ME. *counseiller(e*, etc., a. OF. *conseillere* :—L. *consiliator*, f. *consiliare* to COUNSEL.] 1. One who counsels; an adviser. Also *fig.* 2. An official counsellor. (In this sense now spelt COUNCILLOR, q.v.) 3. (More fully *c.-at-law.*) One whose profession is to give legal advice to clients, and conduct their cases in court; a barrister or advocate. *arch.* in Eng. use. 1531.

1. Wyse conseylyrs and polytyke men STARKEY. 3. Good Counsellors lacke no Clients *Meas. for M.* I. ii. 109. Hence **Cou·nsellorship**, the office of c.; formerly = COUNCILLORSHIP.

Count (kaunt), *sb.*[1] [ME. *counte*, a. OF. *conte, cunte* = It. *conto* :—late L. *computum*, f. *computare* to calculate. Refash. in 14th c., after L., as *compte*.] 1. The action of counting; a computation. 2. The result of reckoning; the reckoning; the sum total 1483. 3. A reckoning as to money or property; *fig.* reckoning (cf. ACCOUNT *sb.*) ME. 4. Estimation; the act or way of estimating; regard, notice (cf. ACCOUNT *sb.*) 1475. 5. *Law.* Each particular charge in a declaration or indictment; also, in a real action, the whole declaration 1588.

1. Infinite..because..out of all c. *Two Gent.* II. i. 62. Phr. *To put one out of c. To keep (lose) c.* 2. Very near double the c. SWIFT. 3. Look, Steward, to your compt 1610. *fig.* When we shall meete at compt, This looke of thine will hurle my Soule from Heauen *Oth.* V. ii. 273. 4. They make no counte of generall councels ASCHAM.

Count (kaunt), *sb.*[2] 1553. [a. AF. *counte* = OF. *cunte, conte* :—L. *comitem* lit. 'companion', subseq. a title of dignity under the empire. Unlike COUNTESS, the word never passed into English till used in 16th c. to represent Fr. *comte*, It. *conte*, as foreign titles. See also COUNTY *sb.*[2]] A foreign title of nobility, corresponding to the English EARL.

Count Palatine: orig. in the later Roman Empire a count (*comes*) attached to the imperial palace, and having supreme judicial authority in certain causes; thence, under the German Emperors, etc., a count having supreme jurisdiction in his fief; in Eng. Hist. =*Earl Palatine*, the proprietor of a county palatine, now applied to the Earl of Chester, and Duke of Lancaster, dignities which are attached to the crown. See PALATINE.

Comb. **C.-bishop**, a bishop holding also the temporal dignity of *count*; so **c.-cardinal.**

Count (kaunt), *v.* [ME. *counten*, a. OF. *cunter, conter* :—L. *computare*; see COMPUTE. A var. *compt*, after the Fr., is also found (15th to 18th c.).]

I. *trans.* 1. To tell over one by one, so as to ascertain the number of individuals in a collection; to number; to reckon up; also, to repeat the numerals one, two, three, etc., as *to c. ten.* 2. To include in the reckoning 1526. 3. To esteem, reckon, hold (a thing) to be (so and so) ME. 4. To reckon, esteem (at such a value); †to hold of account ME. †5. To reckon or impute *to* -1701. †6. To tell, relate -1778.

1. Then must I c. my gaines SHAKS. Phr. *To c. out*: to c. and take out (from a stock), to c. so as to exhaust the stock. *To c. out the House* (of Commons): to bring the sitting to an end by pointing out to the Speaker that the number of members present is less than forty, the number required to 'make a House'; also *to c. out a measure*, etc., i. e. to stop it by this means. 3. Coumptynge all fyshe that cometh to the net 1546. I c. you for a fool TENNYSON. 5. Abram beleued the Lorde, and yt was counted vnto him for righteousnes COVERDALE *Gen.* xv. 6.

II. *intr.* 1. To reckon, make reckoning. *Obs.* exc. in *To c. without one's host.* ME. Also with *on, upon* (†*of*). †2. To make account *of*, think (much, lightly, etc.) *of* -1846. 3. (*absol.* use of 1.) To 'do sums'; to reckon numerically 1588. †4. *Law.* To plead in a court of law. [AF. *counter*, in Law-books from 13th c.] -1809. 5. To admit of being counted 1845. b. To amount to, number 1819. 6. To enter into the account (with *compl.* or *absol.*) 1857.

1. There is less wisdom, honesty, and mercy in men than is counted on FULLER. 2. *Two Gent.* II. i. 65. 3. To c. by tens 1865. 4. The plaintiff was said to 'count' when he declared..the nature of his complaint, while 'plead' and 'plea' were specifically used of the defendant's answer N. E. D. 5. b. The carambole counts two 1820. 6. Many doubt whether good play really counts much at Whist PROCTOR.

Hence **Cou·ntable** *a.* †responsible; †sensitive *to*; proper to be counted, numerable.

Countenance (kau·ntĭnăns), *sb.* [ME. *con-, cun-, countena(u)nce*, a. OF. *con-, cuntenance*, ad. L. *continentia* (see CONTINENCE). The extension of sense from 'mien' to 'face' is Eng.] †1. Comportment, demeanour; conduct -1719. †2. Appearance, look; mere show -1837. †3. A sign, gesture -1568. 4. The expression of a person's face ME. 5. The face ME. 6. Composure of face ME. †7. Demeanour as expressing good or ill will -1632. 8. Appearance on any side; moral support 1576. †9. Repute in the world -1745; position -1784.

4. Their countenances speak a different language JUNIUS. Phr. *To keep one's c.*: to refrain from expressing emotion. 5. A youth, and ruddy, and of a faire c. 1 *Sam.* xvii. 42. 6. I will not be put out of c. *L. L. L.* V. ii. 611. Phr. *To keep (put) in c.*: to keep from being abashed. 8. A doctrine which has no c. in reason or revelation PRIESTLEY. 9. Men of c. and authority 1617. Hence **Countenanced** *ppl. a.* having a (specified) c.

Countenance (kau·ntĭnăns), *v.* 1486. [f. F. *contenancer*, f. *contenance* COUNTENANCE *sb.*] †1. *intr.* To behave, pretend, or make (as if..) -1519. †2. *trans.* To pretend. SPENSER. †3. To set off, grace -1603. 4. To give countenance to; to favour, patronize, support 1568. †5. To keep in countenance. SHAKS.

4. To c. Burnet at the Hague MACAULAY, the practice 1832. 5. As from your Graues rise vp..To c. this horror *Macb.* II. iii. 85. Hence **Cou·ntenanced** *ppl. a.*[2] favoured, supported. **Cou·ntenancer**, one who supports or encourages.

†**Counter** (kau·ntəɹ), *sb.*[1] ME. [aphet. f. *acuntre*, ACOUNTER.] ENCOUNTER, opposition -1591.

Counter (kau·ntəɹ), *sb.*[2] ME. [a. AF. *countour* = OF. *conteor* :—L. *computatorem*; see COUNT.] 1. One who counts or calculates. †2. A serjeant-at-law, etc.; see COUNTOUR. 3. An apparatus for keeping count of revolutions, strokes of a piston, etc. 1803.

Counter (kau·ntəɹ), *sb.*[3] ME. [a. AF. *counteour, countour*, in OF. *conteoir, -eor*, etc., mod. *comptoir* :—L. *computatorium*, f. *computare.*] 1. Anything used in counting or keeping count; as a piece of metal, ivory, or the like, used now *esp.* in games of chance, etc. Also, applied to the 'pieces' or 'men' used in chess, draughts, etc. 2. An imitation coin; a token; money generally (*contempt.*) 1526. †3. A table or desk for counting money -1587. 4. A banker's table; also, the table in a shop on which the money paid by purchasers is counted out 1688. †5. A counting-house -1809. †6. The court or hall of justice of a mayor -1734. 7. The prison attached to such a city court; the name of certain prisons for debtors (see COMPTER). *Obs.* exc. *Hist.* ME.

1. What comes the wooll too?..I cannot do't without Compters *Wint. T.* IV. iii. 38. Counters..at a card-table are used..as signs substituted for money BERKELEY. The noblest aims and lives were only counters on her board GREEN. 2. Silver, not as now a c., but the body of the current coin BURKE. 4. In fair days he would take some £40 over the c. 1889.

Counter (kau·ntəɹ), *sb.*[4] 1575. [f. COUNTER *a.* or *adv.*; in senses 3-4?] 1. *Hunting.* The opposite direction to that taken by the game; see COUNTER *adv.* 2. The contrary (*mod.*). 3. That part of a horse's breast which lies between the shoulders and under the neck 1678. 4. The curved part of a ship's stern 1626.

3. For he was barbed from c. to tail SCOTT. 4. The torpedo exploded under her c. 1864.

Counter (kau·ntəɹ), *sb.*[5] 1809. [ad. F. *contre*, It. *contro.*] 1. *Fencing.* A name applied to all circular parries. Called also *c.-parry*, †*-parade*, †*-caveating parade*. 2. *Pugilism.* A blow delivered as the adversary leads off 1861.

Counter (kau·ntəɹ), *sb.*[6] 1841. [Short f. *counterfort.*] *Shoemaking.* The piece of stiff leather forming the back part of a shoe or boot round the heel.

Counter (kau·ntəɹ), *sb.*[7] 1869. *Mus.* Short for COUNTER-TENOR; also any voice part set in contrast to a principal melody.

Counter, *sb.*[8] 1881. *Mining.* Short for COUNTER-LODE.

Counter (kau·ntəɹ), *a.* 1596. [Arising chiefly from COUNTER- *pref.*] Acting in opposition; lying or tending in the opposite direction; opposed, opposite; duplicate, serving as a check. Mostly *attrib.*

C. orders 1780. The c. doctrine SIR W. HAMILTON, side TENNYSON, sect DE QUINCEY. A c. episcopate BP. WILBERFORCE.

Counter (kau·ntəɹ), *v.*[1] ME. [In senses 1, 2, aphet. f. ACOUNTER, ENCOUNTER; in later senses, cf. COUNTER- *pref.*, and COUNTER *sb.*[5] 2.] †1. *trans.* To meet -1813. 2. *trans.* To encounter ME.; *intr.* (constr. *with*) ME. 3. *trans.* (*fig.*) To go counter to ME. †4. *intr.* (*fig.*) To engage in contest, dispute *against*, *with* -1589. 5. *Boxing.* To strike with a counterblow (*trans.* and *intr.*). Also *fig.*

3. To all which Matters..his Answer countered every Design of the Interrogations NORTH. 5. Of course I countered him there with tremendous effect HUGHES.

†**Counter**, *v.*[2] ME. [f. F. *contre*; cf. OF. *contre-chanter.*] *Mus.* To sing an accompaniment to a melody or plain-song -1562.

Counter (kau·ntəɹ), *adv.* ME. [a. F. *contre*; see COUNTER- *pref.* Due mainly to analysis of verbs, etc. in *counter-*.] 1. In the opposite direction; back again. Also *fig.* †2. In full face -1654. 3. *fig.* In opposition; contrary 1643. †4. In opposite directions to each other -1704.

1. Phr. *To hunt, run, go c.*: *i.e.* in a direction opposite to that taken by the game. *Haml.* IV. v. 110. 3. Let us go c. to tradition rather than to Scripture NEWMAN.

Cou·nter-, *pref.* :—ME. and AF. *countre-*, a. F. *contre-* :—L. *contra* adv. and pref. (see CONTRA-) against, in return. Often viewed as an independent element, written separately, and practically treated as an adjective; see COUNTER *a.*

I. *verbs*, as COUNTERACT, COUNTERMINE, -MURE, q.v. (Stress on the root-word.)

II. *sbs.* (and *adjs.*) 1. With sense '(actor or action) against or in opposition', as in *c.-exercise, -latration* (barking against), etc. 2. Done, directed, or acting against, in opposition to, as a rejoinder or reply to another thing of the same kind already made or in existence; as in *c.-address, -affirmation*, etc. (Stress on the prefix.) Also with agent-nouns, as *C.-appellant.* 3. Acting in reversal of a former action; as in C.-REVOLUTION. 4. Reciprocal; as in *c.-assurance*, etc. 5. Opposite locally; as C.-SEA, -SLOPE, -FISSURE, q. v. 6. Crossing, making an angle with; as in C.-LODE. 7. Forming the opposite one of two, as C.-BALANCE, -FOIL, -POISE, etc.; or constituting a second thing of the same kind standing opposite, parallel to, or side by side with the original, as C.-EARTH, *c.-branch, -pillar*; or denoting the duplicate, substitute, or that which is the 'second' of another, =*rear-, sub-*; as in *c.-base*, etc., C.-DRAIN [cf. †*contre-master*, a boatswain.] 8. Running counter (to something else); as in *c.-hypothesis, -interest, -tendency*, etc. (The stress is usually equal.) 9. In prepositional combination with an object: a. Against, ANTI-; as C.-NATURAL *a.* contrary to nature. b. False, counterfeit, pseudo-, ANTI-, as *c.-apostle, -taste*, etc. 10. Mutually opposed, reciprocal, as C.-CHANGE, reciprocal exchange; C.-BATTERY, etc.; also *c.-curses, -ferments*, etc. 11. *Mus.* See CONTRA-. 12. *Mil.* Applied to works erected to act against the works of the enemy; as in C.-APPROACH, etc. 13. *Her.* (*adjs.*) a. Turned in the contrary direction or in contrary directions, as C.-PASSANT, -SALIENT. b. On the two opposite sides, as *c.-indented*, etc., C.-EMBATTLED, -FLEURY. c. Having the tinctures reversed, as C.-ERMINE. d. Having two ordinaries of the same nature opposite to each other, so that colour is opposed to metal, and metal to colour: cf. *counterchanged* (see COUNTERCHANGE *v.*), etc.

Counter-acquittance; see COUNTER- II. 4.

Counteract (kauntəræ·kt), *v.* 1678. [COUNTER- I.] †1. To act in opposition to; to oppose -1832. 2. To hinder or defeat by contrary action 1678.

2. Neither knowledge nor philosophy is..sufficient to c. the effect of human frailty SIR B. BRODIE. Hence **Countera·ctant** *sb.* a counteracting agency or force. **Countera·cter, -or. Countera·ction**, action in opposition to action, resistance; a counteracting influence or force. **Countera·ctive** *a.* tending to c.; *sb.* a counteracting agent or force. **Countera·ctively** *adv.*

Counter-a·gency. 1838. [COUNTER- II. 1.] Agency in opposition *to.* So **Counter-a·gent**, a counteractant.

Cou·nter-approa·ch. Usu. in *pl.* 1678. [ad. F. *contre-approche.* See COUNTER- II. 12.] *Mil.* A work constructed by the besieged to check and command the works of the besiegers.

Cou·nter-arch, *sb.* 1726. [COUNTER- II. 7.] a. An inverted arch opposite to another arch. b. An arch connecting counterforts at the top. Hence **Counter-a·rch** *v.* to furnish with a c.

Cou·nter-attra·ction. 1763. [COUNTER- II. 2, 8.] Attraction of a contrary tendency.

So Counter-attractive *a.* having counter-attractions.

Counterbalance (kau·ntəɹbæ:lăns), *sb.* Also with hyphen. 1580. [COUNTER- II. 7.] †1. The opposite scale of a balance -1581. 2. A weight used to balance another weight; *spec.* that used to balance the weight of a rotating or ascending and descending part, so as to make it easily moved 1611. 3. *fig.* A power which balances the effect of a contrary one 1640.

3. Freedom was in his eyes a c. to poverty, discord, and war BANCROFT.

Counterbalance (kau·ntəɹbæ·lăns), *v.* 1603. [COUNTER- I.] 1. To act as a counterbalance to; to counterpoise. 2. *fig.* To neutralize the effect of, by a contrary power or influence 1636.

2. A meeting-place to counter-balance the alehouse GEO. ELIOT.

†**Cou·nterband.** *rare.* 1611. = COUNTERBOND -1678.

†**Counter-ba·rry,** *a.* 1611. [a. F. *contrebarré*; see COUNTER- II. 13 d.] Barry per pale counterchanged -1751.

Cou·nter-ba·ttery. 1592. [COUNTER- II. 1, 2, 10.] †1. A counter-attack with artillery -1670. Also *fig.* 2. A battery raised against another. Also *fig.* 1603.

Cou·nter-beam. 1874. *Printing.* A beam connected to the platen by rods, by which the reciprocating motion is communicated to the platen.

Cou·nter-bi·ll. 1598. [COUNTER- II. 2, 7.] †a. The counterpart or duplicate of a bill. b. A (parliamentary) bill forming a set-off to another.

Counterblast (kau·ntəɹblast). 1567. [COUNTER- II. 2.] a. A blast blown in opposition to another. b. A strong declaration against something.

b. A Counterblaste to Tobacco JAS. I. (*title*).

Counterblow (kau·ntəɹblōᵘ:), *sb.* 1655. (COUNTER- II. 2, 4.) A return blow; the back-stroke of a rebound.

Counterbond (kau·ntəɹbǫnd). 1594. [COUNTER- II. 4.] A bond to indemnify one who has entered into a bond for another.

Counter-bore, *v.*; see COUNTER- I.

Cou·nter-brace, *sb.* 1823. [COUNTER- II. 2, 5.] a. A brace which counteracts the strain of another brace. b. *Naut.* The lee-brace of the fore-topsail-yard, when in tacking it is counter-braced to help to bring the ship round.

Cou·nter-bra·ce, *v.* 1867. [COUNTER I.] *Naut.* To brace the head-yards one way, and the after-yards another, so that the sails counteract each other.

†**Cou·nterbuff,** *sb.* 1575. [COUNTER- II. 2, 10.] 1. A blow in return or in the contrary direction -1641. 2. A rebuff -1678. 3. An encounter -1656. Hence **Cou·nterbuff** *v. arch.*, to give a c. to.

Counter-carte (*Fencing*); see COUNTER *sb.*[5]

†**Cou·nter-cast.** An antagonistic artifice. SPENSER.

†**Cou·nter-ca·ster.** One who reckons with counters; 'a word of contempt for an arithmetician' (J.). *Oth.* I. i. 31.

†**Cou·nterchange,** *sb.* 1579. [ad. F. *contrechange* = It. *contracambio*; see COUNTER II. 2, 4, 10.] 1. Exchange -1706; equivalent return -1661. 2. Transposition -1622.

Counterchange (kau·ntəɹ,tʃēⁱ·ndʒ), *v.* 1598. [ad. F. *contrechanger*; see COUNTER- I.] †1. *trans.* To exchange -1646. 2. To change to the opposite (position, state, quality); to transpose 1613. 3. *Her.* To interchange or reverse the tinctures; *transf.* and *fig.* to chequer 1614.

2. When they are counterchanged the Ranter becomes an Hypocrite, and the Hypocrite an able Ranter BUTLER. 3. Witch-elms that c. the floor Of this flat lawn with dusk and bright TENNYSON. So **Cou·ntercha·nged** *ppl. a. Her.* Of a charge: Having the tinctures reversed; transmuted; also *transf.*

Countercharge (kau·ntəɹ,tʃā·ɹdʒ), *sb.* 1611. [COUNTER- II. 2.] A charge brought in opposition to another, or against the accuser. So **Cou·ntercha·rge** *v.* a. To bring a charge against. †b. To oppose with a contrary charge. c. To charge contrariwise.

Cou·ntercharm, cou·nter-cha·rm, *sb.* 1601. [COUNTER- II. 2, 9.] A counteracting charm. So **Cou·ntercha·rm** *v.* to neutralize the effect of a charm upon; to affect with an opposing charm.

Countercheck, counter-check (kau·ntəɹ,tʃek), *sb.* 1559. [COUNTER- II. 1, 2.] †1. A check in return for another -1706. 2. A check that arrests the course of anything 1595. 3. A check that controls a check 1832.

1. If againe, it was not well cut, he wold say, I lie: this is call'd the counter-checke quarrelsome SHAKS.

Countercheck (kau·ntəɹ,tʃe·k), *v.* 1587. [COUNTER- I.] †1. *trans.* To check in reply to a check or rebuke, or in opposition -1598. 2. To arrest by counteraction 1590.

Counter-che·vroned, counter-che·vrony, *a.* 1727. [COUNTER- II. 13 d.] *Her.* Of a shield: Chevrony and divided pale-wise, the half chevrons being of alternate tinctures.

Cou·nter-clai·m, cou·nterclaim, *sb.* 1876. [COUNTER- II. 2.] A claim set up against another, or against the plaintiff. So **Cou·nterclai·m, cou·nterclai·m** *v. trans.*, to claim as against a prior claim, or against the plaintiff; also *absol.*

Cou·nter-clo·ckwise, *a.* and *adv.* 1888. [COUNTER *prep.*] In a direction counter to that of the movement of the hands of a clock.

Counter-co·loured, *ppl. a.* 1572. [COUNTER- II. 13 d.] *Her.* Having the opposite parts of different tinctures; counterchanged.

Counter-compony (kau·ntəɹkǫmpōᵘ·ni), *a.* 1610. [COUNTER- II. 13 d.] *Her.* Composed of two conjoined rows of squares of alternate tinctures. var. †**Counter-compo·ned** *ppl. a.*

Counter-cou·chant, -cou·rant (*Her.*); see COUNTER- II. 13 a.

Cou·nter-cu·rrent, *sb.* 1684. [f. COUNTER- II. 2, 5.] An opposite current. So **Counter-cu·rrent** *a.* running counter.

Cou·nter-deed. 1727. [COUNTER- II. 2.] *Law.* A secret writing or a private act, which annuls or alters some more public act.

Cou·nter-disenga·ge, *v.* 1889. [ad. F. *contre-dégager.*] *Fencing.* To disengage at the same time as the adversary.

†**Cou·nterdisti·nct,** *a.* 1662. = CONTRADISTINCT -1680. So †**Cou·nterdisti·nction,** †**Cou·nterdisti·nguish** *v.*

Cou·nter-drain. 1842. [COUNTER- II. 8.] A drain parallel to a canal or embanked watercourse, for collecting and passing on the soakage water.

†**Counter-draw·,** *v.* 1727. [COUNTER- I.] To copy a design, etc., by means of oiled paper or other transparent material.

Cou·nter-earth. 1857. [COUNTER- II. 7: a tr. of Gr. ἀντίχθων.] An opposite or secondary Earth, in the Pythagorean system; cf. ANTICHTHON.

Cou·nter-emba·ttled, *ppl. a.* 1863. [COUNTER- II. 13.] *Her.* Of an ordinary: Embattled on opposite sides.

Counter-embowed (*Her.*); see COUNTER- II. 13.

Cou·nter-e·rmine. 1727. [COUNTER- II. 13.] *Her.* The reverse of ermine; = ERMINES.

Cou·nter-e·vidence. 1665. [COUNTER- II. 2.] Evidence tending to rebut other evidence.

Cou·nter-exte·nsion. 1860. [COUNTER- II. 5.] *Surg.* The pulling or holding of the upper part of a limb, etc., towards the trunk, while extension is practised on the lower part. So **Cou·nter-exte·nd** *v.*

Counter-faced (*Her.*) = COUNTER-FESSED.

Cou·nter-fa·ller. 1836. [COUNTER- II. 7.] *Spinning.* In a mule, a wire which passes beneath the yarns, when pressed down by the faller-wire, so as to keep the tension uniform. Also *attrib.*

†**Cou·nterfei·sance.** 1590. [ad. F. *contrefaisance*, f. *contrefaire* to counterfeit.] The action of counterfeiting; deceit, dissimulation, fraud, imposture -1656.

Counterfeit (kau·ntəɹfit, -fīt), *a.* (*pa. pple.*) and *sb.* ME. [a. OF. *contrefet, -fait*, pa. pple. of *contrefaire*, f. L. type *contra-facere* to make in opposition, hence in opposing imitation.]

†A. as *pa. pple.* Forged -1631; made to a pattern -1547; disguised CAXTON.

B. *adj.* 1. Made in imitation of something else, 'imitation'; spurious, sham, base (*esp.* of coin) 1449; of writings: Forged ME. 2. Of things immaterial: Pretended, false ME.; †disguised SWIFT. 3. Of persons: Sham 1530; †false, deceitful -1732. †4. Deformed -1575. †5. Represented in a picture (or *transf.* in writing); portrayed -1838.

1. A Bait, which..proves but a c. Fly BOYLE. 2. These C. Terrours often grow..to be Real 1718. 3. This counterfeight Herault HALL. Fabulous or c. writers BERKELEY. 5. *Haml.* III. iv. 54. Hence **Cou·nterfeit-ly** *adv.*, **-ness.**

C. *sb.* 1. A false or spurious imitation ME; a forgery 1613. †2. One who pretends to be another; a pretender, an imposter -1768. 3. †A representation in painting, sculpture, etc.; an image, portrait -1843; *fig.* a copy (*arch.*) 1587. †4. A misshapen person -1578.

1. Neuer call a true peece of Gold a C. 1 *Hen. IV*, II. iv. 540. Els Justice..were..a fals counterfet of that impartial and Godlike vertue MILT. 3. What finde I here? Faire Portias c. *Merch. V*, III. ii. 115.

Counterfeit (kau·ntəɹfit, -fīt), *v.* ME. [f. prec.] 1. *trans.* To make an imitation of, imitate (with intent to deceive); to forge. †2. To disguise, falsify -1722. 3. To put on (with intent to deceive) the appearance of; to feign, simulate ME. †4. To pretend to be (a person, etc.); to personate -1622. 5. *intr.* To feign, practise deceit ME. 6. *trans.* To take, receive, or have the appearance of; to imitate, resemble, be like. (Without implying deceit.) †7. To copy, make a copy of -1621. †8. To depict, delineate, portray -1660.

1. To c. a seal THIRLWALL, coins JEVONS, Mans voice MILT., a Letter 1726, a certificate 1873. 2. I counterfeited my voice DE FOE. 3. To c. a smiling welcome BP. HALL, death CARLYLE. 5. Are you not mad indeed, or do you but c. *Twel. N.* IV. ii. 122. 6. Where glowing embers through the room Teach light to c. a gloom MILTON.

Hence **Cou·nterfeiter,** one who makes fraudulent imitations; *spec.* a coiner; a dissembler; an imitator (without deceit).

Cou·nter-fe·ssed, *ppl. a.* 1486. [COUNTER- II. 13.] *Her.* Barry and divided pale-wise, the half bars being of alternate tinctures. var. **Counter-fe·ssy** *a.*

Cou·nter-fi·ssure. 1656. [COUNTER- II. 5.] *Surg.* A fracture of the skull occurring opposite the place where a blow was received.

Counterfleury, -flory (kau·ntəɹ,flō·ri, -flōᵊ·ri), *a.* 1572. [ad. F. *contrefleuri*; cf. COUNTER- II. 13.] *Her.* Of an ordinary: Having flowers on each side set opposite each other in pairs. So **Counter-flow·ered** *ppl. a.*

Counterfoil (kau·ntəɹfoil). 1706. [COUNTER- II. 7.] 1. A complementary part of a bank cheque, receipt, or the like, containing the particulars of the principal part, to be retained by the person who gives out that part. †2. = COUNTERSTOCK -1708.

Cou·nter-fo·rce, cou·nterforce. 1609. [COUNTER- II. 1, 2.] A force acting in opposition to another.

Counterfort (kau·ntəɹfōᵊɹt). 1590. [ad. F. *contrefort.*] 1. *Arch.* and *Fortif.* A buttress to support and strengthen a wall or terrace. 2. *transf.* A lateral spur of a mountain 1847. †3. A fort raised by the besiegers. *nonce-use.* 1640.

Cou·nter-gauge, *sb.* Also **-gage, -guage** (a mere blunder). 1727. [COUNTER- II. 7.] 'An adjustable, double-pointed gage for transferring the measurement of a mortise to the end of a stick where a tenon is to be made, or *vice versa*' (Knight).

Cou·nter-gea·r. [COUNTER- II. 7.] The driving gear whence power is communicated by a belt, etc., to the separate machine driven by it.

Cou·nter-gua·rd, cou·nterguard, *sb.* 1523. [ad. F. *contregarde*; see COUNTER- II. 7, 12.] †1. An extra guard to check another, or to be a reserve -1651. †2. *Fortif.* 'A narrow detached rampart, placed immediately in front of an important work, to protect it from being breached' (Stocqueler) 1591. 3. Part of a sword-hilt 1874. So †**Cou·ntergua·rd** *v.* to guard against (danger); to safeguard.

Cou·nter-he·m, *sb.* 1882. [COUNTER- II.

7.] *Needlework.* A hem parallel and opposite to a first hem. So **Counter-hem** *v.*

Cou·nter-indica·tion = CONTRA-INDICATION.

Cou·nter-i·nfluence, *sb.* 1834. [COUNTER- II. 2.] An influence in the opposite direction. So **Cou·nter-i·nfluence** *v.* to affect with a counter-influence.

Cou·nter-interroga·tion. 1808. [COUNTER- II. 2.] Cross-examination.

Cou·nter-i·rritant. 1854. [COUNTER- II. 2.] *Med.* An appliance used to produce irritation of the surface of the body, in order to counteract disease of more deeply-seated or distant parts. So **Counter-i·rritate** *v.*; **-irrita·tion,** irritation artificially produced in order to counteract the action of disease.

Cou·nter-jumper. *colloq.* 1841. [f. COUNTER- *sb.*³] *lit.* One who jumps over a counter; used contemptuously of a shopman.

Cou·nter-lath, *sb.* 1659. [COUNTER- II. 6, 7.] *Roofing.* A lath placed by eye between every two gauged ones.

†**Cou·nter-le·tter.** 1603. [COUNTER- II. 2.] 1. A letter of reply. 2. A letter countermanding a letter; a counterdeed –1818.

Cou·nter-lode. [COUNTER- II. 6; cf. CAUNTER.] *Mining.* A lode running across a main lode.

†**Cou·nterly,** *a.* and *adv.* 1486. [f. COUNTER *a.* or *adv.* + -LY.] *Her. adj.* Of the shield, etc.: Divided into two parts of different tinctures –1586. *adv.* In a way that is counter to another; counterwise –1688.

Counterman (kau·ntəɹmæ̆n). 1853. [f. COUNTER *sb.*²] A shopman who serves at the counter.

Countermand (kauntəɹmɑ·nd), *v.* ME. [a. OF. *contremander,* f. L. *contra* + *mandare.*] 1. To command the opposite of; to revoke, annul by a contrary command. Also *intr.* or *absol.* †2. To command in reversal of a previous command –1568. 3. To order back 1464. 4. To revoke an order for 1552. †5. To go counter to –1662; to forbid –1658; to counteract –1711; to control –1654.

1. To declare his will to day, and c. it to morrow HORNECK. 3. Our regiment is countermanded GOLDSM. 4. To c. a movement THIRLWALL. Hence **Counterma·ndable** *a.* that can be countermanded.

Countermand (kau·ntəɹmɑnd), *sb.* 1548. [a. OF. *contremand*; see prec.] 1. A contrary command revoking or annulling a previous one. 2. *Law.* An act that makes void something previously executed 1628. †3. A prohibition –1689.

1. Haue you no c. for Claudio yet? But he must die to morrow? *Meas. for M.* IV. ii. 95.

Countermarch (kau·ntəɹmāɹtʃ), *sb.* 1598. [COUNTER- II. 5.] 1. A march back. Also *fig.* 2. *Mil.* An evolution by which the front and rear, or the right and left file, of a body of cavalry or infantry change places, the original order of the files being retained. Now obs.

Countermarch (kauntəɹmā·ɹtʃ), *v.* 1625. [COUNTER- I.; cf. prec.] 1. *intr.* To march back 1644. 2. *Mil.* To execute a countermarch (sense 2) 1625. 3. *trans.* To cause to countermarch 1658.

2. The Regiment in Line is required to c. on its centre 1832. Hence **Cou·ntermarcher.**

Countermark (kau·ntəɹmāɹk), *sb.* 1502. [ad. F. *contremarque*; cf. COUNTER- II. 7.] 1. An additional mark put on something that has been marked before, for greater security, etc. †2. A mark, letter, etc. on a plan, corresponding to one in a description 1665. 3. An artificial cavity made in the teeth of horses that have outgrown the natural mark, to disguise their age 1727.

1. In goldsmiths works, etc. the *counter-mark* is the mark, or punchion, of the hall, or company, to shew the metal is standard, added to that of the artificer 1727. So **Cou·nterma·rk** *v.* to furnish with a c.

†**Cou·nter-marque.** 1502. [COUNTER- II. 2.] Reprisals against *Letters of Marque* –1755. So †**Counter-mart** (in same sense).

Countermine (kau·ntəɹməin), *sb.* 1548. [COUNTER- II. 2, 12.] 1. *Mil.* A mine or subterranean excavation made by the defenders of a fortress, to intercept a mine made by the besiegers. b. A submarine mine sunk where it may explode the enemy's mines by the concussion of its explosion 1880. 2. *fig.* A plot designed to frustrate another 1570.

2. With secret countermines and open weapons of Law 1611.

Cou·ntermi·ne, *v.* 1580. [f. prec. sb.] 1. *Mil. intr.* To make a countermine 1583; *trans.* to make a countermine against 1684; in naval war: To lay down countermines 1880. 2. *fig.* To defeat by a counterplot 1580. ¶ Erron. for *countermure* 1592.

2. Gods countermining of Hamans plot 1649.

Cou·nter-mo·tion. 1606. [COUNTER- II. 2, 5.] 1. Motion in the opposite direction. 2. A motion or resolution contrary to one already proposed (*mod.*).

Cou·nter-move. 1858. [COUNTER- II. 2.] A move in opposition to another. (Orig. a term of chess.) So **Cou·nter-mo·vement,** a movement in opposition.

Countermure (kau·ntəɹmiūᵊɹ), *sb.* 1524. [ad. F. *contre-mur,* f. *contre* = COUNTER- II. 7 + *mur* wall.] *Mil.* A wall raised within (or outside) another wall for additional defence or to assist the besiegers. Also *fig.* Hence **Cou·ntermu·re** *v.* to defend with a c.; *intr.* to raise a c.

Counter-naiant, *a.* *Her.*; see COUNTER- II. 13 a.

†**Counterna·tural,** *a.* 1666. *rare.* = CONTRANATURAL.

Counter-nebulé, *a.* *Her.*; see COUNTER- II. 13 b.

Cou·nter-o·pening. 1611. [COUNTER- II. 5.] An opening opposite another.

†**Cou·nterpace.** 1580. [COUNTER- II. 5.] 1. A movement in a contrary direction. 2. A step against something –1731.

Cou·nter-pa·led, *a.* 1727. [COUNTER- II. 13.] *Her.* Of a shield: Parted into an even number of divisions pale-wise, and divided fess-wise, the tinctures of the upper and lower halves being counterchanged. var. **Cou·nter-pa·ly.**

†**Cou·nterpane**¹. 1475. [app. a. AF. *countrepan,* f. *contre-* + OF. *pan* piece, part; cf. COUNTER-PAWN.] 1. *Law.* The counterpart of an indenture –1693. Also *fig.* 2. = COUNTERPART 2–4. –1670.

1. Read, Scribe, gi' me the Counterpaine B. JONS.

Counterpane² (kau·ntəɹpēn, -pəⁱn). 1603. [Altered f. COUNTERPOINT², the second element becoming PANE (F. *pan,* L. *pannus*).] The outer covering of a bed, generally woven in raised figures, quilted, or the like; a coverlet.

On which, a Tissue counterpoyne was cast DRAYTON.

Counter-parade, -parry (*Fencing*); see COUNTER *sb.*⁵

Cou·nter-paro·le. 1823. [COUNTER- II. 7.] An extra parole or password given in time of alarm. Cf. COUNTERSIGN.

Counterpart (kau·ntəɹpāɹt). 1617. [COUNTER- II. 7; cf. F. *contre-partie.*] 1. *Law.* The opposite part of an INDENTURE, q. v.; each of the indented parts in its relation to the other; *esp.* that which is not the original. †2. *gen.* A duplicate or exact copy –1712. 3. *fig.* A person or thing appearing to be an exact copy of another 1680. 4. One of two parts which fit and complete each other; a person or thing forming a natural complement to another 1634. 5. *Mus.* A part written to accompany another. [COUNTER- II. 12.] 1706. Also *attrib.*

1. A c. of the lease is to be executed by the lessee LD. ST. LEONARDS. 4. Oh c. Of our soft sex; well are you made our lords DRYDEN.

†**Cou·nter-pa·rty.** 1557. [a. F. *contre-partie.*] An opposite party in a law-suit or contest –1624.

Cou·nter-pa·ssant, *a.* 1610. [COUNTER- II. 13.] *Her.* Passant in opposite directions.

†**Cou·nter-pawn.** 1611. [? f. OF. *contrepan.*] = COUNTERPANE¹ 1. –1634.

Cou·nter-penalty. 1847. [COUNTER- II. 2: tr. Gr. ἀντιτίμησις.] *Gr. Antiq.* The penalty which an accused person who had been pronounced guilty suggested for himself in opposition to that called for by the accuser.

Cou·nterplea. 1565. [COUNTER- II. 2.] *Law.* A replication to a plea or request made, in which arguments are advanced why the same should not be admitted.

†**Counterplea·d,** *v.* ME. [a. AF. *contrepleder,* f. *contre* + *pleder* to PLEAD.] 1. *Law.* To plead in opposition to; to make a counterplea –1642. Also *fig.* 2. *gen.* To oppose in argument; to contradict. (ME. only.)

Cou·nterplot, *sb.* 1611. [COUNTER- II. 2, 1.] 1. A plot contrived to defeat another. †2. A plotting against. MORE.

1. Plot and counter-plot, egad! SHERIDAN.

Cou·nterplo·t, *v.* 1597. [COUNTER- I.] 1. *intr.* To devise a counterplot *against.* 2. *trans.* To plot against; to frustrate by a counterplot 1662.

2. To c. that infamous trickster 1887.

Counterpoint (kau·ntəɹpoint), *sb.*¹ 1530. [In sense 1, a. F. *contrepoint,* in med.L. *contrapunctum, cantus contrapunctus,* lit. 'song or music pointed-against', *i. e.* indicated by notes set *against* (over or under) the notes of the original melody. In senses 3 and 4, f. COUNTER- II. 2, 5, 7.] 1. *Mus.* The melody added as accompaniment to a given melody or plain-song. Also *fig.* 2. The art of adding one or more melodies as accompaniment to a plain-song according to certain rules; this style of composition 1597. †3. A contrary point (in an argument) –1626. 4. The opposite point; †the antithesis 1599.

1. A rainy wind from 'twixt the trees arose, And sang a mournful c. to those MORRIS.

†**Cou·nterpoint,** *sb.*² 1450. [a. OF. *contrepointe,* app. corrupt f. OF. *cuilte-pointe,* repr. L. *culcita puncta* lit. 'quilt stitched through'; cf. QUILT.] A quilted cover for a bed; a COUNTERPANE –1694.

Counterpoi·nted, -poi·nté, *a.* 1727. [F. *contrepointé,* f. *contre* against + *point* point.] *Her.* Said of two chevrons in one escutcheon when they meet in the points.

Counterpoise (kau·ntəɹpoiz), *sb.* ME. [a. OF. *countrepeis, -pais* = mod. *contrepoids,* f. *contre* + *peis, pois* :—L. *pensum* weight.] 1. A weight which balances another weight, or establishes equilibrium against a force. 2. *transf.* and *fig.* That which serves as a counterbalance or set-off ME. 3. The state of being balanced; equilibrium 1591. Also *fig.*

1. These..are of the same weight, and therefore a counterpoize to each other SMEATON. 2. Their Second Nobles..are a Counterpoize to the Higher Nobility, that they grow not too Potent BACON. 3. The pendulous round Earth, with ballanc't Aire In c. MILT.

Counterpoise (kau·ntəɹpoiz), *v.* [ME. *countrepese, -peise,* a. OF. *contrepeser*; assim. to the sb. with *-poise.*] 1. *trans.* To balance by a weight on the opposite side or acting in opposition; to counterbalance 1566. 2. *transf.* and *fig.* To balance in power, quality, or effect ME. †3. *intr.* To be equiponderant (*to, with, against*) –1561. 4. *trans.* To bring into equilibrium (*lit.* and *fig.*) ME. 5. To weigh (a thing) *with, i. e.* against (another) 1685. Also *absol.*

1. One shilling of siluer in those daies did counterpeise our common ounce 1577. 2. And passed wo with ioie [to] countrepese CHAUCER.

Counterpoi·son, cou·nter-poi·son. *arch.* 1578. [a. F. *contrepoison*; see COUNTER- II. 8, 9.] 1. An antidote. Also *fig.* 2. An opposite poison 1789.

Cou·nter-po·le. 1839. [COUNTER- II. 5.] The opposite pole.

Counterpo·se, *v. rare.* = CONTRAPOSE.

Counter-po·tent, *a.* (*sb.*) 1610. *Her.* Of a 'fur': Having the potents arranged as in COUNTERVAIR.

Cou·nter-pre·ssure. 1651. [COUNTER- II. 2, 6.] Contrary pressure.

†**Cou·nter-pri·ce.** 1671. [tr. Gr. ἀντίλυτρον in 1 Tim. ii. 6.] A ransom –1714.

Cou·nter-proo·f, *sb.* 1610. [COUNTER- II. 7, 8.] †1. Proof to the contrary. 2. *Printing.* 'A print taken off from another fresh printed; which, by being passed through the press, gives the figure of the former, but inverted' (Chambers). So **Counterpro·ve** *v.* †to bring proof contrary to; to take a counterproof of.

Counter-qua·rtered, *a.* 1562. [COUNTER- II. 13.] *Her.* 1. Of a charge: Borne counterchanged upon a field quarterly. 2. Of an escutcheon: Quarterly, with each quarter also quartered. var. **Counter-qua·rterly** (in sense 2).

Counter-raguled, -raguly, -rampant, *Her.*; see COUNTER- II. 13.

Cou·nter-reforma·tion. 1840. [COUNTER- II. 3. Applied in *Hist.* to the movement in the Church of Rome which followed on the Protestant Reformation.

Cou·nter-revolu·tion. 1793. [COUNTER- II. 3.] A revolution opposed to a previous revolution or reversing its results.

Counter-ripo·ste. 1889. [F. *contre-riposte*; see COUNTER *sb.*[5]] *Fencing.* A riposte delivered, still on the lunge, after parrying the adversary's first riposte.

†**Cou·nter-ro:ll,** *sb.* 1613. [a. obs. F. *contre-rolle*; see CONTROL and COUNTER- II. 7.] A copy of a roll or document, kept for purposes of checking –1863. So †**Cou:nterro·lment,** the entering in a counter-roll.

Cou·nter-round. ? *Obs.* 1590. [ad. F. *contre-ronde*, f. *contre* + *ronde*.] *Mil.* A patrol of officers to inspect or check the rounds; also *concr.* these officers as a body.

Counter-sa·lient, *a.* 1610. [COUNTER- II. 13.] *Her.* Said of two animals borne as charges: Salient in opposite directions.

Cou·nter-sca·le. 1645. [COUNTER- II. 7.] The opposite scale (of the balance); chiefly *fig.*

Counterscarp (kau·ntəɹskāɹp), *sb.* 1571. [ad. F. *contrescarpe*; see SCARP.] *Fortif.* The outer wall or slope of the ditch which supports the covered way; sometimes the whole covered way with the glacis. Also *transf.* and *fig.* var. Counterscarf(e).

†**Cou·nter-scu·ffle.** 1628. [COUNTER- II. 10.] A scuffle between opposing parties or persons –1674.

†**Cou·nter-sea:.** 1599. [COUNTER- II. 2, 5.] A sea running against the course of a ship, or against another sea –1610.

Cou·nter-sea:l, *sb.* Now *Hist.* 1611. [a. OF. *contre-seel*; cf. COUNTER- II. 7.] A smaller seal impressed upon the reverse of a main seal for further security, or sanction. Also, the reverse side of a seal. Hence †**Cou·nter-sea·l** *v.* to seal with a c.

Cou·nter-secu·re, *v.* 1667. [COUNTER- I.] **1.** *trans.* To secure (any one) against the risk he incurs by becoming security for another. **2.** To give additional security to 1796.

2. You are giving that pledge from the throne, and engaging parliament to c. it BURKE. So **Cou·nter-secu·rity,** security given in return; security given to any one to cover his risk in becoming surety.

Cou·nterse:nse. 1645. [ad. F. *contresens.*] A meaning opposed to the true sense.

Countershaft (kau·ntəɹʃaft). 1864. [COUNTER- II. 7.] *Mech.* An intermediate shaft driven from a main shaft for giving motion to a particular machine.

Countersign (kau·ntəɹsəin), *sb.* 1591. [a. OF. *contresigne*; cf. COUNTER- II. 4.] **1.** A sign or signal used in reply to another sign; *spec.* a private signal, usually a word, to be given to a soldier on guard by any one entitled to pass 1598. **2.** = COUNTERMARK.

Countersign (kau:ntəɹsəi·n), *v.* 1662. [ad. F. *contresigner*; cf. COUNTER- I.] **1.** *trans.* To sign opposite to, alongside of, or in addition to, another signature; to add one's signature to (a document already signed by another) for authentication or confirmation 1696. Also *fig.* †**2.** To mark with a particular sign for authentication, identification, or reference –1665.

1. Charters are signed by the king, and countersigned by a secretary of state or lord chancellor 1806. So **Cou·nter-si·gnature,** the action of countersigning.

Countersink (kau·ntəɹsiŋk), *sb.* 1816. [f. next.] **1.** A tool for countersinking. **2.** The conical enlargement of the upper part of a hole for receiving the head of a screw or bolt.

Countersink (kau:ntəɹsi·ŋk), *v.* Pa. t. and pple. **-sunk.** 1816. [Cf. COUNTER- II. 7.] **1.** *trans.* To enlarge the upper part of (a hole) to receive the head of a screw, bolt, etc.; to bevel the edge of a hole 1831. **2.** To sink the head of (a screw, bolt, etc.) in a depression made to receive it, so that it lies flush with the surface.

Cou·nterslope, *sb.* 1836. [COUNTER- II. 5.] **1.** The opposite slope of a hill, a ridge, etc.; a slope in the opposite direction 1853. **2.** An overhanging slope. So **Cou:nterslo·pe** *v.* to slope on the opposite side.

Cou·nter-spe:ll. 1725. [COUNTER- II. 2, 9.] A spell against something; a spell to dissolve another.

Cou·nterstand, *sb.* [after It. *contrasto.*] Standing against. LONGF.

Cou·nter-sta:tement; see COUNTER-.

Cou·nter-ste:p. 1720. [COUNTER- II. 2, 5.] A step in opposition, or in the opposite direction.

†**Cou·ntersto:ck.** 1706. [COUNTER- II. 7.] That part of a tally retained by the payee –1708.

Counterstroke (kau·ntəɹstrōuk). 1596. [COUNTER- II. 1, 2, 5.] **1.** A stroke given in return. **2.** = CONTRECOUP 2. 1786.

Cou·ntersu:bject. 1854. [COUNTER- II. 11.] *Mus.* A subordinate melody, part of a fugue, written *against*, or as accompaniment to, the subject and answer.

Countersunk (kau·ntəɹsɒ:ŋk). 1794. [pa. pple. of COUNTERSINK *v.*] *ppl. a.* Of a hole: Cut to receive the head of a bolt, screw, etc. Of a bolt, screw, etc.: Sunk so as to lie flush with the surface. As *sb.* = COUNTERSINK *sb.* 2. 1794.

†**Cou·ntersway,** *sb.* [COUNTER- II. 5.] An exertion of opposing force. MILT. So †**Cou:ntersway·** *v. trans.*, to forcibly move to the opposite side; to counterweigh.

†**Cou·ntertai:l.** ME. [a. OF. *contretaille.*] **1.** = COUNTERSTOCK –1617. var. †**Cou·nterta:lly.** **2.** A counter-stroke. (ME. only.)

Phr. **At the c.:** in reply.

Counter-taste; see COUNTER- II. 9.

Counter-tendency, -term; see COUNTER-.

Cou·nter-te·nor. ME. [ad. obs. F. *contreteneur*; see COUNTER- II. 11.] *Mus.* **1.** A part higher in pitch than the tenor, sung by a high male voice; the alto. Also *fig.* **2.** A countertenor voice 1771. **3.** A singer with such a voice 1623. Also *attrib.*

Cou·nter-ti:de. 1570. [COUNTER- II. 5.] A tide running counter to the main current.

Counter-tierce (*Fencing*); see COUNTER *sb.*[5]

†**Cou·nter-time.** 1599. [tr. F. *contretemps.*] **1.** *Fencing.* A pass or thrust made at a wrong moment. Also *fig.* –1676. **2.** *Horsemanship.* Interruption by a horse of the cadence of movement, owing to bad horsemanship or to unruly disposition –1736.

Counter-trench; see COUNTER-.

Cou·nter-tri·pping, *a.* 1610. [COUNTER- II. 13.] *Her.* Said of two stags, hinds, etc.: Walking in opposite directions on the same plain. So **Cou·nter-tri·ppant.**

Cou·nter-tu·rn. 1589. [In senses 1 and 2, tr. Gr. ἀντιστροφή; in 3 and 4 f. COUNTER- II. 5.] †**1.** = ANTISTROPHE. B. JONS. †**2.** *Prosody.* The continued repetition of the same word at the end of successive clauses; = L. *conversio.* PUTTENHAM. **3.** A turn in the contrary direction 1744. **4.** An unexpected development of the plot of a play at the climax 1651.

Cou·nterty:pe. 1624. [COUNTER- II. 2, 7.] †**1.** = ANTITYPE. **2.** A parallel 1855. **3.** An opposite type 1880.

Countervail (kauntəɹvē·l), *v.* ME. [a. AF. *countrevaloir* :—(ult.) L. phrase *contra valere.*] †**1.** *trans.* To be equivalent to in value –1655. **2.** To equal (*arch.*) 1530; †to reciprocate –1633. **3.** †To counterbalance –1669. **4.** To make up for ME. **5.** *intr.* To avail *against*, †*with*, †*for* ME.; †to vie *with* –1581.

3. *fig.* No certificate of a judge was allowed..to c. the oath of the jury BLACKSTONE. **5.** What name.. could c. against the High Priest of Science BREWSTER. Hence **Cou·ntervail** *sb.* that which countervails. †**Countervai·lable** *a.* to be set against as equivalent.

Countervair (kau·ntəɹvēə·ɹ), *sb.* (*a.*) 1766. [COUNTER- II. 13.] *Her.* A variety of vair (one of the 'furs'), in which the bells or cups of the same tincture are placed base to base. So **Countervai·ry** *a.*

Countervalla·tion = CONTRAVALLATION.

†**Counterva·lue,** *v.* 1581. [COUNTER- I.] **1.** = COUNTERVAIL 1. –1656. **2.** *intr.* Of an accused person: To give a counter-estimate 1832.

Cou·nterview. 1590. [COUNTER- II. 7, 8.] †**1.** View from opposite sides –1780. **2.** The opposite opinion. (Better as two words.) 1852.

Counter-vote, etc.; see COUNTER-.

†**Cou:nter-wai·t,** *v.* ME. [a. AF. *countrewaiter*, OF. *contreguaitier*, f. *contre* + *guaitier* to WAIT, watch.] *trans.* To lie in wait against; to watch against –1602.

Cou·nter-wall. 1836. [COUNTER- II. 12.] A line of wall raised against the enemy's wall.

Counterweigh (kau:ntəɹwē·), *v.* ME. [COUNTER- I; cf. COUNTERPOISE *v.*] **1.** *trans.* To weigh (things) against each other; to balance. (Usually *fig.*) **2.** *intr.* To act as a counterpoise (*with, against*). *lit.* and *fig.* 1523. **3.** *trans.* To counterbalance 1825.

Counter-weight, counterweight (kau·ntəɹwēⁱt). 1693. [COUNTER- II. 7; cf. prec.] A counterbalancing weight. Also *fig.*

Cou:nterwhee·l, *v. rare.* 1659. [COUNTER- I.] To wheel round in the contrary direction.

Cou·nterwo:rk, *sb.* 1598. [COUNTER- II. 2, 12.] Any opposing work or operation; *spec.* in *Mil.* a work raised in opposition to those of the enemy.

Counterwork (kau:ntəɹwɒ·ɹk), *v.* Pa. t. and pa. pple. **-wrought** or **-worked.** 1602 [COUNTER- I.] **1.** *intr.* To work in opposition. **2.** *trans.* To work against; to counteract; frustrate 1628. Hence **Cou·nterworker,** a counteracter, an opponent.

Countess (kau·ntės). OE. [a. OF. *cun-, contesse* :—late L. *comitissa*, fem. of *comes*; see COUNT *sb.*[2]] **1.** The wife or widow of a COUNT; in the peerage, the wife or widow of an EARL; also, a lady holding a position in her own right equal to that of count or earl. **2.** A middle size of roofing slate 1803.

Cou·nting, *vbl. sb.* Also **compting.** ME. [f. COUNT *v.* + -ING[1].] The action of COUNT *v.*

Comb. **c.-house,** an office; now *spec.* a building or office in a commercial establishment, in which the book-keeping, correspondence, etc., are carried on; called also (chiefly in U.S.) a **c.-room.**

Countless (kau·ntlės), *a.* 1588. [f. COUNT *sb.*[1] + -LESS.] That cannot be counted: of number, less often of quantity or value.

One sweet kisse shall pay this comptlesse debt SHAKS.

Cou·ntour, -or. ME. [Earlier f. COUNTER *sb.*[2], AF. *countour.*] **1.** *Eng. Hist.* An accountant. (ME. only.) **2.** *Law.* A legal pleader, or serjeant-at-law; cf. COUNT *v.* Now *Hist.* ME.

Countre-, obs. f. COUNTER-.

Countrified, countryfied (kɒ·ntrifəid), *ppl. a.* 1653. [f. next.] **1.** Affected by or smacking of the country and its life; rustic. **2.** Of scenery: Rural 1756.

1. Miss Bell's a little countryfied THACKERAY.

Countrify (kɒ·ntrifəi), *v.* [f. next; cf. *beautify.*] To make rural or rustic.

Country (kɒ·ntri). [ME. *contre(e, cuntre(e,* a. OF. *cuntrée, contrée* = Pr. *contrada* :—late L. *contrata*, f. *contra*, *lit.* that which lies opposite the view. So Ger. *gegend* region, f. *gegen* against. The original stress was on the final syllable, as still in ballads.] **1.** An expanse of land; a region, district. **2.** A tract or district having limits in relation to human occupation, *e.g.* owned by the same lord, or inhabited by people of the same race, dialect, occupation, etc. ME. **3.** The territory or land of a nation ME. **4.** The land of a person's birth, citizenship, residence, etc. ME. **5.** The rural districts as distinct from the town or towns; *occas.*, all outside the capital 1526. **6.** The people of a district or state; the nation ME. **7.** *Law.* Applied to a jury ME. **8.** *Naut.* A region of the sea; also, a station 1748. **9.** *Mining.* (*Cornwall.*) The rock in which a lode of ore occurs 1674. **10.** *attrib.* Of a country, district, or part of the world; national, native. Usu. with a possessive or demonstrative. Now *dial.* ME. **11.** Of or belonging to the rural districts 1525.

1. Marie wente into monteyne contre WYCLIF. **2.** The c. of the Mac-Gregors SCOTT. **4.** To weepe Ouer his Countries Wrongs 1 *Hen. IV*, IV. iii. 82. **5.** God made the c., and man made the town COWPER. **6.** And all countreys came into Egypt to Ioseph, for to buy corne *Gen.* xli. 57. Phr. *To appeal* or *go to the c.*: to appeal to the constituencies from a vote of the House of Commons: see APPEAL *v.* **7.** When the prisoner has..for his trial put himself 'upon the country' (which c. the jury are) H. COX. **11.** A plain C.-fellow TRAPP. **C. cousin,** a cousin or relative of countrified habits; also *gen.* 1770.

Comb.: **c.-box,** small c.-house; **-dance** [cf. CONTREDANCE], an English dance of rural or native origin; *spec.*

applied to dances in which a number of couples stand up face to face in two long lines, as in the *Sir Roger de Coverley*; **-fo·lk**, †compatriots; rustics; **-hou·se**, a house in the c.; a c.-seat; **c. party** (*Politics*): a party which advocates the interests and claims of the c. against the court, etc., or later of c. against town; **c.-peo·ple** = *country-folk*; **-sea·t**, the residence of a c. gentleman or nobleman; a c.-house; **-si·de**, = COUNTRY 2; the inhabitants of a tract of c.; **c. town**, a small town which forms the centre of a rural district, as dist. from a manufacturing town, etc.

Countryman (kɒ·ntrimæ̆n). ME. **1.** A native or inhabitant of a country or district. Often in *comb.* **2.** A man of one's own country; usu. with *possessive* ME. **3.** One who lives in the country; a husbandman 1577.

1. A Disease which seiz'd no Countrymen but English 1708. 2. I am Welch you know, good Countriman SHAKS. So **Cou·ntry·wo·man.**

Countship (kau·ntʃip). 1703. [f. COUNT *sb.*[2] + -SHIP.] The office, dignity, domain, or jurisdiction of a count.

How his C. sulks BROWNING.

County[1] (kau·nti). ME. [a. AF. *counté*, later *counte(e* = mod.F. *comté* :—L. *comitatus*, f. *comes, comitem* COUNT; cf. *ducatus* DUCHY from *dux* DUKE.] †**1.** The domain of a (foreign) count –1665. **2.** One of the territorial divisions of Great Britain and Ireland, forming an important unit for administrative, judicial, and political purposes. Cf. SHIRE. ME. In the United States, the political and administrative division next below the state 1683. **3.** *Eng. Hist.* The shire-moot, shire-court, County-court ME. **4.** The people of a county collectively; the county gentry or county families collectively 1647. **5.** *attrib.* Of a (or the) county; belonging or pertaining to a county 1656.

1. **County palatine**: *orig.* the dominion of a count or earl palatine; in England, a c. of which the earl or lord had originally royal privileges, with exclusive civil and criminal jurisdiction. The counties palatine are now *Cheshire* and *Lancashire*. 2. Of the Old-English kingdoms several still survive as counties FREEMAN. 3. Shires which haue and vse their Counties to bee holden euery six weekes *Act 2–3 Edw. VI*, c. 25.

Comb.: **c. borough**: = *county corporate* (see CORPORATE *ppl. a.* 4); **c. commissioner**, (*a*) a justice of the peace on the commission of a c.; (*b*) in *U.S.*, an elected administrative officer in many counties; **c. council**, a council which conducts the affairs of a c.; **c. court**, *orig.* = COUNTY[1] 3; *now*, a local judicial court for civil actions; hence **cou·nty-cou·rt** *v. colloq.* to sue in the county court; **c. family**, a family belonging to the nobility or gentry, having estates and a seat in the c.; **c. sessions**, the quarter sessions for a c.; **c. town**, the town which is the seat of the administration of a county.

†**Cou·nty**[2]. 1550. [app. ad. AF. *counte*, or OF. and It. *conte*.] = COUNT *sb.*[2] –1848.

Coup (kaup), *sb.*[1] Now only *Sc.* ME. [a. OF. *coup, cop, colp* blow, and from the vb. (COUP *v.*[3]).] †**1.** = COPE *sb.*[2] –1535. **2.** A fall, upset 1535. **3.** A fault by which a coal-seam is tilted up 1795. **4.** The act of tilting rubbish from a cart, etc.; also the right to do this 1887.

Coup, coop (kūp), *sb.*[2] Now *dial.* 1582. [perh. same as COOP *sb.*[1]] A cart or wagon with closed sides and ends, for carting dung, lime, etc.; the load of such a cart. *Comb.* **c.-cart** (in same sense); also a cart with a body which can be tilted.

‖**Coup** (kū), *sb.*[3] [F. *coup* (ku) :—OF. *colp, cop* :—late L. *colpus, colapus*, for L. *colaphus*, a. Gr. κόλαφος cuff, buffet. Naturalized in ME. in a lit. sense (see COUP *sb.*[1]); reintroduced in 18th c. in a fig. sense as Fr.] **1.** A blow (that one sustains) (*rare*) 1793. **2.** A stroke, a move (that one makes); a 'hit' 1791. **3.** *Billiards.* The act of holing a ball without its first striking another ball 1770. **4.** Among N. American Indians: A successful stroke; *esp.* one that captures the weapon or horse of an enemy 1876.

Phrases. *Coup d'état* (kudeta) [F. *état* state]: a sudden and decisive stroke of state policy; *spec.* a change in the government carried out violently or illegally by the ruling power. *Coup de grâce* (kudəgrās) [*lit.* stroke of grace]: a blow by which one condemned or mortally hurt is put out of his misery; hence *fig.* a finishing stroke. *Coup de main* (kudəmæ̃) [*lit.* stroke of hand]: 'a sudden and vigorous attack, for the purpose of instantaneously capturing a position' (Stocqueler); also *transf.* *Coup d'œil* (kudöʸ) [F. *œil* eye]: (*a*) A comprehensive glance; a view as it strikes the eye at a glance. (*b*) *Mil.* The action or faculty of rapidly taking a general view of a position, and estimating its advantages and disadvantages. †*Coup de soleil* (kudəsoleʸ) [F. *soleil* sun]: a sunstroke. *Coup de théâtre* (kudəteʸātr): a theatrical hit; a sensational turn or action in a play; also *transf.*

Coup, cowp (kaup), *v.*[1] *Sc.* and *n. dial.* ME. [a. ON. *kaupa* to buy, barter; see CHEAP *v.* and COPE *v.*[3]] †**1.** To buy; also *fig.* (ME. only.) **2.** To exchange, barter 1610. Hence **Couper, cowper**, one who buys and sells.

Coup, coupe (kūp), *v.*[2] ME. [a. F. *couper*; cf. COPE *v.*[4]] †**1.** *trans.* To cut, slash. (Only in pa. pple.) (ME. only.) **2.** *Her.* To cut off clean (opp. to *erased, slipped*): said *esp.* of the head or any member of an animal; also of an ordinary (*e.g.* a cross) having the extremities cut off.

Coup (kaup), *v.*[3] *Sc.* ME. [prob. same as COPE *v.*[2]] †**1.** *intr.* To strike; to come to blows. (ME. only.) **2.** *trans.* To overturn, upset, tilt 1572. **3.** *intr.* To tumble over; to capsize 1785.

‖**Coupé** (kupe), *a.* 1572. [F., pa. pple. of *couper*.] *Her.* = Couped (see COUP *v.*[2]).

‖**Coupé** (kupe), *sb.* 1834. [F.; see prec.] **1.** A short four-wheeled close carriage with an inside seat for two, and an outside seat for the driver. **2.** The front or after compartment of a continental *diligence* 1834; also, an end compartment in a railway carriage, seated on one side only 1853. **b.** A closed motor car, usually a two-seater 1912. **3.** *Dancing.* = COUPEE, q.v.

Coupee (kupī·, ku·pī), *sb.* Also †*coupie*, †*coupé*. 1673. [ad. F. *coupé* in same sense.] A dance step, in which the dancer rests on one foot and passes the other forward or backward, making a sort of salutation; hence, *occas.*, a bow made while advancing.

Why shall a man practise coupees, who only means to walk 1757. Hence **Coupee** *v. intr.* to make this movement.

‖**Coupe-gorge** (kupgorʒ). ME. [F.; = cut-throat.] †**1.** A cut-throat. (ME. only.) **2.** *Mil.* Any position so disadvantageous that troops occupying it must either surrender or be cut to pieces. Also *fig.*

Couple (kɒ·p'l), *sb.* ME. [a. OF. *cople, cuple*, later *couple* :—L. *copula*; see COPULA.] **1.** That which unites two; *esp.* a brace or leash for hounds, etc. †**2.** Coupling in matrimony; the bond of wedlock; sexual union –1611. **3.** Two of the same sort taken together; a pair, a brace; often loosely = *two*. (The pl. after a numeral is often *couple*.) ME. **4.** A pair of opposite sexes; *e.g.* a wedded or engaged pair ME.; two partners in a dance 1759. **5.** One of a pair of rafters, that meet at the top, and are fixed at the bottom by a tie; a principal rafter, a chevron ME. †**6.** = COUPLET 1 (*rare*) –1589. **7.** *Dynamics.* A pair of equal and parallel forces acting in opposite directions, tending to produce a motion of rotation 1855. **8.** *Electr.* A pair of connected plates of different metals, used for creating either a galvanic or a thermo-electric current 1863.

1. Another company of houndes..had their couples cast off 1602. *transf.* and *fig.* *To go, hunt, run in couples* (now often = *pairs, twos*). 3. A c. of as arrant knaues as any in Messina *Much Ado* III. v. 34. Skilfull Forresters..Do use to say, a C. of Rabbets or Conies GUILLIM. 4. A very loving C. STEELE. I stood two c. above her 1759.

Couple (kɒ·p'l), *v.* ME. [a. OF. *copler, cupler*, later *coupler*, f. *couple*; cf. L. *copulare*.] **1.** *trans.* To fasten (dogs) together in pairs. **2.** *gen.* To fasten or link together (prop. in pairs); to join or connect in any way ME. †**3.** To join in wedlock or sexual union –1754. **4.** *intr.* (for *refl.*) To pair ME. **5.** To associate in pairs (*trans.* and *intr.*) ME.

1. C. Clowder with the deepe-mouth'd brach *Tam. Shr.* Ind. i. 18. 2. Wo that ioynen hous to hous, and feeld to feeld coupleth WYCLIF *Isa.* v. 8. To c. rhimes POPE, trucks together 1874. 3. The Vicar of the next village..hath promis'd to..c. vs *A.Y.L.* III. iii. 45. 4. Begin these wood birds but to c. now *Mids. N.* IV. i. 145. Hence **Cou·pled** *ppl. a.* tied, linked, or associated together in pairs, as *c. columns, windows*; *Her.* = CONJOINED.

†**Cou·ple-be·ggar.** 1702. [f. COUPLE *v.* 3.] A disreputable priest who made it his business to couple beggars (see COUPLE *v.* 3) –1744.

Couple-close. 1572. [app. f. F. *couple* + *close* closed, shut.] **1.** *Her.* A diminutive of the chevron, having one-fourth of its breadth, borne in couples, and usually cotising a chevron. **2.** A pair of rafters or couples in a roof. (See COUPLE *sb.*) 1849.

†**Couplement** (kɒ·p'lmĕnt). 1548. [a. OF.; see COUPLE *v.* and -MENT.] **1.** Union of pairs –1670. **2.** A couple –1816.

Coupler (kɒ·plər). 1552. [f. COUPLE *v.*] **1.** One that couples. **2.** A thing that couples. *spec.* **a.** In an organ: A contrivance for connecting two manuals, or a manual with the pedals, or two keys an octave apart on the same keyboard 1668. **b.** The ring which slips upon the handle of a pair of tongs or a nipping-tool 1874. So **Cou·pleress** (*rare*), a female c.; a bawd.

Couplet (kɒ·plĕt). 1580. [a. F., dim. of *couple*.] **1.** A pair of successive lines of verse, *esp.* when riming with each other. **2.** *gen.* A pair or couple 1601. **3.** *Archit.* A window of two lights 1844. **4.** *Mus.* Two equal notes inserted in a passage of triple rhythm and made to occupy the time of three 1876. Also *attrib.*

1. He [Chaucer] introduces a new metre.. now famous as 'the heroic c.' SKEAT. 2. Weel whisper ore a c. or two of most sage sawes *Twel. N.* III. iv. 412.

Coupling (kɒ·pliŋ), *vbl. sb.* ME. [f. COUPLE *v.* + -ING[1].] **1.** Joining in couples; see the vb. **2.** Sexual union ME. **3.** *concr.* Anything that couples 1549. †**4.** = COUPLE *sb.* 1. –1695. †**5.** = COUPLE *sb.* 5. –1611. **6.** In *Machinery*, etc.: The name of various contrivances for connecting parts of constructions or machinery, *esp.* in order to transmit motion; e. g. *box c., clutch c.*, etc. **7.** Of a dog, etc.: 'The space between the tops of the shoulder-blades and tops of the hip-joints or huckle-bones' (V. Shaw).

Comb.: **c.-box**, a metal box joining the ends of two shafts, so that they may revolve together; **-chain**, the chain which couples railway carriages, trucks, etc.; **-pin**, a pin used for coupling railway carriages, etc.; **-pole**, the pole connecting the fore and hind gear of a wagon; **-reins**, the reins that couple a pair of horses together; **-rod**, the rod that couples the wheels of some locomotive engines.

Coupon (kū·pɒn, ‖kupoṅ). 1864. [a. F. *coupon*, in OF. *colpon, copon* piece cut off, whence the earlier Eng. CULPON.] A separable certificate, of which a series are attached to, and form part of, certain principal certificates, in order that they may be severally detached and given up as required. **b.** A party leader's recommendation to a political candidate 1918.

The coupons for interest annexed to any debenture shall also pass by delivery *Act 37–8 Vict.* c. 3 § 5. The [railway] tickets are..in the shape of small books of coupons *Cook's Excursionist.*

‖**Coupure** (kūpiūə·r). 1710. [a. F., f. *couper* to cut.] *Mil.* A ditch or trench; *esp.* one dug by the besieged for purposes of defence. *Fortif.* A passage cut through the glacis in the re-entrant angle of the covered way.

Courage (kɒ·rĕdʒ), *sb.* [ME. *corage*, a. OF. *corage, curage*, later *courage*, repr. a L. type **coraticum*, f. *cor* heart. See -AGE.] †**1.** Spirit, mind, disposition, nature –1659. †Applied to a person –1647. †**2.** What is in one's mind or thoughts; purpose; inclination –1626. †**3.** Spirit, lustiness, vigour; also *fig.* –1705. †**b.** Wrath; **c.** Pride; **d.** Confidence. –1608. **4.** That quality of mind which shows itself in facing danger without fear; bravery, valour ME.

1. Smale fowles maken melodie.. So priketh hem nature in here corages CHAUCER. 2. I'de such a c. to do him good *Timon* III. iii. 24. 4. What man, corage yet *Merch. V.* IV. i. 111. C. never to submit or yield MILT. *P. L.* I. 108. Phr. *Dutch c.*: bravery induced by drinking (*colloq.*). Hence **Cou·raged** *a.* having c. **Cou·rageless** *a.* without c.

†**Cou·rage**, *v.* 1470. [f. prec. sb.] = ENCOURAGE –1614.

Courageous (kŏrēⁱ·dʒəs), *a.* ME. [a. AF. *corageous*, OF. *corageus*, later *courageux*, f. *corage* COURAGE.] **1.** Having courage; brave, fearless, valiant. †**2.** Eager (*to do* something) –1450. †**3.** Lively, lusty, vigorous –1577.

1. Bee thou strong, and very c. *Josh.* i. 7. Hence **Coura·geous-ly** *adv.*, **-ness.**

Courant, *a.* and *sb.*[1] 1601. [a. F. :—L. *currentem*.] *adj.* †Running; in *Her.* applied to figures of animals represented as running 1727. †*sb.* A running-string. HOLLAND.

Courant (kuræ·nt), *sb.*[2] 1621. [a. F. *courant* runner.] †**1.** ? An express –1727. **2.** A paper containing news. (Now only in names of newspapers.) 1621.

Courant, *sb.*[3]; see COURANTE.

Courante, courant (kurā·nt, kurɑ·nt). 1586. [a. F.; *lit.* running (dance), f. *courir* to run. Cf. CORANTO.] **1.** A dance characterized by a running or gliding step. **2.** *Mus.* The tune used for accompanying this dance, or a similar tune 1597.

‖**Courap** (kūᵊ·răp). 1706. [ad. west. Ind. *khurup* a kind of herpes.] 'Name given in India to cutaneous diseases attended with itching and eruptions' (*Syd. Soc. Lex.*).

Courbaril (kūᵊ·ɹbăril). 1753. [Native Amer.] The West Indian Locust-tree; also its resin (called also ANIMÉ).

Courbash; see KOURBASH.

†**Courbe**, *a.* ME. [a. F.:—L. *curvus* bent.] Bent, crooked –1579.

Her necke is short her shulders c. GOWER. So †Courbe *sb.* (see CURB *sb.*).

†**Courbe, courb**, *v.* ME. [a. F. *courber*:—L. *curvare*; see CURVE *v.*, and CURB *v.*] *intr.* To curve, bend, bow –1602. Also *trans.*

I courbed on my knees and cryed hir of grace LANGL.

‖**Courbette** (kurbɛ·t). 1648. [F.] = CURVET.

Courche, Courchie, obs. ff. CURCH.

Courier (ku·riəɹ, kūᵊ·riəɹ). [ME. *corour, currour*:—(ult.) late L. *curritorem*; also *courier*, F. *courrier*, in med.L. *currerius*; both f. L. *currere.*] **1.** A running messenger; one sent in haste. †**2.** *Mil.* A light horseman acting as scout or skirmisher. Cf. AVANT-COURIER. –1603. **3.** A travelling servant, having the duty of making all the arrangements connected with the journey 1770. **4.** A title of newspapers 1798.

1. He delyuerd his letter to a courrour CAXTON.

‖**Courlan** (kurlaṅ). [Fr.; ad. S. Amer.] A S. Amer. bird of the genus *Aramus*, related to the Rails. (Dicts.)

Course (kōᵊɹs), *sb.* ME. [a. F. *cours* = It. *corso*:—L. *cursum*; also a. F. *course* = It. *corsa*, a fem. form. The two forms are not distinguishable from 15th c.] †**1.** The action of running; a run; a gallop –1687. **2.** Onward movement in a particular path ME. **3.** A race (*arch.*) 1489. †**4.** Violent motion; impetus. (ME. only.) **5.** The charge of combatants in battle or tournament; onset; encounter (*Hist.*) ME. †**6.** A raid –1678. **7.** The action or practice of coursing (see COURSE *v.* 1) ME. †**8.** Running (of liquids); flow, flux –1665. **9.** Faculty of running, flowing, passing current, etc. ME.; †currency (of money, etc.) –1512. **10.** The line, path, or way, along which anything runs or travels ME. **11.** (*Naut.*) The direction in which, or point of the compass towards which, a ship sails 1553; *pl.* points of the compass 1610. **12.** *fig.* The continuous process (of time), succession (of events); progress onward or through successive stages ME. **13.** Habitual or ordinary manner of procedure; way, custom, practice ME. **14.** A line of (personal) action, way of acting 1583. **15.** A planned series of actions or proceedings: as of diet, etc. 1605. **16.** Each of the successive parts or members of a series ME. **17.** *pl.* The menses 1563. **18.** A row, range, or layer; *spec.* in *Building*, a continuous layer of stones, brick, or timber, of the same height throughout, in a wall, the face of a building, etc.; also, a row of slates, tiles, or shingles 1624; in *Mining*, a layer or lode of ore, etc. 1778. **19.** †(One's) turn –1665; one of several sets of persons appointed to serve in their turn 1535. **20.** *Naut.* Each of the sails attached to the lower yards of a ship; now *esp.* the fore-sail (*fore-c.*) and main-sail (*main-c.*) 1515.

2. To slacken one's c. JOHNSON. **5.** We ran our c., my charger fell SCOTT. **9.** Pray for vs, that the word of the Lord may haue free c. *2 Thess.* iii. 1. **10.** The c. of a ship 1665, of the Adige 1757. The round c. at Newmarket 1766. **11.** We sette owre c. south and by East EDEN. Set her two courses off to Sea againe, lay her off *Temp.* I. i. 53. **12.** The yeare hath runne his c. 1576. **13.** Phr. *C. of nature*: the natural order. *C. of Exchange*: see EXCHANGE *sb.* The law must take its c. JUNIUS. **14.** Our wisest c. DISRAELI. Legal and moderate courses MACAULAY. Evil courses 1684. **15.** A c. of study and exercise GIBBON. A long c. of centuries 1828. The four-field or Norfolk c. 1844. **16.** A dinner of many courses O. W. HOLMES. A severe c. of the gout H. WALPOLE. Beare-like I must fight the c. (*i. e.* the successive attacks of dogs, a certain number at a time) *Macb.* v. vii. 2. **19.** A certaine priest, named Zacharias, of the c. of Abia *Luke* i. 5.

Prepositional Phrases. **In course.** †**a.** In turn. **b.** In the regular order. **c.** Naturally; = *of c.* (Now vulgar.) **In course of**: in process of. **Of course.** **a.** *adjectival.* Customary; natural, to be expected. **b.** *advb.* In ordinary or due course. **c.** Hence: Naturally; obviously.

Course (kōᵊɹs), *v.* 1466. [f. COURSE *sb.* in various senses.] **1.** To hunt (game) with hounds; *spec.* to hunt (hares) with greyhounds, by sight 1550. Also *absol.* **2.** *trans.* To chase, pursue 1586. †**3.** To persecute –1600. †**4.** To chase with blows; hence, to thrash –1611. **5.** *intr.* To run, to run as in a race, to career; also *transf.* of liquids, etc. 1533; †*fig.* –1734. Also *trans.* To run over or along 1789. **6.** *intr.* To steer or direct one's course 1555. †**7.** *intr.* To run a course (see COURSE *sb.* 5). SPENSER. **8.** *causal.* To exercise in running 1568.

2. The big round teares Cours'd one another downe his innocent nose In piteous chase *A. Y. L.* II. i. 39. **5.** Coursing like a colt across its lawns W. IRVING. In thoughtless gaiety I coursed the plain WORDSW. **8.** The greyhound ye desired to c. WOLCOTT.

Coursed (kōᵊɹst), *ppl. a.* 1740. **1.** [f. the vb.] Chased, *spec.* as a hare by greyhounds. **2.** [f. the sb.] Of masonry: Laid in courses 1851.

Courser[1] (kōᵊ·ɹsəɹ). ME. [orig. repr. OF. *courseur*: later, prob. f. COURSE *v.* or *sb.*] **1.** One who or a dog which courses (see COURSE *v.*) 1600. †**2.** *Oxford Univ.* A disputant in the schools –1688. **3.** A building stone used in forming a course 1885.

Courser[2] (kōᵊ·ɹsəɹ). ME. [a. F. *coursier*:—L. type **cursarius*, f. *cursus*; see COURSE.] **1.** *orig.* A charger (see COURSE *sb.* 5); since 17th c.: A racer. Now *poet.* or *rhet.* **2.** A stallion. Now *Sc.* 1483.

1. A thousand coursers fleeter than the wind YOUNG.

Courser[3] (kōᵊ·ɹsəɹ). 1766. [ad. L. *cursorius*, used subst.] *Zool.* A bird of the genus *Cursorius*, noted for swift running; esp *C. isabellinus.*

Coursey, -ie, var. of COURSY.

Coursing (kōᵊ·ɹsiŋ), *vbl. sb.* 1538. [f. COURSE *v.* + -ING[1].] **1.** The action of COURSE *v.* 1568. **2.** *spec.* The sport of chasing hares, etc. with greyhounds, by sight 1538. †**3.** *Oxford Univ.* The opposing of a thesis in the schools –1683.

†**Cou·rsy, -sey.** Also **-sie.** 1611. [a. obs. F. *coursie, corsie* = It. *corsia*, f. *corso* COURSE.] A raised passage from prow to poop of a galley over the rowing benches –1693.

Court (kōᵊɹt), *sb.*[1] OE. [Early ME. *curt, court*, a. OF. *cort, curt*, later *court* (from 15th c. *cour*):—L. *cohortem, cortem* court, yard, etc. Assoc. early w. L. *curia* (see III. and IV.).]

I. 1. A clear space enclosed by walls or surrounded by buildings; a yard, a court-yard. Also, a section of the area of a museum, or the like. At Cambridge, a college quadrangle. ME. †**2.** A large building or set of buildings standing in a court-yard; a large house or castle. In early times = BURY. –1887. **3.** In a town: A confined space opening off a street, and built around with houses 1687. **4.** An enclosed quadrangular area, uncovered or covered, with a smooth level floor, for playing tennis, rackets, or fives; the plot of ground marked out for lawn-tennis; also each subdivision of such a plot 1519.

1. Esther..stood in the inner c. of the kings house *Esther* v. 1. My soule..fainteth for the courts of the Lord (*i. e.* the enclosures constituting the temple area round the sanctuary on Mount Moriah) *Ps.* lxxxiv. 2. **2.** This Nutwell C. (which signifies a Mansion-house in a Seigniory) RISDON.

II. 1. The place where a sovereign (or high dignitary) resides and holds state, attended by his retinue ME. **2.** The establishment and surroundings of a sovereign with his councillors and retinue ME. **b.** without article (*at c., to c.*, etc.), including place, persons, and proceedings. Cf. *at church*, etc. ME. **3.** The body of courtiers collectively. (Construed as pl.) ME. **4.** The sovereign with his ministers and councillors. (Construed as sing.) ME.

1. In Courts and Palaces he also Reigns MILT. *P. L.* I. 497. **2.** When the C. lay at Windsor *Merry W.* II. ii. 62. The court's a school, indeed BEAUM. & FL. **4.** The affaires of the French c. 1651.

III. An assembly held by the sovereign at his residence OE.

Arthur..Held c. at old Caerleon upon Usk TENNYSON.

IV. A court of judicature, of law, or of administration. **1.** Applied to Parliament. Cf. Sp. *Cortes.* 1450. **2.** An assembly of judges or other persons legally appointed and acting as a tribunal to hear and determine any cause, civil, ecclesiastical, military, or naval ME.

Justice was formerly administered by judges who followed the king as officers of his court; hence the title *King's Courts* (*curia regis*).

3. The place, hall, or chamber in which justice is administered ME. **b.** without article (*in, into, out of c.*, etc.), including place and proceedings ME. **4.** A session of a judicial assembly ME. **5.** An assembly of the qualified members of a company or corporation, or of the council thereof 1527. **6.** Homage such as is offered at court; attention or courtship to one whose favour is sought: in phr. *to make* or *pay* (*one's*) *c. to* = COURT *v.* 2, 3. 1590.

1. A Prayer for the High C. of Parliament *Bk. Com. Prayer.* **2.** *Supreme C.*: the highest c. of a country or state. *C. of record*: one 'where the acts and judicial proceedings are enrolled in parchment for a perpetual memorial' (Blackstone). *C. of* ADMIRALTY, ARCHES, CHANCERY, COMMON PLEAS, EQUITY, PROBATE, etc.: see those words. **C. of Claims:** a c. in which claims are adjudicated on; in U. S., a c. sitting at Washington for the investigation of claims against the government. **C. of Conscience or of Requests:** a small debt c.; *c. of conscience* (fig.), conscience as a moral tribunal. **3.** Go one and cal the Iew into the C. *Merch. V.* IV. i. 14. **b.** The case was settled out of c. (*mod.*). Phr. *Out of c.*: said of a plaintiff who has forfeited his claim to be heard; now mostly *fig.* **6.** Flatter me, make thy c., and say it did DRYDEN.

V. *attrib.* **a.** Of or belonging to a royal court 1598. **b.** Of or belonging to a court of law 1571.

Comb.: **c.-almanac**, an annual hand-book of royal families and their courts; **-calendar** = *court-almanac*; **-card**, var. of COAT-CARD, q. v.; a picture-card; **c. circular**, a daily record of the doings of the C., published in the newspapers; **-craft**, the art required or practised at c.; **-day**, a day on which a c. (legal, royal, etc.) is held; **-fool, -jester**, a jester kept for the amusement of a prince and his c.; **-guide**, a directory containing the names and addresses of the nobility and gentry; **-hand**, the handwriting in use in the English law-courts from the 16th c. to 1731; **-lands**, 'domains or lands kept in the lord's hands to serve his family' (Wharton); **-man**, a courtier; †**c. marshal**, the marshal of a prince's household; **-newsman**, a person appointed to furnish news of the doings of the C.; **-party**, a party which advocates the interests of the C.; **-room**, a room in which a c. is regularly held; **-suit**, (*a*) a suit preferred at C.; (*b*) a suit worn at C., c.-dress; **-sword**, a light sword worn as part of a man's c.-dress.

Hence **Cou·rtless** *a.* without a c.; without courtliness. **Cou·rtlet.** **Cou·rtlike, cou·rt-like** *a.* **Cou·rtling.**

†**Court**, *sb.*[2] 1576. Some kind of cart –1703.

Court (kōᵊɹt), *v.* 1515. [f. COURT *sb.*[1]; cf. COURTESAN.] †**1.** *intr.* To be or reside at court –1586. **2.** *trans.* To pay courteous attention to 1590. **3.** To pay amorous attention to, woo (with a view to marriage). (Now *homely*; also *poet.*) 1580. *absol.* 1591. Also *fig.* and *transf.* **4.** To entice *into, to, from, out of*, etc. 1602. **5.** To seek to win or attract, to affect (a thing) 1571.

2. To flatter kings, or c. the great GOLDSM. **3.** *absol.* See how they kisse and c. *Tam. Shr.* IV. ii. 27. *fig.* Their broad sheets c. the breeze MOTHERWELL. **5.** Sylla never courted popularity FROUDE. Hence **Cou·rter**, one who courts.

‖**Courtage** (kurtāʒ, kōᵊ·ɹtėdʒ). 1835. [F., f. (ult.) L. *curare* to take charge of.] = BROKERAGE. So ‖**Courtagie.**

Cou·rt-ba·ron. 1542. [a. AF. *court baron*, earlier *court de baroun.*] The assembly of the freehold tenants of a manor under the presidency of the lord or his steward.

Court Christian; see CHRISTIAN *a.*

†**Cou·rt-cupboard.** 1592. A movable cabinet used to display plate, etc. –1821.

Court-customary; = CUSTOMARY court.

Court-dress. 1797. The dress worn by those who attend at Court, and on other state occasions. So †**Court-dresser.**

Courteous (kōᵊ·ɹtyəs, kɒ̄·ɹtyəs), *a.* ME. [a. OF. *corteis, curteis* (later *courtois*).] **a.** Having such manners as befit the court of a prince; graciously polite and respectful in dealing with others; kind and complaisant. **b.** As a formula of address; *orig.* to superiors = Gracious (*arch.*) ME. Also *transf.*

A good man, sage, curtois, and valyaunt CAXTON. *transf.* This is call'd the retort c. *A. Y. L.* v. iv. 75. Hence **Cou·rteous-ly** *adv.*, **-ness.**

†**Cou·rtepy.** ME. [app. a. MDu. *korte pie*; cf. PEA-*coat*.] A short coat of coarse material -1483.

A gay yeman.. He hadde vp-on a c. of grene CHAUCER.

†**Courtesan, -zan,** *sb.*[1] and *a.* ME. [a. F. *courtisan*, ad. It. *cortigiano* a courtier.] *sb.* One attached to the court of a prince -1587. *adj.* The court language (of Italy) -1601.

Courtesan, -zan[2] (kōᵊ·ɹtizæn, kɒ̄·ɹt-). 1549. [a. F. *courtisane*, ad. It. *cortigiana* 'a strumpet', orig. woman attached to the court. Now usually kōᵊɹ-.] A court-mistress; a prostitute. (Somewhat euphemistic.)

Your whore is for euery rascall, but your Curtizan is for your Courtier 1607.

Courtesy (kōᵊ·ɹtėsi, kɒ̄·ɹ-), *sb.* ME. [a. OF. *cur-*, *cortesie* (later *courtoisie*) = It. *cortesia*, from *cortese* COURTEOUS. Now usually kōᵊɹ-, exc. in sense 4.] **1.** Courteous behaviour; graceful politeness or considerateness in intercourse with others; courteous disposition. **2.** *Of, by* (†*at*) *c.*: by favour or indulgence 1587. **3.** *Law.* A tenure by which a husband, after his wife's death, holds certain kinds of property which she has inherited. More fully called *Courtesy (Curtesy) of England* or *of Scotland*. 1523. **4.** (with *pl.*) A courteous act or expression 1450. †**5.** The customary expression of respect by action or gesture, *esp.* to a superior -1645. **6.** = CURTSY *sb.* 3.-1627. †**7.** = CURTSY *sb.* 4.-1627.

1. A Knyght ther was.. he loued chiualrie, Trouthe and honour fredom and curteisie CHAUCER. Courtesie grows in court; news in the citie G. HERBERT. **2.** *C. title*: a title of no legal validity given by social custom; *e.g.* the prefix of *Honourable* to the names of the children of Viscounts and Barons. **3.** No man shall be tenant by the curtesie of Land, without his wife have possession in deed 1531. **4.** That curt'sie with like kindnesse to repay SPENSER. **5.** The Elephant hath ioynts, but none for curtesie SHAKS.

Hence **Cou·rtesy** *v.* †to treat with c.; *intr.* to make a curtsy.

Cou·rt-house. 1483. **1.** A building in which courts of law are held. **2.** A manorial dwelling (*South of Eng.*). **3.** *U.S.* = *County seat* (see COUNTY[1]) 1856.

Courtier (kōᵊ·ɹtiəɹ). ME. [app. f. (ult.) F. *cortoyer* to be at the court.] **1.** One who frequents the court of a sovereign; an attendant at court. Also *transf.* †**2.** A wooer -1766.

1. Reynard the foxe is now asquyer and a courtyer CAXTON. False is the cringing Courtier's plighted word GAY. **2.** Courtiers of beautious freedome *Ant. & Cl.* II. vi 17. Hence **Cou·rtierism,** the practice or quality of a c. **Cou·rtierly** *a.* **Cou·rtiership.** †**Cou·rtiery,** the manners of a c., or ? courtiers as a body B. JONS.

Court leet. 1588. [See LEET.] A court of record held periodically in a hundred, lordship, or manor, before the lord or his steward, and attended by the residents of the district. (Practically superseded.)

Courtly (kōᵊ·ɹtli), *a.* 1450. [f. COURT *sb.*[1]] †**1.** Of or pertaining to the Court -1786. **2.** Having the manners or breeding befitting the Court; polished, of a high-bred courtesy 1450. **3.** Of things: Elegant, refined 1535. **4.** Given to flattery; subservient to the Court 1607.

1. In C. company 2 *Hen. VI*, I. i. 27. **2.** The French are passing c. FORD. **3.** You haue too C. a wit, for me *A. Y. L.* III. ii. 72. **4.** Truth sometimes escapes from the most c. pens H. WALPOLE. Hence **Cou·rtliness.** So **Cou·rtly** *adv.*

†**Court-mantle.** ME. [f. OF. *curt, cort*, now *court* short + MANTLE.] One who wears a short cloak. (Surname of Henry II.) -1677.

Court martial, *sb.* Pl. **courts martial.** 1571. [orig. *martial court*; see MARTIAL.] A judicial court, consisting of military or naval officers, for the trial of military or naval offences, or the administration of martial law.

Drumhead court-martial: a court-martial summoned round an upturned drum, for summary treatment of offenders during military operations.

Hence **Court-ma·rtial** *v. colloq.* to try by court martial.

†**Cou·rtnoll.** 1568. [f. COURT + NOLL.] A courtier. (*contempt.*) -1658.

†**Court of guard.** 1590. A perversion of CORPS DE GARDE, q. v. -1810.

Court-plaster. 1772. [So called from being used for the black patches formerly worn by ladies at Court.] Sticking-plaster made of silk coated with isinglass.

Court roll. 1461. *Law.* The roll kept in connexion with a manorial court, a copy of which constitutes the tenant's title to his holding.

Courtship (kōᵊ·ɹtˌʃip). 1588. [f. COURT *sb.*[1] + -SHIP.] †**1.** Courtliness of manners -1673; courtesy -1719. †**2.** The state befitting a court or courtier -1630. †**3.** Office or position at court -1659. †**4.** Court-craft; flattery, etc. -1734. †**5.** The paying of court or courteous attentions -1729. **6.** The paying of court to a woman with a view to marriage; courting 1596. Also *transf.* and *fig.* **7.** *fig.* Endeavour to win over 1727.

1. *L. L. L.* v. ii. 363. **2.** *Rom. & Jul.* III. iii. 34. **5.** His C. to the common people *Rich. II*, I. iv. 24. **6.** C., and such faire ostents of loue *Merch. V*, II. viii. 44. Hence †**Cou·rtshipment** = COURTSHIP 4. Lovelace.

Cou·rt-ya·rd, cou·rtyard. 1552. An open area surrounded by walls or buildings within the precincts of a large house, castle, etc.

‖**Couscous**[1]**, couscoussou** (ku·skus, -*kusu*) 1600. [a. F. *couscous*, f. (ult.) Arab. *kaskasa* to pound.] An African dish made of flour granulated, and cooked by steaming over the vapour of broth or meat.

‖**Couscous**[2] (ku·skus). 1839. [Fr. form of native word.] A marsupial quadruped, the Spotted Phalanger of the Moluccas (*Cuscus maculatus*).

Cousin (kɒ·z'n), *sb.* ME. [a. F.:-L. *consobrinus* cousin by the mother's side. In ME. often repr. L. *consanguineus.*] †**1.** A collateral relative more distant than a brother or sister; a relative -1748. †**b.** In legal language formerly = the next of kin, or the person to whom one is next of kin. (Here = L. *consanguineus.*) -1642. **2.** *spec.* The son or daughter of an uncle or aunt: = *own, first,* or *full c.*, C.-GERMAN. (The strict modern sense.) ME. Also *fig.* **3.** Used as a term of address by a sovereign of another sovereign, or a nobleman of the same country (in royal writs, etc., of earls and peers of higher rank); also familiarly, *esp.* in Cornwall ME. †**4.** *cant.* A trull. So *C. Betty*. -1863.

1. How now brother, where is my cosen your son *Much Ado* I. ii. 2. **2.** Phr. *First, second c.*, etc.: expressing the relationship of persons descended the same number of steps in distinct lines from a common ancestor; thus the children of *first cousins* are *second cousins* to each other; and so on. **3.** Our brother and c. the King of Scotts EDW. IV in Ellis. C. of Exeter 2 *Hen. VI*, IV. viii. 34. C. Jacky from Redruth 1880.

Phrases: *To call cousins*: to claim kinship (*with*). †*To make a c. of*: ? to beguile. (See COZEN *v.*)

Hence †**Cou·sin** *v. rare*, to call c., claim kinship with. †**Cou·sinage,** cousinhood. **Cou·siness,** a female c. **Cou·sinhood,** cousins or kinsfolk collectively; the relation of being a c. or cousins. **Cou·sinly** *a.* and *adv.* **Cou·sinred,** cousinship, relationship. SCOTT. **Cou·sinry,** a body of kinsfolk. **Cou·sinship,** cousinhood; the action proper to a c.

Cousin-german. Pl. **cousins-german,** †**cousin-germans,** orig. **-s -s.** ME. [a. F. *cousin germain*; see GERMAN *a.*] = COUSIN *sb.* 2. (Now legal or techn.) Also *fig.*

†*Cousin german (once) removed*: = 'first cousin once removed', *i. e.* first cousin's child or *vice versâ*.

‖**Coussinet** (ku·sinet, or as F. kusinę). 1876. [F. dim. of *coussin* cushion.] *Archit.* **a.** 'A stone placed upon the impost of a pier for receiving the first sto e of an arch.' **b.** 'The part of the Ionic capital between the abacus and quarter round, which serves to form the volute,' GWILT.

‖**Couteau** (kuto). 1677. [F.:-OF. *coutel*; see next.] A large knife worn as a weapon. *Couteau de chasse* (F.): a hunting-knife.

†**Coute·l.** 1647. [a. OF. *cotel, coutel*:-L. *cultellum* knife.] 'A short knife or dagger in use during the Middle Ages' (Fairholt) -1654.

Couter, cooter (kū·təɹ). *slang.* 1846. [? f. Danubian-Gipsy *cuta* gold coin.] A sovereign.

Couth (kūþ). Now *Sc.* [OE. *cūð*, pa. pple. of the vb. *cunnan* CAN.] †**1.** *pa. pple.* Known -1613. †**2.** *adj.* Known; well-known, familiar -1557. †**3.** Acquainted (*with, of,* or dative) -1450. **4.** Kind, agreeable. *Sc.* ME. **5.** Snug, cosy. *Sc.* 1749. Hence †**Couth** *adv.* clearly; familiarly. **Cou·thie** *a. Sc.* (in senses 4, 5).

Couth(e, obs. f. *could*, pa. t. of CAN *v.*[1]

Coutil (kuti·l). Also **coutelle, -ille.** 1853. [a. F. *coutil* (kuti) quilt.] A close-woven sort of canvas, used in stay-making, etc.

‖**Couvade** (kuvɑ·d). 1865. [a. obs. F.; f. *couver* to hatch.] Tylor's name for the 'man-childbed' attributed to some uncivilized races, and the customs according to which, on the birth of a child, the man is put to bed, and treated as if he were physically affected by the birth.

†**Couve, cove,** *v.* [a. F. *couver*:-L. *cubare.*] To incubate, hatch. HOLLAND. vars. †**Cou·vey,** covie *v.*

Couvre-feu; see CURFEW.

Cove (kōᵘv), *sb.*[1] [Com. Teut.:-OTeut. **kubon.*] †**1.** In OE.: A small chamber, cell, etc. **2.** A hollow in a rock; a cave, cavern, den (*Sc.* and *n.*) OE. **3.** A recess in the steep flank of a mountain. In U.S. occas. = gap, pass. 1805. **4.** A small bay, creek, or inlet 1590. Also *transf.* **5.** *Archit.* A concave arch or vault; an arched moulding running along the projecting member of a structure; *esp.* the concave arch of a ceiling 1511.

3. It was a c., a huge recess That keeps till June, December's snow WORDSW. **4.** We run our vessel into a little c. DE FOE. *Comb.* **c.-plane,** a plane for cutting coved surfaces.

Cove (kōᵘv), *sb.*[2] *slang* (orig. *Thieves' cant*). 1567. [?] A fellow, chap, customer; *occas.* = Boss.

There's a gentry c. here, Is the top of the shire B. JONS.

Cove (kōᵘv), *v.* 1631. [f. COVE *sb.*[1]] †**1.** *intr.* To shelter in a cove. **2.** *trans.* To arch or vault; *esp.* to arch (a ceiling) at its junction with the wall 1756; to incline inwards (the sides of a fireplace) 1838.

2. The mosques.. are rounded into domes and coved roofs H. SWINBURNE.

Cove, var. of COUVE *v.*; obs. f. COVEY.

Covelline, covellite (kove·ləin, -əit). 1850. [f. *Covelli*, an Italian mineralogist.] *Min.* A native indigo-blue sulphide of copper; often called *blue* or *indigo copper*. var. **Cove·llinite.**

Coven, covin (kɒ·vėn). *Sc.* 1500. [var. of *covent* CONVENT.] A gathering; *esp.* of witches; cf. CONVENT.

†**Co·venable,** *a.* ME. [a. AF. and OF. *covenable*, early var. of *convenable*. Now CONVENABLE, q. v.] **1.** Suitable -1628; consistent. ME. only. **2.** Of persons: Seemly, comely. Cf. *proper*. -1523.

1. Withouten c. cause 1400. Hence †**Co·venableness** (*rare*). †**Covena·blete,** fitness; an opportunity. †**Co·venably** *adv.*

†**Co·venance.** 1475. [a. OF. *covenance*, now *convenance*; see CONVENANCE.] Agreement, covenant, convention -1500.

Covenant (kɒ·vĭnănt), *sb.* ME. [a. OF. *covenant*, later *convenant*, sb. use of adj., orig. pr. pple. of *convenir* to agree.] **1.** A mutual agreement between two or more persons to do or refrain from doing certain acts; sometimes, the undertaking of one of the parties. (Now mainly *legal* or *theological.*) †**2.** A vow. CHAUCER. †**3.** Each of the terms of an agreement -1614. **4.** *Law.* A formal agreement; *esp.* in Eng. Law, a promise or contract under seal ME.; a particular clause of such a contract 1611. †**5.** The matter agreed upon, undertaken, or promised, as covenanted duty, wages, etc. -1596. †**6.** Security. MILTON. **7.** *Theol.* Applied to engagements entered into by and with the Divine Being, as revealed in the Scriptures, etc. ME.; hence *occas.* = Dispensation 1818. **8.** *Eccl. Hist.* The name given *esp.* to the *Solemn League and C.* entered into in 1643 by the Scottish Presbyterians for the defence and furtherance of their ecclesiastical polity. (See also COVENANTER 2.) 1638. Also *attrib.*

1. They made couenaunt that they sholde sle him CAXTON. **4.** Leases.. declared void for non-fulfilment of covenants 1872. **7.** And makes a C. never to destroy The Earth again by flood MILT. *P. L.* XI. 892. *Books of the Old and the New C.*: the O. and N. Testament, belonging to the Mosaic and Christian dispensations respectively. *C. of Works, C. of Grace*: the two relations subsisting between God and man, before and since the Fall. Baptism implieth a c. or league between God and man HOOKER. **8.** *Church C.*: the agreement subscribed by the members of a Congregational Church in order to constitute themselves a distinct religious society.

Hence **Covena·ntal** *a.* of or pertaining to a c.

Covenant (kʋ·vĭnănt), *v.* ME. [f. the sb.] **1.** *intr.* To enter into a covenant; to contract. **2.** *trans.* To agree or subscribe to by covenant ME. **3.** To stipulate 1577.

1. They couenanted with him for thirtie pieces of siluer *Matt.* xxvi. 15. **2.** Nothing is covenanted as to any remainder GROTE. Hence **Co·venantee·**, the person to whom a promise by covenant is made. **Co·venanto·r**, the party by whom the obligation expressed in the covenant is to be performed.

Covenanted (kʋ·vĭnăntėd), *ppl. a.* 1646. **1.** Secured by covenant, as *c. grace, mercies* (Theol.) 1651. **2.** Bound by a covenant 1646. **3.** *Hist.* Having subscribed the Covenant; see COVENANT *sb.* 8. 1660. **4.** *I. C. S.* Applied to the regular members of the service who used to enter into a covenant with the East India Company, and do so now with the Secretary of State for India 1757.

Covenanter (kʋ·vĭnăntəɹ). 1638. [f. COVENANT *v.* + -ER [1].] **1.** *gen.* One who enters into a covenant 1643. **2.** *Sc. Hist.* A subscriber or adherent of the National Covenant signed 28 Feb. 1638, or of the Solemn League and Covenant of 1643. (In Scotland pronounced *covena·nter.*)

†**Covent.** Early f. CONVENT, surviving in *Covent Garden*, etc.

Co·ven-tree, covin-tree. *Sc.* 1823. [f. COVEN.] A large tree in front of old Scottish mansion-houses, where the laird met his guests or assembled his retainers.

Coventry (kǫ·vĕntri, kʋ·v-). An ancient town in Warwickshire.

Phr. *To send (a person) to C.*: to refuse to associate or have intercourse with him. [See CLARENDON *Hist. Reb.* vi. § 83.]

Comb.: †**C. Bells** = *Campanula medium*; also called *C. Rapes*: cf. CANTERBURY BELL. †**C. blue**, a kind of blue thread made at C., and used for embroidery; also simply *Coventry*.

Cover (kʋ·vəɹ), *v.*[1] ME. [a. OF. *cuvrir, covrir*, later *couvrir*:—L. *cooperire*, f. *co-* = *com-* intensive + *operire* to cover.]

I. 1. *trans.* To overlay, overspread *with* something so as to hide or protect. **2.** To put a covering on ME. **3.** To clothe; to put on head-covering; to wrap, wrap up, invest ME. Also *fig.* and *transf.* **4.** To serve as a covering to ME.; to strew, occupy ME. **5.** Of a stallion: To copulate with (the mare); rarely of other animals. Also *absol.* and *casually* 1535. †Of a bird: To sit upon (eggs) –1711.

2. To c. a saucepan SOYER, a roof 1872, a table GRAFTON, a surface with a design JEVONS. Phr. †*To c. his feet* (a Hebraism): to ease himself. **3.** For whan I was a cold thou couerdest me CAXTON. C. thy head..Nay prethee be couer'd *A. Y. L.* v. i. 18. **4.** Feldes..coueryd with deed men LD. BERNERS.

II. 1. To shield, protect, shelter. Also *fig.* ME. **2.** To screen from view; to conceal ME. **3.** *To c.* (*with a gun*, etc.): to present a gun at (something) so as to have it directly in the line of fire 1687. **4.** *Mil.* To stand in line with from a point of sight 1796. **5.** *Cricket.* To take up such a position behind (another man) as to be able to stop the balls missed by him 1840.

1. To c. a march 1684, a retreat 1758. That the flag should c. the merchandise ALISON. **2.** There is nothing couered that shall not be reueiled *Matt.* x. 26. Frank laughed to c. his anxiety (*mod.*).

III. 1. To be extensive enough to include 1793. **2.** To extend over, be co-extensive with, occupy 1864. Also *fig.* **3.** To pass over (ground); to get over (a given distance) 1818. **4.** To be sufficient to defray (a charge), or to meet (a liability); to compensate (a loss or risk); to protect by insurance or the like 1828; *absol.* to provide cover; to insure oneself 1882.

2. This [remark] covers the ground 1887. The loan was covered many times over (*mod.*). **4.** A small charge..to c. the trouble and risk JEVONS. Phr. *To c. short sales*, or *shorts* (Stock Exch.): to buy in shares sold short (*i. e.* without being held by the seller), in order to make delivery, or to guard against loss. *To c. into the Treasury* (U.S.): to transfer the amount into the Treasury.

†**Co·ver,** *v.*[2] ME. [aphetic f. *acover* to recover; but influenced by OF. *covrer, couvrer* to get, acquire; cf. F. *re-couvrer*, L. *recuperare.*] **1.** *trans.* To get, gain, attain –1477. **2.** *trans.* To recover. (ME. only.) Also *refl.* **3.** *intr.* (for *refl.*) To recover; to be relieved –1768.

Cover (kʋ·vəɹ), *sb.*[1] ME. [f. COVER *v.*[1]; cf. OF. *covert.*] **1.** That which covers: anything that is put or laid over, or that overlies or overspreads an object, so as to hide, shelter, or enclose it; *spec.* a lid, the boards of a book, an envelope, a wrapper, etc. **2.** A shelter, a hiding-place ME.; *fig.* a cloak, screen, disguise, pretence 1599. **3.** *Hunting.* Woods, undergrowth, and bushes, that serve to shelter game, etc.; = COVERT 1719. **4.** *Comm.* Funds adequate to meet a liability or secure against loss 1883. **5.** [after F. *couvert.*] The utensils laid for each person's use at table; the plate, napkin, knife, fork, spoon, etc. 1612.

1. [Her Waggon] Couer *Rom. & Jul.* I. iv. 60. Bound up in Past-Board Covers HEARNE. Direct to me..under c. to Alice JANE AUSTEN. **2.** Wisedome.. was vnto them for a couer by day *Wisd.* x. 17. Under c. of the woods 1794. **3.** A c. that is full of foxes P. BECKFORD. **5.** Covers were laid for four THACKERAY.

Comb.: **c.-cloth**, a cloth used as a covering; **-glass**, *spec.* a slip of glass used to cover a microscopical preparation; **-shooting**, shooting in a c.; **-side**, the side of a fox-c., where the hunters congregate.

‖**Cover** (kʋ·vəɹ), *sb.*[2] 1709. [repr. Welsh *cyfair.*] The ordinary measure of land in S. Wales, being $^2/_3$ of an imperial acre.

†**Co·verchief.** ME. [a. F. *couvre-chef*; see COVER *v.*[1] and CHIEF.] Earlier f. KERCHIEF, q.v. –1603.

Covercle (kʋ·vəɹk'l), *sb.* ME. [a. OF., ad. L. *cooperculum.*] †**1.** A cover, a lid –1488. **2.** *Nat. Hist.* An OPERCULUM (*rare*) 1682.

Covered (kʋ·vəɹd), *ppl. a.* 1463. [f. COVER *sb.* and *v.*[1] + -ED.] **1.** Having a cover, covering, or lid. †**2.** Hidden; ambiguous –1581. **3.** Covered with undergrowth. Now only in comb., as *moss-c.*, etc. 1632. **4.** Closed in overhead 1667. **5.** Having one's hat on 1669. **6.** Sheltered, protected, screened; *spec.* in *Fortif. c.-way* (formerly *covert-way*; see COVERT *a.*); see quots. 1685.

4. They walked about in the c. court JOWETT. **6.** The *Covered way* is a space of about 30 feet broad, extending round the counterscarp of the ditch, being covered by a parapet..with a banquette A. GRIFFITHS.

Coverer (kʋ·vəɹəɹ). ME. [f. COVER *v.*[1] + -ER [1].] One who or that which covers.

Covering (kʋ·vəriŋ), *vbl. sb.* ME. [f. as prec. + -ING [1].] **1.** The action of the vb. COVER, q. v. **2.** That which covers or serves to cover; a cover ME.

2. Thicke cloudes are a c. to him that he seeth not *Job* xxii. 14. The geologist..finds its solid c. composed of rocks 1854. *Comb.* **c.-board** = PLANK-SHEER. So **Co·vering** *ppl. a.* (*c. letter*, one sent with another document and indicating its contents).

Coverlet (kʋ·vəɹlėt). ME. [app. repr. OF. *covre-lit (f. *covrir* to cover + *lit* bed).] **1.** The uppermost covering of a bed; a counterpane. **2.** *transf.* A covering of any kind 1551. Also *fig.*

Bitwene hir shete and hir couerlyte of hir bede 1440. var. **Co·verlid.**

Co·ver-poi·nt. 1850. [f. COVER *v.* + POINT *sb.*] **1.** *Cricket.* A fielder who stands behind, and a little to the bowler's side of, point; also, his position in the field. **2.** *Lacrosse.* A player who stands just in front of point.

Co-versed (kou̇vǭ·ɹst), *a.* 1706. [See CO- *pref.*] *Trig.* In *Co-versed sine*: the versed sine of the complement of an angle (see VERSED).

Co·ver-shame. 1629. Something used to conceal shame. **b.** The shrub Savin, used to procure abortion.

Co·ver-slut. 1639. Something worn to cover sluttishness, an apron or pinafore.

Covert (kʋ·vəɹt), *a.* (*pa. pple.*) ME. [a. OF. *covert*, later *couvert*:—L. *coopertum*, pa. pple. of *covrir*:—L. *cooperire.*] **1.** *lit.* Covered, hidden; sheltered. Now *rare*. **2.** *fig.* Concealed, secret; disguised ME. †**3.** Secretive; sly –1673. **b.** Of words: Of hidden meaning. Now *rare*. ME. **4.** *Law.* Said of a married woman: Under the cover, authority, or protection of her husband 1483.

1. A c. nook WORDSW. *C. way* (Fortif.): = COVERED *way*. **2.** A c. threat 1874, glance DICKENS. **3.** Under c. and indifferent words BACON. Hence **Co·vert-ly** *adv.*, **-ness.**

Covert (kʋ·vəɹt), *sb.* ME. [a. F. *couvert*; see prec.] **1.** *gen.* A covering. **2.** = COVER *sb.* 2. ME. **3.** = COVER *sb.* 3. 1494. **4.** *Ornith.* in *pl.* Feathers that cover the bases of the wing and tail feathers of a bird 1774.

1. What c. dare eclipse thy face G. HERBERT. **2.** Holes and coverts RAY. **3.** Like a Deere..to the C. doth himselfe betake DRAYTON. Phr. †*Under c.* (Law) = *Under* COVERTURE.

Co·vert-ba·ron, *a.* (*sb.*) 1512. [a. AF. *couverte baroun*, orig. *coverte de barun.*] *adj.* = COVERT *a.* 4. *sb.* The condition of a *feme covert.* So †**Covert-feme** (*joc.*) DRYDEN.

Coverture (kʋ·vəɹtiŭɹ). ME. [a. OF. *coverture* (now *couverture*):—L. type *coopertura; see -URE.] **1.** Anything used to cover; covering 1450. †**2.** A coverlet –1697. **3.** Shelter; refuge. Also *fig.* 1450. **4.** Disguise, veil. Also *fig.* ME. **5.** *Law.* The condition of a *feme covert* (see COVERT *a.* 4) 1542.

1. Couches..with their rich covertures RAWLINSON. The waggon's c. MRS. BROWNING. **4.** The specious Mantle, and couerture of Religion 1625.

Covet (kʋ·vėt), *v.* ME. [a. OF. *cuveitier, coveiter* (mod. *convoiter*):—L. type *cupiditare, f. *cupiditatem.*] **1.** *trans.* To desire; *esp.* to desire eagerly, long for. Also *fig.* †**2.** To desire with concupiscence –1577. **3.** To desire culpably; to long for (what is another's). (The ordinary sense.) ME. Also *absol.* †**4.** *intr.* To lust; also with *for, after* –1611.

1. Though thou gold coveyte ME. Couet earnestly the best gifts 1 *Cor.* xii. 31. **3.** Thou shalt not couet thy neighbours house *Ex.* xx. 17. Hence **Co·vetable** *a.* greatly desirable. **Co·veter.**

Covetise. *arch.* ME. [a. OF. *coveitise* (later *convoitise*), repr. L. type *cupidititia for *cupiditia; see COVET, COVETOUS.] **1.** Inordinate desire; lust. †**2.** *spec.* Inordinate desire of wealth, or of what is another's –1652.

†**Co·vetiveness.** 1815. *Phrenol.* = ACQUISITIVENESS –1827.

Covetous (kʋ·vėtəs), *a.* ME. [a. OF. *coveitus, -os* (later *convoiteux*):—L. *cupiditosus, f. *cupiditas*; see -OUS.] **1.** Eagerly desirous *of*, †*for, to do, have*, or *be*. **2.** Culpably desirous of wealth or possessions; *esp.* of what is another's; of actions, etc.: Proceeding from cupidity ME. ¶ Occas. written for COVETISE.

1. C. only of a virtuous praise COWPER. **2.** Ryches encreaseth auaryce in a couetous man CAXTON. The couetouse flatery, Which many a worthy king deceiveth GOWER. Hence **Co·vetously** *adv.*

Covetousness (kʋ̄·vėtəsnės). 1486. [f. prec.] **1.** Inordinate desire (*of*) –1595. **2.** Culpable desire of that which is another's 1526.

1. When Workemen striue to do better then wel, They do confound their skill in couetousnesse.

Covey (kʋ·vi), *sb.*[1] [ME., ad. OF. *covée* (mod. *couvée*):—Rom. type *cubata, f. L. *cubare* to sit, hatch.] **1.** A brood or hatch of partridges; a family of partridges keeping together during the first season. (Occas. also of grouse, etc.) **2.** *fig.* and *transf.* A family, party, set 1590.

1. Sinne is..like the Partridges, which flye by Coueys 1614. **2.** A c. of fiddlers BEAUM. & FL., of new doctrines SANDERSON.

†**Covey,** *sb.*[2] 1593. [? f. COVE *sb.*[2]] A pantry.

†**Co·vey,** *v.*; see COUVE.

†**Covid** (kʋ·vid). *Anglo-Ind.* 1685. [ad. Pg. *covado* cubit.] A lineal measure formerly used in India: it varied from 36 to 14 inches –1802.

Covin (kʋ·vin), *sb.* ME. [a. OF. *covin, couvin*, etc.:—late L. *convenium*; see CONVENE.] †**1.** A company –1513. **2.** A privy agreement between two or more to the prejudice of another ME. **3.** Fraud, deceit (*arch.*) ME. So †**Covin** *v.* to agree upon. Hence **Co·vinous** *a.*; **-ly** *adv.* collusively.

Coving (kōu·viŋ), *sb.* 1703. [f. COVE *sb.*[1]] **1.** An arched or vaulted piece of building; coved work. **2.** *pl.* The inclined sides of a fireplace 1796.

Cow (kau), *sb.* [Com. Teut.: OE. *cú*:—OTeut. *kōu-z, *kō-z, fem.; cf. Skr. *gāus*, Gr. *βοῦς*, L. *bos*. OE. pl. *cýe, cý* gave regularly ME. *ky, kye*, and in S. Eng. *kyn*, later *kyne, kine* (cf. *brethren*, etc.). *Cows* hardly appears before 1600.] **1.** The female of the domestic or of any bovine animal OE. Also *transf.* **2.** The female of some other large animals, *e.g.* elephant, whale, seal, etc., the male of which is called a *bull* 1725. **3.** *Mining.* A kind of self-acting brake with two prongs used in ascending an inclined line of rails. (Also called *bull.*) 1834. Also *attrib.*

Comb.: **a c.-baby**, a timorous person; **-bird** (*U.S.*), a name for species of *Molothrus*, esp. *M. ater* or *M. pecoris* (called also *cow blackbird*, *cow bunting*); so called because associated with cattle; also, the Yellow-billed Cuckoo (*Coccyzus americanus*); **-blakes** (*dial.*), dried cow-dung used for fuel; **-calf**, a female calf; **-catcher** (*U.S.*), an apparatus fixed in front of a locomotive engine, to remove straying cattle or obstructions from the line; **-gate, -gait**, pasture for a c.; **-heart**, a pseudo-etym. var. of COWARD; so **-hea·rted** *ppl. a.*; **-hee·l, -heel**, the foot of a c. or ox stewed into a jelly; the dish so made; **-hocked** *ppl. a.*, having hocks that turn inwards like a cow's (said of horses and dogs); **-house**, a shed for cows; **-keeper**, a keeper of cows, a dairyman; **-keeping**; **-la·dy**, a LADY-COW, Lady-bird; a fly used by anglers; **-leech**, a c.-doctor; hence **-leeching**; **-lick**, a tuft of hair which looks as if it had been licked by a c.; **-man**, (*a*) a man who attends to cows; (*b*) a ranchman in the western U.S.; **-milker**, a mechanical contrivance for milking cows; **-paps**, a marine polyp, *Alcyonarium digitatum*; **-path**, a path made or used by cows; **-pen**, a pen for cows; hence **Cowpen-bird** (*U.S.*) = *cow-bird*; also as *v.*; **-pilot**, a fish (*Pomacentrus saxatilis*) of the West Indies, etc.; **-puncher** (*U.S.*), a c.-driver in the western States; **-quakes** (*dial.*), Quaking-grass, *Briza media*; also, Common Spurry; **-run**, a common on which cows pasture; **-shark**, a shark of the family *Hexanchidæ* or *Notidanidæ*; **-troopial** = *cow-bird*; **-woman.**

b. In names of plants, in some of which *cow-* means 'eaten by' or 'fit for cows', or, like 'horse-', indicates a coarse or wild species; **c.-berry**, the shrub *Vaccinium Vitis-Idæa*, and its fruit, called also Red Whortle-berry, Red Huckleberry; **-chervil** = *cow-parsley*; **-cress**, a name for *Lepidium campestre*; **-grass**, a wild species of Trefoil, *Trifolium medium*; also, a cultivated form of Red Clover; **cow's lungwort**, *Verbascum Thapsus*; **-parsley**, an umbelliferous plant, *Anthriscus* (*Chærophyllum*) *sylvestris*, also called *Cow-weed*, *Wild Chervil*, or *Cicely*; **-pa·rsnip**, a coarse umbelliferous plant, *Heracleum Sphondylium*, wild in Britain; **-pea**, a name for *Vigna sinensis*, grown for fodder in the southern U.S.; **c. plant**, a climbing plant of Ceylon, *Gymnema lactiferum*, N.O. *Asclepiadaceæ*, yielding a milky juice used for food; **-thistle** (*Herb.*), *Carduus lanceolatus* or *C. palustris*; **-tree**, one of various trees yielding a milky juice; *esp.* a South American tree, *Brosimum Galactodendron*, N.O. *Artocarpaceæ*; also the Cow-tree of Para, *Mimusops elata*, N.O. *Sapotaceæ*; of British Guiana, *Tabernæmontana utilis*; **-weed**, wild chervil; **-wheat**, a plant, *Melampyrum arvense*, N.O. *Scrophulariaceæ*, which grows in corn-fields; also a name of other species of *Melampyrum*.

Cow, kow (kau), *sb.*² *Sc.* 1500. [?] A hobgoblin; a scarecrow; cf. WORRICOW.

Cow (kau), *sb.*³ *local.* 1736. Phonetic var. of COWL *sb.*¹

Cow (kau), *v.*¹ 1605. [? a. ON. *kúga* to force, tyrannize over; app. often assoc. w. COW *sb.*¹] *trans.* 'To depress with fear' (J.); to dispirit, overawe, intimidate.

We feel faint and heartless..In plain words, we are cowed BURKE. To be cowed into submission 1847.

Cowage, cowhage (kau·édʒ). Also **cowitch.** 1640. [A perversion of Hindī *kiwānch*, *kawānch*, contr. *kawāch*.] The stinging hairs of the pod of a tropical plant, *Macuna pruriens*, N.O. *Leguminosæ*; formerly used as an anthelmintic; also the plant, or its pods.

Cowan (kōu·ăn). 1598. [?] **1.** *Sc.* One who does the work of a mason, but has not been apprenticed to the trade. **2.** Hence, One uninitiated in the secrets of Freemasonry 1707. **3.** *slang.* A sneak, eavesdropper.

Coward (kau·əɹd), *sb.* and *a.* ME. [a. OF. *coart*, f. L. *cauda*, OF. *coe* tail; see -ARD. The reference may be to 'turning tail', or possibly to *Coart*, the name of the hare in the OF. version of *Reynard the Fox*.]

A. *sb.* **1.** One who displays ignoble fear in the face of pain, danger, or difficulty; a pusillanimous person. **2.** Applied to animals 1486.

1. Cowards dye many times before their deaths SHAKS. **2.** Don Juan..ran a c. throughout *Field.*

B. *adj.* **1.** Destitute of courage; faint-hearted ME. **2.** Of actions, etc.; = COWARDLY *a.* 2. 1600. **3.** *Her.* Of a lion, etc. borne as a charge: Having the tail drawn in between the legs 1500. Also as quasi-*adv.*

1. Nor undertake the same for cowheard feare SPENSER *F. Q.* V. x. 15. **2.** Hence with those c. terms; or fight, or fly POPE.

Hence †**Cow·ard** *v.* to make cowardly; to call, or show to be a c. **Cow·ardize** *v.* to make a c. of; to daunt. **Cow·ard-like** *a.* and *adv.* **Cow·ardly** *adv.* †**Cow·ardness**, cowardice. †**Cow·ardous** *a.* cowardly. †**Cow·ardship**, †**Cow·ardy**, cowardice.

Cowardice (kau·əɹdis). ME. [a. OF. *couardise*, f. *couard* COWARD *sb.*] The quality of a coward; cowardliness; want of courage to face danger; pusillanimity.

It is no c. to fly from the rage of persecutors 1703.

Cowardly (kau·əɹdli), *a.* 1551. [f. COWARD *sb.*] **1.** Having the character or spirit of a coward; wanting in courage; pusillanimous. **2.** Befitting a coward; proceeding from a spirit of cowardice 1601.

2. At c. distance..secure thou hast stood COLERIDGE. Hence **Cow·ardliness**, cowardice.

Cow·-bane. 1776. [f. COW *sb.*¹ + BANE *sb.*¹] The Water Hemlock, *Cicuta virosa*, mentioned by Linnæus as fatal to cows. *Spotted c.*: an American species, *C. maculata.*

Cow·-boy, cow·boy. 1725. **1.** A boy who tends cows. **2.** *U.S. Hist.* Applied to some of the tory partisans of Westchester Co., New York, during the Revolutionary war, who were barbarous in the treatment of opponents 1775. **3.** In the western U.S.: A man employed to take care of grazing cattle on a ranch 1882.

3. The rough-and-ready life of men who have cast in their lot among cow-boys 1887.

Cower (kau·əɹ), *v.* ME. [perh. f. Norse; cf. Sw. *kura* to squat; also mod.Ger. *kauern* to cower.] **1.** *intr.* To stand or squat in a bent position; to bend with the knees and back; to crouch. **b.** *pa. pple.* = Cowering (*rare*). 1855. **2.** *trans.* To lower, bend down (*rare*) 1790.

1. They coure so over the coles, theyr eyes be bleard'd with smooke 1575. **2.** My muse her wing maun c. BURNS. Hence **Cow·eringly** *adv.*

Cow·-fish. 1634. [COW *sb.*¹] **1.** The sea-cow or manatee. **2.** A grampus 1860. **3.** A fish, *Ostracion quadricorne*, having two strong spines like horns over the eyes 1885.

Cowhage, var. of COWAGE.

Cow·herd. OE. [See HERD ².] One whose occupation is to tend cows at pasture. So **Cow·herdess** (*rare*), a female c.

Cow·-hi·de, cow·hide, *sb.* 1640. **1.** The hide of a cow, or leather made of it. **2.** *U.S.* A strong whip made of the raw or dressed hide of a cow 1839. **3.** *attrib.* (kau·həid). Made of cow-hide 1840. Hence **Cow·-hide, cowhide** *v.* to flog with a cow-hide.

Cowish (kau·iʃ), *sb.* 1838. [prob. Amer. Indian.] A plant with an edible root found in Oregon.

Cowish (kau·iʃ), *a.* 1570. [f. COW *sb.*¹ + -ISH.] **1.** Like a cow. †**2.** Cowardly -1605.

2. The C. terror of his spirit *Lear* IV. ii. 12.

Cow-itch; see COWAGE.

Cowl (kaul), *sb.*¹ [OE. *cugele*, *cuhle* and *cule*, cogn. w. OHG. *cucula*, *cugula*, a. eccl.L. *cuculla* monk's cowl, from cl.L. *cucullus* hood.] **1.** A garment with a hood (*vestis caputiata*) worn by monks; *occas.*, the hood alone. **b.** Sometimes = Monk 1653. Also *transf.* and *fig.* **2.** A cowl-shaped covering, usually turning with the wind, placed on the top of a chimney or ventilating shaft, to assist ventilation. Also, a wire cage at the top of the funnel of a locomotive, etc. 1812. **b.** = SCUTTLE *sb.*² 3. **c.** (Also **cow·ling.**) A removable cover round the engine of an aeroplane 1917.

1. b. Bluff Harry..turn'd the cowls adrift TENNYSON. *Comb.* **c.-muscle**, the *cucullaris* or trapezius muscle. Hence **Cowl** *v.* to make a monk of; to cover as with a c. **Cowled** *ppl. a.* wearing a c.; (*Bot.*) cucullate.

Cowl, coul (kaul), *sb.*² [ME. **cuvel(e*, *covelle*, app. a. OF. *cuvele* :—L. *cupella*, dim. of *cupa*, F. *cuve* tub, cask, vat. But cf. also Ger. *kübel*.] A tub or the like for water, etc.; *esp.* one with two ears borne by two men on a cowl-staff (*arch.* or *dial.*). *Comb.* **Cowl-staff, coul-staff**, a stout stick used to carry a c., being thrust through the two handles of it; a stang.

Cowle (kaul). *Anglo-Ind.* 1688. [a. Arab.] An engagement, lease, or grant in writing; a safe-conduct or amnesty.

Co-wo·rk, *v.* 1613. *intr.* To work together. **Co-wo·rker**, a co-operator.

Cowperian (kupī·riăn), *a.* 1738. [f. William *Cowper*, the anatomist (1666–1709).] *Cowperian glands*: a pair of glands situated beneath, and with ducts opening into, the urethra in male Mammalia. Also *Cowper's glands.* **Cowperi·tis**, inflammation of Cowper's glands.

Cow·-po·x. 1798. [COW *sb.*¹] A vaccine disease which appears on the teats of cows in the form of vesicles (pocks). The communication of this to the human subject by VACCINATION gives immunity (whole or partial) from small-pox. Occas. called *kine-pox*. (The pl. *pocks* as the name of the disease is conventionally spelt *pox*.) Hence †**Cow·-pox** *v.* to vaccinate.

Cowrie, cowry (kau·ri). 1662. [a. Hindī and Urdū.] Any gastropod (or its shell) of the genus *Cypræa* or family *Cypræidæ*; *esp.* the shell of *Cypræa moneta*, found abundantly in the Indian Ocean, and used as money in parts of Africa and Southern Asia. Also *attrib.*

Cowrie pine; see KAURI.

Cowslip (kau·slip). [OE. *cú-slyppe*, i.e. 'cow-slobber' or 'cow-dung'.] **1.** The common name of *Primula veris*, a well-known wild plant in pastures and grassy banks. Also called *Paigle*. **2.** *U.S.* The Marsh Marigold 1856.

Beyond into the fields, gathering of cowslipps PEPYS. **American C.**, *Dodecatheon Meadia* (N.O. *Primulaceæ*), with umbels of large rose-purple or white flowers, found in woods in N. America. **French** or **Mountain C.**, the Auricula (*Primula Auricula*). **Virginian C.**, *Mertensia* or *Pulmonaria virginica.*

Cowslip'd, cowslipt (kau·slipt), *a.* 1794. [f. prec.] Covered with cowslips.

Cox (kɒks), *sb. colloq.* Abbrev. of COXSWAIN. Hence **Cox** *v.* to act as c. to (a boat); also *intr.* **Co·xless** *a.*

Cox, var. of COKES *Obs.*, fool.

‖**Coxa** (kɒ·ksă). Pl. **coxæ.** 1706. [L.; = hip.] **1.** *Anat.* The hip, or hip-joint; also the ischium, the coccyx. **2.** *Zool.* The joint by which the leg is articulated in insects, arachnida, and crustacea 1826. Hence **Co·xal** *a.*

Coxa·gra [Gr. ἄγρα trap, after *podagra*], *Pathol.* pain in the hip. **Coxa·lgia** [Gr. -αλγία], **Coxa·lgy** [F. *coxalgie*], pain in the hip-joint; hip-disease. **Coxa·lgic** *a.* pertaining to or affected with coxalgia. **Coxarthri·tis** [ARTHRITIS], gout in the hip; coxitis.

Coxcomb (kɒ·kskōum). 1573. [= COCKSCOMB.] †**1.** A cap worn by a jester, like a cock's comb in shape and colour -1605. †**2.** (*joc.*) The head -1866. **3.** A simpleton (*obs.*); now, a foolish, conceited, showy person; a fop 1573. †**4.** *Bot.* See COCKSCOMB -1756. †**5.** ? A kind of lace with an edging like a cock's comb -1760. Also *attrib.*

1. What is your Crest, a Coxcombe *Tam. Shr.* II. i. 226. **2.** *Twel. N.* V. i. 193. **3.** *Oth.* V. ii. 234. Those shallow atheistical coxcombs MACKINTOSH. Hence **Coxco·mbic, -al** *a.* like a c.; of or pertaining to a c. **Coxcombica·lity**, coxcombical quality or act. **Coxco·mbically** *adv.* like a c. †**Coxco·mbly** *a.* like or characteristic of a c. **Cox·combry**, †foolishness; foppery, a piece of foppery (var. **Coxco·mbity** *rare*); coxcombs collectively.

‖**Coxe·ndix.** Pl. **coxe·ndices.** 1615. [L., f. *coxa*.] The hip or hip-bone; also the ischium, the ilium.

Coxitis (kɒksəi·tis). 1878. [f. COXA + -ITIS.] *Pathol.* Inflammation of the hip-joint.

Coxocerite (kɒksɒ·sĕrəit). 1877. [f. L. *coxa* + Gr. κέρας + -ITE.] *Zool.* 'The basal segment of the antenna in Crustacea' (*Syd. Soc. Lex.*). Hence **Coxoceri·tic** *a.*

Coxo-fe·moral, *a.* 1831. [f. L. *coxa* + *femoralis* pertaining to the thigh.] *Anat.* Pertaining to the coxa or ilium and the femur; ilio-femoral.

Coxopodite (kɒksɒ·pŏdəit). 1870. [f. L. *coxa* + Gr. ποδ- + -ITE.] *Zool.* The basal joint which connects the limbs to the body in the Arthropoda. Hence **Coxopodi·tic** *a.*

Coxswain, cockswain (kɒ·ksweᵊn, kɒ·ks'n). Also **coxon, coxen.** 1463. [f. COCK *sb.*³ ship's boat + SWAIN. The spelling *coxswain* (which should be *coxwain*) is now in ordinary use.] The helmsman of a boat; a petty officer having permanent charge of a ship's boat and its crew. Hence **Co·xswainless** *a.* without a c. **Co·xswainship**, skill in steering.

Coy (koi), *sb.* Now *dial.* 1621. [a. Du. *kooi*, †*côye*, in same sense :—WGer. *cawia*, *cauwia*, a. L. *cavea* CAGE.] **1.** A DECOY. **2.** A lobster-trap 1733. **3.** = *Coy-duck*. Also *fig.* 1629. *Comb.* **c.-duck** = DECOY-DUCK; also *transf.*

Coy (koi), *a.* ME. [a. F. *coi* (fem. *coite*),

earlier *quei*:—L. **quetus*, f. *quietus*.] †1. Quiet, still –1632. 2. Not demonstrative; shyly reserved or retiring ME. Of a place or thing: Inaccessible, secluded 1670. Also *fig.* †3. Distant, disdainful –1665.

2. 'Tis but a kiss I beg: why art thou c. SHAKS. [Feining] c. lookes SPENSER *F. Q.* I. ii. 27. The Nile's c. source 1767. Hence **Coy·ish** *a.* somewhat c. **Coy·ly** *adv.* †quietly; in a c. manner; †disdainfully.

Coy (koi), *v.* ME. [f. COY *a.*: or ? aphet. f. *acoy* ACCOY.] †1. *trans.* To calm, appease –1530. †2. To stroke soothingly, caress –1674. †3. To coax, gain over by caresses –1634. 4. *intr.* To behave coyly; to affect shyness or reserve (*arch.*) 1583; †to disdain 1607. 5. *fig.* To withdraw itself 1864.

2. While I thy amiable cheekes doe c. *Mids. N.* IV. i. 2. 3. Phr. *To c. with*: to coax. PEPYS. 4. What! you c. it, my nymph of the high-way SCOTT. If he.. coy'd To heare Cominius speake, Ile keepe at home *Cor.* v. i. 6.

†**Coyn, coyne.** ME. [a. OF. *cooin*, in mod.F. *coing*:—L. *cotoneum*, var. of *cydonium* quince.] A quince –1575.

Coyn(e, obs. f. COIN, QUEAN, QUOIN.

Coyness (koi·nės). 1575. [-NESS.] The quality of being coy; an instance of this.

I scorne men's coynesse, women's stoutnesse hate STIRLING.

Coynye, coignye (koi·nʸi), *sb.* Also *erron.* **coyn, coin.** 1449. [a. Irish *coinnemh* (koinʸev) billeting, one billeted.] *Irish Hist.* The billeting of military followers upon private persons; food and entertainment exacted, by the Irish chiefs, for their attendants; an impost levied for the same purpose.

The damnable custome .. of Coigne and Livory FULLER. Hence †**Coy·nye, coi·gnye** *v. trans.* to billet *upon*; also to exact c. from; *refl.* and *intr.* to quarter oneself *upon*.

‖**Coyote** (ko₍yōᵘ·te, ko₍yōᵘ·t). 1850. [ad. (ult.) Mexican *coyotl*.] *Zool.* The name, in Mexico and now in U.S., of the prairie- or barking-wolf (*Canis latrans*) of the Pacific slope of North America.

Comb. **c.-diggings,** small shafts sunk by miners in California, compared to c.-holes. Hence **Coyo·te** *v.* to mine in irregular openings.

Coypu, coypou (koi·pu). 1793. [Native name.] A S. American aquatic rodent (*Myopotamus Coypus*), nearly as large as the beaver; called also *C. Rat.*

Coystrel; see COISTREL, CUSTRELL.

Coz (kvz). 1559. An abbrev. of COUSIN, used both to relatives and in the wider sense.

Coze (kōᵘz), *v.* 1828. [app. ad. F. *causer*.] To have a long familiar talk. Hence **Coze** *sb.* a cosy friendly chat.

Cozen, obs. f. COUSIN.

Cozen (kv·z'n), *v.* 1573. [Usually associated with COUSIN *sb.*; cf. F. *cousiner.* But ?] 1. *trans.* To cheat, defraud by deceit. 2. To dupe, beguile, impose upon 1583. Also *absol.*

1. He that trusts to a Greek is sure to be couzened HEYLYN. 2. By gar I am cozoned, I ha married oon Garsoon, a boy *Merry W.* v. v. 218. Hence **Co·zenage,** the practice of cozening; deception; a deception. **Co·zener,** a deceiver, cheat.

Cozie, cozily, -ness, Cozy; see COSY, etc.

†**Co·zier.** 1532. [ad. OF. *cousere*, f. *coudre* to sew.] A cobbler –1658.

Cr., abbrev. of *Creditor, Credit.*

Craal, var. of KRAAL.

Crab (kræb), *sb.*¹ [OE. *crabba* = ON. *krabbi* masc. Related to LG. *krabben* to scratch, claw; see CRAB *v.*² and CRAWL.] 1. Any decapod crustaceous animal of the tribe *Brachyura*; *esp.* the edible species found on or near the sea-coast. Also applied with qualifications to other Crustacea and Arachnida.

The common edible crab of Europe is *Cancer pagurus*; the edible or *blue crab* of the United States is *Callinectes hastatus.* Crabs can move in any direction, and frequently walk sideways or backwards: cf. *Haml.* II. ii. 205.

2. *Astron.* = CANCER 2. OE. 3. Short for CRAB-LOUSE 1840. 4. A machine (orig. with claws) for hoisting or hauling heavy weights. **a.** A kind of small capstan. **b.** A portable machine for raising weights, etc., consisting of a frame with a horizontal barrel on which a chain or rope is wound by means of handles and gearing; used in connexion with pulleys, a gin, etc.; a portable winch. 1627. 5. *pl. slang.* The lowest throw at hazard, two aces 1768. 6. *Rowing.* *To catch a c.*: to get the oar jammed under water (as if the rower had caught a crab, which was holding the oar down). Also, *improp.*, the action of missing the water with the stroke, etc. 1785. Also *attrib.*

Comb.: **c.-catcher,** any of several species of herons which feed on small crabs; **-claw,** a claw for grappling or fastening; **-eater,** occas. name for the Little Bittern, *Ardetta minuta*; a scombroid fish, *Elacate canada*; †**-face,** an ugly ill-tempered looking face; so **-faced, -favoured; -lobster,** the porcelain-c.; **-louse,** a parasitical insect, *Phthirus inguinalis*, which infests parts of the body; **-pot,** a trap of wickerwork for taking crabs; **crab's-eye, -eyes,** (usu. *pl.*) a round concretion found in the stomach of the crayfish, etc., consisting mainly of carbonate of lime; used formerly as an absorbent and antacid; (*pl.*) the scarlet seeds of *Abrus precatorius*; also the plant; **-spider,** the name of several species of spiders.

Crab (kræb), *sb.*² ME. [? Cf. Sc. *scrab, scrabbe*, app. from Norse.] 1. Name of the wild apple, especially connoting its sour, harsh quality; applied also to cultivated varieties. 2. The wild apple-tree of northern Europe, the original of the common apple ME. 3. A crabstick 1740. 4. Applied to persons [orig. as *fig.* of 1; later, with reference to CRABBED, or ? to CRAB *sb.*¹] 1580. Also *attrib.*

1. She's as like this, as a Crabbe's like an Apple *Lear* I. v. 15. 4. That sowre c. 1605. That c. of a priest LYTTON.

Comb.: **c.-apple**: see senses 1 and 2; **-stick,** a stick made of the wood of the crab-tree; also *fig.*; **-stock,** a young crab-tree used as a stock to graft upon; also *fig.*; **-tree,** the wild apple-tree; also *attrib.*

Crab (kræb), *sb.*³ 1769. Corruption of CARAP, native name of a S. Amer. tree, *Carapa guianensis*, used in comb.: as **c.-nut,** the nut or seed of this tree; **-oil** (*carap oil*), the oil obtained from C.-nuts, used for lighting and as an anthelmintic; so **-tree, -wood.**

†**Crab** (kræb), *v.*¹ ME. [f. CRABBED *a.* or its source.] 1. *trans.* To go counter to, to cross; to irritate, anger. *Sc.* –1605. 2. *trans.* To sour 1662.

Crab (kræb), *v.*² 1575. [= Du. *krabben* to claw, f. as CRAB *sb.*¹] 1. *Falconry.* Of hawks: To scratch, claw, or fight with each other (*trans.* and *intr.*). 2. *trans.* To criticize adversely, peck at, pull to pieces (*colloq.*) 1812.

2. Men who want to 'c. the new rifle' 1890.

Crab, *v.*³ 1619. [Nonce-uses; see CRAB *sb.*¹ and ².] †1. To cudgel. 2. *Naut.* Of a ship: To drift sideways to leeward 1867. 3. *U.S. colloq.* (*fig.*) To back out; = CRAWFISH *v.* 4. *Dyeing.* To subject to the operation of CRABBING (*vbl. sb.*²) 1892. 5. See CRABBING *vbl. sb.*¹

Crabbed (kræ·bėd), *a.* ME. [orig. f. CRAB *sb.*¹ + -ED; cf. DOGGED. Referred primarily to the crooked gait of the crab; in later use, to the fruit. Cf Ger. *krabbe.*] 1. Of persons: *orig.* Cross-grained, perverse; later: Cross-tempered, churlish 1535. Also *transf.* of things. †2. Proceeding from or expressing a harsh or sour disposition –1641. †3. Unpalatable, bitter –1622. †4. Of trees, sticks, etc.: Crooked; gnarled; cross-grained –1675. 5. Perversely intricate; hard to make sense of; difficult to decipher 1612. 6. Of the nature of the crab-tree or its fruit; also *fig.* 1565.

1. For women are c., þat comes þem of kinde 1440. A cancred c. carle SPENSER. *transf.* How charming is divine Philosophy! Not harsh and c. MILT. *Comus* 477. 2. A c. face 1641. 5. In c. Scholastick style BAXTER. A c. hand 1800. 6. *Wint. T.* I. ii. 102. Hence **Cra·bbedly** *adv.* **Cra·bbedness,** c. quality; asperity or sourness of temper; rugged or perverse intricacy.

Crabber (kræ·bəɹ). 1848. [f. CRAB *sb.*¹] One who fishes for crabs, or the boat he uses.

Crabbery (kræ·bėri). 1845. [f. as prec. + -ERY.] A place abounding in crabs.

Cra·bbing, *vbl. sb.*¹ 1657. [f. CRAB *sb.*¹, ² + -ING¹, implying verb *to crab.*] 1. Crab-fishing. Also *attrib.* 2. Gathering crab-apples; cf. *nutting*, etc. 1877.

Cra·bbing, *vbl. sb.*² 1874. *Dyeing.* The operation of passing a woollen fabric in a state of tension through boiling water, and at once wrapping it on a roller, where it is subjected to great pressure. The object is to prevent unequal contraction, and to give the cloth a certain finish.

†**Cra·bbish,** *a.* 1485. [f. CRAB *sb.*¹ + -ISH.] Cross, crabbed –1606.

Crabby (kræ·bi), *a.*¹ 1583. [f. as prec. + -Y¹.] 1. Crab-like. 2. Abounding in crabs 1622.

Crabby (kræ·bi), *a.*² 1550. [f. CRAB *sb.*² + -Y¹.] †1. = CRABBED 4, 5. –1599. 2. = CRABBED 1, 6. 1776.

†**Cra·ber.** *rare.* [a. F. *crabier* (*raton crabier*), f. *crabe* CRAB *sb.*¹] The water-rat. WALTON.

†**Cra·b-fish.** ME. = CRAB *sb.*¹ 1. –1753.

Cra·b-grass. 1597. [f. CRAB *sb.*¹] 1. The Glasswort, *Salicornia herbacea.* ? *Obs.* 2. The Knot-grass. 3. In *U.S.* A species of grass, *Panicum sanguinale*, and allied species 1881.

Cra·b-harrow. 1796. [f. CRAB *sb.*¹] A harrow with bent teeth for tearing up the ground; its latest form is the *drag-harrow.* Hence **Crab-harrow** *v.*

‖**Crabier.** [F.; f. *crabe.*] = *Crab-catcher* (see CRAB *sb.*¹). WATERTON.

Crabite (kræ·bəit). *rare.* 1847. [a. F.] A fossil crab.

Crablet (kræ·blėt). 1841. [f. CRAB *sb.*¹ + -LET.] A small or young crab. So **Cra·bling.**

Cra·b-sidle, *v.* [f. CRAB *sb.*¹ + SIDLE *v.*] To shuffle sideways like a crab. SOUTHEY.

†**Crabut.** 1626. [?] A kind of fire-arm, used in 17th c. –1659.

Crab yaws. 1740. [f. CRAB *sb.*¹ + YAWS.] In the West Indies, a kind of yaws attacking the soles of the feet, forming ulcers with very hard edges.

Crack (kræk), *sb.* ME. [Goes with CRACK *v.*; originally echoic.]

I. Of sound. 1. A sudden sharp and loud noise; *e.g.* the c. of a rifle, a whip, of thunder, etc.; a sharp, sounding blow (*colloq.*) 1838. 2. The time occupied by a crack or shot; an instant 1725. 3. Loud talk, brag; *occas.*, exaggeration, lie (*arch.*) 1450. 4. Brisk talk; *pl.* news (*Sc.* and *n. dial.*) 1725.

1. What will the Line stretch out to th' cracke (*i. e.* the thunder-peal) of Doome *Macb.* IV. i. 117. A c. on the head DICKENS. 3. That's a damned confounded —c. GOLDSM.

II. Breaking, etc. 1. *Thieves' slang.* House-breaking 1812. 2. A break in which the parts do or do not remain in contact; a fissure; a partial fracture 1530. 3. A flaw, deficiency, unsoundness 1570. 4. The breaking of the voice 1611.

3. I cannot Beleeve this C. to be in my dread Mistresse *Wint. T.* I. ii. 322. 4. *Cymb.* IV. ii. 236.

III. Transf. †1. A lively lad; a rogue. [? short for *crack-hemp.*] –1673. †2. A braggart, liar –1681. 3. One full of conversation. *Sc.* 1827. †4. [? from II. 3.] A prostitute –1785. †5. A crack-brain –1711. 6. That which is 'cracked up'; anything of superior excellence; see CRACK *a.* 1637. 7. = CRACKSMAN 1749. 8. *slang.* Dry wood 1851.

1. When hee was a C., not thus high 2 *Hen. IV*, III. ii. 34. 5. The Parliament..look upon me, forsooth, as a C. and a Projector ADDISON. var. **Crake** (in sense I. 3).

Crack (kræk), *v.* [Com. Teut.: OE. *cracian.* Cf. also F. *craquer.*] *orig.* To make a sharp dry sound in breaking.

I. 1. *intr.* To make a sharp or explosive noise OE. 2. *trans.* To cause (anything, *e.g.* a whip) to make a sharp noise 1647. 3. To slap, smack, box. Now *dial.* 1470. 4. *trans.* To utter briskly or with *éclat*, as in *c. a joke* ME. 5. *intr.* To talk big, brag. Now *dial.* 1460. 6. *intr.* To chat, talk of the news (*Sc.* and *n. dial.*) 1450. 7. *C. up*: to eulogize (*colloq.*) 1844.

1. Moist wood that cracketh in the fire FULKE. 5. Thou art always cracking and boasting ADDISON.

II. Referring mainly to the breaking. 1. *trans.* To break (a skull, a nut, etc.) with a sudden sharp report ME. †b. (from *fig.* use of phr. *to c. a nut*) To puzzle out, discuss –1768. 2. *transf.* To get at the contents of (a bottle, etc.); to empty, 'discuss' 15... 3. *Thieves' slang.* To break open 1725. †4. To snap or split asunder. Also *trans.* –1745. 5. *fig.* To come to pieces, break down 1658. 6. *intr.* To break without complete separation of parts ME. 7. *trans.* To break (anything) so that the parts remain in contact but do not cohere; to break into fissures 1605. 8. To break the clearness of (the voice); to render hoarse. Also *intr.* 1602.

9. *fig.* To render of unsound mind 1614. 10. To damage (credit, etc.) so that it is no longer sound 1567.

1. b. Logic you cannot c. without a tutor WESLEY. 3. Phr. *To c. a crib*: to break open a house. 4. *trans.* Blow windes, and c. your cheekes SHAKS. 6. Heat causes these soils to c. 1855. 7. Glasses that are once crackt, are soon broken 1605. 8. *Timon* IV. iii. 153.

III. To move with a stroke or jerk; to 'whip' *out* or *on* (*colloq.*) 1541; *intr.* to 'pelt' *along* (*colloq.*) 1541.

Crack (kræk), *a. colloq.* 1793. [CRACK *sb.* III. 6, used *attrib.*] Pre-eminent, first-class, as *c. regiments.*

Crack (kræk), *adv., int.* 1767. [The vb. stem so used.] 1. *adv.* with a cracking sound. 2. *int.* 1698.

1. C. went his whip SOUTHEY. 2. C.! all is gone AMORY.

Crack- in comb.:

a. with *crack-* as the vb. stem governing an object, as †**c.-halter**, †**-hemp**, a gallows-bird; **-jaw** *a.*, fit to crack the jaws; †**-rope** = *crack-halter*; **-tryst**, one who breaks tryst. b. with *crack-* for *cracked-*, as **c.-brain(ed**, a crazy fellow, crazy; **-headed** = *crack-brained*; **-skull** = *crack-brain*; **-winded** = BROKEN-WINDED.

Cracked (krækt), *ppl. a.* 1503. [f. CRACK *v.* + -ED.] 1. Broken by a sharp blow 1562. 2. Full of cracks 1570. 3. Fractured; partially broken so as to be no longer sound 1503. 4. *fig.* Damaged, having flaws; †bankrupt 1527. 5. Somewhat deranged, crazy. (Now *colloq.*) 1611. 6. Of the voice: Broken 1739.

1. Bloodie Noses, and crack'd Crownes SHAKS.

Cracker (kræ·kəɹ). 1509. [f. CRACK *v.* + -ER[1].] 1. *gen.* One who or that which cracks; *esp.* a boaster; a liar. 2. *colloq.* A lie 1625. 3. *U.S.* A name for the 'poor whites' in southern States [?short for *whip-cracker*] 1767. 4. A local name for the Pin-tail Duck, and the Corn-crake 1678. 5. A firework which explodes with a succession of sharp reports 1590; also, a *bon-bon*, containing a fulminant, which explodes when pulled at both ends 1841. 6. A thin hard biscuit. (Chiefly in U.S.) 1739.

Crackle (kræ·k'l), *sb.* 1591. [f. the vb.] 1. The act of crackling 1833. †2. A child's rattle 1591. 3. A kind of china ware showing what appear to be minute cracks all over its surface. So *C.-glass*, glass of a similar character.

1. The c. of the blazing faggots 1855. 3. A skin like yellow c.-ware 1881.

Crackle (kræ·k'l), *v.* 1500. [dim. and freq. of CRACK *v.*] 1. *intr.* To emit a rapid succession of slight cracks; to crepitate 1560. 2. *trans.* To crush with slight but rapidly continuous crackling 1611. †3. *intr.* To crack and break *off* in small pieces 1735.

1. Huge logs blazed and crackled 1872.

Crackled (kræ·k'ld), *ppl. a.* 1659. [f. prec.] Marked with cracks upon the surface. b. Of roast pork: Having the skin crisp and hard.

Crackling (kræ·kliŋ), *vbl. sb.* 1599. [f. as prec. + -ING[1].] 1. The action of the verb CRACKLE; crepitation. Also *fig.* 2. The crisp skin or rind of roast pork 1709. 3. The residue of tallow-melting, used for feeding dogs. (Usu. *pl.*) 1621. 4. = CRACKLE *sb.* 3. 1876.

1. The c. of thornes vnder a pot *Eccl.* vii. 6. 2. The crisp, well-watched, not over-roasted, c., as it is well called LAMB. var. **Cra·cklin** (in sense 4).

Cra·ckmans. 1610. [See CRACK *sb.* III. 8.] *Thieves' slang.* A hedge.

Cracknel (kræ·knĕl). ME. [app. for F. *craquelin.*] 1. A light crisp biscuit, of a curved or hollowed shape. 2. *pl.* Small pieces of fat pork dried crisp. 3. = CRACKLE *sb.* 3.

Cracksman (kræ·ksmæ̆n). *slang.* 1812. [f. CRACK *sb.* II. 1.] A housebreaker.

Cra·ck-wi·llow. 1670. [f. CRACK *v.*] A species of willow with brittle branches, *Salix fragilis.*

Cracky (kræ·ki), *a.* 1725. [f. CRACK + -Y.] 1. Having cracks; prone to crack. 2. Crazy 1854. 3. Full of conversation. *Sc.* 1801.

‖**Cracovienne** (krăkŏuvi,e·n). 1844. [F. fem. adj. = Cracovian.] A light and lively Polish dance.

-cracy, formerly also **-cratie, -crasie**, a. F. *-cratie* (-krasi), ad. med.L. *-cratia*, a. Gr. -κρατία power, rule, f. κράτος strength. The *o* which usually precedes the suffix, as in *aristocracy*, etc., has come to be viewed as part of it, whence the form *-ocracy*, which has been added to many English words; as in COTTONOCRACY, etc.

Cradle (krē̆·d'l). [OE. *cradol*: of unkn. deriv.] 1. A little bed or cot for an infant: properly, one mounted on rockers; often a swing-cot. Also *fig.* 2. = Infancy, or the first stage of existence 1555. 3. *fig.* The place in which anything is nurtured in its earlier stage 1590. 4. That which serves as a place of repose (*poet.*) 1590. 5. *Naut.* A standing bedstead for a wounded seaman 1803. 6. Any framework of bars, cords, rods, etc. united by lateral ties; a grating, or hurdle-like structure ME. 7. *Husb.* A light frame of wood attached to a scythe, having a row of long curved teeth parallel to the blade, to lay the corn more evenly in the swathe 1573. 8. *Surg.* A protecting framework of different kinds for an injured limb, etc. 1704. 9. *Naut.* The framework on which a ship rests during construction, etc. Also, that in which a vessel lies in a way or slip, or in a canal-lift; and the like 1627. 10. An appliance in which a person or thing is swung or carried 1839. 11. *Building.* The ribbing for vaulting ceilings, etc. intended to be covered with plaster 1874. 12. *Engraving.* A chisel-like tool with a serrated edge, which is rocked to and fro over the metal plate, to produce a mezzotint ground 1788. 13. *Gold mining.* A trough on rockers in which auriferous earth or sand is shaken in water, in order to separate the gold 1849. 14. See CAT'S CRADLE.

1. Wakynge a nyghtes..to rocke þe cradel LANGL. 2. In the Latine wee haue been exercised almost from our verie c. A.V. *Transl. Pref.* 3. Wessex the c. of the royal house FREEMAN.

Comb.: **c.-holding**, land held in BOROUGH-ENGLISH; **-hole** (*U.S.*), a depression in a road; also a spot from which the frost is melting; **-roof**, a roof, in shape like a half-cylinder, divided into panels by wooden ribs; **-scythe**, a scythe fitted with a c. (sense 7).

Cradle (krē̆·d'l), *v.* ME. [f. prec. sb.] 1. *trans.* To lay in, or as in, a cradle; to rock to sleep; to hold as a cradle 1872. †2. *intr.* (for *refl.*) To lie as in a cradle. SHAKS. 3. To nurture or rear in infancy 1613. 4. *Husb.* To mow (corn, etc.) with a cradle-scythe. Also *absol.* 1750. 5. To support in or on a cradle; to raise a vessel to a higher level by a cradle 1775. 6. To support the back of (a picture, etc.) by ribs and transverse slips 1880. 7. To wash (auriferous gravel) in a miner's cradle. Also *absol.* and *fig.* 1852. 8. *Coopering.* To cut a cask in two lengthwise 1874.

1. Convey'd to earth and cradled in a tomb DRYDEN. 2. Huskes Wherein the Acorne cradled *Temp.* I. ii. 464. 3. A commonwealth..cradled in war BURKE.

Cradling (krē̆·dliŋ), *vbl. sb.* 1818. [f. prec. + -ING[1].] 1. The action of CRADLE *v.* (*lit.* and *fig.*). 2. A framework of wood or iron, *esp.* in *Archit.* 1823.

Craft (kraft), *sb.* [Com. Teut.: OE. *cræft* masc.; ?conn. w. Icel. *kræfr* adj. 'strong'. The transference to 'skill, art, occupation' is English only.] †1. Strength, power, force –1526. 2. Intellectual power; skill; art; ability in planning or constructing, ingenuity, dexterity (*arch.*) OE.; †*spec.* occult art, magic –1483. †3. A device, artifice, or expedient –1533. 4. In a bad sense: Skill or art applied to deceive or overreach; guile, fraud, cunning. (The chief mod. sense.) ME. †5. The learning of the schools; a branch of learning, a science –1530. 6. A calling requiring special skill and knowledge; *esp.* a manual art, a HANDICRAFT OE.; *spec.* the occupation of a hunter or sportsman 1486. Also *fig.* 7. The members of a trade or handicraft collectively; a trade's union, guild, or company ME. 8. *collect.* (constr. as *pl.*) Vessels or boats 1671. 9. *collect.* Implements used in catching or killing fish; now *esp.* in whaling 1688.

2. The lyf so short, the c. so long to lerne CHAUCER. 4. That Crooked Wisdome, which is called C. HOBBES. 5. *The seven crafts*: the 'seven arts' of the mediæval Universities: see ART. 6. And because hee was of the same c., he abode with them *Acts* xviii. 3. The crafts of the shoemaker, tinman, plumber, and potter JOHNSON. Phr. *The c. of the woods* = WOODCRAFT. *Gentle c.*: see GENTLE. 8. There is good lying for small c. 1699. Hence †**Craft** *v. intr.* to use crafty devices; to make a job of it *Cor.* IV. vi. 118. **Craft·less** *a.* without c.

Craftsman (kra·ftsmæ̆n). ME. [Orig. two words.] 1. A man who practises a handicraft; an artisan. Also *transf.* and *fig.* 2. One who cultivates one of the Fine Arts 1876. Hence **Cra·ftsmanship.** So **Cra·ftswoman** (*rare*). vars. †**Cra·ftiman**, †**Craftman.**

Craftsmaster (kra·ftsmastəɹ). *arch.* 1513. [Orig. *craftes master.*] 1. One who is master of his craft; usu. *transf.* an adept. †2. A master of craft or cunning –1734.

Crafty (kra·fti), *a.* [Com. Teut.: OE. *cræftig*; deriv. of *cræft* CRAFT; see -Y.] Having or characterized by CRAFT. †1. Strong, mighty (*rare*) –ME. 2. Skilful, dexterous, clever, ingenious OE. 3. (The current use): Cunning, artful; of actions, etc.: Showing craft ME.

2. The c. Poesie of excellent virgyll BARCLAY. 3. I was c., and toke you with gile TINDALE *2 Cor.* xii. 16. Hence **Cra·ftily** *a.* skilfully; artfully. **Cra·ftiness.**

Crag (kræg), *sb.*[1] ME. [Cf. Ir. and Gael. *creag*, Manx *creg*, Welsh *craig* rock.] 1. A steep rugged rock. 2. A detached or projecting rough piece of rock ME. 3. *Geol.* A name for deposits of shelly sand belonging to the Pliocene and Miocene strata 1735.

1. Bleak Craggs, and naked Hills COTTON. 2. Covered, like the steeps of Helvellin, with a continued pavement of craggs 1786.

Crag (kræg), *sb.*[2] ME. [Chiefly north.; prob. from LG.] 1. The neck. (Chiefly *Sc.*) †2. A neck of mutton or veal. (Cf. SCRAG.) –1767.

1. Like wailefull widdowes hangen their crags SPENSER.

Cragged (kræ·gĕd), *a.*[1] ME. [f. CRAG *sb.*[1] + -ED.] Formed into, beset with, or abounding in crags; *fig.* rugged, rough.

Mountains .. with snowy peaks and c. sides W. IRVING. Hence **Cra·ggedness.**

Cra·gged, *a.*[2] Also *Sc.* **craiged.** 1607. [f. CRAG *sb.*[2]] Chiefly in combs.: Having a .. neck, -necked; as in *narrow-c.*

Craggy (kræ·gi), *a.* 1447. [f. CRAG *sb.*[1] + -Y.] Abounding in crags; of the nature of a crag, steep and rugged. Also *transf.* and *fig.*

fig. Byron 'liked something c. to break his mind upon' EMERSON.

Cragsman (kræ·gsmæ̆n). Also *Sc.* **craigs-.** 1816. [For *crag's man*, f. CRAG[1].] One accustomed to, or skilled in, climbing crags.

Craie, Craier, obs. ff. CRAYE, CRAYER.

Craig, Sc. and north. f. CRAG *sb.*[1] and [2].

Craik, Crail, var. of CRAKE, CREEL.

Crake (krē̆ⁱk), *sb.* ME. [app. a. ON. *krâka* f. crow, *krâkr* m. raven. Echoic; cf. CROAK.] 1. A crow or raven (*n. dial.*). 2. Any bird of the family *Rallidæ*, esp. the CORN-CRAKE 1455. 3. The cry of the corn-crake 1876.

Comb.: **c.-berry** (*north.*), the CROWBERRY; **-needle**, the Shepherd's Needle or Venus's Comb.

Crake (krē̆ⁱk), *v.*[1] ME. [prob. echoic.] *intr.* To utter a harsh grating cry; †to grate harshly, creak –1657.

Crake, *v.*[2] Now *dial.* [var. of CRACK *v.*] To boast, brag.

Cra·ker. *dial.* 1698. [f. CRAKE *v.*[1]] = CRAKE *sb.*[2]

Craker, obs. f. CRACKER, *esp.* a boaster.

Crakow (kræ·kau). Now *Hist.* ME. [f. *Crakow, Krakau*, or *Cracovie*, in Poland.] A boot or shoe with a very long pointed toe, worn in the 14th century.

Cram (kræm), *v.* [OE. *crammian* (:–**krammôjan*), deriv. of *crimman, cram(m, crummen* to insert. The primary meaning was 'to press, squeeze'; cf. CRAMP.] 1. *trans.* To fill (a space, etc.) with more than it properly holds, by compression; to fill quite full or overfull, pack. Const. *with.* 2. To feed with excess of food (*spec.* poultry, etc., to fatten them); to stuff ME.; *intr.* (for *refl.*) to stuff oneself 1609. Also *fig.* 3. To thrust, force, stuff, crowd (anything) *into* a space, etc. which it overfills ME. Also *fig.* 4. *slang.* To stuff with lies, etc. 1794. 5. *colloq.* To prepare (a person), or get up (a subject), hastily for an occasion, by stuffing the memory with facts 1825. Also *absol.* or *intr.* 6. *slang.* To urge on forcibly (a horse) 1830.

1. A room crammed with fine ladies PEPYS. 2. *intr.* Such a bevy of beldames..cramming like so many Cormorants 1634. *fig.* Cram's with prayse *Wint. T.*

I. ii. 91. 3. *fig.* You c. these words into mine eares, against The stomacke of my sense *Temp.* II. i. 106.

Cram (kræm), *sb.* 1614. [f. prec. vb.] 1. Any food used to fatten (*dial.*). 2. A dense crowd, crush, squeeze (*colloq.*) 1858. 3. *slang.* A lie 1842. 4. The action of cramming information for an occasion (see CRAM *v.* 5); the information itself 1853. 5. *Weaving.* 'A warp having more than two threads passing through each dent or split of the reed' (Webster).

†**Crambe** (kræ·mbi). 1565. [a. L., a. Gr. κράμβη a kind of cabbage.] Cabbage: only *fig.*, and usually in reference to *crambe repetita* cabbage served up again (Juvenal VII. 154) -1713. Hence, (Distasteful) repetition -1757.

Cramble (kræ·mb'l), *v.* Now *dial.* 1570. [? Cf. SCRAMBLE.] †1. *intr.* To creep and twist about: said of roots, etc. -1597. 2. To crawl, hobble 1617.

Crambo (kræ·mbo). 1606. [? var. of CRAMBE.] 1. A game in which one player gives a word to which each of the others has to find a rime 1660. 2. *transf.* Rime, riming (*contemptuous*) 1697. †3. = CRAMBE, repetition -1705.

1. From thence to the Hague again playing at C. in the waggon PEPYS. 2. His similies in order set, And ev'ry c. he cou'd get SWIFT.

Dumb c.: a game in which one set of players have to guess a word agreed upon by the other set, after being told what word it rimes with, by acting in dumb show one word after another till they find it. (Occas. = dumb show.)

Crammer (kræ·məɹ). 1655. [f. CRAM *v.* + -ER.] 1. One who or that which crams poultry, etc. 2. *colloq.* One who crams pupils for an examination, etc.; rarely, a student who crams a subject 1813. 3. *slang.* A lie 1862.

Cramoisy, cramesy (kræ·moizi, -ĕzi). *arch.* ME. [a. early It. *cremesi* and OF. *crameisi*, later *cramoisi*, a. (ult.) Arab. *qirmazī* of or belonging to the *qirmiz*, KERMES or ALKERMES; see CRIMSON.] *adj.* Crimson 1480. *sb.* Crimson cloth ME.

adj. A blustering figure .. in .. cramoisy velvet CARLYLE.

Cramp (kræmp), *sb.*1 [ME. *cra(u)mpe*, a. OF. *crampe*, a. OLG. **krampe*; cf. OHG. *chrampf* adj. compressed, bent in.] An involuntary, violent, and painful contraction of the muscles, usually the result of a slight strain, a sudden chill, etc. (Usually spoken of as *cramp*, colloq. *the cramp*; *a cramp* is a particular case or form of cramp.)

Ile racke thee with old Crampes *Temp.* I. ii. 369.

Comb.: **c.-bark** (*U.S.*), the bark of the American Cranberry Tree, having anti-spasmodic properties; also the tree; **-bone**, the patella of a sheep, believed to be a charm against c.; **-fish**, the electric ray or torpedo, called also *c.-ray*, and *numb-fish*; **-ring**, a ring held to be efficacious against c., falling sickness, and the like; *esp.* one of those formerly hallowed by the kings of England on Good Friday for this purpose. Hence **Cra·mper** (*rare*), a kind of fish; a preventative of c.; **Cra·mpy** *a.* liable to, or suffering from, c.; inducing c.; of the nature of c.

Cramp (kræmp), *sb.*2 1503. [app. f. Du. or LG. Orig. the same word as CRAMP *sb.*1, but now differentiated.] 1. = CRAMP-IRON 1. Now *dial.* 2. = CRAMP-IRON 2. 1594. 3. A portable tool or press with a movable part which can be screwed up so as to hold things together. Cf. CLAMP *sb.*1 1669. 4. *Shoemaking.* 'A piece of wood having a curve corresponding to that of the instep, on which the upper leather of a boot is stretched to give it the requisite shape' (Webster). 5. 'A pillar of rock or mineral left for support' (Raymond). 6. *fig.* That which constrains and confines; a cramping restraint 1719. 7. A cramped condition 1864.

6. Crippling his pleasures with the c. of fear COWPER. Attempts to fasten down the progressive powers of the human mind by the cramps of association HALLAM.

Cramp (kræmp), *a.* 1674. [perh. f. CRAMP *sb.* or *v.* But the word is old in Teut.] 1. Difficult to make out; crabbed; cramped. 2. Strait, narrow; cramping 1785.

1. Your Lawyer's .. C. Law Terms 1708. Hence **Cra·mpness**, c. or cramped state or quality.

Cramp (kræmp), *v.* 1555. [f. CRAMP *sb.*1 and 2.]

I. Conn. w. CRAMP *sb.*1 †1. *trans.* To cause to be seized with cramp -1700. 2. To affect with the painful contraction of the muscles which characterizes cramp. Usu. in *pass.* 1639.

1. I'll c. your joints 1610. 2. We stood till we were cramp'd to death, not daring to move 1778.

II. Conn. mainly w. CRAMP *sb.*2 †1. To compress with irons in punishment, etc. Opp. to *to rack*. -1639. Also *fig.* and *transf.* 2. To confine narrowly, fetter. Also *fig.* 1625.

2. *fig.* The want of money cramps every effort JEFFERSON.

III. Conn. w. CRAMP *sb.*2 alone. 1. To fasten or secure with a cramp or cramps; *esp.* in *Building.* Also *fig.* 1654. 2. *Shoemaking.* To form on a boot-cramp 1864.

1. *fig.* The .. fabrick of universal justice, is well cramped and bolted together in all its parts BURKE. Hence **Cra·mpedness.**

Crampet (kræ·mpĕt). 1489. [app. f. CRAMP *sb.*2] 1. The chape of the scabbard of a sword; occas. used in *Her.* as a charge. 2. = CRAMP-IRON 2. (? error.) 1766. 3. *Sc.* = CRAMPON 3; *esp.* one formerly used by curlers 1638.

Cra·mp-iron. 1565. [f. CRAMP *sb.*2] †1. A piece of iron bent in the form of a hook; a grappling-iron -1774. 2. A small metal bar with the ends bent so as to hold together two pieces of masonry, timber, etc. 1598.

†**Cra·mpish,** *v.* ME. only. [f. *crampiss-* stem of OF. *crampir*, f. *crampe* CRAMP *sb.*1] *intr.* To become cramped; *trans.* to cramp.

Crampon (kræ·mpən), *sb.* Also **crampoon** (kræmpū·n). 1490. [a. F. *crampon*, deriv. of **cramp*, f. LG.; cf. CRAMP *sb.*1, 2.] 1. = CRAMP-IRON 1, 2. †2. 'The border of metal which keeps a stone in a ring' (Halliwell). 3. A small plate of iron set with spikes which is fastened to the foot for walking over ice or climbing 1789. 4. *Bot.* Adventitious roots which serve as fulcra or supports, as in the ivy 1870. So †**Cra·mpon** *v.* to fix with crampons. ‖**Crampo·nnee** *a. Her.* Said of a cross having a bend shaped thus, [, at the end of each limb.

Cran1 (kræn). *Sc.* 1797. [?; cf. Gael. *crann* lot.] A measure of fresh herrings; now fixed at 37 1/2 gallons (about 750 fish).

Cran2. *Sc.* 1796. [= the word CRANE.] †1. Applied to the Crane and the Heron. 2. In the South of Scotland, the Swift 1840. 3. An iron instrument, laid across the fire, to support a pot or kettle.

3. *To coup the crans*: *fig.* to have an upset; see COUP *v.*3 (So Jamieson; but perhaps belonging to CRAN 1.)

Cranage (krē·nėdʒ). 1481. [f. CRANE + -AGE.] The use of a crane to hoist goods; dues paid for such use.

Cranberry (kræ·nbĕri). Also **craneberry.** 1672. [app. from some LG. source; cf. G. *kranichbeere, kranbeere*, LG. *krônbere, kranebere*, etc. (all meaning *craneberry*).] The fruit of a dwarf shrub, *Vaccinium Oxycoccos*, growing in turfy bogs: a small, roundish, dark red, very acid berry. Also the similar but larger fruit of *V. macrocarpon* (*Large* or *American Cranberry*). Also the name of the shrubs themselves.

Bush C., High C., or **C. Tree,** *Viburnum Oxycoccos* Pursh (N.O. *Caprifoliaceæ*).

Crance (krɑns). 1846. [Cf. Du. *krans* wreath.] *Naut.* 'A kind of iron cap on the outer end of the bowsprit, through which the jib-boom traverses' (A. Young). Also, any boom-iron.

Cranch, var. of CRAUNCH.

Crane (krēin), *sb.*1 [OE. *cran*, repr. MG. *kran*, MLG. *krân, krôn.*] 1. A large grallatorial bird of the family *Gruidæ*, characterized by very long legs, neck, and bill. The name belongs to the common European crane, *Grus cinerea*, of an ashen-gray colour, formerly abundant in Great Britain, but now extinct. About 15 closely allied species are found in other lands. Also, locally, a name for herons and storks; also for the Shag. 1678. b. *Astron.* The constellation *Grus* 1868. 2. A machine for raising and lowering heavy weights; in its usual form it consists of a vertical post capable of rotation on its axis, a projecting arm or jib over which passes the chain or rope from which the weight is suspended, and a barrel round which the chain or rope is wound. [So F. *grue*, G. *kran*, etc.] ME. 3. A machine for weighing goods, constructed on the principle of the crane described under 2. b. An upright revolving axle with a horizontal arm fixed by a fireplace, for suspending a kettle, etc. c. *Naut.* (*pl.*) Projecting pieces of iron or timber on board a ship, to support a boat or spar. 4. A bent tube for drawing liquor out of a bottle; a siphon. [So G. *kran.*] 1634. 5. An overhanging tube for supplying water to the tender of a locomotive; a water-crane. 6. *attrib.* or as *adj.* †Crane-coloured, ashen-gray; crane-like; pertaining to a c. or the cranes 1517.

Comb.: a. in sense 1, as **c.-fly,** a two-winged fly of the genus *Tipula*; a *daddy-long-legs*; **-colour,** ashy gray; also *attrib.*; hence, **-coloured** *a.*; **-necked** *a.* having a long neck like a crane's; **-vulture,** the Secretary-bird.

b. In sense 2 or 3, as **c.-barge,** a barge carrying a c.; **-post,** the vertical post or axis of a c.; so **-shaft; -wheel,** a tread-wheel by which a c. was formerly worked.

Crane (krēin), *sb.*2 *arch.* 1541. [a. F. *crâne*, ad. med.L. *cranium.*] The skull; = CRANIUM.

Crane (krēin), *v.* 1570. [f. CRANE *sb.*1] 1. *trans.* To hoist or lower with, or as with, a crane. 2. To stretch (the neck) like a crane 1799. 3. *intr.* To lean or bend forward with the neck stretched out 1849. 4. *Hunting.* To pull up at an obstacle and look over before leaping; hence *fig.* to hesitate at a danger, difficulty etc. (*colloq.*) 1823.

1. Being safely craned up to the top of the crag SCOTT. 3. Those who sat above craned forward 1887. 4. A very fat pony, who would have craned if he had attempted to leap over a straw 1844.

Craner (krē·nəɹ). 1869. [f. CRANE *sb.*1 and *v.* + -ER 1.] 1. An official in charge of a crane or public weighing machine 1871. 2. One who cranes at a dangerous leap, etc.

Crane's-bill, cranesbill (krē·nzbil). 1548. [f. CRANE *sb.*1] 1. *Bot.* Any (*esp.* the native British) species of *Geranium*; so called from the long slender beak of the fruit. 2. *Surg.* A kind of forceps with long jaws 1668.

†**Cra·net.** 1548. [Corrupted from OF. *crignete, crinete*, dim. of *crigne*, f. *crin*, L. *crinis.*] A piece of armour covering a horse's neck or mane; a crinière -1611.

Crang (kræŋ). 1821. [A var. of *krang*, KRENG, a. Du.] The carcass of a whale after the blubber has been removed.

Cranial (krē·niăl), *a.* 1800. [f. med.L. *cranium* (a. Gr. κρανίον).] Pertaining to the cranium.

‖**Crania·ta, cranio·ta,** *sb. pl.* 1878. [f. L. *cranium* and Gr. κρανίον. The latter form is Haeckel's.] *Zool.* A primary division of the VERTEBRATA (q. v.), including those which possess a brain and skull.

Cranio- (krē·nio), bef. a vowel **crani-,** comb. f. Gr. κρανίον CRANIUM.

a. In combs., as **c.-fa·cial** *a.*, belonging to the cranium and the face; **-spi·nal** *a.*, belonging to the cranium and the spine; also **-tabes** (-tē·bīz) [L. *tabes* wasting away], 'a form of rickets in which the skull bones are softened' (*Syd. Soc. Lex.*). b. In derivs., as **Cranie·ctomy** [Gr. ἐκτομή], excision of a strip of bone from the cranium to allow the brain to develop. **Cra·niocele** [see CELE *sb.*], 'the protrusion of a part of the encephalon from the cranial cavity' (*Syd. Soc. Lex.*). **Cra·nioclasm** [Gr. κλάσμα breaking], the breaking up of the fœtal head in *craniotomy*; **Cra·nioclast** [Gr. -κλάστης], an instrument for doing this. **Cranio·gnomy** [Gr. γνώμη], 'the science of the form and characteristics of the skull' (*Syd. Soc. Lex.*); hence **Cra:niogno·mic** *a.* So **Cranio·gnosy** [Gr. γνῶσις]. **Cra·niograph** [Gr. -γραφος], an instrument for taking drawings of the skull; **Cranio·grapher; Cranio·graphy,** description of skulls. **Cranio·meter** [Gr. μέτρον], an instrument for taking measurements of skulls; hence **Cra:niome·tric, -al** *a.*; **Cra:niome·trically** *adv.*; **Cranio·metrist; Cranio·metry. Cranio·pathy** [Gr. -πάθεια, f. πάθος], 'disease of the cranium' (*Syd. Soc. Lex.*). **Cra·niophore** [Gr. -φορος bearing], Topinard's instrument for measuring the dimensions of the skull. **Cra·nioplasty** [Gr. -πλαστία, f. πλαστός moulded], an operation for supplying deficiencies in the cranial structures. **Cranio·scopy** [Gr. -σκοπία, f. -σκοπος that views], examination of the size and configuration of the skull; formerly =

PHRENOLOGY; hence **Cra·niosco·pic, -al** *a.*; **Cranio·scopist. Cranio·tomy** [Gr. -τομία, f. -τομος cutting], in obstetric surgery, an operation in which the head of the fœtus is cut open and broken down when it presents an obstacle to delivery.

Cranioid (krēⁱ·ni,oid), *a.* 1849. [See -OID.] *Zool.* Allied to the genus *Crania* of Brachiopods.

Craniology (krēⁱni,ǫ·lŏdʒi). 1806. [f. CRANIO- + Gr. -λογία.] †1. = PHRENOLOGY –1843. 2. The study of the size, shape, and character of the skulls of various races, as a part of anthropology 1851. So **Cra:niolo·gical** *a.* of or pertaining to c. **Cranio·logist**, one versed in c.

Craniota; see CRANIATA.

‖**Cranium** (krēⁱ·niŏm). Pl. **crania** (krēⁱ·niă). 1543. [med.L., a. Gr. κρανίον.] 1. *Anat.*, etc. *strictly*, The bones which enclose the brain, the brain-case; *more widely*, the bones of the whole head; the skull. 2. Used joc. for 'head' 1647.

Crank (kræŋk), *sb.*[1] [OE. *cranc* in *cranc-stæf*, ME. *crank(e*. The primary notion is that of something bent or crooked. Ger. and Du. *krank* 'sick' is a fig. development.] 1. A portion of an axis bent at right angles, used to communicate motion, or to change reciprocal into rotary motion, or the converse. 2. An elbow-shaped device in bell-hanging, whereby the rectilineal motion communicated to a bell-wire is changed in its direction, usually at right angles 1759. 3. An elbow-shaped support or bracket 1769. 4. A revolving disc, to which a regulated pressure can be applied, which criminals sentenced to hard labour are required to turn a certain number of times each day 1847.

Comb.: **c.-axle**, (*a.*) the driving axle of an engine or machine; (*b.*) a carriage-axle with the ends bent twice at a right angle; **-hook**, the rod which connects the treadle and the c. in a foot-lathe; **-pin**, the pin by which the connecting-rod is attached to the c.; **-shaft**, the shaft driven by a c.; **-wheel**, a wheel which acts as a c.; *esp.* one having near its circumference a pin to which the end of a connecting-rod is attached as to a c.-pin; a disc-c.

Crank (kræŋk), *sb.*[2] 1562. [Prob. same word as prec., with sense 'crooking, crook'.] †1. A crook, bend, winding; a crooked path, course, or channel –1630. Also †*fig.* †2. A tortuous hole or crevice; a cranny –1612. Also *fig.* 3. A twist or fanciful turn of speech; a conceit 1594. 4. An eccentric notion or action; a crotchet, whim 1848. 5. *U.S. colloq.* A person with a mental twist; an eccentric; *esp.* a monomaniac. [Prob. f. CRANKY, q. v.] 1881. 6. *dial.* A slight ailment 1847.

1. The turnings and cranks of the Labyrinth NORTH. 3. Quips, and cranks, and wanton wiles MILT. 4. Subject to sudden cranks CARLYLE.

†**Crank**, *sb.*[3] *Thieves' slang.* 1567. [app. a. Du. or G. *krank* sick.] (In full, *counterfeit c.*) A rogue who feigned sickness in order to move compassion and get money –1622.

Crank (kræŋk), *a.*[1] ME. [?] †1. Rank, lusty, vigorous –1659. 2. Lively, brisk; merry; aggressively high-spirited, 'cocky'. Now *dial.* and in U.S. 1499.

2. How came they to grow so c. and confident SOUTH. Hence **Cra·nkly** *adv.*

Crank (kræŋk), *a.*[2] 1696. [? for Du. and Fris. *krengd* (of a ship) laid over on its side.] *Naut.* Liable to lean over or capsize: said of a ship when she is built too deep or narrow, or has too little ballast to carry full sail. Also *fig.*

That c. little boat with its top-heavy sails BLACK. Hence **Cra·nkness. Crank-sided** *a.* (in same sense).

Crank (kræŋk), *a.*[3] 1729. [Senses conn. w. CRANK *sb.*[1] and [2] and CRANKY *a.*] 1. Crooked; augularly bent. *Sc.* 1825. 2. Crabbed, difficult to pronounce, understand, or do. Now *Sc.* 1729. 3. = CRANKY 1 (*dial.*) 1802. 4. Of machinery: Shaky; out of order; CRANKY 1831.

2. Hard, tough, c., gutt'ral, harsh, stiff names SWIFT. Hence **Cra·nkous** *a.* (*Sc.*), irritable, fretful.

Crank (kræŋk), *v.*[1] 1592. [f. CRANK *sb.*[1], [2].] †1. *intr.* To twist and turn about, zigzag –1891. †2. *trans.* To crinkle 1661. 3. *trans.* a. To make crank-shaped. b. To furnish with a crank. 4. To fasten with a crank 1879. 5. To draw *up* by means of a crank, operate by a crank 1883.

1. See, how this Riuer comes me cranking in, And cuts me from the best of all my Land..a monstrous Cantle out 1 *Hen. IV*, III. i. 98.

Crank, *v.*[2] 1827. [App. echoic; cf. CLANK *v.*, and n. dial. CRONK to croak.] To make a jarring or grating sound.

Cranked (kræŋkt), *ppl. a.* 1862. [f. CRANK *sb.*[1]] Formed into or furnished with a crank.

Crankle (kræ·ŋk'l), *v.* 1594. [Freq. of CRANK *v.*[1] Cf. CRINKLE.] 1. *intr.* To run zigzag 1598. †2. *trans.* To zigzag; to crinkle (a surface) –1708.

1. The river crankles round an alder grove SIR H. TAYLOR. Hence **Cra·nkle** *sb.* a bend, twist; an angular prominence.

Cranky (kræ·ŋki), *a.*[1] 1787. [Senses conn. w. CRANK *sb.*[2] and [3], CRANK *a.*[2] and [3].] 1. Sickly (*dial.*). 2. *Naut.* = CRANK *a.*[2] 3. Out of gear; crazy 1862. 4. Cross-tempered, awkward 1821. 5. Crotchety; peculiar 1850. 6. Crooked; full of crannies 1836. Hence **Cra·nkily** *adv.* **Cra·nkiness.**

Cra·nky, *a.*[2] *dial.* 1811. [f. CRANK *a.*[1] + -Y.] = CRANK *a.*[1]

†**Crannel.** 1533. [app. f. F. *cran*; cf. OF. *crenel.*] A cranny, crevice, chink –1640.

Crannied (kræ·nid), *a.* 1440. [f. CRANNY + -ED [2].] 1. Having crannies or chinks. 2. Formed like a cranny. SHAKS.

1. As a Raine doth drench The c. Earth 1639.

†**Crannock.** ME. = CURNOCK, q.v. –1815.

Crannog (kræ·nǫg). Also (*erron.*) **crannoge.** 1851. [a. Irish *crannog*, Gael. *crannag*, deriv. of *crann* tree, beam, etc.] An ancient lake-dwelling in Scotland or Ireland.

Cranny (kræ·ni), *sb.*[1] 1440. [app. related to F. *cran* a notch, etc.; but ?] A small narrow opening or hole; a chink, crevice, crack, fissure. Also *fig.*

Cranny, *sb.*[2] 1662. [?] *Glass Manuf.* An iron rod used in forming the necks of glass bottles.

Cra·nny, *v.* 1440. [f. CRANNY *sb.*[1]] †1. *intr.* To open in crannies or chinks –1607. 2. To penetrate into crannies (*rare*) 1816.

Cranreuch (kra·nrəχ). *Sc.* 1682. [f. Gael. *crann* tree + *reodhadh* freezing.] Hoar-frost.

†**Crants.** 1592. [a. Ger. *kranz.*] A garland, chaplet, wreath –1706.

†**Cra·ny.** 1525. = CRANIUM –1730.

Crap (kræp), *sb.*[1] Now *dial.* ME. [= Du. *krappe*, conn. w. *krappen* to pluck off, cut off. Cf. also OF. *crappe* siftings.] †1. The husk of grain –1483. 2. A name of Buckwheat; also, locally, of Darnel, Rye-grass, Charlock, etc. ME. 3. Residues, as of fat. (Usu. in *pl.*) 1490. 4. Dregs of ale 1879. 5. Money (*slang* or *dial.*) 1700. 6. A SCRAP 1550.

†**Crap**, *sb.*[2] 1721. [a. Du. *krap.*] Madder –1812.

Crap, *sb.*[3] *Thieves' cant.* 1812. [a. Du. *krap* cramp.] The gallows. Hence **Crap** *v. trans.* to hang.

†**Crapaud.** 1440. [a. F.; see Diez, Littré, etc.] 1. A toad –1634. 2. (In full *c.-stone.*) A TOAD-STONE. Cf. SHAKS. *As You Like It* II. i. 13. –1580.

Crapaudine (krapǫdī·n). 1558. [F., f. as prec.] †1. ? = TOADSTONE. †2. *Farriery.* An ulcer on the coronet of a horse –1823. 3. A socket in which the pivot of a swing-door turns; whence *c.-door*, one which turns on pivots at top and bottom 1876.

Crape (krēⁱp), *sb.* 1633. [For mod.F. *crêpe*, in 16th c. *crespe*, sb. use of *crespe* adj. CRISP. See also CRÊPE.] 1. A thin transparent gauze-like fabric, plain woven, of highly twisted raw silk, with a crisped surface. Now chiefly of black silk (or imitation silk), and used for ladies' mourning dresses, etc. b. In the 18th c., 'a sort of thin worsted stuff, of which the dress of the clergy is sometimes made' (Bailey); hence, occas. = the clergy, a clergyman 1699. 2. A band of crape worn round a hat, etc.; a mask of crape 1763. Also *attrib.*

1. b. A Saint in c. is twice a Saint in lawn POPE. 2. A white hat with a c. round it THACKERAY.

Comb.: **c.-myrtle**, a Chinese shrub, *Lagerstræmia indica*, with bright rose-coloured crumpled petals, cultivated in England, and in Southern U.S. **Canton** or **China c.** = *crêpe de Chine* (see CRÊPE).

†**Crape**, *v.*[1] 1786. [a. F. *crêper*:–L. *crispare*; see CRISP *a.*] To make (the hair) wavy and curly; to crimp, to frizzle –1822.

Crape (krēⁱp), *v.*[2] 1815. [f. CRAPE *sb.*] To cover, clothe, or drape with crape. Also *transf.*

Cra·pe-fish. 1856. [Cf. Norse *crappr* compressed.] Cod-fish salted and pressed.

Crappie (kræ·pi). *U.S.* 1861. A species of sunfish, *Pomoxys annularis*, found in the Mississippi.

Cra·ppit-head. *Sc.* 1815. [Cf. Du. *krappen* to cram.] The head of a haddock stuffed with the roe, oatmeal, suet, and spices (Jamieson).

Craps (kræps). *U.S.* 1843. [ad. F. *crabs*, †*craps*, ad. Eng. *crabs* (see CRAB *sb.*[1] 5).] A gambling game with two dice.

‖**Cra·pula.** 1727. [L. *crapula* inebriation, ad. Gr. κραιπάλη drunken headache.] Sickness following upon excess in drinking or eating.

Crapulence (kræ·piŭlĕns). 1727. [f. CRAPULENT; see -ENCE.] 1. = CRAPULA. 2. Gross intemperance; debauchery 1825. var. †**Cra·pulency** (in sense 2).

Crapulent (kræ·piŭlĕnt), *a.* 1656. [ad. L. *crapulentus*, f. *crapula*; see above.] 1. Of or pertaining to crapulence. 2. Given to gross intemperance 1888.

Crapulous (kræ·piŭləs), *a.* 1536. [ad. L. *crapulosus*; cf. F. *crapuleux.*] 1. Intemperate, debauched. 2. Suffering from crapulence; resulting from intemperance 1755. Hence **Cra·pulousness.**

Crapy (krēⁱ·pi), *a.* 1853. [f. CRAPE *sb.*[1] + -Y [1].] 1. Crape-like 1853. 2. Of crape; clothed in crape 1855.

Crare, obs. var. of CRAYER.

Crash (kræʃ), *v.* late ME. [Echoic.] 1. *trans.* To dash to pieces, smash (now *rare*); to cause to come or go with a crash. 2. *intr.* To break or fall to pieces with noise 1535; to move or go with crashing 1694. †3. *trans.* To strike (the teeth) together with noise; to gnash –1646. 4. To make the noise that a hard body does when smashed, or a noise as of many hard bodies dashing and breaking together 1563. 5. *intr.* Of an aeroplane, etc.: To come down violently out of control; also in corresp. trans. sense 1915. Hence *gen.*

1. Crashing the branches as he went DICKENS. 3. He shakt his head and crasht his teeth for ire FAIRFAX. 4. O'erhead the rolling thunders c. SKEAT.

Crash (kræʃ), *sb.*[1] 1549. [f. prec. vb.] 1. A loud and sudden sound, as of a hard body or bodies broken by violent percussion; also *transf.* 1580. 2. *fig.* The action of falling to ruin suddenly and violently; *spec.* sudden collapse of a mercantile undertaking or of credit generally 1817. †3. A short spell, spurt –1767.

1. The whole forest in one c. descends POPE. 2. A great c. is expected..everybody has been over-speculating 1890. 3. A c. at cards BROME.

Crash (kræʃ), *sb.*[2] 1812. [?] A coarse kind of linen, used for towels, etc. Also *attrib.*

‖**Crasis** (krēⁱ·sis). 1602. [Gr. κρᾶσις.] 1. The combination of elements, 'humours', or qualities in the animal body, in herbs, etc.; †constitution –1759; condition. ? *Obs.* 2. *Gr. Gram.* The combination of the vowels of two syllables, *esp.* at the end of one word and beginning of the next, into one long vowel or diphthong; as in κἀγώ for καὶ ἐγώ, etc.

‖**Craspedon, -dum** (kræ·spĭdǫn, -dŏm). Pl. craspeda (-dă). 1869. [Gr. κράσπεδον edge: the form in *-um* is mod.L.] *Zool.* The convoluted filament, charged with thread-cells, forming the border of the mesentery in Actinozoa.

Craspedote (kræ·spĭdǫut), *a.* 1888. [f. Gr. type κρασπεδωτός bordered (see prec.). Hence mod.L. *Craspedota* pl.] *Zool.* Applied to those *Medusæ* which have a velum along the margin of the bell.

Crass (kræs), *a.* 1545. [ad. L. *crassus*. OF. had *cras*, now *gras*.] 1. Coarse, gross, dense, thick. Now *rare.* 2. Grossly dull or stupid; dense; unrefined (*rare*) 1861.

1. A crasse and fumide exhalation SIR T. BROWNE. C. ignorance 1859, minds GEO. ELIOT. Hence **Cra·ss·ly** *adv.*, **-ness.**

†**Cra·ssament.** 1615. [ad. L. *crassamentum* (also used), f. *crassare*, f. *crassus.*] The thick part of a non-homogeneous liquid, which solidifies or settles; *esp.* the coagulum of blood –1666.

†‖**Crassities.** 1659. [L.] Density, materiality -1678.

Crassitude (kræ·sitiūd). ME. [ad. L. *crassitudo*.] †1. Thickness; volume -1703. †2. Density; coarseness -1822. 3. The state or quality of being CRASS 1679.

‖**Cra·ssula.** ME. [med.L., dim. of *crassa* (sc. *herba*); see CRASS.] *Bot.* Formerly, some species of *Sedum*, esp. Orpine; now, limited to a genus of succulent plants, the type of the N.O. *Crassulaceæ*, which includes the Stonecrops, Houseleeks, Echeveria, etc. Hence **Crassula·ceous** *a.* of the N.O. *Crassulaceæ*.

-crat, -ocrat, *suffix*, formerly also *-crate*, after F. *-crate* in *aristocrate*, etc., with the sense 'partisan of an aristocracy', etc. At the French Revolution *aristocrate* came to be used for 'a member of the aristocracy', after which (*-o*)*crat* is now used, as in *plutocrat*, etc. Hence **-cratic, -al.**

Cratch (krætʃ), *sb.*[1] [ME. *crecche*, a. OF. *creche, cresche*; cf. CRIB.] 1. A rack or crib to hold fodder for cattle; in early use sometimes 'a manger' (now *dial.*). 2. A wooden grating or hurdle; a sparred frame or rack ME.

1. A stable was his beste house, and a cratche his cradle KINGESMYLL.

Cratch, *sb.*[2] Now *dial.* ME. [f. CRATCH *v.*] 1. Some form of itch. 2. *pl.* A disease in the feet of horses and sheep; the SCRATCHES 1523.

†**Cratch,** *v.* ME. [? f. Du. or LG.; cf. MDu., MLG. *kratsen*, etc. Cf. also SCRATCH.] 1. *trans.* To scratch -1552. Also *absol.* or *intr.* 2. *trans.* To snatch with, or as with, claws; to grab -1581.

Crate (krēⁱt). 1526. [app. ad. L. *cratis* hurdle. But cf. Du. *krat* basket.] †1. A hurdle. 2. A large basket or hamper of wickerwork, for carrying crockery, glass, etc.; any case or box of open bars or slats of wood, for carrying fruit, etc. 1688. b. A glazier's frame for carrying glass; also measure of glass 1823. Hence **Cra·teman,** a hawker of pottery.

Crater (krēⁱ·təɹ). 1613. [a. L., a. Gr. κρατήρ bowl, lit. 'mixer, mixing vessel', f. κερα-, κρα- to mix.] ‖1. *Gr. Antiq.* 'A large bowl in which the wine was mixed with water, and from which the cups were filled' (Liddell and Scott). Also *krater*. 1730. 2. A bowl- or funnel-shaped hollow at the summit or on the side of a volcano, from which eruption takes place; the mouth of a volcano 1613. ‖3. *Astron.* A southern constellation, situated between Hydra and Leo 1658. 4. *Mil.* The cavity formed by the explosion of a mine or shell 1839. 5. *Electr.* The cavity formed in the positive carbon of an arc light in the course of combustion 1892. Hence **Cra·teral** *a.* of, belonging to, or like, a c. **Cra·teriform, crate·riform** *a.* c.-shaped; in *Bot.* cup- or bowl-shaped. **Cra·terlet,** a small c., *e.g.* on the moon. **Cra·terous** *a.* of the nature of a c.

Cratometer (krătǫ·mĭtəɹ). 1876. [f. Gr. κράτος + μέτρον.] An apparatus for measuring power. (Better *crateometer*.) Hence **Cratome·trical** *a.*

Craunch, cranch (krɑnʃ, krǭnʃ), *v.* 1631. [?an echoic modification of *crush*.] = CRUNCH *v.*

Craunch, cranch, *sb.* 1747. [f. prec.] 1. An act, or the action, of craunching 1806. 2. (*cranch.*) *Mining.* A part of a stratum or vein left in excavating to support the roof.

Cravat (krăvæ·t), *sb.* 1656. [a. F. *cravate*, an application of *Cravate* Croat, Croatian.] *orig.* A piece of lace or linen, or of muslin edged with lace, worn round the neck, and tied in a bow. More recently, a linen or silk handkerchief, or a woollen comforter, worn round the neck, chiefly by men. Also *fig.*

fig. The Gallows comes next..a hempen C. 1685. Hence **Crava·tted** *a.* wearing a c.

Crave (krēⁱv), *v.* [OE. *crafian* :—OTeut. type **kraƀōjan*.] †1. *trans.* To demand, to ask with authority, or by right -ME. 2. To ask earnestly, to beg for, *esp.* as a gift or favour. Const. *of, from.* ME. 3. To dun. *Sc.* 1812. 4. *transf.* Of persons (their appetites, etc.): To long or yearn for; to call for, in order to gratify an appetite; to have a craving for ME. 5. *fig.* Of things: To need greatly, to call for (something necessary) 1576. Also *intr.* and *absol.*

2. Salomon .. craued wisdom from heaven CAREW. I c. leave to observe [etc.] SCOTT. 4. The more you drink, the more you c. 1737. 5. The time craves speed SCOTT. *intr.* Once one may c. for love SUCKLING (J.). Hence **Crave** *sb.* = CRAVING. (Not in general use.) **Cra·ver. Cra·ving-ly** *adv.*, **-ness.**

Craven (krēⁱ·v'n). [ME. *crauant* (rare), etym. obscure.]

A. *adj.* †1. Vanquished. (ME. only.) 2. That owns himself beaten or afraid; abjectly pusillanimous ME.

1. *To cry c.*: to give up the contest, surrender. Also *fig.* Neither King nor Duke was a man likely to cry c. 2. *Haml.* IV. iv. 40. Hence **Cra·venly** *adv.*

B. *sb.* 1. A confessed coward 1581. 2. A cock that is not game 1596.

1. Hee is a Crauen and a Villaine else *Hen. V*, IV. vii. 139. 2. No Cocke of mine, you crow too like a crauen *Tam. Shr.* II. i. 228.

Cra·ven, *v.* 1611. [f. prec.] To make craven.

Craving (krēⁱ·viŋ), *vbl. sb.* ME. [See -ING[1].] †1. Accusation. (ME. only.) 2. Earnest or urgent asking; begging ME. 3. Urgent desire; yearning 16..

3. A c. after prophecies FROUDE.

Craw (krǭ), *sb.* [ME. *crawe*, repr. OE. **craga*, a. Norse *krage* neck. Cf. Du. *kraag*, etc.] 1. The CROP of birds or insects. 2. *transf.* The stomach (of man or animals). *derisive.* 1573.

Craw, Sc. and north. f. CROW.

‖**Craw-craw** (krǭ·krǭ). 1863. [app. Du. Negro, from Du. *kraauw* scratch.] *Pathol.* A malignant species of pustulous itch, prevalent on the African coast.

Crawfish (krǭ·fiʃ), *sb.* 1860. = CRAYFISH, q.v. Cf. also CRAWFISH *v.*

Cra·wfish, *v.* *U.S. colloq.* 1860. [f. prec.] To move backward like a crawfish; hence, to back out of a position.

Crawl (krǭl), *sb.*[1] 1818. [f. CRAWL *v.*[1]] The action of crawling. b. A swimming stroke.

Crawl (krǭl), *sb.*[2] 1660. [a. Colonial Du. *kraal*, a. Sp. *corral*; see CORRAL.] †1. A pen or enclosure for keeping hogs (in the West Indies) -1707. 2. A pen or enclosure in shallow water on the sea-coast, to contain fish, turtles, etc. 1769. 3. = KRAAL, q. v.

Crawl (krǭl), *v.* ME. [prob. from Norse; cf. Da. and Norw. *kravle* to crawl, etc.] 1. *intr.* To move slowly in a prone position, by dragging the body along close to the ground, as a child on hands and knees, a worm, etc.; †*trans.* to crawl upon or over (*rare*) -1796. 2. *transf.* To walk or move with a slow and dragging motion 1460. Also *fig.* 3. Of plants, etc.: To trail, creep (*rare*) 1634. 4. *transf.* To be alive *with* crawling things 1576. 5. To have a sensation as of things crawling over the skin; to feel creepy ME.

1. Slow crawl'd the snail GAY. 2. I can no further crawle *Mids. N.* III. ii. 444. *fig.* Months and seasons crawled along KINGSLEY. Cranmer .. Hath crawl'd into the fauour of the King SHAKS. 4. The whole ground seemed alive and crawling with [ants] GOLDSM. Hence **Craw·ler,** *colloq.* a cab crawling along the streets in search of a fare.

Crawly (krǭ·li), *a. colloq.* 1860. [f. CRAWL +-Y.] Like or having the sensation of insects crawling over the skin.

†**Cray.** ME. [a. F. *craie* :—L. *creta* chalk.] 1. Chalk. (ME. only.) 2. A disease of hawks, in which the excrements become hard and are passed with difficulty -1618.

†**Craye.** 1541. Erron. f. CRAYER -1627.

Crayer, crare (krēᵊɹ). Now *Hist.* ME. [a. OF. *crayer*.] A small trading vessel.

Crayfish (krēⁱ·fiʃ), **crawfish** (krǭ·fiʃ). [ME. *crevice, -visse*, a. OF. *crevice*, a. OHG. *crebiz*, MHG. *krebeʒ*, a deriv. of stem **kraƀ-* in *krabbo* CRAB, q. v. In ME. the second syllable was confounded with *vish* 'fish'. *Crawfish* is chiefly U.S.] †1. *gen.* Any of the larger edible crustacea -1656; *spec.* the crab -1783. †2. A name for large crustacea other than crabs -1624. 3. Now: a. *gen.* A fresh-water crustacean, *Astacus fluviatilis*, resembling a small lobster. Also applied to other species of *Astacus* and of the allied genus *Cambarus*, *e.g.* the blind crawfish of the Mammoth Cave of Kentucky (*C. pellucidus*). 1460. b. In Great Britain: The Spiny Lobster, *Palinurus vulgaris*, the *Langouste* of the French 1748.

Crayon (krēⁱ·ǫ̆n), *sb.* 1644. [a. F., deriv. of *craie* :—L. *creta* chalk.] 1. A pointed stick or pencil of coloured chalk or other material for drawing. 2. *transf.* A drawing in crayons; †*fig.* a sketch 1662. 3. A carbon point in an electric arc lamp. Also *attrib.*

1. Sir Thomas showed me his picture..in c. in little, done exceedingly well PEPYS. 2. *fig.* It is a poor c., which yourself..must fill up T. JEFFERSON.

Cray·on, *v.* 1662. [a. F. *crayonner*; see prec.] 1. *trans.* To draw with a crayon; to cover with drawing in crayons. 2. *fig.* To sketch, chalk *out* 1734.

2. The other [books] will soon follow; many of them are writ, or crayoned out BOLINGBROKE.

Craze (krēⁱz), *v.* ME. [Cf. Sw. *krasa* to crackle, *slå i kras* to dash in pieces. See also ACRAZE.] †1. *trans.* To break in pieces or asunder; to shatter -1667; to bruise, crush, damage -1726. Also †*intr.* 2. *Mining.* To crush (tin ore) in a mill 1610. 3. *trans.* To crack ME.; *spec.* to produce minute cracks on the surface of (pottery) 1874. Also *intr.* 4. *fig.* To destroy the soundness of, impair, ruin. (Usu. in *pass.*) *arch.* 1561. 5. To break down in health; to render infirm. (Usu. in *pa. pple.*) *arch.* 1476. Also †*intr.* 6. To impair in intellect; to render insane, distract. Usu. in *pa. pple.* (The ordinary sense.) 1496. Also *intr.*

1. God..will..c. thir Chariot wheels MILT. *P. L.* XII. 210. 3. I am right siker þat þe pot was crased CHAUCER. 5. Till length of years And sedentary numbness c. my limbs MILT. *Sams.* 570. 6. The greefe hath craz'd my wits *Lear* III. iv. 175. *Comb.* †**c.-mill,** a mill for crushing tin ore. Hence †**Cra·zedness,** the state of being crazed.

Craze (krēⁱz), *sb.* 1534. [f. CRAZE *v.*] †1. A crack, breach, flaw -1645. Also *fig.* 2. An irrational fancy; a mania 1813; craziness 1841. 3. *Mining.* (See quots. and cf. CRAZE *v.* 2.) 1778.

1. *fig.* Would it not argue a c. in the brayne 1608. 2. The miser's c. for gold E. R. CONDER. 3. The tin ..is sorted into 3 divisions..the middle..being named ..the crease 1778.

Crazy (krēⁱ·zi), *a.* 1576. [f. CRAZE *v.* or *sb.* +-Y.] 1. Full of cracks or flaws; impaired; liable to fall to pieces; shaky 1583. †2. Indisposed; broken down, frail, infirm -1847. Also *fig.* and *transf.* 3. Of unsound mind; insane, mad. Often in sense: Mad with excitement, perplexity, etc. 1617. b. Of things, actions, etc.: Showing derangement of intellect 1859.

1. A c. ship 1748, house ADAM SMITH, coach DICKENS. 2. The king somewhat crasie, and keeping his Chamber SPEED. *fig.* A crazie and diseased Monarchy MILT. 3. 'Lord, child, are you c.?' FRANKLIN. b. C. theories 1859. By c. fancies led WHITTIER. c. Used to denote a garden walk or pavement of irregular pieces of flat stone or tile 1923.

Comb.: **c. bone** (*U.S.*), the funny-bone, 'so called on account of the intense pain produced when it receives a blow' (Webster); **c. quilt** (*U.S.*), a patchwork quilt made in fantastic patterns or without any plan.

Hence **Cra·zily** *adv.* **Cra·ziness.**

‖**Creagh, creach** (kreχ), *sb.* 1814. [a. Gael. and Ir. *creach* plunder.] 1. A foray. 2. Booty, prey 1818. Hence **Creagh** *v.* to raid, plunder.

‖**Creaght** (kreχt, krēⁱt), *sb.* 1596. [a. mid.Ir. *caeraigheacht*, f. *caera* sheep.] *Ir. Hist.* A nomadic herd of cattle. (The word often includes the herdsmen.) Also *transf.* Hence **Creaght** *v.* to take cattle about to graze.

Creak (krīk), *v.* ME. [App. echoic.] †1. *intr.* To utter a harsh cry; to CROAK -1669. 2. *intr.* To make a CREAK 1583. Also *transf.* of the noise of crickets, etc. †3. *intr.* To speak in a strident or querulous tone -1661. 4. *trans.* To cause to make a creak 1601.

1. The Henne, the Goose, the Ducke, Might cackle, creake, and quacke 1604. 2. No swinging signboard creaked from cottage elm WORDSW. Where crickets c. BROWNING. 4. Creeking my shooes on the plaine Masonry *All's Well* II. i. 31.

Creak (krīk), *sb.* 1605. [f. CREAK *v.*] A strident noise, as of an ungreased hinge, new boots, etc.; a harsh squeak.

Creaky (krī·ki), *a.* 1834. [f. prec. sb. or v. +-Y.] Apt to creak; crazy

Cream, creme, *sb.*[1] *Hist.* [ME. *creme*, a. OF. *cresme* :—L. *chrisma*; see CHRISM, now the accepted form.] = CHRISM.

Cream (krīm), *sb.*[2] [ME. *creme*, a. F. *crème*, a pop. application of prec.] **1.** The oily or butyraceous part of milk, which gathers on the top when the milk is left undisturbed; by churning it is converted into butter. **2.** *transf.* A fancy dish or sweet made with cream, or so as to resemble cream ME. **b.** A head of scum, froth, etc. 1669. **c.** A cream-like preparation used cosmetically 1765. **3.** *fig.* The most excellent element or part; the quintessence 1581. **4.** *attrib.* Cream-coloured 1861; *ellipt.* cream colour; also, a cream-coloured horse, etc. 1788.

1. *Clotted* or *clouted c.*: see CLOUTED. 2. b. The c. of your champagne BYRON. c. In vain she tries her paste and creams To smooth her face or hide its seams GOLDSM. 3. The c. of the correspondence GOLDSM., of wild-fowl shooting 1890.

C. of tartar: the purified and crystallized bitartrate of potassium, used in medicine and for technical purposes. *C. of lime*: pure slaked lime.

Comb.: **c.-cake**, a cake filled with a custard made of c., eggs, etc.; **-cups**, a papaveraceous plant, *Platystemon californicus*, with c.-coloured flowers; **-faced** *a.*, having a face of the colour of c. (from fear); **-fruit**, the juicy c.-like fruit of a plant found in Sierra Leone; **-laid** *a.*, applied to laid paper of a c. colour; **-nut** = *Brazil nut*; **-separator**, a machine for separating the c. from milk; **-slice**, a knife-like instrument for skimming milk, or for serving frozen c.; **-ware**, c.-coloured pottery ware; **-wove**, wove paper of c. colour.

Cream (krīm), *v.* ME. [f. CREAM *sb.*[2]] **1.** *intr.* Of milk: To form cream 1596; *trans.* to cause to form cream 1883. **2.** *intr.* Of other liquids: To form a scum on the top; to mantle, foam, froth ME. **3.** *trans.* To skim the cream from 1727. **4.** To separate as cream; *fig.* to take the choicest part of. Const. *off.* 1615. **5.** To add cream to tea, etc. 1834.

2. A sort of men, whose visages Do creame and mantle like a standing pond *Merch. V*, I. i. 89. 4. Such a man, truly wise, creams off nature leaving the sour and the dregs, for philosophy and reason to lap up SWIFT. Hence **Creamed** *ppl. a.* having the cream formed or separated; made or flavoured with cream. **Crea·mer**, a flat dish for skimming the cream off milk; a machine for separating cream.

Cream-cheese. 1583. A soft, rich kind of cheese, made of unskimmed milk with added cream; a cheese of this kind. Also *fig.*

Creamery (krī·mĕri). 1879. [prob. ad. F. *crèmerie*.] **1.** A butter-factory (often worked on the joint-stock principle). Also *attrib.* **2.** A shop where milk, cream, butter, and light refreshments are supplied.

Creamometer (krīmǫ·mĭtəɹ). 1876. [after *lactometer*.] An instrument for measuring the percentage of cream in a sample of milk.

Creamy (krī·mi), *a.* 1610. [f. CREAM *sb.*[2] + -Y[1].] **1.** Containing or abounding in cream 1618. **2.** Resembling cream; *fig.* soft and rich 1610.

1. The milk was c. 1861. 2. The..tender curving lines of c. spray TENNYSON. The thickest and creamiest paper VERN. LEE. *fig.* A woman with a c. voice O. W. HOLMES. Hence **Crea·miness.**

Creance (krī·ăns), *sb.* [ME., a. OF. *creance*, f. *creant* pr. pple. of *creire* :—L. *credere*. Cf. CREDENCE.] †**1.** Belief -1490; the thing believed; (one's) faith -1669. †**2.** *Comm.* Credit -1496. **3.** *Falconry.* A long fine cord attached to a hawk's leash, to keep it from flying away when being trained ME. †**b.** Occas. spelt *cranes*, as if pl. -1685.

†**Creance**, *v.* [a. OF. *creancer* to promise, etc.; see above.] *intr.* To pledge oneself to pay; to take credit. CHAUCER. So †**Creancer**, a creditor; a guardian, tutor.

†**Creant**, *a.*[1] ME. [? abbrev. f. OF. *recreant*. Cf. CRAVEN.] In phrases *To yield oneself c.*, *to cry* (or *say*) *c.*: To acknowledge oneself vanquished -1480.

Creant (krī·ănt), *a.*[2] *rare.* [ad. L. *creantem*, f. *creare*.] Creating, creative. MRS. BROWNING.

†**Crease**, *sb.*[1] ME. [f. CREASE *v.*[1]] = INCREASE *sb.* -1575.

Crease (krīs), *sb.*[2] 1578. [?] **1.** The mark produced on the surface of anything by folding; a fold, wrinkle, ridge. **2.** *Cricket.* The name of certain lines marked on the ground to define the positions of the bowler and batsmen 1755. **3.** *Archit.* A curved or ridge tile (app. error for CREST, q. v.) 1703.

2. *Bowling-c.*: a line drawn in the line of each wicket, from behind which the bowler delivers the ball. *Return-c.*: a short line at each end of the bowling-c., and at right angles to it, beyond which the bowler must not go. *Popping-c.* a line in front of each wicket, parallel to the bowling-c., behind which the batsman stands to defend his wicket. Hence **Crea·sy** *a.* full of creases.

Crease, *sb.*[3]; see CREESE.

†**Crease**, *v.*[1] ME. [app. aphet. f. *acrese*, ACCREASE.] = INCREASE *v.* -1547.

Crease (krīs), *v.*[2] 1588. [See CREASE *sb.*[2]] **1.** *trans.* To make a crease or creases in or on the surface of, as by folding, etc. **2.** *intr.* To become creased (*mod.*). **3.** *trans.* To stun (a horse, etc.) by a shot in the crest or ridge of the neck (*U.S.*) 1807.

1. A leafe of paper..cressed in the middes 1588. 2. A material that is apt to c. (*mod.*).

Creaser (krī·səɹ). [f. prec. + -ER[1].] One who or that which creases; *spec.* any contrivance for making creases or furrows in iron or leather, for creasing the cloth in a sewing-machine, etc.

Creasote, var. of CREOSOTE.

†‖**Cre·at.** 1730. [F. *créat*, ad. It. *creato* alumnus :—L. *creatus*.] An usher to a riding-master.

†**Crea·te**, *ppl. a.* ME. [ad. L. *creatus*.] Created -1590.

Statutez..That creat were eternally to dure CHAUCER.

Create (kri,ē·t), *v.* ME. [f. L. *creat-* ppl. stem of *creare*.] **1.** *trans.* Said of God: To bring into being, cause to exist; *esp.* 'to form out of nothing' (J.). Also *absol.* **2.** *gen.* To make, form, constitute, or bring into legal existence 1592. Also *absol.* **b.** Of an actor: To be the first to represent (a rôle) and so to shape it. [F. *créer un rôle*.] 1882. **3.** To invest with rank, title, etc 1460. **4.** To constitute; cause, produce, give rise to (a condition, etc.) 1599.

1. In the beginning God created the heaven and the earth *Gen.* i. 1. C. in mee a cleane heart, O God *Ps.* li. 10. 2. To c. a fee simple CRUISE, wealth MACAULAY. 3. I c. you Companions to our person *Cymb.* V. v. 20. 4. 'Tis only fit to c. Mirth HEARNE.

Creatic (kri,æ·tik), *a.* Also **kr-**. 1891. [f. Gr. κρέας, *κρεατ- + -IC.] Of or pertaining to flesh.

Creatine (krī·ătəin). Also **kr-**. 1840. [f. as prec. + -INE.] *Chem.* An organic base, $C_4H_9N_3O_2$, discovered in 1835 by Chevreul in the juice of flesh.

Creatinine (kri,æ·tinəin). Also **kr-**. 1851. [f. prec. + -INE.] An alkaline crystallizable substance, $C_4H_7N_3O$, a normal constituent of urine and of the juice of muscular flesh.

Creation (kri,ē·ʃən). ME. [a. F., or ad. L. *creationem*.] **1.** The action of creating (see CREATE *v.*); the fact of being created; *absol.* the calling into existence of the world; the beginning, as a date 1593. **2.** *gen.* The action of making, forming, producing, or bringing into existence 1602. **3.** The investing with a title, dignity, or function 1460. **4.** *concr.* That which God has created; the world; creatures collectively 1611. **5.** An original production of human intelligence or power 1605.

1. We can think of c. only as a change in the condition of that which already exists MANSEL. *absol.* From the c. to the general doom SHAKS. *Lucr.* 924. 2. The c. of estates tail BLACKSTONE. 4. *Lord of c.* = man: see LORD. For wee know that the whole c. groaneth *Rom.* viii. 22. 5. Or art thou but A Dagger of the Minde, a false C. *Macb.* II. i. 38. A c. of the ballad-muse 1888. Hence **Crea·tional** *a.* of or pertaining to c. (*rare*).

Creationism (kri,ē·ʃəniz'm). 1847. [f. prec. + -ISM.] A system or theory of creation: *spec.* **a.** The theory that God immediately creates a soul for every human being born (opp. to *traducianism*); **b.** The theory which attributes the origin of matter, species, etc., to special creation (opp. to *evolutionism*). So **Crea·tionist, -ism.**

Creative (kri,ē·tiv), *a.* 1678. [f. CREATE *v.* + -IVE.] **1.** Having the quality of creating; of or pertaining to creation; originative. **2.** Productive *of* 1803.

1. Heav'n's c. hand SHENSTONE. Hence **Crea·tive-ly** *adv.*, **-ness.**

Creator (kri,ē·təɹ). [ME. and AF. *creatour*, *-ur*, ad. L. *creatorem*.] **1.** The Supreme Being who creates all things. **2.** *gen.* One who, or that which, creates or gives origin to 1579.

1. The creatour of euery creature CHAUCER. 2. Since it thus appears that custom was the c. of prelaty MILT. Hence **Crea·torship. Crea·tress**, a female c.; var. ‖**Crea·trix.**

Creature (krī·tiŭɹ, krī·tʃəɹ). ME. [a. F., ad. L. *creatura* thing created.] **1.** Anything created; a created being, animate or inanimate. †**b.** Creation -1611. **c.** Anything that ministers to man's comfort 1614. **d.** *joc.* Strong drink; *esp.* whisky 1638. **2.** An animal; often as distinct from 'man' ME. In *U.S.*, used *esp.* of cattle. **3.** A human being; often in reprobation; also with qualifications expressing admiration, affection, compassion, etc. ME. **4.** *fig.* A result, product, or offspring *of* anything 1651. **5.** One who owes his position to another; one who is actuated by the will of another; an instrument or puppet. [So F.] 1587.

1. These thy gyftes and creatures of bread and wyne *Bk. Com. Prayer.* b. *Rom.* viii. 19. c. Waste of the good creatures of God (cf. 1 *Tim.* IV. 4) 1658. 2. 'Go, from the creatures thy instructions take' POPE. 3. There is no C. loues me *Rich. III*, V. iii. 200. The creatures who govern at Cadiz WELLINGTON. The world hath not a sweeter C. *Oth.* IV. i. 194. 4. Creatures of the fancy HOBBES. 5. Sir Francis Windebank..was a c. of Laud's HUME. *Comb.* **c.-comforts**, material comforts (food, clothing, etc.).

Hence **Crea·tural** *a.* pertaining to creatures; of the nature of a c. **Crea·turehood**, the condition of a c. **Crea·tureless** *a.* (*rare*). **Crea·turely** *a.* of or belonging to creatures; of the nature of a c.; hence **Crea·tureliness. Crea·tureship**, the condition of a c. †**Crea·turize** *v.* to invest with creaturehood.

Creaze (*Mining*); see CRAZE *sb.* 3.

Crebri- (krī·bri), comb. f. L. *creber* closely-placed, as in **Crebrico·state** *a.* [L. *costa*], having closely-set ribs or ridges; **Crebrisu·lcate** *a.* [L. *sulcus*], having closely-set furrows.

Crebrity (krī·briti). *rare.* 1656. [ad. L. *crebritas*.] Frequency.

‖**Crèche** (krēʃ), *sb.* 1882. [F., a. (ult.) OHG. *kripja*, *krippa* CRIB. Cf. CRATCH *sb.*[1]] A public nursery for infants, where they are taken care of while their mothers are at work, etc.

Credence (krī·dĕns), *sb.* ME. [a. F., or ad. med.L. *credentia*, f. *credere*.] **1.** The mental action of accepting as true; belief. †**2.** Faith, confidence *in*, reliance *on* (a person or authority) -1548. †**3.** Trustworthiness, credit, repute -1822. **4.** Credentials; *transf.* the message entrusted to a messenger or embassy. *Obs.* exc. in *letter of c.* ME. †**5.** The tasting or assaying of meats as a precaution against poisoning -1460. †**6.** A side table or sideboard on which dishes, etc. were placed ready to be served at table -1834. **7.** *Eccl.* In R.C. and Anglican churches: A small side table or shelf to hold the eucharistic elements before consecration 1841.

1. Instructions, to which it seems c. was to be given BURKE. 4. *Letter of c.*: a letter of recommendation or introduction. Hence †**Cre·dence** *v.* to give c. to.

‖**Credenda** (kride·ndă), *sb. pl.* 1638. [L.] Things to be believed; matters of faith. (Opp. to *agenda*.)

Is the power of selecting the c. of the nation to be vested in the civil magistrate MIALL.

Credent (krī·dĕnt), *a. rare.* 1602. **1.** Believing, trustful. †**2.** Having credit or repute *Meas. for M.* IV. iv. 29; credible *Wint. T.* I. ii. 142. Hence **Cre·dently.**

Credential (krĭde·nʃăl). 1524. [f. med.L. *credentia* + -AL.]

A. *adj.* Recommending or entitling to credit or confidence, as in phr. †*c. letters.*

B. *sb.* (Usu. in *pl.*) Letters or written warrants recommending or entitling the bearer to credit or confidence; *esp.* a letter of recommendation or introduction given by a government to an ambassador or envoy 1674. Also *transf.* and *fig.*

We will not take a Footman without Credentials from his last Master STEELE. *fig.* There stands The legate of the skies! His theme divine, His office sacred, his credentials clear COWPER.

Credibility (kredĭbi·lĭti). 1594. [ad. med.L. *credibilitas*; cf. F. *crédibilité*.] The quality of being credible; a case of this.

Christianity..rests on the c. of the Gospel history FROUDE.

Credible (kre·dĭb'l), *a.* ME. [ad. L. *credibilis*, f. *credere*.] **1.** Capable of being believed. **2.** Worthy of belief or confidence; trustworthy ME. †**3.** Ready to believe -1675. †**4.** Reputable -1712.

1. Things are made c. either by the known condition

and quality of the utterer, or by the manifest likelihood of truth which they have in themselves HOOKER. 2. Nay tis most c. *All's Well* I. ii. 4. Observations from c. Authors 1671. Hence **Cre·dibleness. Cre·dibly** *adv.*

Credit (kre·dit), *sb.* 1542. [a. F. *crédit*, ad. It. *credito*, ad. L. *creditus*, *-um*, pa. pple. of *credere*.] 1. Belief, confidence, faith, trust. †2. Trustworthiness, credibility –1847; authority –1757. †3. Something believed. *Twel. N.* IV. iii. 6. †4. Trust, charge –1651. 5. The estimate in which the character of a person (or thing) is held; reputation, repute 1576. 6. Influence based on the confidence of others 1549. 7. The commendation bestowed on account of an action, quality, etc. 1607. 8. A source of commendation. (Now only with *a* and *to*.) 1586. 9. *Comm.* a. Confidence in a buyer's ability and intention to pay at some future time, for goods, etc. entrusted to him without present payment 1542. b. Reputation of solvency and probity in business, entitling a person or body to be trusted 1573. 10. A sum placed at a person's disposal in the books of a bank, etc.; any note, bill, etc., on security of which a person may obtain funds 1662. 11. *Parliament.* A sum on account, voted by Parliament in anticipation of the Annual Estimates. Hence *Vote of c.* 1854. 12. *Book-keeping.* The acknowledgement of payment by entry in an account. (with *pl.*) A sum entered on the credit side of an account; this side itself (abbrev. *Cr.*) 1745.

1. Charges like these may seem to deserve some c. GIBBON. 2. On the c. of an excellent witness FULLER. †*Letter of c.* = *letter of credence.* 5. John Gilpin was a citizen of c. and renown COWPER. 6. Buckingham..resolved to employ all his c. in order to prevent the marriage HUME. 7. The c. of inventing coined money 1876. 8. He..may be a Credit to the College HEARNE. 9. a. C. being..the Expectation of Money within some limited Time LOCKE. Phr. *To give c.*; *on* (*upon*) *c.*; *long c.*, i.e. c. for a long time; *six months' c.*, etc. b. Try what my c. can in Venice doe *Merch. V.* I. i. 180. 10. A letter..with a c. for the money DE FOE. *Letter* (*bill*) *of c.*: a letter or document granted by a bank, etc., authorizing a person named therein to draw money to a specified amount from their correspondents in other places.

Credit (kre·dit), *v.* 1541. [f. CREDIT *sb.*, or L. *credit-* ppl. stem of *credere*.] 1. *trans.* To give credit to, put faith in, believe, trust 1548. †2. *trans.* To entrust –1748. †3. To trust (a person) with goods or money on credit –1754. †4. To accredit –1664. 5. To bring into credit; to do credit to (*arch.*) 1596. 6. *Book-keeping.* To enter on the credit side of an account 1682. 7. *fig. To c.* (something) *to* a person, or a person *with* something: to ascribe it to him 1850.

1. Credite not those..that talke that and this 1567. 5. That my actions might c. my profession MABBE. 7. To c. him with a desire to reform the Church FROUDE.

Creditable (kre·dităb'l), *a.* 1526. [f. CREDIT *v.* and *sb.* + -ABLE.] †1. Worthy to be believed –1808; in *Comm.*, having good credit –1822. 2. That brings credit or honour; reputable 1659; †respectable, decent –1860.

1. Persons, sufficiently c., and perfectly informed 1669. The c. traders of any country ADAM SMITH. 2. Clive made a c. use of his riches MACAULAY. Hence **Cre·ditableness. Cre·ditably** *adv.*

Creditor (kre·ditəɹ). ME. [In 15th c. *creditour*, a. AF.] 1. One who gives credit for money or goods; one to whom a debt is owing; correl. to *debtor* 1447. Also *fig.* 2. *Book-keeping. Creditor* (or *Cr.*): applied to the right-hand or credit side of any account, or to what is entered there 1543. Also *attrib.* †3. One who becomes surety for –1523. †4. One who believes 1597.

1. Now unthriftes..byd their creditors go whistle MORE. 2. *attrib.* Cast up the Dr. and Cr. Sides of your Balance 1806. 4. The easie creditours of novelties DANIEL. Hence **Cre·ditress, †-rice, -rix** (? *Obs.*), a female c.

‖**Credo** (krī·do). ME. [L.; = I believe.] 1. The first word of the Apostles' and Nicene creeds, in Latin; hence, either of these Creeds; now *esp.* the name of a musical setting of the Nicene Creed. 2. *gen.* A creed 1587.

Credulity (krĭdiū·lĭti). ME. [ad. L. *credulitas*, f. *credulus*.] †1. Belief, faith, credence; readiness to believe –1794. 2. Readiness to believe on weak or insufficient grounds 1547.

2. A humbug, living on the c. of the people DICKENS.

Credulous (kre·diŭləs), *a.* 1576. [f. L. *credulus* + -OUS.] 1. Disposed to believe. (Now *rare* exc. as in 2.) 1579. 2. Apt to believe on weak or insufficient grounds 1576. *transf.* Of things: Arising from credulity 1648; †believed too readily 1625.

2. Thus c. Fooles are caught *Oth.* IV. i. 46. Hence **Cre·dulously** *adv.* **Cre·dulousness**, credulity.

Cree (krī), *v.* Chiefly *dial.* 1620. [orig. *creve*, a. F. *crever* to burst.] 1. To soften by boiling (*trans.* and *intr.*). 2. *trans.* To pound into a soft mass 1822. Hence **Creed** *ppl. a.*

Creed (krīd), *sb.* [OE. *créda*, ad. L. *credo*; see CREDO.] 1. A brief summary of Christian doctrine. (*The C.* usually = the Apostles' Creed.) More generally: A confession of faith. 1676. 2. A professed system of religious belief 1573; *transf.* a set of opinions on any subject 1613.

1. The thre credes the whyche our moder holy chirche syngeth CAXTON. 2. Every man is better and worse than his c. KINGSLEY. *transf.* The cynical c. of the market EMERSON. So †**Creed** *v. trans.* (also *absol.*) to believe. Hence **Cree·dal, cre·dal** *a.* pertaining to a c. **Cree·dless** *a.* **Cree·dlessness. Cree·dsman**, an adherent of a c. or of the same c. (*rare*).

Creek (krīk), *sb.* [ME. *crike*, *cryke* (ī); also *creke* (whence *creek*), and (since 16th c.) *crick*. Prob. Germanic. Cf. F. *crique*, Du. *kreke*, later *kreek*, and med. (Anglo) L. *creca* (sometimes *crecca*) creek.] 1. A narrow recess or inlet in the coast-line of the sea, or the tidal estuary of a river; a small port or harbour; an inlet within the limits of a haven or port. Also *transf.* 2. In U.S. and British colonies: A branch of a main river, a tributary river; a small stream, or run 1674. †3. A cleft in the face of a rock, etc. –1635. 4. A narrow or winding passage; an out-of-the-way corner. Also *fig.* 1573. †5. A turn, a winding. Also *fig.* –1680.

1. He knew..euery cryke in Britaigne and in Spayne CHAUCER. *transf.* Certain Creeks or corners of Land running into the up-lands BLITHE. 4. A Labyrinth is a place made full of turnings and creekes 1582. They explore Each c. and cranny of his chamber GRAY. Hence **Cree·kward** *a.* towards a c. **Cree·ky** *a.* full of creeks.

†**Creek**, *v.* 1538. [f. prec. sb.] To run (*up*) as a creek; to bend, turn, wind –1610.

Creel (krīl), *sb.*[1] ME. [?] 1. A large wicker basket; now *esp.* a basket used for the transport of fish, and borne upon the back. Hence, An angler's fishing-basket. 1842. 2. A trap of wickerwork for catching fish, lobsters, etc. 1457.

Phr. *To coup the creels* (Sc.): to cause or sustain an upset; in various *fig.* applications. *In a c.* (Sc.): in a state of temporary aberration.

Creel (krīl), *sb.*[2] 1788. [? same word as prec.] 1. A framework, varying in form and use. 2. *Spinning.* A frame for holding the paying-off bobbins in the process of converting roving into yarn, etc. Hence **Cree·ler**, one who attends to a c.

Creep (krīp), *v.* Pa.t. and pple. **crept** (krept). [Com. Teut.: OE. *créopan* :—OTeut. **kreupan*.] 1. To move with the body prone and close to the ground, as a reptile, an insect, a quadruped moving stealthily, etc. (Cf. CRAWL *v.*) OE. 2. To move softly, cautiously, timorously, or slowly; to move quietly and stealthily; to steal (*into*, *away*, etc.) ME. 3. *fig.* (of persons and things). a. To come on slowly, stealthily, or by degrees; to steal insensibly *upon* or *over* ME. b. To move timidly or diffidently; to cringe; to move on a low level 1581. 4. Of plants: To grow extending along the ground, a wall, etc., and throwing out roots or claspers at intervals 1530. Also *fig.* 5. *trans.* = *c. along* or *over* (*rare*) 1667. 6. *intr.* To have a sensation as of things creeping over the skin; to be affected with a shiver ME. 7. *Naut.* To drag in deep water with a creeper 1813. 8. Of metal rails, etc.: To move gradually forward under pressure, or as the result of expansion and contraction on a gradient 1885.

1. [There] the slow-worm creeps TENNYSON. Children must learne to creepe ere they can go 1562. 2. The whining Schoole-boy..creeping like snaile Vnwillingly to schoole *A. Y. L.* II. vii. 146. The mists crept upward WHITTIER. 3. a. Despondency began to c. over their hearts W. IRVING. b. Where men of judgment c. and feel their way COWPER. 4. The Ivy green, That creepeth o'er ruins old DICKENS. 6. You make..my flesh c. DICKENS.

Creep (krīp), *sb.* 1486. [f. the vb.] 1. The action of creeping (*lit.* and *fig.*). 2. A sensation as of creeping things on one's body. Usu. in *pl.* (colloq.). 1862. 3. *Coal-mining.* The slow rising up of the floor of a gallery owing to pressure upon the pillars. 'Also any slow movement of mining ground' (Raymond). 4. A small arch or other opening for an animal to creep through 1875.

4. A c. for cattle, on the Wigtown Railway 1875. *Comb.* **c.-hole**, a hole by which one creeps in and out; 'a hole into which any animal may creep to escape danger' (J.). Also *fig.* (cf. *loop-hole*).

Creeper (krī·pəɹ). OE. [f. CREEP *v.* + -ER[1].] 1. One who creeps. 2. An animal that creeps; a creeping thing 1577. 3. A name for many small birds; *esp.* the common Brown Creeper or Tree-creeper, *Certhia familiaris* 1661. 4. A plant that creeps along the ground, or (more usually) one that climbs trees, walls, etc., as ivy and the Virginian Creeper (*Ampelopsis hederacea*) 1626. b. *pl. Archit.* Crockets (see CROCKET[1] 2) 1864. 5. A kind of grapnel used for dragging the bottom of the sea or other body of water ME. †6. A small iron dog, of which a pair were placed between the andirons –1833. 7. *local.* a. A kind of patten or clog. b. A piece of iron with spikes, worn under the feet to prevent slipping on ice, etc. 8. An apparatus for conveying grain in corn-mills. b. An endless moving feeding-apron, in a carding-machine. 9. A small iron frying-pan with three legs; a *spider.* (*U.S. local.*) 1880.

4. The c., mellowing for an autumn blush KEATS.

Creepie (krī·pi). *Sc.* and *dial.* 1661. [f. CREEP *v.*] 1. A low stool. 2. A small speckled fowl. (*U.S. local.*)

Creeping (krī·piŋ), *vbl. sb.* (and *ppl. a.*) OE. [-ING[1].] 1. The action of the verb CREEP. 2. The sensation as of something creeping on the skin; cf. FORMICATION 1799. 3. In Canada: Stalking the Moose-deer, etc. 1869. *Comb.*: **c.-hole** = *creep-hole*; **-sheet**, the feeding-apron of a carding-machine. Hence **Cree·pingly** *adv.*

Creepy (krī·pi), *a.* 1794. [f. CREEP *v.* or *sb.* + -Y.] 1. Characterized by creeping. 2. Having a creeping of the flesh, caused by horror or repugnance 1831; *transf.* tending to produce such sensations 1883. Also **C.-crawly** 1861.

2. *transf.* A..romance of the c. order 1892.

Creese, crease (krīs), **kris** (kris), *sb.* 1577. [a. Malay *kirīs*, *krīs*, *kres*.] A Malay dagger, with a blade of a wavy form.

Which dagger they [of Java] call a Crise, and is as sharpe as a razor 1586. Hence **Creese, crease, kris** *v.* to stab with a c.

Creesh, creish (krīʃ), *sb. Sc.* ME. [a. OF. *craisse* = *graisse* :—L. *crassa* thick, fat. Cf. GREASE.] 1. Grease, fat. 2. A 'lick', a stroke 1774. Hence **Creesh** *v.* to grease. **Cree·shy** *a.* greasy.

‖**Crémaillère** (kremalyēr). 1828. [Fr.; perh. f. Du. *kram* hook.] *Field-fortif.* An indented or zigzag form of the inside line of a parapet.

Cremaster (krĭmæ·stəɹ). Pl. **-ers**, also ‖**-eres**. 1678. [a. Gr. κρεμαστήρ, f. κρεμα- to hang.] 1. *Anat.* The muscle of the spermatic cord, by which the testicle is suspended. 2. *Entom.* The dorsal process or tip of the abdomen of the pupa of any insect that undergoes complete transformation. Hence †**Crema·steral, cremaste·ric** *a.* of or pertaining to the c.

Cremate (krĭmēⁱ·t), *v.* 1874. [f. L. *cremat-*, ppl. stem.] To consume by fire, to burn; *spec.* to reduce (a corpse) to ashes.

Satt, or a woman who is cremated with her husband 1874.

Cremation (krĭmēⁱ·ʃən). 1623. [ad. L. *cremationem*; see prec.] The action of cremating; *spec.* the reduction of a corpse to ashes in lieu of interment.

When c. was abandoned for inhumation D. WILSON. Hence **Crema·tionist.**

Cremator (krĭmēⁱ·təɹ). 1877. [a. L.] One who, or that which, cremates.

Crematory (kre·mătəri). 1876. [f. L. type **crematorius*; see above.] *adj.* Of or pertaining to cremation 1844. *sb.* A place for cremation; *spec.* an erection for the incineration of corpses; var. **Cremato·rium.** Hence **Cremato·rial** *a.*

Cremocarp (kre·mokāɹp). 1866. [irreg. f. Gr. κρεμα- to hang + καρπός.] *Bot.* A species of fructification, in which the fruit breaks up into two indehiscent one-seeded mericarps, which hang by their summits from the central axis.

Cremona[1] (krǐmōᵘ·nă). 1762. *attrib.* Pertaining to or made at Cremona, a town in Lombardy, as in *C. fiddle, school*; *absol.* A violin made there. Hence **Cremone·se** *a.*

'A Cremona', or 'a Cremonese violin' is often incorrectly used for an old Italian instrument of any make P. DAVID.

Cremo·na[2]. 1660. [Corrupt f. KRUMMHORN, CROMORNE.] An organ reed-stop of 8-foot tone.

‖**Cremor.** 1657. [a. L. (? related to *cremare*).] A thick juice or decoction. **b.** By erron. association with F. *crème*, CREAM *sb.*[2], a scum gathering on the top of a liquid.

Cremosin, -oysin, etc., obs. ff. CRIMSON.

‖**Crena** (krī·nă). [mod.L. *crena* incision, notch; cf. OIt. *crena*, OF. *crene, crenne*.] **1.** An indentation, a notch; *spec.* in *Bot.* one of the notches on a crenated leaf; *Anat.* the groove between the buttocks. **2.** A crenated tooth, a scallop; *spec.* in *Bot.* = CRENATURE, CRENEL; *Anat.* each of the serrations on the cranial bones by which these fit together in the sutures.

Crenate (krī·neᶦt), *sb.* 1838. [f. CREN-IC.] *Chem.* A salt of crenic acid. So **Cre·nated** *a.*

Crenate (krī·nēt), *a.* 1794. [ad. mod.L. *crenatus*, f. CRENA.] *Bot., Zool.*, etc. Having the edge notched or toothed with rounded teeth; finely scalloped. Hence **Cre·nated** *ppl.a.* (in same sense). **Crena·tion,** a crenated formation; a crenature.

Crenato- (krĭnē·to), comb. f. mod.L. *crenatus* CRENATE; crenately, crenate-.

Crenature (kre·nătiŭr, krī·n-). 1816. [f. mod.L. *crenatus*.] *Bot.* and *Zool.* A rounded tooth or denticulation on the margin of a leaf, etc. Also occas. the notches between the teeth.

Crenel, crenelle (kre·nĕl, krĭne·l), *sb.* 1481. [a. OF. *crenel*, app. dim. of *cren, cran* notch; cf. CRANNY.] **1.** One of the indentations of an embattled parapet; an embrasure; see BATTLEMENT. In *pl.* = Battlements, embattled parapet. **2.** *Bot.* = CRENATURE 1835. Hence **Cre·nel** *v.* to crenellate (*rare*). **Cre·nelet,** a small c. (*rare*).

Crenellate, -elate (kre·neleᶦt), *v.* 1823. [f. F. *créneler*.] To furnish with battlements; to furnish with embrasures or loopholes. Hence **Crenella·tion, -elation,** the action of crenellating or condition of being crenellated; a battlement; a notch or indentation.

†‖**Crenellé, -elee,** *a.* 1586. [a. F. *crénelé*.] *Her.* EMBATTLED -1610.

Crengle, obs. f. CRINGLE.

Crenic (krī·nik), *a.* 1839. [f. Gr. κρήνη spring + -IC.] *Chem.* In *C. acid*, an organic acid, existing in humus, and in deposits of ferruginous waters.

Crenulate (kre·niulēt), *a.* 1794. [ad. mod.L. *crenulatus*, dim. of *crenula*, dim. of *crena* (see CRENA).] *Zool.* and *Bot.* Minutely crenate; finely notched or scalloped: said of a leaf, a shell, etc. Hence **Crenula·tion,** a minute crenation.

Creole (krī·oᵘl). 1604. [a. F. *créole*, ad. Sp. *criollo*, native to the locality, 'country'; said to be short for **criadillo*, dim. of *criado*, f. *criar* to breed, etc. :—L. *creare*.]

A. *sb.* In the West Indies and other parts of America, Mauritius, etc.: *orig.* A person born and naturalized in the country, but of European or of African Negro race: the name having no connotation of colour.

a. But now, usually, = *creole white* 1604. **b.** Now, less usually = *creole negro*, as dist. from one freshly imported from Africa 1748.

a. [She] was a c.—that is, born in the West Indies, of French parents MARRYAT. **b.** The term 'Creole' is confined to negroes born in the country BATES.

B. *attrib.* or *adj.* **1.** Of persons: Born and naturalized in the West Indies, etc., but of European (or negro) descent; see A. 1748. Of animals and plants: Born or grown in the West Indies, etc., but not indigenous 1760. **2.** Belonging to or characteristic of a Creole 1828.

1. Fruits..of the C. kind, being European fruits planted there, but which have undergone considerable alterations from the climate *Juan and Ulloa's Voy.*

Hence **Creo·lian,** †*sb.* = CREOLE A.; *adj.* = CREOLE B. ? *Obs.* †**Cre·olism,** Creole descent.

Creophagous (kriˌǫ·fagəs), *a.* Also **kreo-.** 1881. [f. Gr. κρεοφάγος + -OUS.] Flesh-eating; carnivorous.

Creosol (krī·ŏsǫl). Also **crea-.** 1863. [f. CREOS(OTE) + -OL.] *Chem.* A colourless highly refracting liquid ($C_8H_{10}O_2$) with aromatic odour and burning taste, forming the chief constituent of creosote.

Creosote (krī·ŏsōᵘt), *sb.* Also **crea-, kreo-.** 1835. [f. Gr. κρεο-, comb. f. κρέας + σώζειν, and intended to mean 'flesh-saving'.] A colourless oily liquid, with odour like that of smoked meat, and burning taste, obtained from the distillation of wood-tar, and having powerful antiseptic properties. Also *attrib.* **b.** Occas. applied to Carbolic Acid, also known as *coal-tar c.* 1863. *Comb.* **c.-bush, -plant,** a Mexican shrub (*Larrea mexicana*, N.O. *Zygophyllaceæ*) having a strong smell of c. Hence **Cre·osote** *v.* to treat with c., as a preservative.

Crepance. ? *Obs.* 1610. [In 17th c. *crepanches, crepances*, ad. It. *crepacci* pl. :—(ult.) L. *crepare* to crack, chap.] *Farriery.* A wound or chap on a horse's foot. [Misprinted *Crepane* by Johnson and later Dicts.]

‖**Crêpe** (krēp). 1825. [F. :—L. *crispa* curled.] The French word for CRAPE, often borrowed as a term for all crapy fabrics other than black mourning crape.

Crêpe de Chine, a white or coloured crape made of raw silk. *Crêpe lisse*, crape which is not *crêpé* or wrinkled. Also *attrib.* Hence **Crêpe** *v.* to frizz.

†**Crepine, crespin(e.** 1532. [a. OF. *crespine*, f *crespe, crêpe*; see CRÊPE, CRAPE.] A net or caul for the hair, formerly worn by ladies; also, a part of a hood; a fringe of lace or network for a dais, bed, etc. -1721.

‖**Crepita·culum.** [L.] *Zool.* The rattle of the rattlesnake. *U.S.*

Crepitant (kre·pitănt), *a.* 1826. [ad. L. *crepitantem*.] **1.** Making a crackling noise; crepitating 1855. **2.** *Entom.* That crepitates (see CREPITATE 2).

Crepitate (kre·piteᶦt), *v.* 1623. [f. L. *crepitat-*, ppl. stem of *crepitare*, freq. of *crepare* to crack.] †**1.** To break wind -1768. **2.** *Entom.* Of certain beetles: To eject a pungent fluid suddenly with a sharp report 1826. **3.** To make a crackling sound: *spec.* of the tissue of the lungs 1853. **4.** To rattle.

Crepitation (krepitēᶦ·ʃən). 1656. [f. L. *crepitare*; see prec. and -ATION.] **1.** A crackling noise; crackling. **2.** *Med.* and *Path.* The slight sound and accompanying sensation caused by pressure on cellular tissue containing air, or by the entrance of air into inflamed lungs; or observed in the grating together of the ends of fractured bones; the crackling noise sometimes observed in gangrenous parts when examined with the fingers; the cracking of a joint when pulled. **3.** The breaking of wind (*rare*) 1822.

‖**Crepitus** (kre·pitŏs). 1807. [L., f. *crepare*.] **1.** *Med.* and *Path.* = CREPITATION 2. **2.** = CREPITATION 3. 1882. Hence **Cre·pitous** *a.* of the nature of, or such as to produce, c.

‖**Crépon** (kre·poṅ, kre·pən). 1887. [F. :—*crêpe* CRAPE.] A stuff resembling crape, made of fine worsted, silk, or worsted and silk.

Crept (krept). 1628. Pa. pple. of CREEP *v.*; *spec.* in *Coal-mining*, that has been subjected to a creep.

Crepuscle (krĭpɒ·s'l, kre·pŏs'l). 1665. [ad. L. *crepusculum*.] Twilight. var. **Crepuscule** (now *rare*).

Crepuscular (krĭpɒ·skiulăɹ), *a.* 1668. [f. as prec.] **1.** Of or pertaining to twilight 1755; hence *fig.* dim, indistinct; imperfectly enlightened 1668. **2.** *Zool.* Appearing or active in the twilight 1826.

1. *fig.* That c. period when the historical sense was scarcely brought to a full state of activity 1852. **2.** C. insects 1826. So **Crepu·sculine** *a.* (*rare*), **Crepu·sculous** *a.* (in sense 1).

‖**Crepusculum** (krĭpɒ·skiulŏm). ME. [L., related to *creper* dusky, dark.] Twilight, dusk.

The same time..That clerkes call C. at eue LYDG.

†**Crescence.** 1602. [ad. L. *crescentia*; see CRESCENT.] Growth, increase -1736.

‖**Crescendo** (kreʃe·ndo). 1776. [It., pr. pple. of *crescere* to increase; see next.] *Mus.* A direction: To be gradually increased in volume of sound (usu. indicated by the abbrev. *cresc.* or the sign <). As *sb.*: Such an increase; a passage of this description. Also *transf.* and *fig.* Also as vb. (Opp. to DIMINUENDO.)

fig. The intense c. of the catastrophe 1886.

Crescent (kre·sĕnt), *sb.* [ME. *cressant*, a. OF. *creissant*, mod. *croissant* (:—L. *crescentem*, pr. pple. of *crescere* to grow).] **1.** The waxing moon, during the period between new moon and full. Also *fig.* 1530. **2.** The convexo-concave figure of the waxing or waning moon, during the first or last quarter 1578. **3.** A representation of this phase of the moon: **a.** as an ornament ME. **b.** *Her.* as a charge 1486. **c.** As a badge or emblem of the Turkish sultans; hence *fig.* the Turkish power, and used rhetorically to symbolize the Mohammedan religion as a political force 1589. (The attribution of the *crescent* to the Saracens of Crusading times and to the Moors of Spain is an error.) **d.** used as the badge of an order of knighthood or as a decorative order ME. **4.** Anything of this shape, as a row of houses, etc. 1672.

2. *Mids. N.* v. i. 246. **3. c.** The C. gave way to the Cross, the Turks were broken to pieces 1684.

Hence **Crescenta·de,** *prop.*, a religious war waged under the Turkish flag; *rhet.*, a *jihād* or holy war for Islam. **Cre·scented** *ppl. a.* formed as a c. or new moon; ornamented, or charged, with crescents. **Cresce·ntic** *a.* c.-shaped. **Cresce·ntiform** *a.* crescentic.

Crescent (kre·sĕnt), *a.* 1574. [ad. L. *crescentem*; see prec.] **1.** Growing, increasing. (Often with allusion to the moon.) **2.** Shaped like the new or old moon 1603.

1. My powers are Cressent, and my Auguring hope Sayes it will come to th' full *Ant. & Cl.* II. i. 10. **2.** Astarte, Queen of Heav'n, with c. Horns MILT.

Crescive (kre·siv), *a.* 1566. [f. L. *crescere* + -IVE.] Growing.

Vnseene, yet cressiue in his facultie *Hen. V*, I. i. 66.

Cresol (kre·sǫl). Also **cressol.** 1869. [f. *cres-* for CREOS(OTE) + -OL.] *Chem.* An aromatic alcohol of the Benzene group (C_7H_8O), occurring along with carbolic acid in coal-tar and creosote. Hence **Cre·solene,** $C_6H_5CH_3O$, a product of coal-tar, related to carbolic acid. **Creso·tic** *a.* in (*ortho-, para-, meta-*) *cresotic acid* ($C_8H_8O_3$), obtained from the corresponding cresols.

Cress (kres). [OE. *cresse, cerse* :—OTeut. **krasjôn-*, from root of OHG. *chresan* to creep, as if 'creeper'.] **1.** The name of various cruciferous plants, having mostly edible leaves of a pungent flavour. (Until 19th c. almost always in pl.; sometimes construed with a vb. in the sing.) **a.** *spec.* Garden C., *Lepidium sativum*, or WATERCRESS, *Nasturtium officinale*. **b.** With defining words, applied to other cruciferous plants, and occas. to plants merely resembling cress in flavour or appearance. †**2.** As the type of something of little worth. (Cf. *rush, straw.*) -ME.

1. To strip the brook with mantling cresses spread GOLDSM. **2.** Wisdome and witte now is nouȝt worth a carse LANGL. Hence **Cre·ssy** *a.*

Cresset (kre·sĕt). ME. [a. OF. *craicet, craisset, cresset* in same sense.] **1.** A vessel of iron or the like, made to hold grease or oil, or an iron basket to hold pitched rope, wood, or coal, to be burnt for light; usually mounted on the top of a pole or building, or suspended from a roof. Also *transf.* and *fig.* **2.** *Coopering.* A fire-basket used to char the inside of a cask 1874. †**c.-light,** a blazing c.; the light of a c.

‖**Cresson** (krēsoṅ). 1883. [Fr.; = CRESS.] A shade of green used for ladies' dresses.

Crest (krest), *sb.* ME. [a. OF. *creste*, mod. *crête* :—L. *crista* tuft, plume.] **1.** A comb, a tuft of feathers, or the like, upon an animal's head. Also *fig.* (Cf. CREST-FALLEN.) **2.** An erect plume of feathers, horse-hair, etc. fixed on the top of a helmet or head-dress; any ornament worn there as a cognizance ME. **3.** *Her.* A figure or device (orig. borne by a knight on his helmet) placed on a wreath, coronet, or chapeau, and borne above the shield and helmet in a coat of arms; also used separately, as a cognizance, upon seals, plate, note-paper, etc. (Thus it is a vulgar error to speak of the arms or shields of a college or city as *crests*.) ME. Also *fig.* **4.** The apex of a helmet; hence, a helmet ME. **5.** The head, summit, or top of anything ME. **6.** *Archit.* The finishing of stone, metal, etc., which surmounts a roof-ridge, wall, screen, etc.; occas. applied to the finial of a gable or pinnacle ME. **7.** An elevated ridge. **a.** The ridge of a mountain, *col*, bank or the like. **b.** *Fortif.* The top line of a parapet or slope. **c.** The curling foamy ridge of a wave. ME. **8.** The ridge of the neck of a horse, dog, etc. 1592. **9.** A raised ridge on the surface of any object; *spec.* in *Anat.*, etc.

1. Oft he [the serpent] bowd His turret C. MILT. *P. L.* IX. 525. *fig.* Then began the Argives to let fall their crests and sue for peace RALEIGH. 2. Warchiefs with..crests of eagle wings WHITTIER. 3. What is your C., a Coxcombe *Tam. Shr.* II. i. 226. 4. On his c. Sat horror plum'd MILT. *P. L.* IV. 988. 7. First curls the ruffl'd sea With whit'ning crests EARL DERBY. Chuse a horse with a deep neck, large c. MARKHAM.

Comb.: **c.-tile**, a bent tile used to cover the c. or ridge of a roof; **-wreath** (in *Her.*), the wreath or fillet of twisted silk which bears the c.

Crest (krest), *v.* ME. [f. CREST *sb.*[1]] **1.** *trans.* To furnish with a crest. **2.** To serve as a crest to; to surmount as a crest; to crown 1606. **b.** To mark with long streaks, like the streaming hair of a crest 1596. **3.** To reach the crest 1851. **4.** *intr.* To erect one's crest 1713; to form a crest, as a wave 1850.

2. His legges bestrid the Ocean, his rear'd arme Crested the world *Ant. & Cl.* v. ii. 83. **b.** Like as the shining skie in summers night..Is creasted all with lines of firie light SPENSER *F. Q.* IV. i. 13. 3. To c. a hill, a wave, etc. (*mod.*).

Crested (kre·stėd), *ppl. a.* ME. [f. CREST *sb.* and *v.* + -ED.] **1.** Wearing or having a crest; *spec.* applied to animals and plants distinguished by a crest; = L. *cristatus, -a.* Also *fig.* **2.** *Her.* Having a crest of a different tincture from that of the body 1572. **†3.** Ribbed –1834. **4.** Having a raised ridge. (See CREST *sb.* 9.) 1857.

1. Fair dames and c. chiefs SCOTT. *fig.* The c. pride Of the first Edward GRAY. 4. Double-c. skulls WALLACE.

Crest-fallen (kre·st fǭ:lėn), *ppl. a.* 1589. **1.** With drooping crest; *hence*, cast down; humbled, dispirited. **2.** Of a horse: Having the crest or ridge of the neck hanging to one side 1696.

1. Let it make thee Crestfalne, I, and alay this thy abortiue Pride 2 *Hen. VI*, IV. i. 59.

Cresting (kre·stiŋ), *vbl. sb.* 1869. [f. CREST *sb.* (sense 6) + ING[1].] *Archit.* An ornamental ridging to a wall or roof.

Cre·stless, *a.* 1591. Not bearing a crest.

Spring Crestlesse Yeomen from so deepe a Root SHAKS.

Cresyl (kre·sil). Also **cressyl.** 1863. [f. CRES-OL + -YL.] *Chem.* The radical C_7H_7 of cresol. **Cre·sylate**, a salt of cresylic acid. **Cresy·lic** *a.* of cresyl, in *Cresylic acid* = CRESOL.

Cretaceo- (krĭtē̆·ʃio), comb. f. of CRETACEOUS, = 'cretaceous and ——'.

Cretaceous (krĭtē̆·ʃəs), *a.* 1675. [f. L. *cretaceus*, f. *creta* chalk; see -ACEOUS.] **1.** Of the nature of chalk; chalky. **2.** *Geol.* Of or found in the Chalk formation. So *C. group, series, system. C. period*: the period during which these strata were deposited. Hence **Creta·ceously** *adv.*

Cretic (krī·tik). 1603. [ad. L. *Creticus*, f. *Creta* Crete.] *adj.* Belonging to Crete, Cretan; applied in Gr. and L. prosody to a particular metrical foot, or to verse characterized by these. *sb.* (without capital.) A metrical foot consisting of one short syllable between two long; = AMPHIMACER.

†Cre·ticism. 1614. Cretan behaviour, *i.e.* lying –1656.

Cretify (krī·tifəi), *v.* 1859. [f. L. *creta* chalk + -FY.] To impregnate (a tissue of the animal body) with salts of lime. Hence **Cre:tifica·tion**, calcareous degeneration.

Cretin (krī·tin). 1779. [a. F. *crétin*, ad. Swiss patois *crestin, creitin* :—L. *Christianum* CHRISTIAN, *i.e.* 'human creature' as dist. from the brutes. (Cf. *natural.*)] One afflicted with cretinism. Hence **Cre·tinous** *a.* pertaining to a c.; of the nature of cretinism.

Cretinism (krī·tiniz'm). 1801. [f. prec. + -ISM.] The condition of a cretin; a combination of deformity (usually with goitre) and idiocy, endemic in certain Alpine valleys and elsewhere. So **Cre·tinize** *v.* to reduce to c.

Cretion (krī·ʃən). 1880. [ad. L. *cretionem*, f. *cernere* to decide.] *Rom. Law.* Declaration of acceptance of an inheritance; *transf.* the term allowed for this.

Cretize (krī·təiz), *v. arch.* 1653. [ad. Gr. κρητίζειν, f. Κρήτη Crete. (Cf. *Titus* i. 12.)] **1.** *intr.* To play the Cretan, *i.e.* to lie. **†2.** To outdo by lying 1673. So **†Cre·tism** (Dicts.).

‖**Cretonne** (krətǫ·n, kre·tǫn). 1870. [a. F., f. *Creton*, a village of Normandy.] The French name of a strong fabric of hempen warp and linen woof; applied in England to a stout unglazed cotton cloth printed with a pattern in colours, and used for chair covers, curtains, etc.

Creutzer, obs. f. KREUTZER.

Crevasse (krĭvæ·s). 1819. [a. F. *crevasse* = OF. *crevace* CREVICE.] **1.** A fissure or chasm in the ice of a glacier, usually of great depth. Also *transf.* 1823. **2.** *U.S.* A breach in the bank of a river, canal, etc.; used *esp.* of a breach in the *levée* or artificial bank of the lower Mississippi. So **Creva·sse** *v.* to fissure with crevasses. **Creva·ssing** *vbl. sb.* formation of crevasses.

Crevice (kre·vis), *sb.* [ME. *crevace*, a. OF. :—late L. *crepatia*, f. L. *crepare* to creak, crack.] **1.** An opening produced by a crack; a cleft, rift, chink, fissure. **2.** *spec.* (*Mining.*) A fissure in which a deposit of ore or metal is found 1872.

1. A creuisse of an olde cragge ME. Hence **†Cre·vice** *v. trans.* to make crevices in. **Cre·viced** *ppl. a.* having crevices, chinks, or cracks.

Crevis(e, -ish(e, -isse, -ys(e, obs. ff. CRAYFISH, CREVICE.

Crew (krū). 1455. [a. OF. *creue* increase, f. pa. pple. of *croistre* to grow; perh. in part aphet. f. *acrewe*, ACCRUE.] **†1.** An augmentation or reinforcement of a military force; hence, a company of soldiers –1587. **2.** By extension: Any organized band of armed men 1570. **3.** Any body of men organized or associated for a purpose; as, a squad of workmen under a foreman 1699; (*Naut.*) a gang of men under a petty officer, or told off for a particular duty 1692; and *esp.* the whole of the men (inclusive or exclusive of the officers) belonging to and manning a ship, boat, or other vessel afloat (now the leading sense) 1694. **4.** A number of persons associated together; a company 1579. **5.** A number of persons classed together; a lot, set, gang, mob, herd 1570.

3. To order the cooper and his c. to trim the casks SHELVOCKE. Supposing the Captain and Crew would soon be with him DAMPIER. 4. Mirth, admit me of thy c. MILT. *L'Alleg.* 58. 5. All the ravenous c. Of jobbers and promoters 1884.

Crew, pa. t. of CROW *v.*

†Crewe. [a. OF. *crue.*] A pot. SPENSER.

Crewel (krū·ěl), *sb.* 1494. [?] **1.** A thin worsted yarn, used for tapestry and embroidery. **2.** Short for CREWEL-WORK (*mod.*). Also *attrib.*

Crewels (krū·ělz), *sb. pl. Sc.* 1660. [f. F. *écrouelles.*] The king's evil, scrofula.

Crew·el-work. 1863. Embroidery in which a design is worked in worsted on a background of linen or cloth.

Crewet, -ette, obs. f. CRUET.

Crib (krib), *sb.* [Com. WGer.: OE. *crib(b.* Cf. MHG. *krebe* basket, and *korb* CORF.] **1.** A barred receptacle for fodder; a CRATCH OE. **2.** 'The stall or cabin of an ox' (J.) ME. **3.** A cabin, hovel; a narrow room; also *fig.* 1597. **b.** *Thieves' slang.* A dwelling-house, shop, etc. 1812. **4.** *fig.* A berth (*slang*) 1865. **5.** A small bed for a child, with barred sides. (*Occas.* = cradle.) 1649. **6.** *fig.* † ? Provender. *Thieves' cant.* Also a miner's 'bait'. **†7.** A wicker-work basket, pannier, or the like –1676. **8.** *Salt-making.* An apparatus like a hay-rack for draining the salt after boiling 1682. **9.** A framework of bars or spars for strengthening, support, etc. Cf. CRADLE *sb.* 1693. **10.** *Mining.* A framework of timber, etc., lining a shaft, to prevent caving, percolation of water, etc. 1839. **11.** A frame of logs secured under water to form a pier, dam, etc. (*Canada & U.S.*) 1874. **12.** A small raft of boards (*Canada & U.S.*) 1813. **13.** A bin for storing Indian corn (= CORN-CRIB); also for salt, etc. (*U.S.*) 1823. **14.** *Cards.* The cards thrown out from each player's hand, and given to the dealer, in the game of cribbage. Also, = CRIBBAGE (*colloq.*). 1680. **15.** A petty theft. (See CRIB *v.*) (*rare*) 1855. **16.** Something cribbed; a plagiarism (*colloq.*) 1834. **17.** A translation of a classic, etc., for the illegitimate use of students (*colloq.*) 1827.

1. Layd..In a cribbe, bytwen an ox and an asse HAMPOLE. 2. Where no Oxen are, the c. is cleane *Prov.* xiv. 4. 3. Why rather (Sleepe) lyest thou in smoakie Cribs..Then in the perfum'd Chambers of the Great 2 *Hen. IV*, III. i. 9. *fig.* The world.. Whithersoever we turn, still is the same narrow c. CLOUGH.

Comb.: **c.-biter**, a horse addicted to c.-biting; also *fig.*; **-biting**, the morbid habit of seizing the manger (or other object) with the teeth and noisily drawing in the breath; **cribwork**, work consisting of cribs (sense 11); also *attrib.*

Crib (krib), *v.* 1460. [f. CRIB *sb.*] **†1.** *intr.* ? To feed at a crib (*rare*). **2.** *trans.* To shut up as in a crib; to confine within narrow limits; to hamper. (In mod. use as an echo of Shaks.) 1605. **3.** *intr.* To lie as in a crib 1661. **4.** *trans.* To furnish with a crib or cribs (CRIB *sb.* 1, 9–11) 1669. **5.** To make up into cribs (CRIB *sb.* 12) (*U.S.*) 1876. **6.** *colloq.* To pilfer, purloin, steal; to appropriate furtively. [Prob. orig. *thieves' slang.*] 1748. **7.** *colloq.* To take (a passage, etc.) without acknowledgement and use as one's own; to plagiarize 1778. **8.** *intr.* Of horses: To practise crib-biting 1864.

2. Cabin'd, crib'd, confin'd, bound in *Macb.* III. iv. 24. 6. Bits of ground cribbed..at different times from the forest COBBETT. Hence **Cri·bber** (*rare*), one who cribs or uses a CRIB (1, 17) (*colloq.*).

Cribbage (kri·bėdʒ). 1630. [f. CRIB *sb.* and *v.* + AGE.] **1.** A game at cards, played by two, three, or four persons, with a complete pack of cards, and a board with holes and pegs for scoring; the characteristic feature is a CRIB (sense 14). **2.** The action of cribbing, or that which is cribbed (*colloq. rare*) 1830.

1. He proposed a game of four-handed c. DICKENS. *Comb.*: **c.-board**, the board used for marking at c.; **-faced** *a.* pock-marked, and so like a c.-board.

Cribbing (kri·biŋ), *vbl. sb.* 1641. [f. CRIB *v.* (and *sb.*) + ING[1].] **1.** The action of CRIB *v.* 1791. **2.** = Crib-biting; see CRIB *v.* 8. 1864. **3.** That which is cribbed 1837. **4.** *Mining.* Timbering forming the lining of a shaft, etc.; cribwork 1841. **†5.** *Thieves' cant.* Provender 1641.

Cribble (kri·b'l), *sb.* ? *Obs.* 1552. [a. F. *crible*, ad. L. *cribrum* (dim. *cribellum*) sieve.] **1.** A sieve 1565. **†2.** That which is left in the sieve; bran or coarse meal –1691. Also *attrib.* Hence **†Cribble** *v.* to sift. var. **†Cribe** *sb.* and *v.*

Cribrate (krəi·brėt), *a.* 1846. [f. L. *cribrum* + ATE[2].] *Nat. Hist.* Perforated like a sieve.

†Cri·brate, *v.* 1631. [f. ppl. stem of L. *cribrare*, f. as prec.] *trans.* To sift; also *fig.* –1669. Hence **†Cribra·tion**, sifting; also *fig.*

Cribriform (krəi·brifǭɹm, kri·b-), *a.* 1741. [a. mod.L. *cribriformis*; see prec.] Having the form or appearance of a sieve; perforated with small holes.

The c. part of the *Os Ethmoides* MONRO. C. or Sieve-cells, a sort of ducts the walls of which have open slits, through which they communicate with each other GRAY.

Cribrose (krəibrōᵘ·s), *a.* 1857. [f. L. *cribrum* sieve; see -OSE.] Sieve-like, perforated. var. **†Cri·brous.**

Crick (krik), *sb.*[1] 1440. [Prob. echoic; cf. next and STITCH.] A painful spasmodic affection of the muscles of the neck, back, or other part, appearing as a sudden stiffness which makes it almost impossible to move the part.

†Crick, *sb.*[2] 1530. [app. the same as F. *cric.*] The instrument for bending a cross-bow. [1874. A small jackscrew. KNIGHT.]

Crick, *sb.*[3], var. of CREEK *sb.*[1]

Crick (krik), *v.*[1] 1861. [f. CRICK *sb.*[1]] *trans.* To give a crick to (the neck, etc.).

Crick, *v.*[2] 1601. [Echoic.] To make a sharp abrupt sound, as a grasshopper.

Crick-crack, *sb.*, *v.*, *adv.* 1565. [Echoic. Cf. F. *cric-crac.*] A representation of a repeated sharp sound.

Cricket (kri·kėt), *sb.*[1] ME. [a. OF. *criquet, crequet* cicada, from an echoic *krik-*.] Any saltatorial orthopterous insect of the genus *Acheta* or of the same tribe; as, the common house-cricket, *A. domestica*, the field-cricket,

A. campestris, and mole-cricket, *Gryllotalpa vulgaris*. **b.** Used for CICADA.

As cheerful and lively as a c. 1873.

Comb.: **c.-bird**, the grasshopper warbler (*Locustella nævia*); **-frog**, a small tree-frog of the genus *Hylodes*, which chirp like crickets; **-teal**, the garganey (*Querquedula circia*).

Cricket (kri·kėt), *sb.*² 1598. [app. the same as F. *criquet* 'bâton servant de but au jeu de boules' (Godefroy), perh. a deriv. of M.Flem. *krick, kricke*, 'baston à s'appuyer', etc.] A well-known open-air game played with ball, bats, and wickets, by two sides of eleven players each. Also *attrib.* **b.** Used *allus.* for: Fair play 1902. Hence **Cri·cket** *v.* to play c. **Cri·cketer.**

Cricket (kri·kėt), *sb.*³ 1643. [?] A low wooden stool; a footstool. Now *local.*

Crico- (krəi·ko), comb. f. Gr. κρίκος = κίρκος ring, used in *Anat.* in sense 'pertaining to the cricoid cartilage', as **c.-thy·roid** *a.* pertaining to the cricoid and thyroid cartilages; also *sb.* (*sc.* muscle). **Crico·tomy**, the operation of dividing the cricoid cartilage.

Cricoid (krəi·koid). 1746. [ad. mod.L. *cricoides* (formerly also used), a. Gr. κρικοειδής, f. κρίκος = κίρκος ring + -ειδής -form.] *adj.* Ring-shaped; applied *spec.* to the cartilage which forms the lower and back part of the larynx. *sb.* (*sc.* cartilage) 1842.

Cried (krəid), *ppl. a.* 1642. [f. CRY *v.* + -ED.] Proclaimed by crying, announced.

Crier (krəi·əɹ). [ME. *criere*, a. OF. *criere*, nom. of *crieur*, f. *crier* to CRY; see -ER.] **1.** *gen.* One who cries. **2.** *spec.* An officer in a court of justice who makes the public announcements, etc.; a COMMON or TOWN *crier* ME.; one who cries goods for sale 1553.

All common Cryers were excluded from the Temple LEONI.

Crikey (krəi·ki), *int. colloq.* or *slang.* 1842. [perh. orig. an assonant substitute for a sacred name; cf. CRIMINE.] An exclam. of surprise.

Crim. con. 1770. Abbrev. of *criminal conversation, i. e.* adultery. (See CRIMINAL *a.*)

Crime (krəim), *sb.* ME. [a. F. *crime*, in 12th c. *crimne*, ad. L. *crimen*, f. root of *cernere, cretum* to decide, give judgement, etc.] **1.** An act punishable by law, as being forbidden by statute or injurious to the public welfare. (Commonly used only of grave offences.) **b.** *collect. sing.* Violation of law 1485. **2.** An evil or injurious act; a (grave) offence, a sin 1514. **b.** *collect. sing.* Wrong-doing, sin ME. †**3.** Charge, or accusation; matter of accusation –1667.

1. If by this C., he owes the Law his life *Timon* III. v. 83. Men steeped in c. FROUDE. **2.** All yᵉ crymes of yᵉ tonge, as sclaunders..and prevy backbytynges 1526. **3.** That errour now, which is become my c., And thou th' accuser MILT. *P. L.* IX. 1181.

Hence **Crime** *v.* to charge with a c. (*rare*). **Cri·meful** *a.* full of c.; criminal. **Cri·meless** *a.* void of c.

Criminal (kri·minăl). ME. [a. F. *criminel*, ad. L. *criminalis*; see prec. and -AL.]

A. *adj.* **1.** Of the nature of or involving a crime, or a grave offence. **2.** Relating to crime or its punishment 1474. **3.** Guilty of crime or grave offence 1489.

1. *C. conversation* (CONVERSATION 3): adultery, regarded as a *trespass* against the husband at common law. **2.** Good lawes, civil and criminall 1590. An experienced c. lawyer LOWELL. **3.** The neglect..renders us c. in the sight of God ROGERS (J.).

B. *sb.* †**1.** A person accused of a crime –1681. **2.** A person guilty or convicted of a crime 1626.

1. Was ever c. forbid to plead DRYDEN.

Hence **Cri·minalism**, the condition or practice of a c. **Cri·minalist**, one versed in c. law. **Crimina·lity**, the quality or fact of being a c.; a c. act or practice. **Cri·minally** *adv.* according to c. law; so as to constitute crime. †**Cri·minalness**, criminality.

Criminate (kri·mineit), *v.* 1645. [f. L. *criminat-* ppl. stem.] **1.** *trans.* To charge with crime; to represent as criminal. **2.** To prove guilty of crime; to incriminate 1665. **3.** To represent as criminal; to condemn 1677.

1. I suppose the public servants will be criminated GOUV. MORRIS. **2.** Determined not to c. himself by any allusion to the circumstance 1841.

So **Crimina·tion**, the action of criminating; severe accusation or censure. **Cri·minative** *a.* tending to or involving crimination. **Cri·minator**, one who charges with crime. **Cri·minatory** *a.* criminative.

Crimine, -iny (kri·mini), *int.* 1681. [Cf. *jiminy*, GEMINI.] A vulgar exclam. of astonishment: now *arch.*

Criminology (kriminǫ·lŏdʒi). 1890. [f. L. *crimin-* CRIME.] The science of crime; 'criminal anthropology'. So **Criminolo·gical** *a.*, **Crimino·logist.**

Criminous (kri·minəs), *a.* 1483. [a. AFr. *criminous* = OF. *crimineux*, ad. L. *criminosus.*] †**1.** Of the nature of a crime; criminal. **2.** Of persons: Guilty of crime 1535. †**3.** Of or relating to crime; involving crimination –1650.

2. Now only in *c. clerk* (CLERK *sb.* 1). Hence **Cri·minously** *adv.* **Cri·minousness.**

Crimison, crimosin(e, etc., obs. ff. CRIMSON.

Crimp (krimp), *sb.*¹ 1638. [?] †**1.** ? A term of reproach or derision. **2.** An agent who procures seamen, soldiers, etc., *esp.* by decoying or impressing them 1758. Also *transf.* and *fig.* †**3.** A coal broker –1791.

1. Yes, c.; 'tis a gallant life to be an old lord's pimp-whiskin FORD. Phr. †*To play c.*: 'to lay or bet on one side, and (by foul play) to let t'other win, having a share of it' B. E. *Dict. Cant. Crew.* Hence **Cri·mpage**, money paid to a c. for his services.

Crimp, *sb.*² 1632. [? f. CRIMP *v.*¹] An obsolete game at cards.

Crimp (krimp), *sb.*³ 1883. [f. CRIMP *v.*¹] *pl.* Crimped tresses; cf. 'curls'. *U.S.*

Crimp (krimp), *a.* 1587. [app. allied to CRIMP *v.*¹; cf. however MHG. *krimpf* crooked, curved (Kluge). Cf. also CRUMP.] **1.** Friable, brittle; crisp. †**2.** *fig.* 'Not consistent, not forcible' (J.). (But see quot., the sole evidence for this sense.) 1712. **3.** Said of hair, feathers, etc.: Crimped 1764.

1. The grass was c. and white with the hoar frost MRS. CAMERON. **2.** The evidence is crimp (v. l. *scrimp*); the witnesses swear backwards and forwards, and contradict themselves ARBUTHNOT. Hence **Cri·mpness**, friability.

Crimp (krimp), *v.*¹ ME. [= MDu. *crimpen* intr., to contract oneself together, Du. *krimpen* to shrivel, Da. *krympe* trans. to shrink (cloth), etc. See CRAMP *sb.*¹ Not known in OE.; in ME. only in one example.] **1.** *intr.* To be compressed, pinched or indented (as *e.g.* the body of insects). †**2.** *trans.* To curl –1736. **3.** To compress or pinch into minute parallel plaits or folds 1712; to crisp the surface of 1772; to make flutings in (a brass cartridge case). **4.** To cause (the flesh of fish) to contract and become firm by gashing it before *rigor mortis* sets in 1698. Also *transf.* **5.** *spec.* To bend or mould into shape (leather for uppers, etc.) 1874. **6.** 'To pinch and hold; to seize' (Webster).

3. To c. the little frill that bordered his shirt-collar DICKENS.

Crimp (krimp), *v.*² 1812. [f. CRIMP *sb.*¹] To impress (seamen or soldiers); to entrap.

Plundering corn and crimping recruits WELLINGTON.

Crimper¹ (kri·mpəɹ). 1819. [f. CRIMP *v.*¹] **1.** One who crimps. **2.** That which crimps:

a. An apparatus consisting of a pair of fluted rollers, for crimping cloth or the like. **b.** A toilet instrument for crimping the hair. **c.** A machine for crimping leather for uppers. **d.** An apparatus for bending leather into various shapes for saddles and harness. **e.** A small machine for crimping brass cartridge-cases.

Crimper². 1868. [f. CRIMP *v.*² + -ER ¹.] = CRIMP *sb.*¹ 2.

Crimple, *v.* ME. [perh. a dim. and iterative of CRIMP *v.*¹] †**1.** *intr.* To be or become incurved, or drawn together; hence to stand or walk lame from such a cause –1736. **2.** *intr.* and *trans.* To wrinkle, crinkle, curl. Now *dial.* Hence **Cri·mpled** *ppl. a.* (in sense 2).

Crimson (kri·mz'n). ME. [a. (ult.) Arab. *qermazī, qirmazī*; see CRAMOISY. The 15–16th c. F. form was *cramoisin* (Littré).]

A. *adj.* **1.** The name of a colour: of a deep red inclining towards purple (see KERMES). **2.** *fig.* Sanguinary 1681.

1. This cramoysen gowne CHALONER. **2.** C. conquest 1777.

B. *sb.* (The *adj.* used *absol.*) **1.** The colour or pigment ME. †**2.** Crimson cloth –1611.

1. Ros'd ouer with the Virgin C. of Modestie SHAKS.

Crimson (kri·mz'n), *v.* 1601. [f. CRIMSON *a.*] **1.** *trans.* To make crimson. **2.** *intr.* To become crimson; *esp.* in blushing 1805.

1. Heere thy Hunters stand.. Crimson'd in thy Lethee *Jul. C.* III. i. 206. **2.** As the fresh bud a crimsoning beauty shows MRS. NORTON.

Crinal (krəi·năl), *a. rare.* 1656. [ad. L. *crinalis*, f. *crinis.*] Pertaining to the hair.

Cri·nate, by-form of CRINITE, haired. So **Crina·ted** *a.*

Cri·natory, var. of CRINITORY.

Crinc-; see CRINK-.

Crine (krəin), *sb. rare.* 1614. [a. It., or ad. L. *crinis.*] **1.** Hair, head of hair. Also *attrib.* **2.** = CRINET 2. 1883. Hence **Crined** *a.* (*Her.*), having the hair tinctured differently from the body, as a charge.

Crine (krəin), *v. Sc.* 1501. [app. a. Gael. *crion* to wither.] *intr.* To shrink, shrivel.

Crinel, error for CRINET 2.

†**Crinet.** 1486. [dim. of F. *crin.*] **1.** A hair 1572. **2.** *Hawking.* (*pl.*) The small hair-like feathers which grow about the cere of a hawk. (Also written *crinites*; now called *crines.*) –1792. **3.** = CRINIÈRE 1586.

Cringe (krindʒ), *v.* ME. [app. a modification of *crenge, crenche*, f. (ult.) OE. *cringan, crincan*; see CRANK.] †**1.** *trans.* To draw in or contract (any part of the body); to distort (the neck, face, etc.) –1630. **2.** *intr.* To draw in the muscles of the body involuntarily; to shrink; to cower ME. **3.** *intr.* To bend the body timorously or servilely. Const. *to* (a person). 1575. **4.** *fig.* To behave obsequiously; to show base or servile deference 1620. †**5.** *trans.* To bow deferentially to –1660.

1. *Ant. & Cl.* III. xiii. 100. **2.** The Boys that went before were glad to c. behind, for they were afraid of the Lions BUNYAN. **3.** An opinion that to bow or c. (as they profanely call it) before Almighty God is superstition BEVERIDGE. **4.** To teach the people to c. and the prince to domineer MACAULAY.

Hence **Cri·ngeling** (*rare*), a cringing creature; also *attrib.* **Cri·nger.** **Cri·nging-ly** *adv.*, **-ness.**

Cringe (krindʒ), *sb.* 1597. [f. prec. vb.] A deferential, servile, or fawning obeisance. Often applied to a bow. Also *fig.*

Performing cringes and congees like a court-chamberlain THACKERAY.

Cringle (kri·ŋg'l). 1627. [app. of LG. origin; cf. Ger. *kringel*, dim. of *kring* circle, ring. See CRANK *sb.*¹, and cf. CRINKLE.] **1.** *Naut.* A ring or eye of rope, containing a thimble, worked into the bolt-rope of a sail, for the attachment of a rope. **b.** A withe for fastening a gate (*dial.*) 1787. **2.** = CRINKLE (*dial.*) 1807. Hence **Cri·ngle** *v. dial.* to fasten with a c.

Crini-, stem of L. *crinis* hair: used as comb. form:

Crinicu·ltural *a.* of or pertaining to the growth of the hair. **Cri·niger** (*Ornith.*), a genus of African and Asiatic birds allied to the Thrush, having stiff setæ on their bills. **Crini·gerous** *a.* bearing or wearing hair. **Crini·parous** *a.* hair-producing.

Crinid (kri·nid, krəi-). 1862. [f. Gr. κρίνον lily + -ID.] *Zool.* (*pl.*) A family of the *Crinoided* containing the typical crinoids with branching arms.

‖**Crinière** (krinįę·r). 1598. [F., f. *crin* (horse) hair.] The part of the bards of a war-horse which covered the ridge or back of the neck and the mane.

†**Crini·tal**, *a. rare.* 1583. = CRINITE *a.*

He the star c. adoreth STANYHURST.

Crinite (krəi·nəit), *a.* 1600. [ad. L. *crinitus*, f. *crinis.*] Hairy; having a hairy or hair-like appendage; *spec.* in *Bot.* and *Zool.* having hairy tufts on the surface.

How comate, c., caudate starres are fram'd I knew FAIRFAX.

Crinite (kri·nəit, krəi-), *sb.* [f. Gr. κρίνον lily + -ITE.] A fossil crinoid.

Cri·nitory, *a. rare.* 1836. [f. L. *crinitus* + -ORY.] Hairy.

Crinkle (kri·ŋk'l), *sb.* 1596. [prob. f. CRINKLE *v.*] A twist, winding, or sinuosity; a wrinkle or corrugation.

The crinkles in this glass making objects appear double TUCKER. Hence **Cri·nkly** *a.* full of crinkles.

Crinkle (kri·ŋk'l), *v.* ME. [f. OE. *crincan*; see CRANK *sb.*¹ and CRANKLE.] **1.** *intr.* To form many short twists or turns; to wind or twist; to contract wrinkles or ripples; to shrink *up.* **2.** To cringe; *fig.* to recede from one's purpose. Now only *dial.* 1610. **3.** *trans.* To twist or bend to and fro, or in and out; to wrinkle, crumple; to crimp (the hair) 1825. **4.** *intr.* To emit sharp thin sounds 1856.

1. It [a stream] seemed to c. and ripple LOWELL. 2. I like him the worse, he crinkles so much in the hams FORD. 3. And for the hous is krynkeled two and fro And hath so queynte weyis for to go CHAUCER. Her face all bowsy Comely crynklyd Woundersly wrynkled 1529. 4. All the rooms Were full of crinkling silks 1856.

Cri·nkle-cra·nkle. 1598. [Freq. redup. of CRANKLE.] *sb.* A winding in and out, a zigzag. *adj.* and *adv.* Zigzag 1840.

†**Crinkum, crincum.** Also **Grincome,** q.v. 1618. *slang.* In *pl.* The venereal disease –1719.

Cri·nkum-cra·nkum, *sb.* (*a.*) Also **crincum-crancum.** 1761. Anything full of twists and turns, or intricately elaborated (*joc.*).

Crinoid (kri·noid, krəi-). 1836. [ad. Gr. κρινοειδής lily-like.] *adj.* Lily-shaped; applied to an order (chiefly fossil) of echinoderms, having a calyx-like body, stalked and rooted. As *sb.* (with pl. *crinoidea, crinoida*). A member of this order.

Crinolette (krinŏle·t). 1881. [dim. f. CRINOLINE.] A sort of bustle for distending the back of a woman's skirt.

Crinoline (kri·nŏlīn, -ŏlin). 1830. [a. mod. F., f. L. *crinis* hair, in sense of F. *crin* horse-hair + *linum* thread; a trade coinage.] 1. A stiff fabric made of horsehair and cotton or linen thread, formerly used for skirts, and still for lining, etc. 2. A petticoat made of this or any stiff material, worn under the skirt in order to support or distend it; *hence*, a hoop-petticoat 1851. 3. *transf.* A netting fitted round war-ships as a defence against torpedoes. Chiefly *attrib.* 1874.

Crinosity (krəinǫ·sĭti). *rare.* 1656. [f. L. *crinis.*] Hairiness.

Crio- = Gr. κριο-, comb. f. κριός ram:

Crioce·ratite, a fossil of the genus *Crioceras*, a ram's-horn ammonite. **Cri·osphinx,** a sphinx having a ram's head.

Cripple (kri·p'l). [OE. *crypel*:—OTeut. **krupilo-*, f. *krup-* ablaut stem of *kriupan* to CREEP.]

A. *sb.* 1. One who is disabled (either from birth or by accident or injury) from the use of his limbs; a lame person. 2. *techn.* = *Cripple-gap* (see below), where *cripple* = 'creeping' 1648. 3. *slang.* A sixpence 1785.

1. A creeple from his mothers wombe *Acts* xiv. 8. *Comb.* **c.-gap, -hole** (*dial.*), a hole left in walls for sheep to creep through; cf. sense 2. Hence **Cri·ppledom, -hood, -ness. Cri·pply** *a.*

B. *adj.* Disabled from the use of one's limbs, lame. (*Obs.* or *dial.*, exc. as attrib. of prec.) ME.

Cripple (kri·p'l), *v.* ME. [f. CRIPPLE *sb.*] 1. *trans.* To deprive (wholly or partly) of the use of one's limbs; to make a cripple of. 2. *transf.* and *fig.* To disable, impair: a. the action or effectiveness of material objects 1694; b. a person in his resources, efforts, etc., or immaterial things, as trade, schemes, strength, etc. 1702. 3. *intr.* To hobble. (Chiefly *Sc.*) ME.

1. Thou cold Sciatica, C. our Senators *Timon* IV. i. 24. 2. The lower masts, yards and bowsprit all crippled NELSON. The trade..is crippled by the want of transport L. OLIPHANT. Hence **Cri·ppler.**

Crisis (krəi·sis). Pl. **crises,** rarely **crisises.** 1543. [a. L., a. Gr. κρίσις, f. κρίνειν to decide.] 1. *Pathol.* The point in the progress of a disease when a change takes place which is decisive of recovery or death; also, any marked or sudden change of symptoms, etc. †2. *Astrol.* Said of a conjunction of the planets which determines the issue of a disease or critical point in the course of events –1663. 3. *transf.* and *fig.* A turning-point in the progress of anything; also, a state of affairs in which a decisive change for better or worse is imminent 1627. †4. Judgement, decision –1715. †5. A criterion, sign –1657.

1. I had enjoyed a favourable c. SMOLLETT. 3. The ordinary statesman is also apt to fail in extraordinary crises JOWETT.

Crisp (krisp), *a.* [OE. *crisp, cyrps*, ad. L. *crispus* curled. Cf. OF. *crespe* curled, mod.F. *crêpé.* Perh. partly echoic in branch II.]

I. 1. Of the hair: Curly; now *esp.* stiff, closely curling, or frizzy; †also, having such hair. 2. Having a surface fretted into ripples, folds, or wrinkles ME. †3. App. = Smooth, shining, clear –1623.

1. His crispe heer lyk rynges was yronne CHAUCER. 2. The c. white crest of the running waves BLACK. 3. All th'abhorred births below crispe Heauen SHAKS.

II. Brittle or short; said *esp.* of hard things which have little cohesion and are easily crushed by the teeth, etc. 1530. Also *transf.* and *fig.*

The c...not over-roasted crackling C. LAMB. *transf.* The c. frosty air 1883. *fig.* A c. touch on the piano 1857. What he said was c. and decided 1873.

Hence **Cri·sp·ly** *adv.*, **-ness.**

Crisp, *sb.* ME. [app. f. the adj.; cf. OF. *crespe*, mod.F. *crêpe.*] †1. A crape-like material, used for veils, etc.; also a veil, etc. of this –1619. †2. A curl (of hair); *esp.* a short or close curl –1680. 3. The crackling of roast pork. Now *dial.* 1675.

Crisp (krisp), *v.* ME. [f. CRISP *a.*; cf. L. *crispare.*] 1. *trans.* To curl into short, stiff, wavy folds or crinkles; to crimp. 2. *intr.* To curl in short stiff curls 1583. 3. *trans.* To make crisp or brittle. Also *transf.* and *fig.* 1815. 4. *intr.* To become crisp 1805.

1. A cooling breeze which crisps the broad clear river BYRON. 2. The leaues..do somewhat curle or crispe GERARDE. 3. The snow..crisped by..a severe frost SCOTT. 4. The air chilled at sunset, the ground crisped C. BRONTË. Hence **Cri·sper.**

Crispate (kri·spĕt), *a.* 1846. [ad. L. *crispatus.*] Crisped; *spec.* in *Bot.* and *Zool.* having the margin curled or undulated.

Crispation (krispē¹·ʃən). 1626. [f. L. *crispare*; see -ATION.] 1. Curling, curled condition; undulation. 2. A slight contraction of any part, as that of the skin in goose-skin, etc. 1710.

2. Few can look down from a great height without creepings and crispations O. W. HOLMES.

Cri·spature. *rare.* 1745. [f. L. *crispat-*; see prec.] Crisped condition; crispation.

Cri·spin. 1645. A shoemaker, so named in allusion to St. Crispin, the patron saint of shoemakers; also sometimes a member of a union or benefit society of shoemakers.

Crispy (kri·spi), *a.* ME. [f. CRISP *a.* + -Y.] 1. Curly, wavy; undulated. 2. = CRISP *a.* II. 1611. Hence **Cri·spiness,** crispness.

Cri·ssal, *a.* Chiefly *U.S.* 1872. [ad. mod.L. *crissalis*, f. *crissum*; see below.] *Ornith.* 1. Pertaining to the crissum, as the *c. region.* 2. Characterized by the colouring of the under tail-coverts, as *C. thrush* or *thrasher.*

Criss-cross (kri·s,krǫs), *sb.* [A reduction of CHRIST('S)-CROSS: latterly treated as a redup. of *cross.*] 1. = CHRIST-CROSS, q. v. 2. [f. CRISS-CROSS *v.*] A transverse crossing 1876. 3. *U.S.* A children's game, played on a slate; Fox and Geese 1860. Hence **Criss-cross-row**; see CHRIST-CROSS-ROW.

Criss-cross (kri·s,krǫs), *a.* and *adv.* 1846. [See prec.] *adj.* Crossing, crossed; marked by crossings or intersections. *adv.* Crosswise; *fig.* in a contrary way, awry.

Criss-cross (kri·s,krǫs), *v.* 1818. [See prec.] *trans.* To mark or cover with crossing lines.

To c. the letter KEATS.

‖**Crissum** (kri·sŏm). 1874. [mod.L., f. *crissare.*] *Ornith.* The anal region of a bird under the tail; the vent-feathers or lower tail-coverts.

Cristate (kri·stĕt), *a.* 1661. [ad. L. *cristatus.*] *Nat. Hist.*, etc. Crested; in the form of a crest. So **Crista·ted** *a.*

Criterion (krəitīᵊ·riən). Pl. **criteria;** occas. **-ons.** 1613. [a. Gr. κριτήριον a means for judging, f. κριτής.] †a. An organ or faculty of judging –1678. b. A canon or standard by which anything is judged or estimated 1622. †c. A characteristic attaching to a thing, by which it can be judged or estimated –1678.

b. Regular uniformity and the straight line were the criterions of taste and beauty 1788. So ‖**Crite·rium,** L. form of Gr. (occas. used).

Crith (kriþ). 1865. [f. Gr. κριθή barley-corn, the smallest weight.] *Physics.* The weight of 1 litre of hydrogen at standard pressure and temperature; proposed by Hoffmann as the unit of weight for gaseous substances.

Crithomancy (kri·þomænsi). 1652. [f. Gr. κριθή + μαντεία.] Divination by meal strewed over animals sacrificed.

Critic, *a.* 1544. [ad. L. *criticus*, a. Gr., f. (ult.) κρίνειν to decide, judge.] †1. *Med.*, etc. = CRITICAL 4, 5. –1605. 2. Judging captiously or severely, censorious, carping 1598. 3. = CRITICAL 3. 1626.

3. Matters historic, c., analytic, and philologic 1834.

Critic (kri·tik), *sb.*[1] 1588. [ad. L. *criticus* sb. (also used), a. Gr. (see prec.), or ?after F. *critique.*] 1. One who pronounces judgement on any thing or person; *esp.* a censurer, caviller. 2. One skilled in literary or artistic criticism; a professional reviewer; also one skilled in textual or biblical criticism 1605.

1. Take heed of criticks; they bite, like fish, at any-thing, especially at bookes DEKKER. 2. The poet [Milton], we believe, understood the nature of his art better than the c. [Johnson] MACAULAY. You know who the Critics are? The men who have failed in Literature and Art DISRAELI.

†**Critic,** *sb.*[2] 1656. [app. ad. F. *critique* fem., ad. (ult.) Gr. ἡ κριτική the critical art, criticism. Now spelt and pronounced as Fr.; see CRITIQUE.] 1. The art of criticizing; CRITICISM. Also in *pl.* –1773. 2. A CRITIQUE –1766.

1. Grammar and Criticks HOBBES. 2. Make each day a critick on the last POPE.

†**Critic,** *v.* 1607. 1. *intr.* To play the critic, pass judgement (*on*) –1698. 2. *trans.* To criticize; *esp.* (in earlier use) unfavourably –1751.

2. As Helluo..Critick'd your wine and analysed your meat POPE. Hence **Cri·ticable** *a.* (*rare*).

Critical (kri·tikăl), *a.* 1590. [f. L. *criticus* (see CRITIC *a.*) + -AL.] 1. Given to judging; *esp.* fault-finding, censorious. †2. Involving or exercising careful judgement or observation; nice, exact, punctual –1716. 3. Occupied with or skilful in criticism 1641; belonging to criticism 1741. 4. *Med.*, etc. Relating to the crisis of a disease; determining the issue of a disease, etc. 1601. 5. Of the nature of, or constituting, a crisis; involving suspense as to the issue 1664. 6. Decisive, crucial 1841. 7. *Math.* and *Physics.* Constituting or relating to a point at which some action, property or condition passes over into another; constituting an extreme or limiting case 1841. 8. *Zool.* and *Bot.* Of species: Uncertain or difficult to determine 1854.

1. I am nothing, if not criticall *Oth.* II. i. 120. 3. A c. writer 1766. C. acumen FREEMAN. 4. And so the Fever terminates in a c. Abscess CHEYNE. 5. Mrs. H—'s throat was badly cut; her condition is deemed c. 1883. 7. *C. angle* in *Optics*: that angle of incidence beyond which rays of light are no longer refracted but totally reflected. *C. point* or *temperature*: that temperature above which a substance remains in the gaseous state and cannot be liquefied by any amount of pressure. Hence **Critica·lity** (*rare*), c. quality; a criticism; a crisis. **Cri·ticalness.**

Critically (kri·tikăli), *adv.* 1654. [f. prec. + -LY².] 1. Nicely, accurately. †2. Punctually, exactly –1853. †3. At or in relation to a crisis –1670; at a critical moment –1799. 4. Dangerously 1815. 5. *Physics.* In a critical state 1881.

1. To look c. into ourselves 1660. 4. Thus c. circumstanced 1815.

Criticaster (kritikæ·stəɹ). 1684. [See -ASTER.] A petty critic. (Used in contempt.)

I perceived that note to be added by some Jewish C. 1684.

Criticism (kri·tisiz'm). 1607. [f. CRITIC or L. *criticus* + -ISM.] 1. The action of criticizing, or passing (*esp.* unfavourable) judgement upon the qualities of anything; fault-finding. 2. The art of estimating the qualities and character of literary or artistic work 1674; *spec.* the critical science which deals with the text, character, composition, and origin of literary documents 1669. b. *Philos.* The critical philosophy of Kant 1867. 3. (with *pl.*) A critical remark; a CRITIQUE 1608. †4. A nice point or distinction; a quibble –1683.

1. Therfore (reader) doe I..stand at the marke of criticisme..to bee shot at DEKKER. 2. C., as it was first instituted by Aristotle, was meant a standard of judging well DRYDEN. C. and the gospel history FROUDE. *Textual c.*: that which seeks to ascertain the genuine text and meaning of an author. The Higher or Historical C. [of the sacred books] 1881.

Criticize (kri·tisəiz), *v.* Also **-ise.** 1649. [f. as prec. + -IZE.] 1. *intr.* To play the critic; to pass (*esp.* unfavourable) judgement upon something with respect to its qualities. Also with †*on* or †*upon.* 2. *trans.* To discuss critically; to animadvert upon 1665; *esp.* to censure, find fault with 1704.

1. We c. much upon the Beauty of Faces HARTLEY. 2. To c. his gait, and ridicule his dress SWIFT. Hence **Cri·tici·zable** *a.* **Cri·ticizer.**

Critico-, comb. f. (after Gr. κριτικο-), = critically, critical and . . . : as in **c.-historical.**

Critique (kritī·k). 1702. [See CRITIC *sb.*[2]] 1. An essay or article in criticism of a literary (or more rarely, an artistic) work; a review. 2. The action or art of criticizing; criticism 1815.

1. I should as soon expect to see a C. on the Posie of a Ring, as on the Inscription of a Medal ADDISON. 2. The c. of nature in detail is beyond us MARTINEAU. Hence **Criti·que** *v. trans.*, to write a c. upon.

†**Cri·tism.** *rare.* 1651. [f. Gr. κριτής.] = CRITICISM. So †**Cri·tist,** †**Cri·tize** *v* -1677.

Crizzle (kri·z'l), *v.* Now *dial.* 1624. [? dim. of CRAZE *v.*] 1. *intr.* To become rough on the surface, as glass, etc. by scaling 1673. 2. *trans.* To roughen or crumple the surface of 1624.

‖ **Cro** (krō). ME. [Ir. *cró* death, blood, blood-wyte.] 'The compensation or satisfaction made for the slaughter of any man, according to his rank' (Jam.).

Croak (krōᵘk), *sb.* 1561. [See CROAK *v.*] The deep hoarse sound made by a frog or raven. Also *transf.* and *fig.*

Croak (krōᵘ·k), *v.* 1460. [Prob. echoic.] 1. *intr.* To utter a deep, hoarse, dismal cry, as a frog or a raven. 2. *transf.* Of persons: To speak with a hoarse hollow utterance; *fig.* to talk dismally, forebode evil 1460. 3. *trans.* To utter or proclaim by croaking 1605.

1. Th' vnpleasant quyre of frogs still croking SPENSER. 2. They, who c. themselves hoarse about the decay of our trade BURKE. 3. The raven himselfe is hoarse That croakes the fatall entrance of Duncan *Macb.* I. v. 40. Hence **Croa·kery,** croakings collectively. CARLYLE.

Croaker (krōᵘ·kəɹ). 1637. [f. prec. vb. + -ER.] 1. An animal that croaks; applied *spec.* to several N. American fishes, also to the Mole Cricket 1651. 2. *transf.* One who talks dismally, one who forebodes evil.

Croaky (krōᵘki), *a.* 1851. [f. CROAK *sb.* or *v.* + -Y.] Characterized by, or given to croaking. Hence **Croa·kily** *adv.*

‖ **Croc,** †**crock** (krǫk). [OF.; of unkn. origin.] A hook: in *Harquebus à (of) c.*: see HARQUEBUS.

†**Croceous** (krōᵘ·siəs, -ʃiəs), *a.* 1657. [f. L. *croceus*, f. *crocus*.] Saffron-coloured; deep reddish yellow -1688. vars. †**Cro·ceal,** †**Cro·cean, Cro·ceate,** *adjs.*

†**Croche,** *sb.*[1] ME. [= *croce* CROSE.] 1. A pastoral staff, crook, crosier -1563. 2. A CRUTCH, q. v. -1500.

Croche, *sb.*[2] 1575. [a. F. *croche* spur on a fruit-tree, etc.; from same radical as CROC.] One of the buds at the top of a stag's horn.

‖ **Crochet** (kro·ʃe, krōᵘ·ʃi), *sb.* 1848. [F., dim. of *croche*, *croc*.] A kind of knitting done with a hooked needle; work so knitted. Also *attrib.*

A shirt as of c. of women CLOUGH.

Crochet (kro·ʃe, krōᵘ·ʃi), *v.* Pa. t. and pple. **Crocheted** (krōᵘ·ʃed). 1858. [f. the sb.] *intr.* To work with a crochet-needle; *trans.* to knit in crochet.

†‖ **Crocheteur.** 1579. [F.; f. *crochet* hook.] A porter -1613.

Crociary (krōᵘ·ʃiări). [ad. med.L. *crociarius*, f. *crocia* crosier.] *Eccl.* 'The person who carried the crosier before the abbot or bishop' (Ash 1775).

Crocidolite (krosi·dǒləit). 1835. [f. Gr. κροκίς, κροκιδ-, var. of κροκύς nap of woollen cloth + λίθος.] *Min.* A fibrous silicate of iron and sodium, called also *blue asbestos*; sometimes massive or earthy. Also, a yellow fibrous mineral produced by natural alteration from the blue crocidolite, and much used for ornament.

Crocin (krōᵘ·sin). 1863. [f. L. *crocus* saffron + -IN.] *Chem.* A red powder, the colouring matter of Chinese Yellow pods, the fruit of *Gardenia grandiflora.*

Crock (krǫk), *sb.*[1] [OE. *croc(c* and *crocca* masc., earthenware pot, related to Icelandic *krukka* f., in same sense.] 1. An earthen pot, jar, etc. 2. A metal pot. (*S. W. of Eng.*) 1475. 3. A broken piece of earthenware 1850.

1. Like foolish flies about an hony-crocke SPENSER.

Crock (krǫk), *sb.*[2] Now *dial.* 1657. [?] Smut, soot, dirt.

Crock (krǫk), *sb.*[3] Chiefly *Sc.* 1528. [app. related to CRACK *v.*; cf. Norw. *krake*, *krakje* a sickly, weakly, or emaciated beast, Sw. *krake*, Da. *krak*, *krakke*, etc.] 1. An old ewe, or one past bearing. 2. An old broken-down horse 1879; also *transf.*

†**Crock,** *sb.*[4] [?] ?A low stool. ADDISON.

Crock, *v.*[1] Now *dial.* 1594. [f. CROCK *sb.*[1]] To put up in a crock or pot.

Crock, *v.*[2] Now *dial.* 1642. [f. CROCK *sb.*[2]] *trans.* To smut with soot, etc.; to soil, defile.

Crock, *v.*[3] 1893. [f. CROCK *sb.*[3] 2.] *intr.* and *trans.* To (cause to) collapse; often with *up.* So **Cro·cky** *a.*, broken-down.

†**Crockard.** ME. [AF. *crokard*: ?] A foreign coin, decried as base under Edward I. -1769.

†**Crocker.** ME. [f. CROCK *sb.*[1] + -ER[1].] A potter -1703.

Crockery (krǫ·kəri). 1719. [f. CROCKER; see -ERY.] Crocks collectively; *esp.* earthenware vessels. *Comb.* **c.-ware** = CROCKERY.

Crocket (krǫ·kėt). ME. [a. AF. *croket*, *croquet* = F. *crochet*; see CROCHET, CROQUET.] †1. A curl formerly worn. (ME. only.) 2. *Archit.* One of the small ornaments, usually in the form of buds or curled leaves, placed on the inclined sides of pinnacles, canopies, etc. in Gothic architecture 1673. 3. = CROCHE *sb.*[2] 1870. 4. *attrib.* Decorated with crockets 1703.

3. You will discourse.. of the antlers and the crockets BLACK. Hence **Cro·cketing,** c.-work.

Crocodile (krǫ·kǒdəil). [ME. *cocodrille*, *cokadrill*, etc., a. OF. *cocodrille* = med.L. *cocodrillus*, corruption of L. *crocodilus*, a Gr. κροκόδειλος. Refash. after Gr. and L. in 16–17th c.] 1. A large amphibious saurian reptile of the genus *Crocodilus* or allied genera. The name belongs properly to the crocodile of the Nile (*C. niloticus* or *vulgaris*); but is extended to other species, and sometimes to all *Crocodilia*, including the Alligator and the Gavial. 2. *fig.* A person who weeps hypocritically or with a malicious purpose, as the crocodile was fabled to do 1595. 3. *Logic.* = CROCODILITE 1727. 4. *joc.* A girls' school walking two and two in a long file 1870; also *transf.* 5. *attrib.* 1563.

1. Cokadrilles.. Theise Serpentes slen men, and thei eten hem wepynge MAUNDEV. 5. Thence came the Prouerb, he shed C. teares, *viz.* fayned teares 1623. Hence **Crocodi·lian,** *a.* †like a c.; pertaining to a c.: belonging to the c. family; *sb.* an animal of the c. family.

†**Cro·codilite.** 1624. [ad. L. *crocodilites.*] *Logic.* Name of an ancient sophism (see STANLEY *Hist. Philos.*) -1660.

Crocoite (krōᵘ·koˌəit). 1844. [f. Gr. κροκόεις saffron-coloured.] *Min.* Native chromate of lead, a mineral of a red or orange colour.

Croconic (krokǫ·nik), *a.* 1838. [f. L. *crocus* + *-on* (meaningless) + -IC.] In *c. acid* ($C_5H_2O_5$), an inodorous, strongly acid substance, obtained in the form of yellow crystals or powder. Hence **Cro·conate,** a salt of this acid.

Crocus (krōᵘ·kǒs). 1639. [a. L., a. Gr. κρόκος; app. of Semitic origin; cf. Heb. *karkōm* crocus, saffron, Arab. *kurkum* saffron, turmeric. OE. had *croh* saffron, from Latin.] 1. A genus of hardy dwarf bulbous plants, N.O. *Iridaceæ*, with brilliant flowers, usually deep yellow or purple, which appear before the leaves in early spring, or in some species in autumn. The autumnal species, *C. sativus*, yields SAFFRON. †2. Saffron; the stigma of *C. sativus.* (In OE. *croh.*) -1710. 3. *Chem.* A name given to various yellow or red powders obtained from metals by calcination, as *c. of copper* (*c. veneris*), cuprous oxide, etc.; now chiefly to the peroxide of iron obtained by calcination of sulphide of iron, and used as a polishing powder 1640. 4. *slang.* A quack doctor 1785. Hence **Cro·cused** *ppl. a.* bedecked with crocuses.

Croft (krǫft), *sb.*[1] [OE. *croft* enclosed field; cf. Du. *kroft.*] 1. A piece of enclosed ground, used for tillage or pasture: in most parts a small piece of arable land attached to a house. Also *fig.* 2. A small agricultural holding worked by a peasant tenant 1842. 3. *attrib.* 1791.

1. To occupy her husband's cottage, and cultivate.. a c. of land adjacent SCOTT.

Croft, *sb.*[2] *rare.* 1470. [ad. L. *crupta*, *crypta.*] A crypt, vault, cavern.

Croft (krǫft), *v.* 1772. [f. CROFT *sb.*[1]] To bleach (linen, etc.) on the grass.

Crofter (krǫ·ftəɹ). 1799. [f. CROFT *sb.*[1]] One who rents and cultivates a croft; *esp.* in the Highlands and Islands of Scotland, one of the joint tenants of a divided farm. Also *attrib.*

Crofting (krǫ·ftiŋ), *vbl. sb.* 1743. [f. CROFT *sb.*[1] + -ING[1].] 1. The state of being successively cropped; the land so cropped. 2. The system of croft-tenancy; the holding of a crofter 1851.

†**Croh.** [OE. *crōg*, *croh*; cf. Ger. *krug*, and CROCK *sb.*[1]] A pitcher -ME.

Croh, OE. f. CROCUS, saffron.

Crois, early f. CROSS, q. v.

Croisad(e, -ada, -ado, early ff. CRUSADE.

†**Croisard,** a crusader.

†**Croise,** *v.* ME. [a. OF. *cruisier*, *croisier* :—L. *cruciare*, f. *crucem.*] 1. *trans.* To mark with a cross; *esp.* by way of giving sanctity to a vow; *refl.* and *pass.* to take the cross in solemnization of a vow -1639. 2. To crucify -1450. Hence †**Croised** *ppl. a.* having taken the cross.

Croise, *sb.*; see CROISES.

†**Croisee, -ie, -y.** 1482. [a. OF. *croisée*, etc. = med.L. *cruciata*. In 16th c. displaced by *croisade.*] A crusade -1615. So †**Croiserie, -ry,** crusading; a crusade.

†**Croi·ses, croi·sees,** *sb. pl.* 1656. [a. F. *croisés*, in OF. *croisiés* :—L. *cruciatos*; see CROISE *v.* 1.] Those who have been croised, crusaders. (Occas. used as an archaism for *Crusades*; hence an erron. sing. *croise.*) -1846.

Croissant, earlier f. CRESCENT.

†**Cro·ker.** *rare.* 1577. [app. f. CROCUS + -ER[1].] A cultivator or seller of saffron.

Crome, cromb (krōᵘm, krūm), *sb.* Now *local.* ME. [repr. an OE. *cramb, *crǫmb f. :—WG. *kramba*, f. *kramb-* grade of **krimban*; cf. CRAMP *sb.*[1]] A hook, a crook. †In early use, also = claw, talon. Hence **Crome, cromb** *v.* to seize or draw with a c.

Cromlech (krǫ·mlek). ME. [a. Welsh, f. *crom*, fem. of *crwm* crooked, bent, concave, convex + *llech* (flat) stone.] A structure of prehistoric age consisting of a large flat unhewn stone resting horizontally on three or more stones set upright; found *esp.* in Wales, Devonshire, Cornwall, and Ireland. Also applied to similar structures elsewhere.

This is the application of the word in Welsh. In Brittany these structures are called *dolmen* (= table-stones), while *cromlech* is the name of a circle of standing stones. var. (*erron.*) **Crommel.** LYTTON.

Cromorne (kromǭ·ɹn). 1694. [a. F., corrupt f. Ger. *krummhorn* crooked horn.] = KRUMMHORN, CREMONA[2].

Cromwellian (krǫmwe·liăn). 1725.

A. *adj.* Of or pertaining to Oliver Cromwell.

B. *sb.* An adherent of Cromwell; one of the settlers in Ireland at the Cromwellian Settlement of 1652, or of their descendants.

Crone (krōᵘn), *sb.* ME. [In sense 2, conn. w. early mod.Du. *kronje*, *karonje*, a. NF. *carogne* carcass; see CARRION. In sense 1, prob. f. ONF. *carogne* 'a cantankerous or mischievous woman'.] 1. A withered old woman; occas. applied to a man 1630. 2. An old ewe 1552.

1. This olde Sowdones, þis cursed c. CHAUCER. A few old battered crones of office DISRAELI. Hence †**Crone** *v.* to pick out and reject (the old sheep). Also *transf.*

Cronel, obs. f. CORONAL.

†**Cronet, cronett.** 1519. [Syncopated f. CORONET.] 1. = CORONET, q. v. -1602. 2. Some part of the armour of a horse 1633.

Cronian (krōᵘ·niăn), *a.* [f. Gr. κρόνιος belonging to Cronos (Saturn).] *C. sea*: the northern frozen sea. MILT. *P. L.* x. 290.

†**Cronie, crony.** *rare.* Var. of (or ? error for) CRONE. Burton.

Cronk (krǫŋk). *dial.* [Echoic.] The croak of a raven; in U.S., the cry of the wild-goose.

Cronstedtite (krǫ·nstėtəit). 1823. [f. *Cronstedt*, a Swedish mineralogist; see -ITE.] *Min.* A hydrous silicate of iron and manganese.

Crony (krōᵘ·ni), *sb.* 1663. [*orig.*, University slang. Not conn. w. CRONE.] An intimate friend or associate; a chum. Also *attrib.*

Jack Cole, my old schoolfellow .. who was a great chrony of mine PEPYS. Hence **Cro·ny** *v.* to associate (*with*) as a c.

Crood, croud, *v. Sc.* 1513. [Echoic.] *intr.* To coo as a dove. Hence **Croo·dle** *v.*[1] *intr.* (in same sense).

Croodle (krū·d'l), *v.*² *dial.* 1788. [?] *intr.* To cower or crouch down; to draw oneself together, as for warmth; to nestle close together, or cling close to a person.

'There,' said Lucia, as she clung croodling to him KINGSLEY.

Crook (kruk). [ME. *crok, croc*, app. a. ON. *krókr* crook, hook, barb, trident. Unkn. elsewhere in Teut.]

A. *sb.* 1. Any implement of hooked form; a hook. *spec.* **a.** A shepherd's staff, having one end hooked, for catching the hinder leg of a sheep ME. **b.** The pastoral staff of a bishop, etc., shaped like a shepherd's staff; a crosier ME. **2.** Any incurved appendage ME. **3.** An odd corner, nook ME. †4. (*pl.*) Brackets, parentheses –1762. **5.** *Mus.* A piece of curved tubing added to a horn, cornet, etc., to raise or lower the pitch 1842. **6.** The act of crooking ME. **7.** A bending or curve 1486. †8. *fig.* Crooked conduct; a trick, wile –1594. **9.** One whose conduct is crooked; a swindler, sharper; a professional criminal. orig. *U.S.* 1886.

1. Er the bishop hent hem with his c. CHAUCER. 2. The young fronds of the.. Ferns uncurling their crooks 1850. 3. It was full of crooks and nooks W. IRVING. 6. With sacrifice of knees, of crooks, and cringes B. JONSON. 7. The crooks of Tweed STEVENSON.

Phr. *On the c.*: dishonestly (*slang*). *C. in one's lot*: an affliction, trial. *Sc. By hook or by c.*: see HOOK.

B. *adj.* [? shortened f. *crookt, crooked*.] = CROOKED 1508.

Comb.: **c.-back**, †a crooked back; one who has a crooked back; a hunchback; hence, **-backed** *a.*; **-neck** (*U.S.*), a name of varieties of squash (*Cucurbita maxima*) having the neck recurved.

Crook (kruk), *v.*¹ ME. [f. CROOK *sb.*] **1.** *trans.* To distort from a straight line; to bend; to curve. †2. *fig.* To turn out of the straight course; to pervert, twist –1646. **3.** *intr.* To be or become crooked; to bend, curve ME. **4.** *intr.* To bend the body; to bow (*arch.*) ME. †5. *intr.* To turn aside out of the straight course (*lit.* and *fig.*) –1607.

1. And crooke the pregnant hindges of the knee SHAKS. 2. There is no one thinge yat crokes youth more than suche unlefull games ASCHAM. Hee crooketh them to his owne endes BACON. 3. A riuer both large and deepe..goeth crooking on the left hand 1579.

†**Crook**, *v.*² ME. [Echoic; cf. CROAK.] **1.** *intr.* To croak. Rarely *trans.* –1617. **2.** To crood, as a dove –1611.

Crooked (kru·kėd), *a.* ME. [f. CROOK *v.* and *sb.* + -ED.] **1.** Bent from the straight form; curved, bent, awry. **2.** Of persons: Deformed, bent or bowed with age. Hence *transf.* of *age*. ME. **3.** *fig.* Deviating from rectitude; not straightforward; dishonest, perverse; awry ME.; *colloq.* dishonestly come by. (*U.S.* and *Australia.*) 1876. **4.** quasi-*adv.* Not straight 1545.

1. If the drinke..touch my Palat aduersly, I make a c. face at it *Cor.* II. i. 62. 2. A Sybil old, bow-bent with c. age MILT. 3. A peruerse and c. generation *Deut.* xxxii. 5. Of c. counsels POPE. A c. horse R. BOLDREWOOD. Hence **Croo·kedly** *adv.* **Croo·kedness**, the quality or state of being c. (*lit.* and *fig.*).

†**Croo·ken**, *v.* 1552. [f. CROOK *v.*] To make, be, or become crooked; also *fig.* –1828.

Crool (krūl), *v. rare.* 1580. [app. echoic; cf. next.] To make an inarticulate sound more liquid and prolonged than a croak.

Croon (krūn), *v.* Chiefly *Sc.* 1460. [app. f. LG.; cf. Du. *kreunen* to groan, whimper, MLG. *kronen* to growl, etc. There is no trace of the word in OE.] **1.** *intr.* To utter a continued, loud, deep sound; to bellow as a bull, boom as a bell, etc. (*Sc.* or *n. dial.*) 1513. **2.** To sing (or speak) in a low murmuring tone 1460; to make moan (*Sc.* or *n. dial.*) 1823. **3.** *trans.* To sing (a song, etc.) in a low murmuring undertone; to hum 1790.

2. I hear a mother crooning to her baby A. B. EDWARDS. 3. Whiles crooning o'er some auld Scots sonnet BURNS. Hence **Croon** *sb.* a loud deep sound, such as the bellow of a bull, etc.; a low murmuring or humming sound. **Croo·ner**, one who croons; *spec.* in *Sc.*, a fish, the Grey Gurnard, from the noise it makes when landed.

Crop (krǫp), *sb.* [OE. *crop(p*, with Ger. cognates indicating a primitive sense of 'swollen protuberance, bunch'. See also CROUP, GROUP.] **1.** A pouch-like enlargement of the œsophagus or gullet in many birds, in which the food is partially prepared for digestion; the craw. **2.** *transf.* and *fig.* The stomach or maw; also the throat. Now *Sc.* and *dial.* Cf. GIZZARD. ME. †3. The head of a herb, flower, tree, etc.; a cyme; also *fig.* –1785. **b.** *Archit.* A finial 1478. **4.** The upper part of a whip; hence the stock or handle of a whip; *esp.* a whipstock with a handle and a loop instead of the lash; more fully a *hunting-crop* 1562. **5.** [from 3] The annual produce of plants grown or gathered for food; the produce of the field, either while growing or when gathered; harvest ME. **6.** The produce of some particular plant in one season or locality ME. Also *transf.* **7.** The entire hide of an animal tanned 1457. **8.** *transf.* and *fig.* A supply of anything produced or appearing 1575. **9.** *Tin-mining.* The best quality of tin-ore obtained after dressing; more fully *c.-ore, -tin* 1778. **10.** [f. CROP *v.*] The act of cropping or its result; *e.g.* the cutting or wearing of the hair short; a closely cropped head of hair 1795; an ear-mark 1675. **11.** *Min.*, etc. An outcrop 1679. †12. *attrib.* –1825.

3. Take..the crops of Thyme, Savory, Lavender, etc. 1686. 5. The husbandman looks not for a c. in the wild desart BP. HALL. 6. *The crops*: the whole of the agricultural yield of a particular district or season. 8. The annual academical c. of beardless youths 1830. 10. Newgate c. 1878.

Phr. *Neck and c.*: see NECK. *Comb.* **c.-hide**, a hide, *esp.* a cow- or ox-hide, tanned whole and untrimmed.

Crop (krǫp), *v.* ME. [f. CROP *sb.*] **1.** *trans.* To cut off or remove the crop, head, or terminal parts of; to pluck off, cull, browse. Also *fig.* **2.** To reap. Also *fig.* 1601. **3.** *intr.* To bear a crop or crops 1606. **4.** *trans.* To cause to bear a crop; to sow or plant with a crop 1607. **5.** To cut off the top or extremity of 1607; *spec.* to clip short the ears, hair, etc. 1796. **6.** *intr. Min.*, etc. Of a stratum, vein, etc.: To come *up* or *out* 1665.

1. Hee cropt off the top of his yong twigs *Ezek.* xvii. 4. Sheep..that c. the tender grass QUARLES. 5. Having their ears cropped for perjury BP. WATSON.

Phr. *To c. up* (fig.): to turn up unexpectedly. *To c. out* (rarely *forth*): to disclose itself incidentally.

†**Cro·p-ear.** 1596. [Cf. CROP *v.* 5.] An ear that has been cropped; hence, a crop-eared animal or person –1702. Hence **Cro·p-ea:red** *a.* having the ears cropped; also, having the hair cut short, so that the ears are conspicuous, as the Roundheads.

Cro·p-fu:ll, *a.* 1632. [f. CROP *sb.* 1–2.] Having the crop or stomach filled.

Cropper¹ (krǫ·pəɹ). 1655. [f. CROP *sb.* 1 + -ER¹.] A breed of pigeons having the power of greatly puffing up their crops; a pouter.

Cro·pper². 1483. [f. CROP *sb.* or *v.* + -ER.] **1.** One who or that which crops. **2.** One who shears the nap of cloth; also, a machine for doing this 1711. **3.** One who raises a crop 1573. **4.** A plant which yields a crop 1845.

Cro·pper³. 1858. [? f. phr. *neck and crop*.] *colloq.* A heavy fall; often *fig.*

Croppy (krǫ·pi). 1798. [f. CROP *v.* 5.] One who has his hair cut short; applied *esp.* to the Irish rebels of 1798, who thus showed their sympathy with the French Revolution.

Cro·p-sick, *a.* Now *dial.* 1624. [f. CROP *sb.* 1–2.] Disordered in stomach, *esp.* by excess in eating and drinking. Often *fig.* Hence **Cro·p-sickness.**

Croquet (krōᵘ·ke, -ki), *sb.* 1858. [a. North Fr. *croquet*, dial. f. *crochet*, dim. of *croc, croche* crook.] **1.** A game played upon a lawn, in which wooden balls are driven by wooden mallets through hoops fixed in the ground in a particular order. **2.** The action of the verb (see CROQUET *v.*) 1874.

Croquet (krōᵘ·ke, -ki), *v.* Pa. t. and pple. croqueted (krōᵘ·kėd); also **croqueed, -éd, -ed.** 1858. [f. prec. sb.] In the game of croquet: To drive away a ball, after hitting it with one's own, by placing the two in contact and striking one's own with the mallet (*trans.* and *absol.*).

‖**Croquette** (krǫke·t). 1706. [F., f. *croquer* to crunch.] A ball of rice, potato, or finely minced meat or fish, seasoned and fried crisp.

‖**Crore** (krōᵊɹ). *Anglo-Ind.* 1609. [ad. Hindī *karōṛ, kroṛ*:—Prakrit *krodi*, Skr. *koṭi*.] Ten millions, or one hundred lakhs (of rupees).

†**Crose, croce.** ME. [a. OF. *croce* (pronounced krotsə), in *Roland* 11th c.:—late L. type **croccia, croccea*, from late L. **croccus*, in F. *croc.* (See CROC.) A distinct word from L. *crux* CROSS; but confounded with *cross* as *crosse* in 16th c.] **1.** A crosier –1617. **2.** A staff ME.

Crosier, crozier (krōᵘ·ʒiəɹ). ME. [repr. two words: (1) OF. *crocier*, med.L. *crociarius* bearer of a *crocia* (see CROSE); (2) F. *croisier*, L. type **cruciarius* one who bears or has to do with a cross (*crux, croix*). The ME. forms of these were *crocer* or *croser*, and *croiser*; but the distinction was lost, when *cross* and *crose* were confounded as *crosse*. See CROSE.] **1.** One who bears a cross before an archbishop. (prop. **croiser.**) Now *Hist.* †2. The bearer of a bishop's crook or pastoral staff. (prop. **crocer, croser.**) –1558. †**b.** Hence, apparently, *Crosier's staff, crosier staff*, the episcopal staff or crook –1733. **3.** The pastoral staff or crook of a bishop or abbot. (= med.L. *crocea, crocia.*) 1500. ¶ **b.** (*erron.*) The cross of an archbishop. (Chiefly 19th c.) Also *transf.* †4. *Astron.* The Southern Cross; *pl.* its four stars –1751. Hence **Cro·siered** *a.* bearing a c.

Croslet, obs. f. CROSSLET.

Cross (krǫs), *sb.* [From L. *crucem* in several forms: (1) late OE. *crúc*, ad. L. *crucem*; (2) earlier OE. *cros*, a. OIr. = Norse *kross*; (3) *croiz, crois*, etc. The northern *cros* (*crosse, cross*) is the surviving type.] **1.** A kind of gibbet; a stake, generally with a transverse bar, on which anciently certain criminals were put to a cruel or ignominious death ME. **2.** *spec.* The particular structure on which Jesus Christ suffered death; the holy ROOD. (Often written with a capital C.) ME. **3.** The sign of the cross made with the right hand, as a religious act ME. **4.** A representation or delineation of a cross on any surface; used as a sacred mark, symbol, badge, or the like ME. **5.** A figure of a cross as a religious emblem, set up in the open air or within a building, worn round the neck, etc. ME. **6.** A staff surmounted by a cross, borne *esp.* as an emblem of office before an archbishop ME. **7.** A monument in the form of a cross, or having a cross upon it, erected in places of resort, at cross-ways, etc. ME.; *spec.* a market-cross 1465; hence, a market (*local*) 1577. **8.** *fig.* Used as the ensign and symbol of Christianity; the Christian religion ME. **9.** *fig.* The atonement wrought on the cross ME. **10.** A trial or affliction, viewed as to be borne with Christian patience ME.; also *gen.* Anything that thwarts or crosses 1573. **11.** Any cross-shaped object, figure, or mark ME. **12.** A surveyor's instrument; a CROSS-STAFF 1669. **13.** *Her.*, etc. A conventional representation of a cross, or of some modification of it, or of two crossing bars, used as an ordinary or charge, as an ornamental figure in art, etc. 1486. **14.** A figure of a cross used as the ensign of an order of knights; also, a wearer of such a cross 1651. †15. The figure of a cross stamped upon one side of a coin; hence, a coin bearing a cross; a coin generally –1797. †16. A crossing or crossed position: hence *on cross, o cross, a cross*: see ACROSS, CROSS *adv.* –1659. **17.** An intermixture of breeds or races, *esp.* in cattle-breeding; an animal, etc. due to crossing 1760; also *fig.* of men and things 1796. **18.** *slang.* That which is not fair and 'square' 1812. **19.** *Irish Hist.* = CROSS-LAND 1612.

1. The body of Cleomenes was flayed and hung on a c. THIRLWALL. 2. Those blessed feete..nail'd on the bitter Crosse 1 *Hen. IV*, I. i. 26. Phr. *Stations, way of the C.*: see STATION, WAY. 3. Then he shall make a crosse upon the childes forehead and breste *Bk. Com. Prayer* 1548–9. 4. His [the Pope's] slipper of crimson velvet, with a gold c. embroidered on it 1700. 6. Thomas Bourchier archebysshop of Caunterbury..wythe hys crosse before hym, went forthe.. toward Londoun 1465. 7. At the crose in Cheppe 1553. 8. Streaming the Ensigne of the Christian Crosse, Against black Pagans, Turkes, and Saracens *Rich. II*, IV. i. 94. 9. The preaching of the Crosse 1 *Cor.* i. 18. 10. No C. no Crown PENN. After all his losses and crosses ARBUTHNOT. 11. The Southern c.—the pole-star of the South LOCKYER. The body of the Church formes a Crosse EVELYN. In the margent..yee shall set a crosse + 1588. 13. **Greek c.**, an upright c. with limbs of equal length; **Latin c.**, in which the lower limb is longer than the others; **St. Andrew's c.**, or **c. saltier**, an X-shaped c.; **c. of St. Anthony** or *Tau c.*, a T-shaped c.; **c. patée or formée**, in which the limbs are narrow

where they meet, and gradually expand, the whole forming nearly a square; **Maltese c., c. of Malta** or **c. of eight points,** a modification of the preceding, in which the extremity of each limb is indented; **c. of Jerusalem,** a c. having each arm capped by a cross-bar; **c. of St. George,** the Greek c., red on a white ground; **c. of St. Patrick,** the saltier c. of Ireland, red on a white ground, etc. 15. To come and take up an honest house, without c. or coin to bless yourself with GOLDSM. Phr. **C. and (or) pile** [F. *croix et (ou) pile*]. **a.** Head or tail; hence occas.: a coin, money (*arch.*). †**b.** *fig.* A thing and its opposite -1663. †**c.** 'Tossing up'; *fig.* a mere 'toss-up' -1798. †**d.** *advb. phr.* By mere chance -1712. 17. *fig.* A c. between a military dandy and a squire 1852. 18. Phr. *On the c.*: in a dishonest fraudulent manner.

Cross (krǫs), *v.* Pa. t. and pple. **crossed, crost** (krǫst). ME. [f. CROSS *sb.*] †**1.** *trans.* To crucify -1550. **2.** To make the sign of the cross upon or over ME. †**3.** = CROISE **1.** -1610. **4.** To cancel by marking with a cross or by drawing lines across; to erase (*lit.* and *fig.*) Const. *off, out.* 1483. **5.** To lay across; to place crosswise 1489; *Naut.* to set in position across the mast; to hoist (a CROSS-SAIL) ME. **6.** To lie or pass across; to intersect ME.; also *intr.*; *colloq.* to bestride (a horse, etc.) 1760. **7.** To draw a line or lines across; to write across 1703. **8.** To pass over; to pass from one side to the other (*trans.* and *intr.*) 1486. *causal.* To carry across 1804. **9.** To extend across 1577. **10.** To pass in opposite directions; to meet in passing 1782. **11.** To meet (*esp.* adversely) in one's way (*arch.*) 1598; to come across (*rare*) 1684. **12.** *fig.* To thwart, oppose 1555; †to debar *from* (*rare*) -1650; †to contravene -1702. **13.** *trans.* To cause to interbreed; to modify by interbreeding 1754; *intr.* to interbreed (*mod.*).

2. Crossing their hands with coin CLARE. 4. The debt is paid, the score is crossed BP. HALL. 5. Few men ventured to c. swords with him SCOTT. 7. I have ..crossed the t's and dotted the i's THACKERAY. Phr. *To c. a cheque.* 8. How yong Leander crost the Hellespont *Two Gent.* I. i. 22. Phr. *To c. the path of*: to come in the way of, thwart. 10. A letter from me would have crossed yours..on the road MRS. CARLYLE. 11. Ile crosse it, though it blast me *Haml.* I. i. 127. 12. He was crossed in Love STEELE. To crosse me from the Golden time I looke for SHAKS.

Hence **Crossed, crost** *ppl. a.* **Cro·sser.**

Cross (krǫs), *a.* 1523. [Orig. CROSS *adv.* used *attrib.* or *ellipt.*] **1.** Lying or passing athwart; transverse; crossing, intersecting 1602; contrary 1617. Also *fig.* **2.** Contrary, opposite, opposed *to.* (Now rarely predicative.) 1565. **3.** Adverse, thwarting; contrary to one's desire or liking; unfavourable, untoward 1565. **4.** †Given to opposition, contrarious -1770; ill-tempered; out of humour (*colloq.*) 1639. **5.** Involving interchange or reciprocal action 1581; *spec.* in *Book-keeping* 1893. **6.** Cross-bred 1886. **7.** Dishonest; dishonestly come by. (Opp. to *square* or *straight.*) 1892.

1. As crosse as a pair of tailors' legs MARSTON. C. winds DE FOE. *fig.* C. interests DISRAELI. A c. issue M. PATTISON. 2. Answers so very c. to the purpose LOWTH. 3. C. luck 1565, fortune DEKKER, Fate DRYDEN. 4. I have never had a c. word from him in my life JANE AUSTEN. Phr. *As c. as two sticks* (with play on sense 1). 5. For hapning both to Love each other Sisters, They have concluded it in a c. Marriage DRYDEN. C. payments on revenue accounts GLADSTONE. Hence **Cro·ssly** *adv.* †cross-wise; unfavourably; ill-humouredly. **Cro·ssness.**

Cross (krǫs), *adv.* Now *rare.* 1577. [Aphet. f. ACROSS, q. v.] †**1.** Across, transversely -1793. †**2.** In a contrary way *to* -1732. **3.** Awry, amiss. Now *colloq.* 1603.

Cross, *prep.* 1551. [CROSS *adv.* with object expressed.] = ACROSS *prep.* Now *dial.*, or *poet.* (and often written *'cross*).

Hardly could one see crosse the streetes EVELYN. *C. lots*, more usu. *across lots* (U.S.): across the lots or fields as a short cut.

Cross- in *comb.* In some of these relations the use of the hyphen is almost optional.

A. General uses. **1.** From CROSS *sb.* **a.** *objective*: as *c.-adoring, -bearing*, C.-BEARER, etc. 1631. **b.** *instrumental* and *locative*: as C.-FIXED 1839. **c.** *attrib.*: as *c.-days*, C.-BOW, -BUN, etc. ME. **2.** From CROSS *a.*: as *c.-band*, C.-BAR, *c.-vein*, C.-BONES, *c.-current* 1590. **3.** From CROSS *adv.* **a.** with *verbs*: as C.-CUT, -BREED, -QUESTION, *c.-invite* 1590. **b.** with *pr. pples.*: as *c.-pulling*, etc. 1634. **c.** with *pa. pples.*: as C.-GARTERED, etc. 1577. **d.** with *vbl. sbs.* and nouns involving action: as *c.-planking, -entry*, etc. 1684. **4.** From CROSS *prep.* With *object sbs.*: as *c.-country*, C.-COURSE *a.* 1589. **5.** Parasynthetic derivs.: as C.-HEADED, *c.-armed*, C.-LEGGED, etc. 1601.

B. Special combs.: **c.-action** (*Law*), an action brought by the defendant against the plaintiff or a co-defendant in the same action: cf. CROSS-BILL; **-axle,** (1) a shaft, windlass, or roller worked by opposite levers, as the copper-plate printing-press, etc.; (2) a driving-axle with cranks set at an angle of 90° with each other; **-banded** (*Carpentry*), having a veneer laid upon its upper side, with the grain of the wood crossing that of the rail: said of hand-railing; **-bedding** (*Geol.*), apparent lines of stratification crossing the real ones; **-belt,** orig., a belt worn over both shoulders, and crossing in front of the breast; also later, a single belt passing obliquely across the breast; hence **-belted** *a.*; **-birth,** a birth in which the child lies transversely to the uterus; **-bit** = CROSS-PIECE; **-channel** *a.*, passing or situated across the (English or other) channel; **-chocks,** 'pieces of timber fayed across the dead-wood in midships, to make good the deficiency of the lower heels of the futtocks' (Crabbe); **-file,** a file with two convex faces of different curvatures, used in dressing out the arms or crosses of fine wheels; **-finger** *v. intr.*; on wood-wind instruments: to finger out of serial order; **-frog,** a frog adapted for tracks that cross at right angles; **-guard,** a sword-guard consisting of a short transverse bar; **-index** *v.*, to index under another heading as a c.-reference; **-loop,** a loophole in a fort in the form of a cross so as to give free range to an archer, etc.; so *cross-oylet*; **-quarters** (*Arch.*), an ornament of tracery in the form of a cruciform flower; **-sea,** said of the sea, when the waves run athwart the direction of the wind, or when two sets of waves cross each other; **-talk** (*Telephone*), the sputtering noises induced in the telephone line by currents passing through some neighbouring line; **-tining** (*dial.*), cross-harrowing; **-valve,** a valve placed where a pipe has two cross-branches; **-vine,** a climber of the southern U.S., in which a section of the stem shows a cross-like appearance; **-webbing,** webbing drawn over the saddle-tree to strengthen the seat of a saddle; **-wire,** a wire that crosses; spec. = *cross-hair.*

†**Cross-aisle,** transept; see AISLE.

Cross-bar (krǫ·sbāɹ), *sb.* 1557. [CROSS- 2.] **1.** A transverse bar 1562; † = *cross-bar shot* (see below) -1712. **2.** A transverse line or stripe 1599. †**3.** *Her.* The bar sinister -1732. †**4.** *fig.* An impediment; a misfortune -1616.

Comb. **c.-bar shot**; orig. a ball with a bar projecting on each side of it; later, a projectile which expanded on leaving the gun into the form of a cross, with one quarter of the ball at each radial point: cf. *bar-shot* (see BAR). Hence **Cross-bar** *v.* to furnish with cross-bars; to mark with cross-bars.

Cro·ss-beak. = CROSSBILL.

Cross-beam (krǫ·sbīm). 1594. [CROSS- 2.] A beam placed across some part of a structure or mechanism; a transverse beam.

Cross-bearer (krǫ·sbēᵊ:rəɹ). 1540. [CROSS- 1.] **1.** One who bears, wears, or carries a cross; *spec.* one who carries an archbishop's cross before him. **2.** *Cro·ss-bea·rer.* The transverse bars supporting the grate-bars of a furnace 1874.

Cro·ss-bea·rings. 1809. [CROSS *a.* or *adv.*] *Naut.* The bearings of two or more points taken from a point of reference so as to plot the position of a ship on a chart, etc.

Cro·ss-be·nch. 1846. [CROSS *a.*, CROSS- 2.] A bench placed at right angles to other benches. *spec.* In the House of Lords certain benches so placed, on which independent or neutral members sometimes sit. Also *attrib.*

attrib. It would be well for this House if a great majority of its members had the c.-bench mind DK. ARGYLL.

Crossbill (krǫ·sbil). 1672. [CROSS *a.*] A bird of the genus *Loxia* (family *Fringillidæ*) having the mandibles of the bill curved so as to cross each other when the bill is closed. The Common Crossbill is *L. curvirostra.*

Cross-bill, cross bill. 1637. [CROSS *a.*, CROSS- 3 d.] *Law.* A bill filed in Chancery by a defendant against the plaintiff or other co-defendants in the same suit. **b.** A bill of exchange given in consideration of another bill.

†**Cro·ssbi·te,** *v.* 1532. [CROSS- 3 a.] **1.** *trans.* To bite the biter; to take in, gull, deceive -1823. **2.** To censure bitingly or bitterly -1697. Hence †**Cro·ssbite** *sb.* a cheat, trick, deception.

Cro·ss-bond. 1876. [CROSS *a.*] *Bricklaying.* A bond in which a course of stretchers alternates with one of alternate stretchers and headers so as to break joint with it and also with the next row of stretchers.

Cro·ss-bones, *sb. pl.* 1798. [CROSS- 2.] A figure of two thigh-bones laid across each other, usually placed under the figure of a skull, as an emblem of death.

Coffins, 'scutcheons, death's heads and cross-bones CANNING.

Cross-bow (krǫ·sbōᵘ). ME. [CROSS- 1 c.] **1.** A missile weapon consisting of a bow fixed across a wooden stock, having a mechanism for holding and releasing the string; an ARBALEST. **2.** *transf.* (*pl.*) Men armed with cross-bows 1511. Also *attrib.* Hence †**Cro·ssbower, Cro·ssbowman,** a soldier armed with a cross-bow.

Cro·ss-bred, *ppl. a.* 1856. [CROSS- 3 c.] Bred from parents of different species or varieties; hybrid, mongrel. (Also *absol.* as *sb.*)

Cro·ss-bree·d, *v.* 1675. [CROSS *adv.*] To breed from individuals of different species.

Cross-breed (krǫ·sbrīd), *sb.* 1774. [Cf. prec. and CROSS *a.*] A breed produced by crossing; *transf.* an animal of such a breed.

It seems to me a barren thing, this Conservatism, an unhappy cross-breed; the mule of politics that engenders nothing DISRAELI.

Cro·ss-bu·n. 1733. [CROSS- 1 c.] A bun indented with a cross, eaten on Good Friday.

Cro·ss-bu·ttock, *sb.* 1714. [app. f. CROSS *prep.* + BUTTOCK.] A peculiar throw over the hip made use of in wrestling and formerly in pugilism.

†**Cro·ss-cloth.** 1541. [CROSS- 1 c, 2.] **1.** *Eccl.* A cloth or hanging before the rood -1566. **2.** A linen cloth worn across the forehead -1699.

Cro·ss-country, *a.* 1767. [CROSS- 4.] Across the country transversely to the great highways; across the fields, etc.

Cro·ss-course, *sb.* 1802. [CROSS- 2.] *Mining.* A vein (usually barren) intersecting the regular vein at an angle; also = CROSS-CUT **2.**

Cro·ss-cro·sslet. 1486. [Cf. CROSSLET **2.**] *Her.* A cross having the extremity of each arm in the form of a small cross.

Cro·ss-cut, *sb.* 1789. [CROSS- 2.] **1.** (Usually *cross cut.*) A cut across; a direct path, diagonal to the main way 1800. **2.** *Mining.* A cutting across the course of a vein, or the main direction of the workings 1789. **3. a.** A step in dancing. DICKENS. **b.** A figure in skating.

Cro·ss-cut, *a.* 1645. **1.** Adapted for cross-cutting, as a *cross-cut saw.* **2.** [CROSS- 3 c.] Cut across; *esp.* of a file, having two sets of teeth crossing each other diagonally 1833. So **Cro·ss-cu·t** *v.* to cut across.

†**Cro·ss-days,** *sb. pl.* 1501. [CROSS- 1 a.] The three days preceding Ascension Day -1641.

Cro·ss-divi·sion. 1828. [CROSS- 3 d.] The division of any group according to more than one principle at the same time, so that the subdivisions intersect; an instance of this.

A division .. of men into Frenchmen, Asiatics, the unproductive classes, and barbarians, would be a c.-division FOWLER.

Crosse (krǫs). [a. F. :—OF. *croce*; see CROSE.] An implement consisting of a long shank curved round at the end, with a net from the curve to the shank; a *lacrosse-stick.*

‖**Crossette** (krǫse·t). 1730. [F., dim. of *croce, crosse*; see CROSE.] *Archit.* A projection in the architrave or casing round a door- or window-opening, at the junction of the jamb and head; also a ledged projection in the voussoir of a flat arch, which rests in a recess in the adjoining voussoir.

Cro·ss-exa·mine, *v.* 1664. [CROSS- 3 a.] **1.** *trans.* To examine by cross-questioning; to examine minutely and repeatedly. **2.** *spec.* To subject (a witness) to an examination with the purpose of shaking his testimony or eliciting facts not brought out in his direct examination. Hence **Cro·ss-examina·tion,** the action of cross-examining. **Cro·ss-exa·miner, -exa·mining.**

Cro·ss-eye. 1826. [CROSS- 2.] *pl.* Squinting eyes. **b.** Internal strabismus. Hence **Cro·ss-eyed** *a.* squinting.

Cro·ss-fe·rtilize, *v.* 1876. [CROSS- 3 a.] *Bot.* To fertilize by pollen from another flower or plant. Hence **Cro·ss-fertiliza·tion.**

Cro·ss-fi·re. 1860. [CROSS- 3 d.] *Mil.* Lines of fire from two or more positions crossing each other. Also *fig.*

Cro·ss-fish. 1805. [CROSS- 1 c.] A star-fish.

†**Cro·ss-fixed,** *pa. pple.* 1618. [CROSS- 1 b; after L. *crucifixus*.] Fixed on a cross, crucified –1849.

Cro·ss-flower. 1597. [CROSS- 1 c.] Milkwort.

Milke woort..doth specially flourish in the Crosse or..Rogation weeke..in English we may call it Crosse flower GERARDE.

Cro·ss-fox. 1830. [CROSS- 1 c.] A variety of the fox, having dark markings along the back and across the shoulders, forming a cross.

Cro·ss-ga·rnet. 1659. [CROSS- 1 c.] A ⊢-shaped hinge, with the vertical part fastened to the jamb of the doorcase, etc., and the horizontal to the door, etc.

†**Cro·ss-ga·rtered,** *ppl. a.* 1601. [CROSS- 3 c.] Having the garters crossed on the legs. *Twel. N.* II. v. 167.

Cro·ss-grain. 1681. [CROSS- 2.] **1.** A grain running across the regular grain. **2.** The grain cut across 1880.

Cross-grained (krǭ·sˌgreˡnd), *a.* 1647. [f. prec.] **1.** Of wood: Having the grain or fibre arranged in crossing directions, or irregularly 1673. **2.** *fig.* Contrarious; perverse 1647. **3.** *advb.* Across the grain (*lit.* and *fig.*) 1703.

1. Elm..is the most Cross-grain'd Timber: that is, cleaveth so unevenly GREW. 2. So cross-grain'd to all Novelty 1647. Hence **Cross-grai·nedness.**

Cro·ss-ha·tch, *v.* 1822. [CROSS- 3 a.] To engrave or hatch a surface with crossing sets of parallel lines; *esp.* to shade by this method. Hence **Cro·ss-ha·tching** *vbl. sb.* the process of marking thus; the effect so produced.

Cro·ss-hea·d, *sb.* 1827. [CROSS- 2.] **1.** The bar at the end of the piston-rod of a steam-engine, which slides between straight guides, and communicates the motion to the connecting-rods, etc. **2.** A heading to a paragraph printed across the page or column in the body of an article (*mod.*). So **Cro·ss-hea·ded** *a.* having the head in the form of a cross.

Crossing (krǭ·siŋ), *vbl. sb.* 1530. [f. CROSS *v.*] **1.** The marking with or making the sign of the cross. **2.** The action of drawing lines across (see CROSS *v.* 4, 7) 1652. **3.** The action of passing across; intersecting; traversing 1575. **4.** The intersection of two lines, tracks, streets, roads, etc.; in *Eccl. Archit.* that part of a cruciform church where the transepts cross the nave 1695. **5.** A place at which a street, river, etc. is crossed 1632. **6.** A thwarting, opposing, or contravening 1580. **7.** Cross-breeding 1851.

3. The c. of the great and wide sea (*mod.*). 4. Statues..in the c. of streets, or in the squares DRYDEN. 6. Cousin: of many men I doe not beare these crossings 1 *Hen. IV*, III. i. 36. *Comb.* **c.-sweeper,** one who sweeps a (street-) c.

Cross-jack, cro'jack (krǭ·sˌdʒæk, krǭ·dʒĕk). 1626. *Naut.* A square sail bent to the lower yard of the mizen-mast.

Cross keys, cross-keys. 1550. [CROSS- 2.] Keys borne crosswise, as in the Papal arms.

†**Cro·ss-land.** 1568. *Irish Hist.* Land belonging to the Church in the Irish counties palatine.

Cross-legged (krǭ·sˌlegd), *ppl. a.* 1530. [CROSS- 5.] Having the legs crossed.

†**Cro·sslet**¹. ME. [app. dim. of OF. *croiseul* CRUCIBLE.] A crucible –1610.

Crosslet² (krǭ·slėt). 1538. [a. Anglo-F. *croiselette*, dim. of OF. *crois* cross.] **1.** A small cross; *spec.* in *Her.* †**2.** = CROSS-CLOTH 2. –1688. Hence **Cro·ssleted** *ppl. a.* bearing a c.

Cro·ss-light. 1851. [CROSS- 2.] A light which crosses another and illuminates parts which it leaves in shade. Often *fig.*

Cro·ss-multiplica·tion. 1703. [CROSS- 3 d.] = DUODECIMALS.

Crossopterygian (krǫsǫptĕri·dʒiăn). 1861. [f. mod.L. *crossopterygii* or *-ia* (f. Gr. κροσσός tassel, *pl.* fringe + πτέρυξ, πτερύγιον fin).] *adj.* Belonging to the sub-class *Crossopterygia* or sub-order *Crossopterygidæ* of Ganoid fishes, so called from the arrangement of the paired fins to form a fringe round a central lobe. var. **Crossoptery·gious** *a.* *sb.* A fish of this class.

Cross-over (krǭ·sōᵘvəɹ). 1795. [from phr. *to cross over*.] **1.** *Textiles.* A fabric having the design running across from selvedge to selvedge; in *Calico-printing*, a stripe of colour printed across another colour. **2.** A woman's wrap worn crossed upon the breast 1868. **3.** *U.S.* A connexion between the up and down lines of a railway for shunting purposes 1884.

Cro·ss-patch. *colloq.* 1700. [f. CROSS *a.*] A cross ill-tempered person. (Usu. feminine.)

Cross-pawl; see CROSS-SPALL.

Cro·ss-piece. 1607. [CROSS 2.] **1.** A piece of any material placed across anything else. **b.** *Ship-building.* A rail of timber from the knight-heads to the belfry; *pl.* the pieces of timber bolted athwartships to the bitt-pins; *pl.* the pieces placed across the keel, which is let into them 1706. **c.** *Anat.* The corpus callosum connecting the two hemispheres of the brain. †**2.** [CROSS *a.*] A CROSS-PATCH –1694.

Cro·ss-plou·gh, *v.* 1644. [CROSS- 3 a.] To plough (a field) across the former furrows.

Cro·ss-point. 1709. [CROSS *a.*] One of the points of the compass intermediate between two cardinal points.

Cro·ss-pollina·tion. 1882. [CROSS- 3 d.] *Bot.* = CROSS-FERTILIZATION of plants.

†**Cro·ss-post.** 1750. [CROSS- 2.] The post for letters on cross-country routes –1880.

Cro·ss-pu·rpose. 1666. [Orig. f. CROSS *prep.* contrary to the purpose: but now f. CROSS *a.*, CROSS- 2.] **1.** Contrary or conflicting purpose; contradictoriness of intention 1681. **2.** *pl.* A parlour game; cf. CROSS-QUESTION *sb.* Often *fig.* 1666.

2. Then to cross purposes, mighty merry; and then to bed PEPYS. Phr. *To be at cross purposes*: (of persons) to act counter from a misconception by each of the other's purpose. (Perh. from the game.)

Cro·ss-que·stion, *sb.* 1694. [Orig. two words; cf. CROSS *a.*, and CROSS- 3 d.] **a.** A question put by way of cross-examination. †**b.** A question in return. **c.** *Cross questions and crooked answers*: a game in which questions and answers are connected crosswise; as *e.g.* the question asked on one's right with the answer given to another question on one's left, with ludicrous effect.

Cro·ss-ques·tion, *v.* 1760. [CROSS- 6.] *trans.* To interrogate with questions which cross, or tend to check the results of, previous questions; to cross-examine.

Cro·ss-ra·tio. 1881. [CROSS- 3 d.] *Math.* = ANHARMONIC ratio.

Cro·ss-rea·ding. 1768. [CROSS- 3 d.] A reading across the page instead of down the column (of a newspaper, etc.), producing a ludicrous connexion of subjects. Also *fig.*

Cro·ss-re·ference. 1834. [CROSS- 3 d.] A reference made from one part of a book, register, etc. to another part where the same word or subject is treated of. Hence as vb.

Cross-remainder (*Law*); see REMAINDER.

Cro·ss-road. 1719. [CROSS- 2, CROSS *a.* 1.] **1.** A road crossing another, or running across between two main roads. **2.** The place where two roads cross. Also called *the cross roads.* 1812. **3.** *attrib.* Passing by cross-roads; situated at the crossing of two roads 1720.

†**Cro·ss-row.** 1529. [CROSS- 1 c: from the figure (✠) formerly prefixed to it.] The alphabet; = CHRIST-CROSS-ROW.

And from the Crosse-row pluckes the letter G *Rich. III*, I. i. 55.

Cro·ss-ruff. 1592. [CROSS- 3 d.] †**1.** A game at cards; see RUFF –1693. **2.** *Whist.* (See quot.)

2. A Cross-ruff (saw or see-saw) is the alternate trumping by partners of different suits, each leading the suit in which the other renounces CAVENDISH.

†**Cro·ss-sail.** ME. [CROSS- 2.] *Naut.* A square-sail, *i.e.* one placed across the breadth of the ship (not *fore-and-aft*); also a vessel with square-sails –1627.

Cro·ss-spa·ll, cro·ss-spa·le. 1850. [CROSS- 2.] *Ship-building.* One of the deals nailed to the frames of a ship at a certain height, to keep the frames in position until the deck-knees are fastened.

Cro·ss-spri·nger. 1816. [CROSS- 2.] *Archit.* One of the ribs extending diagonally from one pier to another in groined vaulting.

Cro·ss-staff. 1460. **1.** *Eccl.* An archbishop's cross; also, by confusion, used for CROSE-STAFF. Now *Hist.* †**2.** An instrument for taking the altitude of the sun or a star –1669. **b.** A surveyor's cross, used in taking offsets 1874.

Cro·ss-sti·tch, *sb.* 1710. [CROSS- 1 c.] A stitch formed of two stitches crossing each other, thus X; also a kind of needlework characterized by these. Hence **Cro·ss-sti·tch** *v.* to sew with these.

Cro·ss-stone. 1770. [CROSS- 1 c.] *Min.* A name given to CHIASTOLITE; also to STAUROLITE and HARMOTOME, from the cruciform arrangement of the crystals.

Cro·ss-tail. 1839. [CROSS- 2.] *Mech.* In a back-action marine steam-engine: A transverse bar which connects the side levers at the end opposite to the cross-head.

Cro·ss-tree. 1626. [CROSS- 1 c, 2.] **1.** *Naut.* (*pl.*) Two horizontal cross-timbers at the head of the lower and top masts, to sustain the tops, and to spread the top-gallant rigging. †**2.** A gallows 1638; a cross. HERRICK. Also *attrib.*

Cro·ss-vault. 1850. [CROSS- 1 c.] *Archit.* A vault formed by the intersection of two or more simple vaults. Hence **Cro·ss-vau·lting.**

Cro·ss-way, *sb.* 1490. [CROSS- 2, CROSS *a.* 1.] = CROSS-ROAD.

Crosswise (krǭ·swəiz), *adv.* ME. [CROSS- + WISE.] **1.** In the form of a cross. **2.** Across, transversely 1580. **3.** *fig.* Perversely 1594.

1. A church built c. JOHNSON. 2. A frame of logs placed c. JOWETT. vars. **Cro·ssway, Cro·ssways.**

Cro·ssword, cro·ss-word. 1924. [CROSS-A. 2.] A puzzle based on a criss-cross pattern of words for which clues are provided.

Crosswort (krǭ·swɒɹt). 1578. [CROSS- 1 c.] **1.** A name of various plants having leaves in whorls of four; esp. *Galium cruciatum.* **2.** *pl.* A book-name for the N.O. *Cruciferæ* 1861.

‖**Crostarie** (krǫstā·ri). *Sc.* 1685. [a. Gael. *cros-tàraidh, cros-tàra* the cross or beam of gathering.] The FIRE-CROSS or FIERY CROSS, used in the Sc. Highlands to summon the clans.

Crotal (krōᵘ·tăl). 1790. [ad. L. *crotalum*, or F. *crotale*.] **1.** = CROTALUM 1. 1850. **2.** *Irish Antiq.* Applied to a small globular or pear-shaped bell or rattle, the nature and use of which are obscure.

Cro·talid. [f. mod.L. *Crotalidæ*.] *Zool.* A serpent of the *Crotalidæ* or rattlesnake family.

Cro·taliform, *a.* [f. CROTALUS + -FORM.] Structurally like or related to the rattlesnake.

Cro·talin. [f. CROTALUS + -IN.] *Chem.* An albuminoid substance found in the venom of the rattlesnake.

Cro·taline, *a.* 1865. Of or belonging to the rattlesnake family.

‖**Cro·talo.** 1682. [It.] = CROTALUM.

‖**Crotalum** (krǫ·tălǒm). 1727. [L.; a. Gr. κρόταλον clapper, etc.] *Antiq.* A sort of castanet used in ancient religious dances.

‖**Crotalus** (krǫ·tălǒs). 1834. [mod.L.; see prec.] *Zool.* The genus of American serpents containing the typical rattlesnakes.

Crotaphic (krotæ·fik), *a.* 1653. [f. Gr. κρόταφος, *pl.* -οι the temples.] *Anat.* Of or pertaining to the temples. **Cro·taphite** *a.* [F. *crotaphite*], temporal; †*sb.* the temporal muscle. **Crotaphi·tic** *a.* temporal, as in *c. nerve.*

Crotch (krǫtʃ). Now chiefly *U.S.* or *dial.* 1539. [? ; occas. a var. of CRUTCH.] †**1.** A fork –1573. **2.** A stake or pole having a forked top 1573; *Naut.* = CRUTCH 3. **3.** The fork of a tree or bough 1573. **4.** The fork of the human body 1592. †**5.** *fig.* A dilemma 1622. *Comb.* †**c.-tail,** old name of the kite. Hence **Crotched** *a.* forked. (Now *U.S.*)

Crotchet (krǫ·tʃėt), *sb.*¹ ME. [a. F. *crochet* hook; see CROCHET.] **1.** = CROCHET 1, 2. **2.** A hook or hooked instrument; *spec.* (*Surg.*) an instrument used in obstetrical surgery 1754. **3.** A natural hook-like organ or process 1678. **4.** *Mus.* A symbol for a note of half the value of a minim, made in the form of a stem with a round black head; such a note. Also *attrib.* ME. †**5.** *Typogr.* A square bracket –1832. **6.** A whimsical fancy; a perverse conceit; a peculiar notion on some (unimportant) point 1573; a fanciful device 1611. **7.** *Fortif.* A passage formed by an indentation in the glacis opposite a traverse 1853. †**8.** 'The arrangement of a body of troops, either forward or rearward, so as to form a line nearly perpendicular to the general line of battle' (Webster 1864).

2. A c. of 122 Diamonds, set..in Silver STEELE. 6. That castle in the ayr, that c., that whimsie BURTON. *Comb.* c.-monger, a crocheteer. Hence **Crotchet-ee·r**, a person with a c.; *esp.* one who pushes his crotchets in politics, etc.

†**Cro·tchet**, *sb.*[2] 1631. [dim. of CROTCH.] = CROTCH 2. -1764.

Cro·tchet, *v.* 1587. [f. CROTCHET *sb.*[1]] †To break a longer note up into crotchets. **b.** To ornament with crotchets or crockets.

Crotchety (krǫ·tʃėti), *a.* 1825. [f. as prec.] Given to crotchets; of the nature of a crotchet.

All sorts of c. people BRIGHT. Hence **Cro·tchetiness**, c. quality.

Croton (krōu·tǫn). 1751. [mod.L., a. Gr. κροτών a tick, also the Castor-oil plant.] **1.** *Bot.* A large genus of euphorbiaceous plants, mostly natives of tropical regions. **2.** Applied to *Codiæum pictum*, allied to the Crotons 1881.

Comb.: **C. oil**, a fatty oil existing in the seeds of the East Indian species, *C. Tiglium*; it is a drastic purgative; **c. chloral** or **c. hydrate**, a name of *butyl chloral hydrate*, given in error.

Croton-bug. *U.S.* 1842. [f. the *Croton* river, Westchester County, N.Y.] A name given to the Cockroach, *Blatta orientalis*, and other species of the same genus.

Crotonic (krotǫ·nik), *a.* 1838. [f. CROTON + -IC.] Of or derived from croton oil; as in *c. acid*, $C_4H_6O_2$, the second member of the Acrylic series. So **Cro·tonate**, a salt of c. acid. **Cro·tonyle·ne**, a hydro-carbon, C_4H_6 (liquid below 15° C.), homologous with allylene.

Crottels (krǫ·t'lz), *sb. pl.* 1598. [app. dim. f. F. *crote, crotte.*] The globular excrement of hares, etc.

Crottle (krǫ·t'l). *Sc.* 1778. [a. Gael. *crotal, crotan* a lichen.] A name for various species of lichen used in dyeing; cf. CUDBEAR.

†**Crouch**, *sb.*[1] [Early ME. *cruche*, app.:—OE. *crúc*, ad. L. *crux, crucis.*] = CROSS, in its early senses -1463.

Crouch (krautʃ), *sb.*[2] 1597. [f. CROUCH *v.*[1]] An act of crouching.

Crouch (krautʃ), *v.*[1] ME. [? a. OF. *crochir* (Godefroy) to become hooked or crooked.] **1.** *intr.* To stoop or bend low, as in stooping for shelter, in fear, or in submission; to cower with the limbs bent. (To *cower* concerns chiefly the head and shoulders; to *crouch*, the body as a whole.) **2.** To bow or bend humbly or servilely; to cringe fawningly. Chiefly *fig.* 1528. **3.** *trans.* To bow or bend low (the knee, etc.): often with implication of cringing 1705.

1. We sat crouching for the space of three whole days upon this rock 1653. 2. The free spirit must c. to the slave in office 1779. 3. She..crouched her head upon her breast COLERIDGE. Hence **Crou·chant** *a.* crouching. **Crou·cher.**

†**Crouch**, *v.*[2] ME. [f. CROUCH *sb.*[1]] To cross; to sign with the cross -1620.

Crou·chback. Now *Hist.* 1491. [f. stem of CROUCH *v.*; cf. *crook-back.*] **1.** A crooked or hunched back. **2.** A hunchback. Also *attrib.*

Sir Edmunde ye kynges other sone, surnamed Crowch Bak FABYAN.

Crouched, earlier f. CRUTCHED (Friars).

†**Crou·chmas.** ME. [f. CROUCH *sb.*[1] + MASS.] The festival of the Invention of the Cross, observed on May 3. -1706.

Crou·ch-ware. 1817. [?] *Pottery.* A name of the early salt-glazed pottery of Staffordshire.

†**Crouke, crowke.** [OE. *crúce* fem. pot, little pitcher, cogn. w. OS. *krûka.*] A pitcher, a jug -ME.

Croup, croupe (krūp), *sb.*[1] ME. [a. F. *croupe*; of Teut. origin; cf. CROP *sb.*] **1.** The rump or hind-quarters, *esp.* of a beast of burden. **2.** (*crup*). The hinder end of a saddle 1869.

So light to the croupe the fair lady he swung SCOTT.

Croup (krūp), *sb.*[2] 1765. [f. CROUP *v.*, *lit.* a hoarse croaking.] **1.** An inflammatory disease of the larynx and trachea of children, marked by a peculiar sharp ringing cough. **2.** The local name of the Northumbrian 'burr' (*mod.*). Hence **Crou·pal, Crou·pous** *adjs.* relating to, or of the nature of, c.; affected with c. So **Crou·py** *a.*

Croup (krūp), *v.* Now *dial.* 1513. [App. echoic.] **1.** *intr.* To cry hoarsely; to croak. **2.** To make the hoarse ringing cough of the disease called croup 1801. **3.** To pronounce a rough uvular *r* (*r grasseyé*); to have the Northumberland 'burr' (*mod.*).

Croupade (krupē·d). 1849. [a. F., f. *croupe* CROUP *sb.*[1]] *Horsemanship.* A high curvet, in which the hind legs are brought up under the belly of the horse.

Croupe (krūp). 1808. [a. F.] **1.** = CROUP *sb.*[1], q. v. ‖**2.** = CROUPADE. Byron. ‖**3.** The rounded top of a mountain. [So in F.]

Croupier (krū·pi,əɹ, krupī·ə·ɪ). 1707. [a. F. *croupier*, orig. one who rides behind on the croup.] †**1.** One who stands behind a gamester to back him up and help him. **2.** He who rakes in the money at a gaming-table 1731. **3.** One who sits as assistant chairman at the lower end of the table at a public dinner 1785.

1. Since I have such a C. or Second to stand by me as Mr. Pope WYCHERLEY.

Crou·pon. Now *dial.* ME. [a. OF. *croupon*, augm. or dim. of *croupe*; see CROUP[1]. The mod.Sc. form is *curpon.*] The croup or rump; the buttocks; *transf.* the hinder part of a thing; the crupper of the harness.

Crouse (krūs), *a.* *Sc.* and *n. dial.* [ME. north. *crūs, crous*: prob. LG. or Frisian.] †**1.** Angry, cross. (ME. only.) †**2.** Bold, audacious, 'cocky' -1883. **3.** Vivacious; pert, brisk, lively, jolly ME. Also as *adv.*

3. Now they're c. and cantie baith BURNS. Hence **Crou·sely** *adv.*

Crout, *sb.*; see SOUR-CROUT.

Crow (krōu), *sb.*[1] [OE. *cráwe* f., a WG. deriv. of the vb. *cráwan, cráian* to CROW, q.v.] **1.** A bird of the genus *Corvus*; in England usually the Carrion Crow (*Corvus Corone*); in the north of England, Scotland, and Ireland the Rook, *C. frugilegus*; in U.S. *C. Americanus*. Also *fig.* **2.** *Astron.* The southern constellation *Corvus* 1658. **3.** A bar of iron with one end slightly bent and sharpened to a beak, used as a lever or prise; a CROW-BAR ME. †**4.** A grappling-hook, a grapnel -1751. †**5.** A kind of door-knocker. [med.L. *cornix.*] -1846. **6.** *Thieves' slang.* One who keeps watch while another steals 1851. **7.** *Mining.* Used *attrib.* to denote a poor or impure bed of coal, etc. *n.* and *Sc.* 1789.

1. The C. Makes Wing toth' Rookie Wood *Macb.* III. ii. 51. 3. Well, Ile breake in: go borrow me a c. *Com. Err.* III. i. 80. Phrases. *To have a c. to pluck* or *pull* (rarely *pick*) *with any one*: to have something awkward to settle, or some fault to find, with him. *As the crow flies*, etc.: in a direct line.

Comb., etc.: CARRION CROW: see CARRION; **c.-blackbird** (*U.S.*), a name for the Purple Grackle (*Quiscalus purpureus*), and allied species; **-coal** (see sense 7 above); **-iron**, a crow-bar; †**-keeper**, one who guards corn-fields from rooks; also a scarecrow; **crow's-meat**, food for crows, carrion; **c.-sheaf** (*Cornwall*), 'the top sheaf on the end of a mow'; **-shrike**, a bird of the sub-family *Gymnorhininæ* or Piping Crows; **Red-legged C.**, *C. graculus.*

Crow (krōu), *sb.*[2] ME. [f. CROW *v.*] Crowing (of a cock). Also *transf.* and *fig.*

Crow (krōu), *sb.*[3] 1662. [Cf. MHG. *kros*, Du. *kroos* intestines, mod.Du. *kroos* giblets; but also LG. *krage* mesentery.] The mesentery of an animal.

Crow (krōu), *v.* Pa. t. **crew** (krū), **crowed.** Pa. pple. **crowed**, [**crown** (krōun)]. [OE. *cráwan*. Orig. echoic, and prob. of WG. origin.] **1.** *intr.* To utter the loud cry of a cock. Also quasi-*trans.* **2.** *transf.* Of persons. To utter an inarticulate sound of joy or exultation 1579. **3.** *fig.* To exult loudly, boast, swagger 1522.

1. While he yet spake, the cocke crew *Luke* xxii. 60. 2. [The] baby..would..c. with delight THACKERAY. 3. Phr. *To c. over*: to triumph over; I'm not going to be crowed over by you DICKENS.

Crow-bar (krōu·bāɹ). 1825. [f. CROW *sb.*[1] 3.] An iron bar with a wedge-shaped end, used as a lever or prise. Also *attrib.*

Crowberry (krōu·beri). 1597. [prob. tr. Ger. *krähenbeere.*] The fruit of a small evergreen heath-like shrub (*Empetrum nigrum*); the berry is black and insipid. Also the plant itself. Called also *crakeberry* (see CRAKE).

Crow·bill. (Also **Crow's bill.**) 1611. *Surg.* A forceps for extracting bullets, etc. from wounds.

Crowd (kraud), *sb.*[1] Now *Hist.* or *dial.* ME. [a. Welsh *crwth* m. violin, fiddle.] An ancient Celtic musical instrument, having three, or, later, six strings; an early form of the fiddle. Hence, a fiddle. Still *dial.*

Harpes, lutes, and croudes ryght delycyous HAWES.

†**Crowd**, *sb.*[2] ME. [AF. *crudde*, app. corresp. to OF. *crute, crote*, later *croute*:—late L. *crupta*, for L. *crypta*; see CRYPT. The *d* is unexplained.] A crypt. (Also in *pl.*) -1658.

Crowd (kraud), *sb.*[3] 1567. [f. CROWD *v.*] **1.** A number of persons gathered so closely together as to press upon each other; a throng. (The earlier term was *press.*) **2.** *transf.* A large number (*of* persons) 1654; the masses 1683; *colloq.* a company; set, lot (*U.S.* and *Colonies.*) 1857. **3.** *transf.* and *fig.* A number of things crowded together; a multitude 1627.

1. They could not come nigh unto him for the c. *Mark* ii. 4. 2. Far from the madding crowd's ignoble strife GRAY. 3. In the croude of their vnknowne sinnes SANDERSON. *C. of sail* (Naut.): an unusual number of sails hoisted for the sake of speed.

Crowd (kraud), *v.*[1] [OE. *crúdan*, an original str. vb. Rare down to 1600; not in the Bible of 1611.] **1.** *intr.* To press, push, thrust, shove. **2.** *trans.* To press (anything), to push, shove. (Also *absol.*) Now *dial.* ME. **3.** *intr.* To push, or force one's way; to press *forward, up*, etc. Now only *fig.* ME. **4.** *intr.* To congregate closely so as to press upon one another; to throng ME. **5.** *trans.* To press (things) *in* or *into* a confined space; also, to press (things) in numbers *on* a person 1599; to compress, pack closely together 1612. Also *fig.* **6.** To fill *with* a crowd 1695; to throng (a place) 1646; †to beset or crowd upon (a person or place) -1783; *U.S. colloq.* to press by solicitation; to dun 1828.

3. He crowded into a Dancing Room 1687. 4. There croud into his mind the ideas which [etc.] BERKELEY. 5. The experience of years is crowded into hours 1848. 6. A port crowded with shipping 1848. The Men..c. the chearful Fire DRYDEN.

Phrases. *To c. out*: to force out by pressure of a crowd (*obs.*); to exclude by crowding. *To c. sail* (Naut.): to carry a press of sail for speed.

†**Crowd**, *v.*[2] 1589. [f. CROWD *sb.*[1]] To fiddle -1693.

†**Crowd**, *v.*[3] 1575. [Cf. CROOD.] **1.** *intr.* To crow -1752. **2.** Var. of *croud*, CROOD *Sc.*

Crow·der[1]. Now *dial.* 1450. [f. CROWD *sb.*[1] or *v.*[2] + -ER[1].] A fiddler.

Crowder[2] (krau·dəɹ). [f. CROWD *v.*[1] + -ER[1].] One who crowds (see CROWD *v.*).

Crowdie, crowdy (krau·di). *Sc.* and *n. Eng.* 1668. [?] Meal and water made into a thick gruel; hence, brose or porridge generally.

Crow·-flower. 1597. The buttercup. **b.** The Ragged Robin (Gerarde).

Crowfoot (krōu·fut). Pl. **-feet**, in senses 1 and 2 **-foots.** ME. **1.** A name for species of *Ranunculus*; also for the genus. **2.** Any plant of which the leaves or other part resemble a crow's foot; as **C. Cranesbill, C. Plantain**, the wild hyacinth, etc. 1578. **3.** = CROW'S-FOOT 1. 1614. **4.** *Naut.* A number of small cords rove through a long block or EUPHROE, used to suspend an awning, etc. 1627. **5.** *Mil.* A caltrop 1678. **6.** *Mining.* A tool with a side-claw, for recovering broken rods in deep bore-holes (Raymond).

Crow·-garlic. ME. A wild species of garlic, *Allium vineale.*

†**Crowl**, *v.* 1519. [Cf. *growl.*] *intr.* To rumble in the stomach and bowels -1717.

†**Crow-leek.** OE. The wild hyacinth (*Scilla nutans*) -1597.

Crown (kraun). [OE. *corona*, ME. *croun(e*, earlier *crun(e*, syncopated from *coroune*, a. AF. :—L. *corona* crown, *orig.* chaplet.]

I. 1. A fillet, wreath, or other encircling ornament for the head, worn for adornment, or as a mark of honour or achievement ME. Also *fig.* **2.** *spec.* The cincture or covering for the head, worn by a monarch as a mark of sovereignty OE. **3.** *fig.* The rule, position, or empire of a monarch ME. **4.** *fig.* The wearer of a crown; the monarch in his official character 1579. **5.** *fig.* That which adorns like a crown; a chief ornament ME.

1. This aungel had of roses and of lilie Corounes

tuo CHAUCER. *fig.* Be thou faithful unto death, and I will give thee a c. of life *Rev.* ii. 10. The c. of martyrdom 1839. 2. Vneasie lyes the Head that weares a Crowne 2 *Hen. IV*, III. i. 31. 3. Saul from his Asses, and David from his sheepe were called to the crowne 1577. 4. The pardon of the C. was granted 1844. 5. A bisi womman a croune is to hir man WYCLIF *Prov.* xii. 4.

II. 1. Anything having or bearing the figure or the representation of a crown ME. **2.** A name of various coins; originally one bearing the imprint of a crown; *esp.* a coin (now silver) of Great Britain of the value of five shillings; hence the sum of five shillings ME. **3.** A size of paper, orig. watermarked with a crown 1712.

III. Something having the form of an encircling wreath. †**1.** The tonsure of a cleric –1533. **2.** = CORONA **1.** 1563. **3.** †A whorl of flowers. **b.** = CORONA 6a. 1578. †**4.** A ring –1706. **5.** = CORONA 3. 1845. **6.** *Surg.* The circular serrated edge of a trepan 1758.

1. Crounne & cloþ maken no prest WYCLIF.

IV. 1. The top part of the skull; the vertex ME.; hence, the head 1594. **2.** The rounded summit of a mountain or other elevation 1583. **3.** The highest or central part of an arch or arched surface 1635. **4.** The top of a hat; *esp.* the flat circular top of the modern hat 1678. **5.** The flattened or rounded roof of a tent or building 1725. **6.** *Archit.* = CORONA 4. 1611. **7.** In plants: **a.** The leafy head of a tree or shrub; **b.** The flattened top of a seed, etc. **8.** *Farriery.* The CORONET of a horse's hoof 1611. **9.** *Anat.* The part of a tooth which appears beyond the gums 1804. **10.** The part of a cut gem above the girdle 1875. **11.** The part of the shank of an anchor from which the arms proceed 1875. **12.** *Mech.* Any terminal flat member of a structure; the face of an anvil. **13.** *fig.* That which crowns anything; the consummation, completion, or perfection 1611.

1. Crowne is..the top of a mans head where the haire windes about PUTTENHAM. 2. Vpon the crowne o' th' Cliffe *Lear* IV. vi. 67. 3. *C. of the causeway*: the central and most prominent part of the pavement or street. 7. *C. of the root*: the junction of the root and stem. 13. Thou art of all thy gifts thyself the c. COWPER.

V. *attrib.* **a.** Of or pertaining to the Crown (senses 2–4): as *c. demesne, due, duty, rent, revenue, vassal*, etc. **b.** In titles of foreign (chiefly Polish) officials, as *c. chamberlain*, etc. **c.** Pertaining to the coin, as *c. cribbage*, etc. **d.** Used to designate a quality or brand, as *c. soap*, etc. **e.** Pertaining to the top of the head, corona of a plant, etc., as *c. bloom*; *c.-distempered* adj.

Comb.: **c.-agent**, agent for the C.; in Scotland, a solicitor who takes charge of criminal proceedings, under the Lord Advocate; **-antler**, the topmost antler of a stag's horn; **-cases reserved**, criminal cases reserved on points of law for the consideration of the judges; **-colony**, one in which the legislation and the administration are controlled by the home government; **-court**, the court in which the criminal business of an Assize is transacted; **-crane**, the *demoiselle*; **-debt**, a debt due to the C., which has preference over other debts; **-gate**, the upstream gate of the lock of a canal; **-graft**, a graft inserted between the inner bark and the alburnum; hence **-grafting**; **-jewels**, the jewels which form part of the regalia; **c. law**, the criminal law; **c. lawyer**, a criminal lawyer; **c. living**, a church living in the gift of the C.; **c.-pigeon** = *crowned pigeon*: see CROWNED 6; **-saw**, a kind of circular saw with the teeth on the edge of a hollow cylinder, as in a trepan saw, etc.; **-sheet**, the upper plate of the fire-box of a locomotive; **-shell**, a barnacle or acorn-shell; **-side**, the portion of the Court of Queen's Bench which deals with criminal matters, the c. office; **c. solicitor**, a solicitor who prepares criminal prosecutions for the C.; **c.-sparrow**, one of the American genus *Zonotrichia*, with a coloured c.; **-tax**, a tax paid to the C.; **-tile**, a tile of a rectangular form; **-tree**, a support for the roof in coal-mines; **-valve**, a dome-shaped valve which works over a box with slotted sides; **-witness**, a witness for the C. in a criminal prosecution.

Hence **Crow·nless** *a.* **Crow·nlet** *sb.* a tiny c. **Crow·nling**, a scion of the c. (*rare*).

Crown (kraun), *v.*[1] [ME. *crounen*, earlier *crunen*, syncopated from *corunen*, *corounen*, a. AFr. *coruner*, *corouner* :—(ult.) L. *coronare*, f. *corona*.] **1.** *trans.* To place a crown, wreath, or garland upon the head of. **2.** *spec.* To invest with the regal crown, and hence with royal dignity ME.; to enthrone 1596. Also *fig.* **3.** To surmount (something) *with* ME. **4.** To form a crown to 1746. **5.** To adorn the surface of *with* 1697. **6.** To fill to overflowing 1605. **7.** *fig.* To complete worthily 1606. **8.** To bless with a successful issue 1602. **9.** To endow with honour, dignity, plenty, etc. Now *poet.* 1535. †**10.** To mark (a person) with the tonsure. (ME. only.) **11.** *Draughts.* To make (a piece that reaches the opponent's crown-head) into a king by placing another piece upon it 1850. **12.** *Mil.* To effect a lodgement upon, as upon the crest of the glacis, etc. (Webster).

1. A crown of thornes HOBBES. 2. *fig.* Thou..hast crowned him with glory and honour *Ps.* viii. 5. 4. Perugia..crowning a mighty hill HAWTHORNE. 5. Where..vales with Violets once were crown'd DRYDEN. 6. The Bowls were crown'd..and Healths went round PRIOR. 7. No day without a deed to Crowne it *Hen. VIII*, V. v. 59. 9. He that resisteth pleasures, crowneth his life *Ecclus.* xix. 5. Phr. *To c. a knot* (Naut.): to finish a knot by interweaving the strands so as to prevent untwisting.

Crown, *v.*[2] Now *dial.* 1602. [f. CROWNER[2].] To hold a coroner's inquest on.

Crow·nal, *sb. arch.* 1500. = CORONAL *sb.* 1, 2.

†**Crownation.** 1530. = CORONATION –1604.

Crowned (kraund), *ppl. a.* ME. [f. CROWN *v.*[1] and *sb.* + -ED.] **1.** Invested with a crown or with royal dignity. **2.** Surmounted by a crown 1565. †**3.** Consummate; sovereign –1651. **4.** Brimming, bounteous 1605. **5.** Having a CROWN (in various senses) 1665. **6.** Crested 1698.

1. C. and mitred tyranny CAMPBELL. 2. The Harpe C. 1633. 3. His corouned malice CHAUCER. 5. An antick sort of hat which is high crown'd 1665.

Crowner[1] (krau·nəɹ). ME. [f. CROWN *v.* + -ER.] One who, or that which, crowns.

Crowner[2]. Now *dial.* ME. = CORONER.

†**Crow·net.** ME. [A by-form of CORONET.] = CORONET –1842.

Crow·n-gla·ss. 1706. Glass composed of silica, potash, and lime (without lead or iron), made in circular sheets by blowing and whirling.

Crow·n Impe·rial. 1542. **1.** The crown of an emperor. **2.** A species of Fritillary (*Fritillaria Imperialis*) from Levantine regions, bearing a number of pendent flowers forming a whorl round a terminal leafy tuft 1611.

2. Bold Oxlips, and The Crowne Imperiall SHAKS.

Crowning (krau·niŋ), *vbl. sb.* ME. [f. CROWN *v.* + -ING[1].] **1.** Coronation. †**2.** Tonsure. (ME. only.) **3.** Consummation; completion 1598. **4.** *Naut.* The finishing part of a knot made on the end of a rope (see CROWN *v.*) 1769. **5.** That which forms the crown of anything 1704.

Crow·ning, *ppl. a.* 1611. [f. as prec.] **1.** That bestows crowns. *Isa.* xxiii. 8. **2.** That forms the crown or acme 1651. **3.** Arching 1761.

2. The dimensions of this mercy are above my thought. It is for aught I know a c. mercy CROMWELL.

Crown-land, crow·nland. 1625. **1.** (*crow·n-la·nd.*) Land belonging to the Crown Mostly in *pl.* **2.** (*crow·nland* = G. *kronland.*) The name of the administrative provinces of the Austro-Hungarian monarchy.

†**Crow·nment.** [ME., a. AF. *corunement*, after CROWN.] Coronation –1592.

Crown office. 1631. The office in which was transacted, at certain stages, the business of the Crown side of the King's Bench. Now a department of the Central Office of the High Court of Justice. **b.** In Chancery: The office in which the Great Seal is, for most purposes, affixed 1863.

Crown-paper. 1630. = CROWN *sb.* II. 3.

Crown-piece, crow·npiece. 1648. **1.** (*crown-piece.*) = CROWN II. 2. **2.** (*crow·npiece.*) A piece that forms the crown or top 1794.

Crow·n-post. 1703. = KING-POST.

Crown prince. 1791. [tr. Ger. *kronprinz*, etc.] The heir-apparent to a sovereign throne, *esp.* in Germany, etc. Hence **Crown pri·ncess**, the wife of a crown prince.

Crow·n-scab. 1609. A cancerous sore in the coronet of a horse's foot.

Crow·n-wheel. 1647. The balance- or escape-wheel of a vertical watch, the pinion of which is driven by the contrate wheel; but now = a CONTRATE wheel.

Crow·n-work. Formerly **crowned work.** 1677. *Fortif.* A work consisting of a bastion between two curtains, terminated by half bastions, and joined to the body of the place by two long sides.

Crow·-quill. 1740. A quill from a crow's wing, used as a pen for fine writing. Also used for a fine steel pen for map-drawing, etc.

Crow's foot, crow·'s-foot. ME. **1.** One of the wrinkles round the outer corner of the eye. †**2.** *Naut.* = CROWFOOT 4. –1806. **3.** *Mil.* A caltrop 1772. **4.** A three-pointed figure in embroidery (*mod.*). **5.** *Mech.* A bent hook to hold the shoulder of a drill-rod while a section above it is being attached or detached 1874.

Crow-silk. 1721. [CROW *sb.*[1]] A name for the *Confervæ* and other delicate green-spored Algæ with silky filaments.

Crow·'s nest, crow's-nest. 1604. †**1.** *Mil.* ? A fort placed on a height. **2.** A barrel or box fixed to the mast-head of a whaling or other ship, as a shelter for the look-out man 1818.

Crow·-step. 1822. *Archit.* = CORBIE-STEP (see CORBIE).

Crow·-stone. 1677. **1.** The fossil shell *Gryphæa* of the Oolite and Lias. **2.** A kind of hard white flinty sandstone 1778. **3.** 'The top stone of the gable end of a house' (Halliwell).

Crow-toe. Also **crow-toes.** *Sc.* and *n. dial.* 1562. A name of the wild hyacinth (*Scilla nutans*); also of *Orchis mascula*, *Lotus corniculatus*, and the Buttercups.

The tufted crow-toe, and pale jessamine MILT.

†**Crow·-tread**, *v.* 1592. To tread (a fowl) as crows were supposed to do; hence *fig.* to abuse –1652.

A crauen henne that is crow trodden N. BRETON.

Croyl. Now *dial.* 1836. *Geol.* Indurated clay with shells. Hence, perh., †**Croylstone**, native sulphate of barium; cawk.

Croze (krōuz), *sb.* 1611. [? f. F. *creux*, OF. *croz*.] *Coopering.* The groove at the ends of cask staves, etc.; also, the tool for making it.

Croze, *v.*[1] 1880. [f. prec.] *Coopering.* To make the croze in (cask staves, etc.).

Croze, *v.*[2] *Hat-making.* To refold (a hat-body) so as to present a different surface to the action of the felting-machine.

Crozier, -ed; see CROSIER, -ED.

Crub. Now *dial.* 1565. = CURB *sb.*

Cruche, obs. f. CROCHE[1], CROUCH, CRUTCH.

†**Cruche.** [Cf. F. *crochet*.] A small curl lying flat on the forehead. EVELYN.

Crucial (krū·ʃiăl, -ʃăl), *a.* 1706. [a. F., f. L. *crucem* + -AL.] **1.** (Chiefly *Anat.*) Of the form of a cross, as *c. incision*; *spec.* the name of two ligaments in the knee-joint, which connect the femur and tibia. **2.** That finally decides between two hypotheses; relating to, or adapted to lead to, such decision; decisive, critical. [From Bacon's phrase *instantia crucis* (see *Nov. Org.* II. xxxvi); see also CRUX.] 1830. ¶**3.** App. assoc. w. CRUCIBLE 1856.

2. C. experiments for the verification of his theory J. MARTINEAU. 3. The imagination's c. heat MRS. BROWNING. Hence **Cru·cially** *adv.* in a c. manner.

Crucian, crusian (krū·ʃăn). 1763. [f. (ult.) L. *coracinus*, a. Gr. κορακῖνος, a black fish like a perch, found in the Nile.] A species of fish, a native of Central Europe, also called *Crucian Carp*, and (when lean) *German* or *Prussian Carp*; now placed in the genus *Carassius*, being *C. carassius*.

Cruciate (krū·ʃiĕt), *a.* (*sb.*) 1684. [ad. med. L. *cruciatus*, f. *crux*.] *Zool.* and *Bot.* Cross-shaped; arranged in the form of a cross 1826. †*sb.* = CRUCIAL incision.

Cruciate (krū·ʃiĕ[i]t), *v.* 1532. [f. *cruciat-*, ppl. stem of L. *cruciare*, f. *crux*.] **1.** *trans.* To torture, torment, to EXCRUCIATE (*arch.*). †**2.** To crucify (*rare*) –1658.

Cruciation. Now *rare.* 15... [ad. L. *cruciationem*; see prec.] Torture, torment.

Cruciato-, comb. f. L. *cruciatus* CRUCIATE *a.*, as in **c.-complicate**, at the same time crossed and folded, as the wings of insects, *e.g.* of the *Pentatoma*; **-incumbent**, laid upon the abdomen, and crossed but not folded, as in the *Apis*.

Crucible (krū·sib'l), *sb.* 1460. [ad. med. L. *crucibulum*, orig. a night-lamp, later as in sense 1; app. a deriv. of L. *crux* CROSS.] **1.** A vessel, usually of earthenware, made to endure great heat, used for fusing metals, etc.;

a melting-pot. **b.** A basin at the bottom of a furnace to collect the molten metal 1864. **2.** *fig.* Used of any severe test or trial 1645. Also *attrib.*

2. In this Limbec and Crusible of Affliction HOWELL.

Crucifer (krū·sifəɹ). 1574. [a. late L.] **1.** *Eccl.* A cross-bearer. **2.** *Bot.* A CRUCIFEROUS plant 1846.

Cruciferous (krūsi·fĕrəs), *a.* 1656. [a. late L. *crucifer* + -OUS.] **1.** Bearing a cross. **2.** *Bot.* Belonging to the *Cruciferæ*; bearing flowers with four equal petals arranged crosswise. Also said of the flowers; = CRUCIATE 1851.

Crucifier (krū·sifəiəɹ). ME. [f. CRUCIFY.] One who crucifies; one who torments or worries.

†‖**Crucifige.** ME. [L.; = crucify (him)!] The cry of the Jews to Pilate; formerly as sb.: Popular clamour for the death of a victim –1652.

Crucifix (krū·sifiks), *sb.* ME. [a. OF. *crucefix*, now *crucifix*, ad. L. *cruci fixus*, later *crucifixus*, (one) fixed to a cross.] †**1.** The Crucified One; Christ on the cross –1660. **2.** An image (formerly also a pictorial representation) of Christ upon the cross ME.

1. He that sweares by the Crosse, sweares by the Holy C., that is, Jesus crucified thereon JER. TAYLOR. (The conjectured sense 'The Cross or religion of Christ' is merely Todd's misunderstanding of this passage.) So **Cru·cifix** *v.* to crucify (*rare*).

Crucifixion (krūsifi·kʃən). 1648. [ad. mod. L. *crucifixionem*, f. *crucifigere* to CRUCIFY.] **1.** The action of crucifying, or of putting to death on a cross; *spec. The C.*: that of Jesus Christ on Calvary 1649. **2.** *fig.* †Torture; the action of crucifying (passions, sins, etc.) 1648. **3.** A representation of the Crucifixion of Christ 1841.

2. Do ye prove What crucifixions are in love HERRICK.

Cruciform (krū·sifǫɹm), *a.* 1661. [f. L. *crucem* cross; see -FORM.] Of the form of a (right-angled) cross; cross-shaped: *spec.* in *Bot.* of the flowers of cruciferous plants; in *Anat.* = CRUCIAL 1.

Crucify (krū·sifəi), *v.* ME. [a. OF. *crucifier*, repr. pop. L. type **crucificare*.] **1.** *trans.* To put to death by nailing or otherwise fastening to a cross; an ancient mode of capital punishment, considered specially ignominious by the Greeks and Romans. **2.** *fig.* **a.** To mortify; *esp.* to destroy the power of (passions, sins, the flesh, etc.) ME. †**b.** To torture; to excruciate. **c.** To torment, to prove a crux to 1621.

1. Thei cryeden, seyinge, do awey, do awey, crucifie hym WYCLIF *John* xviii. 15. 2. Oure olde man is crucified with him also, that the body of synne myght vtterly be destroyed TINDALE *Rom.* vi. 6. Hence **Cru·cified** *ppl. a.* nailed to a cross; *absol.* a crucified person; *spec.* = Christ.

†**Cruci·gerous,** *a.* [f. L. type **cruciger* + -OUS.] Bearing or marked with a cross. SIR T. BROWNE.

Crud(de, Cruddle, obs. or dial. ff. CURD, CURDLE.

Crude (krūd), *a.* ME. [ad. L. *crudus*.] **1.** In the natural or raw state; 'not changed by any process or preparation' (J.); not manufactured, refined, tempered, etc. **2.** Not, or not fully, digested or concocted 1533; †*transf.* lacking power to digest –1671. **3.** Of fruit: Unripe; sour or harsh 1555. **4.** Of a disease, etc.: In an early stage; not developed 1651. **5.** Not completely thought out or worked up; ill-digested; rough, unpolished; coarse 1611. **6.** Of action or speech: Rough, rude, wanting in amenity 1650. **7.** Of persons: Characterized by crudeness of thought, feeling, action, or character 1722. **8.** *Gram.* In *c. form*: The uninflected form or stem of a word 1805.

1. C. Lead BOYLE, Antimony 1822. Any c. or raw thing, as fruits, herbs COGAN. 2. A c. indigested mass of humours W. BUCHAN. 3. I come to pluck your berries harsh and c. MILT. 5. The *ex tempore* and c. Prayers of the Ministers 1646. C. opinions DISRAELI, efforts JOHNSON, prose LAMB. 6. So c. an answer COTTON. 8. The base or c.-form of an adjective as adverb WHITNEY. **Cru·de-ly** *adv.*, **-ness.**

†**Crude·lity.** 1483. [a. F. *crudélité*.] = CRUELTY –1707.

Crudity (krū·dĭti). 1533. [ad. L. *cruditas*.] **1.** The state or quality of being CRUDE 1638; *concr.* (in *pl.*) raw products 1626. **2.** *Phys.* Indigestion; undigested (or indigestible) matter in the stomach 1533.

2. *fig.* Coryats Crudities, hastily gobled vp in fiue Moneths travells in France, Italy [etc.] 1611 (*title*).

Crudle, obs. f. CURDLE.

Crudy, obs. f. CURDY.

Cruel (krū·ĕl), *a.* ME. [a. F.:—L. *crudelem*, morally rough, cruel; cf. CRUDE.] **1.** Disposed to inflict suffering; indifferent to or taking pleasure in another's pain; merciless, pitiless, hard-hearted. †**2.** Fierce, savage –1600. †**3.** Severe, vigorous –1670. **4.** Painful; distressing; *colloq.* = hard ME. **5.** as *adv.* Distressingly; hence = exceedingly 1573.

1. As c. as a schoolboy TENNYSON. A c. and frowning universe MORLEY. The Puritans had given..c. provocation MACAULAY. 4. Intollerable turmentes.. and moost cruell & bytter deth 1526. Hence **Cru·elly** *adv.* in a c. manner; excessively. †**Cru·elness.**

Cruel(s, var. of CREWEL, -ELS.

Cruelty (krū·ĕlti). ME. [a. OF. *crualté* :—pop. L. type **crudalitatem*, for *crudelitatem*.] **1.** The quality of being cruel; disposition to inflict suffering; delight in or indifference to another's pain; mercilessness, hard-heartedness. Also, an instance of this. †**2.** Severity of pain –1634. †**3.** Severity; rigour –1634.

1. The vice called crueltie, which is contrary to mercye ELIOT. 'Tis a c., To load a falling man *Hen. VIII*, v. iii. 76.

†**Cruentate,** *a. rare.* [ad. L. *cruentatus*, *cruentare*, f. *cruentus*.] Blood-stained. GLANVILL.

Cruentation (krūentēi·ʃən). [ad. L. *cruentationem* (see prec.).] 'A term applied to the oozing of blood which occurs sometimes when an incision is made into the dead body' (*Syd. Soc. Lex.*).

†**Crue·ntous,** *a. rare.* 1648. [f. L. *cruentus*, (f. *cru-* root of *cruor* blood + -OUS).] Bloody. (*lit.* and *fig.*) –1675.

Cruet (krū·ĕt). [ME. *cruete*, *cruette*, app. repr. OF. **cruete*, dim. of OF. *cruie*, *crue* pot.] **1.** A small bottle or vial; now only applied to a small glass bottle with a stopper, to contain vinegar, oil, etc. for the table. **2.** *Eccl.* A small vessel to hold wine or water for use in the celebration of the Eucharist, etc. ME. *Comb.* **c.-stand,** a frame for holding cruets and castors at table.

Cruise (krūz), *v.* 1651. [= Du. *kruisen* to cross, to cruise; also Sp. and Pg. *cruzar*, F. *croiser*; the *ui* is app. after Du., the vowel sound as in Sp. and Pg.] *intr.* To sail to and fro over some part of the sea, on the look out for ships, for the protection of commerce, for plunder, or for pleasure. Also *transf.* and *fig.* **b.** *trans. rare.* To sail to and fro over 1687.

transf. Blackbirds will c. along the whole length of a hedge before finding a bush to their liking JEFFERIES. Hence **Cruise** *sb.* the action of cruising; a voyage in which the ships sail to and fro.

Cruiser (krū·zəɹ). 1679. [f. CRUISE *v.* + -ER[1], or a. Du. *kruiser*.] A person or a ship that cruises. In 18th c. commonly applied to privateers. Now, a class of warships less heavily armed than a battleship (*battle-c.*).

Comb. **c.-weight** (*Boxing*) = light heavy-weight (*colloq.*).

Cruive (krūv). ME. [Orig. *Sc.* (krōv, krūv). Cf. *corve*, CORF, etc.] **1.** A hovel (*Sc.*) 1450. **2.** A pigsty (*Sc.*) 1575. **3.** A coop or enclosure of wickerwork or spars placed in tide-ways, etc. to trap salmon ME.

†**Crull,** *a.* ME. only. [See Grimm *kroll*; cf. CURL.] Curly.

Cruller (krɒ·ləɹ). *U.S.* 1818. [app. a. Du. *cruller*, f. *crullen* to curl.] A cake cut from dough containing eggs, butter, sugar, etc., twisted or curled, and fried crisp in lard or oil.

Crumb, crum (krɒm), *sb.* [OE. *cruma* masc., related to MDu. *crume*, Du. *kruim*, mod. Ger. *krume*, etc. The *b* is late and merely graphic; cf. *dumb*, *thumb*, etc.] **1.** A small particle; *esp.* a small particle of bread, such as breaks off by rubbing, etc. **2.** *fig.* A scrap (of something immaterial) ME. **3.** The soft part of bread; opp. to *crust* ME.

1. Every crumme we put in our mouthes SANDERSON. 2. Crumbs of Comfort D'URFEY. 3. *Lear* I. iv. 217. Phr. †*To gather* (or *pick*) *up one's crumbs*: to pick up strength. *Comb.*: **c.-brush,** a brush for sweeping crumbs from a table; **-cloth,** a cloth laid under the table to catch the crumbs and keep the carpet clean.

Crumb, crum (krɒm), *v.* ME. [f. prec. sb.] **1.** *trans.* To reduce to crumbs or small fragments. Now *rare.* †**2.** *intr.* To crumble –18... **3.** *trans.* To thicken or cover with crumbs 1579. Hence **Cru·mmable** *a.* (*rare*).

Crumble (krɒ·mb'l), *v.* ME. [Earlier *crymble*, *crimble*, f. (ult.) *cruma* crumb; assim. to *crumb*, *crumbly*, etc.] **1.** *trans.* To reduce to crumbs or small fragments; to strew as crumbs. **2.** *intr.* To fall asunder in small particles; to become pulverized 1577.

1. Moisture softens and crumbles the shale PHILLIPS. *fig.* To fritter and c. down the attention BURKE. 2. Marbles with their deepest inscriptions c. away EVELYN. *fig.* His influence was crumbling away FREEMAN. Hence **Cru·mble** *sb. rare*, a small crumb or particle; crumbling substance. **Cru·mbly** *a.* apt to c.

Crumby, *a.*, var. of CRUMMY, q. v.

†**Cru·menal.** *rare.* 1579. [f. L. *crumena* purse.] A purse or pouch –1647.

Crummy (krɒ·mi), *a.* 1567. [f. *crum*, CRUMB *sb.* + -Y.] †**1.** Crumbly –1725. **2.** Like the crumb of bread 1579. **3.** *slang.* Plump; comely; rich 1718. †**4.** Full of crumbs; now CRUMBY.

†**Crump,** *a.*[1] and *sb.* [OE. *crump*, a by-form of OE. *crumb* crooked; cf. CRAMP.] *adj.* Crooked –1783. *sb.* A crooked person, a hunch-back –1765.

Crump (krɒmp), *a.*[2] *Sc.* and *n.* 1787. [A parallel form of CRIMP *a.* 1.] Brittle or friable under the teeth.

†**Crump,** *v.*[1] ME. [f. CRUMP *a.* or its source; cf. CRIMP *v.*[1] and CRAMP *sb.*[1]] *trans.* and *intr.* To bend into a curve, crook, curl up –1818. Hence †**Crumped, crumpt** *ppl. a.* curved, crooked.

Crump (krɒmp), *v.*[2] 1646. [Echoic; cf. *crunch*, *crush*.] *trans.* and *intr.* **1.** To eat with an abrupt but somewhat dulled sound; applied *esp.* to horses and pigs. Also *transf.* **2.** To strike with a brisk or abrupt effect 1850.

2. We could slog to square-leg, or c. to the off 1892. Hence **Crumper** *sb.* a 'whacker'; a 'thumping' lie.

Crumpet (krɒ·mpĕt). 1694. [? f. *crompid*, as in *crompid cake* (WYCLIF), meaning 'curled up'.] †**1.** A thin griddle cake –1830. **2.** A soft cake made of flour, beaten egg, milk, and barm, mixed into batter, and baked on an iron plate 1769. **3.** *slang.* The head 1891.

Crumple, *sb.* 1607. [Cf. CRUMPLE *v.*] A crushed fold or wrinkle.

†**Crumple,** *a.* 1523. [f. next.] = Crumpled: chiefly in comb., as *c.-horned* adj. –1851.

Crumple (krɒ·mp'l), *v.* 1528. [In form, a dim. and iterative of CRUMP *v.*[1]] **1.** *intr.* To become incurved or crushed together; to become creased by being crushed together. **2.** *trans.* To crook, bend together, contort 1613. **3.** To crush into creases 1632. **4.** To crinkle 1858. **5.** To crush together. Also with *up.* 1577.

1. To crompull to gether like parchement cast in the fire 1528. 3. Sir Roger..exposing his palm.. they crumpled it into all shapes and diligently scanned every wrinkle ADDISON. Hence **Cru·mpler.**

Cru·mpy, *a. dial.* 1808. [f. CRUMP *a.*[2] + -Y[1].] = CRUMP *a.*[2]

†**Cru·mster, cromster.** 1596. [f. Du. *krom* crooked.] A kind of galley –1600.

Crunch (krɒnʃ), *v.* 1801. [var. of *cranch*, CRAUNCH, perh. influenced by *crush*, *munch*.] **1.** *trans.* To crush with the teeth; to chew or bite with a crushing noise 1814. Also *intr.* or *absol.* **2.** *trans.* To crush under foot, wheels, etc., with the accompanying noise 1849. Also *intr.* or *absol.* **3.** *intr.* To advance, or make *one's way*, with crunching 1853.

1. A herd of swine crunching acorns KINGSLEY. 2. A sound of heavy wheels crunching a stony road C. BRONTË. 3. The sound of our vessel crunching her way through the ice KANE. Hence **Crunch** *sb.* an act, or the action, of crunching. **Cru·nchy** *a.*

†**Crunk,** *v.* 1565. [Cf. Icel. *krúnka* to croak.] *intr.* Of some birds: To utter a hoarse harsh cry –1617. Hence **Crunk** *sb.* a croak.

Crunkle (krɒ·ŋk'l), *v.*[1] Chiefly *n. dial.* ME. [Parallel to CRINKLE.] *trans.* and *intr.* To crinkle.

†**Crunkle,** *v.*[2] 1611. [dim. of CRUNK *v.*] To cry like a crane.

Crunode (krū·nōud). 1873. [Irreg. f. L. *crux* + NODE.] *Geom.* A point on a curve where it crosses itself; a node with two real tangents. Hence **Crunodal** *a.* having a c.

‖**Cruor** (krū·ǭr). 1656. [L., blood (when out of the body).] *Phys.* and *Med.* Coagulated blood; gore.

Cruorin (krū·ŏrin). 1840. [f. prec.] *Chem.* The red colouring matter of blood-corpuscles; *hæmoglobin.*

Crup, *a. dial.* 1736. [? var. of CRUMP.] Short, brittle; also *fig.*, as a *c. answer.*

Crup(e, var. of CROUP *sb.*[1], hind-quarters.

Crupper (krʊ·pəɹ), *sb.* ME. [a. OF. *cropiere* (mod. *croupière*), f. *crope, crupe* (mod. *croupe*); see CROUP.] 1. A leathern strap buckled to the back of the saddle and passing under the horse's tail, to keep the saddle from slipping forwards. 2. *transf.* The rump of a horse 1591. 3. The buttocks (of a man). Usually *joc.* 1594. 4. a. *Naut.* = *c.-chain.* b. 'The train tackle ring-bolt in a gun-carriage' (Smyth).

Comb. c.-chain (*Naut.*), a chain to secure the jib-boom down in its saddle. Hence **Cru·pper** *v.* to put a c. upon.

Crural (krūᵊ·răl), *a.* 1599. [ad. L. *cruralis*, f. *crus* leg.] 1. Of or belonging to the leg; *spec.* in *Anat.*, as in *c. artery, arch, canal, ring,* etc. 2. Of the nature or form of a leg 1842.

‖**Crus** (krʊs). Pl. **crura** (krūᵊ·ră). 1687. [L. *crus*, pl. *crura*, leg.] †1. *Geom.* A straight line forming one side of a triangle (*rare*). 2. *Anat.* a. The leg or hind limb; *spec.* the part between the knee and the ankle, the shank. b. Applied to parts occurring in pairs and likened to legs, as *crura of the diaphragm*, a pair of muscles connecting the diaphragm with the lumbar vertebræ; *crura of the penis, of the clitoris*, bodies forming the attachments of those organs, one on each side of the pubic arch. 1727.

Crusade (krusēⁱ·d). 1706. [= med.L. *cruciata* (*cruzata*), pa. pple. of *cruciare* to CROSS, used subst. The form *crusade* blends Fr. *croisade* and Sp. *cruzada, crusada.*] 1. *Hist.* A military expedition undertaken by the Christians of Europe in the 11th, 12th, and 13th centuries to recover the Holy Land from the Mohammedans. Also *transf.* of any 'holy war'. 2. *fig.* An aggressive movement or enterprise against some public evil 1786. †3. A papal bull authorizing a crusade –1771. †4. *Span. Hist.* A levy of money, originally for aggression or defence against the Moors –1772. †5. The symbol of the cross, the badge borne by crusaders –1700.

2. A c. against ignorance T. JEFFERSON. Hence **Crusa·de** *v.* to go on a c. **Crusa·der,** one who goes on a c.

‖**Crusado** (krusēⁱ·dǫ). 1544. [ad. Pg. *cruzado.*] A Portuguese coin bearing the figure of the cross; now = about 2*s.* 4*d.* sterling.

†‖**Crusa·do**[2]. 1575. [a. Sp. and Pg. *cruzado*, *lit.* a crossed man.] A crusader –1625.

Crusado[3], var. of *crusada* = CRUSADE.

Cruse (krūs, krūz). *arch.* ME. [Cf. Icel. *krús* pot, tankard. Deriv. unkn.] A small earthen vessel for liquids; a pot, jar, or bottle; also a drinking vessel. Also *fig.*

Neither did the c. of oil fail 1 *Kings* xvii. 16.

†**Cru·set.** 1558. [a. F. *creuset.*] A crucible –1755.

Crush (krʊʃ), *v.* ME. [app. a. OF. *croissir, croisir* to gnash (the teeth), to crash, crack, smash, break: app. of Ger. origin.] †1. To dash together with the sound of violent percussion, to clash, crash. (ME. only.) 2. *trans.* To compress with violence, so as to destroy natural shape or condition ME. Also *intr.* (for *refl.*). 3. To press or squeeze forcibly or violently. (The force, not the effect, being prominent.) 1592. Also *intr.* (for *refl.*). 4. *fig.* a. To break down the power of; to overcome completely 1596. b. To oppress with harshness or rigour 1611. 5. To bruise, bray, break down into small pieces; to comminute (ore, etc.) 1588. 6. To press or squeeze *out.* Also *fig.* 1602.

2. The Ostrich..leaueth her egges in the earth.. And forgetteth that the foot may c. them *Job* xxxix. 15. Some..are crusht to death SIR T. HERBERT. 3. To c. our old limbes in vngentle Steele 1 *Hen. IV*, v. i. 13. 4. His enemies were crushed by his valour GIBBON. Crush'd is thy pride GAY. b. Yea kine of Bashan..which c. the needy *Amos* iv. 1.

Phr. *To c. a cup of wine*, etc.: to drink it: cf. CRACK *v.* Hence **Cru·sher,** one who or that which crushes; *spec.* an apparatus for recording the pressure exerted on a gun by a charge of powder. **Cru·shingly** *adv.*

Crush (krʊʃ), *sb.* ME. [f. prec. vb.] †1. The noise of violent percussion; clashing; a crash. (ME. only.) 2. The act of crushing; destruction by crushing; also *fig.* 1599. †3. A bruise or injury caused by crushing –1702. 4. The crowding together of things, or *esp.* persons, so that they press forcibly upon each other; the mass so crowded together 1806; a crowded social gathering (*colloq.*) 1832.

2. The wrecks of matter, and the c. of worlds ADDISON. 4. I fell in with her at Lady Grey's great c. MACAULAY.

Comb. (? f. verb-stem): **c. hat,** a soft hat which can be crushed flat; *spec.* a hat constructed with a spring so as to collapse; an opera-hat; **-room,** a room or hall in a theatre, etc., in which the audience may promenade between the acts.

Crusily, -illy (krū·sili), *a.* 1572. [a. OF. *crusillié*, var. of *croisillé*, f. *croisille*, dim. of *croix.*] *Her.* Strewn with small crosses, as a charge.

Crust (krʊst), *sb.* ME. [a. OF. *crouste* (mod. *croûte*) or ad. L. *crusta* hard surface, rind, etc.] 1. The hard and dry outer part of bread; a scrap of bread which is mainly crust or is hard and dry 1561. Also *fig.* 2. The paste or cover of a pie 1598. 3. A hard dry formation on the surface of the body, caused by a burn, an ulcer, etc.; a scab, an eschar ME. 4. †The upper or surface layer of the ground (in reference to a supposed molten interior of the earth); hence, *Geol.* the outer portion of the earth 1555. 5. A more or less hard coating or deposit on anything, as the *c. of wine*; an encrustation 1540. 6. The hard external covering of an animal or plant; *spec.* the shell of Crustaceans 1615. 7. *fig.* 1651.

1. You know there can't be c. without crumb 1871. Bring me a cup of beer, and c. of bread 1837. 4. The whole earth, in the opinion of some philosophers, is but a kind of bridge, or c. to the great body of waters included in it 1747. 5. The c. formed over the lava 1869. 7. The c. of his selfishness 1853.

Crust (krʊst), *v.* ME. [f. prec. sb., after F. *crouster, croûter.*] 1. *trans.* To cover as with a crust, to encrust. Also *fig.* 1545. 2. *intr.* To form, or become covered with, a crust. Also *fig.* ME. 3. To make hard like a crust 1671.

1. Snowe..whyche was harde and crusted by reason of the frost ASCHAM. Truth..crusted over with fictions FROUDE. 2. The place that was burnt..crusted and healed in very few days TEMPLE (J.). 3. Dirt.. crusted on the glass 1857.

‖**Crustacea** (krʊstēⁱ·ʃiă), *sb. pl.* 1814. [mod.L. neuter pl. of *crustaceus* adj. (sc. *animalia*).] A large class of Arthropodous animals, mostly aquatic, characterized by a hard, close-fitting, usually chitinous shell or crust which is shed periodically; comprising Crabs, Lobsters, Shrimps, and many others. Hence **Crusta·cean** *a.* belonging to the C.; *sb.* one of the C. **Crusta·ceoid** *a.* crustacean-like (*rare*).

Crustaceo·logy. 1828. [See -(O)LOGY.] The scientific study of Crustacea. Hence **Crustaceolo·gical** *a.* pertaining to c.; **Crustaceo·logist,** one versed in c.

Crusta·ceoru·brin. 1882. [f. L. *Crustacea* + *ruber.*] *Chem.* A red colouring matter found in the bodies of some Crustacea.

Crustaceous (krʊstēⁱ·ʃəs), *a.* 1646. [f. L. *crusta* crust, hard shell; see -ACEOUS.] 1. Pertaining to, or of the nature of, a crust or hard integument 1656. 2. Of animals: Having a hard integument 1659. 3. *Zool.* Belonging to the Crustacea, crustacean 1646; crab-like 1842. Hence **Crusta·ceousness.** (Dicts.)

Crustal (krʊ·stăl), *a. rare.* 1860. [f. L. *crusta* + -AL.] Of or pertaining to a crust. Hence **Crusta·logy,** etc., proposed by Webster for CRUSTACEO·LOGY, etc.

Crustate (krʊ·stēⁱt), *a.* 1661. [ad. L. *crustatus.*] Crusted; crustaceous. So **Cru·stated** *ppl. a.* (in same sense). **Crusta·tion,** the formation of a crust; an encrustation.

Crusted (krʊ·stĕd), *ppl. a.* ME. [f. CRUST *sb.* and *v.* + -ED.] Having or covered with a crust; that has deposited a crust, as old port, etc.; *fig.* antiquated, venerable; with a covered crust of prejudice (*humorous*) 1831.

fig. A fine old c. abuse 1884.

Crusto·se, *a. rare.* 1882. [ad. L. *crustosus.*] Of the nature of a crust; thick-skinned, as mushrooms. var. †**Cru·stous.**

Crusty (krʊ·sti), *a.* ME. [f. CRUST *sb.* + -Y.] 1. Of the nature of a crust; hard like a crust. *spec.* Scabby; crusted (of wine). 2. *fig.* Short of temper; harshly curt; not suave 1570.

1. If þe skyn be c. ME. Good old c. port 1866. 2. Thou c. batch of Nature, what's the newes *Tr. & Cr.* v. i. 5. Hence **Cru·stily** *adv.* **Cru·stiness.**

Crut. 1847. [? ad. F. *croûte.*] The rough part of oak bark. (Dicts.)

Crutch (krʊtʃ), *sb.* [OE. *crycc* fem., a com. Teut. word :—OTeut. *krukjā-, krukjōn-*, f. ablaut stem *kruk-* of *kreuk-* to bend.] 1. A staff for a lame or infirm person to lean upon in walking; now one with a cross-piece at the top to fit under the armpit (usu. *a pair of crutches*). Also *transf.* and *fig.* 2. A support or prop, with a forked or concave top, for various uses; cf. CROTCH 1645. 3. A forked rest for the leg in a side-saddle 1874. 4. *Naut.* A forked support for a boom, mast, spar, etc., when not in use (also called *crotch*) 1769; crooked timbers or iron bands bolted to the stern-post and the sides of a vessel to unite these parts 1769. 5. The fork of the human body 1748; the angle between the two flukes of a whale's tail-fin 1842.

1. Time goes on crutches, till Loue haue all his rites *Much Ado* II. i. 373. From cradle to the c. 1592 *fig.* Hold him fast: He is thy c. *Tr. & Cr.* v. iii. 60.

Comb.: **c.-boots,** tall sea boots; **-handled** *a.*, having a transverse handle like the head of a c.; **-stick,** a c.-handled stick.

Crutch (krʊtʃ), *v.* 1642. [f. prec.] 1. *trans.* To support as with a crutch or crutches, to prop. Also with *up.* 1681. 2. *intr.* To go on crutches, to limp 1828.

1. Two fools that c. their feeble sense on verse DRYDEN.

Crutched (krʊ·tʃĕd), *ppl. a.*[1] 1570. [f. ME. CROUCH *sb.*[1] cross, *crouchen*, CROUCH *v.*[2] to cross.] Having or bearing a cross.

C. or *Crouched* (also *Crossed*) *Friars* (*Fratres Cruciferi* or *Sanctæ Crucis*): a minor order of friars so called from their bearing or wearing a cross. Hence, a name for their quarters, or the part of a town where their convent stood.

Crutched (krʊtʃt, -ĕd), *ppl. a.*[2] 1707. [f. CRUTCH *sb.* or *v.* + -ED.] 1. Furnished with a crutch; crutch-handled. 2. Supported on a crutch or crutches.

Crux (krʊks). 1641. [L.; see CROSS.] ‖1. *Her.*, etc. = CROSS, as *crux ansata*, etc. ‖2. *Astron.* The Southern Cross 1837. 3. A thing that it puzzles one to interpret or explain; *occas.*, a conundrum, riddle 1718.

3. The unity of opposites was the c. of ancient thinkers in the age of Plato JOWETT.

Crwd, crwth; vars. of CROWD *sb.*[1]

Cry (krəi), *sb.* Pl. **cries.** ME. [a. F. *cri*, f. stem of *crier* to CRY.] 1. The loud and chiefly inarticulate utterance of emotion; *esp.* of grief, pain, or terror. 2. †Shouting –1440; a shout ME.; the loud utterance of words; the words as shouted ME. 3. An importunate call, a prayer, entreaty ME. †4. A formal authoritative summons –1483. 5. †A proclamation –1837; the calling of wares for sale in the streets; the words in which wares are cried 1642. †6. Clamour, tumultuous noise, outcry –1440. 7. Public report 1568; the public voice loudly uttered in approbation, denunciation, etc. 1628. 8. An opinion generally expressed 1688. 9. A watchword; a war-cry; a rallying-cry (*lit.* and *fig.*) 1548. 10. A fit of weeping 1852. 11. The vocal utterance of any animal; *e.g.* of wolves, of hounds in the chase, etc. ME. 12. *transf.* A pack of hounds 1590. †13. A pack (*of* people). *contempt.* –1658. 14. The noise emitted by tin, etc., when bent 1882.

1. 'Tis some mischance; the c. is very direful *Oth.* v. i. 48. A c. of triumph SHELLEY, of joy BARRETT. 2. Natives..uttering loud cries 1839. The c. is still they come *Macb.* v. v. 2. 3. Whoso stoppeth his ear at the c. of the poor *Prov.* xxi. 13. 5. The six o'clock cries are not all over HT. MARTINEAU. *Hue and c.*: see HUE. 7. Why, the c. goes, that you marry her *Oth.* IV. i. 127. Vice will always have the C. of her side NORRIS. 9. The C. of *Talbot* serues me for a Sword 1 *Hen. VI*, II. i. 79. The Tory election c... was 'the Church in danger' BREWSTER. 11. *Full c.*: full pursuit; also *fig.* 12. *Mids. N.* IV. i. 131. 13. A crie of Players *Haml.* III. ii. 289.

Phrases. *Great* (or *much*) *c. and little wool*: the proverbial result of shearing hogs; hence, much noise about nothing. *A far c.*: a very long distance.

Cry (krəi), *v.* ME. [a. F. *crier* :—L. *quiri-*

tare to raise a cry.] 1. *trans.* To entreat, beg, beseech, implore in a loud and excited voice. 2. To call in supplication or reverential invocation (*on, upon, unto, to* a person) (*arch.*). Also *fig.* ME. 3. *intr.* To utter the voice loudly and with effort; to call aloud *to*, shout, vociferate ME. 4. *trans.* To utter or pronounce in a loud voice, to call out; *spec.* to shout (a war-cry, or the like) ME. 5. To announce publicly; to proclaim; to appoint by proclamation ME.; to announce (a sale, things for sale); to sell by outcry ME.; to give public oral notice of (things lost or found) 1596; to proclaim the marriage banns of 1775. †6. To call for –1798. †7. To extol –1628. 8. *intr.* To utter inarticulate exclamations; *esp.* to weep and wail ME. 9. Hence, To shed tears 1532. 10. Of an animal: To give forth a loud call or vocal sound ME.

1. To c. QUARTER, TRUCE: see these words. Þe Knyght..cryed iesu mercy LANGL. 2. How he cride to mee for helpe *Wint. T.* III. iii. 97. *fig.* Sir, these Things c. aloud for Reformation STEELE. 3. The watermen do loudly c. and bawl 1684. 4. What cryes the University CORBET. I..cried Mum, and she cride budget *Merry W.* v. v. 209. 5. I will c. broom, or cat's-meat, in Palermo MASSINGER. *To c. stinking fish* Provb. [The strayes] to be..cryed in three markets adjoyning BACON. 8. When the wounded crie *Ezek.* xxvi. 15. An infant crying in the night: An infant crying for the light: And with no language but a cry TENNYSON. 9. And c. my selfe awake *Cymb.* III. iv. 46. 10. Frogs crying..forewarne us of a tempest FULKE.

Phrases. *To c.* AIM, CRAVEN, HALVES, HAVOC, etc.: see these words. **C. against —.** To utter protests or reproofs against; also *fig.* of things. **C. for —.** To call for loudly, or with tears; *fig.* to be in pressing need of. **C. on, upon —**: see senses 2, 3. **C. back.** *intr. Hunting.* To hark back; *fig.* to revert to an ancestral type. **C. down. a.** *trans.* To proclaim as unlawful; to decry. **b.** To condemn loudly, vehemently, or publicly. **c.** To put down by louder or more vehement crying. **C. off.** *intr.* To announce one's withdrawal *from* a treaty, engagement, etc. **C. out.** To exclaim; (of things) to emit a creaking sound. **C. up.** *trans.* To extol; †*intr.* to shout. **C.-baby** *colloq.*, one who cries childishly 1851.

†Cryal. 1565. The Egret or Lesser White Heron –1755.

Cry·ing, *ppl. a.* ME. That cries; of evils: That calls loudly for redress; clamant.

A c. shame (*mod.*). Hence **Cry·ingly** *adv.*

Cryogen (krəi·ŏdʒen). 1875. [f. Gr. κρύος frost + -GEN = producer.] *Chem.* A freezing-mixture.

Cryohydrate (krəiŏ,həi·drēt). 1874. [f. as prec. + HYDRATE.] *Chem.* A solid hydrate formed by the combination of a crystalloid, as salt, with water (ice) at a temperature below freezing-point.

Cryolite (krəi·ŏləit). 1801. [f. Gr. κρύος + -LITE.] *Min.* A native fluoride of aluminium and sodium, found in white or brownish semi-transparent masses or crystals.

‖**Cryophorus** (krəiǫ·fŏrʊs). 1826. [mod.L., f. as prec. + Gr. -φορος.] An instrument for illustrating the freezing of water by evaporation; Wollaston's consists of a glass tube with a bulb at each end.

Crypt (kript), *sb.* ME. [ad. L. *crypta*; see below.] †1. A grotto or cavern. (ME. only.) 2. An underground cell, chamber, or vault; *esp.* one beneath the main floor of a church, used as a burial-place, chapel, or oratory 1789. 3. *fig.* A hiding-place 1833. 4. *Anat.* A small simple tubular or saccular gland; a secretory cavity; a follicle 1840.

2. The chancel..stood upon a large vault or c. BRAND. 3. [The Ballot] is..the c. of political honesty A. FONBLANQUE.

‖**Crypta** (kri·ptă). 1563. [L., a. Gr. κρύπτη vault, f. κρυπτός.] †1. = CRYPT 1, 2. –1703. 2. *Anat.* = CRYPT 4. 1860.

Cryptal (kri·ptăl), *a.* 1842. [f. L. *crypta* (see prec.) + -AL.] Of the nature of or pertaining to a crypt. So **Cry·ptous** (*rare*).

Crypted (kri·ptėd), *a. rare.* 1885. [f. CRYPT + -ED.] Vaulted.

Cryptic (kri·ptik), *a.* (*sb.*) 1605. [ad. L. *crypticus*, a. Gr. κρυπτικός; in sense 2, f. CRYPT.] 1. Secret, occult, mystical 1638. 2. Of the nature of a crypt (*rare*) 1878. †3. *sb.* An occult method. BACON.

1. [Nature's] silent processes and more c. methods 1663. So **Cry·ptical.** Hence **Cry·ptically** *adv.*

Crypto- (kri·ptŏ), bef. a vowel **crypt-**, comb. f. Gr. κρυπτός hidden, secret.

1. In mod. scientific words: **Cry·ptobranch** (-bræŋk), an animal with concealed branchiæ or gills; **Cryptobra·nchiate** *a.*, having the gills concealed. **Cry·ptocarp** = CYSTOCARP; hence **Cryptoca·rpic, Cryptoca·rpous** *a.*, having the fruit or fruiting organs concealed. **Cryptoce·phalous** *a.*, having the head concealed. **Crypto·cerous** *a. Entom.*, having concealed antennæ. **Cryptocla·stic** *a. Min.*, having grains so minute as to conceal the fragmental character of the rock. **Cryptocry·stalline** *a. Min.*, having the crystalline structure concealed; so **Cryptocrystalliza·tion. Crypto·di·rous** *a.*, having a concealed or concealable neck, as some tortoises. **Cry·ptodont** *a.* or *sb.*, having the teeth concealed or suppressed, as certain palæozoic bivalve molluscs. **Cry·ptolite** *Min.*, native phosphate of cerium found enclosed in crystals of apatite. **Cryptoneu·rous** *a.*, having no discernible nervous system. **Cryptopenta·merous** *Entom.*, having one of the five joints of the tarsi minute or concealed. **Crypto·pia, Cry·ptopine** *Chem.*, an alkaloid found in opium. **Crypto·rchid** *Path.*, one whose scrotum contains no testicles; hence **-o·rchidism, -o·rchism. Crypto·zygous** *a.*, in Craniology, having the zygomatic arches not seen when the skull is viewed from above; hence **Cryptozygo·sity.**

2. Prefixed, **a.** to sbs. of any origin, as in **C.-Calvinist,** a name given in the 16th c. to Lutherans and Roman Catholics who secretly held Calvinistic tenets; hence **C.-Ca·lvinism, -Calvini·stic** *a.*; **b.** to adjs. = 'unavowedly', as in *c.-splenetic.*

Cryptogam (kri·ptŏgæm). 1847. [a. F. *cryptogame* adj. and sb.] *Bot.* A plant of the class Cryptogamia.

†**Cry·ptogame,** *a. rare.* [a. F.; see prec.] Breeding in secret. WHITE.

‖**Cryptogamia** (kriptŏgæ·miă). 1753. [mod. L. sb. fem., f. Gr. κρυπτός + γάμος + -ία suffix of state; cf. Gr. ἀγαμία.] *Bot.* A large division of the vegetable kingdom, being the last class in the Linnæan system, comprising those plants which have no stamens and pistils, and therefore no proper flowers; including Ferns, Mosses, Algæ, Lichens, and Fungi. ¶ Erron. treated as pl. = Cryptogams 1813. Hence **Cryptoga·mian** *a.*, **Cryptoga·mic** *a.* (also as *sb.*), **-ga·mical** *a.* of or pertaining to the class Cryptogamia or to cryptogams; **Crypto·gamist,** a botanist who studies cryptogams; **Crypto·gamous** *a.* of the nature of a cryptogam; **Crypto·gamy,** cryptogamic condition or relations.

Cryptogram (kri·ptŏgræm). 1880. [f. Gr. κρυπτός + γράμμα, not on Gr. analogies.] Anything written in cipher.

Cryptograph (kri·ptŏgraf). 1849. [f. as prec. + Gr. -γραφος; see -GRAPH.] 1. = CRYPTOGRAM. 2. A kind of type-writer for writing in cipher 1889. Hence †**Cryptogra·phal** *a.*, **Cryptogra·phic** *a.* of, or of the nature of, cryptography; †**Cryptogra·phical** *a.* dealing or concerned with cryptography; **Crypto·grapher, Crypto·graphist,** one who writes in cipher.

Cryptography (kriptǫ·grăfi). 1658. [a. mod.L. *cryptographia*; see -GRAPHY.] A secret manner of writing intelligible only to those possessing the key; anything written in this way.

Cryptology (kriptǫ·lŏdʒi). 1645. [ad. mod. L. *cryptologia*; see -LOGY.] 'Secret speech or communication' (Blount); enigmatical language.

Cryptonym (kri·ptŏnim). *rare.* 1876. [f. Gr. κρυπτός + ὄνομα; cf. ANONYM.] A private or secret name. So **Crypto·nymous** *a.*

‖**Cryptoporticus** (kriptopǭ·ɹtikʊs). 1681. [L., f. Gr. κρυπτός + L. *porticus* gallery.] *Ancient Arch.* An enclosed gallery having, at the side, walls with openings instead of columns; also a covered or subterranean passage.

Crystal (kri·stăl). OE. [a. OF. *cristal*, ad. L. *crystallum*, ad. Gr. κρύσταλλος clear ice, (rock) crystal, f. (ult.) κρύος frost.]

A. *sb.* †1. Ice, clear ice –1535. 2. A mineral, clear and transparent like ice; *esp.* a form of quartz, now distinguished as *Rock-crystal* OE. Also *transf.* 3. A piece of rock-crystal or similar mineral; *esp.* one used in magic art ME. Also *fig.* of the eyes 1592. 4. Short for *crystal-glass*: a quality of glass of high transparency; also often a synonym for fine cut glass. [Ger. *krystallglas.*] 1594. 5. Anything made of this glass; *esp.* the glass of a watch-case. Also *fig.* 1613. 6. *Chem.* and *Min.* A form in which molecules regularly aggregate by the operation of molecular affinity; it has a definite internal structure, with the external form of a solid enclosed by a number of symmetrically arranged plane faces 1626. **b.** *Crystals*: *pl.* A quality of refined crystallized sugar 1875. 7. *Wireless.* A mineral used in 'rectifying' an oscillatory current. Comb. *c. receiver, set* 1913.

1. He sendis his kristall as morcels HAMPOLE. 2. A sea of glasse like vnto Chrystall *Rev.* iv. 6. *Iceland c.* = Iceland spar. 3. *fig.* Her eye seene in the teares, teares in her eye, Both christals *Ven. & Ad.* 963. 4. Eyeing the plate and c. THACKERAY.

B. *attrib.* and *adj.* Composed of crystal; clear and transparent, like crystal ME.

2. Her crystall eyes full of lowleness HAWES.

Hence **Cry·stal** *v.* to make into c.; to crystallize. **Crysta·llic** *a.* pertaining to crystals or their formation. **Crystalli·ferous** *a.* containing or yielding crystals. **Crysta·lliform** *a.* having the form of a c. **Crystalli·gerous** *a.* bearing a c. or crystals.

Crystallin (kri·stălin). 1847. [f. L. *crystallum* + -IN.] *Chem.* An albuminoid substance contained in the crystalline lens of the eye.

Crystalline (kri·stălin, -əin). ME. [a. F. *cristallin* and L. *crystallinus*, a. Gr. κρυστάλλινος, f. κρύσταλλος. Milton and others use (kristæ·lin), after L.]

A. *adj.* 1. Consisting, or made, of crystal 1509. 2. Clear and transparent like crystal ME. Also *fig.* 3. Of the nature or structure of a crystal 1612. 4. Of or pertaining to crystals and their formation 1866.

1. Cristallyne cuppes EDEN. 2. Nor did the dancing ruby..Allure thee from the cool c. stream MILT. 3. The c. grains are scarcely discernible KIRWAN.

Phr. *C. heaven* (*sphere, circle*): in the Ptolemaic astronomical system, a sphere (later two spheres) supposed to exist between the primum mobile and the firmament, by means of which the precession of the equinox and the motion of libration were accounted for. *C. lens* (formerly *humour*): a transparent body enclosed in a membranous capsule, situated immediately behind the iris of the eye.

B. *sb.* [the adj. used ellipt.] 1. The crystalline heaven; see above (*arch.*) ME. 2. The crystalline lens or humour; see above 1657. 3. A crystal. MRS. BROWNING. †4. = ANILINE 1838.

Crystallite (kri·stăləit). 1805. [f. Gr. κρύσταλλος CRYSTAL + -ITE.] *Min.* †1. A name applied to the somewhat crystalline form and structure taken by igneous rocks, lavas, etc. upon fusion and slow cooling –1852. 2. = MICROLITH 1878.

Crystallization (kri:stăləizē¹·ʃən). 1665. [f. CRYSTALLIZE *v.*] 1. The action of forming crystals, or of assuming a crystalline structure. Also *fig.* 2. *concr.* A crystallized formation or body 1695.

1. *fig.* All systems tend to a certain c. HELPS.

Crystallize (kri·stăləiz), *v.* 1598. [f. CRYSTAL + -IZE.] †1. *trans.* To make into or like crystal –1798. 2. To cause to assume a crystalline form, to form into crystals 1664. 3. *fig.* To give a definite or concrete form to 1663. 4. *intr.* To become crystalline in structure 1641. Also *fig.*

3. The forms of Action..as crystallized in the law POSTE. Hence **Cry·stalli:zable** *a.* **Cry·stallizer.**

Crystallo-, comb. f. Gr. κρύσταλλος crystal: **C.-cera·mic** *a.* pertaining to a method of encrusting a medallion of clay with glass; **-en·gra·ving,** a method of making intaglio designs upon glass by means of casting; **-magne·tic** *a.* pertaining to the magnetic properties of crystals and crystallized bodies.

Crystallod; see OD.

Crystalloge·nesis. 1879. [f. CRYSTALLO- + Gr. γένεσις.] The natural formation of crystals (as a department of science). So **Crystallo·ge·nic** *a.* crystal-forming. **Crystalloge·nical** *a.* relating to the formation of crystals. **Crystallo·geny,** the formation of crystals (as a subject).

Crystallography (kristălǫ·grăfi). 1802. [ad. mod.L. *crystallographia*; see -GRAPHY.] The scientific treatment and classification of crystals; a treatise on this subject.

Dr. Wollaston..almost the originator of the science of c. W. POLE. Hence **Crystallo·grapher,** one who studies c. **Cry:stallogra·phic, -al** *a.* of or pertaining to c.; of or belonging to crystals (as scientifically treated). **Crystallogra·phically** *adv.*

†**Crysta·llogy.** *rare.* 1811. [app. after *mineralogy.*] = prec. Hence †**Crysta·llogist.**

Crystalloid (kri·stăloid). 1861. [See -OID.]

A. *adj.* Crystal-like; *esp.* as opp. to *colloid* 1862.

B. *sb.* 1. A crystalloid or crystalline body or substance, as dist. from a COLLOID 1861. 2. A protoplasmic body resembling a crystal in form, occurring in certain vegetable cells 1875. Hence **Crystalloi·dal** *a.*

Crystallology (kristălǫ·lŏdʒi). 1864. [f. Gr. κρύσταλλος + -λογια.] The scientific study of crystals and crystallization.

Crystallomancy (kri·stălomæ:nsi). 1613. [f. as prec. + -MANCY.] Divination by means of a crystal.

Crystallometry (kristălǫ·mĕtri). 1837. [f. as prec. + -METRY.] The measuring of the angles of crystals, as a part of crystallography.

‖ **Ctenidium** (tĭni·diŏm). 1883. [mod.L., a. Gr. κτενίδιον, dim. of κτεν- (κτείς) a comb.] *Zool.* Each of the respiratory organs or gills of *Mollusca*, consisting of an axis with comb-like processes on each side. Hence **Cteni·dial** *a.* of or pertaining to a c.

Cteno-, comb. f. Gr. κτείς, κτενός a comb: **Ctenobranch**, a ctenobranchiate animal; **Ctenobran·chia, -branchia·ta**, a family of Mollusca, also called *Pectinibranchiata*; **Ctenobra·nchiate** *a.* having pectinate gills. **Cte·nodont** *a.* having ctenoid teeth.

Ctenocyst (tī·nosist). 1861. [f. Gr. κτενο- short for *ctenophora* + κύστις CYST.] *Zool.* The vesicle which constitutes the organ of sense (probably of hearing) in the *Ctenophora.*

Ctenoid (tī·noid), *a.* 1847. [ad. Gr. κτενοειδής.] 1. Having marginal projections like the teeth of a comb; pectinate; as the scales and teeth of certain fishes 1872. 2. Belonging to the *Ctenoidei*, an order of fishes in Agassiz's classification, containing those with ctenoid scales. Also as *sb.* A ctenoid fish. (Now disused.) Hence **Ctenoi·dean** *a.* and *sb.* = CTENOID 2.

‖ **Ctenophora** (tĭnǫ·fŏră), *sb. pl.* 1855. [mod. L., neut. pl. (sc. *animalia*), f. Gr. κτενο- + -φορος.] *Zool.* A division of animals, formerly considered as an order of *Acalepha*, and now made a class of CŒLENTERATA. Hence **Cteno·phoral** *a.* of or pertaining to the C. **Cteno·phoran** *a.* of or belonging to the class C.; *sb.* a member of this class. **Cte·nophore** (tī·nofoəɪ), 1. each of the eight meridionally arranged bands, bearing comb-like fringes, which are the locomotive organs of the Ctenophora; 2. a Ctenophoran. **Ctenopho·ric, Cteno·phorous** *a.*

Cub (kɒb), *sb.*[1] 1530. [?] 1. *orig.* A young fox. 2. Hence: The young of the bear, lion, etc.; also of the whale 1596. Also *transf.* b. A junior member of the Boy Scouts 1922. 3. *fig.* An awkward, unformed youth 1601.

2. Plucke the yong sucking Cubs from the she Beare *Merch. V*, II. i. 29. 3. Like a bashful, great, awkward c. as you were STEELE. *Comb.*: †**c.-drawn** *a.*, drawn (or ?sucked dry) by its cubs; **-hunting**, hunting young foxes at the beginning of the season. Hence **Cu·bbing** *vbl. sb.* cub-hunting. **Cu·bbish** *a.* **Cu·bhood**, the state or condition of a c.

Cub (kɒb), *sb.*[2] Chiefly *dial.* 1546. [Cf. LG. *kübbung, kübje* a shed or lean-to for cattle, Du. *kub* weir-basket, etc.] A stall, pen, or shed for cattle; also, a coop or hutch. b. A crib for fodder.

Cub (kɒb), *v.*[1] 1755. [f. CUB *sb.*[1] Cf. *whelp* vb.] To bring forth cubs (*trans.* and *intr.*).

Cub (kɒb), *v.*[2] Now *dial.* 1621. [f. CUB *sb.*[2]] To coop *up.*

Cuba (kiū·bă). 1837. [An island in the W. Indies, also called Havana.] A cigar made of tobacco grown in Cuba.

Cubage (kiū·bĕdʒ). 1840. [f. CUBE *sb.* or *v.* + -AGE.] Cubature; cubic content.

Cubation (kiubē·ʃən). *rare.* 1727. = CUBATURE.

Cubature (kiū·bătiŭɹ). 1679. [f. mod.L. *cubare to cube, after *quadrature.*] The determination of the cubic content of a solid.

†**Cu·bbridge head.** 1622. *Naut.* A bulkhead across the forecastle and the half-deck of a ship -1642.

Cubby (kɒ·bi). *local.* 1842. [Related to CUB *sb.*[2]] 1. = *Cubby-hole, -house* 1887. 2. In Orkney, etc.: A straw basket. Hence **c.-hole, -house**, a snug place; also a closet.

Cube (kiūb), *sb.* 1551. [a. F., ad. late L. *cubus*, a. Gr. κύβος a cube, *orig.* a die.] 1. *Geom.* A solid figure contained by six equal squares; a regular hexahedron. 2. *Arith.* and *Alg.* The third power *of* a quantity 1557. 3. *attrib.* (= CUBIC *a.* 2), and in *comb.*, as **c.-ore** = PHARMACOSIDERITE; **-root**, that number of which the given number is the c.; **-spar** = ANHYDRITE. b. *Occas.* as in 6 *feet c.* = of cubical form, and measuring 6 ft. in each direction.

Cube (kiūb), *v.* 1588. [Cf. F. *cuber*, and prob. mod.L. *cubare.*] 1. *Arith.* and *Alg.* To raise to the third power. 2. *Mensuration.* To determine the cubic content of 1668.

Cubeb (kiū·beb). ME. [a. F. *cubèbe*, ad. Arab. *kabābah.*] The berry of a climbing shrub *Piper Cubeba* or *Cubeba officinalis*, a native of Java; it resembles a grain of pepper, and has a pungent spicy flavour, and is used in medicine and cookery. (Usually in pl. *cubebs.*) Also *attrib.* Hence **Cube·bene**, the chief constituent of oil of cubebs; **Cube·bic acid**, a resinous acid obtained from cubebs; **Cube·bin**, a crystalline substance existing in cubebs.

Cubi- (kiū·bi), bef. a vowel **cub-** (kiūb), comb. f. L. *cubus* CUBE, now denoting 'of the third degree, cubic', as *c.-cone*, etc.

Cubic (kiū·bik). 1551. [a. F. *cubique*, ad. L. *cubicus*, a. Gr., f. κύβος CUBE.]

A. *adj.* 1. Of the form of a cube; cubical. b. *Crystallography.* = ISOMETRIC, as the *c. system* 1878. 2. *Mensuration.* Of three dimensions; solid; *esp.* used to express the content of a cube whose edge is a given unit, as a *c. foot* 1660. 3. *Arith., Alg.*, etc. Relating to or involving the cube; of three dimensions, of the third degree, as †*c. number* = CUBE number; *c. equation*, an equation of the third degree; *c. curve*, a curve represented by a c. equation.

B. *sb.* (the adj. used ellipt.) *Math.* A cubic expression or equation; a cubic curve.

Cubica (kiū·bikă). 1835. [Sp.] A very fine unglazed shalloon.

Cubical (kiu·bikăl), *a.* 1571. [See CUBIC and -AL.] 1. Of or pertaining to a cube; cube-shaped. (Now more usual than *cubic.*) 1592. 2. *Mensuration.* = CUBIC *a.* 2. (Now less common than *cubic.*) 1571. 3. *Arith., Alg.*, etc. = CUBIC *a.* 3. *Obs.* exc. in *c. parabola, hyperbola*, etc. Hence **Cu·bically** *adv.* **Cu·bicalness** (*rare*).

Cubicle (kiū·bik'l). 1483. [ad. L. *cubiculum*, f. *cubare* to recline.] A bedchamber; in mod. use, one of a series of small separate sleeping chambers, as dist. from an undivided dormitory. So †**Cubi·cular** *sb.* an attendant in a bedchamber. **Cubi·cular** *a.* of or belonging to a bedchamber.

‖ **Cubiculum** (kiubi·kiŭlŏm). Pl. **-a.** 1832. [L. = sleeping-chamber.] A sleeping-chamber. In *Archæol.*, a burial-chamber in the Catacombs; also, a chapel or oratory attached to a church. var. ‖**Cubi·culo.** *Twel. N.* III. ii. 56.

Cubism (kiū·biz'm). 1911. [F. *-isme.*] A form of art based on the cube. Hence **Cu·bist.**

Cubit (kiū·bit). ME. [ad. L. *cubitum* the elbow, f. *cubit-* ppl. stem of *cubare, -cumbere* to recline.] †1. The forearm. b. The ulna, one of the two bones of the forearm. -1847. c. *Entom.* One of the veins or ribs of an insect's wing 1774. 2. An ancient measure of land derived from the forearm; usually about 18–22 inches. Now *Hist.* ME. Also *attrib.*

Cubital (kiū·bităl), *a.* ME. [ad. L. *cubitalis*, f. *cubitus.*] 1. Of the length of a cubit. 2. *Anat.* Pertaining to the CUBIT (sense 1) 1611.

Cubito- (kiū·bito), used as comb. f. L. *cubitus*, in sense 'relating to the ulna and ——', as *c.-carpal, -digital, -radial*, etc.

Cubo- (kiū·bo), bef. a vowel sometimes **cub-** (kiūb), comb. f. Gr. κύβος die, CUBE:

†**cubo-cube** [Gr. κυβόκυβος], the sixth power of a quantity; so †**cu·bic**; †**cubo-cube**, the ninth power; **-cu·neiform** (*Anat.*), relating to the cuboid and cuneiform bones; also in *Solid Geom.*, etc., denoting a solid which combines the form of a cube and another solid, as **cubo-octahe·dron** (*cuboctahedron*), a solid of fourteen faces formed by cutting off the corners of a cube, so as to add eight triangular faces corresponding to those of an octahedron; so **cubo-octahe·dral** *a.*, **cubo-dodecahe·dron, -al.**

Cuboid (kiū·boid). 1829. [ad. Gr. κυβοειδής.] *adj.* Resembling, or approximating to the form of, a cube, as the *c. bone* of the foot, between the calcaneum and the fourth and fifth metatarsal bones. *sb. Anat.* Short for *c. bone*; see prec. 1839. Hence **Cuboi·dal** *a.* cuboid; in *Anat.*, of or belonging to the c. bone.

Cuca, Cucaine, etc., vars. of COCA, etc.

†**Cuck**, *v.*[1] ME. [Cf. Icel. *kúka* cacare.] *intr.* To void excrement -1606.

†**Cuck**, *v.*[2] 1611. [Back-formation from next.] *trans.* To set in the cucking-stool -1648.

Cucking-stool (kɒ·kiŋ-stūl). *Hist.* ME. [f. CUCK *v.*[1] + STOOL.] A chair (sometimes in the form of a close-stool), formerly in use for scolds, disorderly women, fraudulent tradespeople, etc., in which the offender was fastened and exposed to the jeers of the bystanders, or conveyed to a pond or river and ducked.

She..shall..be placed in a certain engine of correction called the trebucket, castigatory, or cucking stool..now it is frequently corrupted into ducking stool BLACKSTONE.

Cuckold (kɒ·kəld), *sb.* [ME. *cukeweld, cokewold* (3 syllables), ad. OF. *cucuald, f. OF. *cucu* cuckoo. The reference is supposed to be to the cuckoo's habit of laying its egg in another bird's nest, but in English *cuckold* is not found applied to the adulterer.] 1. The husband of an unfaithful wife. *derisory.* Also *attrib.* 2. The American cow-bird, *Molothrus ater.* 3. Short for *Cuckold-fish.*

Comb.: †**c.-fish**, a fish with horn-like projections, prob. the cow-fish (*Ostracion quadricorne*); **-maker**; **-knot, neck**, a knot or loop made in a rope by crossing it over itself and binding it together with a cord at the point of crossing.

Hence **Cu·ckold** *v.* to make a c. of; said of a paramour, and of a wife. †**Cu·ckoldize** *v. trans.* to make a c. (*rare*). †**Cu·ckoldly** *a.* having the qualities of a c.; often a mere term of abuse. **Cu·ckoldom**, the state or position of a c.; cuckoldry. **Cu·ckoldry**, the making a c. of a husband; †the position of a c. **Cu·ckoldy** *a. arch.* = *cuckoldly.*

Cuckoo (ku·kū), *sb.* ME. [= F. *coucou*, imitating the cry of the bird. Cf. L. *cuculus*, whence It. *cucu·lo.*] 1. A bird, *Cuculus canorus*, well known by the call of the male during mating time. It is a migratory bird, and does not hatch its own offspring, but deposits its eggs in the nests of other birds. b. The family name of the *Cuculidæ*, including various genera and species 1797. 2. The note of the bird, or an imitation of it ME. 3. = Fool, 'gowk' 1596. 4. (Usu. in *pl.*) A local name of several spring flowers 1878. 5. A species of fish; also called *c.-fish, -wrasse*, etc. (*local*) 1848. 6. *attrib.* Of or pertaining to the cuckoo; resembling the cuckoo and its uniformly repeated call 1650.

1. The merry Cuckow, messenger of Spring SPENSER. 2. Cuckow, Cuckow: O word of feare *L.L.L.* v. ii. 911. 3. The c. I travel with..he also has his uses SCOTT. 6. The c. note..of 'the Bill, the whole Bill, and nothing but the Bill' 1831.

Comb.: **c.-bee**, a genus of bees which deposit their eggs in the nests of other bees; **c.('s) bread**, the Wood-sorrel; also the Lady's Smock; **-dove**, a genus of doves of the East Indies and Australia; **-fish**: see sense 5; also the boar-fish; **c.('s) fool, maid(en, mate**, the Wryneck, which arrives with the c.; **-orchis**, *Orchis mascula*; **-point** = CUCKOO-PINT; **-ray**, a fish, a species of ray; **-wrasse**: see sense 5.

Cuckoo (ku·kū), *v.* 1620. [f. prec.] 1. *intr.* To utter the call of the cuckoo. 2. *trans.* To repeat incessantly 1648.

Cuckoo-bud. 1588. A name of some plant; in Shaks., the buttercup, marsh-marigold, or cowslip.

Cu·ckoo-flow·er. 1578. A name of various spring wild flowers; as the Lady's Smock (*Cardamine pratensis*), the Ragged Robin, etc.

Cu·ckoo-fly. 1868. A name of species of hymenopterous insects belonging to the *Ichneumonidæ* and *Chrysididæ*, which deposit their eggs in the larvæ or nests of other insects.

Cuckoo-pint (ku·kupi:nt). 1551. [Short f. next.] The wild Arum, *A. maculatum.*

†**Cu·ckoo-pi·ntle.** 1450. [From the form of the spadix.] = prec. –1682.

Cuckoo's meat, cuckoo-meat. 1516. Wood-sorrel, *Oxalis Acetosella*; also called *gowk's-meat*.

Cu·ckoo-spi·t. 1592. [f. SPIT, expectoration.] **1.** A frothy secretion exuded by the Frog-hopper and other insects, in which their larvæ lie enveloped on the leaves, axils, etc. of plants. **2.** The Lady's Smock (*local*) 1876.

Cu·ckoo-spi·ttle. 1646. = prec. (sense 1).

†**Cu·ckquean,** *sb.* 1562. [f. stem of *cuck-old*.] A female cuckold –1652. Hence †**Cu·ckquean** *v.* to make a c. of.

†**Cuck-stool.** ME. = CUCKING-STOOL –1769.

Cucu·liform, *a. rare.* [f. L. *cuculus*.] Cuckoo-like in form or structure.

Cu·culine, *a.* [f. as prec.] Pertaining or related to the cuckoo.

Cucullate (kiū·kvlėt, kiukv·lėt), *a.* 1794. [ad. late L. *cucullatus*, f. *cucullus*.] Hooded; shaped like a hood or cowl. So **Cu·cullated** *ppl. a.* (in same sense).

†**Cucu·lle.** ME. [ad. L. *cucullus*.] A hood or cowl of a monk –1677.

Cuculliform (kiukv·lifǭɹm), *a.* 1835. [f. L. *cucullus*.] Cowl-shaped, hood-shaped.

Cucumber (kiū·kvmbəɹ). ME. [a. obs. F. *cocombre*, ad. L. *cucumerem* (nom. *cucumis*) cucumber. In 17th c. *cowcumber* (kau·kvmbəɹ).] **1.** A creeping plant, *Cucumis sativus* (N.O. *Cucurbitaceæ*), long cultivated for its fruit. **2.** The fruit of this plant, commonly eaten as a salad, or pickled when young (see GHERKIN) ME. **3.** Applied to other plants allied to or resembling the common cucumber: as **Bitter C.,** the Colocynth, *Citrullus Colocynthis*; **Indian C.** = *c.-root* (see below); **One-seeded, single-seeded, or Star C.,** the genus *Sicyos*; **Serpent** or **Snake C.,** *Trichosanthes colubrina* and *T. anguina*, also *Cucumis flexuosus* (from the appearance of the fruit); **Spirting** or **Squirting C.,** *Ecbalium agreste* (formerly called *Momordica Elaterium*), the fruit of which when ripe separates from the stalk, and expels the seeds and pulp with force. Also *attrib.*

1. The cowcumber loveth water 1584. **2.** Phr. *Cool* (†*cold*) *as a c.*: perfectly self-possessed; showing no excitement. *Comb.*: **c.-root,** (*a*) the root of the c.; (*b*) the plant *Medeola virginica* (N.O. *Trilliaceæ*), from the taste of its rhizomes; **-tree,** (*a*) *Magnolia acuminata* and other American species, the fruits of which resemble small cucumbers; (*b*) *Averrhoa Bilimbi*, an East Indian tree with an acid fruit resembling a small c.

†‖**Cu·cupha.** 1656. [f. med.L. *cufa*, *cufia* COIF. In F. *cucuphe*.] A cap with spices quilted in it, worn for certain nervous disorders in the head –1665.

†**Cucurbit**[1] (kiukv·ɹbit). ME. [a. F. *cucurbite*, ad. L. *cucurbita* a gourd, etc.] **1.** A vessel or retort, originally gourd-shaped; forming the lower part of an alembic –1823. **2.** A cupping-glass 1541.

Cucurbit[2]. 1866. [mod. ad. L. *cucurbita*.] A cucurbitaceous plant; a gourd.

Cucurbitaceous (kiukǭ:ɹbitēⁱ·ʃəs), *a.* 1853. [f. mod.L. *Cucurbitaceæ*, f. *cucurbita*.] *Bot.* Belonging to the N.O. *Cucurbitaceæ*, comprising trailing or climbing plants with fleshy fruits, as the Gourd, Cucumber, Melon, etc.

Cucurbital (kiukǭ·ɹbităl), *a.* [f. L. *cucurbita*.] *Bot.* Epithet of Lindley's alliance, including the *Cucurbitaceæ* and allied orders.

Cucurbitine (kiukǭ·ɹbitəin, -in), *a.* 1843. [f. as prec.] Gourd-like: applied to a tapeworm, from the resemblance of each segment to the seed of a gourd. var. (erron.) †**Cucurbitive.**

‖**Cucuy, cucuyo** (kukū·i, kukū·yo). Also erron. **cucullo.** 1591. [Sp. *cucuyo*, ad. Haitian.] The West Indian firefly (*Pyrophorus noctilucus*).

Cud (kvd), *sb.* [OE. *cwidu* (*cweodu*, *cwudu*, *cudu*) neut. App. radically identical with OHG. *chuti*, *quiti* glue; stem *kwed-*, cf. Skr. *jatu* resin.] **1.** The food which a ruminating animal brings back into its mouth from its first stomach, and chews at leisure. **2.** Any substance used by men to keep in the mouth and chew. Now a dial. form of QUID. OE.

1. Phr. *To chew the c.* (fig.): to recall and reflect on things past; to ruminate.

Cudbear (kv·dbēᵊɹ). 1766. [Coined from *Cuthbert* by Dr. *Cuthbert* Gordon (who obtained a patent for this powder).] **1.** A purple or violet powder, used for dyeing, prepared from various species of lichens, esp. *Lecanora tartarea* 1771. **2.** The lichen *Lecanora tartarea*.

Cudden (kv·d'n). 1673. †**1.** A born fool –1719. **2.** *local.* The coal-fish [Gael. *cudainn*] 1836.

1. The slavering c., propped upon his staff DRYDEN.

Cuddle (kv·d'l), *v.* 1520. [?f. COUTH *a.* snug, cosy; cf. *fondle* from *fond* adj.] **1.** *trans.* To hug affectionately, to fondle; also *absol.* **2.** *intr.* To lie close and snug 1711; to curl oneself up in going to sleep 1822. Also *fig.*

2. She [a partridge] cuddles low behind the brake PRIOR. **Cu·ddle** *sb.* **Cu·ddlesome, Cu·ddly** *adjs.*

Cuddy[1], **cudeigh.** 1450. [Corruption of Irish *cuid oidhche*, lit. 'evening portion'.] *Irel.* and *Scotl.* **1.** *orig.* A supper and night's entertainment due to the lord from his tenant (*Hist.*). **2.** Hence, a rent or present in lieu of this; a douceur, a bribe (*Hist.*) 15...

Cuddy[2] (kv·di). 1660. [?] **1.** *Naut.* A room or cabin in a large ship abaft and under the round-house. **2.** A small room, closet, or cupboard 1793. Also *attrib.*

Cuddy[3] (kv·di). Chiefly *Sc.* 1714. [?] **1.** A donkey. Also *fig.* **2.** = CUDDEN 2. 1775. **3.** *local.* The hedge-sparrow; also the moor-hen 1802. **4.** *Mech.* A lever mounted on a tripod for lifting stones, etc. 1852.

Cudgel (kv·dʒěl), *sb.* [OE. *cycgel*, *kicgel*; not known exc. in OE.] A short thick stick used as a weapon; a club. **b.** in *pl.* = CUDGEL-PLAY 1630. Also *fig.*

This deponent had a lytell cogell 1566. Phr. *To take up the cudgels* (fig.): to engage in a vigorous contest or debate (*for*, *in behalf of*, etc.). †*To cross the cudgels* (fig.): to forbear the contest. *Comb.*: **c.-play,** the art of combat with cudgels; a contest with cudgels; hence **-pla·yer, -pla·ying.**

Cu·dgel, *v.* 1596. **1.** To beat with a cudgel. **2.** *intr.* To play cudgels *for* 1840.

1. *fig.* Cudgell thy brains no more about it *Haml.* v. i. 63. Hence **Cu·dgelled** *ppl. a.* **Cu·dgeller.**

†**Cuds.** 1599. = CODS –1711.

Cudweed (kv·dwīd). 1548. [f. CUD *sb.*: the plant being administered to cattle that had lost their cud.] The genus *Gnaphalium* of composite plants, having chaffy scales surrounding the flower-heads: originally proper to *G. sylvaticum*; extended to allied or similar plants.

†**Cu·dwort.** 1548. = prec. –1725.

Cue (kiū), *sb.*[1] ME. **1.** The name of the letter Q, q.v. 1755. †**2.** The sum of half a farthing, formerly denoted in College accounts by the letter *q* (orig. for *quadrans*); hence *transf.* a small quantity of bread, or of beer –1831.

2. Hast thou worn Gowns in the university..ate cues, drunk cees? 1605.

Cue (kiū), *sb.*[2] 1553. [? = Fr. *queue* tail; or ? = *q*, first letter of L. *quando* when.] **1.** *Theatr.* The concluding word or words of a speech in a play, serving as a signal to another actor to enter, or begin his speech. **b.** *Mus.* A few notes of some other part immediately preceding his own, printed as a guide to a singer or player to come in at the right time after a long rest 1880. **2.** *fig.* A sign or intimation when to speak or act; a hint 1565. **3.** The part assigned one to play; the proper course to take 1581. **4.** Humour, frame of mind, etc. (proper to any action) 1565.

1. Curst be thy stones for thus deceiuing mee..*Deceiuing me* is Thisbies c.; she is to enter *Mids. N.* v. i. 186. **3.** Pat: he comes..my C. is villanous Melancholly *Lear* I. ii. 147. Hence **Cue** *v.*[1] *trans.* (*a*) to give a cue to as in performing a play; to prompt; (*b*) *Mus.* to insert notes as a cue; usu. with *in*.

Cue (kiū), *sb.*[3] 1731. [var. of QUEUE, a. mod. F.:—L. *cauda*.] **1.** = QUEUE *sb.* 2. **2.** The straight tapering rod with which the balls are struck in billiards 1749. **Cue** *v.*[2] *trans.* to form into a c.; to furnish with a c. **Cue·ist,** a billiard-player. **Cue·less** *a.* without a pigtail.

Cue-·owl. 1855. The Scops-owl (*Scops Giu*).

The Cue-owls speak the name we call them by BROWNING.

†‖**Cuerpo.** 1625. [Sp.:—L. *corpus*.] Only in *in c.*: without the cloak, so as to show the shape of the body; also *fig.* –1748.

Boy: my Cloake and Rapier; it fits not a Gentleman of my ranck to walk the streets *in Querpo* FLETCHER.

Cuff (kvf), *sb.*[1] [ME. *coffe*, *cuffe*; not conn. in sense with ML. *cuffia*, in OE. *cuffie*, COIF.] †**1.** A mitten or glove –1467. **2.** An ornamental part at the bottom of a sleeve, as a fold of the sleeve itself turned back, a band of linen, lace, etc. sewed on, or the like; also, the corresponding part of a shirt-sleeve, or a separate band of linen, etc. worn round the wrist and under the sleeve 1522. **3.** A HANDCUFF 1663.

2. She laid her hand upon the c. of my coat STERNE.

Cuff (kvf), *sb.*[2] 1570. [See CUFF *v.*[1]] A blow; *esp.* a blow with the open hand.

This mad-brain'd bridegroome tooke him suche a cuffe, That downe fell Priest and booke *Tam. Shr.* III. ii. 165. Phr. *At cuffs*: at blows, fighting.

Cuff, *sb.*[3] 1740. Var. (orig. Sc.) of SCUFF, SCRUFF, in *C. of the neck*.

Cuff (kvf), *v.*[1] 1530. [Of unkn. deriv.; cf. G. Rogues' cant *kuffen* to thrash; also Sw. *kuffa* to thrust, push.] **1.** *trans.* To strike with the open hand; to strike, buffet. **2.** *absol.* or *intr.* To deal blows; to scuffle 1611.

1. Prieste..I meane..to cuffe you soundly 1 *Hen. VI*, I. iii. 48. Their opposites with beake and tallons rend; Cuffe with their wings G. SANDYS. Hence **Cu·ffer,** a boxer; †the fist (*joc.*).

Cuff (kvf), *v.*[2] *rare.* 1693. [f. CUFF *sb.*[1]] To put cuffs on; to handcuff.

Cuffin (kv·fin). *Thieves' cant.* 1567. [? Cf. CHUFF[1].] = COVE *sb.*[2]

Cufic (kiū·fik), *a.* Also **Cuphic, Kufic.** 1706. [f. *Cufa* or *Kufa* an ancient city near Babylon.] Of or pertaining to Cufa; applied to a variety of Arabic writing.

‖**Cui bono** (kəi bōᵘ·no). 1604. A Latin phrase, meaning 'To whom for a benefit', *i.e.* 'Who profits by it?' erron. taken in English to mean 'To what good purpose'; hence, occas. *subst.* Practical utility as a principle. As *adj.* or *attrib.* Relating to the question *cui bono?*; *occas.* = utilitarian.

Cuinage, cuynage, obs. ff. COINAGE. As applied to tin it means the official stamping of the blocks.

Cuirass (kwiræ·s, kiuræ·s), *sb.* 1464. [a. F. *cuirasse*, f. *cuir* leather, after Pr. *coirassa*, It. *corazza*, Sp. *coraza*:—L. *coriacea* adj. (fem.), f. *corium*.] **1.** A piece of armour for the body (originally of leather); *spec.* a piece reaching down to the waist, and consisting of a breast-plate and a back-plate, buckled or otherwise fastened together. (The breast-plate alone was sometimes called a cuirass, and the two pieces (*a pair of*) *cuirasses*.) Also *transf.* **2.** *fig.* and *transf.* The buckler of an animal; the armour-plating of a ship, etc. 1863.

1. The Man at Armes..with his cuyrasses of proofe BARRET. *transf.* A dark brown [dress] with a c. of gold lace 1883. var. †**Curats, curiats, curat,** etc. Hence **Cuira·ss** *v.* to cover with, or as with a c. **Cuira·ssed** *ppl. a.* furnished with a c.; of ships, etc.: armour-plated.

Cuirassier (kwirăsīᵊ·ɹ, kiūᵊ-). 1625. [a. F.] A horse soldier wearing a cuirass.

‖**Cuir-bouilli.** ME. [F. (kwir buˡyi) *lit.* 'boiled leather'.] Leather boiled or soaked in hot water, and, when soft, moulded or pressed into any required form, which it retains on becoming dry and hard.

Cuirie, var. of *quiry*, obs. aphet. f. EQUERRY, royal stables, stud.

‖**Cuisine** (kwizī·n). 1786. [F.:—L. *coquina*, *cocina*, f. *coquere*.] Kitchen; culinary department; manner or style of cooking. Hence **Cuisi·nier** [F.], a (French) cook.

Cuisse, cuish (kwis, kwiʃ). ME. [In 14th c. *quyssewes*, *cuissues*, a. OF. *cuisseaux*, *cuisiaux*, pl. of *cuissel* = L. *coxale*, f. *coxa* hip, F. *cuisse* thigh.] *pl.* Armour for protecting the front part of the thigh; in *sing.* a thigh-piece.

†**Cuit, cute.** 1460. [a. F. *cuit*:—L. *coctus*.] Orig. *adj.* in *wine cuit*, subseq. used *absol.*: New wine boiled down and sweetened –1756.

Cuittle (kū·t'l), *v. trans. Sc.* 1565. **1.** To wheedle, coax. **2.** To tickle. (?for *kittle*.) 1790.

‖**Cul** (kü, often kūl). [F. = bottom, anus :—L. *culus*.]

‖**Cul-de-four** (kü-d'fūr, often kŭl də fū·r). Pl. **culs-de-four.** 1727. [F.] *Archit.* 'A low vault spherically formed on a circular or oval plan' (Gwilt).

‖**Cul-de-lampe** (kü-d'lāñp, often kŭl də lāñp). Pl. **culs-de-lampe.** 1727. [F.] **1.** *Archit.* An ornamental support of inverted conical form; a pendant of the same form. **2.** *Printing.* An ornament used to fill up a blank space in a page, as at the end of a chapter.

‖**Cul-de-sac** (kü-d'sak, often kŭl də sæk). Pl. **culs-de-sac.** 1738. [F.]. **1.** *Anat.* A vessel, tube, sac, etc. open only at one end; the closed end of such a vessel, etc. **2.** A passage closed at one end, a blind alley; a place having no outlet except by the entrance; in *Milit.* use, said of the position of an army hemmed in on all sides except behind 1819. Also *fig.*

-cula; see -CULUS.

Culbut, *v. rare.* 1693. [ad. F. *culbuter*, f. *cul* + *buter* to butt.] To overturn backwards; to drive back in disorder.

Culch, cultch (kɒltʃ). 1667. [?a. OF. *culche* (mod.F. *couche*).] Rubbish, refuse; *spec.* the mass of hard material of which an oyster-bed is formed (*local*).

Culdee (kɒ·ldī). [In OIr. *cēle dē*, from *cēle* associate, sometimes servant + *dē* of God. By Hector Boece written *Culdei*, as if = *cultores Dei*, whence *Culdees.*]

A. *sb.* A member of an ancient Scoto-Irish religious order, found from the eighth century onwards. (Orig. a name given to solitary recluses.) ME.

The Culdees thus united in themselves the distinction of monks and of secular clergy PINKERTON.

B. *adj.* Of or belonging to the Culdees 1880. So **Culde·an** *a.*

-cule, *suffix*, corresp. to F. *-cule*, ad. L. *-culus, -cula, -culum* dim. suffix; see -CULUS. In English, both F. endings *-cle* and *-cule* are found, and the L. endings *-culus, -culum* are sometimes retained.

Culerage; see CULRAGE.

Culet[1]. 1550. [a. OF. *cueillete*, semi-pop. ad. L. *collecta.*] A sum collected from a number of persons chargeable; an assessment. *Hist.*

Culet[2] (kiū·lėt). 1678. [a. OF., dim. of F. *cul.*] **1.** The horizontal face forming the bottom of a diamond when cut as a brilliant. **2.** A piece of armour for protecting the hinder part of the body below the waist 1834.

‖**Culex** (kiū·leks). 1483. [L. gnat.] A gnat; in *Entom.* the genus containing gnats and mosquitoes.

‖**Culgee** (kɒlgī·). *Anglo-Ind.* 1688. [a. Urdū *kalghī*, ad. Pers. *kalagī*, of or pertaining to a festive or martial gathering, whence as sb.] †**1.** A rich figured silk, worn as a turban, or otherwise –17... **2.** A jewelled plume surmounting the aigrette upon the turban 1715.

Culinary (kiū·linări), *a.* 1638. [ad. L. *culinarius*, f. *culina.*] **1.** Of or pertaining to a kitchen; kitchen-. **2.** Of or pertaining to cookery 1651; of vegetables: Fit for cooking 1796.

1. A very c. goddess 1856. **2.** The palate undepraved By c. arts COWPER. C. roots and plants MORSE. Hence **Cu·linarily** *adv.* (*rare*).

Cull, *sb.*[1] *dial.* 1490. A fish, the Miller's Thumb.

Cull, *sb.*[2] *slang.* 1698. [? abbrev. of CULLY.] = CULLY.

Cull (kɒl), *sb.*[3] 1618. [f. CULL *v.*[1]] †**1.** The act or product of culling. **2.** *Farming.* An animal drafted from the flock as being inferior or too old for breeding. (Usu. in *pl.*) 1791. **3.** *U.S.* (*pl.*) Any refuse stuff, as timber, etc. 1873.

Cull (kɒl), *v.*[1] ME. [a. OF. *cuillir* and *-er*, later *cueillir*:—L. *colligere.* See also COIL v.[1]] **1.** *trans.* To choose; to select. **2.** To gather, pick, pluck (flowers, etc.) 1634. **3.** *transf.* To subject to the process of selection 1713.

1. Words aptly culled, and meanings well exprest CRABBE. **2.** The Sirens three Culling their potent herbs MILT. *Comus* 255. Hence **Culled** *ppl.a.* chosen; plucked; *spec.* of sheep: Draught (cf. CULL *sb.*[3] 2). **Cu·ller,** one who culls. **Cu·lling** *vbl. sb.* the action of culling; *concr.* a selection; *pl.* portions drafted out.

Cull, *v.*[2] Now *dial.* 1564. [var. of COLL *v.*[1]] To hug.

Cullender; see COLANDER.

Cullet (kɒ·lėt). 1817. [var. COLLET[1].] *Glass-blowing.* Broken or refuse glass for remelting.

†**Cu·llible,** *a.* 1822. [Cf. CULL *sb.*[2], CULLY *v.*[2] No verb *cull* is recorded.] Easily made a cull of; gullible. Hence †**Cullibi·lity,** gullibility.

Cullion (kɒ·lyən). ME. [a. F. *couillon* = Pr. *colho*, Rom. deriv. of L. *coleus, culleus* bag, testicle, a. Gr. κολεός sheath.] †**1.** A testicle –1737. †**2.** A despicable fellow; a rascal –1843. **3.** *pl.* A name of plants of the genus *Orchis*, from the form of the tubers 1611. Hence †**Cu·llionly** *a.* like a c.; rascally, despicable.

Cullis (kɒ·lis), *sb.*[1] Now *rare.* ME. [a. OF. *coleïs* (later *couleïs, coulis*):—L. type **colaticius*, f. *colare* to strain, flow through, etc.] A strong broth of meat, fowl, etc., boiled and strained. Also †*transf.* and *fig.*

Use for a c., a leg of veal and a ham MRS. GLASSE.

Cullis (kɒ·lis), *sb.*[2] 1838. [a. F. *coulisse*, fem. of *coulis* adj., used subst.; see prec.] *Archit.* A gutter, groove, or channel.

Cullisance, -sen, -son, -zan, obs. corruptions of COGNIZANCE, a badge, etc.

Cully (kɒ·li), *sb. slang.* 1664. [?] **1.** One who is cheated or imposed upon; a dupe, gull; a simpleton. **2.** A man; a mate 1676.

1. The whimper of a cheated c. SWINBURNE. Hence †**Cully** *v.* to make a fool of, cheat, take in. †**Cu·llyism,** the condition of a c.

Culm[1] (kɒlm). ME. [= COOM *sb.*[1]; ? conn. w. *col* COAL.] **1.** Soot, smut. Now *Sc.* **2.** Coal-dust, slack 1603; *spec.* the slack of anthracite coal, from the Welsh collieries 1736; hence = anthracite, or the slaty glance coal, one of its varieties 1742. **3.** *Geol.* (= *Culm measures* or *series.*) A name given by some geologists to a series of shales, sandstones, etc. containing, in places, beds of impure anthracite, which represent the Carboniferous series in North Devon. It includes the *calp* of Ireland. 1836.

Culm[2] (kɒlm). 1657. [ad. L. *culmus* stalk.] *Bot.* The stem of a plant; *esp.* the jointed stalk of grasses. Hence **Culm** *v. intr.* to form a c.

†**Culm**[3]. *rare.* 1587. [Short for CULMEN.] The summit, culminating point –1821.

‖**Culmen** (kɒ·lmen). 1647. [L., contr. f. *columen* top, etc.] †**1.** *gen.* The top or summit; *fig.* the culminating point –1856. **2.** *Ornith.* The upper ridge of a bird's bill 1833. **3.** *Anat.* 'The superior vermiform process of the cerebellum' (*Syd. Soc. Lex.*).

Culmiferous (kɒlmi·fėrəs), *a.*[1] 1837. [f. CULM[1].] *Geol.* Containing or producing culm.

Culmi·ferous, *a.*[2] 1704. [f. L. *culmus* CULM[2] + -(I)FEROUS.] *Bot.* Of grasses: Having a jointed stalk.

Cu·lminal, *a. rare.* 1889. [f. L. *culmen.*] Of or pertaining to the summit; apical.

Culminant (kɒ·lminănt), *a.* 1605. [ad. L. *culminantem.*] **1.** Of a heavenly body: That has reached its greatest altitude, that is on the meridian; hence *fig.* at its greatest height. **2.** Forming the highest point, topmost 1849.

Culminate (kɒ·lmineit), *v.* 1647. [f. late L. *culminat-, culminare*, f. *culmen.*] **1.** *intr. Astron.* Of a heavenly body: To reach its greatest altitude, to be on the meridian 1647. Hence *fig.* **2.** *gen.* To reach its highest point; to rise to an apex. Const. *in.* 1665. **3.** *trans.* To bring (a thing) to its highest point; to crown (*rare*) 1659.

1. All Sun-shine, as when his Beams at Noon C. from th' Æquator MILT. *P. L.* III. 617. *fig.* Thus D'Aiguillon rose again and culminated CARLYLE. **2.** The mountain system culminates in Ararat 1869.

Cu·lminate, *a.* 1864. [ad. late L. *culminatus*; see prec.] 'Growing upwards, as distinguished from a lateral growth; applied to the growth of corals' (Dana).

Culmination (kɒlminēi·ʃən). 1633. [f. CULMINATE *v.*] **1.** The attainment by a heavenly body of its greatest altitude; the act of reaching the meridian. **2.** *fig.* The attainment of the highest point; *concr.* that in which anything culminates 1657.

Cu·lmy. ME. [f. CULM[1].] †**1.** = COOMY. (ME. only.) **2.** Of the nature of culm, as *c. beds*, etc.

‖**Culot** (külo). 1683. [F., dim. of *cul.*] A little cup of sheet-iron inserted into the base of the Minié and other projectiles, so as to be driven into and enlarge the diameter of the ball when fired.

Culottic (kiulǫ·tik), *a.* [f. F. *culotte* breeches.] Wearing breeches, respectable; opp. to *sansculottic.* CARLYLE. So **Culo·ttism.**

†**Culp(e.** ME. [a. OF. *coulpe*, f. L. *culpa.*] Guilt, sin, fault, blame –1601.

Culpable (kɒ·lpăb'l), *a.* (*sb.*) [ME. *coupable*, a. OF. :—L. *culpabilis*, f. *culpa* fault, blame. Refash. after L. in 14th c.] **1.** Guilty, criminal; deserving punishment. ? *Obs.* **2.** Blameworthy 1613. †**3.** *sb.* A culprit –1734.

1. Phr. *C. of* (*punishment, death*, etc.): deserving, liable to. **2.** What circumstances make an action laudable or c. HOBBES. Hence **Culpabi·lity, Cu·lpableness,** c. quality. **Cu·lpably** *adv.*

Cu·lpatory, *a. rare.* 1762. [f. L. *culpat-* ppl. stem.] Tending to or expressing blame.

†**Cu·lpon,** *sb.* ME. [a. OF. *colpon*, etc., now *coupon*, f. *colper, couper.*] A piece cut off; a portion, strip, slice, bit, shred –1825. Hence †**Cu·lpon** *v.* to cut up; to ornament with strips of a different-coloured material.

Culpose (kɒlpōu·s), *a.* 1832. [f. L. *culpa* + -OSE, after *dolose.*] *Rom. Law.* Characterized by *culpa* or (criminal) negligence.

Culprit (kɒ·lprit). 1678. [App. a fusion of *cul.*, short f. Anglo-Fr. *culpable* or L. *culpabilis*, and *prit* or *prist* = OF. *prest* 'ready'. See BLOUNT *Law Dict.* s. v.] **1.** *Law.* Used only in the formula 'Culprit, How will you be tried?' formerly said to a prisoner indicted for high treason or felony, on his pleading 'Not guilty'. **2.** Hence assumed to mean, Prisoner at the bar; the accused 1700. **3.** An offender [as if f. L. *culpa*] 1769.

2. An author is in the condition of a c.: the public are his judges PRIOR. **3.** The fled Hungarian, who seems the c. BYRON.

†**Cu·lrage, culerage.** ME. [a. OF. *culrage*, mod. *curage*, f. *cul* + *rage* rabies.] The plant Water-pepper (*Polygonum Hydropiper*) –1611.

Cult (kɒlt), *sb.* 1617. [ad. L. *cultus* worship. In 19th c. often spelt *culte* as in Fr.] †**1.** Worship –1683. **2.** A particular form of religious worship; *esp.* in reference to its external rites and ceremonies 1679. **3.** *transf.* Devotion to a particular person or thing, now *esp.* as paid by a body of professed adherents 1711.

2. The c. of Aphrodite MAHAFFY. **3.** The decay of the Wordsworth c. 1889.

Cultch, var. of CULCH.

Culter, obs. and dial. f. COULTER.

Cultism (kɒ·ltiz'm). 1887. [a. Sp. *cultismo*, f. *culto* polished (:—L. *cultus*).] A kind of affected elegance of style which prevailed in Spanish literature in 16–17th c.; also called *Góngorism* after the poet Góngora. So **Cu·ltist,** a writer affecting c.

Cultivable (kɒ·ltivăb'l), *a.* 1682. [f. F. *cultivable*, f. *cultiver* to CULTIVATE.] Capable of being cultivated.

Cultivate (kɒ·ltiveit), *v.* 1620. [f. *cultivat-*, ppl. stem of late L. *cultivare* to till, f. late L. *cultivus* characterized by being tilled, f. *cultus*, *colere.* Cf. *captivate.*] **1.** *trans.* To bestow labour and attention upon (land) in order to the raising of crops; to till. **2.** To produce or raise by tillage. Also *transf.* 1697. **3.** *fig.* To improve and develop by education and training; to refine 1681. **4.** To promote the growth of; to foster 1662. **5.** To devote one's attention to, practise, cherish 1749.

1. A country..miserably cultivated DE FOE. **2.** To c. pot-herbs DRYDEN. **3.** To c. the wild licentious savage ADDISON. **4.** To c. the Sciences EVELYN, friendship MILT., inward religion BUTLER. **5.** To c. bluntness 1863, [a man's] acquaintance BOSWELL. Phr. *To c. a person* (ellipt.): to court his acquaintance. Hence **Cu·ltiva:table** *a.* cultivable.

Cultivation (kɒltivēi·ʃən). 1700. [a. F., f. *cultiver*; see -ATION.] **1.** The tilling of land; husbandry 1725. **2.** The improvement of a plant by labour and care; the raising of (a crop) by tillage. Also *transf.* 1719. **3.** *fig.* The devoting of attention or study to the development of, or to progress in 1700. **4.** The condition of being cultivated; culture, refinement 1716.

3. Use and c. of reason SOUTH. **4.** Increased cultivation..produces..fastidiousness LECKY.

Cultivator (kɒ·ltiveitəɪ). 1665. [prob. after F. *cultivateur.*] **1.** One who cultivates (*lit.* and *fig.*) **2.** An agricultural implement for loosening the ground, and uprooting weeds between the drills of crops 1759.

†**Cu·ltive**, *v.* 1483. [a. F. *cultiver.*] = CULTIVATE -1635.

Cultrate (kʊ·ltrĕ̆t), *a.* 1856. [ad. L. *cultratus*, f. *culter.*] Formed like a knife or coulter; sharp-edged. So **Cu·ltrated** *ppl. a.* **Cu·ltriform** *a.*

Culturable (kʊ·ltiŭrăb'l), *a.* 1796. [f. CULTURE *v.* + -ABLE.] Capable of culture or cultivation; cultivable. (*lit.* and *fig.*)

Cultural (kʊ·ltiŭrăl), *a.* 1868. [f. L. *cultura* + -AL.] Relating to culture. Hence **Cu·lturally** *adv.*

Culture (kʊ·ltiŭɹ), *sb.* ME. [a. F., ad. L. *cultura*; see CULT.] †1. Worship 1483. 2. = CULTIVATION 1. ME. 3. = CULTIVATION 2. 1626; *spec.* the artificial development of microscopic organisms, *esp.* bacteria, in prepared media; *concr.* the product of such culture 1884. 4. *fig.* Improvement or refinement by education and training 1510. 5. *absol.* The training and refinement of mind, tastes, and manners; the condition of being thus trained and refined; the intellectual side of civilization 1805. 6. = CULTIVATION 3 (*rare*) 1876.

2. The soil is clay, and difficult of c. 1806. 3. The c. of the vine 1856, of silk MORSE, oysters (*mod.*). A c.-fluid..that contains..various species of organisms KLEIN. 4. The education of children [is called] a C. of their mindes HOBBES. 5. C., the acquainting ourselves with the best that has been known and said in the world M. ARNOLD. Hence **Cu·ltureless** *a. rare*, uncultivated (*lit.* and *fig.*). **Cu·lturist**, one engaged in the c. of plants, fish, etc.; an advocate of c.

Culture (kʊ·ltiŭɹ), *v.* Now *rare.* 1510. [a. F. *culturer*, f. *culture*; see prec.] To subject to culture, cultivate. *lit.* (usu. *poet.*) and *fig.*

Cultured (kʊ·ltiŭɹd), *ppl. a.* 1743. [f. CULTURE *v.* and *sb.* + -ED.] 1. *lit.* Cultivated. (Chiefly *poet.*) 2. *fig.* Improved by education and training; refined 1777.

1. Our cultur'd vales SHENSTONE. 2. A c. man of science TYNDALL.

‖**Cultus** (kʊ·ltʊ̆s). 1640. [a. L., f. ppl. stem of *colere*; see CULT.] = CULT *sb.* †1, 2, 3.

Cultus-cod (kʊ·ltʊ̆s,kǫ:d). 1884. [Chinook *cultus* 'of little worth', G. B. Goode.] A chiroid fish (*Ophiodon elongatus*) of the Pacific coast of North America.

-culus, -cula, -culum, a L. dim. suffix of all three genders. See -CULE.

Culver[1] (kʊ·lvəɹ). [OE. *culfre* wk. fem., not known in other Teut. langs.] A dove; now a local name of the wood-pigeon.

The Culuer on the bared bough Sits mourning SPENSER. *Comb.*: †**c.-foot**, Dove's-foot, a species of wild Geranium; †**-house**, a dove-cote; †**-tail** = DOVETAIL; hence **-tailed** *ppl. a.*

†**Cu·lver**[2]. *rare.* Used for CULVERIN (? confused with prec.). SCOTT *Last Minstr.* IV. xx.

Culverin (kʊ·lvĕrin). 1489. [a. F. *coulevrine*, f. *couleuvre*; cf. L. *colubrinus* of the nature of a snake.] *orig.* A kind of hand-gun; later, a large cannon, very long in proportion to its bore.

He found the gate of Say's Court defended by men with culverins SCOTT. He..crouched beneath the carriage of a c. H. AINSWORTH. Hence **Cu·lverineer**, a soldier armed with, or in charge of, a c.

Cu·lverkeys. 1613. [f. CULVER[1] + KEY.] 1. A popular name of plants, the flowers of which suggest a bunch of keys, *e.g.* the wild Hyacinth, *Scilla nutans*, the Cowslip, etc. 2. The seedpods of the ash, ash-keys (*dial.*) 1790.

1. I could..see..there a Girle cropping Culverkeys and Cowslips WALTON.

Culvert (kʊ·lvəɹt), *sb.* 1773. [? *orig.* an Eng. dial. wd.] A conduit or tunneled drain of masonry conveying water across beneath a canal, railway embankment, or road. Hence **Cu·lvert** *v.* to provide with culverts.

Cu·lvertage. 1613. [a. OF., f. *culvert*, late L. *collibertus* fellow-freedman, in Middle Ages a serf, villain.] *Feudal Law.* Villainage; forfeiture and degradation to the position of a *culvert* or serf.

‖**Cum** (kʊm). 1589. L. prep., meaning 'with, together with', used in Eng. in local names, as *Chorlton-cum-Hardy*, etc. Also in several L. phrases, e.g. *cum grano salis* (or *cum grano*), lit. 'with a grain of salt', *i. e.* with some reserve; and in expressions imitating these, as *cum dividend* (*cum div.*) including the dividend announced on stock or shares purchased.

Cumbent (kʊ·mbĕnt), *a.* 1644. [ad. L. *-cumbentem*, pr. pple. of *-cumbere*, used only in comp.] Lying down: *esp.* of figures in statuary.

Cumber (kʊ·mbəɹ), *sb.* ME. [? f. CUMBER *v.* With sense 2 cf. Ger. *kummer.*] †1. Overthrow. (ME. only.) 2. Trouble, distress (*arch.*) 1500. 3. That which cumbers. (*lit.* and *fig.*) ME. 4. The action or quality of encumbering, or fact of being encumbered 1618. †5. Pressure of business -1849.

2. What Gains shall answer all this C., all these pains 1682. 3. A cloke is but a c. in faire weather COTGR. Hence **Cu·mberless** *a.* without c.

Cumber (kʊ·mbəɹ), *v.* ME. [Cf. ENCUMBER *v.*, and OF. *encombrer.*] †1. *trans.* To overthrow -15... †2. To harass, distress, trouble -1666; †to perplex -1616. 3. To hamper, hinder ME. 4. To occupy obstructively, or inconveniently ME. 5. *fig.* (of prec. senses) ME. †6. To benumb. Cf. CUMBLE *v.* -1483.

2. Cumbred about much seruing *Luke* x. 40. 3. The press was thik, and cummerit thaim full fast 1470. 4. Why cumbereth it the ground *Luke* xiii. 7. 5. Cares, that c. royal sway SCOTT.

Comb.: **c.-ground**, a thing or person that uselessly occupies the ground; so †**-world.**

Hence **Cu·mberer. Cu·mberment**, †distress; †perplexity; hindrance; that which cumbers. (Now *rare.*)

Cumbersome (kʊ·mbəɹsəm), *a.* ME. [f. prec. vb.] †1. Of places or ways: Presenting obstruction; difficult of passage -1681. 2. Full of trouble; wearisome, oppressive. Now *dial.* 1535. 3. Troublesome from bulk or weight; unwieldy, clumsy 1594. Also *fig.*

3. That c. Luggage of war MILT. *fig.* Useless and c. Ceremonies H. MORE. **Cu·mbersome-ly** *adv.*, **-ness.**

†**Cu·mble.** [ad. F. *comble* :—L. *cumulum.*] Apex, culmination. HOWELL.

Cu·mble, *v.* Now *dial.* ME. [a. F. *combler* :—L. *cumulare.*] *trans.* To deprive of power; *esp.* to benumb with cold. Also *intr.*

‖**Cumbly, cumly** (kʊ·mli). 1673. [Hind. *kamli* :—Skr. *kambala.*] A blanket, a coarse woollen cloth.

†**Cu·mbrance.** ME. [f. CUMBER *v.* + -ANCE.] The action of cumbering, harassing, hindering; an encumbrance -1671.

Extol not Riches then..The wise man's c. if not snare MILT. *P. R.* II. 454.

Cumbrous (kʊ·mbrəs), *a.* ME. [f. CUMBER *sb.* + -OUS.] †1. = CUMBERSOME 1. -1861. †2. = CUMBERSOME 2. -1667. 3. = CUMBERSOME 3. ME. Also *fig.*

2. A cloud of c. gnattes doe him molest SPENSER. 3. Armour..C. of size, uncouth to sight SCOTT. *fig.* To correct the style where it is c. or incorrect ARNOLD. Hence **Cu·mbrous-ly** *adv.*, **-ness.**

Cumene (kiū·mīn). 1863. [f. L. *cuminum* CUMIN.] *Chem.* A hydrocarbon, C_9H_{12}, found in Roman cumin oil: it is a colourless strongly refracting oil, allied to Benzene; var. **Cumole.** So **Cumic** (kiū·mik) *a.* of or derived from cumin, as in *Cumic acid*, $C_{10}H_{12}O_2$, etc. **Cu·midine**, a base homologous with toluidine, formed by the action of ammonium sulphide on nitrocumene. **Cumi·nic** *a.* = *cumic.* **Cu·myl**, the acid organic radical, $C_{10}H_{11}O$, of Cumic acid, homologous with Benzoyl.

Cumin, cummin (kʊ·min). [OE. *cymen* (:—*cumin*), a. L. *cuminum* (*cym-*), a. Gr. κύμινον, cogn. in origin w. Heb. *kammôn*, Arab. *kammūn*, etc.] An umbelliferous plant (*Cummin Cyminum*) resembling fennel: cultivated for its fruit or seed, which is aromatic and carminative; also called *Common*, *Garden*, or *Roman c.* Also *fig.* (see *Matt.* xxiii. 23).

Rue, myrrh, and cummin for the Sphinx—Her muddy eyes to clear EMERSON.

Black C., a ranunculaceous plant, *Nigella sativa*, with black, acrid, and aromatic seeds; **Sweet C.**, the Anise, *Pimpinella Anisum*; **Wild C.**, an umbelliferous plant, *Lagœcia cuminoides.* *Comb.* **c.-splitting** *a.* skinflint [cf. L. *cuminisector*].

Cummer, kimmer (kʊ·məɹ, ki·məɹ). *Sc.* ME. [a. F. *commère* :—late L. *commater*, f. *com-* + *mater.*] 1. A godmother; a co-mother. 2. A female intimate; a gossip 1500. 3. A woman, a female; applied like 'fellow' to a man, and *spec.* to a witch, wise-woman, midwife, etc. 17...

‖**Cummerbund** (kʊ·məɹbʊnd). *Anglo-Ind.* 1616. [Urdū *kamar-band*, i. e. loin-band.] A sash or girdle worn round the waist.

Cummin; see CUMIN.

‖**Cumquat** (kʊ·m,kwǫt). 1699. [Cantonese dial. f. *kin kü* 'gold orange'.] A small orange (*Citrus Aurantium*, var. *Japonica*), having a sweet rind and acid pulp; used in preserves, etc.

‖**Cumshaw** (kʊ·mʃǫ). Also **kum-.** 1839. [repr. Chinese *kan* to be grateful, *hsieh* thanks = 'grateful thanks'.] In the Chinese ports: A gratuity; a baksheesh. Hence **Cu·mshaw** *v.* to make a present to.

Cumulant (kiū·miŭlănt). 1853. [ad. L. *cumulantem.*] *Math.* 'The denominator of the simple algebraical fraction which expresses the value of an improper continued fraction' (Sylvester).

Cumulate (kiū·miŭlĕ̆t), *a.* 1535. [ad. L. *cumulatus*; see next.] Formed or gathered into a heap.

Cumulate (kiū·miŭlĕ̆it), *v.* 1534. [f. L. *cumulat-*, *cumulare*, f. *cumulus.*] 1. *trans.* To gather in a heap; to heap up; to accumulate. 2. *trans.* To add over and above 1640. 3. To put the crown or summit to (*arch.*) 1660.

1. Sholes of Shells..cumulated..Heap upon Heap WOODWARD. Hence **Cu·mulated** *ppl. a.* heaped up; of clouds: Formed into cumuli. **Cu·mulately** *adv.*

Cumulation (kiūmiŭlē̆·ʃən). 1616. [See CUMULATE.] 1. The action of heaping up; a heap; accumulation. Chiefly *fig.* 2. *Civil Law.* The joining of two or more actions or defences in a single proceeding 1645.

Cumulative (kiū·miŭlĕ̆tiv), *a.* 1605. [f. L. *cumulat-*; see CUMULATE.] †1. Such as is formed by heaping on (as opp. to organic growth). 2. Constituted by accumulation; acquiring or increasing in force by successive additions, as *c. argument*, *evidence*, etc. 1668. 3. *Sc. Law.* Concurrent 1746. 4. That tends to accumulate. H. SPENCER.

1. As for knowledge which man receiveth by teaching, it is c., and not original BACON. 2. The force of character is c. EMERSON. Phr. *C. vote*, or *system of voting*: a system of voting in which each voter has as many votes as there are places to be filled, and may accumulate them upon one candidate or distribute them as he pleases. **Cu·mulative-ly** *adv.*, **-ness.**

Cumulato- (kiūmiulē̆·to), comb. f. L. *cumulatus*, in sense 'cumulately-', 'cumulate and —'.

Cu·mulo-, comb. f. CUMULUS, used in naming cloud-forms which combine the cumulus with other types: *e.g.* **Cu·mulo-stra·tus, -cirro-stra·tus**, etc.

‖**Cumulus** (kiū·miŭlʊ̆s). Pl. **cumuli.** 1659. [L.] 1. A heap, pile; an accumulation; the conical top of a heap. 2. *Meteor.* A form of cloud, consisting of rounded masses heaped upon each other and resting on a nearly horizontal base 1803. 3. *Anat.* The *Discus proligerus* (*Syd. Soc. Lex.*).

2. In the lower cumuli..the groups are..like towers or mountains RUSKIN.

Cun, cunne, *v. Obs.* (or ? *dial.*) [OE. *cunnian*, *-ode*, wk. vb. :—OTeut. type **kunnojan*, deriv. of *kunnan* to know (see CAN).] In OE.: To learn to know; whence **a.** To prove, test try. **b.** To study; see CON *v.*[1] -1688.

Cun; see CAN *v.*[1] and [2], CON *v.*[1] and [2].

‖**Cunabula** (kiunæ·biŭlă), *sb. pl.* 1789. [L. (neut. pl.).] Cf. INCUNABULA.] 1. A cradle; *fig.* the earliest abode. 2. = INCUNABULA 1846.

Cunctation (kʊŋktē̆·ʃən). 1585. [ad. L. *cunctationem.*] The action of delaying; tardy action. Hence **Cuncta·tious** *a. rare*, prone to delay. So **Cu·nctative** *a.* (*rare*).

‖**Cunctator** (kʊŋktē̆·təɹ). 1654. [L., f. *cunctari.*] One who acts tardily, a delayer. Hence **Cu·nctatory** *a.* disposed to delay (*rare*).

Cunctipotent (kʊŋkti·pǫtĕnt), *a. rare.* 1485. [ad. late L. *cunctipotentem* (after cl. *omnipotens*).] Omnipotent.

Cund, var. of COND *v.*, to direct a ship.

‖**Cundurango** (kʊndŭræ·ŋgo). Also **con-.** 1871. [Peruvian, f. *cundur*, *cuntur* eagle, condor + *ango* vine.] A Peruvian climbing shrub,

ö (Ger. Köln). ö̆ (Fr. peu). ü (Ger. Müller). ü̆ (Fr. dune). ʊ (curl). ē (ē·) (there). ē̆ (ē̆) (rein). ẽ (Fr. faire). ɜ (fir, fern, earth).

Gonolobus Cundurango, the bark of which was introduced into therapeutic use in 1871.

Cuneal (kiū·niăl), *a.* ? *Obs.* 1578. [f. L. *cuneus.*] Wedge-shaped, cuneiform.

Cuneate (kiū·niēt), *a.* 1810. [ad. L. *cuneatus*, f. *cuneare*; see prec.] Wedge-shaped, as *c. leaf*, a leaf with a truncated end, tapering gradually to the stipule. So **Cu·neated** *ppl. a.*, **Cunea·tic** *a.*

Cuneator (kiū·niēitəɹ). [= OF. *coigneur* coiner.] An official formerly in sole charge of all the dies used in the various English mints.

Cuneiform (kiunī·ifǫɹm, kiū·nii-). Also **cuniform** (kiū·nifǫɹm). 1677. [f. L. *cuneus* wedge.]

A. *adj.* 1. Wedge-shaped. 2. *spec.* Applied to the wedge-shaped or arrow-headed characters of the ancient inscriptions of Persia, Assyria, etc.; also, to the inscriptions 1818. Also *transf.*

1. *C. bone* (in *Anat.*): (*a*) one of the bones of the carpus; (*b*) each of three bones of the second row of the tarsus, called *internal, middle*, and *external*; (*c*) the sphenoid bone of the skull. 2. *transf.* C. scholars 1862, studies DEUTSCH.

B. *sb.* 1. *Anat.* = *C. bone* in A. 1. 1854. 2. The cuneiform character 1862.

Cuneo- (kiū·nio), comb. f. L. *cuneus*, used in *Anat.*, as **c.-sca·phoid** *a.*, relating to the cuneiform and scaphoid bones, etc.

‖**Cunette** (kiune·t). 1688. [a. F., a. It. *cunetta*, aphæretic f. *lacunetta*, dim. of *lacuna* lagoon, ditch, etc. (Hatzfeld and Darmesteter).] *Fortif.* A trench sunk in a ditch or moat, serving as a drain, etc.

‖**Cuniculus** (kiuni·kiŭlŏs). Pl. **-uli.** 1670. [L.] A burrow, underground passage, or mine; in *Roman Archæol.* applied to the ancient drains of Latium and Southern Etruria. Hence **Cuni·cular** *a.* of or pertaining to cuniculi. **Cuni·culate** *a.*, *Bot.* 'traversed by a long passage, open at one end, as the peduncle of *Tropæolum*' (*Treas. Bot.*). †**Cuni·culous** *a.* full of holes and windings; also, full of rabbits.

Cunner (kʋ·nəɹ). Also **conner.** 1602. [? = CONNER, CONDER of a ship or of herring-boats.] The name of two fishes of the family *Labridæ* or Wrasses: a. The Gilt-head (*Crenilabrus melops*). b. The Blue Perch or Burgall (*Ctenolabrus adspersus*), found on the Atlantic coast of N. America.

Cunning (kʋ·niŋ), *sb.* ME. [vbl. sb. from CAN *v.*[1] to know, hence *orig.* = L. *scientia, sapientia.* Not in OE.] †1. Knowledge; erudition –1670. †2. Intelligence –1532. 3. Knowledge how to do a thing; ability, skill. (Now *arch.*) ME. †4. A science or art, a craft. In early times often = occult art. –1592. 5. Now usually: Skilful deceit, craft; craftiness 1583.

3. Let my right hand forget her c. *Ps.* cxxxvii. 5. More by Chance, than C. 1743. 5. We take C. for a sinister or crooked Wisedome BACON. C. borders very near upon Knavery W. PENN.

Cunning (kʋ·niŋ), *a.* ME. [Orig. type *cunnende, pres. pple. of CAN *v.*[1] to know; hence *orig.* = 'knowing'. Not in OE.] †1. Learned –1667. Also *transf.* of things. 2. Skilful, clever. (Now *arch.*) ME. Also *transf.* of things. †3. *spec.* Possessing magical knowledge or skill, in *c. man, c. woman* –1807. 4. Knowing, clever 1671. 5. In bad sense: Clever in circumventing; crafty, artful, sly. (Now the prevailing sense.) 1599. Also *transf.* of things. 6. *U.S. colloq.* Quaintly interesting or taking. (Cf. CANNY.) 1854.

1. C. Latin books 1519. 2. C. in fence *Twel. N.* III. iv. 312. *transf.* He made the brestplate of c. worke *Ex.* xxxix. 8. 3. A c. man did calculate my birth *2 Hen. VI*, IV. i. 34. 5. The c. will have recourse to stratagem JOHNSON. *transf.* By the sleight of men, and c. craftinesse, whereby they lye in waite to deceiue *Eph.* iv. 14. Hence **Cu·nningly** *adv.* in a c. manner; craftily, artfully. **Cu·nningness.**

Cunningaire, var. CONYGER, rabbit-warren.

Cup (kʋp), *sb.* [OE. *cuppe* wk. fem., supposed to be ad. late L. *cuppa*, var. of *cupa* tub, cask, etc.] I. A small open vessel for liquids, usually hemispherical or hemi-spheroidal, with or without a handle; a drinking-vessel. In forms (*e. g.* a wine-cup, etc.) having a stem and foot, sometimes limited to the concave part that receives the liquid. 2. *spec.* a. The CHALICE in which the wine is administered at the Communion 1449. b. An ornamental vessel offered as a prize for an athletic contest 1640. 3. *Surg.* A vessel used for cupping; a cupping-glass. b. A vessel (holding usually four ounces), used to receive the blood in blood-letting. 1617. 4. Anything having the form of a cup 1545. 5. *Astron.* The constellation CRATER 1551.

1. Monkes haf grete kuppes WYCLIF. 4. Acorne cups *Mids. N.* II. i. 31. The cowslips golden c. 1743.

II. Transf. and fig. uses. 1. A cup with its contents; a cupful ME.; *spec.* the wine taken at the Communion 1597. 2. *fig.* Something to be partaken of; an experience, portion, lot (usually painful). Cf. CHALICE. ME. 3. *pl.* The drinking of intoxicating liquor; potations, drunken revelry ME. 4. A beverage consisting of wine sweetened and flavoured and usually iced; as *claret-c.*, etc. 1773.

1. I did send for a c. of tee (a China drink) PEPYS. 2. Are ye able to drink of the c. that I shall drink of *Matt.* xx. 22. All Foes [shall taste] The c. of their deseruings *Lear* V. iii. 304. 3. Thence from Cups to civil Broiles MILT. *P. L.* xi. 718.

In one's cups: † (*a*) while drinking; (*b*) drunk.

Comb.: †**c. and can**, constant associates (the cup being filled from the can); **c.-and-cone** (*Mining*), an iron hopper with a large central opening, closed by a cone; **-coral** (see CORAL *sb.*[1]); **-gall**, a cup-shaped gall found on oak-leaves; **-lichen**, *Cladonia pyxidata*; = CUP-MOSS; **-man**, a man addicted to drinking; **-mushroom**, a name for species of *Peziza*; **-plant**, *Silphium perfoliatum* of N. America.

Cup (kʋp), *v.* 1482. [f. CUP *sb.*] 1. *Surg.* To apply a cupping-glass to; to bleed by means of a cupping-glass. Also *absol.* †2. To supply with cups, *i. e.* with liquor (*rare*) –1630; *intr.* to indulge in cups 1625. 3. To receive as in a cup 1838. 4. *intr.* To form a cup 1830.

2. C. vs till the world go round *Ant. & Cl.* II. vii. 124.

Cup and ball, cup-and-ball. 1760. 1. = BILBOQUET 2. 2. *attrib.* Of a joint or bones: = *Ball and socket*; see BALL *sb.*[1]

Cup-bearer (kʋ·pbēᵊːrəɹ). 1483. One who carries a cup; an officer of a great household who served his master with wine.

For I was the king's cupbearer *Neh.* i. 11.

Cupboard (kʋ·bəɹd), *sb.* ME. [f. CUP + BOARD.] †1. A board or table to place cups and plate on; a sideboard –1708. 2. A closet or a cabinet with shelves, for keeping cups, dishes, provisions, etc. 1530. 3. *transf.* Food, provisions 1665.

1. A Candlestick on a Cubbert 1663. 2. Lockers to put any thing in, as in little Cupberts 1627. Phr. *Skeleton in the c.*: see SKELETON. 3. Phr. *To cry c.*, to crave for food. ? *Obs.* *Comb.* **c.-love**, love displayed for the sake of what one can get by it. Hence **Cu·pboard** *v.* to keep in or as in a c.

Cupel (kiū·pĕl), *sb.* Also **coppel.** 1605. [a. F. *coupelle*, med.L. *cupella*, dim. of *cupa* cask.] A small shallow porous cup, usually made of bone-ash, and used in assaying gold or silver with lead. Also, a similarly-shaped movable hearth. Also *fig.* *Comb.* †**c.-ashes**, ashes used in purifying metals. Hence **Cu·pel** *v.* to assay or refine in a c. So **Cu·pellate** *v.* (*rare*).

Cupellation (kiūpĕlēi·ʃən). 1691. [f. CUPEL *v.* + -ATION.] The process of assaying or refining the precious metals in a cupel; the separation of silver from argentiferous lead, on a large scale, on a cupel.

Cupful (kʋ·pful). Pl. **cupfuls.** ME. [f. CUP *sb.*] As much as fills a cup.

Cupid (kiū·pid). ME. [ad. L. *Cupido*, personification of *cupido*, f. *cupere* to desire.] *Rom. Mythol.* The god of love, son of Mercury and Venus, identified with the Greek Eros. Also in *pl.* Hence, a representation of the god; a beautiful young boy.

Hir dowves and dan Cupido, Hir blinde sone CHAUCER.

Cupidity (kiupi·diti). ME. [a. F. *cupidité*, ad. L. *cupiditatem.*] 1. *gen.* Inordinate longing or lust; covetousness; (with *pl.*) an inordinate desire (*arch.*) 1542. 2. *spec.* Inordinate desire to appropriate wealth or possessions ME.

2. No property is secure when it becomes large enough to tempt the c. of indigent power BURKE.

‖**Cupidon.** [F. = CUPID.] An Adonis. BYRON.

Cupidone (kiū·pidōᵘn). 1866. [= prec.] Florist's name of a herbaceous border-plant, *Catananche cærulea.*

Cu·p-moss. 1597. A lichen, *Cladonia pyxidata.* b. Locally, the CUDBEAR.

Cupola (kiū·pŏlă), *sb.* 1549. [a. It., ad. L. *cupula*, dim. of *cupa* cask, tun.] 1. *Arch.* A rounded vault or dome forming the roof of a building or part of a building. Often *spec.*: A diminutive dome rising above a roof; also, the ceiling of a dome. Also *transf.* 2. *Mech.* (= *c.-furnace.*) A furnace for melting metals for casting. Also, a furnace for heating shot. 1716. 3. An armour-plated revolving turret to protect mounted guns on an iron-clad ship. Hence *c.-ship.* 1862. 4. In *Anat.*, etc.: A dome-like organ or process; *esp.* the arched summit of the cochlea of the ear 1829. Hence **Cu·polaed, cu·pola'd** *ppl. a.* having a c.

Cupped (kʋpt), *a.* 1796. [f. CUP *sb.* or *v.* + -ED.] Formed like a cup, cup-shaped.

Cupper (kʋ·pəɹ). ? ME. [f. as prec.] †1. = CUP-BEARER –1652. 2. One who performs the operation of cupping 1812.

Cupping (kʋ·piŋ), *vbl. sb.* 1519. [f. CUP *v.* + -ING[1].] 1. *Surg.* The operation of drawing blood by scarifying the skin and applying a CUP (sense 3) the air in which is rarefied by heat or otherwise. (Called distinctively *wet cupping.*) 2. Drinking; a drinking-bout (*arch.*) 1625. 3. The formation of a concavity; a concavity thus formed.

1. *Dry c.*: the application of a cupping-glass without scarification, as a counter-irritant. *Comb.* **c.-glass**, a glass cup with an open mouth to be applied to the skin in the operation of cupping.

Cuppy (kʋ·pi), *a.* 1882. [-Y[1].] Concave like a cup; *esp.* in *Golf*, full of small cavities.

Cu·prate. 1854. [f. L. *cuprum* + -ATE.] A salt of cupric acid.

Cupreo-, comb. f. CUPREOUS 2.

Cupreous (kiū·priəs), *a.* 1666. [f. L. *cupreus* (f. *cuprum*) + -OUS.] 1. Of, of the nature of, or containing copper. 2. Copper-coloured 1804.

Cupric (kiū·prik), *a.* 1799. [f. L. *cuprum* + -IC.] *Chem.* Containing copper in chemical combination; applied to compounds in which copper is divalent, as *c. chloride*, $CuCl_2$.

Cupri·ferous, *a.* 1784. [f. as prec. + -FEROUS.] Yielding copper.

Cuprite (kiū·prəit). 1850. [f. as prec. + -ITE.] *Min.* Native red oxide of copper.

Cupro- (kiūpro), bef. a vowel **cupr-**, used as comb. f. L. *cuprum* COPPER, in *Chem.* and *Min.*, as *cupro-sulphate*; **cuproma·gnesite**, a hydrous sulphate of copper and magnesium; **cupro-nickel**, an alloy comprising 75% copper and 25% nickel established for the so-called silver coinage of Great Britain by the Coinage Act of 1946.

Cuproso- (kiuprōᵘ·so), *Chem.*, comb. f. mod.L. *cuprosus* CUPROUS.

Cuprous (kiū·prəs), *a.* 1669. [f. L. *cuprum* + -OUS.] = CUPREOUS. In *Chem.* applied to compounds in which copper is univalent, e.g. *cuprous chloride*, Cu_2Cl_2.

Cu·p-shake. 1793. An opening between two of the concentric layers of timber. So **Cu·p-shaken, -shaky** *a.*

†**Cup-shot, -shotten**, *a.* ME. [f. CUP + SHOT *pa. pple.*] Intoxicated –1693.

Cupule (kiū·piul). 1826. [ad. L. *cupula* (also used), dim. of *cupa* cask, (later) cup.] 1. *Bot.* A cup-shaped involucre, as in the fruit of the oak, beech, hazel. Also, a cup-like receptacle found in *Peziza* and other fungi. 2. A small cup-shaped depression on a surface 1883. 3. *Zool.* A cup-shaped organ, as a sucker 1826. Hence **Cu·pular** *a.*, *Bot.* c.-shaped. **Cu·pulate** *a.* cupular; having a c.

Cupuliferous (kiūpiuli·fĕrəs), *a.* 1847. [f. L. *cupula.*] *Bot.* Bearing a cupule or cupules; belonging to the N.O. *Cupuliferæ*, including the oak, beech, hazel, etc.

Cur (kɒ̄ɹ). [ME. *curre*; prob. echoic. Cf. ON. *kurra* to grumble, Sw. *kurra* to grumble, rumble, snarl, etc.] 1. A dog: now always depreciative; a low-bred, or snappish dog. 2. *fig.* A surly, ill-bred, or cowardly fellow 1590. †3. A fish: the Red Gurnard, *Trigla cuculus* –1753. 4. The Golden-eye duck, *Clangula glaucion* (*dial.*) 1621.

1. The Mastiues, and such like curres MANWOOD. The beggarly curs of cities W. IRVING. 2. What would you have, you Curres, That like nor Peace, nor Warre *Cor.* I. i. 172. *Comb.* **c.-dog** (in senses 1, 2).

Curable (kiūᵊ·răb'l), *a.* ME. [ad. L. *cura-*

bilis, f. *curare.*] **1.** Capable of being cured; *fig.* remediable. †**2.** Able to cure –1615.
1. C. disorders HAZLITT. Hence **Curabi·lity, †Cu·rableness.**

‖**Curaçao,** (*erron.*) **curaçoa** (kiūᵊrăsōᵘ·). 1813. [Sp., Du., Fr.; name of a Dutch island in the Caribbean sea.] A liqueur consisting of spirits flavoured with the peel of bitter oranges, and sweetened.

Curacy (kiūᵊ·răsi). 1682. [f. CURATE.] The office of a curate, or of a †curator 1734.

‖**Curare** (kiurā·ri). Also **curara, -ri.** 1777. [Corrupt f. Carib name (*wurā·li* or *wurā·ri*) also written *wourali, ourali, ourari, woorara,* etc. In F. *curare.* See OURALI, WOORALI.] A blackish-brown resinous bitter substance, extracted from *Strychnos toxifera*, and other plants; used by Indians to poison their arrows.
When introduced into the blood it is a powerful poison, arresting the action of the motor nerves; used largely in physiological experiments.
Hence **Cu·rarine,** *Chem.* a bitter poisonous alkaloid, $C_{10}H_{15}N$, obtained from c. **Cu·rarize** *v.* to administer c. to.

Curassow (kiūᵊ·răsōᵘ). 1685. [Phonetic sp. of CURAÇAO, q.v.] One of a family of gallinaceous birds found in Central and South America; they resemble the turkey.
The most common species is the Crested C., *Crax alector*, of a greenish-black colour with a white crest; the Galeated C. or Cushew-bird, *Pauxis galeata*, has a large bony protuberance on the upper part of the bill.

Curat, -e, obs. ff. CUIRASS.

Curate (kiūᵊ·rėt). ME. [ad. med.L. *curatus*, in It. *curato*, 'of, belonging to, or having a cure or charge', whence as sb. 'one who has a cure'.] **1.** One entrusted with the cure of souls; orig., any ecclesiastical or spiritual pastor, but now usu. limited to an assistant of a beneficed clergyman. †**2.** A curator, overseer –1660.
1. *Perpetual c.*: the incumbent of the chapel or church of an ecclesiastical district, forming part of an ancient parish, appointed by the patron and licensed by the bishop; he now ranks as a vicar.
Hence **†Cu·rateship,** the office or position of a c.; a curacy.

Curatel (kiūᵊ·rătel). 1875. [ad. med.L. *curatela*, f. *curatus, curator*; cf. *tutela*. In F. *curatelle.*] *Rom. Law.* The position of being under the guardianship of a curator.

†Cura·tion. [ME., a. OF. *curacion*, ad. L. *curationem.*] **1.** Healing, cure –1677. **2.** Curatorship –1774.

Curative (kiūᵊ·rătiv), *a.* (*sb.*) 1533. [a. F. *curatif, -ive*, f. L. *curat-* ppl. stem.] **1.** Of or relating to the curing of disease. **2.** Having the tendency or power to cure disease 1644; *fig.* remedial 1661. Also as *sb.* [sc. *agent.*] Hence **Cu·rative-ly** *adv.*, **-ness.**

Curator (kiurēⁱ·təɹ, kiūᵊ·rătəɹ). ME. [Partly a. AF. *curatour* = F. *-ateur*; partly ad. L. *curatorem.*]
I. (*cu·rator.*) **1.** One appointed as guardian of a minor, lunatic, etc. †**2.** One who has a cure of souls –1450.
II. (*cura·tor.*) **1.** *gen.* One who has charge; a manager, steward 1632. **2.** *spec.* in *Universities.* A member of a board (or an individual) having general or specific charge and powers 1691. **3.** The officer in charge of a museum, library, etc.; a keeper, custodian 1661. **4.** A designation of officials under the Roman Empire 1728. Hence **Curato·rial** *a.* **Cura·torship,** the office or position of a c. **Cu·ratory** *sb.* curatorship; a college of curators.

Cu·ratory, *a.* 1644. [ad. L. *curatorius*; in mod. use referred to *curare.*] Curative.

Curatrix (kiurēⁱ·triks). [L., fem. of *curator.*] †**1.** A female curer. CUDWORTH. **2.** A female curator 1846.

Curb (kɒ̄ɹb), *sb.* 1477. [f. (ult.) F. *courbe* adj.:—L. *curvus*, and F. *courber* :—L. *curvare*; see CURB *v.*[1]]
I. 1. A chain or strap passing under the lower jaw of a horse, and fastened to the upper ends of the branches of the bit; used for checking an unruly horse. **2.** *fig.* Anything that curbs or restrains; a check, restraint 1613.
1. The trot became a gallop soon In spite of c. and rein COWPER. **2.** Service is to the Lofty minde A C., a Spur to th' abiect Hinde 1613.
II. Corresp. to F. *courbe* sb. **1.** A hard swelling on the hock or other part of a horse's leg 1523. †**2.** A curve, an arc (*rare*) –1759. **3.** A mould or template for marking out curved work. (Occas. spelt *kerb.*) 1792.
III. An enclosing framework, orig. of something round. **1.** A frame or 'coaming' round the top of a well 1511. **2.** A curvilinear plate or ring of timber, iron, etc., round the edge of any circular structure, or forming a base for the brickwork of a shaft or well 1811. **3.** A raised margin round an oast, a bed in a garden, a hearth, etc. 1731. **4.** The stone margin of a side-walk. Usu. spelt *kerb.* 1836.
attrib. and *Comb.*: **c.-bit,** bridle, a bit (or bridle) with a c.; **-chain,** a chain acting as a c.; **-pins** (*Horology*), the pins on the lever of a watch-regulator, which control the balance.

†Curb, *v.*[1] *rare.* ME. [Earlier, COURBE *v.*, q.v.] **1.** *trans.* To bend, bow, curve –1662. **2.** *intr.* To bend, bow, cringe –1808.

Curb (kɒ̄ɹb), *v.*[2] 1530. [f. CURB *sb.*] **1.** *trans.* To put a curb on; to restrain with a curb. **2.** *fig.* To restrain, keep in check 1588. **3.** To furnish or defend with a curb or curb-stone. (In the latter case usu. *kerb.*) 1861.
1. Part wield their Arms, part courb the foaming Steed MILT. *P. L.* XI. 643. **2.** To curbe our naturall appetites DONNE. To c. .. our own Subjects from their natural Rights 1719.

Cu·rbless, *a. rare.* 1813. [f. CURB *sb.* + -LESS.] Without restraint.

Cu·rb-plate. 1819. [CURB *sb.* III. 2.] = CURB III. 2.

Cu·rb-roof. 1733. [CURB *sb.*] A roof of which each face has two slopes, the lower one steeper than the other; a mansard-roof.

Cu·rb-, kerb-stone. 1806. One of the stones forming a curb; the stone edge of a side-path.

Curby (kɒ̄·ɹbi), *a.* 1841. [f. CURB *sb.* + -Y.] Liable to be affected with curb, as *c. hocks.*

Curch (kɒ̄ɹtʃ). *Sc.* 1447. [Erron. sing. of *curches*, repr. OF. *couvrechés*, pl. of *couvrechef*; see COVERCHIEF, KERCHIEF.] A covering for the head; a kerchief; formerly worn instead of a cap or mutch.

‖**Curculio** (kɒɹkiū·lio). 1756. [a. L.; 'corn-weevil'.] *Entom.* A Linnæan genus of Beetles, containing the Weevils. Now applied *esp.* to the common fruit-weevils, which are very destructive to plums. Hence **Curcu·lioni·deous** *a.* belonging to the *Curculionidæ* or weevil-family. **Curcu·lionist,** one who studies the *Curculionidæ.*

‖**Curcuma** (kɒ̄·ɹkiumă). 1617. [mod.L., ad. Arab. *kurkum* saffron, turmeric; see CROCUS.] **a.** *Bot.* A genus of *Zingiberaceæ* consisting of plants with perennial tuberous roots. **b.** The substance called Turmeric, prepared from the tubers of *C. longa. Attrib.* as **c. paper,** turmeric paper used as a chemical test. Hence **Cu·rcumin,** *Chem.* the colouring matter of turmeric.

Curd (kɒ̄ɹd), *sb.* [ME. *crud* (also *crod*). Of unkn. deriv.] **1.** The coagulated substance formed from milk by the action of acids; made into cheese or eaten as food. (Often in *pl.*) **2.** *transf.* Any similar substance 1811.
1. The Queene of Curds and Creame *Wint. T.* IV. iv. 161. Hence **Cu·rdiness,** curdy state or quality. **Cu·rdless** *a.* **Cu·rdy** *a.* full of c.; c.-like.

Curd (kɒ̄ɹd), *v.* ME. [f. prec.] **1.** *trans.* = CURDLE *v.* 1. **2.** *intr.* = CURDLE *v.* 2. ME.
1. It doth posset And c., like Aygre droppings into Milke, The thin and wholsome blood *Haml.* I. v. 69.

Curdle (kɒ̄·ɹd'l), *v.* 1590. [Freq. of CURD *v.*] **1.** *trans.* To form into curd; to coagulate, clot, congeal. Also *transf.* and *fig.* **2.** *intr.* To become or form curd; to coagulate 1601. Also *transf.* and *fig.*
1. It will cruddle milk as wel as rennet HOLLAND. An holy horror curdled all my blood 1760. **2.** *fig.* The blood thrills and curdles at the thought COWPER. Hence **Cu·rdly** *a.* apt to c.; of a curdled appearance.

Cure (kiūᵊɹ), *sb.*[1] ME. [a. OF. :—L. *cura* care.] †**1.** Care, heed, concern –1605. †**2.** Care, charge; a duty, office –1641. **3.** *Eccl.* The spiritual charge of parishioners; the office or function of a CURATE. Usu. in *c. of souls.* Hence, A parish; a 'charge'. ME. **4.** †Medical treatment –1725; a particular method or course of treatment, as in *water-c.*, etc. 1842. **5.** Successful medical treatment; the action or process of healing; restoration to health. Also *fig.* ME. **6.** A means of healing; a remedy. Often *fig.* 1613. †**7.** The curing or preserving of fish, pork, etc. –1757.
1. I make of yt no c. CHAUCER. **2.** The c. of the tyllage of the grounde EDEN. **3.** The people committed to your c. and charge *Bk. Com. Prayer.* A small c. was offered me GOLDSM. **5.** Past care, is still past c. *L. L. L.* V. ii. 28. I cast out deuils, and I doe cures *Luke* xiii. 32. **6.** Let the water and the blood ..Be of sin the double c. TOPLADY.

Cure (kiūᵊɹ), *sb.*[2] *slang.* 1856. [app. short for *curiosity*; cf. *curio.*] An odd person; a funny fellow.

Cure (kiūᵊɹ), *v.* ME. [a. F. *curer* :—L. *curare*, f. *cura* care.] †**1.** To take care of; to care for; *intr.* to take trouble; to take care –1623. †**2.** *trans.* (and *absol.*) To take charge of the spiritual interests of (a parish, etc.) –1581. †**3.** To treat surgically or medically –1592. **4.** To heal, restore to health (a sick person). Also *fig.* ME. **5.** To heal (a disease or wound); *fig.* to remedy, remove (an evil) ME. †**6.** *intr.* (for *refl.*) To get well again (*rare*) –1791. **7.** To prepare for keeping, by salting, etc.; to preserve (meat, etc.) 1665. Also *intr.* (for *refl.*).
4. Hee cured many of their infirmities *Luke* vii. 21. *fig.* Time cured him of his grief W. IRVING. **5.** Your tale, Sir, would c. deafenesse *Temp.* I. ii. 106. **6.** One desparate greefe cures with anothers languish *Rom. & Jul.* I. ii. 49. **7.** To c. Sponges 1665, hops 1711, grapes DE FOE, beef 1788, fish 1832.

‖**Curé** (küre). 1655. [F., ad. med.L. *curatus*; see CURATE.] A parish priest in a French-speaking land.

Cu·re-a·ll. 1870. A universal remedy, panacea. Also *fig.*

Cu·reless, *a.* 1541. Without cure; irremediable.

Curer (kiūᵊ·rəɹ). 1581. [f. CURE *v.* + -ER [1].] **1.** One who or that which cures or heals. **2.** One who cures fish, etc. 1791.

Curette (kiūᵊre·t). 1753. [a. F., f. *curer* in sense 'to clear, cleanse'.] *Surg.* A small instrument like a scoop, used in removing morbid matter from the eye, ear, throat, uterine cavity, etc. Hence **Cure·tte** *v.* to scrape with a c.

Curfew (kɒ̄·ɹfiu). ME. [a. AF. *coeverfu* = OF. *covre-feu*, f. *couvre* imper. of *couvrir* + *feu.*] **1. a.** A regulation by which, at a fixed hour in the evening, a bell was rung, as a signal that fires were to be extinguished; also, the hour of ringing, and the bell. (The statement that the curfew was introduced into England by William the Conqueror as a measure of political repression is without early historical support.) **b.** Hence, the practice of ringing an evening (and †morning) bell, in many towns. **2.** A cover for a fire; a fire-plate 1626. Also *attrib.* *Comb.* **c.-bell** (see sense 1). Also *fig.*
1. Well, 'tis nine o'clock, 'tis time to ring c. 1608. **b.** *Rom. & Jul.* IV. iv. 4.

‖**Curia** (kiūᵊ·riă). 1600. [L.] **1.** *Antiq.* **a.** One of the ten divisions of each of the three ancient Roman tribes; also *transf.* **b.** The building belonging to a Roman curia. **c.** The senate-house at Rome. **d.** A name for the senate of ancient Italian towns. **2.** A court of justice, counsel, or administration 1706. **3.** *spec. The C.*: The Papal court, including all its authorities and functionaries 1840. Hence **Cu·rial** *a.* †courtly; of or pertaining to a c.; *sb.* †a courtier; a member of an ancient Roman or an Italian c.; †a treatise on the Court. **Cu·rialism,** a curial or courtly system: *esp.* Vaticanism. **Cu·rialist,** a member of the Papal c.; a supporter of its policy. **Curiali·stic** *a.* of or pertaining to curialists or curialism. **†Curi·a·lity,** what pertains to a court; courtliness; = COURTESY 3.

Curiet, obs. f. CUIRASS.

Curing (kiūᵊ·riŋ), *vbl. sb.* ME. The action of the verb CURE. *Comb.* **c.-house,** a building where curing is carried on; *spec.* in the West Indies, one in which newly potted sugar is placed to harden and drain.

Curio (kiūᵊ·rio). 1851. [Short f. *curiosity.*] An object of art valued as a curiosity or rarity; a curiosity. Also in *comb.*

Curiolo·gic, *a.* 1669. [Better *cyriologic*, ad. Gr. κυριολογικός 'speaking literally', opp. to συμβολικός symbolic.] Pertaining to that form of hieroglyphic writing in which objects are represented by pictures. Also as *sb.* So **Curiolo·gical** *a.*

Curiosity (kiūᵊriǫ·sĭti). ME. [a. OF. *curiosetė*, ad. L. *curiositatem*; see CURIOUS and -TY.] †1. Carefulness –1747; scrupulousness, accuracy –1694; ingenuity –1772; undue niceness or subtlety –1766. 2. Desire to know or learn; inquisitiveness ME.; inquisitiveness about trifles or other people's affairs 1577. †3. Scientific or artistic interest; connoisseurship –1781. †4. A hobby –1661. †5. A fancy, a whim –1718. †6. Careful or elaborate workmanship; nicety of construction –1807. 7. Curiousness 1597. †8. A curious matter of investigation –1700. †9. A vanity, refinement –1705. †10. A curious detail or feature –1747. 11. Anything curious, rare, or strange 1645.

2. A noble and solid c. of knowing things in their beginnings 1632. Curiositie, which I take to be a desire to know the faults and imperfections in other men HOLLAND. 7. Rotterdam, where the c. of the place detained us three days 1686. 11. Japanese goods, lacker ware and curiosities SEMMES

‖**Curioso** (kiūᵊri,ōᵘ·so). *arch.* Pl. **-i, -os.** 1658. [a. It.] In 17th c., one curious in matters of science and art; later, a connoisseur, virtuoso.

Curious (kiūᵊ·riəs), *a.* ME. [a. OF. *curius* :—L. *curiosus.*]

I. †1. Careful –1781; solicitous –1697; nice –1821; accurate –1816; skilful –1771. 2. Desirous of seeing or knowing; inquisitive. Often in bad sense: Prying. (The current subjective sense.) ME. †3. Skilled as a connoisseur or virtuoso –1792. Also *absol.* in pl.

2. He was a man very c., and much inclined to hear of novelties, and rare things H. COGAN. Crowded with c. idlers HALE. She stole a c. look at my face DICKENS.

II. As an objective quality of things, etc. †1. Made with care or art –1772. †2. Elaborate –1674. 3. Of investigations, etc.: Careful, accurate, minute 1526. †4. Inquisitive –1742; abstruse –1664; occult –1619. †5. Exact, precise –1825. †6. Skilled, skilful –1776. 7. Exquisite, choice, fine (in beauty, flavour, etc.). Now *dial.* ME. †8. Noteworthy –1816. 9. Deserving or exciting curiosity; strange, singular; queer. (The current objective sense.) 1715. †10. Such as interests the curioso –1768.

3. A subject, which demands the most c. investigation DISRAELI. 9. A most c. reason, truly! BURKE. No c. shell, rare plant, or brilliant spar, Inticed our traveller CRABBE.

Hence **Cu·rious-ly** *adv.*, **-ness.**

Curl (kɒ̄ɹl), *sb.* 1602. [f. CURL *v.*[1]] 1. A ringlet of hair. 2. Anything of a spiral or incurved shape 1615. 3. The action of curling, or state of being curled 1665. 4. A disease of potatoes, and other plants, in which the shoots, or leaves, are curled up and imperfectly developed 1790.

2. [An oar] which breakes The waues in curles CHAPMAN. Curls of smoke 1832. 3. The lip's least c. BYRON. To keep the hair in c. (*mod.*).

Curl (kɒ̄ɹl), *v.* ME. [conn. w. *croll*, CRULL, curly, corresp. to similar words in Fris., MDu., and MG.] 1. *trans.* To bend round, wind, or twist into ringlets, as the hair. †2. To furnish or adorn with curls; also *fig.* –1667. 3. To twist or coil up into a spiral or incurved shape; to ripple (water) 1562. 4. *intr.* Of hair: To form curls 1530. 5. To take a spiral or incurved form. Often with *up.* 1694. b. To become affected with CURL (*sb.* sense 4) 1793. 6. To move in spiral convolutions or undulations 1791. 7. *Sc.* To play at CURLING, q. v. 1715.

1. They curle their haire and are proud of it SIR T. HERBERT. 2. The snakie locks That curld Megæra MILT. *P. L.* X. 560. 3. Jack [the dog]..curled himself up on the sofa HUGHES. To c. the lip 1816. 5. In stormy Weather little Waves c. on the top of the great ones 1694. b. A..Potatoe that never curls 1793. Phr. *To c. up* (*Sporting*): to collapse. 6. The damp vapours curled round him MRS. RADCLIFFE.

Curler (kɒ̄·ɹləɹ). 1638. [f. CURL *v.* + -ER.] 1. One who or that which curls (hair, etc.) 1748. 2. A player at the game of curling.

Curlew (kɒ̄·ɹliū). ME. [Same as OF. *courlieus, corlys*, said to be echoic; but cf. *corliu* courier, deriv. of *courir.*] 1. A grallatorial bird of the genus *Numenius* (family *Scolopacidæ*), with a long slender curved bill; *esp.* the common European species *N. arquatus* (Sc. *whaup*). †2. Used (*esp.* in the Bible) as tr. L. *coturnix*, Gr. ὄρτυξ, a quail –1508.

Comb., etc.: c.-jack, c. knot, the Whimbrel, *N. phæops*; c. sandpiper, pigmy c., *Tringa subarquata*; stone c., the Norfolk plover (*Œdicnemus scolopax*); also, the whimbrel.

Curlicue (kɒ̄·ɹlikiū). Also **curlycue.** 1858. [f. CURLY + CUE, either = F. *queue*, or the letter Q (2).] A fantastic curl or twist; a caper (*U.S.*).

Curlie-wurlie, curly-wurly (kɒ̄·ɹliwɒ̄·ɹli). 1772. [Redupl. f. *curly.*] A fantastically curled ornament.

Curling (kɒ̄·ɹliŋ), *vbl. sb.* ME. [f. CURL *v.*] 1. The action of the verb CURL, q. v. 2. A game played on the ice in which large rounded stones are hurled along a defined space called the *rink* towards a mark called the *tee* 1620.

Comb.: c.-iron, an instrument which is heated and then used for curling the hair; -stone, a cheese-shaped stone having an iron handle on the upper surface, with which the game of curling is played.

Curly (kɒ̄·ɹli), *a.* 1772. [f. CURL *sb.* + -Y.] 1. Curling or disposed to curl. 2. Having curled hair 1827. 3. Of a curled form; wavy 1795. 4. Of potatoes: Affected with CURL 1791. *Comb.*: c.-pate, a curly-headed person; -pated *a.* Hence **Cu·rliness.**

Curmudgeon (kɒɹmɒ·dʒən). 1577. [?] 'An avaricious churlish fellow; a miser, a niggard' (J.).

A rich uncle..a penurious accumulating c. W. IRVING. Hence **Curmu·dgeonly** *a.* miserly, niggardly, churlish. Also as *adv.* (*rare*).

Curmurring (kɒɹmɒ·riŋ), *vbl. sb. Sc.* 1785. [Echoic.] A low rumbling, growling, or murmuring sound.

Some c. in his guts BURNS.

Curn. *n.* and *Sc.* ME. [? Related to KERN.] †1. *pl.* Grain. (ME. only.) 2. *Sc.* A grain 1474; *transf.* a few 1785. Hence **Cu·rney** *sb. Sc.* a company, lot. **Cu·rny** *a.* granular.

Cu·rple. *Sc.* 1498. [Corrupt f. *curper* CRUPPER.] 1. A crupper. 2. *transf.* The posteriors 1787.

Curr (kɒ̄ɹ, kɒrr), *v.* 1677. [Echoic.] To make a low murmuring sound; to coo, purr.

‖**Currach, -agh** (kɒ·rǎ, ku·rǎχ). 1450. [Ir. *curach* boat, little ship; cf. Welsh *corwg*, also *corwgl* CORACLE.] A boat made of wickerwork covered with hides; a coracle.

Currant (kɒ·rǎnt). ME. [Orig. *raisins of Corauntz* = F. *raisins de Corinthe* raisins of Corinth.] 1. The raisin prepared from a seedless grape, grown in the Levant: used in cookery. 2. The small round berry of certain species of *Ribes* (*R. nigrum, R. rubrum*) called Black and Red Currants. (The White Currant is a variety of the Red.) 1578. b. The shrubs producing this fruit, and other shrubs of the same genus 1665. Also *transf.*

2. b. Corinthes or currans, as they are vulgarly called, are plants well known RAY.

Comb.: c.-borer, -clearwing, the clearwing moth *Ægeria tipuliformis* and its larva; -gall, a small round gall, formed on the male flowers and leaves of the oak by the insect *Spathegaster baccarum*; -moth, the Magpie-moth; -worm, a larva that infests currant-bushes.

Currency (kɒ·rĕnsi). 1657. [ad. L. type *currentia, f. *currentem, currere.*] †1. The fact or condition of flowing, flow; course; *concr.* a current, stream (*rare*) –1758. 2. The course (of time); the time during which anything is current 1726. 3. Of money: The fact or quality of being current as a medium of exchange; circulation. Also *fig.* 1699. 4. The circulating medium; the money of a country in actual use 1729. b. *spec.* Applied to a current medium of exchange when differing in value from the money of account; *e.g.* the former currency and banco of Hamburg (see BANCO) 1755. 5. The fact or quality of being current; prevalence, vogue; *esp.* of ideas, reports, etc. 1722. Also *attrib.*

2. During the whole c. of the lease MCCULLOCH. 3. The c. of Bills 1722, of Wood's copper coin in Ireland POPE. 4. The paper currencies of North America ADAM SMITH. 5. The story..seems to have gained c. FERRIAR. var. †**Cu·rrence** (*rare*).

Current (kɒ·rĕnt), *a.* [ME. *corant, currant*, a. OF. *corant, curant*, pres. pple. of *courir*, OF. *corre* :—L. *currere.*] 1. Running; flowing. Also *fig.* (Now *rare.*) 2. Running in time; in progress; belonging to the week, month, etc. now running 1608. 3. Of money: Passing from hand to hand; in general use as a medium of exchange 1481. †4. Sterling, genuine: opp. to *counterfeit* –1744. 5. Generally reported or known; in general circulation 1563. 6. Generally accepted; in vogue 1593.

1. The c. streame MILT. *P. L.* VII. 67. 2. The c. year 1734, C. services BURKE, expenses RUSKIN. 3. Currant money amonge merchauntes COVERDALE *Gen.* xxiii. 16. 4. To put your love unto the touch, to try If it be currant, or but counterfait 1599. 5. The stories which were c. about..the Speaker MACAULAY. 6. A word which is not c. English DRYDEN.

Phr. *To pass c.* (†*for c.*): to be generally related or accepted. *The 10th c.* (abbreviated *curt.*): the 10th day of the c. month.

Hence **Cu·rrently** *adv.* in a c. manner; flowingly; popularly. **Cu·rrentness.**

Current (kɒ·rĕnt), *sb.* ME. [a. OF. *corant, curant*, sb. use of *courant* adj.; see prec.] 1. That which runs or flows, a stream; *spec.* a portion of a body of water, or of air, etc. moving in a definite direction. 2. The action or condition of flowing 1555. 3. The inclination given to a gutter, roof, etc. to let the water run off 1582. 4. *fig.* The course of time or of events 1586. 5. Tendency, tenor, drift 1595. 6. *Electr.* The apparent flow of electric force through a conducting body 1747. Also *attrib.*

1. Great ocean currents such as the Gulf Stream 1863. 2. There is no great C. in the Bay BURNET. 4. The c. of my speach MARSTON, of our story FREEMAN. 5. The whole c. of modern feeling BRYCE.

Comb.: c.-bedding, the bedding of geological strata in a sloping direction caused by deposition in a c. of water; -gauge, -meter, an apparatus for measuring the flow of liquids through a channel; -mill, a mill driven by a c.-wheel; -wheel, a wheel driven by a natural c. of water. b. Of or pertaining to an electrical c.; as *c.-breaker, -meter*, etc.

Hence **Cu·rrentless** *a.* having no c.

Curricle (kɒ·rik'l). 1682. [ad. L. *curriculum*, f. *currere.*] †1. A course, running –1710. 2. A light two-wheeled carriage, usu. drawn by two horses abreast 1756.

1. Upon a c. in this world depends a long course of the next SIR T. BROWNE.

‖**Curriculum** (kŏri·kiŭlŏm). Pl. **-ula.** 1633. [L.] A course; *spec.* a regular course of study as at a school or (Scottish) University.

Cu·rried, *ppl. a.* 1855. [f. CURRY *sb.*[2] + -ED.] Prepared with curry or curry-powder.

Currier[1] (kɒ·riəɹ). ME. [a. OF. *corier, coryer* :—L. *coriarius*, f. *corium* leather, hide.] 1. One who dresses and colours leather after it is tanned. 2. One who curries horses, etc. 1562.

†**Cu·rrier**[2]. 1557. [?] 1. A fire-arm, of the same calibre and strength as the arquebus, but with a longer barrel –1659. 2. A man armed with a currier –1581.

Currish (kɒ̄·riʃ), *a.* 1460. [f. CUR + -ISH.] 1. Of, relating to, or resembling a cur 1565. 2. *fig.* Like a cur in nature; snappish, quarrelsome, snarling; mean-spirited, base.

2. This c. Iew *Merch. V.* IV. i. 292. Quarrelsome and c. People that bark and snarl at one another 1705. Hence **Cu·rrish-ly** *adv.*, **-ness.**

†**Cu·rry,** *sb.*[1] *rare.* ME. only. [a. F. *corroi*; see CONREY and CURRY *v.*[1]] The currying of leather.

Curry (kɒ·ri), *sb.*[2] 1598. [a. Tamil *kari* sauce.] A preparation of meat, fish, fruit, or vegetables, cooked with bruised spices and turmeric, and used as a relish. Hence, *a curry* = a dish or stew flavoured with this.

†**Cu·rry, currie,** *sb.*[3] 1500. [a. F. *curée*, corresp. to L. type *coriata, lit. hide-ful. Cf. QUARRY.] The portions of an animal slain that were given to the hounds; the cutting up and disembowelling of the game; also *transf.* –1830.

Curry (kɒ·ri), *v.*[1] ME. [a. OF. *correier*, orig. *conreder* to put in order :—early Rom. *conredare; see CONREY.] 1. *trans.* To rub down or dress (a horse, ass, etc.) with a comb. Also *transf.* and *fig.* 2. To dress (tanned leather) by soaking, scraping, paring, beating, colouring, etc. ME. 3. *transf.* To thrash one's hide for him, drub. Also *fig.* 1526. †4. *fig.* To employ flattery, etc., so as to cajole or win favour –1830.

3. He hath well curried thy cote BARET. 4. I would currie with Maister Shallow 2 *Hen. IV*, V. i. 81.

Phr. *To c. favour* (orig. †*to c. favel* = OF. *estriller fauvel* to c. the chestnut horse: cf. FAVEL): to solicit favour by flattery or complaisance.

†**Curry,** *v.*[2] 1608. [? f. *currier*, var. of *courier*,

as if to ride post. Cf. SCURRY.] *intr.* To scurry -1676.

Curry (kʊ·ri), *v.*³ 1839. [f. CURRY *sb.*²] *trans.* To flavour with curry.

Cu·rry-comb, *sb.* 1573. [f. CURRY *v.*¹] A comb or instrument of metal for currying horses, etc. Hence **Cu·rry-comb, cu·rrycomb** *v.* to curry; also *transf.* and *fig.*

†**Cu·rry-favel(l.** 1515. [See CURRY *v.*¹] One who solicits favour by flattery or complaisance -1589. So †**Cu·rry-favour.**

Curse (kɔ̄ɪs), *sb.* [Late OE. *curs* of unkn. origin. Not conn. w. *cross.* Not in Teut., Rom., or Celtic.] 1. An utterance consigning (a person or thing) to evil; *spec.* a formal ecclesiastical anathema. 2. A profane oath, an imprecation OE. 3. An object of cursing ME. 4. The evil inflicted in response to an imprecation, or in the way of retribution ME.; a thing which blights or blasts; a bane 1591.

1. God's c. can cast away ten thousand sail COWPER. A cursse was sent from the pope, which cursssed both the king and the realme HOLINSHED. 2. I giue him curses, yet he giues me loue *Mids. N.* I. i. 196. Phr. *Not worth a c.*: see CRESS. (But *damn* occurs as early as *curse*.) 3. I..will make this city a c. to all the nations *Jer.* xxvi. 6. 4. C. on the stripling! how he apes his sire ADDISON. Phr. *C. of Scotland*: the nine of diamonds in a pack of cards. The origin of the name is doubtful. See N.E.D. Hence **Cu·rseful** *a.* fraught with curses (*rare*).

Curse (kɔ̄ɪs), *v.* OE. [Goes with CURSE *sb.*] 1. *trans.* To utter against (persons or things) words which consign them to evil; to damn ME.; *spec.* to anathematize, excommunicate OE. 2. Hence, To denounce with adjuration of the divine name; to pour maledictions upon; to swear at ME. 3. To speak impiously against; to blaspheme OE. 4. *absol.* or *intr.* To utter curses ME. 5. *trans.* To afflict with such evils as indicate divine wrath or a malignant fate; to blast ME.

1. How shall I c., whom God hath not cursed *Numb.* xxiii. 8. 2. I heard my brother damn the coachman, and c. the maids DE FOE. 3. They shall..c. their King, and their God *Isa.* viii. 21. 4. Then began he to c. and to swear *Matt.* xxvi. 74. 5. To be cursed with a bad temper (*mod.*). Hence **Cu·rser.**

Cursed, curst (kɔ̄·ɪsėd, kɔ̄ɪst), *ppl. a.* OE. [f. prec. + -ED¹.] 1. Under a curse. 2. Deserving a curse; execrable ME. 3. (Usually spelt *curst.*) Malignant; perversely cross (*arch.*) ME.; †savage, vicious -1727.

1. The spot is c. WORDSW. 2. To haue done suilk a cursed dede ME. 3. Curster than she, why 'tis impossible *Tam. Shr.* III. ii. 156. God sends a c. Cow short horns *Much Ado* II. i. 25. Hence **Cu·rsed-ly** *adv.*, **-ness, curstness.**

†**Cu·rsement.** *rare.* ME. only. [f. CURSE *v.* + -MENT.] Cursing.

Cu·rsen, -son, dial. f. CHRISTEN *a.* and *v.*

Curship (kɔ̄·ɪʃip). 1663. [f. CUR.] The estate or personality of a cur: a mock title.

Cursitate (kɔ̄·ɪsiteⁱt), *v. rare.* 1867. [f. L. *cursitare*, freq. of *currere.*] *intr.* To run hither and thither. So †**Cursita·tion,** a running hither and thither.

Cursitor (kɔ̄·ɪsitəɪ). Now *Hist.* 1523. [a. AF. *coursetour*, ad. med.L. *cursitor* = *cursor* runner.] 1. One of twenty-four clerks of the Court of Chancery, who made out all writs *de cursu*, i. e. of common course or routine. †2. A courier -1661. †3. A tramp -1725.

C. baron: the puisne baron of the Exchequer, who attended to matters 'of course' on the revenue side. Abolished in 1856.

Cursive (kɔ̄·ɪsiv), *a.* 1784. [ad. med.L. *cursivus*, f. *currere, curs-.*] Of writing: Written with a running hand, so that the characters are rapidly formed without raising the pen. In ancient manuscripts distinguished from *uncial.* As *sb.* A cursive character or manuscript. Hence **Cu·rsively** *adv.* in c. characters (*rare*). **Cu·rsiveness,** c. quality (*rare*).

Cursor (kɔ̄·ɪsǭɪ). 1566. [a. L., f. *currere, curs-.*] †1. A running messenger -1632. 2. A part of a mathematical instrument, which slides backwards and forwards 1594. ‖3. In mediæval universities, a bachelor of theology who gave the preliminary courses of lectures on the Bible.

†**Cu·rsorary,** obs. f. CURSORY. Shaks.

‖**Cursores** (kɔɪsōᵊ·rīz), *sb. pl.* 1828. [L. pl. of *cursor*; see above.] *Ornith.* An order of birds, containing the ostrich and its allies, which are mostly swift runners; the *Ratitæ.* So **Curso·rial** *a.* adapted for running; *spec.* applied to the *Cursores*, orthopterous insects (*Cursoria*), and crustaceans. **Curso·rious** *a.*

Cursory (kɔ̄·ɪsŏri), *a.* 1601. [ad. L. *cursorius*, f. *cursorem.*] 1. Passing rapidly over a thing or subject; hasty, hurried. †2. Travelling (*rare*) -1650. 3. *Entom.* Cursorious.

1. I had only a c. view of it, and that by accident 1661. Hence **Cu·rsori-ly** *adv.*, **-ness.**

Curst, *a.*; see CURSED.

Curstly, -ness; see CURSED-LY, -NESS.

‖**Cursus** (kɔ̄·ɪsɒs). 1838. [L., f. *currere.*] The Latin word for COURSE; occas. used for a. A running-ground or drive; b. A stated order of daily prayer; c. A curriculum.

Curt (kɔ̄ɪt), *a.* 1630. [ad. L. *curtus.*] 1. Short; shortened 1665. 2. Of words, style, etc.: Concise; terse to a fault; rudely brief 1630.

2. The dry and c. language of a petition in parliament ROGERS. He might have been a little less defiant and c. GEO. ELIOT. Hence **Cu·rt-ly** *adv.*, **-ness.**

†**Curt,** *v.* 1568. [f. L. *curtare*, f. *curtus.*] *trans.* To shorten -1610. Hence †**Cu·rted** *ppl. a.*

Curt., cur^t. An abbrev. of CURRENT *a.*, q. v.

Curtail (kɒɪtēⁱ·l), *v.* 1553. [Orig. *curtal(l*, f. CURTAL *a.*, but later assoc. with *tail*, and perh. with F. *tailler* to cut.] †1. To make a curtal of; to dock -1611. 2. To shorten in length, duration, extent, or amount; to abbreviate, abridge, or reduce 1553.

2. I, that am curtail'd of this faire Proportion *Rich. III*, I. i. 18. To c. salaries 1781, slumbers MRS. CARLYLE, jurisdiction FROUDE. Hence **Curtai·ler. Curtai·lment,** the action of curtailing; abridgement.

Curtail, obs. f. CURTAL *sb.* and *a.*

Cu·rtail-step. Also **curtal-.** 1736. [?] The lowest step (or steps) of a stair, having the outer end carried round in the form of a scroll.

Curtain (kɔ̄·ɪtėn, -t'n), *sb.* [ME. *cortine, curtine*, a. OF.:—L. *cortina*, in Vulgate (*Exod.* xxvi. 1, etc.) a curtain. Of unkn. etym.] 1. A hanging screen of cloth, etc., admitting of being withdrawn sideways, and serving for purposes of use or ornament; *e. g.* to enclose a bed (the earliest English use), to divide a room, to prevent draughts, etc. Also *transf.* 2. In a theatre, etc.: The screen separating the stage from the auditorium, which is drawn up at the beginning and dropped at the end of an act. Also *fig.* 1599. 3. *transf.* and *fig.* Anything that covers or hides ME. 4. *Fortif.* The part of the wall which connects two bastions, towers, gates, etc. 1569; *Archit.* a plain enclosing wall not supporting a roof 1633. Also *attrib.*

1. The Veile or Courtaine of the Temple did rend a sunder GOLDING. Phr. *To draw the c.*: (*a*) to draw it back, so as to disclose an object; (*b*) to draw it forward, so as to cover an object. *C. of mail*: = CAMAIL 1. 2. Phr. *To drop* or *raise the c.*, to end or begin an action. *Behind the c.*: away from the public view.

Comb.: (in sense 2) as *c.-call, -fall, -tune*; **c.-angle,** the angle formed at a bastion, etc., where the c. begins; **-lecture,** 'a reproof given by a wife to her husband in bed' (J.); so †**-sermon**; **-raiser** [Fr. *lever de rideau*], a short piece played before the principal play.

Cu·rtain, *v.* ME. [f. prec.] To furnish, surround, adorn, with a curtain or curtains; *transf.* and *fig.* to cover, conceal, protect, shut *off*, as with a curtain.

fig. Wicked Dreames abuse The Curtain'd sleepe *Macb.* II. i. 51.

Curtal (kɔ̄·ɪtăl). Now *Hist.* 1509. [:—OF. *cortald, curtald*; a deriv. of Romanic *corto.*]

A. *sb.* 1. A horse with its tail docked 1530. 2. *transf.* and *fig.* Anything cut short 1607. 3. *cant.* A rogue who wears a short cloak 1561. 4. A kind of cannon with a short barrel, formerly used 1509. 5. A kind of bassoon; also, an organ-stop of similar tone 1582.

B. *adj.* 1. Having the tail docked 1576. 2. Shortened 1590; abridged; scant, curt 1579. 3. *C. friar*: app. a friar with a short frock; cf. A. 3. 1610. Hence †**Cu·rtalize** *v.* = CURTAIL.

Cu·rtal-ax, -axe. Now *Hist.* or *arch.* 1579. [Perverted f. CUTLASS.] A CUTLASS; any heavy slashing sword.

‖**Curtana** (kɒɪtā·nă, -ēⁱ·nă). Also **curtan.** ME. [A deriv. of L. *curtus*: in AF. *curtein.*] The pointless sword borne before the kings of England at their coronation; emblematically considered the sword of mercy; also called the sword of King Edward the Confessor.

Curtate (kɔ̄·ɪtět), *a.* 1676. [ad. L. *curtatus*; see CURT *v.*] *Geom.*, etc.: Shortened, reduced: applied to a line projected orthographically upon a plane.

C. distance: the distance of a planet or comet from the sun or earth, projected upon the plane of the ecliptic. *C. cycloid*: see CYCLOID.

Curta·tion. 1584. [f. L. *curtare.*] †1. *Alchem.* The shorter process for transmuting metals into gold -1699. 2. *Astron.* The difference between the true and the curtate distance of a planet from the sun 1706.

Curtays(e, -eis(e, obs. ff. COURTEOUS.

Curtein, -teyn; = CURTANA, q. v.

†**Curtelace,** obs. f. CUTLASS.

Curteous, etc.; see COURTEOUS, etc.

Curt-hose (kɔ̄·ɪt,hōᵘz). ME. [OF. *curtehose* short boot; see HOSE.] Short-boot; a surname of Robert, eldest son of William the Conqueror; = med.L. *Curta ocrea.*

Curtilage (kɔ̄·ɪtilėdʒ). ME. [a. AF., OF. *cortillage*, f. *cortil* little court or garth, = med.L. *cortile*, f. *cortis* COURT.] A small court, yard, or piece of ground attached to a dwelling-house, and forming one enclosure with it.

Curtsy, curtsey (kɔ̄·ɪtsi), *sb.* 1528. [var. of COURTESY.] 1. = COURTESY in various senses. 2. An obeisance; now, a feminine movement of respect, etc., made by bending the knees and lowering the body 1575.

Curtsy, curtsey (kɔ̄·ɪtsi), *v.* 1553. [f. prec. sb.] *intr.* To make a curtsy; now said only of women. Also *transf.* and *fig.*

Emma curtsied, the gentleman bowed JANE AUSTEN.

‖**Curucui** (kūᵊrukū·i). 1678. [Native name; echoic.] A bird (*Trogon curucui*) found in Brazil and elsewhere.

Curule (kiūᵊ·rᵢul), *a.* 1600. [ad. L. *curulis, currulis*, referred to *currus* chariot.] 1. *Rom. Antiq. C. chair*: a chair or seat inlaid with ivory and shaped like a camp-stool with curved legs, used by the highest magistrates of Rome 1695. 2. Privileged to sit in a curule chair, as *c. magistrate*, etc. 1600. Also *transf.* of any high civic dignity.

Cu·rval, *a. Her.* = next.

Cu·rvant, *a.* 1830. [ad. L. *curvantem.*] *Her.* Curving.

Curvated (kɔ̄·ɪvētėd), *a. rare.* 1727. [ad. L. *curvatus.*] Curved; of a curved form.

Curvation (kɔ̄ɪvēⁱ·ʃən). 1656. [ad. L. *curvationem.*] Curving, bending.

Curvative (kɔ̄·ɪvătiv), *a. rare.* 1856. [f. L. *curvat-* ppl. stem.] *Bot.* Of leaves: Having the margins slightly curved.

Curvature (kɔ̄·ɪvătiŭɪ). 1603. [ad. L. *curvatura*, f. *curvare, curvat-.*] 1. The action of curving or bending; the fact, or manner of being curved; curved form 1665. 2. *Geom.* The amount or rate of deviation (of a curve) from a straight line, or (of a curved surface) from a plane 1710. 3. *concr.* A curved portion of anything; a curve 1603.

1. A line..of that peculiar c. HOGARTH. *C. of the spine* (Path.): an abnormal curving of the spinal column, of which there are two sorts, *angular* or *Pott's c.*, and *lateral c.* 2. *Circle of c.*: the circle which osculates a curve at any point, and serves to measure the c. of the curve at that point. *Centre of c.*, *radius of c.*: the centre and radius of the circle of c. *Double c.*: that of a curve which twists so as not to lie in one plane, *e. g.* the curve of a screw.

Curve (kɔ̄ɪv). 1571. [ad. L. *curvus.*]

A. *adj.* Curved. Now *rare.*

The tail is c. 1665.

B. *sb.* (Short for *c.-line*, etc.). 1. *Geom.* A curved line: a locus traced by a point, moving in a direction which continuously deviates from a straight line. (In *Higher Geometry*, extended to include the straight line.) 1696. 2. A curved form, outline, etc.; a curved thing or part 1728.

Curve (kɔ̄ɪv), *v.* 1594. [ad. L. *curvare.* Cf. F. *courber.*] 1. *trans.* To bend so as to form a curve; to cause to take a curved form; to inflect 1669. 2. *intr.* To have or take a curved form.

1. Curving a contumelious lip TENNYSON. 2. The tentacles c. inwards DARWIN. Hence **Curved** *ppl. a.* (partly replacing CURVE *a.*). **Cu·rvedness.**

Curvet (kɔ̄·ɪvėt, kɔ̄ɪve·t), *sb.* 1575. [ad.

It. *corvetta*, dim. of *corvo*, now *curvo* :—L. *curvus.*] In the *manège*: A leap of a horse in which the fore-legs are raised together and equally advanced, and the hind-legs raised with a spring before the fore-legs reach the ground. (Also, any frisking motion; cf. CARACOL.)

Curvet (kǭɪve·t, kǭ·ɪvėt), *v.* 1592. [ad. It. *corvettare*, f. *corvetta*; see prec.] **1.** *intr.* To execute a curvet, leap in a curvet; *trans.* to cause to curvet. **2.** *transf.* To leap about, frisk; also *fig.* 1600.

2. Cry holla to the tongue, I prethee: it curuettes vnseasonably *A. Y. L.* III. ii. 258. Hence **Cu·rveting, curve·tting** *vbl. sb.* and *ppl. a.*

Curvi- (kǭ·ɪvi), comb. f. L. *curvus* curved; chiefly in adjs. used in *Nat. Hist.*, as:

Curvicau·date [L. *cauda*], having a curved tail. **Curvico·state** [L. *costa*], having bent ribs. **Curvide·ntate** [L. *dentem*], having curved teeth. **Curvifo·liate** [L. *folium*], having leaves bent back. **Cu·rviform,** of a curved shape. **Curvine·rvate, Curvine·rved** *Bot.*, having veins diverging from the midrib and converging towards the margin; also called *curve-veined.* **Curviro·stral** [L. *rostrum*], having a curved beak. **Curvise·rial,** forming a series disposed in a curve (of leaves on a stem).

Curvili·nead. 1826. [f. CURVI- + L. *linea.*] An instrument for drawing curved lines.

Curvilineal (kǭɪvili·nɪăl), *a.* 1656. = next.

Curvilinear (kǭɪvili·nɪăɪ), *a.* (*sb.*) 1710. [f. CURVI- + L. *linea.*] Consisting of, or contained by, a curved line or lines. (Opp. to *rectilinear*, and in Gothic Archit. to *perpendicular.*) Hence **Curvilinea·rity. Curvili·nearly** *adv.*

†**Cu·rvity.** 1547. [ad. L. *curvitas*, f. *curvus.*] **1.** Curved or bent state; curvature; a curve –1831. **2.** *fig.* Moral obliquity –1678.

Cu·rvograph. 1817. [f. CURVE + -GRAPH.] An instrument for describing curves.

†**Cu·ry.** ME. [a. OF. *keuerie*, f. (ult.) L. *coquus* cook.] Cookery; also, cooked food, a dish –1513.

Cusco-bark. Also **Cuzco-.** A kind of cinchona bark, obtained from Cuzco in Lower Peru. Also called **Cusco-china.**

‖**Cuscus** [1] (ku·skus). 1625. [Same as COUSCOUS.] The grain of the African Millet, *Holcus spicatus* Linn.

‖**Cuscus** [2] (kʋ·skʋs). 1810. [ad. Pers. *khas khas.*] The aromatic root of an Indian grass, *Andropogon muricatus*, used for making fans, screens, etc. Hence *c.-grass, c.-root.*

‖**Cuscus** [3] (kʋ·skʋs). 1662. [See COUSCOUS [2].] A genus of marsupial quadrupeds found in New Guinea.

Cushat (kʋ·ʃăt). Chiefly *Sc.* and *n. dial.* [OE. *cúscute, -scote, sceote* (wk. fem.). Not elsewhere in Teut. Etym. unkn.] The wood-pigeon or ring-dove. So *C.-dove.*

Cu·shew-bird. Also **cashew-bird.** 1758. [From the blue knot on its forehead, which is like the *cashew-nut.*] The Galeated Curassow (*Pauxis galeata*).

Cushion (ku·ʃən), *sb.* [ME. *cuisshin*, a. OF. *coissin* :—L. type *coxinum*, f. *coxa* hip, thigh; also *cusshyn, cushin*, a. F. *coussin*, the surviving form, the history of which is obscure.] **1.** A case of cloth, silk, etc. stuffed with some soft elastic material, used to sit, recline, or kneel upon. **b.** The seat of a judge or ruler. 1659. Also *fig.* **2.** Anything resembling or acting as a cushion 1813; †a swelling simulating pregnancy –1694. **3.** In various specific and technical applications: as, the elastic leathern pad on which gold-leaf is cut 1837; a pad worn by women under the hair 1774; the elastic rim of a billiard-table 1778; *Mech.* a body of steam left in the cylinder of a steam-engine to act as an elastic buffer to the piston 1848. **4.** In a horse, pig, etc.: The fleshy part of the buttock 1710. **5.** *Entom.* A pulvillus 1828; *Bot.* a pulvinus 1870. **6.** *Archit.* = COUSSINET, q. v.

1. They set them downe on cosshyns of sylke LD. BERNERS. *fig.* Idlenesse .. the Devils C., as the Fathers call it 1652.

Attrib. and *comb.*: **c. capital** *Archit.*, a capital used in Romanesque architecture, resembling a c. pressed down by a weight; also, a cap consisting of a cube rounded off at its lower angles, used in the Norman period; †**cloth,** a c. case or covering; **-dance,** a round dance, formerly danced at weddings, in which the women and men alternately knelt on a c. to be kissed; **-star,** a fossil star-fish of the genus *Goniaster*; **-stitch,** a flat embroidery stitch used to fill in backgrounds in old needlework; etc.

Cushion (ku·ʃən), *v.* 1735. [f. prec. sb.] **1.** *trans.* To furnish with a cushion or cushions 1820. Also *fig.* **2.** To rest, seat, or set upon a cushion; to prop *up* with cushions 1735. **3.** *fig.* To suppress (anything) quietly 1818. **4.** *Billiards.* To leave a ball close to, or touching, the cushion. **b.** *intr.* (in U.S.) To make the ball hit the cushion before cannoning or after contact with one of the balls. **5.** To deaden the stroke of (the piston) by a cushion of steam; to form into a cushion of steam 1850.

2. Instead of inhabiting palaces, and being cushioned up in thrones BOLINGBROKE. 3. The way in which complaints are cushioned in official quarters 1887.

†**Cu·shionet.** 1542. [a. F. *coussinet.*] A little cushion; a pin-cushion –1721.

Cushiony (ku·ʃəni), *a.* 1839. [f. CUSHION *sb.* + -Y.] Resembling a cushion in shape, softness, etc., as *a soft c. feel.*

Cushy (ku·ʃi), *a. slang.* 1915. [Anglo-Ind.] Of a job, etc.: Easy. Of a wound: Not serious.

Cusk (kʋsk). 1624. A name for two fishes of the cod tribe: **a.** In Great Britain, the Torsk, *Brosmius vulgaris.* **b.** In U.S., the Burbot, *Lota maculosa.*

Cusp (kʋsp). 1585. [ad. L. *cuspis, cuspidem* point.] **1.** *Astrol.* The beginning or entrance of a 'house'. **2.** *gen.* A point, pointed end, peak 1647. **3.** *Astron.* Each of the horns of the crescent moon (or of Mercury and Venus) 1676. **4.** *Geom.* A point at which two branches of a curve meet, and stop, with a common tangent 1758. **5.** *Archit.* Each of the projecting points between the small arcs in Gothic tracery, arches, etc. 1813. **6.** *Anat.* A projection or point, *e.g.* on the crown of a tooth 1849. **7.** *Bot.* A sharp rigid point, *e.g.* of a leaf 1870. Hence (*erron.*) **Cu·spated** *a. Arch.*, furnished with a c. or cusps. **Cusped** *a.* cuspated. **Cu·sping** *sb. Arch.*, cusp-work.

‖**Cuspa·ria.** 1852. [f. native name *Cuspare.*] *Bot.* A genus of trees, now usually called *Galipea*, species of which yield *Angustura* bark; also = **Cu·sparin** (*Chem.*), a crystalline substance obtained from Angustura bark.

Cuspid (kʋ·spid). 1743. [ad. L. *cuspidem.*] *sb.* †**1.** *Geom.* = CUSP 4. **2.** A cuspidated tooth 1878. *adj.* = CUSPIDATE 1882.

Cuspidal (kʋ·spidăl), *a.* 1647. [f. L. *cuspidem* + -AL.] †**1.** Belonging to the apex. **2.** *Geom.* Having, related to, or of the nature of, a CUSP (sense 4) 1874. **3.** Of teeth, cuspidate 1867.

Cuspidate (kʋ·spidĕt), *a.* 1692. [ad. mod.L. *cuspidatus*, f. *cuspidem.*] Having a cusp or sharp point. *spec.* **a.** Of leaves: Ending in a rigid point. **b.** Applied to the canine teeth. So **Cu·spidated** *a.* **Cuspida·tion,** cusping.

Cuspidine (kʋ·spidəin). 1882. [f. L. *cuspidem* + -INE.] *Min.* A fluo-silicate of calcium from Vesuvius occurring in pale rosy spear-shaped crystals.

Cu·spidor, -ore. *U.S.* 1779. [a. Pg., f. (ult.) L. *conspuere.*] A spittoon.

‖**Cuspis** (kʋ·spis). Pl. **cuspides** (-idīz). 1646. [L.] = CUSP, q. v., in various senses.

Cuss (kʋs), *sb. U.S. colloq.* 1848. [Orig. = *curse*; in sense 2 perh. short for *customer.*] **1.** An execration, etc. **2.** Applied contemptuously, or humorously to persons; also to animals 1775. *Comb.* **c.-word,** an oath. So **Cuss** *v.* = CURSE. **Cu·ssed** *a.* cursed. **Cu·ssedness,** malignity, cantankerousness, contrariness.

Cusser, var. COURSER [2], a stallion. SCOTT.

†**Cust.** [Same as OE. *cyst* choice, excellence, etc.] **1.** Choice. (OE. only.) **2.** = COST *sb.* [1] –ME.

Custard (kʋ·stăɪd). 1450. [Perverted f. †*crustade*, a. F. *croustade.*] †**a.** = DARIOLE. **b.** In modern use, a mixture of eggs beaten up and milk, sweetened, and baked; also a similar mixture served up in a liquid form.

Comb.: **c.-apple,** the fruit of *Anona reticulata*; it has a dark brown rind, and a yellowish pulp resembling c.; also called *bullock's heart*; †**-coffin,** the coffin or crust of a c.

Custode. ME. [Orig. a. OF. *custode*, ad. L. *custodem.* In mod. use, a. It. *custode* (kustō·de), pl. *-odi.*] One who has the custody of anything; a guardian, custodian.

Custodial (kʋstōu·diăl). 1772. [f. L. *custodia* + -AL.] *adj.* Relating to custody or guardianship. *sb.* A vessel for preserving sacred objects, as the host, relics, etc. 1860.

Custo·diam. 1662. [L., from the wording of the grant.] *Irish Law.* A grant by the Exchequer (for three years) of lands, etc., in possession of the Crown.

Custodian (kʋstōu·diăn). 1781. [f. as prec. + -AN.] One who has custody; a guardian, keeper. So **Custo·dier.** (Now *esp.* Sc.) **Custo·dianship.**

Custody (kʋ·stŏdi). 1491. [ad. L. *custodia*, f. *custos.*] **1.** Safe keeping, protection; charge, care, guardianship. **2.** The keeping of an officer of justice; confinement, imprisonment, durance 1611. †**3.** Guardianship –1613.

1. Ships for the c. of the narrow seas BACON (J.). 2. Iaylor, take him to thy custodie *Com. Err.* I. i. 156.

Custom (kʋ·stəm), *sb.* ME. [a. OF. *custume, costume* (now *coutume*) :—L. **costumen*, substituted for **costudne* :—L. *consuetudinem.* Cf. COSTUME.] **1.** A habitual or usual practice; common way of acting; usage, fashion, habit; the being or becoming accustomed 1526. **2.** *Law.* A usage which by continuance has acquired the force of a law or right, *esp.* the special usage of a locality, trade, society, or the like ME. †**3.** Any customary service, rent, or due paid to a lord or ruler –1730. **4.** Duty levied by the lord or local authority upon commodities on their way to market; *esp.* that levied in the name of the king upon exports or imports ME. **5.** The practice of habitually resorting to a particular shop, hotel, etc. to make purchases or give orders 1596.

1. A Custome More honour'd in the breach, then the obseruance *Haml.* I. iv. 15. C. makes all things easy 1867. †*C. of women*: menstruation. 4. *The Customs*: the duties levied upon imports as a branch of the public revenue; the department of the Civil Service that levies these duties. (Now rarely in sing., and never with *a.*) Not to pay c. SWIFT. 5. A tailor, whom I have presented my c. PEPYS.

Comb.: **c.-mill,** (*a.*) a mill belonging to a feudal proprietor at which his tenants are obliged to grind their corn, paying c. for so doing; (*b*) a mill that grinds for customers; **-office** = CUSTOM-HOUSE.

Hence †**Cu·stomed** *ppl. a. arch.*, accustomed; charged with duty; patronized.

†**Custom** (kʋ·stəm), *v.* ME. [a. OF. *costumer*, f. *costume* CUSTOM.] **1.** *trans.* = ACCUSTOM 1. –1626. **2.** To accustom, habituate (oneself or another) (*arch.*) 1510; *pass.* to be used (*to do* something) –1674. **3.** *trans.* To pay duty or toll on –1720. **4.** To bestow one's custom on; to frequent as a customer –1681.

2. Yf he be custommed to doo euylle CAXTON.

Customable (kʋ·stəmăb'l), *a.* ME. [a. OF. *custumable*; see CUSTOM *sb.* and *v.* and -ABLE.] †**1.** Customary, usual –1663. †**2.** Of persons: Accustomed (*to*), wont (*to do*); habitual –1570. **3.** Dutiable (*rare*) 1529.

2. C. Swearers COVERDALE. Hence †**Cu·stomableness.** †**Cu·stomably** *adv.*

†**Cu·stomance, cu·stumance.** ME. [a. OF. *cost-, coustumance.*] Custom, habit –1528.

Customary (kʋ·stəmări), *a.* 1523. [ad. med.L. *custumarius*, repr. L. *consuetudinarius*; see CUSTOM.] **1.** According to custom; commonly used or practised; usual, habitual 1607. **2.** Established by or depending on custom 1660. **3.** *Law.* Subject to customs or dues, as *c. tenants, tenure, lands*, etc. But now taken as: Holding or held by custom (*e.g.* of the manor) 1523.

1. His c. self-possession LYTTON. 2. The family was a religious and c. institution JOWETT. 3. *C. mill* = Custom mill: see CUSTOM. *C. court*: formerly a court which exercised jurisdiction over copyholders, and administered the custom of the manor. *C. holder*, a c. tenant. Hence **Cu·stomari-ly** *adv.*, **-ness.**

Customary (kʋ·stəmări), **custumary** (kʋ·stiumări), *sb.* 1604. [ad. med.L. *custumarius, -um*, repr. L. *consuetudinarius, -um*, subst. uses of the adj.] **1.** *Law.* A collection of customs (see CUSTOM *sb.* 2); *esp.* one reduced to writing. **2.** *Eccl.* = CONSUETUDINARY *sb.* 1882.

1. The earliest written c. in France is that of Bearn HALLAM.

Customer (kɒ·stəməɹ), *sb.* ME. [a. late AF. *custumer*; also in part f. CUSTOM.] †1. A customary tenant 1440. †2. One who collects customs; a custom-house officer –1748. 3. One who customarily purchases anywhere; a buyer, purchaser. (The chief current sense.) 1480. †4. A person with whom one has dealings –1621; a prostitute (SHAKS.). 5. *colloq.* A person to have to do with; chap, fellow 1589.

3. No Milliner can so fit his customers with Gloues *Wint. T.* IV. iv. 192. 5. Queer customers those monks DICKENS. Hence †**Cu·stomership**, the office of a collector of customs.

Custom-house (kɒ·stəmhaus). 1490. [CUSTOM 4.] A house or office at which custom is collected; *esp.* a government office, at which customs are levied on imports or exports. Also, the office of the department which manages the customs. Also *attrib.*

‖**Custos** (kɒ·stɒs). 1465. [L. Formerly treated as Eng.: now Latin, with pl. *custodes.*] A keeper, guardian, custodian.

C. rotulorum: the principal Justice of the peace in a county, who has custody of the rolls and records of the sessions of the peace.

Custrel (kɒ·strĕl). Now *Hist.* 1492. [Cf. OF. *coustillier* lit. a soldier armed with a *coustille* or two-edged dagger.] 1. An attendant on a knight. 2. A term of reproach: Knave. See COISTREL. 1581.

†**Cu·stron.** ME. [a. OF. *coistron* :—late L. *cocistronem*, nom. *cocistro* 'tabernarius' (Papias).] 1. A kitchen-knave; hence a base-born fellow, cad, vagabond –1605. 2. = CUSTREL 1.

Custumal (kɒ·stiumăl), **customal** (kɒ·stəmăl), *sb.* 1570. [f. med.L. *liber custumalis*; see next.] *Law.* = CUSTOMARY *sb.*

Cu·stumal, *a.* 1889. [ad. med.L. *cos-, custumalis*, corresp. to OF. *costumel*, f. *costume* CUSTOM.] Having to do with the customs of a city, etc.

Cut (kɒt), *sb.*¹ Also **cutt, -e.** ME. [Taken usually as a special use of CUT *sb.*², but ?] 1. = LOT: in the phr. *draw cuts*, orig. *draw cut.* (See N.E.D.). †2. (One's) lot; fate or fortune as a ruler of events –1635.

Cut (kɒt), *sb.*² ME. [Mostly f. CUT *v.*]

I. 1. The act of cutting 1808; a stroke or blow with a sharp-edged instrument 1601; a sharp stroke with a whip, cane, etc. 1725. 2. *fig.* An act whereby the feelings are deeply wounded, as a sarcasm, etc.; a severe disaster; a shock 1568. 3. An excision or omission of a part 1604. 4. The act of cutting down rates, prices, salaries, etc.; a reduction of this kind (orig. *U.S.*) 1881. 5. *Card-playing.* The act of cutting a pack; the card so obtained 1598. 6. A step in dancing 1676. 7. A particular stroke in *Cricket, Lawn Tennis*, etc. 1855. 8. *colloq.* The act of cutting an acquaintance 1798.

1. The speech is all whet and no c. COBBETT. *C.-and-thrust adj.*, adapted for both cutting and thrusting; also *fig.* 4. A further c. of two cents 1881. 8. The c. direct THACKERAY.

II. A way straight across. Also *concr.* and *fig.* 1577.

Phr. *Short c.*: a crossing that shortens the distance (*lit.* and *fig.*).

III. The style in which a thing is cut; fashion, shape 1579. Also *fig.*

Attyre of the newe c. LYLY. Phr. *The c. of one's jib*: one's general appearance (*slang*). *A c. above*: a degree or stage above (*colloq.*) 1818.

IV. 1. An opening made by a sharp-edged instrument, an incision; a wound made by cutting, a gash 1530. 2. A slash in the edge of a garment 1563. 3. A passage or channel cut or dug out; a cutting 1548; †a strait –1678. 4. An engraved block or plate; the impression from this; an engraving (see WOODCUT) 1646.

2. Cloth a gold and cut, and lac'd with siluer *Much Ado* III. iv. 19. 3. Through these Fens run great Cuts or Dreyns 1696. 4. Bibles, with cuts and comments CRABBE.

V. 1. A piece cut off, *e.g.* of meat, cloth, yarn, etc. 1591. 2. The quantity cut (*esp.* of timber). Chiefly *U.S.* 1805.

VI. The pa. pple. used subst. †1. A cut-tail horse, or ? a gelding –1612. 2. A term of abuse. (Perh. from prec. sense.) *Obs.* or *dial.* 1490.

2. If thou hast her not i' the end, call me C. *Twel. N.* II. iii. 203. Phr. †*To keep one's c., keep c.*: ? to keep one's distance, be reserved.

Cut (kɒt), *v.* ME. [Prob. f. an OTeut. stem *kut-, *kot-; cf. Sw. dial. *kåta*, (*kutå*) to cut. Not from Welsh *cwta* 'short'.]

I. 1. To penetrate so as to sever the continuity of with an edged instrument; to make incision in; to gash, slash. Said also of the instrument; also *transf.* 2. *absol.* or *intr.* To make incision 1596. 3. To strike sharply as with a whip, etc. Also said of the whip, etc. Also *absol.* 1607. 4. *fig.* (*trans.*) To wound deeply the feelings of 1582.

1. Kyt it wyth a knyf ARNOLDE. 2. C. close to the Stem EVELYN. *fig.* The tongue is not steel, yet it cuts G. HERBERT. 3. Every word in it will c. them to the heart BEVERIDGE.

II. 1. To divide into parts with a sharp-edged instrument; to sever ME. Also *fig.* 2. *spec.* To carve; also *absol.* 1601. 3. To make a narrow opening through, intersect 1590. 4. To break up the viscidity of 1578. 5. To sever for the purpose of taking the part detached; to reap, mow, hew, etc. ME. 6. *intr.* (in *pass.* sense.) To suffer incision; to admit of being cut; to yield when cut 1560.

1. To c. a thread WYATT, asparagus MACAULAY. *fig.* [Friendship] cutteth Griefes in Halfes BACON. Phr. *To c. to* (or *in*) *pieces*: (*fig.*) to rout with great slaughter. 3. To c. a Canal 1677, sea-dykes PALMERSTON, a vein of ore 1778. 5. Thy servants can skill to c. timber in Lebanon *2 Chron.* ii. 8. 6. The trout.. cut red MEDWIN.

III. To separate or remove by cutting; to lop off. Also with *away, off, out.* ME.

Phr. †*To c. a purse*: to steal it by cutting it from the girdle.

IV. 1. *trans.* To pass through as in cutting; to intersect, to cross. Also *intr.* with *through*, etc. ME. 2. *colloq.* To run away; to move sharply. Orig. with *away, off.* 1590.

The old part of the path which the line had cut across 1885.

V. To reduce by cutting; to trim, shear; to prune. Also *fig.* ME.

For cutting my haire, 6d. WOOD. *fig.* To c. rates 1888.

VI. 1. To shape, fashion, form, or make by or as by cutting 1511. 2. To hollow out, excavate 1634. 3. To perform or execute, as in *to c.* a CAPER, a DASH, a FIGURE, a JOKE, etc. (see these words) 1601.

1. Why should a man..Sit like his Grandsire, cut in Alablaster *Merch. V.* I. i. 84. He knows.. when a Coat is well cut STEELE. His features were finely cut S. C. HALL. 2. We do not see how the canals are to be cut 1887. Phr. *To c. one's way*, etc.: to advance by cutting through obstructions.

VII. Special senses. 1. *Surg.* a. To castrate 1465. b. To make an incision in the bladder for extraction of stone; also *absol.* 1566. 2. Of horses: *intr.* To bruise the inside of the fetlock with the opposite foot; to interfere 1660. 3. *Naut.* (*absol.*) To cut the cable 1707. 4. *Card-playing.* To divide (a pack of cards) 1532. 5. *Dancing.* (*intr.*) To spring and twiddle the feet one in front of the other alternately 1603. 6. To execute a particular stroke in *Cricket, Lawn Tennis, Croquet*, etc. 1857. 7. *colloq.* (*trans.*) To break off acquaintance with, affect not to know (a person); to give up (a thing) 1634. Also †*intr.* 8. *Irish Hist.* (*trans.*) To levy (a tax, etc.). Also *absol.* [Cf. F. *tailler.*] –1612.

Phrases. *To c. a tooth, one's teeth*: to have them appear through the gums; also *fig.* to become knowing; so *to c. one's eye-teeth*. *To c. and carve*: see CARVE *v.* *To c. and run* (Naut.): to c. the cable and make sail without waiting to weigh anchor; *colloq.* to hurry off. *To c. short*: *trans.* to curtail; to break off abruptly; to interrupt abruptly; *intr.* to be brief. *To c. one's stick* (slang): to be off. Also *to c. one's lucky*. *To c. the coat according to the cloth*: see CLOTH. *To c. to pieces*: see II. 1 (quots.). *To c. the comb of*: see COMB. *To c. the grass under*, or *ground from under, a person's feet*: see GRASS, GROUND. *To c. the knot*: see KNOT.

Comb. (with adverbs): **C. down. a.** *trans.* To c. and bring down or let fall. **b.** To lay low with the sword. **c.** To take the lead of in a race, etc. **d.** To retrench, curtail. **C. in. a.** To carve or engrave in intaglio. **b.** To penetrate sharply or abruptly. **c.** To strike in. **d.** *Card-playing.* To join in a game by taking the place of a player *cutting out*, q. v. **C. off. a.** *trans.* To c. so as to take off, to sever. **b.** To put a stop to; to break off. **c.** To bring to an untimely end. **d.** To intercept. **e.** To interrupt, stop (communication, passage, etc.) 1599. **f.** To shut out; to debar. **g.** To disinherit. **C. out. a.** *trans.* To c. so as to take out. **b.** To excise, omit. **c.** To carry off (a ship) from a harbour, etc., by getting between her and the shore. **d.** *U.S.*, etc. To detach (an animal) from the herd. **e.** To get in front of a rival so as to take the first place from him. **f.** To excavate, carve out. **g.** To shape by cutting (out of a piece); also *fig.* **h.** To plan; to prepare (*work* to be done). See also WORK *sb.* Phrases. **i.** To form by nature (*for* a purpose). **j.** *intr.* To admit of being cut into shape. **k.** *intr.* (orig. *pass.*) *Card-playing.* To be excluded from a game by cutting an unfavourable card: cf. *c. in.* **C. under.** To c. out by underselling (*colloq.*). **C. up. a.** *trans.* To root up by cutting; also *fig.* **b.** To c. in pieces; also *fig.* **c.** To c. to pieces: see II. 1 (quots.). **d.** To damage by or as by cutting; also *fig.* **e.** To wound deeply the feelings of. (Usu. in *pass.*) **f.** *intr.* To admit of being cut up, to turn out as to amount of fortune (*slang*). **g.** *To c. up rough*, etc.: (*intr.*) to become quarrelsome (*colloq.*). **h.** To behave (*badly*, etc.) in a race (*slang*).

Phraseological combs. **C.-and-come-again.** The act or faculty of helping oneself as often as one likes; hence, abundance; also *fig.* Also *attrib.* **C.-and-cover.** *Engineering.* A method of constructing a tunnel by making a cutting in which the brickwork lining is built and then covered in.

Cut (kɒt), *ppl. a.* ME. [f. CUT *v.*] 1. Gashed or wounded with an edged instrument 1665; slashed, as clothes, etc. 1480. 2. Affected by cutting 1588. 3. Shaped or fashioned by cutting; having the surface shaped by grinding and polishing, as *c. glass* 1677. 4. Divided into pieces by cutting ME. 5. Detached by cutting, as *c. flowers* 1646. 6. Reduced by, or as by cutting; cut down 1646. 7. Castrated 1624. 8. *slang.* Drunk 1673.

Phr. *C. and dried* (also *c. and dry*): orig. of herbs in the herbalists' shops; hence *fig.* ready-made; also, ready shaped on *a priori* notions.

Cutaneous (kiutēⁱ·niəs), *a.* 1578. [f. mod. L. *cutaneus* (f. L. *cutis* skin) + -OUS.] Of, pertaining to, or affecting the skin, as *c. diseases, eruptions*, etc. Also *fig.* var. †**Cuta·nean.**

Cu·t-away, *a.* (*sb.*) 1841. [f. CUT *pa. pple.*] Of a coat: Having the skirt cut back from the waist in a slope or curve. As *sb.* (*ellipt.*) A cut-away coat.

Cutch¹ (kɒtʃ). 1759. [ad. Malay *kachu.*] = CATECHU.

Cutch² (kɒtʃ). 1879. [ad. F. *caucher* :—(ult.) L. *calcare.*] A pile of vellum leaves, between which laminæ of gold-leaf are placed to be beaten.

Cutch, var. of COUCH *sb.*² (*Triticum repens*).

‖**Cutcha** (kɒ·tʃă), *a. Anglo-Ind.* Also **kutcha.** 1834. [a. Hindī *kachchā* raw, crude, uncooked.] Slight, makeshift (opp. to *pucka* solid). As *sb.* = Sun-dried brick.

Cutcher (in *Paper-making*) = COUCHER².

‖**Cutcherry** (kɒtʃe·ri), **cutchery** (kɒ·tʃĕri). *Anglo-Ind.* 1610. [a. Hindī *kachahrī, kachērī*, hall of audience, etc.] 1. A court-house. Also, a business office. †2. A brigade of infantry 1799.

Cute (kiūt), *a. colloq.* Also **'cute.** 1731. [Aphet. f. ACUTE *a.*] 1. Acute, clever, sharp, shrewd. 2. (*U.S. colloq.*, etc.) = CUNNING *a.* 6. 1868. Hence **Cu·teness.**

Cut-grass. 1840. [f. CUT *v.*: *lit.* 'grass that cuts'.] A genus of grasses, *Leersia*, esp. *L. oryzoides.*

Cuticle (kiū·tik'l). 1615. [ad. L. *cuticula*, dim. of *cutis.*] 1. The EPIDERMIS or scarf-skin of the body; also *transf.* of other superficial integuments. 2. *Bot.* Formerly, the primary integumentary tissue; now, a superficial film formed of the outer layers of the epidermal cells 1671. †3. A film or thin coating –1704. var. ‖**Cuti·cula** [L.]. Hence **Cuti·cular** *a.* of, pertaining to, or resembling a c. **Cuti:culariza·tion**, the action or process of forming into c. **Cuti·cularize** *v. trans.*, to form into c.

Cutify (kiū·tifəi), *v.* 1890. [f. L. *cutis* skin; see -FY.] *intr.* To form skin. Hence **Cutifica·tion**, formation of cutis.

Cutikin (kü·tikin). *Sc.* 1816. [f. *cuit, cute* ankle.] A gaiter, a spatterdash.

Cutin (kiū·tin). 1863. [f. CUTIS + -IN.] *Bot.* The cellulose body forming the cuticle of plants, CUTOSE. Hence **Cu·tinize** *v.* = *cuticularize.* **Cutiniza·tion.**

‖**Cutis** (kiū·tis). 1603. [L.] 1. *Anat.* The true skin or derma of the body. 2. *Bot.* The peridium of certain fungi. Hence **Cuti·tis** *Path.*, inflammation of the skin.

Cutlass (kɒ·tlăs). 1594. [a. F. *coutelas*, augm. of *couteau* (*coutel*) knife. See also CURTELACE, CURTAL-AX.] A short sword with a flat wide slightly curved blade; now *esp.* that with which sailors are armed.

Comb.: **c.-fish**, a species of fish, the Silvery hairtail, so named from its shape.

Cutler (kɒ·tləɹ). ME. [a. F. *coutelier* :—L. type *cultellarius*, f. *cultellus*, OF. *coutel* knife.] One who makes, deals in, or repairs knives, etc.

Cutlery (kɒ·tləri). 1449. [a. OF. *coutelerie*, f. *coutelier*; see prec.] **a.** The art or trade of the cutler. **b.** *collect.* Articles made or sold by cutlers, as knives, scissors, etc.

Cutlet (kɒ·tlėt). 1706. [a. F. *côtelette* (formerly *costelette*) double dim. of *coste, côte* rib. In Eng., perh. assoc. w. *cut.*] A small piece of meat, usually mutton cut off the ribs, or veal, used for broiling, frying, etc.

Cutling (kɒ·tliŋ), *vbl. sb. dial.* 1645. [f. as if from a verb *to cutle.*] The making of cutlery. Also *attrib.*

That the men of Toledo..were excellent at c. MILT.

Cut-off (kɒ·t,ǫ·f, *attrib.* kɒ·t,ǫf), *sb.* 1741. [CUT *v.*] **1.** An act of cutting off or portion cut off. **2.** A new and shorter passage cut by a river through a bend. *Western U.S.* 1830. **3.** A stopping of a continuance or flow 1881. **b.** *spec.* (*Steam-engine.*) An arrangement by which the admission of steam to the cylinder is cut off when the piston has travelled part of the stroke, so that the steam during the remainder of the stroke works expansively; a contrivance for effecting this. Also *attrib.* 1849. **c.** Any contrivance for stopping the flow of a liquid, cutting off a connexion, and the like 1874.

Cutose (kiū·tōᵘs). 1881. [f. CUTIS + -OSE.] *Chem.* One of the cellulose bodies; the hyaline substance which forms the cuticle of plants. Also called *cutin.*

Cut-out (kɒt,au·t, kɒ·t,aut), *sb.* 1874. [CUT *v.*] *Electr. Engin.* A device for automatically cutting lamps, motors, etc. out of circuit when the current attains a point at which it is undesirable to work. **b.** In motor-vehicles, an appliance that gives a free opening to the exhaust gases 1905.

Cutpurse, cut-purse (kɒ·tpɒ̄ɹs). ME. [CUT *v.* III.] One who steals a purse by cutting it from the girdle, from which formerly it was suspended; hence, a pickpocket, thief; also *fig.*

How often hast thou seene the C. hanged with the purse about his necke GOLDING.

Cu·ttanee. 1622. [Urdū *kattānī*, f. Arab. *kattān* flax.] Fine linen from the East Indies.

Cutter (kɒ·təɹ), *sb.*[1] ME. [f. CUT *v.* + -ER[1].] **1.** One who cuts; one who shapes things by cutting; as *fustian-, stone-, wood-c.* 1483. **2.** *spec.* †A hair-cutter -1624; a carver, sculptor, engraver 1572; †a tailor; the person in a tailoring establishment who takes the measures and cuts out the cloth 1599; one who castrates animals 1562. †**3.** One over-ready to resort to weapons; a bully; also, a cutthroat -1826. **4.** That which cuts; an implement or tool for cutting; the cutting part of a machine, etc. 1631; †an incisor tooth -1691. **5.** *Mining.* A crack intersecting the lines of stratification; the cleavage of slate (usu. in *pl.*); a crack in a crystal (*dial.*) 1756. **6.** A superior quality of brick, which can be cut and rubbed 1842.

Comb.: **c.-bar**, (*a*) a bar in which cutting-tools are so fastened as to serve for circular cutting; (*b*) the bar in a mowing or reaping machine that bears the knives; **-grinder**, an instrument for sharpening the cutters of reaping machines, etc.; **-head**, the revolving head of a tool with cutters; **-wheel**, one serving for cutting.

Cutter (kɒ·təɹ), *sb.*[2] 1745. [app. a spec. use of prec.] *Naut.* **1.** A boat, belonging to a ship of war, shorter and in proportion broader than the barge or pinnace, fitted for rowing or sailing, and used for carrying light stores, passengers, etc. **2.** A small, single-masted vessel, clinker- or carvel-built, furnished with a straight running bowsprit, and rigged much like a sloop, as a *revenue c.* 1762. **3.** *transf.* A small sleigh or sledge for one or two persons. *Canada* and *U.S.* 1836.

Comb. **c.-brig**, 'a vessel with square sails, a fore-and-aft main-sail, and a jigger-mast with a smaller one' (Smyth).

Cutthroat, cut-throat (kɒ·t,þrout). 1535. [See CUT *v.*] **1.** One who cuts throats; a ruffian who murders or does deeds of violence. Also *transf.* and *fig.* †**2.** A dark lantern -1825. **3.** The Mustang grape of Texas, having an acrid taste. **4.** A West African bird, *Amadina fasciata*, the male of which has a red mark round the throat 1872. **5.** *attrib.* Murderous, ruffianly 1567. **b.** Three-handed, as *c. bridge, euchre.*

1. I am a soldier, sir, and not a cut-throat FROUDE.

Cutting (kɒ·tiŋ), *vbl. sb.* ME. [-ING[1].] **1.** The action of CUT *v.*, in various senses. †**2.** An intersection; also a section -1726. **3.** *concr.* A piece cut off; *esp.* a shred made in trimming an object for use ME. **4.** *spec.* A small shoot bearing leaf-buds cut off a plant, and used for propagation 1664; a piece cut out of a newspaper, etc. 1856. **5.** *Irish Hist.* Tallage 1596. **6.** A carving, etc. 1787. **7.** *Mining.* 'A poor quality of ore mixed with that which is better' (Knight) 1874. **8.** An excavation through ground that rises above the level of a canal, railway, or road which has to cross it 1836.

Comb.: **c.-box**, †(*a*) ?a chaff- or straw-cutter; (*b*) a receptacle for the diamond dust in diamond-cutting; **-shoe**, a special shoe for horses which cut or interfere (see CUT *v.* VII. 2).

Cu·tting, *ppl. a.* ME. [-ING[2].] **1.** That cuts, in various senses, as a *c. blade, wind, employer*, etc. **2.** That acutely wounds the feelings 1583. †**3.** That is a 'cutter' or swaggering blade -1592.

2. He can say the..most c. things in the quietest of tones C. BRONTË. Hence **Cu·ttingly** *adv.*

Cuttle (kɒ·t'l), *sb.*[1] [OE. *cudele*; of unkn. deriv.] A cephalopod of the genus *Sepia* or family *Sepiidæ*, esp. the common cuttlefish, *Sepia officinalis*, also called *ink-fish* from its power of ejecting a black fluid from a bag or sac, so as to darken the water and conceal itself. Thence extended to other decapod, and occas. to octopod, cephalopods. Now usually called **Cuttle-fish.** Also *attrib.*

†**Cuttle**, *sb.*[2] 1546. [app. a. OF. *coutel* (mod. *couteau*).] A knife. Also *fig.* -1661. **b.** *transf.* 2 *Hen. IV*, II. iv. 139.

†**Cu·ttle**, *v. rare.* [? Echoic.] To whisper; to talk privately and confidentially. H. WALPOLE.

Cu·ttle-bone. 1547. The internal calcareous shell of the cuttle-fish; used for pounce, as a polishing material, etc.

Cuttle-fish; see CUTTLE *sb.*[1]

Cuttoe (kɒ·tǫ). *Obs.* exc. *U.S.* 1678. [ad. F. *couteau.*] = COUTEAU.

Cu·ttoo. 1794. *Carriage-building.* One of the projections covering the top of the wheels which shelter the axle-tree arms from the dirt.

Cutty (kɒ·ti). *Sc.* and *n. dial.* 17... [f. CUT *v.*]

A. *adj.* Cut short, curtailed, as *c. knife, pipe, sark*, etc.

B. *sb.* **1.** Short for *c. spoon* (*Sc.*) 17... **2.** Short for *c. pipe* 1776. **3.** A term for a testy or naughty girl or woman; often playful 1816. **4.** A local name for: **a.** The wren. **b.** The Black Guillemot. **c.** The hare. 1776.

Cutty-stool. *Sc.* 1774. [CUTTY *a.*] **1.** A low stool 1820. **2.** Formerly, in Scotland, a seat in a church, where offenders against chastity had to sit, and receive a public rebuke from the minister. Also *fig.*

Cutwal, -waul; see KOTWAL.

Cutwater, cut-water (kɒ·t,wǭ·təɹ). 1644. **1.** The knee of the head of a ship, etc., which divides the water before it reaches the bow; also, the forward edge of the prow. **2.** The wedge-shaped end of the pier of a bridge, which serves to divide the current, break up ice, etc. 1776. **3.** An American sea-fowl, the Skimmer, *Rhynchops nigra* 1732.

Cu·t-work, cu·twork. 1470. **1.** *gen.* Work produced by cutting or carving 1662. **2.** Embroidery with cut-out edges, also a kind of openwork embroidery or lace, formerly worn. **b.** Appliqué work. 1470. †**3.** Flower-beds cut into patterns -1727.

Cu·tworm. 1808. A caterpillar which cuts off by the surface of the ground the young plants of cabbage, maize, melons, etc.; *esp.* in *U.S.* the larvæ of species of *Agrotis*, a genus of moths.

†‖**Cuve.** ME. [F. :—L. *cupa.*] A cask, vat -1673.

‖**Cuvette** (kiüve·t). 1678. [F., dim. of *cuve* (see prec.).] **1.** *Fortif.* = CUNETTE. **2.** An ornamental shallow dish for holding water, etc. 1706. **3.** *Glass-making.* A large clay basin or crucible used in making plate-glass 1832.

Cwt., abbrev. of HUNDREDWEIGHT. [f. *c* = L. *centum* + *wt.* = *weight.*]

-cy, suffix of sbs., originating in L. *-cia, -tia*, Gr. -κια, -κεια, -τια, -τεια. Occurring chiefly in the combined forms -ACY, -ANCY, -ENCY, -CRACY, -MANCY, q. v.

Cya-, shortened f. CYANO-, in names of chemical compounds, as **Cya·melide**, a white crystalline substance polymeric with cyanic acid; etc.

Cy·amid. *Zool.* A crustacean of the family *Cyamidæ*; a whale-louse.

Cyamoid (səi·ămoid), *a. rare.* 1882. [f. Gr. κύαμος.] Resembling a small bean.

Cyan-. **1.** Comb. f. Gr. κύανος and κυάνεος 'dark-blue' bef. a vowel. **2.** *Chem.* = CYANO-2, used as comb. f. CYANOGEN bef. a vowel, as in **Cy·anamide**, the amide of cyanogen, CN_2H_2, a white crystalline body. **Cyanhy·dric** *a.* = hydrocyanic. **Cyanu·rate**, a salt of **Cyanu·ric** [URIC], or **Cyanure·nic** acid, an acid polymeric with cyanic acid, obtained by heating dry urea in a flask.

Cyanate (səi·ăneᵗt). 1845. [f. CYAN- 2 + -ATE.] *Chem.* A salt of cyanic acid.

Cyan-blue. 1879. [f. Gr. κύανος or κυάνεος.] A greenish-blue colour, lying between green and blue in the spectrum.

‖**Cyanea** (səiē·niă). 1883. [fem. of L. *cyaneus*, Gr. κυάνεος dark blue.] A genus of jelly-fishes. Hence **Cya·neid**, one of these.

Cyaneous (səiē·niəs), *a. rare.* 1688. [f. L. *cyaneus* (see prec.) + -OUS.] Deep blue, azure. var. **Cya·nean** (*rare*).

Cyanhydric; see CYAN- 2.

Cyanic (səiæ·nik), *a.* 1832. [f. CYAN- 2 + -IC.] **1.** *Chem.* Of or containing cyanogen. **2.** Blue, azure; *spec.* in *Bot.*, one of the two series into which Candolle divided the colours of flowers (the other being *xanthic* = yellow) 1849.

1. *C. acid*, a colourless, pungent, volatile, unstable liquid (CNHO).

Cyanide (səi·ănəid). 1826. [f. CYAN- 2 + -IDE.] *Chem.* A simple compound of cyanogen with a metal or organic radical, as *potassium c.* (KCy).

Cyanin (səi·ănin). 1863. [f. CYAN- 1 + -IN.] The blue colouring matter of some flowers, as the violet, etc.

Cyanine (səi·ănəin). 1872. [f. as prec. + -INE.] *Chem.* A blue dye-stuff prepared from chinoline with amyl iodide, used in calico-printing.

Cyanite (səi·ănəit). 1794. [f. as prec. + -ITE.] *Min.* **1.** A native silicate of aluminium, usually blue. **2.** A fire-proof priming for paint, etc. 1884.

Cyano- (bef. a vowel or *h* usually **cyan-**). **1.** Used as comb. f. Gr. κύανος a dark-blue mineral, κυάνεος adj. dark-blue, in scientific terms, as:

Cyano·chroite *Min.* [Gr. χροιά], a blue hydrous sulphate of copper and potassium. **Cyano·pathy** *Path.* [Gr. -πάθεια, f. πάθος.] = CYANOSIS. **Cyano·trichite** *Min.* [Gr. θρίξ, τριχ-], a blue fibrous sulphate of copper and aluminium. **2.** *Chem.* (= CYAN- 2): Of or containing cyanogen; in the names of cyanogen compounds.

Cyanogen (səiæ·nǒdʒen). 1826. [ad. F. *cyanogène*, f. Gr. κύανος a dark-blue mineral + -GEN, named from its entering into the composition of Prussian blue.] *Chem.* A compound radical consisting of one atom of nitrogen and one of carbon (symbol CN or Cy). In the form of *di-cyanogen* (C_2N_2), it is a colourless gas, highly poisonous, with an odour like that of prussic acid. It exists in many compounds, the cyanides, cyanates, cyanurets, etc.

Cyanometer (səiănǫ·mǐtəɹ). 1829. [f. CYANO- 1 + -METER.] An instrument for measuring the intensity of the blue of the sky. Hence **Cyanome·tric** *a.* **Cyano·metry.**

Cyanose (səi·ănōus). 1834. [Cf. F. *cyanose.*] *Path.* = CYANOSIS. Hence **Cy·anosed** *ppl. a.* afflicted with cyanosis.

‖**Cyanosis** (səiǎnōᵘ·sis). 1834. [a. Gr. κυάνωσις dark-blue colour.] *Path.* Lividness of the skin owing to the circulation of imperfectly oxygenated blood; blue jaundice. Hence **Cyano·tic** *a.* pertaining to, or affected with, c.

Cyanotype (səiæ·nǒtəip). 1842. [f. CYANO- + TYPE.] A photographic process in which paper sensitized by a cyanide is employed; a print obtained by this process. Also *attrib.*

Cyanu·rate, -uric, etc.; see CYAN- 2.

Cyanuret (səiæ·niŭret). 1827. [-URET.] *Chem.* = CYANIDE.

Cyanurin (səiǎniūᵊ·rin). 1845. [f. CYAN- 1 + URINE.] *Path.* A blue deposit occas. found in urine.

†**Cy·ath.** 1544. [ad. L. *cyathus.*] = CYATHUS 1. -1631.

Cyathiform (səi·ǎþifǭɹm), *a.* 1776. [f. CYATHUS + -(I)FORM.] *Bot.*, etc. Shaped like a cup a little widened at the top.

Cyatholith (səiæ·þoliþ). 1875. [f. CYATHUS + -LITH.] *Biol.* A kind of coccolith resembling two cups placed base to base.

Cyathophylloid (səi:ǎþofi·loid). 1862. [f. mod.L. *Cyathophyllum* (f. Gr. κύαθος + φύλλον) + -OID.] *adj.* Akin to the fossil cup-corals of the genus *Cyathophyllum.* *sb.* A coral of this family 1872.

Cyathozooid (səi,ǎþozōᵘ·oid). 1877. [f. Gr. κύαθος CYATHUS + ZOOID.] *Zool.* An abortive first stage of the embryo of certain compound ascidians, which becomes by gemmation the foundation of a colony.

‖**Cyathus** (səi·ǎþŏs). Pl. **cyathi** (-þəi). ME. [a. L., a. Gr. κύαθος wine-cup, measure.] 1. *Gr. and Rom. Antiq.* A cup or ladle used for drawing wine out of the CRATER or mixing-bowl; also a measure = about $^1/_{12}$ of a pint. 2. *Bot.* The cup-like body which contains the reproductive bodies of *Marchantia* 1866.

Cycad (səi·kǎd). 1845. [ad. mod.L. generic name *Cycas, -adis*, a. supposed Gr. κύκας, scribal error for κόϊκας, acc. pl. of κόϊξ, the Egyptian doum-palm.] *Bot.* A plant of the genus *Cycas* which gives its name to the *Cycadaceæ*, a natural order of Gymnosperms, related to the Conifers. Hence **Cycada·ceous** *a.* of or belonging to the N.O. *Cycadaceæ* or Cycads; var. **Cyca·deous.** **Cyca·diform** *a.* resembling the cycads in form. **Cy·cadite,** a fossil c.

Cyclamen (si·klǎmen). 1550. [med. and mod.L., L. *cyclamīnos* or *-on*, Gr. κυκλάμινος, ?f. κύκλος.] A genus of *Primulaceæ*, cultivated for their handsome early-blooming flowers; the fleshy root-stocks are sought after by swine, whence the name SOWBREAD. Also, a plant of this genus.

Cyclamin (si·klǎmin). 1842. [f. prec.] *Chem.* A poisonous principle extracted from the tubers of Cyclamen; it is a non-azotized glucoside.

‖**Cyclarthrosis** (siklǎɹþrōᵘ·sis). [mod.L., f. Gr. κύκλος + ἄρθρωσις.] *Anat.* A circular or rotatory articulation, as that of the radius with the ulna. So **Cyclarthro·dial** *a.* of, or of the nature of, a c.

‖**Cyclas** (si·klǎs). *Hist.* [L., a. Gr. κυκλάς.] A tightly-fitting tunic anciently worn by women, and occas. by men, *esp.* the tunic or surcoat made shorter in front than behind, worn by knights over their armour in the 14th century. Also confused with CICLATOUN, q. v.

Cycle (səi·k'l), *sb.* ME. [a. F., or ad. L. *cyclus*, a. Gr. κύκλος.] 1. *Astron.* A circle or orbit in the heavens 1631. 2. A recurrent period of a definite number of years ME.; a period in which a certain round of events or phenomena is completed, recurring in the same order in equal succeeding periods 1662; a long indefinite period; an age 1842. 3. A recurrent round or course (of successive events, phenomena, etc.) 1664. 4. *gen.* A round, course, or period through which anything runs to its completion 1821. 5. A complete set; a round 1662. 6. *spec.* A series of poems or prose romances collected round a central event or epoch of mythic history and forming a continuous narrative: as *the Arthurian c.*, (*Mus.*) *c. of songs* 1835. 7. *Bot.* A complete turn of the spire in leaf-arrangement 1857. 8. *Med.* A course of remedies, continued during a fixed series of days 1882. 9. *Zool.* In corals, a set of septa of like age 1877. 10. *Geom.* A closed path in a cyclic region 1881. b. *Thermodynamics.* A series of operations at the end of which the working substance is brought back to its original state 1929. c. *Electr.* A full period of an alternating current. 11. Short for *bicycle, tricycle*, or the like 1881. Also *attrib.*

2. *C. of Indiction*: see INDICTION. *Metonic* or *lunar c.*: a c. of 19 years, established by the Greek astronomer Meton, and used for determining Easter. *Solar c.*: a period of 28 years, at the end of which the days of the week recur on the same days of the month. The c. within which dearths and plenties make their revolution PETTY. A c. of Cathay TENNYSON. 4. Doctrines which have run their c. 1869. Hence **Cy·cled** *ppl. a.* consisting of cycles, as *cycled times.*

Cycle (səi·k'l), *v.* 1842. [f. prec. sb. Cf. Gr. κυκλεῖν.] 1. *intr.* To move in cycles; to pass through cycles. 2. To ride a cycle, to travel by cycle 1883. Hence **Cy·cler** = CYCLIST 1. **Cy·cling** *vbl. sb.*

Cy·clian, *a.* *rare.* 1699. [f. Gr. κύκλιος + AN.] = CYCLIC 2, 3.

Cyclic (si·klik), *a.* 1794. [ad. L. *cyclicus*, a. Gr. κυκλικός, f. κύκλος CYCLE.] 1. Of, pertaining to, or of the nature of, a cycle; moving in cycles. 2. Of or belonging to a cycle of mythic and heroic story; see CYCLE *sb.* 6. 1822. Also *transf.* 3. *Bot.* Of a flower: Having its parts arranged in whorls 1875. 4. *Math.* Of or pertaining to a circle or cycle 1852. 5. *Gr. Prosody.* Of a dactyl or anapæst: Occupying in scansion three instead of four times 1844.

1. Twenty c. years, of ten months each ARNOLD. 2. *C. poet.*: one of the writers of the Epic cycle. 3. *C. region* (*Math.*): a region within which a closed line can be drawn in such a manner that it cannot shrink indefinitely without passing out of the region. Phr. *C. chorus* [Gr. κύκλιος χορός] in *Gr. Antiq.*: the dithyrambic chorus, which was danced in a ring round the altar of Dionysus.

Cyclical (si·klikǎl), *a.* 1817. [f. as prec. + -AL.] 1. Of a line: Returning into itself so as to form a closed curve (*rare*). 2. = CYCLIC 1, 2, 3 (also *transf.* in *Zool.*).

Phr. *C. number*: a number in which the sum of the divisors equals the whole.

Cyclide (səi·klid, si·kləid). 1874. [a. F., f. CYCLE.] *Geom.* 'The envelope of a sphere whose centre moves on a fixed quadric, and which cuts a fixed sphere orthogonally' (Salmon).

Cyclist (səi·klist). 1882. [f. CYCLE *sb.* + -IST.] 1. One who rides a cycle. 2. One who reckons by a cycle or cycles; one who recognizes cycles in the course of phenomena.

‖**Cyclitis** (sikləi·tis). 1861. [f. Gr. κύκλος + -ITIS.] *Path.* Inflammation of the ciliary body.

Cyclo- (səiklo, siklo), comb. f. Gr. κύκλος circle (see CYCLE), as in:

Cyclobra·nchiate *a.* [Gr. βράγχια gills], having gills circularly arranged; applied to a sub-order of gastropodous molluscs (*Cyclobranchia, -branchiata*); also said of the gills. **Cycloce·phalus** [Gr. κεφαλή], a monster having two contiguous eyes, or a double eye in the median line. **Cyclocli·nal** *a.* *Geol.* = QUAQUAVERSAL. **Cyclocœ·lic** *a* [Gr. κοιλία], having the intestines coiled: said of birds. **Cy·clogen** [Gr. -γενης], *Bot.* = EXOGEN; so **Cyclo·genous** *a.* **Cy·clograph** [Gr. -γραφος], an instrument for tracing circular arcs. **Cyclo·grapher,** a writer of a cycle (of legends, etc.). **Cy·clolith** [Gr. λίθος], a name for a prehistoric stone circle. **Cycloneu·rous, -ose** *a.* *Zool.*, having the nervous axis circularly arranged, as in the *Radiata.* **Cyclo·pterous** *a.* [Gr. πτερόν], round-winged, round-finned. **Cy·closcope** [Gr. -σκοπος], (*a*) an apparatus for measuring velocity of revolution; (*b*) an instrument for setting out railway curves. **Cyclospe·rmous** *a.* [Gr. σπέρμα] *Bot.*, having the embryo coiled about the central albumen. **Cyclo·stomate, -sto·matous, -stomous** *a.* [Gr. στόμα], having a round sucking mouth, or a circular aperture of the shell; also belonging to a certain division of the Polyzoa (*Cyclostomata*). **Cy·clostome** *a.* = *Cyclostomous*; *sb.* a cyclostomous fish, as the lamprey; a cyclostomous gastropod. **Cyclosy·stem,** the circular arrangement of the pores in some *Hydrocorallina* (Millepores, etc.).

Cyclode (səi·klōᵘd, si·k-). [f. Gr. κύκλος + ὁδός.] *Math.* The INVOLUTE of any order to a circle. SYLVESTER.

Cycloid (səi·kloid, si·k-), *sb.* 1661. [See next.] 1. *Math.* The curve traced in space by a point in the circumference (or on a radius) of a circle as the circle rolls along a straight line. 2. *Zool.* A cycloid fish; see next 1847.

1. The *common c.* is that traced by a point in the circumference of the circle, and has cusps where this point meets the straight line; that traced by a point within the circle is a *prolate c.* (with inflexions); by a point without the circle a *curtate c.* (with loops).

Cy·cloid, *a.* 1847. [ad. Gr. κυκλοειδής; see CYCLE.] *Zool.* a. Said of the scales of certain fishes: Of a somewhat circular form, with concentric striations. b. Belonging to the *Cycloidei*, or order of fishes with cycloid scales.

Cycloidal (səikloi·dǎl, sik-), *a.* 1704. [f. as prec.] 1. *Geom.* Of, pertaining to, or of the form of a cycloid. 2. *Zool.* = CYCLOID *a.* a.

Cycloi·dean. Also **-ian.** 1837. [f. mod.L. *cycloideus*; see CYCLOID *a.* and -AN.] *adj.* Belonging to the cycloid fishes. *sb.* A cycloid fish.

Cyclometer (səiklǫ·mǐtəɹ). 1815. [f. Gr. κύκλος + μέτρον.] 1. An instrument for measuring circular arcs. 2. An apparatus attached to a wheel, *esp.* of a cycle, for registering its revolutions. So **Cyclo·metry,** measurement of circles.

Cyclone (səi·klōᵘn). 1848. [f. Gr. κύκλος or κυκλῶν.] *gen.* A term for all atmospheric disturbances in which the wind has a circular or whirling course. b. *spec.* A hurricane of limited diameter and destructive violence 1856. c. *Meteorol.* A system of winds rotating around a centre of minimum barometric pressure, the centre and whole system having itself also a motion of translation, which is sometimes arrested, when the cyclone becomes for a time stationary. (Cf. ANTICYCLONE.) Also *transf.* Hence **Cyclo·nal** *a.* of or pertaining to a c. So **Cyclo·nic, -al** *a.* cyclonal; of the nature of a c. **Cyclo·nically** *adv.*

Cyclop; see CYCLOPS.

Cyclopædia, -pedia (səiklopī·diǎ). 1636. [Abbrev. of ENCYCLOPÆDIA, q.v.] †1. = ENCYCLOPÆDIA 1. -1676. 2. = ENCYCLOPÆDIA 2, 3. 1728. Hence **Cyclopæ·dic, -pedic** *a.* pertaining to or of the nature of a c. **Cyclopæ·dically** *adv.* in a cyclopædic manner.

Cyclopean, -ian (səiklopī·ǎn, səiklōᵘ·piǎn), *a.* 1641. [f. L. *Cyclopeus*, f. (ult.) Gr. κύκλωψ a Cyclops.] 1. Belonging to or resembling the Cyclopes; monstrous, huge; single, or large and round, like the one eye of a Cyclops. 2. Applied to an ancient style of masonry in which the stones are immense and irregular in shape; fabled to be the work of a gigantic Thracian race called Cyclopes. Also *transf.* 1835.

Cyclopia (səiklōᵘ·piǎ). 1839. [f. Gr. κύκλωψ; see below.] *Zool.*, etc. The fusion of two eyes into one place in the middle of the forehead, as in a Cyclops.

Cyclopic, †-al (səiklǫ·pik, -ǎl), *a.*[1] 1633. [ad. Gr. κυκλωπικός.] Belonging to or resembling a Cyclops; monstrous; Cyclopean.

Cyclo·pic, *a.*[2] 1879. [f. botanical name *Cyclopia.*] *Chem.* In *c. acid*: an acid obtained from *Cyclopia Vogelii*, a plant used in Africa for the preparation of tea.

Cyclopoid (si·klopoid, səi·-). 1852. [f. mod. L. *Cyclops* (in Zool.) + -OID.] *adj.* Belonging to, or resembling the family *Cyclopidæ* of Copepods, of which the genus Cyclops is the type. *sb.* One of the *Cyclopidæ.*

‖**Cyclops** (səi·klǫps). Also **Cyclop.** Pl. **Cyclopes** (səiklōᵘ·pīz); also **Cyclops, Cyclopses.** 1513. [a. L., a. Gr. Κύκλωψ lit. 'round-eyed', f. κύκλος + ὤψ. In F. *Cyclope*, whence Eng. *Cyclop.*] 1. *Gr. Mythol.* One of a race of one eyed giants who forged thunderbolts for Zeus. 2. *Zool.* A genus of small fresh-water copepods, having an eye (really double) situated in the middle of the front of the head 1849. Also *attrib.*

1. Such an obdurate C., to have but one eye for this text MILT. The Cyclop from his den replies POPE.

Cyclorama (səiklorɑ·mǎ). 1840. [mod. f. Gr. κύκλος + ὅραμα.] A picture of a landscape, etc., arranged on the inside of a cylindrical surface, the spectator standing in the middle. Hence **Cyclora·mic** *a.*

Cyclosis (səiklō·sis). 1835. [a. Gr. κύκλωσις.] **1.** *Biol.* A term for the circulation of latex in the vessels of plants; also for the circulation of protoplasm in certain cells. **2.** *Math.* The occurrence of cycles (see CYCLE 10) 1881.

Cyclostylar (səiklǫstəi·lăɹ), *a.* 1850. [f. Gr. κύκλος + στῦλος + -AR.] *Archit.* Relating to a structure composed of a circular range of columns without a core.

Cyclostyle (səi·klǫstəil). 1883. [f. Gr. κύκλος + STYLE, L. *stilus.*] An apparatus for printing copies of writing. It consists of a pen with a small toothed wheel at the point which cuts minute holes in specially prepared paper; this paper is then used as a stencil-plate from which copies are printed.

Cyclo·tomy. 1879. [f. Gr. κύκλος + -τομια.] **1.** *Math.* The problem of the division of the circle into a number of equal parts. **2.** *Surg.* Division of the ciliary muscle 1889.

‖**Cyclus** (si·klǫ̆s, səi·klǫ̆s). 1810. [L.] = CYCLE 6.

Cyder, var. of CIDER.

‖**Cydippe** (səidi·pī). 1835. [mod.L., a. Gr. Κυδίππη, one of the Nereids.] *Zool.* A typical genus of Ctenophora, including *C. pilosa.* Hence **Cydi·ppian** *a.* **Cydi·ppid,** a ctenophoran of the family of C.

†**Cydon.** *rare.* 1643. [f. L. *cydonia* (sc. *mala*), f. *Cydonia,* Κυδωνία a town of Crete.] Quince. **Cy·donin,** mucilage of quince seeds.

Cyesiology (səi,īsiǫ·lŏdʒi). 1846. [f. Gr. κύησις pregnancy.] That branch of physiology which treats of pregnancy.

Cygneous (si·gni,əs), *a.* 1880. [f. L. *cygnus* swan.] Swan-like; in *Bryology,* curved like a swan's neck.

Cygnet (si·gnėt). ME. [A dim. of F. *cygne* or L. *cygnus* swan.] A young swan; *Her.* a swan borne in coat-armour.

So doth the Swan her downie Signets saue SHAKS.

Cylinder (si·lindəɹ). 1570. [ad. L. *cylindrus,* a. Gr. κύλινδρος, deriv. of κυλίνδειν to roll.] **1.** *Geom.* A solid figure of which the two ends are equal and parallel circles, and the intervening curved surface is such as would be traced by a line moving parallel to itself with its ends in the circumferences of these circles. **2.** Any body or object of cylindrical form 1641. **3.** *Mechanics.* Applied to many cylindrical parts of machines, etc.; *e.g.* the bore of a gun barrel, the part of a revolver which contains the chambers for the cartridges; the barrel of a pump, in which the piston works; the cylindrical chamber in which the steam acts upon the piston; in *Printing,* the roller used in letter-press printing for inking the type (now *inking-roller*), pressing the paper against the type, or carrying the type or printing surface; etc.

Comb.: **c.-axis** = axis-cylinder (see AXIS[1]); **-bore,** (*a*) *sb.* a gun of which the bore is of uniform diameter; (*b*) *vb.* to make with a cylindrical bore; **-cock,** a cock at the end of the c. in a steam-engine to allow water of condensation to escape; **-cover,** the steam-tight lid at the end of a steam-c.; **-escapement,** a form of watch escapement (also called *horizontal escapement*); **-press** (U.S.), **-printing-machine,** a machine in which a c. is used either for carrying the type or giving the impression; **-watch,** one with a c.-escapement.

Cylindra·ceous, *a.* 1676. [Cf. F. *cylindracé.*] Like a cylinder in shape, cylindrical.

‖**Cylindrenchema** (silindre·ŋkimă). 1835. [f. Gr. κύλινδρος + ἔγχυμα infusion.] *Bot.* Tissue consisting of cylindrical cells.

Cylindric (sili·ndrik), *a.* 1688. [ad. mod.L. *cylindricus*; see -IC.] Having the form of a cylinder, cylindrical.

Cylindrical (sili·ndrikăl), *a.* 1646. [f. as prec. + -AL.] **1.** Of the form of a cylinder. **2.** Of, pertaining, or relating to a cylinder 1656.

1. *C. lens*: a lens of which one or both surfaces are portions of c. surfaces. *C. vault*: 'one in the shape of the segment of a cylinder' (Gwilt). **2.** *C. projection*: a form of projection in which part of a spherical surface is projected upon the surface of a cylinder, which is then unrolled into a plane. Hence **Cyli·ndrically** *adv.*

Cylindriform (sili·ndrifǭɹm), *a.* 1870. [f. L. *cylindrus* + -FORM.] Of the form of a cylinder.

Cylindro- (sili·ndro), comb. f. Gr. κύλινδρος CYLINDER, as in **Cylindrome·tric** *a.,* relating to the measurement of cylinders; etc.

Cylindroid (sili·ndroid, si·-). 1663. [f. as prec.; see -OID.] *adj.* Resembling a cylinder; somewhat cylindrical in form 1839. *sb.* A figure resembling a cylinder; *spec.* an elliptic cylinder. So **Cylindroi·dal** *a.*

‖**Cylix** (si·liks). 1850. [Gr. κύλιξ.] *Gr. Antiq.* A shallow cup with a tall stem; a tazza.

‖**Cyma** (səi·mă). 1563. [mod.L., a. Gr. κῦμα anything swollen, a wave, etc.] **1.** *Archit.* A moulding of a cornice, the outline of which consists of a concave and a convex line; an ogee. **2.** *Bot.* = CYME 1, 2. 1706.

1. *C. recta*: a moulding concave in its upper part, and convex below. *C. reversa* (rarely *inversa*): a moulding convex in its upper part, and concave below.

Cymagraph (səi·măgrɑf). 1837. [erron. f. prec. + Gr. -γραφος.] An instrument for copying mouldings.

‖**Cymaise** (simē̆·z). 1656. [F., ad. L. *cymatium.*] = CYMA, CYMATIUM.

Cymar (simā·ɹ). Also †**simar, symar.** 1641. [ad. F. *simarre*; see CHIMER, SIMAR.] **1.** A loose light garment for women, *esp.* a chemise. **2.** = CHIMER 1673.

1. Disrobed of all clothing saving a c. of white silk SCOTT.

Cymatium (simæ·tiǒm, -ē·ʃiǒm). 1563. [a. Gr. κυμάτιον, dim. of κῦμα.] *Archit.* = CYMA.

Cymbal (si·mbəl). OE. [ad. L. *cymbalum,* a. Gr. κύμβαλον, deriv. of κύμβη hollow of a vessel, cup.] **1.** One of a pair of concave plates of brass or bronze, which are struck together to produce a sharp ringing sound. Also *transf.* Also *fig.* (with ref. to *1 Cor.* xiii. 1). **2.** A kind of stop on an organ 1852.

1. In vain with cymbals' ring They call the grisly king MILT. Hence **Cy·mbaled** *ppl. a.,* (*a*) furnished with cymbals; (*b*) produced or accompanied by cymbals. **Cy·mbalist, Cy·mballer,** a player on the cymbals.

‖**Cymbalo** (si·mbălǫ). 1879. [ad. It. *cembalo, cimbalo,* repr. L. *cymbalum,* but applied to the dulcimer.] The DULCIMER, q. v.

Cy·mbiform, *a.* 1836. [f. L. *cymba*; see -FORM.] *Bot.,* etc. Boat-shaped.

Cyme (səim). Also †**cime.** 1725. [a. F. *cime, cyme* 'top, summit':—pop.L. *cima* = L. *cyma* (see above).] †**1.** (*cime.*) A head (of unexpanded leaves, etc.) (*rare*). **2.** *Bot.* (*cyme.*) A centrifugal or definite inflorescence wherein the primary axis bears a single terminal flower which develops first: opp. to RACEME. Applied *esp.* to inflorescences of this type forming a more or less flat head. 1794. **3.** *Archit.* = CYMA 1877. Hence **Cy·mule,** a small c.

Cyme (*Macb.* V. iii. 55, 1st Fol.), ? erron. for *cynne,* SENNA.

Cymene (səi·mīn). 1863. [f. Gr. κύμινον CUMIN.] *Chem.* A hydrocarbon, $C_{10}H_{14}$, discovered in 1840 in oil of cumin, and in other plants. So **Cy·midine,** a base, $C_{10}H_{15}N$. **Cy·mol** = *Cymene.*

Cy·mling; see SIMLIN, a kind of squash.

Cy:mobotryo·se, *a.* 1882. [f. L. *cyma* + BOTRYOSE.] Used of cymes arranged in a racemose manner.

Cymogene (səi·mǫdʒīn). 1882. [f. *cymo-* deriv. of CYMENE + -GENE.] A gaseous substance, consisting chiefly of butane, given off during the distillation of crude paraffin, used condensed as a freezing-mixture.

Cy·moid, *a.* 1815. [f. CYMA + -OID.] Resembling a cyma.

Cymophane (səi·mofēⁱn). 1804. [f. Gr. κυμο, comb. f. κῦμα + -φανης.] = CHRYSOBERYL. Hence **Cymo·phanous** *a.* having a wavy, floating light; chatoyant.

Cymose (səimōᵘ·s), *a.* 1807. [ad. L. *cymosus,* f. *cyma*; see -OSE.] *Bot.* Bearing cymes; of the nature of a cyme; arranged in a cyme. (Of an inflorescence = *centrifugal* or *definite*; opp. to *racemose.*) Hence **Cymo·sely** *adv.* in a c. manner. var. **Cy·mous** (Dicts.).

Cymric (ki·mrik), *a.* 1839. [f. Welsh *Cymru* Wales, *Cymry* the Welsh, pl. of *Cymro,* prob. repr. ancient *Combrox* compatriot (cf. *Allobrox*).] Of or pertaining to the Welsh people or language.

‖**Cynanche** (sinæ·ŋkī). 1706. [L., a. Gr. κυνάγχη, f. κυν- dog + ἄγχειν to throttle; cf. QUINSY.] *Path.* A name for diseases of the throat, marked by inflammation, swelling, and difficulty of breathing, etc.; *esp.* QUINSY.

Cynanthropy (sinæ·nþrǒpi). 1594. [mod. f. Gr. κυνάνθρωπος lit. dog-man.] A species of madness in which a man imagines himself to be a dog.

Cynarctomachy (sinaɹktǫ·măki). [f. Gr. κυν- dog + ἄρκτος bear + -μαχια fighting.] Bear-baiting. BUTLER *Hud.* I. i. 752.

Cynareous (sinēᵊ·riəs), *a.* 1846. [f. mod. L. *Cynareæ,* f. *Cynara* artichoke.] *Bot.* Belonging to the order *Cynaraceæ* proposed by Lindley of Composite plants, including the thistles, artichoke, burdock, etc. So **Cy·naroid** *a.* allied to the artichoke.

†**Cyne-** (künə-, kinə-), in OE. = royal; occurring in many compounds, as **cynebót** (see BOOT *sb.*[1]), the king's boot, compensation paid to the people for the murder of the king; etc.

Cynegetic (sinīdʒe·tik). *rare.* 1646. [ad. Gr. κυνηγετικός, f. κυνηγέτης, f. κυν- dog + ἡγέτης leader.] *adj.* Relating to the chase 1716. *sb. pl.* **Cynegetics**: the chase.

Cynic (si·nik). 1547. [ad. L. *cynicus,* a. Gr., f. κύων, κυνός dog.]

A. *adj.* **1.** Belonging to or characteristic of the sect of philosophers called Cynics; see B. 1. 1634. **2.** Having the qualities of a cynic (see B. 2); pertaining to a cynic; cynical 1597.

2. The c. smile..the signal of a contempt which he was too haughty to express DISRAELI.

Phr. *C. year* or *period*: the canicular cycle of the ancient Egyptians; see CANICULAR. *C. spasm*: a convulsive contraction of the facial muscles of one side, so that the teeth are shown in the manner of an angry dog (*Syd. Soc. Lex.*).

B. *sb.* **1.** One of a sect of philosophers in ancient Greece, founded by Antisthenes, a pupil of Socrates, who contemned ease, wealth, and the enjoyments of life. The most famous was Diogenes, who carried the principles of the sect to an extreme. 1547. **2.** A person disposed to rail or find fault; now usually: One disposed to deny and sneer at the sincerity or goodness of human motives and actions 1596.

1. Like the Cynique shut up alwaye in a Tub HOWELL. **2.** The c., who admires and enjoys nothing, despises and censures everything 1866.

Hence **Cy·nical** *a.* resembling the C. philosophers; surly, currish, misanthropic, captious; now *esp.* disposed to deny human sincerity and goodness; dog-like. **Cy·nically** *adv.*

Cynicism (si·nisiz'm). 1672. [f. CYNIC + -ISM.] **1.** (*with capital C.*) The philosophy of the Cynics; see CYNIC B. 1. **2.** Cynical disposition, character, or quality 1672; an instance of cynicism 1891.

2. The c. of his measured vice LYTTON. var. **Cy·nism** (*rare*).

‖**Cynips** (si·nips). 1777. [Formed by Linnæus from Gr. κυν- dog + ἴψ a kind of cynips (Darmesteter).] *Entom.* The typical genus of the gall-flies, hymenopterous insects which puncture plants in order to deposit their eggs, and thus produce galls or gall-nuts. Hence **Cy·nipid,** an insect of the *Cynipidæ,* or family allied to *Cynips.* **Cynipi·dean, -deous, Cyni·pidous** *adjs.* of or pertaining to the *Cynipidæ.*

Cyno-, a. Gr. κυνο-, comb. f. κύων (κυν-) dog; occurring in many compounds, technical terms, and nonce-words; as **Cy·noclept** [Gr. κλέπτης], a dog-stealer; etc.

‖**Cynocephalus** (sinǫ-, səinǫse·fălǒs). Pl. **-i.** ME. [L., a. Gr., f. κυνο- dog- + κεφαλή head.] **1.** One of a fabled race of men with dogs' heads. **2.** The Dog-faced Baboon. In *Zool.* taken as the name of the genus. 1601. Hence **Cynoce·phalous** *a.* pertaining to or of the nature of a c.; dog-headed.

Cynoid (si·noid), *a.* [ad. Gr. κυνοειδής.] Dog-like; belonging to the *Cynoidea* or canine division of the *Carnivora.*

Cynomorphic (sinǫ-, səinǫmǭ·ɹfik), *a.* 1892. [f. (ult.) Gr. κυνόμορφος, f. κυνο- dog- + μορφή form.] **1.** *Zool.* Belonging to the division

Cynomorpha of catarrhine monkeys. **2.** (after *anthropomorphic.*) Relating to a dog's ways of looking at things. So **Cynomo·rphism.**

Cynosure (si·nŏ-, səi·nŏsiuı). 1596. [a. F., ad. L. *cynosura* (also used), a. Gr. κυνόσουρα dog's tail, Ursa Minor.] **1.** The constellation Ursa Minor, which contains in its tail the Pole-star. **2.** *fig.* **a.** Something that serves to direct 1596. **b.** Something that is a centre of attraction 1601.

2. Some beauty .. The C. of neighbouring eyes MILT. Hence **Cynosu·ral** *a.* relating to or like a c.

Cynthia (si·nþiă). 1632. [L. *Cynthia* (*dea*), the Cynthian goddess, *i. e.* Artemis or Diana, born on Mount Cynthus; hence the Moon.] A name for the Moon personified as a goddess. Hence **Cy·nthian** *a.*

While C. checks her dragon yoke MILT. *Pens.* 59.

Cyperaceous (sipĕrēⁱ·ʃəs), *a.* 1852. [f. Bot. L. *Cyperaceæ*, f. *Cyperus*; see -ACEOUS.] *Bot.* Belonging to the *Cyperaceæ* or Sedges.

‖**Cyperus** (səipī·rŏs, səi·pĕrŏs). 1597. [L., a. Gr. κύπειρος, κύπερος (Herod.), an aromatic marsh-plant.] *Bot.* A large genus of endogenous plants, giving its name to the N.O. *Cyperaceæ*. *C. longus* is the Sweet Cyperus, or English Galingale.

‖**Cyphella** (səife·lă). Pl. **-æ.** 1857. [ad. Gr. κύφελλα (pl.) the hollows of the ears.] *Bot.* A cup-like depression on the under surface of the thallus of some lichens.

Cypher, var. of CIPHER.

Cyphonism (səi·fŏniz'm). 1727. [ad. Gr. κυφωνισμός, f. κύφων, f. κυφός bent.] *Gr. Antiq.* Punishment by the κύφων, a pillory in which slaves or criminals were fastened by the neck.

‖**Cypho·sis.** Also **ky-.** 1847. [mod.L., a. Gr. κύφωσις, f. κυφός bent.] *Path.* Backward curvature of the spine; hump-back. Hence **Cypho·tic** *a.* hump-backed.

‖**Cypræa** (səiprī·ă). [mod.L. f. *Cypria* a name of Venus.] *Zool.* The genus of gastropods containing the cowries. Hence **Cypræ·id,** a gastropod of the cowrie family, *Cypræidæ*. **Cypræ·oid** *a.*

†**Cy·pre.** ME. [ad. L. *cyprus* (also used), a. Gr. (from Κύπρος Cyprus).] **1.** The henna-shrub (*Lawsonia alba* or *inermis*) -1558. ¶ **2.** Confused with CYPRESS[1]. -1632.

‖**Cy pres** (sī prē̩). 1481. [Late AFr. = F. *si près* so near, as near.] *Law.* As near as practicable: applied to a process in equity by which effect is given to the general intention of a trust or charity, when a literal execution of the testator's intention becomes impossible. (Used as *adv.*, *sb.*, and *adj.*)

Cypress[1] (səi·prĕs). [ME. *cipres, cypres,* etc., a. OF. *ciprès*, ad. late L. *cypressus*, ad. Gr. κυπάρισσος.] **1.** A well-known coniferous tree, *Cupressus sempervirens*, with hard durable wood and dense dark foliage. Hence, the English name of the genus. **b.** The wood of this tree. ME. **c.** The branches or sprigs of the tree, used at funerals, or as a symbol of mourning. Also *fig.* 1590. **2.** Applied to various trees and shrubs allied to the true cypress, as **Bald, Black,** or **Deciduous C.,** *Taxodium distichum*; etc. Also, to plants taken to resemble the cypress-tree, as **Field C.,** *Ajuga Chamæpitys*; **Summer C.,** *Kochia scoparia*; etc. **3.** *attrib.* Of cypress; cypress-like; dark, gloomy, funereal 1596.

1. c. But that remorseless iron hour Made c. of her orange-flower TENNYSON. *Comb.* **c.-vine,** a name of several American species of *Ipomæa*, convolvulaceous climbing plants.

†**Cy·press**[2]. ME. [Corrupt f. L. *cyperus*, app. confused with prec.] The Sweet Cyperus or Galingale -1799.

†**Cy·press**[3]. ME. [prob. f. OF. *Cipre, Cypre,* the island of Cyprus.] **1.** A name of textile fabrics originally brought from Cyprus. **a.** A cloth of gold or the like. **b.** A valuable satin, called also *satin of Cypres, satin Cypres*. -1603. **c.** *esp.* (= *C. lawn*) A light transparent material resembling cobweb lawn or crape -1722. **2.** A piece of cypress, used in sign of mourning, and the like -1717. **3.** *attrib.* Of cypress -1678; like cypress in texture or colour -1713.

Cyprian (si·priăn). 1598. [f. L. *Cyprius.*] **A.** *adj.* **1.** Belonging to Cyprus, an island once famous for the worship of Aphrodite 1627. **2.** *transf.* Licentious, lewd 1599.

B. *sb.* An inhabitant or native of Cyprus, a Cypriote; hence *transf.* A licentious person; in later use *spec.* a prostitute 1598.

Cyprine (si·prəin, -in), *a.* 1828. [ad. L. *cyprinus*, a. Gr. κυπρῖνος carp.] *Ichth.* Belonging to the carp genus *Cyprinus*, or the carp family, *Cyprinidæ*

Cyprinid (siprəi·nid). [f. mod.L. *Cyprinidæ*; see prec.] *Ichth.* A fish of the carp family. So **Cypri·niform** *a.* carp-shaped.

Cyprinodont (siprəi·nodǫnt). 1857. [f. L. *cyprinus* carp + Gr. ὀδοντ- tooth.] *sb.* A malacopterygious fish of the family *Cyprinodontidæ*, of which the typical genus is *Cyprinodon*. *adj.* Of or belonging to this family. Hence **Cyprinodo·ntid, -do·ntoid** *a.* of or allied to the Cyprinodonts.

Cyprinoid (siprəi·noid). 1849. [f. as prec. + -OID.] *Ichth. adj.* Resembling or allied to the carp; belonging to the *Cyprinoidea* 1859. *sb* A fish belonging to the *Cyprinoidea*.

‖**Cypripe·din.** 1863. [f. F. *cypripède* = Bot. L. *Cypripedium* Lady's slipper, app. a corruption of *Cypripodium*, f. Gr. Κύπρις Aphrodite + ποδίς shoe.] *Med.* A brown powder prepared from the roots of *Cypripedium pubescens*; used as an antispasmodic.

‖**Cypris** (səi·pris). 1832. [mod.L., a. Gr. Κύπρις Aphrodite.] *Zool.* A genus of minute fresh-water crustacea, having the body enclosed in a delicate bivalve shell. Hence **Cy·proid,** a crustacean allied to the C.

Cyprus, cyprus-lawn; see CYPRESS 3.

Cyprus (*Bot.*); see CYPRE.

‖**Cypsela** (si·psĭlă). 1870. [mod.L., ad. Gr. κυψέλη hollow vessel, chest, etc.] *Bot.* A kind of dry one-seeded fruit; an achene with an adnate calyx, as in the *Compositæ*. Hence **Cy·pselous** *a.* of the nature of a C.

Cypseline (si·psĭləin), *a.* 1874. [f. L. *cypselus*, a. Gr. κύψελος the swift.] *Zool.* Of the family *Cypselidæ* or genus *Cypselus* of birds, comprising the Swifts. So **Cy·pseliform, Cy·pseloid** *adjs.* having the form of a Swift.

Cyrenaic (səirĭnē·ik). 1586. [ad. L. *Cyrenaicus*, a. Gr., f. Κυρήνη Cyrene, a Greek colony in Africa.] *adj.* Belonging to the school of Aristippus of Cyrene, whose doctrine was one of practical hedonism 1641. *sb.* A Cyrenaic philosopher. Hence **Cyrena·icism,** the C. doctrine. So **Cyrene·an, Cyre·nian** *adjs.*

Cyrillic (siri·lik), *a.* 1881. [f. the proper name *Cyril.*] Applied to the alphabet employed by the Slavs of the Eastern Church, and ascribed to St. Cyril. The Cyrillic alphabet is distinguished from the Glagolitic (see Addenda).

Cyriologic, -al (siriolǫ·dʒik, -ăl), *a.* 1655. The analogical form of CURIOLOGIC, -AL.

Cyrto- (sɔ̄ıto-), repr. Gr. κυρτο- from κυρτός curved. Hence **Cyrtoce·ratite** *Palæont.*, a fossil cephalopod of the genus *Cyrtoceras*, having the shell incurved. So **Cyrtocerati·tic, Cyrto·ceran** *adjs.*; **Cyrtoce·ratid. Cy·rtoid** *a.*, resembling a hump on the back. **Cy·rtolite** *Min.*, a variety of zircon with the pyramidal planes convex (Dana). **Cyrto·meter,** an instrument for measuring and recording curves; **Cyrtome·tric** *a.*, **Cyrto·metry. Cy·rtostyle,** a circular portico projecting from a building.

Cyst (sist). 1720. [ad. mod.L. *cystis* (see CYSTIS).] **1.** *Biol.* A thin-walled hollow organ or cavity in an animal body (or plant) containing a liquid secretion; a bladder, sac, vesicle. **2.** *Path.* A closed cavity or sac of an abnormal character, usually containing morbid matter 1731. **3.** *Biol.*, etc. A cell or cavity containing reproductive bodies, embryos, etc.; *e.g* the spore-case of certain fungi 1857.

Cyst-, comb. f. Gr. κύστις CYST bef. vowels (cf. CYSTI-, CYSTO-): as **Cysta·lgia** [Gr. ἄλγος] *Path.*, pain in the bladder, *esp.* of a spasmodic character. **Cyste·ctasy** [Gr. ἔκτασις], dilatation of the bladder.

Cysted (si·stĕd), *a. rare.* [f. CYST + -ED.] Encysted. (Dicts.)

Cysti- (sisti), comb. f. Gr. κύστις CYST; in many modern technical words: as **Cysti·colous** *a.* [L. *-colus*], inhabiting a cyst. **Cy·stiform** *a.*, of the form of a cyst. **Cysti·gerous** *a.* [L. *-ger*], bearing or containing cysts.

Cystic (si·stik), *a.* 1634. [a. F. *cystique*, ad. mod.L. *cysticus*; see CYST and -IC.] **1.** *Anat.* Pertaining to or connected with the gall-bladder: as *c. artery, duct.* **2.** Pertaining to the urinary bladder 1881. **3.** *Path.* Of the nature of a cyst; characterized by formation of cysts, containing cysts (CYST 2) 1713. **4.** Enclosed in a cyst, as a hydatid 1859.

2. *C. oxide* = CYSTINE. *C. calculus*, a urinary calculus containing cystine; so *c. urine.* **4.** In this condition the animal is..a C. worm, or bladder-worm HUXLEY.

‖**Cysticercus** (sistisɔ̄·ıkŏs). Pl. **-ci** (-səi). 1841. [mod.L., f. Gr. κύστις + κέρκος tail.] *Zool.* The scolex or larva of a tape-worm in its encysted state; a hydatid. Hence **Cystice·rcoid** *a.* and *sb.*

Cysticle (si·stik'l). 1855. [dim. of CYST; see -CULE.] A small cyst: applied to an organ, supposed to be that of hearing, in some *Acalephæ*.

Cystid (si·stid). 1862. [f. mod.L. *cystis* CYST + -ID.] **1.** *Geol.* A member of the order *Cystidea* or *Cystoidea* of fossil echinoderms. **2.** *Zool.* 'The sac-like ciliated embryo of some of the *Polyzoa*' 1877. var. (sense 1) **Cysti·dean.**

‖**Cysti·dium.** Pl. **-ia.** 1858. [mod.L., repr. Gr. type *κυστίδιον, dim. of κύστις: occas. **Cystide.**] *Bot.* One of the projecting cells originating among the basidia of hymenomycetous fungi, and supposed to be sterile basidia.

Cystine (si·stəin). Also **-in.** 1843. [mod. f. Gr. κύστις.] *Chem.* An organic base, $C_3NHO_7SO_2$, a yellowish crystalline substance, found in a rare kind of urinary calculus.

‖**Cystis** (si·stis). 1543. [med.L., a. Gr. κύστις.] = CYST.

‖**Cystitis** (sistəi·tis). 1776. [f. prec. + -ITIS.] *Path.* Inflammation of the bladder.

Cysto- (sisto), comb. f. Gr. κύστη = κύστις bladder, cyst; as in:

Cy·stocarp (*Bot.*) [Gr. καρπός], the sexual fruit of the *Florideæ*, a group of *Algæ*; hence **Cystoca·rpic** *a.* **Cy·stocele** [Gr. κήλη tumour, CELE], hernia of the bladder **Cy·stoplast** (*Biol.*) [Gr. πλαστός], a cell having a cell-wall. **Cystorrhœ·a** [Gr. ῥοία flux], vesical catarrh. **Cy·stoscope** [Gr. -σκοπος], *sb.* an instrument for examining the bladder; *v.* to examine (the bladder) with this instrument; hence **Cystosco·pic** *a.* **Cy·stotome** [Gr -τομος], an instrument for the operation of cystotomy. **Cysto·tomy** [Gr. -τομια], cutting into the bladder for extraction of a stone, etc.

Cystoid (si·stoid). 1871. [mod. f. Gr. κύστις.] **A.** *adj.* **1.** *Path.* Of the nature of a cyst. **2.** *Geol.* = CYSTID 1. 1876.

B. *sb. Path.* = CYST 2. 1872.

Cystolith (si·stolip). 1846. [f. CYSTO- + Gr. λίθος.] **1.** *Bot.* A club-shaped stratified outgrowth of the walls of some cells, containing minute crystals 1857. **2.** *Path.* Calculus of the bladder. Hence **Cystoli·thic** *a.*

‖**Cystoma** (sistōu·mă). Pl. **-mata.** 1872. [mod. f. Gr. κύστις.] *Path.* A tumour containing cysts. **b.** A cyst which is a new formation.

-cyte (səit). [ad. Gr. κύτος receptacle.] Frequent in comp. with the sense 'cell', as in *cystocyte*, etc.

Cytherean (siþĕrī·an). 1751. [f. L. *Cytherea* a name of Venus, from *Cythera.*] *adj.* Pertaining to Venus 1866. *sb.* A votaress of Venus; *spec.* a prostitute attached to an Indian temple.

Cytisine (si·tisəin). 1830. [mod. f. next + -INE.] *Chem.* A poisonous alkaloid, $C_{20}H_{23}N_3O$, extracted from the seeds of the Laburnum, *C. Laburnum.*

‖**Cytisus** (si·tisŏs). 1548. [L., a. Gr. κύτισος.] *Bot.* **a.** A shrubby plant mentioned by Greek and Roman writers; now identified with the Shrubby Medic, *Medicago arborea.* **b.** Adopted by Linnæus as the name of a genus of *Leguminosæ*, including the common Broom, the Laburnum, etc. *C. racemosus* is the *Cytisus* of florists.

Cytitis (sitəi·tis). [mod. f. Gr. κύτος skin + -ITIS.] Inflammation of the skin.

Cyto-, comb. f. Gr. κύτος receptacle, etc., taken as = 'cell': as

Cy·toblast (*Biol.*) [+-BLAST], the protoplasmic nucleus of a cell, regarded as the germinal spot from which development proceeds. **Cytoblaste·ma** (*Biol.*) [+ BLASTEMA], the protoplasm from which the cell is produced; hence **Cytoblaste·mal, -te·mic, -te·mous** *adjs.* **Cytococ·cus** [Gr. κόκκος berry], the nucleus of a *Cytula* or impregnated ovum (Haeckel). **Cy·tode** (*Biol.*) [+-ODE], a non-nucleated unicellular mass of protoplasm, the lowest form in which life is exhibited (Haeckel). **Cytoge·nesis**, the generation or production of cells; **Cytogene·tic** *a.*, pertaining to cytogenesis. **Cyto·genic, Cyto·genous** *adjs.*, producing cells. **Cyto·geny** = *cytogenesis.* **Cy·toid** *a.*, cell-like; also *sb.* **Cy·toplasm**, protoplasm; *spec.* the protoplasm of a cell as dist. from the nucleus; **Cytopla·smic** *a.*, pertaining to or consisting of cytoplasm; **Cy·toplast**, the unit of protoplasm contained in a cell. **Cytozo·a** *sb. pl.* (*Zool.*) [Gr. ζῷον], same as *Sporozoa* or *Gregarinida.*

‖**Cytula** (si·tiŭla). 1879. [mod.L., dim. f. CYTE = cell.] *Biol.* The parent cell of an organism; an impregnated ovum. Hence **Cy·tuloplasm**, the protoplasmic substance of a c.

Cyul, cyule. Mod. adaptations of *cyula*, latinized f. OE. *cēol, ciol*:—*ciul* KEEL, boat, etc.

Czar, tzar (tsāɹ, zāɹ). 1555. [Romanized spellings of Russ., repr. (ult.) L. *Cæsar.* The spelling with *cz-* is against Slavonic usage.] The title of the autocrat or emperor of Russia, borne also formerly by Servian rulers. Hence **Cza·rate, Cza·rship, ts-**, the office or position of c. or tsar. **Cza·rdom, ts-**, the dominion, office, or power of a c. or tsar. **Cza·rian, Cza·ric, Cza·rish, ts-** *adjs.* of or pertaining to a or the tsar. **Cza·rism, ts-**, the tsar's system of government.

‖**Czarevitch, -wich, tsar-** (tsā·rĕvitʃ, Russ. tsarē·vitʃ). 1710. [a. Russ. = 'son of a tsar'.] A son of a tsar. (The hereditary prince had the differentiated title *Cesare·vitch, -witch.*)

‖**Czarevna, ts-** (tsare·vna). 1880. [Russ.] A daughter of a tsar. (The title of the wife of the *Cesarevitch* was *Cesare·vna.*)

‖**Czarina, ts-** (tsarī·nă, za-). 1717. [ad. Ger. *czarin, zarin.*] The wife of a or the tsar. Also ‖**Czaritza, ts-** (tsarī·tsă). 1698.

Czech, Czekh (tʃek). 1841. [Boh.] Bohemian. **Cze·chian, Cze·chic, Cze·chish** *adjs.*

Czechoslovak (tʃekoslō·væk). 1917. A native of the state including Bohemia, Moravia, and the northern Slavs of the extinct Austrian Empire. Also as adj.; so **-a·kian.**

D

D (dī), the fourth letter of the Roman alphabet, corresponding to the Phœnician and Hebrew *Daleth*, and Greek *Delta*, Δ, whence also its form. It represents the sonant dental mute, or point-voice stop consonant. Its phonetic value in English is constant, except in pa. pples., where *-ed* after a breath-consonant is pronounced *t.* *pl.* D's, Ds, de's.

II. 1. Used to denote serial order, with the value of *fourth.* 2. *Mus.* The second note of the natural major scale. Also the scale or key which has that note for its tonic 1596. 3. In *Algebra*: see A, II.

III. *Abbreviations*, etc. 1. *d.* stands for L. *denarius*, and so for 'penny', 'pence'; as 1*d.* = one penny. †Formerly also, *d.* = one half (L. *dimidium*). 2. D, the sign for 500 in Roman numerals. [Understood to be the half of CIƆ, earlier form of M = 1000.] 3. D. = various proper names, as David, etc.; *d.* (usu. before a date) = died. D. = Distinguished, as D.C.M. (conduct medal), etc. In *Academical degrees* D. = Doctor, as D.D. (*Divinitatis Doctor*), D.Sc., Doctor of Science. D.B.E., Dame (Commander of Order of) British Empire. D.C. (*Mus.*) = *Da Capo* (q.v.). D.C., or d.c. (*Electr.*), direct current. D.G. = *Dei gratia* (q.v.). D.T., vulgar abbrev. of *delirium tremens.* D.V. = L. *Deo volente*, God willing.

'd, clipped form of *had, would.*

Dab (dæb), *sb.*[1] ME. [f. DAB *v.*[1]] 1. A sharp and abrupt blow; a peck; an aimed blow. Also *fig.* 2. A gentle blow or tap with a soft substance 1755. 3. A flattish mass of some soft or moist substance dabbed on anything 1749. Also *fig.* 4. A wet or dirty clout 1714.

1. Giving us several dabs with its beak SMOLLETT. 3. How can two or three dabs of paint ever be worth such a sum as that MAD. D'ARBLAY. *fig.* Several little dabs of money HERVEY.

Dab (dæb), *sb.*[2] 1577. [?] A species of small flat-fish, *Pleuronectes limanda*, resembling the flounder, common on the British coast; also a street term for any small flat fish.

Dab (dæb), *sb.*[3] 1691. [? a deriv. of DAB *v.*] One skilful *at*, †*of, in* anything; an expert, an adept. Also *attrib.*

A third [writer] is a d. at an index GOLDSM.

Dab (dæb), *v.* ME. [Prob. onomatopœic.] 1. *trans.* To strike somewhat sharply and abruptly; to stick or thrust; to strike with a slight blow. *intr.* Of a bird: To peck with the bill (*mod.*). 2. To strike or cause to strike (usually with something soft) and then withdraw quickly 1562; *spec.* to strike or pat with a dabber 1759. 3. A var. of DAUB *v.* to plaster 1577.

1. To dabbe him in the necke MORE. 2. To d. a brush against paper TYNDALL. To d. glue on his gauzy wings READE. To d. a sore with fine lint 17...

Dab, *adv.* 1608. [The vb.-stem used ellipt.] With a dab.

Dabber (dæ·bəɹ). 1790. [f. DAB *v.*] One who or that which dabs; *spec.* a rounded pad of some elastic material, used by printers, etc., for applying ink, colour, etc., evenly to a surface; in *Printing* = BALL *sb.*[1] 12. Also, a brush used in stereotyping for pressing the damp paper into the interstices of the type, etc.

Dabble (dæ·b'l), *v.* 1557. [Cf. (with sense 2) Du. *dabbelen*, freq. of *dabben.*] 1. *trans.* To wet by splashing; to bespatter, besprinkle, bedabble. Also *causal.* 2. *intr.* To move (with feet or hands, or the bill) in shallow water, mud, etc., so as to cause splashing; to paddle 1611. 3. *fig.* To employ oneself in a dilettante way *in*; to work off and on *at*. Const. *in* (*with*, *at*, etc.) 1625; †to tamper *with*, interfere *in* -1794.

1. With bright hayre Dabbel'd in blood *Rich. III*, I. iv. 54. 2. The long wet pasture grass she dabbles through CLARE. 3. To d. in poetry B. JONS., with the text ATTERBURY. Hence **Da·bbler**, one who dabbles.

Dabby (dæ·bi), *a.* 1581. [f. DAB *sb.*[1] 4.] Damp, moist: (of clothes) wet and clinging.

Dabchick (dæ·bˌtʃik). 1575. [? conn. w. DAB *v.*] The Little Grebe, *Podiceps minor*, a small water-bird, noted for its diving. In U.S., applied to *Podilymbus podiceps. fig.* Of a girl. B. JONS. var. **Dap-, dop-, dip-chick.**

‖**Daboya** (dăboi·ă, dɑ·bɔyā). Also **daboia.** 1872. [Hindī, f. *dabnā* to lurk.] The large viper of the East Indies.

Dabster (dæ·bstəɹ). 1708. [f. DAB *sb.*[3]; see -STER. 1. One skilled at anything; an expert or dab. Chiefly *dial.* 2. Used depreciatively; cf. DAUBSTER 1871.

‖**Dabuh.** 1600. [Arab.] The Striped Hyæna.

‖**Da capo** (da kā·po). 1724. [It. = 'from the beginning'.] *Mus.* A direction: Repeat from the beginning. (The end of the repeat is usually marked with a pause or the word *Fine.*) Abbrev. *D.C.* Also *fig.*

Dace (dēˈs). [ME. *darse*, etc., a. OF. *darz*, *dars*, nom. (and pl.) of *dart*, from *dard* DART, dace: so called from its darting motion; cf. DARE.] A small fresh-water cyprinoid fish, *Leuciscus vulgaris. U.S.* Applied locally to fishes resembling or allied to this: as the genus *Rhinichthys*, and the redfin, *Minnilus cornutus.*

‖**Dachshund** (da·ksˌhund). 1881. [Ger. = badger-dog.] One of a German breed of short-legged long-bodied dogs, used to draw badgers.

‖**Dacoit** (dăkoi·t), *sb.* 1810. [Hindī *ḍakait*, f. *ḍākā* gang-robbery, f. Skr. *dashṭaka* crowded.] One of a class of robbers in India and Burmah, who plunder in gangs. Hence **Dacoi·t** *v.* to plunder as a d.

‖**Dacoity** (dăkoi·ti). 1818. [a. Hindī *dakaitī*, abstr. sb. fem. f. *ḍakait.*] Robbery with violence committed by a gang.

Dacryd (dæ·krid). 1846. [f. mod.L. *Dacrydium*, a. Gr., dim. of δάκρυ tear, in allusion to resinous drops exuded by these trees.] *Bot.* A tree or shrub of genus *Dacrydium.*

Dacryolin (dæ·kriolin). 1875. [f. Gr. δάκρυ + -OL + -IN.] *Chem.* The form of albumin found in the tears.

Dacryolith, -lite (dæ·kriˌolib, -ləit). 1847. [f. as prec. + λίθος.] *Path.* A calculus occurring in the lachrymal passages.

‖**Dacryo·ma.** 1830. [f. as prec.] *Path.* An impervious state of the puncta lachrymalia.

‖**Da·cryops.** 1857. [f. as prec. + ὤψ.] A clear cyst due to the distension of one of the lachrymal ducts. **b.** A watery eye.

Dactyl (dæ·ktil), *sb.* ME. [ad. L. *dactylus*, a. Gr. δάκτυλος a finger, a date, a dactyl (from its 3 joints).] †1. A date -1656. 2. *Prosody.* A metrical foot consisting of a long syllable and two short (or of an accented syllable and two unaccented) ME. 3. A mollusc, the piddock (*Pholas dactylus*) 1802. Hence †**Da·ctylar** *a.* (*rare*). †**Dactyle·t** (*nonce-wd.*), a little d. †**Da·ctylist**, a writer of dactylic verse (*rare*).

Dactylic (dækti·lik), *a.* 1589. [ad. L. *dactylicus*, a. Gr.; see prec.] Of, pertaining to, or of the nature of, a dactyl; consisting of or characterized by dactyls. *sb.* [*sc.* verse].

Dactylio-, comb. f. Gr. δακτύλιος finger-ring [see DACTYL], as in:

Dacty·lioglyph [Gr. δακτυλιογλύφος], an engraver of gems for finger-rings; also, 'the inscription of the name of the artist on a gem' (Brande); hence **Dacty·liogly·phic** *a.*; **Dactylio·glyphist** = *Dactylioglyph*; **Dactylio·glyphy**, the art of engraving gems. **Dactylio·grapher**, one who describes finger-rings, engraved seals, etc.; hence **Dacty·liogra·phic** *a.*; **Dactylio·graphy**, the description of finger-rings, 'the science of gem-engraving' (Brande). **Dactylio·logy**, the study of finger-rings.

Dactyliomancy (dækti·liomæ:nsi). *erron.* dactylo-. 1613. [f. Gr. δακτύλιος + -MANCY.] Divination by means of a finger-ring.

‖**Dactylitis** (dæktiləi·tis). 1861. [-ITIS.] *Path.* Inflammation of a finger or toe.

Dactylo- (dæ·ktilo, dæktilǫ·), comb. f. Gr. δάκτυλος finger, as in:

Dactylo·logy, the art of speaking by signs made with the fingers. **Dactylo·nomy**, the art of counting on the fingers. **Dactylo·podite** (*Zool.*) [Gr. ποδ-], the terminal joint of a limb in Crustacea. **Da·ctylopo:re**, one of the pores in the corallum of Hydrocorallinæ, from which the dactylozoids protrude; hence **Dactylopo·ric** *a.* **Dactylo·pterous** *a.*, having the characters of the genus *Dactylopterus* of fishes, in which the pectoral fins are greatly enlarged and winglike; so **Dactylo·pteroid** *a.* **Da:ctylozo·oid, -zo·id**, a mouthless cylindrical zooid in some Hydrozoa.

Dactyloid (dæ·ktiloid), *a. rare.* 1882. [ad. Gr. δακτυλοειδής.] Resembling a finger.

Dactylose (dæktilōˈs), *a. rare.* 1882. [f. DACTYL + -OSE.] 'Having fingers, or finger-shaped' (*Syd. Soc. Lex.*).

Dad (dæd). *colloq.* 1500. [?] A childish word for father. So **Da·da, Dadda.**

Daddle (dæ·d'l), *sb. dial.* 1785. The fist.

Da·ddle, *v. dial.* 1787. [Stem *dad-* + -LE.] *intr.* To walk totteringly or unsteadily; to dawdle.

Daddock (dæ·dək). *dial.* 1624. [Stem *dad* + dim. -OCK.] Rotten or decayed wood. Hence **Da·ddocky** *a.*

Daddy (dæ·di). *colloq.* 1500. [dim. of DAD.] An endearing form of DAD, father. Hence **Da·ddyism** *U.S.*, respect for ancestry.

Da:ddy-lo·ng-legs. 1814. [From its very long legs.] The CRANE-FLY. (Called also *father-* and *Harry-long-legs.*) **b.** A name for Arachnids of similar appearance, such as those of the genus *Phalangium.*

Dade (dēˈd), *v.* Now *dial.* 1598. [Cf. DADDLE.] 1. *intr.* To move slowly or totteringly, to toddle 1612. 2. *trans.* To lead and support (one who totters). Also *fig.*

1. Which .. No sooner taught to d., but from their mother trip DRAYTON. 2. The little children .. By painefull Mothers daded to and fro DRAYTON.

Dado (dēⁱ·do). 1664. [a. It. *dado* die, cube :—L. *datum*; see DIE.] *Archit.* **1.** The cubical portion of a pedestal, between the base and cornice; the die. **2.** The finishing of wood running along the lower part of the walls of a room, made to represent a continuous pedestal. Hence, Any lining, painting, or papering of the lower part of an interior wall different from that of the upper part. Also *attrib.* Hence **Da·doed** *ppl. a.* having a d.

†**Dæ·dal,** *sb.* Also **de-.** 1630. [ad. L. DÆDALUS.] **1.** Short for Dædalus; a skilful artificer like Dædalus. **2.** A labyrinth. EVELYN.

Dædal (dī·dăl), *a.* Also **de-.** Chiefly *poet.* 1590. [ad. L. *dædalus*, a. Gr. δαίδαλος cunningly wrought, etc.] **1.** Cunning to invent or fashion. **2.** = DÆDALIAN 1. 1630. **3.** Of the earth, etc.: 'Manifold in works'; hence, varied, variously adorned 1596.

1. The d. hand of..Nature 1872. 2. The d. dance LANDOR. 3. What d. landscapes smile 1745.

Dæda·leous, *a.* 1835. [f. as next + -OUS.] *Bot.* Having a point of large circuit, but truncated and rugged.

Dædalian, -ean (dīdēⁱ·liăn), *a.* Also **De-.** 1598. [f. L. *Dædaleus*, Gr. δαιδάλεος + -AN.] **1.** Of or after the style of Dædalus; formed with art; maze-like 1607. †**2.** = DÆDAL *a.* 3.

Dæ·dalist. [See -IST.] An imitator of Dædalus. ADDISON.

Dædalous (dī·dăləs), *a.* Also **de-.** 1828. [f. L. *dædalus* + -OUS.] *Bot.* Of leaves: Having a margin with various windings.

‖**Dædalus** (dī·dalǒs). 1630. [L., a. Gr. Δαίδαλος 'the cunning one', name of the workman who constructed the Cretan labyrinth, and made wings for himself and Icarus.] A cunning artificer (like Dædalus).

Dæmon, Dæmonic, etc.; see DEMON, etc.

Daer-stock (dā·ˌer-stǫk). 1875. [f. MIr. *dáer* servile + STOCK.] *Ir. Antiq.* Stock belonging to the landlord of which the tenant has the use; used *attrib.* in *d. tenant*, etc.

Daff (daf), *sb.* Now *n. dial.* ME. [Cf. DAFT.] One deficient in sense or in spirit; a simpleton; a coward.

Daff (daf), *v.*[1] Chiefly *Sc.* 1535. [f. prec.] **1.** To play the fool; to talk or behave sportively. †**2.** To daunt (*n. dial.*) 1674. Hence **Da·ffing** *vbl. sb.* fooling.

Daff (daf), *v.*[2] 1596. [var. of DOFF.] †**1.** *trans.* To put off (as clothes); to throw off -1606. **2.** To put or turn aside, to thrust aside 1596; †to put off (with an excuse, etc.) *Oth.* IV. ii. 176.

1. Till we do please To daft [= daff't] for our Repose SHAKS. 2. The..Mad-Cap, Prince of Wales..that daft the World aside 1 *Hen. IV*, IV. i. 96.

Daffadowndilly, daffydowndilly. 1573. **1.** = *Daffodilly.* **2.** A shrub: prob. the Mezereon 1591.

Daffodil (dæ·fŏdil). 1548. [var. of AFFODILL, q. v. The initial *d* is obscure.] †**1.** = AFFODILL; the genus *Asphodelus* -1607. †**2.** The genus *Narcissus* -1629. **3.** Now restricted to *Narcissus pseudo-Narcissus* (also called Lent Lily) 1592. **4.** The colour of the daffodil; a pale yellow. Also *attrib.* 1855.

3. Faire Daffadills, we weep to see You haste away so soone HERRICK. *Chequered D.*: the Fritillary, *Fritillaria Meleagris.* var. **Da·ffodilly, daffadilly,** *poet.* (and *dial.*).

Daft (daft), *a.* Now *Sc.* and *n.* [In early ME. *daffte*, corresp. to OE. *gedæfte* mild, gentle :—OTeut. **gadaftjoz*, f. stem *dab-*, in Gothic *gadaban* to become, be fit. Cf. sense-history of SILLY. See also DEFT.] †**1.** Mild, meek, humble. (ME. only.) **2.** Silly; wanting in intelligence, stupid ME. **3.** Of unsound mind, crazy 1536. **4.** Giddy in one's mirth; madly gay 1575.

3. The woman would drive ony reasonable being d. SCOTT. Hence **Da·ftlike** *a.* **Da·ft-ly** *adv.*, **-ness.**

Dag (dæg), *sb.*[1] In 4–5 **dagge.** ME. [?] †**1.** A pendant pointed portion of anything; one of the pointed or laciniated divisions of the lower margin of a garment -1617. †**2.** = AGLET 1, 2. -1616. **3.** One of the locks of wool clotted with dirt about the hinder parts of a sheep 1731. Hence **Da·g-tailed** *a.* having the wool about the tail clotted with dirt.

†**Dag,** *sb.*[2] 1561. [?] A kind of heavy pistol or hand-gun formerly in use -1881.

[The sense 'dagger' (Johnson) is app. a mistake, due to misapprehension of 'dag and dagger'. The sense 'dagger-thrust' is a blunder.]

Dag (dæg), *sb.*[3] 1727. [a. F. *dague.*] **1.** The simple straight pointed horn of a young stag 1859. **2.** A pin or bolt.

Dag (dæg), *sb.*[4] *dial.* 1674. [app. of Norse origin; cf. ON. *dögg* dew.] **1.** Dew. **2.** A drizzle; a mist 1808.

Dag, *v.*[1] ME. [conn. w. DAG *sb.*[1]] †**1.** *trans.* To cut the edge of (a garment) into jags; to slash -1523. **2.** To clog with dirt, bemire. Now *dial.* 1484. **3.** *Farming.* To cut the dags from (sheep) 1706.

†**Dag,** *v.*[2] ME. [Related to F. *dague.* See also DAGGER.] To pierce or stab with or as with a pointed weapon -1794.

†**Dag,** *v.*[3] 1572. [f. DAG *sb.*[2]] *trans.* and *intr.* To shoot with a dag -1580.

Dag (dæg), *v.*[4] *dial.* 1825. [Cf. DAG *sb.*[4] See also DEG.] **1.** *trans.* To sprinkle, wet with sprinkling 1855. **2.** *intr.* To drizzle.

‖**Dagesh, daghesh** (dā·geʃ), *sb.* 1591. [med. Heb., f. Syriac *d'ghash* to prick.] *Heb. Gram.* A point or dot placed within a Hebrew letter, denoting either that it is doubled (*d. forte*), or that it is not aspirated (*d. lene*).

Dagger (dæ·gəɹ), *sb.* ME. [Prob. an English formation (?f. DAG *v.*[2]). Cf. F. *dague.*] **1.** A short stout edged and pointed weapon, used for thrusting and stabbing. **2.** *fig.* Something that wounds grievously 1596. **3.** *Naut.* A piece of timber that faces on to the poppets of the bilge-ways, and crosses them diagonally 1850. †**4.** = DAG *sb.*[3] 1. 1616. **5.** *Printing.* A mark resembling a dagger (†), used for marginal references, etc.; also called *obelisk.* **6.** A name of moths of the genus *Acronycta* having a black dagger-like mark on the fore wing 1832. **7.** *pl.* A name of plants, as Sword-grass (*Poa aquatica*), etc. 1847. †**8.** Name of a tavern in Holborn *c* 1600; hence *d.-ale*, etc. -1610.

1. The Honourable men, Whose Daggers haue stabb'd Cæsar *Jul. C.* III. ii. 157. †*D. of lath*: the weapon worn by the Vice in the old Moralities. Phr. *At daggers drawn*: in a state of open hostility. 2. Phr. *To speak* or *look daggers*: to speak so as to wound. 5. *Double d.*: a mark having each end hilted like a d. (‡), used for references, etc.

Hence **Da·gger** *v.* to stab, or (*Printing*) mark, with a d.

Daggle (dæ·g'l), *v.* 1530. [Freq. of DAG *v.*[1] sense 2; see also DAG *v.*[4]] **1.** *trans.* To trail, so as to clog with wet mud; in later use, To wet by splashing or sprinkling. **2.** *trans.* and *intr.* To drag or trail about (through the mire) 1681.

1. The..plume..Was daggled by the dashing spray SCOTT. 2. You may d. about with your mother, and sell paint VANBRUGH.

Daggle-tail (dæ·g'lˌtēⁱl), *sb.* 1577. Now *dial.* A person (*esp.* a woman) whose garments are bemired by being trailed over wet ground; a slut, slattern. Now DRAGGLE-TAIL. So **Da·ggle-tailed** *a.* (now *dial.*), having the skirts splashed in this way; slatternly.

Dag-lock. 1623. [f. DAG *sb.*[1] 3 + LOCK.] *pl.* Locks of wool clotted with dirt about the hinder parts of a sheep.

Dago (dēⁱ·go). *U.S.* 1888. [Corrupt f. Sp. *Diego* = James.] A name originally given as a generic name to Spaniards; now used of the Latin races generally.

‖**Dagoba** (dā·gŏbă). 1806. [ad. Singhalese *dāgaba.*] In Buddhist countries, a *tope* or dome-shaped structure containing relics of Buddha or some Buddhist saint.

†**Da·gon**[1]. ME. [? conn. w. DAG *sb.*[1]] A piece (of cloth) -1486.

‖**Dagon**[2] (dēⁱ·gǫn). ME. [a. L., a. Gr., a. Heb. *dāgōn* 'little fish, dear little fish', f. *dāg* fish.] The national deity of the ancient Philistines; represented with the head, chest, and arms of a man, and the tail of a fish. Also *transf.* An idol.

†**Da·gswain.** ME. [Etym. unkn. Cf. DAG *sb.*[1], DAGON[1].] A coarse coverlet of rough shaggy material -1577.

Daguerreotype (dăge·rotəip), *sb.* 1839. [f. *Daguerre* name of the inventor + TYPE.] An early photographic process, in which the impression was taken upon a silver plate sensitized by iodine, and then developed by vapour of mercury. Also, a portrait produced by this process. Also †*fig.* and *attrib.* Hence **Dague·rreotype** *v.* to photograph by the d. process; also †*fig.* So **Dague·rreotyper, -ist,** a photographer who uses the d. process. **Da·guerreoty·pic, -al** *a.* relating to the d. process. **Dague·rreotypy** (-təipi), the d. process.

‖**Dahabeeyah, -biah** (dāhăbī·yă). 1877. [Arab., lit. 'the golden': name of the gilded state barge of the Moslem rulers of Egypt.] A large sailing-boat, used by travellers on the Nile.

Dahlia (dēⁱ·liă, prop. dā·liă). 1804. [f. *Dahl*, a Swedish botanist.] **1.** A genus of Composite plants, natives of Mexico, introduced into Europe in 1789. **2.** Name for a particular shade of red 1846.

1. *Blue d.*: *fig.* something impossible.

Dahlin (dā·lin). 1826. [f. prec. + -IN[1].] *Chem.* A name for INULIN from dahlia tubers.

‖**Dail Eireann** (dǭⁱl ē·rən). 1919. [Ir., = assembly of Ireland.] Lower house of Parliament in Irish Free State. Abbrev. **Dail.**

Daily (dēⁱ·li), *a.* [OE. *dæglic*, a deriv. of WGer. *dag* day.] Of or belonging to each day; occurring every day; issued every (week-)day 1470. As *sb.* (*ellipt.*) A daily newspaper.

D. waiter, etc.: one who waits, etc., daily.

Daily (dēⁱ·li), *adv.* ME. [f. DAY + -LY[2].] Every day, day by day; constantly.

With bended knees I dayly beseech God 1635.

‖**Daimio** (dai·mˌyo). 1839. [Jap., f. Chin. *dai* great + *mio, myo* name.] The title of the feudal nobles of Japan; now abolished.

‖**Daimon** (dai·mōᵘn), a transliteration of Gr. δαίμων, one's genius or DEMON.

Dain, *sb.* ME. [Syncop. f. *dedain*, DISDAIN *sb.*] †**1.** Disdain -1591. **2.** Stink. Still *dial.* So †**Dain** *a.* haughty; stinking. †**Dain** *v.* to disdain. †**Dai·nful** *a.* disdainful.

†**Daint,** *a.* and *sb.* 1563. Short f. DAINTY -1633.

†**Dai·nteous,** *a.* ME. = DAINTY *a.* -1556.

Dai·nteth, -ith, *sb.* and *a.* *Sc.* = DAINTY, etc.

Dai·ntify, *v.* [See -FY.] To make dainty. MAD. D'ARBLAY.

Dai·ntihood. *rare.* 1780. Daintiness.

Daintily (dēⁱ·ntili), *adv.* ME. [f. DAINTY *a.* + -LY[2].] †**1.** Handsomely -1640. **2.** In a dainty manner ME. **3.** Delicately, nicely, etc.; elegantly, neatly 1561. †**4.** Rarely -1581.

4. The Auncients..neuer, or very d., match Hornpypes and Funeralls SIDNEY.

Daintiness (dēⁱ·ntinės). 1552. [f. DAINTY *a.* + -NESS.] The quality of being dainty; †choiceness -1627; elegance; neatness 1580; niceness (of taste, sensibility, etc.) 1579; fastidiousness; softness 1530.

More notorious for the d. of the provision..than for the massiness of the dish HAKEWILL. D. of expression in a lyric 1878. Daintinesse of eare *Rich. II*, v. v. 45. The People .. learnt .. of the Flemish d. and softness MILT.

†**Dai·ntrel.** 1575. [?] A dainty -1640.

Dainty (dēⁱ·nti), *sb.* ME. [a. OF. *deintié, daintié, dainté* :—L. *dignitatem*, f. *dignus* worthy.] †**1.** Estimation; regard; affection -1513. †**2.** Liking to *do* or *see* anything; delight -1529. †**3.** Choice quality -1440. †**4.** Fastidiousness -1597. †**5.** *concr.* Anything which is dainty -1798. **6.** *esp.* A choice viand, a delicacy ME.

5. Plenty is no d. HEYWOOD. 6. Let mee not eate of their dainties *Ps.* cxli. 4. Phr. †*To make d. of* (*anything*): to set great store by; hence, to be chary of.

Dainty (dēⁱ·nti), *a.* ME. [f. prec. sb.] **1.** Handsome; choice; delightful. Now *dial.* †**2.** Precious; hence, rare, scarce -1677. **3.** Pleasing to the palate ME. **4.** Of delicate beauty or taste ME. **5.** Of persons, etc.: Nice, fastidious, particular; sometimes, over-nice 1576. Also quasi-*adv.* (*rare*).

1. Full many a deynte hors hadde he in stable CHAUCER. 3. D. bits Make rich the ribs *L. L. L.* I. i. 26. 4. The grassye ground with daintye Daysies dight SPENSER. 5. The hand of little Imployment hath the daintier sense *Haml.* v. i. 78. Let vs not be daintie of leaue-taking, But shift away *Macb.* II. iii. 150. Born with a d. tooth STEVENSON.

‖**Dairi** (dai·rī). 1662. [Jap., f. Chin. *dai* great + *ri* within.] In Japan, prop. the palace or court of the Mikado; also used for the Mikado. Hence **Dairi-sama,** *lit.* lord of the d., an appellation of the Mikado.

Dairy (dēᵊ·ri), *sb.* [ME. *deierie*, etc., f. *deie*, *deye*, DEY female servant + *erie*, -ERY².] **1.** A room or building in which milk and cream are kept, and made into butter and cheese. Occas., in towns, a shop in which these are sold. **2.** That department of farming, or of a farm, which is concerned with the production of milk, butter, and cheese. Hence, occas., the milch cows on a farm collectively. ME. **3.** A dairy-farm 1562.

2. Grounds were turned much in England from breeding either to feeding or dairy TEMPLE. D. of 12 or 16 cows to be let 1882.

Comb.: d.-farm, a farm chiefly producing milk, butter, and cheese; **-farmer, -farming; -school,** a technical school for teaching d.-work or d.-farming; **-woman,** a woman who manages a d.

Dai·ry, *v. rare.* 1780. [f. DAIRY *sb.*] To keep or feed (cows) for the dairy. Hence **Dai·rying** *vbl. sb.* the business of a dairy.

Dairymaid (dēᵊ·rimēᵊd). 1599. A female servant employed in a dairy.

Dai·ryman. 1784. A man who keeps, or works in, a dairy, or sells dairy produce.

Dais (dēᵊs, dēᵊ·is). ME. [a. OF. *deis*, mod.F. *dais* :—L. *discum* (nom. *discus*) quoit, disk, dish, in late L. table.] †**1.** A raised table in a hall, at which distinguished persons sat at feasts, etc.; the high table –1575. **2.** The raised platform in a hall for the high table, or for seats of honour, etc. ME. Also *transf.* **3.** A seat, bench (*n. dial.*) ME. **4.** [after mod.Fr.] The canopy over a throne, etc. 1863.

2. Like the d. or upper part of our old castle and college halls ARNOLD.

Daisied (dēᵊ·zid), *a.* 1611. [f. DAISY + -ED².] Adorned with or abounding in daisies, as *d. lawns.* (Chiefly *poet.*)

Daisy (dēᵊ·zi). [OE. *dæges éage* day's eye, in allusion to the flower opening in the morning.] **1.** The common name of *Bellis perennis*, N.O. *Compositæ*, having small flat flower-heads with yellow disk and white ray, which close in the evening. **2.** Applied to similar plants; as, in N. America, the Ox-eye D., *Chrysanthemum Leucanthemum*; in Australia, various *Compositæ*; **Michaelmas D.,** various cultivated species of *Aster* which blossom about Michaelmas; etc. **3.** *slang.* (chiefly *U.S.*) A first-rate thing or person; also as *adj.* **4.** *attrib.* 1605.

1. The dayeseye, or ellis the eye of day CHAUCER. Hence **Dai·sy** *v.* to cover or adorn with daisies (*rare*).

Dai·sy-cutter. 1791. [*lit.* 'cutter of daisies'.] **1.** A horse that in trotting steps low. **2.** *Cricket*, etc. A ball that skims along the ground without rising 1889.

Dak; see DAWK.

Daker. Also **daiker, dakir.** Var. of DICKER, q. v.

Daker-hen. *dial.* 1552. [?] The Corncrake or Land-rail.

Dakoit, etc.; see DACOIT, etc.

‖**Dal** (dāl). *Anglo-Ind.* 1698. [Hindī.] Split-pulse, *esp.* that of *Cajanus Indicus*, used for food in the East Indies.

‖**Dalai, Dalai-lama**; see LAMA.

Dale¹ (dēᵊl). [OE. *dæl*; Com. Teut. :—OTeut. *dalom* 'deep or low place'.] **1.** A valley. In literary Eng. chiefly *poet.* Also *fig.* †**2.** A hollow, pit, gulf, etc. –1489.

1. By d. and eek by doune CHAUCER. That part of these dales which runs up far into the mountains WORDSW. *Comb.* **d.-land,** the lower ground of a district; so **-lander, -man.**

Dale² (dēᵊl). ME. [Northern var. of DOLE, q. v.] A portion of land; *spec.* a portion of an undivided field indicated by landmarks only.

Dale³ (dēᵊl). 1611. [Cf. LGer. and Du. *daal*; also F. *dalle*, etc.] A wooden tube or trough for carrying off water, as from a ship's pump.

Dalesman (dēᵊ·lzmæn). 1769. [f. DALE¹.] A native or inhabitant of a dale; *esp.* of the dales in Cumberland, Westmorland, etc.

Dalf(e, obs. pa. t. of DELVE.

‖**Dalle** (dal). 1855. [Fr.] **1.** A flat slab of stone, marble, or terra-cotta, used for flooring. **2.** *pl.* In Western U.S.: Rapids where the rivers are compressed into long narrow trough-like channels 1884.

Dalliance (dæ·liăns). ME. [f. DALLY *v.* + -ANCE.] †**1.** Talk, confabulation, chat –1496. **2.** Sport, play; *esp.* amorous or wanton toying ME. **3.** Trifling; playing *with* a matter 1548. †**4.** Idle delay –1590.

2. The Primrose path of d. SHAKS. The lewd d. of the queen of love POPE. 3. Vain d. with the misery Even of the dead WORDSW. 4. *Com. Err.* IV. i. 59.

Dallop, var. of DOLLOP.

Dally (dæ·li), *v.* ME. [a. OF. *dalier* to converse, etc.] †**1.** To talk lightly or idly, chat –1440. **2.** To make sport; to toy, sport *with*, *esp.* in the way of amorous caresses; to wanton ME.; to play *with* (temptation, etc.) 1548. **3.** To trifle *with* a person or thing 1548. **4.** *intr.* To spend time idly; to loiter 1538. †**5.** *trans.* To defer by trifling –1821. †**6.** To move by dalliance –1677.

2. Our Ayerie buildeth in the Cedars top, And dallies with the winde *Rich. III*, I. iii. 265. D. not with her, as Eve with the serpent 1642. 3. Why will you d. with my pain ADDISON. 4. We dallied not, but made all haste we could HEYWOOD. Hence **Da·llier,** one who dallies.

Dalmatian (dælmēᵊ·ʃən), *a.* 1824. Of Dalmatia, the Austrian province on the Adriatic; whence *D. dog*, the spotted coach-dog. Hence *sb.*, A native of Dalmatia; a Dalmatian dog.

Dalmatic (dælmæ·tik), *a.* and *sb.* ME. [The sb. occurs earliest, and is a. F. *dalmatique*, ad. L. *dalmatica*, subst. use (sc. *vestis*) of *Dalmaticus* adj. Dalmatian.]

A. *adj.* Belonging to Dalmatia 1604.

B. *sb.* An ecclesiastical vestment, with wide sleeves, and marked with two stripes, worn in the Western Church by deacons and bishops on certain occasions. **b.** A similar robe worn by kings at coronation.

Cf. ISIDORE *Orig.* XIX. xxii. 9 Dalmatica vestis primum in Dalmatia provincia Græciæ texta est, tunica sacerdotalis candida cum clavis ex purpura.

Dalt (dǭlt). *Sc.* 1775. [ad. Gael. *dalta.*] A foster-child.

Daltonian (dǭltōᵘ·niăn). 1841. [f. the chemist John *Dalton* (1766–1844), who was colour-blind.] *adj.* Relating to John Dalton, or the atomic theory first enunciated by him 1850. *sb.* A person who is colour-blind.

Daltonism (dǭ·ltoniz'm). 1841. [ad. F. *daltonisme*, f. as prec.] A name for colour-blindness, *esp.* as to red. Hence **Da·ltonist** = DALTONIAN *sb.*

Dam (dæm), *sb.*¹ [Com. Teut.] **1.** A bank or barrier of earth, masonry, etc., built across a stream to obstruct its flow and raise its level; any similar work to confine water. Also *fig.* ME. **2.** The body of water confined by a dam. (Now *local.*) ME. **3. a.** *Mining.* A partition of boards, masonry, etc. in a mine to keep out water, fire, or gas. **b.** *Smelting.* 'The wall of refractory material, forming the front of the fore-hearth of a blast furnace' (Raymond). **c.** *Dentistry.* A soft rubber guard to keep a tooth dry during an operation (*U.S.*) 1872.

Comb.: **d.-plate,** the plate upon the d.-stone or front stone of the bottom of a blast furnace RAYMOND.

Dam (dæm), *sb.*² ME. [var. of DAME :—earlier *damme.*] †**1.** = DAME. (ME. only.) **2.** A female parent (now usually of quadrupeds). Correl. to *sire.* ME. **3.** = Mother (human): usually in contempt 1547. Also *fig.*

2. So Kids and Whelps their Sires and Dams express DRYDEN. Phr. *The Devil's dam*, applied opprobriously to a woman. 3. *fig.* That high Priest of Rome, the d. of that..superstitious breed BURTON.

Dam, *sb.*³ Chiefly *Sc.* 1580. [a. F. *dame* lady (DAM², DAME), the name of each piece in the *jeu de dames* or draughts; cf. DAM-BROD.] Each of the pieces in the game of draughts (*obs.*); *pl.* the game itself.

†**Dam,** *sb.*⁴, **damp.** ME. [a. OF. *dam* :—L. *dominus.*] Lord; as a prefix = Sir, Master –1506.

Dam (dæm), *v.* 1553. [f. DAM *sb.*¹, replacing *dem*, OE. *dęmman.*] **1.** *trans.* To furnish with a dam; to obstruct or confine by means of a dam. Usu. with *up.* 1563. **2.** *transf.* and *fig.* To stop up, block, obstruct; to confine.

1. Now d. the Ditches and the Floods restrain DRYDEN. 2. He doth also dambe vp the mercy of God by its contempt SANDERSON.

Damage (dæ·mėdʒ), *sb.* ME. [a. OF. *damage*, mod.F. *dommage*, ad. L. *damnum* + -AGE.] **1.** Loss or detriment caused by hurt or injury affecting estate, condition, or circumstances (*arch.*). **2.** Injury, harm ME. †**3.** A disadvantage –1721; a misfortune, a pity –1612. **4.** *Law.* (Now always in *pl.*) The value estimated in money of something lost or withheld; the sum claimed or awarded in compensation for loss or injury sustained 1542. **5.** *slang.* Cost, expense 1755.

1. As moche to oure d. as to oure profit CHAUCER. 2. The d. done to the monastery HOOK. The damages which the kingdom has sustained by war GOLDSM. 3. And of his deth it was ful gret d. CHAUCER. 4. Damages for breach of contract LD. ST. LEONARDS. Hence †**Da·mageful** *a.* hurtful.

Da·mage, *v.* ME. [a. OF. *damagier*, *-er*, f. *damage*; see prec.] **1.** *trans.* To do or cause damage to; to hurt, harm, injure; now commonly to injure (a thing) so as to lessen its value. **2.** *intr.* To suffer damage (*rare*) 1821.

1. To stop all hopes, whose growth may dammage me *Rich. III*, IV. ii. 60. 2. Her..clothes might d. with the dew CLARE. So **Da·mageable** *a.* †injurious; liable to be damaged.

Damage-feasant. 1621. [OF. *damage fesant.*] *Law.* Said of a stranger's cattle, etc., found trespassing, and doing damage, as by feeding, etc. (Prop. *adj. phr.*; also as *sb.*)

†**Damageous,** *a.* ME. [a. OF. *damageus*, f. *damage*; see DAMAGE *sb.* and -OUS.] Fraught with damage; causing loss or disadvantage –1637.

Damalic (dămæ·lik), **damolic** (dămǫ·lik), *a.* 1863. [f. Gr. δάμαλις, δαμάλη heifer.] *Chem.* In *d. acid*, an acid (C_7H_8O) existing in cows' urine. Hence **Damalu·ric** [URIC] *acid*, an acid ($C_8H_{10}O_2$) of the same origin.

‖**Daman** (dæ·măn). 1738. [From Arab. *daman isrāīl* sheep or lamb of Israel.] The Syrian rock-badger or 'cony' of Scripture (*Hyrax Syriacus*); also *H. Capensis.*

Damascene (dæmăsī·n). ME. [ad. L. *Damascenus* of Damascus.]

A. *adj.* Of or pertaining to Damascus 1543. **2.** Of or pertaining to damask (fabrics), or to the art of damascening metal 1541.

1. *D. plum*: see DAMSON.

B. *sb.* **1.** A native of Damascus ME. **2.** Damascene work; †damask 1481. **3.** See DAMSON.

Damascene (dæmăsī·n), *v.* 1585. [f. prec. adj.] To ornament (metal-work) with inlaid designs in gold or silver, or with a watered pattern. Also *transf* and *fig.* Hence **Damascener.**

Damascus (dămæ·skǒs). Formerly also **Damasco.** 1625. [L., Gr. Δαμασκός, from Semitic.] An ancient city, the capital of Cœle-Syria. Often used *attrib.*, as *D. blade*; also *absol.* = D. steel, etc.

D. iron: a combination of pieces of iron and steel welded together and rolled out, in imitation of D. steel. *D.-twist*: a kind of gun-barrel made of a ribbon of D. iron coiled around a mandrel and welded.

Damask (dæ·măsk). ME. [perh. a. Anglo-Fr. *Damasc = It. *Damasco*, L. *Damascus.*]

I. †**1.** The city of Damascus –1539. **2.** *attrib.* = Made at or brought from Damascus.

2. †**D. plum, prune** = DAMSON. **D. rose,** a variety of rose, app. originally the *Rosa gallica* var. *damascena*, with semi-double pink or light-red (rarely white) flowers, cultivated in the East for attar of roses. †**D. water,** rose-water distilled from D. roses.

II. Substances orig. produced at Damascus. **1.** A rich silk fabric woven with elaborate designs and figures. (Also applied to fabrics of wool, linen, or cotton.) ME. **b.** A twilled linen fabric with designs which show up by opposite reflections of light from the surface; used chiefly for table-linen 1542. **2.** Steel manufactured at Damascus; also steel or a combination of iron and steel exhibiting a similar pattern on the surface: more fully *d. steel* 1603. **b.** The wavy pattern exhibited by these 1818. **3.** The colour of the damask rose 1600.

1. A quantity of China damasks, and other wrought silks DE FOE. 3. She..Blush'd a live d. KEATS.

III. *attrib.* and *adj.* **1.** Made of damask (silk or cloth); furnished with damask 1489. **2.** Made of or resembling Damascus steel 1611. **3.** Of the colour of the damask rose 1588.

Comb: **d. steel** (see above); **d.-stitch,** a name given to satin-stitch on a linen foundation; **-work,** the veining on Damascus-blades; incised patterns inlaid with gold or silver.

Damask (dæ·mǎsk), *v.* 1585. [f. prec. sb. Also *dama·sk* (Milton, etc.).] 1. *trans.* To weave with richly-figured designs 1706. 2. = DAMASCENE *v.* 1585. 3. To ornament with or as with a variegated pattern; to diaper 1610. 4. To deface or destroy, by stamping or marking with figures and lines 1673. †5. To warm (wine) (*slang*) –1778.

2. A faire basen of Copper damasked 1585. 3. As they sat recline On the soft downie Bank damaskt with flowers MILT. *P. L.* IV. 334.

Damasked (dæ·mǎskt), *ppl. a.* 1599. [f. prec.] 1. In senses of DAMASK *v.* 1–3. 2. Having the hue of the damask rose 1600. 3. Furnished with damask 1861.

2. I haue seene Roses damaskt, red and white, But no such Roses see I in her cheekes SHAKS.

†Damaskee·n, -kin. 1551. [a. F. *damasquin, -ine*, ad. It. *damaschino*, f. *Damasco*, Damascus.] *adj.* = DAMASCENE *a.* –1585. *sb.* A Damascus blade –1645.

Damaskee·n, *v.* 1585. [a. F. *damasquiner*; see prec.] = DAMASCENE *v.*

‖**Damassé** (dǎma·se). 1864. [F. = *linge damassé*.] A kind of linen made in Flanders, woven with flowers and figures like damask.

Damassin (dæ·mǎsin). 1839. [f. F. *damas*, DAMASK.] 'A species of woven damask with gold and silver flowers' (Brande).

Dambonite (dæ·mbǒnəit). 1879. [f. *dambo* native name.] *Chem.* A white crystalline substance ($C_4H_8O_3$) found in a kind of caoutchouc obtained from Western Africa.

Dambose (dæ·mbōᵘs). 1879. [f. prec.] *Chem.* A crystallizable sugar ($C_3H_6O_3$) obtained from dambonite.

Dam-brod, dam-board. *Sc.* 1779. [f. DAM *sb.*³ + *brod* (Sc.), BOARD.] A draught-board. *attrib.* Checkered.

Dame (dēᵊm). ME. [a. OF. *dame* :—earlier *damme* :—L. *domina* lady, mistress. Cf. DAM².] 1. A female ruler or head: = 'lady', as fem. of *lord*. Also *fig.* (See also below.) 2. The mistress of a household. Now *arch.* or *dial.*, or used of an aged housewife. ME. Also *transf.* 3. The mistress of a children's school. ? *Obs.* 1649. 4. At Eton: A matron (also a man) who keeps a boarding-house 1737. 5. A form of address; = My lady, Madam: now left to women of lower rank ME. 6. A title given to a woman of rank; = Lady, Mistress, Miss; *spec.* the legal title of the wife of a knight or baronet. Also *fig.*, as in *Dame Nature*, etc. ME. 7. A woman of rank, a lady. Now *Hist.* or *poet.* 1530. b. *spec.* The wife of a knight, squire, citizen, yeoman (*arch.* or *dial.*) 1574. †8. = DAM *sb.*² –1709.

1. The title given to Benedictine nuns who have made their solemn profession; also, any fully professed nun. 7. c. The title of lady members of the Order of the British Empire corresponding to *Knight*: *D. Commander*, *D. Grand Cross* 1917.

Dame's-violet. 1578. [tr. L. *viola matronalis*. Hence by corruption *damas* or *damask v.*] The Garden Rocket, *Hesperis matronalis.*

‖**Dammar** (dæ·mǎɹ). 1698. [a. Malay *damar* resin, whence the genus *Dammara* (N.O. *Coniferæ*), a species of which, *D. orientalis*, yields the resin in Amboyna and the Moluccas.] The name of various resins; *esp.* the cat's-eye resin (*E. India D.*) from *Dammara orientalis*, and the Kauri-gum from *D. australis* of New Zealand; both used for making varnish.

‖**Da·mmara.** 1863. [See prec.] *Bot.* A genus of trees yielding resin.

†Da·mmaret. 1635. [ad. F. *dameret*, f. *dame* lady.] A ladies' man –1649.

Damme (dæ·mi). 1618. I. *int.* Short f. *Damn me!* 1645. 2. as *sb.* The oath itself 1775; †*transf.* one who uses this oath; a profane swearer –1674.

Damn (dæm), *v.* ME. [a. OF. *dampner*, *damner*, ad. L. *damnare*.] †1. *trans.* To affirm to be guilty; to sentence; to CONDEMN (*to*) –1734. 2. To adjudge and pronounce to be bad; to denounce ME.; *spec.* to condemn (a play, etc.) as a failure; to condemn by public expression of disapproval 1654. 3. *transf.* To be the ruin of 1477. 4. *Theol.* To condemn to hell; *transf.* to cause or occasion the eternal damnation of ME. 5. Used profanely (in optative, and with no subject expressed) in imprecations and exclamations. (Now often printed 'd—n', or 'd—'.) 1589. 6. To imprecate damnation upon; to curse (using the word 'damn'). Also *absol.* 1624.

1. See Cromwell damned to everlasting fame POPE. 2. And with faint praises one another d. WYCHERLEY. A comedy..which..in the play-house phrase, was damned BOSWELL. 6. Their proper business is to d. the Dutch DRYDEN.

Damn (dæm), *sb.* 1619. [f. prec. vb.] The utterance of the word 'damn' as an imprecation.

Damns have had their day SHERIDAN. *Not worth a d., not to care a d.*: phrases used vaguely.

Damnable (dæ·mnǎb'l), *a.* (*adv.*) ME. [a. F.; see DAMN *v.*] †1. Worthy of condemnation; reprehensible –1841. 2. Liable to or worthy of damnation ME. †3. Pernicious (*rare*) –1659. 4. = 'Confounded'. (Now vulgar or profane.) 1594. 5. *adv.* Damnably –1735.

1. A d. game 1509, offence PRYNNE. 2. O what must poore lamentable d. I doe to be saved 1614. Hence **Damnabi·lity. Da·mnableness. Da·mnably** *adv.*

Damnation (dæmnēⁱ·ʃən). ME. [a. F.; see DAMN *v.*] 1. The action of condemning, or fact of being condemned; condemnation. 2. *Theol.* Condemnation to eternal punishment in the world to come; perdition (opp. to *salvation*); sin incurring or deserving condemnation ME. 3. In profane use: a. as an imprecation or exclamation 1604. b. as *adj.* or *adv.* = 'Damned' 1757.

1. Nethir thou dredist God, that thou art in the same dampnacion WYCLIF *Luke* xxiii. 40. The d. of a play FIELDING. 2. 'Twere d. To thinke so base a thought *Merch. V.* II. vii. 49. 3. a. *Oth.* III. iii. 396.

Damnatory (dæ·mnǎtəri), *a.* 1682. [ad. L. *damnatorius*; see DAMN *v.*] 1. Conveying or occasioning condemnation. 2. *Theol.* Containing or uttering a sentence of damnation 1738.

2. I do not believe the d. clauses in the Athanasian Creed under any qualification given of them ARNOLD.

Damned (dæmd, *poet.* dæ·mnĕd), *ppl. a.* ME. [f. DAMN *v.* + -ED¹.] †1. Condemned –1710. 2. *Theol.* Condemned or consigned to hell ME.; *absol.* as *sb. pl.* The souls in hell 1507. 3. Lying under, or worthy of, a curse; accursed, execrable 1563. 4. (usually printed 'd—d'.) Used profanely to express reprehension, or as a mere intensive 1596. b. *adv.* Damnably 1607.

2. It was a torment To lay upon the damn'd *Temp.* I. ii. 3. Out d. spot: out I say *Macb.* V. i. 39.

Damnify (dæ·mnifəi), *v.* 1512. [a. OF. *damnifier*, ad. L. *damnificare* (in Itala), f. *damnum*; see -FY.] 1. *trans.* To cause injury, loss, or inconvenience to; to injure; to wrong. (Now *rare*.) †2. To bring to destruction –1693.

1. That the King might not be damnified by the loss of the tributes WHISTON. Hence **†Da·mnifiable** *a.* detrimental (*rare*). **Da·mnifica·tion**, the action of damnifying. (Now only in legal use.)

Damning (dæ·miŋ, dæ·mniŋ), *ppl. a.* 1599. [-ING².] 1. That damns. 2. That leads to condemnation or ruin 1798. 3. Addicted to profane swearing. PEPYS.

2. The d. consciousness of being charlatans DISRAELI. Hence **Da·mning-ly** *adv.*, **-ness.**

Damnous (dæ·mnəs). 1870. [ad. L. *damnosus*.] *Law.* Of the nature of a *damnum*, *i.e.* causing loss or damage of any kind.

Damocles (dæ·mǒklīz). 1747. [L. from Gr.] Name of a flatterer who, having extolled the happiness of Dionysius tyrant of Syracuse, was placed by him at a banquet with a sword suspended over his head by a hair, to impress upon him how precarious that happiness was.

Sword of D., *Damocles' sword*, used of an imminent danger, which may at any moment descend upon one. Hence **Damocle·an** *a.* of or as of D.

‖**Damoiseau** (dæ·mizō). *arch.* 1477. [a. OF. :—L. *dominicellus*; corresp. to *damoisel*, DAMSEL.] A young man of gentle birth, not yet made a knight.

Damoisel, -elle, etc., obs. ff. DAMSEL.

Damolic; see DAMALIC.

Damourite (dǎmūᵊ·rəit). 1846. [f. the F. chemist *Damour*.] *Min.* A hydrous potash mica, with pearly lustre, occurring in small yellowish scales.

Damp (dæmp), *sb.* 1480. [Corresp. with MLG. and Du. and Da. *damp* vapour, steam, smoke, Icel. *dampr* steam, MHG. *dampf*, *tampf*, mod.Ger. *dampf*, etc.] 1. A noxious exhalation; *spec.* in coal mines: (*a*) = CHOKE-DAMP, also called *black d.*, *suffocating d.*; (*b*) = FIRE-DAMP, formerly *fulminating d.* 1626. †2. Visible vapour; fog, mist –1827. 3. Moisture; dampness, humidity. (The ordinary current sense.) 1706; *slang*, a drink. DICKENS. †4. A dazed condition; stupor –1712. 5. Depression of spirits 1606. 6. A check 1587.

3. The morning mist and the evening d. JOHNSON. 4. I felt a general D. and a Faintness all over me ADDISON. 5. He found a great d. upon the spirit of the Governour CLARENDON. *Comb.* **d.-course,** *prop.* **d.-proof course,** a course of some damp-proof material laid slightly above the level of the outside soil, to prevent the damp from rising up a wall.

Damp (dæmp), *a.* 1590. [f. DAMP *sb.*] †1. Of the nature of, or belonging to, a damp; see DAMP *sb.* 1. –1733. 2. Affected with or showing stupefaction or depression of spirits (*arch.*) 1590. 3. Slightly wet; holding water in suspension or absorption; moist, humid. (The ordinary current sense.) 1706.

1. MILT. *Sams.* 8. 2. With looks Down cast and d. — *P. L.* I. 523. 3. A d. bed (*mod.*). Hence **Da·mp-ly** *adv.*, **-ness.**

Damp (dæmp), *v.* 1548. [f. DAMP *sb.* Ger. *dampfen*, Du. *dampen* are of like date.] 1. *trans.* To affect with damp, to stifle; to dull, deaden (fire, sound, etc.). Also *fig.* 1564. †2. To stupefy, benumb, daze –1726. 3. To depress, discourage, check 1548. 4. To make moist or humid, to wet as steam, etc., does; to moisten 1671. 5. *Gardening. To d. off* (intr.): Of plants: To rot from damp; to fog off 1846.

1. All shutting in of Air .. dampeth the Sound BACON. *To d. down* (a fire, etc.): to cover it with small coal, etc., so as to check combustion and prevent its going out. Also *fig.* 3. Sorrow damps my lays CLARE. To d. and spoyl our Trade C. MATHER. 4. They [winds from South] d. linen and paper 1671.

Dampen (dæ·mp'n), *v.* Now chiefly *U.S.* 1630. [f. DAMP *a.* or *v.*] 1. *trans.* = DAMP *v.* 1, 3, 4. 2. *intr.* To become dull or damp 1686.

Damper (dæ·mpəɹ). 1748. [f. DAMP *v.* + -ER.] 1. That which damps (see DAMP *v.*). 2. A contrivance in a pianoforte for damping or stopping the vibrations of the strings; the mute of a horn, etc. 1783. 3. A metal plate in a flue or chimney, used to control the combustion by regulating the draught 1788. 4. *Australia.* A kind of cake or bread made, for the occasion, of flour and water and baked in hot ashes 1833. 5. *Electr.* A device for diminishing or destroying the oscillation of a suspended magnetic needle or freely moving coil 1906.

1. Sussex is a great d. of curiosity H. WALPOLE. *Comb.* **d.-pedal,** that pedal in a pianoforte which raises all the dampers, etc., the 'loud pedal'.

Dampish (dæ·mpiʃ), *a.* 1577. [orig. f. DAMP *sb.* (cf. *boyish*).] †1. Vaporous –1649. 2. Somewhat damp or moist 1641. Hence **Da·mpish-ly** *adv.*, **-ness.**

Dampne, etc., obs. ff. DAMN, etc.

Da·mpy, *a.* 1600. [f. DAMP *sb.*] 1. †Full of vapour or mist –1729; infested with damps, as a mine (*mod.*). 2. Somewhat damp 1691.

Damsel (dæ·mzěl), **damosel** (dæ·mozel). [Early ME. *dameisele*, a. OF., later *damoisele*, *demoiselle* (14th c.), f. *dame*.] 1. A young unmarried lady; orig. one of noble or gentle birth. The 16–17th c. *damosel*, *damozel* is now used by poets, etc., as more stately than *damsel*. 2. A young unmarried woman (sometimes slightingly); a girl, a country lass. (Not now in spoken use.) ME. 3. A maid in waiting (*arch.*) ME. 4. A hot iron for warming a bed. (Cf. 1 Kings i. 1–4.) 1727. 5. A projection on the spindle of a mill-stone for shaking the shoot 1880.

1. Th' adventure of the errant damozell SPENSER *F. Q.* II. i. 19. 2. The damosell is not dead, but sleepeth *Mark* v. 39, 41. *Comb.* **d.-fly,** the slender dragon-fly, *Agrion Virgo*, called in Fr. *demoiselle.*

Damson (dæ·mz'n). [ME. *damascene*, ad. L. *Damascenum* for *Prunum Damascenum* plum of Damascus.] 1. A small plum, black or dark purple, the fruit of *Prunus communis* or *domestica*, variety *damascena*. 2. The tree which bears this ME. 3. *attrib.* Of the colour of the damson 1661.

Comb. **d.-cheese,** an inspissated conserve of damsons and sugar.

†Dan¹. ME. [a. OF. = mod.F. *dom* :—L. *dominus*.] = Master, Sir –1832.

The monke of Bury..Dane Johnn Lydgate SKELTON. D. Chaucer SPENSER.

Dan [2] (dæn). 1687. A small buoy, supporting a pole which bears a flag by day and a lamp by night, used as a mark in deep-sea fishing.

Dan [3]. *local.* 1852. *Coal-mining.* A small truck or sledge on which coal is drawn in mines.

Danaid (dæ·neˌid). [In F. *Danaïde*, ad. Gr. Δαναΐς, pl. Δαναΐδες, the daughters of Danaus king of Argos, who murdered their husbands on the wedding-night, and were condemned eternally to fill sieve-like vessels with water.] A daughter of Danaus; used *attrib.* in reference to the labour of the Danaides: endless and futile. So **Danaide·an** *a.*

Danaide (dæ·neˌəid). 1825. [a. mod.F. *danaïde* (see prec.): so named from analogy to the vessels of the Danaides.] A horizontal water wheel consisting of a vertical axis to which is attached a conical drum and case, with radial spiral floats: also called 'tub-wheel'.

Danaite (dēⁱ·năˌəit). 1833. [f. J. F. *Dana*, U.S. chemist.] *Min.* A variety of arsenopyrite or mispickel, containing cobalt.

Danalite (dēⁱ·năləit). 1866. [f. J. D. *Dana*, U.S. mineralogist.] *Min.* A silicate of iron, glucinum, etc. with sulphide of zinc, occurring in reddish octahedrons in granite.

Danburite (dæ·nbʊ̆rəit). 1839. [f. *Danbury*, Ct., U.S., where it occurs.] *Min.* A boro-silicate of lime, brittle, translucent, and yellowish or whitish in colour.

Dance (dɑns), *sb.* ME. [a. OF. *dance*, *danse*, f. the vb.] 1. A rhythmical skipping and stepping, with regular turnings and movements of the limbs and body, usually to the accompaniment of music; the action or an act or round of dancing. Also *transf.* and *fig.* 2. A tune for regulating the movements of a dance, or composed in a dance rhythm 1509. 3. A dancing party ME. †4. *fig.* Course of action; play, game –1733.

4. Of remedies of loue she knew per chaunce For she koude of that Art the olde daunce CHAUCER.

Phr. *To lead*, occas. *give* (*a person*) *a d.*; *fig.* to cause him to undergo exertion or worry with little result. *D. of death*: an allegorical representation of Death leading men of all conditions in the d. to the grave. Also called *d. of Macabre*, F. *danse macabre*. *St. Vitus's d.* = CHOREA, q.v.; also *fig.*

Dance (dɑns), *v.* ME. [a. OF. *dancer*, *danser*, ad. (see Diez) OHG. *dansôn* to draw, stretch out, whence 'to form a chain or file in dancing'.] 1. *intr.* To leap, skip, hop, or glide with measured steps and rhythmical movements of the body, usually to a musical accompaniment. Also *transf.* and *fig.* 2. To leap, skip, spring, or move up and down from excitement or strong emotion. Also *transf.* and *fig.* ME. 3. Of things inanimate: To bob up and down 1563. 4. *trans.* with cognate object ME. 5. *causal.* a. To cause to dance 1665. b. To toss up and down with a jerky motion; to dandle ME.

1. Many a youth and many a maid Dancing in the chequer'd shade MILT. *L'Alleg.* 96. †*To d. barefoot*: said of an elder sister when a younger one was married before her. *To d. to* (*a person's*) *pipe*, *whistle*, etc.: *fig.* to follow his lead. 2. I haue *Tremor Cordis* on me: my heart daunces, But not for ioy *Wint. T.* I. ii. 110. 3. The mote that daunceth in the beam 1812. *To d. upon nothing*, to be hanged. 4. A minuet, danced by two persons GOLDSM. †*To d. the Tyburn jig*: to be hanged. 5. a. To d. a bear GOLDSM. b. I that danced her on my knee TENNYSON.

Phr. *To d. attendance*: to wait (upon a person) assiduously and obsequiously. See also ATTENDANCE.

Dancer (dɑ·nsəɪ). ME. [f. prec. vb.] 1. One who dances; *spec.* one who dances professionally in public. 2. (*pl.*) A sect of enthusiasts who arose in 1374 in Flanders, and were noted for their wild dancing 1764. 3. *pl.* Stairs (*slang*) 1671. 4. *pl.* The aurora borealis. Also *Merry Dancers.* (Chiefly *Sc.*) 1717. †**Dan·ceress**, a female d.

Dancette (dɑnse·t), *sb.* 1838. [Inferred from next.] 1. *Her.* A fesse with three indentations 1864. 2. *Archit.* A zigzag moulding.

Dancetté, -ee (dɑ·nsĕte, -ti), *a.* 1610. [Corrupt f. F. *danché* (:—late L. *denticatus*).] *Her.* = DANCY.

Dancing (dɑ·nsiŋ), *vbl. sb.* ME. The action of DANCE *v.*

Comb.: **d.-malady, -mania, -plague** = CHOREA; **-master**; **-mistress**; **-school.**

Da·ncing, *ppl. a.* 1563. That dances.

Comb. †**D.-goats** [L. *capræ saltantes*], a species of aurora.

Da·ncing-girl. 1760. [DANCING *ppl. a.*] 1. A female professional dancer; *esp.* in India, a nautch-girl (in Pg. *bailadeira*, BAYADÈRE). 2. *Dancing-girls*: a plant, *Mantisia saltatoria*, having purple and yellow flowers which somewhat resemble a ballet-dancer.

†**Dancy**, *a.* *rare.* 1611. [a. OF. *dansié*, *danché* :—late L. *denticatus.*] *Her.* Toothed, indented –1706.

Dandelion (dæ·ndĭləiən). 1513. [a. F. *dent de lion* 'lion's tooth', from the outline of the leaves.] A well-known Composite plant (*Taraxacum Dens-leonis* or *Leontodon Taraxacum*), with widely toothed leaves, and a bright yellow flower; the leaves, stalk, and root contain a bitter milky juice. Also *attrib.*

Da·nder, *sb.*[1] *Sc.* 1791. [?] A calcined cinder.

Da·nder, *sb.*[2] = DANDRUFF, q.v.

Dander (dæ·ndəɪ), *sb.*[3] *U.S. colloq.* 1837. [? fig. use of prec., or of DUNDER (formerly *dander*) ferment.] Ruffled or angry temper.

Da·nder, *sb.*[4] 1821. [f. DANDER *v.*] 1. *Sc.* A saunter. 2. *dial.* A fit of shivering 1877.

Dander (dæ·ndəɪ), *v.* 1600. [Cf. *blunder*, *wander.*] 1. *intr.* To stroll, saunter (*Sc.* and *n. dial.*). 2. *dial.* To wander in talk; also, to vibrate 1724.

Dandiacal (dændəi·ăkăl), *a.* 1831. [f. DANDY, after *hypochondriacal*, etc.] Of the nature of, or characteristic of, a dandy; dandified.

Arrayed in the most d. manner SALA.

Da·ndie Di·nmont. Also **Dandy.** [From *Dandie Dinmont* in Scott's *Guy Mannering.*] One of a breed of terriers with long bodies, short strong legs, somewhat almond-shaped ears, and a slightly feathered tail carried gaily.

Dandify (dæ·ndifəi), *v.* *colloq.* 1823. [See -FY.] *trans.* To give the character or style of a dandy to; to trim like a dandy. Hence **Da:ndifica·tion** (*colloq.*), the act of dandifying; the being dandified; a dandified ornament. **Da·ndified** *ppl. a.* foppish.

Dandiprat (dæ·ndipræt). *arch.* 1520. [?] †1. A small 16th-c. coin, worth three halfpence –1641. 2. A small, insignificant, or contemptible fellow. Also *attrib.* 1556.

Dandize·tte. 1821. [f. DANDY; after F. *grisette*, etc.] A female dandy.

Dandle (dæ·nd'l), *v.* 1530. [?] 1. To move (a child, etc.) lightly up and down in the arms or on the knee. Also *fig.* and *transf.* 2. *fig.* To make much of, pet, fondle, pamper 1575. †3. To trifle or toy with –1646. 4. *intr.* To play or toy (*with*) (*rare*) 1829. †5. = DANGLE (? erron.) –1687.

1. He sits dandling his child upon his knee 1847. 2. No man or nation was ever dandled into greatness GOLDWIN SMITH. 3. They doe soe d. theyr doinges.. as yf they would not have the Enemye subdued SPENSER. Hence **Da·ndler.** †**Da·ndling** *sb.* a dandled child; a pet.

Dandruff, dandriff (dæ·ndrʊ̆f, -if). 1545. [?] Dead scarf-skin separating in small scales and entangled in the hair; scurf.

Dandy (dæ·ndi), *sb.*[1] (and *a.*) 1780. [?]

A. 1. One who studies ostentatiously to dress elegantly and fashionably; a fop, an exquisite. Also *transf.* 2. *slang* or *colloq.* In phr. *the d.*, 'the correct thing', 'the ticket' 1784. 3. *Naut.* 'A sloop or cutter with a jigger-mast abaft, on which a mizen-lug-sail is set' (Smyth). 4. *dial.* A bantam fowl. (*D. cock*, *d. hen.*) 1828. 5. Short for DANDY-ROLLER 1851.

1. A D. is a Clothes-wearing Man CARLYLE. *transf.* The barque looked a real d. 1885.

B. *attrib.* and *adj.* Of, belonging to, or characteristic of a dandy or dandies; affectedly neat, trim, or smart 1813.

A d. little hand in a kid glove THACKERAY.

Hence **Da·ndily** *adv.* **Da·ndyish** *a.* foppish. **Da·ndyism.**

Dandy, *sb.*[2] Also **dandy-fever.** 1828. See DENGUE.

‖**Dandy, dandi** (dæ·ndi), *sb.*[3] *Anglo-Ind.* 1685. [Hindi *ḍanḍī*, f. *ḍanḍ* staff, oar.] 1. A boatman on the Ganges. 2. (*Dandi.*) A S'aiva mendicant who carries a small wand 1832. 3. 'A kind of vehicle consisting of a strong cloth slung like a hammock to a bamboo staff, and carried by two (or more) men' (Yule).

Da·ndy-brush. 1841. [f. DANDY *sb.*[1]] A stiff brush made of split whalebone, used in cleaning horses.

Dandy-cock, -hen; see DANDY[1] 4.

Da·ndy-horse. 1819. A kind of velocipede.

Da·ndy-line. 1882. A kind of line used in herring fishing, carrying at short intervals transverse pieces of whalebone or cane, having unbaited hooks at either end.

Da·ndy-ro:ller. Also **-roll.** 1839. *Paper-making.* A perforated roller for solidifying the partly-formed web of paper, and for impressing the watermark.

Dane (dēⁱn). [OE. *Dęne* pl.; cf. OE. *Denemearc.*] 1. A native or subject of Denmark; in older usage including Northmen generally. 2. Applied to a breed or breeds of dogs 1774. 3. *attrib.* = DANISH.

2. *Great D.* (also simply *D.*): a large, powerful, short-haired breed of dog, between the mastiff and the greyhound types. *Lesser D.*: the Dalmatian.

Danebrog; see DANNEBROG.

Danegeld, -gelt (dēⁱ·ngeld, -gelt). OE. [Corresp. to ON. **Dana-gjald*, f. *Dana-*, *Dane-* + *gjald*, *gjeld*, payment, tribute.] *Eng. Hist.* An annual tax, imposed originally (as is supposed) to provide funds for the protection of England against the Danes, and continued subsequently as a land-tax.

Dane-law (dēⁱ·nlǭ). [OE. *Dęna lagu* Danes' law.] 1. The Danish law anciently in force over that part of England occupied by the Danes. 2. Hence, The district north-east of Watling Street, where this law prevailed 1837.

Da·nes'-blood. 1607. [f. as DANEWORT, q.v.] The Danewort. b. *Campanula glomerata* 1861. c. *Anemone Pulsatilla.*

Daneweed (dēⁱ·nwīd). 1748. [See next.] †A local name for *Eryngium campestre.* b. = DANEWORT.

Danewort (dēⁱ·nwɒɪt). 1491. [f. DANE + WORT, the plants being supposed to spring up in places where Danish blood was spilt in battle.] The Dwarf Elder, *Sambucus Ebulus.*

Dang, *v.* 1793. A euphemism for DAMN.

Dang, pa. t. of DING *v.*, to drive, push, knock, or dash.

Danger (dēⁱ·ndʒəɪ), *sb.* ME. [a. OF. *dangier*, *danger* :—late L. **dominiarium*, f. *dominium*, f. *dominus.*] 1. Power of a lord, jurisdiction, dominion; power to dispose of, or to harm (*arch.*). †b. Liability (to loss, punishment, etc.) –1689. †2. Difficulty (made or raised); chariness; coyness –1526. 3. Liability or exposure to harm or injury; risk, peril. (From sense 1. Now the main sense.) Also with *a* and *pl.* 1489. †4. Mischief, harm –1601. †5. The lordship over a forest; the rent paid in acknowledgement of this (so OF. *dangier*) 1693.

1. In dawngere had he..The ȝonge girles of þe diocise CHAUCER. Phr. *In* (*a person's*) *d.*: within his power. b. Phr. *Out of debt out of d.* (now taken in sense 3). 2. Phr. †*To make d.* [OF. *faire dangier* (*de*)]: to make a difficulty (about doing anything). 3. Delay breeds D. SHELTON. In d. of their lives, of deth CAXTON, to die NORTH. Blind to the dangers of their country HELPS. 4. *Jul. C.* II. i. 17.

Comb. **d.-signal**, a signal indicating d.; *e.g.* on *Railways*, indicating an obstruction, etc. ahead. Hence †**Da·ngerful** *a.* **Da·ngerless** *a.* (and *adv.*). Now *rare.* **Da·ngersome** *a.* (*dial.*).

†**Da·nger**, *v.* ME. [a. OF. *dangerer*, f. as prec.] 1. To render liable –1633. 2. To endanger –1663. 3. ? To damage. (Cf. DANGER *sb.* 4.) –1614.

Dangerous (dēⁱ·ndʒərəs), *a.* ME. [a. AF. = OF. *dangeros*, *-eus*, f. *danger.*] †1. Difficult to deal with; not affable (ME. only); difficult to please –1577; chary *of* –1598. 2. Fraught with danger or risk; perilous, hazardous, unsafe. (The current sense.) 1490. 3. In danger; dangerously ill. Now *dial.* and *U.S. colloq.* 1616. †4. Injurious. (Cf. DANGER *sb.* 4.) –1576.

1. So fiers & daungerous was he, That he nolde graunte hir askyng CHAUCER. 2. Delay herein is daungerous B. GOOGE. In most of the European nations there are d. classes HELPS. 3. He's d.; they don't think he'll live 1884. 4. Two vices, very daungerous and noysome among men FLEMING. Hence **Da·ngerous·ly** *adv.*, **-ness.**

Dangle (dæ·ŋg'l), *v.* 1590. [app. f. stem *ding-*, *dang-* (DING *v.*).] **1.** *intr.* To hang loosely swaying to and fro 1590; to be hanged 1678. **2.** *trans.* To make (a thing) hang and sway to and fro; to hold or carry (it) suspended loosely 1612. Also *fig.* **3.** *fig.* (*intr.*) To hang *after* or about any one, *esp.* as a loosely attached follower 1607.

1. Our thinne nets dangling in the winde P. FLETCHER. And men [have] as often dangled for't, And yet will never leave the sport BUTLER. 3. Heirs of noble houses..dangling after actresses MACAULAY. *Comb.* **d.-berry**, Blue Tangle, *Gaylussacia frondosa*, an American shrub, N.O. *Vacciniaceæ*.

Hence **Da·ngle** *sb.* act of dangling; that which dangles (*rare*). **Da·ngle** *a.* dangling (*rare*). **Da·ngle-ment**, dangling. **Da·ngler.**

†**Da·nic**, *a.* 1613. = DANISH –1692. Hence **Da·nicism**, a Danish idiom.

Danish (dē¹·nif). [OE. *Dęnisc* :—OTeut. **Danisk-* + -ISH. Thence ME. *Densh*, etc.] *adj.* Of or belonging to the Danes and to Denmark. *sb.* The language of Denmark.

D. ax: a kind of battle-ax with a very long blade. *D. dog*: see DANE. Hence **Da·nishry** [cf. *Irishry*, etc.], the people of Danish race (in Britain). *Hist.*

Danism[1] (dē¹·niz'm). 1886. [f. DANE + -ISM.] Danicism.

†**Da·nism**[2]. 1623. [ad. Gr. δανεισμός.] Money-lending on usury. (Dicts.)

†**Dank**, *sb.* ME. [f. DANK *a.*] Wetness –1602; a wet place –1667.

Dank (dæŋk), *a.* ME. [Etym. unkn.; cf. Sw. *dank* 'marshy spot', Icel. *dökk* (:—*danku-*) pit, pool. Not conn. w. *damp.*] **1.** Wet, watery, wetting. **2.** Damp: as an injurious or disagreeable quality 1573. **3.** Said of weeds, etc. growing in damp places 1820.

1. The d. moisture of the ayre 1601. O'er the d. marsh SOMERVILLE. 2. Vapours, d. and clammy COWPER. The d. and sable earth SCOTT. Hence **Da·nkish** *a.* dank; somewhat moist. **Da·nkish-ness. Da·nkly** *adv.* **Da·nkness.**

Dank (dæŋk), *v.* Now *dial.* ME. [See DANK *a.*] †**1.** To wet, damp, moisten. Also *fig.* **2.** *intr.* To drizzle.

‖**Dannebrog** (dæ·nĕbrǫg). Also **Dane-.** 1708. [Da., f. *Danne-*, *Dane-* + *brog* breech, cloth.] The Danish national flag; hence, a Danish order of knighthood.

‖**Danseuse** (dañsöz). 1845. [Fr.] A female dancer, a ballet-dancer.

†**Dansk**, *a.* Also **Danisk.** 1569. [a. Da., Sw., Icel.] = DANISH –1610.

‖**Da·nsker.** [Da., f. prec.] A Dane. SHAKS.

Dante. 1600. [Cf. It. *dante*; see ANTE.] †**1.** (Also *dant.*) The same as ANTE *sb.*, q. v. **2.** (Also *danta.*) The American tapir 1601.

Dantean (dæ·ntiăn), *a.* 1850. Of, relating to, or resembling Dante or his writings. Also *sb.* A student of Dante. So **Dante·sque** *a.* **Da·ntist**, a Dante scholar. **Danto·philist**, an admirer of Dante.

Dap (dæp), *sb.* Now *dial.* 1583. [?f. DAP *v.*] **1.** *pl.* Ways, modes of action; hence *dial.* likeness, image. **2.** A bounce of a ball, etc. 1835.

Dap (dæp), *v.* Also **dape.** 1653. [app. parallel to DAB, the final *p* expressing a lighter touch. Cf. also DOP.] **1.** *intr.* (rarely *trans.*) To fish by letting the bait dip and bob lightly on the water; to dib. Also *gen.* **2.** To rebound, bounce 1851.

1. How to catch a Chub with daping a Grashopper WALTON.

Daphnad (dæ·fnăd). 1847. *Bot.* Lindley's name for plants of the order *Thymelaceæ*, including *Daphne.*

Daphne (dæ·fnĭ). ME. [Gr. δάφνη the laurel or bay-tree: in *Mythol.* a nymph who was changed into a laurel.] **1.** The Laurel. **b.** in *Bot.* The name of a genus of shrubs containing the Spurge Laurel and Mezereon. **2.** *Astron.* The 41st of the Asteroids. Hence **Da·phnean** *a.*

‖**Daphnia** (dæ·fniă). 1847. [mod.L. f. prec.] *Zool.* A genus of minute fresh-water entomostracans; a water-flea. Hence **Daphnia·ceous** *a.* **Da·phniad**, a member of the order containing the water-fleas. **Da·phnioid** *a.* allied in structure to Daphnia; *sb.* a daphniad.

Daphnin (dæ·fnin). 1819. [f. as prec. + -IN.] *Chem.* A bitter glucoside obtained from two species of Daphne. So **Da·phnetin**, a product of the decomposition of daphnin.

‖**Dapifer** (dæ·pifəɹ). 1636. [f. L. *daps*, *dapi-* + *fer-*.] One who brings meat to table; hence, the official title of the steward of a king's or nobleman's household.

Dapper (dæ·pəɹ), *a.* 1440. [app. ad. Flemish or LG. dial.; cf. MDu. *dapper* powerful, MLG. *dapper* heavy, etc., MHG. *tapfer* heavy, in mod.G., warlike, etc.] **1.** Neat, trim, smart, spruce in dress or appearance. (Formerly, but not now, appreciative.) **b.** *esp.* 'Little and active, lively without bulk' (J.) 1606. **2.** *transf.* Of animals and things 1579. †**3.** as *sb.* A dapper fellow –1747.

1. The spruce and d. importance of his ordinary appearance SCOTT. The d. elves MILT. *Comus* 118. 2. My d. nagg, Pegasus WOOD. Hence **Da·pper-ling**, a d. little fellow. **Da·pper-ly** *adv.*, **-ness.**

Dapple (dæ·p'l), *sb.* 1580. [? conn. w. Icel. *depill* 'spot, dot', app. a dim. of *dapi* pool. Thus perh. originally a 'splash', and, hence, a blotch or speck of colour.] †**1.** One of many spots of colouring on a surface –1611. **2.** Spotting, clouding; dappled condition, dappling 1591. **3.** An animal with a mottled coat 1635.

1. As many eyes upon his body, as my gray mare hath dapples SIDNEY.

Dapple (dæ·p'l), *a.* 1551. [See prec. and DAPPLED.] = DAPPLED.

A third sheykh, with a d. mule LANE.

Dapple (dæ·p'l), *v.* 1599. [? f. the (? ppl.) adj. DAPPLED (q. v.).] **1.** *trans.* To variegate with spots of different colour or shade. Also *fig.* **2.** *intr.* To become dappled 1678.

1. Day .. Dapples the drowsie east with spots of grey *Much Ado* v. iii. 27. 2. To d. into day BYRON.

Da·pple-bay, *sb.* 1835. [After *dapple-grey.*] A dappled bay (horse).

Dappled (dæ·pl'd), *a.* ME. [Cf. OE. *æppled* formed into apples, from *æppel* sb. But DAPPLE *sb.* first appears two centuries later.] Marked with spots of a different colour or shade; speckled. *Comb.* **d.-grey** = DAPPLE-GREY (horse).

Dapple-grey (dæ·p'lˌgrē¹), *a.* (*sb.*) ME. [See DAPPLE *sb.*, *a.*, *v.* and GREY. In such combs., the first element is usually a sb.: *e.g.* in *apple-grey*, etc.; but 'spot-grey' is not satisfactory. Cf. ON. *apalgrár*, Ger. *apfelgrau*, F. *pommelé*, etc., all rendered by *dapple-grey.*] Grey variegated with spots or patches of a darker shade: said of horses. *absol.* A horse of this colour 1639.

His steede was al dappull gray CHAUCER.

Darapti (dăræ·pti). 1551. *Logic.* A mnemonic term for the first valid mood of the third syllogistic figure, in which two universal affirmative premisses (*a*, *a*) yield a particular affirmative conclusion (*i*).

Darby (dā·ɹbi). 1575. A southern (not the local) pronunciation of *Derby*, the English town and shire. Hence an English surname. **1.** *Father Derby's* or *Darby's bands*: app. Some rigid form of usurer's bond 1576. **2.** *pl.* Handcuffs; *occas.*, fetters (*slang*) 1673. †**3.** Ready money (*slang*) –1785. **4.** Short for Derby ale 1704. **5.** *Plastering.* A plasterer's float with two handles, used in levelling surfaces, etc. 1819. **6. Darby and Joan**: an attached couple, *esp.* when old and in humble life. Hence *dial.* a pair of china figures for the chimney-piece. 1773.

Darbyism (dā·ɹbiˌis'm). 1876. [f. Rev. John N. *Darby*, their first leader.] The principles of the Plymouth Brethren, or of a branch of these called Exclusive Brethren. So **Da·rby-ite**, one who holds these principles.

Dardan (dā·ɹdăn). 1606. [ad. L. *Dardanus* Trojan.] *adj.* Trojan, of Troy. *sb.* A Trojan. So **Darda·nian** *a.* and *sb.*; ‖**Darda·nium**, a golden bracelet.

About thy wrist the rich Dardanium HERRICK.

Dare (dē³ɹ), *v.*[1] Pa. t. **durst** (dɒ̄ɹst), **dared** (dē³ɹd); pa. pple. **dared.** [A Teut. preterite-present verb. OE. *durran*, pres. *dearr*, *durron*, pa. *dorste*; belonging originally to the third ablaut series *ders-*, *dars-*, *durs-*; cf. Skr. *dhṛsh-*, perf. *dadhārsha* to be bold, Gr. θαρσ-, θρασ-, in θρασύς, θαρσεῖν.

The 3rd sing. pres. *he dares* and pa. t. *dared* appeared in the south in the 16th c., and are always used in the transitive senses, and now also in the intrans. sense when followed by *to.* When followed by the infinitive without *to*, *dare* and *durst* are still in common use.]

I. *intr.* (Inflected *dare*, *durst*, also *dares*, *dared.*) **1.** To have boldness or courage (*to do* something); to be so bold as OE. **2.** *ellipt.* To dare to go, venture ME.

1. None of the disciples durst aske him, Who art thou *John* xxi. 12. A Spanish Notary dared to appear publickly in the Rota 1619. No one durst to breathe otherwise GALE.

II. *trans.* (Inflected *dares*, *dared.*) **1.** To dare to undertake or do; to venture upon, have courage for 1631. **2.** To venture to meet; to challenge; to defy 1580.

1. To d. all things, but nothing too much 1631. 2. I d. Damnation .. onely Ile be reueng'd *Haml.* IV. v. 133. An English man..[cannot] suffer..to be dared by any LYLY. You..d. me to it MARRYAT.

Dare (dē³ɹ), *v.*[2] Now *dial.* [OE. *darian*, f. stem of MDu. and LG. *bedaren* to appease, calm, Flemish *verdaren* to amaze.] †**1.** *intr.* To gaze fixedly or stupidly –1549; also *fig.* †**2.** To crouch. Also *fig.* –1500. †**3.** To lurk –1440. †**4.** *trans.* To daze; to fascinate –1671. **5.** To daunt, terrify. Now *dial.* 1611.

4. *To d. larks*, to fascinate and daze them in order to catch them.

Dare (dē³ɹ), *sb.*[1] 1594. [f. DARE *v.*[1]] **1.** An act of defying; a challenge. Now *colloq.* †**2.** Boldness –1596.

1. Sin is the d. of God's justice BUNYAN. 2. It lends..A larger D. to your great Enterprize SHAKS.

Dare (dē³ɹ), *sb.*[2] 1860. [f. DARE *v.*[2]] A contrivance for fascinating larks.

†**Dare**, *sb.*[3] 1475. [A sing. f. *dars*, OF. *dars*, *darz*, pl. of *dart*, *dard.*] = DACE –1740.

Dare-devil (dē³·ɹˌde:vil). 1794. [f. DARE *v.*[1] + DEVIL; cf. *cutthroat.*] *sb.* One ready to dare the devil. *adj.* Recklessly daring 1832.

Robert Clive .. an idle dare-devil of a boy GREEN. *adj.* Dare-devil skippers MOTLEY. Hence **Da·re-de·vilry.**

Darer (dē³·rəɹ). 1614. [f. DARE *v.*[1] + -ER.] One who ventures; one who challenges.

Darg (dāɹg). *Sc.* and *n. dial.* ME. [Syncopated f. *daywerk*, or *daywark*, DAYWORK.] A day's work; also, a definite quantity of work. Hence **Da·rger**, **Da·rgsman**, day-labourer.

Daric (dæ·rik). 1566. [ad. Gr. Δαρεικός (sc. στατήρ stater).] A gold coin of ancient Persia, named from the first Darius. Also a Persian silver coin of the same design.

Darii (dē³·riəi). 1551. *Logic.* A mnemonic term for the third valid mood of the first syllogistic figure, in which a universal major premiss (*a*) and a particular affirmative minor (*i*) yield a particular affirmative conclusion (*i*).

Daring (dē³·riŋ), *vbl. sb.* 1611. [-ING[1].] Adventurous courage, hardihood.

Da·ring, *ppl. a.* 1582. [-ING[2].] Bold, adventurous; hardy. Also *transf.* and *fig.*

The most d. of financiers MACAULAY. This d. legal fiction FREEMAN. Hence **Da·ring-ly** *adv.*, **-ness.**

Dariole (dæ·riōul). ME. [a. F.] **1.** A rich meat pie in crust –1664. **2.** A shell or cup of pastry filled with custard, cream, etc.; also = *d. mould* 1846.

Dark (dāɹk), *a.* [OE. *deorc* (repr. earlier **derk*). Not in other Teut. langs.]

I. *literal.* **1.** Devoid of or deficient in light; unilluminated. **2.** Reflecting or transmitting little light; gloomy, sombre OE. **3.** Approaching black in hue; deep in shade (opp. to *light*); of the complexion: the opposite of fair ME.

1. A very darke night HALL. A d. house 1861. Phr. †*To keep (a person) dark*: to keep him confined in a dark room (as madmen were kept formerly). *D. moon* = *d. of the moon.* 2. Cloudy and d. weather 1658. D. hills 1870. 3. D. hair SOUTHEY. On the d green grass THOMSON.

II. *fig.* **1.** Devoid of moral or spiritual light; evil, wicked; foul, iniquitous, atrocious OE. **2.** Gloomy, dismal, sad OE.; of the countenance: clouded, frowning 1599. **3.** Obscure in meaning ME.; indistinct, indiscernible 1592. **4.** Concealed, secret, as in *to keep d.* 1605; of a person: reticent, not open 1675. **5.** Of whom or which little is known 1831. **6.** Not able to see; blind. Now *dial.* ME. **7.** Void of intellectual light; ignorant ME.

1. To darke dishonours vse *Rich. II*, I. i. 169. This darke Conspiracy *Ibid.* V. ii. 96. The darkest and meanest vices MACAULAY. 2. The d. side of things 1849. Men of d. tempers ADDISON. A smile amid d.

frowns SHELLEY. 3. The Cause is d., and hath not been rendred by any BACON. In d. obscurity SHAKS. D. oblivion COWPER. 4. And Lyttelton a d., designing knave POPE. 5. *D. horse* (*Racing slang*), a horse about whose 'form' little is known; hence *fig.* of a candidate or competitor. 7. What in me is d. Illumine MILT. *P. L.* I. 26.

Combs., etc.: **D. Ages,** in its earliest use, the Middle Ages; later, the earlier period to *c.* 1100; **d.-house** = *dark-room* (*a*); **-room,** †(*a*) a room in which madmen were confined; (*b*) *Photogr.* a room from which all actinic rays of light are excluded, used by photographers when dealing with sensitized plates; **†d. tent,** a camera obscura.

Hence **Da·rkful** *a.* full of darkness (*rare*). **Da·rkish** *a.* somewhat d. **Da·rkly** *adv.* in a d. manner.

Dark (dāɹk), *sb.* ME. [f. DARK *a.*; cf. *light* sb. and adj.] 1. Absence of light; darkness; the dark time; night, nightfall; a dark place. Also *fig.* 2. Dark colour or shade; *spec.* in *Art*, a part of a picture in shadow, as opp. to *light* 1675. Also *fig.* 3. Obscurity 1628. 4. *In the d.*: in a state of ignorance 1677.

1. Nights darke approcht apace 1598. One evening after d. 1771. *D. of the moon*: the time near new moon when there is no moonlight. 4. I am entirely in the d. about the designs..of [etc.] BURKE.

Dark (dāɹk), *v. arch.* or *dial.* ME. [f. DARK *a.*] †1. To make or become dark, darken -1715. Also *fig.* †2. *intr.* To lie in the dark, to lie hid -1447.

1. When the nyght darkes SKELTON. My somers day in lusty may is derked before the none 1500.

Darken (dā·ɹk'n), *v.* ME. [f. DARK *a.*, superseding DARK *v.*; see -EN *suffix*⁵.] 1. *intr.* To grow or become dark. (Occas. with *down.*) 2. To grow clouded, gloomy, sad 1742. 3. *trans.* To make dark, to deprive of light. Also *fig.* ME. 4. To deprive of sight, to make blind (*lit.* and *fig.*) 1548. 5. *fig.* To make dark in meaning 1548. 6. *fig.* To cloud; to cast a gloom or shadow over 1553.

1. The Heaven darkens above SHELLEY. 2. His face darkened with some powerful emotion HAWTHORNE. 3. When Night darkens the Streets MILT. *P. L.* I. 501. *To d.* (*a person's*) *door or doors*: emphatic for to appear on the threshold (as a visitor). 4. Let their eyes be darkened, that they see not *Ps.* lxix. 23. 5. Who is this that darkeneth counsel by words without knowledge *Job* xxxviii. 2. 6. To d. The Mirth o' th' Feast *Wint. T.* IV. iv. 41. Hence **Da·rkener.**

Da·rk-la·ntern. 1650. A lantern with an arrangement by which the light can be concealed.

Darkle (dā·ɹk'l), *v.* 1800. [f. DARKLING *adv.*; see next.] 1. *intr.* To show itself darkly 1819. 2. To grow dark 1800. 3. *trans.* To obscure 1884.

Darkling (dā·ɹkliŋ), *adv.* and *a.* [ME. *darkeling*, f. DARK *a.* + -LING.]

A. *adv.* In the dark; in darkness (*lit.* and *fig.*) 1450.

The wakeful Bird Sings d. MILT. *P. L.* III. 39. var. **Da·rklings** (*rare*).

B. *adj.* (taken also as *pres. pple.*) 1. Being, proceeding, etc. in the dark 1763. 2. Showing itself darkly; darksome, obscure 1739.

1. Ye writers..O spare your d. labours SHENSTONE. 2. By the d. forest paths M. ARNOLD. D. was the sense SCOTT.

Da·rkmans. *Thieves' cant.* 1567. [f. DARK *a.*; cf. *lightmans* the day, etc.] The night.

Darkness (dā·ɹknės). [OE. *deorcnes, -nys*, f. *deorc* DARK *a.*] 1. Absence of light (total or partial). 2. The quality of being dark in shade or colour ME. 3. Blindness ME. 4. *fig.* a. Want of spiritual or intellectual sight ME.; b. Death ME. 5. Gloom of sorrow or distress 1645. 6. Obscurity, concealment, secrecy ME. 7. Obscurity of meaning 1553.

1. No light, But rather d. visible MILT. *P. L.* I. 63. 3. His eyes .. Were shrivell'd into d. in his head TENNYSON. 4. a. The prynce of derknes..our goostly ennemy the deuyll 1526. The D. and Superstition of later Ages ADDISON. 5. The d. of deepest dismay SHELLEY. 6. What I tell you in d., that speak ye in light *Matt.* x. 27.

Darksome (dā·ɹksŏm), *a.* 1530. [f. DARK *sb.*; cf. *toilsome.*] 1. Somewhat dark or gloomy. Now chiefly poetic for *dark.* Also *fig.* 2. Sombre in shade or colour 1615.

1. The d. night STERNHOLD & H. *fig.* D. sense BP. HALL, fears HOOD, vices MCCARTHY. 2. A darksom Cloud of Locusts MILT. *P. L.* XII. 185.

Darky, darkey (dā·ɹki). 1789. [f. DARK *a.*] 1. The night (*slang*). 2. A dark-lantern (*slang*) 1812. 3. A negro (*colloq.*). Also *attrib.* 1840.

Darling (dā·ɹliŋ). [OE. *déorling*, deriv. of *déor* DEAR; see -LING.]

A. *sb.* 1. The object of a person's love; a favourite; a pet. Also *transf.* and *fig.* †2. A variety of apple 1586.

1. The idol of my youth, The d. of my manhood TENNYSON. *fig.* The d. of the people STUBBS.

B. *adj.* [attrib. use of sb.] Dearly loved; best-loved, favourite 1596.

His [the devil's] d. sin Is pride that apes humility COLERIDGE.

Darn (dāɹn), *v.* 1600. [?] To mend (stockings, etc.) by filling-in a hole or rent with yarn or thread interwoven. (This is done with a *darning-needle.*) Also *fig.*

Four Pair of Silk-Stockings curiously derned STEELE.

Darn, *sb.* 1720. [f. prec.] The act or result of darning. Hence **Da·rner,** one who darns; a darning-needle.

Darn, Darnation, etc., colloq. f. DAMN, etc. (Chiefly *U.S.*)

Darnel (dā·ɹnĕl). ME. [Cf. Walloon dial. '*darnelle*, ivraie, *lolium temulentum*'; history unkn.] 1. A deleterious grass, *Lolium temulentum*, which grows as a weed among corn. Also, a book-name of the genus *Lolium.* 2. 'Applied to *Papaver Rhœas*' (Britten and Holland) 1612. 3. *fig.* Cf. COCKLE, TARES 1444. Also *attrib.*

1. *Red d.*: Rye-grass, *L. perenne.* 3. [Satan] sowing his d. of errors and tares of discord H. BARROW.

Darning (dā·ɹniŋ), *vbl. sb.* 1611. [-ING¹.] 1. The action of DARN *v.*, or its result. Also *fig.* 2. Articles darned or to be darned (*mod.*).

Comb.: **d.-ball, -last,** an egg-shaped or spherical piece of wood, etc., over which a fabric is stretched while being darned; **-needle,** a long and stout needle used in darning; **-stitch,** a stitch used in darning.

Darnix, darnock, obs. ff. DORNICK.

Daroga, darogha (dărōᵘ·gă). *Anglo-Ind.* 1634. [a. Pers. and Urdū.] A governor, superintendent, chief officer, head of police or excise. Under the Mongols, the Governor of a province or city.

Darraign,-rain(**e**,etc.,var.of DERAIGN *Obs.*

†Darrei·n, *a.* 1555. [a. OF. *darrain, derrein* :—late L. **deretranus* hinder, f. *de retro* (whence F. *derrière*).] *Old Law.* Last, ultimate, final; = DERNIER. *D. ressort*: = *dernier ressort.*

Dart (dāɹt), *sb.* ME. [a. OF. *dart*, accus. of *darz, dars*, in 15th c. *dard.*] 1. A pointed missile thrown by the hand; a light spear or javelin; any pointed missile, as an arrow, etc. Also *fig.* and *transf.* 2. Anything resembling a dart: *spec.* in *Zool.*, the sting of a venomous insect, a dart-like organ in some gastropods (see *d.-sac* below), etc. 1665. 3. *Dress-making.* A seam joining the two edges left by cutting a gore in any stuff 1884. 4. = *d.-serpent, -snake* (see below) 1591. †5. The fish called also DACE or DARE 1655. 6. [f. the vb.] The act of darting, or of casting a dart 1721.

1. As one shuteth deadly arowes and dartes COVERDALE *Prov.* xxvi. 18. b. A light pointed missile thrown at a target in the indoor game of *darts* 1901.

Comb.: **d.-moth,** a moth of the genus *Agrotis*, so called from a mark on the fore-wing; **-sac,** a sac connected with the generative organs of some gastropods, from which the darts are ejected; **-serpent, -snake,** a snake-like lizard of the genus *Acontias*, which dart upon their prey.

Dart (dāɹt), *v.* ME. [f. DART *sb.*; cf. F. *darder.*] †1. *trans.* To pierce with or as with a dart -1752. 2. To throw, cast, shoot (a dart or other missile) 1580. 3. *transf.* and *fig.* To send forth, or emit, suddenly and sharply; to shoot out 1592. 4. *intr.* To throw a dart or other missile 1530. 5. To move like a dart; to spring or start suddenly and rapidly; to shoot. Also *fig.* 1619.

1. To d. a whale BOND. 2. Near enough to d. the harpoon 1839. 3. Her eyes..darted flashes of anger as she spoke THACKERAY. 5. A deer darts out of the copse 1885. Hence **Da·rtingly** *adv.*

†Dartars. 1580. [Corruption of F. *dartre.*] A kind of scab on the chin of lambs -1741.

Darter (dā·ɹtəɹ). 1565. [f. DART *v.* + -ER¹.] 1. One who or that which darts; one who throws or shoots darts. †2. Dart-snake -1820. 3. A name for various birds; *esp.* the web-footed birds of the genus *Plotus*; so called from their way of darting on their prey 1825. 4. A name for various fishes; *esp.* the fresh-water fishes of the N. American subfamily *Etheostominæ*, which dart from their retreats when disturbed 1884.

Dartle (dā·ɹt'l), *v. rare.* 1855. [dim. and iterative of DART *v.*] To dart or shoot forth repeatedly (*trans.* and *intr.*).

Chestnut logs which spit and d. 1893.

Da·rtman. 1605. A soldier armed with a dart.

Dartoid (dā·ɹtoid), *a.* 1872. [f. Gr. δαρτός + -OID; see next.] *Anat.* Like or of the nature of the dartos.

‖**Dartos** (dā·ɹtǫs). 1634. [a. Gr. δαρτός flayed.] *Anat.* The layer of contractile tissue immediately beneath the skin of the scrotum.

Dartre (dā·ɹtəɹ). 1829. [F. *dartre*; see Diez, Littré, etc.] A vague generic name for various skin diseases, *esp.* herpes. Hence **Da·rtrous** *a.* pertaining to or of the nature of d.: applied to a certain diathesis.

Darwinian (daɹwi·niăn), *a.* (*sb.*) 1804. [f. proper name *Darwin.*] †1. Of or pertaining to Erasmus Darwin (1731-1802) -1842. 2. Of or pertaining to the naturalist Charles Darwin (1809-1882), and to his views, *esp.* his theory of the evolution of species; see DARWINISM 2. 1867. 3. *sb.* A follower of Charles Darwin 1871. Hence **Darwi·nianism** = DARWINISM 2; also, a D. idiom or phrase.

Darwinism (dā·ɹwiniz'm). 1856. [-ISM.] †1. The doctrine of Erasmus Darwin (*nonce-use*). 2. The biological theory of Charles Darwin concerning the evolution of species, etc., set forth *esp.* in 'The Origin of Species by means of Natural Selection, or the preservation of favoured races in the struggle for life' (1859), and 'The Descent of Man and Selection in relation to Sex' (1871). So **Da·rwinist,** a Darwinian. **Da·rwinize** *v.* to speculate after the manner of (Erasmus or Charles) Darwin.

‖**Das** (das). 1481. [Du. = Ger. *dachs.*] †1. A badger. CAXTON. 2. The daman or rock-badger of the Cape 1786.

Dase, obs. f. DACE, DAZE.

†Dasewe; see DASWEN *v.*

Dash (dæʃ), *v.* [ME. *daschen, dassen*, perh. from Norse; cf. Sw. *daska* to drub, Da. *daske* to beat, strike; but not known in WGer. Prob. echoic; cf. *clash, crash*, etc.]

I. *trans.* 1. To strike with violence so as to shatter; to strike violently against 1611. 2. To knock, drive, throw, or thrust (*away, down, out*, etc.) with violence ME. 3. To throw or impel into violent contact with 1530. Also *fig.* 4. To splash; to mark as with splashes 1530. 5. To qualify *with* some (usually inferior) admixture. Also *fig.* 1546. 6. *fig.* To destroy, frustrate. Now *Obs.* exc. in *to d.* (*any one's*) *hopes.* 1528. 7. To depress; to daunt 1550; to confound, abash 1563. 8. To write or sketch rapidly without premeditation 1726. 9. To draw a dash through. Now *rare.* 1549. 10. To underline 1836. 11. *colloq.* = 'Damn' 1812.

1. A braue vessell.. Dash'd all to peeces *Temp.* I. ii. 8. To d. on the lips COTG. 2. *Rom. & Jul.* IV. iii. 54. 3. Dashing the salt water in our faces 1839. 4. Floures..poudered or dashte with small spottes LYTE. 5. Vinegar..dashed with water 1684. To d. the Truth with Fiction ADDISON. 7. This hath a little dash'd your Spirits *Oth.* III. iii. 214. 8. Impressions..dashed off with a careless but graceful pen KINGSLEY.

II. *intr.* 1. To move, fall, or throw itself with violence ME. 2. Of persons: To throw oneself with violence; to rush with impetuosity, or with brilliant action. Also *fig.* ME. 3. *colloq.* To 'cut a dash' 1786.

1. The full force of the Atlantic is dashing on the cliffs 1891. 2. Doeg..dashed through thick and thin, Through sense and nonsense DRYDEN. *Comb.*: **d.-pot,** a contrivance for producing gradual descent in a piece of mechanism; a hydraulic buffer; **-wheel** (*Bleaching*), a wheel with compartments, revolving partly in water, to wash and rinse calico in the piece, by dipping it and then dashing it about.

Dash (dæʃ), *sb.*¹ ME. [f. DASH *v.*] I. A violent blow, stroke, impact, or collision. †2. A sudden blow; an affliction, discouragement -1730. 3. A splash; †*concr.* a portion of water splashed up 1677; the sound of dashing 1784. 4. A small portion (of something) thrown upon or into something else. Often *fig.* **5.** A hasty stroke of the pen 1615. **6.** A stroke or line (usually short and straight) made with or as with a pen or the like, drawn through writing for erasure, forming part of a letter, etc., used as a flourish in writing, marking a break in a sentence, a parenthetic clause, an omission, to separate distinct portions of matter, or for other purposes. **b.** *Mus.* A short vertical mark (ˈ) placed above or beneath a note to indicate that it is to be performed *staccato.* 1552. (See also below.) **7.** A sudden impetuous movement, a rush; a sudden onset. Also *fig.* 1809. **8.** Spirited vigour of action; capacity for such action 1796. **9.** A showy appearance, display: usu. in phr. *to cut a d.* 1715. **10.** *Sporting.* A race run in one heat (*U.S.*) 1881. **11.** = DASH-BOARD 1.

1. The d. of oars LYTTON. *fig.* She takes vpon her brauely at first d. 1 *Hen. VI*, I. ii. 71. 4. White relieved by a d. of yellow 1884. 6. c. A stroke drawn through a figure in thoroughbass to indicate that the interval must be raised one semitone. d. The line between notes in old harpsichord music indicating a slur.

Comb.: **d.-guard,** the dash-board which protects the platform of a tram-car; **-lamp,** a carriage-lamp fixed on the dash-board; **-rule** (*Printing*), a strip of metal for printing a d.

‖ **Dash,** *sb.*[2] 1788. [Corruption of Negro word *dashee.*] A gift, present, gratuity.

Dash, *adv.* 1672. [Stem of DASH *v.* used advb.] With a dash.

Da·sh-board. 1859. [f. DASH *v.* and *sb.*] **1.** A board or leathern apron in the front of a vehicle, to catch the mud thrown up by the heels of the horses. Also in motor vehicles, the partition between the engine and front seat. **2.** The spray-board of a paddle-wheel. **3.** *Archit.* A sloping board to carry off rain-water from the face of a wall 1881.

Dasher (dæ·ʃəɹ). 1790. [-ER[1].] **1.** A person who 'cuts a dash' (*colloq.*). **2.** That which dashes or agitates the cream in a churn 1853. **3.** = DASH-BOARD 1 (*U.S.*) 1858.

Dashing (dæ·ʃiŋ), *ppl. a.* ME. [-ING[2].] **1.** That dashes. **2.** Spirited, lively, impetuous 1796. **3.** Given to 'cutting a dash' 1801. Also *transf.* of things.

Hence **Da·shingly** *adv.*

Da·shy, *a.* 1822. [f. DASH *v.* + -Y.] = DASHING 3 (*colloq.*).

‖ **Da·ssy.** 1882. [ad. Du. *dasje*, dim. of *das* DAS.] = DAS 2.

Dastard (da·stăɹd). 1440. [Prob. f. *dast* = *dased*, f. *dase* DAZE + *-ard* suffix; cf. *dullard*, etc.]

A. *sb.* †**1.** A dullard; a sot –1552. **2.** One who meanly shrinks from danger; *esp.* one who does malicious acts in a skulking way 1526.

2. He was, though a dwarf, no d. FULLER.

B. *adj.* Meanly shrinking from danger; showing base cowardice; dastardly 1489.

To waile thy haps, argues a d. minde 1602.

Hence †**Da·stard** *v.* to make a d. of; to cow. †**Da·stardice, -ise,** mean cowardice. **Da·stardize** *v.* = DASTARD *v.* **Da·stardliness,** the quality of being dastardly. **Da·stardly** *a.* †dull; showing despicable cowardice. †**Da·stardness. Da·stardy** (*arch.*), the quality of a d.

†**Daswen,** *v.* Also **dasewe(n.** ME. [Conn. w. *dasen* to DAZE.] *intr.* Of the eyes or sight: To be or become dim –1496.

Dasymeter (dæsi·mǐtəɹ). 1872. [f. Gr. δασύς dense + μέτρον.] An instrument for measuring the density of gases.

Dasyphyllous (dæsifi·ləs), *a.* [f. Gr. δασύς rough + φύλλον.] *Bot.* Hairy- or woolly-leaved.

Dasypod (dæ·sipǫd). [f. generic name *Dasypus*, ad. Gr. δασύπους, hairy-footed.] *Zool.* Of or pertaining to *Dasypus*, a genus of armadillos; an animal of this genus. Hence **Dasy·podid** *sb.* **Dasy·podine** *a.*

‖ **Dasyprocta** (dæsiprǫ·ktă). 1875. [mod.L., f. Gr. δασύπρωκτος having hairy buttocks.] *Zool.* A genus of rodents, the agoutis. Hence **Dasypro·ctid** *a.* (*sb.*). **Dasypro·ctine** *a.*

Dasypygal (dæsipəi·găl), *a.* 1875. [f. Gr. δασύπυγος.] *Zool.* Having hairy buttocks.

Dasyure (dæ·si₍ıū°ɹ). 1839. [ad. mod.L. *dasyurus*, f. Gr. δασύς + οὐρά.] *Zool.* An animal of the genus *Dasyurus* or subfamily *Dasyurinæ*, comprising the small carnivorous marsupials of Australia and Tasmania, also called 'brush-tailed opossums' or 'native cats'. Hence **Dasyu·rine** *a.* belonging to the subfamily *Dasyurinæ*.

Data (dē·ta), pl. of DATUM, q. v.

Datary[1] (dē·tări). 1527. [ad. mod.L. *datarius*, f. *datum* DATE.] **1.** An officer of the Papal Court at Rome, charged with the duty of registering and dating all documents issued by the Pope, and of representing the Pope in matters relating to grants, dispensations, etc. †**2.** A chronologer (*rare*) –1661.

Da·tary[2]. 1645. [ad. mod.L. *dataria*; see prec.] The office or function of dating Papal documents; a branch of the Apostolic Chancery at Rome. Also *attrib.*

Date (dēᵗt), *sb.*[1] ME. [a. OF. *date*, now *datte* :—L. *dactylus*, a. Gr. δάκτυλος date, *orig.* finger.] **1.** The fruit of the date-palm, an oblong single-seeded berry, growing in clusters, with sweet pulp. **2.** The tree which bears dates (*Phœnix dactylifera*) ME.

1. Dates..serve for the Subsistence of more than an hundred Millions of Souls 1712.

Comb.: **d.-palm** = sense 2; **-plum,** the fruit of species of *Diospyros* (N.O. *Ebenaceæ*); also the tree itself; **-shell,** a mollusc of the genus *Lithodomus*; so called from its shape; **-sugar,** sugar from the sap of the wild date-tree of India (*P. sylvestris*); **-wine,** wine made by fermenting the sap of the date-palm.

Date (dēᵗt), *sb.*[2] ME. [a. F. *date* :—L. *data* fem. sing. (or neut. pl.) of *datus* given, the first word of the later L. formula '*Data Romæ*, given at Rome', etc.] **1.** The specification of the time (and often the place) of execution of a writing or inscription, affixed to it. **2.** The precise time at which anything takes place or is to take place; more vaguely, season, period ME. **b.** *U.S. colloq.* An engagement or appointment 1885. **3.** The period to which something ancient belongs ME. **4.** Duration; term of life or existence (*arch.*) ME. **5.** Limit, end ME.

1. A long Letter bearing D. the fourth Instant STEELE. 2. The d. at which he received notice 1893. Not far remov'd the d., When commerce proudly flourish'd through the state GOLDSM. 3. Antiquities of Roman d. FREEMAN. 4. To lengthen out his D. A day DRYDEN. 5. All has its d. below COWPER.

Phr. *Out of d.*: out of season; see also OUT-OF-DATE. Also UP TO DATE.

Comb.: **d.-line,** a line relating to dates; *spec.* the line (theoretically coincident with the meridian of 180° from Greenwich) at which the calendar day is reckoned to begin and end, so that at places east and west of it the d. differs by one day; **-mark** *sb.*, a mark showing the d.

Date (dēᵗt), *v.* ME. [f. DATE *sb.*[2]] **1.** *trans.* To mark with a date. **2.** To fix the date or time of; to reckon as beginning *from* ME.; *absol.* to reckon 1742. †**3.** To put a period to –1618. **4.** *intr.* (for *refl.*) To be dated; to be written *from* 1850. **5.** To assign itself to, or have its origin *from*, a particular time 1828.

1. A Bill dated the 30th of January SCARLETT. A Letter dated from York 1712. b. *pass.* To have its date fixed by some circumstance; *intr.* to bear evidence of or betray one's or its date 1895. 2. I d. from this æra the corrupt method, etc. SWIFT. 4. The letter dates from London (*mod.*). 5. The house dated as far back as the days of Matthew Stach KANE. Hence **Da·t(e)able** *a.* **Da·ter.**

Dateless (dēᵗ·tlės), *a.* 1593. [-LESS.] **1.** Undated 1644. **2.** Having no term; endless 1593. **3.** Immemorial 1794.

2. Thy datelesse fame 1624. 3. The d. hills RUSKIN. Hence **Da·telessness.**

Dation (dēᵗ·ʃən). 1656. [ad. L. *dationem.*] The action of giving. †**a.** *Med.* A dose. **b.** *Civil Law.* The act of giving or conferring.

‖ **Datisca** (dăti·skă). 1863. [mod.L.] *Bot.* The name of a genus of monochlamydeous exogens (N.O. *Datiscaceæ*). Hence **Dati·scin,** a glucoside, $C_{21}H_{22}O_{12}$, obtained from D.

Datisi (dătəi·səi). 1551. *Logic.* A mnemonic term for a valid mood of the third syllogistic figure, in which a universal affirmative major premiss (*a*) and a particular affirmative minor (*i*) yield a particular affirmative conclusion (*i*).

Dative (dēᵗ·tiv). ME. [ad. L. *dativus*, in Grammar rendering Gr. δοτική (πτῶσις).]

A. *adj.* **1.** *Gram.* The name of that case of nouns which denotes the indirect object, expressed in English by *to* or *for* with the objective. †**2.** Of the nature of a gift –1661. **3.** *Law.* **a.** In one's gift. **b.** Of an officer: Removable: opp. to *perpetual.* **c.** *Sc. Law.* Given by a magistrate, not by disposition of law: as in *executor d.*, one appointed by decree of the commissary, an administrator.

B. *sb.* (the adj. used ellipt.) *Gram.* Short for *d. case*; see A. 1520.

Hence **Da·tively** *adv.* in the d. case; as a d.

Datolite (dæ·tǫləit). *erron.* **datholite.** 1808. [irreg. f. part of Gr. δατεῖσθαι to divide + -LITE.] *Min.* A borosilicate of calcium, occurring in glassy crystals of various colours or in masses.

‖ **Da·ttock.** 1884. [Native name.] The hard mahogany-like wood of a W. African tree, *Detarium senegalense*, N.O. *Leguminosæ*; the tree itself.

‖ **Datum** (dēᵗ·tǒm). Pl. **data** (dēᵗ·tă). 1646. [L., neut. pa. pple. of *dare.*] A thing given or granted; something known or assumed as fact, and made the basis of reasoning or calculation. Also in *comb.*, as *d.-line*, *-plane.*

Out of what Data arises the knowledge T. H[ALE].

‖ **Datura** (dătiū°·ră). 1662. [mod.L. ad. Hindī *dhatura.*] *Bot.* A genus of poisonous plants (N.O. *Solanaceæ*), of which *D. Stramonium* is the Strammony or Thorn-apple; it is a powerful narcotic. Hence **Datu·rine** (also **Datu·ria**) = ATROPINE.

Daub (dǭb), *v.* ME. [a. OF. *dauber* :—L. *dealbare* to whiten over, plaster, f. *de-* down, etc. + *albare*, f. *albus.*] **1.** *trans.* To coat or cover *with* plaster, mortar, clay, or the like. **2.** To plaster *with* some sticky or greasy substance, smear 1597. **3.** To soil, bedaub. Also *fig.* 1450. **4.** To paint coarsely and inartistically 1630. †**5.** To bedizen –1760. †**6.** *fig.* To cover with a specious exterior; to whitewash, cloak, gloss –1785. †**b.** *absol.* or *intr.* To put on a false show –1716.

1. Of his shepecote dawbe the walles round about 1515. 2. Whose wrinkled furrows..Are daubed full of Venice chalk BP. HALL. 3. Dawbing eche other with dirte and myer 1535. 4. A trovell will serve as well as a pencill to d. on such thick course colours FULLER. 6. So smooth he dawb'd his Vice with shew of Vertue *Rich. III*, III. v. 29. b. Poore Tom's a cold. I cannot d. it further *Lear* IV. i. 53.

Daub (dǭb), *sb.* ME. [f. DAUB *v.*] **1.** Material for daubing. Also *fig.* **2.** An act of daubing 1669. **3.** A patch or smear of some moist substance 1731. **4.** A coarsely executed painting 1761.

4. The diffrence of a Guido from a d. COWPER.

Dauber (dǭ·bəɹ). ME. [f. DAUB *v.* + -ER[1]]. **1.** One who or that which daubs. **2.** A coarse or unskilful painter 1655. **3.** *U.S.* The mud-wasp 1844. **4.** Anything used to daub with.

2. Rather Dawbers then Drawers FULLER. Hence **Dau·bery, daubry,** the practice of daubing; the work of a d. **Dau·bster,** a clumsy painter.

Daubing (dǭ·biŋ), *vbl. sb.* ME. [-ING[1].] **1.** The action of the vb. DAUB. **2.** Material (*esp.* mortar or clay) used in daubing; rough-cast ME. **3.** (*U.S.*) = DUBBING (Knight).

Daubreelite (dǫ·brīləit). 1892. [f. as next + -LITE.] *Min.* A black sulphide of chromium, found in meteoric iron.

Daubreite (dǫ·bri₍əit). 1876. [f. M. *Daubrée*, a French mineralogist; see -ITE.] *Min.* A native oxychloride of bismuth.

Dauby (dǭ·bi), *a.* 1697. [f. DAUB *sb.* + -Y.] **1.** Sticky. **2.** Given to daubing; dirty, etc. (*dial.*) 1855. **3.** Of the nature of a daub 1829.

Daughter (dǭ·təɹ). [Com. Teut. and Com. Aryan: OE. *dohtor* (*-ur, -er*). Referred (ult.) to **dhugh-*, Skr. *duh-* to milk. The form *daughter* is southern (16th c.).] **1.** *prop.* Female child or offspring. **2.** *transf.* A female descendant; a woman in relation to her native country or place OE. Also *fig.* **3.** A term of affectionate address used by a senior (*arch.*) OE. **4.** A girl, maiden, young woman (*arch.*) ME. **5.** *fig.* Anything (personified as female) viewed in relation to its origin or source ME.

1. Soch a mother, soch a doughter COVERDALE *Ezek.* xvi. 44. 2. Daughters of Jerusalem, weep not for me *Luke* xxiii. 28. *fig.* The daughters of musick *Eccl.* xii. 4, of affliction WESLEY. 3. D., be of good comfort *Matt.* ix. 22. 4. Many daughters haue done virtuously *Prov.* xxxi. 29. 5. Dulness..D. of Chaos and eternal Night POPE.

Comb. **d.-cell** (*Biol.*), one of the cells produced by the fission of a mother-cell.
Hence **Dau·ghterhood**, the condition of being a d.; daughters collectively. **Dau·ghterless** *a.* **Dau·ghterling** (*nonce-wd.*), little d.

Dau·ghter-in-law. ME. [See BROTHER-IN-LAW.] **1.** The wife of one's son. **2.** = STEPDAUGHTER. (Now considered incorrect.) 1841.

Daughterly (dǭ·təɹli), *a.* 1535. Such as becomes a daughter; filial.
Youre very d. dealing MORE. Hence **Dau·ghterliness.**

Dauk (dǭk). 1795. [?] *Mining.* A bed or band of stiff sandy clay.

Dauk; see DAWK.

†**Dauke.** *rare.* 1450. The wild carrot, *Daucus Carota* –1688.

Daun, obs. f. DAN [1].

Daunt (dǭnt), *v.* ME. [a. OF. *danter*, var. of *donter* (mod. *dompter*) :—L. *domitare.*] †**1.** *trans.* To overcome, subdue –1610. †**2.** To tame –1569. Also *fig.* **3.** To abate the courage of, dispirit; to abash; to intimidate. (The current sense.) 1475. **4.** To daze. Now *dial.* 1581. †**5.** To dandle –1483. **6.** *Herring Fishery.* To press down salted herrings with a daunt 1733.
3. Thinke you a little dinne can d. mine eares *Tam. Shr.* I. ii. 200. Hence **Daunt** *sb.* †the act of daunting; a check; *spec.* a disc of wood used to press down salted herrings in the barrels. **Dau·nter.**

Dauntless (dǭ·ntlės), *a.* 1593. [f. DAUNT *v.* + -LESS.] Not to be daunted; bold, intrepid.
Browes Of d. courage MILT. *P. L.* I. 603. Hence **Dau·ntless-ly** *adv.*, **-ness.**

Dauphin (dǭ·fin). 1485. [a. F. = Pr. *dalfin* :—pop.L. **dalphinus* for L. *delphinus* (ad. Gr. δελφίς dolphin). See DOLPHIN.] The title of the eldest son of the King of France, from 1349 to 1830.
According to Littré, the name Dauphin, borne by the lords of the Viennois, was a proper name *Delphinus* (the same word as the name of the fish), whence their province was called *Dauphiné.* The province was ceded to Philip of Valois in 1349, subject to the condition that the title should be borne in perpetuity by the eldest son of the French king.
Hence **Dauphinate**, the rule or jurisdiction of a d. (of Viennois). **Dau·phiness**, the wife of the d.

‖**Dauw** (dāu). 1802. [S. Afr. Du. f. native name.] A species of zebra, *Equus Burchellii.*

Davenport (dæ·v'npōᵊɹt). Also **devonport.** 1853. [From the maker's name.] A kind of small ornamental writing-table filled with drawers, etc.

Da·vidist. 1657. [f. the name *David* + -IST.] **1.** One of a sect founded by David George or Jores, a Dutch Anabaptist of the 16th c. **2.** A follower of David of Dinant.

Davit (dæ·vit, dē̆ⁱ·vit). 1622. [Formerly also *David*, and app. an application of the name. Cf. F. *davier.*] *Naut.* **a.** A curved piece of timber or iron with a roller or sheave at the end, projecting from a ship's bow, and used to fish the anchor; a *fish-d.* **b.** One of a pair of cranes on the side or stern of a ship, fitted with tackle for suspending or lowering a boat.

Davy [1] (dē̆ⁱ·vi). In full **D. lamp, Davy's lamp.** 1817. [f. Sir Humphry *Davy.*] The miners' safety-lamp invented by Davy, in which the flame is surrounded with wire-gauze, so as to prevent contact with explosive gases outside the lamp.

Da·vy [2]. *slang.* 1764. Short for AFFIDAVIT.

Davy Jones (dē̆ⁱ·vi dʒōᵘ·nz). 1751. In nautical slang: The spirit of the sea; the sailors' devil. *Davy Jones's* (or *Davy's*) *locker*: the ocean, *esp.* as the grave of those who perish at sea.

Davyne (dē̆ⁱ·vin). 1826. [ad. It. *davina*, named after Sir H. Davy.] *Min.* A variety of nephelite, from Vesuvius.

Davyum (dē̆ⁱ·viǝm). 1879. [Named as prec. + *-um* as in *platinum*, etc.] *Chem.* A supposed metal of the platinum group, said by Kern to have been found in Russian platinum ore.

Daw (dǭ), *sb.* ME. [OE. **dawe* (:—*dawā* from *dagwā*) in ablaut relation to OHG. *tâha*, MHG. *tâhe.* See CADDOW.] **1.** A bird of the crow kind (*Corvus monedula*); a JACKDAW. **2.** *fig.* †A simpleton –1608; a sluggard, a slut (*Sc.*) 1460. Hence **Daw·ish** *a.* silly, sluttish.

Daw (dǭ), *v.* [1] Now *Sc.* [OE. *dagian*, corresp. to MDu. *daghen*, G. *tagen*, etc., f. WGer. *dag-* DAY.] **1.** *intr.* To dawn. Also *fig.* †**2.** = ADAW *v.* [1] 1, 2. –1612.

†**Daw**, *v.* [2] *rare.* 1616. [Aphet. f. ADAW *v.* [2]] To daunt –1664.

Dawdle (dǭ·d'l), *v.* Also **daudle.** 1656. [var. of DADDLE, ? affected by DAW *sb.* 2.] *intr.* To idle, waste time; to be sluggish; to loiter. Also quasi-*trans.* (usu. with *away*).
To d. over a dish of tea JOHNSON. I..dawdled and fretted the time away until Tuesday evening MAD. D'ARBLAY. Hence **Daw·dle** *sb.* one who dawdles; the act of dawdling. **Daw·dler.**

Dawe, obs. f. DAY.

Dawk (dǭk), *sb.* [1] *dial.* 1703. [?] A depression, furrow, incision. Hence **Dawk** *v.* to make a d. in.

‖**Dawk**, *sb.* [2], **dak** (dǭk, dāk). *Anglo-Ind.* 1727. [Hindī *ḍāk.*] Post or transport by relays; a relay of men or horses for carrying mails, etc., or passengers in palanquins.
Phr. *To travel d.*: to travel in this way. *Comb.* **dak bungalow** (rarely **house**), an inn for travellers on a dāk route.

Dawn (dǭn), *sb.* 1599. [app. f. the verb-stem; see next. ON. had *dagan, dögun* dawn, but no evidence connects the two.] **1.** The first appearance of light before sunrise; the beginning of daylight; daybreak. **2.** *fig.* The beginning, rise, first appearance; an incipient gleam 1633. Also *attrib.*
1. Come away, it is almost cleere dawne SHAKS. *High d.*, d. appearing above a bank of clouds; *low d.*, d. appearing on the horizon. **2.** The d. of manhood 1752, of an idea LAMB, of history 1878.

Dawn (dǭn), *v.* 1499. [App. f. DAWNING, q. v.] **1.** *intr.* To begin to grow daylight; also *transf.* **2.** *fig.* To begin to develop, expand, or brighten 1717. **3.** To begin to appear, become visible or evident 1744.
1. Until the day d. 2 *Pet.* i. 19. As soon as ever the Morning dawned 1726. **2.** In ..1685 his fame.. was only dawning MACAULAY. **3.** Underneath the dawning hills TENNYSON. The idea that [etc.] had never dawned upon her 1852.

Dawning (dǭ·niŋ), *vbl. sb.* [ME. *dawening*, prob. from Norse; Sw. and Da. have *dagning*, from *daga* to dawn.] **1.** The beginning of daylight; dawn; *transf.* the east. **2.** *fig.* The first gleam, appearance, beginning 1612.
1. The Bird of D. *Haml.* I. i. 160. **2.** The dawnings of a literary culture PRESCOTT.

Dawsonite (dǭ·sənəit). 1875. [f. Sir J. W. *Dawson* of Montreal; see -ITE.] *Min.* A hydrous carbonate of aluminium and sodium, in white crystals.

Day (dēⁱ), *sb.* [A Com. Teut. sb.: OE. *dæg.* Not related to L. *dies*; usually referred to an Aryan vb. *dhagh-*, in Skr. *dah* to burn.] **I.** 'The time between the rising and the setting of the sun' (J.); the interval of light between one night and the next; in ordinary usage including the lighter part of morning and evening twilight. **2.** Daylight ME. Also *fig.* †**3.** One of the 'lights' of a mullioned window. [F. *jour.*] –1859. **4.** *Mining.* The surface of the ground over a mine. Hence *d.-coal*, etc. 1665.
1. *Break of d.*: dawn: see BREAK. It was then nyne of the d. LD. BERNERS. *Before d.*: before dawn. **2.** It was broad d. DE FOE. *fig.* I can not yet see d. in the businesse MARVELL.

II. As a unit of time. **1.** The time occupied by the earth in one revolution on its axis, in which the same terrestrial meridian returns to the sun; the space of twenty-four hours OE. **2.** The same space of time treated as a unit of time, on which anything happens, or which fixes a date OE.
1. *Solar* or *astronomical d.*: a period reckoned from noon to noon, and adjusted to its mean length, which is the *mean solar d.* *Civil d.*: the period from midnight to midnight, similarly adjusted. *Sidereal d.*: the time between the successive meridional transits of a star, or, spec. of the first point of Aries, which is about four minutes shorter than the solar day. **2.** The first D. of the Week called the Lord's D. 1704. Phr. *One d.*: on a certain d. in the past; on some future d. So of future time, *some d.*, *one of these days.*

III. A specified or appointed day OE.
New Year's d., *settling-d.*, *D. of Judgement*, *Wrath*, etc. Or if my debtors do not keep their d. (*Sc.* for payment) DRYDEN. We..went on her 'day' (*Sc.* for receptions) MRS. H. WARD. Phr. *To carry, win, lose the d.* (= *day of battle* or *contest*).

IV. A space of time, a period ME.
†*A month's day* (*Sc.*), the space of a month. I'll give no d. (= credit)..I must have present money QUARLES. In the days (= time) of Josephus. The men of our d. JOWETT. Phr. *To this d.*, *at the present d.*, *at some future d.* *The d.*: time (now or then) present. Abbots honour'd in their d. (= lifetime) SOUTHEY. *To end one's days*: to die. Diplomacy has had its d. (= period of power) MIALL.
Phrases. *This d. week, twelve months*, etc.: the same day a week or a year after or before. **D. about**, on alternate days. **D. by d.**, daily, every day in its turn; also *attrib.* **D. after d.**, each day as a sequel to the preceding. **(From) d. to d.**, continuously without interruption; so *d. in* (*and*) *d. out.*
Comb.: **d.-boarder**, see BOARDER; **-boy**, a schoolboy (at a boarding-school) who attends the daily classes without boarding there; **-coal** (see I. 4); **-drift, -hole** (*Coal-mining*), galleries driven from the surface so that men can walk underground to and from their work; **-eye**, a working open to daylight; **-hours** (*pl.*), those offices for the Canonical Hours which are said in the day-time; **-house** (*Astrol.*), a house in which a planet is said to be stronger by night than by day; **dayman**, one employed for the day, or for duty on a special day; **-room**, a room occupied by day only; **-scho·lar** = *day-boy*; **-school**, a week-day school; one carried on in the day (opp. to *night* school); one at which pupils are not boarded; **-shine**, day-light; **-student**, a student who comes to a college, etc., during the day for lectures or study, but does not reside there; **-ticket**, a railway or other ticket covering return on the same day; **-wages**, wages paid by the day; **-water**, surface-water.

†**Day**, *v.* [1] ME. [= DAW *v.*, assim. to *day* sb.] To dawn –1483.

†**Day**, *v.* [2] 1523. [f. DAY *sb.*] **1.** To submit to or decide by arbitration –1580. **2.** To give (a person) time for payment –1573. **3.** To measure by the day; to furnish with days –1839. **4.** *To year and d.*: to subject to the statutory period of a year and a day –1626.

Day·-bed. 1594. A bed to rest on by day; a lounge, sofa, couch.

Day·-blindness. 1834. A visual defect, in which the eyes see badly, or not at all, by daylight, but well by artificial light.

Day·book, day-book. 1580. A diary, journal; *Naut.* a log-book (*obs.*). **b.** *Book-keeping.* Orig., a book in which the transactions of the day, as sales, purchases, etc., are entered at once in the order in which they occur; now usually *Purchases D.*, *Sales D.*, etc.

Day·break. 1530. [Cf. BREAK *v.* and *sb.* [1]] The first appearance of light in the morning; dawn.

Day·-dawn. *poet.* 1813. The dawn of day, daybreak.

Day·-dream. 1685. A dream indulged in while awake; a reverie, castle in the air.
A lover's day-dream SCOTT. So **Day·-dreamer.**

†**Day·-fever.** 1601. A fever lasting a day or coming on in the day-time; the sweating-sickness –1610.

Day·-flower. 1688. A flower that opens by day; *spec.* in *U.S.*, the genus *Commelyna* or Spiderwort.

Day·-fly. 1601. An ephemerid, which in the perfect state lives only a day or so.

†**Day·ing**, *vbl. sb.* 1484. The action of DAY *v.* [2], *esp.* arbitration –1611.

Day labour, day-la·bour. 1449. Labour done by the day or for daily wages.
'Doth God exact day labour, light denied' MILT. So **Day·-la·bourer**, one who works for daily wages.

Dayless (dēⁱ·lės), *a.* ME. [f. DAY *sb.*] †**1.** Without result –1519. **2.** Dark 1816.

Daylight (dēⁱ·ləit). ME. **1.** The light of day; *fig.* the light of knowledge; publicity 1690. **2.** The day-time; *spec.* daybreak ME. **3.** A clear visible interval, as between boats in a race, the rim of a wine-glass and the liquor, etc. 1820. **4.** *pl.* The eyes (*slang*) 1752. Also *attrib.*
1. The day-light fades POPE. Phr. *To let daylight into*: to make a hole in; to stab or shoot (*slang*). **3.** A toast!.. No heel-taps—darken daylights SHELLEY.
Comb. **d.-saving** (cf. SUMMER TIME 2).

Day·-lily. 1597. A lily, the flower of which lasts only for a day; a genus of liliaceous plants, *Hemerocallis*, with large yellow or orange flowers.

Daylong (dēⁱ·lǫŋ). 1855. [f. DAY *sb.*] *adj.* Lasting all day. *adv.* All through the day.

Day·-mare. 1737. [After *nightmare.*] A condition similar to nightmare occurring during wakefulness. Also *attrib.*

†Day·ment. 1519. [f. DAY *v.*²] Arbitration –1580.

†Day·-net. 1608. A clap-net for catching small birds –1766.

Day·peep. 1606. Peep of day; earliest dawn.

†Day·-rawe. ME. [f. DAY + *rawe* ROW.] The first streak of day.

†Day·-rule. 1750. A rule or order of court, permitting a prisoner to go without the bounds of his prison for one day –1813.

Day·-sight. 1834. A visual defect in which the eyes see clearly only in the day.

Daysman (dē¹·zmæ̆n). 1489. **1.** An arbitrator (*arch.*). **2.** A day-labourer 1639.

1. Neither is there any d. betwixt us *Job* ix. 33.

Day·-spring. ME. Daybreak. Now mainly *poet.* or *fig.*

The day-spring from on high hath visited us *Luke* i. 78.

Day·-star. OE. **1.** The morning star. **2.** The sun, as the orb of day (*poet.*) 1598. Also *fig.*

1. Early in the morning, so soone as the day starre appeared 1576. 2. So sinks the day-star in his ocean bed MILT. *Lycidas* 168. *fig.* We lift our Hearts to Thee, O Day-Star from on High WESLEY.

Day's-work (dē¹·z,wǝ̄·ɹk). (Also as two words.) 1594. The work of a day. Also = DAYWORK 2 (*obs.*).

The log-board, the contents of which are termed 'the log',—the working it off, 'the day's work' *Rudim. Navig.* (Weale).

Day-tale, daytal, datal (dē¹·tēl, -tĕl, -t'l). 1530. [f. DAY + TALE reckoning, etc.] **†1.** Day-time. **2.** The reckoning (of work, wages, etc.) by the day. Chiefly *attrib.*, reckoned, paid, or engaged by the day, as in *day-tale labour, wages*, etc. Hence **Day-taler, dataller** (dē¹·tĕlǝɹ) a day-labourer (*local*).

Day·-time. 1535. The time of daylight.

I cry in the day-time..and in the night season *Ps.* xxii. 2.

Day-woman, dairy-woman; see DEY-.

Day·work, day-work. [Cf. DARG.] OE. **1.** = DAY'S-WORK. Now *n. dial.* **†2.** The amount of land that could be worked in a day –1641. **3.** Day labour 1580.

†Day·-writ. 1809. = DAY-RULE.

Daze (dē¹z), *v.* [ME. *dasen*, a. ON. **dasa*, found in Icel. *dasask* refl., to become weary and exhausted, *e. g.* from cold, Sw. *dasa* intr. to lie idle. Not in other Teut. langs.] **1.** *trans.* To stupefy as by a blow on the head, cold, drink, excess of light, etc.; to stun; to benumb; to confuse; to dazzle. **†2.** *intr.* To be or become stupefied –1529. **†3.** Of the eyes, etc.: To become dazzled –1635. **4.** To become dazed (see DAZED 3) 1769.

1. The sudden light Dazed me half-blind TENNYSON. Dazed..by such a calamity MRS. OLIPHANT. 3. Whose more than Eagle-eyes Can..gaze On glitt'ring beams of honour, and not d. QUARLES.

Daze (dē¹z), *sb.* 1671. [f. prec.] **1.** A dazed condition 1825. **2.** *Min.* Mica (from its glitter).

Dazed (dē¹zd), *ppl. a.* ME. [f. DAZE *v.* + -ED.] **1.** Stupefied, bewildered; dazzled. **2.** Benumbed with cold (*north.*) 1513. **3.** Spoiled, as bread, etc.; rotten, as wood 1674. Hence **Da·zed·ly** *adv.*, **-ness.**

Dazy (dē¹·zi), *a. rare.* 1825. [f. DAZE *v.* or *sb.* + -Y.] In a dazed condition. **b.** Chill, chilling (*dial.*).

Dazzle (dæ·z'l), *v.* 1481. [Earlier *dasel, dasle*, freq. and dim. of *dase*, DAZE *v.*] **†1.** *intr.* Of the eyes: To lose the faculty of steady vision, *esp.* from too bright light (*lit.* and *fig.*) –1672. **2.** *trans.* To overpower or confuse (the vision), *esp.* with excess of brightness. (Also *fig.*) 1536. **3.** *fig.* To overpower or confound, *esp.* with brilliant or showy qualities; 'to strike or surprise with splendour' (J.) 1561. Also *absol.* **4.** To outshine, eclipse, dim (*rare*) 1643.

1. Perauenture his eyen daselyd as he loked from aboue doun CAXTON. 3. Rhetorick may dazle simple men 1643. *absol.* Charms that d. and endear GOLDSM.

Hence **Da·zzle** *sb.* an act of dazzling; a brightness or glitter that dazzles; paint put on as camouflage (hence as *v. trans.*, and in *Comb.*, as *d.-painted, -painting*). **Da·zzlement,** the act of dazzling; a cause of dazzling; dazzled condition. **Da·zzler,** one who or that which dazzles. **Da·zzlingly** *adv.*

‖De. 1. (dī) A Latin prep., meaning 'down from, from, off, concerning', occurring in some Latin phrases used in English, as:

a. *de bene esse* (Law), as of 'well-being', as being good, of conditional allowance for the present.

b. *de facto*, in fact, in reality, in actual existence, force, or possession, as a matter of fact. As *adj.* = 'actual'.

c. *de jure*, of right, by right, according to law. As *adj.* = 'legal'. Usu. opp. to *de facto.*

d. *de novo*, anew, afresh, over again. Rarely as *adj.* = 'new, fresh'.

e. *de profundis*, the first words of the L. version of *Ps.* cxxx = 'Out of the depths (have I cried)'; hence subst. (*a*) the name of this psalm; (*b*) a psalm of penitence; (*c*) a cry from the depths of sorrow, misery, etc.

2. The French prep. *de, d'* (dǝ), meaning 'of, from', occurring in place-names, in territorial titles, and in personal surnames; also, in French phrases more or less in English use, as *coup d'état, c. de main*, etc. (see COUP); *de trop*, too much, (one) too many, in the way; etc.

De-, *prefix.* The Latin adv. and prep., used in comb. with vbs., and their derivs.

I. As an etymological element. In the senses: 1. Down, down from, down to, as in DEPRESS, etc. 2. Off, away, aside, as in DECLINE, etc. b. Away from oneself, as in DEPRECATE, etc. 3. Down to the bottom, completely; hence, thoroughly, on and on; as in DECLAIM, DENUDE, DERELICT, etc. b. To the dregs, as in DECOCT, etc. 4. In a bad sense, so as to subject to some indignity, as in DECEIVE, etc. 5. In late L., *decompositus* = 'formed or derived from a compound (word)', 'compounded over again'; hence its sense in DECOMPOSITE, DECOMPLEX, etc. 6. In English, early words taken from OF. with *des-* retained this form (refash. *dis-*), as in *disarm*, etc.; but later words have *de-* (F. *dé-* :—OF. *des-* :—L. *dis*) treated as identical with L. *de-*; e. g. *debauch*, etc. In some words both forms are found, as *disfrock, defrock*, etc. Hence:

II. As a living prefix with privative force.

1. Forming compound vbs. (with their derivs.) having the sense of undoing the action of the simple vb., or of depriving (anything) of the thing or character therein expressed, e. g. *de-acidify, decephalize* (where no simple vb. is in use), etc.

2. Occas., vbs. (and their derivs.) are formed by prefixing *de-* to a noun, with the sense: a. To rid of the thing in question, as DEBOWEL, *depetticoated*, etc. b. To turn out of, as *decart*, DEHUSK, etc. 3. In DEBARE, etc., *de-* is prefixed to adjs.

Deacon (dī·kǝn, -k'n), *sb.* OE. [ad. L. *diaconus*, a. Gr. διάκονος servant, *spec.* in Christian use, minister of the church.] **1.** *Eccl.* The name of an order of ministers or officers in the Christian church. **a.** In Apostolic times (see Acts vi. 1–6) OE. **b.** In Episcopal churches, a member of the third order of the ministry, ranking below bishops and priests, and having the functions of assisting the priest, of visiting the sick, etc. OE. **c.** In the Presbyterian system, one of an order of officers appointed to attend to the secular affairs of the congregation (cf. ELDER *sb.*² 4) 1560. **d.** In Congregational churches, one of a body of officers elected to advise and assist the pastor and attend to the secular affairs of the church 1647. **e.** The cleric who acts as principal assistant at a solemn celebration of the Eucharist; the 'gospeller'. late ME. **†2.** Applied to the Levites –1449. **3.** In Scotland, the president of an incorporated craft or trade in any town ME.; *fig.* a master of his craft 1814. Hence **Dea·conhood,** the office of a d.; deacons collectively. **Dea·conry,** deaconship; deacons collectively; *R.C.Ch.* the chapel in charge of a cardinal d. **Dea·conship,** the office or position of a d.

Dea·con, *v. U.S. colloq.* 1845. [f. prec. sb.] **1.** *trans.* (usually *to d. off.*) To read aloud (a hymn) one line at a time, the congregation singing the lines as read. Hence *fig.* **2.** To pack (fruit, etc.) with the finest on the top; also used of other forms of dishonest dealing 1860.

2. *To d. land*, to filch it from the highway, etc. FARMER. *To d. wine*, to doctor it (*slang*).

Deaconess (dī·kǝnės). 1536. [f. prec., after L. *diaconissa.*] **1.** *Eccl.* A female deacon: **a.** in the early church, with diaconal duties in relation to her sex; **b.** in some modern churches, with functions parallel to those of deacons in the same. **2.** The name taken by certain Protestant orders of women with aims similar to those of Sisters of Mercy 1867. **3.** A deacon's wife. O. W. HOLMES.

Dead (ded), *a.* (*sb., adv.*) [A Com. Teut. adj.; orig. pple.: OE. *dēad*, f. (ult.) OTeut. vb.-stem *dau-*, preserved in ON. *deyja* (:—*daujan*) and in OS. *dôian*, to DIE. The suffix is = L. *-tus*, Gr. -τός, Skr. *-tas.*]

A. *adj.* **I.** Literally, etc. **1.** That has ceased to live; in that state in which the vital functions and powers have come to an end, and cannot be restored. **2.** Bereft of sensation or vitality ME. **3.** As good as dead *to*, or in some respect or capacity; *spec.* in *Law*, cut off from civil rights ME. **4.** Destitute of spiritual life or energy ME. **5.** *fig.* Of things: No longer in existence, or in use; *esp.* of languages 1591. **6.** Inanimate ME. **7.** *transf.* Composed of dead plants, or of dead wood, as *a d. hedge*, etc. 1563. **8.** Of or pertaining to a dead person, animal, plant, etc., or to some one's death 1580. **†9.** Causing death, mortal –1611. **10.** Devoid of life; hence, barren 1577.

1. The maid is not d., but sleepeth *Matt.* ix. 24. D. fleshe EDEN, leaves SHELLEY. My wife is d. (=has died) to night *Rom. & Jul.* v. iii. 210. 2. D. fingers J. HUTCHINSON. In a d. faint (*mod.*). 5. My doubts are d. TENNYSON. 6. D. matter H. MILLER. 8. You breath these d. newes in as d. an eare *John* v. vii. 65. 10. A bottom of d. sand FORSYTH.

II. 1. Wanting some vital quality (see quots.) ME. **2.** Of sound: Without resonance 1530. **3.** Not fulfilling the normal purpose 1806.

1. D. Cider EVELYN. D. (=exhausted) steam 1874. The d. colour of her face DRYDEN. *Electr.* Carrying or transmitting no current, as *d. circuit* 1903. 2. A dull d. sound 1783. 3. *Dead..*False; as of imitation doors or windows KNIGHT.

III. 1. Without animation OE. **2.** Inoperative ME. **3.** Profoundly quiet or still 1548. **4.** Without activity, dull; unproductive; unsaleable 1570. **5.** Of a ball: Out of play 1658.

1. A bare d. description 1665. 2. A d. ordinance J. H. NEWMAN. 3. The d. hours of the night KINGLAKE. 4. In the deadest Vacation 1615. D. stock 1622, goods DRYDEN. 5. *Golf.* So near the hole that it can be holed with certainty at the next stroke 1881.

IV. 1. Without motion OE. **2.** Characterized by abrupt cessation of motion, action, or speech.

1. D. still water WALTON. The wind had fallen d. HUGHES. The d. spindle of a lathe KNIGHT. 2. At a d. stand 1647. D.-stroke hammer KNIGHT.

V. 1. Unrelieved, unbroken, absolute; complete; utmost 1561. **2.** Said of outlay: Unproductive 1715. **3.** Absolute 1660; sure, unerring 1592; direct 1881.

1. A d. wall DRYDEN, level POPE. A d. calm 1673, secret SCOTT. D. low water 1626. A d. pull 1812, strain BAIN. 2. *D. rent*: a fixed rent which remains as a constant charge on a mining concession. 3. A d. bargain GOLDSM., certainty 1878; d. earnest 1883; a d. shot 1776; a d. head-wind 1881.

Phrases. *D. as a door-nail, d. as a herring*: completely or certainly dead. *D. horse*: see HORSE. *To wait for d. men's shoes*: see SHOE.

¶ The compar. *deader* and superl. *deadest* are in use where the sense permits.

B. *sb.*¹ (or *absol.*) **1.** *sing.* A dead person. **b.** *pl. The dead.* ME. **c.** *From the dead* [orig. tr. L. *a mortuis*, Gr. ἐκ νεκρῶν]: from among the dead; hence nearly = from death OE. **2.** = Dead period, season, stage 1548. **†3.** = DEAD HEAT. Quarles. **4.** *Mining. Deads*: earth or rock containing no ore 1653. **5.** *attrib.*, as in *d. list*, list of the dead, etc. 1476.

2. D. of night SHAKS., of winter 1613.

C. *adv.* **1.** To a degree suggesting death; utterly, profoundly (as *d. asleep, calm, drunk*); 'to death' (as *d. run, tired, sick*) 1596. **2.** Hence: Utterly, absolutely, quite 1589. **3.** Directly, straight, as *d. against, d. on end*; also *fig.* 1800.

Combs. (of the *adj.* or *sb.*) 1. With other adjs. or pples. = 'so as to be or seem dead, as if dead, to death, etc.' as in *d.-alive, -set*, etc.

2. Special combs.: **d. angle** (*Fortif.*), 'any angle of a fortification, the ground before which is unseen, and therefore undefended from the parapet' (Stocqueler); **†-birth**: see BIRTH; **-cart,** one in which d. bodies are carried away; **-clothes,** those in which the d. are dressed; **d. dipping,** a process by which a d. surface is given to brass-work; **-end,** a closed end of a water-pipe, passage, etc.; also *attrib.*; **d. fin,** the second dorsal fin of a salmon; **-fire,** St. Elmo's Fire, believed to presage death; **-flat** (*Naut.*), the widest timber or frame in a ship; the midship-bend; **-house,** a mortuary; **-latch,** a latch whose bolt may be so locked by a detent that it cannot be opened from the inside by the handle or from the outside by the key; **d. march,** a piece of solemn music played at a funeral procession; a funeral march; **-office,** the service for the burial of the d.; **d. oil,** a name for those products of the distillation of coal-tar which are heavier than water; *heavy oil*; **-plate,** an ungrated iron plate at the mouth of a furnace, on

which coal is coked before being pushed upon the grate; †-**pledge** = MORTGAGE; -**rising** (*Naut.*), 'those parts of a ship's floor or bottom, throughout her whole length, where the floor-timber is terminated upon the lower futtock' (Falconer); **d. rope**, one that does not run in a block or pulley; **d. sheave**, a score in the heel of a top-mast, through which a second top-tackle pendant can be rove; -**shore**, a piece of timber worked up in brickwork to support a superincumbent mass until the brickwork to carry it is set; †-**slayer**, one guilty of manslaughter; -**smooth** *a.*, said of the finest quality of file; †-**sweat** = *death-sweat*.

Dead, *sb.*[2] The northern form of the word DEATH, still dial. in Sc.

Dead (ded), *v.* Now *local.* [OE. *dēadian* to become dead, f. *dēad* DEAD. Repl. by DEADEN.] 1. *intr.* To die; *fig.* to lose vitality or force; to lose heat ME. 2. *trans.* To make dead (*lit.* and *fig.*) ME. 3. *fig.* To deaden; to deprive of some form of vitality ME.

1 Iron, as soon as it is out of the Fire, deadeth straight-ways BACON. 2. Endlese griefe, which deads my life, yet knowes not how to kill 1586.

Dead beat, dea·d-bea·t, *sb.*[1] (*a.*) 1768. [DEAD *a.*] *Watch-making*, etc. A beat or stroke which stops dead without recoil. Usu. *attrib.* or *adj.*, as in *dead-beat escapement.*

Dead beat, dea·d-bea·t, *ppl. a.* (*sb.*[2]) 1821. [DEAD *adv.*] *adj.* (or *pa. pple.*) Completely beat (*colloq.*). *sb. slang* (U.S.). A worthless sponging idler 1877.

Dea·d-born, *ppl. a.* ME. Born dead, still-born. Also *fig.*

Dea·d-ce·ntre. 1874. *Mech.* 1. = DEAD-POINT. 2. In a lathe, the centre which does not revolve 1879.

Dea·d co·lour. 1658. [DEAD *a.* II. 1.] The first or preparatory layer of colour in a painting. So **Dea·d-co·lour** *v.* to paint in dead colour; **Dea·d-co·louring** *vbl. sb.*

†**Dea·d-do·ing**, *ppl. a.* 1590. Doing to death, murderous –1778.

Deaden (de·d'n), *v.* 1665. [f. DEAD *a.*, repl. DEAD *v.*] 1. *intr.* To become dead (*lit.* and *fig.*); to lose vitality, force, etc. 1723. 2. *trans.* To kill; *spec.* (*U.S.*) to kill (trees) by girdling 1775. 3. To deprive of vitality, force, or sensibility 1684. 4. To deprive of some effective physical quality, as lustre, flavour, etc.; to make (sound) dull; etc. 1666. 5. To destroy or reduce the energy of (motion).

1. The dash Of the out-breakers deaden'd SOUTHEY. 3. To benumb and d. worship MOZLEY. 4. To d. the whiteness of a tissue OWEN, beer WEBSTER, a piercing sound SCOTT. 5. To d. a ship's way SMYTH. Hence **Dea·dener.**

Dead-eye (de·dˌəi). 1748. [DEAD *a.*] *Naut.* A round laterally flattened wooden block, pierced with three holes through which a lanyard is reeved, used for extending the shrouds.

Deadfall, dead-fall (de·dfǫl). Chiefly *U.S.* 1611. 1. A kind of trap used *esp.* for large game, in which a weighted board or the like is arranged to fall upon and kill or disable the prey. 2. A tangled mass of fallen trees 1883. b. A dumping-platform at the mouth of a mine 1874. c. A low drinking- or gaming-place. (*Western U.S.*)

Dea·d-hand. 1612. = MORTMAIN.

Dea·dhead, dead-head, dead head. 1576. †1. *Old Chem.* = CAPUT MORTUUM 2. –1707. 2. *Founding.* The extra head or length of metal at the muzzle end of a gun-casting, which is cut off when cool. b. *Mech.* The tail-stock of a lathe, containing the dead spindle. c. *Naut.* A rough block of wood used as an anchor-buoy. 1867. 3. *colloq.* (orig. *U.S.*) A person admitted without payment to a theatre, a public conveyance, etc. 1853.

Dea·d-hea·rted, *a.* 1642. Dead in feeling, callous, insensible. Hence **Dead-hea·rtedness.**

Dead heat. 1840. [Cf. DEAD *a.* V. 3.] *Racing*, etc. A race in which two or more competitors reach the goal at the same instant.

Deadish (de·diʃ), *a.* Now *rare.* 1450. [f. DEAD *a.* + -ISH.] Somewhat dead (in various senses), as *a d. paleness, sound*; *d. beer*, etc.

Dead letter. 1579. 1. *orig.* A writing taken in a bare literal sense (cf. Rom. vii. 6, 2 Cor. iii. 6). b. A writ, statute, ordinance, etc., which is inoperative, though not repealed 1663. 2. A letter which lies unclaimed for a certain time at a post-office, or which cannot be delivered through any cause 1771.

2. *Dead-letter office*: a department of the Post Office in which dead letters are examined and dealt with; now styled *Returned Letter Office.*

Dead lift. 1551. [DEAD *a.* V. 1.] 1. The pull of a horse, etc., exerting his utmost strength at a dead weight beyond his power to move. 2. *fig.* An extremity, 'a hopeless exigence' (J.). (Now *arch.* or *dial.*) 1567.

2. You must helpe vs at that dead lift J. UDALL.

Dea·d-light. 1726. [DEAD *a.* and *sb.*] 1. *Naut.* A strong shutter fixed outside a port-hole, etc., to keep out water in a storm. 2. A corpse-light or corpse-candle (*Sc.*) 1813.

†**Dea·dlihead.** *rare.* 1612. [f. DEADLY *a.* + -HEAD.] The state of the dead –1642.

Dea·d-line. 1860. [DEAD *a.* IV.] 1. A line that does not move or run. 2. *Mil.* A line drawn round a military prison, beyond which a prisoner may be shot down 1868.

Dead lock, dea·d-lock. 1779. [Cf. DEAD *a.* V. 1.] 1. A position in which it is impossible to proceed or act; a complete standstill. 2. An ordinary lock which opens and shuts only with a key; occas., locally, a padlock. [DEAD *a.* IV. 2.] 1866. Hence **Dea·d-lo·ck** *v.* to bring to a deadlock or stand-still.

Deadly (de·dli), *a.* [OE. *dēadlīc*, f. *dēad* DEAD.] †1. Subject to death –1839; *absol.* a mortal; usu. as *pl.* –1685. †2. In danger of death –1616; of or belonging to death –1483. †3. = DEAD *a.* I. 6 (*rare*) –1440. 4. Causing or having the capacity of causing death; mortal, fatal OE. 5. *Theol.* Of sin: Entailing spiritual death; mortal (opp. to *venial*) ME. 6. Aiming, or involving an aim, to kill or destroy; implacable, mortal ME. 7. Death-like ME. 8. Excessive, 'awful' (*colloq.*) 1660.

4. A d. blow KNOLLES, poison 1866. *D. Nightshade*, the *Atropa Belladonna* (N.O. *Solanaceæ*). 5. The seven d. sins: see SIN. 6. D. imprecations 1703. 7. D. paleness SOUTHEY, faintness LYTTON. Dark and d. SHAKS. 8. A d. drinker PEPYS. Hence **Dea·dlily** *adv.* (*rare*). **Dea·dliness.**

Deadly (de·dli), *adv.* [OE. *dēadlīce*, f. *dēad* DEAD.] †1. In a way that causes death; mortally –1816; *spec.* in *Theol.* –1579. †2. Implacably; to the death –1650. 3. In a manner resembling or suggesting death; as if dead ME. 4. Extremely, excessively (*colloq.*) 1589.

1. So d. cruel 1679. 3. They..look'd d. pale SHAKS. 4. D. slow 1688, dear 1703, dull 1865.

Dea·dman. ME. = *Dead man. Obs.* exc. as in *Deadman's Walk*, etc.

Dead man. 1700. 1. pl. (*dead men.*) Empty bottles (at a carouse, etc.) (*slang*). 2. *Cards.* A dummy at whist 1786. 3. *Naut.* (*pl.*) Reef- or gasket-ends left dangling when a sail is furled.

Dead men's bells, the Foxglove, *Digitalis purpurea Sc.*). **Dead man's (men's) finger(s**: 1. in Shaks. prob. the Early Purple Orchis, *O. mascula*; also other species of *Orchis*, prop. those with palmate tubers. 2. The zoophyte *Alcyonium digitatum.* **Dead man's hand**: 1. *Alcyonium digitatum.* 2. *Orchis maculata*, *O. mascula*; *Nephrodium Filix-mas*, and other ferns; also the seaweed Tangle. **Dead man's thumb**: *Orchis mascula.*

Deadness (de·dnės). 1607. 1. The condition or quality of being dead (see DEAD *a.*). 2. Want of some characteristic physical quality, as lustre, colour, taste, etc. 1707.

1. *fig.* The d. of trade 1642. Inward deadnesses 1749. D. to God 1858. 2. D. in cyder 1707, in complexions 1785.

Dead-nettle (de·dˌne:t'l). ME. A name for plants of the genus *Lamium* (N.O. *Labiatæ*), having leaves like those of a nettle, but stingless.

†**Dead palsy, dea·d-pa·lsy.** 1592. [DEAD *a.* I. 2.] Palsy producing complete local insensibility or immobility –1761.

†**Dead pay.** 1565. [Cf. F. *morte-paye.*] 1. Pay continued to a soldier, etc. no longer in active service; a soldier receiving such pay –1686. 2. Pay dishonestly drawn in the name of a soldier, etc. actually dead or discharged; a person in whose name such pay is drawn –1663.

2. Like a covetous Captain will needs indent for a dead pay 1565.

Dea·d-point, dead point. 1830. [DEAD *a.* IV.] *Mech.* That position of a crank at which it is in a direct line with the connecting rod, and at which therefore the force exerted does not turn the crank.

Dead reckoning. 1613. [DEAD *a.* V.] The estimation of a ship's position from the distance run by the log and the courses steered by the compass, with corrections for current, leeway, etc., but without astronomical observations. Hence *dead* LATITUDE (q.v.), that computed by dead reckoning.

Dead Sea. ME. [tr. L. *mare mortuum*, Gr. ἡ νεκρὰ θάλασσα (Aristotle); ? so called as devoid of life, or of currents, etc.] The inland sea in the south of Palestine, into which the Jordan flows; it has no outlet, and its waters are salt and bitter. Also *attrib.*, as in **Dead Sea apple, fruit** = *Apple of Sodom*; see APPLE.

Dea·d-tongue. 1688. The umbelliferous plant *Œnanthe crocata*, from its paralysing effect on the organs of speech.

Dead water, dead-water. 1561. [DEAD *a.* IV.] 1. Still water 1601. 2. *Naut.* The eddy water just behind the stern of a ship under way 1627. 3. The neap tide 1561.

Dead weight, dea·d-weight. 1660. [DEAD *a.* V.] 1. The heavy unrelieved weight of an inert body (*lit.* and *fig.*). 2. *techn.* A vessel's lading when it consists of heavy goods; the weight of a vehicle, as dist. from the load; etc. 1858. 3. *fig.* A heavy unrelieved weight or burden 1721. †4. An advance formerly made by the Bank of England to Government for the payment of pensions, etc. –1827.

Dead well, dea·d-we·ll. 1852. [DEAD *a.* II. 3, IV.] An absorbing well, to carry off refuse waters.

Dead wood, dea·d-wood. 1727. 1. Wood dead upon the tree; hence *fig.* 2. *Naut.* Solid blocks of timber fastened just above the keel at each end of the ship, to strengthen those parts.

Dea·d-work, dead work. 1653. †1. *Naut.* That part of a ship which is above water when she is laden –1769. 2. *Mining.* Work not directly productive, but only preparatory 1869. 3. Work in hand 1888.

Dea·dy. *slang.* 1819. [Distiller's name.] Gin.

De-aerate; see DE- II. 1 and *aerate.*

Deaf (def), *a.* [Com. Teut. adj.: OE. *dēaf* :—OTeut. *dauƀoz, from an ablaut stem *deuƀ-*, *dauƀ-*, *duƀ-*, pre-Teut. *dheubh-*, to be dull of perception; cf. Gr. τυφλός (:—θυφ-) blind. Still pronounced (dīf) dial. and in U.S.] 1. Lacking, or defective in, the sense of hearing OE. Also *fig.* 2. *fig.* Unwilling to hear or heed, inattentive ME. †3. Of sounds: Dull and indistinctly heard; muffled –1700. 4. Lacking its essential character; hollow, empty, unproductive; insipid. Now chiefly *dial.* OE.

1. But she was somdel deef CHAUCER. Then .. the eares of the deafe shalbe vnstopped *Isa.* xxxv. 5. Phr. *D. and dumb*: also used *absol.* (= DEAF-MUTE) and thence *attrib.* D. to harmony COWPER. 2. Eares .. To Counsell deafe, but not to Flatterie *Timon* I. ii. 257. 3. A d. murmur through the squadron went DRYDEN. 4. *D. nut*: one with no kernel; *fig.* something hollow or worthless.

Comb., etc.: **d.-adder**, the blind-worm, in U.S. a name for certain snakes; -**dumbness**, aphonia arising from deafness; -**nettle** = DEAD-NETTLE.

Deaf (def), *v. arch.* or *dial.* 1460. [f. DEAF *a.*] †1. *intr.* To become deaf 1530. 2. *trans.* To make deaf. Also *fig.* and *transf.* 1460. 3. To drown (a sound) *with* a louder sound 1640.

Deafen (de·f'n), *v.* 1597. [f. DEAF *a.*; see -EN *suffix*[5].] 1. *trans.* To make deaf; to stun with noise. Also *fig.* 2. To render (a sound) inaudible 1823. 3. To make (a floor or partition) impervious to sound by means of pugging. Hence **Dea·fening** *vbl. sb.* material used for this purpose. 1814. †4. *intr.* To become deal (*rare*) 1680.

1. Hunting horns .. that almost d. the company 1717. Hence **Dea·feningly** *adv.*

De-afforest (dīˌăfǫ·rėst), *v.* 1640. [DE- *pref.* II. 1.] = DISAFFOREST. Hence **De-affo·resta·tion.**

Deafly (de·fli), *adv.* ME. [f. DEAF *a.* + -LY[2].] Without hearing (*lit.* and *fig.*). b. Dully, indistinctly.

Deaf-mute, *a.*, *sb.* 1837. [After F. *sourd-muet.*] Deaf and dumb. b. One who is deaf and dumb. Hence **Dea·f-mu·tism**, the condition of a deaf-mute.

Deafness (de·fnės). ME. [See -NESS.] The state or condition of being deaf.

Your tale, Sir, would cure deafenesse *Temp.* I. ii. 106.

Deal (dīl), *sb.*[1] [A Com. Teut. sb.: OE. *dǣl* :—OTeut. **dailiz.*] †1. A part or division of a whole; a portion -1737. 2. A part allowed to any one; a share, dole. Now *dial.* OE. 3. A quantity, an amount; qualified as *good, great, vast, †poor, †small,* etc. OE. Also *absol.* (the thing referred to being implied) 1450. 4. *A deal*: an undefined but large quantity (*rarely* number); a lot (*colloq.*) 15...

1. A meate offering of three tenth deales of flowre *Numb.* xv. 9. Suche godelyhede In speche and neuer a dele of trouthe CHAUCER. †*By a thousand d.*: a thousandfold. 3. To make such a Tragical d. ado about it 1685. 4. Talking a d. of nonsense 1875.

Adverbial phrases. †*Any d.*, any whit. †*Never a d.*, not a whit. *A great, good, vast d.*, considerably, vastly. *A d.*, much (*colloq.*).

Deal (dīl), *sb.*[2] 1588. [f. DEAL *v.*] 1. An act or the act of dealing. 2. *Cards.* The distribution of cards to the players for a round in a game 1607. 3. A business transaction or bargain 1837; *spec.* a secret arrangement in commerce or politics entered into by parties for their mutual benefit; a job (*U.S.*) 1881.

Deal (dīl), *sb.*[3] ME. [From Low German; cf. MLG. *dele* fem. plank, floor (mod.Du. *deel* plank, *dele, delle* floor), etc.] 1. A slice sawn from a log of timber, in Great Britain 9 inches wide, not more than 3 thick, and at least 6 feet long. If shorter, it is a *d.-end*; if not more than 7 inches wide, a BATTEN. 2. The wood of fir or pine, such as deals (sense 1) are made of 1601.

2. *White d.*, the produce of the Norway Spruce (*Abies excelsa*); *red d.*, that of the Scotch Pine (*Pinus sylvestris*); *yellow d.*, that of the Yellow Pine (*P. mitis*), etc.

Comb.: **d.-end** (see sense 1); **-fish**, a genus of fishes of the ribbon-fish family; **-frame**, a gang-saw for cutting deals; **-tree** (*dial.*), a fir-tree.

Deal (dīl), *v.* Pa. t. and pple. **dealt** (delt). [A Com. Teut. vb.: OE. *dǣlan*, f. *dǣl* DEAL *sb.*[1], part, division.]

I. Mainly *trans.* †1. *trans.* To divide -1570. †2. To separate -ME. †3. To distribute in shares; to portion out -1535. 4. To distribute or bestow. Now mostly *fig.* or with *out.* OE. Also †*intr.* 5. To apportion (*to* a person). Also with *out.* ME. 6. To bestow, render, deliver ME. 7. *Cards.* To distribute (the cards) to the players; to give a player (such or so many cards) in distributing. Also *absol.* 1529.

4. The provident hand deals out its scanty dole SOUTHEY. 5. To me.. it deals eternal woe MILT. *P. L.* IV. 70. 6. To d. blows DRYDEN, an ill turn FULLER. By fits he deals his fiery bolts about DRYDEN.

II. Mainly *intr.* †1. To take part *in.* Also with *with* or *of.* -1481. †2. To engage *with*; to contend -1667. 3. *intr.* To have to do *with* (a person); to have dealings *with*; to associate *with* ME. 4. To treat *with*; sometimes implying secret or sinister dealings ME. 5. To do business (*with* a person, *in* an article) 1627. 6. To have to do *with* (a thing) in any way ME. 7. To act towards people generally (in some specified way) ME. †8. To act, proceed (usu. *in* a matter) -1599.

2. Brutish that contest.. When Reason hath to d. with force MILT. *P. L.* VI. 125. 3. [The charge] of dealing with a familiar spirit FREEMAN. 4. It is generally better to deale by speech, then by letter BACON. 5. I d. in dog's leather MIDDLETON. 6. The first question with which I propose to d. HUXLEY. 7. Let us d. justly *Lear* III. vi. 42. 8. Do not you meddle, let me deale in this *Much Ado* V. i. 101.

Phr. *To d. in*: to occupy or exercise oneself in (a thing); to make use of. *To d. on, upon*: to set to work upon (*arch.*). *To d. with*: to act in regard to, handle, dispose of (a thing); b. to handle effectively; to grapple with; c. to treat (in some specified way). Also with *by* (=in regard to) in same sense.

Dea·lable, *a.* 1667. [f. prec.] Capable of being dealt *with*; suitable for dealing.

Dealbate (di͵æ·lbět), *a.* 1866. [ad. L. *dealbatus* (see next).] Whitened; *Bot.* covered with an opaque white powder.

†**Dea·lbate**, *v.* 1623. [f. ppl. stem of L. *dealbare*, f. *de-* + *albare*, f. *albus* white; cf. DAUB *v.*] *trans.* To whiten. Hence **Dealba·tion**, blanching, bleaching.

Dea·l-boa·rd. 1568. [f. DEAL *sb.*[3]] = DEAL *sb.*[3] 1.

Dealer (dī·lər). OE. [f. DEAL *v.*] 1. One who deals (see DEAL *v.*); *spec.* the player who deals the cards. 2. One who deals in merchandise, a trader; *spec.* one who sells articles in the same condition in which he bought them; often in comb., as *corn-, horse-, money-d.* 1611. 3. A dealer on the Stock Exchange 1837.

Dealing (dī·liŋ), *vbl. sb.* ME. [-ING [1].] 1. Distribution (of gifts, blows, cards, etc.); sharing. 2. Friendly or business communication. Now usually *pl.* 1538. 3. Buying and selling 1664. 4. Way of acting, conduct, behaviour 1483. Also with *with.*

†**Dea·mbulate**, *v.* 1623. [f. L. *deambulare.*] To walk abroad. Hence **Dea:mbulation.** †**Dea·mbula·tor**, one who walks abroad.

Dea·mbulatory. ME. [ad. L. *deambulatorius*, whence *-atorium* sb.] A. *adj.* Moving about from place to place; shifting 1607. B. *sb.* A place to walk in for exercise; *esp.* a covered walk or cloister.

Dean[1] (dīn). [ME. *deen, dēn*, a. OF. *deien, dien*, mod. *doyen* :—L. *decanum* one set over ten (cf. Exod. xviii. 21 Vulg.), also Gr. δεκανός.] †1. Repr. late L. *decanus*: A head, chief, or commander of a division of ten -1483. †2. As tr. med.L. *decanus*, applied to the *teoðingealdor*, the headman of a *tenmannetale.* (See Stubbs, *Const. Hist.* I. v. 87.) -1695. 3. As tr. Eccl.L. *decanus*, head of ten monks in a monastery 1641. 4. Hence, The head of the chapter in a collegiate or cathedral church ME. 5. A presbyter invested with jurisdiction or precedence (under the bishop or archdeacon) over a division of an archdeaconry; more fully called a *rural d.*; formerly, *d. of* CHRISTIANITY ME. 6. In other eccl. uses 1647. 7. The officer or officers in the colleges of Oxford and Cambridge appointed to supervise the conduct and discipline of the junior members 1577. 8. The president of a faculty or department of study in a University; in U.S. the registrar or secretary of the faculty 1524. 9. The president, chief, or senior member of any body. [= F. *doyen.*] 1687.

6. *D. of peculiars*: one invested with the charge of a peculiar, *i. e.* a parish or church exempt from the jurisdiction of the ordinary or bishop in whose diocese it lies, *e.g.* the Dean of Battle in Sussex. *D. of the Arches*: the lay judge of the Court of Arches. *D. of the Province of Canterbury*: the Bishop of London. 8. *D. of Faculty*: the president of the Faculty of Advocates in Scotland. 9. *D. of guild*: in Scotland, the head of the guild or merchant-company of a royal burgh, who is a magistrate charged with the supervision of all buildings within the burgh. *D. of the Sacred College*: the chief of the Sacred College, usually the oldest of the Cardinal Bishops, who presides in the consistory in the absence of the Pope.

Dean[2], **dene** (dīn). [OE. *denu*, acc. *dene*, valley :—OTeut. **dani-*; cf. DEN.] A vale; now, usually, the deep, narrow, and wooded vale of a rivulet.

Tauntons fruitfull Deane DRAYTON. *Denes* which débouche upon the coast 1873.

Dean[3]. 1874. *Cornish Mining.* The end of a level.

Deanery (dī·nəri). ME. [f. DEAN[1] + -ERY.] 1. The office of a dean. 2. The group of parishes over which a rural dean presides; formerly, also, the jurisdiction of a dean ME. 3. The official residence of a dean 1598.

Dea·-nettle. Now *dial.* 1523. [? reduced f. *dead-nettle.*] A name for the species of *Lamium* (DEAD-NETTLE) and other Labiates having nettle-like leaves; *esp.* applied to the Hempnettle, *Galeopsis Tetrahit.*

Deanship (dī·nʃip). 1588. [f. DEAN[1].] 1. The office or rank of a dean 1611. 2. Used humorously as a title.

2. I then shall not value his D. a straw SWIFT.

†**Dear**, *sb.*[1] ME. only. [app. repr. an OE. **dīeru*, **dēoru*. Cf. DEAR *a.*[1]] Dearness, dearth.

Dear (dīᵊɹ), *a.*[1] and *sb.*[2] [OE. *dēore*, earlier *dīore*; a Com. Teut. adj., pointing to OTeut. type **deurjo*, **diurjo.*]

I. Of persons. †1. Glorious, honourable, worthy -1606. 2. Regarded with esteem and affection; loved OE. b. Often used *absol.* = 'dear one' ME. †3. Affectionate, fond -1653.

1. *Tr. & Cr.* V. iii. 27. 2. D. to God, and famous to all ages MILT. Deare Sir ABP. USHER. Right dere and welbeloved Q. MARGT. b. Shall I go mourne for that (my deere) *Wint. T.* IV. iii. 15. 3. Sir Henry Wotton, a d. lover of this Art WALTON.

II. Of things. †1. Of high estimation; precious, valuable -1600. 2. Hence, Precious in one's regard, of which one is fond ME.; affectionate (*rare*) 1591. 3. High-priced; costly, expensive: opp. to *cheap* OE.; said of *prices, rates*: = High ME. Also *fig.* †4. 'Heartfelt; hearty; hence earnest' (Schmidt) -1606.

1. My d. time's waste SHAKS. So dangerous and deare a trust 1 *Hen. IV*, IV. i. 34. 2. This Land of such deere soules, this deere-deere Land *Rich. II*, II. i. 57. With d. Love.. I salute thee 1683. Phr. *To ride for d. life.* 3. Sell your face for fiue pence and 'tis deere *John* I. i. 153. *D. year*, a year in which prices are high. 4. *L. L. L.* II. i. 1.

B. *sb.* = Dear one, darling ME.

C. Used interjectionally 1694.

Dear!, Oh dear!, Dear, dear!, Dear me!: exclams. of surprise, anxiety, regret, sympathy, etc. *Dear* (? repr. *dear Lord*) *knows!* goodness knows (*I* do not).

Dear, †**dere**, *a.*[2] *poet.* [OE. *dēor*; not in cogn. langs.] †1. Brave, strenuous, hardy. (OE. only.) 2. Hard, heavy, grievous; fell, dire (*arch.*) OE. †3. Difficult ME.

2. Fortunes dearest spight SHAKS. *Sonn.* xxxvii. My dearest foe *Haml.* I. ii. 180. Sad occasion d. MILT. *Lycidas* 6.

Dear (dīᵊɹ), *adv.* [OE. *dīore, dēore* = OHG. *tiuro*, G. *teuer.*] 1. At a high price. 2. = DEARLY *adv.* 2. ME.

1. The people there [Holland]..eat d. YARRANTON.

Dear (dīᵊɹ), *v.* ME. [f. DEAR *a.*[1]] †1. *trans.* To make dear. *Sc.* (*rare*) -1462. †2. To endear (*rare*) 1603. 3. To address (a person) as 'dear' 1829.

Dea·rborn *U.S.* 1841. [The inventor's name.] A kind of light four-wheeled wagon.

Dea·r-bou·ght, *a.* ME. [DEAR *adv.*] Obtained at great cost, as *dear-bought experience.*

Deare, obs. f. DEAR, DEER, DERE.

†**Dear joy.** 1688. Familiar name for an Irishman -1710.

Dearling, obs. f. DARLING.

Dearly (dīᵊ·ɹli), *adv.* [OE. *dēorlīce*, f. DEAR *a.*[1]] †1. In a precious, worthy, or excellent manner -1606. 2. As one who is held dear; fondly. (Now only with the vb. *love*, or its equivs.) ME. †3. Heartily, earnestly -1606; keenly -1602. 4. = DEAR *adv.* 1. 1489.

2. His dearly-lovèd mate MILT. 3. My father hated his father d. *A. Y. L.* I. iii. 35. 4. He shal derely abye it LD. BERNERS.

Dearn(e, **-ful, -ly**; see DERN, etc.

Dearn, obs. f. DARN *v.*

Dearness (dīᵊ·ɹnės). ME. [f. DEAR *a.*[1]] 1. The quality of being held dear: hence b. Intimacy; c. Affection. 2. Expensiveness, costliness 1530.

1. The d. that was between them, was now turned.. to a most violent enmity BURNET.

Dearth (dəɹþ), *sb.* [ME. *derþe*; abstr. sb. f. WGer. *diuri*, OE. *dīere, dēore*, DEAR *a.*[1]] †1. Glory (*rare*). [= ON. *dyrð.*] (ME. only.) †2. Dearness -1602. 3. A condition in which food is scarce and dear; earlier, a famine ME. Also *transf.* and *fig.*

2. The dearthe of the pryce thairof 1632. 3. In the tyme of d. and famine *Bk. Com. Prayer.* Ther is no grete derthe..of women CAXTON. Hence †**Dearth** *v.* to make dear; to cause a d. of or in anything.

†**De-arti·culate**, *a.* 1650. [Cf. next.] Divided by joints; freely articulated -1651. Also **De-arti·culated** *a.*

De:-articula·tion. 1615. [ad. med.L. *dearticulatio*, used as tr. Gr. διάρθρωσις.] Division by joints; b. = DIARTHROSIS; c. Distinct articulation (of the voice).

†**Dea·rworth, derworth**, *a.* [OE. *dēor-*, *dyrwurþe*, app. f. *dīeru, dēoru* DEAR *sb.*[1] + *wyrþe* worthy.] 1. Precious -ME. 2. = DEAR *a.* I. 1. -ME. 3. Of persons: Dear -1557. var. †**Dea·rworthy, der-**, *a.*; whence †**Dea·rworthily** *adv.* †**Dea·rworthiness.**

Deary, -rie (dīᵊ·ri). 1681. [Dim. of *dear*; see DEAR *a.*[1] + -IE, -Y[6].] A little dear, a darling.

Deas(e, obs. f. DAIS.

‖**Deasil, deiseal** (dye·ʃəl, de·səl), *adv.*, *sb.* 1771. [Gael.] Righthandwise, towards the right; motion as in the apparent course of the sun (a practice held auspicious by the Celts).

Death (deþ). [A Com. Teut. sb.: OE. *dēaþ*, (ult.) an OTeut. deriv. of the verbal stem *dau-*, whence ON. *deyja* to DIE.] 1. The act or fact of dying; the final cessation of the vital functions of an animal or plant. Often personified. OE. 2. The state of being dead OE. 3. The loss or cessation of life in a part 1800. †4. State of unconsciousness, swoon (*rare*) 1596. 5. *fig.* Loss of spiritual life OE.; deprivation of civil life (usually *civil d.*) 1622; end, extinction, destruction ME. 6. Bloodshed, murder 1626. 7. Cause or occasion of death; *poet.* a deadly weapon, poison, etc. OE. †8. A pestilence –1587. †9. *Hunting.* = MORT 1741. 10. As an exclam. 1604.

1. The d. of a deare friend *Mids. N.* v. i. 293. Deth is callyd mors for it is bitter TREVISA. Over them triumphant D. his Dart shook; but delaid to strike MILT. *P. L.* XI. 490. 2. His eyes were closed in d. (*mod.*). 5. *The second d.*: the punishment of lost souls after physical death. (Cf. Rev. xxi. 8.) This banishment is a kind of civil d. 1622. 6. Not to suffer a man of d. to live BACON (J.). 7. The clam'rous lapwings feel the leaden d. POPE. A school would be his d. GOLDSM. 8. **Black d.**, the name given to the Great Pestilence or visitation of the Oriental Plague, which devastated Europe, and caused great mortality in England, in the 14th c.

Phrases. *To death* (Sc. *to deid*): **a.** *lit.* as *to beat, stone,* etc. *to d.*; hence *to do to d.* (arch.), to kill; *to put to d.*, to kill, to execute. **b.** with vbs. of feeling as *hate*, etc., or adjs., as *sick, wearied*: to the last extremity. *To catch one's d.*: see CATCH *v.* *To be the d. of*: see sense 7. *To be* (or *make it*) *d.*: *i.e.* to be (or make it) a matter of capital punishment. *Death's door, the gates* or *jaws of d.* (fig.): a near approach to, or great danger of, d. *To be in at the d.* (in *Fox-hunting*): to be present when the game is killed. *To be d. on* (slang): to be a good hand at dealing with; to be very fond of.

Comb.: **d.-adder**, a name for the genus *Acanthophis* of venomous serpents, esp. *A. antarctica* of Australia; also erron. f. *deaf-adder*: see DEAF *a.*; **-bill** (*Eccl.*), a list of dead for whom prayers were to be said; **-dance**, a dance at or in connexion with d.; the Dance of Death; **-doing** *a.*, doing to d., murderous; **-duty**, a duty levied on the devolution of property in consequence of a d.; legacy, and probate and succession duties; **-feud**, a feud prosecuted to the d.; **-flame** = DEATH-FIRE 1; †**-head** = DEATH'S-HEAD; **-mask**, a cast taken from a person's face after d.; **-moth**, the Death's-head Moth; **-penalty**, capital punishment; **-pile**, a funeral pile; **-rate**, the proportion of deaths to the population; **-rattle**, a rattling sound in the throat of a dying person, caused by the partial stoppage of the air-passage by mucus; so **-ruckle, -ruttle** (*Sc.*); **-tick** = DEATH-WATCH 1; **-trance**, a trance in which reduced action of the heart, lungs, etc. produces the semblance of d.; **-trap**, any place or structure which is unhealthy or dangerous without its being suspected; **-weight**, a small weight placed on the eyelids of a corpse to keep them closed.

Death-bed (de·þbed). OE. The bed on which a person dies. (In OE. the grave.) Also *attrib.*

Death-bell (de·þbel). Also **dead-bell.** 1740. A bell tolled at the death of a person; a passing-bell.

Dea·th-bird. 1821. A carrion-feeding bird; a bird supposed to bode death; a name of a small N. American owl, *Nyctala Richardsoni.*

Dea·th-blow. 1795. A blow that causes death.

fig. The death-blow of my hope BYRON.

Dea·th-day. OE. The day on which a person dies, or its anniversary.

The death-day of the founder .. is still kept THACKERAY.

Dea·th-fire. 1796. 1. = DEAD-LIGHT 2. 2. A fire for burning a person to death 1857.

Deathful (de·þfŭl), *a.* ME. [See -FUL.] 1. Fraught with death; deadly. 2. Subject to death, mortal (*arch., rare*) 1616. 3. Having the appearance of death, deathly 1656.

1. Amidst the d. field COLLINS. 2. That with a deathless goddess lay A d. man CHAPMAN. Hence **Dea·thful·ly** *adv.*, **-ness.**

Deathless (de·þlės), *a.* 1598. [See -LESS.] Not subject to death; immortal. Also *fig.* of things.

D. souls BOYLE, pain MILTON. Hence **Dea·thless·ly** *adv.*, **-ness.**

Deathlike (de·þləik), *a.* 1548. †1. = DEATHLY 2. –1621. 2. Resembling death 1605.

1. D. dragons SHAKS. 2. The d. silence 1856.

Deathling (de·þliŋ). *rare.* 1598. [See -LING.] 1. One subject to death, a mortal. Also *attrib.* 2. *pl.* Young Deaths. SWIFT.

Deathly (de·þli), *a.* [OE. *déaþlic*; cf. DEADLY.] †1. Subject to death, mortal –ME. 2. Causing death, deadly ME. 3. Resembling death, deathlike 1568. 4. Of or pertaining to death (*poet.*) 1850. Hence **Dea·thliness.** So **Dea·thly** *adv.* to a degree resembling death.

†**Dea·th's-face.** = DEATH'S-HEAD 1. *L.L.L.* v. ii. 616.

Death's-head (de·þsˌhed). 1596 [See DEATH 1.] 1. The head of Death figured as a skeleton; a human skull, *esp.* as an emblem of mortality. 2. A South American monkey, *Chrysothrix sciureus*, from the appearance of its face and features.

1. Doe not speake like a Deaths-head: doe not bid me remember mine end *2 Hen. IV*, II. iv. 255.

Death's-head Moth, a large species of hawk-moth (*Acherontia atropos*), having markings on the back of he thorax resembling a human skull.

†**Dea·th's-herb.** 1607. Deadly Nightshade.

Dea·th-sick, *a.* 1628. Mortally sick.

Deathsman (de·þsmæn). *arch.* 1589. An executioner.

Dea·th-struck, *a.* Also **-stricken.** 1622. Smitten with a mortal wound or disease.

Death-throe. ME. The agony of death. Also *fig.*

Dea·thward, *adv.* ME. In the direction of death. var. **Dea·thwards** *adv.* (*adj.*).

Dea·th-wa·rrant. Also 7–8 **dead-.** 1692. A warrant for the execution of the sentence of death. Also *fig.*

Death-watch (de·þˌwǫtʃ). Also 8 **dead-.** 1688. 1. Any of various insects which make a noise like the ticking of a watch, supposed by the superstitious to portend death; *esp.* the small beetles of the genus *Anobium*, and a minute insect, *Atropos pulsatorius*, known as destructive to botanical and other collections. 2. A vigil by the dead or dying.

1. I listened for death-watches in the wainscot GOLDSM.

Dea·th-worm. 1773. †1. = DEATH-WATCH 1. 2. *poet.* A worm of death 1821.

2. How like death-worms the wingless moments crawl SHELLEY.

Dea·th-wound. ME. A mortal wound.

Deathy (de·þi). 1796. [f. DEATH + -Y[1].] *adj.* and *adv.* = DEATHLY *a.* 3, 4, *adv.*

†**Deau·rate,** *a.* ME. [ad. L. *deauratus.*] Gilded, golden –1616. So **Deaurate** (dīˌǭ·reit), *v.* ? *Obs.*, to gild over (1562). Hence **Deaura·tion** (1658).

Deave (dīv), *v.* Now *Sc.* and *n. dial.* [OE. *déafian.*] †1. *intr.* To become deaf (*rare*) –ME. 2. *trans.* To deafen; to stun with din ME.

Deb (deb). 1926. Colloq. abbrev. (orig. *U.S.*) of DÉBUTANTE. Also **De·bby.**

†**Deba·cchate,** *v. rare.* 1623. [ad. L. *debacchari.*] To rage or rave as a bacchanal –1751. Hence †**Debaccha·tion.**

Debacle (dĭbā·k'l). Also **débâcle.** 1802. [a. F., f. (ult.) *dé-* = *des-* + *bâcler* to bar.] 1. A breaking up of ice in a river; in *Geol.* a sudden deluge or violent rush of water, which carries before it blocks of stone and other débris. 2. *transf.* and *fig.* A sudden breaking up; a confused rout, a stampede 1848.

1. They could have been transported by no other force than that of a tremendous deluge or d. of water W. BUCKLAND.

Debar (dĭbā·ɹ), *v.* ME. [a. F. *débarrer*, f. *des-* (see DE- I. 6) + *barer, barrer*, to BAR.] 1. *trans.* To exclude *from* a place or condition; †to shut out, exclude. Also with *of* (*arch.*). 2. To prohibit, prevent, stop 1526.

1. Debarred from voting JOHNSON. 2. Its Egress [would have been] utterly debarr'd WOODWARD. Hence **Deba·rment.**

Deba·rbarize, *v.* See DE- II. 1.

Debark (dĭbā·ɹk), *v.*[1] 1654. [a. F. *debarquer*, f. *dé-* = *des-* (see DE- I. 6) + *barque* BARK *sb.*[2]] = DISEMBARK (*trans.* and *intr.*). Hence **Debarka·tion, debarcation,** the action of landing from a ship.

Debark (dĭbā·ɹk), *v.*[2] *rare.* 1744. [f. DE- II. 2 + BARK *sb.*[1]] To strip of its bark. Also *fig.*

Debarrass (dĭbæ·răs), *v.* 1789. [a. F. *débarrasser*, f. *dé-* = *des-* (see DE- I. 6) + *-barrasser* in *embarrasser* to EMBARRASS.] *trans.* To disembarrass.

Debase (dĭbē¹·s), *v.* 1565. [f. DE- I. 1, 3 + BASE *v.*[1]; cf. ABASE.] †1. *trans.* To lower in position, rank, or dignity; to abase –1827. †2. To decry, depreciate –1746. 3. To lower in quality, or character; to degrade; *spec.* to depreciate (coin) 1591.

1. God sent her to d. me MILT. *Sams.* 999. 3. To d. commodities 1606, words JOHNSON. Hence **Deba·sed** *ppl. a.*, *Her.* reversed. **Deba·sement,** the act of debasing or state of being debased; degradation; †abasement. **Deba·ser.** **Deba·singly** *adv.*

Debatable (dĭbē¹·tăb'l), *a.* Also **debateable.** 1492. [a. OF., f. *debat(t)re.*] Admitting of debate or controversy; subject to dispute; questionable 1581.

The d. Elections 1685, opinions FROUDE.

The D. Land: a tract between the Esk and Sark, claimed (before the Union) by both England and Scotland. Also used *fig.* of regions of thought, etc.

Debate (dĭbē¹·t), *sb.* [ME. *debat*, a. F.; see DEBATE *v.*[1]] 1. Strife, dissension, quarrelling; a quarrel (*arch.*). 2. Contention in argument; dispute, controversy; discussion; *esp.* discussion in Parliament; a discussion ME.

1. To seal the truce and end the dire d. POPE. Their d. was so cruell, that there was slaine v. capitaynes LD. BERNERS. 2. After much d., they concluded unanimously that [etc.] SWIFT. A full D. upon Public Affairs n the Senate STEELE.

Debate (dĭbē¹·t), *v.*[1] ME. [a. OF. *debatre*, f. Rom. *battere* to fight (see ABATE, COMBAT), with L. *de-*, occas. repl. in Rom. by *des-*.] †1. *intr.* To fight, strive, quarrel, wrangle –1665. Also *fig.* 2. *trans.* To contest, dispute; to contend for; to carry on (a fight) (*arch.*) 1489. 3. To dispute about, argue, discuss ME.; *intr.* to engage in discussion; *esp.* in a public assembly 1530. 4. To consider (*trans.* and *intr.*) ME.

1. His cote-armour..in which he wold d. CHAUCER. 2. [To] d. The martial prizes DRYDEN. In many a well debated field SCOTT. 3. The question has been debated among many great Clerks WALTON. Commission to d. of Religion FULLER. 4. I and my Bosome must d. awhile *Hen. V*, IV. i. 31.

Hence †**Deba·teful** *a.* contentious; pertaining to contention. †**Deba·tement,** the action of debating; strife. **Deba·ter,** †one who contends or strives; a controversialist. †**Deba·tive,** relating to, or of the nature of debate or discussion (*rare*). †**Deba·tous** *a.* contentious.

†**Debate,** *v.*[2] ME. [app. f. DE- I. 1, 3 + BATE, aphet. f. ABATE.] To abate (*trans.* and *intr.*) –1658. Hence †**Deba·tement**[2] = ABATEMENT.

Debauch (dĭbǭ·tʃ), *v.* 1595. [a. F. *débaucher*, in OF. *desbaucher* to entice away from service or duty, from a sb. *bauche* = workshop (Littré).] †1. *trans.* To turn or lead away *from* one to whom service, etc. is due –1765. 2. To seduce from virtue or morality; to corrupt 1603. 3. To vitiate (the taste, judgement, etc.) 1664. †4. To vilify; to disparage –1659. †5. To spend prodigally –1649. 6. *intr.* To indulge to excess; to riot, revel. ? *Obs.* 1644.

1. He debauched Prince John from his allegiance HUME. 2. To d. one's conscience 1665, a country girl 1843. 3. A mind not yet debauched by learning BERKELEY. 6. Such as can drink and d. EVELYN. Hence **Debau·cher.** †**Debau·chment,** seduction from duty or virtue; debauched condition; a debauch.

Debauch (dĭbǭ·tʃ), *sb.* 1603. [a. F. *débauche*; see prec.] 1. Excessive indulgence in eating and drinking, or other sensual pleasures. 2. The practice or habit of such indulgence 1673. 3. *transf.* and *fig.* 1672. †4. = DEBAUCHEE –1719.

1. My head akeing all day from last night's d. PEPYS. 2. The first physicians by d. were made DRYDEN.

Debauched (dĭbǭ·tʃt), *ppl. a.* 1598. [f. DEBAUCH *v.* + -ED.] Seduced from duty or virtue; dissolute, licentious.

An vnthriftie, careles, debaucht or mislead man FLORIO. Hence **Debau·chedly** *adv.* **Debau·chedness**; †**Debau·chness.**

Debauchee (debǫʃī·). 1661. [a. F. *debauché.*] One given to excessive indulgence in sensual pleasures.

Debauchery (dĭbǭ·tʃəri). 1642. [f. DEBAUCH *v.* + -ERY.] 1. Vicious indulgence in sensual pleasures. †2. Seduction from duty or virtue; corruption –1790.

1. Youth's deboichery 1647. 2. The republick of Paris will endeavour to compleat the d. of the army BURKE.

†**Debe·l, -ell,** *v.* 1555. [a. F. *débeller*, ad. L. *debellare.*] To vanquish; to expel by force of arms –1825.

†**Debe·llate,** *v.* 1611. [f. L. *debellat-* ppl. stem; see prec.] = DEBEL –1626. Hence

†**Debella·tion**, conquest, subjugation. †**Debella·tor.** SWIFT.

De bene esse; see DE 1.

Debenture (dǐbe·ntiŭɹ). 1455. [prob. L. *debentur* 'there are owing', as the initial word of these certificates.] **1.** A voucher certifying that a sum of money is owing to the person designated in it. **b.** *spec.* At the Custom-house: A certificate given to an exporter of imported goods on which a drawback is allowed, certifying that the holder is entitled to an amount therein stated. 1662. Also †*transf.* and †*fig.* †**2.** A certificate of a loan made to the government for public purposes –1813. **3.** A bond issued by a corporation or company (under seal), acknowledging that it is indebted to the holder in a specified sum of money, bearing interest until repayment of the principal 1847.

1. Certeyn debentur conteynyng the seyd sommes 1455. 3. *Mortgage d.*: a d. the principal of which is secured by the pledging of the whole or a part of the property of the issuing company.

Comb.: **d.-bond** = DEBENTURE 3; **-stock**, debentures in the form of a stock, the nominal capital of which represents a debt of which only the interest is secured by a perpetual annuity.

Hence **Debe·ntured** *a.* furnished with or secured by a d., as *debentured goods, i. e.* goods on which a custom-house d. for a drawback is given.

Debile (de·bil), *a. arch.* 1536. [a. F. *débile*, ad. L. *debilis*, f. *de-* + *habilis*.] Weak.

Debi·litant. 1857. [ad. L. *debilitantem*; see DEBILITATE *v.*]

A. *adj.* Debilitating.

B. *sb. Med.* Debilitating remedies, *e.g.* low diet, etc.

Debilitate (dǐbi·liteᵉⁱt), *v.* 1533. [f. L. *debilitat-* ppl. stem.] To render weak, enfeeble.

A feeble constitution, which he further debilitated by a dissipated life 1871. Hence **Debilita·tion**, the action of debilitating; enfeebled condition. **Debi·litative** *a.* tending to d.

Debility (dǐbi·lĭti). 1474. [a. F. *débilité*, ad. L. *debilitatem*.] **1.** The condition of being weak or feeble; weakness 1484. †**2.** An instance of weakness –1825.

1. D. of body 1563, of mind H. WALPOLE, of the realme of Englande LD. BERNERS.

†**Debi·nd**, *v.* [DE- I. 1.] To bind down. SCOTT.

Debit (de·bit), *sb.* 1450. [ad. L. *debitum*. See DEBT.] †**1.** *gen.* A debt –1614. **2.** *Book-keeping.* An entry in an account of a sum of money owing; an item so entered. **b.** These items collectively; the left-hand side of an account on which debits are entered. (Opp. to CREDIT *sb.*) 1776. Also *attrib.*

Debit (de·bit), *v.* 1682. [f. DEBIT *sb.*] **1.** *trans.* To charge with a debt. **2.** To charge as a debt 1865.

1. He must and may d. the Principal for the said Value SCARLETT. 2. To whom am I to d. it (*mod.*).

†**Debite**, *sb.* 1482. [Corrupt f. DEPUTE.] A deputy –1549. So †**Debity.**

†**De·bitor.** 1484. A by-form of DEBTOR (15–17th c.).

Debitumenize, -ation; see DE- II. 1.

‖**Déblai** (de·blę). 1853. [F., vbl. sb. f. *déblayer* for *déblaer*, orig. to clear from corn.] *Fortif.* The hollow space formed by the removal of earth for parapets, etc.

†**Deboi·se**, *v.* 1632. [A by-form of *debosh* DEBAUCH.] = DEBAUCH *v.* 2, 5. –1662. So †**Deboise** *a.*, †**Deboi·st** *ppl. a.* debauched.

Debonair, -bonnaire (de:bǫ̈nēᵊ·ɹ), *a.* (*sb.*) ME. [a. OF. *débonaire*, prop. *de bonne aire* (11th c.). Now a literary archaism.]

A. *adj.* Of gentle disposition, meek; gracious; courteous (*obs.*); pleasant and affable in address; now often connoting gaiety of heart.

Was neuer Prince so meeke and debonaire SPENSER.

B. *sb.* †**1.** [the adj. used *absol.*] Gracious being or person. (ME. only.) †**2.** = DEBONAIRTY –1748.

Hence **Debonai·r-ly** *adv.*, **-ness.**

†**Debonai·rty, debona·rity.** [ME., a. OF. *debonairetė*, f. *debonaire*.] Debonair character or disposition –1688.

Debo·rd, *v.* ? *Obs.* 1620. [a. F. *déborder*.] Of a body of water: To pass beyond its borders, to overflow. Also †*fig.* Hence †**Debo·rdment**, going beyond bounds, excess.

Debosh, -bosche, obs. or arch. f. DEBAUCH.

Debo·shed, *ppl. a.* 1599. Early var. of DEBAUCHED, repr. the pronunc. of F. *débauché*. Revived by Scott, and now frequent in literary English, with vaguer sense than *debauched*.

Deboshment, obs. f. DEBAUCHMENT.

Debouch (dǐbū·ʃ, debu·ʃ), *v.* Also **debouche.** 1760. [a. F. *déboucher*, f. *dé-* :—*des-*, L. *dis-* (see DE-) + *bouche*.] *Milit.* (*intr.*) To issue from a confined place, as a defile or a wood, into open country; hence *gen.* to emerge. Also *transf.* of a ravine, river, etc.

We saw the column of infantry debouching into Minden plain 1760. Hence **Debou·ch(e)ment**, the action or fact of debouching.

‖**Débouché** (debuʃe). 1760. [Fr.: f. *déboucher* (see prec.).] *Milit.* An opening where troops may debouch: *gen.* an outlet; *fig.* a market for goods.

One gate, as an additional *débouché* for the crowd 1857. var. **Debou·ch** (*rare*).

Debouchure (debuʃū·r). 1844. [Fr. in form only.] The mouth or outlet of a river, a pass, etc.

†**Debou·t**, *v.* 1619. [a. F. *débouter*.] To expel, oust –1644.

‖**Debris, débris** (dēᵊ·brī, de·brī). 1708. [F. *débris*, f. the vb. (see next).] The remains of anything broken down or destroyed; ruins, wreck: in *Geol.* any accumulation arising from the waste of rocks, etc.; hence, any similar rubbish formed by destructive operations.

The *débris* of the ancient rocks MURCHISON.

Debruise (dǐbrū·z), *v.* ME. [a. ONF. *debruisier* = OF. *debrisier*, f. *de-* (DE- I. 1) + *brisier*.] †**1.** *trans.* To break down, break in pieces, crush, smash –1618. **2.** *Her.* (*trans.*) To cross (a charge, *esp.* an animal) with an ordinary so as apparently to press it down; usu. in *pa. pple.* **Debruised.**

2. He..exhibited on his escutcheon the lions of England and the lilies of France without the baton sinister under which..they were debruised in token of his illegitimate birth MACAULAY.

Debt (det), *sb.* [ME. *det, dette*, a. OF. *dete, dette* :—pop.L. **debita* for L. *debitum*.] **1.** That which is owed or due; anything (as money, goods, or service) which one person is under obligation to pay or render to another. **2.** A liability to pay or render something; the being under such liability ME. **3.** *fig.* As the type of an offence requiring expiation, a sin ME.

1. To paye large vsury besides the due det 1559. Love the gift is love the d. TENNYSON. 2. A d. of speciall remembrance and thankefulnesse A.V. *Transl. Pref.* 5. 3. And forgeue vs our debtes euen as we forgiue our debters 1557.

Phrases. *D. of honour*: a d. which depends for its validity solely on the honour of the debtor, *e.g.* a gambling d. *D. of* (or *to*) *nature* the necessity of dying, death. [L. *debitum naturæ*.] *National D.*: a d. owing by a sovereign state to private individuals for money advanced.

†**Debt**, *ppl. a.* ME. [ad. L. *debitus*.] Owed, owing –1602. *Haml.* III. ii. 203.

†**De·bted**, *ppl. a.* ME. [? aphet. f. *an-, en-, indebted* (13th c.).] Owed; of persons, indebted –1590. *Com. Err.* IV. i. 31.

Debtee (de:tī·). 1531. [f. DEBT-OR.] One to whom a debt is due: a creditor.

Debtless (de·tlės), *a.* ME. [See -LESS.] Free from debt.

Debtor (de·təɹ). [ME. *det(t)ur, -our*, a. OF. *det(t)or, -ur, -our* :—L. *debitorem*.] **1.** One who is indebted to another: correlative to *creditor*. **2.** *Book-keeping.* The left hand or debit side of an account, or what is entered there 1714. Also *attrib.* Hence **De·btorship.**

Debunk (dǐbʊ·ŋk), *v.* orig. *U.S.* 1927. [f. DE- II. 2 a + BUNK *sb.*[2]] *trans.* To remove the 'nonsense' or false sentiment from; hence, to remove (a person) from his 'pedestal'.

†**Debu·rse**, *v. Sc.* 1529. [a. F. *débourser*.] To DISBURSE –1705.

Debus (dǐbʊ·s), *v. Army slang.* 1915. [BUS *sb.*] *trans.* and *intr.* To set down, or get down, from a motor vehicle.

‖**Début** (debü). 1751. [F., f. *débuter* to lead off at billiards, etc.] Entry into society; first appearance in public of an actor or other performer. So **Début(e** *v.* to make one's d.

Débutant (debütaṅ). 1824. [F., f. as prec.] A male performer or speaker making his first appearance before the public. So **Débutante** (-taṅt), a girl coming out or presented 1837.

Dec. Abbrev. of DECEMBER; in *Mus.* of DECRESCENDO; in *Med.* of L. *decoctum* (= decoction).

Deca-, dec-, Gr. δεκα- ten, an initial element in many technical words; see below. Also **1. Deca·ca·rbon** *a. Chem.* in *decacarbon series*, the series of hydrocarbon compounds containing C_{10}, as *decane, decene*, etc. ‖**Deca·cera** *sb. pl.* [Gr. κέρας, κερατ-], *Zool.* a name for the ten-armed cephalopods, called also *Decapoda*. **Decadi·anome** [Gr. διανομή], *Math.* a quartic surface (dianome) having ten conical points. **Deca·ngular** *a.* [L. *angulus*], having ten angles. **Decaphy·llous** *a.* [Gr. φύλλον], *Bot.* having ten leaves.

2. *esp.* in the French metric system, the initial element in names of measures and weights, composed of ten times a standard unit. Hence, **De·cagramme, -gram** (F. *décagramme*), the weight of 10 grammes (= 154·32349 troy grains, or ·353 oz. avoird.). **Decalitre** (de·kălītəɹ), [F. *déca-*], a measure of capacity, containing 10 litres (= 610·28 cubic inches, or a little over 2¹/₅ gallons). **Decametre** (de·kămītəɹ), [F. *déca-*], a lineal measure of 10 metres (= 32 ft. 9·7079 inches Eng.). **Decastere** (de·kăstīᵊɹ), [F. *décastère*], a solid measure = 10 steres or cubic metres.

Decachord (de·kăkǫɹd). 1525. [ad. L., a. Gr. δεκάχορδος, -ον, f. δέκα + -χορδή.]

A. *adj.* Ten-stringed.

B. *sb. Mus.* A ten-stringed instrument; var. †**Decacho·rdon.**

Decad (de·kăd). 1616. [ad. Gr. δεκάς, δεκαδ-, f. δέκα.] **1.** The number ten (the perfect number of the Pythagoreans). **2.** Earlier f. DECADE, q.v.

Decadal (de·kădăl), *a.* 1753. [f. L. *decas, decadem*, a. Gr.] Of or relating to the number 10; belonging to a decade.

De·cadarchy, deka-. 1849. [ad. Gr. δεκαδαρχία.] *Gr. Hist.* A ruling body of ten.

Decadary (de·kădĕri), *a.* 1801. [f. L. *decadem* DECADE.] Relating to a DECADE (1 b).

Decade (de·kēd). Also 7–9 **decad.** 1475. [a. F., ad. L. *decas, decad-*. Cf. DECAD.] **1.** A group or series of ten; *spec.* a period of ten years 1594. **b.** A period of ten days, substituted for the week in the French Republican calendar of 1793. **2.** A division of a literary work, containing ten books or parts 1475.

1. So many tens or decads of yeares 1605. 2. The second d. of Livy MACAULAY.

Decadence (de·kădėns, dǐkēᵊ·dėns). 1549. [a. F. *décadence*, ad. med.L. *decadentia*. *De·cadence* is now preferred.] The process of falling away or declining; decay; impaired condition; *spec.* applied to a particular period of decline in art, literature, etc.

The men of the d., not less than the men of the renaissance, were giants of learning STUBBS.

Decadency (de·kădėnsi, dǐkēᵊ·dėnsi). 1632. [f. as prec.] Decaying condition; also = prec.

Decadent (de·kădėnt, dǐkēᵊ·dėnt), *a.* 1837. [f. DECADENCE; see -ENT.] **1.** That is in a state of decay or decline. ‖**2.** Belonging to an age of decadence in literature and art: said of certain French writers, etc. 1888.

‖**Décadi.** 1795. [Fr.: f. Gr. δέκα + *-di* day in *Lundi*, etc.] The tenth day of the DECADE (1 b), superseding Sunday.

Decadic (dǐkæ·dik), *a.* 1838. [a. Gr. δεκαδικός (see DECADE) + -IC.] Reckoning by tens; denary.

Decagon (de·kăgǫn). 1613. [f. (ult.) Gr. δέκα, and γωνία, -γωνος.] *Geom.* A plane figure having ten sides and ten angles. Also *attrib.* Hence **Deca·gonal** *a.* of or pertaining to a d.; ten-sided.

Decagram; see DECA- *prefix* 2.

Decagynous (dǐkæ·dʒinəs), *a.* [f. mod. Bot.L. *decagynus*, f. Gr. δέκα + γυνή (= female organ).] *Bot.* Having ten pistils. So **Decagy·nia**, a Linnæan order of plants having ten pistils.

Decahedron (dekăhī·drǫn). 1828. [Repr. a Gr. *δεκάεδρον, f. δέκα + ἕδρα.] *Geom.* A solid figure having ten faces. Hence **Decahe·dral** *a.* having the form of a d.

Decalcify (dīkæ·lsifəi), *v.* 1847. [f. DE- II. 1 + CALCIFY.] To deprive (*e.g.* bone) of its calcareous matter. Hence **Decalcifica·tion.**

Decalcoma·nia. Also, as Fr., **-manie.** 1864. [ad. F. *décalcomanie.*] A process of transferring pictures from prepared paper to surfaces of glass, porcelain, etc., in vogue about 1862–4. Also *attrib.*

Decalitre; see DECA- *prefix* 2.

Decalogue (de·kălǫg). ME. [a. F. *décalogue*, ad. L. *decalogus*, a. Gr. δεκάλογος (orig. adj. ἡ δεκάλογος, sc. βίβλος), from the phrase οἱ δέκα λόγοι the ten commandments, in LXX, etc.] The Ten Commandments collectively as a body of law. Hence **Deca·logist**, one who expounds the d. (*rare*).

Decameron (dīkæ·mĕrǫn). 1609. [a. It. *Decamerone*, f. Gr. δέκα + ἡμέρα.] The title of a work by Boccaccio containing a hundred tales which are supposed to be related in ten days.

Decametre; see DECA- *prefix* 2.

Decamp (dīkæ·mp), *v.* 1676. [a. F. *décamper*, f. *des-*, *dé-* (see DE- I. 6) + *camp.*] **1.** *intr.* (*Mil.*) To break up a camp; to remove from a camping-place. Hence *gen.* **2.** To go away promptly; to take oneself off 1751. Also *fig.* ¶ **3.** *catachr.* To camp 1698.

2. Probably the rascal is decamped; and where is your remedy 1792.

Deca·mpment. 1706. [a. F. *décampement.*] The raising of a camp; a prompt departure.

Decan (de·kăn). ME. [ad. L. *decanus*; cf. DEAN.] †**1.** A ruler of ten 1569. **2.** *Astrol.* The ruler of ten parts, or ten degrees, of a zodiacal sign; also this division itself 1588. †**3.** = DEAN[1]. –1538.

Decanal (dīkē·năl), *a.* 1707. [f. L. *decanus* + -AL.] **1.** Of or pertaining to a dean or deanery. **2.** In *D. side*: the south side of the choir, on which the dean usually sits 1792.

2. On the D. or Southern side 1877.

†**De·canate.** 1647. [f. DECAN + -ATE.] *Astrol.* One third part, or ten degrees, of each zodiacal sign; = FACE, q.v. –1696.

‖**Deca·ndria.** 1775. [mod. Bot.L. (Linnæus), f. Gr. δέκα + ἀνδρ- (= male organ).] *Bot.* A Linnæan class of plants having ten stamens. Hence **Deca·ndrous** *a.* having ten stamens.

Decane (de·kēn). 1875. [f. Gr. δέκα + -ANE 2.] *Chem.* The saturated hydrocarbon $C_{10}H_{22}$; one of the paraffins found in coal-tar.

†**Deca·nery, -ary.** 1538. [f. L. *decanus* + -ERY.] = DEANERY –1647.

Decangular; see DECA- *prefix* 1.

‖**Decani** (dīkē·nəi). 1760. [L., genitive of *decanus* DEAN.] Dean's; in phrases *d. side*, *stall* (of a choir); = DECANAL 2. In *Mus.*, correlative to *cantoris* in antiphonal singing.

Decant (dīkæ·nt), *v.*[1] 1633. [a. F. *décanter*, ad. med.L. *decanthare*, f. *de-* + *canthus* the angular beak of a jug, a transf. use of Gr. κανθός corner of the eye.] To pour off (the clear liquid of a solution) gently, so as not to disturb the sediment. **b.** To pour (wine, etc.) from the bottle into a decanter; also, *loosely*, to pour out into a drinking vessel 1730. Also *transf.*

†**Deca·nt**, *v.*[2] 1674. = DECANTATE *v.* –1711.

†**Deca·ntate**, *v.* 1542. [f. L. *decantat-* ppl. stem, f. DE- I. 3 + *cantare.*] To sing or say over and over again –1659. So †**Deca·ntate** *pa. pple.* decantated.

Decantation (dīkæntē·ʃən). 1641. [ad. med.L. *decanthatio*; see DECANT *v.*[1]] The action of decanting; *esp.* of pouring off a liquid clear from a deposit.

Decanter (dīkæ·ntəɹ). 1712. [f. DECANT *v.*[1] + -ER.] **1.** One who decants. (Dicts.) **2.** A vessel used for decanting or receiving decanted liquors: *spec.* a bottle of clear flint or cut glass, with a stopper, in which wine is brought to table, and from which the glasses are filled.

Decaphyllous; see DECA- *prefix* 1.

Decapitate (dīkæ·pitēt), *v.* 1611. [f. F. *décapiter* = late L. *decapitare*, f. DE- I. 6 + *caput, capit-*. See -ATE [3].] **1.** To cut off the head of; to behead. **2.** *U.S. politics.* To dismiss summarily from office 1872. Hence **Deca·pitator**, one who or that which decapitates.

Decapitation (dīkæpitē·ʃən). 1650. [a. F. *décapitation*; see prec.] **1.** The action of decapitating; the being decapitated. **2.** *U.S. politics.* Summary dismissal from office 1869.

Decapod (de·kăpǫd). 1835. [a. F. *décapode*, ad. mod.L. *Decapoda*; see next.] *Zool.*

A. *sb.* One of the *Decapoda*; in *pl.* = next.

B. *adj.* Belonging to the *Decapoda.*

‖**Decapoda** (dīkæ·pŏdă), *sb. pl.* [mod.L. (1806), prop. adj. pl. neuter sc. *animalia*, a. Gr. δεκάποδα, neut. pl. of δεκάπους.] *Zool.* **1.** The highest order of *Crustacea*, having ten feet or legs; it includes the lobster, crab, cray-fish, shrimp, etc. 1878. **2.** The ten-armed *Cephalopoda* (order *Dibranchiata*), distinguished from the *Octopoda*. Called also *Decacera.* 1851. Hence **Deca·podal** *a.*; **Deca·podan** *a.* and *sb.*; **Deca·podous** *a.*; **Decapo·diform** *a.* having the form of a decapod crustacean.

Deca·rbonate, *v. rare.* 1831. [Cf. CARBONATE.] = next.

Decarbonize (dīkā·ɹbŏnəiz), *v.* 1825. [DE- II. 1.] To deprive of its carbon or carbonic acid. Hence **Decarboniza·tion.**

Deca·rburize, *v.* 1856. [Cf. CARBURIZE.] = prec. Hence **Decarburiza·tion.**

Decarch, dek- (de·kaɹk), *sb.* 1656. [ad. Gr. δεκάρχης.] *Gr. Hist.* One of a ruling body of ten.

Decarch, dek- (de·kaɹk), *a.* 1884. [f. Gr. δέκα + ἀρχή.] *Bot.* Proceeding from ten points of origin: said of the primary xylem of the root.

Decarchy, dek- (de·kaɹki). 1638. [ad. Gr. δεκαρχία.] *Gr. Hist.* = DECADARCHY.

†**Deca·rd**, *v.* 1550. = DISCARD *v.* –1621.

Decastere; see DECA- *prefix* 2.

Decastich (de·kăstik). *rare.* 1645. [f. Gr. δέκα + στίχος.] A poem of ten lines.

Decastyle (de·kăstəil), *a.* 1727. [ad. L. *decastylus*, a. Gr., f. δέκα + -στυλος.] *Archit.* Of a building: Having ten columns in front. Also *sb.* A portico or colonnade of ten columns.

Decasualize (dīkæ·ziuăləiz), *v.* 1907. [f. DE- + CASUAL *a.* + -IZE.] *trans.* To remove the casual element from (labour). So **Deca·sualiza·tion** (1892).

Decasyllabic (dekăsilæ·bik), *a.* (*sb.*) 1771. [f. Gr. δέκα + SYLLABIC.] Consisting of ten syllables. As *sb.* A line of ten syllables. So **Decasy·llable** *sb.* and *a.*

Decatyl (de·kătil). 1869. [See -YL.] *Chem.* = DECYL.

Decay (dīkē·), *sb.* 1460. [f. DECAY *v.*] **1.** The process of falling off from a thriving condition; progressive decline; decayed condition. †**b.** *Occas.* = Downfall; *poet.* fall, death –1724. †**2.** Falling off; decrease –1816. **3.** Wasting or wearing away; dilapidation 1523; †*pl.* ruins, debris –1777. **4.** Decline of the vital energy or faculties; †(with *pl.*) effect or mark of decay; †*spec.* phthisis –1818. **5.** The wasting of organic tissue; rotting 1594. †**6.** A cause of decay –1690. †**7.** Arrears. [med.L. *decasus redditus.*] –1546.

1. The d. of a town FROUDE. **3.** Who lets so fair a house fall to d. SHAKS. *Sonn.* xiii. 9. *fig.* Contraction and d. ..of a language SAYCE. **6.** My loue was my d. SHAKS. *Sonn.* lxxx.

Decay (dīkē·), *v.* 1483. [a. OF. *decair*, var. of *decaoir*, *dechaoir*, now *déchoir*, f. *de-* down + Rom. *cadēre* = L. *cadĕre* to fall.]

I. *intr.* **1.** To fall off; to deteriorate; †to decrease, dwindle away –1790. **2.** To fall into physical ruin 1494; to rot 1580. **3.** To fall off in vital energy, health, or beauty 1583.

1. Whereby learning .. decaieth STUBBES. Whan the vngodly haue the rule, it [the cite] decayeth COVERDALE *Prov.* xi. 11. **2.** As winter fruits grow mild ere they d. POPE.

II. *trans.* †**1.** To cause to fall off, deteriorate, or dwindle –1691. **2.** †To waste or ruin physically –1703; to rot 1616. **3.** To cause to fail in vital energy, health, or beauty 1540.

1. A High Interest decays trade LOCKE. **3.** A..face more decayed by sorrow than time 1718.

Hence **Decay·able** *a.* **Decay·edness.** **Decay·er**, one who, or that which, causes decay.

Decease (dīsī·s), *sb.* [ME. *deces*, etc., a. F. *décès*, ad. L. *decessus* departure, death, f. *decedere.*] Departure from life; death. (The common term where the mere legal or civil incidence of death is in question.)

The decesse of one Pope..and entrance of another 1654.

Decease (dīsī·s), *v.* ME. [f. prec.; repr. L. *decedere* and F. *décéder*. Cf. the sb.] *intr.* To depart from life; to die; *fig.* to CEASE.

If he discesse without heires ME.

Deceased (dīsī·st, *poet.* dīsī·sĕd), *ppl. a.* 1489. [f. DECEASE *v.* + -ED[1].] **1.** Dead, 'departed'; *esp.* lately dead, 'late'. **2.** *absol.* †**a.** *pl. The d.*: the dead. **b.** The person whose death is in question. 1625.

†**Dece·de**, *v.* 1655. [ad. L. *decedere.*] *intr.* To depart; to secede; to give place, yield –1697.

Decedent (dīsī·dĕnt). 1599. [ad. L. *decedentem.*] A deceased person. *U.S.*, chiefly in *Law.*

Deceit (dīsī·t). [ME. *deceite, deseyte, desaite*, etc., a. OF. *deceite*, etc.: sb. fem. from pa. pple. of *deceveir*, *décevoir*. Cf. CONCEIT.] **1.** The action or practice of deceiving; concealment of the truth in order to mislead; deception, fraud, cheating. Used *spec.* in *Law.* **2.** An instance of deception; a device intended to deceive; a trick, stratagem, wile ME. **3.** Deceitfulness ME.

1. By violence? no..But by d. and lies MILT. *P. L.* v. 243. Accion of desseyte ffor brekynge off promyse 1495. **2.** Venus thought on a d. SWIFT. **3.** Ulexes ..was..full of desseit ME. Hence **Decei·tless** *a.* free from d. (*rare*).

Deceitful (dīsī·tfŭl), *a.* 1483. [f. prec.] Full of deceit; given to deceiving; misleading, false. (As said of things often = DECEPTIVE.)

Appearances are d. LYTTON. Hence **Decei·tful-ly** *adv.*, **-ness.**

Deceivable (dīsī·văb'l), *a.* ME. [a. OF. *decevable*, f. stem of *décevoir.*] **1.** *actively.* Having the quality of deceiving. *Obs.* (or *arch.*) **2.** *passively.* Capable of being deceived; fallible. Now *rare.* 1646.

1. D. speech BUNYAN. **2.** An ignorant and d. majority 1841. Hence **Decei·vabi·lity** (*rare*). **Decei·vableness** (now *rare*). †**Decei·vably** *adv.* deceitfully.

†**Deceiva·nce.** ME. [a. OF. *decevance.*] Deceit, deception –1486.

Deceive (dīsī·v), *v.* ME. [a. OF. *deceveir* :—L. *decipere*, f. DE- I. 1 or 4 + *capere*. Cf. CONCEIVE.] **1.** *trans.* To ensnare; to catch by craft; to overreach; to mislead *Obs.* (or *arch.*) **2.** To cause to believe what is false; to lead into error, delude ME. Also *absol.* **b.** In *pass.* occas. = To be in error ME. †**3.** To be or prove false to; to betray –1658. Also *fig.* †**4.** To overreach; defraud; also with *of* –1761. †**5.** To beguile, wile away (time, etc.) –1841.

1. Giftes the wysest will deceave 1594. **2.** Who [can] d. his mind, whose eye Views all things at one view MILT. *P. L.* II. 189. He was not deceaued in his opinion EDEN. **3.** *fig.* Nor are my hopes deceiv'd 1700. **4.** [He] deceived me of a good sum of money which he owed me 1761. **5.** This while I sung, my sorrows I deceiv'd DRYDEN.

Hence **Decei·ver.** **Decei·vingly** *adv.*

Decelerate (dīse·lĕrēit), *v.* 1899. [f. DE-, after ACCELERATE.] To diminish the speed (of). **Decelera·tion.** **Dece·lerator.**

Decem-, L. *decem* ten, used in comb. as:

Decemco·state *a.* [COSTA], having ten ribs. **Decemde·ntate** *a.* [L. *dens*], having ten teeth or points. **Dece·mfid** *a.* [L. *-fidus*], cleft into ten parts. **Decemfo·liate, -fo·liolate** *a.* [L. *folium, foliolus*], having ten leaves or leaflets. **De:cemnovena·rian**, a man of the Nineteenth Century. **Dece·mpedal** *a.* [L. *pes, ped-*], (*a*) ten feet in length (*obs.*); (*b*) having ten feet.

December (dīse·mbəɹ). Abbrev. **Dec.** ME. [a. OF. *decembre*, ad. L. *December*, f. *decem*; orig. the tenth month of the Roman year. The meaning of *-ber* is obscure.] The twelfth and last month of the year as now reckoned; that in which the winter solstice occurs in the northern hemisphere. Also *attrib.*

December's snow or July's pride SCOTT.

‖**Decemvir** (dīse·mvəɹ). 1600. [L., sing. of *decemviri*, orig. *decem viri.*] **1.** *Rom. Antiq.* (*pl.*) A body of ten men acting as a commission; *esp.* the two bodies of magistrates appointed in 451 and 450 B.C. to draw up a code of laws (the laws of the Twelve Tables) who were, during the time, invested with the supreme government of Rome. **b.** *transf.* Any council or ruling body of ten 1615. **c.** *sing.* A member of such a body 1703. Hence **Dece·mviral** *a.* of or pertaining to the decemvirs. **Dece·mvirate,** the office or government of decemvirs; a body of decemvirs.

Dece·nary, *improp.* **decennary.** 1647. [ad. med.L. *decen(n)arius*; see DECENER.]

A. *adj.* Of or pertaining to a *decena* 1752.

B. *sb.* = med.L. *decena* a tithing.

†**De·cence.** 1678. [a. F. *décence.*] = next -1697.

Decency (dī·sĕnsi). 1567. [ad. L. *decentia*, f. *decentem.*] †**1.** Appropriateness to the circumstances of the case; fitness, seemliness, propriety; what is appropriate -1762. †**2.** Orderly condition of civil or social life -1705. **3.** Propriety of demeanour; due regard to what is becoming; *esp.* freedom from impropriety 1639; respectability 1751. **4.** *pl.* The observances of decorum; proprieties 1667; the outward requirements of a decent life 1798.

1. His discourse on the scaffold was full of d. and courage HUME. 3. Immodest words admit of no defence; For want of d. is want of sense ROSCOMMON. To support oneself with d. JOHNSON. 4. Content to dwell in decencies for ever POPE. Able to command the decencies of life MALTHUS.

Decene (dī·sīn). 1877. [f. Gr. δέκα + -ENE.] *Chem.* The olefine of the decacarbon or DECYL series, $C_{10}H_{20}$. Also called *Decylene.*

†**De·cener.** 1555. [a. Anglo-Fr., in med.L. *decenarius* (improp. *decennarius*), f. *decena* a group of ten, a tithing.] **1.** One in command of ten soldiers -1627. **2.** The head of a *decena* or tithing; a borsholder; **b.** A member of a tithing -1752.

Decennary (dĭse·nări). 1822. [f. L. *decennis*, f. *decem* + *annus* + -ARY.] *adj.* DECENNIAL 1855. *sb.* A decennium.

Decennary; see DECENARY.

Decennial (dĭse·niăl). 1656. [f. L. *decennium* (see next). The L. adj. was *decennalis.*]

A. *adj.* Of or pertaining to a period of ten years; (of persons) holding office for ten years; var. †**Dece·nnal.** Hence **Dece·nnially** *adv.*

B. *sb.* A decennial anniversary. *U.S.*

‖**Decennium** (dĭse·niŏm). Pl. **-ia.** 1685. [L., f. *decennis*; cf. CENTENNIUM.] A decade (of years). Also **Dece·nniad** (-AD 1) 1864.

In the last decennia of the last century PUSEY.

†**Decennoval** (dĭse·nŏvăl), *a.* 1681. [ad. L. *decennovalis*, f. *decem-novem.*] Of or pertaining to nineteen (years) -1694. So †**Dece·nnovary,** †**Decennove·n(n)al.**

Decent (dī·sĕnt), *a.* 1539. [a. F. *décent*, or ad. L. *decentem.*] **1.** Becoming, suitable, or proper to the circumstances of the case; seemly (*Obs.* or *arch.*). †**2.** Comely, handsome -1725. **3.** In accordance with propriety or good taste; *esp.* free from immodesty or obscenity 1545. **4.** Respectable 1696. **5.** Tolerable, passable; good enough in its way 1711. **6.** quasi-*adv.* Decently 1715.

1. A d. solemnity EVELYN. 2. D. and Beautifull Arches BACON. 3. To Praise a Mans selfe, cannot be D. BACON. Men of d. and honourable lives CHATHAM. 4. A d. well-behaved man 1771. A d. suit of clothes 1843. 5. Ability to write d. Latin prose (*mod.*). Hence **De·cent-ly** *adv.*, †**-ness.**

Decentralization (dīse:ntrălaizē^i·ʃən). 1846. [f. next.] The action or fact of decentralizing; decentralized condition.

Decentralize (dīse·ntrălaiz), *v.* 1851. [See DE- II. 1.] *trans.* To undo the centralization of; to distribute administrative powers, etc., which have been concentrated in a single centre.

What you want is to d. your Government BRIGHT.

Decephalize (dīse·fălaiz), *v.* 1861. [DE- II. 1.] *Biol.* To reverse the cephalization of; to reduce, degrade, or simplify the parts of the head of (an animal). Hence **Decephaliza·tion.**

†**Dece·ptible,** *a.* 1646. [? f. L. type *deceptibilis.] Apt to be deceived. Hence **Deceptibi·lity.**

Deception (dĭse·pʃən). ME. [a. F. *déception*, ad. L. *deceptionem.*] **1.** The action of deceiving or cheating; deceived condition. **2.** That which deceives; a piece of trickery; a cheat, sham 1794.

1. D.—a principal ingredient in happiness HOR. SMITH. 2. There is some d., some trick 1794.

Deceptious (dĭse·pʃəs), *a.* Now *rare.* 1606. [a. obs. F. *deceptieux, -cieux.*] That tends to deceive, cheat, or mislead.

D. terms. 1. In the war department—*honour* and *glory* BENTHAM. Hence †**Dece·ptiously** *adv.* So **Decepti·tious** *a.* (Bentham.)

Deceptive (dĭse·ptiv), *a.* 1611. [a. F. *déceptif, -ive*, in mod.L. *deceptivus*, f. *decept-* ppl. stem.] Apt or tending to deceive, having the character of deceiving.

A mere shallow and d. nonentity CARLYLE.

Phr. *D. cadence* (Mus.): false or interrupted cadence: see FALSE *a.* Hence **Dece·ptive-ly** *adv.*, **-ness,** d. quality. **Decepti·vity,** deceptiveness; *concr.* a sham.

†**Dece·ptory,** *a.* ME. [ad. L. *deceptorius.*] Apt to deceive. (Dicts.)

Decern (dĭsə̄·ɹn), *v.* ME. [a. F. *décerner*, ad. L. *decernere* to decide, f. DE- I. 2 + *cernere*; see CERN *v.* Cf. DISCERN.] †**1.** *trans.* To decide, determine -1619. **2.** *trans.* To decree by judicial sentence. Now techn. in *Sc. Law.* 1460. Also *intr.* **3.** *trans.* To distinguish; to discern 1535. Hence †**Dece·rnment.**

Decerniture (dĭsə̄·ɹnitiuɹ). 1632. [f. as prec.] *Sc. Law.* The action of decerning; a DECREE of a (Scotch) court.

†**Dece·rp,** *v.* Pa. pple. **decerped, decerpt.** 1531. [ad. L. *decerpere*; see DE- I. 2. Cf. DISCERP.] To pluck off or out; to excerpt -1678. var. †**Dece·rpt** *v.* So †**Dece·rption** (*rare*), a cropping off, that which is cropped off.

†**Decerta·tion.** 1635. [ad. L. *decertationem*; see DE- I. 3.] Contention, strife, contest; dispute -1661.

Decession (dĭse·ʃən). Now *rare.* 1606. [ad. L. *decessionem*, f. *decedere.*] Departure, secession; diminution (opp. to *accession*).

†**Dece·ssor.** [a. L., f. *decedere.*] = PREDECESSOR. Jer. Taylor.

†**Decha·rm,** *v.* 16... [a. F. *décharmer.*] To undo the effect of (a charm); to disenchant.

De-chri·stianize, *v.* 1834. [DE- II. 1.] To deprive or divest of its Christian character.

Deci- (desi), short f. L. *decimus* tenth, an initial element in names of measures and weights in the French metric system which are one-tenth of the standard unit. (Cf. DECA-.) Thus **Décigramme, -gram, Décilitre, Décimètre, Décistère,** the tenth part of the *gramme, litre, mètre,* and *stère* respectively. (The accents are usually omitted in Eng.)

Decide (dĭsəi·d), *v.* ME. [a. F. *décider*, ad. L. *decidere*, f. DE- I. 2 + *-cædere.* In Eng. also *des-, dis-.*] **1.** *trans.* To determine (a question, controversy, or cause) by giving the victory to one side or the other; to settle, resolve. **2.** To bring to a decision 1710. **3.** *absol.* or *intr.* To settle a question in dispute; to pronounce a final judgement 1732. **4.** *intr.* To come to a conclusion; determine, resolve 1830. †**5.** *trans.* To cut off. FULLER.

1. To the place of difference call the Swords Which must d. it 2 *Hen. IV*, IV. i. 182. Advocates plead causes, and judges d. them BARROW. 3. Who shall d., when Doctors disagree POPE. 4. To d. on a course (*mod.*). Hence **Deci·dingly** *adv.*

Decided (dĭsəi·dĕd), *ppl. a.* 1790. [f. prec.] **1.** Settled; definite; unquestionable. **2.** Resolute, determined 1790.

1. A most d. and complete success DICKENS. 2. He found them vacillating, he left them d. ALISON. Hence **Deci·ded-ly** *adv.*, **-ness.**

†**Deci·dement.** *rare.* [f. as prec. + -MENT.] = DECISION. Fletcher.

†**Decidence** (de·sidĕns). 1646. [f. as DECIDENT. Cf. DECADENCE.] Falling off -1684.

†**De·cident,** *a.* 1674. [ad. L. *decidentem*, *decidere*, f. DE- I. 1, 2 + *cadere*; cf. DECADENT.] Falling.

‖**Decidua** (dĭsi·diu̦ă). 1785. [med.L. for *membrana decidua*; see DECIDUOUS.] *Phys.* The lining membrane of the impregnated uterus in certain Mammalia; it forms the external envelope of the ovum, and is cast off at parturition (whence the name). Also *transf.* Hence **Deci·dual** *a.* of or pertaining to the d.

Deci·duary, *a.* *rare.* [f. as DECIDUOUS + -ARY.] Deciduous. DARWIN.

‖**Deciduata** (dĭsi:diu̦ē^i·tă), *sb. pl.* 1879. [mod.L. adj. pl. neut. (sc. *animalia*); see next.] *Zool.* A term comprising all placental Mammalia which possess a decidua.

Deciduate (dĭsi·diu̦ĕt), *a.* 1868. [ad. med. L. *deciduatus*, f. DECIDUA.] *Zool.* Possessing a decidua; of the nature of a decidua.

Decidu·ity. *rare.* 1846. [f. L. *deciduus*; see -ITY.] Deciduousness.

Deciduous (dĭsi·diu̦əs), *a.* 1656. [f. as prec., f. *decidere*; see DECIDENT.] †**1.** Falling down or off; declining (*rare*). **2.** *Bot., Zool.*, etc. Of leaves, petals, teeth, horns, etc.: Falling off or shed at a particular time, season, or stage of growth. Opp. to *persistent* or *permanent.* 1688. Of a tree or shrub: That sheds its leaves every year; opp. to *evergreen* 1778. Of insects: That shed their wings after copulation, as the females of ants, etc. *Phys.* = Decidual 1829. **3.** *fig.* Transitory 1811. Hence **Deci·duous-ly** *adv.*, **-ness.**

Decigram, -gramme; see DECI-.

De·cil, decile. 1674. [Cf. F. *décile*, app. f. *decem*, after *quintilis*, etc.] *Astrol.* The aspect of two planets when distant from each other a tenth part of the zodiac or 36 degrees.

Decilitre; see DECI-.

Decillion (dĭsi·lyən). 1845. [f. DECI-, after *million.*] The tenth power of a million; = 1 followed by 60 ciphers. Hence **Deci·llionth** *a.* and *sb.*

‖**Decima** (de·simă). 1630. [L., for *decima pars.*] **1.** A tenth part; a tax of one-tenth. **2.** *Mus.* The interval of a tenth (*rare*). var. †**De·cim** (in sense 1).

Decimal (de·simăl). 1608. [ad. med.L. *decimalis*, f. L. *decima* tenth, tithe; in mod. use treated as deriv. of L. *decimus* tenth, or *decem* ten.]

A. *adj.* **1.** Relating to tenth parts, or to the number ten; proceeding by tens. †**2.** Relating to tithes -1662.

1. *D. fraction* (†*number*): a fraction whose denominator is some power of ten (10, 100, 1000, etc.); *spec.* a fraction expressed by figures written to the right of the units figure after a dot (the *d. point*), and denoting respectively so many tenths, hundredths, thousandths, etc. The number of *d. places* is the number of figures after the d. point. *D. coinage* or *currency*: a monetary system in which each successive denomination is ten times the value of that next below it; so *d. system* of weights and measures.

B. *sb.* †**1.** A tenth part -1669. **2.** A decimal fraction (see above); in *pl.* often = the arithmetic of decimal fractions, decimal arithmetic 1651. Also *fig.*

2. *Recurring d.*: one in which one or more decimal figures are continually repeated; called *repeating* when one figure recurs as ·111 etc., written ·i (= 1/9), and *circulating* when two or more recur as ·142857 (= 1/7).

Hence **De·cimalism,** a d. system or theory. **De·cimalist,** an advocate of decimalism (in coinage, or weights and measures). **De·cimalize** *v.* to reduce to a d. system; whence **De·cimalization.** **De·cimally** *adv.* by tens or tenths; into tenths; in the form of a d. fraction.

Decimate (de·simē^it), *v.* 1600. [f. L. *decimare*, f. *decimus* tenth.] †**1.** To exact a tenth or a tithe from -1845. **2.** *Milit.* To select by lot and put to death one in every ten of 1600. **3.** *loosely.* To destroy a large proportion of 1663.

2. To d. a large body of mutineers MACAULAY. 3. Typhus fever decimated the school C. BRONTË.

Decimation (desimē^i·ʃən). 1549. [ad. L. *decimationem.*] **1.** The exaction of tithes, or of a tax of one-tenth; the tax itself. **2.** *Milit.* The selection by lot of one man in every ten as for punishment in cases of mutiny, etc. 1580. **3.** Destruction of a large proportion 1682.

3. The d. which their riot brought upon them 1856.

Decimator, -er (de·simē^itəɹ). 1673. [a. L., or f. DECIMATE *v.* + -ER[1].] One who decimates.

†**De·cime**[1]. 1611. [ad. med.L. *decima.*] A tithing as a division of the *hundred* in the English counties -1630.

‖**Décime**[2] (desī·m). 1810. [F., ad. L. *decima.*] A French coin, one-tenth of a franc.

Decimestrial (desime·striăl), *a.* *rare.* 1842. [f. L. *decimestris*, var. of *decemmestris* (f. *decem* + *mestris*, deriv. of *mensis*) + -AL.] Consisting of ten months, as the *d. year.*

Decimeter, -metre; see DECI-.

De·cimo-se·xto. ? *Obs.* 1599. [f. L. *sexto decimo* (orig. with *in*).] The size of a book, or of the page of a book, in which each leaf is one-sixteenth of a full sheet; prop. SEXTO-DECIMO (abbrev. 16mo). Also *fig.*

Decine, *Chem.*; see DECYL.

Decipher (d*ĭ*səi·fəɹ), *v.* 1528. [f. CIPHER, after F. *déchiffrer*, f. *des-*, *de-* (DE- I. 6) + *chiffre.*] 1. To convert (cipher) into ordinary writing; to interpret by means of the key 1545. 2. *transf.* To make out the meaning of (anything obscure) 1605. †3. To find out, detect –1599. †4. To reveal, make known; to give the key to –1793. †5. To represent verbally, pictorially, or by some kind of cipher –1753.

2. To d. bad hand-writing BAIN, hieroglyphics PRESCOTT, an allusion SPURGEON. 3. You are both decipherd..For villaines *Tit. A.* IV. ii. 8.

Hence **Deci·pher** *sb.* the translation of a cipher. **Deci·pherable** *a.* **Deci·pherer**, one who deciphers (formerly the title of a government official). **Deci·pherment**, deciphering; *esp.* interpretation of hieroglyphics or of obscure inscriptions.

Decipium (d*ĭ*si·pi*ŏ*m). [mod. irreg. f. L. *decipere*, with ending of *sodium*, etc.] *Chem.* A supposed rare metallic element of the cerium earth group. WATTS.

†**Deci·se**, *v.* 1538. [f. L. *decis-*, *decidere.*] = DECIDE *v.* –1662. So †**Deci·sor, -er** 1563–4.

Decision (d*ĭ*si·ʒən). 1490. [a. F. *décision*, ad. L. *decisionem*; see prec.] 1. The action of deciding (a contest, question, etc.); settlement, determination; (with *a* and *pl.*) a conclusion, judgement: *esp.* one formally pronounced in a court of law 1552. 2. The making up of one's mind; a resolution 1886. 3. As a quality: Determination, firmness, decidedness of character 1781. †4. Cutting off, separation –1659.

1. The decisions of the clergy were more satisfactory to themselves than to the laity FROUDE. 3. We want courage and d. of mind BURKE. Hence **Deci·sional** *a.* of, or of the nature of, a d. (*rare*).

Decisive (d*ĭ*səi·siv), *a.* 1611. [ad. med.L. *decisivus*, f. *decis-* ppl. stem. Cf. F. *décisif*, *-ive.*] 1. Having the quality of deciding or determining; conclusive, determinative. 2. = DECIDED 2. 1736. 3. = DECIDED 1. 1794.

1. That sure d. dart CRASHAW. D. experiments 1794. 2. Not an age of d. thought or d. action MAX MÜLLER. 3. A d. leaning towards what is most simple I. TAYLOR. Hence **Deci·sive-ly** *adv.*, **-ness.**

Decistere; see DECI-.

Decitizenize; see DE- II. 1 and *citizenize.*

Decivilize (d*ĭ*si·viləiz), *v.* 1859. [DE- II. 1.] To degrade from a civilized condition.

The decivilizing effect of the wars 1889.

Deck (dek), *sb.* 1466. [In sense 1, prob. a. MDu. *dec* roof, covering, etc.; cf. DECK *v.*] †1. A covering –1712. 2. *Naut.* A platform extending from side to side of a ship or part of a ship, covering in the space below, and also serving as a floor 1513. 3. In U.S. 'A passenger-car roof' (*Standard Dict.*). b. The floor of a tramcar or omnibus 1903; also, of a pier, landing-stage, or jetty 1872. 4. A pack of cards. Now *dial.* and *U.S.* 1593. †5. A pile of things laid flat upon each other –1673.

2. The largest ships of the line had *main-d.*, *middle* and *lower d.*; also the *upper* or *spar-d.*, extending from stem to stern over the main-d., and the *orlop d.* (which carried no guns) below the lower d.; they had also a *poop-d.*, or short d. in the after part of the ship above the spar-d., and sometimes a *forecastle d.*, or similar short d. in the fore-part of the ship, sometimes retained in merchant ships and called the *top-gallant forecastle*. See also HALF-DECK, HURRICANE-DECK, QUARTER-DECK, etc. (N.E.D.). Phr. BETWEEN-DECKS, *on d.*, *under deck(s*; *to clear*, *sweep the decks* (see CLEAR *v.*, SWEEP *v.*). 4. 3 *Hen. VI*, v. i. 44.

Comb. (from sense 2): **d.-beam**, one of the strong transverse beams supporting the d.; **-bridge**, (*a*) a narrow platform above and across the d. of a steamer amidships; (*b*) a bridge in which the roadway is laid on the top of the truss (opp. to *through bridge*); **-chair**, a folding cane-panelled chair, usu. with adjustable leg rest, used in passenger steamers; also, a hammock chair; **-flats** (see FLAT *sb.*); **-hand**, a workman employed on the d. of a vessel; **-house**, a room erected on the d. of a ship; **-plate**, a plate around the chimney of a marine-engine furnace to prevent contact with the wood of the d.; **-tennis**, a game played on the deck of a ship by tossing a ring or quoit of rubber, rope, etc. back and forth over a net.

Deck (dek), *v.* 1513. [app. of Flem. or LG. origin; cf. Du. *dekken*, MDu. *deken*, *decken* to cover. See also THATCH.] †1. *trans.* To cover; *esp.* to clothe –1600. 2. To cover or clothe with what beautifies; to array, attire, adorn 1514. †3. To fit out, equip –1548. 4. *Naut.* To furnish with a deck 1624.

2. Thou deckest thyself with light as with a garment COVERDALE *Ps.* civ. 2. Daisies d. the green CLARE. 4. Phr. *To d. in*, *over*: to cover in with the deck, in ship-building. Hence **Decked** *ppl. a.* adorned, set out; having a deck or decks. **De·cker**[1], one who decks or adorns. **De·cking** *vbl. sb.* the action of the vb.; adornment; planking or flooring forming a deck.

Decker[2] (de·kəɹ). 1781. [f. DECK *sb.* + -ER[1] 1.] 1. A vessel having (so many) decks, as in *two-decker*, etc. Also *transf.* of an oven. 2. A deck-hand; also a deck-passenger (*colloq.*) 1800.

Deckle (dek'l). Also **deckel.** 1810. [a. Ger. *deckel*, dim. of *decke* cover.] *Paper-making.* A thin rectangular frame of wood fitting close upon a hand mould, or a continuous band or strap on either side of the apron in a paper-machine, which confines the pulp and determines the size or width of the sheet.

Comb.: **d. edge**, the rough uncut edge of a sheet of paper, formed by the d.; also *attrib.* = next; **-edged** *a.*

Declaim (d*ĭ*klēⁱ·m), *v.* ME. [Formerly *declame*, ad. L. *declamare*, f. DE- I. 3 + *clamare*: subseq. assim. to *claim.*] 1. *intr.* To speak aloud with rhetorical expression; to make a speech on a set subject as an exercise in elocution. b. To recite with elocutionary effect (chiefly U.S.). 1552. 2. To speak aloud in an impassioned manner; to harangue 1735. †3. *trans.* To discuss aloud. CHAUCER. 4. To utter aloud or repeat rhetorically 1577.

1. Like a schoolboy declaiming EMERSON. 2. Instead of giving a reason you d. BERKELEY. To d. against the growth of luxury L. STEPHEN. 4. To d. a passage with too much emphasis SCOTT. Hence **Declai·mant** (*rare*), **Declai·mer**, one who declaims; one who harangues.

Declamation (deklămēⁱ·ʃən). 1523. [ad. L. *declamationem*; see prec.] 1. The action or art of declaiming (see DECLAIM *v.* 1) 1552. 2. A set speech in rhetorical elocution 1523. 3. Speaking in an impassioned oratorical manner; *spec.* in singing 1614. 4. A harangue 1594.

1. He publicly professed the arts of rhetoric and d. GIBBON. 2. Theams more fit for schollars declamations 1573. 3. In the heat of d. JOHNSON. 4. An insolent d. ..full of fury and indecent invectives 1715.

†**De·clamator.** ME. [a. L.] A declaimer –1710.

Declamatory (d*ĭ*klæ·mătəri), *a.* 1581. [ad. L. *declamatorius.*] Of or pertaining to rhetorical declaiming; of the nature of, or characterized by, declamation; †denunciatory 1589.

A d. theme WOTTON, style 1807, passage L. STEPHEN.

†**Decla·rable**, *a.* 1646. [f. L. *declarare.*] Capable of being declared –1678.

Declarant (d*ĭ*klēᵊ·rănt). 1681. [f. F. *déclarant.*] One who makes a declaration; *esp.* in *Law.*

Declaration (deklărēⁱ·ʃən). ME. [a. F., or ad. L. *declarationem.*] †1. The action of making clear; elucidation –1656. †2. The setting forth of a topic; exposition –1642. 3. The action of setting forth or announcing openly, explicitly, or formally; positive statement or assertion ME. 4. The action of declaring *for* or *against* 1736. 5. A proclamation as embodied in a document, instrument, or public act 1659. 6. *Law.* a. The plaintiff's statement of claim in an action; the writing in which this is made 1483. b. A simple affirmation (as opp. to an *oath*) 1834. c. The creation or acknowledgement of a *trust* or *use* in some form of writing; any writing containing a trust 1626. 7. *Bezique.* The act of declaring a score by placing certain cards on the table 1870. b. *Bridge.* (Cf. DECLARE *v.* 8 b.) 1905.

3. Crosses to be sett vpon mens dores for the declaracion of the plage 1547. Phr. *D. of war*, *peace*, *the poll.* 5. *D. of Indulgence*: see INDULGENCE. *D. of Rights*: see RIGHT. *D. of Independence*: the public act by which the American Continental Congress, on July 4th, 1776, declared the North American colonies to be free and independent of Great Britain; the document embodying this.

Declarative (d*ĭ*klæ·rătiv), *a.* 1536. [ad. L. *declarativus.*] Characterized by declaring (in the various senses of the vb.).

D promises 1646, acts, statutes 1661. The times were too tender to endure them to be d. on either part N. BACON. Hence **Decla·ratively** *adv.*

Declarator (d*ĭ*klæ·rătəɹ). *Sc.* 1567. [repr. F. *déclaratoire* (*acte*, *sentence déclaratoire*); see DECLARATORY.] (*Action of*) *d.* (Sc. Law): a form of action in which something is prayed to be declared judicially, the legal consequences being left to follow as of course.

Declaratory (d*ĭ*klæ·rătəri). 1571. [f. L. *declaratorem*; cf. F. *déclaratoire.*] Having the nature or form of a declaration; affirmatory. †*sb.* A declaration –1691.

D. act or *statute*: one which declares or explains what the existing law is. *D. action* (Sc. Law) = Action of DECLARATOR. Hence **Decla·ratorily** *adv.*

Declare (d*ĭ*klēᵊ·ɹ), *v.* ME. [a. F. *déclarer*, ad. L. *declarare*, f. DE- I. 3 + *clarare* to make clear.] †1. *trans.* To make clear or plain –1691. †2. To make known; to state in detail; to recount, relate –1703. †3. *intr.* To make relation *of* –1533. 4. *trans.* Of things: To manifest, prove ME. 5. To make known or state publicly, formally, or in explicit terms ME. b. *Cricket.* To close an innings before the usual ten wickets have fallen 1897. 6. To state emphatically, to aver 1709. 7. *Law. intr.* To make a statement of claim as plaintiff in an action 1512. b. *trans.* To make a statement constituting or acknowledging a trust or use 1677. c. To make a full statement of or as to goods liable to duty 1714. 8. *Bezique.* To declare a score by laying down certain cards on the table 1870. b. *Bridge.* To name the trump suit or call 'no trumps' 1905.

4. The heavens d. the glory of God *Ps.* xix. 1. 5. To d. an intention JARMAN, oneself a member of the Church of Rome MACAULAY. *To d. war* 1552, *a dividend* (mod.).

Phrases. *To d. oneself*: to avow one's opinions or intentions; to reveal one's true character, etc.; also *fig.* of things. *To d. for* (*in favour of*) or *against*: to avow one's opinion, or resolution to act, for or against. *To d. off*: to withdraw, back out (*colloq.*).

Hence **Decla·red-ly** *adv.*, **-ness.** †**Decla·rement**, declaration. **Decla·rer**, one who or that which declares; one who makes or signs a declaration.

‖**Déclassé** (deklase). 1887. [Fr., pa. pple.] Degraded from one's social class.

Declension (d*ĭ*kle·nʃən). 1565. [Repr. L. *declinationem*, F. *déclinaison.* Perh. a corrupt colloquial form of the F. word.] 1. The action or state of declining; slope, inclination; the dip of the magnetic needle (= DECLINATION). ? *Obs.* 1640. 2. *fig.* Declining from a standard; falling away, apostacy 1594. 3. Declining into a lower condition 1602; sunken condition 1642. 4. *Gram.* a. Inflexion of a noun, adjective, or pronoun, constituting its different cases (see CASE *sb.*[1]). b. Each of the classes into which nouns are grouped according to their inflexions. c. The action of declining, *i. e.* setting forth in order the different cases of a noun, etc. 1565. 5. Courteous refusal (*rare*) 1817.

1. The d. of the land from that place to the sea T. BURNET. 2. A d. from his own rules of life CLARENDON. 3. Symptoms of d. or decay MAURICE. Hence **Decle·nsional** *a.* of or belonging to (grammatical) d.

Declinable (d*ĭ*kləi·năb'l), *a.* 1530. [a. F. *déclinable.*] *Gram.* Capable of being declined; having case-inflexions.

D. adjectives of number ROBY. var. †**Decli·nal** *a.* (*rare*).

Declinate (de·klin*ĕ*t), *a.* 1810. [ad. L. *declinatus.*] *Bot.* Inclined downwards or to one side. So †**De·clinated** *a.*

Declination (deklinēⁱ·ʃən). ME. [a. OF. *declinacion*, ad. L. *declinationem.*] †1. = DECLENSION 2. –1814. †2. A leaning (away *from* or *towards*); a mental bias –1622. 3. A leaning downwards; inclination from the vertical or horizontal position 1594. †4. A sinking into a lower position; descent towards setting –1630. †5. The gradual falling off from a condition of prosperity or vigour; decline; decay –1799. 6. Non-acceptance; courteous refusal. ? *Obs.* 1612. 7. *Astron.* The angular distance of a heavenly body (north or south) from the celestial equator: corresp. to terrestrial *latitude.* (The most usual sense.) ME. 8. Of the magnetic needle: †a. The DIP; b. The deviation from the true north and south line, *esp.* the angular measure of this; also called VARIATION 1635. 9. *Dialling.* Of a vertical plane: The angular measure of its deviation from the prime vertical (if reckoned from east to west), or from the meridian (if reckoned from north to south) 1593. †10. *Gram.* = DECLENSION 4. –1751.

1. The declinations from Religion BACON. 2. The queen's d. from marriage STOW. 3. A d. of the Antiquary's stiff backbone SCOTT. 5. The d. of antient Learning 1673. Hence **Declina·tional** *a.*

Declinator (de·klinēⁱtəɹ). 1606. [f. L. *declinare.*] †1. One who declines; a dissentient –1670. 2. *Dialling.* An instrument for determining the declination of planes 1727.

Declinatory (dǐkləi·nătəri). 1673. [ad. med. L. *declinatorius* (f. *declinat-* ppl. stem) in the legal expression *exceptio declinatoria.*]

A. *adj.* That declines (sense II. 3); expressing refusal.

D. plea (Law): a plea of sanctuary, also pleading benefit of clergy before trial or conviction; abolished in 1826.

B. *sb.* 1. *Law.* A declinatory plea 1693. †2. = DECLINATOR 2. –1751.

Declinature (dǐkləi·nătiŭɹ). 1637. [f. ppl. stem *declinat-.*] 1. *Sc. Law.* A formal plea declining to admit the jurisdiction of a court or tribunal. 2. *gen.* The action of declining; courteous refusal 1842.

Decline (dǐkləi·n), *sb.* ME. [a. F. *déclin*, f. *décliner* to DECLINE.] 1. The process of declining or sinking to a weaker or inferior condition; falling off, decay, diminution, deterioration. b. A gradual failure of the physical powers 1770. c. Any wasting disease; *esp.* tubercular phthisis 1783. 2. Of the sun or day: The action of sinking towards its setting or close ME. 3. A downward incline, a slope (*rare*) 1538.

1. The d. of my daughter's health GOLDSM. The d. of life STEELE. A d. in prices (*mod.*). The D. and Fall of the Roman Empire GIBBON. c. He fell into a rapid d., and died prematurely S. AUSTIN.

Decline (dǐkləi·n), *v.* ME. [a. F. *décliner*, ad. L. *declinare*, f. DE- I. 2 + *-clinare*, cogn. w. Gr. κλίνειν, and Teut. *hlinôjan.]

I. *intr.* †1. To turn or bend aside; to deviate; to turn away –1839. †2. To have DECLINATION (senses 7–9) –1726. †3. *fig.* To turn aside in conduct; *esp.* to swerve (from rectitude, etc.) –1749. †4. *fig.* To lean *to* –1671. 5. To slant or slope downward ME. 6. To bend down ME. †7. To descend, fall –1602. 8. Of the sun, etc.: To sink towards setting ME. Also *transf.* of the day, etc., and *fig.* of one's life. 9. *fig.* To fall morally or in dignity, to sink. (Now only *lit.* and after *Haml.* I. v. 50.) ME. 10. *fig.* To fall off in vigour or vitality; to decay, diminish, decrease; to deteriorate 1530.

3. Yet doe I not d. from thy testimonies *Ps.* cxix. 157. 5. The ground on each side declining gently SIR T. HERBERT. 7. *Haml.* II. ii. 500. 8. The Sun declines, day ancient grows 1607. 10. Who's like to rise, Who thriues, and who declines SHAKS.

II. *trans.* †1. To turn aside (*lit.* and *fig.*) –1750. †2. To turn aside from. (Merged in 3.) –1761. 3. Not to consent to engage in, practise, or do 1631. b. Not to consent or agree to *doing*, or *to do*; hence practically = REFUSE: but a milder expression. (Constr. *vbl. sb.*, *inf.*; also *absol.* or *intr.*) 1691. c. Not to accept (something offered); implying polite refusal 1712. 4. *Sc. Law.* To refuse or object to the jurisdiction of (a judge or court) 1450. †5. To abandon (a practice) –1749. 6. To bend down, bow ME. †7. To depress (*lit.* and *fig.*) –1790. 8. To cause to slant or slope 1578. †9. To undervalue –1649. 10. *Gram.* To inflect or recite in order the cases (or forms) of (nouns, adjectives, pronouns, or, loosely, verbs) ME.; †*transf.* to recite in definite order –1627.

1. Counterfeiting a woman, thereby to d. suspicion HOLLAND. 2. Despairing to d. their Fate KEN. 3. To d. newspaper controversy T. JEFFERSON. b. I declined satisfying his curiosity CARLYLE. Shall we accept or d. (*mod.*). c. The squire said they could not decently d. his visit SMOLLETT. 10. *transf.* SHAKS. *Tr. & Cr.* II. iii. 55.

Hence **Decli·ned** *ppl. a.* **Decli·ner**, one who, or that which, declines.

Declinograph (dǐkləi·nǫgraf). 1883. [irreg. f. L. *declinare* (as etymon of *declination*) + -GRAPH.] *Astr.* An instrument for automatically recording the declination of stars with a filar micrometer.

Declinometer (deklinǫ·mǐtəɹ). 1858. [irreg. f. as prec. + -METER.] 1. *Magn.* An instrument for measuring the variation of the magnetic needle. 2. *Astr.* An instrument for observing and registering declination 1883.

†**Declive** (dǐkləi·v), *a.* 1635. [a. F. *déclive*, ad. L. *declivis*, f. DE- I. 1 + *clivus.*] Sloping downwards –1669.

Declivitous (dǐkli·vitəs), *a.* 1799. [See DECLIVITY and -OUS.] Having a (considerable) declivity; steep.

Declivity (dǐkli·vǐti). 1612. [ad. L. *declivitatem*, f. *declivis*; see DECLIVE.] Downward slope (of a hill, etc.). Also *concr.*

I could see the stones..jumping down the declivities TYNDALL.

Declivous (dǐkləi·vəs), *a.* 1684. [f. L. *declivus*, rare var. of *declivis* (see DECLIVE) + -OUS.] Sloping downwards; slanting.

Declu·tch, *v.* 1905. [DE- II.] *intr.* To disengage the clutch of a motor vehicle.

†**Deco·ct**, *ppl. a.* ME. [ad. L. *decoctus.*] 1. Decocted –1671. 2. Bankrupt 1529.

Decoct (dǐkǫ·kt), *v.* ME. [f. prec.] †1. To boil down or away –1620. Also *fig.* †2. To prepare as food by the agency of fire; to boil, cook –1657; †*transf.* to warm up, as in cooking 1599. †3. To digest in the stomach. (Regarded as a kind of cooking.) Also *fig.* –1608. †4. To prepare or mature (metals, etc.) by heat. (Cf. CONCOCT *v.* 2.) –1653. 5. To boil so as to extract the soluble parts or principles of 1545.

Decoction (dǐkǫ·kʃən). ME. [a. OF., ad. L. *decoctionem*; see prec.] 1. The action of decocting; *esp.* boiling so as to extract the soluble parts or principles of a substance. †2. Maturing or perfecting by heat; *esp.* of metals, etc. –1671. †3. Boiling down; also *fig.* –1655. 4. A liquor in which a substance has been decocted (see DECOCT *v.* 5) ME.

Decode (dǐkōᵘ·d), *v.* 1896. [DE-.] To convert from code into ordinary language.

Decohere (dǐkohīᵊ·ɹ), *v.* 1899. [f. DE- + COHERE.] *Electr.* To restore (a coherer) to its normal condition of sensitiveness. Also *intr.* Hence **Decohe·rence, -cohe·sion. Decohe·rer**, a device for doing this.

†**Deco·ll**, *v.* 1648. [a. F. *décoller.*] *trans.* = DECOLLATE –1653.

†**Decollate**, *ppl. a.* 1470. [ad. L. *decollatus*; see next.] Beheaded –1868.

Decollate (dǐkǫ·lēⁱt, de·kǫlēⁱt), *v.* 1599. [f. L. *decollat-*, *decollare*, f. DE- I. 6 + *collum.*] 1. To behead. 2. *Conch.* To break off the apex of (a shell) 1847. Hence **Decollated** *ppl. a.* **De·collator** *spec.* in *Obstetric Surg.*

Decollation (dǐkǫlēⁱ·ʃən). ME. [a. F., ad. L. *decollationem*; see prec.] 1. The action of beheading; the state of being beheaded; *spec.* in *Obstetric Surg.*, severance of the head from the body of a fœtus. 2. *Conch.* The truncating or truncated condition of a spiral shell 1866.

1. *Feast of the D. of St. John the Baptist*: a festival in commemoration of the beheading of St. John the Baptist, observed on the 29th of August.

‖**Décolleté** (dekǫ·lte), *ppl. a.*; fem. **-ée.** 1831. [F., f. *décolleter*, f. *de-*, *des-* (DE- I. 6) + *collet* collar of a dress, etc.] Of a dress, etc.: Cut low round the neck; low-necked. b. Wearing a low-necked dress. So ‖**Décolletage** (dekoltāʒ) [Fr.], (exposure of neck and shoulders by) low-cut neck of bodice 1894.

Decolorant (dǐkʊ·lərănt). 1864. [a. F. *décolorant*; see DECOLOUR.] *adj.* Decolorizing 1886. *sb.* A decolorizing agent.

Decolorate (dǐkʊ·lərĕt), *a.* 1882. [ad. L. *decoloratus.*] Having lost its colour.

Decolorate (dǐkʊ·lərēⁱt), *v.* 1623. [f. ppl. stem of L. *decolorare.*] †a. = DISCOLOUR. b. = DECOLOUR 2. Hence **Decolora·tion.**

Decolorize, -ourize (dǐkʊ·ləraiz), *v.* 1836. [See DE- II. 1.] To deprive of colour. Hence **Decoloriza·tion, -izing, -izer.**

Decolour, -or (dǐkʊ·ləɹ), *v.* 1618. [a. F. *décolorer*, or ad. L. *decolorare.* Cf. DISCOLOUR.] †1. To discolour; *fig.* to stain –1630. 2. To deprive of colour 1832.

Decomplex (dǐ·kǫmple:ks), *a.* 1748. [See DE- I. 5.] Repeatedly complex; made up of complex parts.

Decomponent (dǐkǫ̆mpōᵘ·nĕnt). ? *Obs.* 1797. [Inferred from *decompose*; see DE- I. 6.] A decomposing agent. So **Decompo·nible** *a.* capable of being decomposed (*rare*).

Decomposable (dǐkǫ̆mpōᵘ·zăb'l), *a.* Also -ible. 1784. [f. next + -ABLE.] Capable of being separated into its constituent elements. Hence **Decomposabi·lity**, d. quality.

Decompose (dǐkǫ̆mpōᵘ·z), *v.* 1751. [a. F. *décomposer*, f. *de-*, *des-* (DE- I. 6) + *composer.*] 1. *trans.* To separate into its constituent parts or elements; to disintegrate; to rot; also *fig.* 2. *intr.* (for *refl.*) To suffer decomposition; to break up; to decay, rot 1793.

1. To d. green light BREWSTER, marble FARADAY, mental operations MILL. Hence **Decompo·sed** *ppl. a.* decayed, rotten. **Decompo·ser**, a decomposing agent. **Decompo·sing** *ppl. a.* that decomposes; usu. *intr* in process of organic decay.

Decomposite (dǐkǫ·mpǒzit). 1622. [ad. late L. *decompositus* for Gr. παρασύνθετος (Priscian); see DE- I. 5.] *adj.* Further compounded; formed by adding an element to something already composite 1665. *sb.* A decomposite thing, word, etc. 1622.

Decomposition (dǐkǫmpǒzi·ʃən). 1659. [f. DECOMPOUND and DECOMPOSE.] †1. with DE- I. 5. Further composition; compounding of things already composite –1690. 2. with DE- I. 6. The action or process of decomposing, separation or resolution (of anything) into its constituent elements; disintegration; putrescence. Also *fig.* 1672.

2. *D. of forces*, in Dynamics = RESOLUTION of forces. The d. of white light BREWSTER, of organic particles DARWIN. *fig.* The d. of society BURKE.

Decompound (dǐ·kǫ̆mpau·nd). 1614. [f. DE- I. 5 + COMPOUND *a.*; cf. DECOMPOSITE.]

A. *adj.* Repeatedly compound; compounded of parts which are themselves compound; *spec.* in *Bot.* of compound leaves or inflorescences whose divisions are further divided (L. *decompositus*, Linnæus) 1691.

B. *sb.* A decompound thing, word, etc. 1614.

De:compou·nd, *v.* 1673. [DE- I. 5, II. 1.] †1. *trans.* To compound further; to form by adding an element to something already compound –1747. 2. To DECOMPOSE 1751.

2. To d. names BOLINGBROKE, the solution of chalk 1766, States 1793. Hence **Decompou·ndable** *a.*

Decompress (dǐ:kǫ̆mpre·s), *v.* 1911. [DE-.] *trans.* To relieve the air pressure on (a worker in compressed air) by means of an air-lock. So **Decompre·ssion** (also in *Surg.*). **Decompre·ssive** *a.* **Decompre·ssor** (in a motor engine).

Deco·nsecrate, *v.* 1867. [DE- II. 1.] To deprive of sacredness. **Deconsecra·tion.**

Deconsi·der, *v. rare.* 1881. [a. F. *déconsidérer.*] To treat with too little consideration.

Decontrol (dǐkǫ̆ntrōᵘ·l), *sb.* 1919. [DE-.] The removal of control, *spec.* the removal of government control. Hence as vb.

‖**Décor** (dekōr). 1656. [Fr., a. L. *decor* DECORE.] 1. Beauty, ornament. 2. The scenery and furnishings of a theatre stage; also, the layout of an exhibition, etc. 1927.

Decorament (de·kǒrămĕnt). *rare.* 1727. [ad. L. *decoramentum* (Tertull.).] Ornament.

Decorate (de·kǒrĕt), *ppl. a. arch.* 1460. [ad. L. *decoratus.*] Adorned, decorated; ornate.

Decorate (de·kǒrēⁱt), *v.* 1530. [f. L. *decorat-*, *decorare*, f. *decus.*] 1. *trans.* To adorn, embellish; to honour (*arch.*). 2. To furnish with anything ornamental 1782. 3. To invest with a military or other decoration 1816.

1. War and plunder were decorated by poetry as the honourable occupation of heroic natures FROUDE. 2. To d. churches with flowers PARKER. The old armour which decorated its walls 1870.

Decorated (de·kǒrēⁱtĕd), *ppl. a.* 1727. [f. prec. + -ED.] Adorned; furnished with anything ornamental; invested with a decoration. b. *Archit.* Applied to the second or Middle style of English Pointed architecture, wherein decoration was increasingly employed.

Decoration (dekǒrēⁱ·ʃən). 1585. [ad. late L. *decorationem.*] 1. The action of decorating (see the vb.); the fact or condition of being decorated. 2. That which adorns; an ornament, embellishment 1678. 3. A star, cross, medal, or other badge conferred and worn as a mark of honour 1816.

1. *D. day* (U.S.): the day (now May 30th) on which the graves of those who fell in the civil war of 1861–65 are decorated with flowers. She..applied all her care to the d. of her person JOHNSON. 2. The Decorations of the Stage 1706.

Decorative (de·kǒrĕtiv), *a.* 1791. [f. L. *decorat-* ppl. stem; cf. F. *décoratif*, *-ive.*] Pertaining to, or of the nature of, decoration. Hence **De·corative·ly** *adv.*, **-ness.**

Decorator (de·kŏreᵗtəɹ). 1755. [f. L. *decorare.* In F. *décorateur.*] One who decorates; *spec.* one who professionally decorates houses, etc., with plaster-work, gilding, and the like. Hence **De·coratory** *a.* (*rare*).

†Deco·re, *sb.* 1513. [ad. (ult.) L. *decor, decorem.*] Grace, honour, glory, beauty, adornment -1616.

†Deco·re, *v.* 1490. [a. F. *décorer.*] To decorate, adorn, embellish -1818. So **†Deco·rement,** ornamentation (*rare*); an ornament.

Decorous (dĕkōᵊ·rəs, de·kŏrəs), *a.* 1664. [In form ad. late L. *decorosus*, f. *decus, decor-*; in sense corresp. to L. *decōrus*, f. *decor.* Bailey 1730 has *de·cōrous*; Johnson *decō·rous.*] †1. Seemly, appropriate -1691. 2. Characterized by decorum or propriety of manners, behaviour, etc. 1792.

2. A d. character 1792, personage HAWTHORNE. D. language BURKE, silence BYRON. Hence **Decorously** *adv.*, **-ness.**

Decorticate (dīkǭ·ɹtikeᵗt), *v.* 1611. [f. ppl. stem of L. *decorticare*, f. DE- I. 6 + *cortex.*] To remove the bark, rind, or husk from; to strip of its bark; also *fig.* b. *intr.* To come *off* as a skin 1805. Hence **Deco:rtica·tion,** the action of decorticating. **Deco·rticator,** a machine, tool, or instrument for decorticating.

Decorum (dīkōᵊ·rŏm). 1568. [a. L. *decorum.*] 1. That which is proper, suitable, or seemly; fitness, propriety, congruity. 2. Hence: †a. Beauty arising from fitness; comeliness -1729. †b. Orderliness -1684. 3. Propriety of behaviour 1572. 4. (with *a* and *pl.*) †a. An appropriate act -1717. b. An act of polite behaviour; chiefly in *pl.* proprieties 1601.

1. If that D. of time and place..be observed BURTON. Maiesty to keepe d., must No lesse begge then a Kingdome *Ant. & Cl.* v. ii. 17. 3. She resolved to keep within the D. of her sex F. GREVILLE.

†Decou·rse. 1585. [a. F. *décours* :-L. *decursum.*] Downward course. Also *fig.* -1597.

†Decou·rt, *v.* 1610. [See DE- II. 2.] To banish from court -1676.

†Deco·y, *sb.*[1] 1550. [?] An obsolete game of cards -1609.

Decoy (dīkoi·), *sb.*[2] 1618. [An extension of COY, a. Du. *kooi.* The origin of the *de-* is undetermined. Cf. prec.] 1. A pond or pool with arms covered with network or the like into which wild fowl, *esp.* ducks, are allured and there caught 1625. Also *fig.* 2. A bird (or other animal) trained to lure others into a trap 1661. 3. Applied to a person: †a. A sharper -1631. b. = DECOY-DUCK 2. 4. Anything employed to allure, *esp.* into a trap; an enticement, bait, trap 1655.

1. The d. has superseded all those ancient methods of taking water fowl STONEHOUSE. *Comb.* **d.-man, decoyman,** one who attends to a d. for wildfowl.

Decoy (dīkoi·), *v.* 1660. [See prec.] 1. To allure or entice (animals) into a snare or place of capture 1671. 2. To entice or allure (persons) by the use of cunning and deceitful attractions *into, away, out, from, to do* 1660.

1. The Wild Elephants are by the tame females of the same kind as 'twere duckoy'd into a lodge with trap-doors 1671. 2. Two of whom the mariners decoyed on ship-board GOLDSM. Hence **Decoy·er.**

Decoy-duck (dīkoi·dvk). 1625. [Cf. Du. *kooieend* in same sense.] 1. A duck trained to decoy others 1651. 2. *fig.* A person who entices another into danger or mischief.

Decra·ssify, *v. rare.* 1855. [f. DE- II. 1 + L. *crassus* + -FY.] To divest of what is gross or material.

Decrease (dīkrī·s, dī·krīs), *sb.* ME. [a. OF. *decreis* (now *décroît*), f. stem of *decreistre* to DECREASE.] 1. The process of growing less; diminution; diminished condition. †2. *spec.* The wane of the moon -1746.

While man is growing, life is in d. YOUNG.

Decrease (dīkrī·s), *v.* ME. [f. OF. *descreiss-*, ppl. stem of *descreistre* (now *décroître*) = It. *discrescere*, repr. L. *decrescere*; see DE- I. 6.] 1. *intr.* To grow less; to diminish, fall off, shrink, abate. (Opp. to INCREASE *v.*) 2. *trans.* To cause to grow less; to diminish 1470.

1. Now ebbe, now flowe, nowe increase, nowe dyscrease SKELTON. He must increace, but I must d. *John* iii. 30. Tyrants fears D. not *Per.* I. ii. 85. 2. Age decreaseth strength 1651. **Decrea·singly** *adv.*

†Decreation (dīkrīˌēᵢ·ʃən). 1647. [See DE- I. 6.] The undoing of creation; annihilation -1678. So **†Decrea·tor.**

Decree (dīkrī·), *sb.* ME. [a. OF. *decré*, var. of *decret*, ad. L. *decretum*; see DECERN.] 1. An ordinance or edict set forth by the civil or other authority; an authoritative decision having the force of law. Also *fig.* 2. *Eccl.* An edict or law of an ecclesiastical council, settling some disputed point of doctrine or discipline, etc.; in *pl.* = DECRETALS ME. 3. *Theol.* One of God's appointments whereby events are foreordained 1570. 4. *Law.* A judicial decision; *spec.* in *Eng. Law*, the judgement of a court of equity (before the Judicature Act of 1873-5), or of the Court of Admiralty, Probate, and Divorce 1622.

1. The decrees of Venice *Merch. V.* IV. i. 102, of the Starre-Chamber 1637. *fig.* Fate's d. DRYDEN. 3. Her Conscience tells her God's D. Full option gave, and made her free KEN.

Decree (dīkrī·), *v.* ME. [f. DECREE *sb.*] 1. *trans.* To command by decree; to order, appoint, or assign authoritatively, ordain. b. *fig.* To ordain as by Divine appointment or by fate 1580. 2. *Law.* To †decide (a cause), order, or determine judicially; to adjudge; *absol.* to give judgement 1530. 3. To pronounce by decree 1571. 4. To determine (*to do* something) (*arch.*) 1526. 5. *absol.* or *intr.* To ordain 1591.

1. The stately triumph we decreed MARLOWE. *fig.* What is decreed, must be; and be this so *Twel. N.* I. v. 330. 4. Here we decreed to rest and dine FIELDING. 5. As the destinies d. *A. Y. L.* I. ii. 111. Hence **Decree·able** *a.* (*rare*). **†Decree·ment,** a decreeing, a decree. **Decre·er,** one who decrees.

Decreet (dīkrī·t), *sb. Obs.* or *arch.* ME. [ad. L. *decretum*; see DECREE *sb.*] 1. Earlier form of DECREE. (Now *Obs.* in Eng., and *arch.* in *Sc. Law.*) †2. A decision, determination (*rare*) -1470.

†Decreet (dīkrī·t), *v.* ME. [a. F. *décréter.* Only *Sc.* after 15th c.] 1. *trans.* To decree -1633. 2. *intr.* To pronounce a decision or judgement -1609.

Decrement (de·krĭmĕnt). 1610. [ad. L. *decrementum*, f. *decre-*, stem of *decrescere.*] 1. The process or fact of growing gradually less, or (with *pl.*) an instance of this; decrease, diminution, waste, loss. (Opp. to *increment.*) b. *Crystall.* 'A successive diminution of the layers of molecules, applied to the faces of the primitive form, by which the secondary forms are supposed to be produced' (Webster) 1805. 2. The quantity lost by diminution or waste; *spec.* in *Math.* a small quantity by which a variable diminishes 1666.

1. Rocks.. suffer a continual D., and grow lower and lower WOODWARD. [The moon's] d. in her waning GUILLIM. *D. of life*: in the doctrine of annuities, etc.: (The annual) decrease of a given number of persons by death. 2. The decrements of heat in each second PLAYFAIR.

Decrepit (dīkre·pit), *a.* 1450. [a. F. *décrépit*, ad. L. *decrepitus*, f. *de-* down + *crepit-*, *crepare* to crack, creak, etc.] Worn out with old age, enfeebled with infirmities; old and feeble. Also *fig.* of things.

To sustayne theyr parents decrepet age 1550. Decrepite superstitions 1646. var. **†Decrepid** (assim. to adjs. in *-id*). Hence **Decre·pit·ly** *adv.*, **†-ness.**

Decrepitate (dīkre·piteᵗt), *v.* 1646. [f. med. or mod.L. *decrepitare*, f. *de-* + *-crepitare*, freq. of *crepare* to crack.] 1. *trans.* To calcine or roast (a salt or mineral) until it no longer crackles. 2. *intr.* Of salts and minerals: To crackle and disintegrate when suddenly heated 1677. Hence **Decrepita·tion** (in both senses).

Decrepitude (dīkre·pitiud). 1603. [a. F. *décrépitude.*] The state of being decrepit; a state of feebleness and decay, *esp.* that due to old age (*lit.* and *fig.*). var. **†Decre·pity.**

‖**Decrescendo** (dēkreʃe·ndo). [It. = decreasing.] *Mus.* A direction: With gradual diminution of force; = DIMINUENDO. Also as *sb.*

Decrescent (dīkre·sĕnt). 1610. [ad. L. *decrescentem.*]

A. *adj.* Decreasing, growing gradually less.

Between the increscent and d. moon TENNYSON.

B. *sb.* The moon in her decrement; in *Her.* represented with the horns towards the sinister side 1616.

Decretal (dīkrī·tăl). ME. [a. F. *décrétal*, *-ale*, ad. L. *decretalis* of or containing a decree, whence med.L. *decretales* (sc. *epistolæ*), *decretale.*]

A. *adj.* 1. Pertaining to, of the nature of, or containing, a decree or decrees 1489. †2. Imperative -1679. †3. Definitive (*rare*) -1697.

1. The canon laws, or d. epistles of the popes BLACKSTONE. A D. Order made in the High Court of Chancery 1714.

B. *sb.* 1. *Eccl.* A papal decree or decretal epistle; a document issued by a Pope determining some point of doctrine or ecclesiastical law ME. b. *pl.* The collection of such decrees, forming part of the canon law ME. 2. *transf.* A decree, ordinance 1588.

1. The false decretals of Isidore 1860.

Hence **†Decretaliarch** [F. *décrétaliarche*], the lord of decretals, the Pope. (A word of Rabelais.) **†Decre·taline** *a.* **Decre·talist,** one versed in the Decretals. **Decre·tally** *adv.* in a d. way.

Decre·te. 1832. 1. Austin's adaptation of L. *decretum.* 2. Obs. var. of DECREET.

†Decre·tion. 1635. [f. L. *decret-*, stem of *decrescere*; cf. *accretion.*] Decrease -1659.

Decretist (dīkrī·tist). ME. [ad. med.L. *decretista.*] A decretalist.

Decretive (dīkrī·tiv), *a.* 1609. [f. L. *decret-*, *decernere* + -IVE.] Having the attribute of decreeing; decretory.

†Decreto·rial, *a. rare.* 1588. [f. L. *decretorius* + -AL.] = DECRETORY 3. -1646.

†Decreto·rian, *a.* 1679. [f. as prec. + -AN.] = DECRETORY 2, 3. -1716.

Decretory (dīkrī·təri), *a.* Now *rare* or *Obs.* 1577. [ad. L. *decretorius*, f. *decret-*, *decernere.*] 1. Of the nature of, involving, or relating to a decree 1631; †(of persons) positive, decided -1680. †2. Decisive -1737. 3. *Old Med.* and *Astrol.* CRITICAL, q. v. (*Obs.* or *arch.*) 1577. Hence **Decre·torily** *adv.* positively, decisively.

†Decrew·, *v. rare.* [f. OF. *décreu*, pa. pple. of *décreistre*, now *décroître*; cf. ACCRUE.] To decrease, wane. SPENSER.

Decrial (dīkrəi·ăl). *rare.* 1711. [f. DECRY *v.* + -AL 5.] The act of decrying; open disparagement. So **Decri·er,** one who decries.

Decrown (dīkrau·n), *v.* ? *Obs.* 1609. [f. DE- II. 2 + CROWN *sb.* Cf. *dethrone.*] To deprive of the crown, to discrown.

Decry (dīkrəi·), *v.* Pa. t. and pple. **decried.** 1617. [a. F. *décrier*, f. *des-*, *de-* (see DE- I. 6) + *crier.* In Eng. the *de-* is taken as = 'down'.] 1. *trans.* To denounce, suppress, or depreciate by proclamation, as coins, etc.; = *cry down* (see CRY *v.*) 1617. 2. To cry out against; to disparage openly; to attack the credit of 1641.

1. The king may..d., or cry down any coin of the kingdom, and make it no longer current BLACKSTONE. 2. The goldsmiths do d. the new Act PEPYS. To d. usury 1872. Hence **†Decry·** *sb. rare*, the decrying (of money).

Decrystallization (dīkri:stăləizēᵢ·ʃən). 1860. [f. DE- II. 1.] Deprivation of crystalline structure.

†Decuba·tion. *rare.* [f. L. *decubare* (*decumbere*).] The action of lying down. EVELYN.

‖**Decubitus** (dīkiū·bitŏs). 1866. [f. L. *decumbere*, after *accubitus*, etc.] *Med.* The manner or posture of lying in bed, as the *dorsal d.* Hence **Decu·bital** *a.* pertaining to or resulting from d.

Decuman (de·kiumăn), *a.* 1659. [ad. L. *decumanus*, var. of *decimanus* of or belonging to the tenth part, or the tenth cohort, f. *decimus*: also, by metonymy, large.] 1. Very large, immense: usu. of waves. 2. *Rom. Antiq.* Belonging to the tenth cohort, as the *d. gate* (*porta decumana*) 1852.

1. That decumane Wave that took us fore and aft MOTTEUX. (See Sir T. Browne *Pseud. Ep.* VII. xvii. 2, on the vulgar error connected with the d. wave.) var. **†Decumanal** *a.* (in sense 1) (*rare*).

Decumbency (dīkv·mbĕnsi). 1646. [f. DECUMBENT; see -ENCY.] 1. Decumbent condition or posture. 2. = DECUMBITURE 2. 1651.

1. The ancient manner of d. SIR T. BROWNE. So **Decu·mbence.**

Decumbent (dīkv·mbĕnt), *a.* (*sb.*) 1641. [ad. L. *decumbentem.*] 1. Lying down (now *rare*); †lying ill in bed -1732. 2. a. *Bot.* Lying or trailing on the ground, but with the extremity ascending; as stems, etc. 1791. **b.** *Nat. Hist.* Of hairs or bristles: Lying flat on the surface 1826. †**3.** *sb.* One lying ill in bed -1699.

1. The d. portraiture of a woman ASHMOLE.

Decumbiture (dǐkɒ·mbitiŭı). ? *Obs.* 1647. [irreg. f. L. *decumbere.* Better *decubiture.*] **1.** Lying down; *spec.* as an invalid in bed 1670. **2.** The act or time of taking to one's bed in an illness. **b.** *Astrol.* A figure erected for the time at which this happens, affording prognostics of recovery or death.

Decuple (de·kiupʼl). ME. [a. F. *décuple*, ad. L. *decuplus.*] *adj.* Tenfold 1613. *sb.* A number ten times another; a tenfold amount ME.

Decuple (de·kiupʼl), *v.* 1674. [ad. L. *decuplare*; see prec.] *trans.* To increase or multiply tenfold. var. **De·cuplate.**

Decurion (dǐkiūᵊ·riǫn). ME. [ad. L. *decurionem*, f. *decem*; see DECURY.] **1.** *Rom. Antiq.* An officer in command of a *decuria* or company of ten horse. Also *gen.* A captain of ten. **2.** *Rom. Hist.* A member of the senate of a colony or municipal town ME. **3.** A member of the Great Council in modern Italian cities and towns 1666. Hence **Decu·rionate, Decu·rionship,** the office of a d.

Decurrence (dǐkɒ·rěns). 1659. [f. DECURRENT.] †**1.** The state or act of running down; lapse -1677. **2.** *Bot.* The condition of being DECURRENT, q. v. 1835. So **Decu·rrency.**

Decurrent (dǐkɒ·rěnt), *a.* ME. [ad. L. *decurrentem.*] †**1.** Running down -1450. **2.** *Bot.* Of leaves, etc.: Extending down the stem below the point of insertion 1753. Hence **Decu·rrently** *adv.*

†**Decursion** (dǐkɒ̄·ɹʃən). 1630. [ad. L. *decursionem*, f. *decurs-* (stem of *decurrere*).] **1.** Downward course, lapse -1680. **2.** *Antiq.* A military evolution, performed under arms -1702.

Decu·rsive, *a.* 1828. [ad. mod. Bot.L. *decursivus*; see -IVE.] = DECURRENT. Hence **Decu·rsively** *adv.*

†**Decu·rt,** *v.* 1550. [ad. L. *decurtare*; see CURT *v.*] To cut down, shorten, curtail -1648.

†**Decu·rtate,** *v.* 1599. [f. stem of L. *decurtare.*] = prec. -1676. So †**Decurta·tion,** shortening, abridging, cutting down.

Decurve (dǐkɒ̄·ɹv), *v. rare.* 1835. [f. L. *de-* + *curvare.*] To curve or bend down. Hence **Decurva·tion, Decu·rvature,** the action of decurving; the condition of being bent downwards.

Decury (de·kiŭri). 1533. [ad. L. *decuria*, f. *decem*, after *centuria* CENTURY.] *Rom. Hist.*, etc. A division, company, or body of ten.

5000 of these citizens were arranged in ten pannels or decuries of 500 each GROTE.

Decus (dī·kɒ̆s). *slang.* 1688. [From the L. motto *decus et tutamen* on the rim.] A crown-piece.

Decuss (dǐkɒ·s), *v. rare.* 1782. [ad. L. *decussare*, f. *decussis*, ? f. *dec(-em)assis.*] = DECUSSATE *v.*

Decussate (dǐkɒ·sět), *a.* 1825. [ad. L. *decussatus*; see prec.] **1.** Having the form of an X. **2.** *Bot.* Of leaves, etc.: Arranged in successive pairs, which cross each other at right angles 1846. Hence **Decu·ssately** *adv.*

Decussate (de·kɒseᶦt, dǐkɒ·seᶦt), *v.* 1658. [f. L. *decussat-* ppl. stem; see DECUSS.] To cross, intersect, so as to form a figure like an X. Also *intr.*

The inner [fibres] always d. or cross the outer 1737. Hence †**Decu·ssative** *a.* crossing (*rare*). †**Decu·ssatively** *adv.*

Decussated (see prec.), *ppl. a.* 1658. [f. prec.] Formed with crossing lines like an X; crossed, intersected; having decussations. **b.** *Rhet.* Consisting of two pairs of clauses or words, in which the terms correspond, but in reverse order; chiastic 1828.

Decussation (dekɒsēᶦ·ʃən). 1656. [ad. L. *decussationem*; see above.] Crossing (of lines, rays, fibres, etc.) so as to form a figure like an X. **b.** *Rhet.* An arrangement of clauses, etc. in which corresponding terms occur in reverse order 1841.

Single and masterly strokes, without decussations EVELYN.

†**Decu·ssion.** *rare.* [ad. L. *decussionem.*] A shaking down or off. EVELYN.

Decyl (de·sil). 1868. [f. Gr. δέκα + -YL.] *Chem.* The univalent hydrocarbon radical $C_{10}H_{21}$; also called *Decatyl.* Also *attrib.* Hence **Decy·lic** *a.* of or pertaining to d., as in *decylic alcohol*, etc. So **De·cine,** the liquid hydrocarbon $C_{10}H_{18}$, the ethine or acetylene member of the d. series.

Dedal, Dedalian, etc.; see DÆDAL, etc.

‖**Dedans** (dədaṅ·). 1706. [F. *dedans* inside, *spec.* gallery of a tennis court.] *Tennis.* The open gallery at the end of the service-side of a tennis-court.

Dedd(e, dede, obs. ff. DEAD, DEATH, DEED.

Dedecorate (dǐde·kŏreᶦt), *v.* 1609. [f. L. *dedecorat-*, ppl. stem of *dedecorare*, f. *dedecus.*] †**1.** To dishonour -1623. **2.** To disfigure 1804.

Dedentition (dǐdenti·ʃən). 1646. [f. DE- II. 1.] *Phys.* The shedding of the teeth.

De·dicate, *pa. pple.* and *ppl. a.* ME. [ad. L. *dedicatus.* Now *arch.*] Dedicated.

Every true Christian.. is a person d. to joy and peace MILT.

Dedicate (de·dikeᶦt), *v.* 1530. [f. L. *dedicat-* ppl. stem, f. DE- + *dicare* to say, make over formally by words, from stem *dic-* of *dicere*; cf. *abdicate.*] **1.** *trans.* To devote (*to* the Deity or to sacred uses) with solemn rites; to surrender, set apart, and consecrate. (The leading sense.) Also *fig.* **2.** *transf.* To give up earnestly, or wholly, *to* a person or purpose; to appropriate; to devote 1553. **3.** To inscribe or address (a book, etc.) *to* a patron or friend 1542. **4.** *Law.* To devote to the use of the public (a highway, etc.) 1843.

1. To whom he buylded and dedicate a chapell and an altare EDEN. 2. To her my thoughts I daily d. SPENSER. Hence **De·dicatee·,** one to whom anything is dedicated. **De·dicative** *a.* having the attribute of dedicating. **De·dicator,** one who dedicates; *esp.* one who inscribes a book to a friend or patron.

Dedication (dedikeᶦ·ʃən). ME. [a. OF. *dédication*, ad. L. *dedicationem.*] **1.** The action of setting apart and devoting to the Deity or to a sacred purpose with solemn rites; the fact of being so dedicated. **b.** The day or feast of dedication (of a church) ME. **2.** *fig.* A devoting (of oneself, one's time, etc.) to a purpose 1601. **3.** The dedicating of a book, etc.; the form of words in which this is done 1598. **4.** *Law.* The action of dedicating (a highway, etc.) to the public use 1809.

1. The founder prepared to celebrate the d. of his city GIBBON. 2. A wild d. of your selues To vnpath'd Waters *Wint T* IV. iv. 577.

Dedicatory (de·dikeᶦtəri, -kětəri). 1565. [f. L. *dedicatorem.* Cf. F. *dédicatoire.*]

A. *adj.* Relating to, or of the nature of, dedication; serving to dedicate.

The epistle Dedicatorie BIBLE. var. **De·dicato·rial.** Hence **De·dicatorily** *adv.*

†**B.** *sb.* A dedicatory inscription or address -1674.

†**Dedigna·tion.** ME. [a. OF. *dédignation*, f. (ult.) DE- I. 6 + *dignari*, f. *dignus.*] **1.** Disdain -1716. **2.** Indignation; *pass.*, state of being under a person's displeasure 1538.

‖**Dedimus** (de·dimɒ̆s). 1489. [From the words of the writ, *dedimus potestatem*, Lat. 'we have given the power'.] *Law.* A writ empowering one who is not a judge to do some act in place of a judge.

Dedition (dǐdi·ʃən). ? *Obs.* 1523. [ad. L. *deditionem.*] Giving up, yielding, surrender.

†**De·dolent,** *a.* 1633. [ad. L. *dedolentem*; see DE- I. 6.] That feels sorrow no more; insensible, callous -1698. Hence †**De·dolence.**

Deduce (dǐdiū·s), *v.* 1528. [ad. L. *deducere*, f. DE- I. 1, 2 + *ducere.* Cf. DEDUCT. In 16-17th c. often confused in form with DIDUCE, q. v.] **1.** To bring, convey; *spec.* (after L.) to lead forth (a colony) (*arch.*). Also *fig.* **2.** To derive *from* (*trans.* and *intr.*). (Now *rare.*) 1565. **3.** *trans.* To trace the course of. †Formerly, also, To conduct (a process), deal with (a matter). 1528. **4.** To show or hold (a thing) to be derived *from* 1536. **5.** To draw as a conclusion *from* something known or assumed; to derive by reasoning; to infer. (The chief current sense.) 1529. †**6.** To deduct -1662. †**7.** To reduce (to another form) -1749.

1. Advising him he should hither d. a colony SELDEN. 2. A ceremony deduced from the Romans SIR T. HERBERT. 4. He cannot d. his descent wholly by heirs male BLACKSTONE. 5. The knowledge of Causes is deduced from their effects 1696. Hence †**Dedu·cement,** a deduction, inference. **Dedu·cible** *a.* that may be deduced; *sb.* a deducible inference. **Deducibi·lity. Dedu·cibleness.**

†**Dedu·ct,** *ppl. a.* ME. [after L. *deductus*; see next.] Deducted -1532.

Deduct (dǐdɒ·kt), *v.* 1524. [f. L. *deduct-*, ppl. stem of *deducere*, f. DE- I. 1, 2 + *ducere.* Cf. DEDUCE.] **1.** *trans.* To take away or subtract from a sum or amount. (The current sense.) †**2.** = DEDUCE 1-5. -1600. †**3.** To reduce. MASSINGER.

1. When we have deducted all that is absorbed in sleep JOHNSON. 2. A people deducted oute of the citie of Philippos COVERDALE. Which by Logicall consequence is not Necessarily deducted out of the Premisses 1609. Hence **Dedu·ctible** *a.* (*rare*).

Deduction (dǐdɒ·kʃən). 1483. [ad. L. *deductionem*, f. *deducere*; see prec.] **1.** The action of deducting or taking away; subtraction; that which is deducted. **2.** A leading forth or away (*spec.* of a colony). ? *Obs.* 1615. †**3.** The action or result of tracing out; a detailed account -1826. †**4.** Derivation -1755. **5.** The process of deducing from something known or assumed; *spec.* in *Logic*, inference by reasoning from generals to particulars 1594; *transf.* that which is deduced 1532.

1. The interest given to them was exclusive of, and with a d. of, that sum JARMAN. 3. A clear d. of the affairs of Europe from the treaty of Munster to this time CHESTERF. 4. The d. of one word from another JOHNSON. 5. D. the process of deriving facts from laws, and effects from their causes ABP. THOMSON.

Deductive (dǐdɒ·ktiv), *a.* 1646. [ad. L. *deductivus*, f. *deduct-*; see DEDUCT, DEDUCE; see -IVE.] **1.** Of or pertaining to deduction; *spec.* in *Logic*, reasoning from generals to particulars (opp. to *inductive*); (of persons) reasoning deductively. †**2.** Derivative. SIR T. BROWNE.

1. All knowledge of causes is d. GLANVILLE. Women naturally prefer the d. method to the inductive BUCKLE. **Dedu·ctively** *adv* var. **Dedu·ctory** *a.* (*rare*).

†**Deduit,** *sb.* ME. [a. F. *déduit*:—L. *deductum* used subst., f. *deducere* in sense of 'divert'.] Diversion, pleasure -1483.

Deduplication (dǐdiūplikēᶦ·ʃən). 1835. [a. F. *déduplication*, latinized deriv. of F. *dédoubler* (*desdoubler*) to separate what is double.] *Bot.* Congenital division of one organ into two (or more); = CHORISIS.

Dee (dī), *sb.* 1794. Name of the letter D; applied to a D-shaped ring or loop used for connecting parts of harness, etc.

Dee (dī), *v.* 1845. Pronunc. of d——, for *damn*; whence *deed* (also *deedeed*) = d——d, damned.

Deed (dīd). [OE. *dǣd, dēd*:—OTeut. **dǣdiz*:—**dhetìs*, f. verb root *dhe*: *dho*, OTeut. *dǣ*: *dō*; see DO *v.*] **1.** That which is done, acted, or performed by an intelligent agent; an act; a feat OE. **2.** Action generally. (Often opp. to *word.*) OE. †**3.** Thing to be done; task or duty -1580. **4.** *Law.* An instrument in writing (or other legible representation of words on parchment or paper), purporting to effect some legal disposition, and sealed and delivered by the disposing party or parties ME.

1. They that haue done this Deede, are honourable SHAKS. Their deeds did not agree with their words 1875. Deedes of Armes 1568. †*Deeds of the Apostles*: the Acts of the Apostles. 2. In som cas the good wylle of a man is accepted for the dede 1500.

Phr. *In d.*: in practice. *In d., in very d.*: in fact, in reality, in truth: hence INDEED.

Deed (dīd), *v.* *U.S.* 1816. [f. prec. sb.] *trans.* To convey or transfer by deed. Also *fig.*

Deed, *adv.* 1547. Aphet. f. *i'deed*, INDEED; now chiefly Sc.

†**Dee·dbote.** [OE. *dǣd* + *bōt* BOOT *sb.*[1]] Amends-deed, penance, repentance -ME.

Deedful (dī·dfŭl), *a.* 1834. [f. DEED *sb.*] Full of deeds, active, effective, as *a d. life.*

Dee·dless, *a.* 1598. Without action or deeds; (of persons) performing no deeds, inactive. *Tr. & Cr.* IV. v. 98.

Dee·d poll, deed-poll. 1588. [See POLL.] *Law.* A deed made and executed by one party only; so called because the paper or parchment is 'polled' or cut even, not indented.

Deedy (dī·di), *a.* *dial.* 1615. [f. DEED *sb.*,

in ILL-DEEDY.] 1. Full of deeds; active. †2. Real (*rare*) -1788. Hence **Dee·dily** *adv.*

Deem (dīm), *v.* [A Com. Teut. derivative vb.: OE. *dǣman, dēman* :—OTeut. **dômjan*, f. *dômoz* DOOM. Cf. DOOM *v.*] †1. *intr.* To pronounce judgement -1579. 2. *trans.* †To judge -1609; to administer (law) (*arch.*) ME. †3. To sentence -1602 Also *fig.* †4. To decree; to decide; to award -1605. †5. To judge of, estimate -1569; *intr.* to judge *of* -1586. 6. To form the opinion, be of opinion; to conclude, consider, hold. (The ordinary current sense.) OE. 7. *intr.* To judge or think (in a specified way) *of* ME. †8. To hope -1819. †9. *trans.* To think of as existent; to surmise -1599; *intr.* to think *of* 1814. †10. To pronounce; to tell, say, declare. [Only poetic, prob. derived from sense 4.] -1547.

2. That..the 24 Keys may be called..to d. the law truly BP. WILSON. 6. Wee may boldly deeme there is neither, where both are not HOOKER. 7. Let vs see how the Greekes..deemed of it [Poetry] SIDNEY. Hence †**Deem** *sb.* judgement, opinion, surmise. **Dee·mer**, one who deems.

Deemster (dī·mstəɹ). 1611. [repr. ME. *dēmestre*, in form fem. of *dēmere* deemer; see also DEMPSTER.] 1. A judge. (*Obs.* or *arch.*) 1748. 2. The title of each of the two judges of the Isle of Man 1611.

Deep (dīp), *a.* [A Com. Teut. adj.: OE. *dīop, dēop* :—OTeut. **deupoz*; pre-Teut. root *dhub*: *dhup*. Cf. DIP *v.*]

I. Literal senses. 1. Having great extension downward OE.; extending far inward from the outer surface or backward from the front OE. 2. Having a (specified) dimension downward OE.; having a (specified) dimension inward from the surface, outer part, or front 1646. 3. Placed far (or a specified distance) down; of a ship, low in the water. b. Far back. OE. 4. Extending to or coming from a depth 1483. †5. Covered with a depth of mud, etc. -1828.

1. The greate deep valleis 1559. Phr. *To go (in) off the deep end*, etc.: to let oneself go. 2. A ditch..eight feet d. 1832. The pleasure is but skin deepe 1646. The Thebans..stood five-and-twenty d. THIRLWALL. 3. The frozen Earth..seven Cubits d. in Snow DRYDEN. The d. veins..of the body 1842. 4. A d. sigh ADDISON, plunge COWPER. 5. We..incountred with such d. sandy ground LITHGOW. [We now say 'd. in sand, mud, etc.']

II. Fig. senses. 1. Hard to fathom; not superficial; profound OE. 2. Solemn; grave; serious OE. 3. Deep-rooted; that affects one profoundly ME. 4. In which the mind is profoundly absorbed 1586. 5. Expensive; heavy 1577. 6. Intense, profound; of actions, powerfully affecting, strong 1547. 7. Of colour, etc.: Intense; highly chromatic. (Opp. to *faint* or *thin.*) 1555. 8. Of sound, etc.: Low in pitch, grave; full-toned, resonant 1591. 9. Penetrating, profound ME. 10. Profound in craft; in *mod. slang*, artful, sly 1513. 11. Of an agent: Who does (what is expressed) deeply 1526. 12. Much immersed *in* 1567.

1. Thy thoughts are very d. *Ps.* xcii. 5. 2. In d. disgrace (*mod.*). 3. A d. Sorrow STEELE, fear SOUTHEY. 4. In d. study LANE. 5. D. taxes FULLER, gaming SWIFT. 6. The d. influence of an anæsthetic 1889. D. silence WORDSW., night HAWTHORNE. 7. All manner of Blues, from the faintest to the deepest 1665. The deepest mourning GOLDSM. 8. And let the bass of heaven's d. organ blow MILT. 9. A deepe clerke, and one that read much HOLINSHED. 10. Deepe, hollow, treacherous, and full of guile SHAKS. 11. Two deepe enemies, Foes to my rest SHAKS. 12. Deepe..in debt 1587.

Deep (dīp), *sb.* [OE. *dēop*, neut. of *dēop* adj. used subst.; see prec.] †1. Depth (*rare*) -1635. 2. That which is deep; the deep part of the sea, etc. (opp. to *shallow*); deep water OE.; a deep place; an abyss ME. Also *fig.* 3. The remote central part (*rare*) ME. †4. The middle (of night, etc.) when the silence, or darkness, is most intense -1682. 5. *Naut.* A term for the fathoms intermediate to those marked on the 20-fathom sounding-line 1769.

2. The Frenchmen..passed by and tooke the deepe of the Sea 1568. And in the lowest d. a lower d. Still..opens wide MILT. 4. *Merry W.* IV. iv. 40.

Phr. *The d.*: a. The deep sea, the main (*poet.* and *rhet.*). b. The abyss or depth of space. c. *Cricket.* (= *the deep field*), the part of the field near the boundary, esp. behind the bowler; also, a fieldsman or his position there.

Deep (dīp), *adv.* [OE. *dīope, dēope.*] 1. *lit.* Deeply; far down, in, on, etc. 2. *fig.* Profoundly, intensely, earnestly, heavily, etc. OE.

1. Waters do ebbe as deepe as they flow R. JOHNSON. 2. That Fooles should be so deepe contemplatiue *A. Y. L.* II. vii. 31.

Comb. Freq. in comb. with pres. and pa. pples., as *d.-thinking*; *d.-cut, -drawn, -felt, -set*, etc. Also formerly, and still sometimes, used with adjs., as *d.-sore, -green*, etc.; d.-dyed, *fig.* 'steeped' in guilt.

Deep (dīp), *v.* *rare.* [OE. *dīepan, dȳpan* trans.] †1. To deepen (*trans.* and *intr.*) -1616. †2. To plunge deeply (*lit.* and *fig.*) -1578.

Deepen (dī·p'n), *v.* 1605. [f. DEEP *a.*, repl. DEEP *v.*] To make or become deep or deeper (in various senses).

To d. trenches STOW, colours PEACHAM, convictions RUSKIN. The shades d. GOLDSM. The combat deepens CAMPBELL. The evening had deepened into ..starlight GEO. ELIOT. Hence **Dee·pener.**

Deep-fetched, †-fet (dī·pˌfeːtʃt, -feːt), *ppl. a.* 1562. [DEEP *adv.*] Fetched from deep in the bosom, etc., as *deepe-fet groanes* (SHAKS.).

Deep-laid (dī·pˌlēⁱːd), *ppl. a.* 1768. [DEEP *adv.*] Deeply laid; planned with profound cunning, as a *deep-laid scheme* (TUCKER).

Deeply (dī·pli), *adv.* [OE. *dīoplīce, dēoplīce*, adv. f. *dēoplic*, deriv. of *dēop*, DEEP.] 1. To a great depth; far downwards, inwards, etc. ME. 2. *fig.* Profoundly, thoroughly OE.; with profound craft 1596. †3. Solemnly -1671. 4. Gravely ME. 5. With deep feeling, etc.; intensely ME. 6. Profoundly; with deep colour; with a deep voice 1632.

1. I..sink in deep affliction, d. down PARNELL. D. he drank SCOTT. 2. Consider it not so d. *Macb.* II. ii. 30. D. you dissemble FLETCHER. 3. Tis deepely sworne *Haml.* III. ii. 234. 4. To commit oneself d. FROUDE. 5. They curst him d. 1634. 6. Some d. Red 1695. A pack of hounds..baying d. 1883.

Comb. Deeply qualifying a pple. is now usually hyphened when the pple. is used attrib., preceding its sb., as 'a deeply-serrated leaf'.

Dee·pmost, *a.* (*superl.*) *rare.* 1810. [f. DEEP *a.*] Deepest.

Deep-mouthed (dī·pˌmauðd, -mauþt), *a.* 1595. [f. *deep mouth.*] Having a deep or sonorous voice: *esp.* of dogs.

Deepness (dī·pnės). Now *rare*; displ. by DEPTH. [OE. *dīopnes, dēopnes*, f. *dēop* DEEP.] 1. The quality of being DEEP (in various senses); depth, profundity. †2. *concr.* A deep place, an abyss; a deep part of the sea, etc. -1502.

1. The d. of his obeisance SCOTT, of the way 1603, of the Sea 1665, thought 1720, Satan 1646.

Deep-read (dī·pˌreˑd), *ppl. a.* 1639. [DEEP *adv.*] Deeply read; skilled by profound reading. Sir Robert, deep-read in old wines BURNS.

Deep-rooted (dī·pˌrūːtėd), *a.* 1669. [DEEP *adv.*] Deeply implanted; chiefly *fig.* of feelings, etc.

Deep sea, deep-sea. 1626. The deeper part of the sea at a distance from the shore. Used *attrib.*: Of or belonging to the deep sea.

Deep-sea lead, line, a lead and line used for soundings in deep water. *Deep-sea fisheries*, fisheries prosecuted at a distance from land.

Deep-seated (dī·pˌsīːtėd), *a.* 1741. [DEEP *adv.*] Having its seat far beneath the surface, as *a deep-seated* abscess.

Deepsome (dī·psŏm), *a.* *poetic.* *rare.* 1615. [f. DEEP *a.* or *sb.*] Having deepness or depths; more or less deep.

Deer (diəɹ). [A Com. Teut. sb.: OE. *dīor, dēor*; generally referred to a root *dhus* to breathe (cf. *animal* from *anima*).] †1. A beast; usually a quadruped -1481. 2. The general name of a family (*Cervidæ*) of ruminant quadrupeds, distinguished by the possession of deciduous branching horns or antlers, and by the presence of spots on the young: the genera and species being distinguished as *reindeer, moose-deer, red deer*, and *fallow deer* OE. Also *attrib.*

1. Se camal þæt micla dear OE. 2. He chaced at the reed dere MALORY.

Phr. *Small d.*: orig. used in sense 1, but now associated with sense 2. Mice, and Rats, and such small Deare SHAKS.

Comb.: **d.-dog** = DEER-HOUND; **-fence**, a high railing such as deer cannot leap over; **-forest**, one reserved for deer; **-neck**, a thin neck (of a horse), like a deer's; **deer's eye** = BUCK-EYE (the tree); **d.-tiger**, the puma or cougar; **-tongue, deer's tongue**, a N. Amer. Cichoraceous plant, *Liatris odoratissima.*

Deerberry (dīə·ɹberi). 1862. A name given to the berry of *Gualtheria procumbens* (N.O. *Ericaceæ*); also to *Vaccinium stamineum* (Squaw Huckleberry); also to the plants.

Dee·r-coloured, *a.* 1611. Tawny red.

Dee·r-hair, deer's hair. 1494. 1. The hair of deer. 2. A small moorland species of club-rush, *Scirpus cæspitosus* 1772.

Dee·r-hound. 1818. A dog used for hunting red-deer; *esp.* a large variety of the rough greyhound, standing 28 inches or more.

Dee·r-lick. 1876. A small spring or spot of damp ground, impregnated with salt, alum, or the like, where deer come to lick.

Dee·r-mouse. 1884. The popular name of certain American mice; *esp.* the white-footed mouse (*Hesperomys leucopus*).

Dee·rskin. ME. The skin of a deer, *esp.* as used for clothing. Also *attrib.*

Dee·r-sta·lker. 1875. [See STALK *v.*] 1. One who stalks deer. 2. A low-crowned close-fitting hat worn by deer-stalkers 1881.

Dee·r-stea·ler. 1640. A poacher who kills and steals deer.

†**De·ess, deesse.** 1549. [a. F. *déesse*, var. of *dieuesse*, fem. of *dieu.*] A goddess -1698.

Dees(se, obs. ff. DAIS, DICE.

De-e·thicize, *v.* 1887. [DE- II. 1.] To deprive of its ethical character; to separate from ethics.

Deface (dĭfēⁱ·s), *v.* ME. [a. obs. F. *defacer*, orig. *desfacier*, f. *des-, dé-* (DE- 6) + *face.*] 1. *trans.* To mar the face, or appearance of; to spoil the form or beauty of; to disfigure. Also *fig.* †2. To destroy, lay waste -1632. 3. To efface ME. Also *fig.* †4. To defame -1641. †5. To cast in the shade -1796.

1. Ancient statues..defaced by modern additions LADY M. W. MONTAGU. 2. Now cleane defaste the goodly buildings fayre 1575. 3. Characters that can never be defaced BENTLEY. *fig.* By false learning is good sense defaced POPE.

Hence †**Defa·ce** *sb.* defacement. **Defa·cement**, the action of defacing; the state of being defaced; *concr.* a disfigurement. **Defa·cer.**

De facto; see DE 1 b.

Defæcate, -cation; see DEFECATE, etc.

†**Defai·l**, *v.* ME. [a. F. *défaillir*: f. DE- 3 + *fallire* Rom. repr. of L. *fallere.* See FAIL.] 1. *intr.* To FAIL (in various senses) -1556. 2. *trans.* To cause to fail; to defeat 1608. So †**Defai·lance, -faillance**, †**Defai·llancy**, †**Defai·lment**, †**Defai·lure**, failure.

Defaisance, obs. f. DEFEASANCE.

†**Defa·lcate**, *ppl. a.* 1531. [See next.] Curtailed.

Defalcate (dĭfæ·lkeⁱt), *v.* 1540. [f. *defalcat-*, ppl. stem of med.L. *defalcare*, f. DE- I. 1, 2 + L. *falx, falcem.*] †1. *trans.* To cut or lop off (a portion from a whole); to retrench, deduct -1817. †2. To curtail, reduce -1817. 3. *intr.* To commit defalcations; to misappropriate property in one's charge 1864.

1. To d. a substantiall part 1624. 3. Head clerks have defalcated 1888. Hence **De·falcator**, one guilty of defalcation.

Defalcation (dīfælkēⁱ·ʃən). 1476. [ad. med. L. *defalcationem*; see prec.] 1. †Diminution by taking away a part -1712; *spec.* reduction of a claim by the amount of a set-off 1622. 2. The action of cutting or lopping off; deduction (*arch.*) 1624; a deduction 1621. 3. Diminution suffered; falling off (*arch.*) 1649. 4. Defection; shortcoming, failure 1750. 5. A fraudulent deficiency in money matters; also *concr.* (in *pl.*), the amount misappropriated 1846.

Defalk (dĭfǭ·lk), *v.* ? *Obs.* 1475. [a. F. *défalquer*, ad. med.L. *defalcare*; see DEFALCATE.] †1. *trans.* To reduce by deductions -1747. 2. To lop off; to abate. *Obs.* exc. locally in U.S. legal use. 1524. †3. To allow (any one) a deduction; to mulct *of* (anything due) -1565.

Defamation (dĕfămēⁱ·ʃən, def-). ME. [ad. OF. *diffamation*, L. *diffamationem*; see DEFAME.] †1. The bringing of ill fame upon any one; disgrace -1711. 2. The action of defaming; the fact of being defamed; also, an act of defaming ME.

2. Diffamation, or D. ..is the uttering of reproachful Speeches, or contumelious Language of any one, with an Intent of raising an ill Fame of the Party thus reproached; and this extends to Writing..and to Deeds AYLIFFE.

Defamatory (dĭfæ·mătəri), *a.* 1592. [ad. med.L. *diffamatorius*, f. L. *diffamat-*, ppl. stem of *diffamare.*] **1.** Of the nature of, or characterized by, defamation; having the property of defaming. **2.** Addicted to defamation 1769.

1. D. writings CLARENDON. 2. D. writers JUNIUS.

Defame (dĭfēⁱ·m), *v.* [ME. *diffamen* and *defamen*, a. OF. *diffamer*, rarely *desfamer*, *defamer* (mod.F. *diffamer*), ad. L. *diffamare*, f. *dif-* = DIS- + *fama*. French retains *dis-*, *des-*, *dé-*, while Eng. has *de-*, prob. after med.L. *defamare.*] **1.** *trans.* To bring ill fame upon, to dishonour or disgrace in fact; to render infamous. **2.** To attack the good name of; to dishonour by report ME. †**3.** To raise an imputation *of* (some offence) against (any one). Const. also with *with*, *by*, or clause. –1820. †**4.** To spread abroad. ME. only.

1. Ioseph, loth to d. her TINDALE *Matt.* i. 19. 2. I am now in certayne she is vntruly defamed MALORY. 3. Rebecca..is, by many..suspicious circumstances, defamed of sorcery SCOTT.

Hence †**Defa·me** *sb.* ill fame; infamy; defamation. **Defa·mer.**

†**Defamous,** *a.* ME. [a. AF. *deffamous.*] Infamous. **b.** Defamatory. –1587. So †**De·famy** = DEFAMATION 1, 2.

†**Defa·tigable,** *a.* 1656. [ad. L. type *defatigabilis.*] Apt to be wearied; capable of being wearied –1662.

†**Defa·tigate,** *v.* [f. L. *defatigat-* ppl. stem.] To weary out –1666.

†**Defatiga·tion.** [ad. L. *defatigationem.*] The action of wearying out or condition of being wearied out –1654.

Default (dĭfǭ·lt), *sb.* ME. [a. OF. *defaute*, deriv. of *defaillir*; see FAULT.] **1.** = FAULT *sb.* 1. *Obs.* or *arch.* **2.** An imperfection, defect, blemish. *Obs.* or *arch.* ME. **3.** Failure to act; neglect; *spec.* in *Law*, failure to perform some legal requirement or obligation; *esp.* to attend court on the proper day ME. †**4.** Culpable neglect of some duty or obligation –1742. Also †*transf.* of things. †**5.** (with *pl.*) A failure in duty; a fault, misdeed, offence –1822. **6.** Failure; *esp.* to meet financial engagements ME.

1. Defalt of mete ME. 2. Grave defaults all the while lay hidden under the surface KINGLAKE. 3. Where a defendant makes d., judgment shall be had against him by d. CROKER. 4. Phr. *To be in d.*: to fail in one's duty. 6. Convicted of fraud or d. JEVONS.

Hence †**Defau·ltive** *a.* faulty, remiss.

Default (dĭfǭ·lt), *v.* ME. [ad. OF. *defaillir*, f. DE- + Rom. *fallire*, L. *fallere*; see FAIL. In Eng. assoc. w. DEFAULT *sb.*] **1.** *intr.* To be wanting; to fail. *Obs.* or *arch.* †**2.** To fail in strength, faint; to suffer failure –1617. **3.** To make DEFAULT (sense 3) 1596. **4.** *trans.* To put in default; in *Law*, to declare (a party) in default and enter judgement against him ME. †**5.** To omit –1656. **6.** To fail to pay 1889.

2. And can your..king D., ye lords, except yourselves do fail GREENE. 3. The Dissenters..in the Weekly Schools .. are grievously defaulting 1845. Last year..44 companies..defaulted 1886.

Defaulter (dĭfǭ·ltəɹ). 1666. [f. DEFAULT *v.* + -ER.] One who is guilty of default; *esp.* one who fails to perform some duty or obligation legally required of him. **b.** *Mil.* A soldier guilty of a military offence. Also *attrib.* 1823. **c.** One who fails properly to account for money or property entrusted to his care 1823. **d.** One who becomes bankrupt 1858. So **Defau·ltress** (*rare*), a female d.

Defeasance (dĭfī·zăns). ME. [a. AF. *defesaunce*, OF. *defesance* undoing, f. (ult.) *des-*, *de-*, DE- I. 6 + *faire.*] **1.** Undoing; ruin, defeat, overthrow. (Now coloured by 2.) 1590. **2.** *Law.* The rendering null and void (of an act, condition, right, etc.) 1592. **3.** *Law.* A condition upon the performance of which a deed is defeated or made void; a collateral deed or writing expressing such condition ME.

1. Where that champion stout After his foes defesaunce did remaine SPENSER *F. Q.* I. xii. 12. Hence **Defea·sanced** *ppl. a.* liable to d.

Defease, *v.* 1621. [repr. OF. *de(s)fes-*, stem of *desfaire*; see prec.] To undo, bring to nought, destroy (*rare*).

Defeasible (dĭfī·zĭb'l), *a.* 1586. [a. AF. Cf. FEASIBLE.] Capable of being undone, defeated, or made void, as a *d. estate.* Hence **Defea·sibleness, Defeasibi·lity.**

Defeat (dĭfī·t), *sb.* 1599. [f. DEFEAT *v.*, prob. after F. *défaite* sb.] †**1.** Undoing; ruin; act of destruction –1636. **2.** Frustration (of schemes, expectations, etc.). Now usu. *fig.* of 3. 1599. **3.** The act of overthrowing in a contest, the fact of being so overthrown 1600. **4.** *Law.* The action of rendering null and void.

1. Vpon whose property, and most deere life, A damn'd defeate was made SHAKS. 3. The D. of the Armada GREEN, of the first Reform Bill 1884.

Defeat (dĭfī·t), *v.* ME. [f. OF. *defeit*, *-fait*, orig. *desfait*, pa. pple. of *desfaire*, f. (ult.) L. *dis-* (see DE- I. 6) + *facere*. App. first taken into Eng. as a pa. pple. (see DEFEIT).] †**1.** *trans.* To unmake, undo; to destroy –1632. †**2.** To cause to waste or languish –1483. †**3.** To disfigure, deface, spoil –1604. **4.** To frustrate 1474. **5.** *Law.* To render null and void 1525. **6.** To do (a person) out *of*; to disappoint, cheat 1538; †to deprive *of* –1677. **7.** To vanquish, beat 1562. Also *transf.* and *fig.*

1. His vnkindnesse may d. my life *Oth.* IV. ii. 160. 4. To thwart its influence, and its end d. COWPER. 5. A condition that defeats an estate CRUISE. 6. Death ..Defeated of his seisure MILT. *P. L.* XI. 254. 7. After this, he defeited Scipio and Ivba HOLLAND. Hence **Defea·ter. Defea·tment** = DEFEAT *sb.* 2, 3.

Defeatism (dĭfī·tiz'm). 1918. [ad. F. *défaitisme.*] Conduct tending to bring about acceptance of defeat, esp. by action on civilian opinion. So **Defea·tist** [F. *défaitiste*] *sb.* and *a.*

Defeature (dĭfī·tiŭɹ), *sb.* ? *Obs.* 1590. [a. OF. *deffaiture*, *desfaiture*, f. *desfaire*, after *faiture*:—L. *factura*. Cf. *defeat.*] †**1.** = DEFEAT *sb.* 1, 2, 3. –1834. **2.** Disfigurement; marring of features.

1. For their first loves d. SPENSER. 2. Carefull houres..Haue written strange defeatures in my face *Com. Err.* v. i. 299. **Defea·ture** *v.* to disfigure.

†**De·fecate,** *ppl. a.* Also †**defæcate.** 1450. [ad. L. *defæcatus.*] Purified from dregs, clarified, clear and pure. Also *fig.* –1742.

A pure and d. Ætherial Spirit MORE.

Defecate (dī·fĭkeⁱt), *v.* Also **defæcate.** 1575. [f. L. *defæcat-* ppl. stem, f. DE- I. 6 + *fæx*, pl. *fæces* dregs.] **1.** *trans.* To clear from dregs or impurities; to purify, clarify, refine. **2.** *fig.* To purify from pollution or extraneous admixture (of things immaterial) 1621. **3.** To purge away (dregs or fæces); to void as excrement 1774; *absol.* to void the fæces 1864.

1. The gum, which they d. in water by boiling and purging SLOANE. 2. To d. life of its misery 1870. Hence **Defeca·tion,** also **defæcation,** the action or process of defecating; cleansing from impurities; the discharging of the fæces. **De·fecator,** *spec.* in *Sugar Manuf.*, an apparatus for removing the feculent matters from a saccharine liquid.

Defect (dĭfe·kt), *sb.* ME. [ad. L. *defectus*, *deficere*; see DEFECT *v.*] **1.** The fact of falling short; lack or absence of something necessary to completeness (opp. to *excess*); deficiency 1589. **2.** A shortcoming; a fault, flaw, imperfection ME. †**3.** Defectiveness –1776. **4.** That by which anything falls short 1660. †**5.** Failure (of the sun, etc.) to shine –1692.

1. Holding on a meane path betweene excesse and d. 1632. Phr. *In d.*: wanting. 2. Ill breeding..is not a single d., it is the result of many FIELDING. 3. When all my best doth worship thy d. SHAKS.

†**Defe·ct,** *a.* 1600. [ad. L. *defectus* pa. pple.] Defective, deficient, wanting –1664.

Defe·ct, *v.* 1579. [f. L. *defect-*, ppl. stem of *deficere*, f. DE- + *facere.*] †**1.** *intr.* To fail, fall short, become deficient –1677. **2.** To fall away *from* (a person or party). Now *rare.* 1596. †**3.** *trans.* To cause to desert –1685. †**4.** To make defective; to dishonour –1639.

2. He defected, and fled to the contrary part GAULE.

Defe·ctible, *a.* 1617. [f. as prec.; cf. *perfectible.*] Liable to fail or fall short. Hence **Defe·ctibi·lity,** liability to become defective.

Defection (dĭfe·kʃən). 1544. [ad. L. *defectionem*; see DEFECT *v.*] **1.** The action or fact of failing, or falling short; failure (*of* anything); †defectiveness; †a defect. **2.** The action of falling away from a leader, party, or cause; desertion 1552. **3.** A falling away from faith, or duty; backsliding; apostasy 1546.

1. Miserable defections of hope C. BRONTË. 2. The d. of Iudas the traitour STUBBES. 3. The d. and disobedience of the first Man HALE. Hence †**Defe·ctious** *a.* having defects; of the nature of d.

Defective (dĭfe·ktiv). ME. [a. F. *défectif*, *-ive*, ad. L. *defectivus*, f. *defect-* ppl. stem; see DEFECT *v.*]

A. *adj.* **1.** Having a defect or defects; imperfect, incomplete 1472. †**2.** At fault –1677. **3.** Lacking (to completeness) 1603. **4.** *Gram.* Wanting one or more of the usual forms of declension, conjugation, etc. 1530.

1. D. weights and measures 1495, buildings 1663, sight COWPER. 3. I wish you had a Fortunatus hat; it is the only thing d. in your outfit CARLYLE. Hence **Defe·ctive·ly** *adv.*, **-ness.**

B. *sb.* †**1.** *gen.* One who is defective 1592; *spec.* in *U.S.*, one who is deficient in one or more of the physical senses or powers 1881. **2.** *Gram.* A defective part of speech. 1612.

Defector (dĭfe·ktəɹ). 1662. [a. L.] One who falls away; a seceder or deserter.

†**Defe·ctuous,** *a.* 1553. [ad. med.L. *defectuosus*, f. *defectus* DEFECT.] Having defects; defective, faulty –1726. So †**Defectuo·sity,** defectiveness, faultiness.

†**Defedation** (dīfĭdēⁱ·ʃən). Also **defœd-.** 1634. [ad. med.L. *defœdationem*, f. (ult.) *fœdus* foul.] The action of making impure; pollution. Also *fig.* –1793.

†**Defei·t, defe·t,** *a.* ME. [a. OF. *defeit*, *desfeit*, *-fait*, pa. pple. of *desfaire*, *defaire*; see DEFEAT *v.*] Marred, disfigured –1605.

Defence, defense (dĭfe·ns), *sb.* [Two forms: ME. *defens*, a. OF., ad. L. *defensum* thing forbidden, etc.; also ME. *defense* prohibition, ad. L. *defensa*. App. the sp. *defence* comes from *defens*; cf. *sithens*, *since*, etc.] The action of defending (see DEFEND *v.*).

I. †**1.** The action of warding off –1588. †**2.** Prohibition –1698.

1. For yᵉ defence of his enemyes FABYAN. 2. Phr. *In d.*: (of fish, or waters) prohibited from being taken or fished in.

II. 1. Protecting from attack; resistance against attack; warding off of injury; protection. (The chief current sense.) ME. †**b.** Capacity of defending –1654. **2.** The art or science of defending oneself (with weapons or the fists); self-defence 1602. **3.** Something that defends; *spec.* (*pl.*) fortifications ME. **4.** The defending by argument ME.; a speech or argument in self-vindication 1557.

1. His d. coude not auayle him LD. BERNERS. **b.** The Citie being but of small d. 3 *Hen. VI*, v. i. 64. 3. The Lord is my d. *Ps.* xciv. 22. The defences of the Austrians on the right bank 1853.

III. *Law.* [Orig. allied to I, but now influenced by II.] The opposing or denial of the truth or validity of the prosecutor's complaint; the defendant's (written) pleading in answer to the statement of claim; the proceedings taken by an accused party or his legal agents, for defending himself 1595.

Hence †**Defence, defense** *v.* to provide with defences; to defend, protect (*lit.* and *fig.*). **Defe·nceless, defenseless** *a.* without d.; unprotected; †affording no d. (*rare*). **Defe·nceless·ly** *adv.*, **-ness.**

Defend (dĭfe·nd), *v.* ME. [a. OF. *defendre* :—L. *defendere*, f. DE- I. 2 + *fendere* (obs.).]

I. †**1.** To ward off, keep off; to avert. (*Obs.* exc. as in III.) –1808. †**2.** To keep (*from* doing something), to prevent –1660. Also *refl.* **3.** To prohibit, forbid. Now *dial.* ME. ¶ In *God defend* = 'God forbid', senses 3 and 1 seem to unite.

II. 1. *trans.* To ward off attack from; to fight for the safety of; to protect, guard ME. Also *absol.* **2.** To support or uphold by speech or argument ME.; †to contend –1620.

1. From Turke and Pope d. vs Lord STERNHOLD. 2. Erronyously defendyng and maynteynyng his seid obstynate opynyons *Act* 4 *Hen. VIII*, c. 19 Preamble. To d. general principles MORLEY.

III. *Law.* (Orig. belonging to I, but also with uses from II.) **a.** Of the defendant: To deny, repel, oppose (the plaintiff's plea, the action raised against him; *absol.* to make defence. **b.** To vindicate (himself, his cause). **c.** Of a legal agent: To take legal measures to vindicate; to appear, address the court, etc. in defence of. ME.

Hence **Defe·ndable** *a. rare*, capable of being protected from assault or injury; capable of being vindicated. **Defe·nder,** one who defends, or wards off an attack; one who upholds or maintains by argument; the party sued in an action at law; = DEFENDANT *sb.* 3. **Defe·nderism** (*Irish Hist.*), the principles or policy of a society of Roman Catholics, formed in the 18th c. to resist the Orangemen.

Defendant (dǐfe·ndănt). ME. [a. F. *défendant*, pr. pple. of *défendre*; see prec.]

A. *adj.* †**1.** Used as *pr. pple.* Defending. (ME. only.) **2.** Defending oneself, or an opinion, cause, etc., against attack. ? *Obs.* 1596. †**3.** Affording defence. *Hen. V*, II. iv. 8.

1. *Him self defendaunt* = in his own defence.

B. *sb.* †**1.** A defender against attack; opp. to *assailant* –1787. †**2.** The party who denies the charge and accepts the challenge of the *appellant* in wager of battle –1828. **3.** *Law.* A person sued in a court of law; the party in a suit who defends (orig. = *denies*); opp. to *plaintiff* ME.

Phr. *In my, his* (etc.) *d.*: in one's defence. [App. a corruption of *me, him, d.* in A. 1.]

Defendress (dǐfe·ndrės). Now *rare.* 1509. [a. F. *défenderesse*.] A female defender or defendant. var. †**Defe·ndrix** (*rare*).

Defenestration (dǐfenėstrēi·ʃən). 1620. [f. L. DE- I. 1, 2 + *fenestra*.] The action of throwing out of a window.

†**Defe·nsative.** Also **-itive.** 1576. [f. L. *defensat-, defensare*, freq. of *defendere*.]

A. *adj.* Having the property of protecting; defensive –1668.

B. *sb.* = DEFENSIVE *sb.* 1. –1783.

A good d. against all venemous humours WOODALL.

Defense, -fenser, var. ff. DEFENCE, DEFENSOR.

Defensible (dǐfe·nsĭb'l), *a.* ME. [ad. L. *defensibilem*; repl. *defensable* :—L. *defensabilem.*] †**1.** Defensive –1828. **2.** Capable of being defended; safe 1600. **3.** *fig.* Capable of being defended in argument. (The chief current sense.) ME.

1. D. men 1549, posts GIBBON, harness ME. 3. A more d., or a juster claim FAWCETT. Hence **Defensibi·lity**, the quality of being d. **Defe·nsibleness. Defe·nsibly** *adv.*

†**Defension** (dǐfe·nʃən). ME. [ad. L. *defensionem*.] = DEFENCE –1555.

Defensive (dǐfe·nsiv). ME. [a. F. *défensif, -ive*, ad. med.L. *defensivus*, f. *defens-* ppl. stem.]

A. *adj.* **1.** Having the quality of defending; protective. **2.** Made, or carried on for the purpose of defence: opp. to *offensive* 1580. **3.** Of or belonging to defence 1643. **4.** Of the nature of a defence 1604.

1. As a Moate d. to a house SHAKS. 2. D. war 1631. 3. A d. position S. AUSTIN. 4. A d. allegation BLACKSTONE. Hence **Defe·nsive-ly** *adv.*, **-ness.**

B. *sb.* **1.** Something that serves to defend or protect ME. **2.** A position or attitude of defence: usu. in phr. *on the d.* (see A. 3) 1601.

1. Wars preventive, upon just fears, are defensives BACON (J.).

Defensor (dǐfe·nsɔɹ, -ǭɹ). [ME. and AF. *defensour* :—L. *defensatorem*, f. *defensare*; subseq. assim. to L. *defensor*, f. *defendere*.] †**1.** A defender –1670. **2.** *Rom. Law.* One who took up the defence and assumed the liability of a defendant in an action 1875.

1. *Chief D. of the Christian Church*, a title formerly bestowed by the Pope, as upon Henry VII.

Defensory (dǐfe·nsǒri). ? *Obs.* 1552. [ad. L. *defensorius*; see prec.]

A. *adj.* That serves to defend; defensive.

†**B.** *sb.* Something defensive; a defence –1677.

Defer (dǐfɜ̄·ɹ), *v.*[1] Inflexions **deferred, deferring.** [ME. *differren*, a. OF. *differer*, ad. L. *differre* to carry apart, put off, etc. Orig. the same word as DIFFER *v.* (q.v.). The forms in *de-, def-*, are against the etymology.] †**1.** *trans.* To put on one side. (ME. only.) **2.** To put off to some later time; to delay, postpone ME. Also *absol.* or *intr.* †**3.** To put off (time) –1633; to protract; *intr.* to linger –1561.

2. Deferre the spoile of the Citie vntill night 2 *Hen. VI*, IV. vii. 141. Be wise to-day; 'tis madness to d. YOUNG. 3. Deferre no tyme, delayes haue dangerous ends 1 *Hen. VI*, III. ii. 33. Hence **Defe·rment**, a putting off; postponement. **Defe·rrer.**

Defer (dǐfɜ̄·ɹ), *v.*[2] Inflexions **deferred, deferring.** 1479. [a. F. *déférer*, ad. L. *deferre*; f. DE- I. 1, 2 + *ferre*.] †**1.** *trans.* To carry down or away; to convey (*rare*) –1654. †**2.** To offer; in *Law*, to offer for acceptance. Const. *to*, rarely *on*. –1832. †**3.** To refer –1691. **4.** *intr.* To pay deference *to* 1686.

2. To deferre to them any obedience, or honour HOBBES. 4. To d. to the judgment of others BURKE.

Deference (de·fėrėns). 1647. [a. F. *déférence*, f. *déférer* to DEFER *v.*[2]] †**1.** The action of offering (*rare*) 1660. **2.** Submission to the acknowledged superior claims, skill, judgement, etc., of another 1647. **3.** Courteous regard, as to one to whom respect is due 1660.

2. Charles often paid a strange d. to minds inferior to his own D'ISRAELI. 3. Their age and learning.. entitle them to all d. CHATHAM.

Phr. *In d. to*: out of practical respect or regard to.

Deferent (de·fĕrĕnt), *a.*[1] and *sb.* ME. [a. F. *déférent*; see DEFER *v.*[2]]

A. *adj.* Carrying or conducting 1626.

The..testes end in a pair of d. ducts HUXLEY.

B. *sb.* **1.** A carrying or conducting agent; *spec.* in *Phys.*, a duct for conveying fluids 1626. **2.** *Ptolemaic Astron.* The circular orbit of the centre of the epicycle in which a planet was conceived to move; corresp. (roughly) to the actual orbit of the planet ME. **3.** One who reports a matter 1670.

1. Though Aire be the most favourable D. of Sounds BACON.

Deferent (de·fĕrĕnt), *a.*[2] 1822. [f. DEFER *v.*[2]] Showing deference, deferential.

His opposition..was always modest, d. 1822.

Deferential (deferė·nʃăl), *a.*[1] 1822. [f. DEFERENCE + -AL.] Characterized by deference; respectful. Hence **Deferentia·lity** *sb.* deference. **Defere·ntially** *adv.*

Defere·ntial, *a.*[2] 1877. [a. F. *déférentiel*, f. *déférent* DEFERENT *a.*[1]] *Phys.* Serving to convey; pertaining to the deferent duct.

Defervescence (dǐfəɹve·sėns). 1721. [f. L. *defervescentem*.] **1.** Cooling down. (Dicts.) **2.** *Path.* The decrease of bodily temperature which accompanies the abatement of fever; the period of this decrease 1866. var. †**Deferve·scency.** So **Deferve·scent** *a.* and *sb.*

Defeudalize; see DE- II. 1 and *feudalize.*

Defial (dǐfəi·ăl). *rare.* 1470. [a. OF. *defiaille*, f. *defier*.] = DEFIANCE.

Defiance (dǐfəi·ăns). ME. [a. OF. *defiance*; see DEFY *v.*[1] and -ANCE.] †**1.** Renunciation of faith, allegiance, or amity; declaration of hostilities –1649. **2.** A challenge; a summons to a combat or contest ME. **3.** The act of setting at nought 1710. †**4.** Declaration of aversion or contempt (*rare*) 1603. †**5.** Distrust [= mod.F. *défiance*.] PEPYS.

1. †*At d.*: at enmity or hostility; The Prouinces at d. with vs GRENEWAY. 2. Shall we..send D. to the Traytor SHAKS. 4. *Meas. for M.* III. i. 143.

Phr. *To bid d. to*: to defy; to brave, set at nought; so *to set at d. In d. of*: setting at nought.

Defiant (dǐfəi·ănt), *a.* 1837. [a. F. *défiant*; see DEFY.] **1.** Showing a disposition to defy. ‖**2.** Feeling distrust. [= mod.F. *défiant*.] 1872.

1. The man's heart that dare rise d...against Hell itself CARLYLE. **Defi·ant-ly** *adv.*, **-ness** (*rare*).

†**Defi·atory,** *a. rare.* 1635. [f. DEFY *v.*[1]; cf. *commendatory*.] Bearing defiance.

Defibrinate (dǐfəi·brineit), *v.* 1845. [f. DE- II. 1 + FIBRIN + -ATE [3].] To deprive of fibrin. Hence **Defibrina·tion**, the process of depriving of fibrin. So **Defi·brinize** *v.* = DEFIBRINATE.

Deficiency (dǐfi·ʃĕnsi). Also †**deficience.** 1634. [f. as prec.] The quality or state of being deficient; failure; lack; insufficiency. Also *attrib.*

In excess as well as in d. GROTE. Where art has to supply the deficiencies of nature NEWMAN.

D. of a curve (Math.): the number by which its double points fall short of the highest number possible in a curve of the same order.

Deficient (dǐfi·ʃĕnt). 1581. [ad. L. *deficientem*, pr. pple. of *deficere*.]

A. *adj.* **1.** Wanting something necessary to completeness; falling short *in* something; defective 1604. **2.** Insufficient; inadequate 1632. †**3.** Failing, fainting –1632.

1. Being not d., blind, or lame of sense *Oth.* I. iii. 63. D. memory JOHNSON. D. in knowledge about health 1861. *D. number*: a number the sum of whose factors is less than the number itself. 3. *Lear* IV. vi. 23.

Phr. †*D. cause*: that failure to act, or absence of anything, which becomes the cause or negative condition of some result. Hence **Defi·ciently** *adv.*

†**B.** *sb.* **1.** Something that is wanting; the want of something; a deficiency –1686. **2.** A defaulter –1719.

Deficit (de·fisit, dǐ·fisit). 1782. [a. F. *déficit*, a. L. *deficit* 'there is wanting', formerly used in inventories, etc.] A falling short; deficiency in amount; the excess of expenditure or liabilities over income or assets.

There was a *surplus*..instead of a d. BENTHAM.

‖**De fide** (dī fəi·di), *predic.* or *attrib. phr.* [L.] That is 'of faith', to be accepted as an article of faith.

Defier (dǐfəi·əɹ). 1585. [f. DEFY *v.*[1] + -ER [1].] One who defies, as a *d. of the Gods.*

†**Defiguration** (dǐfigiŭrēi·ʃən). 1585. [f. med.L. *defigurare*: see DE- I. 6 and *figurare*.] Disfigurement –1830. So †**Defi·gure** *v.*[1]

†**Defigure** (dǐfi·giŭɹ), *v.*[2] 1599. [DE- I. 3.] To figure, delineate. Also *fig.* –1631.

fig. By this defigured they the perplexed life of man 1615.

Defilade (defilēi·d), *sb.* 1851. [f. DEFILE *v.*[3]] = DEFILEMENT.[2]

Defilade (defilēi·d), *v.* 1828. [f. prec.] *Fortif.* To arrange the plan and profile of fortifications, so that their lines shall be protected from enfilading fire, and the interior of the works from plunging or reverse fire.

Defile (dī·fəil, dǐfəi·l), *sb.* 1685. [a. F. *défilé* (also used), f. *défiler* to DEFILE *v.*[3] The final *-é* lost its accent in Eng., and became *e* mute.] **1.** *Mil.* A narrow way along which troops can march only by files or with a narrow front; *esp.* a narrow mountain gorge or pass. **2.** The act of defiling, a march by files 1835.

Defile (dǐfəi·l), *v.*[1] ME. [Altered f. *defoul, defoil*, after FILE *v.* Cf. *foul* and *file* (the latter :—OE. *fȳlan* umlaut deriv. of *fūl* foul); also DEFOUL.] †**1.** To bruise. (ME. only.) **2.** To render foul; to dirty 1530. **3.** To render morally foul; to corrupt, taint, sully ME. †**4.** To violate the chastity of; to debauch –1769. **5.** To render ceremonially unclean 1500. †**6.** To sully the honour of –1708. †**7.** *absol.* To cause defilement; to drop excrement –1596.

2. An evyll birde that defiles hys own nest LATIMER. 3. Defyled with syne 1450. 4. The husband murder'd, and the wife defil'd PRIOR. 5. They have defiled the priesthood *Neh.* xiii. 29. 6. *Mids. N.* III. ii. 410. 7. 1 *Hen. IV*, II. iv. 456. Hence **Defi·ler.**

Defile (dǐfəi·l), *v.*[2] 1705. [a. F. *défiler*, f. DE- I. 6 + *file* sb. FILE.] *Mil.* **1.** *intr.* To march in a line or by files; to file off. Also *transf.* **2.** *trans.* To traverse by files. ? *Obs.* 1762.

Defi·le, *v.*[3] *rare.* 1864. [a. F. *défiler* (14th c. *desfilher*), f. *dé-*, DE- I. 6 + radical part of *enfiler* (= *désenfiler*).] = DEFILADE *v.*

Defilement[1] (dǐfəi·lmĕnt). 1571. [f. DEFILE *v.*[1] + -MENT.] The act of defiling, the being defiled; *concr.* anything that defiles.

When Lust.. Lets in D. to the inward parts MILT. *Comus* 466. Defilements in water 1871.

Defi·lement[2]. 1816. [a. mod.F. *défilement*; see DEFILE *v.*[3]] *Fortif.* The act or operation of defilading.

Defilia·tion. [DE- II. 1.] Deprivation of a son. LAMB.

Definable (dǐfəi·năb'l), *a.* 1660. [f. DEFINE *v.* + -ABLE.] Capable of being defined.

As if infinite were d. DRYDEN. A d. interest GEO. ELIOT. Hence **Defi·nabi·lity. Defi·nably** *adv.*

Define (dǐfəi·n), *v.* ME. [a. OF. *definer*; superseded by F. *définir*, repr. L. *definire* (f. DE- I. 3 + *finire* to FINISH). *Diffinire* is also found in L. texts.] †**1.** *trans.* To bring to an end. Also *intr.* –1677. **2.** To determine the boundary or limits of. Also *fig.* ME. **b.** To make definite in outline or form 1815. †**3.** To limit, confine –1643. **4.** To lay down definitely; †to fix upon 1535; †*intr.* to decide –1612. †**5.** To state precisely –1669. †Also *intr.* **6.** To set forth the essential nature of. (In early use: To describe.) ME. **b.** To set forth what (a word, etc.) means. [Not in J.] 1532. Also *intr.* **7.** *transf.* To make (a thing) what it is; to characterize 1633. **8.** To separate by definition (*from*) (*rare*) 1807.

1. A more ready way to d. controversies BARROW. 2. In nature everything is distinct, yet nothing defined WORDSW. 4. He 'defined his position'.. very clearly E. QUINCY. 6. I wyl descryue and dyffyne it [the courte] to the CAXTON. A lady once asked him how he came to d. *Pastern* 'the *knee* of a horse' BOSWELL. Hence **Defi·nement**, description, definition; †limitation (*rare*). **Defi·ner.**

†**Defi·nish,** *v. rare.* [ad. OF. *definiss-*, stem of *definir*.] *trans.* To define. CHAUCER.

Definite (de·finit), *a.* (*sb.*) 1530. [ad. L. *definitus*; see DEFINE.] **1.** Having fixed limits;

determinate; exact, precise 1553. Also *transf.* of persons, in reference to their actions 1611. **2.** *Gram.* **a.** Applied in German and Early English to those forms of the adjective which are used when preceded by the definite article or an equivalent. **b.** Of verbs: = Finite (*rare*). **c.** *D. article*: the article *the*, as indicating a defined or particularized individual. 1727. **3.** *Bot.* Said of inflorescence having the central axis terminated in a flower-bud which opens first: also called *centrifugal* or *determinate* 1876.

1. In a d. compass 1586. A d. understanding 1691, time 1726, answer DICKENS. Be more d. in your statements (*mod.*). Hence **De·finite-ly** *adv.*, **-ness.**

B. *sb.* **1.** Something that is definite 1530. †**2.** 'Thing explained or defined' (J.) 1726.

Definition (defini·ʃən). ME. [a. OF. *de-, def-, diffinicion*, ad. L. *definitionem*; see DEFINE.] †**1.** The setting of bounds; limitation (*rare*) –1483. **2.** The action of determining a question at issue; *spec.* an ecclesiastical pronouncement ME. **3.** *Logic*, etc. The action of defining (see DEFINE *v.* 6) 1645. **4.** A precise statement of the essential nature of a thing ME. **b.** A declaration of the signification of a word or phrase. (Not in J.) 1500. **5.** The action of making definite; the condition of being made, or of being definite, in form or outline; *spec.* the defining power of an optical instrument 1859.

2. This challenge of infallibility..discrediteth their [councils'] definitions BRAMHALL. 3. *D.* (with *Logicians*), an unfolding of the essence or being of a thing by its kind and difference BAILEY. 4. The old d. of force was, that which caused change in motion GROVE. 5. A d. of a word is any maner of declaration of a word T. WILSON. Hence **Definí·tional** *a.* of or pertaining to a d. (*rare*).

Definitive (dĭfi·nĭtiv). ME. [a. OF. *def-, diffinitif, -ive*, ad. L. *de-, diffinitivus*; see DEFINITE.]

A. *adj.* **1.** Having the function of finally deciding; determinative, final. **2.** Having the character of finality; determinate. In *Biol.* opp. to *formative* or *primitive*, as *d. organs.* 1639. †**3.** *Metaph.* Having a definite position, but not occupying space: opp. to *circumscriptive* –1665. **4.** That specifies the individual referred to; *esp.* in *Gram.* 1731.

1. A d. answer RICHARDSON, treaty WILKES, verdict MACAULAY, †judge 1741. 2. A d. system 1821, result 1865. 4. *D. Article* BAILEY. D. verb W. WARD.

B. *sb.* (the *adj.* used *ellipt.*) †**1.** A definitive sentence, judgement, or pronouncement –1804. **2.** *Gram.* A definitive word 1751.

Hence **Defi·nitive-ly** *adv.*, **-ness.**

Definitor (definəi·tǫɹ). 1648. [ad. L.] **1.** An officer of the chapter in certain monastic orders, who decided points of discipline. †**2.** A kind of surveying instrument –1793.

Definitude (dĭfi·nitiud). 1836. [f. L. *definitus*, after *infinitude*, etc.] The quality of being definite; precision.

Results of remarkable precision and d. LATHAM.

†**Defix** (dĭfi·x), *v.* ME. [f. L. *defix-*, ppl. stem of *defigere.*] To fasten down; to fix firmly or intently (*lit.* and *fig.*) –1679.

In intent and defixed thoughts upon some .. object GLANVILL.

Deflagrable (de·flăgrăb'l), *a. rare.* 1691. [f. L. *deflagrare* + -BLE.] Capable of deflagration. Hence **Deflagrabi·lity,** d. quality, readiness to deflagrate (*rare*). BOYLE.

Deflagrate (de·flăgreˡt), *v.* 1727. [f. L. *deflagrat-* ppl. stem, f. DE- I. 3 + *flagrare.*] **1.** *trans.* To cause to burn away with sudden bursting into flame and rapid combustion. **2.** *intr.* To burst into flame and burn away rapidly 1750.

1. When coal is deflagrated with nitre J. HUTTON. 2. Such a degree of burning heat as would cause the nitre to d. G. ADAMS.

Deflagration (deflăgreˡ·ʃən). 1607. [ad. L. *deflagrationem.*] †**1.** The rapid burning away of anything in a destructive fire –1837. **2.** *Physics.* The action of deflagrating 1666.

1. The fall of a spark on gunpowder, for example, followed by the d. of the gunpowder SIR W. HAMILTON. 2. The metals are sometimes oxidized by what is called d. T. P. JONES.

Deflagrator (de·flăgreˡtəɹ). 1824. [f. L. *deflagrare.*] An apparatus for producing deflagration, *esp.* a voltaic arrangement for producing intense heat.

Deflate (dĭflēˡ·t), *v.* 1891. [f. L. *deflat-*, *deflare*, f. DE- + *flare* to blow.] **1.** *trans.* To release the air from. **2.** To reduce an inflated currency 1919. Hence **Defla·tion.**

Deflect (dĭfle·kt), *v.* 1555. [ad. L. *deflectere*, f. DE- I. 1, 2 + *flectere.*]

I. *trans.* **1.** To bend down 1630. **2.** To bend to one side, or from a straight line 1630; *fig.* 1555. **3.** To turn *to* something different from its natural quality or use 1630.

1. They pray..with their knees deflected under them LORD. 2. If we look at an object through a prism, the rays of light coming from it are deflected HARLAN. *fig.* To d. the judgment by hope or fear LECKY.

II. *intr.* To turn to one side or from a straight line 1646; *fig.* 1612.

At some parts of the Azores it [the needle] deflecteth not, but lyeth in the true meridian SIR T. BROWNE. *fig.* The Mind..can, every moment, d. from the line of truth and reason WARBURTON.

Deflected (dĭfle·ktėd), *ppl. a.* 1828. [f. prec.] **1.** Turned aside; bent to one side 1860. **2.** *Zool.* and *Bot.* Bent downwards; = DEFLEXED 1828. var. **Defle·ct.** MRS. BROWNING.

Deflection; see DEFLEXION.

Deflective (dĭfle·ktiv), *a.* 1813. [f. DEFLECT *v.* + -IVE. (Better *deflexive.*)] Having the quality of deflecting, as *d. forces.*

Deflector (dĭfle·ktəɹ). 1837. [f. as prec. + -OR for -ER. (Better *deflexor.*)] That which deflects; *e.g.* (*a*) a deflecting magnet; (*b*) a diaphragm for deflecting a current of air, gas, etc.

Deflexed (dĭfle·kst), *ppl. a.* 1826. [ad. L. *deflexus* + -ED.] *Zool.* and *Bot.* Bent downwards; deflected. var. **De·flex.**

Defle·xible, *a.* 1796. [f. L. *deflexus.*] Capable of being deflected. Hence **Deflexibi·lity.**

Deflexion, deflection (dĭfle·kʃən). 1603. [ad. L. *deflexionem*, f. *deflex-*, stem of *deflectere.* The sp. *deflection*, now common, is taken from the present-stem *deflect-*.] **1.** The action of bending down; bent condition; a bend or curve 1665. **2.** The action of turning, or state of being turned from a straight line or regular course; the amount of such deviation; a turn or deviation 1605. **3.** The turning of a word or phrase aside from its actual form, application, or use 1603. **4.** *Electr.*, etc. The turning of a magnetic needle away from its zero; the measured amount of this 1646. **5.** *Optics.* The bending of rays of light from the straight line. See DIFFRACTION. 1674. **6.** *Naut.* The deviation of a ship from her true course 1706.

1. The deflection of a beam supporting a lateral weight 1879. 2. The great deflection of the coast southward from Cape Wrath MERIVALE. A deflection from simplicity MOZLEY. 3. A deflexion of a word 1659.

Deflexionize, -ed, -ation; see DE- II. 1 and FLEXIONIZE, etc.

Deflexure (dĭfle·ksiŭɹ, -fle·kʃŭɹ). *rare.* 1656. [f. L. *deflex-* ppl. stem + -URE.] Deflexion; the condition of being bent (down or away).

Deflorate (dĭflōᵊ·rēt, de·florēt), *a.* 1828. [ad. L. *defloratus.*] **1.** *Bot.* Past the flowering state; as anthers that have shed their pollen, etc. **2.** = DEFLOWERED 1883.

Defloration (deflorēˡ·ʃən). ME. [a. OF. *defloracion*, ad. L. *deflorationem*, f. *deflorare.*] **1.** The act of deflowering a virgin. **2.** The culling of the choice parts of a book ME.

2. The *deflorations* or MSS. containing excerpts R. ELLIS.

Deflore, deflour, obs. ff. DEFLOWER.

†**Deflou·rish,** *v.* 1494. [ad. OF. *de(s)flouriss-*, stem of *de(s)flourir*, now *défleurir*; see DE- I. 6.] **1.** *trans.* To deflower; also *fig.* –1538. **2.** *intr.* To cease to flourish 1656.

†**Deflow·,** *v.* [DE- I. 1.] *intr.* To flow down. SIR T. BROWNE.

Deflower (dĭflau·əɹ), *v.* ME. [a. OF. *desflorer*, now *déflorer*, f. DE- I. 6 + *flos, florem.*] **1.** *trans.* To deprive (a woman) of her virginity; to violate, ravish. Also *fig.* †**2.** To cull from (a book) its choice parts –1781. **3.** To deprive of flowers 1630.

1. *fig.* Actual discovery (as it were) rifles and deflowers the newness and freshness of the object SOUTH. Hence **Deflow·erer.**

Defluent (de·fluĕnt). *rare.* 1652. [ad. L. *defluentem.*]

A. *adj.* Flowing down, decurrent.

B. *sb.* That which flows down (from a main body). So †**De·fluency,** fluidity (*rare*).

†**Defluous** (de·fluəs), *a. rare.* 1727. [f. L. *defluus.*] Flowing down; also, falling off –1882.

†**Deflux** (dĭ·flʊks), *sb.* 1599. [ad. L. *defluxus.*] **1.** A flowing down; defluxion –1710. **2.** *concr.* An effluence (*rare*) –1682.

Defluxion (dĭflʊ·kʃən). 1549. [ad. L. *defluxionem*, f. *defluere.*] †**1.** A flowing down –1832. **2.** *Path.* The flow or discharge accompanying a cold or inflammation; a running at the nose; catarrh. Now *rare.* 1576. †**3.** That which flows down –1633; *fig.* an effluence –1678.

Defœdation; see DEFEDATION.

†**Defoi·l,** *v.* [ad. F. *défeuiller.*] *trans.* = DEFOLIATE *v.* Holland.

Defoliate (dĭfōᵘ·lieˡt), *v.* 1793. [f. med.L. *defoliare.*] *trans.* To strip of leaves; also *fig.* So **Defo·liate** *a.* having cast or lost its leaves (*rare*). **Defolia·tion,** loss or shedding of leaves. **Defo·liator,** that which defoliates; an insect which strips trees of their leaves.

Deforce (dĭfōᵊ·ɹs), *v.* ME. [a. AF. *deforcer* = OF. *deforcier*, f. *des-, de-* (DE- I. 6) + *forcier, forcer* to FORCE. Cf. ENFORCE, etc.] **1.** *Law.* To keep (something) by force (*from* the rightful owner) 1470. **2.** To keep (a person) forcibly out of the possession *of* his property 1531. **3.** *Sc. Law.* To prevent by force (an officer of the law) from executing his official duty 1461.

2. He [Stephen] deforced Mawd .. of her right FERNE. Hence **Defo·rcement. Defo·rcer. Defo·rciant,** one who keeps another wrongfully out of possession of an estate †**Deforcia·tion.**

Deforest (dĭfǫ·rėst), *v.* 1538. [DE- II. 2.] **1.** *Law.* To make no longer a forest; = DISAFFOREST 1, DISFOREST 1. **2.** *gen.* To clear of forests or trees 1880. Hence **Deforesta·tion.**

Deform (dĭfǭ·ɹm), *a. arch.* ME. [ad. L. *deformis*; see DE- I. 6.] Deformed; hideous.

Sight so d. what heart of rock could long Drie-ey'd behold MILT. *P. L.* XI. 494. †**Defo·rmly** *adv.*

Deform (dĭfǭ·ɹm), *v.*[1] ME. [a. OF. *deformer*, now *déformer*, ad. L. *deformare*; see DE- I. 6.] **1.** *trans.* To mar the beauty or excellence of; to disfigure, deface (*lit.* and *fig.*) 1450. **2.** To mar the form of; to misshape ME. **3.** To alter the form of; in *Physics*, to change the normal shape of 1702. ¶**4.** Obs. var. of DIFFORM *v.*

1. He..deformed the country with ruine and spoile HAYWARD. 2. Cheated of Feature by dissembling Nature, Deform'd, vnfinish'd *Rich. III*, I. i. 20. Hence **Defo·rmable** *a.* deformed; capable of being deformed; hence **Deformabi·lity. Defo·rmer,** one who or that which deforms.

†**Deform,** *v.*[2] *rare.* ME. only. [ad. L. *deformare.*] To form, fashion.

Deformation (dĭfǫɹmēˡ·ʃən). ME. [ad. L. *deformationem.*] **1.** The action (or result) of deforming; disfigurement, defacement. **2.** Alteration of form for the worse; (often opp. to *reformation*) 1546. **3.** *Physics.* Alteration of shape; an altered form *of* 1846.

3. The d. of the solar disc by refraction 1869.

Deformed (dĭfǭ·ɹmd), *ppl. a.* ME. [f. DEFORM *v.* + -ED.] †**1.** Marred in appearance –1632. **2.** Marred in shape, misshapen; unshapely. Now chiefly of persons. ME. **3.** Shapeless –1677. **4.** *fig.* Perverted; morally ugly 1555. Hence **Defo·rmed-ly** *adv.*, †**-ness.**

Deformity (dĭfǭ·ɹmĭti). ME. [a. OF. *deformité*, ad. L. *deformitas*, f. *deformis*; see DEFORM *a.*] **1.** The quality or condition of being DEFORMED 1450. **2.** Bodily misshapenness or malformation ME. **3.** An instance of deformity; *spec.* a bodily malformation ME. *transf.* A deformed being or thing 1698. **4.** *fig.* Moral ugliness or crookedness ME. ¶**5.** Misused for DIFFORMITY 1531.

1. Disease [small-pox], and its consequent effects, d. 1805. 2. Edmunde..surnamed Crowke backe..for his deformytye FABYAN. 3. The tumour..is merely a d. S. COOPER. 4. The corruption and deformitie of our nature 1561. The deformities of the representative system MACAULAY.

Deforse, etc., obs. ff. DEFORCE, etc.

Defo·ssion. 1753. [mod.L. *defossionem.*] The punishment of burying alive. (Dicts.)

†**Defou·l, defoi·l,** *v.* ME. [a. OF. *defouler*, f. DE- I. 1 + *fouler*:—late L. **fullare*, conn. w. L. *fullo* fuller, etc. Assoc., in senses 5, 6, with FOUL *a.* Cf. DEFILE.] **1.** *trans.* To trample under foot; tread down –1574. **2.** To crush

(*lit.* and *fig.*) -1548. **3.** To deflower, debauch -1596. **4.** To violate (laws, holy places, etc.); to profane -1614. **5.** To render foul; to defile. Also *fig.* -1611. **6.** To make unsightly. ME. only. Hence †**Defou·l**, defoi·l *sb.* oppression; defilement.

†**Defrau·d**, *sb.* ME. [f. next, after FRAUD *sb.*] = DEFRAUDATION -1800.

Defraud (dĭfrǭ·d), *v.* ME. [a. OF. *defrauder* (*des-*, *def-*, *dif-*), ad. L. *defraudare.*] **1.** To take or withhold from (a person) by fraud what is his by right; to cheat, cozen, beguile. Also *absol.* **2.** *fig.* To deprive or cheat (a thing) of what is due to it (*arch.*) 1497.

1. To d. citizens of their rights 1880. 2. Here beggar pride defrauds her daily cheer, To boast one splendid banquet once a year GOLDSM. Hence **Defrau·dment.** ? *Obs.*

Defrauda·tion. 1502. [a. OF., ad. L. *defraudationem*; see prec.] The action (or an act) of defrauding; cheating.

Defray (dĭfrēⁱ·), *v.* 1543. [a. F. *défrayer*, f. *des-*, *de-* (DE- I. 3, 6) + OF. *fraier* to spend, f. *frai*, pl. *frais*, expenses, cost.] †**1.** To pay out, spend -1613. **2.** To discharge by paying; to meet, settle 1570. Also *fig.* **3.** To meet the expense of; pay for. Now *rare* or *arch.* 1581. †**4.** To reimburse (a person); to entertain free of charge -1858.

2. Money to d. their charges FULLER. *fig.* Can Night d. The wrath of thundring Ioue SPENSER *F. Q.* I. v. 42. 4. The State will d. you all the time you stay BACON. Hence †**Defray·**, *sb.* defrayal. **Defray·able** *a.* **Defray·al**, the action of defraying. **Defray·er. Defray·ment**, defrayal.

Defrock (dĭfrǫ·k), *v.* 1581. [Cf. DISFROCK.] To deprive of the priestly garb; to unfrock.

Deft (deft), *a.* ME. [app. a doublet of DAFT, q.v.] †**1.** = DAFT 1 (*rare*). (ME. only.) **2.** Apt, skilful, dexterous, clever or neat in action ME. **3.** Neat, trim; handsome. Still *dial.* 1579. **4.** Quiet. Still *dial.* 1763.

2. To see the lame so d. At that cup service CHAPMAN. Of d. tongue CARLYLE. 3. By the messe, a d. lass HEYWOOD. Hence **De·ft-ly** *adv.*, **-ness.**

Defunct (dĭfɒ·ŋkt). 1548. [ad. L. *defunctus*, or ? a. F. *defunct* (Cotgr. 1611), now *défunt.*]

A. *adj.* Having ceased to live; deceased, dead. Also *fig.* 1599.

The Organs, though d. and dead before, Breake vp their drowsie Graue *Hen. V*, IV. i. 21. The ghost of a d. absurdity COLERIDGE.

B. *sb. The d.*: the deceased; hence, with *pl.* (*rare*), a dead person 1548.

Defunction (dĭfɒ·ŋkʃən). *rare.* 1599. [ad. L. *defunctionem.*] Dying, death. *Hen. V*, I. ii. 58.

†**Defu·nctive**, *a. rare.* [f. L. *defunct-* ppl. stem of *defungi.*] Of or pertaining to dying, as *d. music.* SHAKS.

Defuse, -ed, -edly, Defusion, -ive, obs. ff. DIFFUSE, etc.

†**Defy·**, *sb.* 1580. [a. F. *défi*, earlier *deffy*, f. *deffier*, *defier* to DEFY.] Declaration of defiance; challenge -1734.

Defy (dĭfəi·), *v.*¹ ME. [a. OF. *des-*, *def-*, *defier* :—Rom. **disfidare*, f. DIS- + **fidare* to trust.] †**1.** *trans.* To renounce faith, allegiance, or affiance to; to declare hostilities against; to send a declaration of defiance to -1568. **2.** To challenge to combat (*arch.*) ME. **3.** *trans.* To challenge to a contest or trial of skill. Const. *to* and *inf.* 1674. **4.** To set at defiance; to set at nought ME. †**5.** To reject, renounce, disdain, revolt at -1738. †**6.** *intr.* To have distrust *of.* [OF. *difier de.*] -1613.

2. The knyghtes in the Castel defyen yow MALORY. 3. Defying the Ocean Gods to compete BOWEN. 4. Ha, thou fortune, I the defie GOWER. The fortress defied their attacks THIRLWALL. 5. To d. a bribe GAY.

†**Defy·**, *v.*² ME. [?] **1.** *trans.* and *intr.* To digest -1542. **2.** *trans.* To concoct; to dissolve. (ME. only.)

1. *To d. the stomach, a person*: to *digest* the stomach: see DIGEST *v.*

‖**Dégagé** (degaʒe), *a.*; fem. **-ée.** 1697. [F. pa. pple. of *dégager.*] Easy, unconstrained.

Degarnish (dĭgā·miʃ), *v. rare.* By-form of DISGARNISH; see DE- I. 6.

Degela·tion. *rare.* [f. F. *dégeler.*] Thawing. (Dicts.)

†**Dege·nder**, *v.* 1539. [ad. L. *degenerare*, after GENDER *v.*] *intr.* To degenerate -1597. var. †**Dege·ner.**

Degeneracy (dĭdʒe·nĕrăsi). 1664. [f. DEGENERATE *a.*; see -ACY.] The condition or quality of being degenerate; something that is degenerate (*rare*).

This grand D. of the Church H. MORE. The cathedral of Sens is a sad d. from ours ALFORD.

Degenerate (dĭdʒe·nĕrĕt), *a.* 1494. [ad. L. *degeneratus*; see next.]

A. as *pa. pple.* = degenerated. ? *Obs.*

B. as *adj.* **1.** Having lost the qualities proper to the kind; having declined to a lower type; hence, declined in character or qualities; debased, degraded 1494. Also *fig.* of things. **2.** *transf.* Characterized by degeneracy 1651.

1. Thou art degenerat, & growen out of kynde FABYAN. How then art thou turned into the d. plant of a strange vine *Jer.* ii. 21. Penguins..a d. duck T. HERBERT. Any d. form of active faith MORLEY. 2. These d. days POPE. Hence **Dege·nerate·ly** *adv.*, **-ness** (*rare*).

Degenerate (dĭdʒe·nĕreⁱt), *v.* 1545. [f. ppl. stem of L. *degenerare*, f. *degener* adj., f. DE- I. 1 + *gener-* (*genus*).] **1.** *intr.* To lose the qualities proper to the kind; to fall away from ancestral excellence; hence, to decline in character or qualities, become of a lower type 1553. Also *transf.* and *fig.* of things. †**2.** To show a degeneration or an alteration *from* -1739. †**3.** *trans.* To cause to degenerate -1811.

1. When men d., and by sinne put off the nature of man T. TAYLOR. Plants for want of Culture, d... sometimes so far as to change into another kind BACON. 2. Gods! how the son degenerates from the sire POPE. Hence **Dege·nerative** *a.* of the nature of, or tending to degeneration.

Degeneration (dĭdʒenĕrēⁱ·ʃən). 1481. [a. F. *dégénération*, f. L. *degenerare.*] **1.** The process of degenerating; declining to a lower stage of being; degradation of nature 1607. **b.** *Biol.* A change of structure by which an organism, or an organ, assumes the form of a lower type 1848. **c.** *Path.* A morbid change in the structure of parts 1851. **2.** Degeneracy 1481. †**3.** That which has degenerated -1748.

1. Capable..of D. into any thing harmful COWLEY. Such a d. may take place simply from want of use CARPENTER. Fatty d. 1883. 3. The Degenerations and Counterfeits of Benevolence HARTLEY.

Degenerescence (-e·sĕns). 1882. [a. F. *dégénérescence* (1799 in Hatzf.).] Tendency to degenerate; the process of degeneration.

†**Dege·nerous**, *a.* 1597. [f. L. *degener* (see DEGENERATE *v.*), after GENEROUS *a.*] **1.** Degenerate; characterized by degeneration -1734. **2.** *transf.* and *fig.* of things (*esp.* organisms or organic products) -1748.

1. An upstart and d. race NORTH. A d. feare DANIEL, age BOYLE. Hence †**Dege·nerously** *adv.*

Dege·rm, *v.* [DE- II. 2.] *trans.* To remove the germ from (*e.g.* wheat). So **Dege·rminator**, a machine with iron disks for splitting the grains of wheat and removing the germ. (Dicts.)

Deglaze, *v.*; see DE- II. 2 and *glaze.*

†**Deglo·ry**, *v. rare.* 1610. [DE- II. 2.] To deprive of its glory -1653.

†**Deglute** (dĭglū·t), *v.* 1599. [f. L. *deglutire.*] *trans.* To swallow down. Also *absol.*

Deglu·tinate, *v.* 1609. [f. L. *deglutinare*; see DE- I. 6.] †**1.** *trans.* To unglue; to loosen or separate (things glued together) -1727. **2.** To extract the gluten from (*mod.*). Hence **Deglutina·tion.**

Deglutition (dīglutiʃən). 1650. [a. F. *déglutition*, f. L. *deglutire*; see DEGLUTE.] The action of swallowing. Also *fig.*

In a city feast..what d. PALEY. Hence **Degluti·tious** *a.* pertaining or tending to d. (*rare*). So **Deglu·titory** *a.* pertaining to d.; swallowing (*rare*).

De·go·rder. 1880. [f. DEG(REE) + ORDER.] *Math.* The pair of numbers signifying the degree and order of any form.

†**Dego·rge**, *v.* 1493. [a. F. *dégorger*; see DE- I. 6.] = DISGORGE -1737.

Degradation¹ (degrădēⁱ·ʃən). 1535. [a. F., ad. L. *degradationem*, f. *degradare* to DEGRADE.] **1.** Deposition from some rank, office, or position of honour as an act of punishment; as, the d. of an ecclesiastic, a knight, a military officer, a graduate of a university. **2.** Lowering in honour, estimation, social position, etc.; the state of being so lowered 1752. **3.** Lowering in character or quality; moral or intellectual debasement 1697. **4.** Reduction to an inferior type or stage of development. Also *attrib.* 1850. **b.** *spec. Biol.* Reduction to a less perfect organic condition; degeneration 1849. **c.** *Bot.* A change in the substance of plants, resulting in the formation of degradation-products (see quots.) 1875. **d.** *Physics.* The conversion of (energy) to a form less capable of transformation 1871. **5.** A lowering in strength, amount, etc. 1769. **6.** *Geol.* The wearing down of rocks, strata, etc., by atmospheric and aqueous action 1799.

1. An..active statesman, exposed to the vicissitudes of advancement and d. JOHNSON. 2. The d. of the poor-house JEVONS. 3. The d. of marrying a man she did not love 1866. 4. *D. products*: products which have no further use in the building up of the structures of plants, *e.g.* gum, etc. 5. The d. in the value of silver A. SMITH. 6. The chalk..yields rather easily to d. PHILLIPS. Hence **Degrada·tional** *a.* manifesting structural d.

Degradation² (dīgrădēⁱ·ʃən). 1706. [In sense 1, a. F. *dégradation*, ad. It. *digradazione*, f. *digradare* to come down by degrees. Cf. GRADATION.] **1.** The gradual lowering of colour or light in a painting; *esp.* that which gives the effect of distance. ? *Obs.* †**2.** Diminution by degrees; the part so reduced -1730.

Degrade (dĭgrēⁱ·d), *v.* ME. [a. OF. *degrader*, occas. *desg-*, f. DE- I. 1 + L. *gradus.*] **1.** *trans.* To reduce from a higher to a lower rank, to depose *from* (†*of*) a position of honour or estimation. **2.** To lower in estimation, character, or quality; to reduce in price, strength, purity, tone, etc. 1500. **3. a.** *Biol.* To reduce to a lower organic type. **b.** *Physics.* To reduce (energy) to a form less capable of transformation. 1862. **4.** *Geol.* To wear down (rocks, etc.) by surface abrasion or disintegration 1812. **5.** *intr.* To descend to a lower grade or type; to degenerate 1850. **6.** *Cambridge Univ.* To put off entering the examination in honours for the degree of B.A. for one year 1829.

1. His censure was to be degraded both from her ministry and degrees taken in the University MEADE. 2. How low avarice can d. a man GOLDSM. To d. prices COBDEN. 5. And throned races may d. TENNYSON. Hence **Degra·der. Degra·dingly** *adv.*

Degraded (dĭgrēⁱ·dĕd), *ppl. a.* 1483. [f. prec.] **1.** Lowered in rank, position, reputation, character, etc.; debased. **2. a.** *Biol.* Showing structural or functional degradation 1862. **b.** *Geol.* Worn down 1869. **3.** Of colour: Toned down 1877.

1. A d. race of men MAX MULLER, priest 1885. 2. A d. form of life H. DRUMMOND.

Degra·ded, *a.* 1562. [f. DE- I. + L. *gradus.*] *Her.* Of a cross: Set on steps or degrees.

†**Degra·dement.** [a. obs. F. *dégradement.*] Degradation, abasement. MILTON.

†**De·gravate**, *v.* 1574. [f. L. *degravare*; see -ATE³.] *trans.* To weigh down, burden, load -1727. Hence †**Degrava·tion.**

Degree (dĭgrī·), *sb.* [ME. *degre*, pl. *-ez*, a. OF. *degre*, earlier nom. *degrez* :—late pop.L. **degradus*, f. DE- I. 1 + *gradus.*]

I. 1. A step in an ascent or descent; one of a flight of steps; a rung of a ladder. (*Obs.* exc. in *Her.*) Also *transf.* of anything resembling a step 1611. **2.** *fig.* A step or stage in a process, etc. ME. **3.** A step in direct line of descent; in *pl.* the number of such steps, determining the proximity of blood in collateral descendants of a common ancestor ME. **4.** A stage or position in the scale of dignity or rank; relative social or official rank or station; a rank or class of persons. ? *Obs.* ME. **5.** Manner, way, wise; relation, respect ME. **6.** A step or stage in intensity or amount; the relative intensity, measure, or amount of a quality, attribute, or action. (Cf. sense 2.) ME. **b.** *Crim. Law.* Relative measure of criminality, as in *Principal in the first*, or *second d.* In *U.S. Law*, A grade of crime. 1676.

1. He sawe a ladder whyche had ten degrees or stappes CAXTON. *Jul. C.* II. i. 26. 2. Which recognizance is the first d. to amendment 1550. Phr. *By degrees*: by little and little, gradually. 3. *Prohibited* or *forbidden degrees*: degrees of consanguinity and affinity within which marriage is not allowed. 4. Knyȝte, squiere, ȝoman and knaue, Iche mon in thayre degre ME. 6. Misprision in the highest d. *Twel. N.* I. v. 61. Differing but in d., of kind the same MILT. *P. L.* v. 490. Phr. *To a d.* (colloq.): to an undefined, but serious, extent. *To the last d.*: to the utmost measure.

II. Spec. and techn. senses. **1.** A stage of proficiency in an art, craft, or course of study; *esp.* An academical rank conferred by a university or college as a mark of proficiency in scholarship; honorary distinction ME. **2.** *Gram.* Each of the three stages (POSITIVE, COMPARATIVE, SUPERLATIVE) in the comparison of an adj. or adv. (Cf. I. 6.) 1460. **3.** *Geom.* (*Astron.*, *Geog.*, etc.) A unit of measurement of angles or circular arcs, being an angle equal to the 90th part of a right angle, or an arc equal to the 360th part of the circumference of a circle (which subtends this angle at the centre) ME. **b.** *transf.* A position as measured by degrees (chiefly of latitude) 1647. **4.** *Thermometry.* **a.** A unit of temperature varying according to the scale in use. **b.** Each of the marks denoting degrees on the scale of a thermometer, or the interval between two successive marks. 1727. **5.** *Mus.* Each of the successive lines and spaces on the stave; also applied to tone or interval 1674. †**6.** *Arith.* A group of three figures taken together in numeration –1677. **7.** *Alg.* The rank of an equation or expression as determined by the highest power of the unknown or variable quantity, or the highest dimensions of the terms which it contains 1730.

3. b. He knew the Seat of Paradise, Could tell in what D. it lies BUTLER *Hud.* I. i. 174.

Degree (dǐgrī·), *v.* 1614. [f. prec. sb.] †**1.** *trans.* To lead or bring on by degrees –1670. **2.** To confer a degree upon. *nonce-use.*

‖**Degu** (de·gu). 1843. [Native name.] *Zool.* A S. Amer. genus *Octodon* of hystricomorphous or porcupine-like rodents.

Degust (dǐgɒ·st), *v. rare.* 1623. [ad. L. *degustare.*] To taste. Also *absol.*

Degustate (dǐgɒ·steɪt), *v. rare.* 1599. [f. L. *degustat-* ppl. stem; see prec.] = prec. Hence **Degusta·tion**, the action of degusting.

‖**Déhaché** (deha·ʃe), *a.* 1766. [obs. F., f. DE- I. 1, 2 + *hacher.*] *Her.* = COUPED, q. v.

Dehisce (dǐhi·s), *v.* 1657. [ad. L. *dehiscere*, f. DE- I. 2 + *hiscere*, inceptive of *hiare* to gape.] *intr.* To gape; in *Bot.* to burst open, as seed-vessels.

Dehiscence (dǐhi·sěns). 1828. [ad. mod.L. *dehiscentia*, f. L. *dehiscentem*; see prec.] Gaping, opening by divergence of parts; in *Bot.* the bursting open of capsules, fruits, anthers, etc. in order to discharge their mature contents. Also *fig.* and *gen.* So **Dehi·scent** *a.* gaping open; in *Bot.* opening as seed-vessels.

Deho·nestate, *v. rare.* 1663. [f. ppl. stem of L. *dehonestare*; see DE- I. 6.] *trans.* To dishonour, disparage. Hence **Dehonesta·tion**, dishonouring, dishonour.

‖**Dehors** (dəhō·r). 1701. [a. OF. *dehors*; OF. also *defors*, a late L. comb. of *de* prep. + L. *foras*, *foris* out of doors.]

A. *prep.* (*Law.*) Outside of; not within the scope of.

†**B.** *sb.* (*Fortif.*) All sorts of separate outworks, made for the better security of the main works. (Dicts.)

Dehort (dǐhǭ·ɹt), *v.* Now *rare.* 1533. [ad. L. *dehortari*; see DE- I. 2.] To use exhortation to dissuade from; to advise against. Also *absol.*

Wherby we doe perswade..disswade..exhorte, or dehorte.. any man T. WILSON. Croker dehorts me from visiting Ireland SOUTHEY. So **Dehorta·tion**, earnest dissuasion. **Deho·rtative**, *a.* dehortatory; *sb.* a dehortative address or argument. **Deho·rtatory**, *a.* characterized by dehortation; †*sb.* a dehortatory address. **Deho·rter.**

Dehumanize (dǐhiū·mănəiz), *v.* 1818. [DE- II. 1.] *trans.* To deprive of human attributes.

Turner's face was a good deal de-humanized MOORE.

†**Dehu·sk**, *v. rare.* 1566. [DE- II. 2.] To deprive of the husk.

Dehydrate (dīˌhəi·dreɪt), *v.* 1876. [f. DE- II. 2 + Gr. ὕδωρ + -ATE[3].] *Chem.* **1.** *trans.* To deprive of water, or of its constituents. **2.** *intr.* To lose water as a constituent 1886. Hence **Dehydra·tion**, the removal of water, or of its constituents, in a chemical combination.

Dehydrogenate (dīˌhəi·droˌdʒěneɪt), *v.* 1850. [DE- II. 1.] = next.

Dehydrogenize (dīˌhəi·droˌdʒěnəiz), *v.* 1878. [DE- II. 1.] *Chem.* To deprive of its hydrogen; to remove hydrogen from. Hence **Dehy·drogeniza·tion.**

Deicide[1] (dī·isəid). 1653. [ad. mod.L. *deicida*; see -CIDE 1.] The killer of a god.

Deicide[2] (dī·isəid). 1611. [ad. mod.L. type **deicidium*; see -CIDE 2.] The killing of a god. Hence **De·icidal** *a.* of or pertaining to d.

Deictic (dəi·ktik), *a.* Also **deiktic.** 1828. [ad. Gr. δεικτικός, f. δεικτός vbl. adj. of δεικνύναι. A purely academic word.] Directly pointing out, demonstrative; in *Logic*, applied to reasoning, and opp. to *elenctic*, which proves indirectly. So †**Dei·ctical** *a.* †**Dei·ctically** *adv.*

Deific (dīˌi·fik), *a.* 1490. [a. F. *déifique*, ad. L. *deificus.*] Deifying, making divine; *loosely*, divine, godlike. So †**Dei·fical.**

Deification (dīˌifikēɪ·ʃən). ME. [f. L. *deificare* to DEIFY.] The action of deifying; deified condition; a deified embodiment. **b.** Absorption into the divine nature 1856.

Deiform (dī·ifǭɹm), *a.* 1642. [ad. med.L. *deiformis.*] **1.** Godlike in form. **2.** Conformable to the nature of God; godlike 1654. Hence **Deifo·rmity**, d. quality.

Deify (dī·ifəi), *v.* ME. [a. F. *déifier*, ad. L. *deificare*; see -FY.] *trans.* To make a god of; to exalt to the position of a deity; to enroll among the gods. **b.** To render godlike ME. **c.** To treat, regard, or adore as a god 1590.

[They] were both ystellyfyed In the heauen and there defyed LYDG. **b.** No vertue more deified a Prince then Clemencie SIR T. HERBERT. **c.** The old man deifies prudence JOHNSON. Hence **De·ifier.** **De·ifying** *vbl. sb.* and *ppl. a.*

Deign (dēɪn), *v.* ME. [a. OF. *degnier*, from 14th c. *daigner* :—L. *dignare*, by-form of *dignari*, f. *dignus.*] **1.** *intr.* To think it worthy of oneself (*to do* something); to vouchsafe, condescend. Also †*impers.* **2.** *trans.* with *simple obj.* **a.** To condescend to give or bestow, to vouchsafe. (Now *esp.* with *reply*, *answer*, in neg. sentences.) 1589. †**b.** To vouchsafe to accept. (Opp. to *to disdain.*) –1661. †**3.** To dignify (a person) *with.* [= L. *dignari.*] –1648.

1. Would he daine to wed a Countrie Lasse GREENE. **2.** Nor would we deigne him buriall of his men *Macb.* I. ii. 60. **b.** Thy pallat then did daine The roughest Berry, on the rudest Hedge *Ant. & Cl.* I. iv. 63.

†**Dei·gnous**, *a.* ME. [app. short f. *dedeignous*, DISDAINOUS; cf. DAIN *v.*] Disdainful, haughty –1643.

‖**Dei gratia.** [L.] By the grace of God; see GRACE.

Deil (dīl, dǐl). 1500. [Sc.] **1.** The Devil. **2.** A mischievously wicked fellow 1786.

Deinosaur, Deinothere, etc.; see DINO-.

De-insularize, -integrate, etc.; see DE- II. 1 and INSULARIZE, etc.

‖**Deipara** (diˌi·pără). 1664. [late L., f. *deus* + *-parus*, *-a*; a L. equiv. of Gr. θεοτόκος.] A title of the Virgin Mary, 'Mother of God'. So **Dei·parous** *a.* bearing a god.

Deipnosophist (dəipnǭ·sǒfist). 1656. [ad. Gr. δειπνοσοφιστής, f. δεῖπνον dinner + σοφιστής a master of his craft.] A master of the art of dining: taken from δειπνοσοφισταί, the title of the Greek work of Athenæus, in which a number of learned men discuss dinners, literature, and miscellaneous topics of every kind.

Deis(e, obs. f. DAIS.

Deism (dī·iz'm). 1682. [f. L. *deus* + -ISM. Cf. F. *déisme.*] The doctrine or belief of a deist; usually, belief in the existence of a God, with rejection of revelation; 'natural religion'.

D. being the very same with old Philosophical Paganism BENTLEY.

Deist (dī·ist). 1621. [a. F. *déiste*, f. L. *deus.*] One who acknowledges the existence of a God upon the testimony of reason, but rejects revealed religion.

(The term was originally opposed to *atheist*, and was interchangeable with *theist* even in the end of the 17th c.)

In speaking of a d. they fix their attention on the negative, in speaking of a theist on the positive aspect of his belief 1880. Hence **Dei·stic** *a.* of the nature of or pertaining to deists or deism. **Dei·stical** *a.* (in same sense); also, tending to deism; **-ly** *adv.*

†**De·itate**, *ppl. a.* [repr. a L. **deitatus* (tr. Gr. θεωθείς).] Deified. CRANMER.

Deity (dī·ĭti). ME. [a. F. *déité*, ad. L. *deitas*, *deitatem* (formed by Augustine *De Civ. Dei* VII. i., after L. *divinitas*).] **1.** The estate or rank of a god; godhood; godship; *esp.* with *poss. pron.* **b.** The divine nature of God; Godhood; the Godhead. ME. **2.** *concr.* A divinity, a divine being, a god. Also *fig.* ME. **3.** (*with capital.*) A supreme being as creator of the universe; *the Deity*, the Supreme Being, God. (*Esp.* as a term of Natural Theology.) 1647.

1. The Goddes themselues (Humbling their Deities to loue) *Wint. T.* IV. iv. 26. **b.** The fader the sone & the holy ghost, one essence of deite 1502. **2.** The chief d., the sun SULLIVAN. *fig.* Tobacco (England's bainefull D.) 1630. **3.** Men spoke of the Deity', as a sort of first cause of all things, and..had lost sight of the Personal God PUSEY. Hence **De·ityship.**

Deje·ct, *ppl. a. Obs.* or *arch.* ME. [ad. L. *dejectus*; see DE- I. 1.] **1.** *pa. pple.* Thrown down; †cast away. **2.** *ppl. a.* DEJECTED 1528; abased 1510. Hence **Deje·ctly** *adv.*

Deject (dǐˌdʒe·kt), *v.* ME. [f. L. *deject-*, ppl. stem of *dejicere.*] **1.** *trans.* To cast down; to overthrow. *arch.* or *Obs.* †**2.** To cast away, reject –1633. †**3.** *fig.* To lower in condition or character, to abase –1691. †**4.** To reduce the strength of, weaken –1684. **5.** To depress in spirits; to cast down, dispirit, dishearten. (The ordinary current sense.) 1581.

3. Being loath to d. them whom he had once aduanced 1601. **5.** Good Authours d. me too-too much, and quaile my courage FLORIO *Montaigne.* Hence ‖**Deje·cta** *sb. pl.* excrements. **Deje·ctant** *a. Her.*, bending down. **Deje·cter.**

Dejected (dǐˌdʒe·ktěd), *ppl. a.* 1581. [f. prec.] **1.** *lit.* Cast down (*arch.*) 1682; in *Her.* bent downwards 1889. †**2.** Lowered in estate, condition, or character; abased, lowly –1721. **3.** Downcast, low-spirited 1581. Also *transf.*

3. To-day glad—to-morrow d. LYTTON. *transf.* With a drooping head and d. pace SCOTT. Hence **Deje·cted·ly** *adv.*, **-ness.**

Dejection (dǐˌdʒe·kʃən). ME. [a. OF., ad. L. *dejectionem*; see DEJECT *ppl. a.*] **1.** *lit.* The action of casting down; the fact of being cast down 1681. †**2.** *fig.* A casting down; abasement, humiliation –1659. **3.** Depression of spirits; dejected condition 1450. †**4.** Lowering of force or strength –1732. **5.** *Med.* Fæcal discharge 1605. **6.** That which is dejected 1727.

2. Adoration implies submission and d.; so that, while we worship, we cast down ourselves PEARSON. **3.** What besides Of sorrow and d. and despair Our frailtie can sustain MILT. *P. L.* XI. 301. **6.** Fæcal dejections 1849. Igneous dejections [from a volcano] MURCHISON. So †**Deje·ctive** *a.* characterized by, or betokening, d.; purgative.

Dejectory (dǐˌdʒe·ktəri), *a.* 1640. [f. L. *dejicere* to DEJECT.] *Med.* Capable of promoting evacuation of the bowels; aperient.

Dejecture (dǐˌdʒe·ktiŭɹ). 1731. [f. as prec.] Matter discharged from the bowels; excrement.

†**De·jerate**, *v.* 1607. [f. L. *dejerare*, f. DE- I. 3 + *jurare.*] *intr.* and *trans.* To swear solemnly –1641. So †**Dejera·tion.**

Déjeune, déjuné. *Obs.* or *arch.* 1630 [For earlier *desjeune*, DISJUNE, q. v.] = next.

‖**Déjeuner**, †**déjeuné** (deʒöne). 1787. [mod. F. *déjeuner*, formerly often *déjeune* (cf. COUCHEE), pres. inf. used subst.] The morning meal; breakfast. (In France, often = luncheon.)

De jure; see DE I. c.

Dekadarchy, -drachm, Dekarch, etc.; see DECA-.

Dekle, var. of DECKLE.

Del, obs. f. DEAL *sb.*[1], and of DOLE, mourning.

Dela·bialize, *v.* [DE- II. 1.] To deprive of its labial character. SWEET.

†**Dela·ce**, *v. rare.* [a. F. *délacer.*] To untie, undo. HOWELL.

Delacerate, etc., obs. f. DILACERATE, etc.

Delacrima·tion. Also **delacry-.** 1623. [ad. L. *delacrimationem*; see DE- I. 1.] Weeping (*obs.*); a superabundant flow of an aqueous or serous humour from the eyes; epiphora.

Delacta·tion. 1727. [DE- I. 6.] The act of weaning; **b.** 'artificial arrest of the secretion of milk' (*Syd. Soc. Lex.*).

Delaine (dǐlēɪ·n). 1840. [Short for *muslin delaine*, F. *mousseline de laine* lit. 'woollen muslin'.] A light textile fabric for women's dresses; orig. of wool, now usually of wool and cotton.

Delaminate (dǐlæ·mineɪt), *v.* 1877. [f. DE- I. 1, 2 + L. *lamina.*] *trans.* and *intr.* (*Biol.*)

To split into separate layers. Hence **Delamina·tion**, the process of delaminating: *spec.* applied to the formation of the layers of the BLASTODERM, q. v.

†Dela·pse, *sb. rare.* 1630. [ad. L. *delapsus* (see next).] Downfall, descent -1657.

Delapse (dǐlæ·ps), *v.* ? *Obs.* 1526. [f. L. *delaps-, delabi*, f. DE- I. 1 + *labi*.] *intr.* To fall or slip down, descend, sink (*lit.* and *fig.*).

Nature is delapsed into that dotage and folly BIGGS. So †**Dela·psion**, *spec.* in *Path.* = prolapsus.

†Delassa·tion. *rare.* [f. L. *delassare*.] Fatigue. RAY.

Delate (dǐlēⁱ·t), *v.* 1515. [f. L. *delat-*, ppl. stem of *deferre*; see DEFER *v.*[2]] †1. *trans.* = DEFER *v.*[2] 1. -1626. †2. = DEFER *v.*[2] 2. -1875. †3. To hand down or over; to refer -1858. 4. To accuse, impeach; to inform against; to denounce to a tribunal 1515; to report (an offence, etc.) 1582. 5. To relate 1639.

1. To try exactly the time wherein Sound is delated BACON. 4. To d. sinners from the pulpit JOHNSON. To punish the crimes delated vnto him 1605.

Delate, obs. f. DILATE, DELETE.

Delation (dǐlēⁱ·ʃən). 1578. [ad. L. *delationem*; see DELATE *v.*] †1. Conveyance (to a place) -1626. 2. Handing down, transference. *Obs.* (exc. in *Rom. Law.*) 1681. 3. Informing against; accusation, denouncement 1578.

1. It is certain that the D. of Light is in an Instant BACON.

Delator (dǐlēⁱ·təɹ). 1572. [a. L.; see DELATE *v.*] An informer, a secret or professional accuser. Hence †**Dela·tory** *a.* of the nature of delation.

Delay (dǐlēⁱ·), *sb.* ME. [a. F. *délai*; see DELAY *v.*] 1. The action of delaying; putting off; procrastination; loitering. 2. The fact of being delayed; hindrance to progress 1748.

1. The Lawes d. *Haml.* III. i. 72. Fabius thou, whose timely delays gave strength to the state BOWEN. 2. There will be a d. of a day JOWETT.

Phr. *Without d.*: without loitering, at once.

Delay (dǐlēⁱ·), *v.*[1] ME. [a. OF. *delaier, delayer* to defer. Late L. *dilatare*, freq. of *differre*, accounts for the sense, not for the form.] 1. *trans.* To put off; to defer, postpone. 2. To impede the progress of; to retard, hinder ME. 3. *intr.* To put off action; to linger, loiter 1509.

1. My Lord delayeth his comming *Matt.* xxiv. 48. Delaying as the tender ash delays To clothe herself TENNYSON. 2. Joy and Grief can hasten and d. Time STEELE. 3. So spake th' Eternal Father..nor delaid the winged Saint After his charge receivd MILT. *P. L.* V. 247. Hence **Delay·er** (now *rare*), one who (or that which) delays. **Delay·ingly** *adv.* †**Delay·ment**, delaying; delay.

†Delay·, *v.*[2] 1530. [a. F. *délayer*, in OF. *desleier*:—Rom. **dis-ligare*, f. L. DIS- + *ligare*.] 1. To ALLAY; to temper -1624. 2. To mitigate, assuage -1603. 3. To soak (*rare*) -1580.

‖**Del credere** (del krē·dĕre), *attrib.* and *adv. phr.* 1797. [It. = 'of belief, of trust'.] *Comm.* A phrase expressing the obligation undertaken by a factor, broker, or commission merchant, when he guarantees and becomes responsible for the solvency of the persons to whom he sells. Hence *del credere agent, account*, etc.

Del credere commission: the additional premium charged by the factor for this guarantee.

‖**Dele** (dī·lī). 1841. [L. *dele*, 2nd sing. pres. imper. act. of *delere* to DELETE.] 'Delete (the letter, etc. marked)'. (Commonly written ₰.)

Dele, obs. f. DEAL.

‖**Deleatur** (dīlĭ,ēⁱ·tɒ̆ɹ). 1602. [L. = 'let it be deleted'.] A written mark on a printed proof-sheet directing something to be omitted; hence *fig.*

D., therefore, wherever you meet it EVELYN.

Deleble, var. of DELIBLE.

Delectable (dǐle·ktăb'l), *a.* ME. [a. OF., ad. L. *delectabilis*. In Shaks., stressed *de·lectable*.] Affording delight; delightful. (Now used seriously in poetry only, or elevated prose.)

Trees of God, D. both to behold and taste MILT. *P. L.* VII. 539. Hence **Delectabi·lity**, d. quality. **Dele·ctableness. Dele·ctably** *adv.*

Delectate (dǐle·kteⁱt, dī·lekteⁱt), *v. rare.* 1802. [f. ppl. stem of L. *delectare*.] *trans.* To delight. (Affected or humorous.)

Delectation (dīlektēⁱ·ʃən). ME. [a. OF., ad. L. *delectationem*.] The action of delighting; delight, enjoyment. Also *transf.* (Now restricted to the lighter kinds of pleasure.)

‖**Delectus** (dǐle·ktɒ̆s). 1828. [a. L. = 'selection'.] A selection of passages, *esp.* Latin and Greek, for translation.

Delegable (de·lǐgăb'l), *a.* 1660. [f. L. *delegare* + -BLE.] Capable of being delegated.

Delegacy (de·lǐgăsi). 1533. [f. DELEGATE *sb.*; see -ACY.] 1. The action or system of delegating; commission or authority given to act as a delegate. 2. A body or committee of delegates; †a meeting of such a body 1621.

Delegant (de·lǐgănt). 1627. [ad. L. *delegantem*.] One who delegates; in *Civil Law*, one who, to discharge a debt, assigns his own debtor to his creditor, as debtor in his place.

Delegate (de·lǐgĕt), *sb.* ME. [a. OF. *delegat* (= mod.F. *délégué*), ad. L. *delegatus* pa. pple., used as sb. in Romanic.] 1. A person sent or deputed to act for or represent another or others; a deputy, commissioner. 2. *spec.* A commissioner appointed by the crown under the great seal to hear and determine appeals from the ecclesiastical courts 1554. b. *Oxford Univ.* A member of a permanent committee entrusted with some branch of University business 1604. 3. *U.S.* The representative of a Territory in Congress, where he has a seat and the right of speech, but no vote 1825. b. *House of Delegates*: (*a*) the lower house of the General Assembly in Virginia, West Virginia, and Maryland; (*b*) the lower house of the General Convention of the Protestant Episcopal Church.

Delegate (de·lǐgĕt), *ppl. a.* 1530. [ad. L. *delegatus* pa. pple.] Delegated.

Delegate (de·lǐgeⁱt), *v.* 1530. [f. ppl. stem of L. *delegare*.] 1. *trans.* To send or commission (a person) as a deputy or representative, with power to act for another; to depute 1623. 2. To entrust or commit (authority, etc.) to another as an agent or deputy 1530; †*loosely*, to assign -1774. 3. *Civil Law.* To assign to a creditor as debtor in one's place 1818.

1. Will any man .. think it reasonable my Lord Keeper should, *ad placitum*, d. whom hee will to keep the Seale 1641. 2. Those bodies..to whom the people have delegated the power of legislation T. JEFFERSON. I wish we could d. to women some of this work HELPS. Hence **Delegatee·**, the party to whom a debtor is delegated by the delegant. †**De·legative** *a.* having the attribute of delegating; of delegated nature.

Delegation (delǐgēⁱ·ʃən). 1611. [ad. L. *delegationem*.] 1. The action of delegating or fact of being delegated (see DELEGATE *v.*) 1612. 2. A charge or commission given to a delegate 1611. 3. A delegated body; a number of persons sent or commissioned to act as representatives 1818. 4. *Civil Law.* The assignment of a debtor by his creditor to a creditor of the delegant, to act as debtor in his place and discharge his debt 1721. 5. A letter, etc. not negotiable and unstamped, used by bankers and others for the transfer of a debt or credit 1882. ‖b. A share-certificate. [F. *délégation*.] 1882.

3. The Jersey d. ..presented to congress a number of the counterfeits H. PHILLIPS. 5. b. The English government intended purchasing 200,000 Suez Canal delegations 1882.

Delegator (de·lǐgeⁱtəɹ). 1875. [ad. L.] One who delegates, a delegant. Hence **De·legatory** *a.* of or relating to delegation; of the nature of delegated power; †holding delegated authority.

‖**Delenda** (dǐle·ndă), *sb. pl.* 1645. [L.] Things to be deleted.

†Dele·niate, *v. rare.* 1623. [irreg. f. L. *delenire*.] To soothe, mitigate -1657.

Delete (dǐlī·t), *v.* 1495. [f. L. *delet-, delere*.] †1. *trans.* To destroy, do away with -1851. 2. To strike out, erase, expunge 1605. Also *fig.*

2. Here .. the *and* must be deleted F. HALL. So †**Dele·te** *pa. pple.*, deleted.

Deleterious (delǐtī³·riəs), *a.* 1643. [f. mod. L. *deleterius*, a. Gr. δηλητήριος, f. (ult.) δηλέεσθαι to hurt; see -OUS.] Physically or morally harmful or injurious; noxious.

'Tis pity wine should be so d. BYRON. Politics is a d. profession EMERSON. var. †**Delete·rial** *a.* Hence **Delete·rious-ly** *adv.*, **-ness.**

†Deletery (de·lǐtĕri), *a.* Also *erron.* **-ory, -ary.** 1576. [a. med.L. *deleterius*; see prec. Cf. DELETORY.]

A. *adj.* Deleterious, poisonous -1684.

A certain deletary and poysonous quality 1657.

B. *sb.* 1. A deleterious drug; a poison. Also *fig.* -1653. 2. That which destroys the effect of anything noxious; an antidote. [Assoc. w. L. *delere*.] -1660.

2. Deleteries of sin and instruments of repentance JER. TAYLOR.

Deletion (dǐlī·ʃən). 1590. [ad. L. *deletionem*.] 1. The action of effacing or destroying; destruction. Now *arch.* 1606. 2. The action of deleting; the fact of being deleted; a deleted passage, an erasure 1590.

1. A total d. of the sin JER. TAYLOR. 2. The d. was initialed in the margin KAY.

Deletive (dǐlī·tiv), *a.* [f. L. *delet-, delere*.] Having the property of deleting. EVELYN.

Deletory (dǐlī·təri). 1612. [f. as prec. + -ORY.]

A. *adj.* That is used to delete, effacing.

B. *sb.* That which destroys or effaces. (Cf. DELETERY *sb.* 2.) 1647.

Confession..as a d. of sin JER. TAYLOR.

Delf[1] (delf). Now *local.* [ME. *delf*, late OE. *dælf*, f. (ult.) *delfan* to DELVE.] 1. That which is delved or dug; as, a pit; a trench; a quarry; a mine. †2. That which is or may be dug into; as, a bed of any earth or mineral -1706. 3. *Sc.* A sod 1812; †in *Her.* a square repr. a sod, used as an abatement -1688. †4. A thrust of the spade -1688. Also *attrib.*

1. The fens are divided by embanked upland rivulets or 'delphs' 1851. Quarries or Delfes of Stone or Slate 1588.

Delf[2], **delft** (delf, delft). Also **delph.** 1714. [a. Du. *Delf*, now *Delft*, a town of Holland, named from its chief canal, known as *delf*, *delve* 'ditch'; see prec.] A kind of glazed earthenware made at Delf or Delft in Holland; originally called *Delf ware*. Also *attrib.*

Delian (dī·liăn), *a.* 1623. [f. L. *Delius* (Gr. Δήλιος) + -AN.] Of or belonging to Delos, an island in the Grecian archipelago, the reputed birthplace of Apollo and Artemis.

D. problem, the problem of finding the side of a cube having double the volume of a given cube (*i.e.* of finding the cube root of 2); so called from the answer of the oracle of Delos, that a plague raging at Athens should cease when Apollo's altar, which was cubical, should be doubled.

†Deli·bate, *v.* 1623. [f. L. *delibat-, delibare*; see DE- I. 2.] *trans.* To take a little of, taste, sip; also *fig.* -1660. Hence †**Deliba·tion**, a taste or slight knowledge *of* something; a portion extracted.

†Deli·ber, *v.* ME. [ad. L. *deliberare*, f. DE- I. 3 + *librare* to balance, weigh.] 1. *intr.* To deliberate, consider -1545. 2. *trans.* To determine, resolve -1580.

Deli·berant. *rare.* 1673. [ad. L. *deliberantem*.] One who deliberates.

Deliberate (dǐli·bĕrĕt), *a.* 1548. [ad. L. *deliberatus* pa. pple.] 1. Well weighed or considered; carefully thought out; done of set purpose; studied; not hasty or rash. 2. Of persons: Characterized by deliberation; considering carefully; not hasty or rash 1596. 3. Leisurely, slow, not hurried 1600.

1. Such as .. in stead of rage D. valour breath'd MILT. *P. L.* I. 554. 2. O these d. fooles *Merch. V.* II. ix. 80. 3. D. in his movements (*mod.*). Hence **Deli·berate-ly** *adv.*, **-ness.**

Deliberate (dǐli·bĕreⁱt), *v.* 1550. [f. L. *deliberat-*, ppl. stem of *deliberare*; see DELIBER.] †1. *trans.* To weigh in the mind; to consider carefully with a view to decision; to think over. (Now *to d. upon*.) -1829. 2. *intr.* To use consideration with a view to decision; to think carefully; to take time for consideration. Const. †*of, on, upon*, etc. 1561. †3. To resolve, determine -1633.

2. Two daies the King deliberated vpon an answer 1624. The woman that deliberates is lost ADDISON.

Deliberation (dǐlibĕrēⁱ·ʃən). ME. [a. F., ad. L. *deliberationem*.] 1. The action of deliberating; careful consideration with a view to decision. 2. The consideration and discussion of the reasons for and against a measure by a number of councillors 1489; †a conference -1648. †3. A resolution or determination -1653. 4. Deliberateness of action ME.; absence of hurry; leisureliness 1855.

1. To close tedious d. with hasty resolves JOHNSON.

2. The deliberations of the Royalist Convention MACAULAY. 4. Hee treds with great d. EARLE.

Deliberative (dǐli·bĕrǎtiv). 1553. [ad. L. *deliberativus.*]

A. *adj.* **1.** Pertaining to deliberation; having the function of deliberating. **2.** Characterized by deliberation 1659.

1. Erecting itself into a d. body BURKE. 2. The slower operations of d. reason KAMES. Hence **Deli·berative·ly** *adv.*, **-ness.**

†**B.** *sb.* A discussion of some question with a view to settlement; a deliberative discourse; a matter for deliberation –1650.

In deliberatiues the point is what is good and what is euill BACON.

Deli·berator. 1782. [ad. L.] One who deliberates.

Delible (de·lĭb'l), *a.* 1610. [ad. L. *delebilis*, f. *delere* (see DELETE and -BLE).] Capable of being deleted or effaced (*lit.* and *fig.*).

Delicacy (de·likăsi). ME. [f. DELICATE *a.*; cf. *obstinacy*, etc.]

I. The quality of being DELICATE. †**1.** The quality of being addicted to sensuous delights; voluptuousness, luxuriousness, daintiness –1741. †**2.** Luxury –1725; gratification –1667. †**3.** The quality of being delightful; beauty, daintiness, pleasantness –1650. **4.** Exquisite fineness of texture, substance, finish, etc.; soft or tender beauty 1586. **5.** Tenderness of constitution or health 1632. **6.** The quality or condition of requiring nice handling 1785. **7.** Exquisite fineness of feeling, observation, etc.; sensitiveness 1702. **8.** Exquisite nicety of skill, expression, touch, etc. 1675. **9.** A refined feeling of what is becoming, modest, or proper; sensitiveness; delicate regard for the feelings of others 1712. †**10.** Fastidiousness –1793.

2. He Rome brende for his delicasie CHAUCER. 4. A man .. in whom strong making took not away d., nor beauty fierceness SIDNEY (J.). 5. The d. of her sex 1632, of her Constitution ADDISON. 6. Negociations of the utmost d. (*mod.*). 7. The d. of his sense of right and wrong MACAULAY. 8. D. of expression 1683, of colouring DRYDEN. 9. A false D. is Affectation, not Politeness STEELE.

II. 1. A thing which gives delight; *esp.* a dainty viand 1450. **2.** A delicate trait, observance, or attention 1712. **3.** A nicety 1789.

Delicate (de·likět). ME. [ad. L. *delicatus, -a, -um*; of uncertain etymology; but assoc., if not orig. conn., w. *deliciæ* (DELICE).]

A. *adj.* **I.** = DAINTY *a.* **1.** Delightful, charming, pleasant, nice; *esp.* pleasing to the palate, dainty. †**2.** Characterized by sensuous delight; luxurious, voluptuous, effeminate –1737; of persons, given to pleasure or luxury –1640. †**3.** Self-indulgent, indolent –1601. †**4.** Softly reared; dainty; effeminate –1688. †**5.** Fastidious, nice, dainty –1796.

1. The ayre is d. *Macb.* I. vi. 10. A most fresh and d. creature *Oth.* II. iii. 20. D. meats M. PATTISON. 2. Soft and d. desires *Much Ado* I. i. 305.

II. 1. Fine or exquisite; soft, slender, or slight 1533; of colour, subdued 1822. **2.** Subtle in its fineness 1692. **3.** Tender, fragile 1568; feeble in constitution; weakly ME. **4.** *fig.* Requiring nice handling; critical; ticklish 1742.

1. D. gauze 1825, sea-ferns LOWELL, meats GEO. ELIOT, machines EMERSON. A d. blue light TYNDALL. 2. The most d. differences BAIN. 3. D. mural-Fruit EVELYN. In very d. health MACAULAY.

III. 1. Fine in power of perception, feeling, appreciation, etc.; finely sensitive 1533. **2.** Finely skilful 1589; †finely ingenious –1673. **3.** Finely sensitive to what is becoming, or to the feelings of others 1634; of actions, etc., characterized by feelings of delicacy 1818.

1. A d. ear RUSKIN, conscience MANNING. 2. So d. with her needle *Oth.* IV. i. 199. *Lear* IV. vi. 188. Hence **De·licate·ly** *adv.*, **-ness.**

B. *sb.* †**1.** One who is luxurious, dainty, or fastidious –1709. **2.** A thing that gives pleasure; *esp.* a choice viand, a delicacy 1450.

‖**Delicatesse** (delikăte·s). 1698. [F. *délicatesse*, f. *délicat.*] Delicacy.

‖**Delicatessen** (de:likăte·sən). orig. *U.S.* 1889. [G. *delikatessen*, ad. F. (see prec.).] Delicacies or relishes for the table; esp. *attrib.*, in *d. shop, store.* Also *ellipt.* = d. shop.

†**Deli·ce.** ME. [a. OF. *delice* masc. :—L. *delicium*, and OF. *delices* fem. pl. :—L. *deliciæ.*] **1.** Delight; *esp.* sensual or worldly pleasure –1685. **2.** A delight; a delicacy –1779. ¶Spenser stresses *de·lices.*

†**Deli·ciate,** *v. rare.* 1633. [Formed after OF. *delicier*, med.L. *deliciari.*] *intr.* To take one's pleasure, revel, luxuriate –1678.

Delicious (dǐli·ʃəs), *a.* ME. [a. OF., ad. late L. *deliciosus*; see DELICE and -OUS.] **1.** Affording great pleasure or enjoyment. (Now, less dignified than 'delightful'.) **2.** Highly pleasing to the bodily senses, *esp.* to the taste and smell ME. †**3.** Addicted to sensuous indulgence; voluptuous, luxurious –1681.

1. A green d. plain FARRAR. A d. joke KINGSLEY. 2. The soft d. air MILT. *P. L.* II. 400. 3. Festival and d. Tables JER. TAYLOR. Hence **Deli·ciously** *adv.* **Deli·ciousness,** the quality of being d. (now *esp.* to the senses); luxury.

Delict (dǐli·kt). 1523. [ad. L. *delictum*; see DELINQUENT.] A violation of law or right; an offence, a delinquency.

In flagrant d.: tr. L. *in flagrante delicto*, in the very act of committing the offence. Hence **De·li·ctual** *a.* of or belonging to a d. (*rare*).

Deligation (deligē·ʃən). 1661. [f. L. *deligare*, f. DE- I. 3 + *ligare* to bind.] *Surg.* †**a.** Bandaging; a bandage –1857. **b.** The tying of an artery, etc., with a ligature 1840. So **De·ligated** *ppl. a.* tied with a ligature.

Delight (dǐləi·t), *sb.* [ME. *delit*, a. OF., f. stem of *deliter* vb. The sp. after *light*, etc., is erroneous.] **1.** The fact or condition of being delighted; pleasure, joy, or gratification felt in a high degree. **2.** Anything which affords delight ME. **3.** Delightfulness. Now *poet.* ME. **4.** Cf. TURKISH *delight* 1870.

1. Sounds, and sweet aires, that giue d. and hurt not *Temp.* III. ii. 145. When he hath a delite in that that he doeth KINGESMYLL. 2. Daphnis, the Fields' D. DRYDEN. 3. She was a Phantom of d. WORDSW. Hence **Deli·ghtless** *a.* **Delightsome** *a.*, **-ly** *adv.*, **-ness.** (Now only literary.)

Delight (dǐləi·t), *v.* [ME. *deliten*, a. OF. *delitier* :—L. *delectare*; cf. DELICIOUS. The sp. after *light*, etc., is erroneous.] **1.** *trans.* To give great pleasure or enjoyment to; to please highly. Also *absol.* **2.** *intr.* (for *refl.*) To be highly pleased, take great pleasure, rejoice ME. Also *refl.* †**3.** *trans.* To enjoy greatly –1618.

1. But for I .. was so besy you to delyte CHAUCER. 2. The labour we d. in physicks paine *Macb.* II. iii. 55. I will d. my selfe in thy statutes *Ps.* cxix. 16. **Deli·ghtable** *a.* affording delight (*rare*). **Deli·ghter,** one who takes delight *in.* **Deli·ghtingly** *adv.*

Delighted (dǐləi·tĕd), *ppl. a.* 1603. [f. DELIGHT *v.* and *sb.* + -ED.] **1.** Highly pleased or gratified 1687. †**2.** Attended with delight; delightful –1747.

2. If Vertue no d. Beautie lack *Oth.* I. iii. 290. Hence **Deli·ghtedly** *adv.*

Delightful (dǐləi·tful), *a.* 1530. [f. DELIGHT (*delite*) *sb.* + -FUL.] **1.** Affording delight; highly pleasing, charming. †**2.** Experiencing delight; delighted *with* –1687.

1. Rimmon, whose d. Seat Was fair Damascus MILT. *P. L.* I. 467. D. books LOWELL. Hence **Delight·ful·ly** *adv.*, **-ness.**

Delimit (dǐli·mit), *v.* 1852. [a. F. *délimiter*, ad. L. *delimitare*, f. DE- I. 3 + *limitare*, f. *limitem* boundary.] *trans.* To mark or fix the limits of; to define, as a limit or boundary.

Delimitate (dǐli·mitĕ¹t), *v.* 1884. [f. ppl. stem of L. *delimitare.*] = prec. So **Deli·mitative** *a.* having the function of delimiting.

Delimitation (dǐlimitē·ʃən). 1836. [a. F. *délimitation.*] Determination of a limit or boundary; *esp.* of the frontier of a territory.

†**Deli·ne,** *v.* 1589. [ad. L. *delineare.* Cf. ALINE *v.*] = DELINEATE *v.* **1, 2.** –1734.

Delineate (dǐli·niˌĕ¹t), *v.* 1559. [f. ppl. stem of L. *delineare*; see DE- I. 3.] **1.** *trans.* To trace out by lines, trace the outline of. **2.** To trace in outline, sketch out; 'to make the first draught of' (J.) 1613. **3.** To draw, portray 1610. **4.** *fig.* To portray in words 1618.

1. To d. a triangle BERKELEY. 2. To d. a proposal MARVELL, a process REID, constitution JOWETT. 4. When I d. him without reserve BOSWELL. Hence **Deli·neable** *a.* capable of being delineated (*rare*). †**Deli·neament,** delineation. **Deli·neate** *ppl. a.* delineated (*arch.* or *poet.*).

Delineation (dǐliniˌē·ʃən). 1570. [ad. L. *delineationem.*] **1.** The action of tracing out by lines; *concr.* a drawing, diagram, or figure. **2.** The action of tracing in outline something to be constructed; a sketch, plan, rough draft. Usu. *fig.* 1581. **3.** Pictorial representation; *concr.* a picture 1594. **4.** The action of portraying in words 1603. †**5.** Lineal descent (*rare*) 1606.

2. I call it only a D., or rude draught WOLLASTON. 4. My delineations of the heart are from my own experience COWPER. var. †**Deli·neature.**

Delineator (dǐli·niˌĕ¹tǝɹ). 1774. [f. L. *delineare.*] **1.** One who delineates 1782. **2.** An instrument for tracing outlines. Hence **De·li·neatory** *a.* belonging to delineation.

†**Delini·tion.** *rare.* [irreg. f. L. *delinere* (ppl. stem *delit-*).] The action of smearing. H. MORE.

†**Deli·nquence.** 1682. [ad. L. *delinquentia*; see DELINQUENT *a.*] The fact of being a delinquent; culpable failure in duty –1832.

Delinquency (dǐli·ŋkwĕnsi). 1636. [f. as prec.] **1.** The quality of being a delinquent; failure in or violation of duty; guilt 1648. **2.** (with *pl.*) An act of delinquency; a fault; an offence, misdeed.

2. From these Delinquencies proceed greater crimes 1651.

Delinquent (dǐli·ŋkwĕnt). 1484. [ad. L. *delinquentem.*]

A. *adj.* Failing in, or neglectful of, a duty or obligation; guilty of a misdeed or offence 1603. Also *transf.*

B. *sb.* **1.** One who fails in duty or obligation; more generally, an offender 1484. **2.** *Eng. Hist.* A name for those who assisted Charles I or Charles II in levying war, 1642–1660.

2. Hereupon, they [the Commons] call'd whom they pleased, Delinquents CLARENDON.

†**De·liquate,** *v.* 1669. [f. ppl. stem of L. *deliquare*, f. DE- I. 3 + *liquare.*] **1.** *trans.* To melt down 1673. **2.** *intr.* To deliquesce –1800. Hence †**Deliqua·tion.**

Deliquesce (delikwe·s), *v.* 1756. [ad. L. *deliquescere*; see DE- I. 3.] **1.** *Chem.* To melt or become liquid by absorbing moisture from the air, as certain salts. **2.** *Biol.* To melt away, as some parts of fungi, etc., in the process of growth or of decay 1836. **3.** *gen.* To melt away (*lit.* and *fig.*). (Mostly *humorous.*)

1. This pot-ash .. deliquesces a little in moist air 1780.

Deliquescence (delikwe·sĕns). 1800. [f. DELIQUESCENT.] The process of deliquescing or melting away; the liquid or solution resulting from this process.

The English..hung to the seaside with red, perspiring faces, in a state of combustion and d. HAWTHORNE. So **Delique·scency,** the quality of being deliquescent (*rare*).

Deliquescent (delikwe·sĕnt), *a.* 1791. [ad. L. *deliquescentem.*] **1.** *Chem.* That deliquesces; melting or becoming liquid by absorption of moisture from the air. **2. a.** *Biol.* Melting away in the process of growth or decay 1874. **b.** *Bot.* Dissolved into ramifications, as the trunk of the White Elm, etc. 1866. **3.** *joc.* Dissolving (in perspiration) 1837.

1. Mild fixed alkali is..d. 1791. 3. The dusty and d. pedestrian 1876.

†**Deli·quiate,** *v.* 1782. [irreg. f. L. *deliquare*, or f. DELIQUIUM [2].] *intr.* = DELIQUATE 2, DELIQUESCE –1854. So †**Deliquia·tion.**

Deliquium [1] (dǐli·kwiǒm). *arch.* 1621. [L., f. *delinquere.*] **1.** Failure of the vital powers; a swoon. Also *fig.* †**2.** A failure of light, as in an eclipse –1671. **3.** Confused with next 1711.

†**Deli·quium** [2]. 1641. [L., f. *deliquare*; see DELIQUATE.] = DELIQUESCENCE –1823.

Deli·racy. *rare.* [f. DELIRATE; cf. *accuracy*, etc.] Delirium. SOUTHEY. So **Deli·rament,** †**Deli·rancy** (in same sense). †**Deli·rant** *a.* raving, mad.

†**Deli·rate,** *v. rare.* [f. ppl. stem of L. *delirare*; see DELIRE *v.*] *trans.* = DELIRIATE; *intr.* = DELIRE 2. HOLLAND.

Deliration (delirē·ʃən). 1600. [ad. L. *delirationem*; see DELIRE *v.*] Delirium, aberration of mind; madness. Also *fig.*

An earnestness..which..drove him into the strangest incoherencies, almost delirations CARLYLE.

†**Deli·re,** *v.* ME. [ad. L. *delirare*, f. DE- I. 2 + *lira* ridge, furrow.] **1.** *intr.* To go wrong, err –1633. **2.** To go astray from reason; to be delirious or mad, to rave –1675.

O how green Youth delires QUARLES. So †**De·li·rement** = *delirament.*

Deliriant (dĭli·riănt), *a.* 1883. [f. DELIRIUM.] *Med.* Having power to produce delirium. Also as *sb.* So **Delirifa·cient** *a.* and *sb.*

†**Deli·riate,** *v.* 1658. [f. as prec.] *trans.* To make delirious –1711.

Delirious (dĭli·riəs), *a.* 1599. [f. L. *delirium* + -OUS.] **1.** Affected with delirium, *esp.* as a result or symptom of disease; wandering in mind 1706. **2.** *transf.* and *fig.* Frantic, 'mad' 1599.

1. A d. patient 1871, manner 1809. 2. D. with delight 1855. The d. screech .. of a railway train CARLYLE. Hence **Deli·rious-ly** *adv.*, **-ness.**

Delirium (dĭli·riŏm). Pl. **-iums, -ia.** 1599. [a. L.; see DELIRE *v.*] **1.** A disordered state of the mental faculties resulting from disturbance of the functions of the brain, and characterized by incoherent speech, hallucinations, restlessness, and frenzied excitement. **2.** *fig.* Excitement as of one delirious; frenzied rapture; wildly absurd thought or speech 1650.

2. The gorgeous d. of gladiatorial shows GEO. ELIOT. **D. tremens.** [mod. Medical L. = trembling delirium.] A species of d. resulting from the abuse of alcohol, and characterized by tremblings and delusions.

†**Deli·rous,** *a.* 1656. [f. L. *delirus* + -OUS.] = DELIRIOUS –1722.

Delit, earlier f. DELIGHT. So †**Delitable** *a.* delectable. †**Delitably** *adv.* †**Deli·te** *a.* delightful (*rare*).

Delitescence (delite·sĕns). 1776. [f. DELITESCENT.] **1.** The condition of lying hid; concealment, seclusion. **2.** *Med.* **a.** The sudden disappearance of inflammation by resolution. **b.** = INCUBATION. var. **Delite·scency.**

Delitescent (delite·sĕnt, dĭ-), *a.* 1684. [ad. L. *delitescentem*, f. (ult.) DE- I. 2 + *latescere*, inceptive of *latere.*] Lying hid, latent.

Deli·ver, *a. Obs.* or *arch.* ME. [a. OF. *delivre, deslivre*, f. *delivrer*; see next.] †**1.** Free, at liberty. (ME. only.) **2.** Free from all impediments; active, nimble, quick in action ME. †**3.** Delivered (of a child) –1460.

2. Light and deliuer, voyde of al fatness 1472.

Deliver (dĭli·vəɹ), *v.*[1] ME. [a. F. *délivrer* :—late pop. L. *deliberare* (DE- I. 6), used in sense of L. *liberare* to liberate.] **1.** *trans.* To set free, liberate, rescue, save. Const. *from, out of*, †*of*. †**2.** To free, rid, divest, clear *of, from* –1677; *transf.* to dispel (pain, etc.); to relieve –1610. **3.** To disburden *of* the fœtus; in *pass.*, to give birth to a child or offspring. Rarely said of beasts. (The active is late.) ME. †**b.** *pass.* Of the offspring: To be brought forth (*lit.* and *fig.*) –1604. **4.** To unload. ? *Obs.* 1793. **5.** *refl.* To disburden *oneself of* what is in one's mind; to discourse ME. †**6.** To dispose of quickly; *refl.* to make haste –1530. **7.** To give up entirely, surrender, yield ME. **8.** To hand over to another's possession or keeping; *spec.* to give or distribute to the proper person or quarter; to present (an account, etc.). Const. *to*, or with dative. ME. **b.** *Law.* To give or hand over formally; see DELIVERY 1574. **9.** To give forth, send forth, emit; to discharge, launch; to cast, throw, project 1586. **10.** To give forth in words, utter, pronounce 1576. †**11.** *trans.* To declare, communicate, report, make known; to state, affirm; to set forth, describe –1800. **12.** *Pottery* and *Founding.* To set free from the mould. Also *intr.* 1782.

1. Fro temptacioun deliure me CHAUCER. 2. Phr. *To d. a gaol*: to clear it of prisoners in order to bring them to trial at the assizes. 3. She is, something before her time, deliuer'd *Wint. T.* II. ii. 25. There are many Euents in the Wombe of Time, which wilbe deliuered *Oth.* I. iii. 378. 5. To d. oneself against a bill STEELE. 7. See them deliuered ouer To execution *Rich. II*, III. i. 29. 8. To d. a message 1843, a letter 1881, bill of costs 1892, deed WILLIAMS. 9. To d. water 1633, a harpoon MEDWIN, an assault 1864. Phr. *To d. battle*: to begin an attack. 10. To d a course of lectures 1804, judgment 1882. Hence **Deli·verable** *a.* that can be delivered; to be delivered.

†**Deli·ver,** *v.*[2] var. of DELIBER *v.*

Deliverance (dĭli·vərăns). ME. [a. OF. *delivrance, desl-*, f. *delivrer.*] **1.** The act of setting free, or fact of being set free; liberation, release, rescue. †**2.** The bringing forth of offspring; delivery –1660. †**3.** The action of giving up; surrender –1568. †**4.** The action of handing over, transferring, or delivering; delivery –1631. †**5.** Sending forth, discharge 1626. †**6.** Utterance, enunciation, delivery –1609. †**7.** The action of setting forth in words, or that which is set forth; statement, narration, communication ME. **8.** *Sc. Law.* Judgement delivered; any judicial or administrative order ME.; verdict 1660. †**9.** Deliverness ME.

1. Our d. from the bondage of sin HOBBES. The next generall gaoles deliveraunce 1487. 4. *Writ of second d.* (Law): a writ for re-delivery to the owner of goods distrained or unlawfully taken. 7. The recorded deliverances of the Founder of Christianity MILL.

Deliverer (dĭli·vərəɹ). ME. [a. OF. *delivrere* :—late pop. L. *deliberator.*] **1.** One who sets free or releases; a liberator. **2.** One who hands over, commits, surrenders, etc. 1531. **3.** One who utters, sets forth, etc. (*rare*) 1597.

1. Thy great d., who shall bruise The Serpents head MILT. *P. L.* XII. 149. So **Deli·veress,** a female d. (*rare*). var. (techn.) **Deli·vero·r.**

Deli·verly, *adv. Obs.* or *arch.* ME. [f. DELIVER *a.*] **1.** Lightly, nimbly, quickly. **2.** Deftly 1530. ¶As *adj.* (erron.) SCOTT.

2. Carry it sweetly and d. 1612. So †**Deli·verness,** lightness, nimbleness, quickness.

Delivery (dĭli·vəri). 1480. [a. Anglo-Fr. *delivrée*, fem. sb. f. pa. pple. of *délivrer*; cf. *livery.*] †**1.** The action of setting free; release, rescue, deliverance –1784. **2.** The being delivered of, or bringing forth, offspring; childbirth 1577. Also *fig.* **3.** The act of giving up possession of; surrender 1513. **4.** The action of handing over anything to another; in *Law*, *esp.* the formal transfer of a deed by the grantor 1480. **5.** The act of delivering (a missile, a blow, etc.); throwing or bowling of a ball 1702. †**6.** 'Use of the limbs' (J.); action, bearing, deportment –1771. **7.** Utterance, or manner of utterance or enunciation 1581. †**8.** = DELIVERANCE 7. –1653.

3. The d. of the Castell HALL, of powder and stores 1780. 4. The d. of goods 1799, of letters 1838, a telegram 1879, possession CRUISE, a deed R. COKE. 6. The duke had the neater limbs and freer d. WOTTON (J.). 7. A grave, serious d. PEPYS.

Dell[1] (del). [ME. *delle* :—WGer. **daljâ-*, deriv. of **dalo-* DALE; root meaning 'deep or low place'.] †**1.** A deep hole, a pit –1783. **2.** A small deep natural hollow or vale ME.

2. A green and silent spot, amid the hills, A small and silent d. COLERIDGE.

Dell[2] (del). *Rogues' Cant. arch.* 1567. A wench.

‖**Della Crusca** (de·l,la kru·ska). [It. *Accademia della Crusca*, lit. Academy of the bran or chaff.] The name of an Academy established at Florence in 1582, mainly to sift and purify the Italian language; whence its name, and its emblem, a sieve. Hence **Della-Cru·scan** *a.* of or pertaining to the Academy della Crusca, or its methods; also, applied to an artificial school of English poetry, started at the end of the 18th c.; *sb.* any one of these.

Delocalize (dĭlōu·kălaiz), *v.* 1855. [DE- II. 1.] To detach from its locality, or from local limitations.

‖**Deloo** (dĭlū·). 1861. [Native name (Dor language).] A N. African antelope, akin to the duykerbok.

Delph, var. of DELF.

Delphian (de·lfiăn). 1625. [f. *Delphi* place name.] Of or relating to Delphi, a town of Phocis, in Greece, and to the sanctuary and oracle of Apollo there; hence, of or relating to the Delphic Apollo; and *transf.* oracular. So **De·lphic, De·lphical** *a.*

Delphin (de·lfin). ME. [a. L. *delphin, delphinus*, a. Gr. δελφίν; see DOLPHIN, DAUPHIN.]

†**A.** *sb.* **1.** = DOLPHIN –1633. **2.** *Chem.* Short for *delphinin*: A neutral fat found in the oil of several species of dolphin; called also *phocenin.*

B. *adj.* **1.** [attrib. use of L. *delphini* in phr. *ad usum Delphini.*] Of or pertaining to the Dauphin of France, and to the edition of the Latin classics, prepared 'for the use of the dauphin', son of Louis XIV 1775. **2.** *Chem.* A bad form of DELPHINE, DELPHININE.

De·lphine, *a.* and *sb.* Var. of DELPHIN *a.*, DELPHININE *a.*, DELPHININE *sb.*

Delphinic (delfi·nik), *a.* [f. L. *delphinus*; see DELPHIN *sb.* 2.] In *d. acid*, an acid discovered in dolphin-oil; it is identical with active valeric acid. A salt of it is a **De·lphinate.**

Delphinine (de·lfinəin), *sb.* 1830. [f. Bot.L. *Delphinium* the genus Larkspur.] *Chem.* A poisonous alkaloid obtained from the seeds of *Delphinium Staphisagria* or *Stavesacre.* Called also **Delphi·nia.**

De·lphinine, *a.* Of the nature of a dolphin: in *Zool.*, of or pertaining to the *Delphininæ* or sub-family of Cetacea, containing the Dolphins and Porpoises.

‖**Delphinium** (delfi·niŏm). 1664. [Bot.L., a. Gr. δελφίνιον larkspur, dim. of δελφίν (so named from the form of the nectary).] *Bot.* A genus of plants, N.O. *Ranunculaceæ*, comprising the common Larkspur and other species. In horticultural use the name for the cultivated species and varieties.

De·lphinoid. [ad. Gr. δελφινοειδής.] *Zool.*

A. *adj.* Like or related to a dolphin; belonging to the *Delphinoidea*, a division of the Cetacea, which includes the dolphins and seals.

B. *sb.* A member of the *Delphinoidea.*

Delphinoidine (delfinoi·dəin). 1883. [f. as DELPHININE.] *Chem.* An amorphous alkaloid obtained from the same source as delphinine.

‖**Delphinus** (delfəi·nŏs). 1672. [L., = 'dolphin'.] In *Zool.*, the cetacean genus containing the Dolphin, etc.; in *Astron.*, an ancient northern constellation, figured as a dolphin.

Delta (de·ltă). ME. [Gr. δέλτα (ad. Phœnician *daleth*).] **1.** The fourth letter of the Greek alphabet, having the form of a triangle (Δ), and the power of D. **2.** A Δ-shaped tract of alluvial land enclosed and traversed by the diverging mouths of a river; as the d. of the Nile, the Ganges, etc. 1790. **3.** *Electr.* In a three-phase alternator, the triangular figure formed by connecting the three wires of the transmitting circuit to the junction of the three coils; *attrib.* as *d. connexion, current* 1902.

Comb. **d.-metal,** an alloy of copper, zinc, and iron named in allusion to its *three* constituents; **d. rays** (or *δ-rays*), rays of low penetrative power emitted by radioactive substances. **Deltaic** (deltēi·ik) *a.* pertaining to, or forming a d.; of the nature of a d.

‖**Deltidium** (delti·diŏm). 1851. [mod.L. dim. of Gr. δέλτα, in reference to its shape.] *Conch.* The triangular space between the beak and the hinge of brachiopod shells.

Deltohedron (deltohī·drŏn). 1879. [f. Gr. δελτο-, as comb. f. next + ἕδρα base.] *Crystall.* A solid figure the surface of which is formed by twenty-four deltoids.

Deltoid (de·ltoid), *a.* (*sb.*) 1741. [mod. ad. Gr. δελτοειδής delta-shaped.] **1.** Like the Greek letter Δ in shape; triangular; *esp.* in *Bot.*, of a leaf 1753. **2.** Of the nature of the delta of a river 1837. So **Deltoi·dal** *a.*

1. *D. muscle* (Anat.): the large muscle of triangular shape which forms the prominence of the shoulder.

B. *sb.* The deltoid muscle. Also in L. form *deltoides, deltoideus* 1758.

The d., which caps the shoulder like an epaulette O. W. HOLMES.

‖**Delubrum** (dĭliū·brŏm). 1665. [L., f. *deluere* to cleanse + -BRUM.] **1.** A temple, shrine, or sanctuary. **2.** *Eccl. Archit.* A church furnished with a font; a font 1665.

†**Delu·ce, dely·s.** 1450. Short for *flower de luce* (F. *fleur de lis*, OF. *lys*), *i. e.* lily-flower, the ensign of the Bourbons –1594.

Delude (dĭliū·d), *v.* 1450. [ad. L. *deludere*; see DE- I. 4.] †**1.** *trans.* To play with (any one) to his injury or frustration; to mock; to defraud *of* –1697. **2.** To befool the mind or judgement of, so as to cause what is false to be accepted as true; to cheat, deceive, beguile; to impose upon 1450. †**3.** To frustrate the purpose of; to elude –1680.

2. As arrant imposters as ever deluded the credulous world T. BROWN. 3. The 7. of June she againe deluded us, after two houres chase SIR T. HERBERT. Hence **Delu·der.**

Deluge (de·liudʒ), *sb.* ME. [a. F. *déluge*, early ad. L. *diluvium* (see DILUVIUM).] **1.** A great flood or overflowing of water, an inundation. (Often used hyperbolically.) **2.** *spec.* The great Flood in the time of Noah ME. **3.** *fig.* and *transf.* ME.

1. Together with earthquakes, deluges also, and inundations of the sea HOLLAND. 3. Drowned in the d. of errour EDEN. A fiery D., fed With ever-burning Sulphur unconsum'd MILT. *P. L.* I. 68.

Deluge (de·liudʒ), *v.* 1649. [f. the sb.] **1.** *trans.* To flow over in a deluge; to flood, inundate. Also *absol.* (Often used hyperbolically.) **2.** *fig.* and *transf.* 1654.

1. Sufficient to d. the World, and drown Mankind DE FOE. Deluged in tears MAD. D'ARBLAY. 2. At length Corruption, like a gen'ral Flood .. Shall d. all POPE. Deluged with pamphlets W. IRVING.

†**Delu·mbate**, *v. rare.* 1609. [f. ppl. stem of L. *delumbare*; see DE- I. 6.] To lame, maim, emasculate –1624.

‖**Delundung** (de·ləndʊŋ). 1840. [Native name.] The weasel-cat of Java and Malacca, belonging to the civet family.

Delusion (dǐl'ū·ʒən). ME. [ad. L. *delusionem*, f. *deludere*.] **1.** The action of deluding (see DELUDE *v.* 1, 2); the fact or condition of being deluded. **2.** Anything that deceives the mind with a false impression; a deception; a fixed false opinion with regard to objective things, *esp.* as a form of mental derangement 1552. †**3.** Evasion 1606.

1. God shall send them strong d., that they should believe a lie 2 *Thess.* ii. 11. 2. A juglers d. 1638. The poor fellow was only labouring under a d. C. GEIKIE. Hence **Delu·sional** *a.* of the nature of, or characterized by, d. **Delu·sionist**, one given to deluding; one given up to delusions.

Delusive (dǐl'ū·siv), *a.* 1605. [f. L. *delus-*, *deludere*; see -IVE.] **1.** Having the attribute of deluding, characterized by delusion; deceptive. **2.** Of the nature of a delusion 1645.

1. D. appearances JOHNSON, promises PRESCOTT. 2. Of what d. worth The bubbles we pursue LONGF. Hence **Delu·sive·ly** *adv.*, **-ness.** So **Delu·sory** *a.* of deluding quality; delusive.

De luxe (1819) sumptuous; see LUXE.

Delve (delv), *sb.* 1590. [Partly a var. of DELF *sb.*, partly f. DELVE *v.*] **1.** That which is delved; excavation, pit, den; = DELF *sb.*[1] I. **2.** A depression; a wrinkle 1811. **3.** An act of delving 1869.

1. The very tigers from their delves Look out MOORE. Logs and roots innumerous He gathered in a d. upon the ground SHELLEY.

Delve (delv), *v.* [Com. WGer. vb., orig. strong: OE. *delfan.*] **1.** *trans.* To dig; to turn up (ground) with a spade OE. Also *fig.* and *transf.* **2.** To make by digging, excavate (*arch.*) OE. Also *transf.* and *fig.* †**3.** To put in by digging –1735. **4.** To dig *up* or *out of* (*arch.* or *dial.*) OE. †**5.** To penetrate as by digging –1450. **6.** *absol.* or *intr.* To labour with, or as with, a spade; to dig; to drudge (*arch.* or *poet.*, and *dial.*) OE. **7.** Of a road, etc.: To dip sharply 1848.

1. They delved the soil, they wove the fleece 1845. *fig.* What's his name, and Birth? .. I cannot d. him to the roote *Cymb.* I. i. 28. 2. *fig.* Time .. delues the paralels in beauties brow SHAKS. *Sonn.* lx. 6. Where frigid learning delves In Aldine folios O. W. HOLMES. Hence **De·lver**, one who delves (*lit.* and *fig.*).

Dem, *v.*; formerly **demn.** ME. Minced form of DAMN; so demd for *damned.*

Demagnetize (dīmæ·gnĕtəiz), *v.* 1842. [DE- II. 1.] **1.** To deprive of magnetic quality. †**2.** To free from mesmeric influence; to demesmerize 1850.

1. Hot air traversing the discs and rolls demagnetizes the discs 1887. Hence **Dema:gnetiza·tion.**

Demagogic,-al (demăgǫ·gik, -gǫ·dʒik, -ăl), *a.* 1734. [ad. Gr. δημαγωγικός, f. δημαγωγός DEMAGOGUE, + -AL.] Of, pertaining to, or like a demagogue.

Demagogism, -goguism (de·măgǫgiz'm). 1824. [f. DEMAGOGUE + -ISM.] The practice and principles of a demagogue.

Demagogue (de·măgǫg), *sb.* 1648. [ad. Gr. δημαγωγός a popular leader, a leader of the mob, f. δῆμος + ἀγωγός.] **1.** In ancient times, a leader of the people as against other parties in the state 1651. **2.** In bad sense: A leader of a popular faction, or of the mob; an unprincipled or factious mob orator or political agitator.

2. He despised the mean arts and unreasonable clamours of demagogues MACAULAY. Hence **De·ma·goguery** (*U.S.*), demagogism. **De·magogy**, the action or quality of a d.

Demain(e, early ff. DOMAIN, DEMESNE.

Demand (dǐmɑ·nd), *sb.* ME. [a. F. *demande*, f. *demander.*] **1.** An act of demanding or asking by virtue of right or authority; a peremptory request or claim; also *transf.*, that which is demanded. Also *fig.* **2.** The action of demanding 1602. **3.** *Law.* The action or fact of demanding in legal form; a legal claim 1485. **4.** 'The calling for a thing in order to purchase it' (J.); in *Pol. Econ.* a call for a commodity on the part of consumers, combined with the power to purchase; called also *effectual demand.* Correl. to *supply.* 1776. **5.** An urgent requirement 1790. **6.** A request; a question (*arch.*) ME. **7.** *attrib.*, as *d. note*, a note payable on d.; also, a formal request for payment 1866.

1. A desire that Whitelocke would putt down his demands in writing 1654. *fig.* A d. of nature BUTLER. 2. Phr. *On* (†*at*) *d.*: (payable) on request, claim, or presentation. 4. The English, finding a great d. for tobacco in Europe 1780. Phr. *In d.*: sought after, in request. 5. The demands of a profession destroy the elasticity of the mind JOWETT.

Demand (dǐmɑ·nd), *v.* ME. [a. F. *demander* :—L. *demandare* (f. DE- I. 3 + *mandare* to commission, order).] **1.** *trans.* To ask for with legal right or authority 1489. **2.** *spec.* in *Law.* To make formal claim to (real property) as the rightful owner 1485. **3.** To ask for peremptorily, imperiously or urgently; †to ask (*esp.* in transl. from Fr., etc.) 1484. **4.** *fig.* Said of things: To call for of right, or as necessary 1703. **5.** To ask authoritatively to know 1548; †to ask (a person) to inform one (*of, how*, etc.) –1722. †**6.** With cogn. obj.: To ask (a question, etc.) –1605. **7.** *intr.* To ask, make inquiry ME.

1. I d. my Liberty, being freed by the jury 1670. 3. They demanded a King HOBBES. The offenders are demanded to justice FULLER. 4. Government .. demands skill, patience, energy, long and tenacious grip MORLEY. 5. Then the prieste shall demaunde the name of the child *Bk. Com. Prayer.* *Cymb.* III. vi. 92. 7. Heare .. I will d. of thee, and declare thou vnto me *Job* xlii. 4. Hence **Dema·ndable** *a.* that may be demanded or claimed. **Dema·ndant**, one who demands; *spec.* in *Law*, the plaintiff in a real action; *gen.* any plaintiff or claimant. **Dema·nder.** †**Dema·nderess**, a female demandant.

Dema·ndative, *a.* [f. L. *demandat-* ppl. stem + -ATIVE.] Of the nature of a legal claim; made by the demandant. BENTHAM.

Demarcate (dī·mɑɹkeɪt), *v.* 1816. [f. DEMARCATION.] To mark out the limits of; to mark off *from*; to determine, as a boundary or limit; to define (*lit.* and *fig.*).

To d. a region 1882, a frontier 1884, Reproduction from Growth LEWES.

Demarcation (dīmɑɹkē¹·ʃən). Also **demarkation.** 1727. [ad. Sp. *demarcacion*, f. (ult.) *de-* = DE- I. 3 + *marcar* to MARK.] The action of marking the limits of, or of marking off; delimitation; separation. Usu. in phr. *line of d.* Also *fig.*

As early as the 4th of May (1493) the celebrated bull was signed by Pope Alexander VI, which established 'to all eternity' the line of d. between the Spanish and Portuguese possessions 1849. The lines of d. between the species LYELL.

Demarch (dī·mɑɹk). 1642. [ad. L. *demarchus*, a. Gr., f. δῆμος + ἀρχός.] The chief magistrate of an Attic deme. In mod. Greece: The mayor of a commune. So **De·marchy**, the office of a d.; a popular government; the municipal body of a Greek commune.

‖**Démarche** (demaɹʃ). (In mod. Dicts. **demarch.**) 1658. [F., f. *démarcher*; see DE- I. 3. Now treated as F.] Walk, step; proceeding, manner of action.

Demark (dǐmā·ɹk), *v.* 1834. [f. DEMARCATION.] = DEMARCATE.

Dematerialize (dīmătī°·riăləiz), *v.* 1884. [DE- II. 1.] *trans.* To deprive of material character or qualities; *intr.* to become dematerialized.

†**Deme**, *sb.*[1] [OE. *dǣma, dēma*, f. OTeut. *dôm-* doom.] A judge, arbiter, ruler –ME.

Deme (dīm), *sb.*[2] 1833. [ad. Gr. δῆμος.] **1.** A township or division of ancient Attica. In mod. Greece: A commune. **2.** *Biol.* Any undifferentiated aggregate of cells, plastids, or monads 1883.

†**Demea·n**, *sb.* 1450. [f. DEMEAN *v.*[1]] **1.** Bearing, behaviour, demeanour –1756. **2.** Treatment (of others). SPENSER.

1. Another Damsell .. modest of demayne SPENSER.

Demean (dǐmī·n), *v.*[1] ME. [a. OF. *demener* = Pr. *demenar*, a Rom. deriv. of DE- *pref.* + *menare*, F. *mener* to lead, conduct, etc. :—L. *minare*, orig. (= *minari*) to threaten, in post-cl. L. 'to drive or conduct' cattle, and, later, ships, men, etc.] †**1.** *trans.* To conduct; to manage, deal with, employ –1640; to express (sorrow, etc.) –1607. **2.** *refl.* To comport oneself. (The only existing sense.) ME. Also *fig.* of things.

1. As our obdurat Clergy have with violence demean'd the matter MILT. 2. To d. himself like a Gentleman SHAFTESB. To have a vigilant eye how Bookes d. themselves as well as men MILT. Hence †**Demea·nance**, demeanour. var. †**Demeine.**

Demean (dǐmī·n), *v.*[2] 1601. [f. DE- I. 1 + MEAN *a.*, prob. after *debase.*] *trans.* To lower; esp. *refl.* to lower or humble oneself.

Could a girl so far d. herself as to ask for love BLACK. To d. herself to a common carpenter GEO. ELIOT.

Demean, Demeane, earlier ff. DEMESNE.

Demeanour (dǐmī·nəɹ). Also **-or** (*U.S.*). 1494. [f. DEMEAN *v.*[1] + ? *-ure* :—L. *-atura*, or F. *-er* of the infinitive, taken subst. Cf. BEHAVIOUR.] **1.** Conduct, mode of proceeding, management; practice, behaviour. **2.** Manner of comporting oneself towards others; bearing. (The usual current sense.) 1509.

1. A commission .. to examine Lord Shaftsb[ury's] demeanours 1677. 2. With Goddess-like d. forth she went MILT. *P. L.* VIII. 59. Gravity and almost apathy of d. J. H. NEWMAN.

‖**Démêlé** (demē·le). 1661. [Fr.; = quarrel, etc.] Debate, contention, quarrel.

Demembration (dǐmembrē¹·ʃən). 1597. [ad. med.L. *demembrationem.*] The cutting off of a limb; mutilation; dismemberment. (Chiefly in *Sc. Law.*)

‖**Demembré.** *Her.* 1727. [Fr.] = DISMEMBERED.

Dement (dǐme·nt), *a.* (*sb.*) 1560. [a. F. *dément*, ad. L. *dementem*; see DE- I. 6.] Demented. *Obs.* or *arch.* *sb.* One demented 1888.

Dement (dǐme·nt), *v.* 1545. [ad. L. *dementare*, f. *demens* DEMENT *a.*] To put out of one's mind, drive mad, craze. So **Deme·ntate** *v.* (in same sense); **Dementa·tion**, the action of dementing; the being demented. Hence **Deme·nted** *ppl. a.* crazed; affected with dementia. **Deme·ntedness.**

‖**Dementia** (dǐme·nʃiă). 1806. [L., f. *demens* DEMENT *a.*] **1.** *Med.* [tr. F. *demence* (Pinel).] A species of insanity characterized by failure or loss of the mental powers. **2.** *gen.* Infatuation 1877. var. †**De·mency.**

†**Deme·ntie**, *sb.* 1594. [a. obs. F. *dementie* = mod.F. *démenti.*] The giving any one the lie. [Now only as F., *démenti* (demãnti).]

Demerara (demĕrē°·ră, demĕrā·ră). 1848. The name of a region of British Guiana, used to designate a kind of raw cane-sugar, originally and chiefly brought from Demerara, the crystals of which have a yellowish-brown colour.

†**Deme·rge**, *v.* 1610. [ad. L. *demergere*; DE- I. 1.] *trans.* To plunge, immerse –1669.

Demerit (dǐme·rit), *sb.* ME. [a. F. *démérite*, or ad. L. *demeritum*; see DE- I. 3 (in Rom. app. taken privatively).] †**1.** Merit, desert; a deserving act –1731. **2.** Desert in a bad sense: quality deserving blame; ill-desert; censurable conduct: opp. to *merit* 1509; †a blameworthy act (usu. in *pl.*) –1637. Also *transf.* of things. †**3.** That which is merited (*esp.* for ill doing); desert –1728.

1. Your demerites are so ferre aboue all prayses of man UDALL. 2. Mine is the merit, the d. thine DRYDEN. *transf.* The merits or demerits of hereditary royalty LEWIS.

Demerit (dǐme·rit), *v.* *Obs.* or *arch.* 1538. [f. L. *demerit-* ppl. stem.] †**1.** *trans.* To merit, deserve (*esp.* evil) –1711. †**2.** To disparage –1643. **3.** To fail to merit 1654. †**4.** *intr.* To merit blame, deserve ill –1734.

1. To d. pains 1538, the fauour of God T. TAYLOR, blame 1619. 4. For he was .. the kings servant already, and had not demerited NORTH. Hence **De·merito·rious** *a.* ill-deserving; †undeserving (*rare*).

Demersal (dǐmɔ̄·ɹsăl), *a.* 1889. [f. as next + -AL[1] 1.] Sinking to or living at the bottom of the sea.

†**Demerse** (dǐmɔ̄·ɹs), *v.* 1662. [f. L. *demers-*; see DEMERGE.] *trans.* To immerse, submerge –1691. Hence **Deme·rsion** (*rare*) 1692.

Deme·smerize, *v.* 1855. See DE- II. 1.

Demesne (dǐmē¹·n, dǐmī·n). ME. [a. Anglo-F. *demeyne, -eine, -eigne, -ene*, later *demesne* = OF. *demeine*, etc., orig. the adj. *demenie, de-*

meigne, etc. used subst. :—L. *dominicus*, *-um* of or belonging to a lord or master, f. *dominus*. See DOMAIN. Usu. pronounced dǐmī·n; but dǐmē·ⁱn is historically preferable; cf. *domain.*]

I. Possession. **1.** *Law.* Possession (of real estate) as one's own ME. †**2.** *transf.* and *fig.* Possession; dominion, power -1747.

1. *To hold in d.* (*tenere in dominico*), i.e. in one's own hands as possessor by free tenure. (See II. 1.) *In his d. as of fee* (*in dominico suo ut de feodo*): in possession as an estate of inheritance. (Not applied to things incapable of physical possession.) *In ancient d.*: see below.

II. An estate possessed. **1.** An estate held in demesne: land possessed and held by the owner himself, and not held of him by any subordinate tenant. **b.** In mod. use, The land immediately attached to a mansion, and held along with it for use or pleasure; the park, chase, home-farm, etc. ME. **2.** The territory or dominion of a sovereign or state; a DOMAIN ME.; landed property; usu. *pl.* estates, lands 1584. **3.** *fig.* A district, region, territory; DOMAIN 1592. †**4.** *pl.* Means -1650.

1. *Royal D.*: the Crown-lands. *Ancient d.*: a d. possessed from ancient times; *spec.* the ancient d. of the crown, *i.e.* that property which belonged to the king at the Norman Conquest, as recorded in Domesday-book. Hence *tenants in ancient d.*, etc. 2. A Gentleman.. Of faire demeanes *Rom. & Jul.* III. v. 182. 3. One wide expanse.. That deep-browed Homer ruled as his d. KEATS.

III. *attrib.* or as *adj.* Of or pertaining to a demesne (II. 1); demesnial, as *d. lands* ME.

Demesnial (dǐmē·niăl, -mī·niăl), *a.* 1857. [f. prec., after *manorial*, etc.] Of or pertaining to a demesne.

Demi (de·mi), *sb.*, *a.*, *pref.* ME. [F. :—L. *dimidium*. At first written separately; now almost always hyphened.]

A. As separate word. (Formerly also **demy**.)

I. *adj.* (or *adv.*) Half; half-sized, diminutive. Now *rare*.

†**II.** as *sb.* A half. Chiefly *ellipt.* -1761.

B. Demi- in combination: half, semi-, half-sized, curtailed.

1. In *Heraldry*, etc., as *d.-lion*, *-man*; *d.-belt*, etc.; **d.-vol**, a single wing of a bird used as a bearing.

2. In *Costume*, as *d.-robe*, *-train*; †**d.-crown**, a coronet.

3. In *Arms* and *Armour*, as **d.-brassard**, **-garde-bras**, a piece of plate-armour for the upper arm at the back; **-chamfron**, a chamfron covering part only of the face of the horse; **-cuirass**, a corslet of iron, which only partly protected the body, front and back; **-jambe**, a piece covering the front of the leg; **-mentonniere**, a chin-piece for the tilt covering the left side only. **-pauldron**, the smaller form of shoulder-plate used in the end of the 15th c.; **-pike** = HALF-PIKE; **-placard**, **-placate**, = *demi-cuirass*; **-suit**, the suit of light armour used in and after the 15th c.; **-vambrace**, a piece of plate-armour protecting the outside of the fore-arm.

4. In *Artillery*, as *d.-bombard*; †**d.-cannon**, a gun formerly used, of about 6½ inches bore; †**-culverin**, a cannon formerly in use, of about 4½ inches bore; †**-hake**, †**-haque**, a smaller form of HAQUE or HACKBUT.

5. In *Fortif.*, as **d.-bastion**, a work with one face and one flank, like half a bastion; **-caponier**, a construction across the ditch, having but one parapet and glacis; **-distance** (of polygons), the distance between the outward polygons and the flank; **-gorge**, half of the gorge or entrance to the bastion, taken from the angle of the curtain to the centre of the bastion; **-parallel**, short entrenchments thrown up between the main parallels of attack, to protect the guards of the trenches; **-revetment**, a revetment or retaining wall for the face of a rampart, which is carried only as high as the cover in front, leaving the rest as an earthen rampart at the natural slope.

6. In *Military tactics*, the *Manège*, etc., as **d.-brigade**, a regiment of infantry and artillery, under the first French Republic (Littré); **-volte**, one of the seven artificial motions of a horse: a half-turn made with the fore legs raised.

7. In *Weights, Measures, Coins*, etc., as †*d.-barrel*, †*-groat*; **d.-ame**, half an AAM; **-farthing**, a copper coin of Ceylon, of the value of half a farthing.

8. With names of stuffs, etc., as †**d.-castor**, a mixture of beaver's and other fur; a hat made of this.

9. *Mus.* †**d.-cadence**, an imperfect cadence, a half-close; †**-crochet**, a quaver; †**-ditone**, a minor third (see DITONE); †**-quaver**, a semiquaver; **-semiquaver**, a note of half the value of a semiquaver; the symbol for this note, resembling a quaver, but with three hooks; **-semitone**, a quarter-tone; **-tone** = SEMITONE.

10. With names of material or geometrical figures: Half-, semi-; as **d.-circle**, a semicircle; an instrument of semicircular form for measuring angles; *d.-column*, *-cylinder*, etc.; **-octagonal**, of the shape of half an octagon; †**d.-sphere** = hemisphere.

11. With ordinary class-nouns, as †**d.-island**, †**-isle**, a peninsula; †**-male**, a eunuch; **-tint** (? *Obs.*), a half tint; *d.-wolf*.

12. With nouns of action, state, etc., as **d.-metamorphosis** (*Entom.*), partial metamorphosis, hemimetabolism; **-toilet**, half evening (or dinner) dress.

13. With adjs.: as *d.-Norman*, *-official*; **d.-equitant** (*Bot.*) = OBVOLUTE. (*Semi-* is now usual with most of these.)

14. With vbs., etc.: as †*d.-deify*, †*-natured*.

Demi-bath (de·mibɑþ). 1847. [tr. F. *demi-bain*.] A bath in which the body can be immersed only up to the loins.

Demigod (de·migǫd). 1530. [DEMI- 11: tr. L. *semideus*.] *Mythol.* A being partly of divine nature, as the offspring of a god and a mortal, or a man raised to divine rank; a minor or inferior deity. So **De·migo·ddess** (*rare*).

†**De·migrate**, *v.* 1623. [f. L. *demigrat-*, *demigrare*; see DE- I. 2.] *intr.* To migrate -1651. Hence †**Demigra·tion**.

Demijohn (de·miˌdʒǫn). 1769. [In Fr. *dame-jeanne*, lit. 'Dame Jane'; cf. *Bellarmine*. The Eng. form is a perversion. The Arabic (*damajānah*, etc.) is unfixed in form, and prob. from Levantine use of It. *damigiana*.] A large bottle with bulging body and narrow neck, usually cased in wicker- or rush-work.

Demi-lance (de·miˌlɑns). 1489. [a. F. *demie lance*; cf. DEMI- 3.] **1.** A lance with a short shaft, used in the 15th and 16th centuries. **2.** A light horseman armed with a demi-lance. Hence **Demi-la·ncer** = DEMI-LANCE 2.

Demilune (de·miˌlūn), *sb.* (*a.*) 1727. [a. F., in 16-17th c. *demie lune* half moon; cf. DEMI- 10.] †**1.** *gen.* A half-moon, a crescent 1734. **2.** *Fortif.* An outwork resembling a bastion with a crescent-shaped gorge, to protect a bastion or curtain 1727. **3.** *Physiol.* A granular mass of protoplasm, of semilunar form, found in the salivary glands 1883.

B. *adj.* Semilunar 1885.

‖**Demi-mondaine** (dəmiˌmoṅdēn). 1894. [Fr.; f. next.] A woman of the demi-monde.

‖**Demi-monde** (dəmiˌmoṅd, de·miˌmǫnd). 1855. [Fr.; coined by Dumas the younger.] The class of women of doubtful reputation and social standing, upon the outskirts of society. (Improp. extended to courtesans in general.)

†**Demi-o·stade**, **-ostage**. 1537. [a. OF., f. *demi*, *-e* + *ostade* worsted.] A stuff: app. half-worsted half-linen, linsey-woolsey -1882.

Demi-pique (de·miˌpīk), *a.* (*sb.*) 1695. [DEMI- 3.] **A.** *adj.* Of a saddle: 'Half-peaked'; having a peak of about half the height of that of the older war-saddle. **B.** *sb.* A demi-pique saddle. Hence **De·mi-piqued** *a.* half-peaked.

†**De·mi-pu·ppet**. [DEMI- 10.] A dwarf puppet. *Temp.* V. i. 36.

Demi-rep (de·miˌrep). 1749. [f. DEMI- 11 + '*rep*, for *reputation*'. Cf. also *reputable*.] A woman of doubtful reputation or chastity.

That character which is vulgarly called a demirep, that is to say, a woman.. whom every body knows to be what no body calls her FIELDING. Hence **Demi-re·pdom**.

‖**De·mi-sang**. 1797. [Fr.] *Law.* Half-blood.

Demise (dǐməi·z), *sb.* 1509. [app. of Anglo-Fr. origin: f. OF. *desmettre*, *démettre* (pa. pple. fem. *desmise*, *demise*). In Eng., the *de-* is treated as DE- I. 1.] **1.** *Law.* Conveyance or transfer of an estate by will or lease. **2.** Transference or devolution of sovereignty; usu. in phr. *d. of the crown* 1689. **3.** Transferred to the death or decease which occasions the demise; hence, pop., = Decease, death 1754. Also *fig.*

2. The King James.. had by d. abdicated himself and wholly vacated his right EVELYN. 3. The early d. of this favourite friend of science 1799.

Demise (dǐməi·z), *v.* 1480. [f. prec. sb.] **1.** *Law.* To give, grant, convey, or transfer by will or by lease. **b.** To convey or transfer (a title or dignity); *esp.* said of the transmission of sovereignty, as by abdication or death 1670. †**2.** *gen.* To convey; to 'lease' -1660. †**3.** To dismiss -1615. **4.** *intr.* To resign the crown; to die, decease (*rare*) 1727.

1. To let and demyse fermes ther for the terme of vij yere and undir 1495. To d. the crown 1892. 2. What Honour, Canst thou d. to any childe of mine *Rich. III*, IV. iv. 247.

De·mi-sea·son, *a.* 1890. [ad. F. *demi-saison* (also used).] Of costume: Of a style intermediate between that of the past and that of the coming season.

Demi-semi (de·miˌse·mi), *a.* 1805. [f. DEMI- 13 + SEMI half.] *lit.* Half-half, *i.e.* quarter: usu. a contemptuous diminutive.

Demi-sheath (de·miˌʃīþ). [Cf. DEMI- 3.] *Entom.* A half-sheath; *i.e.* one of the two channelled organs of which the tubular sheaths, covering the ovipositors or stings of insects, are composed.

Demiss (dǐmi·s), *a.* 1572. [ad. L. *demissus*, pa. pple. of *demittere*.] †**1.** Submissive, humble; also in bad sense, Abject, base -1649. †**2.** Hanging down, downcast -1634. **3.** *Bot.* Depressed, flattened.

1. Like a most demisse And abiect thrall SPENSER. With demisse reverence 1612. Hence †**Demi·ss-ly** *adv.*, **-ness**.

Demission[1] (dǐmi·ʃən). 1638. [ad. L. *demissionem*; see DEMISS.] **1.** Abasement, degradation. Now *rare*. †**2.** Dejection, depression -1719. †**3.** *lit.* Lowering -1741.

2. Heaviness and d. of spirit NORRIS.

Demi·ssion[2]. 1577. [a. F. *démission*, in OF. *desmission*, answering to late L. **dismissio*, for *dimissio*, whence DIMISSION, DISMISSION. In Eng. the *de-* is taken as DE- I.] **1.** The action of putting away or letting go from oneself, giving up, or laying down (*esp.* a dignity or office). **2.** Dismission (*rare*) 1811.

1. The queenes d. of hir crowne HOLINSHED.

†**Demi·ssive**, *a.* 1622. [f. L. *demiss-*, *demittere*.] = DEMISS 1, 2. -1763. Hence **Demi·ssively** *adv.*

†**Demi·ssory**, *a.* Var. of DIMISSORY; cf. DEMIT *v.*[2]

Demit (dǐmi·t), *v.*[1] 1556. [ad. L. *demittere*; see DE- I. 1.] **1.** To send, put, or let down; to lower 1646. †**2.** *fig.* To bring down; to humble, abase -1688.

2. By taking on him the nature of man.. he demitted, or humbled himselfe 1656.

Demi·t, *v.*[2] 1529. [ad. F. *démettre*, in OF. *desmettre*, f. *des-*, *dé-* :—L. *dis-* + *mettre*; taking the place of L. *dimittere*; cf. DISMISS. Chiefly *Sc.*] **1.** To dismiss (*arch.*). †**2.** To put away, let go -1678. **3.** To give up, lay down (an office, etc.); to abdicate 1567. Also *absol.* †**4.** To send out -1756.

3. The Ritualists will neither submit nor d. 1880.

Demiurge (de·miǝɹdʒ, dī·mi-). 1678. [ad. Gr. δημιουργός (Latinized *demiurgus*), *lit.* public or skilled worker, f. δήμιος + -εργος.] **1.** A name for the Maker of the world, in the Platonic philosophy; in the Gnostic system, conceived as a being subordinate to the Supreme Being, and sometimes as the author of evil. **2.** *Gr. Hist.* A magistrate in certain Greek states, and in the Achæan league 1844. Hence **Demiu·rgic**, †**-al** *a.* of or pertaining to the D. or his work; creative.

Demi-vill. *rare.* ME. [AF. *demie vile*.] *Constit. Hist.* A half-vill or town; the half of a vill as a political unit.

Demobilize (dīmōᵘ·biləiz), *v.* 1882. [DE- II. 1.] To reduce from a mobilized condition; to disband. Abbrev. **demob** (dīmǫ·b) 1920. Hence **Demo·biliza·tion**, the action of demobilizing, reduction of forces to a peace footing.

Democracy (dǐmǫ·krăsi). 1574. [a. F. *démocratie* (-sī), a. med.L. *democratia*, a. Gr., f. δῆμος + -κρατια in comb. = κράτος rule.] **1.** Government by the people; that form of government in which the sovereign power resides in the people, and is exercised either directly by them or by officers elected by them. In mod. use often denoting a social state in which all have equal rights. 1576. **b.** A state or community in which the government is vested in the people as a whole 1574. Also *fig.* **2.** That class of the people which has no hereditary or special rank or privilege; the common people 1827. **3.** *U.S. politics.* The principles, or the members, of the Democratic party 1825.

1. Those ancient whose resistless eloquence Wielded at will that fierce democraty MILT. *P. R.* IV. 269.

Democrat (de·moˌkræt). 1790. [a. F. *démocrate*, f. *démocratie*, after *aristocrate*.] **1.** An adherent or advocate of democracy; *orig.*

opp. to *aristocrat* in the French Revolution of 1790. **2.** *U.S.* A member of the Democratic party; see DEMOCRATIC 2. 1798. **3.** *U.S.* A light four-wheeled cart with several seats, one behind the other 1873. Also *attrib.* (*rare*).

1. Napoleon, in his first period, was a true d. CARLYLE.

Democratic (demoˌkræ·tik), *a.* 1602. [a. F. *démocratique*, ad. med.L. *democraticus*, a. Gr., f. δημοκρατία.] **1.** Of the nature of, or characterized by, democracy; advocating or upholding democracy. **2.** *U.S. politics.* (With capital D.) Name of the political party originally called *Anti-Federal* and afterwards *Democratic-Republican*, which favours strict interpretation of the Constitution, and the least possible interference with local and individual liberty; opp. to the *Republicans* (formerly called *Federals* and *Whigs*). **b.** Pertaining to the Democratic party, as 'a D. measure'. 1800.

1. Aristocratick gouernment nor Democratick pleas'd 1602. Hence **Democra·tical** *a.* (in sense 1); **-ly** *adj.*

Democratism (dǐmǫ·krætˌiːz'm). 1793. [f. DEMOCRAT + -ISM.] Democracy as a principle or system. So †**Demo·cratist**, a democrat.

Democratize (dǐmǫ·krătəiz), *v.* 1798. [a. F. *démocratiser*, f. *démocrate*, *démocratie*.] To make or become democratic. Hence **Demo·cratiza·tion**, the action of democratizing.

Democritean (dǐmǫ·kritī·ăn), *a.* 1617. [f. L. *Democriteus* (Gr. Δημοκρίτειος) + -AN.] Of, pertaining to, or after the style of Democritus, the Greek philosopher (known as 'the laughing philosopher'), or of his atomistic or other theories. So **Democri·tic**, †**-al** *a.* in same sense; †**Demo·critism**, the practice of Democritus in laughing at everything.

Demo·ded, *ppl. a.* 1887. [f. F. *démodé* + -ED.] That has gone out of fashion. So ‖**Démodé** (demǭ·de, ‖*demode*) [Fr.], demoded.

‖**Demodex** (dī·modeks). 1876. [mod.L.; f. Gr. δημός fat + δήξ wood-worm.] *Zool.* A genus of parasitic mites, including *D. folliculorum*, which infests the hair follicles and sebaceous follicles of man and domestic animals.

Demogorgon (dī·mogǭ·ɹgən). 1590. [late L., of uncertain origin. First mentioned by the Scholiast (Lactantius or Lutatius Placidus, ?*c* 450) on Statius *Theb.* iv. 516, as the great nether deity invoked in magic. Hence perh. a disguised Oriental name.] Name of a mysterious and terrible infernal deity.

Orcus and Ades, and the dreaded name Of D. MILT. *P. L.* II. 965.

Demography (dǐmǫ·grăfi). 1880. [f. Gr. δῆμος + -γραφια (see -GRAPHY).] That branch of anthropology which treats of the statistics of births, deaths, diseases, etc. Hence **Demo·grapher**, one versed in d. **Demogra·phic** *a.* of or pertaining to d.

Demoid (dī·moid), *a.* 1884. [ad. Gr. δημοειδής, f. δῆμος.] Used of a type of animal or plant which by its commonness, etc. characterizes a region or a period of time.

‖**Demoise·lle.** 1520. [mod.F. (dəmwazę·l); see DAMSEL.] **1.** A young lady, a maid, a girl. **2.** *Zool.* The Numidian Crane (*Anthropoides virgo*); so called from its elegance of form 1687. **3.** *Zool.* A dragon-fly 1844.

Demolish (dǐmǫ·liʃ), *v.* 1570. [a. F. *démoliss-*, *démolir*, f. L. *demoliri*, f. DE- I. 6 + *moliri*, f. *moles* mass.] **1.** *trans.* To destroy by disintegration of the fabric of; to pull or throw down, reduce to ruin. †**b.** *intr.* with passive sense (*rare*) –1706. **2.** *fig.* To make an end of. Also *joc.* 1620.

1. To d. a partition wall 1641, the images in cathedrals MACAULAY. 2. To d. a doctrine BERKELEY. Hence **Demo·lishable** *a.* **Demo·lisher.** **Demo·lishment** (now *rare*), the act of demolishing; demolished state or (*pl.*) †remains.

Demolition (demǫli·ʃən, dī-). 1549. [a. F. *démolition*, ad. L. *demolitionem*; see prec.] **1.** The action of demolishing; the fact or state of being demolished 1610; *pl.* demolished remains, ruins 1638. **2.** *fig.* Destruction, overthrow 1549.

1. The d. of the mass-house by Lincoln's Inn JOHNSON. 2. The d. of rights and privileges 1775. Hence **Demoli·tionist**, one who aims at or advocates d.

Demon (dī·mən). Also **dæmon.** ME. [In form, and in sense I, a. L. *dæmon* (med.L. *demon*); in other senses, put for L. *dæmonium*, Gr. δαιμόνιον, used for 'evil spirit'.] **1.** *Gr. Myth.* (= δαίμων): A being of a nature intermediate between that of gods and men; an inferior divinity, spirit (including the souls of deceased persons). Often written *dæmon* for distinction. 1569. **b.** Sometimes, An attendant spirit; a genius ME. **2.** An evil spirit 1706. **b.** *gen.* A malignant being of superhuman nature; a devil ME. Also *transf.* (of persons, animals, or agencies personified), and *fig.* Also *attrib.*

1. In Homer, there is scarcely any distinction between gods and dæmons GROTE. **b.** O Anthony!.. Thy Dæmon, that thy spirit which keepes thee, is Noble, Couragious, high vnmatchable *Ant. & Cl.* II. iii. 19. 2. They sacrificed unto demons, which were no God R. V. *Deut.* xxxii. 17. *transf.* The grim d. of a bull-dog 1821. *fig.* The d. of intemperance (*mod.*). Hence **De·moness**, a female d.; a she-devil. **Demo·nial** *a.* of or relating to, or of the nature of, a d. or demons (*rare*). **Demonia·lity**, the nature of demons; demons collectively (*rare*). **Demo·nian** *a.* = demonial. †**Demo·nianism**, the doctrine of demoniacal possession. †**Demo·niast**, one who has dealings with demons, or with the devil (*rare*).

Demonetization (dǐmǫ·nǐtəizē·ʃən). 1852. [f. next.] The action of demonetizing, or condition of being demonetized.

Demonetize (dǐmǫ·nǐtəiz), *v.* 1852. [ad. mod.F. *demonétiser*, f. DE- I. 6 + L. *moneta* money.] *trans.* To deprive of standard monetary value; to withdraw from use as money.

Demoniac (dǐmōu·niæk). ME. [ad. late L. *demoniacus*, a. Gr. type *δημονιακός, f. δαιμόνιον; see DEMON.]

A. *adj.* **1.** Possessed by an evil spirit. **2.** Of or pertaining to demons 1642. **3.** Befitting a demon; devilish 1820. **4.** = DEMONIC 2. 1844.

1. I hold him certeinly demoniack CHAUCER. 2. The Demoniack legion MILT. 3. D. scorn HAZLITT. 4. The d. element in man 1844. So **Demoni·acal** *a.* (in senses 1–3).

B. *sb.* **1.** One possessed by an evil spirit ME. †**2.** *Eccl. Hist.* One of an Anabaptist sect, who hold that the devils will be saved at the last. (Dicts.)

1. And helyth the demonyackes or madde folk CAXTON.

Demonic (dǐmǫ·nik), *a.* Also **dæm-.** 1662. [ad. L. *demonicus*, a. Gr. δαιμονικός; see DEMON.] **1.** Of, belonging to, or of the nature of, an evil spirit; devilish. **2.** Of, relating to, or of the nature of, supernatural power or genius = Ger. *dämonisch* (Goethe). (Usu. spelt *dæmonic* for distinction.) 1798.

1. D. delusions 1738. 2. The Dæmonic Dickens: as pure an instance of genius as ever lived FITZGERALD. var. **Demo·nical** *a.* (in sense 1). Now *rare.*

Demonifuge (dǐmǫ·nifiūdʒ). *nonce-wd.* 1790. [f. L. *dæmon* (DEMON) + -FUGE.] A charm against demons.

Demonism (dī·mŏniz'm). Also **dæ-.** 1669. [f. DEMON.] Belief in, or doctrine of, demons.

A belief in d. and witchcraft 1891. So **De·monist**, a believer in, or worshipper of, demons.

Demonize (dī·mŏnəiz), *v.* 1821. [f. med.L. *dæmonizare.*] **1.** *trans.* To make into, or like, a demon. **2.** To subject to demoniacal influence 1864. Hence **De:moniza·tion**, the action of making into, or like, a demon.

Demono-, bef. a vowel **demon-**, repr. Gr. δαιμονο-, comb. f. Gr. δαίμων DEMON: as in **Demono·cracy**, the rule of demons. **Demo·nograph(er**, a writer on demons. **Demono·graphy.** **Demono·later**, a worshipper of demons. **Demono·latry.** †**Demono·machy**, fighting with a demon. †**Demono·magy**, magical art relating to demons. †**De·monoma:ncy**, divination by the help of demons. **De:monomama·nia**, a mental disease in which the patient fancies himself possessed by a demon. So **Demono·pathy.** †**Demo·nomist**, a believer in, or worshipper of, demons. †**Demo·nomy**, demon-worship.

Demonology (dīmǒnǫ·lŏdʒi). Also **dæ-.** 1597. [f. Gr. δαίμων + -λογια.] That branch of knowledge which treats of demons, or of beliefs about demons; a treatise on demons. So **Demono·loger**, **Demono·logist**, one versed in d. **Demonolo·gic**, **-al** *a.*; **-ly** *adv.*

†**Demono·manie.** 1623. [a. F. *démonomanie.*] Foolish belief in demons –1638.

De-monopolize (dǐmǫnǫ·pǒləiz), *v.* 1878. [DE- II. 1.] To destroy the monopoly of, withdraw from monopoly.

Demonry (dī·mənri). 1851. [f. DEMON + -RY.] Demoniacal influence or practices.

Demonship (dī·mənʃip). *rare.* 1638. [f. as prec.] The rank or condition of a demon.

Demonstrable (dǐmǫ·nstrăb'l, de·mǫnstrăb'l), *a.* ME. [ad. L. *demonstrabilis*; see DEMONSTRATE.] **1.** Capable of being shown or made evident; *occas.* = Evident (*obs.*). **2.** Capable of being proved conclusively 1551.

2. It being so mathematically d. that [etc.] H. MORE. Hence **Demonstrabi·lity**, **Demo·nstrableness**, d. quality or condition. **Demo·nstrably** *adv.*

†**Demo·nstrance.** ME. [a. OF., f. stem of L. *demonstrantem.*] **1.** A pointing out; indication –1704. **2.** Demonstration, proof –1646.

†**Demo·nstrate**, *ppl. a.* 1509. [ad. L. *demonstratus.*] Demonstrated –1707. As *sb.* A demonstrated proposition 1655.

Demonstrate (dǐmǫ·nstreˈt, de·mǫnstreˈt), *v.* 1552. [f. L. *demonstrat-*, *demonstrare*; see DE- I. 3. For the stress see CONTEMPLATE.] †**1.** *trans.* To point out, indicate; to set forth –1684. †**2.** To manifest, show, display –1803. **3.** To describe and explain by help of specimens, or by experiment; also *absol.* to teach as a demonstrator 1683. **4.** To show or make evident by reasoning; to establish the truth of by deduction; to prove indisputably 1571. Also *absol.* Of things: To prove. 1601. **5.** *intr.* To make a military (or other) demonstration 1827.

3. The anatomist demonstrates, when he points out matters of fact cognisable by the senses 1856. 4. Archimedes demonstrates..that the proportion of the Diameter unto the Circumference is as 7 almost unto 22 SIR T. BROWNE. 5. The habit of demonstrating with bands and banners BRYCE.

Demonstration (demǫnstrē·ʃən). ME. [ad. L. *demonstrationem.*] †**1.** The action of demonstrating; exhibition, manifestation; an instance of this –1668. **b.** An illustration; a sign –1684. **2.** A display, show, manifestation 1556. **3.** The action or process of making evident by reasoning; proving indisputably by deduction or by practical proof; also (with *pl.*) a series of propositions proving an asserted conclusion ME. **b.** That which serves as proof ME. **4.** *Rom. Law.* The statement of the cause of action by the plaintiff at the outset 1864. **5.** The exhibition and explanation of specimens and operations as a method of instruction. Also *attrib.* 1807. **6.** *Mil.* A show of military force or of offensive movement 1835. **7.** A public manifestation of feeling; often taking the form of a procession and mass-meeting 1839.

2. Did your letters pierce the queen to any d. of grief *Lear* IV. iii. 12. 3. A d. is either *Direct* or *Indirect.* In the latter case we prove the conclusion by disproving the contradictory, or shewing that the conclusion cannot be supposed untrue JEVONS. Phr. *To d.*: conclusively. **b.** The Circulation of the Blood is a D. of an Eternall Being 1659. 6. He made last year a d. against Julalabad 1835. 7. Then, besides 'ovations', there are 'demonstrations', the Q. E. D. of which is not always very easy to see 1861. Hence **Demonstra·tional** *a.* of or pertaining to d. **Demonstra·tionist**, one who takes part in a d.

Demonstrative (dǐmǫ·nstrătiv), *a.* and *sb.* ME. [a. F. *démonstratif*, *-ive*, ad. L. *demonstrativus.*]

A. 1. Having the function or quality of demonstrating; making evident; illustrative. **2.** *Rhet.* Setting forth with praise or censure 1553. **3.** Provable by demonstration 1612. **4.** Characterized by outward expression (of the feelings, etc.) 1819. **5.** Teaching by the exhibition and description of examples or experiments (*rare*) 1814.

1. A d. proof..of the fecundity of His wisdom and Power RAY. Logic..is a purely d. science BOWEN. 2. The oracion d. standeth either in praise or dispraise of some one man, or of some one thyng 1553. 3. A d. truth 1798. 4. Englishmen are much less d. than the men of most other European nations DARWIN.

B. *sb. Gram.* An adjective or pronoun having the function of pointing out the particular thing referred to, as *that*, *this*, etc. 1530. Hence **Demo·nstrative·ly** *adv.*, **-ness.**

Demonstrator (de·mǫnstrēˈtəɹ). 1611. [ad. L.; partly after F. *demonstrateur.*] **1.** One who or that which demonstrates, points out, or proves. **2.** An assistant to a professor of science, who does the practical work of exhibiting and describing examples or experiments 1684. **3.**

One who takes part in a public demonstration 1870. Hence **Demo·nstratory** *a.* that has the property of demonstrating.

Demorage, obs. f. DEMURRAGE.

Demoralization (dǐmǫ·răləizē¹·ʃən). 1809. [f. next.] The action of demoralizing; demoralized state.

His army is in a state of utter d. and disorganization 1877.

Demoralize (dǐmǫ·răləiz), *v.* 1793. [a. F. *démoraliser* (f. DE- II. 1 + MORAL *a.*), a word of the French Revolution.] **1.** *trans.* To corrupt the morals or moral principles of. **2.** To lower or destroy the MORALE of: applied *esp.* to an army, etc.; also *transf.* 1848.

2. The long series of English victories had..demoralized the French soldiery GREEN. The market had become demoralized (*mod.*).

‖**Demos** (dī·mǫs). Occas. **demus,** *pl.* **-i.** 1776. [a Gr. δῆμος.] **1.** = DEME² 1. **2.** The people or commons of an ancient Greek state; hence, the populace: often personified 1831.

2. Celtic D. rose a Demon, shriek'd and slaked the light with blood TENNYSON.

Demosthenic (demǫsþe·nik), *a.* 1846. [ad. Gr. Δημοσθενικός.] Of or pertaining to Demosthenes, the Athenian orator; like Demosthenes or his style of oratory. So **Demosthe·ne·an, Demosthe·nian** *adjs.*

Demot (dī·mǫt). [a. Gr. δημότης, f. δῆμος.] A member of a Greek deme. GROTE.

Demotic (dǐmǫ·tik), *a.* 1822. [ad. Gr. δημοτικός; see prec.] **1.** Of or belonging to the people: *spec.* applied to the popular and simplified form of the ancient Egyptian script (as dist. from the *hieratic*): called also *enchorial.* Also *absol.* = The d. character or script. **2.** *gen.* Popular, vulgar. Somewhat *rare.* 1831.

†**Demou·nt,** *v.* 1533. [ad. F. *démonter.*] To dismount.

Dempne, obs. f. DAMN.

Dempster (de·mᵖstəɹ). [ME. *demestre,* in form fem. of *demere* DEEMER; see -STER. Cf. DEEMSTER.] †**1.** A judge; a DEEMSTER (2). (ME. only.) †**2.** *Sc.* 'The officer of a court who pronounced doom or sentence definitively as directed by the clerk or judge' (Jamieson).

†**Demulce** (dǐmɒ·ls), *v.* 1530. [ad. L. *demulcere;* see DE- I. 1.] To soothe or mollify; to soften or make gentle -1831. var. (irreg.) †**Demu·lceate.**

Demulcent (dǐmɒ·lsĕnt). 1732. [f. L. *demulcentem.*] *adj.* Soothing, lenitive, mollifying, allaying irritation. *sb.* A demulcent medicine.

†**Demu·lsion.** [f. L. *demuls-* ppl. stem.] The action, or a means, of soothing. FELTHAM.

Demur (dǐmɒ̄·ɹ), *sb.* ME. [a. F. *demeure* vbl. sb.; see next.] †**1.** Delay, waiting -1675; abode -1673. †**2.** Hesitation; pause; state of irresolution -1824. **3.** The act of demurring 1639. †**4.** *Law.* = DEMURRER¹ -1713.

3. After a little d., he accepted the offer DICKENS.

Demur (dǐmɒ̄·ɹ), *v.* ME. [a. F. *demeurer,* in OF. *demorer, -mourer* :—pop.L. *demorare* = cl.L. *demorari,* f. DE- I. 3 + *morari* to delay.] †**1.** *intr.* To linger, tarry, wait -1653; to abide -1550. †**2.** *trans.* To cause to tarry; to put off, delay -1682. †**3.** *intr.* To hesitate; to suspend action; to pause in uncertainty -1818. **b.** *trans.* To hesitate about -1730. **4.** *intr.* To make scruples or difficulties; to take exception *to* (occas. *at, on*). (The current sense.) 1639. **b.** *trans.* To object to 1827. **5.** *Law.* (*intr.*) To put in a DEMURRER 1620.

1. Yet durst they not demoure vpon the campe NICOLLS. **3.** King Edwine demurred to embrace Christianity FULLER. **b.** Let none d. Obedience to her will 1730. **4.** My host at first demurred..but I insisted TYNDALL. **b.** I d. the inference 1876.

Demure (dǐmiūᵊ·ɹ), *a.* ME. [a. OF. *meur,* now *mûr.* The *de-* is obscure.] †**1.** Calm, still. (ME. only.) **2.** Sober, grave, serious; reserved in demeanour ME. **3.** Affectedly or constrainedly grave or decorous 1693.

2. A face d. and sage BALE. Sober, steadfast, and d. MILT. **3.** This Gentleman, and his d. Psalm-singing Fellows SHADWELL. Demurest of the tabby kind GRAY. Hence **Demu·re·ly** *adv.,* **-ness.**

†**Demu·re,** *v. rare.* [f. prec.] *intr.*? To look demurely. *Ant. & Cl.* IV. xv. 29.

Demu·rity. *rare.* 1483. [Answers to OF. *meurté;* cf. DEMURE.] **1.** Demureness. **2.** A demure character or person. (Cf. *oddity.*) LAMB.

Demurrable (dǐmɒ̄·răb'l), *a.* 1827. [f. DEMUR *v.* or *sb.* + -ABLE.] That may be demurred to; to which exception may be taken.

Demurrage (dǐmɒ·rĕdʒ). 1641. [a. OF. *demorage,* f. *demorer;* see DEMUR *v.*] †**1.** Stay; delay; hesitation; pause-1823; detention-1817. **2.** *Comm.* **a.** Detention of a vessel by the freighter beyond the time agreed on; the payment made in respect of this 1641. **b.** A charge for detention of railway trucks 1858. **c.** A charge of 1½*d.* per ounce made by the Bank of England in exchanging gold or notes for bullion 1875.

2. If the Delay was occasioned by the Merchant, he shall be obliged to pay for the Days of D., to the Captain MAGENS.

Demurral (dǐmɒ̄·răl). *rare.* 1810. [f. DEMUR *v.* + -AL.] The action of demurring; demur.

Demurrant (dǐmɒ·rănt). 1529. [a. OF. *demourant;* see DEMUR *v.*]

A. *adj.* †**1.** Abiding, staying, resident -1587. †**2.** Delaying 1633.

B. *sb.* One who demurs, or puts in a demurrer 1809.

Demurrer¹ (dǐmɒ·rəɹ). 1533. [a. Anglo-Fr. = OF. *demourer,* pres. inf. (see DEMUR *v.*) used as sb.; cf. *user;* see -ER⁴.] **1.** *Law.* A pleading which, admitting the facts as stated in the opponent's pleading, denies that he is legally entitled to relief, and thus stops the action until this point be determined 1547; *transf.* = DEMUR *sb.* 3. 1599. †**2.** = DEMUR *sb.* 2. -1645.

Demurrer² (dǐmɒ̄·rəɹ). 1711. [f. DEMUR *v.* + -ER¹.] One who demurs.

Demy (dimǝi·), *sb.* (and *a.*) Pl. **demies.** ME. [Early f. DEMI- half, retained for the separate word. The uses are all elliptical.] †**1.** A gold coin current in Scotland in the 15th century: app., orig., the half-mark. †**2.** 'A short close vest' (Fairholt) -1599. **3.** *Paper Manuf.* A certain size of paper. (Properly *adj.*; *ellipt.* as *sb.* = demy paper.) 1546.

D. printing paper measures 17½ × 22½ inches; d. writing paper 15½ × 20.

4. A foundation scholar at Magdalen College, Oxford (so called because their 'commons' was orig. half that of a Fellow) 1486. Hence **Demy·ship,** a scholarship at that College.

Den (den), *sb.*¹ [OE. *dęnn,* habitation of a wild beast. Cf. MDu. *dan(n* m. forest, abode of wild beasts, etc. The same root *dan-* appears in *dean,* OE. *dęnu* (:—*dani-*) vale: the root-meaning is uncertain.] **1.** The lair or habitation of a wild beast. **2.** A cavern ME. **3.** *transf.* and *fig.* A place of retreat or abode ME.; a room unfit for human habitation 1837; a small room or lodging in which a man can be alone (*colloq.*) 1771. **4.** A dingle. *Sc. local.* 1552. †**5.** *Anat.* A cavity, hollow -1683.

1. Then the beastes goe into dennes: and remaine in their places *Job* xxxvii. 8. **2.** [They] lurked in dennes and wholes secretly HALL. **3.** A d. of thieves *Matt.* xxi. 13. The frightful dens of some of the Manchester operatives 1840. A small d. for me in particular SCOTT.

Den², in *good den;* see GOOD-DEN.

Den (den), *v.* ME. [f. DEN *sb.*¹] *intr.* To live or dwell in (or as in) a den; to hide oneself in a den 1610.

The sluggish saluages, that d. belowe G. FLETCHER.

†**Dena·me,** *v.* 1555. [DE- I. 3.] To denominate -1640.

Denar, denare (dī·năɹ, dǐnā·ɹ, -ēᵊ·ɹ). 1547. [var. of ME. *dener, denere* (from OF. *dener*), DENIER, assim. to L. *denarius.*] A coin: the Roman DENARIUS; the It. *denaro;* the East Indian DINAR, q.v.

Denarcotize; see DE- II. 1 and *narcotize.*

‖**Denarius** (dǐnēᵊ·riɒs). Pl. **-ii** (-i,əi). ME. [L., f. *d. numus* denary coin, coin containing ten (asses), f. *deni* ten by ten.] **1.** An ancient Roman silver coin, orig. of the value of ten asses (about eightpence) 1579. **2.** A gold coin (*d. aureus*), worth 25 silver denarii 1661. **3.** A (silver) pennyweight ME. ¶ In English reckoning used for 'penny', and abbreviated *d.*

†**Denary, denarie,** *sb.*¹ 1449. [ad. L. *denarius.*] = DENARIUS, the Roman penny -1674.

Denary (dī·nări), *a.* and *sb.*² 1577. [ad. L. *denarius* containing ten.]

A. *adj.* Having ten as the basis of reckoning; decimal 1848.

†**B.** *sb.* **1.** The number ten; a decad -1682. **2.** A tithing 1577.

Denationalize (dǐnæ·ʃənăləiz), *v.* 1807. [a. F. *dénationaliser* (a word of the French Revolution); see DE- II. 1.] *trans.* To deprive (a person, etc.) of nationality; to divest (a country) of national character.

The attempt to..d. the education of the infant poor 1839. Hence **Dena·tionaliza·tion,** the action of denationalizing, denationalized condition.

Denaturalize (dǐnæ·tiŭrăləiz), *v.* 1800. [DE- II. 1.] **1.** To deprive of its original nature; to make unnatural. **2.** To deprive of the status and rights of a natural subject or citizen; the opposite of *naturalize* 1816.

1. The lyrical ballad..is almost always denaturalized by culture PALGRAVE. **2.** The Duque d'Aveiro, having been degraded and denaturalized previous to condemnation KEATINGE. Hence **Dena·turaliza·tion,** the action of denaturalizing; denaturalized condition.

Denature (dǐnē¹·tiŭɹ), *v.* 1685. [a. F. *dénaturer;* see DE- I. 6.] †**1.** *trans.* To render unnatural. **2.** To alter (*e.g.* tea, etc.) so as to change its nature 1878.

2. The denatured nature of London milk 1878.

Denay, obs. var. of DENY *v.* and *sb.*

Dendrachate, etc.; see under DENDRO-.

Dendriform (de·ndrifǭɹm), *a.* 1847. [f. Gr. δένδρον + -FORM.] Of the form of a tree; branching; arborescent.

Dendrite (de·ndrəit). Also in L. form **dendrites** (dendrəi·tīz), pl. **dendritæ** (-tī). 1727. [ad. Gr. δενδρίτης of or pertaining to a tree, f. δένδρον. In F. *dendrite.*] **1.** A tree- or moss-like marking or figure, found on or in some stones or minerals; a stone or mineral so marked. **2.** A crystalline growth of branching or arborescent form, as of some metals under electrolysis 1882. Hence **Dendri·tic, -al** *a.* resembling d.; tree-like; having tree-like markings.

Dendro-, bef. a vowel **dendr-,** comb. f. Gr. δένδρον tree: as in

De·ndrachate [see ACHATE *sb.*¹], a variety of agate with tree-like markings. **De·ndrocœl, -cœle** *a.* [Gr. κοιλία], *Zool.* having a branched or arborescent intestine; belonging to the division *Dendrocœla* of Turbellarian worms; so **Dendrocœ·lan, Dendrocœ·lous** *adjs.,* in same sense. **De:ndrocola·ptine** *a.* [Gr. κολάπτειν to peck], *Ornith.* belonging or allied to the genus of birds *Dendrocolaptes,* or S. American tree-creepers. **Dendrode·ntine,** 'the form of branched dentine seen in compound teeth, produced by the interblending of the dentine, enamel, and cement' (*Syd. Soc. Lex.*). **De·ndrodont** [Gr. ὀδοντ-] *a.,* having, or consisting of, teeth of dendritic internal structure; *sb.* a dendrodont fish. **De·ndrolite,** a petrified or fossil tree or part of a tree. **Dendro·meter,** an instrument for measuring trees. **Dendro·philous** *a.,* tree-loving; in *Bot.* growing on or twining round trees. **De·ndrostyle,** *Zool.* one of the four pillars by which the syndendrium is suspended from the umbrella in the *Rhizostomidæ.*

Dendrobe (de·ndrōᵘb). 1882. [ad. mod.L. *Dendrobium.*] Name of a genus of epiphytal orchids.

Dendrodic (dendrǫ·dik), *a.* 1854. [f. Gr. δενδρώδης + -IC.] Of the form of a tree; *dendritic.* So **De·ndroid, -al** *a.*

Dendrology (dendrǫ·lŏdʒi). 1708. [f. DENDRO- + Gr. -λογια.] The study of trees; the part of botany which treats of trees. So **Dendrolo·gic, -al, Dendro·logous** *adjs.* belonging to d.; **Dendro·logist,** one versed in d.

Dene (dīn), *sb.*¹ Var. of DEAN *sb.*² a (wooded) vale.

Dene (dīn), *sb.*² Also **den.** ME. [?] A bare sandy tract by the sea; a low sand-hill.

†**De·negate,** *v.* 1623. [f. L. *denegat-* ppl. stem.] To deny -1652. Hence **Denegation,** †refusal; denial. So **Dene·gatory** *a.* (*rare*).

Dene-hole, Dane-hole (dī·n-, dē¹·n,hōᵘl). Also Danes' hole. 1768. [app. f. *Dane,* ME. *Dene,* OE. *Dęne* + HOLE. Cf. OE. *Dena-lagu,* ME. *Dene-lawe,* mod. *Danes' law, Dane law.*] The name of a class of excavations, found in chalk-formations in England and France, consisting of a shaft sunk to the chalk, and there widening out into one or more chambers, used probably for concealment in time of war.

Dengue (deŋ·ge). Also **d.-fever, denga.** 1847. [Ult., a Swahili word, *dinga, dyenga, denga* 'sudden cramp-like seizure', pop. identified on its introduction to the West Indies in 1827 with the Sp. *dengue* 'prudery'. Called by the negroes *dandy*, prob. in mockery of the stiffness and dread of motion exhibited by the patients.] An infectious eruptive fever, commencing suddenly, and attended with excruciating pains, especially in the joints, with great prostration and debility, but rarely fatal. Also called *Dandy*, and *Break-bone fever*.

Deni·able, *a.* 1548. [f. DENY *v.* + -ABLE.] That can be denied.

Denial (d*ǐ*nəi·ăl). 1528. [f. DENY *v.* + -AL 2.] **1.** The act of saying 'no'; refusal of anything asked or desired. **2.** The asserting (of anything) to be untrue or untenable; contradiction; also, the denying of the existence or reality of a thing 1576. **3.** Refusal to acknowledge; a disowning, disavowal 1590. **4.** *Law.* †**a.** = DENIER[2] 1628; **b.** The opposing of a plea, claim, or charge advanced 1728.

1. Deniall of buriall 1631. *A d. of one's self*=SELF-DENIAL. 2. The d. of the suppressed premiss WHATELY, of abstract ideas JOWETT. 3. A denyall of the Soveraign Power HOBBES. var. †**Deni·ance.**

Denier[1] (d*ǐ*nəi·əɹ). ME. [f. as prec. + -ER[1].] One who denies.

†**Denier**[2]. 1532. [a. F. *dénier* pres. inf. used subst.; cf. *disclaimer*.] *Law.* The act of denying or refusing –1642.

Denier[3] (d*ǐ*nī°·ɹ, ‖dənye·). *Obs.* or *arch.* ME. [a. OF. *dener*, later *denier* :—L. *denarium*; see DENARIUS.] **1.** A French coin, the twelfth of the sou; orig. of silver; but from 16th c. a small copper coin. Hence, a very small sum. †**2.** Used as tr. L. *denarius* –1606. †**3.** A pennyweight –1706. **4.** A unit of weight, equal to about $8\frac{1}{3}$ troy grains, by which silk yarn is weighed and its fineness estimated 1839. Hence **Denie·r** *v. trans.*, to ascertain the fineness of (silk yarns) in deniers. **Denie·rer.**

1. My Dukedome to a Beggerly d. SHAKS.

Denigrate (de·nigre¹t), *v.* Now *rare.* 1526. [f. ppl. stem of L. *denigrare*; see DE- I. 3.] **1.** *trans.* To blacken, make black or dark 1623. **2.** *fig.* To blacken, defame.

2. This he spake, not to honour Christ, but to d. him TRAPP. Hence **Denigra·tion, De·nigrator,** one who or that which blackens.

Denim (d*ǐ*ni·m, de·nim). 1695. [Short f. *serge de Nim*, F. *serge de Nîmes* or *Nismes*, serge of Nismes in southern France. Cf. DELAINE.] A name orig. of a kind of serge; now in U.S. of a coloured twilled cotton material used for overalls, hangings, etc.

Denitrate (d*ǐ*nəi·tre¹t), *v.* 1863. [DE- II. 1.] To free from nitric or nitrous acid. **Denitra·tion. Deni·trator,** an apparatus for this.

Denitrify (d*ǐ*nəi·trifəi), *v.* 1891. [DE- II. 1.] To deprive of nitrous or hyponitric acid. Hence **Deni·trifier,** a denitrifying agent. **Deni:trifica·tor,** an apparatus used in sulphuric acid works to remove the nitrous vapours from the sulphuric acid previously nitrated in the Gay-Lussac tower. var. **Deni·trize.**

†**De·nizate,** *v.* 1604. [f. ppl. stem of med.L. *denizare*; see DENIZE *v.*] *Law.* To constitute a denizen –1628. Hence **Deniza·tion.**

†**Denize,** *v.* 1577. [f. DENIZ-EN; in med. (Anglo-) L. *denizare*.] **1.** To make (a person) a denizen –1708. **2.** *fig.* To naturalize (a word, a custom, etc.) 1594.

Denizen (de·nizĕn). ME. [a. AF. *deinzein*, etc. = OF. *deinzein*, f. AF. *deinz*, mod.F. *dans* (:—L. *de intus*) + *-ein* :—L. *-aneus*; cf. *foreign, forein*, L. *foraneus*.]

A. 1. One who dwells within a country, as opp. to *foreigners*. Now *rare* in *lit.* sense. **b.** *transf.* and *fig.* Used of persons, animals, and plants. Chiefly *poet.* or *rhet.* 1474. **2.** By restriction: One who lives habitually in a country but is not a native-born citizen; an alien admitted to citizenship by royal letters patent 1576. Also *transf.* and *fig.* 1548.

1. The Charter of London..is the birthright of its own Denisions, not Strangers GURNALL. b. Winged denizens of the crag SCOTT. 2. *fig.* Denisens in heauen UDALL. Hence **De·nizenship.**

B. *adj.* or *attrib.* 1483.

Denizen (de·nizĕn), *v.* 1556. [f. prec. sb.] **1.** To make a denizen; to admit (an alien) to residence and rights of citizenship. Usu. *fig.* 1577. **2.** To furnish with denizens; to people with settlers from without (*rare*).

1. The old denisoned wordes SIR J. CHEKE. The cholera..is denizened among us SOUTHEY.

Dennet (de·nĕt). 1818. [? f. the surname *Dennet*.] A light open two-wheeled carriage akin to a gig; fashionable *c* 1818–1830.

Denominable (d*ǐ*nǫ·minăb'l), *a.* 1658. [f. L. *denominare* + -BLE.] That may be named.

Deno·minant, *sb. rare.* 1889. [ad. L. *denominantem*.] = DENOMINATOR 3.

Denominate (d*ǐ*nǫ·mine̊t), *ppl. a.* and *sb.* 1579. [ad. L. *denominatus*.]

A. *pa. pple.* Named, denominated. *Obs.* or *arch.*

†**B.** *adj. Arith.* Said of a number: CONCRETE, q. v.; opp. to *abstract* –1674.

C. *sb.* †**1.** A name, denomination 1638. †**2.** *Gram.* A denominative –1654.

Denominate (d*ǐ*nǫ·mine¹t), *v.* 1552. [f. L. *denominare*; see DE- I. 3.] **1.** *trans.* To give a name to; to name (orig. *from* or *after* something). Now usually: To call (a thing)... †**2.** To give a name to; to characterize; to constitute –1817. †**3.** To denote –1792.

1. This is what the world..Denominates an itch for writing COWPER. 2. Our general course of life must d us wise or foolish JOHNSON.

Denomination (d*ǐ*nǫminē¹·ʃən). ME. [a. OF. *denominacion*, ad. L. *denominationem* (in cl.L. in the sense of 'metonymy').] **1.** The action of naming *from* or *after* something; naming; calling by a name. **2.** A characteristic name given to a thing or class of things; that which anything is called; an appellation, designation, title ME. **3.** *Arith.* A class of one kind of unit in any system, distinguished by a specific name ME. **4.** A class, sort, or kind distinguished by a specific name 1664. **5.** *spec.* A religious sect or body designated by a distinctive name 1716.

2. The tribes of gypsies, jockies, or cairds—for by all these denominations such banditti were known SCOTT. 3. Weight in which the smallest D. is a Grain 1725. 5. All sects and denominations FRANKLIN.

Denominational (d*ǐ*nǫ·minē¹·ʃənăl), *a.* 1838. [f. prec. + -AL.] Belonging to, or of the nature of, a denomination; sectarian.

Under the dominion of the new law d. schools are the rule M. ARNOLD. Hence **Denomina·tionalism,** adherence to d. principles or a d. system (*e.g.* of education). **Denomina·tionalist,** an adherent of these. **Denomina·tionalize** *v.* to make d. **Denomina·tionally** *adv.* according to a d. method.

Denominative (d*ǐ*nǫ·minĕtiv). 1589. [ad. L. *denominativus*.]

A. *adj.* **1.** Characterized by giving a name to something 1614; connotative 1638. †**2.** Having a distinctive name (*rare*) 1677. **3.** *Gram.* Formed or derived from a noun 1783.

2. The least d. part of time is a minute COCKER. 3. D., that is, derived of a noun, as from *dens* comes *dentatus* 1783. Hence **Deno·minatively** *adv.*

B. *sb.* †**1.** A denominative term –1599. **2.** *Gram.* A word derived from a noun 1638.

Denominator (d*ǐ*nǫ·mine¹təɹ). 1542. [a. med.L., f. *denominare*.] **1.** One who or that which gives a name to something. Now *rare.* 1577. **2.** *Arith.* and *Alg.* The number written below the line in a vulgar fraction, which gives the denomination or value of the parts into which the integer is divided; the corresponding expression in an algebraical fraction, denoting the *divisor*. (Correl. to *numerator*.) 1542. Also *fig.* †**3.** An abstract noun denoting an attribute 1599.

1. The City of Lincoln, the chief d. of the County HEYLIN.

Denotable (d*ǐ*nō^u·tăb'l), *a.* 1682. [f. DENOTE *v.*] That can be denoted or marked.

†**Denotate** (dī·note¹t), *v.* 1597. [f. L. *denotare*; cf. *connotate* vb.] = DENOTE 1–4. –1653.

Denotation (d*ǐ*notē¹·ʃən). 1532. [ad. L. *denotationem*; cf. F. *dénotation*.] **1.** The action of denoting; expression by marks, signs, or symbols; indication; (with *a* and *pl.*) a mark; a sign. **2.** A designation 1631. **3.** The signification of a term 1614. **4.** *Logic.* That which a word *denotes*, as dist. from its *connotation*; the individuals to which a word applies; extension 1843.

3. Time hath brought the word *knaue* to a d. of ill qualities SELDEN.

Denotative (d*ǐ*nō^u·tătiv), *a.* 1611. [f. L. *denotat-* ppl. stem; cf. *connotative*.] Having the quality of denoting; designative, indicative.

Proper names are preeminently d. LATHAM. Hence **Deno·tatively** *adv.*

Denote (d*ǐ*nō^u·t), *v.* 1592. [a. F. *dénoter*, ad. L. *denotare*; see DE- I. 3.] †**1.** *trans.* To note down; to describe –1697. **2.** To mark; to mark out; to distinguish by a mark 1598. **3.** To be the visible sign of; to indicate 1592. **4.** To signify; to stand for 1668; **b.** to express by a symbol 1871. **5.** *Logic.* To be a name of; to be predicated of. (Used by Mill.) 1843.

2. Sun Dialls, by the shadow of a stile or gnomon denoting the hours of the day SIR T. BROWNE. 3. We keep the sea, which denotes a victory PEPYS. Thou hast enough Denoted thy concern SMOLLETT. 4. b. D. by (*X*) the area of the path of *P*. MINCHIN.

Denotement (d*ǐ*nō^u·tmĕnt). 1622. [f. DENOTE *v.* + -MENT.] The fact of denoting; *concr.* a token, sign.

Denotive (d*ǐ*nō^u·tiv), *a.* 1830. [f. as prec. + -IVE.] Serving to denote.

‖**Dénouement** (denū·maṅ). 1752. [F., f. *dénouer, desnouer*, f. (ult.) L. *dis-* + *nodare*, f. *nodus* knot.] Unravelling; *spec.* the final unravelling of the plot in a drama, etc.; the catastrophe; *transf.* the issue of a complication, difficulty, or mystery.

Denounce (d*ǐ*nau·ns), *v.* ME. [a. OF. *denoncier, -noncer* :—L. *denuntiare*, f. DE- I. 3 + *nuntiare*.] **1.** To give formal, authoritative, or official information of; to proclaim, announce, to publish. Also †*transf.* of things. **2.** To proclaim by way of a threat or warning 1632. **3.** To proclaim (a person) to be (something). *Obs.* or *arch.* ME. **4.** To inform against, delate, accuse 1485. **5.** To utter denunciations against 1664. **6.** To give formal notice of the termination of (a treaty, etc.). [So F. *dénoncer*.] 1842.

1. Geving thanks .. at the Cocke-crowing, because at that time the coming of the day is denounced BIBLE (Douay) *Ps.* cxviii. comm. His look denounc'd Desperate revenge MILT. *P. L.* II. 106. 2. To d. fire and desolation T. BROWN. 3. To d. a man as a public enemy DIXON. 4. Archdeacons..shall..d. such of them as are negligent..to the Bishop AYLIFFE. 5. To d. a man as an upstart BRYCE.

Hence **Denou·ncement,** the action of denouncing; denunciation. **Denou·ncer,** one who denounces.

De novo; see DE I d.

†**Densa·tion.** 1615. [ad. L. *densationem*.] Condensation –1729.

Dense (dens), *a.* 1599. [ad. L. *densus*. Cf. F. *dense*.] **1.** Having its constituent particles closely compacted together; thick, compact. **2.** *fig.* Profound, intense, impenetrable, crass 1732. **3.** *Photogr.* Of a negative: Opaque in the developed film, so that the lights and shades are well contrasted.

1. D. fog 1860, tufts 1776. A d. crowd 1836. 2. D. ignorance 1877. Hence **De·nse·ly** *adv.*, **-ness.**

Denshire (de·nʃəɹ), *v.* 1607. [Syncopated f. *Devonshire*.] *trans.* To clear or improve (land) by burning the turf, stubble, etc., and spreading the ashes; = BURN-BEAT.

Densimeter (densi·m*ǐ*təɹ). 1863. [f. L. *densus* + -METER.] An apparatus for measuring the density or specific gravity of a substance.

Density (de·nsĭti). 1603. [a. F. *densité*, ad. L. *densitas*, f. *densus*.] **1.** The quality or condition of being dense; thickness; closeness of consistence. **2.** *Physics.* The degree of consistence of a substance, measured by the quantity of matter in a unit of bulk 1665. **b.** *Electr.* The quantity of electricity per unit of volume or area 1873. **3.** Degree of aggregation 1851. **4.** *Photogr.* Opaqueness of the developed actinized film in a negative 1879.

Dent (dent), *sb.*[1] ME. [var. of DINT, OE. *dynt*.] †**1.** = DINT *sb.* 1. –1603. †**2.** = DINT *sb.* 2. –1600. **3.** A hollow or impression made by a blow or by pressure; a DINT 1565.

1. Ase hit were a d. of þonder ME. 3. Taking his Hammer, he again beat out the d. 1691.

Dent, *sb.*[2] 1552. [a. F. *dent* tooth.] †**1.** An indentation in the edge of anything –1700. **2.** A tooth, in various technical uses 1703.

Dent, *ppl. a.* 1450. [Short for *dented.*] †1. Embossed. †2. *Her.* INDENTED 1610.
D. corn: a variety of Indian corn having a dent in each kernel (*U. S.*).

Dent, *v.* ME. [var. of DINT *v.*] 1. *trans.* To make a dent in; to indent. 2. To impress with a stroke or impact 1450. 3. *intr.* To enter or sink *in*, so as to make a dent. b. To become indented. ME. †4. To aim a penetrating blow (*at*) 1580.
1. Armour..dented at Cressy 1881. 2. The tracks of horses' hoofs deeply dented in the road W. IRVING.

Dental (de·ntăl). 1594. [ad. ? med.L. *dentalis*, f. *dens*; cf. F. *dental.*]
A. *adj.* 1. Of or pertaining to the teeth, or to dentistry; of the nature of a tooth 1599. 2. *Phonology.* Pronounced by applying the tip of the tongue to the front upper teeth, as t, d, n, etc. 1594.
1. *D. formula*, a concise tabular statement of the dentition of a mammal; the numbers of teeth in the upper and the lower row are written above and below a horizontal line: see DENTITION 2.
B. *sb.* 1. *Phonology.* A dental consonant 1794. 2. *Arch.* = DENTIL 1761. 3. *Zool.* A mollusc of the genus *Dentalium* or family *Dentaliidæ*; a tooth-shell 1678. Hence **Denta·lity,** d. quality. **De·ntalize** *v.* to make d. **Dentaliza·tion.**

Dentary (de·ntări). 1830. [ad. L. *dentarius*, f. *dens.*]
A. *adj.* Of, pertaining to, or connected with the teeth; dental.
B. *sb.* A bone forming part of the lower jaw in Vertebrates below *Mammalia*, and bearing the teeth when these are present 1854.

‖**Dentata** (dentē·tă). 1727. [L. fem. of *dentatus* 'toothed' (sc. *vertebra*).] *Anat.* = AXIS[1] 2.

Dentate (de·ntēt), *a.* 1810. [ad. L. *dentatus.*] Having teeth or tooth-like projections; toothed. In *Bot. spec.* of leaves having sharp teeth directed outwards. Hence **De·ntately** *adv.* **Denta·tion,** the condition or fact of being d. So **De·ntated** *ppl. a.*

Denta·to-, comb. f. of L. *dentatus*, prefixed to other adjs. in the sense 'dentately —', 'dentate and —'.

Dented (de·ntėd), *ppl. a.* ME. [f. DENT *v.*] †1. Bent inward; incurved –1607. 2. Having dents, indented, toothed 1552.

De·ntel. 1850. [ad. F. *dentelle.*] = DENTIL.

Dentelated, -ella- (de·ntėlēⁱtėd), *ppl. a.* 1797. [After F. *dentelé.*] Having small teeth; finely indented

Dentelle (dente·l, Fr. dãntę·l). 1859. [a. F., dim. of *dent* tooth.] ‖1. Lace [Fr.]. 2. *Bookbinding.* A tooling resembling lace. Also *attrib.*

Denti-, comb. f. L. *dens, dentem* tooth, *dentes* teeth.
De·ntifactor, a machine for making artificial teeth. **Dentila·bral** *a.*, having relation to teeth and lips. **Dentili·ngual** *a.*, of or formed by teeth and tongue; also as sb. (*sc.* consonant or sound). **Denti·parous** *a.*, producing teeth. **De·ntiphone,** an instrument for conveying sound to the inner ear through the teeth, an AUDIPHONE.

Denticete (de·ntisīt), *a.* 1855. [f. L. *dentem* + *cetus* whale.] Toothed (as a whale).

Denticle (de·ntik'l), *sb.* ME. [ad. L. *denticulus*, dim. of *dentem.* Cf. DENTICULE.] 1. A small tooth or tooth-like projection. 2. *Arch.* = DENTIL 1674. So **Denti·cular** *a.* resembling, or of the nature of, a small tooth; (*Arch.*) having dentils. **Denti·culate** *a.* finely toothed; (*Arch.*) denticular. **Denti·culated** *ppl. a.*

Denticulation (denti:kiulē·ʃən). 1681. [f. L. *denticulus*; cf. *dentation.*] The condition of being denticulate; usu. *concr.* an instance of this; a series of small teeth (mostly in *pl.*).

Denticule (de·ntikiul). 1563. [a. F., ad. L. *denticulus* (also used).] = DENTIL b.

Dentiform (de·ntifǭm), *a.* 1708. [f. L. *dentem*; see -FORM.] Of the form of a tooth; odontoid.

Dentifrice (de·ntifris). 1558. [a. F., ad. L. *dentifricium*, f. *dentem* + *fricare.*] A powder or other preparation for rubbing or cleansing the teeth.

Dentigerous (denti·dʒĕrəs), *a.* 1839. [f. L. type **dentiger* + -OUS.] Bearing teeth.

Dentil (de·ntil). 1663. [a. obs. F. *dentille* :—L. *denticulus*, dim. of *dens.*] *Arch.* Each of the small rectangular blocks, resembling a row of teeth, under the bed-moulding of the cornice in the Ionic, Corinthian, Composite, and sometimes Doric, orders. †b. *transf.* The member of the entablature in which the dentils (when present) are cut –1789. Also *attrib.*

De·ntilated, *ppl. a.* [var. of DENTELATED, after DENTIL.] 'Formed like teeth; having teeth'. So **Dentila·tion,** 'dentition' (Worcester); denticulation, perforation of postage stamps.

Dentile (de·ntil). 1864. [var. of DENTIL.] *Conchol.* A small tooth or tooth-like projection.

Dentine (de·ntīn). 1840. [f. L. *dent-, dens* TOOTH + -INE[4].] *Anat.* The hard tissue, resembling bone but usually denser, which forms the chief constituent of the teeth. Hence **De·ntinal** *a.* pertaining to or of the nature of d.

Dentiro·ster. *rare.* 1847. [a. F. *dentirostre*, ad. mod.L. *dentirostris*, f. DENTI- + *rostrum.*] *Ornith.* A member of the *Dentirostres* or Passerine birds having a tooth or notch on each side of the upper mandible. By later naturalists restricted to the Turdoid or thrush-like *Passeres* or *Insessores.* Hence **Dentiro·stral, Dentiro·strate** *adjs.* belonging to the *Dentirostres*; having a toothed beak.

De·ntiscalp. 1656. [ad. L. *dentiscalpium* toothpick, f. DENTI- + *scalpere.*] An instrument for scaling teeth.

Dentist (de·ntist). 1759. [ad. F. *dentiste*, f. *dent* tooth.] One whose profession it is to treat diseases of the teeth, extract them, insert artificial ones, etc.; a dental surgeon. Hence **Denti·stic, -al** *a.* of, pertaining to, or of the nature of, a d. (*rare*). **De·ntistry,** the profession or practice of a d.

Dentition (denti·ʃən). 1615. [ad. L. *dentitionem*, f. *dentire* to teeth.] 1. The production or cutting of the teeth; teething. 2. The arrangement of the teeth proper to an animal 1849.

Dento-, an incorrect comb. f. L. *dentem* tooth, as in **Dento-li·ngual,** etc.; see DENTI-.

De·ntoid, *a. rare.* 1828. [Bad formation, f. L. *dentem* + Gr. -οειδης, -OID.] Dentiform, ODONTOID.

De·nture[1]. *rare.* 1685. [f. DENT *v.* + -URE.] Indentation, indent.

Denture[2] (de·ntiŭɹ). 1874. [a. F., f. *dent.*] A set of (artificial) teeth.

Denucleate, -ed; see DE- II. 1 and *nucleate, -ed.*

Denudate (dǐniū·dėt, de·niudėt), *a.* 1866. [ad. L. *denudatus.*] Denuded; naked, bare.

Denudate (de·niudeⁱt, dǐniū·deⁱt), *v.* 1627. [f. ppl. stem of L. *denudare.*] = DENUDE.

Denudation (deniudē·ʃən). 1584. [a. F. *dénudation*, ad. L. *denudationem.*] 1. The action of making naked or bare; denuded condition. Also †*fig.* 2. *Geol.* The laying bare of an underlying rock or formation through the *erosion* of that which lies above it by the action of water, ice, etc. 1811. So **Denu·dative** *a.* having the quality of denuding.

Denude (dǐniū·d), *v.* 1513. [ad. L. *denudare*, f. DE- I. 3 + *nudare, nudus.*] *trans.* To make naked or bare; to strip *of* covering; *spec.* in *Geol.*: To lay bare (a rock, etc.) by the wearing away of that which lies above it. Also *fig.*
Rapidly denuded by rain and rivers A. R. WALLACE.

†**Denu·mberment.** 1455. [a. F. *dénombrement.*] The act of numbering; an enumeration –1657.

Denu·merant. 1859. [a. L. *denumerantem.*] *Math.* The number expressing how many solutions a given system of equations admits of.

Denumeration (dǐniū:mĕrē·ʃən). 1623. [ad. L. *denumerationem*, f. *denumerare*, erron. scribal var. of *dinumerare.*] 1. †Enumeration; arithmetical calculation (*rare*); the determination of the denumerant. †2. A present paying down of money –1848.

Denunciant (dǐnɒ·nsiănt, -ʃiănt), *a.* 1837. [ad. L. *denunciantem.*] Denouncing.

Denunciate (dǐnɒ·nsiˌeⁱt, -ʃieⁱt), *v.* 1593. [f. ppl. stem of L. *denuntiare, -nunciare*, f. DE- I. 3 + *nuntiare* (*nunciare*).] To denounce; to utter denunciation against.
He only enunciated and denunciated DE MORGAN. So **Denu·nciative** *a.* characterized by denunciation.

Denunciation (dǐnɒ:nsiˌē·ʃən). 1548. [ad. L. *denunti-, denunciationem.*] †1. Public announcement. 2. Announcement of evil, punishment, etc. in the manner of a warning or menace 1563. 3. Accusation before a public prosecutor 1588. 4. Public condemnation or inveighing against 1842. 5. The action of denouncing a treaty, etc. 1885.
1. D. of Bannes before matrimony BP. HALL. 2. The prophet..by the d. of miseries, weakened the alacrity of the multitude WHISTON.

Denunciator (dǐnɒ·ns-, dǐnɒ·nʃieⁱtəɹ). 1474. [a. F. *dénonciateur*, ad. L. *denuntiatorem.*] One who denounces or utters denunciations; in *Civ. Law*: One who lays an information against another. Hence **Denu·nciatory** *a.* †of or pertaining to denunciation (in various senses); denouncing, accusing, arraigning, condemning.

Denutrition (dǐniutri·ʃən). 1876. [DE- I. 6, or II. 3.] The opposite to nutrition; reversal of the nutritive process; in *Med.* treatment by deprivation of nourishment. Also *attrib.*

Deny (dǐnəi·), *v.* ME. [a. F. *dénier* :—L. *denegare*; see DE- I. 3.] 1. To contradict or gainsay; to declare (anything stated) to be untrue or untenable, or not what it is stated to be. Also *absol.* 2. *Logic.* To assert the contradictory of (opp. to *affirm*) ME. 3. To refuse to admit the truth of (opp. to *assert* or *maintain*) 1630; to reject as non-existent 1621. 4. To refuse to acknowledge; to disown, repudiate, renounce ME. 5. To refuse or withhold; to refuse to give or grant ME. Also *fig.* 6. To say 'no' to ME. †7. To refuse permission to; to forbid (*to do, the doing* of) –1759. †8. To refuse to take –1725.
1. To d. a charge FIELDING. 2. I d. your Maior 1 *Hen. IV*, II. iv. 544. 3. To d. the apparition of ghosts SIR W. HAMILTON, of Witches BURTON. 4. He could not d. his own hand and seal MACAULAY. 5. To d. just requests MARLOWE, a place to art JOWETT. 6. The poor were never at their need denaid GREENE. Too well to d. Company, and too ill to receive them STEELE. Phr. *To d. oneself*; to withhold from oneself the gratification of desire; to practise self-abnegation. Hence **Deny·** *sb.* act of denying or refusing. **Deny·ingly** *adv.* in a way that denies or refuses.

Deobstru·ct, *v.* 1653. [f. DE- I. 6 + L. *obstruere*; see next.] *trans.* To clear of obstruction.

Deobstruent (diˌǫ·bstruĕnt). 1691. [ad. mod.L. type *deobstruentem*, f. as prec.]
A. *adj.* That removes obstructions by opening the natural passages or pores of the body 1718.
B. *sb.* A deobstruent medicine or substance.

Deo·culate, *v.* [f. DE- II. 1 + L. *oculus.*] To deprive of eyes, or of eyesight. LAMB.

Deodand (dī·odænd). 1523. [a. AFr. *deodande*, ad. med.L. *deodandum*, i. e. *Deo dandum.*] A thing to be given to God; *spec.* in *Eng. Law*, a personal chattel which, having been the immediate occasion of the death of a person, was forfeited to the Crown to be applied to pious uses. (Abolished in 1846.) *loosely.* A sum taken in lieu of the deodand 1831.

‖**Deodar** (dī·odāɹ). 1842. [a. Hindī *dēodār, dēwdār* :—Skr. *deva-dāra* tree or timber of the gods.] A sub-species of cedar (*Cedrus Libani*, var. *Deodara*), found native in the Western Himālayas, and now largely grown as an ornamental tree in England. Also applied in India to other trees.

†**Deodate** (dī·odeⁱt). 1600. [ad. L. *deo datum*: in sense 2, = *a deo datum.*]
A. *sb.* 1. A thing given to God. HOOKER. 2. A gift from God. G. HERBERT.
B. *adj* Given by God. GAYTON.

Deodorant (diˌōu·dŏrănt), *sb.* 1869. [f. *odorem* smell, after *decolorare*; see DE- I. 6.] A deodorizer.

Deodorize (diˌōu·dŏrəiz), *v.* 1856. [f. DE- II. 1 + L. *odor.*] *trans.* To deprive of (bad) odour. Also *fig.* Hence **Deodoriza·tion,** removal of (bad) smell. **Deo·dorizer.**

†**Deo·nerate,** *v.* 1623. [f. L. *deonerare*; see DE- I. 6.] To disburden –1651.

Deontology (dīǫntǫ·lŏdʒi). 1826. [f. Gr.

δέον that which is binding + -λογια.] The science of duty or moral obligation

Ethics has received the more expressive name of d. BENTHAM. Hence Deontolo·gical *a.* of, pertaining to, or according to d. De·onto·logist, one who treats of d.

Deoperculate (dī,ōpɔ̄·ɹkiŭlět), *a.* 1866. [f. DE- I. 6 + OPERCULATE.] *Bot.* Having lost the operculum: said of the capsules of mosses, etc. So Deope·rculate *v.* to shed the operculum.

†**Deoppilate** (di,ǫ·pileit), *v.* 1620. [f. DE- II. 1 + OPPILATE.] *trans.* To free from obstruction; *absol.* to remove obstructions -1710. So Deo·ppilant *a.* that removes obstructions; Deo·ppilation, the removal of obstructions; Deo·ppilative, *a.* deobstruent; *sb.* a deobstruent.

Deordination (dī,ǭɹdinē·ʃən). Now *rare.* 1596. [f. (ult.) DE- I. 6 + L. *ordinare.*] 1. Departure from or violation of (moral) order; disorder. 2. Departure from the normal GOAD.

†**Deo·sculate,** *v. rare.* 1623. [f. L. *deosculari*; see DE- I. 3.] To kiss affectionately. Hence †Deoscula·tion, kissing.

De-ossify, -fication; see DE- II. 1 and *ossify*, etc.

Deoxidate (di,ǫ·ksideit), *v.* 1799. [DE- II. 1.] *Chem.* To remove the oxygen from; *intr.* to undergo deoxidation. Hence Deoxida·tion, the removal of oxygen from an oxide or other compound.

Deoxidize (di,ǫ·ksidəiz), *v.* 1794. [DE- II. 1.] *Chem.* = DEOXIDATE. Hence Deoxidiza·tion, Deo·xidizer.

Deoxygenate (di,ǫ·ksidʒėneit), *v.* 1799. [DE- II. 1.] *Chem.* To deprive of (free) oxygen; also = DEOXIDATE. Hence Deoxygena·tion.

Deoxygenize (di,ǫ·ksidʒėnəiz), *v.* 1881. [DE- II. 1.] *Chem.* = DEOXYGENATE.

Deozonize, *v.* to deprive of ozone; see DE- II. 1 and *ozonize.*

†**Depai·nt,** *ppl. a.* [ME. *depeint*, a. F., f. *depeindre*, ad. L. *depingere.*] Depicted; ornamented; coloured. Chiefly as *pa. pple.* -1557.

†**Depaint** (dǐpēɪ·nt), *v.* [ME. *depeinten*, f. prec.] 1. *trans.* To paint; to depict; to delineate -1748. Also *fig.* 2. To depict in words or by comparison -1808. 3. To adorn with or as with painted figures -1706. 4. To stain -1600.

1. Apelles could not d. Motion 1659. 2. Her lips you may in sort d. By cherries ripe 1771. 4. Few siluer drops her vermile cheekes d. FAIRFAX. Hence †Depai·nter one who or that which depaints.

†**Depai·r,** *v.* 1460. [a. OF. *des-, depeirer*, f. (ult.) DE- I. 6 + L. *peiorare*; cf. IMPAIR, etc.] To impair, injure, dilapidate -1568.

Depaire no Church, nor auncient acte T. HOWELL.

†**Depardieu·,** *interj.* ME. [a. OF. *de par Dieu.*] In God's name; by God: used as an asseveration -1634.

Depart (dǐpā·ɹt), *v.* ME. [a. OF. *departir*, f. (ult.) L. *dispertire*, f. DIS- + *partire* to part, divide. See DE- I. 6.]

I. †1. *trans.* To divide into parts -1551; *intr.* to become divided -1577. †2. *trans.* To part among persons; to share; *occas.* to bestow, impart -1651. Also *absol.* †3. *trans.* To separate -1677. †4. *trans.* To sever, break off (a connexion, etc.) -1579. Also *intr.* (for *refl.*).

2. They departed my rayment among them N.T. (Genev.) *John* xix. 24. 3. Till death us d. BARROW. 4. Ye departed the loue bitwene me and my wyf MALORY.

II. †1. *intr.* To go asunder; to separate from each other -1641. 2. *intr.* To go away (*from*); to take one's leave. (The current sense, but chiefly literary.) ME. b. To set out, start. Opp. to *arrive.* (Now commonly to *leave.*) 1489. †c. To go away *to* or *into* -1611. 3. *intr.* To leave this world, die. (Now only *to d. from* (*this*) *life.*) 1501. 4. *trans.* To quit. Now *rare*, exc. in phr. *to d. this life* (= prec.) ME. †5. To send away -1614. 6. *intr.* To withdraw, deviate; to desist (*from*) ME.

2. The Learned Leaches in despair d. DRYDEN. The train departs at 6.30 (*mod.*). 3. Lord, now lettest thou thy servant d. in peace *Luke* ii. 29. 4. The soules of men departing this life HOOKER. 6. They d. from received opinions BERKELEY.

Phrases. †D. with. a. To go away from (*rare*). b. To part with; to give up; to give away. So D. from, in sense b.

Hence †Depa·rtable, -ible *a.* separable; divisible. Depa·rtingly *adv.*

†**Depart,** *sb.* ME. [a. F. *départ*, f. *départir.*] 1. The act of departing; parting; death -1840. 2. *Old Chem* The separation of one metal from another with which it is alloyed -1751.

1. At my d. I gaue this to Iulia *Two Gent.* v. iv. 96. 2. The chymists have a liquor called water of d. BACON (J.).

Departer¹ (dǐpā·ɹtəɹ). ME. [f. as prec.] 1. One who departs (see DEPART *v.*). †2. *Old Chem.* One who separates a metal from an alloy 1656.

†**Depa·rter**². 1628. [sb. use of AF. *departer.*] *Law.* = DEPARTURE 5. -1751.

†**Departition** (dǐpaɹti·ʃən). ME. [f. DEPART *v.*, on L. analogies.] 1. Distribution, partition 1530. 2. Separation -1485. 3. Departure -1485. var. †Depa·rtison.

Department (dǐpā·ɹtmĕnt). [ME., a. OF. *departement*; see DEPART *v.* and -MENT.] †1. = DEPARTURE 1, 2. -1677. 2. 'Separate allotment; province or business assigned to a particular person' (J.); hence, A separate division of a complex whole, *esp.* of activities or studies; a branch, province 1735. b. *spec.* One of the separate divisions or branches of state or municipal administration 1769. 3. One of the districts into which France is divided for administrative purposes 1792. b. A part, section, region (*rare*) 1832.

2. Perfection in every d. of writing but one—the dramatic FOOTE. The D. of War, of State, etc. (*U.S.*) The Paymaster General's D. 4. *attrib.* d. store (orig. *U.S.*), a large shop dealing in a variety of articles. Hence Departme·ntal (dī-) *a.* of or pertaining to a d. Departme·ntally *adv.* Departme·ntalism, attachment to departmental methods.

Departure (dǐpā·ɹtiŭɹ). 1523. [a. OF. *departeüre* :—late L. type **dispartitura*, f. *dispartire.*] †1. Separation, parting -1643. 2. The action of going away 1533; decease, death (*arch.*) 1558. 3. *transf.* and *fig.* Withdrawal, divergence, deviation (from a path, standard, etc.) 1694. 4. The action of starting on a journey; *spec.* the starting of a railway train from a station. Also *attrib.* (Opp. to *arrival.*) 1540. Also *fig.* 5. *Law.* A deviation in pleading from the ground taken by the same party in an antecedent plea 1548. 6. *Navigation.* a. The distance by which a ship in sailing departs east or west from a given meridian 1669. (Abbrev. *dep.*) b. The bearing of an object on the coast, taken at the commencement of a voyage, from which the dead reckoning begins. 1669.

2. D. from this happy place MILT. The time of my d. is at hand 2 *Tim.* iv. 6. 3. D. from evil TILLOTSON, from truth 1832. 4. The d. side of the station (*mod.*). Phr. *New d.*: a fresh start; the beginning of a new course of procedure. 6. We took a new D. from thence [Isle of Ascension] HACKE.

Depascent (dǐpæ·sĕnt), *a. rare.* 1651. [ad. L. *depascentem.*] Consuming.

Depasture (dǐpa·stiŭɹ), *v.* 1586. [f. DE- I. 1 + PASTURE *v.*] 1. *trans.* To consume the produce of (land) by grazing upon it; to use for pasturage. Also *fig.* 1596. 2. *intr.* To graze 1586. 3. *trans.* To pasture or feed (cattle) 1713.

3. A right of depasturing cattle on the land of another WILLIAMS. The run will d. about 4000 sheep 1844. Hence Depa·sturage, Depa·sture *sb.*

†**Depa·triate,** *v.* 1688. [f. DE- I. 2 + L. *patria.*] *intr.* To expatriate oneself -1797.

Depau·perate, *ppl. a.* 1460. [ad. L. *depauperatus*; see next.] †Made poor; †impoverished; in *Bot.*, etc. = DEPAUPERATED.

Depauperate (dǐpǭ·pĕreit), *v.* 1623. [f. (ult.) DE- I. 1 + L. *pauperare*, f. *pauper.*] To render poor, impoverish; to reduce in quality, vigour, or capacity.

Bishops.. had.. depauperated many of the sees CARTE. Hence Depau·perated *ppl. a.* impoverished; in *Bot.*, etc. stunted or degenerate from or as if from want of nutriment. Depau·pera·tion. var. Depau·perize *v.*¹

De-pauperize (dīpǭ·pĕrəiz), *v.*² 1863. [f. DE- II. 1 + *pauperize.*] To free from pauperism; to DISPAUPERIZE.

†**Depe,** *v.* [OE. *dēpan*; OTeut. **daupjan* causal of **deupan* to be deep. In ME. assoc. w. *depe*, DEEP.] 1. To immerse, baptize -ME. 2. To submerge, plunge deeply, dip -1565.

Depe, obs. f. DEEP *a.* and *v.*

†**Depea·ch,** *sb.* 1528. [a. F. *dépêche.*] Dispatch; a message or messengers sent off -1624.

†**Depea·ch,** *v.* 1474. [a. F. *dépêcher*, repr. a late L. type *dis-* (or *de-ex-*)*pedicare*; cf. IMPEACH.] To dispatch -1655.

Depectible, misprint in J. for DEPERTIBLE (Bacon, *Sylva* § 857).

†**Depe·culate,** *v.* 1641. [f. (ult.) DE- I. 1 + L. *peculari.*] *trans.* To plunder by peculation: said of public officials -1648. Hence †Depecula·tion.

†**Depei·nct, depinct,** *v.* 1579. [Cf. DEPAINT and DEPICT.] = DEPICT -1690.

†**Depe·l, depell,** *v.* 1533. [ad. L. *depellere.*] To drive away, expel -1788.

†**Depe·ncil,** *v.* 1631. [f. DE- + PENCIL *v.*] *trans.* To inscribe with a pencil or brush; *fig.* to depict -1766.

Depend (dǐpe·nd), *v.* ME. [a. OF. *dependre*, f. DE- I. 1 + *pendre*, after L. *dependēre.*] 1. *intr.* To hang down, be suspended. (Now literary.) 1510. 2. *intr. fig.* To be contingent on, or conditioned by. Const. *on, upon,* †*of,* occas. *from, to, in.* ME. 3. To belong to as something subordinate 1500. 4. To rest entirely *on, upon* (†*of*) for support, or what is needed 1548. 5. To rely in mind, count *on, upon* (†*of,* etc.) 1500. b. *ellipt.* with following cl.: = 'to depend upon it' (*colloq.*) 1700. †6. To wait in suspense or expectation *on, upon* -1704. 7. To be in suspense or undetermined. (Usu. in pres. pple. = pending.) ME. †8. To impend -1719.

1. As on your boughes the ysicles d. SPENSER. 2. Small things whereunto greater doe d. BAULDWIN. Phr. *That depends* (ellipt.): *i. e.* on circumstances. 3. Hereupon a story depends FULLER. 4. Well directed labour is all we have to d. on HT. MARTINEAU. 5. Faith Miss, d. upon it, I'll give you as good as you bring SWIFT. 6. The hearer on the speaker's mouth depends DRYDEN. 7. Bills of supply were still depending MACAULAY. Hence Depe·ndable, -ible *a.* that may be depended on; trustworthy. Depe·ndably *adv.* Depe·nder, †a dependant; one who depends *on* something.

Dependant, -dent (dǐpe·ndĕnt), *sb.* 1523. [a. F. *dépendant*, pr. pple. of *dépendre.* The spelling *-ent*, after L., is less usual in the sb.; cf. *defendant*, etc.] †1. A subordinate part, appurtenance, dependency -1837. 2. A person who depends on another for support, position, etc.; a retainer, subordinate, servant 1588.

1. With all incidentes, circumstaunces, dependentes or connexes HALL. 2. His own numerous family and dependants CLARENDON

Dependence, -ance (dǐpe·ndĕns). 1535. [a. F. *dépendance*; see prec. The form in *-ance* is rare after 1800.] †1. The action of hanging down; *concr.* something that hangs down (*rare*) 1697. 2. The relation of having existence conditioned by the existence of something else; the fact of depending *upon* something else 1535. 3. The condition of a dependant; subjection, subordination. (Opp. to *independence.*) 1614. †4. *concr.* That which is subordinate to, connected with, or belonging to, something else -1794; a retinue (usu. *-ance*) -1692. 5. The condition of resting in faith or expectation (upon something); reliance; confidence or trust 1627; *transf.* object of confidence or trust (? *obs.*) 1754. 6. The condition of waiting for settlement; pending, suspense. (Now only legal.) 1605. †b. A quarrel 'depending' or awaiting settlement -1820.

2. The chain of dependence which runs throughout creation TYNDALL. 3. To free the Crown from its d. upon Parliament GREEN. 5. Living..in d. on the will of God JOWETT. Your honour, your piety, are my just d. RICHARDSON. 6. Nothing herein contained shall affect any action now in d. 1874.

Dependency, -ancy (dǐpe·ndĕnsi). 1594. [f. as prec.; see -ANCY, -ENCY.] 1. The condition of being dependent; contingent logical or causal connexion; = prec. 2. 1597. 2. The relation of a thing (or person) to that by which it is supported; = prec. 3. 1594. †3. = prec. 5 (*rare*) -1677. 4. Something dependent or subordinate; an appurtenance 1611; †a retinue -1701; a dependent or subordinate place or territory 1684. †5. = prec. 6 b. -1632.

1. Such a dependancy of thing, on thing *Meas. for M.* v. i. 62. 2. The dependency of Ireland upon the crown of England SWIFT. 4. A thorough sifting of this subject, and its dependencies 1852. The earth, and its dependencies T. BURNET. That Sheffield which now, with its dependencies, contains a hundred and twenty thousand souls MACAULAY.

Dependent, -ant (dĭpe·ndĕnt), *a.* ME. [Orig. *dependant*, a. F. *dependant*; now usually *dependent*, after L.] **1.** Hanging down. **2.** That depends *on* something else; having its existence contingent on, or conditioned by, that of something else 1594. **3.** That depends *on* something else for support or what is needed 1643. **4.** Subordinate, subject; opp. to *independent* 1616. †**5.** Impending (*rare*). SHAKS.

1. D. leaves 1880. 2. Effects d. on the same.. Causes POWER. 3. D. upon strangers 1791, on charity TROLLOPE. 4. D. colonies of England BRIGHT. *D. variable* (Math.): one whose variation depends on that of another variable (the *independent variable*). 5. *Tr. & Cr.* II. iii. 21. Hence **Depe·ndently** *adv.*

Depeople (dĭpī·p'l), *v. arch.* 1611. [ad. F. *dépeupler*, after *people*. See DE- I. 6.] To depopulate.

†**Depe·rdit, -ite.** 1608. [ad. L. *deperditus, -um*, see DE- I. 3.]

A. *adj.* Lost, abandoned –1642.

B. *sb.* Something lost or perished 1802. Hence **Depe·rditely** *adv.* So **Deperdi·tion,** loss, destruction by wasting away (*rare*).

Deperition (dĭpĕri·ʃən). *rare.* 1793. [f. L. *deperire*; see DE- I. 3.] Perishing, total wasting away.

Depe·rsonalize, *v.* 1866. [DE- II. 1.] To deprive of personality.

†**Depe·rtible,** *a.* 1626. [f. as if from L. vb. **depertire* = *dispertire* to divide.] Divisible.

†**Dephlegm** (dĭfle·m), *v.* 1660. [ad. mod.L. *dephlegmare*.] = DEPHLEGMATE.

†**Dephlegmate** (dĭfle·gmeᵉit), *v.* 1668. [f. (ult.) DE- I. 6 + Gr. φλέγμα; see PHLEGM.] *Old Chem.* To free (a spirit or acid) from phlegm or watery matter; to rectify –1789; *fig.* to purify BURKE. Hence †**Dephlegma·tion. De·phlegmator,** an apparatus for dephlegmation.

Dephlogi·sticate, *v.* 1775. [DE- II. 1.] †**1.** *trans. Old Chem.* To deprive of PHLOGISTON, q.v. –1788. **2.** To relieve of inflammation 1842. Hence **Dephlogi·sticated** *ppl. a.* (*esp.* in *dephlogisticated air*, Priestley's name for oxygen); **Dephlogi·stica·tion.**

Dephosphorize (dĭfǫ·sfŏrəiz), *v.* 1878. [DE- II. 1.] To free from phosphorus. Hence **Dephosphoriza·tion.**

†**Depi·ct,** *ppl. a.* ME. [ad. L. *depictus*; see next.] Depicted –1598.

Depict (dĭpi·kt), *v.* 1631. [f. L. *depict-*, ppl. stem of *depingere*; see DE- I. 3.] **1.** *trans.* To draw, figure, or represent in colours; to paint; also, to figure anyhow. Also *transf.* and *fig.* **2.** To represent or portray in words; to describe graphically 1740.

1. The history of the Bible..depicted in needle work FULLER. 2. No language can d. the chaos at its base KANE. Hence **Depi·cter, -or,** one who depicts. So **Depi·ction,** the action of depicting; painted representation; graphic description. **Depi·ctive** *a.* having the quality of depicting.

Depi·cture, *sb.* 1500. [f. as prec.] = *Depiction.*

Depicture (dĭpi·ktiŭɹ), *v.* 1593. [f. DE- *prefix* + PICTURE *v.*; influenced by DEPICT *pa. pple.*] **1.** = DEPICT *v.* 1, 2. **2.** *fig.* To picture to one's own mind; to imagine 1775.

1. A paradise or garden was depictured on the ground GIBBON.

Depilate (de·pileᵉit), *v.* 1560. [f. L. *depilat-*, ppl. stem of *depilare*; see DE- I. 2.] **1.** To remove the hair from; to make bare of hair. †**2.** To decorticate (*rare*) 1620. Hence **Depila·tion,** the action of stripping, or condition of being void, of hair; †pillage. **Depi·latory** *a.* having the property of removing hair; var. †**Depi·lative**; *sb.* a depilatory agent or substance.

Depilous (de·piləs), *a.* 1646. [Cf. L. *depilis* and *pilosus*.] Deprived or void of hair.

Deplane (dĭplēᵉ·n), *v.* 1923. [f. DE- II. 2 + PLANE *sb.*³ 1 e(*b*).] To alight from an aeroplane.

Deplete (dĭplī·t), *v.* 1807. [f. L. *deplet-*, ppl. stem; see DE- I. 6.] **1.** To reduce the fullness of; to empty out, exhaust 1859. **2.** *Med.* To relieve the system or vessels when overcharged, as by blood-letting or purgatives 1807.

1. To d. a garrison of troops 1880. So **Deple·te** *a.* emptied out, exhausted. **Deple·tive** *a.* characterized by depletion; *sb.* a drug which produces depletion. **Deple·tory** *a.* depletive.

Depletion (dĭplī·ʃən). 1656. [f. as prec.] **1.** The action of depleting, or condition of being depleted; exhaustion. **2.** *Med.* The relieving of overcharged vessels of the body 1735.

Deplorable (dĭplōᵊ·răb'l), *a.* 1612. [f. L. *deplorare*. Cf. F. *déplorable*.] To be deplored or lamented; lamentable, very sad, grievous, miserable, wretched. Now chiefly used of events, conditions, circumstances.

The storie of Your most d. fortune MASSINGER. A d. want of sense COTTON. Hence **Deplo:rabi·lity,** the quality of being d.; a d. matter (*rare*). **Deplo·rableness. Deplo·rably** *adv.*

†**Deplo·rate,** *a.* 1529. [ad. L. *deploratus*.] Given up as hopeless; desperate –1695.

In a d. or desperate dropsie CROOKE.

Deploration (dĭploᵊrēᵉ·ʃən). 1490. [ad. L. *deplorationem*.] **1.** The action of deploring; lamentation 1533. †**2.** Deplorable condition. CAXTON.

Deplore (dĭplōᵊ·ɹ), *v.* 1559. [ad. L. *deplorare*; see DE- I. 3. Cf. F. *déplorer*.] **1.** To weep for, bewail, lament; to grieve over, regret deeply 1567; to tell with grief (SHAKS.). **2.** *intr.* To lament. ? *Obs.* 1632. †**3.** *trans.* To give up as hopeless (*rare*) –1729.

1. He..left me here his losse for to d. SPENSER. 3. To stay with the patient after the disease is deplored BACON. Hence **Deplo·rer. Deplo·ringly** *adv.*

Deplored (dĭplōᵊ·ɹd, -rĕd), *ppl. a.* 1559. [f. prec.; tr. L. *deploratus*.] **1.** Lamented. †**2.** Given up as hopeless; DEPLORATE –1655. Hence **Deplo·red·ly** *adv.*, **-ness.**

Deploy·, *sb.* 1796. [f. next. Cf. OF. *desploi*, *-ploy*, DISPLAY.] *Mil.* The action or evolution of deploying. So **Deploy·ment** (in same sense).

Deploy (dĭploi·), *v.* 1477. [a. F. *déployer* :—L. *displicare* (in late and med.L.) to unfold. Cf. DISPLAY.] †**1.** (in Caxton) To unfold, display. **2.** *Mil.* To spread out (troops) so as to form a more extended line of small depth 1786. Also *intr.* of a body of troops. Also *fig.*

2. *intr.* The right wing, having deployed into line, began to advance WELLINGTON.

Deplumate (dĭpliū·mĕt), *a.* 1883. [ad. med.L. *deplumatus*.] Stripped of feathers, deplumed. So **Deplu·mated** *ppl. a.*

Deplumation (dīpliumēᵉ·ʃən). 1611. [a. F. *déplumation*, f. *déplumer*.] The action of depluming, or condition of being deplumed; loss of feathers, plumes, or (*fig.*) of honours, etc.; in *Path.*, a disease of the eyelids which causes the eyelashes to fall off.

Deplume (dĭpliū·m), *v.* ME. [ad. F. *déplumer*, or med.L. *deplumare*; see DE- I. 6.] **1.** *trans.* To strip of feathers; to pluck the feathers off. **2.** *fig.* To strip or deprive of honour, wealth, or the like 1651.

1. Thus was the Roman Eagle deplumed, every Bird had its own Feather N. BACON. 2. His favourite amusement of depluming me GIBBON.

Depolarize (dĭpōu·lărəiz), *v.* 1818. [DE- II. 1.] *trans.* To deprive of polarity; to reverse or destroy the effect of polarization. **a.** *Optics.* To change the direction of polarization of (a polarized ray) so that it is no longer arrested by the analyzer in a polariscope 1819. **b.** *Electr.*, etc. To deprive of polarity. Also *fig.* 1860. Hence **Depolariza·tion,** the action or process of depolarizing. **Depo·larizer,** an instrument for producing depolarization.

Depolish (dĭpǫ·liʃ), *v.* 1873. [DE- II. 1.] *trans.* To remove the polish from.

Depone (dĭpōu·n), *v.* Chiefly *Sc.* 1533. [ad. L. *deponere*; in med.L. to testify; f. DE- I. 1, 2 + *ponere*; cf. DEPOSE *v.*] †**1.** *trans.* To lay down (an office, etc.) –1843. **2.** To state or declare upon oath; to DEPOSE 1549. **3.** *intr.* To declare upon oath; to testify. Also *fig.* 1640.

2. Andr. Martin..Depones, that he was present in the house GLANVILL. 3. He could not d. to one fact against the accused ALISON.

Deponent (dĭpōu·nĕnt). 1528. [ad. L. *deponentem*; see prec.]

A. *adj. Gram.* Of verbs: Passive or middle in form but active in meaning.

Both form and meaning were orig. reflexive (e.g. *utor* I serve myself, etc.). What was *laid aside* was, not a passive meaning, as formerly supposed, but the reflexive sense.

B. *sb.* **1.** A deponent verb 1530. **2.** One who deposes or makes a deposition under oath; one who gives written testimony to be used as evidence in a court of justice, etc. 1548. So †**Depo·ner.**

Depo·pularize, *v.*; see DE- II. 1 and *popularize.*

Depo·pulate, *ppl. a.* 1531. [ad. L. *depopulatus*.] Laid waste; deprived (wholly or partly) of inhabitants. Used †**a.** as *pa. pple.*; **b.** as *adj.* (now *arch.* or *poet.*).

Depopulate (dĭpǫ·piŭleᵉit), *v.* 1545. [f. ppl. stem of L. *depopulare* (*-ari*) to lay waste, spoil; *lit.* to pour in a multitude over (a region); but in med.L. to spoil of people, depopulate. See DE- I. 3, and DISPEOPLE, etc.] †**1.** *trans.* To ravage, lay waste –1670. **2.** To deprive wholly or partly of inhabitants; to reduce the population of 1594. Also *transf.* and *fig.* †**3.** To thin –1798. **4.** *intr.* To become less populous 1761. †**5.** *trans.* To destroy, cut off –1650.

2. The late Plague, which did much d. this kingdom CHILD. 4. The kingdom was depopulating from the increase of enclosures HUME. Hence **Depopula·tion,** the action of depopulating; depopulated condition. **Depo·pulator,** one who †ravages or depopulates a district or country.

†**Depo·rt,** *sb.* 1477. [a. OF. *deport, desport*, in mod.F. *déport*.] **1.** = DISPORT. **2.** Behaviour, deportment –1740.

Deport (dĭpōᵊ·ɹt), *v.* 1474. [In branch I, a. OF. *deporter* (mod.F. *dé-*), f. *de-* (DE- I. 1 or 3) + *porter*. In branch II = mod.F. *déporter*, ad. L. *deportare*.]

I. †**1.** *trans.* To bear with; to spare –1481. †**2.** *refl.* To abstain, forbear –1613. **3.** To bear oneself; to behave 1598.

3. He so prudently deported himself, that.. FULLER.

II. *trans.* To carry away, remove; *esp.* to remove into exile, to banish 1641. **b.** In Indian use, to detain (a political offender) 1909.

Hence **Deportee·**, *spec.* in Indian use. = DÉTENU.

Deportation (dīpoɹtēᵉ·ʃən). 1595. [ad. L. *deportationem*; see DEPORT *v.* II.] The action of carrying away; forcible removal, *esp.* into exile; transportation.

Wholesale deportations to Cayenne 1860.

Deportment (dĭpōᵊ·ɹtmĕnt). 1601. [a. OF. *deportement*; see DEPORT *v.*] Manner of conducting oneself; conduct (*of* life); behaviour; carriage, bearing, address. Also *fig.*

His air, his mien, his d., charm'd me so SHADWELL.

Deporture, in Dicts., error for DEPARTURE (Speed, *Hist. Great Brit.* IX. xxiv).

Deposable (dĭpōu·zăb'l), *a.* 1643. [f. DEPOSE *v.* + -ABLE.] That may be deposed; liable to be deposed.

Deposal (dĭpōu·zăl). ME. [prob. a. AFr. *deposaille*.] = DEPOSITION I. 3.

Depose (dĭpōu·z), *v.* ME. [a. F. *déposer*, f. DE- I. 1 + *poser* to place :—Rom. *posare* = late L. *pausare*; see POSE, REPOSE. Associated in idea with derivs. of L. *deponere*.] **1.** *trans.* To lay down; to DEPOSIT (*arch.*). Also †*fig.* **2.** To put down from office, or authority; *esp.* to dethrone. (The prevailing sense.) ME. †**3.** To take away; also to remove (opp. to *impose*) –1617; to divest (a person *of*) –1681. **4.** To testify; to testify to; *esp.* to give evidence upon oath in a court of law, to make a deposition (*trans.* and *intr.*) ME. †**5.** *causally.* To examine on oath; to cite as a witness. *pass.* To bear witness. –1721.

1. A paper which he solemnly deposed on the high altar MILMAN. 2. He was deposed from his kyngly trone COVERDALE *Dan.* v. 20. 3. *Rich. II*, IV. i. 192. 4. He deposed to having fastened up the house at eleven o'clock 1862. When our memory deposes otherwise J. H. NEWMAN. 5. Grant thou hadst a thousand witnesses To be deposed they heard it MASSINGER. Hence **Depo·ser,** one who puts down another from office, etc.; one who makes a statement on oath.

Deposit (dĭpǫ·zit), *sb.* 1624. [ad. L. *depositum*, sb. use of neut. of pa. pple. of *deponere*; see DEPONE, DEPOSE.] **1.** Something laid up in a place, or committed to the charge of a person, for safe keeping. Also *fig.* 1660. **b.** *spec.* A sum of money deposited in a bank 1753. **c.** Something committed to another person's charge as a pledge 1737. **2.** The state of being deposited; in phr. *on, upon,* †*in d.* 1624. **3.** Something deposited, laid, or thrown down; *esp.* matter precipitated from a fluid medium, or collected in one place by natural process. In *Mining*, an accumulation of ore, *esp.* of a somewhat casual character, as in pockets. 1781. 4. The act of depositing; cf. prec. senses, and DEPOSIT *v.* 1773. 5. A depository, a depot. (Chiefly *U.S.*) 1719.

3. Recent deposites of sandstone, clay, and gypsum MACGILLIVRAY. 4. A d. of white powder soon takes place 1823. *Comb.* **d.-receipt**, a receipt for anything deposited, *spec.* for money deposited with a banker at a stated rate of interest.

Deposit (dǐpǫ·zit), *v.* Also †**deposite.** 1624. [a. obs. F. *depositer*; ad. med.L. *depositare*, freq. of L. *deponere.*] 1. *trans.* To lay, put, or set down 1671; *intr.* to be laid down or precipitated, to settle (*rare*) 1831. †2. *fig.* (*trans.*) To lay aside, give up; to lay down (one's life, etc.) –1804. 3. To place in a repository; to commit to the charge of any one for safe keeping or as a pledge; *spec.* to place in a bank at interest 1659. Also *fig.*

1. He deposited his reckoning FIELDING. She flies to some neighbouring pool, where she deposites her eggs GOLDSM. [The water] deposits more or less of the matter which it holds in suspension HUXLEY. 3. The silver..deposited in the bank BERKELEY. *fig.* Christianity is..a trust, deposited with us in behalf of others BUTLER.

Depositary (dǐpǫ·zitări), *sb.* 1605. [ad. L. *depositarius* one who receives or makes a deposit; f. *deposit-* ppl. stem of *deponere.* Often confounded with DEPOSITORY.] 1. A person with whom anything is lodged in trust; a trustee; one to whom anything is committed or confided. In *Law*, a bailee of personal property, to be kept for the bailor without recompense. 1605. 2. = DEPOSITORY 1. 1797.

1. They [Jews]..are the Depositaries of these..Prophecies ADDISON. I am the sole d. of my own secret, and it shall perish with me JUNIUS.

Depositary, *a. rare.* 1839. [f. DEPOSIT *sb.*] 1. *Geol.* Belonging to or of the nature of a deposit. 2. Receiving deposits, as a bank 1886.

Depositation (dǐpǫzitēi·ʃən). Chiefly *Sc.* 1622. [f. med.L. *depositare.*] The action of depositing; a deposit.

Depositee (dǐpǫ·zitī·). 1676. [f. DEPOSIT *v.*: correl. to *depositor.*] A person with whom something is deposited.

Deposition (dǐpozi·ʃən, dep-). ME. [a. OF., ad. L. *depositionem*; see DEPOSE.]

I. 1. The taking down of the body of Christ from the cross; a representation of this 1526. †2. The action of laying down or putting aside or away; usu. *fig.* –1748. 3. The action of deposing from a position of dignity or authority; degradation; dethronement ME. 4. The giving of testimony upon oath in a court of law, or the testimony so given; *spec.* a statement in answer to interrogatories, constituting evidence, taken down in writing to be read in court as a substitute for the production of the witness 1494. b. *transf.* and *fig.* Testimony, statement; allegation 1587.

II. 1. The action of depositing, laying down, or placing in a position of rest; *spec.* interment [med.L. *depositio*], or placing of a saint's body or relics in a new resting-place 1659. 2. The placing of something in a repository, or in the hands of a person for safe keeping; *concr.* a deposit 1592. 3. Precipitation; a deposit, precipitate, sediment 1797.

1. The d. of the eggs by these insect cuckoos 1875. 3. The crystallization, precipitation, and d. of these solids KIRWAN.

Depositor (dǐpǫ·zitəɪ). 1624. [Taken as from DEPOSIT *v.*] One who or that which deposits; *spec.* one who deposits money in a bank.

Depository (dǐpǫ·zitəri). 1656. [f. med.L. *depositorium*, f. *deposit-* ppl. stem.] 1. A place in which things are deposited for safe keeping; a storehouse, a repository 1750. 2. = DEPOSITARY *sb.* 1. Usu. *fig.* 1656.

1. The Jewel Tower..the d. of the Regalia H. AINSWORTH. 2. I think well of her judgment in chusing you to be the d. of her troubles JOHNSON.

†‖**Depositum** (dǐpǫ·zitǒm). Pl. **-a, -ums.** 1582. [L.] 1. = DEPOSIT *sb.* 1 c (*lit.* and *fig.*) –1745. 2. = DEPOSIT 5 (*lit.* and *fig.*) –1796.

Depositure (dǐpǫ·zitiŭ). *rare.* 1635. [Corresp. to a L. type **depositura.*] The action of depositing or placing.

Depot (de·pou, dǐpōu·, dī·pou). Also **depôt, dépôt.** 1794. [a. F. *dépôt* (*depo*), ad. L. *depositum*; see DEPOSITUM, DEPOSIT.] †1. The act of depositing –1836. †2. = DEPOSIT *sb.* 1, 3. –1850. 3. *Mil.* a. A place where military stores are deposited. b. The head-quarters of a regiment, where and whence supplies are received and distributed. c. A station where recruits are assembled and drilled, and where soldiers who cannot join their regiments remain. d. *attrib.* Applied to a portion of a regiment left at home when the rest are on foreign service. 1798. e. A place of confinement for prisoners of war 1806. 4. A place where goods are deposited or stored 1802. 5. *U.S.* A railway station 1842.

†**De·pravate,** *ppl. a.* 152.. [ad. L. *depravatus.*] Depraved, corrupted –1665. So †**Depravate** *v.* = DEPRAVE.

Depravation (dīprăvēi·ʃən, dep-). 1526. [ad. L. *depravationem.* Cf. F. *dépravation.*] 1. The action or fact of making or becoming depraved, bad, or corrupt; deterioration, degeneration, *esp.* moral degeneration 1561. 2. The being depraved; corruption 1577. †3. Depravation or corruption (of a text, etc.) –1849. †4. Detraction, calumny –1606.

1. The total Loss of Reason is less deplorable than the total D. of it COWLEY. 4. A meere deprauation and calumny without all shadowe of truth BACON.

Deprave (dǐprēi·v), *v.* ME. [ad. L. *depravare*; see DE- I. 3. Cf. F. *dépraver.*] 1. To make bad; to pervert; to deteriorate, corrupt. Now *rare*, exc. as in sense 2. 2. *spec.* To make morally bad. (The current sense.) 1482. †3. To represent as bad; to vilify, defame, disparage –1667. Also *absol.* †4. To become bad or depraved. FULLER. ¶ Formerly often erron. for DEPRIVE.

1. To d. the text 1663, the voice of a singer JOHNSON, our money NEAL. 2. Vicious indulgence..depraves the inward constitution and character BUTLER. Hence **Depra·ved-ly** *adv.*, **-ness. Depra·vement** (*arch.*), depravation; †misinterpretation. **Depra·ver,** one who depraves, corrupts, or vilifies.

Depravity (dǐpræ·vĭti). 1641. [An extension of PRAVITY (ad. L. *pravitas*), after DEPRAVE, etc.] The quality or condition of being depraved or corrupt; †perverted quality –1758; moral perversion 1646; *Theol.* the innate corruption of human nature due to original sin (often *total depravity*) 1757; a depraved act or practice 1641.

Both the elect and the non-elect come into the world in a state of total d. and alienation from God, and can, of themselves, do nothing but sin J. H. BLUNT.

†**De·precable,** *a.* 1633. [In form ad. L. *deprecabilis* (Vulgate).] That may be, or to be, deprecated –1648.

Deprecate (de·prǐkeit), *v.* 1624. [f. L. *deprecat-*, ppl. stem of *deprecari*; see DE- I. 2.] 1. To pray against (evil); to seek to avert by prayer; to pray for deliverance from (*arch.*) 1628. 2. To plead earnestly against; to express earnest disapproval of 1641. †3. To beseech (a person) –1822. Also †*absol.* †4. To invoke (evil) –1790.

1. Wise men still d. these mens kindnesses EARLE. 2. To d. such a method of proceeding OUSELEY, panic 1882. Hence **De·precatingly** *adv.*

Deprecation (deprǐkēi·ʃən). 1556. [a. F. *déprécation*, ad. L. *deprecationem*; see prec.] †1. Intercessory prayer. [So in L.] 2. Prayer for the averting or removal (*of* evil, etc.) 1596. 3. Earnest desire that something may be averted or removed; earnest disapproval of 1612. †4. Imprecation (*rare*) –1804.

2. D. of Gods displeasure 1673. 3. A look of d. GEO. ELIOT. So **De·precative** *a.* deprecating; of or pertaining to d.

De·precator. 1656. [a. L.] One who deprecates; †a petitioner.

Deprecatory (de·prǐkeitəri), *a.* 1586. [ad. L. *deprecatorius.*] 1. Serving to deprecate; that prays for deliverance from or aversion of evil. 2. Deprecating anticipated disapproval 1704. Also as †*sb.* [*sc.* word or expression.] –1734.

1. D. Rites to avert Evil 1738. 2. A d. laugh 1872.

Depreciate (dǐprī·ʃieit), *v.* 1646. [f. L. *depretiat-* (*-ciat-*), ppl. stem of *depretiare*; see DE- I. 1.] 1. *trans.* To lower in value, lessen the value of; *spec.* to lower the market value of; to reduce the purchasing power of (money). 2. To represent as of less value; to undervalue, belittle 1666. Also *absol.* 3. *intr.* To fall in value, to become of less worth 1790.

1. To d. the esteeme and value of miracles SIR T. BROWNE, our Silver Standard WOOD. 2. I dont like to hear you d. yourself DICKENS. 3. Conditions which caused property to d. 1884. Hence **Depre·ciatingly** *adv.* **Depre·ciative** *a.* depreciatory. **Depre·ciator.**

Depreciation (dǐprīʃiēi·ʃən). 1767. [f. prec.] 1. Lowering of value; fall in the exchangeable value (of money). 2. Lowering in estimation; disparagement 1790.

Depreciatory (dǐprī·ʃiătəri), *a.* 1805. [f. L. *depretiator.*] Tending to depreciate.

†**Depre·dable,** *a.* 1640. [f. F. *déprédér* (see next).] Liable to be preyed upon –1656.

Depredate (de·prǐdeit), *v.* 1626. [f. ppl. stem of L. *deprædare*; see DE- I. 3. Cf. F. *déprédér.*] †1. *trans.* To prey upon; to plunder, pillage –1677; *fig.* to consume by waste –1662. 2. *intr.* To make depredations. (*affected.*) 1797.

1. *fig.* [Exercise] maketh the Substance of the Body ..less apt to be Consumed and Depredated by the Spirits BACON. Hence **De·predator,** one who, or that which, depredates. **Depre·datory** (also de·prǐ-) *a.* characterized by depredation.

Depredation (deprǐdēi·ʃən). 1483. [a. F. *déprédation*; see prec.] The action of making a prey of; plundering, pillaging; also, †plundered or pillaged condition. Also *fig.*

Habits of d. JOHNSON. *fig.* [They] perished..by the depredations of the lava LYELL.

†**Depre·dicate,** *v. rare.* 1550. [DE- I. 3.] To proclaim aloud; celebrate –1674.

†**Deprehend** (deprǐhe·nd), *v.* 1523. [ad. L. *deprehendere*; see DE- I. 2.] 1. *trans.* To seize, capture; to arrest, apprehend –1834. 2. To take in the act –1677. 3. To detect –1683.

2. Touching the woman deprehended in adultery WHITGIFT. 3. The Motions..are Invisible..but yet they are to be deprehended by Experience BACON.

†**Deprehe·nsible,** *a.* 1653. [f. L. *deprehendere.*] Capable of being detected –1660.

†**Deprehe·nsion.** 1527. [ad. L. *deprehensionem.*] The action of catching in the act; detection; arrest –1649.

Depress (dǐpre·s), *v.* ME. [a. OF. *depresser*, ad. L. type **depressare.* In Eng. taken as repr. L. *deprimere, depress-.*] †1. *trans.* To put down by force –1675. 2. To press down (in space). Often more widely: To lower. 1526. 3. *fig.* To put down, bring low, humble (now *rare*) 1526; †to keep down –1861. †4. To depreciate, disparage –1791. 5. To render weaker or less; to render dull or languid 1647. 6. To cast down mentally, dispirit. (The chief current use.) 1621. †7. *Alg.* To reduce to a lower degree or power –1816.

2. Alternately raising and depressing the piston IMISON. 4. To d. the credit of others HOOKER. 5. When the trade is depressed, and when wages and interest are low JEVONS. To d. the voice SCOTT. 6. This house depresses and chills one DICKENS. Hence **Depre·ssant** *a.* sedative; *sb.* a sedative. **Depre·ssible** *a.* **Depre·ssingly** *adv.*

Depressed (dǐpre·st, *poet.* dǐpre·sėd), *ppl. a.* Also **deprest.** ME. [f. prec. + -ED¹.] 1. Pressed or forced down 1609. 2. Lowered in position, force, amount, or degree ME. 3. Having a flattened or hollowed form, as if produced by downward pressure; *spec.* said of convex things which are flattened vertically (opp. to COMPRESSED); *e.g.* a *d. arch* 1753. 4. Brought low, oppressed, etc.; *esp.* in low spirits 1621. Hence **Depre·ssedly** *adv.*

Depression (dǐpre·ʃən). ME. [ad. L. *depressionem*, f. *deprimere.*] 1. The action of pressing down, or fact of being pressed down; usu. more widely: The action of lowering, or process of sinking; the condition of being lowered. Also *fig.* 1656. 2. *spec.* a. *Astron.* (*a*) The angular distance of a star, the pole, etc., below the horizon (opp. to *altitude*); the angular distance of the visible horizon below the true horizontal plane, the DIP of the horizon. (*b*) The apparent sinking of the celestial pole towards the horizon as the observer travels towards the equator. ME. b. *Surg.* The operation of couching for cataract 1851. 3. A depressed formation on a surface; a hollow, a low place or part 1665. 4. A lowering in quality, vigour, or amount; the state of being lowered; in mod. use *esp.* of trade 1793. b. A lowering of the column of mercury in the barometer or of the atmospheric pressure thereby measured; *spec.* in *Meteorol.* a CYCLONE, q. v. 1881. 5. Dejection 1665. †6.

Alg. Reduction to a lower degree or power –1823.

4. The d. of the public funds VANSITTART. 5. He found her in a state of deep d. GEO. ELIOT.

Depressive (dǐpre·siv), *a.* 1620. [f. L. *depress-*, *deprimere* + -IVE.] Tending to press or force down. Also *fig.* Hence **Depre·ssiveness.**

Depressor (dǐpre·səɹ). 1611. [a. L.] **1.** One who or that which depresses (see the vb.). **2.** *Anat.* and *Phys.* **a.** A muscle which depresses or pulls down the part to which it is attached; also *attrib.*, as *d. muscle.* **b.** *D. nerve*: a branch of the vagus, the stimulation of which lowers the pressure of the blood. 1615.

†**Depressure** (dǐpre·ʃiŭɹ). 1621. [f. L. *depress-* ppl stem.] = DEPRESSION 1, 3, 4. –1774.

†**De·priment,** *a. rare.* 1713. [ad. L. *deprimentem.*] Depressing, as *d. muscles* –1721. As *sb.* That which depresses 1624.

†**Depri·sure.** *rare.* 1648. [See DISPRIZE.] Depreciation.

Deprivable (dǐprəi·văb'l), *a.* 1593. [f. DEPRIVE *v.* + -ABLE.] Liable to be deprived; subject to deprivation.

They [the Bishops]..are..depriuable 1593.

Deprival (dǐprəi·văl). 1611. [f. as prec.; see -AL 2.] The act of depriving; DEPRIVATION.

Deprivation (deprivē·ʃən). 1533. [ad. med. L. *deprivationem.*] **1.** The action of depriving or fact of being deprived; dispossession, loss. **2.** *spec.* The action of depriving of an office, dignity, or benefice; *esp.* the depriving of an ecclesiastic of a benefice or preferment 1551.

1. D. of Ecclesiastical Burial CHANDLER. So **Depri·vative** *a.* of or characterized by d.

Deprive (dǐprəi·v), *v.* ME. [a. OF. *depriver*, f. DE- I. 3 + *privare.*] **1.** To divest, bereave, dispossess *of*, †*from.* **2.** To divest of office; to inflict (*esp.* ecclesiastical) deprivation upon ME. **3.** To keep out *of*; to debar *from* ME. †**4.** To take away; to remove –1654.

1. Thee I have missed, and thought it long, depriv'd Thy presence MILT. *P. L.* IX. 857. 2. The Bp...depriv'd him for three years HEARNE. 3. I am depriued of the residue of my yeeres *Isa.* xxxviii. 10. 4. 'Tis honour to d. dishonour'd life SHAKS. Hence †**Depri·vement,** deprivation. **Depri·ver.**

De profundis; see DE.

†**Depro·me,** *v. rare.* 1652. [ad. L. *depromere*; see DE- I. 2.] To draw out or forth –1657. var. †**Depro·mpt** (*rare*).

†**Depro·strate,** *a. rare.* [DE- I. 3.] Extremely prostrate. G. FLETCHER.

Deprotestantize, deprovincialize; see DE- II. 1 and *protestantize*, etc.

Depth (depþ). late ME. [f. DEEP *a.* + -TH, after *length*: cf. *breadth, width.*]

I. 1. Measurement from the top downwards, from the outer part inwards, or from front to back. **2.** The quality of being DEEP 1526. **3.** *fig.* Profundity; penetration 1590; intensity 1624. **4.** *Logic.* = COMPREHENSION, q. v. 1864.

1. Alle these thre dymensions..that is to seye lengthe, brede and depthe LYDG. Serried Shields in thick array Of d. immeasurable MILT. *P. L.* I. 549. 2. Because it had no d. of erth TINDALE *Matt.* xiii. 5. 3. D. of knowledge BP. HALL. A man of extraordinary d. HEARNE. To sound the d. of this knauerie *Tam. Shr.* V. i. 141. D. of silence 1624, of shadow ROGERS.

II. Concrete senses. **1.** A deep water; a deep part of the sea (usu. in *pl.*; now *poet.* and *rhet.*) late ME.; †the DEEP –1611. **2.** A deep place in the earth, etc.; *pl.* the lowest part of a pit, etc. (*rhet.*) 1523. **3.** An abyss; the deep or remote part. Usu. *pl.* (*poet.* and *rhet.*) 1613. **4.** The inmost part. Also *pl.* late ME. **5.** The middle part 1605. **6.** *fig.* The inmost, remotest, or extreme part. Now often *pl.* late ME.

1. The depths haue couered them *Ex.* xv. 5. 2. The depths of Hell DRYDEN. 3. The Depths of Heav'n above, and Earth below DRYDEN. Measureless depths of air LONGF. 4. In d. of woods embrac'd POPE. 5. The d. of winter BOLTON. 6. The depths of unrecorded time SHELLEY.

Phr. *Beyond* or *out of one's d.*: *lit.* in water too deep for one to touch bottom without sinking; *fig.* beyond one's powers or understanding. *attrib.* **d. bomb, charge,** a bomb to be exploded at a given depth. Hence **De·pthless** *a.* unfathomable; shallow.

De·pthen, *v.* 1587. [f. prec.] = DEEPEN.

†**Depu·cel, -elle,** *v.* ME. [a. F. *dépuceler* :—L. DIS- + F. *pucelle.*] *trans.* To deflower –1483. var. †**Depu·celate** (*rare*).

†**Depu·dorate,** *v.* [DE- II. 1.] To make shameless. CUDWORTH.

†**Depu·lse,** *v.* 1555. [ad. L. *depulsare*, freq. of *depellere.*] *trans.* To drive or thrust away –1623. So †**Depu·lsion,** the action of driving or thrusting away. †**Depu·lsive** *a.* averting; prophylactic. †**Depu·lsory** *a.* depulsive.

Depurant (dǐpiū·ᵊrănt, de·piu-), *a.* 1875. [ad. med. L. *depurantem* (see below).] Purifying; *Med.* Having the quality of purifying the blood or other fluids of the body. Also as *sb.*

Depurate (dǐpiū·rēⁱt, de·piu-), *v.* 1620. [f. ppl. stem of med.L. *depurare*; see DE- I. 3. Cf. F. *dépurer.*] To make or become free from impurities. Also *fig.*

Sufficient to d. the blood 1751.

So †**Depu·rate** *ppl. a.* purified, cleansed, clarified. **Depura·tion,** the action or process of freeing from impurities: in *Med.* the removal of impurities from the humours or fluids of the body. **Depu·rative, de·purative** *a.* depurant; *sb.* a depurant. **De·purator,** an agent or apparatus that purifies. **Depu·ratory** *a.* (*sb.*) = *depurative.*

†**Depu·re,** *v.* ME. [ad. F. *dépurer*; see DEPURATE.] = DEPURATE *v.* –1873.

Depurition, bad f. DEPURATION.

Deputable (dǐpiū·tăb'l, de·piŭ-), *a.* 1621. [irreg. f. DEPUTE *v.* + -ABLE.] Capable of being, or fit to be, deputed.

Deputation (depiutē·ʃən), *sb.* ME. [f. L. *deputare*; cf. F. *députation.*] †**1.** *gen.* Appointment (to an office, function, etc.) –1650. **2.** *spec.* Appointment to act on behalf of another; delegation 1552. †**3.** An appointment by the lord of the manor to the office and rights of a gamekeeper; a document conveying this –1815. **4.** A person or body of persons appointed to go on a mission on behalf of another or others. (The chief current use.) 1732.

2. That we Feed them our selves, and not by Proxy or D. 1698. 4. A d. of the Houses waited on the King D'ISRAELI. Hence **Deputa·tional** *a.* of or belonging to a d.

Deputative (de·piŭtēⁱtiv), *a.* 1625. [f. L. *deputat-* ppl. stem; see prec.] Characterized by deputation; of the nature of a deputy.

De·putator. *rare.* 1669. [f. L. *deputare.*] One who deputes another to act for him.

Depute (de·piut), *ppl. a.* and *sb.* Now only *Sc.* ME. [app. repr. OF. *depute* (mod.F. *député*) pa. pple., the final *e* having become mute.]

†**A.** as *pa. pple.* Deputed; imputed; appointed, assigned; see DEPUTE *v.* –1623.

B. *sb.* = DEPUTY ME.

Depute (dǐpiū·t), *v.* ME. [a. F. *députer*, ad. L. *deputare*; see DE- I. 2.] †**1.** *trans.* To appoint –1683. †**2.** To impute, ascribe –1592. †**3.** To consign –1483. **4.** To assign (a charge); now *spec.* to commit (authority, etc.) to a deputy or substitute 1495. **5.** *spec.* To appoint as one's substitute, delegate, or agent; to ordain to act on one's behalf 1552.

1. He deputed two howres for the matters of Asie LD. BERNERS. 4. The Devil may d. such and such powers..to his confederates DE FOE. 5. To d. Cassio in Othellos place *Oth.* IV. ii. 226.

Deputize (de·piŭtəiz), *v.* 1730. [f. DEPUTE *sb.* or DEPUTY.] **1.** To appoint as a deputy. Chiefly *U.S.* **2.** *intr.* To act as a deputy 1869.

Deputy (de·piŭti), *sb.* ME. [a. F. *député.* Orig. spelt *depute*; the final *e* passed through *-ee, -ie* to *-y*, as in CITY, etc. See also DEPUTE *sb.*] **1.** A person appointed to act for another or others; a substitute, lieutenant, vicegerent. Also *fig.* **2.** A person elected to represent a constituency; a member of a representative legislative assembly 1600. **3.** *attrib.*, etc. Deputed; acting or appointed to act instead of..; vice-.. 1548.

1. For the Greek lecture, the reader therof.. got a d. to do it WOOD. *General d.* (Law): a person authorized to act for another in the whole of his office, but having no interest in the office. *Special d.*: a person similarly authorized to exercise some special function only. Phr. *By d.*: by another person in one's stead. 2. *Chamber of Deputies*: the second house in the national assembly of France, and some other countries. 3. Singing women escorted by d. husbands MACAULAY. Hence **De·putyship,** the office, term of office, or position of a d.

†**Dequa·ntitate,** *v.* [f. DE- II. 1 + L. *quantitatem.*] To diminish the quantity of. SIR T. BROWNE.

Deracinate (dǐræ·sinēⁱt), *v.* 1599. [f. F. *déraciner*, f. *dé-*, *des-*, L. DIS- + *racine.*] To tear up by the roots; to eradicate.

The Culter rusts, That should d. such Sauagery *Hen. V*, V. ii. 47. Hence **Deracina·tion.**

†**Derai·gn,** *sb.* ME. [a. OF. *des-*, *der-*, *deraisne*, *-resne*, etc., f. *desraisnier.*] The action of vindicating one's right, *esp.* by wager of battle; hence, a duel –1658. So **Derai·gnment**[1] (in same sense).

Derai·gn, *v.*[1] Now *Hist.* ME. [a. OF. *deraisnier*, etc., f. *de-*, *des-* (see DE- I. 6) + *raisnier* :—late L. type **rationare*, f. *rationem.* Cf. also ARRAIGN.] *trans. Law.* To justify, vindicate, *esp.* by wager of battle; to contest; to challenge; to determine.

To d. battle (*combat*, etc.): †**a.** To maintain (a wager of battle, etc.); †**b.** To do battle; whence, to set the battle in array; †**c.** To dispose (troops, etc.) in battle array. (Elizabethan archaisms.)

†**Derai·gn,** *v.*[2] 1500. [a. OF. *desregner*, mod.F. *déranger* to DERANGE.] **1.** To derange –1706. **2.** *passive.* To be discharged from (religious) orders –1661. Hence †**Derai·gnment**[2], discharge from a religious order.

Derail (dǐrēⁱ·l), *v.* 1850. [ad. mod.F. *dérailler*; see DE- II. 2. First generally used in U.S.] To run or cause to run off the rails, as a locomotive. Hence **Derai·lment,** the fact of leaving or being thrown off the rails.

Derange (dǐrēⁱ·ndʒ), *v.* 1776. [a. mod.F. *déranger*, f. *dé-*, L. *dis-* + *renc*, mod.F. *rang.* Not in Johnson.] **1.** *trans.* To disturb or destroy the arrangement of; to throw into confusion; to disarrange 1777. **2.** To disturb the normal state, working, or functions of; to cause to act abnormally 1776. **3.** To disorder the mind or brain of 1825. **4.** To disturb 1848.

1. This letter deranged all the projects of James MACAULAY. 2. Habits..which tend..to d. the animal functions SIR B. BRODIE. 3. Minds deranged by sorrow MACAULAY. Hence **Dera·nged** *ppl. a.* disordered, disarranged; insane.

Derangement (dǐrēⁱ·ndʒmĕnt). 1737. [a. mod. F. *dérangement*; see DERANGE.] The act of deranging, or fact of being deranged; disorder; confusion; insanity.

Derate (dǐrēⁱ·t), *v.* 1928. [f. DE- + RATE *sb.*[1]] To diminish the burden of rates upon.

Deray (dǐrēⁱ·), *sb. arch.* ME. [a. OF. *desrei*, etc., f. tonic stem of *desreer*; see DERAY *v.*] **1.** †Disorder –1513; disarray, confusion (*mod. archaism*) 1831. †**2.** Violence, insolent ill-treatment –1550. **3.** Disorderly mirth 1500.

†**Deray** (dǐrēⁱ·), *v.* ME. [a. OF. *desreer*, etc. :—Rom. type **desredare*, f. L. DIS- + -*redare*, f. **redo* order; see ARRAY.] *refl.* and *intr.* To act in a disorderly manner; to rage.

Derby (dā·ɹbi, dɔ̄·ɹbi). The name of a town (in OE. *Déorabý, Déorbý*) and shire of England, and of an earldom named from the shire. See also DARBY. Hence **1.** Name of an annual horse-race, founded in 1780 by the twelfth Earl of Derby, and run at the Epsom races, usually on the Wednesday before, or the second Wednesday after, Whitsunday. **b.** Hence *attrib.* and in *comb.*, as **D. day,** the day on which the Derby is run. Also *transf.* **2.** Short for *D. hat*: a stiff felt hat with a rounded crown and narrow brim (*U.S.*) 1888. **3.** *Plastering.* See DARBY 1823.

Derbyshire (dā·ɹbi-, dɔ̄·ɹbiʃəɹ). [In OE. *Déorbý-scir*, *Déorbí-scir.*] The shire or county of Derby in England. Hence **1. D. neck**: goitre 1802. **2. D. spar,** †**drop**: fluor-spar 1772.

†**Der-do·ing,** *ppl. a.* A pseudo-archaism, app. from *dare-do* (cf. DERRING-DO), in the sense 'Doing daring deeds'. *F. Q.* II. vii. 10.

†**Dere,** *sb.* ME. [f. DERE *v.*] Harm, *esp.* in phr. *to do* (*a person*) *d.* –1674.

†**Dere,** *v.* [OE. *derian*, *derigan* :—WGer. **darjan*, OE. *daru* hurt, etc.] **1.** *trans.* To hurt. Also *absol.* –1613. **2.** To trouble, vex, incommode –1674.

Dereign(e, dereine, var. DERAIGN *v.*

Derelict (de·rǐlikt). 1649. [ad. L. *derelictus*, see DE- I. 3.]

A. *adj.* **1.** Forsaken, abandoned, left by the possessor or guardian; *transf.* said of land left by the sea. **2.** Guilty of dereliction of duty; delinquent (*U.S.*) 1864.

1. A sort of d. possession, to be seized by the occu-

pant HALLAM. *fig.* So as to seize upon the vacant, unoccupied, d. minds of his friends BURKE.

B. *sb.* **1.** That which is abandoned or deserted; *esp.* a vessel abandoned at sea 1670. **2.** One guilty of dereliction of duty (*U.S.*) 1888.

1. I was a D. from my cradle SAVAGE. So †**Dere·li·ct** *v.* to abandon, forsake (*rare*).

Dereliction (derĭli·kʃən). 1597. [ad. L. *derelictionem*, f. *derelinquere*; see prec.] **1.** The action of leaving or forsaking (with intention not to resume); the condition of being forsaken or abandoned. Now *rare*. **b.** *fig.* The leaving of land by the sea; *concr.* the land thus left 1767. **2.** In mod. use implying a reprehensible abandonment or neglect; chiefly in phr. *d. of duty* 1778. **b.** Hence *absol.* Failure in duty, delinquency 1830. †**3.** Failure, cessation; fainting –1807.

1. Imposts..by long d. apparently obsolete BRYCE. Lands newly created..by the alluvion or d. of the sea BLACKSTONE. 2. A d. of every opinion and principle that I have held BURKE.

Dereligionize; see DE- II. 1.

Dereling, -yng, obs. ff. DARLING.

†**Dereli·nquish,** *v.* [Cf. DERELICT.] To relinquish utterly, abandon –1799.

†**Derf,** *sb.* [app. shortened from OE. *gedeorf*, f. *deorfan* to labour.] Trouble, hurt.

†**Derf,** *a.* (*adv.*) ME. [app. a. ON. *djarfr* bold, etc.] Bold; audacious; sturdy; painful; dreadful; difficult –16... †**De·rfful** *a.* ? = DERF *a.* †**De·rf-ly** *adv.*, **-ness.**

Deric (de·rik), *a.* 1878. [f. Gr. δέρος skin.] *Biol.* Pertaining to, or constituting, the skin.

Deride (dĭrəi·d), *v.* 1530. [ad. L. *deridere*; see DE- I. 4.] **1.** To laugh at in contempt; to laugh to scorn; to make sport of, mock. †**2.** *intr.* To laugh scornfully –1675.

1. And the rulers also..derided him *Luke* xxiii. 35. He justly derides the absurd reverence for antiquity GIBBON. Hence **Deri·der. Deri·dingly** *adv.*

Derisible (dĭri·zib'l), *a.* 1657. [f. L. *deris-*, ppl. stem of *deridere*; see -BLE.] To be derided; worthy of derision.

Derision (dĭri·ʒən). ME. [a. F. *dérision*, ad. L. *derisionem*.] **1.** The action of deriding; ridicule, mockery. **2.** *concr.* An object of ridicule; a laughing-stock 1539.

1. Scorne and d. neuer comes in teares *Mids. N.* III. ii. 123. But now they that are younger than I have me in d. *Job* xxx. 1. 2. His word was a reproach and a d. to the profane 1612.

Derisive (dĭrəi·siv), *a.* 1662. [f. L. *deris-*, ppl. stem of *deridere*.] Characterized by derision; scoffing, mocking, as *d. cheers*. Hence **Deri·sive-ly** *adv.*, **-ness.**

Derisory (dĭrəi·səri), *a.* 1618. [ad. L. *derisorius*.] = prec.

Derivable (dĭrəi·văb'l), *a.* 1640. [f. DERIVE *v.*] Capable of being derived (see DERIVE *v.*); †transmissible –1716; obtainable 1711; deducible 1653; traceable *from* (a source) 1682.

The income d. from a capital sum of..twenty-six millions 1884. Hence **Derivabi·lity** (*rare*). **Derivably** *adv.* in a derivative manner.

Derival (dĭrəi·văl). *rare.* 1871. [f. DERIVE *v.*; see -AL 2.] Derivation.

Derivant (dĭrəi·vănt). 1876. [a. F. *dérivant*.]

A. *adj. Med.* = DERIVATIVE 1 b.

B. *sb. Math.* Applied to derived function of a special kind.

Derivate (de·rivĕt). 1494. [ad. L. *derivatus, -um*.]

A. as *pa. pple.* and *a.* Derived.

B. *sb.* Anything derived 1660. So †**De·rivate** *v. rare*, = DERIVE *v.* (*trans.* and *intr.*).

Derivation (derivēi·ʃən). 1530. [a. F., ad. L. *derivationem*.] †**1.** The leading or carrying a current of water, or the like, *from* a source, *to* another part; *concr.* a branch of a river, etc. which does this –1835. **b.** The action of leading away (in a current); diversion; an instance of this; in *Electr.* a fault 1855. **c.** *Med.* The withdrawal of inflammation, etc., from a diseased part of the body, by blistering, cupping, etc. 1600. †**2.** Transmission; communication –1699. **3.** The action of drawing, obtaining, or deducing from a source 1660. **4.** Extraction, origin, descent 1599. **5.** A derivate, a derivative 1641. **6.** *Gram.* Origination as a derivative 1530; the tracing of the origin of a word from its root or radical elements 1596. **7.** *Math.* The operation of passing from any function to any derivative function; *spec.* differentiation 1816. **8.** *Biol.* The theory of evolution of organic forms 1874.

1. The fleet passed from the Euphrates into an artificial d. of that river GIBBON. 3. There was no real d. of English law from Normandy FREEMAN. 4. *Hen. V*, III. ii. 141. 5. The Father is the whole substance, but the Son a d. MILTON. 6. The d. of the word Substance favours the idea we have of it LOCKE. Hence **Deriva·tional** *a.* **Deriva·tionist,** (*Biol.*) one who holds the theory of d. of organic types; one who occupies himself with the d. of words.

Derivative (dĭri·vătiv). 1530. [a. F. *dérivatif, -ive*, ad. L. *derivativus* (Priscian).]

A. *adj.* **1.** †Characterized by transmission –1640. **b.** *Med.* Producing derivation; see DERIVATION 1 c. 1851. **2.** Of derived character or nature 1530. **3.** Of or pertaining to a theory of derivation; derivational 1871.

2. A secondary and d. kind of Fame STEELE. *D. circulation*, term applied to the direct communication which exists between arteries and veins in some parts of the body, so that all the blood does not necessarily pass through the capillaries of these parts (*Syd. Soc. Lex.*). A d. word L. MURRAY, conveyance 1848.

B. *sb.* **1.** A thing of derived character 1593. **2.** *Gram.* Any word which is not a primitive word or root 1530. **3.** *Math.* A function derived from another; *spec.* a differential coefficient 1674. **4.** *Mus.* A chord derived from a fundamental chord, *esp.* by inversion; also, the (assumed) root, from the harmonics of which a chord is derived 1828. **5.** *Chem.* A method or agent that produces DERIVATION (q. v., 1 c) 1843.

1. The third deriuatiue of Delicacie, is sloth NASHE. Hence **Deri·vative-ly** *adv.*, **-ness** (*rare*).

Derive (dĭrəi·v), *v.* ME. [a. F. *dériver*, ad. L. *derivare*, f. DE- I. 2 + *rivus*.]

I. Transitive senses. †**1.** To conduct *from* a source, etc. *to* or *into* a channel, place, etc.; to convey through a channel –1805. †**2.** To draw off, divert the course of; *spec.* in *Med.*, cf. DERIVATION 1 c. –1771. †**3.** To carry (a channel of any kind) –1777. **4.** *transf.* and *fig.* To convey from one to another, as by transmission, descent, etc.; to hand on (*Obs.* or *arch.*) 1526. Also †*refl.* †**5.** To cause to come –1808. **6.** To draw, fetch, obtain. Const. *from*, rarely †*out of*. 1561. Also *refl.*; also *absol.* **b.** *Chem.* To obtain (a compound) from another, as by partial replacement 1868. **7.** To obtain by reasoning; to gather, deduce 1509. **8.** *refl.* To come *from* something as its source 1662. Also *passive* (in same sense) ME. **9.** *trans.* To trace or show the derivation, origin, or pedigree of; to state a thing to be derived *from* 1600.

4. Parents..rich enough to d. unto him the hereditary infirmity of the gout FULLER. 6. O that estates, degrees, and offices, Were not deriu'd corruptly *Merch. V.* II. ix. 42. Sculpture may d. its Pedegree from the infancy of the World EVELYN. *absol.* The grantee whom he derives from BURKE. 7. Rules .. derived from nature 1624. 8. *pass.* A Participle is an Adjective derived of a Verb WESLEY. 9. To d. dream from drama JOHNSON, religion from myths 1874.

II. Intrans. senses. **1.** To have its derivation *from*, rarely *out of* ME. **2.** To proceed (*to* a receiver, etc.) 1559.

1. The Family he derives from 1684. The words *Comus* and *Encomium* d. thence 1866. 2. Puritanism ..derives to this country directly from Geneva M. PATTISON.

Hence †**Deri·vement** (*rare*), derivation; that which is derived. **Deri·ver.**

Derk(e, -ly, etc., obs. ff. DARK, -LY, etc.

Derm (dɜ̄ɹm). 1835. [f. Gr. δέρμα skin; cf. F. *derme*.] *Anat.* The layer of tissue forming the true skin or corium of an animal.

‖**Derma** (dɜ̄·ɹmă). 1706. [mod.L.] *Anat.* = prec. Hence **De·rmad** *adv.* toward the skin. **De·rmal** *a.* pertaining to the skin in general; cutaneous; *occas.*, pertaining to the derma, as opp. to *epidermal*. **Derma·tic, De·rmic** *adjs.* of or relating to the skin; dermal. **De·rmatoid, De·rmoid** *adjs.* resembling or of the nature of skin; *occas.*, dermal.

‖**Dermaptera** (dəɹmæ·ptĕră), *sb. pl.* 1835. [f. Gr. δέρμα skin + πτερόν wing; in mod.F. *dermaptère*.] *Entom.* An order of orthopterous insects, comprising the Earwigs. Hence **Derma·pteran** *a.* belonging to the D.; *sb.* one of the D.; **Derma·pterous** *a.* belonging to the D.

De·rmat-, de·rmato-, comb. stem of Gr. δέρμα, δέρματ- skin, hide, leather, as in ‖**Dermata·lgia** *Path.*, neuralgia of the skin. **Dermatine** (dɜ̄·ɹmătin), *a.* [Gr. δερμάτινος] = DERMATIC. ‖**Dermati·tis,** inflammation of the skin. **Dermatobra·nchia**; see DERMO-. **De·rmatogen** *Bot.*, the primordial cellular layer in the embryo plant, from which the epidermis is developed. **Dermato·graphy** [-GRAPHY], description of the skin. **Dermato·logy** [-LOGY], the branch of science which treats of the skin and its diseases; hence **Dermatolo·gical** *a.*, **Dermato·logist.** ‖**Dermato·lysis** [Gr. λύσις], a relaxed and pendulous condition of the skin. ‖**Dermatomyco·sis** [Gr. μύκης fungus], skin-disease caused by a vegetable parasite, *e.g.* ringworm. ‖**Dermatono·sis** [Gr. νόσος], skin-disease. **Dermato·pathy** [Gr. πάθος], skin-disease. **De·rmatophyte** = DERMO-(*phyte*). **De·rmatopla·sty** [Gr. πλαστός], 'the remedying of skin defects by a plastic operation' (*Syd. Soc. Lex.*). **Dermato·ptera** = DERMAPTERA. **De·rmatopsy,** 'skin-vision', sensitiveness of the skin to light. **Dermato·ptic** *a.* [Gr. ὀπτικός] *Zool.*, having 'skin-vision'. ‖**Dermatorrhœ·a** [Gr. ῥοία], a morbidly increased secretion from the skin. ‖**Dermatosclero·sis** [Gr. σκλήρωσις], induration of the skin; sclerodermia. ‖**Dermato·sis,** the formation of bony plates or scales in the skin; also a skin-disease (*Syd. Soc. Lex.*). **Dermato-ske·leton** = DERMO-(*skeleton*). **Dermato·tomy** = DERMO-(*tomy*). ‖**Dermatozo·a** [Gr. ζῷον], animal parasites of the skin; hence ‖**Dermatozoöno·sis,** skin-disease caused by animal parasites.

‖**Dermestes** (dəɹme·stīz). 1802. [irreg. f. Gr. δέρμα + ἐσθίειν to eat.] *Entom.* A genus of beetles (the type of the family *Dermestidæ*), the larvæ of which are very destructive to leather and other animal substances. Hence **Derme·stid** *a.* belonging to the family *Dermestidæ*; *sb.* one of this family. **Derme·stoid** *a.* resembling the genus *D.*; belonging to the *Dermestidæ*.

‖**Dermis** (dɜ̄·ɹmis). 1830. [mod.L., after ἐπιδερμίς *epidermis*.] *Anat.* = DERM.

Dermo-, repr. Gr. δερμο-, shortened comb. f. δέρμα, δέρματ-, skin, etc. (as in δερμόπτερος); hence

Dermobranchia (dɜ̄ɹmo͜ibræ·ŋkiă), **-branchi·a·ta** [BRANCHIA] *Zool.*, a group of molluscs, having external gills in the form of dorsal membranous tufts; hence **Dermobra·nchiate** *a.* **Dermoga·stric** *a.* [Gr. γαστήρ], pertaining to the skin and stomach, as in *d. pores*, etc. **Dermo·graphy** = DERMATOGRAPHY. **Dermohæmal** (-hī·măl) *a.*, pertaining to the skin of the hæmal or ventral aspect of the body; applied to the ventral fin rays of fishes, in their relation to the hæmal arch. **Dermohæ·mia,** hyperæmia of the skin. **Dermohu·meral** *a.*, pertaining to the skin and humerus, as in the *d. muscle* in some animals. **Dermo·logy, Dermomyco·sis**; see DERMATO-. **Dermomu·scular** *a.*, of skin and muscle. **Dermoneu·ral** *a.*, pertaining to the skin of the neural or dorsal aspect of the body; applied to the dorsal fin rays of fishes, in their relation to the neural arch. **Dermopa·thic, -o·pathy**; see DERMATO-. **De·rmophyte** [Gr. φυτόν], a parasitic vegetable growth in the skin; hence **Dermophy·tic** *a.* ‖**Dermo·ptera** *pl.* [Gr. δερμόπτερος] *Zool.*, a sub-order of Insectivora, containing the *Galeopithecus* or Flying Lemur of the Moluccas (from the wing-like extension of skin, which enables them to take flying leaps). **Dermo·pterous** *a.*, having membranous wings (or fins). **Dermoptery·gian** *a.*, having membranous fins. **Dermorhy·nchous** *a.* [Gr. ῥύγχος snout], having the bill covered by an epidermis, as in the duck. **Dermoscle·rite** [Gr. σκληρός hard], a mass of spicules in the outer layer of the tissue of some Actinozoa. **Dermoske·leton,** the external bony, shelly, crustaceous, or coriaceous integument of many invertebrates and some vertebrates (*e.g.* crabs, tortoises); hence **Dermoske·letal** *a.* **Dermo·tomy** [Gr. -τομια], the anatomy of the skin.

†**Dern.** [OE. *derne, dierne, dyrne*:—OTeut. **darnjo-*.]

A. *adj.* Secret; dark; private –1460.

B. *sb.* A secret –ME.; secrecy –1508; a secret place –1500. Hence †**Derne** *adv.* †**De·rnly**

adv. darkly; dismally (SPENSER). †**De·rnful** *a.* dreary. (A pseudo-archaism.)

Dern, a door-post; see DURN.

Dern, var. of DARN = DAMN.

†**Dern, darn,** *v.* Now *dial.* [OE. *diernan, dyrnan, dernan* :—OTeut. **darnjan*; see prec.] †1. *trans.* To hide –ME. Also *refl.* and *intr.* †2. To cause to hide, run to earth –1637.

Dernier (dǝ·rniǝı, ‖dęrnye), *a.* 1602. [a. F. :—OF. *derrenier*, deriv. of *derrein*; see DARREIN.] Last, ultimate, final. *Obs.*, exc. in *d. ressort*, †*resort*, last refuge; *orig.* last court of appeal; *the* (or *le*) *d. cri* [lit. the last cry], the very latest fashion.

Dero·be, *v. rare.* [DE- II. 1.] To doff.

De·rogate, *ppl. a.* Now *rare.* ME. [ad. L. *derogatus*; see next.] †1. *pa. pple.* Abrogated in part; lessened in authority, etc. –1587. 2. *adj.* Debased 1605. Hence †**De·rogately** *adv.* (*Ant. & Cl.* II. ii. 33.)

Derogate (de·rǒgeit), *v.* 1513. [f. ppl. stem of L. *derogare*; see DE- I. 2.] †1. *trans.* To repeal or abrogate in part; to destroy or impair the force and effect of; to lessen the extent of –1577. †2. To detract from; to disparage, depreciate –1642. 3. To take away (something *from*) so as to lessen or impair (*arch.*) 1561. Also *absol.* or *intr.* 4. *intr.* To do something derogatory to one's rank or position; to degenerate 1611.

2. To d. the author of the booke BILLINGSLEY. 3. Not to d. credit from your owne word BINGHAM. To d. from the Authority of the Ancients 1640, from Pompey ADDISON. 4. I do not d. In loving Romney Leigh MRS. BROWNING. Hence **De·rogator.**

Derogation (derǒgē¹·ʃǝn). 1450. [a. F., ad. L. *derogationem.*] 1. The partial abrogation or repeal of a law, etc. 1548. 2. Impairment of the power or authority *of*; detraction *from* 1450. 3. Lowering in value or estimation, disparagement, depreciation 1520. 4. Falling off in character or excellence; loss of rank 1838.

1. New and subtile inuentions in d. of the Common Law COKE. 2. Papal usurpations, to the d. of the Crown CARTE. 4. He might pretend surely to his kinswoman's hand without d. THACKERAY.

Derogative (dǐrǫ·gătiv), *a.* 1477. [a. OF., f. ppl. stem of L. *derogare.*] Tending to derogation; derogatory.

Derogatory (dǐrǫ·gătǝri), *a.* 1502. [ad. L. *derogatorius*, f. *derogator.*] 1. Having the character of derogating (see DEROGATE *v.* 1). Const. *to, from*, †*of.* 2. Lowering in honour or estimation; depreciatory 1563.

1. Provided there be nothing contain'd in the Law ..d. from his supreme power HOBBES. 2. Conduct.. d. to his rank JAMES.

†*D. clause*: a clause in a will, deed, etc., by which the right of subsequently altering or cancelling it is abrogated, and the validity of a later document, doing this, is made dependent on the correct repetition of the clause and its formal revocation.

Hence **Dero·gatori-ly** *adv.*, **-ness.**

Derotremate (derotrī·mět), *a.* 1849. [ad. mod.L. *derotrematus* (in neut. pl. *Derotremata* name of the group), f. Gr. δέρη neck + τρῆμα(τ-boring.] *Zool.* Of or pertaining to the *Derotremata*, a group of urodele batrachians, having gill-slits. So **Derotre·matous** *a.* **De·rotreme** *a.* and *sb.*

Derout (dǐrau·t), *sb.* 1644. [a. F. *déroute.*] An utter ROUT. So **Derou·t** *v.* to put completely to flight.

Derrick (de·rik), *sb.* 1600. [From the surname of a hangman at Tyburn *c* 1600; *orig.* the Du. *Dirk, Dierryk, Diederik* = Ger. *Dietrich, Theodoric.*] †1. A hangman; hanging; the gallows. (Cf. *Jack Ketch.*) –1656. 2. A contrivance for hoisting or moving heavy weights, consisting of a spar or boom set up obliquely, with its head steadied by guys, and furnished with suitable tackle and purchases; orig. used on board ship. b. A kind of crane (in full *d.-crane*) in which the jib is pivoted to the foot of the central post; a 'jib and tie' crane. 1727.

Derring do, derring-do. *pseudo-archaism.* ME. [f. *durran, dorren* to DARE, and *don, do*, pres. inf. of DO *v.*] *lit.* Daring to do (CHAUCER *Troylus* V. 837); but misconstrued as a substantive phrase, and taken to mean, Daring action or feats, desperate courage. So †**Derring doers,** daring doers (SPENSER).

Derringer (de·rindʒǝı). *U.S.* 1856. [f. the inventor's surname.] A small pistol with large bore, very effective at short range. Also *attrib.*

Derry (de·ri). 1553. A meaningless word used in refrains of songs; *hence*, a set of verses.

Derth(e, obs. f. DEARTH.

Deruralize; see DE- II. 1 and *ruralize.*

†**Derve,** *v.* [ME. *derven* str. and weak; the str. vb. app. = OE. *deorfan* to labour.] 1. *intr.* To labour. (Only in OE.) 2. *trans.* To trouble, hurt, molest –ME.

Dervish (dǝ·ıviʃ). 1585. [a. (ult.) Pers. *darvēsh, darvīsh* poor, a friar, etc. (The native Arabic equiv. is *faqīr* poor, fakir.)] A Mohammedan friar, who has taken vows of poverty and austere life.

Des- in obs. words; see DEC-, DESC-, DESS-, DIS-.

Des-, *prefix.* Regular Romanic form of L. *dis-*; in mod.F. *dés-* bef. a vowel or silent *h*, otherwise *dé-* (OF. *descharge*, mod. *décharge*). Occas. repr. a late L. *de-ex-*, for L. *ex-*. Early OF. words passed into English with the prefix in the form *des-* (*descharge*, ME. *descharge*), but have all a later form in DIS-, under which they are here treated. See also DISPATCH.

‖**Descamisado** (deskamisā·do). 1823. [Sp.; = shirtless. Cf. *sans-culotte.*] A nickname for the ultra-liberals in the Spanish revolutionary war of 1820–23. Also *transf.*

Descant (de·skænt), *sb.* Also 6–9 **dis-.** ME. [a. OF. *deschant*, mod. *déchant*, f. L. *dis-* apart + *cantus.*]

I. *Mus.* Now *Hist.*, or *poet.* 1. A melodious accompaniment to the *plainsong*, sung or played above it: the earliest form of counterpoint. 2. The soprano or highest part of the score in part-singing 1569. 3. *gen.* A melodious strain 1576. 4. Musical composition, harmony; also, a harmonized composition 1565. 5. An instrumental prelude, consisting of variations on a given theme 1644.

1. The merry Larke hir mattins sings aloft; The Thrush replyes; the Mavis d. playes SPENSER. 3. The birds in vain their amorous d. join GRAY. 5. And then a low sad d. rung, As prelude to the lay he sung SCOTT.

II. Transf. uses. †1. Variation from that which is typical or customary –1712. 2. Varied comment on a theme; a comment; †*occas.*, censorious criticism 1594; a disquisition 1622.

1. Running, Leaping, and Dancing, the descants on the plain song of walking FULLER. 2. With merry descants on a nation's woes COWPER.

Descant (dĕskæ·nt), *v.* 1510. [a. OF. *deschanter, descanter*, in med.L. *discantare* (*des-, dē-*), f. prec.] 1. *Mus.* To play or sing an air in harmony with a fixed theme; *gen.* to warble 1538. 2. *intr.* To comment, enlarge (*upon, on*) 1510. †3. *trans.* To comment on; *occas.* to carp at –1649.

2. He used to d. critically on the dishes which had been at table BOSWELL. Hence **Desca·nter.**

Descend (dǐse·nd), *v.* ME. [a. F. *descendre* :—L. *descendere*, f. DE- I. 1 + *scandere* to climb.]

I. Intr. senses. 1. To move or pass from a higher to a lower place; to come or go down, fall, sink. (The general word; the opposite of *ascend.*) Also *fig.* †b. To disembark; to alight –1600. c. *Astron.*, etc. To move towards the horizon; to move southwards ME. 2. *transf.* To slope downwards ME. 3. To come down with or as a hostile force; to fall violently *upon* ME. 4. To proceed to something subsequent in time or order, or (*esp.*) from generals to particulars ME. 5. To come down; to condescend, stoop (*to do* something); usually in a bad sense 1554. 6. *Mus.* To go down the scale 1597. 7. To come *of*, spring *from* (an ancestor or ancestral stock) ME. Also *fig.* 8. *intr.* To come down by way of inheritance 1486. Also *transf.* of personal qualities, etc.

1. The moist droppes of the rein Descenden into middel erthe GOWER. *fig.* Sleep nor quiet upon my eyes descended R. ELLIS. c. The setting Sun Slowly descended MILT. *P. L.* IV. 541. Phr. †*To d. into* or *within oneself*: to betake oneself to deep consideration. 3. That the Turke woulde d. upon the realme of Naples 1600. 5. Wordsworth..descends to such babyisms 1829. 7. We are descended of ancient Families STEELE. 8. The Crowne..descended on her GOUGE.

II. Trans. senses. †1. To cause to descend –1677. 2. To go or come down; to pass downwards over, along, or through 1607.

2. To d. the Hill MILT. steps 1891.

Descendance, -ence (dǐse·ndăns). Now *rare.* 1599. [a. F. *descendance*; see -ANCE, -ENCE.] 1. = DESCENT 7. 2. *concr.* Descendants. (App. a corruption.) var. †**Desce·ndancy, -ency.**

Descendant, -ent (dǐse·ndănt). 1572. [a. F. *descendant*; see -ANT, -ENT. Johnson gives *Descendant* sb., *Descendent* adj., but the distinction is now worth little.]

A. *adj.* 1. Descending (*rare*) 1644; *Her.* descending towards the base of the shield 1572. 2. Descending or originating from an ancestor; also *fig.* 1594.

2. Were not wise sons descendent [*v. l.* -ant] of the wise POPE.

B. *sb.* 1. One who is descended from an ancestor; issue (in any degree) 1600. Also *fig.* and *transf.* †2. *Astron.* The part of the heavens which at any moment is descending below the horizon (opp. to the ASCENDANT) 1690.

1. Abraham s descendents according to the flesh 1729.

Descendental (dǐsende·ntăl), *a. nonce-wd.* 1850. [f. L. *descendentem*: after *transcendental.*] That descends to matter of fact; realistic.

†**Desce·nder** [1]. 1485. [a. F. *descendre*, used subst.; cf. *attainder*, etc.] *Law.* Descent; title of descent –1768.

Descender [2] (dǐse·ndǝı). 1667. [f. DESCEND *v.*] One who or that which descends; in *Typogr.* a letter that descends below the line.

Descendible, -able (dǐse·ndĭb'l, -ăb'l), *a.* 1495. [a. OF. *descendable*: subseq. refash. after L.] 1. That descends or may descend to an heir. 2. Capable of being descended; down which one may go (*rare*) 1730. Hence **Descendibi·lity** (*rare*).

Descending (dǐse·ndiŋ), *ppl. a.* 1642. [f. DESCEND *v.* + -ING [2].] 1. *lit.* Moving downwards 1700. 2. *transf.* Directed downwards, as *d. aorta, colon*, etc. 1737; *spec.* in *Her.* (see DESCENDANT *a.* 1). 3. *fig.* Proceeding to what is lower in position or value, or later in order; in *Math.* of series: Proceeding from higher to lower quantities or powers 1642.

D. node (Astron.): that node of a planet's orbit at which it passes from north to south of the ecliptic. Hence **Desce·ndingly** *adv.*

Descension (dǐse·nʃǝn). Now *rare.* ME. [a. OF., ad. L. *descensionem.*] 1. The action of descending; descent (*lit.* and *fig.*). Now *rare.* †2. Lineage –1523. †3. A coming down from dignity or high station; condescension –1692. †4. *Old Chem.* A method of distillation, in which the vapour was forced to distil downwards –1751. †5. *Astron.* The setting, or descent below the horizon, of a celestial body –1726. †6. *Astrol.* The part of the zodiac in which a planet had least influence (opp. to *exaltation*) 15..

5. *Right d., oblique d.* of a celestial body: the degree of the celestial equator, reckoned from the first point of Aries, which sets with it in a right, or oblique, sphere. Hence **Desce·nsional** *a.* of or pertaining to d. (*rare*).

Descensive (dǐse·nsiv), *a.* 1611. [f. L. *descens-, descendere*; see -IVE.] 1. Having the quality of descending (*lit.* and *fig.*); opp. to *ascensive.* 2. *Gram.* Diminishing the force 1854.

†**Desce·nsory,** *sb.* ME. [ad. OF. *descensoire, -oir*, med.L. type *descensorium.*] *Old. Chem.* A vessel used for distillation by DESCENT –1678. So †**Desce·nsory** *a.* relating to, or of the nature of, distillation by descent.

Descent (dǐse·nt). ME. [a. F. *descente*, after *attente, vente*, etc.] 1. The action of descending; downward motion (of any kind). Also *fig.* †b. *Old Chem.* = DESCENSION 4. –1751. 2. *concr.* A downward slope, a declivity 1591; a means of descending; a way leading downwards 1634; †the lowest part. *Lear* V. iii. 137. 3. A sudden hostile invasion or attack, *esp.* from the sea 1600. 4. *fig.* A coming down to a lower state or condition; fall, decline, sinking; progress downwards to that which is subordinate 1667; a stage or step downward (? *obs.*) 1589. 5. A fall, lowering (of the pitch of sound, temperature, or the like) 1581. 6. The action of proceeding in sequence, discourse, or argument, to what is subsequent; subsequent part or course; succession 1642. 7. The fact of descending from an ancestor or ancestral stock; lineage ME. Also *transf.* (in *Biol.* extended to origination of species) and *fig.* †8. A line of descent, lineage –1618; a descendant (*lit.* and *fig.*); also, issue –1667. 9. A stage in the line of descent; a generation 1513. 10. *Law.* The passing of (real) property to the heir or heirs without disposition by will; transmission by inheritance ME. Also *transf.* and *fig.*

1. The d. to Avernus 1866. 2. At the d. of the mount of Oliues *Luke* xix. 37. 3. Argyle was threatening a d. upon Scotland SCOTT. 4. Her birth was by manie degrees greater than mine, and my woorth by manie discents lesse than hers GREENE. 8. Our d... Which must be born to certain woe, devourd By Death at last MILT. *P. L.* x. 979. 9. Euen twelue descents after the flood BILSON.

Describe (dǐskrəi·b), *v.* 1513. [ad. L. *describere*; see DE- I. 2. In ME. *descrive* (through OF.).] †1. To write down –1667. 2. To set forth in words by reference to characteristics; to give a detailed or graphic account of. (The ordinary current sense.) 1513. 3. To set forth in delineation; to represent, picture, portray. *Obs.* or *arch.* 1526. 4. To delineate, trace the outline of 1552. 5. To form or trace by motion 1559. 6. To mark off or distribute into parts. *Josh.* xviii. 6. ¶ 7. = DESCRY *v.*[1] 1574.

2. D. we next the Nature of the Bees DRYDEN. 3. A Gladiatore .. admirably described in Marble E. BLOUNT. 4. A triangle..described vpon a line 1570. 5. The most northely circle which the Sonne describeth 1559. Hence **Descri·bable** *a.* **Descri·ber.**

Describent (dǐskrəi·bĕnt). 1704. [ad. L. *describentem.*]

A. *adj.* 'Describing, marking out by its motion' (Ash).

B. *sb. Geom.* A point, line, or surface, generating by its motion a line, surface, or solid.

Descrier (dǐskrəi·əɹ). 1599. [f. DESCRY *v.*[1] + -ER [1].] One who descries.

Descri·pt, *ppl. a.* 1665. [ad. L. *descriptus.*] Described; apportioned; inscribed, engraved.

Description (dǐskri·pʃən). ME. [a. F., ad. L. *descriptionem*, f. *describere.*] †1. The action of writing down. CAXTON. 2. The action of setting forth in words by mentioning characteristics; verbal representation or portraiture ME.; (with *pl.*) a graphic or detailed account ME.; in *Logic*, a definition by non-essential attributes. 3. The combination of qualities or features that marks out or describes a particular class; hence, a sort, species, kind, or variety 1596. †4. Pictorial representation (*rare*) –1646. 5. *Geom.* a. The describing of a geometrical figure; see DESCRIBE *v.* 4. ? *Obs.* 1655. b. Tracing out or passing over a certain course or distance 1706.

2. For her owne person, It beggard all discription *Ant. & Cl.* II. ii. 203. 3. A friend of this d. SHAKS. A d. of vehicle, peculiar..to Cuba 1844.

Descriptive (dǐskri·ptiv), *a.* 1751. [ad. (late) L. *descriptivus.* Cf. F. *descriptif.*] Having the quality or function of describing; serving to describe; characterized by description.

D. words JOHNSON, poets HAZLITT, Anatomy (*mod.*). A name..d. of its construction HUXLEY. Hence **Descri·ptive-ly** *adv.*, **-ness.**

Descri·ve, *v.* Now only *Sc.* ME. [a. OF. *descrivre*, full stem *descriv-* (mod.F. *décrire, décriv-*) :—L. *describere.*] = DESCRIBE *v.*, q. v.

Descry (dǐskrəi·), *v.*[1] ME. [app. a. OF. *descrier*, f. *des-, dé-*, L. DIS- + *crier.* Cf. DESCRIBE, and DESCRIVE.] †1. To cry out, announce (*rare*) 1440; to make known –1660; to bewray –1670. †2. To cry out against, challenge to fight –1480; to decry (see DECRY *v.* 1, 2) –1677. 3. To catch sight of, *esp.* from a distance; to espy ME. 4. To discover by observation ME. Also *absol.* †5. To investigate, explore –1742.

1. His purple robe he [Alectus] had thrown aside lest it should d. him MILT. 3. At intervals we descried a maple BLACK. 4. *absol.* Still Hills and Vallies as far as we could d. 1670. 5. The house of Ioseph sent to d. Bethel *Judg.* i. 23. Hence †**Descry·**, discry *sb.* cry, war-cry; perception from a distance.

†**De·secate,** *v.* 1623. [f. L. *desecare*; see DE- I. 2.] *trans.* To cut off, cut away; to cut free –1651.

Desecrate (de·sǐkrеɪt), *v.* 1674. [f. DE- II. 1 + stem of *con-secrate.* L. *desecrare* or *desacrare* meant to consecrate.] *trans.* To take away its sacred character from; to treat as not sacred; to profane 1677. b. To dedicate or devote *to* something evil 1825. c. To dismiss from holy orders (*arch.*) 1674.

To d. Sunday J. H. NEWMAN. b. To d. a spot to Satan SIR J. STEPHEN. c. The [Russian] clergy cannot suffer corporal punishment without being previously desecrated W. TOOKE. Hence **De·secrate** *ppl. a.* **De·secrater, -or. Desecra·tion. De·secrative** *a.*

De:segmenta·tion. 1878. [DE- II. 1.] *Zool.* Union of two or more segments of a body into one. So **Dese·gmented** *ppl. a.*

Dese·nsitize, *v.* 1904. [f. DE-, after *sensitize.*] To reduce or destroy the sensitiveness esp. of a photographic plate, etc.

Desert (dǐzɔ̄·ɹt), *sb.*[1] ME. [a. OF. *desert*, *deserte, desserte*, derivs. of *deservir, desservir* to DESERVE.] 1. Deserving; merit or demerit. b. Meritoriousness ME. 2. That in conduct or character which deserves reward or punishment. Usu. in *pl.* (often = 1.) ME. b. A good deed or quality; a merit. ? *Obs.* 1563. 3. That which is deserved, whether good or evil ME.

1. What constitutes d.?..a person is understood to deserve good if he does right, evil if he does wrong MILL. To behold d. a begger borne SHAKS. 2. To do to each according to his deserts MILL. 3. I shall nother ete nor drynke tyll thou hast thy dysert LD. BERNERS. Hence **Dese·rtful** *a.* deserving. ? *Obs.* **Dese·rtfully** *adv.* **Dese·rtless** *a.*

Desert (de·zəɹt), *sb.*[2] ME. [a. OF. *desert*, ad. eccl.L. *desertum*, adj. neut. used absol.; see DESERT *a.*] 1. An uninhabited and uncultivated tract of country; a wilderness; now *esp.* a desolate and barren region, waterless and treeless, with but scanty herbage :—*e.g.* the *D. of the Sahara*, etc. Also *transf.* and *fig.* †2. *abstractly.* Desert condition; desolation –1523.

1. In our lande is also a grete deserte or forest 1511. The D. ..a wild waste of pebbly soil STANLEY. *fig.* To roam the howling desart of the main POPE.

Comb.: **d.-chough,** a bird of the genus *Podoces*, family *Corvidæ*, found in Central Asia; **-falcon,** a species of falcon inhabiting deserts, a member of the sub-genus *Gennæa*, allied to the peregrines; **-ship,** 'ship of the d.', the camel or dromedary; **-snake,** a serpent of the family *Psammophidæ*, a sand-snake.

Desert (de·zəɹt), *a.* [ME. *dese·rt*, a. OF. *desert* :—L. *desertus*, pa. pple. of *deserere* to sever connexion with, abandon, etc.] 1. Deserted (*arch.*) 1480. 2. Unpeopled, desolate, lonely ME. 3. Barren, waste; of the nature of a desert ME. Also *fig.*

2. When Deucalion hurl'd His Mother's Entrails on the desart World DRYDEN. 3. The Countrey .. is desart, sterile and full of loose sand SIR T. HERBERT.

Desert (dǐzɔ̄·ɹt), *v.* 1603. [a. mod.F. *déserter* = late L. *desertare*, freq. of *deserere*; see prec.] 1. *trans.* To abandon, forsake, relinquish; to depart from. 2. To forsake (a person, cause, etc. having moral or legal claims upon one); *spec.* of a soldier or sailor: To run away from (the service, his colours, etc.) 1647. 3. *intr.* To forsake one's duty, one's post, or one's party; *spec.* of a soldier, etc.: To run away from the service without permission 1689.

1. His slacken'd hand deserts the lance it bore POPE. To d. a ship 1790. 2. A husband deserts his wife if he wilfully absents himself from her society, in spite of her wish SIR H. C. LOPES. 3. The fourth regiment deserted in a body 1792. Hence **Dese·rtedness,** deserted condition.

Deserter (dǐzɔ̄·ɹtəɹ). 1635. [f. DESERT *v.*; after F. *déserteur.*] 1. One who forsakes a person, place, or cause; usually with implied breach of duty. 2. *esp.* A soldier or seaman who quits the service without permission 1667.

Desertion (dǐzɔ̄·ɹʃən). 1591. [a. F. *désertion*, ad. L. *desertionem.*] 1. The action of deserting, forsaking, or abandoning, *esp.* a person or thing that has moral or legal claims to the deserter's support; occas. simply, departure from a place. 2. *Law.* The wilful abandonment of an employment or of duty; *esp.* such abandonment of the military or naval service 1712. 3. Deserted condition 1751; †in *Theol.*, spiritual despondency. SOUTH (J.).

1. The D. of this Island by the Romans 1683. 2. Ranks thinned by frequent desertions THIRLWALL.

Desertness (de·zəɹtnĕs). ME. [f. DESERT *a.*] Desert condition.

†**Dese·rtrice.** *rare.* [f. DESERTER: after F. types.] A female deserter. MILTON. So **Dese·rtress, Dese·rtrix.**

Deserve (dǐzɔ̄·ɹv), *v.* ME. [a. OF. *deservir*, now *desservir* :—L. *deservire*; see DE- I. 3.] 1. To merit by service; to become entitled to or worthy of. *Obs.* or *arch.* 2. To have acquired, and thus to have, a rightful claim to; to be entitled to; to be worthy to have. (Now the ordinary sense.) ME. 3. *absol.* or *intr.* To be entitled to recompense; to merit, be worthy. Often in phr. *to d. ill* or *well of.* ME. †4. *trans.* To earn, win –1628. †5. To serve; to benefit –1634. †6. *trans.* To pay back, requite –1525.

1. 'Tis not in mortals to Command Success, But we'll do more, Sempronius; we'll D. it ADDISON. 2. Mr. Ho...deserves a better fate than to be ever of the loosing side 1668. Books..which d. to last EMERSON. 3. That he, who best deserves, alone may reign DRYDEN. Hence **Dese·rved** *ppl. a.* rightfully earned; merited; † = *Deserving* ppl. a. (SHAKS. *Cor.* III. i. 292.) **Dese·rved-ly** *adv.*, **-ness. Dese·rver,** one who deserves (*esp.* well). **Dese·rving** *vbl. sb.* desert, merit; *ppl. a.* that deserves (*esp.* well); **-ly** *adv.*

†**Dese·sperance, -aunce.** [a. OF. *desesperance.*] Despair –1460.

Deshabille; see DISHABILLE.

Desiccant (de·sikănt, dǐ·sikănt). 1676. [ad. L. *desiccantem*; see DESICCATE.] *adj.* Having the property of drying; serving to dry 1775. *sb.* A medicine or remedy which dries up.

Desiccate (de·sikeɪt, dǐ·sikeɪt), *v.* 1575. [f. L. *desiccat-*, ppl. stem of *desiccare*; see DE- I. 3.] 1. To make quite dry; to deprive thoroughly of moisture; to dry up. Also *fig.* 2. *intr.* To become dry (*rare*) 1679.

1. Wine helpeth to digest and d. the moisture BACON. Desiccated Soup 1884. So **De·siccate** *ppl. a.* (*arch.*). Hence **Desicca·tion,** the action of desiccating; desiccated condition.

Desiccative (de·sikeɪtiv, dǐ·sikătiv). ME. [ad. med.L. *desiccativus*; see above.] *adj.* Having the tendency or quality of drying up 1541. *sb.* A desiccant.

Desiccator (de·sikeɪtəɹ, dǐ·sikătəɹ). 1837. [f. L. *desiccare.*] One who or that which desiccates; a name applied to a chemical apparatus used to dry substances decomposed by heat or by exposure to the air; also, to contrivances for desiccating milk, fruit, etc.

De·siccatory, *a.* 1800. [f. as DESICCATE *v.*] Desiccative.

†**Desi·derable,** *a.* ME. [ad. L. *desiderabilis*; see DESIRABLE.] To be desired; desirable –1675. Hence †**Desi·derably** *adv.*

Desiderata, pl. of DESIDERATUM, q. v.

†**Desi·derate.** 1640. [ad. L. *desideratus*; see next.] *adj.* Desired; desirable. *sb.* A desideratum –1670.

Desiderate (dǐsi·dĕreɪt), *v.* 1645. [f. L. *desiderat-*, ppl. stem of *desiderare*; see DE- I. 1, 2. Cf. CONSIDER.] *trans.* To desire with a sense of want or regret; to feel the want of; to miss.

In an evening I d. the resources of a family or a club GIBBON. The great step which is now desiderated in education SOUTHEY.

Desideration (dǐsi:dĕreɪ·ʃən). 1525. [ad. L. *desiderationem*; see prec.] 1. The action of desiderating. †2. Desideratum (*rare*) 1836.

Desiderative (dǐsi·dĕrĕtiv). 1552. [f. L. *desiderat-* ppl. stem.]

A. *adj.* 1. Having or denoting desire; pertaining to desire 1655. 2. *Gram.* Of a verb, etc.: Formed from another verb to express a desire of doing the act thereby denoted; pertaining to such a verb 1552.

B. *sb. Gram.* A desiderative verb, verbal form, or conjugation 1751.

‖**Desideratum** (dǐsi:dĕrēɪ·tŏm). Pl. **-ata.** 1652. [L.] Something for which a desire is felt; something wanting and required or desired.

The explanation of them was still a d. in geology PLAYFAIR.

‖**Deside·rium.** 1715. [L.; f. stem of *desiderare.*] An ardent desire or wish; a longing, properly for a thing once possessed and now missed; a sense of loss.

†**Desidio·se,** *a.* 1727. = next –1822.

†**Desi·dious,** *a.* 1540. [ad. L. *desidiosus*, f. (ult.) DE- I. 3 + *sedere.*] Idle, slothful –1656. Hence †**Desi·diousness.**

Desight (dǐsəi·t). 1834. [f. DE- + SIGHT; cf. DISSIGHT.] A thing unsightly, an eyesore. So **Desi·ghtment,** disfigurement (*rare*).

Design (dǐzəi·n), *sb.* 1588. [a. 15–16th c. F. *desseing* (mod. *dessein, dessin*), f. *desseigner* to DESIGN.]

I. 1. A plan or scheme conceived in the mind of something to be done; the preliminary conception of an idea that is to be carried into effect by action; a project 1593; 'a scheme formed to the detriment of another' (J.) 1704. 2. Purpose, aim, intention 1588. 3. The thing aimed at 1657. 4. Contrivance in accordance with a preconceived plan; adaptation of means to ends; prearranged purpose; as, the *argument from d.* 1665. 5. In a bad sense: Crafty contrivance; an instance of this (*arch.*) 1704.

1. The d. of insurrection MACAULAY. He had no d. upon your pocket LYTTON. 2. With d. to besiege it 1734. Phr. *By* (†*out of, on, upon*) *d.*: purposely. 3. If Milk be thy D.; with plenteous Hand Bring Clover-grass DRYDEN.

II. 1. A preliminary sketch for a work of art; the plan of a building, or part of it, or of a piece of decorative work, after which the structure or texture is to be completed; a delineation, pattern 1638. 2. The combination of details which go to make up a work of art; artistic idea as executed; a piece of decorative work, an artistic device 1644. Also *transf.* of literary work 1875. 3. The art of picturesque delineation and construction 1638.

2. To admire the designs on the enamelled silver centres GEO. ELIOT. 3. *Arts of d.*: those in which d. plays a principal part, as painting, sculpture, architecture, engraving. *School of d.*: a school in which the arts of d. are specially taught.

Design (dǐzəi·n), *v.* 1548. [a. F. *désigner*, ad. L. *designare, dissignare*, f. DE- I. 2 and DIS- + *signare*.]

I. [after L. *designare*.] †1. To mark out; to indicate -1668. 2. To DESIGNATE (*arch.*) 1603. 3. To appoint or assign. *Obs.* exc. in *Sc. Law.* -1701. 4. To set apart in thought for some one 1664. 5. To destine to a fate or purpose 1593.

2. The writer..is not named or designed 1874. 4. What present I had designed for her DE FOE.

II. [allied to DESIGN *sb.* I.] 1. To plan, plan out 1548. 2. To purpose, intend 1655. Also *intr.* (*rare*). 3. To have in view 1677. 4. *intr.* and quasi-*pass.* (usu. with *for*): To intend to go or start 1644.

1. He can suspend the laws himself designed S. ROGERS. 2 Not for obscurity designed DRYDEN. 4. They d. to Bristol 1688.

III. [allied to DESIGN *sb.* II.] 1. †a. To sketch. b. To trace the outline of, delineate. (App. implied in DESIGNMENT.) 1570. c. To make the preliminary sketch of; to make the plans and drawings necessary for the construction of 1697. 2. To plan and execute; to fashion with artistic skill or decorative device 1666. 3. *intr.* a. To draw, sketch. b. To form or fashion a work of art; less widely, to devise artistic patterns.

2. The Roman bridges were designed on the same grand scale as their aqueducts J. FERGUSSON.

Designable, *a.* 1644. [f. L. *designare*; in sense 2, f. DESIGN *v.*] †1. (de·signăb'l) That can be distinctly marked out -1716. 2. (dǐzəi·năb'l) Capable of being designed.

Designate (de·signĕt), *ppl. a.* 1646. [ad. L. *designatus*.] Marked out for office, etc.; appointed, but not yet installed, as in *bishop d.*

Designate (de·s-, de·zigneᶦt), *v.* 1791. [f. ppl. stem of L. *designare*; see DE- I. 3. *Designate* takes up the senses of the L. verb not expressed by DESIGN.] 1. *trans.* To point out, indicate; to specify 1801. 2. To point out by a name or description; to name, denominate 1818. 3. To appoint, nominate for duty or office; to destine to a purpose or fate 1791.

1. To d. faults 1801, limits WEBSTER. 2. Miriam is almost always designated as the 'prophetess' STANLEY. 3. A clause designating the successor by name MACAULAY. So **De·signative** *a.* having the quality of designating. **De·signator**, one who designates or points out; in *Rom. Antiq.*, an officer who assigned to each person his rank and place in public shows and ceremonies. **De·signatory** *a.* of or pertaining to a designator or designation.

Designation (des-, dezignē·ʃən). ME. [ad. L. *designationem*.] 1. The action of marking or pointing out; indication; *concr.* a distinctive mark. 2. The action of appointing or nominating; the being nominated; appointment, nomination 1605. 3. The action of devoting by appointment to a particular purpose or use; an act of this nature (*arch.*) 1637. †4. Purpose, intention, design -1763. 5. A descriptive name, an appellation; *spec.* in *Law*, the statement of profession, trade, residence, etc., for purposes of identification 1824.

2. The *quasi* d. of Eadward to the crown FREEMAN. 3. To make various designations of their profits BLACKSTONE. 5. The name Argeioi..as a d. of the army before Troy GLADSTONE.

Designed (dǐzəi·nd), *ppl. a.* 1586. [f. DESIGN *v.* + -ED.] †Marked out; planned, purposed; drawn, outlined; fashioned according to design. Hence **Desi·gnedly** *adv.* on purpose.

Designer (dǐzəi·nəɹ). 1649. [f. as prec. + -ER¹.] 1. One who designs or plans; in bad sense, a plotter, schemer, intriguer. 2. One who makes an artistic design or plan of construction; *spec.* one who makes designs or patterns for the manufacturer or constructor 1662.

Designful (dǐzəi·nful), *a.* 1677. [f. DESIGN *sb.* + -FUL.] Full of design; intentional. Hence **Desi·gnfulness**, d. quality.

Designing (dǐzəi·niŋ), *vbl. sb.* 1618. [-ING¹.] The action of DESIGN *v.*; marking out; planning, etc.; plotting, scheming.

Desi·gning, *ppl. a.* 1653. 1. That designs, plans, etc. 2. Scheming, crafty, artful 1671. Hence **Desi·gningly** *adv.*

Designless (dǐzəi·nlės), *a.* 1643. [f. DESIGN *sb.* + -LESS.] Void of design or plan. Hence **Desi·gnlessly** *adv.*

†**Desi·gnment.** 1570. [f. DESIGN *v.* + -MENT.] = DESIGNATION, DESIGN -1738.

Desiliconize (dǐsi·likŏnəiz), *v.* 1881. [DE- II. 1.] To free from silicon.

Desilver (dǐsi·lvəɹ), *v.* 1864. [DE- II. 2.] To remove the silver from, free from silver.

Desilverize (dǐsi·lvərəiz), *v.* 1872. [DE- II. 1.] To extract the silver from (lead, etc.). Hence **Desilveriza·tion.**

Desinence (de·sinĕns). 1599. [a. F. *désinence*, ad. med.L. *desinentia*; see next.] Termination, close; in *Gram.* a suffix or ending of a word. Hence **Desine·ntial** *a.* pertaining to, or of the nature of, a d.

Desinent (de·sinĕnt), *a.* ? *Obs.* 1605. [ad. L. *desinentem*, pr. pple. of *desinere*; see DE- I. 1, 2.] Forming the end, terminal; closing.

Their upper parts human..their d. parts fish B. JONS.

Desipience (dǐsi·piĕns). 1656. [ad. L. *desipientia*, f. *desipientem*, pr. pple. of *desipere*.] Folly; foolish trifling, silliness. var. **Desi·piency.** So **Desi·pient** *a.* foolish, silly; playing the fool (*rare*).

Desirable (dǐzəiᵊ·răb'l), *a.* (*sb.*) ME. [a. F. *désirable*, f. *désirer*, after L. *desiderabilis*.] 1. Worthy to be desired; to be wished for. In early use: Pleasant, delectable, excellent. †2. To be regretted 1650. 3. *sb.* That which is desirable 1645.

1. Horsemen riding vpon horses, all of them desireable young men *Ezek.* xxiii. 12. No evil is in its self d., or to be chosen STILLINGFL. Hence **Desi·rabi·lity. Desi·rableness. Desi·rably** *adv.*

Desire (dǐzəiᵊ·ɹ), *sb.* ME. [a. OF. *desir*, mod.F. *désir*, f. *désirer*; see next.] 1. The fact or condition of desiring; that emotion which is directed to the attainment or possession of some object from which pleasure or satisfaction is expected; longing, craving; a wish. 2. *spec.* Physical appetite; lust ME. †3. = DESIDERIUM. Chapman. 4. A wish as expressed; a request, petition ME. 5. *transf.* That which one desires or longs for ME.

1. Desyre To be clepyd lorde or syre R. BRUNNE. 2. That satiate yet vnsatisf'd d. *Cymb.* I. vi. 47. 4. The House hath been in conference with the Lords upon their d. MARVELL. 5. The d. of all nations shall come *Haggai* ii. 7. Hence **Desi·reful** *a.* (now *rare*), †desirable; desirous; eager; †-ness. **Desi·reless** *a.*

Desire (dǐzəiᵊ·ɹ), *v.* ME. [a. OF. *desirer* (earlier *desidrer*) = Rom. type *desirare*:—L. *desiderare*; see DESIDERATE *v.*] 1. *trans.* To have a strong wish for; to long for, crave. 2. *intr.* (or *absol.*) To have or feel a desire ME. †3. *trans.* Of things: To require, need, demand -1607. 4. To long for (something lost); to desiderate 1557. 5. To express a wish for; to request ME. †6. To request to be told -1708. †7. To invite -1606.

1. Do not all men d. happiness JOWETT. You d. your child to live TENNYSON. 4. And now his chair desires him here in vain TENNYSON. 5. I..thereupon desired to have the Council's letters ABP. PARKER. He desires me to dine with him again on Sunday SWIFT.

Hence **Desi·red** *ppl. a.* wished for, etc. (see above); †desiderated; †desirous [= L. *cupidus*]. **Desi·redly** *adv.* in a desired manner; †according to one's own desire. **Desi·redness. Desi·ringly** *adv.*

Desirous (dǐzəiᵊ·rəs), *a.* ME. [a. AFr. = OF. *desireus* (earlier *desidros*):—late L. or Rom. *desiderosus*, f. stem of *desiderare*. Orig. with stress on third and first syllable.] 1. Having desire or longing; characterized by desire; wishful, desiring; *occas.*, covetous. †2. Eager, ardent (*esp.* in deeds of arms) -1485. †3. Exciting desire; desirable -1728.

1. The Grecians being d. of learning A. V. *Transl. Pref.* 4. Owre men..were desyrous to see the towne EDEN. 3. Places d. to be in BUNYAN. Hence **Desi·rous·ly** *adv.*, **-ness** (now *rare*).

Desist (dǐzi·st), *v.* 1509. [a. OF. *desister* (mod.F. *dé-*), ad. L. *desistere*.] 1. *intr.* To cease *from*; to stop, leave off, forbear 1530. †2. *trans.* To discontinue -1784.

1. I counsayle you desyst from this purpose PALSGR. Request that he would d. in his gallantries to me GOLDSM. 2. Thou foole d. thy wordes vayne BARCLAY. Hence **Desi·stance, -ence,** the action of desisting; cessation, discontinuance of action. **Desi·stive** *a.* ending (*rare*).

Desition (dǐsi·ʃən). 1612. [f. L. *desinere, desit-*; see DESINENT.] Termination or cessation of being; ending.

†**Desitive** (de·sitiv). *rare.* [f. L. *desit-* ppl. stem; see prec. Only in Watts.]

A. *adj. Logic.* Having reference to the ending of any thing, as *d. propositions.*

B. *sb.* A desitive proposition.

Desk (desk), *sb.* [ME. *deske*, app. ad. med. L. *desca*, referred ult. to L. *discus* (also used in med.L. in the sense 'table'). Cf. DAIS, DISH, DISK.] 1. A table, board, or the like, usually with a sloping surface, intended to serve as a rest for a book, writing paper, etc., while reading or writing. Often qualified, as *litany-, music-, writing-desk*, etc. b. In mod. use often a portable box or case, for writing materials, letters, etc. 1548. †c. In early use, also a shelf, case, or press for books -1717. 2. In a church or chapel: A sloping board on which books used in the service are laid. Hence (*esp.* in U.S.), a pulpit. 1449. 3. *fig.* Used for the functions or office of the occupant of a desk 1581; also for clerical or office work 1797.

Comb.: **d.-cloth,** a cloth to cover a reading-d. or lectern; **-knife,** an eraser; **-work,** work at a d., as clerk, book-keeper, etc.

†**Desk,** *v.* 1509. [f. the sb.] 1. To fit up with desks. 2. To place in or as in a desk -1670.

Desma (de·smă). Pl. **-mata, -mas.** 1857. [a. Gr.] *Biol.* 1. A bandage; a ligament. 2. A kind of spicule which unites with others to form the skeletal framework in some sponges.

‖**Desman** (de·smăn). 1774. [Fr. and Ger., from Sw. *desman-råtta* musk-rat, f. *desman* musk.] *Zool.* An aquatic insectivorous mammal, of the genus *Myogale*, nearly allied to the shrew; esp. *M. moschata*, the musk-rat, which inhabits the rivers of Russia. *M. pyrenaica* is a species found in the Pyrenees.

Desmid (de·smid). 1862. [ad. Bot.L. *Desmidium* (generic name), f. Gr. type *δεσμίδιον, dim. of δεσμός.] *Bot.* A plant of the genus *Desmidium*, or order *Desmidiaceæ* of microscopic unicellular algæ; so called because sometimes found united in chains. Hence **Desmidia·ceous** *a.* of the N.O. *Desmidiaceæ*, containing the desmids; **Desmi·dian** *a.* of the desmids; *sb.* a desmid; **Desmidio·logy,** the scientific study of desmids; **Desmidio·logist.**

Desmine (de·smin). 1811. [f. Gr. δέσμη bundle.] *Min.* = STILBITE.

Desmo- (de·smo), comb. f. Gr. δεσμός bond. Hence

Desmo·brya *pl.* [Gr. βρύον; see BRYOLOGY], name for a group of ferns; hence **Desmo·bryoid** *a.*, belonging to or like the *Desmobrya*. **De·smodont** *a.* and *sb.* [Gr. ὀδοντ-], belonging to, or one of, the *Desmodonta*, a group of bivalve molluscs. **Desmo·gnathous** *a.* [Gr. γνάθος], having the type of palatal structure shown in the *Desmognathæ*, a group of birds, in which the maxillopalatine bones are united across the median line; so **Desmo·gnathism,** this type of palatal structure. **Desmo·graphy** *Anat.*, a description of the ligaments of the body. **Desmo·logy,** 'the anatomy of the ligaments of the body; also, a treatise on bandages' (*Syd. Soc. Lex.*). **Desmo·pathy,** disease of the ligaments. **Desmope·lmous** *a.* [Gr. πέλμα sole of the foot] *Ornith.*, having the plantar tendons connected, as some birds, so that the hind toe cannot be moved independently of the front toes. **Desmo·stichous** *a.* [Gr. στίχος row], belonging to or like the *Desmosticha*, a group of echinoids having the ambulacra equal and band-like. **Desmo·tomy** [Gr. -τομια], the dissection of ligaments.

Desmoid (de·smoid), *a.* 1847. [f. Gr. δεσμός and δέσμη.] Resembling a bundle. **a.** *Path.* Applied to the fibrous tissue of certain tumours. **b.** *Zool.*, etc. Ligamentous; tendinous.

†‖**Deso·bligeant.** 1768. [ad. F. *désobligeante* fem. (sc. *voiture*).] A chaise so called in France from its holding but one person. Cf. *sulky.* -1770.

Desocialize, -ation; see DE- II. 1.

‖**Désœuvré** (dezö·vre), *a.* 1750. [Fr.] Unoccupied; languidly idle. So **Désœuvrement,** lack of occupation.

Desolate (de·sŏlĕt), *ppl. a.* ME. [ad. L. *desolatus*, pa. pple. of *desolare*; see DE- I. 3.] †**A.** as *pa. pple.* Brought to desolation; see DESOLATE *v.* ME. only.

B. *adj.* **1.** Left alone, lonely ME. †**2.** Destitute *of*, lacking. With *inf.*: Without means *to.* -1720. **3.** Destitute of inhabitants; uninhabited, deserted ME. **4.** In a ruinous condition; neglected; laid waste; bare, barren; cheerless ME. **5.** Comfortless; forlorn, disconsolate; wretched ME. †**6.** Destitute of good quality, abandoned. (Occas. confounded with *dissolute.*) -1782. Also *absol.*

1. He which hath no wif..lyveth helples, and is al d. CHAUCER. 2. The place..was d. of inhabitants DE FOE. 3. So d. stode Thebes and so bare CHAUCER. 4. No man thinks of walking in this d. place DICKENS. 5. Gyue confort to a d. hert CAXTON. 6. Unhappy men of d. and abandoned principles 1782. Hence **De·solate·ly** *adv.*, **-ness.**

Desolate (de·sŏlē¹t), *v.* ME. [f. prec., after L. *desolare*, F. *desoler.*] **1.** *trans.* To deprive of inhabitants, depopulate. **2.** To lay waste; to make bare, barren, or unfit for habitation ME. **3.** To leave alone, abandon; to make desolate 1530. **4.** To make comfortless 1530.

1. As if the city had been desolated by the plague LYELL. 2. The revolutions of Nature which had desolated France 1796. 4. Desolated by continuous despair 1887. Hence **De·solator, -er,** one who or that which makes desolate. †**De·solatory** *a.* having the quality or tendency of desolating (*rare*).

Desolation (desolē¹·ʃən). ME. [a. F., or ad. L. *desolationem.*] **1.** The action of desolating or laying waste; utter devastation. Also *personified.* **2.** The condition of being left desolate; ruined state; dreary barrenness ME.; a thing or place in this condition 1611. **3.** Solitariness, loneliness 1588. **4.** Deprivation of comfort; dreary sorrow; grief ME.

2. Yon dreary Plain, forlorn and wilde, The seat of d. MILT. *P. L.* I. 181. This house shall become a d. *Jer.* xxii. 5. 3. You have liu'd in d. heere, Vnseene, vnuisited *L. L. L.* v. ii. 357. 4. Euerie thing about you, demonstrating a carelesse d. *A. Y. L.* III. ii. 400.

De·sophi·sticate, *v.* 1827. [DE- II. 1.] To free from sophistication. Hence **Desophistica·tion.**

Desoxalic (desǫksæ·lik), *a.* 1868. [ad. F. *désoxalique*; see DES-.] *Chem.* Formed by the deoxidation of oxalic acid.

D. acid, a synonym of racemo-carbonic acid, $C_5H_6O_8$. Hence **Deso·xalate,** a salt of this acid.

Desoxy-. 1882. [f. as prec.] *Chem.* Without oxygen, deoxidated.

Despair (dĭspē³·ɹ), *sb.* [ME. *des-, dis-peir, -pair*, a. OF. **despeir*, vbl. sb. from *desperer* (tonic stem *despeir-*). Cf. also F. *désespoir.*] **1.** The action or condition of despairing; hopelessness. Also *personified.* **2.** That about which there is no hope 1605.

1. It becomes no man to nurse d. TENNYSON. Hollow-eyed Abstinence, and lean D. COWPER. 2. People.. The meere despaire of Surgery, he cures *Macb.* IV. iii. 152. Hence **Despai·rful** *a.* hopeless, desperate.

Despair (dĭspē³·ɹ), *v.* [ME. *des-, dis-peiren*, a. OF. *despeir-* stem form of *desperer* :—L. *desperare*, f. DE- I. 6 + *sperare.* (Displaced in F. by *désespérer.*)] **1.** *intr.* To give up hope; to be without hope. Const. *of*, rarely †*in, to* with *inf.* ME. Also †*refl.* in same sense. †**2.** *trans.* To cast into despair (*rare*) -1618. †**3.** *trans.* = *despair of* in sense 1. -1773.

1. As long as you hope, I will not d. STEELE. His life was despaired of 1718. 3. *Macbeth.* I beare a charmed Life.. *Macduff.* Dispaire thy Charme *Macb.* v. viii. 13. Hence **Despai·red** *ppl. a.* †desperate; †despaired of. **Despai·rer. Despai·ringly** *adv.*

Desparple, var. of DISPARPLE *v. Obs.*

Despatch, var. of DISPATCH.

†**Despe·che,** *v.* 1531. [var. of DEPEACH, q. v.] To send away, get rid of, dispatch -1550.

De·speci·ficate, *v. rare.* 1872. [DE- II. 1.] To deprive of its specific character. Hence **Despecifica·tion.**

Inaptitude and *ineptitude* have been usefully despecificated; and only the latter now imports 'folly' F. HALL.

†**Despect** (dĭspe·kt), *sb.* 1624. [ad. L. *despectus*, f. *despicere.*] A looking down upon; contempt -1834. So †**De·spection.**

Despe·ctant, *ppl. a.* 1688. [ad. L. *despectantem.*] *Her.* Looking downwards.

†**Despee·d,** *v.* 1611. [DE- I. 2.] To send with speed; to dispatch.

Despend, -pence; see DISP-.

†**De·speracy.** 1628. [f. DESPERATE.] Desperateness -1800.

Desperado (despĕrē¹·do). 1610. [? a refash., after Sp. words in -ADO, of DESPERATE *sb.*] = DESPERATE *sb.* 1, 2.

†**Desperance.** ME. [a. OF., f. *desperer.*] Despair -1560.

Desperate (de·spĕrĕt). 1483. [ad. L. *desperatus*, pa. pple. of *desperare* to DESPAIR.]

A. *adj.* **1.** Despairing, hopeless (*arch.*). **2.** Of conditions, etc.: That leaves little or no room for hope 1555. **3.** Of things (and persons): Given up as hopeless; irretrievable -1871. **4.** Of persons: Driven to desperation. Hence, Reckless, violent, ready to risk or do anything. 1489. **5.** Of actions, etc.: Characterized by the recklessness of despair; applied *esp.* to those done in the last extremity 1579; †involving serious risk -1654. †**6.** Outrageous, extravagant -1661. **7.** Of such a quality as to be despaired of; 'awful' 1604.

1. I am d. of obtaining her *Two Gent.* III. ii. 5. D. sobs DISRAELI. 2. D. diseases EDEN. 3. His d. game FULLER. 4. Want makes Men d. 1718. 5. His look denounc'd D. revenge MILT. *P. L.* II. 107. Marriage is a d. thing SELDEN. 6. The desparate Principles.. of Quakers SANDERSON. 7. D. sots and fools POPE. Hence **De·sperate** *v.* to render d. (*rare*). **De·sperate·ly** *adv.*, **-ness.**

B. *sb.* †**1.** A person in despair -1622. †**2.** One ready for any desperate deed -1718

C. *adv.* Hopelessly; usually (*colloq.* and *dial.*) as an intensive: Excessively, 'awfully' 1636.

Desperation (despĕrē¹·ʃən). ME. [a. F., or ad. L. *desperationem.*] **1.** The action of despairing or losing all hope; the condition of having utterly lost hope; despair. Now *rare.* **2.** *spec.* Despair leading to recklessness, or recklessness arising from despair. (Cf. DESPERATE *a.* 4, 5.) 1531.

1. Horrour of deathe .. and disperation of æternal blisse 1528. 2. Needy and hungry to d. EMERSON.

Despicable (de·spikăb'l), *a.* 1553. [ad. L. *despicabilis*, f. *despicari*, f. DE- I + **specari*, from same root as *specere.*] **1.** To be looked down upon or despised; vile, contemptible; †wretched. †**2.** Contemptuous -1775.

1. All thinges with them are d. and vile EDEN. These poor d. wretches PAGITT. 2. I have a very d. opinion of the present age H. STUBBE. Hence **Despicabi·lity, De·spicableness,** d. quality, worthlessness. **De·spicably** *adv.*

†**Despi·ciency.** 1623. [ad. L. *despicientia*; see DESPISE.] Looking down upon or despising; contempt -1672.

Despiritualize, *v.*; see DE- II. 1.

Despisable (dĭspəi·zăb'l), *a.* [In ME. *despisa·ble*, a. OF., f. stem *despis-* of *despire* to DESPISE.] = DESPICABLE *a.* 1 (now *rare*), †2. Hence †**Despi·sableness.**

Despisal (dĭspəi·zăl). 1650. [f. DESPISE *v.*; cf. *revisal.*] The act of despising; contempt.

Despise (dĭspəi·z), *v.* ME. [f. stem *despis-* of OF. *despire* :—L. *despicere.*] **1.** *trans.* To look down upon; to view with contempt; to scorn or disdain. †**2.** To treat with contempt -1557; †*fig.* of things, to set at nought -1666.

1. He is despised and rejected of men *Isa.* liii. 3. 2. *fig.* [The fire]..despised all the resistance [which] could be made by the strength of the buildings STILLINGFL. Hence †**Despi·se** *sb.* despite, contempt. †**Despi·sedness. Despi·ser. Despi·singly** *adv.*

Despite (dĭspəi·t), *sb.* [ME. *despit*, a. OF. (mod.F. *dépit*) :—L. *despectum*, f. ppl. stem of *despicere.* The 16th c. *dis-*, *despight* was after *sight*, etc.] **1.** The looking down upon anything; contempt, scorn, disdain. *Obs.* or *arch.* **2.** Action that shows contemptuous disregard; insulting action; outrage, injury, contumely ME.; †defiance -1719. **3.** (with *pl.*) An outrage, etc. ME. **4.** Evil feeling, anger. In later use, *esp.* aversion; settled ill-will; SPITE. ME.

1. Any attribute that is given in despight HOBBES. Phr. †*To have in d.* 2. Whi hast thou don despit to Chivalrye CHAUCER. 4. Rancorous d. 1846.

Phr. **In d. of.** †**a.** In contempt of. †**b.** In open defiance of. **c.** Notwithstanding the opposition of. **d.** Notwithstanding. **e.** *In his, her, one's*, etc. *d.*: in the prec. senses. **f.** In later use often **d. of** (senses c, d); whence DESPITE *prep.*, rarely *in d.*

Despite (dĭspəi·t), *v. arch.* ME. [a. OF. *despiter*, mod.F. *dépiter*, app. f. as prec.] **1.** To show contempt for, set at nought; to do despite to. †**2.** To provoke to anger; to spite -1658. †**3.** *intr.* To show despite -1736.

1. Reason..Despiteth love, and laugheth at her Folly DRAYTON.

Despite (dĭspəi·t), *prep.* 1593. [See DESPITE *sb.*] In spite of.

Despiteful (dĭspəi·tful), *a.* 1450. [f. DESPITE *sb.* + -FUL.] †**1.** Contemptuous; insulting -1676. **2.** Cruel; malignant; spiteful 1470.

2. I shalbe called foolishe, curious, despitefull, and a sower of sedition KNOX. The hainous and despightfull act Of Satan done in Paradise MILT. *P. L.* x. 1. Hence **Despi·teful-ly** *adv.*, **ness.**

Despiteous (dĕspi·tiəs), *a.* [Late ME. var. of DESPITOUS, assoc. w. *piteous.*] **1.** *orig.* = DESPITOUS (*arch.*). **2.** Spiteful, malevolent, cruel; later, merciless, DISPITEOUS 1510.

1. The proud, d. rich man MORRIS. 2. Dispitious torture *John* IV. i. 34. Hence †**Despi·teously** *adv.*

†**Despitous,** *a.* ME. [a. AF. *despitous*, f. *despit* DESPITE *sb.*; see -OUS. Orig. stressed on last or first syllable; subseq. on second.] **1.** *orig.* Full of despite; hence insulting, vexing -1494. **2.** Cruel; malevolent -1578. Hence †**Despi·tously** *adv.*

Despoil (dĭspoi·l), *sb.* [ME. a. OF. *despoille*; see next.] **1.** The action of despoiling (*arch.*) 1483. †**2.** *concr.* SPOIL -1619.

Despoil (dĭspoi·l), *v.* [ME. *despuilen*, *-spoilen*, a. OF. *despuillier* (mod.F. *dépouiller*) :—L. *despoliare* (DE- I. 3).] **1.** *trans.* To plunder, rob. **2.** To deprive violently *of*; to rob ME. †**3.** *spec.* To strip of clothes; to undress -1700. †**4.** To strip of value or use; to SPOIL -1685. †**5.** To carry off by violence -1604.

1. The Ebrues well dispoile the Egypcyens MORE. 2. Theeues..dispoiling him of his apparell KNOLLES. Despoild of Innocence MILT. *P. L.* IX. 411. 3. He bad That wommen schuld despoilen hir right there CHAUCER. Hence **Despoi·ler. Despoi·lment.**

Despoliation (dĭspōᵘli,ē¹·ʃən). 1657. [ad. L. *despoliationem.*] The action of despoiling; despoilment.

Despond (dĭspǫ·nd), *v.* 1655. [ad. L. *despondere*; see DE- I. 2.] *intr.* To lose heart or resolution; to become depressed by loss of confidence or hope. (Dist. from *despair* as not expressing entire hopelessness.) Occas. with *of.*

Though he d. that sows the grain 1696. Desponding of their Art DRYDEN. Hence **Despo·nd** *sb.* despondency (*arch.*). **Despo·nder** (*rare*). **Despo·ndingly** *adv.*

Despondence (dĭspǫ·ndĕns). 1676. [f. L. *despondere*; see -ENCE.] The action of desponding; also (less correctly) = DESPONDENCY.

Bear up thyself..from fainting and d. HALE.

Despondency (dĭspǫ·ndĕnsi). 1653. [f. as prec. + -ENCY.] The condition of being despondent; dejection of spirits through loss of resolution or hope.

The d. with which the Greeks viewed the situation THIRLWALL.

Despondent (dĭspǫ·ndĕnt), *a.* 1699. [ad. L. *despondentem.*] **1.** Characterized by despondency; labouring under mental depression. **2.** Of or belonging to despondency 1844.

1. A d. sinner 1699. 2. A d. gesture DICKENS, attitude 1888. Hence **Despo·ndently** *adv.*

[**Desponsage**, error for *despousage* in some modern Dicts.]

†**Despo·nsate**, *a.* 1471. [ad. L. *desponsatus*, pa. pple. of *desponsare* to betroth.] 1. Betrothed, espoused 1483. 2. *fig.* (*Alchem.*) Chemically combined 1471. So †**Desponsa·tion.**

†**Despo·nsories**, *sb. pl.* 1626. [ad. Sp. *desposorios*, f. *desposar* :—L. *desponsare*. Used in relation to the proposed Spanish marriage of Charles I.] 1. Betrothal –1659. 2. A document formally declaring a betrothal –1670.

†**Despo·se**, *v. rare.* 1587. [a. OF. *desposer*, occas. var. of *deposer*; see DE- 6.] To depose, lay down –1603.

Despot (de·spǫt). 1562. [a. OF., mod.F. *despote*, ad. Gr. δεσπότης.] 1. *Hist.* A word which, in its Greek form, meant 'master' or 'lord'; in Byzantine times it was used of the Emperor, and, later, of various subordinate rulers, also as a form of address. 2. An absolute ruler of a country; hence, any ruler who governs absolutely or tyrannically; any person who exercises tyrannical authority; a tyrant, oppressor 1781.

2. Hast thou..returned..A d. big with power obtained by wealth COWPER. Under the primeval despots of Egypt EMERSON. So **De·spotat, -ate**, the dominion of a Greek d. under the Turks; a principality.

Despotic, -al (despǫ·tik, -ăl), *a.* 1608. [a. F. *despotique*, ad. Gr. δεσποτικός, f. δεσπότης, + -AL.] Of, pertaining to, or of the nature of a despot, or despotism; arbitrary, tyrannical. Hence **Despo·tical-ly** *adv.*, †**-ness.**

Despotism (de·spǫtiz'm). 1727. [a. F. *despotisme*; see DESPOT and -ISM.] 1. The rule of a despot; despotic government; the exercise of absolute authority. Also *fig.* 2. A political system under the control of a despot; a despotic state; an arbitrary government 1856.

1. The simplest form of government is d. BURKE. *fig.* The d. of the senses EMERSON. 2. Your empire is a d. exercised over unwilling subjects JOWETT. So **De·spotist**, an advocate of d. **De·spotize** *v. intr.*, to act the part of a d.

†**Despou·se**, *v.* ME. [ad. L. *desponsare*, after *spouse* :—OF. *esposer* :—L. *sponsare*.] To betroth; to marry. Also *fig.* –1609. Hence †**Despou·sage**, betrothal; espousal.

Despraise, Despread, Desprize; see DIS-.

Despumate (dĭspiū·meit, de·spiumeit), *v.* 1641. [f. L. *despumat-*, ppl. stem of *despumare* (DE- I. 2).] 1. *trans.* To skim; to clarify by removing the scum. 2. *intr.* (for *refl.*) To throw off its froth or scum; to become clarified by this process 1733. 3. *trans.* To throw off as froth 1733. Hence **Despu·mate(d** *ppl. a.* clarified. **Despuma·tion**, clarification; the expulsion of impure matter from the fluids of the body; the matter despumated. So †**Despu·me** *v.* to clear of froth or scum; *intr.* to foam.

Desquamate (de·skwămeit), *v.* 1727. [f. L. *desquamat-*, *desquamare*.] †1. *trans.* To take the scales off; to scale, peel 1740. 2. *intr.* To scale off 1828. Hence **Desquama·tion**, the removal of scales or any scaly crust; a coming off in scales, *esp.* that of the epidermis; exfoliation; that which comes off. So **Desqua·mative** *a.* tending to or characterized by desquamation. **Desqua·matory** *a.* of or pertaining to desquamation; *sb.* a desquamatory trepan.

†**Dess**, *sb.* 1552. [a. OF. *deis*, *dais*, DAIS.] 1. Obs. f. DAIS. 2. A desk –1596.

Dessert (dĕzō·ɹt). 1600. [a. F., f. *desservir* to remove what has been served, to clear (the table), f. *des-*, L. *dis-* + *servir*.] A course of fruit, sweetmeats, etc. served after a dinner or supper; 'the last course at an entertainment' (J.). b. In U.S. often including pies, etc. 1848.

Such eating, which the French call desert, is unnaturall W. VAUGHAN. *Comb.* **d.-spoon**, that used for the d.; it is intermediate in size between a table-spoon and a tea-spoon.

‖**Dessiatine, desyatin** (de·syătīn). 1799. [ad. Russ. *desyatina* lit. 'tithe'.] A Russian superficial measure of 2,400 sq. sazhens.

Destemper, obs. f. DISTEMPER.

†**De·stin, destine**, *sb.* 1575. [a. F.] = DESTINY *sb.* –1616. Hence †**De·stinable** *a.* fixed by destiny; fated, fatal. †**De·stinably** *adv.*

†**De·stinal** *a.* of, pertaining, or according to destiny.

†**De·stinate**, *ppl. a.* ME. [ad. L. *destinatus*, pa. pple. of *destinare*.] 1. Fated –1659. 2. Intended, designed –1671.

Destinate (de·stineit), *v.* Now *rare.* 1490. [f. L. *destinat-* ppl. stem; see prec.] To DESTINE, ordain, or design.

That name that God..did d. and appoynt vnto hym UDALL. So †**De·stinate** *ppl. a.* destined.

Destination (destinēi·ʃən). 1598. [ad. L. *destinationem*; cf. F. *destination* (12–13th c.).] 1. The action of destining to a particular use, purpose, or end; the fact of being destined. b. *transf.* The end or purpose for which a person or thing is destined 1656. 2. *spec.* The fact of being bound for a particular place; hence, short for *place of d.*; the intended end of a journey or course. (Now the usual sense.) 1787.

1. Our d. for society KAMES. A d. above the objects, the employments, and the abilities of this world MOZLEY. 2. 'It [the fleet] has as many destinations' he [Nelson] said 'as there were countries' SOUTHEY.

Destine (de·stin), *v.* ME. [a. F. *destiner*, ad. L. *destinare*, f. DE- I. 3 + **stanare*, causal deriv. of *stare* to stand.] 1. *trans.* To ordain, appoint (definitely). *Obs.* (or merged in 3.) 2. To appoint, to predetermine by an unalterable decree. Now chiefly in *pass.*; often without any definite reference to predetermination. (Usu. with *inf.*) ME. 3. To set apart in intention for a particular purpose, use, end, etc.; to design, devote, allot. (Usu. in *pass.*) 1530.

2. Yf god destyneth hym, he shall wynne the pryse CAXTON. He was, however, not destined to escape so easily PEACOCK. 3. Phr. *To be destined*: to be bound (*for* a particular place). Hence **De·stined** *ppl. a.* foreordained, fated (now often merely = 'that is (or was) to be'); intended; *spec.* bound to a particular place.

Destiny (de·stĭni), *sb.* ME. [a. OF. *destinée*, from L. pa. pple. *destinatus*, *-a*; see -ADE suffix.] 1. That which is destined to happen; FATE. 2. That which is destined to happen to a particular person or thing; (one's) FATE ME. 3. In weakened sense: Ultimate condition. (Also in *pl.*) 1555. 4. The power or agency by which events are unalterably predetermined; divine preordination; invincible necessity; FATE. (Often personified.) ME. 5. *Mythol.* The goddess of destiny; *pl.* the three Parcæ ME.

2. Oh, I was borne to it, it was my destonie STUBBES. *Merch. V*, II. ix. 83. 3. Their children also had little better d. 1665. 4. The force Of ruthless D. COWPER. 5. Seuen faire branches..Some..by the destinies cut *Rich. II*, I. ii. 15. Hence **De·stinism**, fatalism. **De·stinist**, a believer in d. †**De·stiny** *v.* to destine, foreordain; to prognosticate.

†**Desti·tuent**, *a.* [ad. L. *destituentem*.] Wanting, lacking. JER. TAYLOR.

Destitute (de·stitiut), *a.* (*sb.*) ME. [ad. L. *destitutus*, pa. pple. of *destituere*, f. DE- I. 1, 2 + *statuere*.] †1. Abandoned; forsaken, forlorn –1755. 2. †Deprived or bereft *of* –1492; devoid *of*, entirely lacking *in* 1500. 3. Bereft of resources, 'in want and misery'; now, without the means of bare subsistence, in absolute want 1535. 4. *sb.* One who is destitute 1737.

1. Great houses long since built Lye d. and wast 1592. 2. A barren waste d. of trees and verdure JOWETT. 3. He will regard the prayer of the d. *Ps.* cii. 17. The deep curses which the d. Mutter in secret SHELLEY. Hence **De·stitute-ly** *adv.*, **-ness.**

Destitute (de·stitiut), *v.* Now *rare. Pa. t.* -ed, †destitute. 1530. [Partly f. prec., partly repr. L. *destituere*; see prec. Cf. F. *destituer*.] †1. *trans.* To forsake, abandon, leave to neglect –1673. 2. To deprive, bereave *of*; to render destitute 1540. 3. *spec.* To deprive of office. [mod.F. *destituer*.] 1653. 4. To lay waste 1593. †5. To frustrate, disappoint –1619.

1. To forsake or d. a Plantation, once in Forwardnesse BACON. 3. Let not the Patriarch think..to d. or depose me 1716. 5. Offended, when his expectation is destituted 1619.

Destitution (destitiū·ʃən). ME. [a. F., ad. L. *destitutionem*; see above.] †1. The action of deserting or forsaking –1727. 2. Deprivation of office 1554. 3. The condition of being destitute (see DESTITUTE *a.* 1, 2) ME. 4. *spec.* The condition of being destitute of resources; want of the necessaries of life 1600.

3. D. in these [food and clothing] is such an impediment HOOKER. 4. Left in a state of d. COBDEN.

‖**Destour, dastur** (dĕstūᵊɹ). 1630. [Pers. *dastūr*, prime minister :—Pahlavi *dastōbār*.] A chief priest of the Parsees.

De·strer, de·strier (de·strəɹ, -iəɹ, destrī·ᵊɹ). *arch.* ME. [a. AF. *destrer* :—late L. *dextrarius* (sc. *equus*); so called from being led by the squire with his right hand.] A war-horse, a charger.

Destroy (dĭstroi·), *v.* [ME. *destruyen*, etc., a. OF. *destruire* (mod.F. *détruire*) :—late pop. L. **destrugere*, for cl.L. *destruere*; see DE- I. 6.] 1. To pull down or undo, as a building; to demolish. †2. To lay waste –1611; to ruin (men) –1621. 3. To undo, break up, reduce into a useless form, consume, or dissolve. (Now the leading sense.) ME. b. To render useless 1542. 4. To deprive of life; to kill ME. 5. To put an end to; to do away with ME. 6. To counteract 1729.

1. The cite of rome shulde haue be dystroyed CAXTON. Like a Torrent, which .. destroies all 1659. 2. That same tyme attila destroyed Italye CAXTON. 3. To d. Skiffs 1700, old houses 1798, works on alchemy GUSTAFSON. b. With Blites d. my Corn DRYDEN. 4. To d. Priam's innocent people BOWEN. 5. And thou destroyest the hope of man *Job* xiv. 19. To d. a contingent remainder CRUISE. Hence **Destroy·able** *a.* **Destroy·ingly** *adv.*

Destroyer (dĭstroi·əɹ). late ME. [f. prec. + -ER [1].] One who or that which destroys. b. abbrev. of TORPEDO-BOAT *destroyer* 1893.

Destructible (dĭstrɒ·ktib'l), *a.* 1755. [ad. L. *destructibilis*; see -BLE.] Capable of being destroyed; liable to be destroyed. Hence **Destructibi·lity, Destru·ctibleness**, d. quality.

Destruction (dĭstrɒ·kʃən). ME. [a. OF. *destructiun*, *-cion*, *-tion*, ad. L. *destructionem*, f. *destruere* to DESTROY.] 1. The action of destroying (see the vb.); demolition; devastation; havoc; slaughter. Often *personified.* 2. The fact or condition of being destroyed; ruin ME. 3. A cause or means of destruction 1526.

1. The dystrucyon of Jerusalem 1520. The d. of clouds 1813, of beasts of prey (*mod.*). D. and death say, We have heard the fame thereof with our ears *Job* xxvii. 22. 2. In horrible d. thus laid low MILT. 3. The d. of the poore is their pouertie *Prov.* x. 15.

Destructionist (dĭstrɒ·kʃənist). 1807. [f. prec. + -IST.] 1. A partisan of a policy of destruction, *esp.* of an existing political system or constitution. (Chiefly dyslogistic.) 1841. 2. *Theol.* One who believes in the final annihilation of the wicked; an annihilationist.

Destructive (dĭstrɒ·ktiv). 1490. [a. OF. *destructif*, *-ive*, ad. L. *destructivus*, f. *destruct-* ppl. stem; see DESTROY.]

A. *adj.* Having the quality of destroying; tending to destroy; pernicious, deadly, annihilative. Const. *to*, *of*. (In political and philosophical use opp. to *constructive* and *conservative.*) b. *Logic.* Applied to conjunctive syllogisms and dilemmas, in which the conclusion negatives a hypothesis in one of the premisses.

D. distillation: see DISTILLATION.

B. *sb.* 1. A destructive agent, instrument, or force; a destructive proposition or syllogism 1640. 2. A destructionist. (Chiefly dyslogistic.) 1832. Hence **Destru·ctively** *adv.* **Destru·ctiveness**, tendency to destroy; in *Phrenol.* a propensity having a bump allotted to it.

Destructor (dĭstrɒ·ktəɹ). 1691. [a. L. In F. *destructeur*.] 1. A destroyer. 2. A furnace for the burning of refuse 1881.

†**Destru·ctory**, *a.* and *sb.* 1614. [f. L. *destructor*.] = DESTRUCTIVE –1644.

Desubstantiate (dīˌsɒbstæ·nʃiˌeit), *v.* 1884. [DE- II. 1.] To deprive of substance.

Desudation (dĭsiudēi·ʃən). 1727. [ad. L. *desudationem*; see DE- I. 3.] *Med.* A profuse and inordinate sweating.

Desuetude (de·swĭtiud). 1623. [a. F. *désuétude*, ad. L. *desuetudo* disuse; see DE- I. 6.] †1. A discontinuance of the use or practice (*of*); disuse; †cessation *from* –1706. 2. The state of disuse 1637.

1. By a d. and neglect of it BOYLE. 2. Rights which had passed into d. GREEN.

Desulphur (dīsɒ·lfəɹ), *v.* 1874. [DE- II. 2.] To free from sulphur. So **Desu·lphurate** *v.* (in same sense); **Desulphura·tion. Desu·lphurize** *v.*; **Desulphuriza·tion.**

Desulphuret (dīsɒ·lfiŭret), *v.* 1878. [DE- II. 2.] To deprive of sulphurets or sulphides.

Desultory (de·sɒ̆ltəri), *a.* 1581. [ad. L. *desultorius*, f. *desultor* leaper down, vaulter.] **1.** Skipping about, jumping from one thing to another; devious; wavering (*lit.* and *fig.*). **2.** Unmethodical 1740; random 1704; motley (*rare*) 1842.

1. I shot at it but it was so d. that I missed my aim G. WHITE. 2. This makes my reading wild and d. WARBURTON. Some d. project HAZLITT. var. **Desulto·rious** *a.* (in sense 1). Hence **De·sultori·ly** *adv.*, **-ness.**

†**Desu·me**, *v.* 1564. [ad. L. *desumere* (DE- I. 2).] To take (*from* some source); to borrow –1697.

Desynonymize (dīˌsinǫ·nimǝiz), *v.* 1817. [DE- II. 1.] **1.** *trans.* To differentiate words previously synonymous; to free from synonyms. **2.** *intr.* To cease to be synonymous 1862. Hence **Desyno·nymiza·tion,** the process of desynonymizing.

Detach (dĭtæ·tʃ), *v.* 1684. [a. F. *détacher*, earlier *destacher*, *destachier*, f. Rom. *des-*, L. *dis-* (DIS-) + Rom. *tacca*, F. *tache* nail, tack, spot, etc. Cf. ATTACH.] **1.** *trans.* To unfasten and separate; to disengage, disunite (*lit.* and *fig.*) 1686. **2.** *Mil.* and *Naval.* To separate and dispatch on special service. Also *transf.* 1684. **3.** *intr.* (for *refl.*) To disengage and separate oneself 1842.

1. [It] only tends..to d. me from the restlessness of human pursuits LAMB. 2. During this the front line detaches skirmishers 1796. 3. Detaching, fold by fold, From those still heights, and slowly drawing near TENNYSON. Hence **Detachabi·lity. Deta·chable** *a.* capable of being detached. **Deta·ched** *ppl. a.* separated; unattached, standing apart, isolated. **De·ta·chedly** *adv.*

Detachment (dĭtæ·tʃmĕnt). 1669. [a. F. *détachement*, f. *détacher*.] **1.** The action of detaching (see DETACH *v.*). **2.** *concr.* That which is detached; *esp.* a portion of an army or navy taken from the main body and employed on some special service 1678. **3.** A standing aloof from objects or circumstances 1798.

1. They confirm the d. of the dauphine with 25,000 men to the Rhine LUTTRELL. 2. A D. of Actors from Drury Lane CIBBER. 3. The d. of a saint J. H. NEWMAN. The d. of the United States from the affairs of the Old World BRYCE.

Detail (dĭ·teⁱl, dĭtēⁱ·l), *sb.* 1603. [a. F. *détail*, f. stem of *détailler*; see next.] **1.** The dealing with matters item by item. **2.** A minute account; a detailed narrative or description of particulars 1695. **3.** An item, a particular; a minute or subordinate portion of any whole 1786. Also as *collective sing.* **4.** *Mil.* **a.** The distribution in detail of the Daily Orders first given in general; hence, the list or table showing the general or particular distribution of duty (*general* or *particular d.*) for the whole force or for any part of it 1703. **b.** The detailing or telling off a small party for a special duty; *concr.* the small body thus detailed 1708.

1. *In d.*, item by item; part by part, circumstantially. He [Brian Boru] defeated his enemies in d. STOKES. 3. The whole d. of private life MILL. The d. of a single weedy bank laughs the carving of ages to scorn RUSKIN. The d. is otherwise denominated the *working drawings* P. NICHOLSON. 4. Details had gone to the front after the wounded GEN. GRANT.

Detail (as prec.), *v.* 1637. [a. F. *détailler*, f. DE- I. 3 + *tailler* to cut in pieces.] **1.** *trans.* To deal with, relate, or describe minutely or circumstantially; to give particulars of; to enumerate, mention, or relate in detail. Also *absol.* **2.** *Mil.* To appoint or tell off for a particular duty 1793. Also *transf.*

1. Certain peculiarities to be detailed hereafter SCRIVENER. Hence **Detailed** *ppl. a.* stated circumstantially; abounding in details; minute, circumstantial. **Detailer.**

Detain (dĭtēⁱ·n), *v.* [Late ME. *deteine*, *-eyne*, a. OF. *detenir* :—Rom. type **detenere* for L. *detinere* to hold off, keep back; see DE- I. 2.] **1.** *trans.* To keep in confinement or custody 1485. **2.** To keep back, withhold. ? *Obs.* 1535. †**3.** To keep, retain –1774; to hold, hold down –1780. **4.** To keep from proceeding; to keep waiting; to stop. (The ordinary current sense.) 1592.

2. To d. servants wages 1535. 3. To d. one's eyes too long upon the same object GOLDSM. 4. The business which then detained him PALEY. Hence †**Detai·n** *sb.* detention. **Detai·nable** *a.* **Detai·nal,** detention (*rare*). **Detai·nment** (now *rare*).

Detainer[1] (dĭtēⁱ·nəɹ). 1531. [f. prec. vb.] One who or that which DETAINS.

Detai·ner[2]. 1619. [a. Anglo-F. *detener* inf. used subst. Cf. *cesser*, etc.] *Law.* The action of detaining, withholding, or keeping in one's possession, *spec.* **a.** The (wrongful) detaining of goods taken from the owner for distraint, etc. 1619. **b.** The detaining of a person; *esp.* in custody or confinement 1640. **c.** A process authorizing the sheriff to detain a person already in his custody 1836.

Phr. *Forcible d.*: the 'violently taking or keeping possession, with menaces, force, and arms, of lands and tenements, without the authority of law' (Blackstone).

Deta·nt, var. of DETENT, q. v.

Detect (dĭte·kt), *ppl. a. arch.* ME. [ad. L. *detectus*; see next.] Detected; disclosed; open.

Detect (dĭte·kt), *v.* *pa. pple.* †**Dete·ct, Detected.** 1447. [f. ppl. stem *detect-* of L. *detegere*; see DE- I. 6.] †**1.** *trans.* To uncover, lay bare, expose, display –1739. †**2.** To expose (a person); to inform against, accuse –1645. **3.** To find out, discover (a person) being or doing something 1581. **4.** To discover the presence, existence, or fact of (something apt to elude notice) 1756. **5.** *Wireless.* To rectify, as in a detector.

1. Secret Confession, wherein Men do d. their sins in the Priests ear FOXE. 2. *Meas. for M.* III. ii. 129. 3. To d. a baker in selling short weight BENTHAM. 4. We d. all the shades of meaning GODWIN. Hence **Dete·ctable, -ible** *a.*

Detection (dĭte·kʃən). 1471. [ad. L. *detectionem.*] †**1.** Exposure, revelation of what is concealed; accusation –1807. **2.** Discovery (of what is unknown or hidden) 1619.

2. It is easy for the author of a lie, however malignant, to escape d. JOHNSON.

Detective (dĭte·ktiv). 1843. [f. L. *detect-* ppl. stem; see DETECT *v* and -IVE.]

A. *adj.* Serving to detect; employed for the purpose of detection; as the *d. police.*

B. *sb.* One whose occupation it is to discover matters artfully concealed; particularly (and as short for *d. policeman*, or the like) a member of the police force employed to investigate specific cases, etc. 1856.

Detector (dĭte·ktəɹ). Also **-er.** 1541. [a. L.] He who, or that which, detects; *esp.* an instrument or device for detecting anything liable to escape observation, abnormal, or the like; as, an arrangement in a lock by which any attempt to tamper with it is indicated; a low-water indicator for a boiler; a coherer 1833.

†**Dete·nebrate**, *v.* 1646. [f. DE- II. 1 + L. *tenebrare.*] To free from darkness –1656.

Detent (dĭte·nt). 1688. [a. F. *détente*, OF. *destente*, f. (ult.) *des-*, L. *dis-* privative (cf. DE- I. 6) + *tendre* to stretch. In Eng., assoc. w. L. *detinere*, *detent-*.] A stop or catch in a machine which checks or prevents motion, and the removal of which brings some motor at once into action; as, in guns, an oscillating tongue to carry the sear over the half-cock; in clocks and watches, the catch which regulates the striking; etc.

Detention (dĭte·nʃən). 1552. [ad. L. *detentionem*, f. *detinere* to DETAIN.] **1.** Keeping in custody or confinement; arrest 1570. **2.** The keeping back of what is due or claimed 1552. **3.** Holding in one's possession or control; retention. ? *Obs.* exc. in *Law.* 1626. **4.** A keeping from going on or proceeding 1600.

1. Her [Q. Mary's] d. under safe custody 1570. 3. The depositary has mere d., the depositor has possession POSTE. Phr. *House of d.*: a lock-up.

‖**Détente** (detānt). 1908. [Fr. 'loosening, relaxation'.] The easing of strained relations.

‖**Détenu** (detənü). 1803. [Fr.; pa. pple. of *détenir* used subst.] A person detained in custody; *spec.* a political prisoner in India (1918).

He was a *d.* for eleven years at Verdun 1815.

Deter (dĭtɜ̄·ɹ), *v.* 1579. [ad. L. *deterrere* (DE- I. 2).] **1.** *trans.* To restrain *from* acting or proceeding by any consideration of danger or trouble. †**2.** To terrify –1634.

1. That degree of severity which is sufficient to d. others 1766. When my own Face deters me from my Glass PRIOR. Hence **Dete·rment,** the action or fact of deterring; a deterring circumstance.

Deterge (dĭtɜ̄·ɹdʒ), *v.* 1623. [ad. L. *detergere*, f. DE- I. 2 + *tergere.*] To wash off or out; chiefly *Med.*, to clear away foul or offensive matter from the body, from an ulcer, etc.

Detergent (dĭtɜ̄·ɹdʒĕnt). 1616. [ad. L. *detergentem*; see prec. Cf. mod.F. *détergent.*]

A. *adj.* Cleansing, purging.

B. *sb.* Anything that cleanses 1676. Hence **Dete·rgency,** d. quality.

Deteriorate (dĭtīᵊ·riŏrēⁱt), *v.* 1572. [f. ppl. stem of L. *deteriorare*, f. *deterior* worse.] **1.** *trans.* To make worse; to lower in quality or value; to worsen. **2.** *intr.* To become worse; to become impaired in quality or value; to degenerate 1758.

1. Not onely not bettered, but much deteriorated G. WALKER. To d. the value of property 1847. 2. Under such conditions the mind rapidly deteriorates GOLDSM. Hence **Dete·riorative** *a.* causing or tending to deterioration. **Dete·riorator.**

Deterioration (dĭtīᵊ:riŏrēⁱ·ʃən). 1658. [a. F. *détérioration.*] The process of growing or making worse; a deteriorated condition. Hence **Deteriora·tionist,** one who holds d., not progress, to be the order of things.

Deterio·rity. *rare.* 1692. [f. L. *deterior* + -ITY; cf. *superiority.*] Poorer or lower quality; worseness.

†**Dete·rm**, *v.* ME. [f. DE- *prefix* + TERM.] By-form of DETERMINE *v.* –1647.

Determinable (dĭtɜ̄·ɹminăb'l), *a.* [In ME., a. OF., ad. L. *determinabilis* that has an end; see also -ABLE.] †**1.** Fixed, definite –1646. **2.** Capable of being determined, authoritatively decided, definitely limited, or definitely ascertained 1485. **3.** Liable to come to an end; terminable (*esp.* in *Law*) 1584.

2. Matters d. by your common law LD. CAMPBELL. Relations .. not d. with Certainty and Precision HARTLEY. 3. In Lease for 99 years, d. on one, two, or three Lives 1707. Hence **Determinabi·lity,** d. quality. **Dete·rminably** *adv.*

Dete·rminacy. *rare.* 1873. [f. DETERMINATE *a.*; see -ACY.] Determinateness.

Determinant (dĭtɜ̄·ɹminănt). 1610. [ad. L. *determinantem*, pr. pple. of *determinare*; cf. F. *déterminant.*]

A. *adj.* Determining; that determines; determinative.

B. *sb.* One who or that which determines. **1.** In *University Hist* (repr. med. L. *determinans*). A determining Bachelor; see DETERMINATION 3. 1864. **2.** A determining factor or agent 1686. **3.** *Math.* The sum of the products of a square block or matrix of quantities, each product containing one factor from each row and column, and having the plus or minus sign according to the arrangement of its factors in the block 1843.

A determinant is commonly denoted by writing the matrix with a vertical line on each side, thus— $\begin{vmatrix} a_1 & a_2 & a_3 \\ b_1 & b_2 & b_3 \\ c_1 & c_2 & c_3 \end{vmatrix}$ Hence **Determina·ntal** *a. Math.*, relating to determinants.

Determinate (dĭtɜ̄·ɹminĕt), *ppl. a.* ME. [ad. L. *determinatus*, pa. pple. of *determinare* to DETERMINE.]

A. as *pa. pple.* = DETERMINED. *Obs.* or *arch.*

My bonds in thee are all d. SHAKS.

B. *adj.* **1.** Definitely limited; definite, fixed; clearly defined; distinct ME. **b.** *Math.* Having a fixed value or magnitude 1722. **c.** *Bot.* Of inflorescence: Definite, centrifugal 1880. **2.** Settled, fixed, so as not to vary 1526. **3.** Finally determined upon; definitive 1533. **4.** Intended 1586. **5.** Fixed in mind or purpose, determined, resolute 1587.

1. The clear and d. meaning of my words BERKELEY. b. *D. problem*, is that which has but one, or at least but a certain number of solutions CHAMBERS. A *d. number* is that referred to some given unit; as a ternary, or three *Ibid.* 2. A d. form of praiyng 1559. 3. No d. reply could be given to the letter WELLINGTON. 4. Men of d. minds and courage BARRET. Hence **Dete·rminate-ly** *adv.*, **-ness.**

†**Dete·rminate**, *v.* 1563. [f. ppl. stem of L. *determinare.*] *trans.* To determine; to end –1788. Also *intr.*

Determination (dĭtɜ̄:ɹminēⁱ·ʃən). ME. [a. F., or ad. L. *determinationem*; see above.] **1.** A bringing, or coming, to an end; ending; termination; *esp.* in *Law*, the cessation of an estate or interest of any kind 1483. **2.** Judicial or authoritative decision or settlement ME. **3.** The resolving of a question or maintaining of a thesis in a scholastic disputation; *spec.* in University history, the name of certain disputations which complete the taking of the degree of B.A. *Obs.* exc. *Hist.* 1665. **4.** The determining of bounds; delimitation; definition 1594; in *Logic*, the rendering of a notion more definite by the addition of attributes; also, a determining attribute 1644. **5.** The action of definitely ascertaining the position, nature, amount, etc. (*of* anything) 1677; the result of this 1570. **6.** Decisive or determining bias (*lit.* and *fig.*) 1660; *spec.* a tendency or flow of the blood, etc., to a particular part 1737. **7.** *Metaph.* The definite direction of the mind or will towards an object or end, by some motive 1685. **8.** The mental action of coming to a decision; the result of this; a fixed intention 1548. **9.** Determinedness, resoluteness 1822.

1. The d. of an estate tail CRUISE. **4.** The d. of the parties who are admissible 1866. **5.** On the D. of the Orbits of Comets 1793. Astronomical determinations 1857. **6.** Heavy bodies have a d. towards the centre of the earth CHAMBERS. **7.** Dr. Hutcheson, considering all the principles of action as so many determinations or motions of the will REID. **9.** Never was.. operation executed with greater..d. 1853.

Determinative (dĭtə̄·ɹminĕtiv). 1655. [a. F. *déterminatif, -ive*, f. ppl. stem of L. *determinare.*]

A. *adj.* **1.** Serving or tending to determine, decide, or fix. **2.** Serving to limit or fix the extent, specific kind, or character of anything: said of attributes or marks 1697.

1. D. of the character of life HOLLAND. **2.** The term ..is d. and limits the subject to a particular part of its extension WATTS.

B. *sb.* **1.** A determinative agent 1832. **2.** That which serves to define the character or quality of something else; *e.g.* in *hieroglyphic writing*, an ideographic sign annexed to a word phonetically represented; in *Gram.*, a demonstrative word 1862.

1. A restraint or d. from wrong AUSTIN.

Hence **Dete·rminatively** *adv.* so as to determine; †determinately. **Dete·rminateness.**

Determinator (dĭtə̄·ɹmineɪtəɹ). 1556. [a. L.] He who or that which DETERMINES (see the vb.); a determiner.

Determine (dĭtə̄·ɹmin), *v.* ME. [a. OF. *determiner*, ad. L. *determinare*; see DE- I. 3.]

I. 1. *trans.* To put an end to; to end. (Now chiefly in *Law.*) 1483. **2.** *intr.* (for *refl.*) To come to an end; to expire ME.; to end *in* (*arch.*) 1605. **3.** *trans.* †To set bounds to, limit –1732; in *Logic*, to limit by adding differences 1838; †to limit *to* –1691.

1. To d. an estate STEPHEN. **2.** The head .. determines in a snout 1767. **3.** It determines his power CROMWELL.

II. 1. *trans.* To settle or decide ME. **2.** *intr.* To come to a judicial decision; to decide. †Const. *of* (*on*). ME. †**3.** To lay down decisively or authoritatively –1486. †**4.** To fix beforehand; to ordain, decree –1758. **5.** *trans.* To fix or decide causally 1651. **6.** To decide upon (one of several) 1659. †**7.** To conclude from reasoning, investigation, etc. –1814. **8.** *trans.* To ascertain definitely; to fix as known 1650. **9.** *Geom.* (*trans.*) To define the position of 1840. **10.** To resolve a question (*determinare quæstionem*), or maintain a thesis, *esp.* in a disputation by which a student entered upon the degree of B.A.; hence, *absolutely*, to perform the exercises of DETERMINATION (sense 3). *Obs.* exc. *Hist.* 1570.

1. Let the lawes of Rome d. all. *Tit. A.* I. i. 407. **4.** For evil is determined against our master 1 *Sam.* xxv. 17. **5.** Not the seller, but the buyer, determines prices HOBBES. **6.** To d. the first passengers by lot 1771. **8.** To d. the velocity of a Glacier TYNDALL.

III. 1. *trans.* To give a terminus or aim to; to direct; to impel *to* ME. Also *fig.* **2.** *intr.* To take its course, go, tend *to* (*arch.*) 1651. **3.** *trans.* To bring to the determination or resolution (*to do* something) 1672. †Also *refl.* [= F. *se déterminer.*] –1701. **4.** *intr.* (for *refl.*) To resolve definitely (*to do* something) 1450.

1. Accidental impulses d. us to different paths JOHNSON. **2.** They all d. and concentre there SANDERSON. **3.** These reflections determined me MRS. SHELLEY. **4.** Phr. *To be determined*: to be finally and firmly resolved.

Hence **Dete·rmined** *ppl. a.* (in various senses of the vb.); resolute; not to be moved from one's purpose; of actions, etc., showing determination. **Dete·rmined-ly** *adv.*, **-ness.**

Determiner[1] (dĭtə̄·ɹminəɹ). 1530. [f. prec. + -ER[1].] **1.** He who or that which determines, in various senses. **2.** = DETERMINANT B. 1. *Obs.* exc. *Hist.* 1574.

Determiner[2]. 1450. [F. *déterminer* inf. used subst.] *Law.* The final determining of a judge or court of justice; in *oyer and d.*, a var. of *terminer*. *Obs.* exc. *Hist.*

Determinism (dĭtə̄·ɹminiz'm). 1846. [f. DETERMINE *v.* + -ISM.] **1.** The doctrine that human action is not free but necessarily determined by motives. **2.** *gen.* The doctrine that everything that happens is determined by a necessary chain of causation 1876. So **Dete·rminist** *sb.* one who holds the doctrine of d.; *a.* of or pertaining to d. **Determini·stic** *a.* of or pertaining to d. or determinists.

†**Deterra·tion.** 1686. [f. L. *de* down + *terra*. (Not conn. w. mod.F. *déterrer.*)] The carrying down of the surface of the earth from hills and higher grounds into the valleys, by rain, landslips, etc.; cf. DEGRADATION[1]. –1704.

Deterrence (dĭte·rĕns). 1861. [f. next.] Preventing by fear.

Deterrent (dĭte·rĕnt). 1829. [ad. L. *deterrentem*, pr. pple. of *deterrere.*]

A. *adj.* Deterring; serving or tending to deter, as *d. weather*.

B. *sb.* Something that deters 1829.

Detersion (dĭtə̄·ɹʃən). 1607. [a. F., or ad. L. *detersionem*, f. *detergere.*] The action of cleansing (a sore, etc.).

Detersive (dĭtə̄·ɹsiv). 1586. [a. F. *détersif, -ive*, f. L. *deters-*, ppl. stem of *detergere.*]

A. *adj.* **1.** Cleansing; tending to cleanse 1601. **2.** *Med.* and *Surg.* Detergent 1586.

B. *sb.* A cleansing agent; a detergent 1634. Hence **Dete·rsive-ly** *adv.*, **-ness.**

Detest (dĭte·st), *v.* 1533. [a. F. *détester*, ad. L. *detestare* (*-ari*), f. DE- I. 1 down + *testari.*] †**1.** *trans.* To curse, calling God to witness; to denounce, execrate –1745. **2.** To hate or dislike intensely; to abhor, abominate 1535. ¶ Misused for *attest, protest, testify*.

1. All posteritie shall..with execrations d. thy fact LE GRYS. **2.** A fashion shee detests *Twel. N.* II. v. 220. The Justice of the Land detesteth that the Judge should himself be an Accuser FULLER. var. †**Dete·state** *v.* (*rare*). Hence **Dete·ster.**

Detestable (dĭte·stăb'l), *a.* 1461. [a. F., ad. L. *detestabilis*; see prec. Orig. *detesta·ble*; in Spenser and Shaks. *de·testable.*] **1.** To be detested; intensely hateful; execrable, abominable. **2.** quasi-*adv.* Detestably 1610.

1. That d. sight SPENSER *F. Q.* I. i. 26. The d. ornamentation of the Alhambra RUSKIN. Hence **Dete·stableness**, d. quality. **Dete·stably** *adv.*

Detestation (dītestē̆ɪ·ʃən). ME. [a. F., ad. L. *detestationem*; see DETEST *v.*] †**1.** Public execration (of a thing) –1683. **2.** The mental state of detesting; intense dislike or hatred; abhorrence 1526. **3.** *concr.* That which is detested 1728.

2. His d. of priests and lawyers JOWETT. **3.** Thou art grown the d. of all thy party SWIFT.

Dethrone (dĭþrōu·n), *v.* 1609. [DE- II. 2; cf. F. *détrôner.*] To remove from the throne; to depose. Also *transf.* and *fig.*

Authoritie to de-Throan and de-Crowne Princes 1609. Love, by dethroning Reason..doth kill the Man BOYLE. Hence **Dethro·nement**, deposition from kingly authority. **Dethro·ner.** var. †**Dethroni·ze**; whence †**Dethroniza·tion**, dethronement.

Detinue (de·tiniū). 1563. [a. OF. *detenue*, f. pa. pple. of *detenir.*] *Law.* The act of detaining (see DETAIN *v.* 2); *spec.* unlawful detention of a personal chattel belonging to another. *Obs.* exc. in *action*, etc., *of d.*

Action of d.: an action at law to recover a personal chattel (or its value) wrongfully detained by the defendant. So *writ of d.* Also *d.* = action or writ of d.

Detonate (de·tŏneɪt, dī-), *v.* 1729. [f. L. *detonat-*, ppl. stem of *detonare*; see DE- I. 1, 2.] **1.** *intr.* To explode with sudden loud report; cf. DETONATION. Also *fig.* **2.** *trans.* To cause to explode with sudden loud report 1801.

1. Saltpeter..detonates, or makes a noise in the fire 1729. Hence **De·tonative** *a.* having the property of detonating. **De·tonator**, that which detonates, as a percussion-cap; a railway fog-signal. var. †**De·tonize** *v.*; whence, †**Detoniza·tion.**

Detonating (de·tŏneɪtiŋ), *ppl. a.* 1808. [f. prec. + -ING[2].] That detonates. **a.** Explosive, as *d. gas*; **b.** That is used in producing detonation, as *d. primer, tube*; **c.** *esp.* That explodes, or is used in explosion, by percussion, as *d. hammer, powder*.

D. bulb, the small glass bulb also called *Prince Rupert's drop*, which flies to pieces on a slight scratch.

Detonation (detŏneɪ·ʃən, dī-). 1677. [a. F., f. *détoner* to DETONATE.] The action of detonating. **1.** The noise produced by the sudden liberation of gas in connexion with chemical decomposition or combination; hence, explosion accompanied with a sudden loud report. **2.** *gen.* A loud noise as of thunder; also, the action of causing a substance to detonate 1727. Also *fig.*

2. The great Crater .. testified by its loud detonations [etc.] LYELL.

†**Detort** (dĭtǭ·ɹt), *v.* 1550. [f. L. *detort-*, *detorquere* (DE- I. 2). Cf. F. *détordre.*] **1.** *trans.* To turn aside from the purpose; to twist, wrest, pervert. (Freq. in 17th c.) 1555. **2.** To derive by perversion 1605. Hence **Deto·rtion, -sion** (?*Obs.*), the action of detorting; distortion.

Detour, ‖**détour** (dĭtūə·ɹ, ‖deɪtūr). 1738. [a. F., f. *détourner*, OF. *destourner*, f. *des-*, L. *dis-* + *tourner* to turn.] A deviation from the direct road; a roundabout way, course, or proceeding. Now usu. *lit.*

To avoid these ruts we make long detours BLACK.

Detract (dĭtræ·kt), *v.* 1449. [f. L. *detract-*, ppl. stem of *detrahere* (DE- I. 2). In some senses app. repr. L. *detractare* or *detrectare.*]

I. 1. *trans.* To take away, withdraw 1509. **2.** *absol.* or *intr.* To take away a portion. Usu. *to d. from.* 1592. **3.** *trans.* To take reputation from; to disparage, belittle, traduce. Now *rare.* 1449. Also †*absol.*

1. That first great grief which..detracts something from the buoyancy of the youngest life DISRAELI. **3.** To..d. his greatest actions B. JONS.

II. †**1.** *trans.* To draw away (*from* an action, etc.); *refl.* and *intr.* To withdraw –1802. †**2.** To draw out, protract –1641; *absol.* or *intr.* To delay –1592.

III. = DETRECT. †*trans.* To draw back from, decline; to give up –1606.

Hence †**Detracta·tion** (*rare*) = DETRACTION 2. **Detra·cter** = DETRACTOR. **Detra·ctingly** *adv.*

Detraction (dĭtræ·kʃən). ME. [a. F., ad. L. *detractionem*; see DETRACT *v.*] **1.** †A taking away, deduction, withdrawal –1817; a detracting *from* (merit, etc.) 1633. **2.** The action of detracting from a person's merit or reputation; the utterance of what is injurious to his reputation; depreciation, defamation, calumny, slander. (The prevalent sense.) ME. †**3.** Protraction (*of time*) –1637.

1. Let it be no d. from the merits of Miss Tox DICKENS. **2.** Enuies abhorred childe, D. MARSTON. Hence †**Detra·ctious** *a.* given to d.

Detractive (dĭtræ·ktiv), *a.* 1490. [a. OF. *detractif, -ive*, f. *detract-*; see DETRACT *v.*] **1.** Conveying, of the nature of, or given to, detraction. **2.** Tending to detract *from* 1654. Hence **Detra·ctiveness.**

Detractor (dĭtræ·ktəɹ). Also **-ter.** ME. [ad. L.; see -OR.] **1.** One who detracts; a defamer, traducer, calumniator. ‖**2.** *Anat.* A DEPRESSOR muscle. ?*Obs.* 1811.

1. Every fashion has its detractors DORAN. So **Detra·ctory** *a.* = DETRACTIVE 1. Hence **Detra·ctress**, a female d.

Detrain (dĭtrēɪ·n), *v.* 1881. [DE- II. 2.] To alight or discharge from a railway train. Hence **Detrai·nment.**

†**Detray·**, *v.* 1509. [ad. OF. *detraire*:—L. *detrahere.*] = DETRACT *v.* 1, 2. –1520.

†**Detre·ct**, *v.* 1542. [ad. L. *detrectare*, freq. of *detrahere.*] = DETRACT *v.* I. 3, III. –1630. Hence **Detrecta·tion**, declinature (*rare*).

†**Detre·nch**, *v.* ME. [a. OF. *detrenchier*, *-cher*; see DE- I. 2.] To cut through –1500; to cut up –1489; *fig.* to retrench 1654.

Detriment (de·trimĕnt), *sb.* ME. [a. F., ad. L. *detrimentum*, f. *deterere* to wear away.] **1.** Loss or damage done to, or sustained by, any person or thing; that which causes a loss 1504. **2.** *Astrol.* The position or condition of a planet when in the sign opposite its house; a condition of weakness 1632. **3.** *Her.* Eclipse (of sun or moon) 1610. **4.** *pl.* Certain small charges made by colleges and similar societies upon their members 1670.

1. To the great D. of our own natural Subjects 1529. Hence **De·triment** *v.* to cause loss or damage to.

Detrimental (detrime·ntăl). 1656. [f. prec. sb. + -AL.]
A. *adj.* Causing loss or damage; prejudicial. **B.** *sb.* A person or thing that is prejudicial; in *Society slang*, a younger brother of the heir of an estate; an ineligible suitor. Hence **Detrime·ntally** *adv.*

Detrital (dĭtrəi·tăl), *a.* 1832. [f. DETRITUS + -AL.] *Physiogr.* Of or pertaining to detritus.

Detrited (dĭtrəi·tėd), *ppl. a.* 1697. [ad. L. *detritus*, pa. pple. of *deterere* + -ED.] **1.** Worn down. **2.** *Geol.* Formed as detritus 1853.

Detrition (dĭtri·ʃən). 1674. [f. ppl. stem *detrit-* of L. *deterere*.] The action of wearing away by rubbing.
D. has made it as smooth as the shingle pebbles on our shores 1890.

Detritus (dĭtrəi·tŏs). 1795. [a. L. *detritus* rubbing away; in (improp.) sense 2, perh. f. Fr.] †**1.** Wearing away or down by detrition –1802. **2.** Matter produced by the detrition of exposed surfaces, *esp.* material eroded and washed away by aqueous agency; a mass of this nature 1802. Also *transf.* and *fig.*
1. The effects of waste and *d.* PLAYFAIR. 2. The quantity of d. brought down by the rivers PLAYFAIR. *fig.* The loose d. of thought, washed down to us through long ages H. ROGERS.

Detrude (dĭtrū·d), *v.* 1548. [ad. L. *detrudere*; see DE- I. 1, 2.] **1.** *trans.* To thrust or force down (*lit.* and *fig.*). **2.** To thrust out or away (*lit.* and *fig.*) 1555. Hence **Detru·sion**, the action of detruding (*lit.* and *fig.*).

Detruncate (dĭtrʊ·ŋkeˈt), *v.* 1623. [f. ppl. stem of L. *detruncare*; see DE- I. 2.] *trans.* To shorten by lopping off a part (*lit.* and *fig.*); to cut short. Hence **Detrunca·ted** *ppl. a.* = TRUNCATED. **Detrunca·tion**, the action of cutting off or cutting short; the being cut short (*lit.* and *fig.*).

Detrusor (dĭtrū·səɹ). 1766. [f. L. *detrudere, detrus-*.] *Anat.* A name for the muscular coat of the bladder, by the contraction of which the urine is expelled.

†**Detruss** (dĭtrʊ·s), *v.* 1475. [a. OF. *destrousser*, mod. F. *détr-*, f. *dé-*, *des-*, L. *dis-* + *trousses* baggage.] To spoil, plunder (of baggage) –1598.

Dette, etc., obs. ff. DEBT, etc.

Detumescence (dĭtiumeˑsĕns). 1678. [f. L. *detumescere*; see -ENCE.] Subsidence from swelling, or (*fig.*) from tumult.

Detur (dī·tŏɹ). 1836. [L. = 'let there be given'.] A prize of books given annually at Harvard College, U.S., to meritorious students: so called from the first word of the accompanying Latin inscription.

†**Detu·rb**, *v.* 1609. [ad. L. *deturbare* (DE- I. 1).] To drive down; to thrust out –1657. var. †**Detu·rbate** (*rare*).

†**Detu·rn**, *v.* 1450. [a. F. *détourner*.] *trans.* To turn away or aside –1745.

†**Detu·rpate**, *v.* 1623. [f. ppl. stem of L. *deturpare* (DE- I. 3).] To make, or become, vile or base –1833. Hence †**Deturpa·tion.**

Deuce[1] (diūs). 1481. [a. F. *deux*, OF. *deus* two. The *-ce* = earlier *-s*, as in *peace*, etc.] **1.** The *two* at dice or cards 1519. **2.** *Tennis.* [= It. *a due*, F. *à deux de jeu.*] A term denoting that the two sides have each gained three points (called 40) in a game, in which case *two* successive points must be gained in order to win the game 1598. *Comb.* **d.-ace**, two and one (*i.e.* a throw that turns up two with one die and ace with the other); hence, a poor throw, bad luck, etc.; **d. game**, the game won, which makes the score in games level when each side has won more than five; so **d. set.**

Deuce[2] (diūs). *colloq.* or *slang.* 1651. [prob. orig. Ger. *das daus* = the DEUCE[1] at dice, changed in gender.] Bad luck, plague; in imprecations, etc. **b.** The spirit of mischief, the devil 1694. **c.** As an exclam. of incredulous surprise; also, as an emphatic negative 1710.
b. The very d. is in them COWPER. c. The d. he is! married to that vengeance SWIFT. Hence **Deuced** (diūst, diū·sėd) *a.* plaguy, confounded; devilish; often advb.; **Deu·cedly** *adv.*

†**Deusan, deuzan.** 1570. [a. F. *deux ans* two years.] = APPLE-JOHN –1741.

Deu·tero-, bef. a vowel **deuter-**, a. Gr. δευτερο-, comb. f. δεύτερος second, as in δευτεραγωνιστής one who plays second, etc. Hence, **Deuterocano·nical** *a.*, of, pertaining to, or constituting a second or secondary canon; opp. to *protocanonical*. **Deutero·gamist** [see next], one who marries a second time, or who upholds second marriages. **Deutero·gamy** [Gr. γάμος], marriage after the death of a first husband or wife. **Deuteroge·nic** *a.* [Gr. γένος], of secondary origin: in *Geol.* applied to rocks derived from the primary or protogenic rocks. **Deutero-Isaiah**, a second or later Isaiah, to whom some attribute c. xl–lxvi of Isaiah. **Deuterome·sal** *a.* [Gr. μέσος] *Entom.*, applied to certain cells in the wings of hymenopterous insects, now usually called the first and third discoidal and first apical cells. **Deutero-Nicene** *a.*, belonging to the second Nicene council. **Deutero·pathy** [Gr. -πάθεια] *Med.*, a secondary affection, sympathetic with or consequent upon another; hence **Deuteropa·thic** *a.*, of or pertaining to deuteropathy. **Deutero·scopy** [Gr. -σκοπία, σκοπιά], †the second view; †an ulterior meaning; second sight (*rare*). **Deutero·stoma** [Gr. στόμα] *Biol.*, a secondary blastopore; hence **Deuterosto·matous** *a.*, having a secondary blastopore. **Deuterozo·oid** (*Biol.*), a secondary zooid produced by gemmation from a zooid.

Deutero·nomist. 1862. [f. next + -IST.] The writer of Deuteronomy, or of the parts of it which do not consist of earlier documents. Hence **Deuteronomi·stic** *a.* of the nature or style of the writer of Deuteronomy.

Deuteronomy (diūtĕrǫ·nŏmi, diū·tĕrǫnǫmi). ME. [ad. eccl.L. *Deuteronomium*, a. Gr., f. δεύτερος + νόμος. The name is taken from the words of the LXX in Deut. xvii. 18 τὸ δευτερονόμιον τοῦτο, a mistr. of the Heb. = 'a duplicate of this law'.] The fifth book of the Pentateuch, which contains a repetition, with parænetic comments, of the Decalogue, etc. Hence **Deuterono·mic, -al** *a.* of or pertaining to, or like, the book of D.

†**Deuterosy.** *rare.* 1641. [ad. Gr. δευτέρωσις repetition.] A 'tradition of the elders' among the Jews –1650.

Deuto-, bef. a vowel **deut-**, shortened f. DEUTERO-, used
1. In Chemistry to distinguish the second in order of the terms of any series. Thus **Deuto·xide**, that which comes next to the *protoxide*, containing the next smallest quantity of oxygen.
2. In *Biology*; as **Deutence·phalon** [Gr. ἐγκέφαλος], the second of the three primary cerebral vesicles of the embryo. Hence **Deutencepha·lic** *a.* ‖**Deutoma·la** [L. *mala* jaw], the second pair of jaws of the Myriapoda; hence **Deutoma·lar** *a.* **Deuto·merite** [Gr. μέρος], the second or posterior cell of a dicystid gregarine, as dist. from the *protomerite*. **Deu·toplasm** [Gr. πλάσμα], Reichert's term for the food-yolk of the meroblastic egg, *e.g.* the yellow yolk of a bird's egg; hence **Deutopla·smic, -pla·stic** *a.* of, pertaining to, or like, deutoplasm; **Deutoplasmi·genous** *a.* producing deutoplasm; **Deutopla·smogen**, that which is converted into deutoplasm. **Deutosco·lex** [Gr. σκώληξ], a daughter-cyst of a scolex or cystic worm. **Deutote·rgite** [L. *tergum*], the second dorsal segment of the abdomen of insects. **Deuto·vum** [L. *ovum*], *pl.* **-ova**, a secondary egg-cell; also called *metovum*, and after-egg.

‖**Deutzia** (diū·tsiă, doi·tsiă). 1837. [f. J. *Deutz* of Amsterdam.] *Bot.* A genus of shrubs (N.O. *Saxifragaceæ*), natives of China and Japan, cultivated for their white flowers.

‖**Deva** (dē·vă). 1819. [Skr., 'a god', *orig.* 'a shining one', f. **div-* to shine.] A god; one of the good spirits of Hindu mythology.

Deva·lue, *v.* 1918. [DE-.] To reduce or annul the value of. **Deva·luate** *v.*, **-a·tion.**

‖**Devanagari** (dē·vănā·gărī). 1781. [Skr.; lit. 'Nāgarī (? town-script) of the gods'.] The formal alphabet in which the Sanskrit is written. Also called *Nagari*. Used both as *adj.* and *sb.*

Devance (dĭvɑ·ns), *v.* 1485. [a. F. *devancer*, after ADVANCE. Obs. early in 17th c.; occas. used in 19th c.] To forestall; to get ahead of; to outstrip.

†**Deva·nt, devau·nt.** ME. [a. F., f. L. *de* + late L. *abante*.]
A. *adv.* In front 1609.
B. *sb.* Front –1599.

Deva·porate, *v.* 1787. [f. DE- II. 1 + L. *vaporem*, after EVAPORATE.] To condense or become condensed. Hence †**Devapora·tion.**

†**Devastate** (de·văsteˈt), *v.* 1634. [f. L. *devastat-*, *devastare* (DE- I. 1, 3). Rare till 19th c.] To lay waste, ravage, render desolate.
A succession of cruel wars had devastated Europe MACAULAY. var. **Deva·st** (now *rare*). Hence **De·vastative** *a.* having the quality of devastating. **De·vastator**, he who or that which devastates.

Devastation (devăstē·ʃən). 1603. [prob. a. F. *dévastation*.] **1.** The action of devastating; devastated condition; laying waste; ravages. **2.** *Law.* Waste of the property of a deceased person by an executor or administrator 1670.
1. The great Devastations made by the Plague HALE.

‖**Devastavit** (dĭvæstē·vit). 1651. [L.; 'he has wasted'.] *Law.* A writ that lies against an executor or administrator for waste of the testator's estate; also, the offence of such waste.

Deve, obs. f. DEAVE *v.* to deafen.

Devel (de·v'l), *sb. Sc.* 1786. [?] A stunning blow. Hence **De·vel** *v.* to strike with such a blow; **De·veller**, a boxer.

Develop (dĭve·lŏp), *v.* Also **develope.** 1592. [a. F. *développer*; cf. mod.It. *sviluppare*. See also ENVELOP.] †**1.** *trans.* To unfold, unroll; to unfurl –1868. **b.** *Geom.* To flatten out (a curved surface); to change the form of (a surface) by bending 1879. †**2.** To unveil; to unfold; to disclose –1837. **3.** To unfold more fully, bring out all that is contained in 1750; in *Mil.*, to open gradually (an attack) 1883. **4.** *Math.* To change the form of a mathematical function or expression without changing the value 1871. **5.** To bring forth from a latent or elementary condition 1813; in *Photogr.*, to bring out and render visible (the latent image produced by actinic action upon a sensitive surface); to apply to (the plate, etc.) the treatment by which this is effected. Also *absol.* 1845. **6.** *trans.* To cause to grow (what exists in the germ); to evolve 1839. Also *transf.* and *refl.* **7.** *intr.* (for *refl.*) To unfold itself, grow from a germ; to grow into a fuller, higher, or maturer condition 1843.
1. To d. the latent excellencies.. of our art SIR J. REYNOLDS, an idea HARE, property SIR R. ROMER. 5. We thus d. both attraction and repulsion TYNDALL. 6. They grow, or in modern phraseology they are developed ARGYLL. Forces have been at work, developing in each great continent animal forms peculiar to itself HAUGHTON. *transf.* Fresh powers.. which.. d. further resources H. MARTINEAU. It is astonishing what ambulatory powers he can d. HELPS. 7. London developed into the general mart of Europe GREEN. The time swine fever takes to d. 1891.

Developable (dĭve·lŏpăb'l), *a.* (*sb.*) 1816. [f. prec. vb.] **1.** Capable of being developed or developing 1835. **2.** *sb.* (*Math.*) A developable surface; a ruled surface in which consecutive generators intersect (Salmon).

Developer (dĭve·lŏpəɹ), *v.* 1833. [f. as prec. + -ER.] He who or that which develops; in *Photogr.*, a chemical agent by which photographs are developed.

Development (dĭve·lŏpmĕnt). Also **-ope-.** 1756. [f. as prec. + -MENT, after F. *développement*.]
I. 1. A gradual unfolding; a fuller working out of the details of anything. Also quasi-*concr.* that in which this is realized. **2.** Evolution; the production of a natural force, energy, or new form of matter 1794. **3.** The growth of what is in the germ; the condition of that which is developed; EVOLUTION 1844. **4.** Growth from within 1836. **5.** A developed or well-grown condition 1851. **6.** The developed result or product 1845.
2. The d. of heat 1794. 3. The d. of buds and flowers SIR B. BRODIE. *D. theory* or *hypothesis* (*Biol.*): the doctrine of Evolution; *esp.* as taught by Lamarck (died 1829). 6. The butterfly.. is the d. of the grub J. H. NEWMAN.
II. Techn. uses. **1.** *Geom.* The unbending of any curved surface into a plane, or of a non-plane curve into a plane curve 1800. **2.** *Math.* The process of expanding any expression into

another of equivalent value or meaning; the expanded form itself 1816. 3. *Photogr.* The process of developing a photograph (see DEVELOP *v.* 5) 1845. 4. *Mus.* The unfolding of the capacities of a musical phrase or subject by modifications of melody, harmony, etc.; *esp.* in a sonata; the part of a movement in which this takes place. Also *attrib.* 1880.

Hence **Deve·lopme·ntal** *a.* of or pertaining to d.; evolutionary. **Developme·ntally** *adv.* **Deve·lopmentist** (*nonce-wd.*), an evolutionist.

†**Devenu·state,** *v. rare.* 1653. [DE- 6.] To deprive of beauty.

Devest (dĭve·st), *v. arch.* 1563. [a. OF. *devester*, f. *des-*, *de-* = L. *dis-* (see DE- 6, DIS-) + *vestir*, mod.F. *vêtir* :—L. *vestire*. Now DIVEST, exc. in sense 4.] †1. *trans.* To unclothe, undress -1649. †2. To strip *of* anything that covers -1809. Also †*fig.* †3. To take off; to put off, lay aside -1765. Also †*refl.* 4. *Law.* To take away (a right, etc. vested in any one), to alienate 1574; †to dispossess of any right, etc. -1810.

2. And Aaron of his Ephod to d. DRYDEN. Hence **Deve·sture,** the action of devesting (*rare*).

†**Deve·x,** *a.* (*sb.*) ME. [ad. L. *devexus* (DE- I. 1).] 1. Bent down, sloping downward -1669. 2. *sb.* = DEVEXITY 1627.

†**Deve·xity.** 1601. [ad. L. *devexitas.*] Downward incline; concavity -1618.

†**De·viant,** *ppl. a. rare.* ME. [ad. late L. *deviantem.*] 1. Deviating -1623. 2. That diverts 1471.

†**De·viate,** *ppl. a. rare.* 1560. [ad. late L. *deviatus.*] Turned out of the way; remote -1638.

Deviate (dī·vi,eit), *v.* 1633. [f. L. *deviat-*, ppl. stem of *deviare* to turn out of the way; see DE- I. 2. Cf. F. *dévier.*] 1. *intr.* To turn aside from the course or track; to turn out of the way; to swerve 1635. Also *fig.* 2. *trans.* To turn (any one) out of the way, divert, deflect (*lit.* and *fig.*) 1660.

1. Neither stand still, nor go back, nor d. QUARLES. *fig.* Shadwell never deviates into sense DRYDEN. 2. To let them d. him from the right path COTTON. Hence **De·viative** *a.* causing or tending to deflexion. **De·viator.** **De·viatory** *a.* deviating.

Deviation (dīvi,ēi·ʃən). 1603. [f. L. *deviare* to DEVIATE.] 1. The action of deviating; turning aside from a track; swerving, deflexion 1646. †b. *Astron.* The deflexion of a planet's orbit from the plane of the ecliptic: attributed in the Ptolemaic astronomy to an oscillatory motion of the deferent 1727. c. *Comm.* Voluntary departure from the intended course of a vessel without sufficient cause 1809. 2. Divergence from the straight line, from the mean, or standard position; variation, deflexion; the amount of this 1675. 3. *fig.* Divergence *from* any course, method, rule, standard, etc. (The usual sense.) 1603. †b. Deviation from rectitude -1831. †c. A digression -1713.

2. *D. of the compass*, the deflexion of the needle of a ship's compass, owing to the magnetism of the iron in the ship, etc. *Conjugate d.* (*Path.*): see CONJUGATE *a.* 3. A d. from the plain accepted meaning of words GROVE.

Device (dĭvəi·s). [ME. *devis*, *devys*, a. OF. *devis* masc.; also *devise*, a. OF. *devise*; Rom. derivs. of L. *divis-*, ppl. stem of *dividere.*] 1. The action, or faculty, of devising; invention, ingenuity. Now *arch.* and *rare.* (orig. *devis*). ME. b. Design (*arch.*) ME. †2. Purpose (orig. *devis*) -1548. 3. Will, pleasure, inclination, desire (orig. *devis*) ME. †4. Opinion, notion; *occas.*, advice -1594. †5. Talk, chat. [F. *devise.*] -1610. 6. Something devised; an arrangement, plan, contrivance; often an underhand contrivance; a plot, stratagem, trick ME. 7. *concr.* The result of contriving; an invention, contrivance ME. 8. Something fancifully devised ME. 9. *spec.* An emblematic figure or design, *esp.* one borne by a particular person, etc., as a heraldic bearing, etc.: usually accompanied by a motto ME.; also, a motto or legend borne with or in place of such a design 1724.

1. Gold, or silver, or stone, graven by art and man's d. *Acts* xvii. 29. 'Tis Plate of rare deuice *Cymb.* I. vi. 189. 3. We will walk after our own deuices *Jer.* xviii. 12. 6. By this happy d. ..[they] screen themselves PRIESTLEY. 7. Devices for baling out hay KNIGHT. 8. A dyvyse of goold for mastres Margret 1465. Ballad, jest, and riddle's quaint d. BEATTIE. Masques and devices, welcome SHIRLEY. 9. The deuice he beares vpon his shield Is a blacke Ethyope, reaching at the sunne. The word, *Lux tua vita mihi* SHAKS. *Per.* II. ii. 19. A banner with the strange d., 'Excelsior' LONGF. Hence **Devi·ceful** *a.* full of d.; ingenious, curious (now *rare*). **Devi·cefully** (†**devisefully**) *adv.* **Devicefulness.**

Devil (de·v'l, de·vĭl), *sb.* [OE. *dēofol*, etc., a. Gr. διάβολος, 'the Devil, Satan', a specific application of διάβολος 'accuser, slanderer, traducer', f. διαβάλλειν to slander, *lit.* to throw across.] 1. *The Devil* [repr. Gr. ὁ διάβολος of the LXX and New Test.]: In Jewish and Christian theology, the supreme spirit of evil, the tempter and spiritual enemy of mankind, the foe of God and holiness, Satan. (In this sense without a pl.) b. In pl. applied to 'the Devil and his angels'; see Matt. xxv. 41. c. As tr. Heb. = 'satyrs'. *Rev.* xviii. 2. 2. = DEMON (sense 2), q. v. OE. Also *fig.*; see BLUE DEVIL. 3. Hence, generically, A fiend, a demon. Also applied to the idols or false gods of the heathen. OE. 4. *transf.* A malignantly wicked man; in ME. occas. a giant OE. b. In later use, a term of reprobation; also used playfully 1601. c. A term of contempt or pity (chiefly with *poor*). [So in It., Fr., etc.] 1698. d. Applied to a vicious beast 1834. 5. *spec. Printer's d.*: the errand-boy in a printing office 1683. b. A junior legal counsel who does professional work for another, usually without fee 1849. 6. *fig.* Applied to qualities 1604. 7. Used (usu. with qualifications) as the name of various animals, on account of their characteristics 1686. 8. A name of various instruments, machines, etc., *esp.* such as work with sharp teeth or spikes 1831. 9. A name for various highly-seasoned broiled or fried dishes; also for hot ingredients 1786. 10. A form of firework; a cracker, squib 1742. 11. A moving sand-spout in Eastern countries 1835. 12. *Naut.* 'The seam which margins the waterways on a ship's hull' (Smyth). 13. *predicatively*: Something as bad as the devil 1710. Also *attrib.*

1. All gathers up in a person, in the d., who has a kingdom, as God has a kingdom TRENCH. The d. appears himself, Armed and accoutred, horns and hoofs and tail BROWNING. 2. Devils they adore for deities MILT. *P. L.* I. 373. He hath a deuill and is mad *John* x. 20. 4. Haue I not chosen you twelue, and one of you is a deuill *John* vi. 70. 6. The diuell drunkennesse *Oth.* II. iii. 297. Evans bowled steadily, but without much 'd.' 1884. 7. *Tasmanian d.*, a carnivorous marsupial of Tasmania (*Sarcophilus ursinus*); *Sea D.*, the DEVIL-FISH. 8. To the paper factory, where they have a horrid machine they call the d., that tears everything to bits O. W. HOLMES. 9. Another holds a curry or d. in utter abomination W. IRVING. 13. These Southern girls are the d. 1885.

Phrases, etc. *To go to the d.*: to go to perdition. So *to wish* any one *at the d.*, etc. *Who, what, how, where, when the d.*: expressions of impatience, irritation, surprise, etc. Used interjectionally in same sense, and, prefixed to a sb., to express strong negation.

In proverbs, etc. a. *The d. to pay*: supposed to refer to bargains made by wizards, etc., with Satan, and the inevitable payment in the end. b. *To play the d.*: to act diabolically, do mischief. c. *The d. among the tailors*: a row going on; also a game.

Comb.: **d.-bird,** a name of various birds, *esp.* the Swift, and the Brown Owl of Ceylon; **-bolt,** a sham bolt; 'a bolt with false clenches, often introduced into contract-built ships' (Smyth); **-carriage, -cart,** one for moving heavy ordnance; **d.-in-a-bush,** a garden flower, *Nigella damascena*, with horned capsules peering from a bush of finely-divided involucre; **d. on two sticks,** a double cone made to spin in the air by means of a string attached to two sticks held in the hand; **-shrieker, -skriker,** the Swift (*local*); **-tree,** an apocynaceous tree (*Alstonia scholaris*) of India, Africa, and Australia, having a powerfully bitter bark and milky juice; **-wood,** *Osmanthus americanus*, N.O. *Oleaceæ*, a small N. American tree with wood of extraordinary toughness and heaviness; **-worship,** the cult of the d., or of a demon; so **-worshipper, -worshipping; -wort,** a plant.

b. Special phrases. **Devil's advocate** [L. *advocatus diaboli*], one who urges the devil's plea against the canonization of a saint, etc.; hence, one who advocates the wrong side, or injures a cause by his advocacy; **devil's bones,** dice; **devil's cow,** a black beetle; **devil's darning-needle** (*U.S.*) = *devil's needle* (see also c); **devil's dirt, devil's dung,** asafœtida; **devil's dozen:** see DOZEN; **devil's finger,** a belemnite; **devil's fingers,** the star-fish; **devil's needle,** the dragon-fly; **'Devil's Own',** the 88th Foot (*the Devil's own Connaught boys*); also the Inns of Court Rifle Corps of Volunteers; **devil's tattoo;** see TATTOO; **devil's toe-nail,** a belemnite.

c. in popular names of plants: **devil's apple,** the thorn-apple (*Datura Stramonium*); **devil's apron,** a U.S. name of species of *Laminaria* and other seaweeds with a large dilated lamina; **devil's club** (*U.S.*), a prickly araliaceous plant, *Fatua horrida*; **devil's cotton,** an East Indian tree, *Abroma*, the fibres of which are made into cordage; **devil's darning-needle,** *Scandix Pecten Veneris*; **devil's ear** (*U.S.*), a species of wake-robin (*Arum*); **devil's fig,** the prickly pear; **devil's leaf,** a virulent species of stinging nettle, *Urtica urentissima*, found in Timor.

Hence **De·vildom,** the rule of the (or a) d.; the domain of the d.; the condition of devils. **De·viless,** a she-devil. **De·vilet,** a little d., in various senses; the Swift. **De·vilhood,** the condition and estate of a d. **De·viling,** a young d.; the Swift (*local*). **De·vilism,** devilish quality; d.-worship. **De·vilize** *v.* to make a d. of; †*intr.* to act as a d. **De·vilkin,** an imp; also *fig.* **De·vil-like** *a.* and *adv.* †**De·villy, devily** *a.* = DEVILISH. **De·vilment,** mischief; a devilled dish; a devilish device. **De·vilry,** †a demon; diabolical art; devilish mischief; *joc.* reckless mischief, hilarity, or daring; demonology; devils collectively. **De·vilship,** the office or condition of a d. **De·viltry** = DEVILRY.

Devil (de·v'l, de·vĭl), *v.* 1652. [f. the sb.] †1. To play the devil with. 2. *trans.* To grill with hot condiments 1800. 3. *intr.* To act as devil to a lawyer (see DEVIL *sb.* 5 b) 1864. 4. To tear to pieces (rags, etc.) with a devil (see DEVIL 8).

De·vil-dodger. *joc.* 1791. [See DODGE *v.*] One who tries to dodge the devil; also, a nickname for (ranting) preachers.

De·vil-fish. 1814. A name of various large and formidable fishes, etc.; *esp.* a. A large pediculate fish (*Lophius piscatorius*), also called ANGLER (q.v.). b. In U.S., a gigantic species of eagle-ray, *Ceratoptera vampyrus*, having expanded sides, the expanse of which is sometimes 20 feet. Less commonly, c. The Californian grey whale. d. The piranha of Uruguay. e. The octopus, cuttle-fish, or other cephalopod.

Devilish (de·v'l,iʃ), *a.* 1494. [f. DEVIL *sb.* + -ISH.] 1. Having the nature or character of the devil; diabolical, execrable. 2. Of or belonging to the devil 1526. 3. *loosely.* Violent; extremely bad; enormous, excessive 1612. 4. *adv.* Very 1612.

1. A diuelish knaue *Oth.* II. i. 249. D. whisperings POLLOK. 2. Devilishe instigacion HALL. Hence **De·vilish-ly** *adv.*, **-ness.**

†**Devi·lity.** 1589. [f. as prec., after *civility*, etc.] Devilism -1609.

De·vil-may-ca·re. 1833 (in *devil-me-Carishness*). [The exclam. used attrib.] Wildly reckless; careless and rollicking.

Devil's-bit. 1450. [tr. med.L. *morsus diaboli.*] *Herb.* 1. A species of Scabious (*Scabiosa succisa*); also *Devil's-bit Scabious.* 2. *transf.* (in U.S.) *Chamælirium luteum*, the Blazing Star, N.O. *Liliaceæ*.

Devil's books. 1729 (Swift). Colloquial expression for playing cards.

Devil's claw. 1. *Naut.* a. A very strong split hook made to grasp a link of a chain cable, and used as a stopper. b. A grapnel. 2. *Conchol.* A Scorpion shell (*Pteroceras Scorpio*) from the Indian Ocean.

Devil's coach-horse. 1840. The large rove-beetle (*Goerius olens*), so called from its defiant attitude when disturbed.

Devil's dust. 1840. The flock made of old cloth by the machine called a devil; shoddy. (Orig. the dust made in this process.)

Devil's guts. 1670. *Herb.* A name of the Dodder (*Cuscuta*), from its pale slender stems which wind round and strangle other plants.

Devil's milk. 1578. [tr. Ger. *Teufelsmilch.*] A name given to plants with acrid milky juice; *e.g.* the Sun-Spurge (*Euphorbia Helioscopia*) and Petty Spurge (*E. Peplus*).

†**Devi·nct,** *ppl. a. rare.* 1573. [ad. L. *devinctus.*] Bounden -1643.

Devious (dī·viəs), *a.* 1599. [f. L. *devius* (f. *de* = DE- I. 2 + *via*) + -OUS.] 1. Lying out of the way; remote, sequestered. 2. Departing from the direct way; following a winding or erratic course 1628. 3. *fig.* Erring, straying 1633. 4. quasi-*adv.* 1782.

1. These d. and untrodden Ice-fields KANE. 2. A

shoal of d. minnows LOWELL. Hence **De·vious·ly** *adv.*, **-ness.**

†Devi·rginate, *v.* 1583. [f. L. *devirginat-*, ppl. stem of *devirginare*; see DE- I. 6.] *trans.* To deprive of virginity; to deflower. Also *fig.* -1680. So **†Devi·rginate** *ppl. a.* Hence **De·virgina·tion. Devi·rginator** (*rare*).

Deviscerate (dĭvi·sĕreʹt), *v. rare.* 1727. [DE- II. 1.] To disembowel, eviscerate. Hence **De·viscera·tion.**

Devise (dĭvəi·z), *v.* ME. [a. OF. *deviser* :—late pop.L. **divisare*, freq. of *dividere* to DIVIDE.] †1. *trans.* To divide -1483. †2. To assign, appoint, order, direct (*absol.* or *trans.*) -1606. 3. *Law.* To give by will. Now only of realty, but formerly = bequeath. ME. 4. To order the plan or design of; to plan, contrive, think out, frame, invent. (The chief current sense.) ME. Also *absol.* 5. *trans.* In a bad sense: To plot, scheme (*arch.*) ME.; to feign, invent (*arch.*) 1513; also *absol.* †6. *trans.* (or *absol.*) To contrive successfully; to 'manage' -1592. †7. To prepare with skill, purvey. (Also *absol.*) -1500. †8. *trans.* (or *absol.*) To conceive; to conjecture -1814. †9. *intr.* (or *trans.* with *obj. cl.*) To think, deliberate -1599. †10. To consider, scan -1509; to discern -1620. †11. To recount -1570. Also †*intr.* (or *absol.*). †12. To confer, converse, talk. [So in mod.F.] *refl.* and *intr.* -1614.

4. The moost..delicate dysshes, that can or may be deuysed for a kynge 1526. Speake all good you can deuise of Cæsar *Jul. C.* III. i. 246. 5. For thirtie pence he did my death d. G. HERBERT. D. fair pleas for delay BOWEN. 12. *intr.* Let us..a little d. of those evils [etc.] SPENSER. Hence **Devi·sable** *a.* that can be devised, bequeathed, or contrived. **Devi·sal** (*rare*), the act of devising; contrivance, invention. **Devi·ser,** one who devises; a contriver, inventor, etc.

Devise (dĭvəi·z), *sb.* 1542. [a. OF. *devise*, *devis* (in same sense) :—Rom. *deviso*, *devisa*, for L. *devisus*, and (late) *divisa*. The same wd. as DEVICE *sb.*, and formerly also so spelt.] The act of devising by will; a testamentary disposition of real property; the clause in a will conveying this. (Cf. DEVISE *v.* 3.)

Devisee (dĭvəi·zī·). 1542. [f. DEVISE *v.* + -EE.] *Law.* The person to whom a devise is made. (Correl. to *devisor.*)

Devisor (dĭvəi·zǭɪ). 1542. [a. AF. *devisour*, f. (ult.) F. *deviser* to DEVISE. Formerly used in all senses of the vb.] One who makes a devise. (Correl. to *devisee.*)

Devitalize (dĭvəi·tăləiz), *v.* 1849. [DE- II. 1.] *trans.* To deprive of vitality or vital qualities. Hence **Devi·taliza·tion.**

†Devita·tion. *rare.* 1614. [ad. L. *devitationem*, f. *devitare.*] Shunning; exhortation to shun: opp. to *invitation* -1623. So **†Devi·te** *v. trans.*, to shun; to ask not (*to do*). LAMB.

Devitrify (dĭvi·trifəi), *v.* 1832. [DE- II. 1; app. after F. *dévitrifier.*] *trans.* To deprive of vitreous qualities; to cause (glass, etc.) to become opaque, hard, and crystalline in structure. Hence **Devi·trifica·tion,** the action or process of devitrifying.

Devocalize (dĭvōᵘ·kăləiz), *v.* 1877. [DE- II. 1.] *trans.* To make (a vowel, etc.) voiceless or non-sonant. Hence **Devocaliza·tion.**

†De·vocate, *v. rare.* 1570. [f. L. *devocat-*, *devocare*; see DE- I. 1, 2.] *trans.* To call down -1633. Hence **†Devoca·tion,** a calling down or away.

Devoid (dĭvoi·d), *a.* ME. [Orig. pa. pple. of DEVOID *v.*, short for *devoided.*] 1. With *of*: Empty, void, destitute; entirely without. (Orig. participial, like *bereft.*) 2. Without *of*: Void, empty. SPENSER.

1. He lay speechlesse, deuoid of sence and motion KNOLLES.

†Devoi·d, *v. rare.* ME. [a. OF. *de-*, *desvoidier*, etc., mod. *dévider*, f. *de-*, *des-* (L. *dis-*) + *vuide*, mod. *vide.*] 1. *trans.* To cast out; to void -1509. †2. To make void or empty -1548.

Devoir (dĕvwǭɪ, de·vwǭɪ), *sb.* ME. [a. OF. *devoir*, subst. use of vb. 'to owe' :—L. *debere*. The old pronunc. is retained in ENDEAVOUR.] 1. One's duty. (Chiefly in phr. *to do one's d.*) *arch.* †2. One's utmost or best -1671. †3. Service due to any one -1742. 4. A dutiful act of civility or respect; usu. in *pl.* 14.. †5. *pl.* Moneys due; dues -1641.

4. I beseech your ladyship instruct me where I may tender my devoirs DRYDEN.

Devolute (de·vŏliūt), *v. rare.* 1534. [f. L. *devolut-* ppl. stem; see DEVOLVE.] *trans.* To pass by devolution; to DEVOLVE. So **†De·volute** *ppl. a.* devolved.

Devolution (devŏliū·ʃən). 1545. [ad. med.L. *devolutionem*; see DEVOLVE.] 1. Rolling down; descending or falling with or as with a rolling motion. 2. *Biol.* (opp. to EVOLUTION): Degeneration 1882. 3. The causing of anything to descend or fall *upon*; the handing (of anything) on to a successor 1621. 4. *spec.* The delegation of portions or details of duties to subordinate officers or committees 1780.

1. This..D. of Earth and Sand from the Mountains WOODWARD. *fig.* A long d. of years 1651. 3. A d. of the right of election for that turn BLACKSTONE. A d. of the crown HALLAM. 4. To lighten the cares of the central Legislature by judicious d. T. JEFFERSON.

Devolve (dĭvǫ·lv), *v.* ME. [ad. L. *devolvere* (DE- I. 1).]

I. *trans.* 1. To roll down; to cause to descend with rolling motion; also to unroll, unfurl (*arch.*). 2. *fig.* To cause to pass *to* or fall *upon* (a person) 1538. 3. *spec.* To delegate to deputies duties for which the responsibility belongs to the principal 1633.

1. His Thames, With gentle course develving fruitful Streams PRIOR. He spake of virtue..And..Devolved his rounded periods TENNYSON. 3. To d. on others the weight of government HUME.

II. *intr.* 1. To roll or flow down or on (*lit.* and *fig.*) 1579. 2. *fig.* To pass to the next in natural or conventional order 1555. 3. Of persons: a. To come *upon* as a charge. b. To sink gradually. ? *Obs.* 1748.

2. The Empire thus deuolued to Dioclesian SPEED. Upon him would d. the chief labour TYNDALL.

Devonian (dĭvōᵘ·niăn), *a.* (*sb.*) 1612. [f. med.L. *Devonia*, latinized form of *Devon*, OE. *Defena-scīr.*] 1. Of or belonging to Devonshire; as *sb.* A native or inhabitant of Devonshire. 2. *Geol.* Name of a system of rocks lying below the Carboniferous and above the Silurian formations; hence, of or pertaining to this formation and its geological period. var. **Devo·nic** *a.* (*rare*).

Devonport; see DAVENPORT.

Devonshire, *v.*; see DENSHIRE.

†Devora·tion. 1528. [a. obs. F., ad. L. *devorationem.*] The action of devouring or consuming -1614.

‖Devo·ta. [It. and Sp.] A female devotee. EVELYN.

†Devo·tary. 1646. [ad. med.L. *devotarius.*] A votary; a devotee -1670.

Devote (dĭvōᵘ·t), *a.* and *sb.* *arch.* 1596. [ad. L. *devotus*, pa. pple. of *devovere*. Repl. by DEVOTEE, or occas. identified with mod.F. *dévote* fem.]

A. *ppl. a.* = DEVOTED.

B. *adj.* = DEVOUT 1625.

C. *sb.* A devotee 1630.

Devote (dĭvōᵘ·t), *v.* 1586. [f. L. *devot-*, ppl. stem of *devovere*; see DE- I. 2.] 1. To appropriate by, or as if by, a vow; to set apart or dedicate solemnly or formally; to consecrate (*to*). 2. To give up, addict, apply zealously or exclusively (*to*); *esp.* refl. *to devote oneself* 1604. 3. To consign to destruction; to pronounce a curse upon 1647.

1. No deuoted thing that a man shall deuote vnto the Lord *Lev.* xxvii. 28. To d. property to charity LD. ELDON. 2. D. this day to mirth ROWE. [He] who devotes himself to some intellectual pursuit JOWETT. Hence **Devo·tement,** the action of devoting, or fact of being devoted; dedication. **Devo·ter,** †a devotee (*rare*); one who devotes (Dicts.). **†Devo·tress,** a female devotee. var. **†Devou·t** *v.*

†Devoté. Erron. f. DEVOTE *sb.*, with pseudo-Fr. spelling. FIELDING.

Devoted (dĭvōᵘ·tĕd), *ppl. a.* 1594. [f. DEVOTE *v.* + -ED¹.] 1. Vowed; dedicated, consecrated. 2. Characterized by devotion 1600. 3. Doomed 1611.

2. Sir, your very d. SHERIDAN. 3. Round our d. heads the billows beat PRIOR. Hence **Devo·ted-ly** *adv.*, **-ness.**

Devotee (devotī·). 1645. [f. DEVOTE *v.* or *a.*, after *assignee*, etc. Repl. DEVOTE *sb.*] 1. *gen.* One who is zealously devoted to a party, cause, pursuit, etc.; a votary 1657. 2. *spec.* One characterized by religious devotion, *esp.* of an extreme or superstitious kind.

1. A d. of vegetarianism BURTON. 2. He grew older, became..from a profligate a d. HARRIS. Hence **Devotee·ism,** the principles or practice of a d.

Devotion (dĭvōᵘ·ʃən), *sb.* ME. [a. OF. *devocion*, *-ciun*, *-tiun*, early ad. L. *devotionem*, f. *devovere.*]

I. In religious use: from eccl.L., through OF. 1. The fact or quality of being devoted to religious observances, etc.; reverence, devoutness ME. 2. Religious worship or observance. b. *spec.* An act of worship; now only in *pl.* c. A form of worship, for private use. ME. †3. An oblation; alms -1662. 4. The action of devoting; solemn dedication, consecration. (A Renascence sense.) 1502.

1. A journey of D. to Rome PRIDEAUX. Devocion ..to Cupido CHAUCER. 2. A splendid book of devotions FREEMAN.

II. In non-religious use; from ancient L. through It. and Fr. 1. The quality of being devoted to a person, cause, etc. 1530. †2. Devoted service; disposal -1839. †3. That to which anything is devoted; object, purpose -1646. 4. The action of applying to a particular use or purpose 1861.

1. This fervid d. to art in Charles D'ISRAELI. 2. Phr. *To be at the d. of*, to be entirely devoted to. 3. *Rich. III*, IV. i. 9. 4. The d. of a few pages to it M. PATTISON.

Hence †**Devotionair** (*rare*), var. of *Devotionary*. **Devo·tional** *a.* of, pertaining to, of the nature of, or characterized by, d. **Devo·tionalist,** one given to d. **Devotiona·lity. Devo·tionally** *adv.* **†Devo·tionary** *a.* pertaining to d.; *sb.* a DEVOTEE. **Devo·tionist,** a devotionalist.

†Devoto (dĭvōᵘ·to), *sb.* Pl. **-oes, -o's, -os;** also (as in It.) **-i.** 1599. [a. It. or Sp. :—L. *devotus.*] A devotee -1712. var. (or ? misprint) **†Devo·tor.**

Devour (dĭvauᵊ·ɪ), *v.* ME. [a. OF. *devorer*, ad. L. *devorare*, f. DE- I. 1 + *vorare* to swallow.] 1. To swallow or eat up voraciously, as a beast of prey. 2. Of human beings: To eat greedily, consume or make away with, as food; to eat like a beast ME. 3. To consume destructively; to waste, destroy, swallow up ME. 4. To take in greedily the sense of (a book, etc.) 1581; to look upon with avidity 1621; to swallow (chagrin, etc.) 1650. 5. Of things: To absorb 1500.

1. Turned, as a wolf to d. the lambs SEWEL. 3. This thy son.. which hath devoured thy living with harlots *Luke* xv. 30. Time hath devoured it [the Monument] SIR T. HERBERT. The quicksand that devours all miserie MARSTON. 4. With eager Eyes devouring .. The breathing Figures of Corinthian Brass DRYDEN. Hence **Devou·rable** *a.* that can be devoured; consumable. **Devou·rer,** one who or that which devours. **†Devou·ress,** a female devourer. **Devou·ringly** *adv.* **Devou·rment,** the action of devouring.

Devout (dĭvau·t), *a.* and *sb.* [ME. *devot*, *devout*, a. OF. *devot*, *devote*, ad. L. *devotus*, pa. pple. of *devovere*. Cf. DEVOTE *a.*] A. 1. Devoted to divine worship or service; reverential in religious exercises; pious, religious; †*gen.* devoted (*to* a person or cause) -1659. 2. Of actions, etc.: Showing or expressing devotion ME. 3. Earnest, sincere, hearty 1828.

1. A shorte orison, saide with good devouute herte 1450. *gen.* The most d. friend of the Church 1659. 2. Uplifted hands, and eyes d. MILT. *P. L.* XI. 863.

B. *sb.* †1. A devotee -1675. 2. The devotional part (of a composition, etc.). MILT.

Hence **Devou·tly** *adv.* in a d. manner; earnestly, sincerely.

†Devou·tful, *a.* 1597. [irreg. f. DEVOUT *a.* + -FUL.] Full of devoutness; pious -1604.

As painfull Pilgrim in deuoutfull wise 1598. So **†Devou·tless** *a.* without devoutness.

Devoutness (dĭvau·tnĕs). ME. [f. DEVOUT *a.* + -NESS.] The quality of being devout; religiousness, piety.

†Devo·ve, *v.* 1567. [ad. L. *devovere*; see DE- I. 2.] To devote -1808.

†Devow·, *v.* 1579. [a. F. *dévouer*, f. DE- I. 2, 3 + *vouer*, after L. *devovere*; see DEVOTE.] 1. *trans.* To dedicate or give up by vow -1609. 2. To devote -1632. 3. To disavow (*rare*) 1610.

Devu·lgarize, *v.* 1868. [DE- II. 1.] *trans.* To free from vulgarity.

Shakespeare, and Plutarch's 'Lives', are very devulgarizing books ABBOTT.

Dew (diū), *sb.* [Com. Teut.: OE. *déaw* :—OTeut. **dauwo-*, Aryan **dháwo-*; cf. Skr.

dhaw to flow, run.] **1.** The moisture deposited in minute drops upon any cool surface by the condensation of the vapour in the atmosphere; plentiful in the early morning. (Formerly supposed to fall softly from the heavens.) **2.** *fig.* Something likened to dew: **a.** as coming with refreshing power or falling gently ME.; **b.** as characteristic of the morning of life 1535. **3.** *transf.* Applied to moisture generally, *esp.* that which exudes from any body ME. **4.** *attrib.* and *comb.* ME.

1. Our day is gone, Clowds, Dewes, and Dangers come *Jul. C.* v. iii. 64. The d. was falling fast WORDSW. 2. The continuall deawe of thy blessinge *Bk. Com. Prayer* 1559. The timely d. of sleep MILT. *P. L.* IV. 614. Thou hast the d. of thy youth *Ps.* cx. 3. 3. The night of d. that on my cheekes downe flowes *L. L. L.* IV. iii. 29. *Mountain-d.*, a term for whisky illicitly distilled on the mountains. 4. Knot-grass, d.-besprent MILT. *Comus* 540. D.-impearled flowers DRAYTON. D.-lit eyes TENNYSON. Hence **Dew·less** *a.*

Dew (diū), *v.* [ME. *dewen*, implying an OE. **dēawian* :—OTeut. **dauwōjan*, f. *dauw-* DEW.] †**1.** *intr.* To give or produce dew; *impers.* to fall as dew (cf. *it rains*, etc.) -1726. **2.** *trans.* To wet with or as with dew; to bedew; to moisten ME. †**3.** To cause to fall as dew -1593.

2. Cold sweat Dew'd all my face OTWAY. [Music] Every sense in slumber dewing SCOTT.

Dew, obs. for DUE.

‖**Dewan** (dĭwā·n). Also **diwan**, etc. 1690. [Arab. and Pers. *dīwān, dīvān*, the same word as DIVAN.] In India: **a.** The head financial minister of a state. **b.** The prime minister of a native state. **c.** The chief native officer of certain Government establishments. **d.** In Bengal, a native servant in charge of a house of business or a large domestic establishment. Hence **Dewa·nship** = next.

‖**Dewani, dewanny, dewaunee** (dĭwā·ni). 1783. [a. Pers. *dīwānī, dīvānī*, the office or function of *dīwān*; see prec.] The office of dewan; *esp.* the right of collecting the revenue in Bengal, Behar, and Orissa, ceded to the E. I. Company by Shāh 'Alam in 1765. Also used occas. for the territory in question.

Dew-berry (diū·beri). 1578. [f. DEW *sb.* + BERRY.] A species of blackberry or bramble-berry: in Great Britain *Rubus cæsius*; in N. America *R. canadensis*, differing from the British plant in its fruit. The name is applied both to the fruit and the shrub. In mod. dialects (and ? in Shaks.), the name is applied to the Gooseberry.

Feede him with Apricocks and Dewberries *Mids. N.* III. i. 169.

Dew-claw (diū·klǫ). 1576. [app. f. DEW *sb.* + CLAW *sb.*] **1.** The rudimentary inner toe or hallux (not reaching the ground) sometimes present in dogs. **2.** The false hoof of deer and other ungulates 1576.

Dewdrop (diū·drǫp). 1590. [f. DEW *sb.* + -DROP.] A drop of dew.

Dew-fall (diū·fǭl). 1622. [f. DEW + FALL *sb.*] The deposition of dew; the time when this begins, in the evening.

†**Dewitt, De-Witt** (dĭwi·t), *v.* 1689. [f. John and Cornelius *De Witt*, Dutch statesmen, who were murdered by a mob in 1672.] *trans.* To lynch -1888.

Dewlap (diū·læp). Also *erron.* **dew-clap.** ME. [f. obsc. element + LAP, OE. *læppa* pendulous piece, lappet, lobe. Cf. Da. *doglæb*, Norw. *doglæp.*] The fold of loose skin which hangs from the throat of cattle. Also *transf.*; and *joc.* of pendulous folds of flesh about the human throat (*Mids. N.* II. i. 50). Hence **Dew·lapped** *a.* having a d.

Dew-point (diū·point). 1833. That point of atmospheric temperature at which dew begins to be deposited.

Dew-pond. 1877. A shallow pond, usu. artificial, fed by the condensation of water from the air, occurring on downs having no other adequate water-supply.

Dew-ret (diū·ret), *v.* Also **-rot, -rate.** 1710. [f. DEW *sb.* + RET *v.*] To ret or macerate (flax, hemp, etc.) by exposure to the dew and atmospheric influence instead of by steeping in water.

†**Dewtry.** 1598. [Cf. Marathī *dhutra, dhotrā*, dial. *dhutrō*.] The Thorn-apple, *Datura Stramonium*; a stupefying drug or drink prepared from this -1711.

Dew-worm (diū·wɒ̄ɹm). 1599. [f. DEW *sb.* + WORM.] The common earth-worm; in OE. ring-worm.

Dewy (diū·i), *a.* [OE. *dēawig*, f. *dēaw* DEW. Not in ME.] **1.** Characterized by, or abounding with, dew; affected by the influence of dew OE. **2.** *transf.* Moistened as with dew. In *Bot.* Covered as with dew. 1577. **3.** Dewlike, moist OE. **4.** Of dew (*poet.*) 1820. **5.** *fig.* Falling gently, vanishing, as the dew (*poet.*) 1611.

1. From Noon to d. Eve MILT. *P. L.* I. 743. Twilight's d. tints S. ROGERS. 2. Her faire deawy eies SPENSER *F. Q.* III. ii. 34. 5. Till dewie sleep Oppressed them MILT. *P. L.* IX. 1044. Hence **Dew·ily** *adv.* **Dew·iness**, d. quality (*lit.* and *fig.*).

Dexiocardia (de·ksi͵okā·ɹdiă). 1866. [a. Gr. δεξιός + καρδία.] An anomaly of development in man in which the heart is on the right side.

Dexiotropic (de·ksi͵otrǫ·pik), *a.* 1883. [f. Gr. δεξιός + -τροπος + -IC.] Turning or turned to the right, as the spire of some shells; opp. to *leiotropic.* var. **De·xiotrope.**

Dexter (de·kstəɹ), *a.* (*sb.* and *adv.*). 1562. [a. L., a compar. form from root *dex-*; cf. Gr. δεξιός, Skr. *daksha*, etc.]

A. *adj.* **1.** Belonging to or situated on the right side; right; *esp.* in *Her.* the opposite of SINISTER. †**2.** = DEXTEROUS -1659.

1. In a representation of a coat of arms, that part of the shield which appears on the *left* side [of a spectator] is called the Dexter, and that on the *right*, the Sinister CUSSANS.

B. *sb.* The right 1814.

C. *adv.* On or to the right. POPE.

†**Dexte·rical,** *a.* 1607. [irreg. f. L. *dexter* (see prec.) + -IC + -AL.] Dexterous -1644.

Dexterity (dekste·rĭti). 1527. [ad. L. *dexteritas*, f. *dexter*; see above. Cf. F. *dextérité.*] **1.** Manual skill, neat-handedness; hence, address in the use of the limbs and in bodily movements 1548. **2.** Mental adroitness or skill; cleverness, address, ready tact. In a bad sense: Sharpness. 1527. †**3.** Handiness, conveniency -1614. **4.** *lit.* Right-handedness (*rare*) 1882.

1. Able to handle his Peece with due dexteritie GARRARD. 2. My admirable dexteritie of wit *Merry W.* IV. v. 120. Dexteritie to cheat and deceive GALE.

Dexterous, dextrous (de·kstĕrəs, de·kstrəs), *a.* 1605. [f. L. *dexter, dextr-* right, *dextra* the right hand. *Dextrous* is the better, *dexterous* the prevailing, form.] †**1.** = DEXTER 1. -1678. †**2.** Handy. BACON. **3.** Deft or nimble of hand; hence skilful in the use of the limbs and in bodily movements 1635. **4.** Having mental adroitness or skill; expert in contrivance or management; clever 1622. †In a bad sense: Clever, crafty -1715. **5.** Of things: Characterized by dexterity; clever 1625. **6.** Right-handed (*mod.*).

3. A dextrous archer GIBBON. 4. Dextrous in Letters MABBE, in business SOUTHEY. Dexterous in the management of temporal affairs MRS. JAMESON. 5. Dexterous conduct SYD. SMITH. var. †**Dexte·rious.** Hence **De·xterously, de·xtrously** *adv.*; var. †**Dexte·riously. De·xterousness, de·xtrousness.**

Dextrad (de·kstræ̆d), *adv.* and *a.* 1803. [f. L. *dextra* right hand + -AD II.] To or toward the right side of the body; dextrally.

Dextral (de·kstrăl), *a.* 1646. [f. L. *dextra* + -AL.] **1.** Situated on the right side of the body; right, as opp. to *left.* **2.** *Conchol.* Of a gastropod shell: Having the whorl ascending from left to right (*i. e.* of the external spectator) 1847. Hence **Dextra·lity**, the condition of having the right side differing from the left, also, right-handedness. **De·xtrally** *adv.* to the right, as opp. to the left.

Dextrane (de·kstrēⁱn). [f. L. *dextra* + -ANE.] *Chem.* An amorphous dextro-rotatory gummy substance, $C_6H_{10}O_5$, found in unripe beet-root, and formed in the lactic fermentation of sugar.

Dextrer(e, dextrier; see DESTRER.

Dextrin (de·kstrin). Also **-ine.** 1838. [a. F. *dextrine*, f. L. *dextra*; see -IN. Named from its property of turning the plane of polarization 138·68° to the right.] *Chem.* A soluble gummy substance into which starch is converted when subjected to a high temperature, or to the action of dilute alkalis or acids, or of diastase. Called also *British gum* and *Leiocome.*

Dextro-, comb. f. L. *dexter, dextra*, in the sense '(turning or turned) to the right', chiefly with reference to the property of causing the plane of a ray of polarized light to rotate to the right. Hence:

a. Dextrogyre (de·kstro͵dʒəiᵊɹ), *a.* [L. *gyrus*, Gr. γῦρος circuit], circling to the right. **Dextrogy·rate** *a.*, characterized by turning the plane of polarization to the right, as a *dextrogyrate crystal.* **Dextrogy·rous** *a.* = *dextrogyre.* **Dextro-rota·tion**, rotation to the right. **Dextroro·tatory** *a.*, dextrogyrous.

b. Dextro-co·mpound, a chemical compound which causes dextro-rotation. **Dextro-glu·cose** = DEXTROSE. **Dextro-race·mic, Dextro-tarta·ric acid**, the modifications of racemic and tartaric acid which cause dextro-rotation.

Dextrorse (dekstrǭ·ɹs), *a.* 1864. [ad. L. *dextrorsum, dextrorsus.*] Turned toward the right hand. (Used by the earlier botanists as = 'to the right hand of the observer'; by modern as = 'to the right hand of the plant', which is to the left of the external observer.) var. **Dextro·rsal** (*rare*).

Dextrose (de·kstrōᵘs). 1869. [f. L. *dexter, dextra*; see -OSE [2].] *Chem.* The form of GLUCOSE which is dextro-rotatory to polarized light; dextro-glucose; ordinary glucose or grape-sugar.

Dextrous; see DEXTEROUS.

Dey [1] (dēⁱ). Now *dial.* [OE. *dæge* :—OTeut. **daigjôn*. The primitive meaning is 'kneader'; cf. OE. *hlæfdige* now LADY.] **1.** A woman having charge of a dairy; in early use, also, female servant. Hence, **2.** A man having similar duties 1483.

Comb.: **d.-house**, a dairy; **-maid**, a dairy-maid; **-wife, -woman**, a dairy woman.

‖**Dey** [2] (dēⁱ). 1659. [a. F., Turkish *dāī* 'maternal uncle', also a friendly title for middle-aged or old people, *esp.* among the Janissaries.] The titular appellation of the commanding officer of the Janissaries of Algiers, who in 1710 deposed the pasha, and became sole ruler. (Disused after the French conquest of 1830.)

Dey, obs. f. DIE *sb.* and *v.*

Deynt, Deynte, -tie, etc.; see DAINT-.

Dezincation (dīziŋkēⁱ·ʃən). 1891. [DE- II. 1.] The removal of zinc from an alloy or composition.

Dezincify, dezinkify (dīzi·ŋkifəi), *v.* 1874. [DE- II. 1.] To remove zinc from an alloy or composition.

Dezymotize (dīzəi·mǒtəiz), *v.* 1884. [DE- II. 1.] To free from disease-germs.

Dh-, in the English spelling of East Indian words, represents the Indian dental sonant-aspirate, written *dha*, also the lingual sonant-aspirate, *ḍha*. It has also been extended erroneously to words having simple *da* dental or *ḍa* lingual, and to words not really Indian, as *dhooly*, etc.

‖**Dhak** (dhāk). Also **dhawk.** 1825. [Hindī *ḍhāk.*] An East Indian tree *Butea frondosa*, N.O. *Leguminosæ*, noted for its brilliant flowers.

‖**Dhal**, var. of DAL Indian pulse.

‖**Dharna, dhurna** (dhɒ·ɹnā). 1793. [Hindī *dharnā* placing, act of sitting in restraint, f. Skr. *dhṛ* to place.] A mode of compelling payment or compliance with a demand, by sitting at the debtor's door, and there remaining without tasting food till the demand shall be complied with; this action is called 'sitting (in) dharnā'.

‖**Dhobi** (dhōᵘbi). 1860. [Hindī, f. *dhōb* washing.] A native washerman in India.

‖**Dhole** (dhōᵘl). 1827. [?] The wild dog of the Deccan in India.

‖**Dhoney, doney** (dōᵘ·ni). Also **doni.** 1582. [ad. Tamil *thōni* (pronounced *dōni*); cf. Pers. *dōnī* a yacht.] A small native sailing vessel of Southern India.

Dhooley, -lie, erron. ff. DOOLIE, a litter.

‖**Dhoti, dhootie** (dhōᵘ·ti, dhū·ti). 1622. [Hindī *dhōtī.*] The loin-cloth worn by Hindus.

Dhourra, dhurra = DURRA, Indian millet.

‖**Dhow, dow** (dau). 1802. [Original language unkn.] A native vessel used on the

Arabian Sea, generally with a single mast, and of 150 to 200 tons burden; more widely, applied to all Arab vessels.

Dhurrie, durrie (dʊ·ri). 1880. [Hindī *darī*.] A kind of cotton carpet of Indian manufacture, usually made in rectangular pieces, and used for sofa-covers, curtains, and the like.

Di- (di, dəi), *pref.*[1], repr. L. *dī-*, short form of *dis-*, used in L. before *b, d, g* (usually), *l, m, n, r, s* + cons., *v*, and sometimes before *j*. In ME. often varying with *de-*, whence *defer, devise*, etc., f. L. *differre, divisa*, etc. For its force in composition see DIS-.

Di- (dəi, di), *pref.*[2], repr. Gr. δι- for δίς twice. Hence, 1. Entering into numerous Eng. words, mostly technical, as *dichromic*, etc.; in Nat. Hist. *Diandria*, etc.; in *Crystallogr. ditetrahedron*, etc. 2. As a living prefix, used in *Chem.* in the general sense 'twice, double', but with special applications, expressing the presence of two atoms, equivalents, molecules, formulas, as the case may be.

Di-, *pref.*[3], the form of DIA- used bef. a vowel, as in *di-optric*, etc.

Dia-, *pref.*[1], bef. a vowel **di-**, repr. Gr. δια-, δι-, the prep. διά through, during, across, by. [orig. *δϝιγα, from root of *δϝο, δύο two, and so related to δίς, and L. *dis-* a-two.] Much used in the senses 'through, thorough, thoroughly, apart'.

Dia-, *pref.*[2], in medical terms. The Gr. phrases διὰ τεσσάρων (in full τὸ διὰ τεσσάρων φάρμακον medicament made up of four ingredients), διὰ πέντε, and the like, were treated in Latin as words, thus *diatessaron, diapente*, etc., and later formations of the same kind were added to the number. Of these a few, *e.g.* DIACHYLUM, survive in modern use.

Diabantite (dəiăbæ·ntəit). 1875. [irreg. f. DIABASE (as if = Gr. διάβας, διαβαντ- having crossed over.] *Min.* A chlorite-like mineral occurring in diabase and giving to this rock its green colour.

Diabase (dəi·ăbēⁱs). 1836. [a. F. *diabase* (improp. for *dibase* 'rock with two bases'); abandoned, and in 1842 re-introduced by Hausmann, perh. with some reference to Gr. διάβασις transition.] *Min.* Brongniart's original name for DIORITE; now applied to a fine-grained, compact, crystalline granular rock, consisting essentially of augite and a triclinic feldspar, with some chloritic matter; a variety of the class of rocks called greenstone and trap. Also *attrib.* Hence **Diaba·sic** *a.* pertaining to or resembling d.

Diabaterial (dəi·ăbătīᵊ·riăl), *a. rare.* 1784. [f. Gr. διαβατήρια (sc. ἱερά) offerings before crossing.] Pertaining to the crossing of a frontier or river.

Diabetes (dəiăbī·tiz). 1562. [a. L., a. Gr. διαβήτης, lit. 'a passer through, a siphon'.] †1. A siphon 1661. 2. *Med.* A disease characterized by the immoderate discharge of urine containing glucose, and accompanied by thirst and emaciation.

Sometimes called *Diabetes mellitus*, to distinguish it from *Diabetes insipidus* which is characterized by an absence of saccharine matter. (In 18th c. with *the* or *a.*) var. †**Di·abete.** **Diabetic** (dəiăbe·tik, -ī·tik) *a.* pertaining to d. or its treatment (var. **Diabe·tical**); affected with d.; *sb.* one who suffers from d.

Diablerie (di̯ā·blĕri). Also **-ery.** 1751. [a. F., f. *diable*; see -ERY.] 1. Dealings with the devil; sorcery or conjuring; devilry. 2. Devil-lore 1824.

‖**Diablotin** (di̯ablotæ̃). 1812. [F., dim. of *diable*.] An imp.

Diabolic (dəiăbǫ·lik). ME. [a. F. *diabolique*, ad. L. *diabolicus*, a. Gr., f. διάβολος.]

A. *adj.* 1. Of, pertaining to, or resembling the devil; having to do with the devil; pertaining to witchcraft or magic. 2. Of the nature of the devil; fiendish; inhumanly wicked 1483.

1. A diabolike instrument 1533. D. pow'r MILT., aspect 1862, possession 1871. 2. No d. delight 1876.

†B. *sb.* An agent of the devil -1638; a person possessed by a devil -1825. var. **Diabo·lical** *a.* and *sb.* Hence **Diabo·lical·ly** *adv.*, **-ness.**

Dia·bolifuge. [See -FUGE.] Something that drives away the devil. O. W. HOLMES.

Diabolify (dəiăbǫ·lifəi), *v.* 1647. [f. L. *diabolus* + -FY.] To make a devil of; to represent as a devil.

Diabolism (dəi,æ·bŏliz'm). 1614. [f. Gr. διάβολος + -ISM.] 1. Dealing with the devil; sorcery, witchcraft. 2. Conduct or action worthy of the devil; devilry 1681. 3. Doctrine as to devils; worship of the devil 1660. 4. The character or nature of a devil 1754. So **Dia·bolist,** a teacher of d. **Dia·bolize** *v.* to render, or represent as, diabolical; to subject to diabolical influence.

Diabolo (diæ·bŏlo). 1907. [It., = devil.] The game 'the devil-on-two-sticks' (see DEVIL).

Diabolology (dəi·ăbǫlǫ·lŏdʒi). 1875. [See -LOGY.] Doctrine of the devil; devil-lore. var. **Diabo·logy.**

Diabolonian (dəi·ăbǫlōᵘ·niăn). 1682. [f. L. *diabolus*, after *Babylonian*, etc.] 'One of the host of Diabolus (the Devil) in his assault upon Mansoul' (Bunyan); also as *adj.*

†**Di·acatho·licon.** 1562. [repr. Gr. διὰ καθολικῶν composed of universal (ingredients). See DIA- *pref.*[2]] Old term for a laxative electuary; hence, a universal remedy or appliance -1665.

Diacaustic (dəiăkǭ·stik). 1704. [f. Gr. διά + καυστικός, f. καίειν.]

A. *adj.* 1. *Math.* Of a surface or curve: Formed by the intersection of refracted rays of light. †2. *Med.* Formerly applied to a double convex lens or burning glass.

B. *sb.* 1. *Math.* A diacaustic curve or surface; a caustic by refraction 1727. †2. *Med.* A double convex lens used to cauterize.

Dia·cetate. *Chem.* See DI-[2] 2 + ACETATE.

Dia·cetin. *Chem.* See DI-[2] 2 + ACETIN.

Diachænium (dəiăkī·niŏm). 1870. [f. DI-[2] + L. *achænium*.] *Bot.* = CREMOCARP.

†‖**Diachore·sis.** 1706. [Gr. = 'excretion'.] *Med.* The act or faculty of voiding excrements -1721. Hence **Diachore·tic** *a.*

Diachylon, -lum (dəi,æ·kilǫn, -lŏm), **diaculum** (dəi,æ·kiŭlŏm). ME. [a. med.L., repr. Gr. διὰ χυλῶν (a medicament) composed of juices. See DIA-[2].] Orig., a kind of ointment composed of vegetable juices; now a name for lead-plaster, *emplastrum plumbi*, made by boiling together litharge (lead oxide), olive oil, and water. It adheres when heated.

†**Dia·chyma.** 1866. [f. Gr. διά- + χύμα that which is poured out.] *Bot.* = PARENCHYMA.

Diacid (dəi,æ·sid), *a.* 1866. [See DI-[2] 2.] *Chem.* Capable of combining with two acid radicals.

Diaclasite (dəi,æ·klăsəit). 1850. [f. Ger. *diaklas*, f. Gr. διακλάειν; on account of its easy cleavage.] *Min.* A bisilicate of iron and magnesium.

†‖**Diacodium** (dəiăkōᵘ·diŏm). Also **-dion.** 1564. [med. and mod.L., repr. Gr. διὰ κωδειῶν (a preparation) made from poppy-heads; see DIA-[2].] A syrup prepared from poppy-heads, used as an opiate -1829.

Diacœlosis (dəi·ăsīlōᵘ·sis). 1888. [f. DIA-[1] + Gr. κοίλωσις hollow, belly.] *Biol.* The separation of the cœlome into several sinuses, as in leeches, etc.

Diaconal (dəi,æ·kŏnăl), *a.* 1611. [ad. late L. *diaconalis*.] Of or belonging to a DEACON.

Diaconate (dəi,æ·kŏnĕt). 1727. [ad. late L. *diaconatus*.] 1. The office or rank of deacon. 2. The time during which any one is a deacon 1880. 3. A body of deacons 1891.

‖**Diaco·nicon.** Also **-um.** 1727. [Gr., neut. adj., f. διάκονος.] *Eccl. Antiq.*, etc. A building or room adjoining the church, where vestments, ornaments, etc., used in the church service are kept; a sacristy, a vestry.

‖**Diacope** (dəi,æ·kopi). 1586. [a. Gr., f. διακόπτειν to cut through.] †1. *Gram.* Tmesis -1678. 2. *Surg.* A cut, fissure, longitudinal fracture; usually an oblique incision made in the cranium by a sharp instrument, without the piece being removed.

Diacoustics (dəiăkau·stiks). 1683. [See DI-[3].] The science of refracted sounds; diaphonics. So **Diacou·stic** *a.* pertaining to d. (Dicts.)

Diacrante·ric, *a.* 1883. [f. Gr. διά + κραντῆρες the wisdom teeth + -IC.] Having the posterior teeth more widely separated than the anterior, as some snakes. So **Diacrante·rian** *a.*

‖**Dia·crisis.** 1684. [mod.L., a. Gr., f. διακρίνειν to separate; *spec.* to mark a crisis in a fever. Cf. F. *diacrise*.] a. The act of separation or secretion. b. 'A critical evacuation'. c. = DIAGNOSIS. Hence **Diacrisio·graphy,** 'a description of the organs of secretion' (*Syd. Soc. Lex.*).

Diacritic (dəiăkri·tik). 1699. [ad. Gr. διακριτικός, f. διακρίνειν.]

A. *adj.* Serving to distinguish, distinctive; in *Gram.* applied to signs or marks used to distinguish different sounds or values of the same letter or character; *e.g.* è, é, ê, ë, etc.

B. *sb. Gram.* A diacritic sign or mark 1866. So **Diacri·tical** *a.* diacritic; also, capable of distinguishing. **Diacri·tically** *adv.*

Diactinic (dəi,ækti·nik), *a.* 1867. [f. DI-[3] = DIA-[1] + Gr. ἀκτίν- a ray.] *Optics.* Having the property of transmitting the actinic rays of light. So **Dia·ctinism,** d. condition.

‖**Diadelphia** (dəiăde·lfiă). 1762. [mod.L., f. DI-[2] + ἀδελφός.] *Bot.* The seventeenth class in the Linnæan Sexual system, including plants with stamens normally in two bundles. Hence **Diade·lphian** *a.*

Diadelphic (dəiăde·lfik), *a.* 1847. [f. as prec.] a. *Bot.* = DIADELPHOUS. b. *Chem.* Of a compound: Having the elements combined in two groups 1866.

Diadelphous (dəiăde·lfəs), *a.* 1807. [f. as prec.] *Bot.* Of stamens: United by the filaments so as to form two bundles. Of plants: Having the stamens so united.

Diadem (dəi·ădem). ME. [a. OF. *dyademe*, mod.F. *diadème*, ad. L. *diadema*, a. Gr., f. διαδέειν to bind round.] 1. A crown. (Now chiefly *poet.* and *rhet.*) b. *spec.* A band or fillet of cloth, worn round the head, originally by Eastern monarchs, as a badge of royalty 1579. c. *Her.* Applied to the circles which close on the top of the crowns of sovereigns, and support the mound 1727. 2. *fig.* Royal or imperial dignity, sovereignty ME. 3. *fig.* and *transf.* 1526. 4. Short for *d.-monkey.*

1. Diocletian..ventured to assume the d...It was no more than a broad white fillet set with pearls, which encircled the emperor's head GIBBON. 3. The crescent moon, the d. of night, Stars countless COWPER.

Comb.: **d.-lemur,** a species of *Indris*; **-monkey,** *Cercopithecus diadematus*; **-spider,** the garden spider, *Epeira diadema.*

Di·adem, *v.* ME. [f. prec. sb.] *trans.* To adorn with or as with a diadem; to crown. Chiefly in *pa. pple.*

And every stalk is diadem'd with flowers SIR W. JONES. The Judge that comes in mercy..To d. the right NEALE. So **Di·ademated** *ppl. a.* diademed. ? *Obs.*

‖**Diadoche** (dəi,æ·dŏki). 1706. [a. Gr.] Succession; *spec.* in *Med.* the exchange of one disease into another of different character and in a different situation.

Diadochian (dəiădōᵘ·kiăn), *a.* 1881. [f. Gr. διάδοχος succeeding, successor.] Belonging to the *Diadochi* or Macedonian generals among whom the empire of Alexander the Great was divided after his death.

†**Di·adrom, -ome.** 1661. [ad. Gr. διαδρομή a running across.] A vibration of a pendulum -1690.

Diæresis (dəi,e·rĭsis, -īᵊ·rĭsis). Also **dieresis.** 1611. [a. L., a. Gr. διαίρεσις, f. διαιρέειν.] 1. The division of one syllable into two, as in *aër*, etc. 1656. b. The sign [¨] marking such a division, or placed over the second of two vowels, to indicate that they are to be sounded separately 1611. 2. *Prosody.* The division made in a line or a verse when the end of a foot coincides with the end of a word 1844. 3. *Surg.* Separation of parts normally united, as by a wound or burn, lancing, etc. 1706.

Diæretic (dəi,ĭre·tik). Also **dieretic.** 1640. [ad. Gr. διαιρετικός; see prec.]

A. *adj.* Of, pertaining to, or by means of diæresis or division.

B. *sb.* A caustic agent 1721.

Diageotropic (dəiăˌdʒīˌotrǫ·pik), *a.* 1880. [f. Gr. διά + γῆ, -γεο- + τροπικός.] *Bot.* Characterized by diageotropism. Hence **Di:ageo·tropism** (*Bot.*), the tendency in parts of plants to grow transversely to the earth's radius.

Diaglyph (dəi·ăglif). *rare.* 1864. [f. stem of Gr. διαγλύφειν.] An intaglio. Hence **Diagly·phic** *a.* pertaining to or of the nature of an intaglio.

Diagnose (dəiăgnōu·z), *v.* 1861. [f. next.] *trans.* To make a diagnosis of; to identify by careful observation. Also *absol.*

Diagnosis (dəiăgnōu·sis). Pl. **-oses.** 1681. [a. L., Gr. διάγνωσις, f. διαγιγνώσκειν to distinguish, discern.] **1.** *Med.* Determination of the nature of a diseased condition; identification of a disease by investigation of its symptoms and history; also, the formal statement of this. Also *transf.* and *fig.* **2.** *Biol.*, etc. Distinctive characterization in precise terms (*of* a genus, species, etc.) 1853.

1. *transf.* Our d. of the character of a person 1868. 2. The 'Genera Piscium' contains well-defined diagnoses of 45 genera GUNTHER.

Diagnostic (dəiăgnǫ·stik). 1625. [ad. Gr. διαγνωστικός, ἡ διαγνωστική (sc. τέχνη); see DIAGNOSIS.]

A. *adj.* **1.** Of or pertaining to diagnosis. **2.** Of value for purposes of diagnosis; specially characteristic, distinctive 1650.

B. *sb.*; occas. in *collect. pl.* **diagnostics.** **1.** = DIAGNOSIS 1. 1625. **2.** A distinctive symptom or characteristic 1646.

Hence **Diagno·stically** *adv.* by means of diagnosis, with reference to diagnosis. **Diagno·sticate** *v.* = DIAGNOSE *v.* **Di:agnosti·cian**, one skilled in diagnosis. var. **Diagnost** (*rare*).

Diago·meter. 1863. [ad. F. *diagomètre*, f. Gr. διάγειν to carry across + μέτρον.] *Electr.* An instrument for measuring the electro-conductive power of various substances.

Diagonal (dəiˌæ·gŏnăl). 1541. [ad. L. *diagonalis*, f. Gr. διαγώνιος from angle to angle, f. διά + γωνία; see -AL I. 2.]

A. *adj.* **1.** *Geom.* Extending, as a line, from any angular point of a quadrilateral or multilateral figure to a non-adjacent angular point. Hence *gen.* Extending from one corner to the opposite corner. **2.** More loosely: Having an oblique direction; inclined at an angle other than a right angle (usually about 45°) 1665. **3.** Marked with diagonal lines, or having some part placed diagonally 1679.

3. *D. cloth*: a twilled fabric having the edges d., *i.e.* running obliquely to the lists. *D. couching* (in needlework): couching in which the stitches form a zigzag pattern. *D. scale*: a scale marked with equidistant parallel lines crossed at right angles by others at smaller intervals, and having one of the larger divisions additionally crossed by parallels obliquely placed: used for measurement of small fractions of the unit of length.

Comb.: **d.-built** *a.*, (a boat or ship) having the outer skin consisting of two layers of planking making angles of about 45° with the keel in opposite directions; **-planed** *a.*, (a crystal) having facets situated obliquely; **-wise** *adv.* = DIAGONALLY.

B. *sb.* **1.** *Geom.* A diagonal line 1571; a diagonal line of things arranged in a square or other parallelogram (*e.g.* of squares on a chessboard); a part of any structure, as a beam, etc., placed diagonally 1837. **2.** = *d. cloth* (see A. 3) 1861.

So **Dia·gonalize** *v.* to move in a d. (*rare*). **Dia·gonally** *adv.* var. †**Dia·gony** *sb.*

†**Diago·nial.** 1624. [f. Gr. διαγώνιος + -AL.] = DIAGONAL; also diagonally opposite; *fig.* diametrically opposed –1678.

Both d. contraries MILT.

Diagram (dəi·ăgræm), *sb.* 1619. [ad. L. *diagramma*, f. (ult.) Gr. δια- + γράφειν.] **1.** *Geom.* A figure composed of lines, serving to illustrate a statement or to aid in a demonstration 1645. **2.** An illustrative figure giving an outline or general scheme of an object and its various parts 1619. **3.** A graphic representation of the course or results of any action or process or its variations. (Often with defining word prefixed, as *indicator-d.* (in the steam-engine, etc.) †**4.** After Gr. usage: A list; a detailed inscription; also, 'the title of a booke' (Cockeram) –1662. †**5.** A musical scale –1751.

2. *Floral d.* (Bot.): a linear drawing showing the position and number of the parts of a flower as seen on a transverse section. Hence **Di·agram** *v.* to make a d. of (*rare*). **Di agramma·tic** *a.* having the form or nature of a d.; of or pertaining to diagrams. **Diagramma·tically** *adv.* in the form of a d.; with diagrammatic representation.

Diagrammatize (dəiăgræ·mătəiz), *v.* 1884. [f. Gr. διαγραμματ- stem of διάγραμμα DIAGRAM.] To put into the form of a diagram.

Diagraph (dəi·ăgrɑf). 1847. [a. F. *diagraphe*, f. stem of Gr. διαγράφειν.] **1.** An instrument for drawing mechanically projections of objects. **2.** A combined protractor and scale used in plotting. So **Diagra·phic**, †**-al** *a.* of or pertaining to drawing or graphic representation. **Diagra·phics**, the art of drawing.

‖**Diagry·dium.** ME. [L., a corruption of Gr. δακρυδίον 'a kind of scammony', dim. of δάκρυ. In F. *diagrède.*] *Pharm.* A preparation of scammony.

Diaheliotropic (dəiăˌhīːliotrǫ·pik), *a.* 1880. [f. Gr. διά + ἥλιος + τροπικός.] *Bot.* Of a plant-organ: Growing transversely to the direction of incident light. So **Diahelio·tropism**, a tendency in plants to do this.

Dial (dəi·ăl), *sb.* ME. [app. a deriv. of L. *dies*, through med.L. *dialis.*] **1.** An instrument serving to tell the hour of the day, by means of the sun's shadow upon a graduated surface; a SUN-DIAL. **2.** With qualifying words: *e.g.* *declining, horizontal, vertical, nocturnal* (= MOON-DIAL), etc. 1605. †**3.** A time-piece of any kind –1676. Also *fig.* **4.** The face of a clock or watch. Cf. *dial-plate.* 1575. **5.** A †mariner's or miner's compass 1523. **6.** An external face on which revolutions, pressure, etc. are indicated by an index-finger or otherwise, as in a gas-meter, etc. 1747. **7.** A lapidary's instrument for holding a gem while exposed to the wheel 1875. Also *attrib.*

Comb.: **d.-bird**, an Indian bird (*Copsichus saularis*); also extended to the genus *Copsichus*; **-lock**, a lock furnished with dials, having pointers which must be set in a given way before the bolt will move; **-piece**, **-plate**, the face-plate of a d.; *spec.* (in *Clock-making*) the sheet of metal, glass, etc. on the face of which the hours, etc. are marked; **-writer**, a type-writer with a d.

Dial (dəi·ăl), *v.* 1653. [f. prec. sb.] **1.** To measure as with a dial 1821. **2.** To survey with the aid of a miner's dial 1653. **3.** To mark as the plate of a dial 1817. **4.** To indicate on a dial (a number required, e.g. on an automatic telephone). Also *absol.* to make a call in this way 1922.

Dialect (dəi·ălekt). 1551. [ad. L. *dialectus*, Gr. διάλεκτος, f. διαλέγεσθαι.] **1.** Manner of speaking, language, speech; *esp.* one peculiar to an individual or class; phraseology, idiom 1579. **2.** A variety of a language arising from local peculiarities. (In relation to modern languages usually *spec.* A variety of speech differing from the standard language; a provincial method of speech.) Also, more widely, a language in its relation to the family to which it belongs. 1577. †**3.** = DIALECTIC *sb.*[1] 1. –1698.

1. By corruption of speech they false d. and misse sound it NASHE. A Babylonish D., Which learned Pedants much affect BUTLER *Hud.* I. i 93. 2. The Durham d. is the same as that spoken in Northumberland HALLIWELL. 3. Logike otherwise called Dialecte T. WILSON. Hence **Diale·ctal** *a.* belonging to or of the nature of a d. **Diale·ctally** *adv.* in dialect; argumentatively.

Dialectic (dəiăle·ktik), *sb.*[1] ME. [a. OF. *dialectique*, ad. L. *dialectica* fem. sing., ad. Gr. ἡ διαλεκτική (sc. τέχνη). The L. *dialectica* was also treated as a neut. pl., whence Eng. *dialectics.*] **1.** The art of critical examination into the truth of an opinion: in earlier Eng. use, a synonym of LOGIC as applied to formal rhetorical reasoning; logical disputation. Also in pl. form **Dialectics.** **2.** In modern Philosophy: Applied by Kant to the criticism which shows the mutually contradictory character of the principles of science, when employed to determine objects beyond the limits of experience (*e.g.* the soul, the world, God); by Hegel (a.) to the process of thought by which such contradictions are seen to merge themselves in a higher truth that comprehends them; and (b.) to the world-process, which, in his view, is but the thought-process on its objective side, and develops similarly by a continuous unification of opposites 1798.

Dialectic (dəiăle·ktik), *a.* and *sb.*[2] 1640. [ad. L. *dialecticus*, a. Gr. διαλεκτικός, f. διάλεκτος; see DIALECT.]

A. *adj.* **1.** Of, pertaining to, or of the nature of logical disputation 1650. **2.** Addicted to logical disputation 1831. **3.** = DIALECTAL 1813.

B. *sb.*[2] [The adj. used absol.] One who pursues the dialectic method; a critical inquirer after truth; a logical disputant 1640.

Hence **Diale·ctical** *a.* = DIALECTIC *a.*; dialectal; *sb.* = DIALECTIC *sb.*[1] 1. **Diale·ctically** *adv.* by means of d.; as regards dialect.

Dialectician (dəi:ălekti·ʃăn). 1693. [a. F. *dialecticien* (Rabelais).] **1.** One skilled in dialectic; a logician. **2.** A student of dialects 1848.

1. An art that..might help the subtile d. to oppose even the man he could not refute BOLINGBROKE.

Diale·ctics, *sb. pl.*; see DIALECTIC *sb.*[1] 1.

Dialectology (dəi:ălektǫ·lŏdʒi). 1879. [See -LOGY.] The study of dialects; that branch of philology which treats of dialects. Hence **Dialecto·loger, Dialecto·logist. Dialectolo·gical** *a.*

Dialing; see DIALLING.

Dialist (dəi·ălist). 1652. [f. DIAL *sb.* + -IST.] A maker of dials; one skilled in dialling.

‖**Diallage**[1] (dəiˌæ·lădʒi). 1706. [mod.L., a. Gr. διαλλαγή interchange.] *Rhet.* A figure by which arguments, after being considered from various points of view, are all brought to bear upon one point.

Diallage[2] (dəi·ălĕdʒ). 1805. [a. F. *diallage*, f. Gr. διαλλαγή (see prec.).] *Min.* A grass-green variety of pyroxene, of lamellar or foliated structure: formerly applied also to hypersthene, bronzite, etc.

‖**Diallelon** (dəiălīˑlǫn). 1837. [mod.L. f. Gr. δι' ἀλλήλων.] *Logic.* Definition in a circle, *i.e.* by means of the term to be defined.

‖**Diallelus** (dəiălīˑlǫs). 1837. [mod.L. f. Gr. (τρόπος) διάλληλος.] *Logic.* Reasoning in a circle.

Dialler, dialer (dəi·ăləɹ). 1747. [f. DIAL *sb.* + -ER[1].] One who surveys mines by the aid of a dial.

Dialling, dialing (dəi·ăliŋ), *vbl. sb.* 1570. [f. DIAL *sb.* and *v.* + -ING[1].] **1.** The art of constructing dials. †**b.** The measurement of time by dials. **2.** The use of a dial in mining 1670.

Di-a·llyl. 1869. [DI-[2].] *Chem. sb.* The organic radical allyl in the free state, C_6H_{10} = $C_3H_5.C_3H_5$; see ALLYL. *attrib.* Containing two equivalents of allyl.

Dialogic, -al (dəiălǫ·dʒik, -ăl), *a.* 1601. [ad. med.L. *dialogicus*, a. Gr., f. διάλογος DIALOGUE; see -IC, -AL.] Of, pertaining to, or of the nature of dialogue. Hence **Dialo·gically** *adv.*

Dialogism (dəiˌæ·lŏdʒiz'm). 1580. [ad. L. *dialogismus*, a. Gr. διαλογισμός, f. διαλογίζεσθαι to DIALOGIZE.] **1.** *Rhet.* The discussion of a subject under the form of a dialogue. **2.** A conversational phrase or speech; a DIALOGUE 1623. **3.** *Logic.* A form of argument having a single premiss and a disjunctive conclusion 1880.

Dialogist (dəiˌæ·lŏdʒist). 1660. [ad. L. *dialogista.*] **1.** One who takes part in a dialogue 1677. **2.** A writer of dialogues. Hence **Dialogi·stic, -al** *a.* having the nature or form of dialogue; taking part in a dialogue; argumentative. **Dialogi·stically** *adv.*

Dialogite (dəiˌæ·lŏdʒəit). Erron. **diall-.** 1826. [Named from Gr. διαλογή 'doubt, selection'.] *Min.* A rose-red carbonate of manganese; = *rhodochrosite.*

Dialogize (dəiˌæ·lŏdʒəiz), *v.* 1601. [ad. Gr. διαλογίζεσθαι, f. διάλογος DIALOGUE.] *intr.* To converse, or carry on a dialogue (*with*).

Dialogue (dəi·ălǫg), *sb.* ME. [a. OF. *dialoge*, mod.F. *dialogue*, ad. L. *dialogus*, Gr. διάλογος, f. διαλέγεσθαι; see DIALECT.] **1.** A conversation between two or more persons; a colloquy; (without *pl.*) conversation. **2.** A literary work in the form of a conversation between two or more persons ME.; (without *pl.*) literary composition of this nature 1589.

1. Feare you not my part of the D. SHAKS.

Dialogue (dəi·ălǫg), *v.* 1597. [f. prec. sb.]

1. *intr.* To hold a dialogue 1607. Also *transf.* and *fig.* 2. *trans.* To express in the form of a dialogue 1597.

2. And dialogu'd for him what he would say SHAKS. Hence **Dia·loguer** (*rare*), = DIALOGIST 1. **Di·a·loguist**, a writer of dialogue.

Di·al-plate. 1690. [f. DIAL *sb.* + PLATE.] = DIAL *sb.* 4.

Dialu·ric, *a.* 1845. [f. DI-² + AL(LOXAN) + URIC.] *Chem.* In *d. acid*, $C_4N_2H_4O_4$, an acid obtained by hydrogenizing alloxan.

Dialy- (dəi·ăli), ad. Gr. διαλυ-, stem of διαλύειν, used with the sense 'separated', or 'non-united'. Thus:

Dialyca·rpel [see CARPEL], 'an ovary or fruit with ununited carpels' (*Syd. Soc. Lex.*). **Dialyca·rpous** *a.* [Gr. καρπός], having the carpels distinct. **Dialype·talous** *a.*, having the petals distinct. **Dialyphy·llous** *a.* [Gr. φύλλον], having the leaves distinct. So **Dialyse·palous, Dialysta·minous** *adjs.*, having the sepals, the stamens, distinct.

Dialyse, -ze (dəi·ăləiz), *v.* 1861. [f. DIALYSIS, after *analyse.*] *Chem.* To separate the crystalloid part of a mixture from the colloid, in the process of chemical dialysis. Hence **Di·aly·sable, -zable** *a.* capable of separation by dialysis. **Dia·lysate** (*Chem.*), that portion of a mixture that remains after dialysis. **Dia·lysa tor, Di·alyser, -zer,** an apparatus for effecting dialysis; a vessel formed of parchment or animal membrane floated on water, through which the crystalloids pass, leaving the colloids behind.

Dialysis (dəi,æ·lisis). Pl. **-lyses.** 1586. [a. Gr. διάλυσις, f. διαλύειν to part asunder.] †1. *Rhet.* **a.** A statement of disjunctive propositions. **b.** = ASYNDETON. -1823. †2. *Gram.* = DIÆRESIS 1. -1818. †3. *Med.* Dissolution of strength -1883. 4. *Path.* Solution of continuity 1811. 5. *Chem.* The process of separating the soluble crystalloid substances in a mixture from the colloid by means of a dialyser 1861.

Dialytic (dəiăli·tik), *a.* 1846. [ad. Gr. διαλυτικός; see prec.] Of or pertaining to DIALYSIS, in various senses.

D. telescope: one in which achromatism is effected by means of two lenses separated and placed at some distance from each other. Hence **Dialy·tically** *adv.* by way of dialysis.

Di·ama·gnet. 1864. [DIA- *pref.*¹] = DIAMAGNETIC *sb.*

Diamagnetic (dəi:ămægne·tik). 1846. [DIA- *pref.*¹]

A. *adj.* 1. Exhibiting the phenomena of DIAMAGNETISM; opp. to *magnetic* or *paramagnetic*. 2. Belonging or relating to diamagnetic bodies, or to diamagnetism 1846.

B. *sb.* A diamagnetic body or substance 1846. Hence **Diamagne·tically** *adv.* in the manner of a d. body, or of diamagnetism.

Diamagnetism (dəi:ămæ·gnĕtiz'm). 1850. [DIA- *pref.*¹] **a.** The phenomena exhibited by a class of bodies, which, when freely suspended and acted on by magnetism, take up a position transverse to that of the magnetic axis, *i. e.* lie (approximately) east and west; the force to which these are attributed; the quality of being diamagnetic. **b.** That branch of science which treats of diamagnetic bodies and phenomena.

Diamagnetize (dəi:ămæ·gnĕtəiz), *v.* 1877. [DIA- *pref.*¹] To render diamagnetic. Hence **Diama:gnetiza·tion.** (Dicts.)

Diama:gneto·meter. 1886. [f. DIAMAGNET(ISM) + Gr. μέτρον.] An instrument for measuring diamagnetic force.

‖**Diamanté** (diăma·nte). 1904. [Fr.: see DIAMOND.] Material scintillating with powdered crystal, etc. Also *attrib.*

Di:amanti·ferous, *a.* 1878. [after mod.F. *diamantifère.*] Diamond-producing.

Diamantine (dəiămæ·ntin). 1591. [a. F. *diamantin.*] **A.** *adj.* 1. Consisting of, or of the nature of, diamond; producing diamonds 1605. †2. Adamantine -1649. **B.** *sb.* A preparation of adamantine or crystallized boron, used as a polishing powder for steel work 1884.

Diamesogamous (dəi:ămĕsǫ·gămǝs), *a.* [f. Gr. διάμεσον the intervening part + γάμος + -OUS.] *Bot* Of flowers: Fertilized by the intervention of some external agency, as that of insects or of wind.

Diameter (dəi,æ·mĭtəɹ). ME. [ad. (ult.) L. *diametrus, -os*, a. Gr. διάμετρος (sc. γραμμή line).] 1. *Geom.* A straight line passing through the centre of a circle (or sphere), and terminated at each end by its circumference (or surface). Hence, a chord of any conic (or of a quadric surface) passing through the centre; also, a line passing through the middle points of a system of parallel chords, in a curve of any order. Also *gen.* 2. The transverse measurement of any geometrical figure or body; width, thickness ME. **b.** *Archit.* The transverse measurement of a column at its base, taken as a unit of measurement for the proportions of an order 1604. **c.** Whole extent from side to side or from end to end 1602.

2. c. [Slander], whose whisper o'er the world's d... Transports his poison'd shot *Haml.* IV. i. 41.

Diametral (dəi,æ·mĭtrăl). 1555. [ad. med. L. *diametralis.*]

A. *adj.* 1. Of or relating to a diameter; of the nature of a diameter. †2. = DIAMETRICAL 2. -1768.

Phr. †*D. number* (Arith.), one that is the product of two factors the sum of whose squares is a square; thus $3^2+4^2=5^2$; then $3 \times 4 = 12$ is a d. number. *D. plane*: (*a*) *Geom.* a plane passing through the centre of a solid; (*b*) *Cryst.* a plane passing through two of the axes of a crystal.

†**B.** *sb.* A diametral line, diameter -1676.

Hence **Dia·metrally** *adv.* in the way of a diameter; †directly; diametrically (*lit.* and *fig.*).

Diametric (dəiăme·trik), *a.* 1802. [ad. Gr. διαμετρικός.] 1. Relating to or of the nature of a diameter 1868. 2. Of opposition, etc.: = DIAMETRICAL 2.

Diametrical (dəiăme·trikăl), *a.* 1553. [f. as prec. + -AL.] 1. Of or pertaining to a diameter; passing through or along a diameter; diametral. 2. Of opposition, etc.: Direct, entire, complete (like that of the ends of a diameter). Usu. *fig.* 1613. †**b.** Directly opposed -1734.

2. b. The Revolution was very quick and d. NORTH. Hence **Diame·trically** *adv.* in the manner or direction of a diameter; directly, entirely.

Diamide (dəi·ămǝid). 1866. [DI-².] *Chem.* An amide formed on the type of two molecules of ammonia, the hydrogen of which is replaced by one or more acid radicals.

Diami·do-. *Chem.* See DI-² and AMIDO-.

Diamine (dəi·ămǝin). 1866. [DI-².] *Chem.* An amine derived from two molecules of ammonia the hydrogen of which is replaced by one or more basic radicals, as *Ethene-diamine* $\left.\begin{matrix}NH_2\\NH_2\end{matrix}\right\}C_2H_4$.

Diamond (dəi·ămǝnd, dəi·mǝnd), *sb.* [ME. *diamant, -aunt*, a. OF. *diamant*, ad. late L. *diamas, diamantem*, an alteration of L. *adamas, -antem*, or ? of its pop. var. *adimantem* (whence OF. *aimant*), after words beginning with DIA-, Gr. δια-. Most recent authorities make the word trisyllabic.] 1. A very hard and brilliant precious stone, consisting of pure carbon crystallized in regular octahedrons and allied forms, and either colourless or variously tinted. It is the hardest substance known. (For TABLE, ROSE, and BRILLIANT cutting, see these words.) †**b.** = ADAMANT -1667. **c.** *Her.* In blazoning by precious stones, the name for the tincture *sable* 1572. 2. *transf.* (usu. with distinguishing epithet) 1591. 3. *fig.* ME. 4. A tool consisting of a small diamond set in a handle; a *glazier's*, or *cutting d.* 1697. 5. A diamond-shaped figure, *i. e.* a plane figure in the form of a section of an octahedral diamond; a rhomb (or a square) placed with its diagonals vertical and horizontal; a lozenge 1496. **b.** *spec.* A figure of this form printed on a playing card; a card of the suit so marked 1594. **c.** The figure formed by the four bases in base-ball; hence, the whole field (*U.S.*) 1894. 6. *Printing.* The second smallest standard size of roman or italian type, a size smaller than pearl. Also *attrib.* [ad. Du. *diamant*: so named by its introducer.] 1778.

This line is a specimen of the type called Diamond.

7. *attrib.* Made or consisting of diamond, as *d. lens*, etc. 1553; †hard as diamond, adamantine -1659; set with a diamond or diamonds, as *d. button, clasp, ring*, etc. 8. *attrib.* or *adj.* Of the shape of a diamond (see sense 5), as *d. fret, netting*, etc.; having a head of this shape, as *d. dibber*, etc. 1598; having a surface cut into facets 1717.

1. b. His vaunting foe, Though huge, and in a Rock of D. Armd MILT. *P. L.* VI. 364. 2. *Bristol d.* (see BRISTOL). 3. Each puny wave in diamonds roll'd O'er the calm deep SCOTT.

Phrases. **a.** *Black d.*: (*a*) a d. of a black or brown colour; (*b*) *pl.* a playful name for coal. **b.** *Rough d.*: a d. before it is cut and polished; hence *fig.* a person of high intrinsic worth, but rude and unpolished. **c.** *D. cut d.*: an equal match in sharpness, finesse, etc.

Combs.: **d.-bird,** an Australian shrike of the genus *Pardalotus*, esp. *P. punctatus*; **-borer** = *diamond-drill* (*b*); **-breaker** = *diamond-mortar*; **-broaching,** broached hewn-work done with a d.-hammer; **-crossing,** a crossing on a railway where two lines of rails intersect obliquely without communicating; **-drill,** (*a*) one armed with one or more diamonds for boring hard substances; (*b*) a drill for boring rocks, having a head set with rough diamonds; **-dust** = *diamond-powder*; **-hammer,** a mason's hammer furnished with pyramidal pick points for stone-dressing; **-knot** (*Naut.*), a kind of ornamental knot worked with the strands of a rope; **-mortar,** a steel mortar used for crushing diamonds; **-plaice,** the common plaice (*local*); **-plough,** (*a*) a d.-pointed instrument for engraving upon glass; (*b*) a small plough having a mould-board and share of a d. shape; **-powder,** the powder produced by grinding or crushing diamonds; **d. rattlesnake,** a rattlesnake (*Crotalus adamanteus*) having d.-shaped markings; **-tool,** a metal-turning tool whose cutting edge is formed by facets; **-weevil** = DIAMOND-BEETLE; **-wheel,** a metal wheel used with d.-powder and oil in grinding hard gems.

Di·amond, *v.* 1751. [f. prec. sb.] To adorn with or as with diamonds.

He plays, dresses, diamonds himself H. WALPOLE. Hence **Di·amonded** *a.* adorned with or as with diamonds; having the figure of a diamond.

Di·amond-back. 1819. [Short for next.]

A. *adj.* = next.

B. *sb.* **a.** The Diamond-back Moth. **b.** The Diamond-backed Turtle.

Di·amond-backed, *a.* 1895. [f. DIAMOND *sb.* + BACKED.] Having the back marked with lozenge-shaped figures.

Diamond-backed turtle or *terrapin*, the fresh-water tortoise of the Atlantic coast of N. America, *Malaclemmys palustris.*

Di·amond-beetle. 1806. A South American beetle, *Curculio* (*Entimus*) *imperialis*, having elytra studded with brilliant sparkling points.

Di·amond-cut, *a.* 1637. 1. Cut into the shape of a diamond. 2. Cut with facets like a diamond, as *diamond-cut glass* 1703.

Di·amond-cutter. 1722. A lapidary who cuts and polishes diamonds. So **Di·amond-cutting** *sb.*

Diamondi·ferous, *a.* 1870. [f. DIAMOND, after *diamantiferous.*] Diamond-producing.

Di·amondize, *v.* 1599. [f. as prec. + -IZE.] To bedeck with or as with diamonds.

Diamond-point. 1874. 1. A stylus tipped with a fragment of diamond, used in engraving, etc. 2. *Railways.* Usually in *pl.* The set of points at a diamond crossing; in *sing.* one of the acute angles formed by two rails at such a crossing 1881. Also *attrib.*

Diamond-snake. 1814. Any snake having diamond-shaped markings, *esp.* **a.** a large Australian serpent, *Morelia spilotes*; **b.** a venomous Tasmanian serpent, *Hoplocephalus superbus.*

‖**Diamorphosis** (dəiămǭ·ɹfǒsis, -mǫɹfōu·sis). 1861. [mod.L., a. Gr.] 1. 'The building up of a body to its proper form' (*Syd. Soc. Lex.*). ¶2. *erron.* for DIMORPHISM.

Dia·myl. 1850. [DI-².] *Chem.* **a.** *sb.* The organic radical AMYL in the free state, $C_{10}H_{22} = C_5H_{11}.C_5H_{11}$. **b.** *attrib.*, etc. Containing two equivalents of amyl.

Dia·mylene. *Chem.* See DI-² and AMYLENE.

†**Di·an.** 1591. [a. F. *diane*, a beating of the drum at day-break, f. *dia* day. Cf. L. *quotidianus.*] A trumpet-call or drum-roll at early morn. Also *attrib.*

The bee.. Beating the d. with its drums MARVELL.

Diana (dəi,æ·nă, dəi,ē·nă), anglicized DIAN (dəi·ăn). ME. [a. L. *Diana* in F. *diane.*] 1. An Italian divinity, the moon-goddess, patroness of virginity and of hunting; subseq. identified with the Greek Artemis, and so with Oriental deities. **b.** *poet.* The moon ME. **2.** In early Chemistry a name for silver 1706.

1. Or on Dianaes Altar to protest For aie, austerity and single life *Mids. N.* I. i. 89. **b.** Meek Dian's crest BYRON.

Diana monkey, *Cercopithecus Diana*, a large African monkey, with a white crescent marked on its forehead.

‖**Diandria** (dəiˌæ·ndriă). 1753. [mod.L., f. Gr. type *δίανδρος; see MONANDRIA, etc.] *Bot.* The second class in the Linnæan sexual system, comprising all plants having two stamens. So **Dia·ndrous** *a.* belonging to the class Diandria; two-stamened.

Dianodal (dəiănōu·dăl), *a.* 1870. [DIA-[1].] *Math.* Passing through nodes.

Dianoetic (dəiănoˌe·tik). 1677. [ad. Gr. διανοητικός, f. (ult.) δια + νοεῖν.] *Metaph.*

A. *adj.* Of or pertaining to thought; intellectual.

B. *sb.* Applied by Sir W. Hamilton to denote the operations of the discursive faculty 1836. Hence †**Dianoe·tical** *a.*; **-ly** *adv.*

Di:anoia·logy. [f. Gr. διάνοια + -LOGY.] *Metaph.* That portion of logic which deals with dianoetic or demonstrative propositions (Sir W. Hamilton).

‖**Dianthus** (dəiˌæ·nþɒs). 1849. [f. Gr. Διός of Jupiter + ἄνθος flower.] *Bot.* A genus of caryophyllaceous flowering plants, which includes the pinks and carnations; one of these. Hence **Dia·nthine**, name of an aniline dye.

‖**Diapa·lma.** 1646. [f. DIA-[2] + L. *palma* palm.] *Pharm.* A desiccating plaster composed originally of palm oil, litharge, and sulphate of zinc, now of white wax, emplastrum simplex, and sulphate of zinc.

Di·apase. 1591. = DIAPASON (*poet.*).

Diapasm (dəi·ăpæz'm). *arch.* 1599. [ad. L. *diapasma*, a Gr., f. διαπάσσειν to sprinkle over.] A scented powder for sprinkling over the person.

Diapason (dəiăpēⁱ·zən), *sb.* ME. [a. L., a. Gr. διὰ πασῶν (sc. χορδῶν), more fully ἡ διὰ πασῶν χορδῶν συμφωνία, the concord through all the notes of the scale. Cf. F. *diapason.*] †**1.** The interval of an octave; the consonance of the highest and lowest notes of the musical scale -1787. †**2.** *fig.* Complete concord or harmony -1719. **3.** More or less vaguely extended, with the idea of 'all the tones or notes' (see quots.) 1501. **4.** *transf.* and *fig.* **a.** A rich outburst of sound 1589. **b.** Entire compass, reach 1851. **5.** A fixed standard of musical pitch; as in F. *diapason normal.* Also *fig.* 1875. **6.** The name of two stops in the organ, the *Open D.*, and the *Closed* or *Stopped D.*, so called because they extend through the whole compass of the instrument; also the name of other stops 1519. Also *attrib.*

2. A d. of vows and wishes BURTON. 3. A full-mouth'd d. swallows all CRASHAW. Through all the compass of the Notes it ran, The D. closing full in Man DRYDEN. 4. a. The D. of thy threates GREENE. b. The whole d. of joy and sorrow HELPS. Hence †**Diapa·son** *v.* (*intr.* and *trans.*) to resound sonorously; (*intr.*) to maintain accord *with.*

‖**Diapedesis** (dəi:ăpidī·sis). 1625. [mod.L., a. Gr. διαπήδησις, f. (ult.) δια- through + πηδᾶν to leap, throb.] *Path.* The oozing of blood through the unruptured walls of the blood-vessels.

†**Diapente** (dəiăpe·ntí). ME. [a. L., Gr. διὰ πέντε; cf. DIAPASON, and DIA-[2].] **1.** *Mus.* The consonance or interval of a fifth -1787. **2.** *Pharm.* A medicine composed of five ingredients -1800; *transf.* punch -1741.

Diaper (dəi·ăpəɹ), *sb.* ME. [a. OF. *dyapre, diapre*, orig. *diaspre*; in Byzantine Gr. δίασπρος adj. 'white at intervals' or ? 'thoroughly white', f. δια- (DIA-[1]) + ἄσπρος white. (Not conn. w. It., Sp., and Pg. *diaspro* 'jasper'.)] **1.** The name of a textile fabric; now, usually, a linen fabric, woven with patterns showing up by opposite reflexions from its surface, and consisting of lines crossing diamond-wise, with the spaces filled up by parallel lines, leaves, dots, etc. **2.** A towel, napkin, or cloth of this material; a baby's clout 1596. **3.** The geometrical or conventional pattern or design forming the ground of this fabric, or any similar pattern 1830. **b.** *Her.* A similar style of ornamentation used to cover the surface of a shield and form the ground 1634. Also *attrib.*

2. Let one attend him with a siluer Bason..Another beare the Ewer: the third a D. *Tam. Shr.* I. i. 57.

Diaper (dəi·ăpəɹ), *v.* ME. [prob. a. F. *diaprer*; see prec.] **1.** *trans.* To diversify the surface of with a diaper pattern; *transf.* and *fig.* to variegate. **2.** *intr.* To do diaper-work; to flourish 1573.

1. *fig.* The rayes Wherewith the sunne doth d. the seas W. BROWNE. Hence **Di·apering** *vbl. sb.* the production of a diaper pattern; a diaper pattern; diaper-work.

Diaphane (dəi·ăfēⁱn). 1561. [a. F., f. Gr. διαφανής, f. δια- through + -φανης showing.]

†**A.** *adj.* = DIAPHANOUS -1824.

B. *sb.* **1.** A transparent body or substance; a transparency 1840. **2.** A silk stuff, having transparent coloured figures 1824.

Hence †**Di·aphaned** *ppl. a.* made diaphanous. **Dia:phane·ity**, †**Diapha·nity**, the quality of being diaphanous. ‖**Dia·phanie**, a French process for the imitation of stained glass. **Diaphano·meter**, an instrument for measuring transparency, *esp.* that of the atmosphere. **Dia·phanoscope**, †a contrivance for viewing transparent positive photographs; also, an instrument used for the examination of internal organs by means of an electric light introduced into the abdomen. **Diaphano·scopy.**

Diaphanous (dəiˌæ·fănəs), *a.* 1614. [f. as DIAPHANE + -OUS.] Permitting light and vision to pass through; perfectly transparent.

Such a d. pellucid dainty body as you see a Crystal-Glasse is HOWELL. **Dia·phanous·ly** *adv.*; **-ness.**

Diaphemetric (dəiˌæ:fīme·trik), *a.* 18.. [f. Gr. δια- (DIA-[1]) + ἀφή touch + -METRIC.] Relating to the measurement of the comparative tactile sensibility of parts, as *d. compasses.*

Diaphonic, -al (dəiăfɒ·nik, -ăl), *a.* 1775. [f. as DIAPHON-Y + -IC, -AL.] **1.** Of or pertaining to DIAPHONY 1822. **2.** = DIACOUSTIC. Hence **Diapho·nics.** ? *Obs.* = DIACOUSTICS.

Diaphony (dəiˌæ·fŏni). 1656. [ad. late L. *diaphonia*, a. Gr., f. διάφωνος, f. δια- apart + φωνεῖν to sound.] *Mus.* †**1.** Discord. **2.** The most primitive form of harmony, in which the parts proceeded by parallel motion in fourths, fifths, and octaves: the same as ORGANUM 1834.

‖**Diaphoresis** (dəi:ăforī·sis). 1681. [L., a. Gr., f. (ult.) δια- through + φορεῖν to carry.] Perspiration, *esp.* that produced artificially.

Diaphoretic (dəi:ăfore·tik). 1563. [ad. L. *diaphoreticus*, a. Gr. διαφορητικός; see prec.]

A. *adj.* Having the property of promoting perspiration; sudorific. var. †**Diaphore·tical** *a.*

B. *sb.* A medicinal agent doing this 1656.

Diaphragm (dəi·ăfræm), *sb.* ME. [ad. L. *diaphragma* (also used), a. Gr., f. δια- through + φράγμα fence, f. φράσσειν. Cf. F. *diaphragme.*]

I. *Anat.* The septum or partition, partly muscular, partly tendinous, which in mammals divides the thoracic from the abdominal cavity; the midriff.

II. Transferred uses. **1.** *gen.* Applied to anything resembling the diaphragm in nature or function 1660. **2. a.** *Zool.* A partition separating the successive chambers of certain shells 1665. **b.** *Bot.* A septum or partition occurring in the tissues of plants; a transverse partition in a stem or leaf 1665. **3.** *Mech.* A thin lamina or plate serving as a partition, or for some specific purpose; also *transf.* 1665.

Hence **Diaphra·gmal** *a.* diaphragmatic. ‖**Dia·phragma·lgia** [Gr. -αλγια], pain in the d. **Di:a·phragma·tic** *a.* of or pertaining to the d.; of the nature of a d.; **Diaphragma·tically** *adv.* by means of the d. ‖**Diaphragmati·tis**, **-mi·tis**, inflammation of the d. **Diaphra·gmatocele**, hernia of the d.

Di·aphragm, *v.* 1879. [f. prec.] *trans.* To fit or act upon with a diaphragm.

To d. down in *Optics*: to reduce the field of vision of (a lens, etc.) by means of an opaque diaphragm with a central aperture.

Diaphysis (dəiˌæ·fisis). 1831. [ad. Gr. διάφυσις, f. δια- + φύειν to produce.] **1.** *Anat.* 'The shaft of a long bone, as distinct from the extremities' (*Syd. Soc. Lex.*). **2.** *Bot.* 'A præternatural extension of the flower, or of an inflorescence' (*Treas. Bot.*) 1866.

‖**Diaplasis** (dəiˌæ·plăsis). 1704. [mod.L., a. Gr., f. διαπλάσσειν to mould.] *Surg.* The setting of a dislocated limb. Hence †**Dia·pla·stic** *a.* good for a dislocated limb; also as *sb.*

†‖**Dia·pnoe.** 1681. [mod.L., a. Gr.] *Med.* An insensible perspiration on the skin -1706. Hence **Diapno·ic** *a.* producing this.

Diapophysis (dəiăpɒ·fisis). Pl. **-physes.** 1854. [f. Gr. δια- + ἀπόφυσις APOPHYSIS.] *Anat.* A term applied to a pair of exogenous segments of the typical vertebra, forming lateral processes of the neural arch. Hence **Diapophy·sial** *a.* of or belonging to a d.

‖**Diaporesis** (dəi:ăporī·sis). 1678. [mod.L., a. Gr.] *Rhet.* A figure, in which the speaker professes to be at a loss, which of two or more courses, statements, etc., to adopt.

Diarch (dəi·aɹk), *a.* 1884. [f. Gr. δι- + ἀρχή.] *Bot.* Proceeding from two distinct points of origin: said of the primary xylem of the root.

Diarchy (dəi·aɹki). 1835. [f. Gr. δι- + -αρχία; cf. μοναρχία.] A government by two rulers **b.** Revived, esp. in the form **dyarchy**, in reference to the reformed Indian constitution of 1919. Hence **Dia·rchal, Dia·rchic** (dy-) *adjs.*

Diarian (dəiˌēə·riăn). 1774. [f. L. *diarium* DIARY *sb.* + -AN.]

A. *adj.* Of or pertaining to a diary; †journalistic. var. **Dia·rial** *a.*

B. *sb.* The writer of a diary (*rare*) 1800.

Diarist (dəi·ărist). 1818. [f. DIARY *sb.* + -IST.] One who keeps a diary. Hence **Diari·stic** *a.* of the style of a d.; of the nature of a diary. So **Di·arize** *v. intr.*, to write a record of events in a diary.

Diarrhœa (dəiărī·ă). Also 6- **diarrhea.** ME. [a. L., a. Gr. διάρροια.] A disorder consisting in the too frequent evacuation of too fluid fæces, sometimes attended with griping pains. Also *transf.*

transf. He..was troubled with a d. of words H. WALPOLE. Hence **Diarrhœ·al, Diarrhœ·ic, Diarrhœ·tic, -rhe·tic** *adjs.* of, pertaining to, or of the nature of d.

Diarthrodial (dəiˌaɹþrōu·diăl), *a.* 1830. [DI- *pref.*[3] (Gr. δια-).] *Anat.* Pertaining to or characterized by diarthrosis.

Diarthrosis (dəiˌaɹþrōu·sis). 1578. [DI- *pref.*[3]] *Anat.* The general term for all forms of articulation which admit of the motion of one bone upon another; free arthrosis.

Diary (dəi·ări), *sb.* 1581. [ad. L. *diarium*, neut. used subst. of *diarius* adj. (see next).] **1.** A daily record of events or transactions, a journal; specifically, a daily record of matters affecting the writer personally. **2.** A book prepared for keeping a daily record; also, applied to calendars containing daily memoranda 1605.

1. Diaries of wind and weather PLOT. 2. This is my d., Wherin I note my actions of the day B. JONS.

Diary (dəi·ări), *a.* 1592. [ad. med.L. *diarius* daily, f. *dies.*] **1.** Lasting for one day; ephemeral 1610. †**2.** Daily -1623.

1. *D.-fever*, a fever lasting one day (*Syd. Soc. Lex.*).

†**Di·ascord.** 1605. [med.L. *diascordium* (also used), for *diascordion*, from Gr. διὰ σκορδίων (a preparation) of scordium; see DIA-[2].] *Pharm.* A medicine made of the dried leaves of *Teucrium Scordium* and many other herbs -1820.

Diaskeuast (dəiăskiu·æst). Also **diasceuast.** 1822. [ad. Gr. διασκευαστής reviser of a poem, interpolator.] A reviser; used *esp.* in reference to old recensions of Greek writings. So ‖**Diaskeu·asis** [Gr.], revision, recension.

†**Dia·sper.** 1582. [ad. med.L. *diasprum.*] = JASPER -1638.

‖**Diaspora** (dəiˌæ·spŏră). 1876. [a. Gr., f. διασπείρειν to disperse.] The Dispersion; cf. John vii. 35, Jas. i. 1, 1 Pet. i. 1. Hence *transf.* (The term originated in Deut. xxviii. 25.)

Diaspore (dəi·ăspōəɹ). 1805. [mod. f. Gr. διασπορά; see prec. So named from its strong decrepitation when heated.] *Min.* Native hydrate of aluminium, an orthorhombic, massive, or sometimes stalactitic mineral, varying in colour from white to violet.

Diastaltic (dəiăstæ·ltik), *a.* 1774. [f. Gr. διασταλτικός serving to distinguish, f. (ult.) διά + στέλλειν.] **1.** *Greek Mus.* Dilated, extended: applied to certain intervals. **2.** *Phys.* Applied to the actions termed reflex, as taking place through the spinal cord 1852.

Diastase (dəi·ăstēⁱs). 1838. [a. mod.F., ad. Gr. διάστασις (see next).] *Chem.* A nitrogenous ferment formed in a seed or bud (*e.g.* in potatoes) during germination, and having the property of converting starch into sugar. Hence **Diasta·sic** *a.* diastatic.

‖**Diastasis** (dəi,æ·stăsis). 1741. [mod.L., a. Gr., f. διά apart + στάσις setting.] *Path.* Separation of bones without fracture, or of the fractured ends of a bone.

Diastatic (dəiăstæ·tik), *a.* 1881. [ad. Gr. διαστατικός separative.] Pertaining to or of the nature of diastase. Hence **Diastatically** *adv.*

Diastem (dəi·ăstem). 1694. [ad. Gr. διάστημα; see next.] In ancient Gr. music, an interval.

‖**Diastema** (dəiăstī·mă). Pl. **diastemata.** ME. [L., a Gr. διάστημα space between.] **1.** *Mus.* = prec. **2.** *Zool.* and *Anat.* A space between two teeth, or two kinds of teeth 1854. Hence **Di:astema·tic** *a.* characterized by intervals (*rare*).

Diaster (dəi,æ·stəɹ). Also **dy-.** 1882. [f. Gr. δι-, DI-² twice + ἀστήρ.] *Biol.* The double star of chromatin filaments which forms the penultimate stage in the division of a single cell-nucleus into two. Hence **Dia·stral** *a.*

‖**Diastole** (dəi,æ·stoli). 1578. [med.L., a. Gr., f. (ult.) διά (DIA-¹) + στέλλειν to put. Cf. F. *diastole.*] **1.** *Phys.* The dilatation or relaxation of the heart, an artery, etc., rhythmically alternating with the *systole* or contraction. Also *fig.* **2.** *Gr.* and *L. Prosody.* The lengthening of a syllable naturally short 1580. **3.** *Gr. Gram.* A mark (originally semicircular) used to indicate separation of words; still occas. used, in the form of a comma, to distinguish ὅ,τι, ὅ,τε, neut. of ὅστις, ὅστε, from ὅτι, ὅτε.

1. *fig.* There must be a systole and d. in all inquiry GEO. ELIOT. **Diasto·lic** *a.* of or pertaining to d.

Diastrophism (dəi,æ·strofizm). 1881. [f. Gr. διαστροφή distortion, dislocation, f. (ult.) διά + στρέφειν to turn.] *Geol.* A general term for the action of the forces which have dislocated the earth's crust, and produced the greater inequalities of its surface. Hence **Diastro·phic** *a.* of or pertaining to d.

Diastyle (dəi·ăstəil). 1563. [mod. ad. L. *diastylos* (also used), Gr. διάστυλος; also ad. Gr. διαστύλιον the intercolumnar space.]

A. *adj.* Of a colonnade, etc.: Having the intercolumnar intervals each of three (or four) diameters (in the Doric order, of 2¾).

B. *sb.* Such a colonnade, etc., or such an intercolumnar interval.

Diasyrm (dəi·ăsəɹm). 1678. [ad. Gr. διασυρμός disparagement.] *Rhet.* A figure expressing disparagement or ridicule.

‖**Diatessaron** (dəiăte·sărǫn). ME. [a. OF., a. L., Gr. διὰ τεσσάρων.] †**1.** *Gr. Mus.* The interval of a fourth –1857. †**2.** *Pharm.* A medicine composed of four ingredients –1698. **3.** A harmony of the four Gospels 1803.

†**Diathermal** (dəiăþɔ̄·ɹmăl), *a.* 1835. [Gr. διά (DIA-¹).] = DIATHERMANOUS.

Diathermancy (dəiăþɔ̄·ɹmănsi). 1837. [ad. F. *diathermansie,* from Gr. διά + θέρμανσις.] †**1.** *orig.* = THERMOCHROSY; also called *heat-colour.* **2.** Now: The property of being diathermic or diathermanous; previous to radiant heat (var. **Diathe·rmacy**) 1837.

Diathermane·ity. *rare.* 1835. [ad. F. *diathermanéité,* f. *diathermane.*] = prec. **2.** So †**Diathe·rmanism** (in same sense).

Diathermanous (dəiăþɔ̄·ɹmănəs), *a.* 1834. [f. F. *diathermane.*] Having the property of freely transmitting radiant heat; previous to heat-rays. (Corresp. to *diaphanous* in relation to light.)

Diathe·rmic, *a.* 1840. [ad. F. *diathermique.*] = prec. So **Diathe·rmous** *a.*

Diathermo·meter. 1883. [f. Gr. διά + θερμόν + μέτρον.] An instrument for measuring the thermal resistance of a body.

Di·athermy. 1910. [f. Gr. διά + θέρμη + -Y³.] Application of electric currents to produce heat in the deeper tissues of the body.

‖**Diathesis** (dəi,æ·þĭsis). Pl. **-theses** (-īz). 1651. [mod. L., a. Gr., f. διατιθέναι to dispose.] *Med.* A permanent condition of the body which renders it liable to certain special diseases.

The epileptic d. 1879. *fig.* The intellectual d. of the modern world MAINE. Hence **Diathe·tic** *a.* of, pertaining to, or arising from d.; constitutional.

Diatom (dəi·ătǫm). 1845. [ad. mod.L. *Diatoma,* f. Gr. διάτομος, f. διατέμνειν to cut through.] A member of the genus *Diatoma,* or of the *Diatomaceæ,* an order of microscopic unicellular Algæ, with silicified cell-walls, and the power of locomotion. The genus *Diatoma* has the frustules, or individual cells, connected by their alternate angles so as to form a kind of zig-zag chain: hence the name. Hence **Di:atoma·ceous** *a.* of or pertaining to the order *Diatomaceæ*; (*Geol.*) consisting of the fossil remains of diatoms. **Diatoma·cean, Diato·mean,** a diatomaceous plant, a diatom.

Diatomic (dəiătǫ·mik), *a.* 1869. [f. DI-² + ἄτομος ATOM + -IC.] *Chem.* Consisting of, or having, two atoms; occas. used as = divalent.

Diatomin (dəi,æ·tŏmin). 1882. [f. mod.L. *Diatoma* + -IN.] The buff-coloured pigment which colours diatoms.

Diatomous (dəi,æ·tŏməs), *a.* 1847. [f. Gr. διάτομος cut through.] *Min.* 'Having crystals with one distinct diagonal cleavage.' (Dicts.)

Diatonic (dəiătǫ·nik), *a.* 1597. [a. F. *diatonique,* f. (ult.) Gr. διά at the interval of + τόνος tone.] **1.** *Gr. Mus.* That scale (the others being CHROMATIC and ENHARMONIC) in which the interval of a tone was used, the tetrachord being divided into two whole tones and a semitone (as in each half of the modern diatonic scale) 1603. **2.** In modern music, denoting the scale which in any key proceeds by the notes proper to that key without chromatic alteration. Also *fig.* Hence **Diato·nically** *adv.* in a d. manner. **Dia·tonism,** diatonic system.

Diatribe (dəi·ătrəib), *sb.* 1581. [a. F., ad. L. *diatriba,* a. Gr. διατριβή a wearing away (of time), study, discourse.] **1.** A discourse, disquisition (*arch.*). **2.** A dissertation directed against some person or work; a bitter and violent criticism; an invective 1804.

2. A rambling, bitter d. on the..sufferings of the labourers 1850. Hence **Di·atribist,** one who writes or utters a d.

‖**Diaulos** (dəi,ǭ·lǫs). 1706. [Gr., f. δι- (DI-²) + αὐλός pipe.] *Gr. Antiq.* **1.** A double course, in which the racers returned to the starting point. **2.** The double flute.

Diazeuctic (dəiăziū·ktik), *a.* 1698. [ad. Gr. διαζευκτικός disjunctive.] Disjunctive; applied, in ancient Gr. Music, to the interval of a tone separating disjunct tetrachords; also to the tetrachords.

Diazo- (dəi,æ·zo). 1873. [f. DI-² + AZO-.] *Chem.* A formative of the names of compounds derived from the aromatic hydrocarbons, which contain two atoms of nitrogen combined in a peculiar way with phenyl (C_6H_5), as *d.-benzine, -naphthaline,* etc. Also used *attrib.,* as in *diazo compounds, reaction,* etc.

‖**Diazoma** (dəiăzōᵘ·mă). 1706. [L., a. Gr. διάζωμα girdle, partition, etc.] **1.** *Gr. Theatre.* A semicircular passage through the auditorium, parallel to its outer border, and cutting the radial flights of steps at a point about half-way up. †**2.** *Anat.* The midriff –1883.

Diazotize (dəi,æ·zǫtəiz). 1889. [DI-².] *Chem.* To convert into a diazo compound.

Dib, *sb.* Usu. in *pl.* **dibs.** 1730. [? f. DIB *v.*² Prob. short for *dibstones.*] **1.** *pl.* A children's game played with pebbles or the knuckle-bones of sheep; also the pebbles or bones so used. **2.** A counter used in playing at cards. **3.** *pl.* Money (*slang*) 1812. **4.** = DIBBLE (*dial.*) 1891.

Dib, *v.*¹ Now *dial.* ME. [? f. DIP *v.,* with duller sound.] = DIP *v.*

Dib, *v.*² 1609. [f. DAB *v.*¹, with weaker vowel.] **1.** *trans.* To dab lightly. **2.** *intr.* To tap lightly 1869. **3.** *intr.* = DAP *v.*¹, DIBBLE *v.*² 2. 1681. **4.** To dibble 1891.

Dibasic (dəibēⁱ·sik), *a.* 1868. [DI-².] *Chem.* Having two bases, or two atoms of a base. *D. acid*: one containing two atoms of displaceable hydrogen. See BIBASIC. Hence **Dibasi·city,** d. quality.

Dibber (di·bəɹ). 1736. [f. DIB *v.*² + -ER ¹.] **1.** An instrument for dibbling; a dibbler. **2.** *Mining.* The pointed end of an iron bar used for making holes (*U.S.*) 1871.

Dibble (di·b'l), *sb.* 1450. [app. conn. w. DIB *v.*²; see -LE 1.] An instrument used to make holes in the ground for seeds, bulbs, or young plants.

Dibble (di·b'l), *v.*¹ 1583. [f. prec. sb.] **1.** *trans.* To make a hole in with or as with a dibble; to sow or plant by this means. **2.** *intr.* To use a dibble; to bore holes in the soil (*mod.*). Hence **Di·bbler,** one who or that which dibbles.

Dibble (di·b'l), *v.*² 1622. [? f. DABBLE, with lighter vowel.] **1.** *intr.* = DABBLE *v.* 2. **2.** = DIB *v.*² 3, DAP *v.* 1. 1658.

Dib-hole. 1883. [app. f. *dib,* var. of DUB.] *Mining.* = SUMP.

Diblastula (dəiblæ·stiŭlă). 1890. [DI-².] *Embryol.* That stage of the embryo at which it consists of a vesicle enclosed in a double layer of cells; = GASTRULA.

Dibrach (dəi·bræk). *rare.* [ad. L. *dibrachys.*] In Gr. and L. prosody: A foot consisting of two short syllables; a pyrrhic.

Dibranchiate (dəibræ·ŋkiĕt). 1835. [ad. mod.L. *dibranchiata,* f. Gr. δι- (DI-²) + βράγχια gills of fishes; see -ATE ².] *Zool.*

A. *adj.* Belonging to the *Dibranchiata,* an order of cephalopods having two branchiæ or gills.

B. *sb.* One of the *Dibranchiata.*

Dibs (pl.); see DIB *sb.*

Di·bstones, *sb. pl.* 1692. [See DIB *sb.*] A children's game; the same as *dibs* or *dabstones.*

Dibu·tyl, Dibutyro-. *Chem.* See DI-².

Dicacity (dikæ·siti). *arch.* 1592. [f. L. *dicax, dicacem* (f. *dic-* stem of *dicere.*] A jesting habit of speech; raillery; pertness; talkativeness.

Given to the humor of dicacitie and iesting BACON.

Dicæology (dəisi,ǫ·lŏdʒi). Also **dice-.** 1656. [ad. L., a Gr. δικαιολογία a plea in defence.] †**1.** A description of jurisdiction 1664. **2.** *Rhet.* Justification.

Dicalcic (dəikæ·lsik), *a.* 1863. [DI-² 2.] *Chem.* Containing two equivalents of calcium.

Dicarbo-, bef. a vowel **dicarb-.** *Chem.* See DI-².

Dicarbon (dəikā·ɹbǫn), *a.* 1869. [DI-².] *Chem.* Containing or derived from two atoms of carbon, as the *d.* series of hydrocarbons.

Dica·rbonate. *Chem.* See DI-².

Dicast (di·kæst). Also **dikast.** 1822. [ad. Gr. δικαστής, f. δικάζειν, f. δίκη.] *Gr. Antiq.* One of the 6,000 citizens chosen annually in ancient Athens to try cases in the several law-courts. Hence **Dica·stic, dik-,** of or belonging to a d. or dicasts.

Dicastery (dikæ·stĕri). Also **dikastery.** 1822. [ad. Gr. δικαστήριον.] One of the courts of justice in which the dicasts sat; the court or body of dicasts.

Dicatalectic (dəi:kætăle·ktik), *a.* [DI-².] *Pros.* Doubly catalectic; wanting a syllable both in the middle and at the end. (Dicts.)

Dice (dəis), *sb.,* pl. of DIE *sb.,* q. v. Much more used than the singular *die.* *Comb.* **d.-coal,** a species of coal easily splitting into cubical fragments; **-shot** = *die-shot* (see DIE).

Dice (dəis), *v.* ME. [f. prec.] **1.** To play with dice; *trans.* to throw *away* by dicing. **2.** To cut into dices: *esp.* in cookery ME. **3.** To mark or ornament with a pattern of cubes or squares; to chequer 1688.

Dice-box. 1552. The box from which dice are thrown in gaming; used typically for gaming.

‖**Dicentra** (dəise·ntră). 1866. [mod.L., f. Gr. δίκεντρος, f. δι- two + κέντρον spur.] *Bot.* A genus of plants (N.O. *Fumariaceæ*) having drooping heart-shaped flowers; several species are cultivated in the flower-garden, esp. *D. spectabilis* (also called *Dielytra*).

Dicephalous (dəise·făləs), *a.* 1808. [f. Gr.

δι-, DI-[2] + κεφαλή.] Having two heads, two-headed.

Dicer (dəi·səɹ). ME. [f. DICE *v.* or *sb.* + -ER [1].] One who plays or gambles with dice. As false as Dicers Oathes *Haml.* III. iv. 45.

Dicerous (dəi·sĕrəs), *a. rare.* 1826. [irreg. f. Gr. δίκερως two-horned.] *Entom.* Having two horns, antennæ, or tentacles.

†**Dich.** *rare.* A corrupt word, app. meaning *do it. Timon* I. ii. 73.

‖**Dichasium** (dəikē·ziŏm). Pl. **-ia.** 1875. [mod.L., f. Gr. δίχασις a division.] *Bot.* A biparous cyme. Hence **Dicha·sial** *a.* belonging to or of the nature of a d.

‖**Dichastasis** (dəikæ·stăsis). 1864. [f. Gr. δίχα + στάσις.] 'Spontaneous subdivision' (Webster). Hence **Dicha·stic** *a.* capable of undergoing d.

Dichlamydeous (dəiklămi·dĭəs), *a.* 1830. [f. Gr. δι- + χλαμύς.] *Bot.* Having two envelopes (calyx and corolla).

Dichloride (dəiklōə·rəid, -rid). 1825. [DI-[2].] *Chem.* A compound of two atoms of chlorine with an element or radical, as mercury dichloride $HgCl_2$.

Dicho-, a. Gr. διχο-, comb. f. δίχα in two, asunder, separately. (The ι is short in Greek.)

Dichogamous (dəikǫ·gămǝs), *a.* 1859. [f. Gr. διχο-, DICHO- + -γαμος, γάμος + -OUS.] *Bot.* Said of those hermaphrodite plants in which the stamens and pistils (or analogous organs) mature at different times, so that self-fertilization is impossible. So **Dicho·gamy**, the condition of being d.

Dichord (dəi·kǭɹd). 1819. [ad. Gr. δίχορδος.] An instrument having two strings. **b.** An instrument having two strings to each note.

Dichoree (dəi·korī). 1801. [f. DI-[2] + CHOREE.] *Pros.* A foot consisting of two chorees or trochees.

Dichotomic (dəikotǫ·mik), *a.* 1873. [f. as DICHOTOMOUS + -IC.] Relating to or involving dichotomy. Hence **Dichoto·mically** *adv.*

Dichotomist (dəikǫ·tŏmist). 1592. [f. DICHOTOMY + -IST.] One who dichotomizes.

Dichotomize (dəikǫ·tŏməiz), *v.* 1606. [f. Gr. διχότομος + -IZE.] **1.** *trans.* To divide into two parts or sections; *esp.* in reference to classification; †*loosely*, to divide. **2.** *intr.* (for *refl.*) To divide into two continuously; *spec.* used of the branching of a stem, root, etc. 1835.

1. That great citie might well be dichotomized into cloysters and hospitals BP. HALL. Hence **Dicho·tomized** *ppl. a.* divided into two branches; *Astron.* said of the moon when exactly half her disk is illuminated.

Dichotomous (dəikǫ·tŏməs), *a.* 1690. [f. L. *dichotomus*, a. Gr. διχότομος; see DICHO- and -OUS.] Divided or dividing into two. The division of arteries is usually d. 1842. Hence **Dicho·tomously** *adv.*

Dichotomy (dəikǫ·tŏmi). 1610. [ad. Gr. διχοτομία a cutting in two; see prec.] **1.** Division of a whole into two parts; *spec.* in *Logic*, etc.: Division of a class or genus into two lower mutually exclusive classes or genera. **2.** *Astron.* That phase of the moon, etc., at which exactly half the disk appears illuminated 1686. **3.** *Bot.*, *Zool.*, etc. A form of branching in which each successive axis divides into two 1707.

1. What is called d. by contradiction, *e.g.* that 'everything must either be red or not red' E. CAIRD.

Dichotriæne (di:ko₁trəi₁ī·n). 1887. [f. DICHO- + Gr. τρίαινα; see TRIÆNE.] *Zool.* A dichotomous triæne; a three-forked sponge spicule, having each fork dividing into two.

Dichro-. In comb. = DICHROIC.

Dichroic (dəikrōᵘ·ik), *a.* 1864. [ad. Gr. δίχροος (f. δι- + χρώς) + -IC.] Having or showing two colours; *spec.* applied to doubly-refracting crystals that exhibit different colours when viewed in different directions. So **Di·chroism**, the quality of being d. Hence **Dichroi·stic** *a.* dichroitic.

Dichroite (dəi·kro₁əit). 1810. [f. Gr. δίχροος (see prec.) + -ITE.] *Min.* A synonym of IOLITE, from its often exhibiting dichroism. Hence **Dichroi·tic** *a.* of, or of the nature of, d.; dichroic.

Dichromate (dəikrōᵘ·mēt). 1864. [DI-[2].] *Chem.* A double CHROMATE (q. v.), as *potassium d.* $K_2 . CrO_4 . CrO_3$. (Also *bichromate*.)

Dichromatic (dəikromæ·tik), *a.* 1847. [f. Gr. δι- + χρωματικός, f. χρῶμα.] Having or showing two colours; *spec.* of animals: Presenting, in different individuals, two different colours or systems of coloration. So **Dichro·matism**, the quality or fact of being d.

Dichromic (dəikrōᵘ·mik), *a.* 1854. [f. Gr. δίχρωμος (see prec.) + -IC.] **1.** Relating to or including (only) two colours; applied to the vision of colour-blind persons including only two of three primary colour-sensations. **2.** DICHROIC 1877.

Dichronous (dəi·krŏnəs), *a.* 1883. [f. late L. *dichronus*, a. Gr. (f. δι-, DI-[2] + χρόνος) + -OUS.] **1.** *Gr.* and *L. Pros.* Having two times or quantities; common. **2.** *Bot.* 'Having two periods of growth in the year' (*Syd. Soc. Lex.*).

Dichroscope (dəi·kro₁skōᵘp). 1857. [f. Gr. δίχροος + -σκοπος.] An instrument for observing or testing the dichroism of crystals, etc. Hence **Dichrosco·pic** *a.*

Dicing (dəi·siŋ), *vbl. sb.* 1456. [f. DICE *v.*] **1.** Gambling with dice; dice-play. **2.** *Bookbinding.* A method of ornamenting leather in squares or diamonds. Also *attrib.* (in sense 1).

Dick (dik), *sb.*[1] 1553. [Playful f. *Ric-*, contr. of Norman Fr. *Ricard*, L. *Ricardus* = *Richard*.] **1.** A familiar form of *Richard*. Hence generically = fellow, lad, man. **2.** *slang.* A riding whip 1873.

1. *Tom, D., and Harry*: any three (or more) of the populace taken at random.

Dick, *sb.*[2] *dial.* 1847. [? conn. w. Du. *dek*.] A leather apron.

Dick, *sb.*[3] *dial.* 1736. [Cf. DIKE and DITCH.] A ditch; a dike.

Dick, *sb.*[4] *slang.* 1860. Abbrev. of *dictionary*; hence, Long words.

Dick, *sb.*[5] *slang.* 1861. [Short for *declaration*; cf. DAVY.] In *To take one's d.* = to take one's declaration.

Dickens (di·kĕnz). *slang* or *colloq.* 1598. [? Substituted for *devil*, or, ?? worn down from *devilkin*.] The deuce, the devil. I cannot tell what (the dickens) his name is SHAKS.

Dickensian (dikeˑnziăn), *a.* 1856. Of or pertaining to Charles Dickens, or his style.

Dicker (di·kəɹ), *sb.*[1] [ME. *dyker*, etc., from a WGer. **decura*, **decora*, ad. L. *decuria*, a company or parcel of ten.] The number of ten; half a score; being the customary unit of exchange, *esp.* in hides or skins; hence a lot of (ten) hides. Also †*transf.*

A dycker of hydes tanned 1526. *transf.* A whole d. of wit SYDNEY.

Dicker (di·kəɹ), *sb.*[2] *U.S.* 1823. [f. DICKER *v.*] The action or practice of dickering; petty bargaining.

Dicker, *v. U.S.* 1845. [? f. DICKER *sb.*[1]; see quot.] *intr.* To trade by barter; to truck; to bargain in a petty way. Also *trans.*

The white men who penetrated to the semi-wilds [of the West] were always ready to d. and to swap F. COOPER.

Dicky, dickey (di·ki), *sb. colloq.*, *slang*, and *dial.* 1753. [cf. *Dicky*, dim. of *Dick*; also DICK *sb.*[2] Some applications are obscure.] **1.** *Naut.* An officer acting in commission 1867. **2.** A (male) donkey 1793. **3.** A small bird (also DICKY-BIRD) 1851. †**4.** An under petticoat -1878. †**5.** A worn-out shirt (*slang*) 1781. **6.** A detached shirt-front 1811. **7.** A shirt collar. (*New England.*) 1858. **8.** A covering worn to protect the dress during work; *e.g.* a leather apron; a child's bib; a 'slop'; an oil-skin suit 1847. **9.** The seat in a carriage on which the driver sits; also one at the back for servants, etc., or for the guard of a mail-coach 1801. **b.** An extra seat at the back of a two-seater motor-car 1912.

Di·cky, dickey, *a. slang* or *colloq.* 1812. [?] Sorry, poor; unsound, shaky, queer.

‖**Diclesium** (dəiklī·ziŏm). 1857. [mod.L., f. Gr. δι- (DI-[2]) + κλῆσις closing.] *Bot.* A dry indehiscent fruit consisting of an achene enclosed within the indurated base of the adherent perianth.

Diclinic (dəikli·nik), *a.* 1864. [f. Gr. δι- + κλίνειν + -IC.] *Cryst.* Having the lateral axes at right angles to each other, but both oblique to the vertical axis.

Diclinism (dəi·kliniz'm). 1882. [mod. f. as next.] *Bot.* The condition of being DICLINOUS.

Diclinous (dəi·klinəs), *a.* 1830. [f. F. *dicline*, f. Gr. δι- (DI-[2]) + κλίνη couch; see -OUS.] *Bot.* Having the stamens and pistils on separate flowers. Also said of the flowers (= unisexual).

Dicoccous (dəikǫ·kəs), *a.* 1819. [DI-[2].] *Bot.* Splitting into two cocci; see COCCUS 2.

Dicondylian (dəikǫndi·liăn), *a.* 1883. [f. Gr. δικόνδυλος (cf. CONDYLE) + -IAN.] *Zool.* Of a skull: Having two occipital condyles.

Dicotyledon (dəi·kǫtilī·dən). 1727. [f. mod. Bot.L. *dicotyledones* pl. (also used), f. Gr. δι- + κοτυληδών; see COTYLEDON.] *Bot.* A flowering plant having two cotyledons or seed-lobes. Hence **Di:cotyle·donary, Di:cotyle·donous** *adjs.* having two cotyledons; belonging to the class of Dicotyledons; of or belonging to a dicotyledonous plant.

Dicrotic (dəikrǫ·tik), *a.* 1811. [f. Gr. δίκροτος double-beating + -IC: in mod. F. *dicrote*.] *Phys.*, etc. Of the pulse (or a tracing of its motion): Exhibiting a double beat or wave for each beat of the heart. **b.** Of or pertaining to a dicrotic pulse or tracing, as a *d. notch* or *wave*. vars. **Dicro·tal, Di·crotous.** So **Di·crotism**, the quality of being d.

Dict (dikt), *sb. arch.* ME. [ad. L. *dictum*.] A saying or maxim.

Dicta, pl. of DICTUM.

Dictaphone (di·ktăfōᵘn). 1907. [irreg. f. DICTATE + *-phone* as in GRAMOPHONE.] A proprietary name for a machine which records and reproduces words spoken into it.

Dictate (di·ktēt), *sb.* 1594. [ad. L. *dictatum*, neut. pa. pple. of *dictare* used subst.] †**1.** That which is dictated -1826; DICTATION -1678. †**2.** A DICTUM -1728; a maxim -1682. **3.** An authoritative direction delivered in words 1618. **b.** Often applied to the monitions of a written law, conscience, reason, nature, experience, self-interest, etc. 1594.

3. I could not receive such dictates without horror JOHNSON. Every man will obey the dictates of Reason and Nature GIBBON.

Dictate (diktē¹·t, di·ktēᵗt), *v.* 1592. [f. L. *dictat-*, *dictare*. The pronunc. *dicta·te* is now usual in England.] **1.** *trans.* To put into words which are to be written down; to pronounce *to* a person (something which he is to write) 1612. Also *absol.* **2.** *trans.* To prescribe; to lay down authoritatively; to order in express terms 1621. **3.** *intr.* To use or practise dictation; to lay down the law, give orders 1651.

1. He dictated them while Bathurst wrote 1783. 2. They dictated the conditions of peace GIBBON. Of all that Wisdom dictates, this the drift COWPER. 3. To cavil, censure, d., right or wrong POPE.

Dictation (diktē¹·ʃən). 1656. [ad. L. *dictationem*; see prec.] **1.** The act of dictating 1727. Also *attrib.* **2.** Authoritative utterance or prescription 1656; arbitrary command 1856. **3.** Something dictated 1841.

1. I will write out the charm from your d. JOWETT. 2. It would have probably been unsafe for the crown to attempt d. or repression FROUDE.

Dictative (diktē¹·tiv, di·ktĕtiv), *a.* 1768. [f. DICTATE *v.* + -IVE.] Of the nature of dictation.

Dictator (diktē¹·təɹ). ME. [a. L.] **1.** A ruler or governor whose word is law; an absolute ruler of a state; *esp.* one invested with absolute authority in seasons of emergency. Also *transf.* **2.** A person exercising absolute authority of any kind or in any sphere 1605. **3.** One who dictates to a writer 1617.

1. As in old Rome, when the D. was created, all inferiour magistracies ceased BURTON. 2. The dictators of behaviour, dress, and politeness SWIFT. Hence **Dicta·torate**, the office of a d.

Dictatorial (diktătōᵊ·riăl), *a.* 1701. [f. L. *dictatorius* + -AL.] **1.** Of, pertaining, or proper to a dictator. **2.** Pertaining to or characteristic of dictation; inclined to dictate; overbearing in tone 1704.

1. D. power 1701. 2. By violent measures, and a d. behaviour SWIFT. Hence **Dictato·rially** *adv.* **Dictato·rialness.** So †**Dictato·rian** *a.* of, proper to, or characteristic of a dictator. var. **Di·ctatory** *a.*; whence **Di·ctatorily** *adv.*

Dictatorship (diktēⁱ·təɹʃip). 1586. [See -SHIP.] 1. The office or dignity of a dictator. 2. Absolute authority in any sphere 16...

Dictatress (diktēⁱ·très). 1784. [f. DICTATOR + -ESS.] A female dictator (*lit.* and *fig.*). So **Dicta·trix.**

Dictature (diktēⁱ·tiūɹ). 1553. [ad. L. *dictatura.*] 1. = DICTATORSHIP. 2. A collective body of dictators 1759.

†**Di·ctery.** *rare.* [ad. L. *dicterium*, in sense assoc. w. L. *dictum.*] A witty saying. BURTON.

Diction (di·kʃən). 1542. [a. F., or ad. L. *dictionem.* Not in Dicts. bef. Johnson.] †1. A word -1697. †2. A phrase, locution -1709. †3. Speech; verbal description -1602. 4. The manner in which anything is expressed in words 1700. 5. *Mus.* Rendition of words in singing, as regards pronunciation, etc.

3. *Haml.* v. ii. 123. 4. Almost all fancy the d. makes the poet HARE. Absolute accuracy of d. and precision of accent in prose RUSKIN.

†**Dictiona·rian.** *rare.* 1846. [f. as next + -AN.] The maker of a dictionary.

Dictionary (di·kʃənări). 1526. [ad. med.L. *dictionarium* lit. a repertory of *dictiones* (see DICTION).] 1. A book dealing with the words of a language, so as to set forth their orthography, pronunciation, signification, and use, their synonyms, derivation, and history, or at least some of these; the words are arranged in some stated order, now, usually, alphabetical; a word-book, vocabulary, lexicon. 2. By extension: A book of information or reference on any subject or branch of knowledge, the items of which are arranged alphabetically; as a D. of *Architecture, Biography*, of *the Bible*, of *Dates*, etc. 1631. Also *fig.* Also *attrib.*

1. Neither is a d. a bad book to read .. it is full of suggestion,—the raw material of possible poems and histories EMERSON. 2. *fig.* Burnet was..a living d. of English affairs MACAULAY.

Dictograph (di·ktŏgraf). 1907. [orig. proprietary name, irreg. f. L. *dictum* thing said + -GRAPH.] An instrument designed to record in one room sounds made in another.

‖**Dictum** (di·ktŏm). Pl. **dicta, dictums.** 1670. [L.] A saying: usu. a formal and authoritative pronouncement 1706. b. *Law.* An expression of opinion by a judge on a matter of law 1776. c. A current saying 1826. d. An award 1670.

A d. of Johnson's 1787. c. The *d.* that truth always triumphs MILL. d. *D. of Kenilworth*, an award made in 1266 between King Henry III and the barons who had taken arms against him.

Dictyogen (di·ktioˌdʒen, diktəi·ŏˌdʒen). 1846. [f. Gr. δίκτυον; see -GEN¹. After ENDOGEN, etc.] *Bot.* Lindley's name for those plants which have a monocotyledonous embryo and reticulated leaf-veins.

Dicy·an(o)-. [DI-².] *Chem.* Combined with two equivalents of the radical cyanogen, CN, replacing two of hydrogen, chlorine, etc.

Dicyanide (dəisəi·ănəid). 1863. [DI-².] *Chem.* A compound containing two equivalents of cyanogen (CN) united to an element or dyad radical, as *mercuric d.* $Hg(CN)_2$.

Dicya·nogen. *Chem.* See DI-². Cyanogen in the free form.

Dicynodont (dəisi·nŏdǫnt). 1854. [f. Gr. δι- + κυν- + ὀδοντ-.] *Palæont.* A fossil reptile having no teeth except two long canines in the upper jaw. *adj.* Having this character.

The typical genus is *Dicynodon*, order *Dicynodontia*. Hence **Dicynodo·ntian** *a.*

Did, pa. t. of Do *v.*, q.v.

‖**Didache** (di·dăkī). 1885. Gr. διδαχή, in the title Διδαχὴ τῶν δώδεκα ἀποστόλων Teaching of the twelve apostles, the name of a Christian treatise of the beginning of the second century.

Didactic (didæ·ktik, dəi-). 1644. [ad. Gr. διδακτικός, f. διδάσκειν to teach.]

A. *adj.* Having the character or manner of a teacher; characterized by giving instruction; instructive, preceptive.

B. *sb.* †1. A didactic author or treatise -1835. 2. *pl.* The science or art of teaching 1846.

2. Life is rather a subject of wonder, than of didactics EMERSON. So **Dida·ctical** *a.* (*rare*). **Dida·ctically** *adv.* **Dida·cticism**, the practice or quality of being d. **Didacti·city** (*rare*), d. quality.

Didactive (didæ·ktiv), *a.* 1711. [irreg. f. Gr. διδακτός + -IVE: after words from L. like *active.*] = DIDACTIC.

Didactyl, -yle (dəidæ·ktil), *a.* 1819. [f. DI-² + Gr. δάκτυλος.] *Zool.* Having two fingers, toes, or claws. var. **Dida·ctylous.**

Didal(l, obs. ff. DIDLE.

Didapper (dəi·dæ:pəɹ). ME. [Reduced f. DIVE-DAPPER.] 1. = DABCHICK. 2. Applied ludicrously to a person 1589.

Didascalic (didæ̆skæ·lik), *a.* 1609. [ad. L. *didascalicus*, a Gr., f. διδάσκειν.] Of the nature of a teacher or of instruction; didactic. Hence **Didasca·lics** *sb. pl.* = DIDACTICS. So **Dida·scalar** *a.* didactic. *nonce-wd.*

Didder (di·dəɹ), *v.* Now *dial.* ME. [? Onomatopœic.] *intr.* To tremble, quake, shake, shiver.

Diddest, rare f. *didst*, 2nd sing. pa. t. of Do *v.*

Diddle (di·d'l), *v.*¹ *colloq.* or *dial.* 1632. [app. parallel to DIDDER. Cf. DADDLE.] †1. *intr.* = DADDLE. 2. To move from side to side by jerks; to shake 1786. 3. *trans.* To jerk from side to side 1893.

Diddle (di·d'l), *v.*² *colloq.* 1806. [? f. OE. *didrian* to delude.] 1. To waste time in mere trifling 1826. 2. *trans.* a. To swindle; to 'do'. b. To do for, ruin; to kill. 1806. Hence **Di·ddler**, a mean swindler or cheat.

Diddle- in comb. 1523. [Conn. w. DIDDLE *v.*¹, *v.*²]

D.-daddle, 'stuff and nonsense'. **D.-dee**, the shrub *Empetrum rubrum.* **D.-diddle**, the sound or action of fiddling. **Diddledum**, used contemptuously for something trifling.

†**Di-decahe·dral,** *a.* 1805. [DI- *pref.*² 1.] *Crystall.* Having the form of a ten-sided prism with five-sided bases, making twenty faces in all.

Didelphian (dəide·lfiăn), *a.* 1847. [f. mod. L. *Didelphia*, f. Gr. δι-, DI-² + δελφύς womb.] *Zool.* Belonging to the subclass *Didelphia* of the class *Mammalia*, characterized by a double uterus and vagina, and comprising the single order of Marsupials. So **Dide·lphic, Dide·lphine, Dide·lphous** *adjs.* in same sense; **Didelph, Dide·lphid**, a member of the subclass *Didelphia*, or of the family *Didelphidæ* (opossums); **Dide·lphoid** *a.* double, as the uterus in the *Didelphia.*

Didine (dəi·dəin), *a.* 1885. [f. mod.L. *didus* the dodo + -INE.] *Zool.* Belonging to the family *Dididæ* of birds, akin to the dodo.

Didle (dəi·d'l), *sb. local.* 1490. [?] A sharp triangular spade, used for clearing out ditches, etc. So **Di·dle** *v.* (*local*), to clean out the bed of (a river or ditch); *intr.* to work with a didle.

Dido (dəi·dŏ). *U.S. slang.* 1843. [?] A prank, a caper; a shindy, *esp.* in phr. *to cut (up) didoes.*

†**Di-do·decahe·dral,** *a.* 1805. [DI- *pref.*² 1.] *Crystall.* Having the form of a twelve-sided prism, with six planes in each base, or twenty-four faces in all.

Didonia (dəidŏu·niă). 1873. [From the story of Dido, who bargained for as much land as a hide would cover, and cut the hide into a long narrow strip so as to inclose a large space.] *Math.* The curve which, on a given surface and with a given perimeter, contains the greatest area.

Didrachm (dəi·dræm). 1548. [ad. L. *didrachma* or *didrachmon.*] An ancient Greek silver coin; a two-drachma piece; see DRACHMA. Hence **Didra·chmal** *a.* of the weight of two drachmæ: applied to the stater.

Didst, 2nd sing. pa. t. of Do *v.*

†**Didu·ce**, *v.* 1578. [ad. L. *diducere.* Sometimes confused with DEDUCE.] 1. *trans.* To pull away or apart -1696. 2. To dilate, expand -1657. Hence †**Didu·ction.**

Diduce, -ment, obs. (erron.) ff. DEDUCE, -MENT.

Diductively, obs. (erron.) f. DEDUCTIVELY.

Didymate (di·dimĕt), *a.* 1843. [f. mod.L. *didymus*, a. Gr. δίδυμος twin + -ATE.] *Zool.*, etc. = DIDYMOUS.

†‖**Di·dymis.** Pl. **-es.** 1543. [f. Gr. δίδυμοι testicles.] = EPIDIDYMIS -1883.

Didymium (didi·miŏm). 1842. [f. Gr. δίδυμος twin. Assoc., like *lanthanium*, with cerium; hence its name.] *Chem.* A rare metal, found only in association with cerium and lanthanium. Symbol Di.

Didymous (di·diməs), *a.* 1794. [f. mod.L. *didymus*, a. Gr. + -OUS.] *Bot.*, etc. Growing in pairs, paired, twin.

‖**Didynamia** (didinēⁱ·miă). 1753. [mod.L. (Linnæus 1735), f. Gr. δι-, DI-² + δύναμις.] *Bot.* The fourteenth class in the Linnæan Sexual System of plants, containing those with four stamens in pairs of unequal length, whence the name. Hence **Di·dynam**, a plant of this class; **Didyna·mian** *a.* didynamous.

Didynamous (dəidi·năməs, did-), *a.* 1794. [f. as prec.] *Bot.* Of stamens: Arranged in two pairs of unequal length. Of a flower or plant: Belonging to the Linnæan class *Didynamia.*

Die (dəi), *sb.* Pl. **dice** (dəis), **dies** (dəiz). [Early ME. *de, dee*, pl. *des, dees*, a. OF. *de*, mod. F. *dé*, pl. *dés*; in form:—L. *datum*, ? in late pop.L. 'that which is given or decreed (sc. by fortune)'; hence applied to the dice which determined this. Cf. *pence* (collective), *pennies* (non-collective).]

I. With pl. *dice.* 1. A small cube, having its faces marked with spots numbering from one to six, used in games of chance by being thrown from a box or the hand. b. *pl.* The game played with these. 2. *fig.* Hazard, chance, luck 1548. 3. A small cubical segment of anything ME.

2. I haue set my life vpon a cast, And I will stand the hazard of the Dye *Rich. III*, v. iv. 10. Phr. *The d. is cast*: the course of action is irrevocably decided. 3. Turnips and carrots cut in dice MRS. RAFFALD.

II. With pl. *dies.* 1. A cubical block; in *Arch.* the cubical portion of a pedestal, between the base and cornice; = DADO 1. 1664. 2. An engraved stamp (often one of two) for impressing a design or figure upon some softer material, as in coining money, striking a medal, embossing paper, etc. 1699. 3. A name of mechanical appliances:

spec. a. One of two or more pieces (fitted in a *stock*) to form a segment of a hollow screw for cutting the thread of a screw or bolt. b. The bed-piece serving as a support for metal from which a piece is to be punched, and having an opening through which the piece is driven. c. *Shoe-making*, etc. A shaped knife for cutting out blanks of any required shape or size: cf. DIE *v.*² 1812.

4. *Sc.* A toy 1808.

attrib. and *Comb.*, as *die-shaped* a.; **d.†-shot**, shot of cubical form; **-sinker**, an engraver of dies for stamping; so **-sinking**; **-stock**, the stock or handle for holding the dies used in cutting screws (see II. 3 a).

Die (dəi), *v.*¹ Pa. t. and pple. **died** (dəid), pr. pple. **dying** (dəi·iŋ). [Early ME. *dēȝen, dēghen*, corresp. to ON. *deyja*, etc. Early lost in OE., and re-adopted in early ME.]

I. Of man and sentient beings. 1. *intr.* To lose life, cease to live, suffer death; to expire. Const. with *of, by, from, through*; also *for* a cause, object, etc., *for* the sake of one, *in* a state or condition, etc. 2. To suffer the pains of death; to face death ME. 3. *Theol.* To suffer spiritual death; 'To perish everlastingly' (J.); cf. DEATH. 4. To languish, pine away with passion; *to d. for*, to desire excessively 1591.

1. In the day thou eat'st, thou di'st MILT. *P. L.* VII. 544. To d. of hunger, by the sword, from inattention, through neglect, at the stake, in battle, in the Romish Communion, etc. (*mod.*). He shall dye a Fleas death *Merry W.* IV. ii. 158. Phr. *To d. the death*: to suffer death, to be put to death. *To d. in one's bed, in one's shoes, in harness* (*i. e.* in full work), *in the last ditch* (*i. e.* to fight till the last extremity). 2. I d. daily 1 *Cor.* xv. 31. 4. Deare, I d. As often as from thee I goe DONNE. I am dying for a drink (*mod.*).

II. 1. Of plants, or organized matter: To cease to be subject to vital forces; to pass into a state of decomposition ME. 2. *fig.* Of substances: To become dead, flat, vapid, or inactive 1612. 3. Of actions, institutions, states, or qualities: To come to an end; to go out, as a candle or fire; to pass out of memory ME. 4. To pass gradually away (*esp.* out of hearing or sight) 1704. 5. To pass by dying (*into* something else) 1633; in *Archit.* to merge *into*; to terminate gradually *in* or *against* 1665.

1. My heart seemed to d. within me SMOLLETT.

The shining daffodils d. TENNYSON. 3. So dies my reuenge *Much Ado* v. i. 301. Art, which cannot d. SHELLEY. 4. I hear soft music die along the grove POPE. 5. The day dyes into night BP. HALL.

Die, *v.*² 1703. [f. DIE *sb.*] *trans.* To furnish with a die; to mould or shape with a die.

Die·-away, *a.* 1802. [from the phr. *to die away.*] That dies away or seems to die away; languishing.

‖**Dieb** (dīb). 1829. [a. Arab. *ðib* 'wolf'.] *Zool.* A North African Jackal (*Canis anthus*).

Die·-back, *sb.* 1886. [from the phr. *to die back.*] The name for a disease affecting orange trees in Florida, etc., in which the tree dies from the top downward.

Diecious, etc., var. DIŒCIOUS, etc.

Diedral, var. DIHEDRAL.

‖**Diegesis** (dəi,idʒī·sis). 1829. [a. Gr., f. διηγέομαι.] A narrative; a statement of the case.

†**Diego** (dyē·go). 1611. [Sp. *Diego*, James, the patron saint of Spain; see also DON *Diego.*] 1. A Spaniard; cf. DAGO. (Also *attrib.*) –1687. 2. A Spanish sword –1867. 3. A variety of pear. EVELYN.

Die·-hard. 1844. [from the phr. *to die hard.*] **A.** *adj.* That resists to the last.

B. *sb.* One that dies hard; *esp.* an extremely conservative politician, etc.; *spec.* (*pl.*) an appellation of the 57th Regiment of Foot in the British Army.

Dielectric (dəi,ile·ktrik). 1837. [DI-³.] **A.** *sb.* A substance or medium through or across which electric force acts without conduction; a non-conductor; an insulating medium.

B. *adj.* 1. Non-conducting 1871. 2. Relating to a dielectric medium, or to the transmission of electricity without conduction 1863.

‖**Diencephalon** (dəi,ense·fălǫn). 1883. [mod. L., f. Gr. δι-, δια- + ἐγκέφαλον. Repr. Ger. *zwischenhirn.*] = THALAMENCEPHALON. Hence **Diencepha·lic** *a.* pertaining to the d.

Dieresis, dieretic, var. DIÆRESIS, -ETIC.

‖**Dies** (dəi·īz). 1607. [L., 'day'.] Used in: **a. Dies iræ**, 'day of wrath', the first words, and hence the name, of a Latin hymn on the Last Judgement, used as the sequence at a mass of requiem. **b. Dies non** (short for *dies non juridicus*), in *Law*, a day on which no legal business is transacted, or which is not reckoned for some particular purpose.

Diesel (dī·zəl). 1894. *D. engine*, a type of oil-engine invented by R. *Diesel* of Munich.

‖**Diesis** (dəi·ėsis). Pl. **dieses** (-īz). ME. [a. L., Gr. δίεσις a quarter-tone, f. διϊέναι to send through.] 1. *Mus.* **a.** In ancient Gr. music, the Pythagorean semitone (ratio 243 : 256). **b.** Now, the interval equal to the difference between three major thirds and an octave (ratio 125 : 128); usually called *enharmonic d.* 2. *Printing.* The sign ‡, usually called 'double dagger' 1706.

Diet (dəi·ĕt), *sb.*¹ ME. [a. OF. *diete*, ad. L. *diæta*, a. Gr. δίαιτα. (Supposed to be conn. w. ζάειν to live.)] †1. Way of living or thinking –1656. 2. *esp.* Way of feeding ME. 3. Prescribed course of food, restricted in kind or quantity; regimen ME. 4. Food; the victuals in daily use ME. 5. †An allowance of food –1671; board (now *Hist.*) 1455. †6. Allowance for the expenses of living –1651.

2. A meat d. is far from satisfying LIVINGSTONE. 3. To preach d. and abstinence to his patients JOHNSON. 4. The Athletick D. was of pulse SIR T. BROWNE.

Comb.: **d.-bread**, special bread prepared for invalids and others; **-kitchen**, a charitable establishment which provides proper food for the helpless poor.

Diet (dəi·ĕt), *sb.*² ME. [ad. med.L. *dieta* in same senses. The association with L. *dies* is prob. later.] †1. A day's journey. Chiefly *Sc.* (So F. *journée.*) –1651. 2. *Sc.* An appointed date or time; *spec.* the day on which a party is cited to appear in court. (So OF. *journée.*) 1568. 3. *Sc.* A session of any assembly occupying a day or part of one 1587. 4. A conference, congress, convention. (So OF. *journée.*) 1450. 5. *spec.* The English name (from the end of the 16th c.) of the former *Reichstag* of the (German) Roman Empire, and of the federal or national assemblies of Switzerland, Poland, Hungary, etc.; later of the *Bundestag* of the Germanic Confederation (1815–66); applied also to the existing *Reichstag* or Imperial Parliament of the Austro-Hungarian and German Empires, and the *Landtag* or local parliament of their constituent states, and sometimes to the parliamentary assemblies of other states of Eastern Europe, of Japan, etc. 1565. 6. The metal scraped or cut from gold and silver plate assayed day by day at the Mint, and retained for the purpose of trial 1700. Hence **Die·tal** *a.* of or belonging to a d.

Di·et, *v.* ME. [a. OF. *dieter*, f. *diete* DIET *sb.*¹] 1. *trans.* To feed; to put to a specified diet. Also *fig.* 2. To prescribe or regulate the food of (a person, etc.) in nature or quantity ME. 3. To board 1635. 4. *intr.* To take one's meals; to feed (*on*) 1566. 5. To regulate oneself as to diet 1660.

1. He that taught Abel how to d. Sheep 1655. 2. Full power .. to pill .. d. .. and poultice all persons FOOTE. 4. At what ordinary .. do they d. FULLER. Hence **Di·eter** (now *rare*), one who diets himself or others.

Dietary (dəi·ĕtări). ME. [ad. L. *dietarius*, *-um*, f. *diæta, dieta.*] **A.** *sb.* 1. A course of diet prescribed; a book prescribing such a course. 2. An allowance and regulation of food, as in a hospital, workhouse, or prison 1838.

B. *adj.* Pertaining to diet, or a dietary 1614.

Dietetic (dəi,ĕte·tik). 1541. [ad. L. *diæteticus*, a. Gr. διαιτητικός, f. δίαιτα.] **A.** *adj.* Of or pertaining to diet, or to the regulation of the kind and quantity of food to be eaten 1579. var. †**Diete·tical** *a.* Hence **Diete·tically** *adv.*

B. *sb.* 1. One who studies dietetics 1759. 2. **Dietetics**, less usually **dietetic**: The part of medicine which relates to diet.

Diethene- (dəi,e·þīn). *Chem.* See DI-².

Diethyl (dəi,e·þil). 1850. [DI-².] *Chem.* 1. as *sb.* A name for the group C_4H_{10} (*butyl hydride* or *butane*), considered as a double molecule of the radical ethyl. 2. in *Comb* Denoting two equivalents of the monad radical ethyl (C_2H_5), replacing two atoms of hydrogen in a compound, as *die·thylami·ne* $NH(C_2H_5)_2$.

Dietic (dəi,e·tik). 1659. [f. DIET *sb.*¹ + -IC.] **A.** *adj.* = DIETETIC *a.* 1716. So **Die·tical** *a.* †**B.** *sb.* A dietetic article or application.

Dietine (dəi·ĕtīn). 1669. [a. F.; = 'little diet'. See -INE.] A subordinate diet; in Polish Hist., a provincial diet which elected deputies for the national diet.

Dietist (dəi·ĕtist). 1607. [f. DIET *sb.*¹ + -IST.] One who professes or practises dietetics. So **Dieti·cian, dieti·tian.**

Dietrichite (dī·trikəit). 1882. [f. *Dietrich*, a German chemist.] *Min.* A fibrous alum, containing zinc and other bases.

†**Dieugard, e.** ME. [F., 'God keep (you)!'] The salutation 'God preserve you!'; a spoken salutation, as contrasted with a nod –1656.

Dif-, prefix of L. origin, = *dis-* before *f*, as in *differre*. In Romanic it became *def-*, whence in OF. *de-*; this occas. appears in Eng., as *defer* from L. *differre*, OF. *defferer*, etc. Usually, however, the L. form is used in Eng. For its force, see DIS-.

Diffame, etc., etymol. f. DEFAME, etc., still occas. used.

Diffarreation (difæri,ē¹·ʃən). 1623. [ad. L. *diffareationem*, f. DIF- + *farreum* a spelt cake; see CONFARREATION.] *Rom. Antiq.* An ancient Roman mode of dissolution of marriage, the undoing of confarreation.

Differ (di·fəɹ), *v.* ME. [a. F. *différer*, ad. L. *differre* to carry apart, defer; also *intr.* to tend apart, to differ. Cf. DEFER *v.*¹ Thus L. *differre* has given two Eng. vbs. *defer* to put off, and *differ* to make or be unlike.] [1. The earlier form of DEFER *v.*¹ in all senses.] 2. *trans.* To make unlike, different, or distinct; to cause to vary; to differentiate. Now *unusual.* 3. *intr.* To be not the same; to be unlike, distinct, or various: two (or more) things are said to differ (absolutely, or *from each other*), one thing differs *from* another ME. 4. *intr.* To be at variance; to disagree. Const. *with*; also *from* (*esp.* when followed by *in*) 1563. †b. To express disagreement; to dispute; to quarrel (*with*) –1737.

2. That differed it from the cases wherein the Court had gone some lengths CRUISE. 3. One star differeth from another star in glory 1 *Cor.* xv. 41. The same man, in divers times, differs from himselfe HOBBES. 4. I d. with him totally 1809. She may..d. from me in opinion J. H. NEWMAN. b. We'll never d. with a crowded pit ROWE. Hence **Di·ffer** *sb.* (*Sc.* and *dial.*) = DIFFERENCE *sb.*

Difference (di·fĕrĕns), *sb.* ME. [a. F. *différence*, OF. also *-ance*, ad. L. *differentia*, abstr. sb. f. *differentem*; see DIFFERENT.] 1. The condition, quality, or fact of being different or not the same; dissimilarity, distinction, diversity; disagreement *between* two or more things. **b.** (with *a* and *pl.*) An instance of unlikeness; a point in which things differ ME. 2. *Math.* The quantity by which one quantity differs from another; the remainder left after subtracting one quantity from another ME. **b.** *spec.* The amount of increase or decrease in the price of stocks and shares between certain dates 1717. 3. A diversity of opinion, sentiment, or purpose; hence, a dispute, a quarrel ME. 4. A mark, device, or feature, which distinguishes one thing or set of things from another. Now *rare*, exc. as in b and c. 1481. **b.** *Her.* An alteration of or addition to a coat of arms, to distinguish a junior member or branch from the chief line 1450. **c.** *Logic.* = DIFFERENTIA 1551. †**d.** *transf.* A division, class, or kind –1682. 5. A discrimination viewed as conceived by the subject ME. Also *attrib.*

1. D. is of two kinds as oppos'd either to identity or resemblance HUME. 3. With full power to concert all matters in d. GOLDSM. 4. An absolute gentleman, full of most excellent differences *Haml.* v. ii. 112. b. Oh you must weare your Rew with a d. — IV. v. 183. 5. He vysyted the seek folke without dyfference CAXTON.

Di·fference, *v.* 1450. [f. prec. sb.; cf. F. *différencier.*] †1. *intr.* To be different (*rare*) –1483. †2. *trans.* To make different –1675. 3. To differentiate (*from* something else). Freq. in *pass.* 1598. 4. To discriminate. Const. *from.* (Now *rare.*) 1570. Also †*absol.* 5. *Math.* To calculate the difference of. †b. To take the differential of. 1670.

3. Every individual has something that differences it from another LOCKE.

†**Di·fferency.** 1607. [see -ENCY.] = DIFFERENCE *sb.* –1812.

Different (di·fĕrĕnt), *a.* (*sb., adv.*) ME. [a. F. *différent*, ad. L. *differentem*, *differre* trans. to bear asunder, etc., *intr.* to DIFFER.]

A. *adj.* 1. Having unlike attributes; not of the same kind; not alike; of other nature, form, or quality. Const. *from*, also *to, than*, †*against*, †*with*. 2. Not identical, distinct 1651. 3. *slang.* Out of the ordinary, special, *recherché* 1912.

1. Persons d. in state and condition PETTIE. Much d. from the man he was *Com. Err.* v. i. 46. Elected for very d. merits than those of skill in war GOLDSM. 2. At d. times ADDISON. Hence **Di·fferent-ly** *adv.*, **-ness** (*rare*).

B. *sb.* †1. = DIFFERENCE *sb.* 3 (*rare*) –1606. 2. That which is different (*rare*) 1581.

C. as *adv.* = *Differently.* Now vulgar.

‖**Differentia** (difĕre·nʃiă). Pl. **-iæ** (-i,ī). 1827. [L.] *Logic.* The attribute by which a species is distinguished from all other species of the same genus; a distinguishing mark.

Differe·ntiable, *a. rare.* 1863. [f. med.L. *differentiare.*] Capable of being differentiated.

Differential (difĕre·nʃăl). 1647. [ad. med. L. *differentialis*, f. *differentia*. Cf. mod.F. *différentiel.*]

A. *adj.* 1. Of or relating to difference; exhibiting or depending on a difference. 2. Constituting a specific difference; special 1652; relating to specific differences 1875. 3. *Math.* Relating to infinitesimal differences (see B. 1) 1702. 4. *Physics* and *Mech.* Relating to, depending on, or exhibiting the difference of two (or more) measurable physical qualities 1768. **b.** Applied esp. to mechanism enabling a motor car's hind wheels to revolve at different rates when turning a corner 1902.

1. D. duties in favour of colonial timber ROGERS. 2. The great D. marks of the Distemper CHEYNE. D. diagnosis 1875. Phr. 3. *D. calculus*: a method of calculation which treats of the infinitesimal differences between consecutive values of continuously varying quantities, and of their rates of change as measured by such differences. *D. equation*: an equation involving differentials. 4. *D. gear, gearing*: a combination of toothed wheels communicating a motion depending on the difference of their diameters or

of the number of their teeth. *D. pulley*: a pulley having a block with two rigidly connected wheels or sheaves of different diameters, the chain or rope unwinding from one as it winds on the other. *D. screw*: a screw having two threads of different pitch, one of which unwinds as the other winds. *D. thermometer*: a thermometer consisting of two air-bulbs connected by a bent tube partly filled with a liquid, the position of the column of liquid indicating the difference of temperature between the two bulbs. *D. winding*: the method of winding two insulated wires side by side in an electric coil, through which currents pass in opposite directions.

B. *sb.* **1.** *Math.* The infinitesimal difference between consecutive values of a continuously varying quantity; either of the two quantities (usually considered to be infinitesimal) whose ratio constitutes a differential coefficient 1704. **2.** *Biol.* A distinction or distinctive characteristic of structure: opp. to *equivalent* 1883. **3.** *Comm.* A differential charge; see A. 1 (*mod.*).

Differentially (diferĕ·nʃăli), *adv.* 1644. [f. as prec.] **1.** Distinctively, specially; see DIFFERENTIAL A. 2. **2.** In relation to the difference of two measurable quantities; in two different directions; see DIFFERENTIAL A. 4. 1862.

Differentiate (diferĕ·nʃi,eⁱt), *v.* 1816. [f. ppl. stem of med.L. *differentiare*.] **1.** To make different; to constitute the difference in or between; to distinguish 1853. **2.** *Biol.*, etc. To make different in the process of development, *esp.* for a special function or purpose; to make unlike by modification; to specialize. (Chiefly in *pass.*) 1858. Also *intr.* (for *refl.*) **3.** *trans.* To ascertain the difference in or between 1876. **4.** *Math.* To obtain the differential or the differential coefficient of 1816.

1. Genius differentiates a man from all other men DE QUINCEY. **2.** 'Protoplasm'.. which is not yet differentiated into 'organs' CARPENTER. Hence **Differe·ntiator,** he who or that which differentiates.

Differentiation (diferenʃi,ēⁱ·ʃən). 1802. [f. prec.] **1.** The action of differentiating, or condition of being differentiated (see prec. 1, 2); *spec.* in *Biol.* the process, or the result of the process, by which in the course of development a part, organ, etc. is modified into a special form, or for a special function; specialization; also the gradual production of differences between the descendants of the same ancestral types 1855. **2.** The action of ascertaining a difference (see prec. 3) 1866. **3.** *Math.* The operation of obtaining a differential or differential coefficient 1802.

1. He [the naturalist] justly considers the d. and specialisation of organs as the test of perfection DARWIN.

†Di·fferingly, *adv.* 1602. [f. DIFFER *v.*] Differently -1691.

†‖Difficile, -il (difi·sil, di·fisil), *a.* 1477. [a. late OF. *difficile*, ad. L. *difficilis*.] Difficult; hard to do -1665; hard to understand -1637; of persons, hard to persuade or satisfy -1855. Hence **Diffici·leness,** the quality of being d.

†Diffici·litate, *v. rare.* 1611. [f. L. *difficilis*.] To render difficult -1648.

Difficult (di·fikŏlt), *a.* Comp. **difficulter,** sup. **difficultest.** ME. [?f. the sb. *difficulty*, or from Old Lat. *difficul* and *difficulty*.] **1.** Not easy; requiring effort or labour; troublesome, hard, puzzling. **2.** Of persons: Not easy to get on with 1589; hard to induce or persuade; obstinate 1502.

1. How d. a thing it is, to love, and to be wise, and both at once 1608. Knowledge..is d. to gain WORDSW. Great things, and d., which thou knowest not *Jer.* xxxiii. 3. **2.** My temper is d. THACKERAY. var. **†Difficul.** Hence **Di·fficult-ly** *adv.*, **†-ness** (*rare*).

Di·fficult, *v.* Now *local.* 1608. [a. obs. F. *difficulter*, f. med.L. *difficultare*.] **†1.** *trans.* To render difficult, impede -1818. **2.** To embarrass. Usu. *pass.* (*Sc.* and *U.S.*) 1686. var. **†Di·fficultate** in sense 1 (*rare*).

Difficulty (di·fikŏlti). ME. [ad. L. *difficultatem* (f. *dif-*, DIS- + *facultas*).] **1.** The quality, fact, or condition of being difficult; the character of an action that requires labour or effort; hardness to be accomplished; the opposite of *ease* or *facility* ME. **b.** The quality of being hard to understand 1529. **2.** with *a* and *pl.* An instance of this quality; that which is difficult; often *spec.* a pecuniary embarrassment (usu. in *pl.*) ME. **3.** Reluctance; demur. *Obs.* exc. in phr. *to make a d.*; formerly *†to make d.*, *i. e.* to show reluctance 1513.

1. If aught..in the shape Of d. or danger could deterre Me MILT. *P. L.* II. 449. The d. and obscurity of the phrase FARRAR. **2.** They mistake difficulties for impossibilities SOUTH. Difficulties in revelation J. H. NEWMAN. Mr. Brunton..is in 'difficulties' (civilized plural for debt) FR. A. KEMBLE.

Diffidation (difidēⁱ·ʃən). 1731. [ad. med.L. *diffidationem*, f. *diffidare*; see DEFY *v.*[1]] The undoing of relations of faith, allegiance, or amity; declaration of hostilities; DEFIANCE.

They sent a..letter of d., in which they renounced their allegiance COXE.

Diffide (difəi·d), *v.* Now *rare.* 1532. [f. L. *diffidere* to distrust.] *intr.* To have or feel distrust. (The opposite of *confide*.) Also *†trans.*

Diffidence (di·fidĕns). 1526. [ad. L. *diffidentia*; see prec.] (The opposite of CONFIDENCE.) **1.** Want of confidence; mistrust, distrust, doubt. Now *rare.* **2.** Distrust of oneself; want of confidence in one's own ability, worth, or fitness; modesty, shyness 1709.

1. A d... of his judgment or his virtue JAS. MILL. **2.** Speak, tho' sure, with seeming d. POPE. var. **†Di·ffidency.**

Diffident (di·fidĕnt), *a.* 1598. [ad. L. *diffidentem*; see DIFFIDE.] (The opposite of CONFIDENT.) **1.** Wanting confidence (*in*); distrustful, mistrustful (*of*). **2.** Wanting in self-confidence; distrustful of oneself; timid, shy, modest, bashful. (The usual current sense.) 1713.

1. In the constancie of his people he was somewhat d. RALEIGH. **2.** He [Dr. Johnson] never..meant to terrify the d. MAD. D'ARBLAY. Hence **Di·ffident-ly** *adv.*, **†-ness** (*rare*).

†Diffla·tion. 1568. [f. L. *difflare*, *difflat-*.] Blowing asunder or dispersion by blowing -1763.

Diffluence (di·fluĕns). 1633. [f. DIFFLUENT; see -ENCE.] **1.** The flowing apart or abroad; dispersion by flowing. Also *fig.* **2.** Dissolution into a liquid state 1847. So **†Di·ffluency,** diffluent condition.

Diffluent (di·fluĕnt), *a.* 1618. [ad. L. *diffluentem*, *diffluere*.] Characterized by flowing apart or abroad; fluid; deliquescent. Also *fig.*

†Difform (difǭ·ɹm), *a.* 1547. [ad. med.L. *difformis*.] **1.** Of diverse forms; differing in shape -1677. **2.** Without symmetry; not uniform; of irregular form -1845.

1. A confused Mixture of d. qualities NEWTON. **2.** If the Parts be dissimilar, then the Substance is d. 1707.

†Difformity (difǭ·ɹmĭti). 1530. [a. F. *difformité*; see prec.] **1.** Want of uniformity between things -1857. **2.** Want of conformity *with* or *to* -1677.

Diffra·ct, *a.* 1883. [ad. L. *diffractus*.] *Bot.* Of lichens: 'Broken into *areolæ* with distinct interspaces'.

Diffract (difræ·kt), *v.* 1803. [f. L. *diffract-*, *diffringere*.] *trans.* To break in pieces, break up; in *Optics*, To deflect and break up (a beam of light) at the edge of an opaque body or through a narrow aperture. Also *fig.*

Diffraction (difræ·kʃən). 1671. [ad. mod.L. *diffractionem*; see prec.] *Optics.* The breaking up of a beam of light into a series of light and dark spaces or bands, or of coloured spectra, due to interference of the rays when deflected at the edge of an opaque body or through a narrow aperture. **b.** *Acoustics.* An analogous phenomenon occurring in the case of sound-waves passing round the corner of a large body.

D. grating, a plate of glass or polished metal ruled with very close equidistant parallel lines, producing a spectrum by diffraction of the transmitted or reflected light.

Diffractive (difræ·ktiv), *a.* 1829. [f. as DIFFRACT *v.* + -IVE.] Tending to diffract. Hence **Diffra·ctively** *adv.*

Diffranchise, error for DISF- in J.

Diffu·gient, *ppl. a.* [ad. L. *diffugientem*.] Dispersing. THACKERAY.

Diffusate (difiū·zeⁱt). 1850. [f. DIFFUSE *v.* + -ATE[4].] *Chem.* The crystalloid portion of a mixture which passes through the membrane in the process of chemical dialysis.

Diffuse (difiū·s), *a.* ME. [ad. L. *diffusus*, *diffundere*; cf. F. *diffus, -use*.] **†1.** Confused; vague, doubtful -1602. **2.** Spread out in space; widespread, dispersed. Also *†fig.* 1643. **3.** Of a style: Using many words to convey the sense; verbose: opp. to *concise* or *condensed* 1742.

1. A mater to me doubtfull and d. 1560. **2.** D. typography JOHNSON, inflammation 1874. **3.** Too strong and concise, not d. enough for a woman JANE AUSTEN. Hence **Diffu·se-ly** *adv.*, **-ness.**

Diffuse (difiū·z), *v.* 1526. [f. L. *diffus-*, ppl. stem of *diffundere*.] **†1.** To pour out as a fluid with wide dispersion; to shed -1734. **2.** To pour or send forth as from a centre of dispersion; to spread widely, shed abroad, disperse, disseminate 1526; *fig.* to dissipate 1608. **3.** To extend or spread out (the body, etc.) freely (*arch.* and *poet.*) 1671. **4.** *intr.* (for *refl.*) To be or become diffused, to spread abroad (*lit.* and *fig.*) 1653. **5.** *Physics.* To intermingle, or (*trans.*) cause to intermingle, by diffusion 1808. **†6.** To distract. *Lear* I. iv. 2.

1. *Temp.* IV. i. 79. **2.** D. thy riches among thy friends JOHNSON. To d. geniality around one MASSON. **3.** See how he lies at random, carelessly diffused MILT. *Sams.* 118. Hence **Diffu·sed** (-zd, *poet.* -ĕd) *ppl. a.* **Diffu·sed-ly** *adv.*, **-ness.** **Diffu·ser,** one who or that which diffuses.

Diffusible (difiū·zĭb'l), *a.* Also **-able.** 1782. [f. as prec. + -IBLE.] Capable of being diffused. Hence **Diffusibi·lity,** capacity of being diffused; *esp.* in *Physics*, as a measurable quality of gases and fluids. So **Diffu·sibleness.**

Diffusio·meter. 1866. [f. L. *diffusio* + -METER.] An apparatus for measuring the rate of diffusion of gases. var. **Diffusi·meter.**

Diffusion (difiū·ʒən). ME. [ad. L. *diffusionem*, f. *diffundere*.] **1.** The action of diffusing; the condition of being diffused; a spreading; dispersion; wide distribution. **2.** *fig.* Spreading abroad, dispersion, dissemination (of abstract things) 1750. **3.** Of writing, etc.: Diffuseness; copiousness of language ME. **4.** *Physics.* The spontaneous molecular interpenetration of two fluids without chemical combination 1808. Also *attrib.*

2. The universal d. of learning among a people HUME. **3.** His d., and affluence of conversation BOSWELL.

Diffusive (difiū·siv), *a.* 1614. [f. as DIFFUSE *v.* + -IVE.] **1.** Having the quality of diffusing, or of being diffused; characterized by diffusion (*lit.* and *fig.*). **†2.** Of a body of people: As consisting of members in their individual capacity. (Common in 17th c.) -1718. **3.** = DIFFUSE *a.* 3. (Occas. in good sense: Copious, full.) 1699.

1. D. of knowledge MILT. Leaven hath..a d. faculty BP. HALL. The strength of some d. thought TENNYSON. **3.** He is less d. and more pointed than usual L. STEPHEN. Hence **Diffu·sive-ly** *adv.*, **-ness.** **Diffusi·vity** = DIFFUSIBILITY.

Dig (dig), *v.* Pa. t. and pple. **dug** (dɒg), formerly **digged** (digd). ME. [Of uncertain origin; prob. ult. a deriv. of OE. *dic* DITCH (cf. *dīcian* to dig, make an embankment). The date of F. *digue* dike, *diguer* to dike, is not appropriate.]

I. *intr.* **1.** 'To work in making holes or turning the ground' (J.); to make an excavation; to work with a spade or similar tool. Also *transf.* and *fig.* **b.** *spec.* To study hard and closely at a subject (*U.S.*) 1789. **2.** To make one's way *into* or *through* by digging; to make an excavation *under* 1535.

1. Digge about þe vyne rotis WYCLIF. They [ants] dug deeper and deeper to deposite their eggs GOLDSM.

II. *trans.* **1.** To penetrate and turn up (the ground, etc.) with a spade or similar tool ME. Also *transf.* **2.** *spec.* To break up and turn over (the soil) with a mattock, spade, or the like, as an operation of tillage ME. **3.** To make (a hole, mine, etc.) by the use of a spade or the like; to form by digging; to excavate ME. **4.** To obtain or extract by excavation. Const *from*, *out of*. ME. **†5.** To put and cover up (in the ground, etc.) by digging; to bury -1647. **6.** To thrust or force *in* or *into* 1553. **7.** To spur vigorously; to thrust, stab, prod 1530.

1. Sone of man, d. the wal WYCLIF *Ezek.* viii. 8. **2.** It [a vineyard] shall not be pruned nor digged; but there shall come up briers and thorns *Isa.* v. 6. **3.** Digge my graue thy selfe 2 *Hen. IV*, IV. v. 111. **4.** I with my long nayles will digge thee pig-nuts *Temp.* II. ii. 172.

In comb. with adverbs. **D. down. a.** To cause to fall by digging. **b.** To lower or remove by digging. **D. in. a.** To put in and cover up by digging. **b.** To drive in deeply. **c.** Also *fig.* To establish oneself in a position. **D. out. a.** To extract or remove by digging. **b.** To excavate. **c.** *intr.* To depart (*U.S.*

colloq.). **D. up. a.** To take or get out of the ground, etc., by digging. **b.** To break up or open by digging. **c.** To break up and open the soil of, by digging.

Dig, *sb.* 1674. [f. prec. vb.] **1.** An act of digging 1887. **2.** A definite quantity to be dug out 1890. **3.** A tool for digging 1674. **4.** A thrust, a sharp poke, as with the elbow, fist, etc. 1819. Also *fig.* **5.** A diligent or plodding student (*U.S. slang*) 1849. **6.** = DIGGING 4. 1893.

Digallic (dəigæ·lik), *a.* 1877. [DI-[2].] *Chem.* In *D. acid*, which contains two molecules of gallic acid, minus one equivalent of water.

Digamist (di·gămist). 1656. [f. as DIGAMY + -IST.] A man or woman who has married a second time.

Digamma (dəigæ·mă). 1698. [a. L., Gr. δίγαμμα, f. δι- twice + γάμμα: so called from its shape Ϝ, resembling two gammas (Γ) set one above the other.] The sixth letter of the original Greek alphabet, corresponding to the Semitic *waw* or *vau*, which was afterwards disused. It was a consonant, probably equivalent to English *w*. So **Diga·mmate** *a.*, **-ated** *ppl. a.* having the d.; formed with a figure like the d.

Digamous (di·găməs), *a.* 1864. [f. L. *digamus*, a. Gr. δίγαμος + -OUS.] **1.** Married a second time; of the nature of digamy. **2.** *Bot.* = ANDROGYNOUS 1883.

Digamy (di·gămi). 1635. [ad. L. *digamia*, a. Gr.] **1.** Digamous condition or state; second marriage. †**2.** = BIGAMY 1. –1766.

Digastric (dəigæ·strik), *a.* and *sb.* 1696. [ad. mod.L. *digastricus* (also used), f. Gr. δι- + γαστήρ.] *Anat.*

A. *adj.* **1.** Having two parts swelling like bellies; *spec.* applied to muscles having two fleshy bellies with a tendon between 1721. **2.** Of or pertaining to the digastric muscle of the lower jaw; see B. 1831.

B. *sb.* A muscle of the lower jaw, fleshy at its extremities, and tendinous at its middle 1696.

Digeneous (dəi,dʒī·niəs), *a.* 1883. [f. Gr. διγενής + -OUS.] **1.** Bisexual. **2.** Of or pertaining to the *Digenea*, a division of the trematode worms or flukes.

Digenesis (dəi,dʒe·nĕsis). 1876. [mod.L., f. Gr. δι- + γένεσις.] *Biol.* Successive generation by two different processes, as sexual and asexual. So **Digene·tic** *a.* relating to or characterized by d.

Digenite (di·dʒĭnəit). 1850. [mod. f. Gr. διγενής of doubtful kind.] *Min.* A variety of CHALCOCITE or copper-glance.

Digenous (di·dʒĭnəs), *a.* 1884. [irreg. f. Gr. δι- + γένος + -OUS.] Of two sexes, bisexual. Hence **Di·geny**, sexual reproduction.

†**Di·gerent.** *rare.* 1477. [ad. L. *digerentem.*]

A. *adj.* Digesting –1755.

B. *sb.* A medicine which promotes digestion or suppuration –1867.

Digest (dəi·dʒest), *sb.* ME. [ad. L. *digesta* 'matters digested'; n. pl. of *digestus*; see DIGEST *v.*] **1.** A digested collection of statements; a methodically arranged compendium or summary of written matter 1555. **2.** *Law.* An abstract of some body of law, systematically arranged 1626; *spec.* the body of Roman laws compiled from the earlier jurists by order of Justinian ME. †**3.** = DIGESTION –1602.

1. His [Milton's] d. of scriptural texts MACAULAY. 2. The Digests of the Jewish Law 1652.

Digest (di,dʒe·st, dəi-), *v.* 1450. [f. L. *digest-*, ppl. stem of *digerere*, f. *di-* = *dis-* (DI-[1]) apart + *gerere* to carry.] †**1.** *trans.* To divide and dispose –1675; to disperse –1727. **2.** To dispose methodically; to reduce into a systematic form, usually with condensation; to classify 1482. **3.** To settle and arrange methodically in the mind; to think over 1450. **4.** To prepare (food) in the stomach and intestines for assimilation by the system; see DIGESTION 1. 1483. Also *absol.* **b.** *intr.* (for *refl.*) To undergo digestion, as food 1574. **c.** *trans.* To cause or promote the digestion of 1607. **5.** *fig.* and *transf.* (from 4) 1576. **6.** To bear without resistance; to 'swallow, stomach' 1553; to get over the effects of (*arch.*) 1576. **7.** To obtain mental nourishment from 1548. †**8.** To mature, *esp.* by the action of heat. Also *fig.* –1708. †**9.** *trans.* To cause to suppurate; also *absol.* to promote suppuration –1767. Also †*intr.* (for *refl.*) **10.** *trans.* To prepare by boiling; to dissolve by the aid of heat and moisture 1616. Also *intr.* (for *refl.*).

2. The Civil Law is digested into general Heads HALE. 3. To d. a plan for keeping accounts SMEATON. 4. *absol.* Each has to..d. for himself CLOUGH. 5. Most of them [leaves] were not able to d. the third fly DARWIN. The Hapsburgs .. have not digested Bosnia completely yet 1889. 6. To d. a wanton attack W. IRVING, a loss COLERIDGE. 7. Read, marke, learne, and inwardly digeste them *Bk. Com. Prayer.* 10. D. the bark in alcohol 1838. Hence †**Dige·st, Dige·sted** *ppl. adjs.* **Dige·stedly** *adv.*

Digester (didʒe·stəɹ, dəi-). Also **-or.** 1578. [f. prec. vb.] He who or that which digests; *esp.* a strong close vessel in which bones or other substances are dissolved by the action of heat.

Digestible (didʒe·stĭb'l, dəi-), *a.* Also **-able.** ME. [a. F., ad. L. *digestibilis.*] Capable of being digested. Hence **Dige·stibleness. Dige·stibly** *adv.*

Digestion (didʒe·styən, dəi-). ME. [a. F., ad. L. *digestionem.*] **1.** The process whereby the nutritive part of food is, in the stomach and intestines, rendered fit to be assimilated by the system. Also *transf.* and *fig.* **2.** The power or faculty of digesting food ME. **3.** *fig.* The action of digesting; see DIGEST *v.* 1610. **4.** *Chem.* †**a.** The operation of maturing by the action of gentle heat –1677. **b.** The operation of dissolving a substance by the action of heat and moisture 1610. †**5.** *Surg.* The process of maturing an ulcer, etc.; disposition to healthy suppuration –1830. †**6.** The action of methodizing and reducing to order; the result of this; a DIGEST –1754.

1. Things sweet to tast, proue in d. sowre *Rich. II*, I. iii. 236. *transf.* Whether they [Drosera]..have the power of d. DARWIN. *fig.* I devoured them [books] with appetite, if not d. W. IRVING. D. of a wrong STERNE. 2. Our digestion would be better, if our dishes were fewer NASHE.

Digestive (didʒe·stiv, dəi-). ME. [a. F. *digestif, -ive*, ad. L. *digestivus.*]

A. *adj.* **1.** Having the function of digesting; engaged in or pertaining to digestion 1532. **2.** Promoting digestion; digestible 1528. **3.** Promoting suppuration.

1. The d. powers 1725, organs 1837, cavity 1841. 2. D. cheese, and fruit there sure will be B. JONS. Applying only a d. warmth DE CRELL.

B. *sb.* **1.** Anything promoting digestion of food ME. **2.** A substance which promotes suppuration in a wound, etc.; digestive ointment 1543.

Hence **Dige·stive-ly** *adv.*, **-ness.**

†**Dige·story.** 1612. [ad. L. *digestorius*, f. *digest-*, *digerere.*]

A. *adj.* = DIGESTIVE.

B. *sb.* A vessel or organ of digestion –1774.

†**Dige·sture.** 1565. [f. L. *digest-*; see prec.] = DIGESTION 1, 2. –1700.

Di·ggable, *a.* 1552. [f. DIG *v.* + -ABLE.] That can be digged.

Digger (di·gəɹ). ME. [f. DIG *v.* + -ER.] **1.** One who or that which digs. **2.** *spec.* A miner; *esp.* one who searches for gold 1531. **b.** One of a tribe of N. American Indians who live chiefly on roots 1837. **c.** *Eng. Hist.* A section of the Levellers in 1649, who began to dig and plant the commons 1649. **3.** An instrument for digging; the digging part of a machine 1686. **4.** A division of Hymenopterous insects, also called *Digger-wasps* 1847.

Comb. **d.-wasp** (see sense 4).

Digging (di·giŋ), *vbl. sb.* 1538. [f. DIG *v.* + -ING[1].] **1.** The action of DIG *v.*, in various senses; an instance of this 1552. **2.** *concr.* The materials dug out 1559. **3.** A place where digging is carried on; in *pl.* (occas. taken as *sing.*) applied to mines, and especially to gold-fields 1538. **4.** *colloq.* in *pl.* Lodgings, quarters 1838.

3. *Wet-diggings* and *Dry-diggings* are terms in gold districts, for mines near rivers or on the higher lands as the case may be FARMER *Americanisms.*

Dight (dəit), *v.* Now *arch.* and *dial.* [OE. *dihtan*, ad. L. *dictare*; see DICTATE *v.*] †**1.** *trans.* To dictate OE.; to ordain –1558; to order –1522; to deal with, treat –1650; *spec.* to have to do with sexually –ME.; to dispose of –1535. †**2.** To compose –1607; to do –1596. **3.** †To put in order –1500; to equip ME.; to dress, array ME.; to make ready, or proper (revived in poet. and romantic use) ME.

1. 'Who checks at me, to death is d.' SCOTT. 3. The hall..With rich array and costly arras d. SPENSER *F. Q.* I. iv. 6. Orion, in golden panoply d. BOWEN. To d. him for earth or for heaven 1821. Hence **Di·ghter** (now *dial.*), one who or that which dights.

Digit (di·dʒit), *sb.* ME. [ad. L. *digitus.*] **1.** One of the terminal divisions of the hand or foot; a finger or toe 1644. **2.** A finger's breadth, three-quarters of an inch 1633. **3.** *Arith.* Each of the numerals below ten (originally counted on the fingers); any of the nine, or (including the cipher, 0) ten Arabic figures ME. **4.** *Astron.* The twelfth part of the diameter of the sun or moon; used in expressing the magnitude of an eclipse 1591.

1. We find among reptiles, all the combinations of digits, from five to one, taken between two pairs of hands or claws 1802. 4. Ye Sun..was darkned 10 digits ½ HEARNE. Hence †**Di·git** *v.* to point out with the finger.

Digital (di·dʒităl). ME. [ad. L. *digitalis*, f. *digitus* DIGIT.]

A. *adj.* **1.** Of or pertaining to a finger, or to the fingers or digits 1656. **2.** Resembling a finger or the impression made by one 1831. **3.** Having digits 1833.

2. The D. Cavity R. KNOX. 3. The d. feet 1887.

B. *sb.* †**1.** = DIGIT *sb.* 3. ME. only. **2.** A finger (*joc.*) 1840. **3.** A key played with the finger in a piano or organ 1878.

Digitalic (didʒitæ·lik), *a.* 1858. [f. DIGITALIS + -IC.] Of or pertaining to digitalis; in *d. acid*, an acid obtained from the foxglove, crystallizing in white acicular prisms.

Digitaliform (-tæ·lifǫɹm), *a.* 1859. [f. L. *digitalis* + -FORM.] *Bot.* Of the form of the corolla of the foxglove.

Digitalin (di·dʒitălin). 1837. [f. DIGITALIS + -IN.] *Chem.* The substance or substances extracted from the leaves of the foxglove, as its active principle. (Originally named *digitalia*, *digitaline.*)

‖**Digitalis** (didʒitē·lis). 1664. [mod.L., f. L. *digitalis*; so named in allusion to the German name *Fingerhut*, i.e. thimble.] **1.** *Bot.* A genus of plants of the N.O. *Scrophulariaceæ*, including the foxglove (*D. purpurea*). **2.** A medicine prepared from the foxglove 1799.

Digitally (di·dʒităli), *adv.* 1832. [f. DIGITAL *a.*] By means of or with respect to the fingers.

Digitate (di·dʒitĕt), *a.* 1661. [ad. L. *digitatus.*] **1.** *Zool.* Having divided digits or toes. **2.** Divided into parts resembling fingers; *spec.* in *Bot.* of leaves, etc.: Having deep radiating divisions, as the compound leaves of the horse-chestnut 1788. Hence **Di·gitately** *adv.* So **Di·gitated** *a.* (in same senses).

Digitate (di·dʒiteit), *v.* 1658. [f. L. *digitus* + -ATE[3].] †**1.** *trans.* To point out with or as with the finger (*rare*). **2.** *intr.* To become divided into finger-like parts 1796.

Digitation (didʒitē·ʃən). 1658. [f. DIGITATE *v.* or *a.*; see -ATION.] †**1.** A touching, or pointing, with the finger –1800. **2.** Division into fingers or finger-like processes; *concr.* one of these processes 1709.

Digiti- (di·dʒiti), comb. f. L. *digitus* (see DIGIT *sb.*).

Di·gitiform *a.* digitate. **Di:gitine·rvate, -ne·rved, -ne·rvous** *adjs.*, *Bot.* having the ribs of the leaf radiating from the top of the leaf-stalk. **Di:gitipa·rtite** *a.* having more than five lobes of a similar character.

Digitigrade (di·dʒitigrē:d). 1833. [a. F., f. L. *digitus* + *-gradus.*]

A. *adj.* Walking on the toes; *spec.* in *Zool.* belonging to the tribe *Digitigrada* of Carnivora. (Opp. to PLANTIGRADE.)

B. *sb.* A digitigrade animal. (Chiefly in *pl.*) 1835. Hence **Di·gitigra:dism**, d. condition.

Digitize (di·dʒitəiz), *v. rare.* 1704. [f. DIGIT.] To treat in some way with the fingers; to finger; as, *to d. a pen.*

Digito-, shortened from *digitalis*, as in *digito·lein*, a fat obtained from digitalis leaves; etc.

†**Digla·diate,** *v.* 1656. [ad. L. *digladiari*, f. *di-*, *dis-* + *gladius.*] *intr.* To cross swords;

to contend. Hence **Digladia·tion** (now *rare*), fighting with swords (*lit.* and *fig.*).

Diglot, Diglott (dəi·glǫt), *a.* 1863. [ad. Gr. δίγλωττος, f. δι-, δισ- + γλῶττα, Attic for γλῶσσα.] Using or expressed in two languages, bilingual; also as *sb.* A diglot book or version. So **Di·glottism,** the use of words derived from two languages.

Diglyph (dəi·glif). 1727. [f. Gr. δι- + γλύφειν; cf. F. *diglyphe.*] *Archit.* A projecting face or tablet with two vertical grooves or channels.

†**Dignation** (dignēⁱ·ʃən). 1450. [ad. (ult.) L. *dignationem*, f. *dignare, -ari.*] The action of deeming worthy; honour conferred –1737.

†**Digne,** *a.* ME. [a. F. *digne*, early ad. L. *dignus.*] 1. Of high worth or desert; honourable –1578. 2. Worthy, deserving. Const. *of* (*to*), or *inf.* –1643. 3. Becoming, fit. Const. *to, unto, of, for.* –1549. 4. Haughty, disdainful (in ME. only). Hence †**Di·gnely** *adv.*

Dignification (di:gnifikēⁱ·ʃən). Now *rare.* 1577. [ad. med.L. *dignificationem.*] The action of dignifying, or fact of being dignified.

Dignified (di·gnifəid), *ppl. a.* 1667. [f. DIGNIFY.] 1. Invested with dignity; exalted 1763. †2. Ranking as a dignitary (*esp.* ecclesiastical) –1860. 3. Marked by dignity; stately, noble, majestic 1812. Hence **Di·gnifiedly** *adv.*

Dignify (di·gnifəi), *v.* 1526. [a. OF. *dignifier*, ad. med.L. *dignificare*, f. *dignus* + *-ficare.*] 1. *trans.* To make worthy or illustrious; to confer dignity or honour upon; to ennoble, honour. b. In lighter use: To give a high-sounding name or title to 1750. †2. To confer a title of honour upon –1727.

1. Such a Day..Came not, till now, to dignifie the Times 2 *Hen. IV*, I. i. 22. To d. letters with the title of Walpoliana H. WALPOLE. Hence **Di·gnifier.**

Dignitary (di·gnitări). 1672. [f. L. *dignitas* + -ARY: so F. *dignitaire* sb.]

A. *sb.* One holding high rank or office, *esp.* ecclesiastical.

B. *adj.* Of, belonging to, or invested with a dignity (*esp.* ecclesiastical).

Dignity (di·gnĭti). ME. [a. OF. *digneté*, F. *dignité*, ad. L. *dignitatem*. Cf. also DAINTY.] 1. The quality of being worthy or honourable; worth, excellence; †desert. 2. Honourable or high estate, position, or estimation; honour; rank ME. Also *fig.* b. *collect.* Persons of high estate or rank 1548. 3. An honourable office, rank, or title; *transf.* a dignitary ME. 4. Nobility of aspect, manner, or style; becoming stateliness, gravity 1667. 5. *Astrol.* A situation of a planet in which its influence is heightened ME. ¶ 6. [Fantastic rendering of Gr. ἀξίωμα.] An axiom. SIR T. BROWNE.

1. It is of the essence of real d. to be self-sustained SIR H. TAYLOR. 2. Gyuyng somewhat to the dygnyte of presthode STARKEY. *collect.* I cannot see the d. of a great kingdom..imprisoned or exiled, without great pain BURKE. 3. *transf.* These filthy dreamers .. speake euill of dignities *Jude* 8. 4. In every gesture dignitie and love MILT. *P. L.* VIII. 489.

†**Digno·sce,** *v.* 1639. [ad. L. *dignoscere.*] To distinguish, discern (*trans.* and *intr.*) –1676.

†**Digno·tion.** 1578. [f. L. *dignot-, dignoscere.*] The action of distinguishing or discerning; a distinguishing sign –1658.

Digoneutic (dəigoniū·tik), *a.* 1889. [f. Gr. δι- + γονεύειν.] *Entom.* Producing two broods in a year. Hence **Digoneu·tism,** d. condition.

Digonous (di·gənəs, dəi-), *a.* 1788. [f. Gr. δι- + -γωνος angled.] *Bot.* Having two angles.

Di·gram. 1864. Proposed synonym of DIGRAPH. Webster.

Digraph (dəi·graf). 1788. [f. Gr. δι- + γραφή.] A group of two letters expressing a simple sound, as *ea* in *head*, etc. Hence **Digra·phic** *a.*

Digress (digre·s, dəi-), *v.* 1530. [f. L. *digress-*, ppl. stem of *digredi*, f. *di-*, DIS- 1 + *gradi.*] 1. *intr.* To go aside from the track; to diverge, deviate, swerve 1552. Also †*fig.* †2. To diverge from the right path; to transgress –1640. 3. To deviate from the subject in discourse or writing. (Now the prevailing sense.) 1530.

1. I find myself in Bond Street .. I d. into Soho, to explore a bookstall LAMB. *fig.* Digresse good sir from such lewd songs 1603. 2. So man .. digressed and fell 1640. 3. I have too long digressed, and therefore shall return to my subject SWIFT. Hence †**Digress** *sb.* = DIGRESSION 2. **Digre·sser.**

Digression (digre·ʃən, dəi-). ME. [ad. (ult.) L. *digressionem*; see DIGRESS *v.*] 1. The action of digressing (*lit.* and †*fig.*). (Now *rare* in *lit.* sense.) 1552. 2. Deviation from the subject in discourse or writing; an instance of this. (The most frequent sense.) ME. 3. *Astron.*, etc. Deviation from a particular line, or from the mean position; deflexion; *e.g.* of an inferior planet from the sun 1646.

1. Then my d. is so vile, so base, That it will liue engrauen in my face SHAKS. 2. It were a long digression Fro my matere CHAUCER. Hence **Digre·ssional** *a.* of, pertaining to, or characterized by d.

Digressive (digre·siv, dəi-), *a.* 1611. [ad. L. *digressivus*; see DIGRESS *v.*] Characterized by, or given to, digression; of the nature of digression. Hence **Digre·ssive-ly** *adv.*, **-ness.**

‖**Digue.** 1523. [F., a. Flem. *dijk.*] = DIKE.

‖**Digynia** (dəidʒi·niă). 1762. [mod.L. (Linnæus) f. Gr. δι- + γυνή + -ia.] *Bot.* The second Order in many classes of the Linnæan Sexual System, comprising plants having two pistils. Hence **Digy·nian, Digy·nious** *adjs.* belonging to the order *D.*; **Di·gynous** *a.* having two pistils.

Dihedral (dəihī·drăl), *a.* 1799. [f. next + -AL.] 1. *Cryst.* Having or contained by two planes or plane faces. 2. *Math.* Of the nature of a dihedron 1893.

1. *D. angle*, the inclination of two planes which meet at an edge; also, the angle formed by any two meeting or intersecting planes or plane faces, *spec.* the angle formed by the wing pairs of an aeroplane. Also as *sb.* = d. angle.

Dihedron (dəihī·drǫn). 1888. [f. Gr. δι-, δισ- + ἕδρα seat, base.] *Math.* The portion of two superposed planes bounded by (or contained within) a regular polygon.

‖**Dihe·lios.** Also **dihelium.** 1727. [mod.L., f. Gr. δι- = διά + ἥλιος.] *Astr.* Kepler's name for that ordinate of the ellipsis, which passes through the focus, wherein the sun is supposed to be placed. CHAMBERS.

Dihexagonal (dəi:heksæ·gŏnăl), *a.* 1864. [DI-².] *Cryst.* Having twelve angles, of which the first, third, fifth, . . eleventh, are equal to one another, and the second, fourth, sixth, . . twelfth, are equal to one another, but those of the one set not equal to those of the other.

Di-hexahe·dron. 1888. [DI-².] *Cryst.* A six-sided prism with trihedral summits, making twelve faces in all. Also occas., a double hexagonal pyramid. So †**Di-hexahedral** *a.* having twice six faces.

Dihydrite (dəihəi·drəit). 1868. [f. Gr. δι-, DI-² + ὕδωρ, ὑδρ- + -ITE.] *Min.* A variety of pseudo-malachite or native phosphate of copper, containing two equivalents of water.

Diiamb (dəi,əiæ·mb). 1753. [ad. L. *diiambus* (also used), Gr. διίαμβος, f. δι-, DI-² + ἴαμβος.] *Pros.* A metrical foot consisting of two iambs (◡–◡–).

Di-iodide (dəi,əi·ŏdəid). 1873. [DI-².] *Chem.* A compound of two atoms of iodine with a dyad element or radical.

†**Diju·dicant.** *rare.* 1661. [ad. L. *dijudicantem*; see next.] One who dijudicates –1691.

Dijudicate (dəi,dʒū·dikeⁱt), *v.* Now *rare.* 1607. [f. ppl. stem of L. *dijudicare*, f. *di-* (DI-¹) + *judicare.*] To judge; to determine, decide; *trans.* to judge of; to pronounce judgement on, decide. Hence **Dijudica·tion** (now *rare*).

‖**Dika** (dəi·kă). 1859. [W. African name.] In *d.-bread*, a cocoa-like substance, prepared from the fruit of a species of mango-tree. *D.-fat, -oil*, the fatty substance of d.-bread.

Di·k-dik. 1895. A small African antelope.

Dike, dyke (dəik), *sb.* [OE. *dīc* masc. and fem., ditch, trench, with Teut. cognates. Cf. DITCH.] 1. †A DITCH –1575; a hollow dug out to hold or conduct water OE. 2. Hence, any water-course or channel 1616. †3. Any hollow dug in the ground; a pit, cave, etc. –1475. 4. An embankment 1487; a wall or fence ME. Also *fig.* 5. An embankment to prevent inundations 1635; a raised causeway 1480. Also *fig.* 6. (*Northumb.*) A fissure in a stratum, filled up with deposited or intrusive rock 1789. Hence, in *Geol.* A mass of mineral matter, usually igneous rock, filling up a fissure in the original strata 1802.

2. Whole sheets descend of sluicy Rain, The Dykes are fill'd DRYDEN. 5. The land here is lower than the waters; for which reason they have the strongest dams or dykes in the whole country 1756. *fig.* The last dike of the prerogative JUNIUS.

Dike, dyke, *v.* [OE. had *dīcian*; but the ME. vb. is prob. a new formation.] 1. *intr.* To make a dike; to dig ME. 2. *trans.* To provide with a dike or dikes, in various senses ME. 3. To place (flax or hemp) in a dike or water-course to steep 1799.

1. He wolde .. dyke and delue .. for euery poure wight CHAUCER. Hence **Di·ker, dy·ker,** one who constructs or works at dikes; *Sc.* one who builds enclosure walls (without mortar).

Di·ke-grave. 1563. [a. MDu. *dijcgrave*, f. *dijk* dike + *graaf* earl.] In Holland, an officer who has charge of the dikes or sea-walls; in England (*esp.* Lincolnshire) = DIKE-REEVE. Now only *dial.*

Di·ke-reeve, dyke-. 1665. [f. DIKE *sb.* + REEVE: perh. an alteration of prec.] An officer who has charge under the Court of Sewers of the drains, sluices, and sea-banks of a district of fen or marsh-land in England.

†**Dila·cerate,** *ppl. a.* 1602. [ad. L. *dilaceratus*; see next.] Rent asunder, torn –1649.

Dilacerate (di-, dəilæ·sĕreⁱt), *v.* 1604. [f. ppl. stem of L. *dilacerare* (f. *di-, dis-* + *lacerare*).] *trans.* To tear asunder, tear in pieces. Also *fig.* Hence **Dila:cera·tion,** the action of dilacerating; the being dilacerated.

Dila·ctic, *a.* 1863. *Chem.* See DI-² and *lactic.*

Dilambdodont (dəilæ·mdǫdǫnt), *a.* [f. Gr. δι-, DI-² + λάμβδα + ὀδοντ-.] *Zool.* Having oblong molar teeth with two Λ- or V-shaped ridges.

Dilamination (dəilæminēⁱ·ʃən). 1849. [f. L. *dilaminare*, f. *di-, dis-* + *lamina.*] *Bot.* Separation into laminæ, or splitting off of a lamina.

†**Dila·niate,** *v.* 1535. [f. L. *dilaniat-, dilaniare.*] To rend or tear in pieces –1653. Hence †**Dilania·tion.**

Dila·pidate, *ppl. a.* *Obs.* or *arch.* 1590. [ad. L. *dilapidatus*; see next.] = DILAPIDATED.

Dilapidate (dilæ·pideⁱt), *v.* Also **de-.** 1570. [ad. L. *dilapidare*, f. *di-, dis-* asunder + *lapidare* to throw stones.] 1. *trans.* To bring (a building) into a state of decay or of partial ruin. Also *fig.* 2. *fig.* To waste, squander (a benefice or estate) 1590. 3. *intr.* To become dilapidated; to fall into ruin, decay, or disrepair 1712.

1. Dilapidated .., to obtain stones to build a house 1706. 2. Those who by overbuilding their houses have dilapidated their lands FULLER. 3. The church of Elgin .. was .. suffered to d. JOHNSON. Hence **Dila·pidated** *ppl. a.* fallen into ruin or disrepair; ruined, broken down (*lit.* and *fig.*). **Dila·pidator.**

Dilapidation (dilæ:pidēⁱ·ʃən). Also **de-.** ME. [ad. L. *dilapidationem*; see prec.] 1. The action of dilapidating; the condition of being in ruins or in disrepair (*lit.* and *fig.*) 1460. 2. *Law.* The action of pulling down, allowing to decay, or in any way impairing ecclesiastical property belonging to an incumbency ME.; also, *loosely*, the sums charged to make good such damage incurred during an incumbency 1553. 3. The falling of stones or masses of rock from mountains or cliffs by natural agency 1794; *concr.* debris 1816.

1. The d. of the national resources MALTHUS, of buildings 1886. The wretched delapidation of the Holy Sepulchre MRS. HARVEY. 2. She hath heard widowes complain of dilapidations OVERBURY.

Dilatable (dəilēⁱ·tăb'l, di-), *a.* 1610. [f. DILATE *v.* + -ABLE.] Capable of being dilated; expansible. Hence **Dila:tabi·lity, Dila·tableness,** capacity of being dilated.

Dilatancy (dəilēⁱ·tănsi, di-). 1885. [f. next.] The property of dilating or expanding; *spec.* that of expanding in bulk with change of shape, exhibited by granular masses.

Dilatant (dəilēⁱ·tănt, di-). 1841. [ad. L. *dilatantem*, pr. pple. of *dilatare* to DILATE.]

A. *adj.* Dilating; expansive.

B. *sb.* a. A substance having the property of dilating. b. A surgical instrument used for dilating.

Dilatate (dəi·lē̆t), *ppl. a.* 1846. [ad. L. *dilatatus.*] *Zool.* Dilated.

Dilatation (dəilē̆tēi·ʃən). ME. [a. OF., ad. L. *dilatationem*; see DILATE *v.*²] 1. The action or process of dilating; the condition of being dilated; expansion, enlargement. (Chiefly in *Physics* and *Physiol.*) b. *concr.* A dilated form, formation, or part of any structure 1833. 2. The spreading abroad (of abstract things) (*arch.*) ME. 3. The action or practice of dilating upon a subject; amplification ME.

3. What needeth gretter dilatacioun CHAUCER.

Dilatator (dəi·lē̆tēi·təɪ). 1611. [a. L.] a. *Anat.* A muscle which dilates a part; also *attrib.* b. *Surg.* An instrument for dilating an opening.

Dilatatory (dəilā̆·tătŏri). 1611. [ad. F. *dilatatoire*, ad. mod.L. *dilatatorium* (also used), f. L. *dilatare.*] *Surg.* An instrument for dilating a part or organ.

†**Dila·te**, *v.*¹ ME. [a. F. *dilater*, ad. med.L. *dilatare*, freq. of *differre* to DEFER; cf. DILATORY.] 1. *trans.* To delay, defer -1620. 2. To protract, prolong, lengthen -1658.

Dilate (di-, dəilē̆·t), *v.*² ME. [a. F. *dilater*, ad. L. *dilatare*, f. *di-*, *dis-* (DIS- 1) + *latus.*] 1. *trans.* To make wider or larger; to expand, amplify, enlarge 1528. Also *fig.* †2. To spread abroad (*lit.* and *fig.*) -1719. 3. *intr.* (for *refl.*) To become wider or larger; to spread out, widen, enlarge, expand 1636. Also *fig.* †4. *trans.* To relate at length; to enlarge or expatiate upon -1801. 5. *intr.* To discourse or write at large. Const. †*of*, *on*, *upon*. 1560.

1. All thynges..are dilated by heate EDEN. 3. The pupil has the property of contracting and dilating HARLAN. 5. She proceeded to d. upon the perfections of Miss Nickleby DICKENS.

Dilate (dəilē̆·t), *a. arch.* 1471. [ad. L. *dilatus*, pa. pple. of *differre*; but in sense of L. *dilatatus.*] = DILATED, widely extended or expanded.

Dilated (dəilē̆·tėd), *ppl. a.* 1450. [f. DILATE *v.*²] Widened, distended, etc.; see the vb.; in *Her.* opened or extended, as a pair of compasses. Hence **Dila·tedly** *adv.*

Dilater (dəilē̆·təɪ). 1605. [f. DILATE *v.*² Now mostly supplanted by DILATOR, q.v.] One who or that which dilates; *spec.* = DILATATOR.

†**Dila·tion**¹. ME. [a. OF. *dilacion*, ad. L. *dilationem*, f. *differre*; cf. DILATE *v.*¹] Delay, procrastination -1665.

Dilation² (dəilē̆·ʃən, di-). 1598. [Improp. f. DILATE *v.*²; better *dilatation.*] = DILATATION 1-3.

The beauty of its d. and contraction SOUTHEY. Frivolous terms, and dilations cut away 1851.

Dilative (dəilē̆·tiv), *a.* 1528. [f. DILATE *v.*² + -IVE.] 1. Having the property of dilating or expanding (*trans.* and *intr.*) 1634. †2. Serving to diffuse (the food) -1634.

Dilatometer (dəiletǫ·mĭtəɪ). 1882. [f. as prec. + -(O)METER.] An instrument for measuring the dilatation or expansion of a liquid by heat. Hence **Dilatome·tric** *a.*

Dilator (dəilē̆·təɪ), *sb.* 1688. [Irreg. f. DILATE *v.*²; the better types are DILATER and DILATATOR.] One who or that which dilates: *spec.* = DILATATOR. Also *attrib.*

Dilatory (di·lătəri). 1535. [ad. L. *dilatorius*, f. *dilatorem*, f. *differre*, *dilat-*; see DILATE *v.*¹]

A. *adj.* 1. Tending to cause delay; made for the purpose of gaining time. 2. Given to or characterized by delay; slow, tardy 1604.

1. This d. sloth and tricks of Rome *Hen. VIII*, II. iv. 237. Phr. *D. plea* (in *Law*), a plea put in for the sake of delay. 2. A d. man 1742, blockade 1843.

B. *sb. Law.* A dilatory plea; see A. 1563.

†**Dildo**¹. Also **dildoe.** 1610. [?] A word used in the refrain of ballads -1698. *Comb.* **d.-glass**, a cylindrical glass.

†**Dildo**². 1696. [prob. same wd. as prec.] A tree or shrub of the genus *Cereus* (N.O. *Cactaceæ*) -1756.

†**Dilection** (dile·kʃən). ME. [a. F., ad. L. *dilectionem* love (of God, etc.).] 1. Love, affection -1683. 2. Choice; *esp.* in *Theol.* = ELECTION 3. -1656.

Dilemma (dile·mă, dəi-), *sb.* 1523. [a. L., a. Gr. δίλημμα, f. δι- (DI-²) + λῆμμα assumption, premiss.] 1. In *Rhet.* A form of argument involving an adversary in choice between two (or, *loosely*, more) alternatives, both equally unfavourable to him. (The alternatives are the 'horns' of the dilemma.) Hence in *Logic*, A hypothetical syllogism having one premiss conjunctive and the other disjunctive. 2. Hence, popularly: A choice between two (or, *loosely*, several) alternatives, which are equally unfavourable; a position of doubt or perplexity 1590.

1. A d., that Bishop Morton .. used, to raise up the benevolence to higher rates. ..'That if they met with any that were sparing, they should tell them that they must needs have, because they laid up; and if they were spenders, they must needs have, because it was seen in their port and manner of living' BACON. 2. In the d. of a swimmer among drowning men, who all catch at him EMERSON. Hence **Dile·mma** *v.* to place or †be in a d. (*rare*). **Dilemma·tic, -al** *a.* of the nature of, or relating to, a d. **Dilemma·tically** *adv.* **Dile·mmist** (*rare*), one who bases his position upon a d.; name of a Buddhist school of philosophy.

Dilettant (di·lėtạnt), *a.* and *sb.* 1851. [var. of next.] = next.

‖**Dilettante** (dilėtæ·nti, It. dı̇letˌta·nte). Pl. **-ti** (-tī), rarely **-es.** 1733. [It., f. *dilettare*:—L. *delectare* to delight.] 1. A lover of the fine arts; orig. = *amateur*; in later use, one who interests himself in an art or science merely as a pastime and without serious study. 2. *attrib.* Amateur 1774; of, pertaining to, or characteristic of a dilettante 1753.

1. [The Romans] cared for art as dilettanti; but no schools either of sculpture or painting were formed among themselves FROUDE. 2. A d. painter T. L. PEACOCK. D. work CARLYLE.

Hence **Diletta·nte** *v.*, **Diletta·ntize** *v.*, to play the d. **Diletta·ntish** *a.*, also **-teish**, somewhat like a d. **Diletta·ntism**, also **-teism**, the practice or method of a d.; the quality or character of dilettanti. **Diletta·ntist**, characterized by dilettantism.

Diligence¹ (di·lidʒėns). Also †**Di·ligency.** ME. [a. F., ad. L. *diligentia.*] 1. The quality of being diligent; industry, assiduity. †2. Speed, dispatch -1781. †3. Careful attention, heedfulness, caution -1795. 4. *Law.* The attention and care due from a person in a given situation 1622. 5. *Sc. Law.* The process by which persons, lands, or effects are attached on execution, or in security for debt; also, the warrant issued to enforce the attendance of witnesses, or the production of documents 1568.

1. The carefull toile and d. of the Bee B. GOOGE. 3. Phr. *To do* or *have d.*, to take care, take heed.

Diligence² (di·lidʒėns; Fr. dı̇lizāns). 1742. [mod.F.: a particular use of *diligence*, DILIGENCE¹ 2.] A public stage-coach; *esp.* in France and abroad. Also *attrib.*

Diligent (di·lidʒėnt), *a.* ME. [a. F., ad. L. *diligentem*, in origin pr. pple. of *diligere.*] 1. 'Constant in application, persevering in endeavour, assiduous', industrious; 'not idle, not negligent, not lazy' (J.). 2. Of actions, etc.: Constantly or steadily applied; prosecuted with activity and perseverance; assiduous ME. †3. Attentive, careful -1756. †4. as *adv.* = diligently -1590.

1. Thei wer d. in here seruice ME. 2. In diligente labourynge 1500. 3. A very d. and observing person DAMPIER. Hence **Di·ligent-ly** *adv.*, †**-ness** (*rare*).

Dill (dil), *sb.* [OE. *dili, dile, (dil) dyle* masc.] An umbelliferous annual plant, *Anethum graveolens*, cultivated for its carminative fruits or 'seeds'. Also called ANET.

Dill, *v. n. dial.* 1450. [Cf. DULL *v.*; also ON. *dilla* intr.] To soothe, lull, quiet down.

‖**Dillenia** (dilī·niă). 1753. [after *Dillenius*, professor of botany at Oxford 1728-1747.] *Bot.* A genus of plants, typical of the N.O. *Dilleniaceæ*, natives of India and the Eastern peninsula, consisting of lofty forest trees with handsome flowers. Hence **Dillenia·ceous** *a.* **Dille·niad**, a member of this N.O.

Di·lligrout. Now *Hist.* 1662. [?] A kind of pottage, of which a mess was offered to the Kings of England on their coronation-day, by the lord of the manor of Addington in Surrey, being the service by which the manor was held.

Dilling (di·liŋ). Now *dial.* 1584. [?] Darling; the last born of a family; *dial.* the weakling of a litter.

†**Di·llue**, *v.* 1671. [a. Cornish *dyllo* to send forth.] *Mining.* To finish the dressing of (tin-ore) by shaking it in a fine sieve in water -1778. Hence **Dilluing-sieve.**

Dilly¹ (di·li). 1786. [Abbrev. of DILIGENCE ².] †1. A public stage-coach -1818. 2. Applied also to other vehicles, *esp.* carts, trucks, etc. used in agriculture 1850.

Di·lly². *colloq.* 1845. A call to ducks; hence, a duck.

Di·lly³. 1878. Short f. DAFFODILLY.

Di·lly⁴. 1895. [Shortened from *Sapodilla.*] In *Wild D.*, a small sapotaceous tree, *Mimusops Sieberi*, found in the W. Indies, etc.

Dilly-dally (di·liˌdæ·li), *v.* 1741. [Redupl. of DALLY *v.*] *intr.* To loiter in vacillation, to trifle. Hence **Di·lly-da·lly** †*sb.*, *a.*

Dilogical (dəilǫ·dʒikăl), *a.* 1633. [f. Gr. δίλογος, διλογία + -IC + -AL.] Of double meaning; equivocal. So **Di·logy**, the use of an equivocal expression; the expression so used.

†**Dilu·cid**, *a.* 1640. [ad. L. *dilucidus.*] Clear to the sight; lucid, plain -1671. var. †**Dilu·cidate** *ppl. a.* Hence **Dilu·cidly** *adv.*

†**Dilu·cidate**, *v.* 1538. [f. L. *dilucidat-*, *dilucidare.*] *trans.* To elucidate -1764. So †**Dilucida·tion.** †**Diluci·dity**, lucidity.

Diluent (di·liuˌėnt). 1721. [ad. L. *diluentem*, pr. pple. of *diluere*; see DILUTE.]

A. *adj.* Diluting; serving to attenuate or weaken by the addition of water, etc. 1731.

B. *sb.* 1. That which dilutes, dissolves, or makes more fluid 1775. 2. *spec.* A substance serving to increase the proportion of water in the blood 1721.

2. Diluents, as Water, Whey, Tea ARBUTHNOT.

Dilute (di-, dəiliū·t), *ppl. a.* 1605. [ad. L. *dilutus*, *diluere.*] 1. Watered down 1658; washed-out 1665. 2. *fig.* Weak, paltry 1605.

Dilute (di-, dəiliū·t), *v.* 1555. [f. L. *dilut-*, ppl. stem of *diluere*, f. *di-*, *dis-* (DIS- 1) + *luere* to wash.] 1. *trans.* To dissolve, or make thinner or weaker by the addition of water; to reduce the strength of by admixture 1664. 2. To weaken the brilliancy of (colour) 1665. 3. *fig.* To weaken 1555. 4. *intr.* (for *refl.*) To suffer dilution; to become attenuated 1764.

1. Replenish it with wine Diluted less COWPER. 2. The chamber was dark, lest these colours should be diluted and weakened by the mixture of any adventitious light NEWTON (J.). Hence **Dilu·ted-ly** *adv.*, **-ness. Dilu·ter.**

Dilution (di-, dəiliū·ʃən). 1646. [f. as prec.] 1. The action of diluting. 2. Dilute condition 1805. 3. That which is diluted 1861.

Diluvial (diliū·viăl), *a.* 1656. [ad. L. *diluvialis*, f. *diluvium*, f. *diluere.*] 1. Of or pertaining to a deluge or flood, *esp.* to the Noachian Flood. 2. *Geol.* Produced by or resulting from a general deluge or periods of catastrophic action of water 1816; of or pertaining to DILUVIUM 1823. Hence **Dilu·vialist**, one who attributes certain geological features to a universal deluge.

Diluvian (diliū·viăn), *a.* Also **de-.** 1655. [f. L. *diluvium* + -AN.] Of or pertaining to a deluge; *esp.* the Noachian Flood. Hence **Dilu·vianism**, a theory which attributes certain phenomena to a universal deluge.

†**Dilu·viate**, *v.* 1599. [f. ppl. stem of L. *diluviare.*] To flow in a deluge.

‖**Diluvium** (diliū·viŏm). 1819. [a. L.; see DILUTE.] Applied to superficial deposits apparently due to some extraordinary movement of the waters; such were at first attributed to the Noachian deluge, whence the name.

†**Dilu·vy.** ME. [ad. L. *diluvium.*] = DELUGE *sb.* -1546.

Dim (dim). [OE. *dim(m.* Only in Teut.]

A. *adj.* 1. Faintly luminous, not clear; somewhat dark, obscure, gloomy. (Opp. to *bright* or *clear.*) Also *fig.* 2. Not clear to the sight; indistinct, faint; misty, hazy OE. Also *fig.* 3. Of colour: Not bright; dull; dusky; lustreless ME. 4. Not seeing clearly ME.; *fig.* dull of apprehension 1729. Also *transf.* of sound, etc.

1. A d. religious light MILT. *Pens.* 160. *fig.* Hope grew pale and d. SHELLEY. 2. Egypt d. in the distance STANLEY. *fig.* A memory d. R. ELLIS. 3. Violets d. *Wint. T.* IV. iv. 119. 4. Jacob..somewhat d. for age 1577. *fig.* The understanding is d., and cannot by its natural light discover spiritual truth 1729.

B. *sb.* Dimness; obscurity; dusk ME.

Comb. **d.-eyed, -sighted**, etc.

Dim, *v.* ME. [f. DIM *a.*] 1. *intr.* To grow

or become dim. **2.** *trans.* To make dim, obscure, or dull; to render less distinct; to becloud (the eyes) ME. Also *fig.*

1. Suddenly mine eyes began to d. 1607. **2.** Windows dimmed with armorial bearings W. IRVING. *fig.* To d. a conqueror's triumph 1659.

Dim., dimin. (*Mus.*), abbrev. of DIMINUENDO.

†**Dima·ne,** *v.* 1610. [ad. L. *dimanare*, f. *di-*, *dis-* + *manare* to flow.] *intr.* To flow forth *from*; to originate *from* -1657.

Dimaris (di·măris). 1827. *Logic.* The mnemonic term designating the third mood of the fourth syllogistic figure, in which a particular affirmative major premiss (*i*), and a universal affirmative minor (*a*), yield a particular affirmative conclusion (*i*).

Dimastigate (dəimæ·stigĕt), *a.* [f. DI-[2] + Gr. μαστιγ- (μάστιξ) whip.] *Zool.* Having two flagella, as certain Infusoria (*Dimastiga*).

Dimble (di·mb'l). Now *dial.* 1589. [? conn. w. DIM or DINGLE.] A deep and shady dell, a dingle.

Dime (dəim), *sb.* ME. [a. OF. *disme*, *dime* :—L. *decima* tithe.] **1.** A tenth part, a tithe. Now *Hist.* **2.** A silver coin of the United States, of the value of 10 cents, or $^1/_{10}$ of a dollar 1786. **3.** *attrib.* Costing a dime; as in *d. novel*, a cheap sensational story.

Dimension (dime·nʃən), *sb.* ME. [a. F., ad. L. *dimensionem*, f. *dimetiri* (*dimens-*).] †**1.** The action of measuring, measurement -1793. **2.** Measurable extent of any kind, as length, breadth, thickness, area, volume; measure, magnitude, size. (Now usu. in pl.) Also *fig.* 1529. †**b.** Extension in time -1677. **3. a.** *Geom.* A mode of linear measurement, or extension, in a particular direction ME. **b.** *Alg.* A term for the (unknown or variable) quantities contained in any product as factors; any power of a quantity being of the dimensions denoted by its index. (Thus x^3, x^2y, xyz are each of three dimensions.) The number of dimensions corresponds to the DEGREE of a quantity or equation. 1557. †**4.** Measurable form or frame; *pl.* material parts; proportions -1667.

1. Things infinite, I see, Brooke no d. GREENE. **2.** Greatness of d. is a powerful cause of the sublime BURKE. **3.** The three dimensions of a body, or of ordinary space, are length, breadth, and thickness (or depth); a surface has only two dimensions (length and breadth); a line only one (length). N.E.D. **4.** Hath not a Iew hands, organs, dementions *Merch. V.* III. i. 62.

Comb.: **d.-lumber, -timber, -stone,** *i.e.* that which is cut to specified dimensions; **-work,** masonry built of d.-stones. (Chiefly *U.S.*)

Hence **Dime·nsion** *v.* to measure or space out (*rare*). **Dime·nsioned** *ppl. a.* having a particular d., or dimensions. **Dime·nsionless** *a.* without d., or dimensions; of no (appreciable) magnitude; vast.

Dimensional (dime·nʃənăl), *a.* 1816. [f. prec. sb. + -AL.] **1.** Of or pertaining to dimension. **2.** *Geom.* Of or relating to (a specified number of) dimensions 1875. Hence **Dimensiona·lity,** d. quality.

Dimensive (dime·nsiv), *a.* Now *rare.* 1563. [f. L. *dimens-* ppl. stem; see DIMENSION *sb.*] †**1.** Having, or related to, physical dimension -1694. †**2.** Serving to measure the dimensions of something -1610. **3.** Dimensional (*rare*) 1845.

2. All Bodies have their measure and their space, But who can draw the Soul's d. Lines DAVIES.

†‖**Dime·nsum.** 1630. [med.L.] A measured portion; a fixed allowance -1643.

†**Dimensura·tion.** 1593. [f. L. *di-* + *mensurare.*] Measuring out or off -1677.

Dimeran (di·mĕrăn). 1847. [f. mod.L. *dimera*, neut. pl. of *dimerus* (see DIMEROUS).] *Entom.* A member of the division *Dimera* of hemipterous insects, having the tarsi two-jointed.

Dimerous (di·mĕrəs), *a.* 1826. [f. mod.L. *dimerus*, f. Gr. διμερής bipartite + -OUS.] Consisting of two parts or divisions: applied to the tarsus of an insect, leaves, etc. So **Di·merism,** d. condition or constitution.

Dimeta·llic, *a.* 1861. [DI-[2].] *Chem.* Containing two equivalents of a metal.

Dimeter (di·mĭtəɹ). 1589. [a. L. *dimetrus* sb., *dimeter*, *-metrus* adj., a. Gr. δίμετρος.] *Pros.* A verse consisting of two measures, *i. e.* either two feet or four feet.

Dimethyl (dəime·þil). 1869. [DI-[2].] *Chem.* A name of Ethane (C_2H_6), regarded as two molecules of the radical methyl (CH_3). Also *attrib.*

Dimetient (dəimī·ʃiĕnt). 1571. [ad. L. *dimetientem.*]

A. *adj.* †**1.** That measures across through the centre -1729. **2.** *Math.* That expresses the dimension 1842.

†**B.** *sb.* (Short for *d. line.*) = DIAMETER -1690.

Dimetric (dəime·trik), *a.* 1868. [f. Gr. δι-, δίς + μέτρον.] *Cryst.* = TETRAGONAL.

Dimication (dimikē·ʃən). Now *rare.* 1623. [ad. L. *dimicationem.*] Fighting; contention.

Dimidiate (dimi·diĕt, dəi-), *a.* 1768. [ad. L. *dimidiatus*, f. (ult.) *di-*, *dis-* asunder + *medius*, *medium.*] **1.** Divided into halves; halved, half. **2.** *Bot.* and *Zool.* **a.** Of an organ: Having one part much smaller than the other, so as to appear to be wanting. **b.** Split in two on one side, as the calyptra of some mosses. **c.** *Zool.* Relating to the lateral halves of an organism: applied to hermaphrodites having one side male and the other female. 1830.

Dimidiate (dimi·dieˈt, dəi-), *v.* 1623. [f. L. *dimidiat-* ppl. stem; see prec.] **1.** *trans.* To divide into halves; to reduce to the half. **2.** *Her.* To cut in half; to represent only half of (a bearing) 1864. Hence **Dimi·dia·tion,** the action of dimidiating; dimidiated condition.

Diminish (dimi·niʃ), *v.* ME. [f. earlier DIMINUE, L. *diminuere*, and MINISH, L. type **minutiare.*] **1.** To make (or cause to appear) smaller; to lessen; to reduce in magnitude or degree. (The opp. of *enlarge, increase, augment, magnify.*) **2.** To lessen in estimation, or power; to put down, degrade; to belittle (*arch.*) 1560. †**3.** To take away *from*; hence *gen.* to take away, subtract -1627. Also †*absol.* †**4.** To deprive in part *of* -1762. **5.** *Mus.* †To make gradually softer. Also, To lessen (an interval) by a semitone. 1674. **6.** *intr.* To become less or smaller; to lessen, decrease 1520; in *Arch.* to taper 1715.

1. Perauenture it diminysshed theyr payne in hell 1526. **2.** I will d. them, that they shall no more rule over the nations *Ezek.* xxix. 15. **3.** Neither add any-thing nor d. 1533. **4.** If now then the builders..be diminished of their wages BP. COX. **6.** Crete's ample fields d. to our eye POPE.

Hence **Dimi·nishable** *a.*, **-ness. Dimi·nisher** (*rare*). **Dimi·nishingly** *adv.* **Dimi·nishment** (now *rare*), the action of diminishing; diminution.

Diminished (dimi·niʃt), *ppl. a.* 1607. [f. prec. + -ED[1].] **1.** Made smaller, lessened; see the vb. **2.** Lowered in estimation, etc. (see DIMINISH *v.* 2); now only in phr. from Milton 1667. **3.** *Mus.* Of an interval: Less by a chromatic semitone than a perfect, or than a minor, interval of the same name 1727.

1. Phr. *D. arch*, an arch which is less than a complete semicircle. *D. bar* in *Joinery*, the bar of a sash that is thinnest on the inner edge. *D. column*, a column decreasing in diameter from the base upwards. **2.** O thou [sun]..at whose sight all the Starrs Hide their diminisht heads MILT. *P. L.* IV. 35.

†**Diminue,** *v.* ME. [a. F. *diminuer*, ad. L. *diminuere* to DIMINISH. Ancient L. had *deminuere.*] = DIMINISH *v.* -1568.

‖**Diminuendo** (dimi:nu,e·ndo). 1775. [It., 'diminishing'; see prec.] *Mus.* A direction: To be gradually decreased in volume of sound (usu. indicated by the abbrev. *dim.* or *dimin.* or the sign >). As *sb.* Such a decrease; a passage of this description. Also *transf.* and *fig.* Also as *vb.* (Opp. to CRESCENDO.)

†**Dimi·nuent,** *a. rare.* 1608. [ad. L. *di-*, *deminuentem.*] Diminishing -1657.

†**Diminu·te,** *a.* 1450. [ad. L. *di-*, *deminutus.*] Diminished, lessened; incomplete -1731. Hence †**Diminu·tely** *adv.* So **Dimi·nute** *v.* to lessen, belittle (*rare*).

Diminution (diminiū·ʃən). ME. [a. F., ad. L. *diminutionem.*] **1.** The action of diminishing or making less; the process of becoming less; reduction in magnitude or degree. †**2.** Extenuation -1659. †**3.** Lessening of honour or reputation; depreciation, belittling -1734. †**4.** Curtailment, abatement -1675. **5.** *Mus.* The repetition of a subject in notes of half or a quarter the length of the original: opp. to *augmentation* 1597. **6.** *Her.* The defacing of part of an escutcheon; later, = DIFFERENCE 1610. **7.** *Law.* An omission in the record of a case sent up to a higher court 1657. **8.** *Archit.* The tapering of a column, etc.; also, the amount of this tapering in the whole length 1706.

1. Change by addition or d. HOOKER. **3.** I shall not much regard the worlds opinion or d. of me *Eikon Bas.* 49. **8.** [The] turret..ends with a fine d. ENTICK.

Diminutival (dimi:niutəi·văl), *a.* (*sb.*) 1868. [f. L. *diminutivus* + -AL.] *Gram.* Of, pertaining to, or of the nature of, a diminutive. As *sb.* A diminutival suffix 1880.

Diminutive (dimi·niŭtiv). ME. [a. F. *diminutif, -ive*, ad. L. *di-*, *deminutivus*, f. (ult.) *di-*, *deminuere.*]

A. *adj.* **1.** *Gram.* Expressing diminution; denoting something little. (Opp. to *augmentative.*) 1580. †**2.** Making less or smaller -1711. †**3.** Depreciative -1791. **4.** Characterized by diminution; hence, of less size than the ordinary; small, little. Now, usu. = minute, tiny. 1602.

2. Anything d. of..national Liberty SHAFTESB. **4.** Small, almost d., in stature E. PEACOCK.

B. *sb.* **1.** *Gram.* A derivative denoting something small of the kind ME. **2.** *Her.* A smaller ordinary corresponding in form and position to the larger, but of less width 1572. **3.** A diminutive thing or person 1606. †**4.** *Med.* Something that abates the violence of a disease -1621.

1. Babyisms and dear diminutives TENNYSON. **3.** Pestred with such water-flies, diminutiues of Nature SHAKS. Hence **Dimi·nutive-ly** *adv.*, **-ness.**

†**Dimi·ss,** *v.* 1543. [f. L. *dimiss-* ppl. stem.] = DISMISS *v.* -1729.

†**Di·missaries,** *sb. pl.* 1494. [? f. L. *demissus.*] Testicles -1577.

†**Dimi·ssion.** 1494. [ad. L. *dimissionem.*] **1.** = DEMISSION[2] 1. -1568. **2.** = DEMISE *sb.* 1. 1495. **3.** Dismissal, discharge -1823.

Dimissory (di·misəri), *a.* (*sb.*) Also **de-.** ME. [ad. L. *dimissorius*, f. *dimiss-* ppl. stem.]

A. †**1.** Pertaining to dismission or leave-taking; valedictory -1656. **2.** *Eccl. D. letter* (usu. in pl. *letters d.*): **a.** Formerly, a letter from a bishop dismissing a clergyman from one diocese and recommending him to another. **b.** A letter from a bishop, authorizing the bearer as a candidate for ordination. 1583.

†**B.** *sb.* = Letters dimissory; see prec. -1725.

†**Dimi·t,** *v.* 1495. [ad. L. *dimittere*; in Branch II, a var. of DEMIT *v.*[1]]

I. 1. *trans.* = DEMIT *v.*[2], in various senses -1678. **2.** *intr.* Of a river: To debouch 16...

II. *trans.* To send, put, or let down, lower -1671; *fig.* to abase 1655.

Dimity (di·mĭti). ME. [f. (ult.) Gr. δίμιτος, f. δι-, δίς twice + μίτος thread of the warp. The final *y* is obscure.] A stout cotton cloth, woven with raised stripes and fancy figures; used undyed for beds and hangings, and sometimes for garments. *attrib.* Made of dimity 1639.

Dimly (di·mli), *adv.* [repr. OE. type **dimlice*, from *dimlic.*] In a dim manner; in or with a dim light; obscurely; faintly.

Di·mmer. 1822. [f. DIM *v.* + -ER[1].] One who or that which dims; *spec.* a device for reducing the brilliance of a light; also, a dim lamp.

Dimmish (di·miʃ), *a.* 1683. [f. DIM *a.*] Somewhat dim. So **Di·mmy** *a.* more or less dim.

Dimness (di·mnės). [OE. *dimnis, dymnys*, f. *dim* DIM.] The quality of being dim.

In proof of the d. of our internal light JOHNSON.

Dimorph (dəi·mǭɹf). [mod. f. Gr. δίμορφος.] One of the two forms of a dimorphous substance; as 'aragonite and calcite are dimorphs'.

Dimo·rphic, *a.* 1859. [f. as prec. + -IC.] Existing or occurring in two distinct forms.

Dimorphism (dəimǭ·ɹfiz'm). 1832. [f. as prec. + -ISM.] The condition of being DIMORPHIC. **a.** *Cryst.* The property of assuming two distinct crystalline forms, not derivable from each other. **b.** *Biol.* The occurrence of two distinct forms of flowers, leaves, etc., on the same plant or in the same species; or of two forms distinct in structure, size, colouring, etc. among animals of the same species 1859. **c.** *Philol.* The existence, in one language, of a word under two different forms, or of doublets 1877.

Dimorphous (dəimǭ·ɪfəs), *a.* 1832. [f. as prec. + -OUS.] = DIMORPHIC. (Mostly in *Chem.* and *Min.*)

Dimple (di·mp'l), *sb.* ME. [? nasalized deriv. of *dip*, or a dim. of *dint*. Cf. OHG. *dumphilo*, mod.G. *dümpfel*, *tümpel* pool.] **1.** A small hollow or dent, formed in the surface of some part of the human body, *esp.* in the cheeks or chin. **2.** *transf.* Any slight surface depression 1632.

1. The Valley, The pretty dimples of his Chin, and Cheeke *Wint. T.* II. iii. 101. 2. In a d. of the hill 1815. Hence **Di·mply** *a.* full of dimples.

Di·mple, *v.* 1602. [f. prec. sb.] **1.** *trans.* To mark with, or as with, dimples. **2.** *intr.* To break into dimples or ripples, to form dimples 1700.

1. With whirlpools dimpl'd DRYDEN. 2. As shallow streams run dimpling all the way POPE. Hence **Di·mplement,** a dimpling (*rare*).

Di·m-si·ghted, *a.* 1561. Having dim sight (*lit.* and *fig.*).

Dimyary (di·miări). 1835. [f. mod.L. *dimyarius* (*Dimyaria* name of group), f. Gr. δι- + μῦς muscle (*lit.* mouse).]

A. *adj.* Double-muscled: said of those bivalve molluscs which have two adductor muscles for closing the shell. Also **Dimyarian** (dimi,ēə·riăn) *a.*

B. *sb.* A d. bivalve.

Din (din), *sb.* [OE. *dyne*, and *dynn*, f. Germanic root *dun-*; cf. Skr. *dhûni* roaring.] A loud noise; *esp.* a continued confused and resonant sound, which stuns or distresses the ear.

Ile..make thee rore, That beasts shall tremble at thy dyn *Temp.* I. ii. 371. I have a perpetual d. in my head and..hear nothing aright COWPER.

Din, *v.* Pa. t. and pple. **dinned** (dind). [OE. *dynnan*, *dynian* :—OTeut. *_dunjan_, from root of DIN *sb.* Also as from the sb.] †**1.** *intr.* (In OE. and ME.) To sound, resound –1513. **2.** *trans.* To assail with din 1674. **3.** To make to resound; to utter continuously so as to deafen or weary 1724. **4.** *intr.* To make a din; to give forth deafening or distressing noise 1794.

2. To have my ears dinned by him and his dotards 1786. 3. This hath often been dinned in my ears SWIFT. 4. The bag-pipe dinning on the midnight moor WORDSW.

‖**Dinanderie** (dīnāndərī). 1863. [Fr.; f. *Dinant*, formerly *Dinand* in Belgium, 'wherein copper kettles, etc., are made'.] Kitchen utensils of brass, made at Dinant; extended recently to the brass-work of the Levant and India.

‖**Dinar** (dīnā·ɪ). 1634. [Arab. and Pers., a. late Gr. δηνάριον, a. L. *denarius*.] A name of various oriental coins: applied to the gold mohur; also to the staple silver coin corresponding to the modern rupee; in Persia a coin of account.

Dindle (di·nd'l, di·n'l), *v.* Now only *Sc.* and *n. dial.* ME. [? onomatopœic.] **1.** *intr.* To tinkle; *trans.* to thrill with sound. **2.** *intr.* To be in a state of vibration from some sound, shock, or percussion 1470. **3.** *intr.* To tingle, as with cold or pain 1483. Hence **Di·ndle** *sb.*[1] a thrill, a tingle.

Di·ndle, *sb.*[2] *dial.* 1787. A name of various yellow Composite flowers; *e.g.* common and corn sow-thistles, hawkweeds, dandelions, etc.

Dine (dəin), *v.* [ME. *dinen*, a. F. *dîner*, in OF. *disner* (*disgner*), held to be :—late L. type *_disjunare_, for *disjejunare*, f. *dis-* + *jejunium* fast. Cf. F. *déjeuner* to DISJUNE.] **1.** *intr.* To eat the principal meal of the day; to take DINNER. Const. *on*, *upon*, *off*. †**2.** *trans.* To eat –1485. **3.** To provide with a dinner; to entertain at dinner; to accommodate for dining purposes ME.

1. They rose & herd masse, & dynid LD. BERNERS. Phr. *To d. with Duke Humphrey* (see N. E. D.). 2. 'Now, maister,' quod the wyf, 'What wil ye dine?' CHAUCER. 3. As much bread as would d. a sparrow ROWLEY. Hence **Dine** *sb.* (now *dial.*), the act of dining; dinner.

Diner (dəi·nəɪ). 1807. [f. prec. + -ER.] **1.** One who dines; a dinner-guest 1815. **b.** **Diner-out**: one who is in the habit of dining from home 1807. **2.** *U.S.* A railway dining car 1890.

1. A brilliant diner out, though but a curate BYRON.

†**Dine·tic,** †**-al,** *a. rare.* 1646. [f. Gr. δινητός whirled round + -IC, + AL.] Of or belonging to rotation; rotatory –1691.

Ding (diŋ), *v. arch.* or *dial.* ME. [Prob. from Norse; cf. Icelandic *dengja* to hammer, etc., Sw. *dänga*, Da. *dænge* to bang, etc.] **1.** *intr.* To deal heavy blows; to knock, hammer, thump (? *n. dial.*). **2.** *trans.* To beat, knock; to thrash, flog. (Now *dial.*) ME. **3.** *fig.* To beat, surpass 1724. **4.** To dash or violently drive (a thing) *away*, *down*, *in*, *out*, *over*, etc. ME. †**5.** *intr.* (for *refl.*) To precipitate oneself, dash, press, drive –1627; to fling, to bounce –1712. **6.** In imprecations: = DASH *v.* 1822.

2. *To d. to death* ME. 3. Duns dings a' *Sc. Prov.* 4. Ready..to d. the book a coits distance from him MILT. 5. They..drive at him as fast as they could d. DRAYTON. Rain dinging on night and day 1663. Hence **Ding** *sb.*[1] *dial.*, the act of dinging.

Ding (diŋ), *v.*[2] 1582. [Echoic. But influenced by prec. and DIN *v.*] **1.** *intr.* To sound as metal when heavily struck 1820. **2.** *intr.* To speak with wearying reiteration 1582.

1. Sledge hammers were dinging upon iron all day long DICKENS.

¶ *To d. into the ears*, 'to drive or force into the ears', unites this with DING *v.*[1] and DIN *v.*

Hence **Ding** *sb.*[2] and *adv.*, used as an imitation of the sound of a bell, etc.

Ding-dong (di·ŋdǫ·ŋ). 1560. [Echoic.]

A. *adv.*, or without constr, **1.** An imitation of the sound of a bell. **2.** With a will 1672.

B. *sb.* **1.** The sound of a bell, a repeated ringing sound; a jingle of rime 1560. **2.** *Horol.* An arrangement for indicating the quarters of the hour by the striking of two bells of different tones. Also *attrib.* 1822.

C. *adj.* **1.** Of or pertaining to the sound of bells or the jingle of rime 1792. **2.** Vigorously maintained, downright, desperate 1864.

Ding-dong theory of language, the theory which refers the primitive elements of language to phonetic expression naturally given to a conception as it first thrilled through the brain, just as a sonorous body when struck naturally emits sound.

Di·ng-do·ng, *v.* 1659. [Echoic.] *intr.* To ring as a bell, or like a bell; also *fig.*

‖**Dinghy, dingey** (di·ŋgi). Also **dingy.** 1810. [a. Hindī *ḍēngī* or *ḍiṅgī*.] **1.** Orig., a native rowing-boat in use upon Indian rivers. **2.** Hence, a small rowing-boat; *spec.* **a.** a small extra boat in men-of-war, **etc.**; **b.** a small pleasure rowing-boat. 1836.

Dingle (di·ŋg'l), *sb.* ME. [?] A deep dell or hollow; now usually, one that is closely wooded; also, a deep narrow cleft between hills (Ray). Hence **Di·ngly** *a.*

Di·ngle-da·ngle. 1598. [redupl. f. DANGLE.]

A. *adv.* In a dangling manner.

B. *sb.* A dangling to and fro; *concr.* a dangling appendage 1622.

C. *adj.* Swinging, dangling 1693.

‖**Dingo** (di·ŋgo). 1789. [Native N.S. Wales name.] The wild or semi-domesticated dog of Australia, *Canis d.*

†**Dingthrift** (di·ŋþrift). ME. [f. DING *v.*[1] + THRIFT.] **1.** A spendthrift –1598. **2.** An obsolete game. ME. only.

The Ding-thrifts proverbe is, Lightly come, lightly goe 1624.

Dingy (di·ndʒi), *a.* 1736. [? orig. *s. e. dial.* Not recognized by Dr. Johnson.] **1.** *dial.* Dirty. **2.** Of a dark and dull colour or appearance; blackish or dusky brown; now usually, dirty as from smoke, grime, dust, etc., or deficiency of daylight 1751. Also *fig.*

2. His clothes getting dingier..summer by summer BLACK. *fig.* D. acquaintances THACKERAY. Hence **Di·ngi-ly** *adv.*, **-ness.**

Dinic (di·nik). *rare.* 1721. [f. Gr. δῖνος.]

A. *adj.* Relating to dizziness. So **Di·nical** *a.*

B. *sb.* A remedy for dizziness.

Dining (dəi·niŋ), *vbl. sb.* ME. [f. DINE *v.* + -ING[1].] The action of DINE *v.*; a dinner. Also in *comb.* with sense 'used for dining', as *d.-hall*, *-room*, *-table*, etc.

Dinitro- (dəinəi·tro-). Bef. a vowel **dinitr-.** 1869. [f. DI-[2] + NITRO-.] **1.** Having two equivalents of the radical NO_2 taking the place of two atoms of hydrogen. **2.** **D.-cellulose,** a substance $C_6H_8(NO_2)_2O_5$, analogous to *gun-cotton* (*trinitro-cellulose*), produced by the action of a mixture of nitric and sulphuric acids on cotton. Also called *soluble pyroxylin.*

Dink (diŋk), *a. Sc.* and *n. dial.* 1508. [?] Decked out; trim. Hence **Di·nkly** *adv.* So **Dink** *v.* (*Sc.*) to dress finely.

Dinky (di·ŋki), *a.* orig. *dial.* and *U.S. colloq.* 1858. [f. prec.] Neat, trim, dainty.

Dinmont (di·nmənt). *Sc.* and *n. dial.* ME. [f. unknown element + *mont* MONTH.] A wether between the first and second shearing.

Dinner (di·nəɪ), *sb.* [ME. *diner*, a. F. *dîner*, subst. use of pres. inf. *dîner* to DINE.] The chief meal of the day, eaten originally, and still by many, about midday (cf. Ger. *Mittagsessen*), but now, by the fashionable classes, in the evening; particularly, a repast given publicly in some one's honour, or the like. Also *attrib.*

Comb. **d.-jacket,** a dress-coat without tails worn in the evening, esp. at dinner; **-wagon,** a tray with shelves beneath, supported by four legs, usually on castors, for the service of a dining-room.

Hence **Di·nnerless** *a.* without d. **Di·nnerly** *a.* of or pertaining to d.; *adv.* in a manner appropriate to d. **Di·nnery** *a.* characterized by d. or dinners.

Dinner (di·nəɪ), *v.* 1748. [f. DINNER *sb.*] **1.** *intr.* To dine, have dinner. **2.** *trans.* To entertain at dinner; to provide dinner for 1822.

‖**Dinoceras** (dəinǫ·sĕræs). 1872. [mod.L., f. Gr. δεινός + κέρας.] A genus of extinct ungulated quadrupeds (*Dinocerata*) of huge size, and having apparently three pairs of horns. Hence **Dino·cerate** *a.* related to the d.

Dinomic (dəinǫ·mik), *a.* 1863. [f. Gr. δι- + νομός district + -IC.] Belonging or restricted to two divisions (of the globe).

‖**Dinornis** (dəinǫ·ɪnis). 1843. [mod.L., f. Gr. δεινός + ὄρνις.] A genus of recently extinct birds of great size, remains of which have been found in New Zealand; the moa of the Maori. Hence **Dinorni·thic, Dino·rnithine** *adjs.*

Dinosaur, deino- (dəi·nǒsǭɪ). 1841. [mod.L. *dinosaurus* (also used), f. Gr. δεινός + σαῦρος (= σαύρα) lizard.] A member of an extinct race of Mesozoic Saurian reptiles (group *Deinosauria*), some of which were of gigantic size; the remains resemble birds in some respects, in others mammals. Hence **Dinosau·rian** *a.* and *sb.*

Dinothere, deino- (dəi·nǒþīəɪ). 1835. [f. mod.L. *dinothe·rium* (also used), f. Gr. δεινός + θηρίον.] A member of a genus of extinct proboscidean quadrupeds of great size, whose remains exist in the miocene formations of Europe and Asia. Hence **Dinothe·rian** *a.*

Di·nsome, *a. Sc.* 1724. [f. DIN *sb.* + -SOME.] Full of din; noisy.

Dint (dint), *sb.* [OE. *dynt*, cogn. w. ON. *dyntr*, *dyttr* in same sense. See also DENT *sb.*[1] and DUNT.] †**1.** A stroke or blow –1837. **2.** The dealing of blows; hence, force of attack or impact (*lit.* and *fig.*); violence, force. Now *rare*, exc. in phr. *By d. of*: by force of. ME. **3.** A mark made by a blow or by pressure; an indentation. Also *fig.* 1590.

1. With d. of Sword, or pointed Spears DRYDEN. Like thunders d. FAIRFAX. 2. The d. of pitty *Jul. C.* III. ii. 198. We..Earned, by d. of failure, triumph BROWNING. 3. Nor d. of hoof, nor print of foot BYRON. Hence **Di·ntless** *a.*

Dint (dint), *v.* [ME. *dynt-*, *dünt-*, *dint-en*, f. DINT *sb.* Not found in OE.] †**1.** *trans.* To strike or knock –1649. †**2.** *intr.* To make a dint *in* something (*rare*) –1590. **3.** *trans.* To mark with dints 1597; to impress with force 1631.

Dinumera·tion. 1626. [ad. L. *dinumerationem*.] **1.** The act of numbering one by one. **2.** *Rhet.* = APARITHMESIS.

Diobol (dəi,ō·bǫl). 1887. [ad. Gr. διώβολον.] *Numism.* A silver coin of ancient Greece equal to two obols.

Diocesan (dəi,ǫ·sĭsăn). ME. [a. F. *diocesain*, f. *diocise*, *diocese*. See also DIOCESIAN.]

A. *adj.* Of or pertaining to a diocese, as *d. synods* 1450.

B. *sb.* **1.** One in charge of a diocese; the bishop of a diocese ME. **2.** One of the clergy or people of a diocese 1502.

1. Prelates who were statesmen rather than diocesans 1881. 2. Humble diocesans of old Bishop Valentine LAMB.

Diocese (dəi·ǒsĕs, -sīs). Also **diocess(e** 6-9. [ME. *diocise*, etc., a. OF., ad. med.L. *diocesis*, for L. *diœcesis*, a. Gr. διοίκησις, f. διοικεῖν to keep house, to manage, administer, govern.] †**1.** Administration (*Sc.*) 1596. **2.**

A division of a country under a governor; a province. Now *Hist.* 1494. 3. *Eccl.* The sphere of jurisdiction of a bishop; the district under the pastoral care of a bishop. (The ordinary sense in English.) ME. Also *transf.* and *fig.* Hence †Diocesener = DIOCESAN *sb.* 2.

†Dioce·sian, *a.* and *sb.* 1686. [f. L. type *diœcesianus*; more regular than DIOCESAN.] = DIOCESAN.

‖Diodon (dəi·ǒdǫn). 1776. [f. Gr. δι- twice + ὀδούς tooth.] *Zool.* A genus of globe-fishes, having the jaws tipped with enamel, forming a tooth-like tubercle in the centre of the beak above and below.

Di·odont. [See prec.] *adj.* Having two teeth; *spec.* of or pertaining to the *Diodontidæ*, of which *Diodon* is the typical genus; *sb.* a fish of this family. So **Diodo·ntoid.** (Dicts.)

‖Diœcia (dəi,ī·ʃiă). 1753. [mod.L., f. Gr. δι- (DI-[2]) + οἶκος. Cf. MONŒCIA.] *Bot.* The twenty-second class in the Sexual System of Linnæus, comprising plants which have male and female flowers on separate individuals. Hence **Diœ·cian** *a.* = DIŒCIOUS.

Diœcious (dəi,ī·ʃiəs), *a.* 1748. [f. DIŒCIA.] 1. *Bot.* Of plants: Having the unisexual male and female flowers on separate plants. 2. *Zool.* Having the two sexes in separate individuals 1826. Hence **Diœ·cious-ly** *adv.*, **-ness.** So **Diœ·cism**, d. condition. **Dioi·cous** *a.*

Diogenes (dəi,ǫ·dʒĕnīz). 1802. A Greek CYNIC philosopher, who showed his contempt for the amenities of life by living in a tub.

D.-crab, a species of W. Indian hermit crab, which chooses an empty shell for its residence. **D.-cup**, the cup-like cavity formed in the palm of the hand by arching the fingers, etc. Hence **Dioge·nic, -al** *a.* of, pertaining to, or of the nature of D.

†Di·onise. 1483. [a. OF., ad. med.L. *dionysia* (also used), f. Gr. Διόνυσος Bacchus.] A precious stone, black, with streaks of red, reckoned, by mediæval writers, a preservative against drunkenness –1855.

Dionysiac (dəi,ǒni·siæk). 1827. [ad. L., a. Gr. Διονυσιακός, f. Διονύσια the feast of Dionysus or Bacchus.]

A. *adj.* Of or pertaining to Dionysus, or to his worship 1844.

B. *sb. pl.* The Dionysiac festivals or *Dionysia*, celebrated periodically in ancient Greece.

Dionysian (dəi,ǒni·siăn), *a.* 1607. [f. L. *Dionysius* + -AN.] 1. = DIONYSIAC 1610. 2. Pertaining to or characteristic of the Elder or Younger Dionysius, tyrants of Syracuse, notorious for cruelty 1607. 3. Pertaining to Dionysius the Little, an abbot of the 6th century, to whom is ascribed the method of dating events from the birth of Christ 1727. 4. Of Dionysius the Areopagite (Acts xvii. 34) 1885.

3. *D. period*, a period of 532 Julian years, after which the changes of the moon recur on the same days of the year; introduced for calculating the date of Easter.

Diophantine (dəi,ofæ·ntin, -əin), *a.* 1700. [f. proper name.] *Math.* Of or pertaining to Diophantus of Alexandria, a celebrated mathematician; *spec.* applied to problems involving indeterminate equations, and to a method of solving them (*D. analysis*).

Diophysite, -ism, improp. ff. DIPHYSITE, DYOPHYSITE, etc.

Diopside (dəi,ǫ·psəid). 1808. [a. F., irreg. f. Gr. δι- + ὄψις; taken later as from Gr. δίοψις a view through.] *Min.* = PYROXENE; now restricted to the transparent varieties.

Dioptase (dəi,ǫ·ptēs). 1804. [a. F., irreg. f. Gr. δι-, δια- + ὀπτός visible.] *Min.* A translucent silicate of copper, crystallizing in six-sided prisms, called emerald copper ore.

Diopter (dəi,ǫ·ptəɹ). Also **dioptra.** 1594. [a. F. *dioptre*, ad. L. *dioptra*, a. Gr. δίοπτρα; cf. also Gr. δίοπτρον spying-glass.] 1. An ancient form of theodolite 1613. 2. = ALIDADE 1594. †3. A surgical speculum –1872. 4. = DIOPTRIC *sb.* 2. 1890.

Dioptric (dəi,ǫ·ptrik). 1635. [mod. ad. Gr. διοπτρικός; in neut. pl. διοπτρικά as sb.]

A. *adj.* †1. Of the nature of, or pertaining to, a DIOPTER (sense 1) –1681. 2. Assisting vision by means of refraction (as a lens, etc.) 1653. 3. Relating to dioptrics (see B. 3); *esp.* (of a telescope, etc.), refractive, refracting. (Opp. to CATOPTRIC.) 1672. †4. Capable of being seen through –1860.

3. *D. system*, in lighthouses, that in which the rays issuing from the flame are collected and refracted in a given direction by a lens placed in front of the light.

B. *sb.* 1. = DIOPTER 1. 1849. 2. A unit for expressing the refractive power of a lens, being the power of a lens whose focal distance is one metre 1883. 3. *pl.* **Dioptrics**: that part of Optics which treats of the refraction of light. (Opp. to CATOPTRICS.) 1644.

Hence **Dio·ptrical** *a.* = DIOPTRIC *a.*; of or belonging to dioptrics; skilled in dioptrics. **Dio·ptrically** *adv.* by means of refraction.

Diorama (dəi,orɑ·mă). 1823. [mod. f. Gr. δι-, δια- + ὅραμα.] A mode of scenic representation in which a picture, some portions of which are translucent, is viewed through an aperture, the sides of which are continued towards the picture; the light, which is thrown upon the picture from the roof, may be diminished or increased at pleasure. Also, the building in which such views are exhibited. Hence **Diora·mic** *a.* (better *dioramatic*) of the nature of, or pertaining to, a d.

Diorism (dəi·ǒriz'm). *rare.* 1664. [ad. Gr. διορισμός, f. διορίζειν.] The act of defining; distinction, definition: in H. More = distinctive application. So **†Diori·stic, -al** *a.* serving to define or distinguish. **†Diori·stically** *adv.*

Diorite (dəi,ǒrəit). 1826. [a. F., irreg. f. Gr. διορίζειν.] *Min.* A variety of GREENSTONE, consisting of hornblende combined with a triclinic feldspar (albite or oligoclase). Hence **Diori·tic** *a.* of the nature of, or containing, d.

‖Diorthosis (dəi,ǫɹþōu·sis). 1704. [mod.L., a. Gr. διόρθωσις.] The act of setting straight: a. in *Surg.*, the straightening of crooked or fractured limbs. b. The recension of a literary work. Hence **Diortho·tic** *a.* corrective.

Dioscoreaceous (dəi,ǫskōə:ri,ēi·ʃəs), *a.* [f. mod.L. *Dioscoreaceæ*, f. *Dioscorea*, the typical genus, containing the yams.] *Bot.* Of or belonging to the N.O. *Dioscoreaceæ* of Monocotyledons.

‖Diosma (dəi,ǫ·zmă). 1794. [mod.L., f. Gr. δῖος + ὀσμή.] *Bot.* A genus of S. African heath-like plants (N.O. *Rutaceæ*), with strong balsamic odour.

‖Diosmosis (dəi,ǫsmōu·sis). Also **di·osmose.** 1825. [mod. f. Gr. δι-, δια- + OSMOSIS.] = OSMOSIS. Hence **Diosmo·tic** *a.*

‖Diota (dəi,ōu·tă). 1857. [L., a. Gr. διώτη two-eared.] *Gr.* and *Rom. Antiq.* A vessel with two ears or handles.

Diothelism, -ite, irreg. ff. DITHELISM, DYOTHELISM, etc.

†‖Dio·ti, dihoti. 1651. [Gr. διότι, f. διὰ (τοῦτο) ὅτι.] A wherefore –1734.

Diotrephes (dəi,ǫ·trĭfīz). 1626. See 3 John 9, 10. Hence used typically of persons loving to have the pre-eminence in the church. Hence **Diotrephe·sian, Diotre·phian, Diotre·phic** *adjs.*

Dioxide (dəi,ǫ·ksəid). 1847. [DI-[2].] *Chem.* An oxide containing two equivalents of oxygen with one of the metal or metalloid, as *Carbon d.* CO_2.

Dip (dip), *v.* Pa. t. and pple. **dipped, dipt,** pr. pple. **dipping.** [OE. *dyppan* wk. vb :—OTeut. **dupjan*, f. *dup-* of ablaut series **deup-*, *daup-*, *dup-*, whence DEEP (:—**deupoz*).]

I. Trans. 1. To put down or let down for a moment *in* or *into*; to immerse; to plunge. Also *fig.* b. To immerse in a colouring solution; to dye 1667. 2. To immerse in baptism; to baptize by immersion (now usu. *contemptuous*). Also *absol.* OE. 3. To suffuse with moisture 1634; to dip into (*rare*) 1842. 4. To obtain or take *up* by dipping 1602. 5. *transf.* To lower or let down for a moment, as if dipping in a liquid; *spec.* to lower and then raise (a flag) as a salute, or (a sail) in tacking 1776. 6. *fig.* To immerse, involve (*in* any affair) 1627; to involve in debt; to mortgage 1640.

1. To d. children in cold water MULCASTER, a garment in bloud HOBBES. With.. colours dipt in Heav'n MILT. *P. L.* v. 283. 3. A cold shuddering dew Dips me all over — *Comus* 802. But, ere he dipt the surface, rose an arm TENNYSON. 4. To d. up shrimps CAREW, water MISS MITFORD. 5. To-day, 'dipping the flag' is an act of courtesy 1894. 6. Sr Steph. Fox is dipt 70,000li deepe in that concerne 1671. Never d. thy Lands DRYDEN.

II. Intrans. 1. To plunge down a little into water, etc., and quickly emerge. Const. *in, into, under.* ME. 2. To plunge one's hand (or a ladle or the like) into water, a receptacle, etc., and take something out 1697. 3. = DAP *v.* 1799. 4. *transf.* To sink, drop, or extend downwards, as if dipping into water ME. 5. To have a downward inclination; to be inclined to the horizon: *spec.* of the magnetic needle, and in *Geol.* of strata 1665. 6. To go into a subject deeply 1755, or cursorily 1682.

1. Her yards would d. into the water 1830. 2. Phr. *To d.* (*deeply*, etc.) *into one's purse, means*, etc. 4. The Sun's rim dips; the stars rush out COLERIDGE. Two turreted precipice blocks D., like walls, to the wave BOWEN. 6. When I dipt into the future far as human eye could see TENNYSON. I have not attentively read him, but only dipp'd here and there GRAY.

Dip (dip), *sb.* 1599. [f. DIP *v.*] 1. An act of dipping; see various senses of the vb. 2. Depth of submergence (*e.g.* of a paddle-wheel); depth below a particular level; depth of a vessel, etc. 1793. 3. *Astron.* and *Surveying.* The apparent depression of the horizon due to the observer's elevation 1774. 4. The angle which the direction of the magnetic needle at any place makes with the horizon 1727. 5. Downward slope of a surface; *esp.* in *Mining* and *Geol.* the downward slope of a stratum or vein, estimated by its angle of inclination to the horizon 1708. 6. A hollow to which the surrounding high ground dips 1789. 7. = *Dip-candle* 1815. 8. A sweet sauce for puddings, etc. (*local Eng.* and *U.S.*) 1825. 9. *Thieves' slang.* A pickpocket; also pocket-picking 1859.

1. A d. in the horse pond JAMES, into a book JAS. GRANT. To keep the signal at the d. MARKHAM. 6. We saw groves and villages in the dips of the hills BECKFORD.

Comb.: **d.-bucket**, a bucket contrived to turn easily and dip into water; **-candle**, a candle made by dipping a wick into melted tallow; **-circle**, a dipping-needle having a vertical graduated circle for measuring the amount of the d.; **-head**, a heading driven to the d. in a coal-mine in which the beds have a steep inclination; **-net**, a small net with a long handle, used to catch fish by dipping in the water; **-pipe**, a valve arranged to dip into water or tar, and form a seal; a seal-pipe; **-sector**, an instrument on the principle of the sextant, used to ascertain the d. of the horizon; **-splint**, a kind of friction-match.

Dipartite (dəipā·ɹtəit), *a.* 1825. [f. DI-[1], L. *dis-* + *partitus.*] Divided into various parts. So **Diparti·tion.**

Dipa·schal, *a.* 1840. [DI-[2].] Including two passovers.

Dipchick, var. of DABCHICK.

Dipetalous (dəipe·tăləs), *a.* 1707. [DI-[2].] *Bot.* Having two petals.

Diphen- in chemical terms; see DI-[2] 2, PHEN-.

Diphenyl (dəife·nil). 1873. [f. DI-[2] + PHENYL.] *Chem.* An aromatic hydrocarbon, $C_6H_5.C_6H_5$, having twice the formula of the radical PHENYL. Also *attrib.*

Diphtheria (difþī°·riă). 1857. [ad. F. *diphthérie*; see DIPHTHERITIS.] *Path.* An acute and highly infectious disease, characterized by inflammation of a mucous surface, and by an exudation therefrom which results in the formation of a false membrane. Its chief seat is the mucous membrane of the throat and air passages.

Hence **Diphthe·rial, Diphthe·rian** *adjs.* of or belonging to d. **Diphthe·ric** *a.* diphtheritic.

Diphtheritis (difþĕrəi·tis). Also ‖(Fr.) **diphtherite.** 1826. [mod. f. Gr. διφθέρα or διφθερίς skin + -ITIS; so named on account of the tough membrane formed upon the parts affected.] = DIPHTHERIA. Hence **Diphtheri·tic** *a.* of the nature of, belonging to, or connected with diphtheria; affected with diphtheria. So **Di·phtheroid** *a.* resembling diphtheria.

Diphthong (di·fþǫŋ), *sb.* 1483. [a. F. *diphthongue*, ad. L., a. Gr. δίφθογγος *a.* and *sb.*, f. δι-, δίς + φθόγγος.] A union of two vowels pronounced in one syllable; the combination of a sonantal with a consonantal vowel. b. Often applied to a combination of two vowel characters, prop. termed DIGRAPH, and applied to the ligatures æ, œ of the Roman alphabet 1587. Also *attrib.*

I and *u* according to our English pronunciation of them, are not properly Vowels, but Diphthongs WILKINS. **b.** When the two letters represent a simple sound, as *ea*, *ou*, in *head* (hed), *soup* (sūp), they have been termed an *improper d.*: properly speaking these are *monophthongs* written by *digraphs.* N.E.D.

Hence **Di·phthong** *v.* to sound as, or make into, a d. **Diphtho·ngal** *a.* of, belonging to, or of the nature of, a d. **Diphtho·ngic** *a.* diphthongal. **Di·phthongize** *v.* to turn into, or (*intr.*) form, a d. **Di phthongiza·tion,** the changing of a simple vowel into a d. **Diphtho·ngous** *a.* diphthongal (*rare*).

Diphy-, ad. Gr. διφυ- from διφυής of double nature or form, double, bipartite: as in

Di·phycerc [Gr. κέρκος tail], *Ichth.* a diphycercal fish. **Diphyce·rcal** *a.*, having the tail divided into two equal halves by the caudal spine. **Di·phycercy,** diphycercal condition. **Di·phyid,** *Zool.* a member of the *Diphyidæ*, a family of Hydrozoa furnished with a pair of swimming-bells. **Di·phyodont** *a.* [Gr. ὀδοντ-], having two sets of teeth; consisting (as teeth) of two sets; as *sb.* a diphyodont animal. **Diphyzo·oid, diphyo-,** *Zool.* a free-swimming organism consisting of a group of zooids detached from a colony of Hydrozoa of the order *Siphonophora.*

Diphyllous (dəifi·ləs), *a.* 1788. [f. mod.L. *diphyllus.*] *Bot.* Having two leaves (or sepals).

Diphyo-; see DIPHY-.

Diphysite (di·fisəit), *sb.* (*a.*) [f. Gr. δι-, δίς + φύσις.] *Theol.* One who held the doctrine (**Di·physiti·sm**), of two distinct natures in Christ, a divine, and a human; opp. to MONOPHYSITE.

Diplarthrous (diplā·ɹþrəs), *a.* 1887. [f. Gr. διπλό-ος + ἄρθρον + -OUS.] *Zool.* Having the carpal or tarsal bones doubly articulated, *i.e.* the several bones of one row alternating with those of the other, as in ungulate mammals: opp. to *taxeopodous.* So **Dipla·rthrism,** d. condition.

Diplasic (diplæ·zik, dəi-), *a.* 1873. [f. Gr. διπλάσιος.] *Pros.* Double, twofold; having the proportion of two to one, as in *d. ratio*, = Gr. διπλασίων λόγος.

‖**Diple** (di·plī). 1656. [Gr. διπλῆ (sc. γραμμή line).] A marginal mark of this form >, to indicate various readings, rejected verses, a paragraph, etc.

‖**Diplegia** (dəiplī·dʒiă). 1883. [mod.L., f. Gr. δι-, δίς + πληγή.] *Path.* Paralysis of corresponding parts on both sides of the body. Hence **Diple·gic** *a.* relating to d., or to corresponding parts on both sides.

Dipleidoscope (diplai·dǭskōᵘp). 1843. [f. Gr. διπλό-ος + εἶδος + -σκοπος viewing, a watcher.] An instrument consisting of a hollow triangular prism, with two sides silvered and one of glass, used for determining the meridian transit of a heavenly body by the coincidence of the two images formed by single and double reflexion.

‖**Dipleura** (dəiplūᵊ·ră), *sb. pl.* 1883. [mod.L., neut. of *dipleurus*, f. Gr. δι-, δίς + πλευρά.] *Morphol.* Bodies with bilateral symmetry having a single pair of antimeres. Hence **Dipleu·ral** *a.* zygopleural with only two antimeres. **Dipleu·ric** *a.* exhibiting bilateral symmetry.

Dipleurobranchiate (dəiplūᵊ·ro,bræ·ŋkiĕt), *a.* [f. mod.L. *Dipleurobranchia* (f. Gr. δι- + πλευρά + βράγχια).] *Zool.* Having the characters of the *Dipleurobranchia* or *Inferobranchiata*, nudobranchiate gastropods having foliaceous branchiæ situated in a fold on each side of the shell-less body.

Diplex (dəi·pleks), *a.* 1878. [altered f. *duplex* after DI-².] *Telegr.* Characterized by the passing of two messages simultaneously in the same direction.

Diplo- (di·plo), bef. a vowel **dipl-**, comb. f. Gr. διπλό-ος, διπλοῦς, twofold, double: as in

Diplobacte·ria *sb. pl.*, bacteria consisting of two cells. **Diplobla·stic** *a.*, *Biol.* having two germinal layers, the hypoblast and epiblast. **Diploca·rdiac** *a.*, *Zool.* having the heart double, *i.e.* with the right and left halves completely separate, as in birds and mammals. **Diploce·phaly,** monstrosity consisting in having two heads. ‖**Diploco·ccus,** *Biol.* a cell formed by conjugation of two cells. **Diplo·dal** *a.* [Gr. ὁδός], *Zool.* of sponges, having both canals, prosodal and aphodal, well developed. **Diplo·docus** [Gr. δοκός beam], a genus of gigantic extinct herbivorous dinosaurs. **Diploga·ngliate** *a.*, having ganglia arranged in pairs. **Diploge·nesis,** the production of double parts instead of single ones; hence **Diploge·netic** *a.*; **Diploge·nic** *a.*, 'producing two substances; partaking of the nature of two bodies' (Craig). **Di·plograph,** an instrument for writing double, *i.e.* in relief for the blind and in the ordinary manner, at the same time; so **Diplogra·phical** *a.*, of or pertaining to writing double; also **Diplo·graphy. Diploneu·ral** *a.*, *Anat.* supplied by two nerves of separate origin, as a muscle; **Diploneuro·se** *a.*, *Zool.* belonging to the *Diploneura* (= *Articulata*); **Diploneu·rous** *a.*, 'having two nervous systems; also, belonging to the *Diploneura*' (*Syd. Soc. Lex.*). **Diplopla·cula,** *Embryol.* a PLACULA composed of two layers; hence **Diplopla·cular, Diplopla·culate** *a.* **Di·plopod** *a.* and *sb.*, *Zool.* belonging to the order of *Diplopoda* (= *Cheilognatha*) of Myriapods, having two pairs of limbs on each segment of the body; a member of this order; hence **Diplo·podous** *a.* **Diplo·pterous** *a.*, *Entom.* belonging to the family *Diploptera* (the true wasps), which have the fore wings folded when at rest. **Diplosphe·nal** *a.*, **Di·plosphene,** *Anat.* = HYPOSPHENAL, HYPOSPHENE. **Diplospondy·lic** *a.*, *Zool.* said of a vertical segment having two centra, or of a vertebral column having twice as many centra as arches, as in fishes and batrachians; hence **Diplospondy·lism. Diplo·stichous** *a.*, arranged in two rows. **Diplosy·ntheme** = DISYNTHEME.

‖**Diploe** (di·plo,ī). 1696. [mod.L., a. Gr. διπλόη, f. διπλόος.] **1.** *Anat.* The light porous or cancellated bone-tissue lying between the inner and outer tables of the skull. **2.** *Bot.* = DIACHYMA 1866. Hence **Diploe·tic** *a.* bad for DIPLOIC. **Diplo·ic** *a.* belonging to the d.

Diploid (di·ploid). [f. Gr. διπλόος + εἶδος.] *Cryst.* A solid belonging to the isometric system, contained within twenty-four trapezoidal planes.

Diploidion (diplo,i·diǭn). 1850. [Gr., dim. of διπλοΐς.] *Gr. Antiq.* A chiton or tunic worn by women, having the part above the waist double with the outer fold hanging loose. So **Diplois** (diplo,is), in same sense.

Diploma (diplōᵘ·mă), *sb.* Pl. **-as,** occas. **-ata.** 1645. [a. L., a. Gr. δίπλωμα (-ματ-), (*lit.* a doubling), a folded paper, a letter of recommendation, etc., f. (ult.) διπλόος double.] **1.** A state paper, an official document; a charter; *pl.* historical or literary muniments. **2.** A document conferring some honour, privilege, or licence; *esp.* that given by a university or college, testifying to a degree taken by a person, and conferring upon him the rights and privileges of such degree, as to teach, practise medicine, etc. Also *attrib.*, as *d. picture*, one given to a society of art by a member on his election. Hence **Diplo·ma** *v.* to furnish with a d. Chiefly in *ppl. a.* **Diplomaed.**

Diplomacy (diplōᵘ·măsi). 1796. [a. F. *diplomatie* (pronounced -*cie*), f. *diplomate*, after *aristocratie*, etc.; see DIPLOMATIC.] **1.** The management of international relations by negotiation; the method by which these relations are adjusted and managed by ambassadors and envoys; the business or art of the diplomatist; skill or address in the conduct of international intercourse and negotiations. †**2.** The diplomatic body. [= F. *diplomatie.*] -1806. **3.** Skill in intercourse of any kind 1848. **4.** = DIPLOMATIC *sb.* 3 (*rare*) 1870.

1. As d. was in its beginnings, so it lasted for a long time; the ambassador was the man who was sent to lie abroad for the good of his country STUBBS. **3.** The lady thought it better to attain her ends by d. (*mod.*).

Diplomat (di·plomæt). Also **-ate.** 1813. [a. F. *diplomate.*] One employed or skilled in diplomacy.

†**Di·plomate,** *v.* 1660. [f. DIPLOMA *sb.*] To invest with a degree, privilege, or title by diploma -1738.

[**Diplomatial:** error in Dicts. for DIPLOMATICAL.]

Diplomatic (diplomæ·tik). 1711. [ad. mod. L. *diplomaticus*, f. Gr. διπλωματ-; see DIPLOMA. In senses A. 2, 3, a. F. *diplomatique.*]

A. *adj.* **1.** Of or pertaining to official or original documents, charters, or manuscripts; textual. **2.** Of the nature of official papers connected with international relations 1780. **3.** Of, pertaining to, or connected with the management of international relations; of or belonging to diplomacy 1787. **4.** Showing address in negotiations or intercourse of any kind 1826.

1. *D. copy*, an exact reproduction of an original. **3.** *D. body* (F. *corps diplomatique*), the body of ambassadors, envoys, and officials attached to the foreign legations at any seat of government. **4.** Conduct which is wily and subtle, without being directly false or fraudulent, is styled 'd.' 1877.

B. *sb.* **1.** = DIPLOMATIST 1791. **2.** The diplomatic art. Also in pl. **diplomatics.** 1794. **3.** The science of diplomas, which has for its object to decipher old writings, to ascertain their authenticity, their date, signatures, etc. Also in *pl.* 1803.

2. Our ministers are not great in diplomatics. var. **Diploma·tical** = DIPLOMATIC *a.* 1, 3; *sb.* 1. Hence **Diploma·tically** *adv.* **Diplomati·cian** (*rare*), diplomatist.

Diplomatics; see DIPLOMATIC B. 2, 3.

Diplomatist (diplōᵘ·mătist). 1815. [f. DIPLOMAT *sb.* + -IST.] One engaged in official diplomacy. **b.** One characterized by diplomatic address.

Diplomatize (diplōᵘ·mătəiz), *v.* 1670. [f. Gr. διπλωματ- DIPLOMA + -IZE; in II, f. *diplomat, -ic, -ist.*]

I. *trans.* To invest with a diploma (*rare*).

II. 1. *intr.* To act or serve as a diplomat; to use diplomatic arts 1826. **2.** *trans.* To act diplomatically towards (*rare*) 1855. Also with *out of.*

‖**Diplopia** (diplōᵘ·piă). Also **diplopy.** 1811. [f. Gr. διπλο- double + -ωπια from ὤψ eye; cf. AMBLYOPIA.] *Phys.*, etc. An affection of the eyes, in which objects are seen double. Hence **Diplopic** (diplǫ·pik) *a.* pertaining to d.

Diplostemonous (diplostī·mǫnəs), *a.* 1866. [f. DIPLO- + Gr. στήμων warp, taken as = στῆμα stamen + -OUS.] *Bot.* Having the stamens in two series, or twice as many as the petals. So **Diploste·mony,** d. condition.

‖**Diplozoon** (diplozōᵘ·ǫn). Pl. **-zoa.** 1835. [f. DIPLO- + Gr. ζῷον.] *Zool.* A genus of trematode worms, parasitic on the gills of fishes; the mature organism is double, and X-shaped.

Dipneumonous (dipniū·mǫnəs), *a.* [f. mod. L. *dipneumonus* (f. Gr. δι-, δίς + πνεύμων lung) + -OUS.] *Zool.* Having two respiratory organs; said of the *Dipneumona* or two-lunged fishes, and of the *Dipneumones* or two-lunged spiders; also of a group of Holothurians.

Dipneustal (dipniū·stăl), *a.* [mod.L. *Dipneusta* (f. Gr. δι- + πνευστός, πνεῖν to breathe) + -AL.] *Zool.* = DIPNOAN.

Dipnoan (di·pno,ăn). 1883. [f. mod.L. *Dipnoi* (see DIPNOOUS).] *Zool.*

A. *adj.* Belonging to the *Dipnoi*, a sub-class of fishes having both gills and lungs.

B. *sb.* A member of this sub-class. var. **Di·pnoid** *a.* and *sb.*

Dipnoous (di·pno,əs), *a.* Also *erron.* **dipnous.** 1811. [f. mod.L. *dipnous* (in pl. *Dipnoi*), a. Gr. δίπνοος, f. δι- + πνοή breathing, breath.] **1.** *Zool.* Having both gills and lungs, as a dipnoan fish 1881. **2.** *Path.* Of a wound: Having two openings for air, etc. 1811.

Dipody (di·pǭdi). 1844. [ad. L. *dipodia* (also used), a. Gr., f. δίπους, διποδ- two-footed.] *Pros.* A double foot; two feet making one measure. Hence **Dipo·dic** *a.* of the nature of a d.

Dipolar (dəipōᵘ·lăɹ), *a.* 1864. [DI-².] Of or pertaining to two poles; having two poles.

Dipolarize, etc., used by some instead of DEPOLARIZE, etc.

‖**Diporpa** (dəipǭ·ɹpă). Pl. **-æ.** 1888. [f. Gr. δι-, δίς + πόρπη pin of a buckle.] *Zool.* The solitary immature form of a DIPLOZOON.

Dipper (di·pəɹ). ME. [f. DIP *v.* + -ER ¹.] **1.** One who dips, in various senses: *spec.* one who immerses something in a fluid 1611. **2.** One who uses immersion in baptism; *esp.* an Anabaptist or Baptist 1617. **3.** A name of birds which dip or dive in water. **a.** The Water Ouzel, *Cinclus aquaticus*; also other species, as, in N. America, *C. Mexicanus*. **b.** *locally* in England: The Kingfisher. **c.** = DABCHICK. ? *Obs.* **d.** in *U.S.* The buffle, *Bucephala albeola*. ME. **4.** That which dips up water, etc.; *spec.* a ladle consisting of a bowl with a long handle 1801. **b.** in *U.S.* A name for the configuration of seven bright stars in Ursa Major. *Little D.*: the seven bright stars in Ursa Minor. 1858. **5.** *Photogr.* An apparatus for immersing negatives in a chemical solution 1859. **6.** A receptacle for oil, varnish, etc., fastened to a palette 1859.

1. I became also a lounger in the Bodleian library, and a great d. into books W. IRVING.

attrib. and *comb.*: **d.-bird** (see 3 a); **-clam** (*U.S.*), a bivalve mollusc, *Mactra solidissima*; **-gourd** (*U.S.*), a gourd used as a d. (sense 4).

Hence **Di·pperful** (*U.S.*), as much as fills a d.

Dipping (di·piŋ), *vbl. sb.* ME. [f. DIP *v.* + -ING [1].] **1.** The action of DIP *v.* **2.** *concr.* A liquid preparation in which things are dipped; a wash for sheep; dubbing for leather (*Sc.*) 1825.

attrib. and *comb.*: **d.-frame**, a frame used in dipping tallow candles, and in dyeing; **-well**, the receptacle in front of an isobath inkstand.

Di·pping-nee:dle. 1667. [See DIP *v.* and *sb.*] A magnetic needle mounted so as to move in a vertical plane about its centre of gravity, and thus indicate by its dip the direction of the earth's magnetism. So *d.-compass* = *dip-circle*.

Dippy (di·pi), *a. slang.* 1922. [?] Mad, crazy.

†Diprisma·tic, *a.* 1821. [DI- [2].] *Min.* Doubly prismatic.

Dipropargyl (dəiprǫpā·ɹdʒil). 1875. [DI- [2] 2.] *Chem.* A hydrocarbon isomeric with benzene, having the constitution of a double molecule of the radical Propargyl ($CH \equiv C.CH_2$); a pungent, mobile, highly refractive liquid.

‖ **Diprotodon** (dəiprōᵘ·tǒdǫn). 1839. [mod.L., f. Gr. δι- + πρῶτος + -οδον, neuter of -οδους, f. ὀδούς tooth.] *Palæont.* A genus of huge extinct marsupials, having two incisors in the lower jaw. So **Dipro·todont** *a.* having the dentition of the genus *D.*; *sb.* a marsupial of this genus.

Dipsacaceous (dipsăkēⁱ·ʃəs), *a.* [f. mod.L. *Dipsacaceæ*, f. *Dipsacus*, Gr. δίψακος teasel, f. δίψα thirst.] *Bot.* Belonging to the N.O. *Dipsacaceæ*, containing the teasels and their allies. var. **Dipsa·ceous** *a.*

Dipsadine (di·psădəin), *a.* [f. L. *dipsad-* stem of *Dipsas* + -INE.] *Zool.* Of or belonging to the family of non-venomous snakes, *Dipsadinæ*, to which belongs the genus *Dipsas* (DIPSAS 2 a).

‖ **Dipsas** (di·psæ̆s). Pl. **dipsades** (di·psădīz). ME. [L., Gr. διψάς, orig. adj., causing thirst, f. δίψα.] **1.** A serpent whose bite was fabled to produce a raging thirst. **2.** *Zool.* **a.** A tropical genus of non-venomous serpents. **b.** A genus of fresh-water bivalves of the family *Unionidæ*, or river-mussels. 1841.

Dipsetic (dipse·tik). 1847. [ad. Gr. διψητικός.]

A. *adj.* Producing thirst.

B. *sb.* A medicine that produces thirst.

‖ **Dipsomania** (dipsomēⁱ·niă). 1843. [f. Gr. διψο-, δίψα + μανία.] A morbid and insatiable craving, often paroxysmal, for alcohol. Also applied to persistent drunkenness. Hence **Dipsoma·niac** *sb.* a person affected with d.; *a.* affected with d. So **Dipsomani·acal** *a.*

Dipsopathy (dipsǫ·păþi). 1883. [f. Gr. διψο-, δίψα + πάθεια, f. πάθος (taken after *homœopathy*, etc.).] The treatment of disease by abstinence from liquids.

‖ **Dipso·sis.** 1851. [irreg. f. Gr. δίψα: the Gr. word was δίψησις.] *Med.* A morbid degree of thirst.

‖ **Di·ptera,** *sb. pl.* 1819. [mod.L. = Gr. δίπτερα, pl. neut. of δίπτερος two-winged.] *Entom.* The two-winged flies, a large order of insects having one pair of membranous wings, with a pair of halteres or poisers representing a posterior pair. Examples are the common house-fly, the gnats, gad-flies, etc.

Diptera·ceous, *a.* 1849. [f. mod. Bot.L. *Dipteraceæ*, f. *Dipter-* contr. of *Dipterocarpus* generic name; see -ACEOUS.] *Bot.* Of or belonging to the N.O. *Dipteraceæ* (*Dipterocarpeæ*); see DIPTEROCARP. So **Dipterad,** a plant of this order.

Dipteral (di·ptěrăl), *a.* 1812. [f. L. *dipteros*, a. Gr. + -AL.] **1.** *Arch.* Having a double peristyle. var. **†Dipte·ric** *a.* **2.** *Entom.* = DIPTEROUS 1828.

Di·pteran, *a.* and *sb.* 1842. [f. as DIPTERA + -AN.] **1.** *adj.* = DIPTEROUS. **2.** *sb.* A dipterous insect.

Di·pterist. 1872. [f. DIPTERA.] One who studies the *Diptera*.

Dipterocarp (di·ptěrǫ,kāɹp). 1876. [ad. mod.L. *Dipterocarpus*, f. Gr. δίπτερος + καρπός.] *Bot.* A member of the genus *Dipterocarpus* or N.O. *Dipterocarpeæ*, comprising E. Indian trees characterized by two wings on the summit of the fruit, formed by enlargement of two of the calyx-lobes. Cf. DIPTERACEOUS. So **Diptero·ca·rpous** *a.* belonging to this genus or order.

Diptero·logy. 1881. [f. DIPTERA; see -(O)LOGY.] That branch of entomology which relates to the *Diptera*. Hence **Di:pterolo·gical** *a.*, **Diptero·logist** = DIPTERIST.

‖ **Di·pteros.** 1706. [a. Gr. δίπτερος (sc. ναός).] *Archit.* A building with a double peristyle.

Dipterous (di·ptěrəs), *a.* 1773. [f. mod.L. *dipterus*, a. Gr. + -OUS.] **1.** *Entom.* Two-winged; of, pertaining to, or resembling the DIPTERA. **2.** *Bot.* Having two wing-like processes, as certain fruits, seeds, etc. 1851.

‖ **Di·pterus.** 1842. [mod.L., f. Gr.; see prec.] *Palæont.* A genus of Palæozoic dipnoous fishes, having two dorsal fins, opposite the ventral and anal respectively. Hence **Dipte·rian** *a.* and *sb.* belonging to, or a member of, this genus.

Dipterygian (diptěri·dʒiăn), *a.* 1847. [f. mod.L. *Dipterygii* (f. Gr. δι-, δίς + πτερύγιον fin).] *Ichth.* Having (only) two fins, as certain fishes. Also **Diptery·gious** *a.*

Diptote (di·ptōᵘt), *sb.* and *a.* 1612. [ad. L. *diptota* (pl.), a. Gr., f. δι-, δίς + πτωτός falling (πτῶσις case).] *Gram.* **1.** *sb.* A noun having only two cases. **2.** *adj.* Having only two cases.

Diptych (di·ptik). 1622. [ad. L. *diptycha* (pl.), a. late Gr. δίπτυχα neut. pl., f. δι-, δίς + πτυχή fold.] **1.** Anything folded, so as to have two leaves; *esp.* a two-leaved, hinged, writing tablet of metal, ivory, or wood, having its inner surfaces covered with wax for writing with the stylus. **2.** *Eccl.* (in *pl.*) Tablets containing a list of those, living and dead, who were commemorated by the early Church at the celebration of the eucharist. Hence, the list of such names; the intercessions in the course of which the names were introduced. 1640. **3.** An altar-piece or painting composed of two leaves which close like a book 1852. So **Di·ptychous** *a.* double-folded.

‖ **Dipus** (dəi·pǒs). 1799. [mod.L., ad. Gr. δίπους.] *Zool.* **a.** The typical genus of the jerboas. **b.** A small marsupial quadruped of Australia, *Chæropus castanotis*.

Dipyre (dipəiᵊ·ɹ). 1804. [mod. ad. L. *dipyros*, Gr. δίπυρος, f. δι- + πῦρ: so named because when heated it exhibits both phosphorescence and fusion.] *Min.* A silicate of alumina with small proportions of the silicates of soda and lime, occurring in square prisms.

Dipyrenous (dəipəirī·nəs), *a.* 1866. [f. Gr. δι- + πυρήν fruit-stone + -OUS.] *Bot.* Containing two fruit-stones.

Diradiation (dəirēⁱdiēⁱ·ʃən). 1706. [f. L. *di-*, *dis-* + RADIATION.] The diffusion of rays from a luminous body.

Dircæan (dəɹsī·ăn), *a.* 1730. [f. L. *Dircæus*, f. *Dirce*, Gr. Δίρκη a fountain in Bœotia.] Of or belonging to the fountain of Dirce: used of Pindar, called by Horace *Dircæus cygnus* the D. swan; Pindaric, poetic.

Dirdum (dɔ̄·ɹdəm). *Sc.* and *n. dial.* ME. [?] **1.** Uproar. **2.** Outcry; blame 1709.

Dire (dəiᵊ·ɹ). 1567. [ad. L. *dirus*.]

A. *adj.* 'Dreadful, dismal, mournful, horrible, terrible, evil in a great degree' (J.).

All monstrous, all prodigious things.. Gorgons and Hydra's and Chimera's d. MILT. *P. L.* II. 628. His direst foe COWPER. D. necessity C. BRONTË.

†B. *sb.* **1.** Direness 1660. **2.** *pl.* = L. *Diræ*, Furies 1610.

Direct (dire·kt, dəi-), *v.* ME. [f. L. *direct-* (*derect-*), ppl. stem of *dirigere* (*de-*), f. *di-* apart (or *de-* down) + *regere* to put or keep straight, to rule. Cf. ADDRESS *v.*] **1.** *trans.* To write (something) directly or specially *to*; to address; *spec.* in mod. usage, To write the direction on (a letter or the like) 1588. Also *absol.* **2.** To address (speech) *to* any one (*arch.*) 1450. **3.** To put or keep straight, or in right order. Also *absol.* 1509. **4.** *trans.* To cause (a thing or person) to move or point straight *to* or *towards* a place; to aim; to make straight (a way) *to*; to turn (the eyes, attention, etc.) straight *to* 1526. **5.** *trans.* To regulate the course of; to guide, conduct; to advise 1559. **6.** To give authoritative instructions to; to ordain, order, or appoint (a person) *to do* a thing, (a thing) *to be done* 1598. **b.** *intr.* or *absol.* To give directions; to order, appoint, ordain 1655.

1. D. to me at Mr. Hipkis's, Ironmonger in Monmouth BURKE. **2.** In the morning will I d. my prayer vnto thee *Ps.* v. 3. **3.** *absol.* Wisedom is profitable to d. *Eccl.* x. 10. **4.** I directed my Sight as I was ordered ADDISON. To d. attention to TYNDALL. **5.** Some God d. my iudgement *Merch. V.* II. vii. 14. **6.** I'le first d. my men what they shall doe with the basket *Merry W.* IV. ii. 98. *absol.* Who can d., when all pretend to know GOLDSM.

Hence **†Dire·ctedly** *adv.* directly.

Direct (dire·kt, dəi-), *a.* and *adv.* ME. [prob. a. F., ad. L. *directus*, pa. pple. of *dirigere*, *de-*; see DIRECT *v.*]

A. *adj.* **1.** Straight; undeviating in course; not circuitous or crooked. **2.** Perpendicular to a given surface, etc.; not oblique 1563. **3.** *Astron.* Of the motion of a planet, etc.: Proceeding in the order of the zodiacal signs, in the same direction as the sun in the ecliptic, *i.e.* from west to east; also said of the planet, etc. Opp. to *retrograde*. ME. **4.** Straightforward, uninterrupted, immediate; *spec.* of succession: Lineal, as opp. to *collateral*; as a *d. heir* or *ancestor* 1548. **5.** Without circumlocution or ambiguity; straightforward; downright 1530. **6.** Without intervening agency; immediate 1596.

2. Phr. *D. fire* (Mil.), fire which is perpendicular to the works attacked. **5.** *A.Y.L.* v. iv. 90. *Oth.* III. iii. 378. **6.** *All's Well* III. vi. 9. *D. narration*: not modified by being reported in the third person. *D. action*, action which takes effect without intermediate instrumentality, as in the *d.-action* or *d.-acting steam-engine*, without the intervention of a working-beam between the piston-rod and the crank; also, the exertion of pressure on the community by strikes, etc., instead of on Parliament through representatives. *D. current* (Electr.), a current running in one direction only (abbrev. *D.C.* or *d.c.*). *D. tax*: see TAX *sb.* 1. **b.** Of or pertaining to the work and expenses actually incurred during production as distinct from subsidiary work and overhead charges; also, applied to labour employed for the construction of works directly (without the intervention of a contractor) 1895.

B. *adv.* = DIRECTLY, q.v. Also in *comb.*

Direct (dire·kt), *sb.* 1615. [app. f. DIRECT *v.*] **1.** *gen.* A direction. **2.** *Mus.* A sign (𝆶) placed on the stave at the end of a page or line to indicate the position of the following note 1674.

Directer; see DIRECTOR.

Direction (dire·kʃən, dəi-). ME. [ad. L. *directionem*, f. *dirigere*; cf. F. *direction*.] **1.** The action or function of directing, aiming, guiding, instructing, or administering; conduct; instruction; management, administration 1509. **†2.** Administrative faculty -1636. **3.** = *Directorate* 1710. **†4.** Arrangement, order. Chiefly in *to take* or *set d.* -1548. **5.** with *a* and *pl.* An instruction how to proceed; an order, a precept 1576. **6.** The action of directing or addressing a letter, or the like; the superscription or address upon a letter or parcel sent, indicating for whom it is intended, and where it is to be taken 1524. **7.** The particular course or line pursued by any moving body, as defined by the region or point towards which it is directed; the relative point towards which one moves, turns the face, the mind, etc.; the line towards any point or region 1665. Also *fig.*

1. A Souldier, fit to stand by Caesar And giue d. *Oth.* II. iii. 128. She felt the need of d. GEO. ELIOT. **2.** *Rich. III*, v. iii. 16. **5.** He..took little or nothing but by the Doctors directions 1654. The stage d. STRUTT. Proper directions for finding me in London GOLDSM. **6.** My d. is—care of Andrew Bruce, merchant, Bridge-street BURNS. **7.** These terms—

north and south, east and west..indicate definite directions HUXLEY. The d. of a force is the line in which it acts 1879. He has gone in the d. of Paris (*mod.*). *fig.* New directions of enquiry JOWETT.

Hence **Dire·ctional** *a.* of or relating to d. in space.

†Dire·ctitude. Humorous blunder, app. for *discredit*. *Cor.* IV. v. 222.

Directive (dire·ktiv, dəi-), *a.* (*sb.*) 1594. [ad. med.L. *directivus*; see DIRECT *v.* and -IVE. In F. *directif, -ive.*] 1. Having the quality or function of directing; see DIRECT *v.* 2. Having the quality, function, or power of directing motion 1625. †3. Subject to direction (*rare*) 1606. †4. *sb.* That which directs -1654.

1. Laws being rules d. of our actions BERKELEY. 2. It is..d., not motive, altering the direction of other forces, but not..initiating them GROVE. 3. *Tr. & Cr.* I. iii. 356. Hence **Dire·ctive·ly** *adv.*, **-ness.**

Directly (dire·ktli), *adv.* ME. [f. DIRECT *a.* + -LY [2].] 1. In a direct manner; in a straight line of motion; straight 1513. Also *fig.* b. *Math.* Opp. to *inversely* 1743. 2. At right angles to a surface; not obliquely 1559. 3. Completely, exactly, just ME. 4. Without the intervention of a medium; immediately; by a direct process or mode 1526. 5. Immediately (in time); straightway 1602. b. *colloq.* as *conj.* As soon as, the moment after. (Ellipt. for *d. that, as,* or *when.*) 1795.

1. To run d. on *Jul. C.* IV. i. 32. *fig.* I asked him his opinion d., and without management BURKE. 2. Take a quadrant..and set it d. upright 1559. 3. The wind .. is d. contrary 1863. I find no decision d. in point 1891. 4. A universal primeval language revealed d. by God to man MAX MÜLLER. 5. I will come d. (*mod.*). b. Iodine and phosphorus combine d. they come into contact 1837.

Directness (dire·ktnės). 1598. [f. as prec.] The quality of being direct (*lit.* and *fig.*).

‖Directoire (dire·ktwāɹ), *a.* and *sb.* 1878. [Fr.; see DIRECTORY *sb.* 5.] (A style of dress) imitating that prevalent at the time of the French Directory.

Director (dire·ktəɹ). Also 6-9 **-er.** 1477. [a. AF. *directour* = F. *directeur*, ad. L. **director.*] 1. One who or that which directs, rules, or guides; a guide, a conductor; a superintendent. b. *spec.* A member of a board appointed to direct the affairs of a commercial corporation or company 1632. c. *Eccl.* (chiefly in *R.C.Ch.*) A spiritual adviser 1669. 2. One who or that which causes something to take a particular direction 1632. b. *Surg.* A grooved probe for guiding a cutting-instrument 1667. c. A metallic rod in a non-conducting handle for applying electric current to a part of the body 1795.

Comb.: **d.-circle** (of a conic), the locus of intersection of tangents at right angles to each other; **-plane**, a fixed plane used in describing a surface, analogous to the line called a DIRECTRIX.

Hence **Dire·ctorate,** the office of a d., or of a body of directors; management by directors; *concr.* a board of directors. **Directo·rial** *a.* of, pertaining to, or of the nature of a d., or of direction; of or pertaining to a body of directors. **Directo·rially** *adv.* **†Dire·ctorize** *v.* to bring under the authority of a directory (*rare*). **Dire·ctorship,** the office or position of a d., guiding.

Directory (dire·ktŏri), *a.* 1450. [ad. L. *directorius*; see -ORY.] Serving or tending to direct; directive, guiding. b. *spec.* Applied *esp.* to a statute or part of a statute which operates merely as advice or direction.

b. There was no necessity..to comply with the d. provisions of the Act as to delivery of copies 1884.

Directory (dire·ktŏri), *sb.* 1543. [ad. mod.L. *directorium* adj. neut. used subst.; see prec. Cf. F. *directoire.*] 1. Something that serves to direct; *esp.* a book of rules or directions. 2. *Eccl.* A book containing directions for the order of public or private worship, *e.g.* that compiled in 1644 by the Westminster Assembly 1640. 3. A book containing one or more alphabetical lists of the inhabitants of any locality, or of classes of them, with their addresses and occupations 1732. †4. *Surg.* = DIRECTOR 2 b. -1764. 5. *Fr. Hist.* [tr. F. *Directoire.*] The executive body in France during part of the revolutionary period (Oct. 1795—Nov. 1799) 1796.

Directress (dire·ktrės). Also **directoress.** 1586. [f. DIRECTOR.] A female who directs. Also *fig.* var. **†Dire·ctrice.**

Directrix (dire·ktriks). Pl. **-ices.** 1622. [a. mod.L. *directrix*, fem. of **director.*] 1. = DIRECTRESS. 2. *Geom.* †a. = DIRIGENT *sb.* 3. b. A fixed line used in describing a curve or surface; *spec.* the straight line the distance of which from any point on a conic bears a constant ratio to the distance of the same point from the focus. 1702.

Direful (dəi·ɹfŭl), *a.* 1583. [f. DIRE *a.* (or *sb.*) + -FUL.] Fraught with dire effects; dreadful, terrible.

Prodigies of d. import MERIVALE. Hence **Di·re·ful·ly** *adv.*, **-ness.**

†Dire·mpt, *ppl. a.* [ad. L. *diremptus, dirimere*, f. *dir-*, DIS- 1 + *emere* to take.] Distinct, divided. STOW. So **†Dire·mpt** *v.* to separate, divide; to break off.

Diremption (dire·mᵖʃən). Now *rare.* 1623. [ad. L. *diremptionem.*] A forcible separation, *esp.* of man and wife.

Direness (dəi·ɹnės). 1605. [f. DIRE *a.*] The quality of being dire.

†Dire·ption. 1483. [ad. L. *direptionem*, f. *diripere*, f. *di-, dis-* + *rapere.*] The action of pillaging, snatching away, or dragging apart violently -1828. So **†Direpti·tiously** *adv.* by way of pillaging.

Dirge (dəɹdʒ), *sb.* ME. [Orig. *dirige*, the first word of the antiphon *Dirige, Domine, Deus meus, in conspectu tuo viam meam*, Ps. v. 8.] 1. In the Latin rite: The first word of the antiphon at Matins in the Office of the Dead, used as a name for that service. 2. *transf.* A funeral song; a song of mourning. Also *fig.* 1500. 3. A funeral feast 1730.

2. D. at an end, the departed is placed in the funeral bed BOWEN. *Comb.* **d.-ale**, an ale-drinking at a funeral. Hence **Di·rgeful** *a.* full of lamentation, mournful.

‖Dirhe·m. 1788. [Arab. *dirham, dirhim*, ad. L. *drachma*; see DRACHM.] An Arabian measure of weight, orig. 44·4 grains troy; in Egypt at present = 47·661 troy grains. Also a small silver coin of the same weight, used still in Morocco, and worth about 4*d.* English.

Dirige (di·ridʒi), original f. DIRGE.

†Dirigent (di·ridʒĕnt). 1617. [ad. L. *dirigentem.*]

A. *adj.* 1. That di·ects. 2. *Pharm.* Formerly applied to certain ingredients in prescriptions which were held to guide the action of the rest -1860. 3. *Geom.* Applied to the line along which the describing line, or surface, is carried in the genesis of any figure 1704.

B. *sb.* 1. = DIRECTOR 1. 1756. 2. *Pharm.* A dirigent ingredient 1854. 3. *Geom.* A dirigent line 1706.

Dirigible (di·ridʒĭb'l), *a.* and *sb.* 1581. [f. L. *dirigere.*] 1. *adj.* Capable of being directed or guided, as a *d. balloon.* 2. *sb.* A dirigible airship. Also *attrib.*, as *d. shed*, etc. (*rec.*).

Dirigo-motor (di:rigo,mōᵘ·tǫɹ), *a.* [irreg. f. L. *dirig-* stem of *dirigere* + MOTOR.] *Physiol.* That both produces and directs muscular motion. H. SPENCER.

Diriment (di·rimĕnt), *a.* 1848. [ad. L. *dirimentem*; see DIREMPT. Cf. F. *dirimant.*] That nullifies; chiefly in *d. impediment*, one that renders marriage null and void from the beginning.

†Di·rity. [ad. L. *diritas.*] Direness. HOOKER.

Dirk (dəɹk), *sb.* 1602. [? Found in 1602 spelt *dork*, then common as *durk*; the spelling *dirk* is Johnson's, and lacks authority.] A kind of dagger or poniard: *spec.* the dagger of a Highlander. *Comb.* **d.-knife**, a large clasp-knife with a d.-shaped blade. Hence **Dirk** *v.* to stab with a d.

Dirk(e, -ness, obs. ff. DARK, -NESS.

Dirl, *v. Sc.* and *n. dial.* 1513. [Onomatopœic modification of Sc. *thirl* to pierce, to THRILL, and to DRILL.] 1. *trans.* To pierce, to thrill. 2. *intr.* To vibrate; to tingle 1715; to ring 1823. So **Dirl** *sb.* a thrill or vibration.

Dirt (dəɹt), *sb.* ME. [By metathesis from ME. *drit*, not known in OE. and prob. a. ON. *drit* neuter, excrement. See DRITE *v.*] 1. Ordure; EXCREMENT. 2. Unclean matter, such as soils any object by adhering to it; filth. Also *fig.* ME. 3. Mud; soil, earth, mould; brick-earth (*colloq.*) 1698; in *Mining, quarrying*, etc., useless material, rubbish 1799; *esp.* the material from which gold, etc. is separated 1857. 4. Dirtiness; uncleanness in action or speech 1774; meanness 1625.

2. The spoiling of my clothes and velvet coat with d. PEPYS. *fig.* The wealth was all like d. under my feet DE FOE. He has too much land: hang it, d. BEAUM. & FL. 4. The Turkish steamer..was in a beastly state of d. C. G. GORDON. Honours..thrown away upon d. and infamy MELMOTH.

Phrases. *To cast, throw,* or *fling d.*: to asperse with scurrilous or abusive language. *To eat d.*: to submit to degrading treatment.

Comb.: **d.-bed,** *Geol.* a stratum consisting of ancient vegetable mould; *spec.* a bed of dark bituminous earth, occurring in the lower Purbeck series of the Isle of Portland; **-bird,** a local name of the skua, *Stercorarius crepidatus*; **-cheap** *a.* (*adv.*), as cheap as d.; exceedingly cheap; **-eater,** one who eats d (see next); **-eating,** the eating of some kinds of earth or clay as food, practised by some savage tribes; a disorder of the nutritive functions characterized by a morbid craving to eat earth; **-pie,** a mud pie; **-track,** a course made of cinders, etc. for motor-cycle racing, or of earth for flat-racing.

Hence **Dirt** *v. trans.*, to dirty.

Dirty (dɔ̄·ɹti), *a.* 1530. [f. DIRT *sb.*] 1. Soiled with dirt; foul, unclean; mixed with dirt; that makes dirty. 2. Morally unclean; 'smutty' 1599; despicable 1670; basely earned 1742. 3. Repulsive, hateful, despicable 1611. 4. Of the weather: Foul, muddy; at sea, wet and squally 1660. 5. Of colour: Inclining to black, brown, or dark grey 1665.

1. A beastly Towne and durtie streets 1630. D. coal 1894, drudgery GOLDSM. 2. One of Swift's d. volumes 1850. A d. trick 1674. D. and dependent bread COWPER. Phr. *To do the d.*: to play a dirty trick. 3. Those Who worship durty Gods *Cymb.* III. vi. 55. Hence **Di·rtily** *adv.* **Di·rtiness. Di·rty** *v.*, to make or become dirty or unclean.

Dirty Allan. 1771. = *Dirt-bird* (see DIRT).

†Diru·ption. *rare.* 1656. [ad. L. *diruptionem.*] Breaking or rending asunder -1680.

Dis- (ME. also **dys-**) *prefix*, of L. origin. [L. *dis-* was related to *bis*, orig. **dvis* = Gr. δίς, from *duo*, δύο, the primary meaning being 'two-ways, in twain'.] In English, *dis-* appears (1) as repr. L. *dis-* in words adopted from L.; (2) as repr. OF. *des-* (mod.F. *dé-, dés-*), the inherited form of L. *dis-*; (3) as repr. late L. *dis-*, Rom. *des-*, substituted for L. *de-*; (4) as a living prefix, used with words without respect to their origin.

I. As an etymological element. In the senses: 1. 'In twain, in different directions, apart, asunder', hence 'abroad, away'; as in *discern, dilapidate, divide*, etc. 2. 'Between'; as in *dijudicate*, etc. 3. 'Separately, singly'; as in *dinumerate*, etc. 4. With privative sense; as in *disjoin, dissuade*, etc. 5. As an intensive, with verbs having already a sense of undoing; as in *disalter, disannul*, etc.

II. As a living prefix, with privative force. 6. Forming compound verbs, etc.; as in DISESTABLISH, DISOWN, etc. 7. With sbs., forming verbs, etc. in the senses: a. To strip of, free or rid of; as in DISFROCK, DISPEOPLE, etc. b. To deprive of the character, rank, or title of; as in DISBISHOP, DISCHURCH, etc. c. To turn out from the place or receptacle implied; as in DISBAR, DISBENCH, etc. d. To undo or spoil; as in DISCOMPLEXION. 8. With adjs., forming verbs in the sense of: To undo or reverse the quality expressed by the adj.; as in DISABLE, etc. 9. With a sb., forming another expressing the opposite, or denoting the lack of (the thing in question); as in DISEASE, DISHONOUR, etc. 10. Prefixed to adjs., with neg. force; as in DISHONEST, etc.

Disability (disăbi·lĭti). 1580. [f. DISABLE *a.*] 1. Want of ability; inability, incapacity, impotence (now *rare* in *gen.* sense); pecuniary inability 1624. 2. Incapacity in the eye of the law, or created by the law; legal disqualification 1641.

1. His disabilitie to performe his promise LUPTON. Disabilities for making a good book 1824. 2. The next legal d. is want of age BLACKSTONE.

†Disa·ble, *a.* ME. [DIS- 10.] Unable; incapable; impotent -1649. Hence **†Disa·bleness,** incapacity; disabled state.

Disable (disē̆·b'l), *v.* 1485. [DIS- 8.] 1. *trans.* To render unable or incapable; to deprive of ability, physical or mental, to incapacitate. Const. *from, †to, for.* 1548. b. *spec.* To render incapable of action or use by injury, etc.; to cripple 1491. 2. *spec.* To incapacitate legally; to pronounce legally incapable 1485. 3. To pronounce incapable; hence, to disparage, depreciate (*arch.*) 1529. †4. To make or pronounce of no force -1693.

1. b. My writeing hand hath been disabled by a

sprain HEARNE. 2. Papists, by the Act of Settlement, are disabled to inherit the crown LUTTRELL. 3. *A.Y.L.* IV. i. 34. Hence **Disa·blement.** **Disa·bler,** one who or that which disables.

Disabuse (disăbiū·z), *v.* 1611. [DIS- 6.] To free from ABUSE (q. v.); to relieve from fallacy or deception; to undeceive.
Wise and disabused persons JER. TAYLOR. [Man] still by himself abus'd, or dis-abus'd POPE.

†**Disacce·ptance.** 1642. [DIS- 6.] Refusal to accept –1720.

Disaccommodate (disăkǫ·mŏdeit), *v.* ? *Obs.* 1611. [DIS- 6.] To put to inconvenience, to incommode. Hence **Disacco:mmoda·tion.** ? *Obs.*

Disaccord (disăkǭ·ɹd), *sb.* 1809. [DIS- 9.] The reverse of accord; disagreement.

Disaccord (disăkǭ·ɹd), *v.* [ME. *disacorden*, a. OF. *desa(c)corder*, f. *des-*, DIS- 4 + *a(c)corder* to ACCORD.] *intr.* To be out of accord; to disagree; to refuse assent. Hence **Disacco·rdance** (*rare*). So **Disacco·rdant** *a.* (*rare*).

Disaccustom (disăkʊ·stəm), *v.* 1484. [a. OF. *desacostumer*, mod.F. *désaccoutumer*, f. *des-*, DIS- 4 + *acostumer.*] 1. *trans.* To render no longer customary; to break off (a habit, etc.) (*arch.*). 2. To cause (a person) to lose a habit. Const. *to*, †*from*. 1530.

Disaci·dify, *v. rare.* [DIS- 6.] To free from acidity.

Disacknowledge (disækn·ledʒ), *v.* 1598. [DIS- 6.] To refuse to acknowledge; to disown.

Disacquai·nt, *v.* ? *Obs.* 1548. [DIS- 6.] To make no longer acquainted; to render unfamiliar. So **Disacquai·ntance.** ? *Obs.*

Disacryl (disæ·kril). 1863. [f. DIS- implying disintegration + ACRYL.] *Chem.* A white flocculent substance into which acrolein changes when kept for some time. Also called *disacrone*. Also *attrib.*

†**Disadju·st,** *v. rare.* 1611. [DIS- 6.] To undo the adjustment of; to unsettle –1747.

†**Disado·rn,** *v. rare.* 1598. [DIS- 6.] To deprive of adornment –1729.

†**Disadva·nce,** *v.* [ME. *disavaunce*, a. OF. *desavancer*, f. *des-*, DIS- 4 + AVANCER to ADVANCE.] To check the advance of; to draw back; to lower. Also *fig.* –1659.

Disadvantage (disădva·ntėdʒ), *sb.* [ME. *des-*, *disavauntage*, a. F. *désavantage*, f. *des-*, DIS- 4 + *avantage.*] 1. Absence of advantage; an unfavourable condition or circumstance 1530. 2. Detriment, loss, or injury to interest; prejudice to credit or reputation ME.
1. Martius we have at d. fought And did retyre to win our purpose *Cor.* I. vi. 49. Every condition has its disadvantages JOHNSON. 2. They speake there.. to the d. of our nation NAUNTON. He sold to d. JOHNSON. Hence **Disadva·ntage** *v.* to cause d. to. †**Disadva·ntageable** *a.* prejudicial.

Disadvantageous (disæ:dvăntēⁱ·dʒəs), *a.* 1603. [DIS- 10.] Attended with disadvantage; unfavourable, prejudicial; depreciative. ? *Obs.*
The English were in a streight d. place MILT. A d. Character SWIFT. Hence **Disadvanta·geous-ly** *adv.*, **-ness.**

†**Disadve·nture.** [ME. *disaventure*, a. OF. *desaventure*, f. *des-*, DIS- 4 + *aventure.*] Mishap, misfortune –1638. Hence †**Disadve·nturous** *a.* unfortunate, disastrous.

Disadvi·se, *v.* 1636. [DIS- 6.] To give advice against; to dehort *from*.

Disaffect (disăfe·kt), *v.*[1] 1621. [DIS- 6.] 1. *trans.* To lack affection for; to dislike. ? *Obs.* 2. To alienate the affection of; to make unfriendly or less friendly; *spec.* to discontent or dissatisfy, as subjects with the government; to make disloyal. (Mostly in *pass.*) 1641.
2. You .. began to raise Cain by disaffecting the other workmen 1893.

†**Disaffe·ct,** *v.*[2] 1625. [DIS- 6.] To affect in an evil manner; to disorder, derange –1688.
It disaffects the bowels HAMMOND.

Disaffected (disăfe·ktėd), *ppl. a.* 1632. [f. DISAFFECT *v.*[1, 2]] 1. Evilly affected; estranged in affection; almost always *spec.* Unfriendly to the government, disloyal. †2. Affected with disease, disordered –1665. Hence **Disaffe·cted-ly** *adv.*, **-ness.**

Disaffection (disăfe·kʃən). 1605. [DIS- 9.] 1. Absence or alienation of affection or good will; *esp.* toward the government. †2. Physical disorder or indisposition –1741.
1. Nor any dis-affection to the state Where I was bred B. JONS.

†**Disaffe·ctionate,** *a. rare.* 1636. [DIS- 10.] Wanting in affection; disloyal –1796.

Disaffirm (disăfɔ̄·ɹm), *v.* 1531. [DIS- 6.] *trans.* To contradict, deny, negative: the contrary of AVER 1548. b. *Law.* To annul or reverse (a decision, etc.); to repudiate (a settlement or agreement): the contrary of CONFIRM.

Disaffirmance (disăfɔ̄·ɹmăns). 1610. [f. prec.] The action of disaffirming; negation; annulment, repudiation.
A Demonstration in d. of any thing that is affirmed HALE. So **Disaffirma·tion.** **Disaffi·rmative** *a.* (Bentham.)

Disafforest (disăfǫ·rėst), *v.* 1598. [ad. med.L. *disafforestare*. Cf. DE-AFFOREST, DEFOREST, DISFOREST.] *trans.* To free from the operation of the forest laws; to reduce from the legal state of forest to that of ordinary land.
The whole inclosed with a Pale, and disaforested 1725. Hence **Disafforesta·tion.** **Disaffo·rest-ment.**

Disa·ggregate, *v.* 1828. [DIS- 6.] 1. To separate (an aggregate) into its component particles. 2. *intr.* (for *refl.*) To separate from an aggregate 1881. Hence **Disaggrega·tion.**

Disagree (disăgrī·), *v.* 1494. [ad. F. *désagréer*; see DIS- 4.] 1. *intr.* To differ; not to AGREE, correspond, or harmonize. Const. *with*, †*to*, †*from*. 2. To differ in opinion; to dissent 1559. 3. To refuse to accord or agree. Const. *to*, *with*, †*from*. 1495. 4. To be at variance, to dispute or quarrel 1548. 5. Of food, climate, etc.: To conflict in operation or effect; to be unsuitable. Const. *with*. 1563.
1. Tradition .. disagreeing to the Scripture STILLINGFL. 2. Who shall decide when Doctors d. POPE. 3. I shall move to d. to that clause GLADSTONE. 4. Men onely d. Of creatures rational MILT. *P. L.* II. 497. 5. So plain a dish Could scarcely d. SHELLEY. Hence **Disagre·er** (*rare*).

Disagreeable (disăgrī·ăb'l), *a.* (*sb.*) ME. [a. F. *désagréable*; see DIS- 4.] †1. Not in agreement. Const. *to*, *with*. –1766. 2. Not in accordance with one's taste or liking; exciting displeasure or disgust 1698. 3. Of persons: Unamiable; offensive 1710. 4. *sb.* A disagreeable †person, thing, or experience 1781.
2. In regard to d. ..things, prudence does not consist in evasion..but in courage EMERSON. 2. A very d. man 1825. 4. The disagreeables of life C. BRONTË. Hence **Disagree:abi·lity,** unpleasantness. **Disagree·ableness,** the quality of being d. **Disagree·ably** *adv.* in a d. manner or degree.

†**Disagree·ance.** 1548. [f. DISAGREE *v.*] = DISAGREEMENT –1597.

Disagreement (disăgrī·mėnt). 1495. [f. DISAGREE *v.* Cf. F. *désagrément.*] 1. Want of agreement or harmony; difference; discordancy 1576. 2. Refusal to agree or assent 1495. 3. Difference of opinion; dissent 1576. 4. Quarrel, dissension, strife 1589. 5. Unsuitableness to the constitution 1702. 6. An unpleasantness. [F. *désagrément.*] *rare.* 1778.

†**Disallie·ge,** *v. rare.* [f. DIS- 6 + **alliege*, deduced from ALLEGIANCE.] To alienate from allegiance. MILTON.

Disallow (disălau·), *v.* ME. [a. OF. *desalouer*, f. *des-*, DIS- 4 + *alouer* to ALLOW. In med.L. *disallocare*.] To refuse to ALLOW (in various senses). †1. *trans.* To refuse to laud; to blame –1656. 2. To refuse to sanction; to disapprove of (*arch.*) 1494. Also †*intr.* with *of*. †3. To refuse to accept with approval –1660. Also †*intr.* with *of*. 4. To refuse to admit (intellectually) ME. 5. To refuse to grant 1555. 6. To forbid the use of 1563.
1. Like errour which wise men disalowe BARCLAY. 2. The auditor also disallowed the refreshments the committee had 1892. 3. What followes if we d. of this *John* I. i. 16. 4. To d. a hypothesis RAY. 5. To d. a claim 1841. 6. He utterly disallowes all hote Bathes in melancholy BURTON. Hence †**Disallow·able** *a.* not to be allowed. **Disallow·ance,** the action of disallowing; disapproval, rejection, prohibition; †in *Mus.*, an irregularity. **Disallow·er.**

Disally (disălai·), *v. rare.* 1671. [DIS- 6.] To free from alliance.

†**Disalte·rn,** *v. rare.* [f. DIS- 5 + L. *alternare.*] *trans.* To alter for the worse. QUARLES.

Disamis (di·sămis). 1551. *Logic.* The mnemonic term for the second mood of the third syllogistic figure, in which a particular affirmative major premiss (*i*), and a universal affirmative minor (*a*), yield a particular affirmative conclusion (*i*).

†**Disana·logy.** *rare.* 1610. [DIS- 9.] Want of analogy –1641.

Disanchor (disæ·ŋkəɹ), *v.* 1470. [a. OF. *desancrer*, f. *des-*, DIS- 4 + *ancrer.*] 1. *trans.* To loosen (a ship) from its anchorage 1477. 2. *intr.* To weigh anchor.

†**Disange·lical,** *a.* 1687. [DIS- 10.] The reverse of angelical –1736.

Disanimate (disæ·nimeit), *v.* 1583. [DIS- 6.] 1. To deprive of life 1646. 2. To deprive of spirit; to discourage, dishearten.
2. Disanimated at disasters C. MATHER. Hence **Disa:nima·tion.**

Disannex (disăne·ks), *v.* 1495. [a. OF. *desannexer*; see DIS- 1.] *trans.* To separate (that which is annexed); to disjoin.
To d. from the Provostship of the College (Oriel) a canonry of Rochester 1869. Hence **Disannexa·tion.**

Disannul (disănʊ·l), *v.* 1494. [DIS- 5.] 1. To cancel and do away with; to bring to nothing, abolish, annul. †2. To deprive by the annulment of one's title; *fig.* to do out *of*. Const. *from*, *of*. –1613.
1. Wilt thou also d. my judgment *Job* xl. 8. Hence **Disannu·ller.** **Disannu·lment.**

Disanoint (disănoi·nt), *v.* 1648. [DIS- 6.] To undo the anointing of; as, *to d. a king*.

†**Disappa·rel,** *v.* 1580. [DIS- 6.] To deprive of apparel; to disrobe, undress. Also *fig.* –1655.
The Cup..does d. the soul FELTHAM.

Disappear (disăpīᵊ·ɹ), *v.* 1530. [DIS- 6. Not in Shaks., nor in A.V.] 1. *intr.* To cease to appear or be visible; to vanish from sight; to be traceable no farther. 2. To cease to be present, to depart; to pass away, be lost 1665.
1. The vysion disapered incontynent PALSGR. A moraine..disappearing at the summit of the cascade TYNDALL. 2. As duly as the swallows d. COWPER. Hence **Disappea·rance,** the action of disappearing. **Disappea·rer.**

†**Disappe·ndancy, -ency.** *rare.* 1760. [DIS- 9.] *Law.* The condition of being disappendant; an instance of this.

†**Disappe·ndant, -ent,** *a.* 1642. [DIS- 10.] *Law.* The opposite of APPENDANT; detached from being an appendancy –1760.

Disappoint (disăpoi·nt), *v.* 1494. [ad. F. *désappointer*; see DIS- 4.] 1. *trans.* To undo the appointment of; to dispossess, deprive. *Obs.* (exc. as *nonce-wd.*) 1586. 2. To frustrate the expectation of; to defeat, balk, or deceive in fulfilment of a desire. Const. †*of*, *in*, *with*. 1494. †3. To break off (what has been appointed); to fail to fulfil an appointment with –1633. 4. To undo or frustrate anything appointed or determined; to defeat; to balk, foil, thwart 1579; †to undo, destroy –1712.
2. [They] were miserably disappointed of their expectations POTTER. 4. The wary Trojan shrinks, and, bending low Beneath his buckler, disappoints the blow POPE. To d. expectations LADY M. W. MONTAGU, good works STEELE. Hence **Disappoi·ntingly** *adv.*

Disappoi·nted, *ppl. a.* 1552. [f. prec.] 1. Having one's expectations frustrated; foiled, thwarted. †2. Improperly equipped; unprepared –1659.
2. Cut off euen in the Blossomes of my Sinne, Vnhouzzled, d., vnnaneld *Haml.* I. v. 77.

Disappointment (disăpoi·ntmėnt). 1614. [f. DISAPPOINT *v.* + -MENT; cf. F. *désappointement.*] 1. The fact of disappointing; the frustration or non-fulfilment of expectation, intention, or desire; an instance of this. 2. The state of being disappointed 1756. 3. *ellipt.* A thing or person that disappoints 1765.
1. Hope will predominate in every mind, till it has been suppressed by frequent disappointments JOHNSON. 2. No one ever lays one [a newspaper] down without a feeling of d. LAMB.

Disappreciate (disăprī·ʃi,eit), *v.* 1828. [DIS- 6.] To regard with the reverse of appreciation; to undervalue. So **Disappre·ciation.** WEBSTER.

Disapprobation (disæ·probēⁱ·ʃən). 1647. [DIS- 9.] The act or fact of disapproving; moral condemnation; disapproval.

Disapprobative (disæ·prŏbeitiv), *a.* 1824. [DIS- 10.] Characterized by or expressing disapprobation. So **Disa·pprobatory** *a.*

Disappropriate (disæprōu·priˌĕt), *ppl. a.* 1613. [ad. med.L. *disappropriatus*; see DIS- 4.] Deprived of appropriation; severed from connexion with a religious corporation.

Disappropriate (disæprōu·priˌeɪt), *v.* 1645. [f. ppl. stem of med.L. *disappropriare*; see DIS- 4.] **1.** *trans.* To dissolve the appropriation of 1656. †**2.** To render no longer the private property or possession of any one. MILT.

1. A Bill for the disappropriating of the Rectory appropriate to Preston 1656. Hence **Disappropria·tion,** the action of rendering disappropriate.

Disapproval (disăprū·văl). 1662. [f. DIS-APPROVE *v.*] The act or fact of disapproving; moral condemnation; disapprobation.

Disapprove (disăprū·v), *v.* 1481. [?f. DIS-4 + F. *approuver*.] †**1.** *trans.* To prove to be untrue or wrong –1793. **2.** To feel or express disapprobation of 1647. Also *intr.* with *of*, †*to* (*rare*).

2. Why must I hear what I d., because others see what they approve STEELE. Hence **Disappro·v-able** *a.* **Disappro·ver,** one who disapproves. **Disappro·vingly** *adv.* in a disapproving manner.

Disard, obs. or arch. f. DIZZARD.

Disarm (disā·ɹm), *v.* ME. [In 15th c. *desarm(e*, a. F. *désarmer*; see DIS- 4.] **1.** *trans.* To deprive of arms; to take the arms or weapons from. Const. *of*. 1481. Also *intr.* (for *refl.*) **2.** *trans.* To deprive of means of attack or defence 1602. **3.** To reduce to the customary peace footing. Usu. *absol.* or *intr.* (for *refl.*) 1727. **4.** *fig.* To deprive of power to injure or terrify; to divest of aversion, suspicion, or the like; to render harmless. Const. *of*, †*from*. ME.

1. A proclamation for disarming papists BLACKSTONE. He may be disarmed by the 'Left Parry' 1833. **3.** On the conclusion of peace it is usual for both sides to d. 1727. **4.** Conscious security disarms the cruelty of the monarch GIBBON. Hence **Disa·rm** *sb.* the act of disarming (an opponent). **Disa·rmer.**

Disarmament (disā·ɹmămĕnt). 1795. [f. DISARM *v.*; cf. F. *désarmement*.] The action of disarming; *esp.* reduction to the customary peace footing.

Disa·rmature. [f. as prec.] The action of disarming. SIR W. HAMILTON.

Disarrange (disărēⁱ·ndʒ), *v.* 1744. [DIS- 6.] *trans.* To undo the arrangement of; to put into disorder. Hence **Disarra·ngement,** the fact of disarranging; disorder.

Disarray (disărēⁱ·), *sb.* ME. [prob. a. OF. *desarei (mod.F. *désarroi*) vbl. sb. from *desareer*; see next.] **1.** The condition of being out of array or regular order; disorder, confusion. **2.** Imperfect or improper attire (*arch.*) 1590.

1. They..put hem to flyght and disaraye CAXTON.

Disarray (disărēⁱ·), *v.* 1470. [?after OF. *desareer*, f. *des-*, DIS- 4 + *areyer* to ARRAY.] **1.** *trans.* To throw out of array or order; to disorganize. (Chiefly of military array.) **2.** To strip or spoil of personal array; to disrobe 1483; to strip *of* any adjunct 1579.

1. At the first skirmish the enemies were disaraied [*fusi*] HOLLAND. **2.** That witch they disaraid, And robd of roiall robes SPENSER *F. Q.* I. viii. 46. My song, its pinions disarrayed of might, Drooped SHELLEY. Hence †**Disarray·ment** (*rare*), the fact of disarraying; derangement.

†**Disarre·st,** *v.* 1528. [ad. OF. *desarrester*; see DIS- 4.] To set free from arrest –1643.

Disarticulate (disaɹti·kiŭleⁱt), *v.* 1830. [DIS- 6.] To disjoint or become disjointed; to separate at the joints. Hence **Disarticula·tion. Disarti·culator,** he who or that which disarticulates.

†**Disasse·nt,** *v.* ME. [ad. OF. *desassentir*; see DIS- 4.] *intr.* To disagree –1692. Hence †**Disasse·nt** *sb.* dissent. †**Disasse·nter.**

†**Disassidu·ity.** 1613. [DIS- 9.] Want of assiduity; slackness –1635.

Disassimilation (disăsi:milēⁱ·ʃən). 1880. [DIS- 9.] The process which reverses assimilation; in *Physiol.* the transformation of assimilated substances into less complex and waste substances; catabolism. So **Disassi·milate** *v.* to transform by catabolism.

Disassociate (disăsōu·ʃiˌeⁱt), *v.* 1603. [DIS-6.] To free or detach from association; to dissociate, sever. Const. *from* (*with*). So **Disasso:cia·tion,** dissociation.

Disaster (diza·stəɹ), *sb.* 1590. [ad. F. *désastre*, f. *des-*, DIS- 4 + *astre*, ad. L. *astrum*, Gr. ἄστρον. Cf. *ill-starred*.] †**1.** An unfavourable aspect of a star or planet; 'an obnoxious planet' –1635. **2.** Anything ruinous or distressing that befalls; a sudden or great misfortune, or mishap; a calamity. Also †*attrib.*

1. Disasters in the sun *Haml.* I. i. 118. **2.** The day's disasters in the morning's face GOLDSM. A record of d. (*mod.*). Hence †**Disa·sterly** *adv.* in an ill-starred manner.

†**Disa·ster,** *v.* 1580. [f. prec. sb.] *trans.* To bring disaster upon; to strike with calamity; to ruin, afflict, endamage –1812.

At his disastred iourney made into Barbary BARRET.

Disastrous (diza·strəs), *a.* 1586. [a. F. *désastreux, -euse*, f. *désastre*; see DISASTER *sb.*] †**1.** Stricken with or subject to disasters; ill-starred, ill-fated; unfortunate –1790. **2.** Foreboding disaster, unpropitious, ill-boding (*arch.*) 1603. **3.** Of the nature of a disaster; fraught with disaster; calamitous 1603.

1. Always desastrous in love MARSTON. **2.** Some dysastrous aspect of the Planets 1648. **3.** Heavy rains followed by d. floods LYELL. Hence **Dis-a·strous-ly** *adv.*, **-ness.**

†**Disatti·re,** *v.* 1598. [DIS- 6.] To divest of attire; disrobe –1677.

†**Disaugme·nt,** *v.* 1611. [DIS- 6.] To diminish –1635.

†**Disauthe·ntic,** *a.* 1591. [DIS- 10.] Not authoritative –1619.

†**Disau·thorize,** *v.* 1548. [DIS- 6.] To strip of authority; to make or treat as of no authority –1689.

Disavai·l, *v.* ? *Obs.* ME. [DIS- 6.] †**1.** *intr.* To be prejudicial –1549. **2.** *trans.* To disadvantage 1471 Hence †**Disavai·l** *sb.* disadvantage.

Disavaunce, Disaventure, obs. ff. DISADVANCE, DISADVENTURE.

†**Disavou·ch,** *v.* 1597. [DIS- 6.] = DISAVOW –1679.

Disavow (disăvau·), *v.* ME. [a. F. *désavouer*; see DIS- 4. In med.L. *disavouare, disadvocare*.] **1.** *trans.* To refuse to avow; to disclaim knowledge of, responsibility for, or approbation of; to disown, repudiate. †**2.** To refuse to acknowledge as true; to deny –1660. †**3.** To decline –1660.

1. Melfort never disavowed these papers MACAULAY. **2.** Yet can they never..d. my blood Plantagenet's FORD. **3.** They..d. to have any further dealing with worldly contentments FULLER. Hence **Disavow·al,** the action of disavowing; repudiation, denial. †**Dis-avow·ance,** disavowal (*rare*). **Disavow·er,** one that disavows. †**Disavow·ment,** disavowal (*rare*). †**Disavow·ry,** disavowal.

Disband (disbæ·nd), *v.* 1591. [ad. 16th c. F. *desbander*, mod.F. *débander*; in military sense after It. *sbandare*.] **1.** *trans.* To break up (a company); to dismiss from service; †to discharge. †**2.** To let loose, turn off or out, send away –1790. †**3.** To break up the constitution of, dissolve –1793. **4.** *intr.* (for *refl.*) To break up as a body of soldiers; to break rank, fall into disorder, disperse; to leave military service 1598. †**5.** To dissolve; to separate, retire from association –1697.

1. The Marquiss of Huntley.. disbanded his forces BP. GUTHRIE. **2.** And therfore .. she [the wife] ought to be disbanded MILT. **4.** I commanded our men not to d., but pursue them SIR F. VERE. **5.** When both rocks and all things shall d. G. HERBERT. Hence **Disba·ndment,** the action or fact of disbanding.

†**Disba·r,** *v.*[1] 1565. [DIS- 1.] = DEBAR *v.* –1598.

Disbar (disbā·ɹ), *v.*[2] 1633. [DIS- 7.] To expel from the bar; to deprive of the status and privileges of a barrister. Hence **Disba·rment.**

†**Disbark** (disbā·ɹk), *v.*[1] 1552. [ad. F. *desbarquer*; see DIS- 4.] = DEBARK *v.*[1] –1842.

Disba·rk, *v.*[2] 1578. [DIS- 7 a.] = DEBARK *v.*[2]

†**Disba·se,** *v. rare.* 1592. [DIS- 5.] = DEBASE –1601.

Before I will d. mine honour so GREENE.

†**Disbeco·me,** *v.* 1632. [DIS- 6.] *trans.* To misbecome –1639.

Disbelief (disbĭlī·f). 1672. [DIS- 9.] The action or an act of disbelieving; mental rejection of a statement; positive unbelief.

Our belief or d. of a thing does not alter the nature of the thing TILLOTSON (J.). A d. in ghosts LECKY.

Disbelieve (disbĭlī·v), *v.* 1644. [DIS- 6.] **1.** *trans.* Not to believe or credit; to refuse credence to. Also *absol.* or *intr.* **2.** *intr.* with *in*: Not to believe in 1834.

Plutarch disbelieved Phanias BENTLEY. It does not rest with any man to determine what he shall believe or what he shall d. CARPENTER. Hence **Disbelie·ver.**

Disbe·nch, *v.* 1607. [DIS- 7 c.] †**1.** To displace from a bench or seat. *Cor.* II. ii. 75. **2.** To deprive of the status of a bencher 1874.

†**Disbe·nd,** *v.* 1607. [DIS- 6.] To unbend, relax –1632.

†**Disbi·nd,** *v. rare.* 1638. [DIS- 6.] To unbind, to loose.

†**Disbla·me,** *v.* ME. [a. OF. *desblamer*; see DIS- 4.] To free from blame, exculpate –1656.

Disbody (disbǫ·di), *v.* 1646. [DIS- 7.] = DISEMBODY. Hence **Disbo·died** *ppl. a.* disembodied.

†**Disbo·gue,** *v. rare.* 1600. [f. DIS- 6 + stem of EM-BOGUE.] *intr.* = DISEMBOGUE –1628.

Disbosca·tion. 1726. [ad. med.L. *disboscationem*.] The clearing away of woods; the conversion of wooded land into arable or pasture.

Disbowel (disbau·el), *v.* ME. [DIS- 7 a.] = DISEMBOWEL (*lit.* and *fig.*).

Disbranch (disbra·nʃ), *v.* 1575. [DIS- 7 a.] **1.** *trans.* To cut or break off the branches of. **2.** To cut or break off, as a branch; to sever 1605.

Disbud (disbʊ·d), *v.* 1725. [DIS- 7 a.] To remove the buds of; to deprive of (superfluous) buds.

Disburden, -burthen (disbɔ̄·ɹd'n, -bɔ̄·ɹð'n), *v.* 1531. [DIS- 7.] **1.** *trans.* To remove a burden from; to relieve of a burden (*lit.* and *fig.*). **2.** *trans.* To get rid of (a burden); to discharge, unload 1586. Also *refl.* **3.** *intr.* (for *refl.*) To discharge its load 1667.

1. I am disburthened and eased of many cares FLEMING. **2.** Obtaining an excuse for disburdening his wrath upon her 1828. **3.** Where Nature..by disburd'ning grows More fruitful *P. L.* v. 319. Hence **Disbu·rdenment, -bu·rthenment,** the act of disburdening; the being disburdened.

†**Disbu·rgeon,** *v. rare.* 1601. [DIS- 7 a.] = DISBUD.

Disburse (disbɔ̄·ɹs), *v.* 1530. [orig. *disbourse*, a. OF. *desbourser*, f. *des-*, DIS- 4 + *bourse*. Now assim. to L. *bursa*.] **1.** *trans.* To pay out or expend; to pay or defray; also *absol.* †**2.** *fig.* To spend, give out or away –1671.

1. Bid my wife D. the summe, on the receipt thereof *Com. Err.* IV. i. 38. Hence †**Disbu·rse** *sb.*, **Disbu·rsement,** the act or fact of disbursing; money paid out; expenditure. **Disbu·rser.**

Disburthen; see DISBURDEN.

Disc, var. sp. of DISK.

†**Disca·binet,** *v.* [DIS- 7.] To disclose, as cabinet secrets. MILT.

Discage (diskēⁱ·dʒ), *v.* 1649. [DIS- 7 c.] To let out as from a cage; to uncage.

Discal (di·skăl), *a.* 1848. [f. L. *discus*.] Of, pertaining to, or of the nature of, a disk; discoid.

Discalceate (diskæ·lsiˌĕt). 1658. [ad. L. *discalceatus*.]

A. *ppl. a.* Barefooted.

B. *sb.* A barefooted friar or nun.

†**Disca·lceate,** *v. rare.* 1623. [f. L. *discalceat-*, ppl. stem of *discalceare*; see DIS- 4.] To pull off the shoes. Hence †**Discalcea·tion,** the action of taking off the shoes.

Discalced (diskæ·lst), *ppl. a.* 1631. [as if from *discalce, repr. L. *discalceare*.] = DISCALCEATE *ppl. a.*

†**Discamp** (diskæ·mp), *v.* 1574. [ad. It. *scampare*, with *dis-* for *s-*; cf. DECAMP.] **1.** *intr.* To raise or break up a camp; to decamp. Also *fig.* –1693. **2.** *trans.* To remove or abandon (a camp); to force to abandon a camp –1658.

†**Disca·ndy,** *v. rare.* [DIS- 6.] *intr.* To melt or dissolve out of a candied condition. SHAKS.

Disca·nonize, *v.* 1605. [DIS- 6.] †**1.** To exclude from the canon –1660. **2.** To undo the canonization of 1797. Hence **Discanoniza·tion.**

Discant, var. of DESCANT.

Discapa·citate, *v. rare.* 1660. [DIS- 6.] To deprive of capacity, to incapacitate.

Discard (diskā·ɹd), *v.* 1586. [DIS- 7 c.] **1.** *Cards.* To throw out (a card) from the hand. Also *absol.* 1591. **2.** To cast off, cast aside, reject 1598. 3. To dismiss from employment, service, or office; to discharge 1586.

2. We have..discarded our faith in astrology and witches SIR B. BRODIE. 3. My man..is a sad dog; and the minute I come to Ireland I will d. him SWIFT. Hence **Disca·rdment**, the action of discarding (*rare*). †**Disca·rdure**, discardment.

Di·scard, *sb.* 1744. [f. prec. vb.] 1. *Cards.* The act of d.scarding; also, the card discarded. 2. That which is discarded (*rare*) 1892.

†**Disca·rnate**, *a. rare.* 1661. [f. (ult.) DIS- 4 + L. *carnem, carnatus.*] Stripped of flesh, as *d. bones.*

Discase (diskē¹·s), *v. arch.* 1596. [DIS- 7 a.] To remove the case of; to uncase, unsheathe, undress. Also *intr.* (= *refl.*)

†**Disca·tter**, *v.* [In ME. *de-scater*, f. F. *de-*, *des-* (DE- 6, DIS- 1) + SCATTER.] *trans.* To scatter abroad, disperse –1635.

†**Disce·de**, *v.* 1650. [ad. L. *discedere*; see DIS- 1.] *intr.* To depart, deviate. –1665.

Discept (dise·pt), *v. rare.* 1652. [ad. L. *disceptare*, f. *dis-* (DIS- 2, 3) + *captare.*] *intr.* To dispute, debate; to express difference of opinion, differ.

Permit me to d. 1818. So †**Discepta·tor** (*rare*).

Disceptation (diseptē¹·ʃən). *arch.* ME. [a. F., ad. L. *disceptationem*; see prec.] Disputation, debate.

Discern (dizɔ̄·ɹn), *v.* ME. [a. F. *discerner*, ad. L. *discernere*; see DIS- 1.] †1. *trans.* To separate as distinct –1645. 2. To recognize as distinct; to separate mentally (*arch.*) 1483. 3. *intr.* To recognize the difference; to discriminate *between* (*arch.*) ME. 4. *trans.* To distinguish (one thing or fact) by the intellect; to perceive distinctly ME.; *intr.* to judge *of* 1622. Also *absol.* 5. *trans.* To distinguish by the sight (or other senses); to make out ME. Also †*intr.* or *absol.* (*rare*). ¶ 6. Formerly sometimes used for DECERN 1494.

2. To discerne the truthe from that whiche is false 1551. 4. His swift pursuers from Heav'n Gates d. Th' advantage MILT. *P. L.* I. 326. 5. We could d. no trace of rupture [in the ice] TYNDALL.

Hence †**Disce·rnance**, difference, discernment. **Disce·rner.** **Disce·rning** *vbl. sb.* discrimination, discernment; *ppl. a.* showing discernment; penetrating. **Disce·rningly** *adv.*

Discernible (dizɔ̄·ɹnĭb'l), *a.* 1561. [orig. a. F. *discernable*, f. *discerner*; refash. after L. *discernibilis.*] 1. Capable of being discerned; perceptible. †2. Distinguishable (*from* something else) –1670.

1. When I behold with mine eyes some small scarce d. Graine or Seed HOOKER. A d. weight 1794. A d. state of danger JER. TAYLOR. Hence **Disce·rnibleness.** **Disce·rnibly** *adv.*

Discernment (dizɔ̄·ɹnmĕnt). 1586. [f. DISCERN *v.* + -MENT.] 1. The act of discerning 168.. 2. The faculty of discerning; discrimination; judgement; keenness of intellectual perception; penetration, insight 1586. †3. The act of distinguishing; a distinction –1648.

2. His d. was expressed in the choice of this important post GIBBON.

Discerp (disɔ̄·ɹp), *v.* Now *rare.* Pa. t. and pple. **discerped, discerpt.** 1482. [ad. L. *discerpere*; see DIS- 1.] 1. To pluck or tear asunder, pull to pieces. Also *fig.* 2. To pluck or tear off, sever 1655. So †**Disce·rpible** *a.* = DISCERPTIBLE.

Discerptible (disɔ̄·ɹptĭb'l), *a.* 1736. [f. L. *discerpt-*, ppl. stem of *discerpere*; see -BLE.] Capable of being plucked asunder, or divided into parts. Hence **Discerptibi·lity**, divisibility.

Discerption (disɔ̄·ɹpʃən). Now *rare.* 1647. [ad. L. *discerptionem.*] 1. The action of pulling to pieces; also *fig.* 2. The action of tearing off, severance; *concr.* a portion torn off or severed 1688.

Disce·rptive, *a. rare.* [f. L. *discerpt-* ppl. stem + -IVE.] Having the quality of dividing or separating; tending to pull to pieces.

†**Discession.** 1521. [ad. L. *discessionem*; see DISCEDE.] Departure; secession; separation –1662.

Discharge (dis,tʃā·ɹdʒ), *v.* ME. [a. OF. *descharger*, (mod.F. *décharger*), f. (ult.) DIS- 4 + *carricare* to load.]

I. 1. *trans.* To unload (a ship, etc.); to rid of a charge or load; to disburden. (Also *absol.*, and *intr.* for *refl.*) b. To disburden (a weapon) by letting fly the missile with which it is charged; to fire off. Also *absol.* 1555. c. *Electr.* (*trans.*) To rid of an electric charge 1748. Also *transf.* and *fig.* (Now *rare.*) 2. *fig.* To relieve *of* (an obligation or charge); to exonerate; to release *from* ME. †b. *refl.* To relieve oneself of an obligation by fulfilling it –1705. 3. *trans.* To relieve of a charge or office; (more usually) to dismiss from office, etc.; to cashier. Const. *from*, †*of.* 1476. †4. *trans.* To clear of a charge or accusation; to exculpate, acquit –1742. 5. To dismiss (one charged with an offence); to release from custody, liberate 1556. b. To send away, let go 1586. 6. To charge not to do; to prohibit, forbid. (Chiefly *Sc.*) 1570. 7. *Archit.* To relieve (some part) of pressure by distributing it over adjacent parts 1667.

1. To d. a Bark 1712, muskets and blunderbusses WESLEY, a Leyden phial 1794, the Earth of its Moisture J. JAMES. 2. Phr. *To d. a bankrupt*: to release him from further legal liability for debts contracted before his bankruptcy. 3. The duke of Yorke was discharged of the office of Regent HALL. To be discharged of employment EVELYN. 4. To d. a constable of suspicion FIELDING. 5. To d. a prisoner JUNIUS, a jury 1893. 7. The arched ceilings.. are made of cane, to d. the Walls LEONI.

II. 1. To remove (that with which anything is charged); to clear out, send out or forth, emit 1479. Also *refl.*; *esp.* of a river, to disembogue (also *intr.*) 1600. 2. *trans.* †To remove (a charge, obligation, etc.); to get rid of –1778; in *Law*, to cancel, annul (an order of a court) 1798. 3. To clear off, or acquit oneself of, by fulfilment or performance; to pay 1525; †to pay for –1842. 4. To acquit oneself of, perform (a charge, office, function, etc.) 1548. 5. *Dyeing*, etc. To remove (the dye) *from* a textile fabric, etc. b. To print (a fabric) with a pattern by discharging parts of the ground colour 1727.

1. To d. cargo R. H. DANA, a shot SHAKS., a dart POPE, a stroke GOLDSM., choler 1600, water 1833. 2. To d. a duty 1741. 3. I will d. my bond SHAKS. To d. one's debts HALLAM, the Jew SHAKS. A shilling to d. his chair SWIFT. 4. Neglygent in dyschargeinge theyr office LATIMER. 5. Wash the Ethiop white, d. the leopard's spots CHURCHILL.

Hence **Discha·rger**, one who or that which discharges; *spec.* an apparatus for producing a charge of electricity; a *discharging rod.*

Discharge (dis,tʃā·ɹdʒ), *sb.* 1460. [f. prec. vb.; cf. OF. *descharge*, mod.F. *décharge.*] 1. The act of freeing from or removing a charge or load; unloading (*of* a vessel, etc.); removal (*of* a cargo, etc.) 1580. 2. The act of discharging a weapon or missile; firing off a fire-arm, letting fly an arrow, etc. Also *fig.* 1596. 3. The act of sending out or pouring forth; emission, ejection; the rate or amount of emission 1600; *concr.* that which is emitted or poured forth 1727. 4. The act of freeing from obligation, liability, or restraint; exoneration; exculpation; dismissal; liberation 1460. b. *concr.* Something that frees from obligation; as, a legal document; an acquittance; a certificate 1495. 5. The act of clearing off a pecuniary liability; payment 1611. 6. Fulfilment, execution 1610. 7. †Dismissal; in *Law*, dismissal or reversal of an order of court 1677. 8. *Archit.* The relieving some part of a building of pressure; *concr.* a contrivance for effecting this 1703. 9. *Dyeing.* The removing the colour with which a textile fabric is charged; *concr.* a mixture used for this purpose 1836.

3. *spec.* (*Electr.*) The emission or transference of electricity between two bodies positively and negatively charged, when placed in contact or near each other 1794. 4. Phr. *D. of a bankrupt*: release from further legal liability for debts contracted before his bankruptcy. His receiving a d. from guilt 1836. There is no d. in that warre *Eccl.* viii. 8. Death, who sets all free, Hath paid his ransom now and full d. MILT. *Sams.* 1573. 5. A penny Cord..of what's past, is, and to come, the d. *Cymb.* v. iv. 173. 6. The d. of our duty 1675.

Discharm (dis,tʃā·ɹm), *v.* 1480. [ad. OF. *des-, décharmer*; see DIS- 4.] *intr.* and *trans.* To undo, or free from the influence of, a charm.

Dischevel, etc., obs. f. DISHEVEL, etc.

†**Dischu·rch**, *v.* 1629. [DIS- 7.] 1. *trans.* To cause to be no longer a church; to unchurch –1656. 2. To exclude from the church 1651.

†**Disci·de**, *v.* 1494. [f. DIS- 1 + *cædere* to cut.] To cut asunder; to cut off or away (*lit.* and *fig.*) –1679.

Disciferous (disi·fĕrəs), *a.* 1883. [f. L. *discus* + -FEROUS.] *Bot.* Bearing a disk or disks.

Discifloral (disiflō̆·răl), *a.* 1873. [f. L. *discus*; cf. *floral.*] *Bot.* Having flowers with the receptacle enlarged into a conspicuous disk surrounding the ovary: *spec.* applied to a series of orders of polypetalous exogens (*Disciflorae*).

Disciform (di·sifǭm), *a.* 1830. [f. as prec. + -FORM.] Discoidal.

Disci·nct, *a. rare.* 1647. [ad. L. *discinctus.*] Ungirt (*lit.* and *fig.*).

†**Disci·nd**, *v.* 1640. [ad. L. *discindere.*] To sever, separate –1691.

Disciple (disəi·p'l), *sb.* [In OE. *discipul*, ad. L. *discipulus.* In early ME. *di-, deciple.*] 1. One who attends upon another for the purpose of learning from him; a pupil or scholar. a. A follower of Christ during his life; *esp.* one of the Twelve. b. In the N.T., an early Christian; hence *absol.*, a Christian ME. c. A follower of any (religious) teacher OE. d. *gen.* A scholar or pupil. (Now *arch.*, *rhet.* or *joc.*) 1489. 2. One who belongs to any 'school' ME. 3. *pl.* The name of a denomination of Christians, a branch of the Baptists; called also Campbellites. (Chiefly in U.S.) 1858.

Hence †**Disci·plehood, Disci·pleship**, the condition or state of a d. †**Disci·pless**, a female d.

Disci·ple, *v.* Now *rare* or *arch.* 1492. [f. prec. sb.] †1. *trans.* To teach, train –1681. 2. To make a disciple of 1647. †3. To subject to discipline; to chastise, correct –1651.

1. He..was Discipled of the brauest *All's Well* I. ii. 28. 2. Go out with Zeal, D. all Mankind KEN.

Disciplinable (di·siplinăb'l), *a.* 1542. [ad. L. *disciplinabilis*; see DISCIPLINE *v.*] 1. Amenable to discipline or teaching; docile. †2. Disciplinary –1677. 3. Subject to discipline or correction 1870.

3. D. offences 1870. Hence **Disciplinableness.**

Disciplinal (di·siplinăl, disipləi·năl), *a.* 1628. [ad. med.L. *disciplinalis.*] †1. = DISCIPLINABLE 1. 2. Of, belonging to, or of the nature of discipline 1853.

Di·sciplinant. 1620. [a. Sp. *disciplinantes* (pl.), or It. *disciplinanti* (pl.).] One who subjects himself to a course of discipline; *spec.* a flagellant.

Disciplinarian (di:siplinē̆·riăn). 1585. [f. as DISCIPLINARY + -AN.]

A. *adj.* 1. *Ch. Hist.* Of or pertaining to the Disciplinarians 1593. 2. Of or pertaining to discipline 1640.

1. The D. or Presbyterian party was extinct 1889.

B. *sb.* 1. *Ch. Hist.* One of the English Puritans, who favoured the Genevan or Presbyterian ecclesiastical polity or discipline 1585. 2. One who enforces discipline 1639. 3. An advocate of strict discipline 1746.

1. All sectaries pretend to scripture; papists, anabaptists, disciplinarians SANDERSON.

Disciplinary (di·siplinări), *a.* 1593. [ad. med.L. *disciplinarius.* Cf. F. *disciplinaire.*] 1. Relating to ecclesiastical discipline. 2. Pertaining to, or promoting discipline 1598. 3. Pertaining to mental training 1644. †4. Acquired by learning (*rare*) –1658.

2. All these restrictions are merely d. 1866. 3. An excellent d. instrument for the formation of character J. MARTINEAU.

†**Di·sciplinate**, *v.* 1586. [f. L. *disciplinat-*, *disciplinare.*] To subject to instruction or discipline –1647. Hence **Di·sciplina:tory, Disci·plinatory** *a.* tending to promote discipline.

Discipline (di·siplin), *sb.* ME. [a. F., ad. L. *disciplina* instruction of disciples, for *discipulina*, f. *discipulus.* Opp. to *doctrine.*] †1. Instruction imparted to disciples or scholars; teaching; learning; education –1615. 2. A branch of instruction; a department of knowledge ME. 3. The training of scholars and subordinates to proper conduct and action by instructing and exercising them in the same; mental and moral training; also used *fig.* ME. b. *spec.* Training in the practice of arms and military evolutions; drill. Formerly, more widely: The art of war. 1489. 4. A trained condition 1509. 5. The order maintained and observed among persons under control or command 1667; a system of rules for conduct 1659. 6. *Eccles.* The system by which order is maintained in a church; the procedure whereby this is carried out; the exercise of penal measures by a Christian Church 1549. **b.** *spec.* The ecclesiastical polity of the Puritan or Presbyterian party (thence styled DISCIPLINARIANS) in the 16th and 17th c. 1574. **7.** Correction; chastisement; in religious use, the mortification of the flesh by penance; also, a beating, or the like ME. Hence *transf.* A whip or scourge 1622. †**8.** Medical regimen (*rare*) 1754.

1. *Tr. & Cr.* II. iii. 31. 2. Professors of arts and disciplines at Paris BURTON. 3. Certainely wife and children are a kind of d. of humanity BACON. A man not ignorant in the disciplyne of warre EDEN. 4. Sound-headed men, Of proper d., and excellent mind POLLOK. 5. The lawless Troops, which d. disclaim DRYDEN. The d. of workshops, of schools, of private families MACAULAY. Submitted to an almost monastic d. M. PATTISON. 7. With a rope's-end..he continued this d. WILLOCK. On the floor lay a d., or penitential scourge SCOTT.

Di·scipline, *v.* ME. [a. F. *discipliner*; see prec.] **1.** *trans.* To subject to discipline; in earlier use, to educate, train; later, *esp.* to bring under control. **b.** *spec.* To train in military exercises and prompt action in obedience to command; to drill 1598. **c.** To subject to ecclesiastical discipline 1828. **2.** To inflict penitential discipline upon; hence, to chastise, thrash, punish ME.

1. Disciplined in the school of adversity BURGON. 2. Ha's he disciplin'd Auffidius soundly *Cor.* II. i. 139. Hence **Di·sciplner,** one who disciplines.

Discipular (disi·piŭlăɹ), *a.* 1859. [f. L. *discipulus* + -AR¹.] Of, belonging to, or of the nature of, a disciple.

Discission (disi·ʃən). 1647. [ad. L. *discissionem*, f. *discindere*; see DISCIND. The var. *discision* (17th c.) is from L. *dis-* and *cædere.*] *Surg.* An incision into a tumour or cataract. *Obs.* in gen. sense.

Disclaim (disklēⁱ·m), *v.* 1560. [a. AF. *des-*, *disclamer*, f. *des-*, *dis-* (DIS- 4) + *clamer* to CLAIM.] **1.** *intr. Law.* To renounce a legal claim. Const. †*in* the thing, †*out of* or *from* the claim of the other party. 1574. †**2.** *intr.* To disavow all part *in* –1637; to proclaim one's renunciation of, or dissent *from* –1644. **3.** *trans. Law.* To renounce a legal claim to; to repudiate a connexion with 1595. **4.** To disavow any claim to or connexion with; to disown formally 1593. **5.** To refuse to admit; to renounce 1659; †to refuse –1805. †**6.** To cry out upon the claims of –1659. **7.** *trans. Her.* To declare not to be entitled to bear arms; to 'make infamous by proclamation' 1634.

1. The lord may disclaime..which signifieth utterly to renounce the seignory COKE. 3. An executor may, before probate, d. the executorship WHARTON. 4. Sir, shee's yours, Or I disclaime her ever HEYWOOD. 5. The troops..disclaimed the command of their superiors GIBBON. 6. Phr. †*To d. against*: to DECLAIM against. Hence †**Disclaim** *sb.* an act of disclaiming.

Disclaimer¹ (disklēⁱ·məɹ). 1579. [a. AF. *disclaimer* inf. used subst.] **1.** *Law.* The action of disclaiming, renouncing, or relinquishing a legal claim; a formal refusal to accept an estate, trust, duty, etc. **2.** *gen.* A disavowal of claims or pretensions 1790. **3.** *Her.* A proclamation of persons not entitled to bear arms 1854.

Disclaimer². 1702. [f. DISCLAIM *v.* + -ER¹.] One who disclaims.

Disclamation (disklămēⁱ·ʃən). 1592. [f. med.L. *disclamare.*] Renunciation, repudiation, disclaimer.

†**Discla·nder,** *sb.* ME. [a. AF. **desclandre*, deriv. of OF. *esclandre* :—L. *scandalum*; see ESCLANDRE.] **1.** Malicious speech bringing opprobrium on any one; slander –1562. **2.** Public disgrace or opprobrium; scandal –1532.

†**Discla·nder,** *v.* [ME. *desclandre*, f. prec. sb.] **1.** *trans.* To slander –1530. **2.** To bring into public disgrace or opprobrium –1483.

†**Discloa·k,** *v.* 1599. [DIS- 6 or 7 a.] To take off the cloak of; to unrobe –1677.

†**Disclo·se,** *sb.* 1548. [f. DISCLOSE *v.*] = DISCLOSURE –1625.

Disclose (disklōᵘ·z), *v.* [ME. *des-*, *dis-closen*, f. (ult.) DIS- 4 + L. *claudere.*] †**1.** *trans.* To open up; to unfasten –1596; to hatch (an egg) 1626. Also *intr.* **2.** *trans.* To uncover; to remove a cover from and expose to view ME.; to uncover (a young bird, etc.) from the egg; to hatch; also *fig.* Rarely, to lay (eggs). 1486. †**3.** To discover –1611. **4.** To open up to the knowledge of others; to reveal ME. Also †*intr.* for *refl.*

1. It [a rosebud] discloseth it selfe and spreadeth abroad B. GOOGE. 2. The parting deep disclos'd her sand TATE & BRADY. Anon as patient as the female Doue, When that her golden Cuplet are disclos'd *Haml.* V. i. 310. 4. Tell me your Counsels, I will not d. 'em *Jul. C.* II. i. 298.

Hence **Disclo·sed** *ppl. a.* in the senses of the vb.; in *Her.* with wings expanded: said of all birds that are not birds of prey. **Disclo·ser,** one who or that which discloses.

Disclosure (disklōᵘ·ʒ'ŭɹ). 1598. [f. DISCLOSE *v.*, after CLOSURE.] **1.** The action of disclosing, opening up to view, or revealing; discovery, exposure. **2.** That which is disclosed; a revelation 1825.

1. A public d. of his motives THIRLWALL. The d. of the insect from the pupa KIRBY. 2. Preparing him for the d. 1825.

Discloud (disklau·d), *v.* 1600. [DIS- 7 a.] To free or clear from clouds; to reveal.

†**Disclou·t,** *v.* [DIS- 7 a.] To take out of a clout. BP. HALL.

†**Disclu·sion.** *rare.* 1656. [ad. L. *disclusionem*, influenced in sense by DISCLOSE *v.*] 'Emission' (J.) –1668.

Disco- (disko), comb. f. Gr. δίσκος quoit, DISK: as in

Discobla·stic *a.* [Gr. βλαστός germ], *Embryol.* (of an ovum), having discoidal segmentation of the formative yolk. **Di·scocarp** [Gr. καρπός], *Bot.* (*a*) a fruit consisting of a number of achenes within a hollow receptacle, as in the rose; (*b*) the disk-like fructification of discomycetous fungi and gymnocarpous lichens; hence **Discoca·rpous** *a.*, relating to, or having, a discocarp. **Discoce·phalous** *a.* [Gr. κεφαλή], *Zool.* belonging to the sub-order *Discocephali* of fishes, having a sucking-disk on the head. **Discoda·ctyl(e, Discoda·ctylous** *adjs.* [Gr. δάκτυλος], *Zool.* having toes dilated at the end so as to form a disk, as a tree-frog. **Discomyce·tous** *a.*, *Bot.* belonging to the order *Discomycetes* of Fungi, having a disk-shaped hymenium or *discocarp.* **Discopla·cental, Discoplacenta·lian** *adjs.*, *Zool.* belonging to the section *Discoplacentalia* of mammals, having a disk-shaped placenta. ||**Discopo·dium,** *Bot.* 'the foot or stalk on which some kinds of disks are elevated'. **Disco·podous** *a.*, *Zool.* having the foot shaped as a disk; belonging to the section *Discopoda* of Gastropods. **Discosto·matous** *a.*, *Zool.* pertaining or belonging to the class *Discostomata* of *Protozoa*, containing the sponges and collar-bearing monads.

†**Discoa·st,** *v.* 1598. [DIS- 6.] **1.** *intr.* To withdraw from the coast or side. **2.** *fig.* To withdraw, depart 1677.

1. Discoasting from England to the coast of Fraunce STOW. 2. Never willingly to discost from truth and equity BARROW.

||**Discobolus** (diskǫ·bŏlŏs). 1727. [L., a. Gr. δισκοβόλος, f. δίσκος + -βολος, f. βάλλειν to throw.] *Class. Antiq.* A thrower of the DISCUS; an ancient statue representing a man in the act of throwing the discus.

†**Discohe·rent,** *a.* 1600. [DIS- 10.] Without coherence –1675.

Discoid (di·skoid). 1794. [ad. L. *discoides*, a. Gr. δισκοειδής, f. δίσκος + -ειδης.]

A. *adj.* **1.** Disk-shaped; (more or less) flat and circular; in *Conchol.* used of spiral shells of which the whorls lie in one plane 1830. **2.** *Bot.* Of composite flowers: Having, or consisting of, a disk only, with no ray, as in Tansy 1794. So **Discoi·dal** *a.*

B. *sb.* A body resembling a disk in shape; in *Conchol.* a discoid shell. Cf. A. 1.

Discolith (di·skoliþ). 1875. [f. DISCO- + -LITH.] *Biol.* A kind of coccolith of the form of a flattened disk. (Cf. CYATHOLITH.)

Discolor (di·skvləɹ, -kŏlŏɹ), *a.* 1866. [a. L., f. DIS- 1 + *color*; cf. *concolor.*] Of different colours; also, of a different colour from some other part or organ. So **Disco·lorous** *a.*

Discolor, *v.*; see DISCOLOUR.

Discolorate (diskv·ləreⁱt), *v. rare.* 1651. [f. med.L. *discolorat-* ppl. stem.] *trans.* = DISCOLOUR *v.* 1.

Discoloration, discolouration (diskvlər-, -kŏlŏrēⁱ·ʃən). 1642. [f. prec.] The action of discolouring or condition of being discoloured; alteration or loss of colour; discolourment. **b.** *concr.* A discoloured marking; a stain. So **Discoloriza·tion** (*rare*).

Discolour, discolor (diskv·ləɹ), *v.* ME. [In senses 1, 2, ad. OF. *descolorer*, f. *des-* (DIS- 4) + L. *colorare.* In sense 3, from L. *discolor* adj.] **1.** *trans.* To alter the proper colour of; *esp.* to make of a dingy or unnatural colour; to stain, tarnish. Also *fig.* **2.** *intr.* (for *refl.*) To become discoloured; to lose or change colour. Also *fig.* 1641. †**3.** *trans.* To render of different colours, or different in colour –1665.

1. We shall your tawnie ground with your red blood D. *Hen. V*, III. vi. 171. *fig.* Some whimsy in the brain..which discoloured all experience to its own shade STEVENSON. So **Disco·lour, disco·lor** *sb.* (now *rare*), discoloured state; loss or change of colour; discoloration, stain. Hence **Disco·loured, -lored** *ppl. a.* altered from the natural colour; †without colours (*nonce-use*); variegated; differently coloured, the one from the other. **Disco·lourment,** discoloration.

Discomfit (diskv·mfit), *v.* ME. [ME. *desconfit*, *-cumfit*, etc., a. OF., f. (ult.) *dis-* + L. *conficere.* Pa. pple. (and pa. t.) (*a*) *disconfit* (also *-confid*) till end of 15th c., (*b*) *discomfited* from the 15th.] **1.** *trans.* To undo in battle; to defeat completely; to rout. **2.** *gen.* To defeat the plans or purposes of; to foil. **b.** To throw into perplexity, confusion, or dejection; to disconcert ME.

1. Hys men..which wer in maner disconfit, and redy to flye HALL. 2. Wel go with me, and be not so discomfited *Tam. Shr.* II. i. 164. Dombey was quite discomfited by the question DICKENS. Hence †**Disco·mfit** *sb.* discomfiture. **Disco·mfiter,** one who or that which discomfits.

Discomfiture (diskv·mfitiŭɹ). ME. [a. OF. *desconfiture*, F. *déconfiture*; see DISCOMFIT.] The action of discomfiting, or fact of being discomfited: **a.** Complete defeat, overthrow, rout; **b.** Defeat or frustration of plans or hopes; **c.** Complete disconcertment.

Sad tidings..Of losse, of slaughter, and d. 1 *Hen. VI*, I. i. 59. To rely upon promises..would end in regret and d. 1828. The d. of the questioner 1885.

Discomfort (diskv·mfəɹt), *sb.* [ME. *disconfort*, a. OF. *desconfort*, mod.F. *déconfort*, f. *desconforter.* Cf. DIS- 9.] †**1.** Undoing of courage; discouragement –1551. †**2.** Absence of comfort or gladness; distress, grief, sorrow, annoyance –1847. **3.** Now: The condition of being uncomfortable; uneasiness 1841.

2. In solitude there is not only d. but weakness also SOUTH. 3. The great d. which attends..a heavy dinner A. COMBE. The troops..had many discomforts to endure MACAULAY.

Discomfort (diskv·mfəɹt), *v.* [ME. *discomfort*, *desconfort*, a. OF. *desconforter*; see DIS- 4.] †**1.** *trans.* To deprive of courage; to dishearten, dismay –1706. **2.** To deprive of comfort or gladness; to distress, grieve, sadden. *Obs.* or *arch.* ME. **3.** Now: To make uncomfortable or uneasy 1856. ¶ Formerly often used for DISCOMFIT, q. v.

1. My Lord, you doe d. all the Hoste *Tr. & Cr.* V. x. 10. 3. The Registrar..was discomforted by a pair of tight boots 1893. Hence **Disco·mforter.**

Discomfortable (diskv·mfəɹtăb'l), *a.* ME. [a. OF. *desconfortable*; see prec.] **1.** Causing discomfort; destroying comfort or happiness. *Obs.* (exc. as in 2). **2.** Wanting in material comfort; causing physical discomfort 1607. **3.** Uncomfortable, uneasy 1844.

2. Pacing to and fro in his d. house STEVENSON. Hence **Disco·mfortableness.**

Discommend (diskǫme·nd), *v.* 1494. [DIS- 6.] **1.** *trans.* To express disapprobation of: the opposite of COMMEND. **2.** To speak of dissuasively: the opposite of RECOMMEND 1533. **3.** To cause to be unfavourably viewed or received. ? *Obs.* 1579.

1. Who else shall d. her choice PATMORE. 2. Savanarola discommends Goats flesh BURTON. Hence **Discomme·ndable** *a.* worthy of censure; †not to be recommended. †**Discomme·ndableness. Discommenda·tion.**

†**Discommi·ssion,** *v.* 1622. [DIS- 7.] To deprive of a commission –1659.

†**Disco·mmodate,** *v.* 1610. [DIS- 6.] = next –1649.

Discommode (diskǫmōᵘ·d), *v.* 1721. [DIS- 6.] To put to inconvenience; to disturb, trouble.

†**Discommo·dious,** *a.* 1540. [DIS- 10.]

Causing trouble or inconvenience; disadvantageous, troublesome–1668. Hence †Discommo·dious·ly *adv.*, †-ness.

Discommodity (diskǫ̆mǫ·dĭti). 1513. [Dis- 9.] The quality of being discommodious; (with *a* and *pl.*) a disadvantage, inconvenience.

Discommon (diskǫ·mən), *v.* 1478. [Dis- 7, 8.] †1. *trans.* To cut off from membership of a community; *esp.* to disfranchise; to excommunicate –1655. 2. At Oxford and Cambridge: To deprive (a tradesman) of the privilege of dealing with undergraduates 1530. 3. To deprive of the right of common; see Common *sb.*[1] Also *fig.* b. To deprive of the character of a common 1597.

Discommons (diskǫ·mənz), *v.* 1852. [f. Dis- 7 a + Commons *sb. pl.*] 1. To deprive of commons in a college 1856. 2. = Discommon 2.

Discommune (diskǫ·miūn), *v.* 1590. [f. Dis- 6 + Commune *v.*, or Dis- 7 a + Commune *sb.*] †1. *trans.* To cut off from community or fellowship –1659. 2. = Discommon 2. 1677. So †Discommu·nion, exclusion from communion or fellowship.

Discommunity (diskǫ̆miū·nĭti). *rare.* [Dis- 9.] Absence of community; the quality of not having something in common. Darwin.

†**Disco·mpanied**, *ppl. a. rare.* 1599. [Dis- 4.] Destitute of company, unaccompanied –1618.

If she bee alone, now, and d. B. Jons.

†**Discomple·xion**, *v. rare.* [Dis- 7 d.] To spoil the complexion or aspect of. Shirley.

Discompli·ance. *rare.* [Dis- 9.] Non-compliance. Pepys.

Discompose (diskǫ̆mpōu·z), *v.* 1483. [Dis- 6.] 1. *trans.* To destroy the composure or calmness of; to ruffle, agitate. 2. To disturb the order or arrangement of; to disarrange, disorder, unsettle. Now *rare.* 1611. †3. To displace, discard –1640.

1. Better for Us.. That never passion discompos'd the mind Pope. No Wind..the Air to d. Cowley. 2. Eve, With Tresses discompos'd Milt. *P. L.* v. 10. Hence Discompo·sed·ly *adv.*, -ness. †Discomposi·tion. †Discompo·sture, discomposure.

Discomposure (diskǫ̆mpōu·ʒiŭɹ). 1641. [f. prec., after Composure.] 1. The fact or condition of being discomposed; disorder; †indisposition; †dismemberment. 2. Agitation, perturbation 1647. †3. Want of harmony; dissension (*rare*) –1673.

2. There was an air of d. about his whole person Scott.

Discompt, obs. f. Discount.

†**Disco·ncert**, *sb. rare.* 1668. [Dis- 9.] Want of concert; disunion, disagreement in action –1839.

Disconcert (diskǫ̆nsə̄·ɹt), *v.* 1687. [a. obs. F. *disconcerter*, mod.F. *déconcerter*; see Dis- 4.] 1. *trans.* To put out of concert; to throw into confusion, derange; now *esp.* to disarrange measures or plans concerted. 2. To disturb the complacency or self-possession of; to ruffle, put out 1716.

1. An unforeseen accident disconcerted all his measures Robertson. 2. He never .. disconcerts a puny satirist with unexpected sarcasms Johnson. Hence Disconce·rtion, Disconce·rtment, the action of disconcerting; the being disconcerted.

†**Discondu·ce**, *v.* [Dis- 6.] To be non-conducive *to*. Donne. Hence †Discondu·cive *a.* not conducive (*rare*).

†**Disconfo·rmable**, *a.* 1603. [Dis- 10.] Unconformable –1823.

Disconformity (diskǫ̆nfǭ·ɹmĭti). 1602. [Dis- 9.] The opposite of conformity or practical agreement; nonconformity.

D. with Rome in the keeping of Easter 1639. Conformity or d. to usage Mill.

Discongru·ity. ? *Obs.* 1624. [Dis- 9.] Absence of congruity; disagreement, inconsistency; incongruity. So †Disco·ngruous *a.* wanting in congruity (*rare*).

Disconnect (diskǫ̆ne·kt), *v.* 1770. [Dis- 6.] 1. To sever the connexion of or between; to disunite, separate. Const. *with, from.* 2. To separate into disconnected parts. *Obs.* exc. in *pa. pple.* 1790.

1. To d. the drains of the defendants from the sewer 1892. 2. They shall not induce me to d. my army Wellington. Hence Disconne·cted *ppl. a.* having no connexion; detached; separate; incoherent. Disconne·cter, -or. Disconne·xion, -ne·ction, the action of disconnecting (*rare*); the being disconnected or unconnected; separation; disconnectedness.

†**Disconse·nt**, *v.* 1530. [Dis- 4.] *intr.* To refuse consent; not to consent; to dissent. Const. *with, from.* –1641.

Disconsider (diskǫ̆nsi·dəɹ), *v. rare.* 1887. [Dis- 6.] To bring into disrepute. So Disconsidera·tion.

†**Disco·nsolacy.** 1653. [f. Disconsolate *a.*] Disconsolate state –1677.

Disconsolance, -cy, errors for prec. in Dicts. (Worcester, etc.).

Disconsolate (diskǫ·nsŏlĕt), *a.* ME. [a. med.L. *disconsolatus*; see Dis- 4.] 1. Destitute of consolation; unhappy, comfortless; inconsolable. 2. Of places or things: Causing or manifesting discomfort; dismal, cheerless, gloomy ME.

1. A poor d. widow 1704. On the nigh-naked tree the robin piped D. Tennyson. 2. The d. darkness of our winter nights Ray. Hence †Disco·nsolate *v.* to make d.; to deprive of consolation. Disco·nsolate·ly *adv.*, -ness. Disco·nsolation.

†**Disco·nsonant**, *a.* 1630. [Dis- 10.] Out of agreement or harmony; discordant –1806. Hence †Disco·nsonancy.

Discontent (diskǫ̆nte·nt), *sb.*[1] 1588. [Dis- 9.] 1. Want of content; dissatisfaction of mind 1591; †vexation –1678. †2. *transf.* An occasion of discontent; a grievance. (Usu. in *pl.*) –1620.

1. Now is the Winter of our D. Made glorious Summer by this Son of Yorke *Rich. III*, I. i. 1. Some inward d. at the ingratitude of the times Bacon. 2. An ill Liuer is my d. 1620. Hence Disconte·ntful *a.* full of d. (*arch.*).

Disconte·nt, *a.* and *sb.*[2] 1494. [Dis- 10.]

A. *adj.* 1. Not content; dissatisfied, discontented. Const. *with, to* with *inf.* 1500. †2. Vexed –1655.

1. He..withdrew, disconcerted and d. M. Pattison.

B. *sb.*[2] A discontented person; a malcontent. Now *rare.* 1596.

Fickle Changelings, and poore Discontents Shaks.

Disconte·nt, *v.* 1494. [Dis- 6.] 1. *trans.* To deprive of contentment; to make unquiet in mind; to dissatisfy. (Now chiefly in pa. pple.) 1549. 2. To vex. *Obs.* or *arch.* 1494. Hence †Discontenta·tion = Discontent *sb.*[1] Disconte·nted·ly *adv.*, -ness. †Disconte·ntive *a.* feeling, showing, or causing discontent. Disconte·ntment = Discontent *sb.*[1]

Discontigu·ity. 1676. [Dis- 9.] Discontinuity of parts.

†**Disconti·nual**, *a.* ME. [Dis- 10.] 1. = Discontinuous –1611. 2. *Math.* Said of *proportion*: = Discontinued –1706.

Discontinuance (diskǫ̆nti·niu͡ăns). ME. [a. AF., f. *discontinuer*; see -ance.] 1. The action of discontinuing; interruption of continuance; cessation; intermission. †2. A (temporary) ceasing to be in a place; absence –1677. †3. *Law.* An interruption of a right of possession or right of entry, consequent upon a wrongful alienation by the tenant in possession for a larger estate than he was entitled to –1768. 4. *Law.* The interruption of a suit, or its dismissal, by reason of the plaintiff's omission of formalities necessary to keep it pending 1540.

1. The cause of the d. of the works at Lisbon Wellington. The d. of agriculture 1875. 4. The devil..is an unwearied sollicitor, and will not lose his claim by d. Sanderson.

Discontinuation (diskǫntiniu͡ē·ʃən). 1611. [a. F., ad. med.L. *discontinuationem.*] 1. = Discontinuance 1. 2. *concr.* A breach of continuity 1728.

1. The d. of the houses T. A. Trollope.

Discontinue (diskǫ̆nti·niu), *v.* ? ME. [a. F. *discontinuer*, ad. med.L. *discontinuare*; see Dis- 4.] 1. *trans.* To cause to cease; to cease from (an action); to break off, put a stop to, give up 1479. Also *ellipt.* To cease to take, pay, etc. (*mod.*). †2. To cease to frequent, occupy, or inhabit 14... 3. *Law.* a. To dismiss or abandon (a suit, etc.) 1487. †b. To alienate land in such a manner as operates to the discontinuance of the heir in tail –1818. †4. To interrupt, disrupt, sunder –1751. 5. *intr.* To cease to continue; to stop 1555; †to cease to reside –1677. †6. To become disrupted 1626.

1. [He] begg'd that they would d. their visits 1726. To d. a subscription (*mod.*). 4. Solid bodies..being once discontinued, are not easily consolidated again Cudworth. 5. To d. a while from labour Baret. And thou, euen thyselfe, shalt d. from thine heritage that I gaue thee *Jer.* xvii. 4.

Hence Disconti·nuee, one to whom an estate is aliened to the discontinuance of the heir in tail. Disconti·nuer, one who discontinues; †an absentee. Disconti·nuo·r (*Law*), the tenant in tail whose alienation of an estate has caused a discontinuance.

Discontinuity (diskǫntiniū·ĭti). 1570. [f. as next + -ity.] The quality or state of being discontinuous; want of continuity; interrupted condition; (with *pl.*) a break or gap 1794.

Discontinuous (diskǫ̆nti·niu͡əs), *a.* 1667. [f. med.L. *discontinuus*; see Dis- 4.] †1. Producing discontinuity; gaping –1703. 2. Not continuous; having interstices or breaks; interrupted, intermittent 1718.

1. The griding sword with d. wound Pass'd through him Milt. 2. Wide spread the d. ruins lie Rowe.

Phr. *D. function* (Math.): one that varies discontinuously, and whose differential coefficient may therefore become infinite. Hence Disconti·nuous·ly *adv.*, -ness.

Disconve·nience, *sb.* ME. [ad. L. *disconvenientia*; see Disconvenient.] †1. Incongruity, inconsistency –1660. †2. Unfitness –1598. 3. Incommodity; (with *pl.*) an inconvenience. Now *dial.* 1553. var. †Disconve·niency. Hence Disconve·nience *v.* to inconvenience (*dial.*).

Disconve·nient, *a.* ME. [ad. L. *disconvenientem*, f. Dis- 4 + *convenire.*] †1. Incongruous; unsuitable –1660. 2. Disadvantageous. Now *dial.* 1450.

Discophoran (diskǫ·fŏrăn). 1878. [f. mod.L. *Discophora*, pl. neut. of *discophorus*, a. Gr. (f. δίσκος + -φορος), taken in sense 'bearing a disk'.] *Zool.*

A. *adj.* 1. Belonging to the subclass *Discophora* of Hydrozoa, comprising the jelly-fishes. 2. Belonging to the order *Discophora* of suctorial worms, synonymous with *Hirudinea* or leeches.

B. *sb.* One of the *Discophora*. Also Di·scophore. So Disco·phorous *a.* of or pertaining to the *Discophora*.

Discoplacental, etc.; see Disco-.

Discord (di·skǫɹd), *sb.* [ME. *des-, discord*, a. OF.; see Discord *v.*] 1. Absence of concord or harmony; dissension; diversity. 2. *Mus.* (The opposite of Concord.) a. Dissonance. b. A combination of notes not in harmony with each other; a chord which requires to be resolved or followed by some other chord. c. The interval between two notes forming a discord. d. A single note which is dissonant with another, or with the others of a chord. 1440. 3. A clashing of sounds, a confused noise; a harsh or unpleasing sound 1590.

1. An Age of d. and continuall strife 1 *Hen. VI*, v. v. 63. Merry and tragicall..How shall wee finde the concord of this d. *Mids. N.* v. i. 60. 3. So musicall a d., such sweet thunder *Mids. N.* iv. i. 123. Hence Disco·rdful *a.* quarrelsome.

†**Di·scord**, *a. rare.* ME. [a. F.] Discordant –1606.

Discord (diskǭ·ɹd), *v.* ME. [a. OF. *des-, discorder*, ad. L. *discordare*, f. *discors*; cf. Concord.] 1. *intr.* To disagree; also, to dissent *from.* 2. Of things (chiefly): To be different (*from*), discordant (*with*) ME.; of sounds, to jar, clash ME.

1. We discorded commonly on two points Carlyle. 2. The one [sound] jarring or discording with the other Bacon.

†**Discordable**, *a.* [ME. *discorda·ble*, a. OF., ad. L. *discordabilis*; see Discord *v.*] Characterized by discord, discordant –1549.

Discordance (diskǭ·ɹdăns). ME. [a. OF. *des-, discordance*; see Discord *v.*] 1. The fact of being discordant; disagreement. 2. Discord of sounds ME.

1. The d. between the action and the law Hobbes. So Disco·rdancy, the condition or quality of being discordant; discord of sounds.

Discordant (diskǭ·ɹdănt), *a.* [ME. *des-, discordant*, a. OF.; see Discord *v.*] 1. Not in accord, not in harmony; at variance; disagreeing, differing; incongruous. Const. *to, from, with.* 2. Of sound: Inharmonious, dissonant, jarring ME.

1. The reasons and resolutions are, and must remain d. Hobbes. A d. family Johnson. 2. War, with d.

notes and jarring noise CONGREVE. Hence **Disco·rdant-ly** *adv.*, **-ness.**

†Di·scordous, *a.* [? f. DISCORD *sb.* + -OUS.] Full of discord. BP. HALL.

Discorporate (diskǭ·ɹpŏrět), *v. rare.* 1683. [DIS- 6.] **1.** *trans.* To deprive of corporate character. **2.** To separate from a corporate body 1891. So **Disco·rporate** *ppl. a.* (*rare*).

†Discorrespo·ndent, *a. rare.* 1654. [DIS- 10.] Lacking in congruity. So **†Discorrespo·ndency.**

Discost, var. of DISCOAST *v. Obs.*

†Discostate (diskǫ·stět), *a.* 1849. [DIS- 1.] *Bot.* Of leaves: Having radiately divergent ribs.

Discostomatous; see DISCO-.

†Discou·nsel, *v.* 1477. [ad. OF. *descon-*, *descunseillier*, f. *des-* (DIS- 4) + L. *consiliare.*] = DISADVISE 1, 2. -1631.

Discount (di·skaunt), *sb.* 1622. [a. 16th c. F. *descompte*, mod.F. *décompte*, f. *descompter* to DISCOUNT. Cf. F. *escompte.*] **†1.** An abatement or deduction from the amount or from the gross reckoning of anything. (Also *fig.*) -1798. **2.** *Commerce.* **a.** A deduction made for payment before it is due, or for prompt payment, of a bill or account; any deduction or abatement from the nominal value or price 1690. **b.** The interest charged for discounting a bill of exchange or promissory note 1683. **3.** The act of discounting a bill, etc. 1839.

2. Here's ready Money: Speak, what D. 1702. The *true* d. is less than the banker's or *mercantile* d. J. BROOK-SMITH.

Phrases. *At a d.*: at less than the nominal value; below par; *fig.* in low esteem, depreciated. *Banker's* or *mercantile d.*: interest on the amount of a bill for the time it has to run. *True d.*: interest on the present worth of a bill.

Comb.: **d.-broker**, one whose business is to cash notes or bills of exchange at a d.; also *d. accommodation, business, house*; (in sense 2 a) *d.-bookseller.*

Discount (diskau·nt, di·skaunt), *v.*[1] 1629. [a. OF. *desconter*, mod.F. *décompter*, med.L. *discomputare*, from *dis-*, DIS- 4 + *computare.*] **†1.** *trans.* To reckon as an abatement or deduction from a sum due -1726; to deduct -1828. **2.** To give or receive the present worth of (a bill or note) before it is due 1694. **3.** *fig.* **a.** To leave out of account; to disregard. **b.** To deduct from. **c.** To part with a future good for some present consideration. **d.** *esp.* To make allowance for exaggeration in. **e.** To take (an event, etc.) into account beforehand. 1702.

1. That the said provisions may be discounted upon the pay of the said army 1645. **3.** Of the three opinions (I d. Brown's), under this head, one supposes [etc.] SIR W. HAMILTON. To d. statements made by the natives 1883. To *d.* news BITHELL. Hence **Discou·ntable** *a.* that may be discounted.

†Discount, *v.*[2] *rare.* 1655. [DIS- 1.] To reckon separately -1662.

Discountenance (diskau·ntǐnăns), *v.* 1580. [DIS- 4 or 7.] **†1.** To put another countenance on, to mask (*rare*) 1587. **2.** To put out of countenance, put to shame, disconcert, abash 1580. **3.** To withdraw one's countenance from, set the countenance against; to show disapprobation of; to discourage 1589.

2. How would one look from his majestic brow..D. her despised MILT. *P. R.* II. 218. He appeared much discountenanced at this last part of my narrative CARLYLE. **3.** Duels are neither quite discountenanc'd, nor much in vogue STEELE. Hence **Discou·ntenancer.**

Discountenance (diskau·ntǐnăns), *sb. arch.* 1580. [partly ad. OF. *descontenance*; partly f. DIS- 9 + COUNTENANCE *sb.*] **1.** The act or fact of discountenancing; unfavourable aspect, disapprobation shown. **†2.** The state of being put out of countenance; abashment -1656.

1. He thought that the estimation of Cato was altogether the d. of his [own] power and greatnesse NORTH.

Discounter (diskau·ntəɹ). 1732. [f. DISCOUNT *v.*[1] + -ER[1].] One who discounts a bill or note; see DISCOUNT *v.* 2.

Discouple (diskɒ·p'l), *v.* 1489. [a. OF. *descupler*; see DIS- 4.] To disunite what is coupled, to uncouple. Also *intr.* (for *refl.*).

Discour, -coure, obs. ff. DISCOVER *v.*

†Discou·rage, *sb.* 1500. [DIS- 9.] Want or failure of courage; discouragement -1611.

Discourage (diskɒ·rědʒ), *v.* 1481. [ad. OF. *descoragier*, mod.F. *décourager*; see DIS- 4.] **1.** *trans.* To deprive of courage; to lessen the courage of; to dishearten, dispirit. The opposite of *encourage.* Also *†transf.* and *fig.* **2.** *transf.* To lessen or repress courage for; to discountenance, express disapproval of, 'throw cold water on' 1641. Also *†intr.* (for *refl.*).

1. I think no Slow of Despond would d. me BUNYAN. To d. from a task 1756. **2.** Idleness should of all things be discouraged BERKELEY. Hence **Discou·rageable** *a.* capable of being discouraged; to be discouraged (*rare*). **Discou·rager,** one who or that which discourages. **Discou·ragingly** *adv.*

Discouragement (diskɒ·rědʒměnt). 1561. [ad. OF. *descouragement*, mod.F. *découragement*; see prec.] **1.** The action or fact of discouraging 1600. **2.** The fact or state of being discouraged; want of spirit or confidence; depression of spirit with regard to effort. (The more usual sense.) 1561. **3.** That which discourages; a deterrent influence 1612.

1. His..d. of that pest of society, Attorneys H. WALPOLE. **2.** Terrour and d. 1561. **3.** The books.. are full of..discouragements from vice SWIFT.

Discourse (diskōᵊ·ɹs), *sb.* ME. [a. F. *discours*, ad. L. *discursus*, f. *discurs-*, ppl. stem of *discurrere*; see next.] **†1.** Onward course; = COURSE -1612. **†2.** 'The act of the understanding, by which it passes from premises to consequences' (J.); reasoning, ratiocination; reason, rationality. (*Obs.* or *arch.*) ME. **3.** Communication of thought by speech; talk, conversation (*arch.*) 1559. **†b.** The faculty of conversing -1641. **c.** (with *a* and *pl.*) A talk; a conversation (*arch.*) 1632. **†4.** Narration; a narrative -1647. **5.** A spoken or written treatment of a subject at length; a dissertation, treatise, sermon, or the like. (The prevailing sense.) 1581. **†6.** Familiar intercourse 1602. **†b.** Conversancy (*in*) 1604.

1. The naturall d. of the sunne ELYOT. **2.** Phr. *†D. of reason*: process or faculty of reasoning; A beast that wants d. of Reason *Haml.* I. ii. 150. **3.** Ample enterchange of sweet D. *Rich. III*, v. iii. 99. I have had a long d. with my father DE FOE. **5.** Authors who have published Discourses of Practical Divinity ADDISON. His discourses in the pulpit MACAULAY. **6.** If you be honest, and fair, your Honesty should admit no d. to your Beautie *Haml.* III. i. 108.

Discourse (diskōᵊ·ɹs), *v.* 1547. [f. DISCOURSE *sb.*; prob. affected by F. *discourir* 'to discourse of'.] **†1.** *intr.* To run or travel over a space, region, etc.; *transf.* to extend -1555. **†2.** *intr.* 'To pass from premises to conclusions' (J.); to reason -1700. Also *†trans.* **3.** *intr.* To hold discourse, to talk, converse; to discuss a matter, confer 1559. Also *fig.* **4.** *intr.* To speak or write at length on a subject 1564. **5.** *trans.* To go through in speech; to treat of in speech or writing; to talk over; to talk of; to tell (*arch.*) 1563. **b.** To utter 1602. **6.** *trans.* To converse with; to talk to; to discuss a matter with; to address. (*Obs.* or *arch.*) 1677.

3. *fig.* She speakes, yet she sayes nothing, what of that? Her eye discourses *Rom. & Jul.* II. ii. 13. **4.** To d. for two hours without intermission BUCKLE. **5.** **b.** Giue it breath with your mouth, and it will d. most excellent Musicke *Haml.* III. ii. 374. **6.** A Friend whom I discoursed on this Point LOCKE. Hence **Discou·rser,** one who discourses. **†Discou·rsist,** one who reasons.

†Discou·rsive, *a.* 1588. [f. DISCOURSE *v.* + -IVE; cf. *discursive.*] **1.** Of or pertaining to discourse or reason; rational -1678. **2.** Discursive -1613. **3.** Disposed to converse; talkative; communicative -1669. **b.** Of the nature of dialogue; conversational -1716.

2. Thou..In thy d. thought, dost range as farre W. BROWNE. **3.** See how these vain D. Bookmen talk DANIEL. **b.** Interlaced with Dialogue or D. Scenes DRYDEN. Hence **†Discou·rsively** *adv.*

†Discou·rt, *v.* 1585. [DIS- 7 b.] To dismiss from court -1722.

Discourteous (diskōᵊ·ɹtyəs, -kɒ̄·ɹtyəs), *a.* 1578. [DIS- 10.] Void of or lacking in courtesy; uncivil, rude. Hence **Discou·rteous-ly** *adv.*, **-ness.**

Discourtesy (diskōᵊ·ɹtěsi, -kɒ̄·ɹ-). 1555. [DIS- 9.] The opposite of courtesy; rude or uncivil behaviour; incivility; an instance of this.

Some jealousies and discurtesies passed lately betweene them and the Pope SANDYS.

†Discou·rtship. *rare.* [DIS- 9.] = DISCOURTESY. B. JONSON.

†Di·scous, *a.* 1706. [ad. mod.L. *discosus*, f. *discus.*] Having a disk or disks; discoid -1794.

†Disco·venant, *v.* 1650. [DIS- 6.] *trans.* To dissolve covenant with; to exclude from a covenant -1861.

Discover (diskɒ·vəɹ), *v.* ME. [a. OF. *descovrir, -couvrir*, ad. med.L. *discooperire*, f. DIS- 4 + *cooperire* to COVER.] **†1.** *trans.* To remove the covering from -1628. **†2.** To remove (anything serving as a cover) -1618. **3.** To disclose or expose to view (anything covered up or previously unseen), to reveal, show. Now *rare.* 1450. **4.** To disclose to knowledge; to make known (*arch.*) ME. **†5.** To reconnoitre. Also *absol.* -1600. **6.** To reveal the identity of; hence, to betray (*arch.*) ME. **†7.** To exhibit, display -1771. **8.** To obtain sight or knowledge of for the first time; to find out 1555; to catch sight of, descry 1576. **†9.** To explore -1850. **†10.** *intr.* To make discoveries; to look; to see -1821. **†11.** *trans.* and *intr.* To distinguish -1796.

1. If the house be discouered by tempest [etc.] COKE. **3.** From those flames No light, but only darkness visible Serv'd only to d. sights of woe MILT. *P. L.* I. 64. **4.** Secrets which Time will d. 1662. **6.** Mercy, and that ye nat discouere me CHAUCER. **7.** The remaining Bones discovered his Proportions SIR T. BROWNE. **8.** Harvey discovered the circulation of the blood H. BLAIR. He discovered that he had made a mistake 1892. Now when we had discovered Cyprus, we left it on the left hand *Acts* xxi. 3. Hence **Disco·verer,** one who discovers (*esp.* in senses 3, 5, 8).

Discoverable (diskɒ·vərăb'l), *a.* 1572. [f. prec. vb. + -ABLE.] Capable of being discovered; discernible, perceptible, ascertainable.

Its effects..are everywhere d. JOHNSON. Hence **Discoverabi·lity,** d. quality. **Disco·verably** *adv.*

Disco·vert. ME. [a. OF. *descovert, -couvert*, mod.F. *découvert* = med.L. *discoopertus.*]

A. *adj.* **†1.** Uncovered, exposed -1525. **2.** *Law.* Of an unmarried woman or a widow: Not covert, not under the cover, authority, or protection of a husband; cf. COVERT *a.* 1729.

†B. *sb.* An uncovered or exposed state -1592. Phr. *†In* or *at d.*, off one's guard. [OF. *à descovert.*]

Discoverture (diskɒ·vəɹtiŭɹ). 1818. [f. prec. after *coverture.*] *Law.* The state of being discovert, or not under coverture; cf. COVERTURE.

Discovery (diskɒ·vəri). 1553. [f. DISCOVER *v.*, app. after *recovery.*] **†1.** The action of uncovering or fact of becoming uncovered 1658. **2.** The action of disclosing or divulging; revelation 1586; in *Law*, disclosure by a party to an action, at the instance of the other party, of facts or documents necessary to maintain his own title 1715. **b.** The unfolding of the plot of a play, poem, etc. 1727. **3.** The finding out or bringing to light of that which was previously unknown; making known; an instance of this 1553; †exploration, reconnaissance -1774. **†4.** Indication that brings anything to light -1705. **5.** That which is discovered, found out, revealed, or brought to light 1632.

2. Resolved..to make a D. of the whole affair 1737. **3.** Show me..a discoverer who has not suffered for his d...whether a Columbus or a Galileo LANDOR. **5.** No indication that the mariner's compass was a recent d. 1837.

†Discra·dle, *v. rare.* 1634. [DIS- 7 c.] *trans.* To turn out of a cradle. *intr.* (for *refl.*) To emerge from the cradle.

Discreate (diskrɪ,ē·t), *v.* 1570. [DIS- 6.] *trans.* To uncreate, annihilate, reduce to chaos.

Thou hast set thine hand to unmake and d. SWINBURNE. Hence **Discrea·tion,** the undoing of creation.

Discredit (diskre·dit), *sb.* 1565. [DIS- 9.] **1.** Loss or want of credit; disrepute, reproach; an instance of this. **2.** Loss or want of belief or credit; disbelief, distrust 1647.

1. Such conduct brings d. on the name of Athens JOWETT. **2.** The answers..[threw] d. upon his previous evidence 1868. The course of the discount market depends upon credit or d. 1885.

Discredit (diskre·dit), *v.* 1559. [DIS- 6.] **1.** *trans.* To refuse to credit; to disbelieve. **2.** To show to be unworthy of belief; to destroy confidence in 1561. **3.** To injure the credit or reputation of; to bring into discredit or disrepute 1579.

1. A statement which there is no reason to d. 1815. **2.** The idea is..discredited by modern science J. MARTINEAU. **3.** Henry is said to have been discredited for the death of Thomas FREEMAN. Hence **†Discre·ditor,** one who discredits anything (*rare*).

Discreditable (diskre·dităb'l), *a.* 1640. [DIS- 10.] The reverse of CREDITABLE; injurious to reputation; disreputable, disgraceful. Hence **Discre·ditably** *adv.*

Discreet (diskrī·t), *a.* [ME. *discret, discrete*, a. F., ad. L. *discretus*, in the late L. sense. A doublet of DISCRETE.] **1.** Showing discernment in the guidance of one's own speech and action; judicious, circumspect, cautious; often *esp.* silent when speech is inconvenient. **2.** In *Sc.* well-spoken, well-behaved 1782. †**3.** Rare 16th c. spelling of DISCRETE, q. v.

1. A wife ought to be discret 1569. You are a d. man, and I make no doubt can keep a secret W. IRVING. A d. silence 1883. Hence **Discree·t-ly** *adv.*, **-ness.**

Discrepance (di·skrīpăns, diskre·păns). ME. [a. OF., ad. L. *discrepantia*; see DISCREPANT.] **1.** The fact of being discrepant; disagreement, difference. †**2.** Distinction, difference –1611. †**3.** Variation, change (of action) (*rare*) 1560.

1. Betwixt us and our Prince there is no d. BAILLIE. 2. Ther hath bene euer a d. in vesture of youthe and age ELYOT. var. **Discrepancy.**

Discrepant (di·skrīpănt, diskre·pănt). 1524. [ad. L. *discrepantem*, pr. pple. of *discrepare*, f. DIS- 1 + *crepare* to creak.]

A. *adj.* **1.** Exhibiting difference; dissimilar, discordant, inharmonious, inconsistent. Const. *from*, †*to*. †**2.** Apart in space (*rare*) –1818.

1. Wherin he is moste d. from brute beastes ELYOT. 2. Further d. than heaven and ground 1649.

†**B.** *sb.* A dissentient. JER. TAYLOR.

Discrete (diskrī·t), *a.* Also 6 **discreet.** ME. [ad. L. *discretus* 'separate, distinct', pa. pple. of *discernere*. A doublet of DISCREET, q. v.] **1.** Separate, detached from others, distinct. Opp. to *continuous*. **b.** *Pathol.* Separate, not coalescent or confluent 1854. **2.** Consisting of individual parts; discontinuous 1570. †**3.** *Gram.* and *Logic.* Of conjunctions: adversative. Of propositions: discretive. –1664. **4.** *Metaph.* Detached from the material, abstract 1854.

1. Of distinct and d. vnits DEE. *D. tones* (Mus.): tones separated by fixed intervals of pitch, as the notes of a piano. 2. *D. quantity*, quantity composed of distinct units, as the rational numbers. Dist. from *continuous quantity* = magnitude. *D. proportion* = DISCONTINUED proportion. 3. A d. sentence, is, which hath a d. conjunction; as, *although, yet, notwithstanding*, etc. Z. COKE. Hence **Discre·te·ly** *adv.*, **-ness.**

Discrete, early f. DISCREET.

†**Discre·te,** *v.* 1646. [f. L. *discret-*, ppl. stem of *discernere*.] To divide into discrete parts; to separate distinctly –1858.

Discretion (diskre·ʃən). ME. [a. OF. *des-, discrecion*, ad. L. *discretionem* distinction, and later, discernment, f. *discernere* (*discret-*).]

I. Separation, disjunction, distinction 1590.

Mind .. has no discretion of parts or capacity of division or determination from without E. CAIRD.

II. [In late L. sense.] †**1.** The action of discerning or judging; judgement; discrimination ME. †**2.** The faculty of discerning –1651. **3.** Liberty or power of deciding, or of acting according to one's own judgement; uncontrolled power of disposal ME.; in *Law*, the power to decide, within the limits allowed by positive rules of law, as to punishments, remedies, or costs, and generally to regulate matters of procedure and administration 1467.

1. Y refer all to your d. MARY Q. SCOTS. 3. As to the form of worship, a large d. was left to the clergy MACAULAY. That the costs of references .. should be in the d. of the arbitrators 1891.

Phr. *At d.*, as one thinks fit, chooses, or pleases.

III. [Cf. DISCREET.] **1.** The quality of being discreet; discernment; prudence, sagacity, circumspection, sound judgement ME. **2.** *Sc.* Propriety of behaviour 1782. †**3.** A title formerly applied to bishops, etc. Cf. *your worship, your honour*. –1555.

1. D. of Speech is more than Eloquence BACON.

Phr. *Age of, years of, d.*: the time of life at which a person is presumed to be capable of exercising d.; in *Eng. Law* the age of fourteen.

Hence **Discre·tional** *a.* discretionary. **Discre·tionally** *adv.* **Discre·tionary** *a.* pertaining or left to d.; †discreet. **Discre·tionarily** *adv.*

Discretive (diskrī·tiv). 1588. [ad. L. *discretivus*, f. *discret-*, ppl. stem of *discernere*.]

A. *adj.* **1.** = DISJUNCTIVE. †**2.** Serving to distinguish or discriminate; diacritic –1819.

†**B.** *sb.* A disjunctive conjunction or proposition –1725.

Hence **Discre·tive·ly** *adv.*, **-ness.**

†**Discri·minable,** *a. rare.* 1730. [f. L. *discriminare* + -BLE.] Capable of being discriminated –1813.

Discri·minal, *a. rare.* 1842. [ad. L. *discriminalis*, f. *discrimen*.] Of the nature of a distinction or division.

D. line in *Palmistry*: the line between the hand and the arm.

Discriminant (diskri·minănt). 1836. [ad. L. *discriminantem*, pr. pple. of *discriminare*.]

A. *adj.* **1.** Discriminating. **2.** *Math.* Implying equal roots or a node (cf. B.). *D. relation*, a one-fold relation between parameters determining a nodal point.

B. *sb. Math.* The eliminant of the *n* first derived functions of a homogeneous function of *n* variables. Hence **Discrimina·ntal** *a.* relating to a d.

Discriminate (diskri·minĕt), *a.* 1626. [ad. L. *discriminatus*; see next.] **1.** Distinct, discriminated (*arch.*). **2.** Marked by discrimination: opp. to *indiscriminate* 1798.

2. Much may be done by d. charity MALTHUS. Hence **Discri·minate-ly** *adv.*, **-ness.**

Discriminate (diskri·mineᶦt), *v.* 1628. [f. L. *discriminat-*, ppl. stem of *discriminare*, f. *discrimen, -crimin-*, f. stem of *discernere*. (Cf. CRIME.)] **1.** To make or constitute a difference in or between; to differentiate. **2.** To perceive or note the difference in or between; to distinguish 1665. **3.** *intr.* or *absol.* To make a distinction 1774.

1. Capacities which d. one individual from another GROTE. 2. To d. the goats from the sheep BARROW. 3. Phr. *To d. against*: to make an adverse distinction with regard to. To d. against certain imports from the United States 1885.

Discri·minating, *ppl. a.* 1647. [f. prec.] **1.** That discriminates (sense 1). **2.** That discriminates (sense 2) 1792.

1. A d. mark of a disease M. BAILLIE. 2. A d. judgment 1794. Phr. *D. duty* or *rate*: one that varies according to the country or place of origin of goods, or according to the persons rated; a differential duty or rate Hence **Discri·minatingly** *adv.*

Discrimination (diskriminēᶦ·ʃən). 1646. [ad. L. *discriminationem*.] **1.** The action of discriminating or distinguishing; a distinction (made with the mind or in action) 1648; the condition of being discriminated or distinguished. ? *Obs.* 1699. **2.** Something that discriminates or distinguishes; a distinction; a distinguishing mark. Now *rare* or *Obs.* 1646. **3.** The faculty of discriminating; the power of observing differences accurately, or of making exact distinctions 1814. †**4.** = RECRIMINATION. *Obs. rare.* –1684.

1. To make a d. between the Good and the Bad 1705. 3. His character was touched with yet more d. by Flora SCOTT.

Discriminative (diskri·minĕtiv), *a.* 1638. [f. L. *discriminat-*.] **1.** Serving to discriminate; distinctive, distinguishing 1677. **2.** Characterized by discriminating; discerning 1638. **b.** *transf.* of things 1826. **c.** Differential 1872.

1. The d. Mark of a True Christian HALE. 2. D. Providence H. MORE. A more d. censure FOSTER. Heavy d. duties 1872. Hence **Discri·minatively** *adv.* So **Discri·minatory** *a.* (*rare*).

Discri·minoid. 1879. [f. after DISCRIMINANT; see -OID.] *Math.* A function of which the vanishing expresses the equality of all the integrating factors of a differential equation. Hence **Discri·minoidal** *a.*

†**Discri·minous,** *a. rare.* 1666. [ad. late L. *discriminosus*.] Critical, hazardous –1727.

Discrive, obs. f. DESCRIVE.

Discrown (diskrau·n), *v.* 1586. [DIS- 6.] To deprive of a crown; *spec.* to depose; also *transf.* and *fig.*

To crown or d. its Monarchs KINGLAKE. Discrowning sovereign reason MORLEY.

†**Discru·ciate,** *v.* 1600. [f. L. *discruciat-, discruciare*; see DIS- 5.] **1.** *trans.* To torture, excruciate –1660. **2.** *nonce-use.* To solve (a crux or riddle) 1745.

2. Pray d. what follows SWIFT.

†**Discuba·tion.** [ad. assumed L. type **discubatio*; cf. CUBATION, ACCUBATION.] Reclining at meals. COWLEY.

†**Discu·bitory,** *a. rare.* [f. *discubit-* ppl. stem of L. *discumbere*.] Adapted for reclining. SIR T. BROWNE.

Disculpate (diskʌ·lpeᶦt), *v.* 1693. [f. *disculpat-* ppl. stem of med.L. *disculpare*; see DIS- 4.] *trans.* To clear from blame or accusation; to exculpate.

Being faithful and just, with the testimony of things to d. him NORTH. Hence **Disculpa·tion.**

†**Discu·mb,** *v. rare.* 1683. [ad. L. *discumbere*; see DIS- 1.] *intr.* To recline (at table) –1699. So †**Discu·mbency,** the reclining posture at meals. †**Discu·mbent** *a.* reclining; *sb.* one who reclines at table; one lying ill in bed.

Discumber (diskʌ·mbəɹ), *v.* 1725. [DIS- 6.] To relieve; to disencumber.

Discure, obs. f. DISCOVER *v.*

†**Discu·rrent,** *a.*[1] [DIS- 10.] Not current. SANDYS.

†**Discu·rrent,** *a.*[2] 1656. [ad. L. *discurrentem*.] Running hither and thither –1710.

Discursion (diskɔ̄·ɹʃən). *rare.* 1535. [ad. L. *discursionem*, f. *discurrere*.] †**1.** The action of running or moving to and fro –1684. Also *fig.* **2.** = DISCOURSE *sb.* 2. 1603. So †**Discu·rsist,** one who practises discoursing.

Discursive (diskɔ̄·ɹsiv), *a.* 1599. [f. L. *discurs-, discurrere* + -IVE.] **1.** Running hither and thither (*rare* in *lit.* sense) 1626. **2.** *fig.* Passing rapidly or irregularly from subject to subject; rambling, digressive; ranging over many subjects 1599. **3.** Passing from premisses to conclusions; ratiocinative. (Cf. DISCOURSE *v.* 2.) Often opp. to *intuitive.* 1608.

2. A most vivid, though very d. and garrulous, history of the time FREEMAN. 3. Reason .. D., or Intuitive MILT. *P. L.* v. 488. The..D. Faculty..has only one operation, it only compares SIR W. HAMILTON. Hence **Discu·rsive·ly** *adv.*, **-ness.**

Discursory (diskɔ̄·ɹsŏri), *a. rare.* 1581. [f. as prec. + -ORY.] †**1.** Of the nature of discourse or reasoning –1614. **2.** Discursive 1881.

†**Discu·rtain,** *v.* 1616. [DIS- 6 or 7 a.] *trans.* To unveil –1659.

‖**Discus** (di·skɒ̆s). 1656. [L., a. Gr. δίσκος quoit.] **1.** *Class. Antiq.* A disk of heavy material used in ancient Greek or Roman athletic exercises; a quoit. Also, *ellipt.*, the game of hurling the discus. †**2.** = DISK in various technical senses –1706.

Discuss (diskʌ·s), *v.* ME. [f. L. *discuss-*, ppl. stem of *discutere*, f. DIS- 1 + *quatere* (in comb. *-cutere*). App. taken from the L. pa. pple. *discussus* Englished as *discussed.*] †**1.** *trans.* To drive away, disperse (*lit.* and *fig.*) –1651; to shake off; also to set free –1590. **2.** *Med.* To dissipate, dispel, or disperse (humours, etc.) (*arch.*) 1533. Also *intr.* (for *refl.*). †**3.** *trans.* To investigate; to try (as a judge) –1613. †**4.** To decide (as a judge) –1771. †**5.** To make known, declare. (This sense is obscure.) –1632. **6.** To investigate or examine by argument; to sift; to debate. (Now the ordinary sense.) 1450. Also *absol.* **7.** To try the quality of (food or drink); to consume. (*Somewhat joc.*) 1815. **8.** *Civil Law.* To 'do DILIGENCE' or exhaust legal proceedings against (a debtor), *esp.* against the person primarily liable, before proceeding against a surety 1681.

1. All regard of shame she had discust, And meet respect of honor putt to flight SPENSER *F. Q.* III. i. 48. 5. Art thou a Gentleman? What is thy Name? discusse *Hen. V*, IV. iv. 5. 6. Several schemes were proposed and discussed MACAULAY. 7. To d. slices of cold boiled beef SCOTT, port wine MARRYAT. Hence †**Discu·ss** *sb.* = DISCUSSION. **Discu·ssable, -ible** *a.* capable of being discussed. **Discu·sser,** one who or that which discusses.

Discussion (diskʌ·ʃən). ME. [a. OF., ad. L. *discussionem*; see prec.] †**1.** Examination, trial (by a judge); judicial decision –1526. **2.** Examination (*of* a matter) by arguments for and against; debate; a disquisition in which a subject is treated from different sides 1556. **3.** Investigation of the quality of food, etc. by consumption of it (*joc.* and *colloq.*) 1862. †**4.** *Med* The dissipation or dispersal of humours, etc. –1758. **5.** *Civil Law.* The exhaustion of legal proceedings against a debtor, *esp.* against the person primarily liable, before proceeding against a person secondarily liable 1681.

2. D. is no prejudice but an honour to the truth H. MORE. This d. is one of the least satisfactory in the dialogues of Plato JOWETT. 3. The d. of a bottle of port 1870. Hence **Discu·ssional** *a.* of the nature of or pertaining to d.

Discussive (diskʋ·siv). 1580. [f. L. *discuss-* ppl. stem; see DISCUSS.]

A. *adj.* †1. *Med.* = DISCUTIENT *a.* -1727. †2. Having the quality of settling; decisive -1644. 3. Pertaining to debate 1644.

†B. *sb. Med.* A DISCUTIENT -1671. Hence †**Discu·ssive·ly** *adv.*, †**-ness.**

†**Discu·stom,** *v.* 1502. [ad. OF. *descostumer*, f. *des-*, DIS- 4 + *costumer*; see CUSTOM *v.*] = DISACCUSTOM -1677.

Discutient (diskiū·ʃiĕnt). 1612. [ad. L. *discutientem.*]

A. *adj.* Having the quality of discussing or dissipating morbid matter; resolvent.

B. *sb.* A discutient agent 1655.

Disdain (disdē¹·n), *sb.* [ME. *dedeyn, desdeyn*, a. OF. *desdeign*, etc., mod.F. *dédain*, Rom. deriv. of *des-, disdegnare*; see next.] 1. The feeling entertained towards anything unworthy of notice or beneath one's dignity; scorn, contempt. †2. Indignation; anger arising from offended dignity; dudgeon -1677. †3. Loathing, aversion; †*transf.* loathsomeness -1655.

1. Disdaine and Scorne ride sparkling in her eyes, Mis-prizing what they looke on *Much Ado* III. i. 51. 2. The great person .. took the neglect in huge d. BARROW. 3. *transf.* Most lothsom, filthie, foul, and full of vile disdaine SPENSER *F. Q.* I. i. 14. Hence †**Disdai·nish** *a.* inclined to be scornful; †**-ly** *adv.* †**Disdai·nous** *a.* disdainful; indignant; †**-ly** *adv.*

Disdain (disdē¹·n), *v.* ME. [a. OF. *desdeignier, -deigner*, later *dédaigner*; a Com. Rom. vb., repr., with *des-* for L. *de-*, L. *dedignare*, f. DE- 6 + *dignare, -ari*; cf. DEIGN.] 1. *trans.* To think unworthy of oneself, or of one's notice; to regard with contempt; to scorn ME.; to think (anything) unworthy *of* 1591. †2. To be indignant, angry, or offended at; to be indignant *that* -1796. †3. *intr.* To be moved with indignation, take offence. Const. *at* (rarely *against, of, on*). -1634. †4. *trans.* To move to indignation or scorn -1817.

1. He laid against me..that I did d. everi mans cumpani G. HARVEY. 2. Ingratitude, which I disdaine as Hell LITHGOW. Disdaining that the enemies of Christ should abound in wealth 1796. Hence **Disdai·nable** *a.* worthy of disdain (*rare*). **Disdai·ner.**

Disdainful (disdē¹·nful), *a.* 1542. [f. DISDAIN *sb.*] 1. Full of or showing disdain; scornful, contemptuous, proudly disregardful. †2. Indignant, displeased; inimical (*rare*) -1550. †3. Hateful; that is the object of disdain -1586.

1. Vnder disdainfull brow WYATT. D. of private ends 1874. Hence **Disdai·nful·ly** *adv.*, **-ness.**

†**Disdecei·ve,** *v.* 1622. [DIS- 6.] To undeceive -1649.

†**Disde·ify,** *v. rare.* [DIS- 6.] To deprive of deity. FELTHAM.

Disdein(e, -deigne, -deyn(e, obs. ff. DISDAIN.

‖**Disdiaclasis** (disdəi,æ·klăsis). 1883. [mod. L., irreg. f. Gr. δίς twice (in comb. regularly δι-) + διάκλασις.] *Optics.* Double refraction.

Disdiaclast (disdəi·ăklæst). 1867. [ad. mod.L. *disdiaclastus* adj. (see next).] Brücke's term for one of the minute doubly-refracting particles of striated muscular tissue.

Disdiacla·stic, *a. rare.* 1670. [f. mod.L. *disdiaclastus* (irreg. f. Gr. δίς twice + *διακλαστός, vbl. adj. of διακλάειν).] Doubly refracting: applied to crystals; also, of the nature of disdiaclasts.

†**Disdiapa·son.** 1609. [a. L., a. Gr. δὶς διὰ πασῶν; see DIAPASON.] *Mus.* The interval of a double octave; a fifteenth -1774.

Disease (dizī·z), *sb.* [ME. *di-, desese*, f. (ult.) OF. *des-*, DIS- 4 + *aise* EASE *sb.*] †1. Absence of ease; uneasiness; inconvenience, annoyance; disturbance; trouble -1623; a cause of discomfort -1712; molestation -1493. 2. A condition of the body, or of some part or organ of the body, in which its functions are disturbed or deranged. Also applied to plants. a. *gen.* Illness, sickness ME. b. An ailment 1526. 3. *fig.* A morbid condition (of mind or disposition, of the affairs of a community, etc.); an evil affection or tendency 1509.

1. Doth sleep thus seize Thy powers, affected with so much dis-ease CHAPMAN. Phr. †*To do d. to*, to molest. 2. The legions of Augustus melted away in d. and lassitude GIBBON. Diseases, desperate growne, By desperate appliance are releeued *Haml.* IV. iii. 9. 3. Bad Latin was a catching d. in that age FULLER.

Phrases. *Addison's d.*, a structural d. of the suprarenal capsules, resulting in anæmia and loss of strength, and commonly characterized by a bronzed discoloration of the skin; first described by Thomas Addison (1793–1860). BRIGHT'S D., FOOT-AND-MOUTH D., FRENCH *d.*, POTATO *d.*, etc.: see these words.

Hence **Disea·seful** *a.* †fraught with discomfort; morbid, diseased (now *rare*); causing or tending to d. †**Disea·sefulness. Disea·sement,** †the action of depriving, or condition of being deprived, of ease; ailment (*nonce-use*). †**Disea·sy** *a.* annoying, troublesome; morbid.

Disease (dizī·z), *v.* ME. [a. AF. **diseaser, -eeser, -aeser*, for OF. *desaaisier*, f. *desaise* sb., after *aaisier, aiser* to ease.] †1. *trans.* To deprive of ease; to trouble, incommode -1697; to disturb (from quiet, etc.) -1653. 2. To bring into a morbid or unhealthy condition; to infect with disease. Usu. in pa. pple. 1467. Also *fig.*

1. What racking cares dis-ease a monarch's bed CONGREVE. 2. D. in body and mind MACAULAY. Evil Ministers D. the Common-wealth 1680.

Diseased (dizī·zd), *ppl. a.* 1467. [f. prec.] Affected with disease. Now usually of the bodily organs or fluids: In a disordered state, infected. b. Characterized by disease; pertaining to disease; morbid 1574. Also *fig.*

His miracles which hee did on them that were d. *John* vi. 2. Hence **Disea·sed·ly** *adv.*, **-ness.**

Disedge (dise·dʒ), *v.* 1611. [DIS- 7 a.] To take the edge off; to blunt, dull.

Served a little to d. The sharpness of that pain TENNYSON.

Disedify (dise·difəi), *v.* 1526. [DIS- 6.] *trans.* To do the reverse of edifying; to shock or weaken the piety of. Hence **Dise:difica·tion.**

Diselder, *v.*; see DIS- 7 b.

Diselectrify (disĭle·ktrifəi), *v.* 1876. [DIS- 6.] *trans.* To render non-electric.

†**Dis-e·lement,** *v.* 1612. [DIS- 7 c.] *trans.* To put out of its element -1727.

Diselenide (dəi,se·lĕnəid), etc., *Chem.*; see DI-² 2, etc.

Disembark (disĕmbā·ɹk), *v.* 1582. [a. F. *désembarquer*; see DIS- 4.] 1. *trans.* To put ashore from a ship; to land. 2. *intr.* To go on shore from a ship; to land 1582.

1. I must vnto the Road, to dis-embarque Some necessaries *Two Gent.* II. iv. 187. 2. Touching Breton Sands, they disembark'd TENNYSON. Hence **Disembarka·tion,** †**Disemba·rkment,** the action of disembarking.

Disembarrass (disĕmbæ·răs), *v.* 1726. [DIS- 6. Cf. DEBARRASS.] *trans.* To free from embarrassment, encumbrance, or complication; to rid; to relieve; to disentangle.

We may at once d. ourselves of those formidable terms—'absolute' and 'unconditioned' E. R. CONDER. Hence **Disemba·rrassment,** disembarrassing or being disembarrassed.

†**Disembay·,** *v.* [DIS- 6.] To bring out of a bay. SHERBURNE.

Disembellish (disĕmbe·liʃ), *v.* 1611. [DIS- 6.] To deprive of embellishment or adornment.

Disembi·tter, *v. rare.* [DIS- 6.] To free from bitterness. ADDISON.

Disembody (disĕmbǫ·di), *v.* 1714. [DIS- 6.] 1. *trans.* To separate (as a spirit) from the body; to free (anything) from that in which it is embodied. 2. To discharge from military embodiment 1762.

1. Our souls, when they are disembodied..will..be always sensible of the divine presence ADDISON. Hence **Disembo·diment,** the action of disembodying; disembodied state.

Disembogue (disĕmbō^u·g), *v.* 1595. [Orig. *disemboque*, ad. Sp. *desembocar*, f. *des-*, DIS- 4 + *embocar*, f. *en* in + *boca* mouth; see EMBOGUE.] †1. *intr.* To come out of the mouth of a river, strait, etc. into the open sea -1633. 2. *intr.* Of a river, lake, etc.: To flow out at the mouth; to empty itself; to flow *into*. Also *fig.* and *transf.* 1598. 3. *trans.* Of a river, lake, etc.: To discharge its waters at the mouth; *refl.* to empty itself. Also *fig.* and *transf.* 1610. †b. To drive out -1632.

2. The Danube disembogues into the Euxine by seven mouths GOLDSM. The presses of Europe are still disemboguing into the ocean of literature DE QUINCEY. 3. Paris disembogues itself.. to witness, with grim looks, the *Séance Royale* CARLYLE. Hence †**Disembo·gue** *sb.* place of disemboguing. **Disembo·guement,** action or place of disemboguing.

Disembo·som, *v.* 1742. [DIS- 6.] To separate from the bosom; to reveal; *refl.* and *intr.* to unburden oneself.

Disembow·el, *v.* 1603. [DIS- 6. In sense 1 an intensive of DISBOWEL.] 1. To remove the bowels or entrails of; to eviscerate. Also *fig.* 2. To take out of the bowels 1703.

2. So her disembowell'd web Arachne .. spreads J. PHILIPS. Hence **Disembo·welment,** the act of disembowelling.

Disembow·er, *v.* 1856. [DIS- 6.] To set free from a bower.

†**Disembra·ce,** *v.* 1638. [DIS- 6.] *trans.* To refrain or withdraw from embracing; also, to undo embracing -1775.

†**Disembra·ngle,** *v.* 1726. [DIS- 6.] To free from complication.

Disembroi·l, *v.* 1622. [DIS- 6. Cf. F. *desbrouiller.*] To free from embroilment or confusion; to disentangle.

To d. a Subject that seems to have perplexed even Antiquity 1741.

Disembu·rden, -bu·rthen, *v.* 1790. [See DISEN-.] = DISBURDEN.

Disemic (dəi,sī·mik), *a.* [f. L. *disemus*, a. Gr. δίσημος (f. δι- (DI-²) + σῆμα a sign).] In *Gr.* and *L. Prosody*: Of the value of two moræ or units of time (cf. TRISEMIC).

Disemploy (disĕmploi·), *v. rare.* 1618. [DIS- 6.] *trans.* To cease to employ, throw out of employment. Hence **Disemploy·ed** *ppl. a.* unemployed. **Disemploy·ment,** absence or withdrawal of employment (*rare*).

Disempow·er, *v. rare.* 1813. [DIS- 6.] To deprive of power conferred.

Disemprison, var. DISIMPRISON.

Disen-, disem-. Verbs in *dis-* are sometimes in sense negative or privative of those in *em-, en-*: e.g. *en-franchise, dis-franchise*; generally, however, verbs in *em-* or *en-* have *dis-* prefixed, as in *dis-embarrass, dis-engage, dis-entwine.*

Disenable (disĕnē¹·b'l), *v.* 1604. [DIS- 6.] To render unable or incapable; the reverse of *enable.*

I am constitutionally disenabled from that vice LAMB.

Disena·ct, *v. rare.* 1651. [DIS- 6.] To repeal.

Disena·mour, *v.* 1598. [DIS- 6.] To free from being enamoured.

Disenchai·n, *v. rare.* 1849. [DIS- 6.] To set free from chains or restraint.

Disenchant (disĕn,tʃɑ·nt), *v.* 1586. [ad. F. *désenchanter*; see DIS- 4.] To set free from enchantment, magic spell, or illusion.

A noble stroke or two Ends all the charms, and disenchants the grove DRYDEN. Hence **Disencha·nter. Disencha·ntment,** the action of disenchanting; disenchanted state. **Disencha·ntress.**

Disencha·rm, *v. rare.* 1651. [DIS- 6.] To deliver from a charm.

†**Disenclo·se,** *v. rare.* 1611. [DIS- 6.] To throw open (that which is enclosed) -1669.

†**Disencou·rage,** *v.* 1626. [DIS- 6.] To DISCOURAGE -1803. Hence †**Disencou·ragement,** disheartenment.

Disencrease; see DISINCREASE.

Disencumber (disĕnkʋ·mbəɹ), *v.* 1598. [DIS- 4.] To relieve or free of encumbrances.

Disencumbered from my villatick bashfulness JOHNSON. Hence **Disencu·mberment** (*rare*), †**Disencu·mbrance,** deliverance or freedom from encumbrance.

Disendow (disĕndau·), *v.* 1861. [DIS- 6.] To deprive of endowments. Hence **Disendow·ment,** the action or fact of disendowing, as, *the d. of the Irish Church.*

Disenfra·nchise, *v.* 1626. [DIS- 6.] 1. To DISFRANCHISE 1664. †2. [f. DIS- 5, or error.] To set free, enfranchise (*rare*) -1654. Hence †**Disenfra·nchisement.**

Disengage (disĕngē¹·dʒ), *v.* 1611. [DIS- 6.] 1. To free from engagement, pledge, contract, or obligation. *Obs.* exc. as *pa. pple.* 2. To loosen from that which holds fast, adheres, or entangles; to detach, liberate, free 1662. Also *fig.* 3. *intr.* (for *refl.*) To free oneself, get loose 1646. 4. *intr. Fencing.* To pass the point of one's blade smartly to the opposite side of the opponent's sword, so as to free it for a thrust 1684.

1. Are you disengaged this evening DICKENS. 2. It slowly decomposes the water, combining with its

hydrogen and disengaging its oxygen HUXLEY. To d. great principles from capricious adjuncts GROTE. 3. The left Troop..must d. ..before it can move 1832. Hence **Disenga·ge** *sb.* (*Fencing*), the action of disengaging.

Disengaged (disĕngē̆·dʒd), *ppl. a.* 1621. [f. prec.] Set free from engagement, ties, or prepossession; detached; not engaged; at liberty. Hence **Disenga·gedness.**

Disengagement (disĕngē̆·dʒmĕnt). 1650. [f. as prec.] The action of disengaging or fact of being disengaged *from* (anything).

A noble D. from the World JER. COLLIER. The d. of a quantity of nitrous gas 1791. Mental d. FERRIER. To parry the d. ROLAND.

Disenme·sh, *v. rare.* 1868. [DIS- 6.] To free from meshes, disentangle.

Disenno·ble, *v.* 1645. [DIS- 6.] To deprive of nobleness; to render ignoble.

An unworthy behaviour..disennobles a man ADDISON.

†**Diseno·rm,** *v.* [DIS- 6 or 8.] To make conformable to a norm or standard. QUARLES.

†**Disenro·l,** *v. rare.* [DIS- 6.] To remove from a roll. DONNE.

Disensanity; see DIS- 5 and INSANITY.

Disenshrou·d, *v. rare.* 1835. [DIS- 6.] To set free from or as from a shroud.

Disensla·ve, *v.* Also †**disin-.** 1649. [DIS- 6.] To set free from enslavement; to liberate from slavery.

Such an one as should d. them from the Roman yoke SOUTH.

Disentail (disĕntē̆·l), *v.* Also †**disin-.** 1641. [DIS- 6.] 1. *Law.* To free from entail; to break the entail of; see ENTAIL *sb.*[2] 1848. †2. To divest *of.* Hence **Disentai·l** *sb.*, **Disentai·lment,** the act of disentailing.

Disentangle (disĕntæ·ŋg'l), *v.* Also †**disin-.** 1598. [DIS- 6.] 1. *trans.* To free from that in or with which a thing is entangled; to disengage, extricate. Const. *from,* †*of.* Also *fig.* 2. To bring out of a tangled state; to unravel, untwist 1805. Also *fig.* 3. *intr.* (for *refl.*) To become disentangled; to disentangle oneself 1607.

1. To d. our line from the water-lilies J. WILSON. To d. our minds from..prejudices BERKELEY. To d. facts from the mass of fable 1874. 2. To d. the knots of my harness KANE. 3. This skein won't d. (*mod.*). Hence **Disenta·nglement,** the fact of disentangling; disentangled state.

†**Dise·nter,** *v.* 1629. [f. DIS- 6 + ENTER *v.*[2]] To eject, oust -1631.

Disenthra·l, -ll, *v.* Also †**disin-.** 1643. [DIS- 6.] To set free from enthralment or bondage; to liberate from thraldom. Hence **Disenthra·lment,** emancipation from thraldom.

Disenthrone (disĕnþrōu·n), *v.* Also †**disin-.** 1608. [DIS- 6.] To put down from a throne; to depose from royal dignity or authority; to dethrone. Hence **Disenthro·nement,** dethroning.

Disentitle (disĕntəi·t'l), *v.* Also †**disin-.** 1654. [DIS- 6.] To deprive of title or right (*to* something).

Every ordinary offence does not d. a son to the love of his father SOUTH.

Disentomb (disĕntū̆·m), *v.* 1626. [DIS- 6.] To take out of the tomb. Also *transf.* and *fig.*

A mummy..which we saw disentombed 1877. Hence **Disentombment** (-tū̆·mmĕnt), the act of disentombing.

†**Disentrai·l,** *v.* 1596. [DIS- 7 a.] To draw forth from the entrails or inward parts -1692.

Disentra·mmel, *v.* 1866. [DIS- 6.] To free from its trammels.

Disentra·nce, *v.* 1663. [DIS- 6.] To arouse from or as from a trance.

Disentwi·ne, *v.* 1814. [DIS- 6.] To free from being entwined; to untwine (*lit.* and *fig.*). Also *intr.* (for *refl.*)

Disenve·lop, -e, *v.* Also †**disin-.** 1632. [DIS- 6 or 7.] To free from that in which it is enveloped; to unfold.

Disepalous (dəise·pălǝs), *a.* 1841. [f. Gr. δι- (DI-[2]) + mod.L. *sepalum.*] *Bot.* Having or consisting of two sepals.

†**Disequa·lity.** 1602. [after *equality.*] Inequality, disparity -1655.

Disequili·brium. 1840. [DIS- 9.] Absence or destruction of equilibrium. So **Disequili·brate, Disequi·librize** *vbs.* to throw out of balance; **Disequilibra·tion.**

†**Dise·rt,** *a.* ME. [ad. L. *disertus,* var. of *dissertus, disserere.*] Well-spoken, eloquent -1675. Hence †**Dise·rtly** *adv.*

†**Disespou·se,** *v. rare.* [DIS- 6.] To undo the espousal or betrothal of. MILT. *P. L.* IX. 17.

Disestablish (disĕstæ·bliʃ), *v.* 1598. [DIS- 6.] To deprive of the character of being established; *spec.* to deprive (a church) of especial State connexion and support.

Disesta·blishment. 1806. [f. as prec.] The act of disestablishing; *spec.* the withdrawal of especial State patronage and control from a church.

From the establishment of Christianity under Constantine, to the beginnings of its d. under Pope Leo X 1806.

Disesteem (disĕstī·m), *sb.* 1603. [DIS- 9.] The action of disesteeming, or position of being disesteemed; low estimation or regard.

Pastorals are fallen into D. DRYDEN.

Disestee·m, *v.* 1594. [DIS- 6.] 1. *trans.* To regard with the reverse of esteem; to hold in low estimation, slight, despise. Also *intr.* with *of.* †b. To take away the estimation of (*rare*) 1637. †2. with *subord. cl.*: To think or believe otherwise than (*rare*) 1677.

1. Strange notes to like, and d. our own DANIEL. Opinions disesteem'd, Impostures branded B. JONS. Hence **Disestee·mer,** one who disesteems.

†**Dise·stima·tion.** 1619. [DIS- 9.] = DISESTEEM *sb.* -1677.

‖**Diseuse** (dĭzöz). 1896. [Fr., fem. = talker.] A female artiste who entertains with monologue. Also less freq. masc. **Diseur.**

†**Dise·xercise,** *v. rare.* [DIS- 6.] To put out of exercise. MILTON.

Disfa·me, *sb. rare.* 1460. [DIS- 9.] Disrepute; defamation. So †**Disfa·me** *v.* to defame.

Disfashion (disfæ·ʃən), *v.* 1535. [DIS- 6.] To mar or undo the fashion of; to disfigure.

Gluttony..disfashioneth the body MORE.

Disfavour, -or (disfē̆·vəɹ), *sb.* 1533. [DIS- 9.] 1. Unfavourable regard, dislike, disapproval. †2. An act or expression of dislike or ill will -1647. 3. The condition of being unfavourably regarded 1581.

1. The kynges disfauoure is like y[e] roaringe of a Lyon COVERDALE *Prov.* xix. 12. 2. To dispense favours and disfavours CLARENDON. 3. Phr. *To be* (*live,* etc.) *in d., to bring, come, fall,* etc. *into d.*

Disfa·vour, -or, *v.* 1535. [DIS- 6.] 1. *trans.* To regard or treat with the reverse of favour; to discountenance; to treat with disapprobation 1570; †to dislike -1740. †2. To mar the countenance or appearance of; to disfigure -1607.

1. Countenanced or disfavoured according as they obey SWIFT. Hence **Disfa·vourer** (*rare*), one who disfavours.

†**Disfa·vourable,** *a.* 1561. [DIS- 10.] Unfavourable; adverse. †**Disfa·vourably** *adv.*

Disfeature (disfī·tiŭɹ), *v.* 1659. [DIS- 7 a or d. Cf. DEFEATURE.] To mar the features of; to disfigure, deface.

Disfe·llowship, *sb.* 1608. [DIS- 9.] Exclusion from fellowship. So **Disfe·llowship** *v.* to exclude from fellowship; to excommunicate. (Now *U.S.*)

Disfigura·tion. 1653. [See -ATION.] = DISFIGUREMENT.

Disfigure (disfi·giŭɹ), *v.* ME. [ad. OF. *desfigurer* (mod.F. *dé-*), f. L. *dis-* + *figura, figurare.* See also DEFIGURE.] 1. *trans.* To mar the figure or appearance of; to deform, deface. Also *fig.* †2. To disguise -1713. †3. *techn.* To carve (a peacock) -1706.

1. Disfiguring not Gods likeness, but thir own MILT. *P. L.* xi. 521. Diction disfigured by foreign idioms MACAULAY. 2. And me so wel d...That..ther shal no man me knowe CHAUCER. Hence †**Disfigure** *sb.* disfigurement. **Disfi·gurer,** one who or that which disfigures.

Disfi·gurement. 1634. [f. prec. vb.] 1. The action of disfiguring; the fact or condition of being disfigured; defacement, deformity. 2. Something that disfigures; a deformity, defacement 1641.

2. A dial is not necessarily a d. to a tower 1874.

Disfle·sh, *v.* 1620. [DIS- 7 a.] To deprive of flesh; also, to disembody.

Disfoliaged; see DIS- 7 a, etc.

Disforest (disfǫ·rĕst), *v.* 1502. [ad. OF. *desforester.*] 1. *trans.* = DISAFFOREST. Also *fig.* 2. To clear of forests or trees 1668. Hence **Disforesta·tion.**

Disform (disfǭ·ɹm), *v. rare.* 1527. [f. DIS- + FORM *v.*; cf. DIFFORM, DEFORM.] †1. To mar the form, character, or condition of; to deform -1658. 2. To alter the form of; *intr.* (for *refl.*) to lose its form (*rare*) 1868.

2. They seem to form, d., and re-form before us, like the squares of coloured glass in the kaleidoscope GLADSTONE.

†**Disfo·rmity.** *rare.* 1494. [var. of DIFFORMITY.] a. = DEFORMITY. b. = DIFFORMITY. -1600.

†**Disfo·rtune.** *rare.* 1529. [ad. OF. *desfortune.*] Misfortune -1592.

†**Disfra·me,** *v.* 1629. [DIS- 6.] To undo the frame or framing of -1644.

Disfranchise (disfræ·ntʃiz, -əiz), *v.* 1467. [DIS- 6.] To deprive of the rights and privileges of a free citizen of a borough, city, or country, or of some franchise previously enjoyed. Also *transf.* and *fig.*

He..shalbe dysfranchesed opynly at Carfox 1535. The decayed burghs were disfranchised, and their members given to the counties LD. BROUGHAM. Wise men are timorous in the disfranchising of their judgement J. HALL. Hence **Disfra·nchisement,** the action of disfranchising or fact of being disfranchised.

†**Disfri·ar,** *v.* 1599. [DIS- 7 b.] To deprive of the order of a friar; also *refl.* -1639.

Disfro·ck, *v.* 1837. [f. DIS- + FROCK; cf. DEFROCK.] To deprive of the clerical garb and character; to unfrock.

Disfu·rnish, *v.* 1531. [ad. OF. *desfourniss-* stem of *desfournir*; see DIS- 4.] To deprive of that wherewith it is furnished; to strip of furniture, etc.; to render destitute (*of*).

These poore habiliments, Of which, if you should here d. me, You take the sum and substance that I haue *Two Gent.* IV. i. 14. Hence **Disfu·rnishment.** So †**Disfu·rniture,** disfurnishment.

†**Disga·ge,** *v.* 1594. [a. 16th c. F. *desgager,* mod.F. *dégager*; see DIS- 4.] To release from pledge or pawn; to disengage -1603.

†**Disga·llant,** *v. rare.* 1599. [DIS- 8.] To deprive of courage; to dispirit -1640.

Disgarland (disgā·ɹlănd), *v.* 1616. [DIS- 7 a.] To divest of a garland or garlands.

Disgarnish (disgā·ɹniʃ), *v.* 1450. [a. OF. *desgarniss-* stem of *desgarnir,* mod.F. *dégarnir*; see DIS- 4.] To deprive of that which garnishes or furnishes; to disfurnish, despoil.

The front .. was .. disgarnished of troops SIR W. NAPIER.

Disga·rrison, *v.* Now *arch.* 1594. [DIS- 7 a.] To deprive of a garrison.

Disgavel (disgæ·vĕl), *v.* 1683. [f. DIS- 7 a + *gavel* (GAVELKIND) sb.] To relieve from the tenure of GAVELKIND.

Disgene·ric, *a.* [DIS- 10.] Of different genera (opp. to *congeneric*). *rec.*

†**Disglo·rify,** *v. rare.* 1577. [DIS- 6.] To deprive of glory; to treat with dishonour -1671.

†**Disglo·ry.** 1547. [DIS- 9.] The opposite of glory; dishonour -1577.

Disgorge (disgǭ·ɹdʒ), *v.* 1477. [ad. OF. *desgorger,* mod.F. *dégorger*; see DIS- 4.] 1. *trans.* To eject or throw out from, or as from, the gorge or throat; to vomit forth (what has been swallowed); *esp.* to give up what has been wrongfully appropriated. Also *absol.* 2. *trans.* To discharge or empty; also *refl.* 1592. †3. *Farriery.* To dissipate an engorgement -1753.

1. Jonah's whale swallowed and disgorged him night after night MISS THACKERAY. D. thy care, abandon feare 1587. Some mode..to make the French Generals d. the church plate which they have stolen WELLINGTON. *absol.* The river Nile..disgorging at seaven mouthes Into the Sea MILT. *P. L.* XII. 158. 2. Several vessels were disgorging themselves HAWTHORNE. Hence **Disgo·rgement. Disgo·rger.**

†**Disgo·spel,** *v.* [DIS- 7 a.] To deprive of the gospel or gospel character; to oust the gospel from life. MILTON.

†**Disgou·t,** *v.* 1611. [DIS- 7 a.] To free from gout -1748.

Disgown (disgau·n), *v.* 1734. [DIS- 7 a.] To strip (any one) of his gown, and thus of his degree or office. Also *intr.* (for *refl.*)

Disgrace (disgrē̆·s), *sb.* 1581. [a. F. *disgrâce,* ad. It. *disgrazia* 'a disgrace, a mishap' (Florio), f. DIS- 4 + *grazia* GRACE.] 1. The disfavour of one in a powerful position; the state of being out of favour and honour; †a disfavour; an affront -1739. †2. The disfavour of Fortune; adverse fortune -1697; a misfortune -1748. 3. Dishonour in public estimation; ignominy, shame 1593. †4. Opprobrium, reproach, disparagement -1676. 5. That which brings into dishonour 1590.

1. I heare Macduffe liues in d. *Macb.* III. vi. 23. The interchange continually of favours and disgraces BACON. 3. Tito shrank..from d. GEO. ELIOT. 4. Then Hector him with words of great d. Reproved HOBBES. 5. I found the two disgraces..are, first, disloyalty to Church and State, and, second, to be born poor EMERSON.

Disgrace (disgrē¹·s), *v.* 1549. [a. F. *disgracier*, ad. It. *disgraziare*; see prec.] †1. *trans.* To undo or mar the grace of; to disfigure -1781. †2. To put out of countenance -1591. 3. To put out of grace or favour; to dismiss from (royal, etc.) favour 1593. †4. To cast shame or discredit upon -1715. †5. To speak of dishonouringly; to disparage, revile -1720. 6. To be a disgrace or shame to; to reflect dishonour upon 1593.

3. Queensbury was disgraced for refusing to betray the interests of the Protestant religion MACAULAY. 4. They never vse reason so willingly as to d. reason HOOKER. 6. I could finde in my heart to d. my mans apparell, and to cry like a woman *A. Y. L.* II. iv. 4. Hence †**Disgra·cement**, the action of disgracing; that which causes disgrace. **Disgra·cer**, one who or that which disgraces; †an opprobrious reviler.

Disgraceful (disgrē¹·sfŭl), *a.* 1591. [f. prec. sb.] †1. Void of grace, unpleasing -1702. 2. Full of, or fraught with, disgrace; shameful, dishonourable 1597. 3. Inflicting disgrace, degrading, opprobrious 1608.

2. Stained with black d. crimes DANIEL. 3. Such d., such contemptible punishment FOOTE. Hence **Disgra·ceful-ly** *adv.*, **-ness**.

‖**Disgracia, -grazia.** 1739. [Sp. *desgracia* (-grāþya), It. *disgrazia* (-gratsya).] An unpleasant accident.

Disgracious (disgrē¹·ʃəs), *a.* 1594. [a. F. *disgracieux*; see DIS- 4.] 1. Ungracious, unkind. ? *Obs.* 1598. †2. In disfavour; disliked -1611. †3. Disgraceful 1615. 4. Uncomely 1870. Hence †**Disgra·ciously** *adv.*

†**Disgra·cive,** *a. rare.* 1602. [irreg. f. DISGRACE *v.*; cf. *coercive.*] Conveying or tending to disgrace -1627.

Disgradation (disgrădē¹·ʃən). ? *Obs.* 1727. [f. DISGRADE *v.*] = DEGRADATION ¹ 1.

Disgrade (disgrē¹·d), *v.* ME. [ad. OF. *desgrader*, by-form of *degrader*, ad. late L. *degradare*; see DE- I. 6.] = DEGRADE *v.* 2.

†**Disgra·duate,** *v.* 1528. [DIS- 7 b.] = DEGRADUATE -1550.

Disgregate (di·sgrĭgeⁱt), *v.* 1593. [f. L. *disgregat-*, *disgregare*; see DIS- 1.] †1. To separate (*from*). 2. To disintegrate 1603. †3. To scatter (the visual rays); hence, to confuse (the sight) -1645. Hence **Disgrega·tion**, disintegration, dispersal; *spec.* in *Chem.* separation of the molecules of a substance by heat, etc.

†**Disgross** (disgrōᵘ·s), *v.* 1611. [ad. 16th c. *desgrossir*, mod.F. *dégrossir*; see DIS- 4.] To make finer or less gross -1823.

If bullion be..disgrost into wire or lace PETTY.

Disgruntle (disgrʊ·nt'l), *v.* Now chiefly *U.S.* 1682. [f. DIS- 5 + GRUNTLE *v.* freq. of GRUNT.] To put into ill humour; to chagrin, disgust. Chiefly in *pa. pple.*

Disguise (disgəi·z), *v.* [ME. *desgisen*, *degisen*, etc., a. OF. *desguisier*, etc., mod.F. *déguiser*, f. *des-*, *de-* (DE- I. 6) + Romanic *guisa*, F. *guise*, a. OHG. *wîsa* WISE, manner, mode (of dress, etc.).] †1. *trans.* To change the usual or natural guise or fashion of; *esp.* of dress -1563. †2. To transform; to disfigure -1697. 3. To change the dress and appearance of so as to conceal identity; to conceal the identity of by dressing *as* or *in*. (Now the leading sense.) ME. Also *refl.* 4. To exhibit (anything) in a false light; to colour; to misrepresent ME. 5. To conceal or hide by a false show, or the like 1591. 6. To intoxicate (with liquor) 1562.

2. Faces..disguised in death DRYDEN. 3. Disguised in the habit of a Turk KNOLLES. Disguised as a monk (*mod.*). 4. To d. and put off a bad commodity 1732. 5. A feint to d. the real intention 1853. 6. Three cuppes full at once shall oft dysgyse thee 1562. Hence **Disgui·sed-ly** *adv.*, **-ness.** **Disgui·ser**, one who disguises; †a masker.

Disguise (disgəi·z), *sb.* ME. [f. prec. vb.] †1. New or strange fashion (*esp.* of an ostentatious kind) -1594. 2. Altered fashion of dress and appearance intended to conceal identity; the state of being thus disguised ME. Also *fig.* 3. A garb assumed in order to deceive 1596. Also *transf.* and *fig.* 4. Any artificial manner assumed for deception 1632. 5. The act or practice of disguising 1603. †6. A masque -1630. 7. 'Disorder by drink' (J.) 1606.

2. The banished Kent; who, in d., Follow'd his enemy king, and did him service *Lear* V. iii. 220. A blessing in d. (*mod.*). 3. Ned, where are our disguises 1 *Hen. IV*, II. ii. 78. 5. Hence false tears, deceits, disguises POPE. 6. Masques (which they then called Disguises) BACON. Hence **Disgui·seless** *a.*

Disgui·sement. 1580. [f. DISGUISE *v.*] 1. The fact of disguising, or of being disguised 1583. 2. That which disguises; a disguise 1580. 3. *pl.* Additions that change the appearance; bedizenments 1638.

†**Disgui·sy,** *a.* ME. [a. OF. *desguisié*; see DISGUISE *v.*] Disguised, altered from familiar guise, mode, or appearance -1430.

Disgu·lf, -gu·lph, *v.* 1635. [DIS- 7 c.] To discharge as from a gulf.

Disgust (disgʊ·st), *sb.* 1598. [ad. 16th c. F. *desgoust*, mod.F. *dégoût*; or ad. It. *disgusto*; see DIS- 4. Not in Shaks.] 1. Strong distaste for food, drink, medicine, etc.; nausea, loathing 1611. (Formerly in milder sense.) 2. Strong repugnance excited by that which is loathsome or offensive; profound instinctive dissatisfaction 1611. †3. An outbreak of mutual ill-feeling; a quarrel -1761. †4. That which causes repugnance; an annoyance. *Obs.* 1654.

1. To this day the [hare]..is an object of d. in certain parts of Russia CLODD. 2. He soon retreated in d. across the Alps S. AUSTIN. 3. Some disgusts happen'd 'twixt Rustan and his brother SIR T. HERBERT. 4. Some disgusts which she had received from the States HUME. Hence **Disgu·stful** *a.* causing disgust; nauseous; displeasing; disgusting; full of disgust. **Disgu·stful-ly** *adv.*, **-ness.**

Disgust (disgʊ·st), *v.* 1601. [ad. F. *desgouster*, or ad. It. *disgustare*; see DIS- 4.] †1. *trans.* To have a strong distaste for or repugnance to -1752. 2. To offend the senses or sensibilities of 1650; *absol.* to be very distasteful 1756.

2. The remedy..disgusts the palate 1650. Want of the usual proportions in men and other animals is sure to d. BURKE. Hence **Disgu·sted** *ppl. a.* †distasteful; feeling disgust. **Disgu·ster** (*rare*). **Disgu·sting-ly** *adv.*, **-ness.**

Dish (diʃ), *sb.* [OE. *disc*, a. L. *discus* quoit, dish (in Vulgate), DISK. Cf. DESK, DAIS.] 1. Any open vessel used to hold food at meals. Often restricted to those of oval, square, or irregular shape, as distinguished from *plates*. b. A hollow vessel of wood or metal, used for drinking, and also *esp.* as a receptacle for alms; a cup; cf. ALMS-DISH ME. 2. The food served on or in a dish; a distinct variety of food 1526. 3. As much as will fill or make a dish; a dishful 1596. Also *fig.* 4. *transf.* Any shallow concave receptacle 1633. 5. A dish-like concavity; *e.g.* a depression in a field, etc. 1810. 6. a. *Tin-mining.* A gallon of ore ready for the smelter. b. *Lead-mining.* A measuring box for lead ore; by statute fixed to contain fifteen pints of water. c. Also, the proportion of ore paid as royalty to the mine landlord, etc. 1531. †7. A quoit; quoit-playing -1552.

1. She brought forth butter in a lordly d. *Judg.* v. 25. I know him as the beggar knows his d. 1605. 2. Let's carue him, as a D. fit for the Gods *Jul. C.* II. i. 173. 3. The Boat returned with a good d. of Fish DAMPIER. He sate him pensive o'er a d. of tea BYRON. *fig.* Roger..had a D. of Chat with her MOTTEUX.

Comb.: **d.-cloth, -clout, -rag, -towel**, a cloth, clout, etc. used for washing dishes; **-wash,** the greasy water in which dishes have been washed; **-washer,** a scullion or scullery-maid; the pied or water wagtail (*Motacilla alba*); **-water** = *dish-wash*; also *attrib.*

Dish (diʃ), *v.*¹ 1586. [f. DISH *sb.*] I. *trans.* To put into a dish, ready for table. Also with *up*. Also *fig.* 2. To make concave like a dish; to hollow *out* 1805. 3. *intr.* To be or become concave; to cave in 1669. 4. *intr.* Of a horse: To move the fore-feet in his trot with a scooping motion 1863. 5. *trans. slang.* To 'do for'; to cheat, circumvent. [From the notion of meat being *done*, and *dished*.] 1798.

1. Jemima, d. up MARRYAT. To d. up a story DORAN. 3. We had much trouble with our wagon, the wheel dishing frequently A. W. GREELY. 5. I believe it [the House of Commons] to be completely used up. Reform has dished it. DISRAELI.

Dish, *v.*² *Sc.* 1821. [var. (ult.) of DASH *v.*] To push violently, thrust.

Dishabilitate (dis,hăbi·liteⁱt), *v.* 1662. [DIS- 6.] *Sc. Law.* To incapacitate, disqualify. Hence **Dishabilita·tion.**

Dishabille (disăbī·l, -bi·l). 1673. [ad. F. *déshabillé* undress, pa. pple. used subst.; see DIS- 4. The final *-é* (or its equivalent) also occurs in English.] 1. Undress; the state of being dressed in a negligent style 1684. 2. A garment of a negligent style 1673. Also *transf.* and *fig.*

1. To surprise his mistress in d. 1684. 2. [Pepys] sets down his thoughts in a most becoming d. MISS MITFORD.

†**Dis,ha·bit,** *v. rare.* [DIS- 6.] To dislodge. SHAKS. *John* II. i. 220.

†**Dis,ha·bited,** *ppl. a.* 1577. [f. F. *déshabité*.] Uninhabited; deserted of inhabitants -1602.

The d. towns afford them rooting CAREW.

Dis,habi·tuate, *v.* 1868. [DIS- 6.] To render unaccustomed.

Dis,hable, obs. f. DISABLE *v.*

Dishallow (dis,hæ·loᵘ), *v.* 1552. [DIS- 6.] To undo the hallowing of; to profane.

God hateth the dishallowing of the Sabboth LATIMER.

Disharmonious (dis,haɹmōᵘ·niəs), *a.* 1659. [DIS- 10.] 1. Not in harmony or agreement. 2. Of sounds: Discordant 1683.

Disharmonize (dis,hā·ɹmŏnəiz), *v.* 1801. [f. DIS- + HARMONIZE; after next.] 1. To put out of harmony; to make discordant. 2. *intr.* To be out of harmony 1863.

Disharmony (dis,hā·ɹmŏni). 1602. [DIS- 9; prob. after *discord*.] 1. Want of harmony or agreement. Also with *a* and *pl.* 2. Discord, dissonance 1655.

1. D. of mind and tongue CARLYLE. Hence **Dis,harmo·nic**, †**-al** *a.*

Dis,hau·nt, *v.* (Chiefly *Sc.*) 1584. [DIS- 4.] To cease to haunt; to absent oneself from.

†**Dis,hea·rt,** *v.* 1603. [DIS- 7 a.] = next -1616.

Dishearten (dis,hā·ɹt'n), *v.* 1599. [DIS- 6.] To deprive of heart or courage; to dispirit. Also with †*from*, or †*to* and *inf.*

Their former losse dishartned them so much WARNER. Hence **Dis,hea·rtenment.**

†**Dis,hei·r,** *v. rare.* 1607. [DIS- 7 b.] 1. To deprive of one's inheritance. 2. To deprive of an heir. DRYDEN.

Dishelm (dis,he·lm), *v.*¹ 1477. [DIS- 7 a, after OF. *desheaulmer*.] To deprive of one's helmet. *intr.* for *refl.* To take off one's helmet.

Sir Raynold dishelmed the Englisshe knyght LD. BERNERS.

Dishelm (dis,he·lm), *v.*² [DIS- 7 a.] To deprive of the helm or rudder.

Disherison (dis,he·rizən), *sb.* ME. [orig. *disheriteson*, a. OF. *des(h)eriteisun*. (The full L. type was **dishereditationem*.)] The action of depriving of, or cutting off from, an inheritance; disinheritance.

Improvident alienations .. to the d. of the lawful heirs WILLIAMS.

†**Disherit** (dis,he·rit), *v.* ME. [a. OF. *desheriter*, etc., mod.F. *déshériter*:—Rom. *desheretare*, for L. **de-*, **dishereditare*; see DE- 6, DIS- 4.] To deprive or dispossess of an inheritance; to disinherit. Const. *of* (rarely *from*). Also *fig.* -1795. So †**Dis,he·ritance**, disinheritance. †**Dis,he·ritor**, one who disinherits.

†**Dishe·vel,** *a.* ME. [var. of DISHEVELY, a. OF. *deschevelé*.] Without coif or head-dress; hence, with the hair unkempt. Sometimes app.: In dishabille. -1470.

Dishevel (diʃe·vĕl), *v.* 1598. [prob. a back-formation from DISHEVELLED.] 1. To loosen and throw about in disorder (hair and the like); to let (the hair) down. †2. *intr.* (for *refl.*) To hang loose or in disorder 1638.

1. The Peacock when he's viewd disheuels his faire traine 1618.

Dishevelled, -eled (diʃe·vĕld), *ppl. a.* 1450. [f. OF. *deschevelé*, mod.F. *déchevelé* (see DISHEVELY.] †a. = DISHEVEL *a.* -1653. b. With disarranged dress 1612. Also *transf.*

1. She, so disheuld blusht SIDNEY. The dishevelled

fair hastily following FIELDING. Our hair dischiveld, not platted nor crisped 1638. Hence **Dishe·velment**, d. condition.

†Dishe·vely, -elee, *ppl. a.* ME. [a. OF. *deschevelé* pa. pple., f. *des-*, DIS- + OF. *chevel, cheveu* hair = med.L. *dis-*, *decapillatus.*] = DISHEVEL *a.*

Dishful (di·ʃful). ME. [See -FUL.] As much as a dish will contain.

Dishing (di·ʃiŋ), *vbl. sb.* 1679. [f. DISH *v.*[1]] The action of the verb DISH; oblique position of the spokes of a wheel.

Dishome (disˌhōu·m), *v.* 1880. [DIS- 7 c.] To deprive of a home.

Dishonest (disǫ·nėst), *a.* ME. [ad. OF. *deshoneste*, mod.F. *déshonnête*; see DE- 6, DIS- 4.] †1. Entailing dishonour or disgrace; dishonourable, shameful –1760. †2. Unchaste, lewd, filthy –1734. †3. Ugly, hideous –1725. 4. Of actions, etc.: Not straightforward or honourable, underhand; now, fraudulent, knavish 1611. 5. Of persons: Wanting in honesty; disposed to cheat or defraud; thievish 1751.

1. The galowes and..dyshonest dethe CAXTON. 2. *Hen. V*, I. ii. 50. 3. Enormous beasts d. to the eye POPE. 4. To get d. gaine *Ezek.* xxii. 27. D. artifices BUTLER. 5. Imposed upon .. by d. brethren JORTIN. Hence **Disho·nestly** *adv.*

†Disho·nest, *v.* ME. [ad. OF. *deshonester.*] 1. To bring dishonour –1670. 2. To defame –1615. 3. To defile –1652.

3. To deflour Virgins, d. Matrons FOXE.

Dishonesty (disǫ·nėsti). ME. [a. OF. *desho(n)nesté*, mod.F. *déshonnêteté*, f. Rom. *dishonestus* for L. *dehonestus*, after *honestatem.*] †1. Dishonour, discredit, shame; also with *pl.* –1596. †2. Unchastity, lewdness –1639. †3. Shameful appearance, ugliness, deformity –1535. 4. Lack of probity; disposition to deceive, defraud, or steal. Also, a dishonest act. 1599.

1. We renounce the hidden things of dishonestie 2 *Cor.* iv. 2. 4. I neuer knew profit in dishonestie SURFL. & MARKH.

Dishonour, -honor (disǫ·nəɹ), *sb.* ME. [a. OF. *deshonor*, mod.F. *déshonneur*; a Rom. formation f. L. *dis-*, DIS- 4 b + *honorem*. In this word, and its derivs., the sp. *dishonor* is usual in U.S.] 1. The reverse of honour; the withholding of honour due to any one; a state of shame or disgrace; ignominy, indignity. Also with *a* and *pl.* 2. A cause or source of shame, a disgrace 1553. 3. *Comm.* Refusal or failure to honour or pay (a bill of exchange, etc.) 1834.

1. He would rather dye .. then live in dishonor H. COGAN. 2. His little daughter, whose sweet face He kissed..Becomes d. to her race TENNYSON. 3. Notice of d. should be given to each indorser CRUMP.

Dishonour, -or (disǫ·nəɹ), *v.* ME. [a. OF. *deshonnorer*, mod.F. *déshonorer* :—late L. *dishonorare*; see DIS- 4.] 1. *trans.* To deprive of honour; to treat with indignity; to violate the honour or respect due to any one. 2. To violate the honour or chastity of; to defile ME. 3. To bring dishonour upon, by one's conduct, etc.; to disgrace 1568. †4. To strip *of* what is an honour –1700. 5. *Comm.* To refuse or fail to accept or pay (a bill of exchange, etc.) 1811.

1. To Value a man .. at a low rate, is to D. him HOBBES. 3. America..dishonours herself by tolerating slavery 1848. 4. His scalp..dishonour'd quite of hair DRYDEN. Hence **Disho·noured, -ored** *ppl. a.* **Disho·nourer, -orer.**

Dishonourable, -honorable (disǫ·nŏrăb'l), *a.* 1533. [orig. f. DISHONOUR *v.*; partly f. DIS- 10 + HONOURABLE.] 1. Entailing dishonour; ignominious, base. 2. Of persons: a. Disesteemed (*rare*). b. Devoid or negligent of honour; unprincipled, base 1611.

1. And peepe about To finde our selues d. Graves *Jul. C.* I. ii. 138. 2. He that is honoured in pouertie, how much more in riches, and he that is d. in riches, how much more in pouertie *Ecclus.* x. 31. Hence **Disho·nourableness.** **Disho·nourably** *adv.*

Disˌho·rn, *v.* 1598. [DIS- 7 a.] To deprive of horns.

Disˌho·rse, *v.* 1859. [DIS- 7 c.] To unhorse.

Dishouse (disˌhau·z), *v.* 1586. [DIS- 6 or 7.] 1. To oust from a house; also, to deprive of a habitation. 2. To clear (ground) of houses 1640.

1. Make them melt as the dishowsed snaile 1586.

†Disˌhu·mour, *sb.* 1712. [DIS- 9.] Ill humour –1795. So **†Disˌhu·mour** *v.* to put out of humour.

Disillu·minate, *v. rare.* 1865. [DIS- 6.] To deprive of illumination; to darken.

Disillusion (disilˌiū·ʒən), *sb.* 1598. [DIS- 5 and 9. Cf. F. *désillusion.*] †1. [DIS- 5.] Illusion, delusion –1603. 2. [DIS- 9.] The action of freeing or becoming freed from illusion; the condition of being freed from illusion; disenchantment. Hence **Disillu·sion** *v.* to free from illusion, disenchant. **Disillu·sionize** *v.* to disillusion. **Disillu·sionment,** the action of disillusioning, or fact of being disillusioned.

Disillu·sive, *a.* 1878. [after *illusive.*] Tending to disillusion.

Disima·gine, *v.* 1647. [DIS- 6.] To imagine not to be.

Disimmu·re, *v.* 1611. [DIS- 6.] To set free from confining walls; to liberate.

†Disimpa·rk, *v.* 1609. [DIS- 6.] To turn out of a park, to free from the enclosure of a park –1675.

Disimpa·ssioned, *ppl. a.* Also **disem-.** 1861. [DIS- 10.] Freed or free from passion.

That pale soft sweet disempassioned moon BROWNING.

Disimpri·son, *v.* Also **disem-.** 1611. [DIS- 6.] To release from imprisonment or confinement.

'All History is an imprisoned Epic'..says Sauerteig there. I wish he had disimprisoned it in this instance CARLYLE.

Disimpro·ve, *v.* 1642. [DIS- 6.] To do the reverse of improving; to render worse in quality. *intr.* To grow worse. Hence **Disimpro·vement,** a change for the worse.

Disinca·rcerate, *v.* 1665. [DIS- 6.] = DISIMPRISON. Hence **Disincarcera·tion.**

Disinclination (disinklinēⁱ·ʃən). 1647. [DIS- 9.] Want of inclination or liking; slight dislike or aversion; indisposition.

His d. to the church CLARENDON. A d. from having recourse to unjust extremities 1813.

Disincline (disinkləi·n), *v.* 1647. [DIS- 6.] To deprive of inclination; to make indisposed, averse, or unwilling. *intr.* To incline not (*to do* something).

It served..to d. them from any reverence or affection to the queen CLARENDON. [He] felt disinclined for any more sleep 1888.

Disinclose; see DISENCLOSE.

†Disinco·rporate, *ppl. a.* 1605. [DIS- 10.] Disunited or separated from a body, corporation, or society –1681.

Disincorporate (disinkǭ·ɹpŏrēⁱt), *v.* 1697. [DIS- 6.] 1. To undo the incorporation of, to dissolve (a corporation). 2. To separate from a corporation or body 1701. Hence **Disincorpora·tion.**

†Disincrea·se, *v.* ME. [DIS- 6.] To decrease, diminish –1430.

Disincru·stant. 1878. [DIS- 10.] Something that removes or prevents incrustation.

Disindivi·dualize, *v.* 1839. [DIS- 6.] To divest of individuality.

Disinfect (disinfe·kt), *v.* 1598. [DIS- 6.] †1. To rid of an infection or infectious disease (*rare*) –1722. 2. To cleanse from infection; to destroy the germs of disease in 1658. Also *absol.*

2. The best mode of disinfecting the clothes of scarlatina patients 1844. Hence **Disinfe·cter, -or,** he who or that which disinfects. **Disinfe·ction,** the action of disinfecting; destruction of the germs of infectious diseases.

Disinfe·ctant. 1837. [ad. F. *désinfectant.*] 1. *adj.* Having the property of disinfecting 1875. 2. *sb.* An agent having this property.

Disinfla·me, *v. rare.* 1611. [DIS- 6.] To make no longer inflamed; to deprive of ardour.

Disinge·nious, etc., 17th c. error for DISINGENUOUS, etc.

Disingenuity (di:sindʒėniū·ĭti). 1647. [f. next.] = DISINGENUOUSNESS (now more usual). Also with *a* and *pl.*

Disingenuous (disindʒe·niuˌəs), *a.* 1655. [DIS- 10.] The opposite of *ingenuous*; lacking in frankness, insincere, morally fraudulent.

A D. Speaker 1718. The d. shift of a protest HALLAM. Hence **Disinge·nuously** *adv.*

Disinge·nuousness. 1674. [f. prec.] The quality of being disingenuous; insincerity, unfairness.

D. and double-dealing JANE AUSTEN.

†Disinha·bit, *v.* 1530. [DIS- 6.] To dispeople –1818. Hence **†Disinha·bited** *ppl. a.* without inhabitants.

Disinhe·rison. Also **disen-.** 1543. [DIS- 9.] = DISHERISON.

Disinherit (disinhe·rit), *v.* Also **disen-.** 1450. [DIS- 6.] To deprive or dispossess of an inheritance; 'to cut off from an hereditary right' (J.); to prevent (a person) from coming into possession of a property or right which in the ordinary course would devolve upon him as heir. Also *fig.*

He was disinherited and turned out of his father's house HOOK. And thou, fair moon..Stoop thy pale visage through an amber cloud, And d. Chaos, that reigns here MILT. *Comus* 334. Hence **Disinhe·ritable** *a.* liable to be disinherited. **Disinhe·ritance,** dispossession from an inheritance.

Disinhume (disinhiū·m), *v.* Also **disen-.** 1821. [DIS- 6.] To unbury, exhume.

Disinsure, Disintail, etc.; see DISEN-.

Disi·ntegrable, *a.* 1796. [f. DISINTEGRATE.] Capable of being disintegrated.

Disi·ntegrant. 1855. [f. as prec.] 1. *adj.* Disintegrating, or becoming disintegrated. 2. *sb.* A disintegrating agent.

Disintegrate (disi·ntĭgrēⁱt), *v.* 1796. [DIS- 6.] 1. *trans.* To separate into its component parts or particles; to reduce to fragments, break up, destroy the cohesion or integrity of. Also *fig.* b. To separate as particles *from* the whole mass 1873. 2. *intr.* To become disintegrated 18...

1. Marlites .. are not disintegrated by exposure to the atmosphere KIRWAN. To d. the Homeric poems GLADSTONE. 2. The Church itself was fast disintegrating FROUDE. Hence **Disi·ntegrative** *a.* tending to d. **Disi·ntegrator,** a machine for reducing substances to powder.

Disintegra·tion. 1796. [f. prec. vb.] The action or process of disintegrating, or the condition of being disintegrated; breaking up; destruction of cohesion or integrity; *spec.* in *Geol.*, the wearing down of rocks by atmospheric influences. Also *fig.*

The d. of clay-slate rocks THOMSON, of nations HT. MARTINEAU, of Roman society MERIVALE.

Disinte·grity. 1785. [DIS- 9.] Want of entireness; disintegrated condition.

Disinter (disintə̄·ɹ), *v.* 1611. [ad. F. *désenterrer*; see DIS- 4.] To take out of the earth in which it is buried; to unbury, exhume. Also *transf.* and *fig.*

†Disinteress, *v.* Pa. pple. **-essed, -est.** 1622. [ad. F. *désintéresser*; see DIS- 4.] = DISINTEREST *v.* –1655. So **†Disintere·ssment,** disinterestedness.

Disinterest, *sb.* 1658. [DIS- 9.] 1. That which is contrary to interest or advantage; prejudice. Now *rare.* 1662. †2. Disinterestedness –1805.

1. Whatever..tends to the D. of the Public, is evil NORRIS.

Disi·nterest, *v.* Now *rare.* 1612. [DIS- 6.] 1. To rid or divest of interest or concern; to detach from the interest or party of. 2. To render disinterested 1681.

Disinterest, var. of DISINTERESSED *ppl. a.*

Disi·nterested, *ppl. a.* 1612. [f. prec. vb.] 1. Without interest or concern. ? *Obs.* 2. Not influenced by interest; now always, Unbiased by personal interest 1659.

1. A careless d. spirit is no part of his character JUNIUS. 2. His d. kindness to us LIVINGSTONE. Hence **Disi·nterested-ly** *adv.*, **-ness.**

Disi·nteresting, *ppl. a.* 1737. [DIS- 10.] Uninteresting.

Disinte·rment. 1790. [f. DISINTER *v.* + -MENT.] The action of disinterring; exhumation; something disinterred.

Disinthrall, Disinthrone; see DISEN-.

Disi·ntricate, *v.* 1598. [DIS- 6.] To free from intricacy; to disentangle, unravel, extricate.

†Disinu·re, *v.* 1613. [DIS- 6.] To disaccustom –1644.

God..dis-inuring his chosen Israel from his wonted call JACKSON.

Disinve·st, *v.* 1630. [DIS- 6.] To deprive of that with which one is invested; to strip, divest (*lit.* and *fig.*). Hence **Disinve·stiture, Disinve·sture,** the action of disinvesting; disinvested state.

Disinvi·gorate, *v. rare.* [DIS- 6.] To enervate. SYD. SMITH.

†**Disinvi·te**, *v.* 1580. [DIS- 6.] To retract or cancel an invitation to –1665. Hence †**Dis·invita·tion**, the opposite of an invitation.

Disinvo·lve, *v.* 1611. [DIS- 6.] To free from an involved condition; to unfold; to disentangle.

Disja·sked, -et, -it, *ppl. a. Sc.* 1816. [? a corruption of *dejected.*] Dilapidated; decayed (*lit.* and *fig.*).

Disject (disdʒe·kt), *v.* 1581. [f. L. *disject-*, *disjicere*; see DIS- 1.] To cast or break asunder; to scatter. Hence **Disje·ction**, forcible dispersion, rout.

‖**Disjecta membra.** *Lat. phr.* An alteration of Horace's *disjecta membra poetæ*, used = Scattered remains.

Disjoin (disdʒoi·n), *v.* [ME. *des-*, *disioyne*, a. OF. *desjoign-*, *desjoindre*, mod.F. *déjoindre* :—L. *disjungere*; see DIS- 4.] 1. To undo the joining of; to disunite; to separate; to sunder 1483. †2. To disjoint –1612. 3. *intr.* (for *refl.*) To part, become separate 1592.

1. Deserts and..mountaines disjoyning the provinces 1601. That mariage therfore God himself dis-joyns MILT. 3. Till breathlesse he disioynd, and backward drew SHAKS.

†**Disjoi·nt**, *sb.* ME. [a. OF. *desjointe*, *dis-* :—L. type **disjuncta*, fem. sb. from *disjunctus* pa. pple.; see -ADE.] A disjointed or out-of-joint condition; a dilemma, fix –1553.

What wyght þat stont in swych disioynte CHAUCER.

†**Disjoi·nt**, *ppl. a.* ME. [a. OF. *desjoint* :—L. *disjunctus*; see prec.] 1. Disjointed, out of joint –1717. 2. In a dilemma 1500. 3. Disjoined; separate –1660.

Disjoint (disdʒoi·nt), *v.* ME. [orig. f. DISJOINT *ppl. a.*; affected by JOINT *sb.*] 1. *trans.* To put out of joint; to destroy the connexion and arrangement of; to dislocate, dismember. Also *fig.* 2. To disjoin, disunite 1583. 3. To separate joint from joint; to take in pieces at the joints 1587. Also *absol.* 4. *intr.* (for *refl.*) To be disjointed; to suffer dislocation; to go out of joint; to come in pieces 1605.

1. To d. the frame of society PUSEY. *fig.* A writer of taste..disjointing the order of his ideas GIBBON. 2. Great Britain, disjointed from her colonies T. JEFFERSON. 3. Like watches by unskilfull men Disjoynted LOVELACE. A good Carver..cuts up, disjoints, and uncases with incomparable Dexterity STEELE. Hence **Disjoi·nted** *ppl. a.* separated joint from joint; disjoined. **Disjoi·nted-ly** *adv.*, **-ness.**

Disjoi·ntly, *adv.* 1621. [f. DISJOINT *a.* + -LY [2].] 1. Separately; disjunctly: opp. to *conjointly* 1634. 2. Disconnectedly 1621.

Disjudication, error in Dicts. for DIJUDICATION.

Disjunct (disdʒʊ·ŋkt), *a.* 1594. [ad. L. *disjunctus.*] 1. Disjoined, separated; †distant. (Now *rare* exc. in techn. senses.) 1599. †2. *Math.* = DISCONTINUOUS –1597. 3. *Mus.* (Opp. to CONJUNCT.) 1694. 4. *Logic*, etc. †a. = DISJUNCTIVE. b. = DISCRETE. c. Applied to the alternative members of a disjunctive proposition.

3. *D. tetrachords*, tetrachords separated by an interval of a tone. Hence †**Disju·nctly** *adv.*

Disjunction (dis,dʒʊ·ŋkʃən). ME. [a. OF., or ad. L. *disjunctionem.*] 1. The action of disjoining or condition of being disjoined; separation, disunion. 2. *Logic*, etc. The relation of the terms of a disjunctive proposition; hence, a disjunctive proposition; an alternative 1588.

1. Death being..a d. of the Soul from the Body H. MORE.

Disjunctive (dis,dʒʊ·ŋktiv). 1570. [ad. L. *disjunctivus*, f. *disjunctus* DISJUNCT, DISJOINT.]

A. *adj.* 1. Having the property of disjoining; characterized by separation. 2. *Logic*, etc. Involving a choice between two (or more) things or statements; alternative 1584. 3. *Gram.* Applied to conjunctions that express an alternative or imply an adversative relation between the clauses which they connect 1628.

2. *D. proposition*, one in which it is asserted that one or other of two (or more) statements is true. *D. syllogism*, one in which the major premiss is d., and the minor affirms or denies one of the alternatives stated in the major; *loosely*, any syllogism containing a d. premiss. 3. The d. conjunctions..which bear this contradictory name, because, while they disjoin the sense, they conjoin the sentences HARRIS.

B. *sb.* 1. a. *Logic.* A disjunctive proposition; see A. 2. Hence generally, b. An alternative 1533. 2. *Gram.* A disjunctive conjunction; see A. 3.

Hence **Disju·nctively** *adv.* alternatively, adversatively.

Disju·ncture. ME. [ad. med.L. *disjunctura*, f. *disjungere.*] The fact of disjoining or disjoined condition; disjunction; breach. Also *fig.*

Disjune (disdʒū·n), *sb.* Chiefly *Sc. arch.* 1491. [a. OF. *desjun*, *-jeün*, f. *desjuner*, *-jeüner* (mod.F. *déjeûner*) to break fast, f. *des-*, *dé-* + *jeün* :—L. *jejunus.*] = DÉJEUNER.

Disk, disc (disk). 1664. [ad. L. *discus*, a. Gr. δίσκος quoit, dish, disk. The better spelling is *disk.*] 1. = DISCUS 1. Now *Hist.* 1715. 2. A thin circular plate of any material 1803. 3. Anything resembling a circular plate 1711. 4. *spec.* The (apparently flat) surface or face of the sun, the moon, or a planet, as it appears to the eye 1664. Also *transf.* 5. *Bot.* A round and flattened part in a plant. *spec.* a. A collection of tubular florets in the flower-head of *Compositæ*. b. An enlargement of the torus or receptacle of a flower, below or around the pistil. c. The flat surface of a leaf, etc. (In these senses always spelt *disk.*) 1727. 6. *Zool.* A roundish flattened part in an animal body. *spec.* a. The central rounded and flattened part containing the oral opening in Echinoderms, Cœlenterates, etc. b. The set of feathers surrounding the eye of an owl. c. The flat locomotive organ or 'foot' of a gastropod. 1761. 7. *Anat.* Applied to various round flat structures, as *blood-disks*, *intervertebral disks*, etc. 8. A phonograph or gramophone record 1888.

1. In empty air their sportive jav'lins throw, Or whirl the disk POPE.

attrib. and *comb.*: **d.-armature**, an armature wound so that its coils lie in the form of a d.; **-barrow**, a flat circular barrow or tumulus; **-dynamo**, a dynamo furnished with a d.-armature; **-engine**, **-steam-engine**, a type of rotary engine in which the steam acts upon a revolving or oscillating d.; **-owl**, the barn-owl; **-valve**, a valve formed by a circular d., with a rotary or reciprocating motion; **-wheel**, a kind of worm-wheel in which the spur-gear is driven by a spiral thread in the face of the d.

Hence **Disked** *a.* having or showing a d. (*rare*). **Di·skless** *a.*

†**Dis,ki·ndness.** 1596. [DIS- 9.] Unkindness; unfriendliness. Also with *a* and *pl.* –1774.

†**Dis,know**, *v.* [DIS- 6.] To fail to know, to ignore. SYLVESTER.

†**Disla·de**, *v. rare.* 1609. [DIS- 6.] *trans.* To unlade, unload –1649.

†**Disla·dy**, *v.* [DIS- 7 b.] To deprive of the rank of a lady. B. JONS.

Dislea·f, -lea·ve, *v.* 1598. [DIS- 7 a.] To strip of leaves.

†**Disle·al**, *a.* [ad. It. *disleale.*] Disloyal. SPENSER *F. Q.* II. v. 5.

Disli·kable, *a.* 1843. [f. DISLIKE *v.* + -ABLE.] Capable of being disliked; exciting dislike, as *d. qualities.*

Dislike (disləi·k), *sb.* 1577. [f. DISLIKE *v.*] †1. Displeasure, disapproval (as directed to some object) –1742. 2. The contrary feeling to liking; distaste, aversion, repugnance. Also with *a* and *pl.* 1597. †3. Discord, disagreement –1632.

1. A letter from the government, in d. of such proceedings PENN. 2. We need not show d. too coarsely LYTTON. Away with these weake dislikes BP. HALL. 3. *Tr. & Cr.* II. iii. 236. Hence †**Disli·keful** *a.* unpleasant; characterized by d.

†**Disli·ke**, *a.* 1596. [DIS- 10.] Unlike, dissimilar –1644.

Dislike (disləi·k), *v.* 1555. [DIS- 6.] †1. *trans.* (Only in 3rd pers.) To displease, annoy –1814. †2. *intr.* To be displeased or dissatisfied (*with*); to disapprove (*of*) –1677. 3. *trans.* Not to like; to regard with aversion; to have an objection to. (The opposite of LIKE *v.*; and so less strong than *hate.*) 1594. †b. To express aversion to –1667.

1. Ile do't, but it dislikes me *Oth.* II. iii. 49. 3. I may neither choose whom I would, nor refuse whom I d. *Merch. V.* I. ii. 26. I neuer heard any Souldier d. it *Meas. for M.* I. ii. 18. Hence **Disli·ker.**

Disli·kelihood. *rare.* [DIS- 9.] Improbability. SCOTT.

†**Disli·ken**, *v.* [f. DISLIKE *a.*, after *liken.*] To make unlike; to disguise *Wint. T.* IV. iv. 666.

†**Disli·keness.** 1623. [DIS- 9.] Unlikeness –1690.

Dislimb (disli·m), *v.* 1662. [DIS- 7 a.] *trans.* To cut off the limbs of; to tear limb from limb.

Dislimn (disli·m), *v.* 1606. [DIS- 6.] 1. *trans.* To obliterate the outlines of; to efface, blot out. 2. *intr.* (for *refl.*) To become effaced, to vanish 1832.

1. That [clowd] which is now a Horse, euen with a thoght The Racke dislimes, and makes it indistinct, As water is in water *Ant. & Cl.* IV. xiv. 10.

Dislink (disli·ŋk), *v.* 1610. [DIS- 6.] To unlink, uncouple, separate (things that are linked) (*lit.* and *fig.*).

†**Dislive** (disləi·v), *v.* 1598. [app. f. DIS- 7 a or c + LIFE.] To deprive of life; to kill –1631.

Disload (dislōᵘ·d), *v.* 1568. [DIS- 6.] *trans.* and *intr.* To unload, disburden.

Dislocable (di·slŏkăb'l), *a. rare.* [f. med.L. *dislocare.*] Displaceable. BENTHAM.

Dislocate (di·slŏkeᵗt), *v.* 1605. [f. *dislocat-* ppl. stem of med.L. *dislocare*; see DIS- 1. In Eng. as pa. pple. in ME.] 1. *trans.* To put out of its proper (or former) place; to displace. Now *rare.* 1623. 2. To put out of proper position in relation to contiguous parts 1660. b. *spec.* To put (a bone) out of joint; to 'put out' (a joint or limb) 1605. Also *fig.*

1. A plant may be dislocated from an old, and removed to a new bed HOLLAND. 2. These hands.. are apt enough to d. and tear Thy flesh and bones *Lear* IV. ii. 65. *fig.* He contrived to d. all their military plans T. JEFFERSON. So **Di·slocate** *ppl. a.*

Dislocation (dislŏkē·ʃən). ME. [a. OF., or ad. med.L. *dislocationem*; see prec.] 1. Displacement; *spec.* displacement of a bone from its natural position in the joint; luxation. b. *Geol.* A displacement in a stratum or series of strata caused by a fracture, with upheaval or subsidence; a fault 1695. c. *Mil.* The distribution of troops to a number of garrisons, camps, etc. 1808. 2. *fig.* Displacement of parts; disarrangement; a disordered state 1659.

2. The utter d. of society PUSEY.

Dislodge (dislǫ·dʒ), *v.* 1450. [a. OF. *desloger*, *-logier*, f. *des-*, DIS- 4 + *loger* to LODGE.] 1. *trans.* To remove or turn out of a place of lodgement; to displace 1500. †b. *Mil.* To shift the position of (a force) –1670. c. *Mil.* To drive (a foe) out of his position 1450. 2. *intr.* (for *refl.*) To go away from one's lodging or abode; to remove 1489.

1. To d. a wilde Bore SIR T. HERBERT, a Ministry J. W. CROKER, a stone L. STEPHEN. To d. the Spaniards from their fortifications 1783. 2. Many of the inhabitants of Paris began to d. HUME. Hence †**Dislo·dge** *sb.* dislodgement. **Dislodgement, -lodgment**, the act of dislodging; displacement.

†**Disloi·gn**, *v.* [a. OF. *desloignier*, f. *des-*, DIS- 1 + *loin* far.] To remove to a distance. SPENSER *F. Q.* IV. x. 24.

†**Dislo·ve.** 1533. [DIS- 9.] Unfriendliness, hatred –1823.

Disloyal (disloi·ăl), *a.* 1477. [a. OF. *desloial*, f. *des-*, DIS- 4 + *loial* LOYAL.] Not loyal; unfaithful to the obligations of friendship or honour, to the marriage tie, etc. (now *rare*); wanting in loyalty to the government or constituted authority; perfidious, treacherous.

Thou do'st suspect That I haue been disloyall to thy bed *Rich. II*, v. ii. 105. Executed by your Lordship as seditious and disloyall PRYNNE.

Disloyalty (disloi·ălti). 1481. [ad. OF. *desloyaute* (mod.F. *déloyauté*), f. *desloyal*; see prec.] The quality of being disloyal; now *esp.* Violation of allegiance or duty to one's sovereign, state, or government.

Dislustre (dislʊ·stəɹ), *v.* 1638. [DIS- 7 a.] 1. To deprive of lustre; to dim, sully. 2. *intr.* To lose its lustre 1890.

Dismai·l, *v. arch.* 1450. [a. OF. *desmailler*; see DIS- 4.] To divest of mail; to break the mail off.

Dismal (di·zmăl). ME. [app. = OF. *dis mal* = L. *dies mali.* Thus orig. a sb. See N.E.D.]

†A. *sb.*[1] (The original use.) The *dies mali*, evil, unlucky days, of the mediæval calendar, called also *dies Ægyptiaci*; hence, Evil days

(generally), days of gloom, the days of old age -1400.

A waytiþ not þeis Egipcian daies, þat we call dysmal 1400.

B. *adj.* [orig. attrib. use of A.] †1. Of days: Of or belonging to the *dies mali*; unlucky -1618. †2. Of other things: Unlucky, sinister, malign, fatal -1632. 3. Disastrous, calamitous. (Now *rare.*) 1592. 4. Causing dismay; dreadful; now, Causing gloom, depressing, miserable 1588. 5. Such as causes gloom or depression; sombre, dreary, or cheerless 1617. 6. (Subjectively) gloomy or miserable 1705.

1. An ugly feend, more fowle than dismall day SPENSER. 4. Dire is the conflict, d. is the din POPE. 5. Blacke is not knowne among them, they say tis dismall and a signe of hell and sorrowe SIR T. HERBERT. The dismallest howlings of the wolves DE FOE. 6. Wrote d. letters to the Court BURNET.

C. *sb.*² [Ellipt. or absol. use of B.] †1. A dismal person; *e.g.* a funeral mute -1708. †2. *pl.* Mourning garments -1778. 3. *pl.* Low spirits 1762. 4. A local name of tracts of swampy land on the eastern sea-board of the U.S. 1763.

Hence **Disma·lity**, d. quality or state; an instance of this. **Di·smalize** *v.* to make d. **Di·smal-ly** *adv.*, **-ness.**

Disman (dismæ·n), *v.* 1627. [DIS- 7.] †1. *trans.* To deprive of what constitutes the man -1651. 2. To deprive of men. KINGLAKE.

Dismantle (dismæ·nt'l), *v.* 1579. [ad. obs. F. *desmanteller*, mod.F. *démanteler*; see DIS- 4.] †1. *trans.* To divest of a mantle or cloak (*lit.* and *fig.*) -1691. Also †*intr.* (for *refl.*). 2. To deprive *of* (clothing, covering, equipment, or fortifications); *esp.* to strip (a fortress) of its defences, (a vessel) of its rigging, etc. 1601. 3. To render useless for its purpose; to pull down, take to pieces, destroy 1579.

1. Muffle your face, Dis-mantle you *Wint. T.* IV. iv. 666. 2. Houses..dismantled of their roofs 1879. 3. The gun was dismounted..the carriage dismantled and conveyed piecemeal to the opposite shore 1853. Hence **Disma·ntlement.**

†**Disma·rch**, *v.* 1596. [ad. F. *desmarcher*; see DIS- 4.] *intr.* To march or fall back, to retreat -1635.

†**Disma·rry**, *v. rare.* [ad. F. *desmarier*; see DIS- 4.] To annul the marriage of. LD. BERNERS.

†**Disma·rshall**, *v. rare.* [DIS- 6.] To derange, throw into confusion. DRUMM. OF HAWTH.

†**Disma·sk**, *v.* 1588. [ad. obs. F. *desmasquer*; see DIS- 4.] To divest of a mask or covering; to unmask -1651.

Dismast (disma·st), *v.* 1747. [DIS- 7 a; cf. F. *démâter.*] To deprive of masts; to break down the masts of.

A furious storm .. dismasted his ship PRESCOTT. Hence **Disma·stment**, the action of dismasting.

†**Dismaw·**, *v.* 1620. [DIS- 7 c.] To empty out from the maw.

Dismay (dismē¹·), *sb.* 1590. [f. DISMAY *v.*] Utter loss of moral courage or resolution in prospect of danger or difficulty; faintness of heart from terror or inability to cope with the situation; †dismaying influence or operation (SPENSER *F. Q.* V. ii 50).

Yet would he not for all his great d. Give over to effect his first intent SPENSER *F. Q.* II. xi. 41. Hence **Dismay·ful** *a.* appalling; **-ly** *adv.*

Dismay (dismē¹·), *v.* ME. [app. repr. Rom. type **dismagare*, f. *dis-*, DIS- 4 + *-mag-*, app. ad. OHG. *magan* to be powerful or able (see MAY *v.*).] 1. *trans.* To deprive of moral courage at the prospect of peril or trouble; to appal or paralyse with fear or apprehension; utterly to discourage, daunt, or dishearten. *refl.* †To be filled with dismay. †2. To defeat by sudden onslaught -1596. †3. *intr.* To become utterly discouraged or faint-hearted -1596.

1. The enemies were dispersed and dismayed GIBBON. 2. SPENSER *F. Q.* VI. x. 13. 3. 1 *Hen. VI*, III. iii. 1. Hence **Dismay·edness**, dismayed condition. **Dismay·er.** †**Dismay·ment**, dismay.

Disme (dəim), var. of DIME *sb.* and *v.*

†**Dismea·surable**, *a.* 1474. [a. OF. *desmesurable*; see DIS- 4.] Beyond measure. Hence †**Dismea·surably** *adv.*

†**Dismea·sured**, *a.* 1483. [f. DIS- + MEASURED.] 1. Unmeasured; unrestrained -1585. 2. In false measure 1574

Dismember (disme·mbəɹ), *v.* ME. [a. OF. *desmembrer*, mod.F. *démembrer*, f. (ult.) DIS- 4 + L. *membrum.*] 1. *trans.* To deprive of limbs or members; to cut off the limbs or members of; to tear or divide limb from limb. Also *transf.* and *fig.* †2. To cut off, sever from the body -1694. Also †*fig.* and *transf.* 3. [f. DIS- 7 b + MEMBER.] To cut off from membership 1649.

1. Fowls obscene dismember'd his remains POPE. To d. (= carve) a Hern FARLEY. Italy..poor Italy lies dismembered, scattered asunder, not appearing in any protocol or treaty as a unity at all CARLYLE. 3. The new members..were soon dismembered by vote of the house NORTH. Hence **Disme·mberer**, one who or that which dismembers.

Disme·mbered, *ppl. a.* 1552. [f. prec.] In the senses of the vb.; *spec.* in *Her.* Depicted without limbs or members; or, with the members separate from the body as if just cut off.

Disme·mberment. 1658. [f. as prec.; cf. OF. *desmembrement.*] 1. The act of dismembering (*lit.* and *fig.*) 1751; quasi-*concr.* a detached part formed by separation from the main body 1830. 2. Cutting off from membership 1658.

1. The present violent d. and partition of Poland 1772. Aversion..to the d. of their country from the Aragonese monarchy PRESCOTT. var. †**Dismembra·tion.**

Di·smembrator. 1877. [f. med.L. *dismembrare.*] Something that disintegrates or dismembers; *spec.* an apparatus for separating flour from bran, after crushing in a roller mill.

†**Disme·rit**, *v.* 1484. [DIS- 6 or 7 a.] To deprive of or lose merit; cf. DEMERIT *v.* -1629.

†**Disme·ttled**, *ppl. a. rare.* 1650. [DIS- 7 a.] Deprived of mettle; spiritless.

Dismiss (dismi·s), *v.* Pa. t. and pple. **dismissed, †-mist.** 1477. [app. f. L. *dimiss-*, ppl. stem of *dimittere* after DISMIT, OF. *desmetre.*] 1. *trans.* To disperse, dissolve; to disband 1582. Also *intr.* (for *refl.*). 2. *trans.* To send away (a person); to bid or allow to depart 1548. Also *transf.* of things. 3. To send away or remove from office, employment, or position 1477. 4. To discard, reject. Also *absol.* 1610. 5. To put away, get rid of 1592. 6. To have done with (a subject), bring to an end; hence, to treat of summarily 1698. 7. *Law.* †a. *refl.* (with *of* or *inf.*) To free or exclude oneself from a burden or advantage -1642. b. To send out of court, reject (a claim or action) 1607.

1. The boys may d. 1809. 2. Please you dismisse me, eyther with I, or no 3 *Hen. VI*, III. ii. 78. 3. *spec.* in the army and navy, not debarring from further employment in public service otherwise than in the army (or navy): cf. CASHIER *v.* 2. To be dismissed of the court LYLY. Dismist the treasury LUTTRELL. 5. He, smiling, said, D. your Fear DRYDEN. Hence †**Dismi·ss** *sb.* a dismissal. **Dismi·ssible, -able** *a.*

Dismissal (dismi·săl). 1806. [f. DISMISS *v.*; cf. *committal*, etc. A recent word, repl. the more regular DISMISSION.] = DISMISSION, q. v.

Dismission (dismi·ʃən). 1547. [f. DISMISS *v.*, corresp. to L. *dimissionem* and OF. *desmission.* See DISMISSAL.] 1. The action of dismissing, or sending away in various directions 1646. 2. Permission to go, leave to depart; earlier, formal leave-taking 1608. 3. Deprivation of office, dignity, or position; discharge from service 1547. 4. Liberation, discharge 1609. 5. Rejection, discarding 1611. 6. Putting aside from consideration 1742.

1. The Diet..had this Day a final D. 1711. 3. To be punished by d. from the public service MACAULAY.

Dismissive (dismi·siv), *a.* 1645. [f. DISMISS *v.*] Tending to dismiss; valedictory.

Dismissory (dismi·səri), *a.* (*sb.*) 1647. [f. DISMISS *v.*] = DIMISSORY.

†**Dismi·t**, *v.* ME. [app. ad. OF. *desmetre*, repr. late pop.L. *dismittere* instead of cl.L. *dimittere* (cf. DIMIT).] 1. *trans.* To send away; to let go. 2. *refl.* To divest oneself of; to relinquish -1496.

†**Dismo·rtgage**, *v.* [DIS- 7 a.] To free from mortgage. HOWELL.

Dismount (dismau·nt), *v.* 1544. [DIS- 6; perh. after OF. *desmonter.*]

I. *intr.* 1. To come down from a height; to descend 1579. 2. To get down, alight (*from* a horse, etc.; formerly, *from* a vehicle) 1588.

1. The bright Sunne gynneth to d. SPENSER. 2. Neither yet in the day of battell ought he to d. BARRET.

II. *trans.* 1. To come down from; to get off, alight from (a horse, etc.) 1589. 2. (*causal*) To unseat, unhorse 1599. 3. To remove from that on or in which it has been mounted, set, or enclosed; to take (mechanism) to pieces 1544. 4. To set, put, or bring down; to lower. ? *Obs.* 1597. †5. *fig.* (largely from 2) -1718.

1. He straight dismounts his throne QUARLES. 3. One of our Ships..had dismounted Two of their Batteries 1707. *Twel. N.* III. iv. 244. 5. But Superstition dismountes all this [Sense, Philosophy, Piety, etc.] BACON. Hence **Dismou·nt** *sb.* an act or method of dismounting.

Disna, *Sc.* = does not; see DO *v.*

†**Disna·tural**, *a.* ME. [ad. OF. *desnaturel*; see DIS- 4.] Contrary to nature -1677.

Disna·turalize, *v.* 1704. [DIS- 6.] = DENATURALIZE *v.* 1, 2.

Disnature (disnē¹·tiŭɹ), *v.* 1450. [ad. OF. *desnaturer*; see DIS- 4.] †1. *intr.* To get into or be in a disordered condition. CAXTON. 2. *trans.* To render unnatural 1450.

Disnest (disne·st), *v. rare.* 1596. [DIS- 7 c.] To dislodge from, or as from, a nest; to void (as a nest) *of* its occupants.

Disobedience (disobī·diĕns). ME. [a. OF. *desobedience*; a Rom. formation for L. *inobedientia*; see DIS- 4.] The fact or condition of being disobedient; neglect or refusal to obey; violation of a command or of a prohibition; an instance of this.

Adam..And Eve..the worlde dampned..By d. HAWES. So †**Disobe·diency**, †**Disobei·sance.**

Disobedient (disobī·diĕnt), *a.* ME. [a. OF. *desobedient*; see prec.] Withholding obedience; refusing or failing to obey; not observant of authoritative command; guilty of breach of prescribed duty; refractory, rebellious. b. *transf.* Intractable, stubborn 1588.

These were not loving subjects, but d. rebels SCOTT. *transf.* D. to any medicine 1588. Hence **Disobe·diently** *adv.* So †**Disobei·sant.**

Disobey (disobē¹·), *v.* ME. [a. F. *désobéir* :—Rom. *dis-*, *desobedire*, for late L. *inobedire*; see DIS- 4.] 1. *intr.* To be disobedient. 2. *trans.* [The obj. repr. an earlier dative.] To refuse or neglect to obey (any one); to neglect wilfully, transgress, or violate, the commands or orders of; to refuse submission to ME.

1. The wish to d. is already disobedience RUSKIN. 2. Ther might nothing hem d. GOWER. Him who disobeyes Me disobeyes MILT. *P. L.* V. 611. To d. a father 1797, God and the law JOWETT. Hence **Disobey·er**, one who disobeys; a rebel.

†**Disobliga·tion.** 1616. [DIS- 9.] 1. Freedom or release from obligation -1770. 2. A slight -1788. 3. The fact or feeling of being disobliged -1754; a grudge 1754.

†**Diso·bligatory**, *a.* 1649. [DIS- 10.] Not binding; releasing from obligation.

Disoblige (disobləi·dʒ), *v.* 1603. [ad. F. *désobliger* :—Rom. **disobligare*, f. DIS- 4 + L. *obligare.*] †1. *trans.* To release from duty or engagement. Const. *of*, *from*. -1678. 2. To refuse or neglect to oblige; not to consult or comply with the wishes of; hence, to put a slight upon, affront 1632. 3. To inconvenience, incommode, annoy 1668.

1. To d. themselves of their greatest duty DRUMM. OF HAWTH. 2. Colonel Lesley..being lately disobliged (as they called it) by the King, that is, denied somewhat he had a mind to have CLARENDON. 3. I must .. get our disobliging neighbours turned out MRS. CARLYLE. Hence **Disobli·gement** = DISOBLIGATION 1, 2. **Disobli·ger** (*rare*). **Disobli·gingly** *adv.*, **-ness.**

Disobstru·ct, *v.* ? *Obs.* 1611. [DIS- 6.] = DEOBSTRUCT.

†**Diso·ccident**, *v.* [DIS- 8.] To throw out of reckoning as to the west; to confuse as to the points of the compass. MARVELL.

Disoccupa·tion. 1834. [DIS- 9.] Lack of occupation, unoccupied condition.

Disomatous (dəisōu·mătəs), *a.* 1857. [f. Gr. δισώματος; see DI-².] Having two bodies.

†**Disopi·nion.** 1598. [DIS- 9.] 1. Adverse or mean opinion (*of*) -1705. 2. Difference of opinion; dissent (*rare*) -1640.

†**Diso·ppilate**, *v.* 1577. [DIS- 6.] *Med.* = DEOPPILATE -1652.

Disorb (disǭ·ɹb), *v.* 1606. [DIS- 7 a, c.] 1. *trans.* To remove from its orb. 2. To deprive of the orb as a symbol of sovereignty 1863.

†**Diso·rdain**, *v.* ME. only. [a. OF. *desordener*, mod.F. *désordonner*, a. Rom. formation f. DIS- 4 + L. *ordinare.*] 1. To deprive of orders. 2.

To disorder, derange. Hence †**Diso·rdained** *ppl. a.* disordered; immoderate.

†**Diso·rdeine, diso·rdeny,** *a.* ME. [a. OF. *desordené*, mod. F. *désordonné*; see prec.] Inordinate, excessive; disorderly –1450.

Disorder (disǭ·ɹdəɹ), *sb.* 1530. [Dis- 9; prob. after F. *desordre* (1530).] **1.** Absence or undoing of order; confusion; confused state or condition. †**b.** Irregularity. Pope. **2.** (with *a* and *pl.*) An irregularity 1574; *spec.* †an irregularity of conduct; a misdemeanour –1772. **3.** Disturbance, commotion, tumult 1532. †**4.** Disturbance of mind –1838. **5.** An ailment, disease. (Usually weaker than Disease, and not implying structural change.) 1704.

1. Light shon, and order from d. sprung Milt. *P. L.* III. 713. Boughs..twined in picturesque d. Praed. b. Pope *Ess. Crit.* 152. 2. The disorders which attended the retreat Sir W. Napier. 3. To prevent all d. the train-bands kept a guard on both sides of the way 1628. 4. *John* III. iv. 102. 5. A slight d. in my eye Cowper.

Disorder (disǭ·ɹdəɹ), *v.* 1477. [app. a modification of earlier *desordene, disordeine* vb., OF. *desordener*, after Order vb.] **1.** *trans.* To put out of order; to throw into confusion; to disarrange, derange, upset. Also †*intr.* (for *refl.*). †**2.** *trans.* To make morally irregular; to corrupt –1585. †**b.** *refl.* To violate moral order; to break loose from restraint; to go to excess –1654. †**3.** *trans.* To disturb the mind or feelings of; to discompose –1819. **4.** To derange the functions of; to 'upset' 1526. †**5.** = Disordain 1. –1681. **6.** [f. Dis- 6 + Order *v.*] To countermand 1643.

1. With..tresses all disorderd Milt. *P. L.* X. 914. 4. The east wind..never fails to d. my head Berkeley. This climate is apt to d. the liver (*mod.*). Hence **Diso·rdered** *ppl. a.* disarranged; †irregular; deranged; morbid. **Diso·rdered-ly** *adv.*, **-ness.**

Disorderly (disǭ·ɹdəɹli), *a.* 1585. [f. Disorder *sb.* + -ly[1].] **1.** Characterized by disorder, or absence of order; in a state of disorder; confused, irregular, untidy 1632. **2.** Violating moral order, constituted authority, or recognized rule; lawless; unruly; tumultuous, riotous 1585. **b.** *spec.* in *Law.* Violating public order or morality; constituting a nuisance; *esp.* in *d. house* 1744. †**3.** Affected with disorder of the bodily functions; morbid 1655.

1. A d. and confused chaos Berkeley. 2. Charged with being drunk and d. (*mod.*). Phr. *D. person*, one guilty of one of a number of offences against public order as defined by various Acts of Parliament 1744. *absol.* as *sb.* a d. person. Hence **Diso·rderliness. Diso·rderly** *adv.*

†**Diso·rdinance.** ME. [a. OF. *desordenance*, later *-on(n)ance.*] Disorder, confusion, irregularity –1502.

†**Diso·rdinate,** *a.* ME. [Latinized f. OF. *desordené.*] **1.** Not conformed to what is right, befitting, or reasonable; inordinate –1693. **2.** = Disorderly *a.* 1. (Only in De Quincey.)

1. D. gestures 1577. A Prince..d. in eating Hellowes. Hence †**Diso·rdinately** *adv.*

†**Disordina·tion.** 1626. [f. Disordain *v.*] = Deordination –1684.

Disorga·nic, *a.* [Dis- 10.] Without organic constitution. Carlyle.

Diso·rganiza·tion. 1794. [ad. F. *désorganisation.* This family of words dates in Eng. from the French Revolution.] The action of disorganizing, or condition of being disorganized; loss or absence of organization.

The total d. of society Ht. Martineau.

Disorganize (disǭ·ɹgănəɪz), *v.* 1793. [ad. F. *désorganiser*; see Dis- 4.] To destroy the organization of; to break up the organic connexion of; to throw into confusion or disorder.

Their ever memorable decree of the 15th of December, 1792, for disorganizing every country in Europe Burke. Hence **Diso·rganizer.**

†**Diso·rient,** *v.* 1655. [ad. F. *désorienter*; see Dis- 4.] *trans.* To turn from the east; to cause to lose one's bearings; to put out –1835.

Disorientate (disōᵊriĕntēᵗt), *v.* 1704. [Dis- 6.] *trans.* To turn from an eastward position; *pa. pple.* not facing due east. Also *fig.*

It has a chancel..strangely disorientated towards the south 1853. Hence **Disorienta·tion.**

Di·sour. Now *Hist.* ME. [a. OF., f. *dire, disant.*] A (professional) story-teller; a jester.

Disown (disōᵘ·n), *v.* 1620. [f. Dis- 6 + Own *v.* Not conn. w. OE. *unnan* to grant.] †**1.** *trans.* To cease to own; to give up, renounce. **2.** To refuse to acknowledge as one's own, or as connected with oneself; not to own; to repudiate, disclaim 1649. †**3.** To refuse to acknowledge or admit; to deny –1726.

2. To own or d. books 1649. Their Mufti..disowns the Emperor's Authority 1726. 3. The Court no longer d. his..Majesty's arrival 1710. Hence **Diso·wnment,** the act of disowning, renunciation.

†**Diso·xidate,** *v.* 1801. [Dis- 6.] *Chem.* = Deoxidate –1817. Hence **Disoxida·tion** = Deoxidation.

†**Diso·xygenate,** *v.* 1800. [Dis- 6.] *Chem.* = Deoxygenate –1831. Hence **Disoxygena·tion** = Deoxygenation.

†**Dispa·ce,** *v.* 1588. [?f. Dis- 1 + Pace.] *intr.* and *refl.* To walk or move about –1610.

Long time he did himselfe d. There round about Spenser.

†**Dispai·nt,** *v.* [Dis- 1.] To paint diversely. Spenser *F. Q.* II. ix. 50.

†**Dispai·r,** *v.* 1598. [Dis- 6.] *trans.* To separate from being a pair.

†**Dispa·nd,** *v.* 1656. [ad. L. *dispandere*; see Dis- 1.] *trans.* To spread abroad, to expand –1732.

Dispansive (dispæ·nsiv), *a.* 1883. [f. L. *dispans-*, ppl. stem of *dispandere.*] A term applied to a system of lenses with negative focal distance; opp. to *collective. Syd. Soc. Lex.*

†**Dispa·radise,** *v. rare.* 1593. [Dis- 7 c.] To turn out of paradise. Also *fig.* –1623.

†**Dispa·rage,** *sb.* [ME. *despara·ge, dispera·ge*, a. OF., f. as next.] **1.** Inequality of rank in marriage; an unequal match –1596. **2.** Disparagement –1615.

1. Her friends .. dissuaded her from such a d. Spenser *F. Q.* IV. viii. 50.

Disparage (dispæ·rēdʒ), *v.* ME. [a. OF. *desparagier*, f. des-, Dis- 4 + *parage* equality of rank.] †**1.** *trans.* To match unequally; to degrade by an unequal match –1781. **2.** To lower in esteem ME. †**3.** To lower in position or dignity; to cast down –1716. **4.** To treat slightingly; to undervalue; to vilify 1536.

1. Moch was this fayr damysel dysparaged sith that she was maryed ayenst al the comune assent of England Caxton. 2. The place oft-times disparages; As, to put the Arke of God into a Cart Bp. Hall. 3. I am disparaged and disheartened by your commendations Pope. 4. It is the fashion..to d. negative logic Mill. Hence **Dispa·rageable** *a.* †tending to d.; to be disparaged. **Dispa·rager,** a detractor. **Dispa·ragingly** *adv.*

Disparagement (dispæ·rēdʒmĕnt). 1486. [a. OF. *desparagement.*] †**1.** Marriage to one of inferior rank; the disgrace or dishonour involved in this –1585. **2.** Lowering of value, honour, or estimation; dishonour, indignity, disgrace, discredit 1486. **3.** Depreciation, detraction, undervaluing 1591.

1. He..thought that match a fowle d. Spenser. 2. Passed sentence may not be recal'd But to our honours great d. *Com. Err.* I. i. 149. 3. A strong bias towards..the d. of the Britons Lewin.

Disparate (di·spărēᵗt). 1586. [orig. ad. L. *disparatus* separated (see Dis- 1); but in use often assoc. w. L. *dispar.*]

A. *adj.* **1.** Essentially different or diverse in kind; dissimilar, unlike, distinct. In *Logic*, used of things or concepts having no obvious common ground or genus in which they are correlated. 1608. **2.** Unequal 1764.

1. As remote in their nature..as any two d. things we can propose or conceive; number and colour T. Burnet. 2. Between ages so very d. Lamb.

B. *sb.* Chiefly *pl.* Things so unlike that they cannot be compared with each other 1586.

Hence **Di·sparate-ly** *adv.*, **-ness.**

†**Dispa·rish,** *v.*[1] ME. [f. F. *disparaiss-, disparaître.*] *intr.* To disappear –1632.

Dispa·rish, *v.*[2] 1593. [Dis- 7.] To oust from one's parish; also, to deprive of the status of a parish.

†**Dispa·rison.** 1609. [ad. L. *disparationem*, after *comparison.*] Depreciatory comparison –1647.

†**Dispari·tion.** 1594. [a. F.] Disappearance –1773.

Disparity (dispæ·rĭti). 1555. [ad. F. *disparité*; see Dis- 4.] **1.** Inequality or dissimilarity in respect of age, amount, number, or quality; want of parity 1597. **2.** The quality of being unlike or different. Also with *pl.* An instance or form of this. 1555.

1. A wife..fit for him without d. 1651. 2. The disparities and differences [of men] North.

Dispark (dispā·ɹk), *v.* 1542. [Dis- 7 b.] *trans.* To divest of the character of a park; to throw open (park-land), or convert (it) to other uses. Also *transf.* and *fig.*

You haue..Dis-park'd my Parkes, and fell'd my Forrest Woods *Rich. II*, III. i. 23. He thereupon disparks his Seralio, and flyes thence Sir T. Herbert.

†**Dispa·rkle, -pa·rcle,** *v.* 1449. [app. a corrupt form of Disparple.] = Disparple –1661.

†**Dispa·rple,** *v.* ME. [a. OF. *desparpelier*, f. Rom. *des-* (Dis-) + **parpaliare*, f. **parpilio*, **parpalio*, app. a changed form of L. *papilio, -onem* butterfly.] *trans.* To scatter abroad, disperse –1615. Also *intr.* (for *refl.*).

Dispart (dispā·ɹt), *sb.* 1578. [?] **1.** The difference between the semi-diameter of a gun at the base ring and at the swell of the muzzle 1588. **2.** *concr.* A sight-mark placed on the muzzle of a gun, to make the line of sight parallel to the bore; called also *d.-sight* 1578.

1. Every Gunner before he shootes must trulie disparte his Peece, or give allowance for the disparte Lucar.

Dispart (dispā·ɹt), *v.*[1] 1590. [In Spenser, app. ad. It. *dispartire*, repr. L. *dispertire* to distribute. Also f. Dis- 1 + Part *v.*] **1.** *trans.* To part asunder, to cleave. **2.** To separate, sever 1633. **3.** To divide into parts; to distribute 1629. **4.** *intr.* To part asunder 1633. †**5.** *D. with*: to part with (*pseudo-arch.*) Scott.

1. The Sea..fled, Disparted by the wondrous Rod Wesley. 2. Till death d. the union Southey. 4. The broken heav'ns d. P. Fletcher.

Dispa·rt, *v.*[2] 1587. [f. Dispart *sb.*] **1.** *trans.* To estimate the dispart in (a gun); to make allowance for this in taking aim. **2.** To furnish with a dispart 1669.

Dispa·ssion, *sb.* 1692. [Dis- 9.] Freedom from passion; dispassionateness; †apathy. So †**Dispa·ssion** *v.* to free from passion. Chiefly in *ppl. a.* **Dispa·ssioned.**

Dispassionate (dispæ·ʃənēᵗt), *a.* 1594. [Dis- 10.] Free from the influence of passion; calm, composed, cool; impartial. Said of persons, their faculties, and actions.

The wise and dis-passionate among them 1594. A d. fairness towards older faiths Green. Hence †**Dispa·ssionate** *v.* to free from passion (*rare*). **Dispa·ssionate-ly** *adv.*, **-ness.**

Dispassioned; see Dispassion *v.*

Dispatch, despatch (dispæ·tʃ), *v.* 1517. [ad. It. *dispacciare*, or Sp. *despachar* to expedite, pointing to a L. type *-pactare* (f. *pactus* 'fastened, fast', pa. pple. of *pangere*). Not related to F. *dépêcher*. *Dispatch* is the better spelling; see N.E.D.]

I. *trans.* **1.** To send off post-haste or with expedition. The word regularly used for the sending of messengers, messages, troops, mails, express trains, etc. **2.** To dismiss (a person) after settling his business; to get rid of. Now *rare.* **3.** To get rid of by putting to death; to kill 1530. **4.** To rid oneself promptly of (a piece of business, etc.); to get through 1533; to dispose of (food) quickly (*colloq.*) 1711. †**5.** To remove; to get rid of –1726. †**6.** To rid (a person, etc. *of, from*) –1641.

1. We..dispached that poste..reservyng thys to be written by my selff at laysor Bp. Tunstall. 3. We are peremptory to dispatch This Viporous Traitor *Cor.* III. i. 286. 4. To my office, where dispatched some business Pepys. 5. Dispatching some by death, and other by banishment Grafton. 6. *Haml.* I. v. 75.

II. *intr.* †**1.** (for *refl.*) To start promptly –1712. **2.** To make haste (*to do something*), be quick (*Obs.* or *arch.*) 1581. †**3.** (*absol.* from 4.) To settle a business; to get through, have done (*with*) –1666.

1. And now dispatch we toward the Court *2 Hen. IV*, IV. iii. 82. Hence **Dispa·tcher.** †**Dispa·tchment,** the act of dispatching, dispatch.

Dispatch, despatch (dispæ·tʃ), *sb.* 1550. [f. Dispatch *v.*, or ad. It. *dispaccio* 'a hastning, a riddance' (Florio). See prec.]

I. 1. The sending off (of a messenger, letter, etc.) 1600. †**2.** Official dismissal; congé –1698. **3.** Making away with by putting to death; killing 1576. **4.** The getting (of business, an affair, etc.) out of hand; (prompt or speedy) settlement 1581. Also, Promptitude in dealing with affairs

1607. **b.** Speed, expedition 1573. †**5.** The act of getting rid (of something) –1653.

1. The d. of a French Embassy to England FROUDE. 2. *Lear* II. i. 127. 4. Clerk-like' despatch of business' 1837. Dispatch is no mean Virtue in a Statesman 1680.

II. Concr. and transf. senses. **1.** A written message sent off speedily; *spec.* an official communication relating to public affairs 1582. **2.** An agency for the quick transmission of goods, etc.; a conveyance by which goods, etc., are dispatched 1694.

1. Excepting upon very important occasions I write my dispatches without making a draft WELLINGTON. *attrib.* and *comb.*: **d.-boat**, a swift vessel used in d. duty; **-box**, a box for carrying dispatches **-rider**, *esp.* motor-cyclist or horseman carrying dispatches; **-tube**, a tube in which letters, etc., are transported by a current of air. Hence **Dispa·tchful** *a.* having the quality of dispatching; speedy, expeditious (*Obs.* or *arch.*).

Dispathy, obs. f. DYSPATHY.

Dispauper (dispǭ·pəɹ), *v.* 1631. [DIS- 7 b.] To deprive of the privileges of a pauper; to disqualify from suing *in formâ pauperis*, i.e. without payment of fees.

Dispau·perize, *v.* 1833. [DIS- 6.] To free from the state of pauperism; to free from paupers.

Dispeace (dispī·s). 1825. [DIS- 9. Orig. *Sc.*] The absence or reverse of peace; uneasiness (of mind); dissension, enmity.

Scotland had elements of d. BURTON.

†**Dispee·d**, *v.* 1603. [app. ad. obs. It. *dispedire*, f. DIS- 1; but in Eng. assoc. w. SPEED.] *trans.* To send off (promptly); *refl.* to get away quickly –1814.

Dispel (dispe·l), *v.* 1631. [ad. L. *dispellere*; see DIS- 1.] *trans.* To drive away in different directions or in scattered order; to disperse by force, dissipate. Also *intr.* (for *refl.*).

He..gently rais'd Their fainted courage, and dispel'd their fears MILT. *P. L.* I. 530. Melt, and d., ye spectre-doubts CAMPBELL. Hence **Dispe·ller**, he who or that which dispels.

Dispence, var. of DISPENSE.

Dispe·nd, *v. Obs.* or *arch.* Pa. t. and pple. **dispended, dispent.** [ME. *des-*, *dispenden*, a. OF. *despendre* (mod.F. *dépendre*) :—late L. *dispendere* to weigh out, etc.; see DIS- 1. Cf. EXPEND, SPEND.] **1.** *trans.* To pay away, expend, spend. **2.** *pass.* To be exhausted or spent; to come to an end ME. **3.** To waste, squander ME. **4.** To DISPENSE ME.

1. To d. shot, time 1582, money 1680, oaths SWIFT. 2. Til hese issue male be dispended 1452. So †**Dispe·nder** = DISPENSATOR.

Dispendious (dispe·ndiəs), *a.* 1557. [ad. L. *dispendiosus*. Cf. mod.F. *dispendieux*.] †**1.** Hurtful. **2.** Expensive; extravagant 1727. So ‖**Dispe·ndium.** [L.] Loss; expenditure; expense.

Dispensable (dispe·nsăb'l), *a.* 1533. [ad. med.L. *dispensabilis*, f. *dispensare* to DISPENSE.] **1.** *Eccl.* Subject to dispensation. **2.** Allowable, excusable. ? *Obs.* 1589. **3.** That can be done without; unessential; unimportant 1649. Hence **Dispensabi·lity. Dispe·nsableness.** var. †**Dispe·nsible** *a.* (in senses 1, 2).

Dispensary (dispe·nsări). 1699. [f. L. type *dispensarium*, *dispensarius* (*liber*); f. *dispens-* ppl. stem of L. *dispendere.*] **1.** A place in which medicines are dispensed. *spec.* A charitable institution, where medicines are dispensed and medical advice given gratis, or for a small charge. †**2.** *transf.* A collection of the drugs, etc., mentioned in the pharmacopœia –1774. †**3.** = DISPENSATORY 1. –1725.

Di·spensate, *v. rare.* 1701. [f. L. *dispensat-*, *dispensare*; cf. *compensate.*] = DISPENSE.

Conceptions of widely dispensated happiness W. IRVING.

Dispensation (dispensē¹·ʃən). ME. [a. F., or ad. L. *dispensationem.*]

I. 1. The action of dispensing or dealing out; distribution; economical disposal. **2.** The process of dispensing medicines or medical prescriptions 1646.

1. The d. of this grace unto all men SELDEN.

II. 1. The action of administering, ordering, or managing; the system by which things are administered. [From the L. use of *dispensatio* as tr. Gr. οἰκονομία in N.T., etc.] **2.** Stewardship (*arch.*) ME. **3.** Ordering, management; *esp.* the ordering of events by divine providence ME.; with *a* and *pl.* 1652. **4.** *Theol.* A religious order or system, conceived as a stage in a progressive revelation, expressly adapted to a particular nation or age, as the *patriarchal*, *Mosaic*, *Christian d.*; also, the age 1643.

3. Mysterious dispensations of Providence DICKENS.

III. 1. *Eccl.* The granting of licence by a pope, archbishop, or bishop, to a person, to do what is forbidden, or omit what is enjoined by ecclesiastical law, etc.; the licence so given ME. Also *transf.* and *fig.* **2.** *Law.* The relaxation or suspension of a law in a particular case 1607. **3.** *transf.* Exemption from any obligation, fate, etc.; remission. ? *Obs.* 1653. **4.** The action of dispensing *with* anything 1593.

2. A way of preventing the King's d. with Acts 1667. 3. A d. from ceremonious visits JOHNSON.

Hence **Dispensa·tional** *a.* pertaining to d., or to a d.

Dispe·nsative, *a.* (*sb.*) 1528. [ad. L. *dispensativus*, f. *dispensare.*] †**1.** Administrative, official; pertaining to a dispensator –1656. **2.** Giving dispensation; dispensatory 1621. Hence **Dispe·nsatively** *adv.*

Di·spensa:tor. Now *rare.* ME. [a. AF. *dispensatour*, ad. (ult.) L. *dispensatorem*. Orig. stressed on final.] One who dispenses; a dispenser, a distributor. †**b.** A steward –1698. So **Dispensa·trix**, a female d.

Dispe·nsatory, *sb.* 1566. [ad. med.L. *dispensatorium*, *dispensatorius* (*liber*); see next.] **1.** A book in which medicinal substances, their composition, method of preparation, and use are described; a pharmacopœia. Also *fig.* †**2.** = DISPENSARY 1. –1799.

Dispe·nsatory, *a.* 1635. [ad. L. *dispensatorius*; see DISPENSATOR.] †**1.** = Of or pertaining to the office of a dispensator, or steward, or to administration –1679. **2.** That gives dispensations 1647. Hence **Dispe·nsatorily** *adv.* by dispensation.

†**Dispe·nse**, *sb.* ME. [a. OF. *despense*, ad. late L. *dispensa*, sb. from pa. pple. of *dispendere*: prob. affected by OF. *despens* :—L. *dispensum*. In sense 4, prob. from the vb.] **1.** The act of spending –1664; *pl.* expenses –1718; money to spend –1652. **2.** The act of bestowing liberally –1596. **3.** = SPENCE 1622. **4.** = DISPENSATION III. 1. –1777.

Dispense (dispe·ns), *v.* ME. [a. OF. *de-*, *dispenser*, ad. L. *dispensare* (freq. of *dispendere*).]

I. from L. in classical senses. **1.** *trans.* To deal out, distribute; to bestow in portions; †to spend (time, talents) –1649. **2.** *Med.* To make up (medicine); to put up (a prescription) 1533.

1. To d. favours and disfavours 1647, equity 1894.

II. from med.L. *dispensare* in eccles. use. **1.** *intr.* To deal dispensatorily, to use dispensatory power ME. †**2.** *trans.* To relax the law in reference to (some thing or person) ME. **3.** To dissolve, relax, or release by dispensation 1532. †**4.** To do without; = *D. with* –1647. †**5.** *intr.* To make amends *for*. SPENSER *F. Q.* I. iii. 30.

1. When he dispenseth he sheweth the case whereon he dispenseth to be contained under the meaning of the law HARPSFIELD. 2. The Pope, dispensing all things for money 1566. 3. Thy holy vow dispensed MASSINGER. Dispensed from all necessity of providing for himself JOHNSON.

Phr. **D. with.** [Orig. = med.L. *dispensare cum aliquo* (*ut possit*), etc.] **a.** To exempt, excuse (a person) from doing something; †to compound with, for an offence, etc. (*rare*). **b.** To give special exemption or relief from; to relax or set aside the obligation of; to do away with; to do without. †**c.** To grant a dispensation for (something illegal or irregular); †to do with, put up with.

Hence **Dispe·nser**, one who dispenses, deals out, or administers. **Dispe·nsing** *vbl. sb.* and *ppl. a.*; also *attrib.*, as in *dispensing power*.

†**Dispe·nsive**, *a.* 1590. [f. L. *dispens-*, *dispendere.*] **1.** Given to spending or distributing –1677. **2.** Subject to dispensation. MARLOWE.

Dispeople (dispī·p'l), *v.* 1490. [ad. OF. *despeupler*, Rom. formation from *des-*, L. *dis-*, DIS- 4 + *populus.*] **1.** = DEPOPULATE 2. †**2.** [DIS- 7 b.] To cut off from being a people –1687.

1. Some cruell Lord..could..d. a whole parish 1649. *transf.* We will d. all the elements To please our palates RANDOLPH. Hence **Dispeo·pler**, one who or that which dispeoples.

†**Dispe·rge**, *v.* 1530. [ad. L. *dispergere.*] = DISPERSE *v.* –1657.

Dispe·rmous, *a.* 1760. [f. DI-[2] + Gr. σπέρμ(ατ- + -OUS.] *Bot.* Having two seeds. var. **Dispe·rmatous.**

Disperple, obs. var. of DISPARPLE *v.*

Dispersal (dispɜ̄·ɹsăl). 1821. [f. DISPERSE *v.*] = DISPERSION.

Disperse (dispɜ̄·ɹs), *v.* 1450. [a. F. *disperser*, f. *dispers*, ad. L. *dispersus*, pa. pple. of *dispergere.*] **1.** *trans.* To scatter in all directions; to rout. **2.** To spread about; to send to, or station apart at, various points. *Esp.* in *pa. pple.* 1529. **b.** *intr.* (for *refl.*) To go different ways 1672. †**3.** *trans.* To divide, dispart –1600. **4.** To distribute from a source or centre 1555. **5.** To spread about; to diffuse 1576. **6.** To dissipate 1563. Also *intr.* **7.** *trans. Optics.* Of a refractive medium: To scatter (rays of light) 1654.

1. Her feet d. the powdery snow WORDSW. 2. Dispersed throughout the museums of Europe YEATS. 4. Wee..find Charles Butler guiltie of dispersing bad monie 1693. 6. At length the sonne..Disperst those vapours that offended vs *Com. Err.* I. i. 90. Hence **Dispe·rsed-ly** *adv.*, **-ness. Dispe·rser**, one who or that which disperses.

Dispersion (dispɜ̄·ɹʃən). ME. [a. F., or ad. L. *dispersionem*; see DISPERSE *v.*] **1.** The action of dispersing or scattering abroad; the state of being dispersed 1450. **2.** The action of diffusing; diffusion 1664. **3.** *Med.* The removal of inflammation, etc., from a part; dissipation 1753. **4.** *Optics.* The divergence of the different-coloured rays of a beam of composite light when refracted by a prism or lens, or when diffracted, so as to produce a spectrum; *esp.* in reference to its amount 1727. Also *attrib.*

1. I conceiv'd that our d. was a necessary circumstance to be fulfil'd BEN ISRAEL. Phr. *The D.*: The Jews living dispersed among the Gentiles after the Captivity (John vii. 35); = DIASPORA ME.

Dispersive (dispɜ̄·ɹsiv), *a.* 1627. [f. L. type *dispersivus.*] Having the character or quality of dispersing; in *Optics*, having the quality of causing the different-coloured rays of light to diverge; see DISPERSION 4. 1802. Hence **Dispe·rsive-ly** *adv.*, **-ness**, d. quality.

Dispersonate (dispɜ̄·ɹsŏnē¹t), *v.* 1624. [DIS- 6.] To divest of personality. So **Dispe·rsonalize** *v.*

Dispersonify (dispəɹsǫ·nifəi), *v.* 1846. [DIS- 6.] To represent or regard as impersonal. Hence **Disperso:nifica·tion.**

Dispe·tal, *v.* 1863. [DIS- 7 a.] To strip of petals.

Disphenoid (dəisfī·noid). 1895. [DI-[2] 1.] *Cryst.* A solid figure contained by eight isosceles triangles.

†**Dispi·cion.** 1510. [? f. L. *dispicere*; but cf. DISPUTISOUN.] Disputation –1553.

Dispie·ce, *v.* 1477. [ad. OF. *despiecer*; see DIS- 1.] To divide into pieces.

Dispirit (dispi·rit), *v.* 1642. [DIS- 7 a.] †**1.** *trans.* To deprive of essential quality; to weaken; to deprive (liquor) of its spirit –1713. **2.** To lower the spirits of, depress 1647. †**3.** To extract and transfuse the essence of. FULLER.

1. He that has dispirited himself by a debauch COLLIER. 2. To d. the sufferer from future exertions COMBE. Hence **Dispi·ritment.**

Dispirited (dispi·ritĕd), *ppl. a.* 1647. [f. prec. + -ED[1].] †**1.** Deprived of essential quality; spiritless –1758. **2.** Cast into low spirits; disheartened, dejected 1647.

1. Flat, D., or Dead Drink 1700. 2. A few unarmed, d. men 1741. Hence **Dispi·rited-ly** *adv.*, **-ness.**

Dispiteous (dispi·tiəs), *a.* 1803. [orig. var. of DESPITEOUS; now taken as f. DIS- 10 + PITEOUS.] Pitiless, merciless. Hence **Dispi·teous-ly** *adv.*, **-ness.**

Displace (displē¹·s), *v.* 1551. [ad. OF. *desplacer*, mod.F. *déplacer*; see DIS- 1, 4.] **1.** *trans.* To shift from its place; to put out of the proper or usual place. **2.** To remove from a position, dignity, or office 1553. **3.** To oust from its place and occupy it instead 1774.

1. Thy diadem displaced, thy sceptre gone COWPER. 2. King Solomon displaced Abiathar the high preest FOXE. 3. To d. by regular garrisons the troops of the Thakurs 1844. In three years..this weed..absolutely displaced every other plant on the ground A. R. WALLACE. Hence **Displa·ceable** *a.* that may be displaced. **Displa·cer**, one who or that which displaces; *Pharm.* a PERCOLATOR.

Displacement (displē¹·smĕnt). 1611. [f. DISPLACE *v.* + -MENT.] **1.** The act of displacing or fact of being displaced. **2.** *Physics.* The amount by which anything is displaced; the difference between the initial position of a body and a subsequent position 1837. **3.** = REPLACEMENT 1868. **b.** *Hydrostatics.* The displacing of a liquid by a body immersed in or floating on it; the amount or weight of fluid so displaced by a floating body, *e.g.* a ship 1802. **c.** *Pharm.* = PERCOLATION 1883.

1. His d. from the Regency of France SPEED. A vertical d. of the strata HAUGHTON. 3. The d. of human labor through .. machinery 1880. b. Phr. *Centre of d.*: see CENTRE *sb.* Her total length is 320 feet..with a d. of 11,407 tons 1876.

Displacency (displē¹·sĕnsi). Now *rare.* 1652. [ad. med.L. *displacentia* (DIS- 4). See also DISPLICENCY.] The condition of being displeased with something; displeasure, dissatisfaction, dislike. (The reverse of *complacency.*) var. †**Displa·cence.**

Displant (displa·nt), *v.* 1491. [ad. OF. *desplanter*:—Rom.**displantare*, for L. *deplantare.*] **1.** *trans.* To remove (a plant) from the ground; to uproot. Also †*fig.* †**2.** To undo the settlement or establishment of (a 'plantation' or colony) –1660.

1. *fig.* He must..d. vices, and plant the contrarie vertues 1612. 2. All those countryes, which .. had bene planted with English, were shortly displanted and lost SPENSER. Hence †**Displanta·tion.**

†**Displa·t,** *v.* [DIS- 6 or 7 a.] *trans.* To unplait. HAKEWELL.

Display (displē¹·), *v.* ME. [a. OF. *despleier* (*-plier, -ployer*) :—L. *displicare.* See also DEPLOY, and SPLAY.] **1.** *trans.* To unfold, expand, spread out; to unfurl (a banner, sail). Now *Obs.* exc. as influenced by sense 3. †**b.** *Mil.* = DEPLOY *v.* 2. –1610. **2.** To lay or place with the limbs extended; to extend (a limb, wing, etc.). *spec.* in *Her.*; see DISPLAYED 2. ME. **3.** To open up to view, exhibit to the eyes, show ME.; in *Printing*, to make more prominent by larger type, spacing, etc. 1888. **4.** To unfold or exhibit to other senses, or to the mind; to make manifest 1575. **5.** *esp.* To exhibit ostentatiously; to make a show of 1628. Also †*intr.* (for *refl.*) *Lear* II. iv. 41. **6.** *trans.* To allow to be seen, to betray 1602. †**7.** To depict, describe; to expound; to unfold (a tale) –1808. †**8.** *Med.* To disperse. TOPSELL. ¶**9.** To discover, descry. [As if 'to unfold to one's own view'.] 1590.

1. [He] displaid his sails to a prosperous west wind EARL MONM. 3. More recently the Royal Banner has always displayed the Arms of England BOUTELL. 4. Their labour to d. QUARLES. To d. insubordination 1885. 5. These few good parts hee has, hee is no niggard in displaying EARLE. 6. He began to d. .. some token of suspition 1632. Hence **Display·er.**

Display·, *sb.* 1583. [f. prec. vb.] **1.** The act of displaying; exhibition, manifestation 1680; †a description –1714. **2.** An exhibition, a show 1665. **3.** Show, ostentation 1816. **4.** *Printing.* The selection and arrangement of types so as to call attention to a word, line, etc. 1824.

1. An occasion for the d. of his powers FROUDE. 2. The d. of dahlias 1845. 3. Fatal to the man of letters, fatal to man, is the lust of d. EMERSON.

Comb.: **d.-letter, -type,** a letter or type used for displaying printed matter; **-stand,** a stand, rack, or shelf, etc. for displaying goods.

Displayed (displē¹·d), *ppl. a.* ME. [f. prec. vb.] **1.** Unfolded, unfurled, spread open to view; expanded, as wings, leaves, etc. 1578. **2.** *Her.* Having the wings expanded: said of a bird of prey ME.

†**Di·sple,** *v.* 1492. [app. f. DISCIPLINE *sb.* or *v.*] *trans.* To subject to discipline; *esp.* as a religious practice –1641.

Bitter Penaunce, with an yron whip, Was wont him once to d. every day SPENSER *F. Q.* I. x. 27.

†**Displea·sance.** ME. [a. OF. *desplaisance*, mod.F. *déplaisance*; see next.] The fact of being displeased; displeasure, dissatisfaction, annoyance; a cause or instance of this –1590.

†**Displea·sant,** *a.* ME. [a. OF. *desplaisant*, ppl. adj. of *desplaire.*] **1.** That displeases; unpleasant, disagreeable –1668. **2.** Displeased –1709. Hence †**Displea·sant-ly** *adv.*, †**-ness.**

Displease (displī·z), *v.* ME. [a. OF. *desplais-*, pres. stem of *desplaisir, desplaire*, refash. repr. of L. *displicere*, Rom. **displacere*; see PLEASE.] **1.** *intr.* To cause displeasure, dissatisfaction, or dislike. **2.** *trans.* [The object repr. an earlier dative.] To be displeasing or disagreeable to; to offend, annoy, vex ME.

1. Ev'n spring displeases, when she shines not here POPE. 2. He put them al to deth that displesid him CAXTON. The world, in the main, displeaseth me ARBUTHNOT. *fig.* My mirth is much displeas'd, but pleas'd my woe *Meas. for M.* IV. i. 13. Hence **Displea·sed-ly** *adv.*, †**-ness. Displea·sing-ly** *adv.*, **-ness.**

Displeasure (disple·ʒiŭɹ), *sb.* 1470. [orig. a. OF. *desplaisir*, mod.F. *déplaisir*, infin. used subst.; later, conformed to PLEASURE.] **1.** The fact or feeling of being displeased or offended; a feeling varying in intensity from dissatisfaction or disapproval to indignation 1484. †**2.** The opposite of pleasure; discomfort, unhappiness; sorrow, trouble –1875. **b.** with *a* and *pl.* –1686. **3.** That which causes offence or trouble; injury; a wrong, an offence (*arch.*) 1470. †**4.** A disagreement –1576.

1. An indication of the d. of Heaven FROUDE. Phr. *To take (a) d.*: to take umbrage. 2. When good is proposed, its absence carries d. or pain with it LOCKE. 3. Hast thou delight to see a wretched man Do outrage and d. to himself *Com. Err.* IV. iv. 119. 4. During the d. betweene him and Earle Godwin LAMBARDE. Hence **Displea·surable** *a.* disagreeable (*rare*). **Displea·sure** *v.* to cause d. to (*arch.*).

Displenish (disple·niʃ), *v. Sc.* 1639. [DIS- 6.] To deprive of furniture, supplies, or (farm) stock. Hence **Disple·nishment.**

†**Di·splicence.** 1605. [ad. L. *displicentia*, f. *displicere.* Cf. DISPLACENCE.] Displeasure, dissatisfaction –1736.

Displicency (di·splisĕnsi). 1640. [f. as prec.] = DISPLACENCY.

†**Displo·de,** *v.* 1667. [ad. L. *displodere*, f. DIS- 1 + *plaudere.*] *trans.* To discharge with an explosion; *intr.* to explode –1812. So †**Displo·sion,** the action of disploding. †**Displo·sive** *a.* eruptive.

Displume (displū·m), *v.* 1480. [f. DIS- 7 a + PLUME *sb.*] †**1.** *trans.* Of birds: To cast (their feathers). CAXTON. **2.** = DEPLUME *v.* (*lit.* and *fig.*) 1606.

2. Wastes where the wind's wings break Displumed by daylong ache SWINBURNE. *fig.* Humblenes may flaring Pride d. SYLVESTER.

†**Dispoi·nt,** *v.*[1] 1483. [a. OF. *despointier*, f. *des-*, DIS- 4 + *-pointier* in *apointier* to APPOINT.] **1.** To dismiss, discard; to deprive *of* –1489. **2.** To disappoint. Const. *of.* –1565.

Dispoi·nt, *v.*[2] [DIS- 7 a.] To deprive of the point. SYLVESTER.

Dispond; see DESPOND.

Dispondee (dəispǫ·ndī). 1706. [ad. L. *dispondeus* (also used); see DI-[2].] A double spondee. Hence **Disponda·ic** *a.*

Dispone (dispōᵘ·n), *v.* Chiefly *Sc.* ME. [ad. L. *disponere*; see DIS- 1.] †**1.** *trans.* To set in order –1588. †**2.** To dispose *to* or *for* (something); to incline –1613. †**3.** To dispose of –1580. **4.** *Sc. Law.* To make over or convey officially or in legal form 1555. †**5.** *intr.* or *absol.* To make disposition, arrange –1605.

Hence **Dispo·nee·,** the person to whom a conveyance is made. **Dispo·ner,** the person who conveys property.

Disponent (dispōᵘ·nĕnt), *a.* 1613. [ad. L. *disponentem*; see prec.] Disposing; inclining towards a particular end.

Disponge, var. f. DISPUNGE.

Dispo·pe, *v.* 1622. [DIS- 7 b.] To deprive of the popedom.

Disport (dispōᵊ·ɹt), *sb. arch.* ME. [a. AF., OF. *desport*; see next.] **1.** Diversion; relaxation; amusement (*arch.*). **2.** A pastime, game, sport (*arch.*) ME. †**3.** Merriment –1801.

Disport (dispōᵊ·ɹt), *v.* ME. [a. AF. *desporter*, f. (ult.) *des-*, DIS- 1 + *porter* :—L. *portare.*] †**1.** *trans.* To divert (from sadness, etc.); to amuse –1665. **2.** *refl.* To cheer, divert oneself; now *esp.* to play wantonly, frolic, gambol ME. **3.** *intr.* (for *refl.*) = prec. 1480. †**4.** *trans.* To turn away (*rare*) 1450.

1. All the way we sail'd .. we were disported by Whales SIR T. HERBERT. 2. Whilst he disported himself at the court of France DRUMM. OF HAWTH. 3. I her caught disporting on the greene SPENSER. Hence **Dispo·rtive** *a.* inclined to d. (*rare*). **Dispo·rtment** = DISPORT *sb.*

Disposable (dispōᵘ·zăb'l), *a.* 1643. [f. DISPOSE *v.*] **1.** Inclinable (*to* something) (*rare*) 1652. **2.** Capable of being disposed of; capable of being put to some use; at (some one's) disposal 1643.

2. A disposeable surplus BURKE. D. as literary ware MASSON.

Disposal (dispōᵘ·zăl). 1630. [f. DISPOSE *v.* + -AL [5].] The act or faculty of disposing. †**1.** The action of arranging, ordering, or regulating by right of power or possession; control, direction; ordinance, appointment, dispensation –1710. **2.** The action of disposing of, settling, or definitely dealing with 1648. **3.** The action of giving or making over; bestowal, assignment 1660. **4.** Power or right to dispose of; control, command, management; usu. in phr. *at* (*in*) *one's d.* 1630. **5.** = DISPOSITION I. 1828.

1. Tax not divine d. MILT. *Sams.* 210. 2. Directions about the d. of your money GAY. 3. The right of d. is suspended STEPHEN. 4. A very pretty young Lady, in her own d. STEELE.

Dispose (dispōᵘ·z), *v.* ME. [a. OF. *disposer*, f. L. *dis-*, DIS- 1 + *poser* (see POSE); substituted for L. *disponere.* Cf. COMPOSE, DEPOSE.]

I. *trans.* **1.** To place suitably, adjust; to arrange in a particular order ME.; to put away; to put in place, distribute (now *rare*) ME.; †to assign, appoint –1697. †**2.** To regulate; to order, control, direct –1677. †**3.** To bestow, make over; to deal out, distribute –1818. **4.** To make fit or ready; to fit, prepare (*to do*, or *to* or *for* something) (*arch.*) ME. **5.** To give a tendency or inclination to; to incline, make prone (*to*, or *to do* something) ME.

1. The sterres .. ben disposed in signis of bestes CHAUCER. The town is..handsomely disposed 1777. Ye Gods, to better Fate good Men d. DRYDEN. 2. I wyll d. this mater as I shall thynke best PALSGR. 4. Therefore will we d. our selves to suffer FLEMING. 5. Not that I imagine geometry disposeth men to infidelity BERKELEY. They ate Lettuse after supper .. to d. them selves to sleepe 1599.

II. *intr.* To make arrangements; to ordain, appoint ME.; †to make terms 1606.

You did suspect She had dispos'd with Cæsar *Ant. & Cl.* IV. xiv. 123.

Phr. **To d. of:** †**a.** = sense I. 2. **b.** To deal with definitely; to get rid of; to get done with, finish. **c.** To make over by way of sale or bargain, sell.

Dispo·se, *sb.* ? *Obs.* 1590. [f. prec.] †**1.** = DISPOSITION I. 1603. †**2.** = DISPOSAL I. –1671. †**3.** = DISPOSAL 4. –1741. †**4.** = DISPOSAL 3. –1673. **5.** †Mental constitution or inclination –1628; air, pose (*rare*) 1601.

2. The unsearchable d. Of Highest Wisdom MILT. *Sams.* 1746. 5. He hath a person, and a smooth d., To be suspected *Oth.* I. iii. 403.

Disposed (dispōᵘ·zd), *ppl. a.* ME. [f. as prec. + -ED [1].] **1.** Arranged, appointed, prepared, etc.; see DISPOSE *v.* 1, 4. †**2.** In a (specified) condition of body or health –1694. **3.** Having a (particular) disposition or turn of mind ME. **4.** Inclined ME.; †*ellipt.* inclined to merriment –1616. Hence **Dispo·sed-ly** *adv.*, **-ness.**

†**Dispo·sement.** 1583. [f. as prec. + -MENT.] Disposition, disposal –1679.

Disposer (dispōᵘ·zəɹ). 1526. [f. as prec. + -ER [1].] One who or that which disposes; see DISPOSE *v.* 1, 5.

My Author and D., what thou bidst Unargu'd I obey MILT. *P. L.* IV. 635.

†**Dispo·sit,** *v. rare.* [f. L. *disposit-* ppl. stem.] To deposit. GLANVILL.

Disposition (dispozi·ʃən). ME. [a. F., ad. L. *dispositionem*, f. *disponere* to DISPONE. Not derivationally related to DISPOSE; cf. COMPOSITION.]

I. 1. The action of setting in order, or condition of being set in order; arrangement, order; relative position 1541. **2.** Arrangement (of affairs, measures, etc.), *esp.* for the accomplishment of a purpose; plan; complexion of affairs ME. **3.** = DISPOSAL 1. ME. **4.** The action of disposing of; *spec.* in *Law*, the action of disponing; power of disposing of: *esp.* in phr. *at* (*in*) *one's d.* (= DISPOSAL 4) ME.

1. The divers d. of the clouds FULKE. *D.*.. in Architecture, is the just placing of all the several Parts of a Building, according to their proper Order PHILLIPS. 2. I craue fit d. for my Wife .. With such Accomodation and besort As leuels with her breeding *Oth.* I. iii. 237. The military dispositions of Julian were skilfully contrived GIBBON. 4. The choice of action or of repose is no longer in our d. GIBBON.

II. †**1.** *Astrol.* The situation of a planet in a horoscope –1590. **2.** Turn of mind ME. **3.**

The state or quality of being disposed (*to*, or *to do* something); inclination (occas. = desire, intention); the condition of being (well or ill) disposed *towards* ME. †b. Mood, humour -1764. †4. Physical constitution -1813. 5. Physical aptitude, or tendency (*to*, or *to do* something) ME. †6. Physical condition -1732; normal condition (*rare*) -1632.

2. [The] saturnine dispositions of the English 1779. 3. Testiness is a d. or aptness to be angry LOCKE. 5. The different dispositions of wool, silk, etc. to unite with the colouring particles 1791.

Hence **Disposi·tional** *a.* relating to d. (*rare*). **Dispositioned** *ppl. a.* having a (specified) d.

Dispositive (dispǫ·zitiv), *a.* 1483. [a. F. *dispositif, -ive*, ad. L. type **dispositivus*, f. *dispositus*.] †1. Characterized by special disposition (*rare*). CAXTON. 2. That disposes or inclines: often opp. to *effective* 1612. 3. Relating to control or disposal 1613. †4. Of or pertaining to natural disposition -1681.

2. Some causes are d., adiuuant, or impetrant 1624. Hence **Dispo·sitively.** ?*Obs.*

Dispositor (dispǫ·zitəɹ). 1598. [a. L., f. *disponere*.] *Astrol.* 'The lord of a sign in its relation to another planet.'

Dispossess (dispǒze·s), *v.* 1494. [ad. OF. *despossesser*, f. *des-*, DIS- 4 + *possesser*.] 1. *trans.* To put out of possession; to deprive of the possession *of*; to dislodge, oust. Also *transf.* and *fig.* †2. To cast out, or rid *of* (an evil spirit) -1845.

1. His father and grandfather had been too powerful for the house of Vicenza to d. them H. WALPOLE. Hence **Disposse·ssion**, the action of dispossessing or fact of being dispossessed; in *Law* = OUSTER; exorcism. **Disposse·ssor**, one who dispossesses.

Dispo·st, *v.* 1577. [DIS- 7.] To deprive of a post.

Disposure (dispōᵘ·ʒiŭɹ). Now *rare.* 1569. [f. DISPOSE *v.*] 1. = DISPOSITION I. 1, 2. 1625. †2. = DISPOSAL 1. -1689. 3. = DISPOSAL 2, 3. 1649. †4. = DISPOSAL 4. -1693.

Dispraise (disprēⁱ·z), *sb.* 1509. [DIS- 9.] 1. The action or fact of dispraising; blame, censure. 2. with *a* and *pl.* An instance or a cause of blame 1535.

1. In praise and in d. the same TENNYSON.

Dispraise (disprēⁱ·z), *v.* ME. [a. OF. *despreisier, -preiser, -priser*:—Rom. type **dispretiare* for cl.L. *depretiare*. Cf. DISPRIZE.] 1. *trans.* To speak of with disparagement, or disapprobation; to blame, censure. †2. To depreciate, despise -1500.

1. Foxes d. the grapes they cannot reach WOODALL. *absol.* When he intends to praise or d., he will doe it to the purpose FULLER. Hence †**Disprai·sable** *a.* worthy of dispraise. **Disprai·ser.**

Dispread, disspread (dispre·d), *v. arch.* 1590. [DIS- 1.] To spread about or out; to extend, open out. Also *intr.* (for *refl.*).

A vine on wall dispred SANDYS. She is the centre from whence all the light Dispreads H. MORE. Hence **Disprea·der**, one who spreads abroad.

Dispre·judice, *v.* [DIS- 7 a.] To free from prejudice. W. MONTAGUE.

Disprepa·re, *v.* [DIS- 6.] To render unprepared. HOBBES.

†**Dispre·ss,** *v.* 1605. [DIS- 1.] To press apart -1627.

Disprince; see DIS- 7 b.

Disprison (dispri·z'n), *v.* [DIS- 7 c.] To set free from prison. LYTTON.

Disprivilege (dispri·vilėdʒ), *v.* 1617. [DIS- 7 a (or 6).] 1. To deprive (a person) of privilege. †2. To undo the privilege of 1622.

†**Dispri·ze,** *sb.* 1560. [a. OF. *despris*:—late L. type **dispretium*. See DISPRIZE *v.*] Disparagement, contempt -1636.

Disprize (disprəi·z), *v. Obs.* or *arch.* 1480. [a. late OF. *despriser*; see DISPRAISE.] 1. *trans.* To depreciate, undervalue (*arch.*). †2. To dispraise, decry -1621.

†**Disprofe·ss,** *v.* [DIS- 6.] To renounce the profession of. SPENSER.

Dispro·fit, *sb. Obs.* or *arch.* 1494. [DIS- 9.] Disadvantage; †a disadvantage -1671.

Dispro·fit, *v. Obs.* or *arch.* 1483. [DIS- 6.] 1. *trans.* To bring disadvantage to. †2. *intr.* (for *refl.*) To fail to profit 1561.

†**Dispro·fitable,** *a.* 1548. [DIS- 10.] Unprofitable; detrimental -1572.

Disproof (disprū·f). 1531. [f. DIS- 9, after DISPROVE.] The proving of a thing not to be what is asserted; refutation; the evidence constituting this. Also with *a* and *pl.*

Allegations..susceptible of specific d. SYD. SMITH.

†**Dispro·perty,** *v. rare.* [DIS- 7 b.] To deprive of property; to dispossess. *Cor.* II. i. 264.

Disproportion (disprɒpōᵊ·ɹʃən), *sb.* 1555. [DIS- 9.] Want of proportion in number, quantity, size, etc.; lack of symmetry or due relation between things or parts; the condition of being out of proportion. Also with *a* and *pl.*

Let there be no great d. in age FULLER. A leg too long, or some other d. JOWETT.

Dispropo·rtion, *v.* 1593. [f. the sb.] To render or make out of due proportion.

To shape my Legges of an vnequall size, To d. me in euery part 3 *Hen. VI*, III. ii. 160. Statutes that d. punishment to crime LYTTON. Hence **Dispropo·rtionable** *a.* out of due proportion. **Dispropo·rtionableness. Dispropo·rtionably** *adv.*

Dispropo·rtional. 1609. [f. prec. sb.] **a.** *adj.* = DISPROPORTIONATE. **b.** *sb.* A disproportional quantity or number 1696.

a. It is very d. to the Understanding of childhood LOCKE. Hence **Disproportiona·lity,** the quality of being d. **Dispropo·rtionally** *adv.*

Dispropo·rtionate, *a.* 1555. [DIS- 10.] Out of proportion; failing to observe or constitute due proportion; inadequately or excessively proportioned. Const. *to.*

A long repentance is a d. price to pay for a short enjoyment WOLLASTON. So †**Dispropo·rtionated.** Hence **Dispropo·rtionate-ly** *adv.*, **-ness.**

†**Dispro·priate,** *v.* [f. DIS- 6 + L. *proprium*, after *appropriate*, etc.] To deprive of the ownership *of*; to dispossess. PURCHAS.

Disprovable (disprū·văb'l), *a.* 1548. [f. DISPROVE *v.*] †1. To be disapproved -1579. 2. Capable of being disproved; refutable 1685.

Dispro·val. *rare.* 1614. [f. as prec. + -AL.] The act of disproving; disproof.

Disprove (disprū·v), *v. Pa. pple.* **disproved, disproven.** ME. [a. OF. *desprover, -prouver*, f. *des-*, L. *dis-* + *prover*.] 1. *trans.* To prove to be false or erroneous; to refute, rebut, invalidate. 2. To convict (a person) of falsehood or error; to refute, confute. ? *Obs.* 1589. †3. To disapprove. Also *intr.* with *of.* -1824.

1. There is a mighty difference between not proven and disproven CHALMERS. 2. *Oth.* v. ii. 172. Hence **Dispro·ver,** a refuter; †a disapprover.

Disprovi·de, *v. arch.* 152.. [DIS- 6.] To fail to provide for; to leave unprovided.

†**Dispu·nct,** *a.* [f. DIS- 4 + L. *punctus*.] The reverse of punctilious; discourteous. B. JONS.

Dispunct (dispɒ·ŋkt), *v. rare.* 1563. [f. L. *dispunct-*, ppl. stem of *dispungere* (DIS- 1).] To mark off with points or pricks of the pen; to erase; to distinguish. Hence †**Dispu·nction,** erasure.

Dispunge (dispɒ·ndʒ), *v.* Also **-sponge.** 1606. [f. *di-*, DIS- 1 + *spunge*, SPONGE *v.* In sense assoc. w. EXPUNGE, L. *expungere*.] 1. To discharge as from a squeezed sponge (*arch.*). †2. To delete, expunge -1662.

1. Oh Soueraigne Mistris of true Melancholly, The poysonous dampe of night d. vpon me *Ant. & Cl.* IV. ix. 12. 2. Thou..that has dispong'd my score 1639.

Dispunishable (dispɒ·nišăb'l), *a.* 1577. [a. AF., f. DIS- 10 + *punishable*.] Free from liability to penalty; not punishable.

†**Dispu·rpose,** *v. rare.* 1607. [DIS- 6.] To defeat of its purpose.

†**Dispu·rse,** *v.* 1593. [altered from DISBURSE.] = DISBURSE -1649.

†**Dispurvey·,** *v.* ME. [a. OF. *desporveeir* (DIS- 4); see PURVEY.] To rob or strip of provision; to render destitute -1609. Hence †**Dispurvey·ed** *ppl. a.* †**Dispurvey·ance** (*rare*).

Disputable (di·spiutăb'l, dispiū·tăb'l), *a.* 1548. [ad. L. *disputabilis*, f. *disputare*.] 1. That may be disputed; liable to be called in question, contested, or controverted; questionable. †2. Disputatious 1600.

1. This is a matter d. in Schooles 1587. 2. He is too disputeable for my companie *A. Y. L.* II. v. 36. Hence **Disputableness. Disputably** *adv.*

†**Disputa·city.** 1660. [irreg. f. DISPUTATIOUS.] = DISPUTATIOUSNESS -1711.

Disputant (di·spiutănt). 1612. [a. L. *disputantem*.]

A. *adj.* Disputing; engaged in controversy 1671.

B. *sb.* One who disputes; *esp.* a public controversialist.

Disputants are rarely..good judges MILL.

Disputation (dispiutēⁱ·ʃən). 1450. [ad. L. *disputationem*; refash. from DISPUTISOUN.] 1. The action of disputing or debating; controversial argument; debate, discussion. **b.** *spec.* An exercise in which parties formally sustain, attack, and defend a thesis, as in the mediæval universities 1551. †2. A dissertation -1615. †3. Doubt -1689. †4. ? Interchange of ideas. SHAKS.

1. In the heat of d. JOHNSON. 4. 1 *Hen. IV*, III. i. 206.

Disputatious (dispiutēⁱ·ʃəs), *a.* 1660. [f. prec.; see -OUS.] Characterized by, or given to, disputation; contentious.

The wine rendered me loquacious, d., and quarrelsome SCOTT. Hence **Disputa·tious-ly** *adv.*, **-ness.**

Disputative (dispiū·tătiv), *a.* 1579. [a. late L. *disputativus*, f. *disputat-*, *disputare*.] 1. Given to disputation; disputatious. †2. That is the subject of dispute; controversial -1708. 3. Pertaining to disputation 1664.

1. The cavils of the d. 1788. 2. D. elections LUTTRELL. Hence **Dispu·tative-ly** *adv.*, **-ness.**

Dispute (dispiū·t), *v.* [ME. *des-*, *dispute*, a. OF. *desputer*, mod.F. *disputer*, ad. L. *disputare*; f. DIS- 1 + *putare*.]

I. *intr.* 1. To contend with opposing arguments or assertions; to discuss, argue, hold disputation; often, to debate with heat, to altercate. †2. To contend with arms, or the like; to strive, struggle -1828.

1. Thou disputes like an Infant: goe whip thy Gigge SHAKS. The Emperor told Josephine that he disputed like a devil on these two points EMERSON.

II. *trans.* 1. To debate, discuss, or argue ME. †2. To maintain by disputation; to argue or contend -1713. 3. To argue against, contest, controvert 1513. 4. To oppose, contest, resist 1605. 5. To contend for or contest a prize, victory, etc. 1654.

1. I will not d. what Gravity is RAY. 3. My right there is none to d. COWPER. He would D. the Devil upon that Question 1687. 4. They..seemed resolved to d. his landing 1748. 5. To d. in arms every inch of ground FREEMAN. Hence **Dispu·ter.**

Dispute (dispiū·t), *sb.* 1594. [f. the vb.; = F. *dispute*.] 1. The act of arguing against, controversy, debate 1638. 2. An argumentative contention, a controversy; also, in weakened sense, a difference of opinion; freq., a heated contention, a quarrel 1611; †a logical argument 1594. †3. Strife; a fight or struggle -1745.

1. That once was in the heat of d. WESLEY. Phr. *In d.*: that is disputed. *Beyond, out of, past, without d.*: indisputably. Hence †**Dispu·teful** *a.* disputatious (*rare*).

†**Dispu·tisoun.** ME. [a. OF. *desputeisun, -on*, etc., early ad. L. *disputationem*; see DISPUTATION.] = DISPUTATION -1450.

Disqualification (diskwǫ:lifikēⁱ·ʃən). 1711. [f. DISQUALIFY.] 1. The action of disqualifying; *spec.* legal incapacitation; also, the being disqualified 1770. 2. That which disqualifies; a ground or cause of incapacitation 1711.

1. D. to hold any office 1789. 2. I hope you don't think good looks a d. for the business DICKENS.

Disqualify (diskwǫ·lifəi), *v.* 1718. [DIS- 6.] *trans.* To deprive of the qualifications required for some purpose; to render unqualified; to unfit, disable. **b.** *spec.* = DISABLE *v.* 2. 1732.

My common illness is of that kind which utterly disqualifies me from all conversation; I mean my deafness SWIFT.

Disquantity (diskwǫ·ntĭti), *v.* 1605. [DIS- 7 a.] To deprive of quantity; to diminish.

†**Disqua·rter,** *v.* [irreg. f. DIS- 1 (or Gr. δίς) + QUARTER *v.*] To halve or divide the quarters of. QUARLES.

Disquiet (diskwəi·ět), *v.* 1530. [DIS- 6.] To deprive of quietness, bodily or mental; to disturb, alarm; to make uneasy or restless.

Yee euery man..disquieteth himself in vayne COVERDALE *Ps.* xxxviii. 5. Hence †**Disqui·etal** (*rare*), the action of disquieting. **Disqui·eter.**

Disquiet (diskwəi·ět), *a.* Now *rare.* 1587. [DIS- 10.] The reverse of quiet; restless, uneasy, disturbed. Hence **Disqui·et-ly** *adv.* in a d. or †disquieting manner; **-ness. Disqui·etude,** disquieted condition or state; restlessness, disturbance; also with *a* and *pl.*

Disquiet (diskwəi·ĕt), *sb.* 1574. [f. DISQUIET *a.* and *v.*] Absence of bodily or mental quietness; disturbance; uneasiness, anxiety; restlessness. Also with *a* and *pl.* (*arch.* or *Obs.*) Hence †**Disqui·etful** *a.* †**Disqui·etive** *a.* tending to d. †**Disqui·etous** *a.* disquieting.

†**Disqui·parancy.** 1697. [ad. med.L. *disquiparantia* for *disæquiparantia* (DIS- 4); see EQUIPARANCE.] *Logic.* The relation of two correlates which are heteronymous, *i.e.* denoted by different names, as father and son: opp. to *equiparancy.* So **Disquipara·tion** (*rare*).

Disquisition (diskwizi·ʃən). 1605. [ad. L. *disquisitionem*, f. *disquisit-* ppl. stem of *disquirere.*] 1. Diligent or systematic search; investigation 1608; †*ellipt.* a subject for investigation –1660. 2. A treatise or discourse in which a subject is investigated and discussed at some length; less correctly, an elaborate dissertation *on* a subject 1647.

1. In this d. into human conduct HARRIS. 2. Puzzling them with scholastical craggy disquisitions TRAPP. Hence **Disquisi·tional** *a.* of the nature of a d. **Disquisi·tionist**, the author of a d.

Disquisitive (diskwi·zitiv), *a.* 1647. [f. L. *disquisit-* ppl. stem; see prec.] Characterized by disquisition; given to research or investigation; inquiring.

A man of great d. powers 1772.

Disquisitor (diskwi·zitəɹ). 1766. [ad. L. **disquisitor.*] One who makes disquisition; an investigator. Hence **Disquisito·rial** *a.* of or belonging to a d.; inquiring (*rare*). So **Disqui·sitory** *a.* (*rare*).

†**Disra·nge**, *v.* 1485. [ad. OF. *desrengier*, *-rangier*, f. *des-*, DIS- 4 + *renc, reng*, now *rang.* Cf. DERANGE.] To disarrange; *refl.* and *intr.* to fall out of rank –1775.

Disrank (disræ·ŋk), *v.* 1597. [DIS- 7 c.] †1. To throw out of rank or into disorder –1654. Also †*transf.* and *fig.* 2. To reduce to a lower rank; to degrade 1599.

Disrate (disrēⁱ·t), *v.* 1811. [DIS- 7 a.] To reduce to a lower rating or rank. Also *fig.*

†**Disray·**, *sb.* ME. [var. of *desray.*] = DERAY, DISARRAY –1610.

†**Disray·**, *v.* ME. [var. of *desray*, a. OF. *desrayer.*] 1. = DISARRAY *v.* 1. –1631. 2. = DISARRAY *v.* 2. –1608.

Disrealize (disrī·ăləiz), *v. rare.* 1889. [DIS- 6.] To divest of reality; to idealize.

†**Disrea·son**, *v.* 1622. [Anglicized from OF. *desraisnier*, var. of *deraisnier.*] To prove, assert, vindicate; = DERAIGN *v.* 1, 2.

Disrecommendation (disre:kǫmendēⁱ·ʃən). 1752. [DIS- 9.] The reverse of a recommendation; that which is unfavourable to any one's claims.

In a Government where trifling qualities are no d. H. WALPOLE.

Disregard (disrĭgā·ɹd), *sb.* 1665. [DIS- 9.] Want of regard; neglect; in earlier use often, slighting, undue neglect; later, the treating of anything as of no importance.

A d. of fame ADDISON, of historical accuracy JOWETT. Hence **Disrega·rdful** *a.* neglectful; **-ly** *adv.*

Disregard (disrĭgā·ɹd), *v.* 1641. [DIS- 6.] To treat without regard. 1. In earlier use, *esp.*, to treat without due regard; to neglect unduly, slight 1641. 2. In later use, *esp.*, to treat as of no importance, to pay no attention to 1793.

1. To make all the people d. and despise the Gospel BAXTER. 2. To d. public opinion 1793, idle rumours MACAULAY, symptoms DICKENS. So **Disrega·rdant** *a.* disregarding. Hence **Disrega·rder.**

†**Disre·gular**, *a.* [DIS- 10.] Irregular. EVELYN.

Disrelish (disre·liʃ), *sb.* 1625. [DIS- 9.] Distaste, aversion, some degree of disgust.

Men .. have an extreme d. to be told of their duty BURKE.

Disrelish (disre·liʃ), *v.* 1548. [f. DIS- 6 or 7 a + RELISH *v.* or *sb.*] †1. *trans.* To destroy the relish of; to render distasteful –1760. 2. To find not to one's taste; to regard with disfavour; to dislike 1604. †3. To prove distasteful to –1708. 4. *intr.* To be distasteful 1631.

2. Her delicate tendernesse wil .. disreelish and abhorre the Moore *Oth.* II. i. 236. Hence †**Disre·lishable** *a.*

Disremember (disrĭme·mbəɹ), *v.* Chiefly *dial.* 1836. [DIS- 6.] To fail to remember; to forget (*trans.* and *absol.*).

Disrepair (disrĭpēᵊ·ɹ). 1798. [DIS- 9.] The being in bad condition for want of repairs.

All spoke neglect and d. SCOTT.

†**Disrepo·rt.** *rare.* [DIS- 9.] Evil report. FULLER.

Disreputable (disre·piŭtăb'l), *a.* (*sb.*) 1772. [DIS- 10.] 1. The reverse of reputable; such as to bring into disrepute; discreditable. 2. In bad repute; not respectable 1828. 3. *sb.* A disreputable person 1853.

1. D. to his character as a Clergyman 1795. 2. A few d. individuals DISRAELI. **Disre·putably** *adv.*

Disreputa·tion. *Obs.* or *arch.* 1601. [DIS- 9.] 1. Privation or loss of reputation; bringing into disrepute; dishonour, disgrace 1601; †a discredit –1751. †2. The condition of being in disrepute –1770.

1. He will..bring d. on the institution T. JEFFERSON.

Disrepute (disrĭpiū·t), *sb.* 1653. [DIS- 9.] Loss or absence of reputation; ill repute.

It brings the administration of justice into d. BUCKLE.

†**Disrepu·te**, *v.* 1611. [DIS- 6.] *trans.* To disesteem; to bring into discredit; to defame; to bring an evil name upon (by one's conduct) –1697.

You quote us the Homilies..I think you d. them BP. MOUNTAGU.

Disrespect (disrĭspe·kt), *sb.* 1631. [DIS- 9; or ? f. the vb.] Want of respect, courteous regard, or reverence; †an instance of this –1714.

My memory fails me, if I have mentioned their names with d. JUNIUS.

Disrespe·ct, *v.* 1614. [DIS- 6.] *trans.* The reverse of *to respect*; to have or show no respect or reverence for.

If he love the one he must d. the other BP. HALL. Hence **Disrespe·cter** (*rare*).

Disrespectable (disrĭspe·ktăb'l), *a.* 1813. [DIS- 10.] The opposite of respectable; not worthy of respect. Hence **Disrespe:ctabi·lity**, the quality of being d.

Disrespectful (disrĭspe·ktfŭl), *a.* 1677. [DIS- 10.] The opposite of respectful; full of or manifesting disrespect.

I must say nothing..that is d. or undutiful RICHARDSON. Hence **Disrespe·ctful-ly** *adv.*, **-ness.**

†**Disrespe·ctive**, *a.* 1623. [after *disrespect.*] = DISRESPECTFUL –1736.

Disrespo·ndency. [DIS- 9.] Absence of response. COKAINE.

†**Disre·st.** 1567. [DIS- 9.] Disquiet, unrest –1726.

†**Disre·verence**, *v.* 1529. [DIS- 6 or 7 a.] To treat with irreverence; to deprive of reverence –1670.

Disrobe (disrōᵘ·b), *v.* 1581. [DIS- 6 or 7 a.] 1. *trans.* To divest of a robe or garment; to undress, strip. Also *transf.* and *fig.* 1590. 2. *refl.* and *intr.* To undress.

1. D. the Images *Jul. C.* I. i. 69. And thou disroab'd of all thy dignitie 1592. Hence **Disro·ber.**

Disroof (disrū·f), *v.* 1837. [DIS- 7 a.] To unroof.

Disroot (disrū·t), *v.* 1612. [DIS- 6.] To pull up by the roots; to uproot; *transf.* to dislodge from the place where it is fixed.

Daun .. could not have disrooted Friedrich this season CARLYLE.

†**Disrou·t**, *v.* 1525. [ad. OF. *desrouter*, mod.F. *dérouter* (DIS- 4). Cf. ROUT *v.*] To put, or be put, to rout –1630.

Disru·ddered, *ppl. a. rare.* 1788. [DIS- 7 a.] Deprived of the rudder.

†**Disru·ly**, *a. rare.* 1570. [a. OF. *desrieulé*, mod.F. *déréglé.*] Unruly. Hence †**Disru·lily** *adv.* in an unruly manner.

Disrump (disrɒ·mp), *v.* 1581. [ad. L. *disrumpere* (DIS- 1).] To break up, DISRUPT (*trans.* and *intr.*).

Disrupt (disrɒ·pt), *ppl. a.* 1730. [ad. L. *disruptus*, pa. pple. of *disrumpere.*] Chiefly as poetic *pa. pple.* = disrupted.

Disrupt (disrɒ·pt), *v.* 1657. [f. L. *disrupt-* ppl. stem; see prec. Only found once before 19th c.] 1. *intr.* To burst asunder. TOMLINSON. 2. *trans.* To break or burst asunder; to shatter 1817. Also *fig.*

2. The attempt..to d. the government 1879. Hence **Disru·pter, -or**, one who breaks up.

Disruption (disrɒ·pʃən). 1646. [ad. L. *disruptionem.*] 1. The action of rending or bursting asunder; forcible severance. 2. A disrupted condition or part 1760.

1. At the sudden d. of the masses of rock above 1816. 2. In the time of weakness and d. 1852.

Phr. *The D.*: the great split in the Established Church of Scotland, 18th May, 1843, when 451 ministers left that Church and formed themselves into the Free (Protesting) Church of Scotland.

Hence **Disru·ptionist**, one who favours d.

Disruptive (disrɒ·ptiv), *a.* 1842. [f. L. *disrupt-* ppl. stem; see DISRUPT *v.* and -IVE.] 1. Causing or tending to disruption; bursting or breaking asunder. 2. Produced by disruption; eruptive 1870.

1. The speedy development of d. tendencies STUBBS. 2. The d. character of these rocks PAGE. Hence **Disru·ptive-ly** *adv.*, **-ness.**

Disrupture (disrɒ·ptiŭɹ), *sb.* 1796. [f. DISRUPT *v.*] = DISRUPTION. Hence **Disru·pture** *v.* to break off or asunder; to divide by a rupture.

Diss (dis). 1855. [a. Arab.] The Algerian name for a Mediterranean grass, *Ampelodesma* (*Arundo*) *tenax*, used for making cordage, etc.

Dissatisfaction (dissætisfæ·kʃən). 1640. [DIS- 9.] The fact or condition of being dissatisfied; discontent; 'want of something to complete the wish' (J.); a cause of this.

The d. you take at the ways of some good men CROMWELL. The d. of being obliged to return home, without [etc.] 1702.

Dissatisfactory (dissætisfæ·ktŏri), *a.* 1610. [DIS- 10.] Not satisfactory; causing dissatisfaction; unsatisfactory; 'unable to give content' (J.).

Things which..were d. to her Subjects SIR J. MELVIL. Hence **Dissatisfa·ctoriness.**

Dissatisfy (dissæ·tisfəi), *v.* 1666. [DIS- 6.] To deprive of satisfaction, to render unsatisfied; to fail to fulfil the desires or wishes of; to displease, discontent. Also *absol.*

Since they [the advantages of life] are not big enough to satisfy, they should not be big enough to d. COLLIER (J.).

Dissa·vage, *v.* [DIS- 8.] To tame, to civilize. CHAPMAN.

Dissceptre (disse·ptəɹ), *v.* 1591. [DIS- 7 a.] To deprive of the sceptre, or of kingly authority.

†**Dissea·son**, *v.* 1583. [DIS- 6.] To take away the flavour of –1621.

Disseat (dissī·t), *v.* 1612. [f. DIS- 6 or 7 c + SEAT *v.* or *sb.*] To remove from or as from a seat; to unseat.

The disseated Parliament-men 1648.

Dissect (dise·kt), *v.* 1607. [f. L. *dissect-*, ppl. stem of *dissecare* (DIS- 1).] 1. *trans.* To cut asunder, cut in pieces, divide by cutting. 2. *spec.* To cut up (an animal, a plant, etc.) for the purpose of displaying the position, structure, and relations of the various internal parts; to anatomize 1611. 3. *transf.* and *fig.* To take to pieces, so as to lay bare every part; to analyse; to criticize in detail 1631.

1. Hee that dissected Gordions knot SIR T. HERBERT. 2. Anatomists d. and mangle, To cut themselves out work to wrangle BUTLER. 3. To d. the human mind JOWETT. Hence **Disse·ctible** *a.* (*rare*).

Disse·cted, *ppl. a.* 1634. [f. prec. + -ED[1].] 1. That has been cut up, or divided into pieces; as, a *d. map.* 2. Cut into many deep lobes; much divided; as, a *d. chin, leaf*, etc. 1652.

Disse·cting, *vbl. sb.* 1767. [f. as prec.] The action of DISSECT *v.*

Comb.: **d.-forceps, -knife, -microscope, -room** (*i.e.* used in anatomical dissection); **-clerk**, one employed in analysing invoices and accounts.

Disse·cting, *ppl. a.* 1854. [f. as prec.] That dissects. *D. aneurism*, one in which the blood passes between the inner and middle and the outer coats of the artery.

Dissection (dise·kʃən). 1581. [ad. L. *dissectionem*, or immed. a. F.] †1. The action of cutting asunder or in pieces; division by cutting –1784. 2. *spec.* The methodical cutting up of an animal or plant for examination of its structure 1605. 3. The action of separating anything into its elements for the purpose of critical examination 1642. 4. *concr.* Anything which is the result or produce of dissecting 1581.

2. For hundreds of years..the d. of human bodies was impeded, and anatomists were confined to the d. of dead animals HUXLEY.

Disse·ctive, *a.* 1860. [f. L. *dissect-* ppl. stem.] Serving to dissect.

Dissector (dise·ktəɹ). Also **-er.** 1578. [f.

L. *dissecare.* Cf. F. *dissecteur.*] One who dissects, *esp.* anatomically.

Disseise, disseize (dissīˑz), *v.* ME. [a. AF *disseisir* = OF. *dessaisir*, f. *des-*, DIS- 4 + *saisir* to SEIZE.] *Law.* To put out of actual seisin or possession; to dispossess (a person) of his estates, etc., usually wrongfully or by force; to oust. Const. *of* (†*from*). Also *transf.* and *fig.*

Where..personnes..be dysseased..from their lawfull inheritance 1540. They..With gentle sleep their fear and care disseised HOBBES.

Hence **Disseiseeˑ, -zeeˑ**, one who is disseised of his estate: correl. to DISSEISOR. **Disseiˑsor, -zor**, one who disseises another of his lands, etc. **Disseiˑsoress.** †**Disseiˑsure, -zure** = next.

Disseisin, -zin (dissīˑzin), *sb.* ME. [a. AF. *disseisine* = OF. *dessaisine*, f. *des-*, DIS- 4 + *saisine, seisine* SEISIN, deriv. of *saisir* to SEIZE.] *Law.* The act or fact of disseising; privation of seisin; usually, the wrongful dispossession of the lands, etc. of another: since 15th c. not used of personalty. †**Disseiˑsin** *v.* = prec.

Dissel-boom (diˑs'lˌbūm). *S. Afr.* 1858. [Du., f. *dissel* shaft + *boom* beam, boom.] The pole of a wagon.

Dissemblance (diseˑmblăns). *arch.* 1463. [ad. OF. *dessemblance.*] 1. Want of resemblance. 2. [var. of DISSIMULANCE.] The action of dissembling, dissimulation 1602.

Dissemble (diseˑmb'l), *v.*¹ 1500. [app. a later form of DISSIMULE *v.*, ? influenced by *resemble.* Not in F.] 1. *trans.* To alter or disguise the semblance of so as to deceive; to give a false semblance to; to cloak or disguise by a feigned appearance 1513. †2. To disguise –1697. 3. To pretend not to see or notice; to ignore 1500. 4. *absol.* or *intr.* To conceal one's intentions, opinions, etc. under a feigned guise; 'to use false professions, to play the hypocrite' (J.) 1523. †5. *trans.* To feign, pretend, simulate –1813.

1. That we shoulde not d. nor cloke them [our sins] before the face of Almighty God *Bk. Com. Prayer.* 2. *Twel. N.* IV. ii. 4. 3. Learn to d. wrongs ROWE. 4. The subtle fiend.. Dissembled, and this answer smooth return'd MILT. *P. R.* I. 467. D. not with me thus SOUTHEY. Hence **Disseˑmbler**, one who dissembles; a deceiver, hypocrite. **Disseˑmblingly** *adv.*

†**Disseˑmble**, *v.*² *rare.* 1586. [a. OF. *dessembler*, f. *des-*, DIS- 4 + *sembler.*] To be unlike, resemble not. So †**Disseˑmblable** *a.* unlike, dissimilar.

Disseˑmbly. *nonce-wd.* A perversion of *assembly. Much Ado* IV. ii. 1.

Disseminate (diseˑmineᶦt), *v.* 1603. [f. L. *disseminat-*, ppl. stem of *disseminare*, f. DIS- 1 + *semen.*] 1. *trans. lit.* To scatter abroad, as in sowing seed; to spread here and there; to disperse, so as to deposit in all parts; †to distribute –1668. b. In *pa. pple.* and *pass.* used of diffused situation, without implying the action 1677. 2. *fig.* To spread abroad, diffuse, promulgate 1643.

1. The mistletoe is disseminated by birds DARWIN. The pantheists supposed life to be disseminated through all the interstices of matter 1869. 2. To d. a Doctrine 1670, opinions BP. WATSON, knowledge 1802. So **Disseˑminative** *a.* having the quality of disseminating or of being disseminated. **Disseˑminator**, one who or that which disseminates.

Dissemination (disemināˑʃən). 1646. [a. L. *disseminationem.*] The action of disseminating; the fact or condition of being disseminated; dispersion, diffusion, promulgation.

The extensive d. of the Scriptures 1829.

Dissension (diseˑnʃən). ME. [a. F., ad. L. *dissensionem*; see DISSENT. Formerly, often *dissention* (cf. *contention*).] 1. Disagreement in opinion; *esp.* such as produces contention; discord; an instance of this. †2. *Med.* Physical disturbance producing ailment –1725. †3. = DISSENT *sb.* 3. –1807.

1. But first among the priests d. springs MILT. *P. L.* XII. 352. There were dissensions..existing within the Church, as well as without J. H. NEWMAN.

Dissensious; see DISSENTIOUS.

Disˌseˑnsualize, *v.* [DIS- 6.] To free from sensual quality or elements. LOWELL.

Dissent (diseˑnt), *v.* ME. [ad. L. *dissentire* (DIS- 1).] 1. *intr.* Not to assent; to disagree with or object to an action. Const. *from*, †*to.* 2. To think differently, disagree, differ *from*, †*with* 1536; *spec.* to differ from the doctrine or worship of a church, *esp.* the Church of England 1553. †3. To be at variance –1743. †4. To differ in sense, or meaning, or in any other respect –1659.

1. Some lords entred their reasons for dissenting to the order LUTTRELL. 2. The Methodists have hitherto been accused of dissenting from the Church of England SYD. SMITH. Hence **Disseˑntingly** *adv.*

Dissent (diseˑnt), *sb.* 1585. [f. prec.] 1. Difference of opinion or sentiment; disagreement; †dissension 1596. 2. Disagreement with a proposal; the opposite of *consent* 1651. 3. *spec.* Difference of opinion in regard to religious doctrine or worship 1585; separation from an established church, *esp.* the Church of England; non-conformity 1772. †4. Want of agreement; difference of sense, nature, etc. –1638.

2. The opposite Lords..desired they might enter their dissents PEPYS. 3. D., not satisfied with toleration, is not conscience, but ambition BURKE. 4. The Consent and D. between Visibles and Audibles BACON.

Dissentaneous (disentēˑniəs), *a.* 1623. [f. L. *dissentaneus*, f. *dissentire* + -OUS.] Disagreeing, discordant; at variance *with*; contrary *to.* var. †**Disseˑntany** *a.*

†**Dissentaˑtion.** 1613. [irreg. f. DISSENT *v.*] Dissension –1623.

Dissenter (diseˑntəɹ). 1639. [f. DISSENT *v.* + -ER¹.] 1. One who dissents in any matter: one who disagrees with any opinion, resolution, or proposal 1647. 2. One who dissents in matters of religious belief and worship 1639; one who separates himself *from* any specified church, *esp.* from the communion of the Established Church of England. Usu. with capital D. (Sometimes restricted to those who disagree with the principle of national or state churches.) 1679.

2. Its discipline is .. so easy, that it allows more freedom to dissenters than any of the sects would allow it DRYDEN. Do you take me for a D., you rascal FIELDING. Hence **Disseˑnterism**, the principles and practice of Dissenters.

†**Disseˑntiate**, *v.* [irreg. f. L. *dissentire.*] *trans.* To move to dissension. FELTHAM.

Dissentient (diseˑnʃĭĕnt). 1621. [ad. L. *dissentientem.*]

A. *adj.* Differing or disagreeing in opinion; *esp.* dissenting from the opinion or sentiment of the majority 1651.

B. *sb.* One who differs or disagrees in opinion. Hence **Disseˑntience** (*rare*).

Dissentious (diseˑnʃəs), *a.* Now *rare.* 1560. [f. DISSENSION, and therefore better *dissensious.*] Of, pertaining to, or characterized by, dissension; *esp.* given to dissension, quarrelsome. Hence †**Disseˑntiously** *adv.*

†**Disseˑntive**, *a.* [irreg. f. DISSENT *v.*] Inclined to dissent. FELTHAM.

Dissepiment (diseˑpimĕnt). 1727. [ad. L. *dissæpimentum*, f. *dissæpire.*] *Bot.* and *Zool.* A partition in some part or organ; a septum. *spec.* a. *Bot.* A partition separating the cells of a syncarpous ovary or fruit. b. *Zool.* One of the horizontal plates connecting the vertical septa in corals. Hence **Dissepimeˑntal** *a.*

Dissert (disɔ̄ˑɹt), *v.* 1623. [f. L. *dissert-*, ppl. stem of *disserere* (DIS- 1).] †1. *trans.* To discuss, examine –1721. 2. *intr.* To make a dissertation. (Now *affected.*) 1657.

2. 'Tis always with a moral end That I d. BYRON.

Dissertate (diˑsəɹteᶦt), *v.* 1766. [f. L. *dissertat-*, ppl. stem of *dissertare*, freq. of *disserere.*] = prec. 2. (Unusual.)

Dissertation (disəɹtēˑʃən). 1611. [ad. L. *dissertationem*; see prec.] †1. Discussion –1709. 2. = DISCOURSE *sb.* 5. 1651.

2. A D. concerning Man HOBBES. Hence **Dissertaˑtional** *a.* belonging to or of the nature of a d. **Disseˑrtationist**, one who makes a d.

Diˑssertator. 1698. [a. L.] One who makes a dissertation.

Disserve (disɔ̄ˑɹv), *v.* 1618. [DIS- 6; cf. F. *desservir* (whence sense 2).] 1. *trans.* To do the contrary of *to serve*; to serve badly, do an ill turn to. 2. To clear a table 1816.

1. In what sort the said Duke had disserved him and abused his trust RUSHW.

Disservice (disɔ̄ˑɹvis), *sb.* 1599. [DIS- 9; cf. F. *desservice.*] The contrary of *service*; the rendering of an ill service or ill turn; injury, detriment; an injury.

The making of religion a notional thing hath been of infinite d. BERKELEY. Hence **Disseˑrviceable** *a.* unhelpful, hurtful, detrimental. **Disseˑrviceableness**, d. quality. **Disseˑrviceably** *adv.*

†**Disseˑttle**, *v.* 1635. [DIS- 6.] *trans.* To unsettle, disturb –1692. Hence **Disseˑttlement**, the action of dissettling; dissettled condition.

Dissever (diseˑvəɹ), *v.* ME. [a. AF. *deseverer*, OF. *dessevrer*, etc. :—L. *disseparare* (DIS- 1, 5).] 1. *trans.* To separate; to divide, disjoin, sever, part. 2. To divide into parts ME.; †to break up –1615. 3. *intr.* To separate, part ME.

1. Disseueringe the bishoprick of Chester..from the iurisdiction of Canturbury 1541. 2. The very name of Crumwell was able to d. insurrections 1615. Hence **Disseveraˑtion**, disseverance. **Disseˑverment**, the action of dissevering; disseverance.

Disseverance (diseˑvĕrăns). ME. [a. OF. *dessevrance*, etc., f. *dessevrer*; see prec.] The action of dissevering; separation.

Disshaˑdow, dish-, *v. rare.* 1583. [DIS- 7 a.] To free from shadow.

Dissheathe (disˌʃīˑð), *v. rare.* 1614. [DIS- 6.] To unsheathe. (Also *intr.* for *refl.*)

†**Disshiˑp**, *v. rare.* 1557. [DIS- 6.] To remove from a ship.

†**Disshiˑver**, *v.* 1586. [DIS- 1.] To shatter or become shattered –1638.

Disshroud (disˌʃrauˑd), *v. rare.* 1577. [DIS- 6 or 7 a.] To deprive of a shroud; *fig.* to expose.

Dissidence (diˑsidĕns). 1656. [ad. L. *dissidentia*, f. *dissidere* (DIS- 1).] Disagreement (in opinion, character, etc.); difference, dissent.

Dissenting for the mere pleasure of d. 1891. var. †**Diˑssidency.**

Dissident (diˑsidĕnt). 1534. [ad. L. *dissidentem*; see DISSIDENCE.]

A. *adj.* Disagreeing (in opinion, character, etc.); at variance, different. Const. *from.*

A forme of prayer d. from the common 1617. D. ejected Priests CARLYLE.

B. *sb.* One who disagrees; a dissentient 1789; a dissenter 1790.

The scruples of such dissidents from public opinion are real SCOTT.

Dissight (dissəiˑt, disəiˑt). 1710. [DIS- 9.] An unsightly object, an eyesore. So **Dissiˑghtly** *a.* unsightly (*rare*).

Dissilient (dissiˑliĕnt), *a.* 1656. [ad. L. *dissilientem*, pr. pple. of *dissilire*, f. DIS- 1 + *salire.*] Leaping asunder, springing apart; *spec.* in *Bot.* bursting open with force, as, a *d. pericarp.* Hence **Dissiˑliency**, d. quality (*rare*).

†**Dissiliˑtion.** 1660. [f. L. *dissilire*; cf. prec.] A leaping or springing apart; a bursting –1685.

Dissimilar (disiˑmilăɹ), *a.* (*sb.*) 1621. [DIS- 10.] 1. Not similar or alike; different in appearance, properties, or nature; unlike. Const. *to* (occas. *from, with*). 2. *sb.* (in *pl.*) Dissimilar things 1654.

1. A new picture..it was d. to all the others C. BRONTË. Hence **Dissimilaˑrity**, unlikeness, difference; an instance of this. **Dissiˑmilarly** *adv.*

Dissimilate (disiˑmileᶦt), *v. rare.* 1841. [f. DIS- 4 + L. *similis*, after ASSIMILATE.] To make or become unlike. Hence **Dissiˑmilative** *a.* tending to or causing dissimilation; *spec.* in *Biol.* katabolic.

Dissimilation (disimilēˑʃən). 1830. [f. prec., after *assimilation.*] The action of making, or process of becoming, unlike: opp. to ASSIMILATION. *spec.* a. *Philol.* The differentiation of two identical sounds occurring near each other in a word, by change of one of them, as in It. *pelegrino* from L. *peregrinus.* b. *Biol.* Katabolism.

Dissimile (disiˑmili), *sb.* 1682. [a. L., after SIMILE.] The opposite of 'simile'; a comparison or illustration by contrast.

Dissimilitude (disimiˑlitiud). 1532. [ad. L. *dissimilitudo.*] 1. The condition of being unlike; unlikeness, dissimilarity; diversity; an instance of this. †2. *Rhet.* A comparison by contrast –1751.

1. D. of life and diuersitie of maners 1564.

†**Dissiˑmulate**, *a.* 1450. [ad. L. *dissimulatus*, pa. pple. of *dissimulare.*] Dissembled, feigned, pretended –1653.

Dissimulate (disiˑmiuleᶦt), *v.* 1533. [f. L. *dissimulat-* ppl. stem; see prec.] †1. *trans.* To pretend not to see, pass over (*rare*). 2. To conceal or disguise under a feigned appearance; to dissemble 1610. Also *intr.* Hence **Dissi·mulative** *a.* given to or marked by dissimulation (*rare*). **Dissi·mulator,** a dissembler.

Dissimulation (disimiulē·ʃən). ME. [a. OF., ad. L. *dissimulationem*; see next.] The action of dissimulating; concealment under a feigned semblance; feigning, hypocrisy; an instance of this (*arch.*).

Let loue be without d. *Rom.* xii. 9. Simulation is a Pretence of what is not, and D. a Concealment of what is STEELE. Smooth D., skilled to grace A devil's purpose with an angel's face COWPER.

†Dissi·mule, *v.* ME. [a. OF. *dissimuler*, ad. L. *dissimulare* (DIS- 4). Hence DISSEMBLE, q.v.] 1. *trans.* = DISSEMBLE *v.* 1-5. -1636. ¶ 2. In the later Wycliffite version repr. *dissimulare* of the Vulgate, where the sense of the original is 'linger' and 'leave off'. Hence **†Dissi·muler, †-our** = DISSEMBLER.

†Dissi·new, *v. rare.* 1640. [DIS- 7 a.] To deprive of sinew or vigour -1641.

†Di·ssipable, *a.* 1603. [ad. L. *dissipabilis.*] That can be dissipated -1710. Hence **†Dissipabi·lity.**

Dissipate (di·sipeᶦt), *v.* 1532. [f. L. *dissipat-*, ppl. stem of *dissipare*, f. DIS- 1 + arch. vb. *supare, sipare* to throw. Cf. F. *dissiper.*] 1. *trans.* To scatter; to cause to go off in all directions; to disperse 1534. Also *intr.* (for *refl.*). †2. *trans.* To scatter in defeat -1789. 3. To dispel by dispersion (mist, clouds, etc.); to cause to disappear 1532. Also *fig.* and *transf.* b. *intr.* To pass away by dispersion; to disappear 1626. 4. *trans.* To disintegrate or dissolve completely, undo, annul 1555. Also *intr.* (for *refl.*). 5. *trans.* To scatter or consume wilfully (money, faculties); to squander 1682. 6. *trans.* To distract by variety of objects; to fritter away 1683. 7. *intr.* To practise dissipation; to engage in frivolous or (now usually) dissolute pleasures 1836.

3. They wil clerely d. and discusse the myst MORE. [It] has dissipated the Fears of that People STEELE. *intr.* Libels neglected quickly..disipat to ayr HOWELL. 4. Shall the Heavens and Earth be wholly dissipated and destroyed RAY. 6. Thought may be dissipated into a number of aperçus 1883. Hence **†Di·ssipate, Di·ssipated** *ppl. adjs.* dispersed, scattered, wasted, frittered away; given to dissipation, dissolute. **Di·ssipater,** one who or that which dissipates. **Di·ssipative** *a.* tending to d. **Dissipati·vity** (in *Physics*), a quantity expressing the rate of dissipation of energy; called also *dissipation-function.*

Dissipation (disipē·ʃən). 1545. [ad. L. *dissipationem.*] †1. The action of dissipating or dispersing; dispersed condition -1760. 2. The wasting of a substance, or form of energy, through continuous dispersion 1615. 3. Complete disintegration or dissolution 1597. 4. Squandering, waste 1639. 5. Distraction of the mental faculties from concentration on serious subjects; diversion, amusement; also with *a* and *pl.* 1733. 6. Waste of the moral and physical powers by vicious indulgence in pleasure; intemperate or dissolute mode of living 1784.

1. Foule d. follow'd, and forc't rout MILT. *P. L.* VI. 598. 3. The d. of the whole frame of Nature into disjoynted dust H. MORE. 4. There had been such a d. of treasure BURNET. 5. Change of place..inevitably produces d. of mind JOHNSON. 6. He died young, worn out by d. 1894.

†Di·ssite, *a.* 1600. [ad. L. *dissitus.*] Situated apart -1657.

Britaine..Far d. from this world of ours HOLLAND.

†Disslander, var. of DISCLANDER.

Dissociable (see below), *a.* 1603. [In sense 1, f. DIS- 10; in senses 2 and 3, f. L. *dissociare.*] 1. (dissōu·ʃăb'l) The reverse of sociable, unsociable. 2. That tends to separate. [= L. *dissociabilis*] (*rare*) 1835. 3. (disōu·ʃiăb'l) Separable 1833.

1. They came in two by two..matched in the most d. Manner ADDISON. Hence **Dissociabi·lity** (*rare*), **Disso·ciableness,** unsociableness.

Dissocial (dissōu·ʃăl), *a.* 1762. [DIS- 10.] Disinclined or unsuitable for society; unsocial.

Hatred and other d. passions KAMES. Hence **Disso·cialize** *v.* to render d.

Disso·ciate, *ppl. a. rare.* 1548. [ad. L. *dissociatus.*] Dissociated.

Dissociate (disōu·ʃiˌeᶦt), *v.* 1611. [f. L. *dissociat-*, ppl. stem of *dissociare* (DIS- 1).] 1. *trans.* To cut off from association or society; to sever, disunite. Const. *from.* b. *Chem.* To separate the elements of, *spec.* by heat 1869. 2. *intr.* (for *refl.*) To cease to associate 1866.

1. Our very wants and desires, which first bring us together, have a tendency likewise to d. us TUCKER. Hence **Disso·ciative** *a.* causing dissociation or decomposition.

Dissociation (disōuʃiˌē·ʃən, -siˌē·ʃən). 1611. [ad. L. *dissociationem*; cf. F. *dissociation.*] 1. The action of dissociating or the condition of being dissociated; disunion. 2. *Chem.* Decomposition, *spec.* by the action of heat. Hence *d.-point*, the temperature at which such decomposition takes place.

1. It will add infinitely to the d., distraction, and confusion of these confederate republics BURKE.

Dissoluble (di·sǫliub'l, disǫ·liub'l), *a.* 1534. [ad. L. *dissolubilis*, f. *dissolvere*; cf. F. *dissoluble.*] 1. Separable into elements or atoms; capable of being destroyed by complete decomposition. †2. Soluble in a liquid -1809. 3. Capable of being loosened, unfastened, or (*fig.*) undone 1600. 4. That may be dissolved, as an assembly 1642.

1. How then should the Gods Being atomic not be d. TENNYSON. Hence **Dissolubi·lity, †Disso·lubleness,** the quality of being d.

Dissolute (di·sŏlᶦut), *a.* (*sb.*) ME. [ad. L. *dissolutus*, pa. pple. of *dissolvere*; cf. F. *dissolu.*] †1. Disjoined, disunited -1651. †2. Relaxed, enfeebled -1816. †3. Slack, negligent, remiss -1619. 4. †Loose, wanton -1713; lawless in style (now *rare*) 1566. 5. Lax in morals, loose-living; licentious, profligate, debauched. The current sense. 1513. 6. *sb.* A dissolute person (*rare*) 1608.

4. The d. dulness of English Flamboyant RUSKIN. 5. Belial, the dissolutest Spirit that fell MILT. *P. R.* II. 150. Hence **Di·ssolute-ly** *adv.*, **-ness.**

Dissolution (disŏlᶦū·ʃən). ME. [a. F., or ad. L. *dissolutionem.*] 1. Separation into parts or constituent elements; disintegration, decomposition. 2. Reduction from the solid to the fluid form; liquefaction; formerly, also, = fusion 1598. 3. Solution in a liquid. ? *Obs.* 1558; †result of this; a solution -1707. †4. Hurtful relaxation or weakening -1683. 5. The condition of being loose from due restraint; †excess; laxity of behaviour or morals; dissoluteness (*arch.*) ME. †b. with *pl.* An instance of this -1653. 6. The relaxation of any tie, bond, or binding power 1534. 7. The breaking up of an assembly, association, or constituted body of persons 1535. 8. Termination of life; death, decease 1522. 9. The action of bringing or condition of being brought to an end 1528. †10. Solution (of a question, etc.) (*rare*) 1549.

1. The d. of flesh, skin, and bones BUTLER. 2. The d. of the great snow FULLER. 6. The cause of the dissolucion of their amitie and league HALL. 7. A d. is the civil death of the parliament BLACKSTONE. The d. of the monasteries LD. BROUGHAM, of the Huguenot party GREEN. 8. The disolucion and seueraunce of the soule fro the body MORE. 9. That realm were like to come to d. GARDINER. Hence **Dissolu·tionism,** the doctrine of dissolutionists. **Dissolu·tionist,** one who advocates d.

Dissolutive (di·sŏlᶦutiv), *a.* Now *rare.* ME. [f. *dissolut-* ppl. stem + -IVE.] 1. Having the property of dissolving. 2. Pertaining to, or of the nature of, dissolution 1886.

Disso·lvable, *a.* Also **-ible.** 1541. [f. DISSOLVE *v.* + -ABLE: repl. (in part) DISSOLUBLE.] 1. Capable of being separated into its elements; decomposable. 2. Capable of being liquefied or melted. ? *Obs.* 1653. 3. Of a connexion, society, etc.: Terminable, destructible 1681.

1. You are but men..and your substance but d. clay 1661. 2. D., by Water, or by Fire 1668. 3. A mere partnership, d...by mutual consent LOWELL. Hence **Dissolvabi·lity, Disso·lvableness.**

†Disso·lvative, *a. rare.* 1577. [f. next + -ATIVE.] a. Having the property of dissolving. b. That tends to dissolve readily -1580.

Dissolve (dizǫ·lv), *v.* ME. [ad. L. *dissolvere* (DIS- 1).]

I. *trans.* 1. To put asunder the parts of; to reduce to its formative elements; to disintegrate, decompose. (Now *rare.*) 2. To liquefy by means of heat, moisture, etc.; to fuse (now *rare*); to melt; to melt (*in* something), make a SOLUTION of ME. Also *fig.* †3. To relax, enfeeble -1563. 4. To loosen, release (*lit.* and *fig.*) (*arch.*) ME. †5. To release from life; usu. in *pass.* to die, depart -1736. 6. To cause to vanish; to bring to nought, destroy ME. †7. *Med.* To dissolve (humours), reduce (swellings), assuage (pains, etc.) -1657. 8. To break up, dismiss, disperse; to terminate the existence of (now *esp.* of Parliament) 1494. Also *ellipt.* = *d. parliament.* 1868. 9. To undo (a tie, etc.); to bring to an end (a relation) ME.; †to sunder -1611. 10. To destroy the authority, force, or influence of; to annul, abrogate 1526. 11. To solve (a question, etc.) 1549. 12. *Cinematogr.* To cause (a picture) to fade away. Also *intr.* 1912.

2. Before the Sunne hath..dissolved the yce HAKLUYT. *fig.* Dissolv'd in Pleasures PENN, tears 1800, Speech CARLYLE. 4. As the soft touch dissolved the virgin zone THOMSON. 6. Each gay phantom was dissolv'd in air SIR W. JONES. 8. To d. his armye HALL, Parliament 1548, a religious house 1586. 9. To d. a jointure BLACKSTONE, marriage LANE, partnership (*mod.*). 10. To frustrate and d. these magic spells MILT. *Sams.* 1149.

II. *intr.* 1. To become disintegrated; to vanish gradually, come to an end ME. 2. To become liquefied; to fuse; to melt; to melt (*in* something), forming a SOLUTION 1450. Also *fig.* 3. Of an assembly, etc.: To break up; to disperse; to lose its corporate character 1513. 4. To lose its binding force 1611.

1. The great Globe it selfe, Yea, all which it inherit, shall dissolue *Temp.* IV. i. 154. 2. While Mountain Snows d. against the Sun DRYDEN. *fig.* I am almost ready to dissolue (= faint away), Hearing of this *Lear* V. iii. 203. 4. The charme dissolues apace SHAKS. Hence **Disso·lve** *sb.* (cf. sense 12 above). **Disso·lver. Disso·lvingly** *adv.*

Dissolvent (dizǫ·lvĕnt). 1646. [ad. L. *dissolventem*; see prec.]

A. *adj.* Having the power to dissolve; solvent.

B. *sb.* One who or that which dissolves. 1. *spec.* A substance having power to dissolve other substances; a solvent, a menstruum; †formerly, in *Med.*, a substance which dissolves morbid concretions, etc. 1646. 2. *gen.* and *fig.* 1835.

1. Fire—the only Catholic D. RAY. 2. Wine is the great d. of distrust 1835.

Dissonance (di·sŏnăns). 1571. [ad. L. *dissonantia.* Cf. F. *dissonance.*] 1. The quality or fact of being dissonant; an inharmonious or harsh sound or combination of sounds; a DISCORD 1597. *spec.* in *Mus.* A combination of tones causing beats (cf. BEAT *sb.*[1]); also, a note which in combination with others produces a harsh effect 1660. 2. Want of concord or harmony (between things) 1571.

1. The..roar..filled the air with barbarous d. MILT. *Comus* 548. So **†Di·ssonancy.**

Dissonant (di·sŏnănt), *a.* (*sb.*) 1490. [a. F., or ad. L. *dissonantem*, pr. pple. of *dissonare*, f. DIS- 1 + *sonare.*] 1. Disagreeing or discordant in sound, inharmonious; harsh-sounding 1573. 2. Disagreeing, discordant, different, in any respect. Const. *from, to* (rarely *with*). 1490. 3. *sb.* A harsh sound of speech 1579.

1. D. and iarring dittyes G. HARVEY. 2. Opinions not altogether d. from the Scriptures PURCHAS. The interests..before that time jarring and d., were..adjusted BURKE. Hence **Di·ssonantly** *adv.*

†Di·ssonate, *a.* 1548. [ad. L. *dissonatus.*] = DISSONANT -1781.

Disspirit, obs. f. DISPIRIT.

†Dissta·te, *v.* 1605. [DIS- 7.] To remove from its state; to deprive of state -1647.

Dissuade (diswē·d), *v.* 1513. [ad. L. *dissuadere* (DIS- 1); cf. F. *dissuader.*] 1. *trans.* To give advice against. ? *Obs.* 2. To advise or exhort (a person) against; to dehort (*from*). ? *Obs.* 1534. 3. To draw a person *from* a course or action by suasion 1576.

1. My friends..With mild entreaties my design d. POPE. 2. Some disswaded him to hunt that day; but he resolved to the contrary CAMDEN. 3. I have tried what is possible to d. him MISS BURNEY. Hence **Dissua·der,** one who dissuades.

Dissuasion (diswē·ʒən). 1526. [ad. L. *dissuasionem*; see prec.] The action, or an act, of dissuading; advice or exhortation against something; dehortation.

Ev'n thy Dissuasions me persuade COWLEY.

Dissuasive (diswē·siv). 1609. [f. L. *dissuas-*, ppl. stem of *dissuadere*; see -IVE.]

A. *adj.* Tending to dissuade; dehortatory; as, *d. ejaculations.*

B. *sb.* A dissuasive speech or argument; that which tends or is intended to dissuade 1629. Hence **Dissua·sive-ly** *adv.*, **-ness.**

†**Dissua·sory**, *a.* and *sb.* 1555. [f. L. *dissuasor.*] = DISSUASIVE –1844.

Dissue, var. of DIZZUE.

Dissunder (dissʊ·ndəɹ), *v.* 1580. [DIS- 1 or 5.] *trans.* To sunder, sever, dissever.

Th' Aethiops, far dissunder'd in their seat CHAPMAN.

†**Disswee·ten**, *v.* 1622. [DIS- 6.] *trans.* To deprive of sweetness –1667.

Dissyllabic, -able, etc.; see DISYLLABIC, -ABLE, etc.

Dissymmetric, -al (dissime·trik, -ăl), *a.* 1867. [DIS- 10.] **a.** The opposite of symmetrical. **b.** Symmetrical, but in opposite directions, like the two hands.

Dissymmetry (dis,si·mĕtri). 1849. [DIS-9.] **a.** Lack or absence of symmetry. **b.** Symmetry between two objects, disposed in opposite directions, such as the two hands, etc.

Distad (di·stæ̆d), *adv.* 1803. [f. DIST(ANT) + *-ad*; cf. DEXTRAD.] In the direction of the end or distal part of a limb, etc.

Distaff (di·stɑf). Pl. **distaffs**, †**distaves.** [OE. *distæf*, for *dis-* or *dise-stæf*; *dis* or *dise* is app. = LG. *diesse* a bunch of flax on a distaff, the second element the sb. STAFF.] **1.** A cleft staff about 3 feet long, on which, in the ancient mode of spinning, wool or flax was wound. **2.** Used as the type of women's work ME.; hence, for the female sex, female authority; also, the female branch of a family; a female heir 1494.

1. Wymen comynly do not entremete but to spynne on the distaf CAXTON. Phr. †*To have tow on one's d.*: to have work in hand. **2.** Some say the Crozier, some say the Distaffe was too busie HOWELL.

attrib. and *Comb.*, as **d. side**, the female branch of a family; **distaff's** or **St. Distaff's day**, the day after the Feast of the Epiphany, on which day (Jan. 7) women resumed their spinning after the holidays; also called *rock-day*, a d. being called a *rock*; **d. thistle**, a name of *Carthamus lanatus* (*Cirsium lanatum*), from its woolly flowering stems.

Distain (distēⁱ·n), *v. arch.* ME. [a. OF. *desteindre* (stem *desteign-*), mod.F. *déteindre*, Com. Rom. f. *des-*, DIS- 1 + L. *tingere.*] **1.** *trans.* To imbue or stain with a colour different from the natural one; to discolour, dye. **2.** *transf.* and *fig.* To defile; to sully, dishonour ME.

1. The tears that so d. my cheeks MARLOWE. **2.** A soul distain'd by earth and gold SHENSTONE.

Distal (di·stăl), *a.* 1808. [f. DIST(ANT) + -AL, after *dorsal*, etc.] *Anat.* Situated away from the centre of the body, or from the point of origin (said of the distant part or of the extremity of a limb or organ); terminal. Opp. to *proximal.* Also *transf.* Hence **Di·stally** *adv.*

Distance (di·stăns), *sb.* ME. [a. OF. *destance, distance*, ad. L. *distantia*, f. *distantem* pr. pple., DISTANT.]

†**I.** [from OF. *destance* discord, quarrel.] The condition of being at variance; discord; dispute, debate –1752; with *a* and *pl.* –1666.

They were in suche vnyte, that there was no dystaunce amonge them LD. BERNERS.

†**II.** [from L. *distantia* 'difference'.] Difference, diversity –1556.

III. [f. L. *distantia*, F. *distance*, in the sense of 'being apart in space'.] **1.** The fact or condition of being far off in space; remoteness 1594. **2.** The space lying between any two objects; the space to be passed over before reaching an object; an intervening space ME. **3.** Techn. applications of 2. **a.** *Mil.* The space between man and man when standing in rank; also that between the ranks 1635. **b.** *Fencing.* A set space to be kept between two combatants 1592. **c.** *Racing.* The space measured back from the winning-post which a horse must have reached, in a heat-race, when the winning horse has covered the whole course, in order not to be 'distanced' 1674. †**d.** *Mus.* An interval –1797. **e.** See also FOCAL *d.*, POLAR *d.*, ZENITH *d.* **4.** *fig.* Remoteness in likeness, relationship, allusion, degree, or the like; 'ideal disjunction' (J.) 1667. **5.** Remoteness in intercourse 1597: hence **a.** Aloofness, excessive reserve 1660; **b.** Deference 1689. **6.** *ellipt.* A point or place at a distance, the region in the distance 1782. **b.** *Painting*, etc. The distant part of a landscape 1706. **7.** *ellipt.* The 'space' of time between two events ME.

1. 'Tis d. lends enchantment to the view CAMPBELL. **2** Within jumping d. TYNDALL. **3.** In these times you stand on d.: your Passes, Stoccado's, and I know not what *Wint. T.* II. i. 233. **4.** The mistake..I conceive to have been an effect of mental d. MAINE. **5.** With safest d. I mine honour shielded SHAKS. A.. courteous Prince..without state or d. 1660. I hope your modesty Will know, what d. to the crown is due DRYDEN. Phr. *To keep one's d.* **6.** Viewed from a d. COWPER. A trumpet in the d. pealing news TENNYSON. Phr. *Middle d.* (in *Painting*): the part of a landscape midway between the foreground and the remote region. **7.** An apprehension not to be mentioned, even at this d. of time, without shame 1849.

Comb.: **d.-flag** (*Racing*), a flag held by the man who is stationed at the d.-post; **-judge**, a judge stationed at the **d.-post**, a post (or flag) placed at the fixed 'distance' in front of the winning-post in a heat-race, to note what horses are 'distanced', through failing to reach this before the winner passes the winning-post.

Di·stance, *v.* 1578. [f. prec. sb.] **1.** *trans.* To place at a distance; to eloign. **2.** To make to appear distant 1695. †**3.** *intr.* To be distant (*rare*) –1658. **4.** *trans.* To outstrip or leave behind in a race. Also *fig.* 1642. **b.** *Racing.* To beat by a distance; see DISTANCE *sb.* III. 3 c. 1674.

1. This insight..distances those who share it from those who share it not EMERSON. **2.** Mountains, which the ripe Italian air distances with a bloom like that on unplucked grapes LOWELL. **4.** [He] had distanced all his competitors LEVER.

Distanced (di·stănst), *ppl. a.* 1644. [f. prec.] †**1.** Put at a distance; remote –1672. **2.** Left behind, outstripped as in a race 1713. **b.** *Racing.* Beaten by a distance; see DISTANCE *sb.* III. 3. 1737.

Distancy (di·stănsi). *rare.* 1628. [ad. L. *distantia.*] Distantness.

Distant (di·stănt), *a.* ME. [a. F., ad. L. *distantem*, pr. pple. of *distare* to stand apart.] **1.** Separate or apart in space. **2.** Widely separated; far apart, not close together 1548. **3.** Standing, lying, or taking place afar off; remote 1590. **4.** Far apart or remote in time 1603. **5.** *transf.* and *fig.* Remote in relations other than those of space and time 1538. †**6.** Different –1710. **7.** Reserved in intercourse; standing aloof; not intimate 1709.

1. One board had two tenons, equally d. one from another *Exod.* xxxvi. 22. **2.** D. from thy blest abode 1760. **3.** Earth's d. ends POPE. D. vision KINGSLEY. **4.** Written..at d. times BERKELEY. **5.** I haven't the most d. idea SHERIDAN. By d. analogy ARGYLL. Not a sister, but a more d. kinswoman FREEMAN. **7.** The d. Behaviour of the Prude STEELE.

So †**Dista·ntial** *a.* distant; differing. Hence **Di·stant-ly** *adv.*, **-ness.**

Distaste (distēⁱ·st), *sb.* 1598. [DIS- 9: prob. as tr. It. *disgusto.*] **1.** Disrelish or dislike of food or drink; nausea. Now *rare.* **2.** Disinclination, dislike 1598. †**3.** Unpleasantness; annoyance, discomfort –1711. †**4.** Offence –1731. †**5.** Mutual aversion, quarrel –1697.

2. An aversion more resembling a d. than a conviction J. MARTINEAU. **3.** Prosperity is not without many Feares and Distastes BACON.

Distaste (distēⁱ·st), *v.* Now *rare.* 1586. [DIS- 6; see prec.] **1.** *trans.* To have no taste for, disrelish, dislike; to regard with aversion or displeasure. †**2.** To offend the taste of; to disgust –1678. Also †*absol.* or *intr.* **3.** *trans.* To displease, offend 1597; †*intr.* to cause displeasure or offence; to be distasteful –1654. †**4.** *trans.* (as f. DIS- 7 a + TASTE *sb.*) To destroy or spoil the taste or savour of –1650.

1. Distasting wholesome meat well dressed FULLER. [He] should d. the society of his class FOSTER. **2.** Let it [the Physicke] distast me so it heale me 1636. Poysons, Which at the first are scarce found to d. *Oth.* III. iii. 327. **3.** Yet loth in anything to d. the King SIR T. HERBERT. Hence †**Dista·stive** *a.* feeling or expressing distaste; disgusting, offensive; also as *sb.* †**Dista·sture**, loathing of food; nausea; vexation.

Distasteful (distēⁱ·stfŭl), *a.* 1607. [f. DISTASTE *sb.*] **1.** Disagreeable to the taste; causing disgust; nasty 1611. **2.** Causing dislike; disagreeable, offensive 1607. †**3.** Full of dislike; showing dislike; malevolent –1646.

1. The green d. fruit DRYDEN. **2.** D. truth 1669. **3.** After distastefull lookes.. They froze me into Silence *Timon* II. ii. 220. Hence **Dista·steful-ly** *adv.*, **-ness.**

Distemonous (dəistī·mŏnəs), *a.* 1883. [f. Gr. δι-, DI-² + στήμων.] *Bot.* Having two stamens; = DIANDROUS.

Distemper (diste·mpəɹ), *v.*¹ Now *rare.* ME. [f. med.L. **distemperare* (DIS- 4).] †**1.** *trans.* To temper improperly; to disturb or derange the due proportion of. (ME. only.) **2.** To disturb or disorder the humour (formerly, the due proportion of the four humours), temper, or feelings of; to render ill-humoured or ill at ease; to upset. (Now *rare.*) ME. **3.** To disorder or derange the bodily or mental condition of; to render unhealthy or diseased; to sicken ME. †**b.** *spec.* To intoxicate –1679. **4.** *transf.* and *fig.* To disorder the condition of; to derange 1494. †**5.** To deprive (a metal) of 'temper' (*rare*) 1795.

3. Vainely distempering himselfe about idle and frivolous questions BP. HALL. **4.** This variable composition of mans bodie hath made it as an Instrument easie to d. BACON. **5.** The malignancie of my fate, might perhaps d. yours *Twel. N.* II. i. 5.

Diste·mper, *v.*² ME. [ad. OF. *destemprer, -tremper* = med.L. *distemperare*, f. DIS- 1 or 5 + L. *temperare.*] †**1.** *trans.* To treat with water or other liquid; to dilute; to steep –1667. **2.** *transf.* and *fig.* To dilute; to allay (*arch.*) 1592. **3.** *Painting.* To paint in distemper 1873.

2. Jealousy.. Distempering gentle Love in his desire, As air and water do abate the fire SHAKS.

Distemper (diste·mpəɹ), *sb.*¹ 1555. [f. DISTEMPER *v.*¹: partly after TEMPER *sb.*] †**1.** 'A disproportionate mixture of parts'; distempered condition –1644. †**2.** A disordered condition of the air, climate, weather, etc.; inclemency –1856. **3.** Derangement of the 'humour' or 'temper' (formerly regarded as due to disturbance in the bodily 'humours'; cf. TEMPER, TEMPERAMENT); ill temper, ill humour; disaffection. (Now assoc. w. sense 4.) 1555. **4.** Deranged condition of the body or mind (formerly regarded as due to disproportion in the four humours); ill health, illness, disease 1598; with *a* and *pl.* 1648. **b.** *spec.* A catarrhal affection of dogs. Also applied to other diseases of animals. 1747. †**c.** Intoxication –1650. **5.** *transf.* and *fig.* Derangement, or disorder (*esp.* in a state) 1605.

2. Exposed to theeves, vermin, and distempers of weather 1655. **3.** Good my Lord, what is your cause of d. *Haml.* III. ii. 351. **4.** Eccentricity Nowise amounting to d. BROWNING. Such plenty of wine as to cause d. 1607. **5.** In these sad times of our Civill Distempers LILLY.

Diste·mper, *sb.*² 1632. [f. DISTEMPER *v.*²] *Painting.* A method of painting in which the colours are mixed with some glutinous substance soluble in water, executed usually upon a ground of chalk or plaster mixed with gum (*d.-ground*): mostly used in scene-painting and in the decoration of walls. Also applied to the pigments and to the ground.

†**Diste·mperance.** ME. [a. OF. *destemprance, -trempance*, f. DIS- 4 + L. *temperantia.*] = DISTEMPERATURE –1620.

Diste·mperate, *a. arch.* ME. [ad. med.L. *distemperatus*, f. DIS- 4 + L. *temperatus*, pa. pple. of *temperare.*] †**1.** Of the air or elements: Not temperate –1647. †**2.** Of the bodily 'humours': Not properly tempered; diseased; ill-conditioned –1658. **3.** Immoderate; intemperate. ?*Obs.* 1557. Hence †**Diste·mperately** *adv*

Distemperature (diste·mpĕrătiŭɹ). Now *arch.* 1531. [Cf. DISTEMPERATE and TEMPERATURE.] **1.** Distempered condition of the air or elements; inclemency, unwholesomeness. **2.** Distempered condition of the 'humours'; disorder, ailment 1533. **3.** Disturbance of mind or temper 1571. Also *transf.* and *fig.* **4.** Excess (*esp.* of heat or cold; cf. sense 1); intemperance 1572.

1. The temperature or d. of the regions ELYOT. **2.** A huge infectious troope Of pale distemperatures *Com. Err.* v. i. 82. **3.** What I uttered through the d. of my passion WARBURTON.

†**Diste·mperment.** 1582. [f. DISTEMPER *v.*¹ + -MENT.] Distempered condition (of the air or humours) –1661.

†**Diste·mperure.** ME. [a. OF. *destemprure.*] = DISTEMPERATURE.

Distend (diste·nd), *v.* ME. [ad. L. *distendere* (DIS- 1).] †**1.** *trans.* To stretch asunder; to spread out. Also *fig.* –1834. †**2.** *intr.* To stretch out, extend –1638. **3.** *trans. spec.* To swell out or enlarge by pressure from within, as a bladder; to expand, dilate by stretching 1650. Also *transf.* and *fig.* **4.** *intr.* To increase in bulk by internal stretching; to swell out, expand 1667.

3. May thy Cows their burden'd Bags d. DRYDEN.

4. Now his heart Distends with pride MILT. *P. L.* I. 573. †**Diste·ndible** *a.* capable of being distended.

Distensible (diste·nsĭb'l), *a.* 1828. [f. L. *distens-*, *distendere* + -IBLE.] Capable of being distended or dilated. Hence **Distensibi·lity**, d. quality.

Distension (diste·nʃən). 1607. [a. F., or ad. L. *distensionem*, var. of *distentionem.*] 1. The action of distending; distended condition; expansion by stretching or swelling out. 2. Extension; straining, racking. ? *Obs.* 1625.

Distensive (diste·nsiv), *a. rare.* 1836. [f. L. *distens-* ppl. stem + -IVE.] Distensible.

†**Diste·nt**, *sb.* 1613. [ad. L. *distentus*, f. ppl. stem of *distendere.*] Distension; breadth –1659.

Distent (diste·nt), *ppl. a.* 1590. [ad. L. *distentus.* Commonly used as a pa. pple. = DISTENDED.] †1. Extended –1773. 2. Swollen out 1605.

Distention, var. of DISTENSION.

Dister; see DISTERR.

†**Diste·rminate**, *v.* 1599. [f. L. *disterminat-*, ppl. stem of *disterminare* (DIS- 1).] To separate as a boundary does; to bound, divide –1676. So †**Diste·rminate** *a.* separated, marked off, divided. †**Distermina·tion**, separation as by boundaries; division.

†**Diste·rr**, *v.* [f. DIS- 7 c + L. *terra.*] To banish from one's country; to exile. HOWELL.

Disthene (di·sþīn). 1808. [f. Gr. δι-, DI-[2] + σθένος.] = CYANITE 1. Named from its different electrical properties in two different directions.

Disthrone (disþrōu·n), *v.* 1591. [DIS- 7 c.] To dethrone. Also *fig.* So †**Disthro·nize** *v.*

Distich (di·stik), *sb.* Pl. **distichs**, †**distiches.** 1553. [ad. L. *distichon* (also used), a. Gr. δίστιχον (neut. of δίστιχος adj.), f. δι- (DI-[2]) + στίχος row.] A couple of lines of verse, usually making complete sense; a couplet.

By far the greater number of verses in the poetry of the Old Testament consist of Distichs DRIVER.

Distich (di·stik), *a. rare.* 1788. [ad. L. *distichus*; see prec.] = DISTICHOUS.

Distichal (di·stikăl), *a.* (*sb.*) 1778. [f. L. *distichus* + -AL; see prec.] 1. *Pros.* Consisting of two lines of verse. 2. *Zool.* Applied to certain joints in the arm of a crinoid; also as *sb.* 1879.

‖**Distichiasis** (distikəi·ăsis). 1875. [mod.L., f. *distichia*, a. Gr., f. δίστιχος; see DISTICH.] *Path.* A malformation in which the eyelid has a double row of eyelashes.

Distichous (di·stikəs), *a.* 1753. [f. L. *distichus* adj.; see DISTICH.] Disposed in two opposite rows; two-ranked; formerly, sometimes = dichotomous. Hence **Di·stichously** *adv.*

Distil, distill (disti·l), *v.* Inflect. **distilled, -illing.** ME. [ad. L. *de-*, *distillare*, f. DE- I. 1 + *stillare* to drop; cf. F. *distiller.*] 1. *intr.* To trickle down or fall in drops; to exude. b. To pass or flow gently (chiefly *fig.*) 1609. c. To drip *with* 1714. 2. *trans.* To let fall or give forth in drops ME. 3. *transf.* and *fig.* To give forth or impart in minute quantities; †to instil ME. 4. To subject to the process of distillation (see DISTILLATION 3) ME.; to extract the essence of by distillation ME.; to transform or convert *into* by distillation 1636. *absol.* 1611. Also *fig.* 5. To obtain, extract, produce, or make, by distillation ME. Also *fig.* 6. *intr.* To undergo distillation; to drop, pass, or condense from the still ME. †7. To melt, dissolve (*lit.* and *fig.*) –1719.

1. Soft showers distill'd, and suns grew warm in vain POPE. My speach shall distill as the deaw *Deut.* xxxii. 2. 2. His dewie locks distill'd Ambrosia MILT. *P. L.* v. 56. 3. Distilling healing virtue into bitter waters MYERS. 4. The Water..Looke thou dystyll B. GOOGE. An herb destill'd, and drunk G. HERBERT. 5. *fig.* Siren tears, Distill'd from limbecks foul as hell within SHAKS. 7. Swords by the lightning's subtle force distill'd ADDISON. Hence **Disti·llable** *a.* capable of being distilled (*lit.* and *fig.*). So **Di·stillate** *sb.* the product of distillation. **Disti·lment**, the process, or produce, of distillation.

Distillation (distilē·ʃən). ME. [ad. L. *de-*, *distillationem.*] 1. The action of falling or flowing down drop by drop. †2. *Path.* A defluxion of rheum –1755. 3. The action of converting any substance into vapour by means of heat, and of again condensing this by means of an alembic, retort and receiver, or a still and refrigeratory; and, generally, the operation of separating by means of fire, and in closed vessels, the volatile from the fixed parts of any substance ME. Also *transf.* and *fig.* 4. *concr.* The product of distilling 1598. Also *fig.*

3. *Dry* or *destructive d.*, the decomposition of a substance by strong heat in a retort, and the collection of the volatile matters evolved, as in the destructive d. of coal in gas-making. *Fractional d.*, the separation of two or more volatile liquids having different boiling-points, so that they pass over at different temperatures and can be collected separately.

†**Di·stillator.** 1576. [f. L. *distillare.*] A distiller –1659.

Distillatory (disti·lătŏri). 1460. [? after F. *distillatoire.*] a. *adj.* Pertaining to, or employed in, distillation 1576. †b. *sb.* An apparatus for distillation; a still, etc. –1736.

Distiller (disti·ləɹ). 1577. [f. DISTIL *v.* + -ER[1].] 1. One who or that which distils; *spec.* one who extracts alcoholic spirit by distillation. Also *fig.* 2. An apparatus for distilling salt water at sea; a *Distilling condenser* 1885.

Distillery (disti·ləri). 1677. [f. prec.; see -ERY.] †1. = DISTILLATION 3. –1807. 2. The establishment or works in which the distilling of spirits is carried on 1759.

Distinct (disti·ŋkt), *ppl. a.* ME. [ad. L. *distinctus*, *distinguere*; cf. F. *distinct*, *-te.*]

A. as *pa. pple.* 1. Distinguished, differentiated –1667. †2. Divided –1526.

B. *adj.* 1. = DIFFERENT 2. ME. b. Not confounded with each other, or with something else 1674. 2. Possessing differentiating characteristics; different in quality or kind; not alike. Const. *from.* 1523. 3. Clearly perceptible or discernible by the senses or the mind; plain, definite ME. 4. Marked; decorated, adorned. (A Latinism, chiefly *poetic.*) 1596.

1. A large Feather..contains neer a million of d. parts HOOKE. The worker from the work d. was known POPE. 2. Holiness..is quite d. from vindictiveness 1836. 3. D. the shaggy mountains lie, D. the rocks SCOTT. The d. expression of thoughts TYNDALL. A d. loss to the stage 1887. 4. The place..was dight With divers flowres d. with rare delight SPENSER.

†**Disti·nct**, *v.* ME. [a. OF. *di-*, *destincter*, f. *distinct.*] = DISTINGUISH; in *pa. pple.* sometimes = DISTINCT *a.* –1583.

Distinction (disti·ŋkʃən). ME. [a. F., ad. L. *distinctionem.*] †1. Division, partition; separation –1729; punctuation; a point or stop –1637. †2. One of the parts of a whole; a division, section; a class, category –1848; class (in relation to status); rank, grade –1763. 3. The action of distinguishing; the perceiving, noting, or making a difference between things; discrimination. Also with *a* and *pl.* ME. 4. The condition of being different; difference; a difference ME. 5. The faculty of distinguishing. ? *Obs.* 1606. †6. The condition of being distinct; distinctness –1712. 7. Something that distinguishes; a distinguishing mark, quality, or characteristic ME. 8. The treating with special consideration or honour; also with *a* and *pl.* 1715. 9. Excellence or eminence that distinguishes from others; elevation of character, rank, or quality 1699.

1. The d. of chapters and verses now in use BOYLE. 3. They rend and tear the scriptures with their distinctions TINDALE. Without d. of rank or creed 1891. 4. Denying a d. of persons in the Godhead 1731. 7. The capital is the great d. of this order RICKMAN. 8. The distinctions..paid us by our betters GOLDSM. 9. Various persons of d. had come there in his train SCOTT. The book..has..d. (*mod.*). Hence **Disti·nctional** *a.* of the nature of d. (*rare*).

Distinctive (disti·ŋktiv). 1583. [f. L. *distinct-* ppl. stem (see DISTINCT) + -IVE.]

A. *adj.* 1. Having the quality of distinguishing; characteristic, distinguishing. 2. Having the power of discriminating; discriminative; discerning (*rare*) 1646. 3. Having a distinct character or position (*rare*) 1867. 4. *Hebr. Gram.* Applied to accents used, instead of stops, to separate clauses 1874.

1. Papist and Protestant now became d. names D'ISRAELI.

B. *sb.* 1. A characteristic 1816. 2. *Hebr. Gram.* A distinctive accent; see A. 4. 1874.

Hence **Disti·nctive-ly** *adv.*, **-ness.**

Distinctly (disti·ŋktli), *adv.* ME. [f. DISTINCT *a.* + -LY[2].] †1. In a distinct or separate manner; separately –1737. 2. Clearly, plainly; without confusion or obscurity ME.; in mod. use (chiefly with adjs. or adjectival phrases): Unmistakably, decidedly, indubitably 1858.

2. I remember a masse of things, but nothing d. SHAKS. An object which was d. not political 1858.

Distinctness (disti·ŋktnės). 1654. [f. as prec. + -NESS.] 1. The condition or quality of being distinct; separateness; individuality 1668. 2. The condition or quality of being clear: a. as a quality of the object 1668; b. as a quality of perception or thought 1654.

1. The soul's..incorporeity or d. from the body CUDWORTH. 2. The absence of all scientific d. of thought WHEWELL.

†**Disti·nctor.** [a. L.] One who draws distinctions. STANYHURST.

†**Disti·ngue**, *v.* [ME. *distingen*, *-guen*, a. F. *distinguer*, ad. L. *distinguere*, f. *di-*, DIS- 1 + *stinguere* orig. 'to prick or stick'.] = DISTINGUISH.

‖**Distingué** (distẽ·ŋge), *a.* 1813. [F.] Distinguished; having an air of distinction.

Distinguish (disti·ŋgwiʃ), *v.* 1561. [f. F. *distinguer*; see -ISH[2]. Cf. DISTINGUE.]

I. *trans.* 1. †To divide or separate –1729; to class, classify 1581. 2. To mark as different or distinct; to separate by distinctive marks; to differentiate 1576. b. To mark; to characterize 1600. 3. To recognize as distinct or different; to separate mentally; to perceive the difference between; to draw a distinction between 1561. †b. To make a distinction in or with respect to –1748. 4. To perceive distinctly or clearly; to 'make out'; to recognize 1593. 5. To single out; to honour with special attention (*arch.*) 1607. 6. To make conspicuous, or eminent in some respect. Now usu. *refl.* or *pass.* 1600.

1. The inhabitants were..distinguished into artisans and soldiers GOLDSM. 2. By the first [Ciuilitie] we are distinguished from bruit-beasts led by sensualitie A. V. *Transl. Pref.* 3. I can d. gold, for example, from iron BERKELEY. 4. No man could d. what he said SHAKS. *Lucr.* 1785. 6. He had distinguished himself on every frontier of the empire GIBBON.

II. *intr.* 1. To make or draw a distinction; to perceive the difference between things; to discriminate. Const. *absol.*, or (usually) with *between.* 1604. †2. *intr.* (for *refl.*) To become distinguished or differentiated (*rare*) 1649.

1. Since I could d. betwixt a Benefit, and an Iniurie *Oth.* I. iii. 314. Phr. *To d. upon* = I. 3 b.

Hence **Disti·nguisher.**

Distinguishable (disti·ŋgwiʃăb'l), *a.* 1597. [f. prec. + -ABLE.] 1. Capable of being distinguished, separated, or discriminated. 2. Capable of being divided or classified; divisible 1658. 3. Discernible, perceptible 1611. †4. Worthy of distinction; noteworthy –1824. †5. Distinctive (*rare*) 1665.

1. Whatever objects are different are d. HUME. 2. A simple idea is not d. into different ideas LOCKE. Hence **Disti·nguishably** *adv.*

Distinguished (disti·ŋgwiʃt), *ppl. a.* 1609. [f. DISTINGUISH *v.* + -ED[1].] †1. Individually distinct –1813. 2. Clearly perceived; clear; pronounced –1782. †3. Differentiated from others; special, distinctive –1813. 4. Possessing distinction; remarkable, eminent; celebrated; of high standing. (Now almost always of persons.) 1714. = DISTINGUÉ 1748.

3. Four or five d. guests, including the Conservative Premier MRS. H. WARD. Mr. Cleveland was tall and d. 1826. Hence **Disti·nguishedly** *adv.* in a d. manner; with distinction.

Disti·nguishing, *ppl. a.* 1670. [f. as prec. + -ING[2].] 1. Constituting a difference; distinctive, characteristic; sometimes, That renders distinguished 1686. 2. Discriminating 1697. †3. That confers special favour –1719.

1. Very probably I shall be ordered to hoist a D. Pendant NELSON. It is Mr. N's d. merit that [etc.] 1893. Hence **Disti·nguishingly** *adv.*

Disti·nguishment. ? *Obs.* 1586. [f. DISTINGUISH *v.* + -MENT.] 1. Distinction; also *concr.* something serving to distinguish. †2. Clear discernment 1642.

†**Disti·tle**, *v.* [DIS- 7 a.] To deprive of title. B. JONS.

‖**Di·stoma, Di·stomum.** 1851. [mod.L., f. Gr. δίστομος, -ον, double-mouthed. *Distoma* has pl. *distomata*; *distomum*, pl. *distoma.* See N.E.D.] *Zool.* A genus of digenetic *Trematoda*, parasitic worms or flukes, having two suckers (whence the name). So **Disto·matous** *a.* belonging to the genus *D.* var. **Di·stome.**

†**Disto·rt,** *ppl. a.* 1588. [ad. L. *distortus*; see next.] Distorted; wry, awry –1642.

Distort (distǭ·ɹt), *v.* 1586. [f. L. *distort-*, ppl. stem of *distorquere* (DIS- 1); cf. EXTORT.] †**1.** *trans.* To twist or wrench to one side, or out of the straight position –1720. **2.** To put out of shape or position by twisting or drawing awry; to change to an unnatural shape 1634. **3.** *fig.* To give a twist to (the mind, thought, views); to pervert (statements, facts) 1586.

1. Headlong he falls, and..Distorts his neck GAY. 2. To d. the limbs JOHNSON. A mirror which distorts the features (*mod.*). 3. Words..distorted from their common use GLANVILL. Hence **Disto·rted-ly** *adv.*, **-ness. Disto·rter. Disto·rtive** *a.* having the quality of distorting.

Distortion (distǭ·ɹʃən). 1581. [ad. L. *distortionem*; see prec. Cf. F. *distorsion.*] **1.** The action of distorting, or condition of being distorted, or twisted awry or out of shape; *spec.* a condition of the body or a limb, in which it is twisted out of the natural shape. **b.** *Math.* and *Optics.* Any change of shape not involving breach of continuity 1879. **c.** *concr.* A distorted form or image 1820. **2.** A twisting or writhing movement; a contortion 1718. **3.** The twisting or perversion of words, facts, history, etc. 1650.

1. The d. or writhing of the mouth MULCASTER. Hence **Disto·rtionist,** a caricaturist; an acrobat who distorts his body.

Distra·ct, *ppl. a. arch.* ME. [ad. L. *distractus, distrahere* (DIS- 1). See also DISTRAIT.] **1.** = DISTRACTED †1, 3, 4. †**2.** Drawn away; having the attention diverted –1553.

Distract (distræ·kt), *v.* ME. [f. L. *distract-* ppl. stem; see prec.] **1.** *trans.* To draw asunder or apart; to separate, divide (*lit.* and *fig.*) 1585. **2.** To turn aside, or in another direction; to divert. (Now only in *to d. the attention, the mind,* or the like.) ME. **3.** To draw in different directions; to perplex or confuse; to cause dissension or disorder in 1597. **4.** To throw into a state of mind in which one knows not how to act 1583. †**5.** To derange the intellect of; to drive mad –1791.

1. A kingdom..divided and distracted into factions ABP. SANDYS. 2. [This] distracts the mind from the sense of danger CARPENTER. 3. How is his tongue distracted between the Spirit of God and the spirit of gold FULLER. 4. I am at present distracted with doubts DICKENS. 5. This is a poore mad soule.. pouerty hath distracted her 2 *Hen. IV*, II. i. 116. Hence †**Distra·ct** *sb.* a distraction. QUARLES. †**Distra·ctful** *a.* fraught with distraction. **Distra·ctingly** *adv.* **Distra·ctive** *a.* of distracting quality or tendency; **-ly** *adv.*

Distracted (distræ·ktėd), *ppl. a.* 1590. [f. DISTRACT *v.* + -ED[1].] †**1.** Drawn apart; divided –1642. **2.** Driven hither and thither; agitated 1632. **3.** Mentally drawn to different objects; perplexed or confused 1633. **4.** Much confused or troubled in mind 1602. **5.** Deranged in mind; crazy, mad. Now *rare* in lit. sense. 1590.

2. A d. Sea 1725. 3. The d. affairs of that kingdom 1799. 5. It [Bethlem] was an Hospital for d. people HOWELL. Hence **Distra·cted-ly** *adv.*, **-ness.**

†**Distra·ctile,** *a.* 1709. [f. L. *distract-*, ppl. stem of *distrahere.*] Capable of being drawn asunder or stretched, extensible. (Cf. *contractile.*) –1835.

Distraction (distræ·kʃən). 1450. [ad. L. *distractionem*; cf. F. *distraction.*] †**1.** A drawing or being drawn asunder; forcible division or severance –1838. **2.** Diversion of the mind or attention (usually in adverse sense) 1450; an instance of this; something that distracts the attention 1614. **3.** The fact or condition of being drawn or pulled in different directions 1598; disorder or confusion caused by internal dissension 1642. **4.** Violent perturbation of mind 1606. †**5.** Mental derangement; craziness, insanity –1794.

2. That you may attend vpon the Lord without d. 1 *Cor.* vii. 35. 3. To settle the Peace of the Kingdom, and compose the present Distractions 1642. 4. The Princess loves you to d. 1802. 5. In the d. of this madding fever SHAKS. Hence †**Distra·ctious** *a.* fraught with distractions.

Distrain (distrē·n), *v.* ME. [a. OF. *destreindre, -aindre* (*destreign-*) :—L. *distringere* (DIS- 1). *Dis-* prob. = *de-* intensive.]

I. General senses: all *Obs.* †**1.** To compress, grasp tightly –1600. †**2.** *fig.* To hold in its grasp, as disease, etc. –1618. †**3.** To constrain or compel (a person *to do* something). (Hence the legal sense II. 1.) –1400. †**4.** To strain out, express –1634. †**5.** To tear off; to rend asunder –1590.

3. Who destreyns þe to swere ofte ME. 5. That same net..neither guile nor force might it distraine SPENSER *F. Q.* II. xii. 82.

II. *Law.* **1.** *trans.* †To constrain or force (a person) by the seizure and detention of a chattel or thing, to perform some obligation; to punish by such seizure for non-performance of an obligation. In later usage: To levy a distress upon (a person) in order by sale of the chattels to obtain satisfaction for a debt, *esp.* for arrears of rent. 1774. **2.** *absol.* or *intr.* To levy a distress. Const. *for*; also *upon, on* a person or thing. ME. **3.** *trans.* To seize (chattels, etc.) by way of distress; to levy a distress upon (*arch.*) 1531.

1. To make sommons, and distreyne for lacke of appearaunce all and every Tenant of the sayd Abbot GRAFTON. 2. To distreyne for the same rentes in the seid Maners 1512.

Hence †**Distrai·n** *sb.* distraint; restraint. **Distrai·nable** *a.* liable to distraint; capable of being distrained for. **Distrai·nee·**, one who is distrained. **Distrai·ner, -or,** one who levies a distress. **Distrai·nment,** the action of distraining; distraint.

Distraint (distrē·nt). 1730. [f. prec. vb.; cf. CONSTRAINT.] The action of distraining (in the legal sense); DISTRESS.

Payment of taxes..was enforced by d. GREEN.

Distrai·t, *a.* ME. [a. F., f. *distraire.*] †**1.** Distracted in mind –1450. **2.** Absent-minded. [from mod.F., with F. fem. *distraite.*]

Distraught (distrǭ·t), *ppl. a. arch.* ME. [var. of DISTRACT *ppl. a.*, L. *distractus*; perh. influenced by *straught.*] **1.** = DISTRACTED 4. **2.** = DISTRACTED 5. †**3.** *lit.* Pulled asunder, drawn in different directions –1642.

1. I lay awake D. with warring thoughts L. MORRIS. 2. D., and mad with terror *Rom. & Jul.* IV. iii. 49. 3. His greedy throte..in two d. SPENSER *F. Q.* IV. vii. 31.

†**Distrau·ghted,** *ppl. a.* 1572. [var. of DISTRACTED.] = DISTRACTED –1603.

†**Distrea·m,** *v. rare.* 1630. [DIS- 1.] To stream down or away –1750.

O'er that virtuous blush distreams a tear SHENSTONE.

Distress (distre·s), *sb.* ME. [a. OF. *destrece*, etc. :—late pop.L. **districtia*, f. *districtus* (cf. *angustia* from *angustus*).] **1.** The action or fact of straining or pressing tightly; strain, stress; *fig.* pressure employed to produce or (less usually) prevent action; compulsion; restraint. Now *dial.* **2.** Anguish or affliction affecting the body, spirit, or community ME. **b.** *Naut.* The condition of a ship when it requires immediate assistance 1659. **c.** Exhausted condition under extreme physical strain 1861. **3.** *Law.* The action of distraining; the legal seizure and detention of a chattel, orig. for the purpose of constraining the owner to do some act; later, in order out of the proceeds of its sale to satisfy some debt or claim, *esp.* for rent unpaid ME. **4.** The chattel or chattels thus seized ME.

2. Sorrow and hearts d. MILT. *P. L.* XII. 613. They fired four Guns as Signals of D. 1745. 3. The Phocians not meaning so to lose their Rent, made a distresse by strong hand RALEIGH. 4. If..no distresse sufficient there can be founde 1512.

Comb.: **d.-gun, -rocket,** signals of a ship in d.; **-sale,** a sale of distrained goods; **-warrant,** a warrant authorizing a d.

Distress (distre·s), *v. Pa. t.* and *pa. pple.* **distressed;** also **distrest.** ME. [a. AF. *destresser* = OF. *destresser*, orig. *destrecier* :—late L. *districtiare*, f. *districtus*; see prec.] **1.** *trans.* To subject to severe strain or pressure; to put to sore straits; now *esp.* to afflict or exhaust. Also *transf.* and *fig.* †**2.** To crush in battle –1796. **3.** To constrain by force or suffering ME. **4.** To cause pain or anxiety to; to afflict, vex, make miserable 1586. †**5.** To rob; to plunder –1568. **6.** To levy a distress upon ME.

1. Wee are troubled on euery side, yet not distressed 2 *Cor.* iv. 8. 3. Men who can neither be distressed nor won into a sacrifice of duty A. HAMILTON. Hence **Distre·ssed-ly** *adv.*, **-ness. Distre·ssingly** *adv.*

Distre·ssful, *a.* 1591. [f. DISTRESS *sb.*] **1.** Fraught with, causing, or involving distress; †gained by severe toil SHAKS. **2.** Of persons, their actions, etc.: Full of distress; sorely distressed 1601.

1. Distressefull Warre 1 *Hen. VI*, V. iv. 126, uncertainty 1860. 2. The most d. districts 1860. Hence **Distre·ssful-ly** *adv.*, **-ness.**

Distributable (distri·biutăb'l), *a.* 1654. [f. DISTRIBUTE *v.*] Capable of being distributed.

Distributary (distri·biutări). 1541. [f. L. ppl. stem *distribut-* (see DISTRIBUTE *v.*).]

A. *adj.* †**1.** Distinct, several. **2.** Distributive 1846.

B. *sb.* Something whose function is to distribute; *e.g.* branch canals 1886.

†**Distri·bute,** *pa. pple.* ME. [ad. L. *distributus.*] Distributed –1562.

Distribute (distri·biut), *v.* 1460. [f. L. *distribut-*, ppl. stem of *distribuere* (DIS- 1).] **1.** *trans.* To deal out or bestow in portions or shares among many; to allot or apportion as his share to each; †to dispense, administer (justice, etc.) –1746. **2.** To spread or disperse abroad through a space or over a surface; more loosely, to spread, scatter. (In *pass.* often with no idea of motion; cf. *diffused*, etc.) 1511. **3.** To divide and arrange 1553. **4.** To divide and place in classes or other divisions; to classify 1664; †in *Arith.* = DIVIDE –1729. **5.** To separate and allocate to distinct places. *spec.* in *Printing.* To remove (type that has been set up) from the forme, and return each letter into its proper box in the case. Also *absol.* 1615. **6.** *Logic.* To employ (a term) in its full extension –1827. **7.** *Gram.* To make distributive 1876.

1. To distribut in almes to an hundred poore men an hundred pence 1574. *absol.* Distributing to the necessity of Saints *Rom.* xii. 13. 2. To d. ink over the form 1875. 6. The middle term..must be distributed once, at least, in the premises WHATELY. Hence **Distributee·** (*Law*), a person to whom a share falls in the distribution of an intestate estate. **Distri·buter, -or,** one who distributes.

Distribution (distribiū·ʃən). ME. [a. F., ad. L. *distributionem*; see prec.] **1.** The action of distributing, dealing out, or bestowing in portions among a number; apportionment, allotment. **b.** *Pol. Econ.* (*a*) The dispersal among consumers of commodities produced: opp. to *production.* (*b*) The distribution of the aggregate produce of any society among its individual members. 1848. **2.** The action of spreading abroad or dispersing to or over every part of a space or area; the condition or mode of being so dispersed or located 1589. **3.** The orderly dividing of a mass into parts; division and arrangement; classification 1605. **4.** *Logic.* †**a.** = DIVISION –1725. **b.** More recently, The application of a term to each and all of the individuals included in its denotation or extension 1827. **5.** *Rhet.* A figure whereby an orderly division or enumeration is made of the principal qualities of a subject 1727. **6.** *Archit.* The arrangement of the parts of a building, *esp.* of the interior divisions 1727. **7.** *Printing.* The action or process of distributing type 1727. **8.** *Steam-engine.* 'The steps or operations by which steam is supplied to and withdrawn from the cylinder at each stroke of the piston; viz. admission, suppression or cutting off, release or exhaust, and compression of exhaust steam prior to the next admission' (Webster 1864).

1. All shall be set right at the final d. of things BUTLER. The laws of Production and D. MILL. The unequal d. of the fruits of industry (*mod.*). 2. This Order..has such and such a geographical d. DAVIDSON. 3. The d. of land into parishes EMERSON. Hence **Distribu·tional** *a.* **Distribu·tionist,** one who advocates a system of d. (*rare*).

Distributive (distri·biutiv). 1475. [a. F. *distributif, -ive*, ad. L. *distributivus.*]

A. 1. Having the property of distributing; dispensing, bestowing, or dealing out in portions; given to distribution. **2.** Having a tendency to diffusion 1627. **3.** Of, belonging to, or arising from, distribution 1616. **4.** Expressing distribution; *spec.* in *Gram.* Having reference to each individual of a number or class 1520. **5.** *Logic.* Referring to each individual of a class separately: opp. to *collective* 1725. **6.** *Math.* Operating upon every part in operating upon the whole; as *d. formula, function*, etc. 1855.

3. *D. justice*, one of the two divisions of Justice, according to Aristotle (the other being COMMUTATIVE). Hence, applied to that part of substantive law, which is concerned with the determination of rights. 4. *D. adjectives*, the words *each, either, neither, every. D. numerals*, in Latin, *singuli*, one by one, *bini*, two by two, etc.

B. *sb.* 1. *Gram.* A distributive word; see A. 4. 1530. †2. That which is distributed 1635. Hence **Distri·butive·ly** *adv.*, **-ness.**

†Distri·ct, *a.* 1526. [ad. L. *districtus*, pa. pple. of *distringere*; see DISTRAIN and STRICT.] Strict; severe; exact -1700. **†Distri·ctly** *adv.*

District (di·strikt), *sb.* 1611. [a. F., ad. med.L. *districtus*, f. L. *district-* ppl. stem; see DISTRAIN.] †1. *Law.* The territory under the jurisdiction of a feudal lord -1670. 2. A portion of territory marked off or defined for some special administrative or official purpose; *e. g.* a *police, postal,* or *registration d.*, etc. 3. *spec.* **a.** A division of a parish, having its own church or chapel, etc. 1818. **b.** A subdivision of a county, having an Urban or Rural District Council 1895. **c.** In British India: A division or subdivision of a province or presidency, having at its head a 'Magistrate and Collector', or 'Deputy-Commissioner' 1776. **d.** In U.S. used in specific and local senses: *e. g.* a political division = election constituency, as an *assembly, congressional,* or *senate d.* 1800. **e.** An allotted sphere of operation; *esp.* a section of a parish allotted to a lay visitor, working under the clergyman 1863. Also †*fig.* 4. A tract of country of vaguely defined limits; a region, locality, quarter 1712.

4. A purely agricultural d. (*mod.*).

attrib. and *Comb.*, in sense 'of, belonging to, or allotted to a particular d.'; as *d.-chapel*, etc.; *d.-judge*, etc. **D.-attorney** (U. S.), the local prosecuting officer of a d.; **-council,** the local council of an Urban or Rural D. as constituted by the Parish Councils Act of 1894; hence **-councillor; -court** (U.S.), a court of limited jurisdiction, having cognizance of certain causes within a d., presided over by a d.-judge; **d. visitor,** a person who does parochial work in a district under a clergyman's direction.

Di·strict, *v.* 1828. [f. prec. sb.] To divide into districts.

†Distri·ction. 1450. [a. OF., ad. L. *districtionem*; cf. DISTRICT *a.*] Strictness, severity, rigour -1660.

‖**Distringas** (distri·ŋgæs). 1467. [a. L., = 'thou shalt distrain', being the first word of the writ.] *Law.* The name of a writ bidding the sheriff distrain in certain cases.

‖**Distrix** (di·striks). 1811. [mod.L., f. Gr. δίς + θρίξ.] *Med.* A disease of the hair, in which it splits at the end.

†Distrou·ble, *v.* ME. [a. OF. *destrobler, -troubler*, f. *des-*, L. *dis-* + *trobler, troubler.*] To disturb (greatly) -1609.

†Distru·ss, *v.* ME. [ad. OF. *destrousser* (mod.F. *détrousser* to unfasten), f. *des-*, DIS- 4 + *trousser.*] *trans.* To strip or plunder; hence, to rout. Also *fig.* -1548.

Distrust (distrɒ·st), *sb.* 1513. [DIS- 9.] **a.** Absence or want of trust; lack of confidence, faith, or reliance; doubt, suspicion. **b.** Loss of credit 1667. **c.** Breach of trust 1667.

1. Eche..in such hatred and d. of other MORE. Foul d. and breach Disloyal on the part of Man MILT. Hence **†Distru·stless** *a.* confident; unsuspecting.

Distrust (distrɒ·st), *v.* ME. [DIS- 6.] †1. *intr.* with *of, in, to*: To be without confidence in -1671. 2. *trans.* To do the opposite of trusting; to withhold trust from; to put no trust in, or reliance on 1548; to entertain doubts concerning 1586. †3. with *infin. phr.* or *cl.*: To suspect -1707.

2. To d. mine eyes *Twel. N.* IV. iii. 13. He..distrusted his ministers GIBBON. Not distrusting mine health 2 *Macc.* ix. 22. I shall not d. to be acquitted of presumption MILTON. Hence **Distru·ster.**

Distrustful (distrɒ·stfŭl), *a.* 1591. [f. DISTRUST *sb.*] 1. Full of distrust in oneself or others; wanting in confidence, diffident; doubtful, suspicious, incredulous. 2. Causing or giving rise to distrust 1618.

1. Faith fortifieth the heart against d. fears TRAPP. Hence **Distru·stful-ly** *adv.*, **-ness.**

Distu·ne, *v.* 1484. [DIS- 6 or 7.] To put out of tune.

Disturb (distǭ·ɹb), *v.* [ME. *destorben, -ourben*, a. OF. *destorber*, etc.:—L. *disturbare* (DIS- 5).] 1. *trans.* To agitate and destroy (quiet, etc.); to break up the quiet, tranquillity, or rest of; to stir up, trouble, disquiet; to agitate 1599; to unsettle 1664. 2. To agitate mentally, discompose the peace of mind or calmness of; to trouble, perplex ME. 3. To interfere with the settled course or operation of; to interrupt, hinder, frustrate ME. 4. *Law.* To deprive of the peaceful enjoyment or possession *of* 1541.

1. No Nonconforming Sects d. his Reign DE FOE. An image in the lake Which rains d. SHELLEY. 2. Disturbed by a dream JOHNSON. 3. Praise..may much d. The bias of the purpose COWPER. 4. An action against a stranger for disturbing the plaintiff in his pew 1870. Hence **†Distu·rb** *sb.* an act of disturbing; a thing that disturbs; disturbance. **Distu·rbedly** *adv.*

Disturbance (distǭ·ɹbăns). ME. [a. OF. *destorbance*, etc., f. *destourber* to DISTURB.] 1. The interruption of tranquillity, peace, rest, or settled condition; agitation (physical, social, or political). 2. Interruption of mental tranquillity; discomposure ME. 3. Interference with the due course of any action or process; molestation ME. 4. *Law.* The hindering or disquieting the owners in their regular and lawful enjoyment of an incorporeal hereditament 1598.

1. Innumerable Disturbances on Earth through Femal snares MILT. The..election passed off without any d. H. WALPOLE. Storms or atmospheric disturbances 1875. 2. To any ones disturbaunce and vexation 1576. 3. That he may let the ship sail on without d. ADDISON. 4. D. of (1) franchise, (2) common, (3) ways, (4) tenure, and (5) patronage WHARTON. Hence **†Distu·rbancy,** state of d. (*rare*).

Disturbant (distǭ·ɹbănt). 1617. [ad. L. *disturbantem.*] **a.** *adj.* That disturbs; agitating. **b.** *sb.* A disturber 1865.

†Disturba·tion. 1529. [ad. L. *disturbationem.*] = DISTURBANCE -1658.

Disturber (distǭ·ɹbəɹ). ME. [a. AF. *destourbour* = OF. *destorbeor*:—L. type **disturbatorem.*] 1. A person or thing that disturbs or disquiets; one who causes tumult or disorder; a troubler. 2. *Law.* (also *disturbor.*) One who disquiets or hinders another in the lawful enjoyment of his right 1498.

1. Only one man, a common d., behaved amiss WESLEY.

Disturbor; see DISTURBER 2.

†Distu·rn, *v.* ME. [a. OF. *destourner* (DE- I. 6).] *trans.* To turn aside or away; to avert, divert, pervert -1631.

Distyle (dəi·stəil), *sb.* (*a.*) 1840. [f. DI-[2] + Gr. στῦλος column: so F. *distyle* sb.] *Archit.* A porch having two styles or columns. Also as *adj. D. in antis*: two circular pillars between two square piers.

Disulphate (dəisɒ·lfět). 1838. [DI-[2].] *Chem.* 1. A salt containing two equivalents of sulphuric acid to one of base. 2. A sulphate containing a hydrogen atom replaceable by a basic element or radical (*Cent. Dict.*). 3. A salt of disulphuric acid, a pyrosulphate 1877.

Disulphide (dəisɒ·lfəid). 1863. [DI-[2].] *Chem.* A compound in which two atoms of sulphur are united with another element or a radical, as *carbon d.*, CS_2.

Disulpho- (dəisɒ·lfo). 1868. [See DI-[2] 2 and SULPHO-.] *Chem.* In composition, denominating acids derived from two molecules of sulphurous acid. Hence **Disulpho·nic** *a.*

Disu·lphuret. 1854. [See DI-[2] 2.] = DISULPHIDE.

Disulphuric (dəisɒlfiū°·rik), *a.* 1875. *Chem.* In *d. acid*, the same as pyrosulphuric or Nordhausen sulphuric acid, $H_2S_2O_7 = 2(SO_2OH) + O$. (So called because the molecule represents two molecules of sulphuric acid deprived of one of water.)

Dis,u·niform, *a.* 1687. [DIS- 10.] Without uniformity.

Disunion (disyū·niən). 1598. [DIS- 9.] 1. Rupture of union; separation; disjunction. 2. Absence or want of union; disunited condition; dissension 1601.

1. Foreigners would..believe..that we are on the very verge of d.; but the fact is otherwise G. WASHINGTON. 2. Ages of d. and disaster CHALMERS.

Disunionist (disyū·niənist). 1846. [f. prec.] One who works for disunion; *spec.* in U.S., for a dissolution of the Union of the States.

Disunite (disyunəi·t), *v.* 1560. [DIS- 6.] 1. *trans.* To undo the union of; to disjoin 1598; to set at variance, alienate 1560. 2. *intr.* (for *refl.*) To separate oneself; to part; to fall or come asunder 1675.

1. A corner-stone, that unites things most disunited DONNE. Goe on both hand in hand, O Nations never to be dis-united MILT. 2. The several joints of the body politick do separate and d. SOUTH. Hence **Dis,uni·ter** (*rare*).

Disu·nity. 1632. [DIS- 9.] Want of unity; a state of separation; dissension.

†Dis,u·sage. 1475. [f. DISUSE *v.*, after *usage.*] = DISUSE *sb.* 1. -1712. So **Disu·sance** (*rare*).

Disuse (disyū·s), *sb.* 1552. [DIS- 9.] 1. Discontinuance of use, practice, or exercise; †unaccustomedness -1792; desuetude 1699. †2. Uselessness. FELTHAM.

1. Mary, strange they [fashions] be by reason of d. HOLLAND. Through long d. of solitude SWIFT.

Disuse (disyū·z), *v.* ME. [DIS- 6.] †1. *trans.* To disaccustom. Chiefly in *pass.* Const. *from, of, to,* or *infin.* -1791. 2. To cease to use; to discontinue the use or practice of 1487. †3. To misuse, abuse -1440.

1. With Bion long disus'd to play BLACKLOCK. 2. Which lawe by negligence is disused 1487. Hence **†Dis,u·ser,** lapse of use.

Disuti·lity. 1879. [DIS- 9.] Injuriousness, harmfulness.

Disutilize (disyū·tiləiz), *v.* 1856. [DIS- 6.] To deprive of utility, render useless.

Disvalue (disvæ·liu), *v.* Now *rare.* 1603. [DIS- 6.] To make or treat as of no value, depreciate, disparage. Hence **†Disvalua·tion, †Disva·lue** *sbs.* depreciation, disparagement.

†Disva·ntage. 1591. [DIS- 9.] = DISADVANTAGE -1619. Hence **†Disvanta·geous** *a.* disadvantageous (*rare*).

†Disve·lop, *v.* 1592. [ad. early F. *desveloper*; see DEVELOP.] To DEVELOP, display heraldically -1755.

†Disve·nture. 1612. [ad. Sp. *disventura.*] A misadventure -1718.

Disvi·sage, *v. rare.* 1603. [ad. OF. *desvisager* (DIS- 4).] To deface, disfigure.

†Disvi·sor, *v.* 1548. [DIS- 7 a.] To uncover (a visored face) -1621.

†Disvou·ch, *v.* [DIS- 6.] = DISAVOUCH. *Meas. for M.* IV. iv. 1.

†Diswa·rn, *v. rare.* 1607. [DIS- 1.] To warn off *from* -1622.

Diswa·rren, *v.* 1727. [DIS- 7 b.] To make no longer a warren.

†Diswea·pon, *v.* 1602. [DIS- 7 a.] To deprive of weapons. Also *fig.*

†Diswe·re. ME. [f. DIS- 5 + WERE doubt.] Doubt -1500.

†Diswi·t, *v.* 1599. [DIS- 7 a.] To deprive of wit -1627. Hence **Diswi·tted** *ppl. a.*

†Diswo·nt, *v.* 1600. [DIS- 6.] To render unaccustomed or unused -1635. Hence **Diswo·nted** *ppl. a.* unwonted, unaccustomed.

†Diswo·rkmanship. [DIS- 9.] Defective workmanship. HEYWOOD.

†Diswo·rship, *sb.* ME. [DIS- 9.] The withholding of esteem, regard, or honour; a disgrace, a dishonour -1644. So **†Diswo·rship** *v.* to do d. or dishonour to; to dishonour. **†Diswo·rshipful** *a.* dishonourable.

†Diswo·rth, *v. rare.* [DIS- 7 a.] To render worthless. FELTHAM.

Disyllabic, dissyllabic (dəi-, disilæ·bik), *a.* 1637. [a. F. *dissyllabique*, f. L. *disyllabus* (DI-[2]), a. Gr., after SYLLABIC. The etymological spelling *dis-* is preferred by scholars.] Consisting of two syllables. var. **†Di·syllabe, dissyllabe.** Hence **Disylla·bically, diss-** *adv*

Disyllabize, diss- (dəi-, disi·lăbəiz), *v.* 1870. [f. L. *disyllabus.*] To make disyllabic So **Disylla·bify, diss-** *v.* Hence **Disy·llabism, diss-,** disyllabic character or state.

Disyllable, dissyllable (dəi-, disi·lăb'l), *sb.* (*a.*) 1589. [f. F. *dissyllabe*; see DISYLLABIC.] A word, or metrical foot, consisting of two syllables; as *adj.* = DISYLLABIC.

Disyntheme (dəisi·nþīm). 1879. [f. DI-[2].] *Math.* A system of groups of elements, each group being so formed, that each element occurs just twice among all the groups. Thus 1·2, 2·3, 3·4, 1·4 is a duadic d.—that is, one composed of pairs.

Disyoke (disyōu·k), *v. rare.* 1847. [DIS- 6.] To unyoke; to free from the yoke.

Dit, *sb. arch.* 1590. [app. taken by Spenser

from ME. *dit* = DITE *sb.*, and mispronounced.] A ditty; see DITE *sb.*

Dit (dit), *v.* Now *Sc.* or *dial.* [OE. *dyttan* :—OTeut. **duttjan.*] *trans.* To stop up, shut; to fill *up.*

Dit, early f. DITE *sb.*

‖**Dita** (dī·tă). 1876. [Native name.] The bark of *Echites* (*Alstonia*) *scholaris.* Usu. **d.-bark.**

Dital (dəi·tăl). 1816. [f. It. *dito* finger, after *pedal.*] A thumb key, by which the pitch of a guitar- or lute-string can be raised a semitone.

†**Dita·tion.** 1612. [f. L. *ditare.*] Enrichment -1659.

Ditch (ditʃ), *sb.* [OE. *dīc*: whence also DIKE, q. v.] **1.** A long and narrow hollow dug in the ground; a trench, a fosse. **2.** *esp.* Such a hollow dug out to receive or conduct water ME.; hence, rhetorically, any watercourse or channel 1589. †**3.** Any hollow dug in the ground; a pit, cave, etc. -ME. **4.** = DIKE 4. Now only *dial.* 1568.

1. Rather a d. in Egypt Be gentle graue vnto me *Ant. & Cl.* v. ii. 57. **2.** A Caue or D., which alwaies was full of water 1582. *Comb.* **d.-water,** the stagnant or foul water that collects in a d.

Ditch (ditʃ), *v.* ME. [f. DITCH *sb.* OE. *dīcian* would give *dike.*] **1.** *intr.* To construct a ditch or ditches. **2.** *trans.* To surround with a ditch ME. **3.** To dig ditches or furrows in for purposes of drainage, etc. ME. **4.** To clean out (a ditch); to cast up and repair (the banks of a ditch) 1576. **5.** To throw into or as into a ditch, *esp.* to throw (a train) off the line or track 1877.

3. Set two men to d. the five roods HOWITT. **5.** The engine was ditched and turned on its side (*U.S.*) 1881.

Ditcher (di·tʃəɹ). ME. [f. prec.] **1.** One who makes and repairs ditches. **2.** A ditching-machine 1862.

†**Dite,** *sb.* (After 1500 only *Sc.*) ME. [a. OF. *dit* :—L. *dictum.* See also DIT *sb.*] **1.** A written or spoken composition -1578. **2.** A song, a ditty -1567. **3.** Diction. *Sc.* -1549.

†**Dite,** *v.* ME. [a. OF. *diter* :—L. *dictare,* freq. of *dicere.* Occas., aphet. f. *endite.*] **1.** *trans.* To compose or put in words; to indite. (Also *absol.*) -1603. **2.** = DICTATE -1643. **3.** To summon, indict -1775. Hence †**Di·tement,** a composition; an indictment. †**Di·ter,** one who indites or indicts.

Diter, obs. f. DIGHTER.

Ditetragonal (dəitĕtræ·gŏnăl), *a.* 1879. [DI-² 1.] *Cryst.* Having eight angles, of which the first, third, fifth, and seventh are equal, and also the second, fourth, sixth, and eighth, but those of the one set are not equal to those of the other; as a *d. pyramid* or *prism.*

†**Di-tetrahe·dral,** *a.* 1805. [DI-² 1.] *Cryst.* Having the form of a tetrahedral prism with dihedral summits.

Dithecous (dəiþī·kəs), *a.* 1880. [f. Gr. δι-, DI-² + θήκη case + -OUS.] *Bot.* Consisting of two cells; bilocular. var. **Dithe·cal.**

Ditheism (dəi·þiˌiz'm). 1678. [DI-².] Belief in two supreme gods; religious dualism; *esp.* the belief in two independent antagonistic principles of good and evil, as in Zoroastrianism and Manicheism. So **Di·theist,** one who holds the doctrine of d. **Di·thei·stic, -al** *a.*

Dither (di·ðəɹ), *v.* 1649. [phonetic var. of DIDDER, q.v.] *intr.* To tremble, quake, quiver (*dial.*). **b.** To vacillate (*colloq.*). Also as *sb.* Hence **Dithering-grass,** *Briza media.*

Dithionic (dəiþəiǫ·nik, diþiǫ·nik), *a.* 1854. [f. DI-² + θεῖον sulphur. (The formative *-thionic* is used for a group of compounds containing H_2O_6, in combination with two or more atoms of sulphur.)] In *d. acid,* $H_2S_2O_6$, a dibasic acid not isolated in the pure state, but forming crystallizable salts, called **Dithionates.**

Dithyramb (di·þiræmb). 1603. [ad. L. *dithyrambus* (also used), a. Gr.] *Gr. Antiq.* A Greek choric hymn, originally in honour of Dionysus or Bacchus, vehement and wild in character; a Bacchanalian song; hence, *transf.* a poem, speech, or writing having this character.

1. The Dithyrambe with clamours dissonant HOLLAND. *transf.* What dithyrambs he went into about eating and drinking GEO. ELIOT.

Dithyrambic (diþiræ·mbik). 1603. [ad. L. *dithyrambicus,* a. Gr.; see prec.]

A. *adj.* Pertaining to, or like, a dithyramb; composing dithyrambs; *transf.* wild, vehement.

Priests..howling chaunt these Dithyrambik charms 1611.

B. *sb.* A dithyrambic verse; a dithyramb; something like a dithyramb in style; a writer of a dithyramb 1646.

†**Dition** (di·ʃən). 1538. [a. OF. *dicion* (*dition*), ad. L. *dicionem*; ? from root *dic-* of *dicere.* Cf. CONDITION.] Rule, dominion -1654; a dominion -1685. Hence †**Di·tionary** *a.* and *sb.* (one) under dominion.

Ditokous (di·tǫkəs), *a.* [f. Gr. δίτοκος (DI-²) + -OUS.] **a.** Having twins. **b.** Laying only two eggs at a clutch. **c.** Producing young of two kinds. (In recent Dicts.)

Ditolyl (dəitǭ·lil). 1877. [DI-².] *Chem.* An aromatic hydrocarbon, a crystalline substance of the composition $2(C_6H_4.CH_3)$; see TOLYL.

Ditone (dəi·tǭn). 1609. [ad. Gr. δίτονον the ancient major third; see DI-².] *Mus.* An interval containing two whole tones; *esp.* the Pythagorean major third.

Ditrematous (dəitrī·mătəs), *a.* [f. mod.L. *ditremata* neut. pl., f. Gr. δι- + τρῆμα opening.] *Zool.* Of or pertaining to the *Ditremata,* a division of gastropod molluscs, having the external male and female orifices far apart; also, having the anal and genital orifices distinct, as in *Ditrema,* a genus of fishes.

Ditremid (dəitrī·mid). [f. mod.L. *Ditremidæ* sb. pl., f. *Ditrema*; see prec.] *Zool.* A fish of the family *Ditremidæ,* of which *Ditrema* is the typical genus.

Di-tri-, short for *di- or tri-, di- and tri-,* in composition, as *di-trichotomous* = dichotomous or trichotomous.

Ditriglyph (dəitrəi·glif). 1727. [a. F. *ditriglyphe,* f. DI-² + *triglyphe.*] *Arch.* **1.** 'The space between two triglyphs.' **2.** A space between columns of the Doric order, admitting the use of two triglyphs in the frieze, between those over the columns 1791. So **Ditrigly·phic** *a.* having two triglyphs in the space over the intercolumniation.

Ditrigonal (dəitri·gŏnăl), *a.* 1878. [DI-².] *Cryst.* Having (dihedral) angles, of which the first, third, and fifth are equal, and also the second, fourth, and sixth, but those of the one set are not equal to those of the other.

Ditrochee (dəitrǭ·kī). 1855. [ad. L. *ditrochæus* (oftener used), a. Gr. διτρόχαιος (DI-²).] *Pros.* A foot consisting of two trochees; a double trochee. So **Ditroche·an** *a.* containing two trochees.

Ditroite (di·trǫˌəit). 1868. [f. *Ditro* in Transylvania.] *Min.* A rock composed of orthoclase, elæolite, and sodalite.

Ditt, obs. f. DIT *sb.* and *v.*

Dittander (ditæ·ndəɹ). ? *Obs.* 1578. [f. as DITTANY + ?.] **1.** A name for Pepperwort, *Lepidium latifolium* 1578. †**2.** Dittany of Crete -1658.

Dittany (di·tăni). ME. [repr. OF. *ditan,* etc. :—med.L. *dictamus, -um,* L. *dictamnus, -um,* Gr. δίκταμνον, said to be f. Δίκτη (Dicte) in Crete, where the herb grew.] **1.** A labiate plant, *Origanum Dictamnus,* called also *D. Creticus* or Dittany of Crete. **b.** *fig.* (From the supposed power of Cretan dittany to expel weapons.) 1623. †**2.** *Marrubium Pseudodictamnus,* also called Bastard Dittany -1671. **3.** The English name for the genus *Dictamnus* (N.O. *Rutaceæ*); esp. *D. Fraxinella* (Bastard Dittany), and *D. albus* (White Dittany) 1605. †**4.** Erron. for DITTANDER 1. -1578. **5.** in U.S. Applied to *Cunila Mariana* (N.O. *Labiatæ*) 1676.

1. *fig.* The shaft sticks still in thee;..None but the Sovereign D. of thy Saviour's Righteousness can drive it out BP. HALL.

Dittay (di·te, di·ti). 1470. [a. OF. *dité, ditté.*] *Sc. Law.* The ground of indictment against a person for a criminal offence; also, the indictment.

Ditto (di·to). 1625. [a. It. *ditto, detto* (:—L. *dictus, -um*). Used in It. with a sb. like 'said' in Eng.] †**1.** Said month -1677. **2.** Hence, The aforesaid, the same; used, in accounts and lists (often in the form *d^o, do.,* or as two dots or commas, or a dash), to avoid repetition; hence in commercial, office, and colloquial language 1678. **3.** Hence as *sb.* **a.** A duplicate; the like 1776. **b.** Cloth of the same material; chiefly pl., in *suit of dittos*: a suit of clothes of the same material throughout 1755. Hence **Di·tto** *v.* to match.

Dittography (ditǫ·grăfi). 1874. [f. Gr. διττός + -GRAPHY.] In *Palæography,* etc.: Double writing; unintentional repetition of a letter, or series of letters, by a copyist. So **Di·ttograph,** a letter or series of letters thus repeated; **Ditto·gra·phic** *a.* of the nature of a dittograph.

Dittology (ditǫ·lŏdʒi). 1678. [ad. Gr. διττο-, δισσολογία; see prec.] A twofold reading or interpretation.

†**Di·tton.** 1572. [a. F. *dicton* :—L. *dictum*; see DICTUM.] A phrase, an expression; *esp.* a motto or proverb -1653.

Ditty (di·ti), *sb.* [ME. *dite, ditee,* a. OF. *dité, ditté,* orig. *ditié* :—L. *dictatum* thing dictated.] †**1.** = DITE *sb.* 1. (ME. only.) **2.** A song, lay; now, a short simple song ME.; †any composition in verse -1614. †**3.** The words of a song; also, the leading theme or phrase; hence, Subject, theme, burden -1672.

2. The lark..doth welcome daylight with her d. SHAKS. **3.** There vvas no great matter in the dittie, yet ye note was very vntunable *A. Y. L.* v. iii. 36. Hence †**Di·tty** *v. intr.* to sing a d.; *trans.* to sing as a ditty; also, to fit words to (music); **Di·ttied** *ppl. a.*

Di·tty-bag. 1860. [?] A bag used by sailors to contain their smaller necessaries. So **Di·tty-box,** a box used similarly by fishermen.

Diureide (dəiˌiūᵊrīˌəid). 1877. [DI-².] *Chem.* A compound of two urea-residues with an acid radical.

‖**Diuresis** (dəiˌiurī·sis). 1681. [mod.L., a. Gr. *διούρησις, f. διά + οὔρησις. Cf. F. *diurèse.*] *Med.* Excretion of urine, esp. when excessive.

Diuretic (dəiˌiure·tik). ME. [ad. L. *diureticus,* a. Gr., f. διουρεῖν; see prec.]

A. *adj.* Having the quality of exciting (excessive) discharge of urine; †of persons, urinating excessively -1812.

B. *sb.* A substance having diuretic qualities ME. var. †**Diure·tical** *a.* (*sb.*)

†**Diu·rn(e,** *a.* ME. [ad. L. *diurnus,* f. *dies.*] = DIURNAL *a.* -1603.

Diurnal (dəiˌǭ·ɹnăl). ME. [ad. L. *diurnalis,* f. *dies.* See JOURNAL.]

A. *adj.* **1.** Performed in one day; daily. **2.** Of or belonging to each day; daily (*arch.*) 1594. **3.** Of or belonging to the day; day-: opp. to *nocturnal.* In *Zool., spec.* of animals active by day only. 1623. **4.** Lasting for a day only; ephemeral (*rare*) 1866.

1. The D. Motion of the Sun DRYDEN. **2.** D. prints 1815. The Laird's d. visits SCOTT. **3.** D. birds WOOD. The d. position [of leaves or petals] 1875.

B. *sb.* **1.** *Eccl.* A service-book containing the day-hours, except matins 1550. **2.** A day-book, diary; *esp.* a journal (*arch.*) 1600. **3.** A newspaper published daily, or (*loosely*) at short periodical intervals 1640. **4.** A diurnal bird, butterfly, or moth. (In recent Dicts.) Hence **Diu·rnalist,** a writer of a d. **Diu·rnally** *adv.*

Diurna·tion. 1836. [f. L. *diurnus,* after *hibernation.*] The habit of sleeping or remaining quiescent during the day.

Diuturnal (dəiˌutǭ·ɹnăl), *a.* Now *rare.* 1599. [f. L. *diuturnus,* f. *diu.*] Of long duration, lasting. var. †**Diutu·rn.**

Diutu·rnity. Now *rare.* ME. [ad. L. *diuturnitatem.*] Long duration; lastingness.

‖**Div** (dīv). 1777. [Pers. :—Zend *daēva* = Skr. *deva* god; see DEVA.] An evil spirit or demon of Persian mythology.

‖**Diva** (dī·va). 1883. [It. :—L. *diva* goddess.] A distinguished female singer, a prima donna.

Divagate (dəi·văgeⁱt), *v.* 1599. [f. L. *divagat-,* ppl. stem of *divagari* (DI-¹, DIS- 1).] *intr.* To wander about; to stray from one place or subject to another.

So does a child's balloon d. upon the currents of the air STEVENSON. Hence **Divaga·tion.**

Divalent (dəi·vălĕnt, di·v-), *a.* 1869. [f. DI-² + L. *valentem,* pr. pple. of *valere* to be worth.] *Chem.* Having two combining equivalents; also *bivalent.* Formerly *dyad.*

Divan (divæ·n). 1586. [Orig. Pers., *dēvān*, now *dīwān*, a brochure; an account-book; a custom-house, etc. An older form is It. *dovana*, *doana*, now *dogana*, F. *douane*; see DOUANE.] 1. An Oriental council of state; *spec.* in Turkey, the privy council of the Porte 1586; a council in general 1619. 2. The hall where the Turkish divan is held; a court of justice; a council-chamber 1597. 3. A continued step, or raised part of the floor, against the wall of a room, often cushioned, so as to form a sofa or couch 1702 4. A room entirely open at one side 1678. 5. A smoking-room furnished with lounges; hence, a cigar-shop 1848. ‖6. A name for a collection of poems; *spec.* a series of poems by one author, the rimes of which usually run through the whole alphabet 1823.

1. In this councell called diuan..audience is open to euery one 1586. 6. The most important diwans are those of..Hafiz, Saadi, and Jami 1877.

†**Divapora·tion.** 1612. [DI-¹, DIS- 1.] The driving out of vapours by heat; evaporation.

Divaricate (di-, dəivæ·rike't), *v.* 1623. [f. L. *divaricat-*, ppl. stem of *divaricare*, f. DI-¹, DIS- 1 + *varicare*, f. *varicus* straddling.] 1. *intr* To stretch or spread apart; to branch off or diverge; in *Bot.* and *Zool.* to diverge widely. 2. *trans.* To stretch or open wide apart or asunder 1672. 3. To cause to spread or branch out in different directions. ? *Obs.* 1670.

1. At the spot where these two [roads] divaricated, the horseman stopped JAMES. So **Diva·ricate** *a.* widely divergent; *spec* applied (in *Bot.* and *Zool.*) to branches which diverge from the stem, etc. almost at right angles. **Diva·ricately** *adv.* Hence **Divarica·tion,** the action of stretching apart; spreading out, divergence; *transf.* divergence of opinion; *concr.* the point at which branching takes place; that which divaricates. **Diva·ricator,** a muscle which draws parts asunder, as that which opens the shells of Brachiopods.

†**Divast,** *a.* [incorrect f. *devast.*] Devastated. T. HARVEY.

Dive (dəiv), *v.* Pa. t. **dived**; *U.S.* and *Eng. dial.* dove. [OE. had: (1) the strong vb. *dúfan*, pa. t. *déaf*, pl. *dufon*, intr. to duck, dive, sink (obs. bef. 1300); (2) the weak vb. *dýfan*, *dýfde* to dip, submerge. The mod. dial. pa. t. *dove* is app. a new formation, after *drive, drove*, etc.]

I. *intr.* 1. To plunge (usually head-foremost) into or under water or other liquid. Also *transf* 2. To penetrate with the hand *into*; *slang* to pick pockets 1700. 3. *fig.* To enter deeply or plunge *into* (a matter) 1583. 4. To dart out of sight, disappear 1844.

1. [The cormorant] from a vast height drops down to d. after its prey GOLDSM. *transf. Timon* IV. i. 2. The fierce soul to darkness dived and hell POPE.

II. *trans.* [In early use OE. *dýfan.*] 1. To dip or plunge (a person or thing) *in*, or *into* a liquid, or the like (*arch.*) OE.; to plunge (the hand, etc.) *into* 1590. Also †*transf.* and *fig.* 2. To penetrate or traverse by diving. Now *rare.* 1615. 3. *slang.* To pick (pockets). B. JONSON.

2. The Curtii bravely dived the gulf of flame DENHAM. He dives the hollow, climbs the steep EMERSON.

Dive (dəiv), *sb.* 1700. [f. prec. vb.] 1. The act of diving (*lit.* and *fig.*). Also *transf.* 2. In *U.S.* An illegal drinking-den, or place of low resort, often situated in a cellar, or the like 1882.

2. Opium-smoking dives H. H. KANE.

Di·ve-dap, -dop. Now *dial.* [OE. *dufe-doppa*, f *dúfan* to dive + *doppa*, agent-n. f. ablaut stem *déop-*, *dup-* (*dop-*) to dip. *Dyve-* replaced *dufe-* when the strong form of the vb. became obs.; see DIVE.] = next.

Di·ve-dapper. 1559. [f. prec.; assim. to agent-nouns in -ER.] = DIDAPPER; also applied to other diving water fowls.

†**Dive·ll,** *v.* 1627. [ad. L. *divellere.*] To tear or rend asunder –1801.

Divellent (di-, dəive·lĕnt), *a.* 1782. [ad. L. *divellentem.*] Drawing asunder; decomposing, separative.

Dive·llicate, *v.* 1638. [f. L. *di-*, *dis-*, DIS- 1 + ppl. stem of *vellicare*, from *vellere.*] To pull to pieces. Also *fig.*

Diver (dəi·vəɪ). 1506. [f. DIVE *v.* + -ER¹.] 1. One who, or that which, dives under water. b. *fig.* One who dives into a subject, etc. 1624. 2. A water bird that dives. a. *spec.* Any of the *Colymbidæ*, as the *Great Northern D.*, the *Red-throated D.*, etc. b. The grebe. c. Various *Anseres*: *Black D.*, the common scoter, *Dun D.*, the female and young male merganser. 1510. 3. A pickpocket 1608.

1. Dyvers, and Fishers for Pearls WOODWARD. b. A d. into causes WOTTON.

†**Di·verb.** 1621. [f. *di-* (? DI-²) + L. *verbum* word.] A proverb, byword; a proverbial expression –1689.

You may define *ex ungue leonem*, as the d. is BURTON.

†**Dive·rberate,** *v.* 1609. [f. ppl. stem of L. *diverberare* (DIS- 1).] *trans.* To cleave asunder; to strike through –1656. Hence **Diverbera·tion,** beating.

Diverge (divə̄·ɹdʒ, dəi-), *v.* 1665. [ad. mod.L. *divergere* (DIS- 1).] 1. *intr.* To proceed in different directions from a point or from each other: opp. to CONVERGE. b. *transf.* and *fig.* To take different courses; to turn off *from* a track or course; to differ in opinion or character; to deviate from a normal form or state 1856. 2. *trans.* To cause (lines or rays) to branch off in different directions; to deflect 1748.

1. The mountains here d., in a fan-like form KEATINGE. Hence **Dive·rgement,** divergence.

Divergence (divə̄·ɹdʒĕns, dəi-). 1656. [ad. mod.L. *divergentia*, or a. F.; see DIVERGENT.] 1. The action of diverging; also *ellipt.* for *amount* or *degree of d.* 2. *transf.* and *fig.* Continuous deviation from a standard or norm 1839. 3. *Math.* In fluid motion, the decrement of density at any point. So **Dive·rgency,** divergent quality or state; also = DIVERGENCE 1.

Divergent (divə̄·ɹdʒĕnt, dəi-), *a.* 1696. [ad. mod.L. *divergentem*; cf. F. *divergent.*] 1. Proceeding in different directions from each other or from a common point; diverging. 2. *transf.* and *fig.* Differing from each other or from a standard or norm 1801. 3. Of, pertaining to, or produced by, divergence 1831. 4. *Math.* = DIVERGING 2. 1837.

1. *D.*, a Term in Opticks, said of the Beams, which having suffered the Refraction, separate one from the other PHILLIPS. 2. Thence arise d. opinions SOUTHEY. 3. *D. squint*: strabismus in which the axes of the eye diverge. Hence **Dive·rgently** *adv.*

Dive·rging, *ppl. a.* 1706. [-ING².] 1. Proceeding in different directions from a common point, so as to become more and more widely separate; turning off from the straight course. 2. *Math.* Applied to a series, the sum of whose terms becomes indefinitely greater as more and more are taken. (Opp. to CONVERGENT.) 1795. Hence **Dive·rgingly** *adv.*

Divers (dəi·vəɹz), *a.* [ME. *divers, diverse*, a. OF. *diviers, divers*, fem. *-erse*:—L. *diversus.* The stress was orig. on the last syllable, as in F.] †1. Different in character or quality; not of the same kind. Now repl. by DIVERSE. –1691. †2. Differing from what is right, good, or profitable; perverse, adverse –1581. 3. (always *pl.*) Various, sundry, several; more than one, some number of. (Thus *variety* gradually becomes *indefinite number.*) ME. Also *absol.* and with *of.* †4. as *adv.* = DIVERSELY –1720.

1. Whether it be lawful to beare Arms for the Service of a Prince that is of d. Religion 1625. 3. At sundry times and in d. manners *Heb.* i. 1. Seised in fee of d. freehold lands JARMAN. 4. MILT. *P. L.* IV. 234. Hence **Di·versly** *adv.*

Diverse (di-, dəivə̄·ɹs, dəi·vəɹs), *a.* ME. [orig. f. as DIVERS, but, later, immed. assoc. w. L. *diversus*. Hence since *c* 1700 distinctly assoc. w. *diversity.*] 1. = DIVERS 1. 2. Multiform, varied, diversified 1541. †3. = DIVERS 2. –1483. †4. Distracting. (In SPENSER.). †5. = DIVERS 3. (rare in this spelling after 1700.) –1728. Also *absol.* †6. *adv.* = DIVERS 4. –1729.

1. With habits so d., we may well expect [etc.] 1841. 2. The d. Moon WYATT. 5. Collected out of d. Authenticall Records 1601. [It] hath been excellently handled by d. BACON. Hence **Diversely** *adv.*, **-ness** (now *rare*).

†**Dive·rse,** *v.* ME. [a. OF. *diverser*:—med.L. *diversare*, freq of *divertere* to DIVERT.] 1. To render, be, or grow, diverse –1634. 2. *intr.* To turn aside (*rare*) 1590.

2. The Redcrosse Knight diverst: but forth rode Britomart SPENSER *F. Q.* III. iii. 62.

Diversi-, comb. element, f. L. *diversus* DIVERSE: as in

Diversiflo·rate, -flo·rous *adjs.*, bearing flowers of different kinds. **Diversifo·liate, -fo·lious** *adjs.*, having leaves of different kinds. **Dive·rsiform** *a.*, of diverse forms. †**Diversi·volent** *a.*, desiring strife or differences (*rare*).

Diversification (divə̄ɹsifikē·ʃən, dəi-). 1603. [f. med.L. *diversificare*; see next.] The action of diversifying; the process of becoming diversified; the fact of being diversified; a diversified condition, form, or structure.

The minuter diversifications are called varieties KIRWAN.

Diversify (divə̄·ɹsifəi, dəi-), *v.* 1481. [a. OF. *diversifier*, ad. med.L. *diversificare*, f. *diversus* + *-ficare*, see -FY.] 1. *trans.* To render diverse, different, or varied, in form, or qualities; to give variety to; to variegate, vary, modify 1490. †2. *intr.* or *absol.* To produce diversity or variety. Also *intr.* (for *refl.*) –1815.

1. The bones of the body..be deuersyfyed in dyuers maners R. COPLAND. We diversifie our selves from him [God] FELTHAM. Hence **Dive·rsifiable** *a.* capable of being diversified (*rare*). **Diversifiabi·lity.**

Diversion (divə̄·ɹʃən, dəi-). 1600. [ad. med.L. *diversio* (vox Medicorum: Du Cange).] 1. The turning aside (*of* any person or thing) from any course, object, or occupation; a turning aside of one's course or attention; deviation, deflexion 1626. 2. *Mil.* A manœuvre to draw off the enemy's attention from a particular operation, by an attack in an unexpected quarter 1647. 3. *spec.* The turning away of the thoughts, attention, etc., from fatiguing or sad occupations; distraction, recreation, amusement. Also with *a* and *pl.* 1648.

1. Fearing the d. of trade YEATS. A d. ..from this rectitude, this uprightness DONNE. The..d. ..was the suggestion of a treaty proposed by the enemy BURKE. 3. Among the in-door diversions were draughts, chess, etc. 1875.

Diversity (divə̄·ɹsiti, dəi-). ME. [a. OF. *diverseté*, *diversité*:—L. *diversitatem*, f. *diversus* DIVERSE.] 1. The condition of being diverse; difference, unlikeness. Also with *a* and *pl.* †b. Divers manners or sorts –1610. †2. Perversity, evil, mischief –1523.

1. Diversitie of circumstance may alter the case RALEIGH. Mo diuersitie of sounds, all horrible SHAKS.

†**Dive·rsory,** *sb.* ME. [ad. L. *di-*, prop. *deversorium* inn.] A place to which one turns in by the way –1681.

Dive·rsory, *a. rare.* 1864. [f. L. *divers-*, ppl. stem of *divertere* + -ORY.] Serving to divert, divertive.

Divert (divə̄·ɹt, dəi-), *v.* ME. [a. OF. *divertir*, ad. L. *di-*, *devertere.*] 1. *trans.* To turn aside from its direction or course; to deflect; to turn *from* one destination *to* another 1548. Also †*refl.* 2. *intr.* (for *refl.*) To deviate, digress (*lit.* and *fig.*). Now *arch.* ME. †3. (?) To turn awry. *Tr. & Cr.* I. iii. 99. 4. To draw off (a person) *from* a course, etc.; to distract (the mind, attention, etc.) 1600. 5. To draw away from fatiguing or serious occupations; to entertain, amuse 1662. Also *refl.* (now *rare*). †6. To while away (time) –1773.

1. The old Channel..for diverting the Thames 1699. Persevering labour, not diverted from one object to another SIR B. BRODIE. 4. Less profitable amusements d. their attention COWPER. 5. I had neither Friends or Books to d. me STEELE. Hence **Dive·rter.** **Dive·rtible** *a.* (*rare*). **Dive·rting·ly** *adv.*, **-ness.** †**Dive·rtment,** diversion.

†**Dive·rticle.** 1570. [ad. L. *diverticulum*; see below.] 1. A byway or bypath; a turning out of the course. Also *fig.* –1782. 2. = DIVERTICULUM 2. 1847.

‖**Diverticulum** (dəivəɹti·kiŭlŏm). Pl. **-a.** 1647. [L. *di-*, *deverticulum*, f. (ult.) DE- 1 + *vertere.*] †1. A byway; a means of exit –1695. 2. A smaller side-branch of any cavity or passage; in *Anat.* applied to a blind tubular process 1819 Hence **Diverti·cular** *a.* pertaining to or like a d. **Diverti·culate**(d *a.* having a d.

‖**Divertimento** (divertime·nto). Pl. **-ti** (-ti), **-tos.** 1759. [It.] †a. Diversion, amusement b. *Mus.* = DIVERTISSEMENT 2.

†**Divertise,** *v.* Also 7 **-ize.** 1597. [f. F. *divertiss-*, lengthened stem of *divertir*; cf. *advertise.* Stressed by Bailey *dive·rtise*; Johnson has *diverti·se.*] = DIVERT 4, 5. Chiefly *refl.*: To enjoy oneself, make merry –1696. So ‖**Di·vertissant** *a.* diverting.

Divertisement (divə̄·ɹtizmĕnt). *arch.* 1642

[ad. F. *divertissement*; see prec.] **1.** = DIVERSION 3. **2.** = DIVERTISSEMENT 2. 1667.

1. Some for d., and some for businesse HOBBES.

‖**Divertissement** (divertisman). 1728. [F.] **1.** An entertainment 1804. **2.** A short ballet or other entertainment given between acts or longer pieces (= F. *entr'acte*); †a piece of music on given *motifs* (Grove).

Divertive (divɜ·ɹtiv, dəi-), *a.* Now *rare.* 1598. [f. DIVERT *v.* + -IVE.] Tending to divert; distractive, amusing, entertaining.

Greatly d. to the inward man 1831.

‖**Dives** (dəi·viz). ME. [L.] **1.** Commonly taken as the proper name of the rich man in the parable (see Luke xvi); and used generically for 'rich man'. **2.** *Law. D. costs*: costs on the higher scale 1849.

Divest (dive·st, dəi-), *v.* 1605. [ad. med.L. *disvestire*, rectified to *divestire*, replacing earlier DEVEST, from OF. *desvestir*, exc. in legal use.] **1.** *trans.* To unclothe; to strip *of* clothing, or of any covering, ornament, etc. 1795. **2.** *fig.* To strip *of* possessions, rights, or attributes; to denude, deprive; occas., to free, rid. Also *refl.* 1605. **3.** To put off. Now *rare.* 1639. **4.** *Law.* To take away (property, etc., vested in any one); to DEVEST 1789.

2. [Monkeys] can never be divested of a mischievous disposition 1769. 3. I will d. all fear BROWNING. Hence **Dive·sted** *ppl. a.* (loosely used for: Devoid *of*). **Dive·stible** *a.* capable of being divested. **Dive·stment**, divestiture.

Dive·stitive, *a.* 1802. [f. as next + -IVE.] Having the property of divesting.

Ablative, or say d. facts BENTHAM.

Divestiture (dive·stitiŭɹ, dəi-). 1601. [f. mod.L. *divestit-*, ppl. stem of *divestire*; cf. *investiture*.] **1.** Deprivation of a possession or right; dispossession; alienation. **2.** Putting off of clothing; also *fig.* 1820. var. **Dive·sture.**

Divet, var. of DIVOT.

Dividable (divəi·dăb'l), *a.* 1587. [f. DIVIDE *v.* + -ABLE.] **1.** Capable of being divided; divisible. †**2.** Having the function of dividing. *Tr. & Cr.* I. iii. 105.

Dividant, var. of DIVIDENT.

Divide (divəi·d), *v.* [ME. *de-, dividen*, ad. L. *dividere*: F. has *diviser* (OF. *deviser*); see DEVISE.]

I. *trans.* **1.** To separate into parts, or into smaller groups; to split up, cleave; to break or cut asunder. **2.** To separate into branches ME. **3.** To separate or mark out into parts (in fact or in thought). Most freq. in *pass.*; sometimes nearly = to consist of (so many) parts. ME. **4.** To separate into classes; to class, classify 1551. **5.** To separate *from*; to cut off, sunder, part ME. **6.** To establish or constitute a boundary between (*lit.* and *fig.*) ME. **7.** To separate in opinion, feeling, or interest; to set at variance; to distract ME. **8.** To distribute among a number; to deal out, dispense ME.; to share 1526; to direct to different things 1611. **9.** *Math.* To perform the process of DIVISION on; also *absol.* ME.; to be a divisor of 1709. **10.** To part (a legislative assembly, etc.) into two groups in order to ascertain the number voting on each side of a question. Also *absol.* and *intr.* 1554. †**11.** *Mus. trans.* To perform with divisions; *intr.* to perform divisions; to descant -1618.

1. And the king said, D. the living child in two 1 *Kings* iii. 25. Phr. *To d. the hoof*: to have cloven hoofs. (A Hebraism.) 3. A ruler divided into inches and small parts HOOKE. Thir songs D. the night MILT. *P.L.* IV. 688. 5. The sick were divided from the rest 1700. 6. What thin partitions Sense from Thought d. POPE. 7. There shall be five in one house divided, three against two, and two against three *Luke* xii. 52. 8. God divided the land of Canaan among the Israelites HOBBES. He stood, This way and that dividing the swift mind, In act to throw TENNYSON.

II. *intr.* (See also I. 9, 10, 11.) **1.** *absol.* To make separation or distinction (*between*) ME. **2.** *intr.* (for *refl.*) To become divided, undergo division; to become separated; to part; to cleave, break up, go to pieces; to branch 1526.

1. Diuide with reason betweene Self-loue, and Society BACON. 2. Loue cooles, friendship falls off, brothers diuide *Lear* I. ii. 15. The river divides and subdivides HUXLEY.

Divi·de, *sb.* 1642. [f. prec. vb.] **1.** Division. **2.** In U.S., etc.: A ridge or line of high ground forming the division between two river valleys or systems; a watershed 1807.

Divi·ded, *ppl. a.* 1565. [f. DIVIDE *v.* + -ED¹.] **1.** Separated into parts; in *Bot.* (of leaves, etc.) cut into segments. **2.** Situated apart; separate 1658. **3.** Discordant; split into factions 1594. **4.** Distributed among a number; directed to different objects 1607. Hence **Divi·ded·ly** *adv.*, **-ness.**

Dividend (di·vidĕnd). Also 6–7 *erron.* **dividente, -ent.** 1477. [a. F. *dividende* in sense 4, ad. L. *dividendum.*] **1.** *Math.* A number or quantity which is to be divided by another. (Correl. to DIVISOR.) 1542. **2.** A sum of money to be divided among a number of persons; *esp.* the total sum payable as interest on a loan, or as the profit of a joint-stock company 1623. **3.** *transf.* A portion or share of anything divided; *esp.* the share that falls to each distributee 1477. †**4.** The action of dividing; distribution -1726.

2. *To declare a d.*: see DECLARE *v.* 3. A very liberal d. of praise JOHNSON. A testatrix gave to trustees certain bank stock, upon trust to pay the dividends to [etc.] JARMAN.

†**Di·vident.** 1450. [ad. L. *dividentem.*]

A. *adj.* **1.** Distributive 1660. **2.** Separate. (In Shaks. *divi·dant.*) *Timon* IV. iii. 5.

B. *sb.* One who or that which DIVIDES; in *Arith.* = DIVISOR -1656.

Divident, -e; see DIVIDEND.

Divider (divəi·dəɹ). 1526. [f. DIVIDE *v.*] **1.** One who or that which divides, or separates a whole into parts 1591. **2.** One who distributes; one who shares something with another 1526. †**3.** One who classifies -1610. **4.** One who or that which causes division 1643. **5.** *pl.* Dividing compasses, worked by means of a screw; a pair of compasses with steel points 1703.

2. Who made me a judge or a d. over you *Luke* xii. 14. 4. Hate is of all things the mightiest d. MILT. Money, the great d. of the world SWIFT.

Divi·ding, *ppl. a.* 1620. [f. as prec.] That divides (see the vb.).

D. engine, a machine for graduating a circle, or for cutting the circumference of a wheel into a number of teeth. *D. ridge* = DIVIDE *sb.* 2. Hence **Divi·dingly** *adv.*

‖**Divi-divi** (di·vidi·vi). 1843. [Carib.] The curled pods of *Cæsalpinia coriaria*, a tree of tropical America; they are highly astringent, and much used in tanning. Also the tree.

Dividual (divi·diuăl), *a.* (*sb.*) 1598. [f. L. *dividuus* + -AL.]

A. **1.** Separable; separate. **2.** Divisible; divided into parts 1619. **3.** Distributed among a number; shared 1667.

†**B.** *sb.* **1.** That which is dividual 1668. **2.** *Math.* One of the parts of the dividend, each of which yields successively one term of the quotient -1811. Hence **Divi·dually** *adv.* separately.

Dividuous (divi·diuəs), *a. rare.* 1766. [f. as prec. + -OUS.] = DIVIDUAL 1, 2.

†**Di·vinail.** ME. [a. OF. *de-, divinail* masc., and *devinaille*, etc. fem., repr. L. types **divinale*, **divinalia* pl.] **1.** Divining, divination -1484. **2.** A riddle -1483.

Divination (divinē¹·ʃən). ME. [a. OF., ad. L. *divinationem.*] **1.** The action or practice of divining; the foretelling of future events or discovery of what is hidden or obscure by supernatural or magical means. Also with *a* and *pl.*, an exercise of this, a prophecy, an augury. **2.** Successful conjecture or guessing 1597. ¶ *catachr.* Divine condition. HOLLAND.

1. The flying of birds, which doe geue a happy d. to things to come NORTH. 2. 2 *Hen. IV*, I. i. 88.

Di·vinator. ? *Obs.* 1607. [ad. L. *divinator*, f. *divinare.*] One who divines; a diviner; soothsayer. So **Divinato·rial** *a.* conjectural (*rare*). **Divi·natory** *a.* prophetic; conjectural.

Divine (divəi·n), *a.* and *sb.*¹ [ME. *devine, divine*, a. OF. *devin*:—L. *divinus.*]

A. **1.** Of or pertaining to God or a god ME. **2.** Given by or proceeding from God ME. **3.** Addressed, or devoted to God; religious, sacred ME. **4.** Partaking of the nature of God; godlike; celestial ME.; †beatified -1632. **5.** More than human, excellent in a superhuman degree. Said of persons and things. 1470. **6.** Connected or dealing with divinity or sacred things. ? *Obs.* 1548. †**7.** Foreboding, prescient. [A Latinism.] 1667.

1. D. acts R. W. DALE. 2. The d. right of kings 1640. An irresistible d. impulse SEELEY. 3. Like prayers d. SHAKS. *D. Office, Service*: see OFFICE 6 a, SERVICE¹ III. 4 b. 4. Or flocks, or herds, or human face d. MILT. *P. L.* III. 40. 5. 1 *Hen. VI*, I. vi. 4. Blackness sits On the divinest wits H. VAUGHAN. 7. Yet oft his heart, d. of something ill, Misgave him MILT. *P. L.* IX. 845.

†**B.** *sb.*¹ **1.** Divine service -1606. **2.** Divinity, theology -1400. **3.** DIVINATION. (ME. only.) **4.** Divine nature. (ME. only.)

Divine (divəi·n), *sb.*² ME. [a. OF. *devin* soothsayer (see prec.); also later *devin, divin* theologian, repr. med.L. *divinus* doctor of divinity; both subst. uses of L. *divinus* adj.] †**1.** A diviner, soothsayer; a seer -1587. **2.** Formerly, any ecclesiastic, clergyman, or priest; now, a theologian ME.

2. It is a good Diuine that followes his owne instructions *Merch. V*, I. ii. 16.

Divine (divəi·n), *v.* ME. [a. F. *deviner*, ad. L. *divinare.*]

I. *trans.* †**1.** To make out by supernatural or magical insight; hence, to interpret, explain, make known -1625. **2.** To conjecture, guess ME. **3.** To have presentiment of (things to come); hence *gen.* to predict by intuition ME. †**4.** To point out, foreshow, prognosticate -1847. †**5.** To render divine; to divinize -1622.

2. To d. the meaning of anything 1696. 3. To shun the danger that his Soule diuines *Rich. III*, III. ii. 18. 4. A certain magick rod .. divines Whene'er the soil has golden mines SWIFT.

II. *intr.* **1.** To use or practise divination; to soothsay ME. **2.** To foretell by divine or superhuman power (*arch.*) ME. **3.** To conjecture ME.

1. You shal not d., nor observe dreames BIBLE (Douay) *Lev.* xix. 26. 3. Something from Cyprus, as I may diuine *Oth.* I. ii. 39. Whereon d. you, Sir GREENE. Hence †**Divi·nement**, divination.

Divinely (divəi·nli), *adv.* 1582. [f. DIVINE *a.*] In a divine manner. **1.** By or as by the agency of God 1594. **2.** As or like God; in a godlike manner; with an excellence more than human 1582. †**3.** In a holy manner -1682.

1. As some d. gifted man TENNYSON. 2. Shee fair, d. fair, fit love for Gods MILT. *P. L.* IX. 489.

Divineness (divəi·nnĕs). 1579. [-NESS.] **1.** The quality or state of being divine. **2.** Superhuman or supreme excellence 1580.

Diviner (divəi·nəɹ). [ME. *de-, divinour* = OF. *devineor*, corresp. to L. *divinatorem.* Till 1500 stressed *de·vinou·r, de·vinou·r.*] **1.** One who practises divination; a successful conjecturer 1690. †**2.** A theologian -1552.

1. The deuynour had told hym that he shold deye within fyue dayes CAXTON. A notable D. of Thoughts LOCKE. So **Divi·neress**, a female d.

†**Divinesse.** 1594. [Compressed var. of *divineness.*] **a.** Divination. **b.** Divineness, divinity. -1605.

Diving (dəi·viŋ), *vbl. sb.* ME. [f. DIVE *v.* + -ING¹.] The action of DIVE *v.*

Comb. **d.-bell**, a strong heavy vessel, originally bell-shaped, with the bottom open, in which persons may descend into deep water, respiration being sustained by compressed air, or by fresh air from above.

Di·ving, *ppl. a.* 1602. [-ING².] That dives.

Comb.: **d.-buck** or **goat**, a S. African antelope (*Cephalophus mergens*); **-duck**, the golden-eye duck (*Clangula glaucion*); **-pigeon**, the black guillemot (*Uria Grylle*); **-spider**, *Argyroneta aquatica*, which lives in a nest under water.

Divinify (divi·nifəi), *v.* 1633. [f. L. *divinus*; cf. *deify.*] To render or regard as divine; to divinize.

Divi·ning, *vbl. sb.* (*ppl. a.*) ME. [f. DIVINE *v.*] The action of DIVINE *v.*; also *attrib.*

D.-rod, a rod used in divination; *spec.* a forked stick, by means of which certain persons claim to be able to discover water and minerals underground. See DOWSING-ROD.

†**Divi·nister.** [f. DIVINE *v.*; see -ISTER.] A diviner. CHAUCER.

Divinity (divi·nĭti). [ME. *de-, divinite*, a. OF. *devinité*, ad. L. *divinitatem*, f. *divinus.*] **1.** The character or quality of being divine; divineness; divine nature; Deity, Godhead. **2.** *concr.* A divine being; a god, a deity ME. Also *fig.* **3.** Divine quality, virtue, or power 1510. **4.** The science of divine things; the science that deals with the nature and attributes of God, His relations with mankind, etc.; theology; the theological faculty ME. Also *transf.* †**5.** = DIVINATION 1 (*rare*) -1601.

1. The veil is rent..That hides d. from mortal eyes

COWPER. 2. There's a Diuinity that shapes our ends, Rough-hew them how we will *Haml.* v. ii. 10. 3. There is Diuinity in odde Numbers *Merry W.* v. i. 3. 4. *Hen. V*, I. i. 38. *attrib.* **d. calf,** dark-brown binding with blind tooling. Hence **Divi·nityship,** the status of a d.; skill in d. (STERNE).

Divinize (di·vinəiz), *v.* 1656. [ad. F. *diviniser.*] To make or †become divine. Hence **Diviniza·tion,** the action of divinizing, or condition of being divinized.

†**Divi·se,** *a.* ME. [ad. L. *divisus*, pa. pple. of *dividere.*] Divided; separate, distinct –1677.

Divisible (divi·zib'l), *a.* (*sb.*) 1552. [ad. L. *divisibilis*, f. *divis-* ppl. stem of *dividere.*] 1. Capable of being divided into parts (actually or in thought). 2. *Math.* Capable of being divided without remainder (*by*) 1709.

1. Every particle of matter is infinitely d. PRIESTLEY. Hence **Divisibi·lity, Divi·sibleness,** d. quality. **Divi·sibly** *adv.*

Division (divi·ʒən). [ME. *de-, divisioun*, a. OF. *devisiun, division*, ad. L. *divisionem.*]

I. As an action or condition. 1. The action of dividing or state of being divided into parts; partition; separation. 2. The action of distributing among a number; distribution, sharing ME. †3. The action of distinguishing; distinction –1611. 4. Disagreement, variance, dissension; a disagreement ME. 5. *Math.* The action or process of finding how many times one quantity or number is contained in another; the inverse of multiplication; a rule or method for doing this ME. 6. *Logic*, etc. Separation of a genus into species; classification. Also, less strictly, b. Enumeration of the parts of a whole, called *partible d.* c. Distinction of the various meanings of a term, called *nominal d.* 1551. †7. *Mus.* The execution of a rapid melodic passage, originally conceived as the dividing of each of a succession of long notes into several short ones; such a passage itself; often nearly = DESCANT *sb.* –1840. 8. The separating of the members of a legislative body, etc. into two groups, in order to count their votes 1620.

1. The D. of Time into Hours, Days, and Weeks 1726. 2. Phr. *D. of labour*, the d. of a process or employment into parts, each of which is performed by a particular person. 4. Mark them which cause divisions..and avoid them *Rom.* xvi. 17. 5. Phr. *Long d.* (in *Arith.*), the method in which the steps of the operation are successively written down. *Short d.*, the method adopted when the divisor is 12 or less, in which the quotient is set down directly, without writing down the steps of the operation. 7. Ditties ..Sung by a faire Queene ..With ravishing Diuision to her Lute SHAKS. 8. Negatived without a d. 1794.

II. What produces, or is produced by, division. 1. What divides or marks separation; a partition ME. 2. One of the parts into which anything is or may be divided; a portion, section ME. *spec.* b. A portion of a country, etc., as marked off for some political, administrative, or other purpose 1640. c. *Mil.* and *Naut.* A portion of an army or fleet, under one commanding officer; also, a definite portion of a squadron or battalion (see quots.); also, a portion of a ship's company appropriated to a particular service 1597. d. *Nat. Hist.* A section of a larger group in classification: used widely, as the divisions of a kingdom, class, order, family, or genus 1833.

2. The leafe jagged in five divisions like a starre B. GOOGE. *Division*—In its strict sense, the fourth part of a Squadron *Regul. Instr. Cavalry.* Two or three battalions are usually formed into a brigade, two brigades into a division 1879. e. A grade of clerk in the Civil Service 1876. f. One of the three grades of imprisonment 1865. **Divi·sional** *a.* of the nature of d.; pertaining to d.; of or belonging to a d. or portion. **Divi·sionally** *adv.* **Divi·sionary** *a.* divisional (*rare*). †**Divi·sioner,** one who makes a d.

Divisive (divəi·siv), *a.* 1603. [f. L. type **divisivus*; see DIVISE and -IVE.] 1. Causing or expressing division or distribution; analytical. 2. Producing or tending to division, dissension, or discord 1642.

2. Vanity is of a d., not of a uniting nature CARLYLE. Hence **Divi·sive-ly** *adv.*, **-ness.**

Divisor (divəi·zəɹ). ME. [ad. L. *divisorem* from *dividere.*] *Math.* A number or quantity by which another is to be divided. (Correl. to DIVIDEND.) b. One that divides another exactly; a measure, factor 1557.

Common d. = common measure or factor.

Divisory (divəi·zŏri), *a.* 1614. [ad. med.L. *divisorius*, f. *divisor.*] Pertaining to distribution among a number.

Divorce (divō³·ɹs), *sb.* ME. [a. F. *divorce* :—L. *divortium* (*divertium*), f. *divertere* (earlier *divortere*) to turn aside, to separate from (a husband).] 1. Legal dissolution of marriage by a court or other competent body, or according to forms locally recognized. 2. *transf.* and *fig.* Complete separation; disunion of things closely united ME. †3. That which causes divorce –1607. Also *attrib.*

1. D. *a mensa et thoro* (from bed and board), now, since 1857, called 'judicial separation'. 2. To suffre devorce or departyng betwene his soule and his body 1532. 3. SHAKS. *Ven. & Ad.* 932.

Divorce (divō³·ɹs), *v.* ME. [a. F. *divorcer* :—med.L. *divortiare*; see prec.] 1. *trans.* To dissolve the marriage contract between, by process of law; to separate by divorce *from* 1494. Also *refl.* and *intr.* 2. *trans.* To put away (a spouse). Also *fig.* ME. 3. To dissolve (a marriage or union) (*arch.*) 1580. 4. *fig.* To separate; to sever ME.

2. *fig.* Say March may wed September And time d. regret SWINBURNE. 4. Divorced from matter, where is life TYNDALL. Hence **Divo·rceable** *a.* that can or may be divorced. **Divo·rcee·** (also as F. *divorcé(e)*, a divorced person. **Divo·rcement,** divorce; complete separation. **Divo·rcer. Divo·rcive** *a.* (also -**sive**), causing or leading to divorce.

Divot (di·vət). *Sc.* and *n. dial.* 1536. A slice of earth with the grass growing on it, a turf, a sod: used for roofing cottages, etc.; in *Golf*, a piece of turf cut out in making a stroke.

†**Divu·lgate,** *ppl. a.* ME. [ad. L. *divulgatus*; see next.] Made public. (Chiefly used as pa. pple. = divulged.) –1574.

Divulgate (dəi·vɒlgeⁱt), *v.* 1530. [f. L. *divulgat-*, ppl. stem of *divulgare.*] To DIVULGE. **Di·vulgater, -ator. Divulga·tion. Di·vulgatory** *a.* tending to publish (*rare*).

Divulge (divɒ·ldʒ, dəi-), *v.* 1460. [ad. L. *divulgare.*] †1. *trans.* To make publicly known –1791; to publish –1709. 2. To declare or tell openly (something private or secret); to disclose, reveal 1602. †3. *transf.* To make common, impart generally. [A Latinism.] (*rare*) 1667. 4. *intr.* (for *refl.*) To become publicly known (*rare*) 1602.

1. Among the Danai thy dreams divulging COWPER. 2. Command him to d. the crimes confessed to him 1797. 3. MILT. *P. L.* VIII. 583. Hence **Divu·lgement,** the act of divulging; also, †*concr.* in *pl.* **Divu·lgence,** disclosure. **Divu·lger.**

†**Divu·lse,** *v.* 1602. [f. L. *divuls-*, ppl. stem of *divellere*, f. *di-*, DIS- 1 + *vellere*; cf. *convulse.*] *trans.* To tear apart or asunder –1691. So **Divu·lsive** *a.* tending to tear apart or asunder.

Divulsion (divɒ·lʃən, dəi-). 1603. [a. F., or ad. L. *divulsionem*; see prec.] The action of tearing, pulling, or plucking asunder; the condition of being torn apart *from.* Also *fig.*

Others [islands] are made by d. from some continent 1684.

Diwan; see DEWAN, DIVAN.

Dixie¹ (di·ksi). 1879 (**dechsie**). [Hind. *degachi*, a. Pers. *degcha*, dim. of *deg.*] An iron pot or kettle for tea or stew.

Dixie² (di·ksi). 1861. The Southern U.S. Also *Dixie Land.*

‖**Dixit** (di·ksit). 1628. [L., = he has said; see *ipse dixit.*] An utterance (quoted as) already given.

‖**Dizain** (dizēⁱ·n). 1575. [a. F., f. *dix* ten.] A poem or stanza of ten lines.

‖**Dizdar, disdar** (dī·zdāɪ). 1768. [Pers. and Turkish.] The warden of a castle or fort.

Dizen (dəi·z'n, di·z'n), *v.* 1530. [Cf. *dis-, dise-* in DISTAFF, and LG. *diesse* the bunch of flax on a distaff.] †1. *trans.* To dress (a distaff) with flax, etc. for spinning –1575. 2. To dress, *esp.* to attire or array with finery, deck *out* (*up*), bedizen. Also *transf.* and *fig.* 1619.

2. Lasses..Sate dizen'd up 1706. Like a tragedy-queen he has dizen'd her [Comedy] out GOLDSM. Hence **Di·zenment.**

Dizz (diz), *v.* 1632. [f. DIZZY, after *craze*, etc.] To make dizzy or giddy.

†**Dizzard** (di·zăɹd). 1529. [? modified f. DISOUR; in sense 2 app. assoc. w. DIZZY.] 1. = DISOUR –1618. 2. An idiot, a blockhead –1886. Also *attrib.* Hence **Di·zzardly** *a.*

Dizzy (di·zi), *a.* [OE. *dysig, dyseg* foolish, stupid, from a root *dus-* found also in LG. *dusen* to be giddy, etc.] 1. Foolish, stupid. Now only *dial.* 2. Having a sensation of vertigo in the head, with proneness to fall; giddy ME. 3. Mentally or morally unsteady, giddy 1501. 4. Producing giddiness 1605. 5. Arising from giddiness; reeling 1715. 6. *fig.* Whirling with mad rapidity 1791.

2. I daunce up and down tyll I am dyssy SKELTON. 3. At thy heels the d. multitude MILT. *P. R.* II. 420. 4. He began..to climb..towards that d. pinnacle MACAULAY. 5. Lost in a d. mist the warrior lies POPE. Hence **Di·zzily** *adv.* **Di·zziness.**

Dizzy (di·zi), *v.* [In sense 1, from OE. *dysigan*, etc. to be foolish; in the trans. sense, f. prec. adj.] †1. *intr.* To act foolishly or stupidly –ME. 2. *trans.* To make dizzy or giddy; to cause to reel 1501. 3. To bewilder or confuse mentally 1604.

2. You turn my head, you d. me COWLEY. 3. A vision to d. and appal J. H. NEWMAN.

Dj-, repr. the Arabic letter *jim*, = English *j* (dʒ), in Arabic, Turkish, or Berber words, which have come to us through a French channel; *e. g.* **djebel, djerid** or **djereed, djin,** etc. For these see under J; for **djowr,** see GIAOUR.

Do (dū), *v.*, *pa. t.* **did** (*2nd pers. sing.* **didst,** †**didest**); *pa. pple.* **done;** *pres. pple.* and *vbl. sb.* **doing.** In the *Present Indicative*: *1st pers. sing.* **do;** *2nd pers. sing.* **doest** (now confined to the principal vb.), **dost** (usu. auxiliary); *3rd pers. sing.* **does** (*arch.* **doth, doeth,** now *liturg.* and *poet.*); *pl.* **do.** [A common WGer. strong vb.: OE. *dōn*; pa. t. *dyde*, pl. *dēdon, dǣdon, dydon*; pa. pple. *gedōn, geden*; OTeut. types *dōn, deda, dǣno-*: *dōno-*, from vbl. stem *dǣ-*: *dō-*, repr. the Aryan verb stem *dhe-*: *dho-* to place, put, etc., in Skr. *dha-*, OPers. *da-*, Gr. θη-, L. *-dĕre* in *abdĕre, condĕre, dedĕre.*]

I. *trans.* 1. To put, place (*lit.* and *fig.*). Now only *dial.* †2. *refl.* To put oneself; to proceed, go. Also †*intr.* –ME. 3. To bestow, impart, render, give (a thing to a person); to cause by one's action (a person) to have (something) OE. 4. To put forth (action or effort); to perform; to perpetrate; to execute OE. 5. To perform duly, carry out OE.; †to deliver (a message, etc.) –1707. 6. (In *pa. pple.* and *perf. tenses.*) To accomplish, finish, bring to a conclusion ME. 7. To put forth (diligence, etc.) in effecting something ME. 8. To bring into existence by one's action 1580. 9. To operate upon or deal with in any way; *e.g.* to clean 1515; to prepare, as food, lessons, a review, etc. 1660; to play the part of 1599; to 'do for' ME.; to swindle (*slang*) 1641; to go over as a tourist (*colloq.*) 1830; to serve out (a term of punishment) 1865; etc. 10. To render *into* another language or form of composition 1660.

1. Take a gallon..of pure water, and d. it into a pot 1600. Phr. *To d. to death*: orig. to put to death; now, often implying a protracted process (*arch.*). 3. It..did me a great deal of good WOOD. To d. him right He was a Man indeed ROWE. 4. He did neuer doe a more pleasing deed A.V. *Transl. Pref.* 2. Phr *To d. good, evil, right, wrong*, etc. We knew not what to d. with this poor girl DE FOE. 5. Thy will be done *Matt.* vi. 10. To d. penance STUBBS. 6. When dinner is done SWIFT. 7. Phr. *To d. one's best, devoir, diligence, endeavour, might*, etc. 8. The sun is a painter. He does the photograph 1860. 9. To d. a room 1883, pastry (*mod.*), a sum (*mod.*), Andromache FOOTE, the amiable (*colloq.*), a mile a minute (*mod.*), Cologne 1854, time 1889. 10. He did his sentences out of English into Johnsonese MACAULAY.

II. *intr.* 1. To put forth action; to act (in some specified way). Now a leading sense of the vb. OE. 2. To perform deeds; to work ME.; *euphem.* to copulate 1601. 3. In perfect tenses: To make an end ME. 4. To fare, get on ME.; *spec.* to be in health 1463. 5. To 'work'; to do what is wanted; to succeed, answer, or serve; to be fitting; to suffice 1596.

1. Send me word how ye wyll that I doo there in MARG. PASTON. 2. Let's meet, and either d. or die FLETCHER. 3. Ha done with words SHAKS. 4. The farmers were doing badly 1832. Flax does well after wheat 1847. All..asked him 'how the Marquess did?' DISRAELI. 5. That will d., thank you (*mod.*).

III. Causal and auxiliary uses. †1. With *that* and subord. clause: To cause (*that* a person or thing shall do something) –ME. 2. With *obj.* and *infin.*: To make or cause a person, etc. to do something OE. 3. Put as a substitute for a verb just used, to avoid repetition OE. 4.

As a *Periphrastic Auxiliary* of the present and past Indicative, and Imperative:

a. In *Affirmative* sentences, orig. = the simple tense; still retained, where the order of pronoun and verb is inverted, and now the normal *Emphatic* form of the present and past Indicative OE. b. In *Interrogative* sentences, now the normal form ME. c. In *Negative* sentences, now the normal form with *not* 1489. d. In *Negative Interrogative* sentences, now the normal form 1581.

5. As auxiliary of the *Imperative*:

a. In the Imperative *positive*, adding force; in earlier times, merely periphrastic OE. b. In *do but* —, perh. not auxiliary, but = *ne do but, do nought but* —: cf. BUT *conj.* 1604. c. In the Imperative *negative do not*, colloq. contracted *don't* (dōᵘnt) is now the normal form.

2. Phr. †*To d. him die*: to make him die, to put him to death. *To d.* (one) *to wit, know*, or *understand*: to cause (one) to know; to give (one) to understand; to inform. 3. He speaks as well as you do BAIN. I chose my wife, as she did her wedding-gown GOLDSM. 4. a. The flowers she most did love LONGF. How bitterly did I repent (*mod.*). I *do* wish you would let me sleep (*mod.*). b. What *do* you mean MRS. STOWE. c. We d. not know (*mod.*). d. Didn't you stop SHERIDAN. 5. a. D., d. be calm 1884. b. D. but hear me GOLDSM. c. Don't you speak DICKENS.

IV. Special uses.

†1. Do, the imperative, was used absol. = Go on! Go it! (Cf. L. *age.*) -1610. 2. To do, the dative infin., after the verb *to be*, also after a *sb.* = Proper or necessary to be done, hence, †the thing to be done. *What's to do?* What is the matter? ME. Hence, as a *subst. phr.* = ADO, business, fuss 1570. *To have to do*, to have business, or concern. *To have to do with*: to have business or dealings with. 3. Doing, the pres. pple. = in action, at work, busy ME. b. *To be doing* ME. *Nothing doing*: nothing going on; no prospect of business or success. 4. Done, the pa. pple., is used *esp.* in the sense 'finished'; hence, in dating an official document, in accepting a wager, etc. 1596.

V. With prepositions.

†1. D. after —. To act in obedience to or compliance with. 2. D. by —. To act towards or in respect of: see BY *prep.* 3. D. for —. To act for or in behalf of; to attend to (now *colloq.*); to ruin, destroy, wear out entirely (*colloq.*). 4. D. to —, unto —. To behave to; to treat. 5. D. with —. To deal with; to manage with. 6. D. without —. To d. one's business without; to dispense with.

VI. With adverbs. (Chiefly *trans.* with *passive.*)

1. D. away. †To put away, dismiss; to put an end to, destroy; also, later, *d. away with* (intr.), in same sense. 1*. D. in. To bring disaster upon, to kill (*slang*). 2. D. off. To put off; to DOFF (*arch.*); to sketch, hit off. 3. D. on. = DON *v.* (*arch.*). 4. D. out. †To put out; to clean out; *to d.* (any one) *out of*: to deprive of, *esp.* by sharp practice. 5. D. over. To overlay, cover, coat. 6. D. up. To raise; *refl.* to arise; to repair, restore; to wrap up (a parcel); to disable, tire out (chiefly in *pa. pple.*); to ruin financially (*colloq.*). †7. D. way (in imperative): to put away; *absol.* to cease. †8. D. withal. *intr.* To d. to the contrary; to help it. (In neg. and interrog. sentences.)

Do (dū), *sb.*¹ 1586. [f. Do *v.*] †1. Stir, fuss, ADO. (Common in 17th c.) 2. The action of doing or that which is done; deed, action, business. Now *rare* or *arch.* 1631. b. *colloq.* A performance, entertainment, jollification 1828. 3. A cheat, swindle, imposture 1835. ¶ See also DERRING-DO.

Do (dōᵘ), *sb.*² 1754. [It. (17th c.).] *Mus.* The syllable now commonly used in solmization instead of UT, to denote the first note (key-note) of the scale (*movable Do*); or in some cases the note C, the key-note of the 'natural scale' (*fixed Do*). (In *Tonic Solfa* commonly *doh.*)

Do., abbrev. of DITTO.

‖**Doab, duab** (dōᵘ·ăb, dū·ăb). 1803. [Pers. and Urdū; lit. 'two waters'.] The tongue or tract of land between two confluent rivers.

The Doab, Entre Rios, or Mesopotamia, bounded by the rivers Obi and Irtish R. G. LATHAM.

Doable (dū·ăb'l), *a.* 1449. [f. Do *v.* + -ABLE.] Capable of being done.

Do-all (dū·ǫl). 1633. [f. Do *v.* + ALL.] A factotum.

Dunstan was the Doe-all at Court, being the Kings Treasurer, Chancellour, Counsellour, Confessour, all things FULLER.

Doand, obs. f. *doing*, pr. pple. of Do *v.*

Doat, -er, -ing, etc.; see DOTE, etc.

Dobber (dǫ·bəɹ). *U.S. local.* 1809. [a. Du.] The float of an angler's fishing-line.

Dobbin (dǫ·bin). 1596. [the proper name *Dobbin* (dim. of *Dob*, altered forms of *Robin, Rob*) as a pet name.] 1. An ordinary draught horse; *contempt.*, a jade. 2. [? a distinct word.] A small drinking-vessel 1792.

Dobby, dobbie (dǫ·bi). 1691. [? playful application of proper name *Dobbie* (f. as prec.).] 1. A silly old man, a dotard (*dial.*). 2. A household sprite or apparition; a brownie (*dial.*) 1811. 3. *Weaving.* A small Jacquard attachment to a loom for weaving small figures 1878.

Dobchick(in, obs. ff. DABCHICK.

‖**Do·bla.** Now *Hist.* 1829. [Sp.] An obs. Sp. gold coin.

Dobson (dǫ·bsən). *U.S.* 1889. An angler's name for the larva of *Corydalus cornutus*.

Do·bule. 1864. [ad. mod.L. *Dobula.*] *Ichthyol.* A N. Amer. species of dace.

Docent (dōᵘ·sĕnt). 1639. [ad. L. *docentem.*]

A. *adj.* Teaching.

B. *sb.* In some American universities, etc., a recognized teacher not on the salaried staff.

‖**Docetæ** (dosī·tī), *sb. pl.* 1818. [med.L., a. Gr. Δοκηταί, f. δοκέ-ειν.] *Eccl. Hist.* A sect of heretics, who held that Christ's body was either a phantom, or of celestial substance. Hence **Doce·tic** *a.* of or pertaining to the D. **Doce·tism**, the doctrine or views of the D. **Doce·tist. Doceti·stic** *a.*

Dochmiac (dǫ·kmiæk). 1775. [ad. Gr. δοχμιακός, f. δόχμιος pertaining to a δοχμή or hand's-breadth.] *Gr. Pros.*

A. *adj.* Of the nature of a *dochmius*; composed of *dochmii*, i.e. of pentasyllabic feet of which the typical form is ◡ — — ◡ —.

B. *sb.* A foot or verse of this description.

Docible (dǫ·sib'l), *a.* ? *Obs.* 1549. [ad. L. *docibilis*, f. *docere.*] 1. Apt to be taught or trained; teachable; tractable. 2. Capable of being imparted by teaching 1659.

1. Their tenderest and most d. age MILT. Hence **Docibi·lity** (? *Obs.*), **Do·cibleness** (? *Obs.*), capacity or aptness for being taught; teachableness.

Docile (dōᵘ·səil, dǫ·sil), *a.* 1483. [a. F., ad. L. *docilis.*] 1. Apt to be taught or trained; teachable; tractable. 2. *transf.* of things: Yielding readily to treatment; tractable 1795.

1. The d. mind may soone thy precepts know B. JONS. 2. The d. wax 1881, ores 1884. Hence **Do·cilely** *adv.*

Docility (dosi·lĭti). 1560. [ad. F. *docilité*, ad. L. *docilitatem.*] Docile quality; aptness to be taught; amenability to training or treatment; tractability, obedience.

The elephant..whose d. is exhibited unto us in the theaters HOLLAND.

Docimasy (dǫ·simăsi). 1802. [ad. Gr. δοκιμασία, f. δοκιμάζειν to examine.] 1. *Gr. Antiq.* A judicial inquiry (*esp.* at Athens) into the character and antecedents of aspirants for public office or citizenship. 2. The art or practice of assaying metallic ores 1802. 3. The art of ascertaining the properties and purity of drugs; also of ascertaining certain physiological facts. Hence **Docima·stic** *a.* of or pertaining to d., *esp.* to the assay of metals; proving by experimental tests.

Docimology (dǫsimǫ·lŏdʒi). 1847. [f. Gr. δόκιμος + -LOGY.] A treatise on the art of assaying metals, etc.; see prec.

Do·city. *dial.* 1682. [?] Docility; gumption.

Dock (dǫk), *sb.*¹ [OE. *docce*; app. Com. WGer or OTeut.; cf. MDu. *docke*, in comb. *docke-blaederen* 'petasites', Ger. *docken-blätter*, etc.] The common name of various species of the genus *Rumex* (N.O. *Polygonaceæ*), coarse weedy herbs with thickened rootstock, sheathing stipules, and panicled racemes of inconspicuous greenish flowers. Without qualifying word usually the common dock (*R. obtusifolius*). **Yellow Dock** is *R. crispus*. Also applied to other coarse plants of similar habit.

Phr. *In d., out nettle* orig. a charm uttered to aid the cure of nettle-stings; †hence, a proverbial expression for changeableness. *Comb.* **d.-cress**, nipplewort.

Dock (dǫk), *sb.*² ME. [Same as mod.Icel. *dockr* short stumpy tail. Etym. unkn.] 1. The solid fleshy part of an animal's tail. 2. A piece of leather harness covering the clipped tail of a horse; also, the crupper of a saddle or harness ME. 3. A cut end of anything, *e.g.* of hair, (?) of a tree-trunk. Now *dial.* 1573. †4. [f. DOCK *v.*¹] The act of docking -1751.

Dock (dǫk), *sb.*³ 1513. [Same as Du. *docke*, mod.Du. *dok.* Of uncertain origin.] †1. The bed (in the sand or ooze) in which a ship lies dry at low water -1633. †2. An artificial inlet, to admit a boat, etc. -1719. 3. An artificial basin excavated, built round with masonry, and fitted with flood-gates, into which ships are received for repair, loading, etc. 1552. 4. (Often *pl.*) A range of dock-basins (sense 3) together with the adjoining wharfs, warehouses and offices (*commercial docks*). b. A DOCKYARD (*naval docks*). 1703. 5. *Railways.* An enclosure in a platform into which a single line of rails runs and terminates.

3. *Dry* or *graving d.*, a narrow basin into which a single vessel is received, and from which the water is then let out, leaving the vessel dry for repairing, etc. *Wet d.*, a large water-tight enclosure in which the water is maintained at the level of high tide, so that vessels remain constantly afloat in it. *Floating d.*, a large floating structure that can be used like a dry d. 4. Cuttle lived .. near the India Docks DICKENS. *Comb.* **d.-warrant**, a warrant given to the owner of goods warehoused in a d.

Dock (dǫk), *sb.*⁴ 1586. [Cf. Flem. *dok* hutch, pen.] The enclosure in a criminal court in which the prisoner is placed at his trial.

attrib. d. brief, a brief undertaken by a barrister in court for a prisoner in the d. without means.

Dock (dǫk), *v.*¹ ME. [f. DOCK *sb.*²] 1. *trans.* To cut short in some part, *esp.* in the tail, hair, or the like. 2. *transf.* and *fig.* To cut short, curtail; to deprive *of* some part ME. 3. To cut away, cut off; also = DAG *v.*¹ 3. ME.

1. His tope was doked lyk a preest biforn CHAUCER. His [a dog's] tail must then be docked JOHNSON. 2. To d. wages by rent 1889. Phr. *To d. the entail* (Law): to cut off or put an end to the entail; also *fig.*

Dock (dǫk), *v.*² 1514. [f. DOCK *sb.*³] 1. *trans.* To take, bring, or receive (a ship) into a dock (see DOCK *sb.*³). 2. To furnish or lay out with docks 1757.

1. And see my wealthy Andrew dockt in sand *Merch. V.* I. i. 27.

Dockage (dǫ·kĕdʒ). 1708. [f. as prec.] Charges made for the use of docks; also, dock accommodation; the berthing of vessels in docks.

Docker (dǫ·kəɹ). 1762. [f. as prec.] 1. A dweller in or near a dock; *spec.* an inhabitant of Devonport. 2. A labourer in the docks (*mod.*).

Docket (dǫ·kĕt), *sb.* Also 6-9 **docquet.** 1483. [Doubtfully derived from DOCK *v.*¹] 1. A brief, summarized statement; an abstract; a digest, minute. Now *Hist.* 1483. 2. *spec.* The abstract of the contents of a proposed Letter-patent, written upon the King's bill which authorized the preparation of such letter, and also copied into a Register or Docket-book 1552. 3. *Law.* A memorandum or register of legal judgements 1668. 4. *Law.* A list of causes for trial, or of names of persons having causes pending. Hence phr. *On the d.* (U.S.) 1790. 5. An endorsement on a document, briefly indicating its contents or subject; a label; a written direction, a ticket 1706. 6. A warrant from the Custom House on entering goods, certifying the payment of the duty 1712.

Phr. †*To strike a d.*: to issue a fiat in bankruptcy; to make a man a bankrupt.

Do·cket, *v.* 1615. [f. prec. sb.] †1. *trans.* To furnish with a docket -1833. 2. *Law.* To make an abstract of (judgements, etc.) and enter them in a list or index 1692. 3. To endorse (a letter, etc.) with a short note of its contents, writer, date, etc. 1750. Also *transf.* and *fig.*

3. Whatever letters and papers you keep, d. and tie them up in their respective classes CHESTERF.

Dockyard (dǫ·kˌyāɹd). 1704. [f. DOCK *sb.*³ + YARD.] An enclosure in which ships are built and repaired, and all kinds of ships' stores are brought together; *esp.* a Government establishment of this character.

Docoglossate (dǫkoglǫ·sĕt), *a.* 1884 [f. mod.L. *Docoglossa* (f. Gr. δοκός balk, bar + γλῶσσα tongue).] *Zool.* Of or pertaining to the *Docoglossa*, a group of gastropod molluscs having transverse rows of beam-like teeth on the lingual ribbon.

Docquet(t, obs. f. DOCKET.

Doctor (dǫ·ktəɹ), *sb.* ME. [a. OF., ad. L. *doctorem*, f. *docere*.] **1.** A teacher, instructor; one who inculcates learning, opinions, or principles. (Const. *of*.) Now *rare*. **2.** One skilled in, and therefore competent to teach, any branch of knowledge; an eminently learned man (*arch.*) ME. Also †*transf.* **3.** *spec.* applied to: *The Doctors of the Church*, certain early 'fathers' distinguished by their eminent learning. **b.** The leading Schoolmen. ME. **4.** One who, in any faculty, has attained to the highest degree conferred by a University; a title originally implying competency to teach such subject, but now merely a certificate of the highest proficiency therein. (Now often conferred by Universities as an honorary compliment.) ME. **5.** Hence: A learned divine ME.; one learned in the law ME. **6.** *spec.* A doctor of medicine; *pop.* any medical practitioner ME. Also *fig.* **7.** *transf.* Any mechanical appliance for curing or removing defects, regulating, adjusting, or feeding 1796. **8.** A fish of the genus *Acanthurus*: also called *d.-fish, surgeon-fish* 1833. **9.** *Naut.* A ship's cook 1860. **10.** *Old slang.* A loaded die 1700.

1. These new Doctors of the rights of men BURKE. 2. Who shall decide, when Doctors disagree POPE. 6. So liv'd our Sires, ere doctors learn'd to kill DRYDEN. 7. (*Calico-printing*)..The cleaning-d., which wipes clean the surface of the roller 1874. The superfluous colour is..wiped off by the colour doctors 1875.

Doctor (dǫ·ktəɹ), *v. colloq.* 1599. [f. prec. sb.] **1.** *trans.* To confer the degree of Doctor upon; to make a Doctor. **2.** To treat, as a doctor; to administer medicine or treatment to 1737; also *transf.* **3.** *fig.* To tamper with, adulterate, sophisticate 1774. **4.** *intr.* To practise as a physician 1865.

2. Brodie..sent me off to d. myself COL. HAWKER. 3. To d. wines 1820, dice DE QUINCEY, narratives 1866. Hence **Do·ctoral, Docto·rial** *adjs.* of or belonging to a d.; †holding the position of a d. **Do·ctorally** *adv.* **Do·ctorly** *a.* like or befitting a d.

Doctorate (dǫ·ktŏrĕt), *sb.* 1676. [ad. med.L. *doctoratus*. Cf. F *doctorat*.] The degree of doctor.

Doctorate (dǫ·ktŏreⁱt), *v.* Now *rare*. 1611. [f. med.L. *doctorare*.] *trans.* To confer the degree of Doctor upon; also *absol.*

Doctoress; see DOCTRESS.

Do·ctorize, *v. rare.* 1600. [f. DOCTOR *sb.* + -IZE.] To confer the degree of Doctor upon; to doctor. Hence **Doctoriza·tion.** (Dicts.)

Doctors' Commons. 1680. [See COMMONS.] The common table of the Association or College of Doctors of Civil Law in London; hence, the buildings occupied by these as an incorporated Society; and now the name of the site of these, to the south of St. Paul's Cathedral.

Literary references to Doctors' Commons in later times usually refer to the registration, etc. of wills, to marriage licences, or to divorce proceedings.

Doctorship (dǫ·ktəɹʃip). 1586. [-SHIP.] **1.** = DOCTORATE *sb.*[1] **2.** The position, character, or function of a DOCTOR 1598.

Doctress (dǫ·ktrĕs), **doctoress** (dǫ·ktŏrĕs). 1549. [f. DOCTOR; cf. F. doctoresse.] **1.** A female doctor. (Now only when sex is emphasized.) **2.** *joc.* A doctor's wife or daughter 1748.

†**Do·ctrinable**, *a.* [f. DOCTRINE *sb.* or *v.*] Fit for instruction; instructive. SIDNEY.

Doctrinaire (dǫktrinēᵊ·ɹ). 1820. [a. F.]

A. *sb.* **1.** *Fr. Hist.* One of a constitutionalist party which arose in France soon after 1815, having for their object to reconcile authority and liberty, royalty and national representation. **2.** Hence, One who tries to apply some doctrine without sufficient regard to practical considerations; a pedantic theorist. (Often used as a term of reproach by practical men.) 1831.

B. *adj.* Pertaining to, or of the character of, a doctrinaire; merely theoretical or speculative 1834. Hence **Do:ctrinai·rism**, the principles or practice of a d.

Doctrinal (dǫ·ktrinăl, dǫktrəi·năl), *a.* and *sb.* 1450. [The sb. was a. F. *doctrinal*; the adj. perh. ad. late L. *doctrinalis*.]

A. *adj.* **1.** Of or pertaining to doctrine; containing doctrine. †**2.** Serving to teach or instruct –1641.

1. He had some d. opinions which they liked not CLARENDON. 2. In the nature of a doctrinall instrument HOOKER.

B. *sb.* †**1.** The title of a text-book on grammar by Alex. de Villedieu; hence, any text-book –1653. **2.** *pl.* Matters of doctrine or instruction 1619.

Hence **Doctrinally** *adv* in a d. manner; by way of, or in respect of, teaching.

Doctrinarian (dǫktrinēᵊ·riăn). 1747. [f. L. type **doctrinarius*.] **a.** *sb.* =DOCTRINAIRE *sb.* **b.** *adj.* = DOCTRINAIRE *a.* Hence **Doctrina·rianism**, doctrinairism.

Do·ctrinate, *v. arch.* 1631. [f. stem of med.L. *doctrinare*; see -ATE[3] 5.] *trans.* To teach or instruct; *absol.* To give instruction *on*.

Doctrine (dǫ·ktrin), *sb.* ME. [a. F., ad. L. *doctrina*, f. *doctor*.] †**1.** The action of teaching or instructing; a lesson, a precept –1710. **2.** That which is taught. **a.** A body of instruction or teaching ME. **b.** *esp.* That which is laid down as true concerning a particular department of knowledge, as religion, politics, science, etc.; a belief, theoretical opinion; a dogma ME. **3.** A body or system of principles; a theory; a science, or department of knowledge. ? *Obs.* 1594. †**4.** Erudition –1601. †**5.** Discipline (*rare*) –1533.

1. He..said unto them in his d., Hearken *Mark* iv. 2. 2. The d. of the equality of all men BURKE. *Monroe d.* (U.S. politics): the principles of policy put forward in the Message of President Monroe to Congress, 2 Dec. 1823, the effect of which is that the United States will regard as an unfriendly act any attempt by any European Power to interfere with for the purpose of controlling, or to plant new colonies in, any part of the American continent. 3. The d. of comets CHATHAM. 4. *All's Well* I. iii. 247. Hence **Do·ctrinism**, adherence to, or setting forth of, d. So **Do·ctrinist**, one who does this.

Document (dǫ·kiumĕnt), *sb.* 1450. [a. F., ad. L. *documentum*.] †**1.** Teaching, instruction, warning –1793. †**2.** A lesson; an admonition, a warning –1800. †**3.** That which serves to show or prove something; evidence, proof –1847. **4.** Something written, inscribed, etc., which furnishes evidence or information upon any subject, as a manuscript, title-deed, coin, etc. 1727.

2. Even bad pictures supply him with useful documents SIR J. REYNOLDS. 3. A d. of Fortunes instabilitie RALEIGH. 4. These frescoes..have become invaluable as documents MRS. JAMESON. Hence **Do:cume·ntal** *a.*

Do·cument, *v.* 1648. [f. prec. sb.] †**1.** *trans.* To teach, instruct –1739; to give a lesson to –1802. **2.** To furnish with documents; to provide (a ship) with the papers required to manifest its ownership and cargo 1807.

1. I am finely documented by my own daughter DRYDEN.

Documentary (dǫ:kiume·ntări), *a.* 1802. [f. L. *documentum*.] **1.** Of the nature of or consisting in documents. **2.** Evidential (*rare*). CARLYLE. **3.** Relating to teaching (*rare*) 1871.

1. Fragments of Letters and other d. scraps CARLYLE.

Documentation (dǫ:kiumentēⁱ·ʃən). 1754. [ad. med.L. *documentationem*.] †**1.** Admonition, 'lecturing' –1844. **2.** The furnishing of a ship with papers 1844. **3.** Use of documentary evidence and authorities 1888.

†**Do·cumentize**, *v.* 1599. [f. DOCUMENT *sb.* + -IZE.] *trans.* To teach, give a lesson to; also, to furnish with evidence –1754.

Dod, *sb.*[1] and *interj. dial.* 1676. Orig. a deformation of *God*.

Dod (dǫd), *sb.*[2] *dial.* 1661. [Cogn. w. Du. *dodde*.] The Reed-Mace or Cat's-tail, *Typha latifolia*.

Dod, dodd, *sb.*[3] *n. dial.* 1878. [Cf. DOD *v.*[1]] A rounded summit or eminence.

Dod (dǫd), *v.*[1] Now *dial.* [ME. *dodden*, from same root as DOD *sb.*[3]] To make the top or head of (anything) blunt, rounded, or bare; hence, to clip, poll, lop, etc.

Dod, *v.*[2] Now *dial.* 1661. [var. of DAD *v.*] *trans.* To beat, knock.

†**Do·ddard.** *rare.* [app. f. DOD *v.*[1]; cf. *pollard*.] A tree that has lost its head of branches by decay. Also *attrib.* DRYDEN.

Do·dded, *ppl. a. n. dial.* ME. [f. as prec.] Polled, lopped; hornless; awnless.

Dodder (dǫ·dəɹ), *sb.* [perh. Com. WGer. ME. *doder*.] **1.** The common name of the genus *Cuscuta*, N.O. *Convolvulaceæ*, comprising slender leafless plants, like masses of twining threads, parasitic on flax, clover, thyme, furze, etc. **2.** = DOD *sb.*[2] *dial.*

Dodder (dǫ·dəɹ), *v.* 1617. [Cf. dial. *dadder* vb., to tremble.] **1.** *intr.* To tremble or shake from frailty. **2.** To move unsteadily, totter 1819. **Do·dderer. Do·ddering** *vbl. sb.* and *ppl. a.*; **Do·ddering-grass**, quaking-grass. **Do·ddery** *a.*

Doddered (dǫ·dəɹd), *ppl. a.* 1697. [app. orig. a deriv. of DOD *v.*[1]; cf. DODDARD.] **1.** Having lost the top or branches, *esp.* through age or decay; hence, remaining as a decayed stump: a conventional epithet of old oaks. Johnson's erroneous explanation 'Overgrown with dodder', has added, in lit. usage, a vague notion of some kind of parasitical accretion accompanying decay. **2.** *dial.* Shattered, infirm 1847.

1. Sere-wood, and firs, and d. oaks DRYDEN.

Doddle (dǫ·d'l), *v.* 1653. [var. of DADDLE.] †**1.** *trans.* To shake, nod (the head). **2.** *intr.* To toddle; to totter; to dawdle 1761.

Doddy, doddie (dǫ·di), *sb. Sc.* 1808. [f. DOD *v.*[1]] A cow or bull without horns; *attrib.* = DODDED.

†**Doddypoll** (dǫ·dipōᵘl). ME. [app. f. DOTE *v.*, referred to DOD *v.*[1]; cf. *roundhead*.] A stupid person; blockhead, fool –1767.

Dodeca-, dodec-, Gr. δώδεκα twelve, a comb. form, as in:

Dode·cadrachm [Gr. δραχμή], an ancient Greek coin worth 12 drachmas. **Dode·cagon** [Gr. -γωνος, γωνία], *Geom.* a plane figure having twelve sides and twelve angles. ‖**Do:decagy·nia** [Gr. γυνή], *Bot.* a Linnæan order of plants having either eleven or twelve pistils; hence, **Dode·cagyn**, a plant of this order; **Do:decagy·nian, -gy·nious, Dodeca·gynous** *adjs.* **Dodecahe·dral** *a.* [see next], having the form of a dodecahedron; twelve-sided. **Do:decahe·dron** [Gr. ἕδρα], *Geom.* a solid figure having twelve faces. **Dodeca·merous** *a.* [Gr. μέρος], consisting of twelve parts or divisions. ‖**Dodeca·ndria** [Gr. ἀνδρ-, ἀνήρ], *Bot.* the eleventh class in the Linnæan system, comprising plants having from twelve to nineteen stamens, not cohering; hence, **Dodeca·nder**, one of the *Dodecandria*; **Dodeca·ndrian** *a.*, belonging to that class; **Dodeca·ndrous** *a.*, having twelve stamens. **Do·decane**, *Chem.* a paraffin of the composition $C_{12}H_{26}$. **Do:decape·talous** *a.*, *Bot.* having twelve petals. **Do·decarchy** [Gr. -αρχία], government by twelve; a ruling body of twelve. **Do:decase·mic** *a.* [Gr. -σημος, σῆμα], *Pros.* consisting of twelve units of time, as a *d. foot*. **Do·decastyle** [Gr. στῦλος], a portico or colonnade of twelve columns. **Do:decasy·llable**, *Pros.* a line or word of twelve syllables; hence, **Do:decasylla·bic** *a.*, of or containing twelve syllables.

†**Dodecate·mory.** 1603. [ad. Gr. δωδεκατημόριον, f. δωδέκατον twelfth + μόριον portion.] *Astron.* A twelfth part; applied chiefly to each of the twelve divisions of the Zodiac –1751.

Dode·cuplet. 1880. [f. DODEC(A-) + (OCT)UPLET.] *Mus.* 'A group of twelve notes to be played in the time of eight' (Stainer and Barrett).

Dodge (dǫdʒ), *v.* 1568. [Of unkn. origin. Wedgewood and Skeat compare an alleged dial. Sc. *dodd* to jog.] **1.** *intr.* To move to and fro, or backwards and forwards; to shuffle 1704; †to use shifts (*with* a person, etc.) so as to baffle or catch him –1816. †**2.** *intr.* To be off and on in one's speech and action; to parley, palter, haggle –1763. **3.** *trans.* To play fast and loose with; to baffle by shifts; to trifle with 1573. **4.** To avoid or elude by changes of position, shifts, etc. 1680. **5.** To follow stealthily 1727. **6.** *trans.* and *intr.* (*dial.*) To jog 1802.

1. The King..had been dodging with Essex eight or ten days DE FOE. Dodging behind the mizzen mast 1756. 2. With Fate's lean tipstaff none can d. PRIOR. 3. He dodged me with a long and loose account TENNYSON. 5. I will d. your steps 1840. Hence **Do·dgy** *a.* evasive, tricky, artful. **Do·dgily** *adv.* **Do·dginess.**

Dodge (dǫdʒ), *sb.* 1575. [f. prec. vb.] **1.** The act of slipping aside and eluding; the slip, the go-by. Now *dial.* **2.** A shifty trick 1638. **3.** *colloq.* and *slang.* A clever expedient or contrivance (cf. *trick*); vulgarly extended to a machine, a natural phenomenon, etc. 1842.

2. 'It was all false, of course?' 'All, sir,' replied Mr. Weller, 'reg'lar do, sir; artful d.' DICKENS. 3. The alternation of green and corn crops is a good d. 1842.

Dodger (dǫ·dʒəɪ). 1568. [f. DODGE *v.*] 1. One who dodges; in early use, *esp.* a haggler; later, *esp.* one who practises artful dodges. 2. *U.S.* A hard-baked corn-cake 1852. 3. *U.S.* A small handbill 1884. So **Do·dgery**, trickery.

†**Dodipole**, var. DODDYPOLL.

Dodkin (dǫ·dkin). ME. [15th c. *doydekyn, doykyn*, a. MDu. *duytken*, dim. of *duyt, doyt*; see DOIT.] = DOIT, q. v. Hence, any small coin. Now *Hist.*

Do·dman. Now *dial.* 1550. [?] A snail; called also *hodman-dod.*

Dodo (dōu·dǫ). 1628. [a. Pg. *doudo* fool, as *adj.* silly.] An extinct bird, *Didus ineptus*, of the order *Columbidæ*, formerly inhabiting Mauritius; it had a massive clumsy body, and small wings, useless for flight.

Dodonæan, -ean (dōudǫnī·ăn), *a.* 1569. [f. L. *Dodonæus*, a. Gr., f. Δωδώνη Dodona.] Of or pertaining to Dodona in ancient Epirus, or its oracle of Zeus situated in a grove of oaks. Also †**Dodo·nian.**

†**Dodra·ntal**, *a. rare.* 1656. [ad. L. *dodrantalis*, f. *dodrans.*] 'Of nine ounces or nine inches in length or weight' (Blount).

Doe (dōu). [OE. *dá*, ? a contracted form, ? a. L. *dama, damma.*] 1. The female of the fallow deer; also, of allied animals, as the reindeer. 2. The female of the hare or rabbit. Also *attrib.*, as *d.-buck*, a male deer.

Doe, obs. f. DO, DOUGH.

Doer (dū·əɪ). ME. [f. DO *v.* + -ER [1].] 1. One who performs some act or deed. 2. One who acts for another; an agent; a factor; an attorney. Now only *Sc.* 1465. 3. An animal or plant that does or thrives (well or ill) 1865.

1. Talkers are no good dooers *Rich. III*, I. iii. 352.

Does, 3rd pers. sing. pres. ind. of DO *v.*

Doeskin (dōu·skin). 1456. [f. DOE + SKIN.] 1. The skin of a doe; also, a kind of leather made from this. 2. A closely-cut thick black cloth, twilled, but dressed so as to show little of the twill. (Cf. BUCKSKIN.) 1851.

Doest (dū·ĕst), 2nd pers. sing. pres. ind. of DO *v.*

Doff (dǫf), *v.* Pa. t. and pple. **doffed** (dǫft). ME. [Fused form of *do off.* In 19th c. freq. in lit. use.] 1. *trans.* To put off or take off, as clothing, the hat, etc. Also †*intr.* with *with. absol.* To raise one's hat (*rare*). 2. *refl.* To undress oneself. Also *fig.* Now only *dial.* 1697. 3. *transf.* and *fig.* To put off, lay aside; hence, to get rid of 1592. †4. To put (any one) *off* (with an excuse, etc.); to turn aside -1659.

1. Thou weare a Lyons hide! d. it for shame *John* III. i. 128. 3. He sometimes d'offeth his owne nature and puts on theirs B. JONS. 4. *Oth.* IV. ii. 176 (Qo. 1).

Doffer (dǫ·fəɪ). 1825. [f. prec. vb.] One who or that which doffs. 1. In a carding machine, a comb or revolving cylinder which strips off cotton or wool from the cards; a *doffing-cylinder.* 2. A worker who removes the full bobbins or spindles 1862.

Dog (dǫg), *sb.* [late OE. *docga* (once in a gloss); previous history unkn. Introduced into continental langs. usually, in early instances, with the attribute 'English'. In Teut. langs., the generic name was *hund*; see HOUND.] 1. A quadruped of the genus *Canis*, of which wild species are found in various parts of the world, and numerous breeds, varying greatly in size, shape, and colour, occur in a more or less domesticated state in almost all countries. These are referred by zoologists to a species *C. familiaris*; but their common origin is disputed. b. *esp.* A dog used for hunting; a hound ME. c. *fig.* ME. d. With qualifications, as BAN-DOG, BULL-DOG, CUR-DOG, etc., q.v. ME. 2. The male of this species; opp. to BITCH. Also, a male fox. 1577. 3. Of a person: a. in contempt: A worthless, surly, or cowardly fellow. (Cf. CUR.) ME. b. playfully: A gallant; a fellow, chap. Usu. with *adj.*, as *sad, sly*, etc. 1618. c. = BULL-DOG 2. 1847. 4. *Astron.* The name of two constellations, the Great and Little D. (*Canis Major* and *Minor*); see DOG-STAR 1551. 5. Short for DOG-FISH 1674. 6. A name for various mechanical devices used for gripping or holding, such as:

a. A grappling-iron for raising the monkey of a pile-driver, or clutching and withdrawing tools used in well-boring or mining. b. A grappling-iron with a fang which clutches an object, as a log, etc. to be hoisted, or to be secured in position for sawing. c. A projection or tooth acting as a detent, *e.g.* in a lock; a catch or click which engages the teeth of a ratchet-wheel. d. An adjustable stop placed in a machine to change direction of motion (Webster).

7. One of a pair of irons for supporting burning wood in a fireplace; a *fire-d.*; = ANDIRON; also, a rest for the fire-irons 1596. 8. *attrib.*, etc. = Canine 1565; = male 1555; = Bastard, as *d.-Latin* 1611; with certain adjs. = As.. as a d. (cf. D.-CHEAP) 1552.

1. *fig.* Cæsars Spirit..Shall..Cry hauocke, and let slip the Dogges of Warre *Jul. C.* III. i. 273. 3. You spurn'd me such a day; another time You cald me d. *Merch. V.* I. iii. 129. I was an unfortunate d. DE FOE.

Phrases, etc. *To the dogs*: to destruction or ruin; as in *to go, send, throw to the dogs. Fight d., fight bear*: *i.e.* till one be overcome. *A hair of the d. that bit you*: formerly thought a specific for the bite of a mad d.; hence allusively, *esp.* of more drink to take off the effects of drunkenness. *To lead a dog's life*: *i.e.* a life of misery, or of miserable subserviency. *Whose d. is dead?* What's the matter? Also in many other proverbs and phrases.

Comb. a. †**d.-ape**, ad.-faced baboon, CYNOCEPHALUS; **-belt**, in *Coal-mining*, a belt worn round the waist, used for drawing sledges, etc. in the workings; †**-chance** = *dog-throw*; **-grate**, a detached fire-grate standing in a fireplace upon supports called dogs; **-iron** = sense 7; **-nap**, a short nap taken while sitting; **-power**, the mechanical power exerted by a d., as in turning a spit, etc.; †**-spasm** = CYNIC spasm; **-stopper** *Naut.*, a strong rope clenched round the mainmast, and used to relieve the deck-stopper when the ship rides in a heavy sea (Smyth); **-stove** = *dog-grate*; **-tent**, a small tent, having a resemblance to a dog's kennel; **-throw**, the lowest throw at dice (L. *canis, canicula*); **-town** (*U.S.*), a colony of prairie dogs.

b. *Comb.* with *dog's*: **Dog's body**, a sailor's name for dried pease boiled in a cloth; †**dog's face**, a term of abuse; **dog's lug** (*Naut.*) = DOG'S-EAR *sb.* 2; **dog's sleep, trick**, see DOG-SLEEP, -TRICK.

c. In names of animals (*a*) resembling dogs in some respect, or (*b*) infesting dogs: as **d.-badger**, one resembling the d. in his feet; **-bat**, one having a head like a dog's; **-flea**, a species of flea (*Pulex serraticeps*) infesting dogs; **-guts**, the fish *Harpodon nehereus*, also called BUMMALO; **-louse**, a kind of louse infesting dogs; also = *dog-tick*; **-tick**, a tick of the genus *Ixodes* infesting dogs.

d. In names of plants (frequently denoting a worthless sort, or one unfit for human food): as **d.-blow**, in Nova Scotia, the Ox-eye daisy; **dog('s) cabbage**, *Thelygonum Cynocrambe*, a succulent herb of the Mediterranean; **d.-daisy**, the common Daisy, *Bellis perennis*; also, locally, and in books, the Ox-eye Daisy; **-lichen**, *Peltidea canina*, formerly used as a cure for hydrophobia; **dog('s)-parsley**, *Æthusa Cynapium*, also called Fool's Parsley; **dog('s)-wheat**, *Triticum caninum* = DOG-GRASS.

Dog (dǫg), *v.* Pa. t. and pple. **dogged** (dǫgd). 1519. [f. prec. sb.] 1. *trans.* To follow like a dog; to follow pertinaciously or closely; to pursue, track. Also *fig.* 2. *intr.* or *absol.* To follow close 1519. 3. *trans.* To drive or chase with, or as with, a dog or dogs 1591. 4. To fasten by means of a dog (see DOG *sb.* 6) 1591. 5. *U.S. slang.* Used in imprecations. Cf. DOG-GONE. 1860.

1. The Bayliffs dog'd us hither to the very door WYCHERLEY. Famine dogs their footsteps SOUTHEY.

Dogal (dōu·găl), *a.* 1848. [ad. It. *dogale.*] Of or pertaining to a doge.

‖**Dogana** (dǫgā·nă). 1645. [It.; see DIVAN and cf. DOUANE.] A custom-house (in Italy); also, customs (in Italy and Spain).

‖**Dogare·ssa.** 1820. [It., irreg. fem. of *doge.*] The wife of a doge.

Dogate (dōu·geit). 1727. [ad. Fr. *dogat*, ad. It. *dogato.*] The office of a DOGE.

Dogbane; see DOG'S-BANE.

Dogberry[1] (dǫ·gberi). 1551. The drupe of the Wild Cornel or DOGWOOD; the shrub itself. Also, in Nova Scotia, the mountain-ash.

Do·gberry[2]. The constable in *Much Ado about Nothing*; thence, allusively, an ignorant consequential official.

Dogbolt, dog-bolt (dǫ·gbōult). 1465. [?] †1. Some kind of bolt or blunt-headed arrow; ? one of little value that might be shot at any dog -1612. †2. A term of contempt; = 'mean wretch' -1690. 3. The bolt of the cap-square over the trunnion of a gun 1867.

Dog-bramble. Also **dog's-.** 1567. A name for various thorny shrubs; *esp.* a kind of currant, *Ribes Cynosbati.*

†**Dog-brier.** 1530. [tr. L. *sentis canis*, Gr. κυνόσβατος.] The wild brier -1682.

Dog-cart. 1668. 1. A small cart drawn by dogs. 2. A cart with a box under the seat for sportsmen's dogs; now, an open vehicle, with two transverse seats back to back, the hinder of these originally made to shut up so as to form a box for dogs.

Dog-cheap, *adv.* and *pred. a. arch.* 1526. [See DOG 8.] Extremely cheap; also *fig.*

Dog-days, *sb. pl.* 1538. [tr. L. *dies caniculares*; see CANICULAR.] 1. The days about the time of the heliacal rising of the Dog-star; noted as the hottest and most unwholesome period of the year. Rarely in *sing.*

Variously calculated, as depending on the greater dog-star (Sirius) or the lesser (Procyon); and on the heliacal, or the cosmical rising of either of these (both of which also differ in different latitudes); and their duration has been variously reckoned at from 30 to 54 days. In the latitude of Greenwich, the cosmical rising of Procyon now takes place about July 27, that of Sirius about Aug. 11. The heliacal rising is some days later. In current almanacs the dog-days begin July 3, and end Aug. 11.

2. *fig.* A time in which malignant influences prevail. Also *attrib.*

†**Dog-draw.** 1598. *Forest Law.* The act of drawing after or tracking venison illegally killed or wounded, by the scent of a dog drawn by the hand -1708.

‖**Doge** (dōudʒ). 1549. [a. F., ad. Venetian *doge* (disyll.):—(ult.) L. *ducem* (*dux*).] The chief magistrate in the republics of Venice and Genoa. Also *transf.* and *fig.* Hence **Do·geless** *a.* without a d.

Dog-ear, var. of DOG'S-EAR.

Dog-faced (dǫ·gfēist), *a.* 1607. Having a face like a dog's.

Dog-fennel. Also **dog's-.** 1523. [from its smell, and fennel-like leaves.] Stinking Camomile, *Anthemis Cotula.*

Do·g-fish, dogfish. 1475. 1. One of various small sharks of the families *Squalidæ* (*Spinacidæ*), *Galeorhinidæ* (*Carchariidæ*), and *Scylliidæ*, or these collectively; *esp.* the Large and Small Spotted Dogfish (*Scyllium catulus, S. canicula*), and in New England, the Picked Dogfish (*Squalus acanthias*). b. Applied also to the mud-fish (*Amia calva*); to the black-fish (*Dallia pectoralis*); and to the mud-puppy (*Necturus maculatus*). 2. *fig.* Opprobriously of persons 1589.

Dog-fisher. The Otter. WALTON.

Dog-fly. ? ME. An English tr. of Gr. κυνάμυια; identified by some writers with British flies troublesome to dogs.

Dog-fox. 1576. 1. A male fox (see DOG *sb.* 2). 2. Applied also to certain small burrowing animals of the genus *Canidæ*, as the CORSAC.

Dogged (dǫ·gĕd), *a.* (*adv.*) ME. [f. DOG *sb.* + -ED [2]; cf. CRABBED.] 1. *gen.* Like a dog. b. Of or pertaining to a dog, canine. Now *rare.* 2. Currish; cruel; surly; sullenly obstinate. Also †*transf.* of things. ME. 3. Obstinate, stubborn; pertinacious. (The current use.) 1779.

1. Now..Doth d. warre bristle his angry crest, And snarleth in the gentle eyes of peace *John* IV. iii. 149. 2. My wife in a d. humour for my not dining at home PEPYS. 3. A d. veracity JOHNSON. Hence **Do·ggedly** *adv.*, **-ness.**

Dogger[1] (dǫ·gəɪ). [ME. *doggere.* Cf. MDu. *dogge* in phr. *ten dogge varen* to go to the cod-fishing.] 1. A two-masted fishing vessel with bluff bows, used in the North Sea deep-sea fisheries. 2. Short for *Dogger Bank* 1887. *Comb.*: **D. Bank**, name of a shoal in the North Sea; **d.-man**, one of the crew of a d.

Dogger[2] (dǫ·gəɪ). 1670. [? deriv. of DOG.] 1. *dial.* A kind of ironstone; = CATHEAD 2. 2. *Geol.* A sandy ironstone of the Lower Oolite; applied to part of the Jurassic series 1822.

Doggerel (dǫ·gərĕl), **doggrel** (dǫ·grĕl). ME. [Origin unkn.]

A. *adj.* An epithet applied to burlesque verse of irregular rhythm; or to mean, trivial, or undignified verse. *transf.* Bastard, burlesque.

This may wel be Rym dogerel quod he CHAUCER.

B. *sb.* Doggerel verse 1630; a piece of doggerel 1857.
He has a happy talent at d. ADDISON. A d. always had a curious fascination for him [Browning] 1892.

Doggery (dǫ·gəri). 1611. [f. DOG *sb.* + -ERY.] †1. Obscene language. 2. Dog-like or mean behaviour 1844. 3. Dogs collectively. Used by Carlyle as tr. F. *canaille.* 1843. 4. *U.S.* (*vulgar*). A low drinking saloon 1860.

Dogget, obs. f. DOCKET.

Doggish (dǫ·giʃ), *a.* ME. [f. DOG *sb.* + -ISH.] 1. Pertaining to or like a dog 1530. 2. Currish; malicious; snappish. Now *rare.* ME. Hence **Do·ggish-ly** *adv.*, **-ness.**

Doggo (dǫ·go), *adv. slang.* 1893. [?] *To lie* (etc.) *d.*: to lie quiet, to remain hid.

Dog-gone (dǫ·ggǫ̆n). *U.S. slang.* Also **dog on.** 1851. [? a deformation of *God damn*, or ? short for *dog on it* (cf. *pox on it*, etc.).] **A.** *vb.* Used imperatively: 'hang!' **B.** *adj.* or *pa. pple.* = C. 1851. **C. Dog·goned** *adj.* or *pa. pple.* 'darned' 1860.

Dog-grass, dog's-grass. 1597. A name for Couch-grass, *Triticum repens*, and for *T. caninum*; also, locally, for *Cynosurus.*

Doggy, doggie (dǫ·gi), *sb.* 1825. [-Y dim. suffix.] 1. A little dog; a pet name for a dog. 2. *Coal-mining* (*colloq.*) A man employed by the BUTTY (q. v.) as his underground manager.

Doggy (dǫ·gi), *a.* ME. [f. DOG *sb.*; cf. *horsy.*] †1. Malicious; vile -1583. 2. Of or pertaining to a dog 1869. 3. Addicted to dogs, as *d. men* 1859.

Dog-head. (See also DOG'S-HEAD.) 1607. †1. A kind of ape with a head like a dog's; the CYNOCEPHALUS. 2. a. The head of a nail formed by a rectangularly projecting shoulder. (Cf. DOG-NAIL.) 1793. b. The hammer of a gun 1812. So **Dog-headed** *a.* (in sense 1).

Dog-hole. 1579. A hole fit only for a dog; a vile or mean dwelling or place.

Dog-hook. 1571. †1. A hook used for leading a dog -1631. 2. A wrench for uncoupling boring-rods; a spanner. b. An iron bar with a bent prong for grappling logs, etc.

Dog-hutch. 1830. A hutch for a dog; a DOG-HOLE.

Do·g-in-the-ma·nger. 1573. A churlish person who will neither use a thing himself nor let another use it; in allusion to the fable of the dog in a manger and the hay.

Dog-Latin. Bad Latin; see DOG *sb.* 8.

†Dog-leech. 1529. 1. A veterinary surgeon who treats dogs -1831. 2. A quack -1652.

Dog-legged (dǫ·glegd), *a.* 1703. *Archit.* Applied to a staircase, without a well-hole, the successive flights of which form a zigzag; also, to a variety of golf-hole.

Dogma (dǫ·gmă). Pl. **dogmas, dogmata.** 1638. [a. L., a. Gr. δόγμα, f. δοκεῖν. At first used with Gr.-L. pl.] 1. That which is held as an opinion; a belief; a tenet or doctrine; sometimes, depreciatingly, an arrogant declaration of opinion. 2. The body of opinion formulated and authoritatively stated; tenets or principles collectively; doctrinal system 1791.
1. Our dogmata and notions about justification 1652. 2. The present .. is a revolution of doctrine and theoretick d. BURKE.

Dogmatic (dǫgmæ·tik). 1605. [ad. L. *dogmaticus*, a. Gr., f. δόγμα, δογματ-; cf. F. *dogmatique.*]
A. *adj.* 1. Pertaining to the setting forth of opinion; didactic (*rare*) 1678. 2. Of, pertaining to, or of the nature of, dogma or dogmas; doctrinal 1706. 3. Proceeding upon *a priori* principles accepted as true 1696. 4. Of persons, writings, etc.: Asserting dogmas or opinions in an authoritative or arrogant manner 1681.
1. He is no longer interrogative but d. JOWETT. 2. Dogmatick jargon learnt by heart GAY. 3. D. philosophy 1696. 4. He wrote against dogmas with a spirit perfectly d. D'ISRAELI.
B. *sb.* †1. A dogmatic philosopher or physician -1771. †2. A dogmatic person. HOBBES. 3. Chiefly in *pl.* form **Dogmatics**: A system of dogma; *spec.* dogmatic theology 1845.
So **Dogma·tical** *a.* (*sb. pl.*). Hence **Dogma·tical-ly** *adv*, **-ness. Dogmati·cian,** a professor of dogmatics.

Dogmatism (dǫ·gmătiz'm). 1603. [a. F. *dogmatisme*, ad. med.L. *dogmatismus*, f. (ult.) Gr. δόγμα DOGMA; see -ISM.] 1. Positive assertion of dogma or opinion; dogmatizing; positiveness in the assertion of opinion. 2. With *pl.* A dogmatic tenet or system (*rare*) 1803. 3. *Philos.* A system of philosophy based upon principles dictated by reasoning alone; opp. to *scepticism.* More generally, a way of thinking based upon principles which have not been tested by reflection. 1858.
1. Where there is most doubt, there is often the most d. PRESCOTT. 3. What Kant meant we may best understand if we consider how he opposes Criticism to two other forms of philosophy, D. and Scepticism E. CAIRD.

Dogmatist (dǫ·gmătist). 1541. [a. F. *dogmatiste*, ad. med.L. *dogmatista*, ad. Gr. δογματιστής; see DOGMATIZE.] 1. One who dogmatizes, or lays down particular dogmas; *esp.* one who does this positively or arrogantly; a dogmatic person 1654. †2. A propounder of new opinions -1797. 3. A philosopher or a physician of the dogmatic school (see DOGMATIC *a.* 3) 1541.
1. I expect but little success of all this upon the d., his opinion'd assurance is paramount to argument GLANVILL.

Dogmatize (dǫ·gmătəiz), *v.* 1611. [ad. F. *dogmatiser*, ad. med.L. *dogmatizare*, ad. Gr. δογματίζειν, f. δόγμα.] 1. *intr.* To make dogmatic assertions; to speak authoritatively or imperiously *upon* without reference to argument or evidence; †to teach new opinions -1696. 2. *trans.* To deliver as a dogma. Now *rare.* 1621.
1. Prompt to impose, and fond to d. POPE. Hence **Do·gmatizer.**

Dog-nail. 1703. A nail having a large and slightly countersunk head; also a large nail with a head projecting on one side.

Dog-rose. 1597. [tr. med.L. *rosa canina*, repr. L. *cynorrodon* (Pliny), Gr. κυνόροδον.] A species of wild rose (*Rosa canina*), with pale red flowers, frequent in hedges.

Do·g's-bane, do·g-bane. 1597. [See BANE.] A name for plants reputed to be poisonous to dogs, chiefly of the orders *Asclepiadaceæ* and *Apocynaceæ.*

Do·g's-ear, *sb.* 1725. [Cf. next.] The corner of a leaf of a book, etc. turned over like a dog's ear, by careless use, etc.

Dog's-ear, *v.* Also **dog-ear.** 1659. [Cf. prec.] To disfigure a book by turning down the corners of the leaves.

Dog-shore. 1805. Each of two blocks of timber used to prevent a ship from starting off the slips while the keel-blocks are being removed in preparation for launching.

Dog-skin. 1676. The skin of a dog, or the leather made from it. Also *attrib.* So **†Dog's-leather.** 2 *Hen. VI*, IV. ii. 26.

Dog-sleep. 1613. †1. Feigned sleep -1711. 2. A light or fitful sleep, easily interrupted 1708.

Dog's letter. 1636. [tr. L. *litera canina*, Persius.] The letter R, as resembling in sound the snarl of a dog.

Dog's-meat, dog's meat. 1593. 1. Food for dogs, prepared from horse-flesh, offal, etc. 2. *transf.* and *fig.* Carrion; offal 1606. Also *attrib.*

Dog's-tail. Also **dog-tail.** 1753. [tr. Bot.L. *Cynosurus.*] 1. (Usu. **Dog's-tail Grass.**) A genus of grasses, *Cynosurus*, and chiefly the species *C. cristatus*, which has the flowers in each panicle all pointing one way, like the hairs of a dog's tail. 2. = CYNOSURE 1. 1867.

Do·g-star. 1579. [after Gr. κύων, L. *canicula* (*canis*).] The star Sirius, in the constellation of the Greater Dog, the brightest of the fixed stars. Also, Procyon (the Lesser Dog-star).
The Dogge starre, which is called Syrius, or Canicula reigneth 1579.

Do·g-stone. 1640. A stone used for a millstone.

Do·gstones. 1597. [tr. med.L. *Testiculus canis*; from the shape of the tubers.] A name for various British species of Orchis.

Do·g's-tongue. Also **dog-.** 1530. [tr. L. *cynoglossum.*] 1. The genus *Cynoglossum* of boraginaceous plants, esp. Hound's-tongue. (From the shape of the leaves.)

Dog's-tooth. Also **dog-.** 1578. [tr. med.L. *dens canis*] 1. (Now **Dog's-** or **Dog-tooth Violet.**) The genus *Erythronium* of liliaceous plants, esp. *E. Dens-canis*; so called from the teeth on the inner segments of the perianth. 2. A species of grass, *Cynodon Dactylon* 1600. ¶ See also DOG-TOOTH.

Dog-tired, *a.* 1809. [See DOG *sb.* 8.] Tired out.

Dog-tooth. Also **dog's-.** ME. 1. A canine tooth; see CANINE *a.* 2. *Archit.* A pointed moulding resembling a projecting tooth, frequent in mediæval architecture. Also *attrib.* 1836.
Dog-tooth spar: a variety of calcite, crystallizing in pointed scalenohedral forms. Hence **Dog-tooth** *v.* to decorate with dog-tooth moulding.

Dog-tree. 1548. [app. as bearing DOG-BERRIES, q. v.] 1. The common Dogwood. 2. Locally applied to the Spindle-tree, the Elder, and the Guelder-Rose 1703.

Dog-trick. ? *Obs.* 1540. A low, treacherous, or spiteful trick; an ill turn.

Dog-trot. 1664. An easy trot like that of a dog. Also †*fig.*

Dog-vane. 1769. *Naut.* 'A small vane, made of thread, cork, and feathers, or buntin, placed on the weather gunwale to show the direction of the wind' (Smyth). Hence, *joc.* A cockade.

Dog-violet. Also **dog's violet.** 1778. [tr. Bot.L.] The common name of *Viola canina.*

Dog-watch. 1700. [Cf. DOG-SLEEP.] *Naut.* The name of the two short or half watches, one from 4 to 6 p.m., and the other from 6 to 8 p.m.

Dog-weary, *a.* 1596. = DOG-TIRED.

Dog-whelk. 1856. [See WHELK.] A name of univalve molluscs of the genus *Nassa.*

Dogwood (dǫ·gwud). 1617. [*lit. wood* of the DOG-TREE, q. v.] 1. The wild Cornel, *Cornus sanguinea*, common in English woods and hedgerows; also, other species of the genus *Cornus*; *esp.*, in N. America, *C. florida*, a tree bearing large white or pink flowers, and scarlet berries 1676. 2. Applied to various other shrubs and trees; as, in Jamaica, to various species of *Piscidia*; in England, improp., to the Spindle-tree, Guelder-Rose, Woody Nightshade, etc. 1725. 3. The wood of any of these; *esp.* that of *C. sanguinea*, which is close and smooth-grained 1664. Also *attrib.*
White D., Guelder-Rose and *Piscidia Erythrina.*

Dohter, -or, -ur, obs. ff. DAUGHTER.

Doiled, doilt, *ppl. a. Sc.* 1513. [cf. DOLD.] Stupid; crazed.

Doily (doi·li), *a.* or *sb.* 1678. [from surname *Doiley* or *Doyley.*] †1. *attrib.* or *adj.* The name of a woollen stuff for summer wear -1714. 2. *sb.* (Orig. **D.-napkin.**) A small ornamental napkin used at dessert 1711.
1. Some D. Petticoats, and Manto's we have DRYDEN.

Doing (dū·iŋ), *vbl. sb.* ME. [f. DO *v.*] 1. The action of the verb Do; *euphem.* copulation. 2. A deed, act, action, performance, transaction, etc. Usu. (now always) *pl.* ME. 3. *pl.* (*U.S.*) Adjuncts of a dish, fancy dish 1838; *gen.* adjuncts, etceteras, anything that is needed or is 'about' 1915. Also *ppl. a.*
2. Even a child is known by his doings *Prov.* xx. 11.

Doit (doit). 1594. [a. Du. *duit*, of unkn. deriv.] 1. A small Dutch coin formerly in use; hence, a very small coin or sum 1728. 2. *transf.* and *fig.* A very small part *of* anything; a bit, jot; *esp.* in *not to care a d.* 1660.

Doi·ted, *a. Sc.* ME. [? var. of DOTED.] Having the faculties impaired.

Doitkin = DODKIN, q.v.

Dokimastic, -asy, var. ff. DOCIMASTIC, -ASY.

†Dola·bre. *rare.* 1474. [ad. L. *dolabra* pickax, f. *dolare* to chip.] An adze. Hence **Do·labrate** *a. Bot.* = DOLABRIFORM.

Dolabriform (dolæ·brifǭrm), *a.* 1753. [f. L. *dolabra* (see prec.) + *forma.*] Ax-shaped, cleaver-shaped; in *Bot.* applied to some fleshy leaves; in *Entom.*, to joints of antennæ, etc.

‖Dolce far niente (do·ltʃe fār nie·nte). 1814. [It.; = 'sweet doing nothing'.] Delightful idleness. Also *attrib.*

Dolcinist, -ite; see DULCINIST.

Doldrum (dǫ·ldrŏm). Usu. in pl. **doldrums.** 1811. [app. a slang term; cf. OE. *dol* DULL. Cf. *tantrum.*] †1. *slang.* A dullard –1824. 2. pl. *The doldrums.* **a.** Dumps, low spirits 1811. **b.** The condition of a ship which is becalmed 1824. **c.** A non-plussed condition 1871. 3. *spec.* A region near the equator, where the trade winds neutralize each other. (App. due to taking the state 'in the doldrums' for a locality.) 1855.

Dole (dōul), *sb.*[1] [OE. *dál*; cf. DEAL *sb.*[1]] †1. The state of being divided –ME. †2. = DEAL *sb.*[1] 1. –1573. **b.** *Mining.* A portion of ore 1823. **c.** = DALE[2] 1. –1787. 3. A share, portion, lot (*arch.*) ME. 4. Lot in life; destiny (*arch.*) 1500. 5. Distribution; *esp.* of charitable gifts ME. 6. That which is doled out ME. **b.** *The d.*: relief paid to the unemployed 1919. †7. Dealing, intercourse –1561. Also *attrib.*

3. What d. of honour Flies where you bid it *All's Well* II. iii. 176. 4. Happy man be his d., say I 1 *Hen. IV*, II. ii. 79. 5. Large doles of death FLETCHER. A d. every Sunday, of 21 two-penny loaves 1778. 6. Recipients of the ordinary d. of grain MERIVALE.

Comb.: **d.-beer,** beer given as alms; **-land, -meadow, -moor,** common land, moor, etc. in which several have portions indicated by landmarks, but not divided off; **-window,** one at which doles were distributed.

Dole, dool, dule (dōul, dūl), *sb.*[2] *arch.* and *dial.* ME. [a. OF. *doel,* mod.F. *deuil* :—late L. *dolium* grief.] 1. Grief, sorrow. 2. Mourning, lamentation; chiefly in phr. *To make d.* ME. 3. That which excites grief or pity; a grief, sorrow ME. †4. *transf.* Mourning garments –1734. 5. A funeral. Now *dial.* 1548. †6. A company of doves 1486.

1. Earth's..joy and dole MRS. BROWNING. 2. She died. So that day there was dole in Astolat TENNYSON.

Dole, *sb.*[3] 1563. [ad. L. *dolus.*] †1. Guile, deceit –1839. 2. *Sc. Law.* Corrupt, malicious, or evil intent 1753.

Dole, *sb.*[4], var. of DOOL, boundary mark, etc.

Dole, *v.*[1] 1465. [f. DOLE *sb.*[1]] 1. *trans.* To give as a dole. 2. To give *out* in small quantities; to portion *out* in a niggardly manner 1749. †3. To deal *about, around* –1766.

2. This comfort..she doled out to him in daily portions FIELDING. 3. Compensations most liberally doled about to one another LD. MANSFIELD.

Dole, *v.*[2] ? *Obs.* ME. [a. OF. *doleir, doloir,* mod.F. (*se*) *douloir* :—L. *dolere.*] 1. *intr.* To sorrow, grieve, lament –1668. †2. *trans.* To mourn, bewail 1567. †3. To grieve. B. JONS.

1. The doling of the dove W. E. AYTOUN.

Dole; see DOOL, DOWEL, DULL.

†**Do·leance.** 1489. [a. F. *doléance,* f. *doleant,* old pr. pple. of *doloir, douloir.*] 1. Grieving; grief –1639. 2. Complaining, complaint –1656.

Doleful (dōu·lfŭl), *a.*[1] ME. [f. DOLE *sb.*[2]] 1. Full of or attended with dole or grief; distressful, sorrowful. 2. Expressing grief, mourning, or suffering ME. Also as *sb.* (*pl.*) *colloq.*

1. Regions of sorrow, d. shades MILT. *P. L.* I. 65. The d. Ariadne so..forsaken stood COWLEY. 2. A d. face 1865. Hence **Do·leful-ly** *adv.*[1], **-ness.**

Do·leful, *a.*[2] *rare.* 1617. [f. DOLE *sb.*[3]] Crafty, malicious. Hence **Do·lefully** *adv.*[2]

Dolent (dōu·lĕnt), *a. arch.* 1450. [a. F., ad. L. *dolentem.*] Grieving; sorrowful.

Dolerin(e (dǫ·lĕrin). 1863. [a. F. *dolérine,* f. Gr. δολερός deceptive.] *Min.* A gneissoid rock in the Alps, consisting of talc and felspar.

Dolerite (dǫ·lĕrəit). 1838. [a. F. *dolérite,* f. as prec.; so called from the difficulty of discriminating its constituents.] *Min.* A mineral allied to basalt, containing feldspar (labradorite) and augite. Hence **Doleri·tic** *a.*

Dolesome (dōu·lsŏm), *a.* Now *rare.* 1533. [f. DOLE *sb.*[2] + -SOME.] = DOLEFUL *a.*[1] Hence **Do·lesome-ly** *adv.*, **-ness.**

Dolf, -en, obs. pa. t. and pple. of DELVE.

Dolichocephalic (dǫ:likosĭfæ·lik), *a.* 1849. [f. Gr. δολιχός long + κεφαλή head.] *Ethnol.* Long-headed; applied to skulls of which the breadth is less than four-fifths of the length: opp. to BRACHYCEPHALIC. var. **Dolikhokephalic.** So **Dolichoce·phali** *sb. pl.* [mod.L.], men with d. skulls. **Dolichoce·phalism,** the quality of being d. **Dolichoce·phalous** *a.* = DOLICHOCEPHALIC. **Dolichoce·phaly** = *dolichocephalism.*

‖**Dolichurus** (dǫlikiūə·rŏs). [mod.L., ad. Gr. δολίχουρος long-tailed.] *Gr.* and *L. Pros.* A dactylic hexameter with a redundant syllable in the last foot. Hence **Dolichu·ric** *a.*

Do-little. 1586. [f. DO *v.* + LITTLE.] *sb.* One who does little; a lazy person. *adj.* Doing little; lazy.

‖**Dolium** (dōu·liŏm). 1483. [L.] 1. *Rom. Antiq.* A large earthenware jar or vessel, for holding wine, oil, or dry commodities; hence, in mod. use, a cask. 2. *Zool.* A genus of gastropod molluscs, having a ventricose shell; also called *tun.*

Doll (dǫl), *sb.* 1560. [Shortened pet-form of *Dorothy*; cf. *Hal = Harry,* etc.] 1. A female pet, a mistress. 2. A girl's toy-baby 1700. 3. *transf.* A pretty but silly woman 1841.

2. I'll carry you and your d. too GARRICK. 3. A sturdy lad..is worth a hundred of these city dolls EMERSON. 4. *Comb.* **doll's house,** a miniature toy house for dolls; hence, a diminutive dwelling-house. Hence **Doll** *v.* to dress up finely (*colloq.*).

Dollar (dǫ·ləɹ). 1553. [In 16th c. *daler, daller,* a. LG. and early mod.Du. *daler,* = HG. *taler, thaler,* in full *Joachimstaler,* lit. '(gulden) of Joachimsthal' (in Bohemia), where they were coined in 1519.] 1. English name for the German *thaler*; *esp.* the unit of the German monetary union (1857–73) equal to 3 marks (about 2*s.* 11*d.*). Also of the *rigsdaler* of Denmark, etc. 2. English name for the peso or Spanish piece of eight (*i.e.* eight reales), largely used in the British N. American Colonies at the time of their revolt 1581. 3. The standard unit of the gold and silver coinage of the United States, containing 100 cents; = about 4*s.* 1½*d.* Eng. Also a coin of the same value in some British colonies. Sometimes abbreviated *dol.,* but usually represented by the dollar-mark $ before the number. 1785. 4. Also a name for various foreign coins of corresponding value; as the *peso* of Mexico, etc., the *piastre* of Arabia, the *yen* of Japan, etc. 1882. **b.** *slang.* A five-shilling piece.

Phrases. *Pillar d.,* a silver coin of Spain, bearing a figure of the Pillars of Hercules: cf. sense 2. *Trade d.,* a silver d. of 420 grains formerly coined by the U.S. mint for purposes of trade with eastern Asia.

Comb.: **d.-bird,** an Australian bird of the genus *Eurystomus,* having a large round white spot on its wing; **-fish, a.** *Vomer setipinnis,* called also *moonfish*; **b.** *Stromateus triacanthus,* called also *butter-* and *harvest-fish.* Hence **Do·llish** *a.*

Dollop (dǫ·ləp). 1573. [Cf. Norweg. dial. *dolp* lump.] †1. *Farming.* A clump of grass, weeds, etc. in a field –1825. 2. *colloq.* or *vulg.* A large quantity; a clumsy lump 1812.

Dolly (dǫ·li), *sb.*[1] 1610. [f. DOLL; see -Y.] 1. A pet-form of *Dorothy.* 2. † A female pet (*slang*). **b.** A slattern (*dial.* or *colloq.*) 1648. 3. A pet name for a child's doll 1790. 4. Applied to contrivances fancied to resemble a doll:

a. *dial.* A wooden appliance with two arms, and legs or feet, used to stir clothes in the wash-tub, called a *d.-tub.* Also applied to an apparatus for agitating and washing ore in a vessel. **b.** *Pile-driving.* A block set on the top of a pile to act as a buffer between it and the ram; a punch. **c.** *Austral. Gold-fields.* An appliance like a pile-driver, used to crush quartz. **d.** A tool used in forming the head of a rivet. *Comb.* **d.-shop,** a marine store, frequently having a black doll hanging outside as a sign, and often serving as a low pawn-shop.

‖**Dolly** (dǫ·li), *sb.*[2] *Anglo-Ind.* 1860. [ad. Hindī *dālī.*] An offering of fruit, flowers, sweetmeats, etc., presented usually on a tray.

Dolly (dǫ·li), *a.* 1852. [f. DOLL *sb.*] Like a doll; babyish. **b.** *Games.* Designating an easy catch, etc. 1895.

Dolly (dǫ·li), *v. dial.* and *techn.* 1831. [f. DOLLY *sb.*[1] 4.] **a.** To stir, as clothes, ore, etc. with a dolly. **b.** *Gold-mining.* To crush (quartz) with a dolly; to obtain (gold) by this process; of the quartz: To yield (so much gold) by this method 1894.

Dolly Varden. 1872. [from the character in Dickens's *Barnaby Rudge.*] **a.** A print dress with a large flower pattern, worn with the skirt gathered up in loops. **b.** A large hat, with one side bent downwards, and abundantly trimmed with flowers. **c.** A Californian species of trout.

Blue eyes look doubly blue Beneath a Dolly Varden A. DOBSON.

Dolman (dǫ·lmăn). 1585. [orig. a. Turkish *dōlāmān* or *dōlāmah.*] 1. A long robe open in front, with narrow sleeves, worn by the Turks. 2. The uniform jacket of a hussar, worn like a cape with the sleeves hanging loose 1883. 3. A mantle with cape-like appendages instead of sleeves, worn by women 1872.

Dolmen (dǫ·lmen). 1859. [a. mod.F. *dolmen* (*dolmin* Latour d'Auvergne, 1796). Prob. repr. the Cornish name *tolmên,* lit. 'hole of stone', misapplied to the *cromlech.* French name for a CROMLECH.

Dolomite (dǫ·lŏməit). 1794. [after M. *Dolomieu,* a French geologist; see -ITE.] *Min.* A native double carbonate of lime and magnesia, occurring crystalline, and in granular masses, white or coloured, called *d. marble*; a rock consisting of this. **b.** pl. *The Dolomites* = the d. mountains; *spec.* those of Southern Tyrol. Hence **Dolomi·tic** *a.* of the nature of or containing d. **Do·lomitize** *v.* (also **Do·lomize**), to convert into d. **Dolomitiza·tion** (also **Dolomiza·tion**), conversion into d.

Dolor, var. of DOLOUR.

†**Dolori·ferous,** *a.* 1599. [f. L. *dolorem* + *-fer.*] = next –1638.

Dolorific (dǫlŏri·fik), *a.* Now *rare.* 1634. [ad. med.L. *dolorificus.*] Causing pain; grievous.

Dolorous (dǫ·lŏrəs), *a.* ME. [a. OF. *doleros, -eus,* mod.F. *douloureux* :—late L. *dolorosus.*] 1. Painful. 2. Causing grief; distressful; doleful, dismal 1450. 3. Of persons, etc.: Full of or expressing sorrow; sad, distressed 1513.

1. A very d. thirst 1731. 2. The death of therle was d. to all Englishmen HALL. 3. Many a d. groan MILT. Hence **Do·lorous-ly** *adv.*, **-ness.**

Dolose (dolōu·s), *a.* 1832. [ad. L. *dolosus,* f. *dolus.*] *Law.* Characterized by criminal intention; intentionally deceitful.

Dolour, dolor (dōu·ləɹ, dǫ·ləɹ). ME. [a. OF. *dolor, -our,* mod.F. *douleur* :—L. *dolorem,* f. *dolere.* Now rare in spoken use.] †1. Physical suffering, pain; a pain, a disease –1720. 2. Mental suffering ME.; *pl.* griefs, sorrows (now *rare*) 1611. †3. Lamentation, mourning –1634. †4. Indignation. [As in L.] –1644.

2. Pitifully behold the dolour of our heart 1544. 3. *To make dolour*: to mourn.

Dolphin (dǫ·lfin). ME. [In the form *delfyn, delphin,* from L. *delphinus*; with the form *dalphyne,* cf. OF. *daulphin,* whence *dolfin*: Littré has *doffin* (15th c.).] 1. A cetaceous mammal (*Delphinus Delphis*), frequently confounded with the porpoise. 2. The dorado (*Coryphæna hippuris*), a fish celebrated for its rapid changes of hue when dying 1578. 3. *Astron.* A northern constellation, *Delphinus* ME. 4. A figure of a dolphin, in painting, sculpture, etc. ME. 5. Applied to various contrivances fancifully likened to a dolphin.

a. In early artillery, each of two handles cast solid on a cannon nearly over the trunnions. **b.** *Naut.* (*a*) A spar or block of wood with a ring-bolt at each end for vessels to ride by. (*b*) A mooring-post or bollard placed along a quay, wharf, or beach. (*c*) A wreath of plaited cordage fastened about a mast or yard 1764. **c.** *Gr. Antiq.* A heavy mass of lead, etc. suspended from a yard at the bow of a war-vessel, to be dropt into an enemy's ship.

6. A black species of aphis or plant-louse (*Aphis fabæ*), very destructive to bean-plants; also called *collier* and *d.-fly* 1731. †7. = DAUPHIN.

1. Like Orion on the Dolphines backe *Twel. N.* I. ii. 15. 2. Parting day Dies like the D., whom each pang imbues With a new colour.. The last still loveliest BYRON.

Comb.: **d.-flower,** the Larkspur (*Delphinium*); **-fly** = sense 6; **-striker** (*Naut.*), a short gaff spar fixed vertically under the bowsprit; also called *martingale.*

Hence †**Dolphine·t,** a female d. SPENSER.

Dolt (dōult), *sb.* 1543. [app. related to OE. *dol, doll,* DULL, and to *dold* stupid.] 1. A dull stupid fellow; a blockhead, numskull. 2. *attrib.* or as *adj.* Doltish, stupid. *Comb.,* as †**d.-head,** a dolt. 1679.

1. Oh Gull, oh d., As ignorant as durt *Oth.* V. ii. 163. Hence †**Dolt** *v.* to make a d. of; *intr.* to act like a d. **Do·ltish** *a.* like a d.; thick-headed. **Do·ltish-ly** *adv.*, **-ness.**

Dolven, obs. pa. pple. of DELVE *v.*

‖**Dom**[1] (dǫm). 1716. [In sense 1, a. Pg. *dom,* = Sp. *don* :—L. *dominus.* In sense 2, short for L. *dominus.* Cf. DON *sb.*[1], DAN[1].] 1. In Portugal and Brazil, a title of dignity conferred only by Royal authority 1727. 2. A title prefixed to the names of certain R.C. ecclesiastical dignitaries and monks 1716. 3. *Dom Pedro* (*U.S.*): a game at cards, a variation of DON, q.v. 1887.

‖**Dom**[2] (dǭm). 1861. [mod.Ger., ad. L. *domus* (*Dei*); see DOME.] A cathedral church.

-dom, *suffix*. [OE. *-dóm* = Du. *-dom*, Ger. *-tum*, etc.] Abstract suffix of state, f. stem *dô-* of Do *v.* + abstract suffix *-moz*, OE. *-m*, as in *hel-m*, *strea-m*, etc. Frequent in OE. as a suffix to sbs. and adjs. Now a living suffix, with the sense of 'condition, state, dignity'; also of 'domain, realm' (*fig.*).

†**Do·mable**, *a. rare.* 1623. [ad. late L. *domabilis*, f. *domare*.] Tamable. Hence †**Do·mableness**.

Domage, -eable, etc., obs. ff. DAMAGE, etc.

Domain (domēⁱ·n), *sb.* ME. [a. mod.F. *domaine*, for OF. *demeine* :—L. *dominicum*, sb. use of *dominicus* of or belonging to a lord. See DEMESNE.] †1. = DEMESNE 1. Also *attrib.* in *d. lands.* -1630. 2. A heritable property; estate or territory held in possession; lands; dominions 1601. b. *transf.* Sphere of activity or dominion 1727. 3. *fig.* A sphere of thought or action; field, province, etc. 1764.

2. These are in the nature of a d. and inheritance, and fall to the next heire in succession HOLLAND. *transf.* He was lord of his library, and seldom cared for looking out beyond his domains LAMB. 3. The d. of Art CARLYLE, of Science 1864.

Phr. *Eminent d.*: ultimate or supreme lordship; the superiority of the sovereign power over all property in the state, whereby it is entitled to appropriate any part required for the public advantage, compensation being made to the owner.

Hence **Domai·nal, Doma·nial** *adjs.* of, pertaining, or relating to d., or to a d.

Domal (dōᵘ·măl), *a.* 1716. [ad. med.L. *domalis*, f. *domus*; see DOME, etc.] 1. *Astrol.* Of or pertaining to a house. 2. Domestic 1728.

Dómbóc, OE. form of DOOMBOOK.

Domdaniel (dǫmdæ·niĕl). 1801. [a. F., app. f. Gr. δῶμα Δανιήλ. Introduced in the French 'Continuation of the Arabian Nights' by Chaves and Cazotte 1788–93.] A fabled submarine hall where a magician met his disciples; used by Carlyle in the sense of 'infernal cave'.

Chief Enchanter..in the D. of Attorneys CARLYLE.

Dome (dōᵘm), *sb.* Also 7 **dosme**, 8 **doom**. 1513. [In sense 1, ad. L. *domus*; in other senses, a. F. *dome* (15–16th c.), ad. It. *duomo* house, house of God, etc. :—L. *domus*.] 1. A house, a home; a mansion. Now chiefly *poet.* †2. = DOM[2]. -1753. 3. A rounded vault forming the roof of a building or chief part of it; a cupola 1656. 4. *transf.* Anything resembling a dome or rounded vault 1727. 5. Technical uses:

a. *Manuf.* The cover of a reverberatory furnace. b. *Cryst.* A trimetric, monoclinic, or triclinic prism, whose faces and edges are parallel to one of the secondary axes. c. *Railways.* The raised conical part of the boiler of a locomotive engine, the *steam-d.*; the raised roof of a railway carriage. d. *Watch-making.* The back part of the inner case of a watch.

1. Dated at my D., or rather Mansion place in Lincolneshire 1553. 4. A bed, with a d. to it COMBE. The d. of the sky MRS. RADCLIFFE. Imbower'd vaults of pillar'd palm..the d. Of hollow boughs TENNYSON. Tabor with its rounded d. STANLEY.

Dome, *v.* 1876. [f. prec. sb.] 1. To cover with or as with a dome. 2. To make dome-shaped 1879. 3. *intr.* To rise or swell as a dome 1887.

1. [He] domes the red-plow'd hills With loving blue TENNYSON.

Dome, obs. f. DOOM, DOUM.

Domed (dōᵘmd), *a.* 1775. [f. DOME *sb.* or *v.*] 1. Dome-shaped; vaulted. 2. Having a dome or domes 1855.

†**Domes-booke**. = DOMESDAY BOOK.

Domesday (dūᵘ·mzdēⁱ, dū·mzdēⁱ). ME. [f. *dómes* genitive of *dóm* DOOM + DAY.] ME. spelling of DOOMSDAY, day of judgement, now used as a historical term, in the following:

D. book, colloq. *D.*: the name of the record of the Great Inquisition or Survey of the lands of England, their extent, value, ownership, and liabilities, made by order of William the Conqueror in 1086. Also *transf.*, *fig.*, and allusively.

The booke..to be called D., bicause (as Mathew Parise saith) it spared no man, but iudged all men indifferently, as the Lord in that great day will do LAMBARDE.

Domestic (dome·stik). 1521. [ad. L. *domesticus*, f. *domus*; orig. through F. *domestique*.]

A. *adj.* †1. Housed -1681; intimate, at home -1750. 2. Of or belonging to the home, house, or household; household, home, family 1611. 3. Of or pertaining to one's own country or nation; internal, inland, home 1545; indigenous; home-grown, home-made 1660. 4. Of animals: Living in or near the habitations of man; tame, not wild 1620; †of men: Not nomad 1632. 5. Attached to home; domesticated 1658.

1. He was..domestick..with all CLARENDON. 2. D. joy GOLDSM., life D'ISRAELI, servants DICKENS. 3. D. Trade 1719, policy MACAULAY, woollens and flannels URE. 4. Domesticke or tame Ducks VENNER. 5. It is praiseworthy and right to be d. J. H. NEWMAN.

B. *sb.* †1. A member of a household (*lit.* and *fig.*) -1737. 2. A household servant 1613. †3. An inhabitant of the same country -1682. 4. *pl.* Articles of home produce or manufacture, *esp.*, in U.S., home-made cotton cloths 1622.

2. His Domesticks are all in Years, and grown old with their Master ADDISON.

Hence †**Dome·stical** *a.* domestic; familiar, homely; *sb.* = DOMESTIC *sb.* 1, 2. **Dome·stically** *adv.* in a d. manner; with regard to d. affairs.

Domesticate (dome·stikeⁱt), *v.* 1639. [f. ppl. stem of med.L. *domesticare*, f. *domesticus*.] 1. *trans.* To cause to be at home; to naturalize. Also *transf.* and *fig.* 2. To make domestic; to attach to home and its duties 1748. 3. To tame or bring under control; *transf.* to civilize 1641. †4. *intr.* (for *refl.*) To live at home (*with*); to take up one's abode -1812.

1. D. yourself there [at Naples] CHESTERF. 2. [They] easily become domesticated 1863. 3. To d. a savage people EARL MONM., the dog DARWIN. So †**Dome·sticant** *a.* making its home (*rare*). Hence **Dome·sticated** *ppl. a.* **Dome·stica·tion**, the action of domesticating; domesticated condition. **Dome·sticator**, one who domesticates.

Domesticity (dōᵘmesti·sĭti). 1721. [f. DOMESTIC *a.* + -ITY; cf. F. *domesticité*.] 1. The quality or state of being domestic; family life; devotion to home; homeliness. 2. *pl.* Domestic arrangements 1824.

Dome·sticize, *v.* 1656. [f. DOMESTIC + -IZE.] *trans.* = DOMESTICATE.

Domett (dǫ·mėt). 1835. [? proper name.] 'A kind of plain cloth of which the warp is cotton and the weft woollen' (Booth).

Domeykite (domēⁱ·kəit). 1850. [after *Domeyko*, a Chilian mineralogist, etc.] *Min.* A native arsenide of copper of a greyish or tin-white metallic appearance.

Domic, -al (dōᵘ·mik, -ăl), *a.* 1823. [f. DOME *sb.* + -IC, + -AL.] 1. Of, pertaining to, or like a dome. 2. Characterized by domes or dome-like structure 1861.

Domicile (dǫ·misil, -səil), *sb.* 1477. [a. F. *domicile*, ad. L. *domicilium*, deriv. of *domus*.] 1. A place of residence or ordinary habitation; a house or home. Also *transf.* and *fig.* 2. *Law.* The place where one has his permanent residence, to which, if absent, he has the intention of returning 1766; residence 1835. 3. *Comm.* The place where a bill of exchange is made payable 1892.

Do·micile (see prec.), *v.* 1809. [f. prec. sb.] 1. To establish in a domicile or fixed residence. Also *transf.* and *fig.* 2. *Comm.* To make (a bill, etc.) payable at a certain place 1809. 3. *intr.* (for *refl.*) To dwell 1831.

†**Domici·liar**. *rare.* 1655. [f. L. *domicilium*.]

A. *adj.* Of or pertaining to one's domicile.

B. *sb.* Short for *d. canon*, a canon of a minor order having no voice in a chapter 1761.

Domiciliary (dǫmisi·liări), *a.* 1790. [f. as prec.] 1. Pertaining to or connected with a domicile. 2. *Zool.* Of or pertaining to the general integument occupied in common by infusoria, and the like. (Dicts.)

1. *D. visit*, a visit to a private dwelling, by official persons, in order to search or inspect it.

Domiciliate (dǫmisi·li,eⁱt), *v.* 1778. [f. as prec.] 1. *trans.* To establish in a place of residence; to domicile. Also *intr.* (for *refl.*). †2. To domesticate (animals) (*rare*) -1816. Hence **Do:micilia·tion**, the action of domiciliating; domestication (*rare*).

Domiculture (dǫ·mikɒltiŭɹ). *rare.* 1860. [f. L. *domus*, after *agriculture*.] The art of housekeeping, cookery, etc.; domestic economy.

†**Do·mify**, *v.* ME. [a. F. *domifier*, ad. med.L. *domificare*, f. *domus*.] *Astrol. trans.* To divide (the heavens) into twelve houses; to locate (the planets) in their respective houses -1751.

‖**Domina** (dǫ·mină). 1706. [L.] †1. A lady of rank. 2. The superior of a nunnery 1751.

Dominance (dǫ·minăns). 1819. [f. DOMINANT *a.*] The fact or position of being dominant; ascendancy, sway. So **Do·minancy**, dominant quality.

Dominant (dǫ·minănt). 1532. [a. F., f. L. *dominantem*.] A. *adj.* 1. Exercising chief authority or rule; ruling, governing; most influential. 2. Occupying a commanding position 1854. 3. *Mus.* [cf. B. b.] Relating to or based upon the dominant 1819. 4. In Mendelism, of a marked parental character transmitted to a hybrid descendant 1900.

1. An odde feaverish sickness d. in the Universitie WOOD. 2. To take possession of the d. parts of the globe 1854.

Phr. *Rom. Law. D. land, tenement*: 'the tenement or subject in favour of which a servitude exists or is constituted' (Bell). Hence **Do·minantly** *adv.*

B. *sb. Mus.* a. In eccl. modes, the reciting note of a tone. b. The fifth note of the scale of any key 1819.

Dominate (dǫ·mineⁱt), *v.* 1611. [f. L. *dominat-*, ppl. stem of *dominari*, f. *dominus*; cf. F. *dominer*.] 1. *trans.* To bear rule over, command, sway; to master. 2. *intr.* To be dominant (*over*) 1818. 3. *trans.* To command as a height; also *fig.* 1833.

1. Hee that..can d. his passions 1613. 2. Republicanism dominates within and without CARLYLE. 3. This hill..dominates the plain BOSW. SMITH.

Domination (dǫminēⁱ·ʃən). ME. [a. F., ad. L. *dominationem*; see prec.] 1. The action of dominating; lordly rule, sway, or control; ascendancy. †2. The territory under rule; a dominion -1654. 3. *pl.* The fourth of the nine orders of angels in the Dionysian hierarchy. Cf. DOMINION 4. ME.

1. The Lordship and d. over thys yle 1585. 2. His subiectes of his saide dominacion of Wales 1535. 3. Thrones, Dominations, Princedoms, Vertues, Powers MILT. *P. L.* v. 601.

Dominative (dǫ·minĕtiv), *a.* 1599. [ad. med.L. *dominativus*, F. *dominatif*, *-ive*.] 1. Of lordly authority. †2. Of predominant importance -1655.

Dominator (dǫ·mineⁱtəɹ). 1450. [a. F. *dominateur*, ad. L. *dominatorem*.] One who or that which dominates; a ruler.

Jupiter..Lord of the ascendant, and great d. GAULE.

†**Domine** (dǫ·mini), *sb.* 1566. [voc. case of L. *dominus*.] 1. Lord, master: a term of address to the clergy or members of the professions -1675. 2. A clergyman or parson; *spec.* = DOMINIE 1, 2, q. v. -1711.

†**Do·mine**, *v.* 1470. [a. OF. *dominer*, ad. L. *dominari*.] *trans.* To rule, DOMINATE -1509; *intr.* to prevail -1614.

Domineer (dǫminiᵊ·ɹ), *v.* 1588. [app. a. Du. *domineren*, a. F. *dominer*; see prec.] 1. *intr.* To rule arbitrarily or despotically; to tyrannize. Now usually, To lord it; †to play the master -1764. †2. To feast riotously. [Du. *domineren* to feast luxuriously.] -1691. †3. To prevail -1725. 4. To tower (*over*, *above*) 1658. 5. *trans.* To govern imperiously, tyrannize over 1764; to tower over 1812.

1. Oligarchies, where a few rich men d. BURTON. He rants and domineers, He swaggers and swears DRYDEN. 2. Goe to the feast, reuell and domineere *Tam. Shr.* III. ii. 226. 5. The entrenchments..were domineered within pistol shot 1812. Hence **Dominee·r** *sb.* a domineering air or manner. **Do:minee·rer** (now *rare*), a tyrant, despot. **Dominee·ring** *vbl. sb.* and *ppl. a.* despotic; overbearing, insolent; †dominant. **Dominee·ring·ly** *adv.*, **-ness**.

Dominial (domi·niăl), *a.* 1727. [f. L. *dominium* + -AL.] Of or pertaining to ownership.

Dominical (domi·nikăl). 1540. [ad. med.L. *dominicalis*, f. L. *dominicus* belonging to a *dominus*.]

A. *adj.* 1. Of or pertaining to the Lord (Jesus Christ); Lord's; as *D. day*, *year* 1553. 2. Of or pertaining to the Lord's day; Sunday -1623. Also *fig.* †3. Belonging to a demesne -1640.

2. Grave D. Postures COWLEY. *D. letter*: the letter used to denote the Sundays in a particular year. The seven letters A, B, C, D, E, F, G are used in succession to denote the first seven days of the year (Jan. 1–7), and then in rotation the next seven days, and so on, so that, *e.g.* if the 3rd Jan. be a Sunday, the d. letter for the year is C. Leap year has two D. letters,

one for the days preceding Feb. 29, the other for the rest of the year. *fig.* For all Cromwells Nose weares the Dominicall Letter [in allusion to the printing of the d. letter in red] 1647.

B. *sb.* †1. *Eccl.* A garment or veil for Sundays [med.L. *dominicale*] -1751. †2. Short for *D. letter* -1686. †3. The Lord's day -1673.

2. My red Dominicall, my golden letter SHAKS.

Dominican (domi·nikăn). 1632. [ad. eccl.L. *Dominicanus*, f. *Dominicus*, L. form of the name of *Domingo* de Guzman, also called St. Dominic; cf. F. *dominicain.*] **A.** *adj.* Of or pertaining to St. Dominic or to the order of preaching friars (and nuns) founded by him. 1680. **B.** *sb.* A friar of this order; a Black friar.

Dominie (dǫ·mini). Also **domine.** 1612. [same word as DOMINE.] 1. A schoolmaster, pedagogue. (Chiefly *Sc.*) 2. In U.S., the title of a pastor of the Dutch Reformed Church; whence, of ministers or parsons of other churches. (Usu. pronounced, after Du., dōu·mini.)

Dominion (dǒmi·nyən). ME. [a. obs. F., ad. L. type **dominionem*, deriv. of *dominium*, f. *dominus.*] 1. The power or right of governing and controlling; sovereign authority; sovereignty; rule; control. Also *fig.* 2. The domains of a feudal lord. b. The territory subject to a king or a ruler, or under a particular government or control. Often in *pl.* 1512. Also *fig.* 3. *Law.* Ownership, property; right of possession. [=*dominium* in Rom. Law.] 1651. 4. = DOMINATION 3. (Usu. in *pl.*) 1611.

2. *The Old D.*, a popular name in U.S. for Virginia. b. Applied to countries outside England or Great Britain under the sovereignty or suzerainty of the English crown; (*b*) (usu. with cap.) designating the larger self-governing British dominions; the title was given *spec.* to Canada in 1867 (1 July; anniversary called *D. day*) and to New Zealand in 1907 (28 Sept.). In the Statute of Westminster (1931) the term includes the Dominion of Canada, the Commonwealth of Australia, the Dominion of New Zealand, the Union of S. Africa, the Irish Free State, and Newfoundland. 3. *Eminent D.* (cf. DOMAIN). 4. *Col.* i. 16.

‖**Domi·nium.** 1823. A term of Roman law, rendered 'lordship', 'ownership', 'property', etc., often retained in legal use: cf. DOMINION 3.

Domino (dǫ·mino). Pl. **-oes.** 1719. [a. F. *domino* a hood worn by priests in winter; cf. Sp. *domino* a masquerade garment. Derived in some way from L. *dominus.*] 1. A kind of loose cloak, chiefly worn at masquerades, with a small mask covering the upper part of the face; *occas.*, the half-mask itself. Also *fig.* 2. A person wearing a domino 1749. 3. One of 28 rectangular pieces of ivory, bone, or wood, having the under side black, and the upper equally divided by a cross line into two squares, each either blank or marked with pips from one to six in number. *pl.* A game played with these, (usually) by placing corresponding ends in contact, the player who has the lowest number of pips remaining being the winner. 1801. b. *interj.* An ejaculation of completion 1882

Domitable (dǫ·mităb'l), *a. rare.* 1677. [f. L. *domitare* + -BLE.] Tamable.

Domite (dōu·məit). 1828. [f. *Puy de Dôme* in Auvergne.] *Min.* A light-grey variety of trachyte.

Dom Pedro; see DOM[1] 3.

Don (dǫn), *sb.*[1] 1523. [a. Sp. *don* :—L. *dominum.*] 1. A Spanish title, formerly confined to men of high rank, but now an appellation of courtesy. 2. A Spanish lord or gentleman; a Spaniard 1610. 3. *transf.* A distinguished man; a leader; an adept (*colloq.*) 1634. 4. Hence, in the English Universities: A head, fellow or tutor of a college 1660. †5. = DAN[1], DOM[1] 2 (*rare*) 1600. 6. More fully, *D. Pedro*, a game at cards 1873.

2. I never turn'd my back upon D. or devil yet TENNYSON. 3. The great dons of wit DRYDEN. 4. An introduction to two Oxford dons BURGON.

†**Don**, *sb.*[2] *rare.* 1524. [a. F. :—L. *donum.*] A gift.

Don (dǫn), *v. arch.* 1567. [contr. from *do on*; see DO *v.*] 1. *trans.* To put on (anything worn, etc.). The opposite of DOFF. 2. *refl.* To dress oneself. Chiefly *n. dial.* 1801.

1. She donned the garment of a nun 1879.

‖**Doña** (do·nʸa), **dona** (dōu·nă). 1622. [Sp. and Pg. :—L. *domina.*] 1. A (Sp. or Pg.) lady. Also prefixed to the name as a courtesy title. 2. *slang.* (*dona*, also vulgarly *donah, doner.*) A woman, a sweetheart 1873.

Donary (dōu·nări). 1582. [ad. L. *donarium*, f. *donum.*] A gift; a votive offering.

†**Donat**, var. of DONET.

Do·natary. 1818. [f. L. *donat-*, ppl. stem of *donare*; cf. F. *donataire.*] The donee of a gift; a DONATORY: spec. in *Sc. Law.*

Donate (donē¹·t), *v.* (Chiefly *U.S.*) 1845. [f. L. *donat-*; see prec.] 1. *trans.* To make a donation of; hence (in U.S.) to give, grant. 2. To present *with* 1862.

Donation (donē¹·ʃən). ME. [a. F., ad. L. *donationem.*] 1. The action or faculty of giving; presentation; grant. 2. *Law.* The action or contract by which a person transfers the ownership of a thing from himself to another, as a free gift 1651. 3. That which is presented; a gift 1577.

1. Many principal church livings are in the d. of the crown SWIFT. 3. The commissioners had anticipated that the donations would fall off (*mod.*).

Donatism (dǫ·nătiz'm). 1588. [f. as next.] The principles of the Donatists.

Donatist (dǫ·nătist). 1460. [ad. med.L. *Donatista*, f. ? *Donatus* of Casæ Nigræ, or ? Donatus the Great.] One of a sect of Christians, named after Donatus, which arose in North Africa in 311; they claimed to be the only true and pure church, and maintained that the baptisms and ordinations of others were invalid. Also *attrib.* or *adj.* Hence **Donati·stic, -al** *a.* pertaining to Donatism or the Donatists.

Donative (dǫ·nătiv). ME. [ad. L. *donativus* adj., whence *donativum* sb.; see DONATE.]

A. *adj.* Of the nature of a donation; *esp.* of a benefice: Vesting or vested by donation; opp. to PRESENTATIVE 1559.

B. *sb.* 1. A donation, gift, present; a largess ME. 2. *spec.* A benefice which the founder or patron can bestow without presentation to or investment by the ordinary 1564.

1. The Romane Emperors custome was at certaine solemne times to bestow on his Souldiers a Donatiue HOOKER.

Donator (donē¹·təɹ). 1449. [a. AF. *donatour*, ad. L. *donatorem.*] One who makes a donation; a donor.

Donatory (dǫ·nătəri). 1617. [ad. med.L. *donatorius.*] The recipient of a donation.

Do-naught; see DO-NOUGHT.

Done (dʊn), *ppl. a.* (*sb.*) ME. [pa. pple. of DO *v.*] Performed, executed, finished, ended, settled; also, used up, worn out; see DO *v.*

Donee (dōunī·). 1523. [f. stem of DON-OR.] One to whom anything is given; *esp.* in *Law*, (*a*) one to whom anything is given gratuitously; (*b*) one to whom land is conveyed in fee tail; (*c*) one to whom a power is given for execution.

†**Do·net, do·nat.** ME. [a. OF. *donet, donnat*, ad. L. *Donatus.*] An introductory Latin grammar; orig. that of Ælius Donatus; hence, any introductory treatise -1535.

Dong (dǫŋ), *v.* 1587. [Echoic.] *intr.* To sound as a large bell. So **Dong** *sb.* (or without construction), the sound itself.

‖**Donga** (dǫ·ŋgă). *S. Afr.* 1879. [Native.] A ravine or watercourse with steep sides.

Doni, var. of DHONEY.

Donjon (dʊ·ndʒən, dǫ·ndʒǒn), arch. sp. of DUNGEON, q. v.; now usual in sense 1, 'The great tower or innermost keep of a castle'.

Donkey (dǫ·ŋki). 1785. [app. of dial. or slang origin. ? A deriv. of *dun* adj., or, prob., a familiar form of *Duncan* (cf. *Neddy*).] 1. An ass. (Now in general use, exc. in scriptural language, and in Nat. Hist.) 2. *transf.* A stupid or silly person 1840.

Comb.: **d.-boy, -man**, one in charge of a d., or of a d.-engine; **-engine**, a small steam-engine, usually for subsidiary purposes, as feeding the boilers, etc.; hence *d.-boiler*; **-pump**, an auxiliary steam-pump; **d.'s years**, a very long time (*slang*).

‖**Donna** (dǫ·nă, It. dǫ·nna). 1670. [It. :—L. *domina.*] A lady; a title of honour or courtesy for an Italian lady.

Prima d.: the principal female singer in an opera.

Donnish (dǫ·niʃ), *a.* 1835. [f. DON *sb.*[1] + -ISH.] Of the character of a (college) don; pedantically stiff in manner. Hence **Do·nnishness.** So **Do·nnism**, d. action or manner.

Donnot; see DO-NOUGHT.

Donor (dōu·nəɹ, -ǭɹ). 1494. [a. AF. *donour*, OF. *doneur*, mod.F. *donneur* :—L. *donatorem.*] One who gives or presents; *esp.* in *Law*, one who grants an estate, or power for execution. Correl. of DONEE.

The doctrine..that a freehold interest in possession must pass instantly from d. to donee DIGBY.

Do-nothing (dū·nɒ:þiŋ). 1579.

A. *sb.* One who does nothing; an idler.

B. *adj.* Characterized by doing nothing; idle, indolent, as *do-nothing folk* 1832. Hence **Do·no·thingism, Dono·thingness**, the habit or practice of doing nothing; idleness, indolence.

Do-nought (dū·nǭt), **donnot** (dǫ·nǭt). Now usu. *dial.* 1594. [app. f. *do nought.*] = DO-NOTHING; also, a good-for-nothing.

Donship (dǫ·nʃip). 1626. [f. DON *sb.* + -SHIP.] The personality of a don; the possession of the title 'don'.

Don't (dōunt), colloq. contr. of *do not.* Also as *sb.* = Prohibition, and *vb.*

Donzel (dǫ·nzĕl). *arch.* 1592. [ad. It. *donzello* :—late L. *dom(i)nicellus*, dim. of *dominus*; cf. DAMOISEAU.] A young gentleman not yet knighted; a squire, a page.

Doo, Sc. form of DOVE.

‖**Doob** (dūb). 1810. [Hindī *dūb* = Skr. *dūrvā.*] The dog's-tooth grass (*Cynodon Dactylon*).

Doodah (dū·dā). *slang.* 1915. *All of a d.*, in a flutter of excitement.

Doodle (dū·d'l), *sb. colloq.* 1628. [Cf. LG. *dudeltopf, -dop*, noodle, lit. night-cap.] A noodle. Hence **Doo·dle** *v.*[1] (*dial.*) to befool, cheat.

Doodle (dū·d'l), *v.*[2] Chiefly *Sc.* 1816. [a. Ger. *dudeln, dudelsack* bagpipe.] To play (the bagpipes). Also **D.-sack**, a bagpipe.

Dook, obs. and Sc. f. DUCK *v.*

Dool[1] (dūl), **dole** (dōul). ME. [= E.Fris. *dôle, dōl*, landmark, boundary-mark.] 1. A boundary or landmark, consisting of a post, a stone, or an unploughed balk of land. 2. *Sc.* (*dūl*). The goal in a game 1550. Also *attrib.*

Dool[2], var. of DOLE *sb.*[2] grief, etc.

‖**Doolie, dooly** (dū·li). 1625. [a. Hindī *ḍōlī* a litter, f. (ult.) Skr. *dōlā*, f. *dul-* to swing.] A rudimentary litter or palanquin used by the lower classes in India, and as an army ambulance. Also *attrib.*, as *d.-bearer.*

Doom (dūm), *sb.* [Com. Teut. sb.: OE. *dóm* :—OTeut. **dômoz*, lit. that which is put or set up, f. *dôn* to place, set; see DO *v.* (Cf. Gr. θέμις, f. stem θη-, L. *statutum*, f. *statuere.*) Cf. -DOM.] 1. A statute; *gen.* an ordinance. Now *Hist.* 2. A judgement; a sentence; mostly in adverse sense OE. †3. Private judgement, opinion -1624; discernment -1697. 4. Fate, lot, destiny. (Rarely in good sense.) ME. b. Final fate, ruin, death 1600. 5. Judgement, trial (*arch.*) OE. 6. The last Judgement (*arch.*) ME. †7. Justice; equity; righteousness. (Chiefly in versions of Scripture.) -1587. †8. Power, authority; *esp.* to judge -ME.

1. The first Dooms of London provide especially for the recovery of cattle GREEN. 2. O! Partial Judge, Thy D. has me undone 1709. 3. With..unerring D., He sees what is, and was, and is to come DRYDEN. 4. The doome of Destiny SHAKS. The minister's d. was sealed GREEN. 6. What will the Line stretch out to' th' cracke of Doome SHAKS. Phr. *Day of d.*: the day of judgement; †*transf.* the last day of one's life. *Comb.*: **d.-ring** (*Archæol.*), a ring of stones delimiting the old Norse courts of judgement; **-tree**, a tree on which the condemned were hanged.

Hence **Doo·mful** *a.* fraught with d.; fateful.

Doom (dūm), *v.* 1450. [f. prec. sb.] 1. *trans.* To pronounce judgement or sentence upon. *arch.* exc. as in 2. 2. To pronounce judgement or sentence against; to condemn *to* 1588. 3. To destine or consign to some (adverse) fate or lot 1602. 4. *U.S.* (*local*). To judge and assess the tax payable by a person who has made no returns 1816. 5. To decree; to fix as a sentence or fate; to adjudge 1588. 6. *intr.* To give judgement (*arch.*) 1591.

2. Tribunes with their tongues d. men to death *Tit. A.* III. i. 47 3. Hopes..doomed to disappointment TYNDALL. 5. The Emperour in his rage will doome her death *Tit. A.* IV. ii. 114. Hence **Doo·mage** (*U.S. local*), assessment in default. **Doo·mer.**

Doombook (dū·mbuk). Also **dome-**, domes-, dooms-. [OE. *dóm-bóc* book of dooms.]

A book or code of (Old Teutonic) laws; *spec.* that attributed to King Alfred. Also *transf.*

Doomsday (dū·mzdē¹). [OE. *dómes dæg*, ME. *domes dei, dai*; see DOOM *sb.*] **1.** The judgement day. **b.** *transf.* A day of judgement or trial. Also, a day of final dissolution. 1579. **2.** = DOMESDAY. **3.** *attrib.* 1649.

1. Hit myght laste til Domesday ME. Why then Al-soules day is my bodies d. *Rich. III*, v. i. 12.

Doo·msman. [ME. *dómes man.*] A judge, deemster.

Doomster (dū·mstəɹ). ME. [var. of *demester*, DEMPSTER, DEEMSTER, after DOOM *sb.* and *v.*] **1.** A judge, doomer (*arch.*). **2.** *Sc.* = DEMPSTER 2. 1609.

Door (dōᵊɹ). [OE. *duru*, fem. *u*-stem, from the base *dur-*. OE. had also *dor* neut., pl. *doru*. Cf. Skr. *dvr, dwār*, Gr. θύρα, L. *fores*. In ME. *dure, dor, dur, dore* the two OE. types are mixed. *Door* appeared in 16th c.] **1.** A movable barrier of wood or other material, usually turning on hinges or sliding in a groove, and serving to close or open a passage into a building, room, etc. **b.** Indicating the room or house to which the door belongs 1669. **2.** The passage into a building or room; a doorway ME. **3.** *fig.* A means of entrance or exit OE.

1. Doors and windows barred fast 1509. Having taken offices a few doors off 1885. 2. They..met the iealous knaue their Master in the doore *Merry W.* III. v. 103. 3. Phr. *To open a d. to* or *for*; *to close the d. upon*· etc.

Phrases. **a.** *In doors*· within doors, in or into the house. *Next d.* (*to*). in the next house (to); hence *fig.* very near (to). *Out of door(s*: out of the house; in the open air; hence *fig.* out of place, irrelevant. *Within door(s* in a house or building, indoors. *Without doors*: out of doors.

b. *To lay, lie,* or *be at the d. of*: to impute, or be imputable or chargeable to. *To darken a d.*: see DARKEN. *To keep open doors*: see OPEN.

attrib. and *Comb.* **a.** attrib. as *d.-arch, -curtain, -handle, -knocker, -ring*, etc. **b.** objective and obj. genitive, as *d.-banging, -opener*, etc.

Comb.: **d.-alarm,** a device attached to a d., to give an alarm when the d. is opened; **-case,** the case lining a doorway, in which the d. is hung; **-cheek** (now *n. dial.*), a d.-post; **-frame,** (*a*) a d.-case; (*b*) the structure forming the skeleton of a panelled d.; **-keeper, doo·rkeeper,** one who keeps or guards a d., a janitor, porter; **-mat; -nail,** a large-headed nail, with which doors were formerly studded: now chiefly in *dead, deaf, dumb, dour as a d.-nail*; **-plate,** a plate on a d., giving the name, etc. of the occupant; **-post,** one of the jambs of a d.; **-sill,** the sill or threshold of a d.; **-stead,** a place for a d.; **-step,** the step at the threshold of a d., raised above the level of the ground outside; **-stone,** a flagstone before a d.; **-stop,** a device to stop a d. from opening too widely; also, the slip of wood against which it shuts in its frame; **-weed,** a name for *Polygonum aviculare*; **-yard** (*U.S.*), a yard or garden-patch about the d. of a house.

Dooring, error for *door-ring*; see above.

Doo·rless, *a.* ME. [-LESS.] Having no door.

Doo·rward. *arch.* Also 4 **durward.** OE. [f. OE. *weard* keeper.] A door-keeper. In *Sc. Hist.* = warder of the palace.

Doo·rway. 1799. The opening or passage which a door serves to close or open; a portal.

†**Dop,** *sb.*¹ 1599. [f. DOP *v.*] A curtsy, dip –1825.

Dop, *sb.*² 1700. [Du.] **1.** A pupa case. **2.** A copper cup into which a diamond is cemented for cutting or polishing 1764. **3.** Cape brandy made from grape-skins 1894.

†**Dop,** *v.* ME. To duck, dip –1692.

Dope (dōᵘp), *sb.* 1880. orig. *U.S.* [ad. Du. *doop*, f. *doopen* to dip.] **1.** Any thick liquid or semi-fluid used as a lubricant or absorbent. **b.** A surface dressing, e.g. varnish for aeroplanes 1912. **3.** A preparation of opium or other narcotic, esp. for doctoring horses; any narcotic (*d.-fiend*, a drug addict) 1889. **4.** Information about a racehorse's condition; hence, fraudulent information and information generally 1901. Hence **Dope** *v.*, to drug, 'doctor', apply 'dope' to (a fabric); *fig.* to make, find, or work *out*.

Do·ppelga·nger. 1895. = DOUBLE-GANGER.

†**Dopper.**¹ ME. [f. DOP *v.*] A didapper.

Dopper ² (dǫ·pəɹ). 1620. [ad. Du. *dooper*, f. *doopen* to dip.] A (Dutch) Baptist.

Dopplerite (dǫ·plərəit). 1863. [f. *Doppler*, a German physicist.] *Min.* A hydrocarbon, amorphous and jelly-like when fresh, and elastic when dried, looking like black pitch.

Dor, dorr (dǭɹ), *sb.*¹ [OE. *dora*: of unkn. origin.] An insect that flies with a loud humming noise. †**1. a.** A humble-bee or bumble-bee. **b.** A drone bee. **c.** A hornet. **d.** *fig.* A drone. –1681. **2.** *spec.* **a.** The common black dung-beetle (*Geotrupes stercorarius*), which flies after sunset. **b.** The cockchafer. **c.** The rose-beetle. Also, vaguely, other species of beetles. 1450. Also †*fig.*

Comb.: **d.-bee, -beetle** (see 1, 2); **-bug** (*U.S.*), a name for various beetles; **-fly** (see 1, 2); **-hawk,** the night-jar.

†**Dor,** *sb.*² 1552. Also **dorre.** [? from ON. *dár* scoff.] Mockery, 'making game' –1855.

[He] brings home the dorre upon himself MILT.

†**Dor,** *v.*¹ Also **dorre.** 1570. [Goes with DOR *sb.*²] To make game of, mock, befool –1675.

Phr. *To d. the dotterel*: to hoax a simpleton: cf. DARE *v.*²

†**Dor(r,** *v.*² 1601. [Cf. Sc. and n. dial. *dirr* to deaden.] To make dim (in colour).

Dora (dōᵊ·rā). 1918. Joc. formation (identical with a female name) on initials of the *D*efence *O*f the *R*ealm *A*ct (August 1914), which gave the Government wide powers in time of war.

‖**Dorado** (dorā·do). 1604. [a. Sp. *dorado* gilded:—L. *deauratus*; see DORY.] **1.** A fish (*Coryphæna hippuris*); also called *dolphin*. **2.** A southern constellation, also called Xiphias or the Sword-fish 1819. †**3.** *fig.* A rich man.

Dorcas (dǭ·ɹkās). 1847. Name of a woman mentioned in Acts ix. 36; hence, *D. society*, a ladies' association in a church for making and providing clothes for the poor.

Doree, dorey, var. of DORY.

Dor-fly, dorhawk; see DOR *sb.*¹

‖**Doria, dorea** (dōᵊ·riă). 1696. [Hindī *ḍoriyā* striped.] A kind of striped Indian muslin.

Dorian (dōᵊ·riăn), *a.* 1603. [f. L. *Dorius* (a. Gr. Δώριος of Doris).] **A.** Of Doris or Doria, a division of ancient Greece.

D. mode in *Mus.*, an ancient Grecian mode, characterized by simplicity and solemnity; also, the first of the authentic ecclesiastical modes.

B. *sb.* A native or inhabitant of Doris 1662.

Doric (dǫ·rik). 1569. [ad. L. *Doricus*, a. Gr. Δωρικός; cf. prec.]

A. *adj.* **1.** = DORIAN; of or pertaining to the Dorians; of a dialect, etc.: Broad; rustic. **2.** *Archit.* The name of one of the three Grecian orders (Doric, Ionic, Corinthian), of which it is the oldest, strongest, and simplest 1614.

1. With eager thought warbling his D. lay MILT.

B. *sb.* **1.** The Doric dialect of ancient Greek 1837. **b.** A broad or rustic dialect of English, Scotch, etc. 1870. **2.** The Doric order of architecture 1812.

Hence **Do·ricism,** a D. form of expression.

Dorism (dōᵊ·riz'm). 1698. [ad. Gr. Δωρισμός; see DORIZE.] **1.** The Dorian character of culture 1870. **2.** A Doricism.

Dorize (dōᵊ·rəiz), *v.* 1678. [ad. Gr. δωρίζειν.] **1.** *intr.* To imitate Doric manners, language, etc. **2.** *trans.* To render Doric in manners, etc. 1846.

Dorking (dǭ·ɹkiŋ), *a.* (*sb.*) 1840. [f. *Dorking* in Surrey.] Name of a breed of poultry of a long square form, and possessing five toes.

Dormancy (dǭ·ɹmănsi). 1789. [f. next.] Dormant condition; cf. next.

The d. of any such prerogative 1789.

Dormant (dǭ·ɹmănt). ME. [a. OF. *dormant*, pr. pple. of *dormir*:—L. *dormire.*]

A. *adj.* **1.** Sleeping, lying asleep or as asleep; hence, *fig.* intellectually asleep 1623. **b.** Of plants: With development suspended 1863. **c.** *Her.* In a sleeping attitude 1500. **2.** In a state of inactivity; quiescent; in abeyance 1601. **3.** Fixed, stationary, as *d. tree* ME. **4.** *D. window*, also *d.* = DORMER 2. 1651.

1. In dry weather they [Mosses] are often completely d. 1863. 2. A d. claim 1792, volcano HUXLEY. Phr. *D. commission, credit, warrant, writing*, etc., one drawn out in blank, to be filled up when required to be used. *D. partner*, a sleeping partner, who takes no part in the working of a concern. 3. *D. table*, one fixed to the floor (*arch.*).

B. *sb.* †**1.** A fixed horizontal beam; a sleeper; a summer. More fully *d. tree* (see A. 3). –1665. **2.** = DORMER window; see A. 4.

Dormer (dǭ·ɹməɹ). 1592. [ad. OF. *dormeor*, etc.:—L. *dormitorium* sleeping-room.] **1.** A dormitory. Now *Hist.* 1605. **2.** A projecting vertical window in the sloping roof of a house. Also *d.-window.* (Orig. the window of a dormitory.) 1592. †**3.** = DORMANT *sb.* 1. –1825. Hence **Do·rmered** *a.* having dormers.

‖**Dormeuse** (dormö·z). 1734. [F.; fem. of *dormeur.*] †**1.** A nightcap –1753. **2.** A travelling-carriage adapted for sleeping in 1825.

Dormient (dǭ·ɹmiĕnt), *a.* 1643. [ad. L. *dormientem.*] Sleeping, dormant.

Dormition (dǫɹmi·ʃən). 1483. [a. F., ad. L. *dormitionem.*] Sleeping; falling asleep; *fig.* death (of the righteous).

Do·rmitive. 1593. [a. F. *dormitif, -ive*, f. (ult.) L. *dormire.*] **A.** *adj.* Causing sleep. **B.** *sb.* A soporific; a narcotic 1619.

Dormitory (dǭ·ɹmitŏri), *sb.* 1485. [ad. L. *dormitorium* sleeping-place.] **1.** A sleeping-chamber; *spec.* a room containing a number of beds, or a gallery or building divided into cells or chambers with beds, as in a monastery, schools, etc. **2.** *fig.* A resting-place 1634. †**3.** A cemetery, vault, grave –1775.

3. We obtained a D. for his Body among the Armenian Christians SIR T. HERBERT.

Dormouse (dǭ·ɹmaus). ME. [? (F. *dormeuse*, occas. given as the etymon, is not known before the 17th c.)] **1.** A small rodent of a family intermediate between the squirrels and the mice; *esp.* the British species *Myoxus avellanarius*, noted for its hibernation. **2.** *transf.* A sleepy person 1568. **3.** *attrib.* Sleepy 1601.

2. A d. against the Devil MILT. 3. Your d. valour SHAKS.

Dormy (dǭ·ɹmi), *a.* 1887. *Golf.* Of a player: As many 'up' as there are holes to play; thus, *d. one*, etc.

Dornick (dǭ·ɹnik). 1489. Applied to certain fabrics originally manufactured at *Doornick*, a Flemish town (in French called Tournay), and used for hangings, carpets, vestments, etc. Also, 'A species of linen cloth used in Scotland for the table' (J.).

(In the latter sense, referred erron. to *Dornoch* in Scotland.)

Dorothy Perkins (dǫ·rəþi pɔ̄·ɹkinz). 1904. [Personal name.] A climbing rose bearing clusters of double pink flowers.

†**Dorp.** 1570. [a. Du. *dorp* = OE. *þorp.*] A (Dutch) village; formerly: = THORP.

No neighb'ring D., no lodging to be found DRYDEN.

Dorr, var. of DOR *sb.*¹ and *v.*²

Dorsad (dǭ·ɹsæd), *adv.* 1803. [f. L. *dorsum* + -AD II.] *Anat.* Towards the back.

Dorsal (dǭ·ɹsăl), *a.* (*sb.*) 1541. [ad. med.L. *dorsalis*, f. *dorsum*; cf. F. *dorsal.*]

A. †**1.** Having a back: of a knife with one edge. **2.** *Anat.* **a.** (*Zool.*) Pertaining to, or situated on or near, the back of an animal, as *d. fin, nerves, vertebræ.* (Opp. to VENTRAL.) 1727. **b.** (*Zool.* and *Bot.*) Pertaining to, or situated on the back (*i.e.* upper, outer, convex, or hinder surface) of any organ or part 1808. **3.** *gen.* Forming a ridge like the back of an animal 1827.

3. The great d. range that in Turkey corresponds to the Apennines G. DUFF. Hence **Do·rsally** *adv.*

B. *sb.* **1.** *Anat.* Short for *d. fin* or *d. vertebra* 1834. **2.** *Eccl.* = DOSSAL b. 1870.

†**Dorse,** *sb.*¹ 1524. [ad. L. *dorsum.*] **1.** = DOSSER ¹ 1. **2.** The back of a book or writing –1691.

2. Books..richly bound with gilt dorses WOOD.

Dorse (dǭɹs), *sb.*² 1610. [ad. LG. *dorsch* = ON. *torskr* codfish.] A young cod. (Formerly supposed to be a distinct species, and named *Gadus* (or *Morrhua*) *callarias.*)

Dorsel; see DOSSAL, DOSSEL.

Dorser; see DOSSER ¹.

Dorsi- (**dors-**), comb. f. L. *dorsum* back = 'back-; of, to, on the back'. (Sometimes used improperly where DORSO- is the correct form.) Hence:

Dorsibra·nchiate *a.*, having gills on the back; belonging to the order *Dorsibranchiata* of Annelids; *sb.* a dorsibranchiate annelid. **Do·rsigrade** *a.*, walking upon the backs of the toes, as certain armadillos. **Dorsi-me·dian** *a.*, situated in the middle line of the back. **Dorsime·sal, dorsome·sal** *a.* [see next] = prec. **Dorsime·son** [Gr. *μέσον*], the middle line of the back. **Dorsispi·nal** *a.*, pertaining to the spinous processes of the vertebræ.

Dorsiferous (dǭɹsi·fĕrəs), *a.* 1727. [L. *-fer* bearing.] **1.** *Bot.* Bearing the fructification (as a fern) upon the back (*i.e.* under side) of the frond. **2.** = DORSIPAROUS b. 1755. **3.** = next.

Dorsigerous (dǭɹsi·dʒĕrəs), *a.* 1839. [L. *-ger* carrying; see -OUS.] Carrying the young upon the back, as a species of opossum.

Dorsiparous (dǭɹsi·părəs), *a.* 1727. [L. *-par-us* bringing forth.] **a.** *Bot.* = DORSIFEROUS. **b.** *Zool.* Hatching the young upon the back, as certain toads.

Dorsi-ventral; see *Dorso-ventral* s. v. DORSO-.

Dorso-, dors-, stem and comb. f. L. *dorsum* back, used in comb. in the sense 'back and —' (and sometimes improperly, where *dorsi-* is the correct form). Hence:

Dorso-abdo·minal, dorsabdo·minal *a.*, relating to the back and abdomen. **Dorso-la·teral** *a.*, relating to the back and the side. **Dorso-ve·ntral** *a.*, (*a*) = *dorsabdominal*; (*b*) *Bot.* having dorsal and ventral halves of different internal structure, as most monosymmetrical organs; whence **Dorso-ve·ntrally** *adv.*, in a dorso-ventral direction or situation.

‖**Do·rsolum, -ulum.** 1826. [mod.L., dim. of *dorsum.*] *Entom.* A piece of the exoskeleton of an insect situated between the collar and scutellum.

‖**Dorsum** (dǭ·ɹsǒm). 1782. [L.] **1.** The back of an animal. **b.** The upper, outer, or convex surface of an organ or part. 1840. **2.** A ridge of high ground (*nonce-use*) 1782.

Dors-umbonal; see DORSO-, etc.

Dortour, dorter (dǭ·ɹtəɹ). Now *Hist.* ME. [a. OF. *dortour, -ur*, etc., vars. of *dortoir* :—L. *dormitorium.*] A dormitory.

Dory (dōə·ri), *sb.*[1] ME. [a. F. *dorée*, fem. pa. pple. of *dorer* used subst.; see prec.] A fish, *Zeus faber.* Also called JOHN DORY, q.v.

Dory (dōə·ri), *sb.*[2] *W. Indies* and *U.S.* 1798. A small flat-bottomed boat much used in sea-fisheries.

Dosage (dōu·sėdʒ). 1867. [f. DOSE *v.* or *sb.* + -AGE.] **1.** The administration of medicine in doses 1876. **2.** The operation of dosing; addition of a dose or doses, *e.g.* to wine, etc.

Dose (dōus), *sb.* 1600. [a. F., ad. med.L. *dosis*; see DOSIS.] **1.** *Med.* A definite quantity of a medicine given or prescribed to be given at one time. **2.** *transf.* and *fig.* A definite quantity of something regarded as analogous to medicine in use or effect; a definite amount of some ingredient added to wine to give it a special character 1607.

1. To administer doses of bark MACAULAY. 2. To repeat and daily increase the d. of flattery MERIVALE.

Dose (dōus), *v.* 1654. [f. prec. sb.] **1.** *trans.* To divide into, or administer in, doses 1713. **2.** To administer doses to; to physic 1654. Also *transf.*

2. A bold, self-opinioned physician .. who shall d., and bleed, and kill him *secundum artem* SOUTH.

Dosimeter (dǫsi·mĭtəɹ). 1881. [f. Gr. *δόσις* + -METER.] An apparatus for measuring doses or the like.

Dosimetric (dǫsime·trik), *a.* 1881. [f. as prec. + -METRIC.] Relating to the measurement of doses. So **Dosi·metry**, the measurement of doses.

Dosio·logy, doso·logy. 1678. [irreg. f. DOSE or DOSIS.] The science of the doses in which medicines should be given.

‖**Do·sis.** 1543. [med.L., a. Gr. *δόσις.*] = DOSE *sb.*

†**Doss,** *sb.*[1] 1482. [a. F. *dos* :—late L. *dossum*, for *dorsum.*] = DORSE *sb.*[1] 1, DOSSER[1] 1. -1533.

Doss (dǫs), *sb.*[2] *slang.* 1789. [Prob. f. as prec.] **1.** A bed; *esp.* a bed in a common lodging-house. **2.** Sleep 1858.

Comb. **d.-house,** a common lodging-house.

Doss (dǫs), *v.*[1] Now *dial.* 1583. [? onomatopœic.] **1.** *intr.* To push with the horns, as a bull; *trans.* to toss. **2.** *Sc.* To throw *down* with force 1745.

Doss, *v.*[2] *slang.* 1785. [See DOSS *sb.*[2]] *intr.* To sleep; *esp.* to sleep at a 'doss-house'.

Dossal, dossel (dǫ·săl, -ĕl). 1658. [ad. med.L. *dossale*, var. of *dorsale* a hanging behind a seat, etc.] **a.** An ornamental cloth forming a cover for the back of a seat (*arch.*). **b.** *Eccl.* An ornamental cloth hung at the back of the altar or at the sides of the chancel.

†**Dossel.** Also 8–9 **dorsel.** 1755. [a. F. *dossel* :—late L. *dorsale* what pertains to the back.] = DOSSER[1] 2. -1827.

Dosser[1] (dǫ·səɹ), **dorser** (dǭ·ɹsəɹ). Now *Hist.* ME. [a. OF. *dossier*, f. *dos* back; cf. med.L. *dorsarium.*] **1.** = DOSSAL b. **2.** A pannier ME.

Do·sser[2]. *slang.* 1866. [f. DOSS *v.*[2]] One who frequents a 'doss-house'.

Dossier (dǫ·siē). 1880. [a. F. *dossier* bundle of papers; likened to a back (*dos*) from their bulging.] A bundle of papers referring to some matter.

Dossil (dǫ·sil). ME. [a. OF. *dosil*, now *doisil, douzil* spigot, etc. :—late L. *duciculus*; dim. of *dux, ducem.*] †**1.** A plug for a barrel, a spigot -1483. **2.** A plug of lint or rag for stopping a wound, etc.; a pledget 1575. **3.** A roll of cloth for wiping ink from the surface of a copper-plate in printing 1874.

Dost (dɒst), 2 sing. pres. ind. of DO *v.*, q. v.

Dot (dǫt), *sb.*[1] [In OE., *dott* 'head of a boil' occurs once; otherwise the word is not known till 16th c. Perh. orig. = 'small lump, clot'.] †**1.** The head of a boil. (Only OE.) **2.** A small lump, clot. Now *dial.* 1570. **3.** A minute spot, speck, or mark 1674. **4.** A minute roundish mark made with or as with a pen 1748. **5.** Specifically:

Orthogr. **a.** A point used in punctuation. **b.** The point over the letters i and j. **c.** A point placed over, under, or by a letter or figure to modify its value 1740. **d.** *Mus.* A point placed after, over, or under a note, after a rest, or before or after a double bar.

6. A little child or other creature 1859. **7.** The act by which a dot is made 1858.

4. A small island..represented in the general chart ..only by a d. 1748. 6. Troops of children, from little dots of four and five..to big girls SALA.

Comb.: **d.-and-dash** *a.*, formed by dots and dashes, as the Morse alphabet, etc.; **-punch** = CENTRE-PUNCH; **-stitch,** a stitch used in making dots in embroidery; **-wheel,** a toothed wheel mounted in a handle, which when rolled over a surface produces a dotted line.

‖**Dot** (dǫt), *sb.*[2] 1855. [a. F., ad. L. *dotem* dower.] A woman's marriage portion, of which the annual income alone is under her husband's control. See also DOTE *sb.*[2]

Some little difficulty about the *dot* 1870.

Dot (dǫt), *v.*[1] 1740. [f. DOT *sb.*[1]] **1.** *trans.* To mark with a dot or dots. **2.** To cover or diversify as with minute spots 1818. **3.** To scatter like dots or specks 1816. **4.** *intr.* To make a dot or dots 1755.

1. *D. in*, to fill in with dots. *To d. the i's* (*fig.*): to particularize minutely; [He] dotted our 'i's' and crossed our 't's'..about the lack of men in the Navy 1896. 2. The whole Channel was dotted with our cruisers MACAULAY.

Phr. *To d. down*, to write down compendiously.

Dot, *v.*[2] *rare.* 1887. [ad. mod.F. *doter*, after DOT *sb.*[2] Cf. DOTE *v.*[2]] *trans.* To dower with a marriage portion.

Dotage (dōu·tėdʒ). ME. [app. f. DOTE *v.*[1] or *sb.*[1] Cf. F. *radotage.*] **1.** The state of one who dotes, now *esp.* through old age; feebleness of mind; folly; second childhood; senility. Also *transf.* **2.** The action or habit of doting upon any one; foolish affection; excessive fondness ME.; that which is doted upon 1662.

1. The world is in its d. 1766. Rabbinical dotages 1825. 2. Merlyn felle in a dottage on the damoisel MALORY. You shall..Become Jove's d. 1662.

Dotal (dōu·tăl), *a.* 1513. [ad. L. *dotalis*, f. *dotem.*] Pertaining to a dower, dowry, or woman's marriage portion.

†**Do·tant.** [f. DOTE *v.* Cf. F. *radotant.*] = DOTARD. *Cor.* v. ii. 47.

Dotard (dōu·tăɹd). ME. [In sense 1, f. DOTE *v.* + -ARD.]

A. *sb.* **1.** An imbecile; now, usually, one who is in his dotage. †**b.** One who dotes (*on* something) 1602. †**2.** (? a different word) A tree that has lost its top or branches, and of which the decayed trunk alone remains -1725.

1. Thou were an olde dooterd and a foole CAXTON.

B. *adj.* [*sb.* used *attrib.*] **1.** Imbecile; in senile decay ME. †**2.** Of a tree: Remaining as a decayed trunk without branches -1787. Hence **Do·tardly** *a.* foolish.

Dotarie, obs. f. DOTERY.

Dotation (dotē¹·ʃən). ME. [a. F., ad. L. *dotationem*, f. *dotare*, f. *dos, dotem.*] The action of endowing; endowment.

A general d. of the poorer citizens MERIVALE.

†**Dote,** *sb.*[1] ME. [f. DOTE *v.*[1]] **1.** A dotard -1630. **2.** Dotage 1619.

Dote (dōut), *sb.*[2] *arch.* 1515. [app. a. 16th c. F. *dote*, var. of *dot*; see DOT *sb.*[2]] **1.** A woman's marriage portion. †**2.** *fig.* (Usu. in *pl.*) A natural gift -1656.

Dote, doat (dōut), *v.* [Early ME. *doten, dotien* = MDu. *doten* to be crazy or silly, to dote.] **1.** *intr.* To be silly, deranged, or out of one's wits; to act or talk foolishly. **2.** Now *esp.* To be weak-minded from old age ME. **3.** To be infatuatedly fond *of*; to be foolishly in love Const. †*of, upon, on.* 1477. **4.** To decay, as a tree. Now *dial.* ME. †**5.** *trans.* To cause to dote; to befool, infatuate -1611. †**6.** To say or think foolishly -1612.

1. Doting about questions, and strifes of wordes 1 *Tim.* vi. 4. 2. The parson..is now old and doates 1710. 3. You doate on her, that cares not for your loue *Two Gent.* IV. iv. 87. Hence **Do·ted, doa·ted** *ppl. a.* †dotard; †infatuated; of a tree, decayed inside (*dial.*). **Do·ter, doa·ter,** one who dotes. †**Do·tery, doterie,** doting.

Doth (dɒþ), arch. 3rd pers. pres. ind. of DO *v.*

Do·ting, doating, *vbl. sb.* ME. [f. DOTE *v.*] The action of DOTE *v.*; an instance of this.

Do·ting, doating, *ppl. a.* 1489. [f. as prec.] That dotes; weak-minded; foolishly fond; of trees, decaying from age. Hence **Do·tingly** *adv.*

Do·tish, doatish, *a. arch.* 1509. [f. DOTE *sb.*[1]] Silly, childish.

Dottard, obs. or dial. f. DOTARD, sense 2.

Dotted (dǫ·tėd), *ppl. a.* 1772. [f. DOT *v.*[1]] **1.** Formed of dots. **2.** Marked with or as with dots 1821. **3.** Furnished with a dot 1837.

1 A d. line 1772. 2. The back-ground..is d. or stippled 1821. 3. Thus a double dotted minim is equal to three crotchets and a quaver 1837.

Dotter (dǫ·təɹ), *sb.* 1832. [f. DOT *v.* + -ER[1].] One who or that which dots; *spec.* a hand-instrument used in embossing letters for the blind.

Put on the eyes [in bird's-eye maple] by dabbing with the d. SPON.

Dotterel (dǫ·tərĕl), **dottrel** (dǫ·trĕl). ME. [f. DOTE *v.*: see -REL.] **1.** A species of plover (*Eudromias morinellus*): said to be so simple that it readily allows itself to be taken. **2.** A silly person (*dial.*) ME. **3.** A doddered tree (*dial.*) 1568.

1. This dotrell is a lytell fonde byrde, for it helpeth in maner to take it selfe 1526. 2. Old idle dottrels tayles 1547.

Dottle (dǫ·t'l). 1440. [f. DOT *sb.*[1] + -LE.] †**1.** A plug -1743. **2.** A plug of tobacco left unsmoked in a pipe 1825.

Dotty (dǫ·ti), *a.* 1812. [f. DOT *sb.*[1]] **1.** Consisting of dots; dot-like. **2.** Of unsteady gait. Hence *fig.* Silly 1870.

Do·ty, *a. dial.* 1883. [conn. w. DOTE *v.* 4, etc.] Of wood: Decayed.

‖**Douane** (duˌa·n, dwan). 1656. [Fr.; see DIVAN.] A custom-house. Hence ‖**Douanier** (dwanye), a custom-house officer (in France or, by extension, elsewhere).

‖**Douar, dowar** (dū·aɹ). 1829. [a. Arab. *dūār.*] A group of Arab tents arranged in a circle round an enclosure for the cattle.

Doub, var. of DOOB.

Double (dɒ·b'l), *a.* (*adv.*) [ME. a. OF. *duble, doble*, later *double* :—L. *duplus* twice as much, f. *duo* + *-plus* from root *ple-* to fill.]

A. *adj.* **1.** Consisting of two combined; twofold; forming a pair, coupled. Often with a sing. sb., = 'two' or 'a couple of' with pl. sb. ME. **b.** Doubled; bent, 'doubled up' 1450. **c.** Having some essential part double 1469. **d.** Of flowers: Having the number of petals doubled or more by conversion of stamens and carpels into petals 1578. **2.** Having a twofold relation; of two kinds; dual; occas. = ambiguous ME.

3. Twice as much or many; multiplied by two. Const. *of*; also *ellipt.* = twice. ME. 4. Of (or about) twice that denoted by the simple word; of extra size, strength, amount 1472. b. *Mus.* Sounding an octave lower in pitch 1674. 5. Acting in two ways at different times; characterized by duplicity; false, deceitful ME.

1. Like to a d. cherry .. Two louely berries molded on one stem *Mids. N.* III. ii. 209. A d. knock DICKENS. Bent d. with pain (*mod.*). Phr. *A d. horse*: see HORSE. 2. Fye on doble entendement, and cloked adulacion HALL. 3. Let a d. portion of thy spirit be vpon me 2 *Kings* ii. 9. 4. Sengle bere, and othir that is dowbile 1500. D. foolscap, 27 by 17 URE. A new coin, to be called a D.-Florin 1887. Phr. *D. time* (Mil.): formerly, a pace of 150 steps in the minute; at present (1896), in the British Army, one of 165 steps of 33 inches to the minute. 5. He was d. in love and nothing pleyne CHAUCER. He was .. either very d. or very inconstant BURNET.

Phrases. *D.-acting* ppl. a. acting in two directions, by two methods, etc.; *spec.* of a steam-engine, worked by application of steam power on both sides of the piston. So *D. action*. *D. algebra*: algebra which deals with two sets of quantities or relations. *D. change* (Bell-ringing): one in which two pairs of bells change places. *D. cone* (Archit.): a moulding composed of truncated cones joined base to base and top to top. *D. consonant* (Phonology): two instances of the same consonant coming together, as in *wholly*; also = *double letter* (*a*) below. *D. feast* (Eccl.): one on which the antiphons are recited in full before and after psalms and canticles. *D. first* (Univ. colloq.): a place in the first class in each of two final examinations in different subjects; one who takes such a place. *D. letter*: (*a*) a letter denoting two sounds, as *x* (= *ks*); (*b*) in *Printing*, two letters combined in one type as ff, fi. *D. point*: in the Higher Geometry, a point common to two branches of a curve, or at which the curve has two tangents; a node, cusp, or conjugate point; also an analogous point on a curved surface. *D. snipe*, the greater snipe, *Gallinago major*. *D. spar*, a name for Iceland spar, as being double-refracting. *D. star* (Astron.): two stars so near as not to be separately visible without a telescope. *D.-stopping* (Mus.): the simultaneous sounding of two (stopped) notes on two strings of a violin, etc.: notes so played are called *d.-stops*. *To work d. tides* see TIDE. *D. time*: see 4 (quots.). *D. U*: name of the letter W.

¶ Also in other phrases, as *d. bar, curvature, entry, Gloucester, question, refraction, shuffle, tooth*, etc., etc., for which see the sbs.

B. *adv.* 1. To twice the amount or extent; in two ways; twice, twice over, DOUBLY; in a couple ME. †2. After a numeral: = (so many) times; -fold. (Occas. pleonastic, as *sevenfold d.* = sevenfold.) –1698.

1. Words brought into the world, to make men see d. HOBBES. To ride d. 1599. To carry d. 1678.

Phr. *D. or quit(s* (Gambling): an expression implying that the stake already due is either to be doubled, or to be cancelled, on the next issue; hence *fig.*

C. Double- in comb.

1. **Double** *adj.* in parasynthetic combs., e. g. *d.-barred* (having a d. bar or two bars), *-chinned, -eyed*, etc.; **d.-brooded**, producing two broods in the year or season, as some insects; **-footed**, †(*a*) two-footed; (*b*) = *diplopod* (see DIPLO-); **-fronted**, d.-faced; **-leaded**, having the lines of type widely separated by means of d. leads; **-lived**, having two lives or manners of life; †amphibious; etc.

2. **Double** *adj.* in comb. with sbs., forming **a.** adjs., as *d.-action, -shift*, etc.; **d.-beat valve**, (*a*) a valve in a pump affording two openings for the water; (*b*) a device in a steam-engine consisting of two connected conical valves between which steam is admitted so as to equalize the upward and downward pressure; also called *d.-seat valve*. **b.** sbs. arising out of the absol. or ellipt. use of those preceding, as D.-FACE, etc. **c.** sbs., as **d.-ripper, -runner** (*U.S.*), two sleds connected by a plank, used by boys for coasting downhill; etc.

3. Vbs. formed from *double* adv. in comb. with vbs. (or from *double* adj. with sbs.), as *d.-arm, -bar* (to secure with d. bars), *-bolt, -damn*, etc.

4. **Double** *adv.* in comb.: **a.** with pa. pples. or ppl. adjs., as *d.-distilled, -stitched*, etc.; **d.-cut**, of a file = CROSS-CUT *a.* 2; **-hung**, of sashes, those of which the window contains two, each movable separately; **-ironed**, loaded with irons on both legs; **-milled**, of cloth, milled twice to make it closer and thicker; **-sunk**, of a dial, having recesses for the hour hand and the seconds hand; **-worked**, of a tree, twice budded or grafted. **b.** with pres. pples. or ppl. adjs., as *d.-refracting*, etc. **c.** with adjs., as *d.-concave, -convex*, etc. **d.** with agent-nouns, as **d.-breather**, an animal that breathes through two nostrils.

Double (dʊ·b'l), *sb.* ME. [In branch I, the adj. used ellipt.; in II, noun of action from DOUBLE *v.*]

I. 1. A double quantity; twice as much or many. 2. A thing that is an exact repetition of another. †a. A duplicate (*of* a writing). Chiefly *Sc.* –1752. b. A counterpart. c. *spec.* A wraith. 1798. 3. Technical senses:

a. *Bell-ringing.* A change, in which two pairs of bells change places. b. Double-headed shot. c. *pl.* A kind of thick narrow black ribbons for shoe-strings. d. Accidental duplication of a word or passage. e. *Mil.* A double pace: see DOUBLE *a.* 4 (quots.). f. *Lawn Tennis.* A game played by two a side; also two faults in succession. g. An actor or singer who takes two parts in the same piece, as in case of absence of another performer. h. *Whist.* A game in which one side scores five before the other scores three. i. Often ellipt.: e.g. = *double bed, feast, flower, line, star*, etc.

1. Ten, which is the d. of five JOWETT. 2. The fetch or d. of the Göttingen student HONE. 3. e. The men cheering, broke out into a d., and at last into a regular race RUSSELL. h. That's two doubles and the rub DICKENS.

II. 1. A fold; a folded piece of stuff. ? *Obs.* 1602. 2. A sharp turn in running, as of a hunted hare; also, of a river; *fig.* an evasive turn or shift 1592.

1. Rowled up in seaven-fould doubles Of plagues MARSTON. 2. Phr. *To give one the d.*, i. e. the slip.

Double (dʊ·b'l), *v.* [ME. *dublen, doblen, doublen*, a. OF. *dubler, dobler, doubler*:—L. *duplare* (less common = *duplicare*).] 1. *trans.* To make double; to make twice as much, as many, or as great; to multiply by two; to put two in place of one. Also *absol.* 2. *intr.* (for *refl.*) To increase twofold ME.; of flowers, to become double 1882. †3. *trans.* To repeat; to redouble; to make a duplicate of (*Sc.*) –1805. †b. *intr.* or *absol.* To speak with repetition of sounds (*rare*) –1621. 4. *Mil.* a. *trans.* To increase (ranks or files) to twice their length by marching others up into them. b. *intr.* Of ranks or files: To march up into the other ranks or files so as to double them 1598. c. *trans.* (*colloq.*) To couple *with* 1837. 5. *Mil. intr.* To go 'at the double' 1890. 6. *trans.* To line or add a second layer of material to ME. 7. To bend over, so as to bring the two parts into contact or proximity; to fold; to close, clench (the hand or fist). Often with *up*. ME. Also *intr.* (for *refl.*). 8. *Naut.* (*trans.*) To sail round or to the other side of (a cape or point) 1548; *intr.* to get round. 9. *intr.* To turn sharply in running; to turn back on one's course 1596; *fig.* to make evasive turns or shifts. ? *Obs.* 1530.

1. I doubled my pace DE FOE. To d. a vowel ROBY. Phr. *To d. a part*: to act as the double of or substitute for another player; also *fig.* 2. The circulation doubled 1882. 3. This knaues tongue begins to d. 2 *Hen. VI*, II. iii. 94. 7. The page is doubled down DRYDEN. Phr. *To d. up*: to make to bend, as by a blow; hence *fig.* to cause to collapse (*slang*). 8. To d. the Cape of Good Hope 1665. Phr. (*intr.*) *To d. upon* (Mil., etc.): to get round so as to enclose between two fires. 9. See how he doubles, like a hunted hare DRYDEN. *fig.* Why hast thou dealt thus craftely And doubled so with mee 1578.

Double-banked (-bæŋkt), *a.* 1697. [parasynth. f. *double bank*.] a. Having pairs of opposite oars pulled by rowers on the same bench; or, having two rowers at each oar. b. *Double-banked frigate*: one carrying guns on two decks; a **Double-banker**. **Double-bank** *v.*, to provide thus with rowers; also *transf.* and *absol.*

Double-barrelled, -eled, *a.* 1709. Of a fire-arm: Having two barrels; *fig.* double, twofold.

Double-bass (dʊ·b'l,bēⁱ·s). 1727. [f. DOUBLE *a.* 4 + BASS, after It. CONTRABASSO.] The largest and deepest-toned instrument of the violin class.

Double-bitt, *v.* 1833. [See BITT.] *Naut.* To pass (a cable) twice round the bitts, or round two pairs of bitts.

Double-bitted, *a.* 1816. [See BIT *sb.*[1]] Having two bits.

Double-breasted, *a.* 1701. Of a coat, etc.: Having the two sides of the breast made alike, so as to button on either side.

Double-cro·ss, *sb. slang.* 1874. [f. DOUBLE *a.* + CROSS *sb.* 18.] An act of treachery to both parties, esp. by pretended collusion with each; also more widely. **Double-cross** *v.*, **-crosser**.

Dou·ble-dealer. 1547. [f. next.] One who acts with duplicity.

Dou·ble-dealing, double dealing, *vbl. sb.* 1529. [See DOUBLE *a.* 5.] Action marked by duplicity. Also as *ppl. a.*

Double-decker. *colloq.* [parasynth. f. *double deck*.] 'A ship with two decks above the water-line.' Also, A street-car having seats on top as well as inside.

Double-dye, *v.* 1602. [f. DOUBLE *adv.*] To dye twice; *fig.* to stain deeply, as, *a double-dyed scoundrel*.

Double-e·nder. 1865. 1. Anything having two ends alike; *spec.* a gun-boat rounded fore and aft (*U.S.*). 2. A cross-cut sawing machine, with two adjustable circular saws, for sawing both ends of timber.

‖**Double entendre** (dūbl antandr). 1673. [rare obs. F. = *double entente*.] A double meaning; a word or phrase having a double sense, *esp.* as used to convey an indelicate meaning.

Double-face. 1892. a. (As two words) 'Duplicity'; double-dealing. b. (*dou·ble-face*) A double-faced person.

Double-faced (-fēⁱst), *a.* 1575. 1. Having two faces or aspects; of a fabric, finished on both sides 1589. 2. *fig.* Facing two ways; insincere.

2. Double-fac'd men God abhorreth 1577.

Dou·ble-ganger (-gæŋəɹ). 1830. [ad. Ger. *doppelgänger*.] The apparition of a living person; a double, a wraith.

Dou·ble-ha·nded, *a.* 1611. 1. Two-handled. 2. Having two hands; *fig.* capable of two applications 1665.

Dou·ble-hea·ded, *a.* 1542. Having a double head or two heads, two-headed (*lit.* and *fig.*).

Double-headed shot: a shot consisting of two balls joined together. *Double-headed snake* = AMPHISBÆNA 2.

Double-hea·der. *U.S.* 1869. a. A kind of firework. b. A railway train having two engines.

Dou·ble-hea·rted, *a.* 1552. [See DOUBLE *a.* 5.] Having a double heart; deceitful, dissembling.

Dou·ble-lo·ck, *v.* 1592. *trans.* To lock by two turns of the key

Bid Suspicion double-lock the door SHAKS.

Double meaning, *sb.* 1551. = DOUBLE ENTENDRE. So **Dou·ble-meaning** *a.*

Dou·ble-mi·nded, *a.* 1552. Having two minds; undecided or wavering in mind; †also, formerly, Having two meanings.

A double minded man is vnstable in all his ways *Jas.* i. 8.

Doubleness (dʊ·b'lnės). ME. [f. DOUBLE *a.*] 1. The quality or state of being double or twofold. 2. The character of being double in action or conduct; duplicity, treachery ME.

Dou·ble-qui·ck, *a.* (*sb.*, *adv.*) 1822. a. *adj. Mil.* Applied to the quickest step next to the run; see DOUBLE *a.* 4 (quots.). b. *sb.* Double-quick pace or time; = DOUBLE *sb.* 3 e; also *gen.* c. *adv.* In double-quick time.

In the U.S. army, Double-quick time is identical with the 'double time' now in force in the British Army, for which see DOUBLE *a.* 4 (quots.).

Doubler[1] (dʊ·bləɹ). Now *dial.* ME. [a. AF. *dobler, dubler*:—L. *duplarium* liquid measure, bag, purse, f. *duplus*.] A large plate or dish.

Doubler[2] (dʊ·bləɹ). 1552. [f. DOUBLE *v.*; cf. F. *doubleur*.] One who or that which makes double; *esp. Electr.* A machine intended to multiply, by repeated doubling, a very small quantity of electricity, till it became sufficient to affect an electrometer, give sparks, etc.

Double-reef, *v.* 1703. *trans.* To reduce the spread of (a sail) by taking in two reefs.

Double-shot, *v.* 1824. To load with a double quantity of shot. Also *fig.*

Doublet (dʊ·blėt). ME. [a. F., f. *double* + -ET.] 1. A close-fitting body-garment, with or without sleeves, worn by men from the 14th to the 18th centuries. Now *Hist.* 2. One of two things precisely alike; one of a pair or couple; a duplicate copy; *pl.* twins. *spec.* b. *Philol.* One of two words (in the same language) representing the same ultimate word but differentiated in form, as *cloak* and *clock*, etc. c. *Printing.* = DOUBLE *sb.* 3 d. 3. *Gaming.* (*pl.*) a. The same number turning up on both the dice at a throw 1450. †b. An old game at tables or backgammon –1684. 4. A pair or couple 1816; *spec.* a combination of two simple lenses 1831. 5. A counterfeit jewel composed of two pieces of 'crystal' cemented together with a layer of colour between them, or of a thin slice of a gem cemented on a piece of glass or inferior stone 1449.

1. Phr. *D. and hose*; *esp.* as the typical masculine attire; also as a sort of undress, or dress for active pursuits. †*Iron* or *stone d.*: a prison.

Doubleton (dɒ·b'ltən). *Cards.* 1906. [After *singleton*.] Two cards only of one suit in a hand.

†Double-tongue. ME. 1. Duplicity of speech. (Prop. two wds.) ME. only. 2. *Herb.* The shrub *Ruscus Hypoglossum* -1601.

Double-tongued (-tɒŋd), *a.* ME. [f. DOUBLE *a.* 5.] Deceitful or insincere in speech.

Thou art but a double-tongued Christian DE FOE.

Doubling (dɒ·bliŋ), *vbl. sb.* ME. [-ING 1.] 1. Twofold increase; multiplication by two. b. 'The second distillation of low wines' (Knight). 2. *concr.* The lining of a garment; *esp.* in *Her.* 1572. 3. *Naut.* a. A piece of timber fitted on to the bitts; fir-lining. b. The lining of a ship with an extra layer of planking; also, the extra layer. c. *pl.* That part of a mast between the trestletrees and the cap. 4. *Building.* 'The double course of shingles or slates at the eave of a house' (Knight). 5. The folding of anything; a fold 1634. 6. A sudden turn in running; *fig.* an evasion; double-dealing 1573.

Doubloon (dɒblū·n). 1622. [a. F. *doublon*, or Sp. *doblon*, augm. of *doble* DOUBLE.] A Spanish gold coin, orig. = 2 pistoles; now = £1.

‖**Doublure** (dublü·r). 1886. [F.; = 'lining'.] An ornamental lining, usually of leather, on the inside of a book-cover.

Doubly (dɒ·bli), *adv.* ME. [f. DOUBLE *a.* + -LY 2.] 1. In two ways, or twice as much. 2. With duplicity ME.

1. Here we synnen doubli WYCLIF. D. sorry 1789. 2. Let him not deale d. with vs 1585.

Doubt (daut), *sb.* [ME. a. OF. *dute, dote, doute*, vbl. sb. f. *douter* to doubt. As to the *b*, see DOUBT *v.*] 1. The (subjective) state of uncertainty as to the truth or reality of anything. With *pl.*: A feeling of uncertainty as to something. b. The condition of being (objectively) uncertain; a state of affairs giving occasion to uncertainty ME. †2. A doubtful matter or point; a difficulty -1693. †3. Apprehension, dread, fear -1659; danger, risk -1596.

1. Your wordes bring me in a d. 1559. Modest D. is cal'd The Beacon of the wise *Tr. & Cr.* II. ii. 16. b. To give the defendant the benefit of the d. 1892. 3. They dare not, for dought of Kyng Charlemayne LD. BERNERS. Well approv'd in many a d. SPENSER. Phrases. *To make d.*: to doubt, to be uncertain. *No d.*: doubtless. *Without d.*: certainly; †fearlessly.

Doubt (daut), *v.* Pa. t. and pple. **doubted.** [ME. *duten, douten*, a. OF. *duter, douter*, etc. :—L. *dubitare*, related to *dubius*. Artificially spelt *doubt-* after L.]

I. 1. *intr.* To be in doubt; to be undecided in opinion or belief. 2. *trans.* To be uncertain or divided in opinion about; to call in question; to mistrust ME. †3. To hesitate, scruple, delay: with *infin.* -1743.

1. Hee that never doubted, scarce ever well-beleeved 1633. 2. Doctors d. that *Merry W.* v. v. 183. It was never doubted but that one partner might bind the rest 1817. 3. Mr. Locke hath not doubted to assert [etc.] FIELDING.

II. 1. *trans.* To dread, fear, be afraid ME. 2. In weakened sense: To apprehend; to suspect (*arch.*) 1509. †3. *refl.* To fear; to be afraid. [= OF. *se douter.*] -1820. †4. To be in fear; to be afraid *of* -1587. †5. *impers.* To make (a person) afraid -1625.

1. I d., I d., I have been beguiled SCOTT. 2. They doubted some sinister motive PRESCOTT. I d. that Thackeray did not write the Latin epitaph TROLLOPE. 5. The virtues of the valiant Caratach, More doubts me than all Britain FLETCHER. So **Dou·btable** *a.* doubtful, questionable; redoubtable. †**Dou·btance**, doubt; dread. Hence **Dou·bter. Dou·bting** *a.*, **-ly** *adv.*, **-ness.**

Doubtful (dau·tfŭl), *a.* ME. [f. DOUBT *sb.* + -FUL.] 1. Of things: Involved in doubt; uncertain; indistinct, ambiguous. b. Of uncertain issue 1562. c. Of questionable character 1838. d. *Pros.* That may be either long or short 1871. 2. Of persons: Divided or unsettled in opinion; in doubt; undetermined, hesitating 1509. †3. To be feared; dread -1556. †4. Giving cause for apprehensions -1776. †5. Full of fear; apprehensive -1791. 6. as *sb.* A doubtful person or thing 1589.

1. Whether he were a God or man, is doutful GALE. The d. Chance of War MANLEY. She never employed d. agents or sinister measures PRESCOTT. 2. The king was d., and could not resolve DE FOE. He was d. of the prospects of the rebellion FROUDE. 4. The d. and dangerous situation of the empire GIBBON. 5. I hear things which make me d. and anxious BURKE. Hence **Dou·btful·ly** *adv.*, **-ness.**

Doubtless (dau·tlės). ME. [f. DOUBT *sb.* + -LESS.]

A. *adj.* Free from doubt; undoubted, indubitable; †free from apprehension.

Pretty childe, sleepe doubtlesse, and secure SHAKS.

B. *adv.* Without doubt; unquestionably, certainly (now generally concessive) ME.; often in a weaker sense; = No doubt 1664.

Of good things, the greater good is most excellent? D. BERKELEY. So **Dou·btlessly** *adv.*

†**Dou·btous, doutous,** *a.* [ME. a. OF., mod. F. *douteux*, f. *doute* DOUBT *sb.*; cf. *despitous*.] 1. Doubtful -1532. 2. Doubting -1490. 3. Fraught with terror -1500.

‖**Douc** (duk). 1774. [a. F., a. Cochin.] A species of monkey (*Semnopithecus nemeus*) found in Cochin China.

Douce (dus), *a.* [ME. *douce, dowce*, a. OF. *dolz, dols, dous*, later *doux*, fem. *douce* :—L. *dulcis* sweet.] †1. Sweet, pleasant -1614. 2. Quiet, steady, sedate. *Sc.* and *n. dial.* 1728.

1. Y-born in d. fraunce ME. 2. A d. woman she was, civil to the customers SCOTT.

Doucepere; see DOUZEPERS.

Doucet (dū·sėt), **dowset** (dau·sėt). ME. [a. F. *doucet, doucette*, dim. of *doux, douce*; also sb. See also DULCET.] †1. A sweet dish -1640. †2. A kind of flute -1450. 3. *Hunting.* (*pl.*) The testicles of a deer 1611.

‖**Douceur** (dusǭr). ME. [a. F. :—Romanic type **dolçore*, **dulçore*, for L. *dulcorem*, f. *dulcis*. In ME. app. naturalized.] †1. Sweetness and pleasantness of manner; amiability -1793. †2. A complimentary phrase or speech -1807. 3. A gratuity; a bribe 1763.

3. Her lord has..added..little douceurs..to her jointure 1763.

Douche (duʃ, dūʃ), *sb.* 1766. [a. F. *douche* spout, stream of water :—(ult.) L. type **ductiare*, f. *ductus*, f. *ducere* to lead.] A jet or stream of water, or the like, applied to some part of the body, generally for medicinal purposes; the application of this; an instrument for administering it. Hence **Douche** *v.* to administer a d. to.

‖**Doucine** (dusī·n). 1726. [F.] *Archit.* = *Cyma recta*; see CYMA.

Doucker, obs. f. DUCKER.

Dough (dōu), *sb.* [A Com. Teut. sb.: OE. *dáh*, gen. *dáges* :—OTeut. **daigoz*, f. stem *dig-, deig-* to form of clay, to knead; cf. Skr. *dih-*, L. *fig-, fingere*; cf. Gr. τεῖχος.] 1. A mass consisting of flour or meal moistened and kneaded into a paste, ready to be baked into bread, etc.; paste of bread. 2. Any soft pasty mass 1559. 3. *U.S. slang.* Money 1851.

1. (*My*) *cake is d.*: my project has failed. See *Tam. Shr.* v. i. 145. *Comb.*: **d.-brake, -kneader, -maker, -mixer,** machines for kneading and mixing d.; **-head** (*U.S.*), a fool; **-raiser,** 'a pan in a bath of heated water, to maintain a temperature in the d. favorable to fermentation' (Knight).

Dou·gh-baked, *ppl. a.* Now *dial.* 1592. [f. DOUGH *sb.* + BAKE *v.*] Imperfectly baked, so as to remain doughy; hence, imperfect; deficient in intellect, etc.; feeble, 'soft'.

Dou·gh-bird. *local U.S.* The Eskimo curlew (*Numenius borealis*).

Dou·gh-boy. 1685. 1. A boiled flour dumpling. 2. *U.S.* An infantry soldier 1867.

Dou·gh-face, doughface. *U.S.* 1833. 1. A face resembling dough. 2. One who is easily moulded or worked upon; formerly, in U.S. politics, applied to Northern politicians who were unduly compliant to the South, in the matter of slavery, etc. So **Dou·gh-faced** *a.*

Doughnut (dōu·nɒt). *local Eng.* and *U.S.* 1809. A small cake made of dough, and fried or boiled in lard.

Dough-trough (dōu·trǫf). ME. A trough or vessel in which dough is placed to rise; also = *dough-raiser*; see DOUGH *sb.*

Doughty (dau·ti), *a.* [OE. *dyhtig*, from an OTeut. sb. **duhtiz*, f. *dugan*; see DOW *v.*1 The phonology is obscure. See N.E.D.] Capable, virtuous; valiant, formidable: now somewhat arch., and often joc.

Kyng Arthur was .. bolde and doubty of body CAXTON. Of his duchtie Deidis and Justice done STEWART. Hence **Dou·ghtily** *adv.* **Dou·ghtiness.**

Doughy (dōu·i), *a.* 1601. [f. DOUGH *sb.* + -Y 1.] Of the nature of dough; like dough 1601.

All the unbak'd and dowy youth of a nation *All's Well* IV. v. 3. Hence **Dou·ghiness.**

Doulocracy, var. of DULOCRACY.

Doum (daum, dūm). Also **doom.** 1801. [Arab.] A palm (*Hyphæne Thebaica*) found in Egypt, having a dichotomously divided trunk, and an edible fruit about the size of an apple. Usu. **d.-palm.**

Dour (dūr), *a. Sc.* and *n. dial.* ME. [ad. L. *durus.*] 1. Hard, stern. 2. Obstinate, sullen 1470.

1. A d. and hard lyfe 1596. 2. D. men 1572. Hence **Dou·r-ly** *adv.*, **-ness.**

Doura, var. DURRA, Indian millet.

Douse (daus), *sb.* 1625. [f. DOUSE *v.*1] A dull heavy blow.

Douse (daus), *v.*1 1559. [In sense 1, ? conn. w. MDu. *dossen.*] †1. *trans.* To strike, punch -1736. 2. *Naut.* To strike (a sail); to lower or slacken suddenly or in haste; to close (a port-hole) 1627. 3. To doff 1785. 4. (? a different wd.) To dout (a light) 1785. 5. To stop 1887.

2. D. the ports 1802. 4. Phr. *Dowse the glim* (slang) = put out the light. Hence **Dou·ser,** a heavy blow.

Douse (daus), *v.*2 1600. [? echoic.] †1. *trans.* To plunge vigorously *in* water or the like -1662. 2. To throw water over; to drench 1606. 3. *intr.* To plunge or be plunged in water 1603. Hence **Dou·ser,** one who drenches.

Douse, Douser, etc.; see DOWSE, etc.

Dousing-chock, -rod; see under DOWSE *v.*

Dout (daut), *v.* Now *dial.* 1526. [fused f. *do out*; see DO *v.*] *trans.* To put out (a fire or light). Hence **Dout** *sb.* an extinguisher. **Dou·ter,** one who or that which douts.

‖**Douzaine** (duzē·n). 1682. [Fr. = DOZEN, q. v.] *Channel Islands.* A body of twelve men representing a parish. Hence **Douzainier** (dūzēnīə·ɪ), one of such a body.

†**Douzepers** (dū·zəpēəɪs), *sb. pl.* ME. [a. OF. *douze per(s*, mod. F. *douze pairs* twelve peers. In Eng. finally treated as one word, with a singular.] In the *Romances*, the twelve peers or paladins of Charlemagne. In *History*, applied to the twelve great peers, spiritual and temporal, of France. (See Du Cange s. v. *Pares Franciæ.*) Also *transf.*

Dove (dɒv). [OE. **dufe*, not found. Perh. a deriv. of *dub-* to dive, dip (see DIVE). See also CULVER.] 1. A bird of the *Columbidæ*, or pigeon family.

Formerly applied to all the species of pigeon native to or known in Britain; but now often restricted to the Turtle-dove, and its congeners. The dove, as the type of gentleness and harmlessness, occupies an important place in Christian symbolism.

2. *fig.* and *transf.* (see quots.) ME. 3. An image of a dove as a symbol of innocence, etc.; also, the vessel enclosing the pyx, formerly used in the East and in France 1513.

1. Voices of the well-contented doves TENNYSON. 2. Holy Spirit, heavenly D. WATTS. He will be a d. of peace to your ark LYTTON. She is coming, my d., my dear TENNYSON.

Comb.: **d.-colour,** a warm grey with a tone of pink or purple; **-dock,** the coltsfoot; **-flower** = *dove-plant*; **dove's-foot,** the plant *Geranium molle*, and some other small species of cranesbill; **-hawk,** the *d.-coloured falcon* or hen-harrier (*Circus cyaneus*); **-plant,** an orchid of Central America, *Peristeria elata*; **-tick,** a blind mite parasite on pigeons.

Dove (dōuv), occas. pa. t. of DIVE *v.*

Dovecot, -cote (dɒ·vkǫt). ME. [f. DOVE *sb.* + COT, COTE.] A house for doves or pigeons; usually placed at a height above the ground, with openings, and internal provision for roosting and breeding. Also *fig.*

Like an Eagle in a Doue-coat *Cor.* v. vi. 115.

Do·ve-ey:ed, *a.* 1717. Having eyes like a dove; meek, or soft-eyed; as, *Dove-eyed Hope.*

Do·vehouse. ME. A house for doves; a dovecot. Also *attrib.*

Dovekie (dɒ·vki). 1821. [Sc. dim. of *dove.*] An Arctic bird, the Black Guillemot.

Dovelet (dɒ·vlėt). 1825. A little dove.

Dovelike (dɒ·vləik), *a.* and *adv.* 1577. Like a dove; after the manner of a dove.

Thou..Dove-like satst brooding on the vast Abyss MILTON.

Dover's powder. 1854. [Name of Thomas Dover (d. 1742).] A pharmaceutical preparation of opium and ipecacuanha.

Dovetail (dɒ·vtēl), *sb.* 1565. **1.** Something in the shape of a dove's tail; *spec.* a tenon cut in the shape of a dove's tail spread, to fit into a mortise of corresponding shape; also, a mortise shaped to receive such a tenon 1674. **2.** = *D. joint*: A joint composed of these.

Comb.: **d.-moulding,** *Archit.* a moulding arranged in the form of a series of figures like dove-tails; **-saw,** a saw employed in making dovetails.

Do·vetail, *v.* 1657. [f. prec. sb.] **1.** *trans.* To fit together or join by means of dovetails. Const. *in, into, to.* **2.** *fig.* To adjust exactly so as to form a continuous whole 1815. **3.** *intr.* To fit into each other, so as to form a compact and harmonious whole 1817.

Dovey (dɒ·vi). 1769. [f. DOVE + -Y⁶.] A term of affection: cf. LOVEY.

†**Do·vish,** *a.* 1537. Of or pertaining to the dove; dovelike –1546.

Doveyshe simplicitie, serpentlike wysdome 1546.

Dow (dau), *v.*[1] Now *Sc.* and *n. dial.* [An original Teut. preterite-present vb. (see CAN, DARE, MAY): OE. *dugan* to avail, be strong, good, worthy:—OTeut. *dugan.*] †**1.** *intr.* To be good, strong, virtuous. Only OE. †**2.** To be valid, or of value; to be good for anything –1788. †**3.** To avail. Chiefly *impers.* –1590. †**4.** To become, behove. Usually *impers.* –ME. **5.** To be able (to do something) ME. **6.** To thrive, prosper 1674.

5. I never dowed to bide a hard turn o' wark in my life SCOTT.

†**Dow,** *v.*[2] ME. [a. F. *douer*:—L. *dotare*, f. *dos, dotem.*] **1.** = ENDOW 2. –1483. **2.** To invest *with* –1450. **3.** To bequeath. CHAUCER.

Dow, earlier f. DHOW, q. v.

Dowable (dau·ăb'l), *a.* 1535. [a. AF. *dowable*, f. F. *douer*, DOW *v.*[2]] Capable of being endowed; entitled to dower.

Dowager (dau·ĕdʒəɹ). 1530. [a. OF. *douagere, -iere*, etc., fem. of *douagier*, etc. (=mod.F. *douairier*), f. *douage* dower.] A widow who is in the enjoyment of some title or some property that has come to her from her deceased husband. Often added to the title so enjoyed, as *princess-, queen-d., d.-duchess*, etc. **b.** *familiarly.* An elderly lady of dignified demeanour 1870.

I haue a Widdow Aunt, a d., Of great reuennew *Mids. N.* I. i. 157. Hence **Dow·agerism,** the condition of a d.

Dowcet(e, obs. ff. DOUCET, DULCET.

Dowd (daud), *sb.*[1] ME. [?] A person whose dress and appearance are devoid of smartness and brightness.

Dowd, *sb.*[2] Now *dial.* 1749. A woman's cap or night-cap.

Dowd, dowed, *ppl. a.*; see DOW *v.*[3]

Dowdy (dau·di). 1581. [A deriv. of DOWD.]

A. *sb.* A woman or girl unattractively dressed, without smartness or brightness.

The Duchesse of Albemarle, who is ever a plain homely d. PEPYS.

B. *adj.* Shabbily dull in colour or appearance; without brightness or freshness 1676.

A dress..d. with age TROLLOPE. A shy, d. young woman 1869. Hence **Dow·dily** *adv.* **Dow·diness. Dow·dyish** *a.* somewhat d. **Dow·dyism,** d. character or quality.

Dowel (dau·ĕl), *sb.* ME. [? answering to MLG. *dovel*, Ger. *döbel* plug, tap (of a cask, etc.). Cf. OF. *doelle, douelle* barrel-stave; but the change of sense is a difficulty.] **1.** A headless pin, peg, or bolt, of wood, metal, etc., serving to fasten together two pieces of wood, stone, etc., by penetrating into the substance of both pieces. **2.** A plug of wood driven into a wall to receive nails. [Ger. *döbel, dübel.*]

Comb.: **d.-bit,** a boring-tool of semi-cylindrical form terminating in a conoidal edge; a *spoon-bit*; **-joint,** a junction formed by means of dowels; **-pin** = sense 1; **-pointer,** a tool for pointing the ends of dowels. Hence **Dow·el** *v.* to fasten with dowels.

†**Dower,** *sb.*[1] ME. [Cf. OF. *douvre*, var. of *douve* ditch, dyke, etc.] A burrow (of rabbits, or the like) –1490.

Dower (dau·əɹ), *sb.*[2] ME. [a. OF. *douaire*, etc., ad. late L. *dotarium*, f. L. *dotare.*] **1.** The portion of a deceased husband's estate which the law allows to his widow for her life. **2.** = DOWRY 2, †**3.** ME. **3.** *fig.* Endowment ME.

1. Her part and dowyer of my godes ME. 2. Choose thou thy husband, and Ile pay thy d. SHAKS. 3. A mortal Song we sing, by d. Encouraged of celestial power WORDSW. *Comb.*, as **d.-house, -land.**

Dower (dau·əɹ), *v.* 1605. [f. DOWER *sb.*[2]] **1.** *trans.* To give a dowry to; to endow. **2.** To endow *with* any gift, talent, or power 1793. **3.** *intr.* To take or receive dower 1848.

2. Dower'd with the hate of hate, the scorn of scorn TENNYSON.

†**Dow·eress.** 1519. [f. DOWER + -ESS.] A widow holding a dower –1823.

Dowerless (dau·əɹlės), *a.* 1605. [f. DOWER *sb.*[2] + -LESS.] Portionless.

Dowie, dowy (dau·i, do·wi), *a. Sc.* and *n. dial.* 1508. [=16th c. *dolly.* Prob. a deriv. of ME. *dol, doll* DULL.] Dully and lonely, dreary, dismal.

Dowl (daul). Now *dial.* ME. [? related to DOWN *sb.*[2]] One of the filaments of a feather; down, fluff.

Dowlas (dau·lăs). 1529. [f. *Daoulas* or *Doulas*, SE. of Brest in Brittany.] †**a.** A coarse kind of linen, much used in the 16th and 17th centuries. **b.** A strong calico, now made in imitation of this. Also *attrib.*

Doulas, filthy Doulas 1 *Hen. IV*, III. iii. 79.

†**Dowment.** 1552. [f. DOW *v.*[2]] Endowment; the giving of dower –1628.

Down (daun), *sb.*[1] [OE. *dūn* fem., hill = ODu. *dūna* (MDu. *dūne*, etc.). ?Of Celtic origin; cf. OIr. *dún* hill, Welsh *din*, etc.] †**1.** A hill –1653. **2.** An open expanse of elevated land; *spec.* in *pl.*, the treeless undulating chalk uplands of the south and south-east of England; serving chiefly for pasturage; also, similar tracts elsewhere ME. **3.** A sand-hill, DUNE 1523. **4.** *The Downs*: the part of the sea within the Goodwin Sands, off the east coast of Kent, a famous rendezvous for ships. (It lies opposite the eastern end of the North Downs.) 1460. **5.** Applied to a breed of sheep raised on the chalk downs of England. Cf. SOUTHDOWN. 1831.

2. My boskie acres, and my vnshrubd downe *Temp.* IV. i. 81. By dale and d. We dwell SCOTT. 3. Over the downs of sand by the sea side CARTE. 4. Sir Simon Mondford..was appoynted to kepe the downes, and the five Portes HALL.

Down (daun), *sb.*[2] ME. [a. ON. *dúnn*, nom. *dúnn* down.] **1. a.** The first feathering of young birds. **b.** The fine soft under plumage of fowls, used for stuffing beds, pillows, etc. Also *fig.* **2.** Hence, **a.** The hair as it first shows itself on the face 1580. **b.** The pubescence on some plants and fruits; the soft feathery pappus of some seeds ME. **c.** Any feathery or fluffy substance 1626.

1. Of downe of pure doves white CHAUCER. *fig.* Must I break from the d. of thy embraces, To put on steel FORD. 2. The callow d. began To shade my chin DRYDEN.

attrib. and *Comb.*, as *d.-bed, -pillow*, etc.; **d.-tree,** the cork-wood, *Ochroma Lagopus*; **-weed,** *Filago germanica.*

Down, *sb.*[3] 1611. [DOWN *adv.*, used subst., or ellipt. for 'downward motion'.] †**1.** The burden of a song –1656. **2.** A descent; a reverse of fortune. Usu. in phr. *ups and downs.* 1710. **3.** *colloq.* A tendency to be 'down *upon*' 1893. **4.** A cry of *down with* 1889.

Down (daun), *a.* 1565. [DOWN *adv.*, used attrib., or by ellipsis of some ppl. wd.] **1.** Directed downwards; descending; of a train or coach: Going down, *i.e.* in Great Britain, away from London. Hence *transf.* 1851. **2.** Downcast, dejected. *Obs.* (exc. predicatively.) 1645.

1. To cross the line to the d. platform 1885.

Down (daun), *adv.* [In late OE. *dūne, dūn*, aphet. f. *adūne* ADOWN, q. v.] **1.** In a descending direction (real or imaginary); from above, or towards that which is below; from a higher to a lower place or position; to the ground. Also vaguely in *up and d.*, often = to and fro; see UP. **2.** In a low or lower situation or position, or one conventionally viewed as lower; on the ground ME. **3.** Into or in a fallen, sitting, or overthrown position or posture ME. **4.** Prostrate with sickness; ill 1710. **5.** Below the horizon ME. **6.** Below the surface or to the bottom of water 1659. **7.** Downstairs, or to the dining-room, to dinner 1592. **8.** Down the throat 1582. **9.** In reference to payment: (Laid) upon the table or counter; (paid) at the instant 1557. **10.** In writing: with *write, note, set*, etc. See the vbs. 1576. **11.** From an earlier to a later time ME. **12.** To or at a lower amount, rate, or price 1573. **13.** Into or in a lower or inferior condition, low spirits, a state of depression, defeat, or the like ME. **14.** To a smaller bulk or finer consistency 1675. **15.** Into or in a state of subsidence 1590. **16.** Into a weaker quality 1816. **17.** *slang.* Aware, wide-awake 1812. **18.** With ellipsis of a verb; *e.g.* of *come, go, sit, kneel, lie* ME.; of *go*, in sense 'be swallowed' (*lit.* and *fig.*) 1580; of *put*, etc. 1820; so *d. with*; also used in ballad refrains, without meaning 1598.

1. He a lighted downe of his horse HALL. In our journey d. GOLDSM. To go d. from Oxford (*mod.*). 2. The tide was d. 1894. 3. Fold it d. 1669. Four d. and three to play 1894. 4. We have now about 50 men d. 1712. 5. The sun had gone d. 1849. 6. When Kempenfelt went d. COWPER. 8. A bitter potion that is soon d. 1660. 9. For a lump sum d. 1894. 10. *Much Ado* IV. ii. 17. 11. D. from the time of Moses 1662. 12. Cutting d. his salary MACAULAY. 13. Who can rayse him, that Fortune will have downe DRAYTON. 14. He..melted it [New Coll. plate] downe WOOD. 15. D. dropt the breeze COLERIDGE. 18. Downe therefore, and beg mercy of the Duke SHAKS.

Phrases. **D. on. a.** Aware of, 'up to' (*slang*). **b.** *To be d. on* (*upon*): to fall upon, attack (from a superior position); to treat severely. **D. east** (*U.S.*): into or in the eastern sea-coast districts of New England, *esp.* Maine. Also as *adj.* and *sb.* Hence **D.-easter. D. south:** into or in the south; in *U.S.* into or in the Southern States. **D. to the ground** (*colloq.*): completely.

¶ For **Down-** in comb., see DOWNCAST, DOWNCOME, etc.

Down (daun), *prep.* 1508. [DOWN *adv.* construed with an object.] **1.** In a descending direction along, through, or into; from a higher to a lower part of 1508; at a lower part of 1769. **2.** To (or at) what is regarded as a lower part of; along the course or extent of 1674. **3.** The prep. and its object may be used as an advb. or attrib. phrase; as in *d.-river, -stream, -town* 1645.

1. Such notes as..Drew iron tears d. Pluto's cheek MILT. Three miles d. the river DE FOE. 2. Phr. *Up and d.*: see UP. *D. town*: Into the town; down in the town. *D.* (*the*) *wind*: see WIND.

Down, *v.* 1682. [f. DOWN *adv.* in ellipt. uses; see above.] **1.** *trans.* To bring, put, throw, or knock down 1778. **2.** *intr.* To descend 1825. **3.** *To d. upon, on*: to fall upon as from a superior position 1852. **4.** *To d. with*: to put down; to have done with 1682.

1. His horse had downed him three times SURTEES. 4. Except they d. with their dust 1682.

Down and out, *adj. phr.* orig. *U.S.* 1889. Completely without resources. Also as *sb.*

†**Downbea·r,** *v.* ME. *trans.* To bear down, press down, cause to sink; also *fig.* –1834.

Downcast (daunkɑ·st), *v.* ME. [f. DOWN *adv.* + CAST *v.*] To cast down (*lit.* and *fig.*); to demolish; to dispirit. (Now only *poet.*)

Downcast (dau·nkast), *sb.* ME. [f. DOWN *adv.* + CAST *sb.*; cf. prec.] **1.** The act of casting down (*lit.* and *fig.*); demolition; downward cast (of the eyes, etc.); in *Geol.* = DOWNTHROW 2. **2.** The throwing down of a current of air into a coal-mine, etc.; *attrib.* in *d. shaft*, the shaft by which this is done, also *ellipt.* called the *down-cast* 1816.

1. I saw the respectful d. of his eyes STEELE.

Downcast (dau·nkast), *ppl. a.* 1602. [f. DOWN *adv.* + CAST *ppl. a.*; also f. DOWNCAST *v.*] **1.** Cast down; ruined, destroyed; *fig.* dejected. **2.** Of looks, etc.: Directed downwards; dejected 1633.

1. A few looked d. 1832. 2. With d. eyes FREEMAN.

Downcome (dau·nˌkɒm), *sb.* 1513. [f. DOWN *adv.* + COME *v.*; cf. *income.*] **1.** The act of coming down (*lit.* and *fig.*); downfall; humiliation; in *Hawking*, a swoop down. **2.** *Metallurgy.* (See quot.) 1881.

2. *Downcome*, the pipe through which tunnel-head gases from iron blast-furnaces are brought down to the hot-blast stoves and boilers, when these are below

the tunnel-head (Raymond). So **Dow·n-coming** (in sense 1).

Down-draught (dau·ndraft). 1849. A descending current of air.

Downfall (dau·nfǭl). ME. **1.** Sudden descent; a fall (of rain, snow, etc.) 1450. †**2.** A steep descent, precipice; an abyss, etc. –1822. **3.** Fall from high estate; ruin. (The current use.) ME. **b.** *concr.* (*pl.*) Ruins 1602. **4.** *attrib.* Descending 1793.

1. The sonne knowyng no downe falle 1450. **2.** Dreadfull downfalls of unheeded rocks DRYDEN. **3.** Histories of the downfal of kingdoms JOHNSON. So **Dow·n-fallen** *ppl. a.* **Dow·nfalling** *ppl. a.*

Down grade, down-grade. 1885. [See GRADE.] *lit.* A downward gradient (on a railway, etc.); hence *fig.* a downward course in morals, etc. Also *attrib.*

†**Down-gyved,** *ppl. a.* Hanging down like fetters. *Haml.* II. i. 80.

Dow·nhaul (-hǭl). 1669. [f. DOWN *adv.* + HAUL *v.*] *Naut.* A rope to pull down a sail when shortening sail. Also *attrib.*

Downhearted (-hāɹtėd), *a.* 1774. [See DOWN *adv.* 13.] Having the heart down; low-spirited (*colloq.*).

Downhill.

A. *sb.* (dau·nhil). [f. DOWN *adv.*] The downward slope of a hill; a declivity, descent (*lit.* and *fig.*) 1591. **B.** *adv.* (daunhi·l). [f. DOWN *prep.*] Down the slope of a hill; on a decline; downwards (*lit.* and *fig.*) 1659. **C.** *adj.* (dau·nhil). Sloping or descending downwards; declining. (Also *fig.*) 1727.

sb. The d. of life 1853. *adv.* A very short cut, and all d. *adj.* The d. side of life COWPER.

Dow·nland. 1842. [Cf. OE. *dūn-land.*] Land forming downs; hilly pasture-land.

†**Dow·nlooked** (-lukt), *a.* 1641. [See DOWN *a.* 1.] Having downward looks; guilty-looking; demure –1814.

Dow·n-lying, *vbl. sb.* 1526. **a.** Lying down, going to bed. **b.** Lying-in of a woman, confinement (*n. dial.*).

Downmost (dau·nmōust). 1790. Superlative degree of DOWN *adv.* and *adj.*

Dow·npour (-pōᵊɹ), *sb.* 1811. A pouring down; *esp.* a heavy, continuous fall (of rain, etc.).

Downright (daunrəi·t, dau·nrəit). ME. [f. DOWN *adv.* + RIGHT *adj.* and *adv.*]

A. *adv.* (Stressed *dow·nright* before, *downri·ght* following, the word it qualifies.) †**1.** Straight down; vertically downwards –1763. **2.** Absolutely, out and out ME. †**3.** In a straightforward manner; plainly –1684. †**4.** Straightway, straight –1712.

2. Killed four d., and wounded several 1724. **4.** Mrs. Bull..fell down right into a fit ARBUTHNOT.

B. *adj.* (Usu. stressed *dow·nright.*) **1.** Descending straight downwards; vertical 1530. **2.** *fig.* **a.** Direct, straightforward. Of persons: Plain and direct (sometimes to bluntness). *Obs.* or *arch.* 1603. **b.** Nothing less than . ., mere, absolute, thorough 1565.

2. A certain d. honesty 1875. A d. atheist 1856.

C. *sb.* (*dow·nright.*) [The *adj.* used *ellipt.*] †**1.** A perpendicular 1674. **2.** (*pl.*) A quality of wool 1793.

Hence **Downri·ght-ly** *adv.* (*rare*), **-ness.**

Dow·nrush (-rʋʃ). 1855. Rapid descent.

Dow·nset, *a.* 1847. *Her.* Of a fess: Broken so that the one half is set lower than the other by its whole width.

Downside (dau·nsəid). 1683. The under side. Also *advb.*

Dow·nshare, corrupt f. DENSHIRE.

Downstairs. Less freq. **downstair.** 1596. **a.** *adv. phr.* (daunstēᵊ·ɹz). On or to a lower floor or (*fig.*) the lower regions. **b.** *attrib.* or *adj.* (dau·nstēᵊɹ(z) 1819. **c.** *sb.* (daunstēᵊ·ɹz). The downstairs part of a building; the lower regions 1843.

†**Dow·nsteepy,** *a.* Steeply descending. FLORIO.

Downthrow (dau·nþrōᵘ). 1615. **1.** A throwing or being thrown down (*rare*). **2.** *Geol.* The depression of strata below the general level on one side of a fault 1858.

Downtrodden (dauntrǫ·d'n), *pa. pple.* and (dau·ntrǫ:d'n), *ppl. a.* 1568. **1.** Trampled down. **2.** Crushed by oppression or tyranny 1595.

The..d. vassals of perdition MILT. var. **Dow·n-trod** *ppl. a.*

Downward (dau·nwǭɹd). ME. [orig. aphet. f. ADOWNWARD, in OE. *adūnweard.*]

A. *adv.* **1.** Towards a lower place or position; towards what is below; with a descending motion. **2.** *fig.* Towards that which is lower in order, or inferior in any way ME. **b.** Onward from an earlier to a later time 1611.

1. A drope..fallyth dounwarde by his owne heuynesse TREVISA. Looking d. 1855. **2.** Things seem to tend d. EMERSON. From Solon d. GROTE.

†**B.** *prep.* = DOWN *prep.* 1 (*rare*) ME. only.

C. *adj.* **1.** Directed towards that which is lower; descending; inclined downward (*lit.* and *fig.*) 1552. **2.** Lying or situated below; lower (*rare*) ME.

1. The d. track DRYDEN. Steps in a d. scale FREEMAN.

Downwards (dau·nwǭɹdz), *adv.* ME. [See -WARDS.] = DOWNWARD *adv.*

Downweigh (daunwē¹·), *v.* 1600. *trans.* To weigh down; to outweigh; to depress.

The gloom..downweighs My spirit MOIR.

†**Down weight, down-weight.** 1524. Full or good weight. *attrib.* Of full weight. Also *fig.* –1698.

Downy (dau·ni), *a.*[1] 1671. [f. DOWN *sb.*[1] + -Y [1].] Characterized by downs.

A..rolling, d. country MOTLEY.

Downy (dau·ni), *a.*[2] 1548. [f. DOWN *sb.*[2] + -Y [1].] **1.** Of the nature of or like down 1578. **2.** Made or consisting of down 1592. **3.** Covered with down 1548. **4.** *transf.* Soft as down 1602. **5.** *slang.* [See DOWN *adv.* 17.] Wide-awake, knowing 1821.

1. Thick d. feathers R. H. DANA. **2.** D. pillows 1712. **3.** D. Peaches DRYDEN. **4.** Shake off this Downey sleepe, Deaths counterfeit *Macb.* II. iii. 81. Hence **Dow·nily** *adv.* (*rare*). **Dow·niness.**

Dowress; see DOWERESS.

Dowry (dauᵊ·ri). ME. [a. AF. *dowarie* fem. = OF. *douaire* masc.; see DOWER.] †**1.** = DOWER 1. –1841. **2.** The portion given with the wife; the dot ME. †**3.** A present given by a man to or for his bride –1611. **4.** *fig.* A gift of nature or fortune; an endowment ME.

3. Aske mee neuer so much dowrie and gift..but giue mee the damsell to wife *Gen.* xxxiv. 12.

†**Dow·sabel.** 1590. An English form (through Fr.) of *Dulcibella.* Applied generically to a sweetheart, lady-love; cf. DOLL. –1675.

Dowse (dauz), *v.* Also **douse.** 1691. [app. a dialect term.] *intr.* To use the divining-rod in search of water or mineral veins. Hence **Dow·sing** *vbl. sb.* **Dowser** (dau·zəɹ), one who uses the dowsing-rod. **Dowsing-rod,** the rod or twig used by dowsers. **Dowsing-cheek, -chock,** one of several pieces fayed athwart the apron and lapped on the knight-heads or inside stuff above the upper deck (Weale).

Dowve, obs. f. DOVE.

Doxastic (dǫksæ·stik), *a.* 1794. [ad. Gr. δοξαστικός, f. δοξάζειν to conjecture.] Of, pertaining to, or depending on opinion.

Doxology (dǫksǫ·lŏdʒi). 1649. [ad. med.L. *doxologia,* a. Gr., f. δοξολόγος, f. δόξα glory + -λογος speaking. So F. *doxologie.*] †**a.** Thanksgiving. **b.** A short formula of praise to God; *spec.* the *Gloria in excelsis* or 'Greater d.', the *Gloria Patri* or 'Lesser d.', or some metrical formula, *e. g.* 'Praise God from whom all blessings flow', etc. Hence **Doxolo·gical** *a.* pertaining to or of the nature of a d. **Doxo·logize** *v. intr.* to say the d.; *trans.* to address a d. to.

Doxy[1] (dǫ·ksi). 1530. [?] A beggar's trull; hence, *slang,* a paramour, prostitute; *dial.* a sweetheart.

Do·xy[2]. *colloq.* 1730. [f. (*ortho*)*doxy,* etc., from Gr. δόξα.] Opinion (*esp.* in theological matters). (Cf. *-ism.*)

'Orthodoxy, my Lord,' said Bishop Warburton.. 'is my d.,—heterodoxy is another man's d.'

‖**Doyen** (dwayæ̃). ME. [F. :—L. *decanus* DEAN.] †**1.** A commander of ten. ME. only. **2.** The senior member of a body 1670.

Doyley, -ly; see DOILY.

Doze (dōᵘz), *v.* 1647. [Perhaps earlier in dialects. The trans. sense = Da. *döse* to make dull, drowsy, etc.] †**1.** *trans.* To stupefy; to make drowsy or dull; to confuse –1818. **2.** *intr.* To sleep drowsily; to be half asleep; to nod. Also *fig.* 1693. **3.** *trans.* (with *away, out*). To pass (time) in dozing 1693.

1. The tobacco had..dozed my head DE FOE. **2.** I have been dozing over a stupid book SHERIDAN. **3.** We d. away our hours 1693. Hence **Doze** *sb.* a short slumber. **Dozed** *ppl. a.* stupefied; drowsy; of timber, decayed inside; doted. **Do·zer,** one who dozes.

Dozen (dʋ·z'n), *sb.* ME. [a. OF. *dozeine, dosaine,* a Com. Rom. deriv. of **dodece, dotze,* etc. :—L. *duodecim* + *-ena,* as in *centena,* etc.] **1.** A group or set of twelve. Orig. as a sb., with *of;* in sing., without *of* = twelve. (Abbrev. *doz.*) †**2.** A kind of kersey. (Usu. in *pl.*) –1721. †**3.** Corruptly, a tithing, or group of ten households (AF. *dizeyne,* Fr. *dizaine*) –1672.

1. A d. of Knives 1726. Six d. pencils (*mod.*). Phr. *Baker's d.* (see BAKER), *devil's, long, printer's d.,* thirteen. *Round d.,* a full d. *To talk nineteen to the d.:* to talk very fast. Hence **Do·zener,** (*a*) a member of a tithing; (*b*) the head of a dozen; (*c*) a local name for constables. **Do·zenth** *a. colloq.* = TWELFTH.

Dozy (dōᵘ·zi), *a.* 1693. [f. DOZE *v.* + -Y [1].] **1.** Drowsy. **2.** Of timber or fruit: In incipient decay; sleepy 1882. Hence **Do·zily** *adv.* **Do·ziness.**

†**Do·zzle,** *v.* [freq. of DOZE *v.*] *trans.* To stupefy. HACKET.

Dr., abbrev. of *Debtor* (in *Book-keeping*), *Doctor.*

Drab (dræb), *sb.*[1] 1515. [Conn. w. Ir. *drabog,* Gael. *drabag* slattern; cf. also LG. *drabbe* dirt.] **1.** A slatternly woman. **2.** A strumpet 1530. **3.** (? a different word.) *Salt-making.* A wooden case into which the salt is put when it is taken out of the boiling pan 1753.

Drab (dræb), *sb.*[2] and *a.* 1541. [Orig. synonymous with *drap* cloth (cf. DRAP-DE-BERRY). ? Applied to a cloth of a natural undyed colour, whence attrib.]

A. *sb.* A kind of hempen, linen, or woollen cloth.

B. *adj.* Of a dull light brown or yellowish-brown 1775; *fig.* dull; wanting brightness 1880.

C. *sb.* [the adj. used absol.] **1.** Drab colour; cloth of this colour; also, in *pl.* = drab breeches 1821. **2.** Name for a group of moths 1819.

Drab (dræb), *v.* 1602. [f. DRAB *sb.*[1]] *intr.* To whore. Also *to d. it.* Hence †**Dra·bber,** a whoremonger.

Drabbet (dræ·bėt, dræbe·t). 1851. [f. DRAB *sb.*[2] + -ET.] A drab twilled linen.

Drabbish (dræ·biʃ), *a.*[1] 1566. [f. DRAB *sb.*[1] + -ISH.] Sluttish.

Dra·bbish, *a.*[2] 1842. [f. DRAB *a.* + -ISH.] Somewhat drab in colour.

Drabble (dræb'l), *v.* [ME. *drabelen* = LG. *drabbeln* to walk in water or mire; cf. *drabbe* dirt, etc.] **1.** To make or become wet and dirty by contact with muddy water or mire. **2.** *Angling.* (*intr.*) To fish for barbel, etc. with a rod and a weighted line 1799. Hence **Drabble-tail,** a draggle-tail.

Drabbler, drabler (dræ·bləɹ). 1592. [f. DRABBLE *v.,* from its position.] *Naut.* A piece of canvas, laced to the bottom of the bonnet of a sail, to give it greater depth.

‖**Dracæna** (drăsī·nă). 1823. [mod.L., a. Gr. δράκαινα, fem. of δράκων.] *Bot.* A genus of *Liliaceæ,* containing the dragon-tree *Dracæna Draco,* and other ornamental species.

Drachm (dræm). See also DRAM. ME. [a. F. *drachme,* earlier *dragme* = L. *drachma,* a. Gr. δραχμή, an Attic coin and weight, prob. orig. 'a handful', f. δράσσεσθαι to grasp.] **1.** An ancient Greek silver coin, the DRACHMA. Its average value was $9^3/_4d.$ English. (Also DRACHMA.) Hence, the Arabic DIRHEM. **2.** A weight about equal to that of the coin; now, in Apothecaries' weight = 60 grains, or $^1/_8$ of an ounce, in Avoirdupois = $27^1/_3$ grains, or $^1/_{16}$ of an ounce. (Spelt *drachm* or *dram.*) Also, the Arabic DIRHEM. ME. **3.** *fig.* A very little 1635.

‖**Drachma** (dræ·kmă). Pl. **-mas,** also **-mæ.** 1579. [a. L., a. Gr. δραχμή DRACHM.] **1.** = DRACHM 1. Also, the Jewish quarter-shekel. **b.** A silver coin of modern Greece, = Fr. *franc,* It. *lira* 1882. **2.** = DRACHM 2. 1527.

ō (Ger. Kōln). ö (Fr. peu). ü (Ger. Müller). ü (Fr. dune). ʋ (curl). ē (ēᵊ) (there). ē (ē¹) (rein). ę (Fr. faire). ɜ (fir, fern, earth).

†Dracin, -ine. *Chem.* = DRACONIN.

Draco·nian, *a.* 1876. [f. as DRACONIC.] = DRACONIC 1, 2.

Draconic (drăkǫ·nik), *a.* 1680. [f. L. *draco*, ad. Gr. δράκων, also f. Δράκων Draco.] **1.** Of, pertaining to, or characteristic of Draco, archon at Athens in 621 B.C., or the severe code of laws attributed to him; harsh, severe, cruel 1708. **2.** Pertaining to, or of the nature of, a dragon 1680. **3.** *Astron.* = DRACONTIC 1876. var. **†Draco·nical** *a.* Hence **Draco·nically** *adv.*

Dra·conin, -ine. 1837. [f. L. *draco.*] *Chem.* The colouring matter in *Dragon's blood.*

‖**Draconites** (drækŏnəi·tīz). 1579. [L., f. *draconem.*] A precious stone fabled to be taken out of the head of a dragon.

Draconi·tic, *a.* *Astron.* = DRACONTIC. (In recent Dicts.)

Dracontic (drăkǫ·ntik), *a.* 1727. [f. Gr. δρακοντ-, stem of δράκων.] *Astron.* Pertaining to the moon's nodes; see DRAGON'S-HEAD, -TAIL.

Dracontine (drăkǫ·ntəin), *a.* 1806. [irreg. f. Gr. δράκων, -οντα + -INE.] Of the nature of, or belonging to, a dragon.

‖**Dracunculus** (drăkv·ŋkiŭlŏs). 1706. [L., dim. of *draco.*] **1.** The Guinea-worm, *D.* (*Filaria*) *medinensis.* **2.** *Ichthyol.* A fish, a dragonet of the genus *Callionymus* 1752. **3.** *Bot.* A herbaceous genus of *Araceæ*, containing the GREEN DRAGON (q. v.) or DRAGONS 1706.

Drad, obs. f. DREAD *a.* and *v.*

Dradge, obs. or dial. f. DREDGE.

Draff (drɑf). [Early ME. *draf*, prob. repr. OE. **dræf* :—OTeut. type **trađaz* neut.] Refuse, lees, dregs; hog's-wash; *spec.* brewer's grains. Also *transf.* and *fig.*

The d. of servile food MILT. *Sams.* 573. The brood of Belial, the draffe of men MILT. Hence **Dra·ffish, Dra·ffy** *adjs.* worthless.

Dra·ffsack. Now *dial.* ME. [f. DRAFF + SACK *sb.*] A sack of draff or refuse; also *fig.* a big paunch; lazy glutton. Hence **†Dra·ff-sacked** *ppl. a.* stuffed with draff; worthless.

Draft (drɑft), *sb.* 1494. A modern phonetic spelling of DRAUGHT *sb.*, now established in the following senses: **1.** The turn of the scale in weighing; hence a deduction from the gross weight allowed for this (= CLOFF, q. v.). **2.** The drawing off or selection of a party from some larger body for some special purpose; *spec.* in military use 1703; the body so drawn off 1756. **3.** The drawing of money by an order in due form. Also DRAUGHT, q. v. 1633. **b.** A bill or cheque drawn; sometimes, *spec.* an order drawn by one branch of a firm upon another, or by one department of an office upon another 1745. Also *fig.* **4.** A plan, sketch, or drawing, *esp.* of a work to be executed. More often DRAUGHT, q. v. 1697. **5.** A rough sketch of a writing or document, from which the final or fair copy is made 1528. **6.** *Masonry.* Chisel-dressing at the margin of the surface of a stone to serve as a guide for the levelling of the surface. Also DRAUGHT, q. v. **b.** 'The degree of deflexion of a millstone-furrow from a radial direction' (*Cent. Dict.*). **7.** *attrib.* **a.** Drafted from the flock, as *d. ewe.* **b.** Drawn up as a rough form whence a fair copy can be made. **c.** *D.-cattle, -horses*; see DRAUGHT.

2. I am .. convinced .. all the drafts [will] quit the service G. WASHINGTON. **3.** *fig.* So great a d. on our patience 1869. **5.** The d. of the petition BURKE. **7.** A d. will 1879.

Draft (drɑft), *v.* 1714. [f. prec. sb. Still spelt DRAUGHT in some senses.] **1.** *trans.* To draw out and remove from a larger body for some special purpose. Chiefly in *Mil.* use, and in *Stock-farming.* **b.** *gen.* To draw off or away 1742. **2.** To draw up in a preliminary form. Rarely *draught.* 1828. **3.** *Masonry.* To cut a draught (or draft) on a stone 1878.

1. The .. Corps out of which they have been drafted 1724. **2.** The Duke .. read me a letter .. which he had drafted J. W. CROKER. Hence **Dra·fter,** one who drafts (animals, a document, etc.).

Draftsman (drɑ·ftsmæn). 1663. [var. sp. of DRAUGHTSMAN.] **1.** One who makes drawings or designs. **2.** One who drafts a document, *esp.* a legal document or a parliamentary bill or clause 1759. Hence **Dra·ftsmanship.**

Drag (dræg), *v.* 1440. [A deriv. of OE. *dragan*, or ON. *draga* to DRAW. See also DRUG *v.*[2]]

I. 1. *trans.* To draw or pull (that which is heavy or resists motion); to haul; hence to draw with force or violence; to draw slowly and with difficulty; to trail. Also *intr.* for *refl.* = *passive.* **2.** *fig.* Said of other than physical force or local motion 1596. **3.** *intr.* To lag behind 1494. **4.** *intr.* To trail; to move with friction on the ground or surface 1666. **5.** To protract or continue tediously; usu. *d. on* 1697. **6.** *intr.* To progress slowly and painfully; to become tedious by protraction 1735.

1. Or Captive drag'd in Chains MILT. *P. L.* VI. 260. To d. one foot after the other (*mod.*). *To d. the anchor* (Naut.): to trail it along the bottom after it is loosened from the ground. **2.** Phr. *To d. in* (*into*), to introduce (a subject) in a forced manner, or unnecessarily. **3.** The tenor dragged (*mod.*). **4.** To raise the Door that it d. not MOXON. **5.** 'Tis long since I .. have dragg'd a ling'ring life DRYDEN. **6.** The day drags through BYRON.

II. To use or put a drag to. **1.** *trans.* To draw some contrivance over the bottom of (a river, etc.); to dredge; to sweep with a drag-net; to search by means of a drag or grapnel. Also *fig.* 1577. *absol.* 1530. **2.** To break up with a drag or heavy harrow 1722. **3.** To put a drag upon (wheels, etc.) 1829.

1. *fig.* While I dragg'd my brains for such a song TENNYSON. Hence **Dra·gger,** one who drags.

Drag (dræg), *sb.* See also DRUG *sb.*[2] ME. [mainly f. DRAG *v.*] **1.** Something heavy that is used by being dragged along the ground or over a surface. **a.** A heavy kind of harrow for breaking up ground ME. **b.** A rough kind of sledge 1576. **c.** A kind of vehicle; often = BREAK; in strict English use, a sort of private stage-coach, with seats inside and on the top 1755. **2.** Something used to pull a weight or obstruction. **†a.** A hook or the like with which anything is forcibly pulled –1789. **b.** A DRAG-NET 1481. **c.** An apparatus for dredging; also for collecting oysters from the bed 1611. **d.** An apparatus for recovering objects, the bodies of drowned persons, etc., from the bottom of rivers or pools 1797. **3.** Something that drags or hangs heavily, so as to impede motion. **a.** *Naut.* 'Whatever hangs over a ship, or hinders her sailing' (Kersey). **b.** A drag-anchor (see below). **c.** An iron shoe, or other device, for retarding the rotation of a carriage wheel 1797. **d.** *fig.* A heavy obstruction to progress 1857. **4.** Techn.: **a.** *Masonry.* A thin plate of steel indented on the edge, used in working soft stone 1823. **b.** *Founding.* The bottom part of a flask; called also *drag-box* 1864. **5.** *Hunting.* **a.** The line of scent left by a fox, etc.; the trail 1735. **b.** Any strong-smelling thing used to leave an artificial scent; *e.g.* a red-herring, etc. 1841. **c.** = *drag-hunt.* **6.** The action or fact of dragging; slow, heavy, impeded motion; progress against resistance 1813; the amount by which anything drags 1864; in *Billiards*, retarded motion given to the cue-ball 1873.

1. c. Behind her came .. a d., or private stage-coach, with four horses THACKERAY. **2. b.** They catch them in their net, and gather them in their d. *Hab.* i. 15. **3. c.** Gently down hill. Put on the d. SYD. SMITH. **5. a.** As the D. or Trail mends, cast off more Dogs that you can confide in 1741. **6.** Working with pleasure, and not with any d. 1887.

attrib. and *Comb.*: **d.-anchor,** a floating frame of wood, or of spars clothed with sails, used to keep the ship's head to the wind in a gale or when dismasted; a drift-anchor; **-bar, -bolt, -chain, -hook, -spring,** those by which locomotive engines, tenders, and trucks are connected; **-box,** (*a*) see 1 c; (*b*) see 4 b; **-hound,** one of a pack used to hunt with a d. (sense 5 b); **-hunt,** a hunt in which a d. (sense 5 b) is used; also, a club for the prosecution of this sport; **-link,** a link for connecting the cranks of two shafts, in marine engines; **-man,** one who uses a drag-net; **-rake,** a large rake, for raking after the cart in hay and corn harvest; **-sheet** = *drag-anchor*; **-twist,** a spiral hook at the end of a rod, for cleaning bore-holes.

Drag-chain (-tʃēⁱn). 1791. **1.** A chain used to retard the motion of a vehicle; *esp.* one with a large hook to hitch on the hind wheel. Also *fig.* **2.** The strong chain by which railway wagons, etc. are coupled.

‖**Dragée** (draʒe). 1866. [F.; see DREDGE *sb.*[2]] A sugar plum containing a drug; now often, a chocolate drop.

Draggle (dræ·g'l), *v.* 1513. [dim. and freq. of DRAG *v.*] **1.** To wet or befoul by allowing to drag through mire or wet grass; to make wet, limp, and dirty; †to trail (through the dirt) –1723. **2.** *intr.* (for *refl.*) To trail (on the ground), hang trailing 1594. **3.** *intr.* To come on or follow slowly and stragglingly 1577.

1. The wet day draggles the tricolor CARLYLE. **3.** With heavy hearts they draggled at the heels of his troop W. IRVING. Hence **Dra·ggle** *sb.* the action of draggling (*rare*).

Draggle-haired, *a.* [after next.] With hair hanging wet and untidy. DICKENS.

Draggle-tail (dræ·g'l₁tēⁱl). 1596. [f. DRAGGLE *v.* + TAIL *sb.*] **1.** A draggle-tailed person. **2.** *pl.* Skirts that drag on the ground in the mud 1858. **3.** *attrib.* = next 1707.

Dra·ggle-tailed, *a.* 1654. Having a tail or skirt that trails on the ground in mud and wet.

Drag-hook. 1530. **1.** A hook used for dragging. **2.** The hook of a drag-chain.

Dragman [1]; see DRAG *sb.*

Dragman [2], obs. f. DRAGOMAN.

Dra·g-net. 1541. [Cf. Sw. *drag-not.*] A net which is dragged along the bottom of a river, etc., as in fishing; also one used to sweep the ground game off a field. Also *fig.*

Dragoman (dræ·gŏmăn). Pl. **-mans, -men.** ME. [a. F. *dragoman, drogman* = late Gr. δραγούμανος, ad. OArab. *targumān* interpreter, f. *targama* to interpret = Chaldee *targēm* (whence *targum*). See also TRUCHMAN.] An interpreter; strictly applied to a guide in countries where Arabic, Turkish, or Persian is spoken. Also *transf.*

Cirus .. All vnpurueyed of drogeman or of guide LYDG. Hence **Dra·gomanate,** the office of a d. **Dragoma·nic** *a.*

Dragon (dræ·gən). ME. [a. F.:—L. *draconem* (nom. *draco*), a. Gr. δράκων, -οντα; usu. referred to δρακ- aorist stem of δέρκεσθαι to see clearly.] **†1.** A huge serpent or snake; a python –1849. **2.** A mythical monster, part serpent, part crocodile, with strong claws, and a scaly skin; it is generally represented with wings, and sometimes as breathing out fire. The heraldic dragon combines reptilian and mammalian form with the addition of wings. ME. **3.** In the Bible versions repr. *draco* of the Vulgate and δράκων of the Septuagint, where the Hebr. has (*a*) *tannīn* a great sea- or water-monster, also a large serpent; or (*b*) *tan*, now understood to be the jackal ME. **4.** An appellation of Satan, the 'Old Serpent' ME.; *transf.* a fiend 1508. **5.** An appellation of Death (*arch.*) 1500. **6.** A fierce violent person; *esp.* a duenna 1755. **7.** A figure of the mythical creature ME. **8.** *Astron.* The constellation *Draco* 1551; †the part of the moon's path which lies south of the ecliptic –1594; †applied to a shooting star with a luminous train –1774. **†9.** = DRAGOON 1, 2. –1849. **10.** *Zool.* A lizard of the genus *Draco*, having on each flank a broad wing-like membrane, which enables it to make long leaps in the air 1819. **11.** *Ichthyol.* (Also *d.-fish.*) **a.** = DRAGONET 2. **†b.** The ANGLER, *Lophius.* 1661. **12.** = DRAGOON *sb.* 3. 1867. **13.** (Also *Green D.*) The plant *Dracunculus vulgaris*; = DRAGONS, DRAGONWORT 1538. **†14.** A disease of the eye in horses –1720. **15.** *attrib.* Of or as of a dragon; dragon-like 1606.

1. Hee .. Now D. grown .. Huge Python MILT. *P. L.* X. 529. **2.** His Armes spred wider than a Dragons Wings 1 *Hen. VI*, I. i. 11. Saint George that swindg'd the D. *John* II. i. 288. Swift, swift, you Dragons of the night (*i. e.* those which drew the chariot of Cynthia or the moon) *Cymb.* II. ii. 48. Phr. *Like a d.*: fiercely, violently. **3.** The lion and the d. [*R. V.* serpent] shalt thou trample under feet *Ps.* xci. 13. It shall be an habitation of dragons [*R.V.* jackals] and a court for owls *Isa.* xxxiv. 13. **7.** *D. china*, a kind of porcelain decorated with designs of dragons. **15.** Cynthia checks her d. yoke MILT. *Pens.* 59.

Comb.: **d. Arum,** the plant *Dracunculus vulgaris* (sense 13); **d.-beam, -piece,** 'a beam bisecting the wall-plate, for receiving the heel or foot of the hip-rafters' (Nicholson); **-fish** (see sense 11); **-shell,** a species of concamerated limpet; **-stone,** DRACONITES; **†-water,** a medicinal preparation popular in 17th c.

Comb. with *dragon's.* **a.** In names of plants, as **dragon's-claw, -herb** (= DRAGONWORT); **-mouth,** the Snap-dragon. **b. Dragon's belly** (*Astron.*), that part of a planet's orbit most remote from the nodes, that is, from the dragon's head and tail; **dragon's skin,** a familiar term among miners, etc., for the stems of *Lepidodendron*; **dragon's teeth,** the teeth of the d. fabled to have been sown by Cadmus, whence sprang armed men.

Dragonade; see DRAGONNADE.

Dragoness (dræ·gŏnės). 1634. A female or she dragon (*lit.* and *fig.*).

Dragonet (dræ·gŏnėt). ME. [a. F.] **1.** A small or young dragon. **2.** A fish of the genus *Callionymus*, esp. *C. dracunculus* 1769. **3.** A S. American lizard, *Crocodilurus*.

Dra·gon-fly, dragon fly. 1626. The common name for neuropterous insects of the group *Libellulina*, characterized by a long, slender body, large eyes, and two pairs of large reticulated wings, and by their strong, swift flight.

Dra·gonish, *a.* 1530. Of the nature or shape of a dragon.

Dragonnade (drægŏnē¹·d), *sb.* 1715. Also **dragonade, dragoonade.** 1715. [a. F.] In *pl.*, a series of persecutions directed by Louis XIV against French Protestants, in which dragoons were quartered upon them. Hence, any persecution carried on with the help of troops. (Rare in *sing.*)

The dragoonades of Claverhouse SPURGEON.

Dra·gon-root. 1621. †**1.** The root of dragonwort or dragons. **2.** In *U.S.*, the tuberous roots of species of *Arisæma*; also, the plants themselves 1866.

†**Dra·gons.** [In late ME. *dragance* :—(ult.) L. *dracontia*, for *dracontium*, a. Gr. δρακόντιον, f. δράκων.] The DRAGONWORT, *Dracunculus vulgaris* –1757.

Dragon's blood. 1599. A bright red gum or resin, an exudation upon the fruit of a palm, *Calamus Draco*. Formerly applied also to the inspissated juice of the dragon-tree, *Dracæna Draco*, and to exudations from *Pterocarpus Draco, Croton Draco*, etc. Also *attrib.*

Dragon's head. 1509. [See DRAGON 8.] **1.** *Astron.* The ascending node of the moon's orbit with the ecliptic (marked ☊); in *Her.*, the name of the tincture *tenné* or tawny, in blazoning by the heavenly bodies 1706. **2.** *Herb.* The name of a genus of plants, *Dracocephalum* 1753.

Dragon's tail. 1605. [See DRAGON 8.] **1.** *Astron.* The descending node of the moon's orbit with the ecliptic (marked ☋) 1605; in *Her.*, the name of the tincture *murrey* or *sanguine*, in blazoning by the heavenly bodies 1706. **2.** *Palmistry.* The discriminal line 1678.

Dra·gon-tree. 1611. The monocotyledonous plant *Dracæna Draco* (N.O. *Liliaceæ*).

†**Dra·gonwort.** 1565. **1.** = DRAGONS –1607. **2.** *Small d.* : the common Arum or Wake-robin 1674. **3.** The Snakeweed (*rare*) 1656.

Dragoon (drăgū·n), *sb.* 1622. [ad. mod.F. *dragon.*] †**1.** A kind of carbine. So called from its 'breathing fire'. –1659. **2.** Orig., a mounted infantryman armed with a dragoon (sense 1); now, a name for certain regiments of cavalry 1622. **b.** A rough and fierce fellow 1712. **3.** A variety of pigeon 1725. *Comb.* **d.-bird,** a Brazilian bird (*Cephalopterus ornatus*), called also *umbrella-bird.*

Dragoo·n, *v.* 1689. [f. prec. sb.] **1.** *trans.* To force or drive by the agency of dragoons; to persecute, as in the DRAGONNADES. **2.** To force (*into* a course) by rigorous and harassing measures 1689.

1. To D. all Men into the Kings Religion 1692. **2.** He dragooned men into wisdom GODWIN.

Dragoonade; see DRAGONNADE.

†**Dragoo·ner.** 1639. [prob. from a Fr. *dragonnier*, not found.] **1.** = DRAGOON *sb.* 2. –1705. **2.** A horse ridden by a dragoon 1642. **3.** [f. DRAGOON *v.*] A rigid persecutor –1826.

Dragsman (dræ·gzmæ̆n). 1812. **1.** The driver of a drag. **2.** One employed to drag a river-bed, etc. 1896.

Dra·g-staff (-stɑf). 1769. A trailing pole hinged to the rear of a vehicle to check backward movement in going up-hill.

†**Drail,** *v.* 1598. [app. var. of TRAIL.] **1.** *trans.* To drag or trail along –1664. **2.** *intr.* To draggle, move laggingly –1716.

Drain (drē¹n), *v.* [OE. *drēahnian*, prob. for **drēagnian*, f. root *drēag-* :—OTeut. **draug-* dry. Found in OE., then not till 16th c.] †**1.** *trans.* To strain through any porous medium –1667. **2.** To draw or carry *off* or *away* gradually 1538. Also *transf.* and *fig.* **3.** To drink to the last drops 1602. **4.** *intr.* Of liquid: To trickle *through*; to flow gradually *off* or *away* 1587. **5.** *trans.* To withdraw the water or moisture from gradually; to leave dry by withdrawal of moisture 1577. **6.** To drink dry 1697. **7.** *transf.* and *fig.* To exhaust; to deprive gradually of resources, strength, etc. 1660. **8.** *intr.* To become dry by percolation or flowing away of moisture 1664.

1. Salt-water drayned through twenty vessels BACON. **2.** The streams . . are now drained drie FULLER. He . . permitted those of Rome to exhaust and d. the wealth of England 1625. **3.** He dreines his draughts of Renish downe *Haml.* I. iv. 10. **5.** Ile dreyne him drie as Hay *Macb.* I. iii. 18. **6.** They had drained the cup of life to the dregs DICKENS.

Drain (drē¹n), *sb.* 1552. [f. DRAIN *v.*] **1.** That by which liquid is drained; *esp.* an artificial channel or conduit for carrying off water, sewage, etc.; in *Surgery*, a tubular instrument used to draw off the discharge from a wound or abscess 1834. **2.** The act of draining; drainage; now only *fig.* constant or gradual outlet or withdrawal 1721. **3.** *slang.* A drink 1836. **4.** *pl.* Dregs from which liquid has been drained; *dial.* brewers' grains from the mash-tub 1820.

1. Through these Fens run great Cuts or Dreyns 1696. The main d. of the country is the Walé nullah 1876. **2.** A sad d. upon my time T. MOORE. A d. on the revenue 1849. *attrib.* and *Comb.*, as *d.-pipe, -tile*, etc.; **d.-cock,** a cock for draining the water out of a boiler; **-trap,** a trap on a d. to prevent the escape of sewer-gas; **-well,** a pit sunk through an impervious stratum of earth to reach a pervious stratum and form a means of drainage for surface water (Knight).

Drainage (drē¹·nėdʒ). 1652. [f. DRAIN *v.* + -AGE.] **1.** The action of draining. Also *fig.* **2.** A system of drains, artificial or natural 1878. **3.** That which is drained off by a system of drains; sewage 1834.

attrib. and *Comb.*, as *d.-area, -district, -shaft*; **d.-tube** (*Surg.*), a small tube, with lateral perforations, passed through a cannula into the cavity to be drained.

Drainer (drē¹·nəɹ). 1598. [f. as prec.] **1.** One who drains; *esp.* one who constructs field-drains 1611. **2.** That which drains; a drain; a vessel for draining moist substances.

Drai·ning, *vbl. sb.* 1565. [f. DRAIN *v.* + -ING¹.] The action of DRAIN *v.*

attrib. and *Comb.*, as *d.-brick, -tile, -well*, etc.

Drai·nless, *a.* 1817. [f. DRAIN *sb.* or *v.* + -LESS.] Exhaustless.

Drake¹ (drē¹k). [OE. *draca* :—Com. WGer. **drako*, a. L. *draco* dragon.] **1.** = DRAGON 2. *Obs.* or *arch.* †**b.** = DRAGON 1. (OE. only.) †**2.** A fiery meteor; see FIRE-DRAKE 2. –1610. **3.** A small sort of cannon. Now *Hist.* 1625. **4.** Angler's name for species of *Ephemera* 1658. **5.** A beaked galley. (Cf. ON. *dreki.*) 1862. *Comb.* **d.-shot** from sense 3.

Drake² (drē¹k). [ME., corresp. to north. and central Ger. dial. *draak, drake, drache* (same sense). Not shortened from an OE. **andrake.*] The male of birds of the duck kind. Also *attrib.* *Comb.* **d.-stone,** a flat stone thrown along the surface of water so as to graze it and rebound.

Drake, obs. f. DRAWK *sb.*

Dram (dræm), *sb.*¹ ME. [phonetic sp. of DRACHM.] †**1.** = DRACHM 1. –1526. **2.** A weight; = DRACHM 2. Also the Arabic DIRHEM. **3.** A fluid dram (= ¹/₈ fluid ounce) of medicine, etc.; hence, **b.** A small draught of spirits or the like. 1590. Hence **dram·shop,** a liquor shop (1761). **4.** *fig.* = DRACHM 3. 1566. **5.** *Canada* and *U.S.* A section of a raft of staves. (? A distinct word.) 1878.

4. Having not one d. of learning HEARNE. Hence **Dram** *v.* to tipple; *trans.* to ply with drams.

Dram, *sb.*² 1663. [Short for *Drammen.*] Timber from Drammen in Norway. Also *attrib.*

Drama (drā·mă). 1515. [a. late L. *drama*, a. Gr. δρᾶμα, f. δρᾶν to do, act, perform. Earlier *drame*, as in Fr.] **1.** A composition in prose or verse, adapted to be acted on the stage, in which a story is related by means of dialogue and action, and is represented with accompanying gesture, costume, and scenery, as in real life; a play. **2.** With *the*: The dramatic branch of literature; the dramatic art 1661. **3.** A series of actions or course of events having dramatic unity, and leading to a final catastrophe 1714.

1. I cannot for the stage a d. lay, Tragic or comic B. JONS. **2.** The received Rules of the D. ADDISON. The lover of the Elizabethan d. M. PATTISON. **3.** The awful d. of Providence now acting on the moral theatre of the world BURKE.

Dramatic (drămæ·tik), *a.* (*sb.*) 1589. [ad. late L. *dramaticus*, a. Gr., f. δρᾶμα, δράματ-; cf. F. *dramatique.*]

A. 1. Of, pertaining to, or connected with the, or a, drama; dealing with or employing the forms of the drama. So **Drama·tical** *a.* (now *rare*). **2.** Characteristic of, or appropriate to, the drama; theatrical 1725.

1. A d. critic 1885. **2.** The destruction of a great and ancient institution is an eminently d. thing LECKY.

B. *sb.* †**1.** A dramatic poet –1741. **2.** *pl.* The drama 1684.

Drama·tically, *adv.* 1652. [f. as prec.] In a dramatic manner; from a dramatic point of view; with theatrical effect.

Drama·ticle, -icule. 1813. [f. L. *drama.*] A miniature or insignificant drama.

‖**Dramatis personæ** (dræ·mătis pəɹsō̆u·ni). Abbrev. *dram. pers.* 1730. [L.] The characters of a play (*lit.* and *fig.*).

Dramatist (dræ·mătist). 1678. [f. Gr. δρᾶμα, δράματ- + -IST.] A writer of dramas or dramatic poetry; a play-wright.

Dramatize (dræ·mătəiz), *v.* 1780. [f. as prec. + -IZE.] **1.** *trans.* To convert into a drama; to put into dramatic form, adapt for the stage. **2.** To represent dramatically 1823. **3.** *intr.* To admit of dramatization 1819.

1. To d. the Lady of the Lake SCOTT. **3.** The story would d. admirably 1836. Hence **Dra:matiza·tion,** conversion into drama; a dramatized version.

Dramaturge (dræ·mătɒ̄ɪdʒ). 1870. [a. F., ad. Gr. δραματουργός, f. δρᾶμα, δράματο- + ἔργειν, -εργος worker.] = DRAMATURGIST.

Fate is the d.; necessity Allots the parts SYMONDS. So **Dramatu·rgic, -al** *a.* pertaining to dramaturgy.

Dra·maturgist. 1825. [f. as prec.] A composer of a drama.

Dra·maturgy. 1801. [ad. Gr. δραματουργία; cf. F. *dramaturgie.*] **1.** Dramatic composition; the dramatic art. **2.** Theatrical acting 1837.

Drank, pa. t. of DRINK.

[**Drank,** erron. f. DRAWK *sb.* brome-grass.]

†**Drap-de-Berry.** Also as three words. [F.; = cloth of Berry.] 1619. A kind of woollen cloth, coming from Berry in France –1818.

Your rotten French camlets now, or your drab-de-berries SCOTT.

Drape (drē¹p), *v.* ME. [a. F. *draper* to weave, f. *drap* cloth.] †**1.** *trans.* To weave into cloth –1683. Also *absol.* **2.** To cover with, or as with, cloth; to hang, dress, or adorn with drapery 1847. Also *transf.* and *fig.* **3.** To adjust artistically. Also *intr.* for *refl.* 1862. †**4.** To reprimand. [Cf. DRESS *v.*] TEMPLE.

1. Flanders doth d. Cloth for thee of thine own Wool 1683. **2.** A red gown draped with old Spanish lace 1882. *fig.* Draped in solemn inanities FROUDE. Hence **Dra·ping** *vbl. sb.*

Drape (drēp), *sb.* 1665. [f. F. *drap* and DRAPE *v.*] **a.** Cloth, drapery. **b.** Draping.

Draper (drē¹·pəɹ), *sb.* ME. [a. AF. *draper* = F. *drapier*, f. *drap.*] **1.** Orig. One who made (woollen) cloth. Subseq., A dealer in cloth, whence, now, in other textile fabrics. **2.** In comb. = *-seller*; see ALE-DRAPER. So †**Dra·per** *v. rare*, to weave into cloth; *absol.* to drape.

Drapery (drē¹·pəri), *sb.* ME. [a. OF. *draperie.*] **1.** Cloth or textile fabrics collectively. **2.** The business of a draper; †cloth-making; now, the sale of cloth, etc. 1488. **3.** The artistic arrangement of clothing in painting or sculpture 1610. **4.** The stuff with which anything is draped; clothing or hangings of any kind; *esp.* the clothing of the human figure in sculpture or painting. Also *fig.* 1686. Also *attrib.*

3. Attitude without action . . dress without d. FUSELI. **4.** To dispose the d., so that the folds shall have an easy communication, and gracefully follow each other SIR J. REYNOLDS. Nature is stripped of all her summer d. HOWITT. Hence **Dra·pery** *v.* to cover with, or as with, d. **Dra·peried** *ppl. a.*

†**Dra·pet.** 1590. [ad. It. *drappetto*, dim. of *drappo.*] A covering –1799.

Drastic (dræ·stik), *a.* 1691. [ad. Gr. δραστικός, f. δρᾶν.] **1.** *Med.* Of medicines: Acting with vigour, violent. Also as *sb.* **2.** *transf.* Vigorously effective; violent 1808.

1. D. purgatives 1789, remedies 1836. 2. So d. a measure MILL. Hence **Dra·stically** *adv.*

Drat (dræt), *int.* 1815. [Aphetic f. *'od rot*, for *God rot!*; see ROT *v.*] An exclam. of angry vexation; = 'Hang', 'dash', 'confound'. Hence **Drat** *v.*; **Dratted** *ppl. a.*

Drat, obs. 3rd pers. sing. pres. of DREAD *v.*

Draught (drɑft), *sb.* [Early ME. *draht*, from Com. Teut. *dragan* to draw. Usually the *gh* passed, in pronunciation, through *wh*, into *f*, whence DRAFT, q. v.]

I. 1. The action, or an act, of drawing or pulling, *esp.* of a vehicle, plough, etc.; pull, traction. (rarely *draft.*) **2.** That which is drawn. †**a.** A load ME. only. **b.** A quantity drawn: used as a specific measure 1740. **3.** Something used in drawing or pulling, as harness for horses 1483. **4.** A team of horses or oxen, together with what they draw. Now *dial.* 1523.

1. The Hertfordshire wheel-plough..is of the easiest d. MORTIMER. 2. *Draught*..sixty-one pounds weight of wool HALLIWELL.

II. *fig.* Drawing, attraction; inclination (*arch.*). (also †*draft.*) ME.

III. 1. The act of drawing a net for fish ME. **2.** The take in one drawing of the net. (rarely *draft.*) ME. **3.** A measure of weight of eels, = 20 lbs. 1859.

1. For he was astonished .. at the d. of the fishes which they had taken *Luke* v. 9.

IV. †**1.** The drawing of a bow; also, a bow-shot –1605. †**2.** The sweep of a weapon –1460. **3.** The drawing of a saw through a block of wood or stone; hence a measure of sawyer's work ME. **4.** See DRAFT 1. 1494.

V. 1. The drawing of liquid into the mouth or down the throat; an act of drinking; the quantity drunk at one pull. (rarely *draft.*) ME. **2.** A dose of liquid medicine; a potion 1656. **3.** Inhaling of smoke or vapour; that which is inhaled at one breath 1621. **4.** *fig.* The drinking in of something by the mind or soul. (Cf. DRINK *v.*) 1560.

1. Our morning d. MASSINGER. 2. Fee the doctor for a nauseous d. DRYDEN. Phr. *Black d.*: a purgative consisting of an infusion of senna with sulphate of magnesia and extract of liquorice. (Also *fig.*) 4. Make the d. of life sweet or bitter JOHNSON.

VI. The action of drawing out to a greater length; that which is drawn out or spun, a thread ME.

VII. *Naut.* The action of drawing or displacing (so much) water; the depth of water which a vessel draws. (sometimes *draft.*) 1601.

A..Vessel..For shallow d. and bulke vnprizable *Twel. N.* v. i. 58.

VIII. †**1.** The action of moving along; course, going –1485. †**2.** A move at chess, etc. [F. *trait*:—L. *tractus.*] –1656. **3.** *pl.* A game played by two persons on a chequer-board, simpler than chess, all the pieces being of equal value and moving alike diagonally. (In U.S. called *checkers*, in Scotl. *dambrod.* (rarely †*drafts.*) ME. **b.** One of the pieces: = DRAUGHTSMAN. (Usu. in *pl.*) 1894.

IX. 1. A current, stream, flow 1601; in *Hydraulics*, the area of an opening for a flow of water. (also *draft.*) 1874. **2.** A current of air, *esp.* in a room or a chimney. (occas. *draft.*) 1768.

2. *Natural d.*: the current of air that passes through the fire in a steam boiler, etc. without mechanical aid, as dist. from *blast, forced d.*, that artificially increased either by rarifying the air above the fire or by compressing it below.

X. †**1.** The drawing of a line or mark with a brush, pen, pencil, etc.; the mark so made; a stroke. [F. *trait.*] –1662. †**2.** Delineation, drawing –1734. †**3.** That which is drawn or delineated. (rarely *draft.*) –1796. †**b.** Representation in sculpture; a sculptured figure –1686. **4.** *spec.* A sketch, preparatory to a work of art 1847. Also *fig.* **5.** A sketch in words. (occas. *draft.*) 1503. **6.** A plan. Also DRAFT, q. v. **7.** See DRAFT 5. 1528. †**8.** Something drawn up; a scheme; a plot. (rarely *draft.*) –1731.

4. Like the first d. of a painter FULKE. 5. Thus I have, in a short d., given a view of our original Ideas LOCKE. 7. What I wrote in the first d. of this work BURNET.

XI. 1. See DRAFT 2. 1703. **2.** *Comm.* See DRAFT 3. 1633.

1. Draughts of labourers were employed in Spain YEATS.

XII. †**1.** *fig.* Derivation; something derived –1561. †**2.** An extract –1601. **3.** The action of drawing liquor from a vessel; readiness to be so drawn ME. **4.** A mild blister, etc. that 'draws' 1828. **5.** *Masonry*, etc. See DRAFT 6. 1859.

XIII. †**1.** (?) A cesspool or sink –1703. †**2.** A privy –1681.

XIV. *attrib.* **a.** Of beasts: Used for draught or drawing. (also *draft.*) 1466. **b.** Of sheep: Drafted from the flock. **c.** Of liquor: On draught; as *d. ale, beer*, etc. 1893. **d.** Of a document: Drawn up as a rough copy. (Commonly DRAFT, q.v. 7.) 1878.

Comb.: **d.-board**, the board on which the game of draughts is played; **-box**, an air-tight tube by which the water from an elevated wheel is conducted to the tail-race; **-engine**, the engine over the shaft of a coal-pit or mine; **-hook**, one of the hooks of iron fixed on the cheeks of a cannon carriage, used for drawing a gun backwards or forwards; †**-hound**, a hound used for tracking by scent; †**-house**, a privy (= sense XIII. 2); **-line**, a line on a ship marking the depth of water she draws; **-net**, a net that is drawn for fish; **-spring**, a spring inserted between the trace and the car so as to relieve the strain of starting; **-way**, a way along which something is drawn; a passage for a current of air.

Draught (drɑft), *v.* 1714. [f. DRAUGHT *sb.*] **1.** *trans.* = DRAFT *v.* 1. **2.** To make a plan or sketch of; to design. (occas. *draft.*) 1828. **3.** To cut a draught upon. (Also DRAFT, q.v. 3.) 1848. **4.** *Weaving.* To draw (the threads of the warp) through the heddles of the loom; see DRAW *v.*

1. The commander..shall d. off an equal number of men..to supply their places 1758.

¶ For other senses see DRAFT *v.*

†**Drau·ght-bridge.** ME. = DRAWBRIDGE –1543.

Draughtsman (drɑ·ftsmæn). Pl. **-men.** See also DRAFTSMAN. 1663. [f. *draught's* + MAN.] **1.** A man employed or skilled in making drawings or designs. **2.** One who draws up, or makes a draft of, legal or other documents. Now oftener DRAFTSMAN, q. v. 1759. **3.** One of the pieces used in the game of draughts; var. DRAUGHTMAN 1894.

1. The d. of the Survey 1875. 2. The actual d. of the Report 1887. Hence **Drau·ghtsmanship.**

Draughty (drɑ·fti), *a.* 1602. [f. DRAUGHT *sb.* + -Y[1].] **1.** Abounding in currents of air, as, a *d. room* 1846. †**2.** Rubbishy; filthy (*rare*) 1602. Hence **Drau·ghtiness.**

Drave, obs. or arch. pa. t. of DRIVE *v.*

Dravidian (drăvi·diăn), *a.* and *sb.* 1856. [Skr. *Dravida*, province of S. India.] Name of a race of S. India and Ceylon, and the group of agglutinative languages spoken by them.

Draw (drǭ), *v.* Pa. t. **drew** (drū); pa. pple. **drawn** (drǭn). [Com. Teut. str. vb.: OE. *dragan.* Only in OE. and ON. with sense 'draw, pull'; in other langs. with that of 'carry, bear'.]

I. Of simple traction. (The most general word for this.) **1.** *trans.* To cause to move toward oneself by the application of force; to pull. Also *absol.* Also *refl.*, and *intr.* for *passive.* **2.** To pull after one; move (a thing) along by traction ME. Also *absol.*, and *intr.* for *passive.* **3.** *transf.* To convey in a vehicle; to cart; to haul ME. ***In specific applications.* **4.** To drag (traitors) at a horse's tail, or on a hurdle, to the place of execution ME. †**5.** To pull or tear *in pieces, asunder* –1700. **6.** To cause to shrink; to distort ME. Also *intr.* for *refl.* †**7.** To mend (a rent) –1611. *** *With specific objects.* **8.** To pull up (a sail, etc.), pull out (a bolt, etc.), haul in (a net), etc. ME. **9.** To bend (a bow); also, to pull back (the arrow) on the string. Also *absol.* ME. **10.** To pull (a curtain, veil, etc.) over something, or aside or off from it. Also *fig.* ME. Also *intr.* for *refl.* = *passive.* **11.** Of a ship, etc.: To displace (so much depth of water); to sink so deep in floating. [So F. *tirer seize pieds d'eau*, etc.] 1555. **12.** In *Cricket*, To divert (the ball) to the 'on' side by a slight turn of the bat 1857. ****In *transf. and fig. applications.* **13.** *trans.* To cause to come, move, or go (from or to some place, position, or condition). *Obs.* exc. in assoc. with other senses. ME. †**14.** To lead (a ditch, wall, etc.) from one point to another. (L. *ducere.*) –1796. †**15.** To render; to translate –1569. †**16.** *fig.* **a.** To adduce. **b.** To attribute. **c.** To pervert, wrest. –1704. †**17.** *Arith.* To add (*to, together*); to subtract (*out of*); to multiply (*into, in*) –1811.

1. A Shark..drew him under Water 1700. The rope drew taut 1866. 2. A locomotive drawing a long train of wagons (*mod.*). Phr. *To d. with*: to be in like case with SHAKS. 4. After the fassyon of treytours to be drawen, hanged and quartred HALL. 6. The face smiling, but drawn and fixed SWINBURNE. 9. A certaine man drew a bow at a venture 1 *Kings* xxii. 34. Phr. *To d. a bead*: see BEAD *sb.* *To d. bit, bridle, rein*: to pull up: also *fig.* 10. When the curtens were drawne, all the people might see it 1631. Phr. *To d. the cloth*: to 'clear away' after a meal. (Now *arch.*) 13. Phr. *To d. into example, precedent, comparison*, etc.

II. Of attraction, drawing in or together. **1.** To take in (air, etc.) into the lungs; to breathe; to cause (a draught) to enter ME. **2.** *absol.* or *intr.* To produce or admit of a draught; said of a chimney, a cigar, etc. 1758. **3.** To attract, as a magnet; to contract (rust, heat, etc.: also *fig.*) ME. **4.** *fig.* To attract by moral force, persuasion, inclination, etc.; to lead, entice, turn (*to, into,* or *from* a course, condition, etc.) ME. Also *absol.* **5.** To induce (*to do* something) 1568. **6.** To bring together. *Obs.* exc. as assoc. with other senses. 1568. Also *intr.* for *refl.* **7.** To bring about as a result, entail, bring on ME. **8.** To cause to fall *upon* ME.

1. Swoln with wind and the rank mist they d. MILT. *Lycidas* 126. 2. The fire does not d. well 1833. 3. Bras draweth soone ruste ME. 4. I was drawn.. therunto through the FLEMING. MILT. *P. L.* II. 308. Mr. Emerson always draws LOWELL. 7. The interest that drawes the freehold BACON. 8. The occasion [that] drew this mischiefe upon him EARLE.

III. Of extraction, withdrawal, removal. **1.** To pull out, take out, extract ME. Also *absol.* **2.** To pull or take out one of a number of things ('lots') ME.; to obtain or select by lot 1709. **3.** To separate or select from a group or heap; *spec.* to separate (seeds) from the husks ME. **4.** To drag or force (a badger or fox) from his hole 1834. †**5.** To withdraw (stakes, a horse, etc.) –1857. **6.** To leave undecided (a game, etc.). [? = *withdraw.*] 1837. **7.** To raise, as, water from a well, etc. ME. **8.** To cause (liquid) to flow from a vessel through an opening, blood from a wound, etc. Also *absol.* to draw liquor. ME. **9.** To extract (a liquor, etc.) by suction, pressure, infusion, or distillation 1550. Also *absol.* (of the teapot), and *intr.* (of the tea). **10.** *Med.* To cause a flow of (blood, etc.) to a particular part; to promote suppuration. Also *absol.* (of a poultice or blister). ME. **11.** To drain off (water); also *absol.*, and *intr.* (for *refl.*) 1607. **12.** To take, obtain, or derive *from* a source ME. Also *intr.* or *absol.* **13.** To elicit, evoke. *spec.* in *Cards*, To cause (a card or cards) to be played out. ME. **14.** *colloq.* To rouse to action, speech, or anger; to 'fetch'; to exasperate 1860. **15.** To deduce 1576. **16.** To extract something from, draw out the contents of; to drain 1576; to draw out the viscera of; to disembowel ME. **17.** To draw a net through or along (a river, etc.) for fish ME. **18.** *Hunting.* To search (a wood, etc.) for game. Also *absol.* 1583. **19.** *colloq.* To 'pump' (a person) 1857.

1. He would have drawn the cork 1828. To d. stumps at cricket 1850, two cards 1870. To d. [= thin] an onion bed (*mod.*). *absol.* D. (*sc.* the sword), if you be men *Rom. & Jul.* I. i. 69. 2. Phr. *To d. cut(s, lot(s*: see CUT *sb.*[1], LOT. The jury is drawn very fairly KEATINGE. 6. To d. a battle 1878. 8. I will entertaine Bardolfe: he shall d.; he shall tap *Merry W.* I. iii. 11. Their Stings d. Blood DRYDEN. Phr. *To d. it mild*: (*a*) *lit.* in reference to beer; (*b*) to refrain from exaggeration. 9. Oil of sweet Almonds newly drawn 1747. 12. The stocke from whence he draweth his descent FLEMING. [He] drew his salary quarterly 1850. 13. He draws all the trumps and wins all the tricks H. H. GIBBS. 16. To d. an oven PEPYS. To pluck and d. a Goose CULPEPPER. 18. Phr. *To d. (a covert) blank*: to search it without success; also *to d. a blank* (with allusion to drawing a blank in a lottery).

IV. Of tension, extension, protraction. **1.** To pull out to a greater length or size; to stretch, distend, extend; to spin (a thread). Also *absol.*, and *intr.* for *refl.* ME. Also *fig.* **2.** *techn.* **a.** To make (wire) by drawing a piece of metal through holes of diminishing size. **b.** To flatten out (metal). **3.** *Naut. intr.* Of a sail: To swell out tightly with the wind 1627.

1. The Skin drew or stretch'd like a Piece of Doe-Leather 1747. *fig.* The anguish..is too long drawn 1885.

V. Of delineation or construction by drawing. **1.** To trace (a line, figure, etc.) by drawing a pencil, pen, or the like, across a surface ME. **2.** To make by drawing lines; to design, delineate; †to model. Also *fig.* ME. Also *absol.* or *intr.* 1530. †**3.** To devise; to set in order, arrange –1663. **4.** To frame (a document, bill, cheque, etc.) in due form; to write out ME. Also *fig.* **5.** To frame, formulate, institute (comparisons, distinctions, etc.) 1789.

1. Like figures drawn upon a dial plate COWPER. Phr. *To d. a line* (*fig.*): to fix a limit or boundary. 2. To d. cartoons on wood 1861. *fig.* To d. a character ADDISON. 4. Clarke, d. a deed of gift *Merch. V.* IV. i. 394. She should d. bills upon me DE FOE. Phr. *To d. against*, to issue drafts in consideration of (value placed in the drawee's hands). 5. I..avoided drawing comparisons between your son and F. 1802.

VI. *refl.* and *intr.* Of motion, moving oneself. †**1.** *refl.* *To d. oneself*: to move oneself, come, go *to* or *towards*; to withdraw *from* –1618. †**2.** *intr.* To move, come, go –1808. **b.** Now only, To move *towards* a place, to come near, approach, to come *together*, to withdraw to one side ME. Also *fig.* **3.** To draw near or approach in time ME. **4.** *Hunting.* Of a hound: To track game by the scent. **b.** To move slowly towards the game after pointing. 1589. **5.** *Racing.* Gradually to gain *on* or get *away from* an antagonist 1823.

2. Our men immediately .. drew together in a body DAMPIER. *fig.* To d. to age CAXTON. 3. To d. to a conclusion 1821. 5. Phr. *To d. level*: to come up with an antagonist.

Comb. with adverbs. See also simple senses and adverbs. **D. back. a.** *Comm.* To recover (the whole or part of the duty on goods) upon exportation: see DRAWBACK *sb.* **b.** *intr.* To move backwards from one's position; also *fig.* **D. in. a.** *trans.* To contract; to cause to shrink. **b.** To inhale. **c.** *fig.* To inveigle, entice; to ensnare. **d.** Of a day or evening: To draw to a close. Also of a succession of days: To become gradually shorter. **D. off. a.** *trans.* To withdraw (troops) from a position; *intr.* to withdraw. **b.** To divert (the mind, etc.). **c.** *trans.* To convey away (liquid) by a tap, a channel, or the like. Also *intr.* (for *refl.*). **D. on. a.** To bring on. **b.** To lead on. **c.** *intr.* To advance, approach. **d.** *Hunting.* = sense VI. 4. **D. out. a.** *trans.* To extract. **b.** *Mil.* To lead out of camp or quarters; also *intr.* for *refl.*; to extend in line; to detach from the main body. **c.** To stretch; to flatten out (metal). **d.** *fig.* To protract. **e.** To elicit. **f.** To induce to talk (*colloq.*). **g.** To draw up; to make out; to delineate. **h.** *intr.* To become longer. **i.** *Racing.* To get gradually further ahead. **D. over.** To convert to one's party or interest. **D. up. a.** *refl.* To assume an erect attitude. **b.** To bring or come to a stand. **c.** To set in array, as troops. Also *intr.* for *refl.* **d.** To frame, write out in proper form. **e.** To come up *with*, come close *to*. **f.** To take up *with*.

Draw (drǭ), *sb.* 1663. [f. DRAW *v.*] **1.** An act of drawing; see DRAW *v.* **2.** Anything having power to draw a crowd (*colloq.*) 1881. **3.** Drawing of lots; a raffle 1755. **4.** A drawn game or match 1871. **5.** 'That part of a bridge which is raised up, swung round, or drawn aside (*U.S.*)' (Webster). **6.** A thing or person employed to draw a person out. Also, one who is easily drawn out (*slang*). 1811.

Draw-, the verb-stem in comb.:

a. used attrib. = drawing-, used for, in, or by drawing: as

d.-arch, a movable arch in a bridge; a drawbridge arch; **-bench**, a machine in which wire or strips of metal are reduced in thickness by drawing through gauged apertures, also called *drawing-bench*; **-bolt**, a coupling-pin of a railway wagon; **-bore**, a pin-hole through a tenon, so bored that the pin shall draw the parts together; hence **d.-bore** *v.*; **-dock**, a creek or inlet in the bank of a navigable river into which boats or barges can be run; **-gear**, (*a*) harness for draught animals; (*b*) the apparatus by which railway carriages and trucks are connected together in a train; **-head**, the head of a draw-bar in a railway-carriage; **-kiln**, a lime-kiln so constructed that the burned lime is drawn at the bottom; **-link**, a link connecting railway carriages or trucks; **-loom**, the loom used in figure-weaving, in which the strings through which the warps are passed were pulled by a d.-boy; **-rod**, a rod connecting the d.-bars of railway carriages; **-shave**, a drawing-knife for shaving spokes, etc.; **-spring**, the spring between a d.-bar and the truck or carriage; **-tap**, a tap for emptying a pipe, cistern, etc.; **-tube**, the compound tube, one part sliding within the other, which carries the object-glass and eye-piece of a microscope.

b. governing an object: as

d.-blood, he who or that which draws blood.

Draw·able, *a.* 1647. Capable of being drawn.

Drawback (drǭ·bæk). 1618. [f. phr. *to draw back.*]

A. *sb.* †**1.** One who draws back or retires. **2.** An amount paid back from a charge previously made; *esp.* a certain amount of excise or import duty remitted when the commodities on which it has been paid are exported; orig., the action of drawing back a sum paid as duty 1697. **3.** A deduction 1753. **4.** A hindrance, disadvantage 1720.

3. A .. d. from the utility of their compilations 1837. 4. Roman citizenship had its drawbacks 1865.

B. *adj.* That is, or has to be, drawn back; as *d.-lock* 1703.

Draw-bar (drǭ·bār). 1839. The bar that bears the draw-links or couplings by which railway carriages and trucks are connected in a train.

Draw·-boy. 1731. The boy who pulls the cords of the harness in figure-weaving; hence, the piece of mechanism by which this is now done.

Draw·bridge. ME. [f. DRAW-; see also DRAUGHT-BRIDGE.] **1.** A bridge hinged at one end and free at the other, which may be drawn up and let down so as to prevent or permit passage over it, or allow passage through the channel which it crosses.

The original form was the *lifting d.*, used to span the foss of a castle or fortification, or the inner part of it; in more recent times a *swing-* or *swivel-bridge* which revolves horizontally is much employed; see also BASCULE. A d. to permit the passage of vessels sometimes forms a small section of a long permanent bridge.

2. A movable bridge or gangway on a ship, etc. 1856.

Drawcansir (drǭkæ·nˌsəɪ). Also **Draw·-cansir.** 1672. [Formed after Dryden's *Almanzor.*] Name of a blustering, bragging character in Villiers's burlesque 'The Rehearsal', who in the last scene enters a battle and kills all the combatants on both sides: hence allusively, and *attrib.*

Such a D., as to cut down both friend and foe TUCKER.

Draw·-cut, *sb.* 1833. A cut made by a drawing movement.

Drawee (drǭˌī·). 1766. The person on whom a draft or bill of exchange is drawn.

Drawer[1] (drǭ·əɪ). ME. [f. DRAW *v.* + -ER[1].] **1.** One who, or that which, draws; see DRAW *v.* **2.** *spec.* One who draws liquor; a tapster at a tavern 1567. **3.** One who draws a draft, bill of exchange, or legal document 1682. **4.** One who makes a drawing; a draughtsman 1579.

Drawer[2] (drǭ·ᵊɪ). 1580. [f. DRAW *v.*; cf. F. *tiroir.*] A box-shaped receptacle, fitting into a space in a cabinet or table, so that it can be drawn out horizontally. **b.** *pl. Drawers* = *Chest of drawers*: a piece of furniture made to contain a number of drawers, arranged in tiers.

Drawers (drǭ·ᵊɪz), *sb. pl.* 1567. [f. DRAW *v.*; orig. low.] A garment for the lower part of the body and legs: now usually under-hose worn next the skin.

Draw-file (drǭ·fəil), *v.* 1884. [f. DRAW-used advb.] *trans.* To file longitudinally, without lateral movement.

Draw·gate. 1791. A sluice-gate.

Draw-glove. ME. †**1.** (Also *draw-gloves.*) An old parlour game, also called *drawing* (*of*) *gloves*, which consisted in a race at drawing off gloves when certain words were spoken. **2.** An archer's drawing-glove.

Drawing (drǭ·iŋ), *vbl. sb.* ME. [f. DRAW *v.*] **1.** *gen.* The action of DRAW *v.* q.v. **b.** *concr.* That which is drawn, or obtained by drawing. *spec.* in *pl.*, the amount of money taken in a shop, or drawn in the course of business 1883. **2.** The formation of a line by drawing some tracing instrument from point to point of a surface; representation by lines; delineation, as dist. from painting; the draughtsman's art 1530; *transf.* the arrangement of the lines which determine form 1753. **3.** That which is drawn; a delineation by pen, pencil, or crayon; a sketch 1668. **4.** *Textile Manuf.* A name given to a number of operations from combing to spinning, to reduce the thickness of the sliver of wool by drawing the warp through the reed 1831.

Comb.: **a.** In various senses, as **d.-awl**, an awl having an eye near the point, so as to carry a thread through the hole bored; **-bench**, a bench or table in the mint on which strips of metal are drawn to the same thickness for coining; also a bench on which a cooper works with his d.-knife; **-bridge** = DRAWBRIDGE; **-frame**, a machine in which the slivers from the carding machine are drawn out and attenuated; **-glove**, a glove worn by archers on the right hand in drawing the bow; **-machine**, a machine through which strips of metal are drawn to be made thin and even, etc.; **-press**, a machine for cutting and pressing sheet metal into a required shape, as for pans, etc.; **-table**, a table extensible by drawing out slides or leaves. **b.** Of or pertaining to delineation, as **d.-block**, a block composed of leaves of drawing-paper, adhering at the edges, so as to be removable one by one; **-board**, a board on which paper is stretched for drawing on; **-book**, a book for drawing in; **-compass, -es**, a pair of compasses having a pencil or pen in place of one of the points; **-paper**, stout paper of various kinds for drawing on; **-pen**, an instrument adjustable by a screw to draw ink lines of varying thicknesses; **-pin**, a flat-headed pin used to fasten d.-paper to a board, desk, etc.

Draw·ing, *ppl. a.* ME. [f. as prec.] **1.** *gen.* That draws, in various senses 1576. **2.** *spec.* Draught- 1551. **3.** That draws out purulent or foreign matter from a wound, etc. ME. †**4.** Attractive –1669. Hence †**Draw·ingly** *adv.* in a slow manner.

Draw·ing-knife. 1737. **a.** A tool, consisting of a blade with a handle at each end, for shaving or scraping a surface. **b.** A farrier's instrument. **c.** A tool used to make an incision on the surface of wood along which the saw is to follow, to prevent the teeth of the saw from tearing the wood.

Draw·ing-master. 1779. A teacher of drawing.

Drawing-room (drǭ·iŋˌrūm). 1642. [Shortening of WITHDRAWING-ROOM.] **1.** *orig.* A room to withdraw to; *spec.* a room reserved for the reception of company, and to which the ladies withdraw after dinner; now sometimes used for an important reception room. **b.** The company assembled in a drawing-room 1841. **2.** A levee held in a drawing-room; that at which ladies are presented at court 1711.

1. The gentlemen..rejoin the ladies in the drawing-room, and take coffee EMERSON. 2. There was a drawing-room to-day at court SWIFT.

Drawk, drauk (drǭk). ME. [Corresponds to OF. *droe, droue*, F. *droc*, mod.Du. *dravig*, etc.] A kind of grass growing as a weed among corn; app. orig. *Bromus secalinus*; but also confounded with cockle, darnel, and wild oats.

Draw-knife. = DRAWING-KNIFE.

Drawl (drǭl), *v.* 1597. [App. an intensive deriv. from DRAW *v.*; cf. Du. *dralen*, mod.Icel. *dralla*, quasi *dragla* to loiter.] **1.** *intr.* To crawl or drag *along*. Now *rare*. **2.** *intr.* To speak slowly, as from indolence or affectation 1598. **3.** *trans.* To utter with lazy slowness: chiefly with *out* 1663. **4.** To cause to pass *on* or *away*, or move along slowly or laggingly; to drag *out, on*, etc. 1758.

2. Such a drawling-affecting rogue *Merry W.* II. i. 145. 4. The Chancery would d. it out till [etc.] COBBETT. Hence **Draw·ler. Draw·lingly** *adv.*

Drawl, *sb.* 1760. [f. prec. vb.] The action of drawling; a slow indolent utterance.

†**Draw·-latch**, *sb.* ME. [f. DRAW *v.* + LATCH.] **1.** A string by which a latch is drawn or raised 1614. **2.** A thief who enters by drawing up the latch; a sneaking thief –1607. **3.** A lazy laggard –1610.

Drawn (drǭn), *ppl. a.* ME. [f. DRAW *v.*] **1.** In the senses of the vb. **2.** Of a sword: Pulled out of the sheath, naked ME. **3.** Of a battle or match: Undecided 1610. **4.** Traced, as a line. Chiefly in *comb.* 1571. **5.** Disembowelled 1789. **6.** Subjected to tension 1879. **7.** Gathered, in needle-work 1852.

Draw·-net. = DRAG-NET; also 'a net with large meshes for catching the larger varieties of fowls'.

Draw·n-work. Also **drawn-thread work.** 1595. Ornamental work done in textile fabrics by drawing out some of the threads of warp and woof, so as to form patterns.

Draw·-plate. 1832. A steel plate pierced with graduated apertures through which wire or metal is drawn to be reduced in thickness.

Draw·-well. ME. **1.** A deep well from which water is drawn by a bucket suspended to a rope. †**2.** A deep drawer. STERNE.

Dray (drēⁱ), *sb.*[1] ME. [A deriv. of OE. *dragan*

to draw.] †1. A sled or cart without wheels –1552. 2. A low cart without sides for carrying heavy loads: *esp.* that used by brewers 1581. 3. *attrib.* and *Comb.*, as d.-cart = sense 2; d.-horse, a large and powerful horse used for drawing a d.

Dray, drey (drēⁱ), *sb.*[2] *local.* 1607. [?] A squirrel's nest.

Drayage (drēⁱ·ėdʒ). 1791. [f. DRAY *sb.*[1]] a. Conveyance by dray. b. The charge for this.

Dray·man. 1581. A man who drives a (brewer's) dray.

Drazel (dræ·z'l). Now *dial.* 1674. [? See DROSSEL.] A slut.

Dread (dred), *v.* [Early ME. *dreden, drǣden*; prob. aphet. f. *adreden*, OE. *an-, ondrǣdan*; see ADREAD.] 1. *trans.* To fear greatly; to regard with awe or reverence. 2. To look forward to with terror ME. †3. *intr.* (or *absol.*) To be greatly afraid or apprehensive –1840; also *refl.* †4. *trans.* To cause to fear; to affright –1681.

1. MILT. *P. L.* I. 464. 2. Leaves look pale, dreading the winter's near SHAKS. 3. D. not, nor be dismayed 1 *Chron.* xxii. 13. Hence †**Drea·dable** *a.* to be dreaded. **Drea·der**, one who dreads.

Dread (dred), *sb.* ME. [f. prec. vb.] 1. Extreme fear; deep awe or reverence; apprehension as to future events. Rarely in *pl.* 2. An object of fear, reverence, or awe ME. †3. Doubt, risk of the thing proving otherwise –1556.

1. The drede of god FISHER. Suspicion ripened into d. WORDSW. 2. Vna his dear dreed SPENSER *F. Q.* I. vi. 2. Their once great d., captive and blind before them MILT. *Sams.* 1473.

†**Dread** (dred), *a.* [Aphetic f. ME. ADRAD.] Afraid, frightened –1450.

Dread (dred), *ppl. a.* [ME. pa. pple. of DREAD *v.*] 1. Feared greatly; hence, to be feared; dreadful. 2. Held in awe; awful, revered ME.

1. Death or aught then Death more d. MILT. *P. L.* IX. 969. 2. Most Dredde Soverayne Lord ME. Your d. command *Haml.* III. iv. 109.

Dreadful (dre·dfŭl). ME. [f. DREAD *sb.*]

A. *adj.* †1. Full of dread, fear, or awe; fearful; reverential –1659. 2. Inspiring dread or reverence; terrible; awful ME. 3. In mod. colloq. use often a strong intensive = Exceedingly bad, great, long, etc.

2. Harsh resounding Trumpets dreadfull bray *Rich. II*, I. iii. 135. 3. The parting was d. (*mod.*).

B. *adv.* = Dreadfully. (Now *vulgar.*) 1682.

C. *sb.* A story of crime written in a morbidly exciting style; a journal or print of such a character (*colloq.*) 1884.

Hence **Drea·dfully** *adv.* in a d. manner; *colloq.* = EXCEEDINGLY.

Drea·dingly, *adv.* 1589. [f. *dreading.*] With dread.

Drea·dless. ME. [See -LESS.]

A. *adj.* Void of dread or fear; fearless. Const. *of.* †b. Exempt from apprehension of danger; secure (*rare*) –1622.

With d. confidence 1854. That which makes death so..dreadlesse to a beleeuer S. WARD.

†B. *adv.* Without doubt of mistake; doubtless –1535.

Hence **Drea·dless·ly** *adv.*, **-ness.**

†**Drea·dly,** *a.* ME. only. [f. DREAD *sb.*] = DREADFUL 1, 2.

Dreadly (dre·dli), *adv.* ME. [f. DREAD *a.*] 1. Dreadfully. 2. With dread or awe (*rare*) 1674.

1. D. sweeping thro' the vaulted sky W. MASON. So **Drea·dness** (now *rare*).

Dreadnought (dre·dnǭt). 1806.

A. *adj.* Dreading nothing, fearless 1836.

B. *sb.* 1. A thick coat worn in very inclement weather; also, the cloth of which such garments are made. 2. Name of a recent type of battleship 1908.

†**Dream,** *sb.*[1] [OE. *drēam* = OS. *drôm* mirth, minstrelsy :—WGer. **draum-*.] 1. Joy, gladness, mirth –ME. 2. Music; noise –ME.

Dream (drīm), *sb.*[2] [Early ME. *dream, drēm*; not in OE. Kluge suggests connexion with *dreug-, draug-, drug-* to deceive, Ger. *trügen.*] 1. A train of thoughts, images, or fancies passing through the mind during sleep; a vision during sleep; the state in which this occurs. 2. *fig.* A vision of the fancy indulged in when awake (*esp.* as being unreal or idle); a reverie, castle-in-the-air; cf. DAY-DREAM 1581. Also *transf.*

1. He interpretid þe kynges dremes ME. Striving, as is usual in dreams, without ability to move 1752. 2. These may seem..but Golden Dreams 1697.

†**Dream,** *v.*[1] [OE. **drieman* = OS. *drômian* 'jubilare'; f. WGer. **draum-*, OE. *drēam* DREAM *sb.*[1]] *intr.* To make a musical or joyful noise –ME.

Dream (drīm), *v.*[2] Pa. t. **dreamed** (drīmd), **dreamt** (dremt). [Appears in 13th c. with DREAM *sb.*[2], q. v.] 1. *intr.* To have visions and imaginary sense-impressions in sleep ME. 2. *trans.* To behold, imagine, or fancy, in, or as in, a dream ME. 3. *intr.* with *of*, †*on*: To think *of* even in a dream; to have any conception *of*; to conceive, imagine. Chiefly in neg. sentences. 1538. 4. *intr.* To fall into reverie; to form imaginary visions *of* (unrealities) 1533. 5. *intr. fig.* To hover or hang dreamily or drowsily 1842. 6. *To d. away* or *out*: to pass or spend in dreaming 1590.

1. Jacob..Dreaming by night under the open Skie MILT. *P. L.* III. 514. 2. Said he not so? Or did I dreame it so *Rom. & Jul.* V. iii. 79. He dreamed that God spake to him HOBBES. Come now, and let me d. it truth M. ARNOLD. 3. *Haml.* I. v. 168. 4. He also dreaming after the empire KNOLLES. 5. Mist..dreamed along the hills HAWTHORNE. 6. Foure nights wil quickly dreame away the time *Mids. N.* I. i. 8. Hence **Drea·mingly** *adv.*

Dreamer (drī·məɹ). ME. [f. DREAM *v.*[2] + -ER [1].] 1. One who dreams; a visionary; an idle speculator. 2. A puff-bird.

1. He is a D., let vs leaue him *Jul. C.* I. ii. 24.

Dreamery (drī·məri). 1838. [f. DREAM *sb.*[2] + -ERY.] Dream-work.

Drea·mful, *a.* 1552. [f. DREAM *sb.*[2]] Full of dreams; dreamy, as *d. slumber.* Hence **Drea·mfully** *adv.*

Dream-hole. 1559. [? f. DREAM *sb.*[1]] One of the holes or slits left in the walls of steeples, towers, barns, etc.

Dreamland. 1834. [f. DREAM *sb.*[2] + LAND.] The land which one sees in dreams; an ideal or imaginary land.

They are real, and have a venue in their respective districts in d. LAMB.

Drea·mless, *a.* 1605. [See -LESS.] Without or free from dreams. Hence **Drea·mlessly** *adv.*

Dreamy (drī·mi), *a.* 1567. [f. DREAM *sb.*[2] + -Y [1].] 1. Abounding in dreams. 2. Given or pertaining to reverie 1809. 3. Dream-like; vague, indistinct; misty, dim, cloudy 1848.

1. A d. slumber KANE. 2. D. moods 1845. 3. A d. recollection JOWETT. Hence **Drea·mily** *adv.* **Drea·miness.**

†**Drear,** *sb.* 1563. [f. DREARY *a.*] Dreariness, sadness, gloom –1775.

Drear (drīəɹ), *a.* Chiefly *poet.* 1629. [Short for DREARY *a.*] = DREARY 3, 4.

A d. and dying sound MILT. *Nativity* 193.

Drearihead (drīə·rihed). *arch.* ME. [See -HEAD.] = DREARINESS. So **Drea·rihood.**

†**Drea·ring.** [irreg. f. *drear.*] Sorrowing, grief. SPENSER.

Dreary (drīə·ri), *a.* [OE. *drēorig* gory, f. *drēor* gore. Generally referred to the stem **dreuz-*, OE. *drēosan* to drop. Cf. Ger. *traurig.*] †1. Gory –1590. †2. Cruel, dire, horrid, grievous –1600. 3. Of persons, etc.: Sad, doleful, melancholy. *Obs.* or *arch.* OE. 4. Dismal, gloomy; repulsively dull. (The ordinary current sense.) 1667.

3. Al drery was his cheere and his lookyng CHAUCER. 4. Seest thou yon d. Plain.. The seat of desolation MILT. *P. L.* I. 180.

Hence **Drea·rily** *adv.* **Drea·riment,** d. or dismal condition or the expression of it. **Drea·riness.** **Drea·risome** *a.* of a d. character.

Dreche; see DRETCH *v.*

Dredge (dredʒ), *sb.*[1] 1471. [? from stem of DRAG *v.*] An instrument for collecting and bringing up objects by dragging. a. *orig.* A dragnet for taking oysters, etc. b. An apparatus for collecting marine objects for scientific investigation. c. A dredging machine. Also *attrib.*

Dredge, *sb.*[2] [Late ME. *dragie, dragé*, a. OF. *dragie, dragee*, mod.F. *dragée*: supposed to derive in some way from L. *tragemata*, a. Gr. τραγήματα spices.] †1. A sweetmeat; cf. DRAGÉE –1616. 2. A mixture of grains, *esp.* of oats and barley, sown together ME. 3. *Mining.* Ore of a mixed quality 1875. *Comb.* **d.-malt,** malt made of oats and barley.

Dredge, *v.*[1] 1508. [Goes with DREDGE *sb.*[1]] 1. *trans.* To collect and bring up by means of a dredge. Also *fig.* 2. *intr.* To make use of a dredge 1681. 3. *trans.* To clean out the bed of (a river, etc.) with a dredging apparatus 1844.

Dredge, *v.*[2] 1596. [app. f. DREDGE *sb.*[2]] 1. *trans.* To sprinkle with powder, *esp.* flour; *orig.* to sprinkle with a powder of mixed spices, sugar, etc. 2. To sprinkle *over* anything 1648. Hence **Dre·dging** *vbl. sb.*; *attrib.* as *dredging-box.*

Dredger [1] (dre·dʒəɹ). 1508. [f. DREDGE *v.*[1] + -ER [1].] 1. One who uses a dredge. 2. A boat employed in dredging for oysters 1600. 3. A dredging machine; see quot. 1863.

3. *D.*, vessels fitted with iron buckets and machinery for deepening rivers or bars [etc.] 1892.

Dre·dger [2]. Also **drudger.** 1666. [f. DREDGE *v.*[2]] A box with a perforated lid for sprinkling powder over anything, as a *flour d.*

Dree (drī), *v.* Now *Sc.* and *n. dial.* or *arch.* [OE. *drēogan.* Revived as a literary archaism by Sir Walter Scott.] 1. To do, endure, suffer. 2. *intr.* To endure, last, hold out ME.

1. *To d. one's weird*: to suffer one's destiny. Hence **Dree** *sb.* suffering. Mostly a mod. archaism.

Dree, dreigh (drī, drīχ), *a.* Now *Sc.* and *n. dial.* or *arch.* [ME. *dreȝ, dregh*; from stem of DREE *v.*] Long; tedious; persistent; difficult to surmount; dreary, doleful.

Dreg, *sb.* Chiefly in pl. **dregs** (dregz). ME. [Cf. Icel. *dreggjar* pl., Sw. *drägg* pl. dregs.] 1. (Usu. pl.) The sediment of liquors; grounds, lees, feculent matters. Also *fig.* †2. *transf.* Fæces, refuse; corrupt or defiling matters –1668. 3. *fig.* The refuse 1531. 4. Small remnant, residue; hence, a small quantity or drop 1577.

1. Phr. *To drink to the dregs.* 3. The very dregs of the population 1876. 4. A d. of the Romish superstition 1789. Hence **Dre·ggish, Dre·ggy** *adjs.* of the nature of dregs; feculent; foul; polluted. Also *transf.* and *fig.*

Dreint, obs. pa. t. and pple. of DRENCH *v.*

Drench (drenʃ), *sb.* [OE. *drenc* draught, drink, drowning :—OTeut. **draŋkiz*, f. *draŋk-* ablaut grade of *driŋkan* to DRINK.] †1. Drink; a draught –ME. 2. *spec.* A potion. From 1600 often (after 3): A large draught, or one forcibly given. OE. 3. A draught of medicine administered to an animal 1552. 4. The act of drenching; such a quantity that drenches 1808.

2. A d. of sack B. JONS. 4. A d. of rain 1893.

Drench (drenʃ), *v.* [OE. *drençan*, f. (ult.) as prec.] 1. *trans.* To make to drink; now *spec.* to administer a draught of medicine forcibly to. †2. To submerge, drown –1621. †3. *intr.* To sink, to be drowned –1570. 4. *trans.* To steep, soak, saturate ME. 5. To wet through and through 1549. †6. *fig.* To drown, immerse, plunge, overwhelm –1818.

4. Good Shepherds after Sheering d. their Sheep DRYDEN. 5. Dark wood-walks drench'd in dew TENNYSON.

Dre·ncher. 1755. [f. DRENCH *v.*] One who or that which drenches; a drenching shower; an apparatus for administering a drench.

Dreng (dreŋ). Also **drench.** [OE. *dreng*, ON. *drengr* young man, fellow.] *Eng. Hist.* A free tenant (specially) in ancient Northumbria, holding by a tenure partly military, partly servile. So **Dre·ngage,** the tenure or service of a d.

†**Drent.** ME. Pa. pple. of DRENCH *v.* –1579.

Dresden (dre·zdən). 1752. Name of a town in Saxony designating a white porcelain of elaborate and delicate kind. Also allusively.

Dress (dres), *v.* Pa. t. and pple. **dressed, drest.** ME. [a. OF. *dresser* (earlier *drecier, drescer*) :—L. type **directiare*, f. *directus.*]

I. †1. *trans.* To make straight or right –1673. †2. To place or set in position; to put on –1530. 3. *Mil. trans.* To draw up (troops) in proper alignment 1746; *intr.* to form in proper alignment 1796. 4. *trans.* To make ready or prepare. *Obs.* exc. as transf. from 5. ME. †b. *refl.* and *intr.* –1596. 5. To array, attire; to deck with apparel; in later use, to clothe ME. b. *refl.* (and *pass.*) To attire oneself with attention to effect; *spec.* to put on dress-clothes; also, simply, to put on one's clothes 1641. c. *intr.* in reflexive sense 1703. 6. To array, equip; to adorn ME. 7. To treat (a person) properly, *esp.* with deserved severity; hence, to chastise; to reprimand. (Now usually with *down.*) ME. 8. To treat with remedies or curative appliances 1471. 9. To treat or prepare (things) in a proper manner; to cleanse, purify, trim, smooth, etc. 1480. 10. To remove (anything) in the process of preparing, etc. 1710. 11. Spec. and techn. uses (see quots.) ME.

2. A coroun on hir heed thay han i-dressed CHAUCER. 3. The battalion dressed its ranks with precision KINGLAKE. *intr.* Soldiers d. by one another in ranks STOCQUELER. 5. Some light housewife..dressed like a May-lady BURTON. I was up and dressed at seven MRS. CARLYLE. b. He was come back to d. himself for a ball JOHNSON. Phr. *To d. up*: to attire elaborately. *To d. out*: to deck out with dress. 6. *To d. a ship*: to deck it out with flags, etc. 7. He would d. my jacket, an [etc.] 1785. 8. He had his wound dressed 1850. 10. Kill your pig, d. off the hair MRS. RAFFALD. 11. a. To prepare for use as food: We d. them with carp sauce T. SHERIDAN. b. To do up (the hair): Her hair dressed *à la negligence* PEPYS. c. To till, cultivate, prune, tend: In planting and dressing the vines DE FOE. †d. To train or break in: That horse, that I so carefully haue drest *Rich. II*, v. v. 80. e. To groom or curry: D. your horse twice a day, when hee rests MARKHAM. f. To curry, as leather. g. To finish, as cloth. h. To cleanse from chaff: Corn Threshed, Winnowed, and Dressed PRIDEAUX. i. To prepare (ore) for smelting by removing the non-metallic portion: Apparatus used for dressing the inferior copper ores 1851.

II. To direct. †1. *trans.* To make straight the course of; to direct, guide -1591. †2. *refl.* and *intr.* To direct one's course; to repair; to proceed, go -1572. †3. To ADDRESS (speech or a writing) *to* any one -1664.

Dress (dres), *sb.* 1565. [f. prec. vb.] †1. The act of dressing -1778. 2. Personal attire: orig. that proper to some special order of person or to some ceremony or function; later, merely: Clothing, costume 1606. b. With *a* and *pl.*: A lady's robe or gown made not merely to clothe but also to adorn 1638. Also *transf.* and *fig.* 3. *techn.* The arrangement of the furrows on the face of a millstone 1870.

2. Phr. *Full d.* (or, simply, *d.*): the elaborate apparel proper to a public ceremony, a dinner, etc. *fig.* Eloquence, the d. of our thoughts BOYLE.

attrib. and *Comb.* a. Of, for, or pertaining to apparel, or to a woman's d., as *d.-goods*, *-gown*, *-skirt*, etc.; **d.-guard**, an appliance fixed to a cycle, etc. to prevent injury to d. from the wheels; **-improver** = BUSTLE *sb.*[2] b. Characterized by, or pertaining to, 'full dress', as *d.-ball*, *-coat*, *-shoes*, *-suit*, *-sword*, *-uniform*, etc.; **d.-circle**, a circular row of seats in a theatre, etc., the spectators in which were originally expected to be in dress-clothes.

Dresser[1] (dre·sər). ME. [a. OF. *dresseur*, *dreceur* (=mod.F. *dressoir*), f. *dresser* to DRESS.] 1. A sideboard or table in a kitchen on which food is or was dressed. 2. A kind of kitchen sideboard surmounted by rows of shelves on which plates, dishes, etc. are ranged 1552. 3. *U.S.* A dressing- or toilet-table 1906.

2. Dressers..with brilliant copper..vessels 1859.

Dre·sser[2]. 1520. [f. DRESS *v.* + -ER[1].] 1. One who dresses (see the vb.). 2. One who attires another 1625. 3. One who attires himself (or herself) elegantly, or in a specified way 1679. 4. A surgeon's assistant in a hospital, whose duty it is to dress wounds, etc. 1747. 5. Any appliance used in dressing things; *e.g.* a shoemaker's tool, a plumber's mallet, a tool for dressing the furrows on a millstone, etc. 1600.

2. A former d. of the Queen's 1884.

Dre·ssing, *vbl. sb.* ME. [f. as prec. + -ING[1].] 1. The action of the vb. 2. Applied to various techn. processes. See the vb. 1540. 3. *ironically.* A beating; chastisement, castigation 1769. 4. *concr.* That which is used in the preceding actions and processes; that with which any thing or person is dressed: *e.g.*

a. *Cookery.* The seasoning substance used in cooking; stuffing; the sauce, etc., used in preparing a dish, a salad. b. Personal decorations; vestments, dress; trimmings. c. *Agric.* Manure or compost spread over or ploughed into land. d. *Surg.* The remedies, bandages, etc. with which a wound or sore is dressed. e. *Arch.* Projecting mouldings on a surface. f. Glaze, size, or stiffening used in the finishing of textile fabrics; etc.

1. There is no elaborate d. for dinner here MRS. CARLYLE. 3. For this he got a very severe d. from Ld. North 1769. Blucher..got a genuine d. down 1876.

attrib. and *Comb.* a. Employed in or connected with attiring the person, as *d.-bag*, *-block*, *-gown*, *-jacket*, *-maid*, *-robe*, *-room*, *-table*, etc.; **d.-bell**, **-gong**, one rung as the signal for dressing for dinner. b. Pertaining or appropriated to the treatment of various articles, as *d.-machine*, *-shed*, etc.; **d.-floors**, a surface works where the tin stuff as it comes from the shaft of the mine is first crushed, and then washed, in order to separate the tin from alien matter.

†Dre·ssing-board. ME. A board on which anything (*esp.* food) was dressed; a dresser -1700.

Dre·ssing-case. 1819. A case of toilet utensils; also formerly called a *dressing-box*.

Dress-maker (dre·s,mē¹kər). 1828. A (female) maker of dresses.

Dre·ss-making, *vbl. sb.* 1837. The action or occupation of making (women's) dresses.

Dressy (dre·si), *a.* 1768. [f. DRESS *sb.*] 1. Attentive to dress; given to showy dressing. 2. Of garments: Stylish 1818.

1. I am a d. man THACKERAY. 2. A d. boot 1845. Hence **Dre·ssiness.**

Drest, var. pa. t. and pple. of DRESS.

†Dretch, *v.* [OE. *drecc(e)an*: not in other Ger. langs.] *trans.* To afflict, torment, vex; in ME. *esp.* to trouble in sleep -1485.

Drevel(l, -ill, -yll, var. of DRIVEL *sb.*[1]

Drew (drū), pa. t. of DRAW *v.*

Drey, obs. f. DRY, DRAY[1]; var. of DRAY[2].

Dreynt, obs. pa. t. and pple. of DRENCH *v.*

†Drib, *v.* 1523. [app. onomatopœic, arising out of DRIP or DROP.] 1. To fall in drops; also *fig.* 2. *trans.* To let fall in or as in drops or driblets -1599; to defalcate 1693; to lead one by little and little *into* 1700. 3. To shoot (an arrow) so that it falls short or wide -1592. Hence **Drib** *sb.* a DRIBLET.

Dribble (dri·b'l), *v.* 1565. [freq. of DRIB *v.*] 1. *trans.* To let flow or fall in driblets (*lit.* and *fig.*) 1589. 2. *absol.* or *intr.* To slaver, as a child or an imbecile; to DRIVEL 1673. 3. *intr.* To flow down in small quantities; to trickle 1599. Also *transf.* and *fig.* 4. *trans.* In *Football*, etc.: To keep (the ball) moving along the ground in front of and close to one by successive short pushes. Also *absol.* 1863. †5. *Archery.* = DRIB *v.* 3. -1615.

1. Dribling Almes by Art WARNER. 3. *transf.* The Reichs Army kept dribbling in CARLYLE.

Dribble, *sb.* 1680. [f. prec. vb.] 1. A small trickling stream; a small drop of liquid. Also *transf.* and *fig.* 2. *Football.* An act of dribbling (sense 4) 1889.

1. *transf.* The little d. of Commerce L. STEPHEN.

Dribbler (dri·blər). 1835. [f. as prec.] One who dribbles; *e.g.* at football.

Driblet, dribblet (dri·blėt), *sb.* 1591. [f. DRIB *v.* + -LET.] 1. 'A small sum, odd money in a sum' (J.) 1632. 2. A petty quantity or part 1678. 3. A DRIBBLE (of liquid) 1860.

1. We..pay in Driblets, or else never pay QUARLES. 3. A d. of sour milk 1860.

Drie, obs. f. DREE *v.*, DRY.

Dried (drəid), *ppl. a.* ME. [f. DRY *v.* + -ED[1].] Deprived of moisture, desiccated. Often with *up*. Also *fig.*

Drier, dryer (drəi·ər). 1528. [f. as prec.] 1. One who or that which dries. 2. (*dryer*) A desiccating substance or apparatus 1840.

Drier, driest, comp. and superl. of DRY *a.*

Drift (drift), *sb.* [Early ME. *drift*; verbal abstract from *drīfan* to DRIVE.]

I. 1. The act of driving; propulsion, impulse, impetus. (Now *rare.*). b. *Forest Law.* The driving of the cattle within a forest to one place on a particular day, for the determination of ownership, levying of fines, etc. 1540. †c. *Arch.* The horizontal thrust of an arch -1823. 2. The condition of being driven, as by a current; the action of drifting; a slow course or current. Also *fig.* 1562. b. *Naut.* The deviation of a ship from its course in consequence of currents 1671. c. *Aeronautics.* The horizontal component of the aerodynamic pressure on all exposed surfaces of an aeroplane in flight 1896. 3. *fig.* Natural or unconscious course; tendency 1549. 4. The conscious direction of action or speech to some end; the end itself; purpose, object, aim. (Now *rare.*) 1526. b. Meaning, tenor, scope. Now the usual sense. 1526. †5. A scheme, plot, device -1674.

1. As the whele gothe by drifte of water FITZHERB. 2. A considerable Frost and d. of Ice..that Winter PERRY. 3. The general d. of affairs on the Continent 1891. 4. My sole d. is to be useful COWPER. b. The main d. and scope of these pamphlets FULLER.

II. That which is driven. 1. A drove, herd, flock, †flight of birds. *Obs.* or *dial.* 1450. 2. A shower (of rain, dust, snow, etc.) driven by the wind ME. b. An accumulation of snow, sand, etc., driven together by the wind. Also *transf* ME. 3. Floating matter, a log, a mass of wood, etc., driven by currents of water 1600. 4. *Geol.* (*a*) Any superficial deposit caused by a current of water or air; (*b*) *spec.* (*the D.*) Pleistocene deposits of glacial and fluvio-glacial detritus; diluvium 1839. 5. A set of fishing-nets. b. A large kind of net, extended by weights at the bottom and floats at the top, and allowed to float with the tide; a *d.-net.* 6. *techn.* a. A tool used for driving or ramming something (*e.g.* for driving piles). b. A steel tool for enlarging or shaping a hole in a piece of metal; a *drift-pin.* c. *pl.* *Ship-building.* Those parts where the sheer is raised, and where the rails are cut off and ended by scrolls. d. The difference between the size of a bolt and the hole into which it is driven, or between the circumference of a hoop and that of the mast on which it is to be driven 1792.

1. Whole driftes of quailes BP. HALL. 2. The city lies Beneath its d. of smoke TENNYSON. 3. Some log perhaps upon the waters swam, An useless d. DRYDEN.

III. 1. *gen.* A track (*poet.* and *rare*) 1711. 2. *Mining.* A passage driven or excavated horizontally; *esp.* one driven in the direction of a mineral vein 1653. 3. = DRIFTWAY 1 (*local*) 1686. 4. *S. Afr.* A ford 1849.

IV. *Naut.* Length of rope paid out before a fastening is made; length that a tackle will reach from its fixed point; distance so estimated 1860.

Comb.: **d.-anchor**, a floating wooden frame or the like, used to keep the ship's head to the wind in a gale or when dismasted; **-bolt**, a long punch used for driving out other bolts; **-keel** = BILGE-KEEL; **-net** = sense II. 5 (also *attrib.*); **-pieces**, solid pieces, fitted at the drifts, to form scrolls (see II. 6 c); **-pin**, **-punch** = sense II. 6 b; **-weed**, (*a*) sea-weed drifted on shore by the waves; (*b*) the gulf-weed (*Sargassa baccifera*) and tangle (*Laminaria digitata*).

Drift, *v.* 1584. [f. prec. sb.] 1. *intr.* To move as driven or borne along by a current; to DRIVE 1600. Also *transf.* and *fig.* 2. *trans.* To drive or carry along, as by a current of water or air; to blow into heaps 1618. 3. *trans.* To cover with drifts; also *intr.* for *refl.* 1851. †4. To drive at, aim at -1618. 5. *Mech.* To form or enlarge a hole with a DRIFT (II. 6 b) 1869. 6. *Mining. intr.* To excavate a DRIFT (III. 2); *trans.* to excavate a drift in 1864.

1. To d. with the current SCOTT. *fig.* Content to let things d. 1885. 2. To be drifted into civil war FROUDE. 3. When Winter drifts the fields With snow MOIR. Hence **Dri·fting** *vbl. sb.* the action of the vb.; also *concr.* that which is drifted.

Driftage (dri·ftėdʒ). 1768. [f. DRIFT *v.* + -AGE.] 1. The process or operation of drifting 1862. 2. *concr.* Drifted material 1768.

Drift-ice. 1600. [f. DRIFT *sb.*] Detached pieces of ice drifting with the ocean currents, etc.

Driftland; see DROF-LAND.

Driftless (dri·ftlės), *a.* 1806. [f. DRIFT *sb.* + -LESS.] 1. Having no drift or purpose; aimless. 2. *Geol.* Free from drift 1873.

Driftway, drift-way (dri·ft,wē¹). 1611. [f. DRIFT *sb.* + WAY.] 1. A lane or road along which cattle are driven; a drove-way. 2. *Naut.* Lee-way 1721. 3. *Mining*, etc. = DRIFT *sb.* III. 2. 1843.

Drift-wood, dri·ftwood. 1633. Wood floating on, or cast ashore by, the water.

[We] made a fire..with the drift-wood R. H. DANA.

Drifty (dri·fti), *a.* 1571. [f. DRIFT *sb.* + -Y.] †1. Wily. 2. Characterized by drifts, of the nature of a drift 1730.

Drill (dril), *sb.*[1] 1641. [Goes with DRILL *v.*[2]] A (?trickling) rivulet; a rill.

Springs.. Whose Drils our plants with moisture feed 1641.

Drill (dril), *sb.*[2] 1611. [a. Du. *dril*, *drille* (in sense 1), and f. DRILL *v.*[3], q.v.] 1. An instrument for drilling or boring; *e.g.* a pointed steel tool for boring holes in metal, stone, and other hard substances; a drilling machine, etc. 2. A shell-fish which bores into the shells of young oysters; a borer 1886. 3. Style in which a hole is drilled 1849. 4. *Mil.* The action or method of instructing in military evolutions;

military exercise or training; with *a* and *pl.* such an exercise 1637. 5. A drill-master 1814. 6. *fig.* Rigorous discipline; exact routine 1815.
1. The ordinary miner's d. is a bar of steel, with a chisel-shaped end RAYMOND. 4. A company of soldiers..at d. 1859. 6. D. in Latin grammar, cricket, boating, wrestling EMERSON.
attrib. and *Comb.* a. Pertaining to a d. (sense 1), as **d.-press,** 'a machine for drilling holes in metal, the drill being pressed to the metal by the action of a screw' (Webster); **-stock,** the holdfast for a metal d.; etc. b. Pertaining to or connected with military d., as *d.-master*; **d.-sergeant,** a non-commissioned officer who trains soldiers in military evolutions.

Drill (dril), *sb.*3 1644. [? ad. native name.] A W. Afr. baboon, *Cynocephalus leucophæus.*

Drill, *sb.*4 1727. [? same as DRILL *sb.*1; cf. Ger. *rille.*] 1. A small furrow in which seed is sown; a ridge having such a furrow on its top; also, the row of plants thus sown. 2. A machine for sowing seed in drills, drawing furrows, and covering the seed when sown 1731.
Comb.: **d.-barrow,** a barrow-like contrivance for sowing in drills; **-harrow,** a harrow used between the drills for extirpating weeds; **-machine, -plough** = sense 2.

Drill (dril), *sb.*5 1743. = DRILLING *sb.*

Drill, *v.*1 Now *dial.* ME. [?] 1. *trans.* and *absol.* To delay, put off. Also with *away, on, out.* 2. To entice (a person) *on* from point to point; and so = to put off 1669. Also with *in, into; on, along, out of.* 3. To slip away, vanish by degrees (*dial.*) ME.
1. This accident hath drilled away the whole summer SWIFT. 2. She drilled him on to Five and Fifty and.. she will drop him in his old Age ADDISON.

†**Drill,** *v.*2 1603. [? altered f. TRILL.] *intr.* To flow in a small stream or in drops; to trickle; to drip. Also *transf.* and *fig.* –1638.

Drill, *v.*3 1622. [prob. f. Du.; cf. Du. *drillen.* Not conn. w. *thrill, thirl,* OE. *þyrelian.*] 1. *trans.* To pierce or bore with or as with a drill; to perforate. 2. To make or bore (a hole, etc.) by drilling 1669. 3. *trans.* To turn round and round. *Obs.* or *dial.* 1681. 4. *trans.* To train or exercise in military evolutions. [Prob. f. sense 3.] 1626. Also *intr.* for *refl.* and *pass.* 5. *transf.* and *fig.* To train or instruct as with military rigour and exactness 1622. 6. To regulate exactly 1877. b. To impart by strict method 1863.
4. He [Frederick the Great] drilled his people as he drilled his grenadiers MACAULAY. 5. He had drilled her in all that she should do or say BLACK.

Drill, *v.*4 1740. [f. DRILL *sb.*4] 1. *trans.* To sow in drills; to raise (crops) in drills. 2. To plant (ground) in drills 1785.
2. He drilled two acres of land with this barley 1894.

Driller (dri·lər). 1652. One who or that which drills.

Drilling (dri·liŋ), *sb.* 1640. [corruption of Ger. *drillich,* ad. L. *tri-* three + *licium* thrum, thread.] A coarse twilled linen or cotton fabric. Also *attrib.*

Dri·lling, *vbl. sb.*1; see DRILL *v.*2

Drilling (dri·liŋ), *vbl. sb.*2 1639. [f. DRILL *v.*3 + -ING1.] 1. Boring; perforation 1698. 2. Training in military evolutions. Also *transf.*

Drily, *adv.*; see DRYLY.

Drink (driŋk), *v.* Pa. t. **drank** (dræŋk); pa. pple. **drunk** (drʌŋk). [Com. Teut.: OE. *drincan*:—OTeut. **driŋkan,* not found outside Germanic. The full form *drunken* of pa. pple. is mostly used as adj., exc. as a poetic archaism. From 17th to 19th c. *drank* was intruded from the pa. t. into the pa. pple.]

I. Trans. senses. 1. To take (liquid) into the stomach; to swallow down, imbibe. Also with *off, out, up,* expressing exhaustion of the liquid. Also *transf.* and *fig.* 2. *transf.* To absorb (moisture); to suck. Often with *up* or *in.* 1530. 3. *fig.* esp. with *in*: To take into the mind; to listen to, or contemplate with rapture 1592. †4. To inhale (tobacco smoke, etc.) –1781. 5. To swallow down the contents of ME. 6. To spend in drinking 1492.
1. I ne're drank sacke in my life SHAKS. *fig.* Dire sorrow drinkes our blood SHAKS. 2. Let the purple Vi'lets d. the Stream DRYDEN. 3. To d. in the beauty of the scene 1859. 4. The first who smoked, or, (as they called it) drank tobacco publickly PENNANT. 5. Phr. *To d. the cup of joy, sorrow,* etc.: see CUP *sb.* 6. He drinks his whole earnings (*mod.*).

II. Absol. and intr. senses. 1. *absol.* To swallow down or imbibe liquid, for nourishment or quenching of thirst OE. 2. To take intoxicating liquor, either convivially, or to gratify appetite; to indulge therein to excess; to tipple; *spec.* to be a habitual drunkard 1440. 3. *intr.* To have a specified flavour when drunk. [F. *se boire,* refl. for pass.] 1607. †4. *fig.* To experience, endure, pay the penalty; to taste the cup of suffering (*trans.* and *absol.*) –1677.
1. Having sufficiently eaten and drunken RUSKIN. Phr. *To d. deep*: to take a large draught, either once or habitually. 2. I have been drinking hard 1611. Poor woman! her husband drinks (*mod.*).
Phr. *To d. to* (a person): †a. To hand beverage for his use. The cup presented was first sipped by the one who offered it, and hence b. To salute by drinking; to invite (any one) to d. by drinking first; to d. in his honour; to d. in honour of (anything desired), with good wishes for its furtherance.

Drink (driŋk), *sb.* [OE. *drinc* and *drinca,* f. *drincan* to DRINK.] 1. Liquid swallowed for assuaging thirst or taken into the system for nourishment. Also *fig.* and *transf.* 2. A beverage OE. 3. *spec.* Intoxicating alcoholic beverage OE. 4. A draught or portion of liquid OE.
1. For d. the Grape She crushes MILT. *P. L.* v. 344. 2. Hiss drinnch wass waterr ORMIN. 3. I doe not speake to thee in Drinke 1 *Hen. IV,* II. iv. 458. [He] shall drink neither wine nor strong d. *Luke* i. 15. 4. A d. of milk KINGSLEY.
Comb.: **d.-offering,** an offering of wine or other liquid poured out in honour of a deity; **-money, -penny,** a gratuity to be spent on d.

Drinkable (dri·ŋkăb'l). 1611. [-ABLE.] a. *adj.* That may be drunk, suitable for drinking. b. *sb.* (usu. *pl.*) That which may be drunk, liquor 1708. Hence **Dri·nkableness.**

Drinker (dri·ŋkər). OE. [f. DRINK *v.*] 1. One who drinks; *spec.* one who drinks to excess; a drunkard. 2. (In full **d.-moth.**) A large European moth, *Lasiocampa* (*Odonestis*) *potatoria,* so called from its long suctorial proboscis 1682.
1. His father was a hard d. (*mod.*).

Dri·nk-hail. Now *Hist.* [Early ME. *drinc hæil, drinc hail,* f. DRINK *v.* in imper. + HAIL *a.* = ON. *heill* HAIL *a.*] The customary reply to a pledge in early English times. The cup was offered with the salutation *wæs hail* 'health or good luck to you' (see WASSAIL), to which the reply was *drinc hail* 'drink health or good luck'.

Drinking (dri·ŋkiŋ), *vbl. sb.* ME. [f. DRINK *v.*] 1. The action or habit denoted by the vb. DRINK; *spec.* the use of intoxicating liquor, *esp.* to excess. 2. An occasion of drinking; a carousal 1515.
Comb. a. with sense 'used for d.', as *d.-bowl, -cup, -horn, -water,* etc. b. 'used for the sale or consumption of drink', as *d.-booth, -house, -room, -saloon.*

Dri·nkless, *a.* ME. [See -LESS.] Without drink or liquor; dry.

Drip (drip), *v.* [OE. *dryppan*:—OTeut. **drupjan,* OE. *dréopan.*] 1. *trans.* To let fall in drops. 2. *intr.* To have moisture or liquid falling off in drops 1508. 3. *intr.* To fall in drops 1670.
1. The lofty barn..Which from the thatch drips fast a shower of rain SWIFT. 2. Pine branches..dripping with moisture L. STEPHEN. 3. The rain .. came through..and dripped from the ceiling TYNDALL.

Drip (drip), *sb.* 1440. [f. prec. vb.] †1. A falling drop –1552. 2. The act or fact of dripping 1669. 3. That which drips; *pl.* drippings 1707. 4. *Arch.* A projecting member of a cornice, etc., from which the rain-water drips and so is thrown off from the parts below; also, a *drip-joint* 1664.
2. On the ear Drops the light d. of the suspended oar BYRON. Phr. *Right of d.* (Law): an easement which entitles the owner of a house to let the water from his eaves drip on his neighbour's land.
attrib. and *Comb.*, as **d.-joint,** a mode of uniting two sheets of metal in roofing where the joint is with the current, so as to form a water conductor (Knight).

Dri·p-drop, *sb.* 1848. [redupl. of DRIP or DROP.] Continuous dripping with alternation of sound.

Dri·pping, *vbl. sb.* 1440. [f. DRIP *v.*] 1. The fall of liquid in drops; the liquid so falling. 2. *spec.* The melted fat which drips from roasting meat. Formerly often in *pl.* 1463. *Comb.* **d.-pan,** a pan used to catch the d. (sense 2).

Dripple (dri·p'l), *v.* 1821. [Fusion of DRIP and DRIBBLE.] 1. *intr.* = DRIBBLE *v.* 3; but connoting a brisker motion. 2. = DRIP *v.* 3. 1822.

Dripstone (dri·pstōun). 1812. 1. A moulding or cornice over a door, window, etc., to throw off the rain. Also *attrib.* 2. A filter composed of porous stone 1858.

Drive (drəiv), *v.* Pa. t. **drove** (drōuv); *arch.* **drave** (drēiv). Pa. pple. **driven** (dri·v'n). [Com. Teut.: OE. *drīfan, drāf.*]

I. 1. *trans.* To force to move on before one, or flee away from one; to urge on or impel with violence; *transf.* to constrain to go or flee 1510. Also *fig.* 2. To chase, pursue; also *fig.* *Obs.* or *arch.* ME. b. To impel game, etc., into nets, traps, or a small area where they can be killed, etc. 1753. 3. With the area as verbal object ME. 4. *spec.* To urge onward and direct the course of (a vehicle or the animal which draws it, a railway train, etc.) ME.; hence, to convey in a vehicle 1662; *absol.* to act as driver; also, to go in a carriage driven or directed by oneself. Also *intr.* for *pass.* of the vehicle. 1592.
1. We droue them to flyghte EDEN. *transf.* Hope of employment drives him up to London 1615. 2. Grouse and partridge driving 1883. 3. To d. the forests: see DRIFT *sb.* I. 1 b. To d. a rocky hill for a tiger BAKER. 4. Where Chineses d. With sails and Wind thir canie Waggons light MILT. *P. L.* III. 438. If they do not like the price, they d. off LANDOR.

II. 1. To cause to move along; to propel, carry along OE. 2. To throw, cast, send, or impel in any direction OE. 3. To force, impel, or expel, by a blow or thrust. Also *fig.* Also *intr.* for *refl.* or *pass.* of a nail, ball, etc. 1703. 4. To cause to penetrate, as a tunnel, etc.; *spec.* in *Mining,* to excavate horizontally (also *absol.*): dist. from SINK 1485. 5. *intr.* (Also *to let d.*): To aim a blow or a missile *at*; *trans.* to aim (a blow) ME. 6. To spread or beat out thin. (Now only in *Painting.*) ME. 7. To set going, supply motive power for 1596.
1. Their ships were driuen on shore 1582. 3. [He] drove his heels into the horse's sides 1816. 5. Driving at him with her stool 1752. 6. When colour is spread thinly and rapidly, it is..' driven' GULLICK & TIMBS. 7. A dynamo driven by belting from the engine 1891. Phr. *To d. a quill* 1793.

III. 1. To impel forcibly; to force (*to, into, from* some action, state, etc.) ME. 2. To urge on to action; to force to work; to overtask 1645.
1. To d. a girl to a decision BLACK, a man out of his senses 1879. 2. To d. a committee GRAY.

IV. *trans.* To carry on vigorously, push (a trade, etc.); to carry through or out; to conclude (a bargain) OE.

V. †1. *trans.* To pass (time); to cause (the time) to pass –1697. 2. To protract (time, etc.); hence, to defer. Also *absol.* ME.
1. To d. the tedious Hours away DRYDEN. 2. To d. a thing to the last minute (*mod. colloq.*).

†VI. To deduce, DERIVE –1674.

VII. *intr.* 1. To run or come with violence; to dash, rush, hasten OE. Also *fig.* 2. To drift ME.; to fish with a drift-net 1677. 3. *fig.* To tend 1460; with *at*: To aim at, mean 1579.
1. They..ran away as fast as they could d. DAMPIER. 2. The clouds that drove before the wind THOMSON. 3. What can he be driving at now FOOTE.

Drive (drəiv), *sb.* 1697. [f. prec. vb.] 1. The action or an act of driving; see the vb. b. An excursion in a carriage driven or directed by oneself 1785. c. A forcible blow or stroke in various games; in *Cricket* one which sends the ball back nearly straight 1857. d. (orig. *U.S.*) An organized effort to collect money for a special purpose 1890. 2. A carriage road; also, a course over which game is driven 1816. 3. *Mining.* = DRIFT *sb.* III. 2. 1864. 4. *Type-founding.* = STRIKE *sb.* II. 1874.
1. Phr. *Full d.*: at full speed. *fig.* The constant d. of work 1854. *Whist-drive*: see WHIST *sb.*2

Drive-, the vb.-stem used in *Comb.*:
d.-bolt = *drift-bolt* (see DRIFT *sb.*); **-pipe,** a pipe conveying water for driving machinery; **-screw,** a kind of screw driven by a hammer; **-shaft,** a shaft for communicating motion so as to drive machinery; **-wheel** = DRIVING-WHEEL.

†**Dri·vel,** *sb.*1 [Early ME.: app. of LG. origin; cf. MDu. *drevel* scullion, etc., OHG. *tribil,* f. MDu. *drīven,* OHG. *trīben* to DRIVE.] 1. A drudge, a menial servant –1580. 2. Hence: a. An imbecile. (Cf. *driveller.*) –1597. b. A dirty or foul person –1596.

Drivel (dri·v'l), *sb.*2 ME. [f. next.] = SLAVER *sb.*1 (now *rare*); *fig.*, twaddle (1852).

Drivel (dri·v'l), *v.* [ME. *drevelen* repr. OE. *dreflian*; ME. *dravelen* indicates an OE. **draflian* (not found); prob. f. OTeut. stem *drab-*

(see DRAFF).] 1. *intr.* To let saliva or mucus flow from the mouth or nose, as infants and idiots do; to slaver. Also †*trans.* †2. *intr.* To flow as saliva from the mouth; to flow ineptly from the lips; also *transf.* of water, etc. –1784. 3. *transf.* To talk childishly or idiotically; to rave. Also *trans.*, and with *away*, *on*. ME.

3. Droning and dreaming and drivelling to a Multitude SWIFT. Hence **Dri·veller, -eler,** one who drivels or slavers; a drivelling idiot. **Dri·velling, -eling** *vbl. sb.* and *ppl. a.*

Driven (dri·v'n), *ppl. a.* 1579. [pa. pple. of DRIVE *v.*] 1. See the vb. 2. Of snow: Drifted. Of feathers or down: Separated from the heavier by a current of air (see DRIVE *v.* II. 2). 1579.

2. As white as the d. snow LYLY. My thrice-driuen bed of Downe *Oth.* I. iii. 232.

Driver (drəi·vəɹ). ME. [f. DRIVE *v.*] 1. *gen.* One who drives (see the vb.). 2. *spec.* a. One who drives cattle 1483. b. One who drives a vehicle or the animal that draws it; a coachman, cabman, etc.; also, one who drives a locomotive 1450. c. The overseer of a gang of slaves 1796. 3. A tool or appliance for driving: a. A tool used in driving on the hoops of casks. b. *Weaving.* The piece of wood which drives the shuttle through the shed of the loom. c. A tamping-iron. d. = DRIFT *sb.* II. 6 b. e. A tool for driving out the piece of a metal plate in punching. f. *Golf.* The *play-club.* 1674. 4. A boat used in fishing with a drift-net 1664. 5. *Naut.* A SPANKER, a fore-and-aft sail used at the aftermost part of a ship 1867. 6. A part of machinery which communicates motion to other parts; the driving-wheel of a locomotive, etc. 1831.

1. Solicitors and Drivers of Bargains 1570.

Comb.: **d.-ant,** a species of ant (*Anomma arcens*) found in W. Africa, so called because they drive before them every living creature; **-boom** (*Naut.*), the boom on which the d. (sense 5) is set.

Driveway (drəi·vˌwēⁱ). Chiefly *U.S.* 1875. [f. DRIVE *v.* + WAY.] A way along which something is driven; a carriage drive.

Driving (drəi·viŋ), *vbl. sb.* ME. [-ING 1.] The action of DRIVE *v.*

attrib. and *Comb.* a. Relating to, adapted for, or devoted to driving (in a carriage), as *d. clubs*, etc. b. In names of mechanical contrivances used for driving, as *d.-block*, *-bolt*, etc.; *esp.* of parts of machinery communicating motion to other parts, as *d.-axle*, *-band*, *-belt*, *-gear*, *-pulley*, *-shaft*; also **d.-iron,** an iron used in golf for playing longish approaches.

Dri·ving, *ppl. a.* ME. [-ING 2.] 1. Impelling, actuating. 2. Moving along rapidly, *esp.* before the wind 1601.

1. The ability of its journals is the d. force EMERSON. 2. Perpetual Sleet, and d. Snow DRYDEN.

Phr. †*D. notes* (*Mus.*): syncopated notes, so named as being driven or prolonged through the accent.

Dri·ving-box. 1794. 1. The box on which the driver of a carriage sits. 2. The journal-box of a driving-axle 1874.

Driving-wheel. 1838. a. A wheel which communicates motion. b. Each of the large wheels of a locomotive engine, to which the power is transmitted through the connecting-rod and crank. c. The wheel of a bicycle, etc. to which the force is directly applied. Also *fig.*

Drizzle (dri·z'l), *sb.* 1554. [Goes with DRIZZLE *v.*] Fine spray-like rain.

Drizzle (dri·z'l), *v.* 1543. [? dim. and freq., f. OE. *drēosan* to fall.] 1. *intr.* To rain in fine spray-like drops; *impers.* to fall, as rain, in fine drops 1566. †2. *trans.* To shed in fine spray-like drops –1642. 3. To wet with minute drops (*rare*) 1810.

1. These tears, that d. from mine eyes MARLOWE. It is even drizzling a little CARLYLE. 2. *Jul. C.* II. ii. 21. 3. Drizzled by the ceaseless spray, The wizard waits SCOTT.

Drizzly (dri·zli), *a.* 1697. [f. DRIZZLE.] Of the nature of, or characterized by drizzling.

During Winter's drisly Reign DRYDEN.

Drof(e, droff(e, obs. ff. *drove*; see DRIVE *v.*

†**Drof-land.** 1660. [f. ME. *drof*, OE. *draf*, DROVE, driving + LAND.] *Old Law.* Land held by the service of driving, as of the lord's cattle from place to place, or to and from markets, fairs, and the like –1664. var. (*erron.*) **Driftland.**

Drogher (drōᵘ·gəɹ). Also **droger, drogger.** 1756. [a. obs. F. *drogueur*, f. 16th c. Du. *drogher*, etc., f. *droogen* to dry.] A W. Indian coasting vessel; hence used of other slow clumsy coasting craft. Also *attrib.*

Drogoman, droguemen, vars. of DRAGOMAN.

Drogue (drōᵘg). 1725. [perh. orig. *drug*, var. of DRAG *sb.*] 1. *Whale-fishing.* A contrivance attached to the end of a harpoon line to check the progress of a whale. 2. *Naut.* A hooped canvas bag towed at the stern of a boat to prevent it from broaching to 1875.

Droh, obs. pa. t. of DRAW *v.*

†**Droil,** *sb.* 1579. [Goes with the vb. Prob. influenced by *toil*, *moil*. Cf. the vb.] 1. A drudge –1668. 2. Drudgery –1645.

†**Droil,** *v.* 1591. [? related to Du. *druilen* to loiter, slumber.] 1. *intr.* To drudge, slave –1660. 2. *trans.* To subject to drudgery. QUARLES.

Droit[1] (droit, or as F., drwa). 1480. [a. F. *droit*, earlier *dreit*:—L. *directum*, in late L. right, legal right, law.] 1. A right; hence, that to which one has a legal claim; a due; a perquisite; *pl.* dues, duties 1481. †2. Law, right, justice; a law –1536.

1. *Droits of Admiralty*: certain rights or perquisites, as the proceeds arising from the seizure of enemies' ships, wrecks, etc., formerly belonging to the Court of Admiralty, but now paid into the Exchequer. Hence **droitsman,** the collector of droits.

†**Droit**[2]. 1601. [?] The four hundred and eightieth part of a grain troy, one twenty-fourth of a mite– 1858.

Droitural (droi·tiŭrăl), *a.* 1850. [f. F. *droiture* (see next) + -AL.] *Law.* Relating to a right to property, as dist. from possession.

†**Droi·ture.** *rare.* [a. F.] Uprightness. CAXTON.

Droll (drōᵘl), *sb.* 1645. [a. F. *drôle*, orig. a sb. See Diez, Littré, Darmesteter.] 1. A funny or waggish fellow; a merry-andrew, buffoon, humorist. †2. A farce; an enacted piece of buffoonery; a puppet-show –1818. †3. Jesting; burlesque writing or style –1842. 4. *attrib.*, as †*d.-house*, a place where drolls were acted 1706.

1. Very merry we were, Sir Thomas Harvy being a very drolle PEPYS.

Droll, *a.* 1623. [f. F. *drôle*; see prec.] 1. Intentionally facetious, amusing, comical. 2. Unintentionally amusing; queer, quaint, odd, funny 1753.

1. The d. inventions of Hogarth 1789. 2. A d. sort of house SCOTT. Hence **Dro·lly** *adv.*

Droll, *v.* 1654. [a. obs. F. *drôler*, f. *drôle* sb.] 1. *intr.* To make sport; to jest; to play the buffoon. 2. *trans.* To jest (a thing) *away*, *off*, †(a person) *out of* or *into*; to bring *forth* like a jester 1663.

1. Whitelocke drolled with them 1654. 2. Men that will not be reasoned into their senses, may yet be laughed or drolled into them L'ESTRANGE. Hence †**Dro·ller,** †**Dro·llist,** a jester; **Dro·llingly** *adv.*

Drollery (drōᵘ·ləri). 1597. [a. F. *drôlerie*, f. *drôle.*] 1. The action of a droll; waggery 1653. 2. Something humorous or funny: †a. A puppet-show; a puppet –1847; †b. a caricature –1641; c. a facetious story 1654. 3. Droll quality; quaint humour 1742.

1. An affected humour of d. GLANVILL. 2. That fatal d. called a representative government DISRAELI. 3. The rich d. of 'She Stoops to Conquer' MACAULAY.

Dromæognathous (drǫmiˌǫ·gnăþəs), *a.* 1867. [f. *Dromæus* emeu (ad. Gr. δρομαῖος swift-running) + γνάθος.] *Ornith.* Having the bones of the palate arranged as in the emeu and its allies. Hence **Dromæo·gnathism,** d. quality.

Dromedary (drɒ·m-, drǫ·mĕdări). ME. [ad. F. *dromedaire* (mod.F. *dromadaire*), late L. *dromedarius* (sc. *camelus*), f. *dromas*, a. Gr. δρομάς running, runner.] 1. A light and fleet breed of the camel, usually of the Arabian or one-humped camel, specially trained for riding. See CAMEL. †2. = DROMOND –1568. †3. A stupid, bungling fellow –1785. 4. *attrib.*, as *d. camel*, etc. 1553.

1. The Dromidory..will ride above 80 miles in the day LITHGOW. Hence **Dromeda·rian** *a.* of the nature of a d.; *sb.* a rider of a d.; also **Dro·medarist.**

Dromic, -al (drǫ·mik, -ăl), *a.* 1850. [ad. Gr. δρομικός, f. δρόμος race-course.] Of, pertaining to, or of the form of a race-course; applied to the basilican type of Eastern churches.

Dromioid (drǫ·miˌoid), *a.* (*sb.*) 1852. [f. mod.L. *Dromia.*] a. Having the form of a *Dromia*, a genus of Anomourous Crustacea, closely allied to the true crab. b. *sb.* A crustacean of this genus.

Dro·mograph. 1883. [f. Gr. δρόμος + -GRAPH.] An instrument for measuring the speed of the blood current. Also *attrib.*

Dromond (drǫ·mŏnd, drɒ·mənd). Also **dromon.** *Hist.* and *arch.* ME. [a. OF. *dromon*, *dromont*, ad. L. *dromonem*, a. Byz. Gr. δρόμων, f. δρόμος racing, course.] A very large mediæval ship. Used both in war and commerce.

The great d. swinging from the quay MORRIS.

‖**Dromornis** (drǫmǭ·ɹnis). Also **Dromæornis.** 1872. [f. Gr. δρόμος, or mod.L. *Dromæus* emeu + ὄρνις.] A genus of extinct Australian ratite birds allied to the emeu.

‖**Dromos** (drǫ·mǫs). 1850. [Gr., f. vbl. stem δρεμ- to run.] *Archæol.* An avenue or entrance-passage to a building, often between rows of columns or statues.

Alleys of..sphinxes form the approach or d. LEITCH.

Drone (drōᵘn), *sb.*[1] [OE. *dran*, *dræn* (? *drán*, *drǽn*). Cf. OS., pl. *drani* (? *drâni*), MLG. *drâne*, *drône*, LG. *drône*, whence mod.Ger. *drohne.* Also OHG. *treno*, etc.] 1. The male of the honey-bee. It is a non-worker. 2. *fig* A non-worker; an idler, a sluggard 1529.

1. Some against hostile drones the hives defend GAY. 2. A Droan of a Husband OTWAY.

Comb.: **d.-beetle** = DOR-BEETLE; **-fly,** a dipterous insect, *Eristalis tenax*, resembling the drone-bee.

Hence **Dro·nage,** the condition of a d.

Drone (drōᵘn), *sb.*[2] 1500. [app. f. DRONE *v.*] 1. A continued monotonous humming or buzzing sound, as that of the bass of the bagpipe, etc. Also *transf.* 2. A bagpipe 1502. 3. The bass pipe of a bagpipe. (The modern Highland bagpipe has three drones.) 1592. 4. The tone emitted by the drone of a bagpipe 1596.

1. Ever .. thrumming the d. of one plaine song MILT. *transf.* The d. of her voice MAD. D'ARBLAY. 4. As Melancholly as..the D. of a Lincolnshire Bagpipe 1 *Hen. IV*, I. ii. 85. *attrib.* The d.-pipe of an humble-bee COWPER.

Drone (drōᵘn), *v.*[1] 1500. [f. DRONE *sb.*[1]; or *sb.*[2], sense 2.] 1. *intr.* To give forth a continued monotonous sound; to hum or buzz; to talk in a monotonous tone. 2. *trans.* To emit in a dull monotonous tone. Also with *out.* 1614. †3. [f. DRONE *sb.*[2]] To smoke (a pipe) (as if playing on a bagpipe). B. JONS.

1. Beetles d. along the hollow lane KINGSLEY. 2. Penitents..droning their dirges THACKERAY.

Drone, *v.*[2] 1509. [f. DRONE *sb.*[1]] 1. *intr.* To proceed sluggishly or indolently. 2. *trans.* To pass *away*, drag *out* sluggishly 1739.

2. To d. out manhood in measuring cloth LYTTON.

Drongo (drǫ·ŋgo). 1841. [a. Malagasy.] A name orig. of a Madagascar bird, *Dicrurus* (*Edolius*) *forficatus*; subseq. extended to the numerous other species of *Dicruridæ*, also called **D.-shrikes.**

D. cuckoo, a species of the cuckoo genus *Surniculus*, a native of Nepaul.

†**Dronkelew,** *a.* ME. [-LEWE.] Drunken –1532.

Dronish (drōᵘ·niʃ), *a.* 1580. [f. DRONE *sb.*[1]] Like a drone; sluggish, inactive. Hence **Dro·nish·ly** *adv.*, **-ness.** So **Dro·ny** *a.*

†‖**Dronte** (drǫ·nt). [Du. and Fr.] A name of the DODO, q. v.

Drool (drūl), *v.* *dial.* and *U.S.* 1847. [Contr. f. DRIVEL *v.*] = DRIVEL *v.*

Droop (drūp), *v.* [ME. *drupen*, *drowpen*, a. ON. *drúpa* to droop, deriv. wk. vb. f. ablaut series *dreup-*, *draup-*, *drup-*; see DROP *sb.*] 1. *intr.* To hang or sink down, as from weariness, etc.; to bend or incline downward. 2. To sink; to decline, draw to a close. Now only *poet.* ME. 3. To decline in vital strength; to languish, flag ME. Also *transf.* and *fig.* 4. To become dispirited or despondent ME. 5. *trans.* To let hang or sink down; to bend downwards; to cast down 1583.

1. Thus droupes this loftie Pyne 2 *Hen. VI*, II. iii. 45. 2. Laborious til day d. MILT. *P. L.* XI. 178. 3. *fig.* The rate of interest droops BON. PRICE. 4. Why droop'st, my soul? Why faint'st thou in my breast P. FLETCHER. 5. I cannot veil, or d. my sight TENNYSON. Hence **Droop** *sb.* the act or fact of drooping. **Droop** *a.* (*rare*) = drooping; *esp.* in combs., as *d.-headed.* **Droo·per,** one that droops. **Droo·pingly** *adv.* in a drooping manner.

Droopy (drū·pi), *a.* [Early ME. *drupi*, referred to DROOP *v.*] Dejected, drooping.

Drop (drǫp), *sb.* [In I repr. OE. *dropa* wk. masc.:—OTeut. **dropon-* and **droppon-*, f. *u* grade of ablaut stem *dreup-*, *draup-*, *drup-*.]

I. The orig. sb. **1.** The smallest quantity of liquid that falls in a spherical form; a globule. Also *fig.* **2.** *ellipt.* or *absol.*: = tear-drop; also drop of blood, sweat, etc. OE. **3.** In dispensing, etc. the smallest separable quantity of a liquid 1772. **4.** *pl.* Medicine to be taken in drops. Rarely *sing.* 1726. **5.** The smallest appreciable quantity ME. Also *transf.* and *fig.* **6.** *spec.* A small quantity of drink 1700. †**7.** A spot of colour; also *fig.* –1674. **8.** Anything resembling a drop of liquid in size, shape, or pendent character. **a.** A pendant, as an ear-drop; a glass pendant of a chandelier, etc. 1502. **b.** *Arch.* The frusta of cones used as an ornament under the triglyphs, and also in the under part of the mutuli, of the Doric Order 1696. †**c.** Small shot 1752. **d.** A sugar-plum, orig. of spherical form 1836. **e.** Applied to flowers with pendent blossoms, as the fuchsia (*dial.*), and in comb., as *snow-d.* 1664.

1. Why raine falleth in round drops W. FULKE. *fig.* To preserve thy sweets Unmix'd with drops of bitter COWPER. Phr. *D. serene*, tr. L. *gutta serena*, an old name for amaurosis. 2. They would be faithful to him to the last d. DE FOE. 5. Phr. *A d. in the* (*a*) *bucket* or *the ocean*: an inappreciable addition. 6 I..had a d. too much J. PAYN. 8. Phr. (*Prince*) *Rupert's Drops*: glass drops with long and slender tails, which burst to pieces, on the breaking off those tails in any parts (Chambers).

II. Secondary sb., f. DROP *v.* **1.** The action or an act of dropping; an abrupt fall or descent 1637. Also *fig.* **2.** That which drops or is used for dropping; *e.g.* in a theatre, the painted curtain let down between the acts; also called *act-d.*, and *d.-curtain* 1779. **3.** A small platform or trap-door on the gallows, which is let fall from under the feet of the condemned 1796. **4.** A contrivance for temporarily lowering a gas-jet (Webster). **b.** A movable plate covering the key-hole of a lock. **c.** The slit of a letter-box (*U.S.*) 1870. **5.** The distance through which anything drops; *e.g.* a criminal when hanged 1879. **6.** The depth to which anything sinks or is sunk below the general level 1794.

1. The d. of the woodland fruit's begun BROWNING. *fig.* A d. in exchanges 1884, in the temperature (*mod.*). 3. The d. fell. They were executed in their irons 1813.

attrib. and *Comb.* (See also DROP-.) **a.** Of, pertaining to, or consisting of a d. or drops, as *d.-earring*, *-pearl*, etc. **b.** Special comb.: **d.-black**, a superior quality of bone-black ground in water, formed into drops, and dried; **-dry** *a.*, watertight; **-meter**, an instrument for measuring out liquid d. by d.; **-sulphur**, **-tin**, *i.e.* that granulated by being dropped in a molten state into cold water.

Drop (drǫp), *v.* Pa. t. and pple. **dropped**, **dropt.** [OE. *dropian*, *droppian*, f. (ult.) as DROP *sb.*]

I. Intr. senses. **1.** To fall in drops. **2.** = DRIP *v.* 2. ME. **3.** To fall, like a drop ME. Also *fig.* **4.** To fall exhausted, wounded, or dead ME.; of a setter, etc.: To squat down at the sight of game 1870. **5.** To fall *into* some condition 1654; *fig.* to die (cf. *d. off*) 1654. **6.** To come to an end; to fall through 1697. **7.** To sink, become depressed 1729. **8.** To descend with the tide or a light wind 1772; to let oneself fall *behind* or *to the rear* 1823. **9.** To come or go casually; to fall upon 1633.

1. The crystal tide that from her two cheeks..Dropt SHAKS. 3. The shell opens, and the nut drops out 1660. *fig.* His words like Honey dropped from his tongue HOBBES. 4. Tho' thousands of their Men dropt, they would not give ground an Inch 1700. 5. To d. into oblivion PRIDEAUX. 6. The matter was let d. HEARNE. 7. Prices dropped afterwards 1866. 8. The Resolution..dropped down the river COOK. Phr. *To d. astern*: to slacken a ship's way, so as to let another pass.

II. Trans. senses. **1.** To let fall or shed in drops; to distil. Also *fig.* ME. **2.** To sprinkle with or as with drops; to bedrop (*arch.*) ME. **3.** To let fall (like a drop or drops). Also *fig.* ME. **4.** To let fall in birth; to give birth to. Also *absol.* 1662. **5.** To let fall (words, a hint, etc.); to utter casually or by the way 1611; to let (a letter, etc.) fall into the letter-box; hence, to send (a note, etc.) in an informal way 1777. **6.** *slang.* To part with (money) 1676. **7.** To cause to fall by a blow or shot 1726. **8.** To set down; also, to leave (a packet) at a person's house 1796. **9.** To omit in pronunciation or writing 1864. **10.** To let droop 1842. **11.** To let move gently with the tide 1805. **b.** *To d. astern*: to leave in the rear 1867. **12.** *Football.* To obtain (a goal) by a drop-kick 1882. **13.** To have done with; to break off acquaintance with 1605.

1. To d. many a teare 1626. 2. Their wav'd coats dropt with Gold MILT. *P. L.* VII. 406. 3. Phr. *To d. anchor*: to let the anchor down, to cast anchor. 4. At the time the ewes d. KEATINGE. 5. D. not thy word against the house of Isaac *Amos* vii 16. 6. We played hazard..And I dropped all the money I had THACKERAY. 8. [He] promised to d. us at the Shetland Islands KANE. 9. He does not d. his *h*'s O. W. HOLMES. 13. She will d. him in his old Age ADDISON. Phr. *To d. a curtsy*: to make a curtsy by lowering the body.

Comb. with adverbs. See also simple senses and advs. **D. away.** *intr.* To fall away drop by drop or one by one. **D. in.** *intr.* **a.** To pay a casual visit. **b.** To come in at intervals. **c.** To become vacant. **d.** To fall in *with*. **D. off.** *intr.* **a.** To withdraw one by one, or by degrees. **b.** To fall asleep. **c.** To die. **d.** To become less frequent *in*. **D. out.** *intr.*, to disappear from one's place in a series or order. **D. short.** *intr.* **a.** To fall short; usu. with *of*. **b.** *colloq.* or *slang.* To die.

Drop-, the vb.-stem used in *Comb.*

a. *attrib.* with sb., in the sense of 'dropping', 'used in dropping', 'arranged so as to drop', forming sbs. or adjs.; as **d.-arch** (*Arch.*), one having a radius shorter than the breadth of the arch; **-bar** (*Printing*), a bar or roller for running the sheet into the machine; **-curtain** = DROP *sb.* II. 2; **-fly** (*Angling*) = DROPPER 3; **-hammer** = *drop-press*; **-handle** *a.*, applied to a form of needle-telegraph instrument which is operated by a handle directed downward; **-lamp**, **-light** (*U.S.*), a portable gas-burner, connected with the gas-fittings by a flexible tube, usually in the form of a lamp, which can stand on a table; **-press**, a machine for embossing, punching, etc., consisting of a weight guided vertically, to be raised by a cord and pulley worked by the foot, and to drop on an anvil; called also *d.-hammer*; **-shutter**, a device consisting of a slide operated by a spring or the like; used in instantaneous photography to secure very brief exposure; **-table**, a machine for lowering weights, and *esp.* for removing the wheels of locomotives. **b.** In vbl. comb. with object, as **d.-seed**, a grass that readily drops its seed, spec. *Muhlenbergia diffusa*.

‖**Dropax** (drōu·pæks). ? *Obs.* 1621. [mod.L., a. Gr. δρῶπαξ, f. δρέπειν to pluck.] A pitch-plaster, a depilatory.

Drop-kick. 1857. [See DROP-.] *Football.* A kick made by dropping the ball from the hands, and kicking it the very instant it rises.

Dro·plet. 1607. [See -LET.] A minute drop.

Drop-letter. *U.S.* 1844. A letter posted in any place merely for local delivery.

†**Dro·p-meal,** *adv.* [OE. *drop-mælum*; see -MEAL.] In drops, drop by drop.

As the cloud dissolves drop-meal upon the earth TRAPP.

Dropped, dropt, *ppl. a.* 1600. [f. DROP *v.*] **a.** See the vb. **b.** Of eggs: Fried or poached, 'dropped into the frying pan' (Jam.) 1824.

Dropper (drǫ·pəɹ). 1700. [f. DROP *v.*] **1.** One who or that drops; *spec.* one who drops seeds into the holes made by a dibbler. **2.** A dog that drops (see DROP *v.* I. 4); a setter. **3.** *Angling.* A fly adjusted to a leader above the stretcher fly. Also *drop-fly*, *d.-fly* 1746. **4.** A pendant 1825. **b.** A glass tube for dropping liquid 1889. **c.** A branch vein which drops off from the main lode 1864.

Dropping (drǫ·piŋ), *vbl. sb.* OE. [f. DROP *v.* + -ING [1].] **1.** The action of DROP *v.* **2.** That which drops; dripping, etc. ME. **3.** Dung of animals. (Now only *pl.*) 1596.

attrib. and *Comb.*, as **d.-bottle**, a bottle used to supply fluid in small quantities; **-tube**, the tubulated stopper of the d.-bottle; **-well**, a well formed by the dropping of water from above.

Dropping, *ppl. a.* ME. [f. as prec. + -ING [2].] **1.** That drops. **2.** Desultory, not continuous, as *a d. fire* 1708. Hence **Dro·ppingly** *adv.*

Dro·p-scene. 1815. Used loosely for *drop* or *act-drop* (DROP *sb.* II. 2); also for the final scene of a drama in real life.

Dropsical (drǫ·psikăl), *a.* 1678. [f. DROPSY, after *hydropical*.] **1.** Of, pertaining to, or like dropsy 1688. **2.** Affected with or subject to dropsy. Also *transf.* and *fig.*

1. D. symptoms 1846. Hence **Dro·psically** *adv.*

Dropsied (drǫ·psid), *a.* 1601. [f. DROPSY + -ED [2].] Having the dropsy; swollen with or as with water; as *the d. clouds* (DRAYTON).

Dropsy (drǫ·psi), *sb.* (*a.*) ME. [aphet. f. ME. *i-*, *ydropsy*, HYDROPSY, q.v.] **1.** *Med.* A morbid accumulation of watery fluid in the serous cavities or the connective tissue of the body. Also *transf.* of young trout and of succulent plants. Also *fig.* †**2.** *attrib.* or *adj.* = DROPSICAL –1683.

†**Drop vie, drop-vie,** *vbl. phr.* or occas. *v.* 1598. [f. DROP *v.* + VIE *sb.*] To drop coins or the like in rivalry; to vie –1616.

Dropwise (drǫ·pwəiz), *adv.* 1673. [See -WISE.] Drop by drop.

The spring..trickling d. from the cleft TENNYSON.

Dropwort (drǫ·pwɒɹt). 1538. [f. DROP *sb.* + WORT; cf. the L. name *Filipendula*, *i.e.* pendulous threads.] A name of plants; esp. *Spiræa Filipendula*, and other species of Spiræa.

‖**Droshky** (drǫ·ʃki), **drosky** (drǫ·ski). Also **droitzschka, droshka, -ke.** 1808. [ad. Russ. *drozhki*, dim. of *drogi* waggon, hearse; properly pl. of *droga* perch.] Prop., a Russian low four-wheeled carriage, in which the passengers sit astride a narrow bench, their feet resting on bars near the ground; hence *transf.*; in some German towns the name of the ordinary fiacre.

Drosometer (drosǫ·mĭtəɹ). 1825. [mod. f. Gr. δρόσος; see -METER.] An instrument for measuring the quantity of dew deposited.

Dross (drǫs), *sb.* [OE. *drós*, f. *dreósan* to drip, also to fall down.] **1.** The scum thrown off from metals in smelting. **b.** An alloy formed in the zinc-bath by the action of the zinc on the iron articles dipped 1884. Also *fig.* **2.** Dreggy, impure, or foreign matter mixed with any substance ME. Also *fig.* **3.** *gen.* Refuse; rubbish; worthless, impure matter ME.

2. *fig.* The Dregs and Lees of the Earth, and Drosse of Mankinde 1677. 3 All treasures and all gain esteem as d. MILT. *P. R.* III. 23. Hence **Dross** *v.* to free from d. **Dro·ssless** *a.* free from d.

†**Dro·ssel, drosell.** 1581. [Cf. DRAZEL.] A sloven, a slut –1617.

Drossy (drǫ·si), *a.* ME. [f. DROSS *sb.*] Of metals, etc.: Full of dross; of the nature of dross; dreggy, feculent. Also *transf.* and *fig.*

Thin brass or d. lead MORRIS. Hence **Dro·ssiness.**

Drou, drough, drouȝ, obs. pa. t. of DRAW *v.*

Drought (draut), **drouth** (drauþ, *Sc.* drūþ). [OE. *drúgað*, *-oð*, f. *drúg-* stem of *drýge* DRY, q.v. Cf. *highth*, *height*. The form *drouth*, *drowth* (Sc. and n. dial.) is often used by Eng. poets; *drouth* is common in U.S.] **1.** The quality of being dry; aridity, lack of moisture (*arch.*). **2.** *spec.* Dryness of the weather or climate; lack of rain. ME. †**3.** Parched land, desert –1671. **4.** Thirst (*arch.* and *dial.*) ME.

1. The burning drouth Of that long desert TENNYSON. 2. The tender dew after drouth SWINBURNE. 3. MILT. *P. R.* III. 274. 4 His carcass, pined with hunger and with droughth MILT. *P. R.* I. 325.

Droughty (drau·ti), **drouthy** (drau·þi, *Sc.* drū·þi), *a.* 1603. [f. prec.; cf. *weighty*, etc.] **1.** Dry, without moisture; arid. Also *fig.* **2.** Characterized by drought 1605. **3.** Thirsty; addicted to drinking 1626.

1. Out of the droughty rocke Moses..bringeth forth water 1643. 2. Drouthy weather SCOTT. 3. The dusty, drouthy wayfarers 1879. Hence **Drou·ghtiness.**

†**Droumy,** *a. rare.* 1605. [? conn. w. Sc. DRUMLY.] Turbid –1640.

Drouth, drouthy, var. of DROUGHT, -Y.

Drove (drōuv), *sb.* [OE. *dráf*, f. *drífan* to DRIVE.] †**1.** The action of driving. (Only OE.) **2.** A number of beasts, as oxen, sheep, etc., driven in a body; a herd, flock OE.; *transf.* a crowd, multitude, shoal OE. Also *fig.* of things. **3.** Locally: **a.** A road along which horses or cattle are driven 1664. **b.** A channel for drainage or irrigation OE. **4.** A stone-mason's chisel with a broad face 1825.

1. A d. of sheep LYTTON. His finny d. SPENSER. A great d. of Heresies..broke loose among them 1692. 3. The major rode in the middle of the D. (so our fen roads are called) 1829. *Comb.* **d.-road**, an ancient road along which there is a free right of way for cattle, but which is not kept in repair.

Drove, *v.* [1] 1632. [f. DROVE *sb.*; or ? f. DROVER.] To follow the occupation of a drover (*trans.* and *intr.*).

Drove, *v.*² 1825. [f. DROVE *sb.* 4.] *trans.* To dress (stone) in parallel lines with a DROVE (sense 4).

Drove, pa. t. (and obs. pa. pple.) of DRIVE *v.*

Drover (drōᵘ·vəɹ). ME. [f. DROVE *sb.* + -ER¹ 1; cf. *gardener*, etc.] **1.** One who drives droves of cattle, sheep, etc., to market; a dealer in cattle. **2.** A boat used for fishing with a drift-net 1465.

1. Why that's spoken like an honest Drouier: so they sel Bullockes *Much Ado* II. i. 201.

Drovy (drōᵘ·vi), *a.* Now *dial.* [f. OE. and ME. *drōf.*] Turbid.

Drow, obs. pa. t. of DRAW *v.*

Drown (draun), *v.* [ME. *drun-*, *droun-*, *drown-*, pointing to an OE. **drūnian*. Connexion with ME. *drunkn-* or ON. *drukn-* is improbable.] **1.** *intr.* To suffer death by suffocation under water, etc.; †to sink (as a ship) –1523. (Now *unusual.*) **2.** *trans.* To suffocate by submersion in water, etc. Also said of the water. ME. Also *fig.* †**3.** To sink in water; to send to the bottom –1632. **4.** To lay under water, etc.; to submerge, inundate; to drench ME. **5.** *transf.* and *fig.* To overwhelm, to overpower (sound, etc.); to smother ME.

2. He..was privety drouned in a But of Malvesey HALL. *fig.* They d. themselves in drink 1659. 4. When the Fens are drowned 1696. Phr. *To d. out*: to stop (works, etc.) or drive (people, etc.) from their houses by flooding. 5. Yells drowned his voice FROUDE. Hence **Drow·nage** (*rare*), drowning. **Drow·ner,** one who, or that which, drowns. **Drow·ningly** *adv.* so as to d.

Drowse (drauz), *v.* OE. [? identical with OE. *drūsian* to be sluggish, from OE. *drēosan* to fall; in current use perh. f. *drowsy*.] †**1.** *intr.* To sink, become slow. (OE. only.) **2.** *intr.* To be drowsy; to be heavy with or as with sleep; to be half asleep. Also *fig.* 1573. **3.** *trans.* To render drowsy; to make heavy or inactive, as with sleep 1600.

2. I drowsed..but I anon wakened PEPYS. *fig.* Let not your prudence..d. TENNYSON. 3. Nations drows'd in peace KEATS.

Drowse, *sb.* 1814. [f. prec. vb.] The action of drowsing; the state of being half asleep.

Drowsy (drau·zi), *a.* 1529. [prob. related to OE. *drūsian*; see DROWSE *v.*] **1.** Inclined to sleep; heavy with sleepiness; half asleep, dozing 1530. **2.** Caused or characterized by sleepiness 1529. **3.** Soporific 1590. **4.** *fig.* Dull, inactive; lethargic 1570.

1. A d. watchman's footsteps DICKENS. 2. D. Diseases, called Coma [etc.] CULPEPPER. 3. A d. posset MIDDLETON. 4. The dead and drowsie fier SHAKS. *Comb.* **d.-head,** a person of a sluggish disposition. Hence **Drow·sihead, Drow·sihood,** drowsiness. **Drow·sily** *adv.* in a d. manner. **Drow·siness,** d. state; also *fig.*

Drowte, drowth, obs. var. DROUGHT.

Droyl, Droyt, obs. ff. DROIL, DROIT.

Drub (drɒb), *v.* 1634. [? repr. Arab. *ḍaraba* (*i.e.* *ḍarɒba*) to beat, bastinado.] **1.** *trans.* To beat with a stick or the like, to cudgel; in early use, *spec.* to bastinado; also, to beat in a fight. Also *transf.* and *fig.* **2.** To beat the ground, stamp (*trans.* and *intr.*) 1855.

1. He is almost drubd (with many terrible bastinadoes on the soles of his feet) to death SIR T. HERBERT. He was most confoundedly drubb'd just now FIELDING. 2. Drubbing with her little feet THACKERAY. Hence **Drub** *sb.* a stroke with a cudgel; a thump. **Dru·bber,** one who drubs or beats. **Dru·bbing** *vbl. sb.* a beating, a thrashing.

Drudge (drɒdʒ), *sb.* 1494. [?] One employed in mean, servile, or distasteful work; a hack; a hard toiler.

Lexicographer, a writer of dictionaries; a harmless d. [etc.] JOHNSON.

Drudge (drɒdʒ), *v.* 1548. [app. f. prec. sb.] **1.** *intr.* To perform mean or servile tasks; to work slavishly; to toil at distasteful work. **2.** *trans.* To subject to drudgery (*rare*) 1847.

1. College-tutors do indeed work; they d. M. PATTISON. Phr. *To d. out*, to perform as drudgery; *to d. away, over*, to pass in drudgery. Hence **Dru·dger,** one who drudges. **Dru·dgingly** *adv.*

Drudgery (drɒ·dʒəri). 1550. [f. DRUDGE *sb.*; cf. *slavery*.] The occupation of a drudge; mean, servile, or wearisome toil; distasteful work. Also *attrib.*

A servant with this clause Makes drudgerie divine G. HERBERT. The d. of his Dictionary BOSWELL.

†**Druery, drury.** ME. [a. OF. *druerie*, etc., f. *dru*, *drut*, friend, app. of Ger. origin; cf. Ger. *traut*.] **1.** Love, *esp.* sexual love; courtship; *often*, illicit love –1460. **2.** A love-token, keepsake –1560. **3.** A sweetheart –1450. **4.** A beloved thing, a treasure. (Only ME.)

Drug (drɒg), *sb.*¹ [ME. *drogges*, *drugge*, a. F. *drogue*, a Com. Rom. word: ult. origin uncertain.] **1.** An original, simple, medicinal substance, organic or inorganic, used by itself, or as an ingredient in Medicine, or, formerly, in the arts generally. In early use always *pl.* **b.** *spec.* A narcotic or opiate 1902. **2.** A commodity which is no longer in demand, and so is unsaleable. (Now usu. *a d. in the market.*) 1661.

1. Tea and other Drugs 1682. What d. can make A wither'd palsy cease to shake? TENNYSON. 2. Horses in Ireland are a D. TEMPLE. A wife's a d. now; mere tar-water..but nobody takes it MURPHY. They told me poetry was a mere d. 1824. 3. Comb. **d.-store** (*U.S.*), a druggist's shop, also dealing in toilet requisites, stationery, etc. 1845. Hence **Dru·ggy** *a.* of, pertaining to, or resembling drugs.

Drug, *sb.*² 1677. [Allied to DRUG *v.*¹; cf. DRAG *sb.*] Truck for the carriage of timber, etc.

Drug, *sb.*³ var. of DROGUE.

Drug, *v.*¹ Now *dial.* ME. [?] To drag.

Drug (drɒg), *v.*² 1605. [f. DRUG *sb.*¹] **1.** *trans.* To mix or adulterate with a drug. **2.** To administer drugs to, *esp.* for the purpose of stupefying or poisoning 1730; to administer something nauseous to 1667. **3.** *intr.* To take drugs habitually 1895.

1. I haue drugg'd their Possets, That Death and Nature doe contend about them *Macb.* II. ii. 7. 2. Whom he has drugg'd to sure repose FENTON. With pleasure drugg'd, he almost long'd for woe BYRON.

Drug, Druggery, etc., obs. ff. DRUDGE, etc.

Drugger (drɒ·gəɹ). 1594. [f. DRUG *sb.*¹, and DRUG *v.*²] †**1.** A dealer in drugs –1845. **2.** One who administers a drug 1836.

Druggery (drɒ·gəri). 1535. [a. F. *droguerie*, f. *drogue* drug.] **1.** Drugs collectively. **2.** A place where drugs are kept 1865.

Drugget (drɒ·gėt). 1580. [a. F. *droguet*. Ult. origin unkn.] **1.** Formerly, a kind of stuff, all of wool, or half wool, half silk or linen, used for wearing apparel. **b.** Now, a coarse woollen stuff used for floor-coverings, etc. **2.** †A garment of drugget; a floor-cloth of drugget 1713. **3.** *attrib.* 1580.

2. He was married in a plain d. STEELE. 3. A d. petticoat BLACK. Hence **Dru·ggeting** = sense 1 b.

Druggist (drɒ·gist). 1611. [a. F. *droguiste*.] One who deals in drugs. In Scotl. and U.S. the name for a pharmaceutical chemist.

Druid (drū·id), *sb.* (*a.*) 1563. [a. F. *druide*, ad. L. **druida*, ? *druis*; a. OCelt. stem *druid-*, whence OIr. *drui*, mod.Ir. and Gael. *draoi* (*draoidh*, *druidh*) magician.] **1.** One of an order of men among the ancient Celts of Gaul and Britain, who, according to Cæsar, were priests, but in native Irish and Welsh legend were magicians, soothsayers, and the like. (The Eng. use follows the L. sources.) Orig. always in *pl.* **2.** Hence: **a.** A priest, chaplain. **b.** A philosophic bard. 1710. **c.** One of certain officers of the Welsh Gorsedd 1884. **3.** *attrib.* Druidic 1670.

1. Mona was a sacred place of the Druids GARDINER. 2. *United Ancient Order of Druids*, a secret benefit society founded in London in 1781, and having now numerous lodges or *groves* in most English-speaking countries. 3. *D. stone, sandstone*, grey-weather, of which Stonehenge is constructed. Hence **Dru·idess,** a female D.; a Druidical prophetess. **Dru·idism,** the religious and philosophical system of the Druids.

Druidic, -al (drui·dik, -ăl), *a.* 1755. [See DRUID + -IC + -AL.] Of or pertaining to the Druids.

Circles of upright stones, like those which in Europe are termed Druidical PRICHARD.

Drum (drɒm), *sb.*¹ 1541. [perh. an Eng. shortening of *drombyllsclad*, *drombeslade*, DRUMSLADE.] **1.** A percussive musical instrument, consisting of a hollow cylinder or hemisphere of wood or metal, with a head of tightly stretched membrane at one or both ends, to be beaten with a stick. Also *fig.* and *transf.* **b.** *Zool.* Applied to the hollow hyoid bone of the howling monkey 1817. **2.** The sound of the instrument, or any similar sound 1646. **3.** *Mil.* One who plays the drum; a drummer. Also, †a small party sent with a drum to parley with the enemy. 1577. **4.** Anything resembling a drum in shape or structure. **a.** The tympanum of the ear 1615. **b.** *Machinery.* A cylinder round which a belt passes or is wound 1776. **c.** A cylinder or cask for steaming printed fabrics in order to fix the colour. **d.** The cylindrical case for the spring of a car-brake. **e.** A cylindrical chamber used in heating apparatus 1888. **f.** A doffer in a carding-machine. **5.** *Arch.* **a.** The vase of the Corinthian and Composite capitals 1727. **b.** The block of stone composing one section of the shaft of a column (Gwilt). **c.** The upright part under or above a cupola 1837. **6.** *techn.* **a.** A sieve 1706. **b.** A cylinder of canvas used as a storm-signal 1867. **c.** The cylindrical part of an urn or the like. **7.** A cylindrical box or receptacle for fruit, fish, etc. 1812. **8.** An evening assembly of fashionable people at a private house; a rout. Later, an afternoon tea-party. Cf. KETTLEDRUM. 1745. **9.** More fully **d.-fish:** Any of various sciænoid fishes which make a drumming noise; as, the 'salt-water d.' (*Pogonias chromis*) found on the Atlantic coast; the 'fresh-water d.' (*Haplodinotus grunniens*) of the Mississippi, etc.; the 'branded d.' or 'sea-boss' (*Sciæna ocellata*) of the Gulf States 1676.

1. And sodainly strake up a Dromme or Drounslade HALL. The large d., beaten at both ends, is called a *double-d.* KNIGHT. *Bass d.* = *double-drum*. 2. Phr. *John D.'s entertainment*: a rough reception, turning an unwelcome guest out of doors. *All's Well* III. vi. 41. 8. We went last night to a d. at Rothschild's 1824. *attrib.* and *Comb.*: **d.-armature,** a dynamo-armature in the form of a rotating hollow cylinder; **-curb,** a cylindrical curb of iron or wood to support the brickwork of a shaft; **-fire,** continuous rapid artillery fire; †**-room,** the room in which a d. or rout is held; **-sieve,** a sieve enclosed in a d.-like box, for sifting fine substances; **-wheel,** (*a*) a cylinder round which a rope is coiled; (*b*) a water-raising current-wheel made in the form of a d., a tympanum.

Drum, *sb.*² 1725. [a. Gael. and Ir. *druim* back, ridge.] A ridge or 'rigg', a long narrow hill often separating two parallel valleys. Hence *Geol.* A long narrow ridge of 'drift' formation.

Drum, *v.* 1578. [f. DRUM *sb.*¹] **1.** *intr.* To beat on or as on a drum 1583. **b.** Applied to the strong beating of the heart 1593. **2.** Of birds or insects: To make a hollow reverberating sound, as by the quivering of the wings 1813. **3.** To sound like a drum; to resound 1638. **4.** 'To go about, as a drummer does, to gather recruits, to secure partisans, customers, etc.; with *for*' (Webster). **5.** *trans.* To summon by or as by beat of drum; to beat *up* as by drumming; *colloq.* to obtain by solicitation 1606. **6.** To expel publicly by beat of drum 1766. **7.** To din or drive *into* by persistent repetition 1820. **8.** To perform (a tune) on or as on a drum 1864.

1. [Her] foot was drumming on the carpet SALA. 2. Flies and gnats d. around you 1873. 6. Another is drummed out of a regiment MACAULAY. 7. To d. a doctrine into the public mind MILL.

Drumble, *sb.* Now *dial.* 1575. [var. of *dumble*, DUMMEL.] An inert or sluggish person; a drone.

Drumble, *v.* Now *dial.* 1579. [f. prec.] **1.** *intr.* To be sluggish; to move sluggishly 1598. †**2.** *intr.* To drone, to mumble –1596.

1. Look, how you d. *Merry W.* III. iii. 156.

†**Drumbler, drumler.** 1598. [a. early mod. Du. *drommeler* a kind of ship.] A small fast vessel used as a transport, etc. –1630.

Dru·mhead. 1622. [f. DRUM *sb.*¹ + HEAD *sb.*] **1.** The skin or membrane stretched upon a drum. **2.** The tympanic membrane 1664. **3.** The circular top of a capstan, into which the capstan bars are fixed 1726. **4.** A flat-topped variety of cabbage 1797. **5.** *attrib.*, as *d. court-martial*, a court-martial round an up-turned drum, for summary trial of offences during military operations. So *d. law, discipline*.

Drumlin (drɒ·mlin). 1833. [app. for *drumling*, dim. of DRUM *sb.*²] = DRUM *sb.*²

Drumly (drɒ·mli), *a.* Orig. *Sc.* 1513. [Cf. DROUMY *a.*] **1.** Of the sky or day: Troubled; cloudy. Also *fig.* **2.** Of water, etc.: Turbid; not clear 1570. Also *fig.* and *transf.*

Dru·m-ma·jor. 1598. [See MAJOR *sb.*] †**1.** The first or chief drummer in a regimental band **b.** A non-commissioned officer who has command of the drummers. **c.** An officer of a band or drum-corps, who leads and directs it on the march. †**2.** *joc.* A large drum or rout 1753.

Drummer (drɒ·məɹ). 1573. [f. DRUM *v.* + -ER¹.] **1.** One who beats a drum for military or other purposes; one who plays the drum in a band. 2. *fig.* A commercial traveller. See DRUM *v.* 4 and 5 (*U.S.*) 1827. 3. A drum-fish. b. The large W. Indian cockroach (*Blatta gigantea*), which drums its head against the woodwork of houses as a sexual call. c. A rabbit.

Dru·mming, *vbl. sb.* 1583. [See -ING [1].] 1. The action of DRUM *v.* 2. Fishing for drum-fish (*U.S.*) 1889.

Drummond light. 1854. The lime-light, or oxyhydrogen light (invented by Capt. T. *Drummond*, R.E., *c* 1825), wherein a blow-pipe flame, *e.g.* of combined oxygen and hydrogen, impinges on a piece of pure lime, and renders it incandescent.

†**Drumslade, dromslade.** 1527. [app. corruption of Du. or LG. *trommelslag*, Ger. *trommelschlag* drum-beat, somehow applied to the instrument.] 1. A drum -1635. 2. A drummer -1777. Hence †**Dru·mslager** = sense 2.

Drumstick (drʊ·mstik). 1589. 1. The stick with a knobbed end used in beating a drum 2. *transf.* (in reference to shape.) a. The lower joint of the leg of a fowl 1764. b. *U.S.* The stilt-sandpiper.

Drungar (drʊ·ŋgăı). *Hist.* 1619. [ad. late L. *drungarius*, f. *drungus* a body of soldiers (Vegetius).] The commander of a troop.

The great drungaire of the fleet GIBBON.

Drunk (drʊŋk), *ppl. a.* and *sb.* ME. [pa. pple. of DRINK *v.*, earlier DRUNKEN. Now only in the predicate, exc. in Sc. and n. dial.]

A. 1. Overcome by or as by alcoholic liquor; intoxicated. Also *fig.* †2. Drenched; soaked with moisture -1697. 3. = DRUNKEN 5. 1884.

1. She was blind d. SIMS. D. with opium 1585, with tobacco 1698. *fig.* D. with success GREEN. 2. I will make mine arrows d. with blood *Deut.* xxxii. 42.

B. *sb.* (*colloq.*) 1. A drinking-bout 1862. 2. A drunken person; a case or charge of being drunk 1882.

Drunkard (drʊ·ŋkărd). 1530. [f. DRUNK *ppl. a.* + -ARD.] One addicted to drinking, *esp.* to excess; an inebriate, a sot.

1. As drunckards..they stagring reele 1586.

Drunken (drʊ·ŋkĕn), *ppl. a.* OE. [pa. pple. of DRINK *v.*; cf. DRUNK. Sc. *drucken* is from Norse.] 1. Intoxicated. Also *transf.* and *fig.* 2. Habitually intemperate. (The more usual current sense.) 1548. 3. Proceeding from or pertaining to drink or drunkenness 1591. 4. *transf.* Soaked with moisture ME. 5. *fig.* Of a thing: Unsteady; off the vertical 1786.

1. Ye fare as folkes that dronken ben of ale CHAUCER. D. with cold KANE. 2. Stephano, my d. butler *Temp.* v. i. 277. 3. To take up a d. brawl MASSINGER. 4. The d. Field DRYDEN. Hence **Dru·nkenly** *adv.*

Drunkenness (drʊ·ŋkĕnˌnĕs). OE. [f. prec. + -NESS.] 1. The state of being drunk; intoxication; the habit of drinking to excess. 2. *fig.* Intoxication of the mind or spirit.

1. D. is frequently a disease NAPHEYS. 2. The d. of factious animosity MACAULAY. vars. †**Dru·nkenship,** †**Dru·nkness,** †**Dru·nkship.**

Drupaceous (drupēı·ʃəs), *a.* 1822. [f. mod. L. *drupa*; see next and -ACEOUS.] *Bot.* Of the nature of a drupe, or bearing drupes; belonging to the *Drupaceæ*.

Drupe (drūp). 1753. [ad. mod. Bot.L. *drupa*, L. *drupa*, *druppa* (sc. *oliva*) over-ripe = Gr. δρύππα; cf. F. *drupe*.] *Bot.* A stone-fruit; a fleshy or pulpy fruit enclosing a stone or nut having a kernel, as the olive, plum, cherry.

Drupel (drū·pĕl). 1835. [ad. mod.L. *drupella*, dim. of *drupa*.] *Bot.* A little drupe: such as those of the blackberry. So **Dru·pelet, Dru·peole.**

Drupose (drū·pōᵘs). 1872. [See -OSE.] *Chem.* A substance ($C_{12}H_{20}O_8$) produced together with glucose, by the action of boiling moderately diluted hydrochloric acid on glyco-drupose, the stony concretions found in pears.

Druse [1] (drūz). 1811. [a. Ger. *druse* = Boh. *druza*.] *Min.* A crust of small crystals lining the sides of a cavity in a rock; also, the cavity. Hence **Dru·sy** *a.* lined with minute crystals.

Druse [2], **druze** (drūz), *sb.* (*a.*) 1786. [ad. Arab. *Durūz*.] One of a political and religious sect of Mohammedan origin, inhabiting the region round Mount Lebanon. Hence **Dru·sian, -ean** *sb.* (*obs.*) and *a.*

Druxy (drʊ·ksi), *a.* 1589. [formerly *dricksie*, f. DRIX.] Of timber: Having decayed spots concealed by healthy wood.

Dry (drəi), *a.* [OE. *drȳge*, f. (ult.) OTeut. ablaut-series **dreug-*, *draug-*, *drug-* to be dry, whence also OE. *drūgian* to dry, etc.]

I. As a physical quality. 1. Destitute of moisture; arid; of the eyes, free from tears. b. Of a season or climate: Free from or deficient in rain ME. 2. That has lost its natural moisture; dried, parched, withered OE.; dried up ME. 3. Of persons: Wanting drink; thirsty. (Now vulgar.) *transf.* Causing thirst. ME. 4. Not yielding liquid; of cows, etc.: Not yielding milk ME. 5. Not under, in, or on water (see also DRY LAND) ME. 6. Of bread, etc.: Without butter 1579. 7. Solid, not liquid; also *transf.* 1688. 8. Of wines, etc.: Not sweet or fruity 1700. 9. Of copper, tin, or lead: Not sufficiently deoxidated in refining 1875. 10. Not associated or connected with liquid; *esp.* (*Med.*) not marked by a discharge of matter, phlegm, etc., as diseases, etc. ME. †11. Of a blow, or a beating: prop., That does not draw blood; also vaguely = Hard, stiff, severe -1774.

1. Among whome was not oon drie eye 1562. A d. year (*mod.*). 2. D. fish from Newfoundland 1677. Some small Rivers..are d. at certain seasons DAMPIER. 3. *transf.* It's d. work (*mod.*). 4. D. milch cows 1658. A d. inkstand 1874. 5. Further d. arches on each shore 1798. The tide leaves them d. 1816. 7. D. wares, as Corn, Seeds, [etc.] HUTTON. Phr. *D. measure*, measure of capacity for non-liquids. 8. Where's the old d. wine? THACKERAY. 10. A d. death *Temp.* I. i. 72. b. Of a country, legislation, etc. (orig. *U.S.*): teetotal, prohibiting sale of intoxicants; also, deprived of intoxicants by prohibition 1888.

II. Fig. senses. 1. Feeling or showing no emotion ME. 2. Of a jest or sarcasm: Uttered in a matter-of-fact tone; of humour: Apparently unconscious; used also of the humorist; in early use, ironical 1542. †3. Yielding no fruit, result, or satisfaction; barren, jejune, unfruitful -1680; of persons: Miserly, uncommunicative -1689. 4. Lacking embellishment; bare; matter-of-fact 1626. 5. Insipid. (*fig.* from food.) 1621. 6. *Art.* Stiff and formal in outline; lacking in softness; frigidly precise 1716. 7. Of money, rent, etc.: Paid in hard cash. [Cf. F. *argent sec*.] 1574. 8. *Dry light* (see Heraclitus, ed. Bywater 30): 'Light' untinged by prejudice or fancy 1625.

1. Noted for an address so cold, [d., and distant [etc.] HUME. 2. [He] was..something of a..d. joker SCOTT. 4. A long catalogue of d. facts DARWIN. 6. A hard and d. manner of execution 1876. 8. The d. light of every day LOWELL.

Combs. a. Parasynthetic, as **d.-eyed** *a.*, having d. eyes, tearless. b. Adverbial, in sense 'in a d. way: without the use of liquid; without drawing blood'; as **d.-cupping**, see CUPPING; **-cure** *v.*, to cure meat, etc. by salting and drying; **-salt** *v.* = *dry-cure*. c. Special attributive combs.: **d.-bob** (see BOB *sb.*); also as *vb.*; **-bone** (U.S.), a name for the silicate and other ores of zinc; **-bones,** a familiar name for a thin and withered person; **-castor,** 'a kind of beaver, called also *parchment-beaver*' (Webster); †**-ditch** *v.*, to work at without result, like one digging a ditch into which no water flows; **-fly** *a.* and *v.* (*Angling*), used to describe a method of fishing in which an artificial fly floats lightly on the water; **-march,** a boundary line not formed by water; **d. multure,** see MULTURE; **d. pack,** see PACK; **-plate** (*Photogr.*), a sensitized plate which may be exposed to the action of light in a d. state; **-point** (*Engraving*), (*a*) a sharp-pointed needle used for engraving without acid on a copper plate from which the etching-ground has been removed; (*b*) this process of engraving, or an engraving so executed; hence **-point** *v.*; †**-rent,** a RENT-SECK; **-stone** *a.*, used of a dike built without mortar; **-stove,** a stove for plants, with d. heat; **d. wall,** a wall built without mortar. Hence **Dry·ish** *a.* somewhat d.

Dry, *sb.* ME. [subst. use of prec.] 1. Dry state, *esp.* of the atmosphere. 2. That which is dry; *spec.* dry land ME. 3. A drying-house 1876. 4. *Masonry.* A fissure in a stone, rendering it unfit to support a load 1825. 5. (orig. *U.S.*) A prohibitionist 1918.

Dry (drəi), *v.* Pa. t. and pple. **dried** (drəid). [OE. *drȳg(e)an*, *drīgean*, f. *drȳge* DRY *a.*] 1. *trans.* To make dry by any means; to rid or deprive of moisture; to desiccate. 2. *intr.* To become dry; to lose or be exhausted of moisture ME.; of moisture, to disappear by evaporation, exhaustion, or draining ME. †3. To be thirsty -1541. 4. *trans.* To render a cow dry; *intr.* to become dry 1780.

1. Thei dryen it at the Sonne MAUNDEV. To d. all teares 1551. The water .. was now dried away DAMPIER. 2. It [a sandbank] drys at Low-Water 1705. Great Seas haue dried *All's Well* II. i. 143.

Comb. **D. up.** *trans.* a. To suck, draw, or take up moisture entirely. b. To exhaust of its moisture. (Chiefly in *pass.*) c. *intr.* Of moisture: To disappear entirely. Of a source: To become quite dry. d. (*slang*) To cease talking; also *gen.* to cease 1855.

Dryad (drəi·ǣd). Pl. **dryads**; also in L. form dryades (drəi·ădīz). 1555. [ad. L. *Dryas* = Gr. Δρυάς, f. δρῦς, δρυός tree.] *Gr.* and *L. Mythol.* A nymph supposed to inhabit trees; a wood-nymph. Also *transf.*

transf. The palm, the loftiest d. of the woods BYRON. Hence **Drya·dic** *a.* of, pertaining to, or resembling a d.

Dryasdust (drəi·ǣzdʊst). 1820. [i. e. *Dry as dust*.]

A. *sb.* Name of a fictitious person to whom Sir W. Scott dedicates some of his novels; hence, a writer or student of antiquities, statistics, etc., who occupies himself with dry details. B. *adj.* Extremely dry 1872.

†**Dry-beat,** *v.* 1567. [See DRY *a.* I. 11.] To inflict dry blows upon -1667.

Drydenian (drəi·dīniăn), *a.* 1687. Characteristic, or in the style, of John Dryden. So **Dry·denism,** a D. phrase, etc.

Dry dock, dry-dock. 1627. See DOCK *sb.*[3] Hence **Dry-dock** *v.* to place in a dry dock for repairs.

Dryer, var. of DRIER, freq. in techn. senses.

†**Dry-fat, dry-fat.** Also as two wds. 1526. [f. DRY *a.* + FAT *sb.*[1] = *vat.*] A large vessel used to hold dry things (as opp. to liquids) -1677.

†**Dry·-fist.** 1604. [Cf. DRY *a.* II. 3.] A niggardly person. So †**Dry·-fi·sted** *a.* niggardly.

Dry-foot (drəi·fut), *adv.* Also as two wds. ME. 1. Without wetting the feet. †2. *To draw* or *hunt dry-foot*: to track game by the mere scent of the foot -1651. Also as *adj.*

2. *Com. Err.* IV. ii. 39. Hence **Dry·-foo·ted** *a.* in sense 1; *fig.* ?passing lightly over a difficulty.

Dry·-fou·nder, *v.* 1611. = FOUNDER *v.* Chiefly in pa. pple.

Dry goods. 1708. A name (chiefly in U.S.) for textile fabrics; articles of drapery, mercery, etc. (as opp. to groceries). Also *attrib.*

Drying (drəi·iŋ), *vbl. sb.* ME. [f. DRY *v.* + -ING [1].] 1. The action of DRY *v.* 2. *attrib.* and *Comb.* Used in or for drying something, as *d.-box*, *-floor*, *-ground*, *-room*, *-yard*, etc. 1502.

Dry·ing, *ppl. a.* ME. [f. as prec.] 1. That dries or renders dry; having the quality of abstracting moisture; as, *a d. wind*. 2. Becoming dry; drying quickly; *spec.* of oils 1758.

2. Some oils, by the absorption of oxygen, become what are termed 'd. oils' 1865.

Dry land. ME. [See DRY *a.* I. 5.] Land not under water; land as opp. to sea. Also *attrib.*

Dryly, drily (drəi·li), *adv.* ME. [f. DRY *a.* The better spelling is *dryly*; cf. *shyly*, *slyly*, etc.] In a dry manner; see DRY *a.* II. 1, 2, 4-6.

Dryness (drəi·nĕs). ME. [f. as prec.] The quality or condition of being dry; see DRY *a.*

Dry-nurse, *sb.* 1598. [Cf. DRY *a.* I. 4.] A woman who looks after a child, but does not suckle it (opp. to *wet-nurse*). Also *fig.* of a man who 'coaches' another in his duties. Hence **Dry-nurse** *v.* to bring up by hand, without the breast; to play the dry-nurse to (*lit.* and *fig.*).

Dry rot, dry-rot. 1795. A decayed condition of timber in confined situations, in which it becomes brittle and crumbles to a dry powder; caused by various fungi, or by slow chemical processes. Also, any fungus causing this. Also *fig.* of hidden moral or social disintegration. Hence **Dry-rot** *v.* to affect with dry rot. **Dry-rotten** *ppl. a.*

Drysalter (drəi·sǫltəı). 1707. [app. f. *dry salt*.] A dealer in chemical products used in the arts, drugs, gums, etc.; occas. also in oils, sauces, pickles, etc. Hence **Dry·sa·ltery,** the store or business of a d.; the articles dealt in by a d. (*sing.* and *pl.*).

Dry-shod (drəi·ʃǫd), *a.* 1535. [= *dry shoed*, with dry shoes.] Without wetting the feet. (With *go*, *walk*, etc.)

Dryster (drəi·stəı). ?ME. [f. DRY *v.*; see -STER.] A workman or woman employed in drying something, *e.g.* the grain in a kiln.

Dryth (drəiþ). Also **drith(e.** Now *s. dial.* 1533. [f. DRY *a.*, after *warmth*, etc.] Dryness, dry condition; drought.

D.T. (dī·tī·), also **D.T.'s**: see D III. 1858.

Duad (diū·æd). 1660. [ad. Gr. δυάς, δυαδ-; normally DYAD.] A combination of two; a couple, a pair. Hence **Dua·dic** *a.* relating to or consisting of duads.

Dual (diū·ăl). 1607. [ad. L. *dualis*, f. *duo*.] **A.** *adj.* **1.** Of or pertaining to two. **2.** Two-fold, double 1654.

1. *D. number* (Gram.), the inflected form expressing two or a pair. 2. Truth is often of a d. character TYNDALL.

B. *sb. Gram.* The d. number 1650.

Dualin (diū·ălin). Also **-ine.** 1874. [f. DUAL + -IN: in reference to the twofold combination with nitre.] *Chem.* A powerful explosive consisting of 20 parts of nitre mixed with 30 of fine sawdust, and 50 of nitro-glycerin. Also *d.-dynamite.*

Dualism (diū·ăliz'm). 1794. [See -ISM; cf. F. *dualisme.*] **1.** The state of being dual; twofold division; duality 1831. **2.** *Gram.* The fact of expressing two in number 1874. **3.** A system of thought which recognizes two independent principles. *spec.* **a.** *Philos.* The doctrine that mind and matter exist as independent entities; opp. to *idealism* and *materialism.* **b.** The doctrine that there are two independent principles, one good and the other evil. **c.** *Theol.* The (Nestorian) doctrine that Christ consisted of two personalities. 1794. **4.** *Chem.* The theory, now abandoned, that every compound is constituted of two parts having opposite electricities 1884.

1. A d. between knowing and being, between the 'me' and the 'not me E. CAIRD. 3. The d.—the existence of matter as the source of evil apart from God—finds a distinct expression in the *Wisdom of Solomon* FARRAR.

Dualist (diū·ălist). 1661. [See -IST; cf. F. *dualiste.*] **1.** One who holds a doctrine of dualism or duality 1822. †**2.** A holder of two offices (*rare*). FULLER.

Dualistic (diūăli·stik), *a.* 1801. [f. prec. + -IC; cf. F. *dualistique.*] **1.** Pertaining to, or of the nature of, dualism. **2.** Dual 1832.

1. Berzelius raised the structure of d. chemistry, which asserted that every compound .. must be constituted of two parts, of which one is positively, and the other negatively electrified MUIR. Hence **Duali·stically** *adv.*

Duality (diu,æ·lĭti). ME. [ad. F. *dualité*, ad. late L. *dualitas*, f. *dualis* DUAL.] **1.** The fact of being dual; twofold condition. †**2.** The holding of two benefices together –1647.

Dualize (diū·ăləiz), *v.* 1838. [See -IZE.] To make or regard as two.

Dually (diū·ăli), *adv.* 1650. [See -LY [2].] In a dual capacity; in the dual number.

Duan (dū·ăn). 1765. [Gael.] A poem or song; a canto.

Till what is call'd, in Ossian, the fifth D. BYRON.

Duarchy (diū·ăɹki). 1586. [f. L. *duo*, after *monarchy*, etc.] A government by two; a diarchy.

Dub (dɒb), *sb.*[1] *Sc.* and *n. dial.* 1500. [?] **1.** A muddy or stagnant pool; a puddle. (Chiefly *Sc.*) **2.** A deep dark pool in a river or stream. (*n. dial.*) 1535.

Dub (dɒb), *sb.*[2] 1572. [Mainly echoic.] **1.** A beat, or the sound, of a drum. **2.** A blow 1664. Hence **Dub-a-dub**, the sound made in beating a drum: used advb., as *sb.*, or as *adj.*; also as *vb.*

Dub (dɒb), *sb.*[3] *East Ind.* 1781. [Telugu *dabba.*] A small copper coin; = 20 cash.

Dub (dɒb), *v.*[1] [Late OE. *dubbian*, ad. OF. *duber*, aphetic of *aduber* (F. *adouber*).] **1.** To confer knighthood by a stroke of a sword. **2.** To invest with a dignity or new title. (Often *joc.*) ME. **3.** To style, nickname (now usu. in pleasantry) 1599. †**4.** To dress, array, adorn –1570. **5.** *Angling.* To dress (a fly, or a hook and line *with* a fly) 1450. **6.** To cut off the comb and wattles of (a cock) 1570. **b.** To trim or crop (hedges, etc.) 1634. **7.** To dress (cloth) 1801. **8.** To smear with fat or grease, as leather 1611. **9.** To trim with an adze 1711. **10.** To beat blunt or flat 1879.

1. Whan my Kyng had doubed me a Knight 1559. So he him dubbed SPENSER *F. Q.* VI. ii. 35. 2. A Man of wealth is dubb'd a Man of worth POPE. 4. Dobbed in his diademe 1450.

Dub, *v.*[2] 1513. [Echoic.] **1.** *trans.* To thrust; now implying a somewhat blunt thrust or poke; *intr.* to make a thrust, to poke (*at*) 1833. **2.** Used *intr.* and *trans.* of the beating or sound of a drum. Also *Dub-a-dub* (DUB *sb.*[2]), *rub-a-dub.*

2. With trumpets sounding, and with dubbing drums 1588.

Dub, *v.*[3] *slang.* 1840. [?] *intr. To d. up*: to pay up.

‖**Dubash** (dubɑ·ʃ). *E. Ind.* 1698. [ad. Hindī *dōbāshī*, f. *dō* two + *bhāshā* language.] An (Indian) interpreter or commissionaire.

‖**Dubba, dubber** (dɒ·bə). *E. Ind.* 1698. [Urdū *dabbah* vessel made of raw skins.] A leather bottle or skin bag, used chiefly in India for holding oil, ghee, and other liquids.

Dubbing, *vbl. sb.* ME. [f. DUB *v.*[1] + -ING[1].] **1.** The act of dubbing, as a knight, etc.; see DUB *v.*[1] 1, 2. **2.** *Angling.* The materials used in dressing a fly 1676. **3.** A preparation of grease for softening leather and making it waterproof. Also *dubbin.* 1781. **4.** The act of smoothing, etc.; *spec.* working timber with an adze 1823.

Dubiety (diubəi·ĕti). 1750. [ad. late L. *dubietas*, f. *dubius.*] The state or quality of being dubious; doubtfulness; also, an instance of this.

The twilight of d. never falls upon him LAMB.

Dubiosity (diūbiǫ·sĭti). 1646. [f. L. *dubiosus*; see -ITY.] = DUBIOUSNESS; with *pl.*, a doubtful matter.

Men swallow falsities for truths, dubiosities for certainties SIR T. BROWNE.

Dubious (diū·biəs), *a.* 1548. [ad. L. *dubiosus*, f. *dubium* doubt.] **1.** Objectively doubtful; uncertain, undetermined; ambiguous, vague. **b.** Of uncertain issue 1635. **c.** Of questionable character 1860. **2.** Subjectively doubtful; wavering or fluctuating in opinion; hesitating 1632.

1. A d. honour STANLEY. b. In d. Battel MILT. *P. L.* I. 104. c. In very d. company 1884. 2. Fluctuations of a d. Will NORRIS. Hence **Du·biously** *adv.*, **-ness**, d. quality.

Dubitable (diū·bităb'l), *a.* 1624. [ad. L. *dubitabilis*, f. *dubitare* to DOUBT.] Liable to doubt or question. Hence **Du·bitably** *adv.*

†**Dubitancy.** 1648. [ad. L. **dubitantia*, f. as prec.] Doubt, hesitation, uncertainty –1669.

Dubitant (diū·bitănt), *a.* 1821. [ad. L. *dubitantem.*] Doubting; having doubts. *absol.* One who doubts.

Dubitate (diū·bitēˡt), *v. rare.* 1827. [f. L. *dubitat-*, *dubitare.*] *intr.* To doubt, hesitate, waver.

If .. he were to loiter dubitating, and not come CARLYLE.

Dubitation (diūbitēˡ·ʃən). 1450. [a. F., ad. L. *dubitationem.*] The action of doubting; doubt; a doubt.

Dubitative (diū·bitĕtiv), *a.* 1615. [ad. L. *dubitativus* (Tertullian); cf. F. *dubitatif.*] Inclined to doubt; expressing doubt or hesitancy. Hence **Du·bitatively** *adv.*

Duboisine (diuboi·səin). 1883. [See -INE.] *Chem.* An alkaloid obtained from an Australian shrub (*Duboisia myoporioides*), having qualities similar to those of hyoscyamine.

Ducal (diū·kăl), *a.* 1494. [a. F., ad. late L. *ducalis*, f. *ducem* (*dux*) leader, DUKE.] **a.** Of or pertaining to a duke or dukedom (also, a doge). **b.** Of the rank of duke, as *d. families* 1796.

Laws, which are for the most part the d. customs of Normandy BLACKSTONE. Hence **Du·cally** *adv.* in a d. manner; as a d.

Ducape (diukēˡ·p). 1678. [?] 'A plain-wove stout silk fabric of softer texture than *Gros de Naples*' (Beck).

Ducat (dɒ·kăt). ME. [a. F., ad. It. *ducato*, in late L. *ducatus* DUCHY, f. L. *dux* DUKE.] **1.** A gold (or silver) coin of varying value, formerly in use in most European countries. First issued by Roger II of Sicily, as Duke of Apulia. The gold ducat was worth about 9*s.* 4*d.*; the silver ducat of Italy about 3*s.* 6*d.* **2.** *loosely.* A piece of money; *pl.* Money, cash 1775.

Ducatoon (dɒkătū·n). 1611. [a. F. *ducaton* a small or half ducat, ? ad. It. *ducatone* (being a bigger coin than the gold ducat); see -OON.] A silver coin formerly current in some European states, worth from 5*s.* to 6*s.* sterling.

‖**Duces tecum** (diū·sīz tī·kɒm). 1617. [L. phrase: more fully *sub pœna duces tecum*, 'Under penalty thou shalt bring with thee'.] *Law.* A writ commanding a person to produce in court documents, etc. required as evidence.

Duchess (dɒ·tʃes). ME. [a. F. *duchesse*, ad. late L. *ducissa*, f. *dux* (*duc-*); see DUKE. Usu. spelt *dutchess* till c 1810.] **1.** The wife or widow of a duke. **b.** A lady holding a DUCHY in her own right. **2.** *slang.* A woman of imposing appearance. [Cf. F. *duchesse.*] 1700. **3.** A size of roofing slate, 24 by 12 inches 1823.

1. *Hen. VIII*, II. iii. 38.

‖**Duchesse** (dɒ·tʃės, ‖düʃęs). 1878. [Fr. (see prec.).] A kind of satin, also of Brussels pillow-lace. *D. dressing chest*, etc., a dressing-table with a swing glass; so *d. toilet set*, a set of covers for a dressing-table.

Duchy (dɒ·tʃi). ME. [a. OF. *duchée*, later *duché*, fem., repr. a L. type **ducitatem* dukeship, and later OF. *duché* masc.:—late L. *ducatus* territory of a duke.] **1.** The territory ruled by a duke or duchess. **2.** *attrib.* **a.** *gen.*, as *d. rights.* **b.** *spec.* Of or relating to the Royal duchies of Cornwall and Lancaster; as *d. land, tenement*, etc.; **d.-chamber,** the court room at Westminster of the **d.-court** of Lancaster, having equitable jurisdiction over lands holden of the Crown in right of the d.

Duck (dɒk), *sb.*[1] [OE. *duce* (? *dūce*), from *u-* (or *ū-*) grade of *dūcan* to DUCK, dive; cf. Da. *duk-and* lit. dive-duck, etc.] **1.** A swimming bird of the genus *Anas* and kindred genera of the family *Anatidæ.*

Without addition, the word is applied to the common *domestic d.*, a domesticated form of the *wild d.* or MALLARD. In its widest technical sense, the name includes golden-eyes, pintails, scoters, sheldrakes, teal, widgeons, and other related groups; the geese, though *Anatidæ*, are not usually called 'ducks'.

b. *spec.* The female of this fowl: the male being the DRAKE ME. **2.** *transf.* A term of endearment 1590. **3.** Short for *lame d.*; see sense 6. **4.** A boy's game, also called *duckstone*; a stone used in this game, and occas. a player 1821. **5.** *Cricket.* Short for DUCK'S EGG 1868. **6.** *Lame d.*: a disabled person or thing: *spec.* (*Stock Exchange*): a defaulter. Also *d.* 1761. **7.** *Bombay d.* = BUMMALO 1860. **8.** *attrib.* 1884.

1. Though thou canst swim like a Ducke, thou art made like a Goose *Temp.* II. ii. 136.

Comb.: **d.-boards,** a narrow slatted path laid over wet ground; **-legged** *a.*, having unusually short legs; so *duck-legs*; **-shot,** shot of a size for shooting wild ducks; **-weight,** a d. of stone or clay used as a weight in ancient Assyria and Babylonia. **b. d.-ant,** the termite: **-eagle,** a S. Afr. species of eagle; **-mole,** the Duck-billed Platypus; **-mud,** Crow-silk; **-snipe,** (Bahamas), the willet. *Symphemia semipalmata*; **-wheat** = D.-BILL wheat; etc.

Duck, *sb.*[2] 1554. [f. DUCK *v.*] **1.** A dip 1843. **2.** A rapid jerky lowering of head or body.

2. The ducks and nods Which weak minds pay to rank LAMB.

Duck, *sb.*[3] 1640. [app. a. 17th c. Du. *doek* linen; = Ger. *tuch*, etc.] **1.** A strong untwilled linen (or later, cotton) fabric, lighter and finer than canvas; used for small sails and men's (*esp.* sailors') clothing. **2.** *pl.* Trousers of duck 1825. **3.** *attrib.* 1849.

Duck (dɒk), *v.* [The ME. forms correspond to an OE. **dūcan* = LG. *dûken* (Da. *duiken*), MHG. *tûchen*, G. *tauchen*, a WGer. strong vb. of 2nd ablaut series (with *ū* in pres. stem). It was shortened in Eng. to *duck* about 1550, prob. after DUCK *sb.*[1] Cf. however Ger. *ducken*:—**dukjan*; also Sw. *dyka* to duck, dive.] **1.** *intr.* To plunge or dive, or suddenly go down under water, and emerge again. Also *fig.* **2.** To bend or stoop quickly; to bob; hence *fig.* to cringe, yield; so, *to d. under* 1530. **3.** *trans.* To plunge momentarily *in*, *into*, or *under* water or other liquid ME. **4.** To lower (the head) suddenly for a moment; to jerk down 1598.

1. (To avoid their Darts) he sometimes ducked HEYLIN. 2. To d. at the whiz of a cannon-ball POPE. Law ducks to Gospel here BROWNING. 3. I say, d. her in the loch, and then we will see whether she is witch or not SCOTT. 4. We ducked our heads, and hurried 1884.

Duck and Drake. 1583. [from the motion of the stone over the water.] A pastime consisting in throwing a flat stone or the like over the surface of water so that it shall skip as many times as possible before sinking. (Often in *pl.*) Also *fig.* Also *attrib.*

Phr. *To make ducks and drakes of* or *with, to play (at) duck and drake with*: to throw away idly and carelessly; to handle recklessly; to squander.

Du·ck-bill, *sb.* 1556. [f. DUCK *sb.* + BILL *sb.*²] **a.** Short for *duck-bill wheat*; red wheat. **b.** = Duck-billed platypus; see below 1840. Hence **Duck-billed** *a.* having a bill like a duck's. **Duck-billed platypus,** the *Ornithorhynchus* of Australia, a monotrematous mammal having a horny beak like a duck's bill; **duck-billed speculum,** a speculum flattened like a duck's bill.

Ducker (dɒ·kəɹ). 1475. [f. DUCK *v.* + -ER¹. In sense 2 = Du. *duiker*, Ger. *taucher* diver (bird).] **1.** A person who ducks; a diver 1483. **2.** A diving-bird; *spec* the little grebe or dabchick 1475. **3.** 'A cringer' (J.).

Duck-hawk. 1812. [f. DUCK *sb.*¹ + HAWK.] **1.** Eng. name of the marsh harrier or moor-buzzard (*Circus æruginosus*). **2.** *U.S.* The American variety of the peregrine falcon (*Falco peregrinus* var. *anatum*) 1884.

Ducking (dɒ·kiŋ), *vbl. sb.*¹ 1539. [f. DUCK *v.* + -ING¹.] **a.** Immersion in water 1581. **b.** Prompt bending of the head or body.

Du·cking, *vbl. sb.*² 1577. [f. DUCK *sb.*¹] The catching or shooting of wild ducks.

Du·cking-pond. 1607. [f. DUCKING *vbl. sb.*¹ and ².] **a.** A pond on which ducks may be hunted or shot. **b.** A pond for the ducking of offenders.

Du·cking-stool. 1597. A chair at the end of an oscillating plank, in which scolds, etc., or dishonest tradesmen, were tied and ducked in water, as a punishment.

Du·ckling. 1440. [-LING.] A young duck.

Duck's bill. 1601. The bill of a duck. Applied to surgical instruments, etc., of this shape. *Comb.*, as **duck's-bill bit,** a form of bit for use in a brace in wood-boring; **duck's-bill limpet,** a limpet of the genus *Parmophorus.*

Duck's egg. Also **duck egg.** ME. **a.** The egg of a duck; hence, **b.** in *Cricket*, the score of zero or 'o'; no runs. **c.** The colour of the egg of a duck; used *attrib.* 1876.

Duck's meat, duckmeat. 1538. = next.

Du·ckweed. 1440. A name for plants of the genus *Lemna*, which float on still water, and cover the surface like a green carpet.

Ducky (dɒ·ki). 1819. [f. DUCK *sb.*¹ + -Y⁶.] A term of endearment; as *adj.*, an emotional epithet of commendation.

Duct (dɒkt). 1650. [ad L. *ductus* leading, etc., in med.L. aqueduct, f. *ducere.*] †**1.** The action of leading; lead -1684. †**2.** Course, direction -1718. †**3.** A stroke drawn or traced or the tracing of it (cf. L. *ductus litterarum*) -1796. **4.** A conduit, channel, or tube for conveying water, etc. 1713. **5.** *Phys.* A tube or canal in the animal body. Now restricted to the vessels conveying the chyle, lymph, and secretions. 1667. **b.** *Bot.* One of the vessels of the vascular tissue of plants 1858. **Du·ctless** *a.*

Ductile (dɒ·ktil, -əil), *a.* ME. [a. F., ad. L. *ductilis* that may be led or drawn, f. *ducere.*] **1.** Malleable; flexible, not brittle. Still freq. in lit. use. **b.** That may be drawn out into wire or thread, tough. (The current techn. use.) 1626. **2.** That may be led or drawn; tractable, pliant; plastic 1622. Also *fig.*

1. All Bodies D. (as Metals that will be drawne into Wire) BACON. 2. D. wax POPE, language H. ROGERS, streams 1834. The man was in truth childishly soft and d. MRS. H. WARD. var. **Du·ctible** (now *rare*). Hence **Du·ctile·ly** *adv.*, **-ness** (*rare*). **Ductili·meter,** an instrument for measuring the ductility of metals.

Ductility (dɒkti·lĭti). 1654. [f. DUCTILE + -ITY.] **1.** Capability of being extended by beating, drawn into wire, worked upon, or bent. Also *fig.* **2.** Tractableness, docility 1654.

†**Du·ction.** ME. [ad. L. *ductionem.*] The action of leading or bringing (*lit.* and *fig.*) -1696.

Ductor (dɒ·ktəɹ, -ǫ̆ɹ). 15.. [a. L.] **1.** A leader. **2.** *Printing.* A roller which conveys the ink from the ink-fountain to the distributing-rollers. Also *d.-roller.* 1851.

†**Du·cture.** 1644. [ad. L. type **ductura.*] **1.** Leading -1716. **2.** Movement in some direction -1691. **3.** A duct 1670.

Dud (dɒd). Chiefly *pl.* **duds** (dɒdz). *colloq.* and *dial.* ME. [?] **1.** Usually (now always) *pl.* = Clothes. (depreciatory or joc.) **b.** 'Things' 1662. **2.** *pl.* Rags, tatters. (Rarely *sing.*) 1508. **3.** A counterfeit thing; a futile person or thing 1825; also as *adj.* 1903. Hence **Du·ddery** (*dial.*), a place where woollen cloth is sold or made.

Dudder (dɒ·dəɹ), *v.* Now *dial.* 1658. [var. of DIDDER.] *intr.* To shudder, shiver.

Dude (diūd). *U.S.* 1883. [?] A name given in ridicule to a man who is ultra-fastidious in dress, speech, deportment, and 'form'; hence, an exquisite, a dandy; as, *a social d.*, *a club d.*, etc. Hence **Dudine** (-ī·n), a female d.; **Du·dish** *a.*

Dudeen (dudī·n). Also **dudheen,** etc. 1841. Irish name for a short clay tobacco-pipe.

†**Dudgen.** 1589. [? same as DUDGEON *sb.*¹] **A.** *sb.* Trash 1592. **B.** *adj.* **1.** Mean, poor -1593. **2.** ? Ordinary, homely -1618.

Dudgeon (dɒ·dʒən), *sb.*¹ ME. [Occurs as *digeon* in AF.: no corresp. wd. is found in French.] †**1.** A kind of wood (according to Gerarde, boxwood) used by turners, *esp.* for handles of knives, daggers, etc. -1660. †**2.** The hilt of a dagger made of this. SHAKS. **3.** Hence **d.-dagger,** and later **d.**: A dagger with a d.-haft; also, a butcher's steel (*arch.*) 1581.

Dudgeon (dɒ·dʒən), *sb.*² 1573. [?] A feeling of anger or resentment; ill humour. Usu. in phr. *in d.*, and *esp.* with *high, great, deep.*

I hope you are not going out in d., cousin CONGREVE.

Due (diū). [ME. *dewe*, a. OF. *deü*, later *dû* :—late L. **debutum* for *debitum.*]

A. *adj.* **1.** That is owing or payable, as a debt. †**2.** Belonging or falling *to* by right -1655. **3.** That ought to be given or rendered; merited ME. **4.** Such as ought to be; fitting; proper; rightful ME. **5.** Such as is requisite or necessary; adequate ME. **6.** To be ascribed or attributed; owing to, caused by, in consequence of (*rare* bef. 19th c.) 1661. **7.** Under engagement or contract to be ready or arrive (at a defined time) 1833.

1. Three thousand Ducats d. vnto the Iew SHAKS. 3. Silent, not wanting d. respect, the crowd CRABBE. 4. In d. Form 1728, time BUDGELL, course 1876. 5. Upon d. consideration LD. BROUGHAM. 6. The difficulty..is really d. to our ignorance JOWETT. 7. The train is d. in London at 5 a.m. (*mod.*). *Comb.*, etc., as **d.-bill** (*U.S.*), a brief written acknowledgement of a debt, not made payable to order, like a promissory note; **d. date,** the date on which a bill falls d.; so †**d. day.** Hence **Due·ness.**

B. *adv.* **1.** = DULY, in various senses. (*arch.*) 1597. **2.** With reference to the points of the compass: Properly; right, straight; directly. (Orig. *Naut.* Allied to A. 4.) 1601.

2. There lies your way, d. West *Twel. N.* III. i. 145.

Due (diū), *sb.* ME. [subst. use of DUE *a.*; cf. F. *dû* sb.] †**1.** That which is due; a debt -1682. **2.** That which is due to any one legally or morally 1582. **3.** That which is due by any one 1738. **4.** *spec.* A legal charge, toll, tribute, fee, or the like. Chiefly in *pl.* 1546. †**5.** Duty -1697. †**6.** A right -1669. **7.** *Naut.* What is duly or thoroughly done: in phr. *for a full d.* = for good and all 1830.

1. *Timon* II. ii. 16. 2. To cheat the hangman of his d. 1612. Phr. *To give the devil his d.*: to do justice to a person one dislikes. 6. *Of* (*by*) *d.*, by right: The key of this infernal Pit by d...I keep MILT.

†**Due,** *v.*¹ ME. [var. of DOW *v.*²; cf. ENDUE.] To endow -1591.

†**Due,** *v.*² *rare.* [f. DUE *a.*] *impers.* To be due. DRAYTON.

Dueful (diū·fŭl), *a. arch.* [Coined by Spenser from DUE *a.*; cf. *rightful.*] Due, appropriate.

Duel (diū·ĕl), *sb.* 1591. [a. F. *duel*, ad. It. *duello* or med.L. *duellum*, ancient form of L. *bellum.*] **1.** A regular fight between two persons; *esp.* one prearranged and fought with deadly weapons, usu. in the presence of two witnesses called seconds, to settle a quarrel or point of honour 1611. **2.** Duelling as a practice 1615. **3.** Any contest between two persons or parties 1591.

1. They fought a Duell, that is, a single combat in a field hard by Spira CORYAT. 3. A d. in the form of a debate COWPER. Hence **Du·elsome** *a.* inclined to duelling THACKERAY.

Duel (diū·ĕl), *v.* 1645. [f. prec.] **1.** *intr.* To fight a duel. †**2.** *trans.* To encounter or kill in a duel -1716. Hence **Du·eller, dueler,** a duelist. **Du·elling, dueling** *vbl. sb.* the fighting of duels; also *attrib.*

Duellist, duelist (diū·ĕlist). 1592. [f. DUEL *sb.* + -IST.] One who fights duels, or practises duelling. Also *fig.*

The blind wrestling of controversial duellists FROUDE.

‖**Duello** (due·lo). 1588. [It.; = DUEL.] **1.** Duelling as a custom; the code of duellists. †**2.** A duel (*lit.* and *fig.*) -1826.

1. But observes not the lawes of the D. OVERBURY.

Duenna (diu,e·nă). 1668. [Sp. *dueña* (dwe·nʸă), formerly spelt *duenna* :—L. *domina.*] **1.** The chief lady in waiting upon the queen of Spain. **b.** An elderly woman, half governess, half companion, having charge over the girls of a Spanish family 1681. **2.** Any elderly woman whose duty it is to watch over a young one; a chaperon 1708.

2. Guarded by a dragon-like d. 1877.

Duet, duett (diu,e·t), *sb.* 1740. [ad. It. *duetto*; see below.] *Mus.* A composition for two voices or two performers. Hence **Due·t, -ett** *v. intr.* to perform a d.

‖**Duettino** (diuettī·no). 1839. [It.: dim. of next.] 'A duet of short extent and concise form' (Grove).

Duetto (due·tto). 1724. [It.: dim. of *duo* a duet.] = DUET.

Duff (dɒf), *sb.*¹ 1840. [orig. a north. pronunc. of DOUGH.] **a.** Dough, paste (*dial.*). **b.** A flour pudding boiled in a bag.

Duff (dɒf), *sb.*² *local.* 1844. [? same as prec.; or echoic.] **1.** *Sc* The spongy part of a loaf, a turnip, etc. **b.** 'A soft spongy peat' (Jam.). **2.** *Sc.* and *U.S.* The decaying vegetable matter which covers forest ground 1844. **3.** Coal-dust; slack. Also *d.-coal.* 1865.

Duff (dɒf), *v.*¹ *slang* or *colloq.* 1838. [? f. DUFFER *sb.*¹] **1.** *trans.* To 'fake up'. **2.** *Australia.* To alter the brands on (stolen cattle); to steal (cattle), altering the brands 1869.

Duff, *v.*² 1897. [f. DUFFER *sb.*²] *Golf.* To perform (a shot) badly. Also *fig.*

‖**Duffada·r.** *E. Ind.* 1800. [Pers. and Urdū.] A petty officer of native police; a non-commissioned officer (= corporal) in regiments of Irregular Cavalry.

Duffel, duffle (dɒ·f'l). 1677. [From *Duffel*, a town near Antwerp.] **1.** A coarse woollen cloth having a thick nap or frieze. **2.** *U.S.* Change of flannels; a sportsman's outfit 1884. **3.** *attrib.*

1. Let it be of duffil grey WORDSW.

Duffer (dɒ·fəɹ), *sb.*¹ 1756. [Conn. w. DUFF *v.*¹] **1.** One who sells trashy articles as valuable, upon false pretences. **2.** A pedlar or hawker 1795. **3.** [f. DUFF *v.*¹] One who 'fakes up' sham articles 1851. **b.** (*Australia.*) One who duffs cattle 1889.

1. Duffers, who vend pretended smuggled goods MAYHEW.

Du·ffer, *sb.*² *colloq.* and *slang.* 1842. [app. conn. w. DUFF *v.*¹] **1.** *colloq.* A person without practical ability or capacity. Also, generally, a stupid or foolish person. **2.** *slang.* Any article that is no good; *esp.* counterfeit coin 1875.

Du·ffer, *v.* 1885. [f. prec.] *intr.* Of a mine: To prove no good, give *out.*

Duffing (dɒ·fiŋ), *ppl. a. slang.* 1851. [f. DUFF *v.*¹] **1.** That passes off a worthless article as valuable 1862. **2.** Rubbishy and offered as valuable 1851. **3.** Duffer-like 1881.

Duffle; see DUFFEL.

Dufoil (diū·foil). 1688. [f. L. *duo* + FOIL; cf. *trefoil*, etc.] *Her.* A two-leaved flower; = TWAYBLADE.

Dufrenite (diufre·nəit). [Named 1833 after M. *Dufrénoy*, a French mineralogist.] *Min.* Hydrous phosphate of iron, occurring in greenish nodules and fibrous masses.

‖**Dufter** (dɒ·ftəɹ). *E. Ind.* 1776. [Urdū *daftar*, ad. Gr. διφθέρα skin.] **a.** A bundle of official papers; a register, record. **b.** A business office. **Dufterda·r,** a Turkish officer of finance 1599.

Dug (dɒg), *sb.*¹ 1530. [? radically conn. w. Sw. *dägga*, Da. *dægge* to suckle.] The pap or udder of female mammalia; also the teat or nipple. As applied to a woman's breast, now contemptuous.

†**Dug**, *sb.*[2] 1607. *Angling.* A kind of red worm used as a bait. Also *d.-worm.* -1674.

Dug (dɒg), *ppl. a.* 1715. [pa. pple. of DIG *v.*] Obtained by digging, etc.; see the vb.

Dugong (diū·gɒŋ). 1800. [a. Malay name *dūyong.*] A large herbivorous mammal (*Halicore dugong*, order *Sirenia*) of the Indian seas.

Dug-out. 1819. [See *dig out*, DIG *v.*]

A. *ppl. a.* Hollowed out by digging 1886.

B. *sb.* (chiefly *U.S.*) 1. A canoe made by hollowing out the trunk of a tree 1819. 2. A rough dwelling formed by an excavation (usually in a slope or bank), roofed with turf, canvas, etc. 1855. b. *spec.* A roofed shelter used in trench warfare 1904. 3. A person who has retired, but whose services are utilized on emergency; a superannuated officer in temporary service (chiefly *Army slang*) 1912.

‖**Duiker, duyker** (dəi·kəɹ). 1777. [Du. *duiker* (dvü·kəɹ) = Ger. *taucher* ducker or diver.] In full *duikerbok*: A small S. Afr. antelope, *Cephalopus mergens*, which plunges through the bushes when pursued.

Duke (diūk), *sb.* [ME. *duc, duk*, a. F. *duc*, in OF. nom. *dux, ducs*, early ad. L. *dux, ducem.*] †1. A leader; a captain or general; a chief, ruler -1591. 2. In some European countries: A sovereign prince, the ruler of a duchy ME. †b. As tr. DOGE -1820. c. Cf. GRAND DUKE. 3. In Great Britain and some other countries: A hereditary title of nobility, ranking next below that of a prince ME. 4. Name of a kind of cherry 1664. 5. *pl. slang.* The hand or fist 1879.

1. Jesus Crist d. of our batel WYCLIF. 2. Thy father was the D. of Millaine and A Prince of power *Temp.* I. ii. 58. The D., and the Senators of Venice greet you *Oth.* IV. i. 230. 3. *Royal d.*, a d. who is a member of the royal family, taking precedence of other dukes. Hence **Duke** *v. intr.* (also *to d. it*), to play the d., act as a d. **Du·keling**, a petty d.; a duke's child. **Du·keship**, the office or dignity of a d.; also (*joc.*) as a title.

Dukedom (diū·kdəm). 1460. [See -DOM.] 1. The territory ruled by a duke; a duchy. 2. The office or dignity of a duke 1534.

Dukery (diū·kəri). 1565. [See -ERY, -RY.] 1. †A dukedom -1596. b. A duchy. (Now only as *nonce-wd.*) 1855. 2. The residence or estate of a duke; *spec.* (usually *pl.*) a district in Nottinghamshire containing several ducal estates 1837.

‖**Dulcamara** (dɒlkămēᵊ·ră). 1578. [med.L., f. L. *dulcis* + *amara* (sc. *herba*).] *Herb.* and *Pharm.* The Woody Nightshade or Bittersweet, *Solanum Dulcamara.* Hence **Dulcama·rin**, *Chem.* the glucoside $C_{22}H_{34}O_{10}$, obtained from d.

†**Dulca·rnon.** ME. [a. med.L. *dulcarnon*, corrupted from Arab. *dhū 'lqarnayn* two-horned.] A dilemma (= med.L. *cornutus*, CORNUTE *sb.*); a non-plus; *at d.*, at one's wit's end -1534.

†**Dulce** (dɒls), *a.* 1500. [ad. L. *dulcis.*] Sweet -1709. Also as *adv.* **Du·lce-ly** *adv.*, **-ness.**

Dulce, *sb.* 1659. [f. prec.] †1. Sweetness, gentleness -1728. ‖2. [Sp.] A sweet substance; must 1870.

†**Dulce**, *v.* 1579. [Refash. from DOUCE, *doulce* v.] *trans.* To sweeten; to soften, soothe -1610.

Dulcet (dɒ·lsėt). ME. [A refash. of *doucet* (from F.), after L. *dulcis.*]

A. *adj.* 1. Sweet to the taste or smell. (*Obs.* or *arch.*) 2. Sweet to the eye, ear, or feelings; pleasing; soothing. Now chiefly of sounds. ME.

1. D. creams MILT. *P. L.* v. 347. 2. My d. frinde 1567. D. Symphonies and voices sweet MILT.

B. *sb.* †1. A dulcet note 1575. †2. ? = DOUCET 3. 3. † = DOUCET 2. b. An organ stop resembling the Dulciana, but an octave higher in pitch 1876.

Dulcian (dɒ·lsiăn). 1852. [f. L. *dulcis.*] *Mus.* = BASSOON 2.

‖**Dulciana** (dɒlsiɑ·nă). 1776. [ad. med.L. *dulciana*, f. *dulcis.*] *Mus.* An 8-foot organ stop of a soft string-like tone.

Dulci·fluous, *a. rare.* 1727. [f. L. *dulcis* + *-fluus.*] Sweetly or softly flowing.

Dulcify (dɒ·lsifəi), *v.* 1599. [ad. L. *dulcificare*, f. *dulcis.*] 1. *trans.* To render sweet to the taste. †2. *Old Chem.* To wash the soluble salts out of; to neutralize the acidity of -1789. Also †*intr.* for *pass.* 3. To sweeten in temper; to mollify; to appease 1669. Hence **Du·lcifica·tion.**

†**Dulci·loquy.** *rare.* 1623. [ad. L. **dulciloquium.*] A soft manner of speaking (Dicts.).

Dulcimer (dɒ·lsiməɹ). 1475. [a. OF. *doulcemer* (Roquefort), *doulcemele* = obs. Sp. *dulcemele*; supposed to represent a L. *dulce melos* sweet air.] a. A musical instrument, having strings of graduated lengths stretched over a sounding board, which are struck with two hammers held in the hands. b. Sometimes applied erron. to wind-instruments, as in *Dan.* iii. 10, where 'bagpipe' would be more correct. 'Psaltery' in the same passage signifies 'dulcimer'. 1567.

‖**Dulcinea** (dɒlsi·nɪ̆ᵢă, dɒlsinī·ă). 1748. [Sp., f. *dulce* sweet.] The name of Don Quixote's mistress; hence, A mistress, sweetheart.

[**Dulciness**, in Dicts., an error for DULCENESS.]

Dulcite (dɒ·lsəit). 1863. [See -ITE.] *Chem.* A saccharine substance ($C_6H_{14}O_6$), isomeric with mannite, obtained from various plants, and known in the crude state as Madagascar manna. Called also **Dulcin, Dulcitol, Dulcose.**

Du·lcitude. 1623. [ad. L. *dulcitudo.*] Sweetness. So †**Du·lcity.**

†**Dulcorate** (dɒ·lkorėit), *v.* 1566. [f. ppl. stem of L. *dulcorare.*] To sweeten, DULCIFY -1675. Hence **Dulcora·tion.**

Duledge (diū·lėdʒ). 1721. [Cf. DOWEL.] A dowel or peg for connecting the felloes of the wheels of gun-carriages.

‖**Dulia** (dulǝi·ă). Also **douleia.** 1617. [med. L., a. Gr. δουλεία.] Servitude, service; *spec.* the inferior kind paid by Roman Catholics to saints and angels; opp. to LATRIA.

Dull (dɒl), *a.* [ME. *dul, dull*, OE. *dol* foolish (:—**dulo-*), from the Germanic *dul-*, ablaut form of *dwel-* to be foolish.] 1. Not quick in intelligence; obtuse, stupid. In early use, occas.: Fatuous, foolish. 2. Wanting sensibility. In dial. use, *esp.* Hard of hearing. ME. Of pain, etc.: Indistinctly felt 1725. 3. Slow in motion or action; not brisk ME. 4. Of persons, or their mood: Depressed; listless; not lively or cheerful ME. 5. Causing depression or ennui 1590. 6. Not sharp or keen; blunt (in *lit.* sense) ME. 7. Of physical qualities: Not clear, vivid, or intense; obscure; muffled; flat. b. Of the weather: Gloomy, overcast ME.

1. Dulle are þi wittes LANGL. A d. child HT. MARTINEAU. 2. When I..sleepe in d. cold Marble SHAKS. A d. ache (*mod.*). 3. A d. Sailer DAMPIER, boy HAZLITT. D. trade FAWCETT, Consols 1895. 4. You are d. to Night; prithee be merry STEELE. 5. A d. Campaign 1798, curate 1838. 6. Thy sithe is d. G. HERBERT. 7. Is not their Clymate foggy, raw, and d. SHAKS. The dawn was d. 1860.

Comb., as *d.-looking*; parasynthetic, as *d.-brained, -browed, -eyed, -headed, -hearted, -sighted, -witted*; also †**d.-house**, a mad-house.

Dull (dɒl), *v.* ME. [f. DULL *a.*] 1. *trans.* To render sluggish or inert; to stupefy. †2. To render dull of mood; the opposite of to enliven -1611. 3. To render less sensitive or less intense 1552. 4. To take off the sharpness of, to blunt ME. 5. To make dim or indistinct; to tarnish. Also *fig.* ME. 6. *intr.* To become stupid, inert, blunt, dim, etc. ME. †7. To grow listless; to tire *of.* (ME. only.)

1. D. not Deuice, by coldnesse and delay SHAKS. 2. I would not d. you with my song SHAKS. 3. To d. the sight LYTE, the inward pain TENNYSON. 4. How quickly the edge of their valour was dulled SOUTH. 6. The day had dulled somewhat BLACK.

Dullard (dɒ·lăɹd). ME. [See -ARD.]

A. *sb.* A stupid or dull person; a dolt, a dunce.

B. *adj.* Stupid, dull 1583.

Du·ller. *rare.* 1611. [See -ER[1].] One who or that which dulls.

†**Du·ll-head.** 1549. A slow-witted person; a fool -1624.

Dullish (dɒ·liʃ), *a.* ME. [See -ISH.] Somewhat dull.

Dullness, dulness (dɒ·lnės). ME. [f. DULL *a.* The former spelling is the more analogical.] The state or quality of being DULL, q. v.

Dully (dɒ·lᵢli), *adv.* ME. [f. DULL *a.* + -LY[2].] In a dull manner (see DULL *a.*).

Honest joggtrot men, who go on smoothly and d. GOLDSM.

Dulness; see DULLNESS.

Dulocracy (diulǫ·krăsi). Also **dou-.** 1656. [ad. Gr. δουλοκρατία.] Government by slaves.

Dulse (dɒls). 1684. [ad. Ir. and Gael. *duileasg*, in W. *delysg.*] An edible seaweed, *Rhodymenia palmata*, having bright red, deeply divided fronds. Also, locally, *Iridæa edulis.*

Duly (diū·li), *adv.* ME. [f. DUE *a.*] In DUE manner, order, form, or season; see quots.

Rent d. paid STEELE. The Man..who d. weighs an Hour YOUNG. Persons duely qualified 1769.

Duma (dū·mă). In Russia, an elective municipal council; *spec.* the elective legislative council of state of 1905-17.

Dumb (dɒm), *a.* (*sb.*) [A Com. Teut. adj.: OE. *dumb.* The original sense may have been 'stupid', 'not understanding'.] 1. Destitute of the faculty of speech. Also *fig.* 2. That does not or will not speak; silent; reticent ME. 3. Unaccompanied by speech 1538. 4. Not emitting sound; silent, mute; unheard 1606. 5. Applied to contrivances which take the place of a human agent. See DUMB-WAITER. 1782. 6. Silent to the understanding; meaningless; stupid. Now *rare.* 1531. b. *U.S. colloq.* (cf. G. *dumm*, Du. *dom*) Foolish, stupid. (Chiefly of persons.) 1823. 7. Lacking something normally belonging to things of the name 1638. †8. Lacking brightness; dull. DE FOE.

1. A dum mouthe SKELTON. The tongue of the dumbe [shall] sing *Isa.* xxxv. 6. *Deaf and d.*: see DEAF *a.* *To strike d.* to deprive for the moment of the faculty of speech. 2. This Spirit dumbe to vs, will speake to him *Haml.* I. i. 171. 3. *D. crambo*; see CRAMBO. *D. cake*, a cake made in silence on St. Mark's Eve, by maids, to discover their future husbands. Excellent d. discourse *Temp.* III. iii. 39. 4. All the while his whip is d. WORDSW. Its thunder made the cataracts d. SHELLEY. *D. peal*: a muffled peal of bells. 6. 'Twas not dumbe chance SIR T. BROWNE. 7. *D. ague*, one in which the paroxysms are obscure.

†B. *absol.* or as *sb.* 1. A dumb person -1596. 2. A state or fit of dumbness -1678.

Comb.: **d.-chalder** or **cleat**, a metal cleat, bolted to the back of the stern-post for one of the rudder-pintles to rest on (Smyth); **d. iron**, either of the two forward ends of the frame-side members of a motor chassis; **-scraping**, 'scraping wet-docks with blunt scrapers' (Smyth); **d. sheave**, a sheaveless block having a hole for a rope to be reeved through; **-tooling** (*Book-binding*) = *blind tooling*; **d. well**, a well sunk into a porous stratum, to carry off surface water or drainage; a *blind* or *dead* well.

Dumb, *v.* ME. [f. prec. adj.] †1. *intr.* To become dumb. (ME. only.) 2. *trans.* To render dumb, silent, or unheard 1608.

Dumb barge. 1869. [DUMB *a.* 7.] A barge without mast or sails, as a Thames lighter.

Dumb-bell (dɒ·mbel), *sb.* 1711. 1. Formerly, An apparatus, like that for swinging a church-bell, but without the bell, 'rung' for exercise. 2. A short bar, weighted at each end with a roundish knob; used in pairs, and swung for exercise 1785. 3. An object of the shape of a dumb-bell; *e.g.* certain crystals found in the urine; also, a diplococcus 1864.

Dumb cane. 1696. A W. Indian araceous plant, *Dieffenbachia Seguine*, which, when chewed, swells the tongue and destroys the power of speech.

Dumbfound, dumfound (dɒmfau·nd), *v.* 1653. [app. f. DUMB *a.* + (CON)FOUND.] *trans.* To strike dumb; to confound; to nonplus. Hence **Dumb-, dumfou·nder** *v.* in same sense.

Dumble-, in names of insects, app. = DUMMEL, but varying with *bumble-, humble-.*

Dumbledore, dumble-dore (dɒ·mb'lᵢdōᵊɹ). *local.* 1787. [f. DUMBLE- + DOR *sb.*[1]] A humble- or bumble-bee; also *dial.* a cockchafer.

Dumbly (dɒ·mli), *adv.* 1552. [See -LY[2].] In a dumb manner; speechlessly, mutely.

Dumbness (dɒ·mnės). ME. [f. DUMB *a.* + -NESS.] Dumb quality or condition; inability to speak; silence, muteness.

There was speech in their dumbnesse SHAKS.

Dumb show. 1561. 1. Formerly, A part of a play represented by action without speech. 2. Significant gesture without speech 1588.

2. Expressing in dumb Show those Sentiments [etc.] ADDISON.

Dumb-waiter. 1755. [See DUMB *a.* 7.] 1. An upright pole with revolving trays or shelves for holding dishes, cruets, etc. 2. (*U.S.*) A movable frame or lift, by which dishes, etc. are passed from one room or story of a house to another.

Dumdum (dɒ·mdɒm). 1897. [*Dum Dum*, name of military station and arsenal near Calcutta.] orig. *Dum Dum bullet*: A soft-nosed bullet which expands on impact.

Dumfound, -er, var. DUMBFOUND, -ER.

Dummel (dɒ·mĕl), *a. dial.* 1570. [app. f. DUMB.] Stupid, dull. Also *sb.*

†**Du·mmerer.** 1567. [f. DUMB *a.*] *Cant.* A beggar who pretended to be dumb -1834.

Dummy, dumby (dɒ·mi), *sb.* 1598. [f. DUMB *a.* + -Y. Cf. BLACKY, etc.] **1.** A dumb person (*colloq.*). **2.** At *Whist*, An imaginary player whose hand is exposed, and played by his partner; a game so played 1736. **b.** *Bridge.* The partner of the player who makes the first call in the accepted declaration, or his hand 1895. **3.** A person who has no active part in affairs; a dolt, blockhead 1796. **4.** One who is a mere tool of another 1866. **5.** A counterfeit object, as a sham package, a lay figure, etc. for showing clothes, a baby's indiarubber teat; etc. 1845. **6.** *attrib.* or *adj.* Counterfeit, sham 1843.

2. *Double d.*: a game in which two hands are exposed so that each of the two players manages two hands. **5.** Phr. *To give* or *sell the d.* (Rugby Football): to deceive an opponent by feigning to pass the ball. **6.** *D. whist*: see **2.**

Dump (dɒmp), *sb.*[1] 1523. [?] †**1.** A fit of abstraction, a reverie; perplexity; absence of mind. (Often in *pl.*) -1698. **2.** A fit of melancholy or depression; now only in *pl.* (*colloq.* and *joc.*): Low spirits 1529. †**3.** A mournful or plaintive melody or song; a tune; *occas.*, a kind of dance -1852.

1. [They] were in a great dumpe and perplexitie J. HOOKER. **2.** His head, like one in doleful d., Between his knees BUTLER. **3.** Some good old dumpe that Chaucers mistresse knew SIDNEY.

Dump, *sb.*[2] 1770. [prob. f. DUMPY *a.*[2]] A familiar term for objects of a dumpy shape.

a. A leaden counter, used by boys in games. **b.** A name of certain small coins; *esp.* a coin worth 1*s.* 3*d.* formerly current in Australia; hence (*slang* or *colloq.*) a small coin or amount; in *pl.* money. **c.** A bolt or nail used in ship-building (also *d.-bolt*, *-nail*). **d.** A globular sweetmeat, a bull's-eye.

Dump, *sb.*[3] *local.* 1788. [perh. from Norse; cf. Norw. *dump* pit, pool.] A deep hole in the bed of a river or pond.

Dump, *sb.*[4] 1825. [f. DUMP *v.*[1]] **1.** (Chiefly *U.S.*) A pile or heap of refuse, etc. dumped or thrown down 1871. **b.** A temporary depôt of ammunitions of war, etc.; hence, material deposited for use later, or the place of such deposit 1915. **2.** (Chiefly *U.S.*) A place where refuse, *esp.* from a mine or quarry, is dumped 1872. **3.** A dull, abrupt blow; a thud; a bump 1825.

Dump (dɒmp), *v.*[1] ME. [perh. from Norse; cf. Da. *dumpe*, Norw. *dumpa* to fall suddenly, to fall plump. But in mod. use partly echoic; cf. *thump*.] †**I.** *intr.* and *trans.* To plunge (down) ME. **II. 1.** *trans.* (Chiefly *U.S.*) To throw down in a lump or mass, as in tilting anything out of a cart; to shoot (rubbish, etc.); to fling down or drop with a bump. Also *fig.* 1828. **b.** To throw on the market in large quantities and at low prices; to send (surplus goods) to a foreign market for sale at low prices 1884. **c.** To deposit in or as in a dump (DUMP *sb.*[4] 1 b) 1919. **2.** *intr.* To strike with a thud 1832. **3.** *trans.* To compress (wool-bales), as by hydraulic pressure. (*Australia.*) 1872.

Hence **Du·mping** *vbl. sb.*; *concr.* that which is dumped; *attrib.* used for dumping, as *d.-bucket*, *-cart*, *-ground*, etc.

†**Dump,** *v.*[2] 1530. [f. DUMP *sb.*[1]] **1.** *intr.* To fall into a reverie; to muse. **b.** To be in the dumps. -1590. **2.** *trans.* To cast into melancholy, grieve, cast down -1614.

Du·mpage. *U.S.* 1864. [f. DUMP *v.*[1]] The work of dumping; the privilege of dumping on a particular spot; the fee paid for the privilege.

Dumper (dɒ·mpəɹ). *U.S.* 1881. **a.** One who dumps. **b.** A dumping-cart or truck.

Dumpish (dɒ·mpiʃ), *a.* 1545. [f. DUMP *sb.*[1] + -ISH.] †**1.** Slow-witted; inert; insensible -1682. **2.** Dejected; in the dumps 1562. Hence **Du·mpish-ly** *adv.*, **-ness.**

Dumple (dɒ·mp'l), *v. rare.* 1625. [? f. DUMPY [2].] To bend or compress into a dumpy shape.

Dumpling (dɒ·mpliŋ). 1600. [prob. related to LG. and EFris. *dump* damp, moist, etc.] **1.** A pudding consisting of a mass of dough, more or less globular in form, either plain and boiled, or inclosing fruit and boiled or baked. **2.** A dumpy animal or person 1617.

Dumpty (dɒ·mpti), *a.* (*sb.*) 1847. By-form of DUMPY *a.*[2]

Dumpy (dɒ·mpi), *a.*[1] 1618. [f. DUMP *sb.*[1]] Dejected.

Dumpy (dɒ·mpi), *a.*[2] (*sb.*) 1750. [app. conn. w. DUMP *sb.*[2]]

A. Short and stout; as, *d. level* (Surveying), a spirit-level having a short telescope with a large aperture.

B. *sb.* **a.** A dumpy person or animal; *spec.* one of a breed of short-legged fowls. **b.** Short for *d. level*; see above 1808.

Dun (dɒn), *a.* [OE. *dun(n*; cf. Ir. and Gael. *donn* brown, Welsh *dwn* dusky.] **1.** Of a dull or dingy brown colour; now *esp.* dull greyish brown, like the hair of a mouse. **2.** Dark, dusky (from absence of light); murky. (Chiefly *poet.*) ME.

1. Its d. or iron-grey colour HUXLEY. **2.** D. Night has veil'd the solemn view COLLINS.

Comb.: **d.-bar**, a d.-coloured moth (*Cosmia trapezina*), having two bars on the fore-wings; **d. cow** (*local*), the shagreen ray, *Raia fullonica*; **d. cur** (*local*), the pochard = DUN-BIRD. Hence **Du·nness.** **Du·nnish** *a.*

Dun (dɒn), *sb.*[1] ME. [subst. use of prec.] **1.** Dun colour 1568. **2.** A dun horse. Formerly, a quasi-proper name for any horse. ME. **3.** *Angling.* A name for various dusky-coloured flies 1681.

Phr. *D.* [the horse] *is in the mire*, i. e. things are at a stand-still CHAUCER.

Dun, *sb.*[2] 1628. [Goes with DUN *v.*[3]] **1.** One who duns. **2.** An act of dunning, *esp.* for debt; a demand for payment 1673.

1. An Vniversitie Dunne..Hee is a sore beleaguerer of Chambers EARLE.

‖**Dun,** *sb.*[3] Also **doon.** 1605. [Ir. and Gael. *dun* (dun), hill, hill-fortress, W. *din.*] An ancient hill-fortress or fortified eminence.

Dun (dɒn), *v.*[1] [OE. *dunnian*, f. *dun(n*, DUN *a.*] *trans.* To make dun, dusky, or dingy. **b.** In New England, To cure (cod-fish) in a particular way, by which they become of a dun colour, and are termed *dunfish* 1828.

†**Dun,** *v.*[2] ME. [app. a. ON. *duna* to thunder, f. Ger. root *dun-*, whence also DIN.] *intr.* = DIN *v.* **1.** -1483.

Dun (dɒn), *v.*[3] 1626. [? same as DUN *v.*[2], or var. of DIN.] **1.** *trans.* To press repeatedly and persistently, to importune; *esp.* for money due. **2.** *transf.* To pester, plague 1659. **3.** Assoc. w. DIN *v.* 1753.

1. I dunn'd him for money and could not get it 1681.

Dun-bird. 1766. [f. DUN *a.* + BIRD.] The pochard, *Fuligula ferina.*

Dunce (dɒns), *sb.* 1527. [From John *Duns* Scotus, the scholastic theologian, called the Subtle Doctor, who died in 1308. The *Dunsmen* or *Dunses* were a predominating sect, until the 16th c., when the system was discredited by the humanists and the reformers.] †**1.** The name *Duns* used attrib. -1641. †**2.** A copy of the works of Duns Scotus; a text-book embodying his teaching; a gloss by him or after his manner -1633. **3.** An adherent of Duns Scotus; a hair-splitting reasoner; a cavilling sophist. Now *Hist.* 1577. †**4.** A pedant -1642. **5.** One who shows no capacity for learning; a dullard, blockhead 1577.

1. †*Duns man* = sense 3. **4.** A d., void of learning but full of books FULLER. **5.** Blockhead! d.! ass! coxcomb ARBUTHNOT.

Hence †**Dunce** *v.* to puzzle; to make a d. of. **Du·ncedom**, the domain of dunces; a dunce's condition or character; dunces collectively. **Du·ncely** *adv.* as a d., or †a follower of Duns Scotus. **Du·ncery, dunsery**, the practice or character of a †Scotist, or of a d. **Du·ncical** *a.* (now *rare*), of or pertaining to duncery. **Du·ncify** *v.* to make a d. of (*rare*). **Du·ncish** *a.* d.-like.

Dunch (dɒnʃ), *v. Sc.* and *n. dial.* ME. [?] *trans.* To push with a short rapid blow; now *esp.* to jog with the elbow. So **Dunch** *sb.*

Dunch, *a.* Now *dial.* 1574. [?] **1.** Deaf. **2.** Blind 16... **3.** Heavy as bread 1842.

Dunciad (dɒ·nsiæ̆d). 1728. [f. DUNCE *sb.*; see -AD.] The epic of dunces; a poem by Pope. Also, the commonwealth of dunces.

Dunder (dɒ·ndəɹ). 1793. [Corrupted from Sp. *redundar* to overflow.] The lees or dregs of cane-juice, used in the W. Indies in the fermentation of rum.

Dunderbolt, dial. f. THUNDERBOLT.

Dunderhead (dɒ·ndəɹhed). 1625. [?] A ponderously stupid person; a numskull. Hence **Du·nder-headed** *a.* So **Du·nderpate.**

Dun-diver. 1678. [f. DUN *a.* + DIVER **2.**] **a.** The female and young male of the goosander (*Mergus merganser*). **b.** *U.S.* The ruddy duck.

Dundreary (dɒndrīə·rī). Name of a character in T. Taylor's comedy *Our American Cousin* (1858); *D. whiskers*, long side whiskers without a beard.

Dune (diūn). 1790. [a. mod.F. *dune*, a. ODu. *dūna* = OE. *dún* DOWN *sb.*[1]] A mound, ridge, or hill of drifted sand on the sea-coast.

By the aid of embankments and the sand dunes of the coast LYELL.

Du·nfish, dun-fish. *U.S. local.* 1828. [f. DUN *a.*] Cod cured by dunning (see DUN *v.*[1]).

Dung (dɒŋ), *sb.* [OE. *dung* = OFris. *dung*, OHG. *tunga* manuring, G. *dung*, *dünger* manure.] **1.** Manure. **2.** (As constituting the usual manure.) The excrement of animals: as *cow-*, *horse-d.*, etc. ME. Also *transf.* and *fig.*

Comb.: **d.-bath** (*Dyeing*), a mixture of d., usually that of cows, with chalk in warm water, used to remove superfluous mordant from printed calico; **-beetle**, the dor-beetle; also, any of the group of beetles which roll up balls of d.; **-bird**, (*a*) the hoopoe; (*b*) = *dung-hunter*; **-chafer** = *dung-beetle*; **-fly**, a two-winged fly of the genus *Scatophaga*, feeding in ordure; **-hunter, -teaser**, the Dirt-bird or Dirty Allan.

Dung (dɒŋ), *v.* [In OE. *dyngian* from *dung* sb. In ME. assim. to the sb.] **1.** *trans.* To manure with dung. **2.** *intr.* Of animals: To eject excrement 1470. **3.** *Calico-printing.* To immerse in a dung-bath in order to remove superfluous mordant 1836.

‖**Dungaree** (dɒ·ŋgărī). Also **dungeree.** 1696. [Hindī *dungrī.*] A kind of coarse inferior Indian calico; *pl.* overalls of such material.

Du·ng-cart. ME. A cart used to convey manure.

Dungeon (dɒ·ndʒən), *sb.* ME. [a. F. *donjon*:—late L. *domnionem* in same sense, f. *domnus* (for *dominus*) lord; cf. DOMINION.] **1.** The great tower or keep of a castle. (Now usually spelt **donjon.**) **2.** A strong close cell; a deep dark vault ME. Also *transf.* and *fig.*

1. The noble tour of Ylion That of the citee was the cheef d. CHAUCER. **2.** Beneath the castle I could discern vast dungeons BERKELEY. A d. of learning (*Mod. Sc.*). *Comb.*: **d.-keep, -tower** = sense **1.**

Dungeon (dɒ·ndʒən), *v.* 1615. [f. prec. sb.] *trans.* To shut *up* in or as in a dungeon. Hence **Du·ngeoner**, one who or that which dungeons.

Du·ng-fork. ME. **1.** A kind of pitchfork used to lift or spread dung. **2.** *Entom.* A fæcifork.

Dunghill (dɒ·ŋhil), *sb.* ME. **1.** A heap of dung or refuse. **2.** *transf.* and *fig. esp.* as the type of the basest station 1526. **3.** *attrib.* Of or pertaining to a dunghill; fit for a dunghill; cowardly, as the *d. cock* ME.

1. Mud hovels, with their dunghills .. around them LEVER. **2.** The condition from which this son of a d. sprung 1768. Out, d.! dar'st thou braue a Nobleman SHAKS. *Comb.*: **d.-cock, -fowl, -hen**, common barndoor fowls, as dist. from the game-cock, etc.

Dungy (dɒ·ŋi), *a.* ME. [See -Y [1].] **1.** Of the nature of dung; abounding in dung 1606. **2.** Filthy or vile as dung.

1. Our dungie earth alike Feeds Beast as Man *Ant. & Cl.* I. i. 35.

‖**Duniwassal** (dū·ni,wa·săl). 1565. [Gael. *duine uasal* lit. gentleman, = *duine* man + *uasal* well-born.] A (Highland) gentleman of secondary rank; a cadet of a family of rank.

Dunker (dɒ·ŋkəɹ), **Tunker** (tɒ·ŋkəɹ). 1756. [ad. Ger. *tunker*, f. *tunken* (*dunken*) to dip.] A member of a body of German-American Baptists, who administer baptism only to adults, and by triple immersion. var. **Du·nkard.**

Dunkirk (dɒ·nkɔ̄ɹk). 1602. Name of a town on the coast of French Flanders; hence, a privateer from that town. Also *transf.* and *fig.* Hence **Du·nkirker**, a D., or one of its crew.

Dunlin (dʊ·nlin). 1531. [dial. f. *dunling*, f. DUN *a.* + -LING.] The red-backed sandpiper (*Tringa alpina*). Also an Amer. species (*T. pacifica*).

Dunnage (dʊ·nėdʒ), *sb.* 1623. [In 17th c. *dynnage, dinnage*. Origin unkn.] *Naut.* Brushwood, mats, or any light material, stowed among and beneath the cargo of a vessel to keep it from injury by chafing or wet. Hence **Du·nnage** *v.* to stow or secure with d. Also *intr.*

Dunner (dʊ·nəɹ). 1700. [f. DUN *v.*[3]] One who duns another, *esp.* for money due; a dun.

Dunnock (dʊ·nǒk). 1475. [app. f. DUN *a.* + -OCK; from its brown plumage. Cf. *dunlin.*] **1.** The hedge-sparrow (*Accentor modularis*). **2.** (form *dinnick*) The Wryneck (*local*) 1863.

Du·nny, *a. dial.* 1708. [? f. DUN *v.*[2]] Dull of hearing, deaf; stupid. Hence **Du·nniness.**

Duns, dunse, etc., obs. ff. DUNCE, etc.

Dunstable (dʊ·nstăb'l). 1549. [A town in Bedfordshire.] †**1.** *attrib.* in phr. *D. way*, app. referring orig. to the road from London to Dunstable, a part of the Roman Road called Watling Street; used proverbially as a type of directness and plainness –1744. †**b.** Hence as *adj.*: Direct, plain, downright –1817. †**c.** as *sb.* in phr. *Plain* (or *downright*) *D.*: plain language –1824. **2.** *attrib.* Made at D., or in the D. manner, as a kind of straw plait 1849.

1. As plain as D. Road FULLER. That's the plain d. of the matter, Miss RICHARDSON.

Dunstone (dʊ·nˌstōun). 1777. [f. DUN *a.*, q. v.] *Geol.* Stone of a dun or dull brown colour; as magnesian limestone, ironstone, sandstone, and sometimes dolerite.

Dunt (dʊnt), *sb. Sc.* and *dial.* ME. [perh. a var. of DINT *sb.*] **a.** A firm but dull-sounding blow. **b.** A beat of the heart 1768.

Dunt (dʊnt), *v. Sc.* and *dial.* 1570. [f. prec.] **1.** To knock with a dull sound. Also *absol.* and *intr.* **2.** *intr.* Of the heart: To beat violently 1724.

Dunter (dʊ·ntəɹ). *local.* 1693. [f. DUNT *v.*] **1.** The eider-duck. Also *d.-goose, -duck.* **2.** A porpoise 1825.

‖**Duo** (dū·o). 1590. [It., a. L.] *Mus.* A duet.

Duo-, L. *duo* = Gr. δύο (*dyo*), 'two'; a combining form. Sometimes improp. used for BI- (or in Gr. wds. DI-); *e.g.* **Duoca·meral** = bicameral; **Du·oglott** = diglott; etc.

Duode·cagon, -he·dron = DODECAGON, -HEDRON.

Duodecahe·dral, *a.* = DODECAHEDRAL.

Duodecim-, L. *duodecim* twelve, an initial element; *e.g.* in **Duodeci·mfid** *a.* [L. *-fidus* cleft], divided into twelve parts.

Duodecimal (diuˌode·simăl). 1714. [f. L. *duodecimus*; see -AL.]

A. *adj.* Relating to twelfth parts or to the number twelve; proceeding by twelves 1727.

B. *sb.* **Duodecimals,** a method of multiplying together quantities given in feet, inches, etc., without reducing them to one denomination; also called *cross-multiplication.*

‖**Duodecimo** (diuˌode·simo). 1658. [L. (*in*) *duodecimo* in a twelfth (*sc.* of a sheet).] **1.** The size of a book, or of a page of a book, in which each leaf is one-twelfth of a sheet: usu. abbreviated 12mo. **2.** A volume of this size 1712. **3.** *attrib.* or *adj.* 1777.

2. The Author of a D. ADDISON. **3.** Lady Betty.. was taking the dust..in a sort of d. phaeton SHERIDAN.

Duode·cuple, *a.* [f. *duodecim*, after DECUPLE.] Twelvefold. ARBUTHNOT.

Duodenal (diuˌodī·năl), *a.* 1843. [ad. mod.L. *duodenalis*, f. *duodenum*.] Pertaining or relating to the duodenum.

Duode·nal, *sb.* 1874. *Mus.* The symbol of the root of a DUODENE.

Duodenary (diuˌodī·nări). 1681. [ad. L. *duodenarius* containing twelve.]

A. *adj.* **1.** *Arith.* Pertaining to twelve; proceeding by twelves 1857. **2.** *Mus.* Relating to duodenes 1874.

1. The d. system of calculation 1890.

B. *sb.* †**1.** A period of twelve years 1681. **2.** *Mus.* A keyboard constructed according to duodenes 1874.

Duodene (diū·odīn). 1874. [f. med.L. *duodena* a group of twelve, f. L. *duodeni* twelve each.] *Mus.* Name for a group of twelve notes having certain fixed relations of pitch, in a proposed scheme for obtaining exact intonation on a keyboard instrument.

‖**Duodenum** (diūˌodī·nɒ̆m). ME. [med.L. (so called from its length, = *duodenum digitorum* space of twelve fingers' breadth, f. *duodeni* (see prec.).] *Anat.* The first portion of the small intestine immediately below the stomach, terminating in the jejunum. Hence **Duodeni·tis,** inflammation of the d.; **Duodeno·stomy** [Gr. στόμα], **Duodeno·tomy** [Gr. -τομία], the opening of the d. through the abdominal walls, to introduce food.

Duologue (diū·ǒlǒg). 1864. [irreg. f. Gr. δύο (*dyo-*) two, after *monologue.*] A dialogue; *spec.* a dramatic piece spoken by two actors. Also *attrib.*

‖**Duomo** (dwōmo). 1549. [It.; see DOME *sb.*] A cathedral church (in Italy); cf. DOM [2].

Vignettes..Of tower or d., sunny-sweet TENNYSON.

Dup (dʊp), *v. dial.* or *arch.* 1547. [contr. from *do up*; cf. *don, doff*, etc.] *trans.* To open. *Haml.* IV. v. 51.

Dupable (diū·păb'l), *a.* Also **dupeable.** 1833. [f. DUPE *v.* + -ABLE.] Capable of being duped. Also as *sb.*

Dupe (diūp), *sb.* 1681. [a. F. *dupe*, †*duppe* deluded person: in 1426 said to be a cant term.] One who allows himself to be deluded; a victim of deception.

The ready d. of astrologers and soothsayers SCOTT.

Dupe, *v.* 1704. [a. F. *duper*; or f. DUPE *sb.*] *trans.* To make a dupe of; to delude; to cheat.

I will not concur to d. and mislead a senseless multitude. Hence **Du·per,** a deluder. **Du·pery,** the act or practice of duping; duped condition.

Du·pion. ? *Obs.* 1828. [ad. F. *doupion* = It. *doppione*, f. *doppio* double.] 'A double cocoon formed by two silk-worms' (Simmonds).

Duplation (diuplē·ʃən). ME. [ad. L. *duplationem*, f. *duplare.*] The operation of doubling.

Duple (diū·p'l). 1542. [ad. L. *duplus.*]

A. *adj.* Double, twofold. *Obs.* in *gen.* sense: in *Math.* applied to the proportion of two quantities one of which is double of the other; in *Mus.*, to time having two beats in the bar.

†**B.** *sb.* = DOUBLE *sb.* I. –1787. So †**Du·ple** *v.* to double. Hence †**Du·plet,** doublet. DRYDEN.

Duplex (diū·pleks), *a.* 1817. [a. L., f. *duo* + *plic-* to fold.] **1.** Composed of two parts; twofold. **2.** *Electric Telegraphy.* **a.** = DIODE. **b.** Now restricted to systems in which two messages are sent simultaneously in opposite directions: opp. to DIPLEX, q.v. 1873.

1. *D. escapement*, one in which the escape-wheel has both spur and crown teeth; *d. gas-burner*, one having two jets so arranged as to combine the two flames into one; *d. lamp*, one with two wicks; *d. lathe*, one having a cutting-tool at the back opposite to that in front, and in an inverted position.

Du·plex, *v.* 1880. [f. prec. **2.**] *Electric Telegraphy.* To render duplex; to arrange (a wire or cable) so that two messages can be sent along it at the same time.

Duplexity (diuple·ksiti). *rare.* [f. DUPLEX *a.*] The quality of being double; doubleness; = DUPLICITY 2.

Duplicate (diū·plikėt). ME. [ad. L. *duplicatus, duplicare.*]

A. *adj.* **1.** Double, twofold, consisting of two corresponding parts. **2.** Double, doubled 1548. **3.** That is the counterpart of something; said of any number of copies or specimens 1812.

3. The d. copy of Florio, which the British Museum purchased EMERSON. Phr. *D. proportion, ratio*: the proportion or ratio of squares, in relation to that of the radical quantities.

B. *sb.* [the adj. used absol.] **1.** One of two things exactly alike, so that one is the double of the other; *esp.* that which is made from or after the other. **a.** A second copy of a letter or official document, having the legal force of the original. **b.** The second copy of a bill drawn in two parts; a 'second of exchange'. **c.** A pawnbroker's ticket. 1532. **2.** *gen.* A thing which is the exact double of another reckoned the original; one of two or more specimens exactly or virtually alike 1701.

1. Two duplicats thereof to be signed 1575. **2.** We will part with duplicates [of coins] HEARNE. As if a man should suddenly encounter his own d. LAMB. Phr. *In d.*: in two exactly corresponding copies.

Duplicate (diū·plikeᶦt), *v.* 1623. [f. L. *duplicat-, duplicare*, f. *duplex.*] **1.** *trans.* To double; to make double or twofold; to redouble. **2.** To make or provide in duplicate; to repeat 1860. Also †*intr.* for *refl.* **3.** *Eccl.* (*absol.*) To celebrate the Eucharist twice in one day 1865.

2. To provide against the possibility of a breakdown ..all the vital parts are duplicated 1880.

Duplication (diuplikē·ʃən). ME. [a. F., ad. L. *duplicationem.*] **1.** The action of doubling. **b.** The repetition of an action or thing; division into two by natural growth or spontaneous division 1590. **2.** A duplicate copy or version; a counterpart 1872. **3.** *Civil* and *Canon Law.* A pleading on the part of the defendant in reply to the replication 1622. †**4.** *Anat.* A folding, a doubling; *concr.* a fold –1748. **5.** *Eccl.* 'A second celebration of the Eucharist by the same priest on the same day' 1866.

1. The d. of their joys JER. TAYLOR. Phr. *D. of the cube* (Math.): the problem of finding the side of a cube having double the volume of a given cube; see DELIAN *a.*

Duplicative (diū·plikėtiv). 1870. [f. L. *duplicat-* ppl. stem.] **a.** *adj.* Having the quality of doubling; producing two instead of one. **b.** *sb.* A doubling addition 1884.

Du·plica to-, comb. f. L. *duplicatus*, prefixed to adjs. in the sense 'doubly'; *esp.* in *Bot.*, as *d.-dentate, -pinnate*, applied to toothed, etc. leaves, of which the teeth are themselves again dentate, etc.

Duplicator (diū·plikeᶦtəɹ). 1894. [See -OR.] A machine for producing copies. Also *attrib.*

Duplicature (diū·plikeᶦtiūɹ). 1686. [a. F.] A doubling; a fold. (Chiefly in *Anat.*)

Duplicidentate (diū:plisidenˑtėt), *a.* [f. L. *duplici-* (comb. f. *duplex*) + DENTATE.] *Zool.* Belonging to the *Duplicidentata*, a division of rodents characterized by two pairs of upper incisor teeth.

Duplicity (diūpli·siti). ME. [a. F. *duplicité*, ad. L. *duplicitatem.*] **1.** The quality of being double in action or conduct; deceitfulness, double-dealing. (The most usual sense.) **2.** *lit.* The quality of being double; doubleness 1589. **3.** *Law.* Double pleading 1848.

1. The d. of the King's conduct D'ISRAELI *Chas. I*, I. vi. 206. **2.** The d. of Saturn's ring 1867.

Duppa, dupper, var. DUBBA.

Duppy (dʊ·pi). 1774. [Afr.] Name among W. Ind. negroes for a ghost or spirit.

Dura (diūᵊ·ră). 1882. [L. adj. fem.] **1.** Short for DURA MATER. **2.** = DURAMEN.

Durability (diūᵊrăbi·līti). ME. [a. obs. F. *durabilité*, ad. late L. *durabilitatem.*] The quality of being durable (senses **1** and **2**).

Durable (diūᵊ·răb'l), *a.* ME. [a. F., ad. rare L. *durabilis.*] **1.** Capable of continuing in existence; persistent; permanent. **2.** Able to withstand change, decay, or wear ME. †**3.** Able to endure toil, etc. –1616.

1. D. remedie 1450, compunction HUME, designs ALISON. **2.** Inscriptions are more d. incised than in relief 1874. **Du·rableness** (*rare*). **Du·rably** *adv.*

Dural (diūᵊ·răl), *a.* 1888. [f. DURA (*dura mater*) + -AL.] Of or pertaining to the dura mater.

Duralumin [diuræ·liumin). 1910. [Trade name, f. L. *durus* hard + ALUMIN(IUM.] A light aluminium alloy, remarkable for its strength and hardness, used esp. in aircraft building.

‖**Dura mater** (diūᵊ·ră mē·təɹ). ME. [med.L. = hard mother; lit. tr. of Arab.; 'mother', etc. in Arab. being used to indicate relations between things.] The dense, tough, outermost membranous envelope of the brain and spinal cord.

‖**Duramen** (diurē·men). 1837. [rare L., f. *durare.*] The heart-wood of an exogenous tree.

Durance (diūᵊ·răns). 1494. [a. OF., f. *durer* to last; see -ANCE.] †**1.** Duration; lastingness –1698. †**2.** Lasting quality –1847. †**3.** A stout durable cloth. (Cf. DURANT *sb.*) –1709. **4.** Endurance (of toil, etc.) (*arch.*) 1579. **5.** Forced confinement, imprisonment; constraint. Now *esp.* in phr. *in d. vile*, 1513.

2. The d. of a granite ledge EMERSON. **4.** Hardinesse .. acquired by practise of their bodies to d. SPEED. **5.** St. Paul being at d. in Rome SANDERSON. var. †**Durancy** (*rare*) in sense **1.**

Durant (diū°rănt). 1455. [a. F. *durant*, pres. pple. of *durer*.] †A. *adj.* Lasting, continuous; current –1653. B. *sb.* A variety of tammy, called by some 'everlasting' 1766.

‖**Durante** (diuræ·ntí), *pres. pple.* and *prep.* 1556. The abl. sing. of L. pres. pple. *durans*, used in absol. constructions. a. In L. phr. *durante beneplacito*, during pleasure; *d. vita*, during life 1621. †b. Hence, in Eng. context, = DURING –1832

Duration (diurē·ʃən). ME. [a. obs. F., ad. late L. *durationem*. Not in Shaks.] 1. Lasting, continuance in time; the continuance of time; the time during which anything continues. †b. Durableness –1753. †2. Hardening –1657.
1. The peace will probably be of short d. COWPER. The average d. of human life..[in] great cities 1862.

‖**Durbar** (dɔ̄·ɹbāɹ). *E. Ind.* 1609. [Pers. and Urdū *darbār* court.] 1. A public audience or levee held by a native prince, or by a British governor or viceroy in India. 2. The hall or place of audience 1793.
1. The Maharanee held durbars daily 1862. A grand D. was held..by Mr. Crosthwaite the Commissioner at Mandalay 1887.

Dure (diū°ɹ), *v. arch.* and *dial.* ME. [a. F. *durer* :—L. *durare*.] 1. *intr.* To last; to continue (*arch.*). †2. To extend in space –1500. †3. *trans.* To endure –1598. Hence †**Du·reful** *a.* lasting. †**Du·reless** *a.* transient.

Dure (diū·°ɹ), *a. arch.* ME. [a. F. *dur, dure* :—L. *durus*; cf. also DOUR.] 1. Hard. (*lit.* and *fig.*) †2. *Mus.* Sharp. [So formerly F. *dur.*] 1609.
Blows with bils most d. was delt *Flodden F.* viii. 80.

Dureresque (dürĕrĕ·sk), *a.* 1860. [See -ESQUE.] In the style or manner of Albert Dürer (1471–1528), famous both as painter and as engraver on copper and on wood.

Duress, duresse (diure·s, diū°rĕs), *sb.* ME. [a. obs. F. *duresse, -esce, -ece* :—L. *duritia* (= *durities*).] †1. Hardness; severity; hardiness of endurance; firmness –1651. †2. Harsh treatment; affliction –1673. 3. = DURANCE 5. ME. 4. Constraint; in *Law*, Constraint illegally exercised to force a person to perform an act 1596.
3. What, then, is the degree of duresse which is to constitute imprisonment WELLINGTON. 4. The man was under duresse, and his act not voluntary, but imposed upon him by force TUCKER. Hence †**Du·ress** *v.* to subject to d. †**Dure·ssor,** he who subjects another to d.

†**Duret.** [?] A kind of dance. BEAUM. & FL.

‖**Dure·tto.** Also **-etta, -ette.** 1619. [a. It., dim. of *duro* :—L. *durum*.] A coarse stout stuff. Also *attrib.* –1660.

‖**Durgah** (dɒ·rgā). *E. Ind.* 1793. [Pers. *dargāh* royal court.] In India, 'The shrine of a (Mohammedan) saint' (Yule).

‖**Durian** (durī·ăn, dūᵊ·riăn). 1588. [Malay; = thorn, prickle.] The oval or globular fruit of *Durio zibethinus*, N.O. *Sterculiaceæ*; it has a hard prickly rind and luscious cream-coloured pulp, of a strong civet odour, but agreeable taste; also, the tree.

During (diū°·riŋ), *pres. pple.* and *prep.* (*conj.*) ME. †1. The pres. pple. of DURE *v.* = enduring, lasting, continuing; used in Fr. and Eng. as tr. L. *durante* in absolute constructions; thus L. *vita durante*, OF. *vie durant*, Eng. *life during*, while life lasts –1545. Hence, 2. *prep.* Throughout the whole continuance of; in the course of ME. †3. *conj.* While, until. (Also *d. that.*) (*rare*) –1693.
2. Trees may live d. the world 1670. D. the course of seven hundred years HUME. D. the night the rain changed to snow TYNDALL. Hence †**Du·ringly** *adv.* lastingly; for a long time.

†**Du·rity.** 1543. [ad. L. *duritas*.] Hardness (*lit.* and *fig.*) –1795.

Durmast (dɔ̄·ɹmɑst). 1791. [f. ? + MAST, fruit of forest tree.] A variety of oak (*Quercus pubescens*, or *Q. sessiliflora*). Usually *d.-oak.*

†**Du·rous,** *a. rare.* 1666. [f. L. *durus*.] Hard.

†**Duroy** (dūroi·). 1619. [? Fr.] A kind of coarse woollen fabric; akin to *tammies*. (Not the same as *corduroy*.) –1807.

‖**Durra, dhurra** (du·ră). 1798. [Arab.] A kind of corn, Indian Millet. Also *attrib.*

Durst, pa. t. (and *dial.* pa. pple.) of DARE *v.*[1]

Dusk (dɒsk). [OE. *dox, dosc* dark.] A. *adj.* (Now more often *dusky*.) 1. Dark from absence of light; dim, gloomy, shadowy; blackish; dusky ME. †2. Obscure, veiled from sight or understanding –1583.
1. Vapour and Exhalation, d. and moist MILT.
B. *sb.* 1. The quality of being dusk; that which is dusk; duskiness; gloom 1700. 2. The darker stage of twilight at night or in the morning 1622.
1. In the d. of thee [Old Yew] TENNYSON. 2. In the duske of the evening MABBE.

Dusk, *v.* ME. [f. DUSK *a.*; OE. had *doxian*, from *dox*.] To make or (*intr.*) become dusky or dark. Also *fig.*
Dusked hise eyen two and failled breeth CHAUCER. That shadow which dusketh the light of the moon HOLLAND. So **Du·sken** *v. rare*, in same senses.

Duskish (dɒ·skiʃ), *a.* 1530. [See -ISH.] Somewhat dusk or dusky, as *a d. red.* Hence **Du·skish·ly** *adv.*, **-ness.**

Dusky (dɒ·ski), *a.* 1558. [f. DUSK *a.*; cf. *worth, worthy*, etc.] 1. Somewhat black or dark in colour; darkish. 2. Somewhat dark or deficient in light; dim, obscure 1580. 3. *fig.* Gloomy, melancholy 1602.
1. No duskie vapour did bright Phœbus shroude GREENE. 2. The duskie hour Friendliest to sleep MILT. *P. L.* v. 667. 3. That d. scene of horror, that melancholy prospect BENTLEY. Hence **Du·skily** *adv.* **Du·skiness.**

‖**Dusserah** (dɒ·sĕrā). 1799. [a. Hindī *dasahrā*.] A Hindu annual festival extending over nine nights (or ten days) in the month Jaishṭha (Sept.–Oct.).

Dust (dɒst), *sb.* [OE. *dūst* (later prob. *dust*), going back to an earlier *dunst*, whence also Ger. *dunst* vapour. The primary notion is that which rises or is blown in a cloud.] 1. Earth or other solid matter so comminuted as to be easily raised and carried in a cloud by the wind; any substance pulverized; powder. (Rarely in *pl.*) Often extended to include ashes, etc., from a house. 2. With *a* and *pl.* a. A minute particle of dry matter 1593. b. in *Cookery*, etc., a small pinch of something powdery 1784. c. (With *a*) A cloud of dust floating in the air 1570. 3. *transf.* and *fig.* That to which anything is reduced by disintegration; *spec.* the ashes of a dead body. Also in phrases denoting the condition of being dead and buried. OE. b. Denoting a condition of humiliation ME. c. As the type of that which is worthless ME. 4. *fig.* (from 2c.) Confusion, disturbance, turmoil 1570. b. Hence (*slang* or *colloq.*) A disturbance, row, shindy 1753. 5. *slang.* Money, cash 1607. 6. = DUST-BRAND. 7. *attrib.* 1580.
1. To clense houses of duste TREVISA. Showers, which..laid the d. WESLEY. 2. A graine, a d., a gnat, a wandering haire *John* IV. i. 93. A d. of grated nutmeg 1784. 3. The Noble d. of Alexander *Haml.* V. i. 225. The Power..that rais'd us from the d. MILT. *P. L.* IV. 416. 4. That quarrel and raise a D. about nothing T. BROWN. 5. He..is not willing to down with his d. 1691.
Phrases. *To shake the d. off one's feet* (see Matt. x. 14, etc.). *To throw d. in the eyes of*: to make blind to the actual facts of the case. *To bite the d.*: to fall to the ground; *esp.* to fall wounded or slain.
Comb.: **d.-bin, du·stbin,** a receptacle for the d. and refuse of a house; **-chamber** (in an ore-roasting furnace), a closed chamber in which the heavier products of combustion are collected; **-colour,** a dull light brown; **-cover, -jacket,** a paper cover in which a book is issued; **-guard,** a contrivance to keep off d. from the axle and bearings of a wheel, etc.; **-hole,** a hole or bin in which d. and refuse are collected; **-louse,** an insect of the genus *Psocus*; **-pan,** a utensil into which d. is swept from a floor, etc.; **-shoot,** a place where d. and refuse are shot; **-storm,** a tempest in which large clouds of d. are carried along.

Dust, *v.* ME. [f. prec. sb.; cf. ON. *dusta* to dust.] †1. *intr.* To be dusty. ME. only. †2. To reduce, or (*intr.*) crumble, to dust –1686. 3. *trans.* To sprinkle with dust or powder 1592. Also *intr.* for *refl.* 4. To make dusty 1530. 5. To strew as dust 1790. 6. To free from dust 1568. 7. To brush, shake, or rub off as dust 1775. 8. To ride or go quickly; also, *to d. it.* (Now *U.S. slang* or *colloq.*) 1655.
6. Phr. *To d. a person's coat, jacket*, etc.: to beat him soundly. (*colloq.*) 1690.

Dust-box. 1581. A box from which dust, *i.e.* fine sand or powder, is sprinkled on something (*e.g.* on writing, etc.).

Dust-brand. 1861. [f. DUST *sb.* + BRAND *sb.*] A disease of corn, in which the ears become filled with a black powder; *smut.*

Duster (dɒ·stəɹ). 1576. [f. DUST *v.* or *sb.*] 1. One who, or that which, dusts or removes dust. 2. An apparatus for sifting dry poisons upon plants to kill insects. 3. A light cloak or wrap worn to keep off dust. Chiefly *U.S.* 1864.

Dusting (dɒ·stiŋ), *vbl. sb.* 1623. [f. DUST *v.* + -ING[1].] 1. The action of DUST *v.* 2. A beating, thrashing; also (*Naut.*) rough weather (*colloq.* or *slang*) 1799. 3. *attrib.*, as *d.-brush, -cloth, -powder*, etc. 1667.

Dustless (dɒ·stlĕs), *a.* 1618. [-LESS.] Free from dust.

Dustman (dɒ·stmæ̆n). 1707. [f. as prec. + MAN.] 1. A man whose occupation is to remove dust and refuse from dust-bins, etc. 2. *slang.* A preacher who uses violent action; a 'cushion-thumper' 1877.

‖**Dustoor** (dɒstū°·ɹ). *E. Ind.* 1680. [Pers. and Urdū *dastūr*.] a. Custom, usage, fashion. b. Customary commission; var. ‖**Dustoo·ry.**

†**Dust-point.** 1611. A boy's game in which 'points' were laid in a heap of dust, and thrown at with a stone –1675.

‖**Dustuck, dustuk** (dɒ·stɒk). *E. Ind.* 1748. [a. Pers. and Urdū *dastak*.] A passport.

Dusty (dɒ·sti), *a.* ME. [f. DUST *sb.*] 1. Full of, abounding with, or strewn with dust. 2. Consisting of dust; powdery 1552. 3. Of colour, etc.: As if strewn with dust. Also *advb.* 1676. 4. *fig.* Mean, worthless; now only in slang phr. *not so d.* 1893. *Comb.* **d. miller,** (*a*) the auricula (*Primula Auricula*), from the fine powder on the leaves and flowers; (*b*) a kind of artificial fly. Hence **Du·stily** *adv.* **Dustiness.**

Dutch (dɒtʃ). ME. [a. MDu. *dutsch, duutsch, duutsc*, Hollandish, Netherlandish, or even German, in early mod. Du. *duytsch*, now *duitsch*, 'German', OHG. *diutisc*, popular, national, vulgar. Since 1600 the term 'Dutch' has been gradually restricted in England to the Netherlanders, with whom the English came most in contact.]
A. *adj.* 1. Of or pertaining to the people of Germany; German; Teutonic. Now *Hist.* 1460. 2. Of, pertaining to, or characterizing the 'Low Dutch' people of Holland and the Netherlands 1606. 3. Of or belonging to the Dutch; native to, or coming from Holland 1592. 4. Characteristic of or attributed to the Dutch; often used in derision or contempt 1608.
1. *High D.*, of or pertaining to the South Germans, High German; *Low D.*, of or pertaining to the Germans of the sea-coast, and of the north and northwest, including the Netherlands and Flanders. 2. The collection of pictures of the D. school 1838. A D. love for tulips TENNYSON. 3. Late as the D. clock showed it to be DICKENS. **D. cheese,** a small round cheese made from skim milk. **D. clinker,** a kind of brick used for paving stables and yards, being exceedingly hard. **D. foil, gold, gilt, gilding, leaf, metal,** a very malleable alloy of 11 parts of copper and 2 of zinc, beaten into thin leaves, forming a cheap imitation of gold-leaf. **D. liquid, oil,** Ethene dichloride, $2(CH_2Cl)$, a thin oily liquid, having a sweetish smell and taste. **D. Rushes,** a species of *Equisetum* or Horse-tail used for polishing; shave-grass. 4. *D. auction, bargain, concert, courage, nightingale*, etc.: see AUCTION, BARGAIN, etc.
B. *sb.*[1] [The adj. used ellipt.] 1. The German language. *Obs.* exc. in *High D.* = German; *Low D.* = Low German, including Netherlandish. 2. The language of Holland and the Netherlands 1706. *Double* (†*high*) *D.*: gibberish 1789. 3. *The D.* †a. The Germans. b. The people of Holland and the Netherlands. 1577.

Dutch (dɒtʃ), *sb.*[2] *slang.* 1889. [abbrev. of DUCHESS.] A costermonger's wife (*old d.*).

Dutch, *v.* 1763. [f. prec. adj.] To clarify and harden (quills) by plunging them in heated sand, or rapidly passing them through a fire.

Dutchify (dɒ·tʃifəi), *v.* 1680. [f. DUTCH *a.* + -FY.] To make Dutch or Dutch-like.

Dutchman (dɒ·tʃmæ̆n). ME. †1. A German –1788. 2. An inhabitant of Holland or the Netherlands 1596. 3. A Dutch ship 1657.
1. *Much Ado* III. ii. 33. 2. Phr. *I'm a D.*, i.e. I'm not myself: as an alternative clause to an assertion (*colloq.*). 3. *Flying D.*: A legendary or spectral ship supposed to be seen near the Cape of Good Hope; also, its captain, said to have been condemned to sail the seas for ever. *Comb.*: **Dutchman's breeches,** (*a*) in U.S., the plant *Dicentra Cucullaria*; (*b*) *Naut.* a very small patch of blue sky often seen when a gale is breaking; **Dutchman's laudanum,** a climbing shrub allied to the Passion-flower, *Passiflora Muru-*

cuja; also, a narcotic prepared from this; **Dutchman's pipe,** (*a*) a climbing shrub, *Aristolochia Sipho*; (*b*) the nest of the S. Amer. wasp.

Duteous (diū·tĭəs), *a.* 1593. [f. Duty + -ous.] Characterized by the performance of duty to a superior; dutiful, submissive, obedient. A daughter d. Dryden. **Du·teous-ly** *adv.*, **-ness.**

Dutiable (diū·ti,ăb'l), *a.* 1774. [See -able.] Liable to duty; on which a duty is levied; as *d. articles.*

Dutied (diū·tid), *a. U.S.* 1771. [f. Duty + -ed².] Subjected to duty.

Dutiful (diū·tiful), *a.* 1552. [See -ful.] 1. Full of duty, *i.e.* that which is due to a superior; rendering the services and attention that are due. †2. Relating to duty (*rare*) 1588.

1. With all duetifull respect unto your Lordship 1590. D. and loyal subjects of the King 1844. Hence **Du·tiful-ly** *adv.*, **-ness.**

Duty (diū·ti). ME. [a. AF. *duetė*, f. *du*, *due* Due; see -ty, and cf. *beauty*, etc.] 1. The action and conduct due to a superior; homage; reverence, due respect. †2. That which is owing to any one; (one's) due; a debt -1642. 3. A payment due and enforced by law or custom 1489. *spec.* †a. Payment for the services of the church. Chiefly *pl.* (repl. by *dues*). -1562. b. A payment to the public revenue; *esp.* one levied upon the import, export, manufacture, or sale of certain commodities. Applied to payments under the heads of customs, excise, licences, stamp-duties, death-duties, inhabited house duty. 1474. 4. Action, or an act, that is due by moral or legal obligation; that which one ought or is bound to do. (The chief current sense.) ME. b. Absolutely: Moral obligation. (Occas. personified.) 1579. 5. Business, office, function ME. 6. *Mech.* The measure of effectiveness of an engine, expressed by units of work done per unit of fuel 1827.

1. Our d. to your Honour *Haml.* I. ii. 252. 2. Take that which is thy d. Tindale *Matt.* xx. 14. To pay their d. unto nature, as their creditor 1540. 3. By taxes they [the American colonists] mean internal taxes; by duties they mean customs Franklin. 4. England expects that every man will do his d. Nelson. Stern Daughter of the Voice of God! O D. Wordsw. 5. *Ministerial* or *clerical d.*, or simply *d.*: the regular ministration and service of a clergyman. *Military d.*: appointed military service (now, where no enemy is to be engaged). Phr. *On d.*: officially engaged. So *Off d.* *Comb.*: **d.-free** *a.* (and *adv.*), free of d.; **-paid** *a.*, on which customs or excise-d. has been paid.

Duumvir (diu,ʊ·mvəɹ). Pl. **-virs**, or as L. **-viri** (-virəi). 1600. [L.; lit. 'man of the two'.] *Rom. Hist.* One of the *duumviri* or pairs of co-equal magistrates, etc. in Rome and in her coloniæ and municipia. Also *transf.*

Here is a compact of iniquity between these two duumvirs [Wheler and Hastings] Burke.

Hence **Duu·mviral** *a.* of or pertaining to duumvirs. **Duu·mvirate,** the joint office of duumvirs; a coalition of two men; a pair of officials.

‖**Duvet** (dü·vę). 1758. [F.] A quilt of eider-down or swan's-down.

Dux (dʊks). 1808. [a. L.] 1. A leader, chief; *spec.* the head pupil in a class: chiefly in Scotland. 2. *Mus.* The subject of a fugue (the answer being called *comes*) 1819.

Duyker; see Duiker.

Dwale (dwēɪl), *sb.* ME. [prob. from Scandinavian; cf. Da. *dvale* dead sleep, stupor, *dvaledrik* soporiferous draught; from same root as prec.] †1. A stupefying or soporific drink. (Prob. the infusion of Belladonna.) -1606. 2. The deadly Nightshade, *Atropa Belladonna* ME. †3. In *Her.* occas. used for *sable* -1751.

Dwang (dwæŋ). *Sc.* 1842. [Cf. Du. *dwang* force.] *Arch.* 'A term used in Scotland to denote the short pieces of timber employed in strutting a floor' (Gwilt).

Dwarf (dwǫɹf). Pl. **-fs.** [Com. Teut.: OE. *dweorȝ*, *dweorh* (:—*dwerg*) :—(ult.) Aryan type **dhwér-gʷhos*, repr. in Gr. by σέρφος midge.]

A. 1. A human being much below the ordinary stature or size; a pygmy. 2. *transf.* Of animals and plants 1664.

B. *adj.* Of or pertaining to a dwarf; dwarfish; pygmy 1634. Also *transf.* of plants, animals, etc. *Comb.* **d.-wall,** any low wall; *spec.* one which forms the basis of a railway, or which supports the joists under a floor.

Hence **Dwa·rfish** *a.* d.-like; of a size below the average; pygmy, puny. **Dwa·rfish-ly** *adv.*, **-ness.** **Dwa·rfling,** a small d. **Dwa·rfy** *a.* dwarfish.

Dwarf (dwǫɹf), *v.* 1626. [f. prec. sb.] 1. *trans.* To render dwarf or dwarfish; to stunt in growth. Also *transf.* and *fig.* 2. To cause to look or seem small (*lit.* and *fig.*) 1850. 3. *intr.* To become dwarf or dwarfed 1833.

1. [We] d. them and stay their growth Bacon. The incessant repetition of the same hand-work dwarfs the man Emerson. 2. An immense chandelier..dwarfing the apartments Disraeli.

Dwell (dwel), *v.* Pa. t. and pple. **dwelt,** now rarely **dwelled.** [OE. *dwęllan* (later also *dwęlian*) :—OTeut. **dwaljan*, causal of strong vb. of ablaut series *dwel-*, *dwal-*, *dwol-* (*dul-*), repr. by OE. pa. pple. *gedwolen* gone astray, perverted; from an Aryan root *dhwel*, *dhul*, appearing in Skr. *dhwr*, *dhūr* to mislead, deceive.] †1. *trans.* To lead into error; to stun, stupefy -ME. †2. To hinder, delay. (Only OE.) †3. *intr.* To tarry; to desist from action -1485. 4. To abide for a time, in a state, place, or condition (*arch.*) ME. 5. *To d. on, upon,* †*in*: to spend time upon or linger over; now *esp.* to treat at length or with insistence; also, to sustain (a note) in music. (The most frequent use in speech.) 1530. †6. To last; to remain. (ME. only.) 7. To remain as in a permanent residence; to have one's abode; to reside. (Now usu. repl. by *live* in spoken use.) ME. †8. *trans.* To inhabit -1799. †9. To cause to abide *in* 1667.

4. Ile rather d. in my necessitie *Merch. V.* I. iii. 157. 5. [Plato] is constantly dwelling on the importance of regular classification Jowett. 7. The King that dwelleth in Heaven Hobbes. *fig.* Farewel happy Fields Where Joy for ever dwells Milt. *P. L.* I. 250. 9. Milt. *P. L.* xii. 487.

Dweller (dwe·ləɹ). ME. [f. as prec. + -er¹.] One who dwells (in a place); an inhabitant, resident. Also with *on.*

The rude dwellers on the mountain-heights Cowper.

Dwelling (dwe·liŋ), *vbl. sb.* ME. [f. as prec. + -ing¹.] 1. The action of Dwell *v.* 2. *concr.* A place of residence; a dwelling-place, habitation, house. Also *fig.* ME.

2. Good will To future men, and in their dwellings peace Milt. *P. L.* vii. 183. *fig.* Enclosed in the narrow d. of the mind 1655 *Comb.*, etc.: **d.-house,** a house occupied as a place of residence; **-place,** a place of abode.

Dwindle (dwi·nd'l), *v.* 1596. [A freq. from Dwine *v.*; cf. Kindle *v.*²] 1. *intr.* To become smaller and smaller; to shrink, waste away, decline. b. *fig.* To degenerate 1678. 2. *trans.* To cause to shrink 1661.

1. Man seems the only growth that dwindles here Goldsm. *fig.* In thy old age to d. to a Whig T. Brown. 2. These Monsters..have dwindled the Wolf into a Fox 1679. Hence **Dwi·ndler.**

Dwi·ndle, *sb. rare.* [f. prec. vb.] The process of dwindling; *concr.* a dwindled object.

Dwine (dwəin), *v.* Now *Sc.*, *dial.*, and *arch.* [OE. *dwīnan*, *dwán*, *dwinen*; an OTeut. strong vb.] *intr.* To waste or pine away. b. *trans.* To cause to pine away (*rare*) 1597.

Dwt., abbrev. for Pennyweight; see D.

Dyad (dəi·æd). 1675. [ad. L. *dyas*, *dyad-*, a. Gr. δυάς, δυάδ-.] 1. The number two; a group of two. 2. *spec.* a. *Chem.* An atom, radical, or element that has the combining power of two units, *i. e.* of two atoms of hydrogen 1865. b. *Biol.* A secondary unit consisting of an aggregate of monads 1883. c. *Pros.* A group of two lines having different rhythms 1885. 3. *attrib.* or as *adj.* = Dyadic 1869.

Dyadic (dəiæ·dik), *a.* 1727. [ad. Gr. δυαδικός.] a. Of or pertaining to a dyad. b. *Chem.* Of the atomic constitution of a dyad 1873.

Phr. *D. arithmetic*: binary arithmetic, in which the radix is 2.

Dyakis-dodecahedron (dəi·ăkis,dōu:dĭkă-hī·drǫn). 1881. [f. Gr. δυάκις twice + Dodecahedron.] *Cryst.* = Diploid.

Dyarchy: see Diarchy.

Dyas (dəi·æs). 1876. [a. Gr. δυάς. After *Trias.*] *Geol.* A name for the Permian system. Hence **Dya·ssic** *a.*

Dye (dəi), *sb.* [OE. had *dēaȝ*, *dēah* fem. (:—OTeut. **daugā-*), ME. *dehe.*] 1. Colour produced by, or as by, dyeing; tinge, hue. Also *fig.* 2. A material used for dyeing; *esp.* colouring matter in solution OE.

1. *fig.* Wings and crests of rainbow dyes J. Wilson. *fig.* Crimes..of the blackest d. Mackintosh.

Comb.: **d.-bath, -beck,** the vessel containing the dyeing liquid; also the colouring matter contained in it; **-house,** the building in which a dyer carries on his work; **-stuff, -ware,** a substance which yields a d.; **-wood,** wood yielding a d.; **-works,** works in which dyeing is carried on.

Dye (dəi), *v.* Pa. t. and pple. **dyed**; pr. pple. dyeing. [OE. *dēaȝian* (:—OTeut. **daugōjan*), f. *dēag* Dye *sb.* The distinction in spelling between *die* and *dye* is recent.] 1. *trans.* To tinge with a colour or hue; to fix a colour in the substance of; to colour, stain. 2. *intr.* for *pass.* To take a colour (well or badly) in the process of dyeing (*mod.*).

1. My hands with blood of innocence are dy'd Gay. The most usual stuffs.. which are required to be dyed, are wool, silk, cotton, and linen 1816. Phr. *To d. in (the) wool, in grain,* to d. while the material is in the raw or primitive state, and therefore more lastingly; hence *dyed-in-the-wool* adj. (*fig.*).

Dye, obs. f. Die *v.* and *sb.*

Dyeing (dəi·iŋ), *vbl. sb.* Also formerly **dying.** OE. [f. Dye *v.* + -ing¹.] The process of impregnating with colour; *esp.* the fixing of colours in solution in textiles, etc.

Dyer (dəi·əɹ). ME. [f. as prec.] One whose occupation is to dye cloth, etc.

Comb., etc.: **dyer's broom, whin,** *Genista tinctoria*, also called **dyer's greenweed,** *Dyer's weed*, and *woadwaxen*; **dyer's moss,** archil; **Dyer's weed,** a name for plants that yield a dye: *esp.* Yellow-weed or Weld, *Reseda luteola*; also Dyer's greenweed or Woadwaxen, and Dyer's woad, *Isatis tinctoria.*

Dyer, obs. f. Dier, one who dies.

Dygogram (dəi·gogræm). 1862. [Contr. for Dynamo-gonio-gram, 'force and angle diagram'.] A diagram showing the variation of the horizontal component of the force of magnetism exerted upon the ship's compass-needle by the iron in the ship's composition while making a circuit or curve.

Dying (dəi·iŋ), *vbl. sb.* ME. [f. Die *v.*¹ + -ing¹.] 1. Ceasing to live, expiring, decease, death. Also *transf.* and *fig.* 2. *attrib.* Of, belonging to, or relating to dying or death, as *d. bed, command, day, declaration,* etc. 1580.

Dy·ing, *ppl. a.* ME. [f. as prec. + -ing².] Departing from this life; at the point of death; mortal. Also *transf.* and *fig.* Hence **Dy·ing-ly** *adv.* in a d. manner, in d.; **-ness,** d. quality.

Dyke, etc., a frequent sp. of Dike, etc.

Dynactino·meter. ? *Obs.* 1851. [f. Gr. δύν(αμις power + ἀκτίς (ἀκτιν-) ray + μέτρον; cf. Actinometer.] An instrument for measuring the intensity of the photogenic rays, and for computing the power of object-glasses.

†**Dy·nam.** 1847. [a. F. *dyname*, f. Gr. δύναμις.] Whewell's proposed term for expressing a pound or other unit, in estimating the effect of mechanical labour.

Dynameter (dəi-, dinæ·mĭtəɹ). 1828. [f. Gr. δύνα(μις + μέτρον.] = Dynamometer 2. Hence **Dyname·tric, -al** *a.* pertaining to a d.

Dynamic (dəi-, dinæ·mik). 1817. [ad. F. *dynamique* (Leibnitz), ad. Gr. δυναμικός, f. δύναμις.]

A. *adj.* 1. Of or pertaining to force producing motion: often opp. to *static* 1827. 2. Of or pertaining to force in action; active 1862. Also *transf.* and *fig.* 3. Of, according to, or pertaining to Dynamics: as the *d.* theory of the tides 1838. 4. *Med.* Functional, as opp. to *organic* 1829. 5. In the Kantian philosophy: Relating to the reason of existence of an object of experience. 6. Relating to the existence or action of some force or forces 1817.

1. According to the d. view..heat is regarded as a motion Tyndall. 2. A mere capacity..potential but not d. Tyndall. 5. *D. relations*, the relations of substance and accident, of cause and effect, and of substances acting on each other. 6. *D. theory of Kant*, a theory according to which matter was constituted by attraction and repulsion.

B. *sb.* 1. = Dynamics, q. v. 1873. 2. = Dynamic theory; see A. 6. 1884. 3. Energizing force 1894.

Dynamical (dəi-, dinæ·mikăl), *a.* 1812. [See -al.] 1. = Dynamic *a.* 1–4. 2. Applied to inspiration conceived as an endowing with divine power 1841. 3. Of or pertaining to DYNAMISM (sense 1) 1845. Hence **Dyna·mically** *adv.* in the way of a force in action or motion; from the point of view of dynamics.

Dynami·city. *Chem.* = VALENCY or ATOMICITY. (Mod. Dicts.)

Dynamics (dəi-, dinæ·miks). 1788. [Pl. of DYNAMIC; see -ICS.] 1. The branch of Physics which treats of the action of Force: in earlier use restricted to *Kinetics*, and thus opp. to *Statics*, but more recently taken as including both. Also called DYNAMIC. b. That branch of any science in which force or forces are considered 1843. 2. *transf.* The moving physical or moral forces in any sphere, or the laws by which they act 1833.

2. The great storehouse of our spiritual d. J. MARTINEAU.

Dynamism (dəi·n-, di·nămiz'm). 1831. [f. Gr. δύναμις; see -ISM.] 1. A philosophical theory, which seeks to explain the phenomena of the universe by some immanent force or energy; *esp.* the doctrine of Leibnitz that all substance involves force 1857. 2. The mode of being of force or energy 1831. 3. *Med.* 'The theory of the origin of disease from change or alteration of vital force' (*Syd. Soc. Lex.*). Hence **Dy·namist,** one who holds the doctrine of d. **Dynami·stic** *a.*

‖**Dynamitard.** 1882. [f. DYNAMITE, after Fr. *communard.* (Not in recognized Fr. use.)] = DYNAMITER. (Newspapers.)

Dynamite (dəi·năməit, di·n-), *sb.* 1867. [f. Gr. δύναμις + -ITE, by Alfred Nobel the inventor.] 1. A high explosive prepared from nitro-glycerine mixed, for safety, with some inert absorptive substance. 2. *attrib.*, as *d. outrage*; **d. cruiser,** a cruiser armed with d. guns; **d. gun,** a pneumatic gun for throwing d. shells, or the like 1880. Hence **Dynami·tic, -al** *a.* **Dynami·tically** *adv.* **Dy·namiti·sm,** the principles or practice of the dynamiter; the use of d., etc., as a means of attacking a government, nation, or person.

Dy·namite, *v.* 1881. [f. prec. sb.] *trans.* To wreck by the explosion of dynamite; to mine or charge with dynamite.

Dynamiter (dəi·năməitəɹ, di·n-). 1883. [f. prec.] One who employs dynamite, etc., for unlawful purposes; *esp.* as a means of attacking a government, nation, or person.

Dynamize (dəi·n-, di·năməiz), *v.* 1855. [See -IZE.] *Med.* To endow with power. In *Homœopathy*, To increase the power of (medicines) by trituration or succussion. Hence **Dynamiza·tion.**

Dynamo-, from Gr. δύναμις 'power, force', a combining form, as in **D.-electric** *a.*, pertaining to current (formerly called dynamic) electricity; also, pertaining to the conversion of dynamical into electrical energy, as *d.-electric machine*; etc.

Dynamo (dəi·nămo), *sb.* Pl. **-os.** 1882. [Short for *dynamo-machine*, itself short for *dynamo-electric-machine.*] *Electr.* A machine for converting mechanical power into electric energy, by setting conductors (usually coils of copper wire) to rotate in a magnetic field.

Dynamogeny (dəin-, dinămǫ·dʒĭni). [mod. f. DYNAMO- + Gr. -γένεια; see -GENY.] Production of increased nervous activity; dynamization of nerve-force. So **Dynamoge·nesis,** in same sense. **Dynamoge·nic** *a.*

Dynamograph (dəi·n-, di·nămograf). 1851. [f. DYNAMO- + Gr. -γραφος.] An instrument for recording the amount of force exerted.

Dynamometer (dəin-, dinămǫ·mītəɹ). 1810. [ad. F. *dynamomètre*, f. DYNAMO- + Gr. μέτρον.] 1. Any instrument for measuring the amount of energy exerted by an animal, or expended by a motor in its work, or by the action of any mechanical force. 2. An instrument for measuring the magnifying power of a telescope 1832. Hence **Dynamome·tric, -al** (also **dynami-**) *a.* of or pertaining to the measurement of force; **Dynamo·metry,** the measurement of force.

Dynast (di·n-, dəi·næst). 1631. [ad. late L. *dynastes*, a. Gr., f. δύνασθαι.] One in power; a ruler, lord, potentate, *esp.* a hereditary ruler; a member or founder of a dynasty. Hence **Dyna·stic, -al** *a.* of, pertaining to, or connected with a dynasty or dynasties. **Dyna·stically** *adv.* **Dyna·sticism,** the dynastic principle; the system of ruling dynasties.

Dynastidan (din-, dəinæ·stidăn). 1835. [f. mod.L. *Dynastidæ*, f. *Dynastes* as a generic name.] *Entom.* A member of the *Dynastidæ*, a family of large beetles including the *Dynastes* or Hercules-beetle.

Dynasty (di·năsti, dəi-). 1460. [a. F. *dynastie*, ad. late L. *dynastia*, a. Gr., f. δυνάστης DYNAST.] 1. Lordship, sovereignty, power; régime. Now *rare.* 1613. 2. A succession of rulers of the same line or family 1460. Also *transf.* and *fig.*

Dyne (dəin). 1873. [a. F. *dyne*, taken from Gr. δύναμις.] *Physics.* The unit of force in the centimetre-gramme-second (C.G.S.) system, *i.e.* the force which, acting for one second on a mass of one gramme, gives it a velocity of one centimetre per second.

Dyophysite (dəi,ǫ·fizəit). 1860. [ad. late Gr. δυοφυσῖται, f. δύο + φύσις.] *Theol.* A holder of the doctrine of the coexistence of two natures, the divine and the human, in Christ: opp. to the Monophysites. Hence **Dyophysi·tic** *a.*

Dyothelete, -ite (dəi,ǫ·þĭlīt, -əit). 1848. [f. Gr. δύο + θελητής: lit. a 'two-willer'.] *Theol.* a. *adj.* Holding the doctrine that Christ had two wills, a divine and a human. b. *sb.* One who holds this doctrine; an opponent of MONOTHELETISM.

Dyphone (dəi·fōun). 1676. [f. Gr. δύο + φωνή. The better form is *diphone*, Gr. δίφωνος.] *Mus.* The 'double lute', invented by Thomas Mace in 1672.

Dys-, obs. spelling of DIS-, in many words.

Dys- (dis), *prefix*, repr. Gr. δυσ- [= Skr. *dus-*, OTeut. **tuz-*, OHG. *zur-* (Ger. *zer-*), ON. *tor-*, OE. *tó-* in *to-break*, etc.] 'inseparable prefix, opp. to εὖ [see EU-], with notion of *hard, bad, unlucky*, etc.; destroying the good sense of a word, or increasing its bad sense' (Liddell and Scott).

Dysgenesis (-dʒe·nĭsis) [Gr. γένεσις], difficulty in breeding; *spec.* a condition of hybrids in which they are sterile among themselves, but capable of producing (sterile) offspring with either of the parental races; so **Dysgenesic** (-dʒĭne·sik) *a.* **Dysphonia** (-fōu·niă), **Dysphony** (di·sfōni) [Gr. δυσφωνία], difficulty of speaking arising from affection of the vocal organs; hence **Dysphonic** (-fǫ·nik) *a.* **Dystocia** (-tōu·siă), **Dystokia,** erron. **-tochia** (-tǫ·kiă) [Gr. δυστοκία], difficult or painful childbirth; hence **Dysto·cial** *a.* **Dystome** (di·stoum), **Dystomic** (distǫ·mik), **Dystomous** (di·stŏməs) *adjs.* [Gr. δύστομος], *Min.* having imperfect fracture; cleaving with difficulty. See also N.E.D.

Dysæsthesia (disĕsþī·siă). 1706. [L., a. Gr. δυσαισθησία, f. δυσ- (DYS-) + αἰσθε- to feel.] *Path.* Difficulty or derangement of sensation, or of any bodily senses.

†**Dyscra·se,** *v.* ME. [a. OF. **discraser*, f. *discrasie.* Later, viewed as conn. w. CRAZE *v.*] To affect with a dyscrasy; to distemper, disorder –1610.

‖**Dyscrasia** (diskrē̆·siă). ME. [med.L., a. Gr. δυσκρασία, f. δυσ- (DYS-) + κρᾶσις mixing.] = DYSCRASY. Hence **Dyscra·sic** *a.*

Dyscrasite (di·skrăsəit). Also **dis-.** 1852. [f. Gr. δυσκρασία + -ITE.] *Min.* Antimonial silver, a native alloy of silver and antimony in various proportions.

Dyscrasy (di·skrăsi). ME. [a. OF. *dyscrasie*, ad. med.L. *dyscrasia.*] A bad or disordered condition of the body (originally ascribed to a disproportionate mixture of the 'humours'); morbid diathesis; distemper. Also *fig.*

Sin is but a disease and d. in the soul CUDWORTH.

Dysenteric, †-al (disente·rik, -ăl), *a.* 1601. [ad. L. *dysentericus*, a. Gr., f. δυσεντερία; see DYSENTERY.] 1. Belonging to or of the nature of dysentery 1727. 2. Affected with dysentery 1822.

1. D. diarrhœa 1846. 2. Twelve d. patients GOOD.

Dysentery (di·sentĕri). ME. [a. OF. *dissenterie*, ad. L. *dysenteria*, a. Gr., f. δυσέντερος, f. δυσ- (DYS-) + ἔντερα bowels.] Inflammation of the mucous membrane and glands of the large intestine, attended with griping pains, and mucous and bloody evacuations.

Dyslogistic (dislǫdʒi·stik), *a.* Also erron. **dis-.** 1802. [f. DYS- + stem of *eu-logistic.*] Having a bad connotation; opprobrious; opp. to *eulogistic.*

The d. names, by which it pleases each side to denominate its opponents 1887. Hence **Dyslogi·stically** *adv.*

Dysluite (di·sl*u*,əit). 1821. [arbitrary f. DYS- + Gr. λύειν.] *Min.* A variety of gahnite or zinc spinel, containing manganese: it is difficult to decompose.

Dyslysin (di·slisin). 1851. [arbitrary f. DYS- + Gr. λύσις.] *Chem.* A substance got from bilin digested with dilute hydrochloric acid with alcohol; it is almost insoluble.

‖**Dysmenorrhagia** (di:smenorē̆·dʒiă). 1885. = next.

‖**Dysmenorrhœa** (-rī·ă). Also **-rhea.** 1810. [See DYS-.] *Path.* Difficult or painful menstruation.

Dysmerism (di·smĕriz'm). 1881. [f. Gr. δυσ- (DYS-) + μερισμός (MERISM).] *Biol.* The aggregation of unlike parts in the formation of an organism. Hence **Dysmeri·stic** *a.* having the character of such an aggregation. **Dysmerogenesis** (di:smĕro,dʒe·nĕsis), the formation of an organism by successive production of parts which are unlike; hence **Dy:smerogene·tic** *a.*

Dysodyle, -ile (di·sodəil). 1809. [a. F. *dysodyle*, f. Gr. δυσώδης ill-smelling + ὕλη; cf. CACODYL.] *Min.* A very inflammable hydrocarbon, yellow, and of foliated structure, which burns with a fetid odour.

Dyspathy (di·spăþi). *rare.* 1603. [= OF. *dyspathie*, taken as the opposite of Gr. συμπάθεια.] The opposite of *sympathy*; antipathy; disagreement of feeling or sentiment.

‖**Dyspepsia** (dispe·psiă). Also **dyspe·psy** (now less usual). 1706. [a. L., a. Gr. δυσπεψία, f. δύσπεπτος.] Difficulty or derangement of digestion; indigestion: applied *esp.* to disorder of the stomach, usually involving weakness, loss of appetite, and depression of spirits.

A French writer calls d. 'the remorse of a guilty stomach' 1862.

Dyspeptic (dispe·ptik), *a.* (*sb.*) 1694. [f. Gr. δύσπεπτος, f. δυσ- (DYS-) + πεπτός cooked, digested; after Gr. πεπτικός.]

A. †1. Difficult of digestion. 2. Of or belonging to dyspepsia; also *fig.* 1809. 3. Subject to or suffering from dyspepsia 1822.

2. D. symptoms 1875. *fig.* No d. politics 1894.

B. *sb.* A person subject to or suffering from dyspepsia 1822. Hence **Dyspe·ptical** *a.* (*rare*). **Dyspe·ptically** *adv.*

‖**Dysphagia** (disfē̆·dʒiă). Rarely **dysphagy** (di·sfădʒi). 1783. [mod.L., f. DYS- + Gr. -φαγία.] *Path.* Difficulty of swallowing (as a symptom of some affection). Hence **Dyspha·gic** *a.*

‖**Dyspnœa** (dispnī·ă). 1681. [L., a. Gr. δύσπνοια, f. (ult.) δυσ- (DYS-) + πνοή breathing.] *Path.* Difficulty of breathing. Hence **Dyspnœ·al** *a.* of or belonging to d.; **Dyspnœ·ic** *a.* of the nature of or affected with d.

Dysporomorph (di·spŏromǭɹf). [f. *Dysporus* name of a genus of gannets + -μορφος -FORM.] *Zool.* A bird of the division *Dysporomorphæ*, including the pelicans, gannets, cormorants, etc. So **Dy:sporomo·rphic** *a.*

Dysteleology (di:stelĭ,ǫ·lŏdʒi). 1874. [ad. Ger. *dysteleologie* (Häckel), f. DYS- privative + *teleologie* TELEOLOGY.] The doctrine of purposelessness in nature (opp. to TELEOLOGY); the study of functionless rudimentary organs as bearing on this doctrine. Hence **Dy:steleolo·gical** *a.* relating to d. **Dy:steleo·logist.**

Dysury (di·siŭri). ME. [a. OF. *dissurie*, ad. L. *dysuria* (also used), a. Gr. δυσουρία, f. (ult.) δυσ- + οὖρον urine.] *Path.* Difficult or painful urination. So **Dysu·ric** *a.* pertaining to or affected with d.

Dyvour (dəi·vəɹ). *Sc.* ? *Obs.* 1508. [?] A bankrupt; hence *gen.* one in debt; a beggar.

‖**Dzeren** (dzīə·ren). Also **-on, -in.** 1834.

[Mongolian, f. *dzĕr* reddish-yellow.] The Mongolian antelope, *Procapra gutturosa*.

‖**Dziggetai, dzh-** (dzi·gĕtai, dʒ-). 1793. [Mongolian, more properly *tchikhitei* long-eared, f. *tchikhi* ear.] A species of equine quadruped, *Equus hemionus*. It approaches the mule in appearance.

E

E (ī), the fifth letter of the Roman and English Alphabet, repr. historically the Semitic ☰ (= *h*), but adopted by the Greeks (and from them by the Romans) as a vowel. In pronunc. it probably varied from the 'mid-front' (*e*) to the 'low-front' (*ę*) vowels of Bell's system.

For its principal sounds in standard English see KEY TO THE PRONUNCIATION.

The silent *e*, due primarily to the ME. obscure *-e*, is still retained: (1) To indicate that the vowel in the syllable is long; *e.g.* in *wine* (wəin), *paste* (pēⁱst), etc. (2) When otherwise *v*, or, after consonants, *l*, or *r* would end the word. (3) To soften the sound of a preceding *c* or *g*. (4) After *s* or *z* preceded by a cons., as in *pulse*, *furze*, etc. (5) In words like *infinite*, *rapine*, etc., and in words adopted from Fr. (6) In certain anomalous cases, as *are*, *were*, *come*, *done*, *gone*, *some*, *one*, *none*.

II. Besides serial order (5th) in the alphabet, or as a vowel (2nd), E, e, or *e* signifies *spec.* **1.** *Mus.* The 3rd note of the diatonic scale of C major. Also the scale or key which has that note for its tonic. **2.** In *Logic*: a universal negative. **3.** E. The second class of rating on Lloyd's books. Cf. A. IV. **4.** In *Math.* e or *e*. **a.** The quantity 2·71828.., the base of Napier's system of logarithms. **b.** The ECCENTRICITY of an ellipse. **5.** In *Electr.* *e* stands for the electromotive force of a single cell, E for the sum of such forces. **6.** In *Chem.* E = the element Erbium.

III. *Abbreviations.* E. = **1.** various proper names, as Edward, etc.; Engineer(s) in C.E. and R.E. **2.** East, a point of the compass. **3.** E.E., E. & O.E. (*Comm.*) = *errors* (*and omissions*) *excepted*. **4.** E.M. = Earl Marshal. **5.** *e.g.* = Lat. *exempli gratia* for example.

E, *prefix*, L. *ē*, shortened form of *ex-* out of; see Ex-[1].

Ea (ī·ă). *dial.* 1781. [repr. OE. *ēa* river.] A river, running water. Also *attrib.*

They rowed away for Crowland, by many a mere and many an e. KINGSLEY.

Each (ītʃ), *a.* and *pron.* [OE. *ǣlc* = OFris. *ellik*, *e*(*l*)*k*, (M)LG., (M)Du. *elk* :—WGerm. **aiwo galīkoz* AYE (ever) ALIKE; for loss of *l* cf. *such*, *which*.]

I. As adj. used *attrib.* Every (one of two or more) regarded separately. **a.** followed immediately by a sb. **b.** with *one* used absol. (Now usually repl. by *every one*, or by *each* absol.) OE.

a. E. night we die, E. morn are born anew YOUNG. **b.** Every e. one respectively 1631.

II. Absol. (quasi-*pron.*) **1.** With reference to a sb. going before, or followed by *of*. Occas. (erron.) with pl. vb. OE. **2.** Distributing a pl. subj. or obj. OE.

1. All and e. ..Did join in the pursuit COWPER. E. has his own place J. H. NEWMAN. **2.** His majesty's heirs and successors, e. in his time and order BURKE. Phr. *E. other* = *one another*. (Now a compound (cf. Du. *elkander*); but orig. *other* was governed by a vb., as still occas. in *e. to other*, etc.)

†**Ea·ch-whe·re.** ME. [f. EACH + WHERE.] Everywhere -1649.

†**Ea·di,** *a.* [Com. Teut.: OE. *ēadig*.] **1.** Wealthy -ME. **2.** Fortunate -ME.

Eadish, obs. f. EDDISH.

Eager (ī·gəɹ), *a.* ME. [a. OF. *aigre* :—L. *acrem* (*acer*) sharp.] †**1.** Pungent, acrid, keen; sharp; severe -1601. Also *fig.* †**2.** *spec.* Acid, tart -1727. †**3.** Of metals: Brittle -1766. †**4.** Of persons, etc.: Strenuous, ardent, impetuous; fierce -1733. Also *transf.* **5.** Full of keen desire or appetite; impatiently longing; impatient ME.; of actions, etc.: Manifesting alacrity or impatient desire 1697. †**6.** *spec.* Hungry -1766.

1. A..more egre medicine CHAUCER. *fig.* The bitter clamour of two e. tongues *Rich. II*, I. i. 49. **2.** It doth posset And curd like Aygre droppings into Milke *Haml.* I. v. 69. **4.** Egre as is a Tygre CHAUCER. **5.** E. of fame BLACKMORE, for war 1769, about your coming BURKE, in plundering the baggage MORSE. E. controversy 1853.

So †**Ea·ger** *v.* to excite, irritate; also *refl.* **Ea·gerly** *adv.*; **-ness,** the state or quality of being e.; keenness of appetite or desire.

Eagle (ī·g'l), *sb.* [ME. *egle*, a. OF. *egle*, *aigle* :—L. *aquila*.] **1.** Any of the larger Diurnal Birds-of-prey which are not Vultures. Two species of Eagle are natives of Britain; the Golden Eagle (*Aquila chrysaëtus*), mainly confined in these islands to the mountainous parts of Scotland and Ireland; and the Sea, or White-tailed Eagle (*Haliaëtus albicilla*), found on the coasts of the same countries. The emblematic bird of the United States is the Bald or White-headed Eagle (*H. leucocephalus*). Also *fig.* **2.** A figure of the bird used for any purpose: **a.** as an ensign in the Roman army, and as an ensign and badge by France under the empire ME. **b.** as an armorial bearing; *esp.* of the Holy Roman Empire, and of the Austrian, French, German, and Russian empires ME. **3.** Anything made in the form of an eagle; as a lectern in a church; a clasp for a belt; etc. 1766. **4.** The constellation *Aquila* 1551. **5.** A coin bearing an image of the bird; *spec.* a base coin current at the accession of Edward I; a U.S. gold coin, value ten dollars. *Double-e.*: a U.S. coin worth twenty dollars. 1753. **6.** *Golf.* A hole played in two strokes under par or bogey 1922.

1. These moyst Trees, That haue out-liu'd the E. *Timon* IV. iii. 224. Can I make mine eye an Eagle's BROWNING. *fig.* Russia's famish'd eagles SHELLEY.

Comb.: **a.** attrib., as *e.-eye*, *-speed*, etc.; **b.** objective, as *e.-bearer*; **c.** parasynthetic, as *e.-sighted*, *-winged* adjs. Also **e.-eyed** *a.*, having an eye like an e.; keen-sighted (*lit.* and *fig.*); **-fisher,** the Osprey; **-hawk,** a S. Amer. bird of prey of the genus *Morphnus* (not in Eng. use); **-owl,** a nocturnal bird of prey (*Bubo ignavus*), the largest European owl; **-ray, -skate,** a species of skate, *Myliobates marginata*; **-stone** = AETITES, q. v.

Eaglet (ī·glėt). 1572. [a. F. *aiglette*, dim. of *aigle*; see -ET.] A young eagle.

Ea·gle-wood. 1712. [tr. F. *bois d'aigle*, f. (ult.) Skr. *aguru*.] = AGALLOCH, CALAMBAC.

Eagre (ēⁱ·gəɹ, ī·gəɹ). 1612. [Of unkn. etym.] A tidal wave of unusual height in a narrowing estuary; = BORE *sb.*[3]

Eam, obs. var. of EME, uncle.

†**Ean,** *v.* [OE. *ēanian*.] Of ewes: To bring forth lambs -1750. Hence **Ea·nling,** a young lamb.

-ean, sometimes varying with **-æan,** suffix repr. L. *-æus*, *-ēus* (corr. to Gr. *-αῖος*, *-ειος*), *-eus*, compounded with -AN; e.g. *Eurōpæus*, EUROPEAN, *Eurīpidēus* (Εὐρωπαῖος, Εὐρῑπίδειος), *Herculeus*; med.L. *empyreus*, *-æus* (ἐμπύριος) EMPYREAN; the use in ANTIPODEAN is irregular.

Ear (īᵊɹ), *sb.*[1] [Com. Teut.: OE. *ēare* wk. neut. :—OTeut. **(au·son-)*, *auzo·n-*, cogn. w. L. *auris* (:—**ausis*), Gr. *οὖς*, etc.] **1.** The organ of hearing in men and animals. Its parts are (1) the *external ear*, consisting of the pinna and the meatus or passage leading thence to (2) the *middle ear*, or tympanum, separated from the external meatus by a membrane called the *membrana tympani*; (3) the *internal ear*, or labyrinth. **2.** The external ear OE. **3.** The internal and middle ear, together or separately ME. **4.** With reference to its function: The organ of hearing OE. Also *transf.* and *fig.* of the mind, heart, etc. **5.** *transf.* Used in *sing.* and *pl.* for: The sense of hearing, auditory perception ME. **6.** (in *sing.*) The faculty of discriminating sounds, and recognizing musical intervals 1526. **7.** Voluntary hearing, favourable attention 1503. **8.** Any object resembling the external ear in shape or position; as, †an auricle of the heart; the handle of a pitcher; the projecting part of anything by which it is hung, as a bell, lifted, as a pile-driver, or handled, as a mortar-shell, a composing-rule, etc. **9.** *Bot.* and *Conch.* = AURICLE 2. 1688.

1. In the lowest animals the e. is reduced to a sack filled with a special fluid 1861. **2.** The jewel That trembles in her e. TENNYSON. Phr. *About one's ears*: said of a shower of missiles, a falling house, etc. Also *fig.* *Button e.*: in dogs, an ear falling forward and hiding the inside. *Rose e.*, one folding at the back, and disclosing the inside. *Over* (*head and*) *ears*, *up to the ears*: *fig.* deeply immersed *in*. *To set* (*persons*) *by the ears*: to put them at variance. †(*Not to dare*) *for one's ears* (in allusion to the loss of ears as a punishment). **4.** They say Walls have Ears (*i.e.* there may be listeners anywhere) SHELTON. *fig.* The ears of fame J. H. BURTON. Phr. *To incline one's ear*(*s*, *lend an e.* *To bow down one's e.*: to listen graciously. *To be all ears*: to be eagerly attentive. **6.** I have no E. for Musick STEELE. **7.** Phr. *To give e.* *To have* (*win*, *gain*) *a person's e.*

attrib. and *Comb.* **a.** attrib., as *e.-drum*, *-lobe*, etc.; *e.-jewel*, etc.; *e.-douche*, *-speculum*, *-syringe*, etc.; **b.** objective, as *e.-protector*, *-catching*, *-deafening*, *-piercing*, *-splitting*, etc.

Special comb.: **e.-bob** (now *vulg.* or *joc.*) = EAR-DROP; **-brisk** *a.*, quick at pricking up his ears, said of a horse; **-brush** = AURILAVE; **-cap,** a covering for the ears against the cold; **-chamber,** the cavity of the internal e.; **-cough,** a cough excited by irritation of the external ear; **-drop,** (*a*) a pendant worn in the e.: (*b*) the flower of the common fuchsia; †**-finger,** the little finger, often put in the e.; **-flap,** the lobe of the e.; the external e. generally; **-lap,** the lobe of the e.; **-lock,** a lock of hair over or above the e.; **-phone,** a head-phone; **-pieces, -plate,** part of a helmet covering the e.; **-shell,** one of the *Haliotidæ*, called also *sea-ears*; also, *Auris marina*, a genus of shell-fish; †**-shrift,** auricular confession; †**-sore** (cf. EYE-SORE); **-sore** *a.* (*dial.*), irritable, ill-tempered; **-stone,** an otolith; **-string** (cf. *heart-strings*); **-worm** ? = EARWIG; **-wort,** a plant, *Dysophila auricularis*, supposed to cure deafness.

Ear (īᵊɹ), *sb.*[2] [OE. *ēar*, Northumb. *eher* :—OTeut. **ahoz-* = L. *acus* (genit. *-ĕris*) neut., husk of corn. Allied to AWN.] A spike or head of corn; the part of a cereal plant which contains its flowers or seeds.

Barley was in the e. *Ex.* ix. 31.

†**Ear,** *sb.*[3] *rare.* 1460. [f. EAR *v.*[1]] The action of ploughing -1693.

Ear (īᵊɹ), *v.*[1] Now *arch.* [Com. Teut.: OE. *ęrian* :—OTeut. **arjan*, f. WAryan root **ar* to plough, whence Gr. *ἀρόειν*, L. *arare*, Ir. *airim*.] **1.** *trans.* To plough, till; also with *up*. Also *absol.* **2.** *transf.* and *fig.* ME.

2. Make the Sea serue them; which they eare and wound With keeles *Ant. & Cl.* I. iv. 49.

Ear (īᵊɹ), *v.*[2] ME. [f. EAR *sb.*[2]] *intr.* Of corn: To come into ear.

Ea·r-ache. 1789. [f. EAR *sb.*[1]] Pain in the the drum of the ear; otalgia.

Ear-cockle (īᵊ·ɹkǫ:k'l). 1836. [f. EAR *sb.*[2] + COCKLE in some sense.] A disease of wheat, etc., caused by vibriones in the seed.

Eared (īᵊɹd), *ppl. a.*[1] ME. [f. EAR *sb.*[1] + -ED.] **a.** Furnished with ears (in various senses); in *Bot.* = AURICULATE. **b.** With defining word: Having (large, open, etc.) ears 1514.

E. owl: a species with ear-like tufts on the head.

Eared (īᵊɹd), *ppl. a.*[2] ME. [f. EAR *sb.*[2] and *v.*[2] + -ED.] Of corn, etc.: Having ears; that has come into ear. In *Her.* having ears of a certain tincture.

†**Ea·ring,** *vbl. sb.*[1] ME. [f. EAR *v.*[1] + -ING[1].] Ploughing; a ploughing -1616.

Ea·ring, *vbl. sb.*[2] 1547. [f. EAR *v.*[2] + -ING[1].] The coming into ear. Also *concr.*

Earing (īᵊ·riŋ), *sb.* 1626. [? f. EAR *sb.*[1]; or ? = EAR-RING.] 'One of a number of small ropes employed to fasten the upper corner of a sail to the yard' (Adm. Smyth). Also *attrib.*

Earl (ɜ̄ɹl), *sb.* [OE. *eorl* = OSax. *erl* a man, ON. *earl*, later *iarl*, nobleman, chieftain :—OTeut. **erloz*.] †**1.** A man of noble rank, as dist. from a *ceorl* CHURL. Only in OE. **b.** In OE. poetry: A warrior, a man. **2.** In late OE.: A Danish under-king (see JARL); hence, later, the governor of one of the great divisions of England, as Wessex, Mercia, etc. (In this sense = ALDERMAN.) *Obs.* exc. *Hist.* **3.** After the Norman Conquest taken as = L. *comes* COUNT. †**a.** Applied to all feudal nobles and princes bearing the Romanic title of Count; also *Hist.* to the officers called *comites* ME. **b.** *spec.* In England, Scotland, and Ireland, a title of nobility ranking next below that of marquis and next above that of viscount, and corresponding to the European *Count* OE.

Earldom (ɜ̄·ɹldəm). OE. [f. prec. + -DOM.] The territory governed by an earl (*Obs.* exc *Hist.*); the rank or dignity of an earl.

Others with Titles and new Earldoms caught DRYDEN.

Earless (īᵊ·ɹlės), *a.* 1611. [f. EAR *sb.*[1] + -LESS.] **1.** Having no ears, as human beings, drinking vessels, bivalve shells, etc. **2.** Without the sense of hearing; without an ear for music; also *poet.*, where nothing is heard 1802.

2. In some deep dungeon's e. den WORDSW.

Earlet (īᵊ·ɹlėt). 1609. [f. EAR *sb.*[1] + -LET.] †**1.** An ear-ring. **2.** Anything resembling a small ear (see EAR *sb.*[1] 8) 1668.

Ea·rl Ma·rshal. ME. A high officer of state, formerly the deputy of the CONSTABLE as judge of the court of chivalry. The title was originally 'marshal'. The office is now hereditary in the line of the Dukes of Norfolk, who, as such, preside over the Heralds' College, appoint its officers, and undertake certain purely ceremonial duties.

Earlship. [OE. *eorlscipe.*] †1. Manliness; nobility, lordship. OE. only. 2. The dignity or office of an earl (*Hist.*) 1792.

Early (ɔ̄·ɹli), *a.* [ME. *earlich*; prob. from the adv.] 1. Near to the beginning of a period of time, as morning, night, the year, a lifetime: opp. to *late*. 2. Belonging or relating to the initial stage of an epoch, of the history of a people, of the world, of a science, etc.; ancient 1672. 3. Connected with the initial part of any continuous action, etc.; also, timely, done or taking place before it is too late. In compar. and superl. = former, foremost (in time). 1767. b. Of future events, etc.: Not remote, near at hand 1857. 4. Near the beginning in serial order 1707.

1. The e. Village Cock *Rich. III*, v. iii. 209. Ev'n in this e. Dawning of the Year DRYDEN. E. rest, rising COWPER. E. Purple Orchis 1861. E. training JOWETT. 2. While yet in e. Greece she sung COLLINS. E. philosophers 1794, engravers 1821, fathers of the Church MACAULAY. 3. No prospect of an e. peace 1857. 4. The e. chapters of the book (*mod.*).

Phr. **e. closing**, designating a movement for the reduction of hours of labour, (later) a system of closing business premises early one day in the week 1847; **E. English** (*Arch.*): the style of English architecture succeeding the Norman, characterized by pointed arches and lancet windows.

Hence †**Ea·rlily** *adv.* **Ea·rliness.**

Early (ɔ̄·ɹli), *adv.* [OE. *ǽrlíce*, f. **ǽr* positive degree of *ǽr* ERE + *líce* -LY[2]. The OE. var. *ǽrlíce* gave rise to *arli*, *erli* (whence the mod. form).] 1. Near the beginning of a period of time (see EARLY *a.* 1). 2. Far back in date, anciently ME. 3. In the initial part of any continuous action, etc. Also, in good time, before it is too late. 1655. 4. Near the beginning in serial order (*mod.*).

1. What misaduenture is so earely vp SHAKS.

Ea·r-mark, *sb.* 1523. [f. EAR *sb.*[1] + MARK *sb.*] 1. A mark in the ear of a sheep or other animal, serving as a sign of ownership. 2. *transf.* and *fig.* A stamp, mark of ownership, identifying mark 1577.

2. Fanatick Money hath no Ear-mark MARVELL.

Ea·r-mark, *v.* 1591. [f. prec. sb.] *trans.* To mark in the ear as a sign of ownership or identity. b. To assign (money, etc.) to a definite purpose 1890.

Sums ear-marked..for the extinction of licences 1890.

Earn (ɔ̄ɹn), *v.*[1] [OE. *earnian*, *ge-earnian*, repr. an OTeut. **aznōjan*, f. **aznā* labour, conn. w. OHG. *aran* (whence mod.G. *ernte*), OE. *esne* serf, etc.] *trans.* To render an equivalent in labour for; hence, to obtain or deserve as the reward of labour. In early use: To deserve. b. Of qualities or actions: To procure as a direct consequence *for* a person 1596.

1. These praises..have been dearly earned JUNIUS. Do they all e. wages HT. MARTINEAU. b. The stern justice of his rule earned the hatred of the disorderly baronage GREEN.

Earn, *v.*[2] 1674. Now *dial.* [same as ME. *erne.*] To curdle (*intr.* and *trans.*).

†**Earn**, *v.*[3] 1579. [var. of YEARN:—OE. *geornian*; but see Skeat (s. v. YEARN).] 1. *intr.* To desire strongly –1596. 2. To grieve –1651. 3. Of hounds, etc.: To utter a prolonged cry.

Earn, var. of ERNE, eagle.

Earnest (ɔ̄·ɹnėst), *sb.*[1] [OE. *eornust* fem. :—OTeut. **ernusti*, perh. f. root **ers*, found also in †*erre* anger. Cf. mod.G. *ernst*, etc.] †1. Ardour in battle; more widely, intense desire –ME. 2. Seriousness, as opp. to jest OE.

2. But in good e., madam, speak 1570. This caitiff, never worth my e., and now not seasonable for my jest MILT.

Earnest (ɔ̄·ɹnėst), *sb.*[2] [ME. *ernes*; prob. conn. w. the synonymous *erles* (see ARLES), †*erres* (a. OF. *erres* pl.). App. confused early with prec. sb.] Money in part payment, *esp.* for the purpose of binding a bargain. Also *fig.* a foretaste, instalment, pledge, of what is to come.

E. given me of something further intended in my favour STEELE. *Comb.*, *e.-money*, etc.

Earnest (ɔ̄·ɹnėst), *a.* (*adv.*) [OE. *eorneste*, f. EARNEST *sb.*[1]] 1. Of persons: Serious; usually in emphatic sense, intensely serious, in purpose, feeling, conviction, or action; sincerely zealous. Of words or actions: Proceeding from intense conviction. Also *transf.* 2. Of things: Demanding serious consideration; weighty 1544.

1. I..haue been An e. aduocate to plead for him *Rich. III*, I. iii. 87. We ought to giue the more e. heede *Hebr.* ii. 1. *transf.* Life is e. LONGF. 2. E. and weightie matters ASCHAM.

†B. *adv.* = Earnestly –1791.

Hence **Ea·rnest-ly** *adv.* in an e. manner; **-ness.**

†**Ea·rnest**, *v.* [f. prec. adj.] To use in earnest; to render earnest –1603.

†**Ea·rnestful**, *a.* ME. [f. EARNEST *sb.*[1] + -FUL.] = EARNEST *a.* 1, 3. –1563.

†**Ea·rnest-pe·nny.** 1508. [f. EARNEST *sb.*[2] + PENNY.] A piece of money paid as earnest to bind a bargain –1760. Also *fig.*

Ea·rnful, *a.* Now *dial.* 1500. [var. of YEARNFUL.] Anxious, full of yearning; sorrowful. Hence **Ea·rnfully** *adv.*

Earning (ɔ̄·ɹniŋ), *vbl. sb.*[1] [OE. *earnung*, *geearnung.*] 1. The action of EARN *v.*[1]; *concr.* in pl. that which is earned by labour, or invested capital 1732. †2. The fact of deserving; what one deserves –ME. †3. *pl.* Gain, profit –1675.

1. The earnings of the peasant MACAULAY. The gross earnings of railways 1888.

†**Ea·rning**, *vbl. sb.*[2] [f. EARN *v.*[3]] = YEARNING –1711.

Earning (ɔ̄·ɹniŋ), *vbl. sb.*[3] *dial.* 1615. [f. EARN *v.*[2] + -ING[1].] 1. The action of EARN *v.*[2] 1782. 2. Rennet. Also *attrib.* Also **e.-grass** = BUTTERWORT.

Ea·r-pi·ck, -pi·cker. 1483. [f. EAR *sb.*[1]] An instrument for clearing the ear of wax, etc.; also *fig.*

†**Ea·r-re·nt.** 1610. [?f. EAR *sb.*[3]] ? Some kind of agricultural rent. Used punningly by B. Jons. for loss of ears in the pillory. –1624.

Ea·r-ring, earring. OE. [f. EAR *sb.*[1]] 1. A ring worn in the lobe of the ear for ornament, etc.; often, a pendant or drop. 2. *dial.* The common fuchsia.

Earsh. Now *dial.* 1622. [A slurred pronunc. of EDDISH.] a. A stubble field. b. Eddish.

Earshot (ī³·ɹʃǫt). 1607. [f. EAR *sb.*[1]; after *bowshot*, etc.] The distance at which the voice may be heard; hearing.

Earth (ɔ̄ɹþ), *sb.*[1] [Com. Teut.: OE. *eorþe*, wk. fem. = OS. *ertha* wk. fem., Du. *aarde*, mod.G. *erde*, ON. *iǫrð*, Sw., Da. *jord*, Goth. *airþa* str. fem. :—OTeut. **erþā*. Cf. Gr. ἔραζε on the ground.]

I. 1. The ground as a mere surface, or as a solid crust. 2. The hole or hiding-place of a burrowing animal, as a fox, etc. Also *fig.* 1575. 3. The soil as suited for cultivation OE. 4. *Electr.* Connexion of a wire conductor with the earth, either accidental (with leakage of current) or intentional (as for providing a return path for a telegraph current, etc.) 1870.

1. They kneele, they kisse the E. *Wint. T.* v. i. 109. Who under e. on human kind avenge Severe, the guilt of violated oaths COWPER. 2. Frighted hare fled to cover, or fox to e. DE FOE. 3. Fatty e. 1751.

II. The world we live on. 1. The dry land OE. 2. The world as including land and sea; as dist. from the (material) heaven OE. 3. The world as the abode of mortals; freq. opp. to heaven and hell. In poet. and rhet. use often without the article. OE. Also *transf.* of the inhabitants of the world 1549. 4. The world as a sphere, orb, or planet ME.; †*transf.* –1841.

1. God clepid the drie erthe WYCLIF *Gen.* i. 10. 3. Those that haue knowne the E. so full of faults *Jul. C.* I. iii. 45. The whole e. was of one language *Gen.* xi. 1. What on e. is the matter (*mod.*). 4. *transf.* He affirmed..the Moon [to be] an e., having Mountains [etc.] CUDWORTH.

†III. A country, land; a portion of the earth's surface –1628.

This blessed plot, this e., this Realme, this England *Rich. II*, II. i. 50.

IV. 1. The material of which the surface of the ground is composed, soil, mould, dust, clay OE. 2. Used for: The body. Cf. *dust*, *clay*. 1600. 3. Earth as one of the four (or more) so-called 'elements' ME. 4. *Chem.* Applied to certain metallic oxides, *e. g.* magnesia, alumina, zirconia, and the 'alkaline earths', baryta, lime, strontia 1728.

2. Poore soule the center of my sinfull e. SHAKS. *Sonn.* cxlvi. 3. You should not rest Betweene the elements of ayre and e. *Twel. N.* I. v. 294.

attrib. and *Comb.*: **e.-bags** = *sand-bags* (Adm. Smyth); **-balls**, truffles; †**-bath**, a medical bath in which the patient was buried up to the shoulders in e. or mud; **-battery** (*Electr.*), a battery formed by burying two voltaic elements some distance apart; **-bed**, a bed upon the ground; the grave; **-bob**, a maggot, the larva of the beetle; **-chestnut** = EARTH-NUT; **-closet**, a closet in which e. is used as a deodorizing agent; **-current** (*Electr.*), an irregular current due to the e., which renders telegraph wires temporarily useless; †**-dog**, a terrier; **-flax**, ? asbestos; **-gall**, the Lesser Centaury; **-hog** = AARD-VARK; **-house**, an underground dwelling; *fig.* the grave; **-hunger**, a disease characterized by a morbid craving for eating e.; *fig.* greed of land or territory; **-oil**, petroleum; **-pillar** (*Geol.*), a pillar-like mass of earth, sometimes capped with a stone; **-plate** (*Electr.*), a metal plate buried in the e., connected with a telegraph battery; **-sack** = *earth-bag*; **-shine** = E.-LIGHT; †**-shrew**, the Shrew-mouse; **-smoke**, the plant Fumitory; **-spring**, in electrical machines a spring connected with the e.; **-star**, a fungus so called from its shape when lying on the ground; **-stopper**, one who stops up the earths of foxes; **-table** (*Arch.*), the plinth of a wall, the projecting course immediately above the ground; **-tongue** (*Bot.*), the genus *Geoglossum*; **-wave**, a seismic wave in the crust of the e.; **-wolf**, tr. Du. AARD-WOLF, q. v.

†**Earth**, *sb.*[2] [OE. *ęrþ*, f. **ar-*: see EAR *v.*[1]] The action of ploughing –1813.

Earth (ɔ̄ɹþ), *v.* ME. [f. EARTH *sb.*[1]] 1. *trans.* To commit to the earth; to bury. Now *dial.* 2. To hide in the earth; to cover *up* with earth. Also *intr.* (for *refl.*). Also *fig.* 1648. 3. *trans.* To conceal in a hole or burrow 1619; *intr.* (for *refl.*) of the fox, etc.: To run to his earth 1622. 4. *trans.* To drive (a fox, etc.) to his earth. Also *fig.* 1575. 5. *Electr.* To connect (a conductor) with the earth 1888.

1. Though earthed be his corps, yet florish shall his fame 1557. 2. Seeds thrive When earth't BENLOWES. E. up the plants frequently 1796. 3. Perhaps some Foxe had earth'd there 1634. 4. We e. and digge a Badgerd TURBERV.

Ea·rth-apple. OE. [f. EARTH *sb.*[1]] 1. In OE. ? A cucumber. 2. ? The potato [tr. F. *pomme de terre*]. Mod. Dicts.

Ea·rth-board. 1649. [f. EARTH *sb.*[1] or [2] + BOARD.] The mould-board of a plough.

Ea·rth-born, *ppl. a. poet.* or *rhet.* 1603. 1. Born by emerging from the earth, as the Titans, etc. Also = AUTOCHTHONOUS. 2. Of earthly or mortal race 1667. 3. Of things: Produced by or arising from the earth 1702.

1. Cadmus and his earth-born men JOWETT. 2. Creatures .. earth-born perhaps, Not Spirits MILT. *P. L.* IV. 360. 3. Earth-born pride ROWE.

†**Ea·rth-din.** OE. [f. EARTH *sb.*[1] + DIN.] An earthquake –1483.

Earthen (ɔ̄·ɹþ'n), *a.* ME. [See -EN.] 1. Made of earth; made of baked clay. 2. *transf.* and *fig.* Characteristic of the earth; merely material *c* 1600.

Earthenware (ɔ̄·ɹþ'nˌwēᵊɹ). 1673. [f. EARTHEN *a.* + WARE; formerly as two words.] 1. Vessels, etc., made of baked clay; in *pl.* kinds of earthenware. 2. The material of which such vessels are made 1799. 3. *attrib.* 1812.

Earthfast (ɔ̄·ɹþfɑst), *a.* OE. [f. EARTH *sb.*[1]] Fixed in the ground.

Earthiness (ɔ̄·ɹþinės). ME. [f. EARTHY *a.*] 1. The quality of being earthy; the properties characteristic of earth; †*concr.* earthy matter –1693. 2. *fig.* = EARTHLINESS 1. 1670.

Ea·rth-light. 1833. *Astron.* The light reflected from the earth upon the dark half of the moon; = *earth-shine*.

Earthliness (ɔ̄·ɹþlinės). 1535. [f. EARTHLY *a.* + -NESS.] 1. The quality of being earthly or terrestrial; worldliness as opp. to *heavenliness* 1583. †2. = EARTHINESS 1. –1642.

1. Each stain of e. Had passed away SHELLEY.

†**Ea·rthling**, *sb.*[1] [OE. *yrþling*; see EARTH *sb.*[2]] A ploughman –1714.

Earthling (ɔ̄·ɹþliŋ), *sb.*[2] 1593. [f. EARTH *sb.*[1]] 1. An inhabitant of the earth. 2. A worldling 1615.

2. Beyond your earthlings gold and siluer mines 1615.

Earthly (ɔ̄·ɹþli), *a.* [OE. *eorþlic*; see EARTH *sb.*[1]] 1. Pertaining to the earth, terrestrial. Now usually opp. to *heavenly*. b. As an expletive; = on earth 1753. †2. Existing or living in or on the ground –1658. 3. =

EARTHY. *arch.* or *Obs.* ME. †4. = EARTHEN (*rare*) -1533.

1. The pageant pomp of e. man SCOTT. Of no e. use ROGERS. c. *Not an e.*: not an e. chance. 2. A Scepter, or an E. Sepulchre 3 *Hen. VI*, I. iii. 17.

Comb.: e.-minded *a.*, having the affections set on the things of the e.; whence -mindedness; -wise *adv.*, in an e. manner.

†**Ea·rth-mad.** *rare.* [OE. *eorþmata* for *eorþmaþa*, f. *eorþe* EARTH *sb.*[1] + *maþe* a worm.] An earthworm -1601.

Ea·rth-nut. OE. 1. The roundish tuber of an umbelliferous plant (*Bunium flexuosum*, including *B. Bulbocastanum*), called also *Earth-chestnut* and *Pig-nut*. 2. Applied also to the truffle (*Tuber*), the ARACHIS, the *Œnanthe pimpinelloides*, and the Heath Pea 1548.

Earthquake (ɔ̄·ɹþkwēɪk). ME. [f. EARTH *sb.*[1] + QUAKE *sb.*] 1. A shaking of the ground; usually *spec.* a convulsion of the earth's surface produced by volcanic or similar forces within the crust. Also *fig.* 2. *attrib.*, as *e.-shock*, *-voice*, *-wave*, etc. 1821.

1. *fig.* In this age, wherein there is an e. of ancient hospitals FULLER. This social and political e. BRIGHT.

†**Ea·rthquave.** ME. [f. EARTH *sb.*[1] + QUAVE *sb.*] = EARTHQUAKE -1541.

Earthward (ɔ̄·ɹþwəɹd), *adv.* ME. Towards the earth.

Earthwork (ɔ̄·ɹþwɒ̄ɹk). 1633. [f. EARTH *sb.*[1] + WORK *sb.*] A bank or mound of earth used as a rampart or fortification.

Earthworm (ɔ̄·ɹþwɒ̄ɹm). 1591. [f. EARTH *sb.*[1] + WORM.] 1. A worm that lives in the ground, *esp.* one of the genus *Lumbricus*. 2. *fig.* A mean grovelling person 1594.

Earthy (ɔ̄·ɹþi), *a.* ME. [See -Y.] 1. Of the nature of earth; resembling, characteristic of, or consisting of earth. Of minerals: Without lustre, friable, and roughish to the touch; also, containing earth, as in *E. Cobalt*, etc. 1667. †2. Having the properties of the 'element' earth; heavy, gross -1677. Also *fig.* 3. *Chem.* Pertaining to an 'earth' or 'earths' (see EARTH IV. 4); in mod. use, pertaining to the class of metallic oxides so named 1718. 4. Pertaining to the ground, or to what is below it; dwelling inside the earth 1665. 5. Dwelling or existing on the earth: opp. to *heavenly* 1595.

1. Starry roofe and e. floore SIDNEY. 2. *fig.* Her e., and abhor'd commands *Temp.* I. ii. 273. 4. Those e. spirits black and envious are DRYDEN. 5. The impious race Of e. giants, that would heaven outface CHAPMAN.

Ea·r-trumpet. 1776. A straight or convoluted conoidal tube, used by persons partially deaf, to collect and intensify sounds.

Ea·r-wax. ME. [f. EAR *sb.*[1]] A viscid secretion which collects in the external meatus of the ear.

Earwig (ī^ə·ɹwig). [OE. *éarwicga*, lit. ear-punner; cf. WIGGLE *v.* to wriggle.] 1. An insect, *Forficula auricularia*, which is supposed to creep into the ear. †2. *fig.* A whisperer, flatterer, parasite -1758.

2. The earwigs of royalty 1758.

Earwig (ī^ə·ɹwig), *v.* 1837. [f. the sb.] a. To pester by private importunities. b. To bias by secret communications; to insinuate oneself into the confidence of.

Each secretary of state is sure to be earwigged by a knot of sturdy beggars 1839.

Ea·r-witness. 1594. [f. EAR *sb.*[1]] One whose testimony is based upon his own hearing.

Strabo himself was an ear-witness of this 1734.

Ease (īz), *sb.* ME. [a. OF. *eise*, *aise* (mod. *aise*); cf. It. *agio*, Pg. *azo*. Of unkn. origin.] †1. Opportunity, means or ability -1500. 2. Comfort, convenience; *formerly* also, enjoyment. Also with *an* and *pl.* (obs.) ME. 3. Absence of pain or discomfort; freedom from annoyance ME. 4. Rest; leisure; in bad sense, idleness, sloth ME. b. Facility; *esp.* in phr. *with e.* 1610. c. Unconcern; absence of hesitation 1808. 5. Freedom from constraint; an unconstrained position; *esp.* in *Mil.* phr., *To stand at e.* 1802. 6. Freedom from awkwardness in social behaviour 1750. 7. Relief; alleviation 1542. Also with *an* and *pl.* (obs.) ME.

2. The e., and benefit the Subjects may enjoy HOBBES. A condition of e. and fortune EMERSON. Phr. *To take one's e.*: to make oneself comfortable. 3. E. of bodie 1597, of Mind STEELE, heart BURKE. 4. E. breedeth vice 1577. 6. A certain graceful e. marks him as a man of the world MACAULAY. 7. Sudden e. from pain BUTLER. Phr. *Chapel of E.*: see CHAPEL.

Phrases (senses 1–6). *At e.*, *at one's e.*: in comfort, without anxiety or annoyance, unconstrained, unembarrassed; formerly also, well-to-do. *Ill at e.*: uncomfortable, uneasy.

Ease (īz), *v.* ME. [virtually f. the sb.] 1. *trans.* To give ease to; to comfort, disburden; †to benefit, help. Also *refl.* Also (rarely) *absol.* 2. To relieve, lighten, set free (a person, etc.) *of*, †*from* a burden, anxiety, etc. ME. b. *joc.* To deprive *of* 1609. 3. To lighten (a burden, etc.); to lessen (an inconvenience); to assuage (pain, etc.) ME. b. *poet.* To relax (labour) 1715. 4. To facilitate (*rare*) 1632. 5. To relax slightly; to shift a little, make to fit (*mod.*). 6. *Naut.* Often with *away*, *down*, *off*: to slacken (a rope, sail, etc.). *E. her!* (in a steam vessel): reduce the speed of the engine. *E. the helm!*: put the helm down a few spokes in a head sea. (Adm. Smyth.)

1. Some scruple rose, but thus he eas'd his thought POPE. The declared intention of easing the dissenters HUME. 2. E. your bosoms of a fear so vain POPE. 3. Is there no play To e. the anguish of a torturing hour SHAKS. 4. [Storks] with mutual wing Easing thir flight MILT. Hence Ea·seless *a.*

Easeful (ī·zful), *a.* ME. [See -FUL.] 1. That gives ease, comfort, or relief. 2. Unoccupied; indolent 1611.

1. E. Death KEATS. 2. Giving the best of their grain to the easefull and idle RALEIGH. Hence Ea·seful-ly *adv.*, -ness.

Easel (ī·zĕl, ī·z'l). 1634. [ad. Du. *ezel* = Ger. *esel* ass. Cf. HORSE *sb.*] A wooden frame to support a picture during its execution, or for exhibition. *Comb.* e.-picture, -piece, one painted at the e., or small enough to stand on an e.

Easement (ī·zmĕnt). ME. [a. OF. *aisement*, f. *aisier* EASE *v.*; see -MENT.] 1. The process or means of giving or obtaining ease or relief; alleviation; †redress of grievances. Now somewhat *rare*. 2. Advantage, convenience, comfort; furtherance; formerly also, enjoyment (*arch.*) ME. b. Accommodation ME. 3. The right or privilege of using something not one's own; *esp.* in *Law*. (See quot.) 1463.

1. I certainly stand in need of every kind of relief and e. BURKE. 3. If the purposes for which the land of another is used merely tend to the more convenient enjoyment of another piece of land, the right is called an e. DIGBY.

Easily (ī·zili), *adv.* Formerly compared easilier, -est. ME. [f. EASY *a.* + -LY[2].] 1. Comfortably; without pain, anxiety, or disturbance. 2. Freely ME. †3. Without hurry. Also, quietly. -1695. 4. With little labour or difficulty ME. 5. With little resistance or reluctance 1649. †6. After *but*: Indifferently, poorly -1536.

1. Persons seeking only to live e. 1562. 2. Sir, your wit ambles well; it goes e. *Much Ado* V. i. 159. 4. Nothing is more e. broken than a mans word HOBBES. 5. To catch Distempers e. STEELE.

Easiness (ī·zinĕs). ME. [See -NESS.] 1. The state or quality of being EASY (see quots.). †2. The being easily influenced; in bad sense, credulity -1797.

1. The e. we enjoy when asleep RAY. E. of Behaviour RICHARDSON, of wit D'ISRAELI. Ruin'd by his E. and Neglect 1699. E. of conquest 1800, of temper BUTLER. 2. Persons..who practised upon their e. 1674.

Ea·ssel, *adv. Sc.* 1810. [f. EAST.] Eastward, easterly.

East (īst). [repr. (1) OE. *éastan* adv. :—OTeut. **aus-to-nô* 'from the east', f. base **aus-* dawn (found in L. *aurora* :—**ausosa*, Skr. *ushas*, Gr. ἠώς, ἕως, ἄυως dawn); (2) OE. *éast* adv. in the east, in compounds repr. OTeut. **aus-to-* (see above).]

A. *adv.* †1. [repr. OE. *éastan.*] From the east -ME. 2. [repr. OE. *éast.*] In the direction of the part of the horizon where the sun rises; in the direction of that point of the horizon which is 90° to the right of the north point; also *due e.* OE. 3. quasi-*sb.*, with *from*, *on*, etc. ME.

B. *sb.* 1. subst. use of A. 2. The portion of the horizon or the sky near the place of the sun's rising; that one of the cardinal points near which the sun rises ME. 2. The orient; the eastern part of a country, district, or town ME. 3. = East wind 1763.

1. The gentle day.. Dapples the drowsie E. with spots of grey *Much Ado* V. iii. 27. 2. Where the gorgeous E...Showrs on her Kings Barbaric Pearl MILT. *P. L.* II. 3. 3. Where the sharp e. for ever.. blows SHENSTONE.

C. as *adj.* That is in, near, or towards the east; oriental, easterly ME.

An E. window welcomes the infant beams of the Sun FULLER. *Comb.*: E.-south-east, E.-north-east: the points of the compass distant $22\frac{1}{2}°$ from due E.; E.-by-South, E.-by-North: the points distant $11\frac{1}{4}°$ from due E.

East (īst), *v.* 1858. [f. prec.] a. *intr.* To move towards the east. b. *refl.* To orientate; to find one's true position.

Ea·st-country. 1701. An eastern country: in 18th c. *spec.* the region of the Baltic; cf. EASTLAND. Also *attrib.*

Ea·st-e·nd. OE. The easterly part of anything. Now often *spec.* The eastern part of London. Hence Ea·st-e·nder.

Easter (ī·stəɹ), *sb.* [OE. *éastre* wk. fem., pl *éastron*. Bæda derives the word from *Eostre* (Northumb. sp. of *Éastre*), a goddess whose festival was celebrated at the vernal equinox.] 1. A festival of the Christian Church, commemorating the resurrection of Christ, and corresponding to the Jewish passover, whence its name in most European langs. (Gr. πάσχα, ad. Heb. *pěsaḥ*, L. *pascha*, Fr. *Pâques*, It. *Pasqua*). It is observed on the first Sunday after the calendar full moon—*i.e.* the 14th day of the calendar moon—which happens on or next after 21 March. Applied colloq. to the week commencing with Easter Sunday. †2. The Jewish passover -1611. 3. *attrib.*, as *e.-holidays*, *-Sunday* (*-Monday*, etc.), *-tide*, *-time*, *-week*, etc. ME.

2. Intending after E. to bring him foorth *Acts* xii. 4. *Comb.*: e.-dues, money payable at E. to the parson of a parish by the parishioners; -eggs, eggs painted in bright colours, which it was (and, now, again is) customary to present to friends at E.; -offering = *easter-dues*; formerly also the paschal sacrifice.

†**Ea·ster,** *a.* ME. [? compar. of EAST *a.*; cf. Du. *ooster-*.] Nearest the east; eastern -1816.

Ea·ster-da·y. [OE. *éastor-dæg*, f. *éastor*, comb. f. *éastron.*] Easter Sunday.

Ea·stering, *ppl. a. rare.* 1876. [Cf. *westering.*] Shifting eastward.

Ea·sterling. Now *Hist.* 1534. [app. f. EASTER *a.* + -LING, ? after Du. *oosterling*. In AFr. and Anglo-L. *sterling(us*, *esterling(us* appear in the 13th c., but only in the sense of 'sterling penny' or 'pennyweight', not as the name of the Easterlings or Hanse merchants. See STERLING.] A native of the east. 1. *spec.* A native of the Baltic coasts; chiefly applied to the citizens of the Hanse towns. Hence *E. money*. b. [tr. Anglo-L. *esterlingus.*] The weight of the easterling or sterling penny; a penny-weight 1605. 2. *gen.* An inhabitant of an eastern country or district; also, a member of the Eastern Church (*arch.*) 1561.

Easterly (ī·stəɹli). 1548. [? f. EASTER *a.* + -LY; cf. Du. *oosterlijk.*]

A. *adj.* 1. Situated towards the east. 2. Coming from the east 1559.

1. E. towns..are more wholesome than the westerly 1655.

B. *adv.* In an eastern position or direction; from the east 1635.

†**Ea·stermost,** *a.* 1555. [f. EASTER *a.* + -MOST.] = EASTERNMOST -1832.

Eastern (ī·stəɹn). [OE. *éasterne* :—OTeut. **austrônjo*, f. **austr-* East + *ônjo-* (? = L. *-aneus*).]

A. *adj.* 1. Of or pertaining to the east; dwelling in the East; Oriental OE. 2. Lying or directed towards the east 1593. 3. Coming from the east (*poet.*) OE.

1. E. priests POPE. An e. tale MORLEY. 2. The e. sky TYNDALL. E. voyages ADDISON.

B. *sb.* An inhabitant of the East OE. b. A member of the Eastern Church 1865.

Hence Ea·sterner, an inhabitant of one of the eastern or New England states of U.S. 1864.

Easternmost (ī·stəɹnməst, -moust), *a.* 1830. [f. prec. + -MOST.] Situated farthest to the east.

Ea·st I·ndia. *Obs.* exc. *attrib.* 1634. Formerly used = (*The*) EAST INDIES.

East India Company, a company formed for carrying on an East Indian trade, *esp.* the English company incorporated in 1600. *E. Indiaman*, a ship of large tonnage engaged in the East India trade.

Ea·st I·ndian. 1553. [f. prec.]

A. as *adj.* 1. Of or pertaining to the East

Indies. **2.** In Anglo-Ind. use; = EURASIAN *a.* 1831. **B.** as *sb.* A Eurasian 1831.

Ea·st I·ndies. 1598. A term including Hindostan, Further India, and the islands beyond. Opp. to the *West Indies* or Central American islands.
They shall be my East and West Indies, and I will trade to them both *Merry W.* I. iii. 79.

Easting (ī·stiŋ), *vbl. sb.* 1628. [See -ING 1.] **1.** *Naut.* 'The course made good, or gained to the eastward' (Adm. Smyth). **2.** An approach to an easterly direction; a shifting or veering eastwards; easterly direction.

Eastland (ī·stlænd). OE. [f. EAST + LAND.] An eastern country or district; †*spec.* the lands bordering on the Baltic. Also *attrib.*

Eastward (ī·stwəɹd). [OE. *ēasteweard(e* adv., *ēastenweard* adj.] **A.** *adv.* **1.** In an eastern direction. **2.** quasi-*sb.* 1695.
1. Turne thee E. 1 *Kings* xvii. 3. 2. To sail to the e. 1828. var. **Ea·stwards** *adv.*
B. *adj.* That moves or looks eastward OE.
The e. posture in prayer SCHAFF.
Hence **Ea·stwardly** *adv.* in an eastern direction; from an eastern quarter. Also as *adj.*

East wind. **1.** (OE. *ēastanwind*) A wind blowing from the east 1398. **2.** A player in the game of mah jong 1922.

Easy (ī·zi). ME. [a. OF. *aisié* (mod. *aisé*), pa. pple. of OF. *aiser*, *aisier* to put at ease.]
A. *adj.* †**1.** At liberty, having opportunity or means (to do something). ME. only. **2.** Characterized by ease or rest; comfortable, quiet ME. **3.** Free from pain or discomfort ME. **4.** Free from constraint or stiffness; without trace of effort; smooth 1711. **5.** Not hard pressed; not hurried, gentle ME. **6.** Free from care, or apprehension 1692. **7.** = EASY-GOING 1649. **8.** Comfortably off 1701. **9.** Conducive to ease ME. **10.** Presenting few difficulties; offering little resistance ME. **11.** Of persons, etc.: Soon yielding, compliant; credulous 1611. **12.** That is obtained with ease 1697. **13.** Not oppressive; not burdensome ME.; †of persons: Not exacting; lenient; not difficult to get on with –1727. †**14.** Indifferent; slight –1648. **15.** Loosely fitting 1594. **16.** *Comm.* (opp. to *tight.*) Of a commodity: Not much in demand. Of the market: Showing little firmness in prices. 1888.
2. To make life e. BEVERIDGE. 3. After an opiate he became easier 1809. 4. Easie and obliging conversation BURNET. An e. Writer STEELE. E. and unstudied writing CHURCH. Phr. *Free and e.* (see FREE). 5. Under e. sail CAUNTER. Of e. motion 1852. 6. I made her e. on that point DE FOE. An e. conscience 1885. 8. In e. circumstances 1879. 9. E. cushions 1879. 10. This easie truth HOBBES. E. of access H. WALPOLE. It is e. to make a solitude and call it peace CARLYLE. 11. An easie King deserves no better Fate DRYDEN. Phr. *Lady of e. virtue.* 12. He obtained an e. pardon 1856. 13. On the easiest terms PEPYS. A generous and easie Governour BENTLEY. In e. confinement 1855. 16. The money-market is e. (*mod.*). Phr. *Honours e.* (Whist): 'honours divided'.
B. *adv.* In an EASY manner. Now mostly *colloq.* ME.
Phr. *To take it e.*, to do no more than one must. *E. ahead!*: (steam) at a moderate speed! *Easy all!* (in Boating): stop (rowing)! Hence as *sb.* A short rest. *To stand e.*: (of a squad, etc. standing at ease) to relax still further.

Ea·sy chai·r, ea·sy-chai·r. 1707. A chair adapted for ease or repose, often with arms and padded.

Ea·sy-go·ing, *ppl. a.* 1674. Of a horse: Having an easy gait. Hence *fig.* That takes things easily; comfort-loving; indolent.

Eat (īt), *v.* Pa. t. **ate, eat** (ēt, et, īt). Pa. pple. **eaten** (ī·t'n). [Com. Teut.: OE. *etan* str. vb.:—OTeut. *etan* = L. *edere*, Gr. ἔδειν, Skr. *ad-*.] **1.** *trans.* To masticate and swallow as food. Used also of liquid food, for which a spoon is used. Also *transf.* and *fig.* Also with *of* in partitive sense. **2.** *intr.* To consume food, take a meal OE. Also quasi-*trans.* **3.** *intr.* with pass. force (chiefly with *adj.* or *adv.*) 1601. **4.** *trans.* To devour, consume; to feed destructively upon (*lit.* and *fig.*) OE. **5.** *trans.* To gnaw, pierce 1611; also *transf.* of the slow action of frost, rust, cancer, corrosives, the waves, etc. 1555. Also *absol.* **6.** To make (a hole, etc.) by fretting or corrosion (*lit.* and *fig.*) 1697. **7.** *intr.* To make a way by gnawing or corrosion (*lit.* and *fig.*) 1606. **8.** *Naut. trans.* and *intr.* (See quots.) 1769.
1. They.. eate rootes for breade NORTH. We eat excellent cream EVELYN. Lest.. thou eate of his sacrifice *Ex.* xxxiv. 15. Phr. *To e. one's terms*: to qualify for being called to the Bar by eating dinners three or more times during each of twelve terms in the Hall of an Inn of Court. *To e. one's words*: to retract humbly. See also HUMBLE PIE. 2. There should be temperance.. in eating EMERSON. Phr. quasi-*trans.* *To e.* (a person) *out of house and home.* 3. If the cakes at tea e. short and crisp GOLDSM. 4. That they may..eate every herbe of the land *Ex.* x. 12. Phr. *To e. one's (own) heart*: to suffer from silent grief or vexation. 5. *transf.* The Rose..eaten with the canker LYLY. 7. Has not the desire of wealth so eaten into our hearts J. H. NEWMAN. 8. *Sourdre au vent*, to hold a good wind; to claw or e. to windward FALCONER. *To e. the wind out of a vessel*: to steal to windward of her by very keen seamanship. Hence **Ea·ter.**

Eat, *sb.* [OE. *ǣt.* In mod. use f. prec.] †**1.** That which is eaten –1609. **b.** Now freq. in pl. *U.S.* 1889. **2.** The action of eating; a meal –ME. Phr. *On the eat* (U.S.) 1879.

Eatable (ī·tăb'l). 1483. [See -ABLE.]
A. *adj.* In a state fit to be eaten.
B. *sb.* An article of food. Chiefly in *pl.* 1672.

Eatage (ī·tėdʒ). *n. dial.* 1641. [f. EAT *v.*; cf. EDDISH.] **1.** Grass available only for grazing; *esp.* the aftermath. **2.** The right of using for pasture 1857.

Eath, eith (īð, īþ). *Obs.* exc. *Sc.* [OE. *ēaþe* adv.] **A.** *adj.* Easy. **B.** *adv.* Easily OE. var. †**Ea·thly** *a.* and *adv.*

Eating (ī·tiŋ), *vbl. sb.* ME. [f. EAT *v.*] **1.** The action or habit of taking food. Also, a meal. **2.** Corrosion 1691. **3.** *attrib.*, as *e.-apple*, etc. ME.
Comb. **e.-house**, a house for e., *esp.* one in which meals are supplied; a restaurant.

‖**Eau** (*o*). 1823. [Fr.; = 'water'.] Hence: **E.-de-Cologne**, a perfume, originally made at Cologne. **E.-de-vie** [lit. 'water of life'], the French name for brandy.

Eave (īv). 1580. [f. EAVES, treated as pl.] Used as sing. of EAVES. Hence **Eave** *v.* to shelter under eaves. **Eaved** *ppl. a.* provided with eaves.

Eaver (ī·vəɹ). Now *dial.* 1732. [?] Rye grass.

Eaves (īvz). [OE. *efes*, fem.; prob. f. same root as OVER. In mod. Eng. commonly treated as pl.; see EAVE.] **1.** The projecting edge of a roof, etc., which overhangs the side. **2.** *transf.* Anything that projects or overhangs slightly; *poet.* the eyelids ME.
1. With minute-drops from off the e. MILT. *Pens.* 130. 2. Closing e. of wearied eyes I sleep TENNYSON.
Comb.: **e.-board** (also *eave-board*), **-catch, -lath,** an arris fillet, when used to raise the slates at the e. of a building (Gwilt); **-martin,** the House Martin (*Hirundo urbica*).

Ea·vesdrip, -drop, *sb.* [OE. *yfesdrype*, f. EAVES + DRIP, subseq. refash. after DROP.] The dripping of water from the eaves of a house; the space of ground on which such water falls.

Eavesdrop (ī·vzdrǫp), *v.* 1606. [f. prec.; or ? f. next.] *intr.* To stand within the 'eavesdrop' of a house in order to overhear secrets; hence, to listen secretly to private conversation. Also *trans.* To listen secretly to; to listen to the secrets of.
It is not civil to e. him SHIRLEY. We must not peep and e. at palace-doors EMERSON. Hence **Ea·vesdropper,** one who eavesdrops.

‖**Ebauchoir.** [F., f. *ébaucher* to sketch out.] **a.** A large chisel used by sculptors to rough-hew their work. **b.** A large hatchel or comb used by ropemakers.

Ebb (eb), *sb.* [OE. *ebba* = OFris. *ebba*, Du. *ebbe, eb*; of unkn. etym.] **1.** The reflux of the tide; the return of tide-water towards the sea. **2.** *transf.* and *fig.* Decline, decay; a change to a worse state ME. **3.** *attrib.* and *Comb.*, as *e.-tide*, etc. 1699. **4.** [? a distinct wd.] The Common Bunting, *Emberizia miliaria* (*dial.*) 1802.
1. During the freshets the e. and flow are little felt DE LA BECHE. 2. Not coueting to make of my floudde, another manes ebbe 1555. Private and public Virtue were at the lowest E. 1763. Hence **E·bbless** *a.*

†**Ebb,** *a.* ME. [? orig. the sb. used attrib.] **1.** Shallow. With *of*: Short. –1747. **2.** Near the surface; also as quasi-*adv.* –1794.

Ebb (eb), *v.* [OE. *ebbian*, f. EBB *sb.*] **1.** *intr.* To flow back or recede, as the water of the sea or a tidal river. Also *transf.* **2.** *fig.* To take a backward course; to decay, decline; to fade or waste away ME. **3.** *trans.* To hem in (fish) with stakes and nets at the ebb-tide 1827.
1. The sea will ebbe and flow *L. L. L.* IV. iii. 216. *transf.* [He] eyed The life-blood e. in crimson tide SCOTT. 2. After full sea, our hopes ebde too 1633.

Ebdomade, -ary, obs. ff. HEBDOMAD, -ARY.

Ebe·neous, *a.* [f. L. *ebeneus.*] Of the nature of ebony. (Mod. Dicts.)

Ebenezer (ebĕnī·zəɹ). 1758. [Heb.; = 'the stone of help'.] **1.** The name of the memorial stone set up by Samuel after the victory of Mizpeh; see 1 *Sam.* vii. 12. Used in fig. phrases, with allusion to the sentiment 'Hitherto hath the Lord helped us'. **2.** Occas. adopted by Methodists, Baptists, etc. as the name of a meeting-house. Hence, contemptuously, A 'dissenting chapel' 1856.

Ebionite (ī·biŏnəit). 1650. [ad. L. *ebionita*, f. Heb. *ebyōn* poor.] One of a body of 1st c. Christians, later, a sect, who held that Jesus was a mere man, and that the Mosaic law was binding upon Christians. Hence **E:bioni·tic** *a.* pertaining to the Ebionites or their doctrine; **E·bioni:tism,** the tenets of the Ebionites; also **E·bionism.** **E·bionize** *v. intr.* to adopt Ebionitism.

Eblis (ĕ·blĭz). Also **Eblees.** [Arab.] In Mohammedan demonology, the chief of the jinns; Satan.

Eboe (ī·bo). 1834. A W. Indian name for the negroes of Benin. ? Hence *attrib.* **E.-tree** (*Dipteryx eboensis*), a tree of Central America, yielding **E. oil.**

Ebon (e·bən). ME. [ad. L. *hebenus, ebenus*, ad. Gr. ἔβενος, whence perh. Heb. *hobnīm* (Ezek. xxvii. 15).]
A. *sb.* **1.** = EBONY. Now only *poet.* †**2.** The tree, *Diospyros Ebenus*, which provides ebony –1623.
1. India black e. and white iv'ry bears DRYDEN.
B. *attrib.* and *adj.* (chiefly *poet.* or *rhet.*) 1592.
Deaths e. dart SHAKS. As blind as E. night HEYWOOD. The tough shaft of heben wood SCOTT.

Ebonist (e·bŏnist). 1706. [f. EBONY. Cf. F. *ébéniste.*] A worker or dealer in ebony and ornamental woods.

Ebonite (e·bŏnəit). 1861. [f. as prec.] = VULCANITE. Also *attrib.*

Ebonize (e·bŏnəiz), *v.* 1880. [f. as prec.] To make (furniture, etc.) look like ebony.

Ebony (e·bŏni). [ME. *hebenyf*, app. ad. L. *hebeninus* (?read as *hebeniuus*), f. *hebenus* ebony. Cf. EBON.] **1.** A hard black wood, obtained from various species of the N.O. *Ebenaceæ*, esp. *Diospyrus Ebenus*, a native of Ceylon, Madagascar, and the Mauritius, and *Diospyrus Melanoxylon*, a native of Coromandel. **b.** The wood of *Brya Ebenus*, a native of Jamaica. Also the trees. **2.** As the type of intense blackness 1834. **3.** *attrib.* 1598.

‖**Eboulement.** [F. *éboulement*, f. *ébouler* to roll like a ball as one falls.] **1.** *Fortif.* The crumbling or falling of the wall of a fortification. **2.** *Geol.* A landslide.

Ebracteate, -ated (ībræ·ktiˌĕt, -eˑtėd). 1830. [ad. mod.L. *ebracteatus*, f. *e-* + *bractea.*] *Bot.* Destitute of bracts.

Ebra·cteolate, *a.* 1870. [ad. mod.L. *ebracteolatus*; cf. prec.] *Bot.* Not furnished with bracteoles.

Ebraick, Ebrew; see HEBRAIC, HEBREW.

Ebriety (ībrəi·ėti). 1582. [ad. F. *ébriété*, f. L. *ebrietatem*, f. *ebrius.*] The state or habit of intoxication; drunkenness. Also *fig.*
fig. The e. of constant amusement JOHNSON.

‖**Ebrillade.** 1753. [Fr.] *Manège.* A check of the bridle by a jerk of one rein, given to a horse when he refuses to turn.

Ebriosity (ībriˌǫ·sĭti). *rare.* 1646. [ad. F. *ébriosité*, L. *ebriositatem*, f. *ebriosus.*] Habitual intoxication; exhilaration.

Ebrious (ī·briəs), *a.* 1569. [f. L. *ebrius* + -OUS.] **a.** Addicted to drink; tipsy. **b.** Characteristic of the intoxicated state. var. **E·brio·se** (*joc.*). Hence **E·briously** *adv.*

Ebu·lliate. *rare.* 1599. [badly f. L. *ebullire.*] *trans.* and *intr.* To boil; to bubble out.

Ebullience (ībʊ·liens). 1749. [f. L. *ebullientem*; see -ENCE.] An issuing forth in agitation, like boiling water; overflow; effervescence. So **Ebu·lliency**, ebullient quality (*lit.* and *fig.*).

Ebullient (ĭbɒ·liĕnt). 1599. [ad. L. *ebullientem, ebullire.*] 1. That boils; agitated, as if boiling. 2. Characterized by heat; causing heat and agitation 1620. 3. *fig.* Bubbling over, overflowing, enthusiastic 1664.

2. They engender e. humours VENNER. The E. Ague 1684. 3. Commentaries..e. with subtlety 1844. Hence **Ebu·lliently** *adv.*

Ebullioscope (ĭbɒ·lioˌskōᵘp). 1880. [hybrid f. L. *ebullire* + Gr. -σκοπος.] An instrument for ascertaining the strength of distilled liquors by observing the boiling point and the atmospheric pressure.

Ebullition (ebɒli·ʃən). 1534. [ad. L. *ebullitionem.*] 1. The process of boiling; the state of agitation occasioned by boiling 1594. Also *transf.* †b. *Path.* A state of agitation in the blood or 'humours' due to heat -1753. 2. The action of rushing forth in a state of agitation or boiling; said of water, fire, lava, etc. 1599. 3. *fig.* A sudden outburst, as of war, passion, sentiment, etc. 1638.

3. Ebullitions of genius JOHNSON, of jealousy 1796.

Eburin (ī·biŭrin). [f. L. *ebur* + -IN.] A substance made of ivory or bone dust mixed with albumen or ox blood and subjected to pressure.

Eburnation (ĭbɒɹnēⁱ·ʃən). 1840. [f. L. *eburnus.*] *Path.* 'The act or process of becoming hard and dense like ivory' (*Syd. Soc. Lex.*). So **E·burnated** *ppl. a.*

Eburnean, -ian (ĭbɒ̄·ɹnĭăn), *a.* 1656. [f. L. *eburneus* + -(i)AN.] Made of or resembling ivory.

Ebu:rnifica·tion. *rare.* 1878. = EBURNATION.

Ecalcarate (ĭkæ·lkărĕt), *a.* 1819. [f. E- *pref.* + L. *calcar.*] *Bot.* Without a spur.

Ecardine (ĭkā·ɹdəin). 1878. [f. E- *pref.* + L. *cardinem.*] A mollusc which has no hinge.

‖**Écarté** (ekarte). 1824. [F., f. *écarter* to discard.] A game of cards for two persons, played with a pack from which the cards from 2 to 6 are excluded. The players may discard any or all of the cards dealt, and replace them from the pack; hence the name. Also *attrib.*

Ecaudate (ĭkǭ·deⁱt), *a.* 1840. [f. E- *pref.* + L. *cauda.*] 1. *Zool.* That has no tail, or a very short one 1847. 2. *Bot.* 'Spikeless, without a stem' (Paxton).

‖**E·cbasis.** 1706. [Gr. ἔκβασις.] 'A going out, an Event; also a Rhetorical Figure call'd Digression' (Phillips).

Ecbatic (ekbæ·tik), *a.* 1836. [ad. Gr. ἐκβατικός, f. ἐκβαίνειν; cf. prec.] *Gram.* Of a clause or conjunction: Denoting a mere result or consequence, as dist. from a purpose or intention.

[The use of ἵνα is sometimes] e. 1836.

‖**Ecblastesis** (ekblæstī·sis). 1866. [mod.L., a. Gr. ἐκβλάστησις.] *Bot.* The production of buds within flowers, or in inflorescences.

‖**Ecbole** (e·kbŏlĭ). 1753. [mod.L., a. Gr. ἐκβολή, f. ἐκβάλλειν to throw out.] *Rhet.* A digression, in which a person is introduced speaking his own words (Webster).

Ecbolic (ekbǫ·lik). 1753. [as if ad. Gr. ἐκβολικός; see prec.] a. *adj.* That promotes the expulsion of the fœtus 1877. b. *sb.* [sc. *drug.*]

Ecca:leobi·on. 1839. [Gr. ἐκκαλέω βίον (in sense 'I evoke life') as one word.] An egg-hatching apparatus.

‖**Ecce** (e·ksi). 1596. Latin for 'lo!' or 'behold!' Used in *Ecce signum!* behold a sign (1 *Hen. IV*, II. iv. 187). Also **Ecce Homo**, 'Behold the Man' (*John* xix. 5); hence *sb.*, a picture of Christ wearing the crown of thorns.

Eccentric (ekse·ntrik). 1551. [ad. late L. *eccentricus*, f. Gr. ἔκκεντρος (f. ἐκ + κέντρον centre); see -IC.]

A. *adj.* 1. Of a circle: Not concentric with another circle (const. *to*); †*fig.* having little in common -1670. 2. That has its axis, its point of support, etc., not centrally placed 1647. 3. Not centrally placed; not passing through the centre 1849. 4. Of orbital motion: Not referable to a fixed centre; not circular. Of a curve, an elliptic, etc., orbit: Deviating from a circular form. Also *transf.* of planets, etc. 1642. 5. *fig.* Regulated by no central control; irregular, anomalous, capricious; of persons, etc., odd, whimsical 1630.

1. *fig.* His owne endes, which must needes be often eccentrique to the endes of his Master or State BACON. 2. That..contrivance the e. wheel 1831. 4. A comet moves round the sun..in..a very e. ellipse SIR J. HERSCHEL. Phr. *E. anomaly*: the true (as opp. to the mean) anomaly of a planet moving in an e. orbit. *E. equation*: see EQUATION. 5. The eccentrick aberration of Charles the Second BURKE. That great, though..e. genius 1836.

B. *sb.* 1. [= *e. circle, orb.*] In Ptolemaic astronomy: A circle or orb not having the earth precisely in its centre. Now *Hist.* 1561. 2. *Mech.* A circular disk fixed on a revolving shaft, some distance out of centre, working freely in a ring (the *e. strap*), which is attached to a rod called an *e. rod*, by means of which the rotating motion of the shaft is converted into a backward and forward motion. (Earlier *e. circle, motion*; see A. 2.) 1827. 3. An irregular, odd, or whimsical person 1832.

attrib. and *Comb.*, as *e.-hook, -rod*, etc.; **e.-hoop, -ring, -strap**, the ring in which the e. revolves. b. = worked by an e. wheel or dependent on an e. arrangement, as *e.-arbor, -chuck, -gear, -pump*, etc.

So **Ecce·ntrical** (in sense A. 1); also *fig.*; exceptional, irregular. Hence **Ecce·ntrically** *adv.*

Eccentricity (eksentri·sĭti). 1551. [See -ITY.] 1. The quality of being abnormally centred; of not being concentric; of not having the axis in the centre. †2. Distance from the centre -1837. 3. Of a curve: Deviation from circular form 1696. b. as a measurable quantity: The ratio of the focal distance (of any point in the curve) to the distance from the directrix 1726. 4. The quality or habit of deviating from what is customary; irregularity, oddity, whimsicality. Also with *a* and *pl.* 1657.

‖**Ecchymoma** (ekimōᵘ·mă). 1541. [mod.L., a. Gr. ἐκχύμωμα; see next.] *Path.* A tumour formed by an effusion of blood under the skin.

Ecchymosed (e·kimōᵘst, -ōᵘzd), *ppl. a.* 1834. [ad. Fr. *ecchymosé*, f. *ecchymose*, F. form of next.] *Path.* Affected with ecchymosis.

‖**Ecchymosis** (ekimōᵘ·sis). 1541. [mod.L., a. Gr. ἐκχύμωσις, f. ἐκχυμόεσθαι to extravasate blood.] *Path.* 'A blotch caused by extravasation of blood below the skin' (*Syd. Soc. Lex.*). So **Ecchymo·tic** *a.* of the nature of e.

Eccles (e·k'lz). 1881. [Name of a town in Lancashire.] *E. cake*, a cake resembling a Banbury cake.

‖**Ecclesia** (eklī·ziă, -ʒiă). *Hist.* 1577. [med. L., a. Gr. ἐκκλησία, f. ἔκκλητος summoned.] A regularly convoked assembly; *esp.* the general assembly of Athenian citizens. Later, the regular word for CHURCH, q.v. Hence †**Eccle·sial** *a.* ecclesiastical. (Freq. in Milton.) **Eccle·siarch**, a ruler of the church.

Ecclesiast (eklī·ziˌæst). ME. [ad. (through L.) Gr. ἐκκλησιαστής one who takes part in an ECCLESIA; used by the LXX. as tr. Heb. *qōhéleth.*] 1. 'The Preacher', *i.e.* Solomon. †2. An ecclesiastic. CHAUCER. 3. A member of the Athenian Ecclesia 1849.

Ecclesiastes (eklīziæ·stīz). ME. [a. Gr.; see prec.] The title of a book of the O.T., written in the person of Solomon, or prop. the designation of Solomon considered as the author of the book.

Ecclesiastic (eklīziæ·stik). 1483. [f. (ult.) Gr. ἐκκλησία church.]

A. *adj.* (Now *rare.*) 1. Of or pertaining to the church; opp. to *civil* or *secular*. 2. Of persons, etc.: Clerical, as opp. to *lay*, as *e. attire* 1603.

1. E. terms HOBBES, writers 1678, architecture 1856.

B. *sb.* 1. A clergyman, person in orders, a 'churchman' as dist. from a 'layman' 1651. †2. *pl.* Matters ecclesiastical. b. The science of church government (*rare*) -1738.

Ecclesia·stical, *a.* 1538. [f. prec. + -AL.] 1. = ECCLESIASTIC A. 1. 2. Of or pertaining to the church as consisting of the clergy 1538. 3. quasi-*sb.* Matters ecclesiastical; *pl.* matters concerning the church 1641.

1. *E. Commission, Commissioners*: a body of commissioners for administering certain portions of the revenues of the Church of England. *E. Courts*: courts for administering e. law and maintaining the discipline of the Church of England. *E. law*: the law, derived from Canon and Civil law, which such courts administer. *E. judge*: a judge of an e. court. 2. †*E. State(s*, the provinces formerly ruled by the Pope as Head of the Roman Church; = *States of the Church, Papal States.*

Hence **Ecclesia·stically** *adv.*

Ecclesiasticism (eklīziæ·stisiz'm). 1862. [f. as prec. + -ISM.] Ecclesiastical spirit, or principles of action.

Ecclesio·graphy. 1881. [f. *ecclesio-*, comb. f. ECCLESIA + Gr. -γραφία.] A descriptive treatise on the church.

Ecclesiolatry (eklīziˌǫ·lătri). 1847. [f. as prec. + Gr. λατρεία.] Worship of the church, church forms, and church traditions.

Ecclesiology (eklīziˌǫ·lŏdʒi). 1837. [f. as prec. + Gr. -λογία.] a. The science of church building and decoration. b. A treatise on churches.

The first phase of e. was simple antiquarianism FREEMAN. Hence **Eccle·siolo·gic, -al** *a.* of or pertaining to e.; **-ly** *adv.* **Eccle:sio·logist**, a student of e.

Eccoprotic (ekǫprǫ·tik). 1656. [f. (ult.) Gr. ἐκ + κόπρος dung.] a. *adj.* Mildly purgative. b. *sb.* A mild aperient.

Eccrinology (ekrinǫ·lŏdʒi). [a. F. *eccrinologie*, f. Gr. ἐκκρίνειν + -λογία.] *Phys.* The doctrine of, or a treatise on, the secretions.

‖**Eccrisis** (e·krisis). 1706. [mod.L., a. Gr. ἔκκρισις; see prec.] *Med.* Old term for an excretion; also the thing excreted.

Eccritic (ekri·tic), *a.* 1681. [ad. Gr. ἐκκριτικός.] *Med.* A remedy which promotes discharges, as an emetic, or a cathartic (Webster).

Ecderon (e·kdĕrǫn). 1859. [irreg. f. Gr. ἐκ + δέρος, δέρμα skin.] Huxley's term for the outer part of the skin and skin-like structures. Opp. to ENDERON. Hence **Ecdero·nic** *a.*

‖**Ecdysis** (e·kdisis). 1854. [mod.L., a. Gr. ἔκδυσις, f. ἐκδύειν.] The action of shedding or casting off an integument, as in serpents, caterpillars, Crustacea, etc. Also *concr.* that which is cast off.

Echelon (eʃəlon̄, e·ʃĕlǫn). Also **echellon.** [a. F. *échelon*, f. *échelle* ladder.] 1. 'A formation of troops in which the successive divisions are placed parallel to one another, but no two on the same alignement' (Stocqueler). Also *attrib.* 2. A division marching in e. 1808.

Echelon (e·ʃĕlǫn), *v.* 1860. [ad. F. *échelonner.*] *trans.* To arrange (troops) in the form of an echelon. Also *fig.*

†**Echene·is.** *rare.* Also **echineis.** 1594. [Gr. ἐχενηΐς, f. ἔχειν + ναῦς (dat. νηΐ), from its supposed power of holding back a ship.] The Remora, or Sucking-fish, which has on the crown of its head an oblong flat sucker -1774.

Echeveria (ekĭvĭᵊ·riă). 1840. [after M. *Echeveri*, draughtsman of the *Flora Mexicana.*] A handsome genus of succulent plants allied to the house-leek (N.O. *Crassulaceæ*).

‖**Echevin** (eʃəvæn̄). 1766. [Fr. *échevin*; of Teut. origin.] The French or Belgian equivalent of an English alderman.

‖**Echidna** (ĭki·dnă). 1847. [mod.L., a. Gr. ἔχιδνα viper.] *Zool.* A genus of Australian toothless burrowing monotremate mammals (family *Echidnidæ*), as large as hedgehogs and like them. The best known species is *E. Hystrix*, the Porcupine Ant-eater. So **Echi·dnine**, the essential principle of the poison of the viper.

Echinal (ĭkəi·năl, e·kinal), *a.* [f. L. ECHINUS.] Of or belonging to a sea-urchin. LYELL.

Echinate (e·kinĕt), *a.* 1668. [ad. L. *echinatus*, f. *echinus* hedgehog.] 1. *Bot.* Furnished with bristles or prickles. 2. *Zool.* Resembling a sea-urchin 1846. So **E·chinated** *ppl. a.*

Echinid (ĭkəi·nid). [mod. f. Gr. ἐχῖνος + -ID.] *Zool.* Any member of the *Echinus* family. As pl. mod.L. **Echi·nida**; also **Echi·nidans.**

Echinite (e·kinəit). 1750. [ad. mod.L. *echinita*; see ECHINUS.] A fossil echinoderm Hence **Echini·tal** *a.* pertaining to or like an e.

Echino- (ĭkəi·no, e·kino), comb. f. Gr. ἐχῖνος hedgehog, sea-urchin.

Echinococcus (-kǫ·kɒs) [Gr. κόκκος seed-grain], *Zool.* a former genus of ACEPHALOCYSTS or hydatids, now known to be the higher larval form of a species of tapeworm, *Tænia*

Echinococcus (formerly *T. nana*). †Echi·nod [Gr. ὀδούς], the fossil tooth of the sea-urchin.

Echinoderm (ĭkəi·no-, e·kinodəɹm). 1835. A member of the class *Echinodermata*; hence **Echinode·rmal** *a.* = ECHINODERMATOUS. ‖**Echinodermata** (-dɜ̄·ɹmătă), *sb. pl.* [f. Gr. δέρμα (δέρματ-) skin], a class of animals formerly included in the *Radiata*, but now placed in the sub-kingdom *Annuloida*, comprising Sea-urchins, Sea-cucumbers, etc. The skin of the typical species is covered with spines. **Echinode·rmatous** *a.*, belonging to or like the echinodermata.

Echinoid (e·kinoid). 1851. [f. ECHINUS + -OID.]

A. *adj.* Like, or having the characteristics of, an Echinus or Sea-urchin.

B. *sb.* An individual of the Order *Echinoidea* (Class *Echinodermata*), characterized by a shell composed of calcareous plates, and locomotion by suckers and spines 1864.

Echinulate (ĭki·niŭlĕt), *a.* 1846. [f. L. **echinulus*, dim. of *echinus*, after ACICULATE.] Having or covered with small prickles. So **Echi·nuliform** *a.* in the form of, or like, small prickles.

Echinus (ĭkəi·nŏs). ME. [a. L., Gr. ἐχῖνος hedgehog, sea-urchin.] *Zool.* **1.** The Sea-urchin; a genus of animals (Order *Echinoidea*, Class *Echinodermata*), inhabiting a spheroidal shell built up from polygonal plates, and covered with rows of sharp spines. (The sense 'hedgehog' is not in Eng. use.) **2.** *Arch.* The ovolo moulding next below the abacus of the capital of a column. [So in Gr. and L.] 1563.

Echites (ĭkəi·tīz). ME. [a. Gr. ἐχίτης f. ἔχις viper.] †**1.** A precious stone, dark-green, red, or violet, with fabulous properties; cf. AETITES –1731. **2.** *Bot.* A genus of climbing plants (N.O. *Apocynaceæ*) 1731.

Echo (e·kou), *sb.* Pl. **echoes**, rarely **echos**. ME. [a. L., a. Gr. ἠχώ, related to ἠχή sound.] **1.** A repetition of sounds, due to the reflection of the sound-waves by some obstacle; hence *concr.* a secondary or imitative sound, as dist. from the original sound. **2.** The cause of this personified, *e.g.* in Gr. Myth. as an Oread 1592. **3.** An artifice in verse, by which one line repeats the concluding syllables of the preceding line. Hence, this kind of verse. Also *attrib.*, as in *e. verse.* 1633. **4.** *fig.* A repetition or close imitation (*e.g.* of a writer's thoughts or style); an enfeebled reproduction; and the like 1622. Also *transf.* of a person. **5.** *Mus.* = *e. organ, stop* (see below) 1711. **6.** *Whist* and *Bridge.* A conventional indication given to a partner of the number of cards held in a suit led, etc. 1862.

1. Echoes softly flung from rock and hill BRYANT. Phr. *To applaud to the e.*: *i.e.* so vociferously as to produce echoes. 2. *Rom. & Jul.* II. ii. 162. 3. But are there cares and businesse with the pleasure? *Echo*, Leisure G. HERBERT. *Comb.* **e. organ**, one of the divisions of a large organ, containing soft stops (**e. stops**) for echo effects. Hence **Echo·ic** *a.* of the nature of an **e.**; **E·choism**, the formation of words imitative of sounds; **E·choist**, one who repeats like an e.; **E·choize** *v.* to form words imitative of sounds. **E·choless** *a.* (*lit.* and *fig.*).

Echo (e·kou), *v.* 1559. [f. the sb.] **1.** *intr.* To resound with an echo. Also *fig.* 1596. **b.** Of a sound: To be repeated by echoes, reverberate, resound; hence *fig.* of rumours, fame, etc. 1559. **2.** *trans.* To repeat by echo 1855. Also *transf.* of light. **3.** *fig.* To play the echo to; to repeat the words of, imitate the style or sentiments of; to resemble 1604. Also *absol.* and *intr.* **4.** *Whist* and *Bridge.* (Cf. ECHO *sb.* 6) 1862.

1. And at every Roar it gave, it made all the Valley Eccho BUNYAN. That sound echoed and reverberated from innumerable cavities among the rocks DE FOE. 2. A sound echoed from many sides BAIN. 3. Posterity have echoed these censures KEIGHTLEY. *intr.* Now e. vnto me, and sing, Thou myne HEYWOOD. Hence **E·choer**. **E·choingly** *adv.*

Echo·meter. 1736. [f. Gr. ἦχος + μέτρον.] *Mus.* A graduated scale for measuring the duration of sounds and ascertaining their intervals and ratios. So †**Echo·metry.**

‖**Éclair** (ekl·ēɹ). 1870. [Fr., lit. lightning.] A small pastry filled with cream and iced.

†**Eclaircise,** *v. rare.* 1754. [f. next.] *trans.* To clear up.

‖**Éclairci·ssement.** 1673. [F. (eklęrsismaṅ), f. *éclairciss-*, *éclaircir* to clear up. Freq. in 18th c.] A clearing up of what is obscure, unknown, or misunderstood; an explanation.

When the e. comes there will be a scene THACKERAY.

Eclampsia, eclampsy (eklæ·mpsiă, -si). 1866. [mod.L., as if a. Gr. *ἐκλαμψία, f. ἐκλάμπειν.] *Path.* 'Epileptiform convulsions dependent on some actual disturbance of the nervous centres caused by anatomical lesion' (*Syd. Soc. Lex.*). So **Ecla·mptic** *a.*; also, *erron.*, **ecla·mpsic.**

‖**Éclat** (ekla·). 1674. [Fr., related to *éclater*, OF. *esclater* to burst out: prob. ad. WGer. **slaitan*, causative of **slītan*; see SLIT.] †**1.** Brilliancy, radiance, dazzling effect –1835. †**2.** Ostentation; publicity; *concr.* public exposure, scandal –1823. **3.** Lustre of reputation; celebrity, renown. In 19th c. often disparaging. 1742. **b.** Conspicuous success; acclamation 1741.

2. He was then a man of e., had many servants CLARENDON. With the view of saving an é. BYRON. 3. A diplomatist of great é. BYRON. b. We get on with great é. BYRON. So ‖**Eclat** *v.* to make or become known (*rare*).

Eclectic (ekle·ktik). 1683. [ad. Gr. ἐκλεκτικός selective, f. ἐκλέγειν.]

A. *adj.* **1.** In ancient use, epithet of a class of philosophers who 'selected such doctrines as pleased them in every school' (Liddell and Scott). In mod. times applied similarly, *e.g.* to V. Cousin and others. **2.** That borrows or is borrowed from various sources. Of persons, etc.: Broad, not exclusive. 1847. **3.** Made up of selections. **b.** That selects. 1814.

1. Some e. system of belief 1796. The E. school of thought MORLEY. 2. The e. phraseology [of] the Shepherd's Calendar CHURCH. 3. b. His mind was in the best sense e. GLADSTONE. Hence **Ecle·ctical** *a.*

B. *sb.* **a.** An adherent of the Eclectic school of philosophy 1856. **b.** One who follows the eclectic method 1817.

Eclecticism (ekle·ktisiz'm). 1835. [f. prec.] The eclectic philosophy; the eclectic method in speculation or practice.

†**Ecle·gme.** 1605. [a. med.L. *eclegma*, for *ecligma*, a. Gr. ἔκλειγμα, f. ἐκλείχειν to lick out.] *Med.* Old term for a linctus, or semifluid medicine, which is licked off the spoon –1710.

Eclipse (ĭkli·ps), *sb.* ME. [a. OF. *eclipse*, *esclipse*, ad. L. *eclipsis*, Gr. ἔκλειψις, f. ἐκλείπειν to fail to appear.] **1.** *Astron.* An interception or obscuration of the light of the sun, moon, or other luminous body, by the intervention of some other body, either between it and the eye, or between the luminous body and that illuminated by it; as of the moon, by passing through the earth's shadow; of the sun, by the moon coming between it and the observer; or of a satellite, by entering the shadow of its primary. **b.** *transf.* Absence of light, temporary or permanent 1526. **2.** *fig.* Obscuration, obscurity; dimness; loss of splendour 1598.

1. Phr. *Annular, partial, total e.*: see these adjs. These late Eclipses in the Sun and Moone portend no good to vs *Lear* I. ii. 112. *transf.* Blind among enemies..Irrecoverably dark, total e. MILT. *Sams.* 80. 2. God oftentimes leaves the brightest men in an e. FULLER. b. Of birds: Change to duller plumage 1838.

Eclipse (ĭkli·ps), *v.* ME. [f. prec.] †**1.** *intr.* To suffer eclipse –1667. Also †*fig.* **2.** *trans.* To cause the obscuration of; said of a heavenly body. Also *transf.* **3.** *fig.* To throw into the shade, *esp.* by surpassing; to obscure, deprive of lustre 1581; †to hide *from* –1653.

1. When the moon eclipses the sun to us, the earth is eclipsed to the moon 1832. 2. The splendour of the House of Argyle had been eclipsed MACAULAY. Hence **Ecli·psable** *a.* **Ecli·pser.**

Ecli·psis. 1538. [ad. Gr. ἔκλειψις; see ECLIPSE *sb.*] †**1.** An omission of words needful fully to express the sense –1589. **2.** In *Irish Grammar*: 'The suppression of the sounds of certain radical consonants, by prefixing others of the same organ' (J. O'Donovan).

Ecliptic (ĭkli·ptik). ME. [ad. L. *eclipticus*, Gr. ἐκλειπτικός in same sense.]

A. *adj.* Of or pertaining to an eclipse 1609. Also *fig.*

Phr. *E. limits*, the limits within which an eclipse is possible. *E. conjunction*, a conjunction of sun and moon which results in a solar eclipse. †*E. circle, line, way* = ECLIPTIC *sb.*

B. *sb.* **1.** The great circle of the celestial sphere which is the apparent orbit of the sun. So called because eclipses can happen only when the moon is on or near this line. Occas. = plane of the ecliptic. 1635. **2.** The great circle on the terrestrial sphere which at any given moment lies in the plane of the celestial ecliptic 1819. Hence **Ecli·ptical** *a.*, **-ly** *adv.*

Eclogite (e·klŏdʒəit). 1852. [f. Gr. ἐκλογή selection.] *Min.* A metamorphic rock, consisting of granular garnet and hornblende, with grass-green smaragdite; so called because the constituents do not exist together in primitive rocks.

Eclogue (e·klǫg). *c.* 1430. [ad. L. *ecloga*, a. Gr. ἐκλογή, f. ἐκλέγειν to select. Also spelt *æglogue*, as if from Gr. αἴξ, αἰγός, in sense 'discourse of goatherds'.] A short poem of any kind, *esp.* a pastoral dialogue, *e.g.* Virgil's Bucolics.

†**Eco·d,** *int.* 1733. [var. of EGAD, q. v.] Used as a mild oath –1865.

Ecology, etc., var. ŒCOLOGY, etc.

Economic (īkonǫ·mik). ME. [ad. L. *œconomicus*, perh. through Fr. *économique*; see ECONOMY and -IC.]

A. *adj.* **1.** †Pertaining to household management (*arch.*) –1791. **b.** Relating to pecuniary position 1831. **2.** Relating to Political Economy 1835. **b.** Practical, industrial (*mod.*). †**3.** = ECONOMICAL 2. –1801. **4.** *Theol.* Pertaining to economy of truth (*mod.*). **5.** Pertaining to a dispensation. Cf. ECONOMY II. 1817.

1. a. Oeconomicke or houshold order 1603. 2. E. problems, subjects, forces (*mod.*). b. E. applications of electricity (*mod.*). 3. E. of her smiles 1801.

B. *sb.* †**1.** *sing.* Housekeeping –1609. **2.** *pl.* (after L. *œconomica*, Gr. τὰ οἰκονομικά a treatise attributed to Aristotle.) The science of †household, rural, and *esp.* political economy 1792. **3.** Financial or material condition (*mod.*).

2. The London school of Economics (*mod.*). 3. The oppression has gone.. into the economics of Ireland CARLYLE.

Economical (īkonǫ·mikăl), *a.* 1577. [f. as prec.] **1.** = ECONOMIC *a.* 1, 2, 4, 5. Now *rare.* **2.** Saving, thrifty (cf. ECONOMY 1) 1780.

1. The e. writers of antiquity GIBBON. 2. An œconomical constitution is a necessary basis for an œconomical administration BURKE. [Pope's] e. habits L. STEPHEN. Hence **Econo·mically** *adv.*

Economist (īkǫ·nŏmist). 1586. [f. Gr. οἰκονόμος + -IST. Cf. Fr. *économiste.*] **1.** One who practises economy (see ECONOMY 1); hence, **a.** A housekeeper (*arch.*). **b.** A thrifty and effective manager *of* money, time, etc. 1710. **2.** A student of, or writer upon, political economy 1804. **b.** One of the French school dubbed *Les Economistes* 1776.

1. a. The perfect e., or mistress of a household RUSKIN. b. A rigid e. of time 1841. 2. a. Facts which form the special study of the e. ROGERS.

Economize (īkǫ·nŏməiz), *v.* 1648. [f. as prec. + -IZE.] †**1.** *intr.* To govern a household. **2.** *trans.* To use sparingly; to save *from* 1820. **3.** *intr.* To practise thrift (*in* a thing) 1790. **4.** *trans.* To turn to account 1832.

4. [Machinery's] object is to e. force supplied from without 1872. Hence **Eco·nomiza·tion**, the action of economizing. **Eco·nomi·zer**, one who, or that which, economizes; in *Mech.* any appliance that effects a saving, *esp.* of heat or fuel.

Economy (īkǫ·nŏmi). 1530. [ad. L. *œconomia*, ad. Gr. οἰκονομία house management, and, in later *Theol.* use, as in II. below.]

I. 1. Management of expenditure: orig. of household (*arch.*), later of any, expenses; often specialized, as *Domestic, Naval, Rural*, etc. **2. Political Economy** [tr. Fr. *économie politique*]: orig. The art of managing the resources of a people and of its government (Adam Smith); later, The theoretical science of the laws of production and distribution of wealth (McCulloch). 1767. **3.** Careful management, frugality, of labour, money, time, etc. Also in *pl.* Savings. 1670.

1. Yconomie, or Howsolde keepynge 1530. His Equipage and Oeconomy had something in them.. sumptuous STEELE. The Œconomy of a Commonwealth HOBBES. Dockyard E. and Naval Power 1863. 3. The e. shown by nature in her resources is striking DARWIN. Saved from bankruptcy by economies (*mod.*).

II. 1. *Theol.* The divine government of the world; *esp.* = DISPENSATION, as the *Mosaic, Jewish, Christian e.* 1664. **2.** *Theol.* Judicious handling, *i. e.* tactful presentation, of doctrine (a tr. of Gr. οἰκονομία as used by the Fathers) 1833. Hence, by confusion (begun by Voltaire) with sense I. 3: *E. of truth* = A (discreditable) reticence 1796.

1. The scheme of the divine e. 1814. 2. An œconomy of truth..a sort of temperance BURKE.

III. *fig.* Organization, like that of a household, in a product of art, in the mind or body, nature or society 1592.

Œconomy of the fable MILT. The e. of the body 1660, of the brain 1704. Phr. *The animal, vegetable e.*; *the e. of nature, of society.*

‖**Écorché.** [pa. pple. of F. *écorcher*, OF. *escorcher*:—L. *excorticare*, to take away the bark, to flay.] An anatomical subject with the skin removed so as to display the muscles for study.

‖**Écossaise.** 1863. [Fr.] A lively dance tune, formerly in 3/4 slow time, now in 2/4 time.

Ecostate (ĭkǫ·stēt), *a.* 1866. [f. E- *pref.* + *costa* + -ATE.] *Bot.* Having no central rib.

‖**Écoute** (ekut). 1815. [F., f. *écouter.*] *Mil.* An excavation in which a miner listens for the working of the enemy's miners.

‖**E·cphasis,** also **E·cphrasis.** 1706. [Gr.] 'A plain declaration'.

‖**Ecphone·ma,** ‖**Ecphone·sis,** exclamation (Puttenham): Greek rhetorical terms now found only in Dicts.

‖**Ecphora** (e·kfŏră). 1715. [Gr., f. ἐκφέρειν.] *Arch.* 'The projecture of a member or moulding of a column' (Gwilt).

Ecphore (e·kfoᵊr), *v.* 1914. [ad. Gr. ἐκφορεῖν.] *Psycho-analysis.* To evoke or revive by means of a stimulus.

†**Ecphra·ctic,** *a.* 1657. [ad. late Gr. ἐκφρακτικός, f. ἐκφράσσειν to remove obstructions.] Aperient, deobstruent. Also as quasi-*sb.* –1883.

‖**Écraseur** (ekrazör). 1859. [F., f. *écraser* to crush.] *Surg.* A blunt chain-saw, tightened by a screw, etc., for removing piles, polypi, etc.

‖**Écroulement.** 1820. [Fr.] The fall of a mass of rock, a building, etc. Also *fig.*

‖**Ecru** (ekrü), *a.* (*sb.*) 1869. [Fr.; = 'raw, unbleached'.] The colour of unbleached linen.

‖**Ecstasis** (e·kstăsis). 1621. = next 2, 3.

Ecstasy (e·kstăsi). ME. [a. OF. *ecstasie*, f. med.L. *extasis*, a. Gr. ἔκστασις displacement, also, in late Gr., a trance, f. ἐκ + ἱστάναι to place.] **1.** The state of being beside oneself with anxiety, astonishment, fear, or passion. **2.** *Path.* †**a.** Any morbid state characterized by unconsciousness, as swoon, trance, catalepsy, etc. –1647. **b.** A nervous state in which the mind is absorbed in a dominant idea, and becomes insensible to surrounding objects 1866. **3.** In mystical writers, the state of rapture in which the soul, liberated from the body, was engaged in the contemplation of divine things. Now *Hist.* 1652. **b.** The state of trance supposed to accompany prophetic inspiration; hence, Poetic frenzy or rapture 1670. **4.** Rapture, transport; rapturous delight 1526. †**b.** An outburst (of feeling, etc.) –1725.

1. Our words will but increase his e. MARLOWE. 2. a. The Ministers of the State..like men in an Extasy..had no Speech or Motion CLARENDON. 3. a. The Emigration of humane Souls from the bodie by E. MORE. b. Certaine women in a kind of ecstasie foretold of calamities to come MILT. In mood Of minstrel e. SCOTT. 4. In the e. of my joy DE FOE. *transf.* The e. of the monk's terror SCOTT.

E·cstasy, *v.* 1624. [f. the sb.] †**1.** *trans.* To throw into a state of frenzy or stupor. Only in *pass.* –1670. **2.** To raise to a high state of feeling; now *esp.* to enrapture 1624.

2. The crowd was again ecstasied T. HARDY.

Ecstatic (ekstæ·tik). 1630. [ad. Gr. ἐκστατικός; see ECSTASY *sb.* and -IC.]

A. *adj.* Of the nature of ecstasy; characterized by or producing ecstasy. Of persons: Subject to trance, catalepsy, rapturous emotion, etc. (See ECSTASY *sb.* 1, 2, 4.)

1. In e. fit MILT. In trance extatic POPE. In e. pain FALCONER, idolatry DISRAELI. Minds of a visionary and e. nature 1878.

B. *sb.* **1.** One who is subject to fits of ecstasy (see ECSTASY *sb.* 2, 3) 1659. **2.** *pl.* Sarcastically used for: Transports 1819.

2. Ecstatics, again, might be spared 1865. Hence **Ecsta·tical** *a.* (*arch.*). **Ecsta·tical-ly** *adv.*, †**-ness.**

‖**Ectasia** (ektēi·ziă). 1876. [f. as next, after Gr. ἀναισθησία, etc.] *Path.* A dilatation; = ANEURISM.

‖**E·ctasis.** 1706. [a. Gr. ἔκτασις, f. ἐκτείνειν to stretch out.] **1.** *Gram.* A figure whereby a short syllable is made long. **2.** *Path.* Any morbid condition of dilatation.

Ecteron, -onic, bad ff. ECDERON, -ONIC.

Ectethmoid (ekte·þmoid), *a.* 1882. [f. ECTO- + ETHMOID.] *Anat.* External to the ethmoid; prefrontal.

‖**Ecthlipsis** (ekþli·psis). 1657. [mod.L., a. Gr., f. ἐκθλίβειν to squeeze out.] *Pros.* 'Crushing out, in verse, of a syllable ending in *m* before an ensuing vowel' (Roby).

‖**Ecthyma** (ekþəi·mă). 1834. [mod.L., a. Gr. ἔκθυμα, f. ἐκθύειν 'to break out as heat or humours' (L. and S.).] Same as *Impetigo.*

Ecto- (e·kto), comb. form, repr. Gr. ἐκτο-, stem of ἐκτός *adv.*, outside:

E·ctoblast [Gr. βλαστός], the membrane composing the walls of a cell. **E:cto-cu·neiform** *a.*, of or pertaining to one of the bones of the tarsus; see CUNEIFORM. **E·ctocyst** [Gr. κύστις], the cell encasing each individual of a colony of Polyzoa. **E·ctoderm** [Gr. δέρμα], the outer layer of the blastoderm, called also *epiblast*; also, the outer layer of the body of the Cœlenterata; hence **Ectode·rmal, -mic** *adjs.* **Ectoge·nesis,** the production of structures or bodies outside the organism. **E:ctopa·rasite,** any parasite which derives its nourishment from the skin. **E·ctoplasm** [Gr. πλάσμα], the outer firm layer of the body of an Amœba, or the like; opp. to *endoplasm*; hence **E:ctopla·smic** *a.* **E:cto-pro·ctous** *a.* [Gr. πρωκτός], belonging to the *Ectoprocta*, an order of *Polyzoa* having the anus outside the mouth-tentacles. **E:cto-pte·rygoid** *a.* [see PTERYGOID], situated externally to the pterygoid; of or relating to an ectopterygoid bone. **E·ctosarc** [Gr. σάρξ, σαρκός], *Zool.* the outer transparent sarcode-layer of certain rhizopods, such as the Amœba. **Ectosto·sis** [f. Gr. ὀστέον, after ἐξόστωσις], an external growth of bone. **Ectozo·on** (pl. -a) [Gr. ζῷον], any parasitic insect that infests the surface of the body; opp. to *Entozoon.*

‖**Ecto·pia.** 1847. [mod.L., f. Gr. ἔκτοπος out of place.] *Path.* 'Displacement; anomaly of situation or relation' (*Syd. Soc. Lex.*).

‖**Ectro·pion, -um.** 1685. [mod.L. *ectropium*, Gr. ἐκτρόπιον, f. ἐκ + τρέπειν.] *Path.* An outward bending; *esp.* applied to eversion of the eyelid.

Ectrotic (ektrǫ·tik), *a.* 1866. [ad. Gr. ἐκτρωτικός pertaining to abortion.] *Med.* Tending to cause abortion of the fœtus. Also tending to produce the abortion of a disease.

Ectypal (e·ktipăl), *a.* 1642. [f. next + -AL.] Of or pertaining to an ectype; of the nature of a copy; opp. to *archetypal.*

Ectype (e·ktəip). 1642. [ad. Gr. ἔκτυπον adj. neut., f. ἐκ + τύπος figure.] **1.** An impression of a seal or medal. ? *Obs.* 1662. **b.** *fig.* A copy: *esp.* as opp. to *archetype* or *prototype* 1646. **2.** *Arch.* An object in relievo or embossed 1876.

1. *fig.* The Complex Ideas of Substances are Ectypes, Copies too; but not perfect ones LOCKE.

Ectypography (ektipǫ·grăfi). 1870. [f. Gr. ἔκτυπος (see prec.) + -γραφία.] A method of etching in which the lines on the plate are produced in relief.

‖**Écu** (ekü). 1704. [Fr.:—L. *scutum*; so called from the three fleurs-de-lis stamped on the coin as on a shield.] A French silver crown piece. Now, a French five-franc piece.

Ecumenacy, -ic, -ical, etc.; see ŒCUMEN-.

Eczema (e·kzĭmă). 1753. [Gr. ἔκζεμα, f. ἐκ + ζέειν to boil.] *Path.* 'A..non-contagious, simple inflammation of the skin, characterized by the presence of itching papules and vesicles which discharge a serous fluid, or dry up' (*Syd. Soc. Lex.*). Hence **Ecze·matous** *a.*, **-ly** *adv.*

†**Ed-,** *prefix*, OE. *ed-* (= L. *re-*). Freq. in OE.; occas. in ME.

-ed, *suffix* [1], in OE. *-ed, -ad, -od* (*-ud*), in ME. *-ed* (*-id, -yd*), the formative of the pa. pple. of wk. vbs. The ppl. suffix proper is *-d*:—OTeut. *-đo-*:—Aryan *-tó-*; cf. Gr. -τός and L. *-tus.* **1.** The written spelling is usually *-ed*, although the pronunc. is now normally vowelless (d), or after a voiceless cons. (t), as in *robed* (rōᵘbd), *hoped* (hōᵘpt). From 16th to 18th c. the suffix was often written *-t*, when so pronounced, as in *jumpt, whipt, stept*, and this is still occasionally done.

2. In 15th, 16th, and 17th c. the suffix was added to adapted forms of L. pples., e. g. *situated*, and to ppl. adjs. in *-ate*, ad. L. *-atus*, e. g. *bipinnate(d, dentate(d*, without difference of meaning.

3. Some of the adjs. formed by the addition of *-ed* to sbs. may be examples of this suffix.

-ed, *suffix* [2], OE. *-ede* = OS. *-ôdi*:—OTeut. type *-ôđjo-* is appended to sbs. in order to form adjs., with the sense 'possessing, provided with, characterized by'; *e.g.* in *toothed, moneyed, jaundiced*, etc. As to pronunciation this suffix follows the same rules as -ED [1].

Edacious (ĭdēi·ʃəs), *a.* 1819. [f. L. *edaci-* (nom. *edax*), f. *edere* + -OUS.] Of or relating to eating; voracious; *fig.* greedy.

E. Flunkies CARLYLE. The e. tooth of Time LOWELL.

Edacity (ĭdæ·sĭti). 1626. [f. as prec.] **1.** The quality of being edacious; capacity for eating. (Now *joc.*) †**2.** Corrosive quality 1657.

Edaphodont (e·dăfodǫnt), *a.* 1854. [ad. mod.L. *edaphodus*, f. Gr. ἔδαφος floor + ὀδούς, ὀδόντος tooth; so named from the shape of the teeth.] *Palæont.* A fish of the fossil genus *Edaphodus*, found in deposits ranging from the Cretaceous to the Eocene.

‖**Edda** (e·dă). 1771. [ON.; ? proper name of the great-grandmother in the 'Rigsþul'; or ? f. *óðr* poetry.] Applied to: **a.** A miscellaneous handbook to Icelandic poetry written *c* 1230, and called since 1642 Snorre's Edda, or the Younger or Prose Edda. **b.** A collection (made *c* 1200) of ancient ON. poems, named 'Elder or Poetic Edda' or 'Edda of Sæmund', and erroneously ascribed to the Icel. historian Sæmund (*d.* 1133). Hence **Edda·ic, E·ddic** *a.* of, pertaining to, or resembling the Eddas.

Edder (e·dəɹ), *sb.* Now *dial.* 1523. [? same as OE. *eodor, eder* enclosure.] Osiers, and the like, used for interlacing hedge stakes at the top. Hence **Edder** *v.*, also **ether,** to interlace or bind (a hedge) at the top with osiers, etc. **E·ddering** *vbl. sb.* the materials used in doing this.

Edder, obs. and dial. f. ADDER *sb.*[1], EIDER.

Eddish (e·diʃ). See also EARSH, ARRISH. [? same as OE. *edisc* park; or ? from OE. *ed-* 'again'. Either conjecture presents difficulties.] †**1.** OE. *edisc*: A park or enclosed pasture for cattle. **2.** Grass (also clover, etc.) which grows again; aftermath. **b.** Stubble; a stubble-field. 1468. **3.** *attrib.*, as in *e.-grass* OE.

Eddoes (e·doᵘz). 1685. [A Gold Coast word.] *Bot.* The tuberous stems of various araceous plants, as *Colocasia esculenta*, etc. *Eddy-root*: the root of the taro (*Colocasia macrorhiza*).

Eddy (e·di), *sb.* 1455. [Of unkn. history; cf. ON. *iða* of same meaning.] The water that runs contrary to the direction of the tide or current; a circular motion in water, a small whirlpool. Also *transf.* of wind, fog, dust, etc. Also *fig.*

The madness of the straiten'd stream Turns in black eddies round THOMSON. Circling eddies of fog DICKENS. *fig.* The eddies of the royal history STANLEY.

Eddy (e·di), *v.* 1730. [f. prec. sb.] **1.** *intr.* To move in an eddy or eddies (*lit.* and *fig.*) 1810. **2.** *trans.* To whirl round in eddies. Also with *in*: To collect as into an eddy (*rare*).

1. Eddying in almost viewless wave SCOTT. The vapour..eddying wildly in the air TYNDALL. 2. The circling mountains e. in From the bare wild the dissipated storm THOMSON.

E·ddy-wind. 1626. A wind that moves in an eddy.

‖**Edelweiss** (ē·dĕlvəis). 1862. [f. Ger. *edel* noble + *weiss* white.] *Bot.* An Alpine plant, *Gnaphalium Leontopodium* or *L. alpinum*, remarkable for its white woolly flower, growing at high altitudes on the Swiss mountains.

Edematose, -ous, var. ff. ŒDEMATOSE, -OUS.

Eden (ī·d'n). ME. [a. Heb.; meaning 'pleasure, delight'.] 1. The first abode of Adam and Eve, Paradise. 2. *transf.* and *fig.* A delightful abode, a paradise ME.

2. This sceptred Isle..This other E., demy paradise *Rich. II*, II. i. 42. Hence **Edenic** (īde·nik) *a.* of or pertaining to E. **E·denize** *v.* to make like E.; to admit into E. or Paradise.

Edental (īde·ntăl), *a.* 1845. [f. E- + L. *dentem* + -AL.] = next.

‖**Edenta·ta,** *sb. pl.* 1834. [mod.L., f. *edentatus, edentare* to render toothless.] *Zool.* An order of Mammalia characterized by the absence of front teeth; represented by the Ant-eater, Armadillo, Sloth, etc.

Edentate (īde·ntēt). 1828. [ad. L. *edentatus*; see prec.]

A. *adj.* Characterized by the absence of front teeth; belonging to the *Edentata*. Occas. = 'toothless'.

He is not truly e., but has teeth PARKER.

B. *sb.* 1. in *pl.* = EDENTATA 1835. 2. *joc.* One who has lost his teeth. KINGSLEY.

Edentulous (īde·ntiŭləs), *a.* 1782. [f. L. *edentulus* toothless.] Having no teeth, toothless.

Edge (edʒ), *sb.* [OE. *ecg* str. fem.:—OTeut. **agjā*, f. OAryan root **ak*, whence also L. *acies*, Gr. ἀκίς point, etc. (The sense 'corner' of the equivalent Du. *egge*, and Ger. *ecke*, is wanting in Eng.).] 1. The thin sharpened side of a cutting instrument or weapon. Hence b. A cutting weapon OE. c. Sharpness ME. 2. *fig.* Power to cut or wound; trenchancy; keenness (of desire, etc.) 1593. 3. The crest of a narrow ridge ME.; *fig.* a sharp dividing line; a critical position or moment 1597. 4. The line in which two surfaces, *e.g.* of a polyhedron, meet abruptly 1823. 5. Any relatively thin terminating border, as of a coin, a book, etc. 1677. 6. A bounding line; a border; also, the part adjacent thereto. Also *fig.* ME. 7. The brink or verge (of a precipice, etc.) ME.

1. [They] escaped the e. of the sword *Hebr.* xi. 34. A tool with a fine e. GODWIN. c. The knife has no e. (*mod.*). 2. Abate the e. of Traitors, Gracious Lord *Rich. III*, v. v. 35. The e. of law SHERIDAN, of appetite 1830. Phr. *On e.*: full of eagerness, ready. *To set the teeth on e.*: 'to cause an unpleasant tingling in the teeth' (J.); also *fig.* 3. *fig.* The perilous e. Of battel MILT. *P. L.* I. 276. 5. The milled e. of a shilling (*mod.*). The top e. of a book (*mod.*). 6. From e. to e. A th' world *Ant. & Cl.* II. ii. 117. *fig.* On the e. of winter JOHNSON. 7. *fig.* Phr. *On the e. of*: on the point of (doing something).

attrib. and *Comb.*

a. locative, as *e.-moulding, -gilt* adj., etc. b. objective, as *e.-cutting*. c. advb., as *e.-view*. Also **e.-joint,** a joint made by two edges, forming a corner; **-mill,** an ore-grinding or oil-mill in which the stones travel on their edges; **-rail,** (*a*) one form of rail-road rail, which bears the rolling stock on its edge (Knight); (*b*) a guard-rail placed by the side of the main rail at a switch; **-roll,** a brass wheel used hot, in running an e. ornament, on a book cover (Knight); **-shot** *a.*, having an e. planed, as a board; **-wheel,** a wheel travelling on its e. in an annular or circular bed (Knight).

Edge (edʒ), *v.* ME. [f. EDGE *sb.*; see also EGG *v.*] 1. *trans.* To give an edge to (a weapon, etc. or tool). b. *transf.* and *fig.* To give keenness or incisive force to 1599. †2. = EGG *v.* (but usu. with more direct reference to the sb.); also, to stimulate –1648. Also with *on*. 3. To set (the teeth) on edge. Now *dial.* ME. 4. To furnish with a border or edging 1555. 5. *intr.* To move edgeways; to advance by almost imperceptible movements. Chiefly *Naut.* 1624. 6. *trans.* To move by insensible degrees; to insinuate *into* a place 1677.

1. *fig.* With spirit of Honor edged More sharper then your Swords *Hen. V*, III. v. 38. To e. the appetite BLAIR. 2. This..will Encourage and e., Industrious and Profitable Improuements BACON. 4. Haunted spring and dale Edged with poplar pale MILT. A balustrade which edges it quite round EVELYN. 5. They..stood edging in for the shore DE FOE. 6. Every one edging his chair a little nearer W. IRVING. Phr. *To e. in* (a word, etc.): to get in edgeways.

Edge-bone, corruption of AITCH-BONE, q.v.

Edgeless (e·dʒlės), *a.* 1617. [See -LESS.] That has no edge.

His sword, which he carried neither edgeles, nor in vaine 1617.

†**E·dgeling, -long,** *adv.* ME. [See -LING; for the corrupt form *-long* cf. *sidelong*, etc.] a. With the edge. b. On the edge. –1611.

b. A dye that stands edgeling, so as tis doubtfull what chance it will yeeld COTGR.

Edge-tool, edged tool. ME. 1. In early use, Any implement having a sharp cutting edge, as a knife or a sword; now (in lit. sense) restricted to industrial tools, as chisels, etc., also (with defining adj. *heavy*) axes, etc. Also *attrib.* 2. *fig.*; *esp.* in phr. *play* or *jest with edge tools* 1579.

E·dge-ways, -wise, (rarely) **-way.** 1566. 1. With the edge towards the spectator. 2. Of motion: With the edge foremost 1794. 3. On the edge. SMEATON.

2. *fig.* Phr. *To get a word*, etc. *in edgeways*, etc.

Edging (e·dʒiŋ), *vbl. sb.* ME. [f. EDGE *v.*] †1. The setting on edge (of the teeth). ME. only. 2. The putting an edge or border to anything. Also *attrib.*, as in *e.-lace, -tile*, etc. 1580. 3. *concr.* That which forms an edge to anything, as the fringe, trimming, etc. on the edge of a garment, a border round a flower-bed, etc. 1664.

Edgy (e·dʒi), *a.* 1775. [See -Y.] 1. Sharp, cutting. Also *fig.* 2. Of a painting: Having the outlines too hard 1825.

1. E. splinters RUSKIN. 2. Less e. .. than previous works 1868. Hence **E·dginess.**

Edible (e·dib'l). 1611. [ad. late L. *edibilis*, f. *edere*.] A. *adj.* That is suitable for food. B. *sb.* Anything edible, an article of food. (Chiefly in *pl.*) Hence **Edibi·lity, E·dibleness,** the quality of being e.

Edict (ī·dikt). ME. [ad. L. *edictum*, f. *edicere*, f. *e* + *dicere*. In 16th and 17th c. stressed on the last syllable.] That which is proclaimed by authority as a rule of action; an order issued by a sovereign to his subjects; an ordinance or proclamation having the force of law; *esp.* the edicts of the Roman emperors, and of the French monarchs. Also *fig.*

fig. The generall Edicts of nature HOOKER.

Phr. *E. of Nantes*, an edict issued by Henry IV of France, granting toleration to the Protestants; revoked by Louis XIV.

Edictal (īdi·ktăl), *a.* 1814. [ad. late L. *edictalis*.] Of or pertaining to an edict or edicts; consisting of edicts.

The e. rights of patronus POSTE. **Edi·ctally** *adv.*

†**Edi·ficant,** *a.* 1642. [ad. L. *ædificantem*.] Edifying –1655.

†**Edi·ficate,** *a.* 1470. [ad. L. *ædificatus*.] Built up –1560.

Edification (e:difikē¹·ʃən). ME. [ad. L. *ædificationem*.] 1. Building (now *rare*) 1549; †*concr.* a building –1584. Also *fig.* 2. *fig.* A building up in faith and holiness of life (cf. 1 *Cor.* xiv.) ME.; mental or moral improvement; instruction (now often *ironical*) 1660.

2. To the e. of God's people 1651. That he might distribute his e. in equal proportions 1857.

Edi·ficative, *a.* ? *Obs.* ME. [f. L. *ædificat-* ppl. stem.] Edifying.

Edificatory (e·difikē¹təri). 1649. [ad. L. *ædificatorius*.] Intended or proper for edification.

Edifice (e·difis). ME. [a. F. *édifice*, ad. L. *ædificium*; see EDIFY.] 1. A (large and stately) building, as a church, palace, fortress. Also *transf.* and *fig.* †2. Style of building. NORTH.

1. *fig.* The corner-stone of Comte's e. MORLEY. Hence **Edifi·cial** *a.* pertaining to, or of the nature of, an e.

Edify (e·difəi), *v.* ME. [a. F. *édifier*, ad. L. *ædificare*, f. *ædes, ædis* a building, orig. a hearth + *-ficare* to make; see -FY.] 1. *trans.* To build; to construct, set up (now *rare*). †b. To build over –1596. †2. *fig.* To build up, establish –1781. †3. *intr.* To take form, grow, prosper –1662. 4. *trans.* To build up in faith and holiness; to strengthen. Also *absol.* ME. b. To instruct, improve (occas. *ironical*) 1534. †5. *intr.* To profit spiritually or mentally –1800

1. To take timber to edifie the house againe 1641. Edified out of the Rib of Adam SIR T. BROWNE. 2. He secretly edified the throne of his successors GIBBON. 4. To edifie the conscience that is weake DRAYTON. b. *Twel. N.* v. i. 298. Hence **E·difier** (*rare*). **E·difying** *ppl. a.* that tends to moral and spiritual improvement; now often *ironical.* **E·difyingly** *adv.*

Edile, var. of ÆDILE.

Edingtonite (e·diŋtənəit). 1825. [f. the surname *Edington*.] *Min.* A greyish white translucent mineral, consisting chiefly of the silicates of alumina, baryta, etc.

Edit (e·dit), *v.* 1791. [f. L. *editus*, pa. pple. of *edere* to give out; also, back-formation from EDITOR.] †1. To publish, give to the world. Chiefly in pa. pple. 2. To prepare an edition of, *e. g.* 'to e. (the works of) Horace,' etc. b. To prepare, set in order for publication (literary material). Sometimes euphemistically for: To garble, 'cook'. c. To be or act as the EDITOR of (a newspaper, etc.). 1793.

2. b. The folly of attempting to 'e.' the news 1885.

Edition (īdi·ʃən). 1551. [a. F. *édition*, ad. L. *editionem*; see prec.] †1. Publication –1663. †2. The action of producing; hence, birth, creation, origin, kind, fashion –1677. 3. *concr.* a. One of the differing forms in which a literary work is published. b. The whole number of copies printed from the same set of types and issued at one time. 1570. Also *fig.*

2. Barons of late e. EARL MONM. 3. a. Above 60 editions of the Orlando Furioso were published in the 16th century HALLAM. b. The latest e. of an evening paper (*mod.*) Hence †**Edi·tioner** (*rare*) = EDITOR.

‖**Editio princeps** (īdi·ʃio pri·nseps). 1802. [mod.L.] The first printed edition of a book.

Editor (e·ditəɹ). 1649. [a. L.; see EDIT.] †1. A publisher (cf. F. *éditeur*). 2. One who edits (a text, newspaper, etc.) 1712.

2. This blunder-headed e. of *Bell's Messenger* COBBETT.

Editorial (editōᵊ·riăl). 1744. [f. prec.] A. *adj.* Of or pertaining to an editor; characteristic of an editor; as *e. criticism, prophecy*, etc. B. *sb.* A newspaper article written by, or by the direction of, the editor 1864. Hence **Edito·rially** *adv.* in an e. manner or capacity.

E·ditorship. 1782. [See -SHIP.] The duties, functions, and office of an editor; editorial superintendence.

Editress (e·ditrės). 1799. [See -ESS.] A female editor.

†**Edi·tuate,** *v.* [f. L. *ædituat-*, ppl. stem of *ædituari*, f. *æditus*, tr. Gr. νεωκόρος in *Acts* xix. 35.] To keep, as a temple. J. G[REGORY].

E·domitish, *a.* 1641. [f. *Edomite* descendant of Esau or Edom, inhabitant of Edom + -ISH.] Pertaining to Edom; characteristic of the Edomites. In 17th c. sometimes used with reference to *Ps.* cxxxvii. 7.

Edriophthalmian (e:dri,ǫfþæ·lmiăn). 1877. [f. mod.L. *Edriophthalma* sb. pl. (irreg. f. Gr. ἕδρα seat + ὀφθαλμός eye).] a. *adj.* Belonging to or resembling the *Edriophthalma*, or sessile-eyed Crustacea (including the Prawns, Shrimps, etc.). b. *sb.* An individual of that order. So **E·driophtha·lmous** *a.*

Educable (e·diŭkăb'l), *a.* 1845. [as if ad. L. **educabilis*.] Capable of being educated. Hence **E:ducabi·lity.**

Educate (e·diŭkeᵗt), *v.* 1588. [f. L. *educat-*, *educare*, related to *educere* to lead forth (see EDUCE).] *trans.* or *absol.* †1. To rear, bring up –1818. 2. To bring up from childhood, so as to form habits, manners, mental and physical aptitudes 1618. b. To provide schooling for 1588. 3. To train generally 1849. 4. To train so as to develop some special aptitude, taste, or disposition. Const. *to*, also *inf.* 1841.

2. Mountaines, among which he had been educated BOLTON. b. It costs 8*d.* a week to e. a child 1863. 3. The question is, not what to teach, but how to e. KINGSLEY. 4. Our ears are educated to music by his rhythm EMERSON. I had..to e...our party DISRAELI.

Educated (e·diŭkeᵗtėd), *ppl. a.* 1670. [f. prec.] That has received education; instructed, trained, etc.; see the vb. Often qualified, as *half-, over-, well-*, etc. Also *transf.*

Education (ediŭkē¹·ʃən). 1531. [ad. L. *educationem*; see EDUCATE *v.*] †1. The process of nourishing or rearing –1661. 2. The process of bringing up (young persons); the manner in which a person has been brought up. *Obs.* exc. with notion of 3. 1531. 3. The systematic instruction, schooling or training given to the young (and, by extension, to adults) in preparation for the work of life. Also, the whole course of scholastic instruction which a person has received. Often qualified, as *classical, legal, medical, technical*, etc. 1616. Also *fig.* 4. Hence, Culture or development of powers, formation of character. Often qualified, as *intellectual, moral*, etc. 1860. 5. *attrib.*, as *E. Society*, etc. 1662.

2. The beste forme of e. or bringing up of noble children ELYOT. 3. If you consent to put your clerical e., or any other part of your e., under their direction or control BURKE. *fig.* The e. of the world TEMPLE. 4. It confounds e. with the knowledge of facts, whereas it really is the possession of method ROGERS. Hence **Educa·tional** *a.* †due to e.; of, pertaining to, or concerned with e. **Educa·tionally** *adv.* **Educa·tionalist, Educa·tionist**, a student of the science or methods of e.; an advocate of e.

Educative (e·diŭkētiv), *a.* 1844. [f. L. *educat-* ppl. stem; see EDUCATE.] 1. Of or pertaining to education 1856. 2. Tending to educate, as, an *educative* knowledge.

Educator (e·diŭkeɪtəɹ). 1566. [a. L.] One who or that which educates. Hence **E·duca-tress**, a female e.

Educe (ĭdiū·s), *v.* ME. [ad. L. *educere* to lead out.] †1. *pass.* To be led forth, as a river, a blood-vessel –1578. †2. *Med.* To draw forth so as to remove –1658. 3. To bring out, elicit, develop 1603. b. *Chem.* To disengage from a compound; contrasted with *produce* 1805. 4. To evoke, give rise to 1665.

3. Chaos was that ancient slime, out of which al things were educed GALE. Notions.. which we e. from experience SIR W. HAMILTON. Hence **Edu·cible** *a.* that may be educed.

Educt (ī·dɒkt). 1799. [ad. L. *eductum*, pa. pple. neut. of *educere* to EDUCE.] That which is educed. 1. *Chem.* A body separated by decomposition from another; as dist. from *product*. 2. A result of inference or of development 1816.

Eduction (ĭdɒ·kʃən). 1649. [ad. L. *eductionem*, f. *educere*.] †1. A leading or putting forth or out –1659. †2. *Med.* Removal by drawing forth –1710. 3. The action of educing. Also *concr.* = EDUCT. 1655. 4. *Steam-engine.* a. = EXHAUST. b. Short for *e.-valve.* 1782.

4. b. An e. valve .. to let the steam escape to the condenser 1859.

Eductive (ĭdɒ·ktiv), *a.* 1657. [f. L. *educt-*, *educere*.] Tending to educe.

Eductor (ĭdɒ·ktəɹ). 1794. [a. L.] He who, or that which, educes.

Edulcorate (ĭdɒ·lkŏrēt), *ppl. a. rare.* 1810. [See next.] Softened, sweetened.

Edulcorate (ĭdɒ·lkoreɪt), *v.* 1641. [f. L. *edulcorat-*, *edulcorare*.] †1. To make sweet –1710. 2. To free from harsh and acrid properties; to purify, soften 1641. 3. *Chem.* To free from soluble particles by washing, etc. 1660.

2. Experiments for edulcorating vicious train-oil 1762. Hence **Edu·lcora·tion**, the action or process of washing away particles soluble in water.

Edulcorator (ĭdɒ·lkoreɪtəɹ). 1669. [f. as prec.] One who, or that which, edulcorates.

Edward (e·dwəɹd). 1598. The 'angel' of Edward IV, or the 'noble' of Edward III.

E. shovelboard, a broad shilling of Edward VI, used in the game of Shovel-board. *Merry W.* I. i. 158.

Edwardian (edwǭ·ɹdiăn), *a.* and *sb.* 1861. [-IAN.] 1. Pertaining to (the reigns of) the three Edwards (1272–1377). 2. Belonging to the reign of Edward VI (1547–1553) 1866. b. Belonging to (an alumnus of) a school of the foundation of Edward VI, St. Edward's School, Oxford, or King Edward VII Schools 1873. c. (A person) of the reign of Edward VII (1901–1910) 1908. Also **Edwa·rdine** (-əin) *a.* belonging to the acts of Edward VI's reign.

Ee, *north.* and *esp. Sc.* f. EYE.

-ee, *suffix* [1], correl. to *-or*; orig. ad. *-é* of certain AF. pa. pples.; used chiefly in technical terms of Eng. law, denoting usually the indirect object of the vbs. from which they are derived; as *vendee*, the person to whom a sale is made; etc. In a few words, as *bargee, devotee*, the use is app. arbitrary.

2. *-ee* also appears in the Eng. spelling of certain sbs. adopted from mod.F. ppl. sbs. in *-é*, as *debauchee, refugee*.

-ee, *suffix* [2], usu. with a dim. force, as in *bootee, coatee*. In other words, as *goatee, settee*, its meaning is vague.

Eel (īl). [Com. Teut.: OE. *ǣl* :—OTeut. **ǣloz*; cf. Du., Ger., and Da. *aal*, etc.] 1. The name of a genus (*Anguilla*) of soft-finned osseous fishes, resembling snakes in appearance; including the Common or Sharp-nosed Eel (*A. anguilla*), and the Broad-nosed Eel or GRIG (*A. latirostris*). b. A name for the *Murænidæ*, comprising the true eels with other genera, notably the CONGER. OE. 2. Applied to other fishes resembling eels in form 1705. 3. The pop. name for the *Entozoa* found in vinegar, and in sour paste 1746.

1. An old yeele is wholsomer than a yong COGAN. †*Salt e.*: a rope's end used for flogging. PEPYS. 2. *Electric e.*: = GYMNOTUS. *Nine-eyed e.*: the River Lamprey.

Comb.: e.-**backed** *a.*, applied to horses having black lists along their backs; -**basket**, a trap of basket-work with funnel-shaped entrance for catching eels; -**buck** (see BUCK *sb.*[4]); -**fork** = EEL-SPEAR; -**grass** (*U.S.*), a name for GRASS-WRACK (*Zostera marina*), and for other grass-like weeds; -**pot** = *eel-buck*; -**ware**, *Ranunculus fluitans*; -**weel** (erron. -*wheel*) = *eel-buck*.

Ee·l-bed. 1483. A pond for eels; *transf.* a bivouac on swampy ground.

Eel-fare (ī·lfēəɹ). 1533. a. The passage of young eels up a river. b. A brood of young eels.

Ee·l-pout. [OE. *ǣlepūta*, corr. to M.Du. *aelpuyt*, G. *aalputte*; see EEL, POUT *sb.*[1]] 1. = BURBOT. b. = BLENNY. 2.? = *eel-ware* 1736.

Ee·l-skin. 1562. [f. EEL + SKIN.] The skin of an eel. Also *attrib.*, as in **eelskin-dress**, a tight-fitting dress.

Ee·l-spear. 1555. [f. EEL + SPEAR.] A pronged instrument for spearing eels.

Eely (ī·li), *a.* 1655. [See -Y.] Eel-like.

Een, obs. and dial. pl. of EYE.

E'en, var. of EVEN *adv.*

Eer, obs. f. ERE, before.

-eer, *suffix*, repr. Fr. *-ier* (= L. *-iarius*, and often replacing *-air* :—L. *arius*), in sense 'one who is concerned with', 'one who deals in', often with a contemptuous implication.

E'er, var. of EVER.

Eerie, eery (ī·ri), *a.* [ME. *eri*, ? var. of *erȝ*, ARGH; or ? f. that word + -Y. Properly *Sc.*] 1. Fearful, timid. In mod. use, expressing the notion of a vague superstitious uneasiness. 2. Fear-inspiring; gloomy, strange, weird 1792.

2. Night comes dark and eerie 1795. Hence **Ee·rily** *adv.* **Ee·riness**, a vague sense of fear; superstitious dread. **Ee·risome** *a.* weird, gloomy.

Eete(n, eette, obs. ff. pres. t., pa. t. and pple. of EAT.

Ef (ef). Name of the letter F, q. v.

Ef-, *pref.*, repr. L. pref. *ex-* used before *f*.

Effable (e·făb'l), *a.* 1637. [a. F., ad. L. *effabilis*, f. *effari* to speak out.] That can be uttered, or expressed in words. Now only *arch.*

Efface (efē·s), *v.* 1490. [ad. F. *effacer*, f. L. *ex* + *facies*.] 1. To rub out, obliterate; more widely, to cause to disappear 1611. 2. To expunge, erase. Now only in fig. sentences. 1737. 3. To wipe out; to blot out, obtain oblivion for; to abolish 1490. 4. *fig.* To reduce to insignificance; also *refl.* [after F. *s'effacer*] 1716.

1. So coin grows smooth.. Till Cæsar's image is effaced at last COWPER. 2. Fluent Shakspeare scarce effac'd a line POPE. 3. All my sins e. WESLEY. 4. As a politician he has completely effaced himself (*mod.*). Hence **Effa·ceable** *a.* **Effa·cement.** **Effa·cive** *a.* (*nonce-wd.*), disposed or tending to e.

‖**Effaré** (efa·re), *a.* 1738. [a. F., f. *effarer.*] *Her.* Salient.

†**Effa·scinate**, *v.* 1616. [f. L. *effascinat-*, *effascinare*.] = FASCINATE –1678. So †**Effa·scina·tion**, = FASCINATION.

†**Effa·te.** 1650. [ad. L. *effatum* (also used), f. *effari* to speak out.] A saying, dictum, maxim –1690.

Effect (efe·kt), *sb.* ME. [a. OF. *effect* (mod. F. *effet*), ad. L. *effectus*, f. *efficere* to work out, f. *ex* + *facere*.] 1. Something caused or produced; a result, consequence. Correl. w. CAUSE. b. Efficacy ME. c. *Mech.* The amount of work done in a given time 1812. 2. Purport, drift, tenor ME. †3. An outward manifestation; a phenomenon –1656. b. A (happy) combination of colour or form in a picture, a landscape, etc. 1884. †4. Something attained or acquired by an action 1602. b. *pl.* Goods and chattels, movable property; also, funds in the bank to meet drafts 1704. 5. Operative influence 1668. b. The state or fact of being operative 1771. 6. The impression produced on the mind 1736. 7. Accomplishment 1483. †b. Reality, fact –1674.

1. We know not at all what death is in itself; but only some of its effects BUTLER. b. This Tree is..of Divine e. To open Eyes MILT. *P. L.* IX. 865. c. Phr. *Useful c.*: the net result, after allowance made for friction, etc. 2. Phr. *To this* or *that e.*, *to the e. that.* 3. What effects of passion shows she *Much Ado* II. iii. 112. 4. *Haml.* III. iii. 54. b. Sale of household effects (*mod.*). 5. Speeches which will have an e. upon the courts JOWETT. b. Phr. *To give e. to*: to render operative. *To take e.*: to become operative. 7. Phr. *To bring to e.*, *to carry into e.* b. *Tr. & Cr.* V. iii. 109. Phr. *In e.*: formerly = in fact, in reality; in mod. use, virtually, substantially. Hence **Effe·ctless** *a.*

Effect (efe·kt), *v.* 1589. [f. prec. sb.] 1. *trans.* To bring about; to accomplish. b. To make (*arch.*) 1791. †2. To give effect to; to fulfil –1660. †3. *absol.* and *intr.* To have an effect, be effectual –1660. ¶ 4. Confused with AFFECT 1494.

1. To e. a marriage SHAKS., Peace 1792, a cure JOWETT. Phr. *To e. a sale, an insurance*; hence, *to e. a policy* (of insurance). 2. *Tr. & Cr.* V. x. 6.

Hence **Effe·cter, -or**, one who or that which effects. **Effe·ctible** *a.* capable of being effected. †**Effe·ction**, production; performance; in *Geom.* a construction, a proposition.

Effective (efe·ktiv). ME. [a. F. *effectif*, *-ive*, ad. L. *effectivus*.]

A. *adj.* †1. That is concerned in the production *of* –1684; having the power of acting upon objects –1652. †2. Concerned with, or having the function of, effecting –1607. 3. That has an effect 1760; *spec.* said of that portion of an agency or force which is actually brought to bear on an object 1798. 4. Efficient ME.; striking 1853. 5. Fit for work or service, as soldiers, etc. 1684. 6. Actual, *de facto*; opp. to *potential, nominal* 1786.

3. An e. voice in legislation ADAM SMITH. *E. range*: the range within which a missile or fire-arm is e. *E. faith, love* (Theol.): that bears fruit in action. 4. An e. speaker 1836. 5. Army of 60,000 on paper; of e. more than 50,000 CARLYLE. Phr. *E. charge*: the expenditure on e. forces, as dist. from pensions, etc. 6. The collection of an e. .. revenue BURKE. Phr. *E.* coin, as dist. from paper money.

B. *sb.* †1. An efficient cause –1686. 2. *Mil.* An effective soldier. (See A. 5.) Usually *pl.* 1722. b. *collect. sing.* The effective part of an army 1885.

2. The garrisons..consist of 1000 Effectives 1722. Hence **Effe·ctively** *adv.* in an e. manner; †in fact; virtually; decisively, completely. **Effe·ctiveness**, the quality of being e.

†**Effectress** (efe·ktrés). 1601. [See -ESS.] A female effecter –1662. So ‖**Effe·ctrix** [sc. *causa, vis*], an efficient cause or power.

Effectual (efe·ktiŭăl), *a.* ME. [a. OF. *effectuel* :—late L. *effectualis*, f. *effectus* EFFECT *sb.*] 1. That produces its intended effect, or answers its purpose. †2. = EFFECTIVE, q. v. –1689. 3. Of prayers: Earnest, urgent ME. †4. ? Actual –1655. †5. To the point, pertinent, conclusive –1677.

1. To make complaints rather e. than loud BURKE. Phr. *E. calling* (Theol.): 'the word of God's Spirit, whereby..he doth persuade and enable us to embrace Jesus Christ' *Shorter Catech.* *E. demand* (Pol. Econ.): demand 'sufficient to effectuate the bringing of the commodity to market' (Adam Smyth). 5. A speedy and e. answer 1625.

Hence **Effectua·lity**, e. quality. **Effe·ctually** *adv.* so as to answer the purpose; †earnestly; †explicitly; †in effect; †in fact. **Effe·ctualness** (now *rare*), efficacy.

Effectuate (efe·ktiuˌeɪt), *v.* 1580. [f. F. *effectuer*, f. L. *effectus*; after ACTUATE.] *trans.* To bring to pass; to carry into effect, accomplish.

To e. a desire SIDNEY, a Cure CHEYNE, purpose JOHNSON, an intention CRUISE, a conclusion (*mod.*).

Hence **Effe·ctua·tion**, accomplishment, fulfilment.

†**Effe·ctuous**, *a.* ME. [ad. OF. *effectueux*, ad. med.L. *effectuosus*; see EFFECT *sb.* and -OUS.] = EFFECTUAL *a.* 1, 3. –1655. Hence †**Effe·ctuous·ly** *adv.*, †**-ness**.

†**Effei·r**, *sb.* ME. [Sc. var. of AFFAIR, q. v.] 1. A 'cause' –1605. 2. Appearance; show; ceremony –1818.

Effeir, effere (in Sc. efī·r), *v. n. dial.* ME. [Usual spelling of AFFEIR, AFFERE.] 1. *impers. intr.* To fall by right, appertain, be proper or meet. *Obs.* exc. in Sc. law phr. 'as effeirs'. †2. As *personal* vb. To pertain properly -1820.

2. In all that effeirs to war SCOTT.

Effeminacy (efe·minăsi). 1602. [f. EFFEMINATE *a.*; see -ACY.] 1. Effeminate quality; unmanly weakness, softness, or delicacy. †2. Addiction to women -1671.

2. But foul e. held me yok't Her Bond-Slave MILT.

Effeminate (efe·minĕt). ME. [ad. L. *effeminatus, effeminare*, f. *ef-* (for *ex-*) + *femina*.]

A. *adj.* 1. That has become like a woman: a. Unmanly, enervated; self-indulgent; delicate or over-refined. b. Of things: Characterized by, or proceeding from, effeminacy 1579. †c. Gentle, compassionate -1594. †d. Of music, odours, etc.: Soft, voluptuous -1692. †2. Addicted to women -1589.

1. a. An e. persone neuer hathe spirite to any hie or noble dedes LD. BERNERS. b. I scorn those e. revenges 1685. c. *Rich. III*, III. vii. 211.

B. *sb.* An effeminate person 1597.

This wanton young e. [Richard II] DANIEL.

Hence **Effe·minately** *adv.* in an unmanly manner or style; †through addiction to women (MILT. *Sams.* 562). **Effe·minateness**, e. quality or condition.

Effeminate (efe·mine^i^t), *v.* ME. [ad. L. *effeminatus*; see prec.] †1. *trans.* To represent as a woman (*rare*) -1739. 2. To make womanish or unmanly; to enervate 1551. 3. *intr.* To become womanish; to grow weak, languish ME.

2. Luxurious living .. Effeminates fools in body SHADWELL. 3. In a slothfull peace both courages will e., and manners corrupt BACON.

Effemination (efe:minē^i^·ʃən). ? *Obs.* 1650. [ad. L. *effeminationem*.] The process of making or of becoming effeminate.

Effeminize (efe·minəiz), *v.* Now *rare.* 1612. [f. EFFEMINATE *a.* + -IZE.] *trans.* To render effeminate.

‖**Effendi** (efe·ndi). 1614. [Turk. *efendī*, a corruption of Gr. αὐθέντης (afþe·ndīs) lord, master.] A Turkish title of respect, chiefly applied to officials and to professional men.

Efferent (e·fĕrĕnt). 1856. [ad. L. *efferentem*, f. *efferre*.] *Phys.* a. *adj.* Conveying outwards; as, *e. vessels, nerves.* Opp. to AFFERENT. b. *sb.* That which carries outwards 1876.

†**E·fferous**, *a. rare.* 1614. [f. L. *ex* + *ferus* + -OUS.] Fierce, violent -1657.

Effervesce (efəɹve·s), *v.* 1702. [ad. L. *effervescere*, f. *ex* + *fervescere*, inceptive f. *fervere* to be hot.] †1. *intr.* 'To generate heat by intestine motion' (J.). 2. To give off bubbles of gas, *esp.* as the result of chemical action 1784. Of the gas itself: To issue forth in bubbles 1830. Also *fig.*

2. *fig.* A number of .. juveniles .. were effervescing in all those modes of .. gambol and mischief MRS. STOWE. Hence **Efferve·scible** *a.* capable of producing effervescence; *fig.* ready to e. **Efferve·scive** *a.* tending to effervescence.

Effervescence (efəɹve·sĕns). 1651. [f. L. *effervescentem*; see prec.] †1. The action of boiling up; heated agitation of the particles of a fluid -1710. 2. The action of bubbling up as if boiling; the rise of bubbles of gas from a fluid; *esp.* as the result of chemical action 1684.

2. That e. observed in the mixture of acids and alkalies BERKELEY. *fig.* The e. of invention JOHNSON. So **Efferve·scency**, effervescent state or condition.

Effervescent (efəɹve·sĕnt), *a.* 1684. [ad. L. *effervescentem*; see above.] †1. That is in a state of bubbling heat. 2. That has the property of rising in bubbles 1875. Also *fig.*

2. *fig.* Nonsense e. with animal spirits MACAULAY.

Effet, obs. or dial. f. EFT *sb.*[1]

Effete (efī·t), *a.* 1621. [ad. L. *effetus*, f. *ef-* (for *ex*) + *fetus* that has brought forth.] †1. Of animals: That has ceased to bring forth offspring -1774. Also *fig.* 2. *transf.* Of substances: That has lost its special quality or virtue; exhausted, worn out 1662. 3. *fig.* Of systems, etc.: That has exhausted its vigour; incapable of efficient action 1790.

3. They find the old governments e., worn out BURKE. Your e. English aristocrat 1857. Hence **Effe·teness.**

†**E·fficace**, *sb.* ME. [a. OF., ad. L. *efficacia*, f. *efficax*.] a. Efficacy. b. Effect. c. Active duty. -1712.

Efficacious (efikē^i^·ʃəs), *a.* 1528. [f. L. *efficaci-* (stem of *efficax*) + -OUS; see -ACIOUS.] That produces, or is certain to produce, the intended effect; effective. (Not said, in prose, of personal agents.)

Lesse e., that is, in plain English ineffectual 1651. Hence **Effica·cious-ly** *adv.*, **-ness.**

Effica·city. ME. [ad. L. *efficacitatem* (see prec.).] = next.

Efficacy (e·fikăsi). 1527. [ad. L. *efficacia*, f. *efficax*; see -ACY.] 1. Capacity to produce effects; power to effect the object intended. (Not used of personal agents.) †2. A mode of effecting a result. LOCKE. †3. Effect -1633.

1. An act, not .. beyond the e. of the Sun SIR T. BROWNE. E. in a distemper BERKELEY. The e. of mirth JOHNSON.

Efficience (efi·ʃĕns). ? *Obs.* 1669. [ad. L *efficientia*; see EFFICIENT and -ENCE.] The exercise of efficient power.

Efficiency (efi·ʃĕnsi). 1593. [ad. L. *efficientia*; see prec.] 1. The fact of being an efficient cause. Now only in philosophical use. †b. Production, causation, creation -1678. 2. Efficient power, effectiveness, efficacy 1633.

2. The greatest dissemination of power consistent with e. MILL. The e. of labour FAWCETT.

Efficient (efi·ʃĕnt). ME. [a. F., ad. L. *efficientem*, f. (ult.) *ef-* (for *ex*) + *facere*.]

A. *adj.* 1. Making, causing to be; that makes (a thing) to be what it is. 2. Productive of effects; operative. Of persons: Adequately skilled and active. 1787.

1. The common e. cause of beauty BURKE. 2. An e. government 1787. An expert and e. workman 1850.

B. *sb.* †1. 'The cause which makes effects to be what they are' (J.). Common in 17th c. -1804. 2. *Mil.* An efficient soldier; a volunteer qualified for service 1864.

1. The E. or Author of it, is .. God himselfe 1649. Hence **Effi·ciently** *adv.* †as by an e. cause; in an e. manner.

†**Effie·rce**, *v.* [f. EF- + FIERCE.] To render fierce. SPENSER *F. Q.* III. xi. 27.

Effi·gial, *a. rare.* 1715. [f. L. *effigies*.] Of the nature of an effigy.

Effigiate (efi·dʒi,e^i^t), *v.* Now *rare.* 1608. [f. late L. *effigiat-, effigiare*, f. *effigies*.] To present a likeness of; to portray. Also *fig.* Also with *into* (obs.).

To effigiat the Emperour Nero 1628. Hence **Effi:gia·tion**, the action of representing; a representation.

‖**Effigies** (efi·dʒi,īz). *arch.* 1600. [L.] Now EFFIGY, q. v.

Effigy (e·fidʒi). 1539. [a. F. *effigie*, ad. L. *effigies*, f. (ult.) *ef-* (for *ex*) + *fingere*.] A likeness, portrait, or image. Now chiefly applied to a sculptured figure or to a habited image; also to a portrait on coins.

Phrases. *In e.*: under the form, or by means of, a representation; also *fig.* *To execute, hang, burn in e.*: to treat thus an image of any one, as an indication of the treatment popularly desired for the original; formerly also done in the case of a criminal who had fled from justice.

†**Effla·gitate**, *v. rare.* 1641. [f. L. *efflagitat-, efflagitare*, f. *ex* + *flagitare* to demand.] To demand eagerly -1676.

†**Effla·te**, *v. rare.* 1634. [f. L. *efflat-, efflare*, f. *ex* + *flare* to blow.] To puff out.

Efflation (eflē^i^·ʃən). 1578. [f. as prec.] 1. A blowing out; expulsion of breath. 2. *concr.* That which is blown or breathed forth 1862.

The *Rig-veda* is the e. of that great being F. HALL.

Effloresce (eflore·s), *v.* 1775. [ad. L. *efflorescere*, inceptive form of *efflorere*, f. *ef-* (for *ex*) + *florere*.] 1. To bloom, burst forth into or as into flowers. 2. *Chem.* a. Of a crystalline substance: To change over the surface, or throughout, to 'flowers' or fine powder, owing to loss of water on exposure to the air 1788. b. Of a salt: To come to the surface, and there crystallize 1820. c. Of the ground, a wall, etc.: To become covered with a powdery crust of saline particles left by evaporation 18.. 3. *fig.* To blossom out; to become manifest 1834.

3. A disposition .. to e. into extremely tall talk 1864.

Efflorescence (eflore·sĕns). 1626. [a. F.; see prec. + -ENCE.] 1. The process, or period, of flowering. Also *fig.* 2. *Path.* 'A morbid redness, or rash of the skin' (*Syd. Soc. Lex.*) 1684. 3. *Chem.* The process of efflorescing (see EFFLORESCE 2); the powdery deposit which results from this 1667.

1. *fig.* His impertinent e. of Rhetorick MARVELL. So †**Efflore·scency** (in senses 1 *fig.* and 3).

Efflorescent (eflore·sĕnt), *a.* 1818. [ad. L. *efflorescentem*.] 1. *Bot.* That is efflorescing or blooming. 2. Resembling, or forming, an efflorescence; also *fig.*

Efflower (eflau^ə^·ɹ), *v. rare.* 1875. [ad. F. *effleurer*.] To deprive a skin of its epidermis with a blunt knife.

Effluence (e·fl^i^ŭĕns). 1603. [f. L. *effluentem* flowing out.] 1. A flowing out (*esp.* of light, magnetism, etc.). Also *transf.* and *fig.* 1628. 2. *concr.* That which flows forth; an emanation. Also *fig.* 1603.

1. A moist e. of vapours 1635. *transf.* That stormful e. towards the Frontiers CARLYLE. 2. Colour is an e. of form JOWETT. So †**E·ffluency.**

Effluent (e·fl^i^ŭĕnt). 1726. [ad. L. *effluentem*; f. (ult.) *ex* + *fluere*.]

A. *adj.* That flows forth or outwards, as an *e. drain.*

B. *sb.* a. A stream flowing from a larger stream, lake, etc. b. The outflow from a sewage tank 1859.

Effluve (efl^i^ū·v). 1881. [a. F., ad. L. *effluvium*, f. *ex* + *fluere*.] *Electr.* The diffusion of electricity from an electrified body by radiation or atmospheric conduction.

†**Efflu·viable**, *a.* [f. EFFLUVIUM + -ABLE.] That can pass off in effluvia. BOYLE.

†**Efflu·viate**, *v.* 1664. [f. EFFLUVIUM + -ATE [3].] *trans.* To throw off effluvium; also *absol.* and *intr.* -1693.

Effluvious (efl^i^ū·viəs), *a.* 1668. [See -OUS.] Of the nature of an effluvium.

Effluvium (efl^i^ū·viŏm). Pl. **-ia**, †**-iums.** 1646. [a. late L. *effluvium*, f. (ult.) *ex* + *fluere*.] †1. A flowing out, an issuing forth -1704. 2. *esp.* The (real or supposed) outflow of material particles too subtle to be perceived by the senses; *concr.* a stream of such particles. (*Obs.* in gen. sense.) 1646. b. An exhalation affecting the sense of smell; *pop.*, a noxious or disgusting exhalation 1656. ¶ 3. In sense 2, the pl. *effluvia* has been ignorantly treated as a sing., with pl. *effluvias* or *effluviæ* 1652.

2. The Effluvia of the Load-stone BOYLE. Quick effluvia darting through the brain POPE.

Efflux (e·flɒks), *sb.* 1641. [ad. L. *effluxus*, f. *effluere*.] 1. A flowing outwards; often opp. to *afflux* or *influx*. Also *attrib.* Hence, a channel of outflow. Also *fig.* 1649. 2. The lapse (of time, etc.); hence, expiry 1647. 3. *concr.* That which flows out; an emanation 1647.

2. In e. of time N. BACON. The e. in 1877 of the time within which the turnpike trust was limited 1884. Hence †**Efflu·x** *v.* to flow or cause to flow forth (*rare*).

Effluxion (eflɒ·kʃən). 1621. [f. prec.] 1. The action or process of flowing out; an outflow. Also *fig.* 1646. 2. = EFFLUX 2. 1621. 3. = EFFLUVIUM 1626.

2. The partnership .. having expired by e. of time 1868. So †**Efflu·xive** *a.* outflowing (*rare*).

†**Effo·liate**, *v. rare.* 1671. [f. EF- + FOLIATE *v.*] To open into leaf. Hence (with different sense) **Effolia·tion**, removal of leaves.

Efforce (efō^ə^·ɹs). 1512. [ad. F. *efforcer* (OF. *esforcer*) :—med.L. *exfortiare*, f. *ex* + *fortis* strong.] †1. *refl.* To make an effort (= Fr. *s'efforcer*) -1543. 2. To force open, to gain by force. SPENSER. 3. To force out (*rare*) 1855. Hence **Effo·rced** *ppl. a.* uttered with effort.

Efform (efǭ·ɹm). 1578. [f. EF- + FORM *v.*] To shape, fashion. Hence †**Efforma·tion.** †**Effo·rmative** *a.* **Effo·rmer.**

Effort (e·fǭɹt), *sb.* 1489. [a. F., f. *efforcer*; see EFFORCE *v.* Formerly stressed *effo·rt*.] †1. Power; also *pl.* powers, properties -1680. 2. A strenuous exertion of power, physical or mental; a laborious attempt; a struggle 1489. b. In oratory, etc.: An achievement 1857.

2. The panting Courser .. Makes many a faint E. SOMERVILLE. It required a considerable e. TYNDALL. Hence †**Effo·rt** *v.* to strengthen. **E·ffortless** *a.* making no e. **E·ffortlessly** *adv.*

†**Effo·ssion.** *rare.* 1657. [ad. L. *effossionem*, f. *effossus, effodere*.] The action of digging out -1714.

Effraction (efræ·kʃən). 1840. [a. F., ad. L. *effractionem*, f. (ult.) *ex* + *frangere*.] Breaking open (a house); burglary.

A riot, with e. and murder MILMAN.

Effranchise (efræ·ntʃəiz), *v.* 1864. [app.

rec.; cf. AFFRANCHISE, ENFRANCHISE.] To invest with franchises or privileges.

†Effray·, *v.* ME. [a. F. *effrayer*; see AFFRAY.] **1.** *trans.* To frighten –1596. **2.** To frighten away; to scare 1588. Hence Effray·able [? misprint for EFFROYABLE] *a.* frightful.

†E·ffrenate, *a.* 1561. [ad. L. *effrenatus*, f. (ult.) *ex* + *frenum*. Cf. F. *effréné*.] Unbridled; violent in action –1657. So †Effrena·tion.

†Effro·nt, *v. rare.* 1643. [(1) from next; (2) ad. OF. *effronter*.] **1.** *trans.* To free from bashfulness. **2.** To put to confusion 1649.

†Effro·nted, *ppl. a.* 1598. [f. F. *effronté*, OF. *esfronté*, f. (ult.) L. *ex* + *frons*, in sense 'ability to blush'.] Shameless, unblushingly insolent –1641. Hence †Effro·ntedly *adv.* Also (irreg.) †Effro·ntuous *a.* characterized by effrontery (North).

Effrontery (efrʊ·ntĕri). 1715. [ad. F. *effronterie*, f. *effronté*; see prec.] Shameless audacity, unblushing insolence.
The happy inheritance of impregnable e. SMOLLETT.

†Effu·de, *v.* 1634. [incorrect ad. L. *effundere*.] To pour out –1657.

Effulge (efʊ·ldʒ), *v.* 1729. [ad. L. *effulgere*, f. *ex* + *fulgere*.] **1.** *intr.* To shine forth brilliantly. Also *fig.* (now humorously pedantic.) 1735. **2.** *trans.* To flash forth (*lit.* and *fig.*).
1. *fig.* He effulges with the sun in velveteen jacket and breeches 1828.

Effulgence (efʊ·ldʒĕns). 1667. [f. next.] The quality of being effulgent, splendid radiance (*lit.* and *fig.*).
On thee Impresst the e. of his Glorie abides MILT.

Effulgent (efʊ·ldʒĕnt), *a.* 1738. [ad. L. *effulgentem*; see EFFULGE.] Shining forth brilliantly; diffusing intense light; radiant.
He is upborne by an e. cloud 1852. Hence Effu·lgently *adv.*

†Effu·mabi·lity. [f. L. *effumare*; see EFFUME and -ITY.] Capability of being converted into vapour. BOYLE.

†Effu·me, *v. rare.* [ad. F. *effumer*, f. L. *effumare*, f. *ex* + *fumus*.] To puff out (smoke). B. JONSON. So †Effuma·tion, the action of converting into vapour; *concr.* a vapour emitted.

Effund (efʊ·nd), *v.* ME. [ad. L. *effundere*.] *trans.* To pour out (*lit.* and *fig.*).

†Effu·se, *sb. rare.* 1593. [f. the vb.] Effusion –1631.
Much e. of blood 3 *Hen. VI*, II. vi. 28.

Effuse (efiū·s), *a.* 1530. [ad. L. *effusus*, pa. pple. of *effundere*.] **1.** Poured out freely; chiefly *transf.* and *fig.* overflowing, unrestrained. ? *Obs.* **2.** *Bot.* Of an inflorescence: Spreading loosely, *esp.* on one side 1870. **b.** *Conch.* Having the lips separated by a groove 1842.
1. No wanton waste amidst e. expence YOUNG.

Effuse (efiū·z), *v.* ME. [f. L. *effus-*; see prec.] *trans.* To pour forth or out; †to shed (blood); in *pass.* to be extravasated. Also *transf.* and *fig.* Also *absol.*
My pitying eye..effus'd a pienteous stream POPE. *fig.* A palpable tranquillity had been effused abroad GALT. Hence Effu·sedly *adv.* unrestrainedly (*rare*).

Effusion (efiū·ʒən). ME. [ad. L. *effusionem*; cf. Fr. *effusion*.] **1.** A pouring out; †shedding (of tears, blood, etc.). **b.** *Path.* The escape of any fluid out of its natural vessel, and its lodgement elsewhere 1732. **2.** *transf.* and *fig.* (see quots.) ME. **3.** *concr.* That which is poured out; *esp.* a speech, or the like. Now often *contemptuous.* 1779.
1. E. of wine JER. TAYLOR, of lava HERSCHEL. Phr. †*E. of spirits* (see ANIMAL SPIRITS): the supposed cause of fainting. **2.** E. of treasure RALEIGH, of joy 1778, of His [Christ's] Spirit FARRAR. **3.** Here ended this wild e. SCOTT.

Effusive (efiū·siv), *a.* 1662. [f. L. *effus-* (see EFFUSE *v.*) + -IVE.] **1.** Pouring out, overflowing. Of emotions, etc.: Demonstrative. **2.** That gives outlet to emotion. BAIN.
1. The floor Wash'd with th' e. wave POPE. Peel.. was not e.; he did not pour out his emotions MCCARTHY. Hence Effu·sive-ly *adv.*, -ness.

‖Efreet (e·frīt). 1841. var. of AFREET.

Eft (eft), *sb.* [OE. *efeta*, of unkn. origin. The form NEWT is now more used.] A small lizard. Now chiefly applied to the Greater Water-Newt (*Triton cristatus*), of the order *Salamandridæ*.

†Eft, *a. superl.* **eftest.** ? Ready, apt. *Much Ado* IV. ii. 38.

†Eft (eft), *adv.* [OE. *eft*, f. (ult.) OTeut. stem *aft*; see AFT.] **a.** Again –1651. **b.** Afterwards –1559.

Eftsoons (eftsū·nz), *adv.* *Obs.* or *arch.* Also eftsoon. [OE. *eftsōna*, f. *eft* EFT *adv.* + *sōna* SOON; extended with advb. *-s* in 14th c.] †**1.** A second time, again –1637. †**2.** Again, moreover –1601. **3.** Afterwards, soon after; forthwith. †**4.** From time to time, repeatedly –1720.

Egad (ĭgæ·d), *interj.* 1673. [prob. f. A *interj.* + GOD, but now assoc. w. *By God!*] Used as a softened oath.

Ega·lity. [ME. *egalite*, a. F. *égalité*.] = EQUALITY. Re-coined by TENNYSON. So Egalita·rian *a.* that asserts e.

†E·gall, *a.* ME. [a. OF. *egal* (mod.F. *égal*) :—L. *æqualem*.] = EQUAL –1596. Hence †E·gal·ly *adv.*, †-ness.

E·gence. *rare.* [f. L. *egentem*, *egere*.] Need. J. GROTE.

Eger, obs. f. EAGER *a.*, EAGRE.

Egest (ĭdʒe·st), *v.* 1607. [f. L. *egest-*, *egerere*.] *trans.* To pass off, expel; *esp.* from within the body, as excrement, perspiration, etc. Hence Ege·stive *a.* pertaining to egestion.

‖Egesta (ĭdʒe·stă), *sb. pl.* 1787. [L., neut. pl. of *egestus*; see prec.] Excreta.

Egestion (ĭdʒe·stʃən). ME. [ad. L. *egestionem*; see prec.] †**1.** The action of emptying out. ME. only. **2.** *Phys.* The passing off of excreta from within the body; excrement 1607.

Egg (eg), *sb.* [ME. a. ON. *egg*; Com.Teut.: = OE. *ǽg*, pl. *ǽgru* (whence ME. *ei*, pl. *eyren*), OS., OHG., etc. *ei* :—OTeut. **ajjoz-* neut., prob. rel. to Gr. ᾠόν, L. *ovum*, Ir. *og*.] **1.** The oval body laid by the female of birds and other animal species, and containing the germ of a new individual, enclosed within a shell or strong membrane. **b.** *spec.* A hen's egg OE. **2.** *fig.* That which contains the germ of anything; usu. in a bad sense 1645. **3.** *transf.* An oval 1589.
1. Thinke him as a Serpents egge *Jul. C.* II. i. 32. **b.** They are vp already, and call for Egges and Butter 1 *Hen. IV*, II. i. 64. **2.** Phr. *To crush in the e.*
Phrases. *To have all one's eggs in one basket*: to risk all one's property on a single venture. *To tread upon eggs*: to walk on delicate ground. *A bad e.*: a person or thing that comes to no good 1853. So *Good e.* (U.S.), used as a commendatory exclamation.
Comb.: **a.** attrib., as *e.-basket*, *-cup* (1837), *-spoon*, etc. **b.** objective, as *e.-beater*, *-boiler*, etc. **c.** similative, as *e.-bald*, *-shaped*, etc.
Special comb.: **e. and anchor, e. and tongue, e. and dart** (*sc.* mouldings), varieties of the ECHINUS, produced by the alternation of vertical with e.-shaped ornaments; **e.-apple**, the fruit of the E.-plant (*Solanum Melongena*); **-bag**, (*a*) the ovary; (*b*) = *egg-case*; **-bird**, a species of tern (*Hydrochelidon fuliginosum*); **-bound** *ppl. a.*, said of fowls unable through weakness or disease to expel their eggs; **-case**, the silken cocoon in which spiders enclose the tubes in which the females lay their eggs; **-cell**, the cell or germ from which an ovum or an individual is subsequently developed; **-dance**, a dance blindfold among eggs; also *fig.*; **-flip** = EGG-NOG; **-glass**, (*a*) a glass for holding an e.; (*b*) a sand-glass for timing the boiling of an e.; †**-hot**, 'a hot drink made of beer, eggs, sugar, and nutmeg'; **-plum**, an egg-shaped plum of a light yellow colour; **-pop** (*U.S.*), ? a kind of *egg-flip*; **-pouch**, **-sac** = *egg-case*; **-Saturday**, the Saturday before Shrove Tuesday (Nares); **-slice**, a slice for removing omelets or fried eggs from the pan; **-stone** = OOLITE; **-sucker**, a bird, the Toucan; **-Sunday**, the Sunday before Shrove Tuesday; **-trot** = *egg-wife's trot*; **-urchin**, the name of species of ECHINUS; †**-wife**, a woman who offers eggs for sale; hence **e.-wife's trot**, her pace in riding to market.

Egg (eg), *v.*[1] ME. [a. ON. *eggja* (Da. *egge*), = EDGE *v.*[1]] *trans.* To incite, encourage; to provoke, tempt. *Obs.* exc. with *on.* 1566.
A man which sharpens his enemy with taunts, when he would e. him to fight H. SMITH. Schemers and flatterers would e. him on THACKERAY. Hence E·gger *sb.*[1]

Egg (eg), *v.*[2] 1833. [f. the sb.] **a.** To cover with yolk of egg. **b.** To pelt with (rotten) eggs. **c.** *intr.* To collect (wild fowls') eggs.
a. To see a sweetbread egged and crumbed 1864. Hence E·gger *sb.*[2] (in sense c).

Egger (e·gəɹ), *sb.*[3] 1705. [app. f. EGG *sb.* + -ER.] A collector's name for moths, *esp.* the Oak Egger-moth (*Bombyx quercus*).

†E·ggment. ME. only. [f. EGG *v.*[1] + -MENT.] Incitement.

Egg-nog(g (e·g·nǫ·g). 1825. [f. EGG + NOG strong ale.] A drink in which eggs are stirred up with hot beer, cider, wine, or spirits.

E·gg-plant. 1767. A name for the *Solanum esculentum*, now including both the white-fruited variety, and the purple-fruited Aubergine.

E·gg-shell. ME. [f. EGG *sb.* + SHELL.] The shell or external covering of an egg; often as a type of worthlessness or of fragility. **b.** *attrib.*, as in *egg-shell china*: a very thin and delicate porcelain ware.

Eglandular (ĭglæ·ndiŭlăɹ), *a.* 1870. [See E- *pref.*] *Bot.* That has no glands. So Egla·ndulose *a.* (in same sense).

Eglantine (e·glăntəin, -tin). ME. [a. F. *églantine*, f. OF. *aiglant*, prob. repr. L. type **aculentus* prickly, f. *acus* needle + *-lentus* suffix.] **1.** The Sweet-briar; also *attrib.* ¶**2.** In Milton: ? The honeysuckle.
1. Quite ouer-cannoped with..E. *Mids. N.* II. i. 252. **2.** Through the sweetbrier or the vine, Or the twisted e. MILT. *L'Allegro* 48.

Eglatere (eglătiᵊ·ɹ). ME. [a. OF. *esglantier*, *aiglantier* (mod.F. *églantier*), f. *aiglant* (see prec.) + *-ier*, as in *rosier*, etc.] = prec. Now only *poet.*

Eglogue, obs. f. ECLOGUE.

†Eglomerate (ĭglǫ·mĕrēᵗt), *v.* 1656. [f. L. *e* + *glomerare*, f. *glomus* clew or ball.] To unwind. (Dicts.)

E·gma. A blunder for ENIGMA. *L.L.L.* III. i. 73.

‖Ego (e·go, ī·go). 1824. [L. The pronunc. (ī·go) is obsolete in England.] *Metaph.* The *I*; the conscious thinking subject, as opp. to the *non-ego* or object. Also *joc.* for 'self'.
In every act of consciousness we distinguish a self or ego 1829. Hence E·hood, individuality. Ego·ical *a.* of or pertaining to egotism.

Egoism (e·g-, ī·goˌiz'm). 1785. [ad. F. *égoïsme*, ad. mod.L. *egoismus*, f. prec.; see -ISM.] **1.** *Metaph.* The belief, on the part of an individual, that there is no proof that anything exists but his own mind: chiefly applied polemically to philosophical systems supposed to involve this conclusion. **2.** *Ethics.* The theory which regards self-interest as the foundation of morality. Also, in practical sense: Regard to one's own interest; systematic selfishness. (Latterly opp. to *altruism*.) **b.** with *an* and *pl.* 1795. **3.** The habit of looking upon all questions chiefly in their relations to oneself. Also, self-opinionativeness 1840. **4.** = EGOTISM **1.** 1807.

Egoist (e·g-, ī·goˌist). 1785. [f. as prec. + -IST.] **1.** An adherent of EGOISM (sense **1**). **2.** A systematically selfish man 1879. **3.** = EGOTIST. Also quasi-*adj.* 1794.
3. I will turn e., and tell you *my* adventures LYTTON. Hence Egoi·stic, -al *a.* pertaining to, or of the nature of, EGOISM (senses 1–3). Egoi·stically *adv.*

E·goistry. *nonce-wd.* = EGOISM. Ld. Shaftesbury.

Egoity (egōᵘ·iti). 1651. [See -ITY.] Selfhood; that which forms the essence of the individual.

Egomania (egomēⁱ·niă). *joc.* 1825. [after *monomania*, etc.] Morbid egotism.

†E·gomism. *rare.* 1730. [a. F. *égomisme*; cf. L. *egomet*.] The belief of one who considers himself the only being in existence –1856.

Egophony, var. of ÆGOPHONY.

Egotheism (egoþī·iz'm). *rare.* 1856. [f. Gr. ἐγώ + θεός + -ISM.] The (mystical) identification of oneself with the deity.

Egotism (e·g-, ī·gǒtiz'm). 1714. [f. as EGOISM, with intrusive *t*.] **1.** The too frequent use of the word *I*; hence, the practice of talking about oneself and one's doings. **2.** Self-conceit; also, selfishness 1800.
1. The e. of personal narrative KANE. **2.** His [Napoleon's] absorbing e. was deadly to all men EMERSON.

Egotist (e·g-, ī·gǒtist). 1714. [f. as prec. + -IST.] One who uses the word *I* too often; one who thinks or talks too much of himself. Also *attrib.* Hence Egoti·stic, -al *a.* pertaining to, or characterized by, egotism. Egoti·stically *adv.*

Egotize (e·g-, ī·gǒtəiz), *v.* 1789. [f. EGO-

TISM; see -IZE.] *intr.* To talk or write egotistically.

Egranulose (ĭgræ·niŭlōᵘs), *a.* 1884. [See E- *pref.*] Without granules.

Egre, obs. f. EAGER.

Egregious (ĭgrī·dʒiəs, -dʒiəs), *a.* 1534. [f. L. *egregius*, f. *e* + *grex, gregis* + -OUS; hence *lit.* chosen out of the flock.] †1. Prominent, projecting 1578. 2. Remarkable: †a. (in a good sense) Distinguished, excellent, renowned -1738. b. (in a bad sense) Gross, flagrant 1573.

2. a. E. Ransome SHAKS., doctrine MILT. An e. mathematician HOBBES. b. E. Liars and Impostors MILT. An e. exercise of tyranny HUME. Hence **Egre·giously** *adv.* in an e. manner (now only in a bad sense). **Egre·giousness,** excellence.

Egremoigne, -moyn, obs. ff. AGRIMONY.

Egress (ī·gres), *sb.* 1538. [ad. L. *egressus*, f. *egredi* to go out.] 1. A going out, or the right or liberty of going out. Also *attrib.* b. *Astron.* The end of an eclipse or transit 1706. 2. A channel of exit, an outlet. Also *fig.* 1604.

1. Free entre, egresse, and regresse tr. *Lyttleton's Tenures.* Gates of burning Adamant..prohibit all e. MILT. *P. L.* II. 437. 2. A lane..an e. from which was shut up SCOTT.

Egress (ĭgre·s), *v.* 1578. [f. the sb.] *intr.* To issue, to go forth. Hence **Egre·ssion,** the action of going out or issuing forth. **Egre·ssive** *a.* tending to go forth.

Egret (e·grėt, ī·grėt). ME. [var. of AIGRETTE, q.v.; see also HERON.] 1. The Lesser White Heron. Also *attrib.*, as in *e.-heron.* 2. = AIGRETTE 3. 1794. 3. *attrib.*, as †**e.-monkey,** a hypothetical species of ape, called by Linnæus *Simia Aygula* 1802.

1. An egript..is all white as the swanne, with legs like to an hearnshaw HAKLUYT.

Egrimonie, -y, obs. ff. AGRIMONY.

†**E·grimony.** *rare.* 1626. [ad. L. *ægrimonia.*] Deep sorrow. (Dicts.)

Egriot, var. of †AGRIOT, a kind of cherry.

Egritude, obs. var. of ÆGRITUDE.

Egurgitate (ĭgɔ̄·ɪdʒitēᶦt), *v.* *rare.* 1656. [ad. L. *egurgitat-, egurgitare*, f. *e* + *gurgitem* whirlpool.] To vomit forth; also *fig.*

Egyptian (ĭdʒi·pʃən). ME. [f. *Egypt* + -IAN.]

A. *adj.* 1. Belonging or relating to Egypt; also *fig.*, as in *E. bondage, darkness*, etc. ME. 2. = GIPSY (*joc.*) 1749.

Phrases. a. *Bot.* **E. Bean:** perh. the fruit of *Nelumbium speciosum.* **E. Lotus** = *Nymphæa Lotus.* **E. Thorn:** *Cratægus Pyracantha.* b. *Min.* **E. Jasper,** †**pebble:** a brown mottled Jasper from Egypt.

B. *sb.* 1. A native of Egypt. Often *fig.* (cf. *Ex.* xii. 36) ME. 2. = GIPSY 1514. 3. *pl.* Short for *E. stocks* (*rec.*).

Hence **Egy·ptianize** *v.* [see -IZE] 1665.

Egyptology (ĭdʒiptǫ·lŏdʒi). 1859. [f. as if ad. Gr. *αἰγυπτολογία (see -LOGY).] The study of Egyptian antiquities. Hence **Egypto·loger, Egypto·logist** (also **Epy·ptologue**), one versed in E. **Egyptolo·gical** *a.* of, pertaining to, or devoted to E.

Eh (ē, ēᶦ), *interj.* 1567. [ME. *ey*; of instinctive origin.] 1. An exclam. of sorrow. Cf. AH 1. 2. An interjectional particle of inquiry, often inviting assent 1773. 3. *Eh?*: colloq. or vulgar = What did you say? 1837.

Ehlite (ē·ləit). 1868. [f. *Ehl* near Lenz on the Rhine.] *Min.* A variety of Pseudomalachite.

Eident (əi·dėnt), *a. Sc.* 1591. [See IDENT.] Diligent; attentive *to.*

Eider (əi·dəɪ). 1743. [a. (ult.) Icel. *æðar* (pron. aiðăr), genit. of *æðr* eider-duck. Hence Sw. †*eider*, now *ejder*, Da. *eder(-fugl)*, etc.] 1. A species of duck, *Somateria mollissima*, of northern regions, that lines its nest with EIDER-DOWN; also, *King-e.* (*Somateria spectabilis*). Chiefly *attrib.*, as in *e.-duck*, etc. 2. The down itself 1766. 3. *attrib.* or *adj.* Resembling eider-down 1791.

Ei·der-down. 1774. [a. (ult.) Icel. *æðar-dún*; see DOWN *sb.*²] 1. The small soft feathers from the breast of the eider-duck. Also *attrib.* 2. = *eider-down quilt.*

Eidograph (əi·dŏgraf). 1801. [f. Gr. εἶδος + γράφειν.] An instrument for reproducing drawings on any scale.

‖**Eidolon** (əidōᵘ·lǫn). Pl. occas. **-a.** 1828. [a. Gr. (see IDOL, IDOLUM).] An (unsubstantial) image, spectre, phantom. Hence **Eido·loclast** [f. Gr. κλάστης], an image-breaker.

†**Eidoura·nion.** 1825. [f. Gr. εἶδος + οὐρανός.] A mechanical contrivance for representing the motions of the heavenly bodies; cf. ORRERY -1829.

Eigh (ēᶦ), *interj. dial.* [Cf. EH, EY.] An exclam. of wonder or asseveration.

Eight (ēᶦt). [Com. Teut. and Aryan: OE. *ahta, eahta, æhte* = ON. *átta*, Goth. *ahtau*, etc.; cf. L. *octo*, Gr. ὀκτώ, Skr. *ashtâu*, etc.] The cardinal number next after seven; symbols 8 or viii.

A. as *adj.* (see quots.).

E. years 1513. Phr. *An e. days* (= a week) *Luke* ix. 28. *ellipt.* We breakfast at e. (*mod.*). *Piece of e.* (*reals*): the Spanish dollar. (Now *Hist.*)

B. as *sb.* 1. The number eight ME. 2. A set of eight persons or things, as, *the e. of hearts, the Oxford e.* Phr. *In eights*: in lines of e. syllables. 1598. 3. The figure (8); hence anything in the form of an 8. 1607.

Comb., as *e.-sided*, etc.; *e.-day* adj., *-fold* adj. and adv.; **e.-day clock,** one that goes for e. days without winding up; **-oar** *a.* (of a boat) manned by e. rowers; also as sb.

Eight, obs. f. AIT.

Eighteen (ēᶦtī·n, ēᶦ·tīn), *a.* (*sb.*) [OE. *eahtatýne, -téne*; see EIGHT and -TEEN.] 1. The cardinal number next after seventeen; symbols 18 or xviii. 2. quasi-*sb.* = **e.-pounder** 1833.

Syxe and twelue makyth eyghtene TREVISA.

Comb.: **e.-knot** *a.*, (a vessel) going e. knots in an hour; **-penny** *a.*, worth or costing e.-pence; also quasi-*sb.*; **-pounder,** a gun throwing an eighteen-pound shot.

Eightee·nmo. 1858. [Eng. reading of 18mo.] Colloq. for OCTODECIMO.

Eighteenth (ēᶦtī·nþ, ēᶦ·tīnþ), *a.* [OE. *eahtatéoða*, f. *eahta* EIGHT + *téoða* tenth. Now taken as f. EIGHTEEN + -TH.] 1. Next in order after the seventeenth. 2. *E. part*: one of eighteen equal parts of anything. Hence **Eightee·nthly** *adv.*

Eighth (ēᶦtþ). [OE. *eahtoða*, repr. OTeut. type *ahto·þon-*, f. **ahtau*, **ahtô* EIGHT.]

A. *adj.* 1. That comes next in order to the seventh. Also *ellipt.*, as *the e. of April.* 2. *E. part*: one of eight equal parts of anything 1523.

B. *sb.* 1. = *eighth part* 1577. †2. *Mus.* = OCTAVE -1706. Hence **Ei·ghthly** *adv.* in the e. place.

Eightieth (ēᶦ·tiėþ), *a.* (*sb.*) ME. [f. EIGHTY; see -TH.] The ordinal number answering to the cardinal eighty.

Ei·ght-squa·re. *Obs.* exc. *Naut.* 1538. [f. EIGHT + SQUARE, after *four-square.*] Having eight equal sides; octagonal.

Eighty (ēᶦ·ti), *a.* (*sb.*) [OE. *hundeahtatig*, f. *hund-* (see HUNDRED) + *eahta* EIGHT + *-tig* :—OTeut. **tigiwiz* pl. of **teguz* decade (see -TY).] 1. The cardinal number equal to eight tens; symbol 80 or lxxx. Also *ellipt.*, as in *now over e.* 2. quasi-*sb.* a. The age of eighty years. b. *The eighties*: the years between eighty and ninety in a century. 1835.

Eigne (ēᶦn), *a.* 1586. [corrupt f. AYNE, ad. Fr. *aîné.*] *Law.* First-born, eldest; see AYNE.

Phr. *E. title*: a prior title. *E. estate*: one that is entailed.

Eikon, var. of ICON.

Eild (īld), *a. Sc.* 1822. [? var. of YELD *a.*] Of a cow: Not giving milk; dry.

Eild, var. of ELD *sb.* and *v.*

Eir(e, obs. f. AIR, EYRE, HEIR.

Eirenarch (əiri·nāɹk). 1641. [ad. Gr. εἰρηνάρχης.] An officer charged with the preservation of the public peace.

Eirenic, irenic (əirī·nik), *a. rare.* 1878. [ad. Gr. εἰρηνικός.] Tending to peace.

‖**Eirenicon** (əirī·nikǫn). 1865. [ad. Gr. εἰρηνικόν, adj. neut.] A proposal tending to reconcile differences.

Eiry, var. of AERY, EERIE.

†**Ei·sell.** OE. [a. OF. *aisil, aissil* :—late L. **acetillum*, dim. of *acetum.*] Vinegar -1634.

Woo't drinke vp Esile, eate a Crocodile SHAKS.

‖**Eisteddfod** (ēᶦste·ðvǫd). 1822. [Welsh; lit. 'session', f. *eistedd* to sit.] A congress of (Welsh) bards.

Either (əi·ðəɹ, ī·ðəɹ), *a.* (*pron.*) and *adv.* [OE. *ǽghwæðer* (contracted *ǽgðer*), f. *á* AY, always + *gehwæðer* each of two. See Y- and WHETHER.]

A. *adj.* (*pron.*) 1. Each of the two. b. with pl. sb.: = 'both' -1608. †2. *absol.* as *pron.* -1759. b. Sometimes = each (of more than two) 1588. 3. One or other of the two ME. 4. *absol.* as *pron.* 1548. b. Sometimes = any one (of more than two) 1616.

1. There was a huge fireplace at e. end of the hall SCOTT. 2. How different has been the fate of e. GOLDSM. b. At e. of the three corners HOWELLS. 3. Spirits when they please Can e. Sex assume MILT. *P. L.* I. 424. 4. E. causes loss CRUMP. b. The furtherance of all or e. of these three HIERON.

B. as *adv.* (*conj.*) †1. In OE. and early ME. = BOTH. 2. Introducing alternatives ME. †3. = OR -1611. 4. As an alternative, 'which you please'. b. In neg. or interrog. sentences: 'Any more than the other'. ME.

2. I never thought treson to your Highnes..ayther in woorde or dede CROMWELL. 3. E. [*R.V.*, Or] how canst thou say to thy brother *Luke* vi. 42. 4. *To.* Wilt thou set thy foote o' my necke? *An.* Or o' mine e. *Twel. N.* II. v. 206. b. The sex cannot help that e. SCOTT.

Ejaculate (ĭdʒæ·kiŭlēᶦt), *v.* 1578. [f. L. *ejaculat-, ejaculari*, f. (ult.) *e* + *jaculum, jacere* to cast.] 1. *trans.* To dart forth; to throw out suddenly and swiftly, eject. *Obs.* exc. *spec.* Also †*transf.* and *fig.* 2. To utter suddenly (a short prayer; now a short exclamation). Also *absol.* 1666.

1. They [Porcupines] have..prickles..which they e. LOVELL. *spec.* To e. its venom into the wound 1816. 2. But where can the Prince be? he kept ejaculating CARLYLE. Hence **Eja·culative** *a.* of the nature of an ejaculation.

Ejaculation (ĭdʒæ:kiulēᶦ·ʃən). 1603. [f. as prec.] †1. The action of ejaculating (missiles, water, etc.) -1818. 2. The sudden ejection or emission (of seed, fluids, etc.) 1603. 3. *transf.* and *fig.* a. The emission of rays, occult influence, etc. b. The hasty utterance of prayers, emotional exclamations, etc. 1625. 4. *concr.* A short hasty emotional utterance 1624.

3. a. There seemeth to be acknowledged, in the Act of Enuy an Eiaculation..of the Eye BACON. 4. Ejaculations of welcome FR. KEMBLE.

‖**Eja·culator.** 1727. [mod.L., f. as prec.] *Phys.* Applied to two muscles of the genitals, which ejaculate the seminal fluid.

Ejaculatory (ĭdʒæ·kiŭlătəri), *a.* 1644. [f. as prec. + -ORY.] 1. †Adapted for, or concerned in, ejection 1655. †2. Given to ejaculation. QUARLES. 3. Of the nature of or resembling an ejaculation 1644. 4. quasi-*sb.* = EJACULATION 4 (*rare*) 1883.

1. E. ducts 1751. 3. E. passages 1644, prayers 1698, petitions SMOLLETT.

Eject (ī·dʒekt), *sb.* 1878. [ad. L. *ejectum*, after *subject, object.*] Something (*viz.* an inferred sensation or mental state) which is neither an actual nor a possible object of one's own consciousness.

My neighbour's mind, feelings, motions are ejects to me; they can never be objects C. L. MORGAN.

Eject (ĭdʒe·kt), *v.* 1555. [ad. L. *eject-*, ppl. stem of *ejicere.*] 1. To throw out from within; also *transf.* and *fig.* 1598. 2. To expel, drive out *from* any place or position 1555. 3. To expel from a dignity or office. Also, To evict *from*; *esp.* in *Law.* 1570.

1. A Diana ejecting a fountain EVELYN. 3. If they can prove their Ministers fit to be ejected, let them there prove it BAXTER. Hence **Eje·ctive** *a.* that has the function or power of ejecting; pertaining to an eject. **Eje·ctively** *adv.*

‖**Ejectamenta** (ĭdʒe:ktăme·ntă), *sb. pl.* 1863. [pl. of L. *ejectamentum*, f. *ejectare.*] *Geol.* Substances ejected by eruptive forces.

Ejection (ĭdʒe·kʃən). 1566. [ad. L. *ejectionem*; see EJECT *v.*] 1. The action of casting out from within. Formerly *spec.* in *Phys.* 1613. b. *concr.* Something ejected; *spec.* by a volcano 1654. 2. Expulsion from a place or position; also from office or possessions; †exile (*rare*) 1566. †3. = ECBOLE 2. 1603.

1. E. of ashes 1813, of gas STOKES. 2. Exorcisme (that is to say, of e. of Devills by Conjuration) HOBBES.

Ejectment (ĭdʒe·ktmėnt). 1567. [f. EJECT *v.* + -MENT.] 1. *Law.* The act or process of ejecting a person from his holding; hence, more widely, = EJECTION 2. 2. 'An action at law whereby a person ousted or amoved from an estate for years may recover possession thereof' (Tomlins); the original writ in this action 1697. †3. *pl.* [after L. *ejectamenta.*] Things cast up or out. SIR T. BROWNE.

Ejector (ĭdʒe·ktəɪ). 1640. [See -OR.] 1. *gen.* One who ejects (*lit.* and *fig.*); *spec.* in *Law*, one who ejects a person from his holding. 2. Any portion of machinery, etc. which ejects; *e.g.* an appliance for discharging empty cartridge cases from a fire-arm; etc. Also *attrib.*

2. *E.-condenser* (steam-engine), a form of condenser worked by the exhaust steam from the cylinder.

†Ejula·tion. 1619. [ad. L. *ejulationem.*] Wailing, lamentation -1708.

Eke (īk), *sb.* Now *dial.* [OE. *ēaca*:—OTeut. **aukon-*, f. same root as ECHE *v.*] 1. An addition. In OE., A reinforcement (of troops). 2. *spec.* a. A tag to a bell-rope; also *attrib.* 1549. b. A cylinder on which a beehive is placed to add to its capacity 1857.

Eke (īk), *v.* ME. [partly f. prec.; partly north. f. ECHE *v.*] 1. *trans.* To increase, add to. Also *absol.* Now *dial.* †2. To add. Also *absol.* -1733.

1. Some patch'd dog-hole ek'd with ends of wall POPE. Phr. *To e. out*: to supplement (const. *with*); *esp.* to make to last, or to suffice, by additions, by economy, by makeshifts, or the like.

Eke (īk), *adv. arch.* [Com. Teut.: OE. *éac*; perh. from EKE *v.*] Also, too, moreover; in addition.

E. therto he was right a mery man CHAUCER.

Ekebergite. 1822. [f. Sw. traveller *Ekeberg* + -ITE.] *Min.* A variety of scapolite.

†E·ke-name. ME. [f. EKE *sb.* + NAME.] An additional name, a NICKNAME, q. v. -1483.

Eking (ī·kiŋ), *vbl. sb.* ME. [f. EKE *v.*] 1. The action of EKE *v.* 2. An augmentation ME. 3. *Naut.* a. 'A piece of wood fitted . . to make good a deficiency in length, as the end of a knee or the like.' b. 'The carved work under the lower part of the quarter-piece, at the aft part of the gallery.' SMYTH.

-el, *suffix* [1], repr. OE. *-el, -ela, -ele* (OTeut. **-ilo*, etc.); in mod.Eng. retained only after *v, th, ch, n*, as in *hovel, brothel*, etc. See -LE.

-el, *suffix* [2], a. OF. *-el* (mod.F. usu. *-eau*), *-elle*, repr. L. *-ello-, -ella-*; used to form diminutives, as (from the masc. *-el*), *tunnel*, etc.; (from the fem. *-elle*) *chapel*, etc.

2. In Eng. wds. adapted from Fr., *-el* may also stand for Fr. *-el*:—L. *-ali-* (see -AL), as in *vowel*; for Fr. *-eil*:—L. *-iculo-* (see -CLE), as in *apparel*; or for Fr. *-il*:—L. *-ile*, as in *kennel*.

Ela (ē·lā·). Now *Hist.* 1580. [f. E + LA.] *Mus.* The highest note of Guido's scale. Often *fig.* as a type of something 'high-flown'.

Why God-a-mercy..this is a note above E La SCOTT.

Elaborate (ĭlæ·bŏrĕt). 1581. [ad. L. *elaboratus*; see next.]

†A. as *pa. pple.* = ELABORATED.

B. as *adj.* 1. Produced by labour; also = ELABORATED. *Obs.* or *arch.* 1592. 2. Worked out minutely; highly finished 1621. Also *transf.* of persons: Painstaking 1649.

2. An e. letter DAVENANT, contrivance DARWIN, study MORLEY. *transf.* An e. Collector 1728.

Hence Ela·borate-ly *adv.*, -ness.

Elaborate (ĭlæ·bŏreⁱt), *v.* 1607. [f. L. *elaborat-, elaborare*, f. e out + *laborare* to LABOUR.] 1. To produce or develop by labour; to work out in detail 1611. 2. *transf.* Of nature, etc.: To produce from elements or sources; to fashion or develop; also, to transmute *into* a developed product 1607.

1. The objects of landscape may be either elaborated or suggested RUSKIN. 2. Honey..is elaborated by the Bee BOYLE. The animal spirits are elaborated from the blood BERKELEY.

Hence Ela·borated *ppl. a.* worked up; worked out in detail, finely wrought, etc. Ela·borative *a.* that has the property of elaborating. Ela·borator.

Elaboration (ĭlæ:bŏrēⁱ·ʃən). 1578. [ad. late L. *elaborationem.*] 1. The process of elaborating (see ELABORATE *v.* 1); the state of being elaborated 1612. 2. The production by natural agencies of chemical substances from their elements or sources; *spec.* in *Phys.* the formation of animal or vegetable tissues, or the process of assimilation of alimentary substances after their reception into the body 1578. 3. *conor.* 1765.

1. The e. of his [Virgil's] verse GLADSTONE. 2. Milk is a chyle which..has received but a light E. 1677. 3. Science is an e. DOVE.

Elaboratory (ĭlæ·bŏrătəri). 1652. [as if ad. L. **elaboratorium.*] = LABORATORY. Now *Hist.* Also *transf.*

transf. The functions of leaves are to..act as elaboratories 1845.

Elæo-, comb. f. Gr. ἔλαιον oil (properly olive-oil); as in Elæopten(e (elī,ǫ·ptīn), also ela- [Gr. πτηνός volatile], the liquid part of a volatile oil, as dist. from stearoptene; etc.

Elæolite (ĭlī·ŏləit). Also elao-. 1816. [f. Gr. ἔλαιον + -LITE.] *Min.* A variety of nephelite occurring massive, or in large crystals, and having a greasy lustre.

Elaic (ĭlē·ik), *a.* 1845. [irreg. f. as prec. + -IC.] *Chem.* = OLEIC.

Elaidic (eleᵢi·dik), *a.* 1865. [f. as prec. + *-idic.*] *Chem.* Designation of an acid $C_{18}H_{34}O_2$, derived from elaic (oleic) acid. So Ela·idate, a salt of e. acid. Ela·idin, a solid isomeric modification of olein, produced by the action of nitrous acid.

Elain (ĭlē·ĭn). 1810. [irreg. f. as prec. + -IN.] = OLEIN.

†Ela·mp, *v.* [? f. E- *pref.* + LAMP *v.*] To shine forth. G. FLETCHER.

‖Élan. 1880. [Fr.; see next.] An impetuous rush (*e.g.* of troops); also (*abstr.*), ardour, dash.

Elance (ĭla·ns), *v.* ? *Obs.* 1718. [ad. F. *élancer*, f. L. *ex* + late L. *lanceare*, f. *lancea* LANCE.] *trans.* To launch; to cast or throw (a lance or dart). Also *fig.* Also *intr.* for *refl.*

Thy unerring Hand elanc'd..another Dart PRIOR.

Eland (ī·lănd). 1786. [a. Du. *eland* elk, ? ad. Lith. *élnis.*] A very large S. Afr. Antelope (*Boselaphus Oreas*), much prized for its flesh. Also *attrib.*

Elanet (e·lănĕt). 1880. [app. f. mod.L. *elanus* (? ad. Fr. *élan*) + -ET.] A species of kite, *Elanus melanopterus.*

Elao-: see ELÆO-.

Elaphine (e·lăfəin), *a.* 1835. [f. L. *elaphus*, a. Gr. + -INE.] Belonging to or like the stag.

‖Elaps (ī·læps). [mod.L. a. Gr. ἔλαψ corrupt var. of ἔλλοψ; see ELLOPS.] A genus of venomous S. African garter snakes.

Elapse (ĭlæ·ps), *v.* 1644. [f. L. *elaps-*, *elabi*; see LAPSE.] 1. *intr.* Of time: To slip or glide away, expire. (Perfect tenses occas. with *be.*) †2. *trans.* To suffer to pass by -1709. †3. *intr.* To lapse -1769.

1. Fourteen months were now elapsed 1792.

Ela·pse, *sb. arch.* 1677. [f. prec. vb.] 1. A flowing out or away; also *fig.* 2. Lapse, slipping away 1793. So †Ela·psion (*rare*).

†Ela·rgement. [Cf. Fr. *élargir.*] = ENLARGEMENT. H. More.

Elasmobranch (ĭlæ·zmobræŋk). 1872. [Shortened f. mod.L. *elasmobranchii*, f. Gr. ἐλασμός metal beaten out + βράγχια gills.] *Zool.* One of the *Elasmobranchii* or *Chondropterygii*, a class of fishes marked by the cartilaginous nature of the bones, and the absence of sutures in the cranium, as the Shark, Sturgeon, Ray, etc. Also *attrib.* or *adj.* var. Elasmobra·nchiate.

Elastance (ĭlæ·stăns). 1890. [irreg. f. ELASTIC + -ANCE.] *Electr.* The capacity of a dielectric for opposing an electric charge or displacement.

Elastic (ĭlæ·stik). 1653. [ad. mod.L. *elasticus*, a. Gr. ἐλαστικός, f. ἐλα- stem of ἐλαύνειν to drive.]

A. *adj.* †1. Pertaining to, causing, or characterized by, spontaneous expansion. Now merged in 2. -1669. 2. That spontaneously resumes its normal bulk or shape after contraction, dilatation, or distortion by external force. Also of motions, forces, etc.: Characteristic of an elastic body. 1674. b. *fig.* Not permanently or easily depressed; buoyant 1778. 3. *pop.* That can be stretched without permanent alteration of size or shape 1781. b. *fig.* Flexible, accommodating 1859. †4. Propulsive. BLACKMORE.

2. His e. bow COWPER. Phr. *E. limit*: the extent to which the particles of a body may be relatively displaced without fracture or other permanent alteration. *E. fluids*: still often used spec. for gases, though the mod. definition applies perfectly to liquids. b. This e. little urchin CARLYLE. 3. *fig.* A very e. conscience. Phr. *E. tissue* (Anat.): a variety of areolar or connective tissue. †*E. gum* [= Fr. *gomme élastique*]: india-rubber. *E. web*: cloth woven with india-rubber threads so as to stretch. *E. boots*: boots with elastic web at the sides.

B. *sb.* Elastic cord or string, usually woven with india-rubber 1663.

Hence †Ela·stical *a.* elastic. Ela·stically *adv.*

Ela·sticin. 1878. [See -IN.] 'The substance composing the elastic fibres of connective tissue' (*Syd. Soc. Lex.*).

Elasticity (ĭ-, elæsti·sĭti). 1664. [See -ITY.] 1. The quality of being elastic (see ELASTIC A. 1, 2). 2. *fig.* Capacity for resisting or overcoming depression 1678; flexibility, accommodatingness 1858.

1. The e. or tension of steam MRS. SOMERVILLE. The e. of the spine DARWIN. 2. Our old men have lost the e. of youth JOWETT. There is no e. in a mathematical fact O. W. HOLMES.

Elastin (ĭlæ·stin). 1875. = ELASTICIN. (*Syd. Soc. Lex.*)

Elate (ĭlēⁱ·t), *a.* ME. [ad. L. *elatus*, pa. pple. of *efferre.*] †1. Lifted (*rare*) 1730. 2. *fig.* a. Exalted, lofty ME. b. Of persons: In high spirits, exultant, flushed (with success, etc.) 1647.

1. With upper lip e., he grins FENTON. 2. a. A fortune more e. 1610. Of an e. spirit SELDEN. b. An army e. with victory CLARENDON.

Ela·te, *v.* 1578. [f. L. *elat-* ppl. stem; see prec.] †1. *trans.* To lift on high, elevate -1772. Also *fig.* 2. To exalt the spirits of; to stimulate, excite; also, to make proud. Also *absol.* 1619.

1. Sometimes they e. a finger, smile and pray to Mahomet SIR T. HERBERT. 2. Elated with the glory of Martyredome 1619. The wine..elateth me LONGF. Hence Ela·ted-ly *adv.*, -ness. †Ela·tement, elatedness. Ela·ter [1], one who or that which elates.

Elater [2] (e·lătəɪ). 1653. [a. mod.L., a. Gr. ἐλατήρ one who or that which drives.] †1. The expansive property inherent in air or gases; hence, = 'spring', 'elasticity'. Also *fig.* 2. *Zool.* Linnæus' name for the family *Elateridæ* of beetles, possessing the power of springing upward from a supine position in order to fall on their feet; also, a beetle of this family, a skip-jack 1802. 3. *Bot.* An elastic spiral filament, or elongated cell, serving to disperse the spores when ripe, as in certain Liverworts, Horsetails, etc. 1830.

1. Persons .. having the e. or spring of their own natures to facilitate their iniquities SIR T. BROWNE.

Elaterin (ĭlæ·tĕrin). Also elatine. 1830. [f. ELATERIUM + -IN.] *Chem.* The active principle of Elaterium ($C_{20}H_{28}O_5$).

†Ela·terist. 1661. [f. ELATER [2] + -IST.] One who explains certain phenomena as due to ELATERY -1674.

Elaterite (ĭlæ·tĕrəit). 1826. [f. ELATER [2] + -ITE.] *Min.* A brown hydrocarbon, usually soft and elastic like india-rubber; elastic bitumen.

‖Elaterium (elătĭᵊ·riŭm). 1578. [a. L., ad. Gr. ἐλατήριον, f. ἐλα- stem of ἐλαύνειν to drive.] †1. A purgative. 2. A precipitate from the juice of the Squirting Cucumber (*Ecballium agreste, Momordica Elaterium*), acting as a drastic purgative and emetic 1578. †3. = ELATER [2]. (Dicts.)

Elaterometer (ĭlæ:tĕrǫ·mĭtəɪ). [ad. Fr. *élatéromètre*; cf. ELATER [2].] An instrument for indicating the pressure of confined air or steam. KNIGHT.

†E·latery. 1653. [f. ELATER [2] + -Y.] The elastic force of the air -1676.

Elation (ĭlēⁱ·ʃən). [ME. *elacion*, ad. OF., ad. L. *elationem*; see ELATE *a.*] †1. (after L.) a. Lifting. b. Carrying out (*e.g.* of a dead body) (*rare*). -1697. 2. Elevation of mind arising from success, etc.; pride, vainglory ME. 3. Elevation of spirits. (The usual current sense.) 1750. b. with *an* and *pl.* 1870.

2. Riches exposes a Man to..a foolish E. of Heart ADDISON. 3. These praises give me but very little E. FOSTER.

Ela·tive, *a. rare.* 1595. [as if ad. L. **elativus.*] That elates (*lit.* and *fig.*).

†Elayl (e·leᵢil). 1865. [f. Gr. ἔλαιs an olive-tree + ὕλη.] *Chem.* = ETHYLENE.

Elbow (e·lbo͡u). [Com. Teut.: OE. *ęlnboga* :—OTeut. **alino-bogon-*, f. **alinâ* arm (see Ell) + **bogon-* bending = Bow *sb.*[1]] 1. The bend of the arm; the outer part of the joint at the bend of the arm. †b. The analogous part in the shoulder or hock of quadrupeds –1789. 2. *transf.* Anything resembling an elbow. a. A sharp bend in the course of a river, road, etc. 1591. b. A forward or outward projection 1626. c. *Mech.* An angle in a tube, etc.; a piece of piping bent at an angle to join two long straight pieces 1777. d. *Arch.* The upright side which flanks any panelled work, as in windows below the shutters, etc. (Gwilt); the projections on the side of stalls (Parker). †3. *transf.* An arm of a chair, made to rest the elbow –1784.

1. A pair of Gloves Up to his Elbows Etheredge. 2. a. The elbows of serpentine rivers H. Walpole. 3. A great Chair with elbows 1679.

Phrases. *At the elbow(s*: very near; in close attendance; also *fig.* *E. in the hawse* (Naut.): a cross in the hawse, when a ship, being moored in a tideway, swings twice the wrong way. *To be out at elbow(s*: to have a coat worn out at the elbows, to be ragged, poor, in seedy condition.

attrib. and *Comb.*, as *e.-cushion*, etc.; also **e.-chair,** a chair with elbows (see 3); **-grease** (*joc.*), vigorous rubbing; hard physical labour of any kind; **-joint,** (*a*) the hinge-joint connecting the fore and the upper arm; (*b*) = Elbow 2 c; **-piece,** (*a*) a piece of armour covering the juncture of the plates meeting at the e.; (*b*) a piece of tubing forming an e.; **-room,** room to move one's elbows; hence, free scope.

Elbow (e·lbo͡u), *v.* 1605. [f. prec. sb.] 1. *trans.* To thrust with the elbow; to jostle; also *fig.* Also with *off*, *out of*. †2. *absol.* and *intr.* To push right and left with the elbow; also *fig.* –1885. 3. quasi-*trans.* To make (one's way) by elbowing 1833. 4. *intr.* To go out of the direct way, zigzag 1804. 5. 'To jut out in angles' (J.).

1. Must our Sides be elbowed, our Shins broken 1710. They [the Dutch] would e. our own Aldermen off the Royal Exchange Macaulay. 3. To e. his way into the bank 1833.

Elbowed (e·lbo͡ud), *ppl. a.* 1825. [f. Elbow *sb.* + -ed[2].] a. Having elbows or bends. b. Provided with elbow-rests, as a seat. c. Bent into the shape of an elbow.

‖**Elchee** (e·ltʃī). Also **elchi, eltchi.** 1828. [Turk. *īlchi* 'from *īl* a (nomad) tribe, hence the representative of the *īl*' (Y.).] An ambassador.

Eld (eld), *sb.* [OE. *ęldo* (abstr. sb. f. *ald*, in WS. *eald*, Old *sb.*).] 1. The age of a person. Now *dial.* †2. Full age; majority –1529. 3. Old age OE. †b. Old men; senate, aristocracy –1592. 4. Antiquity, the olden time ME. †5. A secular period –1513.

1. Gamelyn, that yong was of elde ME. 3. Who scorns at e., peels off his own young hairs B. Jons. 4. Lands that contain the monuments of E. Byron.

Eld (eld), *a. poet.* and *arch.* 1619. [repr. ME. *eld(e*, OE. (WS.) *eald* (see Old).] = Old, q. v.

†**Eld,** *v.*[1] [repr. OE. (WS.) *ealdian* (:—type **aldōjan*), f. *eald*, Old.] To grow or make old. ME. only.

†**Eld,** *v.*[2] [OE. *ęldan* :—OTeut. **aldjan*, f. **aldo-* Old.] *trans.* and *intr.* To defer, delay –ME.

Elder (e·ldəɹ), *sb.*[1] [OE. *ellærn*; cf. MLG. *ellern, elderne, elhorn*, etc.] 1. A low tree or shrub, *Sambucus nigra* (N.O. *Caprifoliaceæ*), called, for distinction, the Common or Blackberried Elder; bearing umbel-like corymbs of white flowers. The young branches are full of pith. 2. Extended to other species of the genus *Sambucus*; in N. America applied chiefly to *S. canadensis*. b. In names of plants superficially resembling the Elder, as **Dwarf E.,** Goutweed (*Ægopodium Podagraria*); **Marsh** or **Marish E.**; etc.

1. My heart of E. *Merry W.* II. iii. 30. 2. **Dwarf E., Ground E., Dog E.** (*S. Ebulus*) = Danewort.

attrib. and *Comb.*, as **e.-berry,** the fruit of the e.; **-gun,** a pop-gun made of a hollow shoot of e.; **-moth,** *Uropteryx Sambucata*.

Elder (e·ldəɹ), *a.* and *sb.*[2] [OE. *ęldra* (fem. and neut. *ęldre*) :—OTeut. **a·lþizon-*, regularly f. **aldo-*, OE. *ald* (WS. *eald*), Old.]

A. *adj.* The comparative degree of Old *a.*; formerly = the mod. Older, but now differentiated. 1. That has lived or existed longer; senior. Now used without *than*, chiefly as denoting the senior of two; otherwise *arch.* †2. Of longer standing, prior; senior –1800. 3. Ancient, earlier, former ME.

1. The said Wil. Rycroft yelder 1478. How much more e. art thou then thy lookes *Merch. V.* IV. i. 251. **E. statesman,** in Japan, one of the *genro* ('old men') retired statesmen and nobles who are consulted by the Emperor; also *transf.* 2. An e. title 1642. Phr. *E. hand* (Cards): the first player. 3. The giant race of e. times Southey.

B. *sb.* An elder person (*lit.* and *fig.*). †1. A parent [cf. mod.G. *eltern* pl.]; a forefather; hence, a predecessor. Usu. in *pl.* –1557. 2. One who is old or older, a senior. Usu. in *pl.* ME. 3. A member of a senate, governing body or class, consisting of men (supposed to be) venerable for age. Now chiefly *Hist.* ME. 4. *Eccl.* = Presbyter 1526. b. In the Presbyterian churches, one of a class of lay officers who, with the minister, compose the Session, and manage the church affairs.

2. I know my duty to my elders *Tam. Shr.* II. 7. 3. The reverend elders nodded o'er the case Pope. 4. That thou..shuldest ordeyne elders in every citie Tindale *Titus* i. 5.

E·lderling. *rare.* 1606. [See -ling.] †1. Contemptuously for Elder *sb.*[2] 4. 2. An elderly person 1863.

Elderly (e·ldəɹli), *a.* 1611. [f. Elder *a.* + -ly[1].] 1. Somewhat old, verging on old age. 2. Of or pertaining to an elderly person 1674.

1. E. Fops, and superannuated Coquets Budgell.

Eldern (e·ldəɹn), *a.*[1] ME. [f. Elder *a.* + -en.] †1. Elderly –1818. 2. Belonging to earlier times (*arch.*) ME.

Eldern (e·ldəɹn), *a.*[2] 1842. [f. Elder *sb.*[1] + -en.] Made of elder.

Eldership (e·ldəɹʃip). 1549. [f. Elder *a.* and *sb.*[2] + -ship.] 1. The position of being elder; seniority. 2. The office of elder in a church; the body of elders; a presbytery 1577.

1. My claim to her by E. I prove Dryden.

Eldest (e·ldėst), *a. superl.* [OE. *ęldest(a*, superl. of OE. *ald* (WS. *eald*), Old; see Elder *a.*] †1. Most aged. Also *absol.* (quasi-*sb.*). Replaced by Oldest. –1611. 2. First-born, or oldest surviving. Also quasi-*sb.* OE. 3. Earliest; most ancient (*arch.*) OE.

2. The Erle of Ruttlandes eldyste daughter 1536. 3. The primall e. curse *Haml.* III. iii. 37. Phr. *E. hand* (Cards): the first player; the right of playing first.

†**E·ldfather.** [OE. (WS.) *ealdfæder*, f. *eald*, Eld *a.* + Father; cf. Ger. *altvater* ancestor.] 1. A grandfather; a forefather –1460. 2. A father-in-law –1634.

E·lding. Now *dial.* ME. [a. ON. *elding*, f. *eldr* fire.] Fuel.

E·ldmother. Now *dial.* [OE. (WS.) *ealdmōdor*; see Eldfather.] †1. A grandmother –ME. 2. A mother-in-law; also, a stepmother ME.

‖**El Dorado** (e:ldorā·do). 1596. [Sp.; = 'the gilded'.] A fictitious country (or city) abounding in gold, believed by the Spaniards to exist upon the Amazon within the province of Guiana. Also *fig.*

Unspoil'd Guiana, whose great Citie Geryon's Sons Call El Dorado Milt. *P. L.* XI. 411.

Eldress (e·ldrės). 1640. [f. Elder *sb.*[2]] A female Elder.

Eldritch (e·ldritʃ, e·lritʃ), *a. Sc.* 1508. [? conn. w. Elf.] Weird, unnatural, hideous.

Eleatic (eli,æ·tik). 1695. [f. L. *Eleaticus*, f. *Elea*, an ancient Greek city in S.W. Italy.]

A. *adj.* Pertaining to Elea or its inhabitants; *spec.* of the philosophy of Xenophanes, Parmenides, and Zeno, who lived or were born there.

The dialectical movement emanated..from the E. school Grote. Hence **Elea·ticism.**

B. *sb.* An Eleatic philosopher.

Elecampane (e:lĭkæmpē·n). 1533. [corrupt ad. med.L. *enula* (= cl.L. *inula*) *campana*. The adj. *campana* prob. means 'growing in the fields'.] 1. A perennial composite plant (*Inula Helenium*), with large yellow radiate flowers and bitter aromatic leaves and root; formerly used as a tonic and stimulant. 2. A sweetmeat flavoured with the root of this plant 1806. 3. *attrib.* 1610.

2. I don't know how he spent it except in hardbake and alycompaine Thackeray.

Elect (ĭle·kt). ME. [ad. L. *electus*, *eligere*.]

A. *adj.* 1. Picked out, chosen; also, chosen by preference; select. Also *absol.* 2. *spec.* in *Theol.* Chosen by God, *esp.* for eternal life. Often *absol.* 1526. 3. Chosen to an office or dignity. Now usually, Chosen, but not installed in office. 1643.

1. The e. o' th' Land *Hen. VIII*, II. iv. 60. 2. The blessed Spirits e. Milt. *P. L.* III. 136. 3. The Bishop e. Ayliffe. So *The bride e.* (mod.).

B. *sb.* †1. One of the elect (see A. 2) –1646. †2. One that has been chosen for an office or function; often *spec.* = *bishop e.* (see A. 3) –1709.

1. Saule..was an e. 1584. 2. Johne Guthre, e. of Ross 1491.

Elect (ĭle·kt), *v.* *Pa. t.* and *pple.* **elected.** 1494. [f. *elect-* ppl. stem; see prec.] †1. *trans.* To pick out, choose. Also *absol.* –1802. 2. To choose in preference to an alternative. In legal use often *absol.* 1509. 3. To choose by vote for any office or position 1494. 4. *Theol.* Of God: To choose as recipients of favour, *esp.* of eternal life. Also *absol.* 1617.

1. 1 *Hen. VI*, IV. i. 4. 2. The daughter..was..incompetent to e. to take the estate as land or money J. Powell. He must therefore e. Cruise. 3. They resolved to e. an Inter-Rex Tindal.

Hence **Ele·ctable** *a.* able or qualified to be elected. **Ele:ctee·**, one chosen or elected.

†**Ele·ctant.** [ad. L. *electantem.*] One who has power of choosing. Tucker.

Electary, var. of Electuary.

†**Ele·ctic,** bad f. Eclectic.

Election (ĭle·kʃən). ME. [a. OF., ad. L. *electionem.*] 1. The action of choosing for an office, dignity, or position; usually by vote. b. *spec.* The choice by popular vote of members of a representative assembly, *e.g.* the House of Commons 1648. 2. The exercise of deliberate choice ME.; †the faculty of discriminative selection –1602. 3. *Theol.* The exercise of God's sovereign will in preferring some of His creatures, *esp.* as recipients of eternal life ME. †b. *concr.* The body of the elect (*rare*) 1611. 4. *Astrol.* The selection of times as fit for any particular business; a time so selected. Now *Hist.* ME. †5. The choosing of things for special purposes, as simples, etc. –1751.

1. In a large society the e. of a monarch can never devolve to the wisest Gibbon. b. Phr. *General e.*: a simultaneous e. of representatives all over the country; opp. to *by-election*. 2. Disseisins of incorporeal hereditaments are only at the e. and choice of the party injured Cruise. 3. The e. of God went to the shepherd, not to the tiller of the ground Bacon. b. The e. hath obtained it *Rom.* xi. 7. 5. An e. of apt words, and a right disposition of them Dryden.

attrib. and *Comb.*, as *e.-address*, etc.; also **e.-committee,** a committee formed to promote the e. of a particular candidate.

Hence **Ele·ctional** *a.* relating to (astrological) e. (*rare*).

Electioneer (ĭle:kʃəniə·ɹ), *v.* 1789. [f. Election + -eer.] *intr.* To busy oneself in (political) elections. Hence **Ele:ctionee·rer.**

Elective (ĭle·ktiv). 1530. [a. F. *électif*, *-ive*; see Elect *v.* and -ive.]

A. *adj.* 1. Appointed by election; derived from or dependent on election. 2. Having the power of election 1632. 3. Pertaining to election; based upon the principle of election 1642. †4. Pertaining to, or proceeding from, choice –1775. †5. = Eclectic. H. More. 6. Of physical forces and agencies: Having a tendency to operate on certain objects in preference to others 1766. Also *fig.*

1. E. Kings Raleigh. An e. sway Milt. 2. An e. body Ld. Brougham. 3. The e. constitution of the new clergy of France Mackintosh. The E. Franchise Carlyle. 4. E. actions Hobbes. 6. Phr. *E. affinity*, also, formerly, *e. attraction*: a tendency to combine with some things and not with others. Light..which has been sifted..by e. absorption Tyndall.

†B. *sb.* An elected representative (*rare*) 1701.

Hence **Ele·ctively** *adv.* by choice. **Electi·vity,** the act or property of selection.

†‖**Ele·cto.** 1609. [Sp.; pa. pple. of *elegir* to Elect.] A leader chosen by mutineers –1650.

Elector (ĭle·ktəɹ). 1467. [a. L.] 1. One who has the right to vote in an election. b. *spec.* In Great Britain and Ireland, one who has the parliamentary vote; in U.S., one of those chosen by the several states to elect the President and Vice-President. 2. One of the Princes of Germany formerly entitled to take part in the election of the Emperor 1529. Hence **Ele·ctorship,** the state or condition of an e.

Electoral (ĭle·ktŏrăl). 1675. [See -al.]

A. *adj.* 1. Relating to, composed of, or holding rank as, electors. ¶ 2. = ELECTIVE 1 (*rare*) 1849.

1. Austria had..friends in the e. college S. AUSTIN.

†**B.** *sb.* = ELECTOR -1707.

Hence **Ele·ctorally** *adv.* with reference to electors or elections.

Electorate (ĭle·ktŏrĕt). 1675. [See -ATE [1].] 1. The dignity of a German Elector. b. The dominions of an Elector. 2. The whole body of electors 1879. So †**Electora·lity** (in sense 1) (*rare*).

Electorial (ĭlektōᵊ·riăl). 1790. [See -IAL.] = ELECTORAL.

†**Ele·ctral,** *a.* 1673. [f. *electrum* amber.] = ELECTRICAL -1708.

†**Ele·ctre.** Also **electar.** ME. [ad. L. *electrum*, ad. Gr. ἤλεκτρον amber, etc.] 1. An alloy of gold and silver; also *attrib.* -1656. 2. Amber. Also *attrib.* -1632.

Electress (ĭle·ktrĕs). Also **ele·ctoress.** 1618. [See -ESS.] 1. The wife of a German Elector of the Empire. 2. A female elector 1869.

Electric (ĭle·ktrik). 1646. [ad. mod.L. *electricus*, f. L. *electrum*, Gr. ἤλεκτρον amber; see -IC.]

A. *adj.* 1. Possessing the property (first observed in amber) of developing electricity. b. Charged with electricity. 2. Of the nature of, or pertaining to, electricity; producing, produced by, or operating by means of, electricity 1675. 3. *fig.* 1793.

1. By Electrick bodies, I conceive..such as conveniently placed unto their objects attract all bodies palpable SIR T. BROWNE. 2. From e. fire (= *fluid*).. spirits may be kindled FRANKLIN. 3. The e. flash, that from the melting eye Darts the fond question COLERIDGE.

Phr. **e. arc,** the luminous electrified space between the points of two electrodes through which a current of electricity is passing; **e. atmosphere,** the space round electrical bodies within which they manifest their special properties; **e. chair,** a chair used for electrocution; **e. charge, circuit** (see the sbs.); **e. current,** the flow of electricity through a conducting body from the positive to the negative pole, or from a high to a low potential; **e. eel** = GYMNOTUS; **e. fishes,** certain fishes that can give electric shocks; **e. fluid,** Franklin's term for a (supposed) all-pervading fluid, the cause of electricity; **e. force,** the force with which electricity tends to move matter: **e. ray** = TORPEDO: **e. resistance,** opposition to the passage of an e. current; **e. spark,** the luminous discharge from the conductor of an electrical machine to a pointed body presented to it; **e. tension,** the strain or pressure exerted upon a dielectric in the neighbourhood of an electrified body.

Also, in names of instruments for developing, measuring, illustrating, or applying electricity, and of machines, etc. actuated or controlled by electricity, as in *e. clock, governor, heater, railway, telegraph*, etc. (see these sbs.); **e. battery** (see BATTERY); **e. candle,** a form of electric-light apparatus in which the carbon pencils are parallel and separated by a layer of plaster of Paris; **e. chimes,** three bells suspended on a metal rod, rung by electricity; **e. column,** a form of the voltaic pile; **e. harpoon,** one in which a bursting charge is exploded by electricity; **e. indicator,** one indicating magnetic currents; **e. log,** a ship's log registering by electricity; **e. machine,** usu. *spec.* a machine for developing frictional electricity; **e. regulator,** one for stopping or starting a machine by electro-magnetic circuit; **e. switch,** a commutator; **e. wires,** those of the electric telegraph.

B. *sb.* 1. A substance in which the electric force can be excited and accumulated by friction 1646. 2. *Positive (negative) electrics*: = electro-positive (-negative) substances 1842.

Electrical (ĭle·ktrikăl), *a.* 1635. [f. prec. + -AL.] 1. = ELECTRIC A. 1. 2. Relating to or connected with electricity; also, of the nature of electricity. (The mod. sense.) Also more usual than *electric* in *electrical machine, electrical eel.* 1747. 3. *fig.* 1775.

3. The atmosphere becomes e. SHERIDAN. Hence **Ele·ctrically** *adv.* (*lit.* and *fig.*).

Electrician (ĭlek-, elektri·ʃăn). 1751. [See -IAN.] One who studies, or is versed in, electricity; one who deals with electrical apparatus.

Electricity (ĭlek-, elektri·sĭti). 1646. [f. ELECTRIC + -ITY.] 1. In early use, The property (first observed in amber) of attracting light bodies when excited by friction; also, the state of excitation produced by friction. Subseq., the name given to the common cause of this phenomenon and of many others, *e.g.* the electric spark, lightning, the galvanic current, etc. This cause Franklin considered to be a subtle fluid diffused through all bodies, which, when in excess of the normal, constituted 'positive electricity', when in defect, 'negative electricity'. The view now current is that electricity is a peculiar condition of the molecules of a body or of the ether surrounding them, developed by friction, etc. (see below); but the term 'electric fluid' is still in popular use. 2. *fig.* 1791. 3. The branch of electricity which deals with the nature and phenomena of electrical action 1734.

1. E. may be called into activity by mechanical power (= *frictional e.*), by chemical action (= *galvanic e.*), by heat (= *thermal e.*), and by magnetic influence (= *magnetic e.*) MRS. SOMERVILLE. 2. The natural e. of youth LOWELL.

Phrases. With adjs. denoting (*a*) the source or mode of production, as *frictional, galvanic, induced, thermal, vital, voltaic*; (*b*) the place of development, as *animal, atmospheric, organic*; (*c*) the quality, as *active, constant, free, negative, positive. Vitreous, resinous e.*: older synonyms for positive and negative electricity, which were first observed as resulting from the friction of glass and of resinous bodies respectively.

Electricize (ĭle·ktrisəi·z), *v. rare.* [See -IZE.] = ELECTRIFY *v.* 1.

Ele·ctric li·ght. 1843. **a.** *gen.* Light produced by electrical action. **b.** *spec.* The same as used for illumination. It is commonly produced by the incandescence of a metallic or carbon filament, or by the arc formed by the passing of electricity between two carbon points.

Electrification (ĭle:ktrĭfikēⁱ·ʃən). 1748. [f. ELECTRIFY *v.*] The act of electrifying, or the state of being charged with electricity.

Electrify (ĭle·ktrifəi), *v.* 1747. [f. ELECTR-IC + -(I)FY.] 1. *trans.* To charge with electricity, or pass the electric current through; to subject to an electric shock or current. b. To introduce electric power into (railways, etc.) 1900. 2. *fig.* To startle, rouse, excite, as though with an electric shock 1752.

1. To e. the body 1796, quicksilver SIR J. HERSCHEL. 2. Those heights of courage which e. an army and ensure victory BURKE. An audience is electrified EMERSON.

†**Electrine,** *a.* 1677. [See ELECTRUM + -INE.] 1. Resembling what exists in amber, electric. H. MORE. 2. Made of ELECTRUM.

Electrize (ĭle·ktrəiz), *v.* 1746. [f. ELECTR-IC + -IZE.] = ELECTRIFY. Hence †**Elec·tri·zable** *a.* **Ele:ctriza·tion.**

Electro (ĭle·ktro), *sb.* or *v. colloq.* 1864. Short for a. ELECTRO-PLATE *v.*, ELECTRO-PLATING *vbl. sb.*; b. ELECTROTYPE *sb.* and *v.*

Electro- (ĭle·ktro), comb. f. Gr. ἤλεκτρον, taken as meaning 'electricity'; hence:

Ele:ctroballi·stic *a.*, relating to the art of timing by electricity the flight of projectiles. **Ele:ctro-bio·scopy** [see BIO- + -*scopy*], the examination of an animal body by means of a galvanic current, to discover muscular contractions as evidence of life. **Ele:ctro-ca·pillary** *a.*, having reference to the influence of electricity on capillary tubes under certain conditions. **Ele:ctro-che·mic, -al** *a.*, pertaining to electricity and chemistry jointly. **Ele:ctro-chro·nograph,** an instrument for recording electrically exact instants of time. **Ele:ctro-depo·sit** *v.*, to deposit by means of electricity; hence **-depo·sit, -deposi·tion,** this process; **-depo·sitor,** one who does this. **Ele:ctro-fu·sion,** the fusion of metals by means of electricity. **Ele:ctro-ge·nesis** [see GENESIS], the state of tetanoid spasm that supervenes in the muscles highly stimulated by galvanism, when the current is withdrawn; so **Ele:ctroge·nic** *a.*, pertaining to electro-genesis. **Ele:ctro-gi·ld** *v.*, to gild by means of an electric current; hence **-gi·lding** *vbl. sb.*, **-gilt** *ppl. adj.* **Ele:ctro-kine·tic** *a.* [see KINETIC], having reference to electricity in motion. **Ele:ctro-ma·ssage,** kneading the body or a limb with a combined roller and small galvanic machine. **Ele:ctro-meta·llurgy,** the application of electrolysis to the deposition of thin coatings of metals; hence **-metallu·rgic, -al** *a.* **Ele:ctro-mu·scular** *a.*, having reference to the relations between electricity and muscular contraction. **Ele:ctro-ne·gative** *a.*, pertaining to, or producing, negative electricity. **Ele:ctro-patho·logy,** the science of morbid conditions as revealed by electricity. **Ele:ctro-po·lar** *a.*, applied to a cylindrical conductor when, on being electrified by induction, the ends become polar. **Ele:ctro-po·sitive** *a.*, pertaining to, or producing, positive electricity. **Ele:ctropu·ncture** = GALVANOPUNCTURE. **Ele:ctrosynthe·tic** *a.*, causing chemical composition by means of the galvanic current; hence **Ele:ctrosynthe·tically** *adv.* **Ele:ctro-tele·graphy** = electric telegraphy; hence **Ele:ctro-te·legraphic** *a.* **Ele:ctro-therapeu·tics,** the treatment of disease by electricity. **Ele:ctro-the·rapy** [Gr. θεραπεία healing] = *electro-therapeutics.* **Ele:ctro-the·rmancy,** also **Ele·ctro-the:rmy** [as if ad. Gr. -θερμία], the science of the electricity developed by heat. **Ele·ctroti:nt** [cf. AQUATINT], a mode of engraving, the design being drawn on copper-plate and transferred by means of an electric bath. **Ele:ctro-vi·tal** *a.*, having reference to the relations of electricity and the vital actions; hence **Ele:ctro-vi·talism.**

Electro-biology (ĭle:ktro‚bəi‚ǫ·lŏdʒi). 1849. [f. prec. + BIOLOGY.] 1. = *Electro-physiology* (see ELECTRO-). 2. A form of hypnotism, in which unconsciousness was induced by causing the patient to gaze steadily at a small disk of zinc or copper; also, 'animal magnetism' generally 1850. Hence **Ele:ctrobiolo·gical** *a.* **Ele:ctrobio·logist.**

Electrocute (ĭle·ktrŏkiūt), *v.* 1889. [f. ELECTRO-, after EXECUTE *v.*] *trans.* To put to death by means of a powerful electric current. Hence **Electrocu·tion.**

Electrode (ĭle·ktrōᵘd). 1834. [f. as prec. + *-ode*, ad. Gr. ὁδός.] One of the poles of a galvanic battery. See ANODE and CATHODE.

Electrodynamic, -al (ĭle:ktro‚dəinæ·mik, -ăl), *a.* 1832. [f. as prec. + DYNAMIC.] Pertaining to the force excited by one magnetic current upon another. Hence **Ele:ctrodyna·mics,** the science of the mutual influence of electric currents. **Ele:ctrody·namism** = *electrodynamics.* **Ele:ctro-dynamo·meter,** an instrument for measuring e. force.

Electrograph (ĭle·ktrograf). 1840. [f. as prec. + Gr. -γράφος that writes.] †1. An instrument for producing electrotypes. 2. An instrument for registering electrical conditions; the automatic record of an electrometer 1881.

Electrolier (ĭle:ktrŏlīᵊ·ɪ). 1882. [f. ELECTRO-, after *chandelier.*] A cluster of electric lamps.

Electrology (ĭ-, elektrǫ·lŏdʒi). [f. as prec. + -LOGY.] The science of electricity. Hence **Electrolo·gic, -al** *a.*

Electrolysis (ĭ-, elektrǫ·lĭsis). 1839. [f. ELECTRO- + Gr. λύσις; after ANALYSIS.] 1. Chemical decomposition by galvanic action; also, the science of this. 2. *Surg.* The breaking up of tumours, also of calculi, by galvanic action 1867.

Electrolyte (ĭle·ktrŏləit). 1834. [f. as prec. + Gr. λυτός, f. λύειν to loose.] 'A body which can be or is being decomposed by ELECTROLYSIS' (*Syd. Soc. Lex.*). Hence **Ele:ctroly·tic, -al** *a.* pertaining to, or capable of, electrolysis. **Ele:ctroly·tically** *adv.*

Electrolyze (ĭle·ktrŏləiz), *v.* 1834. [f. prec., after *analyze*, etc.] *trans.* To treat by ELECTROLYSIS (senses 1, 2). Hence **Ele:ctroly·zable** *a.* capable of being electrolyzed. **Ele·ctrolyza·tion,** the process of electrolyzing.

Electro-magnet (ĭle:ktro‚mæ·gnĕt). 1831. [f. ELECTRO- + MAGNET.] A piece of soft iron surrounded by a coil of wire, through which a current of electricity may be passed, rendering the iron temporarily magnetic.

The first simple electro-magnet was made by Sturgeon [of Manchester] G. PRESCOTT.

Hence **Ele:ctro-magne·tic, -al** *a.* pertaining to electro-magnetism. **Ele:ctro-magne·tically** *adv.* **Ele ctro-magne·tics,** the science of electro-magnetism. **Ele:ctro-ma·gnetism,** the phenomena of the production of magnetism by the electric current; also, the influence of a magnet on the electric current.

Electrometer (ĭlek-, elektrǫ·mĭtəɪ). 1749. [f. as prec. + METER.] An instrument for determining the quality and quantity of electricity. Hence **Ele:ctrome·tric, -al** *a.* **Electro·metry,** measurement of electricity by the e.

Electromotion (ĭle·ktro‚mōᵘ·ʃən). 1803. [f. as prec. + MOTION.] The motion of a galvanic current; also, recently, mechanical motion produced by electricity.

Electromotive (ĭle:ktrǫ,mōᵘ·tiv). 1806. [f. ELECTRO- + MOTIVE *a.*]

A. *adj.* Pertaining to electromotion.

Phr. *E. force*: orig., the force exhibited in the voltaic battery; in mod. use, the difference of potential which is the cause of electric currents.

B. *sb.* [after *locomotive.*] A locomotive engine with electricity for its motive power 1887.

Electromotor (ĭle:ktro,mōᵘ·təɹ). 1827. [f. as prec. + MOTOR.]

A. *sb.* Orig., a metal serving as a voltaic element. In mod. use, a machine for applying electricity as a motive power.

B. *attrib.* or *adj.* = ELECTROMOTIVE.

‖**Electron**[1] (ĭle·ktrǫn). 1856. [a. Gr. ἤλεκτρον.] = ELECTRUM 2.

Electron[2] (ĭle·ktrǫn). 1891. [f. ELECTR(IC + -*on.*] *Physics.* The smallest supposed component of matter, associated with (or consisting of) an invariable charge of negative electricity. Hence **Electro·nic** *a.*

Electrophorus (ĭlek-, elektrǫ·fŏrŭs). 1778. [mod.L., f. ELECTRO- + Gr. -φόρος.] An instrument, invented by Volta, for generating statical electricity by induction. Anglicized as **Ele·ctrophore.**

Electroplate (ĭle·ktrǫpleᶦt), *v.* 1870. [f. ELECTRO- + PLATE.] *trans.* To coat with silver by electrolysis. Hence **Ele·ctro-pla:ter**, one who electroplates. **Ele·ctro-pla:ting** *vbl. sb.* So **Ele·ctro-plate** *sb.* the ware produced by electro-plating.

Electroscope (ĭle·ktrǫskōᵘp). 1824. [f. as prec. + Gr. -σκόπος.] An instrument for ascertaining the presence and quality of electricity. Hence **Ele:ctrosco·pic** *a.* measured by the e.

Electrostatic, -al (ĭle:ktrǫ,stæ·tik, -ăl), *a.* 1867. [f. as prec. + STATIC.] Pertaining to statical electricity. Hence **Electrostatics,** the theory of statical electricity.

‖**Electrotonus** (ĭlek-, elektrǫ·tŏnŭs). 1860. [mod.L., f. ELECTRO- + Gr. τόνος tension; see TONE.] The modified condition of a nerve subjected to a constant current of electricity. Anglicized as **Ele·ctrotone.** So **Ele:ctroto·nic** *a.* relating to or characterized by e.; also applied by Faraday to the peculiar electrical state characteristic of a secondary circuit in the electro-magnetic field. **Ele:ctrotoni·city,** the condition produced by electrotonizing. **Electro·tonize** *v.* to produce e.

Electrotype (ĭle·ktrǫtəip). 1840. [f. as prec. + TYPE.] 1. A copy of a thing formed by the deposition of copper on a mould by galvanic action; also *attrib.* 2. The process of electrotyping 1840.

1. An e. seal 1840. E. cuts 1880. 2. The E. in America 1840.

Ele·ctrotype, *v.* 1847. [f. prec. sb.] *trans.* To copy in electrotype. Also *fig.* Hence **Ele·ctroty:per. Ele·ctroty:pist.**

Electrum (ĭle·ktrŏm). ME. [a. L., ad. Gr. ἤλεκτρον.] †1. Amber –1794; also *fig.* of tears 1591. 2. = ELECTRE 1. Also *attrib.* ME. b. *Min.* Native argentiferous gold containing from 20 to 50 per cent. of silver 1555. 3. An alloy of copper, zinc, and nickel. URE.

1. *fig.* It was her masters death That drew e. from her weeping eyes GREENE.

Electuary (ĭle·ktiŭări). ME. [ad. late L. *electuarium, electarium* (5th c.); cf. Gr. ἐκλεικτόν, f. ἐκλείχειν to lick out.] A medicine, consisting of a powder or other ingredient mixed with honey, jam, or syrup. Also *fig.*

‖**Eledone** (elĭdōᵘ·nĭ). 1835. [mod.L., a. Gr. ἐλεδώνη a kind of polypus.] A cephalopod of the tribe *Octopoda.*

Eleemosynary (e:lĭ,ĭ,mǫ·sinări). 1620. [ad. med.L. *eleemosynarius,* f. *eleemosyna*; see ALMS.]

A. *adj.* 1. Of or pertaining to alms or almsgiving; charitable 1630. 2. Supported by alms 1654. 3. Of the nature of alms; gratuitous 1620.

1. These her eleemosinary acts RISDON. 2. The flock of e. doves HAWTHORNE. 3. E. relief C. BRONTË.

†B. *sb.* 1. One who lives upon alms. Also *fig.* –1673. 2. = ALMONER (*rare*) –1809. 3. = ALMONRY 1688. Hence **Eleemo·synarily** *adv* charitably, by way of charity.

Elegance (e·lĭgăns). 1510. [a. F. *élégance,* ad. L. *elegantia*; see ELEGANT.] 1. The state or quality of being elegant; refined grace or propriety; tasteful correctness; ingenious simplicity, neatness: said of form, movement, manners, style, formulæ, scientific demonstrations, etc. 2. *concr.* That which is elegant; an instance or kind of elegance 1676.

1. With untutored e. she dressed CRABBE. E., by which I always mean precision and correctness LANDOR. 2. A nice contriver of all elegances EVELYN. So **E·legancy** (*esp.* in sense 2).

Elegant (e·lĭgănt), *a.* 1485. [a. F. *élégant,* ad. L. *elegantem,* ? pr. pple. of **elegare,* related to *eligere* to select.] 1. Tastefully ornate in dress. 2. Characterized by refinement, grace, or propriety 1658. 3. Of scientific processes, formulæ, etc.: Neat 1668. 4. Of persons: Correct and delicate in taste. Now only in *e. scholar.* 1667. 5. Graceful, polite, appropriate to persons of cultivated taste 1705. 6. *U.S.* Excellent, first rate 1772.

2. An e. poem BURKE. An e. bedroom 1859. 3. An e. Composition for a troublesome..Cough FULLER. An e. chess problem (*mod.*). 4. Thou art exact of taste, And e. MILT. *P.L.* IX. 1018. 5. Phr. *E. arts*; nearly = 'fine arts'. Eminent for..e. literature JOHNSON. Hence **E·legantly** *adv.*

‖**Elegante** (ele·gaṅt). 1806. [Fr. *élégante* fem.] A fashionable lady.

Elegiac (elĭdʒəi·ăk). 1581. [ad. L. *elegiacus,* ad. Gr. ἐλεγειακός, f. ἐλεγεῖον ELEGY.]

A. *adj.* 1. *Pros.* Appropriate to elegies; as, the *e. distich,* consisting of a (dactylic) hexameter and pentameter; *e. verse* (sometimes applied to the pentameter separately) 1586. 2. Of the nature of an elegy; pertaining to elegies; hence, mournful, plaintive, melancholy 1644. var. **Elegi·acal** (in both senses).

2. E. griefs, and songs of love MRS. BROWNING. Phr. *E. poet*: one who writes a. in e. metre; b. in a pensive strain.

B. *sb.* †a. An elegiac poet 1581. b. *pl.* Elegiac verses 1774.

Ele·giast. [f. ELEGY, after *ecclesiast,* etc.] A writer of elegies. GOLDSM.

†**Ele·gious,** *a.* [f. as prec. + -OUS.] Resembling an elegy; hence, lugubrious, mournful. QUARLES.

Elegist (e·lĭdʒist). 1774. [f. as prec. + -IST.] The writer of an elegy.

Elegit (ĭlĭ·dʒit). 1503. [L.; = 'he has chosen'; from the words in the writ.] *Law.* A writ of execution, issued on the election of a judgement creditor, by which the creditor is put in possession of (formerly half) the goods and lands of a debtor, until his claim is satisfied. Also, the right secured by this writ, as in 'tenant by *elegit*'.

Elegize (e·lĭdʒəiz), *v.* 1702. [See -IZE.] 1. *intr.* To write an elegy; to write in an elegiac strain. 2. *trans.* To write an elegy upon 1809.

2. The bard who soars to elegise an ass BYRON.

Elegy (e·lĭdʒi). 1514. [ad. F. *élégie,* ad. L. *elegia,* ad. Gr. ἐλεγεία, f. ἔλεγος a lament.] 1. A song of lamentation, *esp.* a funeral ode. 2. Any species of classical poetry written in elegiac verse 1600. 3. Poetry, or a poem, written in elegiacs. †b. An elegiac distich. 1589.

1. Their name, their years.. The place of fame and e. supply GRAY. 2. They gave the name of e. to their pleasantries as well as lamentations SHENSTONE.

Eleme (e·lĭmi). 1879. [a. Turk.; = 'something selected'.] *Comm.* Epithet of a kind of dried figs from Turkey.

Element (e·lĭmĕnt), *sb.* ME. [a. OF., ad. L. *elementum*; a word employed as tr. Gr. στοιχεῖον in its various senses.]

I. Component part. 1. One of the simple substances of which all material bodies are compounded: as, a. In ancient philosophy, Earth, water, air, and fire. Now *Hist.* †b. In prescientific chemistry, Water, air, oil, salt, earth, or as variously enumerated –1765. c. In mod. chemistry, Any of seventy or more substances which are provisionally taken to be simple bodies, as having hitherto resisted analysis 1813. 2. More widely: One of the relatively simple parts of any complex substance; in *pl.* the 'raw material' of anything ME. 3. The bread and wine used in the Eucharist. Chiefly *pl.* 1593. 4. *Phys.* A definite small portion of an organic structure 1841. b. One of the essential parts of any scientific apparatus. *Voltaic e.*: usu. = CELL, q.v., but occas. = *electrode.* 1831. 5. A constituent portion of an immaterial whole 1599. 6. One of the facts or conditions necessary to determine the result of a process, calculation, deliberation, or inquiry 1812. 7. *Math.* An infinitesimal part of a magnitude of any kind; a differential 1727.

2. The Elements Of whom your swords are temper'd may as well Wound the loud windes *Temp.* III. iii. 61. 5. These simple Elements of Magnitude, Figure, Site, and Motion CUDWORTH. The elements of feudalism FREEMAN. It had its usual e. of (= consisting of) cant KINGSLEY. 6. The elements of their [comets'] orbits PLAYFAIR, of a crystal GURNEY.

II. The four elements. 1. Used as a general name for earth, water, air, and fire (see I. 1); now merely a survival ME. Also *fig.* †2. The sky; ? also, the air –1714. †b. ? One of the celestial spheres of ancient astronomy; also (rarely) one of the heavenly bodies themselves –1604. 3. *pl.* Atmospheric agencies 1555. 4. That one of the four elements natural to any particular class of living things. Hence *transf.* and *fig.* the surroundings natural to anything, or forming its proper sphere of activity. 1598.

1. The foure elementes menace alle men that thanke not god CAXTON. Those who drink the pure e. G. WHITE. Fire as 'the devouring e.' 1886. 2. b. *Oth.* III. iii. 464. 3. Daunted by the elements PRESCOTT. 4. She workes by Charmes..beyond our e. *Merry W.* IV. ii. 186. My proper e. of prose LAMB. Phr. *in, out of* (*one's*) *e.*

III. Primordial principle, source of origin (*rare*) 1655.

One God, one law, one e. TENNYSON.

IV. *pl.* †The letters of the alphabet. Hence, the 'A, B, C' of learning; also, the first principles of an art or science. ME.

†**E·lement,** *v.* ME. [f. prec. sb.] 1. *trans.* To compound of (the four) elements –1647. Also *fig.* 2. To instruct in the rudiments of learning –1662.

Elemental (elĭme·ntăl), *a.* 1519. [f. as prec. + -AL.] 1. Of or pertaining to the four elements, or to any one of them. †2. Composed of, or produced by, the (four) elements; material, physical –1646. †3. Applied to fire: a. Material. b. As a pure element. –1755. 4. Pertaining to the forces of nature 1821. Also *fig.* †5. Pertaining to the sky –1627. 6. Of the nature of an ultimate constituent 1555. 7. Constituent 1639. 8. Relating to rudiments; elementary. Now *rare.* 1577.

1. All subsists by e. strife POPE. 2. The slaying of an elementall life MILT. 4. E. worship of the grossest kind MERIVALE. *fig.* The freedom and e. grandeur of Byron MORLEY. 6. The primitive e. operations of thought 1863. 8. E. truths 1855.

Hence **Eleme·ntalism** (*nonce-wd.*), worship of the elementary powers of nature. †**E:lementa·lity,** the fact of being an element. †**Eleme·ntally** *adv.*

Elementaloid (elĭme·ntăloid), *a.* 1885. [f. prec. + -OID.] *Chem.* Like an element; having the appearance of an element.

Elementary (elĭme·ntări). ME. [ad. L. *elementarius,* f. *elementum*; see -AR, -ARY.] 1. = ELEMENTAL 1. Now *rare.* 1549. †2. = ELEMENTAL 2. –1750. †3. Applied to air, fire, water, earth: a. Physical. b. As pure elements. –1794. 4. = ELEMENTAL 4, which is now more used 1739. Also *fig.* †5. Congenial 1760. 6. = ELEMENTAL 6. 1622. b. *Math.* Of the nature of an element or infinitesimal part 1882. 7. Of the nature of elements; rudimentary, introductory 1542.

1. E. war—deluges and earthquakes 1856. 4. The e. god of fire H. WALPOLE. 6. The e. substances of which rocks are composed 1813. 7. Phr. *E. books, writers, schools.*

Hence **Eleme·ntarily** *adv.* **Eleme·ntariness,** also †**E:lementa·rity,** the quality of being e.

†**E·lementate,** *v.* 1650. [f. mod.L. *elementat-, elementare,* f. *elementum.*] *trans.* a. To impregnate with an element; to compound out of elements. b. To be elements or an element of (a substance). ASHMOLE.

†**Eleme·ntish,** *a.* 1580. [See -ISH.] Material, physical –1646.

Elemi (e·lĭmi). 1543. [In Fr. *élémi*; ? Oriental.] A resin obtained from various trees, as *Canarium commune* (Manilla), *Icica Icicariba* (Brazil), *Elaphrium elemiferum* (Mexico), used in plasters, ointments, and the manufacture of varnishes. More fully GUM ELEMI. Also *attrib.*

Elemin (e·lĭmin). 1868. [f. prec. + -IN.] *Chem.* A crystalline body extracted from elemi; also, a transparent colourless oil obtained from elemi by distilling with water.

†**Elench** (ĭle·ŋk). 1529. [ad. L. *elenchus*, a. Gr. ἔλεγχος.] **1.** *Logic.* A syllogism in refutation of a syllogistic conclusion; hence, more widely, a logical refutation -1631. **b.** A sophistical argument; a fallacy -1689. **2.** An index 1563. Hence **Ele·nchic, -al** *a.* = ELE·NCTIC, -AL. **Ele·nchically** *adv.* †**Ele·nchize** *v.* to use the elenchus. B. JONS.

‖**Elenchus** (ĭle·ŋkŏs). *Pl.* **elenchi.** 1663. [L., a. Gr. ἔλεγχος cross-examination.] **1. a.** *Logic.* = ELENCH 1. **b.** *Socratic e.*: the Socratic method of eliciting truth by cross-examination. †**2.** = ELENCH 2.

Elenctic, -al (ĭle·ŋktik, -ăl), *a.* 1833. [ad. Gr. ἐλεγκτικός, f. ἐλέγχειν; cf. prec.] Pertaining to elenchus; concerned with cross-examination.

E·lenge, *a.* Now *dial.* [OE. *ǽlenge*, f. Æ- *pref.* + **lęnge* LONG *a.*] †**1.** Very long, tedious -ME. **2.** Remote, lonely; dreary ME. Hence †**E·lengenesse.**

†**E·lephancy.** 1547. [ad. L. *elephantia*; see next.] = ELEPHANTIASIS -1657.

Elephant (e·lĭfănt). [ME. *olifaunt*, a. OF. *olifant*, repr. pop. L. **olifantum* (whence also OE., ME. *olfend* camel), alteration of L. *elephantum* (*-us*), *elephantem* (*-phas*), a. Gr. ἐλέφας, -ντ-; ultimate origin obsc.] **1.** A huge quadruped of the Pachydermate order, having long curving ivory tusks and a prehensile proboscis. Only two species now exist, the Indian and the African; the former of which (the largest of extant land animals) is often used as a beast of burden. Also *fig.* †**2. a.** Ivory [after L. *elephantus*]. **b.** A horn of ivory [after OF. *olifant*]. -1725. †**3.** A species of lizard mentioned by Pliny -1608. †**4.** [after Pg. *elephante.*] = ELEPHANTA -1703. **5.** (more fully **e.-paper**): A size of drawing paper measuring 28 × 23 inches. *Double e.*, one measuring 40 × 26½ inches. 1702. **6.** *attrib.* 1774.

1. *fig.* Shall the E. Aiax carry it thus *Tr. & Cr.* II. iii. **2.** Phr. *White e.*: a burdensome or costly possession (given by the kings of Siam to obnoxious courtiers in order to ruin them. *To see the e.* (U.S.): to see life or the world. **2. a.** Polished E. DRYDEN.

Comb.: **e.-bed,** a stratum at Brighton containing remains of *Elephas primigenius*, etc.; **-beetle,** some S. Amer. beetle, prob. *Dynastes Neptunus*; also applied to the Afr. species *Goliathus giganteus* and *G. cacicus*; **-fish,** the *Chimæra callorhynchus*, named from the proboscis-like process on its nose; **-leg** = ELEPHANTIASIS; **-paper** (see 5); **-seal,** a species of seal (*Macrorhinus proboscideus*), the males of which have the snout somewhat prolonged; also called **Sea elephant**; **-shrew,** *Macroscelides typicus*, a long-snouted burrower of Southern Africa; **-tusk,** the tooth-shell.

b. Also in the names of plants, as **e.-apple,** *Feronia elephantum*, of the genus *Aurantiaceæ*; **-creeper,** *Argyreia speciosa*; **elephant's ear,** the Begonia; **elephant's foot,** a species of Yam (*Testudinaria elephantipes*); **elephant's grass,** a kind of reed-mace (*Typha elephantum*); **elephant's-trunk-plant,** *Martynia proboscidea*; **elephant's vine,** *Cissus latifolia.*

Elepha·nta. Also (erron.) **elephanter.** 1725. [a. Pg. *elephante.*] A name, originally Portuguese, for violent storms which attend the termination, or, some say, the setting in, of the Monsoon.

Elephantiac (elĭfæ·ntiæk). 1868. [ad. L. *elephantiacus.*] One who has elephantiasis.

‖**Elephantiasis** (e:lĭfăntəi·ăsis). 1581. [L., a. Gr., f. ἐλέφας ELEPHANT.] *Med.* One of various skin diseases, which make the part affected resemble an elephant's hide. The best known is *E. Arabum*, called also Elephant, or Barbadoes, Leg, which indurates and darkens the skin of the leg.

Elephantic (elĭfæ·ntik). 1491. [ad. L. *elephanticus.*] **a.** *adj.* = ELEPHANTINE. Now *rare.* 1598. †**b.** *sb.* = prec.

Elephantine (elĭfæ·ntəin, -tin), *a.* 1630. [ad. L., a. Gr. ἐλεφάντινος, f. ἐλέφας.] **1.** Pertaining to an elephant; resembling an elephant (usually in size or gait); huge, unwieldy, clumsy. **2.** *Rom. Antiq.* Made of ivory 1751.

1. Phr. *E. epoch* (Geol.): the period marked by the abundance of huge pachydermata. Misshapen e. bodies 1630. Ungraceful e. play 1860. **2.** Phr. *E. books*: books composed of ivory tablets, wherein were recorded the acts of the Roman emperors and of the senate.

Elephantoid, -al (elĭfæ·ntoid, -ăl), *a.* 1841. [See -OID.] **a.** Elephant-like. **b.** Of or belonging to elephant-like animals.

E·lephantry. 1747. [f. ELEPHANT, after *cavalry.*] Troops mounted on elephants.

Eleusinian (eliusi·niăn). 1643. [f. L. *eleusinius*, Gr. Ἐλευσίνιος.] Belonging to Eleusis in Attica. *E. mysteries*: the mysteries of Demeter there celebrated; also *fig.*

Eleu·therarch. *rare.* 1813. [f. Gr. ἐλεύθερος + -αρχης.] The chief of an (imaginary) secret society, 'the Eleutheri'.

Eleuthe·rian, *a. rare.* 1623. [f. Gr. ἐλευθέριος.] The title of Zeus as protector of political freedom.

Eleuthero- (ĭliū·þəro), comb. f. Gr. ἐλεύθερος free:

Eleu·theroma·nia [see MANIA], frantic zeal for freedom. So **Eleu:theroma·niac** *a.* Also in botanical compounds, as **Eleu:thero-pe·talous** [Gr. πέταλον], **-phy·llous** [Gr. φύλλον], **-se·palous** [see SEPAL] *adjs.*, having the petals, leaves, sepals, free, *i. e.* distinct, not cohering.

†**E·levable,** *a.* [a. F. *élévable.*] That can be elevated. H. MORE.

Elevate (e·lĭvĕt), *pa. pple.* and *ppl. a.* ME. [ad. L. *elevatus.*] Used as pa. pple. of ELEVATE *v.*; also = ELEVATED *ppl. a.* From 18th c. only *poet.*

Apart.. In thoughts more e. MILT. *P. L.* II. 559.

Elevate (e·lĭveit), *v.* 1497. [f. L. *elevat-*, ppl. stem of *elevare*, f. *e* + *levare* (related to *levis* light) to lighten, lift up, etc.] †**1.** *trans.* To lessen the weight of; to depreciate -1788. **2.** To raise, lift up higher. Also *fig.* 1497. **b.** To hold up to view, as the Host 1637. †**c.** Of heat: To evaporate or sublime -1715. **3.** *transf.* To raise (the voice) 1618. **4.** To direct upwards; also *fig.* 1611. **b.** *Gunnery.* To raise the axis of (a gun, etc.) to an angle with the horizon 1692. **5.** To exalt in rank or status 1509. **6.** To raise morally or intellectually 1624. **7.** To elate, exhilarate (now *rare*) 1634. **b.** *spec.* of the effects of liquor (*joc.* or *slang*) 1704.

2. To e. a bucket LARDNER. **b.** To e. the Host for adoration 1660. **4. b.** The mortar must be more elevated 1769. **5.** To e. a plebeian 1835. **6.** Books which e. the Mind above the World STEELE. **7. b.** We were all elevated above the use of our legs 1704.

Elevated (e·lĭveitėd), *ppl. a.* 1553. [f. the vb.] **1.** Raised up; at a high level. Also *fig.* and *transf.* **2.** Exalted in character; lofty, sublime 1604. **3. a.** Elated. **b.** Slightly intoxicated (*joc.* or *slang*). 1624.

1. E. lakes GOLDSM. Phr. *E. railway*: a railway raised on pillars above the street-level; so *e. train.* **2.** One of the most e. passages in Plato JOWETT. Hence **E·levatedly** *adv.*, **-ness.**

Elevation (elĭvē¹·ʃən). ME. [ad. L. *elevationem*; see ELEVATE *v.*]

I. 1. The action of lifting up, raising aloft, or directing upwards 1526. Also †*fig.* and *transf.* **2.** *concr.* A swelling; an eminence 1543. †**3.** Sublimation; vaporization by heat -1677. **4.** The action of raising in rank or dignity; the being elevated in rank 16...

1. But the land is subject also to local elevations and depressions HUXLEY. The E. [of the Host] 1884. *transf.* E. of voice 1668, of the Pulse 1725, of temperature 1882. **4.** A sudden e. in life HARE.

II. 1. Of angular magnitude: **a.** *Astron.* The altitude of the pole, or of any heavenly body, above the horizon. Also in *Dialling*, the angle made by the gnomon with the horizon (= the latitude of the place). ME. **b.** The angle made with the horizontal by any line of direction; *spec.* the angle at which a gun is elevated 1692. **2.** A particular altitude above a given level 1732. **3.** *concr.* A drawing of a building, etc., made in projection on a vertical plane 1731. **4.** Height, loftiness (*lit.* and *fig.*) 1639.

2. Snow at the higher elevations TYNDALL. **4.** E. of style WOTTON (J.), of character LECKY. A building of imposing e. (*mod.*).

Elevator (e·lĭveitəɹ). 1646. [a. L.] One who or that which elevates. **1.** *Anat.* A muscle which raises a limb or an organ 1646. **2.** *Surg.* 'An instrument for raising any depressed portions of bone. Also, an instrument used in Dentistry for the removal of stumps of teeth' (*Syd. Soc. Lex.*). **3. a.** A machine used for raising corn or flour to an upper storey. **b.** *U.S.* A large building (containing one or more of these machines) used for the storage of grain. **c.** A lift, hoist, ascending chamber. 1825. **4.** *Aeronautics.* **a.** An elevating screw. **b.** A rudder device for lifting or steering an aircraft vertically 1871.

Elevatory (e·lĭveitəri). 1612. [See -ORY.] **A.** *adj.* Of or pertaining to elevation; that tends to elevate (*lit.* and *fig.*) 1833. **B.** *sb.* = ELEVATOR 2.

†**Ele·ve.** Now only as Fr. 1736. [a. F. *élève.*] A pupil -1829.

Eleven (ĭle·v'n). [Com. Teut.: OE. *ęndleofon*, corresp. to Goth. *ainlif*:—OTeut. **ainlif-*, f. **ain-* ONE + *-*lif-* (= Lith. *-lika* remaining).] The cardinal number next after ten; symbols 11 and xi.

A. *adj.* **1.** With sb. expressed. **2.** With ellipsis of sb. ME.

2. About a leuen [*sc.* hours] of the clocke UDALL.

B. as *sb.* **1.** The abstract number eleven ME. **2.** A set of eleven persons; *esp.* a side at cricket or football 1800.

Eleventh (ĭle·v'nþ). [OE. *ęndlyfta, ællefta* :—OTeut. **ainliftón-*, f. **ainlif-* ELEVEN + ordinal suffix f. OAryan *-to-*. Recoined (since 14th c.) from ELEVEN + *-th* (after FOURTH).]

A. *adj.* **1.** That comes next after the tenth. **2.** *E. part*: one of eleven equal parts of anything 1797. †**3.** *Mus.* The interval of an octave and a fourth 1597.

1. Phr. *E. hour*: the latest possible time (see *Matt.* xx); Though at the e. hour Thou hast come SOUTHEY.

B. *sb.* = *eleventh part*; see A. 2. 1557.

Hence **Ele·venthly** *adv.*; also quasi-*sb.*

Elf (elf), *sb.* [OE. *ælf* str. masc. = OHG. *alp* nightmare, ON. *álfr* elf:—OTeut. **alƀoz.* (The mod.G. *elf* is prob. from Eng.).] **1.** *Mythol.* The name of a class of supernatural beings, believed to be of dwarfish form, and to possess magical powers, which they exercised either to the help or the hurt of mankind. Now a mere synonym of FAIRY. †**b.** Sometimes dist. from fairies: (*a*) as a subject species; (*b*) as more malignant; also *fig.* 1587. **2.** *transf.* A diminutive being; a dwarf; a mischievous child 1530. **b.** A tricksy, sometimes a malicious, creature 1553. †**3.** A knight of Spenser's 'faerie land'.

1. Ye Elves of hils, brooks, standing lakes and groues *Temp.* v. i. 33.

Comb. **a.** appositive, as *e.-child*, a changeling; **b.** attributive, as *e.-land*, etc. Also **e.-arrow, -bolt,** a flint arrow-head (see ELF-SHOT); also, a belemnite; **-dart** = ELF-SHOT 1; **-dock,** the Elecampane; **-fire,** *ignis fatuus*; **-knot** = ELF-LOCK; **-stone** = ELF-SHOT 2; **-wort** = *elf-dock.*

†**Elf,** *v. rare.* [f. ELF *sb.*] To tangle (hair) as an elf might do. *Lear* II. iii. 10.

Elfin (e·lfin). 1596. [perh. later var. of ME. *elven*, OE. *ælfen* elf.] **A.** *adj.* Pertaining to elves; of elfish nature or origin. Also *transf.*

An e. storm from faery land KEATS.

B. *sb.* **1.** An ELF, or urchin 1596. †**2.** *Sc.* ? Elf-land -1802.

Elfish (e·lfiʃ), *a.* 1542. [See -ISH.] Pertaining to elves; weird, spectral; tricksy, mischievous; †intractable.

The e. light COLERIDGE. Our e. rogue Myouk KANE.

Elf-lock. 1592. [f. ELF + LOCK (of hair).] Hair tangled, *esp.* by Queen Mab: 'which it was not fortunate to disentangle' (Nares).

E·lf-shot. 1681. [f. ELF + SHOT.] **1.** Disease, supposed to be due to the agency of elves. **2.** A flint arrow-head; 'supposed to be shot by fairies at cattle' (Pennant) 1769.

Eliasite (ĭləi·ăsəit). 1852. [f. a mine called *Elias* at Joachimsthal.] *Min.* Hydrous oxide of uranium, like gum in appearance.

†**Elicit** (ĭli·sit), *a.* 1624. [ad. L. *elicitus*, pa. pple. of *elicere* to draw out.] *Philos.* Of an act: Evolved immediately from an active power or quality; opp. to *imperate* -1693.

Not .. the .. elicite acts of conscience, but the imperate, commanded and externall acts 1646.

Elicit (ĭli·sit), *v.* 1641. [f. L. *elicit-* ppl.

stem; see prec.] 1. *trans.* To draw forth (what is latent or potential). Also *fig.* 2. To educe (principles, etc.) *from* data; to draw out (information), evoke (a response, etc.), *from* a person 1677.

1. They e... the innate sense of right and wrong J. H. NEWMAN. 2. He could not e. a syllable from him on the subject 1822. So †**Eli·citate** *v.* (in same sense) H. MORE. **Eli·cita·tion.** Hence †**Eli·citive** *a.* pertaining to, or of the nature of, elicit acts. **Eli·citor.**

Elide (ǐləi·d), *v.* 1593. [ad. L. *elidere*, f. *e* + *lædere* to strike.] †1. *trans.* To destroy (the force of evidence) –1688. 2. To strike out, suppress 1847. 3. *Gram.* To omit (a vowel, or syllable) in pronunciation 1796.

3. Some sounds elided, others exaggerated 1851.

†**E·ligent.** 1670. [ad. L. *eligentem.*] = ELECTOR –1688.

Eligibility (e:lidʒibi·lĭti). 1650. [f. next; see -ITY.] 1. The quality of being eligible. 2. *concr.* in *pl.* Eligible courses of action; qualities that render eligible 1660.

1. E. to a fellowship 1815.

Eligible (e·lĭgib'l), *a.* 1561. [a. F. *éligible*, f. L. *eligere* to pick out.] 1. Fit or proper to be chosen (for an office, etc.). †2. Subject to appointment by election –1739. 3. That deserves to be chosen; desirable, suitable 1603. b. That is a matter of choice 1769. 4. quasi-*sb.* in *pl.* Eligible persons or things 1844.

3. The most e. manner of doubling Cape Horn ANSON. E. property 1871. Hence **E·ligibly** *adv.*

Eliminant (ǐli·minănt). 1876. [ad. L. *eliminantem*; see next.] A. *adj.* Expulsive; throwing off by the excretions 1876. B. *sb. Math.* The result of eliminating *n* variables between *n* homogeneous equations of any degree 1881.

Eliminate (ǐli·mineit), *v.* 1568. [f. L. *eliminat-*, *eliminare*, f. *e* + *limen* threshold.] 1. *trans.* To put out of doors, expel. Now *joc.* 2. a. *Phys.* To get rid of (waste matter, etc.), *esp.* by excretion. b. *Chem.* To disengage, expel (a constituent). 1794. 3. *gen.* To expel, get rid of 1714. b. *fig.* To treat as non-existent 1850. 4. *Algebra.* To get rid of (one or more quantities) from an equation 1845. ¶5. Incorrectly used for: To disengage, isolate, disentangle; hence, to elicit, deduce 1843.

3. To e. middle men and intermediate profits GOSCHEN, the supernatural R. H. HUTTON. *fig.* Eliminating him from the argument THACKERAY. 5. The roots indeed e. nourishment from the soil 1872. Hence **Eli·minable** *a.* **Eli·minative** *a.* that eliminates or tends to e. (*rare*). **Eli·minator** *spec.* an apparatus which eliminates a battery by enabling a wireless set to be worked from a mains current.

Elimination (ǐlimĭnē¹·ʃən). 1601. [f. L. *eliminare*; see -ATION.] †1. The action of turning out of doors or expelling –1809. 2. *gen.* Expulsion, casting out, getting rid of 1627. 3. *Phys.* The process of throwing off (waste matter, etc.) from the tissues 1855. Also *transf.* and *fig.* 4. *Algebra.* The act or process of eliminating (one or more quantities) from an equation or set of equations 1845. ¶5. *catachr.* (See ELIMINATE *v.* 5.) 1869.

†**Eli·nguate,** *v.* [f. L. *elinguat-* ppl. stem, f. (ult.) *e* + *lingua.*] To deprive of the tongue. J. DAVIES.

†**Eli·ngued,** *a.* [as if f. **elingue* v., ad. L. *elinguare* (see prec.).] Deprived of the tongue; hence *fig.* speechless, dumb. FELTHAM.

Eliquate (e·likweit), *v.* 1621. [f. L. *eliquat-*, ppl. stem of *eliquare* to melt out.] †1. *trans.* a. To melt (by heat), fuse. b. To liquefy. c. To cause to flow freely. –1710. 2. To separate by fusion, smelt 1879.

Eliquation (elikwē¹·ʃən). 1651. [ad. L. *eliquationem*; see prec.] †1. The action or process of liquefying; liquefaction –1757. 2. *Metall.* The process of separating the different parts of ores or alloys by the different degrees of heat required to melt them 1753.

†**Eli·quidate,** *v. rare.* [See E- *pref.*] To make clear. HARINGTON.

Elision (ǐli·ʒən). 1581. [ad. L. *elisionem*; see ELIDE.] 1. The action of dropping out or suppressing, as a letter or syllable in pronunciation, a passage in a book, etc. 2. A breaking (so as to make a gap) by mechanical force 1760.

Phr. †*E. of the air*: a cutting, dividing, or attenuating of the air, formerly assigned as the cause of sound. Hence **Eli·sional** *a.* pertaining to e. (*rare*).

Elisor (e·lizər), *sb.* ME. [a. OF. *elisour*, f. *elis-* stem of *elire.*] †1. = ELECTOR –1529. 2. *Law.* One of two persons appointed in certain cases to select a jury 1628.

‖**Élite** (eli·t), *sb.* 1823. [Fr. *élite*:—med.L. *electa* choice, f. L. *eligere.*] The choice part or flower (of society, etc.).

The é. of the Russian nobility 1848.

Elixate (ǐli·k-, e·liksēit), *v.* 1623. [f. L. *elixat-*, ppl. stem of *elixare* to boil, stew.] 1. To boil, seethe; to extract by boiling. 2. To steep (in water); to macerate 1657. Hence **Elixation,** the action of seething; digestion.

†**Eli·xed,** *ppl. a. rare.* 1602. [ad. L. *elixus.*] a. Boiled; hence, distilled. b. Macerated. –1666.

Elixir (ǐli·xəɪ), *sb.* ME. [a. med.L. *elixir*, ad. Arab. *al-iksir* (= sense 1), prob. from Gr. ξηρόν dry (residuum).] 1. *Alchemy.* A preparation by the use of which it was hoped to change the baser metals into gold. Occas. = 'the philosopher's stone'. Also *e.-stone.* Also *transf.* and *fig.* 2. A supposed drug or essence capable of indefinitely prolonging life. More fully, *E. of life* (tr. med.L. *elixir vitæ*). 1605. 3. A strong extract or tincture. Now *Hist.* 1597. b. *fig.* The quintessence of a thing 1638.

2. To toy with magic, and pursue the e. of life DIXON. 3. b. A pure elixar of mischief MILT. Hence †**Eli·xir** *v.* to distil as an e.; to work upon as by an e. (*rare*). Also *absol.* †**Eli·xirate** *v.* to distil; to refine, purify.

†**Elixi·viate,** *v. rare.* 1674. [f. E- *pref.* + LIXIVIATE.] *trans.* To clear from lixivium or lye; to refine –1756.

Elizabethan (ǐli:zăbī·păn). 1817. [See -AN.] A. *adj.* Belonging to, or in the style of, the period of Queen Elizabeth; *esp.* of architecture, literature, etc.

B. *sb.* A poet, dramatist, statesman, etc., of the period of Queen Elizabeth 1881.

Elk[1] (elk). 1486. [prob. ad. MHG. *elch* (:—OHG. *elaho*). The Eng. form *alke* was influenced by L. *alces*, Gr. ἄλκη (cf. ALCE).] 1. The largest existing animal of the deer kind (*Alces malchis*). The American variety is also called MOOSE. 2. Applied also to the 'Irish Elk', an extinct species of deer (*Cervus megaceros*); and to the Wapiti (*Cervus canadensis*) 1884. 3. The ELAND or Cape-elk 1731.

Comb.: **e.-nut,** *Hamiltonia oleifera*; **-wood,** *Magnolia macrophylla.*

†**Elk**[2]. 1541. A kind of yew, of which bows were made –1607.

†**Elk**[3] (elk). 1552. The Wild Swan (*Cygnus ferus*). Also the Wild Goose (*Anas anser*). –1839.

Ell[1] (el). [Com. Teut.: OE. *eln*, str. fem. :—OTeut. **alinâ*, cogn. w. Gr. ὠλένη, L. *ulna.* Cf. ELBOW.] 1. A measure of length varying in different countries. The English ell = 45 in.; the Scotch = 37·2 in.; the Flemish = 27 in. Now only *Hist.* †2. = ELL-WAND –1768.

Ell[2] (el). *dial.* and *U.S.* 1875. [var. of *ele*, AISLE.] = L (the letter) I. 1 a.

Ellagic (elæ·dʒik). 1810. [ad. Fr. *ellagique*, f. *ellag*, anagram of *galle* gall-nut; see -IC. Cf. GALLIC.] In *e. acid*: $C_{14}H_8O_9$; orig. obtained from oak-galls; found also in bezoar, whence called also *bezoartic acid.* Hence **E·llagate,** a salt of ellagic acid.

†**E·llan.** 1613. [a. F. *élan*, a. Ger. *elend*; cf. ELAND.] The Elk –1682.

Ellebore, -bory, obs. ff. HELLEBORE.

Elleck (e·lėk). 1862. A fish: the Red Gurnard, *Trigla cuculus.*

†**Ellinge,** var. of ELENGE *a.*

Ellipse (eli·ps). 1753. [ad. Gr. ἔλλειψις a coming short; so called because the inclination of the cutting plane to the base comes short of the inclination of the side of the cone.] 1. A plane closed curve in which the sum of the distances of any point from the two foci is a constant quantity. 2. *transf.* An object or figure bounded by an ellipse. Also *fig.* 1857. 3. *Gram.* = ELLIPSIS 2 (*rare*) 1843.

1. The dark Earth follows wheel'd in her e. TENNYSON.

‖**Ellipsis** (eli·psis). Pl. **ellipses** (-sīz). 1570. [a. L., ad. Gr. ἔλλειψις; see prec.] 1. = ELLIPSE 1, 2. Now *rare.* 2. *Gram.* The omission of one or more words in a sentence, which would be needed to express the sense completely; *concr.* an instance of this 1612. †3. Formerly applied to the dash (—) as indicating the omission of letters in a word 1824.

Ellipsograph (eli·psŏgrɑf). [See -GRAPH.] An instrument for describing ellipses.

Ellipsoid (eli·psoid). 1721. [See -OID.] A. *sb.* A solid of which all the plane sections through one of the axes are ellipses, and all other sections ellipses or circles.

Phr. *E. of revolution*: a solid generated by the revolution of an e. round one of its axes.

B. *adj.* Having the nature or shape of an ellipse 1861. So **Ellipsoi·dal** *a.*

Elliptic (eli·ptik). 1726. [ad. Gr. ἐλλειπτικός; cf. ELLIPSE.] 1. That has the form of an ellipse; pertaining to ellipses. 2. *Gram.* Characterized by ELLIPSIS (sense 2).

1. *E. chuck*: a chuck for oval or elliptic turning. *E. compass(es*: an instrument for drawing ellipses. *E. integrals* (Math.): a class of integrals discovered by Legendre in 1786, as the result of the investigation of e. arcs. *E. functions* (Math.): certain specific functions of these integrals.

Comb., as *e.-lanceolate a.*, etc, having a form intermediate between e. and lanceolate, etc.

Hence **Elli·ptical** *a.* **Elli·ptically** *adv.*

Ellipticity (elipti·sĭti). 1753. [See -ITY.] Elliptic form; degree of deviation (of an orbit, etc.) from circularity, (of a spheroid) from sphericity.

The e. of the earth..has been found to be 1/299 BREWSTER.

Elliptograph. = ELLIPSOGRAPH.

‖**Ellops** (e·lǫps). *Obs.* in actual use. 1601. [a. Gr. ἔλλοψ or ἔλοψ.] 1. A kind of serpent. MILT. *P. L.* x. 526. 2. A kind of fish mentioned by ancient writers 1601.

Ell-wand (e·lwǫnd). Chiefly *Sc.* and *n. dial.* ME. [f. ELL + WAND.] 1. An ell-measure: sometimes used for 'yard-measure' 1500. †2. = ULNA. ME. only. 3. *Sc.* The group of stars called Orion's Belt 1513.

Elm (elm). [OE. *elm* str. masc. :—WGer. **elmoz*; whence also, with difference of ablaut, ON. *álmr* etymologically = L. *ulmus.*] 1. Any of the trees belonging to the genus *Ulmus*, *esp.*, in England, *Ulmus campestris*; in Scotland, *Ulmus montana* or *Ulmus suberosa*; in U.S. the White Elm (*Ulmus americana*) OE. 2. The wood of these trees 1823.

1. The E. delights in a sound, sweet and fertile Land EVELYN. *Comb.*, chiefly *attrib.*, as *e.-tree*, *-wood*, etc.; **e.-balm,** the fluid contained in elm-galls; **-gall,** that produced on elms by the puncture of *Aphis ulmi.* Hence **E·lmen** *a.* (now *arch.*), of or pertaining to elms or elm-wood. **E·lmy** *a.* consisting of or abounding in elms.

†**Elne, e·llen,** *sb.* [Com. Teut.: OE. *ellen.*] Strength, courage (also, in OE., zeal). So †**E·lne** *v.* to strengthen, comfort.

†**Eloca·tion.** *rare.* 1619. [f. L. *elocare.*] 1. Removal from a person's control. BP. HALL. 2. *fig.* Alienation (of mind).

Elocular (ǐlǫ·kiŭlăɪ), *a.* 1864. [f. L. *e* + *loculus* + -AR.] *Bot.* Without partitions or separate cells.

Elocution (elŏkiū·ʃən). 1509. [ad. L. *elocutionem*, f. *eloqui* to speak out.] †1. Oratorical or literary expression; literary style as dist. from matter –1844. †2. Eloquence, oratory; in *pl.* harangues –1791. 3. Oral utterance 1623. 4. The art of public speaking as regards delivery, pronunciation, tones, and gestures; manner or style of oral delivery. [= L. *pronuntiatio.*] Also *attrib.* 1613.

1. Elocucion is an applying of apte wordes and sentences to the matter 1553. 2. Both e. and address in arms COWPER. 3. Whose taste.. Gave e. to the mute MILT. *P. L.* IX. 747. 4. True theatrical e. CIBBER. Hence **Elocu·tionary** *a.* of or pertaining to e. **Elocu·tionist,** a master of e.

Elocutive (ǐlǫ·kiŭtiv), *a.* 1627. [f. L. *eloqui*; see prec.] Pertaining to utterance or eloquence. FELTHAM.

Elo·ge. 1566. [a. F. *éloge*, ad. L. *elogium.* Now only as F. (elǫʒ).] †1. An encomium –1802. 2. A funeral oration; a discourse in honour of a deceased person 1725.

2. Pronouncing the E. of his old master into whose place he now ascends 1861. So †**E·logist,** one who pronounces an e.

†‖**Elo·gium.** 1570. [L.; app. confused with EULOGIUM.] = next -1789.

†**E·logy.** 1605. [Anglicized f. prec.] **1.** An explanatory inscription, *e.g.* on a tombstone -1663. **2.** A characterization; *esp.* a eulogy -1740. **3.** A biographical notice -1652. **4.** A funeral oration -1689.

‖ **Elohim** (elōu·him, -hīm). 1605. [Heb.; = 'gods', but often construed as sing.] One of the Hebrew names of God, or of the gods. Hence **Elohi·mic** *a.* using the word *Elohim* instead of *Yahveh* (*rare*).

Elohist (elōu·hist). 1862. [f. ELOH(IM) + -IST.] A name for the author (or authors) of those parts of the Hexateuch in which *Elohim* is used as the name of God instead of *Yahveh* (pop. *Jehovah*). Hence **Elohi·stic** *a.* of or pertaining to the E.; using ELOHIM instead of *Yahveh*.

Eloin, eloign (ǐloi·n), *v.* 1535. [a. AF., OF. *esloignier* (mod.F. *éloigner*) :—late L. *exlongare, elongare*; see ELONG.] †**1.** To remove to a distance (*lit.* and *fig.*) -1692. **2.** *Law.* To convey or remove out of the jurisdiction 1558. **3.** To remove, carry off (property) 1622.

1. From worldly cares himselfe he did esloyne SPENSER *F. Q.* I. iv. 20. 2. The sheriff may return that he is eloigned BLACKSTONE. Hence **Eloi·ner** (*Law*). †**Eloi·nment, eloi·gnment,** distance; removal to a distance.

†**Elo·ng,** *v.* ME. [ad. late L. *elongare*, f. *e* + *longe, longus*.] **1.** *trans.* To make longer; to retard -1610. **2.** To remove, separate *from*. Also *fig.* -1609.

Elongate (ī·lǫŋgeⁱt, ǐlǫ·ŋgeⁱt), *v.* 1540. [f. late L. *elongat-* ppl. stem; see prec.] †**1.** *trans.* and *intr.* To remove *from* -1646. **2.** *Astron.* (*intr.*) To recede apparently from the sun; said, *e.g.*, of a star or planet 1646. **3.** *trans.* To lengthen, prolong 1578. **4.** *Bot.* (*intr.*) To grow in length; to be lengthy 1801.

Elongate (ǐlǫ·ŋgĕt), *a.* 1828. [formed as prec.] Lengthened, extended; *esp.* in *Bot.* and *Zool.* long in proportion to its breadth.

Lip e...narrowing towards the point STARK. Hence **E·longato-**, comb. form, as in **e.-conical, -ovate, -triangular** *adjs.*, having the form of a lengthened cone, egg, triangle.

Elongation (ǐlǫŋgēⁱ·ʃən). ME. [ad. late L. *elongationem*.] **1.** *Astron.* The angular distance of a planet from the sun, or of a satellite from its primary. †**2.** Removal to a distance; hence, remoteness; also *fig.* -1787. **3.** The action or process of elongating 1731. **4.** *Surg.* **a.** An imperfect luxation, when the ligaments are lengthened, but the bone is not displaced 1676. **b.** 'The extension of a limb for the purpose of reducing a dislocation' (*Syd. Soc. Lex.*). **5.** The state of being elongated; that which is elongated 1751.

2. His e. and further removal from Court 1654. 3. E. of the boughs on the lee side 1828. 5. The e. of the image WHEWELL.

Elope (ǐlōu·p), *v.* 1596. [In AF. *aloper*, f. ME. **alopen*, pa. pple. of **aleapen* = MDu. *ontlopen*, Ger. *entlaufen* to run away.] **1. a.** *Law.* Of a wife: To run away from her husband with a paramour. **b.** More frequently said of a woman running away from home with a lover for the purpose of being married. **2.** *gen.* To run away, abscond 1596. Also *transf.* and *fig.*

1. If the wife e. from her husband she shall lose her dower COKE. We..must e. methodically, madam GOLDSM. Hence **Elo·per.**

Elopement (ǐlōu·pmĕnt). 1641. [In AF. *alopement*; see prec.] The action of eloping (see ELOPE *v.*).

‖**Elops** (ī·lǫps). [mod.L., a. Gr. ἔλοψ; see also ELLOPS.] *Zool.* A genus of fishes of the Herring family.

Eloquence (e·lŏkwĕns). ME. [a. F. *éloquence*, ad. L. *eloquentia*, f. (ult.) *eloqui* to speak out.] **1.** The action, practice, or art of speaking or writing with fluency, force, and appropriateness, so as to appeal to the reason or move the feelings. Also *fig.* †**2.** Verbal expression in general -1659. **3.** The quality of being eloquent ME. **4.** = RHETORIC 1623.

1. His e. was irresistibly impressive GROTE. *fig.* Her tears her only e. S. ROGERS. 3. A Scantling of Jacks great e. SWIFT. So †**E·loquency** (in sense 3).

Eloquent (e·lŏkwĕnt), *a.* ME. [a. F. *éloquent*, ad. L. *eloquentem*; see prec.] **1.** Of persons: Possessing or exercising the power of fluent, forcible, and appropriate expression. Also *transf.* and *fig.* **2.** Of utterances or style: Characterized by forcible and appropriate expression ME.

1. E. speakers are enclined to Ambition HOBBES. *fig.* Her dark eyes—how e. S. ROGERS. Hence **E·loquently** *adv.* So †**Elo·quious** *a.* (*rare*).

Eloquential (elŏkwe·nʃăl), *a.* *rare.* 1711. [See -AL.] Pertaining to eloquence; rhetorical.

Elrage,-aige,-ich,-itch, var. ff. ELDRITCH.

Elroquite (elrǫ·kəit). 1882. [f. *El Roque*; see -ITE.] *Min.* An apple-green to grey silicate of aluminium and iron.

-els, *suffix*, common in OE. See **-LE.**

Else (els), *adv.* [OE. *ęlles*, advb. use of gen. neut. of OTeut. **aljo-* other = L. *alius*.] **1.** A synonym of *other*, used with pronominal words or phrases, which in mod. use it follows. Also inflected, as in *somebody else's*, etc. (*colloq.*). **2.** = 'in (some, any, what, etc.) other manner, place, or time' ME. †**3.** By other means -1471; = *elsewhither* -1591. **4.** In another case; otherwise; if not; also preceded by *or* ME. **b.** *idiomatically.* = 'If it is not believed'. Now *rare* or *dial.* 1590. †**5.** quasi-*conj.* If only, provided that, so long as. (Cf. Ger. *anders*.) ME. only.

1. Shall he nede any thynge elles 1532. What do they e., but scrape and scramble..for these things BARROW. 2. Here more than anywhere e. MORLEY. 3. *Two Gent.* IV. ii. 125. 4. E. how should any one be saved J. H. NEWMAN. Speak fair words, or e. be mute SHAKS.

Hence †**Elsewhat** *pron.* something or anything else.

Elsewhere (elshwē·ər), *adv.* OE. [f. ELSE + WHERE.] **1.** At some other point; in some other place. **2.** = next 1513.

1. Here as well as e. SCOTT. 2. If ill used..we go e. GOLDSM.

Elsewhither, *adv.* ?*arch.* OE. [f. ELSE + WHITHER.] To some other place, in some other direction; †whithersoever.

Send to the town or e. to buy bread 1616. The dusty fugitives must shrink e. CARLYLE.

Elsewise (e·lsˌwəiz), *adv.* 1548. [See -WISE.] Otherwise.

Elsin (e·lsin). Now *n. dial.* ME. [? a. MDu. *elssene*, f. same root as AWL.] An awl.

†**Elu·cid,** *a.* [See E- *pref.*] That gives out light. BOYLE.

Elucidate (ǐlˡū·sideⁱt), *v.* 1568. [f. late L. *elucidat-*, ppl. stem of *elucidare*, f. *e* + *lucidus*.] To render lucid; now only *fig.* to throw light upon, explain. Also *absol.*

The merit of elucidating the text MACAULAY. Hence **Elu·cidative** *a.* tending to e. **Elu·cidator. Elu·cidato ry** *a.* that elucidates or tends to e.

Elucidation (ǐlˡū sidēⁱ·ʃən). 1570. [f. as prec.] **1.** The action or process of elucidating. **2.** That which serves to elucidate; an explanation, demonstration, illustration 1667.

1. Documents..and the notes..added for their e. FROUDE.

†**Elu·ctate,** *v.* [f. L. *eluctat-*, *eluctari*.] To struggle forth. HACKET.

†**Elucta·tion.** 1627. [ad. L. *eluctationem*; see prec.] The action of struggling forth; *fig.* escape through struggle -1682.

†**Elu·cubrate,** *v.* 1623. [f. L. *elucubrat-*, *elucubrare* to compose by lamplight.] To produce by the use of midnight oil -1656. Hence †**Elu·cubrator.**

Elucubration (ǐlˡū:kiubrēⁱ·ʃən). 1643. [See -ATION.] †**1.** The action of composing by candle-light -1697. **2.** *concr.* Any literary composition 1664.

Elude (ǐlˡū·d), *v.* 1538. [ad. L. *eludere*, f. *e* + *ludere*.] †**1.** To befool; also, to baffle -1656. **2.** *trans.* To escape by dexterity or stratagem 1634. **3.** To evade compliance with or fulfilment of 1651. **4.** To escape adroitly from; to evade 1667.

2. The wary Trojan, bending from the blow Eludes the death POPE. To e. an argument D'ISRAELI. 3. To e. a Treaty STEELE, the obligation of an oath 1769. 4. The glittering gem..ever eludes the grasp 1859. Hence **Elu·der. Elu·dible** *a.*

E·lul. [Heb.] The 6th month of the Heb. sacred, the 12th of the civil year, nearly = September.

Elumbated (ǐlv·mbeⁱtĕd), *ppl. a.* Now only *joc.* 1731. [f. L. *elumbis*, f. *e* + *lumbus* loin.] Weakened in the loins.

Elusion (ǐlˡū·ʒən). 1550. [f. L. *eludere*.] †**1.** The action of befooling; *concr.* an illusion -1695. **2.** The action of escaping dexterously from, evading (now *rare*) 1624; *absol.* †an evasion; †evasiveness 1617.

Elusive (ǐlˡū·siv), *a.* 1719. [f. L. *elus-*, ppl. stem of *eludere*.] That eludes or seeks to elude; also *fig.*

fig. Guérin's e., undulating, impalpable nature M. ARNOLD. Hence **Elu·sive·ly** *adv.*, **-ness.**

Elusory (ǐlˡū·səri), *a.* 1646. [ad. late L. *elusorius*, f. as prec.] Tending to elude; evasive; deceptive.

E. tergiversations 1646. An e. problem 1856.

†**Elu·te,** *v.* 1731. [f. L. *elut-*, *eluere*.] To wash out, cleanse.

Elution (ǐlˡū·ʃən). 1612. [ad. L. *elutionem*; see prec.] *Chem.* Washing from impurity.

All these starches are prepared by e. 1870.

Elutriate (ǐlˡū·triˌeⁱt), *v.* 1731. [f. L. *elutriat-*, ppl. stem of *elutriare* to wash out.] *trans.* To decant; to purify by straining; in *Chem.* to separate the lighter from the heavier particles of a mixture by washing.

Hence **Elu tria·tion,** the action of elutriating.

‖**Eluvies** (ǐlˡū·viˌīz). 1710. [L., f. *eluere*.] **a.** 'The humour discharged in leucorrhœa; an inordinate discharge of any kind'. **b.** 'The effluvium from a swampy place' (Hooper).

Eluvium (ǐlˡū·viŏm). 1882. [mod.L., f. *e* + *luere*, after ALLUVIUM.] *Geol.* Accumulations of débris whether atmospheric or carried by wind-drift. Hence **Elu·vial** *a.* pertaining to, or of the nature of, e.

Eluxate (ǐlv·kseⁱt), *v.* 1731. [f. E- *pref.* + *luxat-* ppl. stem.] To put out of joint. Hence **Eluxa·tion.**

Elvan (e·lvăn). 1791. [Referred to Corn. *elven* spark.] **1.** The Cornish name for intrusive rocks of igneous origin, such as quartz-porphyry, whinstone, etc. Also *attrib.* **2.** A dike of this rock. MURCHISON. Hence **E·lvanite** (*Min.*) = ELVAN. **Elvani·tic** *a.*

Elve, obs. var. of ELF.

Elver (e·lvəɹ). 1640. [var. of EEL-FARE.] A young eel, *esp.* a young conger or sea-eel.

Elves, pl. of ELF.

Elvish (e·lviʃ), *a.* ME. [f. ELF + -ISH.] **1.** Of or pertaining to elves; supernatural, weird. **2.** Elf-like in behaviour: †**a.** Spiteful. **b.** Tricksy (cf. ELFISH). ME.

2. He semeth eluyssh by his contenance CHAUCER.

†**Ely·chnious,** *a.* [f. Gr. ἐλλύχνιον lamp-wick.] Of the nature of a wick. SIR T. BROWNE.

Elysian (ǐli·ziăn, -ʒiăn), *a.* 1579. [f. ELYSIUM + -AN.]

A. 1. Of or pertaining to Elysium. **2.** *fig.* Of the nature of, or resembling, what is in Elysium; beatific, glorious 1750.

1. E. joys MASSINGER. Phr. *E. fields* = ELYSIUM 1.

B. as *sb.* = ELYSIUM. Marlowe.

Elysium (ǐli·ziŏm, -ʒiŏm). 1599. [a. L., ad. Gr. Ἠλύσιον (πεδίον) the abode of the blessed.] **1.** The abode assigned to the blessed after death in Greek mythology. Also *transf.* of other states of the departed. **2.** *fig.* A place or state of ideal happiness 1599.

2. The wretched Slaue all Night sleepes in Elizium *Hen. V*, IV. i. 291.

Elytriform (eli·trifǭɹm), *a.* 1835. [f. as next + -FORM.] That has the form of elytra.

Elytrigerous (elitri·ʒĕrəs), *a.* 1877. [f. *elytri-*, comb. f. ELYTRUM + L. *-ger-* + -OUS.] That has or bears elytra.

Elytrin (e·litrin). [f. ELYTRON + -IN.] 'The form of chitin which composes the elytra of insects' (*Syd. Soc. Lex.*).

Elytroid (e·litroid), *a.* 1864. [ad. Gr. ἐλυτροειδής.] Resembling an elytron, sheath-like.

Elytron (e·litrǫn). Pl. **elytra.** 1774. [a. Gr. ἔλυτρον a sheath.] **1.** The outer hard wing-case of a coleopterous insect, pl. *elytra*. **2.** One of the shield-like dorsal plates of some annelids 1841. **3.** 'A term for the vagina' (*Syd. Soc. Lex.*).

E·lytrum. 1816. [mod.L., ad. prec.] = ELYTRON.

Elzevir (e·lzǐvəɹ). 1710. **1.** The name (properly *Elzevier*, latinized *Elzevirius*) of a family of printers at Amsterdam, Leyden, etc. (1592-

1680), famous chiefly for their editions of the classics. Used *attrib.* or as *adj.*, *e.g.* in *E. edition*; also formerly applied to books published in the style of the Elzeviers. Also *absol.* a book printed by one of them. **2. E. letter, type. a.** The style of type of the small Elzevir editions of the classics. **b.** Now used for a special type—ELZEVIR TYPE.

Hence **Elzevi·rian** *a.* of or pertaining to the Elzeviers; published by or in the style of the Elzeviers; quasi-*sb.* one who collects or fancies E. editions.

Em (em). The name of the letter M. In *Printing*, the square, formerly of the type 'm', now of a pica 'm', used as the unit for measuring the amount of printed matter in a line, page, etc.

'Em (əm), *pron.* ME. Orig. a form of HEM, dat. and accus. 3rd pers. pl. Now regarded as an abbrev. of *them.* Still in colloq. use.

Em-, *prefix*, the form taken by EN- (q. v.) bef. *b*, *p*, and (frequently) *m*. Nearly all the Eng. words with this prefix have (or have had) alternative forms with IM-. Hence:

1. Transitive vbs. **a.** f. *em-*+sb., as **empanoply**, to array in complete armour; etc. **b.** f. *em-*+sb. or adj., as **embeggar**, to bring into a state of beggary; etc. **2.** Verbs f. *em-*+verb, with intensive force, as †**embias**. **3.** Ppl. adjs. f. *em-*+sb.+*-ed*, as **embastioned**, etc.

(For *em-* words not found under E, see IM-.)

†**Ema·cerate**, *v. rare.* 1610. [f. L. *emacerat-* ppl. stem, f. (ult.) *e*+*macerare* to make lean.] *trans.* = EMACIATE -1609. Hence †**Ema:cera·tion. a.** = EMACIATION. **b.** = MACERATION.

Emaciate (ɪ̆mēⁱ·ʃiˌēt), *ppl. a.* 1675. [ad. L. *emaciatus*, *emaciare*, f. *e*+*maci-es* leanness.] Emaciated.

Emaciate (ɪ̆mēⁱ·ʃiˌeⁱt), *v.* 1646. [f. L. *emaciat-* ppl. stem; see prec.] To make or †become lean or wasted in flesh.

Consumption may e. the dimpled cheeks HERVEY. Hence **Ema·ciated** *ppl. a.* made lean, atrophied; also *fig.* **Ema:cia·tion**, the action of emaciating; emaciated state.

†**Ema·culate**, *v.* 1623. [f. L. *emaculat-*, *emaculare*, f. *macula* spot.] *trans.* To free from spots or blemishes, emend -1656.

†**Emai·led**, *ppl. a.* 1480. [?f. F. *émaillé* enamelled, etc.] ?Embossed (with a raised pattern).

Emanant (e·mănănt), *ppl. a. arch.* 1614. [ad. L. *emanantem*; see next.] That emanates or issues from a source.

Filling eminent places, with e. poisons 1614.

Emanate (e·măneⁱt), *v.* 1788. [f. L. *emanat-*, *emanare*, f. *e*+*manare* to flow.] **1.** *intr.* To flow forth, issue *from*, as a source. **2.** To flow forth, issue, originate, from a source 1818. **3.** *trans.* To emit, send out (*lit.* and *fig.*) (*rare*) 1797.

1. His destruction..emanating from himself LAMB. 2. Fissures..from which mephitic vapours emanated LYELL.

Emanation (emănēⁱ·ʃən). 1570. [ad. L. *emanationem*; see prec.] **1.** The process of flowing forth, issuing, or proceeding from as a source (*lit.* and *fig.*). **b.** The action of emitting. Cf. EMANATE *v.* 3. 1742. **2.** That which emanates; an efflux; *spec.* a beam, flash, ray of light 1646. Also *fig.* **3.** A person or thing produced by emanation from the Divine Essence 1650.

1. The E. of the Son BURNET. The pantheistic doctrine of e. 1880. 2. The powerful emanations of the loadstone GOLDSM. Gaseous emanations 1836. A direct e. from the first principles of morals MILL.

Hence **Emana·tional** *a.* pertaining to the theory of e., as dist. from creation.

E·manatist. *rare.* 1838. [f. L. *emanat-* (see EMANATE *v.*).] A believer in EMANATION. Hence **E:manati·stic** *a.*

Emanative (e·mănětiv), *a.* 1651. [as if ad. L. **emanativus.*] **1.** Tending to emanate (see EMANATE *v.* 1-3); of the nature of an emanation; due to emanation. **2.** Relating to or connected with the theory of EMANATION 1839. Hence **E·manatively** *adv.*

Emanatory (e·mănătəri), *a.* 1659. [as if ad. L. **emanatorius.*] **a.** Derivative. **b.** Pertaining to the theory of EMANATION.

Emancipate (ɪ̆mæ·nsipět), *ppl. a.* 1605. [ad. L. *emancipatus*; see next.] = EMANCIPATED. Now usu. *poet.*

Emancipate (ɪ̆mæ·nsipeⁱt), *v.* 1625. [f. L. *emancipat-*, ppl. stem of *emancipare*, f. (ult.) *e*+*manus*+*capere.*] **1.** *trans.* In *Rom. Law*: To set free (a child or wife) from the *patria potestas* 1651. **2.** *gen.* To set free from control; to release from civil, moral, or intellectual restraint 1625. Also *transf.* and *fig.* †**3.** To deliver into subjection; to enslave (because emancipation in Rom. Law was effected by fictitious sale) -1752.

1. The Son discharged from Paternal Power is emancipated MAINE. 2. Emancipated from our civil disabilities HT. MARTINEAU. Emancipated from modern Puritanism KINGSLEY. Hence **Ema:ncipative** *a.* that has the property of emancipating. **Ema·ncipator**, one who emancipates (*lit.* and *fig.*). **Ema·ncipato:ry** *a.* that has the function or the effect of emancipating.

Emancipation (ɪ̆mæ:nsipēⁱ·ʃən). 1631. [a. F., ad. L. *emancipationem*; see prec.] **1.** *Rom. Law.* The action of setting free from the *patria potestas* 1651. **2.** The action of setting free from slavery; and hence, generally, from civil disabilities 1797. Also *transf.* and *fig.* of intellectual, moral, or spiritual fetters 1631.

2. The e. of the Catholicks BURKE. The national e. from superstition T. WARTON.

Hence **Ema:ncipa·tionist**, an advocate of the e. of any class, *esp.* of slaves.

Emancipist (ɪ̆mæ·nsipist). *Australian.* 1834. [f. EMANCIPATE + -IST.] An ex-convict, who has served his term.

Emandibulate (ɪ̆mæ̆ndi·biŭlět), *ppl. a.* 1826. [f. E- *pref.*+L. *mandibulum.*] *Entom.* Destitute of mandibles.

†**Ema·ne**, *v.* 1656. [ad. F. *émaner.*] = EMANATE *v.* -1817.

Emarcid (ɪ̆mā·ɹsid), *a.* 1661. [f. L. *e*+*marcidus* withered.] †**1.** Drooping, limp (*rare*). **2.** *Bot.* Withered, flaccid, wilted. (Dicts.)

Emarginate (ɪ̆mā·ɹdʒinět), *a.* 1794. [ad. L. *emarginatus*; see next.] **1.** Notched at the margin, as a leaf, shell, etc. **2.** *Crystall.* Having the edges of the primitive form cut off.

Emarginate (ɪ̆mā·ɹdʒineⁱt), *v.* 1656. [f. L. *emarginat-*, *emarginare* to remove the edge.] **1.** *trans.* To remove the margin of. **2.** *Optics.* Of the effects of unequal refraction: To double the contour lines of (an object embedded, *e.g.* in a jelly) 1881. Hence **Ema:rgina·tion**, the state of being emarginate.

Emasculate (ɪ̆mæ·skiŭlět), *a.* (quasi-*sb.*) 1622. [ad. L. *emasculatus*; see next.] Emasculated.

Emasculate (ɪ̆mæ·skiŭleⁱt), *v.* 1607. [f. L. *emasculat-*, *emasculare*, f. *e*+*masculus*, dim. of *mas* male.] **1.** *trans.* To deprive of virility, to castrate 1623. **2.** *transf.* and *fig.* To deprive of strength and vigour; to weaken, make effeminate; to enfeeble 1607. **b.** *esp.* To take the vigour out of (literary compositions) by removing what is indecorous 1756. †**3.** To turn woman. SIR T. BROWNE.

2. b. I .. consented to e. my poems KINGSLEY. Hence **Ema·sculator.** (Dicts.) **Ema·sculato:ry** *a.* that tends to emasculation.

Emasculation (ɪ̆mæ:skiŭlēⁱ·ʃən). 1623. [f. L. *emasculare*; see prec.] **1.** The action of depriving of virility; the state of impotence. **2.** *fig.* The depriving of masculine vigour; prudish expurgation of a literary work 1654.

Embace, obs. var. of EMBASE.

Embale (embēⁱ·l), *v.* 1727. [See EN-. Cf. F. *emballer.*] To do up into bales; also *fig.* So †**Emba·ll** *v.*[1] HAKLUYT.

Emball (embǭ·l), *v.*[2] 1580. [f. EN- + BALL *sb.*] **1.** *trans.* To encompass with a sphere. **2.** To invest with the ball as an emblem of royalty. (Or ?indecent.) *Hen. VIII*, II. iii. 47.

Embalm (embā·m), *v.* [ME. *enbaume*, a. F. *embaumer*, f. *en-* (see EN-)+*baume.*] **1.** To impregnate (a dead body) with spices, to preserve it from decay. **2.** *fig.* To preserve from oblivion; to keep in honoured remembrance 1675. **3.** †**a.** To anoint with aromatic spices, oil, etc. **b.** To make balmy. ME.

1. They imbalmed him and he was put in a coffin in Egypt *Gen.* l. 26. 2. That..elegance of language in which he has embalmed so many BOSWELL. 3. The buxom air, imbalm'd with odours MILT. *P. L.* II. 842. Hence **Emba·lmer**, he who or that which embalms; *esp.* one who embalms dead bodies. **Emba·lmment**, the act of embalming; a preparation used for this.

Embank (embæ·ŋk), *v.* Also **im-**. 1649. [f. EN- + BANK *sb.*[1]] **1.** *trans.* To enclose, confine, or protect by banks 1700. †**2.** *intr.* Of a ship: To run aground 1649. **3.** To cover with embankments 1872.

Embankment[1] (embæ·ŋkměnt). 1786. [f. prec. + -MENT.] **1.** The action of embanking 1874. **2.** A mound, bank, or the like, for confining a river, etc. within bounds 1786. **3.** A long earthen bank or mound 1810.

3. A vast e., over which the canal is carried 1810.

†**Emba·nkment**[2]. *rare.* 1813. [f. EM- + BANK *sb.*[3] + -MENT.] A banking speculation; a bank account.

‖**Embaphium** (embæ·fiŏm). 1715. [mod.L., ad. Gr. ἐμβάφιον.] *Med.* A small vessel in which food or medicine is put or measured, or in which it is dipped.

Embar (embā·ɹ), *v.* 1480. [ad. F. *embarrer*, f. *en-* (see EN-)+*barre.*] **1.** *trans.* To enclose within bars; to imprison. Also *fig.* (*arch.*) 1594. **2.** To arrest, stop; to interrupt. ?*Obs.* 1577. †**b.** *Law.* = BAR *v.* -1599. †**3.** To debar *from* an action -1603. †**4.** To lay under embargo -1649. †**5.** To break in the bars of (a helmet). CAXTON.

1. Fast embar'd in mighty brazen wall SPENSER *F. Q.* I. vii. 44. 2. To e. all farther trade for the future BACON. Hence †**Emba·rment.**

‖**Embarcade·ro.** *rare.* 1850. [Sp., f. *embarcar.*] A wharf, quay.

Embarcation, var. of EMBARKATION.

†**Emba·rge**, *sb.* 1574. [ad. Sp. *embargo.*] = EMBARGO -1656.

†**Emba·rge**, *v.* 1600. [f. prec. sb.] *trans.* To lay under an embargo; to sequestrate; to arrest -1657. Hence †**Emba·rgement.**

Embargo (embā·ɹgo), *sb.* 1602. [a. Sp., f. *embargar*, f. (ult.) *in-* (see IN-)+*barra* BAR.] **1.** A prohibitory order, forbidding the ships within a country's ports to sail; generally issued in anticipation of war. **2.** A suspension of commerce, either general or particular, imposed by municipal law 1658. **3.** *transf.* and *fig.* A prohibition, impediment 1692.

1. An e. ..is daily expected 1758. 2. An e. on the export of provisions MAY.

Embargo (embā·ɹgo), *v.* 1650. [f. prec. sb.] **1.** To forbid (a vessel) to leave a port; to lay under an embargo 1755. Also *fig.* **2.** To requisition for the service of the state 1755. **3.** To seize, confiscate 1650.

Embark (embā·ɹk), *v.* 1550. [ad. F. *embarquer*:—late L. *imbarcare*, f. *in-* (see IN-) + *barca* BARK *sb.*[2]] **1.** *trans.* **a.** To put on board ship. **b.** Of the ship: To take on board. **2.** *transf.* and *fig.* 1584. **3.** *intr.* (for *refl.*) To go on board ship (*lit.* and *fig.*) 1580. **4.** To engage *in* a business or undertaking 1649.

1. b. The Osborne will..e. the Prince 1885. 2. To e. money in an ironwork HT. MARTINEAU. 3. A restless impulse urged him to e. SHELLEY. 4. To e. in the most disastrous of wars ROGERS.

Embarkation (embaɹkēⁱ·ʃən). 1645. [a. F. *embarcation*; see prec.] **1.** Embarking. †**2.** *concr.* A body of troops embarked -1757. †**3.** A vessel, boat. [Cf. F. *embarcation.*] -1807.

1. The E. of the Army CLARENDON. 2. Another and much greater e. followed BURKE. So †**Emba·rkage. Emba·rkment** (in sense 1), now *rare.*

Embarque, obs. var. of EMBARK.

Emba·rras, *sb.* 1664. [a. F., rel. to F. *embarrer*, f. *en-* (see EN-[1]) + *barre.*] **1.** Embarrassment. Now only as F. (aṅbara) in phr. *e. de choix*, *e. de richesse* so much choice, wealth, as to be embarrassing. **2.** *U.S.* A place in a river made difficult by accumulation of driftwood 1814.

Embarrass (embæ·răs), *v.* 1672. [ad. F. *embarrasser*, lit. 'to obstruct'; see prec.] **1.** To encumber, hamper, impede (movements, actions, persons) 1683. **b.** *pass.* Of persons: To be encumbered with debts; to be 'in difficulties'. **2.** To perplex (in thought) 1672. **3.** To render difficult; to complicate (a question, etc.) 1736.

1. The state of the rivers..will e. the enemy WELLINGTON. 2. Such a circumstance may e. an operator TRAVERS. 3. This case will [not] be embarrassed by that decision CRUISE. Hence **Emba·rrassedly, Emba·rrassingly** *advs.*

Embarrassment (embæ·răsmĕnt). 1676. [f. EMBARRASS + -MENT.] **1.** Embarrassed state or condition, *esp.* of pecuniary affairs, circumstances, etc. **b.** Perplexity, confusion of thought; hesitation; constraint arising from bashfulness or timidity 1774. **2.** Something which embarrasses. In *pl.* often = 'pecuniary difficulties'. 1729.

1. A state of e. and threatened bankruptcy BRIGHT. 2. There was e. on the maiden's part SCOTT. 2. The embarrassments of that humble household TRENCH.

Embarrel; see EM- *prefix* and BARREL.

†**Emba·rren**, *v.* 1627. [See EN-.] *trans.* To make barren -1808.

†**Em:barrica·do**, *v.* 1603. [f. Sp. *embarricado* sb.] = BARRICADE *v.* -1630.

†**Embase** (embē¹·s), *v.* 1551. [f. EN- + Fr. *bas*, BASE *a.*] **1.** To lower in position or direction -1644. Also *fig.* **2.** To lower in rank, condition, etc.; to humiliate; to degrade. Also *refl.* -1820. **3.** To depreciate (*lit.* and *fig.*) -1698. **4.** To debase (coin) by a mixture of alloy (*lit.* and *fig.*) -1752.

1. When God..Embast the Valleys and embost the Hills SYLVESTER. 2. It is..selfishness that 'embases and embrutes' L. HUNT. 4. It will imbase even the purest metal in man FELTHAM. Hence †**Emba·sement**.

Embassade (embăsē¹·d). ? *Obs.* 1480. [Occas. var. of AMBASSADE, q. v.] **1.** = AMBASSADE 1-3. **2.** quasi-*adv.* On an embassy (*rare*) 1525.

Embassador (embæ·sădəɪ). Var. of AMBASSADOR; now *obs.* in England, but in U.S. still preferred. Cf. EMBASSY. So **Embassadorial** *a.* ambassadorial. †**Embassadress**, ambassadress. †**Embassadry**, ambassadry.

Embassage (e·mbăsĕdʒ). *arch.* 1526. [var. (freq. in mod. archaistic use) of AMBASSAGE, q.v. In ordinary use repl. by EMBASSY.] = EMBASSY 1-3.

Carneades the philosopher came in e. to Rome BACON.

†**Emba·ssiate**. ME. only. [var. of AMBASSIATE, q. v.] = EMBASSY.

Embassy (e·mbăsi). 1579. [A var. (now the prevailing form) of AMBASSY, q.v.] **1.** The function or position of an ambassador; also, the sending of ambassadors. **2.** Hence †**a.** The message or business; **b.** The official residence, of an ambassador. 1595. **3.** The ambassador and his retinue, with their surroundings 1671.

3. Embassies from regions far remote MILT.

Embastardize, mod. var. of IMBASTARDIZE.

Embathe, imbathe (em-, imbē¹·ð), *v. poet.* 1593. [f. EN-, IN- + BATHE.] To bathe, immerse; to bedew, drench.

Embattle (em-, imbæ·t'l), *v.*¹ [ME. *embataile*, a. OF. *embataillier*, f. *en-* (see EN-) + *bataille* BATTLE *sb.*¹] **1.** *trans.* To set in battle array. Also (Spenser) to arm (an individual) for battle. ME. Also *fig.* **2.** *refl.* To form in order of battle 1450. Also †*intr.* for *refl.* **3.** = EMBATTLE *v.*² Also *fig.* ME.

1. One in bright armes embatteiled full strong SPENSER *F. Q.* II. v. 2. As a General..mustereth and embattaileth his troops BARROW. 3. Fear builds castles and embattles cities 1830.

Embattle (embæ·t'l), *v.*² ME. [f. EN- + BATTLE *v.*²; app. not in OF.] *trans.* To furnish with battlements.

Licenses to e. manor-houses 1851. Hence †**Emba·ttle** *sb.*, **Emba·ttlement** = BATTLEMENT.

Embattled (embæ·t'ld), *ppl. a.*¹ 1475. [f. EMBATTLE *v.*¹] **1.** Drawn up in battle array, marshalled for battle. Also *transf.* and *fig.* **2.** Covered with troops in battle array. Also *fig.* 1593. **3.** Fortified 1765.

1. Bondage threatened by the e. East WORDSW. The embattled legions of ignorance HALLAM. 2. Castor glorious on th' e. plain POPE.

Embattled (embæ·t'ld), *ppl. a.*² ME. [f. EMBATTLE *v.*²] **1.** *Arch.* Furnished with battlements, crenellated. **2.** Having an edge shaped like a battlement; crenellated; *spec.* in *Her.* ME.

1. An embatelid Waulle now sore yn ruine LELAND. 2. His comb..Enbateled as it were a castel wall CHAUCER.

Embay (embē¹·), *v.*¹ 1583. [f. EM- + BAY *sb.*²] **1.** *trans.* To lay within a bay. Also, To force into or detain within a bay. 1600. **2.** To enclose (as in a bay); to shut in; also *fig.*

1. He found himself embayed within a mighty head of land C. MATHER. 2. Embayed by the ice COOK.

†**Embay·**, *v.*² *poet.* 1590. [f. EN- *pref.* + BAY *v.* to bathe.] *trans.* To bathe; hence, to drench. Also *fig.* -1762.

fig. In the warme sunne he doth himselfe e. SPENSER.

Embayment (embē¹·mĕnt). 1815. [f. EMBAY *v.*¹ + -MENT.] **1.** The action of forming into a bay; *concr.* a bay. **2.** A bay-like recess 1848.

2. The deep e. of her favourite window 1848.

†**Embeam** (embī·m), *v.* 1610. [f. EN- + BEAM *sb.*] *trans.* To cast beams upon, irradiate -1652.

Embed, imbed (em-, imbe·d). 1778. [f. EN-, IN- + BED *sb.* (*Embed* is now usual.)] **1.** *trans.* To fix firmly in a surrounding mass of material. Also *fig.* and *transf.* **2.** Said of the surrounding mass: To enclose firmly. Also *fig.* 1853.

1. Insects..imbedded in the gum-copal LIVINGSTONE. *transf.* Nemi, imbedded in wood, Nemi inurned in the hill CLOUGH. Hence **Embe·dment**, the action of embedding; embedded state; *concr.* something which embeds.

†**E·mbelif**. ME. [a. OF. phr. *en belif* (:-late L. type **bis-liquus* = *obliquus*).] **a.** *adv.* Obliquely. CHAUCER. **b.** *adj.* Oblique -1413.

Embellish (embe·liʃ), *v.* ME. [a. OF. *embelliss-*, stem of *embellir*, f. *en-* (see EN-) + *bel* beautiful.] **a.** To render beautiful (*obs.* in gen. sense). **b.** To beautify with adventitious ornaments; to ornament. **c.** *fig.* Often = to dress up (a narration) with fictitious additions 1447.

b. Bridles..embellished with bits of yellow gold STRUTT. c. Events..probably..much..embellished 1801. Hence **Embe·llisher**.

Embe·llishment. 1623. [f. prec. + -MENT.] **1.** The action or process of embellishing; decoration, adornment. **2.** That which embellishes or beautifies (*lit.* and *fig.*); an ornament, decoration; also, an exaggeration.

1. They might not tend to the E. of my paper ADDISON. 2. Abatement is made for poetical embellishments FULLER.

Ember¹ (e·mbəɪ). [OE. *ǣmerge* wk. fem., corresp. to OHG. *eimuria*, ON. *eimyrja* (Da. *emmer*) :—OTeut. **aimuzjôn-*. The *b* is euphonic.] A small piece of live coal or wood in a smouldering fire. Chiefly in *pl.*: The smouldering ashes of a fire. Also *fig.*

They heat it [flesh] a little upon imbers of coales HAKLUYT. Hence **E·mbered** *ppl. a.* strewn with, or burnt to, embers.

Ember² (e·mbəɪ). Now only *attrib.* and in *Comb.* [OE. *ymbren* (app. neut.: pl. *ymbren*), perh. a corruption of OE. *ymbryne* masc., period, revolution of time, f. *ymb* round + *ryne* running.] The English name of the four periods of fasting and prayer (L. *quatuor tempora*) in the four seasons of the year. Each of these occupies three days, called *E. days*, and the weeks in which they occur are called *E. weeks*. The Council of Placentia (A.D. 1095) appointed for Ember days the Wednesday, Friday, and Saturday next following (1) the first Sunday in Lent, (2) Whitsunday, (3) 14 Sept., (4) 13 Dec.

†1. As *sb.*; = *E.-day* -1573. 2. *attrib.* and *Comb.*, as *e.-day*, *-fast*, *-tide*, etc.; **e.-eve**, the vigil of an E. day OE. var. **E·mbering**.

Ember³. Also **imber, immer, emmer**, etc. 1744. [a. Norw. *emmer(-gaas)*.] A variety (*Colymbus Immer*) of the Northern Diver or Loon (*Colymbus glacialis*) to which the name is sometimes given. Chiefly in Comb., as *e.-goose*, etc.

†**Embe·tter**, *v.* 1583. [f. EN- + BETTER *a.*] To make better -1680.

Embezzle (embe·z'l), *v.* 1469. [ad. AF. *enbesiler*, f. *en-* + *besiler* = OF. *besillier* to destroy; ? f. L. *bis-*, in late L. used as a pejorative prefix (Paul Meyer). In 16th c. referred to the L. *imbecillare* to weaken.] †**1.** *trans.* To make away with; *esp.* to carry off secretly for one's own use -1750. †**b.** To mutilate, tamper with (a document, etc.) -1691. †**2.** To impair, diminish -1670; to squander -1770. **3.** To divert to one's own use in violation of trust or official duty. (The only current sense.) 1585.

1. b. To imbezill or corrupt a Record 1671. 2. He hath embeazled his estate BURTON. 3. Bellasys, the English General, embezzled the stores MACAULAY. Hence **Embe·zzler**.

Embezzlement (embe·z'lmĕnt). 1548. [f. prec. + -MENT.] The action of embezzling. †**a.** In senses of EMBEZZLE 1, 2. **b.** Fraudulent appropriation of property entrusted to one.

Fraud, peculation, and e. BURKE.

†**Embi·llow**, *v. rare.* 1625. [f. EN- + BILLOW.] *trans.* To raise in billows.

Embind (embəi·nd), *v.* Also **im-**. 1628. [f. EN- + BIND.] *trans.* To confine, hold fast.

Embitter (embi·təɪ), *v.* Also **im-**. 1603. [f. EN- + BITTER *a.*] **1.** *trans.* To make bitter. Now *rare* in *lit.* sense. Also *fig.* **2.** *fig.* To make more bitter or painful 1642. **3.** *fig.* To render virulent, intensely hostile, or discontented; to exacerbate 1634.

1. Brewers e. their beer with hops 1834. *fig.* It would e. all the sweets of life STEELE. 2. His actual misery was embittered by the recollection of past greatness GIBBON. 3. To e. Peoples minds one against another BURNET.

Hence **Embi·tterer**. **Embi·tterment**, the action of embittering; embittered state.

†**Embla·dder**, *v. rare.* 1662. [f. EN- + BLADDER.] **a.** To blister. **b.** To confine in a bladder 1664.

†**Embla·nch**, *v.* ME. [a. OF. *emblanchir*, f. *en-* + *blanc*.] *trans.* To whiten (*fig.*) -1662.

Emblaze (emblē¹·z), *v.*¹ Also **im-**. 1634. [f. EN- + BLAZE *sb.*¹] **1.** *trans.* To light up, cause to glow. **2.** To set in a blaze. Also *fig.* 1728.

1. Th' unsought Diamonds .. e. the forehead of the Deep MILT. *Comus* 733. 2. Where nearer suns e. its veins COLLINS.

Emblaze (emblē¹·z), *v.*² Also **im-**. 1522. [f. EN- + BLAZE *v.*²] †**1. a.** *trans.* To describe heraldically. **b.** To set forth by means of heraldic devices. -1781. **2.** To adorn with heraldic devices. Hence, to make resplendent. 1522. **3.** To inscribe conspicuously 1590. **4.** To celebrate, render famous or infamous 1596.

2. With crowns of gold emblased SKELTON. 3. Where stout Hercules Emblaz'd his trophies on two posts of brass GREENE. Hence **Embla·zer**.

Emblazon (emblē¹·zən), *v.* 1592. [f. EN- + BLAZON *v.*] **1.** *trans.* To inscribe or portray conspicuously, as on a heraldic shield; to adorn *with* heraldic devices, words, etc. (*lit.* and *fig.*). Occas. influenced by EMBLAZE *v.*¹ 1593. **2.** To celebrate, extol; to render illustrious.

1. God..emblazond the aire with the tokens of his terror NASHE. 2. Heraulds to emblazen his Progresse GAULE.

Hence **Embla·zoner**. **Embla·zonment**, the action of EMBLAZON *v.*; *concr.* that which is emblazoned.

Emblazonry (emblē¹·zənri). 1667. [f. prec. vb. + -RY.] **1.** The art of emblazoning; *concr.* heraldic devices collectively. **2.** Display of gorgeous colours; brilliant representation or embellishment (*lit.* and *fig.*) 1805.

1. With bright imblazonrie, and horrent Arms MILT. 2. The Sun..with his gold-purple e. CARLYLE.

Emblem (e·mblĕm), *sb.* Also **embleme**. ME. [OF. *embleme*, ad. L. *emblema*, a. Gr. ἔμβλημα a thing put on, f. ἐμβάλλειν to throw in, on.] †**1.** An ornament of inlaid work -1775. †**2.** A drawing or picture expressing a moral fable or allegory; a fable or allegory such as might be expressed pictorially -1736. **3.** An object, or a picture of one, representing symbolically an abstract quality, an action, a class of persons, etc. 1601. **b.** In wider sense: A symbol, type 1631. **4.** A figured object used symbolically, as a badge 1616.

2. An E. is but a silent parable QUARLES. 3. His sicatrice an E. of warre heere on his sinister cheeke *All's Well* II. i. 44. b. The evening is an e. of autumn JOHNSON. 4. National emblems—a crescent, a lion, an eagle..on an old rag of bunting EMERSON.

Emblem (e·mblĕm), *v.* 1584. [f. prec.] *trans.* To be the emblem of; to express, symbolize, suggest.

All Christianism..is emblemed here CARLYLE.

Emblematic, -al (emblĕmæ·tik, -ăl), *a.* 1644. [f. Gr. ἐμβληματ- (ἔμβλημα).] Pertaining to, of the nature of, or serving as, an emblem; symbolical, typical.

Clothes .. are Emblematic .. of a manifold cunning Victory over Want CARLYLE. Hence **Emblema·tically** *adv.* **Emblema·ticize** *v.* to impart an e. character to (*rare*).

Emblematist (emble·mătist). 1646. [f. as prec. + -IST.] One who delineates or writes emblems.

Emblematize (emble·mătəiz), *v.* 1615. [f.

as prec. + -IZE.] 1. *trans.* To serve as an emblem of. 2. Of persons: To represent by means of an emblem 1830.

1. The goose and little goslings should e. a Quaker poet that has no children LAMB.

Emblement (e·mblĭmĕnt). 1495. [a. OF. *emblaement*, f. *emblaer* (mod.F. *emblaver*) to sow with corn :—med.L. *imbladare*, f. *in* + *bladum* (= F. *blé*).] *Law.* 'The profits of sown land'; occas. used more largely for grass, fruit, etc.

†**Emble·mish**, *v.* ME. [f. EN- + BLEMISH.] *trans.* To damage, injure; also, to deface -1671.

Emblemize (e·mblĕməiz), *v.* 1646. [f. EMBLEM + -IZE.] *trans.* To represent emblematically. So †**E·mblemist** = EMBLEMATIST.

†**Embli·ss**, *v. rare.* ME. [See EN-.] To make happy -1797.

†**Embloo·m**, *v.* 1528. [See EN-.] To cover with bloom -1729.

Emblossom, im- (em-, imblǫ·səm), *v.* 1766. [See EN-.] To load or cover with blossoms.

Embodiment, im- (em-, imbǫ·dimĕnt). 1828. [f. EMBODY *v.* + -MENT.] 1. The action of embodying; embodied state (*lit.* and *fig.*) 1858. 2. *concr.* That in which anything is embodied; the 'vesture' *of* (a soul); the concrete expression (of an idea, a principle, etc.); the incarnation (of a quality, sentiment, etc.).

2. Works of art..the visible e. of the divine JOWETT.

Embody, im- (em-, imbǫ·di), *v.* 1548. [f. EN-, IN- + BODY *sb.* The form *embody* is now usual.] 1. *trans.* To put into a body. 2. To give a material or concrete character or form to 1634. 3. To unite into one body; to incorporate 1601. †4. *Chem.*, etc. a. *trans.* To form into one body. b. *intr.* for *refl.* To draw together, solidify. -1710. 5. *intr.* (for *refl.*) To form or join a body or company 1648.

1. A pale, small person, scarcely embodied at all HAWTHORNE. 2. The custom having been embodied in law GROTE. 3. Livius..embodied the population of the town ARNOLD. The measure embodies..the six points..of the charter 1869. 5. [He] commanded the Horse to E. within the Lines 1681. Hence **Embo·dier.**

Embog (embǫ·g), *v.* Also **embogue.** 1602. [f. EN- + BOG *sb.*] *trans.* To plunge into a bog.

†**Embo·gue**, *v.* 1603. [? corrupt ad. Sp. *embocar*, f. *em-* + *boca* mouth.] = DISEMBOGUE. Hence †**Embo·guing** *vbl. sb.* the place where a lake or river discharges its waters.

†**Emboi·l**, *v.* [f. EN- + BOIL.] *trans.* To cause to boil with rage; *intr.* to be in a boil. SPENSER.

‖**Emboîtement** (aṅbwatmaṅ). 1854. [Fr.; f. *emboîter*, f. *en-* + *boîte* box.] 1. *Anat.* The fitting of a bone into another. 2. *Biol.* Buffon's term for the hypothesis that successive generations proceed from germs, and contain the germs of all future generations. 3. The closing up of a number of men in order to secure the front rank from injury. (Dicts.)

Embolden, im- (em-, imbōu·ldən), *v.* 1571. [f. EN-, IN- + BOLD + -EN.] To render bold or more bold; to incite, encourage.

Thus I embold'nd spake MILT. *P. L.* VIII. 434. So †**Embo·ld** *v.* Hence **Embo·ldener.**

‖**Embole** (e·mbŏlī). 1811. [mod.L., a. Gr. ἐμβολή a putting in.] *Med.* †1. The reducing of a dislocated limb. 2. A plug or wedge (*Syd. Soc. Lex.*). 3. = EMBOLUS (*Syd. Soc. Lex.*).

Embolic (embǫ·lik), *a.* 1866. [f. EMBOLUS + -IC.] *Path.* Relating to or caused by an embolus.

†**Embolimæ·al**, *a. rare.* 1677. [f. Gr. ἐμβολιμαῖος (cf. EMBOLISM) + -AL.] Intercalary. So †**Embolimæ·an, -ar.**

Embolism (e·mbŏliz'm). ME. [ad. L. *embolismus*, a. late Gr. ἐμβολισμός; cf. EMBOLE, EMBOLUS.] 1. *Chronol.* An intercalation or insertion of a day or days in the calendar, to complete a period. *concr.* The time intercalated. 2. *Path.* The occlusion of a blood-vessel by an embolus 1855.

1. The year of the Mahometans consists of twelve lunar months..no e. being employed to adjust it to the solar period MARSDEN.

Hence †**Emboli·smal, Emboli·smic** *adjs.* that pertains to e.; intercalary.

‖**Embolismus** (embŏli·zmŏs). ME. [L.; see prec.] †1. *Chronol.* a. The excess of the solar over the lunar year of twelve synodical months. b. Intercalation. -1796. 2. In the Gr. liturgy: A prayer inserted after the concluding petitions of the Lord's Prayer. SHIPLEY.

Embolite (e·mbŏləit). 1850. [f. Gr. ἐμβόλιον a thing inserted + -ITE; 'because between the chlorid and bromid of silver' (Dana).] *Min.* A chloro-bromide of silver, $Ag_5Br_2Cl_3$. Also *attrib.*

‖**Embolon** (e·mbŏlǫn). 1878. [Gr.] *Path.* = EMBOLUS 2.

‖**Embolus** (e·mbŏlŏs). 1669. [L., a. Gr. ἔμβολος peg, stopper.] †1. *Mech.* Something inserted, as a wedge; *esp.* the piston of a syringe -1739. 2. *Path.* 'The body which causes EMBOLISM' (*Syd. Soc. Lex.*). 3. *Anat.* 'The osseous axis of the horns of the *Ruminantia cavicornia*' (*Syd. Soc. Lex.*).

Emboly (e·mbŏli). 1877. [f. stem of Gr. ἐμβάλλειν.] = INVAGINATION: a. *Surg.* A particular operation for hernia. b. *Phys.* The process of formation of the *gastrula* by involution of the wall of the single-layered segmented ovum.

‖**Embonpoint** (aṅbǫnpwaṅ). 1751. [Fr.; OF. *en bon point* 'in good condition'.]

A. *sb.* Plumpness (*complimentary* or *euphemistic*).

B. as predicative *adj.* Plump, of well-nourished appearance 1806.

†**Embo·rder**, *v.* Also **im-.** 1530. [See EN-.] a. To furnish with a border; to edge. b. To set as a border. -1667.

Embosom, im- (em-, imbu·zəm), *v.* 1590. [f. EN-, IN- + BOSOM.] 1. *trans.* To take to, or place in, the bosom; to cherish; to embrace. Chiefly *fig.* Now *rare.* 2. *transf.* To enclose, conceal, shelter, in the bosom. †b. *refl.* Of a river: To pour itself *into* the bosom. 1685.

1. Anger rests Embosom'd..in foolish brests QUARLES. 2. My..home Which oaks e. SHENSTONE. Deep sleep embosometh their jaded limbs SINGLETON.

†**Embo·ss**, *sb.* [f. EMBOSS *v.*[1]] A boss-like projection. EVELYN.

Emboss (embǫ·s), *v.*[1] ME. [prob. a. OF. **embocer*; see EN- and BOSS *sb.*[1]] 1. *trans.* To cause to bulge; to cover with protuberances 1460. 2. *spec.* To carve or mould in relief. Also *fig.* (The prevailing mod. sense.) ME. b. To adorn with figures, etc. in relief; to represent in relief. Also of the figures, etc.: To stand out as an ornament upon. ME. 3. To ornament with or as with bosses; hence, to decorate sumptuously 1578.

1. Botches and blaines must all his flesh imboss MILT. *P. L.* XII. 180. 2. Fleur-de-lis embossed out of the stone EVELYN. b. The rich bronze which embossed its gates PRESCOTT. 3. Berries that imboss the bramble COWPER.

Hence **Embo·sser. Embo·ssing** *vbl. sb.* the action of the vb., as in *e.-press*, etc.

Embo·ss, *v.*[2] [ME. *embose*, perh. f. EN- + OF. *bos, bois* wood, and (ult.) identical with IMBOSK *v.*] †1. *intr.* To plunge into a wood or thicket -1680. †2. To drive (a hunted animal) to extremity -1768. †3. In *pass.* To be exhausted; *hence*, to foam at the mouth -1651. 4. *trans.* To cover with foam (*arch.*) 1531.

4. Embossed with foam..The labouring Stag strained full in view SCOTT.

†**Embo·ss**, *v.*[3] 1590. [perh. f. EN- + BOSS *sb.*[3]] *trans.* To encase (in armour); to plunge (a weapon) *in* an enemy's body. Also *fig.* in *pass.* To be wrapped (in ease). -1621.

Embossed (embǫ·st), *ppl. a.* ME. [f. EMBOSS *v.*[1]] 1. Carved or moulded in relief, etc. (see EMBOSS *v.*[1]) 1541. 2. Covered with bosses; richly decorated 1591. †3. Humpbacked. ME. only. †4. Bulging, swollen; *fig.* of style -1646. 5. *Bot.* 'Projecting in the centre like the boss of a shield' (*Syd. Soc. Lex.*).

1. The e. alphabet for the blind 1849. 4. 1 *Hen. IV*, III. iii. 177.

Embossment (embǫ·smĕnt). 1610. [f. as prec. + -MENT.] †1. The action of embossing 1801. 2. *concr.* A figure carved or moulded in relief; embossed ornament. Now *rare.* Also *attrib.*, as in *e.-map*, 1620. 3. *gen.* A bulging 1610. So **Embo·sture** [after *sculpture*].

Embottle; see EM- *pref.* and BOTTLE *sb.*

‖**Embouchement** (aṅbuʃmaṅ, embū·ʃmĕnt). 1844. [Fr.; see next.] a. The mouth (of a river). b. *Phys.* The point at which one vessel leads into another.

‖**Embouchure** (aṅbuʃür). 1760. [Fr.; f. *emboucher* to put in or to the mouth, f. *en-* + *bouche.*] 1. The mouth of a river or creek. Also *transf.* of a valley. 1792. 2. *Mus.* The mouthpiece of a wind instrument 1834. 3. *Mus.* 'The disposition of the lips, tongue, and other organs necessary for producing a musical tone' (Grove).

Embound, im- (em-, imbau·nd), *v. poet. arch.* 1595. [f. EN-, IN- + BOUND *sb.*] *trans.* To set bounds to; to confine.

Embow (embōu·), *v.* ME. [f. EN- + BOW *sb.*[1]] 1. To bend or curve into a bow. 2. *Arch.* To arch, vault 1481. 3. To englobe, encircle 1605.

2. The pillared vestibule..the roof embowed WORDSW. Hence **Embow·ed** *ppl. a.* bent into a bow; *Her.* bent or curved; *Arch.* arched, vaulted; also, projecting outward, as in a bow-window. †**Embow·ment**, vaulting BACON.

Embowel (embau·ĕl), *v.* 1521. [In sense 1, ad. OF. *enboweler*, var. of OF. *esboueler*, f. *es-* (= L. *ex-*) + *bouel* BOWEL. In sense 2, f. EN- + BOWEL.] 1. *trans.* = DISEMBOWEL. Also *transf.* and *fig.* †2. To put, convey into the bowels. Usu. *transf.* and *fig.* -1634.

1. Imbowell'd will I see thee by and by 1 *Hen. IV*, v. iv. 109. W[ch] made me..send for a chirurgeon from York to e. him 1640. 2. All was embowelled and enwombed in the waters DONNE. Hence **Embow·eller. Embow·elment**, the action of disembowelling; the inward parts of a thing.

Embower, im- (em-, imbauə·ɹ, -bau·əɹ), *v.* 1580. [f. EN-, IN- + BOWER *sb.*[1]] 1. To shelter, enclose, as in a bower; also *absol.* †2. *intr.* for *refl.* To lodge as in a bower -1610.

1. Him..Whom Sion holds embowered SIDNEY. 2. Small Birds in their wide boughs embowring SPENSER. Hence **Embow·erment**, the action of embowering.

†**Embow·l**, *v. rare.* 1580. [f. EN- + BOWL *sb.*[1]] To make, or grow, into the form of a globe -1886.

Embox (embǫ·ks), *v.* 1611. [f. EN- + BOX *sb.*[2]] To set in or as in a box.

Embrace (embrē[i]·s), *sb.* 1592. [f. EMBRACE *v.*[2]] The action of clasping in the arms, pressing to the bosom. (Sometimes *euphem.* of sexual intercourse.) Also *transf.* and *fig.*

Armes, take your last e. *Rom. & Jul.* v. iii. 113. Pride..by whose embraces she had two daughters JOHNSON.

†**Embra·ce**, *v.*[1] *rare.* ME. [f. EN- + Fr. *bras* arm; see BRACE *sb.*[1]] To put (a shield) on the arm -1592.

Embrace (embrē[i]·s), *v.*[2] ME. [ad. OF. *embracer* to grasp in the arms :—late L. **imbracchiare*, f. *in-* + *bracchium* (pl. *bracchia*); see BRACE *sb.*[2]] 1. *trans.* To clasp in the arms, usually as a sign of affection. Used also of sexual embraces. Also *absol.* 2. *fig.* †a. To compass, gain -1475. †b. To accept as a friend -1635. c. To accept eagerly; now chiefly, to avail oneself of ME. d. To accept, submit to 1591. †e. To cultivate (a virtue, etc.) -1623. f. To adopt (a course of action, a doctrine, etc.). Formerly also, to take (a path) 1639. g. To attach oneself to (a cause, etc.) 1720. †h. To take in hand -1818. 3. To encircle; to clasp, enclose (*lit.* and *fig.*) ME. 4. To include, comprise 1697. 5. To take in with the eye or mind; also with these as subject 1831.

1. The frere..her embracith in his armes narwe CHAUCER. You will say, she did e. me as a husband *Much Ado* IV. i. 50. 2. c. E. we then this opportunitie 1 *Hen. VI*, II. i. 13. d. Thurio give backe, or else e. thy death *Two Gent.* v. iv. 126. f. To e. the monastic life FREEMAN. g. To e. the Reformed faith SMILES. 3. You'l see your Rome embrac'd with fire SHAKS. 4. To e. all the cases in a single formula (*mod.*).

Hence **Embra·ceable** *a.* inviting an embrace; so **Embra·ceably** *adv.* **Embra·ced** *ppl. a.* (*Her.*) braced or bound together. **Embra·cive** *a.* given to embracing THACKERAY.

Embrace (embrē[i]·s), *v.*[3] 1475. [app. f. EMBRACER[2].] *Law.* To attempt to influence (a jury, etc.) corruptly. Also *absol.*

†**Embra·ce**, *v.*[4] 1475. [f. EN- + BRACE *sb.*[2]] To fix with a brace; to fasten, fit close -1596.

Embracement (embrē[i]·smĕnt). 1485. [f. EMBRACE *v.* + -MENT.] 1. = EMBRACE *sb.* †2. An undertaking -1662. 3. A clasping, enclosure; also *fig.* 1599. 4. *fig.* Willing acceptance 1535.

1. After embracements and teares MILT. 4. The favorable embracement of Gods word 1535.

Embracer[1] (embrē̆ⁱ·səɹ). 1547. [f. EMBRACE *v.*[2]] One who embraces (see EMBRACE *v.*[2] 1, 2).

Embracer[2] (embrē̆ⁱ·səɹ). 1495. [a. AF., OF. *embraceor, -aseor* instigator, f. *embraser* lit. 'to set on fire'.] *Law.* One who attempts to influence a jury corruptly.

Embracery (embrē̆ⁱ·sĕri). 1450. [f. as prec.; see -RY.] *Law.* The offence of influencing a jury illegally and corruptly.

†**Embrai·d**, *v.*[1] 1481. [f. EN- + BRAID *v.*[2]] *trans.* To upbraid. Also, to taunt one with. -1582.

†**Embrai·d**, *v.*[2] 1491. [f. EN- + BRAID *v.*[1]] *trans.* **a.** To fasten on like braid. **b.** To plait; to intertwine. -1596.

Embranchment (embra·nʃmĕnt). 1830. [f. EN- + BRANCH *sb.* + -MENT.] A branching off or out, as of an arm of a river, etc.; a branch, ramification. Also *fig.*

Embrangle, im- (em-, imbræ·ŋg'l), *v.* 1664. [f. EN-, IN- + BRANGLE *v.*] *trans.* To entangle, perplex.

Embrangled in inexplicable difficulties BERKELEY. Hence **Embra·nglement.**

†**Embra·se**, *v.* 1480. [a. F. *embraser*, f. *en-* + **brase, braise* live coals.] To set on fire. Also *fig.* -1605.

†**Embra·sure**, *sb.*[1] [f. EMBRACE *v.*[2] + -URE.] = EMBRACE. Shaks.

Embrasure (embrē̆ⁱ·ʒiŭɹ), *sb.*[2] Also **embrazure.** 1702. [a. F., f. *embraser*, f. *em-* (= L. *in-*) + *braser* 'to skue or chamfret oft' (Cotgr.).] 1. A bevelling inwards of the sides of an aperture for a window or door 1753. 2. *Mil.* An opening widening from within made in an epaulement or parapet, so that a gun can be fired through it 1702. 3. *attrib.* 1809.

1. They put me in a chair in the e. of the window CARLYLE. Hence **Embra·sure** *v.* to furnish with embrasures.

Embrave (embrē̆ⁱ·v), *v.* 1579. [f. EN- + BRAVE *a.*] †1. To make brave; to adorn splendidly -1736. 2. To render courageous 1648.

The faded flowres her corse embraue SPENSER.

†**Embrea·ch**, *v.* 1581. [f. EN- + BREACH *sb.*] *intr.* To enter a breach; *trans.* to make a breach in -1610.

Embread, var. of EMBRAID *v.*[2]

Embrea·stment. [f. EN- + BREAST + -MENT.] A swelling of the ground. COLERIDGE.

Embreathe (embrī̆·ð), *v.* 1529. [f. EN- + BREATHE *v.*; cf. IMBREATHE.] 1. *trans.* To breathe *into*; to inspire *with.* Also, to give breath to. 2. To inhale (*fig.*). M. ARNOLD. Hence **Embrea·thement** (*rare*) = INSPIRATION.

Embrew, obs. f. IMBRUE.

†**Embri·ght**, *v.* 1598. [f. EN- + BRIGHT *a.*] To make bright -1766.

Embri·ghten, *v.* 1610. [f. as prec. + -EN.] = BRIGHTEN.

†**Embroca·do**, *v.* [f. EN- + *brocado* = BROCADE, q.v.] ?To adorn with or as with brocade. FELTHAM.

Embrocate (e·mbrŏkeⁱt), *v.* 1612. [f. med.L. *embrocat-*, *embrocare*, f. *embrocha*; see EMBROCH.] *Med. trans.* To bathe or foment (a diseased part) with liquid.

Embrocation (embrokē̆ⁱ·ʃən). 1543. [f. med.L. *embrocare*; see prec.] †1. The action of embrocating -1634. 2. A liquid used for embrocating a diseased part; now usu. one applied by rubbing; a liniment 1610.

2. He bathed the doctor's face with an e. SMOLLETT.

†**Embro·ch(e**, *sb.* 1585. [ad. med.L. *embrocha*, ad. Gr. ἐμβροχή, f. (ult.) ἐν + βρέχειν to wet.] = EMBROCATION 2. -1657. So †**Embro·che** *v.* = EMBROCATE.

Embroglio, bad f. IMBROGLIO. Scott.

Embroider (embroi·dəɹ), *v.* ME. [f. EN- + BROIDER.] 1. *trans.* To ornament with, or (†*transf.*) as with, needlework; to work in needlework upon cloth, etc. Also *absol.* 2. *fig.* †To dignify -1667; †to set forth floridly -1648; to embellish with rhetoric or with exaggerations 1614.

1. The women..e...for the embellishment of their persons BERKELEY. 2. He had embroidered his own story with some marvellous legends H. WALPOLE. Hence **Embroi·derer. Embroi·deress.**

Embroidery (embroi·dəri). [ME. *embrouderie*, f. OF. *embroder* EMBROWD *v.*; see -RY.] 1. The art of embroidering; also *attrib.* 2. Embroidered work or material 1570. 3. *fig.* of any showy or adventitious ornamentation 1640. 4. *transf.* Any ornament or marking compared in appearance to needlework 1644. ¶5. An embroidery manufactory. BURKE.

2. Saphire, pearle, and rich embroiderie *Merry W.* v. v. 75. 3. All the e. of poetic dreams COWPER. 4. An e. of daisies and wild flowers SCOTT.

†**Embroi·l**, *sb.* 1636. [f. EMBROIL *v.*[2]] = EMBROILMENT -1788.

†**Embroi·l**, *v.*[1] *rare.* [f. EN- + BROIL *v.*[1]] To burn up -1726.

Embroil (embroi·l), *v.*[2] 1603. [ad. F. *embrouiller*; cf. EN- and BROIL *sb.* and *v.*] 1. *trans.* To bring into confusion and disorder; to render unintelligible. 2. To throw into uproar or tumult 1618. 3. To entangle in dissension or hostility *with* (any one); to bring into a state of discord 1610.

1. The former..are so embroil'd with Fable ADDISON. 2. More to e. the deep THOMSON. 3. [They] embroiled him with the House of Commons 1680. Hence **Embroi·ler.**

Embroilment (embroi·lmĕnt). 1609. [f. prec.; cf. F. *embrouillement.*] 1. The action of embroiling 1622. 2. A tumult 1609; a state of variance 1667. 3. A state of entanglement or confusion 1856.

2. He was not apprehensive of a new e. BURNET.

Embronze; see EM- *pref.* and BRONZE *sb.*

Embrothelled; mod. sp. of IMBROTHELLED.

†**Embrow·d, embraw·d**, *v.* ME. [f. EN- + BROWD *v.*; cf. OF. *embrodé.*] *trans.* To embroider -1555.

Embrown (embrau·n), *v.* 1667. [f. EN- + BROWN *a.*; cf. F. *embrunir*, used in sense 1.] 1. To make dusky. Chiefly *poet.* 2. To make brown. Also (occas.) *intr.* for *refl.* 1725.

1. The air, Imbrown'd with shadows CARY. 2. The Smith's hardy and embrowned countenance SCOTT.

Embrue, var. of IMBRUE.

Embrute, var. of IMBRUTE.

Embryo (e·mbriˌo). 1590. [med.L. corruption of EMBRYON, q.v.]

A. *sb.* 1. The offspring of an animal before its birth (or emergence from the egg); in the case of man, the fœtus before the fourth month of pregnancy. 2. *Bot.* 'The rudimentary plant contained in the seed' (*Syd. Soc. Lex.*) 1728. 3. *fig.* A thing in its rudimentary stage; a germ 1601. 4. *attrib.* 1835.

3. The project itself was but an E. 1601. Phr. *In e.*: in an undeveloped stage; There a chancellor in e. SHENSTONE. *Comb.*: **e.-bud**, 'an adventitious bud, when enclosed in the bark, as in the cedar of Lebanon' (*Syd. Soc. Lex.*); **-cell**, the first cell of the fecundated animal ovum; **-sac**, *Bot.* a cavity in the archegonium of a plant, within which the e. is produced.

B. *adj.* [The sb. used attrib.] That is still in germ; unformed, undeveloped, as *e. patriots* 1684.

Hence **E·mbryoi·sm**, the state of being an e.

Embryoctony (embriˌǫ·ktŏni). [f. Gr. ἐμβρυοκτόνος.] 'The destruction of the fœtus in the womb' (*Syd. Soc. Lex.*).

Embryoferous (embriˌǫ·fərəs), *a.* 1859. [See -FEROUS.] *Biol.* That bears or contains an embryo.

Embryogenesis (e:mbriˌodʒe·nĕsis). 1830. [f. EMBRYON + Gr. γένεσις.] *Biol.* 'The origin and formation of the embryo; and the science thereof' (*Syd. Soc. Lex.*). Hence **E:mbryogene·tic** *a.* pertaining to e.

Embryogeny (e:mbriˌǫ·dʒĕni). 1835. [f. EMBRYON + Gr. γεν- + -Y.] = prec. Hence **E:mbryogeˈnic** *a.* embryogenetic.

Embryography (embriˌǫ·grăfi). [f. as prec. + Gr. -γραφία.] 'The description of the fœtus or embryo' (*Syd. Soc. Lex.*).

Embryology (embriˌǫ·lŏdʒi). 1859. [f. EMBRYON + -LOGY.] *Biol.* The science relating to the embryo and its development.

Against the belief in such abrupt changes, e. enters a strong protest DARWIN.

‖Hence **E·mbryolo·gic, -al** *a.*; **-ly** *adv.* **Embryologist**, one who studies or is versed in e.

Embryon (e·mbriˌǫn), *sb.* (*a.*) Pl. **embrya, embryons.** 1592. [mod.L., a. Gr. ἔμβρυον, f. ἐν in + βρύειν to be full of.] The original form of EMBRYO; now *rare*, and only in techn. use. Hence **E·mbryonal** *a.* of or pertaining to an e. **E·mbryona·ry** *a.* relating to an e.

Embryonate (e·mbriˌŏnĕt), *a.* 1669. [f. prec. + -ATE[2].] †1. = EMBRYONATED -1675. †2. = *embryonal* 1693. 3. 'Having an embryo in germ' (*Syd. Soc. Lex.*). Hence in *Bot.* **E. plants**, plants which possess seeds.

†**E·mbryonated**, *ppl. a.* 1652. [f. as prec.] Of chemical and mineral bodies: Found with or embedded (like embryos) in other bodies -1676.

Embryonic (embriˌǫ·nik), *a.* 1849. [See -IC.] Pertaining to, or like, an embryo; *fig.* immature, undeveloped.

fig. Every Englishman is an e. chancellor EMERSON. So **Embryo·tic** *a.* (*lit.* and *fig.*).

Embryotomy (embriˌǫ·tŏmi). 1721. [ad. Gr. ἐμβρυοτομία, f. ἔμβρυον + -τομία.] 'The cutting up of the *fœtus in utero* into pieces in order to effect its removal' (*Syd. Soc. Lex.*).

†**E·mbryous**, *a. rare.* 1677. [f. EMBRYON *sb.* + -OUS.] Of or pertaining to an embryo; in germ; undeveloped. (Dicts.)

Embulk; see EM- *pref.* and BULK *sb.*

†**Embu·ll**, *v.* 1480. [f. EN- + BULL *sb.*[2]] *trans.* To publish in a bull, issue a bull against; to affix the Papal (or other) seal to -1589.

Embus (embʊ·s), *v.* 1915. [f. EM- + BUS.] To go or take on board a bus.

Embush, obs. f. AMBUSH.

†**Embu·sy**, *v.* 1484. [f. EN- + BUSY *a.*] To occupy -1693.

Eme. *Obs.* exc. *dial.* [Com. WGer.: OE. *ēam*; cf. Du. *oom*, Ger. *oheim, ohm.*] An uncle; also *dial.* a gossip.

Didna his e. die .. wi' the name of the Bluidy Mackenyie SCOTT.

Emeer(e, var. ff. EMIR.

Emend (ĭme·nd), *v.* ME. [ad. L. *emendare*, f. *e* + *menda* fault.] 1. *trans.* To free from faults, correct. Also *intr.* for *refl.* Now *rare.* **b.** *esp.* To remove errors from (a text), emendate 1768. 2. = MEND -1480.

1. b. Pisistratus..did..collect, arrange, and e. poems LYTTON. Hence **Eme·ndable** *a.* **Eme·nder.** †**Eme·ndment** (*rare*), = AMENDMENT.

†**Emendate**, *a.* 1654. [ad. L. *emendatus.*] Emended, corrected -1677. Hence †**Emendately** *adv.*

Emendate (ī·mendē̆ⁱt), *v.* 1876. [f. L. *emendat-*; see prec.] To remove errors and corruptions from (a text).

Hence **E·mendator. Eme·ndatory** *a.* †corrective; pertaining to EMENDATION 2.

Emendation (īmendē̆ⁱ·ʃən). 1536. [ad. L. *emendationem*, f. *emendare* to EMEND.] †1. *gen.* Correction, reformation -1677. 2. Improvement by alteration and correction; *esp.* of literary and artistic products, methods, systems, etc.; an instance of this 1586. **b.** *esp.* The correction (usually by conjecture) of corruptions in a text; an instance of this 1622.

1. The e. of the Church R. COKE. 2. A better E. of the Calendar 1665. 3. The emendations being more often wrong than right DOWDEN.

†**Eme·ndicate**, *v.* 1611. [f. L. *emendicat-*, *emendicare* (f. *e* + *mendicus*).] To obtain by begging -1681.

Emerald (e·mərăld). [ME. *emeraude*, a. OF. *emeraude, esmeraude, esmeralde* :—Com. Rom. types **smaralda*, **smaraldo*, repr. L. *smaragdus*; see SMARAGDUS.] 1. A precious stone of bright green colour; in mod. use applied only to a variety of beryl (see BERYL *sb.*). 2. *Her.* Eng. name for the colour *vert* 1572. 3. *transf.* = *emerald-green.* 4. *Printing.* A size of type intermediate between nonpareil and minion:

Emerald Type.

5. *attrib.* **a.** Simple *attrib.*, as in *an e. ring* 1877. **b.** quasi-*adj.*, as in *e. meadow* 1598. **c.** Similative, as in *e.-bright, -green*, etc. 1614.

1. The fourth an emeralde (= Heb. *nōphek*, LXX ἄνθραξ, Vulg. *carbunculus*) TINDALE *Rev.* xxi. 19. *Comb.*: †**e. copper** (*Min.*) = DIOPTASE; **e. green**, a vivid light-green pigment, prepared from the arseniate of copper; **E. Isle**, a name given to Ireland

on account of its verdure; **e. moth** (*Entom.*), a name of certain bright green moths, *e.g.* those of the genus *Hipparchus*; **e. nickel** (*Min.*), a native hydrocarbonate of nickel.

Emeraldine (e·mərăldin, -əin). 1855. [See -INE.]

A. *adj.* Like an emerald in colour.

B. *sb.* A dye formed from aniline treated with hydrochloric acid and chlorate of potassium; aniline-green.

†Emeras. 1631. One of a pair of small escutcheons affixed to the shoulders of an armed knight.

Emerge (ǐmɔ̄·ɹdʒ), *v.* 1563. [ad. L. *emergere*, f. *e* + *mergere* to dip.] †1. *intr.* To rise by virtue of buoyancy *from* or *out of* a liquid –1721. 2. To come up out of a liquid in which (the subject) has been immersed. Also *transf.* to rise *from* (under) the earth. 1640. 3. To come forth into view, issue, appear 1563.

2. The Ocean out of which [Great Britain] emerged EMERSON. 3. To e. from the crowd JOHNSON. The satellite.. will e... after.. occultation SIR J. HERSCHELL. *fig.* To e. into distinct notice FROUDE. Here emerges the question as to [etc.] M. PATTISON. Hence †**Eme·rgement** NORTH.

Emerge, bad sp. of IMMERGE *v.*

Emergence (ǐmɔ̄·ɹdʒĕns). 1649. [ad. late L. *emergentia*; see prec.] 1. The rising out of the water 1833. 2. The process of issuing from concealment, confinement, etc. (*lit.* and *fig.*) 1755. 3. An unforeseen occurrence; a sudden occasion (hence erron. used for 'urgent want'). Now repl. by EMERGENCY. 1649. 4. *Bot.* An outgrowth on leaves or stems which arises from the sub-epidermic tissue 1882.

1. The e. of the land CROLL. 2. The e. of refracted light 1704. A glacier's e. from the valley KANE.

Emergency (ǐmɔ̄·ɹdʒĕnsi). 1631. [See prec. + -ENCY.] 1. = EMERGENCE 1. Now *rare.* 1646. †2. = EMERGENCE 2. –1762. †3. The sudden or unexpected occurrence (of a state of things, etc.) –1776. 4. *concr.* A juncture that arises or 'crops up'; a sudden occasion (hence erron. used for 'pressing need') 1631; in *pl.* †casual profits (*a* 1662). 5. *attrib.* or *adj.* Used, issued, called upon, or arising in an emergency. *E. man*: spec. (in Ireland) a bailiff's officer, recruited for special service, *esp.* in evictions.

3. The e. of war..on the frontiers GIBBON. 4. Relief on sudden emergencies BURN.

Emergent (ǐmɔ̄·ɹdʒĕnt). 1528. [a. L. *emergentem*; see EMERGENCE.]

A. *adj.* 1. Rising out of a surrounding medium, *e.g.* water; also *fig.* 1627. 2. That is in process of issuing forth; also *fig.* 1619. 3. Casually or unexpectedly arising (*arch.*) 1593. ¶4. Used (improp.) for 'urgent', 'pressing' 1706.

1. *fig.* Hope, still e., still contemns the wave SHENSTONE. 2. The e. rays will be collected to a focus IMISON. *fig.* Declining all e. controversys 1619. E. parties J. H. NEWMAN. 3. Directions vpon e. occasions DIGBY.

B. *sb.* †1. An outcome –1656. †2. = EMERGENCY 3. –1720. 3. *Science.* That which is produced by a combination of causes, but cannot be regarded as the sum of their individual effects. Opp. to *resultant.* 1874.

Hence **Eme·rgently** *adv.*

Emerick, emeril(l, obs. ff. EMERY.

†Eme·rit, *v.* [f. L. *emerit-*, *emerere*, *-ri.*] *trans.* To earn by service. FAIRFAX.

Emerited (ǐme·ritĕd), *ppl. a. arch.* 1664. [f. L. *emeritus*; see next.] = EMERITUS *a.*; *hence*, skilled, experienced.

‖**Emeritus** (ǐme·ritɒ̆s). 1823. [L., pa. pple. of *emereri* to earn (one's discharge) by service.]

A. *adj.* Honourably discharged from service; that has retired from an office.

An e. Professor of Moral Philosophy DE QUINCEY.

B. *sb.* One who has retired from active service or occupation; an e. professor. (Dicts.)

†E·merods, *sb. pl.* ME. [ad. L. *hæmorrhoïdes*, a. Gr.] = HÆMORRHOID[1] 1. Still occas. used in allusions to 1 *Sam.* v. 6, 7.

Emersed (ǐmɔ̄·ɹst), *ppl. a.* 1686. [f. L. *emersus* pa. pple.; see EMERGE.] Standing out from a medium, *e.g.* water.

Emersion (ǐmɔ̄·ɹʃən). 1633. [as if ad. L. *emersionem; see EMERGE.] 1. The appearing (of what has been submerged) above the surface of the water 1667. 2. The action of issuing (from concealment, etc.). Somewhat *rare.* 1763. †3. A coming into notice –1680.

1. The Immersion and E. of the Globe 1667. 2. The e. of a satellite of Jupiter JOHNSON. 3. The e. of the New Jerusalem into Being 1680.

Emery (e·məri). 1481. [a. F. *émeri*, *émeril*, OF. *esmeril*:—late L. *smericulum*, f. Gr. σμῆρις (σμύρις) a powder for rubbing.] 1. A coarse variety of corundum, used for polishing metals, stones, and glass. 2. *attrib.*, as *e.-stone.*

Comb.: **e.-cloth, -paper,** cloth or paper covered with e.-powder, used for polishing or cleaning metals, etc.; **-powder,** ground e., hence a *vb.*, to rub with e.-powder; **-stick,** 'a stick of wood round which E. paper is glued'; **-wheel,** a wheel coated with e., and used for polishing.

‖**Emesis** (e·mĭsis). 1875. [Gr., f. ἐμέειν to vomit.] *Path.* Vomiting.

Emetia (ǐmī·tiă). 1830. [f. Gr. ἔμετος vomiting + -IA.] = EMETINE.

Emetic (ǐme·tik). 1657. [ad. Gr. ἐμετικός, f. ἐμέειν to vomit.]

A. *adj.* Having power to cause vomiting; *fig.* sickening, mawkish 1670.

fig. Richardson..in his e. history of Pamela 1770.

B. *sb.* A medicine that excites vomiting.

Hence **Eme·tical** *a.* = EMETIC *a.*, **-ly** *adv.*

Emetine (e·mĭtəin). 1819. [f. Gr. ἔμετος vomiting + -INE.] *Chem.* An alkaloid obtained from the root of *Cephaëlis ipecacuanha.*

Emeto-cathartic (e:mĭto,kăþā·ɹtik). 1879. [f. Gr. ἔμετος + καθαρτικός.] *Med.* **a.** *adj.* Able to induce both purging and vomiting. **b.** *sb.* [*sc.* substance.]

Emetology (emĭtǫ·lŏdʒi). 1847. [See -LOGY.] *Med.* 'The doctrine of, or a treatise on, vomiting and emetics' (*Syd. Soc. Lex.*).

Emeu, emu (ī·miu). Also **emew.** 1613. [a. Pg. *ema*, orig. crane, later, ostrich.] †1. = CASSOWARY 1. –1656. †2. ? The American Ostrich, *Rhea americana.* [Perh. an error.] –1796. 3. A genus (*Dromæus*) of birds, peculiar to the Australian continent. The best known species is *D. novæ-hollandiæ.* The Emeu and Cassowary are closely allied. 1842. *Comb.* **e.-wren,** an Australian bird, *Stipiturus* (or *Malurus*) *malacurus*, of the family *Sylviidæ.*

‖**Émeute** (emö̆t). 1862. [Fr.; f. *émouvoir* to set in motion.] A popular rising or disturbance.

†Emfo·rth. ME. only. [f. *em*, EVEN *adv.* + FORTH.] **a.** *adv.* Equally. **b.** *prep.* 1. According to; in proportion to. 2. Equally with.

†E·micant, *a.* [ad. L. *emicantem*; see next.] That darts or flashes forth. BLACKMORE.

†E·micate, *v. rare.* 1657. [f. L. *emicat-*, *emicare* to spring forth.] *intr.* To spring forth, appear. Also *fig.* –1708. Hence **†Emica·tion,** flying off in small particles, as sparkling liquors; shining forth.

Emiction (ǐmi·kʃən). 1666. [f. *emict-*, stem of late L. *emingere*, f. *e* + *mingere* to make water.] 1. The voiding of urine 1847. 2. Urine.

Emictory (ǐmi·ktəri). [f. as prec.; see -ORY.] **a.** *adj.* Diuretic. **b.** *sb.* A diuretic. (Dicts.)

Emigrant (e·migrănt). 1754. [ad. L. *emigrantem*; see EMIGRATE.]

A. *sb.* One who leaves his own country to settle (permanently) in another. Also *attrib.*, as in *e.-ship.* **b.** *spec.* = EMIGRÉ 1792.

The noise of embarking emigrants EMERSON.

B. *adj.* That emigrates. Also (of birds) migratory. 1794.

†Emi·grate, *a.* [ad. L. *emigratus*; see next.] That has migrated (from the body) GAYTON.

Emigrate (e·migre¹t), *v.* 1778. [f. ppl. stem of L. *emigrare* to wander forth.] 1. *intr.* To quit one country, etc. to settle in another. 2. *trans.* To cause or assist to do this 1870.

1. They don't e., till they could earn their livelihood ..at home 1778.

Emigration (emigrē¹·ʃən). 1649. [ad. L. *emigrationem*; see prec.] 1. The action of departing out of a particular place or set of surroundings. 2. *esp.* The departure of persons from their native country, to settle permanently in another. Also *attrib.*, as in *e.-agent.* 1677. 3. Emigrants collectively 1863.

1. The E. of humane Souls from the bodies by Ecstasy MORE. 2. Those melancholy emigrations.. from the Islands..of Scotland 1791. Hence **Emigra·tional** *a.* pertaining to e. **Emigra·tionist,** an advocate of e.

Emigrator (e·migre¹təɹ). *rare.* 1837. [See EMIGRATE *v.*] = EMIGRANT.

Emigratory (e·migre¹təri), *a.* 1839. [See EMIGRATE *v.* and -ORY.] 1. Of animals: = MIGRATORY (*rare*). 2. Engaged in emigrating; pertaining to emigration 1854.

‖**Émigré.** 1792. [Fr.: pa. pple. of *émigrer.*] A French emigrant; *esp.* one of those Royalists who fled at the time of the French Revolution.

Eminence (e·minĕns). 1603. [ad. L. *eminentia*, f. *eminentem* EMINENT.]

I. 1. †Height; an elevated position 1658. †2. A prominence. Chiefly in *Anat.* –1743. 3. A rising ground, hill. Also *fig.* 1670.

3. There is a battery..on an e. ANSON. *fig.* We.. speak..of Age As of a final E. WORDSW.

II. 1. Distinguished superiority as compared with others in rank, station, character, attainments, or the possession of any quality, good or bad 1603. 2. As a title of honour, now borne only by Cardinals 1653. †3. An eminent quality; a distinction –1659. †4. Eminent measure –1710.

1. Satan by merit rais'd to that bad e. MILT. *P. L.* II. 6. Surgeons of e. 1800. E. in science M. PATTISON. 3. So several eminences met in this worthy man FULLER. 4. Men..who had no one Quality in any E. STEELE. So **E·minency** (in same senses).

Eminent (e·minĕnt), *a.* ME. [f. L. *eminentem*, *eminere* to project.] 1. High, towering above other things; projecting, prominent. Also *fig.* 1541. 2. Of persons: **a.** Exalted in rank or station 1603. **b.** Distinguished in character or attainments 1611. †3. Of things or places: Chief, important; especially useful –1748. 4. Remarkable in degree; signal, noteworthy ME. ¶Confused with IMMINENT. 1600.

1. Upon an high mountain and e. *Ezek.* xvii. 22. 2. a. A certain e. rajah BURKE. b. E. cooks are paid 1200*l.* a-year HT. MARTINEAU. E. as a speaker GROTE. 4. His success was e. DISRAELI.

Phr. *Right of e. domain*: see DOMAIN.

Eminently (e·minĕntli), *adv.* 1610. [f. prec. + -LY[2].] In an eminent manner. †1. On high –1675. †2. Conspicuously –1774. 3. In an eminent degree 1641. 4. *Philos.*, etc. In a higher sense than *formally* (*i.e.* according to the definition of things) 1640.

Emir (emī^ə·ɹ, ī·məɹ). 1625. [a. Arab. *amīr* commander; see AMEER, ADMIRAL.] 1. A Saracen or Arab prince, or governor of a province; a military commander 1632. 2. A title of honour borne by the descendants of Mohammed.

2. Mahomet's..kinsmen in greene Shashes, who are called Emers PURCHAS. Hence **Emi·rate,** the jurisdiction or government of an e.

Emissary (e·misări), *sb.*[1] and *a.* 1625. [ad. L. *emissarius* adj., that is sent, also *absol.*, f. *emiss-*, *emittere* (see EMIT) + *-arius*, -ARY[1].]

A. *sb.* A person sent out on a mission to promote the interests of his employer. (Usually in a bad sense, implying something odious or underhand in the mission or its manner.) Also *fig.* **b.** = SPY. (Dicts.)

I am endeavouring to get information by emissaries WELLINGTON. Hence **E·missaryshi·p** B. JONS.

B. *adj.* 1. That is sent forth 1659. 2. *Phys.* Of small vessels: Sent forth from a main trunk 1831.

1. The High-Priest .. offered the e. (= scape-) goat ROCK.

Emissary (e·misări), *sb.*[2] 1601. [ad. L. *emissarium* an outlet, f. *emiss-* (see prec.) + -ARY[1].] An outlet, channel, duct. Also *fig.* *Obs.* exc. in *Rom. Antiq.*

Without any emissaries, tunnels, or holes HOLLAND. *fig.* The common e. of scandal SWIFT.

Emissile (ǐmi·sil), *a.* 1732. [f. L. *emiss-* ppl. stem + -ILE.] That can be thrust out, as *emissile* cornua in snails.

Emission (ǐmi·ʃən). 1607. [ad. L. *emissionem.*] †1. *gen.* The action of sending forth –1827. †2. The issuing (of a book, notice, etc.) –1779. 3. The setting in circulation (of bills, notes, shares, etc.). Also *concr.* 1773. 4. The action of giving off or sending out (of light, heat, gases, etc.). Also *fig.* 1619. 5. *concr.* That which is emitted 1664. 6. *Phys.* = L. *emissio seminis* 1646.

4. The e. of fragrance 1859, of sparks of light 1871. Phr. *Theory of e.*, *E. theory*: the theory that ligth

consists of imponderable particles emitted from luminous bodies.

†**Emissi·tious**, *a.* [f. L. *emissicius* sent out; see EMIT.] Prying, inquisitive, as *emissitious* eyes. BP. HALL.

Emissive (ĭmi·siv), *a.* 1657. [f. L. *emiss-* ppl. stem + -IVE.] 1. Having power to EMIT (sense 1) 1870. †2. That is emitted -1737.

1. Phr. *E. theory*: = *Emission theory*. Hence **Emissi·vity**, emissive or radiating power of heat or light 1880.

Emissory (ĭmi·səri). 1858. [f. as prec. + -ORY.] = EMISSARY *sb.*²

Emit (ĭmi·t), *v.* 1626. [ad. L. *emittere* to send forth.] (Not used with personal obj.) 1. *trans.* To send forth, discharge, exude, give off. †2. To throw out as an offshoot -1756. 3. To utter 1753. †4. To issue, publish -1847. 5. To issue formally and by authority (now *esp.* paper currency, bills, etc.) 1649. †6. To discharge (a missile) 1720.

1. To e. effluvia BENTLEY, light 1794, threads (as spiders) TODD, flames MRS. JAMESON, fluid 1879. 3. To e. sound TYNDALL, thoughts CARLYLE.

So †**Emi·ttent** *a.* that emits. Hence **Emi·tter.**

Emmantle, var. of IMMANTLE.

Emmarble (emā·ɹb'l), *v.* Also **en-**. 1596. [f. EN- + MARBLE *sb.*] *trans.* To turn into marble (*fig.*); to sculpture in marble; to adorn with marble.

Emmarvel (emā·ɹvėl). Also **en-**. 1740. [f. EN- + MARVEL.] *trans.* To fill with wonder.

Emmenagogue (emī·năgǫg). 1702. [f. Gr. ἔμμηνα menses + ἀγωγός drawing forth.] *Med.* †A. *adj.* Having power to promote the menstrual discharge -1830. Hence **Emme:nago·gic** *a.* (in same sense).

B. *sb.* Agents which promote the menstrual discharge 1731.

Emmenology (emīnǫ·lŏdʒi). 1742. [See prec. and -LOGY.] A treatise on, or the doctrine of, menstruation. Hence **Emme:nolo·gical** *a.* relating to menstruation.

Emmet (e·mėt). [repr. OE. *ǣmete* wk. fem. (see ANT). The OE. *ǣ* became in ME. *ă* or *ĕ*, whence ME. *ămete* (*amt*, ANT), and *ĕmete* (EMMET) respectively.] An ANT. Chiefly *dial. Comb.* **e.-hunter** (*dial.*), the Wryneck.

Emmetrope (e·mĕtrōᵘp). 1875. [f. as next.] *Phys.* One whose sight is emmetropic.

‖**Emmetropia** (emĕtrōᵘ·piă). Also **Emme·tropy.** 1864. [mod.L., f. Gr. ἔμμετρος in measure + ὤψ (ὠπ-) the eye + -IA.] *Phys.* The normal condition of the refractive media of the eye in which parallel rays come to a focus upon the retina when the eye is at rest and passive. So **Emmetro·pic** *a.* characterized by e.

Emmew, var. of INMEW *v.*

Emmove, var. of ENMOVE *v.*

Emodin (e·mŏdin). 1858. [f. mod.L. (*Rheum*) *Emodi*, Turkey rhubarb (f. Gr. Ἠμωδός the Himalaya) + -IN.] *Chem.* A constituent of rhubarb root. Its formula is $C_{40}H_{30}O_{13}$.

Emollescence (imǫle·sĕns). 1794. [f. L. *emollescere* + -ENCE.] *Chem.*, etc. 'A state of softening; the softened condition of a melting body before it fuses' (*Syd. Soc. Lex.*).

Emolliate (ĭmǫ·liˌeᶦt), *v.* 1802. [f. L. *emollire* + -ATE.] To soften, render effeminate. PINKERTON. So †**Emo·lliative** *a.* that tends to e. (*rare*).

Emollient (ĭmǫ·liˌĕnt). 1643. [f. L. *emollientem*; see prec.] a. *adj.* That can soften or relax. Also *fig.* b. *sb.* A softening application. Chiefly in *pl.* 1656.

Emolli·tion. ? *Obs.* 1619. [as if ad. L. **emollitionem*; see prec.] The action of softening. Also *fig.*

Emolument (ĭmǫ·liŭmĕnt). 1480. [ad. L. *emolū-*, *emolĭmentum*; usu. said to be f. *emolīri* to work out, but ? f. *emolĕre* to grind out.] 1. Profit or gain from station, office, or employment; dues; remuneration, salary. †2. Advantage -1756.

1. Certain..emoluments unto the said benefice due 1480. Hence †**Emolume·ntal** (*rare*), **Emo:lume·ntary** *adjs.* profitable, advantageous.

†**Emo·ng**, *prep.* and *adv.* ME. = AMONG -1571. Hence †**Emo·nges(t** *prep.* = AMONGST.

Emony (e·mǫ̆ni). 1644. [? taken as *an emony.*] = ANEMONE.

Emotion (ĭmōᵘ·ʃən). 1579. [as if ad. L. **emotionem*, f. *ēmovere* to move away or much.] †1. A moving out, migration -1695. †2. A (physical) moving, stirring, agitation -1822. †3. *transf.* A popular movement, tumult -1757. 4. *fig.* Any vehement or excited mental state 1660. b. *Psychology.* A mental feeling or affection (*e.g.* of pain, desire, hope, etc.), as dist. from cognitions or volitions. Also *abstr.* 'feeling'. 1808.

4. The emotions of humanity JER. TAYLOR. b. He ..almost denounces me..for referring Religion to the region of E. TYNDALL. Hence **Emo·tioned** *ppl. a.* stirred by e.

Emotional (ĭmōᵘ·ʃənăl), *a.* 1847. [f. prec. + -AL.] 1. Connected with the feelings or passions. 2. Liable to, or easily affected by, emotion; having the capacity for emotion. Also as quasi-*sb.* 1857.

1. The e. weaknesses of humanity FROUDE. Hence **Emo:tiona·lity**, e. character or temperament. **Emo·tionally** *adv.* in an e. manner; with reference to the emotions.

Emotionalism (ĭmōᵘ·ʃənăliz'm). 1865. [f. prec. + -ISM.] Emotional character; *esp.* the habit of cultivating or of weakly yielding to emotion.

The religion of e. [is] represented by the negro 1883.

Emotionalist (ĭmōᵘ·ʃənălist). 1866. [f. as prec. + -IST.] a. One who bases his theory of conduct on the emotions. b. Contemptuously: One who is foolishly emotional, or who appeals (discreditably) to the emotions of others.

a. Mill writes..as if he were a mere e. J. GROTE.

Emotionalize (ĭmōᵘ·ʃənăləiz), *v. rare.* 1879. [f. EMOTIONAL + -IZE.] To render emotional; to deal with emotionally.

A pious family, where religion was not..emotionalised FROUDE.

Emotive (ĭmōᵘ·tiv), *a.* 1735. [f. L. *emot-*, *emovere* + -IVE.] 1. †a. Causing movement. b. Tending or able to excite emotion. 2. Pertaining to emotion 1830. Hence **Emo·tively** *adv.* emotionally. **Emo·tiveness.**

Emove (ĭmū·v), *v. rare.* ME. [ad. L. *emovere.*] *trans.* †a. To move (to an action). b. To excite emotion in.

b. Kindly raptures them e. THOMSON.

Empacket, *v. rare.* See EM- *pref.* and PACKET.

Empæstic (empī·stik), *a.* 1850. [ad. Gr. ἐμπαιστική (τέχνη), f. ἐμπαίειν to beat in, emboss.] In phr. *E. art*: the art of embossing.

Empair, Empale, etc.; see IMP-.

†**Empa·le**, *v.* 1604. [f. EN- + PALE *a.*] To make pale -1664.

The heart's still perfect; though empaled the face 1604.

†**Empa·nel**, *sb.* 1501. [f. next.] A list of jurors; a panel -1775.

Empanel, im- (empæ·nĕl), *v.* 1487. [a. AF. *empaneller*; see EN- and PANEL.] *trans.* To enter (the names of a jury) on a panel or official list; to constitute or enroll (a body of jurors).

Jurors duly empannelled and sworn BURKE. Hence **Empa·nelment**, the action of the vb.

†**Empa·nnel**, *v. rare.* 1620. [f. EN- + PANEL.] To put a pack-saddle upon -1881.

Empanoply; see EM- *pref.* and PANOPLY.

Emparadise, Empark, etc.; see IMP-.

†**Empa·sm.** *rare.* 1657. [f. Gr. ἐμπάσσειν to sprinkle on.] A powder to be sprinkled on the body to mask the smell of sweating; also for other purposes.

Empassion, Empawn, etc.; see IMP-.

Empathy (e·mpăþi). *Psychol.* 1912. [Rendering of G. *einfühlung* (f. *ein* in + *fühlung* feeling), after Gr. ἐμπάθεια.] The power of projecting one's personality into, and so fully understanding, the object of contemplation.

Empennage (empe·nėdʒ). 1909. [Fr., f. *empenner* to feather (an arrow).] An arrangement of stabilizing planes at the stern of an aeroplane or airship; also, the tail-surfaces or tail-plane.

†**Empeo·ple**, *v.* 1582. [f. EN- + PEOPLE.] 1. *trans.* To fill with people -1631. 2. *nonce-use.* To establish as the population. SPENSER.

Emperess(e, Emperice, obs. ff. EMPRESS.

†**Empe·rish**, *v. rare.* 1530. [app. f. Fr. *empirer*; perh., later, assoc. w. PERISH.] *trans.* To make worse, impair -1593.

I deeme thy braine emperished bee Through rustie elde SPENSER. Hence †**Empe·rishment.**

†**E·mperize**, *v. rare.* 1598. [f. EMPERY + -IZE.] *trans.* and *intr.* To rule as an emperor -1601.

Emperor (e·mpərəɹ). ME. [ad. OF. *empereor*:—L. *imperatorem*, f. *imperare*, f. *im-* (for *in*) + *parare* to make ready, order.] 1. The sovereign of an Empire: a title considered superior in dignity to that of 'king'. Also *transf.* and *fig.* †2. In the etymol. sense = 'commander'. b. *Rom. Antiq.* As tr. L. *imperator* in its republican sense (now repl. by the L. word). -1741. 3. *attrib.*, as *e.-king*, etc. ME.

1. The grete Cham..is the gretteste Emperour..of alle the parties beȝonde MAUNDEV. Otton the emperour 1529. The E. of Russia was my Father *Winter's T.* III. ii. 120. Since Buonaparte's time the title of E... has ceased to have any particular meaning FREEMAN. 2. Cicero was saluted E. MIDDLETON. *Comb.*: **e.-moth** (*Saturnia pavonia minor*); **Purple E.**: a butterfly, *Apatura Iris*, also called †**E. of the Woods**, and perh. †**E. of Morocco.** Hence **E·mperorshi·p**, the office, dignity, or reign of an e.

Empery (e·mpĕri), *sb.* Now usu. *poet.* ME. [a. OF. *emperie*, ad. L. *imperium* EMPIRE.] 1. †The dignity or dominion of an emperor -1588. b. Absolute dominion 1548. †c. Legitimate government (= L. *imperium*) -1642. 2. The territory of an emperor, or of a powerful ruler; also *fig.* 1550.

1. b. The only God of emperie and of might DRAYTON. 2. *fig.* More than her e. of joys KEATS.

Empetrous (e·mpĭtrəs), *a.* [f. Gr. ἔμπετρος growing on rocks + -OUS.] *Zool.* Of seals, and other short-limbed animals: Lying directly upon the ground.

†**Empha·se**, *v.* [f. EMPHASIS.] ? To lay emphasis upon. B. JONS.

Emphasis (e·mfăsis). Pl. **emphases.** 1573. [a. L., a. Gr. ἔμφασις, f. ἐν + φάσις an appearance, a declaration.] †1. (The Gr. and L. sense.) A figure of speech in which more is implied than is actually said; a meaning conveyed by implication -1764. 2. Vigour of expression. Now as *transf.* from 4. 1573. 3. Force of feeling, action, etc. 1602. 4. Stress of voice laid on a word or phrase to indicate its implied meaning, or simply to mark its importance 1613. 5. *transf.* Stress laid upon, or importance assigned to, a fact or idea 1687. 6. Prominence 1872. †7. A mere appearance. WHARTON.

2. Tertullian doth add the greater E. to his Argument STILLINGFL. 3. *Haml.* V. i. 278. 4. The e. is wrongly placed JOWETT. 5. My laying e. on the previous effect of the vaccine inoculation 1805. 6. The bones which mark the features.. lose their e. BLACKIE. var. †**E·mphasy.**

Emphasize (e·mfăsəiz), *v.* Also **-ise.** 1828. [f. EMPHASIS + -IZE.] To impart emphasis to; to lay stress upon; to add force to; to bring into special prominence.

Gesticulation goes along with speech..to e. it TYLOR.

Emphatic (emfæ·tik), *a.* 1708. [ad. Gr. ἐμφατικός; see EMPHASIS.] 1. Forcibly expressive; bearing the stress in pronunciation. 2. Of persons: That expresses himself with emphasis of voice, gesture, or language 1760. 3. Of actions, etc.: Strongly marked 1846.

1. The e. representation of Scripture 1836. Accented or..e. syllables HALLAM. 2. A little e. man DICKENS. 3. Still more e. honours PRESCOTT. Hence **Empha·tical** *a.* (now *rare*), in senses 1-3; also, †merely apparent. **Empha·tically** *adv.* in an e. manner, forcibly; decisively; †suggestively; †merely in appearance. **Empha·ticalness** (*rare*).

Emphractic, †-al (emfræ·ktik, †-ăl). 1678. [ad. Gr. ἐμφρακτικός, f. ἐμφράττειν to obstruct.] *Med.* a. *adj.* Having power to obstruct 1727. b. *sb.* A medicine which shuts up the pores of the skin.

Emphrensy, obs. var. of ENFRENZY.

‖**Emphysema** (emfisī·mă). 1661. [mod.L., a. Gr. ἐμφύσημα, f. ἐμφυσάειν to puff up.] *Med.* A swelling caused by the presence of air in the connective tissue. So **Emphyse·matous** *a.* of the nature of e.; pertaining to e.

Emphyteusis (emfitiū·sis). 1618. [a. L., a. Gr. ἐμφύτευσις, lit. 'implanting'.] *Law.* A perpetual right in a piece of another's land.

An e. or hereditary lease 1878. Hence **Emphy·teu·tic, -al** *a.* of the nature of, or held by, e.

‖**Emphyteuta** (emfitiū·tă). 1708. [a. L., ad. Gr. ἐμφυτευτής, f. ἐμφυτεύειν.] *Law.* 'A tenant of land which was subject to a fixed perpetual rent' (Maine). So †**Emphyteu·ticary**, in same sense.

Empicture (empi·ktiūr), *v.* Also **en-, im-**. 1520. [f. EN- + PICTURE.] To represent in a picture, portray.

Empierce, im- (em-, impīᵊ·ɹs), *v.* 1578. [f. EN-, IN- + PIERCE *v.*] *trans.* To pierce through keenly; to transfix (*lit.* and *fig.*).

†**Empi·ght,** *v.* ME. [pa. t. and pple. of **empitch*, f. EN- + PITCH *v.*] Fixed in, implanted. Also *intr.* for *refl.* -1746.

Empire (e·mpəiᵊɹ), *sb.* ME. [a. F. :-L. *imperium*; related to *imperare*, whence *imperator* EMPEROR.] 1. Supreme and extensive political dominion. 2. *transf.* and *fig.* Absolute sway, supreme control ME. 3. = EMPERORSHIP 1606. 4. Government by an emperor or emperors, and the period during which it existed 1834. 5. An extensive territory (*esp.* an aggregate of many states) ruled over by an emperor, or by a sovereign state ME. Also *transf.* and *fig.* (Cf. *realm*.) 6. A sovereign state 1532.

1. The establishment of the British e. in India 1845. 2. Thy blood and vertue Contend for E. in thee *All's Well* I. i. 72. 4. The Consulate and the E. CROWE. 5. The approximate population of the British E. is now 321,000,000 *Whitaker's Almanack* 1887. Phr. *The E.*: often *spec.* (*esp.* before 1804) the 'Holy Roman' or 'Romano-Germanic' empire; (*b*) Great Britain with its colonies and dependencies; the British Empire.

Order of the British Empire: an order, open to both men and women, instituted by George V in 1917 to reward services rendered to the Empire, whether at home or abroad.

Comb. **E. City, State**: in U.S., a name for the City and State of New York. **E. Day,** 24th May.

Hence †**E·mpire** *v.* to rule as an emperor.

Empiric (empi·rik). 1541. [ad. L. *empiricus*, Gr. ἐμπειρικός, f. ἔμπειρος, f. ἐν + πεῖρα trial, experiment. In 17th c. usu. (e·mpĭrik).]

A. *adj.* = EMPIRICAL (chiefly in senses of the use as *sb.*) 1605.

B. *sb.* 1. One of the sect of ancient physicians called *Empirici* (Ἐμπειρικοί), who drew their rules of practice only from experience 1541. b. One who, in matters of science, relies solely upon observation and experiment. Also *fig.* 1578. 2. One who practises physic or surgery without scientific knowledge; a quack, a charlatan. Also *transf.* 1562.

Empirical (empi·rikăl), *a.* 1569. [f. prec. + -AL.] 1. *Med.* Based on, or guided by, the results of observation and experiment only. 2. That practises physic or surgery without scientific knowledge; quack 1680. 3. *gen.* That is guided by mere experience, without knowledge of principles. Often *transf.* from 2: Charlatan. 1751. 4. Pertaining to, or derived from, experience 1649.

2. A.. Tinker e. to the Body of Man BUTLER. E. drugs 1839. 3. Hasty and e. measures GOSCHEN. 4. An e. law then, is an observed uniformity, presumed to be resolvable into simpler laws, but not yet resolved into them MILL. Hence **Empi·rically** *adv.*

Empiricism (empi·risiz'm). 1657. [f. EMPIRIC + -ISM.] 1. *Med.* The method or practice of an EMPIRIC; ignorant and unscientific practice; quackery. Also *transf.* 2. The use of empirical methods in any art or science. b. *Philos.* The theory which regards experience as the only source of knowledge. 1803. 3. *concr.* An empirical conclusion 1846.

So **Empi·ricist**, one who upholds philosophical e., or one who follows empirical methods.

Empirism (e·mpiriz'm). 1716. [f. Gr. ἔμπειρος + -ISM.] = EMPIRICISM 2 b. Hence **Empiri·stic** *a.* pertaining to e.

Emplacement (emplē·smĕnt). 1802. [a. F. *emplacement*.] 1. The action of placing in a position; placed condition 1869. 2. Position; site (*rare*) 1802. 3. *Mil.* A platform for guns, with epaulements to protect the gunners 1811.

Hence **Empla·ce** *v.* (*rare*) to put into position.

Empla·ne, *v.* 1923. [f. EM- + PLANE *sb.*[3]] To take or go on board an aeroplane.

†**Empla·ster,** *sb.* ME. [a. OF. *emplastre* (F. *emplâtre*), L. *emplastrum* (also used), ad. Gr. ἔμπλαστρον (used by Galen for ἔμπλαστον), f. (ult.) ἐν + πλάσσειν to mould.] 1. *Med.* or *Surg.* = PLASTER. Also *fig.* -1809. 2. = EMPLASTRATION 1, q. v. -1656.

†**Empla·ster,** *v.* ME. [a. OF. *emplastrer*; see prec.] 1. To cover with a plaster; to plaster over; also *fig.* b. To spread on as a plaster. -1633. 2. To bud trees; see EMPLASTRATION 1. -1656.

1. Als fair as ye his [Solomon's] name emplastre, He was a lecchour CHAUCER.

†**Empla·stic.** 1618. [ad. Gr. ἐμπλαστικός; see EMPLASTER *sb.*] a. *adj.* Fit to be used as a plaster; *hence*, adhesive, glutinous. Also, that stops up the pores. -1756. b. *sb.* An adhesive or glutinous substance -1751.

†**Emplastra·tion.** ME. [ad. L. *emplastrationem*; see EMPLASTER *v.*] 1. A mode of budding trees; so called from the piece of bark surrounding the bud, like a plaster on the tree -1745. 2. The application of a plaster -1633.

Emplead, obs. f. IMPLEAD.

Emplection, bad f. EMPLECTON.

Emplectite (emple·ktəit). 1857. [f. Gr. ἔμπλεκτος inwoven + -ITE, from its appearance.] *Min.* A sulphide of bismuth and copper, occurring in bright tin-white needle-shaped crystals.

‖**Emple·cton.** 1708. [mod.L., a. Gr. ἔμπλεκτον; see prec.] *Arch.* 'A kind of masonry, in which the outsides of the wall are ashlar, and the interval filled up with rubble' (Liddell and Scott).

Emplore, obs. f. IMPLORE.

Employ (emploi·), *sb.* 1666. [ad. F. *emploi*, f. *employer*.] †1. = EMPLOYMENT 1. -1829. 2. The state or fact of being employed 1709. 3. That on which a person or thing is employed; occupation 1678.

2. Phr. *In, out of, e.*; *in the e. of* (the person employing).

Employ (emploi·), *v.* 1460. [a. F. *employer* :-L. *implicare*, orig. 'to involve', in late L. 'to bend upon something', f. *in* + *plicare* to fold. Cf. IMPLY.] 1. *trans.* To apply to a purpose; to use as a means or instrument, or as material. b. To make use of (time, etc.); 'to fill with business' (J.) 1481. 2. To use the services of for some special business; to have or maintain in one's service 1584. 3. To find work or occupation for; in *pass.* often merely to be occupied. Also *refl.* 1579. †4. = IMPLY in various senses -1626.

1. Imploy your chiefest thoughts To courtship *Merch. V.* II. viii. 43. b. Having ten days at my disposal.. I was anxious to e. them TYNDALL. 2. Lessing.. was employed by Voltaire.. in the Hirschel case MORLEY. Scott & Co., employing nine men six months RAYMOND. 3. He was imploy'd in drinking SWIFT. Speculations to e. our curiosity BERKELEY. Hence **Employ·able** *a.*

‖**Employé** (aṅplwaye). 1834. [F., pa. pple. of *employer*.] One who is employed; *esp.* one employed for wages or a salary by a business house or by government. Hence also **Employée**, a female e.

Employee (emploi·ī, emploi,ī·). 1854. [See -EE.] = prec. Also in U.S. **Employ(e.**

Employer (emploi·əɹ). 1599. [f. EMPLOY *v.*] One who employs; *spec.* one who employs servants, workmen, etc. for wages.

Employment (emploi·mĕnt). 1593. [f. EMPLOY *v.* + -MENT.] 1. The action of employing; the state of being employed 1598. †b. Service -1603. 2. That on which (one) is employed; business; occupation; a commission 1597. †b. The use to which a thing is put -1658. †3. A position in the public service -1734.

1. The hand of little Imployment hath the daintier sense *Haml.* v. i. 77. b. *John* I. i. 198. 2. The excuse of not finding e. HOBBES. b. *Rich. II*, I. i. 90.

Emplume (emplū·m), *v.* Also **im-**. 1623. [a. F. *emplumer*.] To adorn with or as with plumes. Hence **Emplu·med** *ppl. a.*

Emplunge, obs. var. of IMPLUNGE.

Empocket (empǫ·kĕt), *v. arch.* Also **im-**. 1728. [f. EN- + POCKET *sb.*] *trans.* To put into one's pocket.

Empoison (empoi·zən, -z'n), *v.* ME. [a. F. *empoisonner*; see EN- and POISON *sb.*] †1. *trans.* To administer poison to. Also *absol.* -1670. †Also *transf.* and *fig.* -1667. 2. To put poison into; also, to dip in poison. Now *rhet.* 1602. 3. *fig.* To vitiate as with poison; to envenom; to embitter ME.

3. *fig.* How much an ill word may impoison liking SHAKS. Hence **Empoi·soner.** *Obs.* or *arch.* **Empoi·sonment**, the act of poisoning or fact of being poisoned (*Obs.* or *arch.*); the action of tainting with, or as with, poison.

Emporetic (empore·tik), *a.* [ad. L. *emporeticus*, a. Gr. *ἐμπορητικός, f. (ult.) ἔμπορος merchant.] *Antiq.* Pertaining to trade. *E. paper*: a coarse kind of papyrus used for wrapping up parcels.

†**Emporeu·tic.** 1612. [ad. Gr. ἐμπορευτικός, f. (ult.) as prec.]

A. *adj.* Of or pertaining to trade.

B. *sb.* a. *sing.* The emporeutic art. b. *pl.* Articles made for sale.

Emporium (empōᵊ·riŭm). Pl. **-iums, -ia.** 1586. [a. L., a. Gr. ἐμπόριον, f. ἔμπορος merchant.] 1. A place in which merchandise is collected or traded in; a principal centre of commerce, a mart. b. A pompous name for: A shop 1839. Also *transf.* and *fig.* †2. 'The common sensory of the brain' (Bailey).

1. The e., or general market, for the goods of all the different countries whose trade it carries on ADAM SMITH. b. Emporiums of splendid dresses DICKENS. var. †**E·mpory.** Hence †**Empo·rial** *a.* pertaining to, or of the nature of, an e.

†**Empo·rtment.** [a. F. *emportement*.] A fit of passion. NORTH.

†**Empo·ver,** *v. rare.* 1474. [a. OF. *enpoverir*.] To impoverish -1528.

Empoverish, obs. f. IMPOVERISH.

Empower (empau·əɹ), *v.* Also **im-**. 1654. [f. EN- + POWER.] 1. *trans.* To invest legally or formally with power; to authorize, license. 2. To impart power (*to do* something); to enable, permit 1681. Also †*refl.* with *over*.

1. To e. (a person) to erect a Colledge 1654, to levy troops MOTLEY. 2. Much less can he e. others to do Miracles SCOTT. Hence **Empow·erment**, the action of empowering; the state of being empowered.

†**Empre·nt,** *v.* Used as tr. L. *impetrare* to obtain by request. CHAUCER.

Empress (e·mprĕs), *sb.*[1] [ME. *emperesse*, a. OF., fem. of *emperere* EMPEROR.] 1. The consort of an emperor. Also, a female sovereign of an empire. 2. A female exercising absolute power. Chiefly *transf.* and *fig.* ME.

2. The pale-faced Empresse of the night HABINGTON. *Comb. E.-cloth*: a woollen fabric resembling merino, but untwilled. (App. not an Eng. trade term.)

†**E·mpress,** *sb.*[2] 1593. [var. of IMPRESS *sb.*[2], ad. It. *impresa*.] A motto or significant device. Also *attrib.* -1688.

†**Empre·ss,** *v.* ME. [a. OF. *empresser*.] To press, oppress. Also *intr.* to crowd *into*. -1475.

‖**Empressement** (aṅprę·smaṅ). 1749. [Fr.] Effusive cordiality.

†**Empri·me,** *v. rare.* 1575. To separate a deer from the herd.

Emprint, obs. f. IMPRINT *sb.* and *v.*

Emprise, emprize (emprəi·z), *sb. arch.* ME. [a. OF. *emprise, emprinse* :—late L. **imprensa*, f. (ult.) *in-* + *prehendere* to take.] 1. An undertaking, an (adventurous or chivalrous) enterprise. 2. *abstr.* Enterprise, prowess ME. †3. Renown -1500; estimation. ME. only.

1. To fighten in this emprise CHAUCER. Dare first The great emprise BROWNING. 2. Giants of mightie Bone and bould emprise MILT. *P. L.* xi. 642.

†**Empri·se,** *v.* ME. [f. prec. sb.] *trans.* To undertake -1608. Hence **Empri·sing** *ppl. a.* enterprising, adventurous.

Emprison, obs. f. IMPRISON.

‖**Emprosthotonos** (emprǫsþǫ·tǫnǫs). 1657. [mod.L., a. Gr., f. ἔμπροσθεν + τόνος.] *Path.* 'A condition in tetanus in which the body is drawn forwards by excessive action of the anterior muscles of the trunk' (*Syd. Soc. Lex.*). Hence **Empro·sthotoˑnic** *a.* characterized by e.

Empt (empt), *v.* Now *dial.* [OE. *ǽmtian*, f. *ǽmta, ǽmetta* leisure; cf. EMPTY *a.* and *v.*] †1. To be at leisure. Only in OE. 2. To make or †become empty (*lit.* and *fig.*) ME. 3. To pour forth or carry out 1606.

Emptiness (e·mptinĕs). 1533. [f. EMPTY *a.* + -NESS.] 1. The condition of being empty or void of contents or of specified contents; *concr.* void space, a vacuum. 2. Want of solidity or substance; inability to satisfy desire; unsatisfactoriness; vacuity, hollowness 1695. 3. Want of knowledge; lack of sense; inanity 1658.

1. No idea of the e. of London 1747. Neglect and e. of form 1875. 2. The E. of Ambition 1710.

Emption (e·mpʃən). 1461. [ad. L. *emptionem*, f. *emere*.] 1. The action of buying, as in *right of emption*. 2. *Rom. Law.* Purchase (L. *emptio*, as correl. of *venditio*) 1555. Hence **E·mptional** *a.* that can be purchased.

‖**Emptor** (e·mptɔɪ, -əɪ). 1875. [L.] A purchaser.

†**E·mptory.** 1641. [ad. late L. *emptorium*.] A mart -1676.

Empty (e·mpti). [OE. *ǣmitig*, f. *ǣmetta* leisure + -*ig*, -Y.]

A. *adj.* †1. At leisure. Also, unmarried. Only in OE. 2. Containing nothing; void of contents or of specified contents; opp. to *full*. Also *fig.* OE. 3. *transf.* †a. Destitute of money. (Only contextual.) -1724. b. Wanting food. Now *colloq.* 1593. †c. Of the body: Emaciated; of the pulse: Weak -1707. 4. Of space, etc.: Unoccupied. Also *fig.* OE. 5. Without anything to bring or carry ME. 6. Lacking knowledge and sense; frivolous, foolish 1611. b. Of things: Wanting solidity and substance; unsatisfactory, vain, meaningless ME.

2. The e. vessel makes the greatest sound *Hen. V*, IV. iv. 73. We..are of ourselves emptie of all good BP. HALL. 4. And dead mens cries do fill the emptie aire 2 *Hen. VI*, v. ii. 4. Dauids place was emptie 1 *Sam.* xx. 25. 5. E. camels MARLOWE. Vessels..e., or loaded with Masts 1714. *fig.* A hollow form with e. hands TENNYSON. 6. A very e. and unprepared design CLARENDON. b. Weighs .. solid pudding against e. praise POPE. Hence **E·mptily** *adv.*

B. *sb.* An empty truck or wagon; an empty box, case, etc. which has contained goods 1865.

Empty (e·mpti), *v.* 1526. [f. EMPTY *a.* The form *ge-ǣmtigian* appears in OE.] 1. *trans.* To make empty; to remove the contents of. Also with †*in*, *into*, *upon*. b. To drain away, pour off. Also *fig.* 1578. 2. To discharge *of*. Chiefly *transf.* and *fig.* 1526. Also *refl.* of persons. 3. *refl.* Of a river, etc.: To discharge itself *into* 1555. Also *intr.* for *refl.* (now chiefly in *U.S.*). 4. *intr.* To become empty 1633.

1. E. the woolly Rack DRYDEN. 2. All The Chambers emptied of delight TENNYSON. 3. The Veins..e. themselves into the Heart HOBBES. Hence **E·mptier.**

E·mpty-ha·nded, *a.* 1613. [See EMPTY *a.*] Bringing no gift; carrying nothing away: chiefly in phrases, *To come, go*, etc. *empty-handed*.

E·mptying, *vbl. sb.* 1605. [f. EMPTY *v.*] 1. The action of making empty. 2. *concr.* a. What is emptied out of any vessel; also *fig.* b. *pl.* Yeast. *U.S.* 1650.

Empurple (empɒ̄·ɹp'l), *v.* Also **im-**. 1590. [f. EN- + PURPLE.] *trans.* To make purple; to redden; to robe in purple (*rare*).

The violets..impurple not the winter DRUMM. OF HAWTH.

Empusa (empiū·ză). Also **empuse.** 1603. [a. Gr. Ἔμπουσα.] 1. A hobgoblin or spectre. 2. *Bot.* A genus of the family *Entomophthoreæ*.

†**Empu·zzle,** *v.* [f. EN- + PUZZLE *sb.* or *v.*] To puzzle. SIR T. BROWNE.

Empyema (empi,ī·mă). 1615. [mod.L., a. Gr. ἐμπύημα, f. ἐμπυέειν to suppurate.] *Path.* 1. 'A collection of pus in the cavity of the pleura, the result of pleurisy' (*Syd. Soc. Lex.*). 2. More widely: Suppuration (*rare*) 1866. Hence †**Empye·matous,** †**Empyema·tic** *adjs.* belonging to or suffering from e.

Empyesis (empi,ī·sis). [mod.L., a. Gr. ἐμπύησις.] *Path.* A pustular eruption.

Empyreal (empi·rĭăl, empirī·ăl, -pəi-), *a.* 1481. [f. med.L. *empyreus*, -*æus* (f. Gr. ἐμπύριος fiery) + -AL.] 1. Of or pertaining to the EMPYREAN. Also *fig.* b. Of or pertaining to the sky, celestial 1744. 2. Fiery; composed of pure fire. Also *fig.* 1601. †3. *Chem.* Capable of supporting combustion -1812.

1. Go soar with Plato to th' e. sphere POPE. 3. Phr. *E. air*: Scheele's name for oxygen. var. †**Empyre.**

Empyrean (empi·rĭăn, empirī·ăn, -pəi-). Also **empyræan.** 1614. [f. as prec. + -EAN.]

A. *adj.* Of or pertaining to the sphere of fire or highest heaven. Also *fig.*

Drenched in e. light WORDSW.

B. *sb.* 1. The highest heaven. Anciently, the sphere of pure fire; in Christian use, the abode of God and the angels. Also *fig.* 1667. 2. *transf.* a. The visible heavens 1808. b. Cosmic space 1880.

1. Divine Interpreter sent Down from the E. MILT.

†**Empyre·um.** Also **empyræum.** 1647. [a. L. (sc. *cælum*).] = EMPYREAN B. 1. -1777.

Empyreuma (empirū·mă). Pl. **-mata.** 1641. [a. Gr. ἐμπύρευμα a live coal covered with ashes.] †1. 'Heat left by the fire in the burned part' (J. Steer) -1656. 2. The burnt smell imparted by fire to organic substances 1641. var. †**Empyreu·m(e.** Hence **Empy·reuma·tic, -al** *a.* pertaining to, or having the quality of, e., as *empyreumatic oil*. **Empyreu·matize** *v.* to taint with an e.

Empyrical (empi·rikăl), *a. rare.* [f. Gr. ἔμπυρος + -IC + -AL.] a. Of or pertaining to burning. b. 'Containing the combustible principle of coal' (Smart 1847).

†**Empyro·sis.** *rare.* 1677. [a. Gr. ἐμπύρωσις.] A general fire, conflagration.

Emrod(e, obs. var. of EMERALD.

Emu, var. of EMEU.

†**E·mulable,** *a. rare.* 1693. [f. L. *æmulare* + -ABLE.] Worthy of emulation.

†**E·mulate.** [ad. L. *æmulatus*.] Ambitious. *Haml.* I. i. 82.

Emulate (e·miŭleˡt), *v.* Also †**æm-**. 1589. [f. L. *æmulat-*, ppl. stem of *æmulari*.] 1. *trans.* To strive to equal or rival; to imitate with the object of equalling or excelling; to vie with, rival. †2. *intr.* To strive in a spirit of rivalry. Const. *inf.* -1649. †3. To desire to rival; *hence*, to be jealous of -1654. †4. To spur (*rare*) 1804.

1. Contemn the bad, and E. the best DRYDEN. I see how thine eye would e. the diamond SHAKS.

Emulation (emiulēⁱ·ʃən). Also †**æm-**. 1552. [ad. L. *æmulationem*.] 1. The endeavour to equal or surpass others in actions or qualities; also, the desire to equal or excel. †2. Ambitious rivalry; contention or ill will between rivals -1651. †3. Jealousy; dislike of those who are superior -1771.

1. This Faire æmulation, & no envy is B. JONS. 2. The dissension and e. that I have seen..between private captains for vainglory 1588. 3. For E. ever did attend Upon the Great DRAYTON.

Emulative (e·miŭlĕtiv), *a.* 1593. [f. as EMULATE *v.* + -IVE.] Characterized by, or tending to, emulation or rivalry. Const. *of*. Also *fig.* 1748.

Noble minds, e. of perfection 1748. Hence **E·mulatively** *adv.*

Emulator (e·miŭleⁱtəɹ). Also †**æm-**. 1589. [a. L.] One who emulates, in good or bad sense.

An enuious e. of every mans good parts SHAKS. A diligent e. of Grocyn..was..Linacre HALLAM.

†**E·mulatory,** *a. rare.* 1621. [f. prec.; see -ORY.] Of the nature of emulation, as *emulatory officiousness* -1627.

†**E·mulatress.** *rare.* 1620. [See -ESS.] A female emulator -1741. So †**Emula·trix.**

†**E·mule,** *v. rare.* Also **æm-**. [ad. L. *æmulari*.] = EMULATE *v.* SPENSER.

Emulge (ĭmɒ·ldʒ), *v.* 1681. [ad. L. *emulgere* to milk out.] *trans.* To drain (secretory organs).

Emulgence (ĭmɒ·ldʒĕns). *rare.* 1674. [See next and -ENCE.] The action of milking out.

Emulgent (ĭmɒ·ldʒĕnt). 1578. [ad. L. *emulgentem*; see EMULGE.]

A. *adj.* That milks out; *esp.* applied to the vessels of the kidneys.

B. *sb.* = *Emulgent vessels* 1612.

Emulous (e·miŭləs), *a.* ME. [f. L. *æmulus* + -OUS.] 1. Desirous of rivalling, imitating, obtaining. Also, formerly, of things (*rare*). 2. Filled with emulation 1617. †3. Covetous of praise or power; also, envious -1660. 4. Proceeding from emulation or rivalry 1535.

1. Of other excellence not e. MILT. *P. L.* VI. 822. 2. Æmulous the royal robes they lave POPE. 3. He is not e., as Achilles is *Tr. & Cr.* II. iii. 243. 4. E. extravagance 1782. Hence **E·mulous-ly** *adv.*, **-ness.**

Emulsic (ĭmɒ·lsik), *a.* [f. EMULSIN + -IC.] *Chem.* Related to EMULSIN.

Emulsify (ĭmɒ·lsifəi), *v.* 1859. [f. L. *emuls-* ppl. stem; see EMULGE *v.*] To convert into an emulsion. Also *absol.*

To e. bromide of silver in liquid gelatine 1881. So **Emu·lsionize** *v.* Hence **Emu·lsifica·tion,** the action of the vb.; *spec.* the last stage of fatty degeneration. **Emu·lsifier,** an emulsifying agent.

Emulsin (ĭmɒ·lsin). 1838. [f. EMULSION + -IN [1].] *Chem.* A neutral substance contained in almonds; called also *synaptase*.

Emulsion (ĭmɒ·lʃən). 1612. [ad. mod.L. *emulsionem*. In Fr. *émulsion*.] †1. The action of emulging (*fig.*) 1658. 2. A milky liquid obtained by bruising almonds, etc. in water. b. *Pharm.* 'A milky liquid, consisting of water holding in suspension minute particles of oil or resin by the aid of some albuminous or gummy substance' (*Syd. Soc. Lex.*). 1612. Also *attrib.* 3. *Photog.* A mixture of light-sensitive silver salts suspended in collodion or gelatin for coating plates, films, etc. 1877.

Emu·lsive, *a.* 1861. [f. L. *emuls-*, ppl. stem + -IVE.] That has the nature of an EMULSION.

†**Emu·nct,** *a. rare.* 1679. [ad. L. *emunctus*, as in L. phrase *emunctæ naris homo*.] Of the judgement: Keen -1697. So †**Emu·nction** (*rare*), the wiping of the nose; whence *transf.* of clearing any of the passages of the body.

Emunctory (ĭmɒ·ŋktəri). 1547. [ad. mod.L. *emunctorius*, *emunctorium*, f. *emungere* to wipe the nose.] *Phys.* A. *adj.* a. Of or pertaining to the blowing of the nose. b. That conveys waste matters from the body 1858. B. *sb.* A cleansing organ or canal. Also *fig.* 1601.

†**Emu·nge,** *v.* 1664. [ad. L. *emungere*.] *trans.* To wipe or clean out; *fig.* to cheat -1846.

†**Emusca·tion.** 1664. [f. L. *emuscare* to cleanse from moss.] The action of cleansing from moss. Also *fig.* -1679.

En (en). 1785. [The name of the letter N.] *Printing.* The half-square, formerly of the type 'n', half the width of an EM.

‖**En** (aṅ). Fr. prep., = in, as (a), used in various phr., many of which are current in Eng., as **en déshabillé**, in undress; **en famille**, among one's family; **en garçon**, as a bachelor; **en pension**, as a boarder; **en règle**, in due form; **en route** (see ROUTE *sb.* 4); **en suite** (see SUITE 4). See also EN BLOC.

En-, *prefix* [1], the form assumed in Fr. (Pr., Sp., Pg.) by L. *in-* (see IN-). In Eng., used chiefly in words adapted from Fr.

A. 1. Before *b* and *p*, and occas. before *m*, it is now (since 17th c.) changed to *em-*. 2. In ME. (as in OF.) *en-*, *em-*, freq. became *an-*, *am-* (cf. AMBUSH), whence *a-* (see APPAIR, APPRAISE). Conversely, *a-* often became *en-* (*em-*), as in *embraid*. 3. From 14th c. onwards IN- (IM-) has taken the place of *en-* (*em-*); and the converse has also occurred. Hence much difficulty in determining in a particular word whether the prefix *en-* or *in-* is Fr., Lat., or purely Eng. in origin.

B. The applications of the prefix in Fr. (Pr., Sp., Pg.), and hence in Eng., are mainly those of the L. *in-*; viz. to form vbs. from sbs., adjs., or from other vbs.

1. Verbs formed by prefixing *en-* to a sb.

a. With sense 'to put into or on what is denoted by the sb.':

†**Enambush**; **enchair**; **enchannel**; †**encoach**; †**engaol**; †**enkennel**; **enkerchief**; **enkernel**; **enmagazine**; **enniche**; †**enseat**; **enshadow**; **enshawl**; †**enshelter**; †**enslumber**; †**enstage**; **enwall**; **enzone**; etc.

b. With sense 'to put what is denoted by the sb. into or on' (a person or thing):

†**Encowl**; **endiadem**; **enmoss**; †**ensilver**; †**enspangle**; †**entackle**; **enverdure**; etc.

2. Verbs formed by prefixing *en-* to a sb. or adj., with sense 'to bring into a certain condition or state':

†**Enanger**; †**encanker**; †**encinder**; **encommon**; **endiaper**; †**endrudge** (*refl.*); †**enfavour**; †**enfierce**; †**enfort**; **enfoul**; **enfree**; **enfreedom**; **enfroward**; †**engallant**; †**engarboil**; **engloom**; **engolden**; †**enlength**; †**enripe**; †**ensafe**; †**ensober**; **entempest**; **envineyard**; †**enwoman**; †**enwrack**; etc.

b. Verbs formed (with sense as above) on adjs. or sbs. with prefix *en-* and suffix -EN [5], as ENLIVEN, ENLIGHTEN.

3. Verbs, mostly transitive, formed by prefixing *en-* to a verb, with additional sense of *in*, or simply intensive; also vbs. formed as in 2 b.

†**Encheck**, †**enchequer**, to arrange chequer-wise; †**enclog**; †**endamnify**; †**endart**; †**en-**

dazzle; enfasten; †enfester; †enfreeze; engladden; †enhedge; †enlengthen; †enmix; †enquicken; †enrive; †enstrengthen; †entwist; †enwallow *intr.*; †enwiden; enwrite; †enyoked; etc.

En-, *prefix* [2], the form taken by the Gr. ἐν. (Before *b, m, p, ph*, it becomes *em-*; before *l, r* it becomes *el-, er-* respectively.)

-en, *suffix* [1] :—OTeut. *-îno(m*, formally the neut. of *-îno-*, -EN [4], is used to form dims. from sbs., as in CHICKEN, etc.

-en, *suffix* [2] :—WGer. *-innja*, repr. OTeut. *-inî*, is used to form feminines, as in VIXEN, the only surviving instance of this. It is also added to the stem of a vb., or of a verbal-abstract sb., as in BURDEN, etc.

-en, *suffix* [3], the ME. form of OE. *-an*, the termination of the nom., accus., and dat. pl. of wk. sbs. Hence the termination *-en* became a formative of the pl., as in *ox-en*, and was also added to the remains of other old plurals, as in *brethren, children, kine.*

-en, *suffix* [4] (reduced to *-n* after *r* in unstressed syllables) :—OTeut. *-îno-*, = Gr. *-ινο-*, L. *-îno-* (see -INE), added to noun-stems to form adjs. with sense 'pertaining to, of the nature of'. In literary English the use of these adjs. is largely superseded by the attrib. use of the sb., as in 'a gold watch'. In a few cases (e. g. *wooden, woollen, earthen, wheaten*) they are still familiarly used.

-en, *suffix* [5], forming verbs. **1.** from adjs., as *darken, deepen*, etc. **2.** from sbs. The majority of these (e. g. *heighten, lengthen, strengthen*, etc.) appear first in mod.Eng., and follow the analogy of verbs f. adjs. LISTEN (OE. *hlystnian* :—OTeut. **hlusinôjan*) is an exception. **3.** In one or two cases (e. g. *waken*) the suffix *-en* represents OTeut. *-na-*, the formative of the present stem in some strong verbs.

Enable (enē¹·b'l), *v.* ME. [f. EN-[1] + ABLE *a.*; cf. ABLE *v.*] †**1.** To invest with legal status –1721. **2.** To empower; to give legal power or licence to 1526. **3.** To make able (to be or to do something); to strengthen; to supply with means, opportunities, or the like 1460. †**4.** To regard as competent –1596. †**5.** To make possible; also, to make effective –1675. †**6.** *intr.* for *refl.* To become able (*rare*) ME.

1. She was restored and enabled in blood STRYPE. **2.** Congress cannot e. a state to legislate 1824. **3.** Exercise to e. the body MULCASTER. A solitude.. which enabled him to work better there MORLEY. Hence †**Ena·blement**, the action or means of enabling. **Ena·bler. Ena·bling** *ppl. a.* that enables: chiefly of legislative enactments.

†**Ena·ct**, *sb.* 1467. [f. next.] That which is enacted; *fig.* a purpose, resolution (*Tit. A.* IV. ii. 118) –1588.

Enact (enæ·kt), *v.* ME. [f. EN-[1] + ACT *sb.* and *v.*] †**1.** (from ACT *sb.*) To enter among the *acta* or public records, or in a chronicle –1641. **2.** Of a legislative authority: To make into an act; hence, to ordain, decree 1464. †**3.** To declare officially –1715. †**4.** (from ACT *v.*) To actuate, influence –1647. **5.** To represent on or as on the stage; to act the part of, play; also *fig.* ME. †**6.** To bring into act, perform –1616. †**7.** *intr.* To act –1684.

2. Wouldst thou His laws of fasting disanull? E. good cheer G. HERBERT. **5.** I did e. Julius Cæsar *Haml.* III. ii. 108. To e. the philosopher DE QUINCEY. Hence †**Ena·ct** = *enacted* pa. pple. **Ena·ctable** *a.* **Ena·cting** *ppl. a.* that enacts; *spec.* in *enacting clauses* (of a statute), viz. those in which new provisions are enacted (opp. to *declaratory*). **Ena·ctive** *a.* enacting. **Ena·ctor**, one who enacts (a law); one who enacts (a part, scene, transaction, etc.). **Ena·ctory** *a.* enacting. †**Ena·cture**, ?fulfilment (*Haml.* III. ii. 207 *Qq.*).

Enaction (enæ·kʃən). 1630. [f. prec.] = ENACTMENT 1, 2.

Enactment (enæ·ktmĕnt). 1817. [f. ENACT *v.* + -MENT.] **1.** The action of enacting (a law); the state of being enacted. **2.** That which is enacted; an ordinance, a statute; one of the provisions of a law 1821.

1. The e. of the Six Articles MILMAN. **2.** Enactments for the regulation of trade GREEN.

†**Ena·ge**, *v.* 1593. [See EN-[1].] To make or cause to look old –1631.

Enaliosaur (enæ·li,osǭɹ). 1863. [f. Gr. ἐνάλιος of the sea + σαῦρος lizard.] A 'marine lizard'; a name for the gigantic fossil reptiles forming the orders *Sauropterygia* and *Ichthyopterygia.* Hence **Ena:liosau·rian** *a.* and *sb.*

Enallage (enæ·lădʒī). 1583. [a. L., a. Gr. ἐναλλαγή, f. ἐναλλάσσειν to change.] *Gram.* The substitution of one grammatical form for another, *e.g.* of sing. for pl., present for past tense, etc.

†**Ena·luron.** 1562. [? a. AFr. phr. **en aileron.*] *Her.* A bordure charged with birds. (According to Porny the word is an adv., = '*orlé*, or in manner of a bordure'.) –1766.

‖**Enam** (ĭnā·m). Also **enaum, inam.** 1803. [Pers. (Arab.); lit. 'favour'.] In India: A grant of land free of the land-tax due to the State; also, the land so held. So ‖**Ena:mda·r**, one who holds an e.

Enambush; see EN- *prefix* [1] 1.

Enamel (enæ·mĕl), *sb.* 1463. [f. ENAMEL *v.*; see AMEL *sb.*] **1.** A semi-opaque variety of glass, applied by fusion to metallic surfaces, either to ornament them in colours, or to form a surface for encaustic painting; now also as a lining for cooking utensils, etc. **b.** *fig. esp.* with reference to the hardness and polish of enamel 1680. **c.** A glassy bead formed by the blowpipe. **d.** In recent use, any composition employed to form a smooth hard coating on any surface. **2.** *Phys.* [after Fr. *émail.*] The substance which forms the hard glossy coating of the teeth; the similar substance coating the bony scales of ganoid fishes 1718. **3.** A work executed in enamel 1861. **4.** *transf.* Any smooth and lustrous surface-colouring 1600. **5.** *attrib.*, as *e.-colour, -painting*, etc. 1754.

1. b. None of the hard and brilliant e. of Petrarch in the style MACAULAY. **4.** On the green e. of the plain Were shown me the great spirits CARY. *Comb.*: **e.-painting,** painting by fusing vitrifiable colours laid on a metal surface; **-paper,** paper covered with a glazed metallic coating. Also (in dental anatomy), **e.-cell**, one of the cells of the *enamel-organ*, sometimes called collectively 'enamel-membrane'; **-germ**, a portion of thickened epithelium, which develops into the **e.-organ.**

Enamel (enæ·mĕl), *v.* ME. [ad. AFr. *enamayller, enameler*; see EN-[1] and AMEL *sb.*] **1.** *trans.* To inlay, cover, or portray with ENAMEL. **b.** *transf.* To variegate like enamelled work; to beautify with varied colours 1650. †**c.** *fig.* To adorn magnificently; to impart an additional splendour to –1670. **2.** To cover with a glossy coating resembling enamel. **b.** To make smooth (the skin of the face) with cosmetics 1868.

1. Brende golde..enaumaylde with azer ME. And therin imagery grauen & enamelyd FABYAN. **b.** Spring ne'er enamell'd fairer meads than thine SHENSTONE. **2.** To e. cardboard, leather, etc. (*mod.*). Hence **Ena·meller, -eler. Ena·melist**, an artist in enamel.

Enamellar, -elar (enæ·mĕlăɹ), *a.* [f. ENAMEL *sb.* + -AR.] Of or like enamel; smooth, glossy. (Dicts.)

Enamelling, -eling (enæ·mĕliŋ), *vbl. sb.* 1449. [f. ENAMEL *v.*] The action or process of covering or adorning with enamel; *concr.* anything so treated. Also *fig.* and *attrib.*

fig. A fair enamelling of a terrible danger LD. BURLEIGH.

‖**Enamora·do.** [Sp.] = INAMORATO. Sir T. Herbert.

†**Ena·morate**, *v. rare.* 1591. [f. It. *innamorat-, innamorare.*] *trans.* To inspire with love –1711. Hence **Ena:mora·tion.**

†**Ena·morate.** 1607. [ad. It. *inamorato.*] **a.** *adj.* Enamoured. **b.** *sb.* A lover. –1711.

Enamour (enæ·məɹ), *v.* ME. [a. OF. *enamourer*; see EN-[1] and AMOUR.] **1.** *trans.* To inspire with love. Chiefly *pass.* Also *fig.* **2.** To charm, delight, fascinate. Chiefly *pass.* Const. *of*, †*on*, †*with*. 1590.

1. Me-thought I was enamoured of an Asse *Mids. N.* IV. i. 82. **2.** Mine eare is much enamored of thy note *Mids. N.* III. i. 141. Hence **Ena·mourment.**

Enantiopathy (enæ:nti,ǫ·păþi). 1852. [f. Gr. ἐναντιοπαθής of contrary properties.] *Med.* = ALLOPATHY; the treatment of disease by contraries. Hence **Ena:ntiopa·thic** *a.*

Enantiosis (enæ:nti,ōᵘ·sis). 1657. [mod.L., a. Gr., f. ἐναντιοῦσθαι to oppose.] *Rhet.* A figure in which the opposite is meant to what is said; irony.

†**Enarch** (enā·ɹtʃ), *v.* ME. [f. EN-[1] + ARCH *sb.*; cf. INARCH.] To build in the form of an arch; to arch in or over; in *Her.* of a chevron: To have an arch within its inner angle –1631. Hence **Ena·rched** *ppl. a.*

Enargite (enā·ɹdʒəit). 1852. [f. Gr. ἐναργής clear (from its cleavage being apparent) + -ITE.] *Min.* A black sulph-arsenide of copper, of metallic lustre.

†**Ena·rm**, *v.* ME. [a. OF. *enarmer* to arm.] = ARM *v.* –1588.

Enarm, var. of INARM, to embrace.

†**Enarration.** 1563. [ad. L. *enarrationem.*] **1.** An exposition –1647. **2.** A description, a detailed narrative –1826.

Enarthrodial (enaɹþrōᵘ·diăl), *a.* 1836. [f. mod.L. *enarthrodia* (f. Gr. ἐν + ἀρθρωδία) = next + -AL.] *Anat.* Of the nature of, or belonging to, the ball-and-socket joint.

Enarthrosis (enaɹþrōᵘ·sis). 1634. [a. Gr., f. ἔναρθρος jointed.] *Anat.* The jointing of the head of a bone into a socket; the ball-and-socket joint.

Enascent (ĭnæ·sĕnt), *a. rare.* 1745. [ad. L. *enascentem*, pr. pple. of *enasci.*] That is just coming into being. Also *fig.*

†**Enatant**, *a. rare.* [ad. L. *enatantem*, pr. pple. of *enatare.*] Floating up, coming to the top. So †**Enata·tion**, a swimming out.

Enate (ī·nēt), *a.* 1666. [ad. L. *enatus*, pa. pple. of *enasci.*] *Phys.* That has grown out, as the apophysis of a bone. So **Ena·tion** (*Bot.*), outgrowth.

†**Enau·nter**, *conj. rare.* ME. [var. of *an, in, on aunter*, Fr. *en aventure.*] In case that; lest by chance. SPENSER.

Enb-, obs. spelling of EMB-.

†**Enbai·ssing**, *vbl. sb.* [corrupt var. of *abaissing.*] Abashment. CHAUCER.

Enbibe, enbibing, obs. ff. IMBIBE, etc.

‖**En bloc** (aṅ blok), *adv. phr.* 1877. [Fr.] In a block, as a whole. Also *attrib.*

‖**Enca·dré.** 1817. [F., pa. pple. of *encadrer* to frame.] *Crystall.* Having 'facets which form kinds of squares around the planes of a more simple form already existing in the same species' (R. Jameson).

Encænia (ensī·niă). Also 4 **encenia.** ME. [a. L., a. Gr. (τὰ) ἐγκαίνια, f. ἐν + καινός new.] †**1.** A renewal; a dedicatory festival. ME. only. **2.** The anniversary festival of the dedication of a temple or church ME. **3.** The annual Commemoration of founders and benefactors at Oxford 1691.

Encage, in- (en-, inkē¹·dʒ), *v.* 1593. [f. EN-[1], IN- + CAGE *sb.*] To confine in, or as in, a cage. Hence †**Enca·gement** (*rare*).

Encalendar; modernized spelling of †INCALENDAR *v.*

Encamp (enkæ·mp), *v.* Also †**in-**. 1549. [f. EN-[1] + CAMP *sb.*[2]] **1.** *trans.* To form into or settle in a camp. Also *intr.* for *refl.* **2.** *transf.* (*intr.* and *pass.*) To lodge in the open in tents or the like 1725.

1. Bid him encampe his Souldiers where they are SHAKS. **2.** We followed up the stream..encamping each night DE FOE. Hence †**Enca·mper** (*rare*).

Encampment (enkæ·mpmĕnt). Also **in-**. 1598. [f. prec. + -MENT.] **1.** The action of encamping, or state of being encamped 1686. **2.** The place where troops are encamped in tents, huts, etc.; a CAMP. Also *attrib.* and *fig.* 1598. **b.** *transf.* The temporary quarters of a body of men on the march, travellers, etc. Also *fig.* 1725. †**3.** A Masonic meeting –1878.

1. A square of about seven hundred yards was sufficient for the e. of twenty thousand Romans GIBBON. **2. b.** Signs of a small Indian e. 1825.

Encanker; see EN- *pref.*[1] 2.

Encanthis (enkæ·nþis). 1586. [a. Gr. ἐγκανθίς, f. ἐν + κανθός corner of the eye.] *Med.* A small red excrescence growing in the inner corner of the eye.

Encapsulate, -ation, var. ff. INCAPSULATE, -ATION.

Encapsule (enkæ·psiul), *v.* 1877. [See EN-[1].] *Phys.* To enclose in a capsule; cf. CAPSULE 2.

Encaptivate; see INCAPTIVATE.

†**Enca·ptive**, *v.* 1592. [f. EN-[1] + CAPTIVE *a.*] To make into a captive; to enthral –1605.

†**Enca·rdion.** [a. Gr. ἐγκάρδιον the heart of wood.] *Bot.* 'The pith of vegetables' (*Syd. Soc. Lex.*).

Encarnadine, var. of INCARNADINE.

Encarnalize (enkā·ɹnăləiz), *v.* Also **in-**. 1847. [f. EN- + CARNALIZE.] To put in flesh and blood; also *fig.* Also, to make gross, sensual.

fig. So incarnalise The strong idea H. COLERIDGE.

‖**Enca·rpa,** *sb. pl.* 1662. [L., a. Gr. ἔγκαρπα; cf. ENCARPUS.] *Arch.* Festoons of fruit (as an ornament).

Encarpus (enkā·ɹpŏs). [ad. Gr. ἔγκαρπος containing fruit, taken as = prec.] *Arch.* 'The festoons on a frieze; consisting of fruit, flowers, leaves, etc.' (Gwilt).

Encase, in- (eŋ-, iŋkēⁱ·s), *v.* 1633. [f. EN-[1], IN- + CASE *sb.*[2]] **1.** *trans.* To put into or enclose within a case 1727. **2.** To overlay, surround, hem in; also, to cover, invest 1633.

1. A little soul is encased in a large body JOWETT. Hence **Enca·sement,** also **in-**, that which encases; in *Biol.* = EMBOÎTEMENT.

Encash (enkæ·ʃ), *v.* 1861. [f. EN-[1] + CASH *sb.*[1]; cf. F. *encaisser.*] **1.** To convert into cash; to CASH. **2.** To receive in cash, realize 1861.

2. The communication of the revenue encashed 1879. Hence **Enca·shable** *a.* **Enca·shment,** the action of encashing; *concr.* the sum received in cash.

†**Encau·ma.** 1708. [a. Gr. ἔγκαυμα result of burning in.] †**1.** 'The scoria of silver' (*Syd. Soc. Lex.*). **2.** A deep foul ulceration of the cornea. (Dicts.) **3.** The mark, or a vesicle, resulting from a burn.

Encaustic (enkǭ·stik). 1601. [ad. Gr. ἐγκαυστικός, f. ἐγκαίειν.]

A. *adj.* Pertaining to, or produced by, the process of burning in: **a.** chiefly with reference to the ancient method of painting with wax colours, and fixing by heat; **b.** applied occasionally to enamelling, painting on pottery, etc. 1656. Also *transf.* and *fig.*

Phr. *E. brick, tile*: one decorated with patterns in different coloured clays, inlaid in the brick, and burnt with it.

B. *sb.* [ad. Gr. ἐγκαυστική τέχνη.] **1.** The art or process of encaustic painting (see A.) 1601. †**2.** A pigment or glaze applied by burning in 1662.

Hence **Encau·stically** *adv.* in e.

†**Encave,** *v.* [a. OF. *encaver.*] To put into a cellar. *Oth.* IV. i. 82.

-ence, *suffix.* [a. F. *-ence*, ad. L. *-entia*, forming abstr. sbs. on ppl. stems in *ent-*, e. g. *sapient-em, sapient-ia.* See also -ANCE. In sense, words in *-nce* are partly nouns of action, as in OFr., partly of state or quality, as in L.]

‖**Enceinte** (aṅsæ̃nt), *sb.* 1708. [Fr.; f. late L. type **incincta*, f. ppl. stem of *incingere* to gird in.] An enclosure; chiefly in *Fortif.*

The 'enceinte' or 'body of the place' is the main enclosure of the fortress 1879.

‖**Enceinte** (aṅsæ̃nt), *a.* 1602. [Fr.:—late L. *in-cincta* ungirt; or ? pa. pple. of *incingere* to gird.] Of women: Pregnant.

Encens(e, obs. ff. INCENSE.

Encense, var. of †ENSENSE *v.*

‖**Encephala** (ense·fălă), *sb. pl.* 1854. [mod.L., f. Gr. ἐν + κεφαλή.] *Zool.* A division of Mollusca, viz. those which have a distinct brain. Hence **Ence·phalous** *a.* belonging to the E.

Encephalic (ensĭfæ·lik), *a.* 1831. [f. Gr. ἐγκέφαλος + -IC.] Pertaining to the brain or ENCEPHALON.

Encephalitis (ensefăləi·tis). 1843. [f. as prec. + -ITIS.] *Path.* Inflammation of the brain; now chiefly of the brain-substance, as dist. from its membranes. Hence **Encephali·tic** *a.*

Encephalocele (ense·fălosīl). 1835. [f. as prec. + Gr. κήλη tumour.] *Med.* Hernia of the brain.

Encephaloid (ense·făloid), *a.* 1846. [a. F. *encéphaloïde*, f. as prec. + -OID.] *Path.* Resembling the brain or brain-structure; the distinctive epithet of soft cancer.

Encephalon (ense·fălǫn). 1741. [a. Gr. (τὸ) ἐγκέφαλον what is within the head.] *Anat.* What is within the skull; the brain.

Encephalopathy (ensefălǫ·păþi). 1866. [f. Gr. ἐγκέφαλος + -πάθεια, f. πάθος.] *Path.* Disease of the brain in general. Hence **Encephalopa·thic** *a.* pertaining to e.

‖**Encephalos** (ense·fălǫs). *rare.* 1708. [a. Gr.] = ENCEPHALON.

Enchafe (en,tʃēⁱ·f), *v.* [ME. *enchaufe*, altered form of *eschaufe*, ACHAFE.] To make or grow hot or warm; also *fig.*

Enchain (en,tʃēⁱ·n), *v.* ME. [a. OF. *enchainer*, f. *en-* (see EN-[1]) + *chaine.*] **1.** To put in, or bind with, chains 1491. **2.** *fig.* To fetter 1751; to hold fast; to bind 1658. †**b.** *intr.* for *refl.* To become closely united. ME. only. †**3.** To link together -1768.

2. Enchained by rules HALLAM. Rachel's acting.. enchained me with interest C. BRONTË.

Hence **Enchai·nment,** the action of enchaining; enchained state.

Enchair, Enchannel; see EN- *pref.*[1] 1.

Enchant (en,tʃɑ·nt), *v.* ME. [a. F. *enchanter* :—L. *incantare*, f. *in* upon, against + *cantare*; cf. CHANT *v.*, INCANTATION.] **1.** *trans.* To exert magical influence upon; to bewitch. Also, to endow with magical powers or properties. Also *fig.* †**2.** *fig.* To influence as if by a charm; to hold spellbound; in bad sense, to delude -1678. **3.** To charm, enrapture 1592.

1. Cockering mothers inchant their sonnes to make them rod-free FULLER. Enchanted amulets 1772. 3. Bid me discourse, I will e. thine ear SHAKS. Hence **Encha·nted** *ppl.a.* bewitched; invested with magical powers or properties; charmed. **Encha·nting** *ppl.a.* that enchants; charming. **Encha·ntingly** *adv.*

Enchanter (en,tʃɑ·ntəɹ). ME. [orig. a. OF. *enchanteor* :—L. *incantatorem.*] One who enchants, uses magic; formerly also, a conjurer.

By this means I knew the foul e. MILT. *Comus* 645.

Enchanter's nightshade, *Circæa lutetiana.*

†**Encha·ntery.** *rare.* ME. [a. OF. *enchanterie.*] Magic -1591.

Enchantment (en,tʃɑ·ntmĕnt). ME. [a. OF. *enchantement*; see -MENT.] **1.** The action of enchanting, or of using magic or sorcery. **2.** *fig.* Alluring or overpowering charm; enraptured condition; (delusive) appearance of beauty 1678.

1. With thyne inchantment [A.V. sorceries] were deceaved all nations TINDALE *Rev.* xviii. 23. 2. 'Tis distance lends e. to the view CAMPBELL.

Enchantress (en,tʃɑ·ntrĕs). ME. [a. OF. *enchanteresse*, fem. of *enchantere, -eor* ENCHANTER.] **1.** A female who uses magic; a sorceress. Also *fig.* **2.** *fig.* A bewitching woman 1713.

1. Endor, famous by reason of the Inchantresse RALEIGH.

†**Encha·rge,** *sb.* [a. OF.; see next.] An injunction. COPLEY.

Encharge (en,tʃā·ɹdʒ), *v.* Also **in-**. ME. [a. OF. *encharger*, f. *en-* (see EN-[1]) + *charge* CHARGE *sb.*] †**1.** *trans.* To impose as a charge or duty -1828. †**2.** To enjoin *to* do something -1681. **3.** To burden, entrust *with* 1640.

3. Encharging them with the flocke over which Christ hath made them Bishops BP. HALL.

†**Encha·rm,** *v.* Also **in-**. 1480. [a. OF. *encharmer.*] To throw a charm over; to enchant -1611.

†**Encha·se,** *v.*[1] ME. [a. OF. *enchacier*, f. *en-* (see EN-[1]) + *chacier* (see CHASE).] To drive away; to hunt, pursue -1741. Hence †**Encha·se** *sb.* chase; hunting (*rare*).

Enchase (en,tʃēⁱ·s), *v.*[2] 1463. [a. F. *enchâsser* 'to enchace or set in gold' (Cotgr.), f. *en-* + *châsse* :—L. *capsa* CASE *sb.*[2]] **1.** To set *in*; also, to serve as a setting for 1534. **2.** To set (gold, etc.) *with.* Also *transf.* and *fig.* 1589. **3.** To inlay *with* 1640. **4.** To adorn with figures in relief. Hence, to engrave. 1463. **5.** *transf.* and *fig.* To adorn as with engraved figures 1590. **6.** To enshrine *in.* [The orig. Fr. sense.] Also *fig.* 1615. †**7.** To shut in, enclose -1715. **8.** To 'let in' to a 'chase' or mortice. Also *transf.* and *fig.* 1611.

1. A gold ring with a ruby enchased 1877. 2. Whose floore with Stars is gloriously inchased DRAYTON. 4. Wherein is enchased many a fayre sight SPENSER. 6. Enchased in a crystal covered with gold EVELYN. *fig.* Thy bright Idea in my Heart E. KEN.

Hence †**Encha·sement,** setting, frame. **Encha·ser,** one who enchases or engraves metal. So ‖**Enchâssure** [F.] (*rare*), the casing of a relic.

Encha·sten, *v.* [See EN-[1].] To make chaste. K. WHITE.

†**Enchea·son.** Also **Anchesoun.** ME. [a. OF. *encheson, encheison*, f. *encheoir*, lit. to fall in, hence to be in fault.] Occasion, cause, reason -1642.

†**Enchea·t,** *sb.* ME. [a. OF. *encheoite*, f. *encheoir*; see prec.] Revenue from escheats or confiscations -1494.

Encheck, Enchequer: see EN- *pref.*[1] 3.

Encheer (en,tʃīə·ɹ), *v.* 1605. [f. EN-[1] + CHEER *v.*] To cheer.

‖**Enchei·ria.** [Gr.] Method of manipulation. NEWTON.

Enchesoun, variant of ENCHEASON.

†**Enche·st,** *v.* Also **in-**. [See EN-[1].] To enclose in, or as in, a chest. VICARS.

Enchiridion (enkəiri·diǫn). 1541. [a. Gr., f. ἐν + χείρ + dim. suff. -ιδιον.] A handbook or manual.

Enchisel; see EN- *pref.*[1] 2.

‖**Enchondroma** (enkǫndrōᵘ·ma). *Pl.* **-mata.** 1847. [mod.L., f. Gr. ἐν + χόνδρος cartilage.] *Path.* A cartilaginous tumour. Hence **Enchondro·matous** *a.*

Enchorial (enkǭ·riăl), *a.* 1822. [f. Gr. ἐγχώριος (f. ἐν + χώρα) + -AL.] That belongs to, or is used in, a particular country; used *esp.* of the popular (as dist. from the hieroglyphic and the hieratic) writing of the ancient Egyptians; = DEMOTIC. In general sense now *rare.*

†**Enchro·nicle,** *v.* 1513. [See EN-[1].] To enter in a chronicle -1593.

†**Enchu·rch,** *v.* 1681. [See EN-[1].] To form into a church -1702.

Enchyma (en·kĭma). [mod.L., a. Gr. ἔγχυμα.] *Biol.* The formative juice of tissues.

Encincture (ensi·ŋktiŭɹ), *v.* 1821. [f. EN-[1] + CINCTURE *sb.*] To surround with, or as with, a girdle. Also as *sb.* (*rare*), enclosure; an enclosure.

Encinder; see EN- *pref.*[1] 2.

Encipher (ensəi·fəɹ), *v.* 1577. [f. EN-[1] + CIPHER *sb.*] *trans.* To write in cipher; also, to combine in a monogram *with.*

Encircle (ensɔ̄·ɹk'l), *v.* ME. [f. EN-[1] + CIRCLE.] **1.** To enclose in a circle, surround; also, to surround *with.* Also *transf.* and *fig.* **2.** To make a circling movement round 1598.

1. Great Britaine .. encircled by the Sea HOWELL. *fig.* Satire and censure encircled his throne GOLDSM. 2. Hermes.. Her brows encircled with his serpent-rod PARNELL. Hence **Enci·rcler** (*rare*).

†**Encla·ret,** *v.* [See EN-[1].] To tinge with claret. HERRICK.

Enclasp (enklɑ·sp), *v.* Also **in-**. 1596. [f. EN-[1] + CLASP *sb.* and *v.*] To hold in or as in a clasp.

‖**Enclave** (enklēⁱ·v, aṅkla·v), *sb.* 1868. [Fr., f. (ult.) L. *in* + *clavis* key or *clavus* nail.] A piece of territory entirely shut in by foreign dominions. Also *fig.*

Encla·ve, *a.* 1661. [a. F. *enclavé* dovetailed; see prec.] *Her.* Of the border of an ordinary: Having a contour like that of a dovetail joint.

†**Enclea·r,** *v.* 1509. [f. EN-[1] + CLEAR *a.*] **1.** To make clear -1556. **2.** To light up (*lit.* and *fig.*) -1580.

Enclitic (enkli·tik). 1656. [ad. L. *encliticus*, a. Gr., f. ἐν + κλίνειν to lean.] *Gram.*

A. *adj.* That 'leans its accent on the preceding word' (Liddell and Scott): in Gr. grammar applied to words which have no accent, and which usually modify the accent of the word they follow. Hence applied analogously to the L. particles *-que, -ve, -ne*, etc., and to similar unemphatic words in mod. langs.

B. *sb.* An enclitic word 1663.

B. When we say 'Give me content', the *me* in this case is a perfect enclitick HARRIS.

So †**Encli·tical** *a.* **Encli·tically** *adv.* **Encli·ticism,** accentual leaning on another word.

Enclog; see EN- *pref.*[1] 2.

†**Encloi·ster,** *v.* 1596. [EN-[1].] To shut up in or as in a cloister; to immure -1710.

†**Enclo·se,** *sb. rare.* 1484. [f. next.] = ENCLOSURE -1648.

Enclose, in- (en-, inklōᵘ·z), *v.* ME. [f. EN-[1] + CLOSE *v.* Eng. usage favours *enclose.*] **1.** *trans.* To surround so as to bar ingress or egress. **b.** To fence in (common land) with a view to appropriation. Also *fig.* 1503. **2.** To seclude, imprison. ? *Obs.* ME. **3.** To insert within a frame, case, envelope, receptacle, or the like. Also *fig.* ME. **4.** To surround, bound on all sides; to contain ME. **5.** Of an army, etc.: To hem in on all sides 1601.

2. The nuns live in community, but are not enclosed SHIPLEY. 3. Onix stones enclosed in ouches of gold *Ex.* xxxix. 6. 4. Two straight lines cannot e. a space 1762. 5. *Jul. C.* v. iii. 27. Hence †**Enclo·sement** (*rare*) = ENCLOSURE.

Encloser (enklōu·zəɹ). ME. [f. prec. + -ER.] **1.** One who encloses; *esp.* one who appropriates common land 1597. †**2.** As tr. L. *clusor* (Vulg.), for Heb. *masgēr*, a smith. ME. only.

Enclosure (enklōu·ʒiŭɹ, -ʒəɹ). Also **in-**. 1538. [a. OF.; see ENCLOSE *v.* and -URE.] **1.** The action of enclosing; *spec.* the action of surrounding (land) with a fence; the action of thus appropriating common land. Also *attrib.*, as in *Enclosure Act.* Also *fig.* **2.** The state of being enclosed (see ENCLOSE *v.* 2) 1816. **3.** That which encloses, as a fence, barrier, wall, envelope 1556. **4.** That which is enclosed: **a.** A space included within boundaries 1580. **b.** Anything enclosed within an envelope (*mod.*).

Enclothe (enklōu·ð), *v.* 1831. [f. EN-[1] + CLOTHE *v.*] To clothe, invest.

Encloud (enklau·d), *v.* 1591. [f. EN-[1] + CLOUD *sb.*] To envelop in a cloud; to overshadow.

Encoach; see EN- *pref.*[1] 1 a.

Enco·ffin, *v.* Now *rare.* 1598. [f. EN-[1] + COFFIN.] To put in or as in a coffin. Hence **Enco·ffinment.**

Encolden; see EN- *pref.*[1] 1, 3.

Encollar; see EN- *pref.*[1] 2.

Enco·lour, *v.* 1648. [See EN-[1].] To colour, tinge.

Encolure (enkoliū·ɹ). [Fr.; the neck of an animal.] Used by Browning for: The mane (of a horse).

Encomiast (enkōu·miˌæst). 1610. [ad. Gr. ἐγκωμιαστής, f. (ult.) ἐγκώμιον ENCOMIUM.] One who composes or utters an encomium; a panegyrist. So †**Encomia·ster.**

Encomiastic (enkōu·miˌæ·stik). 1599. [ad. Gr. ἐγκωμιαστικός; see prec.] **a.** *adj.* Commendatory, eulogistic. †**b.** *sb.* A eulogistic discourse -18... So **Enco:mia·stical** *a.*; **-ly** *adv.* (*rare*).

Encomium (enkōu·miŏm). *Pl.* **-iums**; (now *rarely*) **-ia.** 1589. [a. L., ad. Gr. ἐγκώμιον (ἔπος) eulogy.] A formal or high-flown expression of praise; a panegyric.

Many .. encomia of ancient famous men JOWETT. vars †**Enco·mion**, †**Enco·my.**

Encommon; see EN- *pref.*[1] 2.

†**Enco·mpany**, *v.* 1494. [ad. OF. *encompaignier*; see EN-[1] and COMPANY.] **1.** *trans.* To accompany -1533. **2.** To associate. Const *to.* LD. BERNERS.

Encompass (enkʊ·mpăs), *v.* Also †**in-**. 1553. [f. EN-[1] + COMPASS *sb.*] **1.** To encircle, surround, bound on all sides 1555. **2.** Of persons: To form a circle about. Also *fig.* Also *absol.* 1555. †**3.** To go all round (anything) -1784. **4.** To surround entirely; to contain 1553. †**5.** To 'get round'. SHAKS.

1. The mountains encompassing Borrowdale 1872. 2. Encompass'd by his faithful guard TENNYSON. 5. *Merry W.* II. ii. 158. Hence **Enco·mpasser** (*rare*). **Enco·mpassment** (*rare*), the action of encompassing; encompassed state.

Encorbellment (enkǭ·ɹbĕlmĕnt). 1886. [f. EN- + CORBEL + -MENT; cf. F. *encorbellement.*] *Arch.* The continuous projection of each horizontal course over the one immediately below it.

Encore (aṅkǭ·r, often ǫŋkōᵊ·ɹ). 1712. [a. F. *encore* still, yet; usu. taken as :—L. (*in*) *hanc horam* until this hour. Not used abroad in the Eng. sense.]

A. *interj.* Again, once more: used by spectators or auditors to demand the repetition of a song, piece of music, or the like.

Loud shouts of 'encore' roused him HONE.

B. *sb.* A call for the repetition of a song, etc.; the repetition itself. Also *attrib.* 1763.

Enco·re, *v.* 1748. [f. prec.] To call for a repetition of (a song, etc.), or by (a performer).

They encored it RICHARDSON. The wretches .. encored him [Sir Charles] without mercy 1754.

†**Enco·rpore**, *v.* ME. [a. OF. *encorporer*, ad. L. *incorporare.*] **1.** *intr.* in *Alchemy*: To amalgamate -1470. **2.** To insert in a body of documents. LD. BERNERS.

Encounter (enkau·ntəɹ), *sb.* ME. [a. OF. *encontre* masc. and fem.; f. as next.] **1.** A meeting face to face; a meeting in conflict; *hence*, a battle, skirmish, duel, etc. **2.** A coming upon, *esp.* undesignedly or casually. Const *of*, *with.* 1656. †**b.** An amatory meeting. SHAKS. †**3.** Style of address, behaviour. SHAKS. **4.** Occurrence (*rare*) 1870. †**5.** *Rhet.* = ANTITHESIS. Puttenham.

1. This keene e. of our wittes SHAKS. The e. with death 1853. 2. There was constant risk of an e. which might have produced several duels 1859.

Encounter (enkau·ntəɹ), *v.* ME. [a. OF. *encontrer* :—late L. *incontrare*, f. *in* + *contra.*] **1.** *trans.* To meet as an adversary; to confront in battle. Also *fig.* Also †*intr.* with *with.* †**2.** *trans.* To go counter to, oppose; to contest. Also *absol.* -1786. †**3.** *trans.* To be opposite in position or direction to 1610. **4.** To come upon, *esp.* casually. Occas. *absol.* Also *fig.* ME. Also †*intr.* with *with.* **5.** To meet with; to face resolutely 1814. Also †*intr.* with *with.* †**6.** To go to meet; also *fig.* SHAKS. †**7.** To address -1590.

1. They challenge, and e. Breast to Breast DRYDEN. 2. To e. his [God's] Word GOLDING. 4. We never met before, and never .. may again e. BYRON. 5. The Royal Society .. encountered fierce hostilities D'ISRAELI. 6. I will e. darkness as a bride SHAKS. Hence †**Encou·nterer**, one who or that which encounters; a 'forward' person (*Tr. & Cr.* IV. v. 58).

Encourage (enkʊ·rėdʒ), *v.* 1483. [ad. OF. *encoragier*, mod.F. *encourager*; see EN-[1] and COURAGE.] **1.** *trans.* To inspire with courage, animate, inspirit 1490. **2.** To embolden 1538. **b.** To incite, instigate; to recommend 1483. **3.** To stimulate; to countenance; in bad sense, to abet 1668. **b.** To allow or promote the growth of; to foster 1677.

1. Jack was incouraged at this success STEELE. 2. To be encouraged to do the like EDEN. **b.** To e. individuals to make right or wrong for themselves JOWETT. 3. Paying them [tradesmen] is only encouraging them SHERIDAN. **b.** To e. the Iron Manufacture 1677.

Hence **Encou·rager.** **Encou·raging** *ppl. a.* that encourages or tends to e. **Encou·ragingly** *adv.*

Encouragement (enkʊ·rėdʒmĕnt). Also †**in-**. [a. F.; see prec. and -MENT.] The action or process of encouraging, the being encouraged; that which serves to encourage.

[Plato] gives no e. to individual enthusiasm JOWETT. The e. of saving (*mod.*).

Encover, in- (en-, inkʊ·vəɹ), *v. rare.* 1520. [f. EN-[1], IN- + COVER *v.*] To cover completely.

Encowl; see EN- *pref.*[1]

Encradle (enkrēɪ·d'l), *v.* 1596. [See EN-[1].] To lay in a cradle.

Where he encradled was In simple cratch SPENSER.

Encratism (e·nkrătiz'm). 1885. [f. Gr. ἐγκρατής + -ISM.] The doctrine and practice of the Encratites.

Encratite (e·nkrătəit). Usu. in *pl.* 1587. [ad. late L. *encratita*, f. as prec. + Gr. -ιτης; see -ITE.] One of an early Christian sect that abstained from flesh, wine, and marriage.

Encrease, etc.; see INCREASE.

Encrimson (enkri·mzən), *v.* Also **in-**. 1773. [f. EN-[1] + CRIMSON.] To make or dye crimson; also *fig.*

Encrinital (enkrinəi·tăl), *a.* 1847. [f. ENCRINITE + -AL.] **1.** *Geol.* Of, pertaining to, or resembling, Encrinites. **2.** Containing Encrinites 1876. vars. **E·ncrinal**, **Encri·nic.**

Encrinite (e·nkrinəit). 1808. [f. ENCRINUS + -ITE.] *Geol.*, etc. A fossil crinoid; formerly, *occas.*, any crinoid. Hence **Encrini·tic** *a.* containing fossil Encrinites.

‖**Encrinus** (e·nkrinŏs). 1762. [mod.L., f. Gr. ἐν + κρίνον lily.] *Zool.* †**a.** = ENCRINITE. **b.** A particular (extinct) genus of crinoids, the type of the family *Encrinidæ.* †**c.** One of certain extant animals resembling the fossil encrinus; *esp.* the *Pennatula Encrinus* of Linnæus. Hence **E·ncrinoid** *a.* resembling an Encrinite.

†**Encri·sp**, *v. rare.* ME. [See EN-[1].] *trans.* To curl crisply -1523.

†**Encroa·ch**, *sb. rare.* 1611. [f. next.] Encroachment -1716.

Encroach (enkrōu·tʃ), *v.* ME. [a. OF. *encrochier* to hook away, catch in a hook, f. *en-* (see EN-[1]) + *croc* hook.] †**1.** *trans.* To seize, acquire wrongfully. Also *absol.* -1606. **2.** *intr.* To trench or intrude usurpingly (*esp.* by insidious or gradual advances) on the territory or rights of another. Also *transf.* and *fig.* of things: To make gradual inroads on. Const. *on*, *upon*; also *simply.* 1534. **3.** *intr.* To intrude beyond natural or conventional limits. Also †*refl.* 1555.

2. Bie littell and littell engroched on the sowthe partes of the Ile 1534. The sea encroched upon these cliffs SMEATON. 3. A state which encroaches beyond the boundaries of sleep 1830.

Hence **Encroa·cher.** **Encroa·chingly** *adv.*

Encroachment (enkrōu·tʃmĕnt). 1523. [See -MENT.] The action of encroaching.

Encrochment, when the Lord hath gotten and seised of more rent or seruices of his tenant then of right is due 1613. The encroachments of error SIR T. BROWNE, of the waves 1878.

Encrown (enkrau·n), *v.* 1486. [f. EN-[1] + CROWN *sb.*] To put a crown on; to crown. Hence †**Encrow·nment.**

Encrust, in- (en-, inkrʊ·st), *v.* 1641. [ad. F. *incruster*, ad. L. *incrustare*, f. *in* + *crusta* CRUST. Cf. F. *encroûter.* Actual use favours *encrust.*] **1.** *trans.* To ornament by overlaying with a crust of something precious. **2.** To cover with a crust or thin coating. Also *fig.* 1733. **3.** To form into a crust, as snow 1726. Also *intr.* for *refl.* **4.** *intr.* To form or deposit a crust *upon* 1725. **5.** To shut up as within a crust (*rare*) 1711.

1. A staircase encrusted with jasper MACAULAY. 2. Such .. waters .. incrust vessels in which they are contained 1756. 5. Tho' I should .. In Alps of Ice encrusted, freeze KEN. Hence **Encru·stment**, that which is deposited as a crust; an outer encrusted layer or shell.

†**Encu·mber**, *sb.* ME. [a. OF. *encombre* :—late L. *incumbrum*; see next.] The state of being encumbered; an encumbrance -1642.

Encumber (enkʊ·mbəɹ), *v.* ME. [a. OF. *encombrer*, a. Com. Rom. wd. :—late L. *incombrare*, f. *in* + *combrus*, corrupt f. L. *cumulus* a heap.] **1.** *trans.* To hamper, embarrass *with* or *as* a clog or burden. Also *fig.* †**2.** To entangle *in* -1720. †**3.** To cause trouble to -1605. **4.** To burden with debts, etc.; *esp.* to charge (an estate) with a mortgage 1593. **5.** To load or fill *with* what obstructs or is superfluous; to block up; also *fig.* ME.

1. They marched heavily armed and encombered HOLLAND. To e. branches of trade with high duties 1842. 2. And lefte his scheep encombred in the myre CHAUCER. 4. Encumbered with much serving 1593, with debt BERKELEY. Hence **Encu·mberer.** **Encu·mberingly** *adv.* **Encu·mberment** (now *rare*) = ENCUMBRANCE.

Encumbrance (enkʊ·mbrăns). ME. [a. OF. *encombrance*; see -ANCE.] †**1.** Encumbered state or condition; trouble, molestation -1559. **2.** *concr.* That which encumbers; a burden, clog; a useless addition; an annoyance 1535. **3.** A person dependent on another for support 1742. **4.** *Law.* 'A claim, lien, liability attached to property; as a mortgage, etc.' (Wharton) 1626.

2. To hire incumbents or rather incumbrances for life-time MILT. 3. Phr. *Without e.* = 'having no children'. Hence **Encu·mbrancer**, one who has a legal claim on an estate.

†**Encu·mbrous**, *a.* ME. [a. OF. *encombros*; see ENCUMBER *sb.* and -OUS.] Cumbersome, distressing -1694.

Encurl (enkǭ·ɹl), *v.* Also **in-**. 1647. [See EN-[1].] To twist, entwine.

Encurtain (enkǭ·ɹtėn, -t'n), *v.* ME. [a. OF. *encortiner*, f. *en-* + *cortine* CURTAIN.] **1.** To surround with, or as with, a curtain. †**2.** *Fortif.* To flank with a wall 1598.

-ency, ad. L. *-entia*, a suffix signifying properly quality or state. Where the same word exists in both the *-ence* and the *-ency* forms, the former is usually restricted to action or process, the latter to quality; cf. *coherence* and *coherency*. See also -ANCY.

Encyclic (ensəi·klik). 1824. [ad. late L. *encyclicus*, for *encyclius*, a. Gr. ἐγκύκλιος, f. ἐν + κύκλος.] = ENCYCLICAL.

Encyclical (ensəi·klikăl). 1616. [f. late L. *encyclicus* + -AL; see prec.]

A. *adj.* 1. *Antiq.* Used as tr. Gr. ἐγκύκλιος (παιδεία); *i.e.* general (education); cf. ENCYCLOPÆDIA. 2. Of eccl. letters: Circular, intended for many. Now chiefly of letters issued by the pope. 1647.

2. The apostolical vicars put forth an e. letter forbidding the people..to take the oath 1805.

B. *sb.* An encyclical letter; see A. 2. 1837.

Encyclopædia, -pedia (ensəi:klopī·diă). Also -pedy. 1531. [a. late L. *encyclopædia*, a. pseudo-Gr. ἐγκυκλοπαιδεία, for ἐγκύκλιος παιδεία circular or complete education (cf. ENCYCLICAL *a.* 1).] 1. The circle of learning; a general course of instruction. 2. A work containing information on all branches of knowledge, usually arranged alphabetically 1644. b. Occas. applied *spec.* to the French 'Encyclopédie ou Dictionnaire raisonné des Sciences, des Arts, et des Métiers' (1751–1765) 1773. 3. A work containing exhaustive information on some one art or branch of knowledge, arranged systematically 1801.

Hence Ency:clopæ·diac, -al *a.* = ENCYCLOPÆDIC. Ency:clopæ·dial *a.* pertaining to an encyclopædia.

Encyclopædian (ensəi:klopī·diăn), *a.* 1837. [f. prec. + -AN.] a. Embracing the circle of knowledge, or a wide range of subjects. b. Of the nature of or resembling an encyclopædia.

Encyclopædic, -pedic (ensəi:klopī·dik), *a.* 1824. [f. as prec. + -IC.] Of, pertaining to, or resembling an encyclopædia; hence, embracing all branches of learning; full of information, comprehensive.

Affectation of e. knowledge MERIVALE. An e. statistician 1872. So Ency:clopæ·dical, -pe·dical.

Encyclopædism, -pedism (ensəi:klopī·diz'm). 1833. [f. prec. + -ISM.] 1. Encyclopædic learning. 2. The doctrines of the Encyclopædists 1835.

Encyclopædist, -pedist (ensəi:klopī·dist). 1651. [f. as prec. + -IST.] 1. One who compiles, or writes in, an encyclopædia; *esp.* one of the writers of the French *Encyclopédie* (see ENCYCLOPÆDIA 2 b) 1796. 2. One who takes all knowledge for his province 1871.

1. What Steam-engine..did these Encyclopedists invent for mankind CARLYLE.

Encyclopædize, -pedize (ensəi:klopī·dəiz), *v.* 1824. [f. as prec. + -IZE.] *trans.* To arrange as an encyclopædia. b. To describe in an encyclopædia.

Encyst (ensist), *v.* 1845. [f. EN-[1] + CYST.] To enclose in a cyst; only in *pa. pple.* and *refl.*

Encystation (ensistē[i]·ʃən). 1869. [f. prec.] = ENCYSTMENT.

Encysted (ensi·stĕd), *ppl. a.* 1705. [f. as prec.] That is contained in a cyst or sac. Also *fig.*

E. Tumors 1705. The e. venom, or poison-bag, beneath the adder's fang COLERIDGE.

Encystment (ensi·stmĕnt). 1865. [f. as prec.] a. 'The condition of an encysted tumour' (*Syd. Soc. Lex.*). b. *Biol.* The process of becoming surrounded by a cyst.

End (end), *sb.* [Com. Teut.: OE. ęnde :—OTeut. **andjo-z* :—pre-Teut. **antjo'-s*, cogn. w. Skr. *ánta* end, boundary, and w. AND *prep.*]

I. 1. The extremity or outermost part of a portion of space or of anything extended in space; utmost limit. *Obs.* exc. in *ends of the earth.* b. A limit of multitude OE. †2. A quarter (of the world, of a country or town) –1450. 3. One of the two extremities of a line or of the length of anything; that part of anything which includes either of its two extremities ME. b. ? *transf.* In the game of Bowls: The part of a game which is played from one end of the green 1688. 4. The surface which bounds an object at either of its extremities 1526. 5. A piece broken, cut off, or left; a fragment, remnant 1481. †Also *fig.* 6. *techn.* a. *Coal-mining.* The furthest part of a working 1865. b. Naut. *Cable's e.*, or simply *end*: the last length of a cable. *Rope's e.*: a short length of rope, bound at the ends with thread. *Bitter e.* (see BITTER). c. *A shoemaker's e.*: = WAX-END. d. *Textiles.* (*a*) *Card-e.*: a sliver or carding. (*b*) A worsted yarn in a Brussels carpet.

1. The towns e. GREENE. Earth's distant ends POPE. b. There was no e. to the advantages MILL. 3. At the tables ende LD. BERNERS. Mutton-chops off the worst e. JOHNSON. Phr. *From e. to e.* 4. The ends of a cask (*mod.*). 5. A broker's shop that hath ends of everything BACON. Phr. *Odds and ends* (see (ODDS). 6. b. I beat him, and then went up in to fetch my rope's e. PEPYS.

II. 1. Limit of duration; termination, conclusion OE. b. Latter part ME. 2. Termination of existence; destruction, abolition; death, mode or manner of death OE. 3. Ultimate state. Chiefly in Biblical phrases. OE. †4. A termination of doubt or debate; a settlement –1543. †5. Completion of an action; accomplishment of a purpose –1679. 6. Event, issue, result ME. 7. Intended result; aim, purpose ME. 8. Final cause 1534.

1. To his Life's E. ADDISON. From year's e. to year's e. TREVELYAN. b. In e. of Autumne *Merch. V.* I. iii. 82. 2. A Swan-like e., Fading in musique *Merch. V.* III. ii. 44. There would be an e. of all civil government LOCKE. 3. *Ps.* xxxvii. 37. 6. The e. still crownes the deed HEYWOOD. 7. I have no e. to serve but truth BERKELEY. 8. The flower is the e. or proper object of the seed RUSKIN.

Phrases. 1. a. *At the e.*: at last. *In the e.*: ultimately. *To an e.*: consecutively, all through. b. *On e.* (see also AN-END): consecutively; in an upright position. c. *Without e.* (ME. *buten ende*): for ever; also in adj. sense, endless. *World without e.*: see WORLD I. 6. d. *E. for e.*: each end in place of the other; chiefly *Naut.* to reverse (a rope); to upset (a boat). *E. to e.*: lengthwise. e. *E. on*: with the end directly towards the eye, or towards any object; opp. to *broadside on*. *E. up*: with the end uppermost. f. *No e.*: a vast quantity or number (*colloq.*). Also (*slang*) as adv. = 'immensely'.

2. Proverbial phrases. *To have at one's fingers'* or *tongue's e.*: to know by heart. *At a loose e.*: with no fixed occupation. *To make both, two, ends meet*: to live within one's income. *To come to the e. of one's tether*: see TETHER *sb.* *To keep one's e. up*: to sustain one's part in an undertaking or performance.

Combs., chiefly *attrib.* with sense 'placed at the e.' or 'last used'; as *e.-man, -parlour, -wall*, etc.; also **e.-bulb**, the terminal expansion of a nerve; **-gatherer**, a collector of refuse wool; **-grain**, (*attrib.*) (of wood), placed with the e. of the grain turned outwards; **-iron**, a movable plate in a kitchen range which enlarges or contracts the grate; **-paper** (*Bookbinding*), a sheet of paper folded and pasted to the first or last leaf of a book; **-plate**, the extreme fibres of a muscle or nerve; **-shake**, a freedom of motion in a spindle at its e.; **-stone**, one of the plates of a watch-jewel supporting a pivot; **-stopping**, (of blank verse) a division of the lines such that they end with a pause; so **-stopped** *ppl. a.*; **-wool**, refuse wool.

End (end), *v.*[1] [OE. *ęndian* :—OTeut. **andjōjan*, f. **andjo* END *sb.*]

I. Trans. †1. To finish, complete –1738. 2. To conclude, come to a termination of ME. Also *absol.*; *esp.* with reference to speech. 3. To put an end to OE. †b. To kill (a person) –1623.

1. Pray e. what you began POPE. 2. Not then the drudging Hind his Labour ends DRYDEN. *absol.* To e. with a motion (*mod.*). 3. To e. strife 1808. b. This Sword hath ended him 1 *Hen. IV*, v. iii. 9.

II. Intr. 1. To come to an end. Also with *in* or *by*. OE. 2. To die. Now *rare*. ME. 3. To terminate, have its end or extremity 1611.

1. All's well that ends well, yet *All's Well* v. i. 25. 2. Thus Thisbie ends *Mids. N.* v. i. 353. 3. The plateau ends in a precipice (*mod.*).

End, *v.*[2] Now *dial.* 1607. [? corrupt f. INN *v.*, influenced by prec.] *trans.* To put (corn, etc.) into (a barn, etc.); to get in. Also *fig.*

I.. holpe to reape the Fame Which he did e. all his *Cor.* v. vi. 37.

†**E·ndable**, *a.* 1693. [See -ABLE.] That can be ended. (Dicts.)

End-all (e·nd-ǭl). 1605. [f. END *v.*[1] + ALL.] That which ends all. Now *dial.*, exc. as in *Macb.* I. vii. 5.

Endamage (endæ·mėdʒ), *v.* ME. [f. EN-[1] + DAMAGE *sb.*, or a. OF. **endamagier*.] *trans.* To inflict damage or injury upon; to prejudice, hurt; to spoil (a thing).

Nor was Christianity endamaged by all that fury BURNET. Hence †**Enda·mageance** (*rare*), injury. **Enda·magement**, the action of endamaging; endamaged state; injury.

Endamnify; see EN- *pref.*[1] 3.

Endanger (endē[i]·ndʒəɹ), *v.* 1477. [f. EN-[1] + DANGER *sb.*] †1. To subject (a person) to the will of another –1579. †2. *pass.* To be liable to punishment by another –1596. †3. To put in peril. Const. *of, to* with *inf.* –1737. †4. To cause the danger of (something untoward) –1796. †5. To chance, risk –1771. 6. To put in danger. (The only mod. sense.) 1509.

4. Such ill Courses as will e. his Ruin 1716. 5. To e. being benighted ADDISON. 6. To e. the liberties of the country JUNIUS. Hence **Enda·ngerer**. **Enda·ngerment**, the action of putting in danger; endangered condition.

†**Enda·rk**, *v. rare.* ME. [f. EN-[1] + DARK *a.*] To render dark; to dim –1631. So †**Enda·rken** *v.*

†**Ende.** [OE. *ened.*] A duck –1475.

Endear (endīᵊ·ɹ), *v.* 1580. [f. EN-[1] + DEAR *a.*] †1. *trans.* To enhance the price or value of; also, to exaggerate –1803. 2. To render dear; to create affection for (a person or thing). (The mod. sense.) 1611. †3. To hold dear –1711. †4. To win the affection of. Also, to deepen (affection). –1704.

1. All Victualls and other Provision endeared 1618. 2. Endeared by long companionship GEIKIE. Hence **Endea·rance** (*rare*), the action of endearing or state of being endeared. †**Endea·red-ly** *adv.*, †**-ness**. **Endea·ring** *ppl. a.* inspiring or manifesting affection. **Endea·ringly** *adv.*

Endearment (endīᵊ·ɹmĕnt). 1612. [f. ENDEAR *v.* + -MENT.] 1. The action of endearing or the fact of being endeared; *concr.* something that endears 1663. 2. An action or utterance expressive of affection; a caress. Also *abstr.* 1702. †3. Affection –1821.

2. His Indearments and Tenderness to his Lady RICHARDSON. 3. Pledges of conjugal e. HERVEY.

Endeavour (ende·vəɹ), *sb.* ME. [app. f. next vb.] 1. The action of endeavouring; effort directed to attain an object; a strenuous attempt. †2. *Philos.* Used by Hobbes: = L. *conatus* (see quot.) –1667.

1. On his high e. The light of praise shall shine WORDSW. Phr. *To do one's endeavour(s*: to do all one can; My best endeuors shall be done herein *Merch. V.* II. ii. 182. 2. These small beginnings of Motion, within the Body of Man.. are commonly called E. HOBBES.

Endeavour (ende·vəɹ), *v.* ME. [f. EN-[1] + DEVOIR *sb.*; cf. F. *se mettre en devoir de faire quelque chose* to make it one's duty to do something; hence, to endeavour.] †1. *refl.* To exert oneself –1655; †*trans.* to exert (one's power, etc.) –1642. †2. *intr.* for *refl.* To exert oneself; to direct one's efforts –1624. 3. *intr.* To try, strive, make an effort for a specified object; to attempt strenuously. (The only mod. sense.) 1594. 4. *trans.* To use effort for; to attempt (now *arch.*) 1581; †to try to fulfil (a law) MILT.

3. To e. to compromise matters FROUDE. To e. at eminence JOHNSON, after more riches MILL. 4. To e. the extirpation of Popery CLARENDON. Hence **Endea·vourer**, one who endeavours; an aspirant; also *spec.*, a member of the Christian Endeavour Society founded in U.S. in 1881. †**Endea·vourment**, endeavour.

Endebt, -ed; see IND-.

Endeca-, incorrect f. HENDECA-; as in: **Ende·cagon**, a plane figure of eleven sides; **Endeca·gynous** *a.* (*Bot.*), having eleven pistils; **E:ndecaphy·llous** *a.*, having eleven leaflets; **E:ndecasylla·bic** *a.*, having eleven syllables; **E:ndecasy·llable**, a verse of eleven syllables.

Ended (e·ndėd), *ppl. a.* 1598. [f. END *v.* and *sb.*] 1. That has come to an end. 2. [f. END *sb.*] That has its end (of a certain kind), or (so many) ends.

Endeictic (endəi·ktik), *a.* 1655. [ad. Gr. ἐνδεικτικός, f. (ult.) ἐν + δεικνύναι to show.] Serving to show or demonstrate: a term used in ancient classifications of the Platonic dialogues.

†**Endei·gn**, *v.* [ad. OF. (*s'*)*endaignier* :—L. *indignari*.] *intr.* To be indignant. WYCLIF.

Endemial (endī·miăl), *a.* 1672. [f. Gr. ἐνδήμιος.] = ENDEMIC *a.*

Endemic (ende·mik). 1662. [f. Gr. ἐν + δῆμος + -IC.]

A. *adj.* Peculiar to a people or to a district: *esp.* a. Of plants and animals: Having their habitat in a (specified) district; opp. to *exotic*. b. Of diseases: Habitually prevalent in a certain country, and due to permanent local causes.

Famines are periodical or e. in Hindostan 1776.

B. *sb.* An endemic disease. Also *fig.*

Hence **Ende·mical** *a.* endemic. **Ende·mically** *adv.* **Endemi·city**, the quality or fact of being e.

†**Ende·nize,** *v.* Also **in-**. 1598. [altered f. ENDENIZEN.] 1. *trans.* = ENDENIZEN 1. -1687. 2. To remove into another order of being; to translate. Hence, to metamorphose. -1633. Hence **Endeniza·tion** (*rare*).

Endenizen (ende·nizən), *v.* 1592. [f. EN-[1] + DENIZEN.] 1. *trans.* To make a denizen of; to naturalize, enfranchise. Also *transf.* and *fig.* †2. *intr.* To become a denizen or citizen 1598.

Endent, -ure; see INDENT, etc.

Ender (e·ndəɹ), *sb.* ME. [f. END *v.* + -ER.] He who or that which ends.

Myn hertes lady, e. of my lyf CHAUCER.

Enderma·tic, *a.* = next.

Endermic, -al (endə̄·ɹmik, -ăl), *a.* 1831. [f. Gr. ἐν + δέρμα + -IC, -AL.] That acts on, or through, the skin.

He administers it by the endermic method; that is, applied in the form of a salve on a part deprived of the epidermis 1831. Hence **Ende·rmically** *adv.* by the endermic method.

Enderon (e·ndĕrǫn). 1859. [Irreg. f. Gr. ἐν + δέρος, δέρμα skin.] *Phys.* Huxley's term for the inner derm or true skin, or any homologous structure. Opp. to ECDERON. Hence **Endero·nic** *a.*

†**Endiablee,** *v.* [ad. F. *endiabler.*] To put a devil into. NORTH. So †**Endia·blement,** diabolical possession (*rare*).

Endiadem, Endiaper; see EN- *pref.*[1]

Endict, obs. f. INDICT.

Ending (e·ndiŋ), *vbl. sb.* OE. [f. END *v.*[1]] 1. The action of END *v.*[1]; termination, conclusion, completion; †death, etc. Also *attrib.* 2. Concluding part; *esp.* that of a word, metrical line, piece of music, etc.; also, an inflexional or formative suffix 1599.

1. Time is our tedious song should here have e. MILT.

Endite, etc., obs. f. INDICT, INDITE, etc.

Endive (e·ndiv). ME. [a. Fr.:—late L. **intybea* adj. fem., f. *intibus* (*intubus*).] The name of two species of Chicory, *Cichorium Intybus* or Wild Endive, and (*esp.*) *C. Endivia*, N.O. *Compositæ*. The leaves of the latter are commonly blanched and used as salad, etc.

Endless (e·ndlĕs). [OE. *ęndelēas*, f. *ęnde* END *sb.*; see -LESS.]

A. *adj.* 1. Having no end of duration; unending, eternal. Also *hyperbolically* for: Interminable; incessant. 2. Having no end in space; boundless, infinite; †bottomless ME. 3. Of immaterial things: Limitless, infinite ME. †4. Fruitless. FLETCHER.

1. E. night SHAKS., day STEELE, feast TENNYSON, platitudes 1872. 2. E. Labyrinths COWLEY, passages 1864, miles of moor BLACK. 3. Endeles wisdom WYCLIF.

Phrases. *E. band, cable, chain, strap*: one whose ends are joined for the purpose of continuous motion. *E. screw*: a short length of screw revolving on an axis, used to give continuous motion to a toothed wheel.

†B. *adv.* a. In an infinite degree. b. For ever. -ME. Hence **E·ndless·ly** *adv.*, **-ness.**

Endlong (e·ndlǫŋ). ME. [orig. OE. *andlang* prep. (see ALONG), replaced by ME. *endelong*, f. *ende* END *sb.* + LONG. Prof. Sievers derives *-lang* in *andlang* directly from OTeut. **lingan* to reach, extend.]

A. *prep.* From end to end of; through or over the length of; along (as opp. to *across*). Chiefly of *place*.

The rede blood Ran endelong the tree CHAUCER.

B. *adv.* 1. At one's whole length; horizontally. Now *n. dial.* ME. 2. Lengthwise, as dist. from *crosswise* or *athwart* (*arch.*) ME. †3. Right along, straight on or through -1700. 4. On end, vertically 1600.

2. Galloping.. crossways and e. SCOTT. 3. Spurring at full speed, ran e. on DRYDEN.

C. *adj.* †1. Extended lengthwise -1541. 2. (from B. 4.) Set on end, perpendicular (*rare*) 1716.

E·ndmost, *a. rare.* 1775. [f. END *sb.*; cf. *hindmost.*] Nearest to the end, furthest, most distant.

Endo- (e·ndo; bef. two unstressed syllables endǫ·), also **end-**, *prefix*, comb. f. Gr. ἔνδον within; as in:

E·ndarteri·tis, E·ndo-arteri·tis [see ARTERITIS], *Path.* inflammation of the inner coat of an artery. **E·ndocho·rion** [see CHORION], *Anat.* the inner layer of the chorion. **E·ndochrome,** the colouring matter of vegetable cells except when green. **E·ndocrane** [Gr. κρανίον; also in L. form *endocra·nium*], the inner surface of the skull. **E·ndocyst** [see also CYST and ECTOCYST], the body-wall within the cell in Polyzoa. **Endogna·thal** *a.* [Gr. γνάθος], *Zool.* that is placed within the jaw; *endognathal palp*, a palpiform appendage in certain Crustacea. **E·ndolary·ngeal** *a.* [cf. LARYNGEAL], pertaining to the interior of the larynx. **E·ndolymph** [see LYMPH], *Anat.* the fluid contained in the membranous labyrinth of the ear. **Endome·trial** *a.*, pertaining to **E·ndometri·tis** [Gr. μήτρα womb + -ITIS], *Path.* inflammation of the lining membrane of the womb. **Endo·metry** [see -METRY], *Med.* the measurement of an internal part. **E·ndomorph** [Gr. μορφή], *Min.* a mineral enclosed within another. **Endopa·rasite,** *Zool.* an animal that lives and finds food in the internal organs of another; hence **E·ndoparasi·tic** *a.* **E·ndophragm** [Gr. φράγμα partition], a. *Bot.* a transverse diaphragm or septum; b. *Zool.* the chitinous covering of the neural canal in the thorax of some Crustacea; hence **Endophra·gmal** *a.* **Endophy·llous** *a.* [Gr. φύλλον], evolved from within a sheath, as the young leaves of monocotyledons. **E·ndoplasm** [Gr. πλάσμα something moulded], the inner soft layer of the body of an Amœba, or the like (cf. ECTOPLASM). **E·ndoplast** [Gr. πλαστός formed], 'a large protoplasmic corpuscle in the external parenchyma of the body of the Infusoria' (*Syd. Soc. Lex.*); hence **Endopla·stic** *a.*; **Endopla·stule** [see -ULE], 'a bright rod-like mass lying in the interior or outside of the endoplast of Protozoa; supposed to be a male sexual organ' (*Syd. Soc. Lex.*). **Endopleu·ra** [Gr. πλευρά side], *Bot.* the internal covering of a seed. Hence **Endopleu·rite,** *Zool.* the portion of the apodeme of the thorax in Crustacea, which arises from the interepimeral membrane connecting each pair of somites. **Endo·podite** [Gr. πούς, ποδός + -ITE], 'the innermost of the two processes appended to the basal process of the hinder limbs of some of the Crustacea' (*Syd. Soc. Lex.*). **E·ndor(r)hiz** [Gr. ῥίζα root], *Bot.* 'the sheath-enclosed radicle of an endorrhizous plant' (*Syd. Soc. Lex.*). Hence **Endor(r)hi·zal, -ous** *adjs.* **E·ndosarc** [Gr. σάρξ, σαρκός flesh], *Zool.* the inner sarcode-layer of certain rhizopods, as the Amœba. **E·ndoscope** [Gr. -σκοπος], *Med.* 'an instrument so arranged as to give a view of some internal part of the body through a natural canal' (*Syd. Soc. Lex.*). Hence **Endosco·pic** *a.* **Endo·scopy.** **E·ndoske·letal** *a.*, of or pertaining to the **E·ndoske·leton** [see SKELETON], *Anat.* the interior framework of the *Vertebrata*, consisting of bone and cartilage. **E·ndosperm** [Gr. σπέρμα], *Bot.* the nutritive element, or albumen, enclosed with the embryo in many seeds; hence **Endospe·rmic** *a.* **E·ndospore** [Gr. σπορά sowing], *Bot.* a. the inner coat of a spore in lichens; b. a spore formed inside a theca; hence **E·ndospo·rous** *a.* having spores contained in a case. **Endoste·rnite** [Gr. στέρνον], *Zool.* the portion of the apodeme of the thorax of Crustacea which arises from the intersternal membrane. **Endo·steum** [mod.L., f. Gr. ὀστέον bone], *Anat.* the internal periosteum; hence **Endo·steal** *a.*; **Endo·steally** *adv.* **Endo·stoma** [Gr. στόμα], *Zool.* a plate which supports the labrum in certain Crustacea. **E·ndostome** [see prec.], *Bot.* the orifice in the inner integument of an ovule. **Endosto·sis** [Gr. ὀστέον], an internal growth of bone. **E·ndostyle** [Gr. στῦλος column], *Zool.* 'a rigid, hollow, rod-like structure on the floor of the ventral groove of *Tunicata*' (*Syd. Soc. Lex.*); hence **Endosty·lic** *a.* **Endothe·ca** [Gr. θήκη case], a. *Zool.* the inner layer of the wall of the sac of the gonosome of the *Hydrozoa*; b. *Bot.* the inner membrane of the wall of the cells of the anther. Hence **Endothe·cal** *a.*, (dissepiments) horizontal plates growing inwards from the septa of a corallite (*Syd. Soc. Lex.*). **Endothe·lium** [Gr. θηλή nipple], *Phys.* the layer of cells lining a blood-vessel or serous cavity (cf. EPITHELIUM); hence **Endothe·lial** *a.*; **Endothe·lioid** *a.*

Endocardial (endokā·ɹdiăl), *a.* 1847. [f. ENDO- + Gr. καρδία + -AL.] *Phys.* a. That is within the heart. b. Relating to the endocardium.

Endocarditis (e:ndo‚kaɹdəi·tis). 1836. [f. next + -ITIS.] *Med.* Inflammation of the lining membrane of the heart. Hence **Endocardi·tic** *a.*

‖**Endocardium** (endokā·ɹdiŏm). 1872. [mod. L., f. Gr. ἔνδον (see ENDO-) + καρδία.] *Phys.* The membrane lining the cavities of the heart.

Endocarp (e·ndokāɹp). 1830. [f. as prec. + Gr. καρπός.] *Bot.* The inner layer of a pericarp.

Endocrine (e·ndokrəin). 1913. [orig. adj., f. ENDO- + κρίνειν to separate.] *Anat.* A ductless gland. Hence **Endocrino·logy** [-OLOGY].

Endoderm (e·ndodə̄ɹm). 1835. [f. Gr. ἔνδον (see ENDO-) + δέρμα.] 1. *Bot.* a. The cellular face of the liber. b. The inner layer of the wall of a vegetable cell. 2. *Biol.* a. The inner layer of the blastoderm. b. The lining of the interior cavity of the *Cœlenterata* 1861. Hence **Endode·rmal, Endode·rmic** *adjs.*; **Endode·rmis** [after *epidermis*], *Bot.*

Endogamy (endǫ·gămi). 1865. [f. as prec. + Gr. γάμος; after *polygamy*.] The custom of marrying only within the limits of a clan or tribe. Hence **Endo·gamic, Endo·gamous** *adjs.*

Endogen (e·ndodʒĕn). 1842. [Fr. *endogène* (De Candolle), f. as prec. + Gr. -γενης born, produced.] *Bot.* A plant in which new wood is developed in the interior of the stem, which is not differentiated into wood and bark; opp. to EXOGEN. Also *fig.* Hence **Endogene·ity,** the fact of being ENDOGENOUS. (A bad formation.)

Endogenous (endǫ·dʒĭnəs), *a.* 1830. [f. prec. + -OUS.] a. Growing from within. b. *Path.* Of a contagion: Passing direct from the sick body to the sound. c. Of or pertaining to an ENDOGEN. Hence **Endo·genously** *adv.*

Endorse (endǭ·ɹs), *sb.* 1572. [app. f. next.] *Her.* A vertical division of a shield, one-eighth (or one-fourth) of the breadth of a PALE.

Endorse, in- (en-, indǭ·ɹs), *v.* 1547. [Altered f. ME. *endosse* (see ENDOSS). Commercial and literary use favours *endorse*, legal *indorse*.] 1. *trans.* To write on the back of (a document); *spec.* in *Comm.* to sign one's name on the back of (a bill, promissory note, or cheque). 2. *fig.* To confirm, countenance, as by an endorsement 1847. b. To declare one's approval of, 'crack up' (a person or thing). *U.S.* 1914. 3. To load the back of (an animal) *with.* (Merely literary.) 1671. 4. *Her.* In pa. pple. *endorsed.* a. = ADDORSED. b. Of a pale: Placed between two endorses. c. Of wings: Thrown backwards. 1500.

1. A bundle of letters..indorsed..'Letters from the Old Gentleman' 1709. To e. a bill ROGERS, a chauffeur's licence (*mod.*). 2. This conclusion I unhesitatingly indorse CARPENTER. 3. Elephants indorsed with towers MILT. *P. R.* III. 329. Hence **Endo·rsable,** also **in-** *a.*, that may or can be endorsed. **En·dorsee·**, also **in-**, one to whom a note or bill is endorsed, or assigned by endorsement. **Endo·rser, indorser,** occas. **-or**, one who endorses (*lit.* and *fig.*).

Endorsement, in- (en-, indǭ·ɹsmĕnt). 1547. [See -MENT.] 1. The action of endorsing; *concr.* a signature, memorandum, or remark endorsed upon a document. 2. *fig.* Confirmation, ratification, approving testimony 1633.

1. By his E. he made it his own Bill 1682. 2. This doctrine..bears the e. of the very highest names 1879.

Endosmic (endǫ·zmik), *a.* 1865. [f. Gr. ἔνδον + ὠσμός + -IC.] Of or pertaining to endosmosis. So **Endosmo·dic** *a.* (*rare*).

Endosmometer (endǫzmǫ·mĭtəɹ). 1836. [f. as prec. + -METER.] An instrument for exhibiting and measuring endosmosis.

Endosmose (e·ndǫzmōus). 1829. [a. F., as if ad. mod.L. *endosmosis*; see next.] = next. Hence **Endosmo·sic** *a.* of or pertaining to e.

Endosmosis (endǫzmōu·sis). 1836. [mod.L. (quasi-Gr.), f. Gr. ἔνδον (see ENDO-) + ὠσμός pushing, thrusting.] *Phys.*, etc. The passage of a fluid inwards through a porous septum, to mix with another fluid on the inside of it. So **Endosmo·tic** *a.* of or pertaining to e.

Endosperm, -spore, etc.; see ENDO-.

†**Endo·ss,** *v.* [ME. *endosse*, a. OF. *endosser*, f. (ult.) L. *in* + *dorsum* (F. *dos*) back.] **1.** = ENDORSE *v.* **1.** –1613. **2.** To inscribe or portray on any surface –1596.

2. Her name in euery tree I will endosse SPENSER.

Endoubt; see EN- *pref.*[1] 2.

Endow (endau·), *v.* ME. [f. EN- *pref.*[1] + F. *douer* :—L. *dotare*, f. *dotem* dowry.] **1.** *trans.* To give or assure †a dowry, or dower, to. Formerly with *of*. 1535. **2.** To enrich with property; to provide a permanent income for 1460. **3.** *fig.* To enrich or furnish *with* any gift ME.

1. The wife..shall bee endowed of the thirde parte of such landes tr. *Littleton's Tenures*. 2. With all my worldly goods I thee e. *Bk. Com. Prayer*. To e. an Hospital BURKE, a parrot (*mod.*). 3. To be endowed with ample priviledges 1661, with life and organisation YEATS, speech MORLEY. Hence **Endow·er,** one who endows. †**Endow·ry** = DOWRY.

Endowed (endau·d), *ppl. a.* 1700. [f. prec.] In senses of the vb. Chiefly of societies or institutions: Possessing a permanent income from gifts or bequests.

They are schools e.; with exhibitions .. for the education of youth DR. WALLIS.

†**Endow·er,** *v.* 1606. [ad. OF. *endouairier*; see EN-[1].] To dower (a woman); also *fig.* –1654.

Endowment (endau·mĕnt). 1460. [f. ENDOW *v.* + -MENT.] **1.** The action of endowing (see ENDOW *v.*). **2.** *concr.* The property or fund with which a society, institution, etc. is endowed 1597. †**3.** Property, possessions (*rare*) –1816. **4.** A gift, power, capacity, or the like, with which a person is endowed 1610.

2. Alms, and endowments, the usual fruits of a late penitence BURKE. 3. These women's worldly endowments SCOTT. 4. The King's rare natural Endowments SIR J. MELVIL.

Endrudge; see EN- *pref.*[1] 2.

†**E·ndship.** 1589. [f. END *sb.*] A small suburb –1701.

Endue, in- (en-, indiū·), *v.* ME. [ad. OF. *enduire* :—L. *inducere*, f. *in* + *ducere*. In 16th and 17th c. the verb *endue* had also all the senses of ENDOW.] †**1.** To induct into a living, or into a lordship –1460. †**2.** Of a hawk: To digest. Hence *transf.* Also *fig.* –1618. †**3.** To lead on; to bring up, educate –1604. **4.** To put on as a garment; to clothe; to cover. Also *transf.* ME. **5.** To invest, endow, supply *with* anything; *esp.* with a power or quality, a spiritual gift, etc. ME.

4. Endu'd with robes of various hue DRYDEN. To e. his heavy mail LYTTON. 5. Leah said, God hath endued me with a good dowry *Gen.* xxx. 20. We are endued with capacities of action, of happiness, and misery BUTLER. Hence †**Endue·ment,** the action of enduing; that with which one is endued.

Endungeon (endʊ·ndʒən), *v.* 1599. [See EN-[1] *pref.*] To put into or shut up in a dungeon. Hence *transf.*

Endurable (endiūᵊ·răb'l), *a.* 1607. [f. ENDURE *v.* + -ABLE.] **1.** That can be endured or put up with 1800. **2.** Durable (*rare*). Hence **Endu·rabi·lity** (*rare*). **Endu·rableness** (*rare*).

Endurance (endiūᵊ·răns). 1494. [f. ENDURE *v.* + -ANCE.] **1.** The fact, the habit or the power of enduring; *absol.* longsuffering, patience 1667. **2.** Duration. Also, power of lasting. 1494. **3.** That which is endured; a hardship 1555.

1. Ease out of pain Through labour and e. MILT. 3. Heauie Burthens and Endurances BACON.

Endurant (endiūᵊ·rănt), *a.* 1866. [f. as prec. + -ANT.] That endures or is capable of enduring. Const. *of*.

Doing good, and e. of evil NEALE.

Endure (endiūᵊ·ɹ), *v.* ME. [a. OF. *endurer* :—L. *indurare*, f. *in* + *durare*, f. *durus* hard.] †**1.** To harden. Hence *fig.* to make callous. Also, to strengthen. –1600. **2.** *intr.* To last. Also, to persist, hold out. ME. **3.** *trans.* To undergo, bear, support, sustain; *prop.* to undergo without giving way. Also *absol.* ME. **4.** To suffer without resistance, submit to, tolerate 1475. †**5.** Of things: To permit of (*arch.*) –1823.

2. His lordship and power in this worlde may not long e. EARL RIVERS. Highe wodes and forestes that endured to the cyte of Constances LD. BERNERS. 3. To e. exile, or ignominy, or bonds, or pain MILT. *P. L.* II. 206. To e. the whole weight of the imperial army DE FOE. 4. Brutus, baite not me, Ile not e. it SHAKS. For how can I e. to see the evil that shall come unto my people *Esther* viii. 6. 5. I have that to say..which will not e. your presence SCOTT.

Hence †**Endu·rement,** the action of enduring; hardship. **Endu·rer.** †**Endu·ring** *prep.* = DURING. **Endu·ring·ly** *adv.*, **-ness.**

End-way(s, -wise (endwē̆ⁱ, -wē̆ⁱz, -waiz), *adv.* 1575. [f. END *sb.* + -WAY(S, -WISE.] **1.** Of position: With the end uppermost, foremost, or towards the spectator. Also *Endways on.* 1657. **2.** Of motion: **a.** End on, continuously. (Now *dial.*) 1575. **b.** End foremost 1765. **c.** Lengthwise; also quasi-*adj.* 1790.

-ene, *suffix*, in *Org. Chem.* the termination of names of hydrocarbons, e.g. *benzene*, *camphene*, etc. In systematic nomenclature, proper to compounds of the olefine group, with formula C_nH_{2n}, and also more widely used.

†**E·necate,** *v.* 1657. [f. L. *enecat-*, *enecare*.] To kill outright –1665. Hence †**Eneca·tion.**

En échelon; see ECHELON.

Ened, var. of ENDE.

Eneid, var. of ÆNEID.

Enema (e·nĭma, enī·mă). Pl. **enemas;** (techn.) **enemata.** 1681. [a. Gr. ἔνεμα, f. ἐνιέναι to send in.] **1.** *Med.* A liquid or gaseous substance (either medicinal or alimentary) injected into the rectum; a clyster, an injection. Also *attrib.* **2.** Short for 'enema-apparatus'.

Enemy (e·nĕmi). ME. [a. OF. *enemi* (mod.F. *ennemi* :—L. *inimicus*, f. *in-* + *amicus* friendly, friend.]

A. *sb.* **1.** One that hates, and wishes or seeks to injure another; an adversary, opponent. Also *transf.* and *fig.* **2.** One of a hostile army or nation ME. **3.** The hostile force. Also, a hostile ship. 1601.

1. The man of the world, that worst e. of the world MORLEY. Phr. *The e.*: the Devil. *fig.* So mak'st thou faith an e. to faith *John* III. i. 263. 2. A rebel is not an e. BLACKSTONE. 3. They strike at the e. in his..most vulnerable part BURKE.

B. *adj.* †**1.** Hostile, unfriendly –1726. **2.** Of or pertaining to an ENEMY (sense 2); hostile. Now *rare*. ME.

1. I have been shipwrackt, yet am not e. with the sea or winds SIR T. BROWNE. 2. E. goods 1793.

Enemy, dial. corruption of ANEMONE.

†**Ene·nt, ene·ntes,** *prep.* ME. [var. of ANENT.] = ANENT –1516.

Enepidermic (enepidə̄·ɹmik), *a.* [See EN-[2] *pref.*] *Med.* Of or pertaining to applications to the skin.

Energetic (enəɹdʒe·tik), *a.* 1651. [ad. Gr. ἐνεργητικός active. Now as if from ENERGY.] †**1.** Operative. GREW. **2.** Powerfully operative 1651. **3.** Characterized by energy 1796.

1. A being eternally energetick 1701. 2. An energetick remedy BIGGS. 3. Active and e. respiration 1842. The world belongs to the e. EMERSON. So **Energe·tical.** Hence **Energe·tically** *adv.* **Energe·tics** *sb. pl.* the science of ENERGY.

†**Ene·rgiatype.** 1845. [f. *energia* + TYPE.] = FERROTYPE –1859.

Energic, †-al (enə̄·ɹdʒik, -ăl), *a.* 1665. [f. ENERGY + -IC, -AL.] †**1.** = ENERGETIC 2. –1753. **2.** = ENERGETIC 3. Now *rare*. 1702. **3.** *nonce-uses.* (see quots.) 1796.

2. Cæsar, astute, e., press'd the war 1876. 3. E. reason COLERIDGE. The e. faculty that we call Will 1859.

‖**Energico** (ẹne·rdʒiko), *adv.* [It.] *Mus.* A direction: With energy. In mod. Dicts.

Energize (e·nəɹdʒəiz), *v.* 1752. [f. ENERGY + -IZE.] **1.** *trans.* To rouse into energy, or supply with energy 1753. **2.** *intr.* To be in active operation; to put forth energy 1752.

1. Faith will e. us for any sort of work MCLAREN. 2. We exist only as we energise SIR W. HAMILTON. Hence **E·nergizer,** he who or that which energizes.

Energumen (enəɹgiū·mĕn). 1702. [ad. late L. *energumenus*, a. Gr. ἐνεργούμενος, pass. pple. of ἐνεργέειν; cf. F. *energumène*.] **1.** One possessed by a devil; a demoniac 1706. **2.** An enthusiast, a fanatical devotee 1702.

1. If there was ever an *Energumene*..there is a devil speaking with that woman's tongue SCOTT.

Energy (e·nəɹdʒi). 1599. [ad. late L. *energia*, Gr. ἐνέργεια, f. ἐνεργής, f. ἐν + ἔργον work.] **1.** Force or vigour of expression 1599. **2.** Exercise of power, operation, activity; †*concr.* an effect 1626. †**b.** Effectual operation –1725. **3.** Vigour of action, utterance, etc. Hence: The capacity and habit of strenuous exertion. 1809. **4.** Power actively and efficiently exerted. Occas. in *pl.* 1665. **b.** *pl.* Activities 1742. **5.** Ability or capacity to produce an effect 1677. **6.** *Physics.* The power of doing work possessed by a body or system of bodies. (First used by Young to denote *actual*, *kinetic*, or *motive e.* (cf. sense 4); but now including *potential*, *static*, or *latent e.*, or *e. of position*. Also differentiated as *mechanical*, *molecular*, *chemical*, *electrical*, etc.) 1807.

1. The Liturgy, admired for its e. and pathos EMERSON. 2. Naturalization had a retrospective e. 1798. 3. He took his measures with his usual e. MACAULAY. 4. The disturbing e. of the planets MRS. SOMERVILLE. b. The troublesome energies of Parliament MAY. 5. The e. and power of church music ATTERBURY. 6. 'The term e. may be applied..to the product' (now *half* the product) 'of the mass or weight of a body, into the square of the number expressing its velocity' YOUNG. Phr. *Conservation of e.* (see CONSERVATION). In every case in which e. is lost by resistance, heat is generated THOMSON & TAIT.

Enervate (ĭnə̄·ɹvĕt), *a.* 1603. [ad. L. *enervatus* pa. pple.; see next.] **1.** Wanting in strength or force; debilitated, spiritless, weak. **2.** *Bot.* Ribless.

Enervate (e·nəɹveⁱt), *v.* 1610. [f. L. *enervat-*, ppl. stem of *enervare*, f. *e* + *nervus* sinew (see NERVE *sb.*). In 17–18th c. stressed *ene·rvate*.] †**1.** *trans.* To cut the tendons of; chiefly *spec.* to hamstring, hough (a horse) –1751. †**2.** To emasculate. J. H(EALEY). **3.** To weaken physically; now only of things that impair nervous tone 1668. **4.** To weaken mentally or morally; to destroy the capacity of for action. Also *transf.* of sentiments, expressions, etc. 1614. †**5.** To render ineffectual –1836.

3. The conquerors were enervated by luxury GIBBON. 4. The tendency of abstract thought .. to e. the will M. PATTISON. 5. To e. the force and vigour of all divine injunctions 1702. Hence **E·nervator.**

Enervation (enəɹvē̆ⁱ·ʃən). 1555. [ad. late L. *enervatio*.] †**1.** = L. *enervatio*, used as tr. Gr. ἀπονεύρωσις (see quot.) –1751. **2.** The action of enervating; enervated state 1555.

1. The fibres of the recti of the abdomen..are intersected by several nervous places, called by the antients, enervations: though they be real tendons CHAMBERS *Cycl.* s. v. 2. A love for knowledge without e. of character GROTE.

†**Ene·rve,** *v.* 1613. [ad. F. *énerver*, ad. L. *enervare*.] = ENERVATE *v.* –1799.

†**Ene·rvous,** *a. rare.* 1677. [f. L. *enervis*, f. *e* + *nervus*.] Without nerve or strength; powerless, futile –1734.

Eneuch, eneugh, Sc. f. ENOUGH.

†**Enew·,** *v.* 1486. [ad. OF. *enewer*, *eneauer*, f. *en* (see EN-[1]) + *eau* water.] Of a hawk: To drive (a fowl) into the water. (In SHAKS. *Meas. for M.* III. i. 91, erron. *emmew*.) –1612.

Enface (enfē̆ⁱ·s), *v.* 1861. [f. EN-[1] + FACE *sb.*, after ENDORSE.] *trans.* To write or print on the face of. Hence **Enfa·cement,** what is written or printed on the face of a bill or note.

†**Enfa·mish,** *v.* ME. [Altered f. AFFAMISH; EN-[1].] *trans.* To famish –1491. Hence †**-ment.**

‖**Enfant terrible** (aṅfaṅ tẹrī·bl). 1851. [Fr. 'terrible child'.] A child who embarrasses his elders by his remarks; also *transf.*

†**Enfa·rce,** *v.* ME. [a. F. *enfarcir*, ad. L. *infarcire*.] To stuff. Also *fig.* –1624.

Enfect, obs. f. INFECT *a.* and *v.*

Enfeeble (enfī·b'l), *v.* ME. [a. OF. *enfeblir*, f. *en* + *feble* FEEBLE.] *trans.* To make feeble.

So much hath..paine Infeebled me MILT. *P. L.* IX. 488. Hence **Enfee·blement. Enfee·bler** (*rare*).

†**Enfee·blish,** *v.* ME. [a. OF. *enfebliss-*, *-ir*: see -ISH [2].] To make or become feeble –1576.

Enfe·lon, *v. Obs.* or *arch.* 1475. [ad. OF. *enfelonner*, f. *en-* + *felon* furious.] To make furious, infuriate.

Like one enfelon'd or distraught SPENSER.

Enfeoff (enfe·f), *v.* ME. [a. OF. *enfeffer*, *enfieffer*, f. *en-* + *fief* FIEF.] **1.** *trans.* To invest with a fief; to put in possession of the fee-simple or fee-tail of lands, tenements, etc. Also *absol.* Also *transf.* and *fig.* **2.** *fig.* To hand over as a fief; to give up entirely 1596.

2. The skipping King..Enfeoff'd himselfe to Popularitie SHAKS.

Enfeoffment (enfe·fmĕnt). 1460. [f. ENFEOFF + -MENT.] **a.** The action of enfeoffing. **b.** The deed or instrument by which a person is enfeoffed. **c.** The fief. **d.** The possession of a fief.

Enfester; see EN- *pref.*[1] 3.

Enfetter (enfe·təɹ), *v.* Also **in-**. 1604. [See EN-[1].] To put into fetters (*lit.* and *fig.*); to enslave *to*.

His Soul is so enfetter'd to her Loue *Oth.* II. iii. 351.

Enfever (enfī·vəɹ), *v.* 1799. [See EN-[1].] To throw into a fever; *fig.* to incense.

Enfief (enfī·f), *v. rare.* 1861. [f. EN-[1] + FIEF.] = ENFEOFF.

Enfield (e·nfīld). 1858. A village in Middlesex, near which is a Government manufactory of small-arms. Used *attrib.*, as in *E. rifle*, etc.

Enfierce; see EN- *pref.*[1] 2.

Enfilade (enfilē̆·d), *sb.* 1705. [a. F., f. *enfiler* to thread, f. *en-* (see EN-*pref.*[1]) + *fil* thread.] †1. A suite of rooms, whose doorways are opposite each other; also, a vista, as between rows of trees, etc. –1805. 2. *Mil.* A fire from artillery or musketry which sweeps a line of works or men from end to end. Also *attrib.* in *e. fire.* 1796.

Enfilade (enfilē̆·d), *v.* 1706. [f. prec.] †1. *trans.* To set (trees) so as to form an enfilade 1725. 2. *Mil.* To subject to an enfilade; to rake (a line of works or troops, a road, etc.) from end to end with a fire in the direction of its length 1706. Also *transf.*

2. The bridge..was enfiladed by the enemy's cannon PRESCOTT.

†**Enfi·le**, *v.* ME. [a. Fr. *enfiler*; see ENFILADE *sb.*] 1. To put on a string or thread –1675. 2. *Her.* In pa. pple. (See quot.) 1830.

2. When the head of a man or beast, or any other charge, is placed on the blade of a sword, the sword is said to be enfiled with whatever is borne upon it ROBSON.

†**Enfi·re**, *v.* 1513. [See EN-[1].] *trans.* To set on fire. Also *fig.* –1855.

Enflesh (enfle·ʃ), *v.* Also **in-**. 1548. [See EN-[1], IN-.] *trans.* **a.** To make into flesh. **b.** To cause a growth of flesh upon. **c.** To plant in the flesh, to ingrain. **d.** To give a form of flesh to.

Enflower (enflau·əɹ), *v.* 1523. [See EN-[1].] To cover or deck with flowers.

These odorous and enflower'd fields B. JONS.

Enfold, in- (en-, infōu·ld), *v.*[1] *Pa. pple.* occas. **infold, enfolden.** 1579. [f. EN-[1], IN- + FOLD *sb.* and *v.*] 1. *trans.* To wrap up, envelop *in* or *with*. Also said of the garment, etc. Also *fig.* 1592. 2. To encompass; to clasp, embrace. Also *fig.* 1596. †3. = INVOLVE –1646. 4. To shape as a fold or folds; formerly *fig.* to render involved 1605.

1. The oak is enfolded in the acorn TRENCH. *fig.* Night enfolds the day 1867. 2. [Vines] with lusty stems Their elms infolding SINGLETON. 4. The rim is infolded DARWIN. Hence **Enfo·lder, infolder. Enfo·ldment**, enfolding; that which enfolds.

Enfold (enfōu·ld), *v.*[2] *rare.* 1683. [See EN-*pref.*[1]] To shut up in a fold.

†**Enfo·llow**, *v. rare.* ME. [See EN- *pref.*[1]] **a.** *trans.* To follow after; *fig.* to imitate. **b.** *intr.* To follow on; to result. –1485.

†**Enfo·rce**, *sb.* ME. [f. next.] Effort, exertion –1671.

A petty enterprise of small e. MILTON.

Enforce (enfōə·ɹs), *v.* ME. [ad. OF. *enforcier, enforcir* :—late L. *infortiare, infortire*, f. *in-* (see IN-) + *fortis*; see also EN- *pref.*[1] and FORCE.]

I. †1. *trans.* To strengthen physically or morally; to reinforce, encourage –1685. †2. To add force to –1775. 3. To press home; to urge; †to emphasize 1449. †4. *refl.* To exert oneself, strive –1693. †5. *intr.* for *refl.* To strive, attempt –1595.

1. To e. the Towns of Flanders by..our Troops TEMPLE. 3. In order to e. what he had said JOHNSON.

II. †1. *trans.* To drive by force *to* or *from* –1664. †2. To press hard upon; also *fig.*; also *intr.* in same sense –1662. †3. To overcome by violence; also *fig.* –1631. 4. To compel, constrain 1509.

1. As swift as stones Enforced from the old Assyrian slings *Hen. V*, IV. vii. 65. 2. *Jul. C.* IV. iii. 112. 3. To e. a woman CAXTON, a town 1579. 4. To inforce a Borrower to pay LOCKE.

III. 1. To produce, impose, effect by force 1531. 2. To compel the observance of; to support by force (a claim, etc.) 1603.

1. To e. a brawle B. JONS., a tear 1812, obedience to an order 1844, payment KINGSLEY. 2. To e. a precept GOLDSM., a demand 1841.

Hence **Enfo·rceable** *a.* that can be enforced; also, †forcible. **Enfo·rcedly** *adv.* **Enfo·rcer. Enfo·rcingly** *adv.*

Enforcement (enfōə·ɹsmĕnt). Also **in-**. 1475. [a. OF.; see ENFORCE *v.* and -MENT.] 1. The action of enforcing (see ENFORCE *v.*); *concr.* a reinforcement 1587. 2. Constraint, compulsion; a constraining or compelling influence. Now *rare.* 1475. 3. The forcible exaction of a payment, an action, etc.; the compelling the fulfilment of (a law, obligation, etc.); †*concr.* a means of enforcing, a sanction 1597.

1. What inforcements..to perswade men GOLDING. And his e. of the Citie Wiues *Rich. III*, III. vii. 8. The Prince of Conde was sent..with a great E. TEMPLE. 2. Tuneless numbers, wrung By sweet e. KEATS. 3. The Rewards and Punishments..established as the Enforcements of his Law LOCKE. An e. of domestic discipline SCOTT.

Enforcible, var. of ENFORCEABLE.

†**Enfo·rcive**, *a.* 1606. [f. ENFORCE *v.* + -IVE.] Tending to enforce; forcible, urgent –1693. Hence †**Enfo·rcively** *adv.*

†**Enfo·rest**, *v.* 1619. [See EN-[1].] To turn into forest –1662.

Enform, etc.; see INFORM, etc.

Enfort; see EN- *pref.*[1] 2.

†**Enfortu·ne**, *v.* [See EN-[1].] To invest with a quality. CHAUCER.

†**Enfou·lder**, *v.* [app. f. EN-[1] + OF. *fouldre*, mod.F. *foudre.*] In **Enfou·ldred** *ppl. a.* ? black as a thunder-cloud. SPENSER.

Enframe (enfrē̆·m), *v.* Also **in-**. 1848. [See EN-[1].] To enclose in or as in a frame.

†**Enfra·nch**, *v.* 1581. [a. AF. *enfraunchir.*] = ENFRANCHISE –1633.

Enfranchise (enfrɑ·ntʃiz, -tʃəiz), *v.* 1514. [ad. OF. *enfranchiss-, enfranchir*, f. *en-* + *franc* free; see FRANK *a.*] 1. To set free; to release from slavery or serfdom, confinement, or obligatory payments or legal liabilities 1531. †2. To make free of a municipality or corporation. Also *fig.* –1655. 3. To invest (a city or town) with municipal rights. Now *chiefly* to invest with the right of representation in Parliament. 1564. 4. To admit to political rights; now *esp.* to the electoral franchise 1683. 5. To naturalize; also *fig.* ? *Obs.* 1601.

1. Phr. *To e. a copyhold* or *leasehold*: to convert it into freehold. 3. Verolam-cestre was at this time enfranchised FULLER. 5. By enfranchising strange forein words 1668. Hence **Enfra·nchiser**, one who or that which enfranchises.

Enfranchisement (enfrɑ·ntʃizmĕnt). Also †**in-**. 1595. [f. as prec. + -MENT.] 1. Liberation from imprisonment, servitude, or political subjection. Also *fig.* 2. Admission to the freedom of a city or body politic; admission to political rights. **b.** The conferring of privileges (*esp.* of the electoral franchise) upon a town. 1628. 3. The conversion of copyhold or leasehold lands into freehold 1876.

Enfree, -freedom, -freeze, etc.; see EN-*pref.*[1]

Enfrenzy (enfre·nzi), *v.* 1656. [See EN-[1].] To throw into a frenzy.

Enfroward; see EN- *pref.*[1]

†**Enfu·me**, *v.* 1601. [ad. F. *enfumer* :—L. *infumare*, f. *in* + *fumus.*] To expose to the action of smoke –1658.

Engage (engē̆·dʒ), *sb.* 1589. [f. next.] †1. Bargain; also, entanglement, peril –1626. 2. In Sword-exercise: The preliminary movement in which combatants cross swords 1833.

Engage (engē̆·dʒ), *v.* 1525. [a. F. *engager*, f. *en-* (see EN-[1]) + *gage* (see GAGE, WAGE).]

I. †1. To pledge or pawn; to mortgage –1669. 2. *fig.* To pledge (one's life, honour, etc.); also, to expose to risk. Now *rare.* 1568. †3. To make (a person) security for (a debt, etc.) –1651. 4. To bind by promise, or by legal or moral obligation; *spec.* to betroth 1603. **b.** *pass.* To have made an appointment, etc. (*mod.*). 5. To bespeak 1753. 6. *intr.* for *refl.* To pledge oneself 1613. †7. *trans.* To lay under obligation; in *pass.* to be committed *to* –1667. 8. To urge, induce. Now *rare.* 1647. 9. To gain, win over, as an adherent or helper (*arch.*) 1697. 10. To attract, charm, fascinate. Also *absol.* Now *rare.* 1711.

2. This to be true, I do e. my life *A. Y. L.* v. iv 172. 3. *Merch. V.* III. ii. 264. 4. I am engaged for to-morrow (*mod.*). 5. To e. Balmat as guide TYNDALL, rooms, box-seats, etc. (*mod.*). 6. More than I e. for JANE AUSTEN. 8. O..example high! Ingaging me to emulate MILT. *P. L.* IX. 963. 9. To e. poetry in the cause of virtue 1779.

II. 1. **a.** To entangle. ? *Obs.* 1602. **b.** *Arch.* To fasten, attach. In *pass.* of a pillar: To be partly let into a wall in the rear. 1766. **c.** *Mech.* (*intr.* for *refl.*) of a cog-wheel, etc.: To gear *with* 1884. †2. *trans.* To cause to penetrate *into* a country, a defile, etc.; also *refl.* and *intr.* –1693. †3. To involve, mix up *in*, also occas., *into, to, with.* Also *intr.* for *refl.* –1796. 4. To attract and hold fast 1642. 5. *trans.* To occupy, employ. Now usu. *pass.* 1648. 6. *intr.* for *refl.* 'To embark in any business' (J.) 1646. 7. *trans.* Of combatants: To interlock (weapons). Also *absol.* 1697. 8. **a.** To bring into conflict *with* the enemy 1668. **b.** *intr.* for *refl.* To enter into combat (*with*); also *fig.* 1647. 9. = 'engage with' (see 8); also (now *rarely*) *fig.* 1698.

1. a. *Haml.* III. iii. 69. 4. Her form..engaged the eyes of the whole congregation in an instant STEELE. 5. Engaged with my guitar 1847. 6. To e. in politics JOWETT. 8. a. He had taken care not to e. the whole of his troops (*mod.*). 9. These monsters, Critics! with your darts e. POPE.

Engaged (engē̆·dʒd), *ppl. a.* 1615. [f. prec.] 1. †Entangled. †**b.** Obliged. **c.** Locked in fight. **d.** Betrothed. 2. (See quots.)

1. b. Not as an e. person, but indifferently WALTON. 2. Phr. *E. column*, one partly let into a wall in the rear. *E. wheels* (Mech.), wheels in gear with each other. Hence †**Enga·gedness.**

Engagement (engē̆·dʒmĕnt). Also †**in-**. 1624. [f. as prec. + -MENT.] 1. The action of engaging, in various senses (see ENGAGE *v.*). 2. The state, condition, or fact of being engaged; *spec.* betrothal 1642. 3. A formal promise, agreement, undertaking, covenant 1624; an appointment 1806; in *pl.* pecuniary liabilities 1848. †4. Moral or legal obligation; a tie –1794; attachment, prepossession, bias (*rare*) –1708. 5. A battle, encounter; †a single combat 1665. †6. *concr.* An inducement, motive –1698.

2. Your account of your daughter's e. DICKENS. 3. Mr. A. B. is unable to meet his engagements (*mod.*). 5. We daily expect to hear of an E. between the Swedish and Danish Fleets 1710.

Engager (engē̆·dʒəɹ). 1650. [f. ENGAGE *v.*] 1. One who engages; *esp.* one who enters into an engagement or agreement; †a guarantor 1653. 2. *spec.* One of those who approved of the secret treaty or engagement negotiated at Carisbrooke in 1647 between Charles I and the Scottish commissioners. *Obs.* exc. *Hist.* 1650.

Engaging (engē̆·dʒiŋ), *ppl. a.* 1673. [f. as prec.] That engages; †obliging; †absorbing; winning, attractive.

Phr. *E. and disengaging machinery* (Mech.): that in which one part is alternately united to or separated from another part, as occasion may require (Nicholson). Hence **Enga·gingly** *adv.*, †**-ness.**

Engallant, -gaol, -garboil, etc.; see EN-*pref.*[1]

Engarland (engā·ɹlănd), *v.* 1581. [See EN- *pref.*[1]] To encircle with or as with a garland.

†**Enga·rrison**, *v.* 1612. [f. EN-[1] + GARRISON.] To serve as a garrison in; to protect by a garrison; to station as a garrison (*pass.* only) –1775.

†**Enga·strimyth.** 1598. [f. (ult.) Gr. ἐν + γαστήρ + μῦθος.] A ventriloquist –1708. Hence **Engastrimy·thic** *a.*

Engem (endʒe·m), *v. rare.* 1630. [See EN-[1].] To set with, or as with, gems; to bejewel.

†**Enge·nder**, *sb.* 1528. [a. OF. *engendre*; see next.] The action of engendering; *concr.* offspring, produce –1647.

Engender (endʒe·ndəɹ). ME. [a. F. *engendrer* :—L. *ingenerare*, f. *in* + *generare* to GENERATE, f. *genus* breed.] 1. *trans.* Of the male: To beget. Const. *on, of.* Now *rhet.* or *fig.* †2. Of the female: To conceive, bear –1683. 3. To produce, give existence to ME. †4. *absol.* To copulate. Const. *with.* Also *fig.* –1826. †5. *intr.* To breed, be produced, develop. Also *fig.* –1865.

1. When a man..engenders his like..it is no Miracle HOBBES. 3. Reptiles ingendered in the putrid waters

1777. Taxes..destroy industry, engendring despair HUME. Heat engendered by friction TYNDALL. 5. Thick clouds are spread, and storms e. there DRYDEN. Hence **Enge·nderer. Enge·nderment.**

Engendrure (endʒe·ndriŭɹ). *arch.* ME. [a. OF. *engendreure*, f. *engendrer*; see prec.] †1. The action of engendering –1555. 2. Descent, origin ME. var. **Enge·ndure** (a bad form).

Engild (engi·ld), *v.* ME. [f. EN-[1] + GILD *v.*] To gild; also *fig.*

Faire Helena; who more engilds the night SHAKS.

Engine (e·ndʒin), *sb.* ME. [a. OF. *engin* :—L. *ingenium* (whence INGENIOUS), f. *in* + *gen-* root of *gignere* to beget.] †1. Mother wit; genius. (Stressed *engi·ne.*) –1632. †2. Ingenuity; also, artfulness, trickery –1628. †3. An instance or product of ingenuity; a contrivance, plot; a snare, wile (cf. GIN *sb.*[1]); also, an appliance, means –1781. 4. A mechanical contrivance, machine, implement, tool; also short for *beer-, fire-, garden-e.*, etc. (see BEER-, FIRE-, etc.). Also *fig.* of persons and things. ME. 5. *spec.* a. A machine or instrument used in warfare ME. †b. An engine of torture –1689. †6. As tr. L. *machina* (see MACHINE) –1654. 7. = STEAM-ENGINE. (The prevailing sense.) 1816. 8. Applied also to analogous machines, including in themselves the means of generating power, as *caloric-, gas-e.*, etc. (*mod.*).

1. A man hath sapiences thre, Memorie, engin, and intellect also CHAUCER. 3. The hidden engines, and the snares that lie So undiscovered QUARLES. 4. Our modern e., the microscope POWER. An e. to grind knives and scissars ARBUTHNOT. *fig.* Empson and Dudley, the wicked engines of Henry VII BLACKSTONE. Two great engines, punishment and reward BENTHAM. 6. Phr. *E. of the world* (after L. *machina mundi* Lucr.): the 'universal frame'. 7. His iron might the potent e. plies CLOUGH.

attrib. and *Comb.*: a. attrib., as *e.-room*, etc.; b. objective, as *e.-driver*, etc.; also **e.-lathe**, a lathe worked by machinery; **-sized (paper)**, sized by a machine, not by hand; **-turning**, the engraving of symmetrical patterns upon metals by machinery.

Engine (e·ndʒin), *v.* ME. [orig. a. OF. *enginier* :—med.L. *ingeniare*, f. *ingenium* (see prec.); later, f. ENGINE *v.*] †1. *trans.* To contrive, plan. Also *absol.* with inf. –1611. †2. To take by craft, ensnare. Only in ME. †3. To put on the rack ME.; to assault with engines 1613. 4. To supply with engines 1868.

3. Enemies to e. and batter our walls T. ADAMS.

Engineer (endʒinīᵊ·ɹ), *sb.* [ME. *engyneour*, a. OF. *engigneor* (mod.F. *ingénieur*) :—late L. *ingeniatorem*, f. *ingeniare*; see prec. The forms in *-ier(e, -eer* may be ad. It. :—L. type **ingeniarius*, or f. ENGINE *sb.* + *-ier, -eer.*] †1. One who contrives, designs, or invents; an inventor, a plotter –1702. 2. One who designs and constructs military †engines or works. Also *fig.* ME. 3. One who designs and constructs works of public utility. (From 18th c. also *Civil E.*, dist. orig. from 2, but now from 4.) Often specialized, as *electric, gas, mining, railway, telegraph e.* 1606. 4. A contriver or maker of engines (see ENGINE *sb.*); now spec. *mechanical e.* 1575. 5. One who manages an engine; now in England only a marine engine; in U.S. often applied to the driver of a locomotive 1839.

Engineer (endʒinīᵊ·ɹ), *v.* 1681. [f. prec. sb.] 1. *intr.* To act as an engineer. 2. *trans.* To employ the art of the engineer upon; to construct or manage as an engineer 1843. b. *fig.* To contrive, plan, superintend. Also (U.S.) to carry through a measure or enterprise 1873.

2. The roads are admirably engineered OLMSTED. b. The corner in grain engineered .. in Chicago JAY GOULD.

Engineering (endʒinīᵊ·riŋ), *vbl. sb.* 1720. [f. prec.] 1. The work done by, or the profession of, an engineer. Often specialized as *civil, mechanical, military e.*; *agricultural, electric, gas, hydraulic, railway, sanitary, telegraph e.*; see ENGINEER *sb.* 2–4. 1720. b. *fig.* Contriving, manœuvring 1780. 2. *attrib.* 1739.

1. b. Party e. and the trickery of elections 1884. 2. E. slang BYRON.

Engineership (endʒinīᵊ·ɹʃip). 1649. [See -SHIP.] The business or position of an engineer.

†**Enginee·ry.** [f. ENGINEER *sb.* + -Y.] The science of engineering. SMEATON.

Engineman (e·ndʒinmæ̆n). 1835. [f. ENGINE *sb.* + MAN.] One who works or attends to an engine (see ENGINE *sb.*).

Enginery (e·ndʒinəri, -nri). 1605. [f. ENGINE *sb.* + -(E)RY.] †1. The art of constructing engines (see ENGINE *sb.*), or military works. Also *attrib.* –1672. 2. Engines collectively; machinery; engines of war. Often *fig.* 1641. 3. The work of an engine. Also *fig.* 1804.

2. In hollow Cube, Training his devilish Enginrie MILT. *P. L.* vi. 553.

†**E·nginous**, *a.* ME. [a. OF. *engineus* :—L. *ingeniosus*; see ENGINE *sb.*] 1. Clever, crafty; deceitful –1615. 2. Of, or of the nature of, an engine (*lit.* and *fig.*) –1630.

1. Open force, or projects e. CHAPMAN. 2. Some e. strong words B. JONS.

Engird (engə̄·ɹd), *v. Pa. pple.* **engirt.** 1566. [f. EN-[1] + GIRD *v.*] To surround with, or as with, a girdle.

Engirdle (engə̄·ɹd'l), *v.* 1602. [f. EN-[1] + GIRDLE.] = prec.

†**Engi·rt**, *v.* 1590. [f. EN-[1] + GIRT *v.*] 1. To gird *with.* Also *simply.* –1634. 2. To surround as a girdle does –1742; to enclose or hem in –1634.

1. The wat'ry zone Ingirting Albion W. BROWNE.

Engiscope; see ENGYSCOPE.

Engladden; see EN- *pref.*[1]

England (i·ŋglănd). [OE. *Engla land*, lit. 'the land of the Angles'; see ENGLISH, ANGLE[3].] †1. The territory of the Angles. Only in OE. 2. The southern part of the island of Great Britain. Occas. loosely: Great Britain. Often: The English (or British) nation or state. OE. Also *transf.* 3. Short for *The King of England*, also for the English, or a portion of them, as in 'Young England' (see YOUNG) 1595. Hence **E·nglander** (*rare*), an Englishman.

‖**Englanté**, *a.* 1731. [Fr., f. *en-* (see EN-[1]) + *gland* :—L. *glandem* acorn.] *Her.* Bearing acorns. (Dicts.)

Engle, obs. f. INGLE.

†**Englei·m**, *v.* ME. [f. EN-[1] + obs. *gleim* slime.] To make slimy; to set fast with, or as with, slime. Also to clog, surfeit –1470.

English (i·ŋgliʃ). [OE. *englisc, ænglisc* :—OTeut. **anglisko-*, f. **Angli-* (OE. *Engle*) pl., the Angles; see ANGLE[3].]

A. *adj.* 1. Of or belonging to the *Angelcynn* ('Angle-kin' = Bæda's *gens Anglorum*); or, later, to the pre-Norman inhabitants of England or their descendants. Now only *Hist.* 2. Of or belonging to England or its inhabitants ME. b. *ellipt.* = 'English people, soldiers', etc. 1599. 3. *transf.* Marked by the characteristics of an Englishman 1539. 4. As the designation of a language (see B. 1). Hence: Belonging to, written or spoken in, the English language. OE.

2. Phr. †*E. Disease* (*Malady*), *E. Melancholy*: the spleen. 3. He will find the design to be truly E., that is, sincere and honest 1695. 4. The E. Classics MACAULAY.

B. *sb.* 1. The English language. Also *attrib.*, as *E. scholar.* OE. b. The 'English' of any special period, district, or author ME. 2. Means of expression in English; the English word or equivalent (*for*). 3. *transf.* The plain sense (*of*) 1645. 4. *Printing.* a. A size of type intermediate between Great Primer and Pica.

English Type.

b. *Old E.*: a form of Black Letter, now occas. used for ornamental purposes.

1. Wych I purpose now to declare On (= *in*) ynglysh BOKENHAM. Phr. *The king's, the queen's E.* (cf. 'to deface the king's coin). b. The *Old E.* period, that ending about 1100–1150. The *Middle E.* period, that ending about 1500, when the period of *Modern E.* begins. The term *Old E.* is also popularly applied to all obsolete forms of the language. 2. Myn Englissh eek is insufficient CHAUCER. 3. When they unmask cant, they say, 'The E. of this is', etc. EMERSON.

English (i·ŋgliʃ), *v.* ME. [f. prec. adj.] 1. To translate into English. †2. To describe in plain English –1671. 3. To make English, to anglicize 1824.

1. I Englishe it thus WYCLIF. 2. Those gracious Acts..may be english'd more properly Acts of feare MILT. 3. Clive—he..Conquered and annexed and Englished 18·0. Hence †**E·nglishable** *a.* (Dicts.) **E·nglisher**, one who translates into English.

Englishism (i·ŋgliʃiz'm). *rare.* 1855. [See -ISM.] The characteristics of the English; English ways or manifestations; attachment to what is English.

Englishly (i·ŋgliʃli), *adv.* Now *rare.* 1529. [See -LY[2].] In an English manner; †in English; like an Englishman or Englishmen.

Englishman (i·ŋgliʃmæ̆n). OE. [f. ENGLISH + MAN.] A man who is English by descent, birth, or naturalization.

Englishry (i·ŋgliʃri). 1470. [ad. AF. *englescherie*, f. *englesche*, ad. ME. *englisch*, ENGLISH; see -RY.] 1. The fact of being an Englishman 1620. 2. That part of the population, *esp.* in Ireland, that is of English descent. *Hist.* 1470. b. English people; an English quarter (*rare*) 1867.

1. *Presentment of E.* (Law): the offering of proof that a slain person was an Englishman, in order to escape the fine levied (in Norman times) upon the hundred for the murder of a Norman.

E·nglishwoman. 1530. [f. ENGLISH + WOMAN.] A woman who is English by descent, birth, or naturalization.

Englobe (englōᵘ·b), *v.* Also †**in-**. 1611. [f. EN-[1] + GLOBE. Cf. Fr. *englober.*] To form into a globe; also, to enclose in, or as in, a globe. Usu. *fig.*

Engloom; see EN- *pref.*[1] 2.

†**Englue·**, *v.* ME. [a. F. *engluer*, f. *en-* + *glu* birdlime.] 1. To fasten down with, or as with, glue; *fig.* to connect closely –1475. 2. To ensnare, fascinate. Only in ME.

Englut (englʊ·t), *v. arch.* 1491. [orig. ad. OF. *englotir*, mod.F. *engloutir* :—L. *ingluttire*; also f. EN-[1] + GLUT *v.*] 1. To swallow; to gulp down. 2. To glut, satiate (*lit.* and *fig.*) 1571.

1. Inveterate wolf! whose gorge ingluts more prey, Than any beast beside CARY.

‖**Engobe** (engōᵘ·b). 1857. [Fr.] A white coating of pipe-clay, used to cover pottery.

Engolden; see EN- *pref.*[1]

Engore (engōᵊ·ɹ), *v.*[1] 1593. [f. EN-[1] + GORE *sb.*] To steep in gore; to make gory.

†**Engo·re**, *v.*[2] *rare.* 1590. [f. EN-[1] + GORE *v.*] To gore, wound deeply; *fig.* to infuriate. SPENSER.

Engorge (engǭ·ɹdʒ), *v.* 1515. [a. F. *engorger*, f. *en* + *gorge* GORGE.] 1. *trans.* To gorge, feed or fill to excess; chiefly *refl.* Also *transf.* in *pass.* 2. To put into the gorge; to devour greedily. Also *transf.* and *fig.* 1541.

1. *transf.* These vessels are congested, or engorged with blood 1869. 2. Prepare not to ingorge The eternal Pyramids 1798. Hence **Engo·rger.**

Engorgement (engǭ·ɹdʒmĕnt). 1611. [f. prec.] a. The action of engorging. b. Engorged state; esp. *Path.* congestion (of a tissue or organ) with blood, secretions, etc.

‖**Engouement** (añgūmañ). 1848. [Fr.; lit. 'obstruction in the throat'.] Unreasoning fondness.

Engouled (engū·ld), *a.* [ad. F. *engoulée*, f. *en* + OF. *goule* (mod.F. *gueule*) mouth.] *Her.* An epithet of bends, crosses, saltiers, etc.: Entering the mouths of animals. var. (in mod. Dicts.) engoulée.

Engrace (engrē̆ᵢ·s), *v.* Also †**in-**. 1610. [f. EN-[1] + GRACE *sb.*] †a. To introduce into favour –1641. b. To put grace into. PUSEY.

†**Engra·ff, in-**, *v.* ME. [f. EN-[1], IN- + GRAFF *v.*] = ENGRAFT *v.* 1, 2. –1739. Hence **Engra·ffment** = ENGRAFTMENT.

Engraft, in- (en-, ingra·ft), *v.* 1585. [f. EN-[1], IN- + GRAFT.] 1. *trans.* To insert (a scion of one tree) as a graft *into* or *upon* (another). Also *absol.* 1677. b. *transf.* To set firmly in. SMEATON. 2. *fig.* To implant; to incorporate; to superadd 1585. 3. To graft (a tree) 1794. †4. = INOCULATE 1717.

2. This word .. would root out vice and ingraft virtue ABP. SANDYS. To e. trade on a national bank BERKELEY. 4. The boy was engrafted last Tuesday 1717. Hence **Engrafta·tion** (*rare*).

Engraftment (engra·ftmĕnt). Also **in-**. 1647. [f. prec.] 1. The action of engrafting (*lit.* and *fig.*); also *concr.* a graft. †2. = INOCULATION 1722. †3. The issuing of additional stock in a trading company –1776. So

†**Engra·fture**, also **in-**, the action of engrafting; engrafted state.

Engrail (engrēⁱ·l), *v.* [ME. *engrele*, a. OF. *engresler*, mod.F. *engrêler*, f. *en-*+*gresle*, *grêle* hail.] **1.** To indent the edge of with curvilinear notches; *spec.* in *Her.* Mainly in pa. pple. **2.** *transf.* To give a serrated appearance to; †to render prickly 1576. †**3.** To indent –1602. †**4.** ?To variegate –1611. **5.** *Occas.*, To ornament *with* (metal) (*poet.*) 1814.

1. They also e. the bend itself BOUTELL. **2.** Hills with peaky tops engrail'd TENNYSON. **5.** The car Engrailed with brass BRYANT. Hence **Engrai·led** *ppl. a.* in the senses of the vb.; *spec.* in *Her.* curvilinearly notched, as an ordinary. †**Engrai·ling** *vbl. sb.* the action of the vb.; *concr.* an engrailed edge. **Engrai·lment**, the state of being engrailed; the engrailed circle round the margin of a coin, etc.

Engrain, in- (en-, iŋgrēⁱ·n), *v.* ME. [perh. *orig.* a. F. *engrainer* to dye, f. *en*+*graine* the cochineal dye; later, assoc. w. *grain*, a. F. *grain*, the fibre or minute structure of a thing. The form *engrain* is now preferred.] **1.** *trans.* To dye with cochineal; hence, to dye in fast colours, dye in grain. Also *transf.* and *fig. Obs.* or *arch.* **2.** To work into the fibre or minute structure of a thing. Chiefly *fig.* of habits, convictions, tastes, etc. 1641. **3.** *nonce-use.* To form a granular surface on. BURTON *Bk.-Hunter.*

1. Hire robe..of red scarlet engreyned LANGL. **2.** The stain hath become engrained by time SCOTT. *fig.* The feeling .. so deeply engrained in human nature MAX MÜLLER. Hence **Engrai·ned** *ppl. a.* in the senses of the vb.; *fig.* incorrigible. †**Engrai·ner**, in-.

†**Engra·ndize, -ise**, *v.* 1625. [a. F. *engrandiss-*, lengthened stem of *engrandir*, f. (ult.) L. *in-* (see IN-) + *grandis.*] *trans.* To make great, increase in estimation, etc. –1670.

Engrapple, obs. var. of INGRAPPLE *v.*

Engra·sp, *v.* 1593. [See EN-¹.] To embrace, grasp; also *fig.*

Engrave (engrēⁱ·v), *v. Pa. pple.* **engraved, engraven.** 1509. [f. EN-¹+GRAVE *v.*, after F. *engraver.*] †**1.** *trans.* To sculpture –1614. **2.** †To cut into (*rare*). **b.** To mark by incisions. 1590. **3.** To carve upon a surface; hence, to record by incised letters; also *fig.* 1542. **b.** *fig.* To impress deeply, fix indelibly 1509. **4.** To represent by incisions upon wood, metal, stone, etc. with the view of reproducing by printing 1667.

1. Lysippus engraued Vulcan with a streight legge LYLY. **2. b.** This fruit, whose gleaming rind engrav'n 'For the most fair' TENNYSON. **3.** Crimes..ingraven in some Plate of Iron or Brass BUNYAN. *fig.* To e. them on his memory OUSELEY. **4.** Maps..engraven in Copper PETTY. Hence †**Engra·vement**, the action of engraving; that which is engraved; also *fig.* a record, trace.

Engrave, var. of †INGRAVE, to entomb.

†**Engra·ven**, *v.* 1605. [?altered f. ENGRAVE.] = ENGRAVE –1713.

Engraver (engrēⁱ·vəɹ). 1586. [f. ENGRAVE *v.*] **1.** One who engraves; *spec.* one who engraves pictures on metal or wood from which to take prints. **2.** A graver (*rare*) 1821. So †**Engra·very**, the art or work of the e.; also *concr.* engravings, (*rarely*) an engraving.

Engraving (engrēⁱ·viŋ), *vbl. sb.* 1601. [f. as prec.] **1.** The action of ENGRAVE *v.*; the art of the engraver. **2.** *concr.* That which is engraved; an engraved figure or inscription (*rare*) 1611. **3.** An impression from an engraved plate 1803.

2. The worke of an engrauer in stone; like the engrauings of a signet *Ex.* xxviii. 11.

†**Engrea·ten**, *v.* 1614. [f. EN-¹+GREAT *a.* + -EN⁵.] To make great –1684.

†**Engre·ge**, *v.* ME. [ad. OF. *engregier*, f. late L. **ingraviare*, f. *in-*+*gravis* heavy. See AGGREGE.] To make heavy; hence, to harden (the heart, etc.); also, to aggravate –1600.

†**Engrie·ve**, *v.* ME. [ad. OF. *engrever*:—L. *ingravare*, f. *in-* (see IN-)+*gravis.*] **1.** To cause grief to; also *absol.* –1626. **2.** To aggravate –1592. **3.** To make a grievance of. HOLINSHED.

Engroove, in- (en-, ingrū·v), *v.* 1842. [f. EN-¹, IN-+GROOVE *sb.* or *v.*] *trans.* To work into a groove, or form a groove in.

Let the change which comes be free To ingroove itself with that which flies TENNYSON.

Engross (engrōᵘ·s), *v.* ME. [Two formations: (1) a. AF. *engrosser* (med.L. *ingrossare*) to write in large letters, f. Fr. phr. *en gros* in large, f. L. *in-*+*grossus.* (2) a. Fr. *engrosser* :—late L. *ingrossare* to make gross, f. *in-*+*grossus* GROSS.] **1.** To write in large letters; now usually, to write in a large, fair, legal hand; *hence*, to express in legal form. Also *absol.* †**b.** To include in a list –1660. **2.** To buy up wholesale; *esp.* to buy up the whole, or as much as possible, of (a commodity) for the purpose of 'regrating'. Now *Hist.* ME. **3.** *transf.* and *fig.* †To collect from all quarters (also with *up*); to monopolize 1596. **4.** To occupy wholly, absorb 1602. **5.** To render gross, dense, or bulky. Also *intr.* for *refl.* 1561. †**6.** *Mil.* To add to the numbers of (an army); also, to draw up (a battalion) in a compact body –1654.

1. For engrossing his will, twice unto paipar, after unto parchment 1591. **b.** T'ingross their names within his Register QUARLES. **2.** Forestallyng, regratyng..ingrossing of marchaundise CRANMER. **3.** To e. the sovereign powers AUSTIN, the conversation BUCKLE. **4.** If man alone e. not Heaven's high care POPE. The degree in which self-love engrosses us BUTLER. **5.** To e. the body 1587, the minde 1628, a bill 1663. **6.** They went on in ingrossing the Militia HOWELL. Hence **Engro·ssedly** *adv.* **Engro·ssing·ly** *adv.*, **-ness.**

Engrosser (engrōᵘ·səɹ), *vbl. sb.* 1460. [f. prec.] **1.** †One who buys in large quantities; †a forestaller; a monopolist. **2.** One who copies (a document) in large, fair characters 1607.

Engrossment (engrōᵘ·smĕnt). 1526. [f. as prec. + -MENT.] **1.** The action of engrossing; also that which is engrossed; also *fig.* **2.** The state or fact of being engrossed 1837.

1. An e. of grain 1818, of a charter SIR F. PALGRAVE. **2.** Amidst the e. of other studies CAIRNS.

Enguard; see EN- *pref.*¹ 3.

Engulf, in- (engʊ·lf), *v.* 1555. [f. EN-¹+GULF; cf. OF. *engoulfer.*] *trans.* To swallow up in, or as in, a gulf; *transf.* to bury completely. Also *refl.* and *intr.* for *refl.*

They were engulfed by chance in the great sea EDEN. Hence **Engu·lfment.**

Engyscope (e·ndʒiskōᵘp). Also (badly) engiscope. 1684. [f. Gr. ἐγγύς + -σκοπος; see -SCOPE.] In 17th and 18th c.: = MICROSCOPE; subseq. restricted to reflecting microscopes.

Enhalo (enhēⁱ·lo), *v.* 1842. [f. EN-¹+HALO.] To surround with, or as with, a halo.

Enhance (enhɑ·ns), *v.* ME. [a. AF. *enhauncer*, ?corrupt f. OF. *enhaucer* :—late L. **inaltiare*, f. *in-*+*altus.*] †**1.** *trans.* To lift, raise, set up –16.. Also †*fig.* **2.** To raise in degree, heighten, intensify 1559; to make to appear greater ME. **3.** To raise, increase (prices, charges, etc.) 1542. Also †*intr.* to rise –1671. **4.** To raise or increase *in* price, value, importance, attractiveness, etc. Also †*simply.* 1526.

1. Who, nought agast, his mightie hand enhaunst SPENSER. *fig.* To inhaunce with favours this thy reign DRUMM. OF HAWTH. **2.** To e. an injury RAY, delights GIBBON, the infirmity of Philip 1832. **3.** Taxes and customs daily enhansed 1649. **4.** Base Mony, may easily be enhansed, or abased HOBBES.

Hence **Enha·nced** *ppl. a.* raised, etc.; *spec.* in *Her.* put higher in the field, as a bend, etc. **Enha·ncement.** **Enha·ncer.**

†**Enha·ppy**, *v.* 1626. [See EN-¹.] To make happy or prosperous –1742.

†**Enha·rbour**, *v.* 1596. [f. EN-¹+HARBOUR *sb.* or *v.*] To harbour within itself; to dwell in, as in a harbour –1616.

Enharden (enhɑ·ɹd'n), *v.* ? *Obs.* 1502. [f. EN-¹+HARDEN *v.*] To make hard, harden (*fig.*); to embolden (*rare*).

†**Enha·rdy**, *v.* 1483. [f. EN-¹+HARDY *a.*] To make hardy, embolden –1525.

Enharmonic, -al (enhaɹmǫ·nik, -ăl), *a.* 1603. [ad. L. *enharmonicus*, a. Gr., f. ἐν + ἁρμονία; see HARMONY.] *Mus.* **1.** Pertaining to that scale of Greek music which proceeded by quarter tones and major thirds. **2.** Pertaining to, or concerned with, intervals smaller than a semitone; *esp.* with reference to the interval between those notes (belonging to different keys) which in instruments of equal temperament are rendered by the same tone: *e. g.* between G♯ and A♭. 1794.

2. Phr. *E. change* or *modulation*: that in which 'advantage is taken of the fact that the same notes can be called by different names, which lead .. into unexpected keys' PARRY. Hence **Enharmo·nically** *adv.* **Enharmo·nics** *sb.pl.* e. music.

†**Enhau·lse**, *v.* [ad. OF. *enhalcer*, *enhaucer.*] = ENHANCE, q.v. HOLLAND.

†**Enhau·nt**, *v.* ME. [ad. F. *enhanter*, f. *en-*+*hanter* to haunt.] **1.** *trans.* To practise. WYCLIF. **2.** To haunt; *intr.* to keep company *with* –1658.

†**Enha·zard**, *v.* 1562. [f. EN-¹+HAZARD *sb.*] To expose to hazard, to risk –1611.

Enhearse, in- (en-, inhɔ̄·ɹs), *v.* 1600. [f. EN-¹+HEARSE.] To put into, or as into, a hearse.

Enhearten (enhā·ɹt'n), *v.* Now *rare.* Also †in-. 1610. [f. EN-¹+HEARTEN *v.*] To make courageous; to strengthen, cheer.

Enhea·ven, in-, *v.* 1652. [See EN-¹.] To place in or as in heaven.

Enhedge; see EN- *pref.*¹ 3.

†**Enho·rt**, *v.* ME. [a. OF. *enhorter* :—L. *inhortari.*] *trans.* To encourage, incite. Also with sb. as obj.: To recommend. –1483. Hence †**Enho·rtment**, an exhortation.

†**Enhui·le**, *v.* [ad. OF. *enhuilier.*] = ENOIL. Holland.

Enhungered (enhʊ·ŋgəɹd), *ppl. a.* 1480. [Alteration of AHUNGERED, ANHUNGERED by substitution of EN-¹ for the prefix.] Hungry.

For he was sore enhongred 1480.

Enhydrite (enhəi·drəit). [f. as next + -ITE.] A mineral containing water occluded in its cavities. Hence **Enhydri·tic** *a.* of the nature of an e., as *enhydritic agates.*

Enhydrous (enhəi·drəs), *a.* 1812. [f. Gr. ἔνυδρος.] Containing water or other fluid.

Enhypo·statize, *v. rare.* [f. EN-²+HYPOSTATIZE.] To unite in one hypostasis or 'person'. SCHAFF.

Enigma (ĭni·gmă). 1539. [a. L. *ænigma*, Gr. αἴνιγμα (pl. αἰνίγματα), f. αἰνίσσεσθαι to speak allusively or in riddles, f. αἶνος apologue, fable. Cf. F. *énigme.*] **1. a.** A riddle. †**b.** An obscure or allusive speech; a parable. (Now only *transf.* from a.) **2.** *fig.* Something as puzzling as an enigma 1605.

1. a. Some e., some riddle, come, thy Lenuoy begin SHAKS. **2.** A person both God and Man, an ænigma to all Nations, and to all Sciences JER. TAYLOR. Hence †**Eni·gmatist**, one who writes, or speaks in, enigmas. **Eni·gmatize** *v.* †to symbolize; to render enigmatical; *intr.* to make, or talk in, enigmas.

Enigmatic, -al (ĭnigmæ·tik, -ăl), *a.* 1576. [ad. late L. *ænigmaticus*; see prec. Cf. F. *énigmatique.*] Pertaining to, of the nature of, or containing, an enigma; ambiguous, obscure, perplexing. Of persons: Mysterious.

He saw the figure of the enigmatic Jew GEO. ELIOT. Hence **Enigma·tically** *adv.* ambiguously obscurely.

Enigmato-, comb. f. ENIGMA, as in **Enigmato·grapher** [Gr. -γράφος], a maker or explainer of enigmas. **Enigmato·graphy** [Gr. -γραφία], the making or collecting of enigmas. **Enigmato·logy** [see -LOGY], the study of enigmas.

Enisle, in- (en-, inəi·l), *v.* 1612. [f. EN-¹, IN-+ISLE.] **a.** To make into an isle 1630. **b.** To place or settle on an isle; *fig.* to isolate, sever.

a. Mine eyes en-isle themselves with floods DRUMM. OF HAWTH. **b.** An inisled kingdom of fisherfolk 1880.

Enjail, in- (en-, indʒēⁱ·l), *v.* 1631. [f. EN-¹, IN-+JAIL. See also ENGAOL.] To shut up in, or as in, a jail.

†**Enja·mb**, *v.* 1600. [ad. F. *enjamber.*] To encroach.

Enjambment (endʒæ·mbmĕnt). Also **enjambement.** 1837. [ad. F. *enjambement*; see prec.] *Pros.* The continuation of a sentence beyond the second line of a couplet.

It [the couplet] was turned by enjambements into something very like rhythmic prose SAINTSBURY.

Enjewel (endʒ¹ū·ĕl), *v.* 1648. [See EN-¹.] To adorn with jewels; to adorn as a jewel does.

Faire injewel'd May Blowne out of April HERRICK.

Enjoin (endʒoi·n), *v.* ME. [a. F. *enjoign-*, stem of *enjoindre* :—L. *injungere* to bid, ordain, orig. to join on, f. *in-*+*jungere.*] †**1.** *trans.* To join together –1684. **2.** In early use: To impose (a penalty, duty, etc.); said *esp.* of a spiritual director. Hence: To prescribe authoritatively and with emphasis. ME. †**b.** To impose rules on (oneself). BACON. **3.** To prohibit, forbid. Now only in *Law*: To prohibit or restrain by an INJUNCTION. 1589.

2. The Lords .. have enjoyned their clerks secrecy MARVELL. The pope..enjoined him to return to his duties FROUDE. 3. To e. an action LD. ELDON, a person from infringing a right SIR C. BOWEN. Hence **Enjoi·ner. Enjoi·nment.**

Enjoy (endʒoi·), *v.* ME. [a. OF. *enjoier* to give joy to, *refl.* to enjoy, f. *en-* + *joie* JOY.] †1. *intr.* To be in a joyous state; to rejoice -1549. †2. *trans.* To put into a joyous condition -1610. b. *refl.* To experience pleasure, be happy 1656. 3. *trans.* To possess, use, or experience with delight; also, to relish. Also *absol.* 1462. 4. To have the use of, have for one's lot 1460. †b. To have one's will of (a woman) -1667.

2. b. Creatures are made to e. themselves, as well as to serve us H. MORE. To e. oneself at the seaside (*mod.*). 3. No one can long Enyoy plesure STARKEY. 4. To hold and e. the same as a place of inheritance CRUISE. At best she enjoys poor health 1834. Hence **Enjoy·able** *a.* capable of being enjoyed; affording pleasure. **Enjoy·ably** *adv.* **Enjoy·er.**

Enjoyment (endʒoi·mĕnt). 1553. [See -MENT.] 1. The action or state of enjoying anything. Also, the possession and use of something which affords pleasure or advantage. Const. *of*. 2. Gratification, pleasure; *concr.* that which gives pleasure 1665.

1. Injoyment of many Lands MANLEY, of one's legal rights MACAULAY. 2. Food, drink, sleep, and the like animal enjoyments BERKELEY.

†**Enke·nnel,** *v.* 1577. [See EN-[1].] To lodge as in a kennel -1603.

Enkindle (enki·nd'l), *v.* 1548. [f. EN-[1] + KINDLE *v.*] 1. *trans.* To cause to blaze up. Chiefly *fig.* (to excite passions, war, etc.) 1583. 2. To set on fire. In lit. sense *Obs.* 1548. b. *transf.* To light up 1870. †3. *intr.* To take fire; to burst forth in flame -1747.

1. To e. rage JOHNSON. 2. Inkindled to an indeauour of good BP. HALL. Hence **Enki·ndler.**

Enlace (enlē^i·s), *v.* ME. [a. F. *enlacer*:—late L. **inlaciare*, f. *in-* + **lacius* :—L. *laqueus* noose. Now as if f. EN-[1] + LACE.] 1. *trans.* To lace about, encircle tightly with, or as with, lace; *transf.* to enfold, embrace. 2. To interlace, entangle. Also *fig.* ME.

1. They will e. him in the coils of their red tape (*mod.*). Hence **Enla·cement.**

†**Enla·rd,** *v.* 1556. [f. EN-[1] + LARD.] *trans.* a. To lard -1606. b. = INTERLARD -1621.

Enlarge (enlā·ɹdʒ), *v.* ME. [a. OF. *enlarger, enlargir*, f. *en-* + *large* (see LARGE).] 1. *trans.* To make larger; to increase the size of; to extend the limits of; to magnify, exaggerate. b. *Photog.* To reproduce on a larger scale. Also *absol.* 1871. 2. *fig.* To extend the scope of 1553; to widen, to expand 1665; †to grant or obtain an extension of time for (an action, a lease, an order, etc.) -1863. 3. *intr.* for *refl.* To increase or widen in extent, bulk, or scope. Also *refl.* ME. 4. *intr.* for *refl.* To speak at large, expatiate 1659. 5. To set at large, release. Now *arch.* or *U.S.* 1494. †6. To bestow liberally. [So OF. *enlargir*; cf. L. *largiri.*] -1657.

1. That..his honour [might be] inlarged FLEMING. Any Prince willing to inlarge his Territories PETTY. Report generally inlarges matters 1728. Phr. †*To e. on* (intr.): to add to (a plan); to amplify (a hint) -1800. 2. To e. the Christian fayth EDEN, the legal operation of an instrument 1884, our conceptions of Time MᶜCOSH. Phr. *To e. the heart*: now usu., to increase its capacity for affection. *To e. an estate* (Law): to convert a lease for years or a life-interest into a fee-tail or fee-simple. 4. I shall e. upon the point BUTLER. 5. He was enlarged upon sureties 1878. Hence **Enla·rgeable** *a.* **Enla·rgeableness. Enla·rged** *ppl. a.* increased, expanded, set free; also *fig.* liberal. †**Enla·rgedly** *adv.* †**Enla·rgedness. Enla·rger. Enla·rgingly** *adv.*

Enlargement (enlā·ɹdʒmĕnt). 1540. [f. ENLARGE *v.* + -MENT.] 1. The action of enlarging; an increase in extent, capacity, magnitude, or amount 1564. b. *Photog.* (Cf. ENLARGE *v.* 1 b.) 1871. 2. The widening or expanding of the mind, of a person's sympathies, affections, etc.; the quality of being enlarged in mind, etc. 1806. 3. Expatiation on a subject (*arch.*) 1659. 4. Release from confinement, limitation, or bondage 1540; liberty (*arch.*) 1611.

3. I restrain my pen from all e. MALLET. 4. The e. of the deer 1875, of Mr. Parnell from prison 1883.

Enlay; see INLAY.

Enleague (enlī·g), *v.* 1602. [f. EN-[1] + LEAGUE *sb.* or *v.*] *trans.* To unite in, or as in, a league.

Enlength, -en; see EN- *pref.*[1] 2, 3.

Enlevement (enlī·vmĕnt, aṅlɛ̄vmaṅ). 1769. [Fr.; f. *enlever.*] *Sc. Law.* An abduction.

Enle(v)en, -enth, obs. ff. ELEVEN, -TH.

†**Enlight** (enləi·t), *v.* [OE. *inlīhtan*, f. *in-* + *līhtan* to shine (see LIGHT *v.*); subseq. f. EN-[1] + LIGHT *v.*] To shed light upon, illuminate. Also *fig.* and *absol.* -1709.

Enlighten (enləi·tən), *v.* ME. [f. EN-[1] + LIGHT *sb.* + -EN[5].] †1. *trans.* To put light into, make luminous -1763. 2. To illuminate; to give light to. Also *absol.* Now *poet.* or *rhet.* 1611. †3. To light -1817. 4. *fig.* To impart knowledge, wisdom, or spiritual light to; to instruct. In mod. colloq. use: To inform. 1577.

2. His lightnings inlightned the world *Ps.* xcvii. 4. Shadow and sunshine..darkning and enlightning.. every spot COWPER. 4. [The Seuentie] were .. enlightened by propheticall grace A.V. *Pref.* To e. their minds JOHNSON. Hence **Enli·ghtener,** one who or that which enlightens. (Rare exc. *fig.*)

Enlightened (enləi·t'nd), *ppl. a.* 1611. [f. prec.] †1. Blazing, light-giving -1803. 2. Illuminated 1638. 3. Possessed of mental light; instructed, well-informed; free from superstition or prejudice 1663. Hence **Enli·ghtenedness.**

Enlightenment (enləi·t'nmĕnt). 1669. [f. as prec. + -MENT.] 1. The action of enlightening; enlightened state. Only in *fig.* sense. 2. [after Ger. *Aufklärung.*] Shallow and pretentious intellectualism, unreasonable contempt for authority and tradition, etc.; applied *esp.* to the spirit and aims of the French philosophers of the 18th c. 1865.

2. The individualistic tendencies of the age of E. CAIRD.

†**Enli·mn,** *v.* 1453. [f. EN-[1] + LIMN.] *trans.* To illuminate (a book); also, to paint in bright colours -1603.

Enlink (enli·ŋk), *v.* 1560. [f. EN-[1] + LINK.] *trans.* To fasten as with links; to connect closely (*lit.* and *fig.*).

Enlist (enli·st), *v.* Also †**in-.** 1698. [f. EN-[1] + LIST *sb.* or *v.*] 1. *trans.* To enrol on the list of a military body; to engage as a soldier. 2. *transf.* and *fig.* To secure the support or aid of; to make available for a purpose 1753. 3. *intr.* for *refl.* To have one's name inscribed in a list of recruits; to engage for military service. Also *transf.* and *fig.* 1776.

2. It was clever to inlist on your side those venerable prejudices 1826. To e. the aunt as his friend DISRAELI. 3. A bounty to induce men to e. 1865.

Enlistment (enli·stmĕnt). 1765. [f. prec. + -MENT.] 1. The action of enlisting men for military service; the action of engaging for military service. Also *fig.* and *attrib.* 2. 'The document by which a soldier is bound' (Webster). ? *U.S. only.*

†**Enli·ve,** *v.* 1593. [f. EN-[1] + LIFE; cf. the pl. *lives.*] = next -1659.

Enliven (enləi·v'n), *v.* 1633. [f. as prec. + -EN[5].] †1. *trans.* To give or restore life to; to animate -1732. 2. To give fuller life to; to inspirit, invigorate; to quicken 1644. 3. To make lively, cheer; to relieve the monotony of; to brighten 1691.

2. To inliven Trade 1677, to e. old trees PLOT, the circulation DUNDAS. 3. To e. Morality with Wit ADDISON. A sage to consult, rather than a companion to e. DIBDIN. Hence **Enli·vener,** one who or that which enlivens. **Enli·venment,** the action of enlivening; the being enlivened; that which enlivens.

Enlock (enlǫ·k), *v.* Also **in-.** 1596. [f. EN-[1] + LOCK *v.*] To lock up, shut in, hold fast. Also *fig.*

†**Enlu·mine,** *v.* ME. [a. OF. *enluminer*, ad. late L. *inluminare*, f. *in-* + *lumen, luminis.* See LIMN.] 1. To light up, illuminate; also *fig.* -1596. 2. To illuminate (MSS.) -1579.

†**Enlu·re,** *v.* 1486. [See EN-[1].] To entice by a lure; also *fig.* -1613.

†**Enlu·te,** *v.* ME. [f. EN-[1] + L. *lutare*, f. *lutum* clay.] *Alch.* To stop or cement with clay -1584.

Enmagazine; see EN- *pref.*[1] 1 a.

†**Enma·nché, emma·nché.** 1586. [a. F. *emmanché*, f. *en-* + *manche* handle.] *Her.* 1. Of the field: = *barry-pily.* (Not in Eng. use.) 2. Of a chief: Having 'lines drawn from the upper edge of the chief on the sides' (Bailey).

Enmarble, etc.; see EMM-.

‖**En masse** (aṅmas). 1802. [Fr.] In a mass or body; all at once.

Enmesh, emm-, imm- (enme·ʃ, eme·ʃ, ime·ʃ), *v.* 1604. *trans.* To catch or entangle in, or as in, meshes.

I got immeshed in a network of turns unknown C. BRONTË. Hence **Enme·shment,** entanglement.

Enmew; see INMEW.

Enmity (e·nmĭti). ME. [ad. OF. *enemistié* :—late L. **inimicitatem*, f. *inimicus*; see ENEMY.] 1. The disposition or the feelings of an enemy; ill-will, hatred. 2. The condition of being an enemy; a state of mutual hostility ME. Also *transf.*

1. For enymyte and hate are contrary to frendship and concorde CAXTON. 2. An age at e. with all restraint LOCKE (J.).

Enmoss; see EN- *pref.*[1] 1 b.

Enmove, obs. var. of INMOVE *v.*

†**Enmu·ffle,** *v.* [f. EN-[1] + MUFFLE *v.*] To muffle up. FLORIO.

[**Ennation,** 'the ninth segment of insects' is a blunder for *ennaton* (a. late Gr. ἔνvατον ninth).]

E·nneacontahe·dral, *a. rare.* 1817. [f. Gr. ἐνενήκοντα (erron. for ἐνενήκοντα) ninety + ἕδρα.] Of a crystal: Having ninety faces.

Ennead (e·nĭæd). 1653. [ad. Gr. ἐννεάς, f. ἐννέα nine.] †1. The number nine 1655. 2. A set of nine; *spec.* one of the six divisions in Porphyry's collection of Plotinus' works, each of which contains nine books. Hence **Ennea·dic** *a.* pertaining to an e.

Enneaeteric (e:nĭă‚ĭte·rik), *a.* [f. Gr. ἐννέα + ἔτος year, after τριετηρίς, etc.] Consisting of nine years. GROTE.

Enneagon (e·nĭ‚ăgǫn). 1660. [f. Gr. ἐννέα + γωνία.] *Geom.* A plane figure with nine angles. Hence **Ennea·gonal** *a.* having nine angles.

Enneagynous (enĭæ·dʒinəs), *a.* [f. Gr. ἐννέα + γυνή.] *Bot.* Having nine pistils. (Dicts.)

Enneahedral (e:nĭăhī·drăl), *a.* 1802. [f. Gr. ἐννέα + ἕδρα + -AL.] Having nine faces.

Ennea·ndrian, *a.* [f. mod.L. *enneandria* (f. as next) + -AN.] *Bot.* = next.

Enneandrous (enĭæ·ndrəs), *a.* 1870. [f. Gr. ἐννέα + ἀνδρ- male + -OUS.] *Bot.* Having nine stamens.

Enneapetalous (e:nĭăpe·tăləs), *a.* 1847. [f. Gr. ἐννέα + πέταλον + -OUS.] *Bot.* Having nine petals. So **Enneaphy·llous** *a.* [Gr. φύλλον], having nine leaves. **Ennease·palous** *a.* [see SEPAL], having nine sepals. **Enneaspe·rmous** *a.* [Gr. σπέρμα], having nine seeds.

Enneatic, -al (enĭæ·tik, -ăl), *a. rare.* [f. Gr. ἐννέα + -ATIC (+ -AL).] Occurring once in nine times, days, years, etc.; ninth.

Phr. †*Enneatical day*: every ninth day of a disease. †*Enneatical year*: every ninth year of life.

†**Ennew·,** *v.*[1] ME. [f. EN-[1] + NEW.] To make new or anew -1623.

†**Ennew·,** *v.*[2] ME. [? f. EN-[1] + F. *nuer* to shade.] *trans.* To shade; to graduate (colours). Also *fig.* -1573.

Enniche; see EN- *pref.*[1] 1 a.

Ennoble (enōᵘ·b'l), *v.* 1502. [ad. F. *ennoblir*, f. *en-* (see EN-[1]) + *noble.*] 1. To give the rank of nobleman to 1594. 2. To impart nobility to; to dignify, elevate, refine 1502. †3. To render illustrious or conspicuous -1775.

1. His [Columbus'] family were ennobled 1791. 2. The Son of God .. ennobling all that he touches TRENCH. 3. Bear Thy death, ennobl'd by Ulysses' spear POPE. Hence **Enno·blement,** the action of ennobling; the state or fact of being ennobled; †that which ennobles. **Enno·bler. Enno·blingly** *adv.* var. †**Enno·blish,** †**Enno·blize.**

†**Ennoy·,** var. of ANNOY *sb.* and *v.*

‖**Ennui** (aṅnüi), *sb.* 1758. [a. F. *ennui*, OF. *enui* :—L. *in odio*; see ANNOY.] Mental weariness and dissatisfaction arising from want of occupation, or lack of interest.

Ennui, *v.* 1805. [f. prec. sb.; only in pa. pple.] To affect with ennui; to bore, weary.

They [animals] rejoice, play, are ennuied as we are 1805.

‖**Ennuyé** (aṅnüiye), *a.* 1757. [Fr.; pa. pple.

of *ennuyer.*] Affected with ennui. As quasi-*sb.* (also *fem.* -ée), one who is troubled with ennui.

†Eno·date, *v.* 1656. [f. L. *enodat-, enodare*, f. *e*+*nodus.*] To free from knots; *fig.* to unravel, make clear -1681. Hence †Enoda·tion.

†Eno·de, *v. rare.* 1623. [ad. L. *enodare*; see prec.] To untie (a knot); *fig.* to solve (a riddle) -1684.

†Enoi·l, *v.* ME. [f. EN-¹+OIL *sb.*] To anoint, or mix, with oil -1647.

Enoint, obs. f. ANOINT.

Enology; see ŒNOLOGY.

Enomotarch (enǫ·mǒtaɪk). 1623. [ad. Gr. ἐνωμοτάρχης, f. ἐνωμοτία + ἄρχειν.] *Gr. Antiq.* The commander of an ENOMOTY.

Enomoty (enǫ·mǒti). 1623. [ad. Gr. ἐνωμοτία a band of sworn soldiers, f. ἐν + ὀμνύναι.] *Gr. Antiq.* A division in the Spartan army.

Enoptromancy (enǫ·ptrǒmænsi). Also (erron.) enopto-. 1855. [f. Gr. ἔνοπτρον + μαντεία; see -MANCY.] Divination by means of a mirror.

Enorganic (enǫɪgæ·nik), *a.* [See EN-².] Inherent in the organism. SIR W. HAMILTON.

Enorm (ǐnǭ·ɪm). 1481. [a. Fr. *énorme*:—L. *enormis*, f. *e*+*norma.*] †1. Abnormal, extravagant -1734. †2. Outrageous -1639. 3. Abnormally large (*arch.*) 1581.

†Eno·rmious, *a.* 1545. [f. L. *enormis*; see prec.] = ENORMOUS -1665.

Enormity (ǐnǭ·ɪmǐti). 1475. [ad. F. *énormité*, ad. L. *enormitatem*; see ENORM.] 1. Deviation from a normal standard or type; *esp.* from moral or legal rectitude. In later use: Monstrous wickedness. 1538. 2. *concr.* That which is abnormal; an irregularity; a crime; in later use, a monstrous offence 1475. †3. Excess in magnitude. (An incorrect use.) -1846.

1. Deeds of peculiar e. and rigour ROBERTSON. 2. Other enormities Catiline had been guilty of FROUDE.

Enormous (ǐnǭ·ɪməs), *a.* 1531. [f. L. *enormis*+-OUS.] †1. Deviating from ordinary rule or type; abnormal; hence, monstrous -1818. †2. Of persons, deeds, etc.: Disorderly. Hence, excessively wicked, outrageous. -1827. 3. Extraordinary in size or quality; huge, vast, immense. (The only current sense.) 1544.

1. E. appetite VENNER, bliss MILT., faith POPE. 2. Oh great corrector of e. times 1612. E. wickedness, guilt SOUTHEY. 3. E. woe POLLOK, cracks and fissures 1836. Hence Eno·rmous-ly *adv.*, -ness.

†Eno·rn, *v.* ME. [var. of ANORN, q.v.] = ANORN -1513.

Eno·rthotrope. [f. Gr. ἐν + ὀρθός + -τροπος.] A toy; a card on which confused objects are transformed into regular figures or pictures, by causing it to revolve rapidly. (Dicts.)

Enostosis (enǫstǭᵘ·sis). 1874. [f. Gr. ἐν + ὀστέον, after ἐξόστωσις.] *Anat.* A bony tumour growing inward into the medullary canal of a bone.

Enough (ǐnʊ·f). [OE. *genóg*, later *genóh* adj. :—OTeut. **ganógo-z*, related to the impers. vb. (pret.-pres.) OE. *geneah* 'it suffices', f. OTeut. **ga-* (see Y-) + **nah* :—Aryan **nak*, Skr. *naç* to reach.]

A. *adj.* 1. Sufficient in quantity or number: used in concord with sb., which it usually follows, or predicatively. 2. *absol.* in *sing.* That which is sufficient OE. b. *ellipt.* = 'Enough has been said,' etc.; quasi-*interj.*; also with *of* ME.

1. With payne and trauayle anough LD. BERNERS. Prisoners mo than Inough 1500. It is ynough, holde now thy hande COVERDALE 2 *Sam.* xxiv. 16. 2. I have had e. of fighting DE FOE.

B. *adv.* (In mod. Eng. *enough* normally follows the word it qualifies.) 1. Sufficiently; in a quantity or degree that satisfies or is effectual OE. 2. In vaguer sense. a. With intensive, or slightly intensive, force OE. b. Belittling what is conceded 1606.

1. He [Dauid] himselfe was olde, and had lyued ynough COVERDALE 1 *Chron.* xxiii. 1. Good e. for me JOWETT. 2. a. This poynte is..metely playn inough MORE. Phr. *Aptly e., oddly e.* b. A good e. man in his way MRS. CARLYLE.

Enounce (ǐnau·ns), *v.* 1805. [ad. F. *énoncer*, ad. L. *enuntiare*, after ANNOUNCE.] 1. *trans.* = ENUNCIATE. 2. To state publicly, proclaim 1807. 3. To utter, pronounce; cf. ENUNCIATION 1829.

3. The student should be able to e. these [sounds] independently A. M. BELL. Hence Enou·ncement.

Enow (ǐnau·), *a.* and *adv.*¹ Now only *arch.* [See ENOUGH, of which, in many dialects, ENOW served for the pl.] = ENOUGH *a.* and *adv.*

Enow (ǐnau·), *adv.*² *dial.* [? Short for *e'en* (= *even*) or for *the now.*] Just now (*Sc.*); presently.

Enp-; see EMP-.

‖ **En passant** (aṅ pasaṅ), *adv.* 1665. [Fr.] In passing; by the way.

†Enqua·rter, *v.* 1622. [f. EN-¹+QUARTER *sb.*] 1. To put into quarters; to billet. Also *absol.* -1673. 2. *Her.* To quarter -1635.

Enquere, obs. var. of ENQUIRE, INQUIRE.

Enquicken; see EN- *pref.*¹ 3.

Enquire (enkwəi·ɹ), *v.* An alternative form of INQUIRE; used *esp.* in the sense 'to ask a question'. Hence Enquirer, Enquiry, etc., for which see IN-.

†Enra·ce, *v. rare.* 1577. [f. EN-¹+RACE *sb.*] To introduce into a race; to implant -1596.

Enrage (enrēⁱ·dʒ), *v.* 1500. [ad. OF. *enrager*, f. *en-* (see EN-¹)+*rage.*] †1. *intr.* To be distracted. Const. *for.* -1557. †2. To rage -1782. †3. *Pa. pple.* Maddened; inspired. Also, affected with rabies. -1719. 4. *trans.* To put into a rage; to exasperate; also *absol.* 1589. †5. *transf.* To cause heat or fever in -1693.

3. His love, perceiving how he is enraged, Grew kinder SHAKS. 4. Question enrages him *Macb.* III. iv. 118. 5. To e. the blood 1626, a wound 1635. Hence Enra·ged-ly *adv.*, -ness. Enra·gement, the action of enraging; enraged state or condition; †rapture.

†Enrai·l, *v.* 1523. [f. EN-¹+RAIL *sb.* and *v.*] To enclose with, or as with, a railing -1607.

†Enra·nge, *v.* [f. EN-¹+RANGE *sb.* and *v.*] 1. To arrange. 2. To range or ramble in. ? In Spenser only.

Enra·nk, *v.* 1591. [f. EN-¹+RANK *sb.*] To set in ranks, or in order (of battle).

‖ **En rapport** (aṅrapǭr). In relation (*with*); in mesmeric 'rapport'; see RAPPORT.

Enrapt (enræ·pt), *pple.* 1606. [f. EN-¹+RAPT.] Carried away in an ecstasy; hence, absorbed in contemplation, enraptured. ¶Sometimes undistinguishable from *enwrapt* (fig.).

Enrapture (enræ·ptiŭɹ), *v.* 1740. [f. EN-¹+RAPTURE.] 1. To throw into a poetic rapture 1742. 2. To delight greatly.

Enravish (enræ·viʃ). Now *rare.* 1596. [f. EN-¹+RAVISH.] To transport with delight; to enrapture. Hence †Enra·vishingly *adv.* Enra·vishment, enravished condition; ecstasy.

Enregiment (enre·dʒměnt), *v.* 1831. [ad. F. *enrégimenter.*] To form into, or as into, a regiment; hence, to discipline.

Enregister (enre·dʒistəɹ), *v.* 1523. [ad. F. *enregistrer*, f. *en-*+*registre.*] 1. *trans.* To enter in a register or official record. Also *transf.* and *fig.* (Revived in recent use as a gallicism.) 2. To put on record as law 1651.

Hence Enregistra·tion, the registering, on the brain, of previous actions, so that performance becomes automatic or instinctive 1922. †Enre·gistry, the action of enregistering.

†Enrheu·m, *v.* 1666. [ad. OF. *enrheumer*, f. *en-*+*rheume*, ad. Gr. ῥεῦμα RHEUM.] *trans.* To affect with rheum; to give a cold to.

Enrich (enri·tʃ), *v.* ME. [a. F. *enrichir*, f. *en-*+*riche.*] 1. *trans.* To make rich with material, or (*fig.*) mental or spiritual, wealth. Also *absol.* 2. To add to the valuable contents of. Also *fig.* 1579. 3. To make (the soil, etc.) rich; to fertilize 1601. 4. To make rich with (costly) decoration. Also *fig.* 1601. 5. To make richer; to heighten 1620.

1. To enrych the Corowne FORTESCUE. *fig.* E. them with thy heauenly grace *Bk. Com. Prayer.* 2. E. thy cofers LYLY. *fig.* The English tongue is mightily enriched 1598. 4. The hilt and scabbard were gold enriched with diamonds SWIFT. Hence Enri·cher. Enri·chingly *adv.*

Enrichment (enri·tʃměnt). 1626. [f. prec. +-MENT.] 1. The action or process of enriching; the condition of being enriched; *concr.* that which enriches. 2. *spec.* The ornament used for enriching a building, etc. 1664.

†Enridged, *ppl. a.* Thrown into ridges, ridged. *Lear* IV. vi. 71 *Qo.* 1 & 2.

Enring (enri·ŋ), *v. poet.* 1589. [f. EN-¹+RING *sb.*] *trans.* To put within a ring; to encircle.

The female Iuy so Enrings the barky fingers of the Elme SHAKS.

Enripen (enrəi·p'n), *v. rare.* 1631. [See EN-¹.] To mature.

Enrive; see EN- *pref.*¹ 3.

Enrobe (enrǭᵘ·b), *v.* 1593. [f. EN-¹+ROBE *sb.*] To put a robe upon, dress in a robe. Also *transf.* and *fig.*

Enro·ckment. 1846. [f. EN-¹+ROCK+-MENT.] A mass of large stones thrown into water at random to form the bases of piers, breakwaters, etc.

Enrol, enroll (enrǭᵘ·l), *v.* [ME. *enrolly*, ad. OF. *enroller* (mod.F. *enrôler*); see EN-¹ and ROLL.] 1. To write, inscribe the name of, on a roll, list, or register. 2. To place upon a list; *esp.* to enlist, incorporate in the ranks of an army; to levy (an army) 1576. 3. To enter among the rolls, *i. e.* upon the records of a court 1495. 4. To record (*lit.* and *fig.*); also, to celebrate 1530. 5. To form into rolls; to wrap up *in* or *with*; also *transf.* and *fig.* 1530.

1. Our Sea-men..were carefully enroll'd T. HALE. 2. Enrolled among the wittes BARROW, as guards to the Caliph J. H. NEWMAN. 3. Indentures..inrolled in your Courte of the Chauncery of recorde 1495. Hence Enro·ller.

Enrolment (enrǭᵘ·lměnt). 1535. [f. prec. +-MENT.] 1. The action of enrolling; the process of being enrolled 1552. 2. The action of recording in official archives; *esp.* registration 1535. b. *concr.* An official entry; a record 1603.

Enroot (enrū·t), *v.* Only in pa. pple. 1490. [f. EN-¹+ROOT.] 1. To fix by the root; *fig.* to implant deeply in the mind. 2. To entangle root by root. 2 *Hen. IV*, IV. i. 207.

Enrough (enrʊ·f), *v.* 1601. [f. EN-¹+ROUGH *a.*] To make (the sea) rough; also *fig.*

†Enrou·nd, *v.* ME. [f. EN-¹+ROUND *sb.*] To surround -1600.

‖ **En route** (aṅrut). [Fr.] On the way; see ROUTE.

Ens (enz), *sb.* *Pl.* **entia** (e·nʃiă). 1581. [Late L., f. L. *esse*, after *absens*, etc.] 1. *Philos.* a. A being, entity, as opp. to an attribute, quality, etc. 1614. b. An entity as an abstract notion 1581. †2. = ESSENCE -1730. †b. *Alch.* 'The most efficacious Part of any natural Mixt Body' (Kersey) -1715.

1 a. Men have needlessly multiplied *Entia* HALE.

Ensafe; see EN- *pref.*¹

Ensample (ensa·mp'l), *sb. arch.* ME. [Altered f. obs. *asaumple*, a. OF. *essample*; see EXAMPLE *sb.*] = EXAMPLE.

An ensampelle of deseytte ME. As ye haue vs for an e. *Phil.* iii. 17. Making them [Sodom and Gomorrha] an e. vnto those that after should liue vngodly 2 *Peter* ii. 6.

†Ensa·mple, *v.* ME. [f. prec. sb.] 1. To exemplify -1599. 2. To give an example to. Also, to model (something) *by, upon.* -1654. Hence †Ensa·mpler, a copy, pattern.

Ensanguine (ensæ·ŋgwin), *v.* 1667. [f. EN-¹+L. *sanguinem.*] To stain with blood. Also *fig.* and *transf.*

Th' ensanguind Field MILT. *P. L.* XI. 654. Ensanguined fury 1806, hues BARHAM.

Ensate (e·nsēⁱt), *a.* 1830. [ad. mod.L. *ensatus*, f. L. *ensis*; see -ATE.] *Bot.* Sword-shaped.

†Ensca·le, *v.* [? f. EN-¹+SCALE (in music).] *trans.* ? To attune. G. DANIEL.

†Ensche·dule, *v.* [f. EN-¹+SCHEDULE *sb.*] To insert in a schedule; to schedule. SHAKS.

Ensconce (enskǫ·ns), *v.* 1590. [f. EN-¹+SCONCE *sb.*, prob. ad. OF. *esconse* hiding-place, shelter.] †1. *trans.* To furnish with earthworks -1752. †2. To shelter within or behind a fortification; also *transf.* and *fig.* -1734. Also †*intr.* for *refl.* 3. To conceal or place securely. Chiefly *refl.* 1598.

3. I will e. mee behinde the Arras SHAKS. Ensconcing themselves in the warm chimney-corner DICKENS.

Enseal (ensī·l), *v. arch.* ME. [a. OF. *enseeler*, f. *en-* (see EN-¹)+*seel* (mod. *sceau*) SEAL.] *trans.* To put a seal upon; to confirm by sealing. *fig.* For every thing he said there, Seemed as it insealed were CHAUCER.

†**Ensea·m**, *v.*[1] 1450. [ad. OF. *ensaimer, altered f. *essaimer*, f. *es-*, L. *ex-* + OF. (**saim*) *saïn* grease :—med.L. *sagimen* stuffing.] To cleanse or become clear of superfluous fat: said of a hawk, and later a horse –1774.

†**Ensea·m**, *v.*[2] 1562. [ad. F. *enseimer* (now *ensimer*); OF. **ensaimer* (see prec.).] To load with grease.

In the ranke sweat of an enseamed bed SHAKS.

Enseam (ensī·m), *v.*[3] 1605. [f. EN-[1] + SEAM *sb.* and *v.*] †1. To sew or stitch up in. 2. To mark as with a seam 1611.

2. His lechery inseam'd upon him BEAUM. & FL.

†**Ensea·m**, *v.*[4] *rare.* 1596. [?] a. To include. b. To introduce to company 1607.

†**Ensea·r**, *v.* [f. EN-[1] + *sear* SERE *a.*] *trans.* To dry up. *Timon* IV. iii. 187.

Ensearch (ensɔ̄·ɹtʃ), *v. Obs.* or *arch.* [ME. *encerche(n, enserche(n*, ad. OF. *encerchier, enserchier*; see SEARCH.] *trans.* and *intr.* To search; to seek (for); to inquire (into). Hence **Ensea·rcher.**

†**Enseel** (ensī·l), *v. rare.* 1486. [f. EN-[1] + SEEL *v.*[2]] To stitch up the eyelids of (a hawk).

Ensemble (aṅsāṅb'l). ME. [a. F. :—late L. *insimul*, f. *in* + *simul*.] †A. *adv.* Together, at the same time –1528. ‖B. *sb.* (Only as Fr.) All the parts of anything taken together so that each is considered only in relation to the whole; the general effect. Also **Tout ensemble** (tutaṅsāṅb'l) in same sense. b. *Mus.* The united performance of all voices or all instruments in a piece of concerted music, or of a chorus and orchestra; also the manner in which this is done 1844.

†**Ense·mble**, *v.* ME. [a. OF. *ensembler*.] To bring together, assemble –1533.

They ensembled themselfe together MORE.

Ensepulchre (ense·pɒ̆lkəɹ), *v.* 1820. [f. EN-[1] + SEPULCHRE.] To put into a sepulchre; to entomb. Also *transf.*

Cities.. ensepulchred beneath the flood POLLOK.

Enshadow, Enshawl; see EN- *pref.*[1] 1 a.

Ensheath(e (enʃī·þ, -ð), *v.* 1593. [f. EN-[1] + SHEATH, SHEATHE.] To enclose in, or as in, a sheath.

Enshelter; see EN- *pref.*[1] 1 a.

†**E·nshield**, *a.* [? f. EN-[1] + SHIELD *sb.*] ? Shielded, concealed.

These blacke Masques Proclaime an e. beauty *Meas. for M.* II. iv. 80.

Enshield (enʃī·ld), *v. rare.* 1855. [f. EN-[1] + SHIELD *v.*] To guard as with a shield.

Enshrine (enʃrəi·n), *v.* Also †in-. 1583. [f. EN-[1] + SHRINE.] 1. *trans.* To enclose in, or †as in, a shrine. 2. To serve as a shrine for. Also *fig.* 1621.

1. We will e. it as a holy relic MASSINGER. 2. The greatest God of all My brest inshrines 1621.

Enshroud (enʃrau·d), *v.* 1583. [f. EN-[1] + SHROUD.] To cover as with a shroud; to envelop, hide completely.

They lurk enshrouded in the vale of night CHURCHILL.

Ensient (ensie·nt), *a.* 1827. *Law.* Later sp. of *enseint* = ENCEINTE.

Ensiform (e·nsifɔ̄ɹm), *a.* 1541. [f. L. *ensis*; see -FORM.] *Biol.* Sword-shaped. (Often said of leaves.)

E. cartilage, a cartilage appended to the sternum.

Ensign (e·nsəin). ME. [a. OF. *enseigne* :—L. *insignia*, pl. of *insigne*, adj. neut., f. *in* + *signum* sign.] †1. A signal; a battle-cry. Chiefly *Sc.* –1513. 2. A sign or token (*arch.*) 1474. 3. An emblem, badge 1579. 4. *esp.* A badge or symbol of office or dignity; chiefly *pl.* = L. *insignia*; also, heraldic bearings 1513. 5. A naval or military standard; a banner; *spec.* in British nautical use, a flag with a white, blue, or red field, and the union in the corner ME. Also *transf.* †6. A company, troop, serving under one banner –1650. 7. The soldier who carries the ensign (see ANCIENT *sb.*[2]). Formerly a commissioned officer of the lowest rank in the infantry, now a sub-lieutenant, 1513. 8. †a. Midshipman (tr. F. *enseigne de vaisseau*) 1708. b. In the U.S. navy, a commissioned officer of the lowest rank 1886.

2. We see no Ensigns of a Wedding here B. JONS. 3. Those ensigns of authority, the keys MISS MITFORD. 4. Having in his hands the Ensigne meet.. A Golden Scepter and a Crown of Bays HOBBES. 5. We are wont to fight cheerfully under this e. abroad BP. HALL. Hence **E·nsigncy**, †**E·nsignship**, the rank or position of an e. *Comb.* †**E.-bearer** = ENSIGN 7.

Ensign (ensəi·n), *v. Obs.* exc. *Her.* 1474. [a. OF. *ensignier, enseigner* :—med.L. *insignare*, f. *in* (see IN-) + *signum* sign.] †1. *trans.* To indicate. Also *absol.* –1576. †2. To direct *to* an object; to instruct; to teach –1598. 3. To mark with a distinctive sign or badge; *esp.* in *Her.* with a crown, coronet, or mitre. *Obs.* in gen. sense. 1572.

3. Henry but join'd the roses, that ensign'd Particular families B. JONS. Archbishops.. e. their Shields with their Mitres BOUTELL.

†**Ensi·gnment.** ME. [a. OF. *enseignement*; cf. ENSIGN *v.* and -MENT.] 1. Instruction; a lesson; also a means of instruction –1600. 2. = ENSIGN 4. –1611.

Ensilage (e·nsilėdʒ), *sb.* 1881. [a. F.; see ENSILE *v.*] 1. The process of preserving green fodder in a silo or pit, without previously drying it. 2. The fodder thus preserved 1881. 3. *attrib.* 1883.

2. About 3 in. of the e. was found to be mouldy 1882.

Ensilage (e·nsilėdʒ), *v.* 1883. [f. prec. sb.] To subject to the ensilage process. So **E·nsilate.**

Ensile (ensəi·l), *v.* 1883. [ad. F. *ensiler*, ad. Sp. *ensilar*, f. *en-* (see EN-[1]) + *silo* (see SILO), repr. L. *sirus*, a. Gr. σιρός, σειρός underground granary.] *trans.* To put into a silo for preservation; to convert into ensilage.

The ensiling of immature fodder 1885. Hence **E·nsilist**, one who preserves his crops by ensilage.

Ensilver; see EN- *pref.*[1] 1 b.

†**Ensi·ndon**, *v.* [See EN-[1].] To wrap in a sindon or linen cloth. DAVIES.

Ensisternal (ensistɔ̄·ɹnăl), *a.* [f. L. *ensis* + mod.L. *sternum* + -AL.] 'Relating to the ensiform cartilage' (*Syd. Soc. Lex.*).

Ensky (enskəi·), *v.* 1603. [See EN-[1].] To place in the sky or in heaven; *pass.* only. *Meas. for M.* I. iv. 34.

Enslave (enslē·v), *v.* 1643. [f. EN-[1] + SLAVE.] *trans.* To reduce to slavery; to make a slave of. Also *transf.* and *fig.*

Prevent them from.. enslaving their brethren, of whatever complexion MORSE. *fig.* All spirits are enslaved which serve things evil SHELLEY. Hence **Ensla·vement. Ensla·ver.**

Enslumber; see EN- *pref.*[1] 1 a.

Ensnare (ensnēᵊ·ɹ), *v.* Also in-. 1593. [f. EN-[1] + SNARE.] *trans.* To catch in a snare. Chiefly *transf.* and *fig.*

She ensnar'd Mankind with her faire looks MILT. *P. L.* IV. 717. Hence **Ensna·rement. Ensna·rer.**

†**Ensna·rl**, *v.* 1593. [f. EN-[1] + SNARL *sb.*[1]] To entangle in, or as in, a snarl or ravelled knot –1675.

Ensober; see EN- *pref.*[1] 2.

†**Enso·phic**, *a.* 1693. [f. late Heb. *ēn sōph* 'no end' + -IC.] *Cabbala.* Infinite.

Enso·rcell, *v.* 1541. [a. OF. *ensorceler*.] *trans.* To bewitch.

†**Enso·rrow**, *v.* [ME. *insorwen*, f. IN- + *sorwen* SORROW *v.*; later, f. EN-[1] + SORROW *sb.*] To sorrow or render sorrowful –1603.

Ensoul, in- (en-, insōᵘ·l), *v.* 1633. [f. EN-[1] + SOUL.] 1. *trans.* To take into the soul. 2. To infuse a soul into; to dwell in as a soul 1652.

Enspangle; see EN- *pref.*[1] 2.

Ensphere (ensfīᵊ·ɹ), *v.* Also in-. 1612. [f. EN-[1] + SPHERE.] 1. To place in, or as in, a sphere; to enclose. 2. To make into a sphere. Also *fig.* 1640.

1. His ample shoulders in a cloud enspher'd Of fierie chrimsine CHAPMAN. Hence **Ensphe·rement.**

Enstamp (enstæ·mp), *v.* 1611. [f. EN-[1] + STAMP *v.*] To stamp, imprint (marks, etc.) *on* anything. Also *fig.*

On the other side were enstamped the towers of Zion C. MATHER.

Enstate; see INSTATE.

Enstatite (e·nstătəit). 1857. [f. Gr. ἐνστάτης adversary (from its refractory nature) + -ITE.] *Min.* A variety of diallage, varying from greyish-white to olive-green and brown. Hence **Enstati·tic** *a.*

†**Enstee·p**, *v.* [f. EN-[1] + STEEP *v.*] To station under water. *Oth.* II. i. 70.

†**Ensto·re**, *v.* ME. [var. of ASTORE; see also EN-[1] and STORE.] 1. *trans.* To repair (tr. L. *instaurare*). WYCLIF. 2. To store *with* –1633.

Enstrengthen; see EN- *pref.*[1] 3.

†**Ensty·le**, *v.* 1599. [f. EN-[1] + STYLE.] To style, name –1648.

Ensue (ensiū·), *v.* ME. [ad. OF. *ensu-*, stem of *ensuivre* :—late L. *insequere*, L. *insequi* to follow after.] †1. *trans.* To follow. Also *absol.* and *intr.* –1626. †2. *fig.* To imitate; to conform to (advice, inclination, etc.) –1599. 3. †To pursue –1569; *fig.* to seek after (*arch.*) 1483. 4. †*trans.* To succeed, be subsequent to –1649; *intr.* to be (immediately) subsequent; to arise subsequently 1485. 5. †To result from –1754; *intr.* to result 1483. 6. *intr.* To follow as a conclusion. Usu. *impers.* Now *rare.* 1581.

3. *fig.* Let him seke peace and e. it COVERDALE *Ps.* xxxiii. 14. 4. *intr.* Now dreadful deeds Might have ensu'd MILT. *P. L.* IV. 991. 5. *intr.* From the wound ensued no purple Flood DRYDEN. 6. *A. Y. L.* I. iii. 36. Hence †**Ensu·able** *a.* following naturally or logically, sequent. †**Ensu·ant** *a.* **Ensu·er. Ensu·ing** *ppl. a.* and †quasi-*prep.* †**Ensu·ingly** *adv.*

‖**En suite** (aṅ swī·t, Fr. aṅ süi·t), *adv.* So as to form a suite; see SUITE.

†**Ensu·rance**; see INSURANCE.

Ensure (enʃūᵊ·ɹ), *v.* ME. [ad. AF. *enseurer*, f. *en-* (see EN-[1]) + OF. *seur* (mod.F. *sûr*) sure. See also INSURE.] †1. *trans.* To convince –1674. †2. To pledge one's credit to –1642. †3. To warrant; to guarantee –1738. †4. To betroth –1606. 5. To secure, make safe 1704. †6. *Comm.* To INSURE –1747. 7. To make certain, ASSURE 1742. Hence **Ensu·rer.**

Enswathe, in- (enswē·ð), *v.* 1597. [f. EN-[1] + SWATHE.] To bind or wrap in a swathe or bandage. Also *transf.* and *fig.*

fig. Inswathed sometimes in wandering mist TENNYSON. Hence **Enswa·thement.**

Ensweep; see EN- *pref.*[1] 3.

†**Enswee·ten**, *v.* 1607. [f. EN-[1] + SWEETEN *v.*] To sweeten. Also *fig.* –1640.

Ensynopticity (e·nsinǫpti·siti). [f. EN-[2] + SYNOPTIC + -(I)TY.] A capacity for taking a general view of a subject. WHATELY.

-ent, *suffix*, a. Fr. *-ent*, ad. L. *-entem*, the ending of pr. pples. of vbs. of the 2nd, 3rd, and 4th conjugation. In sense the words in *-ent* are primarily adjs., sometimes ppl., as *obsolescent*, etc., and some are used as sbs., meaning an agent, personal or material, as *president, regent, coefficient, aperient*, etc.

Entablature (entæ·blătiŭɹ). 1611. [ad. (through F.) It. *intavolatura*, prop. 'something laid flat', f. *in* + *tavola* table.] 1. *Arch.* That part of an order which is above the column; including the architrave, the frieze, and the cornice. 2. *Mech.* a. In the marine steam-engine: A strong iron frame supporting the paddle-shaft. b. The platform which supports the capstan. 1867. Hence **Enta·blatured** *ppl. a.* furnished with an e.

Entablement (entē·b'lmĕnt). 1664. [a. F., f. *entabler*, f. *en-* + *table*.] a. = prec. b. The platform or series of platforms supporting a statue and placed above the dado and the base.

†**Enta·ch, ente·ch**, *v.* ME. [a. OF. *entachier, entechier*, f. *en-* + *tache, teche* spot, etc.; see ATTACH.] 1. To stain; to infect –1509. 2. To imbue with any quality. Only in ME.

Entackle; see EN- *pref.*[1] 1 b.

†**Entai·l**, *sb.*[1] ME. [a. OF. *entaille*, f. *entailler* ENTAIL *v.*[1]; cf. It. *intaglio*.] 1. Ornamental carving –1530. 2. *transf.* Cut, fashion of a garment; shape; figure, stature –1570.

1. Carven in Cristall by crafte of Entaile ME. Phr. (Persons) *of entaile*: of quality.

Entail (entē·l), *sb.*[2] ME. [f. ENTAIL *v.*[2]] 1. *Law.* The action of entailing; the state of being entailed. 2. *transf.* and *fig.* a. The securing (an office, etc.) to a predetermined line of successors; a predetermined order of succession ME. b. The transmission, as an inalienable inheritance, of qualities, conditions, etc. 1706. c. Necessary sequence 1662. d. *concr.* That which is entailed 1822.

1. To his heires male by an especial Entaile aforesaid POWEL. Phr. *To break, cut (off) the e.* 2. b. An e. of dependence is a bad reward of merit BURKE.

†**Entai·l**, *v.*[1] ME. [a. OF. *entailler* :—late L. *intaleare*, f. *in* + *taleare* (F. *tailler*) to cut.] 1. *trans.* To carve; to ornament with carvings;

to represent by carving –1500. 2. To engrave in intaglio (*rare*) –1587. 3. To cut into 1601.

2. Costlie stones alreadie intailed for seales 1577.

Entail (entē·l), *v.*² ME. [f. EN-¹ + AF. *tailé* TAIL *a.* or *taile* sb. entail. See TAIL *a.*] 1. *Law.* To convert into 'fee tail' (*feudum talliatum*); to settle (land, an estate, etc.) on a number of persons in succession, so that it cannot be dealt with by any one possessor as absolute owner. 2. *transf.* and *fig.* To bestow as if by entail 1509. †3. *gen.* To tack on, attach –1713. 4. To impose (labour, expense, etc.) *upon* a person 1665. 5. *simply.* To necessitate; to involve logically 1829.

1. They cannot sell them [houses], because they are entailed 1856. 2. The benefits of the Gospell are intayled vpon them alone 1630. 5. A conquest which brought with it no evil and entailed no regret 1829.

Hence **Entai·lable** *a.* **Entai·ler.** **Entai·lment.**

†**Enta·lent,** *v.* ME. [a. OF. *entalenter*, f. *en-* + *talent* (ad. L. *talentum* a weight, that which inclines the balance, hence) inclination.] To inspire with desire or passion; to excite –1616.

†**E·ntally,** *adv.* 1691. [f. med.L. *ent-*, stem of *ens.*] Really.

†**Enta·me,** *v.*¹ ME. [a. F. *entamer* = *attamer*; see ATTAME.] 1. To make a cut into; also *fig.* –1490. 2. *fig.* To open –1500.

Enta·me, *v.*² 1600. [f. EN-¹ + TAME.] To make or †become tame. *A. Y. L.* III. v. 48.

Entangle (entæ·ng'l), *v.* 1555. [f. EN-¹ + TANGLE *sb.* or *v.*] 1. To catch or impede with a tangle; to involve in coils, network, or the like, or in anything from which extrication is difficult. b. *esp.* To ensnare. Also *fig.* 1568. †c. *intr.* To become entangled –1673. 2. *fig.* To involve in difficulties; to embarrass; to perplex, bewilder 1540. 3. To make tangled; to twist, interlace, or mix up in a tangle; *fig.* to complicate (a subject, etc.) 1555.

1. Lest she should e. her Feet in her Petticoat ADDISON. Entangled in the meshes of political parties D'ISRAELI, in the defiles of the mountains PRESCOTT. 2. Entangled in a complimentary speech 1833. 3. The obscure and intangl'd Wood of Antiquity MILTON. Hence **Enta·ngler.**

Entanglement (entæ·ŋg'lmĕnt). 1637. [f. prec.] 1. The action of entangling; the fact or condition of being entangled, confused medley 1687. 2. That which entangles 1637.

‖**Entasis** (e·ntăsis). 1753. [mod.L., a. Gr. ἔντασις, f. ἐντείνειν to strain.] 1. *Arch.* An almost imperceptible swelling of the shaft of a column 1827. †2. *Path.* 'Old term for tonic spasm' (*Syd. Soc. Lex.*). Hence †**Enta·tic,** also (erron.) †**Enta·stic,** *adjs.* of or pertaining to e.

Enta·ssment. [ad. F. *entassement*, f. *en-* + *tas* heap.] A heap, accumulation. (Dicts.)

Entelechy (ente·lĕki). Also **entelecheia, entelechia.** 1603. [ad. Gr. ἐντελέχεια, f. ἐν + τέλει, dat. of τέλος perfection + ἔχειν.] 1. In Aristotle's use: The condition in which a potentiality has become an actuality. 2. a. That which gives form or perfection to anything. b. The soul, as opp. to the body. 1603. 3. A monad in the system of Leibnitz.

‖**Entellus** (ente·lŏs). 1843. [Proper name; see Virg. *Æn.* v. 437–472.] *Zool.* An E. Indian species of monkey of the genus Semnopithecus.

Entemple (ente·mp'l), *v.* 1603. [f. EN-¹ + TEMPLE.] To enclose as in a temple.

†**Ente·nder,** *v.* 1594. [f. EN-¹ + TENDER *a.*] To make tender; to weaken –1765.

‖**Entente** (aṅtā·ṅt). 1877. [Fr.] An understanding; most freq. used as a shortening of ‖**Entente cordiale** (1844). b. A group of states or powers connected by an entente cordiale.

†**E·nter,** *sb.* ME. [f. the vb.] 1. The action, power, or right of entering; *concr.* a passage –1588. 2. Grafting. EVELYN.

Enter (e·ntəɹ), *v.* ME. [a. F. *entrer* :—L. *intrare*, related to *inter, intro, intra.*]

I. *intr.* (Often conjugated with *be.*) 1. To go or come into; to pass within the boundaries of. Also *fig.* b. *simply.* To make entry. ME. 2. *Law.* To make entry (into lands); to take possession 1523. 3. To penetrate *into*; to be plunged deeply. Also †*fig.* ME. 4. To become a member in a society, etc. ME. †5. To come into a state or condition –1710. 6. To make a beginning, engage. Const. *in* (arch.), *into.* 1450. †b. Of a period, state of things, etc.: To begin –1688.

1. We..entered into a noble forest MARRYAT. b. The Air..entring by the Furnace-pipes EVELYN. 3. The iron entered into his soul BIBLE (Great) *Ps.* cv. 18. 5. Entre thou into the ioye of thi lord WYCLIF *Matt.* xxv. 21. 6. E. not into iudgement with thy seruant *Ps.* cxliii. 2.

II. *trans.* (formerly occas. conjugated with *be.*) 1. To go or come into or within; to step upon (a path, a bridge) ME. b. To take up one's abode in. *Meas. for M.* I. ii. 182. c. To force an entrance into 1586. 2. To pierce; to penetrate 1613. 3. To become a member of (*mod.*). 4. To begin 1515. 5. To come into a state or condition; to embrace (a profession). *Obs.* exc. in *To e. religion.* 1563. 6. To turn to a particular place in (a mathematical table). Still in *Naut.* use. 1593.

1. To e. a Gaol STEELE, a carriage DICKENS. 3. Phr. *To e. the army, the church, a university.* 5. To e. wedlocke 1576, the profession of a monke SPEED.

III. To cause to enter. 1. *trans.* To put or bring into something (*arch.*); also †*fig.* 1523. 2. To instruct initially; to initiate; to train; to put (a young dog) on the scent of 1481. 3. To put *into*, insert, introduce. Now chiefly *techn.* ME. 4. To put into a list in writing, a description, a record; to write down ME. b. To hand in at the Custom House a statement of the amount and value of (goods exported or imported). Also, to register (a vessel) as arriving or leaving. 1634. c. To insert by name on the list of competitors. Also *intr.* 1684. 5. To admit; to engage; to procure admission for. Also *refl.* and *intr.* for *refl.* 1651.

1. *fig.* Baptism..enters us into covenant with God 1658. 2. To e. children in the Rudiments of the Latin Tongue ELLWOOD. To e. young hounds to fox STONEHENGE. 3. To e. shot or shell and ram home 1859. 4. To e. his answer on the records BURKE. Phr. *To e. up*: a. To enter in regular form. b. *Law.* To cause (judgement, etc.) to be written down on the records of a court. *To e. an action, caveat, writ,* etc.: to bring it before the court in due form, usu. in writing. *To e. a protest*: to record a protest on the minutes; hence *gen.* to protest. 5. He was entred into Ch. Ch. WOOD. He therefore entered himself as a clerk to a solicitor E. PEACOCK.

Comb. (with preps.). **To e. into** (†**in**): a. To take upon oneself; as, *to e. into matrimony*, etc. b. To become a party to; to bind oneself by; as, *to e. into a treaty*, etc. (See also RECOGNIZANCE, SECURITY.) c. To consider. †d. To intermeddle with. e. To take an interest in. f. To form part of; to be a constituent element in. g. In Bible phrase, *To e. into* (another's) *labours*: to reap where another has sown. **To e. on, upon:** a. (*Law.*) To make an entry into (land); to assume possession of. b. To take the first steps upon or in; also *fig.* c. To begin to deal with (a subject).

Enter-, entre-, *prefix*, a. F. *entre-*:—L. *inter* (see INTER-), with senses 'between', 'among', 'mutually'. Since *c* 1650 the compounds in which this prefix occurs are either obs. or have been refashioned with *inter-*.

Enteradenography,-ology; see ENTERO-.

Enterate (e·ntĕrĕ̄t), *a.* 1877. [ad. mod.L. *enteratus*, f. Gr. ἔντερα; see -ATE.] *Zool.* Having an intestine distinctly separated from the outer body-wall.

†**E·nterclose, i·nter-.** ME. [a. OF. *entreclos*, f. *entre* + *clos*; see CLOSE *sb.*] 1. A partition. TREVISA. 2. *Arch.* ?A screen, partition; a space partitioned off –1853.

†**Enterfea·t.** 1614. [ad. F. *entrefaite.*] *pl.* Deeds (of arms) on both sides –1662.

Enteric (ente·rik), *a.* 1869. [ad. Gr. ἐντερικός, f. ἔντερον.] *Anat.*, etc. Of or pertaining to the intestines. *E. fever*: typhoid fever.

b. *Pharm.* Of or designating a medicinal preparation that becomes disintegrated in the intestines, after passing through the stomach unaltered.

Entering (e·ntəriŋ), *vbl. sb.* ME. [f. ENTER *v.*] 1. The action of the vb. †2. An entrance; a door, etc.; an opening –1541. 3. *attrib.* esp. *Naut.* with reference to the means of entrance to a vessel, as *e.-port, -rope*, etc.; and *Mech.*, as *e.-chisel*, etc.

Enteritis (entĕrəi·tis). 1808. [f. Gr. ἔντερον + -ITIS.] *Path.* Inflammation of the (small) intestines.

†**Enterme·te,** *v.* ME. [a. OF. *entremetre* (mod. F. *entremettre*); cf. L. *intermittere* and *intromittere.*] 1. *refl.* To intermeddle; to have dealings. Also, to undertake *to* (do something). Also *intr.* for *refl.* –1548. 2. To put (oneself) *between* 1541.

†**Entermi·se.** 1490. [a. F. *entremise*; see prec.] a. Business. b. Interposition. –1638.

Entero- (e·ntĕro, entĕrǫ·, bef. a vowel sometimes *enter-*), comb. f. Gr. ἔντερον intestine: as in

Enteradeno·graphy [see ADENOGRAPHY], *Anat.* 'a description of the intestinal glands' (*Syd. Soc. Lex.*). **Enteradeno·logy** [see ADENOLOGY], *Anat.*, etc. 'an account of the intestinal glands' (*Syd. Soc. Lex.*). **E·nterocele** [Gr. κήλη tumour], *Surg.* a hernial tumour whose contents are intestine. Hence **Enteroce·lic** *a.* **E·nteroepi·plocele** [see EPIPLOCELE], *Surg.* a hernia in which portions of intestine and omentum are both protruded. **E·nteroga·strocele,** *Surg.* an abdominal hernia containing intestine. **Entero·graphy,** 'a description of the intestines' (*Syd. Soc. Lex.*). **E·nterohy·drocele** [see HYDROCELE], *Surg.* 'intestinal hernia conjoined with hydrocele' (*Syd. Soc. Lex.*). **E·nteroli·te,** altered f. **E·nteroli·th** [Gr. λίθος], *Path.* a stony concretion in the intestines. **Entero·logy** [+ -LOGY], *Anat.* a treatise on, or the science of, the intestines. **Entero·pathy** [Gr. -πάθεια, f. πάθος], *Path.* intestinal disease. **E·nteropla·sty** [Gr. πλάστης fashioner + -Y], *Surg.* the restoration by plastic operation of a solution of continuity of the intestine. **Entero·tomy** [Gr. -τομία cutting], *Surg.* the opening of the intestine to release its contents, or to remove a foreign body.

Enterodelous (e:nterodī·ləs), *a.* 1847. [f. mod.L. *enterodela* sb. pl., f. ENTERO- + Gr. δῆλος.] *Biol.* Having an intestine plainly visible; applied to certain Polygastria.

‖**Enteron** (e·ntĕrǫn). 1878. [mod. L. a. Gr. ἔντερον intestine.] The alimentary canal.

Enteropneustal (e:ntĕro,pniū·stăl), *a.* 1877. [f. Gk. ἔντερον + πνευστ-, f. πνέειν to breathe + -AL.] Of or pertaining to the *Enteropneusta*, worm-like animals having the breathing apparatus borne on the intestinal canal.

†**Enterpa·rlance.** 1603. [ad. AF. *entreparlaunce.*] A conference –1643. So †**Enterpa·rle** *v.* to confer. †**Enterpa·rley.**

Enterprise (e·ntəɹprəiz), *sb.* ME. [a. OF. *entreprise, -prinse*, f. *entreprendre* to take in hand.] 1. A design of which the execution is attempted; a piece of work taken in hand; now only, a bold, arduous, or dangerous undertaking. 2. Disposition to engage in undertakings of difficulty, risk, or danger; daring spirit 1475. †3. Management –1803.

1. The enterprizes of fancy CHALMERS. Those enterprises which we call joint-stock undertakings HELPS. 2. Times of national e. 1783. Contempt for his lack of e. FREEMAN.

Enterprise (e·ntəɹprəiz), *v. arch.* 1450. [partly f. prec.; partly f. Fr. *entrepris* pa. pple.] 1. *trans.* To take in hand, attempt, run the risk of (*arch.*) 1485. †2. *intr.* To make an attempt, form a design, make an attack (*upon*) –1813.

1. This was enterprized by a Prince, who [etc.] LOCKE. To e. a road RUSKIN. 2. Be sure of the court, before you e. any other where UDALL. Hence **Enterpri·ser,** one who attempts an undertaking; †an adventurer.

Enterprising (e·ntəɹprəiziŋ), *ppl. a.* 1611. [f. prec.] That undertakes. In early use, foolhardy, also scheming; now, full of enterprise.

An enterprizing foole needs little wit 1611. A company of e. Venetian merchants J. H. NEWMAN. Hence **Enterpri·singly** *adv.*

†**Entertai·n,** *sb.* 1591. [f. next; cf. F. *entretien.*] = ENTERTAINMENT –1686.

Entertain (entəɹtē·n), *v.* [late ME. *entertene*, ad. F. *entretenir* :—late L. *intertenere*, lit. 'to hold or keep among'.] †1. *trans.* To hold mutually –1578. †2. To keep in a certain state or condition –1714. 3. To keep up, maintain. *Obs.* or *arch.* 1475. †4. To keep in one's service; to be at the charges of; to hire; to retain –1771. †5. To support; to provide sustenance for –1771. †6. To deal with; to treat in a (specified) manner –1662. 7. To engage, keep occupied the attention of. Hence, to discourse to *of* something. 1598. †b. To occupy (time) -1673. 8. To engage agreeably the attention of; to amuse. Now often *ironical.* Also *refl.* and *absol.* 1626. †9. To accommodate -1721. 10. To receive as a guest; to show hospitality to. Also *absol.* 1490. 11. †To give reception to; to receive -1710; to admit to consideration 1614; to harbour; to cherish; to experience 1576. †12. To encounter (*rare*) -1634. †13. To take upon oneself; to engage in -1719.

3. To e. Discourse SOUTHEY, a correspondence MILMAN. 4. With princely wagies dyd me enterteyne 1559. Sweet Lady, entertaine him for your Seruant *Two Gent.* II. iv. 110. 7. To entertaine him with hope *Merry W.* II. i. 68. b. The weary time she cannot e. SHAKS. 8. My favourite occupations..now cease to e. LAMB. 11. To e. a novell opinion BP. HALL, thoughts of Death BOYLE, the Addresses of a Man STEELE. To e. resentment LANGHORNE, a purpose SCOTT. Hence **Entertai·nable** *a.* capable of being received into the mind. **Entertai·ner.**

Entertaining (entəɹtē·niŋ), *ppl. a.* 1651. [f. prec.] †1. Affording sustenance (*rare*) 1691. 2. Interesting; now chiefly, amusing 1697. †3. Hospitable (*rare*) 1659.

Hence **Entertai·ning·ly** *adv.*, **-ness.**

Entertainment (entəɹtē·nmĕnt). 1531. [f. as prec. + -MENT.] †1. The action of taking into service; service, employment -1662. Also †*concr.* pay, wages -1709. †2. Support; sustenance -1761. †3. Treatment -1660. 4. Occupation (of time). Now *rare.* 1551. 5. The action of occupying attention agreeably; that which affords interest or amusement; *esp.* a public performance of a varied character 1612. †6. Accommodation -1721. †7. Reception; manner of reception -1692. 8. The action of receiving a guest 1594. b. *concr.* Hospitable provision for the wants of a guest (now *arch.*) 1540. c. A meal; *esp.* a banquet. Now *rare.* 1607. 9. The action of receiving, of taking into consideration, or of harbouring 1586.

1. The Saxons..desirous of intertainment to serue in warres HOLINSHED. 3. The savage e. He met with in it [the World] BOYLE. 4. *L. L. L.* v. i. 126. 5. An Oration..to giue the visitours intertainment 1612. Importunate for dramatic entertainments EMERSON. 7. *Ant. & Cl.* III. xiii. 140. 8. Hezekiah's e. of them with gladnesse 1649. b. Great deal of company, but poor e. PEPYS. *Comb.* **Entertainment tax** 1918.

Enterta·ke, *v.* [cf. F. *entreprendre.*] *trans.* To entertain. SPENSER.

Entertissue; see INTER-.

†**E·nthean,** *a.* 1635. [f. Gr. ἔνθεος (see ENTHEOS) + -AN.] Divinely inspired -1652.

†**E·ntheasm.** 1751. [f. Gr. ἐνθεάζειν, f. ἔνθεος ENTHEOS.] = ENTHUSIASM. So †**Enthea·stic, -al** *a.* agitated by a divine energy. †**Enthea·stically** *adv.*

†**E·ntheate,** *a.* Also **entheat.** 1630. [ad. L. *entheatus*, f. *entheus*; see next.] Possessed by a god -1640.

†‖**E·ntheos, -us.** 1594. [a. L. *entheos, -us*, Gr. ἔνθεος, f. ἐν + θεός.] An indwelling divinity; inspiration -1782.

Enthetic (enþe·tik), *a.* 1867. [ad. Gr. ἐνθετικός, f. ἐνθε- aor. stem of ἐντιθέναι to put in.] *Med.* Put in; introduced from without. Said *esp.* of syphilitic diseases.

Enthral(l (enþrǭ·l), *v.* Also **in-.** 1576. [f. EN-[1] + THRALL *sb.*] To hold in thrall; to enslave. Also *fig.* now chiefly in sense 'to hold spellbound by pleasing qualities'.

Ingrateful Cæsar who could Rome e. COWPER. *fig.* So is mine eye enthralled to thy shape *Mids. N.* III. i. 142. Hence **Enthra·ldom** (*rare*), the condition of being enthralled. **Enthra·ller. Enthra·lment,** the action of enthralling; slavery. Chiefly *fig.*

†**Enthri·ll,** *v.* 1559. [f. EN-[1] + THRILL *v.*] *trans.* To pierce -1593.

Enthrone (enþrōu·n), *v.* Also **in-.** 1606. [f. EN-[1] + THRONE.] 1. *trans.* To seat on a throne; *esp.* to set (a king, bishop, etc.) on a throne as a formal induction to office; to invest with regal or episcopal authority. Also *fig.* 2. To set as on a throne; to exalt 1699.

1. [The] Bishop of Norwich was..enthroned as Primate 1876. *fig.* There pride, enthroned in misty errours, dwels 1628. Hence **Enthro·nement,** the action of enthroning; the fact of being enthroned. **Enthro·niza·tion,** enthronement. var. **Enthro·nize** (*Obs.* exc. *arch.*).

Enthuse (enþiū·z), *v.* orig. *U.S. slang.* 1859. [Back-formation from ENTHUSIASM.] To make or grow enthusiastic.

Enthusiasm (enþiū·zi,æ̆z'm). 1603. [ad. late L. *enthusiasmus*, Gr. ἐνθουσιασμός, f. ἐνθουσιάζειν, f. ἐνθουσία the fact of being possessed by a god.] †1. Possession by a god, supernatural inspiration, prophetic or poetic ecstasy -1807. †b. Poetical fervour -1781. 2. Fancied inspiration; a conceit of divine favour or communication. In 18th c. often: Ill-regulated religious emotion or speculation (*arch.*) 1660. 3. Rapturous intensity of feeling on behalf of a person, cause, etc.; passionate eagerness in any pursuit. (The current sense.) 1716.

1. Doth he think they knew it by E. or Revelation from Heaven BAXTER. 2. Everywhere the history of religion betrays a tendency to e. 1841. 3. E. is very catching, especially when it is very eloquent 1817.

Enthusiast (enþiū·zi,æst). 1609. [ad. Gr. ἐνθουσιαστής; see prec.] †1. One who is (really or seemingly) possessed by a god. Also *fig.* -1700. 2. †a. *Eccl. Hist.* One of a set of 4th c. heretics who laid claim to special revelations -1639. b. *gen.* One who imagines himself to receive special divine communications 1609. 3. One who is full of enthusiasm (see ENTHUSIASM 3). Occas., A visionary self-deluded person. 1764. 4. *attrib.* or *adj.* 1681.

2. b. It is the believing those to be Miracles which are not, that constitutes an E. WESLEY. 3. Paracelsus..an astrological e. 1793.

Enthusiastic (enþiū·zi,æ·stik). 1603. [ad. Gr. ἐνθουσιαστικός; see prec.]

A. *adj.* †1. Pertaining to, or of the nature of, possession by a deity. Also *fig.* -1849. †2. Characterized by mystical delusions in religion; *transf.* quixotic -1775. 3. Of the nature of, characterized by ENTHUSIASM 3. 1786.

2. *transf.* An e. contempt of interest JOHNSON. 3. E. admirers of literature LANE. Hence **Enthusia·stical** *a.* (in same senses). **Enthusia·stically** *adv.*

†B. *sb.* = ENTHUSIAST 1, 2 b. -1707.

Enthymematic, -al (e:nþimīmæ·tik, -ăl), *a.* 1588. [ad. Gr. ἐνθυμηματικός (see next).] Of, pertaining to, or containing, an enthymeme; consisting of enthymemes.

Enthymeme (e·nþimīm). 1588. [ad. L. *enthymema* (also used), a. Gr., f. ἐνθυμέεσθαι, f. ἐν + θυμός mind.] †1. *Rhet.* An argument based on probable premisses, as dist. from a demonstration -1841. 2. *Logic.* A syllogism with one premiss unexpressed; as, *Cogito, ergo sum.* (A misapprehension of 'imperfect syllogism' applied to 1.) 1588.

2. The common form of Argumentation is E., which consists of but two propositions BOWEN.

Entice (entəi·s), *v.* ME. [a. OF. *enticier, enticher*; perh. f. (ult.) L. *in-* (see IN-) + *titio* brand, in sense 'to add fuel to (a fire)'; cf. ATTICE, and TICE.] †1. *trans.* To stir up, instigate -1628. 2. To allure, attract by the hope of pleasure or profit; *esp.* to allure insidiously or adroitly. Also *absol.* ME.

2. My son, if sinners e. thee, consent thou not *Prov.* i. 10. Beer mingled with Honey, to e. the Wasps EVELYN. Hence †**Enti·ceable** *a.* seductive. **Enti·cer. Enti·cing** *ppl. a.* alluring. **Enti·cingly** *adv.*

Enticement (entəi·smĕnt). ME. [a. OF.; see prec. and -MENT.] †1. Incitement; *concr.* that which incites -1587. 2. The action of alluring or attracting; attractive quality; *concr.* a means or method of enticing; an allurement 1549.

2. What inticement is there in common profane Swearing BENTLEY.

Entier, Entierty, obs. ff. ENTIRE, etc.

Entify (e·ntifəi), *v. rare.* 1882. [f. *enti-*, crude form of L. ENS + -FY.] To make into an entity, attribute objective existence to. Hence **Entifica·tion.**

Entire (entəi°·ɹ). ME. [a. OF. *entier* :—L. *integrum*, f. *in-* not + **tag-* root of *tangere* to touch.]

A. *adj.* I. 1. Whole; with no part excepted. 2. Complete; †perfect ME. †b. Applied about 1722 to 'porter' -1839. 3. Thorough, total ME. †b. Of persons: Wholly devoted; unreserved -1718. 4. Unbroken, intact; undiminished 1601. b. *spec.* Not castrated 1834. c. Of persons: Not fatigued, fresh. [So L. *integer.*] (*arch.*) 1590. 5. Of one piece; continuous; in *Bot.*, etc. without notches or indentations 1590. †6. Homogeneous; unmixed -1699.

1. A day e. MILT. The e. Creation WESLEY. Phr. *E. tenancy* (Law): a sole possession in one man. E. control of a business (*mod.*). 2. An e. farm 1804. 3. E. liberty of conscience MACAULAY. b. It is best to be courteous to all; e. with few BP. HALL. 4. With all the Fortifications e. 1727. Apprehension, Memory, Reason, all e. BUTLER. 5. Of one entyre and perfect Chrysolite *Oth.* v. ii. 144. Last segment of the abdomen e. or notched STARK. Phr. *Rank e.* (Mil.): *i. e.* forming an unbroken body.

II. †1. Morally whole, blameless -1779. †2. Of integrity; honest, upright -1707. †3. Of feelings, etc.: Unfeigned, sincere -1716. †4. ? Inward. SPENSER *F. Q.* IV. viii. st. 48.

B. *sb.* 1. The whole. Now *rare.* 1597. 2. Entirety 1622. 3. An entire horse 1881. 4. Short for *entire beer*; see A. I. 2 b. 1825.

Hence **Enti·rely** *adv.* in an e. state or manner. **Enti·reness,** the quality, state, or condition of being e.

Entirety (entəi°·ɹti). 1548. [ad. AF. *entiertie*, OF. *entiereté* :—L. *integritatem*, f. *integer*; see prec.] 1. The state or condition of being entire; in *Law*, the entire and undivided possession of an estate. 2. The whole; the sum total 1856.

1. The Christian Church taken in its e. ROBERTSON. They shall not haue the land by entierties, but by moities ioyntly SIR H. FINCH.

Entitative (e·ntitētiv), *a.* 1600. [ad. med.L. *entitativus*, f. *entitatem*; see ENTITY.] 1. Pertaining to the mere existence of anything. 2. Having real existence 1862. Hence **E·ntitatively** *adv.*

Entitle (entəi·t'l), *v.* ME. [a. AF. *entitler*, OF. *entituler*, mod.F. *intituler*, f. (ult.) L. *in* + *titulus.*]

I. 1. *trans.* To furnish with a heading, name, or designation (see TITLE *sb.*). †b. To ascribe *to* an author -1724. 2. To speak of by a title or designation ME. †3. To write down under titles or headings -1582.

1. I will intitle this boke the Golden boke LD. BERNERS. b. A booke, entitled to sainct Augustine CRANMER.

II. 1. To furnish with a title *to* an estate. Hence *gen.* to give a rightful claim *to* anything. 1468. †2. To regard as having a title *to* something, or as being the agent, cause, or subject of anything -1690. †b. To impute (something) *to* -1665.

1. Entitled to any timber felled by the tenant for life CRUISE. Entitled to complain of neglect HT. MARTINEAU. 2. b. Intitling the Opinion of Intentional Species to Aristotle GLANVILL.

Entitule, obs. var. of INTITULE *v.* (*arch.*).

Entity (e·ntĭti). 1596. [ad. late L. *entitatem*, f. *ens, entis*; see ENS.] 1. Being, existence, as opp. to non-existence; the existence, as dist. from the qualities or relations, of anything. 2. That which makes a thing what it is; essence, essential nature 1643. 3. *concr.* An ENS, as dist. from a function, attribute, relation, etc. 1628. 4. 'Being' generally 1604.

1. Both Night and Coldnesse..have reall entitie H. MORE. 3. An ideal E., like the Utopia BOLINGBROKE.

Ento- (e·nto), *prefix* (bef. a vowel usually *ent-*), repr. Gr. ἐντός within, inside: as in **E·ntoblast** [Gr. βλαστός sprout], the nucleolus of a cell. **Entocu·neiform** *a.* [see CUNEIFORM], the innermost of the three cuneiform bones. **E·ntocyst** [see CYST], 'the inner layer of the cuticular envelope of the Polyzoa' (*Syd. Soc. Lex.*). **E·ntoderm** [Gr. δέρμα], the outer layer of the blastoderm, also called *hypoblast.* **Entoga·stric** *a.* [see GASTRIC], pertaining to the interior of the gastric cavity. **Entoglo·ssal** *a.* [Gr. γλῶσσα + -AL], a term applied to one of the bones of the hyoidean arch in some fishes, which supports the tongue. **Entome·tatarse** [mod.L. *metatarsus*], the bones between the tarsus and the toes. **E·ntoperi·pheral** *a.* [see PERIPHERAL], a term applied to feelings initiated within the body, as hunger. **E·ntophyte** [Gr. φυτόν], a plant growing within the substance of other plants or animals; hence **Entophy·tic** *a.* **Entopro·ctous** *a.* [Gr. πρωκτός anus], belonging to the *Entoprocta*, a class of Polyzoa, in which the anus lies within the circle of tentacles. **Entopte·rygoid** *a.* [see PTERYGOID], 'an oblong and thin bone attached to the inner border of the palatine and pterygoid' (Gunther). **Ento·ptic** *a.* [see OPTIC], relating to the appearance of the different internal structures of the eye; hence **Ento·ptics** *sb.* **Entoste·rnal** *a.* [see STERNAL], pertaining to the *entosternum* or median piece of the breastbone, very largely developed in birds. **Ento·tic** *a.* [see OTIC], pertaining to or occurring in the inner ear. **E:ntotympa·nic** *a.* [see TYMPANIC], situated within the tympanum.

Entoil (entoi·l), *v. arch.* 1621. [f. EN-[1] + TOIL *sb.*[2]] To bring into toils or snares; to entrap. Chiefly *fig.*

So mused awhile, entoyled in woofed fantasies KEATS.

Entomb (entū·m), *v.* 1576. [a. OF. *entoumber*, mod. *entomber*, f. *en* + *tombe*.] **1.** To place in, or as in, a tomb; to bury. **2.** To serve as a tomb for (*lit.* and *fig.*) 1631. Hence **Ento·mbment**, the action of entombing.

Entomic (entǫ·mik), *a.* 1862. [f. Gr. ἔντομα insects + -IC.] Of or pertaining to insects. So **Ento·mical.** (Dicts.)

Entomo- (entŏmǫ·-, entǫ·mŏ-, e·ntŏmo-), comb. f. Gr. ἔντομος adj. 'cut up', in neut. pl. 'insects'; see INSECT.

Entomo·genous *a.* [Gr. -γενής + -OUS], *Bot.* having its growth in the body of insects. **Ento·molite** [Gr. λίθος], *Geol.* a fossil insect. **Entomo·meter** [Gr. μέτρον], an instrument for measuring insects. **Entomo·phagan** [Gr. φαγεῖν + -AN], *Zool.* one of the *Entomophaga* or insect-eaters—in mammals, a division of the *Marsupialia*, in insects of the *Hymenoptera*. **Entomo·phagous** *a.* [Gr. φαγεῖν + -OUS], insect-eating. **Entomo·philous** *a.* [Gr. φίλος + -OUS], *Bot.* used of plants in which fertilization is effected through the agency of insects. **Entomo·stracan** *a.* [Gr. ὄστρακον shell + -AN], *Zool.*, etc. of or belonging to the *Entomostraca*, one of the orders of the *Crustacea*; also as *sb.* So **Entomo·stracous** *a.* **Entomo·tomy** [Gr. -τομία], *Zool.* the science of the dissection of insects; hence **Entomo·tomist,** one who dissects insects.

Entomoid (e·ntŏmoid), *a.* 1835. [f. as prec. + -OID.] Insect-like. Also quasi-*sb.*

Entomology (entŏmǫ·lŏdʒi). 1766. [ad. F. *entomologie*, f. (ult.) ENTOMO- + Gr. λογία (see -LOGY).] That branch of natural history which deals with insects.

Hence **E:ntomolo·gical** *a.* of or pertaining to e. or insects. **Entomo·logist,** one who studies e. **Entomo·logize** *v.* to study e.; to collect specimens, or observe the habits, of insects.

Entone (entōu·n), *v.* 1485. [a. F. *entonner.*] = INTONE.

Entonic (entǫ·nik), *a.* [f. Gr. ἔντονος strained + -IC.] *Med.* 'Having exaggerated action, or great tension' (*Syd. Soc. Lex.*).

†**Ento·rtill,** *v.* 1629. [ad. F. *entortiller*, f. *en* + *tortiller* to twist, ad. late L. *tortillare*, f. (ult.) L. *torquere.*] To entwine, coil -1653. Hence †**Entortilla·tion,** the action of twisting.

Entosthoblast (entǫ·sþoblast). 1884. [f. Gr. ἔντοσθε + -BLAST.] A granule within the nucleolus of a nucleated cell.

Entour, *v.* 1623. [ad. F. *entourer.*] †**1.** To surround (with a halo or the like) -1653. **2.** *Her.* Said (in *pa. pple.*) of a shield decorated with branches 1847.

‖**Entourage** (äntūra·ʒ). 1832. [Fr.; f. (ult.) *en* in + *tour* circuit.] Surroundings, environment; *esp.* the set of persons who are in attendance on a superior.

The e. which surrounded Elizabeth FROUDE.

Entozoon (entozōu·ǫn). 1834. [f. ENTO- + Gr. ζῷον animal.] *Zool.* A parasitic animal that lives within another. Also *attrib.* In *pl.* **entozo·a**, an artificial class of animals, taking their name merely from their mode of existence.

Also **Entozo·al** *a.* of or pertaining to the *Entozoa*; also, caused by the presence of *Entozoa.* So **Entozo·ic** *a.* **E:ntozoolo·gically** *adv.* with reference to entozoology. **E:ntozoo·logist.** **Entozoo·logy,** that part of zoology which treats of the *Entozoa.*

‖**Entr'acte** (äntrakt). 1863. [Fr., f. *entre* + *acte.*] **a.** The interval between two acts of a play. **b.** A dance, piece of music, etc. performed between the acts.

†‖**Entra·da.** 1618. [Sp. *entrada.*] Income, revenue -1654.

Entrail (e·ntrẹ̄l), *sb.*[1] Chiefly in pl. ME. [a. OF. *entraille* = Pr. *intralia* :—late L. *intralia*, neut. pl. of **intralis* inward, f. *inter*; see INTERIOR. Cf. L. *interanea* entrails.] †**1.** *collect. sing.* The intestines or internal parts -1652. **2.** *sing.* An internal organ; = L. *viscus* 1483. **3.** *pl.* The internal parts of man or other animals; *spec.* the bowels, the intestines ME. †**4.** *transf.* = 'heart', 'soul' -1790. **5.** The inner parts of anything. Now *rare.* 1490.

4. In her entrayles all malice was enclosed LYDG. **5.** The other entralles of the earth; as Pitch, Chalke, lyme FULBECKE. To look into the entrals of this Sacrament 1655.

†**Entrai·l,** *sb.*[2] [f. next.] The action of ENTRAIL *v.*; a coil. SPENSER.

†**Entrai·l,** *v.* 1577. [ad. OF. *entreillier*, f. *en-* + *treille* trellis-work.] *trans.* To entwine, interlace -1736.

Entrain (entrẹ̄·n), *v.*[1] 1568. [ad. F. *entraîner*, f. *en-* (L. *inde*) away + *traîner* to drag.] *trans.* To drag away with or after oneself. Now *rare.* Also †*fig.*

Yeares entraine me if they please, but backward FLORIO.

Entrai·n, *v.*[2] 1881. [f. EN-[1] + TRAIN *sb.*] To put into or board a railway-train.

Entrammel (entræ·mĕl), *v.* 1598. [f. EN-[1] + TRAMMEL.] To put into trammels; to entangle, fetter.

Entrance (e·ntrăns), *sb.* 1526. [a. OF., f *entrer* to enter; see -ANCE.] **1.** The action of coming or going in; the coming (of an actor) upon the stage 1600. **b.** *fig.* 1526. **c.** Short for *entrance money* 1681. **2.** Power, right, or opportunity of entering (*lit.* and *fig.*) 1576. †**3.** The beginning or commencement; the first part -1765. **4.** *concr.* A door, gate, avenue, passage, etc. for entering. Also, the point at which anything enters or is entered. 1535. **5.** *Naut.* The part of a ship that comes first (in the water); 'the bow of a vessel, or form of the fore-body under the load-water line' (Smyth) 1781. †**6.** The action of entering in a record; an entry -1620. **7.** *attrib.*, as *entrance-hall*, etc. 1681.

1. The e. of the Royal party 1839. They haue their Exits and their Entrances *A. Y. L.* II. vii. 141. **b.** Before they made an e. upon more solemn debates CLARENDON. **2.** Free e. and safe egress LYTTON. **3.** At the E. of the Spring EVELYN. **4.** The e. of a tent SHAKS., of a harbour 1849.

Entrance (entra·ns), *v.* 1593. [f. EN-[1] + TRANCE.] **1.** *trans.* To throw into a trance 1608. **2.** To put 'out of oneself'; to overpower with delight, fear, etc. 1598; to carry away in or as in a trance (*from, to*) 1593.

1. Angel Forms, who lay intrans't MILT. *P. L.* I. 301. **2.** So stand the Sea-men .. Entraunch'd with what this man of God recited QUARLES. Hence **Entra·ncedly** *adv.* **Entra·ncement,** the action of entrancing; entranced state. **Entra·ncing** *ppl. a.* transporting. **Entra·ncingly** *adv.*

Entrant (e·ntrănt). 1635. [a. F. *entrant*, pr. pple. of *entrer*; cf. INTRANT.]

A. *sb.* One who or that which enters (see ENTER *v.*). Also *fig.*

B. *adj.* That enters 1640.

Entrap (entræ·p), *v.* 1534. [ad. OF. *entraper, entrapper*, f. *en-* + *trappe* TRAP.] **1.** *trans.* To catch in or as in a trap; to bring unawares into difficulties or dangers; to beguile (*to, into*). **2.** To involve in contradictions 1611.

1. To e. the wild elephant GOLDSM. Manuel .. was .. intrapped in the straights of Cilicia, and his Army miserably cut off WANLEY. Hence **Entra·pment.** **Entra·pper.** **Entra·ppingly** *adv.* so as to e.

Entreasure (entre·ʒiŭɹ), *v.* 1597. [f. EN-[1] + TREASURE *v.*] **1.** To store up in or as in a treasury. †**2.** To stock with treasure. CHAPMAN.

†**Entrea·t,** *sb.* 1485. [f. next.] Entreaty, supplication -1650.

Entreat (entrī·t), *v.* Also **in-** (*arch.*) ME. [ad. OF. *entraiter*, f. *en-* (see EN-[1]) + *traiter* to TREAT.]

I. 1. To treat (a person, etc.) in a (specified) way. *Obs.* or *arch.* †**2.** To handle -1681. †**3.** *intr.* To treat *of* or *upon* -1681. †**4.** *intr.* To treat *with* a person; *of*, occas. *about, for*; also *simply* -1603.

1. Their authors .. spitefully entreated as monomaniacs 1864. **4.** To intreat with him of peace KNOLLES.

II. †**1.** *intr.* To plead *for* -1818. **2.** *trans.* To ask earnestly for; chiefly with *clause* as obj. 1600. **3.** To request earnestly; to beseech, implore 1502. †**4.** To prevail on by supplication or solicitation; to persuade by pleading. Also, to induce. -1638.

1. The prisoners entreated for their release JAS. MILL. **2.** To e. of the gods what they will not give 1878. **3.** I e. my reader to think BERKELEY. **4.** God was intreated and Moses prevailed 1638.

Hence †**Entrea·table, intrea·table** *a.* that can be handled; manageable; placable. **Entrea·tableness.** †**Entrea·tance,** also **in-**, treatment; intercession. †**Entrea·ter.** †**Entrea·tful** (*rare*), supplicating. **Entrea·tingly** *adv.* †**Entrea·tive** *a.* of the nature of, or characterized by, entreaty. **Entrea·tment** (now *arch.*), treatment; †negotiation; †conversation.

Entreaty (entrī·ti). 1523. [f. ENTREAT *v.*] †**1.** Treatment; handling; management -1670. †**2.** Negotiation -1607. **3.** Earnest request, solicitation, supplication 1573.

3. The poore vseth intreaties *Prov.* xviii. 23.

‖**Entrechat** (äntrəʃa). 1775. [Fr., ad. It. (*capriola*) *intrecciata* a complicated caper.] A feat in dancing, in which the dancer leaps from the ground and strikes the heels together a number of times.

‖**Entrée** (äntre). 1782. [Fr.] **1.** The action or manner of entering; also, privilege of entrance; admission. **2.** *Cookery.* A made dish, served before the joint 1850. **3.** *Mus.* 'The opening piece (after the overture) of an opera or ballet' (Grove).

†**E·ntremess.** ME. [a. OFr. *entremès* (mod. F. *entremets*), f. *entre* + *mès* (mod. F. *mets*) :—L. *missum* something placed.] Something served between the courses of a banquet -1708.

‖**Entremets** (äntrəmẹ). *pl.* 1475. [mod. F.; see prec.] **1.** Side dishes. **2.** *Antiq.* A spectacular interlude between the courses of a banquet 1863.

Entrench, in- (en-, intre·nʃ). 1555. [f. EN-[1], IN- + TRENCH *sb.* and *v.* In recent use *entrench* is favoured.] **1.** *Mil.* To place within a trench; to surround or fortify with trenches. Also *transf.* and *fig.* †**2.** To make by cutting -1601. **3.** *intr.* To encroach or trespass; to TRENCH, q.v. Now *rare.* 1633.

1. Here he found the enemy strongly entrenched BURKE. *fig.* Entrenched within tradition, custom, authority, and law BERKELEY. **2.** *All's Well* II. i. 45. **3.** To e. upon the privileges of parliament 1831.

Entrenchment, in- (en-, intre·nʃmĕnt). 1590. [f. prec. + -MENT.] **1.** The action of entrenching (Dicts.); *concr.* a line of trenches, a post fortified by trenches; *loosely*, a fortification. †**2.** Encroachment, intrusion -1694.

1. The 52nd regiment .. carried the **e.** with the bayonet WELLINGTON. **2.** An e. upon their Prerogative SELDEN.

‖**Entrepôt** (äntrəpo). 1721. [Fr.; f. L. *inter* + *positum* neut. pa. pple. of *ponere.*] **1.** Temporary deposit of goods, etc.; chiefly *concr.* a storehouse, depot. Also *fig.* **2.** A commercial centre; a place to which goods are brought for distribution. Also *attrib.*, as in *entrepôt-trade.* 1758. **3.** A mart or place where goods are deposited, free of duty, for exportation.

‖**Entrepreneur** (äntrəprənör). 1878. [Fr., f. *entreprendre* to undertake.] **a.** The director or manager of a public musical institution. **b.** One who gets up entertainments. **c.** *Pol. Econ.* A contractor acting as intermediary between capital and labour 1885.

‖**Entresol** (e·ntəɹsǫl, F. äntrəsol). 1711. [Fr.; f. *entre* + *sol* the ground.] A low story placed between the ground floor and the first floor of a building; a mezzanine.

†**Entri·ke,** *v.* ME. [a. OF. *entriquer* :—(ult.) L. *intricare*, f. *in* + *tricæ* quirks, tricks. Cf. INTRICATE, INTRIGUE.] **1.** To ensnare, beguile -1545. **2.** To complicate -1549.

‖**Entrochus** (e·ntrŏkŏs). Pl. **entrochi.** 1676. [mod. L., f. Gr. ἐν + τροχός wheel.] *Palæont.* A name for the wheel-like plates of which certain crinoids are composed. Hence **E·ntrochal** *a.* pertaining to, or containing, entrochi. var. **E·ntrochite.** (Dicts.)

‖**Entropion, entropium** (entrōu·pi,ǫn, -ŏm).

1875. [mod.L., f. Gr. ἐντροπή, f. ἐν + τρέπειν to turn.] *Path.* Introversion of the eyelids.

Entropy (e·ntrŏpi). 1868. [f. Gr. τροπή transformation, after ENERGY. First proposed by Clausius (1865) in sense 'transformation-contents' of a system.] *Physics.* The name given to one of the quantitative elements which determine the thermodynamic condition of a portion of matter.

A portion of matter at uniform temperature retains its entropy unchanged so long as no heat passes to or from it, but if it receives a quantity of heat without change of temperature, the entropy is increased by an amount equal to the ratio of the mechanical equivalent of the quantity of the heat to the absolute measure of the temperature on the thermodynamic scale. The entropy of a system..is always increased by any transport of heat within the system; hence 'the entropy of the universe tends to a maximum' (Clausius).

Entrust, in- (en-, intrɒ·st), *v.* 1602. [f. EN-¹ + TRUST *sb.* The form *intrust* is obsolescent.] **1.** *trans.* To invest with a trust; to commission or employ (a person) in a manner implying confidence. **2.** To confide the care or disposal of *to*, †*with* 1618.

1. Those entrusted in the fleete to inform us PEPYS. To e. new universities with power to confer degrees M. ARNOLD. 2. To e. an errand to a boy DE FOE, one's safety to a boat (*mod.*). Hence **Entru·stment**, the action of entrusting; the fact of being entrusted; †that with which one is entrusted.

Entry (e·ntri). [ME. *entre(e*, a. F. *entrée* :—late L. *intrata*, f. *intrare* (F. *entrer*) to ENTER.] **1.** The action of coming or going in or into; the coming (of an actor) upon the stage. Also *transf.* and *fig.* **2.** *Law.* **a.** The actual taking possession of lands and tenements, by entering or setting foot on the same 1491. **b.** An act essential to complete the offence of burglary 1769. **3.** †**a.** A dance introduced between the parts of an entertainment –1675. **b.** *Mus.* = ENTRÉE 3. 1728. †**4.** = ENTRANCE 2. –1615. **5.** *concr.* That by which entrance is made; a door, a gate; a passage; the mouth (of a river). Also *fig.* ME. **b.** *transf.* A passage common to two or more houses; an alley (now *dial.*); also, †an avenue ME. **6.** The action of entering something in a list, record, account-book, etc. Also *concr.* that which is so entered. 1553. **b.** The list of competitors entering (for a race, etc.) 1885. **c.** The entering at the custom-house of the nature and quantity of goods in a ship's cargo 1692. **7.** *attrib.*, as in *entry-clerk*, etc. 1471.

1. Since our e. into the ice KANE. *fig.* To find e. into the mind CHALMERS. 4. Free entree, egresse, and regresse 1574. 5. At the entrie of which riuer he stayed his course HAKLUYT. 6. A notary made an e. of this act BACON. Phr. *Double E.*: the method of bookkeeping in which every item is entered twice, once to the credit of one account in the ledger, and once to the debit of another. *Single E.*: the method in which each item (as a general rule) is entered only in one account. **c.** Phr. *Port of e.*: the port at which imported goods are entered.

†**Entu·ne**, *v.* ME. [var. of ENTONE, q. v.] **1.** *trans.* To intone. Also *absol.* –1627. **2.** To bring into tune –1530. Hence †**Entu·ne** *sb.* tune; melody (*rare*).

Entwine, in- (en-, intwəi·n), *v.* 1597. [f. EN-¹, IN- + TWINE *v.*] **1.** *trans.* To twine, twist, or wreathe together or round 1616; to form by twining 1700. Also *intr.* for *refl.* Also *fig.* **2.** To clasp; to enfold, embrace. Also *fig.* 1633.

1. Intwine..the flesh-like Columbine With Pinckes W. BROWNE. For him may Love the myrtle wreath e. LANDOR. Hence **Entwi·nement**.

Entwist, in- (en-, inˌtwi·st), *v.* 1590. [f. EN-¹, IN- + TWIST *v.*] To clasp with, or form into, a twist; to twist in *with*.

†**Entwi·t(e**, *v.* 1542. [Altered f. ATWITE; cf. TWIT.] To twit or twit with –1608.

Enucleate (ɪ̆niū·kliˌeⁱt), *v.* 1548. [f. L. *enucleat-*, *enucleare*, f. *e* + *nucleus* kernel.] **1.** *fig.* To extract the kernel from; to lay open, clear, explain. **2.** *Surg.* To extract (a tumour, etc.) from its capsule. Also *absol.* 1878.

1. Enucleating the sense which underlies a difficult construction 1859.

Enucleation (ɪ̆niū:kliˌēⁱ·ʃən). 1650. [f. L. *enucleare*.] **1.** The action of enucleation; unfolding, explanation. **2.** *Surg.* The shelling out of a tumour, etc. from its capsule 1874.

Enula campana; see ELECAMPANE.

Enumerable, Enumerate, erron. ff. INNUMERABLE, INNUMERATE.

†**Enu·merate**, *pa. pple.* 1646. [ad. L. *enumeratus*; see next.] = ENUMERATED –1711.

Enumerate (ɪ̆niū·mĕreⁱt), *v.* 1647. [f. L. *enumerat-*, *enumerare*, f. *e* + *numerare* to count.] *trans.* To count, ascertain the number of; more usually, to mention separately, as if for counting; to specify as in a catalogue or list.

The priest pardons no sins but those which are enumerated JER. TAYLOR. The enumerated population of London..was 3,251,804 *Census* 1871. Hence **Enu·merative** *a.* that enumerates; concerned with enumeration. **Enu·merator**, one who enumerates.

Enumeration (ɪ̆niū:merēⁱ·ʃən). 1551. [a. F., ad. L. *enumerationem*; see prec.] **1.** The action of ascertaining the number of something; *esp.* a census 1577. **2.** The action of specifying seriatim; *concr.* a catalogue, list 1551. **3.** *Rhet.* tr. L. *enumeratio*: A recapitulation, in the peroration, of the heads of an argument.

2. The e. of these circumstances is not to restrict the generality of the enactment LD. ST. LEONARDS.

Enunciable (ɪ̆nɒ·nʃiăb'l), *a.* 1652. [f. L. *enuntiare*; see next.] That admits of being enunciated.

Enunciate (ɪ̆nɒ·nʃiˌeⁱt), *v.* 1623. [f. L. *enuntiat-*, ppl. stem of *enuntiare*, f. *e* + *nuntius* messenger.] **1.** *trans.* To give definite expression to (a proposition, etc.). **2.** = ENOUNCE 2. 1864. **3.** = ENOUNCE 3. 1759.

1. The dogmas enunciated in the Lambeth articles 1853. 3. Each enunciates with a human tone 1759. Hence **Enu·nciative** *a.* that serves to e.; declaratory; pertaining to vocal utterance. **Enu·nciatively** *adv.* **Enu·nciator**, one who or that which enunciates. †**Enu·nciatory** *a.* enunciative.

Enure (eniūə·ɹ), *v.* 1489. [f. EN-¹ + URE, a. OF. *œuvre* operation. Now repl. by INURE, exc. in sense 3.] †**1.** = INURE *v.* 2. –1612. **2.** = INURE *v.* 1. 1489. **3.** *intr.* Chiefly *Law.* To come into operation; to have effect; to be available; to be applied (to the use of) 1607.

2. Troops enured to toil ADDISON. 3. The dignity enures only to the grantee for life BLACKSTONE.

‖**Enuresis** (eniurī·sis). 1800. [mod.L., f. Gr. ἐνουρεῖν to urinate in.] *Path.* Incontinence of urine.

†**Enva·ssal**, *v.* 1605. [f. EN-¹ + VASSAL.] *trans.* To make a vassal of. Also *fig.* –1660. Hence †**Enva·ssalage** (*rare*).

†**Envau·lt**, *v.* 1523. [f. EN-¹ + VAULT *sb.*] To arch over; also, to entomb –1745.

Enveigle; see IN-.

Enveil (envē·l), *v.* 1555. [f. EN-¹ + VEIL *sb.*] To cover with, or as with, a veil.

Envelop (enve·ləp), *v.* ME. [a. OF. *envoluper*, *enveloper* (mod.F. *envelopper*), f. *en-* (see EN-¹) + **volup-*, **velop-*, of unkn. origin.] **1.** *trans.* To wrap up in, or as in a garment, etc.; to serve as a wrapping or case for 1595. Also *fig.* **2.** To wrap, surround on all sides. Const. *in*, *with*. Also *fig.* 1474. **b.** *Mil.* To effect the surrounding of (the enemy). †**3.** *catachr.* To line. SPENSER *F. Q.* II. vii. 4.

1. Envoliped in synne CHAUCER, in cotton LYELL, by the earth 1870. 2. A cloud of smoke envelops either host DRYDEN. Invelloped in vapours 1762.

Envelope (e·nvĕlōᵘp, ăṅv'lōp), *sb.* 1707. [ad. F. *enveloppe*, f. *envelopper*; see prec.] **1.** That in which anything is enveloped; 'a wrapper, integument, covering' (J.) 1715. Also *fig.* **2.** *spec.* The cover of a letter 1714. **3.** *Bot.* The calyx or the corolla, or both together 1830. **4.** *Astron.* The nebulous covering of the head of a comet, the coma 1830. **5.** *Fortif.* 'A work of earth, sometimes in form of a single parapet, and at others like a small rampart' (Stocqueler). **6.** *Math.* The locus of the ultimate intersections of consecutive curves in a system of curves 1871.

Envelopment (enve·ləpmĕnt). 1763. [f. ENVELOP *v.* + -MENT.] The action of enveloping; the state of being enveloped; *concr.* a covering, wrapper. Also *fig.*

Envenom (enve·nəm), *v.* [ME. *envenimen*, ad. OF. *envenimer*, f. *en-* (see EN-¹) + OF. *venim* (mod. *venin*) :—L. *venenum* poison.] †**1.** *trans.* To poison by contact, bite, inoculation, etc. Also *absol.* –1725. **2.** To put venom or poison on; to taint with poison; to render noxious ME. **b.** To infuse venom or bitterness into; to embitter, make virulent 1533. **3.** *fig.* To corrupt, vitiate ME.

1. A Toad may envenome outwardly 1665. 2. To e. arrowes EDEN. To e. thoughtes GRAFTON, a crime 1658, hatred MILL. 3. A universall tetter of impurity had invenom'd every part MILTON.

Enve·nomed, *ppl. a.* ME. [f. prec.] **1.** †Charged with venom; smeared with venom; poisoned –1810. **2.** *fig.* Virulent, malignant, embittered ME.

1. As when Alcides..felt th' envenom'd robe MILT.

†**Enve·nomous**, *a.* ME. [ad. OF. *envenimeus.*] Poisonous –1624.

†**Enve·rmeil**, *v.* ?ME. [ad. OF. *envermeiller*, f. *en-* (see EN-¹) + *vermeil*; see VERMEIL.] *trans.* To tinge as with vermilion; to make ruddy –1822.

Enviable (e·nviăb'l), *a.* 1602. [See -ABLE.] That is to be envied.

An e. mediocrity of fortune CAREW. Hence **E·nviableness**. **E·nviably** *adv.*

Envier (e·nviəɹ). 1509. [f. ENVY *v.* + -ER¹.] One who envies.

Never bride had fewer enviers 1762.

Envigor, var. INVIGOUR *v.*

†**Envi·ned**, *ppl. a.* [ad. F. *enviné*.] Stored with wine. CHAUCER.

Envious (e·nviəs), *a.* ME. [a. AF. *envious*, OF. *envieus* (mod.F. *envieux*) :—L. *invidiosus*, f. *invidia* ENVY.] **1.** Full of envy, affected or actuated by envy; vexed at the good fortune or qualities of another. Const. †*against*, †*at*, *of*, †*to* with *sb.* or *inf.* †**2.** Full of ill-will; malicious –1713. †**3.** Full of emulation –1821. †**4.** Grudging, excessively careful –1667. †**5.** Invidious; odious –1640. †**6.** Enviable –1665.

1. Neither be thou enuious at the wicked *Prov.* xxiv. 19. E. of my diamond LYTTON. The e. who but breathe in others' pain BYRON. 3. Foremost in the e. race KEATS. 4. No men are so e. of their health JER. TAYLOR. 6. So e. a place PEPYS. Hence **E·nviously** *adv.* **E·nviousness**.

Environ, *sb.* *Obs.* in *sing.* ME. [a. OF. sing. *environ* (subseq. a. mod.F. pl. *environs*), f. the adv.] †**1.** *sing.* Compass, circuit. Only in ME. **2.** In mod. Eng. *pl.* **Environs** (envəi·rənz, e·nvirənz). The outskirts, surrounding districts, of a town 1665.

2. London and its Environs EVELYN. Hence **Envi·ronage** (*rare*), surroundings. **Envi·ronal** *a.* arising from relations to the environment.

Environ (envəi·rən), *v.* ME. [a. F. *environner*, f. *environ* round about; see next.] **1.** *trans.* To form a ring round, surround, encircle; to beset; to beleaguer. Also *fig.* of circumstances, dangers, etc. **2.** To envelop, enclose ME. †**3.** To go round in a circle –1647.

1. Ilands environed by the sea GOUGE. Colonel Pride..had environed the house with two regiments HUME. *fig.* What Perils do environ The Man that meddles with cold Iron BUTLER *Hud.* I. iii. 1. 2. Gravely-gladsome light environed them LANDOR.

†**Envi·ron**. ME. [a. F. *environ*, f. *en* + OF. **viron* circuit, related to *virer* to VEER.]

A. *adv.* Round about; in the neighbourhood –1600.

B. *prep.* Round, about –1450.

Environment (envəi·rənmĕnt). 1603. [f. ENVIRON *v.* + -MENT.] **1.** The action of environing; the state of being environed. **2.** That which environs; *esp.* the conditions or influences under which any person or thing lives or is developed 1827.

2. In such an element with such an e. of circumstances CARLYLE. The organism is continually adapted to its e. 1874.

Environs; see ENVIRON *sb.*

Envisage (envi·zėdʒ), *v.* 1820. [a. F. *envisager*, f. *en-* (see EN-¹) + *visage* face.] **1.** *trans.* To look in the face of; also *fig.* **2.** To set before the mind's eye; to contemplate 1837.

1. To e. circumstance, all calm KEATS. 2. From the very dawn of existence the infant must e. self McCOSH. Hence **Envi·sagement**, envisaging.

†**Envolume** (envǫ·lium), *v. rare.* 1632. [f. EN-¹ + VOLUME.] To form into, or incorporate with, a volume.

Envolupe(n, obs. f. ENVELOPE *v.*

Envoy (e·nvoi), *sb.*¹ Also (in Fr. form) l'envoi; see L'ENVOY. ME. [a. OF. *envoy(e* (mod.F. *envoi*), f. OF. *envoiier* (mod. *envoyer*) to send, f. *en voie* on the way.] **1.** The final stanza of a poem containing an address to the reader or the person to whom it is dedicated;

the concluding strophe, as of a ballade or chant royal, having a prescribed metrical form (*arch.*). **2.** The action of dispatching a messenger or parcel; hence, a mission, errand (*arch.*) 1795.

Envoy (e·nvoi), *sb.*[2] 1666. [an altered form of F. *envoyé* (previously used unchanged).] **1.** A public minister sent by one sovereign or government to another for the transaction of diplomatic business. Now *esp.* a minister plenipotentiary, ranking below an ambassador, and above a 'chargé d'affaires'. **2.** An agent, commissioner, deputy, messenger, representative 1696. Hence **E·nvoyship**, the office, position, or function of an e.

Envy (e·nvi), *sb.* [ME. *envie*, a. F. :—L. *invidia*, f. *invidus*, related to *invidere* to look upon (in a bad sense), f. *in* + *videre*.] †**1.** Ill-will, malice, enmity –1707. **b.** as tr. L. *invidia*: Odium, unpopularity –1679. †**2.** Harm, mischief –1460. **3.** Mortification and ill-will occasioned by the contemplation of another's superior advantages ME.; *concr.* the object of envy 1836. **4.** †**a.** Emulation –1635. **b.** A longing for another's advantages 1723. †**5.** Desire; enthusiasm –1607.

1. No lawful meanes can carrie me Out of enuies reach *Merch. V.* IV. i. 10. 3. E. .. es joye of oþer mens harme and sorowe of oþer mens welefare 1440. All..saue only hee, Did that they did, in enuy of great Cæsar *Jul. C.* V. v. 70. Enuie striketh most spitefully at the fairest A.V. *Transl. Pref.* 2. The little envies of them [women] to one another DRYDEN. 4. b. Your success excites my e. (*mod.*).

Envy (e·nvi), *v.*[1] ME. [ad. F. *envier*:—med. L. *invidiare*, f. L. *invidia* ENVY *sb.* The stress (envəi·) still survives *dial.*, *esp.* in Sc.] **1.** *trans.* To feel envy at the superior advantages of; to regard with discontent another's possession of (some superior advantage). Also in more neutral sense: To wish oneself on a level with (another) in some respect, or possessed of (something which another has). †**2.** To feel a grudge against –1630. †**3.** *trans.* To begrudge; to treat grudgingly. Also *absol.* –1770. †**4.** *intr.* To have envious, grudging, or malevolent feelings 1477.

1. I..owe no man hate, enuie no mans happinesse *A. Y. L.* III. ii. 78. I e. him for walking .. with you MIDDLETON. Ah! much I e. thee thy boys CRABBE. 3. But that sweet Cordiall..She did to him e. SPENSER *F. Q.* III. v. 50. Antiquity enuieth there should be new additions BACON. 4. Phr. *To e. at* = senses 1–3; But now I enuie at their libertie SHAKS.

†**Envy·**, *v.*[2] ME. [a. OF. *envier* :—L. *invitare* to challenge; cf. VIE.] **a.** *intr.* To vie. **b.** To vie with, seek to rival –1621.

As thogh the erthe enuye wolde To be gayer than the heuen CHAUCER.

Enwall, in- (en-, inwǭ·l), *v.* 1523. [f. EN-, IN- + WALL.] To enclose within a wall; also, to serve as a wall to. Also *fig.*

Enwallow; see EN- *pref.*[1] 3.

†**Enwhee·l**, *v. rare.* 1604. [f. EN-[1] + WHEEL *sb.*] To encircle –1621.

Enwiden; see EN- *pref.*[1] 3.

Enwind, in- (en-, inwəi·nd), *v.* 1850. [f. EN-, IN- + WIND *v.*] *trans.* To wind itself around; to encircle (*lit.* and *fig.*).

Let her great Danube rolling fair E. her isles TENNYSON.

Enwoman; see EN- *pref.*[1] 2.

Enwomb (enwū·m), *v.* 1590. [f. EN-[1] + WOMB.] **1.** *trans.* To make pregnant; also *fig.* **2.** To hold in or as in the womb. ? *Obs.* 1601. **3.** *transf.* To plunge *into*, bury *in*, the womb or bowels of 1591.

Enwrap, in- (en-, inræ·p), *v.* ME. [f. EN-[1], IN- + WRAP *v.*] **1.** *trans.* To wrap, envelop, enfold. Also *transf.* and *fig.* **2.** *fig.* **a.** To contain implicitly 1642. **b.** To wrap in slumber, engross in thought, etc. 1589. †**c.** To involve, implicate (in danger, difficulty, etc.) –1826.

2. b. If such holy song E. our fancy long MILTON. Hence †**Enwra·pment**, also **in-**, *rare*, the action of enwrapping; the being enwrapped; a wrapping, covering.

Enwreathe, in- (en-, inrī·ð), *v.* 1620. [f. EN-[1], IN- + WREATHE *v.*] To surround or encircle with or as with a wreath.

Enzootic (enzo,ǫ·tik). 1880. [f. Gr. ἐν + ζῷον + -IC, after *chaotic*, etc.] **A.** *adj.* 'Applied to diseases of cattle peculiar to a district, climate, or season' (*Syd. Soc. Lex.*). **B.** *sb.* An enzootic disease.

Enzyme (e·nzəim). 1881. Also *U.S.* enzym. [ad. G. *enzym*, f. mod. Gr. ἔνζυμος leavened.] *Biochem.* Any of a class of complex organic substances that cause chemical transformations of material in plants and animals; formerly called *ferment*. Hence **Enzy·mic** *a.*

Eo-, *prefix*, comb. f. Gr. ἠώς dawn, as in: **Eoli·thic** *a.* pertaining to the earliest age of man that is characterized by the use of worked flint instruments. **Eozoic** (ī,ozōᵘ·ik) *a.* [Gr. ζῷον animal], characterized by the earliest appearance of animal life; said of the Laurentian strata and their period.

Eoan (i,ōᵘ·ăn), *a.* 1619. [f. L. *eous*, a. Gr. ἠῷος, f. ἠώς dawn.] Of or pertaining to the dawn; eastern.

Eocene (ī·ŏsīn), *a.* 1833. [f. Gr. ἠώς (see EO-) + καινός new.] *Geol.* **1.** The epithet applied to the lowest division of the Tertiary strata, and to the geological period which they represent. Also *fig.* **2.** quasi-*sb.*, as *Upper E.*, etc.

Eol-, Eon, varr. ÆOL-, ÆON.

Eolienne (iōᵘlie·n). 1902. [a. F. *éolienne*, f. Gr. αἰόλος sheeny.] A fine dress fabric of silk and wool.

Eosin (ī·ŏsin). 1866. [f. Gr. ἠώς dawn + -IN.] *Chem.* A red dye-stuff produced by the addition of bromine to a solution of fluorescin in glacial acetic acid. Its potassium salt is used as a rose-coloured dye. Also *attrib.*

-eous, *suffix*, occurring in adjs., is chiefly f. L. *-eus* + -OUS, in the sense 'of the nature of, resembling'.

Eozoic, etc.; see EO- *pref.*

Ep-, *prefix*; see EPI-.

Epacrid (epæ·krid). 1881. [ad. mod.L. *epacridem*, f. Gr. ἐπί + ἄκρις summit; so named by Forster (1776), because 'generally found on mountain tops'. In sense b, f. mod.L. *Epacrideæ*.] **a.** A plant of the genus *Epacris*. **b.** A plant of the N.O. *Epacrideæ*, consisting of corollifloral dicotyledons, growing in Australia and the Indian Archipelago, and resembling heaths.

Epact (ī·pækt, e·pækt). 1552. [ad. F. *epacte*, L. *epacta*, Gr. ἐπακτή, f. ἐπακτός, vbl. adj. of ἐπάγειν to intercalate.] **1. a.** (Also pl. *epacts*.) The number of days by which the solar exceeds the lunar year of 12 months. **b.** The number of days of the moon's age on the first day of the year (now Jan. 1st, formerly March 1st or 22nd). **2.** Any intercalated day or days (*rare*) 1603.

Epactal (ĭpæ·ktăl, epæ·ktăl), *a.* 1878. [f. Gr. ἐπακτός (see prec.) + -AL.] *Anat.* 'Imported; foreign' (*Syd. Soc. Lex.*).

E. bone: the Wormian bone at the superior angle of the occipital bone.

†**Epæne·tic**, *a.* 1675. [ad. Gr. ἐπαινετικός.] Panegyrical –1736.

‖**Epagoge** (epăgōᵘ·gī). [Gr. ἐπαγωγή, f. ἐπάγειν to bring in.] *Logic.* The bringing forward of particular instances to lead to a general conclusion; argument by induction. Hence **Epago·gic** *a.* inductive. (Dicts.)

Epagomenic (e:păgome·nik), *a.* 1839. [f. Gr. ἐπαγομενή (ἡμέρα).] Intercalary.

Epalpate (ipæ·lpĕt), *a.* 1884. [f. E- *pref.*[3] + L. *palpus*.] *Entom.* Having no palpi or feelers.

Epalpebrate (ĭpæ·lpĭbrĕt), *a.* 1884. [f. as prec. + L. *palpebra*.] Having no eyebrows.

Epana-, bef. a vowel *epan-*, comb. of Gr. ἐπ(ί) upon, in addition + ἀνά up, again, occurring in some rhetorical terms, adopted from Gr. **Epa:nadiplo·sis** [Gr. δίπλωσις], a figure in which 'a sentence begins and ends with the same word; as Severe to his servants, to his children severe' (Phillips). **E:panale·psis** [Gr. λῆψις], a figure by which the same word or clause is repeated after intervening matter. **Epana·phora** [Gr. φορά] = ANAPHORA. **Epana·strophe** [Gr. στροφή], a figure by which the end-word of one sentence begins the next. **Epa·nodos** [Gr. ὁδός], **a.** the repetition of a sentence in inverse order; **b.** a return to the regular thread of discourse after a digression.

E:panortho·sis [Gr. ὄρθωσις], a figure in which a word is recalled, in order to substitute a more correct term. Hence **E:panortho·tic** *a.*

Epanthous (epæ·nþəs), *a.* [f. Gr. ἐπ(ί) + ἄνθος.] *Bot.* Growing upon flowers, as certain fungi. (Dicts.)

Eparch (e·paɹk). 1656. [a. Gr. ἔπαρχος, f. ἐπ(ί) + ἀρχός.] **1. a.** *Hist.* = L. *præfectus* prefect. **b.** The governor of an eparchy in modern Greece. **2.** *Eccl.* A metropolitan (bishop) in the Greek (Russian) Church 1882.

Eparchy (e·păɹki). 1796. [ad. Gr. ἐπαρχία; see prec.] **1.** A district or province under an eparch; in mod. Greece, a division of a nomarchy 1838. **2.** In the Russian (Greek) Church: A diocese. Hence **Epa·rchial** *a.*

‖**Epaule** (epǭ·l). 1702. [a. F. *épaule*, OF. *espaule*.] *Fortif.* The shoulder of a bastion, *i.e.* the place where the face and flank meet.

Epaulement (epǭ·lmĕnt). 1687. [a. F., f. *épauler* to protect by an epaulement; see prec.] *Fortif.* 'A covering mass raised to protect from the fire of the enemy' (Smyth).

Epaulet, epaulette (e·pǫlet). 1783. [a. F. *épaulette*, dim. of *épaule*; see EPAULE. The better form is *epaulet*, that in *-ette* is more common.] **1.** A shoulder-piece; an ornament worn on the shoulder as part of a military, naval, or (occas.) civil uniform. **2.** *Entom.* The plate that covers the base of the anterior wings in hymenopterous insects 1834. **3.** = PAULDRON, q.v. 1824. **4.** An ornament for the shoulder of a lady's dress 1865.

1. Obliged to borrow from Rothschild, the banker, the epaulettes he wore as Austrian consul 1848. Hence **E·paule:tted** *ppl. a.*

Epaxial (epæ·ksiăl), *a.* 1872. [f. EP- + L. *axis* + -AL.] *Anat.* On or above the axis (of the body): said of muscles, cartilages, etc. that lie upon or above the vertebral column viewed horizontally. Hence **Epa·xially** *adv.* in an e. position or direction.

Epencephalon (epense·fălǫn). 1854. [f. EP- + ENCEPHALON.] *Anat.* The anterior of the two enlargements into which the posterior primary vesicle of the brain divides. Also called *hind-brain*. Hence **Epe:ncepha·lic** *a.* pertaining to or covering the e.

Ependyma (epe·ndimă). 1872. [a. Gr. ἐπένδυμα, f. ἐπενδύειν, f. ἐπί + ἐν + δύειν.] 'Virchow's name for the lining membrane of the cerebral ventricles and of the central spinal canal' (*Syd. Soc. Lex.*).

Epenthesis (epe·nþĭsis). 1657. [late L., a. Gr., f. ἐπί + ἐν + θέσις.] *Gram.* The insertion of a letter or sound in the middle of a word. var. †**Epe·nthesy**.

Epenthetic (epenþe·tik), *a.* 1831. [ad. Gr. ἐπενθετικός; see prec. and -IC.] Pertaining to epenthesis. Of a letter or sound: Inserted in the middle of a word.

Epergne (ĭpǭ·ɹn). 1761. [? a corruption of Fr. *épargne* saving. The meaning is not accounted for.] A centre-dish for the dinner-table, now often in a branched form, each branch supporting a small dish, or a vase for flowers.

Grand Epergnes filled with fine Pickles 1761.

Epexegesis (epe:ksĭdʒī·sis). 1621. [a. Gr., f. ἐπεξηγεῖσθαι; see EXEGESIS.] The addition of a word or words by way of further elucidation; that which is so added. Hence **Epe:xege·tic, -al** *a.* pertaining to or of the nature of an e. **Epe:xege·tically** *adv.*

Ephah (ī·fă). ME. [a. Heb.; ? Egyptian.] *Heb. Antiq.* A Hebrew dry measure; = BATH *sb.*[3]; variously said to have contained $4^1/_2$ to 9 gallons. Also *fig.*

Ephebe (efī·b). 1880. [ad. L. *ephebus* (also used), a. Gr. ἔφηβος, f. ἐπί upon + ἥβη early manhood.] *Gr. Antiq.* A young citizen from eighteen to twenty years of age, which period he spent chiefly in garrison duty. Hence **Ephe·bic** *a.*

Ephectic (efe·ktik), *a.* 1693. [ad. Gr. ἐφεκτικός, f. ἐπέχειν to hold back, suspend.] Characterized by suspense of judgement.

†**Ephe·mera**, *a.* and *sb.*[1] ME. [a. med.L. *ephemera* (sc. *febris*), adj. fem., a. Gr. ἐφήμερος, f. ἐπί (see EPI-) + ἡμέρα.]

A. *adj.* Of a fever: Lasting only for a day. **B.** *sb.* (sc. *fever*) –1813.

Ephemera (ɪ̆fe·mĕră), *sb.*² Pl. **ephemeræ, -as.** 1677. [a. mod.L. *ephemera* (?sc. *musca*); see prec.] *Zool.* An insect that (in its imago) lives only for a day. In mod. entomology, a genus of pseudo-neuropterous insects belonging to the *Ephemeridæ* (Day-flies, May-flies). Also *transf.* and *fig.*

These papers of a day, the Ephemeræ of learning JOHNSON.

Ephemeral (ɪ̆fe·mĕrăl). 1576. [f. Gr. ἐφήμερος (see prec.) + -AL.]

A. *adj.* **1.** Beginning and ending in a day; existing only for a day, or for a few days. **2.** Short-lived, transitory 1639.

1. An e. fever 1866. E. insects HELPS. **2.** Their e. liberty SYD. SMITH. May I, the e., ne'er scrutinize Who made the heaven and earth BROWNING.

B. *sb.* in *pl.* Insects which live only for a day. Also *transf.* of books, persons, etc. 1817.

Hence **Ephe:mera·lity,** e. quality; in *pl.* e. matters. var. †**Ephe·meran** *a.* (in sense A. 1) and *sb.*

Ephe·meric, *a.* [f. EPHEMERA + -IC.] = EPHEMERAL. (Dicts.)

Ephemerid (ɪ̆fe·mĕrid). 1872. [ad. mod.L. *Ephemeridæ*, f. *ephemera.*] One of the *Ephemeridæ*; see EPHEMERA ².

‖**Ephemeris** (ɪ̆fe·mĕris). Pl. **ephemerides** (efɪ̆me·ridɪ̄z), formerly used as *sing.* 1551. [mod. L. *ephemeris*, a. Gr. ἐφημερίς diary, f. ἐφήμερος daily.] †**1.** A diary, journal –1682. **2.** A table showing the computed (rarely the observed) places of a heavenly body for every day of a given period. †Also, in *pl.* the tabulated positions of a heavenly body for a series of successive days, 1551. †**b.** *pl.* A collection of such tables –1635. **3.** A book giving the places of the planets and other astronomical matters in advance for each day of a certain period; an astronomical almanac 1647. †**4.** An almanac or calendar of any kind. (Used in bibliographical works, in *pl.*, as a general heading for Almanacs, Calendars, etc.) –1796. ¶ **5.** *catachr.* = EPHEMERA ².

5. Honour is venerable to us because it is no e. EMERSON. Hence †**Ephe·merist,** one who makes or uses an e.

Ephemeromorph (ɪ̆fe·mĕro͵mǭɹf). *rare.* [f. Gr. ἐφήμερος + μορφή.] *Biol.* A general name for the lowest forms of life, which are not definitely either animal or vegetable. BASTIAN.

Ephemeron (ɪ̆fe·mĕrǫn). *Pl.* **ephemera, -ons.** 1578. [a. Gr. (ζῷον) ἐφήμερον, neut. of ἐφήμερος; see EPHEMERA ².] **1.** An insect, which, in its winged state, lives only for a day. Also *fig.* and *attrib.* 1626. †‖**2.** A plant described by ancient writers –1661. Hence **Ephe·merous** *a.* like an e.; transitory.

Ephesian (ɪ̆fɪ̄·zăn). ME. [f. L. *ephesius* (ad. Gr., f. Ἔφεσος) + -AN.]

A. *adj.* Of or pertaining to Ephesus.

B. *sb.* **1.** An inhabitant of Ephesus ME. †**2.** A boon companion. *Merry W.* IV. v. 19.

Ephesine (e·fɪ̆sin), *a.* 1579. [ad. L. *Ephesinus* f. *Ephesus.*] Of or pertaining to Ephesus; chiefly *Eccl.*

†**Ephe·stian,** *a.* [f. Gr. ἐφέστιος of the hearth.] Domestic. URQUHART.

Ephete (e·fɪ̄t). *rare.* 1839. [ad. Gr. ἐφέτης, f. ἐφιέναι to impose, etc.] In *pl.* A body of magistrates at Athens. More usu. in L. form *ephetæ.*

Ephialtes (efi͵æ·ltɪ̄z). 1601. [a. Gr. ἐφιάλτης, ? agent-n. f. *ἐφιάλλεσθαι to leap upon.] Nightmare.

‖**Ephippium** (efi·piŏm). 1841. [L., ad. Gr. ἐφίππιος adj. 'that is for putting on a horse'.] **1.** *Anat.* A saddle-shaped depression of the sphenoid bone 1842. **2.** *Zool.* The envelope enclosing the winter ova of the Daphniidæ (a genus of the Crustaceans). It is probably a development from the carapace.

Ephod (e·fǫd). ME. [Heb., f. *āphad* to put on.] **1.** A Jewish priestly garment, without sleeves, slit at the sides below the armpits, fastened with buckles at the shoulders, and by a girdle at the waist. The ephod worn by the priests was of linen; that of the high-priest was of 'gold, purple, scarlet, and byssus'. **2.** *transf.* A typical priestly garment; hence, †the priestly office, etc. 1603.

2. The holy e. made a cloak for gain DRAYTON.

Ephor (e·fǭɹ). 1586. [ad. Gr. ἔφορος overseer, f. ἐπί upon + root of ὁράειν to see. Also in L. form **ephori.**] **1.** One of a body of five magistrates at Sparta, elected annually by popular vote, who exercised control over the kings. **2.** In mod. Greece: An overseer 1890. Hence **E·phoral** *a.* of or pertaining to the ephors. **E·phoralty,** the office of e.; the body of ephors. **E·phorship,** term of office as e.

Ephy·driad. [ad. Gr. ἐφυδριάς, f. ἐπί + ὕδωρ.] A water-nymph. L. HUNT.

Epi-, *prefix*, repr. Gr. ἐπι- (bef. an unaspirated vowel ἐπ-, bef. an aspirate ἐφ-, in Eng. EP-, EPH-) in senses 'upon, at, or close upon, on the ground or occasion of, in addition'.

Epibasal (epibē̆·săl), *a.* 1882. [f. EPI- + BASAL *a.*] *Bot.* Epithet of the upper cell in the oospore of certain cryptogams.

Epiblast (e·piblast). 1866. [f. EPI- + BLAST.] **1.** *Bot.* A small transverse plate found on the embryo of some grasses. **2.** *Biol.* The outermost layer of the wall of the blastoderm when fully formed 1877.

‖**Epiblema** (epiblɪ̄·mă). 1870. [mod.L., a. Gr. ἐπίβλημα that which is thrown over, f. ἐπί + βάλλειν.] *Bot.* A modified epidermal tissue investing the roots of plants.

Epic (e·pik). 1589. [ad. L. *epicus*, a. Gr. ἐπικός, f. ἔπος.]

A. *adj.* **1.** Pertaining to that kind of narrative poetry (see EPOS) which celebrates the achievements of some heroic personage of history or tradition. **2.** Such as is described in epic poetry 1847.

1. My poem's E., and is meant to be Divided in twelve books BYRON. Phr. *E. dialect*: that form of the Greek language in which the e. poems were written.

B. *sb.* †**1.** An epic poet. B. JONS. **2.** An epic poem. Also *transf.* and *fig.* 1706.

2. Phr. *National e.* (transf): any imaginative work embodying a nation's conception of its own past history, or of incidents in it.

Hence **E·pical** *a.* **E·pically** *adv.* **E·picism,** the mental habit characteristic of the e. poet. **E·picist,** a writer of e. poetry.

Epicalyx (epikæ·liks). 1870. [f. EPI- + CALYX.] *Bot.* A whorl of leaf-like organs surrounding the true calyx in some plants.

Epicarp (e·pikāɹp). 1835. [f. Gr. ἐπί + καρπός.] *Bot* In fruits: The outermost layer of the pericarp. Cf. ENDOCARP.

Epicede (e·pisɪ̄d). *arch.* 1549. Anglicized f. EPICEDIUM.

‖**Epicedium** (episɪ̄·diŏm, -sɪ̆dəi·ŏm). Pl. epicedia, -ums. 1587. [L., a. Gr. ἐπικήδειον adj. neut., f. ἐπί + κῆδος care, *esp.* funeral observance.] A funeral ode. Hence **Epice·dial** *a.* elegiac (*arch.*). **Epice·dian** *a.* elegiac, funereal; †*sb.* an epicedium. var. †**Epice·dion.**

Epicene (e·pisɪ̄n). 1528. [ad. L. *epicœnus*, a. Gr. ἐπίκοινος, f. ἐπί + κοινός common.]

A. *adj. Gram.* In L. and Gr. grammar, said of nouns which have but one form to denote either sex. Hence (improp.) *epicene gender.* Loosely, = *common.* Also *transf.* and *fig.* 1601.

fig. In an Epicœne fury B. JONS. An e. creature, a bundle of languid affectations BLACK.

B. *sb.* One who shares the characteristics of both sexes 1609.

E., or The Silent Woman B. JONS. (*title*).

Epicentral (epise·ntrăl), *a.* 1866. [f. Gr. ἐπίκεντρος (see EPICENTRUM) + -AL.] **1.** Situated upon a (vertebral) centrum. Also quasi-*sb.* **2.** Pertaining to an epicentrum 1887.

‖**Epicentrum** (epise·ntrŏm). 1879. [mod.L., a. Gr. ἐπίκεντρον, adj. neut., f. ἐπί + κέντρον CENTRE.] The point over the centre: applied in *Seismology* to the point of outbreak of earthquake shocks. var. **E·pice:ntre.**

†**Epicera·stic,** *a. rare.* 1684. [ad. Gr. ἐπικεραστικός.] Emollient. Also as *sb.* in *pl.*

Epicerebral (epise·rɪ̆brăl), *a.* [f. EPI- + CEREBRAL.] *Anat.* Situated upon the brain.

‖**Epicheirema** (e:pikəirɪ̄·mă). 1721. [mod.L., a. Gr., f. ἐπιχειρέειν to undertake, f. ἐπί + χείρ.] A name given to a syllogism when to either premiss, or to both, is annexed a reason implying the existence of a prosyllogism. In Aristotle the word denotes a dialectical proof, which is something short of a demonstrated conclusion.

Epichile (e·pikəil). [ad. mod.L. *epichilium*, f. Gr. ἐπί + χεῖλος lip.] *Bot.* 'The upper half of the lid of an orchid, when that organ is once jointed or strangulated' (*Treas. Bot.*).

Epichordal (epikǭ·ɹdăl), *a.* [f. EPI- + CHORD + -AL.] *Anat.* Situated upon or about the intercranial part of the notochord; applied to certain segments of the brain.

Epichorial (epikō°·riăl), *a.* 1840. [f. Gr. ἐπιχώριος + -AL.] Proper to a country or district.

The local or e. superstitions from every district DE QUINCEY.

Epichristian (epikri·styăn), *a.* [f. EPI- + CHRISTIAN. Coined by DE QUINCEY.] Pertaining to the age not long after Christ.

‖**Epiclesis, -klesis** (epiklɪ̄·sis). 1878. [Gr. ἐπίκλησις, f. ἐπικαλεῖν to invoke.] In some Christian liturgies, a part of the prayer of consecration in which the Holy Spirit is invoked.

Epiclinal (epikləi·năl), *a.* [f. Gr. ἐπί + κλίνη couch + -AL.] *Bot.* 'Placed upon the disk or receptacle of a flower' (*Treas. Bot.*).

Epicœle (e·pisɪ̄l). 1877. [f. EPI- + Gr. κοιλία the cavity of the belly.] In the Tunicata, a kind of perivisceral cavity, formed by an invagination of the ectoderm. **Epicœ·lous** *a.*

Epicolic (epikǫ·lik), *a.* [f. EPI- + Gr. κόλον COLON.] *Anat.* Of or pertaining to the region over, or beside, the colon.

Epico·ndyle. 1836. [a. F.: see EPI-.] *Anat.* The external CONDYLE of the humerus.

Epicoracoid (epikǫ·răkoid). 1839. [f. EPI- + CORACOID.] **A.** *adj.* A bone, or pair of bones, found in reptiles, etc., and forming a continuation of the coracoid. **B.** *sb.* The epicoracoid bone. Hence **Epico:racoi·dal** *a.*

Epicorolline (epiko·rǫlin, -əin), *a.* [f. EPI- + COROLLA + -INE.] *Bot.* Inserted in or upon the corolla.

Epicotyl (epikǫ·til). 1880. [f. EPI- + Gr. κοτύλη; see COTYLEDON.] *Bot.* The stem immediately above the cotyledons.

Epicotyle·donary, *a.* 1884. [f. EPI- + COTYLEDON + -ARY.] *Bot.* Immediately above the cotyledons.

Epicranial (epikrē̆·niăl), *a.* 1831. [f. EPI- + CRANIUM + -AL.] *Anat.* Pertaining to the epicranium.

‖**Epicranium** (epikrē̆·niŏm). 1888. [mod.L., f. Gr. ἐπί + κρανίον CRANIUM.] *Anat.* All that overlies the cranium; the scalp. **b.** In insects: The upper surface of the head.

†‖**Epicra·sis.** [mod.L., a. Gr., f. ἐπικεραννύναι; see EPICERASTIC.] The use of epicerastics. G. HAKEWIL.

Epicure (e·pikiuɹ), *sb.* 1545. [?ad. L. *Epicurus*, a. Gr. Ἐπίκουρος an Athenian philosopher *c* 300 B.C. Or ?ad. late L. *epicurius* (= L. *epicureus*) Epicurean, f. *Epicurus.*] †**1.** A follower of Epicurus; an EPICUREAN –1722. †**b.** *loosely*, One who disbelieves in the divine government of the world and in a future life –1691. †**2.** One who gives himself up to sensual pleasures; a glutton, a sybarite –1774. **3.** One who cultivates a refined taste for the pleasures of the table. (The current sense.) Also *transf.* 1586.

3. *transf.* The little E., the Bee STILLINGFL. An e. in words 1872. Hence †**E·picure** *v.* to indulge as an e.

Epicurean (e:pikiurɪ̄·ăn). 1572. [f. L. *epicureus*, late L. *epicurius* (ad. Gr. ἐπικούρειος, f. Ἐπίκουρος Epicurus) + -AN.]

A. *adj.* **1.** Of or pertaining to Epicurus, or to his system of philosophy 1586. **2.** Devoted to the pursuit of pleasure. Now chiefly: Devoted to refined sensuous enjoyment 1641.

1. It was no E. speech of an Epicure BURTON. The Atomical or E. Hypothesis STILLINGFL. **2.** The sober majesties Of settled, sweet, E. life TENNYSON.

B. *sb.* **1.** A disciple of Epicurus 1605. **2.** One who makes pleasure the object of his life 1572.

1. The very Epicureans allowed the being of gods BERKELEY. **2.** A voluptuary and an e. SCOTT.

†**Epicu·reous, -ious, E·picurish** (*rare*) *adjs.*

Epicureanism (e:pikiurɪ̄·ăniz'm). 1751. [f. prec. + -ISM.] **1.** The philosophical system of

Epicurus. **2.** Adherence to the principles of Epicurus; hence, devotion to a life of ease and luxury. Also *transf.* 1847.

Epicurism (e·pikiuriːz'm). 1575. [Two formations: (1) f. *Epicurus*; cf. F. *Épicurisme*. (2) f. EPICURE + -ISM. Stressed in Johnson *epicu·rism*; in SHAKS. (*Lear* I. iv. 165) *epi·cur-ism*.] **1.** The philosophical system of Epicurus, and allied doctrines; attachment to such doctrines. Now usu. EPICUREANISM. 1575. †**2.** The pursuit of pleasure; sensuality; gluttony –1775. **3.** The disposition and habits of an epicure. Also *transf.* 1619.

2. Epicurisme and Lust Make it [our Court] more like a Tauerne, or a Brothell Than a grac'd Pallace SHAKS. So †**Epicurist** = EPICUREAN *sb.*

†**Epi·curize**, *v.* 1621. [f. *Epicurus* (or EPICURE) + -IZE.] **1.** *intr.* To profess or practise the doctrines of Epicurus –1688. **2.** To play the epicure. Const. *on.* Also *fig.* –1711.

Epicycle (e·pisəik'l), *sb.* ME. [ad. L. *epicyclus*, a. Gr. ἐπίκυκλος, f. ἐπί + κύκλος circle.] **1.** A small circle, having its centre on the circumference of another circle. Chiefly *Astron.*

In the Ptolemaic system each of the 'seven planets' was supposed to move in an epicycle, the centre of which moved along a greater circle called a deferent. This conception is still occas. used with reference to the geocentric hypothesis.

2. *Mod. Astron.* The curve described by a planet moving in an epicycle, *i. e.* its geocentric path 1854.

Epicyclic, -al (episi·klik, -ăl), *a.* 1837. [f. prec. + -IC.] Of or pertaining to epicycles.

Phr. *E. train*: one in which the axes of the wheels revolve around a common centre.

Epicycloid (episəi·kloid). 1790. [f. EPICYCLE + -OID.] A curve generated by a point in the circumference of a movable circle, which revolves on the exterior of a fixed circle; formerly called an *exterior epicycloid*, and dist. from the *interior epicycloid* (now *hypocycloid*). Hence **E:picycloi·dal** *a.* of the form or nature of an e.

Epideictic, -ktic (epidəi·ktik), *a.* Also epidictic. 1790. [ad. Gr ἐπιδεικτικός, f. ἐπί + δεικνύναι to show.] Adapted for display; chiefly of set orations. Hence **Epidei·ctical** *a.*

Epidemic (epide·mik). 1603. [ad. F. *épidémique*, f. *épidémie* (see EPIDEMY).]

A. *adj.* **1.** Of a disease: 'Prevalent among a people or a community at a special time, and produced by some special causes not generally present in the affected locality' (*Syd. Soc. Lex.*). †**2.** Widely prevalent, universal –1745.

1. E. diseases BACON, fever COWPER. *fig.* The e. terror of an imaginary danger SCOTT. 2. A toleration of epidemick whordom MILTON.

B. *sb.* An epidemic disease; also *fig.* 1757.

fig. An epidemick of despair BURKE.

var. †**Epide·mial** *a.* (in sense A. 1). Hence **E:pidemi·city**, e. quality.

Epidemical (epide·mikăl), *a.* 1621. [f. prec. + -AL.] **1.** Epidemic; also, characterized by epidemics. †**2.** = EPIDEMIC A. 2. –1813. Hence **Epide·mical-ly** *adv.*, **-ness.**

Epidemiography (e:pidīːmiɒ·grăfi). [f. Gr. ἐπιδήμιος + -γραφία.] A treatise on, or history of, epidemic diseases. Hence **E:pidemio·graphist**, a writer on e.

Epidemiology (epidīːmiɒ·lŏdʒi). 1873. [f. as prec. + Gr. -λογία (see -LOGY).] That branch of medical science which treats of epidemics. Hence **Epide:miolo·gical** *a.* of or pertaining to e. **Epide:mio·logist**, one who studies e.

†**Epidemy.** 1472. [a. OF. *ydipime*, mod.F. *épidémie*, ad. L. *epidemia*, *epidimia*, Gr. ἐπιδημία, f. ἐπιδήμιος, f. ἐπί + δῆμος people.] An epidemic disease –1809.

Epidendral (epide·ndrăl), *a.* 1882. [f. EPI- + Gr. δένδρον + -AL.] *Bot.* That grows upon trees. So **Epide·ndric** *a.*

Epiderm (e·pidɜːm). 1835. [ad. F. *épiderme*.] = EPIDERMIS. Hence **Epide·rmal** *a.* of or pertaining to the epidermis.

†‖**Epide·rma.** 1582. [mod.L. *epiderma*.] = EPIDERMIS.

Epidermatoid (epidɜ·ımătoid), *a.* [f. as next + -OID.] Resembling an epidermis. (Dicts.)

Epidermatous (epidɜ·ımătəs), *a.* [f. EPI- + Gr. δέρμα (δερματ-) + -OUS.] Pertaining to the epidermis.

Epide·rmic 1830, †**-ical** 1693, *adjs.* [f. EPIDERM + -IC, -ICAL.] Of, pertaining to, or of the nature of an epidermis. **-ically** *adv.*

Epidermis (epidɜ·ımis). 1626. [a. mod.L. *epidermis*, a. Gr., f. ἐπί + δέρμα.] **1.** *Anat.* The outer (non-vascular) layer of the skin; the cuticle or scarf-skin. **b.** = ECTODERM. (Huxley.) **2.** *Conch.* The outer animal integument of a shell 1755. **3.** *Bot.* 'The true skin of a plant below the cuticle' (*Treas. Bot.*) 1813.

Epidermoid (epidɜ·ımoid), *a.* 1835. [f. EPIDERM + -OID.] Of the nature of epidermis. So **E:pidermoi·dal** *a.*

Epide·rmose. 1847. [f. EPIDERM + -OSE.] *Chem.* The insoluble matter in the epidermis.

Epidiascope (epidəi·ăskōup). 1903. [f. EPI- + DIA-¹ + -SCOPE.] A kind of magic lantern for projecting images both of opaque and transparent objects. Hence **Epidiasco·pic** *a.*

Epidictic, obs. f. EPIDEICTIC.

Epididymis (epidi·dĭmis). 1610. [a. Gr. ἐπιδιδυμίς, f. ἐπί + δίδυμοι testicles.] *Anat.* A long narrow structure attached to the dorsal surface of the testicle, and consisting chiefly of coils of the efferent duct. Hence **Epidi·dymal** *a.* pertaining to the e. **E:pididymi·tis**, *Path.* inflammation of the e.

Epidi·orite. [f. EPI- + DIORITE.] *Min.* A mineral differing from diorite in that the hornblende it contains is fibrous.

Epidote (e·pidōut). 1808. [a. F. *épidote*, f. Gr. ἐπιδιδόναι to superadd, f. ἐπί + διδόναι.] *Min.* A mineral common in many crystalline rocks, consisting largely of the silicate of iron and lime. It usually takes the form of flattened needles, and has a yellowish-green (pistachio) colour. Hence **Epido·tic** *a.* **E:pidoti·ferous** *a.* containing e.

Epigæous, var. of EPIGEOUS.

†**Epiga·ster.** 1653. [ad. F. *épigastre*.] = EPIGASTRIUM.

Epigastric (epigæ·strik), *a.* 1656. [f. EPIGASTRIUM + -IC.] Of or pertaining to the epigastrium. So **Epiga·strial** *a.*

Epigastriocele (epigæ·striosīːl). [f. Gr. ἐπιγάστριος + κήλη tumour.] *Path.* An abdominal hernia near the epigastrium.

‖**Epigastrium** (epigæ·striɒ̆m). 1681. [mod.L., ad. Gr. ἐπιγάστριον, adj. neut., f. ἐπί + γαστήρ stomach.] *Anat.* That part of the abdomen which is immediately over the stomach' (*Syd. Soc. Lex.*).

Epigeal (epidʒī·ăl). = EPIGEOUS. (Dicts.)

Epigee (e·pidʒī). [ad. Gr. ἐπίγειον, adj. neut., f. ἐπί + γῆ.] = PERIGEE. (Dicts.)

Epigene (e·pidʒīn), *a.* 1823. [a. F. *épigène*, ad. Gr. ἐπιγενής, f. ἐπί upon, after + -γενής born.] **1.** *Crystall.* Of crystals: Chemically altered in substance subsequently to their formation (Haüy). By some used for *pseudomorphous*. **2.** *Geol.* Produced on the surface of the earth; opp. to *hypogene*. GEIKIE.

Epigenesis (epidʒe·nĭsis). 1807. [f. Gr. ἐπί upon + γένεσις.] *Biol.* The formation of an organic germ as a new product.

Phr. *Theory of e.*: the theory that the germ is brought into existence (by successive accretions), and not merely developed, in the process of reproduction. (The opposite theory is now spoken of variously as the theory of 'preformation', of 'encasement', or of 'emboîtement'.)

Hence **Epige·nesist**, one who holds the theory of e. **E:pigene·tic** *a.* of or pertaining to, or of the nature of, e. **Epigene·tically** *adv.*

Epigenist (ĭpi·dʒĭnist). 1875. [f. Gr. ἐπί + γεν- + -IST.] = EPIGENESIST.

Epigenous (ĭpi·dʒĭnəs), *a.* 1866. [f. as prec. + -OUS.] *Bot.* 'Growing upon the surface of a part, as many fungals on the surface of leaves' (*Treas. Bot.*).

Epigeous (epidʒī·əs), *a.* 1835. [f. Gr. ἐπίγειος (f. ἐπί + γῆ) + -OUS.] Of plants: Growing on the ground.

†**E·piglot.** 1547. Anglicized f. EPIGLOTTIS –1594.

Epiglottis (epiglɒ·tis). 1615. [a. Gr. ἐπιγλωττίς, f. ἐπί + γλῶττα (γλῶσσα) tongue.] 'The erect, leaf-like cartilage at the root of the tongue, which during the act of swallowing is depressed, and forms a lid, or cover for the glottis' (*Syd. Soc. Lex.*). Hence **Epiglo·ttic**, **E:piglotti·dean** *adjs.* of or pertaining to the e.

Epigone¹ (e·pigōun). *rare.* 1865. [In pl. a. F. *épigones*, ad. L. *epigoni* (also used), a. Gr. ἐπίγονοι, f. ἐπί + -γονος, root of γίγνεσθαι.] One of a succeeding (and less distinguished) generation. Applied *esp.* to the sons of the 'Seven against Thebes'; and hence allusively.

Epigone² (e·pigōun). 1866. [ad. mod.L. *epigonium*, f. Gr. ἐπί + γονή, γόνος seed.] *Bot.* The membranous bag which encloses the spore-case of a liverwort or scale-moss when young.

Epigram (e·pigræm). 1538. [ad. F. *épigramme*, ad. L. *epigramma*, Gr. ἐπίγραμμα, f. ἐπί + γράφειν.] †**1.** = EPIGRAPH 1. –1699. **2.** A short poem leading up to and ending in a witty or ingenious turn of thought 1538. **3.** A pointed or antithetical saying 1796. **b.** Epigrammatical expression (*mod.*).

1. The E., that was written upon the public Sepulchre at Athens BENTLEY. 2. The force and vertue of an e. is in the conclusion TOPSELL. 3. He [Bacon] liked .. to generalise in shrewd and sometimes cynical epigrams CHURCH.

†**E:pigrammata·rian.** 1597. [f. late L. *epigrammatarius*.] A writer of epigrams –1607.

Epigrammatic, -al (e:pigrămæ·tik, -ăl), *a.* 1605. [f. L. *epigrammat-*, Gr. ἐπιγραμματ-, stem of ἐπίγραμμα (see EPIGRAM) + -IC, + -AL.] Of or pertaining to epigrams; of the nature, or in the style, of an epigram; concise, pointed.

The sting is very e. H. WALPOLE. Smart e. speeches EMERSON. E. terseness BANCROFT. Hence **E:pigramma·tically** *adv.* So **Epigra·mmatism**, e. style. **Epigra·mmatist**, a maker of epigrams.

Epigrammatize (epigræ·mătəiz), *v.* 1691. [ad. Gr. ἐπιγραμματίζειν; see EPIGRAM.] **1.** *intr.* To compose epigrams; to write or speak in an epigrammatic style 1811. **2.** *trans.* To express epigrammatically 1691. **3.** To make the subject of an epigram 1862.

1. Men do not e. .. with the bitterness of Voltaire LIDDON. Hence **Epigra·mmatizer.**

‖**Epigramme** (epigram). 1736. [Fr.; app. a use of *épigramme* = EPIGRAM.] A small cutlet, dressed in a certain way.

Epigraph (e·pigrɑf). 1624. [ad. Gr. ἐπιγραφή, f. ἐπιγράφειν, f. ἐπί + γράφειν.] **1.** An inscription; *esp.* one placed upon a building, tomb, statue, etc., to indicate its name or purpose; a legend on a coin. †**2.** The superscription of a letter, book, etc.; the imprint on a title-page –1826. **3.** The short quotation or motto placed at the commencement of a book, a chapter, etc. 1844.

1. And this E., *Quid me Persequeris* EVELYN. 2. Geneva was adopted for the e. of the title-page 1812. Hence **E·pigraph** *v.* to furnish with an e. **Epigra·phic, -al** *a.* **Epigra·phically** *adv.*

Epigraphy (ĭpi·grăfi). 1851. [f. prec.; see -GRAPHY.] **1.** Inscriptions collectively. **2.** The science concerned with the interpretation, classification, etc. of inscriptions. Often, the palæography of inscriptions. 1863. Hence **Epi·grapher**, **Epi·graphist**, a student of, or authority on, inscriptions.

Epigynous (ĭpi·dʒinəs), *a.* 1830. [f. EPI- + *gyn-*, a. Gr. γυνή in sense 'female organ' + -OUS.] *Bot.* Placed upon the ovary; growing upon the summit of the ovary. Said of the stamens or corolla. Hence **Epi·gyny**, e. character or quality.

Epihyal (epihəi·ăl), *a.* 1854. [f. EPI- + HY(OID) + -AL.] *Anat.* That is placed upon the hyoid bone. Applied to the upper part of the hyoid arch; also, to a bone found in certain fishes.

†**E·piky.** 1508. [ad. Gr. ἐπιείκεια.] Reasonableness, equity –1549.

Epilate (e·pileit), *v.* 1886. [f. F. *épiler* (f. *é-* for *es-*, L. *ex* + *pilus* hair +) -ATE³.] *trans.* To pull out (hair). Hence **Epila·tion.**

†**E·pileny.** [ad. Gr. ἐπιλήνιον (μέλος), f. ἐπί + ληνός wine-vat.] A song in praise of wine; a drinking song. MOTTEUX.

Epilepsy (e·pilepsi). 1578. [a. OF. *epilepsie*, ad. L. *epilepsia*, a. Gr., f. ἐπιλαμβάνειν to take hold of.] *Path.* A disease of the nervous system, characterized by paroxysms, in which the patient falls to the ground unconscious, with general spasm of the muscles, and foaming at the mouth; the *falling sickness*. var. †**E·pilency**; whence †**Epile·ntic** *a.*

Epileptic (epile·ptik). 1605. [a. F. *épileptique*, ad. L. *epilepticus*, a. Gr., f. ἐπιλαμβάνειν; see prec.]

A. *adj.* **1.** Of, pertaining to, or of the nature of, epilepsy 1608. **2.** Affected with epilepsy 1605.

2. A plague vpon your Epilepticke visage SHAKS.

B. *sb.* **1.** An epileptic person 1651. **2.** In *pl.* Medicines for epilepsy. (Dicts.)

Hence **Epile·ptical** *a.* (in sense A. 1); also *fig.* **Epile·ptiform** *a.* resembling epilepsy. **Epile·ptoid** *a.* resembling, or of the nature of, epilepsy.

Epilobe (e·piloub). 1861. [ad. mod.L. *epilobium* (also used), f. Gr. ἐπί + λοβός lobe, pod, capsule; named with reference to the position of the corolla.] *Bot.* A plant of the genus *Epilobium* (N.O. *Onagraceæ*): *e.g.* the Willowherb.

†**Epi·logate**, *v.* 1652. [f. F. *épiloguer* + -ATE[3].] To speak the epilogue of (a play). Hence †**Epiloga·tion**, a final summing up.

†**Epilogism.** 1646. [ad. Gr. ἐπιλογισμός, f. ἐπιλογίζεσθαι to reckon over or in addition; also, to EPILOGIZE.] **1.** Computation; *concr.* number reckoned; also, excess in reckoning. **2.** Something said by way of epilogue 1671.

Epilogize (ĭpi·lŏdʒəiz), *v.* 1623. [ad. Gr. ἐπιλογίζεσθαι, f. ἐπίλογος EPILOGUE.] *intr.* To serve as an epilogue; also, to write or speak an epilogue. *trans.* To put an epilogue to.

Epilogue (e·pilǫg), *sb.* 1564. [a. F., ad. L. *epilogus*, a. Gr., f. ἐπί in addition + λόγος speech.] †**1.** *Rhet.* The peroration of a speech; a summary 1644. **2.** The concluding part of a literary work; an appendix 1564. **3.** A speech or short poem addressed to the spectators by one of the actors after a play is over. Also *transf.* and *fig.* 1590.

3. No E., I pray you; for your play needs no excuse SHAKS. Hence **Epilo·gic**, **-al** *a.* pertaining to, or like, an e. **Epi·logist**, the writer or speaker of an e. **E:pilogi·stic** *a.* of the nature of an e.

†**Epiloguize** (ĭpi·lŏgəiz), *v.* 1634. [f. EPILOGUE *sb.* + -IZE. Cf. EPILOGIZE.] *intr.* To deliver an epilogue, or speak as though delivering one. *trans.* To put an epilogue to. -1750.

Epi·macus. 1830. *Her.* = OPPINICUS, an imaginary beast resembling a griffin.

Epimeron (epimiᵊ·rǫn). *Pl.* **epimera.** 1872. [f. Gr. ἐπί + μηρός thigh.] *Anat.* That part of the lateral wall of a somite of a crustacean which is situated between the articulation of the appendage and the pleuron. Hence **Epime·ral** *a.* of or pertaining to the e.

Epimyth (e·pimiþ). 1866. [ad. Gr. ἐπιμύθιον.] The moral of a fable.

Epinasty (e·pinæsti). 1880. [f. EPI- + Gr. ναστός (f. νάσσειν to squeeze close) + -Y[3].] *Bot.* (See quot.)

The term e. ..implies that the upper surface of an organ grows more quickly than the lower surface, and thus causes it to bend down C. & F. DARWIN. Hence **Epina·stic** *a.* of the nature of, or influenced by, e.

Epineural (epiniūᵊ·răl), *a.* 1866. [f. EPI- + NEURAL.] *Anat.* Situated upon a neural arch, as a spine of a fish's backbone. Also quasi-*sb.*

‖**Epinglette.** [F., dim. of *épingle.*] 'An iron needle with which the cartridge of any large piece of ordnance is pierced before it is primed' (Stocqueler).

Epinician (epini·siăn), *a.* 1652. [f. next + -AN.] Celebrating victory. vars. †**Epini·cial**, **Epini·kian.**

Epinicion (epini·siǫn). Also **epinikion**, **epinicium.** 1613. [a. Gr. ἐπινίκιον, adj. neut., f. ἐπί + νίκη.] In Greece, an ode in honour of a victor in the games; also generally.

†‖**Epinyctis** (epini·ktis). 1676. [mod.L., a. Gr. ἐπινυκτίς, f. ἐπί + νύξ.] *Med.* A pustule which appears only at night.

Epiotic (epiǫ·tik), *a.* 1870. [f. Gr. ἐπί + οὖς, ὠτός ear + -IC.] *Anat.* Situated above the ear; epithet of one of the three bones which together form the periotic bone. Also quasi-*sb.*

†**E:pipedo·metry.** [f. Gr. ἐπίπεδος, in *Geom.* = plane, superficial + -μετρία.] Measurement of plane surfaces. Explained in Dicts. as 'The mensuration of figures standing on the same base'.

Epiperipheral (e:pipĕri·fĕrăl), *a.* [f. EPI- + PERIPHERY + -AL.] Of sensations: Externally initiated. H. SPENCER.

Epipetalous (epipe·tăləs), *a.* 1845. [f. EPI- + PETAL + -OUS.] *Bot.* Of stamens: 'United separately to the corolla' (Bentley).

Epiphanous (ĭpi·fănəs), *a.* [f. Gr. ἐπιφανής + -OUS; cf. next.] Resplendent. LAMB.

Epiphany[1] (ĭpi·făni). ME. [a. OF. *epiphanie*, ad. late L. *epiphania*, neut. pl., a. late Gr. ἐπιφάνια, adj. neut. pl., f. ἐπιφαίνειν, f. ἐπί + φαίνειν to show.] *Eccl.* The festival commemorating the manifestation of Christ to the Gentiles in the persons of the Magi; observed on Jan. 6th, the 12th day after Christmas.

Epiphany[2] (ĭpi·făni). 1667. [ad. Gr. ἐπιφάνεια manifestation (in N.T. applied to the 'appearing' of Christ), f. ἐπιφανής, related to ἐπιφαίνειν; see prec.] A manifestation or appearance of some divine or superhuman being. Also *transf.* and *fig.*

An e. of Vishnu F. HALL. Epiphanies of the Grecian intellect DE QUINCEY.

Epipharyngeal (e:pifări·ndʒĭăl), *a.* 1871. [f. Gr. ἐπί + φάρυγξ + -(E)AL.] Situated above the pharynx.

Epiphenomenon (e:pifĭnǫ·mĭnǫn). 1706. [f. EPI- + PHENOMENON.] *Path.* A secondary appearance or symptom.

‖**Epiphonema** (e:pifonī·mă). 1579. [L., a. Gr. ἐπιφώνημα, f. (ult.) ἐπί + φωνή voice.] **1** *Rhet.* An exclamatory sentence or striking reflection, which sums up or concludes a discourse or a passage. **2.** Acclamation 1654.

1. The e. to the daughters of Jerusalem 1870. Hence **E:pipho:nema·tical** *a.*, **-ly** *adv.* var. †**E:pipho·ne·me.**

‖**Epiphora** (epi·fŏră). 1657. [L., a. Gr. ἐπιφορά a bringing to or upon.] **1.** A sudden afflux of humours; *esp.* a flow of an aqueous or serous humour from the eyes. **2.** *Rhet.* A figure, in which one word is repeated impressively at the end of several sentences 1678. **3.** *Logic.* The conclusion of a syllogism or consequent of a hypothesis. (Dicts.)

Epiphragm (e·pifræm). 1854. [ad. mod.L. *epiphragma*, a. Gr., f. ἐπιφράσσειν to fence up.] **1.** *Zool.* The secretion with which a snail closes the aperture of its shell during hibernation. **2.** *Bot.* A membrane closing the mouth of the spore-case in urn-mosses and fungi 1882.

†**Epiphy:llospe·rmous**, *a.* 1704. [f. EPI- + Gr. φύλλον + σπέρμα + -OUS.] *Bot.* Having the seeds on the back of the leaves. Cf. DORSIFEROUS. -1760.

Epiphyllous (epifi·ləs), *a.* 1835. [f. EPI- + Gr. φύλλον + -OUS.] *Bot.* That grows upon a leaf, as *epiphyllous fungi.*

‖**Epiphysis** (epi·fĭsis). Also (in F. form) **epiphyse.** *Pl.* **epiphyses.** 1634. [a. Gr. ἐπίφυσις, f. ἐπί upon + φύσις growth.] *Anat.* **1.** An extremity or other portion of a long bone originating in a separate centre of ossification; opp. to APOPHYSIS. **2.** *abstr.* The process of developing such a growth 1862. Hence **Epi·physary**, **Epiphy·sial** *adjs.* pertaining to, or of the nature of, an e.

Epiphyte (e·pifəit). 1847. [f. Gr. ἐπί upon + φυτόν plant.] **1.** *Bot.* A plant which grows on another plant; usually restricted to those which do not derive nutrition from other plants 1861. **2.** *Path.* A vegetable parasite on the surface of the animal body 1847.

Hence **Epiphy·tal** *a.* having the distinctive property of an e. **Epiphy·tic**, **-al** *a.* epiphytal. **Epiphy·tically** *adv.* **Epi·phytous** *a.* epiphytal.

Epipleural (epipliūᵊ·răl), *a.* 1866. [f. Gr. ἐπίπλευρος + -AL.] Situated upon a rib. Also quasi-*sb.*

‖**Epiplexis** (epiple·ksis). 1678. [L., a. Gr. ἐπίπληξις, f. ἐπί upon + πλήσσειν to strike.] *Rhet.* A figure of rhetoric which endeavours to convince by a kind of upbraiding. Hence †**Epiple·ctic** *a.* of the nature of e.

‖**Epiploce** (epi·plŏsī). 1678. [mod.L., a. Gr. ἐπιπλοκή plaiting together.] *Rhet.* A figure by which one striking circumstance is added, in due gradation, to another. (Dicts.)

Epiplocele (epi·plosīl). 1721. [ad. Gr. ἐπιπλοκήλη, f. ἐπίπλοον + κήλη rupture.] *Path.* A hernia in which a part of the omentum is protruded.

Epiploön (epi·plŏǫn). 1541. [mod.L., a. Gr., f. ἐπιπλέειν to sail or float on.] The caul or omentum, a fatty membrane enwrapping the intestines. Hence **Epiplo·ic** *a.* of or pertaining to the e.

Epipodial (epipōᵘ·diăl), *a.* 1877. [f. EPIPODIUM + -AL.] Pertaining to or like the epipodium.

Epipodite (epi·pŏdəit). 1869. [f. next + -ITE.] *Anat.* A long, curved appendage to the basal joint of the anterior limbs of some Crustacea. Hence **Epi:podi·tic** *a.* like an e.

Epipodium (epipōᵘ·diǒm). *Pl.* **-a.** 1866. [mod.L., ad. Gr. ἐπιπόδιον, adj. neut., f. ἐπί + πούς.] **1.** *Zool.* A lobe developed from the lateral and upper surfaces of the foot of some molluscs 1877. **2.** *Bot.* A form of disk consisting of glands upon the stipe of an ovary; also, the stalk of the disk.

Epipolic (epipǫ·lik), *a.* 1845. [f. Gr. ἐπιπολή surface + -IC.] *Physics.* **a.** Of, pertaining to, or taking place upon the surface. **b.** Of or pertaining to epipolism. Hence **Epi·polism**, e. dispersion; = FLUORESCENCE. **Epi·polize** *v.* to change into the e. condition; to cause to exhibit the phenomena of fluorescence.

Epipterous (ĭpi·ptĕrəs), *a.* 1866. [f. Gr. ἐπί + πτερόν + -OUS.] *Bot.* Of seeds: Bearing wings at the summit.

Epirhizous (epirəi·zəs), *a.* 1866. [f. Gr. ἐπί + ῥίζα + -OUS.] *Bot.* Growing on a root.

†**Epi·rot.** [ad. Gr. ἠπειρώτης, f. ἤπειρος mainland.] One who dwells inland. JER. TAYLOR.

Episcleral (episklīᵊ·răl), *a.* 1861. [f. EPI- + Gr. σκληρός hard + -AL.] *Anat.* Belonging to or placed upon the sclerotic coat of the eye.

Episcleritis (e:pisklīᵊrəi·tis). 1861. [f. as prec. + -ITIS.] Inflammation of the connective tissue covering the sclerotic coat of the eye.

Episcopable (ĭpi·skŏpăb'l), *a.* 1676. [f. L. *episcopus* + -ABLE.] Capable of being made a bishop.

Episcopacy (ĭpi·skŏpăsi). 1647. [f. late L. *episcopatus*; see EPISCOPAL + -ACY.] †**1.** Supervision 1659. **2.** Government of the church by bishops; the system of church government which comprises three distinct orders, bishops, priests, and deacons 1647. **3.** The office, or period of tenure, of a bishop. Now *rare.* 1660. **4.** *concr.* The body of bishops 1757.

3. Aldhelm died..in the fifth year of his e. LINGARD. 4. An aggressive e. 1885.

Episcopal (ĭpi·skŏpăl). 1485. [a. F., ad. late L. *episcopalis*, f. *episcopus* BISHOP.]

A. *adj.* **1.** Of or pertaining to a bishop or bishops, or to episcopacy; †advocating episcopacy. **2.** Of a church: Governed by bishops. Often *spec.* (with capital E) of the Anglican Church; also of other bodies, specialized as *Methodist E.*, *Reformed E.*, etc. Hence of buildings: Belonging to such a church. 1752.

1. An E. See 1675. E. government 1704. 2. The established clergy were e. HUME. The e. chapel 1806.

†**B.** *sb.* = EPISCOPALIAN -1823.

Hence **Epi·scopally** *adv.*

Episcopalian (ĭpi:skopē·liăn). 1738. [f. late L. *episcopalis*; see prec.]

A. *adj.* **1.** Belonging to an episcopal (*esp.* the Anglican) church 1768. **2.** Of an episcopal character (*rare*) 1822.

B. *sb.* **a.** An adherent of episcopacy. **b.** One who belongs to an episcopal church. 1738.

Hence **Episcopa·lianism**, the principles of an E. as such.

Episcopalism (ĭpi·skŏpăli:zm). [f. EPISCOPAL + -ISM.] That theory of church polity which places the supreme authority in the hands of an episcopal or pastoral order, and regards any recognized head of the church who exercises this authority as merely the delegate of this order. Held in the Church of Rome by the Gallicans, but rejected by the Vatican Council in 1870.

†**Epi·scopant.** [ad. med.L. *episcopantem.*] A bishop. MILTON.

†**Episcopa·rian.** 1649. [f. L. *episcopus* + *-arius* + -AN.]
 A. *adj.* Of or pertaining to episcopacy -1691.
 B. *sb.* An adherent of episcopacy -1691.

Episcopate (ĭpi·skŏpět), *sb.* 1641. [ad. L. *episcopatus.*] 1. The office or dignity of a bishop. 2. An episcopal see 1807. 3. The time a bishop holds office 1868. 4. The body of bishops 1842.

†**Epi·scopate,** *v.* 1641. [f. ppl. stem of med. L. *episcopare*, f. *episcopus.*] To make, or become, a bishop; also, to act as a bishop -1705.

†**Epi·scopici·de.** *rare.* 1692. [f. L. *episcopus* + -(I)CIDE 2.] The murdering of a bishop -1751.

Episcopize (ĭpi·skŏpəiz), *v.* 1649. [f. as prec. + -IZE.] 1. *trans.* To make or consecrate (a person) a bishop. Also *absol.* 2. To rule as a bishop; also *intr.* 1679. 3. To render Episcopalian 1767. **Epi·scopiza·tion** (*rare*).

Episcopy (ĭpi·skŏpi). 1641. [ad. Gr. ἐπισκοπία, f. ἐπίσκοπος overseer.] †1. Survey; superintendence. MILTON. †2. Government of the church by bishops. JER. TAYLOR. 3. The bench of bishops 1874.

Epise·palous, *a.* 1882. [f. EPI- + SEPAL + -OUS.] *Bot.* Growing upon the sepals.

Episiorrhaphy (e:pisəi,ǫ·răfi). 1872. [f. Gr. ἐπίσειον the region of the pubes + -ραφία, f. ῥάπτειν to sew.] *Surg.* An operation for the relief of prolapsus uteri by a suture.

Episkeletal (episke·lĭtăl), *a.* 1871. [f. EPI- + SKELETON + -AL.] *Anat.* Of muscles: Situated upon the skeleton, *i.e.* epaxial.

Episodal (e·pisōᵘdăl), *a.* 1876. [f. next + -AL.] = EPISODIC.

Episode (e·pisōᵘd). 1678. [a. Gr. ἐπεισόδιον, adj. neut., f. ἐπί in addition + εἴσοδος entering, f. εἰς into + ὁδός way. Cf. Fr. *épisode.*] 1. In the Old Greek Tragedy, the interlocutory parts interpolated between two choric songs. 2. An incidental narrative or digression in a poem, story, etc., separable from, but arising naturally out of, the main subject 1679. 3. *transf.* An incidental passage in a person's life, in a history, etc. 1773. 4. *Mus.* In ordinary fugues, a certain number of bars allowed to intervene from time to time before the subject is resumed 1869.

3. Like the Glacial e. before mentioned LYELL. Hence **Episo·dial, Episo·dic** *adjs.* of, pertaining to, or of the nature of an e.; incidental; casual. **Episo·dical** *a.* **Episo·dically** *adv.* by way of e.

Epispastic (epispæ·stik). 1657. [ad. mod.L., a. Gr. ἐπισπαστικός, f. (ult.) ἐπί towards + σπάειν to draw.]
 A. *adj.* Drawing out humours; blistering.
 B. *sb.* A blister; a substance used for blistering 1675.

Episperm (e·pispɔ̄ɪm). [f. EPI- + Gr. σπέρμα.] *Bot.* The outer covering of a seed.

Epispore (e·pispōᵊɪ). 1835. [f. EPI- + SPORE.] *Bot.* The outer membrane on the spore of a lichen or fern.

‖**Epistaxis** (epistæ·ksis). 1793. [mod.L., a. Gr., f. ἐπιστάζειν, f. ἐπί + στάζειν to let fall in drops.] Bleeding from the nose.

Epistemology (e:pistīmǫ·lŏdʒi). 1856. [f. Gr. ἐπιστημο-, comb. f. ἐπιστήμη + -λογία; see -LOGY.] The theory or science of the method or grounds of knowledge. Hence **E:pistemolo·gical** *a.*

†**E:pistemo·nical,** *a.* [f. Gr. ἐπιστημονικός + -AL.] ?Capable of becoming an object of knowledge. CUDWORTH.

Episternum (epistɔ̄·ɪnɒ̆m). 1855. [f. EPI- + STERNUM.] *Anat.* In mammals, the upper part of the sternum or breast-bone; in other animals, applied to various structures adjoining the breast. Hence **Episte·rnal** *a.* situate upon the sternum; also, pertaining to the e.; of the nature of an e.

‖**Epistho·tonos.** 1811. [Erron. formation, after OPISTHOTONOS.] = EMPROSTHOTONOS.

Epistilbite (e:pisti·lbəit). 1826. [f. EPI- + STILBITE.] *Min.* A zeolitic mineral, a hydrous silicate of aluminium, calcium, and sodium.

Epistle (ĭpi·s'l), *sb.* OE. [a. OF. *epistle, epistole* (mod.F. *épître*), ad. L. *epistola*, a. Gr. ἐπιστολή, f. ἐπιστέλλειν, f. ἐπί on the occasion of + στέλλειν to send.] 1. A communication made to an absent person in writing; a letter. Chiefly applied to those letters written in ancient times which rank as literature. Now used only rhetorically, playfully, or sarcastically. 2. *spec.* A letter from an apostle, forming part of the canon of Scripture ME. 3. *Eccl.* *The Epistle*: The extract from an apostolical Epistle read in the Communion Service ME.

1. What seyth also the epistelle of Ouyde CHAUCER. Some obscure Epistles of Loue *Twel. N.* II. iii. 169. *Comb.* **e.-side** (of the altar), the south side, from which the e. is read. Hence **Epi·stle** *v. trans.* to write as a preface (*rare*); †to write a letter to; to write in a letter. **Epi·stler,** one who writes an e.; also, = EPISTOLER 2.

†**Epistolar** (ĭpi·stŏlăɪ), *a.* 1579. [ad. L. *epistolaris.*] = EPISTOLARY -1715.

Epistolary (ĭpi·stŏlări), *a.* 1656. [ad. F. *épistolaire*, ad. L. *epistolaris.*] 1. Of or pertaining to letters or letter-writing. 2. Contained in, or carried on by, letters; of the nature of letters 1706.

1. I seek no e. fame SWIFT. 2. Intercourse, personal and e. T. JEFFERSON. Hence **Epi·stola·rian** *a.* given to or occupied in letter-writing; *sb.* a letter-writer. var. **Epi·stolatory** *a.* (*arch.*)

Epistole·an. A writer of epistles or letters. MRS. C. CLARKE.

Epistoler (ĭpi·stŏləɪ). 1530. [ad. F. *épistolier*, ad. L. *epistolaris.*] 1. A letter-writer 1637. 2. *Eccl.* One who reads the epistle.

Epi·stolet. [f. L. *epistola* + -ET.] A small epistle. LAMB.

†**Episto·lic,** *a.* 1741. [a. Gr. ἐπιστολικός, f. ἐπιστολή; see EPISTLE.] a. = EPISTOLOGRAPHIC. b. = EPISTOLARY.
 Hence †**Episto·lical** *a.* (in sense b).

†**Epi·stolist.** 1743. [f. L. *epistola* + -IST.] One who writes epistles -1853.

Epistolize (ĭpi·stŏləiz), *v.* 1634. [f. as prec. + -IZE.] 1. *intr.* To write a letter. 2. *trans.* To write a letter to 1739.
 Hence **Epi·stolizable** *a.* that may form the subject of a letter. **Epi·stoliza·tion,** the writing of letters. **Epi·stolizer.**

Epistolographic (ĭpi·stŏlogræ·fik), *a.* 1699. [ad. Gr. ἐπιστολογραφικός, f. ἐπιστολή + γράφειν.] Used in the writing of letters; = DEMOTIC, ENCHORIAL, q.v. So **Epi·stolo·grapher, Epi·stolo·graphist,** a writer of letters. **Epi·stolo·graphy,** letter-writing.

Epistom(e (e·pistǫm, e·pistōᵘm). 1852. [ad. mod.L. *epistoma*, f. Gr. ἐπί + στόμα.] *Zool.* An appendage in front of the mouth in Crustacea and certain insects.

‖**Epistrophe** (epi·strŏfī). 1647. [mod.L., a. Gr., f. ἐπί + στροφή, f. στρέφειν to turn.] *Rhet.* A figure in which each sentence or clause ends with the same word.

E. ..as 'we are born to sorrow, pass our time in sorrow, end our days in sorrow' 1845.

Epistyle (e·pistəil). 1615. [ad. L. *epistylium*, a. Gr. ἐπιστύλιον, f. ἐπί + στῦλος a pillar.] *Arch.* = ARCHITRAVE.

Episyllogism (episi·lŏdʒiz'm). 1860. [ad. mod.L. *episyllogismus*; see EPI- and SYLLOGISM.] *Logic.* A syllogism the major premiss of which is proved by a preceding syllogism, called in this relation the *prosyllogism*.

Epitactic (epitæ·ktik), *a.* 1845. [ad. Gr. ἐπιτακτικός, f. ἐπιτάσσειν to enjoin.] Of the nature of an injunction.

Epitaph (e·pitaf), *sb.* ME. [ad. L. *epitaphium*, a. Gr. ἐπιτάφιον, adj. neut., f. ἐπί + τάφος tomb. Cf. F. *épitaphe.*] An inscription upon a tomb. Hence, occas., a brief composition written on the occasion of a person's death. Also *transf.* and *fig.*

Such a epitaphie as shall be devised by me or my executours 1520. A Booke of Epitaphes made upon the Death of Sir William Buttes 1583 (*title*).

Epitaph (e·pitaf), *v.* 1592. [f. prec. sb.] 1. *trans.* To describe in an epitaph (with *compl.*); to furnish with an epitaph. †2. *intr.* To speak or write as in an epitaph -1661.

1. Epitaph'd an honest man 1818. 2. The commons .. e. vpon him as on that Pope, 'He lived as a wolfe, and died as a dogge' BP. HALL. Hence **E·pita·pher,** the writer of an e.

Epitaphial (epitæ·fiăl), *a. rare.* 1862. [f. Gr. ἐπιτάφιος + -AL.] Contained in sepulchral inscriptions.

The e. assertions of heathens LOWELL. So **Epita·phian** *a.* (MILTON), **Epita·phic, -al** *adjs.* pertaining to, or of the nature of, an epitaph. **E·pitaphist,** a writer of epitaphs.

‖**Epitasis** (epi·tăsis). 1589. [mod.L., a. Gr., f. ἐπιτείνειν to intensify, f. ἐπί + τείνειν.] 'That part of a play where the plot thickens' (Liddell and Scott). Hence †**Epita·tical** *a.* intensive (*rare*). †**Epita·tically** *adv.*

‖**Epithalamium** (e:piþălē̆·miɒ̆m). Pl. **-iums, -ia.** 1595. [L., a. Gr. ἐπιθαλάμιον, adj. neut., f. ἐπί + θάλαμος bride chamber.] A nuptial song or poem in praise of the bride and bridegroom.

To sing Epithalamions to our marriage Feasts 1653. Hence **E:pithala·mial** *a.* of the nature of an e. **Epithala·miast** *rare*, a writer of an e. **E:pithala·mic** *a.* of or pertaining to an e. var. †**Epitha·lamy.**

‖**Epitheca** (epiþī·kă). 1861. [L., a. Gr. ἐπιθήκη, f. ἐπί + θήκη case.] *Zool.* A continuous layer surrounding the thecæ in some corals. Hence **Epithe·cal** *a.* of, or pertaining to, an e. **Epithe·cate** *a.* provided with an e.

‖**Epithelioma** (epiþī:li,ōᵘ·mă). *Pl.* **-mata.** 1872. [mod.L., f. next.] *Path.* Epithelial cancer.

‖**Epithelium** (epiþī·liɒ̆m). 1748. [mod.L., f. Gr. ἐπί + θηλή teat.] 1. *Anat.* A non-vascular tissue forming the outer layer of the mucous membrane in animals. 2. *Bot.* An epidermis consisting of young thin-sided cells, filled with homogeneous transparent colourless sap. (*Treas. Bot.*) 1870.

Hence **Epithe·lial** *a.* of, pertaining to, or of the nature of, e. **Epithe·liate** *v.* to become covered with e., as a wound when beginning to heal. **Epithe·lioid** *a.* resembling e.

Epithem (e·piþĕm), *sb.* 1559. [ad. Gr. ἐπίθεμα, f. ἐπί + τιθέναι to put.] *Med.* 'Any kind of moist, or soft, external application' (*Syd. Soc. Lex.*). Hence †**E·pithem** *v.* to put an e. upon. †‖**E:pithema·tion,** a small plaster.

‖**Epithesis.** [Gr., f. as prec.] ?

And make his heart E. of sinne TOURNEUR.

Epithet (e·piþĕt), *sb.* 1579. [ad. L. *epitheton*, a. Gr. ἐπίθετον, adj. neut., f. ἐπί + τιθέναι to place. Cf. F. *épithète.*] 1. An adjective expressing some quality or attribute regarded as characteristic of a person or thing 1588. 2. A significant appellation 1579. †3. A term, phrase, expression. SHAKS.

1. Hollow, empty—is the e. justly bestowed on Fame GEO. ELIOT. 2. We..employ the French term ennui, for want of an equally appropriate e. in English SIR B. BRODIE. 3. *Oth.* I. i. 14. Hence **E·pithet** *v.* to apply an e. to; to term. **Epithe·tic, -al** *a.* †full of epithets; pertaining to, or of the nature of, an e.; -ly *adv.* **E·pitheti·ze** *v.* to apply an e. *to* (*rare*).

†‖**Epi·theton.** 1547. [late L., a. Gr.; see EPITHET *sb.*] 1. An attribute. HOOPER. 2. = EPITHET 1, 2. -1720.

†**E·pithyme.** 1585. [ad. L. *epithymon*, a. Gr., f. ἐπί + θύμον thyme.] *Bot.* The *Cuscuta Epithymum* or Dodder, a parasitic plant growing on thyme, etc. -1725.

Epithymetic (e:pi,þime·tik), *a.* Also **epithumetic.** 1631. [ad. Gr. ἐπιθυμητικός, f. ἐπιθυμεῖν to desire.] Connected with desire or appetite. So †**Epithyme·tical** *a.*

†**Epi·tomate,** *v.* 1702. [f. ppl. stem of L. *epitomare* to abridge; see EPITOME.] = EPITOMIZE. So **Epi·toma·tic** *a.* [badly f. EPITOME], pertaining to, or of the nature of, an epitome. **Epi·toma·tor,** one who epitomizes a larger work.

Epitome (ĭpi·tŏmi), *sb.* 1529. [a. L., a. Gr. ἐπιτομή, f. ἐπιτέμνειν, f. ἐπί upon + τέμνειν to cut.] 1. A brief statement of the chief points of a larger work; an abridgement, abstract. b. A summary of anything; a compendium 1621. 2. *transf.* A condensed record or representation in miniature 1593.

1. In general nothing is less attractive than an e. MACAULAY. b. To number his virtues is to give an e. of his life MRS. HUTCHINSON. 2. The world's epitomy, man 1666. Hence †**Epi·tome** *v.* to make an e. **Epito·mic, -al** *a.* of the nature of an e. **Epi·tomist,** one who writes an e.

Epitomize (ǐpi·tŏməiz), *v.* 1599. [f. EPITOME *sb.* + -IZE.] **1.** *trans.* To make an epitome of; to abridge; to summarize; to concentrate. **2.** To comprise in brief 1628. †**3.** To reduce to a smaller scale –1713.

1. To e. Hooker D'ISRAELI, a pamphlet 1868. To e. the evidence of Theism E. CONDER. 2. A Carpet, a Pan, and a Platter, epitomizes all their Furniture SIR T. HERBERT. Hence **Epi·tomi:zer.**

Epitonic (epitǫ·nik). 1879. [f. Gr. ἐπίτονος on the stretch.] Overstrained.

Epitrite (e·pitrəit). 1609. [ad. L. *epitritos* containing the unit and one third, a. Gr., f. ἐπί in addition + τρίτος the third.]

†**A.** *adj.* In the ratio of 4 to 3; *spec.* in ancient music.

B. *sb. Pros.* A foot consisting of three long syllables and one short one, and called first, second, third, or fourth epitrite, according as the short syllable stands first, second, third, or fourth 1678.

Epitrochoid (epitrǫ·koid). 1800. [f. Gr. ἐπί + τροχός wheel + -OID.] *Math.* The curve described by a point rigidly connected with the centre of a circle which rolls on the outside of another circle. Cf. EPICYCLOID. Hence **Epitrochoi·dal** *a.*

‖**Epitrope** (epi·trŏpī). 1657. [L., a. Gr., f. ἐπιτρέπειν to give up, yield.] *Rhet.* A figure by which permission is granted to an opponent, either seriously or ironically, to do what he proposes to do.

Epitympanic (e:pitimpæ·nik), *a.* 1849. [f. EPI- + Gr. τύμπανον drum + -IC.] *Anat.* Pertaining to or forming the uppermost subdivision of the tympanic pedicle which supports the mandible in fishes. Chiefly quasi-*sb.*

‖**Epizeuxis** (epiziū·ksis). 1589. [mod.L., a. Gr., f. ἐπί upon + ζευγνύναι to fasten.] *Rhet.* A figure by which a word is repeated with vehemence or emphasis.

‖**Epizoon** (epizōu·ǫ̆n). *Pl.* **-oa.** 1836. [mod. L., f. Gr. ἐπί + ζῷον.] *Zool.* A parasite that lives on the exterior of the body of another animal. Opp. to ENTOZOON.

Hence **Epizo·al, Epizo·an** *adjs.* of or pertaining to epizoa. **Epizo·ic** *a.* of or pertaining to epizoa; living upon animals; *sb.* an epizootic disease.

Epizootic (e:pizo,ǫ·tik). 1748. [ad. Fr. *épizootique*, f. *épizootie*, irreg. f. on Gr. ἐπί + ζῷον.]

A. *adj.* **1.** Of diseases: Temporarily prevalent among animals; opp. to *enzootic* 1865. †**2.** *Geol.* Containing animal remains, as *e. strata* –1840.

B. *sb.* An epizootic disease 1748.

Epizooty (epizōu·ŏti). 1781. [ad. F. *épizootie*; see prec.] An epizootic disease.

Epoch (e·pǫk, ī·pǫk). 1614. [ad. late L. *epocha* (also used), ad. Gr. ἐποχή stoppage, pause, fixed date, f. ἐπέχειν to hold, stop. Cf. F. *époque*, It. *epoca*.]

I. A point of time. **1.** *Chron.* The initial point assumed in a system of chronology, or in reckoning a series of years; *e. g.* the date of the birth of Christ; an ERA. Now *rare.* **2.** The beginning of a new era or distinctive period in the history of anything 1673. †**b.** The date of origin of anything –1824. **3.** A fixed point of time 1661. **4.** *Astron.* An arbitrarily fixed date for which the elements necessary for computing the place of a heavenly body are tabulated. Also, the heliocentric longitude of a planet at such a date. 1726.

1. In divers..ages, divers epochs of time were used USSHER. The Epocha of the Olympiads 1726. 2. Men that mark out Epocha's 1673. The epochs of our life EMERSON. b. The year 1629 is reckoned the epocha of long perukes E. NARES. 3. The precise e. on which they [the designs of the court] were to be executed BURKE. Up to the present e. SCRIVENER.

II. A period dated from an epoch in sense I. **1.** Later, a period of history defined by the prevalence of some particular state of things. 1628. **b.** A period in the life of an individual, or in the history of a process 1768. **c.** *Geol.* Any distinct portion of geological time 1802.

Two epochs of terrible civil discord STUBBS. The Addisonian e. 1883. b. Actions unsuitable to the e. of life DRAPER. c. The glacial e. TYNDALL. *Comb.* **e.-making** *a.* said chiefly of scientific discoveries or treatises. Hence **E·pochal** *a.* pertaining to, or of the nature of, an e.; e.-making. **E·pochism,** the practice of dividing time into epochs. **E·pochist,** †a philosopher of the Ephectic School; also, one who holds the days of creation in *Genesis* to be epochs.

Epode (e·pəud). 1598. [a. OF., ad. L. *epodos*, a. Gr. ἐπῳδός after-song.] **1. a.** A kind of lyric poem, invented by Archilochus, in which a long line is followed by a shorter one, of metres other than the elegiac; as, the *Epodes* of Horace. **b.** An incantation. **c.** A grave poem. **2.** The part of a lyric song which follows the strophe and antistrophe 1671. Hence **Epo·dic** *a.*

Epoist (e·po,ist). [badly f. Gr. ἔπος + -IST.] A writer of epic poetry. BROWNING.

Eponym (e·pŏnim). 1846. [ad. Gr. ἐπώνυμος, f. ἐπί upon + ὄνομα, Æol. ὄνυμα name.] **1.** One who gives, or is supposed to give, his name to a people, place, or institution. Also in L. form **eponymus. b.** *transf.* One whose name is a synonym of something 1873. **2.** *Assyriology.* A functionary who gave his name to his year of office. Cf. EPONYMOUS 2. Also *attrib.* 1864. **3.** [ad. Gr. ἐπώνυμον.] A distinguishing title 1863.

1. Pelops is the e. or name-giver of Peloponnesus GROTE. b. Charles [the Great]..had become, so to speak, an e. of Empire BRYCE.

Hence **Epony·mic** *a.* of or pertaining to an e.; that is an e. **Epo·nymism,** the practice of referring names of places or peoples to supposed prehistoric eponyms. **Epo·nymist** = EPONYM 1. **Epo·nymize** *v.* to serve as an e. to.

Eponymous (epǫ·niməs), *a.* 1846. [See prec.] **1.** That gives (his) name to anything. **2.** Giving his name to the year, as did the chief archon at Athens 1857.

1. The e. hero or protagonist of the play SWINBURNE.

Eponymy (epǫ·nimi). 1865. [ad. Gr. ἐπωνυμία; see EPONYM.] **1. a.** = EPONYMISM. **b.** Eponymic nomenclature. **2.** The year of office of an (Assyrian) eponym 1875.

Epopee (e·pŏpī). Now *rare.* 1697. [a. F. *épopée* (also used), ad. mod.L. *epopœia*; see next.] An epic poem; epic poetry. Also *transf.*

transf. A sort of historical e. GROTE.

Epopœia (epopī·iă). *arch.* 1749. [a. mod.L., a. Gr. ἐποποιΐα, f. (ult.) ἔπος (see EPOS) + -ποιος maker.] = EPOPEE. Hence **Epopœ·ist,** one who writes epic poetry.

Epopt (e·pǫpt). 1696. [ad. late L. *epopta*, ad. Gr. ἐπόπτης, f. ἐποπ- (f. ἐπί + root ὀπ- to see).] A beholder; in *Gr. Antiq.* one initiated into the Eleusinian mysteries. Also *transf.* Hence **Epo·ptic** *a.* of or pertaining to an e. var. **Epo·ptist.**

‖**Epos** (e·pǫs). 1835. [L., a. Gr. ἔπος, f. ἐπ- stem of εἰπεῖν.] **1. a.** *collect.* Early unwritten narrative poetry celebrating incidents of heroic tradition 1839. **b.** = EPIC B. 2. 1855. **c.** Epic poetry 1835. **2.** A series of events worthy of epic treatment 1848.

1. a. The ancient E. hardly survived. b. Every age .. expects a morn And claims an e. MRS. BROWNING. c. Almost rises into e. CARLYLE.

†**Epota·tion.** 1627. [f. L. *epotare.*] The drinking up or off –1677.

‖**Eprouvette** (epruve·t). 1781. [F., f. *éprouver* to try.] **1.** An apparatus for testing the strength of gunpowder. **2.** A spoon used in assaying metals 1874.

Epsom (e·psəm). 1770. **1.** *attrib.* and *Comb.*, as **E.-water,** the water of a mineral spring at Epsom in Surrey. **E.-salt** (*colloq.* **-salts**), orig. the salt (chiefly magnesium sulphate) obtained from Epsom-water; now magnesium sulphate however prepared. **2.** Short for Epsom-salt 1803. Hence **E·psomite,** native magnesium sulphate.

Epulary (e·piŭlări), *a.* 1678. [ad. L. *epularis*, f. *epulum.*] Of or pertaining to a feast or banquet.

Epulation (epiulē·ʃən). Now *rare.* 1542. [ad. L. *epulationem.*] The action of feasting.

‖**Epulis** (epiū·lis). 1859. [mod.L., a. Gr. ἐπουλίς, f. ἐπί + οὖλον gum.] *Path.* A tumour of the gums.

Epulotic (epiulǫ·tik). 1634. [ad. Gr. ἐπουλωτικός, f. (ult.) ἐπί + οὐλή scar.] *Med.*

A. *adj.* Having power to cicatrize 1761.

B. *sb.* in *pl.* Epulotic medicines or ointments.

Epurate (e·piŭrēit), *v. rare.* 1799. [f. F. *épurer* + -ATE 6.] *trans.* To purify (*lit.* and *fig.*). Hence **Epura·tion.**

Equability (īk-, ekwăbi·lĭti). 1531. [ad. L. *æquabilitas*, f. *æquabilis* EQUABLE.] **1.** The quality of being equable; freedom from fluctuation or variation. †**2.** Capability of being compared on equal terms –1817. †**3.** Well-balanced condition –1605.

1. Such an equabilitie of mind HOLINSHED. E. of the Sun's motion RAY, of the climate HOOKER.

Equable (ī·k-, e·kwăb'l), *a.* 1643. [ad. L. *æquabilis*, f. *æquare* to make uniform or equal, f. *æquus.*] **1.** Uniform, free from fluctuation or variation: said of motions, temperature, the feelings, etc. 1677. **2.** Free from inequalities; uniform throughout; equally proportioned 1692. †**3.** = EQUITABLE. Sir T. Browne.

1. An e. pulse 1799. E. climates MAURY. E. in style JOWETT. 2. A more e. system of taxation THIRLWALL. Hence **E·quableness** = EQUABILITY. **E·quably** *adv.*

Equæval (ĭkwī·văl), *a.* Also **equiæval.** 1867. [f. L. *æquævus* (f. *æquus* + *ævum*) + -AL.] Of equal age; belonging to the same period. So †**Equæ·vous** *a.*

Equal (ī·kwăl). ME. [ad. L. *æqualis*, f. *æquus* even, just.]

A. *adj.* **1.** Identical in amount, magnitude, number, value, intensity, etc.; neither less nor greater. **2.** Possessing a like degree of a quality or attribute; on the same level in dignity, power, excellence, etc.; having the same rights or privileges. Const. *to, with.* 1526. **3.** Adequate or fit in quantity or degree; adequately fit or qualified. Of persons: Having competent strength, endurance, or ability. Const. *to.* 1674. **4.** Evenly proportioned; uniform in effect or operation 1661. †**5.** [= L. *æquus.*] Fair, equitable, impartial –1769. **6.** Of surfaces: Level, on the same level (*arch.*) 1649. **7.** †Uniform throughout –1793; in *Bot.* symmetrical 1876. **8.** = EQUABLE 1. 1626. †**9.** Of numbers: Even (*rare*) 1806. †**10.** quasi-*adv.* Equally –1659.

1. Three hils, not in equall distaunce GRAFTON. Of equall height DIGBY. Of e. Profit DRYDEN. In nearly e. ratios 1846. 2. Equall in glory to the father 1526. He meant his children to be all e. CRUISE. Phr. *E. voices* (Mus.): voices either all male or all female. 3. To make my commendations e. to your merit DRYDEN. Phr. *E. to the occasion.* 4. The army dreaded his e. and inexorable justice GIBBON. E. laws 1836. Phr. †*It is e. to me* (*whether*): = 'it makes no difference'. 5. E. heauen hath denied that comfort GREENE. 6. The e. plains of fruitful Sicily MRS. BROWNING. 8. Try them by boiling upon an e. fire BACON. An even or e. trot 1761. In a firm and e. tone GIBBON. To keep an oath with an e. mind TENNYSON.

B. *sb.* **1.** One who is equal to another; as, in rank, in power or performance, or †in age 1573. **2.** abstr. *An e.*: a state of equality. Now *dial.* 1596.

1. A minister who never had his e. ..for wisdom and integrity 1792. 2. SPENSER *F. Q.* v. ii. 34.

Equal (ī·kwăl), *v.* 1586. [f. prec.; cf. F. *égaler.*] **1.** To make equal or level, to equalize 1594. †**2.** To represent as equal; to liken, compare –1805. **3.** *trans.* To be or become equal to; to come up to, match 1590. **4.** To produce or achieve something equal to. Also †*intr.* To cope on equal terms *with* (*rare*). 1597.

1. Cities .. equalled with the ground 1629. Those other two equal'd with me in Fate MILT. *P. L.* III. 33. 2. To e. robbery with murder JOHNSON. 3. The golde and the chrystall cannot equall it *Job* xxviii. 17. 4. To e. art with art W. BROOME. *intr.* A Body strong enough..to equall with the King 2 *Hen. IV*, I. iii. 67.

Equalist (ī·kwălist). *rare.* 1661. [f. EQUAL + -IST.] One who asserts the equality of certain (indicated) persons or things.

Equalitarian (ĭkwǫ:litē·riăn). 1799. [f. EQUALITY; cf. *humanitarian*, etc.]

A. *adj.* Of or pertaining to the doctrine of the equality of mankind.

B. *sb.* One who holds this doctrine.

Equality (ĭkwǫ·lĭti). ME. [a. OF. *équalité* (mod.F. *égalité*), ad. L. *æqualitatem*, f. *æqualis.*] **1.** The condition of being equal in quantity, amount, value, intensity, etc.; *esp.* in *Math.* exact correspondence between magnitudes and numbers in respect of quantity (sometimes expressed by the sign =) 1570. **2.** The condition of being equal in dignity, privileges, power, etc. with others ME. †3. Fairness, impartiality, equity; in things, proportionateness -1845. 4. Evenness, uniformity. Now *rare*. ME.

1. Pleading e. of years COWPER. 3. E. is of the essence of such taxes McCULLOCH. 4. E. of Motion 1664, temper 1762, wear HT. MARTINEAU.

Equalize (ī·kwălaiz), *v.* 1590. [f. EQUAL + -IZE.] †1. = EQUAL *v.* 3. -1826. †2. To represent as equal; to place on an equality -1751. 3. To make equal in magnitude or degree 1622. †4. To level -1653. 5. To render uniform 1822. 6. *intr. Football*, etc. To bring the score to an equality with the opponent's.

1. The Scythians..do e. the grass in multitude 1595. 2. The Virgin..they do at least equalize to Christ H. MORE. 3. Intending to e. it [Babel] with the Starres SIR T. HERBERT. Those who attempt to level, never e. BURKE. Office of itself does much to e. politicians MACAULAY. 5. To e. the motion of a machine IMISON. Hence **E:qualiza·tion. E·qualizer**, one who, or that which, makes equal.

E·qualler. *rare.* 1630. [f. EQUAL *v.*] One who, or that which, makes equal.

Equally (ī·kwăli), *adv.* ME. [f. EQUAL *a.*] 1. To an equal degree or extent. Const. *with*; occas. *as*. 1634. 2. In equal shares ME. 3. According to one and the same rule or measure; impartially, justly 1526. †4. On a level; uniformly; in a line *with* -1721. 5. In uniform degree or quantity 1664.

1. And e. of Fear and Forecast void DE FOE. 2. To her other sisters e. between them CRUISE. 3. To deal e between man and man HOBBES.

Equalness (ī·kwălnės). Now *rare*. 1530. [f. as prec. + -NESS.] 1. = EQUALITY 1, 2. †2. Fairness, equity -1556. †3. Evenness, uniformity -1799.

Equanimity (īkwăni·mĭti). 1607. [ad. L. *æquanimitas*, f. *æquanimis* having an even mind, f. *æquus* + *animus*.] †1. Fairness of judgement, impartiality -1752. 2. Evenness of mind or temper; the quality of being undisturbed by good or ill fortune 1663.

2. To bear odium with e. BURKE.

Equanimous (īkwæ·nimŏs), *a.* 1656. [f. L. *æquanimis* (see prec.) + -OUS.] 1. Even-tempered; not easily elated or depressed. †2. Impartial 1670. Hence **Equa·nimous·ly** *adv.*, **-ness**.

Equant (ī·kwănt). 1621. [ad. L. *æquantem*, pr. pple. of *æquare*.]

A. *adj.* That equalizes. *E. circle* [med.L. *circulus æquans*], in ancient astronomy, a circle imagined in order to reconcile the planetary movements with the hypothesis of the uniform velocity of celestial motion.

B. *sb.* = *E. circle*.

Equate (īkwē·t), *v.* ?ME. [f. L. *æquat-* ppl. stem, see prec.] †1. To make bodies equal; to balance (*rare*) -1755. 2. †To take the average of; in *Astr.* to reduce to an average 1633. 3. *Math.* To state the equality of; to put in the form of an equation 1799. 4. *transf.* and *fig.* To treat as equivalent 18..

2. To e. solar days, that is to convert apparent into mean time [etc.] 1751. 4. Boudicca might perhaps be equated.. with such a Latin name as Victorina J. RHYS.

Equation (īkwē·ʃən). ME. [ad. L. *æquationem.*] 1. The action of making equal or balancing; equilibrium, equality 1656. †*spec.* in *Astrol.* Equal partition. Only in ME. 2. *Astron.* Reduction to a normal value or position by making compensations for a known cause of irregularity or error. Chiefly *concr.* the quantity added or subtracted for this purpose. 1666. †3. *Math.* The act of stating the identity in value of two quantities or expressions -1673. 4. A formula affirming the equivalence of two quantitative expressions, connected by the sign =. Also *transf.* 1570.

1. Again the golden day resum'd its right, And ruled in just e. with the night ROWE. Phr. *E. of demand and supply, e. of trade*, etc. (*mod.*). 2. The difference between true and mean solar time..is called the e. of time MOSELEY. Phr. *Annual e.*: see ANNUAL. *E. of the centre*: the difference between the mean and the true anomaly of a heavenly body. *E. of the equinoxes*: the difference between the mean and the apparent places of the equinoxes. *E. of time*: the difference between the time shown by a clock (mean time) and that shown by a sundial. *Personal e.*: the correction required in astronomical observations in consequence of greater or less inaccuracy habitual to individual observers. Also *transf.* *E. of payments*: the process of finding a mean time for the payment in one amount of sums due at different times. 4. The two chief kinds of equations are: (1) Those which contain symbols denoting one or more unknown quantities.. (2) Those which indicate a constant relation between variables: as *E. to a curve*, an equation expressing a relation between coordinates or the like, which is constant for every point of the curve; *e. of motions*, etc. Equations are distinguished as *simple, quadratic, cubic*, etc. (or as of the 1st, 2nd, 3rd, etc. degree) according to the highest power which they contain of any unknown or variable. N.E.D. Phr. *To solve an e.*: to discover the numerical values of the symbols denoting unknown quantities.

Equational (īkwē·ʃənăl), *a.* 1864. [f. prec. + -AL.] Pertaining to, or involving the use of, equations. Hence **Equa·tionally** *adv.*

Equator (īkwē·toɹ, -əɹ). ME. [a. late L. *æquator* one who makes equal, hence (*circulus*) *æquator diei et noctis* 'the equalizer of day and night'.] 1. *Astron.* A great circle of the celestial sphere, whose plane is perpendicular to the axis of the earth. Called also the EQUINOCTIAL, q. v. 2. *Geog.* A great circle of the earth, in the plane of the celestial equator, and equidistant from the two poles 1612. Also *transf.* 1746.

2. *transf.* The solar e. LOCKYER. Phr. *Magnetic e.* = *Aclinic line* (see ACLINIC). *E. of the magnet*: the portion of the magnet midway between the two poles, which is apparently less magnetic.

Equatorial (īkwătō·riăl). 1664. [f. L. *æquator* (see prec.) + -(I)AL.]

A. *adj.* Of or pertaining to an equator, *esp.* the terrestrial equator.

Phr. *E. instrument* or *telescope*: a telescope attached by an arm to an axle revolving in a direction parallel to the plane of the equator. By a uniform motion given to this axle the telescope follows the diurnal apparent motion of any point in the heavens to which it is directed. *E. circle*: a graduated circle (also called *hour-circle, right-ascension-circle*) revolving in a plane parallel to the equator, forming part of the e. instrument.

B. *sb.* = *E. instrument*; see A. 1793.

Hence **Equato·rially** *adv.*

Equerry (e·kwĕri, īkwe·ri). Also *aphet.* †querry. 1526. [ad. F. *écurie*, earlier *escurie* (also *escuierie*, by assoc. with *escuyer* ESQUIRE), med.L. *scuria* stable, f. OHG. *scûr* shed, shelter. The stress (e·kweri) is favoured, and is due to an imagined connexion with L. *equus* horse.] †1. The stables of a royal or princely household, or the body of officers in charge of them -1731. 2. [Short for 'gentleman of the e.' or 'groom of the e.'] †a. A groom 1708. b. An officer charged with the care of the horses of a royal or exalted personage. At the English Court, an officer of the household, in occasional attendance on the sovereign. 1526.

Hence **E·querryship**, the position of an e.

Equestrial (īkwe·striăl), *a.* Now *rare*. 1553. [f. as next + -AL.] = next.

Equestrian (īkwe·striăn). 1656. [f. L. *equestris* (f. *eques*, f. *equus*) + -AN.]

A. *adj.* 1. Of or pertaining to horse-riding. Also, skilled in horse-riding. 2. Mounted on a horse. Also, representing a person so mounted. 1711. 3. *Rom. Antiq.* Of or pertaining to the order of *Equites* 1696.

1. Candidates for e. glory JOHNSON. 2. An e. lady appeared upon the plains 1711. The Antique E. Statue of Marcus Aurelius ADDISON.

B. *sb.* One who rides on horseback; also, one who publicly performs on horseback 1791.

Hence **Eque·striani:sm**, the art or practice of riding on horseback. So **Equestrie·nne**, a female e.

Equi- (ī·kwi-), repr. L. *æqui-*, comb. f. *æquus*, in sense 'equal', or (advb.) 'equally, in an equal degree'. Hence:

E:qui,anharmo·nic *a.*, *Math.* equally anharmonic: applied when two ranges, each of four points, are projective; **-ly** *adv.* **E:qui,arti·culate** *a.*, having equal joints with another. **Equiba·lance** *sb.* = EQUILIBRIUM. †**Equiba·lance** *v.*, to counterpoise. **Equicha·ngeable** *a.*, equally varying. **Equico·nvex** *a.*, having two convex surfaces with equal curves. **Equicre·scent** *a.*, having equal increments. **E:quidia·gonal** *a.*, having the diagonals equal. **E:quidiu·rnal** *a.* *nonce-word*, [tr. Gr. ἰσημερινός], pertaining to the time when days and nights are equal: applied to the equinoctial line. **Equigra·phic** *a.* = HOMOLOGRAPHIC. **Equilo·bate** *a.*, having equal lobes. **E:quimome·ntal** *a.* *Physics*, having equal moments of inertia about parallel axes. †**Equipe·nsate** *v.*, to weigh or esteem equally. **E:quiperio·dic** *a.*, having equal periods. **Equipro·babilism**, the doctrine of the equiprobabilists. **Equipro·babilist**, one of those who hold that of two opinions the less safe may be followed provided it be as probable, or nearly as probable, as the opposite. **Equira·dial** *a.*, having equal radii. **Equira·dical** *a.*, 'equally radical' (W.). **E:quisegme·ntal** *a.*, *Math.* having equal segments. **E:quitange·ntial** *a.*, having a tangent equal to a constant line; said of a certain curve. **Equiva·lue** *v.*, to make or be equal in value. **E·quivalved** *a.*, *Conch.* having both valves alike. †**E:quivelo·city**, equality in velocity. **Equivo·te** (*U.S.*), a tie in voting.

†**Equia·ngle.** 1570. [a. F., f. *équi-* EQUI- + *angle* ANGLE.]

A. *adj.* = EQUIANGULAR -1611.

B. *sb. pl.* Equal angles. *By equiangles*: at right angles. 1593. So †**Equia·ngled** *a*.

Equiangular (īkwi,æ·ŋgiŭlăɹ), *a.* 1660. [f. EQUI- + ANGULAR.] Having equal angles, as an *e.* figure, mutually *e.*

Phr. *E. spiral*, a name for the logarithmic spiral, in which the angle between the radius vector and the tangent is constant. Hence **E:quia:ngula·rity**, the condition or fact of being e.

Equiaxe (īkwi,æks), *a.* 1810. [a. F., f. L. *æqui-* + *axis*.] *Crystall.* Having equal axes. So **E·quiaxed** *a.*

Equicrural (ī:kwi,krūᵊ·răl), *a.* 1650. [f. L. *æquicrurus* (f. *æqui-* + *crus, cruris*) + -AL.] Having equal legs or sides; isosceles. var. †**E·quicrure.**

Equidifferent (īkwi,di·fĕrĕnt), *a.* 1695. [f. EQUI- + DIFFERENT.] Having equal differences; arithmetically proportional.

Equidistant (īkwi,di·stănt), *a.* 1570. [a. F., ad. late L. *æquidistantem*, f. *æqui-* (see EQUI-) + *distantem* standing apart.] 1. Separated by an equal distance. Also *fig.* 1593. 2. Of lines: Parallel.

Hence **Equidi·stantly** *adv.* at an equal distance.

Equiform (ī·kwifǫɹm), *a.* [ad. L. *æquiformis*, f. *æquus* + *forma*.] Having one and the same form. (Dicts.) So **Equifo·rmal** *a.* Hence †**Equifo·rmity**, uniformity. SIR T. BROWNE.

†**Equila·ter.** 1570. [ad. F. *équilatère*, ad. late L. *æquilaterus*, f. *æqui-* (see EQUI-) + *latus, lateris*.]

A. *adj.* Having equal sides -1715.

B. *sb.* A square or cube, or a square or cube number -1636.

Equilateral (īkwi,læ·tĕrăl), *a.* 1570. [ad. late L. *æquilateralis*, f. as prec. + -AL.] Having all the sides equal.

Phr. *E. arch*: an arch in which the chords of the sides form with the base an e. triangle. *E. hyperbola*, one whose axes are equal. *E. shell*, one in which a transverse line drawn through the apex of the umbo divides the valve into two equal and symmetrical parts. Hence **Equila·terally** *adv.*

Equilibrant (īkwi·librănt). 1883. [a. F. *équilibrant*, f. *équilibrer*.] *Physics.* 'Any system of forces which if applied to a rigid body, would balance a given system of forces acting on it' (Thomson & Tait).

Equilibrate (īkwi,ləi·brēɪt), *v.* 1635. [f. ppl. stem of late L. **æquilibrare*, f. *æqui-* (see EQUI-) + *libra* balance.] 1. *trans.* To bring into or keep in equipoise or equilibrium; to balance. 2. To counterpoise 1829. 3. *absol.* and *intr.* To be in a state of equilibrium; to balance. Const. *with*. 1829.

3. The forces neutralise each other and mutually e. 1830. So †**Equili·brate** *a.* equally balanced. **Equili·bratory** *a.* tending to produce equilibrium. var. **Equili·briate** *v.*

Equilibration (īkwi,ləibrē·ʃən). 1612. [f. as prec.; see -ATION.] The action of bringing into or keeping in equilibrium; the state of being in equilibrium. Const. *to, with*.

Drowsy equilibrations of undetermined counsel JOHNSON. var. †**Equili·bre.**

Equilibriate (īkwi,li·bri,ĕt), *a.* 1649. [f. EQUILIBRIUM + -AL.] = EQUILIBRATE.

Equilibrist (īkwi·librist, īkwi,li·-). 1760. [a. F. *équilibriste*, f. *équilibre*.] One skilled in feats of balancing; *esp.* a rope-dancer. Hence E·quilibri·stic *a.*

Equilibrity (ĭkwi₁li·briti). 1644. [ad. L. *æquilibritas.*] The state of being equally balanced; equilibrium.

Equilibrium (ĭkwi₁li·brĭŏm). 1608. [a. L. *æquilibrium*, f. *æquus* + *libra* balance.] **1.** *Physics.* The condition of equal balance between opposing forces; that state of a body in which the forces acting upon it are so arranged that their resultant at every point is zero. **2.** The state of balance between powers of any kind 1677. **b.** The condition of indecision or indifference produced by opposing influences of equal force 1685.

1. The Fluids, pressing equally and easily yielding to each other, soon restore the Æquilibrium 1697. 2. So to balance their [the Spaniard and the French] Power, as to keep both in an E. 1677. b. There is an end of the Doubt or Æquilibrium 1685.

Hence **Equili·brial** *a.* of or pertaining to e.; constructed on the principle of e. **Equili·brious** *a.* that is in a state of e. †**Equili·briously** *adv.* **Equi·librize** *v.* to bring to an e. var. **Equili·brio** [the L. ablative, treated as Eng.]

Equimultiple (ĭkwi₁mʊ·ltip'l). 1656. [ad. mod.L. *æquimultiplex*; see EQUI- and MULTIPLE.]

†**A.** *adj.* Produced by multiplying by the same number. HOBBES.

B. *sb.* One of a set of numbers or quantities which each have a common multiplier. Thus 14 and 28 are equimultiples of 2 and 4. Chiefly *pl.* 1660.

Equine (ĭ·kwəin), *a.* 1778. [ad.L. *equinus*, f. *equus.*] Of, pertaining to, or resembling a horse.

The mule is apt to forget all but the e. side of his pedigree LOWELL. So †**Equi·nal** *a.* Hence **Equi·nity.** LANDOR.

Equinoctial (ek-, ĭkwinǫ·kʃăl). ME. [ad. L. *æquinoctialis*, f. *æquinoctium* EQUINOX.]

A. *adj.* **1.** Pertaining to a state of equal day and night. **2.** Pertaining to the period or point of the equinox 1570; happening about the time of the equinox 1792. **3.** = EQUATORIAL; also, pertaining to the regions near the terrestrial equator 1594.

1. Phr. *E. line, circle* (*road* MILTON), the celestial or terrestrial equator. Cf. B. 1 and 2. *E. point* = EQUINOX 2. 2. Six houres, which is the one halfe of an Equinoctiall day BLUNDEVIL. The e. rains WELLINGTON, gales LIVINGSTONE. Phr. *E. colure*: see COLURE. *E. month*: a month which includes one of the equinoxes.

B. *sb.* **1.** The celestial equator: so called because, when the sun is on it, day and night are of equal length ME. **2.** The terrestrial equator. Now *rare.* 1584. Also *transf.* and *fig.* †**3.** = EQUINOX -1665. **4.** An equinoctial gale 1748.

2. As if, when you have crossed the e., all the virtues die BURKE. Hence **Equino·ctially** *adv.* in the direction of the e. or equator.

†‖**Equinoctium.** *rare.* Pl. **-ia, -iums.** ME. [L., f. *æquus* + *nox, noctis.*] Equinox -1688.

Equinox (ĭ·k-, e·kwinǫks). 1579. [ad. L. *æquinoctium* (in med.L. spelt *equinoxium*); see prec.] **1.** One of the two periods of the year when day and night are of equal length, owing to the sun's crossing the Equator. Hence, the time of this crossing, that is, the 20 March, and the 22 or 23 September. 1588. **b.** The condition of equality of day and night. Also *fig.* 1604. **2.** One of the two points at which the sun's path crosses the Equator, *viz.* the first points in Aries and Libra 1594. †**3.** = *Equinoctial line* or EQUATOR -1728. †**4.** An equinoctial gale (*rare*) DRYDEN.

1. Live long, nor feel..Our changeful equinoxes TENNYSON.

Equip (ĭkwi·p), *v.* 1523. [a. F. *équiper*, *esquiper*, prob. ad. ON. *skipa* to man (a vessel), fit up, arrange, ?f. *skip* = SHIP.] **1.** *trans.* To fit out (a ship) 1580. **2.** 'To furnish for service' (T.); to provide with what is requisite for action, as arms, instruments, or apparatus. Hence *fig.* Const. *with.* **b.** To finance 1690. **3.** To array; to dress, fit out (*for* a journey) 1695.

1. Equipping the ship for these two different voyages ANSON. 2. To e. Horses 1605, a man as a writer 1793, a new theory 1879. 3. It is Dr. Donne, equipped for the expedition to Cales H. WALPOLE.

Equipage (e·kwipĕdʒ), *sb.* 1579. [a. F. *équipage*, f. *équiper*; see EQUIP and -AGE.] †**1.** = EQUIPMENT -1684. **2.** Furniture, apparatus, or outfit, including all that is needed for an army, a ship, an establishment, a journey or expedition, etc. 1579. †**3.** Uniform, accoutrements -1818; costume, dress, 'get up' -1823. **4.** Articles for personal ornament or use; a case of these 1716. †**5.** Apparatus in general (*lit.* and *fig.*) -1734. †**6.** Formal state or order; ceremonious display -1756. †**7.** Train, retinue, following -1731. **8.** A carriage with or without horses and the attendant servants 1721. †**9.** The crew of a ship [tr. F. *équipage.*] (*rare*) -1751. †**10.** [as if f. L. *equi-.*] = EQUIPACE; also *fig.* -1655.

2. How war may..Move..In all her e. MILT. Our e. for the night 1858. Phr. *Breakfast-, tea-e.*: a breakfast-, tea-service (*arch.*). 7. The young Prince of Orange, with a splendid E. EVELYN. 8. Here..roll and rumble all kinds of equipages HAWTHORNE. 10. To march in e. with better wit W. BROWNE.

†**E·quipage**, *v.* 1590. [f. prec.] **1.** *trans.* To furnish with an equipage; to fit out -1784. **2.** To rank (*trans.* and *intr.*). HEYWOOD.

†**Equiparable**, *a.* 1611. [a. F., ad. L. *æquiparabilis*, f. *æquiparare*, f. (ult.) *æquus* + *par.*] Equal in comparison, equivalent -1695.

†**Equi·parate**, *a.* 1632. [f. L. *æquiparat-* ppl. stem; see prec.] To level; to treat as on the same level -1671.

Equiparation (ĭkwi·părē̆·ʃən). 1615. [ad. L. *æquiparationem*; see prec.] The action of placing on an equality; †the action of comparing; *concr.* a parallel.

Equipedal (ĭkwipĭ·dăl), *a.* [f. L. *æquipedus* + -AL.] Having equal feet; *Zool.* having the pairs of feet equal. (Dicts.)

Equipede (ĭ·kwipĭd). 1835. [f. L. *æquus* + *pes, pedis.*] *Zool.* Having legs of equal length. Also as *sb.* in *pl.*

†**Equipe·ndent**, *a.* 1640. [f. EQUI- + PENDENT.] Hanging in equipoise -1681. Hence †**Equipe·ndency.**

Equipment (ĭkwi·pmĕnt). 1717. [f. EQUIP *v.* + -MENT.] **1.** The action of equipping; the state of being equipped; the manner in which a person or thing is equipped 1748. **2.** *concr.* Anything used in equipping; furniture, outfit, warlike apparatus; necessaries for travelling, etc.; *fig.* intellectual outfit 1717.

1. The e. of an expedition 1809, of Arctic ships EMERSON. 2. The e. of a female archer STRUTT, of a soldier 1870, a railroad (*mod.*).

Equipoise (ĭ·kwipoiz), *sb.* 1658. [f. EQUI- + POISE *sb.*] **1.** Equality or equal distribution of weight; a condition of perfect balance or equilibrium; *esp.* in intellectual, moral, political, or social forces or interests. **2.** A counterpoise; an equivalent force. Chiefly *fig.* 1780.

1. To live in a continual e. of doubt JOHNSON. 2. The e. to the clergy [*i.e.* the aristocracy] being removed, the Church became so powerful BUCKLE.

Equipoise (ĭ·kwipoiz), *v.* 1647. [f. prec. sb.] **1.** *trans.* To serve as an equipoise to; to counterbalance 1664. **2.** To place or hold in equipoise 1764. †**3.** *intr.* To balance *with* 1647.

Equipollence (ĭkwi₁pǫ·lĕns). ME. [a. OF. *equipolence* (mod.F. *équipollence*), ad. L. *æquipollentia.*] **1.** Equality of force, power, or signification. **2.** *Logic.* An equivalence between two or more propositions ME. var. **Equipo·llency.**

Equipollent (ĭkwi₁pǫ·lĕnt). ME. [a. OF. *equipolent* (mod.F. *équipollent*), ad. L. *æquipollentem*, f. *æquus* + *pollentem*, pr. pple. of *pollere* to be strong.]

A. *adj.* **1.** Of equal power, weight, importance, or significance. *Obs.* of persons. **2.** Identical in meaning or result; equivalent; in *Logic*, said *esp.* of propositions expressing the same thing but differently 1577. Hence **Equipo·llently** *adv.*

1. A considerable and e. muscular force PALEY.

B. *sb.* Something that has equal power, weight, etc.; an equivalent 1611.

Equiponderance (ĭkwi₁pǫ·ndĕrăns). 1775. [f. next; see -ANCE.] Equality of weight; equilibrium. var **Equipo·nderancy.**

Equiponderant (ĭkwi₁pǫ·ndĕrănt). 1630. [ad. L. *æquiponderantem* pr. pple.; see next.]

A. *adj.* Of equal weight; evenly balanced.

The quantity of air to a quantity of water e. thereto, is as 1300 to 1 BOYLE. E. strife 'twixt Good and Evil 1882.

B. *sb. pl.* Things of equal weight 1852.

Equiponderate (ĭkwi₁pǫ·ndĕrē̆it), *v.* 1641. [f. ppl. stem of med.L. *æquiponderare*, f. *æquus* + *ponderare* to weigh.] †**1.** *intr.* To be in equipoise -1822. **2.** *trans.* To counterbalance 1661. **3.** To make well-balanced 1810.

2. Both e. (a pound, suppose) in air 1766. Hence †**Equipo·nderate, Equipo·nderated** *ppl. adjs.* **Equipo·nderation.**

†**Equipo·nderous**, *a.* 1656. [f. EQUI- + L. *pondus, ponderis* + -OUS.] Of equal weight or specific gravity; also *fig.* -1729.

†**Equipo·ndious**, *a.* [f. L. *æquipondium* (f. as prec.) + -OUS.] Of equal weight on both sides; nicely-balanced. GLANVILL.

Equi·potent, *a. rare.* 1875. [f. EQUI- + POTENT.] Of equal power.

Equipotential (ĭkwi₁pote·nʃăl), *a.* 1678. [f. EQUI- + POTENTIAL.] †**1.** Of equal authority. **2.** Having equality of potential 1880.

2. When a potential function exists, surfaces for which the potential is constant are called E. surfaces MAXWELL.

Equirotal (ĭkwi₁rōᵘ·tăl), *a.* 1839. [f. EQUI- + L. *rota* + -AL.] **1.** Having fore and hind wheels of equal diameter. **2.** 'Having equal rotation'. (Dicts.)

Equisetaceous (e:kwi₁sĭtē̆·ʃəs), *a.* 1867. [See EQUISETUM and -ACEOUS.] *Bot.* Belonging to the order *Equisetaceæ.*

Equisetic (ekwisĭ·tik), *a.* 1838. [f. EQUISETUM + -IC.] *Chem.* Derived from Equisetum. *E. acid* = ACONITIC acid.

Equisetum (ekwisĭ·tŏm). *Pl.* **-ums, -a.** 1830. [a. L. *equisetum* (prop. *equisætum*), f. *equus* + *sæta* bristle.] *Bot.* The typical genus of the N.O. *Equisetaceæ*; Horsetail. Hence **Equise·tiform** *a.* (Dicts.)

Equison. [ad. L. *equisonem*, f. *equus.*] A groom. LANDOR.

Equisonant (ĭkwisōᵘ·nănt), *a.* [f. EQUI- + SONANT, after L. *æquisonus.*] *Ancient Mus.* Consonant in the octave. Hence **Equiso·nance.**

Equitable (e·kwităb'l), *a.* 1646. [a. F., f. *équité* EQUITY.] **1.** Characterized by equity or fairness: now *rarely* of persons. **2.** Pertaining to the department of jurisprudence called EQUITY; valid in equity as dist. from law 1720.

1. E. Judges BURNET. In all literal and e. construction CROMWELL. Upon e. grounds 1654. 2. A trust estate..is good as an e. jointure CRUISE. Hence **E·quitableness. E·quitably** *adv.*

Equitant (e·kwitănt), *a.* 1830. [ad. L. *equitantem*, pr. pple. of *equitare* to ride, f. *equitem* horseman, f. *equus.*] *Bot.* Overriding: said of leaves which successively overlap each other according to age, as in the iris.

Equitation (ekwitē̆·ʃən). 1562. [ad. L. *equitationem.*] The action, art, or habit of riding on, or as on, horseback; horsemanship.

Broomsticks..the..instruments of their nocturnal e. LOWELL.

Equity (e·kwĭti). ME. [a. OF. *equité*, ad. L. *æquitatem*, f. *æquus* even, fair.] **1.** *gen.* The quality of being equal or fair; impartiality; even-handed dealing. **2.** That which is fair and right. *rarely* in *pl.* ME. **3.** *Jurisp.* The recourse to general principles of justice (= L. *naturalis æquitas*) to correct or supplement the ordinary law 1574. **4.** In England, Ireland, and U.S., a system of law existing side by side with the common and statute law (together called 'law' in a narrower sense), and superseding these, when they conflict with it 1591. Also *transf.* of analogous systems. **5.** An equitable right, *i.e.* one recognizable in a court of equity. Often in *pl.* 1626. **b.** The ordinary shares of a company as opposed to the preference shares 1904. **6.** *attrib.* 1832.

1. E. was my crowne *Job* xxix. 14. 2. To do equyte and justice CAXTON. 3. Chancellors..moderated the rigour of the law according .. to e. LD. ST. LEONARDS. 4. There are settled and inviolable rules of e., which require to be moderated by the rules of good conscience LD. ST. LEONARDS. In England, e. was formerly administered by a special class of tribunals, of which the Court of Chancery was chief; but since 1873 all the branches of the High Court administer both 'law' and 'equity', it being provided that where the two differ, the rules of e. are to be followed. N.E.D. 5. The wife's e. to a suitable provision for the maintenance of herself and her children KENT. Phr. *E. of redemption*: the right of a mort-

gagor who has in law forfeited his estate to redeem it within a reasonable time by payment of the principal and interest. *E. to a settlement*: a wife's equitable right to have settled upon her any properties coming to her after marriage. *Comb.* **e.-draftsman**, a barrister who draws pleadings in e.

†**E·quivale**, *v.* 1608. [ad. F. *équivaloir*, ad. late L. *æquivalere*.] *trans.* To be equivalent to; to provide an equivalent for -1695.

Equivalence (ĭkwi·vălĕns), *sb.* 1541. [a. F., ad. med.L. *æquivalentia*, f. *æquivalentem* EQUIVALENT.] 1. The condition of being equivalent; in *Physics*, equality of energy or effect. 2. *Chem.* The doctrine that differing fixed quantities of different substances are equivalent in chemical combinations 1880.

1. To reduce propositions to identity or e. LEWES. Phr. *E. of force*. the doctrine that force of one kind becomes transformed into force of another kind of the same value. Hence †**Equivalence** *v. nonce-wd.* to balance SIR T. BROWNE. **Equi·valency** [see -ENCY] = EQUIVALENCE; *Geol.* correspondence of strata in serial order and characteristics.

Equivalent (ĭkwi·vălĕnt). 1460. [ad. late L. *æquivalentem*, pr. pple. of *æquivalere*, f. *æquus* + *valere* to be worth.] **A.** *adj.* 1. Equal in value, power, efficacy, or import; having equal or corresponding significance. *Obs.* of persons. 2. Tantamount 1639. 3. Corresponding 1634. 4. *Chem.* Equal in combining value; having the same degree of quantivalence 1850. Also **Equi-valent** (ĭkwivē¹·lĕnt).

1. No Fair to thine E. or second MILT. *P. L.* IX. 609. To pay an e. penalty JAS. MILL. Here he makes a republic e. to a democracy LEWIS. 2. His presence..would be e. to an army of ten thousand men AUSTIN. 3. The Cadi, or some e. officer MORSE. Hence **Equi·valently** *adv.*

B. *sb.* 1. Something equal in value or worth; also, something tantamount 1502. 2. A word, expression, sign, etc. of equivalent import 1651. 3. a. *Chem.* = *e. proportion* (see quot. and A. 4) 1827. b. That which corresponds in relative position or function; as, (*Biol.*) analogous and homologous structures; (*Geol.*) a stratum or formation in one country answering to one in another 1839. c. Physics. *Mechanical e.*: the amount of mechanical effect resulting from the operation of a force. *Mechanical e. of heat*: taken as, the amount of mechanical energy required to raise 1 lb. of water through 1° C. 1842.

1. Belleisle alone .. was a sufficient e. for Minorca 1792. Phr. *The E.* (Eng. Hist.): the sum ordered, by the Act of Union of 1807, to be paid to Scotland as a set-off against additional excise-duties, loss on coinage, etc. 3. a. The term e. was subsequently introduced to indicate the proportional weights of analogous substances found to be of equal value in their chemical action WILLIAMSON.

Comb.: **e.-money** (see B. 1, quot.); **e. number** (*Chem.*) atomic weight.

Equivalue; see EQUI- *pref.*

†**Equi·vocacy**. *rare.* [f. L. *æquivocus* + -ACY.] Equivocal character. SIR T. BROWNE.

Equivocal (ĭkwi·vŏkăl). 1601. [f. late L. *æquivocus* ambiguous (f. *æquus* + *vocare*) + -AL.]

A. *adj.* †1. Equal or the same in name but not in reality; nominal -1744. 2. Having two or more significations equally appropriate; capable of double interpretation; ambiguous 1601. 3. Of uncertain nature; undecided (chiefly in neg. sentences) 1658. 4. Of persons, callings, etc.: Doubtful in character; questionable, suspicious 1790.

2. Without ambiguous or equiuocall tearmes FULBECKE. E. sentences SHAKS., answers 1756, proofs JUNIUS. 3. The sentiments of London were not e. BURKE. Phr. *E. generation*: the (supposed) production of plants or animals without parents; spontaneous generation. *E. chord* (Mus.): one which may be resolved into different keys without changing any of its tones. 4. A Churchman..whose sanctity was e. H. WALPOLE. An e. mode of life LYTTON.

Hence **Equi·voca·lity**, e. quality; an equivoque. **Equi·vocally** *adv.* **Equi·vocalness**, e. quality.

†**B.** *sb.* An equivocal word or term; a homonym -1734.

Equivocate (ĭkwi·vŏkeᶦt), *v.* 1590. [f. low L. *æquivocat-*, *æquivocare* to call by the same name, f. late L. *æquivocus*; see prec.] †1. *intr.* To have the same sound *with* 1611. †2. To use words of more than one sense; to deal in ambiguities -1686. 3. In bad sense: 'To mean one thing and express another' (J.); to prevaricate 1590. †4. *trans.* To evade (an oath, etc.) by equivocation -1649.

3. The witness shuffled, equivocated, pretended to misunderstand the questions MACAULAY. Hence **Equi·vocatingly** *adv.* **Equi·vocator**. **Equi·vocato·ry** *a.* indicating or containing equivocation.

Equivocation (ĭkwi:vokē¹·ʃən). ME. [ad. late L. *æquivocationem*; see prec.] †1. The using (a word) in more than one sense; ambiguity of meaning in words -1810. b. *Logic.* As = Gr. ὁμωνυμία: The fallacy of using the same term in different senses in a syllogism 1605. 2. The use of words or expressions susceptible of a double signification, in order to mislead. Also *concr.* 1605.

2. The Subtle difference.. Betwixt Æquivocation and a Lye 1634.

Equivoque, -voke (ī·kwi-, e·kwivoᵘk). ME. [ad. L. *æquivocus*; see EQUIVOCAL.]

†**A.** *adj.* = EQUIVOCAL -1650.

B. *sb.* †1. A thing which has the same name as something different -1660. 2. An expression capable of more meanings than one; word-play, punning 1614. 3. Ambiguity of speech. Also *transf.* 1809. 4. = EQUIVOCATION 2 (*rare*) 1616.

Equivorous (ĭkwi·vŏrəs), *a. rare.* 1828. [f. L. *equus* + *-vorus* + -OUS.] Feeding on horseflesh.

Er (ɔ̄ɹ). 1862. Representing the inarticulate murmur of a hesitant speaker.

-er¹, *suffix*, ME. *-er(e*, *-ar(e*, OE. *-ere*, forming sbs., represents WGer. *-ări* :—OTeut. *-ărjo-z*. The relation between OTeut. *-ărjo-z* and L. *-arius* is obscure.

1. In its original sense 'a man who has to do with', it designates persons according to their profession or occupation, as in *hatter*, *slater*, etc. Exceptions to this are *cottager*, *villager*, and the like; also *header*, *back-hander*, *fiver*, etc. In some other words, e. g. *Londoner*, *foreigner*, *southerner*, *-er* indicates place of origin or residence.

2. The suffix became also a formative of agent-nouns. These normally denote personal (*orig.* male) agents; but they may be things; e. g. *blotter*, *poker*, *roller*, etc.

3. In some words, chiefly of Fr. origin, *-er* appears to be a mere extension of earlier words in *-er* denoting trades or offices; e. g. *caterer*, *fruiterer*, etc.

4. The suffix *-er* is also used to form sbs. serving as adaptations of L. types in *-logus*, *-graphus*; e. g. *chronologer*, *biographer*, etc.

-er², *suffix*, of various origin, occurring in sbs. and adjs. adopted from OF.

1. ME. *-er*, repr. OF. *-er* :—L. *-arem*, *-ar*: see -AR, and *sampler*.

2. ME. *-er*, a. AF. *-er* (OF. *-ier*) in sbs. which descend from L. forms in *-arius*, *-arium* (see -ARY). The sense is 'a person or thing connected with', 'a receptacle for', as in *mariner*, *garner*, etc.

3. In mod. Eng. *-er* represents occas. other OF. suffixes, as OF. *-ëure* (:—L. *-aturam*), e. g. in *border*; OF. *-ëor*, now *-oir* (:—L. *-atorium*), e.g. in *laver*; and OF. nom. forms in *-ere* (:—L. *-a·tor*).

-er³, *suffix*, the formative of the comparative degree.

A. In *adjs.* ME. *-er*, *-ere* (*-ore*, *-ure*), *-re*, OE. *-ra* (fem., neut. *-re*) represents two different OTeut. suffixes; viz. *-izon-*, and *-ōzon-*, f. the adverbial *-iz*, *-ōz*; see B. In mod. Eng. the use of *-er* is almost restricted to words of one or two syllables.

B. In *adverbs*. The OE. form was *-or* :—OTeut. *-ōz*, ? f. *-ō* adverbial suffix + *-iz*, corresp. to L. *-is* in *magis*, *nimis*. The inflexional comparison still occurs in poetry, as in *keenlier* (Tennyson).

-er⁴, *suffix*, the ending of certain AF. infs. used as sbs.; e. g. *dinner*, *supper*; *user*, *waiver*.

-er⁵, *suffix*, forming frequent. and iterative vbs., e. g. *chatter*, *patter*, *scatter*.

-er⁶, *suffix*, in Oxford Univ. slang used in joc. formations, as *brekker* (f. *breakfast*), *footer* (f. *football*), SOCCER.

Era (ī³·ră). 1615. [a. late L. *æra* fem. sing. 'a number expressed in figures', prob. f. *æra* counters (for calculation), pl. of *æs* brass, money.] 1. A system of chronology, numbering years from some particular point of time 1646. 2. = EPOCH I. 1. 1615. 3. A date or an event, which begins a new period in the history of anything; an important date. Cf. EPOCH II. 2. 1703. 4. A period marked by the prevalence of some particular state of things 1741. b. = EPOCH II. b, c. 1796. 5. The approximate date of an event, etc. 1714.

1. Dionysius the Abbot.. brought in the Æra of Christ's Incarnation 1646. In the year 570 of our E. ..the man Mahomet was born CARLYLE. 2. Some three centuries before our e. HERSCHEL. 3. The landing of this English Governor was an e. in their lives DIXON. 4. The polished æra of Queen Anne H. WALPOLE. b. The worst e. of architecture 1870.

Eradiate (ĭrē¹·di,eᶦt), *v.* 1647. [f. L. *e* + RADIATE *v.*] 1. *intr.* To shoot forth, as rays of light. †2. *trans.* To give forth like or in rays -1794. Hence **Era:dia·tion**, the action of eradiating; also *concr.*

Eradicate (ĭræ·dikeᶦt), *v.* 1564. [f. L. *eradicat-*, *eradicare*, f. *e* + *radicem* root.] 1. *trans.* To pull or tear up by the roots; to root out. 2. To extirpate, get rid of 1647.

1. Okes eradicated By a prodigious whirlwind 1635. 2. In hopes of eradicating mendicancy LECKY. Hence **Era·dicable** *a.* **Era·dica·tion**, the action of eradicating; total destruction; extirpation. **Era·dicator**, one who or that which eradicates. **Era·dicatory** *a* tending to e.

Eradicative (ĭræ·dikătiv). 1543. [f. L. *eradicat-* ppl. stem (see prec.) + -IVE.]

A. *adj.* Tending or serving to root out or expel (disease, etc.). Const. *of*.

†**B.** *sb.* An eradicative medicine 1654.

Erase (ĭrē¹·z, -s), *v.* 1605. [f. L. *eras-*, *eradere*, f. *e* + *radere* to scrape. (Perh. occas. a var. of ARACE to uproot.)] 1. *trans.* To scrape or rub out; to efface, expunge. 2. *fig.* To obliterate from the mind or memory 1695. 3. *transf.* To destroy utterly 1728.

1. To e. a letter 1778, a mark 1858, an obnoxious protestation 1863. 2. To e. events from the memory SIR B. BRODIE. Hence **Era·sable** *a.* **Era·sement**. **Era·sion**, the action of erasing; an instance of it. **Era·sive** *a.* tending to e. (*rare*).

Erased (ĭrē¹·zd, -st), *ppl. a.* 1572. [f. prec.] 1. In senses of the vb. 1848. 2. *Her.* Of the head or other part of an animal: Represented with a jagged edge, as if torn off.

Eraser (ĭrē¹·zəɹ, -səɹ). [f. as prec.] One who, or that which, erases; anything used to erase writing, blots, etc.

Erasmian (ĭræ·zmiăn). 1758. [f. *Erasmus*, literary name of the eminent Dutch scholar (1466-1536) + -IAN.] **A.** *adj.* Pertaining to, or after the manner of, Erasmus 1881.

B. *sb.* A follower of Erasmus; *spec.* one who follows the system of pronunciation of ancient Greek advocated by him; opp. to *Reuchlinian*. Hence **Era·smianism**, the doctrines of Erasmus.

Erastian (ĭræ·stiăn). 1651. [f. *Erastus*, Swiss physician and theologian (1524-1583) + -IAN.]

A. *adj.* Of or pertaining to Erastus or his doctrines 1837.

B. *sb.* An adherent of the doctrines attributed to Erastus; one who maintains the theory of the supremacy of the State in ecclesiastical affairs.

Many most respectable persons have been .. Erastians GLADSTONE. Hence **Era·stianism**. **Era·stianize** *v.* to organize (a church) on, or incline to, E. principles.

Erasure (ĭrē¹·ʒiŭɹ). 1734. [f. as ERASE + -URE.] 1. The action of erasing, or an instance of it. 2. The place where a word or letter has been erased (*mod.*). 3. Total destruction 1794.

1. The devise to the trustees was not revoked by the e. 1817. 2. The word was written over an e. (*mod.*). 3. E. of cities GIBBON.

Erbia (ɔ̄·ɹbiă). 1869. [mod.L., f. (*Ytt*)*erby*, where gadolinite is found, in which it occurs.] *Chem.* One of the three earths formerly called YTTRIA.

Erbium (ɔ̄·ɹbiɒm). 1843. [mod.L., f. prec.; cf. *sodium* f. *soda*, etc.] The metallic radical of erbia.

Erce-, Erche-, obs. ff. ARCH-.

†**Erd**, *sb.* [OE. *eard* :—OTeut. **ardu-z*, *ardâ*, prob. f. WAryan **ar* to plough.] 1. Native land; a country -ME. 2. In OE.: ? State, condition. Hence (in ME.) disposition. So †**E·rde** *v.* to dwell; to be or be found; *trans.* to inhabit.

Erd(e, etc., obs. ff. EARTH, etc.

Ere (ē³ɹ). [OE. *ǽr* :—OTeut. **airiz*, compar. of **air* adv., early.]

A. *adv.* 1. Early. Now only *Sc.* †2. Earlier -1650. †3. Rather, in preference -1536. †4. Before, formerly; just now -1647.

2. He that commeth after me, was before me because he was yer than I TINDALE *John* i. 15. 4. He myght not do as he dyd are 1557.

B. *prep.* 1. Before (in time) OE. 2. In the advb. phrases *ere then*, *ere this*, etc., before then, before this. Also ERELONG, ERENOW, EREWHILE. OE.

1. E're that time CLARENDON.

C. *conj.* **1.** Of time: Before. Also with *ever.* OE. **2.** Rather than OE.

1. Syr, come downe e. my child die *John* iv. 49. This heart shal break..Or ere Ile weepe SHAKS.

†**D.** *adj.* Only in late OE. and ME. = 'early', 'former'.

Ere, var. of †EAR to plough.

Erebus (e·rĭbŏs). 1596. [a. L., a. Gr. Ἔρεβος; cf. Goth. *riqis* darkness.] *Myth.* Name of 'a place of darkness, between Earth and Hades' (Liddell and Scott); usu. in *dark as E.*

Erect (ĭre·kt), *a.* ME. [ad. L. *erectus*, pa. pple. of *erigere* to set up, f. *e* out, up + *regere* to make straight, rule.] **1.** Upright; not bending forward or downward; vertical. Also used *Bot.* and *Her.* in general sense. Also *fig.* **2.** Chiefly participial: †**a.** Of the face: Uplifted, unabashed. **b.** Of the hair, etc.: Rigid, bristling. 1618. †**3.** *fig.* Of the mind: Uplifted; alert –1756.

1. The e. or vertical diameter of the Luminary 1726. *fig.* A spirit as e. as the king's tiara THIRLWALL. Phr. *E. dial*: see DIAL. 2. Her front e. with majesty she bore DRYDEN. With Ears and Tail e., neighing he paws the ground SOMERVILLE. 3. It conduceth much to haue the Sense Intentiue and E. BACON. Hence **Ere·ct·ly** *adv.*, **-ness.**

Erect (ĭre·kt), *v.* ME. [f. L. *erect-* ppl. stem; see prec.]

I. †**1.** To direct upwards; to lift up –1696. †**2.** To raise in consideration; to exalt; elevate to office –1709.

1. E. your Heads, eternal Gates 1696. 2. We have seen..Monarchs erected and deposed STEELE.

II. 1. To raise, set upright; to prick up (the ears); also *Phys.* (chiefly in pass.) to render turgid and rigid any organ containing erectile tissue 1573. †**b.** *intr.* for *refl.* To straighten oneself BACON. †**2.** *fig.* To rouse, excite, embolden –1734.

1. Erecting one most like to fall TUSSER.

III. 1. To set up (a building, etc.); to build ME. Also *fig.* Also *absol.* **2.** *Geom.*, etc. To set up (a perpendicular, a figure of the heavens, etc.) 1646. **3.** To set up or found (an office, institution, etc.); to initiate (a project). *Obs.* or *arch.* exc. in *Law.* 1565.

1. To e. a statue SHAKS., a stove EVELYN, a House of Prayer DE FOE, an engine 1825. *fig.* Malebranche erects this proposition LOCKE (J.). 2. On B e. the perpendicular BA 1828. 3. Two Courts of High Commission were erected BUCKLE.

Phr. *To e. into* [cf. F. *ériger en*]: to form into, set up as; To e. the town into a staple for wool SCOTT. Hence **Ere·ctable** *a.* **Ere·cter**: see ERECTOR.

Erectile (ĭre·ktil), *a.* 1830. [a. F. *érectile*, f. as prec.] Capable of being erected or set upright.

E. tissue: a kind of tissue found in animals, capable of being distended and becoming rigid under excitement; also, a similar tissue in vegetables. Hence **Erecti·lity.**

Erection (ĭre·kʃən). 1503. [ad. late L. *erectionem*; cf. F. *érection.*] †**1.** A lifting up; also, an elevated condition –1692. †**2.** Advancement in condition; elevation to office –1661. **3.** A setting upright; an upright position 1622. **4.** *Phys.* The action of making rigid any organ containing erectile tissue; the condition of being so erected 1594. †**5.** Exaltation, excitement, invigoration –1651. **6.** The action of setting up (a building, column, etc.); *concr.* a building, structure. Also *fig.* 1609. †**7.** *Astrol.* The construction of a figure of the heavens. B. JONS. **8.** Constitution (of an office, institution, etc.). Also with *into.* 1508.

5. It must be a wonderful e. of their spirits, to know that God will be a father of those fatherless CLARENDON.

Ere·ctive, *a.* 1611. [See -IVE.] Tending to erect or set upright.

Erectopatent (ĭre·ktoˌpæ·tĕnt, -pē·tĕnt), *a.* 1848. [f. *erecto-* as comb. f. L. *erectus* + PATENT.] **a.** *Bot.* Having a position intermediate between erect and spreading. **b.** *Entom.* Having the primary wings at rest and the secondary horizontal.

Erector (ĭre·ktəɹ). Also **-er.** 1538. [f. ERECT *v.* + -OR.] **1.** One who, or that which, erects. †**2.** One who sets up a candidate or a pretender –1611. **3.** *Optics.* A tube with two lenses, slipped into the inner end of the draw-tube of a microscope, serving to erect the inverted image; an *erecting-glass* (*mod.*). **4.** A muscle which causes erection in any part. Also *attrib.* as in *erector-muscle.* 1831.

Erelong (ēəlǫ·ŋ), *adv.* Also as two wds. 1577. [f. ERE *prep.* + LONG *adv.*] Before the lapse of a long time; soon. Of future time; also (*arch.*) of past.

E. he had not only gotten pity but pardon 1586.

‖**Eremacausis** (e:rĭmăkǭ·sis). 1847. [mod.L., f. Gr. ἠρέμα quietly + καῦσις burning, f. καίειν.] *Chem.* 'A slow combustion taking place in presence of air and water, and accompanied by a kind of fermentation' (Watts).

Eremite (e·rĭmait). ME. [ad. late L. *eremita*, ad. eccl. Gr. ἐρημίτης, f. ἐρημία a desert, f. ἔρημος uninhabited. Orig. used indiscriminately with HERMIT, but now mainly poet. or rhet.] **1.** A recluse, an anchoret. Also *transf.* **2.** A (?quasi-religious) mendicant, a vagabond (see HERMIT) 1495.

1. Heremytis..þat flees þe felaghshipe of men HAMPOLE. *transf.* Who ledst this glorious E. (='desert-dweller') Into the Desert MILT. *P. R.* I. 8. Hence †**E·remitage**, the condition, or dwelling, of a hermit. **E·remiteship**, the condition of being a hermit. **E·remitism**, the state of a hermit. (Dicts.)

Eremitic, -al (erĭmi·tik, -ăl), *a.* 1483. [f. prec. + -AL.] Of or pertaining to an eremite; characteristic of or habitual to an eremite.

Affecting much an Eremiticall and solitarie life 1601. So **E·remitish** *a.* resembling, or befitting, an eremite.

Erenow (ēəˌnau·), *adv.* Also as two wds. ME. [See ERE and NOW.] Before this time.

Ereption (ĭre·pʃən). 1633. [ad. L. *ereptionem*, f. *eripere.*] The action of snatching away.

†**E·rer.** OE. [See ERE.]

A. *adj.* Former –ME.

B. *adv.* **1.** Formerly –ME. **2.** Sooner, in preference –1560.

Erethism (e·rĭþiz'm). 1800. [ad. F. *éréthisme*, ad. Gr. ἐρεθισμός, f. ἐρεθίζειν to irritate.] *Path.* Abnormal excitement of an organ or tissue; also *transf.* Hence **Erethi·smic** *a.* resembling e. **Erethi·stic** *a.* relating to e.

Erewhile (ēəˌhwai·l), *adv.* ME. [See ERE and WHILE.] A while before, some time ago.

The faces weeping lay That e. laughed the loudest MORRIS. So †**Erewhi·les** *adv.* [see WHILES].

†**Erf**[1]. [Com. Teut.: OE. *ęrfe*:—OTeut. **arbjo(m* neut. 'inheritance', related to Gr. ὀρφανός, L. *orbus* bereft.] Cattle –ME.

Erf[2] (ɔ̄ɹf). *S. Afr.* 1887. [a. Du. *erf*; see prec.] 'A garden plot, usually containing about half an acre' (Webster).

Erg (ɔ̄ɹg). 1873. [ad. Gr. ἔργον (also used as Eng.).] *Physics.* A unit of work or energy in the centimetre-gramme-second system.

‖**Ergo** (ɔ̄·ɹgo), *adv.* ME. [L.; = 'therefore'.] *Logic.* A word used to introduce the conclusion of a syllogism. Hence †**E·rgo** *sb.* a conclusion, a conclusive authorization. **E·rgoism**, pedantic adherence to logically constructed rules.

Ergometer (əɹgǫ·mĭtəɹ). 1879. [f. Gr. ἔργον + μέτρον.] An instrument for measuring work or energy.

Ergosterol (əɹgǫ·stĕrǫl). 1906. Earlier **ergosterin** (1889). [f. ERGOT + *-sterol* as in CHOLESTEROL: see -OL.] *Biochem.* An inert alcohol derived orig. from ergot, but now obtained from yeast and other sources.

Ergot (ɔ̄·ɹgǫt), *sb.* 1683. [a. F., OF. *argot* cock's spur; see ARGOT[1].] **1.** A diseased transformation of the seed of rye and other grasses, being the *sclerotium* of a fungus (*Claviceps purpurea*), in colour dark-violet, and in form resembling a cock's spur. Also, the disease. **b.** The diseased seed of rye used as a medicine 1860. **2.** *Farriery.* 'A small horny capsule on each side of the claw..in Ruminants and Pachyderms' (*Syd. Soc. Lex.*). **3.** *Anat.* A projection in the floor of the posterior extremity of the lateral ventricle of the brain; the *hippocampus minor* 1840.

†**E·rgot,** *v. rare.* 1653. [a. F. *ergoter* 'to rise on his toes, wrangle' (Cotgr.), f. *ergot* (cf. ARGOT[1]); but assoc. w. ERGO.] *intr.* To argue, wrangle –1658. Hence ‖**Ergoteur,** a wrangler.

Ergotic (əɹgǫ·tik), *a.* 1875. [f. ERGOT *sb.* + -IC.] Of, pertaining to, or resulting from ergot.

E. acid: 'a volatile acid said to exist in Ergot of rye' (*Syd. Soc. Lex.*).

Ergotine (ɔ̄·ɹgǫtin). 1851. [f. as prec. + -INE.] The active principle of ergot of rye. Hence **Ergo·tinine**, 'an unstable alkaloid existing in very small quantity in ergot' (Watts).

Ergotism[1] (ɔ̄·ɹgǫ̆tiz'm). 1853. [f. as prec. + -ISM.] **1.** The formation of ergot in grasses. **2.** The disease produced by ergotized grain, when eaten 1869. **3.** Poisoning by ergot 1884.

Ergotism[2] (ɔ̄·ɹgǫ̆tiz'm). 1656. [a. F. *ergotisme*, f. L. *ergo*, assoc. w. *ergoter*; see ERGOT *v.*] Arguing, wrangling; also, logical conclusions.

Ergotize (ɔ̄·ɹgǫ̆taiz), *v.* 1860. [f. ERGOT *sb.* + -IZE.] To affect with or transform into ergot. Hence **E·rgotiza·tion.**

Eria (ī·riă). 1868. [Assamese *eriya* adj., f. *era* the castor-oil plant.] In *eria silk*: silk obtained from the cocoons of a silkworm (*Phalæna Cynthia*), which feeds on the leaves of the castor-oil plant.

‖**Eric** (e·rik). 1586. [Ir. *eiric.*] *Hist.* A blood-fine or pecuniary compensation for the crime of murdering an Irishman.

‖**Erica** (ĭrai·kă). 1826. [L., ad. Gr. ἐρείκη heath.] *Bot.* The genus of plants called in Eng. HEATH.

Ericaceous (erikē·ʃəs), *a.* 1882. [See prec. and -ACEOUS.] *Bot.* Belonging to the N.O. *Ericaceæ*, of which the *Erica* is the typical genus. So **Erici·neous** *a.* in same sense.

Ericetal (erĭsī·tăl), *a.* 1876. [as if f. L. **ericetum* place where *erica* grows + -AL.] *Bot.* Moorland.

Ericolin (eri·cŏlin). 1876. [f. ERICA + -OL + -IN.] *Chem.* A resinous substance found in *Ericaceæ.*

†‖**Eri·geron.** 1601. [Gr. ἠριγέρων, f. ἦρι early + γέρων old man.] Gr. name of the Groundsel –1666.

Erigible (e·rĭdzib'l), *a.* 1803. [f. L. *erigere* + -IBLE.] Capable of being erected.

Erinaceous (erinē·ʃəs), *a.* [f. L. *erinaceus* hedgehog + -OUS.] *Zool.* Pertaining to the hedgehog family; of the nature of a hedgehog. (Dicts.)

Eringo, var. of ERYNGO.

Erinite (e·rinait). 1828. [f. *Erin* ancient name of Ireland + -ITE.] *Min.* A green arseniate of copper found in Ireland and in Cornwall.

Eri·nnic, *a.* [f. L. *Erinnys*, Gr. Ἐρινύς a Fury + -IC.] Characteristic of a Fury. SOUTHEY.

Eriometer (eriǫ·mĭtəɹ). 1829. [f. Gr. ἔριον wool + μέτρον.] An instrument for measuring by optical means the diameter of small fibres, such as wool, cotton, etc.

Eristic (eri·stik). 1637. [ad. Gr. ἐριστικός, f. (ult.) ἔρις strife.]

A. *adj.* Of or pertaining to disputation; controversial.

Polemicke and Eristicke discourses 1637. So †**Eri·stical.**

B. *sb.* **1.** One given to disputation; a controversialist 1659. **2.** = Gr. ἡ ἐριστικὴ (τέχνη), the art of disputation 1866.

1. Phr. *The Eristics*: the school of Megara.

Erke, obs. f. IRK.

Erl-king (ɔ̄·ɹlˌkiŋ). 1797. [tr. Ger. *erlkönig* (lit. alder-king), Herder's (erron.) tr. Da. *ellerkonge* king of the elves.] 'A goblin that haunts the Black Forest in Thuringia.'

†**Erme,** *v.* [OE. *yrman, ięrman*, f. *earm* miserable.] To be or make miserable –1481.

E·rmelin. Now *arch.* 1555. [? See ERMINE.] = ERMINE 1, 2.

Ermine (ɔ̄·ɹmin), *sb.* ME. [a. OF. (*h*)*ermine* (mod.F. *hermine*), ?ad. OHG. *harmîn* adj., f. *harmo* ermine, stoat, weasel = OE. *hearma*; or ? from *Armenius* (*mus*), the mouse of Armenia.] **1.** An animal of the weasel tribe (*Mustela Erminea*), found in northern countries, called in England a *stoat*, whose fur is reddish brown in summer, but in winter wholly white, except the tip of the tail, which is always black.

2. The fur of the ermine, often with the black tails arranged upon it for the sake of effect; also in *pl.*, trimmings, or garments, made of ermine ME. **3.** *fig.* With reference to the ermine worn by judges and peers 1794. **4.** *Her.* A heraldic fur; white marked with black spots of a triangular shape 1562. **5.** *attrib.* 1450; also quasi-*adj.* white as ermine 1610.

1. Fair ermines, spotless as the snows they press 1744. 3. Skilful lawyers..were rewarded with e. 1856. 5. †*E. cross*: = cross ERMINEE. E. snow 1821.

Comb.: **e. white** *a.*, white as e.; **e. moth** (*Hyponomeuta padellus*), a moth with white wings spotted with black.

Hence **E·rmine** *v.* to clothe with or as with e. **E·rmined** *ppl. a.* trimmed with or made to resemble e.; robed in e., *i.e.* made a judge or a peer.

Erminee (ɜ·ɹmini), *a.* 1736. [a. heraldic Fr. (*croix*) *erminée*, f. *ermine.*] *Her.* Composed of four ermine spots placed in the form of a cross.

E·rmines. 1562. [? a. OF. *hermines*, pl. of *herminet*, dim. of *hermine.*] *Her.* A fur forming the reverse of ERMINE, *i.e.* with white spots on a black ground.

Erminites (ɜ·ɹminəits). 1562. [ad. F. *herminite.*] *Her.* A heraldic fur resembling ermine, with the addition of a red hair on each side of the spots.

Erminois (ɜɹminoi·z). 1562. [a. OF. (*h*)*erminois*, f. *hermine.*] A heraldic fur, Or with Sable spots.

Ermit(e, Ermitage, obs. ff. HERMIT, -AGE.

†Ern, *v.* [ME. *ernen*, OE. *irnan*, by metath. for *rinnan.*] *intr.* To run; to flow -1600.

Ern, dial. f. EARN *v.*[1] to glean. So **Ernes** *sb. pl.* gleanings.

Erne (ɜɹn), *sb.* [OE. *earn* :—OTeut. **arnu-z.* Cf. Gr. ὄρνις bird.] An eagle; *esp.* the *Sea-Eagle* (see EAGLE). *Comb.* **e.-stone** = AËTITES.

Erne, obs. f. EARN *v.*[2]

Ernes(se, -st(e, etc., obs. ff. EARNEST.

Erode (ĭrōu·d), *v.* 1612. [a. F. *éroder*, ad. L. *erodere*, f. *e* + *rodere* to gnaw.] **1.** To gnaw away; to destroy by slowly eating out. **2.** *Geol.* To wear away; to eat out 1830.

1. The process of ulceration..eroding the middle coat [of the vessel] TODD. 2. The materials through which the channel is eroded LYELL. Hence **Ero·ded** *ppl. a.* in senses of the vb.; *Bot.* = EROSE.

Erodent (ĭrōu·dĕnt). [ad. L. *erodentem*; see prec.] **A.** *adj.* 'Applied to medicines which cause erosion' (*Syd. Soc. Lex.*). **B.** *sb.* A substance which erodes. (Dicts.)

†E·rogate, *v.* 1531. [f. L. *erogat-*, *erogare* f. *e* EX-[1] + *rogare.*] *trans.* To pay out, expend. Also *absol.* -1692. Hence **†Eroga·tion,** expenditure; in *pl.* money expended.

Eros (ĭə·rǫs, e·rǫuz). 1775. Pl. **Erotes** (erōu·tez); Eroses (ĭə·rǫsèz, e·rǫuzèz). [L. *Erōs*, a. Gr. ἔρως.] Love, the god of love: = CUPID.

Erose (ĭrōu·s). 1793. [ad. L. *erosus*, pa. pple. of *erodere*; see ERODE.] *Bot.*, etc. Having the margin irregularly denticulated, as if bitten by an animal.

Erosion (ĭrōu·ʒən). 1541. [a. F. *érosion*, ad. L. *erosionem*; see ERODE.] **1.** The action or process of eroding; the state of being eroded; *spec.* in *Geol.* Also *transf.* and *fig.* Also *concr.* **2.** *attrib.* 1879.

2. *E. theory*: the theory which accounts for the contour of the land by superficial denudation. Hence **Ero·sionist,** one who upholds this theory.

Erosive (ĭrōu·siv), *a.* 1830. [f. L. *eros-*, *erodere* + -IVE.] Having the property of eroding.

Eroso- (ĭrōu·so-), comb. f. L. *erosus* (see EROSE) in **Ero:so-de·ntate** *a.*, toothed irregularly, as if bitten; etc.

Erostrate (irǫ·streit). 1866. [f. E- *pref.*[3] + L. *rostrum* + -ATE.] *Bot.* Without a beak.

‖Erote·ma. 1589. [mod.L., a. Gr., f. as next.] = next.

‖Erotesis (erotī·sis). 1657. [mod.L., a. Gr., f. ἐρωτάειν to question.] *Rhet.* A figure in which a speaker, in the form of a question, boldly asserts the opposite of what the question asks; as in 'Shall I be frighted when a madman stares?' Hence **Erote·tic** *a.* interrogatory.

Erotic (erǫ·tik). 1651. [ad. Gr. ἐρωτικός, f. ἔρως, ἔρωτος.] **A.** *adj.* Of or pertaining to the sexual passion; treating of love; amatory. **B.** *sb.* An erotic poem; also [= ἐρωτική (τέχνη)], a doctrine or science of love. Hence **†Ero·tical** *a.* **Ero·tically** *adv.* **Ero·ticism,** e. spirit or character. So **E·rotism,** *Path.* sexual excitement; eroticism.

Erotomania (erōu:tomē·niă). 1874. [f. Gr. ἔρως + μανία.] *Path.* Melancholy or madness caused by imaginative love or by sexual excitement.

Erpetology, -ist; see HERP-.

Err (ɜɹ), *v.* [ME. *erre*, a. F. *errer*, L. *errare* :—prehistoric **ersare*, cogn. w. Goth. *airzjan* trans. to lead astray. Cf. Ger. *irren.*] **†1.** *intr.* To ramble, roam, stray -1697. **2.** To go astray; to miss, fail (*rare*) ME. **3.** To go wrong in judgement or opinion; to be incorrect ME. **4.** To go astray morally; to sin ME. **†5.** *trans.* To do or go wrong in -1644.

2. We haue erred and strayed from thy wayes, lyke loste shepe *Bk. Com. Prayer.* The arrows e. not from their aim SOUTHEY. 3. Possibly the man may e. in his judgement of circumstances JER. TAYLOR. 4. So Manasseh made Iudah..to erre 2 *Chron.* xxxiii. 9. Hence **†Err** *sb.* an error, fault; also heresy. **E·rringly** *adv.*

Errable (e·răb'l), *a. arch.* 1665. [f. ERR *v.* + -ABLE.] Fallible, liable to err. Hence **Errabi·lity,** liability to err. **†E·rrableness.**

Errabund (e·răbŏnd), *a.* [ad. L. *errabundus.*] Erratic; as, *e.* guesses. SOUTHEY.

Errancy (e·rănsi). 1621. [f. ERRANT *a.*; see -ANCY.] The condition of erring or being in error.

Mr. Gladstone's e. 1864.

Errand (e·rănd). [OE. *ǽrende*; perh. conn. w. Goth. *áirus*, ON. *árr*, OE. *ár* messenger.] **†1.** A message; a verbal communication for a third party -1754. **2.** A going with a message or a commission; *esp.* a short journey on which an inferior is sent to convey a message or do something for the sender OE. **3.** The business on which one goes; a purpose, intention ME.

1. Tel your King, from me, this e. 1583. 2. The Doctor came on a fool's e. 1840. 3. He had another errant to Persia, than buying of Slaves BENTLEY.

Errant (e·rănt), *a.* (*sb.*) ME. [a. F. *errant*: in branch I, pr. pple. of OF. *errer* :—vulgar L. *iterare* to travel, f. *iter*; in branch III, ad. L. *errantem*; in branch II, qy. Cf. ARRANT.]

I. A. *adj.* **1.** Itinerant, travelling (in quest of adventure, or like a knight-errant) (*poet.*). **†2.** In bailiff-errant (see BAILIFF); **justice-errant,** a justice who travels on circuit -1641. Also *gen.*

B. *sb.* A knight-errant, or the like -1643.

II. 1. In phr. *errant* (*arrant*) *thief*: in Chaucer, the leader of a band of thieves; subseq., a notorious thief. *Obs.* exc. as ARRANT. **†2.** As an intensive: Unmitigated; thorough, downright -1776.

2. An errand grosse hypocrite 1619. So e. a whig 1710.

III. Astray, wandering; straying from the proper course, place, or standard ME.

Planets or e. Starres SIR T. BROWNE. The famous beauty and e. lady the Dutchesse of Mazarine 1676. With e. foot 1861.

Hence **†Erra·ntic** *a.* of or pertaining to knights errant. **E·rrantly** *adv.* at random.

Errantry (e·rǎntri). 1654. [f. prec. + -RY.] The condition of being errant; the condition or characteristics of a knight-errant.

Errata; see ERRATUM.

Erratic (eræ·tik). ME. [ad. L. *erraticus*, f. *errare.* Cf. F. *erratique.*]

A. *adj.* **1.** Wandering; first used of the planets, and of certain diseases, as gout, rheumatism, etc. **†2.** Vagrant; nomadic -1816. **3.** Having no fixed course 1841. **4.** Eccentric, irregular 1841.

1. The Erratick [stars] are seven STANLEY. A slow E. Fever 1725. 2. My erratick industry JOHNSON. Phr. *E. blocks, boulders* (Geol.): masses of rock, that have been transported from their original locality, apparently by glacial action. 3. E. puffs of wind 1879. 4. An e. genius 1841.

B. *sb.* **1. †a.** A vagabond. **b.** An eccentric. 1623. **†2.** An erratic star, a planet (*rare*) 1714. **3.** *Geol.* An erratic block 1849.

Hence **Erra·tical** *a.*, **-ly** *adv.*, **-ness.**

Erratum (erē·tŏm). Pl. **-ta.** 1589. [a. L., f. *errare*; see ERR.] **1.** An error in writing or printing. Also *transf.* **¶2.** In the forms *errata's*, or *erratae*s pl., and *errata* sing. = 'list of errata', with *-es* in *pl.* 1635.

2. A page Fill'd with Errata's of the present age QUARLES.

Errhine (e·rəin), *sb.* (*a.*) 1601. [ad. mod.L. *errhinum*, ad. Gr. ἔρρινον, f. ἐν + ῥίν nostril. Cf. F. *errhin* adj.] **1.** A medicine to be snuffed up the nose in order to increase the natural secretions and produce sneezing 1626. **†2.** A plug of lint steeped in this for insertion in the nose -1758. **3.** *adj.* Having the action of an errhine 1876.

Erroneous (erōu·niəs), *a.* ME. [f. L. *erroneus*, f. *erronem* vagabond; see -OUS.] **†1.** Wandering, roving; moving aimlessly. Also quasi-*adv.* -1777. **†b.** Straying from the proper course, as an *e.* circulation 1731. **2.** Straying from the moral, or wise course; misguided. *Obs.* or *arch.* 1512. **3.** Containing errors; of the nature of error; mistaken, wrong ME.; faulty in law, vitiated by error (see ERROR) 1495.

1. The Moon, e. in her course 1777. 2. 'Tis difficult getting of good Doctrine in e. Times BUNYAN. That e. clemency JOHNSON. 3. E. opinions 1494, spelling 1711. An e. supposition 1822, impression 1845. Hence **Erro·neous·ly** *adv.*, **-ness.**

Error (e·rəɹ). [ME. *errour*, a. OF. (mod.F. *erreur*) :—L. *errorem*, f. *errare* to ERR. The form *error*, now universal, dates from 1753.] **1.** The action of wandering; hence a devious or winding course. Now only *poet.* 1594. **†2.** Chagrin, fury; extravagance of passion -1460. **3.** The condition of erring in opinion; the holding of mistaken beliefs; a mistaken belief; false beliefs collectively. Also *personified.* ME. **4.** Something incorrectly done through ignorance or inadvertence; a mistake ME. **†b.** A flaw, malformation; a miscarriage -1791. **c.** *Law.* A mistake in matter of law appearing on the proceedings of a court of record 1495. **d.** *Math.* The difference between an approximate result and the true determination 1726. **5.** A departure from moral rectitude; a transgression ME.

1. His e. by sea, the sack of Troy B. JONS. 3. In Religion, What damned e., but some sober brow Will blesse it *Merch. V.* III. ii. 78. Phr. *To be, stand in, lead into e.*; †*without e.* = 'doubtless'. 4. Errors of the press 1710. Phr. *Clerical e.* (see CLERICAL). b. *Nature's e.* = L. *lusus naturæ*; Sure, thou art an errour of nature BOSWELL. c. *Writ of e.*: a writ brought to procure the reversal of a judgement, on the ground of e. (Now, since 1875, limited to criminal cases.) 5. The errors of a very wild life BERKELEY.

Hence **E·rrorful** *a.* faulty. **E·rrorist,** one who is inclined to e.; one who encourages e. **E·rrorless** *a.* **E·rrorlessness.**

†Ers. ? *Obs.* 1578. [a. F. *ers*, app. cogn. w. It. *ervo* :—L. *ervum.*] The Bitter Vetch (*Ervum Ervilia* L.).

Erse (ɜɹs), *a.* ME. [Early Sc. var. of IRISH.] **†1.** In early Sc. use: = IRISH. **2.** Applied by Sc. Lowlanders to the Highland Gaelic dialect, people, customs, etc. In 18th c. literary use, the Gaelic of Scotland, and occas. of Ireland; now, *occas.*, the Irish Gaelic alone. Nearly *Obs.* Hence **†E·rseman,** one who is E. by birth or descent.

Ersh; = EARSH *dial.*, eddish.

Erst (ɜɹst). [OE. *ǽrest*, superl. of *ǽr* (see ERE).]

A. *adj.* **†1.** First -ME. **†2.** *absol.* in advb. phrases -1596.

2. Phr. *Now at e.*: now and not sooner. (By Spenser taken erron. as = 'at once'.)

B. *adv.* **†1.** Earliest, soonest -ME. **†2.** In the first place. (Occas. pleonastically before *ere.*) -1587. **†3.** At first, as opp. to *afterwards* -1605. **†4.** Sooner, earlier; *esp.* with negs. -1588. **5. a.** Of old ME. **†b.** Not long ago -1791.

5. b. The.. horrid spectacle, Which e. my eyes beheld, and yet behold MILT. *Sams.* 1543.

Erstwhile (ɜ·ɹst,hwəil), *adv. arch.* 1569. [f. ERST + WHILE.] Some while ago, formerly. Also *adj.* 1901. So **†E·rstwhiles** [see WHILES].

Erubescence (erube·sĕns). *rare.* 1736. [a. F., ad. late L. *erubescentia*; see next.] Erubescent quality or state.

Erubescent (erube·sĕnt), *a.* 1736. [ad. L. *erubescentem*, *erubescere*, f. *e* + *rubescere* to redden.] Reddening, blushing.

Erubescite (erube·səit). 1850. [f. L. *erubescere* (see prec.) + -ITE.] *Min.* A copper sulphide, purple copper.

‖**Eruca** (ĭrū·kă). *rare.* 1609. [L.; = 'a caterpillar'.] The larva of a butterfly or the like; a caterpillar. Hence **Eru·ciform** *a.* caterpillar-like.

Erucic (ĭrū·sik), *a.* 1869. [f. L. *eruca* a kind of cabbage + -IC.] *Chem.* Of or pertaining to *eruca.*

E. acid, 'an acid ($C_{22}H_{42}O_2$) obtained by the saponification of the fixed oil of white mustard (Sinapis alba)' (Watts).

Eruct (ĭrʊ·kt), *v.* 1666. [ad. L. *eructare*, f. *e* + *ructare* to belch.] **1.** *intr.* To void wind noisily from the stomach through the mouth. **2.** To emit by eructation; also *fig.* 1774. Hence **Eru·ction** (*rare*).

Eructate (ĭrʊ·kteɪt), *v.* Now *rare.* 1638. [f. L. *eructat-* ppl. stem: see prec.] **1.** *trans.* To belch, vomit forth. Chiefly *transf.* and *fig.* **2.** *intr.* = ERUCT 1.

Eructation (ĭrʊktēɪ·ʃən). 1533. [ad. L. *eructationem*; see prec.] **1.** The action of belching wind from the stomach through the mouth; belching. Also *transf.* and *fig.* **2.** *concr.* That which is belched forth. Also *fig.* 1607.

1. *transf.* The Ætna, whose eructations throw whole stones from its depths 1652.

Erudite (e·rŭdəit). ME. [ad. L. *eruditus*, *erudire*, f. *e* + *rudis* rude, untrained.]

A. *adj.* **1.** †**a.** Trained. **b.** Learned, scholarly. (Now chiefly sarcastic.) **2.** Of books, etc.: Characterized by erudition 1533.

1. An e. Pedant MARSTON. **2.** E. theology JER. TAYLOR. Hence **E·rudite-ly** *adv.*, **-ness.**

B. *sb.* [So Fr. *érudit.*] An erudite person (*rare*) 1865.

Erudition (erudi·ʃən). ME. [ad. L. *eruditionem*; see prec.] †**1.** The action of training or instructing; education –1749. †**2.** *concr.* Imparted instruction; also, a doctrine, maxim –1574. **3.** †**a.** Trained condition. **b.** Later: Acquired book learning; scholarship. 1530. †**4.** Of a coin: Perfect workmanship –1747.

3. b. Exhibiting a little e. in such a manner as to make it look like a great deal MACAULAY. Hence **Erudi·tional** *a.*

†**E·rugate**, *v. rare.* 1656. [f. L. *erugat-*, *erugare*, f. *e* + *ruga* wrinkle.] *trans.* To take out wrinkles from; to smooth –1657. So †**E·rugate** *ppl. a.* having the wrinkles rubbed out, smooth.

†**Eru·ginous**, *a.* 1646. [ad. L. *æruginosus*, f. *æruginem* rust of copper.] Partaking of the nature or substance of verdigris, or of copper itself; resembling verdigris –1666. var. †**Eru·ginary.**

†**Eru·mp**, *v.* 1657. [ad. L. *erumpere*, f. *e* + *rumpere* to break forth.] To break out as an eruption. So **Eru·mpent** *a.* that bursts forth.

Erupt (ĭrʊ·pt), *v.* 1657. [f. L. *erupt-* ppl. stem; see prec.] **1.** *intr.* Of the teeth: To break through the skin of the gums. **b.** *trans.* To force through the gums 1859. **2.** *intr.* To break out in eruption, be in a state of eruption; to burst forth 1770. **b.** *trans.* To throw out in an eruption 1769.

2. The showers continued to e. 1866. The Don.. erupts into..a large inland lake 1864. **b.** The volcanic rocks of Tuscany..have been chiefly erupted beneath the sea LYELL.

Eruption (ĭrʊ·pʃən). 1555. [ad. L. *eruptionem*; see ERUMP.] **1.** A bursting forth from natural or artificial limits; also *concr.* that which bursts forth. Also *fig.* **2.** An outbreak of volcanic activity 1740. **3.** Of persons: The action of breaking forth from within boundaries; *e.g.* a hostile movement of armed men from a stronghold, or from their own country, etc. Now *rare.* 1615. **4.** *Path.* A breaking out of a rash, or of pimples on the skin; an efflorescence, rash 1596.

1. *concr.* The streets of Naples..paved with the matter of eruptions BERKELEY. *fig. L. L. L.* v. i. 121. **2.** Iceland chronicles give a list of 63 eruptions 1794. **3.** The eruptions of Barbarians BARROW. Hence **Eru·ptional** *a.* of or pertaining to volcanic e.

Eruptive (ĭrʊ·ptiv), *a.* 1646. [a. F. *éruptif*, *-ive*, f. L. *erupt-*, *erumpere*; see -IVE.] **1.** Bursting forth. **2.** Of or pertaining to volcanic eruption. Of rocks: Formed or forced up by eruption, showing traces of eruption. 1799. **3.** *Path.* Attended with or producing efflorescence 1790.

1. The sudden glance [lightning]..e. through the cloud THOMSON. **2.** Crystalline rock, both e. and metamorphic MURCHISON. **3.** Illness of an e. kind 1852. Hence **Eru·ptive-ly** *adv.*, **-ness. Erupti·vity.**

†**Eruptu·rient**, *a.* 1664. [f. L. *erupt-* ppl. stem, after *esurient*, and the like.] On the point of bursting forth –1685.

-ery, *suffix*, ME. *-erie*, forming sbs., orig. in words adopted from Fr., and by extension in other words.

1. The Fr. *-erie* represents: **a.** Com. Rom. *-arīa*, f. the L. suffix *-ario-* (Fr. *-ier*, *-er*) + the suffix *-ia* (Fr. *-ie*, -Y[3]); **b.** the addition of the suffix *-ie* to agent-nouns in OF. *-ere*, *-eor* (mod.F. *-eur*) :—L. *-ator*, *-atorem.*

2. The derivs. of sbs. in *-er* and of vbs. denote the place where an employment is carried on, as *bakery*, *brewery*, etc.; or classes of goods, as *ironmongery*, etc.; with an extension in a general collective sense (= '*-ware*', '*-stuff*'), as in *machinery*, *scenery.* The wds. formed by adding *-ery* to sbs. signify a state or condition, as *slavery*; or 'that which is connected with the sb.', as *popery*; or often the place where certain animals are kept or plants cultivated, as *swannery*, *vinery.* In the pl. form the suffix has of late given rise to various jocular nonce-wds.; *e.g.* 'the Fisheries' for the Fisheries Exhibition of 1883, and the like. Cf. 'The Dukeries'.

3. See also the contracted form -RY.

Eryngo (iri·ŋgo). 1596. [? (ult.) ad. L. *eryngion*, a. Gr. ἠρύγγιον, dim. of ἤρυγγος name of the plant.] †The candied root of the Sea Holly (*Eryngium maritimum*), formerly used as an aphrodisiac –1709. Also, the plant itself, or any allied plant. (In this sense in L. form *eryngium.*) 1668. var. †**Ery·nge.**

Erysipelas (erisi·pĭlæs). ME. [a. Gr. ἐρυσίπελας, ? f. ἐρυσι- (for ἐρυθρός red) + πελ- in πέλλα skin.] *Path.* A local febrile disease accompanied by diffused inflammation of the skin; often called St. Anthony's fire, or 'the rose'.

Hence **E:rysi·pela·tic** *a.* of the nature of or resembling e. **E:rysipe·latoid** *a.* resembling e. †**Erysi·pelous**, †**E:rysipe:lato·se** *adjs.* = ERYSIPELATOUS.

Erysipelatous (e:rĭsipe·lătəs), *a.* 1646. [f. stem of ἐρυσίπελας (see prec.) + -OUS.] Pertaining to, of the nature of, or affected with, erysipelas.

Erythema (eriþī·mă). 1766. [a. Gr. ἐρύθημα, f. ἐρυθαίνειν to be red, f. ἐρυθρός.] *Path.* A superficial inflammation of the skin, showing itself in rose-coloured patches. Hence **E:rythema·tic, Erythe·matous** *adjs.* of, pertaining to, or of the nature of, e.

Erythrean, -æan (eriþrī·ăn), *a.* [f. L. *erythræus*, a. Gr. ἐρυθραῖος, f. ἐρυθρός red + -AN.] Red; as in the *E.* main. MILTON.

Erythric (eri·þrik), *a.* 1840. [f. Gr. ἐρυθρός + -IC.] *Chem.* In *E. acid*: = ERYTHRIN.

Erythrin (eri·þrin). 1838. [f. as prec. + -IN.] *Chem.* 'An acid ($C_{20}H_{22}O_{10}$) discovered by Heeren in *Roccella tinctoria*; it appears also to be contained in most of the lichens from which archil is prepared' (Watts).

‖**Erythrina** (eriþrəi·nă). 1865. [mod.L., f. as prec.] *Bot.* The Coral-tree, a tropical genus of leguminous plants bearing clusters of blood-red flowers.

Erythrine (eri·þrəin). 1837. [f. as prec. + -INE.] = COBALT-BLOOM.

Erythrite (eri·þrəit). 1844. [f. as prec. + -ITE.] **1.** *Min.* **a.** = prec. **b.** 'A flesh-coloured feldspar, containing 3 per cent. magnesia, found in amygdaloid' (Watts). **2.** *Chem.* An organic substance obtainable from erythrin 1865.

Erythro- (eri·þro-) (bef. a vowel *ery·thr-*), comb. f. Gr. ἐρυθρός red, in compounds occurring in *Chem.* and *Min.*; as,

Ery·thro-benze·ne, a red dye obtained from nitrobenzene. **Erythro·lein** [see OLEIN]. **Ery:throli·tmin** [see LITMUS and -IN], 'red substances obtained from litmus' (Watts). **Ery·throphyll** [Gr. φύλλον leaf], the red colouring matter of leaves in autumn; so **Ery:throphy·llin. Ery:throphy·toscope** [Gr. φυτόν plant + -σκοπος] = ERYTHROSCOPE. **Ery:thropro·tid** [see PROTEID or PROTIDE], 'a red extractive matter obtained by Mulder from albumin and allied substances'. **Ery:throre·tin** [see RETENE and -IN], 'a resinous constituent of rhubarb-root, soluble with purple-red colours in alkalis' (Watts). **Ery·throscope** [Gr. -σκοπος], an optical contrivance, by which the green of leaves is caused to appear red, while other green objects retain their hue. **Ery·throsi·derite** [Gr. σίδηρος + -ITE], a hydrous chloride of potassium and iron formed by sublimation in the lavas of Vesuvius. **Ery·throzyme** [Gr. ζύμη leaven], 'an azotised substance which exists in madder root, and gives rise to a peculiar transformation of rubian' (Watts).

Erythrogen (eri·þrodʒen). 1846. [f. ERYTHRO- + -GEN[2] 'producer'.] **1.** *Bot.* A variety of Chromogen, so called because it produces a red colour with acids (*Syd. Soc. Lex.*). **2.** *Chem.* 'A crystalline, fatty substance obtained from diseased bile; so called from the reddish or purple colour of some of its compounds' (Watts).

E·rythroid, *a.* [f. Gr. ἐρυθρός + -OID.] Of a red colour. (Dicts.)

Es-, *prefix*, = OF. *es-* :—L. *ex-* out, as in *escape*, *escheat.* In a few words refashioned, after L., as *esample*, now *example*, *eschange*, now *exchange*; otherwise obsolete. See also A- *pref.* 9.

†**Esba·tement.** 1475. [a. OF. (mod.F. *ébattement*) :—(ult.) late L. type **exbattere*, f. *ex* + *battere* to beat. Cf. ABATE.] Amusement; an amusement –1531.

†**Esbay·**, *v.* 1480. [a. OF. *esbaïr*, mod.F. *s'ébahir*; see ABASH.] *trans.* To dismay –1531.

Escalade (eskălēɪ·d), *sb.* 1598. [a. F., ad. Sp. *escalada*, f. (ult.) L. *scala* ladder.] The action of scaling the walls of a fortified place by means of ladders; also *transf.* and *fig.*

The wall had been protected against such an e. by.. old bottles STEVENSON. var. **Escala·do** (*arch.*).

Escalade (eskălēɪ·d), *v.* 1801. [f. prec. sb.] To climb up and get over (a wall, etc.) by means of ladders; to scale. Hence **Escala·der.**

Escalator (e·skălēɪtəɹ). orig. *U.S.* 1904. [f. stem of ESCALADE, after *elevator.*] A moving staircase for carrying passengers up and down.

‖**Escallonia** (eskălōu·niă). 1882. [mod.L., f. *Escallon* the discoverer.] *Bot.* A genus of flowering shrubs (N.O. *Saxifragaceæ*) found in the temperate parts of S. America.

Escallop (eskæ·ləp). 1610. [a. OF. *escalope* shell, of Teut. origin. The var. SCALLOP is earlier.] **1.** = SCALLOP 1. **2.** *Her.* = ESCALLOP-SHELL 1671. **3.** One of a series of segments of circles forming a scalloped edge. Usu. SCALLOP. 1691.

3. The figure of the leaves..divided into so many jags or Escallops RAY. Hence **Esca·lloped** *ppl. a.* = SCALLOPED 1, 2.

Esca·llop-she·ll. 1610. [See prec.] **1.** The shell (usu. one valve) of the escallop 1628. **2.** An imitation of this for ornamental purposes; *e.g.* in the collar of the order of St. Michael 1664. **3.** *Her.* The figure of an escallop borne as a charge 1610.

1. The escalop-shell, the device of St. James, was adopted as the universal badge of the palmer 1846.

†**Esca·ndalize**, *v.* 1574. [ad. Sp. *escandalizar.*] = SCANDALIZE, q.v. –1640.

Escapade (eskăpēɪ·d). 1653. [a. F., ad. Sp. *escapada*; see ESCAPE *v.*] **1.** An act of escaping from confinement; *fig.* an act in disregard of restraint or rules; a prank. †**2.** Of a horse: A fit of plunging and rearing (*rare*). DRYDEN.

1. *fig.* Lord R. Churchill's latest e. 1885.

‖**Escapado** (eskăpā·do). [Sp.] An escaped prisoner. MAYNE REID.

Escape (ĕskēɪ·p), *sb.*[1] ME. [f. ESCAPE *v.*; cf. OF. *eschap.*] **1.** The action of escaping, or fact of having escaped from custody, danger, etc.; *spec.* in *Law* (see quot.). **2.** *concr.* A garden plant growing wild 1870. **3.** A means of escape; also, short for FIRE-ESCAPE 1810. **4.** Leakage, as of water, gases, etc. 1874. †**5.** A sally –1796. †**6.** An inadvertence, mistake; a clerical error –1844. †**7.** A transgression (SHAKS.); a peccadillo –1678.

1. What, has he made an e.! which way B. JONS. E. is where one that is arrested commeth to his liberty before that he be delivered by award of any Justice, or by order of Law *Termes de la Ley* 142. **5.** *Meas. for M.* IV. i. 63. **7.** Rome will despise her for this foul e. *Tit. A.* IV. ii. 113.

Comb.: **e.-pipe**, the pipe through which steam passes from an e.-valve; **-valve** (*Steam-engine*), a relief valve to provide for the exit of steam or water when necessary; **-warrant**, a process addressed to sheriffs, etc., to retake an escaped prisoner' **-wheel,** an *escapement-wheel.*

Escape (ėskē¹·p), *sb.*² 1846. [a. F., ad. L. *scapus*; see SCAPE ².] *Arch.* Properly, the shaft of a column; occas. = APOPHEGY.

Escape (ėskē¹·p), *v.* [ME. *escape*, a. ONF. *escaper* :—late L. type **excappare*, f. *ex* + *cappa* cloak.] **1.** *intr.* To gain one's liberty by flight. **b.** Of fluids, etc.: To issue, find egress 1450. †**2.** *trans.* To effect one's flight from; to free oneself from; to get safely out of –1667. **b.** To issue unawares from (a person, his lips) ME. **3.** *intr.* To flee and get off safely; to avoid any threatened evil; to go unpunished ME. **4.** *trans.* To get clear away from; to succeed in avoiding; to elude ME.

1. Such sure watch layd vpon him that he cannot eskape MORE. **b.** Common electricity escapes when the pressure of the atmosphere is removed MRS. SOMERVILLE. **2. b.** No word of courtesy escaped his lips 1870. **3.** They escaped all safe to land *Acts* xxvii. 44. **4.** To e. the multitude DANIEL, mistakes 1669, suspicion JORTIN, observation 1821. The name of which escapes me DICKENS.

Hence **Esca·pable** *a.* that can be escaped. **Esca·peless** *a.* that cannot be escaped. **Esca·per.** **Esca·pingly** *adv.*

Escapement (ėskē¹·pmĕnt). 1779. [f. ESCAPE *v.* + -MENT; cf. F. *échappement.*] **1.** The action of escaping (*rare*) 1824; an outlet 1856. **2.** In a watch or clock, the mechanism which intervenes between the motive power and regulator, and which alternately checks and releases the train, thus causing an intermittent impulse to be given to the regulator. (So named with reference to the regulated escape of the toothed wheel from its detention by the pallet.) 1779.

2. 'Escapements are of various kinds, as the *anchor-*, *chronometer-*, *crown-*, *dead-beat-*, *lever-*, etc. *escapement*' (N.E.D.). **3.** *Mus.* In a piano action, the contrivance which causes the hammer to rebound after striking. **4.** The mechanism which controls the movement of the carriage in a typewriter.

Escarbuncle (ėskā·ɹbʊŋk'l). 1572. [a. OF.; see CARBUNCLE.] *Her.* = CARBUNCLE 2.

‖**Esca·rgatoire.** [Misspelling of F. *escargotière.*] A place for rearing snails. ADDISON.

†**Esca·rmouche,** *sb.* 1475. [a. F.; see SKIRMISH.] A skirmish; a fit of anger –1820.

Escarp (ėskā·ɹp), *sb.* 1688. [a. F. *escarpe*, ad. It. *scarpa*. Cf. SCARP.] *Fortif.* 'A steep bank or wall immediately in front of and below the rampart . . generally the inner side of the ditch' (Adm. Smyth). Also *transf.*

Escarp (ėskā·ɹp), *v.* 1728. [ad. F. *escarper*; see prec.] *trans.* To form into a steep slope or escarp; to furnish with scarps.

The Glacis was all escarp'd upon the live Rock 1728.

Escarpment (ėskā·ɹpmĕnt). 1802. [ad. F. *escarpement*; see prec.] **1.** Ground cut into the form of an escarp for the purpose of fortification. **2.** *Geol.* 'The abrupt face or cliff of a ridge or hill range' (Page). Also *transf.* 1813.

2. *transf.* A naked e. of ice, twelve hundred feet high KANE.

†**Escarteled, escartelee.** 1688. [ad. and a. OF. *escartelé* pa. pple., f. (ult.) *es-* (:—L. *ex*) + med.L. *quartellus*, dim. of *quartus* fourth.] *Her.* **1.** Quartered or quarterly. (Dicts.) ¶ **2.** Having a square notch. R. HOLME.

-escent, *suffix*, forming adjs., repr. *-escentem*, the ending of pr. pples. of verbs in *-escere*, chiefly inceptives. The general sense is 'beginning', 'beginning to be'. Hence used to form adjs. upon sbs., as in *alkalescent*, etc.

Eschalot (eʃălǫ·t). 1707. [ad. F. *eschalotte* (now *échalotte*).] = SHALLOT.

Eschar (e·skaɹ). 1543. [ad. L. *eschara*, a. Gr. ἐσχάρα lit. 'hearth', hence mark of a burn. Cf. SCAR.] *Path.* 'A . . dry slough, resulting from the destruction of a living part, either by gangrene, by burn, or by caustics' (*Syd. Soc. Lex.*). Also *transf.* Hence †**E·scharous** *a.* full of eschars; resembling an e.; scabby.

Escharotic (eskărǫ·tik). 1612. [ad. late L. *escharoticus*, a. Gr.; see prec.]

A. *adj.* Tending to form an eschar, caustic. **B.** *sb.* An e. drug; a caustic 1655.

Eschatology (eskătǫ·lŏdʒi). 1844. [f. Gr. ἔσχατος last + -LOGY.] *Theol.* The science of 'the four last things: death, judgement, heaven, and hell'.

E., the science of the last things, is, as a science, one of the most baseless BALDW. BROWN. Hence **E:schatolo·gical** *a.* of or concerned with e. **Eschato·logist,** one who treats of e.

†**Eschau·fe,** *v.* ME. [a. OFr. *eschaufer*; see ACHAFE.] *trans.* To heat, warm; also *fig.* –1530.

Eschaunge, obs. var. of EXCHANGE.

Escheat (es,tʃī·t), *sb.* [ME. *eschete*, a. OF. *eschete, escheoite* (orig. fem. pa. pple.), f. OF. *escheoir* (mod. F. *échoir*) :—late L. **excadēre*, f. *ex* + *cadĕre* (vulg. L. *cadēre*) to fall.] **1.** *Law.* An incident of feudal law, whereby a fief reverted to the lord when the tenant died seised without heir. (See also ATTAINDER.) Hence, the lapsing of land to the Crown (in U.S. to the state), or to the lord of the manor, on the death of the owner intestate without heirs. **b.** In Scotland: Confiscation or forfeiture of property, real or personal 1457. **2.** Property falling by e. to the lord, king, or state ME. **3.** The right of appropriating escheats 1570. †**4.** A writ to recover escheats. Now abolished. –1842. **5.** Forced contribution, plunder; in *pl.* booty. –1609.

1. Escheats were frequent in England, because there was no power of willing away land BUCKLE. **5.** To make one great by others losse is bad excheat SPENSER.

Escheat (es,tʃī·t), *v.* ME. [f. prec. sb.] **1.** *trans.* To make an escheat of, confiscate; †*Sc.* to forfeit. Also *transf.* and *fig.* **2.** *intr.* To become an escheat; to revert by escheat to the lord, king, or state. Also *fig.* 1531.

Hence **Eschea·table** *a.* liable to escheat. **Eschea·tage,** the right of succeeding to an escheat. **Eschea·tor,** an officer formerly appointed to take notice of the escheats in his county, and to certify them into the Exchequer; hence **Eschea·torship,** the office of escheator.

†**Eschel** (e·ʃĕl). 1753. [a. Ger., dim. of *esche* ashes.] A grey substance resembling ashes, used to mix with smalt when in fusion.

†**Eschele.** ME. [? OF. var. of *eschiere* = It. *schiera*; cf. Ger. *schaar.*] A troop (of soldiers) –1460.

†**Esche·ve,** *v.* ME. [a. OF. *eschever*; see ACHIEVE.] = ACHIEVE –1533.

Eschevin, obs. var. of ÉCHEVIN.

†**Eschew·,** *a.* ME. only. [a. OF. *eschieu* :—Com. Rom. **skivo*, of Teut. origin; cf. mod. Ger. *scheu*, OE. *scéoh* SHY.] Loth, unwilling.

Eschew (es,tʃū·), *v.* ME. [a. OF. *eschiver*, *eschever* :—Com. Rom. **skivare*, f. **skivo* (see prec.); cf. SHY *v.*] **1.** *trans.* To avoid, shun; to abstain carefully from. †**2.** *intr.* To get off, escape –1560.

1. They must not only e. evil but do good in the world BEVERIDGE. **2.** I promit . . That he sall not e. away, nor fle 1560. Hence **Eschew·al,** a keeping clear of (evil). **Eschew·ance,** avoidance. **Eschew·er.** **Eschew·ment,** eschewance.

†‖**Escho·ppe.** [F. (now *échoppe*) :—L. *scalprum.*] A graver. EVELYN.

‖**Eschscholtzia** (eʃǫ·ltsiă). 1857. [mod.L.; after J. F. v. *Eschscholtz*, a German botanist.] *Bot.* A Californian genus of herbaceous plants (N.O. *Papaveraceæ*); *E. californica*, the best-known species, has large bright yellow flowers, saffron-coloured in the centre.

‖**Esclandre** (ęsklăndr'). 1855. [F. :—L. *scandalum*; see SCANDAL and SLANDER.] Unpleasant notoriety; a scandalous occurrence; a scene.

†‖**Esclavage** (esklavāʒ). 1758. [Fr., used in same sense.] A necklace composed of rows of gold chains, beads, or jewels, so called as resembling the fetters of a slave –1834.

Escocheon, obs. f. ESCUTCHEON.

Escopette (eskope·t). *U.S.* 1805. [ad. Sp. *escopeta*, ad. It. *schioppetto*, f. *schioppo* a sort of fire-arm, L. *sclopus, stlopus.*] A sort of carbine. var. **Escope·tto.**

Escort (e·skǫɹt), *sb.* 1579. [a. F. *escorte*, ad. It. *scorta*, f. *scorgere* to conduct :—L. *ex* + *corrigere* to set right.] **1.** *Mil.* A body of armed men accompanying a traveller or travellers for protection, surveillance, or as a mark of honour, or serving as a convoy for baggage, provisions, etc. Also *transf.* **2.** *abstr.* Attendance in the capacity of an e. 1833.

1. The e. of the military chest WELLINGTON. *transf.* The courier and his e. 1847. **2.** To make him desire Cooper's e. HT. MARTINEAU.

Escort (eskǫ·ɹt), *v.* 1708. [f. prec. sb.] *trans.* To act as an escort to; to accompany for the purpose of protection or guidance, or as a civility.

Catharine, escorted by old Henshaw and a groom of the Knight of Kinfauns SCOTT.

Esco·t, *sb.* [AFr. f. SCOT.] = SCOT (as in *scot and lot*). JOHNSON.

†**Esco·t,** *v.* [a. OF. *escoter*; see prec.] To pay a reckoning for, maintain. *Haml.* II. ii. 362.

†**Escou·t,** *sb.* 1560. [a. OF. *escoute* fem.] Look-out 1630; a SCOUT –1603. Also as *v.* HOLLAND.

Escribe (īskrəi·b), *v.* 1558. [f. E- *pref.*³ + L. *scribere.*] †**1.** *trans.* To write or copy out. **2.** *Math.* To describe (a circle) so as to touch one side of a triangle exteriorly, and the other two produced 1870.

†**Escri·me.** *rare.* 1652. [a. F., f. *escrimer.*] Fencing; swordsmanship. So †**Escri·mer,** a fencer, a swordsman.

†**E·script.** 1483. [a. OF. *escript* for *escrit* (mod. *écrit*) :—L. *scriptum.*] A writing; *spec.* a writ –1724.

Escritoire (ęskrītwā·r, e·skritwǭɪ). 1706. [a. F. (now *écritoire*) :—late L. *scriptorium* apparatus or place for writing.] A writing-desk; a bureau, secretary. Hence **Escrito·rial** *a.* COWPER.

Escrod (eskrǫ·d). = SCROD. D. Webster.

Escroll (eskrōu·l). 1610. [ad. OF. *escroele*, dim. of *escroe*; see next and SCROLL.] †**1.** *Law.* = ESCROW –1736. **2.** *Her.* = SCROLL 1610.

Escrow (eskrōu·). 1598. [a. AF. *escrowe*, OF. *escroe, escroue* scrap, scroll :—med.L. type **scroda* of Teut. origin; cf. SHRED.] *Law.* A deed, bond, or other engagement delivered to a third party to take effect upon a future condition, and not till then to be delivered to the grantee.

†**Escry·,** *sb.* 1483. [f. next.] **a.** Outcry; notoriety. **b.** Battle-cry (*lit.* and *fig.*). –1538.

†**Escry·,** *v.* 1475. [a. OF. *escrier*, f. *es-* (:—L. *ex*) + *crier.*] **1.** *intr.* To cry out –1533. **2.** *trans.* To call out to; to invoke –1530. **3.** *trans.* = DESCRY –1625.

Escuage (e·skiuĕdʒ). Now *Hist.* 1513. [a. F., f. OF. *escu* (mod. *écu*) :—L. *scutum.* Cf. SCUTAGE.] **1.** A form of feudal tenure (*lit.* shield-service), personal service in the field for forty days in each year. **2.** = SCUTAGE 1577.

‖**Escudero** (eskudē·ro). 1637. [Sp.; f. *escudo* shield.] A shield-bearer; an esquire; hence, an attendant.

Esculapian, var. of ÆSCULAPIAN.

Esculent (e·skiŭlĕnt). 1625. [ad. L. *esculentus*, f. *esca* food.]

A. *adj.* Suitable for food, edible. Also as quasi-*sb.* 1626. Hence †**E·sculency,** e. quality.

B. *sb.* Anything fit for food; *esp.* vegetables.

An e. something like the cabbage YEATS.

Esculic, -in(e, var. ff. ÆSCULIC, -IN.

Escu·rialize, *v. nonce-wd.* 1843. [f. *Escurial* (better *Escorial*), name of the chief palace of the Spanish kings, about 30 miles from Madrid.] *trans.* To subject to influences like those which prevailed at the Escurial.

Escutcheon (eskʊ·tʃən). 1480. [a. ONF. *escuchon* (mod. *écusson*) :—late L. type **scutionem*, f. *scutum* shield.] **1.** *Her.* The shield or shield-shaped surface on which a coat of arms is depicted; also, the shield with the bearings; a representation of this. Also *fig.* †**2.** A hatchment –1820. **3.** Anything shaped like, or resembling, an e., as: **a.** *Arch.* A shield-shaped ornament, chiefly in Gothic buildings 1875. **b.** A name-plate, a keyhole-plate, etc. 1655. **c.** *Naut.* 'The compartment in the middle of a ship's stern, where her name is written' (Smyth). **d.** *Zool.* An oval depression behind the beaks of certain bivalves 1854.

1. *fig.* A dark blot on the e. of the House of Godwine FREEMAN. Phr. *E. of pretence*: the small e. bearing the arms of an heiress placed in the centre of her husband's shield. **2.** Mrs. Veal was . . dead, and her escutcheons were making DE FOE.

-ese, *suffix*, forming adjs. from names of countries and towns; ad. OF. *-eis* (mod. *-ois*, *-ais*) :—Rom. **-ese* :—L. *-ensem*, with the sense 'belonging to, originating in'. These adjs. may be used as sbs. From the use with authors' names, e.g. *Carlylese*, arose JOURNALESE, etc.

Ese, esement, etc., obs. ff. EASE, etc.

Esemplastic (esemplæ·stik), *a.* 1817. [f. Gr. ἐς into + ἕν, neut. of εἷς one + πλαστικός, f. πλάσσειν to mould; an irreg. formation after Ger. *ineinsbildung* forming into one.] Moulding into unity; unifying.
Nor I trust will Coleridge's.. word e... ever become current HARE.

Eserine (e·sĕrəin). 1879. [a. F. *éserine*, f. *éséré* native name; see -INE.] *Chem.* A crystalline alkaloid obtained from the Calabar bean, the fruit of *Physostigma venenosum*. It is used in ophthalmic surgery to produce contraction in the pupil of the eye.

†**Esguard.** 1616. [a. OF. *esgard* (mod. *égard*) lit. 'look, attention'; see Es- and GUARD.] A tribunal of the Knights of St. John, which settled differences within the order.

Esker (e·skəɪ). 1852. [a. Ir. *eiscir.*] *Geol.* An Irish name for ridges of post-glacial gravel.

Esloign, -loin(e, obs. ff. ELOIN.

†**Esmay·le, emayle.** 1589. [ad. OF. *esmail* (mod. *émail*); see AMEL.] Enamel -1594.

Esne (e·zni). Now *Hist.* [OE. *ęsne* :— OTeut. **aznjo-z* harvestman, f. **asano-z* harvest.] A serf, hireling.
Theow and E. art thou no longer SCOTT.

†**E·snecy.** 1607. [ad. med.L. *æsnecia*, repr. OF *ainsneece* (mod. *aînesse*), ad. **antenatitia*, f. *antenatus* one born before another.] A prerogative allowed to the eldest coparcener to choose first after the inheritance is divided (Dicts.)

Eso- (e·so-), *prefix* [Gr. ἔσω within], comb. form, as in:

Esoenteri·tis [see ENTERITIS], *Path.* inflammation of the intestinal mucous membrane. **Esogastri·tis** [see GASTRITIS], *Path.* inflammation of the mucous lining of the stomach. **Esona·rthex** [see NARTHEX], the inner vestibule of a Greek church.

Esodic (esǫ·dik), *a.* 1850. [f. Gr. ἔσω + ὁδός + -IC.] Of nerves: Proceeding to or into the spinal marrow; afferent.

Esophageal, Esophagus, etc.; see ŒS-.

Esoteric (esote·rik). 1655. [ad. Gr. ἐσωτερικός, f. ἐσωτέρω, compar. of ἔσω within.]

A. *adj.* 1. Designed for, or appropriate to, an inner circle of disciples; communicated to, or intelligible by, the initiated only. Hence of disciples. Opp. to EXOTERIC, q.v. 2. *transf.* Not openly avowed; pertaining to a select circle 1866. 3. *Phys.* 'Applied to things which relate to, or have origin within the organism' (*Syd. Soc. Lex.*).
1. A hidden stream of e. truth HALLAM. Phr. *E. Buddhism*: a body of theosophical doctrine handed down by secret tradition among the initiated. 2. An exoteric and an e. motive 1866.

B. *sb.* 1. *pl.* (after Gr. τὰ ἐσωτερικά.) Esoteric doctrines or treatises 1711. 2. One initiated in esoteric doctrines 1655.

So **Esote·rical** *a.*, **-ly** *adv.*

Esoterism (esǫ·tĕriz'm). 1835. [f. Gr. ἐσωτέρω (see prec.) + -ISM.] The holding of esoteric doctrines. var. **Esote·ricism.** So **Eso·terize,** to hold esoteric doctrines (*rare*). **E·sotery,** esoteric doctrine, secret lore.

‖**Esox** (ī·sǫks). 1520. [L.; a Gaulish word.] A large fish mentioned by Pliny, = *lax*, i. e. salmon. In mod. Ichthyology, the Pike.

†**Espa·ce.** 1483. [a. F. *espace* :—L. *spatium.*] = SPACE -1490.

‖**Espadon.** [a. F., app. a. Sp. *espadon*, augm. of *espada* sword.] A long two-handed sword used in 15-17th c.

‖**Espagnolette.** 1870. [Fr., f. *Espagnol* Spanish.] A bolt for French casements; also *attrib.*

Espalier (ėspæ·liəɪ), *sb.* 1662. [a. F., ad. It. *spalliera*, f. *spalla* shoulder.] 1. A kind of framework of stakes upon which fruit-trees or shrubs are trained; also the stakes singly 1741. 2. A fruit-tree or †row of trees so trained 1662. 3. *attrib.* 1717.
2. Plant your fairest Tulips .. under Espaliers EVELYN.

Espalier (espæ·liəɪ), *v.* 1810. [f. prec. sb.] To train as an espalier; also, to furnish with an espalier.

†**Espa·rcet.** 1669. [a. F.] A kind of sainfoin -1708.

Esparto (ėspā·ɪto). 1868. [a. Sp. *esparto* :—L. *spartum*, ad. Gr. σπάρτον a rope made of σπάρτος.] A kind of rush (*Macrochloa tenacissima*), called by some Spanish grass, of which paper, and, in Spain, cordage, shoes, and other articles are made. Also called **esparto grass.**

Espathate (ispē·pet), *a.* 1866. [f. E- *pref.*[3] + L. *spatha* + -ATE[2].] *Bot.* Not having a spathe.

Especial (ėspe·ʃăl), *a.* ME. [a. OF. *especial* (mod. *spécial*), ad. L. *specialis* (see SPECIAL), f. *species* SPECIES.] 1. = SPECIAL. *arch.* or *Obs.* 2. Pre-eminent, distinguished; exceptional ME. 3. Pertaining chiefly to one particular person or thing 1855.
1. Phr. †*E. pleading*, *e. tail.* 2. My most especiall good friend Sir Peter Hamond KNOLLES. 3. I must repeat one thing.. for your e. benefit JOWETT.
Phr. *In e.*: in particular; especially. Hence **Espe·cially** *adv.* in an e. manner or degree; principally. **Espe·cialness.** †**Espe·cialty,** an e. degree (of anything); in *Law* = SPECIALTY.

†**E·sperance.** ME. [a. F.:—late L. **sperantia*, f. *sperare.*] Expectation, hope -1651. Used as a battle-cry 1 *Hen. IV*, v. ii. 97.

Esperanto (espĕræ·nto). [Pen-name (= Hoping-one) of its inventor, Dr. L. L. Zamenhof, 1887.] Name of an artificial language invented for universal use. Hence **Espera·ntist.**

Espial (ėspəi·ăl). ME. [a. OF. *espiaille* the action of spying (in pl. 'spies'), f. *espier*, mod. F. *épier*; see ESPY *v.*] 1. The action of espying or spying; the fact of being espied. †2. *concr.* A body of spies; hence (with *pl.*) a spy, scout -1653.
1. The Captain.. cut a small hole of e. in the wall DICKENS. 2. Ful prively he had his espiaile CHAUCER.

‖**Espiègle** (ęspiẹgl), *a.* 1816. [Fr., of hist. origin; a corruption of Ger. *Eulenspiegel.*] Frolicsome, roguish. So ‖**Espièglerie,** roguishness.

Espier (ėspəi·əɪ). ME. [f. ESPY *v.*] One who espies; †a spy. Hence **Espi·ery,** the action or habit of espying.

†**Espine·l.** 1595. [ad. F. *espinelle.*] = SPINEL -1677.

†**Espine·tte.** [a. OF. *espinete.*] = SPINET. Pepys.

Espionage (e·spiŏnėdʒ). 1793. [ad. F. *espionnage*, f. *espionner*, f. *espion* spy, of Teut. origin.] The practice or employment of spies.

†**Espi·ritual,** *a.* ME. [a. OF. :—L. *spiritualem.*] = SPIRITUAL -1477.

Esplanade (esplănē·d). 1681. [a. F., ad. Sp. *esplanada*, f. *esplanar* :—L. *explanare* to level, f. *ex* + *planus.*] 1. *Fortif.* a. The glacis of the counterscarp, or the sloping of the parapet of the covered way toward the country 1696. b. 'An open, level space of ground, separating the citadel of a fortress from the town' (Stocqueler) 1708. 2. A levelled piece of ground; *esp.* one used for a public promenade 1682; *transf.* a level open space 1681; a grass-plot 1818.

Esplees (esplī·z), *sb. pl.* 1598. [ad. AF. *esplez, espletz*, pl. of OF. *esplet, esploit* revenue :—L. *explicitum*. Cf. EXPLOIT.] The products which ground or lands yield; as the hay of meadows, herbage of pasture, corn of arable, rents, services, etc.; also, the lands, etc. themselves (Wharton).

†**Espo·ntoon.** 1772. [ad. F. *esponton*, ad. It. *spuntone.*] = SPONTOON -1838.

†**Espou·sage.** 1549. [a. OF., f. *espouser.*] The action of espousing or betrothing; also, spousehood, marriage -1599.

Espousal (ėspau·zăl), *sb.* Somewhat *arch.* ME. [a. OF. *espousailles* :—L. *sponsalia*, neut. pl. of *sponsalis* adj., f. *sponsus*. The sense 'marriage' was prob. the earliest in Eng.] 1. In *pl.*, formerly also in *sing.* a. The celebration of a marriage. b. The formal plighting of troths; betrothal. Also *fig.* 2. [as if f. the vb.] The action of espousing; hence *fig.* the espousing a cause, a principle, etc. Now *rare.* 1674. †3. An espoused person, a husband or wife -1620. 4. *attrib.* 1598.
1. a. Though it [the childe] were borne but one day after the espousels solemnized *Termes de la Ley* 39. 2. Political reasons forbid the open e. of his cause H. WALPOLE.

†**Espou·se,** *sb.* 1475. [a. OF. *espous, espouse* :—L. *sponsus*; see ESPOUSE *v.*] = SPOUSE -1654. Hence †**Espou·sess,** a bride.

Espouse (ėspau·z), *v.* 1475. [a. OF. *espouser* (mod. *épouser*) :—L. *sponsare*, f. *sponsus*, pa. pple. of *spondere* to betroth. Cf. SPOUSE *v.*] †1. *trans.* To contract or betroth (*gen.* a woman). Usually said of the parents. -1626. Also †*fig.* 2. To take as spouse; to marry. Of the father: To give in marriage *to*. Also *transf.* and *fig.* 1475. †3. To unite in marriage (*lit.* and *fig.*) SHAKS. Also †*absol.* DRYDEN. 4. *trans.* To attach oneself to; to take to oneself, make one's own; to adopt, embrace 1622.
1. To a virgine espoused to a man whose name was Ioseph *Luke* i. 27. 2. On Ascension Day the Duke [of Venice] .. solemnly espouseth the sea 1615. 3. Espous'd to death *Hen. V*, IV. vi. 26. 4. To e. a quarrel BACON, a Party ADDISON, a cause 1759, a doctrine PRIESTLEY. Hence **Espou·ser.**

‖**Espressivo** (espressī·vo), *adv.* [It.] *Mus.* A direction: With expression.

Espringal. Now *Hist.* 1605. [ad. OF. *espringale*, ?f. Ger. *springen* SPRING *v.*] A mediæval military engine for throwing stones, bolts, or the like.

†**Espri·se,** *v.* 1474. [f. OF. *espris*, pa. pple. of *esprendre*, f. *es-* (:—L. *ex-*) + *prendre* to take.] *trans.* To enkindle (with love, etc.); also *lit.* -1567.

‖**Esprit** (ęsprī). 1591. [Fr., ad. L. *spiritus* SPIRIT.] Spirit, mind; hence, lively wit; cleverness
Phr. **Esprit de corps** (ęspri d'kor). [*corps* body.] A spirit of jealous regard for the corporate honour and interests, and for those of each member of the body as belonging to it. **Esprit fort** (ęspri fǫr). Pl. *esprits forts*. [F. *fort* strong.] A 'strong-minded' person, *esp.* a 'freethinker'.

†**Espy·,** *sb.* ME. [a. OF. *espie*, f. *espier*; see ESPY, SPY *vbs.*] 1. Espial; in WYCLIF, 'snare' -1607. 2. A spy -1656.

Espy (ėspəi·), *v.* ME. [a. OF. *espier* (mod. *épier*) :—Com. Rom. **spiare*, ad. OHG. *spehôn* (Ger. *spähen*) to SPY. Cf. L. *specere*, Gr. σκέπτεσθαι to look.] 1.† *trans.* To act as a spy upon, to watch; to examine closely. Also, to look out for. -1667. Also *absol.* or *intr.* (*arch.*) ME. 2. *trans.* To discover by looking out; to catch sight of; to detect ME. b. To perceive by chance 1483.
1. Now question me no more, we are espied *Tit. A.* II. iii. 48. He sends angels to e. us in all our ways JER. TAYLOR. 2. If I could in any place e. a word of promise BUNYAN. b. As one of them opened his sack .. he espied his money *Gen.* xlii. 27. Hence †**Espy·ingly** *adv.* insidiously.

Esq., Esqr., abbrevs. of ESQUIRE.

-esque, *suffix*, repr. Fr. *-esque*, ad. It. *-esco* :—med.L. *-iscus*, forming adjs., with sense 'resembling in style or characteristics', as in *arabesque, burlesque*, etc.

Esquire (ėskwəi·ɪ), *sb.*[1] 1460. [a. OF. *esquier* (mod. *écuyer*), lit. 'shield-bearer' :—L. *scutarius*, f. *scutum* shield. In Fr. assoc. wrongly with *écurie* (OF. *escurie*), see EQUERRY. See also SQUIRE.] 1. *Chivalry.* A young man of gentle birth, an aspirant to knighthood, who attended on a knight, and carried his shield. Now *arch.* Cf. ARMIGER. 1475. 2. A title of dignity next in degree below 'knight' 1460.
Esquires, legally so called, are: (1) younger sons of peers and their eldest sons; (2) eldest sons of knights and their eldest sons; (3) chiefs of ancient families (by prescription); (4) esquires by creation or office, as judges, officers, justices of the peace, barristers-at-law; (5) esquires who attend the Knight of the Bath on his installation.

3. A title allowed by courtesy to all who are regarded as gentlemen. In U.S. it belongs officially to lawyers and public officers, and is freely used in the addresses of letters. 1552. 4. [transf. use of 1.] A gentleman who attends or escorts a lady in public 1824.

Esquire (ėskwəi·ɪ), *sb.*[2] 1562. [app. a. OF. *esquire* (mod. *équerre*) square.] *Her.* a. *Based esquire*: the lower of the halves into which a canton is divided diagonally. Hence, b. = GYRON.

Esquire (ėskwəi·ɪ), *v. rare.* 1652. [f. ESQUIRE *sb.*[1]] To attend (a lady) as a squire.

‖**Esquisse.** 1731. [Fr., ad. It. *schizzo*; see

SKETCH.] The first rough sketch of a picture or design.

Ess. Pl. **esses.** 1540. The name of the letter S; anything S-shaped. See COLLAR *sb.* I.2.

-ess, *suffix* 1, a. F. *-esse* :—Com. Rom. *-essa* :—late L. *-issa*, a. Gr. *-ισσα* (:— *-ikya*), forming sbs. denoting female persons or animals; as *authoress, actress*, etc. But the agent-nouns in *-er*, and the sbs. indicating profession, etc., are now treated as of common gender, whenever possible.

-ess, *suffix* 2, ME. *-esse*, in sbs. a. Fr., repr. OF. *-esse, -ece* :—L. *-itia*, forming nouns of quality from adjs.; as *duress, largess*, etc.; it is spelt *-es* in *laches, riches.*

Essart (esā·ɹt), *sb.* 1851. [a. OF. *essart.*] = ASSART *sb.* 1. So **Essa·rt** *v.* = ASSART *v.*

Essay (e·sei), *sb.* 1597. [a. OF. *essai*; see ASSAY *sb.*] 1. The action or process of trying or testing; an ASSAY 1598. 2. An attempt, endeavour 1598. †3. A first attempt in learning or practice -1734; a first draft -1793. 4. A short composition on any particular subject; orig. 'an irregular undigested piece' (J.), but now said of a finished treatise 1597.

1. By way of triall and e. HEYLIN. A small e. of my zeal for .. your Majesty CLARENDON. 2. My second e. at authorship 1865. 4. For Senacaes Epistles..are but Essaies—that is dispersed Meditations BACON.

Hence **Essaye·tte, E·ssaykin, E·ssaylet,** dims.

Essay (esei·), *v.* 1483. [refash. f. ASSAY, after F. *essayer.*] 1. *trans.* To put to the proof, try; to test the nature, excellence, fitness, etc. of. †2. To ASSAY (an ore, etc.) -1816. 3. To attempt (anything difficult) 1641. 4. with *inf.* To set oneself, undertake (*to do* something). Also *absol.* 1530.

1. To e. the world 1593, one's powers MACAULAY. 3. To e. a Task 1712, a method LOWELL. 4. To e. to dissipate the cloud of error M. ARNOLD. Hence **Essay·er**, one who essays (something); †an essayist.

Essayist (e·sei,ist). 1609. [f. ESSAY *sb.* and *v.*] 1. One who makes trials or experiments. Now *rare.* 1736. 2. A writer of essays.

2. Meere Essaists! a few loose sentences, and that's all B. JONS.

‖**Esse** (e·sĭ). 1592. [L., inf. of *sum*, used subst.] 1. In phr. *in esse*, in being; opp. to *in posse*, in potentiality. 2. Essence 1642.

1. Persons..*in esse* at the time when a will is made CRUISE. See also DE BENE ESSE.

†**Essee.** ME. [ad. L. *Essæi* pl., Gr. Ἐσσαῖοι.] = ESSENE -1613.

Essence (e·sĕns), *sb.* ME. [a. F., ad. L. *essentia*, f. **essentem*, fictitious pr. pple. of *esse*, after Gr. οὐσία, f. ὀντ-, εἶναι.] †1. Being viewed as a fact or as a property of something -1688. 2. *concr.* Something that *is*; an entity. Now only a spiritual entity. 1587. †b. In *fifth e.*: an element distinct from the four elements; see QUINTESSENCE -1837. c. 'Constituent substance' (J.) ME. †3. Specific being, 'what a thing is'; nature, character -1664. 4. *Metaph.* Substance; the substratum of phenomena; absolute being 1646. 5. That by which anything subsists 1585. †6. Essentiality -1652. 7. That which constitutes the being of a thing, either (*a*) as a conceptual, or (*b*) as a real, entity (Locke's *nominal* and *real e.*); that by which it is what it is 1667. 8. *loosely.* The specific difference of anything 1656. 9. An extract obtained by distillation or otherwise from a plant or drug, and containing its specific properties in a reduced form. In pharmacy, an alcoholic solution of the volatile elements or essential oil. Also *fig.* 1660. 10. *spec.* A perfume, scent. Somewhat *arch.* 1627.

2. As far as Gods and Heav'nly Essences Can perish MILT. *P. L.* I. 138. Commonwealths are not physical but moral essences BURKE. c. So soft And uncompounded is their [Spirits'] E. pure MILT. *P. L.* I. 425. 5. *Two Gent.* III. i. 182. 7. We may exactly know the several Ideas that go to make each Law-term, and so their real Nature and E. may be known 1714. The e. of the mind being equally unknown to us with that of external bodies HUME. 9. *fig.* It [a love-letter] was the e. of nonsense MARRYAT. Hence **E·ssence** *v.* to pour like an e.; to perfume with an e. var. †**E·ssency.**

Essene (esī·n). 1553. [ad. L. *Esseni* pl., a. Gr. Ἐσσηνοί; of Heb. origin.] One of an ancient Jewish sect, remarkable for ascetic practices and a cenobitical life. Hence **Esse·nian** *a.* pertaining to, or resembling, the Essenes. **Esse·nic, -al** *a.* of the nature of Essenism. **E·ssenism,** the doctrine and practice of the Essenes, or a tendency thereto.

Essential (ése·nʃăl). ME. [ad. late L. *essentialis*, f. *essentia* ESSENCE.]

A. *adj.* 1. Of or pertaining to the essence of anything (see ESSENCE *sb.* 1-4). 2. Of or pertaining to specific being, or intrinsic nature ME. 3. Constituting, or forming part of, the essence of anything; necessarily implied in its definition 1546. b. Material, important 1770. 4. Indispensably requisite 1526. 5. Of the nature of, or resembling, an essence or extract (see ESSENCE 10); in a state of essence 1674.

1. Anye reall and essenciall presence *Bk. Com. Prayer.* E. poetry COLERIDGE. Phr. *E. disease* (Path.), an idiopathic disease. 2. Phr. *E. difference* (Logic) = 'specific difference', DIFFERENTIA. *E. character*: the marks which distinguish a species, genus, etc. from the others included with it in the next superior division. *E. proposition* (Logic): one which predicates of a subject part of its connotation. *E. form* (Metaph.): see FORM. 3. By the Law of Nature as an e. right of Soveraignty BRAMHALL. b. You have done e. service to the cause JUNIUS. 4. Silica..is an e. ingredient in mortar 1807. Phr. *E. chord* (Mus.), in early use = *common chord*; later, = FUNDAMENTAL, opp. to *accidental.* 5. Phr. *E. oil*, a volatile oil, obtained by distillation, and having the characteristic odour of the plant from which it comes; as the oil of turpentine, etc. Now often = 'volatile oil'.

B. *sb.* †1. What exists; existence 1667. 2. That which is essential; an indispensable element or adjunct; a leading point. Orig. only in *pl.* 1513. †3. *pl.* Vitals. SOUTH.

1. MILT. *P. L.* II. 93. 2. 'Well, well', said Glossin, 'no occasion to be particular, tell the essentials' SCOTT.

Hence **Esse·ntial·ly** *adv.*, **-ness.**

Essentiality (ése:nʃi,æ·lĭti). 1616. [f. prec.] 1. The quality or fact of being essential 1640. 2. Essence 1616. 3. An essential quality (*rare*); also *pl.* essentials 1649.

†**Esse·ntiate,** *v.* 1561. [f. as if on L. **essentiat-*, ppl. stem of **essentiare*, f. *essentia*; see ESSENCE.] 1. *trans.* To make into an essence or being; to constitute the essence of -1687. 2. *intr.* To become essence. B. JONS.

†**Essera.** 1706. [med.L., ad. Arab.; cf. F. *essère.*] *Path.* A variety of nettle-rash -1811.

Essoin, essoign (esoi·n), *sb.* ME. [a. OF. *essoine, essoigne* (mod. *exoine*) vbl. sb., f. *essoigner*; see next. See also ASSOIN *sb.*] 1. *Law.* The allegation of an excuse for non-appearance in court at the appointed time; the excuse itself. 2. *gen.* An excuse, parleying, delay ME. ¶3. = ESSOINEE. (App. a misunderstanding of AF. *essonié.*) COWELL.

2. SPENSER *F. Q.* I. iv. 20. *Comb.* **e.-day,** the first general return day of the term, on which the court sat to receive essoins.

Essoin (esoi·n), *v.* 1495. [a. OF. *essoignier, essoinier*, f. *essoyne* :—med.L. *exsoniare*, f. *ex* + *sonia, sunnis* lawful excuse, f. OHG. *sunna, sunnia*, corresp. to ON. *syn* refusal, denial; cf. Goth. *sunjōn* to excuse.] 1. *Law. trans.* To offer an excuse for the non-appearance of in court. 2. To excuse, let off. QUARLES.

2. Away with wings of time, (I'll not e. thee) 1620. Hence **Essoi·nee**, a person excused for non-appearance in court. **Essoi·ner**, one who essoins another. **Essoi·nment**, the action of essoining.

Essonite, var. of HESSONITE, cinnamon-stone.

Est, obs. var. of EAST.

-est, *suffix*, forming the superl. degree of adjs. and advbs., repr.: (1) OE. *-ost-, -ust-, -ast-* :—OTeut. *-ōsto-*; (2) OE. *-est-, -st-*, with umlaut :—OTeut. *-isto-*. The OTeut. suffixes are combs. of the two compar. suffixes *-ōz-, -iz-* with OAryan *-to-*; cf. Gr. *-ιστο-*, Skr. *ishtha-*. The only surviving umlaut forms are *best, eldest.*

†**Esta·ble,** *v.* ME. [ad. F. *establir* (mod.F. *établir*) :—L. *stabilire*, f. *stabilis.*] = ESTABLISH in various senses -1533.

Establish (ėstæ·bliʃ), *v.* [ME. *establissen*, a. OF. *establiss-*, stem of *establir*; see prec.] 1. To render stable or firm; †to ratify; to confirm, settle; to restore (health) permanently. 2. To fix, settle, institute or ordain permanently; also with †*to*, †*upon* ME. 3. To set up on a secure basis; to found 1460. 4. To place in a secure or permanent position; to set up in business; to settle (a person) in or at a place. Also *refl.* and †*intr.* for *refl.* 1557. 5. To set up or bring about permanently; to create (a precedent). Also to create for oneself (a reputation, a position). 1597. 6. To place beyond dispute; to prove 1704. 7. To place (a church or a religious body) in the position of a state church 1558.

1. To conferme, ratefie and astablishe this my deyd 1537. The great Pensioner's Health seems to be Establish'd 1708. 2. Behold, I e. my couenant with you *Gen.* ix. 9. To e. an edict STRUTT, the lodger franchise GLADSTONE. 3. To e. Knighthode HAWES, a manufactory 1863, a throne FREEMAN. 4. To e. Cæsar as a king SHAKS., the daughters of the house 1872. 5. To e. a price in the market 1801, liberty of worship MACKINTOSH, order DICKENS. Phr. *To e. a suit* (Cards): to give it the command by drawing all the best cards in it which were against the player. 6. To e. a point FREEMAN, a case 1885. Hence **Esta·blisher.**

Establishment (ėstæ·bliʃmĕnt). 1481. [f. prec. + -MENT. Cf. OF. *establissement*, mod.F. *établissement.*]

I. 1. The action of establishing; the fact of being established (see the vb.) 1596. †2. Established or stable condition -1777; organization, footing -1799. †3. That which establishes or strengthens -1646. 4. Settlement in life; (formerly often) marriage 1684; settled income or provision 1727.

1. The e. of Christianity in any place BUTLER.

II. †1. That which is established; a settled constitution or government -1793. 2. The ecclesiastical system established by law; the *Church E.* 1731. 3. a. A permanent military, naval, or civil organization. b. The quota of officers and men in a regiment, ship, etc. 1689. 4. An organized staff of employés or servants, including, or occas. limited to, the building in which they are located 1832. b. A household, family residence 1803.

2. To meddle with the Church E. PITT. 3. b. Phr. *Peace E.*, the reduced numbers of an army in a time of peace. So *War E.* The usual e. of officers for ships of the same class 1828.

Phr. *E. of a port* [Fr. *établissement d'un port*]: the interval between the instant of the moon's transit across the meridian on the day of new or full moon, and the subsequent high water.

Hence **Esta:blishmenta·rian** *a.* advocating the principle of an established church; characteristic of those who advocate this principle; *sb.* one who belongs to, or supports the principle of, an established church. **Establishmenta·rianism. Esta·blishmentism,** the principle of a State Church.

‖**Estaca·de.** 1663. [Fr., ad. Sp. *estacada*, f. *estaca* stake.] *Mil.* A dike of piles in the sea, a river, etc., to check the approach of an enemy. Cf. STOCKADE.

‖**Estafe·tte.** 1792. [Fr., ad. It. *staffetta*, dim. of *staffa* stirrup, f. OHG. *stapho* step.] A mounted courier.

†**Esta·ll,** *v.* 1577. [app. ad. OF. *estaler* to place, fix; cf. INSTALL.] *trans.* To arrange the payment of by instalments -1643.

Estamin (e·stămin). 1701. [a. F. *estamine* (now *étamine*) :—late L. **staminia*, L. *staminea*, f. *stamen* warp, thread.] An open woollen fabric, used for making sieves, etc. In 18th c. also applied to a silk fabric.

‖**Estaminet** (estaminé). 1848. [Fr.] A café in which smoking is allowed.

Estampede (estæmpī·d), *sb. rare.* [ad. Sp. *estampido* a sudden crash.] = STAMPEDE. Marryat. Hence **Estampe·de** *v. trans.* to stampede (cattle, etc.). ‖**Estampede·ro** [Sp.], a stampeded animal. **Estampe·do** *v. intr.* (of cattle, etc.) to run off in a panic.

‖**Estancia** (esta·nsiă, in Sp. -þiă). 1704. [Sp.; *lit.* station, f. (ult.) L. *stare.*] A cattle-farm in Spanish America. So ‖**Estancie·ro** [Sp.], the keeper of an e.

†**Esta·ng.** 1628. [a. OF.] A pool, fish-pond -1673.

†**Esta·ntion.** 1697. [app. a fusion of Sp. *estacion* and ESTANCIA.] A cattle-farm -1707.

Estate (ėstēi·t), *sb.* ME. [a. OF. *estat*, ad. L. *status*, f. *stare.*] 1. *gen.* State or condition. b. A special state or condition. *Obs.* exc. in *Man's, woman's estate.* ME. 2. Condition as regards worldly prosperity, fortune, etc. (*arch.*) ME. 3. Status; degree of rank or dignity ME. 4. Display of one's condition; pomp, STATE. Now *arch.* ME. †b. *ellipt.* A canopy, chair, dais, etc., of state -1607. †5. A class or order in a community or nation -1643. 6. An order or class as part of the body politic, participating in the government directly or by representation ME. †7. Political constitution, form of government -1670. †8. = STATE -1750. 9. *Law.* The interest which any one has in lands, tenements, or other effects ME. 10. Property, fortune, capital 1563. b. The collective assets and liabilities of a person (*esp.* of a deceased person, a bankrupt, or a *cestui que trust*) 1830. 11. A landed property; usually, a considerable one. (Now the commonest sense.) 1760.

1. We pray for the good e. of the Catholick Church *Bk. Com. Prayer.* b. Phr. *The (holy) e. of matrimony.* 2. Distressed in mind, body, or e. *Bk. Com. Prayer.* 3. The e. of a clerke in the chyrche CAXTON. Their [Princes'] high e. *Bk. Com. Prayer.* 4. Phr. *Cap of e.* (Her.): see CAP *sb.*[1] b. Princes..sitting upon their e. TOPSELL. 6. Phr. *Third E.*, a designation of the English 'commons', as dist. from the Lords Spiritual and the Lords Temporal. *The Fourth E.*, the Press. 9. Phr. An *e. upon condition, in fee, for life, of inheritance, tail, from year to year, at will,* etc. *Real e.*, an interest in realty. *Personal e.*, an interest in personalty. 10. They were..of no great e. OUIDA. b. If his [a bankrupt's] e. pay 10s. in the pound MCCULLOCH. 11. Lord of the broad e. and the Hall TENNYSON.

Estate (ĕstēⁱ·t), *v.* 1590. [f. prec. sb.] 1. *trans.* To put into an estate; to endow. Now *rare.* 1609. †2. To furnish with an estate or property (*lit.* and *fig.*) -1653. †3. To bestow as an estate *on* or *upon* -1669. †4. To put into a certain state -1701.

†**Esta·tely.** [f. as prec. + -LY[1] and [2].]
A. *adj.* Stately.
B. *adv.* In a stately manner. Only in ME.

Estatesman (ĕstēⁱ·tsmæ̆n). 1820. [Cf. *beadsman*, etc.] A perversion of STATESMAN, a Cumberland or Westmoreland yeoman.

Esteem (ĕstī·m), *sb.* 1450. [f. next; cf. F. *estime.*] †1. Estimate, valuation; estimated value -1680. 2. Estimation, opinion (? *arch.*) 1588. 3. Favourable opinion; regard; respect 1611. †4. Account; reputation -1824.

1. Of the substance of your realme..I wyll make an esteame SKELTON. 2. Yourself, held precious in the worlds esteeme *L. L. L.* II. i. 4. 3. Whist had engaged her maturer e. LAMB. 4. 1 *Hen. VI*, III. iv. 8.

Esteem (ĕstī·m), *v.* 1460. [ad. OF. *estimer*, ad. L. *æstimare* to ESTIMATE. See also AIM.] †1. *trans.* To estimate the value of; to assess, appraise -1776. 2. To attach value (subjectively) to; to think highly of; to feel regard for, respect 1530. †b. *intr.* To have a (specified) opinion *of* -1697. †3. *trans.* To estimate. Const. *at*, *to* (an amount); also *simply.* -1717. †4. To judge of -1624. 5. To consider, hold 1526. †b. *intr.* To account *of* -1633; to be of opinion *that* 1548. †6. To purpose, aim (*rare*) -1557.

1. What do you esteeme it at *Cymb.* I. iv. 85. 2. Have much and thou shalt be esteem'd much SKELTON. 5. Esteeming these virtues to be in me HOBBES. b. E. of things as they really are BP. HALL. Hence †**Estee·mable** *a.* = ESTIMABLE. **Estee·mer.** (*Obs.* exc. w. *of.*)

Ester (e·stəɹ). 1852. [Coined arbitrarily by L. Gmelin, German chemist, perh. 'to recall the sound of' *Essigäther*, at that time the name of the commonest representative of the group. Not in general Eng. use till *c* 1880.] *Chem.* An ethereal salt; a compound of an alcohol radical with an acid.

Esthete, -ic, var. ff. ÆSTHETE, -IC.

†**Esthiomene.** 1541. [a. F. *esthiomène*, ad. Gr. ἐσθιόμενος pr. pple. pass. or middle of ἐσθίειν.] *Path.* A gangrenous sore.

Estimable (e·stimăb'l). 1460. [a. F., ad. L. *æstimabilis*, f. *æstimare*; see ESTEEM, ESTIMATE *vbs.*]
A. *adj.* †1. Capable of being estimated or appraised -1805. †2. Valuable; of worth -1803. 3. Worthy of esteem or regard 1698.

2. A pound of mans flesh .. Is not so e., profitable neither As flesh of Muttons, Beefes, or Goates *Merch. V.* I. iii. 167. 3. A lady said of her two companions, that one was more amiable, the other more e. 1698.

†B. *sb. pl.* Things estimable. Cf. *valuables.* SIR T. BROWNE.
Hence **E·stimableness. E·stimably** *adv.*

Estimate (e·stimĕt), *sb.* 1563. [ad. L. *æstimatus* (only in abl.), vbl. sb. f. *æstimare*; see next and ESTEEM *v.*] †1. The action of valuing or appraising; a valuation; also *fig.* -1677. b. Repute -1657. 2. An approximate calculation based on probabilities; the result of this 1630. b. The sum stated by a builder, etc., as that for which he is prepared to execute a specified piece of work 1796.

1. Of my love he makes no e. DEKKER. 2. There is a design of building a Church..which by e. will cost [etc.] 1702. This e. both of interest and fitness varied from day to day FROUDE.

Estimate (e·stimeⁱt), *v.* 1532. [f. L. *æstimat-*, ppl. stem of *æstimare.* Cf. ESTEEM.] †1. *trans.* To assign a value to; to appraise, assess. Const. *at.* -1751. b. To value (subjectively); to esteem 1597. 2. To form a notion of (quantities, numbers, magnitudes, etc.) without actual enumeration or measurement; to fix by estimate *at* 1669. †3. = ESTEEM *v.* 5 (*rare*) -1794. 4. To gauge; to judge of 1651.

1. It is by the weight of silver .. that men e. commodities LOCKE (J.). To e. securities JOHNSON. 2. The difference of declination was only estimated 1765. To e. the amount of injury inflicted PRESCOTT, defalcations 1885. 4. To e. the powers of an author JOHNSON, of Shakespeare LANDOR. Hence **E·stimator. E·stimatory** *a.* for a price or valuation.

Estimation (estimēⁱ·ʃən). [ME. *estimacion, -cioun*, a. OF., ad. L. *æstimationem*, f. *æstimare*; see ESTIMATE.] †1. The action of estimating; valuation -1792; estimated value -1775. 2. Appreciation, esteem 1530; †repute -1828. 3. The process of forming a notion of without using precise data ME. 4. Opinion, judgement ME.; †conjecture. 1 *Hen. IV*, I. iii. 273.

2. An hie estimacion of our self MORE. Phr. *To have or hold in e.* How in estimacion a chaste life is 1569. Phr. *To grow out of e.* 3. If a ship sail 8 Miles South in an Hour, by Log or E. STURMY. 4. The dearest of men in my e. LANE.

Estimative (e·stimătiv), *a.* ME. [ad. late L. *æstimativus*; see ESTIMATE and -IVE.] 1. Serving for estimating; having the power of estimating. †2. Based upon approximate calculation -1651.

1. The errour is not in the eye, but in the e. faculty BOYLE.

‖**Estivage.** [Fr., f. *estiver*, ad. It. *stivare* :—L. *stipare* to pack close.] The practice of pressing or screwing the cargo into a vessel by means of a capstan machinery, as in American and Mediterranean ports.

Estival, Estivate, Estivation, var. ff. ÆSTIVAL, etc.

‖**Estoc** (e·stǫk). 1830. [Fr.] A kind of short sword. Hence †**Estoca·de**, a blow with an e.; the weapon itself.

Estoil(e (ĕstoi·l). 1572. [a. OF., mod.F. *étoile.*] *Her.* A charge in the form of a star with wavy points or rays. So **Estoilée** *a.* shaped like a star with wavy rays, as a *Cross Estoilée.*

Estop (ĕstǫ·p), *v.* ME. [a. OF. *estoper*, *estoupper*, and AF. *estopper*, f. OF. *estoupe* (mod. *étoupe*) :—L. *stuppa* tow. Cf. STOP *v.*] 1. *trans.* To stop with or as with a dam, plug, or bar (*arch.*). 2. *Law.* To impede or bar by ESTOPPEL 1531. 3. *gen.* To stop, prevent (*rare*) 1876.

2. A man may ..ot deny .. that whereof he wilfully estopped or excluded himselfe by deed indented WEST. Hence **Esto·p** *sb.* a stop or stoppage. **Esto·ppage**, stoppage; in *Law*, the condition of being estopped.

Estoppel (ĕstǫ·pĕl). 1531. [app. ad. OF. *estoupail* bung or cork, f. *estouper*; see prec.] †1. An obstruction (to a watercourse) -1638. 2. *Law.* An impediment or bar to a right of action arising from a man's own act, or where he is forbidden by law to speak against his own deed (Wharton) 1531. †b. *gen.* Prohibition 1583.

2. No e. can bind the king 1667.

Estovers (ĕstōᵘ·vəɹz), *sb. pl.* 1523. [a. OF., subst. use of *estovoir* to be necessary.] 'Necessaries allowed by law' (J.); *esp.* wood for repairs allowed to a tenant from off the landlord's estate; alimony for a widow or for a wife separated from her husband; maintenance for an imprisoned felon. (Cf. BOOT *sb.*[1])
Phr. *Common of e.*: see COMMON *sb.*

Estrade (ĕstrā·d). 1696. [a. F., ad. Sp. *estrado*; see ESTRADO.] A slightly raised platform; a dais.

†**Estra·diot.** 1577. [a. F. = It. *stradiotto*, f. Gr. στρατιώτης soldier.] One of a class of light cavalry, originally raised in Greece and Albania, who served as mercenaries in the 15th and 16th centuries -1596.

‖**Estrado** (estrā·do). 1588. [Sp. :—L. *stratum* neut., pa. pple. of *sternere* to spread (with carpets).] a. In Sp. sense: Drawing-room 1748. b. = ESTRADE.

Estramazo·ne. [var. of STRAMAZON.] A slashing cut in fencing. SCOTT.

†**Estra·nge.** *rare.* ME. [a. OF.; see STRANGE.]
A. *adj.* a. Distant, reserved. ME. only. b. Strange -1587; in *Law*, not privy *to* -1721.
B. *sb.* A stranger, foreigner. ME. only.

Estrange (ĕstrēⁱ·ndʒ), *v.* 1485. [ad. OF. *estranger* (mod. *étranger*) :—L. *extraneare*, f. *extraneus*; see STRANGE.] 1. *trans.* To remove from what is accustomed; to keep apart from acquaintance with. Const. *from* (*arch.*). 2. To render or regard as alien; to remove from the ownership or dominion of any one (*arch.*) 1523. 3. To alienate in feeling or affection. †Also *intr.* for *refl.* 1494. †4. To change from one's usual condition; hence, to put beside oneself, madden -1622. 5. To disguise (*arch.*) B. JONS.

1. Estranged from politics POPE. The room waits for its master long estranged B. TAYLOR. 2. He should not e. or cut off all the Churches of God which retained the tradition of old custome HANMER. 3. To e. and alienate the Saints from their God FLAVEL. 4. Being mad and sodainely estranged and bereft of his wits HANMER.

Hence **Estra·ngedness**, alienation in feeling or affection. †**Estra·ngeful** *a.* foreign in appearance.

‖**Estrangelo, estranghelo** (estræ·ŋgĕlo). 1730. [Syriac; ? a. Gr. στρογγύλος rounded.] An archaic form of the Syriac alphabet. Also *attrib.*

Estrangement (ĕstrēⁱ·ndʒmĕnt). 1660. [f. ESTRANGE *v.* + -MENT.] The action of estranging; the condition of being estranged; alienation. E. from God's house 1736.

Estranger[1] (ĕstrēⁱ·ndʒəɹ). 1623. [f. ESTRANGE *v.*] One who or that which estranges.

†**Estra·nger**[2]. 1471. [a. OF. *estranger*; see STRANGER.] 1. One belonging to another nation, family, or district -1641. 2. *Law.* = STRANGER. -1714.

†**Estra·ngle,** *v.* 1483. [ad. OF. *estrangler.*] = STRANGLE *v.*

Estrapade (estrăpēⁱ·d). 1730. [a. F., ad. It. *strappata*, f. *strappare* to pull with violence.] 1. The attempt of a horse to get rid of his rider by rearing and kicking. 2. *Hist.* = STRAPPADO. 1856.

Estray (ĕstrēⁱ·). 1581. [a. AF. *estray* vbl. sb., f. *estraier*; see ASTRAY.]
A. *sb. Law.* 'Any beast not wild, found within any Lordship, and not owned by any man' (Cowell) 1594. Also *transf.*
B. *adj.* That is astray (*rare*).
So **Estray·** *v.* to STRAY (*arch.*).

†**E·stre.** ME. [a. OF. *estre* (mod. *être*) being, condition.] 1. Condition, way of life. ME. only. 2. *concr.* A place; a region; also *pl.* apartments; inner rooms, or divisions -1485.

Estreat (ĕstrī·t), *sb.* ME. [a. AF. *estrete*, OF. *estraite* (in law L. *extracta*) :—L. *extrahere* to EXTRACT.] *Law.* 1. 'The true extract, copy, or note of some original writing or record, *esp.* of fines, amercements, etc., entered on the rolls of a court to be levied by the bailiff or other officer' (Wharton). †2. *transf.* in *pl.* The fines, etc., themselves -1640.

Estreat (ĕstrī·t), *v.* 1523. [f. prec.] *trans.* To extract or take out the record of (a recognizance, etc.) and return it to the court of exchequer to be prosecuted.

Estrepe (ĕstrī·p), *v.* 1672. [ad. OF. *estreper* :—L. *exstirpare* to root up.] *Law. trans.* To commit waste in lands or woods, to the prejudice of the reversioner (Dicts.).

Estrepement (ĕstrī·pmĕnt). 1503. [a. AF., f. *estreper*; see prec.] Wasting of lands; *esp.* waste committed by a tenant for life to the prejudice of the reversioner; 'also, making land barren by continual ploughing' (Wharton).

E·strich, e·stridge. 1450. [var. of OSTRICH, q.v.] †1. = OSTRICH -1687. 2. *Comm.* The fine down of the ostrich 1842.

†**E·striche.** [OE. *éast-ríce*, f. EAST + *ríce* kingdom.] **1.** An eastern kingdom; in OE. *spec.* the East Frankish kingdom –ME. †**2.** *attrib.* in *Estrich board*: applied to timber coming from Norway or the Baltic –1514.

†**E·stuant,** *a.* ME. only. [ad. L. *æstuantem*, f. *æstuare* to boil.] Boiling hot. So †**E·stuance,** heat, warmth.

Estuarial (estiu̯ēə·riăl), *a.* [f. L. *æstuarium* + -AL.] Of or pertaining to an estuary. So **Estua·rian, E·stuarine** *adjs.* (in same sense).

Estuary (e·stiuări). 1538. [ad. L. *æstuarium* adj. 'tidal', used subst., f. *æstus* heat, boiling, tide.] **1.** *gen.* A tidal opening; an arm of the sea. **2.** *spec.* The tidal mouth of a great river, where the tide meets the current. STOW. †**3.** A place where liquid boils up –1825. †**4.** A vapour-bath 1657. **5.** *attrib.* 1832.

1. La Plata .. is rather an e. of the sea than a river 1880 **2.** Estuaries (a term which we confine to inlets entered both by rivers and tides of the sea) LYELL.

Estuate, -ation, var. ff. ÆSTUATE, -ATION.

‖ **Estufa** (estū·fă). 1875. [Sp., corresp. to OF. *estuve* (mod. *étuve*); see STOVE.] An underground chamber, in which a fire is kept always burning; used as a place of assembly by the Pueblo Indians.

†**Estuo·sity.** 1657. [f. L. *æstuosus* + -ITY.] Heated condition –1730.

Esture, var. of ÆSTURE, *Obs.*

Esurience (ɨsiūə·riĕns). 1825. [See ESURIENT and -ENCE.] Hunger; 'neediness and greediness'. So **Esu·riency.**

Esurient (ɨsiūə·riĕnt), *a.* and *sb.* 1672. [ad. L. *esurientem*, pr. pple. of *esurire*, desiderative vb. f. *edere*.]

A. *adj.* **1.** Hungry. Now often in Juvenal's sense 'needy and greedy'. ¶ **2.** *catachr.* Gastronomic 1821.

1. An e. unprovided Advocate; Danton by name CARLYLE.

B. *sb.* A greedy person 1691.

†**Esurine.** 1651. [ad. mod.L. *esurinus*, app. irreg. f. *esuries* hunger.]

A. *adj.* Promoting appetite; also, voracious. Of salts: Corrosive. –1687.

B. *sb.* A medicine which provokes appetite 1775.

-et, *suffix*, forming dims. from sbs., repr. OF. *-et* masc., *-ete* (mod.F. *-ette*) fem. :—Com. Rom. *-itto, -itta*, ? of non-Latin origin; as in *bullet, fillet, pullet, sonnet*, etc., chiefly Fr. words, the original dim. sense of which is no longer felt.

Etacism (ē·tăsiz'm). 1833. [f. Gr. ἦτα, *eta*, the letter η, after LAMBDACISM.] The Erasmian pronunciation of the Gr. letter η as (ē) or (ẹ̄), and not as (ī). So **E·tacist,** one who favours e.

‖ **Étagère** (etaʒẹr). 1858. [Fr., f. *étage* shelf, story.] A piece of furniture having a number of shelves or stages, one above another, for holding ornaments, etc.

Et cetera, etcetera (et₁se·tĕră). Also **et** cætera; often abbrev. as etc., &c. ME. [a. L. *et cetera* (*cætera*).] **1.** As phr.: And the rest, and so forth, and so on, indicating that other things which can be inferred are included in the statement. **2.** As *sb.* Also pl. **etceteras. a.** A number of unspecified things or (improp.) persons 1656. **b.** *pl.* only: Usual additions, extras, sundries 1817.

Etch (etʃ), *sb.* 1573. [contr. f. EDDISH.] = EDDISH 2, 3.

Etch, *v.*[1] Now *dial.* 1806. [f. prec.] *intr.* To sow an after-crop.

Etch (etʃ), *v.*[2] 1634. [a. Du. *etsen*, a. Ger. *ätzen* :—(ult.) OTeut. **atjan*, causative of **etan* to EAT.] **1.** *trans.* To engrave by eating away the surface of with acids; chiefly, to engrave (a metal plate) by this process for the purpose of printing from it. Hence, to copy or represent (figures, designs) by this method. Also *transf.* and *fig.* **2.** *absol.* or *intr.* To practise the art of etching 1634. **3.** To corrode 1664.

1. All the Illustrations, which were formerly etched on copper, have been newly etched on steel MRS. JAMESON. **2.** The operation of etching upon glass 1854. Hence **E·tcher,** one who etches.

†**Etch,** *v.*[3] 1682. Var. of obs. *eche* vb., to increase. *To etch out*, to eke out. LOCKE. –1698.

Etching (e·tʃiŋ), *vbl. sb.* 1634. [f. as prec.] **1.** The action of ETCH *v.*[2]; the art of the etcher. **2.** *concr.* A copy or representation produced by etching; an impression from an etched plate 1762. **3.** *attrib.*, as *e.-needle*, etc.; **e.-ground,** the composition with which the plate, etc. is covered, preparatory to etching 1790.

1. Prince Rupert..was the inventor of e. HUME.

†**E·ten, e·ttin.** [OE. *eoten, eten* :—OTeut. **ituno-z.*] A giant –1611.

†**Eteo·stic, eteo·stichon.** [f. Gr. ἐτεος, gen. of ἔτος year + στίχος row.] = CHRONOGRAM. B. JONS.

†**Ete·rminable,** *a.* [f. E- *pref.*[3] (= IN-) + TERMINABLE.] Without end; eternal. SKELTON.

Eternal (ɨtɔ̄·ɹnăl). ME. [a. OF. *eternal, -el* (mod. *éternel*), ad. late L. *æternalis*, f. *æternus*; see ETERNE and -AL.]

A. *adj.* **1.** Without beginning or end; that has always existed and always will exist; *esp.* of God 1470. **b.** *Metaph.* Not conditioned by time 1651. **2.** Infinite in past duration 1690. **3.** Infinite in future duration. Also *rhet.* ME. **b.** *transf.* Pertaining to eternal things; having eternal consequences 1605. **4.** *familiar.* Perpetual, incessant, always recurring 1787. **5.** Valid through all eternity, immutable 1688. **6.** Infernal, damned. Now *vulgar.* 1601. **7.** quasi-*adv.* 1611.

1. The eternall God is thy refuge *Deut.* xxxiii. 27. **3.** Judgment upon the e. soul 1834. Phr. *E. life, death, punishment. rhet.* That eternall citie Rome 1609. **b.** Things of such e. moment LAW. **4.** Sipping her e. tea THACKERAY. **5.** A Treatise concerning E. and Immutable Morality CUDWORTH (*title*). **6.** I will be hang'd, if some eternall Villaine Haue not deuis'd this Slander SHAKS. **7.** To be Boy eternall SHAKS.

B. quasi-*sb.* and *sb.* **1.** *The E.*: God. 1582. †**2.** = ETERNITY, as in phr. *from eternal* –1742. **3.** Eternal things 1649.

1. The lawe whereby the Eternal himselfe doth worke HOOKER. Hence †**Ete·rnalist,** one who believes in the e. duration of the world. †**Eterna·lity,** eternalness. **Ete·rnalize** *v.* to make e.; to perpetuate; to immortalize. **Ete·rnal-ly** *adv.*, **-ness.**

Eterne (ɨtɔ̄·ɹn), *a.* Now *arch.* (*poet.*) ME. [a. OF., ad. L. *æternus* for *æviternus*, f. *ævum.*] **1.** = ETERNAL *a.* **2.** *absol.* †**a.** In *fro e.* (= L. *ab æterno*), from eternity. **b.** *The e.*: that which is eternal. **c.** *The E.*: the Eternal.

1. In them, Natures Coppie's not e. *Macb.* III. ii. 38. Hence **Ete·rnify** *v.* to make eternal.

†**Ete·rnish,** *v. pa. pple.* **eternest.** 1579. [ad. F. *éterniser*; see -ISH.] To make eternal or eternally famous –1594.

Eternity (ɨtɔ̄·ɹnĭti). [ME. *eternite*, a. F. *éternité*, ad. L. *æternitatem*, f. *æternus*; see ETERNE.] **1.** The quality, condition, or fact of being eternal; eternal existence. **b.** Indefinite continuance ME. **2.** Infinite time: **a.** without beginning or end 1587; **b.** without beginning 1651; **c.** without end ME. **3.** Time felt as endless, or indefinitely remote 1703. **4.** In contrast with *time*. **a.** *Metaph.* (cf. ETERNAL 1 b): Timelessness 1662. **b.** The condition which begins at death; the future life 1602.

1. He wants nothing of a god but E. *Cor.* V. iv. 25. **b.** A desire he had..of æternity and perpetuall fame HOLLAND. **2. b.** 'Natural' are those which have been Lawes from all E. HOBBES. **c.** Eternitie, whose end no eye can reach MILT. *P. L.* XII. 556. **4. a.** E. is a permanent now HOBBES. **b.** All that liues must dye, Passing through Nature to E. *Haml.* I. ii. 73.

Eternize (ɨtɔ̄·ɹnəiz, ī·tɔɹnəiz), *v.* 1568. [a. F. *éterniser*, ad. med.L. *æternizare*, f. *æternus*; see ETERNE.] **1.** *trans.* To make eternal or everlasting 1580. **2.** To make lasting 1568. **3.** To make eternally famous; to immortalize 1610.

1. This other [immortality] serv'd but to e. woe MILT. *P. L.* XI. 60. **2.** To e. quarrels 1716. **3.** Monuments to e. the men who have thus become great BRIGHT. Hence †**Ete·rnizement,** immortal fame. †**Ete·rnizer.**

Etesian (etī·ʒiăn), *a.* (*sb.*) 1601. [f. L. *etesius*, a. Gr. ἐτήσιος annual, f. ἔτος year + -AN.] **1.** Epithet of certain winds in the region of the Mediterranean, which blow from the NW. for about 40 days annually in the summer. Hence *transf.* of the trade-winds, monsoons, etc. †**2.** quasi-*sb.* –1684.

Eth- (eþ-). *Chem.* The first syllable of ETHER, used to form names for the members of the bi-carbon or ETHYL series of hydrocarbons.

Ethal (e·þăl). 1839. [f. ETH- + -AL.] *Chem.* The same as *Cetyl* or *Cetylic Alcohol* (see CET-). Hence **Etha·lic** *a.*

Ethane (e·þēⁱn). 1873. [f. ETH- + -ANE.] *Chem.* The saturated hydrocarbon, C_2H_6, forming the second member of the series C_nH_{2n+2}; also called *Ethyl hydride* and *di-methyl*; a colourless, inodorous gas.

‖ **Ethanim** (e·pănim). 1535. [Heb.] The 7th month of the Heb. sacred, and 1st of the civil year, called also Tisri.

E·thel, *sb.* Now *Hist.* [Com. Teut.: OE. *æðel, éðel.*] Ancestral land or estate, patrimony.

†**E·thel,** var. of ATHEL *a.* Hence **ethelborn** *a.* nobly born.

Etheling, obs. f. ATHELING.

Ethene (e·þīn). 1873. [f. ETH-YL + -ENE.] *Chem.* A fatty hydrocarbon, C_2H_4, forming the second member of the series C_nH_{2n}; known as Ethylene, Olefiant Gas, or Heavy Carburetted Hydrogen. Also *attrib.*

Ether (ī·þəɹ). Also **æther.** ME. [a. L. *æther*, ad. Gr. αἰθήρ, f. root of αἴθειν to burn, glow. In the *Chem.* sense, *ether* is the recognized form.] **1.** The clear sky; the medium filling the upper regions of space. Now *poet.* or *rhet.* 1587. **2.** In ancient cosmology, an element filling all space beyond the sphere of the moon, and constituting the substance of the stars and planets. It was conceived as a purer form of fire or of air, or as a fifth element. ME. **3.** Air 1713. †**4.** = AURA 2, 3. –1791. **5.** *Mod. Physics.* An elastic and subtle substance believed to permeate all space; the medium through which the waves of light are propagated. Sometimes called *the luminiferous ether.* Also *fig.* Also *attrib.* 1644. **6.** *Chem.* **a.** The colourless, light, volatile liquid ($C_4H_{10}O$), resulting from the action of sulphuric acid upon alcohol, and hence known as *Sulphuric ether.* In commercial use the term ether refers to this substance, which is now called technically *Common ether*, or *Ethyl oxide*. It is an anæsthetic and a powerful solvent of fats, etc. 1757. **b.** Hence, the generic name of a class of compounds, formed by the action of acids upon alcohols, divided into (1) *Simple ethers*, which comprise the oxides, sulphides, chlorides, etc. of alcohol radicals; and (2) *Compound ethers*, in which an acid radical replaces the hydrogen of the hydroxyl of an alcohol 1838.

1. All the unmeasured æther flames with light POPE. A land..Where every breath even now changes to e. divine CLOUGH.

Hence **E·theric** *a.* of or pertaining to e. So †**Ethe·rical** *a.* **E·therifica·tion,** the process of converting alcohol into e. **E·theriform** *a.* having the form of e. **E·therify** *v.* to convert into an e. **E·therous** *a.* e.-like.

Ethereal, -ial (ɨþī³·riăl), *a.* 1513. [f. L. *ætherius* or *æthereus* (ad. Gr. αἰθέριος) + -AL.] **1.** Of the nature of the ether; hence, light, airy, attenuated 1598. **2.** Celestial. Chiefly *poet.* 1667. **3.** Pertaining to the higher region of the atmosphere; also, to the terrestrial atmosphere, relatively to the lower regions 1513. **4.** Spirit-like, impalpable 1647. **5.** *Physics.* Of, pertaining to, or having the nature of 'ether' (see ETHER 5) 1692. **6.** *Chem.* Resembling 'ether' (see ETHER 6), or its qualities 1800. **7.** *absol.* The ethereal principle, the spirit or essence 1661.

2. Go, Heavenly Guest, Ethereal Messenger MILT. *P. L.* VIII. 646. **3.** Near the Confines of Etherial Light .. Th' unwary Lover cast his Eyes behind DRYDEN. **4.** Her e. nature seemed to shrink from coarse reality DISRAELI.

Phr. *E. oil* = Essential or Volatile oil.

Hence **Ethe·realism,** e. quality or state (Dicts.). **Ethe·rea·lity, -iality,** the quality of being e. or incorporeal; something that is e. **Ethe·really, -ially** *adv.* **Ethe·realness.**

Etherealize, -ialize (ɨþī³·riăləiz), *v.* Also æther-. 1829. [f. prec. + -IZE.] To make or render ethereal in various senses. Hence **Ethe·realiza·tion, -ialization,** the action or process of etherealizing.

Etherean, -ian (ɨþī³·riăn), *a. rare.* 1651. [f. L. *æthereus* or *ætherius* + -AN.] = ETHEREAL.

Etherene (ī·þĕrīn). Also **-ine.** 1850. [f. ETHER + -ENE.] *Chem.* = ETHYLENE.

Ethereous, -ious (ɨþī³·riəs), *a.* 1667. [f. L.

æthereus + -OUS.] Composed, or of the nature, of ether, or of the upper element of the universe.

Etherin (ī·þĕrin). 1882. [f. ETHER + -IN.] *Chem.* A substance which separates, mixed with etherol, from heavy oil of wine when warmed with water. Both etherin and etherol are polymeric with ethylene.

Etherism (ī·þĕriz'm). [f. ETHER + -ISM; cf. *alcoholism.*] 'The successive phenomena developed in the animal body by the administration of the vapour of ether' (*Syd. Soc. Lex.*).

Etherize (ī·þĕrəiz), *v.* 1748. [f. ETHER + -IZE.] **1.** To convert (alcohol, etc.) into ether 1828. **2.** To mix or compound with ether 1800. **3.** To put (a patient) under the influence of ether. Also *transf.* 1864. †**4.** = ELECTRIFY. 1748. Hence **E:theriza·tion**, the administration of ether (also *fig.*); the becoming, or being, etherized. **E·therizer**, an apparatus for administering ether.

Etherol (ī·þĕrǫl). 1876. [f. ETHER + -OL.] *Chem.* See ETHERIN.

Ethic (e·þik). ME. [ad. L. *ethicus*, Gr. ἠθικός, f. ἦθος character, *pl.* manners. Cf. F. *éthique.*]

A. *adj.* (Now usu. ETHICAL.) **1.** Relating to morals 1581. **2.** Treating of moral questions or of moral science 1589. **3.** Characterized by 'ethos' (see ETHOS 2) 1848.

1 Æthique precepts 1644, doctrine SAVAGE. 2. E. epistles POPE. Dr. Hutcheson is the principal E. writer of this country [Ireland] MORSE.

B. *sb.* **1.** *sing.* [Gr. ἡ ἠθική (τέχνη).] The or a science of morals ME. **2.** *pl.* **Ethics** (after Gr. τὰ ἠθικά). The science of morals 1602. **b.** A treatise on the science; *spec.* that of Aristotle ME. **3. a.** The moral system of a particular writer or school of thought 1651. **b.** The rules of conduct recognized in certain limited departments of human life 1789. **4.** The science of human duty in its widest extent, including, besides ethics proper, the science of law whether civil, political, or international 1690.

1. An attempt to construct an e. apart from theology 1886. 3. a. Christian ethics 1855. The zoölogical ethics of Combe MARTINEAU. b. Sea rights and sea ethics 1864. The ethics of dining 1870. Church ethics MOZLEY. Medical ethics 1884.

Ethical (e·þikăl), *a.* 1607. [f. prec. + -AL.] **1.** = ETHIC *a.* 1, 3. **2.** = ETHIC *a.* 2. 1665. **3.** *Gram.* In *Ethical dative*: the dative when used to imply that a person, other than the subject or object, has an interest in the fact stated. Hence **E·thical-ly** *adv.*, **-ness**.

Ethician (eþi·ʃăn). *rare.* 1889. [f. L. *ethicus.*] One versed in ethics. So **E·thicist**. (Dicts.)

Ethicize (e·þisəiz), *v.* 1816. [f. as prec. + -IZE.] **1.** *intr.* To discuss ethics; to moralize. COLMAN. **2.** *trans.* To make ethical 1885.

2. The idealizing process which .. ethicizes nature MARTINEAU.

Ethico- (e·þiko-), repr. Gr. ἠθικο-, comb. f. ἠθικός; as in **E.-physical, -political, -religious**, pertaining jointly to ethics, and physics, politics, or religion.

Ethide (e·þəid). 1865. [f. ETH- + -IDE.] *Chem.* A compound of an element or radical and the monad radical ethyl.

Ethine (e·þəin). 1877. [f. ETH- + -INE.] *Chem.* = ACETYLENE.

Ethionic (īþi,ǫ·nik), *a.* 1838. [f. E(THER) + Gr. θεῖον sulphur + -IC.] (*Chem.*) *E. acid*: $C_2H_6S_2O_7$ produced by the action of water on *E. anhydride*, $C_2H_4 2SO_3$, formerly called *Sulphate of carbyl*, which is obtained by bringing together olefiant gas and vapour of sulphuric anhydride in a tube.

Ethiop (ī·þi,ǫp). *arch.* ME. [ad. L. *Æthiops*, *Æthiopis*, ad. Gr. Αἰθίοψ, Αἰθίοπος, Ethiopian, ? f. αἴθειν to burn + ὤψ face. (In Eng. with initial capital.)]

A. *sb.* lit. = ETHIOPIAN; hence, a black.

To wash an (the) E. (white): to attempt the impossible.

B. *attrib.* and *adj.* **1.** = ETHIOPIAN. 1667. **2.** Black 1600.

2. E. vvords, blacker in their effect Then in their countenance *A. Y. L.* IV. iii. 35.

Hence †**Ethiopesse**, a female Ethiopian.

Ethiopian (īþi,ōᵘ·piăn). 1552. [f. prec. or *Ethiopia*; see -IAN, -AN.]

A. *adj.* **1.** Of or belonging to Ethiopia, or to the *Æthiopes.* Often = 'negro'. **2. a.** *Anthropology.* Name of one of the races of man 1861. **b.** *Biol.* Epithet of one of the biological regions 1880.

1. The E. guards LYTTON, serenaders 1861.

B. *sb.* A native of Ethiopia; †a negro 1552.

Ethiopic (īþi,ǫ·pik), *a.* 1659. [ad. L. *æthiopicus.*] **1.** Of or belonging to Ethiopia. Now only with reference to language. **2.** *absol.* The Ethiopic language 1867.

†**E·thiops.** Also **æ-**. 1706. [a. L. *æthiops* lit. 'ETHIOP, negro'.] A name given formerly to certain black or dark-coloured compounds of metals. *E. martial*: the black oxide of iron. *E. mineral*: the black sulphide of mercury, prepared by triturating mercury with sulphur. -1854.

Ethmo- (e·þmo-), comb. f. Gr. ἠθμός sieve, with sense 'pertaining to the ethmoid bone and ——'; as in

Ethmo-turbinal (plates) or **Ethmo-turbinals** [see TURBINAL], the lateral masses of the ethmoid bone, connected horizontally with each other at the upper surface by the cribriform bone. **Ethmo-vomerine** (plate), 'a cartilaginous plate beneath the front of the fetal brain, from which the ethmoid region of the skull is developed' (Webster).

Ethmoid (e·þmoid). 1741. [ad. Gr. ἠθμοειδής sieve-like, cribriform; see -OID.]

A. *adj.* Sieve-like, finely perforated.

E. bone: a square-shaped cellular bone, situated between the two orbits, at the root of the nose, containing many perforations, through which the olfactory nerves pass to the nose.

B. quasi-*sb.* or *sb.* = *ethmoid bone.*

Hence **Ethmoi·dal** *a.* of or pertaining to the e. bone; ETHMOID.

Ethmose (eþmōᵘ·s). [f. Gr. ἠθμός sieve.] *Phys.* Cellular tissue

Ethnarch (e·þnaɹk). 1641. [ad. Gr. ἐθνάρχης, f. ἔθνος + -αρχος.] A governor of a people or province. So **E·thnarchy**, the office or dominion of, or the province ruled by, an e.

Ethnic (e·þnik). ME. [ad. Gr. ἐθνικός heathen, f. ἔθνος nation; in the LXX, etc. τὰ ἔθνη = the (non-Israelitish) nations, Gentiles.]

A. *adj.* **1.** Pertaining to nations not Christian or Jewish; Gentile, heathen, pagan 1470. **2.** Ethnological 1851.

†**B.** *sb.* A Gentile, heathen, pagan -1728.

Hence **E·thnical** *a.* †heathenish; †pagan; ethnological. **E·thnically** *adv.* **E·thnicism**, †heathenism, paganism; in mod. use, the religions of the Gentile nations or their common characteristics.

†**E·thnish**, *a.* 1550. [f. Gr. ἔθνος (see prec.) + -ISH.] = HEATHENISH. -1563.

Ethnize (e·þnəiz), *v. rare.* 1847. [f. as prec. (see ETHNIC) + -IZE.] To favour Gentile views or practices.

Ethnodicy (eþnǫ·disi). *rare.* 1889. [f. Gr. ἔθνος + -δικία, f. δίκη justice.] Comparative jurisprudence as a branch of ethnology.

Ethnogeny (eþnǫ·dʒĭni). [f. as prec. + Gr. -γένεια birth.] The branch of ethnology which treats of the origin of races and nations. Hence **Ethnoge·nic** *a.* pertaining to e.

Ethnography (eþnǫ·grăfi). 1834. [f. Gr. ἔθνος + -γραφια.] The scientific description of nations or races of men, their customs, habits, and differences.

E. embraces the descriptive details .. of the human aggregates and organizations RECLUS.

Hence **Ethno·grapher**, one who studies or is versed in e. **Ethnogra·phic, -al** *a.* of or pertaining to e. **Ethnogra·phically** *adv.* **Ethno·graphist**, ethnographer.

Ethnology (eþnǫ·lŏdʒi). 1842. [f. Gr. ἔθνος + -λογια; see -LOGY.] The science which treats of races and peoples, their relations, their distinctive characteristics, etc.

General e.; [viz.] ethics, ethnodicy, and sociology 1889. Hence **Ethno·loger** = ETHNOLOGIST. **Ethnolo·gic, -al** *a.* of or pertaining to e. **Ethnolo·gically** *adv.* **Ethno·logist**, one who studies or is versed in e. **Ethno·logize** *v. intr.* to speculate on ethnological questions.

Ethnomaniac (eþnomēⁱ·niæk). 1863. [f. Gr. ἔθνος + MANIAC.] One who is crazy about racial autonomy.

Ethnopsychology (e:þno,səikǫ·lŏdʒi). 1886. [f. as prec. + PSYCHOLOGY.] The study of the psychology of races and peoples. Hence **E:thnopsycholo·gical** *a.*

Ethology (iþǫ·lŏdʒi). 1656. [ad. L. *ethologia*, a. Gr., f. ἦθος character + -λογια; see -LOGY.] †**1.** The portrayal of character by mimicry. (Dicts.) †**2.** The science of ethics; also, a treatise on morals. (Dicts.) **3.** 'The science of character' (J. S. Mill). Hence **Etholo·gic, -al** *a.* pertaining to e. **Etho·logist**, one who practises, studies, or is versed in e.

†**E:thopoe·tic**, *a.* [ad. Gr. ἠθοποιητικός, f. ἦθος character + ποιητικός.] Intended to represent character or manners. URQUHART.

‖**Ethos** (ī·þǫs). 1851. [mod.L., a. Gr. ἦθος character.] **1.** [After Arist. *Rhet.* II. xii–xiv.] The prevalent tone of sentiment of a people or community; the genius of an institution or system. **2.** *Gr. Æsthetics* and *Rhetoric.* Character; ? ideal excellence; in *Gr. Rhet.* often opposed to *pathos*, emotion 1875.

1. The e. of Catholic sacerdotal life 1882. 2. By e., as applied to the paintings of Polygnotus, we understand a dignified bearing in his figures, and a measured movement throughout his compositions A. S. MURRAY.

Ethyl (e·þil). Also †**ethule.** 1840. [f. ETH(ER) + -YL = Gr. ὕλη matter.] The hypothetical radical of the dicarbon series (C_2H_5), the base of common alcohol, ether, and acetic acid, and of a large series of compounds, as *E. hydride* C_2H_6 (= C_2H_5H), *E. chloride* C_2H_5Cl, *E. iodide* C_2H_5I, *E. alcohol* C_2H_6O.

Hence **E·thylami·ne**, a compound ($NH_2C_2H_5$) of the ammonia type in which one of the hydrogen atoms of ammonia is replaced by ethyl; called also *e. ammonia.* **E·thylate**, a salt of the radical ethyl, in which ethyl takes the place of the oxygenated group in a metallic salt. **E·thylene**, the diatomic hydrocarbon or olefine of the ethyl series, C_2H_4; also known as Ethene, Olefiant gas, or Heavy Carburetted Hydrogen, an important constituent of coal gas. **Ethy·lic** *a.* of ethyl; = ETHYL used attrib., as in *Ethylic cyanate* = Ethyl cyanate = Vinic cyanate.

Etiolate (ī·tiolᵉⁱt). 1791. [f. F. *étioler*, of dial. origin :—(ult.) L. *stipula* straw.] **1.** *trans.* To blanch or make colourless (a plant) by excluding the light from it. **2.** *transf.* To give a pale and sickly hue to (a human being or his skin) 1842. Also *fig.* **3.** *intr.* To become white or whiter; to blanch; to be whitened by exclusion of sunlight, as plants 1828.

1. Celery is in this manner blanched or etiolated WHEWELL. 2. *fig.* These industries .. are sickly, nerveless, and etiolated 1879. Hence **Etiola·tion**, the action of etiolating, or the becoming, or being, etiolated.

Etiolin (ī·tiŏlin). 1882. [f. ETIOL(ATE) + -IN.] A yellow modification of chlorophyll formed in plants growing in the dark.

Etiological, var. of ÆTIOLOGICAL.

Etiology, var. of ÆTIOLOGY. Hence **Etio·logist**, one who studies etiology, or the science of causes.

Etiquette (e·tiket). 1750. [a. F. *étiquette* ticket, label (:—OF. *estiquette*). Cf. TICKET.] **1. a.** The prescribed ceremonial of a court; the usages of diplomatic intercourse. **b.** The order of procedure established by custom in the army and navy, in parliament, etc. **c.** The conventional rules of behaviour and ceremonies observed in polite society. **d.** The unwritten code of honour which discountenances certain practices in some of the professions. †**2.** A rule of etiquette. Chiefly *pl.* -1816. **3.** A label (*rare*) 1867.

c. Man is..a slave..to e. ROBERTSON.

Etna (e·tnă). Also **ætna.** 1832. [f. the name of the volcano.] A vessel for heating liquids by burning some kind of spirit.

Eton (ī·t'n). *E. College*, a public school for boys, on the Thames opposite Windsor.

E. collar, a broad stiff collar orig. and esp. worn outside the *E. jacket*, a short black broadcloth jacket pointed at the back (so *E. suit*, also called *Etons*). *E. crop*, a fashion of cutting women's hair close to the head all over.

Etonian (ītōᵘ·niăn). 1749. [f. *Eton* + -IAN.] **a.** *adj.* Of or pertaining to Eton or Eton College. **b.** *sb.* One educated at Eton College 1770.

Etrurian (ĭtrūᵊ·riăn). 1623. [f. *Etruria.*]

A. *adj.* Of or belonging to Etruria. **B.** *sb.* A native of Etruria.

Etruscan (ĭtrʊ·skăn). 1706. [f. L. *Etruscus* + -AN.] **A.** *adj.* Of or belonging to ancient Etruria or its people; *absol.* their language. **B.** *sb.* One belonging to the Etruscan people.

Et seq. and the following: see SEQ.

-ette, *suffix*, forming dims., repr. OF. *-ette* fem.; see -ET.

Ettercap (e·təɹkæp). *Sc.* 1721. [var. f. ATTERCOP.] = ATTERCOP.

Ettle (e·t'l), *v.* Now only *n. dial.* ME. [a. ON. *ætla* to think, conjecture, purpose, etc. :—prehist. **ahtila*, f. OTeut. **ahtā* (OE. *eaht*, Ger. *acht*) consideration, f. root of Goth. *aha* 'νοῦς', understanding, *ahma* soul.] **1.** *trans.* To purpose, plan; to endeavour. **2.** To assign ME. **3.** To direct (speech or actions) to an object; *absol.* or *intr.* to take aim (*at*) ME.; *intr.* to make an effort *at* 1725. **4.** *trans.* To guess, conjecture ME. Hence **E·ttle** *sb.* aim, intent; opportunity.

Etui, etwee (etwī·). 1611. [a. F. *étui*, OF. *estui*, ?f. *estuier* (:—late L. type **stugare*) to keep, hold in custody. Cf. TWEEZE.] A case for small articles, as bodkins, needles, toothpicks, etc.; †a case for surgical instruments.

Etymologer (etimǫ·lŏdʒəɹ). 1650. [f. Gr. ἐτυμολόγος, f. ἔτυμον ETYMON + -λογος one who discourses + -ER.] = ETYMOLOGIST.

‖**Etymologicon** (e:timolǫ·dʒikǫn). 1645. [mod.L., a. Gr. ἐτυμολογικόν adj. neut.; see prec.] An etymological word-book.

Etymologize (etimǫ·lŏdʒəiz), *v.* 1530. [ad. late L. *etymologizare*, f. *etymologia* ETYMOLOGY; see -IZE.] **1.** *trans.* To give or trace the etymology of; to suggest an etymology for. **2.** *intr.* To study etymology; to suggest etymologies for words 1652. Hence **Etymologiza·tion.**

Etymology (etimǫ·lŏdʒi). ME. [a. OF. *ethimologie* (mod. *étymologie*), ad. L. *etymologia*, a. Gr., f. ἐτυμολόγος; see ETYMOLOGER.] **1. a.** The process of expounding the elements of a word with their modifications of form and sense. Also with *an* and *pl.* 1588. **b.** The facts relating to the formation and derivation (of a word) ME. †**c.** Etymological sense –1714. **2.** The branch of linguistic science which treats of the origin of words 1646. **3.** *Gram.* The part of grammar which treats of the parts of speech, their formation and inflexions 1592.

1. E. is sometimes a very precarious..thing WATTS. c. This name [widowes]..hath received one constant E.; 'deprived' or 'destitute' BRATHWAIT.

Hence **E:tymolo·gic, -al** *a.* of, pertaining to, or in accordance with e. **E:tymolo·gically** *adv.* **Etymo·logist,** one who treats of, or is versed in, e.

‖**Etymon** (e·timǫn). 1570. [L., a. Gr. ἔτυμον (orig. neut. of ἔτυμος true).] †**1.** The 'true' or primitive form of a word –1793. **2.** The primary word from which a derivative is formed 1659. †**3.** 'True' or original signification –1834.

1. Blew hath his E. from the high Dutch Blaw PEACHAM. 2. Logic is nothing more than a knowledge of words, as the Greek e. implies LAMB.

Eu-, *prefix*, repr. Gr. εὐ-, comb. f. ἐύς good, used in neut. εὖ as adv. = well. In Eng. the prefix occurs mostly in words of Gr. derivation, with the senses 'good', 'well', 'easily'.

Euboic (yubōᵘ·ik), *a.* 1667. [ad. L. *Euboicus*, a. Gr., f. Εὔβοια Eubœa.] Belonging to Eubœa. MILT. *P. L.* II. 546.

Eucairite (yūkē̆ᵊ·rəit, yūkai·rəit). Also **eukairite.** 1822. [f. Gr. εὔκαιρος opportune + -ITE.] *Min.* A mineral, consisting principally of selenium, copper, and silver; so named because found about the time Berzelius discovered selenium.

Eucalyn (yū·kălin). 1864. [f. EUCALY(PTUS) + -(I)N.] *Chem.* A saccharine substance, obtained by the decomposition of melitose, under the influence of yeast.

Eucalyptus (yūkăli·ptǫs). *Pl.* **-i, -uses.** 1809. [mod.L., as if f. Gr. εὐκάλυπτος for 'well-covered'; the flower before it opens having a sort of cap.] *Bot.* A genus of plants of the N.O. *Myrtaceæ*; the Gum-tree of Australia; a tree of this kind. **b.** = *e. oil*, an antiseptic and disinfectant 1885. Hence **Eucaly·ptene, Eucaly·ptin,** a product ($C_{12}H_{18}$), yielded when eucalyptol is heated with phosphoric anhydride and gives up water. **Eucaly·ptol,** a compound contained largely in the volatile oil of *E. globulus*.

Eucharis (yū·kăris). 1866. [a. Gr. εὔχαρις gracious, f. εὐ- (see EU-) + χάρις.] *Bot.* A South Amer. bulbous plant (N.O. *Amaryllidaceæ*), bearing white bell-shaped flowers. Also *attrib.*

Eucharist (yū·kărist). ME. [a. OF. *eucariste*, ad. late L. *eucharistia*, a. Gr., f. εὐ- (see EU-) + χαρίζεσθαι to offer willingly.] **1.** *Eccl.* The sacrament of the Lord's Supper; the Communion. **2.** The consecrated elements, *esp.* the bread 1536. †**3.** The box containing the bread; the pyx –1560. **4.** Thanksgiving 1613.

1. The efficacy of the E. in both kinds was more complete S. AUSTIN. 2. The corporal presence of our Lord in the E. HOOK. 4. To pay their e. to the Holy Ghost JER. TAYLOR.

Hence **Euchari·stic, -al** *a.* of, pertaining to, or of the nature of, the E.; of or pertaining to thanksgiving. **Euchari·stically** *adv.* **Euchari·stize** *v.* to affect (the elements) by an act of thanksgiving.

Euchite (yū·kəit). 1585. [ad. late L. *euchita*, *eucheta*, f. (ult.) Gr. εὐχή prayer.] One of a 4th c. sect which believed that perpetual prayer was the only means of salvation. Also applied to later sects holding these views.

†**Euchlo·ric,** *a.* 1811. [f. next + -IC.] In *Euchloric gas* = EUCHLORINE.

Euchlorine (yū·klōᵊrin). 1812. [f. Gr. εὐ- (see EU-) + χλωρός green + -INE. Coined by Davy after CHLORINE.] *Chem.* 'A gaseous mixture of chlorine and oxide of chlorine, obtained by the action of hydrochloric acid on chlorate of potassium' (Watts).

Euchlorite (yū·klōᵊrəit). 1876. [f. as prec. + -ITE.] *Min.* A deep green variety of magnesia mica, found at Chester (Mass.) in 1876.

‖**Euchologion** (yūkolōᵘ·dʒiǫn). Also in L. form **-um.** 1651. [ad. Gr., f. εὐχή prayer + λογ- stem of λέγειν.] A prayer-book; also, a book of ritual, primarily that of the Greek Church. vars. †**Eu·chologue, Eucho·logy.**

Euchre (yū·kəɹ), *sb.* 1846. [?] **1.** A game of cards, of American origin, played by 2, 3, or 4 persons, with a pack of 32 cards (the 2, 3, 4, 5, 6 of each suit not being used). A player may 'pass', but if he plays, and fails to take 3 tricks, he or his side is 'euchred' and the other side gains two points.

The highest card is the knave of trumps, called *right bower*, and the next highest the other knave of the same colour, called *left bower*, but in *Railroad Euchre* an extra blank card called the *joker* is used, which takes any other.

2. An instance of euchreing or being euchred 1880.

1. We had a small game, And Ah Sin took a hand: It was e. The same he did not understand B. HARTE.

Hence **Eu·chreist,** a player at e.

Euchre (yū·kəɹ), *v.* 1866. [f. prec. sb.] *trans.* To get the better of (the adversary) by his failure to take three tricks; see the sb. Hence *transf.* to outwit, 'do'.

Euchroite (yū·kro,əit). 1825. [f. Gr. εὔχροος well-coloured, f. εὐ- (see EU-) + χροά + -ITE.] *Min.* A hydrous arsenate of copper of a bright emerald-green colour.

†**Euchy·mous,** *a.* 1651. [f. mod.L. *euchymus*, f. (ult.) Gr. εὐ- (see EU-) + χυμός CHYME.] Conducive to a good state of the fluids of the body. So †**Eu·chymy,** a good state of these.

†**Euchysiderite.** 1823. [f. Gr. εὐ- + χύσις melting + σίδηρος iron + -ITE.] *Min.* = PYROXENE.

Euclase (yū·klēⁱs). 1804. [a. F., f. Gr. εὐ- (see EU-) + κλάσις breaking; so named from its easy cleavage.] *Min.* A silicate of aluminium and glucinum occurring in light-green, transparent crystals.

Euclid (yū·klid). 1581. [ad. Gr. Εὐκλείδης.] A geometer of Alexandria (*c* 300 B.C.): hence, his works, *esp.* the Elements.

Euclidean (yukli·dĭăn, yūklidī·ăn), *a.* Also **-ian.** 1660. [f. L. *Euclideus* (see prec.) + -AN.] Of or pertaining to Euclid; that is according to the principles of Euclid.

Phr. *E. space*: space as known to us, for which the axioms of Euclid are valid, as opp. to hypothetical kinds of space.

Eucolite (yū·kŏləit). 1847. [f. Gr. εὔκολος easily satisfied (f. εὐ + κόλον food) + -ITE. So named 'because it *contented itself* .. with iron oxide in default of zirconia' (Scheerer).] *Min.* A variety of eudialyte.

Eucrasy (yū·krăsi). 1607. [ad. Gr. εὐκρασία, f. εὐ- (see EU-) + κρα-, κεραννύναι to mix.] Such a due mixture of qualities as constitutes health or soundness.

†**Euctical** (yū·ktikăl), *a.* 1638. [f. Gr. εὐκτικός pertaining to prayer + -AL.] Pertaining to prayer; supplicatory –1745.

Eudemon, -dæmon (yudī·mən). 1629. [a. Gr. εὐδαίμων fortunate, happy, f. εὐ- + δαίμων genius. Sense 2 is of mod. origin.] **1.** *Astrol.* The eleventh house of a celestial figure, so called as the source of many good things 1706. **2.** = AGATHODEMON.

Eudemonic, -dæmonic (yūdīmǫ·nik), *a.* 1832. [ad. Gr. εὐδαιμονικός, f. εὐδαιμονία happiness.] **1.** Viewed as conducive to happiness 1865. **2.** *pl.* 'The art of applying life to the maximization of wellbeing' (Bentham). So **Eudemo·nical** *a.*

Eudemonism, -dæmonism (yudī·mənizm). 1827. [f. Gr. εὐδαιμονία + -ISM.] That system of ethics which finds the moral standard in the tendency of actions to produce happiness.

Eudemonist, -dæmonist (yudī·mənist). 1818. [f. as prec. + -IST.] One who believes in eudemonism. Hence **Eudemoni·stic, -al** *a.* of or pertaining to eudemonism.

Eude·mony, -dæ·mony. *rare.* 1730. [ad. Gr. εὐδαιμονία.] Happiness, prosperity.

Eudialyte (yudəi·ăləit). 1837. [f. Gr. εὐ-διάλυτος easily dissolved; see DIALYSE. So named because easy to dissolve in hydrochloric acid.] *Min.* A vitreous bisilicate of zirconium, iron, calcium, sodium, and other elements, occurring in rhombohedral crystals, rose pink or brownish red.

Eudiometer (yūdi,ǫ·mĭtəɹ). 1777. [f. Gr. εὔδιος clear (weather), (f. εὐ- + διϝ- stem of Ζεύς, Διός the god of the sky) + μέτρον.] An instrument for testing the purity of the air, or rather the quantity of oxygen it contains. It is also used, now chiefly, in the analysis of gases. Hence **Eudiome·tric, -al** *a.* of, pertaining to, or requiring the use of the e. or eudiometry. **Eudiome·trically** *adv.* by the use of the e. **Eudio·metry,** the art or practice of using the e.

Eudipleural (yūdiplūᵊ·răl), *a.* 1878. [f. Gr. εὐ- + δίς + πλευρά the side + -AL.] Having two equal and symmetrical halves.

†**Eue·ctic.** Also **evectic** in Dicts. 1574. [ad. Gr. εὐεκτική (τέχνη), f. (ult.) phr. εὖ ἔχειν to be well; see EU- and HECTIC.] That part of medical science which teaches how to get a good habit of body. Hence in same sense **Eue·ctics** *pl.*

Euemerism, etc., obs. f. EUHEMERISM, etc.

Euge (yū·dʒi). 1655. [a. L., a. Gr. εὖγε well done.] An exclam. of commendation.

Eugenesis (yudʒe·nĭsis). [f. Gr. εὐ- + γένεσις; see GENESIS.] The quality of breeding well and freely. Hence **Eugene·sic** *a.* having this quality; applied *esp.* to hybrids that are fertile.

Eugenia (yudʒī·niă). 1775. [mod.L.; named in honour of *Eugene*, Prince of Savoy.] *Bot.* A genus of tropical trees (N.O. *Myrtaceæ*), of which the most important is *E. Pimenta* or Allspice Tree. Hence **Euge·nic** (acid), $C_{10}H_{12}O_2$, oxidized essence of cloves. **Eu·genin,** clove-camphor; a crystalline substance deposited from water which has been distilled from cloves. **Eu·genol** = eugenic acid.

Eugenic (yudʒe·nik). 1833. [f. Gr. εὐ- + root γεν- to produce + -IC.] **A.** *adj.* Pertaining or adapted to the production of fine offspring. **B.** *sb.* in *pl.* The science which treats of this. Hence **Euge·nically** *adv.* So **Eu·genist,** a student or advocate of eugenics.

‖**Euha·ges, euba·ges,** *sb. pl.* 1609. [L. (Ammianus Marcellinus). The form *euhages* is due to a misreading of Gr. οὐατεῖς, Strabo's rendering of a Gaulish wd. = L. *vates*. The other form is a scribal error.] *Celt. Antiq.* An order of priests, or natural philosophers, among the ancient Celtæ.

Euharmonic (yūhaɹmǫ·nik), *a.* 1811. [f. Gr. εὐ- + ἁρμονία + -IC.] Producing perfect harmony.

Euhemerism (yuhī·meriz'm). 1846. [f. L. *Euhemerus*, Gr. Εὐήμερος, a Sicilian (*c* 316 B.C.), who maintained that the gods of Greek mythology were deified men and women.] The method of interpretation which regards myths as traditional accounts of real incidents in human history. So **Euhe·merist**, one who follows the method of Euhemerus; also *attrib.* **Euhemeri·stic** *a.* inclined to e.; of the nature of, or like, e. **Euhe·merize** *v.* to subject to or to follow the method of Euhemerus.

Eukairite; see EUCAIRITE.

Eulerian (yulīə·riăn), *a.* 1882. [f. *Euler*, the Swiss Mathematician (1707–83) + -IAN.] Of, pertaining to, or discovered by, Euler; as *Eulerian constant, function, integral.*

‖**Eulogia** (yulōu·dziă). 1751. [Eccl.L., a. Gr. εὐλογία in N.T. 'blessing'; see EULOGY.] **a.** *orig.* The Eucharist. **b.** A portion of the consecrated bread reserved for those who were not present at the communion. **c.** In the Greek church, the unconsecrated bread remaining after communion, blessed and given to the non-communicants.

Eulogic, †-al (yulǫ·dzik, -ăl), *a.* 1656. [f. EULOGY + -IC + -AL.] Pertaining to eulogy; containing praise. Hence **Eulo·gically** *adv.*

Eulogism (yū·lŏdziz'm). 1761. [f. EULOGY + -ISM.] A eulogistic speech; eulogistic language.

Eulogist (yū·lŏdzist). 1808. [f. as prec. + -IST.] One who eulogizes; a panegyrist.

Eulogistic, -al (yulŏdzi·stik, -ăl), *a.* 1825. [f. prec. + -IC + -AL.] Pertaining to or conveying eulogy; of the nature of eulogy; commendatory, laudatory; as, *eulogistic inscriptions.* Hence **Eulogi·stically** *adv.*

Eulogium (yulōu·dziŏm). *Pl.* **-iums**; also **-ia.** 1706. [a. med.L. *eulogium*, app. a fusion of *elogium* (see ELOGIUM) and *eulogia* (see EULOGY).] = EULOGY 1 and 1 b.

Eulogize (yū·lŏdzəiz), *v.* 1810. [f. next + -IZE.] *trans.* To pronounce a eulogy upon; to speak or write in commendation of; to extol.

Eulogy (yū·lŏdzi). 1591. [ad. (ult.) Gr. εὐλογία praise, in N.T. blessing (f. εὐ- + -λογια speaking). Cf. EULOGIUM.] **1.** A speech or writing in commendation of the qualities, etc., of a person or thing; *esp.* a set oration in honour of a deceased person. **b.** Commendation, praise 1725. **†2.** *Eccl.* = EULOGIA –1782.

Eulysite (yū·lisəit). 1868. [f. Gr. εὐλυσία easy solubility + -ITE.] *Min.* 'A granular mixture of augite, garnet, and nearly 50 per cent. of a mineral allied to olivine' (Watts).

Eulytin (yū·litin). 1850. [f. Gr. εὔλυτος (f. εὐ- + λυτός soluble, f. λύειν) + -IN.] *Min.* Native silicate of bismuth, usually occurring in brownish crystals with a resinous lustre. var. **Eulytite** (yū·litəit).

Eunomy (yū·nŏmi). *rare.* 1721. [ad. Gr. εὐνομία, f. εὐ- + νόμος.] A condition of good law well administered.

Eunuch (yū·nŏk), *sb.* ME. [ad. L. *eunuchus*, a. Gr. εὐνοῦχος, f. εὐνή bed + -οχ- stem of ἔχειν to keep; thus, one who had charge of the bedchamber.] **1.** A castrated male person; also, such a person employed as a harem attendant, or charged with important affairs of state. **b.** = CASTRATO 1732. **2.** *attrib.* and *fig.* 1666.

Hence **†Eu·nuch** *v.* to make a eunuch of; also *fig.* **†Eunu·chate** *v.* to castrate; to deprive of virility. SIR T. BROWNE. **Eu·nuchism**, the custom of making eunuchs; the condition of being a eunuch. **Eu·nuchize** *v.* to castrate; to emasculate (*lit.* and *fig.*).

Euodic (yū,ōu·dik), *a.* 1873. [f. Gr. εὐώδης, f. εὐ- + ὠδ- stem of ὄζειν to smell + -IC.] Aromatic; as *euodic aldehyde.*

Euonymus (yu,ǫ·nimŏs). 1767. [ad. L. *euonymos* (Plin.), subst. use of Gr., f. εὐ- + ὄνομα, in Æolic ὄνυμα name.] *Bot.* A genus of shrubs (N.O. *Celastraceæ*), of which the only British species is the Spindle-tree. The bark of an American species (*E. atropurpureus*) is used as a cathartic.

Euosmite (yu,ǫ·zməit). 1868. [f. Gr. εὔοσμος sweet-smelling + -ITE.] A fossil resin, giving an aromatic odour when burned.

Eupathy (yū·păþi). 1603. [ad. Gr. εὐπάθεια happy condition of the soul, f. εὐπαθής.] *Stoical Philos.* Good affections of the mind; as, joy, caution, will.

Eupatorine (yupæ·tŏrəin). Formerly also **-in, -ina.** 1838. [f. as next + -INE.] *Chem.* An alkaloid contained in the flowers and leaves of the water-hemp (*Eupatorium cannabinum*).

‖**Eupatorium** (yūpătōə·riŏm). 1578. [mod.L., a. Gr. εὐπατόριον, *Agrimonia Eupatorium*, first used by Mithridates *Eupator*, king of Pontus.] *Bot.* A genus of the N.O. *Compositæ*, of which the only British species is *E. cannabinum*, Hemp Agrimony. Also, a plant of the same. So **†Eu·patory**, Hemp Agrimony.

Eupatrid (yupæ·trid, yū·pătrid). *Pl.* **-ids**; also in L. form **-idæ.** 1833. [ad. Gr. εὐπατρίδης, f. εὐ- + πατήρ.] A member of the first of the three orders in the Athenian Constitution. Hence (rarely) *gen.* A patrician. Also *attrib.*

‖**Eupepsia** (yū·pe·psiă). 1706. [mod.L., a. Gr., f. εὔπεπτος (see EUPEPTIC).] Healthy action of the digestive organs; good digestion. Anglicized as **Eupepsy.**

Eupeptic (yupe·ptik). 1699. [f. Gr. εὔπεπτος (f. εὐ- + πέπτειν to digest) + -IC.]

A. *adj.* **†1.** Promoting digestion. EVELYN. **2.** Having a good digestion 1831. **3.** Of, pertaining to, or resulting from, good digestion 1845. **4.** Easy of digestion. (Dicts.)

2. E'en after dinner, e., would rush yet again to his reading CLOUGH. 3. Wrapt in lazy e. fat CARLYLE.

†B. *sb.* Anything that promotes digestion. (Dicts.)

Hence **Eupepti·city**, the state of feeling resulting from eupepsy (Carlyle).

Euphemious (yufī·miəs), *a. rare.* 1853. [f. Gr. εὔφημος (f. εὐ- + φήμη speaking, fame) + (I)OUS.] **a.** = EUPHEMISTIC. **b.** Well reputed.

Euphemism (yū·fĭ,miz'm). 1656. [ad. Gr. εὐφημισμός, f. εὐφημίζειν; see prec.] **1.** *Rhet.* A figure by which a less distasteful word or expression is substituted for one more exactly descriptive of what is intended. **2.** An instance of this figure 1793.

2. A shorn crown..a e. for decapitation FROUDE. var. **Euphemi·smus** (now *rare*).

Euphemistic, -al (yūfĭ,mi·stik, -ăl), *a.* 1856. [f. Gr. εὔφημος (see EUPHEMIOUS) + -IST + -IC, + -AL.] Pertaining to euphemism; of the nature of, or containing, a euphemism. Hence **Euphemi·stically** *adv.*

Euphemize (yū·fĭ,məiz), *v.* 1857. [ad. Gr. εὐφημίζειν, f. εὔφημος.] To speak or speak of euphemistically.

‖**Euphonia** (yū:fōu·niă). 1591. [late L., a. Gr.] = EUPHONY, q.v.

Euphoniad (yufōu·niăd). 1854. [irreg. f. prec.] *Mus.* An instrument said to combine the tones of the organ, clarinet, horn, bassoon, and violin.

Euphonic, -al (yufǫ·nik, -ăl), *a.* 1814. [f. EUPHONY + -IC, + -AL.] **1.** Euphonious. **2.** Of or pertaining to euphony 1816.

2. Purely e. influences WHITNEY. Hence **Eupho·nically** *adv.*

Euphonious (yūfōu·niəs), *a.* 1774. [f. as prec. + -OUS.] Full of or characterized by euphony; pleasing to the ear. Hence **Eupho·niously** *adv.* var. **Eu·phonous.**

Euphonism (yū·fŏniz'm). 1774. [f. as prec. + -ISM.] The habit of using euphonious words; a well-sounding combination or expression.

Euphonium (yufōu·niŏm). 1865. [as if L., f. Gr. εὔφωνος.] *Mus.* A bass instrument of the Saxhorn family, usually tuned in B♭ or C.

Euphonize (yū·fŏnəiz), *v.* 1774. [f. EUPHONY + -IZE.] *trans.* To render euphonious; to alter for euphony.

Euphonon (yūfōu·nǫn). 1824. [ad. Gr. εὔφωνον adj. neut.; see EUPHONY.] *Mus.* A musical instrument which resembled the upright piano in form and the organ in tone.

Euphony (yū·fŏni). 1623. [a. F. *euphonie*, ad. Gr. εὐφωνία, f. εὔφωνος, f. εὐ- + φωνή voice, sound.] **a.** The quality of having a pleasant sound; the pleasing effect of sounds free from harshness. **b.** *Philol.* The tendency to ease of pronunciation, formerly explained as an endeavour after a pleasing acoustic effect.

E. then is the mother of many lies HELPS.

‖**Euphorbia** (yūfǭ·ɹbiă). ME. [a. L. *euphorbea*, f. *Euphorbus*, physician to Juba king of Mauretania.] *Bot.* The name of the Spurge genus (N.O. *Euphorbiaceæ*), comprising many species, secreting a viscid milky juice, and having a peculiar inflorescence. Cf. SPURGE.

The lofty candelabra-shaped euphorbias towering above the copses of evergreens PRINGLE. Hence **Eu.phorbia·ceous** *a.* of the N.O. *Euphorbiaceæ.* **Eupho·rbial** *a.* (Dicts.).

Euphorbine (yufǭ·rbəin). 1838. [f. EUPHORBIA + -INE[4].] *Chem.* A non-volatile poisonous principle contained in the milky juice of *Euphorbia myrtifolia.*

‖**Euphorbium** (yūfǭ·ɹbiŏm). ME. [a. L. *euphorbeum* = *euphorbea.*] **†1.** = EUPHORBIA. –1767. **2.** A gum resin obtained from certain species of *Euphorbia*, and formerly used as an emetic and purgative.

Euphory (yū·fŏri). 1684. [ad. Gr. εὐφορία, f. (ult.) εὐ + φέρειν to bear.] Well-bearing or well-being.

Euphotide (yufōu·təid). 1836. [a. F., f. Gr. εὐ- + φῶς, φωτός light.] *Geol.* 'A crystalline rock consisting essentially of Labrador felspar and diallage, with subordinate intermixtures of hornblende and augite' (Page). Called also GABBRO, q.v.

‖**Euphrasia** (yūfrē·ziă). 1706. [L. form of next.] **1.** *Bot.* = next. **2.** Cheerfulness 1882.

Euphrasy (yū·frăsi). 1475. [ad. med.L. *euphrasia*, a. Gr. εὐφρασία, f. εὐφραίνειν to cheer, f. εὐ- + φρήν mind.] *Bot.* A plant, *Euphrasia officinalis* (N.O. *Scrophulariaceæ*), formerly in repute for the treatment of diseases of the eye; = EYE-BRIGHT. Also *fig.*

Michael .. purg'd with Euphrasie and Rue The visual Nerve MILT. *P. L.* XI. 414.

Euphroe (yū·fro). Also **uphroe.** 1815. [a. Du. *juffrouw*, also *juffer* dead-eye, lit. 'maiden'.] *Naut.* A crowfoot dead-eye; a long cylindrical block perforated to receive the cords composing the crowfoot.

Euphues (yū·fiu,īz). 1578. [Gr. εὐφυής well-grown, f. εὐ- + φυή growth, f. φύειν.] Name of the chief character in John Lyly's books, *Euphues, The Anatomy of Wit* (1578), and *Euphues and his England* (1580). Hence, the book so named.

Euphuism (yū·fiu,iz'm). 1592. [f. prec. + -ISM.] **1.** Properly, the type of diction and style of Lyly's *Euphues*, fashionable in literature and polite conversation in the 16th and beginning of the 17th c. Hence, any similar affectation in writing or speech; high-flown language. **2.** A euphuistic phrase or composition 1871. ¶ **3.** Erron. for EUPHEMISM. 1865.

1. That Beautie in Court, which could not Parley Euphueisme, was as little regarded; as shee which now there, speakes not French E. BLOUNT.

Euphuist (yū·fiu,ist). 1820. [f. as prec. + -IST.] One whose writing or speech is characterized by EUPHUISM.

Elizabeth was the most affected and detestable of Euphuists GREEN. Hence **Euphui·stic, -al** *a.*, **-ly** *adv.* **†Eu·phuize** *v.* to talk or make like Euphues.

Euphyllite (yufi·ləit). 1849. [f. Gr. εὔφυλλος well-leaved + -ITE.] *Min.* A white hydrous silicate, micaceous in structure.

Eupione (yū·pi,ōun). Also **eupion.** 1838. [a. Gr. εὐπίων very fat, f. εὐ- + πίων; assim. to derivs. in -ONE.] *Chem.* A volatile, oily liquid produced by the distillation of wood, tar, etc.

Euplastic (yuplæ·stik). 1847. [f. Gr. εὔπλαστος easily moulded + -IC.]

A. *adj.* Easily formed into an organic tissue. **B.** *sb.* Euplastic matter. (Dicts.)

‖**Eupnœa** (yūpnī·ă). 1706. [mod.L., a. Gr. εὔπνοια, f. εὖ + πνέειν to breathe.] Normal breathing; easy respiration; opp. to *dyspnœa.* Hence **Eupno·ic** *a.* relating to e.; breathing easily.

Eupractic (yupræ·ktik), *a.* [f. Gr. εὖ + πρακ-, πράσσειν to act.] Inclined to act rightly. CARLYLE.

†**Eupy·rion.** 1827. [f. Gr. εὐ- + πυρεῖον fire-stick.] A contrivance for obtaining a light easily. Also *fig.*

‖**Euraquilo** (yuᵊræ·kwilo). Also **Euro-aquilo.** 1582. [L., f. *Eurus* east-wind + *Aquilo* north-wind.] A stormy NE. or NNE. wind, blowing in the Levant. R.V. *Acts* xxvii. 14.

Eurasian (yūᵊrēⁱ·ʃăn). 1844. [f. *Eur-ope* + *Asia* + -AN.] A. *adj.* 1. Of or pertaining to Europe and Asia considered as one continent 1868. 2. Of mixed European and Asiatic (*esp.* Indian) parentage 1844. B. *sb.* A person of mixed European and Asiatic (*esp.* Indian) blood 1845. Cf. ANGLO-INDIAN.

So **Eurasia·tic** *a.* = EURASIAN A. 1.

†**Eure,** *sb.* ME. [a. OF. *eure, heur, aür* :—L. *augurium.* Cf. F. *bonheur.*] Destiny; luck -1525. Hence †**Eure** *v.* to destine. †**Eu·rous** *a.* lucky, prosperous.

Eureka (yuᵊrī·kă), *interj.* 1603. [Gr.; = 'I have found (it)'.] The exclam. of Archimedes when he found out how to determine (by specific gravity) the proportion of base metal in Hiero's crown. Hence *allusively*, with reference to any discovery. Often *attrib.*

Eurhythmy (yuri·þmi). 1624. [ad. L. *eurythmia* (also used), a. Gr. (f. εὐ- + ῥυθμός proportion, RHYTHM).] 1. *Arch.* Harmony in the proportions of a building. 2. *Path.* Regularity of the pulse 1721. 3. a. Rhythmical order or movement; b. graceful proportion and carriage of the body 1706. Hence **Eurhy·thmic** *a.*, in or of harmonious proportion, esp. in architecture. B. *sb. pl.* A system of rhythmical bodily movements, esp. with the aid of music, used with an educational object 1915.

Euripus (yuᵊrai·pŏs). *Pl.* **-pi.** 1601. [L., a. Gr., f. εὐ- + ῥιπή rush.] *orig.* The proper name of the channel between Eubœa (Negropont) and the mainland, where the currents are violent and uncertain. Hence *gen.* a strait or sea-channel of this character. Also *transf.* var. †**Euri·pe.** Hence †**Eu·ripize** *v. intr.* to be whirled hither and thither' (Sir T. Browne).

Eurite (yuᵊ·rəit). 1844. [a. F., f. Gr. εὔρυτος, f. εὖ + ῥέειν to flow; so named as 'melting when exposed to fire'.] *Min.* 'A variety of syenite occurring near Christiania, of a blue colour and stratified' (Watts). **Euri·tic** *a.*

†**Euro-boreal,** *a.* [f. late L. *Euro-* (see EURUS) + BOREAL.] North-easterly. EVELYN.

Euroclydon (yuᵊrǫ·klidǫn). 1611. [a. Gr. εὐροκλύδων (only in *Acts* xxvii. 14, if genuine), f. εὖρος east wind + κλύδων wave.] = EURAQUILO, q.v. Occas., a tempestuous wind. Also *fig.*

E. bellows down the chimney LOWELL.

Europæo-, -eo- (yuᵊrǫpī·o-), comb. f. L. *Europæus* European in **Europe·o-Asia·tic**, etc.

European (yuᵊrǫpī·ăn). 1603. [ad. F. *européen*, f. L. *Europæus*, f. *Europa*, a. Gr. Εὐρώπη Europe.] A. *adj.* Belonging to Europe or its inhabitants; extending over Europe. B. *sb.* A native of Europe 1632.

A. *E. plan* (U.S.), the practice at a hotel of charging for lodging and service without inclusion of meals (contrasted with *American plan*) 1847. A scholar of E. celebrity 1897.

Europeanism (yuᵊrǫpī·ăniz'm). 1828. [f. prec. + -ISM.] a. Tendency to adopt what is European, *e.g.* ideas, manners, methods, etc. b. Anything peculiar to or characteristic of Europe or Europeans.

Europeanize (yūᵊrǫpī·ănəiz), *v.* 1849. [f. as prec. + -IZE.] *trans.* To make European in appearance, habit, mode of life, or extent.

The reaction thus originated in Germany was.. Europeanized by France 1857. Hence **Europe·anization.**

†‖**Eurus** (yuᵊ·rŏs). ME. [L., a. Gr. Εὖρος the east wind.] The east wind, ESE. or SE.; the god of the east wind -1727.

Eurycephalic (yūᵊri₁sĭfæ·lik), *a.* 1878. [f. Gr. εὐρύς wide + κεφαλή head + -IC.] *Ethnol.* Broad-headed; applied to a subdivision of the brachycephalic races of man.

Eurycerous (yuᵊri·sĕrəs), *a.* 1836. [ad. Gr. εὐρύκερως, f. εὐρύς + κέρας horn + -OUS.] Broad-horned. (Dicts.)

Eurygnathous (yuᵊri·gnăþəs), *a.* 1878. [f. F. *eurygnathe* (f. Gr. εὐρύς + γνάθος jaw) + -OUS.] Having a broad upper jaw.

Eurypterid (yuᵊri·ptĕrid). 1871. [ad. mod. L. *Eurypteridæ* pl., f. *Eurypterus* name of the typical genus, f. Gr. εὐρύς + πτερόν feather, wing.] *Palæont.* One of a group of fossil Crustacea, abundant in the Silurian and Devonian periods. So named as having a pair of broad swimming appendages, the hindmost of a series attached to the cephalo-thorax.

Eurystomatous (yūᵊri₁stǫ·mătəs), *a.* 1878. [f. Gr. εὐρύς broad + στόμα mouth + -OUS.] Wide-mouthed. Chiefly of serpents: Having a distensible mouth.

Eurythmic, etc., var. EURHYTHMIC, etc.

Eusebian (yusī·biăn). 1730. [ad. L. *Eusebianus*, f. *Eusebius*: see -IAN.] A. *adj.* Of or pertaining to Eusebius, bishop of Nicomedia, leader of the Arians 1882. b. Pertaining to Eusebius of Cæsarea, or his historical works 1860.

b. *E. canons*: an arrangement of the contents of the four Gospels into ten classes of passages, according as they occur in one of the evangelists alone or in any one of the possible combinations of two or three out of the four.

B. *sb.* A member of the Eusebian sect 1730.

Euskarian (yŭskēᵊ·riăn), *a.* and *sb.* 1864. [f. Basque *Euskara, Eskuara, Uskara*, the Basque language.] Basque; used by some ethnologists to designate a pre-Aryan element in Europeans typified by the Basques.

Eusol (yū·sǫl). 1915. [f. *E*dinburgh *U*niversity *sol*ution.] A solution of free hypochlorous acid used as an antiseptic and bactericide.

Eustachian (yŭstēⁱ·kiăn), *a.* 1741. [f. *Eustachius*, an Italian anatomist (died 1574) + -AN.] *Anat.* Of structures discovered by him.

E. tube (occas. *E. canal*): a canal leading from the pharynx to the cavity of the tympanum; hence *E. catheter*, an instrument for inflating the E. tube with air. *E. valve*: a membranous fold at the orifice of the vena cava inferior, which in the fœtus directs the current of blood from this vessel to the foramen ovale and left auricle.

Eustyle (yū·stəil). 1696. [ad. L. *eustylos*, a. Gr. εὔστυλος with pillars well placed, f. εὐ- + στῦλος.] *Arch.* A. *adj.* Of a colonnade, etc.: Having the space between each successive pair of columns equal to two diameters of a column and a quarter or half diameter. B. *sb.* This distance itself.

Eutaxite (yutæ·ksəit). 1879. [f. Gr. εὐ- + τάξις arrangement + -ITE.] *Geol.* A rock consisting of layers of different kinds of lava lying regularly one above the other. Hence **Eutaxi·tic** *a.* of the nature of e.

†**Eutaxy.** 1614. [a. F. *eutaxie*, ad. Gr. εὐταξία; see prec.] Good or established order or arrangement -1677.

‖**Euterpe** (yŭ:tə̄·ɪpī). 1866. [mod.L., a Gr. Εὐτέρπη, the Muse of music, f. εὖ + τέρπειν to delight.] 1. *Bot.* A genus of graceful palms, sometimes of great height. 2. *Astron.* The 27th asteroid. Hence **Eute·rpean** *a.* pertaining to E., or to music.

Eutexia (yute·ksiă). 1884. [a. Gr. εὐτηξία, f. εὐ- + τήκειν to melt.] The quality of melting readily, *i.e.* at a low temperature. Hence **Eute·ctic** *a.* melting readily; *sb.* a eutectic substance.

Euthanasia (yūþănēⁱ·siă, -ziă). 1646. [a. Gr., f. εὐ- + θάνατος death.] 1. A quiet and easy death. 2. The means of procuring this. Also *transf.* and *fig.* 1742. 3. The action of inducing a quiet and easy death 1869.

1. Not a torture death, but a quiet e. CARLYLE. 2. The true e. she discovered..in the bite of an asp MERIVALE. 3. An e., an abridgment of the pangs of disease LECKY. var. (in sense 1) **Eutha·nasy.**

†**Eu·thymy.** 1623. [a. Gr. εὐθυμία.] Cheerfulness of mind -1671.

Eutopia (yŭtōᵘ·piă). 1556. [f. Gr. εὐ- (see EU-) + τόπος place. First used by Sir T. More, with a play on UTOPIA (f. Gr. οὐ τόπος = nowhere), the country described in his book with that title.] A place of ideal happiness or good order.

Eutrophy (yū·trǫfi). 1721. [ad. Gr. εὐτροφία, f. εὖ + τρέφειν to nourish.] *Path.* Good nutrition. Hence **Eutro·phic** *a.* promoting nutrition; *sb.* [sc. *medicine*]. (Dicts.)

Eutychian (yuti·kiăn). 1556. [f. L. *Eutyches* + -IAN.]

A. *adj.* Of, pertaining, or adhering, to the doctrine of Eutyches (5th c.), who held that the human nature of Christ was lost in the divine.

B. *sb.* A follower of Eutyches.

Hence **Euty·chianism,** the E. heresy.

Euxenite (yū·ksĭnəit). 1844. [f. Gr. εὔξενος hospitable + -ITE. So named as harbouring many rare constituents.] *Min.* A mineral found in Norway, consisting mainly of niobate and titanate of yttrium.

[**Evacate**: a spurious Dict. word.]

Evacuant (ĭvæ·kiŭănt). 1730. [f. pr. pple. of L. *evacuare*; see next.] *Med.*

A. *adj.* That promotes evacuation, cathartic, purgative 1800.

B. *sb.* A purgative, emetic, diaphoretic 1730.

Evacuate (ĭvæ·kiu₁eⁱt), *v.* 1526. [f. L. *evacuat-*, *evacuare* (Pliny), f. *e* + *vacuus* empty. Cf. F. *évacuer.*] 1. *trans.* To empty, clear out the contents of 1542. Also *fig.* 2. Of an army: To relinquish the occupation of 1710; also *gen.* to quit, withdraw from 1809. Also *absol.* †3. To make void -1785. †4. To get rid of (a disease or humour). Also *fig.* -1790. 5. To void, discharge, throw off, vent. Also *absol.* 1607. 6. To take out mechanically, leaving a vacuum; to pump out; to exhaust. Also *fig.* *Obs.* exc. in surgical use. 1719. Also *intr.* for *refl.* 7. To clear out (inhabitants, troops, etc.) 1639.

1. To e. the stomach 1875. *fig.* To e. the mind of all ill thoughts 1653. 2. The garrison, in a panic, evacuated the fort MACAULAY. 3. To euacuate a Marriage BACON. 6. To e. the contents of abscesses 1877. Hence **Eva·cuative** *a.* that evacuates (the bowels); purgative; *sb.* an evacuant. **Eva·cuator,** one who or that which evacuates. †**Eva·cuatory** *a.* and *sb.* (*rare*) = EVACUANT A and B.

Evacuation (ĭvæ:kiu₁ēⁱ·ʃən). ME. [ad. L. *evacuationem*; see prec.] 1. *spec.* a. *Med.* The action of depleting or of clearing out by medicine or other artificial means. Now *rare.* b. *Phys.* The process of discharging (waste matter) through the excretory organs (now *esp.* from the bowels) 1532; *concr.* evacuated matter 1625. 2. *gen.* The action of emptying, or of removing so as to make empty. Also *fig.* 1598. †b. A depleting (of population, etc.) -1755. 3. *Mil.* The withdrawal from occupation of a country, etc.; the removal (of a garrison, inhabitants, etc.) 1710. 4. Cancelling, nullification 1650.

3. *E. day*, the anniversary of the day on which the British army evacuated New York, Nov. 25, 1783.

Evade (ĭvēⁱ·d), *v.* 1513. [a. F. *évader*, ad. L. *evadere*, f. *e* out + *vadere* to go.] 1. *intr.* To get away, escape. Const. *from, out of.* Now *rare.* 2. *trans.* To escape by artifice from; to avoid, save oneself from; to elude, avoid encountering 1535. 4. *absol.* or *intr.* To practise evasion 1716. 5. *trans.* Of things: To elude, baffle (efforts, vigilance, etc.) 1716.

2. To e. her father's anger POPE, payment 1832, enquiries 1832, the force of an obligation LD. BROUGHAM. 5. Some offences e. definition J. MARTINEAU. Hence **Eva·dable** *a.* **Eva·der.** **Eva·dingly** *adv.*

Evagation (ĭvăgēⁱ·ʃən). ME. [a. F., ad. L. *evagationem*, f. (ult.) *e* out + *vagari* to wander.] 1. The action of wandering away; rambling, roving 1691. †Also *fig.* of the mind, thoughts, etc. -1677. †2. A diversion; an extravagance -1649.

Evaginate (ĭvæ·dʒineⁱt), *v.* 1656. [f. L. *evaginat-*, *evaginare* to unsheath, f. *e* + *vagina.*] †a. To unsheath. b. *Phys.* To turn (a tubular organ) inside out; to protrude by eversion. Hence **Eva·ginable** *a.* that can be evaginated. **Evagina·tion,** the action or result of evaginating.

Eval (ī·văl), *a. rare.* 1791. [f. L. *ævum* + -AL.] Of or pertaining to age; age-long.

Evaluate (ĭvæ·liu₁eⁱt), *v.* 1842. [f. F. *évaluer* (see next) + -ATE [3].] *trans.* a. *Math.* To work out the value of; to find a numerical expression for. b. *gen.* To reckon up, ascertain the amount of; to express in terms of the known. Hence **Eva·luable** *a.*

Evaluation (ĭvæ:liu₁ēⁱ·ʃən). 1755. [a. F., f. *évaluer*, f. *é-* = *es-* (:—L. *ex*) + *value* VALUE.] 1. = VALUATION. Now *rare.* 2. The action of evaluating 1779.

Evanesce (evăne·s), *v.* 1822. [ad. L. *evanescere*, f. *e* + *vanescere* to vanish, f. *vanus*

VAIN. Cf. EVANISH.] *intr.* To fade out of sight, disappear; chiefly *fig.*

Evanescence (evăne·sĕns). 1751. [f. next; see -ENCE.] 1. The process or fact of vanishing away. 2. Evanescent quality; tendency to vanish away (*mod.*). 3. *concr.* An evanescent thing (*rare*) 1830.

2. This e. and lubricity of all objects..lets them slip through our fingers EMERSON.

Evanescent (evăne·sĕnt), *a.* 1717. [a. F., ad. L. *evanescentem* pr. pple.; see EVANESCE.] 1. That is on the point of vanishing; in *Math.* on the point of becoming zero, infinitesimal. Hence *transf.*: Imperceptibly minute. 2. That quickly vanishes; fleeting 1738; in *Bot.* of parts of plants: Not permanent 1776.

1. To render the crime e., or almost nothing WOLLASTON. 2. A scene Of e. glory COWPER. Hence **Evane·scently** *adv.*

Evangel[1], **evangile** (ĭvæ·ndʒĕl, -il). Now *arch.* or *rhet.* [ME. *evangile*, a. OF. *evangi(l)le*, repr. Eccl. L. *evangelium*; see EVANGELY.] 1. The GOSPEL (in various senses); *esp.* the Gospel record; also, one of the Four Gospels. 2. *pl.* Copies of the Gospels; used to impart sanctity to an oath. Also *attrib.* ME. 3. *transf.* †Something 'as true as gospel' –1681; a doctrine or principle of saving efficacy 1831. 4. A message of glad tidings 1842.

1. The spirit of the Evangile R. WILLIAMS. Lukes Evangel GALE. 3. That..Merline's prophesies [are] evangels COLVIL.

Evangel[2] (ĭvæ·ndʒĕl). 1593. [ad. Gr. εὐάγγελος, f. εὖ + ἀγγέλλειν to announce.] = EVANGELIST.

Evange·lian, *a.* [f. Gr. (τὰ) εὐαγγέλια.] In *E. sacrifice*: tr. Gr. τὰ εὐαγγέλια, the sacrifice offered on receipt of good news. MITFORD.

Evangelic (īvæn-, evændʒe·lik). 1460. [ad. late L. *evangelicus*, a Eccl. Gr. εὐαγγελικός; see EVANGELY.]

A. *adj.* 1. Of or pertaining to the Gospel narrative, to the Four Gospels, or to the Gospel faith, precepts, or dispensation 1502. †b. ? Pious 1460. 2. = EVANGELICAL 2 a, b. 1583.

B. *sb.* †1. The adj. used *absol.* 1617. †2. = EVANGELICAL B. 1, 2. –1812.

Evangelical (īvæn-, evændʒe·likăl). 1531. [f. prec. + -AL.]

A. *adj.* 1. = EVANGELIC A. 1. 2. As the designation of a sect or party. a. = PROTESTANT. Now only with reference to Germany and Switzerland. 1532. b. Applied to those Protestants who hold that the essence of the Gospel consists in the doctrine of salvation by faith in the atoning death of Christ, and deny the saving efficacy of either good works or the sacraments 1791. 3. Of or pertaining to an evangelist (*rare*) 1651.

1. Phr. *E. prophet*: a designation of Isaiah, as prophetically describing the life of Christ and anticipating Gospel doctrines. 2. b. The Wesleyans, the orthodox Dissenters of every description, and the Evangelical churchmen may all be comprehended under the generic name of Methodists SOUTHEY.

B. *sb.* 1. A Protestant; now *esp.* a German Lutheran, or an adherent of the national church of the German Empire 1532. 2. A member of the evangelical party, *esp.* a Low churchman 1804.

Hence **Evange·licalism**, the doctrines peculiar to the E. party, or adherence to them. **Evange·lical, -ly** *adv.*, **-ness** (*rare*). **Evangeli·city**, the quality of being e. **Evange·licanism**, **Evange·licism** (*rare*) = EVANGELICALISM.

Evangelism (ĭvæ·ndʒĕliz'm). 1626. [f. EVANGEL + -ISM.] 1. The preaching or promulgation of the Gospel. 2. a. = EVANGELICALISM (chiefly in hostile use) 1812. b. The faith of the Gospel (*rare*) 1842.

Evangelist (ĭvæ·ndʒĕlist). ME. [a. F. *évangéliste*, ad. L. *evangelista*, ad. Gr. εὐαγγελιστής; see EVANGELIZE.] 1. One of the writers of the Four Gospels, Matthew, Mark, Luke, and John. †2. The book of the Gospels –1713. 3. a. *gen.* One who preaches the, or a, gospel 1535. b. *orig.* One of a class of teachers, mentioned in *Eph.* iv. 11 after 'apostles' and 'prophets'; *later*, an itinerant preacher having no fixed pastoral charge; *now*, a layman who does home missionary work ME.

2. We swere on the holy euangelist, by vs corporally touched LD. BERNERS. 3. The French Revolution found its E. in Rousseau CARLYLE. b. Timothie and Titus..were Euangelists, a degree aboue ordinarie ministers J. UDALL.

Hence **Eva·ngeli·stic** *a.* of or pertaining to the Four Evangelists, or to preachers of the Gospel. **Eva·ngelistship**, the office or dignity of an e.

Evangelistary (ĭvæ:ndʒĕli·stări). 1646. [ad. med.L. *evangelistarium* (also used), f. *evangelista* EVANGELIST.] a. A book containing the parts of the Gospels used in the liturgy. b. A copy of the Four Gospels 1865.

Evangelize (ĭvæ·ndʒĕlaiz), *v.* ME. [ad. Eccl. L. *evangelizare*, ad. Gr. εὐαγγελίζεσθαι, f. εὐάγγελος; see EVANGEL[2].] †1. *intr.* To bring or tell good tidings; *spec.* to preach, proclaim the Gospel –1808. †2. *trans.* To proclaim as glad tidings; to preach –1698. 3. To preach the Gospel to; to win over to the Christian faith 1652. 4. To make evangelic in spirit or sense 1677.

3. His [Messiah's] Apostles, whom he sends To e. the Nations MILT. *P. L.* XII. 499. Hence **Eva·ngeliza·tion**, the action or process of evangelizing; the condition of being evangelized. **Eva·ngelizer.**

†**Evangely** (ĭvæ·ndʒĕli). ME. [ad. Eccl. L. *evangelium* (also used), ad. Gr. εὐαγγέλιον, f. εὐάγγελος, f. εὖ + ἀγγέλλειν to announce.] = EVANGEL[1] 1, 2, 4. –1683.

Evanid (ĭvæ·nid), *a. arch.* 1626. [ad. L. *evanidus* vanishing; see EVANESCE.] 1. Vanishing away; evanescent. 2. Faint, weak 1646. †3. EMPHATICAL, illusory –1751.

1. Those Animal Spirits are of such an E. and Subtile Nature BURNET. 3. E. colours 1751. Hence †**Eva·nidness.** H. MORE.

Evanish (ĭvæ·niʃ), *v.* ME. [a. OF. *evaniss-*, lengthened stem of *evanir* :—pop. L. *exvanire = cl. L. *evanescere*; see EVANESCE.] *intr.* To vanish.

And cares e. like a morning dream RAMSAY. Hence †**Eva·nishment, Evani·tion**, disappearance.

Evansite (e·vănzəit). 1864. [f. Brooke *Evans* who brought it from Hungary + -ITE.] *Min.* A hydrous phosphate of aluminium occurring in white reniform masses.

Evaporable (ĭvæ·pŏrăb'l), *a.* 1541. [f. L. *evaporare* to EVAPORATE + -ABLE.] Capable of being evaporated. Hence **Evaporabi·lity.**

Evaporate (ĭvæ·pŏreᵢt), *v.* 1545. [f. L. *evaporat-*, *evaporare*, f. *e-* + *vapor* steam, VAPOUR. Cf. F. *évaporer*.] 1. *trans.* To convert or turn into vapour; to drive off in the form of vapour. Also *fig.* 1555. 2. *intr.* To become vapour; to pass off in vapour 1567. 3. *fig.* To pass off like vapour; to be wasted or dissipated; also *joc.* of persons, to become missing 1631. 4. *trans.* To subject to evaporation; to drive off the liquid part of. Also *absol.* 1646. 5. *intr.* To part with liquid particles by evaporation 1799. †6. *trans.* To emit in the form of vapour; to give vent to, exhale. Also *absol.* and *intr.* –1799.

1. In the leaves much of the water of the sap is evaporated SIR H. DAVY. 3. These hostile menaces evaporated without effect GIBBON. 4. E. to the consistence of honey 1799. 6. *fig.* To e. the Spleen ADDISON.

Hence **Eva·porative** *a.* pertaining to or producing evaporation. **Eva·porator**, one who or that which evaporates; *esp.* an apparatus for drying fruits, etc. var. **Eva·porize** *v.* (in sense 1).

Evaporation (ĭvæ:pŏrē¹·ʃən). ME. [a. F., ad. L. *evaporationem*; see EVAPORATE *v.*] 1. The process of conversion into vapour; the action of passing off in vapour; an instance of this. Also *fig.* 2. The action of driving off the liquid part of a substance by means of heat; an instance of this 1718. 3. The action a. of exhaling moisture; †b. of emitting (breath, etc.); †c. of perspiring insensibly. Also *fig.* 1551. 4. *concr.* The product of evaporation; vapour; the amount evaporated 1533. †5. *Med.* Treatment by means of vapour –1610.

1. By e., water is carried up into the air PALEY. 3. a. E. takes place through the leaves 1887. 4. *fig.* The vain evaporations of his discontentment FULLER.

Evapori·meter. Also **-ometer.** 1828. [f. prec. + -(I)METER.] An instrument for measuring the quantity of a liquid evaporated in a given time; an atmometer.

Evasible (ĭvē¹·sĭb'l), *a.* [f. L. *evas-*, *evadere* + -IBLE.] That may be evaded. OGILVIE.

Evasion (ĭvē¹·ʒən). ME. [a. F., ad. late L. *evasionem*; see EVADE.] 1. The action of evading or escaping, as by artifice or contrivance; escape (now *rare*); dodging, prevarication 1460. b. Means of evading; shuffling excuse, subterfuge ME. 2. Going out, exit (*rare*) 1659.

1. Hope of euasion from Purgatorie 1601. E. from the strength of an Argument H. MORE. The king's licence for the e. of the act J. H. BLUNT. b. Evasions and delays 1874.

Evasive (ĭvē¹·siv), *a.* 1725. [ad. F. *évasif*, *-ive*, f. L. *evas-* (see EVADE) + -IVE.] 1. Seeking to evade; shuffling. 2. Tending to, or characterized by, evasion 1744. 3. Elusive 1881. 4. as *sb.* An evasive expression. NORTH.

1. Thus he .. Answer'd e. of the sly request POPE. 2. E. promises of future service SHERIDAN. Hence **Eva·sive·ly** *adv.*, **-ness.** So †**Evaso·rious** H. MORE.

Eve (īv), *sb.* ME. [Short for EVEN *sb.*; cf. *morrow*.] 1. = EVENING *sb.*[1] *lit.* and *fig. poet.* or *rhet.* 2. The evening, hence the day, before a Saint's day or church festival, or *gen.* before any date or event. ME. 3. *transf.* The time immediately preceding some action, event, etc. 1780.

1. From Noon to dewy E. MILT. *P. L.* I. 743. 2. St. Bartholomewes Eeve HANMER. 3. The hull on the e. of sinking DUNCAN. Hence †**Eve** *v.* to be the EVE (sense 2) of.

Eve-churr. 1658. [f. prec. + CHURR.] †1. The Mole-Cricket, or Churr-Worm –1668. 2. The Nightjar 1837.

†**E·veck.** 1585. [?] A kind of wild goat –1611.

Evectant (ĭve·ktănt). 1876. [f. L. *evect-* (see EVECTOR) + -ANT.] *Math.* A contravariant formed by operating upon an invariant or contravariant with an evector.

Eve·cted, *ppl. a. rare.* 1861. [f. L. *evect-* ppl. stem (see EVECTOR).] Of the edge of a tube: Turned outwards, trumpet-shaped.

Evectic, a dictionary spelling of EUECTIC.

Evection (ĭve·kʃən). 1656. [ad. L. *evectionem*, f. *evehere* to carry out.] †1. A lifting up (*rare*) –1659. 2. *Astron.* a. An inequality in the moon's longitude (see quot.) 1706. †b. Used for LIBRATION –1796.

2. a. E., an inequality in the motion of the moon, by which, at her quarters, her mean place differs from her true one by about 2½ degrees more than at her conjunction and opposition BONNYCASTLE. Hence **Eve·ctional** *a.* relating or belonging to the e.

Eve·ctor. [f. L. *evehere*, f. *e-* out + *vehere* to carry.] *Math.* An operator formed by substituting the differential operators d/da_0, d/da_1, d/da_2, etc. for the coefficients a_0, na_1, $\frac{1}{2}n(n-1)a_2$, etc. of a binary quantic.

Eve-jar. 1789. [f. EVE *sb.* + JAR.] = EVE-CHURR 2.

Even (ī·v'n), *sb.* [OE. *ǽfen*, *ēfen*, cogn. w. AFTER.] 1. The latter part of the day. 2. = EVE 2. ME. *Comb.* **e.-fall**, the fall or commencement of the evening.

Even (ī·v'n), *a.* [Com. Teut.: OE. *efen*, *efn* :—OTeut. *ebno-.] 1. Flat, plane, level; b. horizontal (now only *Naut.* in phr. (*On*) *an even keel*) ME. 2. Of surfaces or lines: Uniform, without inequality ME. 3. Uniform throughout (in quality, etc.) 1821. †4. Straight, direct –1602. 5. Level *with*, †*to* ME.; in the same plane or line with; parallel ME. 6. Accurately coincident; exactly adjusted ME. †7. Exact, precise –1601. 8. Uniform; free from variations; equable OE. 9. Equally balanced 1579. 10. Of accounts, etc.: 'Square' 1551. 11. Medium ME. 12. Equal, just OE. †13. On a par, on equal terms –1754. 14. Equal in magnitude, number, quantity, etc. ME. 15. Divisible integrally by two; opp. to *odd* ME. 16. Expressible in integers; containing no fractions 1638.

1. E. ground SHAKS. A fair and e. ridge TENNYSON. 2. Cut close and e. EVELYN. 3. A light e. tint 1821. 5. And shall lay thee euen with the ground *Luke* xix. 44. 7. *All's Well* v. iii. 326. 8. At a steady e. trot JOHNSON. 9. The two scales hang e. BENTHAM. 10. E. reckoning makes lasting friends SOUTH. Phr. *To be e. with*: to be quits with; I will be e. with you for this scorn 1655. 14. Three even parts 1660. Phr. *Of e. date*: of the same date (in Eng. chiefly legal). 15. Death..makes these oddes, all euen *Meas. for M.* III. i. 41. 16. Down to e. money (*mod.*).

Even (ī·v'n), *adv.* [OE. *efne* :—OTeut.

*ebnô (see prec.). The form *e'en* (īn) is now *poet.* or *n. dial.*]

†I. 1. Evenly; regularly, uniformly -1728. 2. In exact agreement -1645. 3. Equally -1577. 4. Directly, straight; due (east, etc.); directly (contrary, etc.) -1550.

2. I .. rather shun'd to go e. with what I heard *Cymb.* I. iv. 47.

II. As an intensive or emphatic particle. 1. Exactly, precisely, just: a. of manner OE; b. of time ME.; †c. of place -1578. 2. Quite, fully (now only *arch.* in *Even to*) OE. 3. Emphasizing identity (now *arch.*); also formerly epexegetical; = 'namely' OE. b. (Chiefly *e'en.*) Before vbs. in sense 'just', 'nothing else but'; also 'forsooth' (L. *scilicet*). Now *arch.* and *dial.* 1553. 4. Introducing an extreme case of something more general implied (= F. *même*). (The prevailing use; not found exc. in Eng.) 1577.

1. E. thus..the warlike god embraced me SHAKS. Let your love e. with my life decay SHAKS. 3. E. she I meane *Two Gent.* II. i. 49. b. I e'en let him out DE FOE. 4. Make sacred euen his styrrop *Timon* I. i. 82. E. on that memorable occasion, his stay did not exceed two months GIBBON.

Even- (in early combs. repr. OTeut. stem *ebno-; in later use combining directly as *adj.* or *adv.*).

1. Chiefly in parasynthetic derivs., as *e.-handed, -tempered*, etc. †2. Prefixed to sbs. in sense 'fellow-', L. *co-*, as in *e.-servant*, etc. 3. In senses of the *adv.* †a. = 'Equally', 'similarly', as in *e.-clad, -high, -mighty*, etc. b. = 'Evenly', as in *e.-spun*, etc. †c. With quasi-prep. sense, in e.-deed *adv.*, indeed. d. Straight, directly; see EVENDOWN.

Even (ī·v'n), *v.* [OE. *efnan*, f. *efen* EVEN.] 1. *trans.* To level; to make even, level, smooth, or †straight ME. †2. To level *to, with* -1632. †3. To make (a balance) even -1718. †4. To make (accounts, etc.) even -1856. 5. To †make, treat, or represent as equal. Const. *to, with.* Also *absol.* Now chiefly *Sc.* ME. 6. To liken, compare. Now *dial.* OE. 7. *intr.* To be equal, comparable, or †in a line *with* ME. 8. *trans.* To equal (*rare*) 1583; †to act up to *Cymb.* III. iv. 184.

1. And e. the erthe above ME. E. your Ranks 1688. 8. A daughter who eveneth thee in beauty BURTON.

†**E·ven-Chri·stian.** OE. [See EVEN-.] A fellow-Christian -1602.

E·vendown. *north.* (Often hyphened, or as two wds.) ME. [f. EVEN *adv.* (sense I. 4) + DOWN *adv.*]

A. *adv.* †1. Straight down. 2. *dial.* Downright; quite 1869.

B. *adj.* 1. Coming straight down, as rain 1801. 2. Downright; straightforward 1786.

†**Eve·ne,** *v.* 1654. [ad. L. *evenire.*] *intr.* To happen -1702.

Evener (ī·v'nəɹ). ME. [f. EVEN *v.*] One who or that which makes even. b. An apparatus for equalizing the draught upon two or three horses working abreast.

†**E·venhead, e·venhood.** ME. [OE. *efenhád, f. *efen* EVEN *a.* + *hád* rank; see -HEAD, -HOOD.] 1. Equality; equal dignity or rank -1483. Also *concr.* one who or that which is equal -1570. 2. Impartiality; well-balanced state (of mind) -1496.

Evening (ī·vniŋ), *sb.*[1] [OE. *æfnung*, f. *æfnian* to grow towards evening, f. *æfen* EVEN *sb.*] †1. The coming on of even; the time about sunset -ME. 2. The close of the day; usu., the time from about sunset to bedtime ME. Also *transf.* and *fig.* 3. An evening spent in a particular way. Cf. F. *soirée*. 1870. 4. *attrib.*, as in *evening-gun*, etc. 1535.

2. I shall fall Like a bright exhalation in the Euening *Hen. VIII*, III. ii. 226. *fig.* The sad e. of a stormy life POPE. 3. Occasional 'evenings out' 1870.

Comb.: e. dress; e. flower, a genus of plants (*Hesperantha*, N.O. *Iridaceæ*) with flowers which expand in the e.; e. primrose: see PRIMROSE; e.-star, (with def. art.) Venus, (with indef. art.) Venus, Jupiter, or Mercury, also *fig.*; e.-tide = EVENTIDE.

†**E·vening,** *sb.*[2] ME. [f. EVEN *v.*] 1. The action of making even, level, or smooth, or ?of comparing -1670. 2. Equality ME.

†**E·venlong.** ME. [f. EVEN- + LONG *a.*]

A. *adj.* Oblong -1565.

B. *adv.* Straight along; in an oblong form. Only in ME.

Evenly (ī·v'nli), *a.* Now *Sc.* only. [OE. *efenlic*, f. *efen*, EVEN *a.* + -*lic*, -LY[1].] †1. Equal -1513. 2. Even; equitable; level ME.

Evenly (ī·v'nli), *adv.* [OE. *efenlíce*; see -LY[2].] In an even manner or degree; smoothly; †directly; †exactly; uniformly; with equanimity; without inclination to either side; equally.

Evenness (ī·vĕnˌnĕs). [OE. *efenniss*; see -NESS.] The quality or state of being even; smoothness, levelness; uniformity; equability; †equipoise (*lit.* and *fig.*); equitableness; †equality.

To carry a full cup with evennesse 1646. E. of Voice and Delivery STEELE. The e. .. in a beautiful set of teeth 1878.

†**Even-old.** [OE. *efeneald*; see EVEN- and OLD.]

A. *adj.* Of the same age.

B. *sb.* One who is of the same age. -1483.

Evensong (ī·vˈnˌsǫŋ). OE. [f. EVEN *sb.* + SONG.] 1. *Eccl.* Before the Reformation, the service (also called *vespers*) celebrated towards sunset. Later, the 'Evening Prayer' of the Church of England, including vespers and compline. b. The time of evensong (*arch.*) ME. 2. *gen.* A song sung in the evening ME.

1. b. Let hir fast till euensong 1486. 2. Thee, chauntress, oft the woods among I woo, to hear thy even-song MILT.

†**Even-star.** [OE. *æfensteorra.*] Evening-star -1552.

Event (ĭve·nt), *sb.* 1573. [a. OF. *event*, ad. L. *eventus*, f. *evenire* to come out.] 1. The occurrence *of*. Now chiefly in phr. *In the event of*. 1602. 2. An incident, occurrence; *esp.* (in mod. use) an occurrence of some importance 1588. b. In the doctrine of chances: Any one of the possible (mutually exclusive) occurrences, one of which must happen under stated conditions, and the relative probability of which may be calculated 1838. c. One of the items in a programme of sports 1855. 3. The outcome, issue, of a course of proceedings; that which results from the operation of a cause; a consequence 1573. †4. What becomes of (a person or thing); fate -1674.

2. Coming events cast their shadows before CAMPBELL. Phr. *The course of events*: see COURSE. *Quite an e.* (colloq.). 3. Causes best friended haue the best euent HEYWOOD. The e. of his enterprise was doubtful MACAULAY. 4. There is one e. to the righteous and to the wicked *Eccl.* ix. 2.

†**Event,** *v.*[1] 1590. [f. L. *event-*, *evenire.*] *intr.* To come to pass -1650.

†**Eve·nt,** *v.*[2] 1559. [ad. F. *éventer*, f. *es-* :—L. *ex* + *vent.*] a. To expose to the air; hence, to cool. b. *intr.* for *refl.* To find a vent. -1606.

†**Eve·nterate,** *v.* [irreg. f. L. *e* + *venter*; cf. F. *éventrer.*] *trans.* To open the bowels of; to disembowel. SIR T. BROWNE.

Eventful (ĭve·ntfŭl), *a.* 1600. [See -FUL.] 1. Full of striking events. 2. Fraught with important issues 1773. 3. Eventual. BENTHAM.

1. This strange euentfull historie SHAKS. 2. Thalaba .. waited calmly for the e. day SOUTHEY.

Eventide (ī·v'ntəid). *arch.* [OE. *æfen-tíd*, f. *æfen* EVEN *sb.* + *tíd* time, TIDE.] The time of evening; evening. Also *fig.*

†**Eve·ntilate,** *v.* 1623. [f. L. *eventilat-*, *eventilare* to fan; see VENTILATE.] 1. To expose to the wind or air; to fan; to winnow -1684. 2. *fig.* To discuss; to VENTILATE -1669.

2. Copiously..elsewhere eventilated 1669. Hence †Eventila·tion.

Eventless (ĭve·ntlĕs), *a.* 1815. [See -LESS; cf. *eventful.*] Without (noteworthy) events.

Eventration (īventrē·ʃən). 1836. [a. F. *éventration*, f. *éventrer*, f. *é* + *ventre.*] 1. The action of opening the belly (of an animal) 1875. 2. a. The condition of a fœtus in which the abdominal viscera are extruded 1860. b. 'The condition of a large ventral hernia' (*Syd. Soc. Lex.*). c. The escape of a large amount of intestines from an abdominal wound 1847.

Eventual (ĭve·ntiuăl), *a.* 1612. [ad. F. *éventuel*, f. L. *eventus*; see EVENT.] †1. Of or pertaining to events; of the nature of an event -1684. †2. That happens to exist -1794. 3. That will arise or take effect in a certain contingency 1683. 4. Ultimately resulting 1823.

3. Nothing is provided for it, but an e. surplus to be divided with one class of the private demands BURKE. 4. An e. denial of God's omnipotence FABER.

Eventuality (ĭveˑntiuˌæ·lĭti). 1828. [f. prec. + -ITY.] 1. A possible event; a contingency 1852. 2. *Phrenol.* The faculty of observing the order of succession in events; the 'organ' of this faculty 1828.

Eventually (ĭve·ntiuăli), *adv.* 1660. [f. as prec. + -LY[2].] 1. In a certain event 1830; †conditionally -1785. 2. †In result -1729; in the event, ultimately 1680.

2. Other vices e. do mischief: this alone aims at it as an end BUTLER.

Eventuate (ĭve·ntiuˌeˈit), *v.* First used in U.S. 1789. [f. L. *eventus* + -ATE; cf. *actuate.*] 1. *intr.* To have a (specified) event or issue; to turn out; to result *in*. 2. To be the issue 1834. 3. *trans.* To bring to the issue 1837.

1. Discussions which eventuated in Acts of Parliament SMILES. Hence **Eve·ntua·tion,** the action of eventuating; realization; issue.

†**Ever,** *sb.* [OE. *eofor* = (OH)G. *eber* :—OTeut. *eburoz, rel. to OSl. *veprĭ*, L. *aper.*] A wild boar; †e. fern, (*a*) polypody, *Polypodium vulgare*, (*b*) flowering fern, *Osmunda regalis.*

Ever (e·vəɹ), *adv.* [OE. *æfre.* ? Conn. with OE. *á*, AY.]

I. Always, at all times; in all cases. 1. Throughout all time, all past or future time, one's life, etc.; perpetually (*arch.*). b. With limiting adv., prep., or conj., as in *ever after (-ward), before, since* ME. 2. = ALWAYS 1. *arch.* and *n. dial.* OE. So in *Ever and again, ever and anon* (see AGAIN, ANON). 3. Constantly; with perpetual recurrence (*arch.*) OE. So with comparatives, *esp.* before *the—the.* 4. quasi-*sb.* use of 1, in phr. *For ever, for ever and ay* (arch.) ME.

1. He liveth and reigneth e. one God *Bk. Com. Prayer.* 1. b. The Coffee-houses have e. since been my chief Places of Resort ADDISON. 2. The Prelate of the Garter..is e. the Bishop of Winchester R. HOLME. And e. and anon some falling shaft Proves his divinity BYRON. 3. Pedants..will e. be carping STEELE. 4. It was the fate of Charles, for e. to aim at projects which were..impracticable GOLDSM.

II. At any time; whence: In any case, in any degree. 1. At any time OE. 2. On any supposition, at all OE. a. In *Ever, e'er a(n* (vulgar) OE. b. In comparative and relative clauses, introduced by *as, than*, by a superlative with *that*, or by *all, the only*, etc. 1523. c. For emphasis with the conjs. *as soon as, before, ere, or* (= *ere*) ME. d. After interrog. pronouns, advs., etc. (*how, who, what, where, why*) 1595. 3. In any degree. a. In *Ever the* with comparatives (*colloq.*); = 'at all', 'any' 1622. b. In *Ever so* = 'in any conceivable degree' 1690; 'vastly' 1858.

1. The first time that e. I remember to have heard the..singing men in surplices in my life PEPYS. 2. a. A Man of my Turn enjoys a Holiday with as high a Relish as e'er a Prentice-Boy..within the Bills of Mortality 1746. b. As lowd as e're thou canst, cry 1 *Hen. VI*, I. iii. 72. 3. a. A Mine undiscovered, from which neither the Owner of the Ground or any Body else, are e. the Richer COLLIER.

Combs.: e.-being *a.* that always is; -blessed *a.* always blessed; to be always adored; -during *a.* everlasting.

Everglade (e·vəɹˌgleˈd). *U.S.* 1827. [?f. EVER (= 'interminable') + GLADE.] A marshy tract of land mostly under water and covered in places with tall grass; chiefly in *pl.*, as, *the everglades of Florida.*

Evergreen (e·vəɹgrīn). 1644. [f. EVER *adv.* + GREEN.]

A. *adj.* 1. Always green; also *fig.* 1796. 2. Having green leaves all the year through; opp. to *deciduous.* Also *transf.* of the leaves. 1671.

1. E. valleys 1796. 2. Shade Of laurel ever-green, and branching palm MILT. *Sams.* 1735.

B. *sb.* An evergreen tree or shrub 1644. Also *attrib.*, as in **Evergreen Oak,** the Holm Oak (*Quercus Ilex*).

Everlasting (evəɹla·stiŋ). ME. [f. EVER *adv.* + LASTING.]

A. *adj.* 1. Lasting for ever; infinite in future (or, contextually, past) duration. 2. Used hyperbolically or in relative sense; *esp.* as implying weariness or disgust; cf. ETERNAL 4. ME. 3. That will never wear out 1590. 4. In plant-names: **a.** Retaining shape and colour when dried; as in *Everlasting Flower*, a name given to the Cudweeds and various species of *Helichrysum*. **b.** Perennial; as in Everlasting Pea (*Lathyrus latifolius*). **5.** quasi-*adv.* Very, excessively (*U.S. slang.*) ? 18..

1. The Primrose way to th' euerlasting Bonfire *Macb.* II. iii. 22. The mightie God, The euerlasting Father *Isa.* ix. 6. 2. See Cromwell, damn'd to e. fame POPE. The e. Din of Mother-in-law S. PENTON. 3. E. wear (*mod.*).

B. *absol.* (quasi-*sb.*) and *sb.* **1.** *absol.* In phrases *For, to, from everlasting* ME. **2.** *The Everlasting*: God, the Eternal ME. **3.** *sb.* **a.** = DURANCE 1590. **b.** = LASTING 1822. **4.** = Everlasting Flower. See A. 4. 1794.

1. Euen from e. to e. thou art God *Ps.* xc. 2. 2. *Haml.* I. ii. 131. 3. a. *Com. Err.* IV. ii. 33.

Hence **Everla·sting·ly** *adv.*, **-ness.**

E·ver-li·ving, *a.* 1547. **1.** That lives or will live for ever. Also *fig.* **2.** quasi-*sb.* 1601.

Evermore (evəɹmōᵊ·ɹ), *adv.* Occas. as two wds. ME. [Later form of †*evermo*, OE. *æfre mā*; see EVER and MO.] Emphatic for EVER. **1.** For all future time. *Obs.* exc. *arch.* **2.** Always, at all times, constantly ME. **3.** With negatives expressed or implied: **a.** At any future time 1600. **b.** Ever again, any longer 1832.

1. Lord, euermore giue vs this bread *John* vi. 34. 2. The minde of man desireth euermore to know the truth HOOKER.

†**Eve·rse,** *v.* ME. [f. L. *evers-* ppl. stem; see EVERT.] = EVERT –1661.

Eversible (ĭvə·ɹsib'l), *a.* 1877. [f. as prec. + -IBLE; see EVERT.] Capable of being everted or turned inside out.

Eversion (ĭvə̄·ɹʃən). 1470. [a. OF., ad. L. *eversionem*; see EVERT.] †**1.** The action of overthrowing; the condition of being overthrown; an overthrow. *lit.* and *fig.* –1820. **2.** *Path.* and *Phys.* The action of everting or turning (an organ or structure) inside out; the condition of being everted; as, *eversion of the eyelids* = ECTROPION 1751.

Eversive (ĭvə̄·ɹsiv), *a.* 1717. [f. L. *evers-* ppl. stem + -IVE; see EVERT.] Tending to eversion or overthrow. Const. *of.*

A maxim e. ..of all justice and morality GEDDES.

Evert (ĭvə̄·ɹt), *v.* 1533. [ad. L. *evertere* to overturn.] †**1.** *trans.* To turn upside down. *lit.* and *fig.* –1693. †**2.** To overthrow –1599. Also *fig.* †**3.** To turn aside –1650. **4.** To turn inside out or outwards 1804.

1. The very thought Everts my soul with passion B. JONS. 4. To e. the eyelid HARLAN.

Evertebral (ivə̄·ɹtĭbrăl), *a.* 1878. [See E- *pref.*[3] and VERTEBRAL.] *Anat.* Not vertebral.

The anterior, or e. portion [of the cranium] BELL.

Evertebrate (ivə̄·ɹtĭbrĕt), *a.* and *sb.* 1883. [See E- *pref.*[3] and VERTEBRATE.] *Zool.* = INVERTEBRATE.

Evertebrate (ivə̄·ɹtĭbreˡt), *v.* 1880. [f. as prec. + L. *vertebra* + ATE [3].] To deprive of the backbone.

Every (e·vəri, ev'ri), *a.* (quasi-*pron.*). [OE. *æfre ælc*, **æfre ylc*; see EVER *adv.* and EACH.

I. As *adj.* used *attrib.* **1.** Each of a group; all taken one by one. Occas. with vb. in *pl.* †**2.** With plural sb.: All severally –1671. **3.** = 'All possible' (*mod.*). †**4.** = ANY; in sentences expressing possibility –1760.

1. In my euerie action to be guided by others experiences *Cymb.* I. iv. 49. Euery the least remembrance 1620. Phr. *Every now and then, every once in a while* [corruption of *ever*, etc.]: from time to time. 2. *Temp.* V. i. 249. 3. I feel e. respect for him (*mod.*).

II. *absol.* (quasi-*pron.*). †**1.** Everybody –1502. **2.** Each, or every one, *of* (several). Formerly often with vb. in *pl.* *Obs.* exc. *Law.* ME. †**3.** = EACH –1485.

1. E. hath of God a propre gift CHAUCER. 2. To all and e. the children and child of the said intended marriage BENTHAM.

Comb. **1.** **Every one.** †**a.** *adj.* = sense I. 1. 1548. **b.** *adj. absol.* (e·vri wʊ·n). Distributing a sb. or pron. going before; or followed by *of.* Often (erron.) w. pl. vb. Occas. = Each (of two). ME. **c.** *pron.* (e·v'ri,wʊn). Everybody; occas. written as one word. The pron. referring to *every one* is often (? unavoidably) *pl.* ME. ¶ **2.** The form *ever each* (orig. *evereche, everych*) was corrupted into *every each*, and has occas. been used *arch.* by recent writers.

Everybody (e·vəri-, e·v'ri,bǫdi, -bǫ̆di), *pron.* 1530. [f. EVERY + BODY (= *person*). Formerly as two wds.] Every person. Occas. (incorrectly) with *pl. vb.* or *pron.*

Everyday (e·vəri,-, e·vri,deˡ, e·vri,deˡ·). ME. [f. EVERY + DAY.]

A. *sb.* Each day in succession; *dial.* a week-day, as opp. to Sunday.

B. *attrib.* **1.** Daily 1647. **2.** Worn on ordinary days, as opp. to Sundays or high-days 1632. **3.** To be met with every day; common 1763.

1. Of e. occurrence 1880. 2. In his every-day garments DICKENS. 3. This was no every-day writer JOHNSON.

†**E·verydeal.** ME. [f. EVERY + DEAL.] **1.** as *sb.* Every part, the whole; also, subjoined to a sb. or sb. pron. for emphasis: Every whit –1560. **2.** as *adv.* Entirely, wholly –1714.

Every one: see EVERY.

Everything (e·vəri-, e·vri,þiŋ), *pron.* ME. [f. EVERY (sense I. 1) + THING.] **1.** = a neut. absol. use of the adj. A current substitute for *all* (absol.), *all things.* Formerly as two wds. **b.** as *pred.* Of supreme importance. *colloq.* **2.** *sb. rare* in *sing.*; in *pl.* (*joc.*) Things of every kind 1797.

2. Patent everythings going of themselves everywhere RUSKIN.

Everyway (e·vəri,-, e·v'ri,weˡ), *adv.* 1570. [Cf. ALWAY, ANYWAY. Occas. as two wds.] In every way, manner, or direction; in every respect.

You wrong me every way: you wrong me Brutus *Jul. C.* IV. iii. 55.

Everywhen (e·vəri,-, e·v'ri,hwe·n), *adv.* 1843. [f. EVERY + WHEN; after *everywhere.*] At all times, always.

Everywhere (e·vəri,-, e·v'ri,hwēᵊɹ), *adv.* [repr. **1.** ME. *Ever-ywhere* (OE. *ȝehwǽr*) anywhere, everywhere. **2.** *Every-where*, f. EVERY (ME. *everille*) + WHERE. Formerly often as two wds.] **1.** In every place; in every part. †**2.** quasi-*adj.* All-pervading 1674. Hence **Everywhereness**, omnipresence.

Everywhither (e·vəri,-, e·v'ri,hwi·ðəɹ), *adv.* ME. [f. EVERY + WHITHER.] In every direction.

Eves(e, obs. f. EAVES.

E·ve-star. *Obs.* exc. *poet.* ME. [f. EVE *sb.*[1] + STAR.] = *Evening star.*

Evet, e, evett, obs. ff. EFT *sb.*

†**Evibrate,** *v. rare.* 1583. [f. L. *evibrat-* ppl. stem; see VIBRATE.] To vibrate. *trans.* and *intr.* Hence †**Evibra·tion.**

Evict (ĭvi·kt), *v.* 1503. [f. L. *evict-*, ppl. stem of *evincere*, f. *e-* + *vincere* to conquer. See EVINCE.] **1.** *Law.* To recover by a judicial process, or in virtue of a superior title. **2.** To expel by legal process; in recent use, to eject (a tenant) from his holding. Also *transf.* 1536. †**3.** *gen.* To conquer; to overcome –1667. †**4.** To extort by force –1648. †**5.** To confute, refute; to convict or convince *of* –1660. †**6.** To prove –1722; to settle by argument –1660.

1. If land is evicted, before the time of payment of rent on a lease [etc.] TOMLINS. 2. Two of the principal tenants..were evicted 1889. Hence **Evi·cted** *ppl. a. spec.* (a farm) from which the tenant has been evicted. **Evi·ctor**, also **-er**, one who evicts.

Eviction (ĭvi·kʃən). 1583. [ad. L. *evictionem*, f. *evincere*; see EVICT, EVINCE.] **1.** *Law.* The action of recovering lands or property by legal process. **2.** The action of evicting or dispossessing a person of property, etc. Also *attrib.* 1626. †**3.** *gen.* The action of conquering –1611; of confuting –1703; of eliciting or establishing by argument –1776.

3. Upon E. I shall freely yield 1703. The sole and ultimate end of logic is the e. of truth 1776.

Evidence (e·vidĕns), *sb.* ME. [a. F. *évidence*, ad. L. *evidentia*, f. *evidentem*; see EVIDENT.] **1.** The quality or condition of being evident; evidentness 1665. †**2.** Manifestation –1611. **3.** That which makes evident; an indication, mark, trace ME. †**4.** Example. Only in ME. **5.** Ground for belief; that which tends to prove or disprove any conclusion ME. **6.** *Law.* Information that is given in a legal investigation, to establish the fact or point in question. Also, *An evidence* = a piece of evidence. 1503. **b.** Statements or proofs admissible as testimony in a court of law 1817. **7.** One who, or that which furnishes proof; a witness; title-deeds. *Obs.* exc. *Hist.* and *Law.* ME.

1. Phr. *In e.* [after F. *en évidence*]: actually present; conspicuous; The sister..was in e. (*mod.*). 3. The evidences of ancient glacier action TYNDALL. 5. Phr. *External, Internal, Moral, Probable E.* (see these adjs.). 6. Phr. *To call in e.*: to call as a witness. *Circumstantial, Parole, Presumptive, Primâ facie, Verbal*, etc. *E.* (see these adjs.). 7. Phr. *To turn King's* (*Queen's, State's*) *e.*: to appear as a witness for the prosecution against one's accomplices in a crime. var. †**E·vidency** (in senses 1, 3).

Evidence (e·vidĕns), *v.* 1610. [f. prec. sb.] **1.** *trans.* To attest; bear witness to 1619. †**2.** To make evident, demonstrate, prove –1807. **3.** *Law.* †**a.** To give evidence against –1695. †**b.** To relate as a witness –1812. **c.** *intr.* To give evidence 1656. **4.** To manifest 1610.

1. I invoke Heav'n, earth, and men to e. my truth 1721. 3. c. Her maid..will e. against her LUTTRELL. 4. Expressions evidencing an intention 1876. Hence †**E·videnceable** *a.* that may be evidenced or proved. †**E·videncer**, a witness.

Evident (e·vidĕnt). ME. [ad. L. *evidentem*, f. *e-* out + *videntem*, *videre*.]

A. *adj.* **1.** †**a.** Conspicuous. **b.** Obvious to the sight. **2.** Clear to the understanding or the judgement; obvious, plain ME. †**3.** Indubitable, certain, conclusive –1653.

1. E. marks of small-pox 1806. 2. Why, this is e. to any formall capacitie *Twel. N.* II. v. 128.

B. *sb.* Something that serves as evidence; *spec.* in *Sc. Law*; usu. in *pl.* title-deeds ME.

Hence **E·vident·ly** *adv.*, **-ness.**

Evidential (evide·nʃăl), *a.* 1610. [f. L. *evidentia* + -AL.] **1.** Of, pertaining to, or based upon evidence; relying on evidence; *esp.* the Evidences of Christianity 1654. **2.** Furnishing evidence; of the nature of evidence 1641. †**3.** Resting on documentary evidence. W. FOLKINGHAM.

1. Phr. *E. method, school, system.* Hence **Evide·ntially** *adv.* So **Evide·ntiary** *a.* (in senses 1, 2).

†**Evigila·tion.** 1720. [ad. late L. *evigilationem.*] Awakening.

Evil (ī·vil). [ME. *uvel* (*ü*), OE. *yfel* :— OTeut. **ubilo-z*; ? conn. w. root of *up, over.*]

A. *adj.* The antithesis of GOOD. Now little used, exc. in literary English.

I. Bad in a positive sense. **1.** Morally depraved. Also *absol.* *Obs.* as applied to persons. OE. **2.** Doing or tending to do harm. Of an omen, etc.: Boding ill. ME. **3.** Combining senses 1 and 2. OE. **4.** Causing discomfort, pain, or trouble OE.; †hard, difficult –1551. **5.** †Unfortunate, miserable –1614; unlucky, disastrous ME.

1. Ivel men ME. The imagination of mans heart is euil from his youth *Gen.* viii. 21. 2. Evyl ensaumple WYCLIF. Euill counsel 1584. The Owle shriek'd at thy birth, an euill signe SHAKS. 3. Much evil-will.. shall happen unto you COVERDALE. Phr. *The E. One*: the Devil; Deliver us from the e. one R.V. *Matt.* vi. 13. 4. A house of e. repute (*mod.*). 4. Of an evill savour LYTE. 5. In euill case *Ex.* v. 19, plight RALEIGH. To anticipate the e. day (*mod.*). Phr. **Evil eye. a.** A look of ill will. **b.** A malicious or envious look, popularly supposed to inflict material harm; also, the supposed faculty of injuring by a look.

II. Bad in a privative sense: Not good. †**1.** Unsound, corrupt; diseased; unwholesome –1611. †**2.** Inferior –1799.

1. The horse had an euill foote 1591. An euill Diet SHAKS. The water whereof was so evill HAKLUYT. 2. Appoint when you come to take an e. dinner with me GRINDAL. E. workmanship 1799.

B. *sb.* The adj. used *absol.*

1. That which is the reverse of good, physically or morally; whatever is censurable, painful, disastrous, or undesirable OE. **2.** The evil portion or element of anything OE. **3.** Any particular thing that causes harm or mischief, physical or moral ME. †**4.** A wrong-doing, sin, crime. Usu. *pl.* –1614. †**5.** A calamity, disaster, misfortune –1791. †**6.** A disease, malady –1725.

1. All partial E., universal Good POPE. E. haunts The birth, the bridal TENNYSON. The greatest of all mysteries—the origin of e. TAIT & STEWART. 2. I pray..that thou shouldest keepe them from the euill *John* xvii. 15. 3. There are evils to which the calamities of war are blessings BURKE. Phr. *The social e.*: prostitution. 4. *Rich. III*, I. ii. 76 (Qo.). 6. †*The falling e.* (= sickness): epilepsy. **King's evil**: scrofula.

Comb., of the *adj.*, as *e.-minded*, etc.; of the *sb.*, as *e.-doer*, etc.

Hence **E·vil·ly** *adv.*, **-ness.**

†**Evil** (ī·v'l), *adv.* [ME. *uvele* (*ü*), *ivele*,

evele, OE. *yfele*, f. *yfel*; see prec.] In an evil manner; ill; harmfully; badly –1841.

Phr. *To speak e.* (OE. *be*) *of*: to speak maliciously *of*; now taken as a *sb.*, but in OE. and ME. an *adv.* *Comb.*: **e.-liking**, ill-favoured; **-sounding**, harsh-sounding; **-sained**, lit. 'ill-blessed', *i.e.* accursed.

†**E·vil-fa·voured**, *a.* 1530. [f. EVIL + FAVOUR.] = ILL-FAVOURED –1612. Hence †**E·vilfa·vouredness.**

Evince (*ĭ*vi·ns), *v.* 1608. [ad. L. *evincere*; see EVICT.] †1. *trans.* To overcome, subdue –1678. †2. To convince –1670; to confute –1672. †3. To extort by argument or persuasive motives –1658. †4. To prove by argument or evidence. Also, *rarely*, To vindicate. Also *absol.* –1767. 5. To indicate, make evident or manifest 1621.

1. Error by his own arms is best evinc't MILT. *P. R.* IV. 235. 4. The Accuser complaines, the Witnesse evinceth, the Judge sentences BP. HALL. 5. His answers .. evinced both wisdom and integrity C. BRONTË.

Hence †**Evi·ncement**, the action of evincing; proof. **Evi·ncible** *a.*, also †**-eable**, demonstrable; †convincing. **Evi·ncibly** *adv.* **Evi·ncive** *a.* indicative.

Evirate (*ī*·vireɪt), e·vireɪt), *v.* 1621. [f. L. *evirat-* ppl. stem of *evirare* to castrate, f. *e* + *vir.*] To deprive of virility or manhood. Hence †**E·virate** *ppl. a.* castrated, emasculated. **Evira·tion**, emasculation.

‖**Evirato** (*evirā·to*). Pl. **-ti.** 1796. [It.; see prec.] = CASTRATO.

†**Evi·rtuate**, *v.* 1640. [f. F. (*s'*) *évertuer*, f. *é-* (for *es-*) :—L. *ex-* + *vertu* + -ATE [3].] 1. *intr.* To put forth virtue, exert influence; also *refl.* –1675. 2. *trans.* To deprive of virtue, strength, or power –1644.

Eviscerate (*ĭ*vi·sĕreɪt), *v.* 1607. [f. L. *eviscerat-*, *eviscerare*, f. *e-* + *viscera* VISCERA.] *trans.* To take out the entrails of; to disembowel; to gut. Also *absol.* 1623. Also *transf.* and *fig.*

A Paper-Warehouse eviscerated by axe and fire. CARLYLE. Hence **Eviscera·tion.**

Evitable (e·vităb'l), *a.* 1502. [ad. L. *evitabilis*; see EVITE *v.*] Avoidable. (Now chiefly with neg. contexts.)

†**E·vitate**, *v.* 1588. [f. L. *evitat-*, *evitare*; see EVITE *v.*] = EVITE *v.* –1603. Hence **Evita·tion**, avoidance, shirking.

E·vite, *sb.* [f. EVE + -ITE. Cf. ADAMITE.] A name for a woman wearing little clothing. ADDISON.

Evite (*ĭ*vəi·t), *v. arch.* 1503. [ad. F. *éviter*, ad. L. *evitare.*] To avoid, shun. (Now mostly *Sc.*)

†**Evite·rnal**, *a.* Also **Æviternal.** 1596. [f. L. *æviternus* (whence *æternus*) + -AL.] = ETERNAL; everlasting –1652. Hence †**Evite·rnally** *adv.* So **Evite·rnity**, eternity, everlastingness.

Evittate (*ĭ*ˌvi·tăt), *a.* 1866. [f. E- *pref.*[3] + VITTA + -ATE [2].] *Bot.* Without vittæ or oil-canals.

Evocable (e·vǒkăb'l), *v.* [a. F. *évocable*; see EVOKE.] That may be called forth.

Evocate (e·vǒkeɪt), *v.* 1639. [f. L. *evocat-* ppl. stem; see EVOKE.] †1. *trans.* To call forth –1665. 2. To call up from the dead, from past times 1675. Hence **Evo·cative** *a.* tending to draw forth. **E·vocator**, one who evocates. **Evo·catory** *a.* having the function of evoking.

Evocation (evokē¹·ʃən). 1612. [ad. L. *evocationem*; see EVOKE.] †1. A calling out or forth; *esp.* of spirits –1656. †2. Avocation –1810. 3. The calling out of a cause from a lower to a higher court 1644. †4. *Gram.* A 'reduction of the third person either to the first or second' –1696.

‖**Evoe**, *interj.* (*sb.*) Also **evohe.** 1586. [a. L., a. Gr. εὐοῖ.] The Bacchanalian cry 'Evoe!'

Evoke (*ĭ*vōu·k), *v.* 1623. [ad. F. *évoquer*, ad. L. *evocare*, f. *e-* + *vocare* to call.] 1. *trans.* To call forth; *esp.* to summon up (spirits, etc.) by the use of magic. Also *transf.* and *fig.* 2. To summon (a cause) from a lower to a higher tribunal 1752.

1. To e. the Queen of the Fairies WARTON. *transf.* etc. To e. sleeping energies EMERSON, a smile MAX MÜLLER. 2. Authority to e. causes to Rome HUSSEY.

†**E·volate**, *v. rare.* [f. L. *evolat-*, *evolare.*] To fly forth or away. TOMLINSON. Hence †**Evola·tion.**

Evolute (*ī*·vǒliūt), *v.* orig. *U.S.* 1868. [Back-formation from EVOLUTION.] 1. *intr.* To develop by evolution. 2. *trans.* To evolve, develop (*journalese*) 1896.

Evolute (e·vǒliūt). 1730. [ad. L. *evolutus* pa. pple.; see EVOLVE.] A. *adj.* a. *Evolute curve* = B. 1. b. *Bot.* Fully developed 1835.

B. *sb.* 1. *Math.* A curve which is the locus of the centres of curvature of another curve (its *involute*), or the envelope of all its normals. (So called because the end of a stretched thread unwound from the evolute will trace the involute.) 1730. 2. The development of a cone or cylinder. SMEATON.

Evolutility (*ĭ*vǫ:liuti·lĭti). 1884. [f. L. *evolut-*, ppl. stem of *evolvere*; cf. *contractility.*] *Biol.* Capability of manifesting change as a result of the nutritive processes.

Evolution (evŏliū·ʃən, *ī*vŏliū·ʃən). 1622. [ad. L. *evolutionem*, f. *evolvere*; see EVOLVE.]

I. 1. The process of evolving, unrolling, opening out, or disengaging from an envelope. Also *concr.* 'the series of things unfolded or unrolled' (J.). Also *fig.* 1647. 2. *Math.* a. *Geom.* The unfolding of a curve, so that from it is produced an involute 1700. b. *Arith.* and *Alg.* The extraction of any root from any given power; the reverse of involution 1706. 3. *Biol.* a. Of animal and vegetable organisms or their parts: The process of developing from a rudimentary to a complete state 1670. b. The hypothesis that the embryo or germ is a development of a pre-existing form, which contains the rudiments of all the parts of the future organism. (Now better called 'the theory of Preformation'.) 1831. c. The origination of species conceived as a process of development from earlier forms, and not as due to 'special creation'. Often in phrases *Doctrine, Theory of Evolution.* 1832. 4. Development or growth as of a living organism (*e.g.* of a polity, science, language, etc.). Also 'growing' as opp. to 'being made'. 1807. 5. The formation of the heavenly bodies by the concentration and consolidation of cosmic matter 1850. 6. In recent speculation used in a more general sense, of which 3a, 3c, 4, 5 are regarded as special applications 1862.

1. The e. of the child 1800, the larva 1817, of light and heat LYELL, of an argument 1870. 3. a. The .. e. of this part of the brain 1805. c. The e. of one species out of another 1863. 4. The tardy e. of the British constitution 1807. 6. E. is an integration of matter and concomitant dissipation of motion; during which the matter passes from an indefinite, incoherent homogeneity to a definite, coherent heterogeneity; and during which the retained motion undergoes a parallel transformation H. SPENCER.

II. *Mil.* and *Naut.* The opening out of a body of troops or squadron of ships; hence *gen.* any tactical movement or change of position 1622. Also *transf.* and *fig.*

Hence **Evolu·tional** *a.* of, pertaining to, or produced by e. **Evolu·tionary** *a.* of, pertaining to, or in accordance with e.; evolutional. **Evolu·tionism**, the theory of e. or development. **Evolu·tionist**, an adherent of evolutionism; also *attrib.* **E·volutioni·stic** *a.* tending to support the doctrine of e.; tending to produce e.

Evolutive (e·vǒliūtiv), *a.* 1874. [f. L. *evolut-* ppl. stem; see EVOLVE.] Pertaining, tending to, or promoting evolution.

Evolve (*ĭ*vǫ·lv), *v.* 1641. [ad. L. *evolvere* to roll out, f. *e* + *volvere.*] 1. *trans.* To unfold, unroll; to open out, expand. Usu. *fig.* 2. To disengage from wrappings; to disentangle 1664. 3. To give off, emit, as vapours 1800. 4. To bring out (what exists implicitly or potentially) 1831. 5. To give rise to 1851. 6. To produce or modify by evolution (see EVOLUTION 3–6). Also *intr.* for *refl.* 1799.

1. To e. the powers of the mind 1839. 2. Time.. Evolves their secrets, and their guilt proclaims 1744. 4. The new diseases that human life Evolves in its progress LONGF. 6. Societies are evolved in structure and function as in growth H. SPENCER.

Hence **Evo·lvable** *a.*, also **-ible**, that may be evolved. **Evo·lvement**, evolution. **Evo·lvent** *a.* that evolves; *sb.* the involute of a curve. **Evo·lver.**

‖**Evo·lvulus.** 1847. [f. L. *evolvere*. Cf. CONVOLVULUS.] *Bot.* A genus of the N.O. *Convolvulaceæ*, containing about 60 species.

†**Evo·mit**, *v.* ME. [f. L. *evomit-*, *evomere*; see VOMIT.] *trans.* To vomit, eject. Also *transf.* and *fig.* –1714. Hence †**Evomi·tion**, the action of vomiting forth.

Evulgate (*ĭ*vɒ·lgeɪt), *v.* ? *Obs.* 1563. [f. L. *evulgat-*, *evulgare*, f. *e* + *vulgus.*] To make publicly known; to publish. Hence **Evulga·tion**, publishing, publication. So †**Evu·lge** *v.*

Evulsion (*ĭ*vɒ·lʃən). 1611. [ad. L. *evulsionem.*] The action of pulling out by force.

‖**Evviva** (evˌvī·va). 1887. [It., f. *e* (:—L. *et*) intensive + *viva* (:—L. *vivat*).] The cry 'Long live (the king)'; hence, a shout of applause.

Ew, obs. f. YEW.

Ewe (yū), *sb.* [Com. Teut. and Aryan: OE. *eowu* :—OTeut. **awi-z* :—OAryan **owi-s*; cf. L. *ovis*, Gr. ὄ(ϝ)ις, Skr. *avi.*] A female sheep. Also *attrib.* *Comb.* **e.-neck**, a thin hollow neck (in a horse).

Ewe, *v.* 1579. [f. prec.] †1. To give birth to (a lamb) –1660. 2. *trans.* To give a 'ewe-neck' look to 1848.

†**Ew·er** [1]. ME. [a. OF. *ewer* (Cotgr. *eauïer*) :—L. *aquarius.*] = EWERER –1601.

Ewer [2] (yū·əɹ). ME. [ad. AF. **ewiere*, repr. L. type **aquaria*: cf. prec.] 'A pitcher with a wide spout, used to bring water for washing the hands' (W.). Now, a bedroom water-jug.

Ew·erer. 1450. [f. EWER [1].] A servant who supplied guests, etc. at table with water to wash their hands.

Ewery, ewry (yūᵊ·ri). 1460. [f. EWER + -Y [3].] The apartment or office for ewers, *esp.* in former times, in the royal household.

Ewt(e, obs. f. EFT.

Ex (eks), *prep.* 1845. [a. L. *ex* out of (arch. also *ec*). Bef. consonants occas. reduced to *e.*] 1. In L. phrases, as EX ANIMO, EX OFFICIO, EX PARTE, EXTEMPORE, EX-VOTO, etc., q. v. 2. *Comm.* a. In sense 'out of' (a ship, the warehouse). b. In sense 'exclusive of'; *esp.* in phr. *Ex dividend* (*ex div.*, *e. d.*). So *ex new* (*ex n.*, *x. n.*), exclusive of the right to an allotment of new shares or stock.

Ex- *prefix* [1], of L. origin.

1. repr. L. *ex-*, the prep. *ex* (see prec.) in combination.

a. In L. (and hence in English) the form *ex-* appears before vowels and *h*; also before *c*, *p* (usually), *q*, *s*, *t*; before *f* it becomes *ef-* (in inscriptions *ec-*); before other consonants (exc. in *exlex*) *e.* An *s* following the prefix is commonly omitted, exc. in some English scientific terms, as *exsert* (= *exert*), *exsanguineous*, etc. See also ES-. b. In English, as in Latin, *ex-* in composition signifies 'out', 'forth', as in *exclude*, *exit*; 'upward' as in *extol*, 'thoroughly' as in *excruciate*; 'to bring into a certain state' as in *exasperate*; 'to remove, expel, or relieve from' as in *expatriate*, *exonerate*; 'to deprive of' as in *excoriate*; 'deprived of' as in *exsanguineous*. The non-Latin sense 'destitute of', as in *exalbuminous*, is more usually expressed by *e-* (see E- *pref.*[3]).

2. Ex- (with hyphen) prefixed to English words.

Prefixed to titles of office or dignity, to designate previous holders of the position. Hence in the sense 'former', 'sometime', 'quondam', with respect to calling, station, character, or the like.

Ex- *prefix* [2], of Gr. origin.

The Gr. ἐξ out of, etymologically = L. *ex-* (see prec.), occurs only bef. vowels, as in *exodus*, *exorcize*, etc. Bef. consonants it is replaced by ἐκ- (L. *ec-*).

Exacerbate (egz-, eksæ·səɹbeɪt), *v.* 1660. [f. L. *exacerbat-*, *exacerbare*, f. *ex-* intensive + *acerbus.*] To increase the smart or bitterness of; to embitter, aggravate. Also, to irritate, provoke. Also *intr.* for *refl.*

To e. the growing moodiness of his temper POE.

Exacerbation (egz-, eksæ:səɹbē¹·ʃən). 1582. [ad. L. *exacerbationem*; see prec.] 1. The action of exacerbating; the condition of being exacerbated; embitterment, irritation. 2. Increase in severity (of disease, sufferings, etc.). Chiefly *Path.*, a paroxysm (of a fever, etc.); also *transf.* 1625. var. †**Exacerbe·scence** (in sense 2).

†**Exa·cerva·tion.** 1730. [f. L. *exacervare*.] The action of heaping up. (Dicts.)

Exacinate, *v.* 1656. [f. med.L. *exacinat-*, *exacinare*, f. *ex-* + *acinus* grape-stone.] *trans.* To remove kernels from. Hence †**E:xacina·tion.** (Dicts.)

Exact (egzæ·kt), *a.* 1533. [ad. L. *exactus*, pa. pple. of *exigere*; see EXACT *v.*] †**I.** Consummate, finished, perfect –1727; of persons, accomplished, refined –1725.

The hearing is most e. in the hare LOVELL. An e. philosopher HAKLUYT. E. of taste MILT.

II. **1.** Admitting of no deviation 1538. **2.** Accurate in detail, strict 1533. **3.** Perfectly corresponding, strictly correct, accurate 1645. **4.** Precise; not admitting of vagueness or uncertainty 1601. †**5.** As *adv.* = EXACTLY. –1791.

1. The troops were kept in such e. discipline, that [etc.] JAS. MILL. **2.** Suche exacte cyrcumspeccion MORE. Writing [maketh] an exacte man BACON. Our most e. Observer Mr. Flamstead WHISTON. **3.** A piece e. to the life COWLEY. An e. translation PRIESTLEY. **4.** An e. Minute of the Moon EVELYN. Phr. *E. sciences*: those which admit of absolute precision in their results; *esp.* the mathematical sciences.

Exact (egzæ·kt), *v.* 1529. [f. L. *exact-*, *exigere*, f. *ex* + *agere* to drive. Thus lit. 'to drive or force out'.] **1.** To demand and enforce the payment of; to extort. **2.** To require by force or with authority; to insist upon. Const. *from*, *of*. 1564. **3.** To call for, demand, require. Const. *from*, *of*. 1592. †**4.** *intr.* To practise exactions. Const. *on*, *upon*. –1727. **5.** To force out, extract. *arch.* 1639. **6.** *Law.* To call to appear in court 1607.

1. To e. from Passengers..arbitrary..Sums 1703. **2.** To e. an Account of Wealth 1665. To e. Obedience from every creature SHERLOCK. **3.** Their gray hairs e. of us a particular respect 1683. Hence **Exa·cter** = EXACTOR.

Exacting (egzæ·ktiŋ), *ppl. a.* 1583. [f. EXACT *v.*] That exacts; *esp.* that requires too great advantages, exertions, or sacrifices.

Naturally jealous and e. BLACK. Hence **Exa·cting·ly** *adv.*, **-ness.**

Exaction (egzæ·kʃən). ME. [a. F., ad. L. *exactionem*; see EXACT *v.*] **1.** The action of demanding and enforcing payment, performance, etc. **2.** An illegal or exorbitant demand; extortion 1494. **3.** That which is exacted; an arbitrary or excessive impost ME. **4.** *Law.* A calling to appear in court 1816.

1. E. of the forfeiture *Merch. V.* I. iii. 166, of respect 1674. **2.** Tyrannous e. brings on servile concealment BURKE.

Exactitude (egzæ·ktitiūd). 1734. [a. F., f. *exact*; see -TUDE.] The quality of being exact; †exactness.

Exactly (egzæ·ktli), *adv.* 1533. [f. EXACT *a.*] †**1.** In a perfect manner; to perfection; completely –1726. **2.** In an exact manner; accurately; with strict conformity to rule; 'just' 1658. **b.** *colloq.* expressing agreement 1869.

1. Arm'd at all points e., *Cap a Pe* SHAKS. **2.** Let it be..e. weighed 1756. E. the man for the post (*mod.*).

Exactness (egzæ·ktnės). 1564. [f. as prec. + -NESS.] †**1.** Consummate skill; perfection of workmanship –1697. †**2.** Strictness, rigour –1747. **3.** Minute attention to detail; accuracy, precision; †punctuality 1645.

3. Every writer who aims at e. has to begin with definitions WHITNEY.

Exactor (egzæ·ktəɹ). ME. [a. L., f. *exigere*; see EXACT *v.* and -OR.] **1.** One who exacts; a tax-collector (*arch.*); †an officer of justice –1582; a taskmaster 1563. **2.** One who makes illegal or extortionate exactions ME. **3.** One who insists upon (something) as a matter of right 1619.

3. Unmerciful exactors of adulation JOHNSON. So **Exa·ctress,** a female e. (*rare*).

†**Exa·cuate,** *v.* 1632. [irreg. f. L. *exacuere* to sharpen.] *trans.* To make keen or sharp –1684. Hence †**Exacua·tion.**

†**Exæ·stuate,** *v.* [f. *exæstuat-*, *exæstuare*, f. *ex-* + *æstuare* to boil up.] *trans.* To overheat. TOMLINSON. Hence †**Exæstua·tion,** a boiling up; fermentation.

Exaggerate (egzæ·dʒĕreᶦt), *v.* 1533. [f. L. *exaggerat-*, *exaggerare*, f. (ult.) *ex-* intensive + *ag-* (= *ad*) to + *gerere* to bring.] †**1.** *trans.* To heap or pile up; to accumulate –1677. †**2.** To emphasize –1734. **3.** To magnify beyond the truth. Also *absol.* 1613. **4.** To enlarge abnormally 1850.

1. The water.. exaggerating and raising Islands and Continents in other parts HALE. **3.** A Friend exaggerates a Man's Virtues ADDISON.

Hence **Exa·ggeratingly** *adv.* **Exa·ggerative** *a.* marked by, or prone to, exaggeration. **Exa·ggeratively** *adv.*, **-ness.** **Exa·ggerator,** one who or that which exaggerates. **Exa·ggeratory** *a.* exaggerative.

Exaggerated (egzæ·dʒĕreᶦtėd), *ppl. a.* 1725. [f. prec.] **1.** Unduly magnified or inflated. **2.** Abnormally enlarged 1860.

1. Heroes were e. men BUCKLE. **2.** An e. zigzag TYNDALL. Hence **Exa·ggeratedly** *adv.* unduly.

Exaggeration (egzæ:dʒĕrēᶦ·ʃən). 1565. [ad. L. *exaggerationem*; see EXAGGERATE.] †**1.** The action of heaping or piling up; also *concr.* the result. HALE. †**2.** The action of emphasizing –1745. **3.** The action of magnifying unduly in words; an instance of this 1565. **4.** *Painting*, etc. A heightened representation of a subject either in design or colouring; *concr.* an exaggerated copy 1734. **5.** Aggravation (of a condition, etc.); also *concr.* 1661.

1. Lakes grow by the e. of Sand by the Sea 1677. **3.** Such exaggerations will be reduced to their just value GIBBON.

†**Exa·gitate,** *v.* 1532. [f. L. *exagitat-*, *exagitare*, f. *ex-* + *agitare* to put in motion, AGITATE.] **1.** *trans.* To stir up; to AGITATE –1732. **2.** To harass, worry –1677. **3.** To attack violently –1685. **4.** To discuss –1749. Hence †**Exagita·tion,** excitement; discussion.

Exalbuminous (eksælbiū·minəs), *a.* 1830. [f. EX- *pref.*[1] + L. *albumen* + -OUS.] *Bot.* Having no albumen in the seed. var. **Exalbu·minose.**

Exalt (egzǫ·lt), *v.* ME. [ad. L. *exaltare*, f. *ex-* + *altus*; cf. F. *exalter*.] **1.** *trans.* To raise on high; to lift up, elevate. Now *arch.* in physical sense. 1535. **b.** *transf.* To lift up (the voice, etc.) (*arch.*) 1611. **2.** *fig.* **a.** To raise in rank, honour, estimation, power, or wealth ME. †**b.** To elate. Also *intr.* for *refl.* –1708. **c.** To extol. Also *absol.* ME. **d.** To dignify, ennoble 1711. **e.** To stimulate (powers) 1744. †**3.** *Alchemy.* To raise (a substance, etc.) to a higher 'degree'; hence, to refine, mature; to intensify. Also *fig.* –1813. **4.** To heighten (colours) 1842. **5.** *Astrol.* (in *pass.*): To be in the position of greatest influence 1647.

1. *Jul. C.* I. iii. 8. **b.** Against whome hast thou exalted thy voyce 2 *Kings* xix. 22. **2.** **a.** E. him that is low *Ezek.* xxi. 26. **c.** My tonge shall..Dewly exalte thy iustice styll 1545. **d.** I shall not lower but e. the Subjects I treat upon STEELE. **3.** *fig.* This is Jacobinism sublimed and exalted into most pure.. essence BURKE. Hence **Exa·lter.**

†**Exaltate,** *pple.* ME. [ad. L. *exaltatus* pa. pple.] Exalted. –1500.

Exaltation (egzǫltēᶦ·ʃən). ME. [a. F., ad. L. *exaltationem*; see EXALT.] **1.** The action of lifting up or raising on high; the state of being lifted up. *lit.* and *fig.* **2.** *Astrol.* The place of a planet in the zodiac in which it was supposed to exert its greatest influence. Also *fig.* ME. †**3.** *Alchemy*, etc. The action or process of refining or subliming; an instance of this –1751.

1. The E. of this Pope happen'd upon Ascension day 1670. The..e. of our best faculties LAW.

Exalted (egzǫ·ltėd), *ppl. a.* 1594. [f. EXALT *v.*] **1.** Raised or set up on high; elevated; highly placed. **2.** Impassioned 1712. **3.** Intense; sublime, noble 1601. †**4.** *Chem.*, etc. Refined, sublimed, concentrated. Of flavour, etc.: Strong. –1796.

1. The Great King..from an e. throne beheld the misfortunes of his arms GIBBON. **3.** E. piety BOYLE, powers EMERSON. Hence **Exa·lted-ly** *adv.*, **-ness.**

†**Exa·ltment.** 1660. [f. as prec.] Exaltation –1677.

Exam (egzæ·m). *colloq.* 1877. Short for EXAMINATION.

Examen (egzēᶦ·men). 1606. [a. L. *examen* tongue of a balance, *fig.* examination, for **exagmen*, f. **exag-*, *exigere* to weigh accurately; see EXACT *v.*] **1.** Examination; investigation. Now *rare.* 1618. †**2.** A critical disquisition –1738. **3.** A test, assay –1765. **4.** The tongue of a balance (*rare*) 1833.

2. An E. of Mr. Pope's Essay, &c. JOHNSON.

Exameter, -tron, obs. ff. HEXAMETER.

Examinable (egzæ·minăb'l), *a.* 1594. [f. EXAMINE *v.* + -ABLE.] Capable of being examined; in *Law*, cognisable.

Examinant (egzæ·minănt). 1588. [ad. L. *examinantem* pr. pple.; see EXAMINE *v.* and -ANT.]

A. *sb.* **1.** One who examines; an examiner 1620. †**2.** One who is being examined; a deponent; also, an examinee –1812.

†**B.** *adj.* That examines. MILT.

Examinate (egzæ·minĕt). 1471. [ad. L. *examinatus*; see EXAMINE *v.*] †**A.** *pple.* Examined –1818. **B.** *sb.* A person who undergoes examination 1537.

Examination (egzæ:minēᶦ·ʃən). ME. [a. F., ad. L. *examinationem*; see EXAMINE *v.*] †**1.** A trial, proof, assay. Also *fig.* –1552. **2.** The action of testing or judging by a standard. Cf. *Self-examination.* ME. **3.** Investigation by inspection or experiment 1630. **4.** Scrutiny 1538. **5.** The process of testing knowledge or ability by questions 1612. **6.** Formal interrogation, *esp.* of a witness, or an accused person 1555. **b.** The depositions of the witness or accused person 1533.

3. Phr. *Post-mortem e.*, autopsy. **4.** Such an account now claims our e. 1878. **5.** To day..I went through part of my e. for Orders 1783. Phr. *Honour, Local, Pass, Senate-House Examinations* (see these words). **6.** The party is brought before the magistrate for e. 1861. Phr. *E.-in-chief* (Law), that made by the party calling the witness. CROSS-, RE-EXAMINATION (see CROSS-, RE-). **b.** Phr. *To take the e. of*: to interrogate and note down the answers.

Hence **Examina·tional** *a.* of or pertaining to an e. or examinations. **Examina·tionism,** belief in examinations as the test of fitness, knowledge, etc.

Examinator (egzæ·mineᶦtəɹ). 1621. [a. late L.] One who examines; an examiner. Mostly *Sc.*

Examine (egzæ·min), *v.* ME. [ad. F. *examiner*, ad. L. *examinare*, f. *examen*; see EXAMEN.] †**1.** To try, test, assay. Also *fig.* –1440. **2.** To test judicially or critically; to try by a standard ME. **3.** To investigate by inspection or manipulation; to inspect in detail, scan, scrutinize ME. **4.** To inquire into, investigate; to discuss critically ME. **5.** To test (a person) by questioning (see EXAMINATION 5) ME. **6.** To interrogate formally (*esp.* a witness, an accused person) ME. **7.** *intr.* †**a.** To 'see to it' *that*, etc. (*rare*) –1712. **b.** To inquire *into* 1764.

2. E. me, O Lord, and proue me; try my reines and my heart *Ps.* xxvi. 2. **3.** Doss examined the books, and found the following entry 1776. **4.** To e. whether things be good or euill HOOKER, a theory REID, a plea MORLEY. **5.** I was examined in Hebrew and History LD. ELDON. Hence **Exa·minee·,** a person under examination. **Exa·miningly** *adv.* searchingly.

Examiner (egzæ·minəɹ). 1530. [f. prec.] **1.** One who looks into the nature or condition of; an investigator 1561. †**2.** One who interrogates; one who conducts an official inquiry –1686. **3.** A person appointed to examine pupils, candidates for a degree, etc. 1715. Hence **Exa·minership.**

Examplar (egza·mplăɹ), *sb.* Now *rare.* ME. [a. OF. *examplaire*, *exemplaire* :—late L. *exemplarium*, f. *exemplum*. Now repl. by EXEMPLAR.] **1.** A pattern, model. **2.** †A copy, transcript. **b.** An exemplar of a book. 1475. †**3.** = SAMPLER –1583. Hence †**Exa·mplary** *a.* exemplary.

Example (egza·mp'l), *sb.* ME. [a. OF. *example*, *exemple* :—L. *exemplum*, f. *exem-*, *eximere* to take out: see EXEMPT. Thus lit. 'something taken out, a SAMPLE'.] **1.** A typical instance; a fact, etc. that forms a particular case of a principle, rule, state of things, or the like; a person or thing that illustrates a quality. **b.** *Math.* A problem framed to illustrate a rule 1674. **c.** A specimen (of workmanship). Also, a copy of a (rare) book, etc. 1530. **2.** *Logic.* = Gr. παράδειγμα. (See quot.) 1679. **3.** A signal instance of punishment; a person whose fate serves as a deterrent; a warning, caution ME. **4.** A parallel case 1530. **5.** A precedent. *arch.* or *Obs.* 1509. **6.** Action or conduct that induces imitation ME.

1. The will is to Science the first e. of power 1885. **c.** Examples of the great masters (*mod.*). **2.** The E.

is an argument which proves some thing to be true in a particular case from another particular case ABP. THOMSON. 3. Brought to the barre to be punished for e. sake 1631. 4. A Discipline and Generosity without e. FREIND. 6. Well, you know what e. is able to do WALTON.

Example (egzɑ·mp'l), *v.* ME. [f. prec. sb.] 1. *trans.* To exemplify; to find or give an instance of. *Obs.* exc. in *pass.* †2. To hold forth as an example -1654. †3. To furnish a precedent or precedents for; to justify -1595. 4. To set an example to 1631. †5. *intr.* a. To serve as a warning 1571. b. To quote an example. B. JONS.

1. Of an interest .. not in this degree exampled in recent literature CARLYLE. 3. That I may e. my digression by some mighty president SHAKS.

†**Exa·mpleless**, *a. rare.* 1603. [See -LESS.] Without a precedent; unexampled -1603.

Exanguin, -guious, -guous, etc.: see EXS-.

Exanimate (egz-,ˈeksæ·nimět), *ppl. a.* 1534. [ad. L. *exanimatus*; see next.] 1. = INANIMATE. 1552. 2. Destitute or deprived of animation; spiritless.

1. Ships..stuck with carcases e. SPENSER *F. Q.* II. xii. 7. 2. Out of heart, crest-faln, e. 1668.

Exanimate (egz-, eksæ·nimeɪt), *v.* Now *rare.* 1552. [f. L. *exanimat-*, *exanimare*, f. *ex-* + *anima* breath of life.] †1. *trans.* To deprive of life, or of animation -1657. †2. To dispirit -1667. Hence **Exa:nima·tion**, deprivation of life; apparent death from swooning; disheartenment.

‖**Ex animo** (eks æ·nimo). 1612. [L.] *lit.* From the soul; hence, heartily, sincerely.

Exannulate (eksæ·niŭlět), *a.* 1861. [f. EX- priv. + ANNULUS + -ATE ².] *Bot.* Having no *annulus* or ring round the sporangium, as certain ferns.

Exanthalose (eksæ·nþălōs). 1837. [f. Gr. ἐξανθέειν (see next) + ἅλς salt + -OSE.] *Min.* 'Native sulphate of sodium' (Watts).

‖**Exanthema** (eksěnþī·mă). Pl. **-ata.** 1657. [late L., a. Gr. ἐξάνθημα, f. ἐξανθέειν, f. ἐξ- + ἀνθέειν to blossom, f. ἄνθος blossom.] 1. *Path.* An efflorescence, or rash such as takes place in measles, small-pox, etc. Also, an eruptive disease. Chiefly *pl.* 2. *Bot.* Eruptive excrescences on leaves 1866. var. **Exa·nthem.** Hence **Ex-a·nthem·atic, Exanthe·matous** *adjs.* of, pertaining to, or of the nature of, an e. **E:xanthemato·logy**, the doctrine of the exanthemata; a treatise on eruptive fevers.

Exanthine (eksæ·nþəin). 1875. [f. Gr. ἐξανθέειν (see prec.) + -INE.] The Purree or Indian yellow of India.

†**Exa·ntlate**, *v.* 1650. [f. L. *exantlat-*, *exantlare*, ? ad. Gr. ἐξαντλεῖν, f. ἐξ + ἄντλος hold of a ship. But the better attested form of the L. word is *exanclare.*] *trans.* To draw out as from a well; *fig.* to exhaust -1680. Hence †**Exantla·tion** (only *fig.*).

Exappendiculate (e:ksæpĕndi·kiŭlět), *a.* 1870. [f. EX- *pref.*¹ + L. *appendicula* (APPENDICLE) + -ATE ².] *Bot.* Having no appendicles.

Exarate (e·ksărět), *a.* 1870. [ad. L. *exaratus*; see next.] *Entom.* Applied to a variety of pupa in which the larval skin is simply thrown off.

†**E·xarate**, *v.* 1656. [f. L. *exarat-*, *exarare*, f. *ex-* + *arare* to plough.] 1. *trans.* To plough up. 2. To write or note down -1657. Hence **Exara·tion** (now *rare*).

Exarch (e·ksaɹk). 1588. [ad. L. *exarchus* a. Gr., f. ἐξάρχειν, f. ἐξ (see EX-pref.²) + ἄρχειν.] 1. Under the Byzantine Emperors, the governor of a distant province, as Africa or Italy. 2. *Eccl.* In the Eastern Church, orig. = 'archbishop', 'metropolitan', 'patriarch'; later, a deputy of the patriarch, entrusted with some special charge or mission.

Exarchate (e·ksaɹkeɪt, eksā·ɹkět). 1561. [ad. late L. *exarchatus*, f. *exarchus* EXARCH.] The office, or the province, of an exarch. *var.* †**E·xarchy.**

Exareolate (eks,ărī·ŏlět), *a.* 1866. [f. EX- *pref.*¹ + AREOLA + -ATE ².] *Bot.* Not areolate.

Exarillate (eks,æ·rilět), *a.* 1830. [f. EX- *pref.*¹ + L. *arillus* + -ATE ².] *Bot.* Not arillate.

Exaristate (eks,ări·stět), *a.* 1866. [f. EX- *pref.*¹ + ARISTA + -ATE ².] *Bot.* Not aristate.

Exarticulate (eks,aɹti·kiŭlět), *a.* 1835. [f. EX- *pref.*¹ + L. *articulus* + -ATE ².] *Entom.* Not jointed; not consisting of two parts.

Exarticulate (eks,aɹti·kiŭleɪt), *v.* 1656. [f. as prec. + -ATE ³.] †a. To put out of joint. b. To amputate at a joint 1884. Hence **E:x-articula·tion**, †dislocation; amputation at a joint.

Exasperate (egzɑ·spĕrět), *pa. pple.* and *ppl. a.* 1540. [ad. L. *exasperatus*; see next.] †A. *pa. pple.* Exasperated -1609.

B. *ppl. a.* 1. *Bot.* Covered with short stiff points 1866. 2. In senses of EXASPERATE *v.* 2, 3 (*arch.*) 1601.

2. Swallows which the e. dying year Sets spinning in black circles MRS. BROWNING.

Exasperate (egzɑ·spĕreɪt), *v.* 1534. [f. L. *exasperat-*, *exasperare*, f. *ex-* + *asper* rough.] †1. To make harsh or rugged -1765. 2. To make more fierce or violent 1611. †b. To make, or represent as, worse -1750. 3. To embitter, intensify 1548. 4. To irritate; to incense 1534. †5. *intr.* To become enraged; of things, diseases, etc.: To become worse -1734.

2. To e. and inflame a sore BARROW. 3. A temper exasperated by disease PRESCOTT. 4. The poor are exasperated against the rich FRANKLIN. 5. The Distemper exasperated NORTH. Hence **Exa·sperated** *ppl. a.* in same senses; *Her.* depicted in a furious attitude. **Exa·sperater, -or. Exa·speratingly** *adv.*

Exasperation (egzɑspĕrē¹·ʃən). 1547. [ad. L. *exasperationem*; see prec.] 1. Exacerbation 1633. 2. The action of exasperating. Also, a cause or means of exasperating. 1631. 3. The condition of being exasperated; irritation, violent passion or anger 1547.

1. Iudging..by the e. of the fits WOTTON. 2. Their ill usage and exasperations of him ATTERBURY. 3. The e. of his spirits SOUTH.

†**Exau·ctorate**, *v.* 1593. [f. L. *exauctorat-*, *exauctorare* to dismiss from service, f. *ex-* + *auctor.*] 1. *trans.* To dismiss from service; to deprive of office, authority, or rank 1623. 2. To destroy the authority of (a law, etc.) 1593.

1. They did e. and depose the Protector Richard Cromwell W. ROW. Hence †**Exau·ctorate** *ppl. a.* †**Exauctora·tion**, the action of exauctorating.

†**Exau·gurate**, *v.* 1600. [f. L. *exaugurat-*, *exaugurare* to profane; see AUGUR.] a. To undo the inauguration of; to make profane -1695. b. To augur evil to 1652. Hence †**Exaugura·tion**, the action of unhallowing.

†**Exau·n.** [repr. (ɛgzãn), pronunc. of Fr. *exempt.*] = EXEMPT *sb.* BUTLER *Hud.*

Exauthorate, -ation, var. ff. EXAUCTORATE, etc.

†**Exau·thorize**, *v.* 1546. [f. EX- + AUTHORIZE.] = EXAUCTORATE *v.* Hence †**Exauthoriza·tion.**

Excalcarate (eks,kæ·lkărět), *a.* 1884. = ECALCARATE.

†**Exca·lceate**, *v.* 1623. [f. L. *excalceat-*, *excalceare*, f. *ex-* + *calceus* a shoe.] *trans.* To take off the shoes of. Hence †**Excalcea·tion**, the action of taking off the shoes, *e.g.* as a mark of worship.

†**Excalfa·ction.** *rare.* 1607. [ad. L. *excalfactionem*, f. (ult.) *ex-* + *calefacere* to heat.] Calefaction. Hence †**Excalfa·ctive**, †**Excalfa·ctory** *adjs.* tending to warm; heating.

Excalibur (ekskæ·libəɹ). [a. OF. *Escalibor*, corrupt f. CALIBURN, in Geoffrey of Monmouth (*c* 1140) *Caliburnus.* Cf. the name of the Irish sword *Caladbolg* ? = 'hard-belly', *i.e.* 'voracious' (Rhys).] The name of King Arthur's Sword.

Excamb (ekskæ·mb), *v.* 1629. [ad. med.L. *excambiare*; see EXCHANGE *v.*] *Sc. Law.* To exchange (land). Also *absol.* var. **Exca·mbie.** So **Exca·mbion**, exchange, *spec.* of land.

Excandescence (ekskænde·sĕns). 1684. [ad. L. *excandescentia*, f. (ult.) *ex-* + *candescere* to grow white-hot.] a. Heat, the state of growing hot. †b. Anger, passion. var. †**Excande·scency.** So **Excande·scent** *a.* white-hot. (Dicts.)

†**Excanta·tion** (ekskæntē¹·ʃən). *rare.* 1580. [f. L. *excantare.*] The action of removing (anything) by enchantment -1863.

†**Exca·rnate**, *v.* 1648. [f. late L. *excarnat-*, *excarnare* to deprive of flesh.] *trans.* To remove the flesh of -1709. Hence **Exca·rnate** *a.* divested of flesh, or of a human body; opp. to *incarnate.*

Excarnation (ekskaɹnē¹·ʃən). 1847. [f. prec.; see -ATION.] 1. *Anat.* A method of isolating the blood-vessels after injection, by the agency of putrefaction or immersion in an acid (Craig). 2. Separation from the flesh and from fleshly conditions 1858.

†**Excarnificate** (ekskaɹni·fikeɪt), *v.* 1563. [f. L. *excarnificat-*, *excarnificare* to tear to pieces; see CARNIFEX.] *trans.* a. To torture, rack. b. To do the office of an executioner upon. -1664. Hence **Exca:rnifica·tion**, the action of taking away the flesh.

Ex cathedra: see CATHEDRA. Hence **Excathe·dral** *a.* authoritative. †**Exca·thedrate** *v.* to condemn authoritatively (HERRICK).

Excavate (e·kskăveɪt), *v.* 1599. [f. L. *excavat-*, *excavare* to hollow out; see CAVE.] 1. *trans.* To make hollow by removing the inside; to dig out leaving a hollow. 2. To form (a hole, channel, etc.) by hollowing out 1839. 3. To lay bare by digging; to unearth. Also *fig.* 1840. 4. To get out by digging 1848.

1. The ground is excavated in a circular shape, so as to make a pit PHILLIPS. 2. To e. a canal 1873. 5. Copper was..excavated in this place 1848. Hence **E·xcavate** *ppl. a.*

Excavation (ekskăvē¹·ʃən). 1611. [ad. L. *excavationem*; see prec.] 1. The action of excavating or of digging out a hollow or hollows in; an instance of this. 2. An excavated space; a cavity or hollow 1779. 3. The process of laying bare by excavating; an unearthing 1864.

2. The wine-press was an oblong e. in the rock 1848.

Excavator (e·kskăveɪtəɹ). 1815. [f. EXCAVATE *v.* + -OR.] 1. One who, or that which, excavates. 2. *spec.* A machine for digging out earth, etc.; also, an instrument for removing the carious parts in a tooth 1864. Hence **Excavato·rial, Exca·vatory** *adjs.* pertaining to excavation.

Excave (eks,kē¹·v), *v. rare.* 1578. [ad. L. *excavare.*] To scoop or hollow out. Also *absol.*

†**Exce·cate**, *v.* 1540. [f. L. *excæcat-*, *excæcare* to make blind, f. *ex-* + *cæcus.*] To make blind. *lit.* and *fig.* -1665. Hence †**Exce·cate** *ppl. a.* blinded. **Exceca·tion**, punishment by blinding (*arch.*); also †*fig.*

†**Exce·dent.** *rare.* 1655. [ad. L. *excedentem*; see EXCEED.] That which exceeds; excess -1811.

Exceed (eksī·d), *v.* [ME. *exceden*, ad. F. *excéder*, ad. L. *excedere* to go out, f. *ex-* + *cedere.*] 1. *trans.* To pass out of; to transcend the limits of; to go beyond. *Obs.* or *arch.* 2. To be greater than; to be too great for ME. 3. To surpass, outdo ME. †4. *intr.* To pass the bounds of propriety or of truth -1815. 5. To be pre-eminent; to surpass others; to preponderate 1482. 6. Chiefly in Cambridge use: To have more, or better fare, than usual. Also of the 'commons': To be in extra quantity. 1590.

1. Do not exceede The Prescript of this Scroule *Ant. & Cl.* III. viii. 4. 2. Such griefe..as did exceede all consolation 1635. Each part exceeds the whole SHELLEY. 3. How much a Chintz exceeds Mohair POPE. 4. You cannot possibly e. in your love to him 1758. 5. Punish so, as pity shall e. DRYDEN.

Hence **Excee·dable** *a.* that may be exceeded. **Excee·der.**

Exceeding (eksī·diŋ), *vbl. sb.* 1480. [f. prec.] 1. The action of EXCEED *v.* 2. *concr.* a. *pl.* In Cambridge use: Extra commons allowed on festival occasions. Also *transf.* 1629. †b. An excess, a surplus -1833.

Excee·ding, *ppl. a.* and *adv.* 1494. [f. as prec.]

A. *adj.* †1. Going to extremes -1742. 2. Extremely great, excessive 1547. †3. Of surpassing excellence -1599.

3. Christ tooke..our nature vpon him..Oh, what an e. thing is this LATIMER.

B. *adv.* = next. Now somewhat *arch.* 1535. My heart is e. heauy *Much Ado* III. iv. 25.

Exceedingly (eksī·diŋli), *adv.* 1470. [f.

prec.] †**1.** So as to surpass others. **2.** Above measure, extremely 1535.

Excel (ekse·l), *v.* Also †**Excell.** ME. [ad. F. *exceller*, ad. L. *excellere*, f. *ex-* + **cellere* to rise high, from the same root as *celsus.*] **1.** *intr.* To be superior or pre-eminent, usu. in good qualities or praiseworthy actions; to surpass others. **2.** *trans.* To be superior to (others) in some respect; usu. in a good sense; to outdo, surpass 1493. **b.** To surpass (another's qualities or work) (*rare*) 1611. †**3.** To be too hard or great for –1703.

1. Vnstable as water, thou shalt not excell *Gen.* xlix. 4. To e. at a game 1802. 2. A babe all babes excelling SHELLEY. 3. She op'nd, but to shut Excel'd her strength MILT. *P. L.* II. 884.

Excellence (e·ksĕlĕns). ME. [a. F., ad. L. *excellentia*, f. *excellentem.*] **1.** The state or fact of excelling; the possession chiefly of good qualities in an unusual degree; surpassing merit, virtue, etc.; dignity, eminence. **2.** That in which a person excels ME. †**3. a.** An excellent personality –1790. **b.** = EXCELLENCY 3 b. –1796.

1. Sir, you are not ignorant of what e. Laertes is at his weapon *Haml.* v. ii. 143. 2. The adoration due to your other excellences LOCKE.

Excellency (e·ksĕlĕnsi). ME. [See prec. and -ENCY.] †**1.** = EXCELLENCE 1. –1783. **2.** = EXCELLENCE 2. 1601. †**3. a.** = EXCELLENCE 3 a. 1688. **b.** As a title of honour. (Applied, formerly, to royal personages, to ladies, and others; now, only to ambassadors, governors (and their wives), and certain other high officers.) 1532.

1. They onely consult to cast him downe from his e. *Ps.* lxii. 4. 2. Cram'd (as he thinks) with excellencies *Twel. N.* II. iii. 163.

Excellent (e·ksĕlĕnt). ME. [a. F., ad. L. *excellentem*; see EXCEL.]

A. as *pr. pple.* Excelling.

B. *adj.* **1.** That excels or surpasses in any respect; pre-eminent, superior. *Obs.* or *arch.* ME. †**2.** Excelling in rank or dignity; exalted, highly honourable –1702. **3.** Extremely good. (The current sense.) 1604.

1. The e. brightnesse of the Sunne BLUNDEVIL. Elizabeth..was an e. hypocrite HUME. 2. His Name alone is e. *Ps.* cxlviii. 13. 3. An e. song SHAKS., Gard'ner EVELYN, Drink ARBUTHNOT. The e. of the Earth HERVEY.

†**C.** *adv.* Excellently –1756.

Hence **E·xcellently** *adv.* in an e. manner or degree.

†**Exce·lse.** 1568. [ad. L. *excelsus*; see EXCEL.]

A. *adj.* Lofty, high; *esp.* in fig. sense –1657.

B. *sb.* [tr. L. *excelsum.*] A high place (*rare*) –1609.

Excelsior (ekse·lsiǫɹ). 1778. [L., compar. of *excelsus* high.] ‖**1.** The Latin motto ('higher') on the seal of the State of New York. (The adverbial meaning is not justified.) Hence *attrib.* in *The Excelsior State*, New York. **2.** *U.S.* A trade name for short thin curled shavings of soft wood used for stuffing cushions, mattresses, etc. Also *attrib.* 1868.

†**Exce·lsitude.** 1470. [f. L. *excelsus.*] Highness –1599.

Excentral (ekse·ntrăl), *a.* 1847. [f. L. *ex-* + *centrum* + -AL.] *Bot.* Out of the centre; ECCENTRIC. (Dicts.)

Excentric, -al, etc.: see ECCENTRIC, -AL.

Except (ekse·pt), *v.* ME. [ad. F. *excepter*, f. L. *except-*, *excipere*, f. *ex-* + *capere.*] **1.** *trans.* To take or leave out (of any aggregate or whole); to exclude; to omit 1530. **2.** *intr.* To object or take exception 1577. †**3.** *trans.* To object. Const. with simple obj. or cl., *against*, *to.* –1753. †**4.** To protest against. SHAKS. †**5.** Erron. for ACCEPT –1635.

1. He was excepted from the general pardon BLUNT. The Church excepted, no agent [etc.] BRYCE. 2. I may be allowed to e. to the witnesses brought against me BACON. 3. Others excepted, that this e. was nothing worth FULLER.

Except (ekse·pt). ME. [ad. L. *exceptus* pa. pple.; see EXCEPT *v.*]

†**A.** *pple.* = Excepted. (Often in nominative absol. following the sb.; = '(being) excepted'.)

B. *prep.* **1.** Excepting, with the exception of, save, but. (Orig. the pa. pple. preceding the sb.) ME. †**2.** Leaving out of account; hence, in addition to, besides (*rare*) –1756.

1. The rabble..know nothing of liberty e. the name GOLDSM.

C. *conj.* **1.** (more fully) *Except that* (the only form now used) 1568. **2.** = 'unless', 'if not' ME. *arch.* **3.** Otherwise (or elsewhere, etc.) than 1586.

1. *Rich. II*, I. iv. 6. 2. E. my memory fails me, these are all MOXON. No drama..will be [written] e. it be by the same hand SOUTHEY. 3. The city was strongly fortified on all sides, e. here (*mod.*).

Exceptant (ekse·ptănt). 1697. [ad. L. *exceptantem*; see EXCEPT *v.*]

A. *adj.* That excepts 1846.

B. *sb.* One who excepts; *esp.* in *Law*, an accused person who excepts to a judge or juror.

Excepting (ekse·ptiŋ). 1549. [f. EXCEPT *v.*]

A. *prep.* **1.** quasi-*prep.* = 'If one excepts' 1549. **2.** With the exception of, except 1618.

2. All young Persons, e. my self HALES.

B. *conj.* = EXCEPT C. 1–3. 1641.

Exception (ekse·pʃən). ME. [(ult.) ad. L. *exceptionem*; see EXCEPT.] **1.** The action of excepting from the scope of a proposition, rule, etc.; the state or fact of being so excepted. Const. *from*, *to.* **2.** Something that is excepted; a person, thing, or case to which the general rule is not applicable. Const. *to*, †*from.* 1483. **3.** *Law.* [cf. EXCEPT *v.* 2.] **a.** A plea made by a defendant in bar of the plaintiff's action; in *Sc. Law* = DEFENCE. ME. **b.** An objection made to the ruling of a court in the course of a trial 1715. **c.** In Courts of Equity (now *Obs.*): An objection by the plaintiff to the defendant's answer as insufficient. †**4.** *transf.* **a.** A plea tending to evade the force of an opponent's argument –1643. **b.** A formal objection –1689. **5.** Objection, demur, cavil; an instance of this. *Obs.* or *arch.* 1571.

1. Phr. *The e. proves the rule*: orig. a legal maxim, in full 'Exception proves the rule in the cases not excepted', but now abbreviated and taken in sense 2. 2. Egypt was an e. from the rules of all other countries FULLER. 3. Phr. *Bill of exceptions*: a statement of objections to the ruling or direction of a judge drawn up on behalf of the dissatisfied party, and submitted to a higher Court. 5. To expose themselues to many exceptions and cauillations A.V. *Transl. Pref.* 4. Phr. *To take e. against*, *at*, *to*; to object to; also (chiefly with *at*) to take offence at.

Exceptionable (ekse·pʃənăb'l), *a.* 1664. [f. prec. + -ABLE.] **1.** Open to exception or objection. ¶**2.** Occas. misused for EXCEPTIONAL. 1801. Hence **Exce·ptionableness. Exce·ptionably** *adv.*

Exceptional (ekse·pʃənăl), *a.* 1846. [f. as prec. + -AL.] Of the nature of or forming an exception; unusual.

Documents or records of e. value 1875. Hence **Exce·ptiona·lity,** e. character. **Exce·ptional-ly** *adv.*, **-ness.**

Exce·ptionary, *a. rare.* 1783. [f. as prec. + -ARY [1].] Of, pertaining to, or indicative of, an exception; EXCEPTIONAL.

†**Exce·ptioner.** One who takes exception; an objector. MILTON.

Exceptionless (ekse·pʃənlės), *a.* 1782. [See -LESS.] Without an exception.

A renewed act of..indispensable, e. disqualification BURKE.

Exceptious (ekse·pʃəs), *a.* 1602. [f. EXCEPTION + -OUS, after *captious.*] Disposed to make objections; cavilling, captious.

It is the character of Country ladies to be e., and suspicious of slights CHESTERF. Hence **Exce·ptiousness.**

Exceptive (ekse·ptiv). 1563. [ad. late L. *exceptivus*; see EXCEPT *v.*]

A. *adj.* **1.** *Logic*, etc. That excepts something (see quots.). **2.** Of persons, etc.: Disposed to take exception; captious 1621.

1. E. Conjunctions are, if it be not..unless that, etc. 1751. E. propositions JEVONS. An e. clause introduced into the act FROUDE. **Exce·ptively** *adv.*

B. *sb.* [The adj. used *absol.*] *Logic.* An exceptive word or proposition 1563.

†**Exce·ptless,** *a.* [irreg. f. EXCEPT *v.* + -LESS.] Making no exception. *Timon* IV. iii. 502.

Exceptor (ekse·ptǫ̆ɹ, -əɹ). 1641. [a. late L.; see EXCEPT *v.*] †**1.** An objector –1690. **2.** †**a.** A shorthand writer –1732. **b.** *Hist.* A clerk of the Court of Chancery under the later Roman Empire 1728.

†**Exce·rebrate,** *v.* 1621. [f. L. *excerebrat-*, *excerebrare*, f. *ex-* + *cerebrum.*] **1.** *trans.* To clear out from the brain. **2.** To beat out the brains of. Hence **Excerebra·tion,** the action of beating out the brains; also, the removing of the contents of the skull.

†**Exce·rn,** *v.* 1578. [ad. L. *excernere*, f. *ex-* + *cernere* to sift.] = EXCRETE. –1738. So **Exce·rnent** *a.* = EXCRETORY.

†**Exce·rp,** *v.* 1563. [ad. L. *excerpere.*] = EXCERPT *v.* 1. –1697.

Excerpt (e·ksəɹpt, eksɔ̄·ɹpt), *sb.* L. *pl.* **excerpta.** 1638. [ad. L. *excerptum* pa. pple. neut.; see next.] **1.** A passage taken out of a book or manuscript; an extract. **2.** An article from the 'Transactions' of a society, a periodical, etc. printed off separately. Cf. *off-print.* 1883.

Excerpt (eksɔ̄·ɹpt), *v.* 1536. [f. L. *excerpt-*, *excerpere*, f. *ex-* + *carpere* to pluck.] **1.** *trans.* To take out as an extract; to extract, quote. Also *absol.* †**2.** To pluck out; to remove. Also *fig.* –1612.

1. He had excerpted..many notes and precedents HEYLIN. Hence **Exce·rption,** the action of excerpting; that which is excerpted. **Exce·rptive** *a.* inclined to e. †**Exce·rptor,** one who excerpts.

Excess (ekse·s). ME. [ad. F. *excès*, ad. L. *excessus*, f. *excedere* to EXCEED.] †**1.** The action of going out or forth; adjournment –1621. †**b.** *fig.* Departure *from* custom, reason, etc. –1738. †**2.** 'Violence of passion' (J.); extravagant feeling –1742. **3.** The action of overstepping (a limit); going beyond (one's rights, decency, moderation, etc.) ME. **4.** Intemperance, *esp.* in eating and drinking ME. **5.** The fact of exceeding something else in amount or degree 1618. **b.** The amount by which this is done 1557. †**c.** Usury. *Merch. V.* I. iii. 63. **6.** The fact or state of being greater in amount or degree than is usual, necessary, or right; an excessive amount or degree (of anything) ME.

1. Phr. †*E. of mind*, ecstasy, trance, stupefaction. 3. The full wrath beside Of vengeful justice bore for our e. MILT. Driven into excesses little short of rebellion JUNIUS. E. of jurisdiction on the part of the House 1891. 4. The excesses of the preceding night BARHAM. 5. When..one or more muscles act in e. of their opponents, a squint is produced HARLAN. Phr. *Spherical e.*: the quantity by which the sum of the degrees in the angles of spherical triangles exceeds 180°. 6. So distribution should vndoo excesse, And each man have enough *Lear* IV. i. 73. Parsimony.. is the more pardonable e. of the two ATTERBURY. Hence †**Exce·ss** *a.*, †**Exce·ssful** *a.* = EXCESSIVE.

Excessive (ekse·siv). ME. [a. F. *excessif*, *-ive*, f. L. *excess-*, *excedere*; see EXCEED.]

A. *adj.* Characterized by, or exhibiting EXCESS, in various senses.

Excessiue greefe [is] the enemie to the liuing *All's Well* I. i. 65.

†**B.** *adv.* = EXCESSIVELY *adv.* –1796.

Hence **Exce·ssively** *adv.* in an e. manner, amount, or degree. **Exce·ssiveness.**

Exchange (eksₜ₁ʃē¹·ndʒ), *sb.* [ME. *eschaunge*, a. AF. *eschaunge* (mod.F. *échange*) :– late L. *excambium*; see EXCHANGE *v.*] **1.** The action, or an act, of reciprocal giving and receiving. **2.** *Law.* 'A mutual grant of equal interests, the one in consideration of the other' (Blackstone) 1574. **3.** The action of giving or receiving coin for coin of equivalent value, for bullion, or for notes or bills; the trade of a money-changer ME. **4.** The system of transactions by which the debts of individuals residing at a distance from their creditors are settled without the transmission of money, by the use of 'bills of exchange' 1485. **5.** = Bill of Exchange (see BILL *sb.*[3]) 1485. **6.** = CHANGE ME. **7.** That which is offered or given in exchange, e. g. a newspaper sent in return for another 1490. **8.** A place of exchange; *esp.* a building in which the merchants of a town assemble for the transaction of business. Also *fig.* Cf. BURSE, CHANGE. 1569. **b.** = *telephone exchange* (TELEPHONE *sb.*).

1. E. of gold for silver 1552, of goods for money BLACKSTONE, of prisoners SMYTH, of salutations STANLEY, of commissions 1875, of pieces captured (in *Chess*) 1878. 3. Well couthe he in eschaunge scheeldes [*i. e.* Fr. *écus*] selle CHAUCER. 4. I haue bils for monie by e. From Florence, and must heere [at Padua] deliuer them *Tam. Shr.* IV. ii. 89. Phr. *Par of e.*: the recognized standard value of the coinage of one country in terms of the coinage of another; *e. g.* £1 sterling at par = 25·22½ francs French money.

Rate or *Course of e.* (also simply *exchange*): (*a*) the price at which foreign bills may be purchased; (*b*) sometimes, the percentage by which this differs from par. (If the price of a foreign bill is above par, *the exchange* is *against* the country in which the bill is drawn; if below par, *in its favour*.) *Arbitration of e.*: see ARBITRATION. 8. Sir Thomas Gresham.. named it the Burse, whereunto afterward Queene Elizabeth gave the name of Royall E. 1593.

Exchange (eks,tʃē¹·ndʒ), *v.* ME. [a. OF. *eschangier* (mod. *échanger*):—late L. *excambiare*; see CHANGE *v.*] 1. *trans.* To change away; to dispose of by exchange; to give or part with (something) for something in return. Also *absol.* 1484. 2. To give and receive reciprocally; to interchange. *Const.* obj. *with* (a person). 1602. 3. *Mil.*, etc. a. To give up a prisoner in return for one taken by the enemy 1726. b. *absol.* To pass, by exchange with another officer, *from* or *out of* one regiment *into* another 1787. 4. *intr.* Chiefly of coin: To be received as an equivalent *for* 1776. 5. *trans.* To CHANGE. ME.

1. They shall not..e., nor alienate the first fruits of the land *Ezek.* xlviii. 14. Old money exchanged for new CAMDEN. 2. E. forgiuenesse with me, Noble Hamlet *Haml.* v. ii. 340. 4. An English sovereign exchanged a little while ago for thirteen rupees 1890.

Exchangeable (eks,tʃē¹·ndʒăb'l), *a.* 1575. [f. prec. + -ABLE.] 1. That may be exchanged. Const. *for.* 1651. †2. = COMMUTATIVE 1 (*rare*) 1575.

1. On condition of General Lee being declared e. WASHINGTON. Phr. *E. value*: value estimated by what will be given for a thing. Hence **Excha·ngeabi·lity.**

Exchanger (eks,tʃē¹·ndʒəɹ). Also †**-or.** 1531. [f. as prec. + -ER¹.] One who exchanges or makes an exchange; †a banker (*Matt.* xxv. 27).

Exchequer (eks,tʃe·kəɹ). [ME. *escheker*, a. OF. *eschequier* (mod. *échiquier*) = med.L. *scaccarium* chess-board; see CHEQUER, CHECK. The *es-* has been mistaken for the OF. *es-*:—L. *ex-*.] †1. A chess-board –1474. 2. Under the Norman kings: An office or department of state managed by the Treasurer, the judges of the King's Court, and certain Barons appointed by the King. Its functions, which were both administrative and judicial, were divided later into two distinct branches; see 3, 4. (So called with reference to a table covered with a cloth divided into squares, on which the accounts of the revenue were kept by means of counters.) ME. 3. (More fully *Court of E.*, *E. of pleas.*) A court of law, historically representing the Anglo-Norman exchequer in its judicial capacity. Its jurisdiction was extended, by a legal fiction, from matters of revenue to all kinds of cases. Its equitable jurisdiction was abolished in 1841. (Now merged in the King's Bench Division.) 1489. 4. The department of state charged with the receipt and custody of the moneys collected by the revenue departments ME. 5. Pecuniary possessions in general 1565. Also *fig.* and *joc.*

2. Phr. *Chancellor of the E.*: originally, an assistant to the treasurer; now, the responsible finance minister of the United Kingdom; see CHANCELLOR. 4. The e. being so exhausted with the debts of king James CLARENDON. 5. The..impoverished state of my e. THACKERAY.

Comb.: e.-bill, a bill of credit issued by authority of Parliament, bearing interest at the current rate; hence e.-bill-office, the office where these are issued and received; -bond, a bond issued by the E. at a fixed rate of interest, and for a fixed period; -tallies, the notched sticks with which the accounts of the E. were formerly kept.

Exchequer (eks,tʃe·kəɹ), *v.* 1705. [f. prec.] 1. *trans.* To place in an exchequer (*rare*). 2. To proceed against in the Court of Exchequer 1809.

Exchequer-chamber. 1494. 1. The chamber devoted to the business of the royal exchequer. 2. 'A tribunal of error and appeal' (WHARTON); now merged in the Court of Appeal 1528.

Excide (eksəi·d), *v.* 1758. [ad. L. *excidere*, f. *ex-* + *cædere* to cut.] *trans.* To cut out. Also *fig.*

Exci·pient. 1726. [ad. L. *excipientem*, pr. pple.; see EXCEPT *v.*]

†A. *adj.* That takes exception.

B. *sb.* 1. One who takes up in succession (*rare*) 1852. 2. That ingredient in a compound medicine which takes up or receives the rest, as the syrup in boluses, etc. 1753. 3. The material or surface that receives the pigments in painting 1855.

Exciple (e·ksip'l), **Excipule** (e·ksipiul), vars. of next.

‖**Excipulum** (eksi·piŭlŏm). 1857. [L., = 'a receptacle'; cf. EXCIPIENT.] *Bot.* A layer of cells partially enclosing, as a cup, the APOTHECIUM in lichens.

Excise (eksəi·z), *sb.* 1494. [app. a. MDu. *excijs*, also *accijs*:—late L. type **accensum*, f. *accensare* to tax, f. *ad* + *census* tax; see CENSUS.] 1. *gen.* Any toll or tax. 2. *spec.* 'A duty charged on home goods, either in the process of their manufacture or before their sale to the home consumers' (*Encycl. Brit.*) 1596. Also *transf.* and *fig.* 3. Payment or imposition of excise 1710. 4. The government department charged with the collection of the excise. Now known as the Board of Customs and Excise. 1784.

2. *Excise*, a hateful tax levied upon commodities, and adjudged not by the common judges of property, but wretches hired by those to whom e. is paid JOHNSON. *Comb.* E. duties, those collected by the Board of Inland Revenue, comprising many improperly so named, *e.g.* the tax for armorial bearings, game licences, etc.

Excise (eksəi·z), *v.*¹ 1578. [f. L. *excis-*, *excidere*, f. *ex-* + *cædere* to cut.] †1. *trans.* = CIRCUMCISE 1. –1650. 2. To cut off or out. Also *fig.* 1647. 3. To notch 1578.

2. To e. a tumour, a reference (*mod.*).

Excise (eksəi·z), *v.*² 1652. [f. EXCISE *sb.*] †1. *trans.* To impose an excise or tax upon. Also *transf.* and *fig.* –1765. 2. To force to pay an excise-due; hence, to overcharge 1659.

Exciseman (eksəi·zmæ̆n). 1647. [f. EXCISE *sb.* + MAN.] An officer who collects excise duties and prevents evasion of the excise laws.

Excision (eksi·ʒən). 1490. [ad. L. *excisionem*; cf. F. *excision.*] 1. The action or process of cutting off or out; extirpation; destruction. Also *fig.* 2. The action of cutting off from a religious society; excommunication 1647.

1. E. of ears had indeed gone out of fashion 1864. The e. of a clause (*mod.*).

Excitability (eksəi:tăbi·lĭti). 1788. [f. next.] 1. The quality of being excitable, or easily excited 1803. 2. *Phys.* Of an organ or tissue: The capacity of being excited to its characteristic activity by the action of a specific stimulus.

1. Romola..shrank..from the shrill e. of those illuminated women GEO. ELIOT.

Excitable (eksəi·tăb'l), *a.* 1609. [ad. L. *excitabilis*; see EXCITE *v.*] Capable of being excited; easily excited. Const. *to.*

Excitant (e·ksitănt, eksəi·tănt). 1607. [ad. L. *excitantem*; see EXCITE *v.*]

A. *adj.* That excites or stimulates (see EXCITE *v.*).

B. *sb.* An agent which excites (organs or tissues) to increased vital activity; a stimulant. Also, an agent for inducing electrical action. 1833.

†**E·xcitate,** *v.* 1548. *Pa.t.* **excitate.** [f. L. *excitat-* ppl. stem of *excitare.*] = EXCITE –1660. Hence **Exci·tative, Exci·tatory** *adjs.*, able or tending to excite.

Excitation (eksitē¹·ʃən). ME. [a. F., ad. L. *excitationem*; see prec.] 1. The action of exciting (see EXCITE *v.*). 2. A means of excitement; a stimulus, instigation (*arch.*) 1627. 3. The state of being excited, excitement. Now *rare*. ME. 4. *Electr.*, etc. The process of inducing an electric or magnetic condition; also, the condition 1656.

†**Excita·tor.** *rare.* 1688. [a. L.; see EXCITATE and -OR.] One who, or that which, excites; *spec.* in *Electr.*, an instrument for discharging a Leyden jar, etc., without exposing the operator to the shock.

Excite (eksəi·t), *v.* ME. [a. F. *exciter*, ad. L. *excitare*, freq. of *exciere* to call forth, f. *ex-* + *ciere.*] 1. *trans.* To set in motion, stir up, incite. 2. To rouse up; to call forth or quicken ME. 3. To induce, elicit, occasion ME. 4. To move to strong emotion, stir to passion 1850. 5. a. *Electr.*, etc. To induce electric or magnetic activity in; to set (a current) in motion. b. *Photogr.* To sensitize (a plate). 1646.

1. We e. children by praising them WOLLASTON. [H] eexcited his attendants to resist JAS. MILL. 2. With Shouts, the Coward's Courage they e. DRYDEN. 3. To e. an insurrection FROUDE. 4. The only result ..had been to e. the Under-Secretary for India L. STEPHEN. Hence **Exci·tedly** *adv.* **Exci·tive** *a.* tending to e.

Excitement (eksəi·tmĕnt). 1604. [f. EXCITE *v.* + -MENT.] 1. The action of exciting; the fact of or state of being excited; excitation. Somewhat *rare.* 1830. 2. *Path.* A state of abnormal activity in any organ 1788. 3. Something that excites; an incentive *to* action (*arch.*); an occasion of mental excitement 1604.

1. The e. and propagation of motion HERSCHEL. 2. The e. it [Tractarianism] caused in England NEWMAN.

Exciter (eksəi·təɹ). ME. [f. as prec. + -ER¹.] One who, or that which, excites; *spec.* in *Med.*, a stimulant.

Exciting (eksəi·tiŋ), *ppl. a.* 1811. [f. as prec.] That excites. Phr. *E. cause*: (chiefly *Path.*) that which immediately causes disease, etc.; opp. to *predisposing cause.*

Excito-motory (eksəi:tomōᵘ·təri), *a.* 1836. [f. EXCITOR + MOTORY.] *Phys.* Of or pertaining to the spinal group of nerves, composed of the excitor and the motor nerves. Often applied to the reflex actions produced by these. var. **Exci·to-mo·tor.**

Excitor (eksəi·tŏɹ, -əɹ). 1816. [f. EXCITE *v.*, after *motor.*] a. = EXCITER. b. An afferent nerve belonging to the spinal group.

Exclaim (ekskle¹·m), *v.* 1570. [ad. F. *exclamer*, ad. L. *exclamare*, f. *ex-* + *clamare* to call, shout.] 1. To cry out with sudden vehemence; to cry out from pain, anger, delight, surprise, etc. Rarely with *out.* †2. *trans.* To proclaim loudly –1782.

1. What makes you thus exclame 1 *Hen. VI*, IV. i. 83. 'Spoke like an oracle', they all exclaimed COWPER. To e. against inconsistencies 1860. Hence **Exclai·m** *sb.* outcry (*rare*). **Exclai·mer.**

Exclamation (eksklămē¹·ʃən). ME. [a. F., ad. L. *exclamationem*; see EXCLAIM *v.*] 1. The action of exclaiming; emphatic or vehement outcry; clamour, vociferation. Also, an instance of this. 2. A loud complaint or protest; a 'vociferous reproach' (J.) ME. †3. Proclamation –1631. 4. a. *Rhet.* = ECPHONESIS. 1552. b. *Gram.* = INTERJECTION. 1862.

1. Huge exclamations burst abruptly out STIRLING. 2. Exclamations against the follies..of those things DE FOE. 4. b. *Note, point of e.*, also (U.S.) *E.-mark* or *point* = *Note of Admiration*; see ADMIRATION.

Exclamative (ekskl æ·mătiv), *a. rare.* 1730. [f. L. *exclamat-* (see EXCLAIM *v.*) + -IVE.] Exclamatory. Hence **Excla·matively** *adv.*

Exclamatory (ekskl æ·mătəri), *a.* 1593. [f. as prec. + -ORY.] 1. That exclaims, or vents itself in exclamation. 2. Pertaining to exclamation; of the nature of, or containing, an exclamation 1716.

1. An intemperate and e. Sorrow DONNE. 2. An e. O! GEO. ELIOT. Hence **Excla·matorily** *adv.*

Exclude (eksklū̆·d), *v.* ME. [ad. L. *excludere* to shut out, f. *ex-* + *claudere.*] 1. *trans.* To bar or shut out; to prevent the existence, occurrence, or use of; not to admit of. 2. To shut off, debar *from*; to preclude 1495. 3. To leave out, except ME. 4. To put out, banish, expel ME. 5. After L. *excludere ova.* To draw or put forth from (a receptacle); to hatch; also *fig.* to give birth to ME.

1. To e. the pouer of the feende ME., lowd noises 1598, all Pittie 1604. 2. And none but such from mercy I e. MILT. *P. L.* III. 202. 4. They excluded him out of their counsayle ELYOT. 5. The method of excluding the Fœtus 1754.

Phr. *Law of Excluded Middle, Third* (Logic): the principle that between two contradictories, *e.g.* A and not-A, no third or middle term is possible—we must think either the one or the other as existing. Hence **Exclu·der**, one who or that which excludes.

Exclusion (eksklū̆·ʒən). 1614. [ad. L. *exclusionem*; see EXCLUDE.] 1. The action of excluding, in various senses; see the verb. 2. The action of putting or thrusting forth from a receptacle (see EXCLUDE *v.* 5) 1646. †3. The action of discharging (excrement). Also *concr.* excrement. –1664.

1. His sad e. from the dores of Bliss MILT. The e. of the Bishops out of the House of Lords LUDLOW. Phr. *Method of Exclusion(s)*: the process of discovering a cause, or the solution of a problem, by disproving all but one of the conceivable hypotheses.

Hence **Exclu·sionary** *a.* of, pertaining to, or characterized by e. **Exclu·sioner**, one who upholds e. **Exclu·sionism**, the character, manners, or principles of an exclusionist. **Exclu·sionist**, one who favours e.; esp. (*Eng. Hist.*) a supporter of the Exclusion Bill.

Exclusive (ekskl*ū*·siv). 1515. [ad. med.L. *exclusivus*, f. *exclus-*, *excludere*; see -IVE.]

A. *adj.* 1. That excludes; †debarring from participation; not admitting of the existence or presence of, not including. Also quasi-*adv.* (and *adv.*) So as to exclude. 2. Excluding all but what is specified 1581. 3. Single, sole 1790. 4. Disposed to resist the admission of outsiders to membership of a body, social intercourse, etc. 1822. b. Of a pattern exclusively claimed by a particular establishment 1901.

1. An E. Voice 1706. On grounds..not e. of each other BURKE. quasi-*adv.* From 25th Decemb. last e. 1679. 2. E. propositions WATTS. The English E. particles are, one, only, alone, exclusively, etc. 1864. Phr. *E. dealing*: the practice of dealing only with certain special tradesmen. 3. The e. channel BURKE. 4. The literary class is usually proud and e. EMERSON.

B. *sb.* 1. An exclusive proposition or particle. (Cf. A. 2.) 1533. 2. An exclusive person 1825. Hence **Exclu·sively** *adv.* in an e. †sense or manner; solely. **Exclu·siveness.** **Exclu·sivism**, systematic exclusiveness. **Exclusivist**, one who maintains the e. validity (of a theory).

Exclu·sory (ekskl*ū*·səri), *a.* 1585. [ad. late L. *exclusorius*; see EXCLUDE *v.* and -ORY.] = EXCLUSIVE A. 1. Const. *of.*

†**Exco·ct**, *v.* 1563. [f. L. *excoct-*, *excoquere*, f. *ex-* + *coquere* to boil, melt.] 1. To extract by heat -1671. 2. To drive off the moisture of; to elaborate -1710. Hence †**Exco·ction**, extraction or elaboration by heat.

Excogitate (ekskǫ·dʒiteᶦt), *v.* 1530. [f. L. *excogitat-*, *excogitare* to find out by thinking; see COGITATE.] 1. *trans.* To think out; to contrive, devise. ¶2. *intr.* = COGITATE. 1630.

1. We here e. no new, no occult principle SIR W. HAMILTON. Hence **Exco:gita·tion**, the action, or result, of excogitating.

†**Excomme·nge**, *v.* 1502. [:—(ult.) L. *excommunicare*.] To excommunicate -1641. Hence †**Excomme·ngement.**

†**Exco·mmune**, *v.* 1483. [ad. F. *excommunier*, ad. L. *excommunicare*.] To EXCOMMUNICATE; *transf.* to exclude from -1654.

transf. Poets..were excommun'd Plato's Common Wealth GAYTON.

Excommunicate (ekskǫmi*ū*·nikeᶦt), *v.* 1526. [f. late L. *excommunicat-*, *excommunicare* lit. 'to put out of the community', f. *ex-* + *communis*; see COMMUNICATE.] *Eccl.* To cut off from communion; to exclude, by an authoritative sentence, from the communion of the Church, or from religious rites. Also *transf.*

transf. He was excommunicated; put out of the pale of the school LAMB.

Hence **Excommu·nicable** *a.* liable, or deserving, to be excommunicated; punishable by excommunication. **Excommu·nicant**, one who excommunicates or is excommunicated. **Excommu·nicative** *a.* that excommunicates; disposed to e. **Excommu·nicator.** **Excommu·nicatory** *a.* of or pertaining to excommunication; excommunicative.

Excommunicate (ekskǫmi*ū*·nikĕt). 1526. [ad. L. *excommunicatus*; see prec.]

A. *pa. pple.* and *ppl. a.* Excommunicated (*arch.*).

Phr. *E. things* (tr. Heb. *ḥērem*): objects devoted to destruction.

B. *sb.* An excommunicated person 1562. Also *transf.*

Excommunication (ekskǫmiūnikēᶦ·ʃən). 1494. [ad. late L. *excommunicationem*; see EXCOMMUNICATE *v.*] 1. *Eccl.* The action of excluding an offender from the sacraments (*lesser excommunication*), or from all communication with the Church or its members (*greater e.*). Also *transf.* 2. Short for 'sentence of excommunication' 1647.

2. The Pope fulminated an e. against him KINGSLEY. So †**Excommu·nion.** MILT.

Excoriate (ekskō̤·riˌeᶦt), *v.* 1497. [f. L. *excoriat-*, *excoriare* to strip off the hide, f. *ex-* + *corium*.] †1. *trans.* To flay -1826. 2. To remove parts of the skin, etc., from; *esp. Path.* by the use of corrosives, abrasion, etc. 1497. Also *transf.* and *fig.* 3. To strip or peel off (the skin) 1547.

3. To prevent..the matter..from excoriating the skin GOOCH. Hence **Exco·riable** *a.* that may be rubbed or stripped off. **Exco·riate** *pple. arch.* having the skin or rind rubbed or stripped off.

Excoriation (ekskō̤:riˌēᶦ·ʃən). 1447. [f. EXCORIATE *v.*; see -ATION.] 1. The action of excoriating; the state of being excoriated. Also *fig.* 2. An excoriated place; a sore 1540.

2. He had a grievous e. behind, with riding post 1751.

Excorticate (ekskǭ·ɹtikeᶦt), *v.* 1600. [f. L. *ex-* + *cortic-* stem of *cortex* bark + -ATE³.] *trans.* To pull or strip off the bark or shell from. Also *fig.* Hence **Exco:rtica·tion.**

†**Excreation.** 1556. [ad. L. *ex(s)creationem*, *ex(s)creare*, (f. *ex-* + *screare* to hawk, hem).] The action of coughing or spitting out; expectoration -1620.

Excrement¹ (e·kskrĭmĕnt). 1533. [a. F. *excrément*, ad. L. *excrementum* what is sifted out, f. (ult.) *ex-* + *cernere*.] †1. That which remains after sifting; the lees, refuse -1698. 2. *Phys.* 'That which is cast out of the body by any of the natural emunctories' (*Syd. Soc. Lex.*); *esp.* the alvine fæces 1533. Also *fig.*

†**E·xcrement**². 1549. [ad. L. *excrementum*, f. (ult.) *ex-* + *crescere* to grow.] 1. That which grows out or forth; an outgrowth. Also *fig.* -1705. 2. *abstr.* Growth, augmentation -1609.

1. It will please his Grace..to dallie with my e., with my mustachio *L. L. L.* v. i. 109.

Excremental (ekskrĭme·ntăl), *a.*¹ 1574. [f. EXCREMENT¹ + -AL.] †1. Pertaining to, or consisting of, dregs or refuse matter -1662. 2. = EXCREMENTITIOUS 2. 1574.

Excreme·ntal, *a.*² *rare.* 1644. [f. EXCREMENT² + -AL.] Of the nature of an outgrowth or excrescence -1656.

Her whitenesse is but an excrementall whitenesse MILT.

Excrementitial (ekskrĭmenti·ʃăl), *a.* 1620. [f. as next.] = next.

Excrementitious (ekskrĭmenti·ʃəs), *a.* 1586. [f. L. *excrementum* EXCREMENT¹ + -OUS.] †1. Of the nature of dregs or refuse matter -1661. 2. Of the nature of, pertaining to, or arising from excrement 1586. So †**Excreme·ntuous** *a.*

†**Excreme·ntive**, *a.* [f. EXCREMENT¹ + -IVE.] Fitted to carry off or discharge excrement. FELTHAM.

†**Excreme·ntize**, *v.* 1670. [f. as prec. + -IZE.] *intr.* To void excrements.

†**Excre·sce**, **-crea·se**, *v.* 1570. [ad. L. *excrescere*.] *intr.* To grow out or forth; to constitute an excrescence -1691.

Excrescence (ekskre·sĕns). 1533. [ad. L. *excrescentia*, f. *excrescentem*; see prec. and -ENCE.] 1. †The action of growing out or forth. Also, abnormal increase. -1752. b. Exuberance (now *rare*). 1629. 2. A natural outgrowth or appendage 1633. 3. An abnormal, morbid, or disfiguring outgrowth. Also *transf.* and *fig.* 1548.

1. The e. of Insects HALE. b. Excrescences of joy JER. TAYLOR. 3. Tumours, wens, and preternatural excrescences BERKELEY. So **Excre·scency**, excrescent state or condition; excrescence.

Excrescent (ekskre·sĕnt), *a.* 1609. [ad. L. *excrescentem* pr. pple.; see EXCRESCE *v.*] †1. That grows out -1843. 2. Growing abnormally; constituting an excrescence; redundant 1633. 3. *Gram.* Of a sound in a word: Due only to euphony, and of no etymological value 1868.

2. We pare off such e. blemishes that the body may be perfect T. ADAMS. The e., or the superinduced population 1832. So **Excresce·ntial** *a.* (in sense 2).

†**Excre·ssion.** 1610. [irreg. f. L. *excrescere*.] An outgrowth; = EXCRETION² -1647.

‖**Excreta** (ekskrī·tă). 1857. [L.; see EXCRETE.] Excreted matters; now *esp.* the fæces and urine.

Excrete (ekskrī·t), *v.* 1620. [f. L. *excret-*, *excernere*, f. *ex-* + *cernere* to separate.] 1. *trans.* To separate and expel from the system; to discharge 1668. Also *absol.* †2. Of drugs, etc.: To cause the excretion of -1651.

1. Certain plants e. sweet juice DARWIN. 2. They loose the belly and e. out choler VENNER. Hence **Excre·tive** *a.* having the power of excreting or promoting excretion.

Excretin [ekskrī·tin). Also **-ine.** 1854. [f. as prec. + -IN.] *Chem.* A crystalline body, $C_{20}H_{36}O$, obtained by exhausting fresh excrements with boiling alcohol.

Excretion¹ (ekskrī·ʃən). 1605. [ad. L. *excretionem*; see EXCRETE.] 1. The action or process of excreting. 2. *concr.* That which is separated and ejected from the body 1630.

1. E. of urine RAY, of the Blood 1732.

†**Excre·tion**². 1612. [f. L. *excrescere*; see EXCRESCE.] = EXCREMENT², EXCRESCENCE. Also *fig.* -1725.

Excretolic (ekskrĭtǫ·lik), *a.* 1867. [f. EXCRET-IN + -OL + -IC.] *Chem.* In *Excretolic acid*: a fatty acid obtained from the alcoholic extract of human excrements.

Excretory (ekskrī·təri, e·kskrĭtəri). 1681. [f. L. *excret-* (see EXCRETE *v.*) + -ORY.]

A. *adj.* Having the function of excreting; pertaining to excretion.

B. *sb.* An excretory vessel or duct 1715.

†**Excri·minate**, *v. rare.* 1661. [f. L. *ex-* + *crimin-* stem of *crimen* charge + -ATE³.] *trans.* To clear from an imputation -1796.

Excruciate (ekskr*ū*·ʃiˌeᶦt), *v.* 1570. [f. L. *excruciat-*, *excruciare*, f. *ex-* intensive + *cruciare* to torment, f. *crucem* cross.] To subject to torture, put on the rack; hence, to cause intense pain or anguish to (often *hyperbolical*).

They .. by pining and excruciating their bodies, liue in hell here on earth NASHE. To e. the mind with cares 1655. Hence **Excru·ciable** *a.* liable to, or deserving of, torment. †**Excru·ciate** *ppl. a.* excruciated; excruciating. **Excrucia·tion**, the action of causing or the state of suffering extreme pain.

Excruciating (ekskr*ū*·ʃiˌeᶦtiŋ), *ppl. a.* 1664. [f. prec.] That excruciates or causes extreme pain or anguish; agonizing. Often *hyperbolical.*

E. deaths 1833. An e. chorus 1876. Hence **Excru·ciatingly** *adv.*

Excubant (e·kski*u*bănt), *a.* [ad. L. *excubantem*, *excubare* to lie on guard, f. *ex-* + *cubare*.] Keeping watch. PEACOCK. So †**Excuba·tion**, the action of keeping guard. (Dicts.) †**Ex·cubitor**, a sentinel. G. WHITE.

Exculpate (e·ksk*ŭ*lpeᶦt, ekskɒ·lpeᶦt), *v.* 1656. [f. EX- *pref.*¹ + L. *culpa* + -ATE³. Cf. med.L. *exculpatio*.] 1. *trans.* To free from blame; to clear *from* an accusation or blame. 2. Of things: †a. To justify 1706. b. To furnish ground for exculpating 1783.

1. The latter stood exculpated on both charges GROTE. 2. b. Evidence, which may .. tend to .. e. every person BURKE. Hence **Excu·lpable** *a.* capable of being exculpated (*rare*). **Excu·lpate** *ppl. a.* declared guiltless. **Exculpa·tion**, the action of exculpating from blame, or from a crime; that which exculpates; an excuse, a vindication. **Excu·lpative**, **Excu·lpatory** *adjs.* adapted or intended to e.

†**Excur** (eksˌkɒ̄·ɹ), *v. rare.* 1656. [ad. L. *excurrere*.] *intr.* To go out or forth; to digress; to go to an extreme -1672.

Excurrent (ekskɒ·rĕnt), *a.* 1826. [ad. L. *excurrentem*.] 1. That runs out or forth 2. Affording an exit 1854. 3. *Bot.* a. (See quot.) 1835. b. Projecting beyond the tip or margin, as when the midrib of a leaf is continued beyond the apex 1847.

1. The residue..is carried out by the e. water 1887. 3. a. Excurrent; in which the axis remains always in the centre, all the other parts being regularly disposed round it; as the stem of abies LINDLEY.

Excurse (ekskɒ̄·ɹs). *v.* 1748. [f. L. *excurs-*; see EXCUR.] 1. *intr.* To run off, wander, digress. 2. To make, or go upon, an excursion 1775. 3. To journey through. (Dicts.)

Excursion (ekskɒ̄·ɹʃən). 1574. [ad. L. *excursionem*; see EXCUR.] †1. The action of running out or forth; escape from bounds; hence formerly *concr.*: Anything that runs out or projects -1852. †2. *fig.* An outburst; a sally (of wit); an escapade -1793. †3. *Mil.* A sally, sortie, raid -1701. 4. A journey from any place with the intention of returning to it. Also *fig.* 1665. b. *transf.* in *Physics*, etc.: One movement of any body or particle in oscillating or alternating motion; the length of such a movement 1799. 5. *spec.* A journey for pleasure or health. Now often: A pleasure-trip taken by a number of persons. 1779. 6. Deviation from a definite path or course; †a digression 1574. 7. *attrib.* (sense 5), as in *e.-train*, etc. 1850.

1. What roaring of flooddes, what e. of riuers 1579. 4. A long aëronautic e. 1816. *fig.* An e. into the historical domain BRYCE. 5. A delightful e. on the

lake 1832. 6. Pardon this long e. on this subject BAXTER.

Hence **Excu·rsion** *v. intr.* to make, or go on, an e. **Excu·rsional** *a.* of or pertaining to an e. †**Excu·rsioner, Excu·rsionist,** one who goes on an e.; one who travels by an e.-train; also (*colloq.*) an e.-agent. **Excu·rsionize** *v. intr.* to make, or go on, an e.

Excursive (ekskʊ̄·ɹsiv), *a.* 1673. [f. L. *excurs-* ppl. stem (see EXCUR) + -IVE.] 1. Of the nature of an excursion. Of reading, etc.: Desultory. 2. Capable of, or addicted to, excursions; also, digressive 1744.

1. Johnson's e. reading SOUTHEY. 2. An intelligence ..e., vigorous, and diligent JOHNSON. E. black cattle SCOTT. Hence **Excu·rsive-ly** *adv.*, **-ness.**

Excursus (ekskʊ̄·ɹsʊ̆s). Pl. **excursus,** (now usually) **excursuses.** 1803. [a. L.: see EXCUR.] 1. A dissertation appended to a work, in which some point is discussed at length. 2. A digression 1845.

Excurvation (ekskʊɹvēⁱ·ʃən). 1877. [f. EX- *pref.*¹ + CURVATION.] A curving or bending outwards.

Excurved (ekskʊ̄·ɹvd), *ppl. a.* 1884. [f. EX- *pref.*¹ + CURVED.] Curved outwards, as antennæ.

Excusable (ekskiū·zăb'l), *a.* ME. [a. F., ad. L. *excusabilis*; see EXCUSE *v.*] That may be excused; deserving to be acquitted; admitting of palliation.

The excuseablest kind of pagans HOWELL. An e. curiosity LYTTON. Hence **Excu·sableness. Excu·sably** *adv.*

Excusal (ekskiū·zăl). Now *rare.* 1584. [f. EXCUSE *v.* + -AL.] The act or fact of excusing.

†**Excusa·tion.** ME. [a. F., ad. L. *excusationem*; see EXCUSE.] 1. The action of excusing or defending –1677. 2. Release from a duty, obligation, etc. –1540. 3. = EXCUSE *sb.* 2, 3. –1662.

Excuse (ekskiū·s), *sb.* ME. [a. OF. *excuse*, f. *excuser*; see EXCUSE *v.*] 1. The action of excusing; justification, indulgence; pardon; release. 2. That which is offered as a reason for being excused; *occas.*, a (mere) pretext 1500. 3. That which serves to excuse, or to extenuate (a fault or offence); *esp.* in phr. *without e.* 1494.

1. Hence with denial vain and coy e. MILT. *Lycidas* 18. He pray'd e. for mirth broke short SCOTT. 2. A bad e. is better, they say, then none at all GOSSON. 3. My Nephewes trespasse.. hath the e. of youth SHAKS. Hence **Excu·seless** *a.* without e.

Excuse (ekskiū·z), *v.* [ME. *escusen, excusen*, ad. OF. *escuser, excuser*, ad. L. *excusare*, f. *ex-* + *causa* CAUSE, charge.]

I. 1. *trans.* To offer an apology for (a person); to seek to extenuate (a fault). Also *absol.* †2. To maintain the innocence of (a person); to justify (an action) –1696. 3. To obtain exemption or release for ME.; †to decline with apologies –1754. †4. To screen, exempt –1711. 5. To serve as an exculpation for 1538. b. In *pass.*: To be held blameless ME.

1. To e. a step, which it is not possible to justify 1793. 3. Clarence e. me to the King my Brother 3 *Hen. VI*, v. v. 46. 4. Faults he took upon him to e. others STEELE. 5. The wife's presence will not e. the husband ADDISON.

II. 1. To accept a plea in exculpation of; to judge indulgently; to overlook, condone ME. 2. To free from a task, obligation, etc.; to dispense from payment, etc. ME. 3. 'To remit; not to exact' (J.) 1646.

1. He is totally Excused, for the reason next before alledged HOBBES. E. my glove, Thomas SHERIDAN. Phr. *E. me* (colloq.): used parenthetically to carry off a strong expression, to indicate politely a difference of opinion, in addressing a stranger, or in interrupting the speech of another. 2. He was excused the entrance-fee (*mod.*). 3. I beg you to e. my waiting on you for a little while 1726. Hence **E·xcusator,** an excuser; *esp.* a person officially authorized to present an excuse. **Excu·satory** *a.* tending, or intended, to e.; apologetic. **Excu·ser,** one who excuses; one who extenuates (a fault).

†**Excu·ss,** *v.* 1570. [f. L. *excuss-, excutere*, f. *ex-* + *quatere* to shake.] 1. *trans.* To shake off, get rid of –1668. 2. To shake out; hence, to discuss –1726. 3. *Mod. Civ. Law.* To seize, take in execution 1726.

†**Excu·ssion.** 1607. [ad. L. *excussionem*; see prec.] 1. The action of shaking off or getting rid of –1698. 2. *Mod. Civ. Law.* Seizure of goods for debt, etc. –1726.

Ex div., abbrev. *Ex dividend*: see EX *prep.* 2.

Exeat (e·ksiˌæt). 1485. [L.; = 'let (him) go out'; see EXIT.]

‖A. In L. use as vb. A stage direction; = later EXIT. (So also **E·xeant,** 'let (them) go out'; = later EXEUNT.)

B. *sb.* 1. A permission to leave the diocese, granted to a priest by the bishop 1730. 2. A permission for temporary absence, as in colleges, religious houses, etc. 1727.

Execrable (e·ksĭkrăb'l), *a.* ME. [ad. L. *execrabilis*, (*exsecrabilis*), f. *execrari* (*exsecrari*); see EXECRATE.] †1. Expressing or involving a curse; hence, of an imprecation: Fearful –1630. 2. Deserving to be execrated; detestable; †accursed; †horrifying. Often *hyperbolical.* 1490.

2. That e. Fraternity of Blasphemers BERKELEY. The e. image of this scene FOSTER. What e. weather MISS BRADDON. Hence **E·xecrableness. E·xecrably** *adv.*

Execrate (e·ksĭkreⁱt), *v.* 1561. [f. L. *execrat-* (*exsecrat-*), *execrari*, f. *ex-* + *sacrare* to devote religiously, f. *sacrum* (*sacer*).] †1. *trans.* To pronounce a curse upon; to declare accursed (*rare*) –1691. 2. To imprecate evil upon; to abhor, detest 1561. 3. *intr.* To utter curses 1786.

2. To e. the idolatrie of the Chaldeans 1561, their lot COWPER. So **Execra·tion** late ME. **E·xecrative** *a.* of or pertaining to execration; prone to execration; characterized by an execration. **E·xecratively** *adv.* **E·xecrator. E·xecratory** *a.* of or pertaining to execration; of the nature of an execration; †*sb.* 'a formulary of execrations' (Todd).

Exect, etc.: see EXSECT, etc.

Executant (ekse·kiŭtănt). 1858. [a. F. *exécutant*, pr. pple. of *exécuter* to EXECUTE.]

A. *adj.* That performs (music) 1865.

B. *sb.* Any one who executes, or performs; *esp.* a musical performer. Hence **Exe·cutancy,** e. power.

Execute (e·ksĭkiut), *v.* ME. [ad. F. *exécuter*, ad. med.L. *executare*, f. L. *ex(s)ecut-* ppl. stem of *ex(s)equi* lit. 'to follow out', f. *ex-* + *sequi.*] 1. To follow out, carry into effect; to give effect to. 2. To carry out, perform (a plan, work, movement, etc.) 1477; †to celebrate (religious service, etc.) –1737. 3. *Law.* To go through the formalities necessary to the validity of. Hence, to complete and give validity to, as by signing, sealing, etc. 1737. 4. To fulfil, discharge (an office, a function). Also formerly †*absol.* or *intr.* ME. 5. To carry out the design of (a work of art or skill); to perform (a piece of music) 1735. 6. To put to death in pursuance of a sentence; hence, †to put to death, kill (*rare*) 1483.

1. To e. the biddyng of the Kyng LYDG., his enuye CAXTON, a Testament 1641, the sentence of the law PRESCOTT. 2. Moreau executed a change of front ALISON. 3. To e. a treaty of peace WELLINGTON, a mortgage CRUMP. 5. I saw executed in marble the Mercury and the Hope B'NESS BUNSEN. 6. Sir Thomas Blonte and all the other prysoners were executed HALL.

Hence **Exe·cutable** *a.* that can be executed, performed, or carried out. †**E·xecute** *ppl. a.* executed. **E·xecuter** = EXECUTOR 1.

Execution (eksĭkiū·ʃən). [ME. *execucion*, a. AF., ad. L. *executionem*; see EXECUTE *v.*] 1. The action of carrying out or carrying into effect; accomplishment; †the giving effect to. –1652. 2. The manner in which a plan, piece of music, etc. is executed 1534. b. Excellence of execution 1795. 3. The performance or fulfilment of (an office or function) 1576. †4. Executive ability –1601. 5. Effective action, or its result. Also *fig.* 1588. 6. *Law.* The due performance of all formalities, as signing, sealing, etc., necessary to give validity to a legal instrument 1776. 7. The enforcement by the sheriff of the judgement of a court 1503. b. Short for *Writ of Execution* 1777. 8. The infliction of (*esp.* capital) punishment in pursuance of a judicial sentence ME. 9. 'The ravaging and destroying of a country that refuses to pay contribution' (Smyth). Also *military e.* 1618.

1. His intention and e. are not very near each other JOHNSON. To put the law in e. GOLDSM. 4. He was a man of much valour and e. HOLLAND. 5. The shot ..did great e. PRESCOTT. 7. *Writ of e.*: the process under which the sheriff is commanded to execute a judgement. 8. The small Remainder of his Ears, left after his first E. W. PRYNNE.

Execu·tionee·ring, *ppl. a.* That executes (criminals). LAMB.

Executioner (eksĭkiū·ʃənəɹ). 1561. [f. EXECUTION *sb.*] 1. One who executes (a plan, law, justice, †the duties of an office, etc.) 1587. 2. *gen.* One who carries out a (capital) sentence 1561. 3. *transf.* and *fig.* One who puts another to death 1594.

Executive (ekse·kiŭtiv). 1646. See EXECUTE *v.* + -IVE. Cf. F. *exécutif.*]

A. *adj.* †1. Operative. 2. †Active, or (U.S.) skilful, in execution 1708. 3. Pertaining to execution; having the function of executing; *esp.* as concerned with carrying out the laws, decrees, and judicial sentences; opp. to 'judicial' and 'legislative' 1649. 4. Of or pertaining to the EXECUTIVE (see B. 1) 1811.

3. The e. government could undertake nothing great without the support of the Commons MACAULAY. Hence **Exe·cutively** *adv.*

B. *sb.* 1. That branch of the government which is charged with the execution of the laws 1790. b. The person or persons in whom the supreme executive magistracy of a country or state is vested. Chiefly U.S. 1787. 2. *transf.* Any administrative body 1868.

1. b. That a national e. to consist of a single person be instituted *Jrnl. Fed. Conv.* (1819) 89.

Executor (eks-, egze·kiŭtəɹ in sense 3, e·ksĭkiutəɹ in sense 1). ME. [a. AF. *executour*, a. L. *ex(s)ecutorem*; see EXECUTE *v.*] 1. One who executes or carries out; an agent, doer. Now *rare* exc. in *Law.* †2. = EXECUTIONER –1614. 3. A person appointed by a testator to execute or give effect to his will after his decease. Also *transf.* and *fig.* ME.

1. Such basenes Had neuer like E. *Temp.* III. i. 13. 2. *Hen. V*, I. ii. 203. Hence **Exe·cuto·rial** *a.* of or pertaining to an e.; executive. **Exe·cutorship.**

Executory (ekse·kiŭtəri). 1483. [ad. L. *ex(s)ecutorius*; see prec. Cf. F. *exécutoire.*]

A. *adj.* 1. Of or pertaining to the execution of a command, decree, law, etc. 1658. b. Of a law, etc.: In force, operative 1483. 2. = EXECUTIVE A. 3. 1649. 3. *Law.* Designed to take or capable of taking effect only at a future time. Opp. to *Executed.* 1592.

1. The question is only e., not declarative 1658. 2. Mere e. agents of the British Government 1829. 3. An e. contract BLACKSTONE, trust J. POWELL.

B. *sb.* †1. = EXECUTORSHIP (*rare*) 1496. 2. An executive body (see EXECUTIVE B. 2) 1868.

Executrix (ekse·kiŭtriks). Pl. **-trixes** (triksĕz), **-trices** (trisīz). 1502. [a. med.L.] A woman appointed by a testator to execute his will. vars. **Exe·cutress,** †**Exe·cutrice.**

†**Exe·de,** *v.* 1669. [f. L. *exedere.*] *trans.* To eat out, corrode –1754. So **E·xedent** *a.* 'eating up; consuming; ulcerating' (*Syd. Soc. Lex.*).

‖**Exedra, exhedra** (e·ksĭdră, eksī·dră). Pl. **-dræ.** 1706. [a. L. *exedra*, f. Gr. ἐξ- + ἕδρα a seat.] 1. *Ancient Archit.* The portico of the palæstra or gymnasium in which disputations were held; also, in private houses, the pastas or vestibule. 2. The APSIS, or bishop's throne 1725. 3. A porch or chapel, or a recess in a wall, which projects 1850.

Exegesis (eksĭdʒī·sis). 1619. [a. Gr. ἐξήγησις, f. (ult.) ἐξ- out + ἡγέεσθαι to guide, lead.] 1. Explanation, exposition; *esp.* the interpretation of the Scriptures 1823. †2. *Algebra.* Extraction of roots out of adfected equations –1796.

Exegete (e·ksĭdʒīt). 1730. [ad. Gr. ἐξηγητής an interpreter; see prec.] An expounder, interpreter. var. **Exege·tist.**

Exegetic (eksĭdʒe·tik). 1655. [ad. Gr. ἐξηγητικός; see EXEGESIS.

A. *adj.* Of, pertaining to, or of the nature of, EXEGESIS or interpretation; *esp.* of the Scriptures; expository. Const. *of.*

B. *sb.* 1. = Gr. ἐξηγητική (τέχνη), the art of interpretation 1838. 2. *pl.* (after Gr. τὰ ἐξηγητικά) that branch of theology which deals with the interpretation of the Scriptures 1838.

Hence **Exege·tical** *a.* = EXEGETIC A. **Exege·tically** *adv.*

Exembryonate (ekse·mbriˌŏnĕt), *a.* 1866.

[See Ex- *pref.*[1]] *Bot.* Not containing an embryo, as cryptogams.

Exemplar (egze·mplăɹ), *sb.* [ME. *exemplaire*, a. OF.; see EXAMPLAR.] 1. A model for imitation; an example. Formerly also, †a SAMPLER. 2. An archetype whether real or ideal 1618. 3. An instance; a parallel 1677. 4. A type, specimen 1656. 5. A copy of a book, etc. 1539.

1. Intimate converse with the great E. 1744. 4. Sisyphus, the legendary e. of cunning THIRLWALL.

†**Exe·mplar**, *a.* 1475. [ad. L. *exemplaris*, f. *exemplum.*] = EXEMPLARY *a.*, in various senses -1739.

Exemplarily (see EXEMPLARY), *adv.* 1611. [f. EXEMPLARY *a.*] †1. In senses of EXEMPLARY 2, 4 -1703. 2. By way of deterrent example 1627. 3. So as to deserve imitation 1611.

2. Some he punisheth e. in the world HAKEWILL. 3. E. religious DONNE. So **Exemplariness.**

Exemplarity (egzemplæ·rĭti), 1619. [f. L. *exemplar* + -ITY.] 1. Exemplariness. †2. The quality or fact of acting as a deterrent example -1660.

Exemplary (egze·-, e·gzemplări). 1589. [f. late L. *exemplaris*, f. *exemplum.*]

A. *adj.* †1. Of or pertaining to an example or examples -1822. 2. That may serve as a type or an illustration 1614. 3. Fit to serve as a deterrent 1603. 4. Serving or fit to serve as an example or pattern 1589.

2. The two Cato's are e. instances 1683. 3. E. severity 1809, damages BRYCE. 4. An e. parish priest MACAULAY.

†B. *adv.* In an e. manner or degree -1772.

†**Exemplary**, *sb.* ME. [ad. L. *exemplarium.*] 1. A type; a typical instance; an example -1583. 2. A copy of a book; a transcript (of a writing) -1706.

Exemplification (egze:mplifikē¹·ʃən). 1542. [a. AF., ad. med.L. *exemplificationem*; see EXEMPLIFY.] 1. The action of exemplifying; showing or illustrating by example 1548. 2. That which exemplifies; an illustration; an example 1582. 3. An attested copy or transcript of a record, etc. 1542.

Exemplificative (egze·mplifikătiv), *a.* 1826. [See next.] Tending to exemplify; furnishing an example.

Exemplify (egze·mplifəi), *v.* ME. [ad. med.L. *exemplificare*, f. *exemplum* and *-ficare*; see -FY.] †1. trans. To instruct by example -1513. †2. To make an example of -1642. †3. To set an example of -1673. †4. To fashion after an example -1681. †5. To adduce as an example -1794. 6. a. To illustrate by examples; to be or serve as an example of. (The current sense.) ME. b. *intr.* To quote instances in illustration 1582. 7. †To copy -1709; to make an attested copy of (a legal document) under seal 1523.

6. a. The rules I sent you concerning the hyperbola I cannot well e. BARROW. The roads to the Highlands e. the correctness of this remark MᶜCULLOCH. Hence **Exe·mplifi·able** *a.* that may be exemplified. **Exe·mplifier.**

Exempt (egze·mpt). ME. [a. F., ad. L. *exemptus*, *eximere* to take out, f. *ex-* + *emere.*]

A. *pple.* and *adj.* 1. = *exempted* pa. pple and ppl. adj. (see EXEMPT *v.*) 2. Not subject to superior authority; privileged, as an *exempt monastery*. Now *Hist.* 1460. 3. Freed *from*; not exposed or subject to ME. 4. Clear, free *from* (a defect, stain, etc.) 1586.

1. Blessed Sleep! in which e. From our tired Selves long hours we lie HOLLAND. 3. To live e. From Heav'ns high jurisdiction MILT. *P. L.* II. 318. E. from the frost EVELYN, Passions STEELE, public concerns and duties 1794, from serving in the militia 1853. 4. From custom's evil taint e. and pure SHELLEY.

B. *sb.* 1. An exempted person 1846. 2. *Eccl.* A person or establishment not subject to episcopal jurisdiction. Now *Hist.* 1532. 3. †A sub-officer of cavalry -1739; also, = EXON, q. v. 1700.

Exempt (egze·mᵖt), *v.* *Pa. pple.* **exempt.** ME. [ad. F. *exempter*, f. *exempt* adj.; see prec.] †1. *trans.* To take out or away; to remove; to single out -1648. †2. To omit; to except -1731. †3. To debar *from* something -1689. 4. To grant to (a person, etc.) immunity or freedom from a liability to which others are subject ME.

2. Thy worth and skill exempts thee from the throng MILT. *Sonn.* xiii. 4. To e. from paying tribute 1573, from the Iurisdiction of the Bishop FULLER, from the general law 1829, military service LANE, the penalties of their crimes FROUDE. So **Exe·mptile** *a.* that may be taken out. †**Exempti·tious** *a.* separable. **Exe·mptive** *a.* tending to procure exemption.

Exemption (egze·mᵖʃən). ME. [a. F., ad. L. *exemptionem*; see prec.] 1. The action of exempting; the state of being exempted. 2. Immunity from a liability, obligation, penalty, law, or authority; freedom ME. 3. Freedom, immunity *from* a defect, disadvantage, or weakness 1662.

2. We take Liberty, for an e. from Lawes HOBBES. An e. from punishment already incurred is a pardon BENTHAM. 3. E. from humane frailty HEYLIN.

‖**Exence·phalus** eks,ense·fălɒ̆s). *Pl.* **-li.** 1884. [mod.L., f. Gr. ἐξ out + ἐγκέφαλος brain.] A term for 'a monstrosity in which the brain lies wholly or chiefly outside the cranial cavity at the back of a very flattened head' (*Syd. Soc. Lex.*).

Exenterate (ekse·ntĕreⁱt), *v.* 1607. [f. L. *exenterat-*, *exenterare*, f. *ex-* + Gr. ἔντερον intestine; cf. Gr. ἐξεντερίζειν.] To take out the entrails or internal parts of; to eviscerate, disembowel. Now only *fig.* or *transf.*

transf. They unlawfully e. and eate out the bowels of poore mens purses J. COTTON. Hence **Exe·nterate** *ppl. a.* exenterated. **Exentera·tion**, the action or process of exenterating.

Exenteritis (eks,entĕrəi·tis). 1847. [f. Ex- *pref.*[2] + ENTERITIS.] *Path.* Inflammation of the outer coat of the intestines.

Exequatur (eksĭkwē¹·tɒ̆ɹ). 1788. [a. L.; = 'he may perform'; see EXECUTE.] 1. An official recognition of a consul or commercial agent by the government of the country to which he is accredited, authorizing him to exercise his functions. 2. An authorization granted by a sovereign for the publication of Papal bulls, etc. Hence, the necessity of such authorization. 1859.

Exequy (e·ksĭkwi), now always in pl. **exequies** (e·ksĭkwiz). ME. [a. OF., a. L. *ex(s)equias*, acc. of *ex(s)equiæ* pl., lit. 'train of followers', f. *exsequi* to follow out.] Funeral rites; *occas.*, funeral train, bier. Formerly *sing.*; with *pl.* in sense 'funerals'.

The E. of Joan Queen of Spayne WOOD. His exequies were solemnized with great pomp 1771. Hence **Exe·quial**, †**Exe·quious** *adjs.* of or pertaining to a funeral.

†**Exerce**, *v.* Chiefly *Sc.* ME. [a. OF. *exercer*, ad. L. *exercere.*] 1. *trans.* To EXERCISE -1578. 2. To employ; to discipline, train -1596. So †**Exe·rcent** *a.* exercising, practising.

Exercise (e·ksəɹsəiz), *sb.* ME. [a. OF. *exercice*:—L. *exercitium*, f. *exercere* to drive out of an enclosure, set to work, f. *ex-* out + *arcere* to shut up.] 1. The action of exercising; the condition of being in active operation. †2. Habitual employment -1738. 3. The practice (of virtues or vices, or of any particular kind of conduct); the execution of (functions) ME. 4. The performance of rites and ceremonies, worship, etc. 1658. †5. The training or drilling of scholars, troops, etc. -1819. 6. Practice for the sake of training or improvement, either bodily, mental, or spiritual; also, a painful mental struggle (now *rare*) ME. 7. Bodily exertion with a view to its effect on the subject, *esp.* in the way of health ME. 8. That which is done for the sake of attaining proficiency, for training body or mind, or as a test of proficiency or skill 1533. 9. A religious observance; an act of worship; a discourse 1560.

1. Their conversation is merely an e. of the tongue BUTLER. The e. of the judge's discretion 1890. 3. The e. of Trades HOBBES, of cruelty 1773. 4. The E. of the Confession of Auxbourgh 1658. 5. A Camp of e. 1819. 6. An army of e. was assembled on the Gwalior frontier STOCQUELER. 7. By e...the health of man is preserued ELYOT. Phr. *Horse-*, *open air*, *walking*, etc., *e.* 8. The public exercises for a degree EMERSON. To prepare their lessons and exercises for the following day HEWLETT. attrib. *e. book.* 10. A formal act or ceremony on some special occasion (*U.S.*) 1863.

Exercise (e·ksəɹsəiz), *v.* ME. [f. prec. sb.] 1. *trans.* To put in operation; to employ, apply, make use of. 2. To employ habitually, practise (now only *refl.* and *pass.*) ME.; †to till (the ground) -1697. 3. To train by practice; to drill (soldiers, etc.); to put (the limbs, the body) through a course of movements for the sake of strength or health ME.; †to habituate -1607. 4. To give employment to; to tax the attention, feelings, or powers of; *esp.* to harass, vex, worry 1538. 5. To carry on, carry out, perform ME.; to fulfil (functions); to exert, possess (dominion, jurisdiction, force, etc.) 1590. 6. *absol.* or *intr.* for *refl.* †a. To ply one's calling -1565. †b. To perform one's office *upon* -1703. c. To go through exercises; to drill 1606. †d. To take exercise -1734. 7. *intr.* To conduct or take part in a religious exercise; to expound Scripture. Now *Hist.* 1561.

1. That right of Punishing, which is exercised in every Common-wealth HOBBES. To e. a trust for sale 1891. 2. A people exercised in arms GIBBON. 3. To e. the body with some labour 1557. To e. all one's powers CARLYLE. 4. The situation was calculated to e. Hindu duplicity and address JAS. MILL. 5. To e. Heroic Games MILT., pasture GOLDSM., oppression JAS. MILL, an influence on politics SMILES. Hence **E·xerci·sable**, †**-ible** *a.* capable of being exercised; as, an office, power, right, etc. **E·xerciser**, one who or that which exercises; *esp.* an apparatus for exercising the limbs, etc.

Exercitation (egzɜ̄ːɹsitē¹·ʃən). ME. [ad. L. *exercitationem*, f. *exercitare*, freq. of *exercere*; see EXERCISE *v.*] 1. EXERCISE, in various senses; practice. 2. An exercise or display of skill; *esp.* a written or spoken disquisition, essay, discourse 1632.

1. Asclepiades [held the soul to be] an e. of the senses FLORIO. 2. The superb exercitations of Bossuet M. ARNOLD.

†**Exercite**, *sb.*[1] 1485. [a. OF., ad. L. *exercitus.*] An army -1550.

†**Exe·rcite**, *sb.*[2] 1485. [a. OF., ? f. as prec.] = EXERCISE *sb.*, in various senses -1533. So †**Exercite** *v. trans.* to exercise.

‖**Exercitor** (egzəːɹsitǫɹ). 1850. [L., f. *exercere.*] *Rom. Law.* The person entitled to the daily profits of a ship. Hence **Exercito·rian** *a.*

Exergue (e·ksɜ̄ɹg, egzɜ̄·ɹg). 1697. [a. F., app. f. Gr. ἐξ + ἔργον work; cf. F. *hors-d'œuvre.*] *Numism.* A small space on the reverse of a coin or medal, below the principal device, for the date, engraver's initials, or the like. Also, what is there inscribed. Hence **Exe·rgual** *a.*

Exert (egzɜ̄·ɹt), *v.* 1660. [f. L. *ex(s)ert-*, pa. pple. of *exserere* to put forth, f. *ex-* + *serere* to bind; see EXSERT *v.*] †1. *trans.* To thrust forth; to push out or up; to emit -1708; to exhibit, reveal -1743. 2. To bring into vigorous action; to exercise, bring to bear 1681. †3. To perform, practise -1757.

1. Apple Trees..e. themselves in air DRYDEN. 2. I should have exerted every nerve for Mr. Laurens BURKE. All bodies are capable of exerting electrical attraction 1816. Phr. *To e. oneself*: to employ one's powers; to use efforts; to strive. Also †*intr.* (for *refl.*). Hence **Exe·rtive** *a.* tending to e. or rouse to action.

Exertion (egzɜ̄·ɹʃən). 1668. [as if ad. L. **exertionem*; see prec.] †1. The action of putting forth; manifestation -1796. 2. The action or habit of exerting, exercising, or putting into operation. Const. *of.* 1677. 3. The action of exerting oneself; effort 1777.

1. A proper e. of chearfulness SECKER. 2. The full e. of one's faculties BURKE. A skilful e. of strength and address SCOTT. 3. Unequal to the e. of pleading 1876. var. †**Exe·rtment** (*rare*).

Exes (e·ksĕz). *pl. colloq.* 1865. [abbrev.] Expenses.

†**Exe·sion.** 1646. [f. L. *exedere.*] The action of eating out -1684.

Exestuate, -ation: see EXÆSTUATE.

‖**Exeunt** (e·ksi,ɒnt), *v.* 1485. [L.; = 'they go out'; see EXIT.] A stage direction (*orig.* Exeant) = 'Here two or more actors leave the stage'. So in *Exeunt omnes* 'all go out'.

Exfetation (eksfītē¹·ʃən). Also **-fœt-.** 1858. [f. Ex- *pref.*[1] + L. *fetare*; see -ATION.] *Med.* 'Imperfect fetation in some organ exterior to the uterus' (Hoblyn).

Exfoliate (eksfōu·li,eⁱt), *v.* 1612. [f. late L. *exfoliat-*, *exfoliare* to strip of leaves, f. *ex-* + *folium.*] 1. *trans.* a. *Path.* To cast off in the form of 'leaves' or scales. b. *Surg.* To remove the surface of by exfoliation. 2. *intr.* To come off in layers or scales; to peel off

1676. 3. *trans.* To unfold the leaves of; to open out 1808.

2. Down with a frozen heel; the bone exfoliating KANE. Before the blowpipe it [anhydrite] does not e. like gypsum DANA. Hence **Exfo·lia·tion**, the action or process of exfoliating; that which is exfoliated; a coat or layer in the stem of a tree. **Exfo·liative** *a.* capable of causing, or favourable to, exfoliation; *sb.* something that causes exfoliation.

Exh-. In words beginning with these letters, the *h* is usually silent. To avoid repetition the more frequent pronunciation is alone indicated.

†**Exhalate**, *v.* 1598. [f. L. *exhalat-* ppl. stem; see EXHALE.] 1. *trans.* To evaporate; to produce by evaporation -1643. 2. *intr.* = EXHALE 2. -1623.

Exhalation (eksălē·ʃən). ME. [ad. L. *exhalationem*; see EXHALE.] 1. The action or process of exhaling, breathing forth, or throwing off in the form of a vapour; evaporation. Const. *of.* 2. *concr.* That which is exhaled; a mist, vapour, etc.; an emanation or effluvium ME. 3. A body of (usually enkindled) vapour; a meteor (*arch.*) 1561.

2. Nero's golden house had risen like an e., and like an e. it disappeared MERIVALE. Pulmonary and cutaneous exhalations 1869. 3. The star of the shepherds was a meteoric e. FARRAR.

Exhale (egz-, eks,hē¹·l), *v.*[1] ME. [ad. F. *exhaler*, ad. L. *exhalare* to breathe out, f. *ex-* + *halare.*] 1. *trans.* To breathe out; to send up (fumes, vapour, etc.); to give off in vapour. Also *fig.* 1626. 2. *intr.* To pass off into the air; to be given off as vapour; to evaporate. Also *fig.* ME. 3. *Phys.* and *Path.* Of animal fluids: To ooze through a membrane or blood-vessel. Also in *pass.* ME. 4. *trans.* To draw up or drive off in vapour; to evaporate. Also *fig.* 1588. 5. To breathe or blow forth from within. Also *fig.* 1589. 6. *intr.* To make an expiration; opp. to INHALE. 1863.

1. Weight .. exhaled by insensible Transpiration 1664. 2. For ofte of it [the floode] exaleth myst impure ME. *fig.* His Hopes exhal'd in empty Smoke DRYDEN. 4. Yon Light..is some Meteor that the Sun exhales *Rom. & Jul.* III. v. 13. 5. I could not e. my wrath before his grace 1867.

Hence **Exha·lable** *a.* that can be exhaled or evaporated. **Exha·lant** *a.* that exhales; *sb.* an exhalant vessel or organ. **Exha·lement**, exhalation.

†**Exha·le**, *v.*[2] 1594. [f. EX- *pref.*[1] + HALE *v.*] To drag out or draw forth or up -1647.

†**Exha·nce**, *v.* 1450. = ENHANCE. -1667.

Exhaust (egzǭ·st), *sb.* 1848. [f. EXHAUST *v.*] The process or means of exhausting. 1. a. *Steam-engine.* The exit of steam from the cylinder after propelling the piston; the passage through which it escapes; EDUCTION. b. The expulsion of combustion products from the cylinder of a petrol engine; also, the valve by which it escapes. c. The process of exhausting (a vessel) of air; the degree to which exhaustion is carried 1880. 2. The production of an outward current of air by creating a partial vacuum; also, any apparatus for effecting this 1852.

attrib. and *Comb.* (chiefly in sense 1 a), as *e.-passage, -pipe, -valve*; also **e.-fan**, a fan for producing a current by creating a vacuum; **e. injector**, an injector for feeding a steam-boiler with water, worked by e. steam; **e.-port**, the opening in the slide-valve of a steam-engine for the escape of e. steam (= *e.-passage*); **-steam**, the waste steam discharged from the cylinder of a steam-engine.

Exhaust (egzǭ·st), *v.* 1533. [f. L. *exhaust-*, *exhaurire*, f. *ex-* + *haurire* to draw.] 1. *trans.* To draw off or out (now only, air); *lit.* and *fig.* 1540. 2. To use up completely; to expend or account for all of 1533. 3. To empty by drawing the contents off or out; to drain; to empty *of* 1614. Also *intr.* of steam. 4. To draw out all that is essential or interesting in (a subject, etc.) 1704. 5. To drain of strength, resources, etc.; to weary out, enfeeble greatly 1631.

2. Whatever relief was given .. the same was soon exhausted BURKE. To e. all the possible combinations MILL. 3. A tube which could be exhausted of air TYNDALL. 4. To e. the history of the Roman Republic M. PATTISON. 5. The Kingdome was much exhausted of men and mony GOUGE.

Hence †**Exhau·st** *pa. pple.* and *ppl. a.* exhausted. **Exhau·stedly** *adv.* **Exhau·ster**, one who, or that which, exhausts; *spec.* in *Gas-making*, a contrivance for pumping the gas in a continuous flow out of the retorts. **Exhau·stible** *a.* that can be exhausted; whence **Exhau·stibi·lity.** **Exhau·stingly** *adv.*

Exhaustion (egzǭ·stʃən). 1646. [as if ad. L. **exhaustionem*; see prec. Cf. F. *exhaustion.*] 1. The action or process of exhausting; the condition of being exhausted. b. *spec.* (*Steam-engine*) The discharge of waste steam from the cylinder 1782. 2. *Chem.* 'Applied to any process, such as percolation, whereby the active constituents of a drug [etc.] are removed in solution, leaving it exhausted' (*Syd. Soc. Lex.*). 3. a. *gen.* A process of proof by exhausting all conceivable hypotheses, except one, relating to the question 1877. b. *Method of Exhaustions* (Math.): an application of a., as in proving the equality of two magnitudes, by showing that if one is supposed to be greater or less than the other a *reductio ad absurdum* is involved 1685.

1. The e. of the air incumbent on the water BOYLE. The rapid sale and e. of a work KNOX. E. ..is an occasional cause of death after severe operations ERICHSEN. vars. †**Exhau·stment** (*rare*). †**Exhau·sture.**

Exhaustive (egzǭ·stiv), *a.* 1786. [f. L. *exhaust-* ppl. stem (see EXHAUST *v.*) + -IVE.] 1. Tending to exhaust 1818. 2. Characterized by exhausting; complete, comprehensive.

2. An e. survey GLADSTONE. Phr. *E. method* = EXHAUSTION 3 a. **Exhau·stive-ly** *adv.*, **-ness.**

Exhaustless (egzǭ·stlės), *a. poet.* and *rhet.* 1712. [f. EXHAUST *v.* + -LESS.] Inexhaustible.

Exhedra, var. of EXEDRA.

Exheredate (eks,he·rĭdeⁱt), *v.* Now *rare.* 1552. [f. L. *exheredat-*, *exheredare* to disinherit.] *trans.* To disinherit. Also *fig.* Hence **Exhereda·tion**, †**Exheredita·tion**, disherison.

Exhibit (egzi·bit), *sb.* 1626. [ad. L. *exhibitum*, *exhibere*; see EXHIBIT *v.*] 1. *Law.* a. Any writing identified in court, and marked by the Examiner accordingly. b. Any document (or object) produced in court and referred to and identified in written evidence. 2. Anything exhibited or presented to view; *esp.* an object, or collection of objects, in an exhibition 1862. 3. A showing, display 1654.

2. An e. in the Peruvian section 1876.

Exhibit (egzi·bit), *v.* 1490. [f. L. *exhibit-*, *exhibere*, f. *ex-* out + *habere* to hold.] †1. *trans.* To offer; to administer (an oath) -1657; †to furnish; hence to defray (expense) -1654; †*intr.* to provide maintenance; to give an exhibition -1868. 2. *trans.* (*Med.*) To administer (a remedy, etc.) 1601. 3. To submit for inspection or consideration; *esp.* to produce, put in (a document) in a court of law, to append as an exhibit to written evidence 1529. 4. To expose to view; to show; *esp.* to show publicly for the purpose of amusement or instruction, or in a competition; *rarely*, to perform in public 1534.

2. To e. Scammony for a purgation HOLLAND. 3. Accept this Scrowle .. Which .. we doe exhibite to your Maiestie 1 *Hen. VI*, III. i. 151. To e. a charge of high treason against the duke CLARENDON. 4. To e. a solo on the violin 1845.

Hence †**Exhi·bit** *pa. pple.* exhibited. **Exhi·bitable** *a.* **Exhi·biter**, **-or** (now more usual).

Exhibition (eksibi·ʃən). ME. [a. OF. *exhibicion*, ad. late L. *exhibitionem*; see EXHIBIT *v.*] †1. Maintenance, support -1711. †2. A pension, salary; a gift -1741. 3. An endowment for a term of years given to a student in a school, college, or university. Cf. BURSARY, SCHOLARSHIP. 1525. 4. *Med.* The administration of a remedy 1785. 5. The action of exhibiting, submitting for inspection, displaying, or holding up to view 1633; *concr.* something that is exhibited 1786. 6. A public display (of works of art, manufactures, etc.); also, the place of the display 1761.

5. An e. of presumption MRS. JAMESON. Phr. *To make an e. of oneself* (colloq.): to show oneself in an unfavourable aspect. 7. The examination of the pupils of a school or college; an instance of this (*U.S.*) 1829.

Hence **Exhibi·tional** *a.* of or pertaining to an e. **Exhibi·tioner**, one who holds an e. at a university; one who exhibits. **Exhibi·tionism**, indecent exposure of the person, esp. as a manifestation of sexual perversion; also *fig.* and *gen.* tendency towards display or extravagant behaviour; so **Exhibi·tionist.**

Exhibitive (egzi·bitiv), *a.* 1596. [ad. mod.L. *exhibitivus*; see EXHIBIT *v.* and -IVE.] Having the property of exhibiting or showing forth. Const. *of.* Hence **Exhibitively** *adv.*

Exhibitory (egzi·bitəri). 1607. [ad. L. *exhibitorius*; see EXHIBIT and -ORY.]

A. *adj.* Intended to exhibit or cause to be exhibited; of or pertaining to exhibition 1772.

†B. *sb.* A procedure with regard to the exhibition of remedies.

Exhilarant (egzi·lărănt). 1803. [a. F., ad. L. *exhilarantem*; see next.]

A. *adj.* That exhilarates; exhilarating 1866.

B. *sb.* An exhilarating medicine.

Exhilarate (egzi·lăreⁱt), *v.* 1540. [ad. L. *exhilarat-*, *exhilarare*, f. *ex-* (see EX- pref.[1]) + *hilaris*); see HILARITY.] 1. *trans.* To make cheerful or merry; to cheer, enliven, gladden. †2. *intr.* To become cheerful 1620.

1. To e. the spirits with a glass of wine SMOLLETT. Hence **Exhi·larating** *ppl. a.* cheering, inspiriting. **Exhi·laratingly** *adv.* **Exhi·larative** *a.* tending to e. **Exhi·larator.**

Exhilaration (egzi:lărē·ʃən). 1623. [ad. late L. *exhilarationem*; see prec.] 1. The action or means of exhilarating; an enlivening influence. 2. Exhilarated condition 1626.

1. E. hath some Affinity with Joy BACON.

Exhort (egzǭ·ɹt), *v.* ME. [ad. L. *exhortari*, f. *ex-* intensive (EX-[1]) + *hortari* to encourage; see HORTATORY. Cf. F. *exhorter.*] 1. *trans.* To admonish earnestly; to urge by words to laudable conduct. Of circumstances, etc.: To serve as an incitement. Also *absol.* 2. With *obj.* a thing: To recommend earnestly 1500.

1. Examples, gross as earth, e. me *Haml.* IV. iv. 46. *absol.* He that exhorteth, to his exhorting R.V. *Rom.* xii. 8. 2. What I exhorte Not herde is 1500.

Hence †**Exho·rt** *sb.* exhortation. **Exho·rtative** *a.* of, pertaining to, or containing exhortation: intended to e. **Exho·rtatory** *a.* exhortative.

Exhortation (egzǭɹtē·ʃən). ME. [ad. L. *exhortationem*; see prec.] 1. The action or process of exhorting, of earnestly admonishing or urging to what is good and laudable. 2. A set speech delivered for the purpose of exhorting; a discourse 1450.

2. The E. before the Communion 1704.

Exhorter (egzǭ·ɹtəɹ). 1513. [f. EXHORT *v.*] 1. One who exhorts or urges on to action 1552. 2. *spec.* In various churches, a person appointed to give religious exhortation under the direction of his pastor.

Exhumate (e·ks,hiumeⁱt), *v.* 1548. [f. med.L. *exhumat-*, *exhumare*; see EXHUME *v.*] = EXHUME *v. lit.* and *fig.* Hence **Exhuma·tion**, the action or process of removing a body from beneath the ground.

Exhume (eks,hiū·m), *v.* 1783. [ad. F. *exhumer*, ad. med.L. *exhumare*, f. *ex-* out + *humus* ground.] 1. *trans.* To dig out or remove (something buried) from beneath the ground; *transf.* and *fig.* to unearth. 2. To remove the overlying soil from (*rare*) 1872.

Exibilate, exiccate, etc.; see EXS-.

Exies (e·ksiz). 1816. [Sc. and north. f. of ACCESS.] a. An ague fit. b. Hysterics. SCOTT.

‖**Exigeant** (ęksiʒaṅ), *a.* 1803. [Fr.; cf. EXIGENT.] Exacting. Also in fem. **Exigeante** (ęksiʒaṅt).

Exigence (e·ksidʒĕns). 1589. [a. F., ad. L. *exigentia*, f. *exigentem*, *exigere*; see EXIGENT.] 1. The state or fact of being exigent; urgent want; need, necessity. †b. = EXIGENCY 2. -1818. 2. A case demanding immediate action or remedy; an emergency; an extremity 1643.

1. In time of e. 1691. 2. Falstaff..is equal to any e. MRS. C. CLARKE.

Exigency (e·ksidʒĕnsi). 1581. [ad. L. *exigentia*; see prec.] 1. Pressing state (of circumstances); stringency (of requirements) 1769. b. Pressing necessity; in *pl.* pressing needs, straits 1630. 2. That which is needed; demands, needs, requirements 1581.

2. The various e. of time and occasion *Bk. Com. Prayer.* The exigencies of theology 1857.

Exigent (e·ksidʒĕnt), *a.* and *sb.*[1] ME. [ad. L. *exigentem*, *exigere*, f. *ex-* out + *agere* to drive; see EXACT *v.*]

A. *adj.* 1. Requiring immediate action or aid; pressing, urgent 1670. 2. Requiring too much; exacting 1828.

1. That e. cry for help CLARENDON. 2. A love that clings not, nor is e. SIR H. TAYLOR.

†B. *sb.*[1] 1. A state of pressing need; an occasion that requires immediate action or remedy; an extremity, strait -1729; end, last extremity -1631. 2. *pl.* Needs, requirements -1677.

1. The duke seeing himselfe to be driuen to such an

e. HOLINSHED. These Eyes..Waxe dimme, as drawing to their E. 1 *Hen. VI*, II. v. 9. **2.** The present exigents of the Kingdom CHAS. I.

†**E·xigent**, *sb.*² 1464. [In 15th c. *exigend*, ad. (ult.) med.L. *exigenda*, see prec.] *Law.* A writ commanding the sheriff to summon the defendant to appear upon pain of outlawry; also called *writ of e.* –1768.

†**Exi·genter.** 1512. [a. AF. *exigenter*, f. as prec.] *Law.* An officer of the Court of Common Pleas (in 18–19th c., of the Court of King's Bench) who made out all exigents –1837.

‖**Exigi facias** (e·ksidʒəi fē·ʃiæs). 1577. [L.; lit. 'that you cause to be exacted'.] = EXIGENT *sb.*²

Exigible (e·ksidʒib'l), *a.* 1610. [as if ad. L. **exigibilis*; see EXACT *v.* Cf. F. *exigible.*] That may be exacted; demandable.

There is no part of our debt e. at this time T. JEFFERSON.

Exiguity (eksigiū·iti). 1623. [ad. L. *exiguitas*; see EXIGUOUS.] The condition of being exiguous; scantiness; smallness, littleness.

Exiguous (egzi·giu,əs), *a.* 1651. [f. L. *exiguus* (f. *exigere* to weigh strictly; see EXACT *v.*) + -OUS.] Scanty in size or number; extremely small, diminutive. Hence **Exi·guousness.**

Exile (e·ksəil, e·gzəil), *sb.*¹ ME. [a. OF. *exil*, semi-popular ad. L. *exsilium*, f. *ex-* out + *sal-* root of *salire* to leap; cf. *consilium* COUNSEL. Or ? f. *ex-* + *solum* (Skeat). Formerly stressed *exi·le.*] **1.** Enforced removal from one's native land according to an edict or sentence; banishment; also *gen.*, prolonged voluntary absence from one's native land. Also *transf.* and *fig.* †**2.** Waste; ruin –1700.

1. He was put to exyle in to yᵉ yle of Sardeyn 1529. **2.** Her cite and landes of Cartage are all dystroied and tourned in exyll CAXTON.

Exile (e·ksəil), *sb.*² ME. [? concrete use of prec.; or f. EXILE *v.*] A banished person; one compelled by circumstances to reside away from his native land. Also *transf.* and *fig.*

Tit. A. III. i. 285. *transf.* An e. from the paternal roof 1820.

Exile (e·ksəil, e·gzəil), *a.* ? *Obs.* ME. [ad. L. *exilis* thin, lank.] **1.** Slender, shrunken, thin; small. **2.** Meagre; poor ME.

Exile (e·ksəil, e·gzəil), *v.* ME. [ad. OF. *exilier* :—late L. *exiliare*, f. *ex(s)ilium* EXILE *sb.*¹ Formerly stressed *exi·le.*] **1.** To compel (a person) by decree or enactment to leave his country; to banish. Also *transf.* and *fig.* †**2.** *gen.* To banish, expel –1700. †**3.** To devastate, bring to ruin. Cf. EXTERMINATE. –1533.

1. The emperour exyled Iohan.. into the yle of Pathmose 1493. **3.** He..exiled diuerse townes LD. BERNERS. Hence **E·xilement**, banishment, exile. †**Exiler.**

Exilic (egz-, eksi·lik), *a.* 1888. [f. EXILE *sb.* + -IC.] Of or pertaining to exile; *esp.* to that of the Jews in Babylon. So **Exi·lian** *a.* 1882.

†**Exili·tion.** 1646. [f. L. *ex(s)ilire*, f. *ex-* + *salire* to leap.] A leaping up or forth –1711.

Exility (eksi·lĭti). 1528. [ad. L. *exilitatem*, f. *exilis* EXILE *a.*] **1.** Thinness, slenderness, meagreness 1528; †poverty –1774. **2.** Tenuity; subtlety 1626.

Eximious (egzi·miəs), *a.* Now *rare.* 1547. [f. L. *eximius*, (f. *eximere*; see EXEMPT *v.*) + -OUS.] Excellent, distinguished, eminent. Hence †**Exi·miously** *adv.*

†**Exi·nanite**, *v.* 1555. [f. L. *exinanit-*, *exinanare* to make empty, f. *ex-* + *inanis.*] **1.** *trans.* To make of none effect –1661. **2.** To reduce to emptiness; to humble –1624.

Exinanition (eksi·năni·ʃən). Now *rare.* 1603. [ad. L. *exinanitionem*; see prec.] **1.** The action of emptying or exhausting; emptied or exhausted condition. **2.** Humiliation 1627.

1. Fastings to the e. of spirits JER. TAYLOR.

Exindusiate (eksindiū·si,ēt), *a.* 1866. [f. EX- *pref.*¹ + INDUSIUM + -ATE ³.] *Bot.* Not having an indusium.

Exi·nguinal (eksi·ŋgwinăl). 1884. [f. EX- *pref.*¹ + L. *inguin-* (*inguen*) + -AL.] *Entom.*

A. *adj.* Situated outside the groin.

B. *sb.* 'The second segment or trochanter of the limbs of the Arachnida' (*Syd. Soc. Lex.*).

Exintine (eksi·ntin, -təin). 1852. [f. L. *ex-* + *intus* + -INE ¹.] 'The membrane of the pollen grain which lies between the *Extine* and the *Intine*' (*Syd. Soc. Lex.*).

Exion. Blunder for 'action'. 2 *Hen. IV*, II. i. 32.

Exist (egzi·st), *v.* 1602. [ad. F. *exister*, ad. L. *ex(s)istere* to stand out, f. *ex-* + *sistere*, f. *stare.*] **1.** To be, to have objective being 1605. **2.** To have being in a specified mode. With advb. phr. or *as.* Also, to subsist, occur 1602 **3.** To live 1828. **4.** To continue to be 1790.

1. To conceive the world..to have existed from eternity SOUTH. **2.** A space of a foot existed between the ice and the water TYNDALL. **4.** How does he contrive to e. here 1797.

Hence **Exi·ster** (*rare*). **Exi·stibi·lity**, also **-ability**, capability of existing. **Exi·stible** *a.* (*rare*) capable of existing. **Exi·sting** *ppl. a.* 1762.

Existence (egzi·stĕns). ME. [a. OF., ad. med.L. *existentia*; see EXIST and -ENCE.] †**1.** Reality; opp. to *appearance.* Only in ME. **2.** Being; the fact or state of existing ME.; continuance in being 1736; life 1634. **3.** A mode of existing 1763. **4.** *concr.* All that exists 1751; a being, an entity 1605.

2. Matter is not necessary to the Soul's e. GLANVILL. We know not at all upon what the e. of our living powers depends BUTLER. A wretched e. DICKENS. **4.** An enumeration of Existences, as the basis of Logic MILL. var. †**Exi·stency** (in senses 2, 4).

Existent (egzi·stĕnt). 1561. [ad. L. *existentem*; see EXIST.] **A.** *adj.* **1.** That exists, existing; having being. Also *absol.* **2.** Now existing; present-day 1791.

1. There is but one necessarily e. Being JACKSON. **2.** Types of e. Frenchmen RUSKIN. Hence **Exi·stently** *adv.*

B. *sb.* An existent person or thing 1644.

Existential (egziste·nʃăl), *a.* 1693. [ad. late L. *existentialis.*] **1.** Of or pertaining to existence. **2.** *Logic.* Of a proposition: Predicating existence 1837. **Existe·ntially** *adv.*

†**Existima·tion.** 1538. [ad. L. *existimationem*, f. (ult.) *ex-* + *æstimare*; see ESTEEM *v.*] = ESTIMATION 2, 4. –1712.

Exit (e·ksit). 1538. [a. L. *exit*, *exire.*] **I.** Replacing EXEAT, q. v. **2.** *sb.* The departure of a player from the stage. Also *transf.* and *fig.*; *esp.* departure from the scene of life; death. 1588. **3.** A going out or forth; liberty to go out; egress 1659. **4.** An outlet; esp. said of the doors affording exit from a public building 1695.

2. They haue their Exits and their Entrances SHAKS. He scorn'd an E. by the common means FELTHAM. **4.** An enclosure..which..had no e. JOWETT. Hence **E·xit** *v. intr.* to make one's e.; *fig.* to die.

Exitial (egzi·ʃăl), *a.* ? *Obs.* 1534. [ad. L. *exitialis*, f. *exitium.*] Hurtful; destructive to life, fatal. So †**Exi·tious** *a.*

†**E·xiture.** ME. [ad. med.L. *exitura*, f. *exire.*] **1.** Passage out or forth –1615. **2.** A running abscess. [So in OF.] –1657.

Exitus (e·ksitŏs). 1664. [L., f. *exire.*] †**1.** A going out or forth; a departure –1706. **2.** *Path.* A prolapsus 1811; also, 'the termination of a disease' (*Syd. Soc. Lex.*) 1884.

‖**Ex-libris** (eks ləi·bris). Used also as *pl.* 1880. [L.; lit. 'out of the books' (of ——).] An inscription, label, or stamp indicating the owner of a book; *esp.* a book-plate or the like. Hence **Ex-li·brist**, one who collects these.

Exo- (e·kso, bef. two unstressed syllables eksǫ-), *prefix* (bef. a vowel sometimes *ex-*), repr. Gr. ἔξω without; as in:

Exoca·rdial *a.*, *Phys.* pertaining to the exterior of the heart. **E·xocarp** [Gr. καρπός] = PERICARP. **Exocœ·lar** *a.* [see CŒLOM], pertaining to the outer side of the body-cavity. **E·xoderm** [Gr. δέρμα] = ECTODERM; also the external crust of the body of an insect. **E·xogene·tic** *a.* [Gr. γενετικός, f. γένεσις], that arises from without. **Exona·rthex** [see NARTHEX], the outer vestibule of a Greek church. **Exopa·thic** *a.* [Gr. πάθος], (of disease) originating outside the body. **Exophy·llous** *a.* [Gr. φύλλον], (of dicotyledons) having the young leaves naked, i. e. not enclosed in a sheath. **E·xoplasm** [Gr. πλάσμα], the outermost layer of the cuticular protoplasm of some Protozoa. **Exo·podite** [Gr. ποδ- πούς], 'the outermost of the two processes appended to the basal process of the hinder limbs of some of the Crustacea' (*Syd. Soc. Lex.*); hence **Exopodi·tic** *a.* **Exo·ptile** *a.* [Gr. πτίλον feather], *Bot.* having a naked plumule. **Exo(r)rhi·zal** *a.* [Gr. ῥίζα root], *Bot.* (of plants) having the radicle naked; also **Exorrhi·zous** *a.* **Exosco·pic** *a.* [Gr. -σκοπος], viewing from the outside; hence **Exosco·pically** *adv.* **Exoske·letal** *a.*, *Anat.* of or pertaining to the **Exoske·leton**, the external integument, whether bony, or calcified, or leathery; also *fig.* **E·xosperm** Gr. σπέρμα], **E·xospore** [see SPORE], *Bot.* the outer coat of a spore or oosphere in fungi or lichens; hence **Exospo·ral** *a.* pertaining to an exospore; **Exospo·rous** *a.* having its spores on the outer surface of the sporangium. **E·xostome** [Gr. στόμα], *Bot.* the aperture in the outer integument of the ovule. **Exothe·ca** [Gr. θήκη case], *Zool.* the hard exterior wall of the gonosome of the Hydrozoa; hence **Exothe·cal** *a.* **Exothe·cium**, *Bot.* 'the cuticular or outer layer of the anther' (*Syd. Soc. Lex.*).

Exoccipital (eks,ǫksi·pităl). 1847. [f. Gr. ἔξω (see EXO-) + L. *occiput* (*occipit-*) + -AL.]

A. *adj.* That is outside the occipital bone.

B. *sb. pl.* Those parts of the occipital bone which form the sides of the foramen magnum and support the condyles 1854.

Exoculation (eks,ǫkiulē·ʃən). 1630. [f. L. *exoculare* to put out the eyes, f. *ex-* + *oculus.*] The action of putting out the eyes; blinding.

Exode (e·ksoud), *sb.*¹ Also **exod.** ME. [anglicized f. EXODUS.] †**1.** = EXODUS **1.** ME. only. **2.** = EXODUS 2 (*rare*) 1751.

Exode (e·ksōud), *sb.*² 1684. [a. F., ad. late L. *exodium.*] = EXODIUM **1**, **2.**

Exodic (eksǫ·dik), *a.* 1850. [f. Gr. ἔξοδος + -IC.] **1.** Of or pertaining to an exodus. (Dicts.) **2.** *Phys.* Proceeding from the spinal marrow 1850.

Exodist (e·ksŏdist). *rare.* 1849. [f. EXODE *sb.* + IST.] **1.** One who makes an exodus 1883. **2.** An emigrant 1849.

‖**Exodium.** 1600. [a. L., ad. Gr. ἐξόδιον, f. ἐξόδιος of or belonging to an exit; see EXODUS.] **1.** *Gr. Drama.* The end or catastrophe of a play 1842. **2.** *Rom. Drama.* A comic interlude or farce following something more serious.

Exodus (e·ksŏdŏs). OE. [a. L., a. Gr. ἔξοδος, f. ἐξ out + ὁδός way.] **1.** The book of the O.T. which describes the departure of the Israelites out of Egypt. **2.** A going out or forth; *esp.* the departure of the Israelites from Egypt; emigration. Also *fig.* 1623. var. **E·xody.**

‖**Ex officio, ex-officio,** *advb. phr.* 1533. [L.] In discharge of duty, in virtue of one's office; hence = OFFICIAL.

Exogamy (eksǫ·gămi). 1865. [f. Gr. ἔξω (see EXO-) + γάμος marriage + -OUS.] The custom by which a man is bound to take a wife from outside his own clan or group; opp. to *endogamy.* Hence **Exoga·mic** *a.* pertaining to e. **Exo·gamous** *a.* practising, of the nature of, or pertaining to, e.

Exogen (e·ksodʒĕn). 1838. [in Fr. *exogène*, mod.L. *exogena*, *-us* adj., used in fem. as sb., f. Gr. ἔξω + -γενής.] *Bot.* A plant whose stem grows by deposit on the outside; opp. to ENDOGEN.

Exogenous (eksǫ·dʒĭnəs), *a.* 1830. [f. mod.L. *exogena*, *-us* (see prec.) + -OUS.] **a.** *Bot.* Growing by additions on the outside; of the nature of an exogen; pertaining to or characteristic of the exogens. **b.** *Path.* = EXOGENETIC. 1883. **c.** *Anat.* (Of a portion of bone) growing out from a previously ossified part; opp. to *autogenous* 1854.

Hence **Exo·genously** *adv.*

†**E·xolete**, *a.* 1611. [ad. L. *exoletus*, *exolescere*, f. *ex-* + *ol-* to grow; cf. *adolescere.*] Obsolete; effete, insipid; faded –1736.

†**Exolu·tion.** Also **exsolution.** 1615. [ad. L. *ex(s)olutionem*, f. *exsolvere.*] The action of loosening or setting free; relaxation; *esp.* the emission of 'animal spirits', formerly assumed as the cause of swooning; faintness –1662.

†**Exo·lve**, *v.* 1578. [ad. L. *ex(s)olvere*, f. *ex-* + *solvere* to loosen.] *trans.* To slacken; also 'to pay clear off' (Bailey). *intr.* for *refl.* To dissolve. –1657.

||**Exomis** (eksōu·mis). 1850. [Gr., f. ἐξ + ὦμος shoulder.] A vest without sleeves, leaving the shoulders bare; worn by artisans and slaves. So **Exo·mion**. Browning.

||**Exomologesis** (eks₁ǫ̈mǫlǫgī·sis). 1592. [Gr., f. ἐξ intensive + ὁμολογέειν to confess.] A full or public confession.

Exomphalos (eksǫ·mfălǫs). 1574. [Gr., f. ἐξ + ὀμφαλός navel.] A rupture or protrusion at the navel.

||**Exon** (e·xǫ̈n). 1767. [repr. the pronunc. (ɛgzañ) of Fr. *exempt*. Cf. EXAUN.] Title of the four officers of the Yeomen of the Royal Guard, styled *corporals* in their commissions, and ranking below the 'Ensign'.

Exonerate (egzǫ·nĕreᶦt), *v.* 1524. [f. L. *exonerat-*, *exonerare*, f. *ex-* + *onus* (*oner-*) burden. Cf. F. *exonérer*.] **1.** *trans.* To take off a burden from; to relieve *of*; to unload, lighten. **2.** To discharge, get rid of 1542. **3.** To free from (a duty, obligation, payment, charge, etc.; also, from blame) 1548.

1. Success would certainly e. our finances WELLINGTON. **2.** To exonerat the blader..whan nede shall requyre BOORDE. Neither did this riuer e. itself into any sea HAKLUYT. **3.** Mr. Hastings .. offered to e. the company from that 'charge' BURKE. To e. myself of a greater crime W. IRVING.

Hence **Exo·nerate** *pple*. exonerated. **Exonera·tion**, the action of discharging, disburdening, or relieving, or the state of being relieved from a duty, office, obligation, payment, etc.; also, from blame; a formal discharge. **Exo·nerative** *a.* tending to give relief (from an obligation). **Exo·nerator**.

||**Exoneretur** (egzǫnĕrī·tɔɪ). 1824. [L.; = 'let him be discharged'; see prec.] *Law.* 'An entry made upon the bail-piece upon render of a defendant to prison in discharge of his bail' (Wharton).

Exophtha·lmia. 1721. [mod.L., f. EXOPHTHALMUS.] = EXOPHTHALMUS.

Exophthalmus, -os (eks₁ǫfþæ·lmǫ̈s, -ǫs). 1872. [mod.L., a Gr., f. ἐξ out + ὀφθαλμός eye.] *Path.* Protrusion of the eye-ball. Hence **Exophtha·lmic** *a.* of, pertaining to, or characterized by, e. var. **Exophtha·lmy**.

†**Exo·pt**, *v.* [ad. L. *exoptare*.] To desire greatly. FORREST. So †**Exopta·tion**, earnest desire.

Exorable (e·ksŏrăb'l), *a.* Now *rare*. 1563. [ad. L. *exorabilis*; see next.] Capable of being moved by entreaty. Hence **E·xorableness**.

†**E·xorate**, *v.* 1599. [f. L. *exorat-*, *exorare*, f. *ex-* + *orare* to pray.] *trans.* To entreat; to prevail upon by entreaty -1654. Hence †**Exora·tion**.

Exo·rbital, *a.* 1876. [f. EX-*pref.*[1] + ORBIT + -AL.] Outside the orbit.

Exorbitance (egzǭ·ɹbităns). 1611. [f. EXORBITANT; see -ANCE.] †**1.** Aberration from the due or ordinary track; eccentricity, irregularity, anomaly. Also, aberration of mind. -1842. **2.** Transgression of law or morality; misconduct, lawlessness, criminality (*arch.*) 1611. **3.** Excessiveness; now chiefly, of demands, charges, prices, etc. 1646.

2. The Border robbers..had committed many exorbitances SCOTT. **3.** The e. of the duties on tea and tobacco MᶜCULLOCH. So **Exo·rbitancy**.

Exorbitant (egzǭ·ɹbitănt). 1460. [ad. late L. *exorbitantem*, *exorbitare*, f. *ex-* + *orbita* wheel-track; see ORBIT. Cf. F. *exorbitant*.]

A. *adj.* †**1.** Leaving a specified track -1674. **2.** Deviating from the normal track; †eccentric; anomalous; abnormal 1460. †**3.** Forsaking, or apt to forsake, the right path; erring -1716. **4.** Exceeding ordinary or proper bounds; excessive; outrageously large 1621.

2. Causes e., and such as their lawes had not provided for HOOKER. **4.** E. appetites BURTON, Impositions R. COKE, tributes GIBBON, influence J. FLETCHER. Hence **Exo·rbitantly** *adv.*

†**B.** *sb.* One who or something which exceeds proper limits (*rare*) -1714.

Exorbitate (egzǭ·ɹbiteᶦt), *v.* ? *Obs.* 1600. [f. L. *exorbitat-*, *exorbitare*; see prec.] *intr.* To deviate from the usual course or orbit. Hence **Exorbita·tion**.

Exorcise: see EXORCIZE.

Exorcism (e·ksǭɹsiz'm, egzǭ·ɹsiz'm). ME. [ad. late L. *exorcismus*, a. Eccl. Gr. ἐξορκισμός; see EXORCIZE. Cf. F. *exorcisme*.] **1.** The action of exorcising or expelling an evil spirit by adjuration, etc. †**2.** *improp.* conjuration; the ceremonies observed in calling up spirits -1652. **3.** A formula employed in exorcizing 1550.

Exorcist (e·ksǭɹsist, egzǭ·ɹsist). ME. [ad. late L. *exorcista*, ad. Gr. ἐξορκιστής; see EXORCIZE.] **1.** One who drives out evil spirits by adjuration, etc.; *spec.* one of the four lesser orders in the R. C. Church. †**2.** One who calls up spirits by magical rites -1621.

1. Exorcists, that served to dispossess such as were possessed by the Devil SELDEN. **2.** *Jul. C.* II. i. 323.

Exorcize, -ise (e·ksǭɹsəiz, egzǭ·ɹsəiz), *v.* 1546. [ad. late L. *exorcizare*, ad. Gr. ἐξορκίζειν, f. ἐξ + ὅρκος oath. The better form *exorcize* is least in use.] **1.** *trans.* To drive out (an evil spirit) by the use of a holy name; to call forth, expel. **2.** To clear of evil spirits; to purify 1645. **3.** To adjure (an evil spirit). Also, to conjure up. Now *rare*. 1584.

1. Touched him on the shoulder with his staff and exorcised the demon MRS. JAMESON. **2.** Monks huddled together..as if to e. the land of a demon LYTTON. Hence **Exorciza·tion**, the action of exorcizing. **Exorcizer**, one who exorcizes.

||**Exordium** (egzǭ·ɹdiǫ̈m). Pl. **-iums, -ia.** 1581. [L., f. *exordiri* f. *ex* + *ordiri* to begin.] The beginning of anything; *esp.* the introductory part of a discourse, treatise, etc.

I shall consider them jointly, by way of e. to the rest SELDEN. Hence **Exo·rdial** *a.* introductory.

†**Exo·rnate**, *v.* 1539. [f. L. *exornat-*, *exornare*.] To adorn, embellish -1589. Hence †**Exorna·tion**.

†**Exo·rtion**. 1657. [f. L. *exoriri*.] The action of arising or emerging; point of emergence.

†**Exoscula·tion**. 1560. [ad. L. *exosculationem*.] **1.** A hearty kiss -1652. **2.** *Anat.* Anastomosis 1634.

Exosmose (e·ksǫzmōus). 1828. [a. F., formed as if ad. mod.L. *exosmosis*; see next.] = next.

Exosmosis (eksǫzmōu·sis). 1839. [mod.L., f. Gr. ἔξω + ὠσμός pushing. Cf. ENDOSMOSIS.] *Phys.*, etc. The passage of a fluid outwards through a porous septum, to mix with external fluid. Hence **Exosmo·tic** *a.*

Exossate (eks₁ǫ·seᶦt), *v.* 1721. [f. L. *exossat-*, *exossare* to bone, f. *ex-* + *os* (*oss-*).] *trans.* To deprive of bones; †to cause (fruits) to grow without stones. Hence **Exossa·tion**.

†**Exo·sseous**, *a.* [f. L. *exossis* + -EOUS.] Boneless. SIR T. BROWNE.

||**Exostosis** (eksǫstōu·sis). 1736. [mod.L., a. Gr. ἐξόστωσις outgrowth of bone, f. ἐξ + ὀστέον.] **1.** *Path.* The formation of bone on another bone, or on some other structure in the body. Also *concr.* a bony tumour found upon a bone or cartilage. **2.** *Bot.* A diseased condition of plants, in which hard woody projections grow from the main stem or roots 1866. Hence **Exo·stosed** *ppl. a.* affected with e. **Exosto·tic** *a.* pertaining to e.; of the nature of an e.

Exostracize (eksǫ·străsəiz), *v.* 1838. [ad. Gr. ἐξοστρακίζειν.] To banish by ostracism; also *fig.* Hence †**Exo·stracism**.

Exoteric (eksote·rik). 1655. [ad. late L., a. Gr. ἐξωτερικός, f. ἐξωτέρω, compar. of ἔξω outside.]

A. *adj.* **1.** Pertaining to the outside; external 1662. **2.** Suitable to the uninitiated. Hence, of disciples, etc.: Belonging to the outer circle. Opp. to ESOTERIC, q. v. 1655. **3.** *transf.* Current among the outside public; popular 1813.

2. Plato like Pythagoras had e. and esoteric opinions LEWES.

B. *sb.* **1.** *pl.* (After Gr. τὰ ἐξωτερικά) Exoteric doctrines or treatises 1738. **2.** One of the uninitiated; an outsider 1697.

Hence **Exote·ric·al** *a.*, **-ly** *adv.*

Exo·tery. 1763. [? a misprint.] Exoteric doctrine or instruction.

Exotic (egzǫ·tik). 1599. [ad L., a. Gr. ἐξωτικός, f. ἔξω outside.]

A. *adj.* **1.** †Alien; introduced from abroad, not indigenous. †**b.** Drawn from outside -1727. **2.** Foreign (now *rare*); hence †outlandish, barbarous 1629.

1. An exotick and forain territory 1650. An e. plant 1660. **2.** An e. habit and demeanour SWIFT.

B. *sb.* **1.** A plant or †animal of foreign extraction; a foreign plant not acclimatized. Also *transf.* and *fig.* 1645. **2.** A foreigner (*rare*) 1651.

Hence †**Exo·tical** *a.* †**Exo·tical·ly** *adv.*, **-ness**. **Exo·ticism**, tendency to adopt what is e.; e. character; a foreign idiom or expression.

Expand (ekspæ·nd), *v.* ME. [ad. L. *expandere*, f. *ex-* + *pandere* to spread; (cf. *patere*).] **1.** *trans.* To spread out; to open out, unfold; to spread out smooth; also, to display. *lit.* and *fig.* **b.** To develop; to write out in full; in *Alg.* to state at length in a series 1802. **2.** *intr.* for *refl.* To spread itself out; to unfold, open out; to develop 1560. **3.** *trans.* 'To spread out every way' (J.); to cause to increase in bulk; to dilate, enlarge. Also *refl.* 1645. **4.** *intr.* for *refl.* To increase in bulk, swell; to dilate; also *fig.* 1791.

1. E. thy sails POPE. Sicily then lay expanded like a map beneath our eyes L. HUNT. **2.** Streams..expanding..to deep green lakes TYNDALL. **3.** To e. the Spirits 1707, a volume MACAULAY, the chest (*mod.*). **4.** When the air is warmed, it expands 1854. Hence **Expa·nder**, one who, or that which, expands.

Expanding, *ppl. a.* 1776. [f. prec.] **1.** That opens out or is opening out. **2.** That becomes enlarged 1874.

2. *E.-alloy*, such as expands in cooling; *E. bit*, a boring-bit whose diameter is adjustable KNIGHT.

†**Expa·nse**, *a.* ME. [ad. L. *expansus*, *expandere*.] **1.** *Bot.* Expanded, spread out 1819. **2.** Separate; opp. to COLLECT. (See Skeat in *Chaucer's Astrolabe* (1872) Gloss.)

Expanse (ekspæ·ns), *sb.* 1667. [ad. L. *expansum* neut. sb., f. as prec.] **1.** That which is expanded or spread out; a wide extent of anything; *esp.* in *The expanse*: the firmament. **2.** Enlargement, expansion. Also, the amount or distance of expansion. 1860.

1. Let there be Lights High in th' e. of Heaven MILT. *P. L.* VII. 340. The broad e. of brow SCOTT.

†**Expa·nse**, *v.* 1477. [f. L. *expans-*, *expandere*.] = EXPAND *v.* 1, 3. -1800.

Expansible (ekspæ·nsĭb'l), *a.* 1691. [f. as prec.; see -IBLE.] That can be expanded.

Readily e. .. by Heat BOYLE. An e. system of theology 1850. Hence **Expa·nsibi·lity**, e. quality. **Expa·nsibleness**. **Expa·nsibly** *adv.*

Expansile (ekspæ·nsil, -əil), *a.* 1730. [f. L. *expans-* + -ILE.] **1.** Capable of expansion 1776. **2.** Of, or of the nature of, expansion.

1. E. and contractile by heat and cold FORDYCE.

Expansion (ekspæ·nʃən). 1611. [ad. late L. *expansionem*.] **1.** The action or process of expanding or spreading out; the state of being expanded or spread out 1646. **b.** Development; writing out in full; in *Alg.* the process or result of working out a contracted expression 1858. **2.** Anything that is spread out; an expanse 1611. †**3.** Extent; space to which anything is extended; also, pure space -1712. **4.** Dilatation; an instance of this 1664. **b.** *Comm.*, etc. An extension (of business transactions); also, an increase of the circulating medium 1847. **5.** The amount or degree of dilatation 1790. **6.** *concr.* An expanded portion; what (a thing) is expanded into 1860. **7.** *Steam-engine.* The increase in bulk of the steam which takes place in a partially filled cylinder after communication with the boiler is cut off 1782.

1. The easie e. of the wing of a bird GREW. **2.** All that lies Beneath the starr'd e. of the skies BEATTIE. **4.** The love of liberty is simply the instinct in man for e. M. ARNOLD.

attrib. and *Comb.*, as *e.-theory*; **e.-coupling**, one consisting of an e.-drum of thin copper between the extremities of two pipes, which, in elongating, press the sides of the drum in, and draw them out in cooling; **-curb**, in *Horology*, a contrivance for counteracting expansion and contraction; **-drum**, an arrangement by which an occasional change of speed may be effected; **-engine**, one in which the piston is propelled, during the latter part of its course, by the expansion of the steam first introduced; **-gear**, an apparatus for cutting off steam from the cylinder at a given point of the stroke; **-joint**, 'a stuffing-box joint connecting the steam pipes, so as to allow one of them to slide within the enlarged end of the other when the length increases by expansion' (Weale); **-slide**, a slide belonging to the **e.-valve**, a valve which shuts off the steam in its passage to the cylinder.

Expansionist (ekspæ·nʃənist). 1862. [f. prec. + -IST.] One who advocates expansion. Also *attrib.*

Expansive (ekspæ·nsiv), *a.* 1651. [f. L.

expans-, *expandere* + -IVE.] 1. Tending or adapted to expand. 2. Of or pertaining to expansion; depending upon the principle of expansion 1782. 3. Having wide bounds, or a wide range; broad, extensive; comprehensive 1806.

1. E. ether 1805, utterance 1858. An e. force 1886. 2. The said new or e. engine *Watt's Patent* No. 1321. 4. 3. An e. intellect D'ISRAELI, forehead 1834. Hence **Expa·nsive·ly** *adv.*, **-ness. Expansi·vity** (*rare*).

†‖**Expa·nsum.** 1635. [L.] = EXPANSE *sb.* -1794.

†**Expa·nsure.** 1606. [f. L. *expans-* ppl. stem + -URE.] The process of expanding; also, = EXPANSE *sb.* 1. -1611.

‖ **Ex parte, ex-parte** (e:kspā·ɹtė), *advb. phr.* used as *adj.* 1672. [L. Ex, abl. of *pars* side, PART.] 1. orig. *Law.* Made or executed on one side only. 2. *gen.* Of statements, etc.: Made by or in the interest of one side only 1812.

Expatiate (ekspē̆·ʃi͵eⁱt), *v.* 1538. [f. L. *ex(s)patiat-*, *ex(s)patiari*, f. *ex-* + *spatiari* to walk about, f. *spatium* space.] 1. *intr.* To walk about at large, wander at will. Also *transf.* and *fig.* 2. To speak or write at some length; to be copious in description or discussion. Const. *on*, *upon.* 1612. †3. *trans.* To enlarge, extend; to spread abroad; to magnify. Also †*refl.* and *intr.* for *refl.* -1738. †b. 'To allow to range' (J.). *refl.* only. -1695.

1. Winter-flies..crawl out..to e. in the sun LOWELL. 2. Ancient orators used to e. in praise of their country BERKELEY. 3. The Jordan..expatiateth itself into the waters of Merom FULLER.

Hence **Expa·tiater, -or. Expa·tia·tion,** the action of expatiating. **Expa·tiative** *a.* expansive. **Expa·tiatory** *a.* characterized by expatiation.

Expatriate (ekspē̆·tri͵eⁱt), *v.* 1768. [f. ppl. stem of L. *expatriare*, f. *ex-* + *patria* + -ATE[3]. Cf. F. *expatrier.*] 1. *trans.* To drive (a person) away from his native country; to banish 1817. 2. *refl.* (rarely *intr.* for *refl.*) To withdraw from one's native country; to renounce one's allegiance 1784.

1. He apologized at length for proposing to e. the negroes 1856. Hence **Expa·triate** *ppl. a.* expatriated; *sb.* an expatriated person.

Expatriation (ekspē̆:tri͵ē̆ⁱ·ʃən). 1816. [f. prec.; see -ATION.] 1. The action of banishing a person from his own country; the state of being banished. 2. The action of withdrawing from one's country; emigration. Also, renunciation of one's allegiance. 1825.

2. The bishops and clergy sought refuge in e. YEOWELL.

Expect (ekspe·kt), *v.* 1560. [ad. L. *ex(s)pectare* to look out for, f. *ex-* + *spectare*, freq. of *specere* to see.] †1. *intr.* To wait -1765. †2. *trans.* To wait for, await -1822. 3. To look for mentally; to look forward to, regard as about to happen; to anticipate the occurrence or the coming of. Const. with simple *obj.*, *obj.* and *inf.*, or clause as *obj.*; also *absol.* 1601. 4. a. with *can* = 'to look for with likelihood' 1650. b. To look for as due from another; to look for and require 1634. 5. To suppose, surmise *that.* Now *dial.* or *colloq.* 1592.

1. *Heb.* x. 13. 2. Prisons e. the wicked COWPER. 3. They expected us, and we expected to come DE FOE. They did not e. she could ever recover CHETWOOD. 4. b. England expects every man to do his duty NELSON.

Hence †**Expe·ct** *sb.* expectation. **Expe·ctable** *a.* to be expected. **Expe·ctedly** *adv.* according to expectation. **Expe·cter,** †**-or,** one who expects.

Expectance (ekspe·ktăns). 1602. [f. L. *expectantia*, f. *expectantem*; see EXPECTANT.] 1. The action or state of waiting for anything. Somewhat *arch.* 1603. 2. The action of looking for mentally. *Obs.* or *arch.* 1631. †b. The condition of being expected; as, *in expectance* -1640. †3. Ground, reason, or warrant for expecting something -1793. †4. That which is expected 1684.

3. A good estate in possession; fine expectances besides RICHARDSON. So **Expe·ctancy.**

Expectancy (ekspe·ktănsi). 1598. [ad. L. *expectantia*; see prec. and -ANCY.] †1. = EXPECTANCE 1. (*rare.*) 1649. 2. = EXPECTANCE 2; also, an instance of this 1600. b. *esp.* The position of being entitled to anything at some future time, either as a remainder, or reversion, or on the death of some one 1811. c. That from which much is expected (*arch.*) 1602. 3. = EXPECTANCE 2 b; also, anything in expectance 1598. 4. The extent of reasonable expectation 1620.

2. c. Th' expectancie and Rose of the faire State *Haml.* III. i. 160.

Expectant (ekspe·ktănt). ME. [a. F., or ad. L. *expectantem*; see EXPECT.]

A. *adj.* 1. In a state of expectation; waiting, looking out; *esp.* that expects a succession, appointment, or the like. 2. Existing in expectancy; reversionary 1628.

1. An anxious and e. eye SOUTHEY. An e. occupier 1886. An e. (= pregnant) mother 1882. 2. A fee simple e. COKE. Hence **Expe·ctantly** *adv.*

B. *sb.* One who expects an arrival, occurrence, etc.; one who looks to receive something; *esp.* in *Law*, an *expectant heir* 1625.

Expectation (ekspektē̆ⁱ·ʃən). 1538. [ad. L. *expectationem*; see EXPECT.] 1. The action or state of waiting, or of waiting for (something). Now only: Expectant waiting. 1550. b. *Med.* The method of waiting upon the efforts of nature in the treatment of a disease 1628. 2. The action of mentally looking for something to take place; anticipation 1552. 3. Expectancy 1538. 4. Ground or warrant for expecting 1611; *pl.* prospects of inheritance or of testamentary gifts 1669. 5. The condition of being expected; only in phr. *in expectation* 1657. 6. That which is expected or looked forward to 1596. 7. The degree of probability of the occurrence of any contingent event 1832.

2. Our expectations that others will act so and so in such circumstances BUTLER. 3. I have what are called expectations LYTTON. 7. Phr. *Expectation of life* that duration which may reasonably be expected from a life of a given age.

Expectative (ekspe·ktătiv). 1488. [ad. late L. *ex(s)pectativus.*]

A. *adj.* 1. Of or pertaining to expectation; †of prospective effect. 2. Characterized by waiting for events 1611.

B. *sb.* †1. Something in expectation; an expectancy -1758. 2. A mandate given by the pope or king conferring the expectation of a benefit; also called *expectative grace* 1563.

†**Expe·ction.** 1532. [erron. f. EXPECT.] = EXPECTATION. -1658. So **Expe·ctive** *a.* (*rare*) = EXPECTATIVE.

Expectorant (ekspe·ktŏrănt). 1782. [ad. L. *expectorantem*; see next.]

A. *adj.* That promotes expectoration 1811.

B. *sb.* An expectorant medicine.

Expectorate (ekspe·ktŏreⁱt), *v.* 1601. [f. L. *expectorat-*, *expectorare*, f. *ex-* + *pectus* (*pector-*) the breast.] 1. *trans.* †To clear out from the chest or lungs -1678; to eject (phlegm, etc.) from the chest or lungs by coughing, hawking, or spitting 1666. Also *absol.* = to spit 1827. †2. To expel from the breast or mind -1656. Also *refl.* and *intr.* for *refl.*

Expectoration (ekspe·ktŏrē̆ⁱ·ʃən). 1672. [f. prec.; see -ATION.] 1. The action of expectorating; discharge of phlegm from the chest by coughing, etc. 2. *concr.* That which is expectorated, as phlegm 1817.

Expectorative (ekspe·ktŏrătiv). 1666. [f. as prec.; see -IVE.]

A. *adj.* Of or pertaining to expectoration 1883.

B. *sb.* = EXPECTORANT *sb.*

Expede (ekspī·d), *v. Sc.* 1513. [ad. L. *expedire.*] = EXPEDITE *v.* 4.

†**Expe·diate** *a.* [f. F. *expédié*, pa. pple. of *expédier*, ad. med.L. *expediare* (= L. *expedire*).] Expeditious. EVELYN.

[**Expediate** *v.*, prob. error for EXPEDITE.]

Expedience (ekspī·diĕns). 1593. [a. F. *expédience*; see EXPEDIENT.] †1. Dispatch; also, that which requires dispatch; an expedition, etc. -1606. 2. = EXPEDIENCY 1. ? *Obs.* 1619. 3. = EXPEDIENCY 2; *pl.* interested motives, etc. 1608.

Expediency (ekspī·diĕnsi). 1612. [f. EXPEDIENT; see -ENCY.] 1. The quality of being expedient; suitability to the conditions; fitness, advantage; †an advantage. 2. The consideration of what is expedient, as a rule of action; what is politic, as dist. from what is just or right 1612. b. occas. in *pl.* The requirements of expediency 1843.

1. In some perplexity..about the e. of the voyage MIDDLETON. 2. Matters of mere e., that affect neither honor, morality, or religion CHATHAM. Following his duty instead of consulting e. JANE AUSTEN.

Expedient (ekspī·diĕnt). ME. [a. F. *expédient*, ad. L. *expedientem*; see EXPEDITE *v.*]

A. *adj.* †1. Expeditious. SHAKS. 2. Advantageous; fit, proper, or suitable to the circumstances of the case ME. 3. Useful, politic, as opp. to just or right. Often *absol.* 1774.

1. *Rich. III*, I. ii. 217. 2. Those things to know for me be full e. 1519. The most e. settlements for a trading country 1806. 3. Too fond of the right to pursue the e. GOLDSM. Hence **Expe·diently** *adv.*

B. *sb.* †1. That which helps forward, or conduces to an object; a means to an end (*rare*) -1667. 2. A device adopted in an exigency; a resource, shift 1653.

2. Finding out expedients..for shifting from one to another all personal Punishments BREVINT.

Expediential (ekspe:di͵e·nʃăl), *a.* 1850. [see EXPEDIENCY and -AL.] Of, pertaining to, or having regard to, what is expedient. Hence **Expedie·ntially** *adv.*

Expe·diment. 1547. [ad. med.L. *expedimentum*; see EXPEDITE.] †1. An expedient -1677. 2. 'The whole of a person's goods and chattels, bag and baggage' (Wharton).

Expeditate (ekspe·diteⁱt), *v.* 1502. [f. med. L. *expeditat-*, *expeditare*, f. *ex-* + *pedem* foot.] To cut off from (a dog) three claws or the ball of the forefoot; to law. Now *Hist.* Hence **Expedita·tion.**

†**E·xpedite,** *a.* 1545. [ad. L. *expeditus*; see next.] 1. Free of impediments; unimpeded -1694. 2. Of soldiers, etc.: Lightly equipped so as to move quickly -1792. 3. Ready, prompt, expeditious -1792. Hence †**E·xpedite·ly** *adv.*, †**-ness.**

Expedite (e·kspĭdəit), *v.* 1471. [f. L. *expedit-*, *expedire*, f. *ex-* + *pedem* foot.] †1. *trans.* To clear of difficulties -1681. 2. To help forward, hasten the progress of 1618. 3. To perform quickly, dispatch 1471. 4. To dispatch, issue officially; *transf.* to send out (an army, munitions, etc.). Now *rare.* 1606.

1. MILT. *P. L.* x. 474. 2. To e. one's desires RALEIGH, destruction FULLER, a local bill MACAULAY. 3. To e. an order SMEATON. 4. Though such charters be expedited of course BACON. Hence **E·xpediter.**

Expedition (ekspĭdi·ʃən). ME. [ad. L. *expeditionem*; see prec.] †1. The action of expediting; the condition of being expedited; prompt execution or supply; dispatch -1649. 2. A sending or setting forth for some definite purpose; *esp.* a warlike enterprise ME. 3. *concr.* What is thus sent out, e.g. a body of persons, a fleet, etc. 1693. 4. The quality of being 'expedite'; promptness, haste, speed 1529.

1. A bill against Pluralityes is committed. Several other things in e. MARVELL. 2. Mean while the Son On his great E. now appear'd MILT. *P. L.* VII. 193. 3. An e. may consist of a single ship CORY. 4. With winged e., Swift as the lightning glance MILT.

Hence **Expedi·tionary** *a.* of, pertaining to, or sent on an e.; †*sb.* a papal officer who took care of dispatches. †**Expedi·tioner,** one engaged in an e. **Expedi·tionist,** one who goes on an e.

Expeditious (ekspĭdi·ʃəs), *a.* 1599. [f. prec.; see -TIOUS.] 1. Characterized by expedition; performed with expedition 1610. 2. Acting or moving with expedition; speedy.

1. E. measures 1832, travelling 1866. 2. An e. set of workmen 1771. **Expedi·tious-ly** *adv.*, **-ness.**

†**Expe·ditive,** *a.* [f. EXPEDITE + -IVE.] Expeditious. BACON.

Expel (ekspe·l), *v.* ME. [ad. L. *expellere*, f. *ex-* + *pellere* to drive; cf. COMPEL.] 1. *trans.* To drive out; to eject by force. Const. *from* (occas. *out of*); also with double obj. (*from* omitted). 2. To turn out, eject from a society, etc. 1534. †3. To reject from consideration -1742. †4. To keep out. *Haml.* V. i. 239.

1. Power to expell and cast out devils 1577. He sent..two knights..to e. them the convent HUME. To e. an idea from consciousness H. SPENCER. 2. To be expell'd the University 1648.

Hence **Expe·llable** *a.* capable of being, or liable to be, expelled. **Expe·llent** *a.*, also **-ant,** that expels or tends to e.; *sb.* an expellent medicine. **Expe·ller.**

Expend (ekspe·nd), *v.* ME. [ad. L. *expendere*, f. *ex-* + *pendere* to weigh, pay. Cf. also SPEND.] 1. *trans.* To pay away, lay out, spend (money); *esp.* for determinate objects. Const. *in*, *upon.* Also *absol.* Also *transf.* and *fig.* 2. To use up (material or force) in any operation; also *refl.* 1745. **b.** *Naut.* To lose (spars, masts, etc.); to pay out (rope) 1801. †**3.** To weigh mentally -1677.

1. To e. money in beer 1867. *transf.*, etc. To e. time SHAKS., care 1728, wisdom EMERSON, blood 1854. **2.** The English archers .. having expended their arrows, drew their swords JEPHSON.

Hence **Expe·ndable** *a.* **Expe·nder.**

†**Expe·nditor.** 1499. [a. med.L., irreg. f. *expendere*; see prec.] *Law.* One who has charge of expenditure; *spec.* formerly an officer appointed to disburse the money collected by tax for the repair of sewers -1847.

Expenditure (ekspe·nditiŭɹ). 1769. [f. med.L. *expenditus* pa. pple. (irreg. formed after *venditus*) of *expendere* + -URE.] **1.** The action or practice of expending; disbursement; consumption. **2.** The amount expended from time to time 1791.

1. Our e. purchased commerce and conquest BURKE. A vast e. of pains BROWNING. **2.** The Income and E. of Great Britain 1791.

Expense (ekspe·ns). ME. [a. AF., ad. late L. *expensa*, pa. pple. fem. used subst.] †**1.** The action of expending; the state of being expended; disbursement; consumption; loss -1797. †**2.** Money, or a sum, expended -1765. **3.** Burden of expenditure; the cost or sacrifice involved in any course of action, etc. 1632. **b.** In *pl.* esp.: 'Money out of pocket', or its reimbursement ME. **c.** An occasion of expense (*mod.*).

1. All of them..dread a woman of expence FORDYCE. The sun is not wasted by e. of light FRANKLIN. **2.** Where a People thrive, there the income is greater than the expence PETTY. **3. b.** There's expences for thee SHAKS. **c.** His sons are an e. to him (*mod.*).

Comb. **e.-magazine**, a magazine in which a small portion of ammunition is kept for immediate use.

Hence †**Expe·nseful** *a.* costly; also, extravagant. †**Expe·nseless** *a.* without e.

Expensive (ekspe·nsiv), *a.* 1628. [See EXPEND and -IVE; assoc. early with EXPENSE.] **1.** Given to expenditure; lavish; extravagant (now *rare*). **2.** Attended with expense; costly, dear. Also *transf.* 1634.

1. E. of ink BP. HALL, Health and Fortune STEELE, time 1817. Sir Oliver, likewise an e. man CARLYLE. **2.** An e. remedy EVELYN, education FROUDE.

Hence **Expe·nsively** *adv.* **Expe·nsiveness**, the quality of being e.; costliness; extravagance (now *rare*).

Expergefaction (ekspɔ̄ːɹidʒǐfæ·kʃən). Now *rare.* 1638. [ad. late L. *expergefactionem.*] The action of awakening or rousing; the state or fact of being awakened.

Experience (ekspǐ·riĕns), *sb.* ME. [a. F. *expérience*, ad. L. *experientia*, f. *experientem*, *experiri* to put to the test.] †**1.** The action of putting to the test; trial -1668; an experiment -1763. †**2.** Proof by trial; demonstration -1715. **3.** The observation of facts or events, considered as a source of knowledge ME. **4.** The fact of being consciously the subject of a state or condition, or of being consciously affected by an event. Also, an instance of this. ME. **b.** A state of mind or feeling forming part of the inner religious life 1674. **5.** What has been experienced 1607. **6.** Personal knowledge 1553; †an experimental fact, maxim, rule, or device -1698. **7.** The state of having been occupied in any study or practice, in affairs, or in the intercourse of life; the duration or extent of such occupation; the qualifications thereby acquired 1483.

1. Make E. of my loyalty, by some service SHIRLEY. **3.** E. informs us only of what has been, but never of what must be REID. **4.** Experiens..were ynough for me To speke of wo that is in mariage CHAUCER. **b.** A repetition of Christiana's e. BUNYAN. **5.** Profound study of Indian e. MILL. **6.** Most men have the generosity to pay for their own e. 1791. **7.** His yeares but yong, but his e. old *Two Gent.* II. iv. 69.

Experience (ekspǐ·riĕns), *v.* 1533. [f. prec. sb.] †**1.** *trans.* To make experiment of; to test, try -1780; to prove by experience -1750. **2.** To have experience of; to feel, suffer, undergo 1588; to find by experience 1580. †**3.** To give experience to; to train (soldiers). Also in *passive*: To be taught by experience. -1654.

2. What we e. in the present world BUTLER. Phr. *To e. religion* (U.S.): to be converted. **3.** The Footmen..being experienced to run suddenly with the Horse men, leaped into the battail TOPSELL.

Hence **Expe·rienced** *ppl. a.* having experience; wise or skilful through experience; †tested; felt, suffered, undergone. **Expe·riencer**, one who experiences, or †makes experiments.

†**Expe·rient**, *a.* ME. [ad. L. *experientem.*] Experienced -1630.

Experiential (ekspǐᵊri,e·nʃăl), *a.* 1816. [f. L. *experientia* + -AL.] Of, pertaining to, or derived from, experience or observation.

Phr. *E. philosophy*: the system which derives all knowledge from experience.

Hence **Experie·ntialism**, the doctrine that all knowledge is derived from experience. **Experie·ntialist**, an adherent of experientialism. **Experie·ntially** *adv.*

Experiment (ekspe·rimĕnt). ME. [a. OF., ad. L. *experimentum*, f. *experiri* to try.] **1.** The action of trying anything; a test, trial. Now *arch.* **2.** A procedure adopted in uncertainty whether it will answer the purpose 1594. **3.** An action or operation undertaken in order to discover something unknown, to test a hypothesis, or establish or illustrate some known truth ME. **4.** Experimentation 1678. †**5.** Experience; an instance of this. Const. *of.* -1741. †**6.** Practical proof; an example -1684.

2. It is good..not to try Experiments in States BACON. **4.** This is proved by e. 1678. **5.** I know by som experiments which I have had of you HOWELL.

Experiment (ekspe·rimĕnt), *v.* 1481. [f. prec. sb.] †**1.** *trans.* To experience -1727. †**2.** To ascertain or establish by trial -1812. †**3.** To make an experiment upon, test, try -1776. **4.** *intr.* To make an experiment or experiments. Const. *on.* 1787.

4. A person who has experimented with a reflector 1837. Hence **Expe:rimenta·tion**, the action or process of experimenting; a series of experiments. **Expe:rime·ntative** *a.* inclined to make an experiment; of the nature of an experiment. †**Expe·rimenta:tor** (*rare*), an experimenter; also, an empiric. **Expe·rimenter, -or, Expe·rimentist**, one who makes or tries experiments.

Experimental (ekspe:rime·ntal). ME. [f. as prec. + -AL.]

A. *adj.* **1.** Based on or derived from experience; founded on experience only. **2.** Based on, derived from, or ascertained by experiment 1570. **3.** Tentative 1818. **4.** Relating to experiments; used in or for making experiments 1792.

2. Phr. *E. philosophy*: (*a*) the philosophy which insists on experiment as the necessary foundation of all reasoned conclusions; (*b*) Physics or 'natural philosophy' as demonstrated by means of experiments (now *rare*). So also, *e. chemistry, physics, science.* Hence *e. philosopher*, etc. Hence **Expe:rime·ntally** *adv.* by experience; by means of experiment.

B. *sb.* A trial; an experimental proof; a datum of experience; in *pl.* experimental knowledge 1628.

Hence **Expe:rime·ntalism**, the principles of the e. school in philosophy or science; e. research. **Expe:rime·ntalist**, one who experiments in some branch of science; one who is fond of trying experiments. **Expe:rime·ntalize**, *v. intr.* to make or try experiments.

†**Expe:rimenta·rian.** 1661. [f. EXPERIMENT *sb.* + -ARIAN.]

A. *adj.* Relying on experiment -1816.

B. *sb.* An experimental philosopher 1690.

Experimented (ekspe·rimĕntĕd), *ppl. a.* 1477. [f. EXPERIMENT *v.*] **1.** Experienced; practised *in* (an art). Now *rare.* †**2.** Proved or known by experience -1807. †**3.** Met with in experience -1812.

†**Experre·ction.** [f. L. *experrect-*, *expergisci* to wake up.] The action of waking up. HOLLAND.

Expert (ekspɔ̄·ɹt), *a.*[1] ME. [a. OF., ad. L. *expertus*, *experiri*; see EXPERIENCE *sb.*] †**1.** Experienced (*in*), having experience (*of*) -1672. **2.** Trained by practice, skilled. Const. *at*, *in*, †*of*, *to* with *inf.* ME. †**3.** Tried, proved by experience -1612.

1. A Militia..e. in war PETTY. **2.** Maystres..That were of lawe e. and curious CHAUCER. An e. Arithmeticien DEE. E. Mariners 1632. E. Valour 1665. **3.** His Pylot Of verie e., and approu'd Allowance *Oth.* II. i. 49. Hence **Expe·rt-ly** *adv.*, **-ness.**

†**Expe·rt**, *a.*[2] ME. [ad. L. *expertem*, f. *ex-* + *pars* (*part-*).] Devoid of, free from -1660.

Expert (e·kspɔ̄ɹt), *sb.* 1825. [a. mod.F. *expert* (the adj. used subst.); see EXPERT *a.*[1]] **1.** One who is EXPERT (sense 2) 1853. **2.** One whose special knowledge or skill causes him to be an authority; a specialist; also *attrib.* 1825.

1. An e. at hurdle-making ROGERS. **2.** My writing was well known; experts swore that the forgery was by me BESANT. *attrib.* E. evidence, witness, etc.

†**Expe·rt**, *v.* ME. [f. L. *expert-*, *experiri* to try.] To experience; to know by experience -1587.

‖**Expertise** (ekspəɹtī·z). 1869. [Fr.] Expert opinion or knowledge; also, the quality or state of being expert.

†**Expe·tible**, *a.* 1569. [ad. L. *expetibilis*, f. (ult.) *ex-* + *petere* to seek.] To be wished for; desirable -1679.

Expiable (e·kspiăb'l), *a.* 1570. [a. F., ad. L. *expiabilis*; see EXPIATE.] Capable of being *expiated*; as, *an e. wrong.*

†**E·xpiate**, *ppl. a.* [ad. L. *expiatus*; see next.] Of an appointed time: Fully come. *Rich. III*, III. iii. 23.

Expiate (e·kspi,eᶦt), *v.* 1594. [f. L. *expiat-*, *expiare* to atone for fully, f. *ex-* + *piare* to propitiate, f. *pius* devout.] **1.** *trans.* To avert by religious ceremonies. *Obs.* exc. *Antiq.* 1611. †**2.** To purify with religious rites -1660. **3.** To extinguish the guilt of 1608. **4.** To pay the penalty of 1665. **5.** To make reparation for 1626. Also †*intr.* with *for.* †**6.** To extinguish by suffering to the full; to end by death -1615.

2. To Lustrate and E. a City STANLEY. **3.** An Affront that nothing but Blood can e. ADDISON. **4.** To e. the act with one's life STUBBS. **5.** To e. wrongs by benefits EMERSON. **6.** SHAKS. *Sonn.* xxii.

Hence **E·xpiatist, E·xpiator**, one who atones fully for.

Expiation (ekspi,ēᶦ·ʃən). 1482. [ad. L. *expiationem*; see prec.] **1.** The action of expiating or making atonement for, etc.; also, the condition of being expiated. **2.** The means by which atonement is made 1538.

1. I will found masses for his soul, in e. of my guilt SCOTT. Phr. *Fast* (or *feast*) *of Expiation*: a Jewish ceremony observed on the 10th day of Tisri, when the High Priest made e. for his own sins and those of the people. **2.** Human victims as an e. for guilt ROBERTSON. Hence **Expia·tional** *a.* pertaining to e.

Expiatory (e·kspiătəri), *a.* 1548. [ad. L. *expiatorius*; see EXPIATOR and -ORY.] Having the attribute of expiating; serving to expiate. Const. *of.* So †**Expiato·rious** *a.*

†**E·xpilate**, *v.* [f. L. *expilat-*, *expilare*, f. *ex-* + *pilare* to plunder.] *trans.* To pillage, plunder. BP. HALL.

Hence **Expila·tion**, the action of pillaging; *concr.* plunder. †**E·xpilator**, a pillager.

Expirant (ekspəi·rănt). *rare.* 1836. [ad. L. *ex(s)pirantem*; see EXPIRE.] A name for a supposed vessel in plants, which assists in evaporation.

Expiration (ekspirēᶦ·ʃən). 1526. [ad. L. *ex(s)pirationem*; see EXPIRE.] **1.** The action of breathing out (air, etc.); emission 1642. **2.** The action of breathing out air from the lungs. Also *transf.* of plants. 1603. †**3.** Exhalation; that which is expired; an exhalation -1667. †**4.** The action of breathing one's last; death -1807. Also †*transf.* and *fig.* **5.** The coming to an end; termination, close 1562.

1. Regular inspirations and expirations of air, by caverns and fissures MORSE. **3.** The true Cause of Cold, is an E. from the Globe of the Earth BACON. **4.** The Lord Treasurer..had notice of the Clark's e. 1647. **5.** A fortnight after the e. of the treaty 1647.

Expiratory (ekspəiᵊ·rătəri), *a.* 1847. [f. L. *ex(s)pirare*; see EXPIRE *v.* and -ORY.] Of or pertaining to expiration.

Expire (ekspəiᵊ·ɹ), *v.* ME. [ad. F. *expirer*, ad. L. *ex(s)pirare* to breathe out, f. *ex-* + *spirare.*] **1.** *trans.* To breathe out (air, etc.) from the lungs. Also *absol.* †**2.** To give out, emit, exhale -1808. †**3.** *intr.* To pass out in, or like, breath; hence, of the winds, etc.: To rush forth -1729. †**4.** *trans.* To breathe out in the article of death -1720. **5.** *intr.* To breathe one's last, die ME. Also *transf.* **6.** To come to an end; to terminate; to become void; to become extinct 1450. †**7.** To cause to expire or cease; to put an end to -1612.

1. *absol.* [The Whales] expired with a rushing sound, the instant the blow-hole was exposed GOSSE. **2.** Ev'ry shrub expires perfume CHURCHILL. **3.** The linstocks touch, the ponderous ball expires DRYDEN. **5.** God onely knows..what becomes of a mans spirit, when he expireth HOBBES. *transf.* A lamp that was just expiring GOLDSM. **6.** Until your date e. SHAKS.

A truce which expired in .. 1635 B. HARRIS. The title of the daughters expired on the birth of a son BURKE. 7. *Rom. & Jul.* I. iv. 109.
var. †E·xpirate (in sense 1). Hence †**Expi·re** *sb.* expiry. **Expi·ree·**, an ex-convict. **Expi·rer,** one who expires; also, an *expiree*.

Expiring (ekspəi·riŋ), *ppl. a.* 1609. [f. prec.] That expires; breathing out air from the lungs, etc.; breathing his or its last, dying; coming to an end.
Thy e. breath HABINGTON. *fig.* Bubbles in e. foam RUSKIN. The e. year 1705, lease BYRON.

Expiry (ekspəi·ri). 1752. [f. EXPIRE *v.* + -Y.] = EXPIRATION 4, 5.
The e. of a term 1862, a contract SMILES.

Expiscate (ekspi·skeit), *v.* Chiefly *Sc.* 1611. [f. L. *expiscat-*, *expiscari*, f. *ex-* + *piscari* to fish, f. *piscis*.] *trans.* To fish out; hence, to find out by scrutiny.
To e. intelligible reasons 1864. Hence **Expisca·tion**, the act of expiscating. **Expi·scator. Expi·scatory** *a.* tending to fish out (*rare*).

Explain (eksplē·n), *v.* 1513. [ad. L. *explanare* to make plain, f. *ex-* + *planus* flat, PLAIN.] †1. To make smooth -1650. †2. To open out, spread out flat. Also *refl.* and *intr.* for *refl.* -1721. 3. To unfold; to make plain or intelligible 1513. 4. To interpret 1608. 5. To account for 1736. 6. *refl.* To make oneself understood, speak plainly 1624. 7. *intr.* a. To say in explanation *that* 1867. †b. To speak one's mind *against*, *upon* -1764.
2. The Horse-Chesnut is..ready to e. its leaf 1684. 3. To e. what is meant by the nature of man BUTLER. 4. To define fire by heat would be to e. a thing by itself BERKELEY. Phr. *To e. away*: to do away with by explanation.
Hence **Explai·nable** *a.* capable of explanation. **Explai·ner.**

†**Explai·t**, *v.* Also explat(e. [? f. Ex- + PLAIT *v.*] To unravel. B. JONS.

E·xplanate, *a.* 1846. [ad. L. *explanatus*; see EXPLAIN.] *Entom.*, etc. Spread out flat.

Explanation (eksplănē·ʃən). ME. [ad. L. *explanationem*; see EXPLAIN.] 1. The action or process, or an instance, of explaining. 2. That which explains, makes clear, or accounts for; a method of explaining 1610. 3. A mutual declaration of the sense of spoken words, motives of actions, etc., with a view to adjust a misunderstanding and reconcile differences; hence, a mutual understanding or reconciliation 1840.
1. I pass to the E. of the following Table EVELYN. 2. My E. of the Mystery of Godliness H. MORE. The e. offered..proves to be erroneous SIR B. BRODIE. 3. To come to an e. with one's father (*mod.*).

Explanative (eksplæ·nătiv), *a.* 1750. [f. L. *explanare*.] Explanatory.

Explana·to-, comb. f. L. *explanatus* EXPLANATE, in sense 'spread, or spreading out, in a plane'.

Explanatory (eksplæ·nătəri), *a.* 1618. [f. L. *explanatus* + -ORY.] Serving to explain, containing an explanation; having the function of explaining.
A short essay, accompanied with two e. prints HOGARTH. Hence **Expla·natorily** *adv.* **Expla·natoriness**, e. quality.

†**Explees**, obs. f. ESPLEES, *Law*.

†**Exple·te**, *v.* Also †**explea·t.** ME. [f. L. *explet-*, *explere*, f. *ex-* + *plere* to fill.] 1. *trans.* To fill out; to complete (a period of time) -1657. 2. To do fully -1611. Hence †**Exple·tion**, fulfilment.

Expletive (e·ksplĭtiv, eksplī·tiv). 1612. [ad. L. *expletivus* serving to fill out; see prec.]
A. *adj.* 1. Serving to fill out; introduced merely to fill up; *occas.*, redundant 1656. 2. Tending or seeking to supply a loss; compensative. HALLAM.
1. He useth them [oaths] as e. phrases .. to plump his speech BARROW. 2. E. justice HALLAM.
B. *sb.* 1. An expletive word or phrase; *esp.* an oath 1612. 2. A person or thing that merely serves to fill up space 1688.
1. Expletives he very early ejected from his verses JOHNSON. 2. A sort of e. at the table, serving to stop gaps 1872.
Hence **Expletive-ly** *adv.*, **-ness.** So **E·xpletory** *a.* serving to fill up.

Explicable (e·ksplikăb'l), *a.* 1556. [ad. L. *explicabilis*.] That may be explained or accounted for.

Explicate (e·kspliкeit), *v.* 1531. [f. L. *explicat-*, *explicare*, f. *ex-* + *plicare* to fold, PLY.] †1. *trans.* To unfold; to expand; to display -1710. †2. To disentangle -1713. 3. To bring out what is implicit in 1628. 4. = EXPLAIN *v.* 3. Now *rare.* 1531. †5. = EXPLAIN *v.* 5. -1729.
1. The leaves..e. themselves SHARROCK. 4. To e. obscure passages S. CLARKE. 5. Perceptions..which ..it may not be very easy at first view to e. BUTLER.
Hence †**E·xplicate** *ppl. a.* unfolded; fully stated; explained. †**E·xplicator** (*rare*).

Explication (eksplikē·ʃən). 1528. [a. F., ad. L. *explicationem*; see prec.] 1. The action or process of expanding, developing, or explaining; explanation, interpretation; †an exposition; †a paraphrase. †2. = EXPLANATION 3. -1745.
1. A better e. of a controverted line JOHNSON.

Explicative (e·ksplikeitiv), *a.* 1627. †1. Tending to unfold (itself). 2. Explanatory; explicit; in *Logic*, = ESSENTIAL. 1649.
2. The new judgments..are all e. or analytic E. CAIRD. Hence **E·xplicatively** *adv.*

Explicatory (e·ksplikătəri), *a.* 1625. [See -ORY [2].] Having the function of explaining.

‖**E·xplicit.** ME. [med.L.; app. short for *explicitus* (*est liber*) lit. 'the book is unrolled'. Also taken as a vb. in 3rd pers. sing., 'Here ends', with pl. *expliciunt*.] A word used to indicate the end of a book, etc. b. as *sb.* The last words or lines of a volume or section of a book; *fig.* conclusion, finis 1658.

Explicit (ekspli·sit), *a.* 1613. [a. F. *explicite*, ad. L. *explicitus*, *explicare*; see EXPLICATE *v.*] †1. Free from folds or intricacies -1697. 2. Developed in detail; hence, clear, definite 1651. 3. Of declarations, etc.: Distinctly expressing all that is meant; leaving nothing merely implied; express 1613. 4. Of persons, etc.: Speaking out fully all that is meant; having no reserves; outspoken 1726.
1. The plot, whether intricate or e. MILT. 2. *E. faith, belief* (Theol.): acceptance of a doctrine with distinct apprehension of all that it involves; opp. to *implicit faith*. 3. There was an e. consent and an implicit consent CROMWELL. Hence **Expli·citly** *adv.* expressly. **Expli·citness.**

Explode (eksplōu·d), *v.* 1538. [ad. L. *explodere*, *explaudere* to drive off the stage by noise, f. *ex-* + *plaudere* to clap; cf. APPLAUD, PLAUDIT.] †1. *trans.* To clap and hoot off the stage; hence *gen.* to drive away with expressions of disapprobation. Also *fig.* -1849. 2. To reject with scorn; also, to discard. Still used occas. in *pass.* with sense: To be disused as obsolete. 1538. 3. To cause to be rejected; to discredit; †to bring into disuse 1635. †4. To drive forth (air); to drive out with violence and sudden noise -1826. 5. *intr.* To go off with a loud report, or to fly in pieces, under the influence of suddenly developed internal energy. Also *transf.* and *fig.* 1790. 6. *trans.* To cause to go off with a loud noise; to blow up. Also *transf.* and *fig.* 1794. 7. *Phonetics.* To utter with a puff of breath, as one of the stop consonants *p*, *b*, *t*, *d*, *k*, *g*.
1. Vertue and Wisdom..were hissed out, and exploded by the common people BURTON. 2. But the court *una voce* exploded this reason, and said [etc.] BACON. 3. To e. a lie LIDDON, a fallacy 1881. Hence **Explo·dent** (*Phonetics*) = EXPLOSIVE B. 1. **Explo·der**, one who or that which explodes; a contrivance for exploding gunpowder, etc.

Exploit (eksploi·t), *sb.* ME. [a. OF. *esplait*, *esploit*:—(ult.) L. *explicitum* pple. neut.: see EXPLICATE.] †1. Advantage; furtherance. Const. *of.* -1525. †2. The endeavour to gain advantage or mastery over; hence, a military or naval enterprise -1755. 3. An act or deed; a brilliant feat 1538. †4. *Law.* A citation or summons; a writ -1682.
2. *All's Well* IV. i. 41. 3. For many years it was counted a great e. to pass this strait DE FOE.

Exploit (eksploi·t), *v.* ME. [ad. F. *exploiter*:—L. **explicitare*, freq. of *explicare*; see EXPLICATE.] †1. *trans.* To achieve -1687. †2. To act with effect; to get on -1602. 3. To work (a mine, etc.); to turn to account 1838. 4. *transf.* To utilize for selfish purposes; to make capital out of 1847. 5. *intr.* To conduct mining operations *for* 1887.
1. They knewe wel that they shold no thyng exployte of their entente CAXTON. 3. To e. mineral resources 1865, the riches of the East 1890.
Hence **Exploi·table** *a.* capable of being exploited. **Exploi·tative** *a.* concerned with exploiting. **Exploi·ter. Exploi·ture**, the action of exploiting, †achieving, or developing.

Exploitation (eksploitē·ʃən). 1803. [a. F.; see prec.] The action of turning to account; the action of utilizing for selfish purposes.
The e. of the credulous public 1868. So **Exploi·tage.**

†**Explo·rate**, *v.* 1549. [f. ppl. stem of L. *explorare*.] = EXPLORE. -1646. Hence **Explo·rative** *a.* exploratory; inclined to make explorations. **Explo·ratively** *adv.*

Exploration (eksplorē·ʃən). 1543. [ad. L. *explorationem*; see EXPLORE.] †1. The action of examining; scrutiny -1655. 2. *Med.*, etc. The examination of an organ, a wound, etc. by the use of the finger, a probe, or the like 1860. 3. The action of exploring; an instance of this 1823.
2. E. of the Rectum 1880. 3. E. of the sources of the Nile 1880.

Explorator (e·ksplorē:təɹ). 1450. [a. L.; see EXPLORE.] One who or that which explores; †a scout; an 'electrical explorer'.

Exploratory (eksplǫ·rătəri), *a.* 1620. [ad. L. *exploratorius*; see EXPLORE.] Of or pertaining to exploration; serving or intended for exploration; bent on exploration.

Explore (eksplōə·ɹ), *v.* 1585. [ad. F. *explorer*, ad. L. *explorare*, ? f. *ex-* + *plorare* to make to flow, f. *pluere* to flow.] 1. *trans.* To seek to find out; †to search for; to make proof of (MILT. *P. L.* II. 632). 2. To look into closely, scrutinize; to pry into 1592; to probe (a wound) 1767. 3. *esp.* To search into (a country, etc.); to go into or range over for the purpose of discovery 1616. 4. *intr.* To conduct operations in search *for* 1823.
1. To e. The city's strength MASSINGER, a fit opportunity 1822. 2. To e. a bookstall LAMB. 3. He..recommended us to e. Wapping BOSWELL. Hence **Explo·rable** *a. rare.* **Explo·rement**, exploration.

Explorer (eksplōə·rəɹ). 1684. [f. prec.] One who explores (a country, etc.); that which examines or †tests; *spec.* an apparatus for exploring a wound or a cavity in a tooth.
Phr. *Electrical e.*: an apparatus for detecting a bullet or other metallic substance in the tissues.

Exploring (eksplōə·riŋ), *vbl. sb.* 1841. [f. as prec.] The action of EXPLORE *v.* Also *attrib.*, as in *exploring needle, trochar*, etc.

Explosible (eksplōu·zib'l), *a.* 1799. [f. L. *explos-* ppl. stem + -IBLE; see EXPLODE.] Capable of being exploded.

Explosion (eksplōu·ʒən). 1656. [ad. L. *explosionem*; see EXPLODE.] †1. The action of rejecting with scorn -1796. 2. The action of driving out, or of issuing forth, with violence and noise 1667; *spec.* explosive utterance (of a sound) 1879. 3. The action of going off with a loud noise, or of bursting, under the influence of suddenly developed internal energy 1744; the resulting noise 1775. Also *transf.* 4. A bursting forth into sudden activity; an outburst (of anger, laughter, etc.) 1817.
2. Frequent explosions of fire and smoke, emitted from the mountain MORSE. 3. The e. of a bomb 1762, of a glass jar, battery, etc. IMISON, of powder 1816. 4. A desperate conspiracy which threatened an e. LD. CASTLEREAGH.

Explosive (eksplōu·siv). 1667. [f. L. *explodere*; see EXPLODE and -IVE.]
A. *adj.* 1. Tending to drive or burst forth with violence and noise. 2. *spec.* Of a consonant-sound: Produced by explosion of breath; stopped 1854. 3. Of, pertaining to, or of the nature of, an explosion 1844.
1. E. power 1667, nitre BURKE. 2. The e. consonants *b*, *d*, *g*, *p*, *t*, and *k* 1854. 3. E. laughs DICKENS.
B. *sb.* 1. An explosive consonant (see A. 2) 1878. 2. An explosive agent or compound 1874.
2. The principal explosives used in mining are gunpowder..nitroglycerin [etc.] RAYMOND.
Hence **Explo·sive-ly** *adv.*, **-ness.**

Expoliate, -ation: see EXSPOLIATE, -ATION.

†**Expo·lish**, *v.* [ad. L. *expolire*; assim. to *polish*.] *trans.* To polish thoroughly. HEYWOOD.

†**Expo·ne**, *v.* ME. [ad. L. *exponere*, f. *ex-* +

ponere to put, place. Since 16th c. chiefly *Sc.*] **1.** *trans.* To expound -1632. **2.** To expend (effort, money) -1587. **3.** To expose -1651.

Exponent (ekspōᵘ·nĕnt). 1581. [ad. L. *exponentem*; see prec.]

A. *adj.* That sets forth or interprets.

B. *sb.* **1.** One who sets forth in words, expounds, or interprets. Also, that which serves to interpret. 1812. **2.** *Algebra.* A symbol denoting a power; an index. Now written at the right hand of and above the symbol of the quantity affected by it. 1706. **3.** He who or that which sets forth as a representative or index 1825.

1. This form of discontent found its e. in John Wycliffe FROUDE. 2. Phr. †*E. of the Ratio*: the quotient which arises when the antecedent is divided by the consequent. 3. Price is the e. of exchangeable value 1833.

Exponential (ekspone·nʃăl). 1704. [f. prec. + -(I)AL.]

A. *adj.* **1.** That sets forth or exhibits (*rare*) 1730. **2.** *Math.* Involving the unknown quantity or variable as an exponent. So *e. equation, function, quantity*, etc.

2. *E. series*, the infinite series $1 + x + \frac{1}{2}x^2 + \frac{1}{6}x^3$ etc.

B. *sb. Math.* An exponential quantity or function; *spec.* the Napierian base *e* raised to the power denoted by the variable; the Napierian antilogarithm of the variable 1784.

Exponible (ekspōᵘ·nib'l). 1569. [ad. med. L. *exponibilis*; see EXPONE and -BLE.]

A. *adj.* That admits or requires explanation; *spec.* in *Logic*, of a proposition, that requires restatement for use in a syllogism 1788.

B. *sb.* An exponible proposition.

Export (ekspōᵊ·ɹt), *v.* 1485. [ad. L. *exportare*, f. *ex-* + *portare* to carry.] †**1.** *trans.* To take away, carry off. Also *fig.* -1691. **2.** *Comm.* To send out (commodities) from one country to another. Also *transf.* and *fig.* 1665.

1. They e. honour from a man and make him a returne in Enuy BACON. 2. To e. Corn MANLEY, black cattle PETTY, olives 1841. Hence **Expo·rtable** *a.* and *sb.*

Export (e·kspoɹt), *sb.* 1690. [f. prec.] *Comm.* That which is exported; also, the action of exporting, exportation.

1. Our commerce, the imports and exports of the nation BURKE. 2. The e. of arms to Spain 1874.

Comb.: **e. bill**, a bill drawn against exported goods; **e. duty**, a duty paid on exported goods.

Exportation (ekspoɹtēⁱ·ʃən). 1610. [a. F., ad. L. *exportationem*; see EXPORT.] †**1.** The action of carrying or sending out -1789. **2.** *Comm.* The sending out (of commodities) from one country to another 1641. **3.** quasi-*concr.* That which is exported; †*pl.* exports 1664.

Exporter (ekspōᵊ·ɹtəɹ). 1691. [f. as prec.] One who exports; an export trader.

Expose (ekspōᵘ·z), *v.* 1474. [a. F. *exposer*, f. L. *ex-* + *pausare*, taken as repr. L. *ponere* in compounds. See COMPOSE.] **1.** *trans.* To put out; 'to cast out to chance' (J.); *esp.* to abandon (an infant) 1611. **2.** To leave without shelter or defence; †to imperil 1477. **3.** To lay open (to danger, ridicule, etc.); to render accessible or liable *to* action or influence 1474. **4.** To exhibit openly 1623; *Eccl.* to exhibit (the Host, relics, etc.) for adoration or veneration 1644. **5.** To put up *for* (or *to*) sale. Now chiefly *Sc.* 1610. **6.** To make known, disclose (secrets, etc.). Formerly: To set forth, explain. 1483. **7.** To unmask, show up 1693. †**b.** In 17-18th c.: To hold up to ridicule (what is not ridiculous) -1772. **8.** *Photog.* To subject (a plate, etc.) to the action of actinic rays 1848.

1. This practice of exposing children HUME. 2. To e. the gunners 1885. 3. Exposed to severe trials 1865, to inharmonious influences J. MARTINEAU. 4. The Beggar, who exposes his Sores STEELE. To e. a card 1870, a vein of quartz RAYMOND. 6. The whole truth is not always to be exposed BOSWELL. 7. To e. the Follies of Men DRYDEN, an imposture MOZLEY. Hence **Expo·sal**, exposure. **Expo·sedness. Expo·ser.**

‖**Exposé** (ekspoze). 1803. [Fr.; pa. pple. of *exposer*.] **1.** A recital of facts and particulars. **2.** A showing up of something discreditable 1831. (Also written **Expose** (ekspōᵘ·z) *U.S.* 1715.)

Exposition (ekspozi·ʃən). ME. [a. F., ad. L. *expositionem*; see EXPONE.] **1.** The action of exposing, or the condition of being exposed 1530. †**2.** = EXPOSURE 3. -1834. **3.** The action of putting out to public view; a display, show, exposure 1649; an EXHIBITION 1868. **b.** *Eccl.* in spec. use: see EXPOSE *v.* 4. **4.** The action of setting forth, or of explaining; a detailed explanation or interpretation ME. **5.** *Logic.* As tr. Gr. ἔκθεσις: the selection of some sensible object, in order to prove a general relation apprehended by the intellect 1588.

2. An Easterly E. EVELYN. 3. An e. of the holy wafer BECKFORD. E. on the pillory 1836. The World's Columbian E. at Chicago 1891. 4. The exposicioun of this holy praier CHAUCER. You know the Law, your e. Hath beene most sound SHAKS. The great expositions of feudal custom STUBBS. Hence **Exposi·tional** *a.* of the nature of an e.

Expositive (ekspǫ·zitiv), *a.* 1535. [ad. L. *expositivus*, f. *exposit-*, *exponere*.] Descriptive; explanatory.

Expositor (ekspǫ·zitəɹ). ME. [ad. (ult.) L. *expositorem*; see EXPOUND.] One who, or that which, sets forth in detail, explains, or expounds.

Expository (ekspǫ·zitəri), *a.* 1628. = [ad. med.L. *expositorius* (Boethius); see prec.] Of, pertaining to, or of the nature of, exposition; containing an exposition; explanatory.

A glossary or e. index to the poetical writers JOHNSON.

‖**Ex post facto** (eks pōᵘst fæ·kto). 1649. [med.L.; = 'from what is done afterwards'. *Post facto* for *postfacto* is erroneous.] From an after act or deed; = 'after the fact'. **b.** As quasi-*adj.* Done after another thing, and operating retrospectively, *esp.* in *Ex post facto law* 1789.

b. They might have objected to the tax had it been *ex post facto* McCULLOCH.

Expostulate (ekspǫ·stiŭlēⁱt), *v.* 1534. [f. L. *expostulat-*, *expostulare*, f. *ex-* + *postulare*; see POSTULATE.] †**1.** *trans.* To demand -1670. †**2.** To complain of; to plead *with* a person about; to debate (a matter) as an aggrieved person -1789. †**3.** *intr.* To complain; to discourse -1773. **4.** To reason earnestly and kindly *with* (a person), *about, for, on*, or *upon* (a thing), for the purpose of reprehension or dissuasion 1574.

3. 3 *Hen. VI*, II. v. 135. 4. He expostulated with him on the impropriety of such conduct to strangers LIVINGSTONE. Hence **Expo·stulator.**

Expostulation (ekspǫ·stiulēⁱ·ʃən). 1586. [ad. L. *expostulationem*; see prec.] **1.** The action of expostulating; earnest and kindly protest. **2.** An uttered remonstrance, protest, or reproof 1597.

2. That pathetick E. ..of Ezekiel. Why will ye die! 1748.

Expostulatory (ekspǫ·stiŭlătəri), *a.* 1586. [f. EXPOSTULATE + -ORY.] Characterized by, or of the nature of, expostulation.

Mr. Jane..wrote me an e. letter BP. WARBURTON.

†**Expo·sture.** [f. EXPOSE, after *posture*, etc.] = EXPOSURE. *Cor.* IV. i. 36.

Exposure (ekspōᵘ·ʒiŭɹ). 1606. [app. f. EXPOSE, after *enclosure*, or the like; see -URE.] **1.** The action of exposing; the fact or state of being exposed (see EXPOSE *v.*). **2.** *concr.* A surface laid open to view, or to the operation of any agency 1611. **3.** The manner or degree in which anything is exposed; *esp.* situation with regard to sun and wind; aspect 1664.

1. Our naked Frailties..That suffer in e. *Macb.* II. iii. 133. Free e. to cold 1844. The e. of a forgery 1873. *Photog.* Ten seconds of e. 1847 (cf. EXPOSE *v.* 8). 3. The Fruits of the Northern E. ripen last of all 1710.

Expound (ekspau·nd), *v.* [ME. *expounen*, *expounde*, ad. OF. *espondre* :—L. *exponere*. The *d* is excrescent.] **1.** *trans.* To set forth in detail. **2.** To explain; *esp.* to interpret (Scripture, religious formularies, etc.) ME. †**3.** To expose to view -1664.

1. I have..an excellent interpretation..which I will e. to you JOWETT. 2. To e. an Ambiguyte 1511, a parable UDALL. The Pope was forced to e. himself BRAMHALL. 3. First, he expounded both his Pockets BUTLER *Hud.* II. iii. 1087. Hence **Expou·nder**, one who or (occas.) that which expounds.

Express (ekspre·s), *a. adv.* and *sb.*[1] ME. [ad. F. *exprès* (fem. *expresse*), ad. L. *expressus*, *exprimere*; see EXPRESS *v.*]

A. *adj.* **1.** Exactly resembling, exact. Now chiefly with reminiscence of *Heb.* i. 3. 1513. †**2.** Stated -1686. **3.** Expressed and not merely implied; definite, explicit; unmistakable in import ME. Hence of persons, a state of mind, etc.: †Explicit, fixed -1778. **4.** Done, made, or sent on purpose ME.

1. Hee Created thee, in the Image of God E. MILT. *P.L.* VII. 528. 3. E. testimony 1662, contracts, malice BLACKSTONE. Sometimes by e., more often by tacit understanding BRYCE. 4. E. laws were made to prevent [it] PRIESTLEY.

Phrases. *E. train*: orig. = 'special train'; later, a passenger train running expressly to one particular place; now, a fast train stopping only at important stations. Hence *E. speed. E. delivery*: (in the Postal service) immediate delivery by special messenger; so *e. fee, messenger, packet*, etc. *E. rifle*: one with a high initial velocity and a low trajectory.

B. *adv.* †**1.** Clearly; distinctly -1712. †**2.** Directly *against*; exactly; completely -1513. **3.** Specially, on purpose; hence, with speed; now, by express messenger or train ME.

3. A piece of news worth sending e. LOWELL.

C. *sb.*[1] **1.** = *E. messenger*: see A. 4. Hence *transf.* The message sent by an express 1642. **2.** Short for *e.-train, e. rifle* 1848. **3.** *U.S.* An institution or agency for the transmission of parcels 1858.

Hence **Expre·ss** *v.* to send by express. (*U.S.*) **Expre·ssage**, the sending of a parcel by express; the charge for this. **Expre·ssly** *adv.* in an e. manner. **Expre·ssness.**

†**Express** (ekspre·s), *sb.*[2] 1513. [f. the vb. Cf. late L. *expressus*.] **1.** The action of expressing; an instance of this. Const. of. -1716. **b.** A manifestation. (Revived by Kingsley with stress *e·xpress*.) -1663. **2.** A phrase; an utterance; an injunction -1677. **3.** A graphic representation, image; also *fig.* -1646.

1. b. Making all Thy creatures to be expresses of Thy power JER. TAYLOR.

Express (ekspre·s), *v.* [ME. *expresse*, a. OF. *espresser*, *expresser*, f. L. *ex-* + *pressare*, freq. of *premere* to press. Taken as Eng. repr. of L. *exprimere*.]

I. **1.** *trans.* To press or squeeze out; hence *fig.*, to extort or elicit by pressure ME. **2.** To press out the contents of. Now *rare.* 1633.

1. E. the juice and spirit 1757. *fig.* The truth was by torture expressed HOLLAND. So affliction Expresseth virtue fully WEBSTER.

II. **1.** To portray, represent. *Obs.* or *arch.* in general sense. ME. †**b.** To be an image of, resemble -1697. **2.** To represent symbolically 1649. **3.** To reveal by external tokens; to betoken. Now chiefly with reference to feelings or personal qualities. 1549. **4.** To represent in language; to set forth; to give utterance to. (The prevailing use.) ME. **b.** *refl.* To put one's thoughts into words; to state one's opinion 1601. †**5.** To mention, specify; to describe -1798. **6.** To state or mention explicitly; opp. to *imply* 1596.

1. Loggan used long strokes in expressing flesh H. WALPOLE. b. Man expresseth God..as the childe doeth resemble hys father or mother UDALL. 2. A child to e. coming into the world, an old man for going out of it STILLINGFL. Phr. *To e. a quantity in terms of another*. 3. Never did tone e. indifference plainer JANE AUSTEN. 4. A phrase they have got among them, to e. their no-meaning by VILLIERS (Dk. Buckhm.). No words can e. too strongly the caution which should be used BUTLER. 6. Hints and allusions expressing little, insinuating much BERKELEY. Hence †**Expre·ssedly** *adv.* statedly; expressly. **Expre·sser, -or. Expre·ssible, †-able** *a.*

Expression (ekspre·ʃən). 1460. [a. F., ad. L. *expressionem*; see EXPRESS *v.*] **1.** The action of pressing or squeezing out; †an expressed drink, juice, etc. 1594. **2.** The action of representing in words or symbols; utterance 1460. **b.** The action of manifesting by action or other external tokens 1647. **3.** quasi-*concr.* An utterance, declaration, representation; a sign, token. (Now only with *of*.) 1628. **4.** Manner or means of representation in language; diction 1628; a word, phrase, or form of speech 1646; in *Alg.* a collection of symbols together expressing a quantity 1796. **5.** Of the countenance, voice, attitude, etc.: Expressive quality 1774. **b.** Look, intonation, etc., as indicating a state of feeling 1830. **6.** *Fine Arts.* The fact or way of expressing character, sentiment, action, feeling, etc., in a work of art 1715.

1. The crushing of the coco-nut for the e. of the oil TENNENT. 2. To encourage the fullest e. of public feeling FROUDE. Phr. *Beyond, past e.*; *to seek, find e.* 3. An unguarded e. 1714. 4. A great range of e. 1859. Ambiguous expressions FROUDE. 5. His eyes

possessing wonderful..e. MEDWIN. 6. Raphael's feeling for e. 1816. She played with e. 1864.

Hence **Expre·ssional** *a.* of or pertaining to e., *esp.* in the fine arts. **Expre·ssionism**, the methods, style, or attitude of expressionists, esp. in artistic technique. **Expre·ssionist**, an artist whose work aims chiefly at 'expression'; now esp. in reference to artistic technique. **Expressioni·stic** *a.* **Expre·ssionless** *a.*

Expressive (ekspre·siv), *a.* ME. [a. F.; see EXPRESS *v.* and -IVE.] †1. Tending to press out. ME only. 2. Concerned with expression 1747. 3. Serving to express 1711. 4. Full of expression; formerly also, †explicit 1690. 5. Open in expressing (sentiments). Const. *of* (*rare*). 1601. †6. Expressing itself in action -1747.

2. The e. arts REID, powers 1891. 4. The e. term of Bung, as signifying a public-house landlord 1859. E. features D. WILSON. 5. Not enough e. of our pleasure LAMB. Hence **Expre·ssively** *adv.*, **-ness.**

Expressless (ekspre·slės), *a. arch.* 1586. [f. EXPRESS *a.*] That cannot be expressed.

Expressman (ekspre·smæn). 1847. [f. EXPRESS *sb.*[1] 3.] A man employed in receiving and delivering parcels; *esp.* an employé of one of the U.S. express companies.

†**Expre·ssure.** 1598. [f. L. *express-, exprimere* + -URE.] = EXPRESSION -1850.

An operation more diuine, Than breath or pen can giue e. (= description) to SHAKS. Th' e. (= image) that it beares: Greene let it be *Merry W.* v. v. 71.

†**E·xprobrate**, *v.* Also **exprobate** (app. after *reprobate*). 1543. [f. L. *exprobrat-, exprobrare* to make a matter of reproach, f. *ex-* + *probrum.*] 1. To make (a thing) a matter of reproach. Const. *to, unto*, or dat. -1670. 2. To reproach (a person). Const. *with.* -1638.

Hence **Exprobra·tion** (*arch.*), the action of upbraiding; reproachful language. †**Expro·brative**, †**Expro·bratory** *adjs.* reproachful.

‖**Ex professo** (eks profe·so). 1823. [L.] Professedly, by profession.

Expromission (ekspromi·ʃən). 1818. [ad. mod.L. *expromissionem*; see next.] *Civil Law.* The act by which a new debtor undertakes the debt of a former one, who is thereby released.

Expromissor (ekspromi·sǫ̈ɹ). 1695. [a. L., f. (ult.) *ex-* + *promittere* to PROMISE.] *Civil Law.* One who promises to pay; *spec.* one who undertakes the debt of another, thereby releasing him; dist. from a 'surety' or 'bail'.

Expropriate (eksprōu·pri,eᶦt), *v.* 1611. [f. late L. *expropriat-, expropriare*, f. *ex-* + *proprium.* Cf. F. *exproprier.*] 1. *trans.* To dispossess of ownership; to deprive of property. (Now chiefly to deprive of property for the public use, generally with compensation.) †2. To put out of one's own control. BOYLE.

1. A power to e. the owner of the land required 1875. 2. When you have..Consign'd your expropriated will to God 1660.

Expropriation (eksprōu:pri,ēᶦ·ʃən). 1449. [See prec.; cf. F. *expropriation.*] †a. The action of giving up one's whole property -1648. b. The action of depriving of property 1848. c. The action of taking (public) property out of the owner's hands, *esp.* by public authority 1878.

c. The e. of the railways 1889. So **Expro·priator.**

†**Expu·gn**, *v.* ME. [ad. OF. *expugner*, ad. L. *expugnare*, f. *ex-* + *pugna.*] 1. To take by fighting; to storm -1640. 2. To overcome or expel by force of arms; to vanquish -1699.

Hence †**Expu·gnable** *a.* that may be taken by force, conquered, or overcome. †**Expu·gnance**, storming, conquest. †**Expugna·tion**, the action of taking by storm; conquest; assault. †**Expu·gnative**, †**Expu·gnatory** *adjs.* tending to e.; offensive. †**Expu·gner.**

†**Expulse** (ekspʊ·ls), *v.* ME. [ad. L. *expulsare*, freq. of *expellere*; see EXPEL.] *trans.* = EXPEL; sometimes with a stronger notion of violence -1842.

Adam our first parent was expulsed paradise STUBBES. Hence †**Expu·lser.**

Expulsion (ekspʊ·lʃən). ME. [ad. L. *expulsionem*; see EXPEL.] The action of expelling, or driving out by force. Also the fact or condition of being expelled.

The e. of the Spaniards 1659, of a member from the House of Commons 1816, of air 1851.

Expulsive (ekspʊ·lsiv), *a.* ME. [a. F., ad. med.L. *expulsivus*; see EXPULSE and -IVE.] 1. Tending or having power to expel. Chiefly of the action of drugs, etc. †2. Subject to expulsion; hence, driven out. HAWES. †3. = REPELLENT -1662.

1. Of poysons most expulsyfe RIPLEY. So **Expu·lsory** *a.* pertaining to expulsion (*rare*). †**Expu·lsure**, expulsion.

Expunction (ekspʊ·ŋkʃən). 1606. [ad. L. *expunct-* ppl. stem; see next.] The action of expunging; an erasure; †removal.

Expunge (ekspʊ·ndʒ), *v.* 1602. [ad. L. *expungere* to mark (a word) for deletion by dots above or below, f. *ex-* + *pungere* to prick; see PUNCTURE, POINT.] 1. *trans.* To strike out, blot out, erase, omit. 2. *fig.* To wipe out, efface, destroy, put an end to 1628. 3. To get rid of, remove (a person) 1616.

1. Having expunged the Passages which had given him offence ADDISON. 2. To e. an offence 1638. 3. To e. God from Science MANNING.

Expurgate (e·kspɒɹgeᶦt, ekspɒ̄·ɹgeᶦt), *v.* 1621. [f. L. *expurgat-, expurgare*, f. *ex-* + *purgare* to cleanse.] †1. *trans.* To purge or clear out -1652. 2. To purify or amend (a book, etc.) by removing what is objectionable. Also *absol.* 1678.

The best edition Expurgated by learned men BYRON. Hence **Expurgator**, one who expurgates or purifies. **Expu·rgato·rial** *a.* of or pertaining to an expurgator; tending to e. or clear of guilt. **Expu·rgatory** *a.* of or pertaining to expurgation; tending to e. or clear of impurity, guilt, etc.

Expurgation (ekspɒɹgēᶦ·ʃən). ME. [ad. L. *expurgationem*; see prec.] 1. The action of expurgating, cleansing, or amending, by removal of what is objectionable; an instance of this. †2. *Astr.* The reappearance of the sun after an eclipse; emersion -1862.

1. Arts and Learning want this e. SIR T. BROWNE. The e. of the History of the Quakers SOUTHEY, of those members opposed to the Fronde 1839.

Expurge (ekspɒ̄·ɹdʒ), *v.* Now *rare.* 1483. [a. F. *expurger*, refash. from *espurger*:—L. *expurgare*; see EXPURGATE.] = EXPURGATE.

†**Exqui·re**, *v.* 1607. [ad. L. *exquirere* to search out diligently, f. *ex-* + *quærere.*] To search out, seek for -1652.

Exquisite (e·kskwizit). ME. [ad. L. *exquisitus* pa. pple. of *exquirere*; see prec.]

A. *adj.* 1. Sought out, 'recherché'. †2. Careful, exact, minute -1757. 3. Carefully or highly elaborated 1552. †4. Of a person: Consummate -1823. 5. Such as to excite intense delight or admiration. (The prevailing sense.) 6. Of pain, pleasure, etc.: Keen, intense 1644. 7. Of the senses, etc.: Keenly sensitive to impressions; delicate, finely-strung 1643.

1. I haue no e. reason for't, but I haue reason good enough SHAKS. With e. thanks 1650. The most e. morsels 1715, fish GIBBON. 2. Accuracy or e. digestion of their laws BURKE. 3. E. workmanship 1561, torments 1603, cookery HUME, ignorance and stupidity JAS. MILL. 4. A most e. sloven DE FOE. 5. A babe of e. beauty 1632. 7. A person of an e. Palate STEELE.

B. *sb.* One who is over-nice in dress; a dandy, fop 1819.

Hence **E·xquisitely** *adv.* in an e. manner or degree. **E·xquisiteness.** **E·xquisiti·sm**, dandyism, foppishness.

†**Exqui·sitive**, *a. rare.* 1660. [f. L. *exquisit-* ppl. stem (see EXQUISITE) + -IVE.] Tending to search out; curious. Hence **Exqui·sitively** *adv.* = EXQUISITELY (*rare*). **Exqui·sitiveness** = EXQUISITENESS (Sterne).

Exsanguinate (eks,sæ·ŋgwineᶦt), *v.* 1800. [f. L. *exsanguinat-, exsanguinare*, f. *ex-* + *sanguinem.*] To drain of blood.

Exsanguine (eks,sæ·ŋgwin), *a.* 1647. [f. Ex- *pref.*[1] + L. *sanguis* (*sanguin-*).] Bloodless; anæmic. Also *fig.* So †**E·xsangui·neous** *a.* bloodless. **Exsangui·nity**, anæmia. **Exsa·nguinous**, **Exsa·nguious**, **-eous** *adjs.* bloodless.

Exscind (eksi·nd), *v.* Also *erron.* **excind.** 1662. [f. L. *exscindere*, f. *ex-* + *scindere* to cut.] To cut out, excise (*lit.* and *fig.*); †to cut off, destroy.

The exscinding..of the Amorites BARROW.

†**Exscribe**, *v.* 1607. [ad. L. *exscribere*, f. *ex-* + *scribere.*] To copy or write out; to transcribe -1716. Hence †**Exscript**, a copy, written extract. †**Exscri·ption.**

†**Exscu·lp**, *v. rare.* 1578. [ad. L. *exsculpere*, f. *ex-* + *sculpere* to cut, carve.] To cut out. Hence †**Exscu·lption** (*rare*).

Exsect (ekse·kt), *v.* 1641. [f. L. *exsect-, exsecare*, f. *ex-* + *secare* to cut.] To cut out. Also *fig.* **Exse·ction**, a cutting out or away.

Exsert (eks,sǝ̄·ɹt), *v.* 1665. [f. L. *exsert-*; see EXERT.] †a. To manifest in action, exercise. b. (chiefly *Biol.*) To thrust forth or out 1836. Hence **Exse·rt** *ppl. a.* exserted.

Exserted (eks,sǝ̄·ɹtėd), *ppl. a.* 1816. [f. prec.] *Biol.* Stretched forth or out; thrust out from, or as from, a sheath; projecting.

Phr. *E. sting*: one that cannot be drawn within the body. Hence **Exse·rtion**, the action of exserting; the being exserted.

Exsertile (eks,sǝ̄·ɹtil), *a.* 1828. [a. F.; see -ILE.] Capable of being exserted.

Ex-se·rvice, *a.* 1907. [Ex-[1] 2.] Having formerly belonged to one of the fighting services.

Exsi·bilate, *v. rare.* 1601. [f. L. *exsibilat-, exsibilare*, f. *ex-* + *sibilare* to hiss; see SIBILANT.] To hiss off the stage. Hence **Exsibila·tion** (*rare*).

Exsiccant (eksi·kănt). 1657. [ad. L. *exsiccantem*; see next.]

A. *adj.* Drying; having the power of drying up.

B. *sb.* An exsiccant drug or medicine 1676.

Exsiccate (e·ksikeᶦt, eksi·keᶦt), *v.* 1545. [f. L. *exsiccat-, exsiccare*, f. *ex-* + *siccus* dry.] To dry up. *trans.* and *intr.* for *refl.*

Bodies..that have been exsiccated into Mummy HALE. Hence **Exsicca·tion**, the action of drying what is moist; thoroughly dried condition. **E·xsiccator**, an apparatus for exsiccating.

Exsiccative (e·ksikeᶦtiv, eks,si·kătiv). ME. [See prec.]

A. *adj.* Tending to make dry or to produce dryness.

B. *sb.* An exsiccative medicine or substance.

Exsolution: see EXOLUTION.

†**Exspolia·tion.** 1612. [ad. L. *exspoliationem*, f. (ult.) *ex-* + *spolium* spoil.] The action of spoiling; a stripping off or removal -1678.

Exspuition (ekspu,i·ʃən). 1650. [ad. L. *exspuitionem*, f. *ex-* + *spuere* to spit.] The action of spitting out from the mouth. Also *transf.* and *concr.* So **Exspu·tory** *a.* that is spit out or ejected (*rare*).

†**Exsti·ll**, *v.* 1651. [ad. L. *exstillare*, f. *ex-* + *stilla* a drop.] To come or send out in drops -1819.

†**Exsti·mulate**, *v.* 1603. [f. L. *exstimulat-, exstimulare*; see STIMULATE.] To stimulate; to provoke; to spur on, incite -1683. Hence †**Exstimula·tion.**

Exstipulate (eks,sti·piŭlėt), *a.* 1830. [f. Ex- *pref.*[1] + L. *stipula* stalk.] *Bot.* Having no stipules.

Exstrophy (e·kstrǒfi). Also **extrophy.** 1836. [f. Gr. ἐκ-, ἐξ- + στροφ-, στρέφειν to turn.] *Path.* A turning inside out of a part; *esp.* a congenital malformation in which the bladder appears to be turned inside out.

†**Exstru·ct**, *v.* 1534. [f. L. *exstruct-, exstruere*, f. *ex* + *struere.*] To build or pile up -1657. Hence †**Exstru·ction.** †**Exstru·ctive** *a.* (*rare*).

Exsuccous (eks,sʊ·kəs), *a.* 1646. [f. L. *exsuccus* + -OUS.] Without juice, sapless. Also *fig.*

Exsuction (eksʊ·kʃən). 1660. [f. L. *exsugere* to suck out. Cf. SUCTION.] The action of sucking out.

Exsudate, obs. f. EXUDATE.

Exsufflate, *v.* Now *Hist.* 1666. [f. L. *exsufflat-, exsufflare*, f. *ex-* + *sufflare* to blow up, f. *sub-* + *flare.*] To blow out or away. Hence **Exsuffla·tion** (now *Hist.*), the action of blowing out; *spec.* in *Eccl.* exorcism, or renunciation of the devil, by the action of blowing.

†**Exsu·fflicate**, *a. rare.* [app. arbitrary f. EXSUFFLATE.] ? Puffed up, inflated. *Oth.* III. iii. 182.

†**Exsu·perance.** 1603. [a. F., ad. L. *exsuperantia*; see EXSUPERATE *v.*] The condition or fact of exceeding; excess -1682.

†**Exsu·perate**, *v.* 1559. [f. L. *exsuperat-, exsuperare* to rise above, f. *ex-* + *super.*] To overtop, surpass; to overcome -1708. So †**Exsu·perant** *a.* excessive.

Exsurge (eks,sɒ̄·ɹdʒ). 1578. [ad. L. *ex-*

surgere.] *intr.* To rise up, start out. Hence **Exsu·rgent** *a.* rising up above the rest.

†**Exsu·scitate**, *v.* 1574. [f. L. *exsuscitat-*, *exsuscitare*, f. *ex-* + *suscitare*.] *trans.* To rouse up, awaken. Hence †**Exsu·scita·tion.**

‖**Exta** (e·kstă). 1663. [L.] The viscera; *spec.* (*Antiq.*) the entrails of a victim from which auguries were taken by soothsayers.

Extacie, -cy, obs. ff. ECSTASY.

†**E·xtance.** [ad. L. *ex(s)tantia*; see EXTANT.] Emergence. SIR T. BROWNE.

†**E·xtancy.** 1644. [f. as prec.] The quality or state of standing out; *concr.* a protuberance –1689.

Extant (e·kstænt, ekstæ·nt). 1545. [ad. L. *ex(s)tantem*, f. *ex(s)tare*, f. *ex-* out + *stare* to stand.]

A. *adj.* 1. Standing out or above any surface; projecting, protuberant. *arch.* 2. Standing forth to the view; conspicuous. *rare.* 1557. 3. In existence; existing 1561; continuing to exist 1581.

1. In St. Paul's it is e. out of the wall ENTICK. 2. E. to the eie 1570. 3. In this e. moment SHAKS. None of his letters during those years are e. BOSWELL.

†B. *sb.* An extant copy 1592. b. *pl.* Remains 1659.

Extatic, obs. f. ECSTATIC.

Extemporal (ekste·mpŏrăl), *a.* Now *rare.* 1570. [ad. L. *extemporalis*, f. *ex tempore*; see EXTEMPORE.] Extemporary, impromptu. var. †**Exte·mporate.**

Extemporaneous (ekste:mpŏrēⁱ·nĭəs), *a.* 1656. [f. late L. *extemporaneus*, f. as prec.; see EXTEMPORE.] 1. Not premeditated, off-hand, extempore. Rarely of a person. 2. Made for the occasion 1725.

1. E. pulpiteers 1812, prayer MACAULAY. 2. An e. supper YEATS. var. †**Extempora·nean.** Hence **Extempora·neous-ly** *adv.*, **-ness.**

Extemporary (ekste·mpŏrări). 1610. [f. EXTEMPORE + -ARY.]

A. *adj.* 1. Unpremeditated; EXTEMPORE. Occas. of a speaker. †2. Arising at the moment –1758. 3. Made for the occasion; hastily provided; makeshift 1631.

1. I have never known a truly e. preacher LD. COCKBURN. 3. An E. Collation EVELYN.

†B. *sb.* An extemporary speech or action. FULLER.

Hence **Exte·mporarily** *adv.* **Exte·mporariness.**

Extempore (eks,te·mpŏrĭ). 1553. [a. L. *ex tempore* lit. 'out of the time'.]

A. *adv.* 1. At the moment, without preparation; off-hand. †2. On the instant; at once –1663.

1. Phr. *To speak, pray e.* †*To live e.*: to live from hand to mouth. 2. I'd yeeld e. my breath 1663.

B. *adj.* 1. Arising out of the moment; casual; sudden 1639. 2. Made or done at the moment, without preparation. Occas. of a speaker, etc. 1637. 3. Makeshift 1694.

1. Such a slight e. business SOUTH. 2. E. translation into English STANLEY. An e. preacher 1886. 3. An e. sofa 1856.

†C. *sb.* Extempore speech, writing, or performance; an impromptu –1815.

Extemporize (ekste·mpŏrəiz), *v.* 1717. [f. prec. + -IZE.] 1. *intr.* To speak, compose, or perform extempore. 2. *trans.* To compose off-hand 1817. 3. To invent for the occasion 1858.

2. To leave half of the dialogue to be extemporised 1880. 3. Gunners..cannot be extemporized 1858. Hence **Exte·mporiza·tion**, improvisation; an extempore performance. **Exte·mporizer.**

†**Exte·mpory**, *adv.* and *a.* Var. of EXTEMPORE –1775.

Extend (ekste·nd), *v.* [ME. *extenden*, ad. L. *extendere*, f. *ex-* + *tendere* to stretch.]

I. 1. *trans.* To stretch, pull, or straighten out, to strain; to expand 1639. 2. To stretch, draw in a specified direction, or for a specified distance. Also *refl.* and *intr.* for *refl.* 1481. †b. To tend –1605. 3. *trans.* To lengthen; to carry further 1569. 4. To spread out in area 1675. b. *Metaph.* To possess extension 1666. c. *intr.* To cover an area; to have a certain range or scope 1481. 5. *trans.* To enlarge in area, range, or scope. Also *intr.* for *refl.* 1580. †6. To exaggerate. *Cymb.* I. i. 25.

1. To e. a vine ME., one's nerves POPE, a horse's stride 1753. Hector's Corps extended on a Bier CONGREVE. To e. shorthand notes 1826, contractions 1874. b. esp. *pass.* and *refl.* of a horse: To exert itself to the full; to go 'all out'; hence *gen.* 1856. 3. To e. a Sermon DONNE, a railway line 1854. 5. To e. the bounds BARET, the law of reason HOOKER, the Sight ADDISON.

II. 1. To stretch forth, hold out; to accord 1601. †2. To display (malice), inflict (vengeance), issue (process) *against*, *upon* –1597. b. *Law.* To present (a protest) 1889.

1. Let there be none to e. mercy to him *Ps.* cix. 12.

III. 1. To assess, value ME. 2. *Law.* To take possession of by a writ of extent; to levy upon 1585; *transf.* to take possession of by force 1606.

Hence †**Exte·ndant** *a.* amounting *to*; *Her.* = DISPLAYED. **Exte·ndible** *a.* extensible; in *Law*, subject to seizure under a writ of extent. **Extendibi·lity.** †**Exte·ndure**, extension; extent.

Extended (ekste·ndėd), *ppl. a.* 1450. [f. prec.] 1. Stretched or spread out; †strained 1552. 2. Continued, prolonged 1450. 3. Enlarged in area, comprehension, or scope; extensive 1700. 4. Having extension 1666. 5. *Law.* Valued; seized upon and held in satisfaction of a debt 1625. Hence **Exte·nded-ly** *adv.*, **-ness.**

Extender (ekste·ndəɹ). Also **-or.** ME. [f. as prec.] 1. One who or that which extends; †*spec.* the EXTENSOR muscle 1611. †2. A surveyor or valuer –15..

†**Exte·ndlessness.** App. in sense 'boundlessness'. HALE.

Exte·nse. *Obs.* or *arch.* 1614. [ad. L. *extensus*, *extendere*.]

A. *adj.* Having 'extension' (H. MORE); extensive 1644.

†B. *sb.* What is extended, an expanse 1614.

Extensible (ekste·nsib'l), *a.* 1611. [a. F., ad. L. **extensibilis*; see EXTEND.] 1. Capable of being extended in any dimension or direction; capable of being protruded. 2. Capable of being enlarged in scope or meaning 1654.

1. An artery is an e., elastic tube GOOCH. Hence **Extensibi·lity**, e. quality. **Exte·nsibleness.**

Extensile (ekste·nsil), *a.* 1744. [f. L. *extens-*, *extendere* + -ILE.] 1. Capable of being stretched out. 2. Of a tentacle, etc.: Capable of being protruded 1802.

Extension (ekste·nʃən). ME. [ad. L. *extensionem.*] 1. The action of extending; extended state or condition. 2. *Law.* The extending of a protest (see EXTEND II. 2. b) 1889. 3. The action or process of spreading out in area; the condition of being so spread out. Also †*concr.* An expanse. 1684. †4. Extent –1708. b. *Physics* and *Metaph.* The property of being extended; spatial magnitude 1624. c. An extended body or space 1739. 5. The range over which anything extends 1604. 6. *Logic.* The range of a term as measured by the number of objects to which it applies; opp. to *intension* or *comprehension* 1725. 7. Enlargement in length, duration, area, or scope 1590; *concr.* an extended portion 1854.

1. Extention of the Synnues 1599. You must use Extention almost to every Dislocation WOODALL. Fullnesse of Meat.. causeth an E. of the Stomacke BACON. 4. b. Our perceptions of the specific e. of the body—its size and shape H. SPENCER. 6. A Bowl, in its E., includes a wooden Bowl, a brass Bowl, etc. WATTS. 7. *University E.*: the extending of the scope and work of the universities, *e.g.* to non-resident students.

Hence **Exte·nsional** *a.* of, pertaining to, or possessed of e. **Exte·nsionist**, one who advocates the e. of anything, *e.g.* of University Teaching; also *colloq.* one who attends the meetings of the University E. Association.

Extensity (ekste·nsĭti). 1834. [f. L. *extensus* + -ITY.] The quality of having (a certain) extension; in *Psychol.* of the breadth of sensation, as opp. to *intensity.*

Extensive (ekste·nsiv), *a.* 1605. [ad. late L. *extensivus*; see EXTEND and -IVE.] †1. Extensible –1691. 2. That enlarges in scope. AUSTIN. 3. Having a wide extent, comprehension, or scope. Of purchases, etc.: Large in amount. 1706. 4. Of, pertaining to, or possessed of extension; occupying space 1624. 5. *Logic.* Denoting a large number of objects; opp. to *intensive* 1686.

1. Silver beaters chuse the finest coin, as .. most e. under the hammer BOYLE. 3. E. plantations PENNANT, markets ADAM SMITH, capital ALISON, quotation 1846. Hence **Exte·nsive-ly** *adv.*, **-ness.**

Extensor (ekste·nsəɹ). 1713. [a. late L., f. *extendere.*] 1. A muscle which serves to extend or straighten any part of the body; opp. to *flexor.* 2. *attrib.* 1830.

‖**Exte·nsum.** [L.; neut. of *extensus.*] A body possessed of extension. CUDWORTH.

†**Exte·nsure.** 1594. [f. L. *extens-* ppl. stem (see EXTEND) + -URE.] The condition of being extended; the action of extending; extent –1631.

Extent (ekste·nt), *sb.* [ME. *extente*, a. AF. *extente*, *estente*, f. *estendre* (F. *étendre*) :—L. *extendere*; see EXTEND.] 1. *Hist.* The valuation of land or other property; assessment; also, assessed value; = STENT. ME. 2. *Law.* A writ to recover debts of record due to the Crown, under which the body, lands, and goods of the debtor may be seized to compel payment 1630. b. Seizure of lands, etc., in execution of a writ; sequestration; also, the right of seizure; also, execution 1592. †c. *transf.* An assault –1601. †3. Rents, etc., arising from extended lands –1626. 4. 'Space or degree to which anything is extended' (J.); thus, dimensions, compass, size 1624; breadth of comprehension, scope 1594. 5. *concr.* An extended space 1627. †6. The action of extending –1719.

4. The Serpent..Of huge e. MILT. *P. L.* VII. 496. The e. of the power which was to be exercised by the Sovereign MACAULAY. 6. *Haml.* II. ii. 390.

†**Exte·nt**, *a.* ME. [ad. L. *extentus.*] = EXTENDED –1664.

Extenuate (ekste·niu,eⁱt), *v.* 1529. [f. L. *extenuat-*, *extenuare*, f. *ex-* + *tenuis* thin.] 1. To make thin or lean. Somewhat *arch.* 1533. 2. To thin out, render thinner 1559. †3. To lessen in size, number, amount, or degree; to weaken the force of, mitigate –1773. †4. To disparage –1705. 5. To estimate or state at a low figure; to underrate. Somewhat *arch.* 1529. 6. Hence: To lessen, or seem to lessen, the seeming magnitude of (guilt or offence) by partial excuses. Also of circumstances: To serve as an extenuation of. 1570. ¶b. Improp.: To extenuate the guilt of 1741.

1. To e. the body by fasting SOUTHEY. 2. To e. gold into plates HAKLUYT. To e. humours MARKHAM, the air VINCE. 4. Just are thy ways..Who can e. thee MILT. *P. L.* X. 645. 5. Cuffe extenuated both the Danger and Difficulty 1625. 6. Fortune, there, extenuates the Crime. What's Vice in me, is only Mirth in him CONGREVE.

Hence †**Exte·nuate** *ppl. a.* and *a.* extenuated. **Exte·nuative** *a.* tending to e.; *sb.* something serving to e. guilt, or to emaciate. **Exte·nuator.** **Exte·nuatory** *a.* characterized by extenuation.

Exte·nuating, *ppl. a.* 1607. [f. prec.] That extenuates. Chiefly in *Extenuating circumstances*: circumstances that tend to diminish culpability. Hence **Exte·nuatingly** *adv.*

Extenuation (ekste:niu,ēⁱ·ʃən). 1542. [ad. L. *extenuationem*; cf. F. *exténuation.*] 1. The action of extenuating; extenuated condition. 2. The action of lessening the guilt of (an offence) by partial excuses; a plea in mitigation of censure 1651.

2. In e. of a noble error MACKINTOSH.

Exterior (ekstīᵊ·riəɹ). 1533. [a. L., compar. of *exterus* outside.]

A. *adj.* 1. Outer; pertaining to or connected with the outside; visible on the outside 1570. 2. Situated outside (an object); coming from without; concerned with what is without; external, extrinsic. Const. *to.* 1533. †b. Foreign (*rare*) 1540.

1. Not th' e., nor the inward man Resembles that it was *Haml.* II. ii. 6. Phr. *E. angle* (Geom.): the angle included between any side of a triangle or polygon and the production of the adjacent side; also, an angle included between a straight line falling upon two parallel lines and either of the latter on the outside. 2. Without e. help sustaind MILT. *P. L.* IX. 336. b. Other exteriour potentates 1540.

B. *sb.* (Not in Johnson.) 1. An exterior thing (*rare*); in *pl.* = EXTERNALS 1591. 2. The outside; outward aspect or demeanour 1695.

2. The engaging e. of urbanity HAN. MORE. The most pious e. MOZLEY.

Hence **Exterio·rity**, outwardness; devotion to

the external instead of to the spiritual; 'the psychical act by which sensations are referred to the external world' (*Syd. Soc. Lex.*). **Exte·riorize** *v.* to attribute an external existence to (states of consciousness); hence **Exte·rioriza·tion.** **Exte·riorly** *adv.* on the outside or surface; as regards externals; in an e. position or direction.

Exterminate (ekstɜ̄·ɹmineᵢt), *v.* 1541. [f. L. *exterminat-*, *exterminare* to drive beyond the boundaries, f. *ex-* + *terminus*.] †1. *trans.* To drive, force *from*, *of*, *out of* the boundaries or limits of; to banish, put to flight -1692. 2. To destroy utterly; to root out, extirpate 1649. †3. To get rid of, destroy; in *Math.*, to ELIMINATE -1827.

1. To e. rank Atheism out of the world BENTLEY. 2. The Holy League..was to e. heresy MOTLEY. 3. A remorse that..exterminated his peace GODWIN.

Hence **Exte·rminable** *a.* that may be exterminated; illimitable (SHELLEY) (*rare*). **Exte·rminative** *a.* tending to e. **Exte·rminator.** **Exte·rminatory** *a.* tending to e.; characterized by attempts at extermination.

Extermination (ekstɜ̄:ɹminēɪ·ʃən). 1549. [ad. L. *exterminationem*; see prec.] †1. Expulsion from the bounds or limits of a country; banishment, excommunication -1664. 2. Total extirpation; utter destruction 1549. †3. *Math.* = ELIMINATION. -1827.

2. The e. of religion 1790, of the Small-pox 1803, the Talmud 1867.

†**Exte·rmine,** *v.* 1539. [ad. F. *exterminer*.] = EXTERMINATE. -1637.

Extern (ekstɜ̄·ɹn). Also **externe.** 1533. [ad. L. *externus* outward; cf. F. *externe*.]

A. *adj.* = EXTERNAL A. 1-4.

B. *sb.* †1. Outward appearance, exterior (*rare*) 1600. 2. An outsider; *esp.* a day-pupil in a school (F. *externe*) 1610.

External (ekstɜ̄·ɹnăl). 1556. [f. L. *externus* + -AL.]

A. *adj.* (Opp. to *internal*.) 1. Situated outside; pertaining to, connected with, or lying towards, the outside 1591. 2. Outwardly visible or perceptible 1556. 3. Situated outside the object under consideration (const. *to*) 1595; †foreign -1599; in *Metaph.*, belonging to the world of phenomena, as opp. to the 'ego' 1667. 4. Arising or acting from without 1651. 5. Having an outside, or foreign, object or sphere of operation 1770.

1. Her vertues graced with externall gifts 1 *Hen. VI*, v. v. 3. E. warmth 1799. The e. meatus 1878. Phr. *E. angle*: one made by producing outwardly a side of a figure. 2. The e. worship of God BUTLER. 3. The e. air 1801. The e. world LOTZE. 4. Not by externall violence, but intestine disorder HOBBES. Phr. *E. evidence*: evidence derived from circumstances outside of the thing discussed. 5. Phr. *E. perception*, *senses*. The e. debt of the Republic of Chili 1891. Hence **Exte·rnally** *adv.*

B. *sb.* 1. *sing.* The outside 1792. 2. That which is external. In *pl.* a. Outward aspect; bodily qualifications; outward observances 1635. b. External circumstances or conditions; also, non-essentials 1652.

2. a. Adam was glorious in his externals .. he had a beautiful body SOUTH. The Externals of religion JORTIN. b. The subordination of externals to essentials 1883.

Exte·rnalism. 1856. [f. prec. + -ISM.] 1. Excessive regard for non-essentials, *esp.* in religion. 2. The worship of the external world 1874.

1. Pharisaic formalities and externalisms 1875. So **Exte·rnalist,** one who has undue regard for externals.

Externality (ekstəɹnæ·lĭti). 1673. [f. as prec. + -ITY.] 1. The quality of being EXTERNAL. 2. *Metaph.* The quality or fact of being external to a conscious subject 1790. 3. An external object or characteristic; *collect.* outward things in general 1839. 4. Absorption in externals 1833.

2. While looking at a solid object they cannot help having the conception..of its e. MILL. 4. Enchained hopelessly in the grovelling fetters of e. LAMB.

Externalize (ekstɜ̄·ɹnăləiz). *v.* Also **-ise.** 1852. [f. as prec. + -IZE.] *trans.* To make external; to embody in outward form; to attribute external existence to.

The universe is the process whereby spirit externalises itself E. CAIRD. Hence **Exte·rnaliza·tion,** the action of externalizing; *concr.* an embodiment. var. **Exte·rnize** *v.*; whence **Exte·rniza·tion.**

‖**Externat** (eksterna). 1853. [F., f. *externe*; see EXTERN.] A day-school.

Externate (e·kstɜ̄ɹneᵢt), *v. rare.* 1890. [f. EXTERN + -ATE[3].] To embody in outward form. Hence **Externa·tion.**

Externity (ekstɜ̄·ɹnĭti). 1713. [f. med.L. *externare* to make external + -ITY.] Outwardness; also, the external part.

†**E·xterous,** *a. rare.* 1570. [f. L. *exter* + -OUS.] Outside -1647.

Exterrestrial (ekstĕre·striăl), *a.* [f. EX-*pref.*[1] + TERRESTRIAL.] Originating or located outside the earth. PROCTOR.

Exterritorial (eksteritō·riăl), *a.* 1880. [f. EX- *pref.*[1] + TERRITORIAL.] Of or pertaining to exterritoriality.

Exterritoriality (eksteritōᵊ:riˌæ·lĭti). 1836. [ad. F. *exterritorialité*; see prec. + -ITY.] The privilege accorded by the *Law of Nations* to ambassadors and their families, of being considered outside the territory, and therefore the jurisdiction, of the state to which they are sent. Also EXTRATERRITORIALITY.

†**Exte·rsive,** *a. rare.* 1657. [f. L. *extersi-*, *extergere* + -IVE.] Cleansing -1661.

Extill, -ation, -atious, var. ff. EXSTILL, etc.

Extimulate, -ation, -atory, obs. ff. EXSTIMULATE, etc.

Extinct (eksti·ŋkt). ME. [ad. L. *ex(s)tinctus*; see EXTINGUISH.]

A. *pple.* Extinguished. Now *rare.*

It tooke fire..but was quickly e. 1631.

B. *adj.* 1. Of a fire, etc.: Extinguished. Of a volcano: No longer in eruption. ME. 2. *fig.* Quenched; that has ceased to burn or shine 1494. †3. Of a person: Cut off; dead; vanished -1675. 4. That has died out or come to an end 1581.

1. A sparke or two not yet e. COWPER. 2. Young Arthurs eies are blinded and e. 1591. 3. My dayes are e. *Job* xvii. 1. 4. All the family e. DE FOE. Phr. *After possibility of issue e.*

†**Exti·nct,** *v.* 1483. [f. L. *ex(s)tinct-*, *ex(s)tinguere* to EXTINGUISH.] = EXTINGUISH *v.*, in various senses -1631.

‖**Extincteur** (ękstæṅtör, ekstiŋktǭɹ). 1878. [F., ad. L. *ex(s)tinctor*.] An apparatus for extinguishing fire.

Extinction (eksti·ŋkʃən). 1494. [ad. L. *ex(s)tinctionem*; cf. F. *extinction*.] 1. The quenching, putting out (of anything); also *fig.*; the process of becoming, or fact of being, extinct. b. *spec.* The slaking (of lime) 1646. 2. Suppression, abolition; the complete wiping out (of a debt) 1651. 3. Destruction, annihilation; †utter disgrace 1542. 4. Of a race, etc.: A coming to an end or dying out; the condition of being extinct 1602.

1. E. of heat 1672, of volcanoes 1843, of a lamp CARLYLE. 2. The gradual e. of the national debt MCCULLOCH. 4. The e. of the male line BRYCE. var. †**Exti·ncture.** SHAKS.

Extinctive (eksti·ŋktiv), *a.* 1600. [f. L. *ex(s)tinguere*; cf. F. *extinctif*.] Tending, or able, to extinguish.

Extine (e·kstin, -təin). 1835. [f. L. *ext(imus)*, f. *ex-* + -INE[1].] *Bot.* The outer membrane of the pollen grain. Also EXINE.

Extinguish (eksti·ŋgwiʃ), *v.* 1545. [ad. L. *ex(s)tinguere*, f. *ex-* intensive + *stinguere* to quench; see -ISH[2].] 1. *trans.* To put out, quench. Also *transf.* and *fig.* 2. To put a total end to, blot out of existence 1548. †3. *intr.* for *refl.* in various senses: To die out -1797.

1. They would e. the very light of nature BERKELEY. Extinguishing his reason, instead of putting out his eyes LAW. 2. To e. all memory thereof MARVELL. To e. a title, right, action, instrument (*Law*). To e. a debt 1777, a bishopric 1839, the Red man 1837. 3. His alacrity suddenly extinguishes HUME. Hence **Exti·nguishable** *a.* able to be extinguished.

Extinguisher (eksti·ŋgwiʃəɹ). 1560. [f. prec.] One who or that which extinguishes; *esp.* a hollow conical cap for extinguishing the light of a candle or lamp. Also *transf.* and *fig.*

Extinguishment (eksti·ŋgwiʃmĕnt). 1503. [f. as prec. + -MENT.] 1. The quenching (of fire, etc.); also *transf.* and *fig.* 2. The putting a total end to, blotting out of existence. Cf. EXTINGUISH *v.* 2, and quots. 1535.

1. An e. of love WHATELEY. 2. The e. of a house 1612, of Ambiguities and doubts 1648, of a contract, right, etc. (*Law*), of a debt MORSE.

Extirp (ekstɜ̄·ɹp), *v. Obs.* or *arch.* 1483. [ad. F. *extirper*, ad. L. *ex(s)tirpare*; see EXTIRPATE.] = EXTIRPATE *v.* Hence †**Exti·rpable** *a.* that may be extirpated. **Exti·rper.**

Extirpate (e·kstəɹpeᵢt, ekstɜ̄·ɹpeᵢt), *v.* 1539. [f. L. *ex(s)tirpat-*, *ex(s)tirpare*, f. *ex-* + *stirps* stem, stock.] 1. To pull or pluck up by the roots; to root up, eradicate 1650. 2. To root out, exterminate; to render extinct. Const. *out of*, *from*. 1586. 3. *fig.* 1539.

1. E. noxious and unprofitable Herbs RAY. To e. a tumor GOOCH. 2. The breed ought to be extirpated out of the island LOCKE (J.). To e. gangs of thieves MACAULAY. 3. To e. superstition LATIMER, drunkenness BENTHAM, heresy SCOTT.

Hence **E·xtirpative** *a.* tending to e. **Extirpator,** one who, or that which, extirpates.

Extirpation (ekstəɹpēɪ·ʃən). 1526. [ad. L. *ex(s)tirpationem*; see prec.; cf. F. *extirpation*.] The action of extirpating or rooting up or out; total destruction; extermination.

The joint e. of woods and men MORSE. The e. of heresy 1602, of the smallpox 1846, of the buffalo 1877.

‖**Extispex** (eksti·speks). Pl. **exti·spices.** 1727. [L.; f. *exta* (see EXTA] + *-spex*, f. *specere* to look at.] A HARUSPEX, q. v. So †**Extispi·cious** *a.* of or pertaining to extispicy (*rare*). **Exti·spicy,** haruspicy.

Extol (ekstǫ·l), *v.* 1494. [ad. L. *extollere*, f. *ex-* + *tollere*.] †1. *trans.* To lift up, elevate -1650. †2. To lift up with pride, joy, etc. -1664; to raise too high; to exaggerate, boast of -1796. 3. To praise highly; to magnify 1509.

1. A begger from the dunghill once extold, Forgets him selfe 1601. 2. The Hors and Foot and the Sea-Souldiers..extoll'd every one their own hazards 1652. 3. S. John extolleth charitie in his Epistle BENTLEY. Hence **Exto·ller,** one who extols. **Exto·lment,** the action of extolling; eulogy.

Extorsive (ekstǭ·ɹsiv), *a. rare.* 1669. [f. L. *extors-* rare form of ppl. stem of *extorquere* + -IVE.] Serving or tending to extort; obtained by extortion. Hence †**Exto·rsively** *adv.*

Extort (ekstǭ·ɹt), *v.* 1529. [f. L. *extort-*, *extorquere*, f. *ex-* + *torquere* to twist.] 1. *trans.* To wrest from a reluctant person by force, violence, torture, intimidation, or abuse of legal authority, or by importunity, argument, or the like. 2. To extract forcibly (a sense or conclusion) *from* (a passage, etc.) 1601. †3. To practise extortion on (a person); to strain (a law) -1681.

1. To e. treasure 1529, Tribute SHAKS., taxes 1820, compassion JAS. MILL, power 1863. 2. Do not e. thy reasons from this clause *Twel. N.* III. i. 165.

Hence †**Exto·rt** *ppl. a.* extorted; extortionate. †**Exto·rt** *sb.* extortion, torture. **Exto·rter, -or.**

Extortion (ekstǭ·ɹʃən). ME. [ad. L. *extortionem*; see prec. Cf. F. *extorsion*.] 1. The action or practice of extorting or wresting anything, *esp.* money, from a person by force or by undue exercise of authority or power; an act of illegal exaction. b. *Law.* The act of any officer 'unlawfully taking, by colour of his office, any money or thing of value, that is not due to him, or more than his due, or before it is due' (Blackstone) 1607. †2. A wresting of the sense of a word or phrase 1652; a straining (of the nerves) 1725.

Hence **Exto·rtion** *v.* to practise extortion; *trans.* to overcharge. **Exto·rtionable** *a.* extortionate (*rare*). **Exto·rtionary** *a.* given to or marked by e. **Exto·rtionate** *a.* characterized by e.; oppressive; exorbitant. **Exto·rtioner,** one who practises e. †**Exto·rtious** *a.* characterized, or gained, by e.

Extortive (ekstǭ·ɹtiv), *a.* 1646. [f. L. *extort-* ppl. stem (see EXTORT) + -IVE.] Of extortion; disposed to extort.

Extra (e·kstră). 1776. [? short for EXTRAORDINARY. So in Fr.]

A. *adj.* Beyond or more than the usual, agreed, or stated amount or number; additional.

Money for any e. wants 1780. E. pay LECKY.

B. *adv.* Unusually; in excess of the usual or specified amount. 1823.

E. strong binding. E.-special edition. Is there anything e.-special for tea? Three maps e. (*mod.*).

C. *sb.* What is extra or additional; anything given in addition or for which an extra charge is made; the extra charge itself; an extra fee; an additional issue of a newspaper; *spec.* at cricket, a run scored otherwise than off the bat 1803.

'With extras?'..'Yes.. we learned French and music' L. CARROLL. Hourly extras were issued 1888. The builder hoped to recoup himself by extras (*mod.*).

‖**Extra** (e·kstrā), *prep. rare.* 1852. [L.; contr. f. *exterā*, abl. fem. of *exter.*] Outside, externally to; as, *extra* the voltaic circuit.

Extra- (e·kstrā), *prefix*, forming adjs. (in L. from phrases, as *extraordinarius* f. *extra ordinem*) with general sense 'situated outside something', 'lying outside the province or scope of'.

Extra-a·cinous, *Anat.* outside the ACINUS or racemose gland. **Extra-alime·ntary,** situated outside the alimentary canal. **Extra-analo·gical,** outside the range of analogy. **Extra-arti·stic,** out of the range of art. **Extra-atmosphe·ric,** of or pertaining to space beyond the atmosphere. **Extra-a·xillar, Extra-a·xillary,** *Bot.* growing from above or below the axils. **Extra-brita·nnic. Extra-cano·nical,** not classed among the canonical books. **Extra-ca·psular,** 'outside a capsule, having special reference to the articular capsules' (*Syd. Soc. Lex.*). **Extra-ce·llular,** *Biol.* situated or taking place outside the walls of a cell. **Extra-chri·stian,** outside the province of Christian thought. **Extra-co·nstellary,** *Astron.* not classed under any constellation. **Extra-co·rial** [L. *corium* hide], pertaining to the outside skin or epidermis. **Extra-corpo·real,** outside the body. **Extra-co·smical,** acting outside the cosmos or universe. **Extra-cu·taneous,** outside the true skin as opp. to the epidermis. **Extra-decre·tal,** not included in the Decretals. **-du·ral** (see DURAL). **Extra-folia·ceous,** *Bot.* external to the leaf. **Extra-galac·tic,** *Astron.* outside the Milky Way. **Extra-governme·ntal. Extra-gramma·tical. Extra-histo·ric, -al. Extra-hu·man. Extra-hu·ndredal,** not included in any hundred. **Extra-juda·ical,** outside the conditions of the Jewish dispensation. **Extra-ju·ral,** 'outside the court' (Poste). **Extra-le·gal. Extra-li·mital** [L. *limes, limit-*], beyond the limits of a country or district. **Extra-li·mitary,** situated beyond the limit or bounds. **Extra-lo·gical,** lying outside the domain of logic; hence, **Extra-lo·gically** *adv.* †**Extra-mari·ne,** from beyond the sea. **Extra-ma·trical** [L. *matrix, matric-*], situated outside the MATRIX of a parasitical plant. **Extra-matrimo·nial. Extra-me·dial,** lying outside or beyond the middle line. **-medu·llary. Extra-meri·dional,** *Astron.* of or pertaining to deviation from the meridian. **Extra-metaphy·sical. Extra-me·trical** = HYPERMETRICAL. **Extra-na·tional,** outside the limits of a nation. **Extra-nu·clear,** placed outside the nucleus of a cell. **Extra-o·cular,** situated or occurring outside the eyes. **Extra-offi·cial,** outside the legitimate duties or emoluments of an office. **Extra-o·rbital,** *Zool.* situated outside the eye-cavity (of a crustacean). **Extra-patria·rchal,** outside the conditions of the patriarchal dispensation. **Extra-peritone·al,** 'outside the peritoneum' (*Syd Soc. Lex.*). **Extra-phy·sical,** not subject to physical laws or methods. **Extra-pla·netary,** beyond the region of the planets' movements. **-po·lar. Extra-profe·ssional,** outside the ranks of a profession; outside the course of professional duties. **Extra-red,** said of rays outside the visible spectrum at its red extremity. **Extra-re·gular,** outside of, or transgressing, the rule. **Extra-sacerdo·tal. Extra-sci·entific,** beyond the scope of science. **Extra-scri·ptural,** drawn from sources outside the Scriptures; hence **Extra-scriptura·lity. Extra-se·nsible, Extra-se·nsuous,** beyond the reach of sensuous perception. **Extra-spe·ctral,** lying outside the visible spectrum. **Extra-sto·machal,** taking place outside the stomach. **Extra-syllogi·stic. Extra-te·rrene. Extra-terre·strial. Extra-the·cal,** *Zool.*, etc. situated outside the theca. **Extra-to·rrid,** existing outside the torrid zone. **Extra-tro·pical. Extra-unive·rsity. Extra-u·rban. Extra-u·terine,** existing, formed, or taking place outside the uterus. **Extra-violet,** said of rays outside the visible spectrum at its violet extremity. **Extra-zodi·acal,** *Astron.* situated outside the zodiac. See also Main words.

Extract (e·kstrækt), *sb.* 1549. [partly ad. L. *extractum, extrahere*; partly repr. L. *extracta* pa. pple. fem. (= AF. *estrete*).] †**1.** *gen.* Something extracted or drawn out; *fig.* the pith –1651. **2.** 'The substance extracted' (J.); in mod. use 'applied to the tough or viscid matter obtained by treating any matter with solvents and then evaporating the solvent' (Watts). Also loosely, any preparation containing the essential principle of a substance in a concentrated form. 1590. Also *fig.* †**b.** = EXTRACTIVE B. 2. –1813. †**3.** A summary; an outline –1681. **4.** An excerpt, quotation 1666. **5.** *Law.* †**a.** = ESTREAT *sb.* **b.** *Sc. Law.* The warrant on which execution on a judicial decree may issue; also, a properly authenticated copy of a deed or other writing of record 1606. †**6.** EXTRACTION, descent –1796.

6. Every Soul, who gets to be rich, immediately enquires into his E. NORTH.

Extract (ekstræ·kt), *v.* 1489. [f. L. *extract-*, *extrahere*, f. *ex-* + *trahere*. Cf. F. *extraire*.] **1.** *trans.* 'To draw out of any containing body or cavity' (J.) 1570. **2.** 'To take from something of which the thing taken was a part' (J.); *esp.* to copy out, make extracts from 1607. **3.** To get out by force, effort, or contrivance; to draw forth against a person's will 1599. **4.** To obtain (elements, juices, etc.) from a thing or substance by any chemical or mechanical operation. Also *fig.* 1594. †**5.** Only in *passive*: To be derived or descended –1678.

1. To put the hand in the pocket, and e. it clutch'd *Meas. for M.* III. ii. 50. 2. To e. Falsehoods out of a Pamphlet SWIFT. 3. To e. an arrow 1767, consent H. WALPOLE, teeth 1878. 4. Extracting of the oiles out of the hearbes PLAT. *fig.* To e. happiness out of ills YOUNG, pleasure out of life GEO. ELIOT. Phr. *To e. the root of a number or quantity* (Math.): to obtain the root by a mathematical operation. Hence **Extra·ct** *ppl. a.* extracted. **Extra·ctable** *a.*, also **-ible. Extra·cting** *ppl. a.* that extracts; also, ?distracting (*Twel. N.* V. i. 288).

Extraction (ekstræ·kʃən). 1477. [a. F., ad. med.L. *extractionem*; see prec.] **1.** The action or process of extracting 1530. †**2.** That which is extracted; extract –1698. **3.** *Math.* The process or method of extracting (a root) 1557. **4.** Origin, descent; †source 1477.

1. The e. of gold from mines MORSE, of corn from Sicily NELSON, of a fœtus 1799. Phr. *Spirit of the first e.*: that which comes off at the first distillation. 2. This rare e...hath .. power to disperse all malignant humours B. JONS. 4. The memory of their common e. GIBBON.

Extractive (ekstræ·ktiv). 1599. [f. L. *extrahere*; see EXTRACT *v.* Cf. F. *extractif*, *-ive*.]

A. *adj.* **1.** Tending to draw out. **2.** Capable of being extracted; of the nature of an extract 1789.

1. Phr. *E. industry*: an industry (*e.g.* agriculture, mining, fisheries, etc.) that is concerned with extracting natural productions. 2. Separating the e. acid.. from wine 1816.

B. *sb.* **1.** An extractive substance 1844. **2.** 'The brown insoluble mass of doubtful composition, left after the preparation of vegetable extracts' (Wagstaffe) 1807.

1. The separation [of the viscous liquor] into..albumen, aqueous e., and alcoholic e. TODD.

Extractor (ekstræ·ktəɹ). 1611. [f. as prec. + -OR.] One who, or that which, extracts; *esp.* that part of a breech-loading gun which removes the cartridge.

†**Extradi·ctionary** *a. rare.* [f. L. *extra dictionem* + -ARY.] Of fallacies: Not consisting in expression; real. SIR T. BROWNE.

Extradite (e·kstrădəit), *v.* 1864. [f. next.] **1.** To give up (a fugitive foreign criminal) to the proper authorities, in pursuance of a treaty. **b.** To obtain the extradition of 1883. **2.** *Psychol.* To localize (a sensation) at a distance from the centre of sensation (*rare*) 1887.

1. b. The effort of England to e. Sheridan, of the Irish World, New York 1883. Hence **Extradi·table** *a.* liable, or rendering liable, to extradition.

Extradition (ekstrădi·ʃən). 1839. [a. F., f. *ex-* + *traditionem* the action of delivering up; see TRADITION.] **1.** The action of giving up a fugitive criminal to the authorities of the state in which the crime was committed. Hence *gen.*: Surrender (of a prisoner) by one authority to another. **2.** The process of localizing a sensation at a distance from the centre of sensation 1874. **3.** *attrib.*, as in **Extradition treaty,** a treaty by which two nations mutually agree to surrender any fugitive criminal who has committed in the other's territory any of certain specified offences. 1852.

Extrados (ekstrē¹·dǫs). 1772. [a. F., f. L. *extra* outside + F. *dos* the back.] *Archit.* The upper or exterior curve of an arch; *esp.* the upper curve of the voussoirs or stones which immediately form the arch. Cf. INTRADOS. Hence **Extra·dosed** *a.* having an e. (of a certain kind); used of an arch in which the curves of the intrados and e. are concentric and parallel.

Extradotal (ekstrădōᵘ·tăl), *a.* 1827. [f. L. *extra* + *dotem* + -AL.] *Law.* Forming no part of the dowry.

Extra-foraneous (e:kstrăfǫrē¹·nĭəs), *a.* 1781. [f. EXTRA- + med.L. *foraneus* (f. *foris* door) + -OUS.] Outdoor.

†**Extrait,** *pa. pple.* [a. F.; see EXTRACT *v.*] Extracted; descended. CAXTON.

Extrajudicial (e:kstrăˌdʒudi·ʃal), *a.* 1630. [f. L. *extra* + *iudicium* + -AL.] **1.** Forming no part of the case before the court; not delivered from the bench; informal. **2.** Outside the ordinary course of justice; unwarranted 1641.

1. The opinion of the judge.. is considered e. MARKBY. Hence **E:xtrajudi·cially** *adv.*

Extrality (ekstræ·lĭti). 1926. Syncopated form of EXTRATERRITORIALITY (in its extended use).

†**Extrami·ssion.** 1630. [See EXTRA and MISSION.] Emission –1674.

Extramundane (ekstrămɒ·ndē¹n), *a.* 1665. [ad. late L. *extramundanus*, f. *extra mundum*; see EXTRA- and MUNDANE.] **1.** Of or pertaining to a region outside of our world; *fig.* remote, not of this world. **2.** Of or pertaining to what is outside the universe 1706.

1. Aerolites..were proved to be of e. origin 1879.

Extramural (ekstrămiūᵊ·răl), *a.* 1854. [f. L. *extra muros* + -AL; see EXTRA- and MURAL.] Outside the walls of a city or town; *esp.* in *extramural* interment.

Extraneity (ekstrănī·ĭti). *rare.* [f. L. *extraneus* + -ITY.] The quality of being extraneous. ABP. THOMSON.

Extraneous (ekstrē¹·nĭəs), *a.* 1638. [f. L. *extraneus* (f. *extra*) + -OUS. Cf. STRANGE.] **1.** Of external origin; foreign. **2.** External *to* something specified 1655.

1. E. interference BURKE, circumstances HARE, rock LYELL. 2. Points clearly e. to religion PALEY. Persons e. to the church ROBERTSON. Hence **Extra·neous-ly** *adv.*, **-ness.**

Extraordinary (ekstrǭ·ɹdinări, ekstraˌǭ·ɹdinări). 1460. [ad. L. *extraordinarius*, f. *extra ordinem* outside (the usual) order. Cf. F. *extraordinaire.*]

A. *adj.* Out of the usual course or order; often opp. to *ordinary*; in *Mus.* †ACCIDENTAL, q. v. –1731. **2.** Out of or additional to the regular staff; supernumerary. Formerly with the notion of being specially employed for a temporary purpose. 1585. **3.** Of a kind, amount, degree, or measure not usually met with; exceptional. Now with emotional sense, expressing astonishment, etc. 1572. †**5.** = EXTRA. Often following the sb. –1812.

1. E. judgements 1553, occasions FULLER, measures 1745. 2. The first audience of the Russian E. Embassadour, at which he made his Emperour's Presents BOYLE. 3. These signes haue markt me extraordinarie 1 *Hen. IV*, III. i. 41. The e. influence of divine Grace 1656. An e. nose 1798. 5. A glass e. after dinner 1812. Hence **Extrao·rdinarily** *adv.* **Extrao·rdinariness.**

†**B.** *adv.* = EXTRAORDINARILY *adv.* –1778.

C. *sb.* **1.** †That which is extraordinary –1754; in *pl.* esp. extraordinary receipts or payments (now *arch.*) 1599. **2.** = EXTRA *sb.* 1660. †**3.** An extraordinary envoy; a supernumerary official –1671.

1. Not only the king's ordinary revenues, but the extraordinaries CARLYLE. 2. A few extraordinaries for the house PEPYS.

Extra-parochial (e·kstră părōᵘ·kiăl), *a.* 1674. [f. EXTRA- + Eccl. L. *parochia* (see PARISH) + -AL.] Outside the parish, or parish obligations. Hence **Extra-paro·chial-ly** *adv.*, **-ness.**

Extrapolation (e:kstrăpolē¹·ʃən). 1878. [f.

EXTRA + (INTER)POLATION.] The action or method of finding by a calculation based on the known terms of a series, other terms, whether preceding or following. Also *transf.*

Extraprovincial (e:kstrăˌprǫvi·nʃăl), *a.* 1685. [ad. med.L. *extraprovincialis*, f. *extra provinciam.*] Outside the limits of a province.

E:xtrate:rritoria·lity. 1836. [f. mod.L. phrase *extrā territōri-um* outside the territory + -AL + -ITY.] = EXTERRITORIALITY; extended later to denote the right or jurisdiction of a country over all its nationals abroad. So **E:xtraterrito·rial** *a.*

†**Extrau·ght,** *pa. pple.* 1523. [var. of EXTRACT *ppl. a.*; cf. *distraught.*] 1. Extracted, descended -1593. 2. Distraught -1575.

1. 3 *Hen. VI*, II. ii. 142.

Extravagance (ekstræ·văgăns). 1643. [a. F.; see EXTRAVAGANT and -ANCE.] †1. A going out of the usual path; an excursion, digression -1656. 2. The quality of being extravagant or of exceeding just or prescribed limits, *esp.* those of decorum, probability, or truth; unrestrained excess; also, an instance of this 1650. 3. Excessive prodigality in expenditure, household management, etc. 1727.

2. You will accuse me of e. in this description LADY M. W. MONTAGU. The extravagances of ignorance and credulity COLERIDGE. 3. The e. of cooks (*mod.*).

Extravagancy (ekstræ·văgănsi). 1601. [f. EXTRAVAGANT; see -ANCY.] = EXTRAVAGANCE 2, 3. 1625; also †vagrancy -1669.

Extravagant (ekstræ·văgănt). ME. [ad. med.L. *extravagantem*, *extravagari* (or *extra vagari*); infl. later by F. *extravagant*, and It. *stravagante.*]

A. *adj.* †1. That wanders out of bounds; vagrant; keeping no fixed place -1672. 2. *Canon Law.* Applied to certain 'stray' decrees not originally codified or collected in the decretals ME. †3. Straggling -1669. †4. Widely divergent (*from*); remote *from*, irrelevant *to* a purpose or subject -1665. †5. Unusual, abnormal; unsuitable -1701. 6. 'Roving beyond just limits or prescribed methods' (J.); excessive, irregular, fantastically absurd. Now: Astonishingly or flagrantly excessive or extreme. 1588. 7. Prodigal, wasteful 1707.

1. At his [the cock's] warning.. Th' e., and erring Spirit hyes to his Confine *Haml.* I. i. 154. 3. Too thick and e. Roots EVELYN. 6. E. in their accounts of themselves STILLINGFL. E. demands 1769, opinions 1809; e. whimsies about dress MACAULAY. 7. An e. interest of 20 per cent FREIND. E. of time 1739. Hence **Extra·vagantly** *adv.*

B. *sb.* 1. *Canon Law.* An 'extravagant' decree; see A. 2. 1502. †2. A vagrant -1650. †3. An eccentric -1768; a spendthrift -1825. †4. An extravagancy -1700.

Extravaganza (ekstræ:văgæ·nză). 1789. [ad. It. *estravaganza*, refash. after L.] 1. A composition, literary, musical, or dramatic, of a fantastic character 1794. 2. Bombastic extravagance of language or behaviour.

Extravagate (ekstræ·văgeit), *v.* 1600. [f. med.L. *extravagat-*, *extravagari* (or *extra vagari*), f. *extra* outside + *vagari* to wander.] 1. *intr.* To stray *from, into.* 2. To wander at will 1766. 3. To exceed what is proper or reasonable 1829. Hence †**Extravaga·tion.**

Extravasate (ekstræ·văseit), *v.* 1669. [f. L. *extra* + *vas* vessel + -ATE[3]; cf. F. *extravaser.*] 1. To let or force out (*esp.* blood) from its proper vessel. 2. *intr.* for *refl.* To flow out; to escape 1686.

2. Blood sometimes extravasates into the arachnoid sac TODD. Hence †**Extra·vasate** *a.* extravasated; formed by extravasation. var. †**E·xtravase.**

Extravasation (ekstræ:văsēi·ʃən). 1676. [f. prec.; cf. F. *extravasation.*] 1. *Path.* The escape of an organic fluid from its proper vessels; a mass or spot of extravasated blood. 2. *Geol.* Effusion (of molten rock) from a subterranean reservoir 1842.

Extravascular (ekstrăvæ·skiŭlăɹ), *a.* 1804. [f. EXTRA- + VASCULAR.] Outside the vascular system; not vascular.

†**Extrave·nate,** *v. rare.* 1650. [f. L. *extra* + *vena* + -ATE[3].] To let (blood) out of the veins -1668. Hence †**Extrave·nate** *a.* extravasated. **Extravena·tion.**

†**Extrave·rsion.** *rare.* 1691. [ad. mod.L. *extraversionem*, f. L. *extra* + *versionem*, f. *vertere* to turn.] A turning out; a rendering manifest -1732. So †**Extrave·rt** *v.* to turn out so as to be visible.

†**Extrea·t,** *sb.* 1489. [var. of ESTREAT, q. v.] 1. = ESTREAT *sb.* -1631. 2. Extraction. SPENSER *F. Q.* V. x. I. Hence †**Extrea·t** *v.* to estreat; to eliminate.

Extreme (ekstrī·m). 1460. [a. OF., ad. L. *extremus*, superl. of *exterus* (see EXTERIOR). The adj. is not always equivalent to a superlative; hence, it is properly compared.]

A. *adj.* 1. Outermost; endmost, situated at either of the ends (opp. to *mean*) 1503. 2. Farthest, or very far advanced in any direction; utmost, uttermost 1600. 3. Last, latest. *Obs.* or *arch.*, exc. in *Extreme unction* (see quots.). 1477. 4. Going to great lengths; opp. to *moderate* 1460. 5. *Mus.* Augmented; as in *extreme interval* 1876.

1. The fruitful continent's extremest bound POPE. *E. and mean ratio* (Math.): the relation of a line and its parts, when the whole is to the greater part, as the greater part is to the less. 2. The Sea's extreamest Borders ADDISON. The e. point reached 1860. 3. The e. day 1513. Phr. *Extreme unction*: in the R. C. Church, 'a sacrament in which the sick in danger of death are anointed by a priest for the health of soul and body, the anointing being accompanied by a set form of words' (*Cath. Dict.*). 4. The most e. Povertie 1460. E. necessity 1550. E. Idolaters 1634. In dress E. COWPER. E. cases JOWETT.

†B. *adv.* In an extreme degree; extremely -1816.

C. *sb.* 1. quasi-*sb.*, as *In* (*the*) *extreme*: extremely 1604. †2. *sb.* The extreme point or verge; an end, extremity -1808. 3. One of two things removed as far as possible from each other, in position, nature, or condition 1555. b. *Logic.* In a proposition the subject or predicate, as distinct from the copula; in a syllogism the major or minor term, as dist. from the middle 1628. c. *Math.* The first or last term of a ratio, series, or set of numbers 1571. 4. A very high degree of anything 1593; †*pl*, extremities, straits, hardships -1667. 5. An excessive degree; also, something carried to excess, an extreme measure 1588.

1. Of one.. Perplex'd in the e. *Oth.* v. ii. 347. 3. Two extremes of passion, ioy and greefe *Lear* v. iii. 198. Phr. *Extremes meet.* 4. Enthusiastical to an e. 1791. 5. To go to the e. of a lock-out 1867.

Hence **Extre·meless** *a.* having no extremities; infinite (*rare*). **Extre·mely** *adv.* †to the uttermost degree; in an e. degree; very much. **Extre·meness.** **Extre·mist**, one who goes to extremes, or who holds e. opinions or advocates e. measures; also as *adj.*; so **Extre·mism.** **Extremi·stic** *a.*

Extremity (ekstre·mĭti). ME. [ad. F. *extrémité*, ad. L. *extremitatem*; see EXTREME *a.*] 1. The extreme point or portion of anything; the end; in *pl.* the hands and feet 1460. †2. The 'extremes' as opp. to the 'mean' -1598. 3. The extreme or utmost degree; = EXTREME *sb.* 4. 1543. †4. Extreme intensity of anything -1797. †5. Extravagance -1712. †6. Extreme severity or rigour -1639. 7. A condition of extreme urgency or need ME. 8. A person's last moments (*arch.*) 1602. 9. An extreme measure. Chiefly in *pl.* 1639. 10. Extremeness. Somewhat *rare.* 1848.

1. Antennæ thickening towards their e. STARK. 3. Extremities of Penury and Want 1638. 4. The e. of the weather BEWICK. 6. *Com. Err.* v. i. 307. 7. Phr. *To drive, reduce to* (*the last*) *e.* or *extremities.* 9. To push matters to the e. of a civil war 1862.

Extricable (e·kstrikăb'l), *a.* 1623. [See next and -ABLE.] That can or may be extricated, †unravelled, or got out.

Extricate (e·kstrikeit), *v.* 1614. [f. L. *extricat-*, *extricare*, f. *ex-* + *tricæ* perplexities.] 1. *trans.* To unravel; *fig.* to clear of intricacies or perplexities. Now *rare.* 2. To disentangle; to set free *from, out of* (anything that entangles, confines, or perplexes) 1631. b. *Chem.* To disengage (gas, etc.) from a state of combination 1790.

1. Some method of extricating public affairs ALISON. 2. A thicket, out of which he knows not how to e. himself 1732. b. To e. water from an acid 1838. Hence **Extrica·tion**, the action of extricating; disentanglement; disengagement (of gas, etc.) from something containing it.

Extrinsic (ekstri·nsik), *a.* 1541. [ad. F. *extrinsèque*, f. (ult.) L. *extrinsecus* adv., f. *exter* outside + *-in* suffix of locality + *secus* prep. 'beside', f. root of *sequi* to follow; thus = 'on the outside'. The ending is assim. to -IC.] 1. †Exterior; external. 2. Pertaining to an object in its external relations. Now *rare.* 1617. 3. Lying outside the object under consideration 1666; operating from without 1613. 4. Not inherent or essential; adventitious; opp. to *intrinsic* 1622.

1. E. ornaments JOHNSON. 2. The e. muscles which serve to move the whole external ear DARWIN. 3. Things extrinsick from.. the main matter 1678. E. stimuli 1878. 4. E. advantages of birth HAZLITT. Hence **Extri·nsical** *a.* extrinsic; †*sb.* something that is e. **Extri·nsical-ly** *adv.*, **-ness.** **Extri·nsicate** *v.* to exhibit outwardly; to express (*rare*).

Extro-, a quasi-L. prefix, an altered form of L. *extra*, with the sense 'outwards'. Used only in compounds, by way of antithesis to *intro-*.

Extroitive (ekstrǫu·itiv), *a. rare.* [f. prec. + L. *it-*, *ire* + -IVE; cf. *introitive.*] Directed to external objects. COLERIDGE.

†**Extrom·it,** *v.* [f. as prec. + L. *mittere.*] To send out. KEN. Hence †**Extromi·ssion.**

Extrorsal (ekstrǭ·ɹsăl), *a.* 1842. [f. next + -AL.] *Bot.* = next.

Extrorse (ekstrǭ·ɹs), *a.* 1858. [a. F., f. L. *extrorsus*, f. *extra* adv. + *versus.*] *Bot.* Turned or opening outwards; said of anthers that look away from the pistils.

Extroversion (ekstrovɔ̄·ɹʃən). 1656. [f. EXTRO- + L. *vertere* to turn; cf. *introversion.*] Turning or being turned outwards; as, *extroversion* of the bladder. So **Extrove·rt** *v.* to turn outwards 1671. Hence **E·xtrovert** *sb.* one who is concerned mainly with what is external or objective: opp. to INTROVERT *sb.* 2. 1918.

Extruct, -ion, -ive: see EXSTRUCT, etc.

Extrude (ekstrū·d), *v.* 1566. [ad. L. *extrudere*, f. *ex-* + *trudere* to thrust.] *trans.* To thrust forth; to urge out; to expel; also, *occas.*, to protrude out. Also *intr.* for *refl.* (*rare*).

Presbyterianism was only extruded gradually M. ARNOLD. Hence **Extru·sive** *a.* tending to e.; characterized by extrusion.

Extrusion (ekstrū·ʒən). 1540. [f. L. *extrudere*; see prec.] The action of extruding; the fact of being extruded.

Extuberance (ekstiū·bĕrăns). ? *Obs.* 1607. [f. EXTUBERANT; see -ANCE.] The quality of being extuberant; *concr.* a swelling, projection, protuberance. *lit.* and *fig.* So †**Extu·berancy.**

Extuberant (ekstiū·bĕrănt), *a.* Now *rare.* 1578. [ad. L. *extuberantem*, *extuberare*, f. *ex-* + *tuber* a swelling.] Swelling out, protuberant.

†**Extu·berate,** *v. rare.* 1623. [f. L. *extuberat-* ppl. stem; see prec.] To swell, or make to swell, out or up -1768. Hence †**Extu·beration,** protuberance.

Extume·scence. 1611. [a. F., f. (ult.) L. *ex-* + *tumere* to swell.] A swelling up or out. So †**Extume·scency** (*rare*).

Extund (ekstɔ̄·nd), *v.* 1610. [f. L. *extundere.*] To beat or hammer out; only *fig.*

†**Exty·pal,** *a.* Var. of ECTYPAL. Cudworth.

Exuberance (egziū·bĕrăns). 1638. [a. F., ad. L. *exuberantia*; see EXUBERANT and -ANCE.] 1. The quality or condition of being EXUBERANT; abundant productiveness; luxuriance; copiousness; redundance 1664. 2. An overflowing quantity; a superabundance 1638. †3. *concr.* An overflow; an excrescence, protuberance -1825.

1. A happy e. of animal spirits SCOTT. An e. of the metaphysical imagination JOWETT. 2. An e. of life 1868. So **Exu·berancy.**

Exuberant (egziū·bĕrănt), *a.* 1503. [ad. L. *exuberantem*, *exuberare*, f. *ex-* + *uberare* to be fertile, f. *uber* adj., conn. w. *uber* udder.] 1. Luxuriantly fertile or prolific; abundantly productive. Also *fig.* 1645. 2. Growing or produced in superabundance 1513. 3. Overflowing, as a fountain, etc. 1678. Also *fig.* 1503.

1. E. vines EVELYN, fancy 1788. 2. E. branches EVELYN. An e. population BUCKLE. 3. *fig.* E. goodness BOYLE, eloquence FULLER, narrative GEO. ELIOT, charities LECKY. Hence **Exu·berantly** *adv.*

Exuberate (egziū·bĕreit), *v.* 1471. [f. L. *exuberat-* ppl. stem; see prec.] 1. *intr.* To be exuberant; to abound, overflow 1623. †2. *trans. Alchem.* ? To render fruitful (mercury, the alkahest) -1671. Hence **Exubera·tion.**

Exuccous, -ction, obs. ff. EXSUCCOUS, -SUCTION.

Exucontian (eksiukǫ·ntiăn). 1844. [f. Eccl. Gr. ἐξουκόντιος, f. phr. ἐξ οὐκ ὄντων from things that once were not + -AN.] *Eccl.* A name for Arians as holding Christ to be 'of a substance that once was not'.

†**E·xudate,** *v.* 1646. [f. L. *ex(s)udat-*, *ex(s)udare* to EXUDE.] = EXUDE *v.* -1796

Hence **Exuda·tion,** the process of exuding; also, *erron.*, percolation; that which is exuded. **Exu·dative** *a.* of, pertaining to, or characterized by exudation. †**Exu·datory** *a.* characterized by exudation; *sb.* a means of exuding.

Exude (egziū·d, eks-), *v.* 1574. [ad. L. *ex(s)udare*, f. *ex-* + *sudare* to sweat.] **1.** *intr.* To ooze out like sweat; to pass off in drops through the pores, an incision or orifice. **2.** *trans.* To sweat out or give out like sweat, to discharge through the pores, etc. Also *fig.* 1798.

1. Gum, which exudes from incisions in thick viscid drops VINES. Hence **Exu·dence** (*rare*).

†**E·xul,** *sb.* 1566. [a. L. *ex(s)ul.*] = EXILE *sb.*², q. v.

†**E·xulate,** *v. rare.* 1535. [f. L. *ex(s)ulat-*, *ex(s)ulare* to be in exile.] To exile or go into exile -1640.

†**Exu·lcerate,** *a.* 1545. [ad. L. *exulceratus*; see next.] Exulcerated. *lit.* and *fig.* -1684.

Exulcerate (egzʊ·lsĕrẽⁱt), *v. arch.* 1533. [f. L. *exulcerat-*, *exulcerare*, f. *ex-* intensive + *ulcerare.*] †**1.** *trans.* To cause ulcers in -1732. **2.** *fig.* To fret; to irritate; to aggravate 1594. †**3.** *intr.* To break out into ulcers -1659.

1. It [the reume] doth e. the lunges ELYOT. 2. I must lye perpetually and e. my conscience CHILLINGW. Hence **Exu·lcera·tion,** ulceration, *esp.* in its early stage; *concr.* an ulcerated place; also *fig.* †**Exu·lcerative,** †**Exu·lceratory** *adjs.*, tending to produce ulcers.

Exult (egzʊ·lt), *v.* 1570. [ad. F. *exulter*, ad. L. *ex(s)ultare*, f. *ex-* + *salire* to leap.] †**1.** *intr.* To spring or leap up; to leap for joy -1727. **2.** To rejoice exceedingly; to be elated; to triumph. Const. *in, at, on, over,* and *inf.* 1594.

1. The whales exulted under him CHAPMAN. 2. Who can..not e. in being born a Briton 1756. Hence **Exu·ltance, Exu·ltancy,** exultant state or condition; gladness; triumph. **Exu·ltingly** *adv.*

Exultant (egzʊ·ltănt), *a.* 1653. [ad. L. *ex(s)ultantem*; see prec.] Exulting, triumphantly joyful.

The wild e. cry 1844. Hence **Exu·ltantly** *adv.*

Exultation (egzʊltẽⁱ·ʃən). ME. [ad. L. *ex(s)ultationem*; see EXULT. Cf. F. *exultation.*] †**1.** The action of springing or leaping up 1599. **2.** The action of exulting; triumph, joyousness, rapturous delight. Also *concr.* an object exulted over. ME. **b.** *pl* Shouts of joy. HOOKER.

2. The e. of the Court over the decision of the judges GREEN.

Exu·ndate, *v. rare.* 1721. [f. L. *exundat-*, *exundare*, f. *ex-* + *undare* to rise in waves, f. *unda.*] *intr.* To overflow. Hence **Exunda·tion,** overflow (now *rare*).

†**Exu·ngulate,** *v.* 1623. [f. late L. *exungulat-*, *exungulare* to lose the hoof, f. *ex-* + *ungula.*] To pare off the nails, the hoofs, the white part from rose-leaves, etc. -1775.

Exuperable, -ate, etc.: see EXSU-.

Exurge, -ence, -ent: see EXSU-.

Exuscitate, -ation: see EXSU-.

†**Exu·st,** *v. rare.* 1623. [f. L. *exust-*, *exurere.*] *trans.* To burn up. Hence †**Exu·st** *a.* burnt or dried up. †**Exu·stible** *a.* capable of being burnt up (*rare*). †**Exu·stion,** the action or process of burning or burning up.

Exuviable (egziū·viăb'l), *a.* 1839. [a. F., f. next + -ABLE.] Capable of being exuviated or sloughed off. Hence **Exu·viabi·lity,** the property of being e. (In Dicts. explained as the power of casting off exuviæ.)

‖**Exuviæ** (egziū·vi,ī). 1653. [a. L. *exuviæ* things stripped off, f. *exuere.*] Cast skins, shells, or coverings of animals; any parts of animals which are shed or cast off, recent or fossil. Also *transf.* and *fig.*

Hence **Exu·vial** *a.* pertaining to, or of the nature of e.; *sb. pl.* things stripped off; spoils. †**Exu·vious** *a.* exuvial.

Exuviate (egziū·vi,eⁱt), *v.* 1855. [f. prec. + -ATE.] *intr.* To cast off or shed exuviæ; *trans.* to cast off as exuviæ.

The young crayfish e. two or three times in the course of the first year HUXLEY. Hence **Exu·via·tion.**

‖**Ex-voto** (eks,vōu·to). 1787. [L. *ex voto.*] An offering made in pursuance of a vow. Hence **Ex-votive** *a.* pertaining to, or performed by, ex-voto offerings.

Ey, obs. f. AY; see also EGG.

‖**Eyalet** (ẹyā·let). 1853. [Turk., a. Arab., f. *āl* to preside.] An administrative division of the Turkish empire; now called VILAYET, q. v.

Eyas (əi·ăs). 1486. [Altered f. NYAS, a. F. *niais*:—L. **nid(i)acem*, f. *nidus* nest; *a nyas* = *an(e)yas*; the spelling being infl. in form by ME. *ey* = EGG and *eyry*; see ADDER.] **1.** A young hawk from the nest, or one incompletely trained. **2.** *attrib.*, as *e.-hawk*; in sense 'unfledged' as *e.-thoughts, -wings.* Also **e.-musket** (see MUSKET), a sprightly child. 1596.

2. Ere flitting Time could wag his e. wings SPENSER.

Eye (əi), *sb.*¹ [OE. *ēage*, wk. neut. :—OTeut. **augon-*. The original pl. was in *-an*, ME. *-en*, whence n. dial. *een, ene*, arch. *eyne.*]

I. The organ of sight, sometimes including the surrounding parts: **a.** in man and vertebrate animals; **b.** in invertebrate animals 1665. **2.** The eye as possessing the power of vision. Often used pleonastically for emphasis. ME. **b.** *fig.*; esp. as applied to a city, country, etc. 1599. **3.** Used in *sing.* and *pl.* for: The action or function of the eyes; the sense of seeing; 'ocular knowledge' (J.); sight ME. †**b.** Range of vision, view, sight -1711. **c.** *fig.* 1602. **4.** With reference to the direction of the eye: Look, glance, gaze OE. **5.** Observation; attention, regard ME. **6.** (in *sing.* only). The faculty of perception or discrimination of visual objects 1657. **7.** *fig.* Point of view; estimation, opinion, judgement ME.

1. Youre two eyn will sle me sodenly, I may the beaute of them not sustene CHAUCER. The pyrates.. bounde his handes..and iyen LD. BERNERS. **b.** The compound eye..consists essentially of a series of transparent cone-like bodies, arranged in a radiate manner against the inner surface of the cornea 1878. Phrases. *To cry one's eyes out* (colloq.). *To wipe the e. of another shooter* (Sporting): to kill game that he has missed. *All my e.* (slang): all humbug. *My eye(s!* an exclam. of astonishment, etc. 2. I have seen him..with my own eyes take off his seal 1776. Phr. *Half an e.*: the smallest power of vision. *To lose an e.*, freq. = to become blind of one eye. *To put out the eyes*, freq. = to deprive of sight *The naked e.*: see NAKED. **b.** Sorrowes eie SHAKS. Athens, the e. of Greece MILT. *P. R.* IV. 240. The e. of faith 1687. 3. Is this face Heroes? are our eies our owne *Much Ado* IV. i. 72. Thy well-study'd marbles fix our e. POPE. **c.** I see my father..In my minds e. *Haml.* I. ii. 184. 4. Phrases. *To see e. to e.* (*Isa.* lii. 8): often misused for to be of one mind. *Eyes right, left, front* (Mil.). *The glad e.*: an amorous or festive glance (*slang*). 5. Phrases. *To give an e. to, have an e. upon. To have an e. to. With an e. to. To be all eyes.* 6. To have the e. of a great captain MACAULAY. Phrases. *To estimate by e. To have, get, one's e.* (*well*) *in*: to be or become able to judge distance accurately. 7. Phr. *In the e. of (the) law, logic,* etc.

†**II.** Slight shade, tinge. (Cf. F. *œil.*) -1699.

III. 1. An object resembling the eye in appearance, shape, or position; as: **a.** the axillary bud on plants; the leaf-bud of a potato; **b.** the remains of the calyx on fruit; **c.** the centre of a flower; **d.** one of the spots near the end of the tail-feathers of a peacock; **e.** a small dark spot in the eggs of a fish and insects while hatching ME. **2.** The opening through which the water of a fountain wells up 1857. **3.** A central mass; the brightest spot (of light) 1864. **4.** The centre of revolution 1760. **5.** A hole or aperture: **a.** in a needle OE.; **b.** in a tool or implement, for the insertion of some other object 1554; **c.** in the upper stone of a mill, in a kiln, etc.; also for exit or ingress, as in a fox's earth, a mine, etc. 1686; **d.** in bread or cheese, etc. (now *dial.*) 1528. **6.** A loop of metal or thread in a 'hook and eye'. Also a metal ring for holding a rod or bolt, or for a rope, etc. to pass through 1599. **b.** A loop of cord or rope; *esp.* 'the circular loop of a shroud or stay, where it goes over the mast' (Smyth) 1584. **7.** *Archit.* The centre of any part, as the *eye* of a dome, etc. Also *transf.* in *Conchology.* 1727. **8.** *Typog.* †**a.** = the FACE of a type. [Fr. *œil.*] **b.** The enclosed space in the letters *d, e, o,* etc. 1676.

5. **a.** So much wit..As will stop the e. of Helens needle *Tr. & Cr.* II. i. 87. **d.** Bad cheese..full of Eyes, not well prest 1688.

Phrases. *Eyes of her* (Naut.): 'the foremost part of the bay, or in the bows of a ship' (Smyth). *In the wind's e.* (Naut.): in the direction of the wind. *Glass e.*: a glass imitation of the natural eye; also, *pl.* a pair of spectacles; also = BULL'S-EYE.

Comb.: **e.-baby,** the image of the spectator seen in another's e.; **-bar,** a metal bar with an e. or hole at either end, used in bridges; **-bone,** the bony circle round the e., the orbit; **-copy,** a copy made by e.; **-dotter,** a small brush used in graining wood in imitation of bird's-eye maple; **-drop,** a tear; †**-flap** = BLINKER, q. v.; **-handle** (of a spade, etc.), a handle having an eyelet or hole; **-lens,** the lens nearest the eye in an optical instrument; **-line,** (*a*) the field or range of vision, (*b*) in *pl.* the lines above and below the e. of a bird; **-memory,** 'the impressing by will on memory things which we have seen'; **-opener,** (*a*) *U.S.* a dram, *esp.* one taken in the morning, (*b*) something that throws light on what was dark or ambiguous, (*c*) something which causes keen surprise; **-pedicel, -peduncle,** *Zool.* a pedicel or peduncle supporting an e.; **-point** = EYE-SPOT; **-probe,** *Surg.* a probe having an e. or small hole at one end; **-shade,** a shade for the eyes; **-speck,** an e. consisting of a single speck, a rudimentary e.; **-stalk** = *-peduncle*; **-stone,** (*a*) a stone resembling an e., (*b*) a calcareous body which being put into the inner corner of the e. works its way out at the outward corner and brings out any strange substance with it; **-trap,** something to catch or deceive the e.; **-tube,** the tube of the e.-piece in a telescope; **-wages,** such wages as e.-service calls for; **-waiter** = EYE-SERVANT; **-wash,** (*a*) lotion for the eye 1866; (*b*) *slang*, humbug, blarney 1884; **-wise** *a.*, wise in appearance; **-worship,** adoration performed by the e.

†**Eye,** *sb.*² ME. [From *an eye*, for *an eye*; see NYE.] A brood (of pheasants) -1725.

Eye (əi), *v.* 1566. [f. EYE *sb.*¹] †**1.** To see. *lit.* and *fig.* -1779. **2.** To direct the eyes to, look at or upon, behold, observe 1566. **3.** To keep an eye on; to observe narrowly 1586. †**4.** To have or keep in view -1771. †**5.** *intr.* To look or appear to the eye 1606. **6.** *trans.* To furnish with eyes 1854.

2. They eyed the prisoners with curiosity 1797. 3. And Saul eyed Dauid from that day 1 *Sam.* xviii. 9. 5. *Ant. & Cl.* I. iii. 97. Hence **Eye·able** *a.* that may be seen by the eye; sightly.

Eye-ball (əi·bǫl). 1590. [f. EYE *sb.*¹ + BALL.] **a.** The apple or pupil of the eye 1592. **b.** The eye itself.

Eye-beam (əi·bīm). 1588. [f. EYE *sb.*¹ + BEAM.] A beam or glance of the eye.

Eye-bolt (əi·bōult). 1769. [f. EYE *sb.*¹ + BOLT *sb.*] A bolt or bar eyed to receive a hook, ring, etc.

Eye·-bree. Now *Sc.* and *dial.* OE. [f. EYE *sb.*¹ + BREE *sb.*¹] = †EYE-LID, †-LASH, -BROW.

Eyebright (əi·brəit). 1533. [f. EYE *sb.*¹ + BRIGHT.]

†**A.** *adj.* Bright to the eye (*rare*) 1607.

B. *sb.* **1.** = EUPHRASY; also *attrib.* prepared from euphrasy 1533. **2.** ? 'A kind of ale in Elizabeth's time' (Latham) 1610.

2. In days of Pimlico and Eye-bright B. JONS.

Eyebrow (əi·brau). 1585. [f. EYE *sb.*¹ + BROW. Not in OE.] **1.** The brow or arch of hair along the upper orbit of the eye. **2.** *Archit.* A moulding over a window; also, *occas.*, the fillet 1703.

Eyed (əid), *ppl. a.* ME. [f. EYE *sb.*¹] **1.** Furnished with eyes; often with *adj.* prefix, as *Argus-, blue-*, etc. **2.** Furnished with an eye, as *eyed-hooks* 1804. **3.** Marked as with eyes; spotted 1815.

Eye·-draught. 1773. [f. EYE *sb.* + DRAUGHT.] A drawing or plan made by eye, without measurement.

Eye·ful, *sb.* 1832. [f. EYE *sb.*¹ + -FUL.] As much as fills the eye. So **Eye·ful** *a.* conspicuous; observant (now *dial.*).

Eye-glass (əi·glas), *sb.* 1611. [f. EYE *sb.*¹ + GLASS.] †**1.** The crystalline lens of the eye. *Wint. T.* I. ii. 268. **2.** †**a.** A microscope. **b.** Now, a lens of glass or crystal to assist the sight. 1767. **3.** The eyepiece of any optical instrument 1664. **4.** A glass for applying lotions to the eye 1842.

Eyehole (əi·hōul). 1637. [f. EYE *sb.*¹ + HOLE.] The cavity containing the orbit of the eye; a hole to look through 1856; one of the depressions in a potato from which the buds spring (*dial.*) 1884.

Eye-lash (əi·læʃ). 1752. [f. EYE *sb.*¹ + LASH.] The row of hairs fringing the edge of the eyelid; also, a single one of these.

Eyeless (əi·lės), *a.* 1570. [f. EYE *sb.*¹ + -LESS.] 1. Without eyes (in various senses). 2. Deprived of the eyes 1592. 3. Blind; undiscriminating 1627.

2. Ask for this great deliverer now, and find him E. in Gaza MILT. *Sams.* 38. 3. An e. destiny MORLEY.

Eyelet (əi·lėt), *sb.* [ME. *oilet*, a. F. *œillet*, dim. of *œil* eye.] 1. A small round hole in cloth, sail-cloth, etc., worked like a button-hole, for the passage of a lace, ring, or rope, an EYELET-HOLE; also, a short metal tube, having its ends flattened for the same purpose. 2. An aperture or loophole, usually for observation ME. 3. A small eye. *lit.* and *fig.* 1799. 4. *attrib.* 1864.

4. *E.-ring*, a small metal ring, inserted in an e. to prevent wearing. *E.-punch*, a device for punching e.-holes and attaching papers together. Hence **Eye·let** *v.* to make eyelets in. **Eyeletee·r**, a stabbing instrument for piercing e.-holes.

Eyelet-hole (əi·lėt,hōul), *sb.* 1497. [f. EYELET *sb.* + HOLE.] = EYELET 1, 2.

Eyelid (əi·lid). ME. [f. EYE *sb.*¹ + LID.] One of the covers of the eye, dist. as *upper* and *lower*; one of the movable folds of skin with which an animal covers or uncovers the eye at pleasure.

Phr. *To hang by the eyelids*: to be in a dangerous position.

Eyepiece (əi·pīs). 1790. [f. EYE *sb.*¹ + PIECE.] *Optics.* The lens or combination of lenses at the eye-end of a telescope or other optical instrument, by which the image, formed by the mirror or object-glass, is viewed and magnified. Also *attrib.*

The principal kinds of eyepieces are (*a*) the *Huyghenian*, or so-called *negative* from the fact of its forming the image between the lenses; (*b*) the *Ramsden*, or common astronomical, called *positive* because the image is formed outside the field-glass; (*c*) the *erecting* or *terrestrial* for ordinary telescopes, which presents the object in an erect position.

attrib. E. micrometer, a graduated slip of glass introduced through slits in the eyepiece tube, so as to occupy the centre of the field.

Eye-pit. ME. [f. EYE *sb.*¹ + PIT.] The socket of the eye; also, the depression between the eye and the orbit.

Eyer (əi·əɹ), *sb. rare.* ME. [f. EYE *v.*] One who eyes or observes.

Eyer, obs. f. HEIR.

Eyer(e, obs. f. AIR.

†**Ey·(e)rer.** ME. [f. *eyre*, var. of AYRE *sb.*²] A brood falcon –1494.

Eye·salve. *Obs.* exc. *fig.* OE. [f. EYE *sb.*¹ + SALVE.] Eye-ointment.

Eye-servant (əi·sɔ̄ɹvănt). *Arch.* 1552. [f. EYE *sb*¹ + SERVANT.] One who serves the eye; one who does his duty only when under the eye of his master.

Eye·-se:rvice. 1526. [f. EYE *sb.*¹ + SERVICE.] a. The conduct of an eye-servant. †b. Service seen by the eye MILT. c. The homage of the eye 1869.

Eye·shot. 1599. [f. EYE *sb.*¹ + SHOT.] 1. The range of the eye, seeing distance, view. 2. A 'shot' or glance from the eye, prospect 1615.

1. Phr. *To come within e. of.*

Eye·sight. ME. [f. EYE *sb.*¹ + SIGHT.] 1. The power of seeing; sight. 2. The action of looking; a look. *Obs* exc. in *By, from, in (a person's) e.* ME. 3. The range of the eye ME.

2. That in Josephus which he sets down from his own e. 1641.

Eyesore (əi·sōəɹ). ME. [f. EYE *sb.*¹ + SORE.] †1. A soreness of the eyes –1562. 2. Something offensive to the eye; a blemish; a defect 1530. 3. A cause or object of dislike or disgust 1548.

2. Not an E. in his whole body DRYDEN. 3. Thou shalt be a burthen, and an Eye sore to thy friends RALEIGH.

Eye·-splice. 1769. [f. EYE *sb.*¹ + SPLICE *sb.*] A splice made by turning up the end of a rope, and interlacing its strands with those of the upper part.

Eye·spot. 1801. [f. EYE *sb.*¹ + SPOT *sb.*] 1. a. A spot resembling an eye 1879. b. A rudimentary eye 1877. 2. A kind of lily having a red spot in the middle of a violet leaf. Hence **Eye·spotted** *a.* having spots resembling eyes.

Eye·string. 1601. [f. EYE *sb.*¹ + STRING *sb.*] In *pl.* The strings (i.e. tendons, etc.) of the eye. *Cymb.* I, iii. 17.

Eye·-tooth. 1580. [f. EYE *sb.*¹ + TOOTH.] A tooth immediately under or next to the eye, a canine tooth.

Phr. *To cut one's eye-teeth*: to get out of babyhood.

Eye·water (əi·wǭtəɹ). 1590. [f. EYE *sb.*¹ + WATER *sb.*] a. Water flowing from the eye. Rare in *pl.* b. A lotion for the eye 1679. c. The humours of the eye 1874. d. *Slang.* = Gin 1869.

Eye·-wink. 1598. [f. EYE *sb.*¹ + WINK *sb.*] A wink or motion of the eye, a glance; an instant. So **Eye·-winker**, eyelash or eyelid.

Eye·witness. 1539. [f. EYE *sb.*¹ + WITNESS.] †1. One whose evidence is of what he has seen with his own eyes –1591. 2. One who has seen a thing done or happen 1590. †3. The result of actual observation –1671.

2. Wee..were eye witnesses of his Maiestie 2 *Pet.* i. 16. 3. Give us..Eye-witness of what first or last was done MILT.

Eyght(e, obs. f. AIT, EIGHT.

Eyl(e, obs. f. AIL *sb.*²; also of AIL *v.*

Eyne: see EYE *sb.*¹

Eyot, more usual var. of AIT, q.v.

Eyr, obs. f. AIR; also of EAR *v.*¹

Eyrant (ē·rănt). [f. *eire*, var. of AIRE *v.* + -ANT.] *Her.* Applied to birds in their nests.

†**Ey·rar.** 1551. [f. *eyrie* = AERIE.] A brood (of swans).

Eyre (ēəɹ). Now *Hist.* [ME. *eire*, a. OF. *eire*, *erre*, f. *errer*:—late L. *iterare* to journey.] 1. Itineration, circuit: in *Justices in eyre* (= L. *in itinere* on a journey). 2. The circuit court held by these officers. Also *E. of justice*, *Justice e.*, *Commission of E.* ME. b. The record of such a court 1614.

Eyren, -ron(e, -roun, obs. pl. ff. EGG.

Eyrie, commoner spelling of AERIE.

Eyst, Eyster, obs. ff. YEAST, OYSTER.

‖**Ezan.** 1753. [Arab.] The formula chanted by the Muezzin at the hour of prayer.

E·zod, obs. var. of IZZARD, the letter Z.

F

F (ef), the sixth letter of the Roman alphabet, repr. Semitic *waw*, which expressed the sounds of *w* (approximately) and *u*. In early Greek writing the form F (retaining the 6th place in the alphabet) came to be appropriated to the consonantal use, while V or Y served for the vowel. Later, in the classical period, both the sound *w* and its sign *F* (called the DIGAMMA from its form) were lost. In the Roman adoption of the Gr. alphabet, and thence in OE., the sound given to the sixth letter was the voiceless labiodental spirant (f), or, between two vowels, the corresponding voiced spirant (v). In mod. Eng. F is always sounded (f), exc. in *of*, where it is voiced to (v) through absence of stress.

In MSS. a capital F was often written as ff. Hence, by a misunderstanding, the spelling of certain family names, *e.g.* Ffiennes, Ffoulkes, etc.

II. As a symbol. 1. F, f, *f* signifies 6th in serial order. 2. *Mus.* F is the 4th note of the diatonic scale of C major. Also, the scale or key which has that note for its tonic. *F clef*: the bass clef (see CLEF ¹).

III. Abbreviations. 1. F = Fellow in F.G.S., F.R.S., etc. 2. = FATHER, as a title of R.C. priests. 3. *F.* = Fahrenheit (thermometer). 4. *Comm.* F.A.A. or f.a.a. = *free of all average*; f.o.b. = *free on board.* 5. In Music *f* = *forte* (loud), *ff* = *fortissimo* (very loud), or occas. *più forte* (louder) with *fff* for *fortissimo*. 6. F (on a black-lead pencil) = 'fine'; also *attrib.* 7. *Chem.* F = fluorine.

Fa (fā), *sb.* ME. [f. L. *fa*(*muli*); see GAMUT.] Name of the fourth note in Guido's hexachords, retained in solmisation as the 4th note of the octave. Hence as vb. SHAKS.

Fabaceous (făbē¹·ʃəs), *a.* 1727. [f. late L. *fabaceus* (f. *faba*) + -OUS.] 'Of or belonging to a bean' (Blount).

‖**Fabella** (făbe·lă). *Pl.* -æ. 1854. [mod.L. dim. of *faba* bean.] 'A name for the sesamoid bones in the tendon of the gastrocnemius muscle of the dog and other animals' (*Syd. Soc. Lex.*).

Fabian (fē¹·biăn). 1598. [ad. L. *Fabianus.*] A. *adj.* 1. Of or belonging to the Roman gens Fabia 1842. 2. Pertaining to, or after the manner of, Q. Fabius Maximus, surnamed Cunctator ('Delayer'), who, in the Second Punic War, foiled Hannibal by dilatory tactics and avoidance of direct engagements 1808.

2. *F. Society*: a society of Socialists, founded in 1884, who deprecate immediate attempts at revolutionary action.

B. *sb.* †1. In *Flaunting Fabian* (? = L. *licens Fabius*), a swashbuckler, a roysterer –1599. 2. One who belongs to, or holds the doctrines of, the Fabian Society 1891. Hence **Fa·bianism.**

Fabiform (fē¹·bifǭɹm), *a.* 1852. [f. L. *faba.*] Bean-shaped.

Fable (fē¹·b'l), *sb.* ME. [a. F., ad. L. *fabula* discourse, etc., f. *fari* to speak; see FATE.] 1. A narrative or statement not founded on fact; a myth or legend (now *rare*); a foolish story; a fabrication, falsehood. 2. A short story devised to convey some useful lesson; an apologue. (The most common sense.) ME. 3. The plot or story of a play or poem; *occas.*, †a play 1678. †4. Talk; discourse, narration (*rare*) –1598. 5. The subject of common talk; a byword 1535.

1. It seems a F., tho' the Fact I saw DRYDEN. The old f. of Seth's pillars 1756. The fables of Oates MACAULAY. Phr. *Old wives'* (*women's*) *fables.* 2. His F. of the Belly and its Members 1796. 3. The Intricacy and Disposition of the F. ADDISON. 5. He ..was the f. of the place THACKERAY.

Fable (fē¹·b'l), *v.* ME. [a. OF. *fabler*:—L. *fabulari* to talk; see prec.] †1. *intr.* To talk, converse. [A Latinism.] –1570. †2. To romance –1814; to talk idly –1653. 3. To talk falsehoods, lie 1530. 4. *trans.* To say or talk about fictitiously; to relate as in a fable; to fabricate, invent 1553.

2. Let Æsop f. in a Winters Night 3 *Hen. VI*, v. v. 25. Fabling about moods and figures 1653. 3. To say verity, and not to f. 1612. 4. Turn this Heav'n itself into the Hell Thou fablest MILT. *P. L.* vi. 292. Hence **Fa·bler**, one who fables.

‖**Fabliau** (fabli,o). Pl. -aux. 1804. [f. *fabliau*, assumed sing. to OF. *fabliaux*, pl. of *fablel*, dim. of *fable.*] A metrical tale, belonging to early French poetry.

The interesting *fabliaux* of the Anglo-Norman *trouveurs* SCOTT.

Fabric (fæ·brik, fē¹·brik), *sb.* 1483. [a. F. *fabrique*, ad. L. *fabrica*, f. *faber* a worker in metal, etc. See FORGE *sb.*] 1. A product of skilled workmanship; as: a. An edifice, a building (also *fig.*); †b. An engine or appliance –1657; c. A frame, structure (also *fig.*) 1633; d. A manufactured material (now only a 'textile fabric') 1753. 2. The action or process of framing or constructing (something specified) 1611. 3. Kind or method of construction or formation; style; texture; also *fig.* 1644. 4. *concr.* Tissue, fibre (also *fig.*) 1823; *occas.*, structural material 1849. 5. A place where work is carried on; a factory, manufactory 1656.

1. The august fabriq of Christ Church EVELYN. c. The wonderful f. of the human body 1848. *fig.* The f. of knowledge REID. d. Woollen fabrics GREEN. 2. The fabricke, reparation, or maintenance of a Church 1611. 3. The f. of the Church is Gothic EVELYN. *fig.* He used almost always the same f. of verse JOHNSON. 4. *fig.* The very f. of our nature CONDER. Hence †**Fa·bric** *v.* to construct, fashion, frame, make.

Fabricant (fæ·brikănt). Now *rare.* 1757. [a. F., ad. L. *fabricantem*, *fabricare.*] A maker or manufacturer.

Fabricate (fæ·brikē¹t), *v.* 1598. [f. L. *fabricat-*, *fabricare*, f. *fabrica* FABRIC *sb.*] 1. *trans.* To make anything that requires skill; to construct, manufacture. Now *rare.* 2. To 'make up'; to frame or invent (a legend, lie, etc.); to forge 1779.

1. To f. hinges PENNANT, clocks WHEWELL, silk YEATS, words WHITNEY. 2. Numerous lies, fabricated by the priests.. were already in circulation 1855. Hence **Fa·bricative** *a.* tending to fabrication.

Fa·bricator. †Fa·bricature, construction; method or style of construction.

Fabrication (fæbrikē¹·ʃən). 1677. [ad. L. *fabricationem*; see prec.] **1.** The action or process of fabricating; construction, manufacture. Now *rare*. **2.** The action of 'making up'; *concr.* an invention; a forgery 1790.

1. The f. of the body HALE, of a government BURKE, of implements LYELL. 2. The common account..is a mere f. 1846.

†Fa·brile, *a.* 1611. [a. OF., ad. L. *fabrilis*, f. *faber*.] Of or belonging to a craftsman or his craft –1678.

Fabular (fæ·biŭlăɹ), *a.* 1684. [ad. L. *fabularis*.] Fabulous.

Fabulate (fæ·biŭlēⁱt), *v.* 1616. [f. L. *fabulat-*, *fabulari*.] †**1.** *trans.* To relate as a fable; *intr.* to talk in fables –1624. **2.** *trans.* To concoct, fabricate 1856. Hence **Fa·bulator,** a story-teller.

Fabulist (fæ·biŭlist). 1593. [ad. F. *fabuliste*, f. L. *fabula*.] **1.** One who relates fables; a story-teller. **2.** One who invents falsehoods 1625.

†Fa·bulize, *v.* 1612. [f. L. *fabula* + -IZE.] **a.** *intr.* To invent fables. **b.** *trans.* To concoct, invent; to dress up as a fable; also, to relate as legend *that* [etc.]. –1818.

Fabulosity (fæbiŭlǫ·sĭti). 1599. [ad. F. *fabulosité*, ad. L. *fabulositatem*; see FABLE *sb.*] **1.** The quality of being fabulous; fabulousness. †**2.** quasi-*concr.* A fabulous statement, fable –1807.

Fabulous (fæ·biŭləs), *a.* 1546. [ad. L. *fabulosus*, f. *fabula*; see FABLE *sb.* and -OUS.] **1.** Of persons: Fond of fabling, or of listening to fables. **2.** Of the nature of, or belonging to fable, full of fables, mythical, legendary, unhistorical 1555. **3.** Spoken of in fable, fabled. [So in L.] 1601. **4.** Resembling a fable (*rare*) 1561; astonishing, incredible 1609.

1. As old Wives, f. COWLEY. 2. The dark and f. Ages 1712. Dragons and other f. monsters JOWETT. 4. Houses..let at f. rents 1857.

Hence **Fa·bulous-ly** *adv.*, **-ness.**

Faburden. Now *Hist.* ME. [a. F. *fauxbourdon*, i. e. *faux* false + *bourdon* BOURDON ².] *Mus.* **1.** A sort of counterpoint; 'a term for a sort of harmony consisting of thirds and sixths, added to a canto fermo' (Stainer and Barrett). **2.** The undersong 1587; the refrain 1580. **3.** A legend, motto. NASHE.

Façade (făsā·d). 1656. [a. F., f. *face*, after It. *facciata*.] The face or front of a building, *esp.* the principal front. Also *transf.* and *fig.*

The f. of the palace is unequalled 1839.

Face (fēⁱs), *sb.* ME. [a. F.:—pop. L. *facia*, altered form of *facies*, referred to *facere* to make, or, by some, to the root *fa-*, to shine (cf. *facem* torch).]

I. 1. The front part of the head, from the forehead to the chin; the visage, countenance; also *transf.* **2.** With reference to its position, often without any reference to the lit. sense ME. **3.** = Sight, presence ME. **4.** The countenance as expressive of feeling or character; a countenance having a specified expression ME. Hence *colloq.* A grimace. 1570. **5.** Command of countenance; *esp.* a bold face; impudence, effrontery 1537. **6.** *Lacrosse.* (Also *f.-off.*) The action of facing (see FACE *v.* I. 3 b), corresponding to the bully in hockey 1900.

1. The f. of a lion, and..the f. of an eagle *Ezek.* x. 14. His f. Deep scars of Thunder had intrencht MILT. *P. L.* I. 600. *transf.* Grotesque masks or faces W. IRVING. Phr. *To have two faces. To look a person in the f.*: to confront. *To shew one's f.*: to appear (*lit.* and *fig.*). *F. to f. To throw in a person's f.* (*lit.* and *fig.*). *To set one's f.*: to give a settled expression to the countenance. *To save one's f.* (fig.): to save appearances; to escape a manifest 'slap in the f.' 2. Phr. *To have the wind in one's f.* (*lit.* and *fig.*). *To fly in the f. of* (*lit.* and *fig.*). 3. Thou fleddest from the f. of Esau *Gen.* xxxv. 1. Thy very children ..curse thee to thy f. COWPER. 4. They weare their faces to the bent of the kings lookes *Cymb.* I. i. 13. Leaue thy damnable Faces, and begin *Haml.* III. ii. 263. 5. With what f. then..shal ye heare these wordes *Bk. Com. Prayer.*

II. 1. External appearance, look; also semblance *of*. Now *rare*, exc. of immaterial objects. ME. ¶**b.** = PHASE. 1646. **2.** Visible state or condition; aspect; configuration (of a country) 1587. **3.** Outward show; disguise, pretence; a pretext ME.

1. A plan..which has a very good f. SCOTT. The problems of the world..are always putting on new faces BRYCE. 2. The arrival of so many ships..caused a new f. of affairs 1781. 3. Phr. *To put a good f. on* (a matter). They..set a F. of civil Authority on Tyranny BUTLER. Phr. *To save one's f.*: see SAVE *v.* I. 6. *To lose f.* [tr. Chinese *tiu lien*]: to lose one's credit, good name, or reputation.

III. 1. The surface or one of the surfaces of anything ME. †**b.** *Astrol.* The third part of a sign of the zodiac, extending over 10 degrees in longitude –1819. **2.** The principal side presented by an object, as: **a.** The front or slope (of a cliff, a fault, etc.) 1632; **b.** *Arch.* The façade of a building; the exposed surface of a stone in a wall; the front of an arch 1611. **3.** The side of anything usually presented outwards or upwards 1611; the obverse (of a coin or medal) 1515; the inscribed side (of a document) 1632; the dial-plate (of a clock or watch) 1696. **4.** Each of the surfaces of a solid 1625. **5.** The working surface or edge (of implements, tools, etc.) 1703. **6.** An even or polished surface 1881.

1. Phrases (*orig.* Hebraisms), *The f. of the earth, the deep, the waters.* 2. The f. of a steep incline of snow TYNDALL. **b.** The Face of the Building is narrow, and the Flank deep WOTTON. 3. The carpet's velvet f. KEATS. The f. of an old Roman coine *L.L.L.* v. ii. 617. It ought to appear on the f. of the plea that [etc.] W. SELWYN.

IV. Technical.

1. *Fortif.* **a.** *Face of a place*, the front that is comprehended between the flanked angles of two neighbouring bastions 1489. **b.** *Faces of a work*, those parts which form a salient angle projecting towards the country 1676. 2. **a.** *Mil.* Each of the sides of a battalion when formed into a square 1853. **b.** *Ordnance. Face of a gun*, the surface of metal at its muzzle 1727. 3. *Mining.* **a.** The end of any adit, tunnel, slope, etc., at which work is progressing, or was last done 1708. **b.** 'The principal cleaving-place at right angles to the stratification' (Raymond) 1867. 4. *Steam-engine.* The flat part of a slide-valve; also, the corresponding flat part on a cylinder, on which the slide-valve travels 1838. 5. *Typog.* That part of a type (or punch) which has the form of the letter. Also, the printing surface of type. 1683.

Comb.: **1.** General: as *f.-sponge, -levelling, -flatterer*, etc. **2.** Special: as **f.-ache**, pain in the facial nerves; **-ague**, an acute form of face-ache, tic douloureux: †**-bone** = CHEEK-BONE; †**-bread** (Heb.) = SHEWBREAD: **-card**, = COAT-CARD; **-cloth**, a cloth laid over the f. of a corpse; **-guard**, a contrivance for protecting the f., *esp.* in fencing, etc.; **-hammer**, one with a flat f.; **-joint**, that joint of a voussoir which appears on the f. of the arch; **-lathe**, one mainly used for surfacing; **-lifting**, a form of face-massage; **-mould**, a mould for drawing the proper figure of a hand-rail on both sides of the plank; **-painter**, (*a*) a painter of portraits, (*b*) one who applies rouge, etc., to the f.; **-painting** *vbl. sb.*, portrait-painting; **-plan**, the front or principal elevation; **-plate** (*Mech.*), an enlargement of the end of the mandrel (of a lathe), to which work may be attached in order to be faced; also *attrib.*; **-stone** (*Archit.*), the slab of stone forming the f. or front, *esp.* in a cornice, entablature, etc.; **-value**, the amount stated on the f. (of a note, etc.), the apparent value; also *fig.*; **-wall** (*Building*), front wall; **-wheel** (*Mech.*) = *contrate wheel* (see CONTRATE); also, a wheel whose disk-face is adapted for grinding and polishing.

Face (fēⁱs), *v.* ME. [f. prec. sb.]

I. †**1.** *intr.* To show a bold or a false face –1601. †**2.** *trans.* To confront with assurance or impudence –1632. **3.** To meet face to face; to oppose with confidence; to stand fronting 1632. **b.** *Lacrosse.* To put (the ball) in play by placing it between the crosses of two opposing players 1867. **4.** To look steadily at 1795.

2. Phr. *To f. down, out* (a person, a matter). 3. Facing fearful odds MACAULAY. 4. The need for external supplies of food..must be faced 1883.

II. 1. *intr.* To look, front, in a certain direction; also *fig.* 1594. **2.** *trans.* To look or front towards 1632; of letterpress, etc.: To stand on the opposite page to 1766. **3.** *intr.* Chiefly *Mil.* To turn the face in a stated direction 1634. **4.** *trans.* (*Mil.*) To cause (soldiers) to face 1630. **5.** To turn face upwards 1674.

1. The little chapel that faced eastwards THACKERAY. *fig.* He steadfastly faced towards peace KINGLAKE. 2. Stand facing the light JOHNSON.

III. 1. To cover a certain breadth of (a garment) with another material; to trim, turn up. Also †*transf.* and *fig.* 1561. **2.** To cover the surface with some specified material 1670. **3.** To dress the surface of 1848. **4.** To coat (tea) with some colouring substance 1850.

1. Blue cloth, trimmed and faced with white 1759. *fig.* Rebellion, faced with publick Good DRYDEN.

Faced (fēⁱst), *ppl. a.* 1500. [f. FACE *sb.*] **1.** Furnished with or having a face; often in comb., as *bare-faced*, etc. **2.** *Arch.* '*Faced work*, thin stone, otherwise called bastard ashlar, used to imitate squared stone work. In painting, the rubbing down each coat with pumice before the next is laid on. Used also of superior plastering' (*Arch. Dict.* 1892).

Facer (fēⁱ·səɹ). 1515. [f. FACE *v.* and *sb.*] †**1.** One who puts on a bold face; a braggart, bully –1611. **2.** A blow in the face 1810.

2. *fig.* I've had a good many facers in my life 1872.

†Fa·cet, *sb.*¹ ME. [ad. L. *facetus* used as a proper name.] The book *Facetus de Moribus*, formerly used in schools for instruction in manners –1483.

Facet (fæ·sėt), *sb.*² Also **facette.** 1625. [a. F. *facette*, dim. of *face* face.] **1.** A little face; *orig.* one of the small cut and polished faces of a diamond. Often in comb., as *skew-f.*, etc. **2.** *Anat.* **a.** A small flat and smooth articular surface of a bone 1836. **b.** One of the segments (*ocelli*) of a compound eye 1834. Hence **Fa·ceted** (also *erron.* facetted) *ppl. a.* cut into, or furnished with, facets.

Facete (făsī·t), *a.* Now *rare.* 1603. [ad. L. *facetus* graceful, pleasant, witty.] **1.** = FACETIOUS. *arch.* †**2.** Elegant, graceful, polished –1662.

1. A man of..a f. and affable countenance WOOD. Hence †**Facete·ly** *adv.*, †**-ness.**

Facetiæ (făsī·ʃiˌī), *sb. pl.* 1529. [a. L., f. *facetus* FACETE.] Humorous sayings or writings, pleasantries, witticisms.

Facetious (făsī·ʃəs), *a.* 1592. [ad. F. *facétieux*, f. *facétie*, ad. L. *facetia* + -OUS.] †**1.** Of manners, etc.: Polished, urbane. **2.** Characterized by, or given to, pleasantry; jocose, waggish. Formerly also: witty, humorous, amusing, gay. 1599.

2. I am no way f. nor disposed for the mirth..of Company SIR T. BROWNE. A nudge..designed to be immensely f. MRS. STOWE. Hence **Face·tious-ly** *adv.*, **-ness.**

Facia (fæ·ʃ'a). 1900. [var. FASCIA.] The tablet over a shop-front with the occupier's name, etc.

Facia, var. of FASCIA, q. v.

Facial (fēⁱ·ʃiăl, -ʃăl), *a.* 1609. [a. F., ad. med.L. *facialis*, f. *facies* FACE.] Of or pertaining to the face; as in *f. artery, nerve*, etc.

Phr. *F. angle*: the angle formed by two lines, one horizontal from the nostrils to the ear, the other (called the *f. line*) more or less vertical from the nostrils to the forehead. Hence **Fa·cially** *adv.* †face to face; with reference to the face.

†Fa·ciata, Fa·ciate. [a. and ad. It. *facciata*.] A façade. EVELYN.

Facient (fēⁱ·ʃiĕnt), *sb. rare.* 1670. [ad. L. *facientem*, pr. pple. of *facere*.] One who does anything; a doer.

-facient, formative element repr. L. *-facientem* 'making', as in *rubefacient*, etc., and in similar words not formed in L., as *absorbefacient*, etc.; also in *calorifacient*, and the like, for which the L. vbs. would have been in *-ficare*, and adjs. in *-ficus*.

‖**Facies** (fēⁱ·siˌīz). 1611. [L.; see FACE.] †**1.** *joc.* Face. **2.** *Nat. Hist.* General appearance 1727.

Facile (fæ·səil, -il), *a.* 1483. [a. F., ad. L. *facilis* easy to do, easy of access, f. *facere*.] **1.** That can be accomplished with little effort. (Now somewhat disparaging.) **2.** Presenting few difficulties; †easy to understand or to use 1531. **3.** Moving without effort; fluent, ready 1605. **4.** †Easy of access, affable, courteous; characterized by ease of behaviour 1590; not harsh or severe 1541. **5.** Easily led or wrought upon 1511. †**6.** quasi-*adv.* Easily –1560.

1. It is facyle to scape out of the handes of the blynd CAXTON. 2. This f. and ready course TOPSELL. A f. and useful machine 1676. 3. A f. and ready expression 1657. Deaths..with f. feet avenged SWINBURNE. 4. F. and debonair in all his deeds GREENE. A Princesse most facil to forgive injuries FULLER. 5. Adam and his facil consort Eve Lost Paradise MILT. *P. R.* I. 51. *transf.* The facil gates of hell too slightly barrd *P. L.* IV. 967. Hence **Fa·cile-ly,** *adv.*, **-ness.**

Facilitate (făsi·litēⁱt), *v.* 1611. [f. F. *faci-*

liter (= It. *facilitare*, f. *facilis*, after L. *debilitare*, etc.) + -ATE [3].] 1. *trans.* To render easier; to promote, help forward. ¶2. To lessen the labour of, assist (a person) 1646.

1. It will..f. the present negociation 1621. To f. the animal or natural Motions ARBUTHNOT. Hence **Facilitaˑtion**, the action, process, or result of facilitating; help (now *rare*). **Faciˑlitator.**

Facility (făsiˑlĭti). 1519. [a. F., ad. L. *facilitatem*; see FACILE and -ITY.] 1. The fact or condition of being easy or easily performed; freedom from difficulty, ease 1531. 2. Opportunity for the easy or easier performance of anything; usu. in *pl.* opportunities 1519. 3. In action, etc.: Ease, readiness; aptitude, dexterity. Of style: Fluency. 1532. †4. Easiness of access or converse, affability, courtesy -1793. 5. Easiness to be led or persuaded to good or bad, pliancy. Also *transf.* of things (*rare*). 1533. 6. Indolent ease, indifference 1615.

1. The great facilitie of their language HOOKER. The f. with which government has been overturned in France BURKE. 2. The facilities given to the exportation of goods manufactured at home McCULLOCH. 3. Famous for f. in discourse 1596. 5. The f. of Charles was such as has perhaps never been found in any man of equal sense MACAULAY.

Facing (fēˑsiŋ), *vbl. sb.* 1523. [f. FACE *v.*] The action of FACE *v.* †1. The action of boasting, swaggering, or brow-beating; a defiance -1647. 2. *Mil.* The action of turning in another direction. Also *transf.* 1635. 3. *concr.* (chiefly in *pl.*): Something with which a garment is faced; *esp.* the cuffs and collar of a military jacket, when of a different colour from the rest of the coat. Also *transf.* and *fig.* 1566. 4. The action of putting a new face on or of covering or protecting the face of (anything) 1549. 5. *concr.* a. A superficial coating or layer; also the material of this 1586. b. *esp.* The external layer of stone, etc., which forms the face of a wall, bank, etc. 1823. c. An external cover or protection 1849. d. *Founding.* Powder, as charcoal, etc., applied to the face of a mould, or mixed in with sands for heavy casting, to give a fine smooth surface to the casting 1874.

2. Phr. *To put* (one) *through* (his) *facings* (*lit.* and *fig.*). 5. a. Of Facing Timber-buildings with Bricks 1703. The f. of tea 1875. *Comb.* **f.-loam, -sand,** that used to form the face of the mould.

Facinorous (făsiˑnŏrəs), *a. arch.* 1548. [ad. L. *facinorosus*, f. *facinus* (*facinor-*, *faciner-*) a (bad) deed, f. *facere*; see -OUS.] Extremely wicked. Common in 17th c.

Hence †**Faciˑnorous-ly** *adv.*, **-ness.**

Faconde, -ound, var. of FACUND.

Facsimile (fæksiˑmilĭ), *sb.* Pl. **facsimiles.** [Orig. two words, L. *fac*, imper. of *facere* + *simile* adj. neut.] †1. Copying; imitation. FULLER. 2. An exact copy, counterpart, or representation. Also *transf.* and *fig.* 1691. 3. *attrib.* 1767.

2. A fac simile might easily be taken 1691. Hence **Facsiˑmile** *v.* to make or (*rarely*) serve as a f. **Facsiˑmilist,** one who makes facsimiles.

Fact (fækt). 1539. [ad. L. *factum* thing done, f. *facere*. See also FEAT.] 1. A thing done or performed: †a. An action, deed. Also, action in general. -1815. †b. An exploit; a feat -1730. c. An evil deed, a crime. Now *obs.* exc. in *after, before the f.*, etc. 1539. †d. An action cognizable in law BACON. †2. The making, doing, or performing -1808. 3. Something that has really occurred or is the case; hence, a datum of experience, as dist. from conclusions 1632. 4. *loosely*, Something that is alleged to be, or might be, a 'fact' 1729. 5. (Without *a* and *pl.*) Truth; reality 1581. 6. *Law.* In *sing.* and *pl.* The circumstances and incidents of a case, as dist. from their legal bearing 1718.

1. a. Gracious in f., if not in word JANE AUSTEN. b. He who most excels in f. of Arms MILT. *P. L.* II. 124. c. Accessories after the f. BLACKSTONE. 2. I caught him in the f. GOLDSM. 3. One f. destroys this fiction THIRLWALL. The f. of resemblance MILL. 4. The writer's facts are untrustworthy (*mod.*). 5. Imagination is often at war with reason and f. JOWETT. Phr. *Matter of f.* *In f.*: in reality. *In point of f.*: in fact. 6. A jury..decides all the issues of f. 1892.

Faction (fæˑkʃən), *sb.* 1509. [a. F., ad. L. *factionem*, f. *facere*.] †1. A doing or making; cf. FASHION -1689. 2. †A class, sort, or set of persons -1606; *spec.* in *Rom. Antiq.* one of the companies of contractors for the chariot races in the circus 1606. 3. A party in the state or in any community or association. Always with imputation of selfish or mischievous ends or unscrupulous methods. Also *transf.* and *fig.* 1509. 4. Factious spirit or action; party strife or intrigue; dissension 1538; †an instance of this -1662.

2. I will..leaue the f. of fooles *Tr. & Cr.* II. i. 130. 3. The public tranquillity was disturbed by a discontented f. GIBBON. 4. F. hath no Regard to national Interests 1738. Hence †**Faˑction** *v. intr.* to act in a factious spirit; *trans.* to form into factions. **Faˑctional** *a.* of or belonging to a f. or factions; factious. **Faˑctionary** *a.* active as a partisan; belonging to a f.; *sb.* a partisan. **Faˑctioneeˑr,** †**Faˑctioner, Faˑctionist,** a party-man.

-faction, repr. L. *-factionem*, forming nouns of action related to vbs. in -FY repr. L. *-facere*, F. *-faire*; also occas. used (instead of -FICATION) where *-fy* repr. L. *-ficare*, F. *-fier*, as in *petrifaction*.

Factious (fæˑkʃəs), *a.* 1532. [ad. L. *factiosus*; see FACTION and -OUS.] 1. Given to faction; inclined to form parties or to act for party purposes; seditious 1535. 2. Pertaining to or proceeding from faction; characterized by party spirit.

1. The censure of f. and seditious persons 1624. 2. His F. indignation at the Princes faults BOYLE. Hence **Faˑctious-ly** *adv.*, **-ness.**

Factitious (fæktiˑʃəs), *a.* 1646. [f. L. *facticius* made by art (f. *facere*) + -OUS.] †1. Made by or resulting from art; artificial -1801. †2. Of soil, etc.: Produced by special causes -1808. 3. Got up; not natural or spontaneous; artificial, conventional 1678.

1. Beer, Ale, or other f. drinks BOYLE. 2. The f. soil of the Gangetic provinces 1808. 3. F. wants created by luxury MORSE. Hence **Factiˑtious-ly** *adv.*, **-ness.**

Factitive (fæˑktitiv), *a.* 1846. [ad. mod.L. *factitivus*, irreg. f. *fact-*, *facere*.] *Gram.* a. Of a verb: Expressing the notion of making a thing to be of a certain character in deed, word, or thought; taking a complementary object. b. Causative.

a. Phr. *F. object, predicate, accusative*, the complementary accusative governed by a factitive verb. To make a man king (*mod.*). To call one a fool (*mod.*).

Factive (fæˑktiv), *a.* 1612. [f. L. *facere*.] †1. Tending or able to make; concerned with making -1649. 2. *Gram.* = FACTITIVE. 1880.

Factor (fæˑktəɹ). 1485. [ad. F. *facteur*, ad. L. *factor*, f. *facere*.] 1. One who makes or does (anything). *Obs.* or *arch.* 1563. †2. A partisan, adherent, approver. [Cf. L. *facere cum aliquo* to side with any one.] -1715. 3. One who acts for another; an agent, deputy. Now *rare.* 1485. 4. *Comm.* One who buys or sells for another; a commission merchant 1491. b. One of the third class of the East India Company's servants. Now *Hist.* 1675. 5. A bailiff, land-steward. *Obs.* exc. *Sc.* 1561. 6. *U.S. Law.* = GARNISHEE. 1878. 7. *Math.* One of the numbers, expressions, etc., which when multiplied together produce a given number, expression, etc. 1673. 8. *transf.* One of the circumstances, facts, or influences which produce a result 1816. b. *Biol.* = GENE. 1907.

3. They..Authorised..the Vicechancellor, to be the common F. for the University FOXE. 4. A F... for Norwich Hose or Stockings 1683. 8. The first f. in the making of a nation is its religion GLADSTONE.

Hence **Faˑctor** *v. intr.* to act as a f.; *trans.* to deal with (goods, etc.) as a f. **Faˑctorage,** the action of a f.; his commission; factors collectively. †**Faˑctoress,** a female f.

Factorial (fæktōˑriăl), *a.*[1] and *sb.* 1816. [f. prec. + -IAL.] A. *adj.* 1. *Math.* Pertaining to a factorial or factorials 1837. 2. Of or pertaining to a factor (sense 4) 1881.

B. *sb. Math.* a. *gen.* The product of a series of factors in arithmetical progression. Also, in later usage: The product of a series of factors which are similar functions of a variable that changes by a constant difference in passing from any factor to the next. 1816. b. *spec.* The product of an integer multiplied into all the lower integers; e.g. the *factorial* of 6 (written |6 or 6!) is $6 \times 5 \times 4 \times 3 \times 2 = 720$.

Factoˑrial, *a.*[2] *rare.* 1864. [f. FACTORY + -AL.] Pertaining to, or consisting in, a factory.

Factorize (fæˑktōrəiz), *v.* 1864. [f. as prec. + -IZE.] 1. *trans.* (*U.S. Law*) = GARNISH. 2. *Math.* To break up into factors.

Factorship (fæˑktəɹʃip). 1599. [See -SHIP.] The office or position of FACTOR (senses 3, 4).

Factory (fæˑktŏri). 1560. [repr. med.L. *factoria*, f. *factor*; also partly f. *factorium*.] 1. An establishment for traders carrying on business in a foreign country 1582. †2. The body of factors in any one place -1777. †3. The action or process of making anything -1678. 4. A building, or buildings, with plant for the manufacture of goods; a manufactory; works. Also *transf.* and *fig.* 1618. 6. *attrib.* 1841.

Vancouver..the main f. of the Hudson's Bay Company W. IRVING. 2. Chaplain to the British f. at St. Petersburg MAD. D'ARBLAY. *fig.* Oxford is a Greek f. EMERSON. *Comb.* **f.-cotton** (*U.S.*), unbleached cotton cloth of home manufacture.

Factotum (fæktōˑtɒm). 1566. [ad. med.L. *factotum* (f. *fac*, imper. of *facere* + *totum*) in phrases *Johannes Factotum*, etc. Source unkn.] A man of all-work; also, a servant who manages all his master's affairs. Also formerly, a busybody. Hence **Factoˑtumship,** the office of a f.

Factual (fæˑktiuăl), *a.* 1834. [f. FACT, after ACTUAL.] Concerned with facts; of the nature of fact, actual, real.

Factum (fæˑktɒm). 1748. [a. L.; see FACT.] 1. *Civil Law.* 'A person's act or deed; anything stated or made certain' (Wharton). 2. A memorial, or statement of facts. [After F. legal use.] 1773. †3. *Math.* The product of two or more factors -1817. var. †**Faˑctus** (in sense 3). NEWTON.

Facture (fæˑktiŭɹ). Now *rare.* ME. [a. F., ad. L. *factura*, f. *facere*. See also FEATURE.] 1. The action, manner, or style of making (a thing); also, the thing made. ‖2. *Comm.* = INVOICE. (F.; perh. never used in Eng.) 1858.

1. The f. or framing of the inward parts BACON.

‖**Facula** (fæˑkiŭlă). Chiefly *pl.* **-læ.** 1706. [L., dim. of *fax* (*fac-*) a torch.] *Astron.* One of the bright spots on the surface of the sun, as dist. from the dark spots or *maculæ*. Hence **Faˑcular** *a.* of or pertaining to faculæ.

Facultate (fæˑkɒlteit), *v. rare.* 1648. [See FACULTY and -ATE [3].] To empower; to authorize.

Facultative (fæˑkɒlteitiv), *a.* 1820. [a. F. *facultatif, -ive*, f. L. *facultatem*; see FACULTY and -ATIVE.] 1. a. Of enactments. etc.: Conveying a faculty or permission; permissive; hence of actions, etc.: Optional. b. *transf.* In scientific use: That may or may not take place, or have a specified character 1874. 2. Of or proceeding from a faculty 1866.

1. a. Creating what is called 'occasional', 'accidental' or 'facultative' contraband 1839. Hence **Faˑcultatively** *adv.* (*rare*).

Faculty (fæˑkɒlti). [ME. *faculte*, a. F. *faculté*, ad. L. *facultatem*, f. *facilis*, easy (cf. early L. *facul* adv.).]

I. 'The power of doing anything' (J.). 1. An ability or aptitude, whether natural or acquired, for any special kind of action; formerly also, ability in general. Occas. limited to a natural aptitude. 1490. †b. Disposition -1613. c. General executive ability. (Chiefly U.S.) 1859. †2. Of things: A power or capacity -1707. 3. A physical capacity or function 1500. 4. One of the powers of the mind; *e.g.* the will, the reason, memory, etc. 1588. †5. Means, pecuniary resources; property -1797.

1. Excelling in Poeticall facultie CAMDEN. I devoted all my faculties to [etc.] JOHNSON. 3. Sight and hearing, for example, I should call faculties JOWETT. 4. The Moral F. MACKINTOSH.

II. †1. A department of knowledge -1757. 2. *spec.* One of the departments of learning at a University. Hence *Dean of a F.* ME. 3. An art, trade, occupation, profession. Now *Hist.* ME. 4. The whole body of Masters, Doctors (and, occas., students), in any one of the studies, Theology, Law, Medicine, Arts ME. 5. *transf.* The members of a profession regarded as one body, *e.g.* of the medical profession (called pop. 'The Faculty') 1511.

1. The greate learned clerkes in al faculties 1553. 2. At Bonn there is a Protestant f. of theology

M. ARNOLD. 4. b. The whole teaching staff of a college or university (*U.S.*) 1829.

III. 1. Power, liberty, or right of doing something, conferred by law or favour 1534. b. A dispensation, licence; esp. *Eccl.* a licence granted by an eccl. superior to some one to do something which otherwise he could not legally do 1533.

1. Duncane Hath borne his Faculties so meeke *Macb.* I. vii. 17. b. Private rights to particular seats, conferred by a f., *i.e.* a license from the ordinary PHILLIMORE.

Comb.: **f.-pew, -seat,** a pew or seat in a church appropriated to a particular person by a f.; †**-tax,** a property or income tax (BURKE).

†**Fa·cund,** *sb.* ME. [ad. F. *faconde*, semi-pop. ad. L. *facundia*.] Eloquence –1483.

Facund (fæ·kʊnd, fă̆kʊ̆·nd), *a. arch.* [ME. *faconde*, ad. OF. *facond*, ad. L. *facundus*, f. *fari* to speak.] Eloquent; also *fig.* of beauty, etc. So †**Facu·ndious** *a.* (in same sense). †**Facu·ndity,** eloquence.

Facy (fē̆ⁱ·si). Now *dial.* [f. FACE *sb.*] Impudent. B. JONS.

Fad (fæd), *sb.* Chiefly *dial.* 1834. [?] A crotchety notion; a pet project, *esp.* of social or political reform; a craze.

Slöjd..the last new 'fad' 1884. Hence **Fa·ddish** *a.* given to fads; of the nature of a f. **Fa·ddist,** one who has a f. **Fa·ddy** *a.*

Fad (fæd), *v.* 1847. [Cf. prec. sb.] *intr.* To be busy about trifles; hence *nonce-use*, to advocate fads.

Faddle (fæ·d'l), *v.* Now *dial.* 1688. [Cf. FAD *v.* and FONDLE, etc.] 1. *trans.* To make much of, fondle, pet. 2. *intr.* To trifle; to play 1755. Hence **Fa·ddle** *sb.* nonsense, trifling; usu. FIDDLE-FADDLE.

Fade (fēⁱd), *a.* ME. [a. F. *fade*; repr. L. *vapidum* (Gaston Paris).] 1. Of colour, etc.: Dull, wan, sombre. *Obs.* exc. *arch.* †2. Faded, languishing –1752. ‖3. [F. *fade*.] Insipid, commonplace 1715.

3. F. and feeble sentimentality 1862.

Fade (fēⁱd), *v.* ME. [a. OF. *fader*, f. *fade* FADE *a.*] 1. *intr.* To lose freshness and vigour; to droop, wither. †2. To grow small or weak; to decline, decay; to shrink. *lit.* and *fig.* –1585. †3. *trans.* To weaken; to corrupt, taint –1775. 4. *intr.* To grow dim, faint, or pale ME. 5. *trans.* To dim, dull, wither. Now *rare*. 1559. 6. *intr.* To pass away gradually; vanish, die out 1590. 7. *Cinematogr. trans.* Tc cause (a picture, etc.) to pass gradually *in* or *out* of view on the screen 1918. b. *transf.* of sound-films and broadcasting 1927. Also *intr.*

1. Elisian Flours..that never f. MILT. *P. L.* III. 360. 4. Thy eternal summer shall not f. SHAKS. *Sonn.* xviii. 6. Like this insubstantiall Pageant faded *Temp.* IV. i. 155. Religious animosity..would of itself f. away MACAULAY. Hence **Fade** *sb.* (also *f.-in* or *f.-out*): cf. sense 7 above. **Fa·ded** *ppl. a.* that has lost its freshness; withered, decayed, worn out. **Fa·dedly** *adv.* **Fa·deless** *a.*, unfading. **Fa·delessly** *adv.* **Fa·dingly** *adv.*, **-ness.**

Fader, obs. and dial. f. FATHER.

Fadge (fædʒ), *sb.*¹ *dial.* and *techn.* 1588. [?] A bundle of leather, sticks, wool, etc.; a bale of goods.

Fadge, *sb.*² *Sc.* 1609. A large flat loaf.

Fadge (fædʒ), *v.* 1573. [perh. based on FAY *v.*¹ and some word ending in *-dge*.] †1. *intr.* To fit, suit, be suitable –1711. †2. To put up *with* (a thing); to agree, rub on (with a person) –1678. †3. *trans.* To fit (the parts of) *together* N. FAIRFAX. †4. *intr.* To succeed –1809. 5. To trudge (*rare* exc. *dial.*) 1658.

2. MILT. *Divorce* Pref.

†**Fa·ding, fa·dding,** *sb.* 1611. [?] The name of a dance, app. Irish. 'With a fading' was the burden of a song. –1672.

Fadme, -om, etc., obs. ff. FATHOM.

Fady (fēⁱ·di), *a.* 1730. [f. FADE *v.*] Tending to fade.

Fæces (fī·sīz), *sb. pl.* Also **feces.** 1460. [a. L. *fæces* pl. of *fæx* dregs.] 1. Sediment; dregs. 2. Excrement 1639. Hence **Fæcal, fe-** (fī·kăl) *a.*, of the nature of or containing f.

Fæcula, fecula (fe·kiŭlă). *Pl.* **-æ.** 1684. [a. L. *fæcula* crust of wine, dim. of *fæx*. Cf. F. *fécule*. The erron. spelling *fecula* is usual.] 1. 'The sediment or lees which subsides from the infusion of many vegetable substances, *esp.* applied to starch' (*Syd. Soc. Lex.*). 2. *gen.* Sediment, dregs. *sing.* and *pl.* (*rare*). 1816.

Fæculence, -ency, -ent: see FEC-.

Faerie, faery (fē̆ⁱ·ĕri), *sb.* (*a.*) *arch.* 1590. [A var. of FAIRY, first employed *arch.* by Spenser.] = FAIRY; *esp.* the imaginary world of Spenser's *Faerie Queene*. Also *attrib.*

Fa·ffle, *v. Obs.* or *dial.* 1570. [Echoic.] To stutter; to flap idly in the wind, as a sail.

Fag (fæg), *sb.*¹ 1780. [f. the vb.] 1. That which causes weariness (*colloq.*). 2. In Eng. schools, a junior who performs certain duties for a senior. Also *transf.* a drudge.

1. Not worth the f. of going and coming MRS. CARLYLE. 2. *transf.* The diminutive f. of the studio THACKERAY.

Fag (fæg), *sb.*² 1486. [See FAG *v.*] = FAG-END. b. A cigarette (*slang*) 1888.

Fag (fæg), *sb.*³ 1464. [?] 1. A knot in cloth. 2. [? a different word.] A sheep-tick; hence, a disease of sheep 1789.

Fag (fæg), *v.* 1530. [Said to be a corruption of FLAG *v.*] 1. *intr.* To flag, droop (*lit.* and *fig.*). *Obs.* exc. *dial.* 2. To do something that wearies one; to toil 1772. 3. *trans.* To make fatigued; to tire 1826. 4. In Eng. schools. *intr.* To be, or act as, a fag 1806; also *trans.* to make a fag of 1824. 5. *Naut.* To untwist or wear out the end of a rope or the edge of canvas 1841.

2. All day I am fagging at business 1772. 3. Correcting manuscript..fags me exceedingly SCOTT. 4. Phr. *To f. out*: to go as fag, *esp.* in cricket, to field.

Fage, *v.* Now *dial.* ME. [?] To coax, flatter. *trans.* and *absol.* or *intr.*

Fag-end (fæ·gˌe·nd). 1613. [f. FAG *sb.*² + END.] 1. The last part of a piece of cloth; the coarser part that hangs loose; an untwisted end of rope 1721. 2. *transf.* The last and poorest part of anything; the extreme end.

2. The fag-ends of cigars C. BEDE.

Faggot, fagot (fæ·gət), *sb.* ME. [a. F. *fagot*; origin unkn.] 1. A bundle of sticks, twigs, or small branches of trees bound together for use as fuel, in fascines, or the like. 2. *fig.* The punishment of burning alive, as heretics 1555. 3. A bundle in general; *fig.* a collection 1489. 4. A bundle of iron or steel rods bound together 1540. 5. A term of abuse applied to a woman (*dial.*) 1591. †6. A person hired to supply a deficiency at the muster; a dummy –1802. 7. = FAGGOT-VOTE. 1817.

3. My faggot of compliments H. WALPOLE.

Faggot (fæ·gət), *v.* 1543. [f. prec. sb. Cf. F. *fagoter*.] 1. *trans.* To make a faggot of; to bind up in or as in a faggot 1598. 2. *Metall.* To fasten together bars or rods of iron to be reheated and welded 1861. 3. To set (a person) on the faggots to be burnt alive; also *fig.* 1543. 4. *intr.* To make or bind faggots 1874.

Fa·ggoting, *vbl. sb.* [f. prec.] 1. The action of FAGGOT *v.* 2. *Embroidery.* The process by which a number of threads in the material are drawn out and cross threads tied together in the middle. Hence, the work done thus.

Faggot-vote (fæ·gətˌvōᵘt). 1817. [App. a transf. use of FAGGOT *sb.* 6, but taken as referring to the primary sense.] A vote manufactured for party purposes, by the transfer to persons not otherwise qualified of sufficient property to qualify them as electors. Hence **Faggot-voter.**

‖**Fagotto** (făgǫ·tto). 1724. [It.] = BASSOON, q. v.

‖**Fahlband** (fā·lband). 1880. [Ger.; f. *fahl* ash-coloured + *band* stripe.] *Geol.* A stratum in crystalline rocks.

‖**Fahlerz** (fā·lĕrts). 1796. [Ger.; f. as prec. + *erz* ore.] *Min.* Grey copper or copper ore, tetrahedrite. So **Fa·hlore** (in same sense).

Fahlunite (fā·lŭnəit). 1814. [f. *Fahlun* in Sweden + -ITE.] *Min.* A hydrous silicate of aluminium and iron, resulting from the alteration of iolite.

Fahrenheit (fæ·rənhəit, fā·rənhəit). 1753. The name of a Prussian physicist (1686–1736), inventor of the mercurial thermometer. Used *attrib.* and *ellipt.* to denote the scale introduced by him and still in use in England and U.S., which gives the freezing-point of water as 32° and the boiling-point as 212°. Often abbreviated *F.*, *Fah.*, or *Fahr.*

‖**Faience** (faˌyāṅs). 1714. [a. F. *faïence*, prob. f. †*Fayence*, Faenza in Italy, where much ceramic ware was made.] A general term for all kinds of glazed earthenware and porcelain.

Faikes (fēⁱks). Also **fakes.** 1865. *Geol.* 'A Scotch miner's term for fissile sandy shales, or shaly sandstones' (Page).

†**Fail,** *sb.*¹ *Sc.* 1513. [? a. Gael. *fàl* a sod.] A turf, a sod. Also turf, as a material. –1816. *Comb.* **f.-dyke,** a wall built of sods. SCOTT.

Fail (fēⁱl), *sb.*² ME. [a. OF. *faile*, *faille*, f. *faillir* to FAIL.] 1. = FAILURE 1; now only in *without f.* = certainly. †2. = FAILURE 2, 3. –1734. †b. Death. *Hen. VIII*, I. ii. 145.

Fail (fēⁱl), *v.* ME. [a. OF. *faillir* to be wanting, miss :—vulgar L. **fallire* (for L. *fallere* to deceive), used *absol.*]

I. 1. *intr.* To be absent or wanting; to be insufficient. 2. To become exhausted, come to an end, run short, die out ME. 3. To lose power or strength; to break down ME. †b. To die. *Hen. VIII*, I. ii. 184. 4. To prove deficient on trial ME. 5. To be wanting at need. Chiefly with *dat.* of the person, rarely with *to*. quasi-*trans.* To disappoint ME.

1. If suche heyres shulde fayle 1543. Failing proof then BROWNING. Phr. *Time would f. me to* [etc.]. 2. Neither shall the cruse of oile faile 1 *Kings* xvii. 14. Thy yeeres shall not fayle *Heb.* i. 12. The eldest line failing 1647. 3. My voice suddenly fail'd WESLEY. The wind failed 1833. *fig.* Her heart within her did not f. TENNYSON. 4. In general this rewle may not fayle CHAUCER. Loop and button failing both COWPER. 5. Here again chronology fails us FREEMAN.

II. 1. *intr.* To be wanting or deficient *in* ME. 2. *trans.* To lack, want. Now *rare*. ME. 3. *To fail of*: to lack; also, †to miss, escape ME.

1. Men þat failen in charite WYCLIF. The Dialogue fails in unity JOWETT. 2. I f. words to express my utter contempt JEFFERIES. 3. A weak prince..seldom fails of having his authority despised GOLDSM.

III. 1. *intr.* To fall short in performance or attainment; to make default; to miss the mark, err ME. 2. *trans.* To make default in; to disappoint; to miss. *Obs.* exc. with *inf.* as object. ME. 3. *intr.* To become insolvent or bankrupt 1682.

1. Their bull gendereth, and faileth not *Job* xxi. 10. Our envious Foe hath fail'd MILT. *P. L.* VII. 139. The year in which our olives failed TENNYSON. His action would f. SIR N. LINDLEY. 2. To f. trust GOUGE, expectation 1699. He failed to keep his word 1885. 3. If that Endorser f. and be insolvent SCARLETT. Twelve capital houses have failed 1796.

†IV. *trans.* To deceive, cheat (L. *fallere*). SPENSER *F. Q.* III. xi. 46.

†**Fai·lance.** 1612. [f. prec. + -ANCE.] The quality or fact of failing; failure, neglect, falling off –1686.

Failing (fēⁱ·liŋ), *vbl. sb.* ME. [f. FAIL *v.*] 1. The action of FAIL *v.*; a failure. 2. A defect, fault, weakness 1590.

2. E'en his failings lean'd to Virtue's side GOLDSM.

Failing (fēⁱ·liŋ), *prep.* 1810. [The pr. pple. of FAIL *v.*, used either intr. or trans.] In default of.

F. all else, what gossip about one another CARLYLE.

Faille (fāy, fēⁱl). 1530. [a. F. in same senses.] †1. A kind of head-dress –1694. 2. A light ribbed silk 1869.

Failure (fēⁱ·liŭɹ). 1643. [Orig. in form *failer*, a. AF. *failer*, for F. *faillir*; cf. *cesser*, *trover*, etc. The ending was subseq. confused with -OR, -OUR, -URE.] 1. A failing to occur, be performed, or be produced; non-performance; default; also, †a lapse; †an infirmity. 2. The fact of failing, becoming exhausted, giving way under trial, etc. (see FAIL *v.*) 1695. 3. Want of success; *concr.* a thing or person that fails of success 1643. 4. The fact of failing in business; bankruptcy, insolvency 1702.

1. A failer of full performance 1648. Failures of the press R. COKE. 2. Utter f. of intellect 1841. 3. Efforts ending in..f. SEELEY. Educated failures 1889.

Fain (fēⁱn). [OE. *fægen*, *fægn*; allied to OE. *gefēon* (pa. t. *feah*) to rejoice.]

A. *adj.* 1. Glad, rejoiced, well-pleased; content ME.; hence: Necessitated, obliged 1513.

2. Disposed, willing, eager (*arch.* or *dial.*) ME. †**3.** Well-disposed –ME.

1. Glad and faine by flight to saue themselves SHAKS. Men were faine to eate horse-flesh GOUGE. He was f. to acknowledge [etc.] 1884. 3. I..saw Love coming towards me, fair and f. ROSSETTI.

B. *adv.* Gladly, willingly, with pleasure. *Obs.* or *arch.* ME.

I would faine dye a dry death *Temp.* I. i. 72.

Hence **Fai·nly** *adv.* (*rare*).

†**Fain,** *v.*[1] [OE. *fæȝnian* (f. prec.).] **1.** *intr.* To be glad, rejoice –1596. **2.** *trans.* To make glad –1480. **3.** To rejoice in, enjoy –1606.

1. [She] faynes to weave false tales SPENSER.

Fain (fēin), *v.*[2] 1870. orig. *dial.* [var. FEN *v.*] In *fain(s) I*, etc., expressing intention to decline participation in a task, etc.

‖**Fainéant** (fēneˌaṅ). 1619. [F.; f. *fait* he does + *néant* nothing.] **A.** *sb.* A do-nothing; an idler. **B.** *adj.* That does nothing; idle, sluggard 1855.

Hence **Fai·neance, -cy,** f. quality or condition. ‖**Faineantise,** 'do-nothing-ness'; indifference.

Faint (fēint), *sb.* ME. [f. FAINT *a.* and *v.*] †**1.** Faintness –1600. **2.** A swoon –1808.

2. The Saint, Who propped the Virgin in her f. SCOTT.

Faint (fēint), *a.* [ME. *feint*, a. OF. *feint*, pa. pple. of *feindre* to FEIGN, q.v.] †**1.** Feigned –1568. †**2.** Sluggish –1680. **3.** Wanting in courage, spiritless. Now chiefly in *f. heart.* ME. **4.** Wanting in strength or vigour; languid, feeble ME. **5.** Striking the senses or the mind feebly; dim, indistinct, hardly perceptible 1552. **b.** *F. lines*, pale or indistinct lines to guide writing. **6.** Feeble through inanition, fear, or exhaustion; inclined to swoon ME. **7.** Producing faintness; sickly; oppressive 1525.

3. F. heart ne'er won fair lady *Provb.* 4. Damn with f. praise POPE. 5. F. reflections HOOKE, odours SHELLEY. Not the faintest chance 1884. 7. The Weather was very wet, hot, and f. 1712.

Hence **Fai·ntish** *a.* somewhat f., **-ness. Fai·ntly** *a.* and *adv.* **Fai·ntness. Fai·nty** *a.* faintish.

Faint (fēint), *v.* ME. [f. FAINT *a.*] **1.** *intr.* To lose heart or courage, become depressed, give way. Now only *arch.* after Biblical uses. **2.** To become faint, grow weak, decline. *Obs.* exc. *poet.* ME. **3.** To swoon. Also with *away.* ME. **b.** To droop, sink *into. lit.* and *fig.* (*rare*) 1712. **4.** To lose colour or brightness; to fade, die away. Now *rare.* ME. **5.** *trans.* To make faint, depress, weaken. Now *rare.* ME.

1. As we have received mercy, we f. not 2 *Cor.* iv. 1. **2.** To f. in courage 1623. 3. Oh, I shall f. ETHEREDGE. He fainted away GROTE. b. There Affectation..Faints into airs POPE. 5. It faints me To thinke what followes *Hen. VIII*, II. iii. 103.

Faint-heart (fēi·nthāɹt). 1580. [f. FAINT *a.* + HEART.] **A.** *sb.* †**1.** The condition of having a faint heart. NORTH. **2.** One who has a faint heart; a coward 1870.

B. *adj.* Faint-hearted, spiritless 1590.

So **Fai:nt-hea·rted** *a.* wanting energy, courage, or will to do anything; timid, cowardly. **Fa:int-hea·rtedly** *adv.* **Fai:nt-hea·rtedness.**

Fainting (fēi·ntiŋ), *vbl. sb.* ME. [f. FAINT *v.*] The action of FAINT *v.*; *esp.* swooning. Also *attrib.* in *f. fit.* So **Fai·ntingly** *adv.*

†**Fai·ntise.** ME. [a. OF. *feintise*, f. *feint* feigned, etc.; see FAINT.] Deceit; hypocrisy; feebleness; cowardice –1470.

†**Fai·ntling.** 1614. [f. FAINT *sb.* + -LING.] **A.** *sb.* One who is faint or faint-hearted. **B.** *adj.* Faint-hearted 1712.

Faints (fēints), *sb. pl.* 1743. [pl. of FAINT *a.* (quasi-*sb.*).] The impure spirit which comes over first and last in the process of distillation. Also *attrib.*

Fair (fēəɹ), *sb.*[1] ME. [a. OF. *feire* (mod.F. *foire*):—L. *feria* holiday.] A periodical gathering of buyers and sellers, in a place and at a time ordained by charter or statute or by ancient custom. Often specialized, as *cattle-, horse-, ram-*, etc., *f.*; *Easter-f.* Also (*fancy f.*) applied *transf.* to a bazaar or sale of fancy goods for a charitable purpose. Also *attrib.*

Phr. *A day after the f.*: too late.

Fair (fēəɹ), *a.* and *sb.*[2] [Com. Teut.: OE. *fæȝer.*]

A. *adj.* (No longer opp. to *foul* exc. with the sbs. *weather, means.*)

I. 1. Beautiful to the eye; of pleasing form or appearance. †**b.** Used as a term of address –1588. **2.** †Desirable, reputable –1676; considerable ME. †**3.** Of language, etc.: Elegant. Hence *f. speaker.* –1477. **4.** Attractive at first sight or hearing; specious, flattering OE.

1. The fairest of her Daughters Eve MILT. *P.L.* IV. 324. Two f. eyes GOWER. Tweed's f. river SCOTT. Phr. *The f. sex.* b. Faire sir, God saue you *L.L.L.* v. ii. 310. 2. A f. fortune 1654, heritage 1859. 4. A fayre speaker, and a deepe dissembler GRAFTON.

II. Of complexion, etc.: Light as opp. to *dark* 1551.

Are Violets not sweet, because not f. DRYDEN.

III. 1. Free from blemish or disfigurement; clean, clear. Of a line, curve, or surface: Free from irregularities; smooth, even (now chiefly *Naut.*). ME. **2.** Free from moral stain, unblemished ME. **3.** Free from bias, fraud, or injustice; equitable, legitimate ME. **4.** Tolerable; passable; average 1860.

1. A fayre white lynnen clothe 1552. A faire cleer water GOUGE. A very f. hand 1697. 2. My f. fame SHELLEY. Phr. *To stand f.* 3. A f. subject of presumption PALEY. F. game for ridicule BENTHAM. Phr. *A f. field and no favour. F. play.* 4. A person in f. health 1875.

IV. 1. Favourable ME. **2.** 'Likely to succeed' (J.); promising, advantageous, suitable ME. **3.** Gentle, peaceable, not violent ME. **4.** Free from obstacles; unobstructed, open 1523. **5.** Clear, distinct, plainly to be seen. Now chiefly *dial.* 1577.

1. Faire weather *Matt.* xvi. 2. The f. season 1671. To proceed..with the first f. wind 1790. 2. So faire an opportunitie KNOLLES. F. pretensions BURKE. 3. By f. meanes or foul 1659. 4. The fairest though farthest way about FORD. 5. F. on the face [God] wrote the index of the mind P. FLETCHER.

Comb.: *Fair-haired*, etc.; **f.-curve** (*Naut.*): in delineating ships, a winding line which varies according to the part of the ship it is intended to describe; **-world,** a state of prosperity (MILT.).

B. *sb.*[2] [The adj. used *absol.* or *ellipt.*] **1.** That which is fair (in senses of the adj.) ME. **2.** One of the fair sex; *esp.* a beloved woman. Now *arch.* or *poet.* ME. †**3.** Beauty; also *pl.* points of beauty –1633.

1. Can we not Partition make..Twixt faire and foule? *Cymb.* I. vi. 37. *To see f.* (colloq.): to see fair play. 2. O happie faire! Your eyes are loadstarres *Mids. N.* I. i. 182.

Fair (fēəɹ), *adv.* [OE. *fæȝre*, f. *fæȝer* FAIR *a.*] In a fair manner or degree: beautifully; civilly (now only in *to speak* (*a person*) *f.*) OE.; clearly, legibly 1513; equitably, impartially ME.; †becomingly –1665; favourably, as in *f. befall*, etc. OE.; †gently –1804; †'due (north, etc.)' –1720; 'clean', 'full' ME.

Fair (fēəɹ), *v.* [ME. *feiren*, OE. *fæȝrian*, f. *fæȝer* FAIR *a.*; also, later, f. FAIR *a.*] **1.** *intr.* To appear or become fair. †**2.** *trans.* To make fair –1600. **3.** *Ship-building.* To make fair or level; to ascertain the correctness of curvature in the parts of a ship. Also, to fit according to the curvature. 1867. Also of an aeroplane (cf. FAIRING *vbl. sb.*[2]).

2. Fairing the foul with art's false borrow'd face SHAKS. *Sonn.* cxxvii.

Fair and square. 1604.

A. *adj.* Honest, just, straightforward 1649.

B. *adv.* In a just or straightforward manner.

Fair-copy, *sb.* 1840. A copy of a document, etc. after final correction. Hence **Fair-copy** *v.* to write out in fair-copy.

Fai·r-faced, *a.* 1588. **1.** Having a blonde, or a beautiful, countenance. **2.** Having a fair appearance; in bad sense, specious 1595.

Fairfieldite (fēə·ɹfīldəit). 1879. [f. *Fairfield* (in Connecticut) where found; see -ITE.] *Min.* A hydrous phosphate of calcium, manganese, and iron.

†**Fai·rhead.** ME. [f. FAIR *a.* + -HEAD.] Beauty –1560. var. †**Fai·rhood.**

Fairing (fēə·riŋ), (*vbl.*) *sb.*[1] 1574. [f. FAIR *sb.*] A complimentary gift; *orig.* one given at or brought from a fair. Also *fig.*

Fairing, *vbl. sb.*[2] 1916. [f. FAIR *v.* + -ING[1].] The making of a flying machine's surface smooth and stream-like; the structure added for this purpose.

Fairish (fēə·riʃ). 1611. [f. FAIR *a.* and *adv.* + -ISH.] **A.** *adj.* Somewhat fair, passable; fairly large (*colloq.*). **B.** *adv.* In a fair manner; to a fair degree (*colloq.*) 1836.

Fair Isle (fēə·ɹəil). 1851. Name of one of the Shetland islands used attrib. to designate woollen articles knitted in certain designs characteristic of the island.

Fair-lead (fēə·ɹlīd). 1860. *Naut.* **a.** Such leading of a rope through the block or sheave aloft, that it does not cut or chafe any of the rigging or cross any other ropes. **b.** (Also **Fair-leader.**) A strip of board, with holes in it, for running rigging, to lead through; also, a block or thimble for the same purpose.

Fairly (fēə·ɹli), *adv.* ME. [f. FAIR *a.*] †**1.** Beautifully; in bad sense, speciously –1819. **2.** Equitably, candidly, impartially 1676. **3.** Becomingly; proportionably 1596; legitimately, opp. to *foully* 1632. †**4.** Gently –1634. **5.** Clearly, distinctly 1661. **6.** Completely, 'clean'; actually, really 1596. **7.** Moderately 1805.

1. Raiment..Most f. woven MORRIS. 2. Treated f. 1851, f. considered 1862. 3. His time will be f...employed 1800. She came f. by her death MRS. RADCLIFFE. 4. I f. step aside, And hearken MILT. 6. We were f. in the trap 1873. 7. F. safe WORDSW.

Fai·r-mai·d. 1776. **1.** = FUMADE, q.v. 1848. **2.** In various names of plants; as **Fair maid(s of February,** the Snowdrop; etc.

Fairness (fēə·ɹnės). OE. [f. FAIR *a.* + -NESS.] The quality or condition of being fair; beauty; lightness of colour, as of the skin, etc.; fair dealing; etc.

Fai·r-spo·ken, *a.* 1460. Of persons: Courteous; smooth-tongued; of words: Bland.

F. sword-men..whose words are softer than butter 1647.

Fai·r-tra·de. 1774. **1.** Trade carried on legally, as opp. to *contraband*. Also, in the 18th c., euphemistic for smuggling. **2.** The principle that reciprocity should be the principle of free-trade 1881.

Hence **Fair-tra·der.**

Fai·rway. Also **fare-way.** 1584. [See FAIR *a.* IV. 4.] A navigable channel in a river or between rocks, sandbanks, etc. **b.** *Golf.* The smooth (trimmed) part of a golf-course between tee and putting-green (cf. ROUGH *sb.* I. 1 c) 1910.

Fai·r-weather, *a.* 1736. **1.** Fit or suitable only for fair weather 1810. **2.** *fig.* 1736.

1. F. craft 1883. 2. A f. service..of God E. IRVING.

Fairy (fēə·ri). ME. [a. OF. *faerie* (mod.F. *féerie*), f. *fae* (mod.F. *fée*) FAY *sb.*[2]]

A. *sb.* †**1.** Fairy-land; see FAERIE. –1610. †**2.** The fays collectively –1603. †**3.** Enchantment, magic; an illusion –1533. **4.** One of a class of supernatural beings of diminutive size, popularly supposed to have magical powers, and to meddle for good or evil in the affairs of man. See ELF and FAY *sb.*[2] ME. **5.** *transf.* An enchantress *Ant. & Cl.* IV. viii. 12; a small graceful woman or child 1838.

1. The Queene of Faerie B. JONS. 3. Hit nis but fantum and feiri ME. 4. Twilight fairies tread the circled Green COLLINS. *F. of the mine* (MILT.): a goblin supposed to inhabit mines; used later as=Ger. *kobold* or *gnome*.

B. *adj.* **1.** Of, pertaining to, or of the nature of fairies; enchanted, illusory 1640. **2.** Fairy-like; delicate, finely formed or woven 1788.

2. F. palms..f. pines TENNYSON. F. textures 1883.

Comb.: **fairies'-arrow** = ELF-SHOT; **f.-bird,** the Little Tern; **-cheeses,** *Malva rotundiflora* from the shape of the seeds; **-circle,** (*a*) = FAIRY-RING, (*b*) a fairy-dance, (*c*) a circle of fairies dancing; hence **-circled** *a.*; **-cups,** *Primula veris*; hence **-cupped** *a.*; **-dart** = ELF-SHOT; **-flax,** *Linum catharticum*; **-grass,** *Briza media*; **-lights,** small coloured lights used esp. for outside illumination; **-loaf,** a fossil sea-urchin said to be made by the fairies; **-martin,** Australian name for *Hirundo ariel*; **-money,** money given by fairies, said to crumble away rapidly; **-mushroom,** a toadstool; **-shrimp** = *Chirocephalus diaphanus*, a British freshwater crustacean; **-stone,** (*a*) a fossil sea-urchin, (*b*) a flint arrow-head; **fairies'-table,** various fungi; **-treasure, -wealth** = *fairy-money*; †**-walk** = FAIRY-RING.

Hence **Fai·rily** *adv.* **Fai·ryhood.**

Fairyism (fēə·riˌiz'm). 1715. [f. prec. + -ISM]. **a.** Fairy power. Hence *transf.* of a poet. **b.** The conditions of fairy existence; fairyland 1763. **c.** Belief in fairies, fairy-lore 1835.

Fairyland (fēə·rilænd). 1590. [f. as prec.

+ LAND.] The country of the fairies.

Fairy-ring (fēᵊ·ri͵riŋ). 1559. A circle of grass of a different colour from the grass surrounding it, a phenomenon caused by the growth of certain fungi, but popularly supposed to be produced by fairies when dancing.

Fai·ry-tale. 1750. [After F. *conte de fée*.] A tale about fairies. Also *transf.*

‖**Fait accompli** (fęt akonpli). 1845. [Fr. 'accomplished fact'.] A thing that is over and done with.

Faith (fēᵢþ), *sb.* ME. [a. OF. *feid, feit* (pronounced *feiđ, ?feiþ*) :—L. *fidem*, f. root of *fidere* to trust. See also FAY *sb.*¹]

I. 1. Confidence, reliance, trust. In early use, only with reference to religious objects. Const. *in*, †*of*. **b.** Belief proceeding from reliance on testimony or authority 1551. **2.** *Theol.* **a.** Belief in the truths of religion as contained in Holy Scripture or in the teaching of the Church. **b.** Saving or justifying faith, as a conviction operative on the character and will; opp. to *speculative faith*. **c.** The spiritual apprehension of divine truths. Often ascribed to the exercise of a special faculty in man, or to supernatural illumination. ME. **3.** That which is or should be believed ME.

1. F. in Ward's pills TUCKER, in the constancy of a law CHALMERS, in God J. H. NEWMAN. **b.** The absolute rejection of authority .. the annihilation of the spirit of blind f. HUXLEY. Phr. *To pin one's f. to or upon.* **2. a.** Abraham the father of fayth EDEN. **b.** Even so f., if it hath not works, is dead, being alone *Jas.* ii. 17. **c.** F. .. the faculty by which we realize unseen things GOULBOURN. **3.** *The Christian, Jewish, Mohammedan*, etc., *f.* *The f.*: the true religion; usu. = the Christian f. *Of f.*: part and parcel of the f. †*Act of the f.*: = AUTO-DA-FÉ.

II. †1. Power to produce belief, credit –1808. †2. Attestation, confirmation, assurance –1730. 3. Assurance given, formal declaration, pledge, promise. *Obs.*, exc. in *on the f. of*. ME.

3. Phr. *To give (one's) f.* On the f. of his oath they had placed themselves in his power THIRLWALL.

III. 1. The duty of fulfilling one's trust; fealty; the obligation of a promise or engagement ME. **2.** The quality of fulfilling one's trust; fidelity, loyalty ME.

1. Vpon the feyth that ye owe to me CAXTON. Phr. *To engage, pledge, plight (one's) f.*; *to perjure (one's) f.*; *to keep, break, violate (one's) f.*; *breach of f.* **2.** Confidence .. in our f. and probity T. JEFFERSON. Phr. *Good f.*: fidelity, loyalty, BONA FIDES. *Bad f.*: faithlessness; intent to deceive. *Punic* (occas. *Carthaginian*) *f.* (= L. *fides Punica*): faithlessness. *In (good) f.*: in truth. *By* or *on my, thy*, etc., *f.*; *my f.* (= F. *ma foi!*): quasi-oaths.

Comb.: **f.-cure**, a cure wrought by means of 'the prayer of faith' (*Jas.* v. 15); **-healer**, one who believes in or practises f.-cure; **-healing**, healing by f.-cure.

Hence †**Faith** *v. trans.* to provide with a f.; to utter on one's f.; to give f. to, believe, trust. †**Faithed** *ppl. a.* having (feeble, etc.) f.; given on one's f.

Faithful (fēᵢ·þfŭl). ME. [f. prec. + -FUL.] **A.** *adj.* †1. Full of or characterized by FAITH (sense I. 2); believing –1759. **2.** Firm in fidelity or allegiance to a person to whom one is bound by any tie; constant, loyal, true. Also *transf.* of things. ME. **3.** True to one's word or profession ME.; †of a covenant, etc.: Binding –1601. **4.** Conscientious in the fulfilment of duty; *esp.* of the duty of telling unwelcome truths ME. **5.** Trustworthy, veracious; reliable ME. **6.** True to the fact or the original, accurate 1529. **7.** *absol.* Chiefly *pl.* = 'True believers'; the orthodox of any religious community 1558.

1. F. Abraham *Gal.* iii. 9. **2.** F. allies DE FOE. His f. dog shall bear him company POPE. Whose hand was f. to his sword SCOTT. **3.** The faithfull God *Deut.* vii. 9. **5.** Memoirs scarcely more f. than romances SCOTT. **6.** A f. report FIELDING. **7.** The faithfull which departed this life before the comming of Christ HOOKER. Phr. *Father of the f.* (after *Rom.* iv. 11): Abraham. *Commander* or *Father of the F.*: Mohammedan titles of the Caliph.

†**B.** *adv.* = FAITHFULLY. –1651. **C.** *sb.* **a.** A true believer 1571. **b.** A trusty follower 1648. Hence **Fai·thfully** *adv.* confidingly; loyally; accurately; with binding assurances. *Yours f.*: one of the more formal phr. used in subscribing a letter, now regular in business use. **Fai·thfulness.**

Faithless (fēᵢ·þlės), *a.* ME. [f. FAITH *sb.* + -LESS.] **1.** Without belief or trust; unbelieving. **b.** Without religious faith; without Christian faith. Also absol. *The f.*: unbelievers. Now *rare*. 1534. **2.** Destitute of good faith; false to vows, etc., perfidious, disloyal ME. **3.** Not to be trusted or relied on; unstable, treacherous, delusive 1603.

1. And bee not faithlesse, but beleeuing *John* xx. 27. **2.** A man..of a..f. disposition 1678. **3.** The midnight murd'rer bursts the f. bar JOHNSON. Hence **Fai·thless-ly** *adv.*, **-ness.**

Fai·thworthy, *a.* 1535. [f. FAITH + WORTHY *a.*] Worthy of belief or trust, trustworthy.

Faitour (fēᵢ·tǝɹ). Now *arch.* ME. [a. AF. *faitour*, OF. *faitor* :—L. *factorem*; see FACTOR.] An impostor, cheat; *esp.* a vagrant who shams illness or pretends to tell fortunes.

These faytours that ben called sothe sayers 1496.

Fake (fēᵢk), *sb.*¹ 1627. [?] *Naut.* One of the circles or windings of a cable or hawser, as it lies in a coil.

Fake (fēᵢk), *sb.*² *slang.* 1827. [See FAKE *v.*²] **1.** An act of faking; a trick, invention; a faked or cooked report. **2.** That which is used for faking 1866.

Fake (fēᵢk), *v.*¹ ME. [app. f. FAKE *sb.*¹] *Naut.* To lay a rope in fakes; to coil.

Fake (fēᵢk), *v.*² *slang.* 1812. [? (ult.) ad. Ger. *fegen* to furbish up, clean, sweep.] **1.** *trans.* In thieves' language: To perform any operation upon; to 'do', 'do for'; to plunder, wound, kill; to do up; to tamper with, for the purpose of deception. **2.** *absol.* or *intr.* To steal 1812.

1. A horse faked up for sale 1874. Faked diamonds 1887. A faked report (*mod.*). Hence **Fa·kement** (*slang*), a piece of manipulation, dodge; vaguely, a thing, 'concern'; a trimming. **Fa·ker.**

‖**Faki.** 1872. [Arab. *faqih* one learned in the law.] A title given in Africa to schoolmasters.

Fakir (fākīᵊ·ɹ, fēᵢ·kiᵊɹ). Also **faquir**, fakeer, etc. 1609. [a. Arab. *faqīr* lit. 'poor, poor man'.] A poor man; *spec.* a Mohammedan religious mendicant; applied loosely to Hindu devotees and naked ascetics. **b.** (fēᵢ·kǝɹ). Erron. f. FAKER (*U.S.*) 1902.

Fa-la (fālā). 1595. Used as a refrain. Also, a sort of madrigal or ballet in vogue in the 16th and 17th c.

‖**Falbala** (fæ·lbălă). 1704. [?] A trimming for women's petticoats, scarves, etc.; a flounce.

Falcade (fælkā·d). 1730. [a. F., ad. It. *falcata*, L. *falcata*, fem. of *falcatus*; see next.] *Manège.* The action of a horse when the haunches and the legs bend very low, as in curvets. (Dicts.)

Falcate (fæ·lkēᵢt), *a.* 1826. [ad. L. *falcatus*, f. *falx* (*falc-*), sickle.] *Anat.*, etc. Bent or curved like a sickle. So **Fa·lcated** *a.* †**Falca·tion**, the condition of being f.; *concr.* that which is f.

Falchion (fǭ·lʃ'ǝn), *sb.* [ME. *fauchoun*, a. OF. *fauchon* :—vulg. L. **falcionem*, f. (ult.) as prec.] **1.** A broad sword more or less curved with the edge on the convex side. Later: A sword of any kind. †**2.** = Bill *sb.*¹ 4 or BILLHOOK. –1664.

1. Phr. *Single, double f.*, *case of falchions*: obs. species of sword-play.

Falcidian (fælsi·diăn), *a.* 1656. [f. *Falcidius* + -AN.] In *F. law* (*Lex Falcidia*), a law carried by P. Falcidius, by which a Roman citizen was obliged to leave at least a fourth part of his estate to his legal heirs. Hence *F. portion.*

Falciform (fæ·lsifǭɹm), *a.* 1766. [f. L. *falx* (*falc-*) + -(I)FORM.] Sickle-shaped, curved, hooked. Freq. in *Anat.*, as in *f. cartilage, ligament, process*, etc.

Falcon (fǭ·kǝn, fǭ·lkǝn). [ME. *faucon* (*faukun*), a. OF. *faucon, falcun*, ad. late L. *falconem*, ? f. *falx* (*falc-*), from the shape of the hooked talons.] **1.** *Ornith.* One of a family of the smaller diurnal birds of prey, characterized by a short hooked beak, strong claws, and great destructive power; *esp* one trained to the pursuit of other birds or game, usually the Peregrine Falcon. In *Falconry*, applied only to the female, the male being called the *tercel* or *tiercel*. **2.** An ancient kind of light cannon 1496.

1. A Faulcon towring in her pride of place *Macb.* II. iv. 12. *Comb.*, chiefly *attrib.*, as (sense 1) *f.-face*; *-eyed*, a.; (sense 2) *-shot*.

Falconer (fǭ·kǝnǝɹ, fǭ·lkǝnǝɹ). ME. [a. OF. *fau(l)connier*, f. *fau(l)con*; see prec.] **1.** One who hunts with falcons. **2.** A keeper and trainer of hawks ME.

1. Thise ffauconers..with hir haukes han the heron slayn CHAUCER.

Falconet (fǭ·kǒnėt). 1559. [In sense 1, ad. It. *falconetto*, dim. of *falcone*; in sense 2, f. FALCON + -ET.] **1.** A light cannon used in the 16th and 17th c. **2.** A species of Shrike (order *Passerinæ*) 1851.

Fa·lcon-ge·ntle. ME. [After F. *faucon gentil*.] The female or young of the Goshawk (*Astur palumbarius*).

Falconine (fæ·lkǒnǝin), *a.* [f. L. *falconem* + -INE.] Like a falcon or hawk, belonging to the *Falconidæ*. (Dicts.)

Falconry (fǭ·kǝnri). 1575. [a. F. *fauconnerie*; see FALCON.] The art of breeding and training hawks; also, *occas.*, the practice of hawking.

Falculate (fæ·lkiŭlēᵢt), *a.* 1847. [f. L. *falcula*, dim. of *falx* (*falc-*) + -ATE.] Of the form of a little sickle, small and curved.

Faldage (fæ·ldėdʒ). 1692. [ad. law-L. *faldagium*, f. OE. *fald*, FOLD *sb.*¹ Cf. FOLDAGE.] *Law.* An old privilege by which a lord of the manor could set up folds in any fields within the manor, in which his tenants were obliged to put their sheep, to manure the land.

Falderal, falderol (fæ·ldəræ·l, fǫ·ldǝrǫ·l). **1.** As a refrain in songs 1701. **2.** A gewgaw, trifle; a flimsy thing 1820.

‖**Faldetta** (falde·tă). 1834. [It., dim. of *falda* fold of cloth, skirt.] A combined hood and cape, worn by women in Malta.

†**Fa·ldfee.** *rare.* [app. f. OE. *fald*, FOLD *sb.*¹ + *feoh* (see FEE).] *Law.* Some kind of manorial dues. BLOUNT. (Possibly an error.)

†**Fa·lding.** ME. A kind of frieze, or a garment of the same –1526.

†**Faldi·story.** 1675. [ad. med.L. *faldistorium*, var. of *faldistolium*; see FALDSTOOL.] The seat or throne of a bishop within the chancel –1768.

Faldstool (fǭ·ldstūl). OE. [ad. med.L. *faldistolium*, ad. OHG. *faldstuol*, f. *faldan* to fold and *stuol* seat, chair; see FOLD and STOOL. Cf. FAUTEUIL.] **1.** *Eccl.* An armless chair used by bishops and other prelates when they do not occupy the throne or when officiating in any but their own church. **2.** A movable folding-stool or desk at which worshippers kneel; *esp.* one used by the sovereign at the coronation 1603. **3.** A small desk at which the Litany is said or sung 1626.

Falern(e (fălǭ·rn), *a.* and *sb.* *poet.* 1601. [ad. L. (*vinum*) *Falernum*.] = next.

Falernian (fălǭ·rniăn), *a.* 1726. [f. as prec. + -IAN.] Of or pertaining to the *ager Falernus* in Campania, celebrated for its wine. Also *absol.* Falernian wine.

Falk (fǭk), *sb.* 1698. A name applied dial. to the Razor-bill.

Fall (fǭl), *sb.*¹ ME. [f. FALL *v.*] An act or instance of falling.

I. 1. A dropping down by the force of gravity; also *fig.* ME.; *concr.* that which falls; also *pl.* 1742. **2.** (Earlier †*F. of the leaf*.) The season when leaves fall from the trees; autumn. Chiefly U.S. Now *rare* in Eng. literary use. 1545. **3.** The manner in which anything falls 1535. **4.** Birth or production by dropping from the parent; the quantity born or produced 1796.

1. A green plum that .. falls .. before the f. should be SHAKS. *fig.* The f. of the Stuarts HALLAM. *concr.* A large aerolitic f. LOCKYER. **2.** In the spring and f. he was alwaies disturbed LUTTRELL. **3.** The f. of the cards 1885. **4.** The principal f. of lambs HOWITT.

II. 1. A sinking down, subsidence; also *fig.* decline, decay 1571. **2.** The discharge or disemboguement of a river; †the place of this, the mouth 1577. **3.** The falling of a stream of water down a declivity; hence, a cascade, cataract, waterfall. Freq. in *pl.* 1579. **4.** Downward direction of a surface or outline; a slope or declivity 1565. **5.** The distance through which anything falls; the difference in the levels (of ground water, etc.) 1686. **6.** The sinking down of the fluid in a meteorological instrument; hence, of temperature, and of the instrument 1806. 7. *Mus.* A lowering of the note or voice; cadence 1601. 8. A sinking down in price, value, etc.; depreciation 1555.

1. The rise and f. of the spring-tides LYELL. *fig.* The f. of Venice OTWAY, of day BLACKMORE. 2. The Po..before its F. into the Gulf ADDISON. 3. The falls of Clyde 1806. 4. The f. of the hills SCOTT, of the shoulders 1847. 5. Hart's Weir..has a f. of 3 ft. 1881. 7. That straine agen, it had a dying f. *Twel. N.* I. i. 4. 8. The f. of the market BP. HALL, of Interest PETTY, of rents MACAULAY.

III. 1. A falling to the ground; also *fig.* of an institution ME. **2.** *Wrestling.* The fact of being thrown by one's opponent; hence, a bout at wrestling 1553. **3.** A felling of trees; *concr.* the timber felled at one time 1572. **4.** The capture or surrender of a city, fortress, etc. 1586. **5.** *fig.* A succumbing to temptation; moral ruin ME. **6.** Death, destruction, overthrow ME.

1. [The house] fell: and great was the f. of it *Matt.* vii. 27. The hero's f. W. IRVING. 2. You shall trie but one f. *A. Y. L.* I. ii. 216. 4. The f. of Londonderry MACAULAY. 5. Phr. *The f., the f. of man* (Theol.): the sudden lapse into a sinful state produced by Adam's transgression. 6. Now happened the f. of..Oliver Cromwell B. HARRIS.

IV. As a measure (orig. = *perch, pole, rod*), the 40th part of a furlong 1597.

†**V.** What befalls a person –1853.

Black be your fa BURNS.

VI. 1. a. A band or collar worn falling flat round the neck 1599. **b.** A kind of veil worn by women 1611. **2.** *Mech.* The loose end of the tackle, to which the power is applied in hoisting 1644; an apparatus for lowering bales, etc; also *Naut.* in *pl.* 1832.

Comb.: **f.-board,** a shutter hinged at the bottom; **-trap** = FALL *sb.*[2]

Fall (fǭl), *sb.*[2] [OE. (*mūs-*) *fealle* wk. fem., f. *feallen* to FALL.] Something that falls; a trap-door, trap. Cf. PITFALL.

Fall (fǭl), *sb.*[3] 1694. [? local Sc. pronunc. of *Whale.*] **a.** The cry given when a whale is sighted or harpooned. **b.** The chase of a whale or school of whales 1820.

Fall (fǭl), *v.* Pa. t. **fell** (fel); pa. pple. **fallen** (fǭ·l'n). [Com. Teut.: OE. *feallan*:—pre-Teut. **phal-n-* cogn. w. L. *fallere* to deceive; the Gr. σφάλλειν is prob. unconnected. In the intr. senses often conjug. with *be.*]

I. 1. *intr.* To descend (primarily by gravity); to drop from a high or relatively high position; also *fig.* **2.** To become detached and drop off; also *fig.* ME. **3.** Of the young of animals: To be dropped or born ME. **4.** Of speech, etc.: To issue or proceed *from* 1605.

1. The Priest let f. the booke *Tam. Shr.* III. ii. 163. What if heaven f., say you BP. HALL. *fig.* Falne from his first perfection BURTON. Most fiercely fell their fury on the Dutch FULLER. The evening fell SCOTT. Provb. *F. back, f. edge*: come what may. 2. *fig.* My fevered mood fell from me 1890. 3. The lambs should f. in May 1864. 4. Wisdom falling from his Tongue 1770.

II. 1. To descend, sink *into, to*; to decline ME. **2.** Of land: To slope 1573. **3.** Of a river, etc.: To discharge itself, issue *into.* Also *transf* of a road. ME. **4.** To subside; also *fig.* ME. **5.** Of the countenance: To lose animation; to assume a look of dismay or disappointment. [Orig. a Hebraism.] ME. **6.** To be lowered in direction 1586. †**7.** To shrink; to become lean –17.. **8.** To sink to a lower point, as the mercury in a barometer; to be reduced, as temperature 1658. **9.** *Mus.* To sound a lower note 1597. **10.** To decrease; to be diminished in price or value 1580.

1. The obsequious billows f. OTWAY. We f. below our position TRENCH. 3. Rivers that f. into Lake Huron 1825. 4. It fell calm 1670. *fig.* What though wit, like ocean, rose and fell SHELLEY. 5. Cain was very wroth, and his countenance fell *Gen.* iv. 5. 6. His eyes fell 1889. 7. A good leg will f. SHAKS. 10. The Rents of Land are generally fall'n PETTY. The exchange fell below par 1812.

III. 1. *intr.* To lose the erect position; to become suddenly prostrate; also *fig.* ME. **2.** To prostrate oneself. [Hebr. idiom.] OE. **3.** To yield to temptation; *esp.* of a woman: To surrender her chastity ME. **4.** To drop down wounded or dead; to die by violence; *rarely,* by disease; also *fig.* ME. **5.** Of a building, etc.: To come down in fragments ME.

1. Starting aside I slipped and fell DICKENS. *fig.* When proud Granada fell BYRON. The proposition fell to the ground MACAULAY. 2. I fell at his feete to worship him *Rev.* xix. 10. 3. It is their Husbands faults If wiues do f. *Oth.* IV. iii. 88. 4. Sheo fallethe dede as any stoone CHAUCER. Seven lions fell to his rifle in one day 1892. Phr. *To f. a prey, sacrifice, victim to. To f. in a snare, into danger, error,* etc. 5. Babylon is fallen, is fallen *Isa.* xxi. 9. Phr. *To f. in* or *to pieces, powder. To f. in two, asunder.*

IV. To move precipitately or with violence; to rush ME.

His master fell about his ears and beat him PEPYS.

V. 1. To have or take its direction; to be directed; to settle or impinge 1570. **2.** Of a lot, etc.: To light *upon* a particular object ME. **3.** To come as a lot, portion, or possession; rarely *impers.* ME. **4.** To come as a burden or duty 1599. †**5.** To appertain or belong; also *impers.* –1563.

1. The rays falling on the pupil BERKELEY. His eye fell..upon Cissy 1886. 2. The lot fell vpon Matthias *Acts* i. 26. 3. The whole fighting fell to Sir Horace CARLYLE. 4. The expense..must f. upon the purchaser 1885.

VI. 1. To come by chance or casually ME. **2.** To come naturally ME.; to be naturally divisible *into* 1641.

1. As for riches, if they f. in my way, I refuse them not BP. HALL. You f. 'mongst Friends SHAKS. The degenerate days on which he had fallen DISRAELI. 2. The subject..falls into four divisions 1862.

VII. 1. To pass (suddenly) †*in, into,* †*to* some specified condition or relation ME. **2.** With compl.: To become (what the complement signifies) ME. **3.** To lapse, as a benefice, etc.; †to become vacant, as a living 1530. †**4.** To change *to, into* (something worse) –1586.

1. To f. into the travaile of childe birthe LAMBARDE. My way of life is falne into the Seare, the yellow Leafe *Macb.* v. iii. 23. Phr. *To f. in love.* 2. His horse fell lame SOUTHEY. To f. heir to an estate 1891. 3. When the living fell, it was given elsewhere 1796.

VIII. To occur, come to pass, befall, result ME.

The xlij day of March fil vp-on a Saterday CHAUCER. Oft..sorrows f. GOLDSM. *impers.* As it fell..an elder 'gan to tell The story MORRIS. Phr. *Fair f., Foul f.*: may good *or* evil befall.

IX. Transitive senses. **1.** To let fall, drop. *Obs.* exc. in *Bellringing.* 1475. †**2.** To lower –1795. †**3.** To bring or throw to the ground. *lit.* and *fig.* –1625; to cut down (trees). *Obs.* exc. *dial.* or *U.S.* ME. †**4.** To direct (*upon*) GOLDSM. †**5.** = 'To fall from' SIR T. HERBERT. **6.** To have as one's share, come in for, obtain. Now *dial.* ME.

1. To f. an axe SHAKS., an argument DRYDEN, a drawbridge 1808. 2. To f. a Gun 1692, the voice 1748, the value of land BURKE. 3. To f. the vnder wode FITZHERB. 5. To f. the precipice 1665.

Special Combs. **1.** With prep. (and prepositional phrases).

F. a-. To set about, begin. Now only *arch.* with vbl. sbs. in *-ing.* **F. across —.** To come upon by chance. **F. behind —.** To be outstripped or left behind by. **F. down —. a.** See DOWN *prep.* **b.** To drop down (a river, etc.). **F. for —.** To be captivated or carried away by; to yield to the attractions of (orig. *U.S. slang*). **F. from —. a.** See simple senses. †**b.** To disagree with. †**c.** To drop away from, forsake; to renounce one's allegiance to. †**d.** To drop out of, give up (a practice, etc.); to break (a commandment). **F. in** (= *into*) **—. a.** = *F. into.* **b.** *To f. in hand to*: see HAND. **F. into —.** †**a.** To drop into. †**b.** To make a hostile inroad upon. **c.** To take (one's place), take one's place in (*lit.* and *fig.*). **d.** To enter upon (*esp.* talk), to begin the discussion of. †**e.** To come within (the range of). †**f.** To be included among. **g.** To take up with, accommodate oneself to. **h.** To drop into (a habit, etc.). **To f. off —. a.** Of an animal: To lose appetite for; to refuse. **b.** Of a vessel: To deviate from (her course). **F. on —.** †**a.** To break out into, set about (an action or state). **b.** *Mil.* To make a descent or attack upon; to rush upon, assault. **c.** To come across; †to hit upon (an expedient). **d.** To have recourse to. **e.** *To f. on one's feet*: *fig.* to fare fortunately. **F. to —.** †**a.** To attach oneself to; also, to make one's peace with. †**b.** To agree with, accede to (a proposal, etc.). **c.** To apply or betake oneself to; to begin. **F. under —. a.** To come or be classed under. **b.** To be subjected to. **F. unto —.** = *F. to,* in various senses. **F. upon —. a.** = *F. on* †a, b, c. †**b.** To begin upon, set about. **c.** To come (casually) to, take up with. **d.** *Geom.* Of a line, point, etc.: To cover, come exactly upon. †**e.** To become chargeable to (the parish). †**F. with —.** To come upon in due course; esp. *Naut.* to make (land). **F. within —.** To be included in; to come within the operation or scope of.

2. With adverbs.

F. aboard. a. To strike or encounter; see ABOARD. †**b.** To make a beginning. **F. astern.** See VI. 2, and ASTERN. **F. away. a.** See simple senses and AWAY. **b.** To draw off, desert, revolt. **c.** To become a backslider, to apostatize (*from*). †**d.** To lose flesh. **e.** To decay, pine away, perish, vanish. **F. back. a.** See simple senses and BACK. **b.** To step back, give way; to retreat. †**c.** To fall into arrear (in payments, etc.). **F. back on, upon. a.** *Mil.* To retire to. **b.** *fig.* To have recourse to (something) when other things fail. **F. down. a.** See simple senses and DOWN. **b.** Of a ship, etc.: To drop down towards the sea. †**c.** To swoop down. †**d.** To sicken. **F. foul. a.** To come into collision. **b.** *fig.* To clash, come into conflict (with); to quarrel. **c.** To make an attack. **F. in. a.** See simple senses and IN. **b.** To drop to pieces inwardly, as a building; also *transf.* of a cliff. †**c.** To make one's way in. Of a ship: To take a course (to land). **d.** To happen, occur, take place. Now *rare.* **e.** *Mil.* To get into line, take one's place in the ranks. **f.** To form (troops) in line; to parade. **g.** To agree, fit in. †**h.** To make up a quarrel. Cf. *F. out.* †**i.** To give way. **j.** To come to an end, terminate; to become due, as a debt; to become available. **To f. in with. a.** To come upon by chance, meet with. Also, †To arrive at (land). **b.** To drop into the views of, agree with; to make common cause with. **c.** To accede to (a proposal), join in (a project). **d.** To harmonize, match. Of a point, etc., of time: To coincide with. **e.** To concur with; to conform to; to humour. **F. off. a.** See simple senses and OFF. **b.** To drop off in position; to step aside or back, withdraw. **c.** *Naut.* Of a vessel: To fail to keep her head to the wind. **d.** *Naut.* To part company; to move away. Of a coast-line: To trend away. **e.** To become estranged, draw off; to revolt. **f.** To decrease in amount, intensity, or number. **g.** To decline; to degenerate. **F. on.** †**a.** To come on, as night. **b.** To make an attack, join battle. **c.** To set to work, begin. Now *rare.* **F. out. a.** *intr.* See simple senses and OUT. **b.** *Mil.* To drop out of the ranks; to drop behind. **c.** To disagree, quarrel. Also with *with.* **d.** To come about by chance (*rare*). **e.** To happen, occur, arise. Now chiefly *impers.* **f.** To prove to be, turn out. **F. out of. a.** See simple senses and OUT. **b.** *Mil.* To drop out of the ranks. **F. over. a.** See simple senses and OVER. †**b.** To go over *to* (the enemy). **F. short. a.** To give out, fail. **b.** Of a shot, etc.: Not to reach the mark. **F. short of. a.** To fail to obtain; to fail in performing. **b.** To fail of attaining to; not to reach the same amount, degree, etc. as. **F. through.** To break down, come to naught, miscarry. **F. to. a.** Of a gate, etc.: To shut automatically. **b.** To set to work, begin; *esp.* to begin eating; also, to come to blows. †**F. together. a.** Of the eyes: To close. **b.** To collapse, contract. **c.** †*F. together by the ears*: To quarrel.

†**Falla·ce.** ME. [a. F. *fallace,* ad. L. *fallacia.*] = FALLACY 1–3. –1634.

Fallacious (fălē¹·ʃəs), *a.* 1509. [f. L. *fallacia* + -OUS.] **1.** Containing a fallacy. **2.** †Deceitful –1769; deceptive, misleading 1651. **3.** Disappointing expectation, delusive 1667.

1. F. syllogisms REID. 2. F. Muse COWLEY, evidence FROUDE. 3. That f. Fruit MILT. *P. L.* IX. 1046. Hence **Falla·cious-ly** *adv.*, **-ness.**

Fallacy (fæ·lăsi). 1481. [ad. L. *fallacia,* f. *fallax* deceptive; see also FALLACE.] †**1.** Deception, trickery; a deception; a lie –1749. **2.** †Deceitfulness –1654; deceptiveness, unreliability 1800. **3.** A deceptive argument, a sophism. In Logic *esp.* a flaw which vitiates a syllogism; any of the types of such flaws. Also, sophistry. 1562. **4.** An error, *esp.* one founded on false reasoning. Also, error. 1590. **5.** Unsoundness (of arguments); delusiveness (of opinions, etc.); †fallibility (*rare*) 1651.

1. Winning by Conquest what the first man lost By F. surpriz'd MILT. *P. R.* I. 155. 2. The f. of human friendship K. WHITE. 4. Absurd and mischievous fallacies SYD. SMITH. 5. The f. of expectations 1850. vars †**Fa·llax.** †**Falla·xity.**

Fal-lal (fæ·l,læ·l). 1706. [? suggested by FALBALA.] **A.** *sb.* **1.** A piece of finery or frippery. Chiefly *pl.* **2.** = FA-LA. 1864.

†**B.** *adj.* Affected, finicking, foppish –1818. Hence **Falla·lery,** tawdry finery.

†**Falla·tion.** [?f. FALLACY.] = FALLACY 3. ASCHAM.

Fallen (fǭ·l'n), *ppl. a.* ME. [See FALL *v.*] **1.** That has come or dropped down. **2.** Of the sun: Having set. TENNYSON. **3.** Shrunken, emaciated, as flesh 1722. **4.** Laid low, or brought to the ground (*lit.* and *fig.*) 1631. **b.** *absol.* with *the*: Those who have died in battle 1914. **5.** *fig.* **a.** Morally ruined. **b.** That has come down in fortune. 1628.

4. Midst f. palaces 1835. The f. king FREEMAN.

†**Fallency.** 1603. [ad. med.L. *fallentia*, f. *fallere*; see -ENCY.] An instance of the failure of a rule; an exception –1660.

Faller (fǭ·ləɹ). ME. [f. FALL *v.*] One who or that which falls; *esp.* any of various appliances in spinning machines.

Fallible (fæ·lib'l), *a.* ME. [ad. late L. *fallibilis*, f. *fallere*; see -BLE. Cf. F. *faillible.*] **1.** Liable to be deceived or to err. **2.** Liable to be erroneous, unreliable ME.

1. A f. being will fail somewhere JOHNSON. 2. Hopes that are f. *Meas. for M.* III. i. 170. Hence **Fallibi·lity**, liability to err or †to mislead. **Fa·llibly** *adv.*

Falling (fǭ·liŋ), *vbl. sb.* ME. [f. FALL *v.*] **1.** The action of FALL *v.* **2.** *Path.* In *F. of the womb*: a pop. term for *prolapsus uteri* (*Syd. Soc. Lex.*). †**3.** A depression; a hollow, declivity –1712. **4.** *concr.* That which falls or has fallen; also *fig.* ME.

Comb., as *f. off*, decadence, defection, diminution; *f. out*, disagreement, quarrel; †ending.

Falling (fǭ·liŋ), *ppl. a.* ME. [f. as prec.] That falls, in various senses of the vb.

Comb. **a.** *F.-†disease*, *†-evil*, *†-ill*, *-sickness* (now *rare*) = EPILEPSY. **b. f.-band** = FALL *sb.*¹ VI. 1 a; †**-door** = *folding-door*; †**-hinge**, one by which a door, etc. rises vertically when opened; **-moulds** (*Arch.*), the two moulds applied to the vertical sides of the rail-piece, in order to form the back and under surface of the rail and finish the squaring (Gwilt); **-sluice**, a flood-gate which opens automatically in the event of a flood; **-star**, a meteor; a shooting star.

Fallopian (fălōᵘ·piăn), *a.* 1706. [f. *Fallopius* (latinized name of an Italian anatomist 1523–1562) + -AN.] *Anat.* Discovered by, or named after, Fallopius; as *F. tubes*, 'two canals inclosed in the peritoneum.. communicating from the sides of the *Fundus Uteri* to the ovaries' (MAYNE); *F. canal*; etc.

Fallow (fæ·lou), *sb.* ME. [? f. OE. **fealh* harrow, or f. **fealgian* (= FALLOW *v.*).] †**1.** A piece of ploughed land; also *collect.* –1713. **2.** Ground ploughed and harrowed, but left uncropped for a year or more 1523. **3.** The state, or interval, of being fallow; also *fig.* 1523. **4.** *attrib.* 1678.

1. All our Vineyards, Fallowes, Meades, and Hedges ..grow to wildnesse *Hen. V*, v. ii. 54. 2. Phr. *Summer f.*: so called because summer is chosen for the sake of killing the weeds. *Green*, *cropped*, or *bastard f.*: one from which a green crop is taken. 3 *fig.* Your f. adds to your fertility BURKE. 4. *F.-chat*, *-finch*, the Wheatear (*Saxicola œnanthe*).

Fallow (fæ·lou), *a.*¹ [OE. *falu*, *fealo*, *fealu* :—OTeut. **falwo-*, prob. cogn. w. Gr. πολιός grey, L. *pallere.*] **1.** Pale brownish or reddish yellow. Now chiefly in FALLOW-DEER. **2.** *absol.* Name of a colour 1741.

1. Many a dere both rede and falowe FABYAN.

Fallow (fæ·lou), *a.*² 1460. [See FALLOW *sb.*] Of land: **a.** That is uncropped for the current year. **b.** Uncultivated. †**c.** Ploughed ready for sowing. Also *transf.* and *fig.*

a. Her f. Leas SHAKS. b. Breake vp your f. ground *Jer.* iv. 3. Hence **Fa·llowness**, f. condition; idleness.

†**Fa·llow**, *v.*¹ [OE. *fealuwian*, f. *fealu*; see FALLOW *a.*¹] To become pale or yellow; hence, to wither. Of the face: To blanch, grow pale. –1584.

Fallow (fæ·lou), *v.*² ME. [? OE. **fealgian*; see FALLOW *sb.*] **1.** *trans.* To plough or break up; to prepare for sowing. **2.** To lay fallow, for the purpose of destroying weeds, and for mellowing the soil; also *fig.* ME.

2. Scarce any f., a few sow clover A. YOUNG. Hence **Fa·llowist** (*nonce-wd.*), one who favours the practice of fallowing land.

Fallow-deer (fæ·lou,dīəɹ). 1500. [f. FALLOW *a.*¹ + DEER.] A species of deer (*Cervus dama* or *Dama vulgaris*) smaller than the stag or *red* deer. So called from its colour.

†**Fa·lsary.** ME. [ad. late L. *falsarius*, f. *falsus* FALSE.] **1.** One who falsifies (a document) –1828; a forger –1697. **2.** A deceitful person –1652.

1. The ground for our f. to forge this Epistle BENTLEY.

False (fǭls, fǫls). [late OE. *fals* adj. and sb., ad. L. *falsus* (neut. *falsum* used subst.), orig. pa. pple. of *fallere* to deceive; cf. ON. *fals* sb. Cf. OF. *fals*, *faus* (mod.F. *faux*).]

A. *adj.* **I. 1.** Erroneous. **2.** Not according to rule, principle, or law; wrong ME. **3.** Incorrect; unfair ME. **4.** Defective 1523.

2. Phr. *F. concord* (Gram.): a breach of any rule for the agreement of words in a sentence. *F. cadence* (Mus.): an interrupted or deceptive cadence. *F. relation* (Mus.): the separation of a chromatic semitone between two parts. *F. imprisonment* (Law): the trespass committed against a person by imprisoning him contrary to law. **b.** *Mus.* Inaccurate in pitch; out of tune 1597. **c.** *Her.* Voided 1864. 3. F. dice 1551. A f. ballance *Prov.* xx. 23. F. play DONNE. A f. step (= F. *faux pas*) 1700. *F. start* (in a race): a wrong start; often *transf.* and *fig.* 4. *F. bearing* (Arch.): 'any bearing which is not directly upon a vertical support' (Webster).

II. 1. Purposely untrue; mendacious ME. **2.** Deceitful, treacherous. Formerly often pleonastically, as in *f. traitor*, etc. ME. **3.** Fallacious, deceptive; distorting 1531.

1. And they said, It is f. 2 *Kings* ix. 12. F. Accusation SHAKS., Prophets STILLINGFL. 2. F. as hell, and cruel as the grave SOUTH. The Ground is f. under us 1692. 3. The Devill makes us f. spectacles 1641. Looking..through a f. medium MACAULAY. Phr. †*F. door*, *postern.*

III. 1. Counterfeit, sham OE.; pretended ME.; artificial 1591; spurious 1600. **2.** *Nav.* and *Mil.* Counterfeited to deceive an enemy; feigned ME. **3.** Improperly so called 1578. **4.** In *f. dyes*, *colours* (= F. *teint faux*): fugitive dyes. **5.** (Chiefly *Mech.*) Subsidiary, supplementary 1552.

1. F. charter parties 1558, wreits 1609; f. prophets HULOET; f. learning POPE. Phr. *F. key*: a skeleton key. 2. Phr. *Under f. colours. To hang out f. colours. F. alarm*: an alarm without foundation. *F. attack*: a feigned movement, intended to divert the attention of the enemy from the real attack. *F. fire*: †(*a*) a blank discharge of firearms; (*b*) a fire made to deceive an enemy, or as a signal by night. 3. *F. ribs*: the five inferior ribs on each side. F. topaz, *i. e.* Yellow Quartz 1776. F. acacia 1861. 5. Phr. *F. bottom*: a horizontal partition in a vessel. *F. keel*, *keelson*, *post*, *rail*, *stay*, *stem*, *stern*, *stern-post* (Shipbuilding). *F. deck*: a grating or the like supported above the main deck by the 'close fights'. *F. pillar*, *roof* (Arch.). Hence **Fa·lsely** *adv.* **Fa·lseness.**

B. *adv.* †**1.** Untruly –1621. **2.** Improperly; in the wrong direction; incorrectly 1591. **3.** Faithlessly, perfidiously; chiefly in *To play* (*a person*) *f.* 1590.

1. *Hen. VIII*, II. iv. 136. 2. The Musitian..plaies f. *Two Gent.* IV. ii. 59. 3. His mother plaid f. with a Smyth *Merch. V.* I. ii. 48.

C. *sb.* †**1.** Fraud, falsehood, treachery –ME. **2.** One who or that which is false ME. **3.** *Fencing.* = FEINT. 1637.

2. My f., ore-weighs your true SHAKS.

Comb. 1. Of the adj., as *f.-coiner*, etc.; *f.-faced*, *-hearted* (whence *-heartedness*), etc. 2. Of the adv., as *f.-boding*, *-promising*, etc.; *f.-derived*, *-imagined*, etc.; *f.-colour*, *-play* vbs., etc.

†**False**, *v.* ME. [a. OF. *falser* (mod.F. *fausser*):—late L. *falsare*, f. *falsus* FALSE *a.*] **1.** To fail, or cause to fail, or give way. Only in ME. **2.** *trans.* To counterfeit (money); to forge (a document) –1553. **3.** To falsify; to corrupt –1598. **4.** To be or prove false to. Also *absol.* –1624. **5.** To maintain to be false, impugn –1708.

2. All that falsen the popes lettres 1450. 4. He..hath his trouthe falsed CHAUCER. *absol.* All that falsen or use false measures 1450. 5. To f. a principle ME. Hence †**Fa·lser.** So †**Fa·lsery**, falsification, deception.

Falsehood (fǫ·lshud). late ME.; earlier + -head. [f. FALSE *a.* + -HEAD, -HOOD.] †**1.** Falseness, deceitfulness, mendacity, faithlessness –1534. **2.** Want of conformity to fact or truth; (intentional) falsity; an untrue proposition, doctrine, etc.; untrue propositions, etc. generally ME. **3.** Deception, falsification, imposture; a forgery, counterfeit (*Obs.* or *arch.*) ME. **4.** Intentional assertion of what is false; lying 1662. **5.** A lie. Also, lies in general ME.

2. In your answeres there remaineth falshood *Job* xxi. 34. Each age has to fight with its own falsehoods HELPS. 3. No falshood can endure Touch of Celestial temper MILT. *P. L.* IV. 122. 4. Herodotus was..suspected of falshood STILLINGFL. 5. To tell a f. RUSKIN. An edifice of f. 1856.

‖**Falsetto** (fǫlse·to). 1774. [It., dim. of *falso* FALSE; cf. F. *fausset.*] **1.** A forced voice of a register above the natural; the head voice; also *fig.* **2.** One who sings with a falsetto voice 1789. **3.** *attrib.* 1826.

1. *fig.* The mock heroick f. of stupid tragedy BURKE. var. (anglicized) †**Falset.**

Falsification (fǫ·lsifikēⁱ·ʃən). 1565. [f. late L. *falsificare*; see -ATION.] **1.** The action of making (something) false; fraudulent alteration; perversion (of facts); counterfeiting. **2.** The showing (something) to be groundless or wrong, as assurances, an item of charge in an account, etc. 1845.

1. By f. of the wordes, wittingly to endeuour that anything may seeme diuine which is not HOOKER. Their..manifest falsifications both of manners and history 1799.

Falsificator (fǫ·lsifikēⁱtəɹ). 1609. [f. late L. *falsificare.*] One who deals in falsification; a falsifier.

Falsify (fǭ·lsifəi, fǫ·-), *v.* 1449. [ad. F. *falsifier*, ad. late L. *falsificare*, f. L. *falsificus* making false, f. *falsus*; see -FY.] **1.** *trans.* To make false or incorrect 1502. †**2.** To counterfeit –1699. **3.** To declare or prove to be false; *esp.* in *Law* 1449. **b.** To fail in fulfilling, or prevent the fulfilment of (a prediction, expectation, etc.) 1596. †**4.** *intr.* To deal in falsehoods –1777. †**5.** *trans.* To prove false to (one's faith, word, etc.) –1670; †*intr.* to give way (PEPYS). †**6.** *Fencing.* To feign (a blow); to make (a blow) under cover of a feint. Also *absol.* –1680.

1. To falsifie the Scriptures HOBBES, facts and dates EMERSON, our standards 1848, the relation between parties M. PATTISON. 3. No man can f. any material fact here stated T. JEFFERSON. Conclusive evidence to f. the warranty W. SELWYN. b. By so much shall I falsifie mens hopes 1 *Hen. IV*, I. ii. 235. 6. As th' are wont to f. a Blow BUTLER.

Hence **Fa·lsifiable** *a.* that may be falsified. **Fa·lsifier**, one who falsifies. †**Fa·lsify** *sb.* a feint (in *Fencing*).

Falsism (fǭ·lsiz'm, fǫ·-). 1840. [f. FALSE *a.* + -ISM.] **a.** A statement which is evidently false. **b.** A platitude which is not even true. (Opp. to *truism* in both senses.)

Falsity (fǫ·lsiti, fǫ·-). ME. [a. OF. *falseté* (mod.F. *fausseté*), ad. L. *falsitas*, f. *falsus*; see -ITY.] **1.** The quality or condition of being false: **a.** Contrariety or want of conformity to truth or fact 1576; **b.** Deceitfulness, insincerity 1603. **2.** That which is false 1557. **3.** False conduct; treachery, fraud –1581.

1. a. Between veritie & falsitie there is no meane FULKE. b. Cressids falsitie 1603. 2. Every f. that could be devised MARRYAT.

Falstaffian (fǫlstæ·fiăn), *a.* 1808. Characteristic of or resembling Falstaff in Shaks. *Hen. IV*, *Hen. V*, and *Merry Wives*; fat, jovial, humorous. Also, resembling his 'ragged regiment' (*Hen. VI*, III. ii).

Falter (fǭ·ltəɹ, fǫ·-), *v.*¹ ME. [? freq. of ME. *falden*, FOLD *v.* 'to give way, fail, falter', after *balter*, *welter*, etc. The deriv. from *fault* is untenable.] **1.** To stumble, stagger; of the limbs, to give way ME; of the tongue, to speak unsteadily 1533. **2.** To stumble in one's speech; to stammer. Of the voice, etc.: To come forth incoherently. Also *trans.*, with quoted words as obj. ME. **3.** To waver; to flinch, hesitate in action; to give way 1521. Also *transf.* of inanimate things (U.S.) 1745.

1. Which [mare] now suddenly faultring under him KNOLLES. Wee find the tongue more apt to f. 1671. 2. Her speach falters MARSTON. Even in the middle of his song He falter'd TENNYSON. *trans.* Faltering, 'I am thine' TENNYSON. The Dean faltered out that he meant no harm MILMAN. 3. A part of the army faultered considerably JAMES MILL. His hopes began to f. 1802. Hence **Fa·lter** *sb.* a faltering; a faltering sound. **Fa·lteringly** *adv.*

Falter (fǫ·ltəɹ), *v.*² 1601. [? a. OF. **faltrer* (*fautrer*) to strike, beat.] *trans.* To thrash (corn) clean; hence, to cleanse.

‖**Falun** (falön). Usu. in *pl.* 1833. [F.] *Geol.* 'A French provincial term for the shelly Tertiary strata of Touraine and the Loire' (Page). Hence **Falu·nian** *a.* Upper Miocene.

‖**Falx** (fælks). Pl. **falces.** 1706. [L.; = 'sickle'.] *Anat.* A process of the *dura mater*, sometimes called *F. cerebri.*

Famatinite (fămæ·tinəit). 1875. [Named from the *Famatina* mountains in the Argentine Republic; see -ITE.] *Min.* An antimonial variety of enargite.

Famble (fæ·mb'l), *sb. slang.* 1567. [? f. next.] **1.** A hand. †**2.** A ring –1691. Hence

†Fa·mbler, a glove; also, one who goes about selling counterfeit rings.

Fa·mble, *v.* ME. [? = FUMBLE, to grope.] 1. *intr.* To stammer. Now *dial.* 2. To eat without an appetite (*dial.*) 1877.

Fa·mble-cro:p. *dial.* 1825. [Cf. FAMBLE *v.* 2.] The first stomach in ruminating animals.

Fame (fēⁱm), *sb.*[1] ME. [a. F. *fame*, ad. L. *fama* report, = Gr. φήμη, f. root *fā-*, *φā-* (OAryan **bhā-*) in L. *fari*, Gr. φάναι to speak.] 1. That which people say; public report, common talk; a rumour. 2. Reputation. Usu, in good sense. ME. 3. The condition of being much talked about. Chiefly in good sense: Celebrity, honour, renown ME. †4. Evil repute –1592.

1. As the f. runneth MORE. A mischefe F... That mouing growes, and flitting gathers force SURREY. 2. His virtues passed his f. TREVISA. Phr. *House of ill f.*: see HOUSE. 3. The f. of Achilles EDEN, of English valour MACAULAY. Hence **Fa·meful** *a.* renowned. **Fa·meless** *a.* undistinguished; -ly *adv.*

†Fame, *sb.*[2] [ad. F. *faim*:—L. *famem*.] Hunger. LD. BERNERS.

Fame (fēⁱm), *v.* Now *rare.* ME. [a. OF. *famer*, f. *fame* FAME *sb.*[1]] 1. *trans.* To tell abroad, report 2. To make famous ME. 3. Short for DEFAME, DIFFAME. ME.

1. His prayse to f. ABP. PARKER. Thou art famed ..To have wrought.. wonders with an ass's jaw MILT. *Sams.* 1094. 2. His name on every shore Is famed and feared BYRON.

†Fame·lic, *a.* 1614. [ad. L. *famelicus* hungry, f. *fames*.] Pertaining to hunger; appetizing –1653.

Familiar (fămi·liăr, -lyăr). ME. [a. OF. *familier*, ad. L. *familiaris*, f. *familia*; see FAMILY.]

A. *adj.* 1. Of or pertaining to a family or household; domestic. Now *rare.* 2. On a family footing; intimate; in bad sense, unduly intimate. Const. *with* ME. 3. Of animals: Domesticated; also *fig.* 1483. †4. Of food, etc.: Suitable –1661. 5. Well or habitually acquainted. Const. *with.* 1508. 6. Known from constant association; well known 1490; common, current, usual. Const. *to.* 1599. †7. Affable; courteous, sociable –1751. 8. Free, unceremonious *with*; *occas.*, too free ME.

1. Nothyng is werse .. than .. a famyliar enemye ME. 2. A f. and privileged guest 1847. Phr. *F. †devil, spirit*: a demon supposed to attend at a call. 3. *fig.* Good wine, is a good familiar Creature, if it be well vs'd *Oth.* II. iii. 313. 5. Men f. with all ancient and modern learning MACAULAY. 6. An experiment f. to nurses 1756. An article of general and f. supply ROGERS. 7. Be thou f.; but by no meanes vulgar *Haml.* I. iii. 61. Hence **Fami·liarly** *adv.* **Fami·liarness.**

B. *sb.* 1. A member of a person's family or household (*Obs.* in gen. sense); in *R. C. Ch.*, a person who belongs to the household of the Pope or a bishop, and renders domestic services 1460; an officer of the Inquisition, chiefly employed in arresting and imprisoning the accused 1560. 2. An intimate friend or associate ME. 3. A familiar spirit (see A. 2, quot.) 1584. Also *transf.* and *fig.*

2. Hugh Capet .. was his famulyer and chief counceler FABYAN. 3. A flie, otherwise called a divell or f. 1584. Hence **†Fami·liarist,** an authority on f. spirits DE FOE.

Familiarity (fămiliæ·rĭti). ME. [a. F. *familiarité*, ad. L. *familiaritatem*; see prec. and -ITY.] †1. The quality proper to a member of a family; hence, devotion, fidelity –1576. †2. Suitableness (of food, etc.) –1646. 3. The state of being familiar; intimacy 1450; undue intimacy ME. †b. *concr.* A familiar person or persons Also *collect.* –1665. 4. Close or habitual acquaintance *with* (a thing); habituation 1601. 5. Absence of ceremony, free intercourse, *esp.* with inferiors ME. b. Something allowed or justified only by intimacy. Usu. in *pl.* 1641. 6. *Astrol.* An aspect 1819.

3. The old f. and kindness between the two kings MARVELL. b. The leaving of Parents, or other f. whatsoever MILT. 5. Familiaritie bringeth contempt UDALL. b. Guilty of a f. 1875.

Familiarize (fămi·liăraiz), *v.* 1608. [f. FAMILIAR *a.* + -IZE.] 1. *trans.* To make (a thing, *rarely* a person) familiar or well known. 2. a. To put (a person) on a footing of intimacy 1754. b. *refl.* (and *intr.* for *refl.*) To adopt a familiar demeanour; also, 'to make oneself cheap'. Now *rare.* 1685. 3. To accustom (*to*, †*into, to do*). Now *rare.* 1646. b. To make well acquainted, at home *with* 1687. †4. To domesticate (an animal) –1682.

1. Shakespeare..familiarizes the wonderful JOHNSON. 3. b. Familiarized with Hardships and Hazards PETTY. Hence **Fami·liariza·tion,** the action of familiarizing; an instance of this. **Fami·liarizer. Fami·liari:zingly** *adv.*

†Fami·liary, *a.* [See FAMILY and -ARY[2].] Pertaining to the control of a family; domestic. MILT.

†Fami·lic, *a.* 1660. [f. FAMILY + -IC.] Pertaining to a family; also, domestic, familiar –1684.

Familism (fæ·miliz'm). 1642. [f. L. *familia* + -ISM.] 1. The doctrine and practice of the Familists. 2. In Fourier: The tendency to form a group existing among members of a family 1848.

Familist (fæ·milist). 1592. [f. as prec. + -IST.] †1. The head of a family, a family-man –1658. †2. One of the same household –1638. 3. A member of the sect called the *Family of Love*; see FAMILY. 1592. Hence **†Famili·stic, -al** *a.*, pertaining to the Familists or Familism, or to a family.

Familistery (fæmili·stĕri). *rare.* 1865. [ad. F. *familistère*, f. *famille*, f. L. *familia*, after *phalanstère*.] The abode of a community living together as one family.

Family (fæ·mĭli), *sb.* ME. [ad. L. *familia* household, f. *famulus* servant.] 1. The servants of a house; the household. *Obs.* exc. in *f. of servants.* –1794. b. The staff of a military officer, or (in India) state official 1808. 2. The body of persons who live in one house or under one head, including parents, children, servants, etc. 1545. 3. The group consisting of parents and their children, whether living together or not; in wider sense, all those who are nearly connected by blood or affinity 1667. b. A person's children regarded collectively 1732. 4. Those descended or claiming descent from a common ancestor; a house, kindred, lineage ME.; a race; a people or group of peoples 1583. 5. *transf.* and *fig.* (with mixed notion of 3 and 4) 1611. 6. A group of objects, connected together and distinguished by the possession of some common features or properties 1626. b. In scientific classification: A group of allied genera. (Usually, a 'family' is a subdivision of an 'order'; but in botany 'family' is synonymous with 'order'.) 1753. 7. *F. of Love*: a sect which originated in Holland, and found a footing in England about 1580; they held that religion consisted chiefly in love, and that absolute obedience was due to all established governments 1579. 8. *attrib.*, as in *f. life, butcher, plate,* etc. 1602.

1. b. The Staff Officers of Sir John Moore's f. 1809. 2. Phr. *Happy F.*: a collection of birds and animals of different natures living together peaceably in one cage. 3. We pass..through the love of our f... to love Mankind 1796. Phr. *The Holy F.*: a group usually consisting of Joseph, Mary, and the child Jesus. 4. Let vs assayle the Family of Yorke 3 *Hen. VI*, II. ii. 129. People of no family BENTHAM. The great Teutonic f. MACAULAY. 5. Of all the Familys and Societys of Christians, they are most hated 1650. 6. The classification of simple minerals into families 1813. Phr. *F. of curves*: a group of curves of different kinds, all defined by the same equation of an indeterminate degree.

Phrases. a. *In a f. way*: without ceremony. b. (*To be*) *in the f. way*: pregnant.

Comb.: **f. Bible,** a large Bible for use at f. prayers (often containing on its fly-leaves a f. record or register of births, etc.); **f.-compact,** a treaty made in the 18th c. between the Bourbon dynasties of France, Spain, and the Two Sicilies for common action, *esp.* against England and Austria; **-tree,** a genealogical tree.

Famine (fæ·min). ME. [a. F. *famine* = Pr. *famina*, f. late L. type **famina*, f. *fames* hunger.] 1. Extreme and general scarcity of food; an instance of this. Also *transf.* 2. Hunger; hence, starvation ME. Also *fig.*

1. By reason wherof ensued a great famyne FABYAN. *transf.* The threatened water f. 1888. 2. To die of f. 1773. *Comb.* **f.-fever,** (*a*) typhus; (*b*) relapsing fever. Hence **†Fa·mine** *v.* to starve.

Famish (fæ·miʃ), *v.* ME. [f. L. *fames* hunger, after vbs. in -ISH. Cf. AFFAMISH.] 1. *trans.* To reduce to the extremities of hunger; to starve; also *fig.* 2. To kill with hunger, starve to death ME. †b. To deprive *of* anything necessary to life. MILT. 3. *intr.* To suffer the extremity of want of food; to be intensely hungry. Const. *for.* 1535. †b. To perish from want of food –1796.

1. Till Paris was besieg'd, famisht, and lost SHAKS. *fig.* To f. affection HOWELL. 2. b. MILT. *P. L.* XII. 78. 3. Resolu'd rather to dy then to f. *Cor.* I. i. 5. b. Now none f. who deserve to eat DRYDEN.

Hence **Fa·mishment** (now *rare*), the state, condition, or process of being famished; general dearth.

†Famo·se, *a.* ME. [ad. L. *famosus*.] = FAMOUS –1625.

Famo·se, *v.* *Obs.* exc. *arch.* 1590. [f. prec.] To make famous.

Famous (fēⁱ·məs), *a.* ME. [a. AF. *famous*, OF. *fameus*, (mod.F. *fameux*), ad. L. *famosus*, f. *fama*; see FAME and -OUS.] 1. Celebrated in fame or public report; much talked about, renowned. Const. *for.* 2. In bad or neutral sense: Notorious. *Obs.* exc. *arch.* ME. †3. Common, ordinary –1744. 4. As a strong expression of approval (chiefly *colloq.*): Excellent, 'capital' 1798.

1. His .. fadre of famouse memorye 1512. Of f. London town COWPER. 2. That f. infamous English Rebel Stuckley 1680. 4. 'Twas a f. victory SOUTHEY. Hence **†Fa·mous** *v.* to make f. **Fa·mously** *adv.* †openly; †notoriously; excellently, capitally (*colloq.*). **Fa·mousness,** the state of being f.

Famp (fæmp). 1836. [Of unkn. etym.; orig. *n. dial.*] *Geol.* 'An indurated wavy calcareous shale' (Phillips) found among limestone rocks. Also *attrib.*

Famulary (fæ·miŭlări), *a.* *rare.* 1840. [ad. L. *famularis*, f. *famulus*.] Of or belonging to servants.

†Fa·mulative, *a.* [f. L. *famulat-*, *famulari* to be a servant.] Having the attribute of serving. CUDWORTH.

‖**Famulus** (fæ·miŭlŏs). *Pl.* **-li.** 1837. [L.; = 'servant'.] An attendant; *esp.* on a scholar or a magician.

Fan (fæn), *sb.*[1] [OE. *fann*, str. fem., ad. L. *vannus*, fem. Cf. F. *van*.] 1. An instrument for winnowing grain; *orig.* a basket of special form (also, earlier, a wooden shovel) used for separating the corn from the chaff by throwing it into the air; *now*, a fanning-machine 1669. Also *transf.* and *fig.* (occ. with allusion to *Matt.* iii. 12) 1559. †b. A quintain. CHAUCER. 2. An instrument for agitating the air, to cool the face, etc. with an artificial breeze; *esp.* one constructed so as to fold up in small compass and to take, when expanded, the form of a sector of a circle 1555. 3. *poet.* A wing [? After It. *vanni*.] 1640. 4. Anything spread out in the shape of a fan (sense 2); *e.g.* a leaf, the tail of a bird, a window, etc. 1599. 5. A rotating apparatus, usu. consisting of an axle or spindle, with arms bearing flat or curved blades: a. for producing a current of air for ventilation, etc. 1835; b. for regulating the throttle-valve of a steam-engine 1887; c. in a windmill 1825; etc. 6. a. The flukes of the whale's tail. b. *Naut.* The screw (or a blade of the screw) of a propeller. c. *Angling.* A similar device on spinning-bait. 1785. †7. Confused with FANE *sb.*[1] –1650. 8. [f. the vb.] The action or result of fanning. *Tr. & Cr.* V. iii. 41.

1. The oxen..shall eat clean provender, which hath been winnowed with the shovel and with the f. *Isa.* XXX. 24. *fig.* The fire and f. of iudgment and discretion LAMBARDE. 3. The fans Of careless butterflies KEATS.

Combs. 1. General: as *f.-stick, -shell, -painter, -shaped,* etc. 2. Special: **f.-fly** (*Mech.*), an instrument to decrease speed by its action on the air; **-governor** = FAN 5 b; **-groining** (*Arch.*) = *fan-tracery*; **-mount** [= F. *monture d'éventail*], the frame upon which a f. is mounted; **-palm,** any palm having f.-shaped leaves; **-plant,** the palmetto; **-tracery** (*Arch.*), a kind of vaulting composed of pendent semi-cones covered with foliated panel-work; **-vaulting** = *fan-tracery*; **-window,** 'a semicircular window with radial sash' (Knight); **-work** = *fan-tracery.*

Fan (fæn), *sb.*[2] orig. *U.S.* 1889. (In earlier use *fann*, 1682.) [abbrev. of FANATIC.] An enthusiast (orig. a keen spectator of a sport, in early use esp. baseball).

Fan (fæn), *v.* OE. [f. prec. Cf. F. *vanner.*] **1.** *trans.* To winnow (corn, etc.); to drive away by or as by the action of a fan ME. **2.** *intr.* †To make a fan-like movement; to flap. Of the wind: To blow. Now *rare.* ME. **3.** *trans.* To move or drive with or as with a fan ME. **4.** To drive a current of air upon, with or as with a fan 1607. **5.** To blow or breathe gently upon 1590. **6.** To spread out like a fan. Also, *To f. out.* 1592.

1. To f. corne GOUGE. As chaff, which, fanned, The wind drives MILT. 2. Fanning in his face with a Peacocks feather *Hen. V*, IV. i. 212. 3. Fanning their joyous leaves to thy soft lays MILT. *Lycidas* 40. 4. a. Fanned into Slumbers STEELE. By slow Degrees he fans the gentle Fire 1709. 5. High Taurus snow, Fan'd with the Easterne wind *Mids. N.* III. ii. 142.

Fanal (fēⁱ·năl). *Obs.* exc. *arch.* 1471. [a. F. *fanal*, med.L. *fanale, fanalis*, f. Gr. *φανός* lantern; f. *φαν-* stem of *φαίνειν* to show.] A beacon, a lighthouse; a ship's lantern.

‖**Fanam** (fənā·m). 1555. [Corrupt f. Malayālam *paṇam*, f. Skr. *paṇa* wealth.] A small coin, formerly the usual money of account in South India.

Fanatic (fănæ·tik). 1533. [ad. L. *fanaticus*, f. *fanum* temple; see -ATIC. Cf. F. *fanatique.*]

A. *adj.* †1. Of an action or speech: Such as might result from possession by a deity or demon; frantic. Of a person: Frenzied. –1660. **2.** Of persons, etc.: Affected by excessive and mistaken enthusiasm, *esp.* in religious matters 1647.

1. Persons Divinely inspired, and Fanatick STANLEY. 2. All our lunatic f. Sects BUTLER.

B. *sb.* †1. A (religious) maniac –1806. **2.** A fanatic person; an unreasoning enthusiast; applied about 1650 to Nonconformists. Also with *of.* 1644.

2. A new word coined, within few months, called fanatics..seemeth well..proportioned to signify..the sectaries of our age FULLER.

Fanatical (fănæ·tikăl), *a.* 1550. [f. prec. + -AL.] †1. Possessed by a deity or by a devil; frantic, mad –1633. **2.** = FANATIC *a.* 2. 1550. †b. Extravagant. *L. L. L.* V. i. 20. †3. Of or pertaining to the Nonconformists –1703. Hence **Fana·tical-ly** *adv.*, **-ness.**

Fanaticism (fanæ·tisiz'm). 1652. [f. FANATIC + -ISM.] †1. The condition of being possessed. SHAFTESB. **2.** Excessive enthusiasm, *esp.* in religious matters, frenzy; an instance or form of this 1652.

2. Dark F. rent Altar, and screen, and ornament SCOTT.

Fanaticize (fănæ·tisəiz), *v.* Also **-ise.** 1715. [f. as prec. + -IZE.] To make, or become, fanatical.

†**Fa·natism.** 1680. [ad. F. *fanatisme.*] = FANATICISM. –1800.

Fancied (fæ·nsid), *ppl. a.* 1568. [f. FANCY *v.*] **1.** Formed or portrayed by the fancy; imaginary. †2. Artistically designed –1782. **3.** Favourite 1589.

2. The prettiest f. [buckles] I ever saw 1782.

Fancier (fæ·nsiəɹ). 1765. [f. as prec.] **1.** One who fancies; a dreamer 1828. **2.** One who makes artistic designs 1856. **3.** One who fancies, and has a critical knowledge of, some class of curiosities, plants, animals, etc.; as in *dog-, flower-, pigeon-f.* 1765.

Fanciful (fæ·nsifŭl), *a.* 1627. [f. FANCY *sb.* + -FUL.] **1. a.** Endowed with fancy (*rare*). **b.** Disposed to indulge in fancies; whimsical. 1695. **2.** Displaying fancy in design; fantastic, odd 1627. **3.** Imaginary, unreal 1697.

1. a. A careful and f. pattern-drawer POPE. b. Cowley [had] a very f. mind COLERIDGE. 2. A petticoat of a f. pattern SCOTT. 3. F. claims 1868. Hence **Fa·nciful-ly** *adv.*, **-ness.**

Fanciless (fæ·nsilės), *a.* 1753. [f. FANCY *sb.* + -LESS.] Destitute of fancy; as, *f. compositions.*

Fancy (fæ·nsi). 1465. [A contr. of FANTASY, q. v.]

A. *sb.* †1. = FANTASY *sb.* 1. –1722. †2. = FANTASY *sb.* 2. –1659. **3.** Delusive imagination; an instance of this 1597. **4.** In early use = IMAGINATION (see FANTASY 4). In later use, *fancy* signifies aptitude for the invention of illustrative or decorative imagery, while *imagination* is the power of giving the consistency of reality to ideal creations. Often *personified.* 1581. **b.** A mental image 1663. **5.** Inventive design; an invention 1665; †*esp.* in *Music*, a composition in an impromptu style –1789. **6.** An arbitrary notion 1471. **7.** Caprice; a caprice, a whim; a whimsical thing 1579; †fantasticalness –1823. **8.** Capricious preference; an inclination 1465; †*spec.* amorous inclination, love –1712. **9.** Taste, critical judgement in matters of art or elegance 1665. †10. 'Something that pleases or entertains' (J.) –1721. **11.** *The fancy*: all who fancy a particular amusement or pursuit; *esp.* the prize-ring or its frequenters 1811; also, pugilism; sporting in general 1820. **12.** The art or practice of breeding animals so as to develop particular points; also, one of these points; also *attrib.* 1862.

3. Phancies of a deluded mind 1693. 4. Pleasures of the Imagination or F. (which I shall use promiscuously) ADDISON. The f. sees the outside.. The imagination sees the heart and inner nature, and makes them felt RUSKIN. 6. As wild a f. as [etc.] COLERIDGE. 7. The fancies of patients 1860. 8. The tune..caught the f. of the nation MACAULAY. Phr. *To have, take a f. for, to.* *spec.* Tell me where is fancie bred *Merch. V.* III. ii. 63. 9. They possess.. f. for form RUSKIN. 10. London-Pride is a pretty F. for borders 1712. 11. A great book sale..had congregated all the *F.* DE QUINCEY.

Comb.: **f.-free**, free from the power of love; **-sick** *a.*, love-sick; **-woman**, a kept mistress.

B. *adj.* [The sb. used attrib.; rarely predicative.] **1.** Fine, ornamental; opp. to *plain* 1761. **b.** Of flowers, etc.: Parti-coloured 1793. **c.** *ellipt.* That deals in fancy goods 1821. **2.** Added for ornament or extraordinary use 1794. **3.** Calling forth or resulting from the exercise of fancy or caprice 1646. **4.** Based upon conceptions of the FANCY (*sb.* 3) 1800.

1. F. breads 1853, stitches 1866, types 1888. b. Webbs' F. Pansy 1893. c. *F. fair*: see FAIR *sb.*[1] *F. ball* = *F. dress ball* (see FANCY DRESS *sb.*). 2. F. stops [in an organ] 1874. Phr. *F. roller* (in Cotton Spinning): a roller that overruns the periphery of the cylinder, and thereby admits heavy carding. 3. F. shooting DICKENS, prices MACAULAY, pigeons 1881. Phr. *F. franchise*: one based on an arbitrary qualification. *F. stocks*: stocks estimated by caprice. 4. A f. portrait 1873.

Fancy (fæ·nsi), *v.* 1545. [f. prec. sb.] **1.** *trans.* To frame in fancy; to portray in the mind; to conceive, imagine. Also, to suppose oneself to perceive. 1646. **2.** To believe without being able to prove; to have an idea *that* 1672. †3. To contrive, devise, design, plan –1759. **4.** To have a good conceit of (oneself, etc.). *colloq.* 1866. **5.** To take a fancy to; to like 1545. **b.** To breed (animals or birds), to grow (plants) so as to develop in them particular points 1851.

1. She fancies musick in his tongue SWIFT. We read Bingham, and f. we are studying ecclesiastical history M. PATTISON. F., now! 1881. 2. The estate is, I f., theirs yet COBBETT. 4. I..fancied my game at whist 1886. 5. I neuer yet beheld that speciall face, Which I could fancie *Tam. Shr.* II. i. 12. The patient may eat anything that he fancies (*mod.*).

Fancy dress. 1770. A costume arranged fancifully, usually representing some fictitious or historical character. *attrib.*, in *f. d. ball.*

Fancy man. a. A man who is fancied; a sweetheart 1835. **b.** *pl.* = *The fancy* (see FANCY *sb.* 11) 1847. **c.** *slang.* A man who lives on the earnings of a prostitute 1821.

Fa·ncy work. 1842. Ornamental, as opp. to plain, work, *esp.* in needlework, etc.; *rarely*, a piece of such work.

Fanda·ngle. *colloq.* 1880. [? f. next.] Fantastic ornament; tomfoolery. Also as *adj.*

Fandango (fændæ·ngo). 17... [a. Sp. *fandango*; perh. of negro origin.] **1.** A lively dance in ¾ time; also, the tune for this. **2.** A social assembly for dancing; a ball. Now *U.S.* 1760.

†**Fane**, *sb.*[1] [Com. Teut.: OE. *fana* wk. masc.] **1.** A flag, banner; pennant –1806. **2.** A weathercock. See VANE. –1773.

Fane (fēⁱn), *sb.*[2] *poet.* ME. [ad. L. *fanum.*] A temple. Also *transf.* and *fig.*

Old Iona's holy f. SCOTT.

‖**Fanega** (fanē·gă). 1502. [Sp. *fanega*, also *hanega.*] A Spanish dry measure, usually equal to a bushel or a bushel and a half.

‖**Fanfare** (fænfēⁱ·ɹ, fanfar). 1605. [Fr.; ? echoic.] A flourish, call, or short tune, sounded by trumpets, bugles, or hunting-horns. Also *transf.* and *fig.*

fig. After all his Fanfares about a separate Peace TEMPLE.

‖**Fanfaron** (fæ·nfărǫn), *sb.* (*a.*) 1622. [Fr., f. *fanfare.*] **1.** A blusterer, boaster, braggart; *attrib.* or *adj.* braggart 1670. ¶2. = FANFARE. 1848.

1. An excellent f., a Major Washington H. WALPOLE.

Fanfaronade (fæ:nfărǫnēⁱ·d, fanfaronād), *sb.* 1652. [ad. F. *fanfaronnade*, f. *fanfaron.* Cf. Sp. *fanfarronada.*] **1.** Boisterous or arrogant language, brag; ostentation; an instance of this. ¶2. = FANFARE. 1812.

1. The Gasconads of France, Rodomontads of Spain, Fanfaronads of Italy URQUHART. Hence **Fa·nfarona·de** *v.* to bluster, swagger.

Fang (fæŋ), *sb.* [OE. *fang*, repr. OTeut. **fango-*, f. root of *fanhan* (see FANG *v.*).]

I. †1. A capture, catch; also, a grip –1600. **2.** *concr.* That which is caught or taken; plunder, spoils. (*Obs.* exc. *Sc.*) OE.

1. The Icie phange..of the winters winde SHAKS.

II. An instrument for catching or holding. †1. A noose, trap; also *fig.* –1794. **2.** A canine tooth, a tusk. In *pl.* teeth (of dogs, etc.). Also *fig.* and *transf.* 1555. **b.** The venom-tooth of a serpent; also the claws, provided with poison-ducts, which terminate the chelicerae of a spider 1800. †3. A claw or talon (Dicts.); in *Bot.*, the shoots or tendrils by which hold is taken 1768. **4. a.** A spike; the tang of a tool 1769. **b.** The root of a tooth, or one of its prongs 1666. †c. A prong of a divided root –1727.

2. The fatal F. drove deep within his Thigh. DRYDEN. *fig.* The verie phangs of malice *Twel. N.* I. v. 196. *transf.* Fangs of broken ice KANE. b. Each horn is tubular, like an adder's f. DARWIN.

III. Technical. **1.** *Naut.* **a.** = VANG. 1513. **b.** *pl.* The valves of a pump-box 1769. **2.** *Mining.* An air-channel 1661.

Fang (fæŋ), *v.*[1] Now *arch.* or *dial.* [Com. Teut.: OE. *fōn*, redupl. str. vb.:—OTeut. **fanhan*, pa. pple. *fangano-*, whence, later, the present stem *fang-* (inf. *fangen*), which gradually supersedes the older form.] **1.** *trans.* To lay hold of, grasp, hold, seize; to clasp. *Obs.* exc. *arch.* **2.** To receive, accept. *Obs.* exc. *dial.* OE. **3.** = TAKE in various uses; *esp.* with obj. *arms, counsel, leave, a name, one's way* OE. **4.** *intr.* To seize, lay hold *on*; to take *to*; to set upon OE. **5.** To begin *on* OE. †6. *intr.* To take one's way, go; also, to swerve *from* –1536.

1. Hee's in the lawes clutches, you see hee's fanged DEKKER & WEBSTER. 2. Phr. *To f. cristendom*: to receive baptism, become Christian.

Fang (fæŋ), *v.*[2] 1808. [f. FANG *sb.*] **1.** *trans.* To strike one's fang or fangs into (*rare*). **2.** *To f. a pump*: to give it a grip of the water; to prime 1819.

Fanged (fæŋd), *a.* 1602. [f. FANG *sb.*] Furnished with fangs.

Whom I wil trust as I will adders fang'd SHAKS.

†**Fa·nger.** ME. [f. FANG *v.*] One who takes another under his protection, a guardian; one who catches or captures; that with which one catches hold (*e.g.* a tooth) –1763.

Fanging (fæ·ŋiŋ), *vbl. sb.* 1493. [f. as prec.] **1.** The action of FANG *v.* **2.** *Mining.* (A main of) air-pipes used for ventilation in mines 1747.

Fangle (fæ·ŋg'l), *sb.* 1548. [Erron. f. NEW-FANGLED, later form of *newfangle* 'eager for novelty'.] **1.** *New fangle*: a new fashion or crotchet; a novelty. (Always contemptuous.) Now *rare.* †2. A fantastic, foppish, or silly contrivance; a piece of finery; foppery, fuss –1695. So **Fa·ngle** *v.* to fashion, fabricate; to trick out. *Obs.* exc. *dial.* **Fa·nglement**, the action of fangling; hence, a contrivance.

†**Fa·ngled**, *ppl. a.* 1587. [f. prec.] Characterized by fopperies –1611.

Our f. world *Cymb.* v. iv. 134.

Fangless (fæ·ŋlės), *a.* 1597. [f. FANG *sb.* + -LESS.] Without a fang or fangs.

Like to a Fanglesse Lion SHAKS.

Fangot (fæ·ŋgǫt). 1673. [ad. It. *fangotto*, var. of *fagotto* FAGGOT.] A quantity of wares, *esp.* raw silk, from 1 to 3 cwt.

Fanion (fæ·nyǫn). 1706. [a. F., f. as *fanon* (see FANON).] A banner carried at the head of the baggage of horse brigades; also, a small flag used in surveying stations, named after these.

Fa·n-light. 1819. A fan-shaped, or (*loosely*) any, window over a door.

Fannell (fæ·nĕl). Now *Hist.* 1530. [ad. med.L. *fanula* or *fanonellus*, dim. of *fano* (see FANON).] = FANON.

Fanner (fæ·nəɹ). 1515. [f. FAN *sb.* or *v.*] 1. One who fans. 2. Any kind of contrivance to blow away the chaff (*lit.* and *fig.*) 1788. 3. A ventilating or cooling apparatus 1874. 4. A kind of hawk so called from the motion of its wings. Also *vanner-hawk.* 1875.

Fanning (fæ·niŋ), *vbl. sb.* 1577. [f. FAN *v.*] 1. The action of FAN *v.* in various senses. 2. = *Fan-tracery.* RUSKIN. Comb.: *f.-machine, -mill* (= FANNER 2).

Fanon (fæ·nǫn). ME. [F. *fanon*, ad. med. L. *fanonem*, *fano* banner, napkin, a. OHG. *fano*; see FANE *sb.*[1]] 1. A maniple. 2. A veil of four colours in stripes, worn by the Pope; formerly called the 'orale' 1844.

Fan-tail (fæ·ntē¹l), *sb.* 1728. [f. FAN *sb.*[1] + TAIL.] 1. A tail or lower end in the shape of a fan. 2. A variety of the domestic pigeon, so called from the shape of its tail 1735. 3. A genus (*Rhipidura*) of Birds found in Australia 1848. 4. *Mech.* A kind of joint. Cf. *dove-tail.* 1858. 5. 'A form of gas-burner in which the burning jet has an arched form' (Knight). 6. *attrib.*, as *fan-tail-hat*, also *fantail*, a sou'-wester 1850. Hence **Fan-tail** *v.* to work its tail like a fan: said of a whale. **Fan-tailed** *a.*

Fan-tan (fæ·ntæn). 1878. [Chinese *fan t'an* repeated divisions.] A Chinese gambling game, in which the number of coins, etc. placed in a bowl has to be guessed after a large handful has been counted off in fours; also, a gambling game of cards.

Fantasia (fantazī·a, fæntā·ziă). 1724. [a. It. *fantasia* (see FANTASY).] 1. *Mus.* 'A composition in a style in which form is subservient to fancy' (Stainer and Barrett). ‖2. In the Levant and N. Africa: a. Pomp, self-importance; b. An Arab dance; also, a set of evolutions on horseback by a troop of Arabs. 1838.

Fantasied, phantasied (fæ·ntasid), *ppl. a. arch.* 1561. [f. FANTASY *sb.* and *v.*] Framed by the fancy; full of (strange, new) fancies; imaginative; whimsical.

I finde the people strangely f. *John* iv. ii. 144.

Fantasm(a, etc.: see PHANTASM(A, etc.

Fantasque (fæntæ·sk). 1698. [a. F. *fantasque*:—L. *fantasticus.*] A. *adj.* Fanciful, fantastic (*rare*) 1701. †B. *sb.* Fancy, whim –1703.

Fantassin (fæ·ntæ̆sin). 1835. [a. F., ad. It. *fantaccino*, dim. of *fante* foot-soldier.] A foot-soldier.

Fantast, phantast (fæ·ntæst). 1588. [ad. med.L. *phantasta*, Gr. φανταστής a boaster.] 1. A visionary; a flighty, impulsive person. 2. A fantastic writer 1873.

Fantastic (fæntæ·stik). ME. [ad. med.L. *fantasticus*, late L. *phantasticus*, a. Gr. φανταστικός, f. φαντάζειν to make visible; see FANTASY. Cf. F. *fantastique.* The form *phantastique* is now obs.]

A. *adj.* 1. Existing only in imagination, unreal (*Obs.*); perversely or irrationally imagined. †2. Of the nature of a phantasm –1716. †3. Of or pertaining to phantasy (see FANTASY *sb.* 1, 4); imaginative –1793. 4. Of persons, etc.: †Imaginative –1847; fanciful, capricious; foppish in dress –1702. Now: Extravagantly fanciful, odd in behaviour. 5. Arbitrarily devised. Now *rare.* 1658. 6. Eccentric, quaint, or grotesque in design or conception 1616. b. Making fantastic movements (in the dance). An arbitrary sense. 1632.

B. *sb.* 1. One who has fanciful or wild ideas. *Obs.* exc. *arch.* 1598. †2. A fop –1680.

1. A F., whose brain was turned with monkish fancies 1882. Hence **Fanta·stical** *a.* and †*sb.* (in same senses). **Fanta·stica·lity**, fantasticalness; *concr.* a whim, crotchet. **Fanta·stically** *adv.* **Fanta·sticalness**, the condition or fact of being fantastical; whimsicality. **Fanta·sticate** *v.* †*trans.* to fancy; *intr.* to frame fantastic notions (*rare*). **Fanta·sticism**, †subjectivism (CUDWORTH); the following of caprice in art or speculation. †**Fanta·sticly** *adv.* **Fanta·sticness** (now *rare*). †**Fanta·stico**, an absurd or irrational person.

†**Fa·ntastry.** 1656. [f. FANTAST + -RY.] a. Fantastic display or show; showy trappings. b. Visionary delusion. c. Deceptiveness. –1710.

c. The Phantastry of Sense CUDWORTH.

Fantasy, phantasy (fæ·ntăsi), *sb.* ME. [a. OF. *fantasie*, ad. L. *phantasia*, a Gr. φαντασία lit. 'a making visible', f. (ult.) φαίνειν to show. The shortened form FANCY soon became differentiated in sense.] †1. Mental apprehension of an object of perception –1669. †2. A phantom; an illusory appearance –1583. 3. Delusive imagination, hallucination. ? *Obs.* ME. 4. Imagination; the process, the faculty, or the result of forming representations of things not actually present. (Cf. FANCY *sb.* 4.) Also *personified.* Now usually: Visionary fancy. 1553. b. *esp.* in *Music*; a fantasia 1597. 5. A supposition resting on no solid grounds. (Now emphatically contemptuous.) ME. 6. Caprice; a caprice, a whim 1450. †7. Inclination, liking, desire –1618.

2. All is but fantesey and enchauntementes LD. BERNERS. 3. You tremble and look pale: Is not this something more then Fantasie *Haml.* I. i. 54. 4. By the power of phantasy we see Colours in a Dream NEWTON. A monstrous f. of rusty iron DICKENS. 5. Less than fancy—mere f. WHITNEY.

Fantasy, phantasy (fæ·ntăzi, -ăsi), *sb.* ME. [a. OF. *fantasier*, f. *fantasie.*] 1. *trans.* = FANCY *v.* 1. Now *arch.* with sense: To imagine in a visionary manner. Also *absol.* †2. To take a fancy or liking to. Also with *inf.*, to 'take it into one's head' –1641. 3. *intr.* To play fantasias. CARLYLE.

Fantee (fæ·ntī). 1819. Also **Fanti.** A member, or the language, of a negro tribe inhabiting the Gold Coast. b. Phr. *To go f.*: to join the natives or a district and conform to their habits 1886.

†**Fa·nterie.** 1577. [a. OF., ad. It. *fanteria*, f. *fante* = *infante*: see INFANTRY.] Infantry –1601.

‖**Fantoccini** (fæ:ntǫtʃī·ni). 1771. [It., pl. of *fantoccino*, dim. of *fantoccio* puppet, f. *fante* boy; see prec.] 1. *pl.* Puppets (see PUPPET *sb.* 3). 2. A puppet show.

Fantom, Faquir; see PHANTOM, FAKIR.

†‖**Far**, *sb.* ME. [L.] A coarse kind of wheat; spelt –1624.

Far (fāɹ), *adv.* [OE. *feor(r*:—OTeut. **ferr-*, f. OTeut. root *fer-*:—OAryan *per-*, whence Gr. πέραν, Skr. *paras* beyond. Comp. orig. *ferrer, -or, farrer, -est*; now *farther, farthest*: see FARTHER.] 1. At a great distance: a. in space; b. in past time ME. Also *fig.* 2. To a great distance; widely OE. 3. To or at an advanced point of progress: a. in space; also *fig.* ME.; b. in time ME. 4. By a great interval, widely OE. 5. Preceded by *as, how, so, thus*, with the notion of *definite* quantity ME. 6. quasi-*sb.* ME.

1. a. Sum ferrer and sum nerrer WYCLIF. Things near seem further off; farst off, the nearest at hand H. MORE. Phr. *F. and near* or *nigh*; *f. or near.* *fig.* In a f. from unfriendly fashion BLACK. 2. He.. remov'd his Tents farr off MILT. *P. L.* XI. 727. 3. a. We travell'd fast and f. SOUTHEY. *fig.* This was going too f. CRUISE. b. With genitive: It is f. nights (= Gr. πόρρω τῆς νυκτός) HOLINSHED. But the day is farre spent 1602. 4. Following not f. after himself KNOLLES. They were not f. wrong JOWETT. Phr. *F. (and) away*; *f. other.* 5. Thus f. Josephus CRUISE. To decide how f. he deserved it THIRLWALL. 6. *From f.*: at a distance. *By f.*: by a great interval. *In so f.*: to such an extent.

Comb., as *f.-beaming*; *-withdrawal*; **-back** *a.*, ancient; **-eastern** *a.*, belonging to the extreme east; **-gone** *a.*, advanced to a great extent; **-northern** *a.*, lying in the extreme north; **-seeing** *a.*, far-sighted; **-seen** *a.*, seen at a distance; **-southern** *a.*, at the extreme south; so **-western** *a.*

Far (fāɹ), *a.* [OE. *feorr*; prob. f. the adv.] 1. Remote: a. in space; b. *fig.* 1531. 2. Extending to a distance, long ME. 3. The remoter of two; in early use also in the comparative ME.

1. a. Folke cam.. from ferre ways for to seke hym CAXTON. A f. whisper SHELLEY. Phr. *The F. West*: now *esp.* the western parts of U. S. or of N. America. b. A vice.. farrest from humanitee ELYOT. His own f. blood TENNYSON. F. landmarks of time HAWTHORNE. 2. Her grete & ferre Journey FISHER. As one farre in elde SPENSER. 3. The farre end of high holborn 1540.

Far, *v.* Now *dial.* [OE. *feorran, fyrran* :—OTeut. type **firrjan*, f. **ferr-*, FAR *a.*] *trans.* To put far off, remove.

Pooh, wench! latter days be farred! MRS. GASKELL.

Far, obs. var. of FARROW, young pig.

Fa·r-abou·t.

A. *adv.* †To a great distance around; †at a great distance; †far astray; by far, very much (*dial.*) ME.

†B. *sb.* A digression, wandering 1639.

Farad (fæ·răd). 1881. [Short f. *Faraday* the electrician.] *Electr.* The capacity of a conductor in which the electrical pressure is raised one volt by the addition of one coulomb.

Faradaic (færădē¹·ik), *a.* 1875. [f. *Faraday* (see prec.) + -IC.] Distinctive epithet of inductive electricity and of the phenomena pertaining to it. var. **Fara·dic.**

Faradism (fæ·rădiz'm). 1876. [a. F. *faradisme*, f. *Faraday*; see -ISM.] Inductive electricity; also, its therapeutic application. var. **Fa·radaism.**

Faradization (fæ:rădəizē¹·ʃən). 1867. [f. next.] The application of induced currents of electricity to the body.

Faradize (fæ·rădəiz), *v.* 1864. [ad. F. *faradiser*, f. *Faraday*; see -IZE.] *trans.* To stimulate by means of faradaic currents. Hence **Faradi·zer.**

Farand, etc.: see FARRAND.

†**Fa·randine.** 1663. [a. F. *ferrandine*, f. *Ferrand* the inventor *c* 1630.] A fabric of silk, wool, and hair; also, a dress made of this. Also *attrib.* –1673.

‖**Farandole** (farandǫl). 1863. [Fr., ad. Pr.] A Provençal dance in 6/8 time.

Far-away (fāɹ,ăwē¹·, fā·ɹ,ăwē¹). ME. [f. FAR *adv.* and AWAY.] A. *adj.* 1. Remote in space, time, or relationship 1816. 2. Of a look, etc.: Absent, dreamy 1881.

1. 'Pate's a far-awa cousin o' mine' SCOTT.

B. *adv.* A long way off ME.

C. *sb.* What is far away; the distance 1823.

Fa·r-betwee·n, *a.* 1743. Occurring at long intervals.

Like angel-visits, few and far between CAMPBELL.

†**Farce**, *sb.*[1] ME. [a. OF. *farce*, f. *farcir* :—L. *farcire* to stuff.] Force-meat, stuffing –1823.

Farce (fāɹs), *sb.*[2] 1530. [a. F. *farce*, app. an application of prec.] 1. A dramatic work (usually short) intended only to excite laughter; the species of the drama constituted by these. 2. Anything fit only to laugh at; a hollow pretence, a mockery 1696.

1. Suche as writte farcis and contrefait the vulgare speche PALSGR. Those Nauseous Harlequins in F. may pass DRYDEN. 2. The f. of fashion W. IRVING.

Farce (fāɹs), *v. Obs.* or *arch.* ME. [ad. OF. *farsir* :—L. *farcire* to stuff.] To stuff. Const. *with.* †1. *trans.* To stuff with force-meat, herbs, spices, etc. –1736. †2. To cram with food; also, to fill out –1669. †3. *gen.* To cram *full of*; also, to overlay thickly –1634. 4. *fig.*; *esp.* to season, spice (a speech, etc.) ME.

1. To f. Cucumbers 1736. 2. If thou would'st f. thy leane ribbes with it too B. JONS. 3. A Helmet.. full farsed with Mayle SPEED. 4. Stale apothegmes ..to f. their Scenes withall B. JONS. Hence †**Fa·rcement**, stuffing. **Fa·rcer**, one who writes or acts a farce.

‖**Farceur** (farsör). 1828. [F., f. *farcer.*] A joker, wag.

Farcical (fā·ɹsikăl), *a.*[1] 1716. [f. FARCE *sb.*[2] + -AL.] 1. Of, belonging to, or of the nature of farce. 2. That is fit only to be laughed at; extremely ludicrous or futile 1739.

1. The Comedy of Errors is Shakespere's one f. play DOWDEN. Hence **Fa·rcical-ly** *adv.*, **-ness.** **Farcica·lity**, f. quality.

Farcical (fā·rsikal), *a.*[2] 1762. [f. FARCY + -IC + -AL.] Pertaining to the farcy. STERNE.

†**Fa·rcilite.** 1799. [f. FARCE *sb.*[1] + -(I)LITE.] *Min.* Pudding-stone –1811.

Fa·rcin. Now *dial.* ME. [a. F. :—L. *farciminum* farcy.] = FARCY 1.

Farcing (fā·ɹsiŋ), *vbl. sb.* 1532. [f. FARCE *v.*[1]] 1. The action of FARCE *v.* 1540. 2. *concr.* Forcemeat.

Farctate (fā·ɹktĕt), *a.* 1832. [f. L. *farctus*,

farcire + -ATE [2].] *Bot.* 'Stuffed, crammed or full; without vacuities' (Webster).

Farcy (fā·ɹsi), *sb.* 1481. [var. of FARCIN.] 1. A disease, *esp.* of horses, closely allied to glanders. 2. The same disease as communicated to man 1762.

Comb.: **f. bud**, one of the small tumours which occur during the progress of f.; **f. button** = *f. bud.*

Fard (fāɹd), *sb. Obs.* exc. *arch.* 1540. [a. F. *fard*; etym. unkn.] Paint (*esp.* white paint) for the face. Also *fig.*

Rouge and f. 1766. *fig.* The f. of Eloquence 1663.

†**Fard** (fāɹd), *v.* 1450. [ad. F. *farder*, f. *fard*; see prec.] *trans.* To paint (the face) with fard; *transf.* and *fig.* to embellish or gloss over anything –1816.

†**Fa·rdage.** 1578. [a. F., f. *farde*; see FARDEL.] 1. Impedimenta, baggage –1600. 2. = DUNNAGE –1860.

Fardel (fā·ɹdĕl), *sb.*[1] ME. [a. OF. *fardel* (later *fardeau*), dim. of *farde* burden, ?f. Arab. *fardah*.] 1. A bundle, a little pack. Also *collect.* 2. *fig.*; *esp.* a burden of sin, sorrow, etc. ME. †3. A wrapping –1649.

2. None sees the f. of his faults behind HERRICK.

†**Fa·rdel,** *sb.*[2]. Also *Sc.* FARL. ME. [repr. OE. *fēorða dǣl* fourth part.] A fourth part of anything. Also in *pl.* Fragments. –1883.

†**Fa·rdel,** *sb.*[3] 1523. [a. Du. *voordeel.*] Profit –1569.

†**Fa·rdel,** *v.* 1582. [f. the *sb.*] 1. *trans.* To make into a bundle –1701. 2. *Naut.* = FURL *v.* –1704.

Fare (fēᵊɹ), *sb.*[1] [Orig. two wds.: OE. *fær* str. neut., and OE. *faru* str. fem.; both f. root of FARE *v.*] †1. A going, journeying; way; voyage –1751; an expedition, as in *herring-f.* –1530. 2. †A road, track; *esp.* the track of a hare or rabbit (now *dial.*) 1509. †3. A number of persons prepared for a journey; also *transf.* –1634. 4. †A passage for which a price is paid; hence, cost of conveyance (now only of persons) ME. Also *transf.* of the person or (now *rarely*) persons conveyed 1562. b. A load or catch of fish. *U.S.* †5. Bearing; aspect –1540; doings –1548; display; commotion –1475. †6. Condition; state of things, success –1611. 7. Food; supply of food; also *fig.* ME.

1. Nought the morrow next mote stay his f. SPENSER *F.Q.* v. x. 16. 4. Making the whole f. (or passage) worth foure shillings LAMBARDE. What's your f. FOOTE. *transf.* The f. was taken up in Grivell-Street 1696. 6. Phr. *What f.* (cf. *What cheer?*); How now faire Lords? What faire? What newes abroad SHAKS. 7. After such delicious f. MILT. *P. L.* IX. 1028. *Bill of f.*: see BILL.

Comb. **f. indicator**, a device for registering fares paid in a public conveyance.

Fare (fēᵊɹ), *sb.*[2] Now *dial.* 1557. [f. FARE *v.*[2]] A litter of pigs.

†**Fare,** *sb.*[3] 1628. [ad. It. *faro*, ad. L. *pharus*, Gr. φάρος PHAROS.] A promontory (marked by a lighthouse) at the entrance of the Strait of Messina. Hence, the strait itself. –1739.

Fare (fēᵊɹ), *v.*[1] Pa. t. and pple. **fared.** [Com. Teut. str. vb.: OE. *faran* :—OTeut. **faran, fōr, farano-*, f. pre-Teut. **por, pōr-*, f. Aryan root **per, por, pər* to pass through; cf. Skr. *par, pṛ* to carry through or across, Gr. πόρος, L. *portare.*] 1. *intr.* To make one's way, travel. Now *arch.* or *poet.* 2. In wider sense = GO. OE. 3. rarely *trans.* Of a horse: To take along. CARLYLE. 4. †To 'go on', act –1697; to bid fair (*dial.*) 1849. 5. *impers.* To 'go'; to turn out ME. 6. To 'get on' OE. 7. *spec.* To 'get on' in respect of food; to feed (*well, ill,* etc.) ME. 8. Used in imperative with *well*: a. with the person as *subj.*; b. *impers.*; = FAREWELL *interj.* (*arch.*) ME.

1. Sadly they fared along the sea-beat shore POPE. 2. One..in would f. SPENSER. Phr. *To f. astray.* 3. The good pony 'Larry' faring us 1867. 4. He fared as one out of his wits FOXE. To f. angerly with anyone RALEIGH. 5. How fares it with the happy dead TENNYSON. 6. Ill fares the traveller now COWPER. Phr. *To go farther and f. worse.* 7. A certaine rich man .. fared sumptuously euery day *Luke* xvi. 19. 8. a. F. ye well *Acts* xv. 29. b. For ever, f. thee well BYRON.

†**Fare,** *v.*[2] [var. of FARROW *v.*] *intr.* Of a sow: To litter. TUSSER.

Farewell (fēᵊɹwe·l), *interj.* Also *sb.* (*a.*) and *adv.* ME. [*Fare* (see FARE *v.* 8) + *well* as one word.]

A. *interj.* 1. An expression of good wishes at parting, originally addressed to the one setting forth, but now = Good-bye! Adieu! *poet.* or *rhet.* ME. 2. *fig.* = Good-bye to, no more of (anything) ME.

1. And now farewel DRYDEN. 2. Farewel my book and my devocioun CHAUCER.

B. *sb.* 1. a. The *interj.* used subst., as a name for itself. So now in *To bid f.*, where *farewell* was orig. the *infinitive.* b. An utterance of the word 'farewell'; a parting salutation, adieu. ME. †2. A payment on quitting a tenancy. FITZHERB. 3. *attrib.* or *adj.* Pertaining to or signifying a farewell. (In this use commonly stressed *fa·rewell.*) 1711.

1. a. I take my farewel of this subject ADDISON. b. I cannot think the thing f. TENNYSON. A few final or f. farewells DE QUINCEY.

†C. *adv. To go f.*: to go away. CHAUCER.

Farewell (fēᵊɹwe·l), *v.* 1580. [f. prec.] To bid or say good-bye to; also *intr.*

Far-famed (fā·ɹ,fēᵢ·md), *a.* 1624. [f. FAR *adv.* + FAMED.] Famed to a great distance; well known, celebrated.

†**Fa·r-fet,** *a.* 1533. [f. FAR *adv.* + *fet*, pa. pple. of FET *v.*] 1. = FAR-FETCHED –1680. 2. as *sb.* The figure *Metalepsis* (*rare*) 1589.

†**Far-fetch,** *sb.* 1562. [f. FAR-FETCHED.] 1. A deeply-laid stratagem –1678. 2. Fondness for far-fetched ideas 1813. So †**Far-fetch** *v.* to derive in a far-fetched manner (*rare*).

Far-fetched (fā·ɹ,fetʃt, fāɹ,fe·tʃt), *ppl. a.* 1583. [f. FAR *adv.* + FETCHED.] 1. Brought from far. *Obs.* exc. *arch.* 2. Studiously sought out; not easily or naturally introduced; strained 1607.

1. A far fetch'd Pedigree, through so many hundred years CLARENDON. 2. Some far-fetched conceit 1844.

Far-forth, *adv.* Now usu. as two wds. ME. [See FAR and FORTH.] †1. Far, far on –1590. 2. To a definite degree or distance. *Obs.* exc. in *So far forth.* ME.

1. The humid night was farforth spent SPENSER. 2. Soffre ye thus farre forthe TINDALE *Luke* xxii. 51. Know thus far forth SHAKS. Hence **Far-fo·rthly** *adv.* to a great or definite extent; entirely.

Fargite (fā·ɹgəit). 1868. [f. (Glen) *Farg* in Fifeshire + -ITE.] *Min.* A red natrolite, containing about 4 p. c. of lime. DANA.

Farina (fărəi·nă, fărī·nă). 1707. [a. L., f. *far* corn.] 1. The flour or meal of any species of corn, nut, or starchy root 1800; a powdery substance, dust 1707. b. A preparation of maize used for puddings (*mod.*). 2. a. *Bot.* = Pollen 1721. b. *Chem.* Starch 1813. c. *Entom.* A mealy powder found on some insects 1828. d. *Fossil f.*: 'a white infusorial or microphytal earth—the Berg-mahl of the Swedes and Laplanders' (Page) 1816.

Farinaceous (færinēᵢ·ʃəs), *a.* 1656. [f. L. *farinaceus*, f. *farina* (see prec.) + -OUS.] 1. Consisting or made of flour or meal. 2. Yielding flour or starch; starchy 1667. 3. Of a mealy nature 1664. 4. Having a mealy appearance 1646.

1. A mild f. diet 1807. 2. F. vegetables 1732, seeds 1873. 3. Cotyledons thick, fleshy or f. HOOKER. 4. All f. or mealy winged animals, as Butter-Flies, and Moths SIR T. BROWNE. **Farina·ceously** *adv.*

‖**Farinha** (farī·nʸă). 1726. [Pg. :—L. *farina.*] = CASSAVA 2.

Farinose (færinōᵘ·s). 1727. [ad. L. *farinosus.*] A. *adj.* Mealy; *spec.* in *Bot.*, *Zool.*, etc. (see FARINA). B. *sb. Chem.* One of the constituents of a starch grain 1882.

‖**Fario** (fēᵊ·riₒ). 1753. [L.] A salmon when about half-grown.

Farl (fāɹl), *sb. Sc.* 1724. [Contr. f. FARDEL *sb.*[2]] A thin cake made of flour or oatmeal; *orig.*, the fourth part of such a cake.

†**Farl,** *v.* 1622. [Contr. f. FARDEL *v.*; cf. FURL.] = FARDEL *v.*

Farleu (fā·ɹliu). 1670. [?] *Law.* A money payment in lieu of a heriot; also, 'the best good' as dist. from 'the best beast'.

Farley, -i(e, -ik, -y(e: see FERLY.

†**Farm,** *sb.*[1] [OE. *feorm* str. fem. :—prehistoric **fermā.*] Food, provision; hence, a banquet –1500.

Farm (fāɹm), *sb.*[2] ME. [a. F. *ferme* :—med. L. *firma* fixed payment, f. *firmare*, f. *firmus*. See also FIRM *sb.*] †1. A fixed yearly amount (whether in money or in kind) payable as rent, tax, or the like. Also *Rent and f.* –1767. 2. A fixed yearly sum accepted as a composition for taxes or other moneys to be collected; also, a fixed charge imposed on a town, county, etc. to be collected as taxes within its limits. Now *Hist.* ME. b. The letting-out of a tax or taxes to a 'farmer'; the privilege thus conferred. Now *Hist.* 1667. 3. Hence: The condition of being 'farmed out' ME. †4. A lease –1647. 5. A tract of land held (orig. on lease) for the purpose of cultivation; sometimes specialized as *dairy-, grass-, poultry-f.* 1523. Also a tract of water used as a preserve, as *fish-, oyster-f.*, etc. 1865. 6. A farm-house 1596. 7. A place where children are 'farmed' 1869.

1. The usual .. feorm or rent BLACKSTONE. 2. b. The first f. of postal income was made in 1672 EDWARDS. 3. Districts which were in a condition to be let to f. BURKE. 4. To refuse to make any longer farmes unto Tenants SPENSER. 5. The pleasant Villages and Farmes MILT. *P. L.* IX. 448. 6. A ferme or mannor house HOLLAND.

Comb.: **f.-crossing**, a railway-crossing from one part of a f. to another; **-hand**, any person that works on a f.; **-stock**, the cattle, etc., implements, and produce of a f.; **-store**, farm-produce.

Farm, *v.*[1] Now *dial.* [OE. *feormian*; etym. unkn.] To cleanse, empty.

Farm (fāɹm), *v.*[2] ME. [f. FARM *sb.*[2]] 1. *trans.* To take or hold for a term at a fixed payment. 2. To let to another for a fixed payment; as, land to a tenant (now *rare*) 1593; the proceeds of customs, taxes, tithes, etc. 1602; labour 1607. 3. To contract for the maintenance and care of (persons, an institution, etc.) at a stipulated price. Also *To f. out.* 1666. 4. To cultivate, till 1806. 5. *intr.* To be a farmer; to till the soil 1719.

1. Abram .. farmed .. some ground of them BP. PATRICK. To f. a lottery JOHNSON, tin-mines M. PATTISON. 2. We are inforc'd to farme our royall Realme SHAKS. If I be minded to f. out my Tythes 1704. They farmed out the Indians ROBERTSON. 5. I farmed upon my own land DE FOE. Hence †**Fa·rmage,** the system of farming; leasehold tenure; the profits from a farm; cost of cultivation.

Farmer (fā·ɹməɹ). ME. [a. AF. *fermer*, F. *fermier* :—med.L. *firmarius*, f. *firma* (see FARM *sb.*[2]); also partly f. FARM *v.*[2]] 1. One who undertakes the collection of taxes, revenues, etc., paying a fixed sum for the proceeds. b. *Mining.* The lessee of 'the lot and cope of the king' (see COPE *sb.*[3]) 1653. †2. *gen.* One who has a lease of anything 1523. 3. *spec.* One who rents land for the purpose of cultivation 1487. 4. One who 'farms' land, whether as tenant or owner 1599. 5. One who undertakes to perform (a work or service) at a fixed price 1838. †6. A farm-bailiff –1580.

1. Speculators, farmers of revenues, and others 1864. 4. I eat like a f. 1771. 5. The f. of infants 1838.

Fa·rmeress. 1672. [See -ESS.] A woman who farms land; also, a farmer's wife.

Farmer-general. 1711. [tr. F. *fermier général.*] One who, under the old French monarchy, farmed the taxes of a district.

†**Fa·rmerly,** *a.* 1674. [f. FARMER + -LY [1].] Like a farmer –1793.

†**Fa·rmership.** 1551. [f. as prec. + -SHIP.] The state or occupation of being a farmer; stewardship –1624.

Farmery (fā·ɹməri), *sb.* 1656. [f. FARM *sb.* + -ERY.] The buildings, yards, etc., belonging to a farm.

Farmhold (fā·ɹmhōᵘld). 1449. [f. FARM *sb.*[2] + HOLD *sb.*] A quantity of land held as a farm.

Fa·rm-hou·se. 1598. [f. FARM *sb.*[2] + HOUSE.] The chief dwelling-house attached to a farm.

Farming (fā·ɹmiŋ), *vbl. sb.* 1591. [f. FARM *v.*[2]] 1. The action or system of farming (out) or letting out to farm (the revenue, etc.). 2. The business of cultivating land, raising stock, etc. 1733. 3. *attrib.* 1764.

2. When I am told that f. answers to gentlemen .. I never believe it A. YOUNG.

†**Fa·rmost,** *a.* 1618. [f. FAR + MOST.] Irreg. superl. of FAR –1700.

Farm-stead (fā·ɹm,sted). 1807. [f. FARM *sb.*[2] + STEAD.] A farm with the buildings upon it, a homestead. So **Fa·rm-stea·ding.**

Fa·rm-ya·rd. 1748. The yard or enclosure attached to a farm-house or surrounded by farm-buildings. Also *attrib.*

Farness (fā·ɹnės). ME. [See -NESS.] The state of being far (or, *occas.*, far-reaching); *concr.* distant parts.

F. of sight and fixedness of purpose BANCROFT.

Faro (fēᵊ·ro). 1713 (farroon). [ad. F. *pharaon*, It. *faraone* PHARAOH: said to be so called from the King of Hearts being so named.] A gambling game at cards, in which the players bet on the order in which certain cards will appear when taken singly from the top of the pack.

Comb. f. bank, (*a*) a gambling-house where f. is played; (*b*) the money staked by the banker against the other players.

Faröelite (fā·ro,ėləit). 1858. [f. *Faröe* + -LITE.] *Min.* A variety of Thomsonite occurring 'in spherical concretions, consisting of lamellar radiated individuals, pearly in cleavage' (Dana).

Far-off (fā·ɹ,ǫ·f), *a.* 1590. [f. FAR *adv.* + OFF *adv.*, orig. as two words.] Far distant, remote.

The far-off Curfeu MILT. Those far-off days 1877.

‖**Farouche** (faruʃ). 1765. [Fr.; said to be f. L. *ferocem.*] Sullen, shy and repellent in manner.

Farraginous (fărǣ·dʒinəs), *a.* 1615. [f. L. *farrago*, (*farragin-*), FARRAGO.] Hotchpotch.

A f. concurrence of all conditions, tempers, sex, and ages SIR T. BROWNE.

Farrago (fărē̆ⁱ·go). 1632. [a. L. *farrago* mixed fodder for cattle, hence *fig.* a medley, f. *far* spelt, corn.] A confused group; a medley, mixture, hotchpotch.

This f. of cowardice, cunning, and cant CANNING.

Fa·rrand, farrant, *a. Sc.* and *n. dial.* ME. [? an application of *farande*, north. pr. pple. of FARE *v.*[1]] †1. Of a person: well favoured, comely; of things: Becoming. Only in ME. 2. Having a specified appearance, disposition, or temperament; as, *auld-*, *fighting-*, *foul-f.* Hence **Fa·rrandly, farrantly** *adv.*

Farreation (færi,ēⁱ·ʃən). 1656. [ad. L. *farreationem.*] = CONFARREATION.

Farrier (fæ·riəɹ), *sb.* 1562. [a. OF. *ferrier* :—L. *ferrarius*, f. *ferrum*, in med.L. horseshoe.] 1. One who shoes horses; a shoeing smith; hence, one who treats the ailments of horses. 2. An official who has care of the horses in a cavalry regiment 1832.

Hence **Fa·rrier** *v.* (*rare*), to treat (an animal) as a f. does; *intr.* to practise farriery. **Fa·rriery,** the art of the f.; now = veterinary surgery.

Farrow (fæ·rou), *sb.* [OE. *fearh* :—OTeut. **farhoz* boar :—pre-Teut. **porkos* = Gr. πόρκος, L. *porcus*; see PORK.] †1. A young pig -ME. 2. An act of farrowing. [Prop. f. the vb.] 1601. 3. Hence *concr.* A litter of pigs; occas. in sing. with numeral (after Shaks.) 1577.

2. That hath eaten Her nine F. *Macb.* IV. i. 65.

Farrow (fæ·rou), *a.* Chiefly *Sc.* 1494. [? Cf. Flem. *verwekoe*, a cow that has ceased to bear offspring.] Of a cow: That is not with calf. Also in *To be, go,* or *run f.*

Farrow (fæ·rou), *v.* ME. [f. FARROW *sb.*] 1. *trans.* Of a sow: To bring forth (young). 2. *intr.* To produce a litter ME.

‖**Farsang** (fā·ɹsæŋ). 1613. [Pers.; see PARASANG.] 'A Persian measure of distance—the *Parasang* of the ancients—about four miles' (H. H. Wilson).

Farse (fāɹs), *sb.* 1842. [ad. med.L. *farsa* (see FARCE *sb.*[2]).] *Eccl. Antiq.* An amplification inserted into a liturgical formula; also, each of the hortatory or other passages in the vernacular interpolated between the Latin sentences in chanting the lesson or epistle. So **Farse** *v.* to amplify by the insertion of certain words; to provide (an epistle) with a f. Also *transf.*

Far-sighted (fāɹ,səitėd), *a.* 1641. [f. FAR *adv.* + SIGHT.] 1. *fig.* Looking far before one; forecasting, shrewd. 2. *lit.* Hypermetropic 1878.

1. The fair and far-sighted eye of his natural discerning MILT. Hence **Far-sighted-ly** *adv.*, **-ness.** So **Far-sight,** ability to see far; also *attrib.*

Fart (fāɹt), *sb.* Not in decent use. ME. [f. the vb.] A breaking wind.

Fart (fāɹt), *v.* Not in decent use. ME. [Com. Teut. and Indo-Germ.: OE. **feortan* :—OTeut. **fertan* :—OAryan **perd-* (Skr. *pard, prd*, Gr. πέρδειν, etc.).] 1. *intr.* To break wind. 2. *trans.* To send forth as wind from the anus 1632.

Farther (fā·ɹðəɹ). [ME. *ferþer* (whence *farther*) is a mere var. of FURTHER. The primary sense of these, 'more forward, more onward', being coincident with that of the comparative of *far*, the forms *further, farther*, ultimately displaced the regular comparative *farrer.* The form *farther* is now preferred as the comparative of *far*, while *further* is used where the notion of *far* is absent.]

A. *adv.* 1. More forward; to or at a more advanced point: a. in space, a course of procedure, etc.; b. in time 1548. 2. To a greater extent 1513. 3. In addition ME. 4. To or at a greater distance; by a greater interval ME.

1. a. To walk f. 1460. b. To argue f. MAR. EDGEWORTH. 2. To know f. *Temp.* I. ii. 33. 3. Nay f., [etc.] DE FOE. 4. Phr. *To wish any one f.*

B. *adj.* †1. = FURTHER *a.* 1. -1534. 2. More extended, additional, more 1520. 3. More distant 1568.

2. Down he sat without f. bidding DICKENS. 3. The f. syde of London GRAFTON

Farther (fā·ɹðəɹ), *v.* Now *rare.* [:—ME. *ferþren*; see FURTHER *v.*] *trans.* = FURTHER *v.*

†**Fa·rtherance.** *rare.* 1785. [See -ANCE.] = FURTHERANCE.

†**Fa·rtherer.** 1494. [See -ER [1].] = FURTHERER -1655.

†**Fa·rthermore.** ME. [See -MORE.] A. *adv.* = FURTHERMORE -1535. B. *adj.* More remote 1610.

Farthermost (fā·ɹðəɹmoᵘst), *a.* 1618. [var. of FURTHERMOST.] Farthest, most remote or distant.

Farthest (fā·ɹðėst). ME. [var. of FURTHEST; used as superl. of FAR; see FARTHER.]

A. *adj.* 1. Most distant or remote. Also with *off.* 2. Longest 1633. 3. *absol.* of space, future time, or degree 1596.

3. At the f. by fiue of the clocke *Merch. V.* II. ii. 122.

B. *adv.* To or at the greatest distance. Also with *off.* 1598.

Farthing (fā·ɹðiŋ), *sb.* [OE. *fēorðing, fēorðung*, f. *fēorða* FOURTH.] 1. The fourth part of a penny; the coin of this value. In N.T. used for the two Roman coins *as* and *quadrans.* 2. *transf.* and *fig.* A very little, a bit ME. †3. The fourth a. of an acre; b. of a hide -1630.

2. In hire cuppe was no ferthing sene Of grees CHAUCER. *Comb.* **f.-land,** 'commonly thirtie acres' (Carew); 'the fourth part of an Acre' (Worlidge).

Farthingale (fā·ɹðiŋ,gēⁱl). 1552. [ad. OF. *verdugale, vertugalle*, corruption of Sp. *verdugado* a farthingale, f. *verdugo* rod, stick.] A frame-work of hoops, usually of whalebone, formerly used for extending the skirts of women's dresses; a hooped petticoat.

The Women wear great Vardingales, standing..far out at each side RAY.

†**Fa·rthingdeal.** ME. [repr. OE. *fēorðan dǽl*, accus. of *fēorða dǽl* fourth part. 1. *gen.* A fourth part. ME. only. 2. *spec.* The fourth part of an acre; a rood -1607. b. A quarter of a yard of land 1640. var. **Far(r)-undell.**

‖**Fasces** (fæ·sīz), *sb. pl.* 1598. [L., pl. of *fascis* bundle.] 1. A bundle of rods bound up with an axe in the middle, its blade projecting. 2. *transf.* and *fig.* The ensigns of authority or power; hence, authority 1619.

The senʳ proctor..laid down the f. of his authority WOOD.

Fascet (fæ·sėt). 1662. [?] A tool used to introduce glass bottles into the annealing oven.

Fascia (fæ·ʃiă). *Pl.* **-iæ**; in *Arch.* **-as.** 1563. [a. L.] †1. in *Lat.* sense: A band, fillet -1606. 2. *Arch.* Any long flat surface of wood, stone, or marble, *esp.* in the Ionic and Corinthian orders, each of the three surfaces which make up the architrave. (Cf. FACIA.) 1563. 3. *Anat.* A thin sheath of fibrous tissue investing a muscle or some special tissue or organ; an aponeurosis 1788. 4. Anything resembling a band or stripe: a. *Astron.* The belt of a planet 1704; b. *Conchol.* A row of perforations 1877; c. *Bot., Zool.*, etc. A band of colour 1752; d. *Her.* = FESSE. 1880.

Fascial (fæ·ʃiăl), *a.*[1] *rare.* 1832. [f. FASCES.] Of or pertaining to the (Roman) fasces.

Fascial (fæ·ʃiăl), *a.*[2] [ad. L. *fascialis*; see FASCIA and AL.] *Anat.* Of or pertaining to the fasciæ; aponeurotic.

Fasciate (fæ·ʃi,ėt), *a.* [ad. late L. *fasciatus, fasciare.*] *Bot.* = FASCIATED.

Fasciate (fæ·ʃi,eⁱt), *v.* 1658. [f. late L. *fasciat-* ppl. stem; see prec.] To bind with or as with a fascia.

Fasciated (fæ·ʃi,eⁱtėd), *ppl. a.* 1715. [f. prec.] 1. *Bot.*, etc. Compressed or massed together 1811. †2. Of a roof: Coved on two opposite sides only 1715. 3. Marked with bands or stripes 1752.

Fasciation (fæsi,ēⁱ·ʃən). 1650. [a. F.; see FASCIA and -ATION.] 1. The binding up of a limb, etc., with bandages; †a bandage -1658. 2. The process of becoming fasciated; also, fasciated condition (see FASCIATED 1) 1677.

Fascicle (fæ·sik'l). 1622. [ad. L. *fasciculus*, dim. of *fascis*; see FASCES.] 1. A bunch, bundle. Now only in scientific use. b. *Bot.* A number of leaves, flowers, roots, etc. growing or occurring in a bunch, bundle, or tuft 1794. c. *Anat.* A bundle of fibres, chiefly applied to nerve structures 1738. 2. A part, number, instalment (of a printed work) 1647.

Hence **Fa·scicled** *ppl. a.* (*Bot.*), growing in a f.

Fascicular (făsi·kiŭlăɹ), *a.* 1656. [f. FASCICULUS + -AR.] †1. Belonging to a bundle. (Dicts.) 2. Pertaining to, or of the nature of, a FASCICLE, as, *f. tissue, fibres* 1805. Hence **Fasci·cularly** *adv.*

Fasciculate (făsi·kiŭlėt), *a.* 1794. [f. as prec. + -ATE [2].] Arranged in a FASCICLE; fascicle-like. So **Fasci·culated** *ppl. a.*

Fasciculation (făsi·kiulēⁱ·ʃən). [See -ATION.] The state of being fasciculate; that which is fasciculated.

Fascicule (fæ·sikiŭl). 1609. [a. F., ad. L. *fasciculus.*] †1. A handful. EVELYN. 2. = FASCICLE 2. 1880. 3. = FASCICLE 1 c. 1745.

Fasciculite (făsi·kiŭləit). 1823. [f. prec. + -ITE.] *Min.* Tufted fibrous hornblende.

‖**Fasciculus** (făsi·kiŭlŏs). *Pl.* **-li.** 1713. [L., dim. of *fascis*; see FASCES.] 1. = FASCICLE 1; chiefly in scientific use. 2. = FASCICLE 2. 1844.

Fascinate (fæ·sineⁱt), *v.* 1598. [f. L. *fascinat-, fascinare*, f. *fascinum* spell, witchcraft.] †1. *trans.* To affect by witchcraft; to enchant, lay under a spell -1657. 2. To cast a spell over by a look (said *esp.* of serpents); to render unable to move or resist 1641. 3. *fig.* To attract and hold the attention of by an irresistible influence 1651.

1. To f. and cure stinking breaths 1657. 2. The serpent fascinates its prey, apparently by the power of its eyes 1845. 3. A wit that would f. sages MOORE. The eye of the Ancient Mariner fascinated the wedding guest BURTON. Hence **Fa·scinating** *ppl. a.* irresistibly attractive, charming. **Fa·scinatingly** *adv.* **Fa·scinative** *a.* tending to f. **Fa·scinator.**

Fascination (fæsinēⁱ·ʃən). 1605. [ad. L. *fascinationem*; see prec.] 1. The casting of a spell; sorcery, enchantment; an instance of this. *Obs.* exc. *Hist.* †b. The state of being under a spell -1767. 2. The action or faculty of fascinating, as serpents are said to do 1796. 3. Fascinating quality, irresistibly attractive influence; an instance or mode of this 1697.

2. The f. of the serpent on the bird held her mute and frozen LYTTON. 3. That perilous f. which haunts the brow of precipices HAWTHORNE.

Fascine (fæsī·n), *sb.* 1688. [a. F., ad. L. *fascina*, f. *fascis* a bundle.] 1. *Mil.* A long cylindrical faggot of brushwood or the like, firmly bound together, used in filling up ditches, constructing batteries, etc. Usu. in *pl.* 2. *transf.* in non-military uses 1712.

2. A large Dike or Peer made of Fachines and Earth 1723. *Comb.* **f.-dwelling,** a lacustrine habi-

tation supported on fascines. Hence **Fasci·ne** *v.* to fill up with fascines.

Fascist (fæ·ʃist). **1921.** [ad. It. *fascista*, f. *fascio* group.] One of a body of Italian nationalists organized in 1919 under Benito Mussolini to oppose Bolshevism. Hence **Fa·scism,** their principles and organization.

Fash (fæʃ), *sb. Sc.* and *n. dial.* 1794. [f. the vb.] Trouble, vexation; bother. So **Fa·shery** (in same senses).

Fash (fæʃ), *v.* Chiefly *Sc.* and *n. dial.* 1533. [a. OF. *fascher* (F. *fâcher*).] **1.** *trans.* To trouble, vex, bother, weary. **2.** *intr.* for *refl.* To weary; to bother oneself; to take trouble 1585.

1. Never f. yoursel' wi' me..but look to yoursel' SCOTT.

Fashion (fæ·ʃən), *sb.* ME. [a. OF. *façon*, *fazon* (mod.F. *façon*) :—L. *factionem*; see FACTION *sb.*] †**1.** The action or process of making –1762. **2.** Make, build, shape; hence, appearance (*arch.*) ME. †**b.** Form as opp. to matter –1614. **3.** A particular make, shape, cut, etc. ME. **4.** Kind, sort. Now *rare.* 1562. **5.** Manner, mode, way (*rare* in *pl.*) ME. **6.** Mode of action, behaviour, demeanour, air (now *rare*) ME.; *pl.* actions, gestures, ways (now *rare*) 1569. †**7.** Outward action; pretence –1816. **8.** A current usage 1489; †in *pl.* often = 'manners and customs', ways –1721. **9.** Conventional usage in dress, mode of life, etc., *esp.* as observed in the upper circles of society; conformity to this. Often *personified.* 1602. **b.** Fashionable people 1807.

1. They judge the f. to be worth about 5*s.* per oz. more PEPYS. 2. The f. of his countenance was altered *Luke* ix. 29. 3. I do not like the f. of your garments *Lear* III. vi. 84. 4. Phr. *In f. to*: of a sort to (*Merch. V.* I. ii. 23). 5. After quite another f. DE FOE. Phr. *After, in, a* or *some f.*: not too well. 6. With such a grace, with such a f. THACKERAY. 8. The mind still turns where shifting f. draws GOLDSM. Dressed in country f. 1859. 9. The glasse of F., and the mould of Forme *Haml.* III. i. 161.

Phrases. *The f.* **a.** The mode of dress, etiquette, style of speech, etc., adopted in society for the time being. **b.** The person or thing that is fashionable to admire or discuss. *In, out of (the) f.*: in, out of, vogue; according or contrary to the customary rule. (*Man, woman*) *of f.*: †**a.** Of high quality, breeding, or repute. **b.** *Now*, That moves in good society, and conforms to its rules.

Comb.: **f. paper,** a journal of the fashions or of fashionable life; **f.-piece** (*Naut.*), one of the 'two Timbers which describe the breadth of the Ship at the Stern' (Harris); **f.-plate,** 'a pictorial design showing the prevailing style or new style of dress' (W.).

Hence **Fa·shionless** *a.* without f. or shape.

Fashion (fæ·ʃən), *v.* ME. [f. prec. sb.; cf. F. *façonner*.] **1.** *trans.* To give fashion or shape to; to form, mould, shape. Also with *out.* **2.** **a.** To frame, make (*rare*) 1549. †**b.** To contrive, manage 1604. †**3.** To change the fashion of; to transform –1753; †to counterfeit, pervert SHAKS. **4.** To accommodate, adapt *to.* Also *refl.* and *intr.* for *refl.* Now *rare.* 1526.

1. Did not one f. vs in the wombe *Job* xxxi. 15. A smith to f. his steel into picks and awls ROGERS. 2. b. His going thence, which I will f. to fall out betweene twelue and one *Oth.* IV. ii. 242. 3. F. thyself to Paul 1592. *Much Ado* I. iii. 31. 4. Doctrines fashioned to the varying hour GOLDSM.

Fashionable (fæ·ʃənăb'l). **1606.** [f. FASHION *v.* and *sb.* + -ABLE.]

A. *adj.* †**1.** Capable of being fashioned, shaped, or moulded –1656. †**2.** Pertaining to the outward form; merely formal –1616. †**3.** Of a good fashion or appearance; stylish –1720. **4.** **a.** Of persons: Observant of or conforming to the fashion 1606. **b.** Of things: Conformable to fashion; in accordance with prevailing usage; current (now in depreciatory sense) 1608. **5.** Of, pertaining to, or characteristic of the world of fashion; patronized by people of fashion 1712.

4. Like a f. Hoste, That slightly shakes his parting Guest by th' hand *Tr. & Cr.* III. iii. 165. **b.** His..attire more f. FULLER. 5. In f. or political saloons EMERSON.

B. *sb.* A fashionable person. Usu. in *pl.* 1800.

Our fair fashionables 1800.

Hence **Fa·shionableness,** f. quality. **Fa·shionably** *adv.* in a f. manner.

†**Fa·shional,** *a.* 1617. [f. FASHION *sb.* + -AL.] = FASHIONABLE *a.* 2, 3. –1629.

Fashioned (fæ·ʃənd), *ppl. a.* 1577. [f. FASHION *sb.*] Having a fashion of a specified kind, as *old-f.*, etc.

Fashioner (fæ·ʃənər). 1548. [f. FASHION *v.*] One that fashions; *esp.* a tailor, costumier, modiste (now *arch.*).

A f. of doublets SCOTT.

Fashionist (fæ·ʃənist). 1616. [f. as prec. + -IST.] **1.** A follower of the fashions. **2.** One who sets the fashions. MILMAN.

Fa·shion-monger. 1599. [f. FASHION + MONGER.] One who studies and follows the fashions. Hence †**Fashion-monging** *ppl. a.*

Fashious (fæ·ʃəs), *a. Sc.* and *n. dial.* 1536. [ad. OF. *fascheux* (F. *fâcheux*), f. *fascher* (F. *fâcher*) to FASH.] Causing anxiety or trouble; tiresome, vexatious.

Fassaite (fæ·sɛ,əit). 1814. [f. *Fassa* (in the Tyrol) + -ITE.] *Min.* †**a.** Foliated zeolite. **b.** A variety of pyroxene, containing a little alumina.

Fast (fɑst), *sb.*[1] [Early ME. *faste*, prob. a ON. *fasta*, f. OTeut. *fastêjan* to FAST. Cf. FASTEN *sb.*] **1.** An act of fasting: **a.** as a religious observance, or as an expression of grief; **b.** in general ME; †**c.** Abstinence from food; also *personified* –1795. **2.** A day or season appointed for fasting ME.

1. b. *To break (one's) f.*: see BREAK *v.* **c.** Surfet is the father of much f. *Meas. for M.* I. ii. 130. 2. The people of Nineueh..proclaimed a f. *Jonah* iii. 5.

Comb.: **f.-day,** a day to be observed as **a f.**; **-mass,** Shrovetide.

Fast (fɑst), *sb.*[2] [ME. *fest*, a. ON. *festr*, f. *festa* to fasten, f. *fastr* FAST *a.*] *Naut.* A rope, etc. by which a ship or boat is fastened to a wharf.

Fast (fɑst), *sb.*[3] 1836. [The adj. used *absol.*] That which is fast or fixed; *esp.* shore or land ice.

†**Fast,** *sb.*[4] [ad. F. *faste*, ad. L. *fastus*.] Arrogance, pompousness. H. WALPOLE.

Fast (fɑst), *a.* [Com. Teut.: OE. *fæst*; prob. repr. OTeut. **fastu-*, cogn. w. Goth. *fastan* to keep, observe, guard.]

I. Firm. **1.** Firmly fixed; not easily moved or shaken; settled, stable. *Obs.* or *arch.*, exc. as in sense 4. **b.** Not easily turned aside, constant, steadfast. Now only in *f. foe* (arch.), *f. friend.* OE. **c.** Of sleep: Deep, sound, unbroken. *Obs.* exc. *dial.* 1592. **d.** Of a colour: Permanent 1658. **2.** Firmly or closely knit together, compact, dense, solid. *Obs.* exc. *dial.* OE. †**3.** Strong; secure against attack or access. Cf. FASTNESS. –1633. **4.** Firmly attached to something else; that cannot easily escape or be extricated; fixed to the spot. *lit.* and *fig.* ME. **b.** Of a knot, band, etc.: Not easily loosed. Also *fig.* 1553. **5.** Of a door, etc.: Close shut, bolted, or locked ME. **6.** Tenacious. *Obs.* exc. in *f. hold of.* –1724.

1. b. England must be the f. friend, or the determined enemy, of France BURKE. **c.** All this while in a most f. sleepe *Macb.* v. i. 9. Phr. *F. aground, ashore, asleep*: fixed on the ground, the shore, in sleep. 2. In close array and f. SCOTT. 4. F. in preson 1535. F. with the gout SCOTT. Phr. *To make f.*: to connect or fix firmly; also *absol.* (Naut.). 6. Roses Damask & Red are f. Flowers of their Smels BACON.

II. Rapid. [App. a sense developed first in the adv.] **1.** Of action, motion, etc.: Quick, swift. Hence of an agent: Moving, or causing to move, rapidly. ME. **b.** Coming in quick succession. SHELLEY. **c.** Of a watch, etc.: Ahead of the true time 1840; also of scales: indicating more than the actual weight 1908. **2.** Adapted to, or productive of, quick movement; *spec.* in *Cricket, Football,* and *Billiards* 1857. **3.** Living too fast; dissipated; dissolute. Often applied to women in milder sense: Disregardful of restraint. Also *transf.* 1745.

1. Idle Weeds are f. in growth *Rich. III*, III. i. 103. A good f. bowler 1886. 2. A f. line of railway (*mod.*). The ground [at a football match] was very f. (*mod.*). 3. All the f. men were anxious to make their acquaintance 1841. Lucknow is a f. place L. OLIPHANT.

Comb.: **f.-pulley,** also in *f. and loose pulley*, a contrivance for disengaging and re-engaging machinery, consisting of two pulleys, one fixed on an axle, the other, having a bush, loose, so that the band conveying the motion may be shifted from one pulley to the other at pleasure; **f.-shot,** in *Mining*, a shot that has discharged without disturbing the coal.

Fast (fɑst), *adv.* [OE. *fæste*:—OTeut. **fastô*, f. *fastu-* FAST *a.*] **1.** In a fast manner, so as not to be moved or shaken; *lit.* and *fig.*; firmly, fixedly. **2.** With firm grasp, attachment, or adhesion; tightly, securely. *lit.* and *fig.* OE. **3.** In a close-fitting manner; so as to leave no opening ME. **4.** Of proximity: Close, hard; very near. Now only in *f. beside, f. by* (arch. or poet.). ME. †**5.** Closely, at once –1782. **6.** Quickly, rapidly, swiftly ME.; in quick succession 1591.

1. Stand f. in the faith 1 *Cor.* xvi. 13. Phr. *To sleep fast*, i.e. soundly. 2. F. binde, f. finde *Merch. V.* II. v. 53. Phr. *To stick f.*: often *fig.* to be nonplussed. 3. Substantial dores, Cross-barrd and bolted f. MILT. *P. L.* IV. 190. 4. F. by Hell Gate MILT. *P. L.* II. 725. 6. His health was breaking f. TREVELYAN. My thoughts come f. SHELLEY. Phr. *To live f.*: **a.** to expend quickly one's vital energy; **b.** to live a dissipated life.

†**Fast,** *v.*[1] [OE. *fæstan* (rare) :—OTeut. **fastjan*, f. **fastu-* FAST *a.*] **1.** To make fast to something; to bind together. Also *refl.* and *intr.*, for *refl.* –1665. **2.** To fix in something else; to fix firmly –1664. **3.** To confirm (a covenant); to pledge (faith, etc.) –1470.

Fast (fɑst), *v.*[2] [Com. Teut.: OE. *fæstan* to make fast, observe, be strict :—OTeut. **fastêjan.*] **1.** *intr.* To abstain from food, or to 'eat meagre', either as a religious observance or as an expression of grief. **2.** *gen.* To go without food (or drink). Const. *from.* Also *transf.* OE. †**3.** *trans.* To pass (time) fasting –1681.

1. We f. by way of penitence J. H. NEWMAN. *fig.* To f. from sinne SIR T. HERBERT. 2. Fasting he went to sleep, and fasting wak'd MILT. *P. R.* II. 284. Phr. *To f. against, upon* (a person) (*Irish Antiq.*): to sit without food or drink at the door of a debtor, or any person who refused to satisfy a lawful demand.

Fast and (†**or**) **loose.** 1557. **a.** An old cheating game played with a stick and a belt or string 1578. **b.** *fig.* Slippery or inconstant, as in *To play (at) fast and loose* 1557. **c.** Shiftiness 1648.

Fa·sten, *sb. Obs.* exc. in *Comb.* [OE. *fæsten* str. neut. :—OTeut. type **fastunjo-m*, f. *fast-êjan* to FAST.] = FAST *sb.*[1] 1, 2.

Fasten (fɑ·s'n), *v.* [OE. *fæstnian* :—OTeut. **fastinôjan*, f. **fastu-* FAST *a.*] To make FAST. †**1.** *trans.* To make firm or stable; to confirm –1643. †**2.** To make firm or solid; to strengthen –1557; *intr.* to set –1730. †**3.** To make fast (in fetters). Also *intr.* –1632. **4.** *trans.* To make fast to something else; to attach by a tie or bond. Also *absol.* or *intr.* ME. **5.** To make fast, secure. Also †*intr.* ME. †**6.** To close (the hands, teeth) with a grip –1607. †**7.** To deliver effectively (a blow) –1697. **8.** *fig.* in senses 4, 5: To fix (something) *upon* a person ME. **9.** intr. *To f. on, upon*: †**a.** To obtain a firm hold upon; **b.** to seize on, lay hold of. ME.

2. *intr.* Buildings..are taken with the Frost..before ever they have fasten'd LEONI. 4. My wife and I, Fastned our selues at eyther end the mast SHAKS. 5. Breeches fasten'd with Buttons 1696. To f. the door FIELDING. Sit at the helm—f. this sheet SHELLEY. 7. Wee could never come once to f. a blow on him 1632. 8. If I can f. but one Cup vpon him *Oth.* II. iii. 50. The eyes of all..were fastened on him *Luke* iv. 20. Phr. *To f. a quarrel upon.*

Fastener (fɑ·s'nəɹ). 1628. [f. prec.] **1.** One who or that which fastens 1755. †**2.** *slang.* A warrant for arrest –1785.

Fastening (fɑ·s'niŋ), *vbl. sb.* ME. [f. as prec.] **1.** The action of FASTEN *v.* †**2.** The condition of being fastened. Only in ME. **3.** *concr.* That which fastens or makes secure ME.

3. Sash Fastenings 1769. The fastenings of a cuirass 1850.

Fastens. 1616. Short for next.

Fastens-een, -eve, even. *Sc.* and *n. dial.* ME. [f. OE. *fæstenes*, genitive of *fæsten* FASTEN *sb.* + EVEN, EVE.] The eve of or day before the fast (of Lent); SHROVE-TUESDAY.

Faster (fɑ·stəɹ). ME. [f. FAST *v.*] One who fasts or abstains from food.

‖**Fasti** (fæ·stəi). 1611. [L., pl. of *fastus* (*dies*) a lawful day, a day on which the courts sat.] **a.** *Rom. Antiq.* A calendar or calendars, indicating the lawful days for legal business, and also the festivals, games, anniversaries, etc., connected with each day of the year. **b.** *transf.* A chronological register of events.

Fastidio·sity. [f. L. *fastidiosus* + -ITY.] Fastidiousness. SWIFT.

Fastidious (fæsti·diəs), *a.* ME. [ad. L. *fastidiosus*, f. *fastidium*; see -OUS.] †1. That creates disgust -1734. †2. That feels disgust -1678; full of pride; disdainful -1796. 3. Easily disgusted, squeamish; over-nice 1612.

1. Folly is..f. to society BARROW. 2. Proud youth! f. of the lower world YOUNG. 3. A f. age..and one of false refinement TRENCH. Hence **Fasti·dious-ly** *adv.*, **-ness.**

Fastidium (fæsti·diǒm). *rare.* 1734. [a. L.] Disgust; ennui.

Fastigiate (fæsti·dʒi,ět), *a.* 1662. [f. L. *fastigium* summit of a gable, top, vertex + -ATE².] 1. Sloping up to a point like a cone or pyramid; in *Bot.* having flowers or branches whose extremities form a cone-like outline. 2. †a. *Bot.* Formerly (after F. *fastigié*): Having a horizontal surface at the top, as in an umbel or corymb -1794. b. Hence, of a zoophyte: = CORYMBED 1846.

Fastigiate (fæsti·dʒi,eit), *v.* 1647. [f. as prec. + -ATE³.] *trans.* To make pointed at the top like a gable; *intr.* to taper to a point. Hence **Fasti·giated** *ppl. a.* 'roofed, narrowed up to the top' (J.).

†**Fasti·gious,** *a.* 1670. [f. next + -OUS.] With gables; *fig.* pretentious -1697.

‖**Fastigium** (fæsti·dʒiǒm). 1677. [L.] 1. Apex, summit; in *Arch.* the ridge of a house. 2. The gable end (of a roof); a pediment 1849. 3. The acme of intensity (of a disease) 1876.

Fasting (fa·stiŋ), *vbl. sb.* ME. [f. FAST *v.*²] 1. The action of FAST *v.*² †2. A season of abstinence from food -1656. 3. *attrib.*, as in **f.-spittle**, the saliva that is in the mouth before one's fast is broken 1460. Hence **Fa·sting-day** = FAST-DAY.

Fastish (fa·stiʃ), *a* 1854. [See -ISH.] Somewhat fast.

Fa·stland. 1883. [f. FAST *a.* + LAND; after Ger. *festland.*] The mainland, as dist. from the islands; the continent.

Fastly (fa·stli), *adv. arch.* OE. [f. FAST *a.* + -LY².] Now repl. by FAST *adv.*] †1. = FAST *adv.* -1817. 2. Rapidly; hence, readily. Now *rare.* ME.

Fastness (fa·stnės). OE. [f. as prec.] 1. The quality or state of being FAST, in various senses. †2. Of style: Conciseness, pithiness. ASCHAM. †3. That which fastens or keeps fast -1676. 4. A place not easily forced; a stronghold OE.

4. They would rather tempt us to attempt them in their f. CROMWELL.

Fastuous (fæ·stiu,əs), *a.* Now *rare.* 1638. [ad. L. *fastuosus*, f. *fastus* arrogance; see -OUS.] Haughty, arrogant, pretentious, ostentatious. Hence †**Fastuo·sity,** f. quality. **Fa·stuous-ly** *adv.*, **-ness.**

†**Fat** (fæt), *sb.*¹ [OE. *fæt* str. neut.:—OTeut. **fatom*. f. Teut. root **fat-* to hold, contain.] 1. A vessel; *esp.* a large vessel for liquids -1755. 3. A cask or barrel to contain dry things -1812. 4. A measure of capacity -1706.

1. In thy Fattes our Cares be drown'd SHAKS.

Fat (fæt), *a.* and *sb.*² [OE. *fǽtt*:—OTeut. **faitido-*, pa. pple. of **faitjan* to fatten, f. **faito-* adj. fat.]

A. *adj.* I. 1. Of an animal used for food: Fatted, ready to kill. 2. In well-fed condition, plump; well supplied with fat; in bad sense, corpulent, obese. Also *fig.* OE. 3. *transf.* Of things: Thick, full-bodied; *spec.* of printing types ME.

1. A feste of fatte bestes WYCLIF *Isa.* xxv. 6. 2. A f. baby 1864. So f. a man one rarely sees 1856. 3. *F. Letter* is a letter with a broad stem 1841.

II. 1. Containing much fat; greasy, oily, unctuous OE. Of wood, etc.: Resinous (*U.S.*) 1831. Of coal: Bituminous 1883. 2. Of mould, clay, etc.: Containing much plastic matter; sticky. Of limestone: Pure. 1502. 3. Of fluids: Charged with solid or extraneous particles ME.

1. Cloid with F. Meate SHAKS. F. Amber DRYDEN. 2. A f. Earth full of Allom MOXON. 3. F. standing water 1587. A f. mist 1659. F. ale SCOTT.

III. 1. Yielding rich returns ME. 2. Well supplied with what is needful or desirable 1563.

1. The broad f. fields of Kent 1851. A f. Lawsuit 1854. F. jobs, livings (*mod.*). 2. In a f. pasture *Ezek.* xxxiv. 14. A f. Cit 1764. Phr. *F. work* (Typog.), work especially paying to the compositor who works by the piece. *F. page*: one having many blanks. *A f. lot* (colloq.): a great deal (often *iron.*).

IV. Like a fat animal; slow-witted, inert, self-complacent 1588.

Make the heart of this people f. *Isa.* vi. 10.

Comb.: **f.-bird,** (*a*) the Pectoral Sandpiper (*U.S.*); (*b*) the Guacharo; **-trained** (sense I. 2 or IV); **-headed** *a.*, having a f. head; dull, stupid; **-lute,** a mixture of pipeclay and linseed oil for filling joints.

Hence **Fa·tly** *adv.* †greasily; largely; clumsily. **Fa·ttish** *a.* somewhat f.. †somewhat greasy.

B. *sb.*² 1. The adj. used *absol.* The fat part of anything ME. b. *transf.* The richest part of anything. Hence, Plenty, superabundance. *Obs.* exc. in *The f. of the land.* 1570. 2. a. The oily concrete substance of which the fat parts of animal bodies are chiefly composed. Often specialized as *beef-*, *mutton-*, etc. *f.* b. *Chem.* Any of a class of organic compounds of which animal fat is the type. 1539. 3. Corpulence, obesity 1726. 4. In various trades, etc., applied to especially paying kinds of work 1700.

4. *Fat* among printers means void spaces GROSE. A piece of 'fat' (that is, a good piece of exclusive news) 1890. Phr. (*All*) *the f. is in the fire*: in early use, the design has irremediably failed; now used when something has been said or done which is sure to provoke an explosion of anger.

Fat (fæt), *v.* [OE. *fǽttian*, f. *fǽtt* FAT *a.*] †1. *trans.* As tr. Heb. *dishshēn*: To anoint (the head); to load (an altar) with fat -1698. 2. *intr.* To become fat. Also *fig.* ME. 3. *trans.* To make fat, fatten; to fertilize (the soil) ME.

2. The hogs which have been fatting 1704. 3. Numbers of black cattle are fatted here GRAY. This ..fatted the sheep 1829. Which with the ashes left after the burning fatteth the ground GAGE.

Fatal (fēⁱ·tăl), *a.* ME. [ad. L. *fatalis*, f. *fatum* FATE. Cf. F. *fatal.*] †1. Allotted or decreed by fate; destined, fated -1713. †2. Doomed *to* -1668. 3. Of the nature of fate; inevitable, necessary 1605. 4. Concerned or dealing with destiny ME.; †prophetic -1635; †ominous -1658. 5. Fateful ME. 6. Deadly, destructive, ruinous. Const. *to.* 1514. 7. Hence, in a weakened sense: Disastrous, gravely mischievous 1681.

3. Nature is a blind and f. Agent 1663. 4. The Parcæ (or fatall Goddesses) are three 1624. The f. thread of life 1704. 5. The f. spot SCOTT. 6. A f. instrument GOLDSM., stroke COWPER, disease 1803, error H. SPENCER, accident (*mod.*). 7. Wars had also a f. influence on population 1794. Hence **Fa·tally** *adv.*

Fatalism (fēⁱ·tăliz'm). 1678. [f. -ISM. Cf. F. *fatalisme.*] 1. The doctrine that all things are determined or arbitrarily decreed by fate. (In early use not distinguished from 'necessitarianism'.) 2. Submission to the decree of fate 1734.

Fatalist (fēⁱ·tălist). 1650. [f. as prec. + -IST. Cf. F. *fataliste.*] 1. One who holds the doctrine of fatalism. 2. One whose conduct is regulated by fatalism 1734. 3. *attrib.* or *adj.* = next 1843.

Fatalistic (fēⁱtăli·stik), *a.* 1832. [f. prec. + -IC.] Of, pertaining to, or of the nature of fatalism.

Fatality (fătæ·lĭti). 1490. [ad. F. *fatalité*, ad. late L. *fatalitatem*, f. *fatalis*; see -ITY.] 1. The condition of being predetermined by or subject to fate or destiny; the agency of fate or necessity; also *fig.* 1631. b. That which a person or thing is fated to 1589. 2. Predestined liability to disaster 1654. 3. Fatalness; a fatal influence 1490. 4. A calamity 1648; a disaster resulting in death 1840.

1. The blind impulses of F. and Fortune BENTLEY. 2. The f. attending an accursed house SYMONDS. 3. The insidious f. of hot countries KANE. 4. Fatalities to which the human race is liable 1815.

Fatalness (fēⁱ·tălnės). 1651. [f. as prec. + -NESS.] 1. 'Invincible necessity' (J. and mod. Dicts.). 2. Disastrous nature; deadly quality.

‖**Fata Morgana** (fā·tă mǫɹgā·nă). 1818. [It. *fata* a fairy; *Morgana*, sister of the legendary Arthur, app. located in Calabria by Norman settlers.] A kind of mirage most frequently seen in the Strait of Messina, attributed formerly to fairy agency. Also *fig.*

attrib. Cloud mountains, and fatamorgana cities CARLYLE.

Fate (fēⁱt), *sb.* ME. [ad. L. *fatum* lit. 'that which has been spoken', pa. pple. neut. of *fari*. The L. sense was, primarily, a sentence of the gods (= Gr. θέσφατον); subseq., 'lot' or 'portion' (= Gr. μοῖρα), and hence as in sense 1. See also FAY.] 1. The principle, power, or agency by which events are unalterably predetermined from eternity. Often *personified.* 2. *Mythol.* a. The goddess of Fate; in Homer Μοῖρα. b. *pl.* In Gr. and Rom. mythol., the three goddesses, Clotho, Lachesis, and Atropos, supposed to determine the course of human life (Gr. Μοῖραι, L. *Parcæ*, *Fata*) 1590. 3. That which is fated to happen; in *pl.* Predestined events 1667. b. An oracle. MRS. BROWNING. 4. What will become of, or has become of (a person or thing); ultimate condition, destiny 1768. b. Death, destruction, ruin ME. c. An instrument of death or destruction (*poet.*) 1700.

1. F. was something that even the gods often endeavoured..to resist PRIESTLEY. 2. We three Sat muffled like the Fates TENNYSON. 3. What I will is F. So spake th' Almightie MILT. He deserves a better f. 1668. 4. Anxiety for the f. of the Edystone SMEATON. The f. of a minister who..had thwarted the popular will FROUDE. Phr. *To decide, fix, seal one's f.* c. Hissing fly the feather'd fates POPE.

Fated (fēⁱ·tėd), *ppl. a.* 1601. [f. prec. sb.] 1. Appointed by fate 1715. 2. Doomed to destruction 1817. 3. Fateful. SHAKS. 4. Guided or driven on by fate 1801. ¶5. Of armour: Made proof by spells. DRYDEN.

2. Cavalry.. were fast approaching the f. city MACAULAY.

Fateful (fēⁱ·tfŭl), *a.* 1715. [f. as prec. + -FUL.] 1. Prophetic of destiny. 2. Fraught with destiny; decisive 1800. 3. Controlled as if by fate 1876. 4. = FATAL 6. 1764. 5. Of eventful history 1886.

1. That f. Hebrew Prophecy CARLYLE. 2. Each minute seemed f. to her 1861. 4. The soldier's f. steel 1808. Hence **Fa·teful-ly** *adv.*, **-ness.**

Fat-faced, *a.* 1632. [f. FAT *a.* + FACE.] Having a fat face; *spec.* in *Printing*, as *fat-faced Egyptian.*

Fat-head. 1842. [f. FAT *a.* + HEAD.] 1. A stupid dolt. 2. a. A labroid fish, *Semicossyphus* or *Pimelometopon pulcher*. b. The Black-headed Minnow, *Pimephales promelas.*

Fat-hen (fæ·t,hen). 1795. A name for certain plants of the Goosefoot tribe, *Chenopodium Bonus-Henricus* and *Atriplex patula.*

Father (fā·ðəɹ), *sb.* [Com. Teut. and Aryan: OE. *fæder* :—OTeut. *fader*, ?*fadēr* :—OAryan *pəte·r*, whence Skr. *pitṛ*, Gr. πατήρ, L. *pater*, etc.] 1. One who has begotten a child, a male parent, the nearest male ancestor. Also *fig.* and *transf.* 2. A male ancestor more remote than a parent, *esp.* the founder of a race or family, a progenitor. In *pl.* ancestors. Also loosely for 'a man of old', 'a patriarch'. OE. 3. One who institutes, originates, calls into being; a designer, framer, originator. Also, the first or a distinguished example of (an immaterial thing). ME. 4. One who performs the offices of a father by protecting care, etc.; one to whom filial reverence and obedience are due OE. 5. a. Applied to God, expressing His relation to Jesus, to mankind in general, or to Christians (as His children by regeneration or adoption) OE. b. Theol. *The F.*: the First Person of the Trinity OE. 6. *Eccles.* a. A confessor or spiritual director ME. b. A priest; a superior of a monastic house 1571. c. Applied to bishops 1508. d. *The Holy F.*: the Pope ME. e. Prefixed to the name of a priest. Also abbrev. (chiefly in R.C. use) F., Fr. 1529. 7. A respectful title given to an old man; also in personifications, as *F. Christmas, F. Thames, F. Time* (cf. TIME *sb.* III. 2) 1559. 8. The oldest member of a society, etc. 1705; the leading individual of a number 1600. 9. *pl.* The leading men or elders of a city or an assembly 1590.

1. His Fathers own Son 1670. *fig.* Thy wish was F. (Harry) to that thought 2 *Hen. IV*, IV. v. 93. The child is f. of the man WORDSW. 2. One man alone, the f. of us all, Drew not his life from woman COWPER. Phr. *To be gathered to* or *sleep with one's fathers.* 3. Abraham the f. of fayth EDEN. The F. of Lies himself (cf. *John* viii. 44) 1826. Plato as the f. of Idealism JOWETT. Phr. *F. of Lights*, etc.: God. *The Fathers* (*of the Church*): the early Christian writers. *The Fathers* (U.S.): the framers of the

constitution. 4. A. F. of the Common-weale 1 *Hen. VI*, III. i. 98. I will be a f. to thee MASSINGER. 6. a. Penance, f., will I none SCOTT. b. A F. of a Convent ADDISON. 7. In vain on f. Thames she calls for aid POPE. 8. The F. of the City HEARNE. The F. of Waters JOHNSON. 9. The fathers of the council GIBBON.

Comb.: **f.-dust** = POLLEN; **-general**, the chief of the Society of Jesus; **†-queller**, a parricide.

Father (fā·ðəɹ), *v.* ME. [f. prec. sb.] 1. *trans.* To be or become the father of; to beget. Also *fig.* 1483. 2. To appear or acknowledge oneself as the father (or, hence, as the author) of; to adopt, take the responsibility of ME. 3. To act as a father to, look after 1577. 4. To provide with a father; to fix the paternity of *on* or *upon*. Also *fig.* 1542.

1. Cowards f. Cowards, & Base things Syre Bace SHAKS. *fig.* Shall Error .. still f. Truth TENNYSON. 2. Men of wit, Who often father'd what he writ SWIFT. 4. The Lady fathers her selfe SHAKS. *fig.* This saiying ..is fathered on Socrates UDALL.

Phr. *To f.* (a thing) *upon* (something else): to trace to (something) as a source or origin.

Fatherhood (fā·ðəɹ,hud); also **†-head.** ME. [f. FATHER *sb.* + -HOOD, -HEAD.] 1. The relation of a father to a child; paternity. Also *fig.* †2. Authority of or as of a father -1690. †3. The personality of a father, as a form of address -1682.

Father-in-law (fā·ðərinlǭ). ME. [App. *in law* = in Canon law.] 1. The father of one's husband or wife. 2. = STEPFATHER. (A misuse.) 1552. 3. as *vb.* FIELDING.

1. Gerard..called to hym his father in law, his wyfes f. LD. BERNERS.

†Fa·therkin. [OE. *fæder cyn*, f. *fæder* genitive + *cyn* KIN.] Descent by the father's side -1556.

Fatherland (fā·ðəɹlænd). 1623. [f. FATHER *sb.* + LAND.] 1. The land of one's birth. 2. The land of one's fathers; mother-country 1822.

1. *The F.*: now usually = Germany.

Fa·ther-la·sher. 1674. The name of two species of sea-fish, *Cottus bubalis* and *scorpius*.

Fatherless (fā·ðəɹlės), *a.* ME. [See -LESS.] 1. Having no father. 2. Of a book, etc.: Without a known author 1611.

1. A father of the f. *Ps.* lxviii. 5. 2. F. essays 1803.

Fatherlike (fā·ðəɹləik). ME. [See -LIKE.] A. *adj.* 1. †Like one's father -1614. 2. Like a father; fatherly 1570. B. *adv.* In a fatherly manner, as a father 1604.

Father-long-legs. 1796. = **Daddy-long-legs.**

Fatherly (fā·ðəɹli), *a.* [OE. *fæderlic*, f. *fæder* + *-lic*; see -LY¹.] †1. Paternal -1633; ancestral; also, venerable -1634. 2. Resembling a father 1577. 3. Such as is proper in or from a father ME.

3. With my fatherlie blessing JAS. I. Hence **Fa·therliness.** So **Fa·therly** *adv.* in a f. manner

Fathership (fā·ðəɹʃip). 1583. [See -SHIP.] The position of a father; paternity, fatherhood.

Fathom (fæ·ðəm), *sb.* [OE. *fæðm* str. masc. (also fem.) :—OTeut. **faþmoz*, f. Teut. root *feþ-*, *faþ-* :—pre-Teut. *pet-*, *pot-*, whence also Gr. πετάννυναι to spread out.] †1. In *pl.* The embracing arms (OE. only); †*fig.* grasp, power -1622. 2. †a. A stretching of the arms in a straight line to their full length -1785. b. *fig.* Breadth of comprehension, grasp; ability (*arch.*) 1604. 3. A measure of length: †a. A CUBIT -ME.; b. The length of the outstretched arms; hence, 6 feet; now chiefly used in taking soundings OE. 4. In *Mining*, 6 feet square by the whole thickness of the vein 1778. 5. A quantity of wood 6 ft. square in section 1577.

2. b. Another of his Fadome, they haue none *Oth.* I. i 153. 3. b. Full fadom fiue thy Father lies SHAKS.

Fathom (fæ·ðəm), *v.* [OE. *fæðmian*, f. (ult.) as prec.] 1. *trans.* To encircle (and, hence, to measure) with extended arms. Also *transf.* and *fig.* ME. 2. To measure with a fathom-line; to sound; also *fig.* 1613. b. To get to the bottom of, thoroughly understand 1625. 3. *intr.* To take soundings (*lit.* and *fig.*) 1607.

1. Stocks of Vines .. as big in bulk as two men can f. HEYLYN. *fig.* Cæsar..in his arms Fathoming the earth MASSINGER. 2. *fig.* O God, who can fadome thy eternity 1642. b. [His] character I am..unable to f. MAD. D'ARBLAY.

Hence **Fa·thomable** *a.* **Fa·thomer,** one who fathoms; an instrument for taking soundings.

Fathomless (fæ·ðəmlės), *a.* 1606. [f. prec. + -LESS.] 1. That cannot be measured or fathomed. 2. *fig.* That cannot be penetrated; incomprehensible 1645.

1. F. and unquiet deeps MILT. 2. The f. mystery of the universe 1883. Hence **Fa·thomlessly** *adv.*

Fatidic, -al (feiti·dik, -ăl), *a.* 1607. [f. L. *fatidicus*, f. *fati-* comb. f. *fatum* FATE + *dic-* wk. root of *dicere* (+ -AL).] Of or concerned with predicting fates; gifted with the power of prophecy; prophetic.

The Ancients write of some Trees, that they are Fatidical HOWELL. Hence **Fati·dically** *adv.*

Fa·tigable, Fati·guable, *a.* 1608. [a. OF. *fatigable*, ad. L. *fatigabilis*, f. *fatigare.*] Capable of being fatigued; easily tired. Hence **Fa·tigableness, Fati·guableness.**

†Fa·tigate, *pa. pple.* 1471. [ad. L. *fatigatus.*] Fatigued -1607.

His doubled spirit Requickened what in flesh was f. *Cor.* II. ii. 121.

†Fa·tigate, *v.* 1535. [f. L. *fatigat-*, *fatigare.*] To FATIGUE -1749. Hence **Fatiga·tion,** the action of fatiguing; weariness.

Fatigue (fătī·g), *sb.* 1669. [a. F., f. *fatiguer*; see next.] 1. Weariness resulting from bodily or mental exertion 1719. 2. *transf.* The condition of weakness in metals caused by repeated blows or continued strain 1854. 3. That which causes weariness; labour, toil 1669. 4. The extra-professional duties of a soldier 1776. b. Short for *f.-party* 1876.

1. Extremities of famine and f. PRESCOTT. 3. The fatigues of the election are over BURKE.

Comb.: **f.-call**, the call to f.-duty; **-dress**, the dress worn on f.-duty; **-duty** = FATIGUE *sb.* 4; **-party**, a party of soldiers on f.-duty.

Hence **Fati·gueless** *a.* **Fati·guesome** *a.* wearisome.

Fatigue (fătī·g), *v.* 1693. [ad. F. *fatiguer*, ad. L. *fatigare*, f. stem **fati-* (in *ad-fatim* enough), prob. meaning 'yawning'; cf. FATISCENT.] 1. *trans.* 'To tire, weary; to harass with toil; to exhaust with labour' (J.). 2. To weaken by straining 1794.

Fatiloquent (feiti·lǒkwĕnt), *a.* 1656. [f. L. *fati-* comb. f. *fatum* FATE + *loquentem*; after L. *fatiloquus.*] Declaring fate; prophetic. So **†Fati·loquency** (*rare*). **†Fati·loquist**, a fortune-teller.

Fatiscent (făti·sĕnt), *a.* 1807. [ad. L. *fatiscentem*, *fatiscere*, f. *fati-* yawning (see FATIGUE *v.*).] Having chinks or clefts; cracked. Hence **Fati·scence** (*Geol.*), the condition of being f.

Fatling (fæ·tliŋ), *sb.* 1526. [f. FAT *v.* + -LING; cf. *nurseling*.] A calf, lamb, or other young animal fatted for slaughter.

Fatling (fæ·tliŋ), *a.* [dim. of FAT *a.*, after prec.] Small and fat. TENNYSON.

Fatness (fæ·tnės). OE. [f. as prec. + -NESS.] 1. The quality or state of being fat; fullness of flesh, corpulence. †Of a tree: Oiliness, juiciness. Of soil: Unctuous nature; hence fertility. †2. That which makes fertile -1738. †3. *concr.* Fat -1697. †4. The richest or best part of anything -1665.

1. God giue thee the dew of heauen, and the fatnesse of the earth *Gen.* xxvii. 28. 2. Thy paths drop fatnesse *Ps.* lxv. 11. 4. Cities, which..devoured the f. of the whole Kingdom 1644.

Fatted (fæ·tėd), *ppl. a. arch.* 1552. [pa. pple. of FAT *v.*] Made or grown fat, fattened. Now only in *to kill the f. calf*, after Luke xv.

Fatten (fæ·t'n), *v.* 1552. [f. FAT *a.* + -EN⁵.] 1. *trans.* To make fat or plump; usually, to make fit to kill. Also *transf.* and *fig.* 2. *intr.* To become fat; also *fig.* 1638. 3. *trans.* To enrich (the soil); to fertilize. Also *transf.* and *fig.* 1563.

1. To f. turkeys .. give them mashed potatoes [etc.] SOYER. 2. *fig.* Persons, who f. on the calamities of their country HUME. 3. The river Nilus, whose overflowings doe marveylously f. the earth FULKE. Hence **Fa·ttener,** one who or that which fattens.

Fattrels (fæ·trělz), *sb. pl. Sc.* [ad. F. *fatraille* trash.] Ribbon-ends. BURNS.

Fatty (fæ·ti), *a.* ME. [f. FAT + -Y¹.] 1. Resembling, or of the nature of, fat, oleaginous, greasy. 2. Consisting of or containing fat 1615. 3. Marked by morbid deposition of fat 1866.

1. F. ink 1879. 2. A *F. tumour* is a mass of soft yellow fat, generally enclosed in a .. thin fibrous capsule *Syd. Soc. Lex.* 3. *F. degeneration*, that condition in which a part or the whole of any tissue or organ is replaced by fat *Syd. Soc. Lex.* *F. heart* or *kidney* = f. degeneration of the heart or kidney.

Phrases. *F. oil* = fixed oil. *F. acids*, a group of acids extracted from fats and fixed oils in saponification. *F. acid series* = *acetic series of acids*.

Hence **Fa·ttily** *adv.*, only in *fattily-degenerated.* **Fa·ttiness,** f. condition or quality.

†Fa·tuate, *ppl. a.* [ad. L. *fatuatus*, *fatuari*, f. *fatuus.*] Rendered fatuous. B. JONS.

Fatuitous (fătiū·itəs), *a.* 1734. [f. L. *fatuitas* + -OUS.] Characterized by fatuity.

Fatuity (fătiū·iti). 1538. [ad. F. *fatuité*, ad. L. *fatuitatem*, f. *fatuus.*] 1. Folly. Now chiefly: Idiotic folly; mental blindness caused by infatuation. Also, that which is fatuous. 2. Idiocy, dementia. Now *rare.* 1621.

1. O strange f. of youth THACKERAY. var. **Fa·tuism** (in sense 2).

Fatuous (fæ·tiŭəs), *a.* 1608. [f. L. *fatuus* + -OUS.] 1. Foolish, vacantly silly, stupid, besotted 1633. 2. That is imbecile; idiotic. Now *rare* exc. in *Sc. Law.* 1773. †3. In L. sense: Insipid, vapid -1624.

1. F. commonplaces MORLEY, disregard for intellect 1878. Phr. *F. fire*: = IGNIS FATUUS. So *f. light*, *vapour*, etc. Hence **Fa·tuous-ly** *adv.*, **-ness.**

Fat-witted, *a.* 1596. [f. FAT *a.* + WIT.] Dull, slow, thick-headed.

Faubourg (fōbur). [late ME. *faubourg*, *fabo(u)r*, a. F. *faubourg*. Now usu. semi-anglicized as fōu·būᵊr, -būᵊɹg.] A portion of a town or city lying outside the gates; a suburb. (In Paris still applied to parts of the city now included within the walls.)

Faucal (fǭ·kăl). 1864. [f. next + -AL.]

A. *adj.* Of or pertaining to the fauces or throat. Applied chiefly to certain deep guttural sounds, *esp.* in the Semitic languages.

B. *sb.* A faucal sound 1883.

‖**Fauces** (fǭ·sīz), *sb. pl.* 1541. [L.] 1. *Anat.* The cavity at the back of the mouth, from which the larynx and the pharynx open out. 2. *Bot.* The throat of a calyx, corolla, etc. 1840. 3. *Conch.* That portion of the chamber of a shell which can be seen from the aperture.

Hence **Fau·cial** *a.* of, pertaining to, or proceeding from, the f.

Faucet (fǭ·sėt), *sb.*¹ ME. [a. F. *fausset* (in sense 1); etym. unkn.] †1. A peg or spigot to stop the vent-hole in a cask or in a tap; a vent-peg -1741. 2. A tap for drawing liquor from a barrel, etc. Now *dial.* and *U.S.* ME. †b. A tapster. B. JONS. 3. *U.S.* 'The enlarged end of a pipe to receive the spigot end of the next section' (Knight).

†Fau·cet, Fau·set, *sb.*² 1684. [Corrupt f. FACET.] = FACET. Also used of a faceted stone. -1712.

Faucitis (fǭsəi·tis). 1875. [f. FAUCES + -ITIS.] *Path.* Inflammation of the fauces.

†Fau·fel(l. 1594. [a. Arab.] = ARECA -1693.

Faugh (fǭ). *interj.* 1542. An exclam. of abhorrence or disgust.

Fough, he smells all lamp-oyle B. JONS.

Fauld, Sc. and dial. f. FOLD.

Fauld (fǭld). 1874. [? = prec.] *Min.* 'The tymp-arch or working arch of a furnace' (Knight).

Fault (fǭlt, fǫlt), *sb.* [ME. *faut(e)*, a. OF. *faute* (also *faut*) :—pop. L. **fallita* a failing, coming short, f. **fallitus*, pop. L. pa. pple. of *fallere*; see FAIL. Still pronounced dial. (fǭt).] †1. Deficiency, want *of* (something specified). Also *absol.* -1591. †2. Default, failing, neglect -1587. 3. A defect, imperfection. (In *Morals*, something less serious than a *vice.*) ME. †4. A flaw, crack; *Mil.* a gap in the ranks -1698. 5. Something wrongly done: a. A misdeed, transgression, offence ME.; b. A slip, error, mistake 1523. 6. *spec.* in *Tennis* and *Rackets.* A stroke which fails to make the ball fall within the prescribed limits 1599. 7. Responsibility for an untoward occurrence; also, the defect in things, conditions, etc., to which such an occurrence is attributable ME. 8. *Hunting.* Loss of scent; a check caused by this 1592. b. *fig.* *At f.*: at a loss 1833. 9. *Geol.*, etc. A break in continuity of the strata or vein. In coal-seams, coal rendered worthless by its condition in the seams, as *slate-f.*, *dirt-f.*, etc. 1881. 10. *Telegr.* An imperfect insulation; a leakage 1863.

2. Phr. *Without f.* (= F. *sans faute*): without fail. 3. Great men too often have greater faults than little men can find room for LANDOR. An essential f. of the Pythagorean theory 1884. Phr. *To a f.* (qualifying an adj.): so much so that it becomes a f.; excessively. *With all faults* (occas. abbrev. 'A.F.'): with all defects, *i.e.* the seller will not make them good. 4. *John* IV. ii. 33. 5. a. The f. of telling a lie JOWETT. b. A f. in the deduction WATTS. 7. Lay the f. on me DE FOE. Phr. *To be in f.*: to be to blame. Voiceless through the f. of birth TENNYSON. 8. Bad hounds never *hit off a f.* (= recover a lost scent) themselves FIELDING. The wisest antiquarians were at f. 1886.

Phrases. *To find (a) f.*: to discover or perceive a f. (senses 3–5) *in* a person or thing. Hence, idiomatically, *To find f.* (*with*, †*at*): to express dissatisfaction (with), censure.

Comb.: f.-finder *sb.*; **f.-reader**, one who can trace the correspondence of strata interrupted by a f.; **-rock, -stuff**, the fragmentary rock, formed into a belt or wall-like mass, which marks the line of fracture; **-slip**, the smooth surface of the fractured rocks in some types of faults.

Fault (fǭlt, fǫlt), *v.* ME. [f. prec. sb.; cf. OF. *fauter.*] †1. *intr.* To be wanting or absent –1525. †2. To be lacking *in* –1606. †3. *trans.* To stand in need of –1475. †4. *intr.* To come short of a standard; to make default, fail –1677. 5. *intr.* To do or go wrong; hence, sometimes, to sin. *Obs.* exc. *arch.* ME. †6. To make a mistake, err, blunder –1765. 7. *trans.* To find fault with, to blame or censure (*rare*) 1559; to impugn or mark as faulty (*rare*) 1585. 8. *Hunting.* To put (a hound) at fault; to throw off the scent (*rare*) 1873. 9. *Geol.*, etc. To cause a fault in, dislocate (chiefly *pass.*) 1849.

2. He faulted in common civilitie HOLLAND. 5. Had I died for thee I had faulted more BROWNING. 9. Phr. *To f. down* or *through*: to cause a fault by driving (part of a stratum) *through* (another).

†**Fau·lter.** 1535. [f. prec.] One who commits a fault –1840.

Faultful (fǭ·lt-, fǫ·ltful), *a.* 1591. [f. FAULT *sb.* + -FUL.] Faulty, culpable. Hence **Fau·ltfully** *adv.*

Faulting (fǭ·lt-, fǫ·ltiŋ), *vbl. sb.* 1450. [f. FAULT *v.*] †1. The action of FAULT *v.* –1679. 2. *Geol.* Dislocation of strata; an instance of this 1849.

Faultless (fǭ·lt-, fǫ·ltlės), *a.* ME. [f. FAULT *sb.* + -LESS.] 1. Without defect. 2. That has committed no fault 1513; *transf.* not caused by any fault –1752.

1. A f. piece POPE. The f. model of a ruler FREEMAN. 2. For our sinnes he faultlesse suffered paine FAIRFAX. b. *F. pardon*, a pardon for an alleged offence never committed. Hence **Fau·ltless-ly** *adv.*, **-ness.**

Faulty (fǭ·lti, fǫ·lti), *a.* ME. [f. as prec. + -Y[1].] 1. Containing faults; defective, imperfect, unsound. 2. Of persons, etc.: Having imperfections; apt to come short of duty 1574. †3. That has committed a fault; also, that is in fault or to blame –1614. 4. Of the nature of a fault; censurable 1548.

1. He [the colt] came of a f. Mare DRYDEN. A f. digestion BERKELEY. 2. F. morals RICHARDSON. 4. A f. habit of mind GOULBURN.

Hence **Fau·ltily** *adv.*, **Fau·ltiness.**

Faun (fǭn). ME. [ad. L. *Faunus*, a god or demigod worshipped by shepherds and farmers = Gr. Pan; also in pl. *fauni* (Chaucer's *fauny*).] *Myth.* One of a class of rural deities; represented as men with horns and the tail of a goat, and, later, with goats' legs, and lustful, like the Satyrs.

The reeling F., the sensual feast TENNYSON.

Fauna (fǭ·nă). Pl. **-æ**; also **-as.** 1771. [mod.L.; an application of the name of *Fauna*, sister of *Faunus* (see prec.). Cf. *Flora.*] 1. A collective name for the animals or animal life of any particular region or epoch. 2. A treatise upon these animals 1885.

1. The f. of tropical America 1846. The carboniferous f. 1851. Hence **Fau·nal** *a.* of or pertaining to the f. of a country. **Fau·nist**, one who studies or treats of the f. of a district. **Fauni·stic, -al**, *a.* of or pertaining to a faunist; hence, relating to a f. **Fauno·logy**, that branch of zoology which treats of the geographical distribution of animals; hence, **Faunolo·gical** *a.*

Faurd, Sc. pronunc. of *favoured*, as in *well-f.*

Fause, Sc. and dial. f. FALSE *a.*

Fau·se-house. *Sc.* [f. prec. + HOUSE.] A hollow made in a corn-stack, with an opening on the most windy side, for the purpose of drying the corn. BURNS.

Fau·sen. 1547. A kind of eel; variously applied. Now *dial.*

Faussebraie, -braye (fosˌbrę̄). 1489. [a. F., f. *fausse* fem. of *faux* + *braie*; see BRAYE.] *Fortif.* An artificial mound or wall thrown up in front of the main rampart. In early use, a covered way.

Fauterer (fǭ·tərəɹ). 1662. [f. *fauter* for FAUTOR.] = FAUTOR.

‖**Fauteuil** (fotöy). 1744. [a. F., f. OF. *faudeteuil*, *faldestoel*; see FALDSTOOL.] An arm-chair. b. pop. (fōu·til). A seat in a theatre, omnibus, etc. designed to resemble an arm-chair 1901.

Fautor (fǭ·tǒɹ, -əɹ). ME. [ad. F. *fauteur*, ad. L. *fautor*, f. *favere* to favour.] 1. A partisan, abettor. †2. A patron –1691.

1. Apologists and fautors of tyranny AUSTIN. So †**Fau·tress**, †**Fau·trix**, a female f.

‖**Fauvette** (fove·t). 1797. [F., f. *fauve* fallow.] A warbler, *esp.* the garden warbler.

‖**Faux** (fǫks). *rare.* 1828. [Assumed nom. sing. to L. *fauces.*] = FAUCES.

‖**Faux pas** (foˌpā). 1676. [F.] A false step (*fig.*); a slip, a trip; *esp.* a woman's lapse from virtue.

†**Fava·ginous**, *a.* 1658. [f. L. *favus* honeycomb.] Resembling a honeycomb –1686.

†**Fa·vel.** ME. [a. OF. *fauvel*, f. *fauve* fallow, a. Teut. **falwo-*; see FALLOW *a.*[1]]

A. *adj.* Of a horse: = FALLOW *a.*[1] 1489.

B. *sb.* 1. As the proper name of a horse. Only ME. 2. The fallow horse proverbial as the type of cunning or duplicity. Only in *To curry F.*: see CURRY *v.* 3. Hence, a personification of duplicity –1576.

‖**Favella** (făve·lă). *Pl.* **-æ.** 1857. [mod.L.; prob. an incorrect dim. of L. *faba* bean, infl. by F. *fève.*] *Bot.* See quot.

F., a form of the conceptacular fruit of florideous Algæ in which the spores are collected into spherical masses which lie on the outer surface of the frond *Syd. Soc. Lex.* Hence **Favelli·dium**, a compound f.

Faveolate (făvī·olėⁱt), *a.* 1866. [f. mod.L. *faveolus*, dim. of *favus* + -ATE[3].] Honeycombed, cellular.

Faverel (fæ·vĕrĕl). 1597. [var. of next.] a. An onion. b. Whitlow-grass 1770. c. *Veronica Anagallis* 1884.

†**Faverole.** ME. [a. OF. *faverolle* (in Normandy the broad bean).] A name of various plants; esp. Water Dragons.

†**Faviform** (fēⁱ·vifǫɹm), *a.* 1753. [f. L. *favus* + -FORM.] Formed like a honeycomb; *spec.* in *Surg.* of certain ulcers.

Favillous (făvi·ləs), *a.* [f. L. *favilla* hot ashes + -OUS.] Consisting of or resembling ashes. SIR T. BROWNE.

Favonian (făvōu·niăn), *a.* 1656. [ad. L. *favonianus*, f. *Favonius* the west wind.] Of or pertaining to the west wind; hence, gentle, propitious.

Favosites (fævosəi·tīz). Also in Eng. form **fa·vosite.** 1832. [mod.L., f. (ult.) L. *favus.*] *Geol.* A genus of fossil zoophytes, resembling a honeycomb.

Favour, favor (fēⁱ·vəɹ), *sb.* [ME. *favor*, *-our*, a. OF.:—L. *favorem*, f. *favere*, to befriend. In U.S. *favor* is usual; in Eng. *favour.*] 1. Propitious or friendly regard, goodwill, *esp.* on the part of a superior or a multitude; approving disposition towards a thing 1827. †b. The object of favour –1667. 2. Exceptional kindness; an instance of this ME. b. *Comm.*, etc. Communication, letter 1645. 3. Kind indulgence: a. Leave, permission, pardon 1580; †b. 'Lenity, mitigation of punishment' (J.); a lenient act –1780; †c. An indulgence, privilege –1737. 4. Partiality, bias ME. 5. Aid, support, furtherance ME. 6. (*concr.* of 1.) Something given as a mark of favour; *esp.* a knot of ribbons, a glove, a ribbon, cockade, etc. 1588. 7. That which wins goodwill; attractiveness, comeliness; an attraction, charm. *Obs.* exc. *arch.* ME. 8. Appearance, aspect, look (now *arch.* or *dial.*) 1450; countenance, face (now *arch.*) 1525; †a feature –1655.

1. Is he inconstant, sir, in his fauours *Twel. N.* I. iv. 7. To look with f. on an enterprise 1884. Phr. *To curry f.*: corruption of *to curry Favel*; see CURRY *v.* and FAVEL *sb.* b. Man, His chief delight and f. MILT. *P. L.* III. 664. 2. I have a friend..who will.. do me so much f. SCOTT. I came to ask a f. of you TENNYSON. b. Your favor of June the 14th T. JEFFERSON. 3. a. Phr. *By*, *with* (your, etc.) *f. Under f.*, I say it's an Anapæst BENTLEY. 4. Withoute fauour iuge the trouthe LYDG. Phr. *Challenge to the f.* (Law): see CHALLENGE *sb.* 5. Under favor of the night, to surprise the Bellerophon 1854. 6. This f. shalt thou wear *L. L. L.* V. ii. 130. A f. of blue, green, and white ribbons 1859. 7. Thine eye desireth fauour and beautie *Ecclus.* xl. 22. 8. In thy Face, one F. from the rest I singled forth DRAYTON.

Phr. **In f. of** (= F. *en faveur de*), used as a prep. with senses: a. On the side of; b. To the advantage of; in *Comm.* so as to be payable to; c. Out of a preference for.

Hence †**Fa·vourize** *v.* = next. †**Fa·vourless** *a.* without bias or beauty. †**Fa·vourous** *a.* obliging, pleasing. †**Fa·voursome** *a.* acceptable.

Favour, favor (fēⁱ·vəɹ), *v.* ME. [a. OF. *favorer*, med. L. *favorare*, f. *favorem*; see prec.] 1. *trans.* To regard with favour or kindness; to approve. 2. To countenance, encourage; to oblige (a person) *with* something ME. 3. To treat with partiality; also, to side with ME.; in *Comm.* to be at prices favourable to (*mod.*). 4. To aid, support; to point in the direction of 1526. 5. To prove advantageous to; to facilitate 1634. 6. To deal gently with; to ease, save, spare. Now *colloq.* and *dial.* 1526. 7. To resemble in features. Now *colloq.* 1609.

1. Men fauour Wonders BACON. 2. To f. a deceit BUTLER. 3. Oats favoured buyers (*mod.*). 4. If Providence should..f. the allied arms BURKE. To f. a Suspicion STEELE. 5. The Wind favours them 1699. 6. Walking in the dark, in the garden, to f. my eyes PEPYS. 7. He favours you in the face 1690.

Hence **Fa·vourer**, one who favours. †**Fa·vouress** (*rare*). **Fa·vouringly** *adv.*

Favourable, favorable (fēⁱ·vŏrăb'l), *a.* ME. [ad. F. *favorable*, ad. L. *favorabilis*; see FAVOUR and -ABLE.] †1. Winning favour; hence, pleasing, comely –1590. 2. Well-disposed, propitious ME.; gracious (now *arch.*) 1502. †3. Partial –1460. 4. Approving, commendatory 1655; †palliative –1772. 5. Of an answer, etc.: That concedes what is desired. Of appearances: Promising. 1734. 6. Facilitating one's purpose or wishes 1460.

2. Bee fauourable to thy people 1548. 4. Giving a f. account of the place DE FOE. F. circumstances.. may justify a doubt [etc.] JUNIUS. 5. A f. oracle GIBBON, aspect SCOTT. 6. A f. breeze 1774.

Hence **Fa·vourableness. Fa·vourably, fa·vorably** *adv.*

Favoured (fēⁱ·vəɹd), *ppl. a.*[1] 1725. [f. FAVOUR *v.*] In senses of the vb.

Most f. nation: that to which the greatest privileges are granted by the terms of a treaty 1758; also *attrib.*

Favoured (fēⁱ·vəɹd), *ppl. a.*[2] [f. FAVOUR *sb.*] 1. Having an appearance or features of a specified kind; as, *evil-*, *hard-*, *ill-*, *well-*, etc. *f.* 2. Provided with rosettes, or the like. Only in *comb.* 1850. Hence **Fa·voured-ly** *adv.*, **-ness.**

Favourite, favorite. 1583. [a. OF. *favorit*, var. of *favori*, pa. pple. of *favorir* to favour.]

A. *sb.* 1. A person or thing regarded with peculiar favour, one preferred above others 1583; in *Racing*, etc. the competitor or competing animal 'fancied', as being most likely to win 1813. 2. One who stands unduly high in the favour of a prince, etc. 1599. 3. A curl or lock of hair hanging loose upon the temple: worn in the 17th and 18th centuries. [Cf. F. *favoris* whiskers.] 1690. †4. = FAVOURER –1591.

1. This new Favorite Of Heav'n, this Man of Clay MILT. *P. L.* IX. 175. 2. Like fauourites, Made proud by Princes *Much Ado* III. i. 9.

B. *adj.* Regarded with especial favour, liking, or preference 1711.

[Fortune's] spoiled and favorite child BYRON.

Phr. *Favorite son* (U.S.): a politician admired in his own State, but little regarded beyond it.

Favouritism (fēⁱ·vŏritiz'm). 1763. [f. prec. + -ISM.] 1. A disposition to show, or the practice of showing, undue partiality to an individual or class. 2. The condition of being a favourite; favour 1808.

1. We conduct war upon the principles of f. BURKE.

‖**Favus** (fēⁱ·vɒs). 1706. [L.] *Path.* A contagious disease of the skin, characterized by pustules, so called as resembling a honeycomb. Also *attrib.* Hence Fa·vous *a.* resembling a honeycomb, or this disease.

Fawe(n, -er, obs. ff. FAIN, FAVOUR.

Fawkener(e, obs. f. FALCONER.

Fawn (fǭn), *sb.*[1] ME. [a. OF. *faon*, also *feon* :—med.L. **fetonem*, f. *fœtus* offspring.] †1. A young animal, cub -1603. 2. A young fallow deer, a buck or doe of the first year ME. 3. Short for *f.-colour* 1892.

1. The Fawne [of a seal] at the first is white OWEN. *Comb.* **f.-colour**, a light yellowish brown (hence *f.-coloured* adj.).

†**Fawn,** *sb.*[2] 1590. [f. FAWN *v.*[1]] An act of fawning; a servile cringe, a wheedling courtesy -1744.

Fawn (fǭn), *v.*[1] ME. [app. a var. of FAIN *v.* to rejoice.] 1. *intr.* To show delight or fondness (by wagging the tail, whining, etc.) as a dog does. Often with *on, upon.* 2. To affect a servile fondness ME.

1. He can both fawne like a Spaniell, and bite like a Mastiue DEKKER. A puppy fawns upon its dam 1776. 2. How the knave fawned when I was of service to him LAMB. Hence **Faw·ner,** a toady. **Faw·ning-ly** *adv.*, **-ness.**

†**Fax,** *sb.* [OE. *feax*. Still found in *Fairfax, Halifax.*] The hair of the head -1606. Hence †**Faxed** *a.* having hair, as *f. star*, a comet.

Fay (fēɪ), *sb.*[1] *Obs.* or *arch.* ME. [ad. later OF. *fei* :—earlier *feit, feid*; see FAITH.] = FAITH, in various senses. Used esp. in asseverative phrases and quasi-oaths; as, *By my f.*, etc.

Fay (fēɪ), *sb.*[2] Also formerly in F. form **fée.** ME. [ad. OE. *fae, faie* :—Com. Rom. *fata* fem. sing., f. L. *fata* the Fates.] = FAIRY *sb.* 4.

Fay (fēɪ), *sb.*[3] 1747. [f. FAY *v.*[2]] The clearings from the surface; the dross of metals, the surface soil.

Fay (fēɪ), *v.*[1] [OE. *fēgan* :—OTeut. **fōgjan* to fit, adapt, join, f. **fōg-*, ablaut-form of Teut. root *fag-*.] †1. *trans.* To fit, adapt, or join; to put together; to fix in position -ME. 2. *intr.* Of a coat: To fit. *U.S.* 1866. 3. To suit, do. Now *dial.* ME. 4. *Ship-building.* a. *trans.* To fit closely and exactly *to* 1754. b. *intr.* To fit close 1794.

Fay, feigh (fēɪ), *v.*[2] ME. [a. ON. *fægja* to cleanse, polish :—OTeut. type **fægjan.*] *trans.* To cleanse, polish; to clear away. Now only *dial.*

Fay, obs. var. of FEY *a.*

Fayalite (fēɪ·ăləit). 1844. [f. *Fayal*, one of the Azores; see -ITE.] *Min.* A silicate of iron and other bases.

Fayence, var. of **Faience.**

†**Fayles.** ME. [Said to be connected with FAIL *v.*] An obs. form of Backgammon -1598.

Fayto(u)r: see **Fait-.**

Faze (fēɪz), *v.* 1890. *U.S. trans.* To discompose. Cf. FEEZE *v.*

‖**Fazenda** (faze·ndă). 1825. [Pg.; = Sp. *hacienda.*] An estate or large farm. Also the homestead belonging to it.

Feaberry (fī·bĕri, fē·bĕri). *dial.* 1597. [? for **theve-berry*, f. ME. THEVE :—OE. *þēfe* prickly shrub + BERRY.] A gooseberry. Also *attrib.*

†**Feague,** *v.* ? 1589. [Prob. ad. Ger. *fegen* lit. to polish, furbish, sweep.] 1. *trans.* To beat, whip. Also *fig.* -1691. 2. = FAKE *v.* -1690.

Feal (fīl), *a. arch.* 1568. [a. OF. *feal*, altered f. *feil* :—L. *fidelem*, f. *fides.*] Faithful, constant, loyal.

Fealty (fī·ălti). ME. [ad. OF. *fealte* = Pr. *fealtad* :—L. *fidelitatem*, f. (ult.) *fides* FAITH.] 1. The obligation of fidelity on the part of a feudal tenant or vassal to his lord. 2. The recognition of this obligation by taking an oath upon a book. Also *pl.* ME. 3. *transf.* and *fig.* 1530.

2. Phr. *To do, make, receive, swear,* etc. *f.* 3. We all to him [God] owe f. and service 1530.

Fear (fīəɹ), *sb.* [OE. *fǣr* str. masc., sudden calamity, danger; cf. Ger. *gefahr* danger. Prob. from the base *fǣr-* (see next).] †1. In OE.: A peril. 2. The emotion of pain or uneasiness caused by the sense of impending danger, or by the apprehension of evil. In early use applied to the more violent extremes of the emotion. Often *personified.* ME. b. A state of alarm or dread ME. 3. The state of fearing (something); *esp.* a mingled feeling of dread and reverence towards God (or, formerly, any rightful authority) ME. 4. Solicitude, anxiety for the safety of a person or thing 1490. 5. In objective senses: a. Ground for alarm 1535; †b. Capability of inspiring fear -1654; †c. Something that is, or is to be, feared -1667.

2. Feare and dread shall fall vpon them *Ex.* xv. 16. Needless Fears DE FOE. b. In f. and trembling 1771. 3. Phr. *For f.*, where in mod. use the sense of the sb. is often weakened; thus *for f. that* or *lest* = 'lest'. The feare of the Lord is the beginning of wisedome *Ps.* cxi. 10. 4. Phr. *For, in, f. of one's life.* 5. a. They are afrayed, where no feare is COVERDALE *Ps.* liii[i]. 5. b. *Jul. C.* II. i. 190. c. I wil mocke when your feare cometh *Prov.* i. 26.

Fear (fīəɹ), *v.* [OE. *fǣran* wk. vb., to terrify, f. *fǣr-* (:—pre-Teut. *per-*) prob. an ablaut form of the Aryan root *per* to go through (see FARE *v.*[1]).]

I. 1. *trans.* To inspire with fear; to frighten. Now *arch.* or *vulgar.* †2. To frighten away, deter *from* -1632.

1. Warwicke was a Bugge that fear'd vs all SHAKS. 2. A scar-crow..to feare the birds of prey SHAKS.

II. 1. *intr.* (and *refl.*) To feel fear, be afraid ME. 2. *trans.* To regard with fear, be afraid of 1460; also with *inf.* (*vbl. sb.*, etc.) as object 1603. 3. To regard with reverence and awe ME. 4. To have an uneasy sense of the probability of; to apprehend (opp. to *hope for*) 1597. b. with *subord. clause.* To be afraid *that* (in neg. sentences *but* or *but that* = that.. not) 1526. 5. To be apprehensive about, to fear something happening to. †*trans.* and *intr.* with *for*, †*of.* 1526. †6. To doubt or distrust -1607.

1. Phr. (colloq.) *Never f. I f. me* (arch.). I feared lest I should drop down 1823. 2. Nor Fate I f. DRYDEN. Dorothee..feared to obey 1794. 3. Who..feared nought but God POLLOK. 4. I feared it would be..two hundred Pounds 1726. 5. Let the greedy merchant f. For his ill-gotten gain DRYDEN.

Hence **Feared** *ppl. a.* (esp. in senses II. 2, 4). †**Fea·redness. Fea·rer,** one who fears.

†**Fear-babe.** 1580. [f. FEAR *v.* + BABE.] A thing fit only to scare a baby -1621.

Fear(e, var. of FERE. *Sc.*

Fearful (fīə·ɹful), *a.* ME. [f. FEAR *v.* + -FUL.] 1. Causing fear; dreadful, terrible, awful; often *hyperbolical.* 2. Frightened, timid, apprehensive. Now usually with *of*, or with *lest* or *that.* ME. †b. Anxious, concerned; with *about, of* -1593. 3. Of looks, words, etc.: Indicating fear or terror 1535. †4. Cautious, wary -1791. 5. Full of awe or reverence 1567.

1. Death is a fearefull thing SHAKS. He complained of f. thirst TYNDALL. 2. Chubs..be a very f. fish WALTON. F. to offend POPE. A f. joy KEBLE. 3. Cold fearefull drops stand on my trembling flesh SHAKS. Hence **Fea·rful-ly** *adv.*, **-ness.**

Fearless (fīə·ɹlĕs), *a.* ME. [f. FEAR *sb.* + -LESS.] 1. Without fear. †2. Not feared; free from danger -1745.

1. A man..fearelesse of what's past, present, or to come SHAKS. Hence **Fea·rless-ly** *adv.*, **-ness.**

Fearnought (fīə·ɹnǭt). 1772. [FEAR *v.* (in imper.) + NOUGHT.] 1. A stout, thick woollen cloth, used chiefly for seamen's coats, also as a covering for portholes, the doors of powder magazines, etc. Cf. DREADNOUGHT. 2. A drink to keep up the spirits 1880.

Fearsome (fīə·ɹsŏm), *a.* 1768. [f. FEAR *v.* or *sb.* + -SOME.] 1. Fear-inspiring; dreadful. ¶2. ? *erron.* Timid, apprehensive 1863.

1. War's a f. thing SCOTT. 2. I'm but a silly f. thing 1871. Hence **Fea·rsome-ly** *adv.*, **-ness.**

†**Fea·sance.** 1538. [ad. AF. *fesance, -aunce*, f. *faire* to do.] The execution of a condition, obligation, etc. -1741.

†**Fea·straw.** 1595. [Corruption of *festue* FESCUE.] = FESCUE -1660.

Feasible (fī·zib'l), *a.* 1460. [a. OF. *faisable, -ible*, f. *fais-* impf. stem of *faire* (:—L. *facere*); see -BLE.] 1. Capable of being done, carried out, or dealt with successfully in any way; possible, practicable. 2. Of a proposition, theory, story, etc.: Likely, probable 1656.

1. To an infinite power all things are equally faisable 1647. I know all Lands are not so Fecible as others are BLITHE. 2. The only f. theory..proposed LYELL. Hence **Fea·sibi·lity,** the quality or fact of being f. **Fea·sibly** *adv.*, **Fea·sibleness.**

Feast (fīst), *sb.* ME. [a. OF. *feste* (F. *fête*) :—Com. Rom. *festa* fem. sing., a. L. *festa* festal ceremonies, neut. pl. of *festus* adj., prob. containing the same root as *feria*; see FAIR *sb.*] 1. A religious anniversary appointed to be observed with rejoicing (hence opp. to a *fast*). b. A village festival held annually on the feast of the saint to whom the parish church is dedicated 1559. 2. A sumptuous meal or entertainment for many guests; a banquet, *esp.* one of a more or less public nature ME. 3. An unusually abundant and delicious meal; something delicious to feed upon; a treat. Also *fig.* ME. †4. Rejoicing, festivity -1667.

1. You shall keepe it a f. by an ordinance for euer *Ex.* xii. 14. Phr. *Movable feasts*: those of which the date varies from year to year; opp. to *immovable feasts*, as *Christmas*, etc. 2. The nexte day she made them a great feest at dyner LD. BERNERS. 3. This makes thy morsell a perpetuall F. QUARLES. Enough's a F. POPE. How little of a f. for the senses M. ARNOLD. 4. Ministring Spirits, traind up in F. and Song MILT. *P. L.* vi. 167.

Phrase. *To make f.* (= F. *faire fête*): a. To make merry, rejoice; later, to feast (*arch.*). †b. To make much of (a person).

Comb. **f.-day,** a day on which a f. (senses 1, 2) is held.

Feast (fīst), *v.* [ME. *festen*, ad. OF. *fester* (F. *fêter*), f. *feste* FEAST *sb.*] 1. *intr.* To make or partake of a feast, regale oneself. Also *fig.* ME. 2. *trans.* To provide a feast for, regale. Also *refl.* Also *fig.* ME. 3. To entertain hospitably and sumptuously 1490.

1. There festen they, there dauncen they and synge CHAUCER. *fig.* With my love's picture then my eye doth f. SHAKS. *Sonn.* xlvii. 2. The Lorde Bartholomew..magnificently feasted there the Queene LAMBARDE. *fig.* F. your eares with the Musicke awhile SHAKS. Hence **Fea·ster,** one who provides, or one who partakes of, a feast; a luxurious liver.

Feastful (fī·stful), *a. arch.* ME. [f. prec. + -FUL.] 1. Occupied in or given to feasting; of the nature of feasting; festive. 2. Filled with feasting. LAMB.

1. The Bridegroom and his f. friends MILT.

†**Fea·stly,** *a.* [f. FEAST *sb.* + -LY[1].] Festive, jolly. CHAUCER.

Feat (fīt), *sb.* ME. [a. OF. *fait, fet* (later *faict*) :—L. *factum*; see FACT.] †1. = FACT 1 a -1732. 2. An exceptional act or achievement; *esp.* a deed of valour. Now somewhat *arch.* ME. 3. A surprising trick, a 'tour de force' 1564. †4. A kind, or department, of action -1652. †5. The art or knack of doing anything -1681. †6. Fact, actuality -1500.

2. Wonderfull in feates of warre *Judith* xi. 8. 3. Feats of balancing IMISON. A wonderful f. of architectural skill LADY HERBERT. 4. *The f. of merchandise*: mercantile business. (*The*) *f. of war*: warfare. *Feats of war*: military duties or exercises.

Feat (fīt), *a.* and *adv.* Now *arch.* or *dial.* ME. [a. OF. *fait* made :—L. *factus.*]

A. *adj.* 1. Fitting (*for, to*). 2. Apt; adroit; dexterous 1519. 3. Neat, elegant; hence, neatly attired ME. 4. Affected, finikin 1540.

2. Neuer Master had A Page..So feate *Cymb.* v. v. 88. 3. Looke how well my Garments sit vpon me, Much feater than before *Temp.* II. i. 273. 4. I hold such to be but f. boldness 1647.

B. *adv.* In a feat manner 1455.

†**Feat,** *v.* ME. [f. prec. adj.] 1. *trans.* To equip, make fit -1613. 2. *Falconry.* To wipe (the beak) -1575. 3. ? To constrain to propriety. *Cymb.* I. i. 49.

Feateous, obs. var. of FEATOUS *a.*

Feather (fe·ðəɹ), *sb.* [Com. Teut.: OE. *feðer* str. fem. :—OTeut. **feþrā* :—pre-Teut. **petra* fem., f. root **pet-*, whence Skr. *pat*, Gr. πέτεσθαι to fly.]

I. 1. One of the epidermal appendages of a bird, usually a central shaft or midrib, of a horny nature, in part tubular, for the rest square in section and solid, fringed on either side with a 'vane', *i.e.* a row of thin narrow plates mutually adpressed (the 'barbs'), which form a rounded outline at the end. Often specialized as *contour-, covert-, pin-, quill-*, etc. *f.* 2. *collect.* Plumage; also *transf.* (of plants); and *fig.*: Attire, 'get-up' ME. b. Description of plumage; species (of bird). Often *transf.* 1581. †3. *pl.* Wings -1614. 4. A feathered animal. Also *collect.* Feathered game. 1601

1. She proyneth & setteth her feders in ordre FISHER.

Phr. *To smooth one's rumpled feathers*: to recover one's equanimity. *To mount, show the white f.*: to perceive, show signs of cowardice (a white feather in a game-bird's tail being a mark of inferior breeding). *Fine feathers make fine birds.* **2.** In full clerical f. THACKERAY. Phr. *In fine, good, high*, etc. *f.*: in good health, spirits, etc. **b.** I am not of that F., to shake off My Friend when he must neede me *Timon* I. i. 100. Provb. *Birds of a f. flock together.* **3.** Set feathers to thy heeles *John* IV. ii. 174. **4.** Like the Haggard, checke at euery F. *Twel. N.* III. i. 71.

II. 1. Simply; or *pl.* as a commodity OE. **2.** A portion, or (*sing.* and *pl.*) portions, of a feather attached to the base of an arrow. Also *collect.* 1631. **3.** A plume, *esp.* in *ostrich-f.* 1473. **4.** As a type of an object weighing little, and easily moved; hence, a trifle 1562. **b.** = FEATHER-WEIGHT 1760.

3. Phr. *A f. in the cap, hat*: a mark of honour (*lit.* and *fig.*). *Prince of Wales's feathers*, also *The f.*: the plume of three ostrich feathers, first adopted as a crest by the Black Prince. **4.** I am a F. for each Wind that blows *Wint. T.* II. iii. 154.

III. Something resembling a feather. **1.** A tuft or ridge of hair standing more or less upright: **a.** on human beings 1530; **b.** on horses 1580. **2.** A flaw having a feather-like appearance in a precious stone 1866. **3.** In techn. uses: **a.** A longitudinal rib added to a shaft, etc. to increase its strength 1823. **b.** *Mining*, etc. One of two slightly curved pieces of iron, placed in a hole drilled in a stone, with the concave surfaces towards each other, which are forced apart with an iron punch, and thus break the stone asunder 1865. **c.** A projection on a board, implement, or piece of machinery; *esp.* one intended to fit into some other part 1765.

IV. [f. the vb.] *Rowing.* The action of feathering 1865.

attrib. and *Comb.* **1.** General, as *f.-bolster, -beater, -tasselled, -legged, -nerved, -wise* adv., etc. **2.** Special: **f.-alum**, see ALUM; **-brain**, a person with a light or weak brain, whence **-brained** *a.*; **-cloth**, a mixture of cloth and feathers woven together; **†-driver**, (*a*) = QUILL-DRIVER, (*b*) 'one who cleanses feathers by whisking them about' (J.); **-duster**, a brush made of feathers, for dusting; **-heeled** *a.* = -FOOTED; **-joint**, 'a mode of joining the edges of boards by a fin or f. let into opposite mortises on the edges of the boards' (Knight); **-mail**, the dress of feathers resembling a coat of mail formerly worn by the Indians of Mexico; **†-maker**, one who dresses or deals in feathers; **-man**, one who deals in feathers; **-ore**, the capillary form of native sulphantimonite of lead; **-pated** *a.* = *feather-brained*; **-poke**, (*a*) a bag of feathers, (*b*) a name of the Willow Warbler, the Long-tailed Titmouse, and the Wren, perh. from the appearance of their nests; **-pulp**, the pulp or matrix from which the f. is formed; **-shot copper**, that made by pouring melted copper into cold water; **-spray**, that thrown off, like a pair of wing feathers, by the cut-water of fast steamers; **-spring**, the spring in a gun-lock which causes the *sear* to catch in the notch of the tumbler; **-star**, a star-fish (*Comatula rosacea*); **-top**, nickname of a parrot (also *attrib.* = next); **-topped** *a.*, (of a wig) frizzed at the top; **-tuft**, an edible mushroom, *Clavaria cristata*.

b. In plant-names, as **F.-bow** = FEVERFEW; **-fern**, *Spiræa Japonica*; **-grass**, a perennial feathery grass (*Stipa pennata*); **-top grass**, *Calamagrostis Epigejos*; etc.

Feather (fe·ðəɹ), *v.* [OE. *gefiðrian*, f. the sb.] **†1.** *trans.* To give wings to. *lit.* and *fig.* –1825. **2.** To fit, clothe, or provide with or as with a feather or feathers, as an arrow, a hat, etc. ME. Also *refl.* and *intr.* for *refl.* (now *dial.*) 1450. **3.** To cover with feathers: **a.** internally, in phr. *To f. one's nest*: to enrich oneself 1583; **b.** externally, in phr. *To tar and f.* 1774. **†4.** Of a cock: To cover with outspread feathers; to tread –1700. **5.** *intr.* To move, grow, extend, etc. in a feathery form 1770. **b.** *U.S.* Of cream: To rise upon the surface of tea, etc. like small flakes or feathers 1860. **6.** To be marked with feather-like lines, as tulips, etc. 1833. **7.** *trans.* To cut (wood, etc.) down gradually to a thin edge 1782. **8.** To turn (an oar) as it leaves the water so that it may cut the air edgeways 1740. **9.** *Shooting.* To knock a few feathers from (a bird) without killing 1890. **10.** *Hunting.* **a.** Of a hound: To make a quivering movement with the tail and body, while searching for the trail 1803. **b.** Of the huntsman: To set the hounds direct on the trail 1884.

2. An arrow feathered with his own wing ARBUTHNOT. A craggy hill, feathered with birch SOUTHEY. **5.** The snow came feathering down G. COLMAN. The ripple feathering from her bows TENNYSON. **9. a.** See that old bitch how she feathers—how her stern vibrates with the quickened action of her pulses 1839.

Fea·ther-be·d. OE. **1.** A bed stuffed with feathers. Also *fig.* **2.** The Willow Warbler; also the Whitethroat 1854.

Feathered (fe·ðəɹd), *ppl. a.* OE. [f. FEATHER *sb.* and *v.*] **1.** Provided with feathers. Also in comb., as *black-, well-*, etc. *f.* ME. **2.** Winged, fleet 1587. **3.** Of an arrow: Fitted with a feather. Of a wound: Inflicted by an arrow. OE. **4.** Adorned with a feather or plume of feathers 1624. **5.** Furnished with something feather-like 1686. **6.** Of an oar: That is or has been turned so as to feather 1812.

1. A f. wanderer SMILES. **2.** I saw young Harry.. Rise from the ground like f. Mercury 1 *Hen. IV*, IV. i. 106. **3.** Across the shoulders came the feather'd wound DRYDEN. **5.** The f. grass KEATS. The arch.. is richly feathered (cf. FEATHERING *vbl. sb.*) RICKMAN.

Fea·ther-e·dge, *sb.* 1785. [f. as prec. + EDGE.] The fine edge of a board, etc. that thins off to one side, so as to resemble a wedge in section. Hence **Fea·ther-e·dge** *v.* to cut to a feather-edge. Also *transf.* to turn (oneself) sideways. **Fea·ther-e·dged** *ppl. a.*

Fea·therfew. ME. [Corrupt var. of FEVERFEW.] = FEVERFEW.

Fea·ther-foo·ted, *a.* 1565. Having feet covered with feathers 1580. **b.** *fig.* Moving silently and swiftly.

Fea·ther-head. 1831. An empty or light head; an empty-headed person. Hence **Fea·ther-hea·ded** *a.*

Featheriness (fe·ðərinės). 1689. [See -NESS.] Feathery state or condition; *fig.* lightness, fickleness.

Feathering (fe·ðəriŋ), *vbl. sb.* 1530. [-ING [1].] **1.** The action of FEATHER *v.* 1640. **2.** *concr.* The plumage of birds; the feather of an arrow; feather-like structure or marking 1530; *Arch.* tracery consisting chiefly of small arcs and foils 1816.

Feathering (fe·ðəriŋ), *ppl. a.* 1740. [+-ING [2].] That feathers; in senses of the vb. 1789. **b.** Of an oar, paddle-wheel, float, etc.: see FEATHER *v.* 8.

b. *F. Paddle-wheel*, a wheel whose floats have a motion on an axis, so as to descend nearly vertically into the water and ascend the same way, avoiding beating on the water in the descent and lifting water n the ascent. KNIGHT.

Featherless (fe·ðəɹlės), *a.* ME. [See -LESS.] Without feathers, in various senses.

Fea·ther-stitch. 1882. A kind of stitch in needlework, producing an ornamental zigzag line. Hence as vb.

Fea·ther-weight. 1812. **1.** A weight no greater than that of a feather; hence, a very small thing 1838. **2.** *Racing.* The lightest weight a horse may carry in a handicap; a jockey not over 4st. 7. 1812. **3.** *Boxing.* A boxer whose weight is from 9st. to 8st. 6, as dist. from a *heavy-, middle-*, or *light-weight* 1889.

Fea·ther-work. 1665. [f. FEATHER *sb.* + WORK.] The art of working in feathers; also *concr.*; also = FEATHERSTITCH.

Feathery (fe·ðəri), *a.* 1580. [f. as prec. + -Y.] **1.** Of birds: Feathered 1634. **2.** Fringed, tipped, or flecked with something feather-like 1792. **3.** Resembling feathers or plumes 1580.

1. His [the cock's] f. dames MILT. **2.** The f. canes 1826, pine-branches 1876. **3.** The f. snows COWPER.

Featly (fī·tli), *adv.* (*a.*) *arch.* ME. [f. FEAT *a.* + -LY [2].] **1.** Fitly; neatly; †exactly. **2.** Cleverly, deftly; nimbly ME. **3.** *adj.* Graceful; neat 1801.

2. She dances f. *Wint. T.* IV. iv. 176. **3.** In f. cloak 1822. So **Fea·tness**, elegance, trimness.

†Fea·tous, *a.* [ME. *fetys*, a. OF. *fetis, feitis, faictis*, f. L. *factitius*; see FACTITIOUS. In 15–17th c. apprehended as a deriv. of FEAT *a.*, and variously ended *-ish, -ous, -eous, -uous.*] **1.** Well-formed, handsome, becoming. Often of dress: Artistically fashioned. –1648. **2.** 'Dexterous' (J.).

1. Ye think it fine and f. to be called roses..and Lilies 1570. Hence **†Fea·tously** *adv.*

Feature (fī·tiŭɹ), *sb.* ME. [a. OF. *feture, faiture*:—L. *factura*; see FACTURE.] **1.** Make, form, fashion, shape; proportions. Now *arch.* **†b.** Good form or shape; comeliness –1594. **†c.** *concr.* Something formed or shaped. Cf. CREATURE. –1667. **†2.** In *pl.* and distributively: The build or make of the various parts of the body. **b.** *concr.* A part of the body; a limb. –1752. **3. a.** In *pl.* and in *sing.* with distrib. adj.: The lineaments of the face, the form or mould of its parts. Also *collect.* in *sing.* ME. **b.** *concr.* Any one part of the face 1828. **4.** *transf.* A distinctive part of anything 1692.

1. Horses of fine f. 1600. An image, huge of f. as a cloud KEATS. **b.** Cheated of F. by dissembling Nature SHAKS. **c.** So sented the grim F., and upturn'd His Nostril wide MILT. *P. L.* x. 279. **3.** Under such simple and homly f., lay..a most subtil..wit KNOLLES. *fig.* The Features of the Mind BUTLER. **4.** Anything exhibited or advertised as particularly attractive; *spec.* the principal attraction in a cinema programme; a prominent article, etc. in a newspaper.

Feature (fī·tiŭɹ), *v.* 1755. [f. prec. sb.] **1.** *trans.* = FAVOUR *v.* 7. **2.** To affect or mould the features of; to stand as a feature upon 1810. **3.** To sketch the features of 1791. **4.** To make a special feature of; *spec.* to exhibit as a prominent feature in a dramatic piece 1888.

Featured (fī·tiŭɹd), *ppl. a.* 1500. [f. FEATURE *sb.* and *v.*] **†1.** Fashioned, formed, shaped; well-formed; comely –1774. **2.** Shaped into or expressed by features 1742. **3.** Furnished with features of a specified cast 1790.

3. That hard-f...old forester 1861.

Featureless (fī·tiŭɹlės), *a.* 1600. [See -LESS.] Without (good) features; having no marked feature. Of business: Uneventful.

Featurely (fī·tiŭɹli), *a.* 1819. [See -LY [1].] Having marked features; characteristic.

Feaze (fīz), *v. Obs.* exc. *Naut.* 1568. [? f. MDu. *vese, veze* fringe, frayed edge.] *trans.* To unravel (a rope, etc.); *intr.* of a rope or thread: To unravel at the end. Hence **Fea·zings** *vbl. sb. pl.* the fagging out of an unwhipped rope.

Feaze, var. of FEEZE *sb.* and *v.*

Febricitant (fĭbri·sitănt). Now *rare.* 1541. [ad. L. *febricitantem, febricitare* to have a fever, f. *febris.*] **A.** *adj.* Affected with fever; feverish 1599. **†B.** *sb.* One affected with fever –1650.

†Febri·cita·tion. 1584. [f. L. *febricitare*; see prec. and -ATION.] The state of being in a fever, feverishness. So **Febri·city.** BROWNING.

Febricula (fĭbri·kiŭlă). 1746. [a. L., dim. of *febris.*] A slight fever, soon over. Hence **Febri·culose, †Febri·culous** *adjs.* having a slight fever. **Febriculo·sity**, feverishness.

Febrifacient (fĭbrifēɪ·ʃiĕnt). 1803. [f. L. *febri-* (*febris*) + -FACIENT.] **A.** *adj.* Fever-producing. **B.** *sb.* Something that produces fever.

Febriferous (fĭbri·fĕrəs), *a.* 1874. [f. as prec. + -FEROUS.] Producing fever, as a *f. locality.*

Febrific (fĭbri·fik), *a.* 1710. [ad. F. *febrifique*, f. as prec. + *-ficus* making.] Producing fever; also, FEVERISH.

Febrifuge (fe·brifiŭdʒ). 1686. [a. F. *fébrifuge*, f. as prec. + *fugare* to drive away.]

A. *adj.* Anti-febrile 1707.

B. *sb.* An anti-febrile medicine; hence, a cooling drink. Also *transf.* and *fig.* Hence **Febri·fugal, febrifu·gal** *a.* **†Febrifugous** *a.*

Febrile (fī·bril, fe·bril), *a.* 1651. [a. F., ad. L. *febrilis*, f. *febris.*] Of or pertaining to fever; produced by or indicative of fever. †Of a person: Suffering from fever.

F. heat 1666, irritation KINGLAKE. Hence **Febri·lity**, feverishness.

Febronian (febrōu·niăn), *a.* 1856. [f. *Febronius* + -AN.] Of or pertaining to (Justinus) Febronius; a pseudonym of J. N. von Hontheim of Treves (18th c.), who wrote maintaining the independence of national churches. Hence **Febro·nianism**, the doctrine itself.

February (fe·bruări). Also abbrev. *Feb.* [ME. *feverer*, ad. OF. *feverier*:—pop. L. **febrarius*, L. *februarius*, f. *februa* pl. a festival of purification held on Feb. 15th.] **1.** The second month of the year, containing twenty-eight days, except in bissextile or leap-year, when it has twenty-nine. **2.** *attrib.* 1599.

2. You have such a Februarie face SHAKS.

Februa·tion. Now *rare.* 1652. [ad. L. *februationem*, f. *februare* to purify; see prec.] A ceremonial purification.

Fecal, feces, etc.: see FÆCAL, etc.

Fecial, var. of FETIAL.

Fecifork (fī·sifǭɹk). 1826. [f. L. *fæci-* comb. f. FÆCES + FORK.] *Entom.* The anal fork on which the larvæ of *Cassida*, etc., carry their fæces.

Feck (fek). *Sc.* and *n. dial.* 1470. [aphet. f. EFFECT *sb.*] †1. Effect, tenor, substance -1600. 2. Efficacy, value; hence, vigour, energy 1535. 3. Amount, quantity. *The (most) f.*: the bulk, the greatest part.
Hence **Fe·ckful** *a.* efficient, powerful. **Fe·ckfully** *adv.* **Fe·ckless** *a.* ineffective, futile, weak. **Fe·ckless-ly** *adv.*, **-ness**. **Fe·ckly** *adv.* mostly; almost.

Fecket (fe·kėt). *Sc.* An under waistcoat. BURNS.

Feculence (fe·kiŭlĕns). 1648. [a. F. *féculence*, ad. L. *fæculentia*; see FECULENT.] 1. The quality or state of being feculent; foulness 1860. 2. *concr.* Feculent matter; dregs, dross, scum. Now chiefly, filth. So †**Fe·culency**.

Feculent (fe·kiŭlĕnt), *a.* 1471. [a. F. *féculent*, ad. L. *fæculentus*, f. *fæc-*, *fæx*; see FÆCES and -ULENT.] 1. Containing or of the nature of fæces or dregs; abounding with sediment or impurities; thick, turbid. Now usually: Foul, fetid. Also *fig.* †2. Covered with fæces. SPENSER *F. Q.* II. vii. 61.
1. *fig.* Every word here is f. and stinks NORTH.

Fecund (fe·kvnd, fī·kvnd), *a.* ME. [a. F. *fecond*, ad. L. *fecundus.*] 1. Fruitful in offspring or vegetable growth; prolific, fertile. Now chiefly *transf.* and *fig.* 2. Fertilizing 1686.
1. This is..f. of other fault and misfortune RUSKIN.
var. †**Fecu·ndous**.

Fecundate (fe-, fīkvndeit), *v.* 1631. [f. L. *fecundat-*, *fecundare*, f. *fecundus.*] *trans.* To render fruitful or productive; *esp.* to make the female (individual or organ) fruitful by the introduction of the male element; to impregnate.
Nature has something else in view than that its own proper males should f. each blossom DARWIN.

Fecundation (fe-, fīkvndē¹·ʃən). 1541. [See prec. and -ATION.] The process of fecundating; fertilization, impregnation.

†**Fecu·ndify**, *v. rare.* 1730. [f. FECUND + -(I)FY.] = FECUNDATE.

Fecundity (fīkv·nditi). ME. [ad. L. *fecunditatem*; see FECUND and -ITY. Cf. F. *fécondité.*] 1. The faculty of reproduction, the capacity for bringing forth young; productiveness. 2. *Bot.* The power of germinating 1691. 3. The quality of producing abundantly; fertility ME. 4. Productiveness in general 1555. 5. Fertilizing power 1642.
4. The extreme f. of the press W. IRVING. 5. The River Nilus is famous for its..Fœcundity 1680.

Fed (fed), *ppl. a.* 1483. [pa. pple. of FEED *v.*] Supplied with food, nourished. b. *F. up*: surfeited, disgusted, bored (*slang*) 1900.

†**Fe·darie.** 1603. [var. of *feodary* FEUDARY, q. v.] A confederate -1611.
Camillo is A Federarie [? a misprint or correction] with her *Wint. T.* II. i. 90.

‖**Feddan** (fedā·n). Also **fedan.** 1817. [Arab. *faddān*, *faddān* a yoke of oxen, an acre.] An Egyptian measure of land, rather more than an English acre.

Federacy (fe·dĕrăsi). 1647. [f. late L. *fœderatus* FEDERATE *ppl. a.*; see -ACY.] 1. The state of being joined by a treaty; an alliance. 2. A CONFEDERACY 1803.

Federal (fe·dĕrăl). 1645. [a. F. *fédéral*, f. *fœdus* (*fœder-*) covenant, cogn. w. *fides* FAITH.]
A. *adj.* 1. Of or pertaining to a covenant, compact, or treaty; *spec.* (*Theol.*) pertaining to the Covenant of Works or Covenant of Grace. 2. Of or pertaining to, or of the nature of, that form of government in which two or more states constitute a political unity while remaining independent as to their internal affairs; of or pertaining to the political unity so constituted 1777. 3. *U.S. Hist.* a. Favouring a strong federal, i. e. central government 1788. b. Of or pertaining to the Northern or Union party in the American Civil War of 1861-65. 1861. 4. United in a league, allied 1867.
1. *F. theology*: the system based on the doctrine of covenants made by God with Adam as repr. mankind, and with Christ as repr. the Church. 2. There was not..any f. bond among the several tribes STUBBS. A F. coinage 1876. 3. a. He [Hamilton] is the..impersonation of the national or F. School CALHOUN.
B. *sb.* Chiefly *pl.* One on the side of the Union in the American Civil War 1870.
Hence **Fe·derally** *adv.* on the basis of a covenant; after the manner of a federation.

Federalism (fe·dĕrăliz'm). 1793. [ad. F. *fédéralisme*; see prec. and -ISM.] The federal principle or system of political organization (see FEDERAL *a.* 2); advocacy of this principle. In *U.S. Hist.* the principles of the Federal party (see FEDERAL *a.* 3).

Federalist (fe·dĕrălist), *sb.* 1787. [ad. F. *fédéraliste*; see FEDERAL and -IST.] 1. One who advocates federalism or federal union 1792. 2. *U.S. Hist.* A member of the Federal party 1787. 3. *attrib.* 1801.
2. The advocates of a central national authority had begun to receive the name of Federalists BRYCE.
Hence **Federali·stic** *a.* inclined to federalism.

Federalize (fe·dĕrăləiz), *v.* 1801. [f. FEDERAL *a.* + -IZE.] a. *trans.* To unite in federal union. b. To decentralize; to take from the central authority and hand over to federal bodies in the state or states in a union. Hence **Fe:deraliza·tion**, the action of federalizing or the state of being federalized.

Federarie: see FEDARIE, *Obs.*

Federate (fe·dĕrĕt). 1671. [ad. L. *fœderat-*, *fœderare*; see next.] A. *adj.* Federated, confederate, allied, in league 1710.
In a f. Alliance, the two Societies still subsist intire WARBURTON.
B. *sb.* 1. One of the parties to a covenant 1671. 2. *French. Hist.* Used as tr. F. *fédéré* 1792.
2. They invited armed federates, as they were called, in July 1791, to Paris 1792.

Federate (fe·dĕreit), *v.* 1814. [f. L. *fœderat-*, *fœderare*, f. *fœdus*; see FEDERAL.] 1. *intr.* To enter into a league for a common object 1837. 2. *trans.* To band together as a league; to organize on a federal basis.
1. Thus, at Lyons..we behold..sixty thousand, met to f. CARLYLE. 2. To f. the Continent against England LOWE. Hence **Fe·deratist** = FEDERATIONIST.

Federation (fedĕrē¹·ʃən). 1721. [a. F., ad. L. *fœderationem*; see prec.] 1. The action of uniting in a league or covenant. Now chiefly *spec.* the union of several states, etc. under a federal government, each retaining control of its own internal affairs. 2. A society; a league; a federated body 1791.
1. *F. of the (British) Empire*, *Imperial F.*: a project under which the colonies would form one state with the mother country in relation to all that concerns the safety and well-being of the empire as a whole. 2. The Miners' F., the Shipping F. (*mod.*). Hence **Federa·tionist**, an advocate of f.

Federative (fe·dĕrĕtiv), *a.* 1690. [f. as FEDERATE *v.* + -IVE.] 1. Of or pertaining to the formation of a covenant, league, or alliance. Now *Hist.* 2. Pertaining to, or forming part of, a federation; of the nature of a federation 1781. 3. Inclined to form federations 1885.
2. Argos, with the f. cities attached to her GROTE.

†**Fe·dity.** 1539. [ad. L. *fœditatem*; see -ITY.] 1. Foulness, moral or physical -1657. 2. *pl.* Loathsome practices -1755.

†**Fee**, *sb.*[1] [Com. Teut. and Aryan: OE. *feoh*, *fioh*, *fēo*, str. neut. :—OTeut. **fehu* :—OAryan **peku-*, whence also Skr. *paçu* masc., L. *pecu* neut. cattle (cf. L. *pecunia* money).] 1. Live stock, cattle -1535. 2. Movable property -1596. 3. Money -1677.

Fee (fī), *sb.*[2] ME. [a. AF. *fee*, *fie* = OF. *fé*, *fié*, *fief*, *fieu*, *fiu*, med.L. *feodum*, *feudum*, commonly said to be f. OHG. *fehu* cattle, etc. (= FEE *sb.*[1]) + *ōd* wealth. But the etym. is uncertain.] 1. *Feudal Law.* An estate in land (in England always a heritable estate) held on condition of homage and service to a superior lord; a fief, feudal benefice. Now *Hist.* 2. *Common Law.* An estate of inheritance in land. (In Eng. Law understood to be held feudally of the Crown, and thus = sense 1. In U.S. the holder of the fee is the absolute owner of the land.) 1535. 3. A territory held in fee; a lordship ME. †4. The heritable right to an office of profit, held feudally, or to a pension or revenue -1700. †5. Employment, service -1596.
1. Phr. *Ecclesiastical f.*: one held by an eccl. person or corporation, owing only spiritual service. *Knight's f.*, *lay f.*: see KNIGHT *sb.*, LAY *a.* 2. Phr. *F.-simple*, *-tail* (see those words). *In f.*, usu. = 'in fee simple'. *Base f.*: see BASE *a.* *To hold in f.* (fig.): to hold as one's absolute and rightful possession; Once did she hold the gorgeous East in f. WORDSW. *At a pin's f.*: at the value of a pin. 5. Venus Damzells, all within her f. SPENSER *F. Q.* VI. x. 21.
II. †1. A tribute to a superior -1602. 2. Payment to a public officer (? orig. one who held his office 'in fee') for the execution of his functions 1450; hence, professional or other remuneration 1583; charge, pay ME. †3. A perquisite; any allotted portion -1736. 4. A fixed salary or wage. Also *pl.* Wages. Now *Sc.* or *Hist.* ME. 5. †A reward -1633; a gratuity 1592; †in bad sense, a bribe -1643.
2. To the Auditor for his F. xiiij *s.* 1546. What f., doctor MAR. EDGEWORTH. 3. I, heere's a Deere, whose skins a Keepers F. 3 *Hen. VI*, III. i. 23. 5. Unstain'd with gold or f. MILT.
Comb.: **f.-estate**, lands or tenements for which some service is paid to the chief lord; **-expectant** (see EXPECTANT *a.*); **-fund** (*Sc. Law*), certain dues of Court out of which the officers of the Court are paid; **-royal** (see ROYAL).

Fee (fī), *v.* ME. [f. prec.] †1. *trans.* ? To invest with a fief 1483. 2. *trans.* To give a fee to; *Sc.* to hire (servants, etc.) 1529. 3. To engage for a fee; †in bad sense, to bribe ME.
2. The writings drawn, the lawyer feed SWIFT. 3. Without Feeing the Journalists DE FOE.

Feeble (fī·b'l). ME. [a. OF. *foible*, later form of *fleible*:—L. *flebilis* doleful; hence, weak. Cf. It. *fievole.*]
A. *adj.* 1. Lacking strength; weak; infirm; having little power of resistance. 2. Lacking moral or intellectual strength ME. 3. Wanting in energy, force, or effect ME. 4. Of a phenomenon, etc.: Faintly perceived 1860.
1. His heed may be harde, but feble his brayne SKELTON. Bunches lateral..stem f. WITHERING. F. folk EMERSON. 2. F. and without volition CARLYLE. F. minds MACAULAY. 3. The old, f., and day-wearied Sunne *John* V. iv. 35. My f. Reason HOBBES. F. conduct 1862. *Comb.* **f.-minded** *a.* (whence **-mindedness**). Hence **Fee·bleness**. **Fee·bling** [-LING[1]], a f. person. **Fee·blish** *a.* somewhat f. **Fee·bly** *adv.*
B. *sb.* †1. A feeble person -1826. 2. = FOIBLE 1. 1678. 3. *Fencing.* = FOIBLE 2. 1645.
1. The most forcible of feebles DISRAELI. 2. Modesty's my forte, And pride my f. BYRON.

Feeble (fī·b'l), *v.* ME. [f. the adj.] †1. *intr.* To become feeble -1496. 2. *trans.* To enfeeble. Now *arch.* ME. var. (in sense 2) †**Fee·blish.**

Feebless. *arch.* ME. [a. OF. *foiblesce* (F. *faiblesse*), f. *foible*, FEEBLE *a.*] Feebleness; infirm health.

Feed (fīd), *sb.* 1573. [f. the vb.] 1. The action of feeding; also, the giving of food 1576. 2. †Feeding-ground; pasturage, pasture; green crops 1573. 3. Food (for cattle); fodder, provender 1588; also, an allowance or meal given to a horse, etc. 1735. 4. *colloq.* A meal; a feast 1808. 5. The action or process of feeding a machine, or supplying material to be operated upon; also, the material, or the amount, supplied; the charge of a gun 1839. b. Short for *f.-gear*, *-pump*, etc.; a feeder 1839.
1. Birds coming late from F. 1686. Phr. *To be off one's f.* (of animals, and *colloq.* of persons); to have lost one's appetite. *On the f.* (said of fish): on the look-out for food; eating. 2. For such pleasure till that hour At F. or Fountain never had I found MILT. *P. L.* IX. 597. 3. One f. of oats in the nose-bag 1859.
Comb. 1. General: as *f.-bag*, *-pipe*, *-pump*, *-cutter*, etc. 2. Special: **f.-apron** = *feed-cloth*; **-cloth**, a revolving cloth which carries the cotton, etc., into a spinning, carding, or other machine; **-door**, the door through which a furnace is supplied with fuel; **-head**, (*a*) a cistern of water for supplying the boiler from above; (*b*) *Founding*, 'the metal above and exterior to the mold which flows into the latter as the casting contracts' (Knight); **-motion**, a contrivance for giving a forward motion to material in a machine; **-screw** (*Lathe*), 'a long screw employed to impart a regular motion to a tool-rest or to the work' (Knight); **-trough**, a trough containing a supply of water for a locomotive; **-water**, a supply of water for a steam boiler, etc.; **-wheel**, a revolving wheel or disk which carries forward an object or material.

Feed (fīd), *v.* Pa. t. and pple. **fed.** [OE. *fēdan* :—OTeut. **fōdjan*, f. **fōd-ā-*; see FOOD.] 1. *trans.* To give food to; to supply with food; to put food into the mouth of; to suckle (young). 2. *fig.* To gratify, minister to the demands of, any sense, passion, feeling, hope, desire, or the like OE. 3. *intr.* To take food, eat. Of persons now only *colloq.* Also *fig.* ME. 4. *trans.* To yield, be, or serve as, food for (*lit.* and *fig.*) ME. 5. To nourish, cause to grow, support, sustain OE. 6. To fill with food, to pamper; to fatten; occas. of the food (*dial.*) 1552; *intr.* to grow fat (*dial.*) 1727. Also *fig.* 7. *trans.* To keep supplied 1582; to supply (a machine, a workman) continuously with material to work upon. Also *intr.* of the material. 1669. 8. To cause to be eaten by cattle; to use (land) as pasture. Often *to f. bare, close, down, off.* 1651. Also *transf.* To supply continuously (material to be consumed, etc.) 1860. b. To deal out (food) *to* animals, etc. (*U.S.*) 1883. 9. Of cattle: To eat, eat off, feed upon 1725.

1. Fede your hawke and sey not geve here mete 1450. Pelias..was fed by a mare 1821. He is too weak to f. himself (*mod.*). 2. Þe soule is fedde wiþ charite WYCLIF. To f. my humour *Rich. III*, IV. i. 65. Phr. *To f. the eyes, sight, ear.* 3. *fig.* Cholera feeds on impurities of every sort 1883. 4. Phr. *To f. the fishes* (slang): to be drowned. 5. A mountain-spring that feeds a dale SHAKS. 6. *Sports.* To pass the ball, etc. to a player. *Theatr.* To supply an actor with a cue. Phr. *To f. off*: to fatten for sale or slaughter. 7. The warm springs that f. the Baths ADDISON. She..fed the turning spindle with the twisting thread 1808. 8. b. Mangel-wurzel..is fed to the cows in winter 1883. 9. The sheep have fed it too close for a grip of the hand JEFFERIES.

Feed (fīd), *ppl. a.* 1460. [f. FEE *v.*] †1. Bound to feudal service. Only in *f. man*; see FEEDMAN. 2. Paid by fees; hired; bribed; *Sc.* employed for wages 1579.

Feeder (fī·dəɪ). ME. [f. FEED *v.* + -ER [1].] 1. One who feeds or supplies food to; †one who maintains (a parasite, etc.). Also *transf.* and *fig.* 1579. 2. One who or that which eats or takes food; also *transf.* of a plant, a flame 1562; *pl.* cattle for fattening 1796. 3. An organ or appliance for feeding (senses 1 and 2); *spec.* in *Entom.* 1811. 4. One who feeds up cattle for slaughter ME. 5. A stream which flows into another body of water; a tributary; also *transf.* and *fig.* 1795. b. *spec.* 'A water course which supplies a canal or reservoir by gravitation or natural flow' (W.) 1825. 6. *Mining.* a. A smaller lode falling into the main lode or vein 1728. b. An underground spring 1702. c. A stream of gas escaping from a fissure in the ground; a blower 1881. 7. One who or that which supplies material for consumption or elaboration; *esp.* one who or that which supplies material to a machine 1669. 8. *Electr. Engin.* A wire bearing a subsidiary current; a branch-wire to supply a house, etc. 1892.

1. The horsse remembers..his f. 1616. *fig.* The Tutor and the F. of my Riots SHAKS. 2. He [the barbel] is a curious f. WALTON. 5. The Kennet.. is one of the main feeders of the Thames 1878.

Feeding (fī·diŋ), *vbl. sb.* OE. [f. as prec.] 1. The action of FEED *v.* 2. *concr.* That which is eaten; food. Now *rare.* ME. 3. Grazing-ground; pasturage. Now *dial.* ME.

1. The f. of singing-birds RAY. 2. His [the Pike's] f. is usually fish or frogs RAY. 3. Lands or feedings, apt for milch kine 1554.

Comb.: f.-bottle, a bottle for supplying milk or the like to infants; also *attrib.* in fig. sense; -cloth = *feed-cloth*; -tube, 'an elastic tube .. which is passed into the stomach' (*Syd. Soc. Lex.*).

†**Fee·dman.** 1460. [f. FEED *ppl. a.* + MAN.] 1. One holding a FEE (*sb.*[2]); a vassal -1565. 2. A soldier serving for pay -1722.

Fee-farm (fī·fārm). ME. [a. AF. *fee-ferme*, OF. *feuferme, fiofferme*; see FEE *sb.*[2] and FARM *sb.*[2]] *Law.* 1. The tenure by which land is held in fee-simple subject to a perpetual fixed rent, without other services; the estate of the tenant in land so held; *rarely*, the land itself. Also *fig.* 2. The rent paid for an estate so held ME. 3. *attrib.*, esp. in *fee-farm-rent* 1638. Hence Fee-farmer.

Fee-faw-fum (fī fǭ fɒm). 1605. 1. Doggerel spoken by the giant in 'Jack the giant killer' upon discovering the presence of Jack. 2. a. An exclam. indicating a murderous intention 1690. b. Nonsense, fit only to scare children. Also *attrib.* 1811. 3. A term for 'a blood-thirsty person' 1678.

1. *Lear* III. iv. 188. 2. b. This is all fee-faw-fum (*mod.*).

Feel (fīl), *sb.* ME. [f. next vb.] 1. The action of feeling (see FEEL *v.*); an instance of this 1461. 2. The sense of touch. Now only in *to the f.* ME. 3. A feeling or sensation, mental or physical 1737. 4. Ascribed as a quality to a material object: The kind of sensation which it produces 1739.

2. A rough texture to the f. 1874. 3. With all sorts of queer feels about me H. WALPOLE. 4. The general f. of the air is very mild MRS. PIOZZI.

Feel (fīl), *v.* *Pa. t.* and *pple.* **felt** (felt). [Com. WGer.: OE. *fēlan* :—WGer. type *fōljan, f. root *fōl-*:—OAryan *pāl-, pl-*, occurring in OE., Gr. παλάμη, L. *palma*, Skr. *pāni*, etc.]

I. 1. *trans.* To handle in order to experience a tactual sensation; to examine by touching; hence, to try by touching 1833. 2. *absol.* and *intr.* a. To touch with the hand or finger. Const. *at, of* (now *dial.* and *U.S.*), †*to.* 1599. b. To search, try to ascertain, by handling or touch; to grope. Const. *after, for.* Also †*fig.* ME. 3. *Mil. trans.* To examine by cautious trial the nature of (ground), the strength of (an enemy) 1793. Also *intr.* with *for*: To try to locate (the enemy) 1839.

1. Suffer me, that I may feele the pillars *Judg.* xvi. 26. To f. the bit gently with the bridle-hand 1833. Phr. *To f. one's way*: to find it by groping; also *fig.* 2. b. If haply they might feele after him, and finde him *Acts* xvii. 27. Come neere .. that I may feele thee..whether thou bee my very sonne Esau, or not *Gen.* xxvii. 21.

II. 1. *trans.* To perceive by the sense of touch ME.; more widely, to perceive through those senses which are not referred to any special organ; to have a sensation of (heat or cold, a blow, a wound, etc.) OE. b. *absol.* and *intr.* To have sensations of touch, etc. ME. 2. To perceive by smell or taste (now *dial.*) ME. †3. To perceive mentally -1483. 4. To be conscious of; to experience ME. b. *intr.* (for earlier *refl.*) with *complement*: To be consciously; to regard oneself as 1816. 5. To undergo consciously. †Also *intr.* const. *of.* ME. 6. To be sensibly affected by. Also *transf.* and *fig.* of inanimate objects. ME. 7. *intr.* To have sympathy *with*, compassion *for*, or the like 1605. 8. †a. To think, hold as an opinion (after L. *sentire*) -1544. b. To believe on grounds not distinctly perceived; to have a conviction of (a fact) 1613.

1. The lawyer can not vnderstond the matter tyl he fele his mony 1545. We..felt not the cold 1662. Phr. *To f. one's legs.* b. The meanest thing that feels WORDSW. 4. He best can paint 'em [woes] who shall f. 'em most POPE. b. I don't f. myself MRS. H. WOOD. Phr. *To f. up to* (one's work, etc.): see UP. *To f. like* (doing something): to have an inclination for (?orig. *U.S.*; now common). 5. To f. inconvenience from heat 1767. 6. I was too young to f. my loss 1726. Phr. *To f. the helm*, said of a ship when she begins to obey the helm. 7. No man can see his army perish by want without feeling for them WELLINGTON. 8. b. Legislation felt to be inexpedient (*mod.*).

III. In quasi-passive sense with complement: To be felt as having a specified quality; to seem 1581.

The air felt chilly 1825.

Hence Fee·lable *a.* that may or can be felt.

Feeler (fī·ləɪ). 1526. [f. FEEL *v.*] 1. One who or that which feels. 2. *Biol.* One of the organs with which certain animals are furnished, for trying objects by the touch or for searching for food; a palp 1665. Also *transf.* and *fig.* 3. One sent out to feel the enemy; *transf.* a proposal or hint put forth or thrown out in order to ascertain the opinions of others 1830.

2. Her ships were the feelers with which she touched on Greece and Italy MERIVALE.

Feeling (fī·liŋ), *vbl. sb.* ME. [f. FEEL *v.*] 1. The action of FEEL *v.* in various senses. Chiefly *gerundial.* 2. The faculty or power by which one feels (in sense II. 1 of the vb.); the general sensibility of the body, as dist. from the special senses ME.; a physical sensation or perception due to this ME. 3. The condition of being emotionally affected; an emotion ME.; *pl.* emotions, susceptibilities, sympathies 1771. 4. Capacity or readiness to feel; susceptibility to the higher emotions; *esp.* tenderness for the sufferings of others 1588. 5. Pleasurable or painful consciousness ME. 6. What one feels in regard to something; also, the objective quality occasioning this. Also *transf.* of a language. 1449. 7. *Pyschol.* a. 'A fact or state of consciousness' (J. S. Mill and others). b. As a generic term comprising sensation, desire, and emotion only. c. (After Kant's *gefühl*) The element of pleasure or pain in any state. d. An intuitive cognition or belief. 1739. 8. In *Fine Art*; cf. senses 3-5. a. *Painting.* That quality in a work of art which depicts the mental emotion of the painter 1854. b. *Arch.* The general tone of a building or style of architecture; the impression produced on a spectator 1859.

1. The first f. of a febrile attack 1805. 2. There is not a living creature..but hath the sence of f., although it have none else HOLLAND. 3. All classes were agreed in one common f. of displeasure FROUDE. 4. She has ..not one grain of F. SWIFT. 6. The apprehension of the good, Giues but the greater f. to the worse *Rich. II*, I. iii. 301.

Feeling (fī·liŋ), *ppl. a.* ME. [f. as prec.] That feels. 1. Sentient; capable of sensation. 2. Accessible to emotion; sympathetic, compassionate 1618; of language: Indicating emotion 1568. 3. That is deeply or sensibly felt or realized, heart-felt, vivid 1530.

2. His f. wordes SPENSER. 3. A f. sense Of all your royal favours 1721. Hence Fee·lingly *adv.*

Feer(e, var. of FERE *sb.*, *Obs.* companion; also obs. f. FEAR.

Fee-si·mple. 1463. [a. AF.; see FEE *sb.*[2] and SIMPLE.] *Law.* An estate in land, etc. belonging to the owner and his heirs for ever, without limitation to any class of heirs. *In fee-simple*: in absolute possession. Also *transf.* and *fig.*

fig. He will sell the fee-simple of his saluation *All's Well* IV. iii. 311.

Feet, *pl.* of FOOT.

Fee-tai·l. 1495. [a. AF. *fee taillé* = Anglo-L. *feudum talliatum*; *taillé* is from OF. *taillir* (mod.F. *tailler*) to cut, to limit.] *Law.* An estate of inheritance entailed or limited to some particular class of heirs; a limited fee. *Fee-tail expectant*: see EXPECTANT *a.*

Feetless (fī·tlės), *a.* 1605. [See -LESS.] Without feet.

Feeze (fīz), *sb.* ME. [f. next vb.] 1. A rush; hence, a violent impact. Also, a rub. Now *dial.* and *U.S.* 2. *U.S. colloq.* A state of perturbation 1846.

1. Phr. *To fetch* or *take (one's) f.*: to take a short run before leaping.

Feeze (fīz), *v.*[1] Now *dial.* [OE. *fēsian*, *fȳsian* to drive = ON. **feysa.*] †1. *trans.* To drive; to drive off or away -1689. 2. To frighten ME. 3. a. *vaguely*, To 'do for' (a person) 1596. b. To beat, flog 1610.

3. a. Ile pheeze you infaith *Tam. Shr.* Induct. i. 1

Feeze (fīz), *v.*[2] *dial.* 17.. 1. *trans.* To turn, as a screw; also *fig.* 1806. 2. *intr.* for *refl.* To wind in and out; to hang off and on.

Feff, Feffment: see FEOFF.

Fegary (fĭgēə·ri). 1600. A corruption of VAGARY, q. v.

Fegs (fegz). Now *Sc.* and *dial.* 1598. [Distortion of FAY *sb.*[1], FAITH, ? + -KIN(S.] An exclam., expressing asseveration or astonishment. Also as an (unmeaning) sb.

Feign (fēⁱn), *v.* [ME. *feinen, feignen*, ad. OF. *feindre* (pr. pple. *feignant*) :—L. *fingere*, whence FICTION, FIGMENT.] 1. *trans.* To fashion, form, shape. Now only after L. 2. To invent; to forge ME. 3. To relate in fiction; to fable. Now *rare.* ME. †b. *absol.* and *intr.* To indulge in fiction -1636. 4. To suppose arbitrarily or erroneously. Now *rare.* ME. 5. *trans.* To assert or maintain fictitiously; to pretend ME. †6. To practise dissimulation, dissemble (*refl.* and *intr.* for *refl.*) -1559. Also *trans.* To conceal. SPENSER. 7. *trans.* To make a show of, pretend, simulate, sham; also *absol.* ME. 8. *refl.* and *intr.* To pretend, make oneself appear ME. 9. To counterfeit 1484. †10. To make a feint -1632. †11. *Mus.* To sing softly; also, to sing with due regarded to the 'accidentals' -1553. †12. To shirk (*trans.* and *intr.*) -1535.

2. Thou hast feigned This tale GOWER. 3. Things.. worse Than Fables yet have feign'd MILT. *P. L.* XI. 627. 4. The Straights, where they fained Hercules his pillars to be STILLINGFL. 7. Escaped death, onely by feigning it 1741. *absol.* She cannot f. C. BRONTË. 8. Faine thy selfe to be a mourner 2 *Sam.* xiv. 2. 12. There they made a great assaut. The Englysshmen fayned nat LD. BERNERS. Feigned *ppl.a.* Fei·gnedly *adv.*, -ness. Fei·gner. Fei·gningly *adv.*

Feint (fē̆int), *sb.* 1679. [a. F. *feinte* ppl. sb., f. *feindre* to FEIGN.] 1. A feigned or false attack; *esp.* in *Mil.* a movement made with the object of deceiving an enemy as to a general's real plans 1683. 2. *transf.* and *fig.* An assumed appearance; a pretence, stratagem 1679.

1. A f. at the head BAKER. An attack on India by way of f. G. DUFF.

Feint (fē̆nt), *a.* ME. [a. Fr. *feint*, pa. pple. of *feindre*.] Feigned, false, or counterfeit; sham. Now *rare*. b. In commercial use: = FAINT *a.* 5b.

The Major..made a f. Retreat 1702.

Feint, *v.* ME. [In sense 1, f. F. *feint* (see prec.); in sense 2, f. FEINT *sb.*] †1. To deceive. ME. only. 2. *Mil.*, etc. a. *intr.* To make a feint or sham attack. b. *trans.* To pretend to make (a pass or cut). 1833.

†**Fei·rie**, *a. Sc.* ME. [? Cf. FERE *a.*] Fit to travel; hence, nimble, vigorous. –1794.

Felanders, obs. f. FILANDERS.

Fela·pton. 1551. *Logic.* A mnemonic word representing the fourth mood in the third syllogistic figure, in which a universal negative major premiss and a universal affirmative minor yield a particular negative conclusion.

Feldspar, felspar (fe·ldspaɹ, fe·lspaɹ). 1757. [= Ger. *feldspat(h*, f. *feld* FIELD + *spat(h* spar. The form *felspar* (as if f. *fels*) is corrupt, but is the prevailing form.] *Min.* Name of a group of minerals, usually white or flesh-red in colour, occurring in crystals or in crystalline masses. They consist of a silicate of alumina with soda, potash, lime, etc. Also *attrib.* Hence Fe·ldsparite = FELDSPAR.

Feldspathic, felspathic (feld-, felspæ·þik), *a.* 1832. [f. *fel(d)spath* (see prec.) + -IC.] Of the nature of or containing feldspar. var. Fe·l(d)spatho·se.

†**Fele.** [OE. *feolo, feolu, feola, fela* :—OTeut. **felu* :—pre-Teut. **pélu* (with ablaut-var. **polú*) much; cf. Skr. *puru*, Gr. πολύς.]

A. *adv.* (and quasi-*sb.*) Much –1598.

B. *adj.* (Indeclinable) 1. With *sb.* in *pl.* Many –1598. b. With *sb.* in *sing.* Much –1535. 2. In predicative use: Much, many. Also in compar.: more in number. Only ME. 3. *absol.* in *pl.* Many persons –1450. Hence †Fe·lefold *a.* (*adv.*) = MANIFOLD. Chaucer.

Felicific (fīlisi·fik), *a.* 1865. [ad. L. *felicificus*, f. *felix* (*felic-*) + *-ficus*; see -FIC.] Making happy; productive of happiness.

†**Feli·cify,** *v. rare.* 1683. [f. L. *felix* (*felic-*) + *-ficare*; see -FY.] To render happy; also *absol.* –1698.

†**Feli·citate,** *pa. pple.* [ad. L. *felicitatus*, *felicitare*; see next.] Made happy. *Lear* I. i. 77.

Felicitate (fīli·site¹t), *v.* 1628. [f. ppl. stem of L. *felicitare*, f. *felix* (*felic-*) happy.] 1. To make happy; also *absol.* Now *rare.* 2. To reckon or pronounce happy; to congratulate (now only a person). Const. *on, upon.* 1634. †3. To offer congratulations on 1684.

1. Since I cannot make myself happy, I will have the glory to f. another DRYDEN. 2. A great poet felicitated himself that poetry was not the business of his life D'ISRAELI. 3. To f. his Majesties happy return 1684. Hence **Felicita·tion,** the action of congratulating; a congratulatory speech or message; also *attrib.* **Feli·citator.**

Felicitous (fīli·sitəs), *a.* 1735. [f. FELICITY + -OUS.] 1. Characterized by felicity, blissful (*rare*) 1824; †prosperous, successful 1735. 2. Strikingly apt; of persons: Happy in expression, manner, or style 1821.

2. A f. adaptation of the organ to the object PALEY. F. in jests upon his own figure LAMB. Hence **Feli·citous·ly** *adv.*, **-ness** (Dicts.).

Felicity (fīli·siti). ME. [a. OF. *felicité*, ad. L. *felicitatem*, f. *felix*.] 1. The state of being happy; happiness (in mod. use, intense happiness, bliss). 2. That which causes happiness; a source of happiness, a blessing ME. 3. Prosperity (now *rare*) ME.; †*pl.* prosperous circumstances; successes –1731; a fortunate trait 1761. 4. A happy faculty in art or speech 1605; a strikingly apt expression 1665. †5. Of a planet: A favourable aspect. Only ME.

1. Absent thee from felicitie awhile *Haml.* v. ii. 358. 2. His coine..is his only hope and felicitie 1597. 3. The felicities of Salomon BACON. 4. Those felicities which cannot be produced at will by wit and labour JOHNSON.

Felid (fī·lid). [ad. mod.L. *felidæ*, f. *feles* cat.] One of the *Felidæ* or cat-tribe.

Feliform (fī·lifǭɹm), *a.* [f. L. *feles* (*feli-*) + -FORM.] Having the form of a cat.

Feline (fī·ləin, -lin). 1681. [ad. L. *felinus*, f. *feles*.]

A. *adj.* 1. Of or pertaining to cats or their species, cat-like in form or structure. 2. Resembling a cat in character or quality 1843.

1. The f. quadrupeds SIR C. BELL. 2. The f. care with which he stepped aside from any patches of mire LYTTON.

B. *sb.* An animal of the cat tribe 1861.

Hence **Fe·line·ly** *adv.*, **-ness. Feli·nity,** f. quality; a cat-like disposition; the typical qualities of the cat tribe.

Fell (fel), *sb.*¹ [Com. Teut.: OE. *fel, fell* :—OTeut. **fello-*:—pre-Teut. **pello-*:—**pelno-*, cogn. w. Gr. πέλλα, L. *pellis* skin. Hence also FILM.] 1. The skin or hide of an animal, usu. with the hair, wool, etc. Also *transf.* of the human skin OE. 2. A covering of hair, wool, etc., *esp.* when thick or matted; a fleece 1600.

1. They carie furth..purple died felles 1551. A light brown f. stood out very clearly H. M. STANLEY. 2. We are still handling our Ewes and their Fels you know are greasie SHAKS. My F. of haire SHAKS.

Fell (fel), *sb.*² ME. [a. ON. *fiall* (Sw. *fjäll*, Da. *fjeld*) mountain; cf. Ger. *fels* rock.] 1. A hill, mountain. *Obs.* exc. in *Bowfell, Scawfell*, etc. 2. A moorland ridge, down. Now chiefly *north.* and *Sc.* ME. ¶b. In 16–17th c.: A marsh, fen 1514.

†**Fell,** *sb.*³ [a. L. *fel* (*fell-*) gall.] Gall; hence, rancour. SPENSER.

Fell (fel), *sb.*⁴ 1625. [f. Fell *v.*; see FALL *sb.*] 1. The action of FELL *v.*: a. A knock-down blow (*dial.*) 1877. b. A cutting down of timber; also *concr.* 1650. c. The sewing down (a fold, etc.) level with the cloth; *concr.* a felled seam 1874. d. A fall of lambs B. JONS. 2. The line of termination of a web, formed by the last weft-thread 1874.

Fell (fel), *sb.*⁵ 1653. *Mining.* Lead ore in its rough state; also, lead ore siftings.

Fell (fel), *a.* and *adv.* ME. [a. OF. *fel* :—pop. L. *fello*, nom. of *fellonem* sb.: see FELON.]

A. *adj.* 1. Fierce, savage; cruel, ruthless; terrible. Now *poet.* or *rhet.* 2. Dire, intensely painful or destructive. Now *poet.* or *rhet.*; also *dial.* ME. †3. Hot, virulent –1590. 4. Full of spirit, doughty (now *dial.*) ME.; eager (*for, on*, †*to*); intent *upon* 1666. †5. Shrewd; clever, cunning –1725. 6. 'Mighty'. *Obs.* exc. *Sc.* 1515.

1. My f. hate DEKKER. The..Ban-dog..is fierce, is f. 1688. 2. Despair and f. Disease GRAY. Biting Boreas, f. and doure BURNS. 3. *Mids. N.* II. i. 20. 4. I am so f. to my business that I..will not go PEPYS. 6. A f. time FERNE.

B. *adv.* In a fell manner; †cruelly, fiercely; eagerly, vigorously, excessively (now *dial.*) ME.

Fell (fel), *v. Pa. t.* and *pple.* **felled** (feld). [OE. *fellan, fællan, fyllan* :—OTeut. **falljan*, causative of **fallan* FALL *v.*] 1. To cause to fall; to knock or bring down; †to kill –1681. †Also *fig.* 2. To cut down (a tree) OE. †3. To bring or let down, lower –1620. 4. To stitch down (the wider of the two edges left projecting by a seam) so that it lies flat and smooth on the under-side of the seam. Also, *to f. a seam.* 1758.

1. Oak or Firr..in Wood or Mountain fell'd MILT. *P. L.* VI. 575. Hence **Fe·llable** *a.* **Fe·ller,** one who or that which fells; a wood-cutter; an attachment to a sewing machine for felling.

Fellah (fe·lā). *Pl.* **fellaheen, fellahs.** 1743. [a. Arab.; = 'husbandman'.] A peasant in Arabic-speaking countries; in *Eng.* used *esp.* of those of Egypt.

Fell-fare, var. of FIELDFARE.

Fellic (fe·lik), *a.* 1884. [f. L. *fel* (*fell-*) gall + -IC.] Only in *Fellic acid*: an acid, $C_{23}H_{40}O_4$, said to accompany cholic acid in human bile.

Fellifluous (feli·fluəs), *a.* 1656. [f. late L. *fellifluus* (f. *fel* + *fluere*) + -OUS.] Flowing with gall.

Fellinic (feli·nik), *a.* 1845. [f. L. *fel* (*fell-*) + -IN + -IC.] *Chem.* In *Fellinic acid*: a. an acid, $C_{50}H_{36}O_6 4HO$, obtained by treating bile with hydrochloric acid (Berzelius); b. a new acid discovered by Schotten in human bile.

Fe·llmo:nger. 1530. [f. FELL *sb.*¹ + MONGER.] A dealer in skins or hides, *esp.* sheep-skins; now, an operative who works skins.

Fellness (fe·lnės). ME. [See -NESS.] 1. The quality of being fell; fierceness, cruelty; †sternness; keenness (of wind). †2. Shrewdness, wisdom. WYCLIF.

Felloe (fe·lo^u), **felly** (fe·li). [OE. *felg* str. fem., perh. cogn. w. OTeut. **felhan* to fit together. In Eng., both forms are in use; in U.S., *felly* is preferred.] The exterior rim, or a part of the rim, of a wheel, supported by the spokes. In *pl.* the curved pieces of wood, which, joined together, form the rim.

Breake all the Spokes and Fallies from her wheele *Haml.* II. ii. 517.

Fellon(e, obs. ff. FELON.

Fellow (fe·lo^u), *sb.* [Late OE. *fēolaga* wk. masc., a. ON. *félaga*, f. *fé* = OE. *feoh* FEE *sb.*¹ + *lag-* to LAY. Primarily 'one who lays down money in a joint undertaking with others'.] †1. One who shares with another in anything; a partner, colleague, co-worker –1626; in bad sense: An accomplice –1667. Also with *of* ME. 2. More vaguely: A companion, associate, comrade. †Also *fig.* and *transf.* ME. †Occas. of women –1611. 3. One of a pair; the mate, marrow; a counterpart, match ME. 4. An equal: a. in rank (now chiefly *pl.*) ME.; b. in ability, etc. ME.; c. in kind 1477; d. in date (chiefly *pl.*) 1874. 5. A member of a company or party with common interests ME. 6. In college or university use: a. *orig.* One of the company or corporation who, with their head, constitute a college, and receive emoluments from the corporate revenues 1449. Hence b. One of the holders of certain stipendiary positions (called 'Fellowships') tenable for a limited period, on condition of pursuing some specified branch of study 1888. c. A member of the governing body, e.g. in the University of London 1837. 7. A member, or one of certain privileged members, of various learned societies, e.g. the Royal Society, etc. 1664. 8. Familiar for: man, male person ME. 9. A term of address: †a. orig. = 'comrade' –1594; b. *contemptuously* ME.

1. The fellows of his crime MILT. *P. L.* I. 606. 2. Fellows in arms 1653. Phr. *Good* or *jolly f.* = 'boon companion'. *To be (hail) f. well met*: to be on free and easy terms *with* (a person). 3. Giue me thy Gloue Souldier; Looke, heere is the f. of it *Hen. V*, IV. viii. 42. 4. a. His fellowes late, shall be his subjects now FAIRFAX. b. In reasonynge..he had few fellowes 1551. 8. A worthy F. *Timon* I. i. 229. Phr. *Poor f.*: an exclam. of pity. *My dear f., my good f.* (implying a tone of remonstrance), *old f.* *A f.*: often = 'one', 'anybody' (e.g. the speaker himself). 9. b. You..have so disdainfully called him f. FIELDING.

attrib. and *Comb.*, as *f.-apostle, -Christian, -communicant, -man, -traveller, tribesman*, etc.; also, **f.-ci·tizen,** a citizen of the same city or polity as another; **-cou·ntryman; -craftsman,** one of the same craft; **-subject,** a subject of the same sovereign.

Fellow (fe·lo^u), *v.* ME. [f. prec. sb.] 1. *trans.* †To join in partnership or companionship *with, to* –1594; to make an equal *with, to* 1450. †2. To be associated with; to be a partner in –1639. 3. To match 1656. 4. *nonce-use.* To address as 'fellow'. FIELDING.

4 Don't f. me FIELDING.

Fe·llow-co·mmoner. 1591. [f. FELLOW *sb.*] †1. A joint-partaker with others; *esp.* one who eats at the same table; see COMMONER *sb.* –1642. 2. A class of undergraduates in Oxford, Cambridge, and Dublin, who dine at the Fellows' table. (Practically *Obs.*) 1637. 3. One who has a right of common with others. LOCKE.

Fe·llow-crea·ture. 1648. [f. as prec.] A production of the same Creator; now used only of human beings and (occas.) animals.

Yon worm, man's fellow-creature BROWNING.

†**Fe·llow-fee·l,** *v.* 1611. [f. FELLOW-FEELING.] 1. *intr.* To share the feelings of others; to sympathize *with* –1641. 2. *trans.* To share the feeling of. ROGERS.

Fe·llow-fee·ling, *vbl. sb.* 1613. [tr. L. *compassio*, Gr. συμπάθεια SYMPATHY.] 1. Sympathy. 2. Sense of community of interest 1712.

2. A fellow-feeling makes us wond'rous kind BYRON.

Fe·llow-hei·r. 1585. A joint heir.

Fellowless (fe·lo^ulės), *a.* ME. [-LESS.] Without a fellow; †solitary; peerless (*poet.*).

†**Fe·llowlike.** 1526. [f. as prec. + -LIKE.] **A.** *adj.* Like a companion or mate; companionable -1633. **B.** *adv.* Like one's fellows; similarly -1569; sociably -1678.

Fe·llowly. ME. (Revived in poet. and rhet. use.) [f. as prec. + -LY.] **A.** *adj.* **1.** Like or pertaining to a fellow; social -1578. **2.** Companionable -1688.

2. Mine eyes ev'n sociable to the shew of thine Fall f. drops *Temp.* v. i. 64.

B. *adv.* On equal terms; sociably; hence, familiarly -1631.

†**Fe·llowred.** Only ME. [f. FELLOW *sb.*: see -RED.] **1.** Company, fellowship. **2.** Intercourse. **3.** A company of fellows.

Fellowship (fe·loᵘʃip), *sb.* ME. [f. FELLOW *sb.* + -SHIP.] **1.** †Partnership -1623; participation, community of interest, sentiment, nature, etc. ME. **2.** Companionship, company, society ME. **3.** †Dealing -1613; intercourse, *esp.* spiritual ME. **4.** = COMMUNION 3. ME. **5.** The spirit of comradeship ME. **6.** A body of fellows or equals; a company. Now *arch.* ME. **7.** A guild, corporation, company; also †*collect.* ME.; an association of any kind 1541. **8.** The position, or the emoluments, of a fellow in a college, university, learned society, etc. 1536; †*collect.* the body of fellows in a college, etc.; the society constituted by them -1796. **9.** *Arith.* The process by which gain or loss is divided among partners 1561. **10.** *pl.* = *Fellowship porters* (see *Comb.*) DICKENS.

1. A F. in a crie of Players *Haml.* III. ii. 289. I feel by proof That f. in pain divides not smart MILT. *P. R.* I. 401. 2. To renounce f. with anyone MACAULAY. 3. F. with the Saints A.V. *Transl. Pref.* 3. 4. Phr. *To give the right hand of f.* (after Gal. ii. 9): to acknowledge as entitled to communion (a literal giving 'the right hand of f.' being in some Protestant denominations a part of the ceremony); also *transf.* 5. A point of good f. JAS. I. 6. The goodly felowship [L. *numerus*] of the Prophetes *Bk. Com. Prayer* 1549. 7. Land is sometimes leased to a small f. JOHNSON. *Comb.* **F. porter,** a member of the f. of the Porters of Billingsgate, a guild having certain monopolies in the City of London.

Fellowship (fe·loᵘʃip), *v.* ME. [f. prec. sb.] †**1.** *trans.* To unite in fellowship. Also *refl.* -1561. †**2.** To accompany -1483. **3.** To admit to fellowship. Now only in religious use. ME. **4.** *intr.* To join in (religious) fellowship. Chiefly U.S. ME.

Fe·llow-so·ldier. 1526. A companion-in-arms.

Felly (fe·li), *adv.* ME. [f. FELL *a.*] In a fell manner; fiercely, cruelly, malignantly; †terribly, hence (*dial.*) exceedingly; †craftily, cunningly -1530.

Felly: see FELLOE.

‖**Felo-de-se** (fe·lo di sī·). *Pl.* **felones-, felos-de-se.** 1651. [Anglo-L. *felo* FELON, *de se* of himself.] **1.** One who 'deliberately puts an end to his own existence, or commits any unlawful malicious act, the consequence of which is his own death' (Blackstone). Also *fig.* **2.** Hence, Self-murder, suicide 1771.

Felon (fe·lŏn), *a.* and *sb.*¹ ME. [a. OF. *felon* adj. and sb.:—vulgar L. **fellonem*; prob. a deriv. of L. *fel* (*fell-*) gall, with sense 'one who, or that which, is full of bitterness or venom'. See N. E. D.]

A. *adj.* **1.** Cruel, fierce, terrible; wicked, base. Now *poet.* Also *transf.* of things and places. †**2.** Courageous -1596. †**3.** 'Terribly' great. *Sc.* -1605. †**4.** Stolen. FULLER.

1. Courtesies .. No gratitude in f. minds beget DRYDEN. *transf.* The f. winds MILT. *Lycidas* 91.

B. *sb.*¹ †**1.** A vile or wicked person. Sometimes applied to the Devil. -1814. **2.** *Law.* One who has committed felony. Also *attrib.* as *f. blow.* ME. †**3.** Villany, baseness; perfidy. ME. only.

1. He, the King of Heav'n .. Down to the deep abyss the flaming F. strook DRYDEN.

Hence **Fe·loness,** a female f. BROWNING. †**Fe·lonly** *adv.* in a f. manner. **Fe·lonry,** the whole class of felons. (Applied orig. to the convict population of Australia.)

Felon (fe·lŏn), *sb.*² ME. [Perh. a. OF. *felon*; see prec.] **1.** A small abscess or boil, an inflamed sore; *esp.* a whitlow under or near the nail of a finger or toe. **2.** *attrib.* in names of plants, herbs, etc., as **F.-wort,** (*a*) *Solanum Dulcamara*; (*b*) *Chelidonium majus*; (*c*) *Geranium Robertianum.* 1715.

Felonious (felōᵘ·niəs), *a.* 1575. [f. FELONY + -OUS.] **1.** Wicked, atrociously criminal. Now chiefly *poet.* **2.** *Law.* Of or pertaining to, or of the nature of, felony. Hence *pop.*: Thievish. 1634. Of a person: That has committed felony 1857.

1. F. outrages HOLLAND. 2. O thievish night! Why should'st thou, but for some f. end, In thy dark lantern thus close up the stars MILT. *Comus* 196.

Hence **Felo·nious-ly** *adv.*, **-ness.**

†**Fe·lonous,** *a.* ME. [f. FELON + -OUS.] Of the nature of a felon; like a felon -1596. Hence †**Fe·lonously** *adv.*

Felony (fe·lŏni). ME. [ad. F. *felonie*:—Com. Rom. **felloni·a*, f. *fellone* FELON; see -Y.] †**1.** Wickedness, baseness -1489; wrath (after OF.) -1523. †**2.** Guile, perfidy -1533. †**3.** A crime, misdeed, sin -1523. **4.** *Feudal Law.* An act on the part of a vassal which involved the forfeiture of his fee ME. **5.** *Common and Statute Law.* Any of a class of crimes regarded by the law as of a graver character than misdemeanours. (Including, besides statutable offences, those which formerly involved forfeiture of lands and goods, and corruption of blood; sometimes also, misprision of treason, which is a misdemeanour.) ME.

Felsite (fe·lsəit). 1794. [f. FELS(PAR) + -ITE.] *Min.* = FELSTONE; also *attrib.* Hence **Felsi·tic** *a.* consisting of or containing f.

Felspar, Felspath-: see FELDS-.

Felstone (fe·lstŏn). 1858. [ad. Ger. *felsstein*, f. *fels* rock + *stein* stone. First used vaguely for amorphous rocks; now = FELSITE.] *Min.* A designation of compact feldspar occurring in amorphous rock-masses.

Felt (felt), *sb.*¹ [OE. *felt*:—OTeut. **feltoz-, filtiz-*:—pre-Teut. **peldos, -es-*. Cf. FILTER.] **1.** A kind of cloth or stuff made of wool, or of wool and fur or hair, fulled or wrought into a compact substance by rolling and pressure, with lees or size. Also *pl.* **2.** A piece of this; something made of this, *esp.* a felt hat (whence †*transf.* a hat of any material) 1450. **3.** A thickly matted mass of hair or other fibrous substance ME.

1. Mute Silence with her feet in f. WOLCOTT. 2. The bed Of rugs and felts M. ARNOLD. *Comb.* **f.-grain,** 'the grain of wood whose direction is from the pith to the bark; the direction of the medullary rays in oak and some other timber' (KNIGHT).

Felt (felt), *sb.*² *dial.* 1708. [? a confusion of FELL *sb.*¹, FELT *sb.*¹, PELT *sb.*] A skin or hide.

Felt (felt), pa. pple. of FEEL *v.*

Felt (felt), *v.* ME. [f. FELT *sb.*¹] **1.** *trans.* To make into felt; to mat or press together into a felt-like consistence 1513; to make of felt ME. **2.** *intr.* for *refl.* To form into felt-like masses, to become matted together 1791. **3.** To cover with felt (*mod.*).

1. They fal to beat, to f., and thicken it close with their feet HOLLAND. 3. To f. the cylinder of a steam-engine (*mod.*).

Fe·lter, *v.* Now *dial.* ME. [ad. OF. *feltrer*, f. *feltre* felt = It. *feltro*:—med.L. *filtrum*; see FILTER *sb.*] **1.** *trans.* To tangle; to mat together. **2.** To entangle 1567. †**3.** = FILTER *v.* B. JONS.

Felting (fe·ltiŋ), *vbl. sb.* 1686. [f. FELT *v.*] **1.** The action or process of making felt. **2.** *concr.* Felted cloth 1849. **3.** *attrib.* 1805.

Felucca (felʊ·kă). 1628. [a. It. *felu(c)ca*, f. (ult.) Arab. root *falaka* to be round.] A small coasting vessel propelled by oars or lateen sails, or both, used chiefly in the Mediterranean.

Brancaccio.. fled in a f. [a boat about as big as a Gravesend barge] J. BARGRAVE. Hence **Felu·cca** *v.* to put on board a f. DE FOE.

Felwort (fe·lwʊɹt). [OE. *feldwyrt*, f. *feld* field + *wyrt* root.] **a.** *Gentiana lutea*, and other species of gentian. **b.** *Swertia perennis.*

Female (fī·mēˡl). [ME. *femelle*, a. OF.:—L. *femella*, dim. of *femina*.]

A. *adj.* **1.** Belonging to the sex which bears offspring. **2.** *Bot.* **a.** Of the parts of a plant: Fruit-bearing; resulting in a new individual 1791. **b.** Of a blossom or flower: Having a pistil and no stamens; pistillate; fruit-bearing 1796. **c.** Of plants, trees: Applied arbitrarily, *esp.* in **Female hemp** = *fimble-hemp* (see FIMBLE *sb.*) 1548. **3.** Consisting of females 1552. **4.** Of or pertaining to a woman or women 1635. **5.** Characteristic of womankind 1632. †**6.** Womanish -1771. **7.** Epithet of various material and immaterial things, denoting simplicity, inferiority, weakness, or the like ME. **8.** Applied, *esp.* in *Mech.*, to that part of an instrument or contrivance which receives the corresponding or male part 1669.

1. Who is this, what thing of Sea or Land? Femal of sex it seems MILT. *Sams.* 711. The Femal Bee — *P. L.* VII. 490. 2. c. The male [pympernel] hath a crimsin floure, and the f. hath a blewe TURNER. The f. Iuy so Enrings the barky fingers of the Elme *Mids. N.* IV. i. 48. 3. Heifars from his F. Store he took DRYDEN. 4. The force of f. lungs POPE. A f. reign GIBBON. 5. Femal charm MILT. *P. L.* IX. 999. 7. The ancients called sapphires male and f. .. the pale blue, approaching the white, [was] the f. EMANUEL. *F. rime*: = *feminine rime*: see FEMININE. 8. *F. screw, socket*, a circular hole or socket having a spiral thread adapted to receive the thread of the male screw.

B. *sb.* **1.** A female animal ME. **2.** A female person; as a synonym for 'woman' now only contemptuous ME. **3.** *attrib.* 1599.

1. Conception and Parturition, in the Human f. CARPENTER. 2. The females.. incapable of performing any military service CRUISE. They are no ladies. The only word good enough for them is the word of opprobrium—females 1889. 3. A f. foe HOWELL.

†**Femalist.** [See -IST.] One devoted to the female sex. MARSTON.

Femality (fīmæ·lĭti). 16.. [f. FEMALE *a.* + -ITY.] **1.** Female nature; *pl.* females 1754. **2.** Unmanliness.

Femalize (fī·măləiz), *v.* 1674. [f. as prec. + -IZE.] †**1.** *intr.* To become effeminate. **2.** *trans.* To give a feminine ending to 1709.

2. The following femalized Christian names: Alexandrina, Andrewina.. and Williamina 1887.

Feme (fem). Also (exc. techn.) **femme.** ME. [a. OF. *feme*, Fr. *femme*.] **1.** *Law.* (Chiefly conjoined with *baron*.) Wife. †**2.** In 16th c. often playfully for: Woman -1653.

1. The feme is entitled to dower BACON.

Phr. *Law.* **Feme covert** (fe·m kʊ·vəɹt), a woman under cover or protection of her husband; a married woman. **Feme sole** (fe·m sōᵘ·l), an unmarried woman, a spinster; a widow. Also, a married woman who with respect to property is as if she were unmarried. Also *attrib.*, as *feme-sole merchant, trader.*

Femerell (fe·mĕrĕl). ME. [ad. OF. *fumeraille* altered f. *fumerole*:—L. *fumariolum*, dim. of *fumarium*, f. *fumus*.] A lantern, louvre, or covering placed on the roof of a kitchen, hall, etc., for ventilation or escape of smoke.

Femicide (fe·misəid). 1801. [See -CIDE 2.] The killing of a woman.

†**Fe·minal,** *a.* ME. [a. OF., f. L. *femina*.] Of or pertaining to a woman -17..

Feminality (feminæ·lĭti). 1646. [f. prec. + -ITY.] **1.** The quality of a female; female nature. Now *rare.* **2.** *pl.* only *concr.* or quasi-*concr.* A female trait or peculiarity; also, a knick-knack such as women like 1825.

†**Fe·minate,** *a. rare.* 1533. [ad. L. *feminatus*, f. *femina*.] Effeminate; feminine -1633.

Femineity (feminī·ĭti). 1820. [f. L. *femineus* + -ITY.] Womanliness; womanishness. So **Femini·lity.**

Feminie (fe·mini). *arch.* ME. [a. OF., f. L. *femina*.] Womankind; a set of women, *esp.* the Amazons.

He conquered all the regne of F. CHAUCER.

Feminine (fe·minin). ME. [a. OF. *feminin, -ine*, ad. L. *femininus*, f. *femina*.]

A. *adj.* **1.** Belonging to the female sex; female. Now *rare.* **2.** Hence *transf.* of objects to which sex is attributed 1601. **3.** Of or pertaining to a woman or to women; carried on by women 1489. **4.** Characteristic of women; womanlike, womanly ME. **5.** Depreciatively: Womanish, effeminate. ? *Obs.* ME. **6.** *Gram.* Of the gender to which appellations of females belong ME.

1. Those Male, These F. MILT. *P. L.* I. 423. 2. They say that the Moone is a planet Fœminine HOLLAND. 3. F. society DISRAELI, discussion 1865. 4. Of a fœminine and delicate body HOLLAND. 5. He was of so unhappy a f. temper, that he was always in a terrible fright CLARENDON. 6. Every noun denoting a female animal is f. 1845. Phr. *F. rime*: in French verse, one ending in a mute *e* (as being the feminine suffix); hence, a rime of two syllables of which the

second is unstressed. So *f. ending*; *f. cæsura*, one which does not immediately follow the ictus.

B. *sb.* **1.** The adj. used absol. ME. **2.** *Gram.* A word of the feminine gender 1607.

1. The fond F. GLANVILLE. The eternal f. 1892. 2. Seamstress and songstress are double feminines 1885. Hence **Fe·minine·ly** *adv.*, **-ness. Fe·mininism**, the state of being f.; a woman's expression.

Femininity (fėmini·nĭti). [ME. *femininite*, f. FEMININE + -ITY.] **1.** Feminine quality; in early use also, female nature. **2.** Womanishness 1863. **3.** *concr.* Womankind 1865.

1. O serpent under femynynytee CHAUCER.

Feminism (fe·miniz'm). 1850. [f. L. *femina* + -ISM; cf. F. *féminisme*.] **1.** The qualities of women (*rare*). **2.** Advocacy of the claims and rights of women 1895. So **Fe·minist.**

Feminity (fĭmi·nĭti). [ME. *feminitie*, a. OF. *feminité*, f. L. *femina*.] = FEMININITY.

The mirrhor of feminitie SPENSER.

Feminize (fe·minəiz), *v.* 1652. [f. L. *femina* + -IZE.] To make or become feminine.

‖**Femme de chambre** (fam də ʃāñbr). 1762. [Fr.] **1.** A lady's maid. **2.** A chambermaid 1890.

Femoral (fe·mŏrăl). 1782. [f. L. *femur* (*femor-*) thigh + -AL.] **A.** *adj.* Of or pertaining to the femur or thigh. Chiefly *Anat.*, as *f. artery*, etc. **B.** *sb.* [sc. *artery*] 1859.

Femur (fī·mɔ̆ɹ). *Pl.* **femurs** (fī·mɔ̆ɹz), **femora** (fe·mŏră). 1563. [a. L.; see prec.] **1.** *Anat.* The thigh-bone in vertebrata 1799. **2.** *Entom.* The analogous part in an insect; the third articulation of the foot 1834. **3.** *Arch.* 'The space between the channels [of the Triglyph]' (Gwilt) 1563.

Fen (fen), *sb.*¹ [OE. *fen*, *fenn* = OHG. *fenna* fem., *fenni* neut., marsh, ON. *fen* neut., quagmire, Goth. *fani* neut., mud :—OTeut. **fanjom*.] **1.** Low land covered wholly or partially with shallow water, or frequently inundated; a tract of such land, a marsh. †**2.** Mud, clay, mire, filth –1535.

1. The margin of the broad reedy f. STEVENSON. *The fens*: certain low-lying districts in Cambridgeshire, Lincolnshire, and adjoining counties.

attrib. and *Comb.*, as *f.-boat*, *-duck*, *-fowl*, *-grass*, *-land* (whence *-lander*), etc.; also **f.-berry**, the cranberry (*Vaccinium Oxycoccus*); **-cricket**, the mole cricket (*Gryllotalpa vulgaris*); **-fire** = IGNIS FATUUS; **-goose**, usually the Gray-Lag Goose (*Anser cinereus*); **-man**, an inhabitant of the fens; **-reeve**, an officer having charge of f. lands; etc.

Fen (fen), *sb.*² *dial.* [OE. *fyne* mildew; cf. VINEWED.] A mould that attacks the hop-plant.

‖**Fen**, *sb.*³ ME. [ad. Arab. *fann* species, class.] A section in Avicenna's Canon. CHAUCER.

Fen (fen), *v.* 1823. [? Corrupt f. FEND *v.*] *trans.* To forbid. Used chiefly by boys at marbles, etc.

'I'm fly,' says Jo. 'But f. larks, you know!' DICKENS.

Fence, *sb.* ME. [aphet. f. DEFENCE.] †**1.** = DEFENCE –1664. **2.** The action, practice, or art of fencing, or use of the sword. Also *transf.* 1533. †**3.** Means or method of defence; protection, security –1756. **4.** *concr.* That which serves as a defence; a bulwark, defence. (*arch.*) ME. **5.** An enclosure or barrier (*e.g.* a hedge, wall, railing, etc.) along the boundary of any place which it is desired to defend from intruders. Often qualified, as *gun-*, *ring-*, *wire*, etc. *f.* (see these words). Also *transf.* and *fig.* 1512. **6.** *Mech.* A guard, guide, or gauge designed to regulate the movements of a tool or machine 1703. **7.** A state of prohibition (cf. L. *in defenso*). STUBBS. **8.** *Thieves' slang.* A receiver of stolen goods; a house where they are received 1700.

1. *Cap, coat of f.*: see CAP *sb.*, COAT *sb.* 2. The wager at f. with Laertes 1863. *transf.* The Sophists were cunning masters of f. BLACKIE. 4. Deer-hides.. made a rude f. against the blast SCOTT. 5. The famished lion..O'erleaps the fences of the nightly fold DRYDEN. *fig.* The strong fences of shame and awkwardness LAMB. Phr. *Sunk f.*: one placed along the bottom of a depression in the ground; also, a ditch. *To be on the f.* (U.S.): to be undecided in opinion, or neutral in action. *To make a Virginia f.* (U.S.): to walk like a drunken man.

Comb.: **f.-lizard**, the common small lizard or swift of the United States; †**-man**, a gladiator; **-month**, (*a*) orig. the fawning-time of deer, a period of about 30 days, during which hunting was forbidden; (*b*) the close season for fishing, etc., not restricted to one month; **-play**, †a gladiatorial combat; *transf.* discussion; †**-roof**, a roof for defence (= L. *testudo*); **-season**, **-time**, a close season or time for fish, swans, etc.; **-shop**, a shop at which stolen goods are sold.

Hence **Fe·nceful** *a.* affording defence. **Fe·nceless** *a.* unenclosed; defenceless.

Fence (fens), *v.* ME. [f. the sb.] **1.** *intr.* To practise the use of the foil or sword; to use the sword scientifically. Also *fig.* of a witness, etc. 1598. **2.** *trans.* To screen, shield, protect. Const. *against*, *from*. 1510. †**3.** *intr.* To provide protection *against* –1759. **4.** *trans.* To keep out, ward off, repel (*arch.*) 1592. **5.** To surround with or as with a fence; to enclose, fortify. Also *fig.* ME. **6.** *intr.* Of a horse: To leap a fence 1884. **7.** *trans.* To close for hunting or fishing. BLACKSTONE. **8.** *slang.* To purchase or sell with guilty knowledge (stolen goods). Also *absol.* 1610.

1. Alas sir, I cannot f. *Merry W.* II. iii. 14. *fig.* For several months .. diplomatists fenced among themselves MOTLEY. 2. A place well fenced from the wind HAKLUYT. He fenced his royal promise with an *if* TENNYSON. 3. To f. against the infirmities of ill health STERNE. 4. A cup of sack shall f. the cold SCOTT. 5. Well fenced either with hedge or pale DE FOE. Fenced round by trees B. CORNWALL. *fig.* Fenced by etiquette EMERSON.

Phr. *To f. the tables* (in Sc. Presbyterian Churches): to deliver an exhortation calculated to deter unworthy persons from communicating.

Hence **Fe·ncer**, one who fences; a swordsman; a horse that jumps fences; a receiver of stolen goods (*slang*).

Fencible (fe·nsib'l). ME. [Short for *defensable*, DEFENSIBLE.]

A. *adj.* **1.** Fit and liable for defensive military service. Chiefly *Sc.* **2.** Capable of being defended 1590. **3.** The sb. used *attrib.*: Belonging to the *Fencibles* 1795.

1. Let f. men..keep watch and ward CARLYLE. 2. Houses..fensible against the Arabs LITHGOW.

B. *sb.* A soldier liable only for service at home. Also *land-*, *river-*, *sea-f.* 1796.

Fencing (fe·nsiŋ), *vbl. sb.* 1489. [f. FENCE *v.*] **1.** The action or art of using the sword scientifically; the practice of this art with a blunted sword, foil, or stick. Also *fig.* 1581. **2.** The action of protecting, or of setting up a defence *against* 1489. **3.** The action of putting up fences or enclosing with a fence 1628; *concr.* an enclosure or railing; fences collectively; also (U.S.) the materials for these 1585. **4.** The action of leaping a fence 1827. **5.** *slang.* The receiving of stolen goods 1851.

1. F. is warre without anger FULLER. *fig.* A piece of diplomatic f. FREEMAN.

Fend (fend), *sb. Sc.* and *dial.* 1658. [f. next vb.] **1.** A shift or venture 1724. **2.** Fare 1804. †**3.** *Naut.* = FENDER.

Fend (fend), *v.* ME. [Shortened from DEFEND.] **1.** *trans.* = DEFEND *v.* (*arch.* or *poet.*) Also *refl.* and *intr.* for *refl.* **2.** *intr.* In *To f. and prove*: To argue 1575. **3.** *trans.* To ward or keep off; *esp.* with *off* ME. **4.** *intr.* To make a shift (*Sc.* and *dial.*) 15.. **b.** = FARE. (*dial.*) 1781.

1. Freedom..shall..f. you with his wing EMERSON. To f. aff the weather SCOTT.

Fend(e, obs. f. FIEND.

Fender (fe·ndəɹ). ME. [f. FEND *v.* + -ER.] **1.** = DEFENDER. Now *dial.* **2.** Something that fends or wards off something else: *spec.* **a.** *Naut.* A piece of old cable, or other device, hung over or fixed on a vessel's side to preserve it from damage, e. g. by collision with another vessel or with a wharf 1626. **b.** A large piece of timber placed as a guard in front of a pier, dock-wall, etc. 1739. **c.** A mud-guard on a carriage-step 1884. **3.** A metal frame placed in front of a fire to keep falling coals from rolling into the room 1688. **4.** A sluice-gate; *occas.*, the whole sluice 1847.

Comb.: **f.-beam**, (*a*) a beam suspended over a vessel's side to ward off ice, etc.; (*b*) = *f.-stop*; **-pile** = FENDER 2 b; **-stop**, the beams fixed at the end of a line of rails to stop the carriages and prevent their running off.

Fe·ndy, *a. dial.* 1782. [f. FEND *v.*] Resourceful; managing.

†**Fe·nerate**, *v.* [f. L. *fænerat-*, *fænerare*, f. *fænus* interest; see -ATE.] To lend on interest. (Dicts.) Hence †**Fenera·tion**, the action or practice of fenerating; usury.

Fenestella (fenėste·lă). 1797. [a. L., dim. of *fenestra* window.] **1.** *Arch.* A small window-like niche on the south side of the altar, containing the piscina and often the credence. **b.** A small window 1848. **2.** *Zool.* 'A polyzoon; known by many fossil remains in Devonian limestones and other rocks' (Rossiter) 1894.

Fenestellid (fenėste·lid). 1882. [f. L. *fenestella* + -ID.] *Palæont.* One of the *Fenestellidæ*, a family of palæozoic polyzoans.

†**Fene·ster.** ME. [a. OF. *fenestre* :—L. *fenestra* (see next).] A window –1548.

‖**Fenestra** (fĭne·stră). *Pl.* **-træ.** 1844. [L., f. root of Gr. φαίνειν to show.] **1.** *Anat.* A small hole or opening in a bone, etc. **2.** *Bot.* A small mark or scar, indicating the part at which the seed has separated from the ovary (Stark) 1828. Also, 'an opening through a membrane' 1866.

1. The f. ovalis or opening into the vestibule [of the ear] and the f. rotunda or opening into the cochlea BARR.

†**Fene·stral**, *sb.* ME. [a. OF., f. *fenestre* (see FENESTER).] A window-frame or lattice, often fitted with cloth or paper instead of glass; *rarely*, a window-pane –1530.

Fenestral (fĭne·străl), *a.* 1674. [ad. L. *fenestralis.*] **1.** Of or pertaining to a window. **2.** *Anat.*, etc. 'Having small openings like windows' (Wagstaffe).

Fenestrate (fĭne·strėt), *a.* 1835. [ad. L. *fenestratus*, *fenestrare*, f. *fenestra.*] **1.** Having small window-like openings or perforations. Chiefly *Bot.* and *Zool.* **2.** *Entom.* = FENESTRATED 3. 1842.

Fenestrated (fĭne·strėtėd), *ppl. a.* 1826. [f. L. *fenestratus* (see prec.) + -ED¹.] **1.** *Arch.* Furnished with windows 1849. **2.** = FENESTRATE 1. 1849. **3.** *Entom.* Having transparent spots 1826.

Fenestration (fenėstrēⁱ·ʃən). 1846. [f. L. *fenestrare.*] **1.** *Arch.* The arrangement of windows in a building. **2.** *Anat.* The becoming, or the being, fenestrated 1870.

Fenestrule (fĭne·strul). 1872. [ad. L. *fenestrula*, dim. of *fenestra.*] *Zool.* One of the openings in the zoarium of Fenestella, Polypora, and allied species.

Fengite: see PHENGITE.

Fenian (fī·niăn). 1816. [f. OIr. *féne* 'one of the names of the ancient population of Ireland' (Windisch), confused in mod. times with *fiann* fem. collect., a body of warriors who defended Ireland in the time of Finn, a legendary Irish king.]

A. *sb.* **1.** Applied to mercenary tribes acting as a permanent force for the support of the Ard Rig, or king of Eire. **2.** One of a 'brotherhood' formed among the U.S. Irish for the overthrow of English rule in Ireland 1864.

B. *sb.* Of or pertaining to the Fenians or to Fenianism 1861.

Hence **Fe·nianism**, the principles, purposes, and methods of the Fenians.

Fenks (fenks), *pl.* 1820. The fibrous parts of the blubber of a whale, which contain the oil; the refuse of the blubber when melted.

‖**Fennec** (fe·nėk). 1790. [Arab. *fenek.*] *Zool.* A small African fox-like animal (*Canis zerda*) having very long ears.

Fennel (fe·nĕl). [OE. *finugl*, *finule*, *fenol*, *fenul*, ad. pop.L. *fenuclum*, *fenoclum* (for L. *fœniculum*, dim. of *fœnum* hay).] *Bot.* **1.** A fragrant perennial umbellifer (*Fœniculum vulgare*) having yellow flowers, made use of in sauces, etc. **2.** Applied to plants resembling fennel 1523.

1. There's F. for you *Haml.* IV. iv. 180. **Sweet F.**, *Fœniculum dulce* or *officinale*, grown in kitchen gardens for the sake of its leaves. 2. Dog or **Dog's F.**, *Anthemis Cotula.* **Hog's F.**, *Peucedanum officinale.* **F.-flower**, a herb of the genus *Nigella.* **F.-giant**, a plant of the genus *Ferula* = *Giant-f.*

Comb.: **f. oil**, 'the oil of common fennel containing anethol and a terpene' (Watts); **f. water**, a spirituous liquor prepared from fennel seed.

Fennish (fe·niʃ), *a.* 1574. [f. FEN *sb.*¹ + -ISH.] **1.** = FENNY *a.*¹ 1. 1577. **2.** Belonging to or produced from a fen 1574.

Fenny (fe·ni), *a.*¹ [OE. *fennig*, f. *fenn* FEN.] **1.** Of the nature of fen; boggy, swampy.

2. = FENNISH **2.** 1543. †**3.** Muddy, dirty –1635.

2. Fillet of a f. snake SHAKS. F. rushes KEATS.

Fe·nny, *a.*² Now *dial.* [OE. *fynig*, f. *fyne* FEN *sb.*²] Mouldy.

†**Fenouille·tte.** 1706. [a. F., f. *fenouil* FENNEL.] Fennel water –1758.

†**Fe·nsive,** shortened f. DEFENSIVE.

Fent (fent), *sb.* ME. [ad. F. *fente*, f. *fendre* :—L. *findere*.] **1.** A short slit or opening in a robe. Also a placket-hole. Now chiefly *dial.* **2.** A remnant (of cloth) 1847.

Fenugreek (fe·niŭgrīk). [OE. *fenogræcum*, L. *fænugræcum* for *fænum Græcum* Greek hay, so called by the Romans.] A leguminous plant (*Trigonella Fœnum Græcum*), the seeds of which are used by farriers. Also *attrib.*

Feodary, Feodatory: see FEU-.

Feoff, var. of FIEF *sb.*

Feoff (fef), *v. P. t.* and *pple.* **feoffed.** [Early ME. *feoffen*, ad. AF. *feoffer*, OF. *fieuffer*, *fieffer*, f. *fieu*, *fief*; see FEE *sb.*², FIEF *sb.*] **1.** *Law.* = ENFEOFF *v.* **1.** ? *Obs.* †Also *fig.* –1636. †**2.** To confer (a heritable possession) *upon*. Chiefly *fig.* –1649.

Feoffee (fefī·). ME. [ad. OF. *feoffé*, pa. pple. of *feoffer*.] *Law.* **1.** The person to whom a feoffment is made 1542. **2.** *spec.* One of a board of trustees holding land for charitable or other public purposes.

Feoffment (fe·fmĕnt). ME. [a. AF. *feoffement*; see FEOFF *v.*] *Law.* **1.** The action of investing with a fief or fee. Applied *esp.* to conveyance by livery of seisin (at common law usually evidenced by a deed). †**2.** The deed or instrument by which corporeal hereditaments are conveyed –1672. **3.** The fief conferred ME.

1. Phr. *F. in, of, upon trust, f. to uses*: a grant of land in trust for another, or for certain uses.

Feoffor, feoffer (fe·fəɹ). ME. [ad. AF. *feoffour*; see FEOFF *v.*] **1.** One who makes a feoffment to another. ¶**2.** Misused for FEOFFEE. –1603.

†**Fer,** *v.* App. meaningless. See context of *Hen. V.* IV. iv. 29.

Fer, obs. f. FAR; FEAR *sb.*; FIRE.

Feracious (fĕrēⁱ·ʃəs), *a.* 1637. [f. L. *ferax* (*feraci-*), f. *ferre* to bear + -OUS.] Bearing abundantly; fruitful.

Feracity (fĕræ·sĭti). *rare.* ME. [ad. L. *feracitatem*; see prec. and -ACITY.] The quality of being feracious.

Feral (fīᵊ·răl), *a.*¹ 1621. [ad. L. *feralis* pertaining to funeral rites or to the dead.] **1.** Deadly, fatal. Freq. in *Astrol.* **2.** Funereal, gloomy 1640.

1. F. diseases BURTON, Signes LILLY. **2.** Ferall Birds that love Darknesse GAUDEN.

Feral (fīᵊ·răl), *a.*² 1604. [f. L. *fera* wild beast + -AL.] **1.** Wild, untamed; uncultivated. Often of animals and plants that have run wild. 1659. **2.** Of, pertaining to, or resembling a wild beast; brutal, savage.

‖**Ferash** (fera·ʃ). *Anglo-Ind.* 1600. [Urdū from Arab. *farrāsh* spreader.] A menial servant who spreads carpets, pitches tents, etc.

Ferberite (fɔ̄·ɹbĕrəit). 1811. [f. *Ferber* proper name + -ITE.] †**1.** (After J. J. Ferber.) A variety of gneiss. **2.** (After R. Ferber.) A variety of wolfram from Southern Spain 1868.

Ferd, obs. f. FEARED *ppl. a.*

‖**Fer-de-lance** (fęr də lāns, fēᵊɹ də lɑns). 1880. [Fr.; = 'head (*lit.* iron) of a lance'.] **1.** *Her.* A lance-head used as a charge 1892. **2.** A venomous serpent (*Trigonocephalus lanceolatus*) of Brazil 1888.

‖**Fer-de-moline** (fēᵊɹ də mǫ·lin). 1741. [Fr.; = 'iron of a mill'.] *Her.* A bearing: The iron support for the moving mill-stone.

Fere, *sb.*¹ Now *arch.* [ME. *fere*, aphet. f. OE. *gefēra* (Y-FERE) :—(ult.) pre-Eng. *gi-* (Y-) + **fōrā* going, f. ablaut-root of *faran*.] **1.** A companion, mate; whether male or female. **2.** A husband or wife ME. **3.** An equal ME.

2. The nuptial f. Of famous Vulcan CHAPMAN.

†**Fere,** *sb.*² ME. [aphet. f. OE. *gefēr* neut., f. as prec.] Companionship; chiefly *concr.* a company. Only ME.

Phr. *In f.*, *I f.* (often written *yfere*): together; in common.

†**Fere,** *a.* Now *Sc.* ME. [a. ON. *fœrr*, f. (ult.) OTeut. **fōrā* (OE. *fōr*, ME. FORE *sb.*) going, f. *faran* FARE *v.*¹] Able to go, in health; hence *gen.* able; sound, whole.

I trust to find ye baith haill and f. SCOTT.

†**Fere,** *v.*¹ [OE. *fēran* wk. vb. :—OTeut. **fōrjan*, f. **fōra*, f. ablaut-root of *faran* FARE *v.*¹] *intr.* = FARE *v.*¹ (exc. in senses 3, 5) –1483.

†**Fere,** *v.*² ME. [aphet. f. AFFEIR, EFFEIR.] *intr.* To fall by right, appertain, become. Chiefly *impers.* –1513.

Fere, obs. f. FAR, FEAR, FEER, FIRE.

Feretory (fe·rĭtŏri). ME. [A perversion of ME. *fertre*, a. OF. *fiertre* :—L. *feretrum*, ad. Gr. φέρετρον, f. φέρειν to bear.] **1.** A portable or stationary shrine, often richly adorned, in which were kept the relics of saints; a tomb. **2.** A bier ME. **3.** The part of an abbey or a church in which shrines were deposited 1449.

1. Porphyry stones for Edward the Confessor's f. H. WALPOLE. var. ‖**Fe·retrum** (in sense 1).

Ferforth, obs. f. FAR-FORTH.

Fergusonite (fɔ̄·ɹgəsənəit). 1827. [f. *Ferguson* (of Raith) + -ITE.] *Min.* 'A metaniobate (and tantalate) of yttrium with erbium, cerium, uranium, iron, calcium, etc.' (Dana).

‖**Feria** (fīᵊ·riă). 1853. [L.; see FAIR *sb.*¹] *Eccl.* A week-day, *esp.* an ordinary week-day as opp. to a festival.

Ferial (fīᵊ·riăl). ME. [a. F. *férial*, ad. med.L. *ferialis*, f. *feria*; see prec.]

A. *adj.* **1.** Pertaining to the days of the week, or to a week-day as dist. from a festival. **2.** Pertaining to a holiday 1500.

Phr. *F. day, time* (Sc. Law): in which the courts were closed and legal process was invalid.

B. *sb.* A week-day not a feast or festival 1877.

†**Feria·tion.** 1612. [f. L. *feriari*, f. *feria*.] Holiday keeping; cessation of work –1822.

†**Fe·rie,** *sb.* ME. [a. OF. *ferie*, ad. L. *feria*.] **1.** A festival, holiday. Also *attrib.* –1616. **2.** = FERIA. –1588.

Ferine (fīᵊ·rəin). 1640. [ad. L. *ferinus*, f. *fera* wild beast.]

A. *adj.* **1.** Pertaining to, or of the nature of, wild animals; wild, untamed 1677. **2.** Of human beings, etc.: Bestial, beast-like 1640. **3.** Of a disease: Malignant (*rare*) 1666.

1. Some in f. Venation take delight MOTTEUX.

B. *sb.* A wild beast. (Dicts.)

Hence **Fe·rine-ly** *adv.*, **-ness.**

Feringhee (fĕri·ŋgi). 1634. [Oriental ad. FRANK, with Arab. ethnic suffix *-i*; in Arab. *faranjī*, in Pers. *farangī*.] Formerly, the Indian term for a European; now used chiefly of the Indian-born Portuguese, and contemptuously of other Europeans.

Ferio (fe·ri,o). 1551. *Logic.* A mnemonic word representing the fourth mood of the first syllogistic figure, in which a universal negative major premiss and a particular affirmative minor yield a particular negative conclusion.

Ferison (ferəi·sǫn). 1509. *Logic.* A mnemonic word representing the sixth mood of the third syllogistic figure, in which a universal negative major premiss and a particular affirmative minor yield a particular negative conclusion.

Ferity (fe·rĭti). 1534. [ad. L. *feritatem*, f. *ferus*; see -ITY.] **1.** The quality of being wild or savage. **2.** Savage or barbarous condition 1646. †**3.** Barbarity, savage cruelty –1718.

2. The ancient Rudeness and F. of our Country STANHOPE.

Fe·rling. Now *Hist.* [OE. *fēorðling*, f. *fēorða* FOURTH + -LING.] = FARTHING.

Ferly (fɔ̄·ɹli). [OE. *fǣrlic* sudden, f. *fǣr* (see FEAR) + *-lic*, -LY¹]

†**A.** *adj.* **1.** Sudden –ME. **2.** Terrible –1577. **3.** Strange, wonderful –1650; wonderfully great –1450.

2. Furres of f. bestes 1460. Hence †**Fe·rly** *adv.*

B. *sb.* Now *Sc.* and *dial.* **1.** A marvel ME. **2.** Wonder, astonishment ME.

Fermacy, obs. f. PHARMACY.

Fermage, Ferm(e, etc., var. of FARMAGE, FARM, etc.

Fermail (fɔ̄·ɹmĕl). 1480. [a. OF. *fermaille* :—med.L. *firmaculum*, f. *firmare* to fix.] *Her.*, etc. A buckle or clasp; a setting.

Ferment (fɔ̄·ɹmĕnt), *sb.* ME. [a. F., ad. L. *fermentum*, f. root of *fervere* to boil.] **1.** *orig.* Leaven or yeast; hence *gen.* that which causes fermentation. Also *fig.* **2.** = FERMENTATION 1. 1605. **3.** *fig.* Agitation, tumult 1672.

1. Pasteur .. proved the real 'ferments' .. to be organised beings TYNDALL. *fig.* This hypothesis lays a f. for frequent rebellion LOCKE. **2.** The first f. of new wine 1744. **3.** To allay the general f. 1781.

Ferment (fəɹme·nt), *v.* ME. [a. F. *fermenter*, ad. L. *fermentare*, f. *fermentum*; see prec.] **1.** *intr.* To undergo the action of a ferment; to suffer fermentation; to 'work'. (In early use primarily of dough or saccharine fluids.) Also *fig.* **2.** *trans.* To subject to fermentation; to cause fermentation in 1672. **3.** *transf.* and *fig.* To work up into an agitation; to excite, stir up 1660.

1. *fig.* My griefs .. f. and rage MILT. *Sams.* 619. **2.** *fig.* Fanaticism .. fermented with the leaven of earthly avarice HURD. **3.** Ye vig'rous swains, while youth ferments your blood POPE.

Hence **Ferme·ntable** *a.* capable of fermentation. **Fermente·scible,** (also *erron.* **-ible**), *a.* capable of causing or of undergoing fermentation.

†**Ferme·ntal,** *a.* 1650. [f. FERMENT *sb.* + -AL.] Pertaining to, or of the nature of, a ferment or fermentation –1694.

Fermentarian (fɔ̄ɹmĕntēᵊ·riăn). 1775. [f. L. *fermentarius*, f. *fermentum* + -OUS.] A term of reproach applied by Latin to Greek Christians, as using fermented bread in the Eucharist.

†**Fe·rmentate,** *v.* 1599. [f. L. *fermentat-*, *fermentare*.] *trans.* To cause to ferment; to leaven –1670.

Fermentation (fɔ̄ɹmĕntēⁱ·ʃən). ME. [ad. L. *fermentationem*; see prec.] The action or process of fermenting. **1.** A process of the nature of that resulting from the operation of leaven on dough or on saccharine liquids.

The features of the process are an effervescence, with evolution of heat, in the substance operated on, and a resulting alteration of its properties. In early use, the term was applied to all chemical changes exhibiting these characters. In modern science it is restricted to a definite class of chemical changes peculiar to organic compounds, and produced in them by a 'ferment' (see FERMENT *sb.* 1), and variously qualified as *acetous, alcoholic, butyric, lactic, putrefactive*, etc. (see these words). In popular language the term usually conveys the notion of a sensible 'working', which is not involved in the chemical sense, but its application is now similarly restricted.

2. *fig.* The state of being excited by emotion or passion; agitation; working (sometimes towards a better condition of things) 1660.

2. Predicting .. the happy, future State of our Country; and that the then F. would be perfective to it 1682. The intellectual f. of Germany MILL.

Fermentative (fəɹme·ntătiv), *a.* 1661. [f. as FERMENTATE *v.* + -IVE.] **1.** Of, pertaining to, or of the nature of fermentation; developed by fermentation 1665. **2.** Tending to cause or undergo fermentation.

1. F. changes 1869. Hence **Ferme·ntative-ly** *adv.*, **-ness.** So **Ferme·ntatory** (in sense 1).

Fermentive (fəɹme·ntiv), *a.* 1672. [f. FERMENT *sb.* or *v.* + -IVE.] Tending to produce fermentation.

†**Fe·rmerer.** ME. [f. FERMERY.] The superintendent of a (monastic) infirmary. CHAUCER.

Fe·rmery, fa·rmery. Now *Hist.* ME. [aphet. f. OF. *enfermerie*; see INFIRMARY.] = INFIRMARY.

†**Fe·rmillet.** 1475. [a. OF. *fermillet*, *fermaillet*, dim. of *fermail* FERMAIL.] A clasp, buckle, or setting –1633.

†**Fern,** *a.* and *adv.* [OE. *fyrn* formerly.]

A. *adj.* Former, ancient, of old –1571.

B. *adv.* Long ago, formerly –ME.

Fern (fɔ̄ɹn), *sb.* [OE. *fearn* str. neut. :—OTeut. **farno-* :—OAryan **porno*, whence Skr. *parṇa* neut., wing, feather, leaf. The orig. sense is doubtless 'feather'.] *Bot.* One of a large group of vascular cryptogamous plants constituting the N.O. *Filices*; a single plant or frond; also *collect.* in *sing.*

Flowering or **Royal F.**: *Osmunda regalis*; see OSMUND². **Hard f.** = *Blechnum*. **Lady-f.** = *Athyrium Filix-femina*. **Male f.** = *Lastrea Filix-mas*. **Prickly f.** = *Polystichum aculeatum*. See also *bladder-, buckler-*, etc. *f.*

Comb.: **f.-bracken** = BRACKEN; **-brake** = prec.; also, a thicket of f.; **-chafer**, a beetle (*Scarabæus* or *Amphimalla solstitialis*); **-gale**, the Sweet F. (*Myrica Comptonia*); **-tree** = *tree-f.*; **-web**, a beetle (*Scarabæus* or *Melorontha horticola*).

†**Ferna·mbuck.** 1595. [Corruptly f. *Pernambuco*.] = BRAZIL *sb.* 1. Also *attrib.* -1722.

Fernery (fɔ̄·ɹnəri). 1840. [f. FERN *sb.* + -ERY.] A place or a glass case in which ferns are grown.

Fe·rn-owl. [f. FERN *sb.* + OWL.] **a.** The Nightjar or Goatsucker 1678; **b.** the Short-eared owl 1885.

Fe·rn-seed. 1596. [f. as prec. + SEED.] The seed of the fern; once popularly supposed to be an invisible seed and to confer invisibility upon its possessor.
1 *Hen. IV*, II. i. 96.

Ferntickle (fɔ̄·ɹntik'l). Now *dial.* 1483. 'A freckle on the skin, resembling the seed of fern' (Webst.).

Ferny (fɔ̄·ɹni), *a.* 1523. [f. FERN *sb.* + -Y[1].] 1. Abounding in fern. 2. Of, pertaining to, or consisting of fern 1710. 3. Resembling fern 1791.

†**Fe·rnyear, fern year.** [OE. *fyrngēar*; see FERN *a.* and YEAR.]
A. *sb.* 1. A past year -1562. 2. Last year -1737.
2. Farwel al the snowgh of ferne yere CHAUCER.
B. *adv.* In past years; in the course of last year -1806.

Ferocious (fĕrōu·ʃəs), *a.* 1646. [f. L. *ferox* (*feroci-*) + -OUS.] 1. Fierce, savage; savagely cruel or destructive. 2. Indicating ferocity 1728.
1. The Lyon a..f. animall SIR T. BROWNE. 2. F. eyes 1826. Hence **Fero·cious-ly** *adv.*, **-ness.**

Ferocity (fĕrǫ·sĭti). 1606. [ad. F. *férocité*, ad. L. *ferocitatem*; see prec.] The quality or state of being ferocious; habitual fierceness or savageness.
It [fear] is always joined with f. RUSKIN.

†**Fe·rous,** *a. rare.* 1653. [f. L. *ferus* + -OUS.] Wild, savage.

-ferous, in use always **-iferous** (i·fĕrəs), an adjectival suffix f. L. *-fer* producing (f. *ferre* to bear) + -OUS; as, *auriferous, frugiferous, lucriferous*, etc.

Ferox (fe·rǫks). 1867. [a. L. (*salmo*) *ferox*, the scientific name.] A fish (*Salmo ferox*), the great Lake Trout.

†**Fe·rrament.** ME. [a. OF. *ferrement*, ad. L. *ferramentum* implement of iron.] *pl.* Articles of iron; *e.g.* instruments, tools, irons, shackles, fittings, etc. -1660.

Ferrandin, var. of †FARANDINE.

†**Ferra·ra,** *rare.* 1762. A broadsword; an 'Andrea Ferrara'. Cf. ANDREW 1. -1785.

†**Fe·rrary.** 1609. [ad. L. (*ars*) *ferraria*.] The smith's art -1611.

Ferrate (fe·rėⁱt). 1854. [f. L. *ferrum* + -ATE [4].] *Chem.* A salt of ferric acid.

Ferrateen. *rare.* Cf. FERRETING *sb.* Scott.

Ferr(e, obs. ff. of FAR *sb.*, *a.*, and *v.*

†**Fe·rren,** *adv.* and *a.* [OE. *feorran*, f. OTeut. **ferr-* FAR *adv.*]
A. *adv.* 1. From far -ME. 2. Afar -ME. 3. With preps. *of, on* (*o*), *from ferren*: from or at a distance -1470.
B. *adj.* Distant, far -1548.

Ferreous (fe·rĭ,əs), *a.* 1646. [f. L. *ferreus* + -OUS.] 1. Pertaining to, consisting of, or containing iron. 2. Like iron: **a.** in hardness 1822; **b.** in colour (*mod.*).

†**Fe·rrer, fe·rrour.** ME. [a. OF. *ferreor*:—med.L. *ferratorem*; see FARRIER.] 1. A worker in iron -1609. 2. = FARRIER 1. -1798.

Ferret (fe·rėt), *sb.*[1] ME. [a. OF. *fuiret*, *furet*:—late L. *furonem*, said to be f. L. *fur* thief.] A half-tamed variety of the common polecat (*Putorius fœtidus*), kept for driving rabbits from their burrows, destroying rats, etc. Also *transf.* and *fig.*
Comb. **f.-eye,** 'the spur-winged goose, so called from the red circle around the eyes' (Webst.).
Hence **Fe·rrety** *a.* like a f. or a ferret's.

Ferret (fe·rėt), *sb.*[2] 1576. [Cf. It. *fioretti* floss-silk, and F. *fleuret*.] †1. attrib. *F.-silk* = floss silk -1612. 2. A stout cotton (or silk) tape. Also *attrib.* 1649.

†**Fe·rret,** *sb.*[3] *rare.* 1662. [a. F. *ferret*, *feret*, dim. of *fer* iron.] *Glass-making.* An iron used for trying whether the melted glass is fit to work; also, an iron for forming the ring at the mouth of bottles. (Now only in Dicts.)

Ferret (fe·rėt), *v.* 1450. [f. FERRET *sb.*[1]; cf. F. *fureter*.] 1. *intr.* To hunt with ferrets; *trans.* to clear out by means of a ferret. 2. *trans.* To take (rabbits, etc.) with ferrets. Also, to drive forth by means of a ferret. 1577. 3. To hunt after; to worry 1599; to drive *from, off, out of* 1601; to search (a place) 1583. 4. *intr.* To rummage, search about 1580. 5. *trans.* With *out, up*: To search out, bring to light 1577.
3. And..vow'd He'd f. him, lurk where he wou'd BUTLER *Hud.* I. iii. 236. To f. this vermin brood out of the colonies W. IRVING. 5. I have ferreted out evidence, got up cases DICKENS. Hence **Fe·rreter.**

Ferreting (fe·rėtiŋ), *sb.* 1670. [f. FERRET *sb.*[2]] = FERRET *sb.*[2]

Ferretto (fere·to). Also **feretto.** 1662. [a. It. *ferretto* (*di Spagna*), dim. of *ferro* iron:—L. *ferrum*.] Copper calcined with brimstone or white vitriol, used to colour glass.

Ferri- (fe·ri), formerly **ferrid-,** comb. f., indicating the presence of iron in the 'ferric' state (cf. FERRO-). **Ferricyanhy·dric** or **Ferricya·nic acid,** an acid, H_4FeCy_6, procured from various ferricyanides, and crystallizing in lustrous brownish-green needles. **Ferricy·anide,** a salt of ferrianhydric acid, e.g. *potassium ferricyanide*, red prussiate of potash; *ferrous ferricyanide*, Turnbull's blue. **Ferricya·nogen,** the hypothetical radical $FeCy_2$ supposed to exist in ferricyanhydric acid.

Ferriage (fe·ri,ėdʒ). ME. [f. FERRY *sb.* and *v.* + -AGE.] 1. The action or business of ferrying; conveyance over a ferry 1450. 2. The fare or price paid for the use of a ferry.
1. We were detained..waiting f. 1880.

Ferric (fe·rik), *a.* 1799. [f. L. *ferrum* + -IC.] 1. Of, pertaining to, or extracted from iron. 2. *Chem.* Applied to compounds in which iron exists in its higher valency, as *ferric acid*, a hypothetical acid H_2FeO, assumed to exist in the salts called ferrates.

Ferrier (fe·ri,əɹ). ME. [f. FERRY *v.*] = FERRYMAN.

Ferriferous (feri·fĕrəs), *a.* 1811. [f. L. *ferrum* + -(I)FEROUS.] Producing iron, as *f. rocks.*

Ferris (fe·ris). 1893. [f. the name of G.W.G. *Ferris*, U.S. engineer.] *F. wheel*, an amusement device consisting of an enormous revolving vertical wheel supporting passenger cars on its periphery.

Ferrite (fe·rəit). 1879. [f. L. *ferrum* + -ITE.] 1. *Min.* Amorphous hydroxide of iron of undetermined composition. 2. *Chem.* 'A combination of ferric oxide with a metallic oxide more basic than itself, as *barium ferrite*, $BaFe_2O_4$; etc.' (Muir).

Ferro- (fero). 1. Used as comb. f. of L. *ferrum* iron, chiefly *Min.* in the names of species containing iron, as **ferro-calcite,** a variety of calcite which contains carbonate of iron and turns brown on exposure; **ferromagne·tic** *a.*, = PARAMAGNETIC; **ferromagnetism,** = PARAMAGNETISM; **ferromanganese,** an alloy of iron and manganese (containing 15 per cent. and upward of manganese); **ferro-tungsten,** iron containing a certain percentage of tungsten.
2. *Chem.* Now applied to designate 'ferrous' as opp. to 'ferric' compounds of iron (cf. FERRI-). **Ferrocyanhy·dric** or **ferrocya·nic acid,** a tetrabasic acid, H_4FeCy_6, forming a white crystalline powder. **Ferrocy·anide,** a salt of ferrocyanhydric acid, as *potassium ferrocyanide*, popularly yellow prussiate of potash. **Ferrocya·nogen,** the hypothetical radical $FeCy_2$ supposed to exist in ferrocyanides. †**Ferropru·ssiate** = *Ferrocyanide.* †**Ferropru·ssic acid** = *Ferrocyanhydric acid.*

Fe·rro-co·ncrete. 1900. = REINFORCED *c.*

Ferroso- (ferōu·so), comb. f. of mod.L. *ferrosus* FERROUS, in *ferroso-ferric oxide*, Fe_3O_4.

Ferrotype (fe·rŏtəip). 1879. [f. FERRO- + TYPE.] A process by which positive photographs are taken on thin iron plates; a photograph so taken. Also *attrib.*

Ferrous (fe·rəs), *a.* 1865. [f. L. *ferrum* + -OUS.] *Chem.* A term applied to compounds in which iron combines as a divalent, e.g. *ferrous oxide*, FeO.

Ferruginate (fĕrū·dʒinėⁱt), *v.* [f. L. *ferrugo* (*ferrugin-*) + -ATE [3].] To give the colour or properties of iron rust to. Hence **Ferru·ginated** *ppl. a.* (Dicts.)

Ferrugineous (ferudʒi·nĭ,əs), *a.* = next.

Ferruginous (fĕrū·dʒinəs), *a.* 1656. [f. as FERRUGINATE + -OUS.] 1. *orig.* Of the nature of, or containing, iron rust; *now*, Of the nature of iron; containing iron 1661. 2. Of the colour of iron rust; reddish brown.

Ferrule, ferrel (fe·rəl), *sb.* 1611. [Corrupted spelling (as if dim. of L. *ferrum*) of the older form *verrel, verril*, ad. OF. *virelle, virol*, med. L. *virola*:—L. *viriola*, dim. of *viriæ*, pl. bracelets.] 1. A ring or cap of metal put round the end of a stick, tube, etc. to strengthen it, or prevent splitting and wearing. 2. A ring or band for strengthening anything, or holding the parts of anything together 1632. 3. *Steam-Engine.* 'A bushing for expanding the end of a flue' (Webst.).
Hence **Fe·rrule, fe·rrel** *v.* to fit or furnish with a f. **Fe·rruled** *ppl. a.* provided with a f.

Ferruminate (fĕrū·minėⁱt), *v.* ? *Obs.* 1623. [f. L. *ferruminat-*, *ferruminare*, f. *ferrumen* cement, f. *ferrum*.] To cement, solder, unite. Hence **Ferrumina·tion.**

Ferry (fe·ri), *sb.* ME. [f. the vb. Cf. ON. *ferja*.] †1. A passage or crossing. ME. only. 2. *esp.* A place where boats pass over a river, etc. to transport passengers and goods ME. 3. Provision for conveyance by boat from one shore to the other 1489. †**b.** = FERRY-BOAT. -1798. 4. *Law.* The right of ferrying men and animals across a river, etc., and of levying toll for so doing 1721.
3. A f. was established where London Bridge now stands GARDINER. **b.** The French had sunk divers Ferries and other Boats in the River 1701.
Comb.: **f.-bridge,** a form of ferry-boat in which a railway-train is transported across a river or bay; **-railway,** 'one whose track is on the bottom of the watercourse and whose carriage has an elevated deck which supports the train' (Knight).

Ferry (fe·ri), *v.* [OE. *ferian*:—OTeut. **farjan*, f. *far-ᵒᵐ*; see FARE *sb.*] †1. *trans.* To convey from one place to another -1583. 2. *esp.* To transport over water (formerly including the sea) in a boat or ship, etc. OE. **b.** To work (a boat, etc.) *across* or *over* 1771. 3. *intr.* for *refl.* To go; now only, to pass over water in a boat or by a ferry; of a boat: To pass to and fro OE.
2. Charon is tyr'd, with ferring soules to hell HEYWOOD. 3. Crist seide to hem verie we over þe water WYCLIF. Upon these waters doe f. fiftie thousand Boats 1630.

Fe·rry-boat. ME. [f. FERRY *sb.* + BOAT.] A boat for conveying passengers, etc. across a ferry.

Fe·rryman. 1464. [f. FERRY *sb.* + MAN.] One who keeps or looks after a ferry.

†**Fers.** ME. [a. OF. *fierce, fierche*, etc., ad. (ult.) Pers. *ferzēn* 'counsellor'.] *Chess.* 1. The queen -1676. 2. A pawn which has passed to the eighth square. CAXTON.
Phr. *The ferses twelve*: all the men exc. the king (Skeat).

Fers, obs. f. FIERCE *a.*, VERSE.

Fe·rter, *v.* ME. [f. ME. *fertre*; see FERETORY.] To put in a shrine.

Ferth, obs. f. FOURTH.

Ferther, obs. f. FURTHER.

Fertile (fɔ̄·ɹtil, -təil), *a.* 1460. [a. OF. *fertil*, ad. L. *fertilis*, f. *ferre*.] 1. Producing in abundance; fruitful, prolific. Also *transf.* and *fig.* 2. Causing or promoting fertility 1597. †3. Copiously produced, abundant -1667.
1. A soil..f. ..of weeds 1785. F. plains C. BRONTË. *fig.* F. in resources T. JEFFERSON. A land f. in warriors FREEMAN. 2. F. slime EMERSON. 3. With adorations, fertill teares *Twel. N.* I. v. 274. Hence **Fe·rtilely** *adv.* **Fe·rtileness** = FERTILITY (*rare*).

†**Ferti·litate,** *v.* 1634. [f. next, after *debilitate*.] To render fertile, fertilize -1650.

Fertility (fəɹti·lĭti). 1490. [a. F. *fertilité*, ad. L. *fertilitatem*, f. *fertilis* FERTILE.] The quality of being FERTILE; fecundity, fruitfulness, productiveness; *pl.* productive powers. Also *transf.* and *fig.*
Thy waste More rich than other climes' f. BYRON.

The f. of this clover absolutely depends [etc.] DARWIN. *fig.* I found some .. f. of fancy JOHNSON. F. of invention PLAYFAIR, thought MACAULAY, resource 1878.

Fertilization (fəːrtiləizēⁱ·ʃən). Also **-isation.** 1857. [f. FERTILIZE + -ATION.] The action or process of rendering fertile; *spec.* in *Biol.* fecundation (see FERTILIZE 2).

These species require the aid of insects for their f. DARWIN.

Fertilize (fəː·rtiləiz), *v.* 1648. [f. FERTILE + -IZE.] 1. *trans.* To make fertile; to enrich (the soil). b. *gen.* To render productive. (*lit.* and *fig.*) 1828. 2. *Biol.* To make (an ovum, an oospore, a female individual or organ) fruitful by the introduction of the male element; to fecundate. Chiefly *Bot.* 1859.

1. He..fertilised bogs, and cultivated barren sands DERRICK. Intense religious conviction fertilizes intellect LIDDON. 2. I have not found a single terrestrial animal that can f. itself DARWIN.

Hence **Fe·rtili·zable** (also **-isable**), *a.* that can be fertilized or fecundated.

Fertilizer (fəː·rtiləizəɹ). 1661. [f. prec.] 1. One who or that which fertilizes land; said *esp.* of manures. 2. An agent of fertilization in plants 1844.

2. Flies are good fertilizers DARWIN.

Ferula (fe·rulă). ME. [a. L.; = giant fennel, a rod.] 1. *Bot.* The giant fennel. 2. A rod, cane, or other instrument of punishment, *esp.* a flat ruler; *fig.* school discipline 1580. 3. *Surg.* A long splint 1688.

Hence **Ferula·ceous** *a.* resembling a f.; having a stalk like a f.

Ferula·ic, feru·lic, *a.* 1876. [f. FERULA + -IC.] *Chem.* In *Ferul(a)ic acid*: $C_{10}H_{10}O_4$, contained in Assafœtida.

†**Fe·rular.** 1594. [ad. L. *ferularis* belonging to the giant fennel.] = FERULA 2. -1688.

Ferule (fe·riul), *sb.* ME. [ad. L. *ferula*; see FERULA.] 1. = FERULA 1. 2. = FERULA 2. 1599. Hence **Fe·rule** *v.* to beat, strike with a f.

†**Fe·rvence.** ME. [a. OF., f. L. *ferventem*; see -ENCE.] 1. Boiling or glowing heat. Also, Violent ebullition. -1634. 2. *fig.* Warmth of the emotions, fervency ME.

2. My f. of love *Hen. VIII.*

Fervency (fəː·rvĕnsi). 1554. [f. as prec.; see -ENCY.] 1. The state or quality of being FERVENT; intensity of heat. Now *rare.* 1598. 2. *fig.* Heat of mind; warmth of devotion, zeal, ardour, eagerness.

2. Peter in a feruencie first left his bote KNOX.

Fervent (fəː·rvĕnt), *a.* ME. [a. F. *fervent*, ad. L. *ferventem*, *fervere* to boil, glow.] 1. Hot, burning, glowing, boiling. †b. Of cold: Intense -1634. 2. Of persons, etc.: Ardent, intensely earnest ME. b. Of conflict, uproar, etc.: Hot fierce, raging. Now *rare.* 1465.

1. The Elements shall melt with feruent heat 2 *Pet.* iii. 10. b. The f. frost so bitter wes 1535. 2. Feruent to fight ME. My Heart in f. Wishes burns WESLEY. b. A moment ends the f. din WORDSW. Hence **Fe·rvent-ly** *adv.*, **-ness.**

Fervescent (fəɹve·sĕnt), *a.* 1683. [ad. L. *fervescentem*, *fervescere*, inceptive verb f. *fervere.*] Growing hot.

Fervid (fəː·rvid), *a.* 1599. [ad. L. *fervidus*, f. *fervere.*] 1. Burning, glowing, hot. Now *poet.* or *rhet.* 2. *fig.* Glowing, impassioned 1656.

1. The mounted Sun Shot down direct his f. Raies MILT. *P. L.* v. 301. 2. He is warm rather than f. JOHNSON. F. loyalty MACAULAY. A f. preacher 1872.

Hence **Fervi·dity**, intense heat (*lit.* and *fig.*). **Fe·rvid-ly** *adv.*, **-ness.**

Fervour, fervor (fəː·rvəɹ). [ME. *fervor*, *-our*, a. OF., ad. L. *fervorem*, f. *fervere.* In U.S. *fervor* is usual; in Eng. *fervour.*] 1. Glowing condition, intense heat. 2. Warmth or glow of feeling, passion, vehemence, zeal ME.

1. The f. of an African climate 1794. 2. She..had more feruor of deuocion CAXTON.

Fesapo. *Logic.* A mnemonic word representing the fourth mood of the fourth syllogistic figure, in which a universal negative major premiss and a universal affirmative minor yield a particular negative conclusion.

Fescennine (fe·senəin). 1601. [ad. L. *Fescenninus* pertaining to *Fescennia* in Etruria, famous for scurrilous dialogues in verse.]

A. *adj.* Pertaining to Fescennia; usually, licentious, obscene, scurrilous.

†B. *sb.* A song or verses of a licentious or scurrilous character -1660.

Fescue (fe·skiu), *sb.* ME. [a. OF. *festu* (F. *fétu*) a straw :—pop.L. **festucum* = L. *festuca.*] †1. A straw, rush, twig; hence, a thing of little importance -1610. 2. A small stick, pin, etc. used as a pointer in teaching children their letters 1513. †3. *transf.* a. The shadow on a sun-dial 1607. b. A plectrum for use with the harp 1616. 4. More fully *Fescue-grass*: A genus (*Festuca*) of grasses. *Hard, Sheep's, Meadow F.*: tr. *F. duriuscula, ovina, pratensis*, botanical names of species. 1794.

1. Thin strawes and fescues small HOLLAND. 2. Play schoolmaster, point as with a f. BROWNING. Hence †**Fescue** *v.* to direct or assist in reading with a f.

Fesels, var. of FASELS.

Fesse[1] (fes). 1486. [a. OF. *fesse* :—L. *fascia* band; mod.F. has *fasce.*] *Her.* An ordinary formed by two horizontal lines drawn across the middle of the field, and containing between them one third of it.

Phr. *Party per f.*: (of the shield) divided by a horizontal line through the middle. *Comb.*: **f.-point**, the exact centre of the escutcheon; **-ways, -wise** *adv.* horizontally.

Fesse[2]. Now *dial.* 1577. A pale blue colour.

Fest, fest-, obs. ff. FAST, FAST-, FEAST, FIST.

‖**Festa** (fe·stă). 1818. [It. :—*festa* (see FEAST *sb.*).] A feast, festival, holy day.

Festal (fe·stăl), *a.* (*sb.*) 1479. [a. OF., f. L. *festum*; see FEAST and -AL.] 1. Of or pertaining to a feast or festivity; festive, joyous. 2. Befitting a feast 1749. 3. *sb.* A feast, festivity 1818.

1. A f. Day 1740, dress 1838. F. people HAWTHORNE. 2. F. mirth 1749. Hence **Fe·stally** *adv.*

Fester (fe·stəɹ), *sb.* ME. [a. OF. *festre* :—L. *fistula*; see FISTULA.] 1. *orig.* = FISTULA; *later*, a rankling sore, an ulcer. In mod. use: 'A superficial suppuration resulting from irritation of the skin' (Quain). †2. A scar -1541. 3. [from the vb.] = FESTERING *ppl. a.* 1860.

3. Used to the f. of the chain upon their necks I. TAYLOR.

Fester (fe·stəɹ), *v.* ME. [f. prec. sb.] 1. *intr.* Of a wound or sore: To become a fester, to gather or generate pus, to ulcerate. Of an arrow, poison, etc.: To envenom the surrounding parts; to rankle. Hence *fig.* of grief, etc. 2. To putrefy, rot 1540. 3. *trans.* To cause festering in (*lit.* and *fig.*); to allow to rankle 1579. †4. = CICATRIZE 1. -1541.

1. A prick or cut that festers WESLEY. The troubles of Saxony..were already festering in silence FREEMAN. 2. Lillies that f. smell far worse then weedes SHAKS. 3. That will heal, instead of festering, the wounds of our minds MRS. SHELLEY. Hence **Fe·sterment**, the process or state of festering; *dial.* a rotting mass.

Festilogy (festi·lŏdʒi). Also **festo-.** 1845. [ad. med.L. *festilogium*, f. L. *festum.*] A treatise on ecclesiastical festivals.

†**Fe·stinate,** *a. rare.* 1605. [ad.L. *festinatus*: see next.] Hasty, hurried -1822.

Lear III. vii. 10. Hence **Fe·stinately** *adv.*

Festinate (fe·stineⁱt), *v.* 1652. [f. L. *festinatus*, *festinare.*] To hasten (*trans.* and †*intr.*). Hence **Festina·tion**, haste, speed. ? *Obs.*

†**Festi·n(e.** 1520. [ad. Sp. or Fr. and It.; see next.] = next. -1819.

†**Festino** (festī·no). 1741. [a. It. *festino*, dim. of *festa* FEAST *sb.* Hence Fr. and Sp. *festin.*] An entertainment or feast -1865.

How..obliging to go to Madame Grifoni's f. H. WALPOLE.

Festino (festəi·no). 1551. *Logic.* A mnemonic word, representing the third mood of the second syllogistic figure, in which a universal negative major premiss and a particular affirmative minor yield a particular negative conclusion.

Festival (fe·stivăl). ME. [a. OF., ad. med. L. *festivalis*, f. L. *festivus* FESTIVE.]

A. *adj.* 1. Of or pertaining to a feast, befitting a feast-day. (Now felt as the sb. used *attrib.*) †2. Glad, joyful, merry -1686.

1. Such dayes are festiuall to those Saincts, that [etc.] FULKE. 2. Our most f. and freeer joys JER. TAYLOR.

B. *sb.* A time of festive celebration, a festal day; also, *occas.*, a merrymaking 1589. b. A musical performance, or series of performances, at recurring periods, e.g. the *Handel Festival*; also in extended use, e.g. a *Shakespeare F.*

The morning trumpets f. proclaim'd Through each high street MILT. *Sams.* 1598.

Hence †**Fe·stivally** *adv.* joyously, gaily; in a f. or holiday manner.

Festive (fe·stiv), *a.* 1651. [ad. L. *festivus*; see FEAST and -IVE.] 1. Pertaining to, or befitting, a feast; mirthful, glad, cheerful. 2. Convivial, jovial; devoted to feasting 1735.

1. The glad Circle .. yield their Souls To f. mirth THOMSON. The f. board PRAED. 2. *The f. season*: = 'Christmas-tide'. Hence **Fe·stively** *adv.* So **Fe·stivous** *a.* (in all senses).

Festivity (festi·vĭti). ME. [a. OF. *festivité*, ad. L. *festivitatem*; see prec.] 1. †Festive quality, condition, or nature; (of writing, etc.) agreeable elegance -1681; rejoicing, mirth, gaiety 1756. 2. A festive celebration, an occasion of feasting. *pl.* Festive proceedings. ME.

1. The f. of his poems FULLER. A time of general f. 1756. 2. To share in the festivities of the day LYTTON.

Festoon (festū·n), *sb.* 1676. [ad. F. *feston*, ad. It. *festone*, ? f. *festa* FEAST, with sense 'decoration for a feast'.] 1. A chain or garland of flowers, leaves, etc. hanging in a curve between two points. Also *transf.* 1686. 2. *Arch.* A carved or moulded ornament representing this 1676. 3. *Ornith.* A lobe on the cutting edge of a hawk's beak 1855.

1. Here..see..vines, trained in festoons, from tree to tree A. YOUNG. 2. Flora and boys in alto-relievo supporting festoons H. WALPOLE. Hence **Festoo·nery**, a group of objects arranged in festoons. **Festoo·ny** *a.*, of, pertaining to, or like a f. (*rare*).

Festoon (festū·n), *v.* 1789. [f. prec.] †1. *intr.* To hang in festoons. 2. *trans.* To adorn with or as with festoons 1800. 3. To form into festoons. Also with *up.* 1801. 4. To connect by festoons 1832.

4. Growths of jasmine turn Their humid arms festooning tree to tree TENNYSON.

Festucine (fe·stiūsəin), *a.* 1646. [f. L. *festuca* stalk + -INE.] 1. Straw-coloured. 2. *Min.* Epithet for a splintery fracture 1823.

1. A little insect of a f. or pale green SIR T. BROWNE.

†**Festu·cous,** *a.* [f. as prec. + -OUS.] Straw-like. SIR T. BROWNE.

†**Fe·sty,** *v.* ME. [ad. OF. *festier*, *festeier* :—vulg. L. **festicare*, f. *festum* FEAST *sb.*] = FEAST *v.* in various senses -1500.

Fet, *v.* Now *dial.* [OE. *fetian*, of obscure affinities. See FETCH *v.*] A synonym of FETCH *v.* in various senses.

Dauid sent, and fet her to his house 2 *Sam.* xi. 27.

Fet, obs. f. FAT.

Fetch (fetʃ), *sb.*[1] 1530. [f. FETCH *v.*] 1. The action of fetching (*lit.* and *fig.*); a long stretch, a far-reaching effort 1549. 2. A contrivance, dodge, trick 1530. 3. *Naut.* a. An act of tacking 1555. b. The line of continuous extent from point to point, *e. g.* of a bay or of open sea 1867. 4. *dial.* An indrawn breath; also, a difficulty in breathing 1832.

2. The crafty fetches of the wilie Prince 1635.

Fetch (fetʃ), *sb.*[2] 1787. [?] The apparition, double, or wraith of a living person.

Fetch, obs. f. VETCH.

Fetch (fetʃ), *v.* [OE. *fecc(e)an*, said to be an altered form of *fetian* (see FET *v.*). Cf. OE. *orceard* orchard from *ort-geard.*] 1. *trans.* To go in quest of, and bring back. 2. To cause to come; to succeed in bringing; to draw forth, elicit. Now *rare.* ME. †b. To restore to consciousness -1744. 3. Of a commodity: To bring in, sell for. †Also *rarely* of money: To purchase. 1605. 4. To move to interest, attract irresistibly. Also *absol.* Not in dignified use. 1605. †5. To go and receive; to get, 'come by' -1656. 6. To draw from a (remote) source (now *rare*) 1552; †to derive as from a cause or origin; to infer -1691. 7. To draw (breath); hence, to heave (a sigh); to utter (a groan); to drain (a draught) 1552. 8. To deal (a blow); to make (a stroke). Now *colloq.* ME. †b. Hence, To 'have at', reach (a person) -1625. 9. To make or perform (a movement, etc.). Now *arch.* 1530. 10. *Naut.* a. To arrive at, reach; to come up with 1556. **b.** To get into (? *Obs.*) 1630. **c.** *intr.* To take a course; to bring one's vessel up 1586.

1. Ile goe f. thy sonnes To backe thy quarrell *Tit. A.* II. iii. 53. Goe f. me Wine LITHGOW. Phr. *To f. and carry*: *lit.* chiefly of dogs; *fig.* to run to and fro with news, tales, etc. 2. Thy hounds shall..f. shrill ecchoes from the hollow earth *Tam. Shr.* Induct. ii. 48. To f. butter in a churn 1844. Phr. *To f. the water*, and (hence) *to f. the pump*: to obtain a flow of water by 'priming'. b. She..then fainted againe, and againe they fetched her 1621. 3. The Guido, what did that f. FOOTE. 6. To f. a fashion from the French 1631, a parallel case out of Roman history 1806. 7. Fetching such dreadful Groans 1707. 8. His hand fetcheth a stroke with the axe *Deut.* xix. 5. 9. Colts, Fetching mad bounds *Merch. V.* v. i. 73. Phr. *To f. a circuit, compass*: see CIRCUIT, COMPASS *sb.* 10. a. To f. the bridges 1835. b. To f. the wind 1630, the wake of a vessel STURMY. Phr. *To f. headway* or *sternway*: to gather motion ahead or astern. *To f. way*: to break loose. c. To f. to windward 1836. *Comb.* with advs. **F. away.** *intr.* To get loose. **F. down.** *trans.* = *bring down* (see BRING *v.*). **F. off.** †a. To bring out of a difficulty. †b. To do or do for; to make an end of. †c. To drink off. **F. out.** To draw forth; to develop and display. **F. up.** †a. To raise. b. To vomit or promote expectoration of. c. To recall. d. To make up (lee-way, lost ground, time, etc.). †e. To come up with. f. *Naut.* To come or get to (a place). g. *intr.* for *refl.* To 'pull up'; to stop.

Fetch-, the vb.-stem in *comb.*, as in *f.-water*, a water-carrier, etc.

Fetch-candle. = FETCH-LIGHT. (Dicts.)

Fetcher (fe·tʃəɹ). 1552. [f. FETCH *v.*] One who or that which fetches.

Fetching (fe·tʃiŋ), *ppl. a.* 1581. [f. as prec.] †1. That contrives; crafty, designing –1583. 2. Fascinating, 'taking' 1880.

Fetch-light. 1692. [? f. FETCH *sb.*[2], or f. FETCH *v.*] A name for the 'corpse-candle' supposed to be seen before a person's death travelling from his house to his grave.

Fête (fēt, fēⁱt), *sb.* 1754. [a. F.; see FEAST *sb.*] 1. A festival, an entertainment on a large scale. 2. The festival of the saint after whom a person is named; in R.C. countries observed as a birthday is in England 1840. Also *attrib.*, as *f.-day*.

Fête (fēⁱt), *v.* 1819. [ad. F. *fêter*, f. *fête*; see prec.] *trans.* To entertain at a fête; to feast; to give a fête in honour of.

Fete, obs. f. FEET.

‖**Fête-champêtre.** 1774. [F.; f. *fête* (see FÊTE *sb.*) + *champêtre*:—L. *campestrem*, f. *campus* field.] An outdoor entertainment, a rural festival.

Fetial, fecial (fī·ʃăl). 1533. [ad. L. *fetialis* (erron. *fec-*): origin unkn.]

A. *adj.* Of or pertaining to the *fetiales* (see B.); heraldic, ambassadorial 1553.

B. *sb.* One of the *fetiales*, a Roman college of priests or heralds, who performed the rites connected with the declaration of war and the conclusion of peace.

Feticide: see FŒ-.

Fetid, fœtid (fe·tid, fī·tid). 1599. [ad. L. *fetidus* (often erron. *fœtidus*), f. *fetere* to stink.]

A. *adj.* Having an offensive smell, stinking. †B. *sb. pl.* Fetid drugs –1748. Hence **Feti·dity**, f. quality, state, or condition; foulness, offensiveness. **Fe·tid-ly** *adv.*, **-ness.**

Fetiferous: see FŒ-.

Fetis(e, obs. var. of FEATOUS *a.*

Fetish, fetich(e (fe·tiʃ, fī·tiʃ). 1613. [a. F. *fétiche*, ad. Pg. *feitiço* sb charm, sorcery; a subst. use of *feitiço* adj.:—L. *factitius* FACTITIOUS.] 1. a. *orig.* Any object used by the negroes of the Guinea coast and neighbourhood as an amulet or means of enchantment, or regarded by them with dread. b. *Anthropol.* An inanimate object worshipped by savages as having magical powers or as being animated by a spirit. c. *fig.* Something irrationally reverenced 1837. †2. Incantation; a magical or religious rite or observance; an oath –1828.

1. a. The chief fetiche is the snake 1761. c. Public opinion, the fetish even of the nineteenth century LOWELL. *Comb.* **f.-man, -woman**, (*a*) one who claims to have power over fetishes; (*b*) a fetish-worshipper.

Hence †**Fe·tish** *v.* to provide or adorn with a f.; *intr.* for *refl.* to dress up. **Fetishee·r, fe·tisher**, a medicine-man; a priest; also = FETISH *sb.* 1. **Fe·tishism, fetichism**, the worship of fetishes, or the superstition of which this is the feature. **Fe·tishist, fetichist**, one who worships a f.; also quasi-*adj.* **Fetishi·stic, fetichistic** *a.* of, pertaining to, characterized by, or resembling fetishism.

Fetlock (fe·tlǫk), *sb.* [ME. *fetlak, fytlok*, of unkn. formation. Popularly taken as f. FOOT *sb.* and LOCK (of hair).] 1. That part of a horse's leg where the tuft of hair grows behind the pastern-joint; the tuft itself. 2. = FETTERLOCK. 1695.

1. Fetlocks shag and long SHAKS. Steeds..fetlocke deep in gore *Hen. V*, IV. vii. 82. Hence **Fe·tlocked** *a.* having a f.; hobbled by the f., hampered, shackled.

Fetor, fœtor (fī·toɹ). 1450. [a. L. *fetor* (erron. *fœtor*), f. *fetere*; see FETID.] An offensive smell; a stench.

Fetter (fe·təɹ), *sb.* [OE. *feter* fem., f. (ult.) OTeut. *fet-* (:—OAryan *ped-*) ablaut-form of *fōt* FOOT. Cf. L. *pedica*, Gr. πέδη.] 1. A chain or shackle for the feet of a man or animal; hence *gen.* a bond, shackle (rare in *sing.*). In *pl* = Captivity 1704. 2. *transf.* and *fig.* Anything that confines or impedes; a check, restraint OE.

1. His feters that were on his fete CAXTON. To escape fetters and the sword ADDISON. 2. Passion's too fierce to be in Fetters bound DRYDEN. Hence **Fe·tterless** *a.* that is not or cannot be fettered.

Fetter (fe·təɹ), *v.* ME. [f. prec. sb.] 1. *trans.* To bind with or as with fetters; to chain, fasten, shackle. 2. *transf.* and *fig.* To impose restraint upon; to confine, impede 1526.

1. Elles had I dweld..I-fetered in his prisoun for evere moo CHAUCER. 2. The generality of the World are fettered by Rules STEELE. Fettered by superstition 1788. Hence **Fe·ttered** *ppl. a.* in senses of the vb.; *spec.* in *Biol.* 'applied to the limbs of animals when, by their retention within the integuments, or by their backward stretched position, they are unfit for walking' (*Syd. Soc. Lex.*). **Fe·tterer.**

Fetterlock (fe·təɹlǫk). ME. [f. FETTER *sb.* + LOCK.] 1. As a corruption of FETLOCK (sense 1) 1587. 2. An apparatus fixed to the foot of a horse to prevent his running away ME. b. *Her.* A representation of this 1605.

Fettle (fe·t'l), *sb.* 1750. [f. next vb.] 1. Condition. 2. The material used for fettling a furnace 1894.

1. A Shetland pony in good f. E. WAUGH.

Fettle (fe·t'l), *v.* ME. [? f. OE. *fetel*, f. (ult.) OTeut. *fat-* to hold; thus primarily 'to gird up'.] 1. *trans.* To make ready, put in order. Now only *dial.* b. *techn.* To line (a puddling furnace, etc.); to scour (rough castings) 1881. †2. *refl.* and *intr.* for *refl.* To get (oneself) ready; to address oneself to battle –1674. b. To busy oneself 1745. Hence **Fe·ttler.** *dial.* and *techn.*

‖**Fettstein** (fe·tstəin). 1815. [Ger., f. *fett* fat + *stein* stone.] *Min.* = ELÆOLITE.

Fetus: see FŒTUS.

‖**Fetwa** (fe·twă). 1625. [Arab (pronounced by the Turks *fetfa*).] A decision given (usually in writing) by a Mufti.

Feu (fiū), *sb.* 1497. [a. OF.; see FEE *sb.*[2]] *Sc. Law.* 1. = FEE *sb.*[2] 1; also a tract of land held in fee 1609. 2. A feudal tenure of land in which the vassal makes a return of grain or money (opp. to WARD and BLANCH; see these words); a grant of land on these conditions; in mod. use, = FEU-FARM. 1497. b. A piece of land held in f. 1791. Hence **Feu** *v.* to grant upon f. **Feu·ar**, one who holds land upon f.

†**Feu·age.** *rare.* 1618. [a. OF., f. *feu* fire.] A tax upon chimneys or hearths –1706.

Feud[1] (fiūd). [ME. *fede*, a. OF. *fede, feide, faide* = OE. *fæhþ(u* enmity, f. (ult.) OTeut. **faiho* adj.; see FOE. The change of form to *food(e, feood, fuid, fewd* (whence *feud*) is unexplained. FEUD *sb.*[2] occurs too late to account for it] †1. Active hatred, hostility, ill will –1787. 2. A state of bitter and lasting mutual hostility; *esp.* such a state existing between two families, tribes, or individuals, marked by murderous assaults in revenge for some previous insult or wrong. More fully *deadly f.* 1568. 3. A quarrel, contention, bickering 1565.

2. He [Argyle] was at F. with all his Superiors in Scotland 1661. A tribe which was at deadly f. with the Joasmis H. H. WILSON. *Comb.* **f.-bote** [ad OE. *fæhþ-bōt*] a recompense for engaging in a feud, a compensation for homicide.

Feud[2], **feod** (fiūd). 1614. [ad. med.L. *feudum, feodum*; see FEE *sb.*[2]] = FEE *sb*[2] 1, 3.

His Majesty conferred on him the title of Duke of Bronte, annexing to it the f. of that name 1806.

Feudal (fiū·dăl), *a.*[1] †Also **feodal.** 1614. [ad. med.L. *feudalis, feodalis*, f. *feudum, feodum* FEUD. Cf. F. *féodal*.] 1. Of, pertaining to, or of the nature of, a feud or fief. 2. Of or pertaining to the holding of land in feud 1639. 3. Of or pertaining to the feudal system; existing or such as existed under that system 1665.

1. The conversion of allodial into f. estates KEMP. 2. The feodal polity BLACKSTONE. F. tenures GIBBON. Phr. *F. system*: the system of polity which prevailed in Europe during the Middle Ages, based on the relation of lord and vassal arising out of the holding of lands in feud. 3. Two ancient f. castles 1840. Hence **Feu·dally** *adv.* in a f. manner or under f. conditions. **Feu·dalism**, the f. system or its principles. **Feu·dalist**, a representative, or an adherent, of the f. system. **Feudali·stic** *a.* of the nature of feudalism; inclined to feudalism.

Feudal (fiū·dăl), *a.*[2] *rare.* [f. FEUD[1] + -AL.] Of or pertaining to a (deadly) feud. SCOTT.

Feudality (fiū·dæ·lĭti), *a.* 1790. [ad. F. *feudalité, feodalité*; see FEUDAL *a.*[1] and -ITY.] 1. Feudal quality or state; the principles and practice of the feudal system; *pl.* feudal principles. 2. A feudal regime; a feudal-like power; a fief 1800. †3. *Law.* Fealty. (Dicts.)

2. Capital in Great Britain has become a f. 1821.

Feudalize (fiū·dăləiz), *v.* 1828. [f. FEUDAL *a.*[1] + -IZE.] *trans.* To bring under the feudal system; to convert (lands) into feudal holdings; also, to reduce (persons) to the condition of feudal vassals. Hence **Feu·daliza·tion.**

Feu·dary, feo·dary. Now *arch.* ME. [ad. med.L. *feodarius*, f. *feodum, feudum*; see FEUD *sb.*[2] and -ARY.]

A. *sb.* 1. One who holds lands of an overlord on condition of homage and service; a feudal tenant, a vassal. b. A subject, dependant, servant 1620. †2. An officer of the ancient Court of Wards, who received the rents of the wards' lands –1736. ¶3. A confederate. (See FEDARIE.)

B. *adj.* Feudally subject. Const. *to.* 1577.

†**Feu·datary.** 1586. [ad. med.L. *feudatarius*, f. *feudat-, feudare* to enfeoff.]

A. *adj.* = FEUDATORY A. 1. –1674.

B. *sb.* = FEUDATORY B. –1818.

Feudatory (fiū·dătəri). Also †**Feodatory.** 1592. [f. med. L. *feudare*; see prec.]

A. *adj.* 1. Owing feudal allegiance *to*; subject. 2. Of or pertaining to vassals or retainers 1861.

1. He is F. to the Pope 1680.

B. *sb.* 1. One who holds his lands by feudal tenure; a feudal vassal 1765. 2. A feud, fief, fee; a dependent lordship 1644.

‖**Feu de joie** (fö də ʒwa). 1609. [Fr.; = 'fire of joy'.] †1. A bonfire; also *fig.* –1771. 2. A salute fired by musketry on occasions of public rejoicing, so that it passes from man to man rapidly and steadily, giving one continuous sound 1801.

Feudist[1] (fiū·dist). 1607. [f. FEUD[2] + -IST.] 1. A writer on feuds; one versed in feudal law. †2. One living under the feudal system. BLACKSTONE.

Feu·dist[2]. *U.S.* 1901. [f. FEUD[1] + -IST.] A person who has a feud with another.

Feu-farm (fiū·fāɹm). ME. [ad. OF. *feu-ferme*; see FEE-FARM.] *Sc. Law.* That kind of tenure by which land is held of a superior on payment of an annual rent. Hence, the annual rent itself.

† **Feuille** (föy). [Fr.] A thin plate, a leaf. PETTY.

‖ **Feuillemorte** (föymort), *a.* 1690. [Fr.; = 'dead leaf'. See FILEMOT.] Of the colour of a dead leaf, brown or yellowish brown.

†**Feuillet**[1]. [a. F. *feuillette*:—med. L. *folietta* a measure of wine.] A half-hogshead. BURKE.

‖ **Feuillet**[2] (föyę). 1845. [F., dim. of *feuille* leaf.] *Diamond-cutting.* 'The projecting points of the triangular facets in a rose-cut diamond, whose bases join those of the triangles of the central pyramid' (Knight).

‖**Feuilleton** (föytoṅ). 1845. [F., f. *feuillet*; see prec.] In French (and other) newspapers, the part of one or more pages (usually at the bottom) appropriated to light literature, criticism, etc.; an article or work printed in that part.

Hence **Feuilletonist**, a writer of feuilletons.

†**Feute, fewte.** ME. [ad. OF. *fuite*, f. *fuir* :—L. *fugere*.] The traces or track (of an animal) –1485.

Feuterer: see FEWT-.

Fever (fī·vəɪ), *sb.* [OE. *fēfor* str. masc., ad. L. *febris*, of obscure etym.] **1.** *Path.* A morbid condition of the system, characterized by increased heat, and excessive change and destruction of the tissues. Often specialized as *intermittent, puerperal, scarlet, typhoid, yellow*, etc. *f.* (see these words). †**2.** In *pl.* with sing. sense –1605. **3.** A state of intense nervous excitement, agitation, heat 1586.

1. Have a care of coming neare those that have the feavour 1678. 3. An enuious Feauer Of pale and bloodlesse Emulation *Tr. & Cr.* I. iii. 133. A mode of life free from..f. of mind J. H. NEWMAN.

Comb.: **f.-blister**, the herpes of the lips often produced by f. or catarrh; **-bush**, the *Benzoin odoriferum*; also the *Prinos verticillatus*; **-fly**, the *Dilophus vulgaris*; **-heat**, the high temperature of the body in f.; also *fig.*; **-nut**, the seeds of *Cæsalpina Bonducella*; **-root**, the *Pterospora andromedea*; also the *Triosteum perfoliatum*; **-sore**, name of a species of caries or necrosis; **-tree**, the *Eucalyptus globulus*; also the *Pinckneya pubens*; **-twig**, the *Celastrus scandens*; **-weed**, a plant of the genus *Eryngium*; **-wort**, the *Triosteum perfoliatum*.

Fever (fī·vəɪ), *v.* 1606. [f. prec. sb.] **1.** *trans.* To throw into a fever; also *fig.* **2.** *intr.* To be seized with a fever; also *fig.* 1754.

1. The white hand of a Lady Feauer thee *Ant. & Cl.* III. xiii. 138. 2. She fevered and died 1754.

Feveret (fī·verĕt). 1712. [f. as prec. + -ET.] A slight fever.

Feverfew (fī·vəɪfiū, fe·v-). [OE. *fēferfuge, -fugie*, ad. late L. *febrifuga*, L. *febrifugia*, f. L. *febri-* (*febris*) + *fugare* to drive away.] *Bot.* **a.** The plant *Pyrethrum Parthenium.* **b.** *dial.* The *Erythræa Centaurium.*

Feverish (fī·vəriʃ), *a.* ME. [f. FEVER *sb.* + -ISH.] **1.** Having the symptoms constituting fever; †ill of a fever 1647. **2.** *fig.* Excited, fitful, restless 1634. **3.** Of the nature of fever; pertaining to or resembling fever ME. **4.** Apt to cause fever. **Of a country**: Infested by fever. 1669.

1. [I] have had a restless f. night PENN. 2. Men.. Strive to keep up a frail and f. being MILT. *Comus* 8. 3. F. Thirst 1695, Rigors 1732, exacerbations 1802. 4. The f. shore of St. Domingo 1803. Hence **Fe·verish-ly** *adv.*, **-ness.**

Feverous (fī·vərəs), *a.* ME. [f. as prec. + -OUS.] **1.** = FEVERISH †1, 2, 3. **2.** Apt to cause fever 1626. Hence **Fe·verously** *adv.*

†**Fe·very** *a.* [f. as prec. + -Y[1].] Affected by fever. B. JONS.

Few (fiū), *a.* *compar.* **Fewer.** *superl.* **Fewest.** [Com. Teut.: OE. *fēawe* pl. (usu. *fēawa*), contracted *fēa*; repr. OTeut. **fawo-*, cogn. w. L. *pau-cus*, Gr. *παῦ-ρος*, L. *pau-llus*, *pau-per*, and perh. w. Gr. *παύειν* to stop.] **1.** Not many; amounting to a small number. (In *a few, some few* opp. to 'none at all'.) *absol.* = *few persons.* OE. **b.** Followed by a partitive genitive, and later by *of* OE. **2.** Used with a pl. sb. to form a virtual collective noun, preceded by *a, every*, (rarely) *that*, but construed with pl. verb ME. †**3.** Of a company or number: Small –1828. **4.** Of quantity: Not much ME.

1. Man that is borne of a woman, is of f. dayes *Job* xiv. 1. F. espied him HALL. b. Ye were the fewest of all people *Deut.* vii. 7. Phr. *Some f.*: an inconsiderable number of. Also *ellipt., absol.*, and with *of. The f.*: a specified company small in number. Now often = 'the minority'; opp. to *the many.* †*In f.*: in few words, in short. 2. Thieves, of which, it seems, there were not a f. DE FOE. Phr. *A faithful, select* etc. *f. A good f.*: a fair number. *Every f. (hours, miles*, etc.). 3. So f. company, that [etc.] SWIFT. 4. *A f. broth, gruel, porridge* (now *dial.*). *A f.*: 'a good bit' (*colloq.* or *slang*).

Hence **Few·ness**, the quality or fact of being f.

Fewmets: see FU-.

†**Few·terer.** [ME. *vewter*, corrupt ad. AF. *veutrier*, f. OF. *veutre, vautre, veltre* :—pop.L. **veltrum*, corruption of L. *vertragum* (nom. *-us*) greyhound, a Gaulish word.] A keeper of greyhounds; hence, an attendant –1801.

Fewtrils (fiū·trilz), *sb. pl. dial.* 1750. Little things, trifles.

Fey (fēi), *a.* Chiefly *Sc.* [Com. Teut.: OE. *fǣgi* :—OTeut. **faigjo-*, of unkn. etym.] **1.** Fated to die, doomed; also, dying. †**2.** Presaging death –1799. †**3.** Accursed, unlucky –1513. †**4.** Feeble, timid; weak –1513.

Fey, Feyn(e(n: see FAY, FEIGN *v.*

Fez (fez). 1802. [a. Turk. *fes, fês*; said to be so called from the town *Fez* (in Morocco).] A skull-cap in the form of a truncated cone, of a dull crimson colour, with a black tassel; the national head-dress of the Turks.

ff. = and the following, *et seq.*; also abbrev. of FORTISSIMO.

‖**Fiacre** (fiakr). 1699. [Fr.; so named from the Hôtel de St. *Fiacre*, where these carriages were first stationed.] A small four-wheeled carriage for hire, a French hackney-coach.

†**Fiançailles**, *sb. pl.* 1477. [a. F., f. *fiancer.*] A betrothal –1655.

†**Fi·ance**, *v.* 1450. [f. F. *fiancer*, f. *fiance* a promise.] **1. a.** = AFFIANCE *v.* 2. –1618. **b.** To take as one's betrothed –1587. **2.** To put on one's parole 1592.

‖**Fiancé** *masc.*, **Fiancée** *fem.* (fiāṅse). 1853. [F.; see prec.] A betrothed person.

Fiant (fəi·ant). 1534. [L.; the first word in the formula *fiant literæ patentes* 'let letters patent be made out'.] A warrant addressed to the Irish Chancery for a grant under the Great Seal.

†**Fi·ants**, *sb.* 1576. [a. OF. *fient, fiente* dung, repr. (ult.) L. *fimus.*] The dung of certain animals, *e. g.* the badger, fox, etc. –1741.

Fiar (fī·ăɪ), *sb. Sc.* 1597. [? f. FEE *sb.*[2]] The owner of the fee-simple of a property, as opp. to the life-renter.

Fiasco (fi,æ·sko). 1855. [a. It. (see FLASK).] ‖**1.** A bottle, flask 1887. **2.** A failure or breakdown, *esp.* in a dramatic or musical performance.

Fiat (fəi·ăt). 1631. [a. L.; = 'let it be done', 'let there be made'; 3rd pers. sing. pres. subj. of *fieri.*] **1.** *orig.* The word 'fiat', alone or in a formula, by which a competent authority sanctioned the doing of something; hence, an authorization 1636. **b.** *gen.* An authoritative pronouncement 1750. **2.** With reference to '*Fiat lux*' (let there be light) Gen. 1. 3 in the Vulgate: A command having for its object the creation of something 1631.

1. Nothing can be concluded without the King's F. 1647. b. Whose f. in matters of fashion was law 1883. 2. If it be a Spirit that immediately produces every effect by a *fiat* or act of his will BERKELEY. *Comb.* **f.-money**, *U.S.* money (such as an inconvertible paper currency) which is made legal tender by a f. of the government. **Fi·at** *v.* to attach a f. to; to sanction (*rare*). **Fi·atist** *U.S.*, an advocate of f.-money.

Fiaunt, obs. var. of FIANT.

Fib (fib), *sb.*[1] *colloq.* 1568. [? Shortened f. FIBLE-FABLE.] **1.** A trivial falsehood; often *euphem.* for 'a lie' 1611. **2.** A fibber.

1. No one was used to..telling polite fibs H. JAMES.

Fib (fib), *sb.*[2] 1814. [f. FIB *v.*[2]] A blow.

Fib (fib), *v.*[1] 1690. [f. FIB *sb.*[1]] *intr.* To tell a fib; to lie.

I do not say he lyes.. but his Lordship fibbs most abominably DRYDEN. Hence **Fi·bber.**

Fib (fib), *v.*[2] *slang.* 1665. *trans.* To deliver blows in quick succession upon, as in pugilism. Also *absol.* or *intr.*

fig. I have fibbed the Edinburgh (as the 'fancy' say) most completely SOUTHEY.

Fi·ble-fa·ble. Now *dial.* 1581. [Redupl. of FABLE.] Nonsense.

†‖**Fibra.** Pl. **-ræ, -ra's.** 1641. [L.] A fibre, filament –1661.

Fibre (fəi·bəɪ), *sb.* ME. [a. F., ad. L. *fibra*; of unkn. origin. Formerly spelt *fiber* in England, as still in U.S.] †**1.** After L.: **a.** A lobe or portion of the liver. **b.** *pl.* The entrails. –1601. **2.** *Phys.* One of the thread-like bodies or filaments, that in part compose animal and vegetable tissue 1607. **3.** One of the thread-like filaments which form a textile or other material substance 1827. **4.** *collect.* A substance consisting of fibres. Also, Fibrous structure. 1810. **5.** A subdivision of a root; occas. of a twig 1656.

2. The optic nerve..might contain as many as a million of fibres BAIN. The fibres of the cocoa-nut LUBBOCK. *Fibres of Corti*: see CORTIAN *a.* *fig.* Every f. of him is Philistine CARLYLE. 3. A silk f. FARADAY. Fibres of glass 1832. 4. Bone and f. EMERSON. *fig.* There is an improvement in our f.—moral if not political BAGEHOT.

Comb. **f.-gun**, 'a device for disintegrating vegetable fiber' (Knight).

Hence **Fi·bred** *ppl. a.* furnished with fibres; chiefly in comb. **Fi·breless** *a.* without fibres or strength. **Fi·briform, Fi·brine,** *adjs.* f.-like.

Fibril (fəi·bril). 1664. [ad. mod.L. *fibrilla*; see next.] **1.** *Phys.* A small fibre; the subdivision of a FIBRE in a nerve, muscle, etc. 1681. **2.** *Bot.* The ultimate subdivision of a root.

Fibrilla (fəibri·lă). *Pl.* **-læ** (-lī). 1665. [mod.L., dim. of L. *fibra* FIBRE.] = prec.

The ultimate fibrillæ of muscles J. HOGG. Hence **Fi·brillar** *a.* of, pertaining to, composed of, or characteristic of, a f. or fibrillæ. **Fi·brillary** *a.* fibrillar. **Fi·brillate** *v. intr.* (of the blood) to turn into fibrillæ. **Fi·brillated** *ppl. a.* having a fibrillar structure. **Fibrilla·tion**, the becoming, or the being, fibrillated; *concr.* a fibrillated mass. **Fibri·lliform** *a.* **Fi·brillo·se** *a.* supplied with, or composed of, fibrils; finely striate. †**Fi·brillous** *a.* full of fibrils; pertaining to a f.

Fibrin (fəi·brin). Formerly also **fibrine**, **fibrina**. 1800. [f. FIBRE + -IN.] An albuminoid or protein compound substance found in animal matter; coagulable lymph. Also, a similar substance found in vegetable matter.

The f. of flesh appears to differ from that of blood HUXLEY. Hence **Fibrina·tion**, the action or process of adding f. to the blood. **Fi·brinous** *a.* composed of, pertaining to, or of the nature of, f.

Fibrino- (fəi·brino), comb. form of FIBRIN, as in:

Fi·brino-albu·minous *a.*, consisting of fibrin and albumen. **Fi·brinogen** [see -GEN], a proteid substance, entering into the composition of fibrin. **Fi·brino-gene·tic, -ge·nic, Fibrino·genous** *adjs.*, producing fibrin. **Fi·brino-pla·stic** *a.*, concerned in the formation of fibrin. **Fi·brino-pla·stin** = GLOBULIN. **Fi·brino-pu·rulent** *a.*, containing a mixture of fibrin and pus.

Fibro- (fəi·bro), comb. form of FIBRE, indicating a fibrous condition.

Fi·bro-are·olar *a.*, consisting of fibrous and areolar or connective tissue. **Fi·bro-bla·st** [see -BLAST], one of the cells in which fibrous tissue is immediately formed. **Fi·bro-calca·reous** *a.*, consisting of fibrous tissue and containing calcareous bodies. **Fi·bro-ca·rtilage**, a firm elastic material partaking of the structure and character of fibrous tissue and cartilage; hence **Fi·bro-cartila·ginous** *a.* **Fi·bro-ce·llular** *a.*, composed of fibrous and cellular tissue. **Fi·bro-chondri·tis**, 'inflammation of a fibro-cartilage' (*Syd. Soc. Lex.*). **Fi·bro-cy·stic** *a.*, consisting of fibrous tissue and cysts. **Fi·bro-cysto·ma**, a tumour containing fibrous tissue and cysts. **Fi·bro-fe·rrite**, *Min.* ferric sulphate occurring in fibrous silky tufts and masses of a yellow colour. **Fi·bro-inte·stinal** *a.*, in '*fibro-intestinal layer*, the innermost of the two layers into which the mesoderm of some Invertebrata divides' (*Syd. Soc. Lex.*). **Fi·bro-myo·ma**, 'a myoma in which the tumour contains a large proportion of fibrous connective tissue (*Syd. Soc. Lex.*); hence **Fi·bro-myo·matous** *a.* **Fi·bro-neuro·ma**, 'the form of neuroma which consists chiefly of fibrous connective tissue' (*Syd. Soc. Lex.*). **Fi·bro-nu·cleated** *a.*, composed of fibrous tissue mixed with elongated nuclei. **Fi·bro-pla·stic** *a.*, fibre-forming; said *esp.* of a tissue organized from the lymph exuded on wounds. **Fi·bro-sarco·ma**, a tumour intermediate between a fibroma and a sarcoma. **Fi·bro-se·rous** *a.*, possessing the nature of both fibrous and serous membranes. **Fi·bro-va·scular** *a.*, *Bot.* composed of a mixture of fibrous tissue and vascular tissue.

Fibroid (fəi·broid). 1852. [f. FIBRE + -OID.] **A.** *adj.* Resembling fibre or fibrous tissue; *f. change, degeneration*, a morbid change into fibre or fibrous tissue.

B. *sb. Path.* A fibroid tumour 1872.

Fibroin (fəi·brouin). 1861. [f. FIBRO- + -IN.] A chemical substance which is the chief constituent of silk, cobwebs, and the horny skeleton of sponges.

Fibrolite (fəi·brŏləit). 1802. [f. FIBRO- + Gr. λίθος stone; see also -ITE.] A fibrous mineral consisting chiefly of aluminium silicate. Hence **Fibroli·tic** *a.*

Fibroma (fəibrōu·mă). Pl. **-mata** (-mătă). 1847. [mod.L., f. L. *fibra* + *-oma*; cf. CYSTOMA.] A fibrous tumour. var. **Fi·brome.**

Fibrosis (fəibrōu·sis). 1873. [mod.L., f. L. *fibra* FIBRE: see -OSIS.] *Path.* Fibroid degeneration. Hence **Fibro·tic** *a.*

Fibrous (fəi·brəs), *a.* 1626. [ad. mod.L. *fibrosus*; see FIBRE and -OUS.] **1.** Full of fibres; formed of fibres. **2.** Fibre-like 1707.

1. F. flesh 1657, gypsum 1813, bark 1846. Hence **Fi·brous-ly** *adv.*, **-ness.** var. †**Fibro·se** *a.*

Fibster (fi·bstəɹ). 1848. [f. FIB *v.*[1] + -STER.] One who fibs.

Fibula (fi·biŭlă). *Pl.* **-læ, -las.** 1673. [a. L., f. *figere* to fix.] ‖**1.** *Antiq.* A clasp, buckle, or brooch. **2.** *Anat.* The long or splint bone on the outer side of the leg (app. as resembling the tongue of a clasp) 1706.

1. The F., whose shape.. Still in the Highland broach is seen WORDSW. Hence **Fi·bular** *a.* of, pertaining to, or †resembling the f.

-fic, *suffix*, repr. L. *-ficus* '-making, -doing' (f. weakened root of *facere*), forming adjs. (1) from sbs., with sense 'making, causing, producing', as in *pacificus*, or 'performing', as *sacrificus*; (2) from adjs., with sense 'performing actions of a specified kind', as *magnificus*, also, later, 'bringing into a specified state', as *beatificus*; (3) from vbs., with sense 'causing to', as *horrificus*; (4) from advs., only in *beneficus, maleficus*, from the phrases *bene, male facere.*

-fication (fikēi·ʃən), *suffix*, repr. L. *-ficationem*, the regular formative of nouns of action from vbs. in *-ficare*: see -FY. In scientific language the suffix forms many sbs., some of which have no corresponding vb.; as, *acetification, dentification*, etc.

Ficelle (fise·l). 1882. [a. F.; = 'packthread'.] Only in comb., as *f.-lace*, string-coloured lace.

Fichu (fiʃü, fi·ʃiu). 1803. [a.F.; app. *fichu* adj. used subst.] A triangular piece of muslin, lace, or the like, worn by ladies to cover the neck, throat, and shoulders, formerly also the head.

Fickle (fi·k'l), *a.* [OE. *ficol*, f.* *fician* to deceive, cogn. w. *gefic* deceit.] †**1.** False, deceitful, -1533. **2.** Changeable, changeful, inconstant, uncertain, unreliable ME.

2. O Fortune, Fortune, all men call thee f. *Rom. & Jul.* III. v. 60. The f. heart of man SCOTT. F. health URE. Hence **Fi·ckleness. Fi·ckly** *adv.* (now *rare*), in a f. manner, †deceitfully.

‖ **Fico** (fī·ko). 1577. [It. :—L. *ficus* FIG *sb.*[1]] †**1.** = FIG *sb.*[1] 2. -1630. **2.** = FIG *sb.*[1] 4. *arch.* 1598. †**3.** = FIG *sb.*[2] -1602.

2 A f. for the phrase *Merry W.* I. iii. 33.

Ficoid (fəi·koid). 1741. [ad. mod. L. *ficoïdes*, f. L. *ficus*; see -OID.] **A.** *adj.* Related to or resembling the genus *Ficus*; also, fig-like 1884.

B. *sb.* A plant of the N. O. *Mesembriaceæ.*

Ficoidal (fikoi·dăl). 1846. [f. as prec. + -AL.]

A. *adj.* **1.** Related to or resembling the genus *Ficus* 1884. **2.** Pertaining to, or of the nature of, the N. O. *Ficoideæ* or *Mesembriaceæ* 1846.

2. *F. alliance*: a group containing the Mesembriaceæ and three other orders. (Lindley.)

B. *sb.* A plant belonging to the *Ficoidal Alliance* 1846.

‖**Ficoides** (fikoi·dīz). 1753. [mod. L. *ficoïdes*; see FICOID.] A botanical name applied to various plants, e.g. the Ice-plant (*Mesembrianthemum crystallinum*).

Fictile (fi·ktil), *a.* 1626. [ad. L. *fictilem*, f. *fingere*; see -ILE.] **1.** Capable of being moulded. Now *rare.* 1675. **2.** Moulded into form by art; made of earth, clay, etc. by a potter 1626. **3.** Having to do with pottery 1854.

1. The several F. clays EVELYN. 2. A f. deity 1655. F. coffins 1825. 3. F. Craft 1888. Hence **Fi·ctileness. Ficti·lity,** f. quality; *concr.* an article of f. ware.

Fiction (fi·kʃən). ME. [a. F. ad. L. *fictionem*, f. *fingere*; see FEIGN.] †**1.** The action or product of fashioning or imitating -1784. †**2.** Feigning; deceit, dissimulation, pretence -1609. **3.** The action of feigning or inventing imaginary existences, events, states of things, etc. 1605. **b.** That which is feigned or invented; invention as opposed to fact ME. **c.** A statement proceeding from mere invention; such statements collectively 1611. **4.** Fictitious composition. Now usually, prose novels and stories collectively, or the composition of such works 1599. **5.** A supposition known to be at variance with fact, but conventionally accepted: **a.** in *Law* 1590; **b.** *gen.* (chiefly *transf.*) 1828.

1. *concr.* The unscented fictions of the loom COWPER. 3. To be pleased in the f. of that, which would please a man if it were reall, is a Passion..adhærent to the Nature..of man HOBBES. F. and Fraud HARTLEY. b. The fictions of the Virgilian age GLADSTONE. c. Let us cast away all f. 1655. 4. Old people like history better than f. LYTTON. 5. a. A..f. of our law that all real property was originally granted by the king CRUISE. b. To reduce debt by borrowing..is a manifest f. in finance LD. GRENVILLE.

Hence **Fi·ctional** *a.* pertaining to, or of the nature of f. **Fi·ctionally** *adv.* by means of a work of f. **Fictionee·r, Fi·ctioner, Fi·ctionist,** a writer of f.

†**Fi·ctious,** *a.* 1641. [f. L. *fictionem.*] **1.** = FICTITIOUS. -1813. **2.** Characterized by fiction -1813.

Fictitious (fikti·ʃəs), *a.* 1615. [f. L. *ficticius*, (f. *fingere*) + -OUS; see -ITIOUS.] **1.** †Artificial; counterfeit, sham, not genuine. **2.** Feigned, assumed; not real 1633. **3.** Feigned to exist; imaginary 1621. **4.** Of the nature of fiction 1773. **5.** Created by a fiction (legal or conventional) 1837.

1. By shedding f. tears 1734. 2. A f. character SCOTT, name DICKENS. 3. A company of f. Saints BURTON. 4. A f. narrative THIRLWALL. 5. Adoption, as a method of obtaining a f. son MAINE.

Hence **Ficti·tious-ly** *adv.*, **-ness.**

Fictive (fi·ktiv), *a.* 1491. [a.F. *fictif, -ive*, f. (ult.) L. *fingere.*] **1.** †Given to feigning; imaginatively creative 1865. **2.** Fictitious, feigned, sham 1612.

2. Dabbling in the fount of f. tears TENNYSON.

†**Fictor** (fi·ktəɹ, -oɹ). 1665. [a. L., f. *fingere.*] One who frames or fashions; *esp.* an artist or modeller in clay, etc. -1677.

Ficus (fəi·kŏs). ME. [a. L. *ficus* fig, fig-tree.] *Path.* 'A fleshy substance or kind of Condyloma resembling a fig' (Mayne).

Fid (fid), *sb.* chiefly *Naut.* 1615. [?] **1.** A conical pin of hard wood, used to open the strands of a rope in splicing. **2.** A square bar of wood or iron, with a shoulder at one end, used to support the weight of the topmast 1644. **3.** A plug of oakum for the vent of a gun; also (? *transf.*) a plug or quid of tobacco 1623. **4.** *dial.* A small thick piece of anything 1838. **5.** 'A wooden or metal bar or pin, used to support or steady anything' (Webster). Hence **Fid** *v.* to fix (a topmast, etc.) with a f.

‖**Fidalgo** (fidæ·lgo). 1638. [Pg., contr. for *filho de algo* son of something.] A Portuguese noble.

Fiddle (fi·d'l), *sb.* [ME. *fiþele*, OE. * *fiðele* wk. fem., of obscure origin. Cf. med. L. *vitula, vidula*, whence VIOL.] **1.** A stringed musical instrument of the viol kind; usu. a violin. **2.** One who plays the fiddle; a fiddler; hence *transf.* a mirth-maker, jester 1600. **3.** Something resembling a fiddle: **a.** *Naut.* A rack or frame to prevent things from rolling off the table in bad weather 1865; **b.** *Agric.* A long wooden bar, attached by ropes at its ends to the traces of a horse, and used to drag loose straw or hay on the ground, [etc.] 1874. **4.** *slang.* **a.** A writ to arrest 1700. **b.** *Scotch* († *Welsh*) f.: the itch 1700. **c.** *Stock Exch.* A sixteenth (of a pound) 1825. **5.** As an exclam. = FIDDLESTICK. 1695.

3. a. A heavy sea, which..caused the production of 'fiddles' on the saloon tables at lunch time 1865. 4. c. To do business with me at a f. 1825.

Phrases. *As fit as a f.*: in good form. *To play first* (or *second*) *f.*: to take a leading (or inferior) position; so *to play third f.*

Comb.: **f.-back,** a back (of a chair) shaped like a f., also *attrib.*; **-block,** *Naut.* a block with two sheaves, one over the other, the smaller one underneath; **-bow** = FIDDLESTICK; **-dock,** the *Rumex pulcher* of Linnæus; **-fish,** (*a*) the Angel-fish or Monk-fish; (*b*) the king-crab (*Limulus polyphemus*); **-pattern,** the pattern of f.-headed spoons and forks; **-patterned** *a.* = FIDDLE-HEADED b.; **-wood,** (*a*) the *Citharexylon*; (*b*) *Scrophularia aquatica.*

Fiddle (fi·d'l), *v.* ME. [f. prec. sb.] **1.** *intr.* To play the fiddle; now *familiar* or *contemptuous.* Also *fig.* **b.** quasi-*trans.* ME. **2.** To make aimless or frivolous movements; to act idly or frivolously. Also with *about.* 1530. **3.** *trans.* To cheat. Now only *slang.* 1604.

1. Others..Teach Kings to f., and make Senates dance POPE. 2. He took a pipe in his hand, and fiddled with it till he broke it SWIFT. Fiddling with Franchise Bills 1884.

Fiddlededee (fi·d'ldidī·). 1784. [f. FIDDLE *sb.* or *v.* with a nonsensical addition.] **A.** *interj.* Nonsense! **B.** *sb.* Nonsense (*mod.*).

Fiddle-faddle (fi·d'l,fæ·d'l). 1577. [Redupl. of FIDDLE or FADDLE.]

A. *sb.* **1.** Trifling talk or action; in *pl.* trivial matters. **2.** A trifler; a chatterbox 1602.

B. *adj.* Trifling, fussy 1617.

C. *interj.* Nonsense! Bosh! 1671. Hence **Fi·ddle-fa·ddle** *v. intr.* to fuss, mess about.

Fi·ddle-head. 1799. [f. FIDDLE *sb.* + HEAD.] **1.** *Naut.* The ornamental carving at the bows of a vessel, which ends in a scroll turning inward like the head of a violin. **2.** A head as empty as a fiddle 1887. Hence **Fi·ddle-hea·ded** *a. Naut.* Having a fiddle-head. **b.** Having the handle made after the pattern of a fiddle, as a fork, spoon. **c.** Empty-headed.

Fiddler (fi·dləɹ). [OE. *fiðelere* = ON. *fiðlari*; see FIDDLE *sb.*] **1.** One who plays on the fiddle, *esp.* for hire. †**2.** A trifler -1735. **3.** *slang.* A sixpence 1885. **4. a.** A fly resembling a cockroach 1750. **b.** The angel or shark-ray 1887. **c.** The sandpiper (*local*) 1885. **d.** A small crab of the genus *Gelasimus*; also called *fiddler-crab* 1714.

1 *Fiddler's Green* (Naut.): 'a sailor's elysium, in which wine, women, and song figure prominently' (Farmer). 4. d. A 'Fidler-Crab' (as it is sometimes called from the rapidity with which it works its elbows) W. B. LORD.

Fiddlestick (fi·d'lstik), *sb.* ME. [f. FIDDLE *sb.* + STICK *sb.*] **1.** The bow strung with horsehair with which the fiddle is played. **2.** *joc.* Something insignificant or absurd. Often substituted for another word in derision. 1621. **3.** As *interj.* Nonsense! Often in *pl.* 1600.

Fi·ddle-string. 1728. [f. as prec. + STRING.] One of the strings on a fiddle. Also *fig.*

I do but..fret myself to fiddlestrings MRS. CARLYLE.

Fiddling (fi·dliŋ), *ppl. a.* 1580. **1.** That plays the fiddle. **2.** Of persons: Busy about trifles. Of things: Petty, futile. 1652.

Fidei-commissum (fəi:di,əi,kǫmi·sŏm). 1727. [a. L., f. *fidei* to faith + *commissum* entrusted.] *Rom. Law.* A bequest which a person made by begging his heir or legatee to transfer something to a third person.

Fideism (fəi·di,iz'm). 1885. [f. L. *fides* faith + -ISM.] A mode of thought according to which knowledge is based on a fundamental act of faith.

Fidejussor (fəidi,dʒǫ·səɹ, -oɹ). 1539. [a. L., f. *fide-jubere*, f. *fide*, abl. of *fides* faith + *jubere* to order.] *Civil Law.* One who authorizes the bail of or goes bail for another; a surety. So **Fideju·ssion** 1657. **Fideju·ssory** *a.*

Fidelity (fəi-, fide·lĭti). 1494. [a. F. *fidélité*, ad. L. *fidelitatem.*] **1.** The quality of being faithful; faithfulness, loyalty to a person, party, etc. 1508. **b.** Conjugal faithfulness 1694. †**c.** Word of honour -1598. **2.** Strict conformity to truth or fact; †veracity; exact correspondence 1534.

1. F. to engagements BENTHAM. †*To make f.*: to take an oath of fealty. c. By my f. this is not well *Merry W.* IV. ii. 160. 2. The principall thing required in a witnesse is fidelitie HOOKER. The F. of the Translation POPE.

Fidepromissor (fəi:di,promi·soɹ). 1875. [a. L., f. *fides* faith + *promittere* to promise.] *Rom. Law.* One who pledges himself as security for another; a bail, surety.

Fidge (fidʒ), *sb. colloq.* or *dial.* 1731. [f. next vb.] **1.** The action or habit of fidgeting; the state of being fidgety; also, a commotion, fuss. **2.** A restless person 1884.

Fidge (fidʒ), *v.* Now *dial.* 1575. [?] *intr.* and *trans.* To fidget; to twitch.

Fidget (fi·dʒĕt), *sb.* 1674. [f. FIDGE *v.*] **1.** A condition of vague physical uneasiness, seeking relief in irregular bodily movements. App. first used in *the fidget(s* (now always pl.)

as if the name of a malady. Hence *transf.* uneasiness, restlessness. 2. [From the vb.] One who fidgets, or who gives others the fidgets 1837. 3. [From the vb.] The act of fidgeting 1860.

Fidget (fi·dʒėt), *v.* 1754. [f. prec. sb.] 1. *intr.* To move restlessly, impatiently, or uneasily to and fro; also, to worry. 2. *trans.* To cause to fidget; to trouble, worry 1785.

2. She says I f. her to death JANE AUSTEN.

Fidgety (fi·dʒėti), *a.* 1730. [f. FIDGET + -Y¹.] Inclined to fidget; uneasy, restless. Hence **Fi·dgetily** *adv.* **Fi·dgetiness.**

Fidibus (fi·dibŏs). 1829. [G.] A paper spill for lighting a pipe, etc.

†**Fidi·cinal,** *a.* [f. L. *fidicen* (*fidicin-*) + -AL.] Of or pertaining to a player on stringed instruments. SIR J. HAWKINS.

Fiducial (fəidiū·ʃăl, fidiū·ʃăl), *a.* 1571. [ad. L. *fiducialis*, f. *fiducia* trust; see -AL.] 1. *Theol.* Of or pertaining to, or of the nature of, trust or reliance. †2. Trusted, trusty. H. MORE. 3. In *Surveying, Astron.* etc. Of a line, point, etc.: Assumed as a fixed basis of comparison 1571. 4. = FIDUCIARY (Webster).

1. Faith..a fiduciall assent to diuine Promises 1625. Hence **Fidu·cially** *adv.*

Fiduciary (fəidiū·ʃiări). 1593. [See prec. and -ARY.]

A. *adj.* 1. **a.** Of a person: Holding something in trust. *Obs.* exc. in *Rom. Law.* 1647. **b.** Of or pertaining to a trustee or a trusteeship 1795. 2. Of a thing: Held or given in trust 1641. 3. Of the nature of, proceeding from, or founded on trust or confidence 1640.

2. Uses of land .. were considered as f. deposits BLACKSTONE. 3. The f. currency of the United States 1892.

B. *sb.* 1. One who holds anything in trust; a trustee 1631. †2. One who identifies justifying faiths with assurance of one's own salvation –1684. †3. Credentials. ABP. BANCROFT.

1. Persuade .. Sir Hugh to make me his .. f. in this SCOTT. Hence **Fidu·ciarily** *adv.*

Fie (fəi), *interj.* [ME. *fi, fy*, app. a. OF.:—L. *fi.*] 1. An exclam. expressing disgust or reproach. Not now in dignified use. 2. quasi-*sb.* or *sb.* 1550.

Fief (fīf), *sb.* 1611. [a. F.; see FEE *sb.*²] = FEE *sb.*² 1. Also *transf.* and *fig.*

Male f., f. masculine: one that could be held by males only. Hence †**Fief** *v.* to grant as a f.

†**Fiel,** *a.* *Sc.* [?] Comfortable. BURNS.

Field (fīld), *sb.* [Com. WGer.: OE. *feld*:—OTeut. **felþu-z.*]

I. Ground. †1. Open land as opp. to woodland; a plain –1697. 2. The country as opp. to a town or village. *Obs.* exc. *arch.* ME. 3. Land or a piece of land appropriated to pasture or tillage OE. 4. A piece of ground put to a particular use; as, a *bleach field* (see BLEACH). 5. An extent of ground containing some special natural production; as *coal, oil*, etc. *fields* 1859. 6. The ground on which a battle is fought; a battle-field. Also *fig.* ME. 7. More widely: The scene of military operations 1612. 8. A battle; as *a hard-fought field* ME.; †order of battle –1678. 9. The ground on which some outdoor games are played 1788; in *Baseball*, the ground in which the fielders stand 1875. 10. *collect.* Those who take part in any outdoor contest or sport. **a.** *Sporting.* All the competitors except the favourite 1771. **b.** *Cricket.* The side who are in the field; also the players on both sides 1850. 11. *Cricket* and *Baseball.* = FIELDSMAN. 1830.

2. *Mids. N.* II. i. 238. 3. The fields!..All spring and summer is in them RUSKIN. COMMON, OPEN *field*: see these words. 6. They haue vs'd Their deerest action, in the Tented F. *Oth.* I. iii. 85. *fig.* To drive the sophists from the field 1848. Phr. *To keep, maintain the f.*: to continue the fight. *To hold the f.*: to hold its ground; to remain in possession. 7. Esmond ..took the field..under Webb's orders THACKERAY. 8. Phr. *To pitch, set a f.*: to choose one's battle-ground, order one's men for fighting. 10. **a.** Phr. *To bet, back, lay against the f.*

II. An extended surface. 1. A large stretch; an expanse 1577. 2. **a.** *Her.* The surface of a shield, or of one of its divisions ME. **b.** The groundwork of a picture, etc. 1634. **c.** *Numism.* The plain part of a coin 1876. **d.** Of a flag: The ground of each division 1867.

1. Yon f. of stars *Per.* I. i. 37. Fields of Air DRYDEN, of ice 1813. The whole f. of English history 1867. 2. **a.** Sir Lancelot's azure lions .. Ramp in the f. TENNYSON.

III. 1. An area or sphere of action, operation, or investigation ME. 2. *Physics.* The area or space under the influence of, or within the range of, some agent 1863.

1. As for the increase of Vertue generally..it is a large F. BACON. [A] wide f. for trade 1750. The f. of a telescope 1765. Phr. *F. of view*: the space to which observation is limited. 2. *Magnetic f.*: any space possessing magnetic properties, either on account of magnets in its vicinity or on account of currents of electricity passing through or round it.

Comb. 1. General: as *f.-dew, -dweller, -fortification, -husbandry, -movements, -service*, etc.

2. Special: **a.** Prefixed to names of animals, birds, insects, etc., often with sense 'wild', and opp. to *house* or *town*, as *f.-cricket, -mouse, -spider*; **f.-duck,** the little bustard (*Otis tetrax*); **-lark** (*Alauda arvensis*); **-martin** (*Tyrannus carolinensis*); **-plover** (*U.S.*), a name for two species of plover, and for a sandpiper (*Bartramia longicauda*); **-sparrow** (U.S.) (*Spizella pusilla* or *S. agrestis*); **-titling,** the Tree Pipit (*Anthus arboreus*); **-vole** (*Arvicola arvensis*).

b. In names of plants growing in the fields, as **f.-ash** (*Pyrus aucuparia*); **-basil:** see BASIL¹; **-madder,** †(*a*) rosemary, (*b*) book-name for *Sherardia arvensis*; **-southernwood** (*Artemisia campestris*).

c. f.-allowance, an allowance to officers and (formerly) privates, when in the field, to meet extra expenses; **-artillery,** light ordnance fitted for travel and use in active operations; **-battery,** a battery of f.-guns; **-carriage,** the carriage for a f.-gun, its ammunition, etc.; **-club,** a society for the outdoor study of Natural History; **-colours** (*Mil.*), small flags for marking out the ground for the squadrons and battalions; also the colours used by an army when in the field; **-cornet,** 'the magistrate of a township in Cape Colony' (Simmonds); **-driver** (U.S.), a civil officer whose duty it is to take up and impound stray cattle; **-events,** athletic events, such as weight-putting, etc. as distinguished from events on the running track; **-gun** = *f.-piece*; **-hand,** (*a*) a slave who works on a plantation; (*b*) a farm-labourer; **-hospital,** (*a*) an ambulance; (*b*) a temporary hospital erected near a field of battle; **-ice,** ice that floats in large tracts; **-lens** = FIELD-GLASS 3; **-magnet,** part of a dynamo, 'usually a massive stationary structure of iron surrounded by coils of insulated copper wire', the function of which is to provide the *magnetic field*; **-naturalist,** one who studies out of doors; **-park,** 'the spare carriages, reserved supplies of ammunition, tools, etc., for the service of an army in the field' (Wilhelm); **-piece,** a light cannon for use on a field of battle; **-practice,** 'military practice in the open field' (Ogilvie); **-show** = *f.-trial*; **-sports,** outdoor sports, *esp.* hunting; **-telegraph,** one used in military operations; **-train,** a body of men consisting chiefly of commissaries and conductors of stores, which belong to the Royal Artillery; **-trial,** a trial in the open field, *esp.* of hunting-dogs.

Field (fīld), *v.* 1529. [f. prec. sb.] 1. *intr.* To go into the FIELD (sense I. 2.) 1868. 2. *trans.* To expose (corn, malt, etc.) to the action of the air 1844. †3. *intr.* To take the field (see FIELD *sb.* I. 7) –1590. 4. *intr.* To back the field against the favourite 1886. 5. *intr.* To act as fielder in cricket, etc.; *trans.* to stop and return the ball 1824. 6. *Sports.* To put into the field 1922.

3. Who, soone prepard to f., his sword forth drew SPENSER.

Fie·ld-bed. 1580. 1. A bedstead for use in the field. 2. A bed upon the ground 1592.

Fie·ld-book. 1616. A book for use in the field, as by a land-surveyor for taking notes, or by a naturalist for preserving collected specimens.

Fie·ld-conve·nticle. 1678. An open-air religious meeting.

Fie·ld-day. 1747. 1. *Mil.* A day on which troops are drawn up for exercise in field evolutions; a military review; hence *transf.* and *fig.* a day occupied with brilliant or exciting events. 2. A day spent in the field, e.g. by the hunt, or by field-naturalists, etc. 1823.

Fielded (fī·ldėd), *ppl. a.* 1607. [f. FIELD *v.*] 1. Engaged in a field of battle. *Cor.* I. iv. 12. 2. Of a ball, in *Cricket*: Stopped and returned 1884.

†**Fie·lden.** 1604. [f. FIELD *sb.*] **A.** *adj.* Open; consisting of fields; rural, rustic –1669. **B.** *sb.* Field land –1712.

Fielder (fī·ldəɹ). ME. [f. FIELD *sb.* and *v.*] †1. One who works in the field. ME. only. 2. FIELDSMAN. 1853.

Fieldfare (fī·ldfēəɹ). [ME. *feldefare* (4 syll. in Chaucer) :—? OE. **feldefare*; app. = 'field-goer', f. *feld* + *far-* (see FARE *v.*).] A species of Thrush (*Turdus pilaris*), which spends the winter in the British Islands.

Hollies..with scarlet berries gemm'd, the fell-fare's food M. ARNOLD.

Fie·ld-glass. 1831. [f. FIELD *sb.* + GLASS.] 1. A binocular telescope for use in the field 1836. 2. 'A small achromatic telescope, usually from 20 to 24 inches long, and having from three to six joints' (Ogilv.). 3. That one of the two lenses forming the eye-piece of an astronomical telescope or compound microscope, which is the nearer to the object glass 1831.

Fie·ld-ma·rshal. 1614. [After G. *feldmarschall.*] The title of a military officer of the highest rank in German-speaking and other armies. (First conferred in the British army in 1736.)

Fie·ld-meeting. 1603. [f. FIELD *sb.* + MEETING.] 1. A duel. 2. *Hist.* A religious meeting in the open air 1649.

Field officer. 1656. 'An officer above the rank of captain, and under that of general' (Stocqueler).

Fie·ld preaching. 1739. [f. FIELD *sb.* + PREACHING.] The practice of preaching in the open air.

Fieldsman (fī·ldzmæ̆n). 1823. [f. FIELD *sb.* + MAN.] **a.** *Cricket.* One of the side which is fielding; a fielder 1824. **b.** *Sporting.* One who habitually backs the field.

Fie·ld-work. 1777. [f. FIELD *sb.* + WORK.] 1. Work done in the field, or in the fields. 2. *Mil.* A temporary fortification thrown up by troops operating in the field 1819.

†**Fie·ldy,** *a.* ME. [f. FIELD *sb.* + -Y¹.] Level, open; exposed; that grows in the fields –1598.

Fiend (fīnd). [Com. Teut.: OE. *fēond*; orig. the pr. pple. of OTeut. **fijējan* (OE. *feogean*) to hate. Cf. FRIEND.] †1. An enemy, foe. ME. only. 2. *spec.* The arch-enemy of mankind; the devil OE. 3. An evil spirit generally; a demon, devil OE. 4. *transf.* A person of superhuman wickedness or cruelty ME. **b.** †A grisly monster (e.g. a dragon). Also applied to baleful agencies personified, or hyperbolically. ME. **c.** With qualifying word: A devotee or addict, esp. to something injurious, as *dope f., opium f.* (orig. *U.S. slang*) 1889.

2. The Gates..belching outrageous flame..since the F. pass'd through MILT. *P.L.* x. 233. 3. Goethe's scoffing f. MACAULAY. 4. Where human fiends on midnight errands walk CAMPBELL. **c.** The botany-f., cyclist-f., interviewer-f. (*mod.*).

Hence †**Fie·ndful** *a.* wrought by fiends (*rare*). **Fie·ndlike** *a.* resembling, or characteristic of, a f. **Fie·ndly** *a.* †hostile; fiendish.

Fiendish (fī·ndiʃ), *a.* 1529. [f. prec. + -ISH.] Resembling, or characteristic of, a fiend; superhumanly cruel or malignant.

F. brutalities FREEMAN. **Fie·ndish-ly** *adv.*, **-ness.**

Fierce (fīᵊɹs), *a.* ME. [a. OF. *fers, fiers*, old nom. of *fer, fier*:—L. *ferus* wild, untamed.] 1. Violent and intractable in temper; vehement and merciless in anger or hostility. (Less emphatic than FEROCIOUS, q.v.) †2. High-spirited, valiant –1533. †3. Proud, haughty –1593. 4. Of natural agents, disease, passions, etc.: Vehemently raging ME. 5. Ardent; furiously zealous or active ME. 6. quasi-*adv.* Fiercely ME.

1. Moloc..the fiercest Spirit that fought in Heav'n now fiercer by despair MILT. *P.L.* ii. 44. F. Tigers couched around DRYDEN. 4. The f. anger of the Lord *Jer.* xxv. 37. F. cold 1863; discussion 1874. 5. Vengeful slaughter, f. for human blood POPE.

Hence **Fie·rce-ly** *adv.*, **-ness.**

Fie·rding. *pseudo-arch.* 1768. [a Sw. *fjerding*:—ON. *fjórðungr*; see FARTHING.] An alleged name for a quarter of a hundred or a shire.

‖ **Fieri** (fəi·ĕrəi). 1640. [L. inf.; = 'to be made, come into being'.] In med. L. phr. *in fieri*: in process of being made or coming into being.

The contract is still *in fieri* AUSTIN.

‖ **Fieri facias** (fəi·ĕrəi, fē·ʃiæs). 1463. [L.; = 'cause to be made', f. *fieri* (see prec.) + *facias*, 2nd pers. sing. pres. subj. of *facere* to do, make.] *Law.* 'A writ wherein the sheriff is commanded that he cause to be made out of the goods and chattels of the defendant, the sum for which judgement was given' (Blackstone); the common process for executing a judgement. Often abbrev. *Fi. fa.* (fəi·fēⁱ).

‖**Fierté** (fyęrte). 1673. [F., f. *fier.*] Haughtiness; high spirit.

Fiery (fəiᵊri), *a.* ME. [f. FIRE *sb.* + -Y¹.] **1.** Consisting of or containing fire; fire-bearing. **2.** Wrought, tested, or performed by the agency of fire; in *f. trial* with reference to the testing of metals ME. **3.** Resembling fire; glowing, of a blazing red ME. **4.** Hot as fire; red hot, burning ME.; acting like fire 1535. **5.** Of persons, etc.: Ardent, eager, fierce, spirited ME.; fiercely irritable 1590. Also *transf.* of a horse 1593. **6.** Of a vapour: Liable to take fire. Hence of a mine, etc.: Containing inflammable gas. 1751.

1. Where no volcano pours his f. flood COWPER. 2. The f. trial which England went through FREEMAN. 3. Purple or f. clouds MORLEY. 4. The f. Suns too fiercely play DRYDEN. A red f. tumour 1758. 5. A f. Soul, which working out its way, Fretted the Pigmy-Body to decay DRYDEN. The f. Courser DRYDEN. 6. The seam of coal was known to be f. 1866. Hence **Fie·rily** *adv.*, **Fie·riness.**

Fiery-cross: see FIRE-CROSS. Also *fig.*

Fife (fəif), *sb.* 1548. [? a. HGer. *pfeife* (see PIPE *sb.*), or ? a corruption of F. *fifre*, f. (ult.) OHG. *pfifan* to PIPE.] **1.** *Mus.* A small shrill-toned instrument of the flute kind, used chiefly to accompany the drum in military music 1555; also, its sound 1627. **2.** A fifer 1548.

1. Their step was regulated by the f. GROTE.

Comb.: **f.-major** (*Mil.*), a non-commissioned officer who superintends the fifers of a regiment.

Fife (fəif), *v.* 1817. [f. prec. sb.] *intr.* To play on a fife; *trans.* to play (a tune) on or as on a fife. Hence **Fi·fer.**

Fife-rail (fəif,rēᵢl). 1721. †**a.** 'Rails forming the upper fence of the bulwarks on each side of the quarter-deck and poop in men-of-war' (Smyth). **b.** The rail round the main-mast, furnished with belaying pins for the running rigging.

Fifish (fəi·fiʃ), *a. Sc.* [f. the county of *Fife* + -ISH; applied orig. to people from that county.] Somewhat deranged. SCOTT.

Fifteen (fiftī·n, fi·ftīn). [OE. *fīftēne, -týne*, f. OTeut. **fimfi* FIVE + **tehun* TEN; see -TEEN.] The cardinal number made up of ten and five; symbols 15, XV.

A. as *adj.* **1.** with *sb.* (*a*) expressed, or (*b*) omitted. †**2.** = Fifteenth *a.* -1623.

1. *The F.*: the Court of Session (formerly) consisting of fifteen Judges. Also, the Jacobite rising in 1715.

B. as *sb.* †**1.** *Eng. Hist.* = FIFTEENTH *sb.* 1. -1643. **2.** A set of fifteen persons or things 1674.

Fifteenth (fiftī·nþ, fi·ftīnþ). [OE. *fīftēoða*, f. *fīftēne* FIFTEEN, after *teoða* TENTH. The ending -TH dates from the 14th c. only.] The ordinal belonging to the cardinal fifteen.

A. *adj.* With sb. (*a*) expressed, or (*b*) omitted.

F. part: one of fifteen equal parts of any quantity.

B. *sb.* **1.** A fifteenth part; *esp.* in *Eng. Hist.* A tax of one-fifteenth formerly imposed on personal property ME. **2.** *Mus.* The interval of a double octave 1597. Also, a stop in an organ sounding two octaves above the Open diapason 1613.

Hence **Fiftee·nthly** *adv.* in the f. place.

Fifth (fifþ). [OE. *fīfta*:—OTeut. **fimfton-*, f. pre-Teut. **penqto-* (Gr. πεμπτός, L. *quin(c)tus*), f. **penqe* FIVE. Refashioned in 14th c. after *fourth.*] The ordinal belonging to the cardinal five.

A. *adj.* With *sb.* (*a*) expressed, or (*b*) omitted.

F. part: one of five equal parts of any quantity. *The f. wheel of a coach*, etc.: used for something superfluous.

B. *sb.* **1.** = *fifth part.* Also, a fifth part of movable goods granted to the king. 1557. **2.** *Mus.* The interval of three tones and a semitone, embracing five diatonic degrees of the scale 1597. **b.** The concord of two tones separated by this interval 1656. **3.** *pl.* Articles of the fifth degree in quality 1881.

Comb.: **f.-wheel**, 'a wheel or segment above the fore-axle of a carriage and beneath the bed..[forming] an extended support to prevent the careening of the carriage bed' (Knight).

Fifth monarchy. 1657. The last of the five great empires referred to in the prophecy of Daniel (Dan. ii. 44), in the 17th c. identified with the millennial reign of Christ predicted in the Apocalypse. Also *attrib.*, *esp.* in **Fifth-monarchy man**, one of those in the 17th c. who believed that the second coming of Christ was near at hand, and that it was their duty to establish his reign by force.

Fiftieth (fi·ftiėþ), *a.* (*sb.*) [OE. *fīftigoða*:—earlier **fīftigunþa*, f. FIFTY, after TENTH.] The ordinal belonging to the cardinal fifty.

F. part: one of fifty equal parts of any quantity.

Fifty (fi·fti). OE. *fīftig* = OTeut. **fimfi* FIVE + **tigiwiz*, pl. of **teguz* decade; see -TY.]

A. *adj.* The cardinal number equal to five tens; symbols 50, l. Also with sb. omitted. **b.** A large number 1818.

B. *sb.* **1.** A set of fifty persons or things OE. **2.** The age of fifty years 1714. **b.** *The fifties*: The years between fifty and sixty in a century or in one's life 1880. †**3.** A fifty-gun ship -1799.

Fifty-fifty *adv.*, on a basis of fifty per cent. each; equally; *a.*, equal, shared equally, half-and-half (*colloq.*, orig. *U.S.*) 1913.

Fig (fig), *sb.*¹ ME. [a. OF. *fige, figue*, ad. Pr. *figa, figua*:—pop. L. **fica* fig, f. L. *ficus* fig-tree, fig.] **1.** The fruit of the fig-tree or *Ficus*, esp. of *F. carica.* **b.** = FIG-TREE. ME. **c.** In the E. and W. Indies applied to the Banana, also to the Cochineal Cactus 1582. †**2.** = A poisoned fig; often *F. of Spain*, *Italian f.* -1691. **3.** As the name of a disease, from the resemblance in shape. †**a.** The disease *Ficus* or the piles. Also *pl.* -1550. **b.** *Farriery.* An excrescence on the frog of a horse's foot 1607. **4.** As a type: Anything small, valueless, or contemptible ME. **5.** A small piece (of tobacco). *U.S.* 1837.

1. The F. which..gave our first Parents Cloaths CHURCHILL. **b.** *Indian F.*: the Banyan (*F. indica*), or the Pipal (*F. religiosa*). 2. Tamberlaine..did cause a F. to be given him, and after his death married his widow NORTH. 4. And so a f. for Miss Edgeworth THACKERAY. Phr. *To care, give a f., or fig's end for, to value* (*a person or thing*) *a f.*, etc.

Comb.: **f.-apple**, a kind of apple without a core; **-bird**, (*a*) = BECCAFICO; (*b*) the chiff-chaff (*local*); **-cake**, a round cake made of figs and almonds worked up into a hard paste; **-dust**, finely ground oatmeal, used as food for caged birds (*Cent. Dict.*); **-eater**, (*a*) one who eats figs; (*b*) = BECCAFICO; **-fauns** = L. *fauni ficarii* (see Forcellini s.v. *ficarius*); **-finch** = BECCAFICO; **-gnat**, a gnat, *Culex ficarius*, injurious to the f.; **-marigold**, a name of species of *Mesembrianthemum*; **-pecker** = BECCAFICO; **-shell**, a shell somewhat resembling a f.

†**Fig** (fig), *sb.*² 1579. [ad. F. *figue* (in phr. *faire la figue*), ad. It. *fica.* By some identified with prec. (see Littré s.v. *figue*).] A contemptuous gesture in which the thumb is thrust between two of the closed fingers or into the mouth. Also *f. of Spain.* -1600.

Hen. V. III. vi. 62.

Fig (fig), *sb.*³ 1841. [f. FIG *v.*⁴ 2.] **1.** Dress, equipment, only in phr. *in full f.* **2.** Condition, form 1883.

†**Fig**, *v.*¹ *rare.* 1609. [f. FIG *sb.*¹] *trans.* Only in †*To f. away* (a person): To get rid of by means of a poisoned fig.

†**Fig**, *v.*² [f. FIG *sb.*²] *trans.* To insult by giving the fig to. 2 *Hen. IV*, v. iii. 123.

†**Fig**, *v.*³ 1595. [var. of FIKE *v.*¹; cf. FIDGE *v.*] *intr.* To move briskly to and fro.

Fig (fig), *v.*⁴ 1692. [var. of FEAGUE.] **1.** *trans.* = FEAGUE *v.* 2. 1810. **2.** *To f. out*: to dress, get up. Also with *up.* 1837. †**3.** ? To stuff. R. L'ESTRANGE.

Figary, var. f. FEGARY, vagary.

†**Fi·gent**, *a.* 1598. [? f. FIDGE *v.* + -ENT.] Fidgety, restless -1672.

A wrangling advocate, Such a f. little thing 1613.

Fi·ggery, *sb.* [f. FIG *sb.*³ or *v.*⁴] Dressy ornament. THACKERAY.

†**Figgum.** ? Juggler's tricks. B. JONS.

Fight (fəit), *sb.* [OE. *feohte, feoht, gefeoht*, f. next vb.] **1.** The action of fighting. Now only *arch.* **2.** A combat, battle: **a.** = BATTLE **1.** Now *arch.* or *rhet.* OE. **b.** A combat between two or more persons or animals. Not now applied (exc. *rhet.*) to a duel. ME. **3.** *fig.* Strife, conflict, struggle for victory OE. **4.** Strength or inclination for fighting; pugnacity 1812. †**5.** A kind of screen to conceal and protect combatants on shipboard. Usu. in *pl.* -1678.

1. Fall'n in f. TENNYSON. 2. **a.** This was the issue of Hornsby F. LD. FAIRFAX. **b.** An Eagle and a Serpent wreathed in f. SHELLEY. Phr. *Running f.*: one kept up while one party flees and the other pursues. *Sham f.*: a mimic battle (to exercise troops, or for display). 3. Fight the good f. of faith 1 *Tim.* vi. 12. 4. Their country had f. enough in her yet 1886. Phr. *To show f.* 5. Vp with your fights Giue fire *Merry W.* II. ii. 142.

Fight (fəit), *v.* *Pa. t.* and *pple.* **fought** (fǭt). [Com. WGer.: OE. *feohtan*:—OTeut. type **fehtan.*] **1.** *intr.* To contend in battle or single combat. Const. *against, with* (a person); hence, *to f. together.* OE. **2.** *transf.* and *fig.* To contend, strive for victory, engage in conflict OE. **3.** quasi-*trans.* with cogn. object ME.; also to maintain (a cause, etc.) by fighting 1600; to make (one's way) by fighting 1859. **4.** *trans.* To engage or oppose in battle; to war against. Also *transf.* and *fig.* 1697. **5.** To contend for (a prize) 1826. **6.** To cause to fight 1680. **7.** To manage, or manœuvre (troops, a ship, guns, etc.) in battle 1779.

1. We..fought a long houre by Shrewsburie clocke 1 *Hen. IV*, v. iv. 151. To f. for a principle 1847. Phr. *To f. with one's own shadow*: to struggle vainly; to talk at random. *To f.* (*for*) *one's own hand, to f. tooth and nail*: see HAND, TOOTH. 2. For Modes of Faith let graceless zealots f. POPE. 3. F. the good fight of faith 1 *Tim.* vi. 12. To f. a business 1784, an action (at law) 1893. 6. To f. cocks SCOTT, dogs DICKENS.

Phrases. *To f. down*: to overcome. *To f. off*: *trans.* to repel; *intr.* to try to back out of. *To f. out*: to settle by fighting, to fight to the end; often *to f. it out.* *To f. shy*: to avoid intercourse with a person, evade an undertaking, etc.

Fighter (fəi·tər). ME. [? OE. *feotere*; see FIGHT *v.* and -ER¹.] **1.** One who fights; *occas.* a combatant, a warrior. †**2.** A pugnacious person; a brawler -1557.

Fighting (fəi·tiŋ), *vbl. sb.* ME. [f. FIGHT *v.*] The action of FIGHT *v.*, in various senses.

Warres and fightinge COVERDALE. The reward of their fightings FREEMAN.

Comb.: **f.-cock**, see COCK *sb.*¹; **-field** = BATTLE-FIELD.

Fighting (fəi·tiŋ), *ppl. a.* ME. [f. as prec.] That fights, able and ready to fight, bearing arms, warlike.

xxᵗⁱ thousand fyghtyng men 1500. Phr. *A f. chance*: a chance of gaining something by fighting.

Comb.: **f. crab**, *Gelasimus bellator*; **f. fish**, a Siamese fish (*Betta pugnax*); **f. sandpiper**, the ruff. Hence **Fi·ghtingly** *adv.* pugnaciously.

Fi·g-leaf. 1535. [f. FIG *sb.*¹ + LEAF.] The leaf of a fig-tree; chiefly with reference to Gen. iii. 7. Also *fig.*

They sewed fig leaves together *Gen.* iii. 7. *fig.* The fig-leaves of decent reticence KINGSLEY.

Figment (fi·gmĕnt). ME. [ad. L. *figmentum*, f. *fig-* stem of *fingere.*] †**1.** Something moulded or fashioned, e.g. an image -1664. **2.** A product of invention; a fiction ME.; an arbitrarily framed notion of the mind 1624.

2. To defend [God's] justice with false tales and figments 1639. Beauty, virtue, and such like are not figments of the mind BERKELEY.

Hence **Figme·ntal** *a.* of the nature of a f.

†**Fi·go.** 1599. [a. OSp. and Pg. *figo.*] = FICO. -1640.

Fi·g-tree. ME. [f. FIG *sb.*¹ + TREE.] A tree of the genus *Ficus*, esp. *F. carica.*

Figuline (fi·giŭlin, -əin). 1657. [ad. L. *figulinus*, f. *figulus* potter.]

A. *adj.* Made of earthenware.

B. *sb.* **1.** An earthen vessel; in *pl.* pottery 1878. **2.** Potter's clay 1859.

Figurable (fi·giŭrăb'l), *a.* 1605. [f. FIGURE *v.* + -ABLE.] Capable of receiving a definite figure or form, or of being represented figuratively.

Lead is f., but not water JOHNSON. Hence **Fi·gurabi·lity.**

Fi·gural, *a.* 1450. [a. OF., ad. late L. **figuralis*, f. *figura.*] †**1.** = FIGURATIVE 1, 4. -1621. †**2.** *Arith.* Of numbers: Representing some geometrical figure, as a square, cube, etc.; consisting of factors -1674. **3.** Pertaining to †figure, or figures (*rare*) 1650. **4.** *Mus.* = FIGURATE *a.* 4. (Dicts.) Hence †**Fi·gurally** *adv.*

‖**Figurant** (figŭran) *masc.*, **Figurante** (figŭrānt) *fem.* 1775. [F., pr. pple. of *figurer* to FIGURE.] **1.** A ballet-dancer 1790. **2.** One who figures on the stage but has little or nothing to do or say.

‖ **Figurante** (figura·nte). *Pl.* **-ti**, *occas.* **-tes.** 1782. [It.] = prec. 1. Also *transf.*

Figurate (fi·giŭrĕt). 1530. [ad. L. *figuratus*, *figurare*, f. *figura*.]

A. *ppl. a.* †1. Based on, or involving the use of figures or metaphors; metaphorical –1728. 2. Having definite form or shape. Now only *Med.* 1626. 3. *Math.* †a. = FIGURAL 2. –1674. b. *F. numbers*: numbers, or series of numbers, formed from any arithmetical progression in which the first term is a unit, and the difference a whole number, by taking the first term, and the sums of the first two, first three, first four, etc., terms as the successive terms of a new series, from which a third series may be formed in the same manner, and so on. So *F. arithmetic*, the science of such numbers.

Thus from the series 1, 2, 3, 4, etc., a second series 1, 3, 6, 10, etc. ('triangular' numbers) may be formed; and from this a third series, 1, 4, 10, 20 ('pyramidal' numbers).

4. *Mus.* a. Involving passing discords by the freer melodic movement of one or more voice parts. b. = FLORID 3 a. 1708.

B. *sb.* That which is figurate; *esp.* a figurate number 1610.

Hence †**Fi·gurately** *adv.* in a f. manner.

†**Fi·gurate,** *v.* 1450. [f. L. *figurat-*, *figurare*.] 1. *trans.* To give shape to –1623. 2. To represent by a figure –1654; to treat as figurative 1806.

Figuration (figiŭrē¹·ʃən). ME. [a. F., ad. L. *figurationem*.] 1. The action or process of giving shape to; determination to a certain form; also quasi-*concr.* the resulting form or shape. 2. *Mus.* Employment of florid counterpoint; alteration by the introduction of passing-notes, rapid figures, etc. 1597.

Figurative (fi·giŭrătiv), *a.* ME. [a. F. *figuratif*, *-ive*, ad. L. *figurativus*, f. *figurare*.] 1. Representing by a figure or emblem; symbolic, typical. 2. Pertaining to, or of the nature of, pictorial or plastic representation 1607. 3. Of speech: Based on figures or metaphors; metaphorical, not literal ME. b. Metaphorically so called ME. 4. Abounding in figures of speech 1589. †5. *Mus.* = FIGURATE *a.* 4. 1744.

1. F. and mystic ceremonial 1853. 2. Both geometric as well as animal and f. decorated forms 1889. 3. By a f. and borrowed speech he declareth the horror..of the damned COVERDALE. b. To confound real with f. sovereignty LEWIS. 4. F. expressions DRYDEN, authors 1740. Hence **Fi·gurative·ly** *adv.*, **-ness.**

Figure (fi·gəɹ, -iŭɹ), *sb.* ME. [a. F., ad. L. *figura*, f. **fig-* stem of *fingere*; see FEIGN. The ordinary tr. of Gr. σχῆμα.]

I. Form, shape. 1. The form of anything as determined by the outline; shape generally ME.; hence, †posture –1684. 2. *Geom.* A definite form constituted by a line or lines so arranged as to enclose a superficial space, or by a surface or surfaces enclosing a space of three dimensions; any of the classes of such forms, as the triangle, cube, sphere, etc. ME. 3. Of persons, etc.: Bodily shape; the bodily frame ME. 4. A person as seen or (*transf.*) thought of ME. 5. Conspicuous appearance 1691. 6. Importance, mark (now only in *man*, *woman of f.*) 1692. b. Style of living. *arch.* 1602.

1. The F. of a Bell partaketh of the Pyramis BACON. Solidity and Extension, and the Termination of it, F. LOCKE. 3. Wise Nestor then his reverend f. rear'd POPE. 4. What a f. of a man is there! DRYDEN. Phr. *F. of fun* (colloq.): an oddity. The disappearance of this brilliant f. [Hamilton] BRYCE. 5. Phr. *To make* (colloq. *cut*) *a f.* 6. b. He obliged her not to increase her f., but to live private DE FOE.

II. Represented form. 1. The image, likeness, or representation *of* something; *esp.* of the human form in sculpture, painting, etc. ME. †2. Represented character; part; hence, position, capacity –1721. 3. An emblem, type ME.

1. A..playne f. of idlenesse ELYOT. Carued figures of Cherubims 1 *Kings* vi. 29. Pourtraitures and Figures of those who had been Travellers 1676. 2. Brauely the f. of this Harpie, hast thou Perform'd *Temp.* III. iii. 83. 3. The Rock..was a Type and F. of Christ 1651.

III. Devised form. 1. A diagram, an illustration. Abbrev. *fig.* ME. 2. *Astrol.* A diagram of the aspects of the astrological houses; a horoscope ME. 3. An arrangement of lines, etc., forming an ornamental device; one of the devices combined into a decorative pattern; also *transf.* of natural markings. Also *collect.* 1597. 4. *Dancing.* Any of the evolutions or movements of a dance or dancer; also, a set of evolutions 1636. 5. *Skating.* 'A movement, or series of movements, beginning and ending at the centre' (*Badm. Libr.*) 1869.

1. For the more declaracioun, lo here the f. CHAUCER. 2. Phr. *To cast, erect, set a f.*: see the vbs. 3. His bonnet sedge, Inwrought with figures dim MILT.

IV. †1. A written character; e.g. a letter, etc. –1660. 2. A character or symbol representing a number ME. 3. Hence, An amount, number, sum of money expressed in figures 1842.

2. Phr. *Two* (or *double*), *three*, *four*, etc. *figures*: ten or more, a hundred or more, a thousand or more, etc., a sum of money so expressed. *F. of eight*: see EIGHT. 3. An uncommonly stiff f. THACKERAY.

V. Repr. Gr. σχῆμα. 1. *Rhet.* Any form of expression which deviates from the normal; e.g. Aposiopesis, Hyperbole, Metaphor, etc. ME. b. Less widely: A metaphor or metaphorical expression ME. 2. *Grammar.* Any permitted deviation from the normal form of words (e.g. Aphæresis, Syncope, Elision), or from the ordinary rules of construction (e.g. Ellipsis) 1669. 3. *Logic.* The form of a syllogism as determined by the position of the middle term in the premisses 1551. 4. *Mus.* 'Any short succession of notes, either as a melody or a group of chords, which produces a single, complete, and distinct impression' (Grove).

1. Your termes, your coloures, and your figures, kepe hem in store, til [etc.] CHAUCER. b. That.. destroyer of fine figures..common sense POPE.

Comb. 1. General: as, *f.-painting*, *-training*, *-weaving*, etc.

2. Special: **f.-servant**, *nonce-wd.*, a commercial clerk; **-skating**, the art or practice of skating in figures (see sense III. 5); **-stone** (*Min.*) = AGALMATOLITE. See also Main Words.

Figure (fi·gəɹ, -iŭɹ), *v.* ME. [f. prec. *sb.*] †1. *trans.* To give figure to; to shape –1790. 2. To represent in a diagram or picture ME. 3. To picture in the mind, imagine 1603. 4. To represent by speech or action 1475. 5. 'To prefigure, foreshow' (J.) 3 *Hen. VI*, II. i. 32. 6. To represent typically ME. †7. To resemble in form –1779. †8. To represent as resembling –1523. 9. To express by a metaphor or image ME. 10. To adorn or mark with figures 1480. 11. a. *trans.* To mark with (numerical) figures 1683. b. *intr.* To use figures in arithmetic 1854. c. *trans.* (*Mus.*) To write figures over or under (the bass) in order to indicate the intended harmony 1674. 12. *intr.* (*Dancing.*) To perform a figure or set of evolutions 1744. 13. *intr.* To appear; often with *as* 1602; also to make a distinguished appearance 1736. 14. *U.S.* To reckon, calculate 1865.

2. The sacred Cross; and figured there The five dear wounds our Lord did bear WORDSW. 3. You cannot . a duller season H. WALPOLE. 4. *Rich. III*, I. ii. 194. 6. Soft Peace they [olives] f. DRYDEN. 10. Blue velvet figured with tawny 1480. 11. a. Your draft is worded for twenty pounds, and figured for twenty-one COWPER. b. Phr. *To f. up*: to reckon up with figures. *To f. out*: to work out by means of figures; also, more widely, to estimate or calculate (chiefly *U.S.*). 13. Persons who figured..in the rebellion 1736.

Fi·gure-ca·ster. 1584. †1. One who casts figures (see FIGURE *sb.* III. 2); 'a pretender to astrology' (J.) –1642. 2. One who casts up figures 1831. So **Fi·gure-ca·sting** *vbl. sb.*

Figured (fi·gəɹ'd, -iŭɹd), *ppl. a.* ME. [f. FIGURE *v.* and *sb.*] 1. In senses of the vb. 1552. 2. Having a particular shape ME. †3. Having definite shape; also, formed into patterns –1789. 4. Adorned with patterns or designs 1489. 5. Adorned with rhetorical figures; figurative 1500. 6. *Mus.* a. = FIGURATE *a.* 4 a. b. *F. bass* = THOROUGHBASS 1879.

3. Geese and cranes..move in f. flights G. WHITE. 4. F. Satin 1611. *F. card* = COURT CARD. 5. The f. language of which he is a master M. ARNOLD.

Fi·gure-fli·nger. 1587. Contemptuous for FIGURE-CASTER I.

Fi·gure-hea·d. 1765. 1. A piece of carving, usually a bust or figure, placed over the cut-water of a ship. 2. Said depreciatingly of one who is the nominal but not the real head of an enterprise, etc. Also *attrib.* 1883. 3. *Arch.* A corbel-head 1874.

Figurine (figiŭrī·n). 1854. [a. F., ad. It. *figurina*, dim. of *figura*; see FIGURE and -INE.] A small carved or sculptured figure.

Figuring (fi·gəriŋ, -iŭriŋ), *vbl. sb.* ME. [f. FIGURE *v.*] 1. The action of FIGURE *v.* Also with *out.* 1534. †2. ? Configuration, form (or perh. emblematic significance). CHAUCER.

†**Fi·gurist.** 1585. [f. as prec. + -IST.] One who explains something as figurative (e.g. the presence of Christ in the Eucharist) –1737.

Fi·g-wort. 1548. [See Fig.[1] *sb.* 3 a.] The name of plants reputed to cure the 'fig'. a. The pilewort. b. The genus *Scrophularia.* 1597.

Fike (fəik), *sb.* *Sc.* 1605. [f. FIKE *v.*] †1. The itch, or anything that causes one to fidget. Also, *the fikes* = the fidgets. –1758. 2. Anxiety about trifles, fuss, trouble 1719. 3. Flirtation 1808.

Fike (fəik), *v.* *Sc.* and *n. dial.* ME. [? a. ON. *fíkja* to move briskly or restlessly.] 1. *intr.* To move restlessly, fidget; also *fig.* Also, to flinch. b. To flirt 1804. 2. *trans.* To vex, trouble 1572. Hence **Fi·kery,** fidgetiness; fuss.

†**Filace.** ME. [a. AF. *filaz*, ad. med. L. *filacium*, ? f. L. *filum* thread.] *Law.* = FILE *sb.*[2] I. 3 b. –1537. var. Filaze.

†**Fila·ceous,** *a.* 1626. [f. L. *filum* thread + -ACEOUS.] Consisting of thread-like parts –1694.

Filacer, Filazer (fi·lăsəɹ, -zəɹ). 1512. [f. FILACE.] *Law.* A former officer of the superior courts at Westminster, who filed original writs, etc., and issued processes thereon.

Filament (fi·lăment). 1594. [ad. mod. L. *filamentum*, f. late L. *filare* to spin, f. *filum* thread.] 1. A tenuous thread or thread-like body; a minute fibre; also *transf.* b. *spec.* The infusible conductor placed in the glass bulb of an incandescent electric lamp 1881. 2. *Bot.* That part of the stamen which supports the anther 1756.

1. *transf.* Slender as a f. of air DE QUINCEY.

Hence **Filame·ntary** *a.* of, pertaining to, or of the nature of a f. or filaments. **Fi·lamenti·ferous** *a.* provided with filaments. **Filame·ntoid** *a.* like a f. **Fi·lamento·se, Filame·ntous** *adjs.* composed of or containing filaments; thread-like; bearing filaments. **Filame·ntule,** a small f. (*rare*).

Filander[1] (filæ·ndəɹ). Chiefly *pl.* 1486. [a. OF. *filandre* :— pop. L. **filandula*, dim. of (*lana*) *filanda* wool to be spun.] In *pl.* Thread-like intestinal worms causing a disease in hawks; also, the disease.

†**Fila·nder.**[2] 1737. A name given to a species of *Macropus* (*M. Brunii*). Also *F. Kangaroo.*

Filander, *v.*: see PHILANDER.

Filar (fəi·lăɹ), *a.* 1874. [f. L. *filum* thread + -AR.] Of or pertaining to a thread; *esp.* in *f. micrometer*, *microscope*, one having threads across its field of view.

Filarial (filē°·riăl), *a.* 1881. [f. mod. L. *filaria*, f. as prec. + -AL.] Of or pertaining to the genus *Filaria* of parasitic worms. Hence **Fila·riform** *a.* of the form of *Filaria*. **Fila·rious** *a.* infected with *Filaria*.

Filate (fəi·lĕt), *a.* 1826. [f. L. *filum* thread + -ATE[2].] *Entom.* Of inversatile antennæ; Having neither a terminal nor a lateral bristle.

Filatory (fi·lătəri). [ad. med. L. *filatorium.*] A machine for forming or spinning threads. TOOKE.

Filature (fi·lătiŭɹ). 1759. [a. F., f. late L. *filare* to spin; cf. It. *filatura.*] 1. The action of spinning into threads; the reeling of silk from cocoons 1783. 2. An establishment for reeling silk.

1. Buying up the cocoons for the Italian f. BURKE.

Filaze, Filazer: see FILACE, FILACER.

Filbert (fi·lbəɹt). ME. [prob. short for *filbert* (i.e. *Philibert*) *-nut*, from being ripe near St. Philibert's day, Aug. 22 (O.S.). Cf. dial. F. *noix de filbert.*] 1. The fruit or nut of the cultivated hazel (*Corylus avellana*). 2. The tree bearing the nut ME.

1. Something bigger, and more oval than a Fillbeard 1712. *attrib.* F. nails TROLLOPE.

Filch (filʃ, filtʃ), *sb.* 1622. [f. next vb.] †1. A staff with a hook at one end, used to steal things from hedges, open windows, etc. –1700. 2. That which is filched 1627. †3. A filcher –1810.

Filch (filʃ, filtʃ), *v.* 1561. [? Orig. slang.] 1. *trans.* To steal, *esp.* things of small value; to pilfer; *occas.*, to carry off furtively. 2. To rob (*of* something) 1567.

1. Or els filtch Poultry, carying them to the Alehouse 1561. To f. a book out of a Library PALEY. Hence **Fi·lcher**, a petty thief. †**Fi·lchingly**, stealthily, surreptitiously.

File (fəil), *sb.*¹ [OE. *fíol*, with Teut. cognates.] 1. A metal (usually steel) instrument, having one or more of its faces covered with small cutting edges or teeth, for abrading, reducing, or smoothing surfaces. Also *fig.* OE. 2. *slang.* An artful or shrewd person. Also, a 'cove'. 1812.

1. She [the serpent] fond a fyle whiche she beganne to gnawe with her teethe CAXTON. *fig.* The critic's f. AKENSIDE. 2. Old Blow-hard was a dry old f. HUGHES.

Combs. 1. General: as *f.-chisel*, *-cleaner*, *-cutter*, *-cutting*, *-grinder*, *-grinding*, etc.

2. Special: as **f.-blank**, a piece of soft steel, ready for cutting, to form a f.; also *attrib.*; **-shell**, a species of *Pholas*, so named from the roughness of its shell.

File (fəil), *sb.*² 1525. [Two wds.: (1) a. F. *fil*; (2) a. F. *file*; both f. (ult.) L. *filum* thread.]

I. Senses repr. F. *fil.* †1. A thread; also *fig.* and *transf.* –1607. †2. The thread, course, or tenor (of a story, etc.) –1647. 3. A string, wire, or other contrivance, on which papers are placed for preservation and reference 1525. b. *esp.* one in a court of law to hold proceedings or documents in a cause, etc.; the list of documents, etc., in a cause 1607. †c. A list or roll –1795. 4. A collection of papers placed on a file, or merely arranged in order of date or subject for reference 1626. 5. *Her.* = Label 1562.

2. Let me resume the F. of my Relation WOTTON. 3. Keep the tradesmen's notes upon a f. 1732. b. Causes unjudg'd disgrace the loaded f. PRIOR. c. Our present Musters grow vpon the f. SHAKS. 4. A f. of the *Times* LD. HOUGHTON.

II. Senses repr. F. *file.* 1. *Mil.* The number of men (in mod. Eng. formation of infantry now only two) constituting the depth of a formation in line. Also *transf.* and *fig.* 1598. b. A small body of men, formerly from two to twelve or more, but now usually two. Also, when 'marching in files', two soldiers abreast. 1616. 2. A row of persons, animals, or things placed one behind another 1603. 3. *Chess.* One of the eight lines of squares extending from player to player 1614. 4. The run or track of a hare 1815.

1. Phr. *In f.*: one behind the other. INDIAN, SINGLE *f.* (see the adjs.). *Rank and f.*: see RANK. *To close their files*: see CLOSE *v.* b. I shall send a sergeant and a f. of mariners to fetch you MARRYAT. 2. Phr. *The common f.* = 'the common herd'. *Cor.* I. vi. 43. *Attrib.* and *Comb.*, as *f.-leader*, the soldier at the front of a f. Also, **f.-fire, -firing**, firing by files, now called independent (opp. to volley-) firing; **-marching**, marching in files, by turning from a formation in line to the right or left, so that the line becomes a series of files facing to the right or left flank.

†**File** (fəil), *sb.*³ *slang.* 1673. [?] A pickpocket –1743. So †**File** *v.*

File (fəil), *v.*¹ ME. [f. FILE *sb.*¹] 1. *trans.* To rub smooth, reduce the surface of, with a file; (contextually) to sharpen. 2. *fig.* To smooth or polish, as with a file ME.

1. To f. the edges of new shillings LUTTRELL. 2. Precious phrase by all the Muses fil'd SHAKS. And f. your tongue to a little more courtesy SCOTT.

File (fəil), *v.*² [OE. **fýlan* :— OTeut. **fûljan*, f. **fûlo-* FOUL *a.*] 1. *trans.* To render foul; to DEFILE ME. †2. To charge with a crime, accuse –1759.

1. For Banquo's Issue haue I fil'd my Minde *Macb.* III. i. 65. To f. my hands in villain's blood 1611.

File (fəil), *v.*³ 1450. [f. FILE *sb.*²] 1. *trans.* †To string upon a thread; to place on a file; to place in consecutive order for preservation and reference. Also *transf.* and *fig.* 1601. b. *spec.* To place in due manner among the records of a court or public office 1511. †2. To arrange in consecutive order –1676. †3. To arrange (men, etc.) in a file or files –1643. 4. *intr.* To march or move in file. Also with *away*, etc. 1616. 5. *trans.* To cause to file off 1831.

1. Miss Abbey filed her receipts DICKENS. *fig.* Dan Chaucer..On fames eternall beadroll worthie to be fyled SPENSER. b. Phr. *To f. a bill (in Chancery), an information.* 2. I would have my several courses and dishes well filed FLETCHER. 4. Phr. *To f. off*: 'to wheel off by files from moving on a spacious front, and march in length' (Stocqueler). The Enemy filed off..towards the Thickets 1708. †*To f. with*: to march in line *with*.

File-fish. 1774. [f. FILE *sb.*¹ + FISH *sb.*] A fish of the genus *Balistes*, having its skin granulated like a file.

Filemot (fi·lĭmǫt). 1647. [corrupt f. FEUILLEMORTE.] A. *adj.* = FEUILLEMORTE *a.* B. *sb.* The name of a colour, viz. that of a dead or faded leaf 1655.

Filer (fəi·lǝɹ). 1598. [f. FILE *v.*¹, ³.] One who files or works with a file.

Filet (fi·lět). 1904. [a. F. *filet* thread, lace.] A kind of net or lace with a square mesh. Also *attrib.*

Filial (fi·liăl), *a.* ME. [ad. late L. *filialis*, f. *filius, filia.*] 1. Of or pertaining to a son or daughter; due from a child to a parent. 2. 'Bearing the character or relation of a son or daughter' (J.). Now only *transf.* and *fig.* of a thing: That is the offspring of something else. 1667.

1. F. respect 1759. 2. Thus the f. Godhead answering spake MILT. *P. L.* vi. 722. Hence **Filia·lity**, f. quality or relation. **Fi·lial-ly** *adv.*, **-ness**.

Filiate (fi·li,eⁱt), *v.* 1791. [f. med. L. *filiat-*, *filiare* to have a child, f. *filius*; see -ATE³.] *trans.* = AFFILIATE *v.*

Filiation (fili,ēⁱ·ʃǝn). 1529. [a. F., ad. med. L. *filiationem*, f. *filiare*; see prec.] 1. *Theol.* The becoming, or the being, a son. 2. Sonship 1659. 3. A person's parentage, 'whose son one is' 1611. 4. Descent, transmission *from* 1799. 5. Genealogical relationship 1794. 6. Formation of branches or offshoots; chiefly *concr.* an offshoot of a society or language 1777. 7. = AFFILIATION 3. 1561.

3. Mr. Cust's reasoning, with respect to the f. of Richard Savage 1799. 5. The true f. of the sciences H. SPENCER. 7. *fig.* The f. of a literary performance is difficult of proof BOSWELL.

Filibeg (fi·libeg). *Sc.* 1746. [ad. Gael. *feileadh-beag*, f. *feileadh* a fold + *beag* little, as dist. from *feileadh-mor* the large kilt of primitive form.] A kilt.

Filibuster (fi·libɒstǝɹ), *sb.* 1587. [Earlier *flibutor*, ad. Du. *vrijbuiter* (see FREEBOOTER). The F. form *flibustier*, adopted about 1790, was superseded about 1850 by *filibuster*, ad. Sp. *filibustero.*] †1. *gen.* = FREEBOOTER (*rare*). 1587. 2. *spec.* One of a class of piratical adventurers who pillaged the Spanish colonies in the West Indies in the 17th c. 1792. b. Applied to the lawless adventurers from the United States who between 1850 and 1860 followed Lopez in his expedition to Cuba, and Walker in his expedition to Nicaragua. 1854. 3. Hence, One who engages in unauthorized and irregular war against foreign states 1860. 4. *nonce-use.* A pirate craft. MOTLEY. 5. *U.S.* One who practises obstruction in a legislative assembly 1889.

Filibuster (fi·libɒ:stǝɹ), *v.* 1853. [f. prec. *sb.*] 1. *intr.* To act as a filibuster. Also *trans.* To subject to the methods of a filibuster 1862. 2. *U.S.* To obstruct progress in a legislative assembly 1882.

2. The objectionable practices of 'filibustering' and 'stone-walling' SIR M. H. BEACH.

Filibusterism (filibɒ·stǝriz'm). 1862. [see -ISM.] The practice of filibustering; inclination to filibustering.

Filical (fi·likăl), *a.* 1835. [f. L. *filix* (*filic-*) fern + -AL.] Of or pertaining to ferns.

Filicide¹ (fi·lisəid). 1823. [f. L. *filius*, *filia*; see -CIDE 1.] One who kills a son or a daughter.

Filicide² (fi·lisəid). 1665. [f. as prec.; see -CIDE 2.] The action of killing a son or a daughter.

Filiciform (fili·sifǭɹm), *a.* 1846. [f. as FILICAL + -(I)FORM.] Fern-shaped.

Filicoid (fi·likoid). 1847. [f. as prec. + -OID.] A. *adj.* Resembling a fern. B. *sb.* A fern-like plant 1847.

Filiety (filəi·ěti). [ad. late L. *filietatem* sonship.] = FILIATION 2. J. S. MILL.

Filiferous (fəili·fěrǝs), *a.* 1841. [f. L. *filum* thread + -(I)FEROUS.] Having thread-like parts.

Filiform (fəi·lifǭɹm), *a.* 1757. [f. as prec. + -(I)FORM; cf. F. *filiforme.*] Having the form of a thread.

F. crystals of felspar 1811.

Filigrane (fi·ligrēⁱn), *sb.* 1668. [a. F., ad. It. *filigrana*, f. L. *filum* thread + *granum* grain.] 1. = FILIGREE *sb.* 1. Also *transf.* of architectural ornament, etc. 2. *attrib.* = FILIGREE *a.* 1680.

1. For airy towers of almost filigraine we have none to be compared with those of Rheims H. WALPOLE. Hence †**Fi·ligraned** *ppl. a.* made of f.

Filigree, filagree (fi·ligri, -ăgri), *sb.* 1693. [Abbrev. f. *filigreen*, var. of prec.] 1. 'Jewel work of a delicate kind made with threads and beads, usually of gold and silver' (*Encycl. Brit.*). 2. *attrib.* Made of, or worked in, filigree 1747.

2. Gold f. baskets containing flowers 1886. Hence **Fi·ligreed** *ppl. a.* ornamented with, or worked in, f.

Filing (fəi·liŋ), *vbl. sb.* ME. [f. FILE *v.*¹] 1. The action of FILE *v.*¹ 2. *concr.* usu. *pl.* One of the particles rubbed off by the action of the file, as *iron filings* ME.

‖**Filioque** (fili,ōᵘ·kwi). 1876. [L.; = 'and from the Son'.] The word inserted in the Western version of the Nicene Creed to assert the doctrine of the procession of the Holy Ghost from the Son as well as from the Father. Also *attrib.*, as *filioque clause*, etc.

‖**Filipendula** (filipe·ndiulă). *Obs.* exc. *Bot.* 1540. [mod. L., fem. of *filipendulus* hanging by a thread, f. *filum* + *pendulus*. Cf. F *filipendule.*] The drop-wort (*Spiræa Filipendula*). So **Filipe·ndulous** *a* hanging by or as by a thread.

Fill (fil), *sb.*¹ [OE. *fyllo, fyllu* fem. :— OTeut. **fullin-*, f. **fullo* FULL *a.* But in Eng. assoc. w. FILL *v.*] 1. A full supply; enough to satisfy want. 2. A filling, charge. *lit.* and *fig.* 1555. †3. Of a river: The head-waters; opp. to *fall.* DRAYTON.

1. Thou mayest eate grapes thy f. *Deut.* xxiii. 24. Talk your f. to me GRAY. 2. A f. of tobacco STEVENSON.

Fill (fil), *sb.*² Now *dial.* 1596. [var. of THILL.] 1. *pl.* = THILLS. *Sing.* 'The space between the shafts' (J.). *Comb.* **f.-horse** = shaft-horse.

Fill (fil), *v.* *Pa. t.* and *pple.* **filled** (fild). [ME. *fullen* (*ü*) :— OE. *fyllan* :— OTeut **fulljan*, f. **fullo-* FULL *a.*]

I. To make full. 1. To supply with as much as can be held or contained; to put or pour into till no more can be received. †2. To impregnate –1645. 3. *intr.* To become full Of the bosom: = *fill out.* 1607. 4. *Naut.* a. *trans.* Of the wind: To distend (the sails) 1610 b. *intr.* Of a sail: To become full of wind 1835. Also *absol.* 5. To stock abundantly OE. 6. To make up with some foreign material; to adulterate 1887.

1. A vessel filled to the lip 1645. Ely's Sons, who fill'd with lust and violence the house of God MILT. 3. In a few weeks, when the town fills 1713. 4. a. South winds filling the sails BOWEN. Phr. *To f. the sails*: 'to brace the yards so that the wind strikes the after side of the sails' (Smyth). 5. Be fruitful, and multiply, and f. the waters of the seas *Gen.* i. 22.

II. 1. To occupy the whole capacity or extent of; also, to pervade ME. 2. To hold or occupy; to discharge the duties of ME. 3. To put a person or thing into (a vacant place) 1593.

1. Glaciers which once filled the valley TYNDALL. Their fame filled Europe (*mod.*). Phr. *To f. the bill* (slang): (*a*) *Theatr.*: 'To excel in conspicuousness, as a star actor whose name is "billed" to the exclusion of the rest of the company' (Farmer). (*b*) *U.S.* To meet all the requirements of the case. 2. I f. a place, I know't *All's Well*, I. ii. 69. †*To f. the time*: to meet the needs of the moment *Ibid.* III. vii. 33. 3. To f. an episcopal chair FREEMAN.

III. 1. To produce a sense of fullness in; to satisfy ME. Also †*intr.* 2. To execute, perform; to fulfil (a prophecy, engagement, etc.); to complete (a period of time, etc.).

1. To see meate f. Knaues, and wine heat fooles *Timon* I. i. 271. 2. To f. an order (*mod.*). An olde man, that hath not filled his dayes *Isa.* lxv. 20.

IV. 1. To put into a vessel to fill it; hence, to pour out. *Obs.* exc. *arch.* –1710. Also *absol.*

2. To fill a receptacle with; to put or take a load of on board a ship ME.

1. *absol.* In the cup which she hath filled f. to her double *Rev.* xviii. 6. 2. Here we filled water, and after set saile 1557.

Combs. 1. With advs. **F. in. a.** *trans.* To complete (an outline). **b.** To put in what will fill a vacancy or blank space. **F. out. a.** *trans.* To enlarge or extend to the desired limit. **b.** *intr.* To become distended or rounded in outline. **c.** *trans.* To pour out. **F. up. a.** *trans.* To fill to repletion. **b.** To complete the filling of. **c.** To supply (a deficiency, a vacancy). **d.** = *fill in* b. **e.** To stop up; to do away with by filling. **f.** *intr.* 'To grow full' (J.).

2. Special. Prefixed to sbs., with sense 'he who or that which fills something', as **f.-basket**, a name of certain large or prolific kinds of peas, etc.; **-belly**, a glutton; **-(the)-dike** *a.* epithet of February; etc.

Filler[1] (fi·ləɹ). 1496. [f. FILL *v.*] **1.** One who or that which fills (see FILL *v.*). **2.** Something used for filling 1591.

2. It [an epithet] is a mere f., to stop a vacancy in the Hexameter DRYDEN.

Filler[2] (fi·ləɹ). 1692. [f. FILL *sb.*[2]] A thill- or shaft-horse. Also *attrib.*, as **f.-horse.**

Fillet (fi·lėt), *sb.* ME. [a. F. *filet*, dim. of *fil* :— L. *filum* thread.] **1.** A head-band of any material, used for binding the hair, for keeping the head-dress in position, or for ornament. Also *fig.* with reference to the *vitta* with which in antiquity the heads of sacrificial victims were adorned. **2.** A strip of any material suitable for binding; a band or bandage 1601. **3.** A thin narrow strip of any material; e.g. of metal in *Coining*, of card-clothing in the *Carding-engine*; a curb to confine the curds in making cheese; etc. 1663. †**4.** (after F. *filet*): A thread or string. *lit.* and *fig.* –1735. **5.** A band of fibre; a flap of flesh: †**a.** A muscle –1543; **b.** 'A tract of obliquely-curved white nerve-fibres seen on the surface of the pons Varolii' (*Syd. Soc. Lex.*); †**c.** A lobe of the liver –1692; **d.** *pl.* The loins (of an animal, *rarely* of a man) ME. **6.** *Cookery.* **a.** A fleshy portion of meat, easily detachable; *esp.* the undercut of a sirloin; one of the thick slices into which a fish is easily divided ME. **b.** The middle part of a leg of veal, boned, rolled, and tied with a string or 'fillet'; a piece of beef, fish, etc. similarly treated 1700. **7.** Any object resembling a fillet or band 1611. **8.** *Arch.* **a.** A narrow flat band separating two mouldings; a fascia. **b.** A small band between the flutes of a column. 1473. **9.** *Her.* A horizontal division of a shield, one-third or one-fourth of the depth of a CHIEF 1572. **10.** *Entom.* and *Ornith.* **a.** A coloured band or stripe. **b.** In a spider: The space between the eyes and the base of the mandibles or chelicerae. 1668. **11.** In techn. uses: **a.** A raised rim or ridge on any surface, *esp.* 'a ring on the muzzle and cascabel of a gun' (Smyth); also, the thread of a screw 1703. **b.** *Carpentry.* A narrow strip of wood fastened upon any surface to serve as a support, etc., or to strengthen an angle formed by two surfaces 1779. **c.** *Bookbinding.* A plain line impressed upon the cover of a book. Also, a tool for doing this. 1641.

Fillet (fi·lėt), *v. Pples.* **filleted, filleting.** 1604. [f. FILLET *sb.*] **1.** *trans.* To bind with or as with a fillet. **2.** *Cookery.* To divide into fillets 1846. **3.** To mark or ornament with fillets; now chiefly in *Bookbinding* 1621.

Filleting (fi·lėtiŋ), *vbl. sb.* 1598. [f. prec.] **1.** The action of FILLET *v.* **2.** *concr.* **a.** Tape for binding; a band or bandage 1639. **b.** A head-band 1648. **c.** Fillets or ornamental lines 1747.

2. b. Put on thy holy fillitings HERRICK.

Filli-: see also FILI-.

Filling (fi·liŋ), *vbl. sb.* ME. [f. FILL *v.*] **1.** The action of FILL *v.* **2.** *concr.* Also *pl.* That which fills or is used to fill a cavity or vacant space, to stop a hole, to make up a bank or road, the interior of a wall, etc. ME. **b.** Something of inferior quality put in to occupy space 1640. **3.** *Brewing.* In *pl.*: Prepared wort, added to casks of ale to cleanse it 1858.

Fillip (fi·lip), *sb.* 1530. [app. echoic.] **1.** A movement made by bending the last joint of a finger against the thumb and suddenly releasing it; a smart stroke or tap given by this means. **b.** A trifle; a moment 1621. **2.** A smart blow (with the fist, etc.). Now *rare.* 1543. **3.** That which serves as a stimulus 1700.

1. The Prince..by a f., made some of it [wine] fly in Oglethorpe's face BOSWELL. **b.** Not worth a f. BYRON. 3. The filip of a little scandal 1847.

Fillip (fi·lip), *v.* 1543. [See prec. sb.] **1.** *trans.* To put into motion by a fillip; hence, to stimulate. **2.** To strike with a fillip 1580. **3.** *gen.* To strike smartly 1577. **4.** *intr.* To make a fillip with the fingers 1577.

1. To f. off crumbs from a muff MAD. D'ARBLAY. 2. If you f. a Lute-string, it sheweth double or treble BACON. 3. If I do, fillop me with a three-man-Beetle 2 *Hen. IV*, I. ii. 255.

Fillipeen, var. of PHILIPPINE.

Fillister (fi·listəɹ). 1819. [?] A rabbeting plane used in making window-sashes, etc.; also, 'the rabbet on the outer edge of a sash-bar, to hold the glass and the putty' (Knight).

Filly (fi·li), *sb.* ME. [? a. ON. *fylja* :— **fuljôn-*, f. *fulfol-*; see FOAL.] **1.** A young mare, a female foal. **2.** *transf.* A young lively girl 1616. **3.** *attrib.* 1523.

2. I believe nobody will be very fond of a Hide-park f. for a wife SEDLEY. Hence †**Fi·lly** *v.* to give birth to a f.

Film (film), *sb.* [OE. *filmen*, f. the same root as FELL *sb.*[1]] †**1.** A membrane –1764. **2.** A thin pellicle or lamina of any material 1653. **3.** *Photogr.* A thin pellicle or coating of collodion, gelatin, etc., spread on photographic paper or plates, or used by itself instead of a plate 1845. **4.** A morbid growth upon the eye. Also *fig.* 1601. **b.** A celluloid roll of film used for a cinema picture 1897. **c.** A cinema performance; *pl.* the cinema 1911. **5.** *transf.* A slight veil of haze, mist, or the like. *lit.* and *fig.* 1833. **6.** A fine thread or filament 1592. **7.** Comb., as *f. actress, -camera, -pack, star.*

2. An icy gale..o'er the pool Breathes a blue f. MANSON. 4. He from thick films shall purge the visual ray POPE. Phr. *The f. of death.* 6. When ..floating films envelope every thorn COWPER.

Film (film), *v.* 1602. [f. prec. sb.] **1.** *trans.* To cover with or as with a film. **2.** *intr.* for *refl.* To become covered with a film; to grow dim as if covered with a film 1844. **3.** *trans.* To make a cinema film of, put on the films 1915.

1. It will but skin and filme the Vlcerous place SHAKS.

Filmy (fi·lmi), *a.* 1604. [f. FILM *sb.* + -Y[1].] †**1.** Of membranous structure –1665. **2.** Forming a thin pellicle or coating 1628. **3.** Gauze- or gossamer-like 1604. **4.** Covered with or as with a film 1825.

2. The area of f. ice KANE. 3. A veil of f. lawn SCOTT. 4. The f. orb of the moon HT. MARTINEAU. Hence **Fi·lmily** *adv.* **Fi·lminess.**

Filoplume (fəi·lŏplūm). 1884. [ad. mod. L. *filopluma*, badly f. L. *filum* thread + *pluma* feather. Better **filipluma.*] *Ornith.* A thread-feather; the nearest approach to hairs that birds have. Hence **Fi:lopluma·ceous** *a.*

Filose (fəilōu·s), *a.* 1823. [as if ad. L. **filosus*, f. *filum* thread.] *Bot.* and *Zool.* Having a thread-like termination.

Filoselle (fi·lŏsel). 1612. [a. Fr.] A silk thread less glossy than floss silk.

Filosofe, -phie, obs. ff. PHILOSOPHE, -Y.

Filter (fi·ltəɹ), *sb.* [ME. *filtre*, a. OF., ad. med. L. *feltrum*; see FELT.] †**1.** = FELT *sb.* **2.** A piece of felt, woollen cloth, paper, or other porous substance, through which liquids are passed to free them from matter held in suspension. Now only *Chem.* 1563. **b.** Any contrivance for freeing liquids from suspended impurities; *esp.* a vessel in which the liquid is made to pass through sand, charcoal, or some porous substance. Also *transf.* and *fig.* 1791. **3.** A material for filtering *rare.* 1823.

2. *Capillary f.*: 'a mode of freeing water of its larger impurities by means of a cord of loose fiber' (Knight).

Comb.: **f.-bed**, a pond or tank with a false bottom covered with sand or gravel, serving as a large filter; also *fig.*; **-faucet**, 'one having a chamber containing sand, sponge, or other material to arrest impurities' (Knight); **-paper**, porous paper for filtering; **-press**, (*a*) a filter in which the liquid is forced through by pressure; (*b*) a machine for extracting oil from fish.

Filter (fi·ltəɹ), *v.* 1576. [ad. mod. L. *filtrare*, f. *filtrum* FILTER *sb.* Cf. F. *filtrer.*] **1.** *trans.* To pass (a liquid) through a filter in order to free it from impurities. Also *absol.* Also *transf.* and *fig.* **b.** Said of the filtering material 1854. **2.** To cause to percolate through a porous medium (now only in *pass.*) 1583. **3.** *intr.* To pass as through a filter; to percolate 1798. **4.** To obtain by filtering. Also *transf. rare.* 1794.

3. *transf.* Filtration. When you are held up at a road junction by a person regulating traffic, do not turn to the left—that is, filter—unless [etc.] *Highway Code* (Ministry of Transport) § 85. 1935.

Filter, var. of PHILTRE.

Filtering (fi·ltəriŋ), *vbl. sb.* 1830. [f. FILTER *v.*] The action of FILTER *v.*

Comb.: **f.-basin**, the chamber in which water from the reservoir is received and filtered before entering the mains; **-cup**, a cup of porous wood used to illustrate the pressure of the atmosphere; **-press** = *filter-press*; **-stone**, any porous stone used in filtering water; **-tank** = *f.-basin.*

Filth (filþ). [OE. *fȳlð* :—OTeut. **fûliþô*, f. **fûlo-* FOUL *a.*] †**1.** The quality or state of being foul; in *pl.* indignities –1579. **2.** *concr.* Foul matter; †rottenness; †pus –1696; dirt. Now only: Loathsome dirt. Rarely in *pl.* ME. **3.** *fig.* Moral defilement; corruption; pollution; obscenity OE. **4.** Said of a person: A vile creature; a scoundrel; a drab. *Obs.* exc. *dial.* ME.

4. *Lear* (Qo. 1) IV. ii. 39.

Filthy (fi·lþi), *a.* ME. [f. FILTH + -Y[1].] **1.** Full of filth; besmeared with filth; dirty, foul, nasty, unclean. Now *rare* in polite speech. **2.** Fond of filth 1526. **3.** Morally foul; obscene 1535. †**4.** Low, mean, scurvy, disgusting –1828. **5.** quasi-*adv.* 1616.

1. Stinking streates and f. lanes 1581. The fogge and filthie ayre *Macb.* I. i. 12. 3. He which is f., let him be f. still: and he that is righteous, let him be righteous still *Rev.* xxii. 11. 4. Doulas, f. Doulas 1 *Hen. IV*, III. iii. 79. Phr. *F. lucre*: dishonourable gain = Gr. αἰσχρὸν κέρδος (Tit. i. 11). Also *joc.* for 'money'. Hence **Fi·lthify** *v.* to make f. (*lit.* and *fig.*). **Fi·lthily** *adv.* **Fi·lthiness.**

Filtrate (fi·ltreʹt), *sb.* 1845. [ad. mod. L. *filtratum*; see FILTER *v.* and -ATE[1].] The liquor which has been passed through a filter.

Filtrate (fi·ltreʹt), *v.* 1612. [ad. mod. L. *filtrat-*, *filtrare.*] **1.** *trans.* = FILTER *v.* 1. **2.** = FILTER *v.* 2. 1661. **3.** *intr.* = FILTER *v.* 3. 1725.

Filtration (filtrēⁱ·ʃən). 1605. [a. F., f. *filtrer.*] **1.** The action or process of filtering. Also *fig.* **2.** Percolation 1664.

1. *transf.* See s.v. FILTER *v.* quot.

Fimble (fi·mb'l). 1484. [a. Du. *femel*, a.F. (*chanvre*) *femelle*, lit. 'female hemp', now used as a name for what botanists call the male plant.] **1.** The male plant of hemp. More fully *f. hemp.* **2.** *attrib.* 1519.

‖**Fimbria** (fi·mbriă). 1752. [L.; = thread, fibre, fringe.] A fringe: *spec.* **a.** *Anat.* the fringed end of the Fallopian tube; **b.** *Bot.* the fringe-like ring of the operculum of mosses. Hence **Fi·mbrial** *a.* (Dicts.)

Fimbriate (fi·mbri,eʹt), *a.* 1829. [ad. L. *fimbriatus.*] **a.** *Her.* = FIMBRIATED. **b.** *Bot.* and *Zool.* Fringed.

Fimbriate (fi·mbri,eʹt), *v.* 1486. [f. L. *fimbria* + -ATE[3].] *trans.* To finish with a border of any kind.

Fimbriated (fi·mbri,eʹtėd), *ppl. a.* 1486. [f. prec.] **a.** *Her.* Of a bearing: Bordered with a narrow band or edge. **b.** *gen.* Having a fringe; fringed 1698.

Fimbriation (fimbri,ēⁱ·ʃən). 1864. [f. as prec.; see -ATION.] The condition or fact of being fimbriated; *concr.* a fringe or border.

Fi·mbricate *a.*, erron. var. of FIMBRIATE *a.*

Fimetarious (fimitēᵊ·riəs), *a.* 1866. [f. L. *fimetum* dunghill + -IC.] Growing on or amidst dung. So **Fime·tic** *a.* pertaining to or concerned with dung. RUSKIN.

Fin (fin), *sb.* [OE. *finn*, cogn. w. MDu. *vinne*, MLG. *finne*; and prob. the same word with L. *pinna.*] **1.** An organ attached to various parts of the body in fishes and cetaceans, which serves for propelling and steering in the water. Qualified as *anal, caudal, dorsal, pectoral, ventral*, etc., according to position. Applied also to analogous organs in other animals, as seals, penguins, etc. **2.** Something resembling a fish's fin: **a.** *joc.* The arm and hand (of a man), or simply the hand 1785. †**b.**

The lid (of the eye) –1623. **c.** The baleen of a whale; hence, a strip of whalebone 1634. **3.** A projecting part: †**a.** A lobe of the liver or lungs 1615. **b.** A lateral projection on the coulter of a plough 1653. **c.** *Mech.* 'A slip inserted longitudinally into a shaft or arbor, and left projecting' (Knight). Also, 'a tongue on the edge of a board' (Knight). **d.** An additional keel-surface in aircraft 1836. **4.** *dial.* The herb rest-harrow. Also *fin-weed.* 1649.

1. All fish..of shell or f. MILT. Fish of every f. (= of every species) POPE. 2. a. Tip us your f. (*slang*).

Comb.: **f.-back** = FINNER; also *attrib.*; **-fish** = FINNER; **-foot,** (*a*) a swimming-foot; a pleiopod; (*b*) a name for birds of the genera *Heliornis* or *Podica*; **-footed** *a. Ornith.*, (*a*) web-footed; (*b*) lobate-footed; (*c*) 'in Mollusca, pteropod' (*Cent. Dict.*); **-keel,** a keel shaped like a dorsal f. inverted; **-ray,** one of the processes which support the skin of the fins; **-spine,** a spine or spiny ray of a fish's f.; **-spined** *a.*, acanthopterygious; **-toed** *a.* = *-footed*; **-weed** (see sense 4); **-whale** = FINNER.

Fin (fin), *v.* 1513. [f. prec.] To cut off the fins from (a fish); to cut up (a chub).

Fin, obs. f. FINE.

Finable, fineable (fəi·năb'l), *a.*[1] 1485. [f. FINE *v.* + -ABLE.] **1.** Liable to a fine. **2.** Of a tenure: Subject to a fine on renewal 1600.

1. A f. offence 1860, offender (*mod.*). 2. F. Copyhold 1641.

Finable (fəi·năb'l), *a.*[2] [f. FINE *v.*[2] + -ABLE.] That can be clarified, refined, or purified. (Mod. Dicts.)

Final (fəi·năl), *a.* ME. [a. F., ad. L. *finalis*, f. *finis*.]

A. *adj.* **1.** Coming at the end; marking the last stage; ultimate. **2.** Putting an end to something; conclusive ME. **3.** Having regard to end or purpose; chiefly in *Final Cause* (see CAUSE *sb.*) ME.

1. The f. debt to Nature MILT., chapter 1865. Phr. *F. process* (*Law*): process of execution; opp. to *mesne process*. 2. Examples, where Sea-Fights have beene Finall to the warre BACON.

B. *sb.* **1.** The adj. used *absol.* Completion, end, finish. Now *rare.* 1582. **2.** The adj. used *ellipt.*: e.g. **a.** The final letter of a word 1627. **b.** *Athletics.* The deciding game, heat, or trial 1880. **c.** The last of a series of examinations; also *pl.* (Oxford *colloq.*) 1894.

Hence **Fi·nalism,** the belief that the end has been reached. **Fi·nalist,** one who holds this belief; also, a competitor left in for the final contest.

‖**Finale** (fīnā·le). 1783. [It. *finale* adj. (used subst.):— L. *finalem*; see prec.] **1.** *Mus.* **a.** 'The last movement of a symphony, sonata, concerto, or other instrumental composition'. **b.** 'The piece of music with which any of the acts of an opera are brought to a close' (Grove). **2.** The closing part of a drama or any other public entertainment 1814. **3.** The end; the final catastrophe 1785.

3. In the real battle..we are most pleased with the *finale* 1816.

Finality (fəinæ·lĭti). 1541. [ad. F. *finalité*, ad. late L. *finalitatem*; see FINAL and -ITY.] †**1.** An end in view. *rare.* 1541. **2.** The relation of being an end or final cause; the principle of final cause viewed as operative in the universe 1859. **3.** The quality, condition, or fact of being final; also, the belief that something is final (first used in this sense of the Reform Bill of 1832) 1833; *concr.* something that is final 1833. **4.** *attrib.* 1839.

3. Althorp's explanations as to the f...of the Bill CROKER. 4. John Russell.. He is our own F. John 1839.

Finally (fəi·năli), *adv.* ME. [f. FINAL *a.*] **1.** In the end, lastly, at last, ultimately. **2.** So as to make an end; decisively, conclusively ME.

1. Evil prevailing f. over good BUTLER. 2. Many men are f. lost SOUTH.

Finance (fi-, fəinæ·ns), *sb.*[1] ME. [a. OF. *finance*, f. *finer* to end, to settle a debt, pay ransom, furnish, procure, etc., f. *fin*; see FINE *sb.* Stressed *fi·nance* by Johnson.] †**1.** Ending. *rare.*–1616. †**2.** Payment of a debt, or of compensation; *esp.* a ransom –1597. †**3.** Supply (of goods); stock of money; substance –1502. †**4.** Borrowing of money at interest –1721. †**5.** A tax; taxation; crown or state revenues –1670. **6.** *pl.* The pecuniary resources of a sovereign or state; hence, of a company or individual 1739. **7.** The management of money; *esp.* the science of levying and applying revenue in a state, corporation, etc. 1770. **8.** *attrib.*, as *f. committee*, etc. 1467.

5. All the finances or revenues of the imperial crown ..be either extraordinary or ordinary BACON. 7. No scheme of f. can be bottomed on sound principles which [etc.] MCCULLOCH. Hence †**Fina·ncer.**

†**Finance,** *sb.*[2] *Sc.* 1473. [? a. F., f. *finer* to refine.] Fineness (of gold, etc.) –1555.

Finance (fi-, fəinæ·ns), *v.* 1478. [f. FINANCE *sb.*[1]] †**1.** *trans.* To put to ransom; *intr.* to pay ransom –1494. **2.** *trans.* To furnish with finances; to find capital for 1866. **3.** *intr.* To engage in financial operations; to provide oneself with capital 1827.

Financial (finæ·nʃăl), *a.* 1769. [f. as prec. + -(I)AL.] Of or pertaining to finance or money matters.

Phr. *F. year*: the annual period for which accounts are made up. Hence **Fina·ncially** *adv.* from a f. point of view.

Financier (finæ·nsiəɹ). 1618. [a. F., f. *finance*; see FINANCE *sb.*[1]] †**1.** *Fr. Hist.* An administrator, collector, or farmer of taxes before the Revolution –1755. **2.** One who is skilled in levying and managing public money 1618. **3.** A capitalist concerned in financial operations 1867.

2. The objects of a f. are..to secure an ample revenue; to impose it with judgment..to employ it economically [etc.] BURKE.

Finary, obs. f. FINERY[2] a puddling furnace.

Finch (finʃ). [OE. *finc*; possibly echoic. Cf. MDu. *vinke*, OHG. *fincho*; also SPINK, the chaffinch = Gr. σπίγγος and σπίζα.] A name for many birds of the order *Passeres*, esp. those of the genus *Fringilla* or family *Fringillidæ*.

Phr. †*To pull a f.* = 'to pluck a pigeon'. CHAUCER. *Comb.* †**f.-egg,** a contemptuous epithet. SHAKS.

Fi·nch-backed, *a.* ? *Obs.* 1796. = next.

Finched (finʃt), *ppl. a.* 1786. [? f. FINCH + -ED.[2]] Of cattle: Streaked with white along the back.

Find (fəind), *sb.* 1825. [f. next vb.] **1.** An act or instance of finding; e.g. the finding of a fox, of minerals, treasure, etc. Somewhat *colloq.* **2.** *concr.* That which is found 1847.

1. Phr. *A sure f.*: in *Sporting*, a place where a f. is sure to be made; *colloq.* one who is sure to be found.

Find (fəind), *v.* *Pa. t.* and *pple.* **found** (faund). [Com. Teut.: OE. *findan*; f. Teut. root **finþ-* :— pre-Teut. **pent-*, ? a nasalized form of the root *pet-* of L. *petere.*]

I. 1. *trans.* To come across, fall in with, light upon. Primarily of persons; hence of things viewed as agents. **2.** To discover the whereabouts of (something hidden or not previously observed) ME. **3.** To come to have, receive, get OE. **4.** To gain or recover the use of 1535. **5.** To discover on inspection or consideration (cf. F. *trouver*). Also *refl.* ME. **6.** To learn by experience or trial; also to feel to be (cf. F. *trouver*) ME.

1. Which impels the water it findes in its way BOYLE. Affliction never leaves us as it finds us BP. HALL. 2. A curse on him who found the Oare COWPER. 3. Phr. *To f. favour, grace, mercy* (see the sbs.). *To f. one's account in*: to experience to be profitable. 4. Phr. *To find one's feet*: lit. of a child: To be able to stand; *fig.* to develop or feel one's powers. 5. Phr. *To f. fault* (see FAULT *sb.*). I f. no sense..in what you say BERKELEY. *refl.* To f. oneself perplexed 1633. Pray, Sir, How d'ye F. your self 1692. 6. *Dan.* v. 27. Phr. *To f. it impossible*, etc., *to do so and so.*

II. 1. To discover or attain by search or effort OE.; also *refl.* 1647. **2.** To succeed in obtaining ME. **3.** Of things: To obtain as if by effort 1810; to arrive at ME.; to come home to the understanding or conscience of 1834. †**4.** To contrive, devise, invent; to discover –1660. **5.** *Law.* To determine and declare to be ME.; to agree upon and bring in (a verdict) 1574; to ascertain the validity of (an instrument) 1512.

1. To f. a hole in a Lease 1553, the centre of a circle WHISTON. *refl.* Browning may be said almost to have found himself in [etc.] 1889. 2. To f. Security for Expenses 1868, time to read a book 1868, courage to speak (*mod.*). Phr. *To f. in one's heart*: to be inclined; now usu., to be hard-hearted enough. 3. Phr. *To f. expression, ingress, outlet, place*, etc. Whatever *finds* me, bears witness for itself that it has proceeded from a Holy Spirit COLERIDGE. *To f. one's way*: to go or be brought to a place in spite of difficulties, or not quite as a matter of course. 5. The Crowner..finds it Christian buriall SHAKS. Is he found guilty SHAKS. The jury..found a verdict of guilty MACAULAY. Phr. *To f. a (true) bill*: see BILL *sb.*[3]

III. 1. To supply ME. **2.** To support, provide for (a person) ME.

1. The hotels do not f. breakfast 1814. Wages £18, *all found* but beer 1884. 2. Phr. *To f. in*: to supply with. *To f. oneself*: to provide for one's own living or needs. †Also *transf.* of a war. The war in continuance will finde it selfe BACON.

Comb. with adv. **F. out. a.** To discover; to invent; to unriddle, solve. **b.** To come upon by searching. **c.** To detect; to penetrate the disguise of.

Hence **Fi·ndable** *a.* that may be found. **Fi·nd-fault** (*dial.*), a censorious person.

Finder (fəi·ndəɹ). ME. [f. FIND *v.* + -ER[1].] **1.** One who or that which finds. **2.** *spec.* A small telescope attached to the large one for the purpose of finding an object more readily 1784. **b.** A microscopic slide divided by crossed lines, so that any point in the field can be identified readily 1867. **c.** *Photogr.* A supplementary lens attached to a camera, to locate the object in the field of view 1894.

‖**Fin de siècle** (fæṅ də syɛkl'). 1890. [Fr.] A phrase used as an adj.: Characteristic of the end of the (nineteenth) century; advanced, modern; also, decadent.

Findhorn: see FINNAN.

Finding (fəi·ndiŋ), *vbl. sb.* ME. [f. FIND *v.*] **1.** The action of FIND *v.*; that which is found; also, a find. **2.** The action of maintaining or supporting ME; †keep, provision, support –1573. **b.** in *pl.* Tools, materials, accessories, etc. used by shoemakers, dressmakers, and jewellers 1846. **3.** The result of a judicial enquiry; the verdict of a jury 1859.

1. When a man..in the deep mines of knowledge, hath furnisht out his findings MILT. 3. The court-martial still adheres to its f. of murder 1859.

Findon: see FINNAN.

†**Fi·ndy** *a.* [ME. *findig, fundi* (*ü*); cf. Da. *fyndig*, f. *fynd* strength, substance.] Firm, solid, weighty –1677.

A May cold and windie maketh the barn full and fyndie 1677.

Fine (fəin), *sb.*[1] [ME. *fin*, a. OF. :—L. *finem* (*finis*) end. With senses in branch II cf. the med. L. and OF. senses 'ending of a dispute, settlement, payment by way of composition'.]

I. End. (*Obs.* exc. in *in fine.*) †**1.** Cessation, end, conclusion –1839. †**2.** End of life, death –1556. †**3.** End in view, aim –1603. †**4.** Final issue, result –1605.

1. Still the fine's the Crowne *All's Well* IV. iv. 35. Phr. *In f.*: †(*a*) at last; (*b*) to conclude; also, in short. 3. To what f. is soche loue, I can not seen CHAUCER.

II. *Law.* A 'final agreement'; 'an amicable composition or agreement of a suit, either actual or fictitious, by leave of the king or his justices' (Blackstone) ME. **b.** *spec.* The compromise of a fictitious or collusive suit for the possession of lands; formerly in use as a mode of conveyance ME. †**c.** Hence *gen.* A contract, agreement. ME. only.

b. The cognizor (= the defendant who acknowledged the right of the plaintiff to the land) was said *to acknowledge* or *levy a fine.* Also *to sue a fine.* N.E.D.

III. A composition paid. **1. a.** *Feudal Law.* A fee (as dist. from rent) paid by the tenant or vassal to the lord on the transfer or alienation of the tenant-right, etc. ME. **b.** *Mod. Law.* A sum of money paid by the tenant on the commencement of his tenancy in order that his rent may be small or nominal 1523. **2.** A sum of money paid to make one's peace, settle a matter, obtain one's release, etc. ME. **b.** A certain sum of money imposed as the penalty for an offence; hence, a penalty of any kind (*arch.*) 1503. †**3.** A fee paid for any privilege; probate duty on a will –1744.

2. b. Fines to the amount of £85,000..were imposed on the Covenanters HALLAM.

Comb. **f.-rolls** (= *rotuli oblatorum* or *finium*): the Rolls on which were entered the sums of money, etc., offered to the king by way of oblation or fine for the passing of charters or grants, etc.

‖**Fine** (fi·nĕ), *sb.*[2] 1873. [Irish.] An Old Irish family or sept.

Fine (fəin), *a.* ME. [a. F. *fin* :—Com. Rom. *fino* (med. L. *finus*), prob. f. *finire* (pa. pple. *finito*) to FINISH.]

I. 1. Of superior quality. 2. Free from dross or impurity; clear, pure, refined ME. Of gold or silver: Containing so many 'carats' (see CARAT) or 'ounces' (*sc.* per lb. troy) of pure metal 1594. †3. Pure, sheer, absolute; perfect –1706. †4. Consummate –1604. 5. Admirably skilful ME.

1. With pelure þe finest vpon erthe LANGL. 2. The air subtle and f. 1567. Two vessels of f. copper, precious as gold *Ezra* viii. 27. The purest gold, 24 carats f. 1862. 5. Pope was a really f. judge of literature L. STEPHEN.

II. 1. Exquisitely fashioned; delicate ME. 2. Not COARSE; delicate in structure or texture ME.; comminuted 1535; attenuated, subtle, rare 1626; very thin or slender ME.; in *Athletics*, reduced in fat to the proper point by training 1815. 3. Sharp-pointed, keen-edged, as a weapon, etc. ME. 4. Of reasoning, etc.: Subtle, refined. Of senses, instruments, etc.; Capable of delicate discrimination; sensitive 1567. †5. Ingenious. In bad sense, cunning, artful –1766.

1. They .. with f. fingers cropt .. The tender stalks SPENSER. A moment of finer joy 1797. 2. F. linen 1721. F. feathery snow SHELLEY. The exudation of a f. fluid POTT. Long f. lashes SHELLEY. *fig.* F. margins of profit (*mod.*) Trained too f. R. L. STEVENSON. 4. F. Raillery DRYDEN. A f. balance 1879. 5. Some of the finer Iesuits 1610.

III. Eng. senses (chiefly = F. *beau*). 1. Excellent; admirable. Often *ironical.* ME. 2. Handsome ME.; of the features, etc.: 'Beautiful with dignity' (J.) 1801. 3. Of handsome size 1590. 4. Of the weather, a day, etc.: Bright or cloudless. Often merely: Free from rain. 1704. 5. Of dress: Smart. Hence of persons: Smartly dressed. 1526. 6. Polished, refined, fastidious, etc. 1546. 7. Of speech, writing, etc.: Affectedly ornate or elegant 1720; complimentary 1848.

1. Saying f. Things STEELE. F. lessons CHATHAM, times KINGSLEY. Your f. goings-on 1890. 2. A monstrous f. woman 1867. A man of f. presence 1878. 3. A f. slice of bread 1833. A f. child 1870. 4. Was ever a May so f. TENNYSON. Phr. *One of these f. days* (= F. *un de ces beaux jours*): often *playful* or *derisive*. 5. F. feathers make f. birds *Prov.* F. as a col'nel of the guards SWIFT. 6. Soft Adonis, so perfum'd and f. POPE. 7. A f. name for self-indulgence MORLEY.

B. *sb.* (The adj. used absol.) That which is fine; e. g. fine weather, etc.

C. *adv.* = Finely ME.

Combs.: 1. General: *f.-looking, -featured, -grained, -spirited, -timbered, -woolled*, etc.

2. Special: **f.-arch**, 'the smaller fritting-furnace of a glass-house' (Knight); **-boring** *vbl. sb.*, the process of giving a f. bore to a gun; **-cut** *a.*, (*a*) delicately chiselled; (*b*) cut so as to be f., as tobacco, etc.; **-stuff**, finely sifted lime and sand mixed with hair, to form the second coat of plaster for a room; **-world** = BEAU-MONDE.

†Fine, *v.*[1] ME. [ad. OF. *finer* = Com. Rom. *finare*, f. L. *finis*.] To come or bring to an end; to finish –1593.

Time's office is to f. the hate of foes SHAKS.

Fine (fəin), *v.*[2] ME. [f. FINE *sb.*[1]] †1. *trans.* To pay as a fine or composition –1599. 2. *intr.* To pay a fine or sum of money ME. 3. *trans.* To punish by a fine; to mulct. Hence simply, †to punish. 1559.

2. Mr. Crow..hath fined for (i.e. to escape the duties of) Alderman PEPYS. In England, women.. fined to the crown for leave to marry whom they would HALLAM. 3. He was..fined five talents 1662, fined in 400 Pound BURNET.

Phrase. *To f. down* or *off*: to arrange for a reduction of (rent) upon payment of a fine.

Fine (fəin), *v.*[3] ME. [f. FINE *a.*] To make or become fine. 1. To make fine or pure; to clarify, refine. Now only of beer. Also with *down.* 2. *intr.* To grow or become fine. *lit.* and *fig.* Also with *down.* 1552. †3. To make beautiful or handsome –1664. 4. To make small, thin, or slender 1548. 5. *intr.* To become fine, thin, etc.; esp. with *away, down, off* 1858.

1. To f. and thin the blood DOWNING. To f. down Spirits 1823. 2. [The ale] hadn't had quite time to f. down HUGHES.

Fine art. 1767. (Orig. in *pl.* as tr. F. *beaux-arts*; cf. FINE *a.* III.] 1. In *pl.* The arts which are concerned with 'the beautiful', or which appeal to taste. Often restricted to the arts of design, as painting, sculpture, architecture. Hence in *sing.* one of these arts; also *transf.*, e.g. of poaching, parliamentary obstruction, etc. 2. *Collect. sing.* The fine arts as a department of study or practice (*mod.*).

Fine-draw, *v.* 1755. [f. FINE *a.* and *adv.* + DRAW *v.*] 1. *trans.* To draw and sew together so finely that the join is not noticed; to mend neatly. 2. To draw out to minute fineness. *lit.* and *fig. rare.* 1761. Hence **Fine-drawn** *ppl. a.* drawn fine; drawn out to extreme fineness. Also in *Sporting*: Reduced in weight or fat by exercise or training.

†Finee·r, *v.*[1] 1708. [early form of VENEER.] = VENEER. –1832.

†Fineer, *v.*[2] [app. ad. Du. *fineeren, fijneren* to collect riches, ad. OF. *finer*; cf. FINE *v.*] To run into debt by getting goods made up in such a fashion as to be unfit for every other purchaser, and then refusing to take them except upon credit. GOLDSM.

Fineless (fəi·nlės), *a. rare.* 1604. [f. FINE *sb.*[1] + -LESS.] Boundless, infinite.

Oth. III. iii. 173.

Finely (fəi·nli), *adv.* ME. [f. FINE *a.* + -LY[2].] In a fine manner (see senses of the adj.).

Wee'll betray him f. *Merry W.* v. iii. 22.

Fineness (fəi·nnės). ME. [f. FINE *a.* + -NESS.] 1. The quality or state of being FINE. 2. In metals: Comparative freedom from alloy 1487.

Finer (fəi·nəɹ). 1489. [f. FINE *v.*[3]] One who or that which fines or refines, a refiner.

Finery[1] (fəi·nĕri). 1680. [f. FINE *a.* + -ERY; ?after BRAVERY.] 1. Smartness, ostentatious elegance or splendour 1729. 2. *concr.* Gaudy decoration; showy dress. Also in *pl.* 1680. †3. *pl.* Things which are finely wrought. DERHAM.

2. My sisters envied my new f. JOHNSON.

Finery[2] (fəi·nĕri). 1607. [a. F. *finerie*, f. *finer* FINE *v.*[2]; see -ERY.] A hearth where cast iron is made malleable, or in which steel is made from pig-iron. Also, the action of refining iron (*rare*).

Fi·ne-spu:n, *a.* 1647. [f. FINE *adv.* + SPUN *ppl. a.*] Spun or drawn out to extreme tenuity; flimsy. *lit.* and *fig.*

Fine-spun theories EMERSON.

Finesse (fine·s), *sb.* 1528. [a. F.:—Com. Rom. **finitia*, f. *fino* FINE *a.*] †1. = FINENESS in various senses –1701. 2. Delicacy of manipulation or discrimination; refinement, refined grace. (Now *rare*, exc. as Fr.) 1564. 3. Artfulness, subtle strategy 1530. 4. An artifice, stratagem 1562. 5. *Whist.* An attempt, by the second or third player, to get or keep the command of a suit by heading a trick with an inferior card, though holding a higher one of the suit not in sequence 1862.

1. Cobwebs of learning, admirable for the f. of thread and work BACON. 2. The f. of her smile 1791. 3. The f. of love JANE AUSTEN.

Finesse (fine·s), *v.* 1746. [f. prec. sb.] 1. *intr.* To use finesse, artifice, or stratagem 1778; *trans.* to bring by artifice *into* (a specified state). Also with *away.* 1814. 2. *Whist. intr.* To attempt to take a trick by finesse 1746; also *trans.* To play (a card) for the purpose of finessing 1837.

1. But our author can hector as well as f. 1803.

Fine-still, *sb.* 1731. [f. FINE *a.* + STILL *sb.*] A vessel used in distilling spirit from treacle. Hence **Fine-still** *v.* to distil spirit from treacle, etc. **Fine·stiller.**

Fi·new, *sb.* Now *dial.* 1556. [f. next.] Mouldiness, mould.

Fi·new, *v.* Now *dial.* [OE. *fynegian*, f. *fynig* mouldy, f. *fyne*; see FEN *sb.*[2]] To become or cause to become mouldy or musty. Hence **†Fi·newed** *a.*

‖**Fingan, Finjan** (fingā·n, -dʒā·n). 1609. [Arab. *finjān.*] A small porcelain coffee cup, used in the Levant.

Finger (fi·ŋgəɹ), *sb.* [Com. Teut.: OE. *finger*:— OTeut. **fingro-z*; perh. conn. w. pre-Teut. **penqe* FIVE.]

I. 1. One of the five terminal members of the hand; *esp.*, one of the four excluding the thumb. 2. *transf.* and *fig.* 1612. 3. One of the divisions of the foot in reptiles, or of the articulations of a bat's wing; also, one of the two parts forming a chelate or forceps-joint 1607. 4. As a measure. a. The breadth of a finger; ¾ inch ME. b. *U.S. slang.* A 'nip' of liquor. [So F. *doigt.*] 1888. c. In U.S., the length of a finger (about 4½ inches). 5. The part of a glove which receives a finger 1565. 6. Skill in fingering (a musical instrument); touch 1741.

1. The fingers are 5 in number in each hand; they are named thumb, index, middle, ring, and little f. 1861. *Fore-f.*: the index f. 2. This is the f. (= 'instrument of work') of God *Ex.* viii. 19. Phrases. a. *To lay* or *put one's f. upon*: to indicate with precision. *To twist* (a person) *round one's* (*little*) *f.*: to make him do anything. b. *His fingers are all thumbs*: he is extremely clumsy. *With a wet f.*: with perfect ease. c. *To burn one's fingers*: see BURN *v.* *To have a f. in*: to take some part in; so *to have a f. in the pie.* See also FINGER-END. 6. An admirable f. upon the harpsichord RICHARDSON.

II. 1. A finger-like projection 1702. 2. A short and narrow piece of anything; also, short for *f.-biscuit* 1846. 3. Something that does the work of a finger: the 'hand' of a clock (now *dial.*); in *Mech.*, any small projecting rod, wire, or piece which is brought into contact with an object to initiate, direct, or arrest motion, or to separate materials 1496. 4. *Printing.* A gripper to hold the paper in a printing-machine 1869. 5. In a reaping machine, the pointed sheaths through which the knife passes in cutting laid corn 1860.

1. Our fig tree.. has furled her five fingers BROWNING. 2. Fingers of toast 1865. 3. Fancy, like the f. of a clock, Runs the great circuit COWPER.

Combs. 1. General: as *f.-ring, -tip*, etc.; *-biscuit, prayer-book*; *-shaped*, adj.

2. Special: **f.-alphabet** (cf. *dactylology*); **-bar**, = cutter-bar (*b*); **-board**, (*a*) 'the flat or slightly rounded piece of wood attached to the neck of instruments of the violin and guitar class, on to which the strings are pressed when stopped by the fingers' (Stainer and Barrett); (*b*) a key-board, manual; **-bowl** = *f.-glass*; **-breadth** (also *finger's breadth*), = DIGIT *sb.* 2; **-brush**, a brush of stiff hairs cut square at the ends, which bookbinders draw across the fingers, so as to jerk colour off in spots; **-coral**, a millepore (*Millepora alcicornis*); **-cymbals**, castanets; **-fern**, a kind of Spleenwort (*Asplenium Ceterach*); **-fish**, the star-fish; **-flower**, the foxglove; **-glass**, a glass vessel to hold water, for rinsing the fingers after dessert; **-grass**, grass of the genus *Digitaria* (N.O. *Gramineæ*); **-guard**, the quillons of a sword recurved towards the pommel as a protection to the fingers; **-hole**, (*a*) one of a series of holes in a wind-instrument, which are opened and closed by the fingers in playing; (*b*) *Bowls*, either of two holes in a bowling ball, to give players a hold; (*c*) any of the small holes in the disk of a dial telephone; **-mark**, the mark left upon a surface where a f. has touched it; **-mark** *v.*, to mark with a (dirty) f.; **-mirror**, a dentist's mouth-mirror fitted with an attachment to the f.; **-nut** (cf. *f.-screw*); **-orchis**, *Palma Christi*; **-parted** *a.*, *Bot.* divided into finger-like lobes; **-plate**, a plate of metal or porcelain on a door, above and below the handle, to prevent f.-marks; **-print** = *f.-mark*, also *fig.*; with specific reference to the recording by the police of impressions taken from the finger-tips of criminals and suspects; also *attrib.*; hence **-print** *v. trans.*, to take the finger-prints of; **fingers-and-thumbs**, *Lotus corniculatus*; **fingers-and-toes**, (*a*) = prec.; (*b*) = ANBURY 2; **-screw**, one made with wings so that it may be turned with the fingers; a thumb-screw; **-shield**, a silver appliance worn on the first f. of the left hand, to protect it from the needle; **-sponge**, one with finger-shaped branches; **-steel**, a steel for whetting a currier's knife; **-watch**, a watch that can be set forwards or backwards by the f. See also Main Words.

Finger (fi·ŋgəɹ), *v.* 1450. [f. prec. sb. Cf. Ger. *fingern.*] 1. *trans.* To point at with the finger –1483. 2. To hold or turn about in one's fingers; also, to do this repeatedly 1590; to receive or handle (money) with unworthy motives 1581. 3. *intr.* To make restless or trifling movements with the fingers 1655. 4. *trans.* To touch thievishly; to pilfer, filch. Also with *from.* 1530. 5. To play upon (an instrument) with the fingers 1515. b. To mark (a piece of music) with figures indicating the fingers with which the notes are to be played 1816. 6. *fig.* To elaborate. *rare.* 1816.

2. To f. the fine needle and nyce thread SPENSER. The Cardinals have finger'd Henry's gold TENNYSON. Hence **Fi·ngerer**, one who fingers; *esp.* a thief.

Fingered (fi·ŋgəɹd), *a.* 1529. [f. FINGER *sb.*] 1. Having or provided with fingers; as *light-, rosy-, three-f.* 2. *Bot.* Of a leaf or plant: Digitate. Of the fruit or root: Shaped like a finger. 1668.

Finger-e·nd, finger's e·nd. *Pl.* **finger-ends, fingers' ends.** ME. The end or tip of the fingers.

Phr. *At one's finger(s' ends*: ready at hand. *To have at one's finger(s' ends* or *tips*: to be thoroughly familiar with.

Fingering (fi·ŋgəriŋ), *sb.* 1681. [Earlier *fingram*, etc.; ? a corruption of F. *fin grain*, lit. 'fine grain' (cf. *grogram* from *gros grain*).] 1. A kind of wool or yarn used chiefly in knitting stockings. †2. A kind of woollen cloth. *Sc.* -1733.

Fingering (fi·ŋgəriŋ), *vbl. sb.* ME. [f. FINGER *v.*] 1. The action of FINGER *v.* 2. *Mus.* a. The action or method of using the fingers in playing upon an instrument ME. b. The indication, by figures set against the notes of a piece of music, of the fingers to be used in playing them 1879. 3. *attrib.* 1603.

1. The Directors..had expected the f. of the money JAS. MILL.

Fingerling (fi·ŋgəɹliŋ). ME. [f. FINGER *sb.* + -LING.] †1. A finger-stall -1580. 2. A name for the parr (*Salmo salmulus*) 1705.

Fi·nger-post. 1785. A post set up at the parting of roads, often with a pointing finger, to indicate the directions of the roads. Also *transf.* and *fig.*

F. post (slang): a parson, so called, because like the finger post, he points out a way he..probably will never go, i.e. the way to heaven GROSE.

Fi·nger-stall. 1483. A cover or protection for the finger, usually of leather, used when the finger is hurt, in dissections, etc.

Fi·nger-stone. 1773. A cylindrical stone, convexly tapering to a point; a belemnite.

†**Fingle-fangle.** 1652. [redupl. of FANGLE.] A trifle; something whimsical. Also *attrib.* -1710.

Fingram, obs. var. of FINGERING *sb.*

Fingrigo, (fi·ŋgrigo). 1707. [Jamaican name.] A prickly climbing shrub, *Pisonia aculeata.*

Finial (fi·niăl). ME. [A var. of FINAL, app. of Eng. origin.]

A. *adj.* †1. = FINAL, -1486. 2. Crowning. *rare.* 1888.

B. *sb. Arch.* An ornament placed upon the apex of a roof, pediment, or gable, or upon each corner of a tower, etc. Also *fig.* 1448.

fig. The absolute perfection and finiall of many noble and excellent Actions HOLLAND.

Finical (fi·nikăl), *a.* 1592. [prob. f. (ult.) FINE *a.*] Over-nice, or particular, affectedly fastidious or precise; of things, over-scrupulously finished.

F. Style..consists of the most curious, affected, mincing metaphors POPE. Such a pretty, little, delicate, ladylike, f. gentleman MISS MITFORD. Hence **Fi·nically** *adv.* **Fi·nicalness**, f. quality; also, a f. thing. **Finica·lity**, finicalness.

Finicking, Finikin (fi·nikiŋ, -in). 1661. [?]

A. *adj.* Finical; dainty, fastidious, mincing; excessively precise in trifles; of things, over-delicately finished; also, trifling. var. **Fi·nicky.** *dial.* and *U.S.*

†B. *sb.* 1. A finicking person 1744. 2. A variety of pigeon -1867.

Finific (fəini·fik), *a.* [f. L. *finis* + -FIC.] Putting a limit to. COLERIDGE.

†**Fi·nify**, *v.* 1586. [f. FINE *a* + -(I)FY.] *trans.* To make fine; to trick up -1708.

Finikin, var. of FINICKING.

Fining (fəi·niŋ), *vbl. sb.* 1502. [f. FINE *v.*[3]] 1. The operation or process of refining (metals); *esp.* that of converting cast iron into wrought iron by heating it in contact with charcoal. 2. The operation or process of clarifying (a liquid; *esp.* beer, wine, etc.) 1607; *concr.* anything used for this purpose (usu. *pl.*) 1772.

Comb. f.-pot, a crucible in which metals are refined.

Finis (fəi·nis). 1460. [a. L.] The L. word for 'end', often placed at the end of a book. Hence, end of life, death 1682.

Finish (fi·niʃ), *sb.* 1790. [f. next vb.] 1. The conclusion, end; *ellipt.* in *Sporting.* 2. That which finishes, completes, or perfects 1793; in *Building*, the last coat of paint or plaster 1823. 3. Finished condition or quality 1805. 4. *slang.* A house of entertainment, where the night is finished. THACKERAY.

1. Phr. *To be in at the f.* (i.e. the death of the fox). 2. To put an American f. to her education 1890. 3. A want of f. in the manufacture 1805.

Finish (fi·niʃ), *v.* [ME. *fenys*, *finisch*, a. OF. *feniss-* (F. *finiss-*) lengthened stem of *fenir* (*finir*) :—L. *finire*, f. *finis.*] 1. *trans.* To bring to an end; to go through the last stage of. Often: To make an end of, cease (doing something). 2. To bring to completion; to complete ME. 3. To deal with or dispose of the whole or the remainder of 1526; to dispatch, kill; also, to complete the discomfiture of; to reduce to exhaustion (now chiefly *colloq.*) 1611. 4. To perfect finally or in detail 1551. 5. *intr.* To come to an end; to cease, leave off 1450; †to die *Cymb.* v. v. 36.

1. His Griefs with Day begun, Nor were they finish'd with the setting Sun DRYDEN. 2. F. sowing greenhouse plants 1816. 3. Five Germans, who were resolved to f. me 1755. 4. To f. the plastering 1703, a pretty woman JANE AUSTEN. 5. Exeter doth wish His dayes may f., ere the haplesse time SHAKS.

Finished (fi·niʃt), *ppl. a.* 1583. [f. prec.] 1. In senses of the vb. 2. Consummate, perfect, accomplished 1709.

2. A f. naturalist HENSLOW, gentleman DISRAELI.

Finisher (fi·niʃəɹ). 1526. [f. as prec.] 1. One who or that which finishes (see the vb.). 2. a. In various trades: The workman, or machine, that performs the final operation in manufacture 1691. b. *colloq.* Something that 'does for' any one; 'a settler'; in *Pugilism*, a blow that ends a fight; also one who gives this.

1. O Prophet of glad tidings, f. Of utmost hope MILT. 2. Phr. *F. of the law* (joc.): the hangman.

Finishing (fi·niʃiŋ), *vbl. sb.* 1535. [f. as prec.] 1. The action of FINISH *v.* 2. *concr.* That which completes or gives a finish to anything 1663.

attrib. and *Comb.*, as *f. governess*, etc.; also **f. cloth**, calico prepared for f.; **-coat**, in *Building*, the last coat of plaster; **-press**, in *Bookbinding*, a small press used in 'finishing'; **-rolls**, i.e. in a rolling-mill; **-school**, a school where young ladies are 'finished'.

Fi·nishing, *ppl. a.* 1705. [f. as prec.] That finishes; *esp.* in *the f. stroke* or *touch.*

Finite (fəi·nəit). 1493. [ad. L. *finitus*, *finire*, f. *finis.*]

A. *adj.* †1. Fixed, definite -1680. 2. Having bounds, ends, or limits; bounded, limited; opp. to *infinite* 1587. 3. *Math.* Of a line: Terminated. Of a quantity, number, distance: Limited. Of a solution: Resulting in a finite quantity. 1570. 4. *Gram.* Of a verb: Limited by number and person 1795.

2. Whatsoever we imagine, is F. HOBBES. F. Duration BENTLEY. A f. nature JOWETT.

B. quasi-*sb.* 1. The adj. used absol. 1687. 2. A finite thing; a finite being 1619.

Hence **Fi·nite** *v.* to make f.; to subject to limitations. **Fi·nite·ly** *adv.*, **-ness.**

Finiteless: a spurious Dict. wd.; a misreading of 'fruitlesse' in SIR T. BROWNE.

Finitesimal (fəinite·simăl), *a.* [f. FINITE *a.*, after *millesimal*, etc.] *Math.* Denoted by the ordinal of a finite number. H. J. S. SMITH.

Finitude (fi·nitiūd). 1644. [f. FINITE + -TUDE.] Finiteness.

Finless (fi·nlės), *a.* 1596. [See -LESS.] Without fins.

Finlet (fi·nlėt). 1874. [dim. of FIN.] A small fin.

Finn (fin). [OE. *Finnas* pl. = ON. *Finnar*; cf. L. *Fenni* (Tacitus), Gr. Φίννοι (Ptolemy). Germanic name of a people of North-Eastern Europe and Scandinavia calling their country Suomi and speaking a Ural-Altaic language; applied also to peoples allied thereto.

Finnan (fi·năn). Also **findhorn, findon, finnon.** 1774. [app. *Findhorn* used *attrib.*; but confused with *Findon* in Kincardineshire.] A haddock cured with the smoke of green wood, turf, or peat earth. More fully *f.-haddock* (*-haddie*).

Finned (find), *a.* ME. [f. FIN *sb.*] Having a fin or fins; as *prickly-f.*, etc.

Finner (fi·nəɹ). 1793. [f. FIN *sb.*] 1. A whale of the genus *Balænoptera*, esp. the Rorqual, so named as having a dorsal fin. 2. A white trout, called also *finnoc.* 1803.

Finnic (fi·nik), *a.* 1668. [f. FINN + -IC.] Pertaining to the Finns, or to the group of peoples ethnically allied to the Finns; Finnish. Also **Finno-**, as in *Finno*-UGRIAN.

Finnicking, Finnikin: see FINICKING.

Finnish (fi·niʃ), *a.* 1789. [f. FINN + -ISH.] Pertaining to the Finns, or (*rarely*) to the Finnish group. Also *absol.* the Finnish language.

Finny (fi·ni), *a.*[1] 1590. [f. FIN *sb.*] 1. Having fins. 2. Of the nature of a fin; fin-like 1648. 3. Of or pertaining to fish; also, teeming with fish 1764.

3. He..With patient angle, trolls the f. deep GOLDSM.

‖**Finochio** (finǫ·kio). 1723. [It. *finocchio* :— pop. L. *fenoclum*; see FENNEL.] The sweet fennel (*Fœniculum dulce*); also called the dwarf or French fennel.

Fiord, fjord (fyōᵊɹd). 1674. [a. Norw.] A long narrow arm of the sea, running up between high banks or cliffs, as on the coast of Norway.

Fiorin (fəi·ŏrin). 1809. [Corruption of Ir. *fiorthán* long coarse grass.] A species of grass (*Agrostis alba*). Also *f.-grass.*

Fiorite (fiōᵊ·rəit). 1808. [f. *Santa Fiora*, its locality; see -ITE.] *Min.* An incrustation formed from the decomposition of the siliceous minerals of volcanic rocks about fumaroles, or from the siliceous waters of hot springs.

‖**Fioritura** (fiǫritū·rā). *Pl.* **-re.** 1841. [It., f. *fiorire* to flower.] A florid ornament or embellishment in music. Usu. *pl.*

Fip (fip). U.S. 1844. [short for *fippenny bit.*] See quot.

Fippenny Bit, or contracted, *Fip*, fivepence. In Pennsylvania..the vulgar name for the Spanish half-real BARTLETT. Hence **Fi·psworth.**

Fi·ppence. 1607. [Corruption of *five pence.*] = Five pence. *colloq.*

†**Fipple** (fi·p'l). [Cf. Icel. *flipi* lip of a horse.] The plug at the mouth of a wind-instrument, by which its volume was contracted. BACON.

Fir (fəɹ). [ME. *firr*, *firre*, perh. repr. OE. *fyre or ON. *fyri-*; prob. cogn. w. L. *quercus* oak.] 1. The name given to a number of coniferous trees, of different genera. **Scotch F.** (*Pinus sylvestris*), a native of arctic Europe and Asia; called also *Scotch Pine.* **Silver F.** (*Abies pectinata*), a native of middle and southern Europe. *Silver F. of Canada* (*Abies balsamea*), a small tree which furnishes 'Canada balsam'. Spruce F. (*Picea excelsa*); called also *Norway Spruce.* 2. The wood of any of these trees ME.

2. Phr. *F.-in-bond*: a name given to all timbers built in walls.

Fire (fəiᵊɹ), *sb.* [Com. WGer.: OE. *fȳr.* The OTeut. **fūir-* (cons. stem) corresponds to Gr. πύ-ρ, πῦρ; cf. Skr. *pū*, *pāvaka* fire.] 1. The active principle operative in combustion; popularly conceived as a substance visible in the form of flame or of ruddy glow or incandescence. b. as one of the four elements ME. c. Volcanic heat, flame, or glowing lava 1582. †d. *Farriery.* = Cautery -1737. 2. State of ignition or combustion ME. 3. Fuel in a state of combustion, e.g. on a hearth or altar, in a furnace, etc. Also *transf.* and *fig.* OE. †4. The means of lighting a fire; fuel -1793. 5. Destructive burning, *esp.* of a building, forest, etc.; a conflagration. Also *fig.* ME. b. As an exclam. 1682. 6. Torture or death by burning 1646. 7. Lightning; a thunderbolt OE. 8. A combustible composition for producing a conflagration; a firework 1602. 9. *Coal Mining.* = FIREDAMP 1883. 10. Luminosity, fire-like glow 1591. 11. Heating quality (in liquors) 1737. 12. Fever, inflammation; disease as a consuming agency ME. 13. *fig.* (sense 1). a. Ardour of passion, *esp.* of love or rage ME. b. Ardour of temperament; courage, zeal, enthusiasm, spirit 1601. c. Glowing imagination, brightness of fancy; genius; inspiration 1656. 14. The action of firing guns, etc. 1590.

1. As red as þe fuyr ME. b. The force of f. ascended first..Then air succeeds DRYDEN. Phr. †*F. of Helt* (Alchem.) = ALKAHEST. *To set f. to*: to apply f. to, ignite. *There is no smoke without f.*: there is no strong rumour without some ground for it. 2. Phr. *On f.*: ignited, burning; also *fig.* *To set the Thames on f.*: to make a brilliant reputation. *To catch, take f.* (see the vbs.). 3. Cold weather; forced to have a f. BERKELEY. *A burnt child dreads the f.*

Provb. *The fat is in the f.*: see FAT *sb.*² 5. A narrative of the late dreadful f. in London 1667. Phr. *F. and sword.* *To go through f. and water*: to face the greatest dangers. 6. *F. and faggot*: see FAGGOT. 8. *Greek f.*: a combustible composition first used in warfare by the Greeks of Constantinople. *Wild f.*: see WILDFIRE. 10. Starres, hide your fires *Macb.* I. iv. 51. *Fires of St. Elmo*: see CORPOSANT. *Fires of heaven*: (*poet.*) the stars. 12. *St. Anthony's f.*: erysipelas. 13 a. The wicked f. of lust *Merry W.* II. i. 68. b. Full of f. and courage 1814. c. Corneille's noble f. POPE. 14. Phr. *To open f.*: to begin firing. *Between two fires*: lit. and fig. *Under f.*: within the range of an enemy's guns. *False f.*, *Running f.* (see the adjs.). *Kentish f.*: see KENTISH.

Fire- in Comb.

1. General: as, *f.-ordeal*, etc.; *-beacon*, *-signal*, etc.; *-basket*, a portable grate; *-bellows*, *-cheek*, *-grate*, *-stove*, etc.; *-bell*, *-main*, etc.; *-darting*, etc.; *-kindler*, etc.; *-extinguisher*, *-extinguishing*, etc.; *-baptism*; *-crowned*, *-lit*, *-scarred*, *-seamed*, etc.; *-hollowing*, etc.

2. Special: **f.-action**, the action of firing, *esp.* skirmishing in line; **-alarm**, an automatic arrangement by which notice of f. is given, also *attrib.*; **-ant**, one of certain small emmets, whose bite is painful; **-back**, a pheasant of the genus *Euplocamus* (*E. ignitus*); **-balloon**, one whose buoyancy is derived from a flaming combustible suspended at its mouth; **-bar**, a bar of a grate or of a boiler furnace; **-barrel**, a cylinder filled with combustibles, used in f.-ships; **-blast**, a disease of certain plants, giving them a scorched appearance; **-blight**, a disease of hops; **-board**, a board used to close up a fireplace in summer, a chimney-board; **-boat** = FIRE-SHIP 1; **-boom** (*Naut.*), one of the long spars swung out from a ship's side to prevent the approach of f.-ships, or of vessels on f.; **-brick**, one capable of resisting great heat without fusion; **-bridge**, a 'plate or wall at the back of the furnace to prevent the fuel being carried over' (Knight); **-brigade**, an organized body of firemen; **-clay**, a clay capable of resisting great heat, used for f.-bricks, etc.; **-company**, (*a*) a f.-brigade; (*b*) a f. insurance company; **-dog** = ANDIRON; **-drill**, (*a*) drill practised by firemen and others in view of fires; (*b*) a primitive contrivance, consisting of an obtuse-pointed stick which is twirled between the hands with the point in a hole in a flat piece of soft wood till f. is produced; **-escape**, an apparatus for facilitating escape from burning buildings; **-flag**, (*a*) a meteoric flame; (*b*) a flag of distress, when a ship is on f.; **-flair**, the sting-ray, *Trygon Pastinaca*; **-guard**, a wire frame, or the like, put in front of a fireplace for the protection of children or others; also a grating to keep the coals from coming out of the bars of a f.; **-hose**, a hose-pipe for conveying water to a f.; **-insurance**, insurance against losses by f.; also *attrib.*; **-office**, an office for issuing f.-policies; a f. insurance company; **-opal**, a variety of opal showing flame-coloured internal reflections; **-piece**, (*a*) = FIRE-ARM; (*b*) a picture of a conflagration; **-plug**, a contrivance for connecting a hose with a water-main, in case of f.; **-policy**, the instrument received from an insurance office, guaranteeing the insurer against loss by f.; **-raft**, a raft for setting an enemy's shipping on f.; **-roll** (*Naut.*), a peculiar beat of the drum on an alarm of f.; **-setting**, the softening or cracking of the working-face of a lode, to facilitate excavation, by exposing it to the action of f.; **-shovel**, a shovel for placing coals on a f., etc.; **-stick**, (*a*) a burning brand; (*b*) = *f.-drill*; **-stink** (*Mining*), the stench from decomposing iron pyrites, caused by the formation of sulphuretted hydrogen; **-swab** (*Naut.*), the wet bunch of rope-yarn used to cool a gun in action and swab up any grains of powder; **-teazer**, a stoker; **-trap**, a place difficult to get out of in case of f.; **-tree**, (*a*) a kind of firework; (*b*) = *flame-tree*; (*c*) in New Zealand the *Metrosideros tomentosa*; **-tube**, a pipe-flue; **-water**, (*a*) = ALKAHEST; (*b*) ardent spirits; **-wood**, wood for burning; fuel; **-worship**, the adoration of f.; hence **-worshipper.**

b. In various plant-names, as **f.-bush**, *Embothrium coccineum*, etc.; and in local names of birds and insects, as **f.-crest**, the golden-crested wren; **-tail**, (*a*) the redstart; (*b*) one of the insects termed *Chrysididæ*; etc.

Fire (fəiəɹ), *v.* OE. [f. FIRE *sb.*] †1. *trans.* To supply with firing. OE. only. 2. *trans.* To set on fire, so as to destroy; to ignite, kindle. Also *transf.* ME. 3. *fig.* to inflame, heat, kindle (a person; also a passion, etc.) ME. 4. *intr.* To catch fire, to be kindled or ignited; also *fig.* and *transf.* 1568. 5. To drive *out*, *out of*, *from*, etc. by fire. Also *fig. rare.* 1530. 6. To subject to the action of fire, as pottery, bricks, etc. 1662. 7. *Farriery.* To cauterize 1607. 8. To supply with fuel; to attend to the fire of; also *absol.* 1760. 9. To apply fire to, so as to explode; to let off 1530. 10. *intr.* or *absol.* To discharge a gun or other fire-arm 1645. 11. *intr.* Of a gun, etc.: To go off. Also *fig.* 1668. 12. To propel (a missile) from, or as from, a gun. Also *fig.* 1588. 13. *U.S. slang.* To eject, expel, or dismiss peremptorily. Often with *out.* 1873.

2. He fired his camp THIRLWALL. 2. They..firen lecherie HOCCLEVE. Fired was each eye SCOTT. 4. *fig.* Women are flax, and will f. in a moment. Phr. *To f. up*: to show sudden heat. *transf.* [The sun] fires the prowd tops of the Easterne Pines SHAKS. 5. *Lear* v. iii. 23. 8. Phr. *To f. up*: to light up the fire of a furnace; hence *colloq.* to light one's pipe. 9. *To f. a broadside*: to f. all the guns on one side of a ship; also *fig.* 10. He fired, and hit two DE FOE. Phr. *To f. away* (fig.): to go ahead. *colloq.*

Fi·re-arm. Usu. *pl.* 1646. [f. FIRE *sb.* + ARM *sb.*] A weapon from which missiles are propelled by an explosive, e.g. gunpowder. (The sing. is late and rare.)

Fi·re-ball. 1555. [f. FIRE *sb.* + BALL *sb.*¹] 1. A ball of fire or flame; *esp.* a large luminous meteor, or lightning in a globular form. 2. *Mil.* A ball filled with combustibles or explosives, used as a projectile, to damage an enemy or set fire to his works 1595. 3. *Her.* A ball represented with fire issuing from the top 1830. 4. A ball of coal-dust and clay, used for kindling fires.

Fi·re-bird. 1593. The Baltimore oriole, *Icterus galbula*.

Fi·re-boot, -bote. Now *Hist.* 1484. [f. FIRE *sb.* + BOOT *sb.*¹] *Law.* The mending of a fire; wood used for this purpose; the right of a tenant to take fire-wood from the landlord's estate.

Fi·re-box. 1555. [BOX *sb.*²] †1. A tinder-box –1840. 2. The chamber of a steam-boiler in which the fuel is burnt. 1830.

Fi·re-brand. ME. [f. FIRE *sb.* + BRAND *sb.*] 1. A piece of wood kindled at the fire. 2. *fig.* One who, or that which, kindles strife or mischief, inflames the passions, etc. ME. †3. = BRAND-MARK –1704.

Fi·re-cross, fi·ery-cro·ss. 1547. A cross or piece of wood burnt at one end and dipped in blood at the other—symbolical of fire and sword—used anciently in Scotland to summon the clans for war.

Fi·re-damp. 1677. [See DAMP *sb.*] Carburetted hydrogen or marsh-gas, which is given off by coal and is explosive when mixed in certain proportions with air.

Fi·re-drake. [OE. *fyr-draca* fire-dragon.] 1. A 'fiery dragon'; a creature of Germanic mythology. †2. A fiery meteor; also, a will-o'-the-wisp –1851. †3. A kind of firework –1634. †4. *transf.* a. An alchemist's assistant B. JONS. b. A man with a fiery nose SHAKS. c. = FIRE-EATER 2. 1626.

Fi·re-ea·ter. 1672. 1. A juggler who eats fire. 2. One who is fond of fighting; a duellist; one who seeks occasion to fight 1804.

Fi·re-engine. 1680. [f. FIRE *sb.* + ENGINE.] 1. A machine for throwing water to extinguish fires. 2. A steam-engine. *Obs.* exc. *local.* 1722.

Fi·re-eyed, *a.* 1596. Having eyes glowing as with fire.

The fire-ey'd Maid of smoakie Warre SHAKS.

Fi·re-fang, *v.* Now *dial.* 1513. [f. FIRE *sb.* + FANG *v.*¹] *trans.* To lay hold of with fire; to singe, scorch. Hence **Fi·re-fanged** *ppl. a.*, †(*a*) caught by the fire, singed, scorched; (*b*) *spec.* of barley, etc.; also of cheese: Having a scorched or singed appearance, smell, or taste, as if overheated.

Fi·re-flaught. Orig. *Sc.* ME. [f. FIRE *sb.* + FLAUGHT.] Lightning; a flash of lightning; hence *transf.* a sudden burst or rush.

Fi·re-fly. 1658. [f. FIRE *sb.*] A lampyrid or elaterid insect which has the property of emitting phosphorescent light. Also *attrib.*

Fi·re-hook. 1467. [f. as prec.] A hook used in pulling down burning buildings; also, one used for raking and stirring the furnace fire.

†**Fi·re-ho·t,** *a.* OE. [f. as prec.] Hot as fire; also *fig.* –1678.

Fi·re-iron. ME. †1. An iron (or steel) for striking a light –1530. 2. *pl.* Implements for tending the fire, usu. shovel, tongs and poker 1812.

Fireless (fəiəˑɹlės), *a.* 1598. [see -LESS.] †1. Unlit 1649. 2. Devoid of fire; without a fire; also *fig.* 1598.

Fi·re-light. OE. The light given by a fire; †lightning.

Firelock. 1547. [See LOCK *sb.*] 1. A gun-lock in which sparks were produced to ignite the priming; orig. the WHEEL-LOCK, later the FLINT-LOCK. 2. A musket having such a lock 1590. 3. A soldier armed with this 1645. 4. *attrib.*, as *f. musket*, etc. 1577.

Fireman (fəiəˑɹmăn). 1626. †1. One who uses fire-arms –1727. 2. One who attends to the fire of a steam-engine, etc.; a stoker 1657. 3. One who is employed to extinguish fires 1714. 4. One who examines the workings of a mine for fire-damp, attends to the blasting, etc. 1866.

†**Fi·re-master.** 1622. An officer of artillery who superintended the manufacture of explosives or fireworks –1824.

Fi·re-new, *a. arch.* 1594. [Cf. Ger. *feuerneu.*] †Fresh from the fire or furnace; hence, brand-new.

Your f. stampe of Honor is scarce currant SHAKS.

Fi·re-pan. [OE. *fyrpanne*, f. *fyr* FIRE + *panne* PAN.] 1. A pan for holding or carrying fire, e.g. a portable grate. †2. The pan which held the priming of a flint-lock gun 1613. 3. *Mining.* A kind of fire-lamp 1883.

Fi·re-place. 1702. A place for a fire, *esp.* the open recess at the base of the chimney appropriated to the fire; a hearth.

Fi·re-pot. 1627. a. *Hist.* An earthen pot filled with combustibles used as a missile. b. The receptacle for the fire in a furnace, etc. 1871. c. A crucible 1874.

Fi·re-proof, *a.* 1638. [f. FIRE *sb.* + PROOF *a.*] Proof against fire; incombustible. Hence **Fire-proofing** *vbl. sb.* the process of rendering f.; also, material for use in making anything f.; also *attrib.*

Firer (fəiəˑrəɹ). 1602. One who, or that which, FIRES: an incendiary (now only with *of*) 1602; one who fires a gun; also the gun itself, usu. in *comb.*, as *quick-f.* 1868.

Fi·re-rai·sing, *vbl. sb.* Orig. techn. in *Sc. Law.* 1685. [f. FIRE *sb.* + RAISING *vbl. sb.*] Arson, incendiarism.

Fi·re-screen. 1758. 1. A screen to intercept the heat of the fire. 2. A fire-guard 1874. 3. *Naut.* A piece of fearnought used as a screen where it is necessary to pass the powder. 1815.

Fi·re-ship. 1588. 1. A vessel filled with combustibles, and sent adrift among ships, etc. to destroy them. 2. *slang.* One suffering from venereal disease 1672.

Fireside (fəiəɹsəiˑd, *attrib.* fəiəˑɹsəid). 1563. [f. FIRE *sb.* + SIDE.] The side of a fire-place; hence, the space about the fire; the hearth. 2. *transf.* Home, home-life 1848; †one's household –1785. 3. *attrib.* 1740.

Fi·re-stone. [OE. *fyrstán*, f. *fyr* FIRE + *stán* STONE.] †1. Iron pyrites, formerly used in striking fire; also, a flint –1865. 2. A stone that resists the action of fire; one used for lining furnaces and ovens 1475. b. A local name for the soft calcareous sandstone sold under the name of hearthstone 1707.

Fi·re-work, fi·rework. 1560. †1. Work done by, in, or with fire –1686. †2. An apparatus for working with fire, a furnace –1674. 3. †A combustible or explosive composition for use in war; a projectile or the like charged with this 1560. 4. Any contrivance for producing with fire a pleasing or scenic effect; *esp.* a rocket, squib, etc. 1611; *pl.* (formerly also *sing.*) a pyrotechnic display 1588. Also *fig.* 5. *attrib.* 1885.

3. The construction of all fireworks is understood at the ordnance-office BURKE. 4. *fig.* He has neither squibs nor fireworks..the curs'd carrier lost his best book of phrases 1670.

Fi·re-wo·rker. 1626. †1. An artillery officer, or other person, who has to do with explosives in war –1800. 2. A pyrotechnist 1772.

Firing (fəiəˑriŋ), *vbl. sb.* 1485. [f. FIRE *v.*] 1. The action of setting or (*rarely*) of becoming on fire 1548. 2. The action of subjecting to the operation of fire 1782. 3. *Farriery.* Cauterizing 1644. 4. Name of a disease in tobacco and in flax 1688. 5. The feeding and tending of a fire or furnace 1892. 6. The discharging of fire-arms, a mine, etc. 1603. 7. *concr.* Fuel 1555; †a quantity of burning fuel 1485.

2. The glazing and f. of pottery 1885. The..'firing' of tea is a kind of roasting 1888. 6. Night coming on, the f. on both sides ceased 1790.

Combs., as *f.-line, -party*, etc.; also **f.-point**, the temperature at which an inflammable oil is liable to spontaneous combustion.

†Firk, ferk, *sb.* 1611. [f. next vb.] **1.** A flick, flip -1679. **2.** A trick, dodge; also, a prank -1682.

Firk, ferk (fəːɹk), *v.* [OE. *fercian, færcian*, prob. f. *fær* (see FARE *sb.*[1]).] †1. *trans.* To bring, conduct -ME. **2.** To drive, force, or move sharply and suddenly *off, out, up* ME. †b. To contrive to get; also, to cheat, rob (any one) -1709. †3. *refl.* and *intr.* To move quickly, hasten; also (*intr.*) to move about briskly -1679. 4. *trans.* To beat, trounce, drub 1567.

2. b. As from poor clients lawyers f. money DEKKER. 3. How would he f... up and about B. JONS. 4. M. Fer: Ile fer him, and firke him *Hen. V*, IV. iv. 29.

Firkin (fəːɹkin), *sb.* ME. [In 15th c. *ferdekyn*, app. a. MDu. **vierdekijn*, dim. of *vierde* fourth part; see -KIN.] **1.** A small cask for liquids, fish, butter, etc., orig. holding a quarter of a barrel. Also applied joc. to a person. **2.** As a measure of capacity: Half a kilderkin (varying according to the commodity) 1465. *Comb.* ale-f.: see ALE.

Firlot (fəːɹlǫt). *Sc.* ME. [First in L. *fertheļota*, app. repr. ON. *fiórþe hlotr* fourth part; see LOT.] **1.** A measure of capacity for corn, etc., the fourth part of a boll; also, a great quantity. **2.** A vessel used to measure a firlot 1573.

2. The old castle, where the family lived, in their decadence, as a mouse lives under a f. SCOTT.

Firm (fəːɹm), *sb.* 1574. [ad. It., Sp. and Pg. *firma*, f. L. *firmare* to confirm, f. *firmus* FIRM *a.*] †1. Signature -1755. **2.** The style or name under which a commercial house transacts business; hence, a partnership of two or more persons for carrying on a business. Also *transf.* (chiefly in sarcastic use). 1744.

1. The Grand Signior's F. or Name 1688. 2. Trading under the f. of 'Grant & Co.' 1864. A f. of solicitors 1882.

Firm (fəːɹm), *a.* and *adv.* [ME. *ferme*, a. OF. :—L. *firmus.*]

A. *adj.* **1.** Having a close consistence; solid; not readily yielding to pressure or impact 1611. **2.** Securely fixed, not easily moved, stable 1597. **3.** Steady in motion or action; not relaxed or nerveless 1593. **4.** Healthy; sound. ? *Obs.* 1577. **5.** Fixed, settled, established; immutable; †secure; †sure; well-founded ME. **6.** Constant, steadfast; unwavering; resolute ME.; indicating steadfastness 1802. **7.** *Comm.* Of prices: Not drooping. Of commodities: Not depressed in market value. Also *transf.* of the market, season, etc. 1883.

1. Down they light On the f. brimstone MILT. 2. As possitiue, as the earth is firme SHAKS. 3. Moving nigh, in slow But f. Battalion MILT. So f. a touch on the piano 1834. 5. Firme and irreuocable is my doombe *A.Y.L.* I. iii. 85. 6. F. Roman Catholicks 1659. A f. friendship 1751, belief 1873. F. eyes 1878. 7. Phr. *A f. offer*: one which the offerer will not improve upon.

Phr. †**F. land, f.-land**: dry land, solid earth; the mainland (opp. to an island).

B. *adv.* and quasi-*adv.* Chiefly in phr. *to stand f.* (lit. and fig.), and *to hold f. (to)* ME.

Firm (fəːɹm), *v.* Now *rare* exc. techn. ME. [Partly ad. L. *firmare*; partly f. FIRM *a.*] **1.** *trans.* To make firm or solid; †to establish, confirm -1682; †to make (a title, etc.) secure -1669. †2. To make (a document) valid by seal, signature, or the like -1690; to affix (one's name) to a document -1620. **3.** *intr.* To become firm 1882.

1. As pilot.. Upon his card and compas firmes his eye SPENSER. Jove has firm'd it with an Awfull Nod DRYDEN. 2. He..firmed therevnto his name 1582.

Firmament (fəːɹmămĕnt). ME. [ad. L. *firmamentum*, f. *firmare*, f. *firmus*. Adopted in the Vulgate, in imitation of the στερέωμα of the LXX (prop. 'firm or solid structure'), as = a Heb. word probably meaning 'expanse'.]

1. The arch or vault of heaven; the sky. Now only *poet.* or *rhet.* Also *transf.* and *fig.* †2. *Old Astron.* The sphere containing the fixed stars; the eighth heaven of the Ptolemaic system -1665. †b. Hence, *occas.*, any of the other spheres -1551. †3. A substratum, a firm support or foundation. *lit.* and *fig.* -1701.

1. Bright was the day, and bliew the f. CHAUCER. Praise him in the f. of his power *Ps.* cl. 1. *transf.* This F. of Hell MILT. 2. b. *First f.*: the *Primum mobile*. CHAUCER. 3. This duty to parents is the very f. and bond of commonwealths JER. TAYLOR.

Hence **Firmame·ntal, †Firmame·ntary** *adjs.* pertaining to the f.; of the nature of a permanent substratum.

Firman (fəːɹmăn, ‖fermā·n). 1616. [a. Pers. = Skr. *pramāṇa* command.] An edict or order issued by an Oriental sovereign, *esp.* the Sultan of Turkey; a grant, licence, passport, permit.

†Firma·tion. 1646. [ad. L. **firmationem.*] A making firm.

Firmer (fəːɹməɹ). 1688. [ad. F. *fermoir* chisel for making mortices, altered f. *formoir*, anglicized as FORMER.] In *f.-chisel*: a broad thin chisel, with the sides parallel to a certain length, and then tapering; used in making the sides of mortices. *F.-tools* are the ordinary short chisels and gouges of wood-workers; opp. to *paring tools*.

†Fi·rmitude. 1541. [ad. L. *firmitudo*, f. *firmus.*] The quality or state of being FIRM; strength; resolution -1701.

†Fi·rmity. 1450. [a. OF. *fermeté*; refashioned after FIRM and -ITY.] Firmness, solidity, stability. Also *fig.* -1729.

†Firmless (fəːɹmlĕs), *a.* 1598. [f. FIRM *a.*] Shifting -1744.

Does passion still the f. mind control POPE.

Firmly (fəːɹmli), *adv.* ME. [f. as prec.] In a firm manner.

Firmness (fəːɹmnĕs). 1561. [f. as prec. + -NESS.] **1.** The state or quality of being FIRM. **2.** *Comm.* Steadiness in price or of prices 1880.

1. Constauncye and firmnes of minde 1561. Fluidity and F. BOYLE. By f. I mean not only strength but stability PALEY.

‖Firn (firn). 1853. [Ger. *firn, firne*, lit. 'last year's' (snow); see FERN *a.*] The imperfectly consolidated granular snow of the glaciers.

Firring: see FURRING.

Firry (fəːri), *a.* 1833. [f. FIR + -Y[1].] Of or pertaining to the fir; abounding in firs.

The tender dove In f. woodlands making moan TENNYSON.

First (fəːɹst). [OE. *fyrst, fyrest* (= *for-est*) :— Com. Teut. **furisto-*, a superlative formation on the stem **fur-, for-*, repr. OAryan *pr-*, whence Skr. *prathama*, Gr. πρῶτος, L. *primus*. See FORE *adv.*, FOR *prep.*] **A.** *adj.*

I. 1. That is before all others in time; earliest. Hence used as the ordinal of ONE. **2.** Preceding all others in serial order OE. **3.** Foremost in position ME. **4.** Foremost in rank, importance, or excellence ME.

1. Our f. father DUNBAR. The f. writer of history 1662. The f. to find fault (*mod.*). Phr. *At f. sight, at (the) f. blush. (The) f. thing*: = as the f. thing that is done; The f. thing in the morning DICKENS. 2. The f. blow is half the battle GOLDSM. The f. turning on the right (*mod.*). Phr. *The F.* (sc. *day*), spec. the f. of September (when partridge-shooting begins). *The f. two (three*, etc.); also, earlier, *the two (three*, etc.) *f.* (= F. *les deux premiers*). 3. To plunge head f. into the lasher (*mod.*). The f. row of seats (*mod.*). 4. *The F. Lord of the Admiralty.* (*Mus.*) Highest or most prominent in carrying the melody, among several voices or instruments of the same class; as *f. violin*.

II. *absol.* (quasi-*sb.*) **1.** *The f.*: a. the person or thing first mentioned; b. the beginning, as *the f. of the ebb*, etc. 1586. **2.** *From the f.*: from the beginning. *From f. to last*: from beginning to end. 1611. *At f.*: at the beginning or first stage. **3.** *ellipt.* Anything that is first; e.g. a place in the first class; a man who has taken such a place; the best quality of butter, etc.; in *Mus.* the upper part of a duet, trio, etc. 1587. *F. of Exchange*: the f. of a set of bills of exchange of even tenor and date.

B. *adv.* [OE. *fyrst*, accus. neut. of the *adj.*] **1.** Before any other person or thing in time, serial order, position, rank, etc. OE. **2.** For the first time ME.

1. Who f. offend will f. complain PRIOR. I wounded one who f. assaulted me GOLDSM. Phr. *F. and last*: reckoned altogether, in all. *F. or last*: sooner or later. 2. Whan seyntes felle fryst from hevene 1461.

Combs. **1.** General, chiefly of *adv.* with ppl. adjs.: as *f.-begotten, mentioned, -named*, etc.; *-comer*, etc. Also **f.-movable, -moved, -mover, moving**; = *primum mobile*.

2. Special: as *f.-cause, -chop, -cousin*, etc. (see the sbs.). Also **f.-aid**, assistance given in the case of street-accidents, etc., pending the arrival of a doctor; **-birth**, a f.-born child; also *fig.*; **f.-coat**, the f. layer of plaster or paint; **-cost**, prime cost; also *attrib.*; **-foot** (*north.*), the f. person to enter a house in the new year; hence *-footing*; **f. form**, the lowest form in a school; **f. night**, the night on which a play is f. produced on the stage; also *attrib.*; hence *f.-nighter, -nighting*; **f. story** = FIRST FLOOR. See also Main Words.

†First: see FRIST *sb.* and *v.*

Fi·rst-born, *a.* ME. [f. FIRST *adv.* + BORN *a.*] That is born first, eldest. Also *absol.*

The first borne sonne *Deut.* xxi. 15. Her first-born MILT. *P.L.* I. 489.

Fi·rst class, first-class.

A. (as two wds.) The first (and usually the most important) of a series of classes in which things or persons are grouped. Also *ellipt.* A place in the first class of an examination list; one who has taken such a place. 1807.

B. *attrib.* or *adj.* (with the hyphen). **1.** Of or belonging to the first class 1846. **b.** In *U.S.* occas. used of the lowest grade; as a first-class clerk. **2.** *gen.* Of the highest grade; of the first or best quality 1858. *colloq.* Extremely good 1879. **3.** quasi-*adv.* 1895.

1. An Oxford first-class man 1860. A first-class carriage (*mod.*). 2. A question of first-class importance 1885. 3. To look, travel, get on first-class (*mod.*).

First-day. 1690. Sunday; so called by the Quakers.

First-floor. 1663. **1.** The floor next above the ground-floor 1865. **2.** The ground-floor. Now only *U.S.*

Fi·rst-fruit. Chiefly *pl.* ME. [Orig. as two wds.; = L. *primitiæ.*] **1.** The earliest products of the soil; hence *transf.* and *fig.* of anything; e.g. of a man's work. **2.** *Eccl.* and *Feudal Law.* The first year's income or profits, formerly paid by each new holder of a benefice, or any office of profit, to some superior ME.

1. The first-fruits to the gods he gave POPE. One of the first-fruits of the great national reaction FREEMAN.

First hand. 1732. **1.** adv. phr. *At first hand*: From the first source or origin; direct from the maker, etc. Also without *at*. **2.** *adj.* (*first-hand*). Of or belonging to the first source, original 1748.

1. Matters we cannot well know at first hand M. ARNOLD. 2. First-hand information 1890.

Firstling (fəːɹstliŋ). 1535. The first of its kind to be produced, or appear. Usu. *pl.*, like *first-fruits*. **b.** *esp.* The first offspring of an animal, the first-born of the season 1593. Also *attrib.*

Lord Chancellor Bacon..procured the firstlings of the species [piane] from Sicily 1830. b. The firstlings of my woolly breed DRYDEN. *attrib.* The f. males *Deut.* xv. 19.

Firstly (fəːɹstli), *adv.* 1532. [f. FIRST *a.*] **1.** In the first place, before anything else, first. (Used only in enumerating heads, etc. of discourse. Many prefer *first*.) **2.** quasi-*sb.* The word *firstly* 1698.

1. First (for I detest your..pedantic neologism of *firstly*) DE QUINCEY.

First rate, first-rate. 1666.

A. As *phr.* and *adj.* **1.** *First rate*: the highest of the rates (see RATE *sb.*) by which vessels of war are distinguished. **2.** *attrib.* *First-rate*: of the first rate (said of vessels); hence *gen.* Of the highest class 1671. **3.** Hence, Extremely good 1812. **4.** quasi-*adv.* (*colloq.*) Excellently, very well 1844.

2. A question of first-rate importance 1853. A first-rate power DUFF.

B. *sb.* **1.** *Naut.* A war vessel of the first rate 1708. **2.** *transf.* A person or thing of the highest class 1663. Hence **First-rater.**

Firth[1] (fəɹþ). Chiefly *north.* ? *Obs.* ME. [Metathesis of FRITH *sb.*[2]] = FRITH *sb.*[2], q. v.

Firth[2] (fəɹþ). Orig. *Sc.* ME. [app. a. ON. *fiǫrðr*: see FIORD.] An arm of the sea; an estuary of a river.

Fi·r-tree. ME. [f. FIR + TREE.] = FIR 1.

Firy, obs. f. FIERY.

Fisc, fisk (fisk). 1598. [a. F. *fisc* or ad. L. *fiscus*. Spelt *fisk* in Sc. Law.] **1.** *Antiq.* The public treasury of Rome; the imperial treasury or privy purse of the Emperor. **b.** An exchequer. Now *rare.* 1599. **2.** *Sc. Law.* The public treasury or 'Crown' to which estates lapse by escheat. †Hence incorrectly: The right of the Crown to the estate of a rebel. 1680. **3.** [after It. *fisco.*] = FISCAL *sb.* (BROWNING.)

Fiscal (fi·skăl). 1539. [a. F., Sp. *fiscal*, It. *fiscale*, ad. late L. *fiscalis*, f. *fiscus* FISC.]
A. *adj.* **1.** Of or pertaining to the treasury of a state or prince 1563. **2.** Of or pertaining to financial matters. (Chiefly *U.S.*) 1865.

1. The king's f. prerogatives, or such as regard his revenue BLACKSTONE. 2. The work of the past f. year 1880.

B. *sb.* †**1.** = FISC 1. **b.** 1590. **2.** †**a.** A treasurer -1676. **b.** In Italy, Spain, etc., a legal official, having the function of public prosecutor; under the Holy Roman Empire, the highest law officer of the crown 1539. **c.** In Holland, etc.: A magistrate who takes cognizance of offences against the revenue 1653. **d.** *Sc.* Short for PROCURATOR FISCAL. 1681. **3.** In Cape Colony, the name of a shrike (*Lanius collaris*) 1822.

Hence **Fisca·lity**, exclusive regard to f. considerations. **Fi·scally** *adv.*

‖**Fiscus** (fi·skɒ̆s). 1650. [L.] = FISC 1.

Fish (fiʃ), *sb.*[1] [Com. Teut.: OE. *fisc* :— OTeut. **fisko-z* :— pre-Teut. **pisko-s*, cogn. w. L. *piscis.*] **1.** In pop. language, any animal living exclusively in the water, including cetaceans, crustaceans, molluscs, etc. In scientific language any vertebrate animal provided with gills throughout life, and cold-blooded; the limbs, if present, being modified into fins. (The collect. *sing.* is often used as *pl.*) OE. **2.** *fig.* 1722. **3.** The flesh of fish, *esp.* as used for food; opp. to *flesh* (i.e. of land-animals) and *fowl* ME. **4.** *Astron. The F.* or *Fishes* (L. *Pisces*), a zodiacal constellation, between Aquarius and Aries ME.

1. The whale, the limpet, the tortoise, and the oyster ..as men have been willing to give them all the name of fishes, it is wisest for us to conform GOLDSM. Phr. *A pretty kettle of f.* (colloq.): a fine muddle. *To feel like a f. out of water. To drink like a f.*: to be always drinking. *All is f. that comes to (his) net*: he turns everything to account. *Royal F.*: whale and sturgeon. 2. The f. [a rich young booby] is hook'd FOOTE. He was an odd f. FRANKLIN. 3. Phr. *Neither f. nor flesh* (*nor good red herring*), also *neither f., flesh, nor fowl*: neither one thing nor another. *To have other f. to fry*: to have other things in hand.

attrib. and Comb. 1. General: as *f.-bone*; *-ball*; *-curer*; *-dinner*; *-market*; *-woman*, etc.

2. Special: **f.-backed** *a.*, swelling upwards, like a fish's back; **-bed**, a deposit containing the fossil remains of fishes; **-bellied**, curved underneath, like a fish's belly; **-bone-thistle** = *f.-thistles*; **-carver**, a carving knife for f.; *pl.* a carving knife and fork for f.; **-crow** (*U.S.*), a crow (*Corvus ossifragus*) that feeds mainly on f.; **-culture**, the artificial breeding of f.; hence, **-cultural** *a.*, **-culturist**; **-eagle**, an eagle that preys upon f.; †**-ears**, gills; **-eater**, (*a*) one who lives chiefly on f.; (*b*) *pl.* a knife and fork to eat f. with; **-fag**, a fishwife; **-farm**, a place where f.-culture is carried on; hence **-farmer**, **-farming**; **-flour**, (*a*) = *f.-meal*; (*b*) a dry inodorous fertilizer made from fishes; **-gaff**, a pole with an iron hook at the end for securing heavy f. when caught with a line; **-globe**, a spherical glass vessel in which f. are kept; **-glue**, glue obtained from the bladders and sounds of f., isinglass; **-guano** = *f.-manure*; **-hawk**, the osprey, or bald buzzard (*Pandion haliaëtus*); **-kettle**, a long oval vessel for boiling f.; **-knife**, a broad knife for carving f. at table; also, a knife for eating f. with; **-ladder**, a series of steps to enable f. to ascend a fall or dam; **-liquor**, the liquid in which a fish has been boiled; **-lock** = *f.-weir*; **-louse**, any crustacean parasitic on fishes; **-manure**, a fertilizer composed of f.; **-maw**, the sound or air-bladder of a f.; **-meal**, dried f. ground to a meal; **-oil**, oil obtained from fishes and marine animals, *spec.* cod-liver oil and whale oil; **-owl**, an eared fishing owl, of the genus *Ketupa*, with rough feet; **-pass** = *f.-way*; **-pearl**, an artificial pearl, manufactured in Germany; **-pomace**, the refuse of f., used as a fertilizer; **-pool**, a fishpond; **-pot**, a wicker basket for catching f., *esp.* eels, crabs, lobsters, etc.; **-room**, a place parted off in the after-hold of a man-of-war, formerly used for stowing salt-fish; **-sauce**, a sauce to be eaten with fish; **-scrap** = *f.-pomace*; **-slice**, a f.-carving knife; also, an instrument for turning f. in the pan; **-slide**, 'a f.-trap for shallow rivers and low waterfalls' (*Cent. Dict.*); **-sound**, the swimming-bladder of a f.; **-story**, an incredible 'yarn'; **-strainer**, (*a*) 'a metal cullender with handles for taking f. from a boiler'; (*b*) 'an earthenware slab with holes, placed at the bottom of a dish to drain the water from cooked fish' (Simmonds); **-tongue**, an instrument occas. used by dentists for removing wisdom-teeth; so named from its shape; **-torpedo**, a f.-shaped torpedo, having an automatic swimming action; **-trowel**, a trowel-shaped f.-carver; **-way**, an arrangement for enabling f. to ascend a fall or dam; **-weir**, a weir on a river for taking or preserving fishes; **-wood**, (*a*) *Piscidia erythrina*, used to intoxicate f.; (*b*) *Euonymus americanus*; **-works**, (*a*) 'the appliances and contrivances used in f.-culture'; (*b*) 'a place where the products of the fisheries are utilized, a f.-factory' (*Cent. Dict.*); **-yard** = *fish-weir.*

Fish (fiʃ), *sb.*[2] 1666. [? a. F. *fiche*; or ? transf. use of prec.] **1.** *Naut.* 'A long piece of hard wood, convex on one side and concave on the other' (Smyth), used to strengthen a mast or yard; a fish-piece. **2.** A flat piece of iron, wood, etc. laid upon a beam, rail, etc., or across a joint, to protect or strengthen it; in railway work = *fish-plate* 1847.

Comb.: **f.-bar**, 'the splice bar which breaks the joint of two meeting objects, as of railroad rails' (Knight); **-beam**, 'a composite beam, where an iron plate is sandwiched between two beams'; **-bolt**, a bolt for fastening f.-plates and rails together; **-joint**, a joint or splice made with fish-plates; hence **-joint** *v.*; **-front**, **-paunch**, = sense 1; **-piece** = 1, 2; **-plate**, one of two pieces bolted together through the ends of two rails on either side of their meeting-point to cover and strengthen the joint; hence **f.-plating.**

Fish (fiʃ), *sb.*[3] 1728. [ad. F. *fiche*; *f.* *ficher* to fix.] A small flat piece of bone or ivory, sometimes fish-shaped; used as a counter in games. (Pop. confused with FISH *sb.*[1]; hence the collect. *sing.* is used for *pl.*)

Fish (fiʃ), *sb.*[4] 1825. [f. FISH *v.*] **1.** An act of fishing (*mod. colloq.*). **2.** The purchase used in 'fishing' an anchor 1825.

Comb. (chiefly *Naut.*); **f.-back**, a rope attached to the hook of the f.-block, and used to assist in fishing the anchor; **-block**, the block of a f.-tackle; **-davit**, a davit for fishing the anchor; **-fall**, the tackle depending from the f.-davit; **-tackle**, that used for fishing the anchor. Also FISH-HOOK 2.

Fish (fiʃ), *v.*[1] *Pa. t* and *pple.* **fished** (fiʃt). [OE. *fiscian* :— OTeut. **fiskōjan*, f. **fisko-z* FISH *sb.*[1]]
I. *intr.* **1.** To catch or try to catch fish; to use nets, etc. for taking fish. **2.** *transf.* 1655. **3.** To use artifice to obtain a thing, elicit information, etc. Const. *after*, *for*. 1563.

2. To f. for silver at a wreck LUTTRELL. Phr. *To f. in troubled waters*: to seek one's account in other people's troubles. 3. The first woman who fishes for him, hooks him. 1848 To f. for compliments (*mod.*).

II. *trans.* **1.** To catch or try to catch (fish); to take as fish are taken; to collect (corals, pearls, etc.) from the bottom of the sea 1585. **2.** *transf.* To draw or pull *out*, *up*, *out of* 1632. **3.** To try and catch fish in ME.; *transf.* to search through *for* 1727. **4.** Chiefly with *out*: To get by artifice or patient effort ME.

2. Phr. *To f. the anchor* (Naut.): to draw up the flukes to the gunwale. 3. To f. a stream 1838. 4. I could not f. from him..what was the matter PEPYS.

III. [f. the sb.] *trans.* To dress (land) with fish-refuse. *U.S.* 1651.

Fish (fiʃ), *v.*[2] 1626. [f. FISH *sb.*[2]] **1.** *trans.* To fasten a fish upon (a beam, mast, etc.) so as to strengthen it; to mend with a fish or fishes. Also *To f. together.* **2.** To join (the rails) with a fish-joint 1850.

Fi·sh-day. ME. [f. FISH *sb.*[1] + DAY.] A day on which fish is eaten; a fast-day.

Fisher (fi·ʃəɹ). [OE. *fiscere* :— OTeut. **fiskārjo-*; see FISH *sb.*[1] Now an agent-n. of FISH *v.*[1]] **1.** = FISHERMAN 1. Also *transf.* and *fig.* Now *arch.* **2.** An animal that catches fish 1562; *spec.* the pekan or Pennant's marten (*Mustela pennanti*) of N. America; also its fur 1796. **3.** A fishing-boat 1864. **4.** *attrib.* (*esp.* in sense 'that is a fisher'), as *f.-boat*, *-boy*, *-folk*, *-girl*, *-woman*, etc. 1525.

Fisherman (fi·ʃəɹmæ̆n). 1526. [f. prec. + MAN.] **1.** One whose occupation is to catch fish. **2.** An animal that catches fish 1634. **3.** A fishing-boat 1604. *Comb.* **fisherman's ring**, the Pope's ring of investiture, 'wherein is represented St. Peter, drawing his net full of fishes' (Chambers).

Fishery (fi·ʃĕri). 1677. [f. FISH *v.*[1], or f. FISHER.] **1.** The business of catching fish, or of taking other products of the sea or rivers from the water. Often specialized as *bank-*, *bay-*, *cod-*, *pearl-*, etc. *f.* **2.** A fishing-ground 1699. **3.** A fishing establishment 1710. **4.** *Law.* The right of fishing in certain waters. **5.** *attrib.*, as *fisheries school*, etc. 1528.

4. Phr. *Free f.*, an exclusive right of fishing in public water, derived from royal grant; *several f.*, an exclusive right to fish derived from ownership of the soil; *common of f.*, the right of fishing in another man's water; *common f.*, the right of all to fish in public waters.

Fishful (fi·ʃful), *a.* 1550. [see -FUL.] Abounding in fish.

Not far from a F. Lake HEYLIN.

Fi·sh-gig. 1642. [var. of FIZGIG.] = FIZGIG 4.

Fi·sh-hook. ME. [f. FISH *sb.*[1] and *v.* + HOOK.] **1.** A hook for catching fish. **2.** *Naut.* An iron hook forming part of the tackle used to fish the anchor 1627.

Fishify (fi·ʃifəi), *v.* 1592. [f. FISH *sb.*[1] + -(I)FY.] *trans.* To turn (flesh) into fish.

Fishing (fi·ʃiŋ), *vbl. sb.*[1] ME. [f. FISH *v*.][1] **1.** The action, art, or practice of catching fish. **2.** = FISHERY 2, 4. 1495.

Comb.: **f.-float** (*U.S.*), 'a scow used in seine-fishing, from which an apron is let down to the bed of a river for the more convenient handling of the seine'; **-rod**, a long slender tapering rod to which a line is attached for angling; **-room**, a portion of the shore set apart for the curing and storing of fish; **-tube** (*Microscopy*), an open-ended glass tube for selecting a microscopic object in a fluid.

Fi·shing, *vbl. sb.*[2] 1798. [f. FISH *v.*[2]] The action of strengthening or supporting with a fish.

Fishing (fi·ʃiŋ), *ppl. a.* 1688. [f. FISH *v*[1].] **1.** That catches fish. **2.** Of an accusation, inquiry, etc.: Preferred in order to elicit information which cannot be gained directly 1831.

2. Colourable and f. Articles of accusation 1863.

Fishmonger (fi·ʃmɒŋgəɹ). 1464. [f. FISH *sb.*[1] + MONGER.] One who deals in fish.

Fishpond (fi·ʃpǫnd). ME. [f. as prec. + POND.] **1.** A pond in which fish are kept; also *joc.* the sea (cf. *herring-pond*). **2.** A depression in a card-table to hold counters (see FISH *sb.*[3]). COWPER.

Fi·sh-scale. 1661. [f. as prec.] One of the scales of a fish's skin. Chiefly *attrib.*

Fish-skin (fi·ʃ͵skin). 1651. [f. as prec.] The skin of a fish.

attrib. and *Comb.*: **fish-skin disease**, ichthyosis; **fish-skin grain**, grain (in leather) resembling a fish's skin.

Fi·sh-tail. 1840. [f. as prec.] The tail of a fish. Chiefly *attrib.*, as in *fish-tail burner* (also *fish-tail*), a kind of gas-burner with a spreading flame; **fish-tail wind**, a shifting breeze, blowing now on this side, now on that, of its main direction.

Fishwife (fi·ʃwəif). 1523. [f. as prec. + WIFE.] A woman who sells fish.

Fishy (fi·ʃi), *a.* 1547. [f. as prec. + -Y[1].] **1.** Abounding in fish. Now *poet.* or *joc.* 1552. **2.** Fish-like; (of the eye) dull, vacant 1611. **3.** Proceeding from fish 1616. **4.** Having the savour, smell, or taint of fish 1547. **5.** Consisting of, or produced from, fish 1699. **6.** *colloq.* or *slang.* **a.** Of dubious quality, questionable, 'shady'. **b.** Having fishy eyes; hence, languid or 'seedy'. 1844.

1. The f. flood POPE. 2. A pallid young man with a f. eye SALA. 6. F. about money matters 1882.
Hence **Fi·shily** *adv.* **Fi·shiness.**

Fisk: see FISC.

†**Fisk**, *v.* ME. [? freq. of OE. *fȳsan* to hurry, or of *fȳsian* FEEZE *v.*] To move briskly, frisk, whisk -1700.

Than he is busi..then he fyskes a brode LATIMER.

Fissi-, less correctly **fisso-**, comb. f. L. *fissus*, *findere* to split, used to indicate the condition of being cleft.

Fi:ssigemma·tion, a mode of reproduction intermediate between fission and gemmation. **Fi:ssili·ngual** *a.* [L. *lingua*], having the tongue cleft; said of a sub-order of saurian reptiles, the *Fissilinguia.* **Fi:ssipa·lmate** *a.* [see PALMATE], partially web-footed; semipalmate. Hence **Fi:ssipalma·tion**, partial palmation. **Fi:ssiro·stral** *a.* [L. *rostrum*], having a deeply cleft beak; belonging to the *Fissirostres.* **Fi:ssiro·strate** *a.* = prec.

Fissile (fi·sil), *a.* 1661. [ad. L. *fissilis*, f. *findere*; see -ILE.] Capable of being split; cleavable; inclined or tending to split. Hence **Fissi·lity**, f. quality.

Fission (fi·ʃən). 1841. [ad. L. *fissionem.*] 1. The action of splitting or dividing into pieces 1865. 2. *Biol.* The division of a cell or organism into new cells or organisms, as a mode of reproduction.

Fissiparous (fisi·pǎrəs). 1835. [f. FISSI- + L. *parere* to bring forth (irreg. after *viviparus*) + -OUS.] Producing new individuals by fission; relating to reproduction by fission.

Hence **Fi·ssipa·tion, Fissi·parism,** the process of f. reproduction. **Fi·ssipa·rity,** the attribute of being f.

Fissiped, fissipede (fi·siped, -pīd). 1646. [ad. late L. *fissipedem*, f. *fissus* split + *pedem* (*pes*).]

A. *adj.* Having the toes separated 1656.

B. *sb.* An animal having its toes divided.

Hence **Fissi·pedal** *a.*, **Fissi·pedate** *a.* = FISSIPED *a.*

Fissive (fi·siv), *a.* 1875. [f. L. *fissus, findere.*] Pertaining to, or of the nature of, fission.

Fissuration (fiʃiurē¹·ʃən). 1864. [a. F.; see FISSURE *v.* and -ATION.] 1. The action of fissuring; the being fissured. 2. *Biol.* = FISSION. 1867.

Fissure (fi·ʃiŭɹ), *sb.* ME. [a. F., ad. L. *fissura*, f. *findere* (*fissus*).] 1. A cleft or opening (usu. long and narrow) made by splitting, cleaving, or separation of parts; 'a narrow chasm where a breach has been made' (J.) 1606. Also *fig.* 2. *spec.* a. *Path.* A narrow solution of continuity produced by injury or ulceration; also, an incomplete fracture of a bone, without separation of parts ME. b. *Anat., Bot.*, etc. A natural cleft in an organ or part; e. g. one of the *sulci* which separate the convolutions of the brain 1656. c. *Her.* A diminutive of the bend sinister 1486. 3. = FISSURATION 1. 1633.

1. The gaping fissures to receive the rain THOMSON.

Comb.: **f.-needle**, a spiral needle for catching together the gaping lips of wounds; **f.-vein**, a f. in the earth's crust filled with mineral (RAYMOND).

Hence **Fi·ssural** *a.* of or pertaining to a f.; inclined to form fissures.

Fissure (fi·ʃiŭɹ), *v.* 1656. [f. prec. *sb.*] 1. To make a fissure or fissures in; to cleave, split. 2. *intr.* To become cleft or split.

Fist (fist), *sb.* [OE. *fȳst* :— WGer. **fūsti.*] 1. The hand clenched or closed tightly, with the fingers doubled into the palm, *esp.* for the purpose of striking a blow. b. Hence, grasp, grip, clutches. Now chiefly *joc.* ME. 2. The hand. *Obs.* exc. *joc.* ME. b. *Printer's slang.* An index mark 1488. 3. Handwriting. Now only *joc.* 1553.

1. The Queen..brake the glasse windowes with her fiste 1626. b. More light then Culver in the Faulcons f. SPENSER *F.Q.* II. vii. 34. Phr. *Hand over f.*: see HAND. 2. Give us your f., old fellow (*colloq.*). 3. To write a tolerable f. 1864.

Hence **Fi·sted** *ppl. a.*, having fists, as *close-f.*, etc. **Fi·stful** *sb.*, a handful. **Fistia·na** (*joc.*), matters relating to boxing. **Fi·stic** *a.* (*vulgar*), pugilistic.

Fist (fist), *v.* ME. [f. FIST *sb.*¹] †1. *intr.* To fight with the fists -1705. 2. *trans.* To strike with the fist 1597. 3. To grasp with the fist; to handle. Now *esp. Naut.* 1607.

2. To the choleric fisting of every rogue Thy ear is liable *Per.* IV. vi. 177.

†**Fi·stic**, *sb.* 1548. [ad. (through med. L.) Arab. *fistuq*, a. Pers. *pistah*, whence (ult.) PISTACHIO.] = PISTACHIO. -1708. Also *f. nut.*

Fisticuff (fi·stikɒf), *sb.* Also **fisty-**. 1605. [f. FIST *sb.* + CUFF *sb.*²] In *pl.* Blows or fighting with the fists. Also *attrib.* Hence **Fi·sticuff** *v. trans.* to cuff with the fists (also *fig.*); *intr.* to fight or spar with the fists.

†**Fi·stinut.** 1676. [corrupt f. *fistic nut*: see FISTIC *sb.*] -1775.

‖**Fistula** (fi·stiŭlǎ), *sb.* 1481. [a. L.; = 'pipe, flute'; in OF. *festre* FESTER *sb.*] 1. *Path.* A long, narrow, suppurating canal of morbid origin in some part of the body; a long, sinuous, pipe-like ulcer with a narrow orifice. Also *fig.* and *transf.* 2. A natural pipe or spout in cetaceous animals, insects, etc. 1646. 3. *Eccl.* A tube through which in early times communicants received the consecrated wine; now used by the Pope only 1670. ‖4. *Mus.* A reed instrument or pipe of the ancient Romans 1717.

1. Henry, notwithstanding his f. and his fever, was able to sit on horseback GREEN. 2. The f. or spout [of the Whale] SIR T. BROWNE.

Hence **Fi·stular** *a. Bot.* hollow or cylindrical like a pipe or reed; *Path.* pertaining to, or of the nature of, a f. So †**Fi·stulary** *a.* **Fi·stuliform** *a.* of the form of a reed or tube. **Fistulo·se, Fi·stulous** *adjs.* fistular; resembling a pipe or tube in form.

†**Fi·stulate,** *v.* 1607. [f. L. *fistulat-, fistulare*; see FISTULA *sb.* and -ATE³.] 1. *intr.* To form or grow to a fistula. 2. *trans.* To make tubular 1751.

Fit, fytte (fit), *sb.*¹ *Obs.* exc. *arch.* [OE. *fitt* = OS. **fittia*; see next.] 1. A part or section of a poem or song; a canto. 2. A strain of music, stave 1500.

1. Lo, lordes, heer is a fyt CHAUCER.

Fit (fit), *sb.*² [OE. *fitt* conflict; ? cogn. w. prec., with primitive sense 'juncture', 'meeting'. Cf. Icel. *fitja* to knit, early mod. Du. *vitten* to accommodate, etc.] †1. Conflict. Only in OE. †2. A position of hardship or danger; an exciting experience; in 16th c. occas., a mortal crisis -1601. 3. a. A paroxysm; also, later, a sudden and severe but transitory attack (of illness) 1547. †b. *spec.* A paroxysm of lunacy -1722. c. A sudden seizure, such as fainting, hysteria, apoplexy, paralysis, or epilepsy; in recent use, *esp.* an epileptic or convulsive fit. 1621. 4. Hence *transf.* a. A sudden and transitory state of activity, inaction, etc. 1586. b. A spell, a short period. *Obs.* exc. *dial.* 1583. c. A mood, humour 1680. d. A violent access of laughter, rage, etc. 1654.

2. Feeling the f. that him forewarnd to die 1591. 3. He had a Feauer..and when the F. was on him, I did marke How he did shake *Jul. C.* I. ii. 120. A f. of rheumatism or gout BAIN. b. *Tit. A.* IV. i. 17. c. Fits are a mighty help in the Government of a good-natured Man STEELE. Phr. *To beat into fits* (colloq.): to 'beat hollow'. *To give* (a person) *fits*: to inflict humiliating defeat on; also, to scold vigorously. 4. a. We have our hot and cold fits alternately FLAVEL. Phr. *By fits* (*and starts*): fitfully, spasmodically. d. A prolonged f. of grumbling 1874.

Fit (fit), *sb.*³ 1688. [f. FIT *v.*¹] 1. The process of fitting or rendering fit. 2. A fitting or adaptation of one thing to another, e. g. the adjustment of dress to the body; *concr.* a garment that fits 1823. 3. *Soap-making.* The condition of the liquid soap in the operation of fitting (see FIT *v.*) 1885.

1. Phr. †*Out of f.*: fitted out, settled in life; Till my children are out of F. BUNYAN. 2. *concr.* It's rather a tight f. 1831. *Comb.* **f.-rod**, a small iron rod with a hook at the end, used in *Shipbuilding* to ascertain the length of the bolts or treenails to be driven in.

Fit (fit), *a.* ME. [Of unkn. origin. Partly influenced by FEAT *a.*] 1. Suited to the circumstances of the case, answering the purpose, proper or appropriate. Const. *for*, or *to* with *inf.* Also *absol.* 2. Becoming, convenient, proper, right. Now only in predicative use. ME. †3. Of the right measure or size -1703. 4. Properly qualified 1573. 5. In a suitable condition; prepared, ready. Const. *for* or *to* with *inf.*; otherwise *Obs.* exc. *dial.* 1568. b. Inclined, disposed. Now chiefly *colloq.* and *dial.*: Angry enough *to*; ready *to.* 1580. 6. *Sport.* In good form or condition; hence *colloq.* perfectly well 1869. 7. quasi-*adv.* = FITLY. ME.

1. Prethee call Gardiner to me, my new Secretary, I find him a f. fellow *Hen. VIII*, II. ii. 117. A f. opportunity 1852. *absol.* Survival of the fittest 1867. 2. What is setled by Custome, though it be not good, yet at least it is f. BACON. Phr. *To think, see f.* 4. F. to command TEMPLE. Phr. *F. to hold a candle to*: see CANDLE. 5. F. for treasons SHAKS., for service 1823. b. Standing till you are f. to sink J. H. NEWMAN. 6. Phr. *As f. as a fiddle*: see FIDDLE *sb.*

Fit (fit), *v.*¹ ME. [Exc. in sense 1, which is of unkn. etym., app. f. FIT *a.*]

†I. *trans.* To array, marshal (soldiers). *Morte Arth.*

II. †1. *intr.* To be fit, or suitable. Chiefly *impers.* -1725. b. To harmonize *with* -1594. 2. *trans.* To befit. Chiefly *impers.* 1586. †3. To answer, suit -1749. 4. To be correctly shaped or adjusted to. Said *esp.* of dress; also *fig.* Often *absol.* 1581. b. *intr.* with *in* (adv. and prep.), *into, in with* 1694.

2. b. Why dost thou laugh? it fits not with this houre SHAKS. 2. This insolence other kind of answer fits MILT. 3. Phr. †*To f.* (= serve) *one's turn*. 4. Euerie true mans apparrell fits your Theefe SHAKS. Phr. *The cap fits*: see CAP *sb.*¹ *To f. to a T*: see T. *intr.* A statement which curiously fits in with our story FREEMAN.

III. *trans.* 1. To make fit or suitable; to adapt to the object in view; to qualify; to make ready. Const. *for, to* with *sb.* or *inf.*; otherwise *dial.* only. 1600. 2. To arrange so as to conform or correspond 1580. 3. To fix, apply, adjust, or insert exactly 1611. 4. *Soap-making.* To bring (fluid soap) into such a condition that it will separate into two strata, the upper purer than the lower 1866.

1. The vessels of wrath fitted to destruction *Rom.* ix. 22. To f. a man for a particular calling 1647. 2. To f. words to a thought BOYLE. 3. Let each..F. well his Helme MILT. *P. L.* vi. 543. Phr. *To f. on*: to try on (a garment, etc.). *To f. the cap on*: to take an allusion as applying to oneself.

IV. 1. To supply *with* what is fit or suitable 1591. 2. To visit with a fit penalty; to punish. *Obs.* exc. *Australian.* 1625.

1. I wil f. him to morrow with a Trout for his breakfast WALTON. Phr. *To f. out*: to equip, rig out. *Obs.* exc. *Naut.* or *transf.* *To f. up*: to supply with necessary fitting or stores. 2. With a look that implied—I'll f. you for this MISS BURNEY.

†**Fit,** *v.*² [f. FIT *sb.*²] To force by fits or paroxysms *out of* (the usual place) SHAKS. *Sonn.* cxix.

Fitch (fitʃ), *sb.*¹ Now *dial.* ME. [var. of VETCH.] = VETCH; the plant *Vicia sativa*, or its seed. Also *attrib.*

Fitch (fitʃ), *sb.*² 1502. [a. med. Du. *visse, fisse*, whence OF. *fissel* FITCHEW.] 1. = FITCHEW. 1550. 2. The fur of a polecat 1502. 3. A brush made of the hair of a polecat; also, a small hog's-hair brush 1873.

Fitché, -ée (fi·tʃe), *a.* Also **Fitchy.** 1572. [ad. F. *fiché, fichée* fixed.] *Her.* Fixed; applied to a cross, the lower extremity of which is sharpened to a point. Also **Fitched** *a.*

Fitchet (fi·tʃėt). 1535. [dim. of FITCH *sb.*²] 1. = FITCHEW 1, 2. 2. *erron.*: The weasel. *Obs.* exc. *dial.* 1693.

Fitchew (fi·tʃū). ME. [a. OF. *fissel* (pl. *fissiaulx*), later *fissau*, dim. formed on MDu. *fisse.*] 1. A foumart, polecat. 2. The fur of the polecat ME. var. †**Fi·tchock.**

†**Fi·tchy,** *a.*¹ 1610. [f. FITCH *sb.*¹] Resembling a vetch.

Fitchy (fi·tʃi), *a.*² 1650. *Her.* Anglicized f. FITCHÉ, q. v.

Fitful (fi·tful), *a.* 1605. [f. FIT *sb.*² + -FUL. A word used once by Shaks.; popularized since 1800.] 1. Characterized by paroxysms. *Obs.* exc. in Shaks. 2. Coming and going by fits and starts; irregularly changeable; spasmodic, shifting, capricious 1810.

1. Life's fitfull Feuer *Macb.* III. ii. 23. 2. The f. breeze SCOTT. Hence **Fi·tful-ly** *adv.*, **-ness.**

Fitly (fi·tli), *adv.* 1550. [f. FIT *a.*] In a way that is fit; properly, becomingly, suitably; †opportunely.

A word f. spoken *Prov.* xxv. 11.

Fitment (fi·tmĕnt). 1608. [f. FIT *v.* + -MENT.] †1. A making fit. *Cymb.* v. v. 409. †2. That which is fitting. *Per.* IV. vi. 6. 3. A piece of furniture. Usu. *pl.* Fittings. 1851.

Fitness (fi·tnės). 1580. [f. FIT *a.* + -NESS.] 1. The quality or state of being fit, or of being fitted. †2. The quality of fitting exactly -1793. †3. Readiness. *Haml.* v. ii. 209.

1. Haue you, I say, an answere of such f. for all questions SHAKS. To insist..on a mere moral f. 1858. Phr. *The* (*eternal*) *f. of things*: 'fitness' or conformity to the relations inherent in the nature of things: an 18th c. phrase referring to Clarke's ethical theory. Hence pop.: What is fitting or appropriate.

Fitted (fi·tėd), *ppl. a.* 1736. [f. FIT *v.*¹] In the senses of the vb.; also *fitted-up.* Often predicatively: Adapted, calculated, likely. Const. *to* with *inf.*

Circumstances..f. to be, to them, a state of discipline 1736. Hence **Fi·ttedness.**

†**Fi·tten,** *sb.* ME. [?] An untruth, an invention -1825. Hence †**Fi·tten** *v. intr.* to fib, tell lies.

Fitter (fi·təɹ), *sb.*¹ 1660. [f. FIT *v.*¹] 1. One who or that which fits (see the vb.). 2. *spec.* in various trades. Also in *Comb.*, as *gas-, hot-water-*, etc. *f.* 1858.

Fitter (fi·təɹ), *sb.*² *local.* 1678. [?] A coal-broker who vends and loads coals.

Fi·tters, *sb. pl.* Now *dial.* 1532. [?] Fragments, pieces.
Which Image..was with Fire from Heaven broken into f. RALEIGH.

Fitting (fi·tiŋ), *vbl. sb.* 1607. [f. FIT *v.*[1]] 1. The action of FIT *v.*[1] 2. *concr.* Anything used in fitting. Usu. in *pl.*: Fixtures, apparatus, furniture. 1823. 3. *Mech. Engin.* The bringing together and adjusting of the parts of engines, machines, etc. 1878.
2. All the roofs, floors, and fittings were burnt FREEMAN.

Fitting (fi·tiŋ), *ppl. a.* 1535. [f. as prec.] That fits; becoming, proper, suitable; that fits exactly. Hence **Fi·tting-ly** *adv.*, **-ness.**

‖**Fitz** (fits). ME. [AF. spelling of OF. *fiz* (pronounced *fits*) :— earlier *filz* :— L. *filius.*] The AF. word for 'son'; chiefly *Hist.* in patronymic designations, e. g. *Fitzherbert, Fitzwilliam*, etc., which survive as surnames. In later times new surnames of the kind have been given to the illegitimate sons of princes. Used by Macaulay to designate an Irishman of Anglo-Norman extraction.

‖**Fiumara** (fiūmā·ra). 1820. [It.] A mountain torrent; also the dry bed left by it.

Five (fəiv). [Com. Teut. and Aryan: OE. *fīf* (ME. *five*) :— OTeut. **fimf*(*i* :— pre-Teut. **pempe*, modified from OAryan **penqe*, whence Skr. *pañca*, Gr. πέντε, πέμπε, L. *quinque*, etc.] The cardinal number next after four; symbols 5, V.

A. as *adj.* 1. With sb. expressed. 2. With ellipsis of sb. OE.
1. Lord Warden of the fiue (= Cinque) ports 1631. Phr. *The five senses, wits*: see the sbs. *F. Nations* (Amer. Hist.), the five confederated tribes of Indians. 2. Ffiue of the clocke, *hora quinta* HULOET. Let me haue Claudios head sent me by fiue SHAKS.

B. as *sb.* 1. The abstract number five ME. 2. A set of five things 1764. 3. *pl.* a. The five fingers 1825. b. Gloves, shoes, etc., of the fifth size 16.. c. Short for *five-pound note* 1837. d. Short for *five-per-cents.* 1848. e. (See FIVES.[2])
2. (*Cards*) A f. of spades 1870. (*Cricket*) To hit a ball for f. 1859. 3. c. Ten to one in fives 1860.

Combs. 1. General: as *f.-act, -guinea, -year-old*, etc.; *-barred, -foiled, -lobed, -rayed*, etc.; *-cleft*.
2. Special: as **f.-acre,** a plot consisting of five acres; **-finger exercise,** a piece of music to practise the fingers in pianoforte playing; **-lined** *a.*, consisting of or marked with five lines, *esp.* of an urgent parliamentary whip; **-mile Act,** an act passed in 1665 forbidding Non-conformist teachers who refused to take the non-resistance oath to come within five miles of any town, etc.; **-per-cents.,** stock or shares paying five per cent. on their nominal value; **-stroke** (*Billiards*), a stroke by which five points are scored. Also, **f.-o'clock** (see A. 2, quots.), used *attrib.* in **f.-o'clock tea** (colloq. *a f.-o'clock*).

Fi·ve-fi·nger. [OE. *fīffingre*, f. *fīf* FIVE + FINGER.] 1. A name of plants: a. The cinquefoil (*Potentilla reptans*, etc.). b. The oxlip (*Primula elatior*). c. *Lotus corniculatus.* 2. A species of star-fish 1678. †3. *Cards.* The five of trumps –1674. *Comb.* **five-finger-grass** = 1 a.

Fivefold (fəi·vfōuld). [OE. *fīffeald*, f. *fīf* FIVE + *-feald* -FOLD.]
A. *adj.* 1. Consisting of five together. 2. Five times as great or numerous; quintuple 1557.
1. Thy tongue, thy face, thy limbes, actions, and spirit, Do giue thee fiue-fold blazon *Twel. N.* I. v. 312.
B. *adv.* In fivefold proportion 1571.

Fi·ve-leaf. [OE. *fīflēafe*, f. *fīf* FIVE + *lēaf* LEAF.] The plant cinquefoil (*Potentilla reptans*).

Fiveling (fəi·vliŋ). [-LING, dim. suffix.] 'A twin crystal consisting of five individuals' (*Cent. Dict.*).

Fivepence (fəi·vₚpĕns). Also *colloq.* FIPPENCE. [f. FIVE + PENCE.] The value of five pennies. In U.S. the value of 5 cents or 2½*d.*

Fivepenny (fei·vpəni), *a. Mod.* [f. FIVE *a.* + PENNY.] Valued at fivepence. *A fivepenny rate*: one at fivepence in the pound.

Fiver (fəi·vəɹ). *colloq.* 1853. [f. FIVE + -ER[1].] 1. A five-pound note. In U.S. a five-dollar note. 2. Anything that counts as five, as a hit for five at cricket.

†**Fives** [1]. 1596. [corrupt f. AVIVES.] The strangles. *Tam. Shr.* III. ii. 54.

Fives [2] (fəivz). 1636. [pl. of FIVE *sb.*, used as *sing.* The reason for the name is obscure.] A game in which a ball is struck by the hand against a wall of a prepared court. The number of 'points' in the game is variously 11, 15, 20, or 25.
Comb. **f.-court,** a prepared court where fives is played.

Fi·ve-twe·nty. *U.S.* Used *attrib.* in *Five-twenty bonds* (or *five-twenties*), certain bonds issued by the U.S. government in 1862, 1864, and 1865; so called from being redeemable at any time after *five* years from date of issue and payable in full at the end of *twenty* years.

Fix (fiks), *sb.* 1839. [f. the vb.] 1. orig. *U.S.* A position from which it is difficult to move, a 'tight place'; a predicament. 2. The material used for lining a puddling-furnace 1871.

†**Fix,** *a.* ME. [ad. L. *fixus, figere*, perh. through OF. *fix.*] = FIXED in various senses –1673.

Fix (fiks), *v. Pa. t.* and *pple.* **fixed** (fikst). ME. [f. (ult.) L. *fixus, figere* to fix, fasten.]

I. 1. *trans.* To fasten, make firm or stable; to set or place and secure against displacement. In immaterial sense: To attach firmly; to implant securely (principles, etc.) 1533. 2. To give stability or constancy to 1604. 3. To direct steadily and unwaveringly, fasten, set (one's eyes, attention, etc.) *on, upon*, †*to* ME. Also *absol.*, and *intr.* for *refl.* b. Of an object of vision or thought: To rivet (the eye, the attention, etc.) 1752. c. To make immobile or rigid. Also *intr.* for *refl.* 1664. 4. *trans.* To deprive of volatility or fluidity. Also *intr.* for *refl.* 1460. 5. *trans.* To make (a colour, a drawing, etc.) fast or permanent 1665. 6. To 'corner' 1736; to hold (a person) occupied 1668.
1. His head to be fixed on a poole HALL. I resolved ..to f. his Face in my memory BUDGELL. To f. an imputation on a person BERKELEY. 2. To f. fluctuating opinions 1793. 3. Why are thine eyes fixt to the sullen earth? SHAKS. To f. the mind upon Heaven 1665. *absol.* Nothing on which attention can f. JOHNSON. c. Ere death her charms should f. 1842.

II. 1. To place definitely and permanently 1568; to establish; to locate 1638. 2. *intr.* for *refl.* To settle permanently 1638. 3. To take up one's position mentally (? *Obs.*) 1623; to decide, determine *to* 1788. 4. To determine the place, time, incidence, etc. of 1833. 5. To settle or assign definitely; to determine 1660. 6. To give a permanent form to 1712. 7. To adjust, make ready for use 1663. 8. To line with a fix (see FIX *sb.* 2) 1881.
1. Phr. *To fix a person up* (colloq.): to provide him with quarters. We are fixed here for some time SOUTHEY. 2. I had..thoughts of fixing in town JANE AUSTEN. 3. Phr. *To f. on* or *upon*: to decide upon, choose. 4. Here will I f. the limits of transgression JOHNSON. Phr. *To f.* (a person) *with costs, liability*, etc.: to put upon him the obligation of meeting them. 5. The opening of the session..is fixed for next Tuesday FRANKLIN. 6. It [Wycliffe's Translation of the Bible] has fixed the language MAURICE. 7. To f. the press for copying WASHINGTON.
Hence **Fi·xable** *a.* **Fixer,** one who or that which fixes.

Fixation (fiksē¹·ʃən). ME. [ad. med. L. *fixationem* (used in *Alchemy*), f. *fixare* to FIX.] 1. The action of fixing (see FIX *v.*) 1652; the fact or condition of being fixed 1631; a fixed †location, proportion or standard 1614. 2. *esp.* in scientific uses: The action of depriving of volatility or fluidity. In mod. use: The process of rendering solid a liquid or semi-liquid substance; also, the process of causing (a gas) to combine with a solid. ME. †b. The condition of being non-volatile or able to resist the action of fire –1721.
1. The f. of the Popes in the Metropolis HEYLIN. The F. of Colours 1671. The f. of the punishment BENTHAM, of Thought 1864. On locomotion and f. in plants and animals 1894.

Fixative (fi·ksătiv). 1644. [f. FIX *v.* + -ATIVE. Cf. F. *fixatif.*]
A. *adj.* Tending to fix.
B. *sb.* That which serves to set or fix colours, charcoal drawings, etc. 1870.

Fixature (fi·ksătiuɹ). 1860. [f. as prec.] A gummy preparation for fixing the hair.
A stick of f. for the moustachios 1860.

Fixed (fikst), *ppl. a.* ME. [f. FIX *v.*] 1. Placed or attached firmly 1577. b. *Her.* Of a cross := FIRME. 1688. 2. In immaterial sense: Firmly attached or implanted. Now rarely of persons: Firmly resolved; constant. 1580. 3. Made rigid or immobile 1608. 4. a. Deprived of volatility 1766. b. Not easily volatilized 1641. c. Of acids and oils: That cannot be evaporated or distilled without decomposition 1800. 5. Fast, permanent, as a colour, etc. 1791. 6. Stationary or unchanging in relative position ME. 7. Not fluctuating; definite, permanent 1698. 8. Prepared, put in order 1638.
1. Where the firm or f. Ice lies 1694. 2. *Fixed idea*: an idea unduly dominant in the brain [F. *idée fixe*]. *Fixed fact*: a well-established fact (*U.S.*). A man of no fixt Resolution HEARNE. 3. Her eyes ..were f. and staring W. BLACK. 4. a. †*Fixed air*: Black's name for *carbonic dioxide* (*carbonic acid*); see AIR *sb.* b. *Fixed alkali*: see ALKALI. 6. *Fixed point*: a place where a policeman is permanently stationed. *Fixed star*: a star which appears always to occupy the same position in the heavens (cf. *planet*). *Fixed capital*: see CAPITAL *sb.* 7. One loves f. Laws, and the other arbitrary Power SIR W. TEMPLE. 8. '*Fixed ammunition*: a charge of powder and shot enclosed together in a wrapper or case ready for loading' (Knight).
Hence **Fi·xedly** *adv.* **Fi·xedness,** the quality or condition of being f.; †the quality of being non-volatile.

Fixidity (fiksi·dĭti). Now *rare.* 1762. [badly f. FIXED *ppl. a.*, after *fluidity.*] = FIXITY.

Fixing (fi·ksiŋ), *vbl. sb.* 1605. [f. FIX *v.*] 1. The action of FIX *v.* in various senses; *concr.* that which fixes. 2. *concr.* In *pl.* (orig. *U.S.*) Apparatus, equipment; trimmings; garnishing 1827. b. = FIX *sb.* 2. 1874. *Comb.* **f.-bath** (*Photogr.*), the bath in which a developed negative or positive is plunged in order to fix it.

†**Fi·xion.** 1555. [ad. med. L. *fixionem.*] = FIXATION 2. –1631.

Fixity (fi·ksĭti). 1666. [f. L. *fixus*; see FIX *a.* and -ITY.] 1. Orig. *spec.*: The property of enduring heat without volatilization or loss of weight. 2. *gen.* The quality or condition of being fixed (see FIXED) 1791.
2. *Fixity of Tenure*: the condition of having a permanent tenure.

Fixive (fi·ksiv), *a. rare.* [L. type **fixivus.*] Adapted or tending to fix. COLERIDGE.

Fixture (fi·kstiŭɹ). 1598. [Altered f. FIXURE, after *mixture.*] 1. The action of fixing; the process of becoming fixed; fixedness. 2. Anything fixed, or made firm, stable, or immobile; *U.S.* in *pl.* 'fixings' 1812. 3. *Law.* In *pl.*, 'Things of an accessory character annexed to houses or lands, which become, immediately on annexation, part of the realty itself' (Wharton) 1758. 4. A person or thing permanently established in a particular place or position 1788. 5. *Sports*, rarely *Comm.* An appointment or date for a meet, race, etc.; hence, the meet, race, etc. itself. 1825.
1. The firm f. of thy foote *Merry W.* III. iii. 67 [*F.* 1 and *Q.* of 1630]. 2. There are no fixtures in nature. The universe is fluid and volatile. EMERSON. 4. Miss Goldsworthy was a f. at her side MAD. D'ARBLAY. 5. Fixtures of the principal..yachting clubs 1869.

Fixure (fi·ksiŭɹ). *Obs.* or *arch.* See prec. 1603. [ad. late L. *fixura*, f. *figere* to FIX.] Fixed condition, position, or attitude; fixedness, stability.

Fizgig, fisgig (fi·zgig). 1529. [f. ? + GIG. Sense 3 is app. f. FIZZ only; sense 4 f. Sp. *fisga* harpoon.] 1. A frivolous gadabout woman; = GIG. 2. A whipping-top 1656. 3. A kind of firework; a squib 1644. 4. A kind of harpoon. Also FISH-GIG. 1565. 5. A gimcrack; a crotchet 1822.

Fizz, fiz (fiz), *sb. colloq.* 1734. [f. next vb.] 1. A hissing sound 1842. 2. A fuss 1734; 'go' 1856. 3. Something that fizzes; *esp.* champagne 1864.

Fizz, fiz (fiz), *v.* 1665. [Echoic.] To make a hissing or sputtering sound; to move with a hissing sound. Hence **Fi·zzy** *a.*, effervescent 1855.

Fizzle (fi·z'l), *sb.* 1598. [f. next vb.] 1. The action of breaking wind quietly; the action of hissing or sputtering. 2. A failure or fiasco 1846.

Fizzle (fi·z'l), *v.* 1532. [See -LE. Cf. FIZZ.] †1. *intr.* To break wind quietly –1739. 2. *intr.*

To niss or sputter 1859. 3. *fig.* (chiefly *U.S. colloq.*) To fail, make a fiasco 1847.

2. The black oil fizzles 1859.

‖**Fjeld** (fyeld). 1860. [a. Norw. *field* :— ON. *fiall*; see FELL *sb.*²] An elevated rocky plateau, almost bare.

Fjord, var. of FIORD.

Flabbergast (flæ·bəɹgɑ·st), *v. colloq.* 1772. [? An arbitrary formation suggested by FLABBY and AGHAST.] *trans.* To put to confusion and embarrassment; to astonish utterly, confound. Hence **Fla·bbergast** *sb.* gasconade (*rare*).

Flabby (flæ·bi), *a.* 1598. [A modification of FLAPPY with a feebler sound.] 1. Hanging loose by its own weight, yielding to the touch and easily moved or shaken, flaccid, limp. 2. Weak, wanting back-bone; nerveless 1791. 3. Clammy 1780.

1. His f. Flanks decrease DRYDEN. 2. An indolent f. kind of creature CARLYLE. 3. F. weather 1780.
Hence **Fla·bbily** *adv.* **Fla·bbiness.**

†**Fla·bel.** 1552. [ad. L. *flabellum* fan, f. (ult.) *flare* to blow.] A fan –1681.

Flabellate (flăbe·lĕt), *a.* 1819. [f. L. *flabellum* (see prec.) + -ATE ².] *Bot.* and *Zool.* Fan-shaped.

Flabellation (flæbĕlē·ʃən). 1658. [a. F., f. L. *flabellare.*] *Surg.* The action of fanning.

Flabe·lli-, comb. f. L. *flabellum* fan, indicating a fan-like form or arrangement, as in *flabellifoliate, flabellinerved* adjs.

Flabelliform (flăbe·lifǭɹm), *a.* 1777. [f. L. *flabellum* + -(I)FORM.] Fan-like.

‖**Flabellum** (flăbe·lŏm). Pl. **-la** (erron. **-i**). 1867. [L.; see FLABEL.] 1. A fan; *esp.* used of a fan carried in religious ceremonies 1875. 2. *Science.* A fan-shaped part of anything.

†**Fla·bile,** *a. rare.* 1727. [ad. L. *flabilis*, f. *flare* to blow.] Of musical instruments: Wind-. Also *transf.*

Flaccid (flæ·ksid), a. 1620. [a. F. *flaccide*, ad. L. *flaccidus*, f. *flaccus* flabby.] 1. Wanting in stiffness, hanging or lying loose in wrinkles; limp; flabby; relaxed. Chiefly of flesh. 2. Wanting vigour and energy, limp, feeble 1647.

1. His double chin over his f. whitey-brown shirt collar THACKERAY. 2. A scheme that has left us f. and drain'd TENNYSON. Hence **Fla·ccid·ly** *adv.*, **-ness.**

Flaccidity (flæksi·dĭti). 1676. [f. prec. Cf. F. *flaccidité.*] 1. The quality or condition of being flaccid. 2. A disease of silkworms. [tr. It. *flaccidezza*, F. *flacherie.*] RILEY.

‖**Flacherie** (flaʃərī). 1885. [F.] = FLACCIDITY 2.

Flacian (flē·ʃiăn). 1565. [f. *Flacius* + -AN.] A. *adj.* Of or pertaining to Flacius Illyricus, a Protestant divine of the 16th c., who opposed the adiaphorist views of Melanchthon.
B. *sb.* A follower of Flacius Illyricus; an anti-Adiaphorist. Hence **Fla·cianism,** the doctrine of the Flacians.

Flacker (flæ·kəɹ), *v.* Now *dial.* [ME. *flakeren*; a frequentative f. the echoic stem *flak-.*] *intr.* To flap, flutter, throb. Also *trans.* To flap (the wings). ME.

Flacket (flæ·kĕt). Now *dial.* ME. [a. ONF. **flaquet, flasquet*, dim. of *flasque*; see FLASK.] A flask, or bottle; now, a barrel-shaped vessel for holding liquor.

‖**Flacon** (flakoñ). 1824. [F.; see FLAGON.] A small stoppered bottle; *esp.* a smelling-bottle.

Flag (flæg), *sb.*¹ ME. [Of obscure origin; cf. Du *flag*, also mod. Da. *flæg.*] 1. One of various endogenous plants, with a bladed or ensiform leaf, mostly growing in moist places. Now properly, a member of the genus *Iris* (esp. *I. pseudacorus*). b. In *pl.* or *collect. sing.* A kind of coarse grass 1577. 2. The blade of a plant, e g. of *Iris* and of cereals 1578.

1. The greene flagge [will] smoke in the flame LD. BERNERS. 2. The wheat was then showing a beautiful f. JEFFERIES.

Comb.: **f.-basket** (*dial.*), a basket made of reeds; **-broom,** a broom commonly made of birch-twigs, or of the leaves of the dwarf palm; **-leaf,** an iris; **-worm,** a worm found in the roots of flags and used by anglers.

Flag (flæg), *sb.*² ME. [Cf. Icel. *flag* the spot where a turf has been cut out, ON. *flaga* slab of stone; also FLAKE *sb.*²] 1. A turf, sod. Also *collect.* Now *dial.* 2. A flat slab of any fine-grained rock which may be split into flagstones; a flagstone 1604. In *pl.* A flagged foot-pavement. 1802.

Flag (flæg), *sb.*³ 1486. [? subst. use of FLAG *a.*] a. *pl.* The quill-feathers of a bird's wing. b. The crural feathers of a hawk 1890.

Flag (flæg), *sb.*⁴ 1481. [First found in Eng.; prob. onomatopœic. Cf. Da. *flag*, Sw. *flagg*, *flagga*, Du. *vlag*, Ger. *flagge* (17th c.).] 1. A piece of stuff (usually bunting), varying in size, colour, and device, but usu. oblong or square, attached by one edge to a staff or to a halyard, used as a standard, ensign or signal, and also for display. Also *transf.* and *fig.* 2. *Naut.* A flag carried by a flagship, as an admiral's emblem of rank afloat 1695. b. A flagship 1652. c. Applied to the admiral 1665. 3. *slang.* An apron 1851. 4. *Sporting.* The tail of a setter or Newfoundland dog. Also occas. of a horse. 1859. 5. *Printing.* A mark indicating an omission by the compositor; an 'out'.

1. *Black, red, white, yellow f.*, see the adjs. *fig.* Beauties ensigne yet Is Crymson in thy lips.. And Deaths pale f. is not aduanced there *Rom. & Jul.* v. iii. 96. Phr. *F.* (*of truce*): a white flag, carried or displayed by an enemy, to express a wish for a parley. Hence, the person or the ship dispatched with it. *To lower* or *strike one's f.*: to take it down, *esp.* in token of respect, submission, or surrender. 2. *To hoist* or *strike one's f.*: (of the admiral) to enter upon or relinquish command.

Comb.: **f.-boat,** a mark-boat in sailing or rowing matches; **-captain,** the captain of a flagship; **-day,** a day on which money is raised for a cause by the sale of small flags or other tokens as evidence of having given; **-lieutenant,** an officer acting as aide-de-camp to an admiral; **-list,** the roll of flag-officers or admirals; **-pay,** the pay of a flag-officer or admiral; **-rank,** the rank of admiral; **-share,** an admiral's share (one-eighth) of prize-money; **-station** (*Railways*), a place where trains stop only when signalled to do so; **-wagging** (*Mil. slang*), signalling with flags held in the hand.

†**Flag,** *a.* 1591. [? a. OF. *flac* (:— L. *flaccus*).] Hanging down, drooping, pendulous –1765.

Flag (flæg), *v.*¹ 1545. [? f. prec.; cf. OF. *flaquir* to become flaccid. But perh. partly onomatopœic.] 1. *intr.* To hang down; to flap about loosely. †b. *trans.* To allow to droop; to drop –1757. 2. *intr.* To become flaccid. Now only of plants: To droop, fade. 1611. †3. *intr.* Of wings: To move feebly or ineffectually. Of a bird: To move its wings feebly. Also *fig.* –1764. 4. *transf.* To lag through fatigue; to lose vigour or energy 1639. b. Of an author, a game, conversation, etc.: To grow dull or languid 1678. †5. *trans.* a. *lit.* Of a bird, etc.: To cease to ply vigorously (its wings) from fatigue. Of conditions, etc.: To clog, impede –1715. b. Hence To depress, enfeeble –1757.

1. Its sails were flagging in the breathless ocean SHELLEY. 2. The white crops f., and the turnip-leaves turn yellow 1846. 3. The Wings of Time flagg'd dully after it COWLEY.

Flag (flæg), *v.*² 1685. [f. FLAG *sb.*¹] †1. *trans.* To plant *about* with reeds. EVELYN. 2. To tighten (the seams of a barrel) with rushes 1757. 3. To cut off the blade of (wheat) 1846.

Flag (flæg), *v.*³ 1615. [f. FLAG *sb.*²] *trans.* To pave with or as with flagstones.

Flag (flæg), *v.*⁴ 1875. [f. FLAG *sb.*⁴] 1. To place a flag over or upon; to decorate with flags. 2. a. To inform, communicate, or warn by flag-signals 1886. b. To decoy (game, *esp.* deer) by waving a flag or the like 1884.

Flagellant (flădʒe·lănt, flæ·dʒĕlănt). 1563. [ad. L. *flagellantem*, *flagellare*, f. *flagellum.*]
A. *sb.* 1. One of a 13th c. sect of fanatics (L. *flagellantes*) who scourged themselves by way of religious discipline or penance. Usu. *pl.* 2. *transf.* One who flagellates (himself or others). Also *fig.* 1785.
B. *adj.* Given to flagellation. Also *fig.* 1880.
The f. head-master of Eton SWINBURNE.
Hence **Flage·llantism.**

Flagellate (flæ·dʒĕlĕt), *a.* 1877. [f. FLAGELLUM + -ATE ².] 1. *Biol.* Furnished with vibratile flagella; also, = FLAGELLIFORM. 2. *Bot.* Having runners or runner-like branches 1882.

Flagellate (flæ·dʒĕleⁱt), *v.* 1623. [f. L. *flagellat-*, *flagellare*, f. *flagellum.*] *trans.* To scourge, whip. Also *fig.*

[That] the angels were created only to f. and burn us LANDOR.

Flagellated (flæ·dʒĕleⁱtĕd), *a.* 1887. [f. FLAGELLATE *a.*] *Zool.* and *Biol.* Provided with flagella.

Flagellation (flæ:dʒĕlē·ʃən). ME. [ad. L. *flagellationem.*] The action of scourging; *esp.* the scourging of Christ, or a picture of this.

Flagellator (flæ·dʒĕleⁱtəɹ). 1691. [f. L. *flagellare.*] One who scourges or flogs; a FLAGELLANT. Hence **Fla·gellato:ry** *a.* pertaining to flagellation.

Flagelliform (flădʒe·lifǭrm), *a.* 1826. [f. FLAGELLUM + -(I)FORM.] *Zool.* and *Bot.* Having the form of a FLAGELLUM.

‖**Flagellum** (flădʒe·lŏm). *Pl.* **-la.** 1807. [L.; = 'scourge'.] 1. *joc.* A whip, scourge. 2. *Bot.* A runner 1887; *Zool.* and *Biol.* a lash-like appendage 1852.

Flageolet (flædʒŏle·t, flæ·dʒŏlĕt). 1659. [a. F., dim. of OF. *flajol.*] 1. A small wind instrument, having a mouthpiece at one end, six principal holes, and sometimes keys. 2. An organ-stop with the tone of a flageolet 1852.

Phr. *F. tones*, the natural harmonics of stringed instruments, so called from the quality of their tone.

‖**Flageolet**² (flædʒole·t, flaʒole). 1885. [F., corruption of *fageolet*, dim. of *fageol* :— L. *faseolus.*] A species of kidney-bean.

Flagging (flæ·giŋ), *vbl. sb.*¹ 1611. [f. FLAG *v.*¹] The action of FLAG *v.*¹

Fla·gging, *vbl. sb.*² 1622. [f. FLAG *v.*³] 1. The action of paving with flagstones 1656. 2. *concr.* The material used in paving; hence, the pavement.

Flagging (flæ·giŋ), *ppl. a.* 1545. [f. FLAG *v.*¹] That flags; drooping; failing. Hence **Fla·ggingly** *adv.*

Flaggy (flæ·gi), *a.*¹ ME. [f. FLAG *sb.*¹] 1. Abounding in flags or reeds; made of flags or reeds; flag-like. 2. Of corn, straw, etc.: Having a large FLAG 1842.

1. Old Chamus f. banks G. FLETCHER.

Flaggy (flæ·gi), *a.*² Now *dial.* 1565. [f. FLAG *v.*¹] 1. Hanging down limply, drooping 1576. 2. Flaccid, flabby.

1. His f. winges when forth he did display, Were like two sayles SPENSER. Hence **Fla·gginess.**

Flaggy (flæ·gi), *a.*³ 1847. [f. FLAG *sb.*²] Readily split into flags, laminate.

Flagitate (flæ·dʒiteⁱt), *v.* 1623. [f. L. *flagitat-* ppl. stem, f. (ult.) root *flag-*: see FLAGRANT.] *trans.* To entreat earnestly; to importune (*rare*).

Carteret himself shall go and f. the Dutch CARLYLE. Hence **Flagita·tion,** earnest or passionate importunity.

Flagitious (flădʒi·ʃəs), *a.* ME. [ad. L. *flagitiosus*, f. *flagitium* shameful act; related to *flagitare.*] 1. Of persons: Guilty of or addicted to atrocious crimes; *loosely*, infamous. 2. Of actions, character etc.: Extremely wicked; heinous, villainous 1550.

1. Crimes shall.. whelm in ruin yon f. town POPE. 2. The f. life of the Pontiff BRYCE.
Hence **Flagi·tiously** *adv.* **Flagi·tiousness.**

Flag-man. 1666. [f. FLAG *sb.*⁴ + MAN.] †1. An admiral, a flag-officer –1713. 2. One who carries or signals with a flag 1832.

Flag-officer. 1665. [f. FLAG *sb.*⁴ + OFFICER.] *Naut.* An officer who carries a flag. a. An admiral, vice-admiral, or rear-admiral. b. In *U.S.* navy 1857–1862, an officer in actual command of a squadron.

Flagon (flæ·gǭn). [ME. *flakon*, ad. OF. *flacon* :— earlier *flascon* :— med. L. *flasconem*; see FLASK *sb.*] 1. A large bottle for holding wine or other liquors; now often, a glass bottle of flattened globular shape with a neck 1470. 2. A large vessel containing a supply of drink for use at table; now *esp.* one with a handle and spout 1512. 3. As much as a flagon will hold; also, a flagon and its contents 1602.

2. He set the f. on the table, and sat down SCOTT. 3. He had..drank many a flaggon JOHNSON.

Flagrance (flē·grăns). *rare.* 1612. [ad. L. *flagrantia*, f. *flagrantem* FLAGRANT.] = next.

Flagrancy (flē·grănsi). 1599. [See prec. and -ANCY.] 1. *lit.* Glowing or blazing condition. *Obs.* or *arch.* Also *fig.* 2. Of an offence, evil, etc.: Heinousness, enormity 1714.

1. Lust causeth a Flagrancie in the Eyes BACON. 2. The f. of the provocation H. WALPOLE.

Flagrant (flē·grănt), *a.* 1500. [ad. L. *flagrantem, flagrare*, f. root *flag-*, Aryan *bhleg-* to blaze.] 1. *lit.* Blazing, glowing. *arch.* Also *fig.* 1513. 2. Actually in progress. *rare.* 1818. †3. Of feelings, etc. (*rarely* of persons): Ardent, burning –1784. 4. †Resplendent 1500; †burning (from the lash) –1838; flaring 1858. 5. Of an offence, etc.: Glaring, scandalous, 'flaming into notice' (J.) 1706. †6. = FRAGRANT. –1611.

1. Forthwith burst The f. lightnings T. AIRD. 2. In moments of f. civil war HALLAM. Phr. *In f. delict* (= L. *flagrante delicto*): in the act. 3. F. Rage 1708, zeal COWPER. 4. T[utchin] f. from the lash POPE. 5. A f. violation of religion THIRLWALL. Hence **Fla·grantly** *adv.*

†**Fla·grate**, *v.* 1705. [f. L. *flagrat-* ppl. stem.] To burn; also (*intr.*) to DEFLAGRATE. –1756. Hence †**Flagra·tion**, burning; a conflagration.

Fla·g-root. *U.S.* 1851. [f. FLAG *sb.*[1]] The root of the sweet flag (*Acorus Calamus*); also the plant.

Fla·g-ship, fla·gship. 1672. [f. FLAG *sb.*[4] + SHIP *sb.*] A ship bearing an admiral's flag.

Fla·g-staff, fla·gstaff. *Pl.* **-staves.** 1613. [f. FLAG *sb.*[4] + STAFF.] A staff on which a flag is hung.

Fla·g-stone, fla·gstone. 1730. [f. FLAG *sb.*[2] + STONE.] 1. A flag suitable for paving, etc.; hence often in *pl.* = pavement. 2. Sandstone capable of being split up into flags 1812.

Flail (flēl), *sb.* [late OE. *fligel*, prob. ad. (ult.) L. *flagellum.* Cf. OF. *flael* (mod. F. *fléau*).] 1. An instrument for threshing corn by hand, consisting of a wooden staff or handle, at the end of which a stouter and shorter pole or club, called a swingle or swipple, is so hung as to swing freely. Also *fig.* 2. A military weapon resembling a threshing-flail, but usually of iron, and often having the striking part armed with spikes 1475. Also *transf.* 1475.

1. Nor did great Gideon his old F. disdain, After won Fields COWLEY. 2. *Protestant f.* (Eng. Hist.): a short staff, loaded with lead, carried by Protestants at the time of the 'Popish Plot' (1678–81).

Comb.: **f.-stone**, an elongated stone with a hole at one end, for use as a flail-swingle.

Hence †**Flai·ly** *a.* acting like a f. (*rare*).

Flail (flēl), *v.* ? ME. [f. prec. sb.] 1. *trans.* To scourge, whip; to thrash. 2. To strike with or as with a flail 1583. 3. To thresh (corn) with a flail 1821.

Flain, obs. pa. pple. of FLAY.

Flair[1] (flēᵊɹ). ME. [a. OF. and F. *flair*, f. *flairier, flairer* to smell :— pop. L. *flagrare*, var. of *fragrare*: see FRAGRANT.] †1. An odour, a smell. ME. only. ‖2. [mod. F.] Power of 'scent', instinctive discernment 1881.

Flair[2] (flēᵊɹ). Also **flare.** 1668. [Cf. OF. *flair.*] The ray or skate.

Flair, var. of FLARE.

Flake (flēk), *sb.*[1] ME. [? a. ON. *flake, fleke* hurdle, wicker shield. Prob. cogn. w. L. *plaga* net.] 1. A (wattled) hurdle; sometimes used as a temporary gate. Now *dial.* 2. A frame or rack for storing provisions ME.; a frame for drying fish, etc. 1623. 3. *Naut.* 'A small shifting stage, hung over a ship's side to caulk or repair a breach' (Smyth) 1867. 4. *Mining.* A framework of boards, used as a shelter against wind and rain 1653.

2. Flakes whereon men yeerely dry their fish 1623.

Flake (flēk), *sb.*[2] ME. [? f. (ult.) Aryan root *plag-* (cf. Gr. πλήγνυναι to beat), parallel with *plak-* (cf. Lith. *plakù* I beat), and allied with FLAW.] 1. A light fleecy tuft or mass; a flock; a fleecy streak. 2. A portion of ignited matter thrown off by a burning or incandescent body; a flash ME. 3. A scale 1500. 4. A thin broad piece peeled, split, or torn off from something 1591. 5. A stratum, lamina, or layer; a floe 1555. 6. A bundle of parallel threads or fibres; a lock or band of hair. *arch.* 1592. 7. A kind of carnation with striped petals 1727. 8. *attrib.*, as in *f.-tobacco*, etc. 1886.

1. As flakes fallen in great snowes CHAUCER. Flying flakes of foam KINGSLEY. 2. Huge Flakes of Flames DRYDEN. 3. Little Flakes of Scurfe ADDISON. 4. The shells..scaling off in flakes DARWIN. Flint Flakes having a fine cutting edge LYELL. Flakes of flesh 1894. 5. Flakes of ice 1820, of Salmon 1892.

Comb.: **f.-knife**, a chip of hard stone used in pre-historic times as a cutting instrument; **-stand**, the cooling-tub of a still-worm; **-white**, a pigment made from the purest white-lead in the form of flakes or scales.

Flake (flēk), *v.* ME. [f. prec. sb.] 1. *intr.* To fall †in or as in flakes. 2. *trans.* To cover with or as with flakes; to fleck 1602. 3. To chip; to break *away*, or take *off* in flakes or layers 1627. 4. *intr.* for *refl.* To come *away* or *off* in flakes 1759. 5. *trans.* To mark with streaks 1615.

4. Its stuccoed cupola was flaking off piecemeal 1877. **Flaked** *ppl. a.* arranged in or formed into flakes or layers; marked with streaks. **Fla·king** *vbl. sb.*

Flaker (flē·kəɹ). 1871. [f. prec.] 1. One who flakes flint for gun-flints. 2. An instrument for flaking flint 1891.

Flaky (flē·ki), *a.* 1580. [f. FLAKE *sb.*[2]] 1. Consisting of flakes, or of what resembles flakes. 2. Separating easily into flakes; flake-like 1672.

1. A snow, moist and f. KANE. 2. A flat, luscious and f. Fish like the Salmon 1758. Hence **Fla·kiness**, f. quality or condition.

Flam (flæm), *sb.*[1] and *a.* 1625. [See FLAM *v.*] †1. A caprice, whim –1672. †2. A conceit –1755. 3. A fabrication, falsehood; a piece of deception, a trick 1632; humbug; 'blarney' 1692.

2. Philips writes little flams .. on Miss Carteret SWIFT. 3. The letter's a f. 1888.

†B. *adj.* Counterfeit, fictitious, sham –1692.

Flam (flæm), *sb.*[2] 1796. [Prob. echoic.] A signal by beat of drum.

Flam (flæm), *v.* 1500. [? short for FLIM-FLAM.] †1. *trans.* ? To counterfeit, mock. 2. To deceive by a lie or trick, or by flattery; also with *off, up.* Now *dial.* or *U.S.*

2. A God, who is not to be flamm'd off with Lyes SOUTH.

Flamb(e, obs. ff. FLAME.

Flambeau (flæ·mbo). *Pl.* **-eaus, -eaux**, etc. 1632. [a. F. (= med. L. *flambellum*), f. *flambe* FLAME *sb.*] A torch; *esp.* one made of several thick wicks dipped in wax; a lighted torch.

An open grave, with four tall flambeaus..placed at the corners SCOTT.

Flamboyant (flæmboi·ănt). 1832. [a. F., pr. pple. of *flamboyer*, f. *flambe* FLAME *sb.*]

A. *adj.* 1. *Arch.* Characterized by waved lines of contrary flexure in flame-like forms (Gwilt): of the style prevalent in France in the 15th and early 16th c. Also *absol.* (quasi-*sb.*). Hence, *loosely*, Florid, floridly decorated 1879. 2. Of wavy form, like the outline of a flame. Said chiefly of a sword. 1876. 3. Flamingly or gorgeously coloured 1851.

1. Etchingham church, with its..curious f. window 1883. F. perorations 1883. 2. With massive face, f. hair GEO. ELIOT.

B. *sb.* A name of plants with flame-coloured flowers; e.g. *Poinciana regia* 1879.

Flame (flēm), *sb.* ME. [a. OF. *flambe, flamme* :— L. *flamma*; ? for **flagma*, f. root **flag-* in *flagrare* to blaze; or ? for **flama*, f. *flare* to blow.] 1. Vapour heated to the point of combustion; ignited gas. Also *fig.* b. *pl.* (with *the*) = fire 1483. 2. The condition of visible combustion. Also *transf.* of a wound, etc., inflamed; and *fig.* 1490. 3. *transf.* A bright beam or ray of light ME. 4. *fig.* Brilliance, brilliant colouring 1781. 5. Something resembling a flame of fire 1602. 6. *fig.* (of sense 1): a. A burning feeling or passion, *esp.* of love ME. b. quasi-*concr.* The object of one's love. Now only *joc.* 1647. †c. Brightness of fancy, power in writing –1702. 7. A name of certain British moths, e.g. *Geometra rubidata*, etc. 1819.

1. The flames ascended above my head SEWEL. Flame consists of particles of carbon brought to a white heat—an opinion of Sir Humphry Davy's BREWSTER. *fig.* Let me not liue..After my f. lackes oyle SHAKS. 2. [My heart] 'tis all on f. COWLEY. His face was all over in a f. 1790. 4. That jewel of the purest f. COWPER. 5. A f. of colour 1888. 6. a. So true a f. of liking SHAKS. b. Euphelia serves to grace my Measure; But Cloe is my real F. PRIOR.

attrib. and *Comb.*

1. General: as *f.-banner; -breathing; -bred, -robed, -uplifted, -winged; -shaped; -proof*; etc.

2. Special: **f.-bearer**, a humming-bird of the genus *Selasphorus*; **-bed** (*Steam-engine*), the fire-brick floor of a f.-chamber; **-bridge**, 'a wall rising from the floor of a furnace to cause the flame to impinge upon the bottom of the boiler' (Knight); **-chamber** (*Steam-engine*), 'the space immediately behind the bridge in which the combustion of the inflammable gases that pass over the bridge is..completed' (Rankine); **-engine**, an early name for the gas-engine; **-furnace**, one in which the ore or metal is exposed to the action of flame, but is not in contact with the fuel; **-kiln** (cf. *f.-furnace*). b. in names of plants with vivid scarlet or crimson flowers: **f.-flower**, a species of *Kniphofia* (*Tritoma*); **-tree**, (*a*) the *Sterculia acerifolia* of N.S. Wales; (*b*) the *Nuytsia floribunda* of W. Australia; (*c*) the *Butea frondosa* or palash tree.

Hence **Fla·meless** *a.* devoid of f.; burning without f. **Fla·melet**, a small f.

Flame (flēim), *v.* [ME. *flambe, flamme*, a. OF. *flamber, flam(m)er*; see prec.] 1. *intr.* To burn with a flame or with flames; to emit flames; to blaze. Also *fig.* 2. *fig.* Of the passions, etc.: To burn like flames. Of persons: To burn; to look angrily or passionately *upon.* Also with *out, up.* 1548. 3. *transf.* To glow like flame or as with flames ME. 4. *intr.* To move as or like flame 1633; *trans.* to convey by flaming ME. †5. To burn, set on fire –1737. †6. To kindle, inflame, excite, animate –1640. 7. To subject to the action of flame. 1875.

1. His left Hand which did f...Like twentie Torches *Jul. C.* I. iii. 16. *fig.* The Republic..flames out.. with Civil War 1793. 2. He flamed with indignation MACAULAY. 3. The rising sun Flames on the ruins DYER. 4. *trans.* In euery Cabyn, I flam'd amazement *Temp.* I. ii. 200. 6. Flam'd with zeal of vengeance inwardly, He ask'd [etc.] SPENSER, *F.Q.* V. i. 14.

Fla·me-co:lour. 1608. The colour of flame; a bright reddish yellow or orange. Hence **Fla·me-coloured** *a.*

Flamen (flē·men). ME. [a. L.; ? for *flagmen*, he who burns the sacrifices, f. root *flag-*.] 1. *Rom. Antiq.* A priest devoted to the service of a particular deity. Hence *transf.* of other priests. 2. The L. *flamen* and *archiflamen* (see ARCH-FLAMEN) were used by Geoffrey of Monmouth to denote two grades of priests in heathen Britain, who were alleged to have been replaced on the conversion of the island by bishops and archbishops. Hence pseudo-*Hist.* ME.

1. No person is elected to the office of one of the greater flamens, i.e. a f. of Jupiter, Mars, or Quirinus.. unless [etc.] MUIRHEAD. *transf.* Let the poor guardless natives never feel The flamen's fraud 1808.

Flaming (flē·miŋ), *ppl. a.* ME. [f. FLAME *v.*] 1. That flames; in flames or on fire. Also *fig.* 2. Burning hot, inflamed 1697. 3. *transf.* Flashing, glowing, brilliant; very bright or vivid ME. 4. *fig.* Highflown; startling; flagrant 1606. 5. Flamboyant ME.

1. A f. sword *Gen.* iii. 24. 2. Under a f. sun 1871. 3. †*F. fly* = FIREFLY. F. poppies 1863. 4. A f. attack against some poor man HELPS. Hence **Fla·mingly** *adv.*

Flamingo (flămi·ŋgo). 1565. [a. Pg. *flamingo*, Sp. *flamenco*, Pr. *flamenc*, f. Rom. *flama* FLAME *sb.* + suffix *-enc* (a. Teut. *-ing*). The Fr. name is *flamant*, lit. '*flaming*'. So called from the colour.] A bird of the genus *Phœnicopterus*, with bright scarlet plumage, long and slender legs and neck, and a heavy bent bill. Also *attrib.* in **f. flower** or **plant**, a name for *Anthurium scherzerianum.*

†**Flami·nical**, *a.* [f. L. *flamin-, flamen* + -IC + -AL.] Of or pertaining to a flamen. MILTON.

Flammable (flæ·măb'l), *a.* 1813. [f. L. *flammare* to set on fire; see -ABLE.] = INFLAMMABLE. Hence †**Flammabi·lity.**

†**Flamma·tion.** [f. as prec.] Exposure to fire. SIR T. BROWNE.

Flammeous (flæ·mĭəs), *a.* Now *rare.* 1646. [f. L. *flammeus* + -OUS.] 1. Of the nature of flame 1664. 2. Flame-like; hence, shining, resplendent 1646. 3. Flame-coloured 1656.

Flammi·gerous, *a. rare.* 1592. [f. L. *flammiger* + -OUS.] Bearing flame. Usu. *fig.*

Flammi·vomous, *a. rare.* 1663. [f. L. *flammivomus* (f. *flamma* + *-vomus*) + -OUS.] Vomiting out flame.

Flamy (flē·mi), *a.* 1494. [f. FLAME *sb.* + -Y[1].] 1. Of or pertaining to flame or flames; consisting of, or beset with, flames. 2. Flame-like 1626. †3. Effected by flame –1635.

Flan (flæn). 1868. [a. F. *flan*, orig. a round cake.] *Coining.* A disk of metal before stamping; a blank. b. (Also ‖flan) An open tart containing fruit, etc. (cf. FLAWN) 1846.

Flanch (flanʃ), *sb.*[1] Also **flanque.** 1562. [? a. OF. *flanche* fem., = *flanc* masc., FLANK.] *Her.* A sub-ordinary formed on each side of the shield by a line convex towards the centre, always borne double. Hence **Fla·nched** *ppl. a.*

Flanch (flanʃ), *sb.*[2] Also **flaunch.** 1726. [prob. f. FLANCH *v.*] = FLANGE 2.

Flanch (flanʃ), *v.* Also **flaunch.** 1776. [? with primary sense 'to extend laterally', f. F. *flanc* FLANK.] *intr.* To spread, widen out; to slope outwards towards the top. Also with *out, off.*

Flanconade (flæ·ŋkŏnēⁱ·d). 1664. [a. F., f. *flanc.*] *Fencing.* A thrust in the side.

†**Fla·nderkin.** 1694. [f. next + -KIN.] A Fleming. Also *attrib.* = Flemish. -1821.

Flanders (fla·ndəɹz). 1460. [ad. Du. *Vlaanderen* pl.; an ancient countship now broken up.] †Short for: **a.** *Flanders-lace*; **b.** *Flanders-horse.* 1718.

‖**Flâneur** (flanör). 1872. [F. f. *flâner* to stroll.] A lounger or saunterer, an idle man about town. Hence ‖**Flânerie** (flan'rī), the disposition or practice of a f.

Flang (flæŋ). 1858. A miner's two-pointed pick.

Flange (flændʒ), *sb.* 1688. [f. FLANCH *sb.*[2]] **1.** A widening or branching out, as of a vein of ore; the part that widens out. **2.** A projecting flat rim, collar, or rib, used to strengthen an object, to guide it, to keep it in place, to facilitate its attachment to another object, etc. 1735. **3.** Hence, any rim or projecting surface; also, a flattened-out disk for covering the end of a pipe or cylinder. Also *blank-f.* 1876.

attrib. and *Comb.*, as **f.-joint,** a joint in pipes, etc., made by two flanges bolted together; **-pipe** (*U.S.*), pipe in sections with flanges for fixing together; **-rail,** (*a*) *U.S.* a rail having on one side a flange to keep wheels, etc., from running off; (*b*) a rail with a flanged base.

Flange (flændʒ), *v.* 1820. [See FLANCH *v.*, and prec. *sb.*] **1.** *intr.* To widen out. Also with *out.* **2.** *trans.* To supply with a flange, form a flange upon 1873. Hence **Flanged** *ppl. a.* made or fitted with a flange.

Flank (flæŋk), *sb.* ME. [a. F. *flanc* :— pop. L. **flancum*, (according to Diez) a nasalized form of L. *flaccus*; hence, lit. 'the weak part of the body'.] **1.** The fleshy or muscular part of the side of an animal or a man between the ribs and the hip. †**2.** The belly; the womb -1481. **3.** *Farriery. pl.* A wrench or other grief in the back of a horse 1706. **4.** The side or lateral part of anything, e.g. of a building, etc. 1624. **5.** *Mil.* The extreme left or right side of an army or body of men in military formation; a wing 1548. **6.** *Fortif.* Any part of a work so disposed as to defend another by a flanking fire; *esp.* the part of a bastion reaching from the curtain to the face and defending the opposite face 1590. **7.** *Mech.* The straight part of the tooth of a wheel which receives the impulse 1842.

1. Marking-irons to brand the flanks of colts and cattle ROGERS. **4.** Mountains..With cities on their flanks TENNYSON. **5.** He scarce Had ended, when to Right and Left the Front Divided, and to either F. retird MILT. Phr. *To turn the f. of*: see TURN.

attrib. and *Comb.* (senses 5, 6), as *f. attack, company, defence, file, fire, march, movement,* etc.; *f.-wise* adv. Also, **f.-bone,** the ilium; **-wall,** a side wall.

Flank (flæŋk), *v.* 1548. [f. prec. sb.] †**1.** *intr.* To shoot on the flank or sideways. **2.** *trans.* To strengthen or protect on the flank. Also *fig.* 1596. **3.** To menace or attack the flank of; to take in flank 1599. **4.** To be placed or situated at the flank of. Also pass. *To be flanked by* or *with*: to have on the flanks. 1651. †**b.** *intr.* To border *on* or *upon* -1828. **5.** *trans.* To march past or go round the flank of; *U.S. slang,* to dodge, etc. 1872. **6.** Of a ship: To present the broadside to (a gale) 1762.

2. A strong intrenchment, flanked with bastions 1783. **3.** The ball [of one of our guns] flanked our own trenches 1782. **4.** A mountain, flanked by real precipices L. STEPHEN.

Flanker (flæ·ŋkəɹ), *sb.* 1550. [f. FLANK *v.*] **1.** Anything which flanks; *esp.* a fortification placed so as to command the flank of an enemy. **2.** One posted on either flank; esp. *Mil.* one of a body of skirmishers thrown out upon the flanks of an army, to guard the line of march 1827.

2. Their services as scouts and flankers proved invaluable 1863.

Flanker (flæ·ŋkəɹ), *v.* 1598. [f. prec. sb.] **1.** *trans.* To support or protect on the flanks; to defend or command from a flanker; to strengthen with flankers. **2.** *intr.* To make an attack on the flank 1603.

Flannel (flæ·nĕl), *sb.* 1503. [First recorded in Eng. Orig. *flannen*; ? a corruption of Welsh *gwlanen*, f. *gwlân* wool.] **1.** An open woollen stuff, of loose texture, usually without a nap. **b.** *joc.* A Welshman. *Merry W.* V. v. 172. **2.** *pl.* Underclothing, bandages, or garments of flannel 1722. **3.** *attrib.* Made of, or resembling, flannel 1585.

2. Phr. *To get* or *receive one's flannels* (Harrow slang): to get into the school cricket or football eleven. *Comb. f.-cake,* a thin griddle-cake.

Hence **Flannele·tte,**† (*a*) a very soft flannel measuring 28 inches in width; (*b*) an imitationflannel made of cotton. **Fla·nnelly** *a.* f.-like; also *fig.*

Flannel (flæ·nĕl), *v.* 1784. [f. prec. sb.] *trans.* To wrap in flannel; to rub with flannel. Hence **Fla·nnelled** *ppl. a.*

Flanning (flæ·niŋ). 1849. [? Cf. FLANGE *v.*] The internal flare or splay of a window-jamb or fireplace.

Flap (flæp), *sb.* ME. [f. next vb.; cf. Du. *flap* blow, lid of a can, etc.] **1.** The action of FLAP *v.*; *esp.* the motion of something broad and loose, or a blow given with it; also the resulting noise. †**2.** Something broad to strike with; e.g. a fly-flapper -1726. **3.** 'Anything that hangs broad and loose, fastened only on one side' (J.) 1522. **4.** Something broad and flat, hanging or working (vertically) on or as on a hinge; e.g. a valve 1565. **b.** *Anat.* †(*a*) The epiglottis -1802; (*b*) in fishes: The operculum or gill-cover 1881. **5.** A broad and loose piece of anything 1603. **6.** *Surg.* A portion of skin or flesh, separated from the underlying part, but remaining attached at the base 1807. **7.** *pl. Farr.* A disease in the mouth of horses 1587.

1. The f. of a swan's wing would break a man's leg GOLDSM. Slang phr. *In a flap*: in a state of agitation. **3.** Thou greene Sarcenet f. for a sore eye *Tr. & Cr.* V. i. 36. The flaps of a hat 1892. **4.** One Table, the F. broken 1754. *Tide f.*: a valve used to shut off the tide water from a sewer. **5.** The damn'd flat flaps of a shoulder of mutton FOOTE.

Comb.: **f.-fracture** = *compound fracture*; **-mouth,** one with broad hanging lips; **-sight,** in a rifle, one that turns up or down on a hinge.

Flap (flæp), *v.* ME. [prob. echoic; cf. *clap, slap,* etc.] **1.** *trans.* To strike with a sudden blow. *Obs.* exc. *dial.* **2.** To strike with something flexible and broad ME. **b.** *intr.* To make a flap or stroke 1581. **3.** *trans.* To toss smartly (now *dial.*) ME.; *intr.* to flop *down* (colloq.) 1660. **4.** *intr.* To swing or sway about loosely; to flutter 1529. **b.** *trans.* (*causal*) To cause to flap 1565. **5.** *intr.* Of a hat: To have the flaps swaying up and down 1679; *trans.* to pull down the flaps of 1751. **6.** *trans.* To move up and down, beat (the wings) 1567. Also *absol.* and *intr.* Also of wings. **7.** *intr.* (with adv.) To make way by flapping 1775.

1. †*To f. in the mouth* (*with a lie*): to tell a barefaced falsehood to. **2.** They flapp'd my light out as I read TENNYSON. **4.** The cheery deep-red curtains flapped and fluttered idly in the wind DICKENS. **5.** *trans.* They had flapped their hats over their eyes SMOLLETT. **7.** A slate-blue heron flapped fifty yards up the creek KINGSLEY.

Flapdoodle (flæpdū·d'l), *sb. colloq.* 1833. [Arbitrary.] **1.** 'The stuff they feed fools on'. MARRYAT. **2.** Nonsense; 'bosh'; also, a gewgaw 1878. Hence **Flapdoo·dle** *v. intr.* to talk nonsense.

†**Flap-dragon** (flæ·pdræ:gən), *sb.* 1588. [f. FLAP *v.* + DRAGON.] 'A play in which they catch raisins out of burning brandy and, extinguishing them by closing the mouth, eat them' (J.). Also, that which is thus caught and eaten -1622.

1. Thou art easier swallowed then a f. SHAKS. Hence **Fla·pdragon** *v.* to swallow, as a f. SHAKS.

Flapjack (flæ·pˌdʒæk). Now *dial.* or *U.S.* 1600. [f. FLAP *v.* (sense 3) + JACK.] **1.** A pancake; also, an apple turnover. **2.** *dial.* The lapwing 1847.

Flapper (flæ·pəɹ), *sb.* 1570. [f. FLAP *v.* + -ER[1].] **1.** One who flaps or strikes another. Hence (after Swift): One who arouses the attention or jogs the memory; a remembrancer. Also, a reminder. 1726. **2.** That which flaps 1570. **3.** A young wild duck 1773. **4.** A broad fin or flipper; the tail of a crustacean 1836. **5.** Applied to young girls who have not yet 'put their hair up': sometimes with implication of flightiness or lack of decorum (*slang* or *colloq.*) 1903.

1. [The absent-minded philosophers of Laputa] always keep a *F*...in their family..And the Business of this Officer is..gently to strike with his Bladder the mouth of him who is to speak, and the Right Ear of him..to whom the Speaker addresseth himself SWIFT, *Gulliver,* III. ii. 17.

Comb. **f.-skate,** *Raia intermedia.*

Flare (flēᵊɹ), *sb.*[1] Also (in sense 4) **flair.** 1814. [f. FLARE *v.*] **1.** A dazzling but unsteady light; a sudden outburst of flame. Also *fig.* Ostentation. **2.** *Naut.* = FLARE-UP 3. Also *transf.* 1883. **3.** *Photogr.* An indistinct image of the diaphragm in the camera 1868. **4.** *Shipbuilding.* Gradual swelling or bulging outwards and upwards 1833; *transf.* of a skirt, etc.

Flare (flēᵊɹ), *sb.*[2] *dial.* 1847. [?] The fat about a pig's kidney. Also *attrib.*

Flare (flēᵊɹ), *v.* 1550. [? Some compare mod. Norw. *flara* 'to blaze'.] **1.** *trans.* To spread out, display. Hence, To wave to and fro. 1550. †**2.** *intr.* To spread out conspicuously -1837. **3.** To spread or cause to spread gradually outwards 1644. **4.** *intr.* To burn with a spreading, unsteady flame; to shine as such a flame does; to glow with or as with flame. Also *transf.* and *fig.* 1632. **b.** *trans.* To light up with a flare 1745.

2. *Merry W.* IV. vi. 42. **3.** Their gunwales f. outwards W. IRVING. A skirt slightly flared about the hem 1930. **4.** Phr. *To f. up*: to burst into a sudden blaze; hence, to break out into sudden anger.

Flare-up (flēᵊrˌɒp). 1837. [f. the phr.; see prec. Usu. stressed on first syll.] **1.** A sudden breaking out into flame 1859. **2.** *fig.* A violent commotion 1837. **3.** *Naut.* A night-signal made by burning something highly inflammable 1858.

2. Some of our young citizens..got into a flare-up with a party of boatmen..a desperate row it was too HALIBURTON.

Flaring (flēᵊ·riŋ), *ppl. a.* 1593. [f. FLARE *v.*] **1.** That flares; †spreading out conspicuously -1641; glaring, showy, gaudy 1610. **2.** Of a vessel, etc.: That has its sides curving gradually outwards from the base 1627. **3.** Blazing irregularly; shining brightly and fitfully 1632.

3. F. tapers brightening as they waste GOLDSM. Hence **Fla·ringly** *adv.* (Dicts.).

Flash (flæʃ), *sb.*[1] ME. [Of echoic origin. Cf. PLASH.] A pool, a marshy place. Now *local.*

Flash (flæʃ), *sb.*[2] 1566. [f. FLASH *v.*[1]] **I. 1.** A sudden outburst of flame or light; a sudden, quick, transitory blaze. **2.** *transf.* The brief period during which a flash is visible 1625. **3.** A brief outburst of something regarded as resembling a flash 1602. **4.** Superficial brilliancy; ostentation 1605. †**5.** A brilliant or showy person; usually, a coxcomb, fop -1808. **6.** A preparation of cayenne pepper or capsicum with burnt sugar, for colouring spirits 1820. **7.** *U.S.* A brief telegraphic news dispatch.

1. Three flashes of blue Light'ning DRYDEN. Phr. *F. in the pan*: *lit.* an explosion of gunpowder without any communication beyond the touch-hole: *fig.* an abortive effort or outburst. **2.** *In a f.*: instantaneously. **3.** Flashes of Merriment *Haml.* V. i. 210.

II. (cf. FLASH *v.* I.) †**1.** A sudden movement of water; a splash; a breaker -1713. **b.** A sudden rush of water, let down from a weir, to take a boat over shallow places 1677. †**2.** *transf.* A sudden burst of rain, wind, etc. -1808. **3.** A contrivance for producing a 'Flash' (senses II. 1, 1 b.) 1768.

Comb.: **f.-flue,** the flue underneath an egg-end or similar externally fired boiler; **-lamp,** (*a*) *Photogr.* a lamp used to give a f.-light; (*b*) an electric torch (see TORCH *sb.*); **-light,** (*a*) a light so arranged as to give forth sudden flashes, used for signals and in light-houses; (*b*) *Photogr.* a sudden light, usually made by blowing magnesium powder through a small flame; **-pan,** (*a*) the pan for holding the priming in an old flint-lock; (*b*) a pan in which powder is flashed as a signal; **-point** = *flashing-point*; **-test,** a test to determine the flashing-point of kerosene, etc.; **-wheel,** a sort of paddle-wheel revolving in a chase or curved water-way, by which the water is raised from the lower to the higher level.

Flash (flæʃ), *a.* Chiefly *colloq.* 1700. [f. FLASH *sb.*[2]] 1. Gaudy, showy; 'swell' 1785. 2. Counterfeit, sham 1812. 3. *slang.* Knowing, wide-awake, 'fly' 1812. 4. Connected with or pertaining to the class of sporting men, or that of thieves, tramps, and prostitutes 1700. b. Thieves' cant, slang 1746.

1. F. fellows, who live nobody knows where 1785. Meurice's f. hotel 1841. 2. F. notes 1837. 4. Poor Tom was..Full f., all fancy BYRON. A f. crib 1839.

Flash (flæʃ), *v.* ME. [app. echoic; cf. *plash, dash, splash, slash.*]

I. 1. *intr.* Of the sea, waves, etc.: To rush along the surface; to rise and dash. Also with *up.* †2. *trans.* To dash or splash (water) *about, abroad, upon* –1813. 3. To send a flash or rush of water down (a river); also *absol.* Also, to send (a boat) down by a flash. 1791.

1. The Tivy..flashed in a sheet of foam through the chasm MEDWIN.

†II. *trans.* To slash; also, to dash –1548.

III. [app. transf. from sense I. 1.] 1. *intr.* Of fire or light: To break forth suddenly. Of lightning: To play. ME. b. Of a hydro-carbon: To give forth vapour at igniting temperature 1890. 2. To emit or reflect light suddenly or intermittently; to gleam 1791. 3. *trans.* To emit or convey (light, fire, etc.) in a sudden flash or flashes. Also *transf.* and *fig.* 1592. 4. *intr.* To come, move, or pass, like a flash of light 1590. 5. To break out *into* sudden action; to pass abruptly *into* a specified state 1605. 6. *trans.* To cause to flash; to kindle or illuminate with a flash 1632. 7. To express or communicate by a flash or flashes 1789. 8. *intr.* To make a display, show off. Now *colloq.* or *slang.* 1607. 9. a. *Glass-making. trans.* and *intr.* To expand into a sheet. Also *trans.* To cover (colourless glass) with a film of coloured glass. 1839. b. *Electr.* To make (a carbon filament) uniform in thickness, by plunging it when heated into a heavy hydro-carbon gas 1883.

1. Lightning flashed about the summits of the Jungfrau TYNDALL. Phr. *To f. in the pan*: *lit.* said of a gun, when the priming is kindled without igniting the charge; *fig.* to fail after a showy effort. 2. Flash'd all their sabres bare TENNYSON. Her eyes flashed 1857. 3. His eyes flashed fire 1854. 4. Ever and anon the rosy red Flasht through her face SPENSER *F. Q.* III. ii. 5. 5. Phr. *To f. up*: to burst into sudden passion or anger. 7. The intelligence was flashed next day all over England BURGON.

Fla·sh-board. 1768. [f. FLASH *v.* + BOARD *sb.*] A board set up on edge on a mill-dam, when the water is low, to throw more water into the mill-race.

Flasher (flæ·ʃəɹ). 1611. [f. FLASH *v.* + -ER.] 1. One who or that which flashes. †2. A person of brilliant appearance or accomplishment –1780. 3. a. 'A name of the lesser butcher-bird: see *Flusher*' (Ogilvie). b. A fish (*Lobotes surinamensis*) 1882.

Flash-house. 1816. [f. FLASH *a.*[2] + HOUSE.] A resort of thieves; also, a brothel.

Flashily (flæ·ʃili), *adv.* 1730. [f. FLASHY.] In a flashy manner.

Flashiness (flæ·ʃinės). 1626. [f. as prec.] The quality of being flashy.

Flashing (flæ·ʃiŋ), *vbl. sb.* 1573. [f. FLASH *v.*] 1. The action of FLASH *v.* 2. The process of letting down a flash of water to carry a boat over shallow places 1791. 3. *techn.* a. *Glass-making.* (See FLASH *v.* III. 9 a.) 1832. b. *Electr.* (See FLASH *v.* III. 9 b.) 1892.

attrib. and *Comb.*, as *f.-furnace* (sense 3 a); **f.-point**, the temperature at which the vapour given off from an oil or hydrocarbon will flash or ignite.

Flash-man. (Also as two wds.) 1789. [f. FLASH *a.*[2]] a. One who is flash; a companion of thieves; a fancy-man. b. A patron of the ring; a 'swell' 1812.

Flashy (flæ·ʃi), *a.* 1583. [f. FLASH *sb.*[2] and *v.* + -Y[1].] †1. Splashing –1611. †2. watery, frothy –1771; †insipid –1847; †*fig.* trifling; void of meaning, trashy –1745. 3. Giving off flashes; sparkling, brilliant. *lit.* and *fig.* Also, lasting only for a flash. 1609. b. Showy, but shallow; cheaply attractive 1690. †4. Excited –1781. 5. Showy; gaudy, glaring 1801. 6. Of persons: Fond of cutting a dash 1687.

3. A fine, f., disagreeable day SCOTT. b. A f. rhetorician DE QUINCEY. 6. Veteran topers, f. young men, visitors from the country HAWTHORNE.

Flask (flask), *sb.*[1] [OE. *flasce*, more usually *flaxe.* First recorded in med. L. in the form *flasco*, (according to Diez) for *vlasko, a metathesis of **vasclo*, from L. *vasculum.* ? Of Rom., or of Teut., origin.] †1. In OE.: A vessel for carrying liquor. 2. A case of leather or metal (or formerly of horn) to carry gunpowder in. Now *powder-f.* 1549. 3. A bottle, usually of glass, of bulbous shape, with a long narrow neck; often covered with wicker-work or plaited grass, etc., for protection, as in *Florence flasks*, in which wines, oil, etc. are exported from Italy. In verse occas. = bottle. Also, the contents of a flask. 1693. b. A flat bottle of glass or metal for the pocket; used to carry wine or spirits for a journey 1814. c. *Mining.* An iron bottle, of 76½ pounds capacity, in which quicksilver is sent to market 1872. 4. *Founding.* A frame or box used to hold a portion of the mould for casting. [? a distinct wd.] 1697.

Comb.: **f.-leather**, a fastening for a powder-f.; **-shell**, a mollusc whose shell is f.-shaped.

†**Flask**, *sb.*[2] 1578. [ad. F. *flasque*, var. of *flaque* beam, plank.] The bed of a gun-carriage. –1800.

Flask (flask), *v.* 1707. [f. FLASK *sb.*[1]] *trans.* To put into a flask. BROWNING.

Flasket (fla·skėt). 1460. [a. OF. *flasquet*, dim. of *flasque* FLASK *sb.*[1]] 1. 'A long shallow basket' (J.); also, a similar article made of metal. b. *dial.* A shallow washing tub 1814. 2. A small flask 1577.

1. They gathered flowers to fill their f. SPENSER. The silver stands with golden flaskets graced POPE.

Flat (flæt), *sb.*[1] 1801. [Altered f. FLET; orig. *Sc.*] 1. A floor or story in a house. 2. A suite of rooms on one floor, forming a complete residence 1824.

2. The rents of these flats seem to be extortionate 1887.

Flat (flæt), *a.*, *adv.*, and *sb.*[2] ME. [a. ON. *flatr* :— OTeut. **flato-*.]

A. *adj.* I. Lit. senses. 1. Horizontally level; without inclination. Of a seam of coal: Not tilted. 2. Spread out, stretched or lying at full length (*esp.* on the ground); usu. predicative (often quasi-advb.) with *fall, fling, lie,* etc. ME.; levelled, overthrown 1560; lying in close apposition 1559. b. *Paper-making.* Packed without folding 1890. 3. Without curvature, indentation, or projection of surface; plane; level ME. 4. *transf.* in *Painting.* Without relief or projection 1755. 5. Broad and thin; of a vessel, wide and shallow ME.

1. Houses..f. a-top SIR T. HERBERT. *F. arch* (Arch.): 'an arch in which the sides of the voussoirs are cut so as to support each other, but their ends form a straight line top and bottom' (Shipley). 2. What ruins kingdoms and lays cities f. MILT. *P. R.* IV. 363. 3. Thy..f. Medes *Temp.* IV. i. 63. *Chest, flat.* A chest which has lost its rounded front *Syd. Soc. Lex.* 4. *F. tint*: one of uniform shade. 5. Her feet are f. like a Ducks Feet 1697.

II. Senses of fig. origin. 1. Absolute, downright, unqualified, plain; peremptory. Now chiefly of a denial, contradiction, etc. 1551. 2. Prosaic, dull, uninteresting, lifeless, monotonous, insipid 1573. 3. Deficient in sense or vigour; stupid, dull, slow-witted 1599. 4. Wanting in spirit; dull. Also, out of spirits, depressed. 1602. b. Of trade, etc.: Dull, inactive 1831. 5. Of drink, etc.: Dead, insipid, stale 1607. 6. Of sound, etc.: Not clear and sharp; dead, dull 1626. b. *Mus.* Of a note or singer: Relatively low in pitch; below the true pitch. Of an interval or scale: = MINOR. 1591. 7. *Gram.* †a. Of an accent, a syllable: Unstressed –1612. b. Of a consonant: Voiced 1874. 8. *Comm.* Unvarying, fixed 1898.

1. That in the Captaine's but a chollericke word, which in the souldier is f. blasphemie SHAKS. A f. calm 1880. F. disobedience 1891. Phr. *That's f.*: an expression of one's final resolve. 2. How weary, stale, f., and vnprofitable Seemes to me all the vses of this world SHAKS. A dull, f. Presbiter preached PEPYS. My news falls f. DICKENS. 4. A f. market for maize. 5. A scent of f. ale GEO. ELIOT. 6. Arions Harpe, Now delicately f., now sweetly sharp DRUMM. OF HAWTH. *B, D, E,* etc. *flat*: a semitone lower than B D, E, etc. 8. The f. cost, a f. fare, a f. rate (*mod.*).

Comb.: **f. arch** (see I. 1, quot.); **-bedded** *a.* (*Geol.*), having a naturally plane cleavage; **-bill**, a bird having a broad flat bill, *e.g.* one of the genus *Platyrhynchus*; **-car** (*U.S.*), a railroad car consisting of a platform without sides or top; **f. chisel**, a smoothing chisel; **f. impression** (*Printing*), see *flat pull*; **f. nail**, a small sharp-pointed nail, with a flat thin head; **flat pull**, (*Printing*) 'a simple proof without under or over-laying' (Jacobi); **f. race**, a race over clear and level ground; **-rail**, 'a railroad rail consisting of a simple flat bar spiked to a longitudinal sleeper' (Knight); **f. rod** (*Mining*), one of a series of rods for communicating motion from the engine, horizontally, to the pumps or other machinery in a distant shaft; **f. rope** (for mining-shafts), one made by sewing together a number of ropes, making a wide flat band; **-sheets** *pl.* (*Geol.* and *Mining*), 'thin beds, flat veins, or blanket veins or deposits of some mineral usually different from the adjacent layers; often contact-deposits' (*Standard Dict.*); **-tool**, (*a*) 'a turning chisel which cuts on both sides and on the end, which is square' (Knight); (*b*) an elongated conical tool used in flat chasing; **-ware**, plates, dishes, saucers and the like, collectively, as distinguished from hollow ware. See also Main Words.

B. *adv.* †1. By horizontal measurement 1663. 2. Downright, absolutely, positively, plainly; entirely, fully, quite. Now *rare.* 1577. †3. Directly, exactly –1654.

2. Sir Harry contradicted him f. JENNER.

C. *absol.* and *sb.*[3] 1. *absol.* (quasi-*sb.*) That which is flat; e.g. the flat surface of a sword, etc. ME. b. Level ground. Also, A race-course without hedges or ditches. 1836. 2. A horizontal plane; a level as opp. to a slope 1605. †b. A geometrical plane; an even surface –1674. 3. *Building.* The horizontal part of a roof, usually covered with lead 1842. 4. *Mining.* A horizontal bed or stratum of coal, stone, etc.; a horizontal vein or portion of a vein of metal 1747. 5. A piece of level ground; a plain; also *fig.* ME.; a swamp 1610. 6. Usu. *pl.* A nearly level tract, over which the tide flows; a shallow, shoal 1550. 7. Something broad and thin (see quots.) 1545. 8. Something broad and shallow (see quots.) 1640. 9. *Ship-building.* a. *pl.* 'All the floor-timbers that have no bevellings in mid-ships' (Smyth) 1815. b. The partial deck or floor of a particular compartment 1869. 10. *Theatr.* A part of a scene mounted on a wooden frame which is pushed horizontally or lowered on to the stage 1807. 11. *House-Painting.* A surface painted so as to appear dead (see DEAD *a.*). Also, the pigment employed for this. 1823. 12. *slang.* A person who is 'only half sharp'; a simpleton 1762. 13. *Mus.* a. A note lowered half a tone below the natural pitch. b. The sign ♭ which indicates this lowering of the note. 1589.

1. The f. of the hand SCOTT, of the back DICKENS. b. In steeple-chases, hurdle races, and on the f. 1886. 5. The Cambridgeshire flats or marshes 1859. 6. The boat grounded on the flats a little to the east of the pier 1813. 7. *Flats*, a cant name for playing cards J. H. VAUX. Small drawings..greatly injured by the ..deep gold flats brought close up to them 1886. 8. a. A broad flat-bottomed boat 1749. b. A broad shallow basket for packing produce for market 1640. c. *U.S.* = *flat-car* (see A. *Comb.*) 1864. d. *U.S.* A low-crowned hat 1859. 13. Phr. *Sharps and flats*: the black keys of the keyboard of a piano; also punningly, sharpers and their victims.

Flat (flæt), *v.* 1607. [f. FLAT *a.*] †1. *trans.* To lay flat, raze, overthrow –1637. 2. *Naut.* To force (the sail) flat against the mast 1642. 3. *trans.* To make flat in shape. Now ordinarily FLATTEN. 1613. †4. *intr.* To become flattened –1725. †5. *trans.* To make dull, insipid, or spiritless –1710; *intr.* to become dull, depressed or feeble –1718. †6. *Mus.* To lower by one semitone –1685. 7. To cover (a surface) with lustreless paint; in *Carriage-building*, to remove the gloss from (a surface) 1842. 8. *U.S.* To reject (a lover) 1859.

4. U.S. *To f. out*: to become gradually thinner. Hence *fig.* to prove a failure, to collapse, etc. 5. *intr.* Their loyalty flatteth and deadeth by degrees FULLER.

Hence **Fla·tted** *ppl. a.*

Fla·t-boat. (Also as two wds.) 1660. 1. A flat-bottomed boat, used for transport, *esp.* in shallow waters. b. *U.S.* A large roughly-made boat formerly much used for floating goods, etc. down western rivers 1837.

Fla·t-bottom, *sb.* 1579. A boat with a flat bottom. Also *attrib.*

Fla·t-bo·ttomed, *a.* 1582. Having a flat bottom: chiefly of a boat.

Fla·t-cap. 1598. †1. A round cap with a low, flat crown, worn in 16–17th c. by London citizens –1891. †2. One who wears a flat-cap *esp.* a London citizen or 'prentice –1822. 3. A size of writing paper, 14 × 17 inches 1875.

Flated (flē¹·tėd), *a.* 1887. [as if pa. pple. of *flate v., f. FLATUS.] *Phonetics.* Of consonant-sounds: Produced by *flatus*, i.e. by breath without vibration of the vocal chords.

Flat fish, fla·t-fish. 1710. Fish of the family *Pleuronectidæ*, which includes the sole, turbot, plaice, etc.

Fla·t-foot. 1870. A condition of the foot in which the tarsus possesses little or no arch.

Fla·t-foo·ted, *a.* 1601. [Stress variable.] 1. Having flat feet (see prec.); splay-footed. 2. *U.S. colloq.* Downright, plain and positive 1846.

Fla·t-head. 1832. 1. One who has a flat head; *spec.* a member of a tribe of N. American Indians erroneously supposed to flatten their children's heads artificially 1837. 2. *Australia.* A fish of the genus *Ceratodus* 1832. 3. *U.S.* 'A snake which flattens its head, as a species of Heterodon' (*Cent. Dict.*) 1888. 4. *Arch.* An ornament of an archivolt with a flat uncarved surface 1883. Hence **Fla·t-hea·ded** *a.*

Fla·t-iron, *sb.* 1810. An iron with a flat face for smoothing linen, etc. Also *attrib.* Hence **Fla·t-iron** *v.* to smooth with a flat-iron.

†**Fla·tive,** *a.* 1599. [f. L. *flare* to blow.] Flatulent –1607.

Fla·tland. 1884. An imaginary land in space of two dimensions.

Fla·tling(s. Now *arch.* or *dial.* ME. [f. FLAT *a.* + -LING(S.]

A. *adv.* 1. At full length, flat. 2. With the flat side 1470. 3. Of motion: Horizontally 1598. 4. *dial.* Plainly, peremptorily 1847.

2. So that the blade struck me flatlings SCOTT.

B. *adj.* (*flatling.*) Of a blow: Dealt with the flat side of a weapon –1609.

†**Fla·tlong,** *adv.* 1570. [var. of prec.] 1. In or into a prostrate position –1632. 2. With the flat side; with the flat sides in contact –1648.

Flatly (flæ·tli), *adv.* ME. [f. FLAT *a.* + -LY².] 1. In a prostrate position. ? *Obs.* 2. a. with small curvature 1797. b. Without relief 1883. 3. Plainly, bluntly; decisively 1562; absolutely, completely, 1577. 4. Spiritlessly; without zest 1644.

3. F. against Scripture MILT. 4. We shall but f. relish the most poinant meates DIGBY.

Flatness (flæ·tnės). ME. [See -NESS.] 1. The quality or condition of being flat. 2. The quality of having a small curvature 1683. 3. 'Want of relief or prominence' (J.) 1702. 4. Plainness (of speech) 1887; absoluteness 1611. 5. Want of interest or incident 1882. 6. Deadness 1626. 7. Want of spirit or energy 1641. 8. Of an author, etc.: Prosaic dullness 1649.

2. The f. of the Earth at the Poles 1796. 4. The flatnesse of my miserie *Wint. T.* III. ii. 123. 6. Flatnesse of Sound BACON. F. in Cyder 1707. 7. The f. of being content with common reasons PALEY.

Fla·t-nose. 1636. A. *sb.* One who has a flat nose. B. *adj.* = **Fla·t-nosed** *a.* (1530) having a flat nose.

Flatten (flæ·t'n), *v.* 1630. (f. FLAT *a.* + -EN⁵.] †1. *trans.* To lay flat on the ground. *rare.* 1712. 2. = FLAT *v.* 3. 1630. 3. *intr.* (for *refl.*) To become flat or more flat. Also with *out.* 1721. Of a wind or storm: To decrease in force 1748. 4. = FLAT *v.* 5. 1631. 5. To lower (a note) in pitch; also *absol.* 1824. 6. To deprive (paint) of its lustre 1823. 7. *Aviation. To f. out* (intr.), to bring an aeroplane into a position parallel with the ground; also, of the aeroplane, to assume such a position 1913.

Phr. *To f. in a sail* (Naut.): to extend it more nearly fore-and-aft of the vessel.

Hence **Fla·ttener,** one who flattens; something used for flattening.

Fla·ttening, *vbl. sb.* 1726. [f. prec.] The action or process of making, or of becoming, flat. In *Glass-making*, the process of laying out (sheet-glass) flat 1879. b. Flattened condition.

attrib. and *Comb.* (chiefly in *Glass-making*), as *f. arch, furnace, iron, kiln, oven, stone, tool.*

Flatter (flæ·tər), *sb.* 1714. [f. FLAT *v.*] 1. A workman who makes something flat. 2. A tool used in making things flat, e.g. a very broad-faced hammer used by smiths 1874.

Flatter (flæ·tər), *v.*¹ [ME. *flatteren*, in the earliest instance a various reading for *flakeren*. Cf. ON. *flaðra*, MSw. *flakra, flikra* to flatter, all prob. of onomatopœic origin.] †1. *intr.* To show delight or fondness, e.g. as a dog does by wagging its tail –1607. 2. *trans.* To try to please or win the favour of by obsequiousness; to court, fawn upon ME. 3. To praise or compliment unduly or insincerely. Also *absol.* ME. 4. To gratify the vanity or self-esteem of; to cause to feel honoured ME. 5. To play upon the vanity of; to beguile with artful blandishments; to coax, wheedle 1500. 6. To beguile (sorrow, etc.); also with *to.* Now *arch.* 1580. 7. To inspire with hope, usually on insufficient grounds. Also, To foster (hopes). ME. b. To please with the idea *that.* Now chiefly *refl.* 1592. 8. To gratify (the eye, ear, etc.) 1695. 9. To represent too favourably; to exaggerate the good points of. Also *absol.* 1581.

1. Lyk to the scorpioun.. That flaterest with thin heed whan thou wilt stynge CHAUCER. 2. To f. kings, or court the great GOLDSM. 4. When I tell him, he hates Flatterers, He says, he does; being then most flattered SHAKS. 5. Priests and women must be flattered 1591. 6. F. my sorrows with report of it SHAKS. 7. Hope..doth f. thee in thoughts unlikely SHAKS. 9. Yet the Painter flatter'd her a little SHAKS. Hence **Fla·tterer,** one who flatters; *esp.* one who employs false praise to serve his own purposes.

†**Fla·tter** *v.*² ME. [Onomatopœic.] *intr.* To float, flutter –1803.

Fla·ttering, *ppl. a.* ME. [f. FLATTER *v.*] That flatters, in senses of the vb.

That f. tongue of yours wonne me *A. Y. L.* IV. i. 188. A flatt'ring dreame SHAKS. Opinions..f. to national vanity BURKE. A f. painter GOLDSM. Hence **Fla·tteringly** *adv.*

Flattery (flæ·tėri). ME. [ad. F. *flatterie*, f. *flatteur*, f. *flatter* to smooth down, to caress.] 1. The action or practice of flattering; false or insincere praise; adulation; blandishment. 2. *fig.* Gratifying delusion 1600.

1. F. is the destruction of all good fellowship DISRAELI. 2. My friend and I are one: Sweet f. SHAKS.

Flatting (flæ·tiŋ), *vbl. sb.* 1611. [f. FLAT *v.*²] 1. The action or process of making flat, *spec.* the process of rolling metal into plates; in *Glass-making*, the process of flattening a split glass cylinder. †2. The process of becoming flat –1675. 3. *Gilding* and *House-painting.* The action of FLAT *v.* 7. Also *concr.* The overlaid coat. 1823.

attrib. and *Comb.*, as *f. furnace, hammer, hearth, stone, tool* (chiefly in *Glass-making*: see 1); *f. coat, colour, white* (sense 3); **f.-mill,** a mill for flattening *esp.* one for rolling metal into sheets and forming the ribbon from which the planchets are cut in coining.

Flattish (flæ·tiʃ), *a.* 1611. [See -ISH.] Somewhat flat.

Flatulence (flæ·tiŭlėns). 1711. [a. F.; see FLATULENT and -ENCE.] 1. The condition of being charged with gas 1816. 2. The state of having the alimentary canal charged with gas; also, the tendency in foods to produce this state 1858. 3. *fig.* Windiness, vanity; pomposity 1711. So **Fla·tulency** (in senses 2, 3).

Flatulent (flæ·tiŭlėnt), *a.* 1599. [a. F., ad. mod. L. *flatulentus*, f. *flatus* a blowing; see -ULENT.] †1. Of a windy nature. Of a tumour: Turgid with air. –1745. 2. Generating or apt to generate gas in the alimentary canal 1599. 3. Attended with or caused by the accumulation of gases in the alimentary canal. Of persons: Troubled with flatulence. 1655. 4. *fig.* Puffed up, windy; empty, vain, pretentious 1658.

2. Peas and Beans are f. meat BLOUNT. 3. A f. Asthma 1655. 4. F. with fumes of self-applause YOUNG. Hence **Fla·tulent·ly** *adv.*, **-ness.**

†**Flatuosity** (flæ:tiu,ǫ·sĭti). 1597. [ad. F. *flatuosité*; see FLATUOUS and -ITY.] 1. = FLATULENCE 2. –1727. 2. *concr.* A quantity of wind, air, or gas –1601.

†**Fla·tuous,** *a.* 1580. [ad. F. *flatueux*, f. L. *flatus* a blowing; see -OUS.] 1. = FLATULENT 1. –1720. 2. Caused by inflation. SIR T. BROWNE. Hence †**Fla·tuousness.**

Flatus (flē¹·tŏs). *Pl.* **flatuses.** 1669. [a. L., f. *flare.*] ‖1. A blowing; a breath, a puff of wind 1692. 2. *Path.* Wind accumulated or developed in the stomach or bowels 1669. 3. A morbid inflation. *lit.* and *fig.* 1702.

Flat-ways, -wise (flæ·twē¹z, wəiz). 1601. [f. FLAT *a.* + -WAYS, -WISE.] With the flat side uppermost, foremost, or applied to another surface; not EDGE-WAYS.

Flaught (flǭt, *Sc.* flaχt), *sb.* Chiefly *Sc.* [ME. *flaȝt*, prob. f. same root as FLAKE *sb.*², q.v.] 1. = FLAKE *sb.*² 1, 2. 2. A sudden blast. *Sc.* 1802.

1. When your eyes wax red and dark, with flaughts of fire between SWINBURNE.

Flaunt (flǭnt), *sb.* Now *rare.* 1590. [f. FLAUNT *v.*] 1. The action or habit of making a display 1625. †2. Showy dress, finery –1611.

2. In these my borrowed Flaunts *Wint. T.* IV. iv. 23.

Flaunt (flǭnt), *v.* 1566. [? onomatopœic, after *fly, flout, vaunt.*] 1. *intr.* Of plumes, etc.: To wave gaily 1576. 2. Of persons: To move about or display oneself ostentatiously, impudently, or defiantly. Of things: To be extravagantly gaudy or conspicuous. 1566. 3. *trans.* To parade, show off 1827.

1. Orange and lemon trees f. over the walls 1789. 2. One flaunts in rags, one flutters in brocade POPE. 3. [The pirates] flaunted their sails in front of Ostia itself FROUDE. Hence **Flau·nting** *ppl. a.* waving gaily or proudly; making an obtrusive display. **Flau·ntingly** *adv.*

‖**Flautino** (flautī·no). 1724. [It.; dim. of *flauto* flute.] *Mus.* a. A small flute, piccolo, or flageolet. b. A small accordion 1876. c. An organ flute-stop 1852.

Flautist (flǭ·tist). 1860. [ad. It. *flautista.*] One who plays the flute; a flutist.

‖**Flauto** (flau·to). 1724. [It.; = 'a flute'.] A flute; also, a name for several organ-stops.

F. piccolo, an octave flute. *F. traverso*, a traverse, or German flute. DANNELEY.

Flavaniline (flē¹væ·niləin). 1882. [f. L. *flavus* yellow + ANILINE.] *Chem.* A yellow colouring matter, $C_6H_{14}N_2ClH$, obtained by heating acetanilide with zinc chloride for several hours to 250–260°.

Flavescent (flē¹ve·sėnt), *a.* 1853. [ad. L. *flavescentem, flavescere*, f. *flavus* yellow.] Turning a pale yellow; yellowish.

Flavin (flē¹·vin). Formerly also *flavine.* 1853. [f. L. *flavus* + -IN.] *Chem.* A yellow dye-stuff prepared from quercitron bark.

Flavo- (flē¹vo), comb. f. L. *flavus*, indicating a yellow tint.

Flavorous (flē¹·vərəs), *a.* Also **flavourous.** 1697. [f. next + -OUS.] 1. Full of flavour; 'fragrant, odorous' (J.) 2. *fig.* Having a flavour *of* (*rare*) 1885.

Flavour, flavor (flē¹·vəɹ), *sb.* ME. [app. an adoption of OF. *flaur, fleiur*, **flaor, fraor* smell; referred (ult.) by some to L. *fragrare*, by others to L. *flare.* As to *-our, -or*, see FAVOUR.] 1. A smell, odour. In mod. use: A trace of a particular odour. 2. The element in the taste of a substance which depends on the co-operation of the sense of smell; a slight peculiarity of taste distinguishing a substance from others; a trace of a particular kind of taste; a savour 1697. 3. *fig.* a. An undefinable characteristic quality instinctively apprehended. b. Piquancy, zest. 1699.

1. An earthy f. DICKENS. 2. The Flavor of Canary 1745. Oak..smoke gives the peculiar f. to that bacon MRS. PIOZZI. 3. The f. of Socratic irony JOWETT. Hence **Fla·vourless** *a.*

Flavour (flē¹·vəɹ), *v.* ME. [f. prec. sb.] †1. *intr.* To be odorous, savour, smell. ME. only. 2. To give flavour, taste, or scent to; to season 1545. 3. To try the flavour of. LAMB.

Flavoured (flē¹·vəɹd), *ppl. a.* 1740. [f. FLAVOUR *sb.* and *v.*] a. Mixed with something to impart a flavour. b. Having (a specified) flavour 1764.

a. Herbs, or flavour'd fruits DODSLEY. b. Nicely-flavoured mince-meat 1867.

Flavouring (flē¹·vəriŋ), *vbl. sb.* 1845. [f. FLAVOUR *v.*] 1. The action of FLAVOUR *v.*; also *attrib.* 2. *concr.* Something used to impart flavour 1845.

Flavous (flē¹·vəs), *a.* 1666. [f. L. *flavus.*] Yellow.

Flaw (flǭ), *sb.*¹ ME. [Perh. a. ON. *flaga*, recorded in sense 'slab of stone'. Cf. FLAKE *sb.*²]

I. †1. A flake (of snow); a flake or spark (of fire) –1597. 2. A fragment. *Obs.* exc. *Sc.* 1605. 3. a. A turf, or *collect.* turf 1811. †b. A slab of stone 1570.

1. 2 *Hen. IV*, IV. iv. 35. 2. But this heart shal break into a hundred thousand flawes *Lear* II. iv. 288.

II. 1. A crack, breach, fissure, rent, rift.

Also *fig.* 1606. **2.** A defect, fault 1586. **b.** *esp.* An invalidating defect in a legal document or procedure, a title, etc. 1616.

1. Or some frail China-jar receive a f. POPE. 2. Thou hast a Crack, F., soft Place in thy Skull BUTLER. Health without a f. C. BRONTË. b. A f. in the indictment 1883.

Hence **Flaw·less** *a.* **Flaw·less·ly** *adv.*, **-ness.**

Flaw (flǭ), *sb.*[2] 1513. [? :— OE. **flagu* = MDu. *vlaghe*, Sw. *flaga*, of same meaning; ? primary sense 'stroke' (Aryan root **plak-*: see FLAY *v.*).] **1.** A sudden blast or gust, usually of short duration. Also *fig.* **b.** A short spell of rough weather 1791. †**2.** *fig.* A sudden onset; a burst of feeling or passion; a sudden uproar or tumult –1676.

1. It blew..not only by squalls and flaws but a settled terrible tempest DE FOE. 2. O, these flawes and starts.. would well become A woman's story *Macb.* III. iv. 63.

Flaw (flǭ), *v.*[1] 1613. [f. FLAW *sb.*[1]] **1.** *trans.* To make a flaw in; to crack. Also *fig.* **2.** *intr.* To become cracked. †Also, to break *off* in flakes. 1648.

1. The Brazen Cauldrons with the Frost are flaw'd DRYDEN. *fig.* France hath flaw'd the League SHAKS.

Flaw (flǭ), *v.*[2] 1805. [f. FLAW *sb.*[2]] *intr.* To blow in gusts; *trans.* to ruffle as a flaw of wind does. *rare.*

Flaw, obs. f. FLAY.

Flawn (flǭn). *arch.* ME. [a. OF. *flaon* (Fr. *flan*) :—med. L. *fladonem*, a. OHG. *flado* flat cake :—W.Ger. **flaþon-*; cf. Gr. πλάθανον, πλατύς.] A kind of custard or cheese-cake. Also, a pancake.

Flawy (flǭ·i), *a.* 1712. [f. FLAW *sb.*[1] and [2] + -Y[1].] **1.** Full of defects. **2.** Gusty 1828.

Flax (flæks), *sb.* [Com. W.Ger.: OE. *fleax* :— OTeut. **flahsom*; ? f. OTeut. root **fleh-*, to plait :— OAryan **plek-, plok-*; cf. Ger. *flechten*, L *plectere*, Gr. πλέκειν. Some make the root *flah-* (:— OAryan **plak-*) as in FLAY *v.*] **1.** The plant *Linum usitatissimum* bearing blue flowers which are succeeded by pods containing the seeds known as linseed. It is cultivated for its textile fibre and for its seed. **2.** The fibres of the plant whether dressed or undressed. Also *transf.* ME. †**3.** As a material of which a candle or lamp wick is made; the wick itself –1632. **4.** Cloth made of flax; linen OE.

1. F...is called of the Northern men lynt TURNER. **Mountain F.,** (1) *Linum catharticum*; (2) *Erythræa Centaurium.* **New Zealand F.,** *Phormium tenax* (also called *f.-bush, -lily, -plant*), a native of New Zealand, the leaves of which yield a textile fibre. 3. The smoking f. shall he not quench *Isa.* xlii. 3. *attrib.* and *Comb.* **1.** General: as in *f.-culture, -fibre, -mill, -sandal, -thread*, etc. **2.** Special: as **f.-brake,** a toothed instrument for bruising f.-stalks; **-comb,** a f.-hackle; **-cotton,** cottonized flax; **-hackle,** an instrument for hackling or straightening the fibres of the flax; **-wench, -wife, -woman,** a female f. worker.

b. In plant-names, as **f.-weed,** *Linaria vulgaris*, toad-flax; etc.

Flaxen (flæ·ksĕn, flæ·ks'n). 1520. [f. as prec.]

A. *adj.* **1.** Made of flax 1521. **2.** Of the colour of dressed flax 1523. **3.** Of or pertaining to flax 1707.

1. A f. thread 1825. 2. All F. was his Pole *Haml.* IV. v. 196. 3. The f. trades of the United Kingdom 1875.

†**B.** *sb.* Material made of flax; linen; a linen cloth –1696.

Fla·x-seed, fla·xseed. 1562. **1.** The seed of flax, linseed. **b.** The plant *Radiola Millegrana* 1848.

Flaxy (flæ·ksi), *a.* 1634. [f. FLAX *sb.* + -Y[1].] Like flax; made of flax.

Flay (flēⁱ), *v.* *Pa. t.* and *pple.* **flayed.** [Com. Teut.: OE. *flēan* :— OTeut. **flahan*, f. Aryan root **plak-*, whence Gr. πλήσσειν to strike. Cf FLAKE *sb*[2], FLAW *sb.*[1] and [2].] **1.** *trans.* To strip off the skin of; to skin. **b.** To excoriate ME **2.** *fig.* and *transf* 1584. **3.** To strip or peel off (skin); also *transf.* ME.

1. No doubt, they would have flea'd me alive CONGREVE. b. With a back flayed and an eye knocked out MACAULAY. 2. To f. the people with requisitions FROUDE To f. an author 1884. 3. It [the frost] flaw d the very skin of my face EVELYN.

Hence **Flay·er,** one who flays or fleeces. **Flay·-flint,** a skin flint.

Flea (flī), *sb.* [Com. Teut.: OE. *flēah, flēa*; repr OTeut. **flauh-*, or more prob. **plau-* (cons -stem) cogn. w. FLEE *v.*] A small wingless insect (or genus of insects, *Pulex*, the common flea being *P. irritans*), well known for its biting propensities and its agility in leaping; it feeds on the blood of man and of other animals. **b.** = *flea-beetle* (see *Comb.*) 1805. **c.** *transf.* of small crustaceans which leap like a flea 1888.

A f. Hath smaller fleas that on him prey; And these have smaller still to bite 'em SWIFT. c. SAND-F., WATER-F. (see those wds.).

Phr. *A f. in one's ear*: a stinging or mortifying reproof, rebuff, or repulse: chiefly in phr. *to go (send, etc.) away with a f. in one's ear.*

Comb.: **f.-beetle,** a small leaping beetle of the genus *Haltica*, destructive to hops, grape-vines, turnips, etc.; **-louse,** a leaping plant-louse of the genus *Psyllidæ*; †**-seed,** *Plantago Psyllium*; **-wood,** bog myrtle, *Myrica Gale.*

Flea (flī), *v.* Also *dial.* **fleck.** 1610. [f. prec.] To rid of fleas.

Flea·-bane. 1548. [See BANE.] A name of plants: *esp.* **a.** the genus *Inula* (or *Pulicaria*); **b.** the genus *Erigeron*; **c.** *Plantago Psyllium* (from the appearance of the seed).

Flea·-bite. 1570. [f. FLEA *sb.* + BITE *sb.*] **1.** The bite of a flea, or the red spot caused by it. **2.** *fig.* A trifling inconvenience or discomfort 1582.

Flea-bitten, *a.* 1570. [f. as prec. + BITTEN *ppl. a.*] **1.** Bitten by (or full of) fleas 1621. **2.** Of the colour of a horse, etc.: Having bay or sorrel spots or streaks, upon a lighter ground.

2. [Pointers] of a flea-bitten blue or grey E. JESSE.

Fleak(e, obs. or dial. f. FLAKE.

Fleam, obs. and dial. var. of PHLEGM.

Fleam (flīm), *sb.* 1552. [a. OF. *flieme* (Fr. *flamme*), from late L. *flebotomum*, ad. Gr. φλεβοτόμον; see PHLEBOTOMY.] **1.** A surgical instrument for letting blood or for lancing the gums; a lancet. *Obs.* or *arch.* exc. in *U.S.* **2.** A lancet for bleeding horses 1616.

Comb. **f.-tooth,** a fleam-shaped tooth of a saw.

Fleamy, obs. and dial. var. of PHLEGMY.

Flear, obs. f. FLEER.

Fleawort (flī·wɒɹt). [OE. *flēawyrt*, f. FLEA *sb.* + WORT.] A name of plants: *esp.* **a.** *Inula Conyza*, and some species of *Cineraria* and *Erigeron*, supposed to destroy fleas; **b.** *Plantago Psyllium*, the seeds of which resemble fleas. Cf. FLEABANE.

Flebotomy: see PHLE-.

‖**Flèche** (fleʃ). 1710. [Fr., primarily 'arrow'.] **1.** *Fortif.* = ARROW 7. **2.** *Arch.* A slender spire 1848.

Fleck (flek), *sb.*[1] 1598. [Cogn. w. ON. *flekkr* blow, spot :— OTeut. **flekko-, -kon-*. Cf. L. *plaga* a blow.] **1.** A blemish, freckle, spot. Also *fig.* **2.** A flake, speck 1750.

1. *fig.* Flecks of sin TENNYSON. 2. Flecks and scraps of snow EMERSON.

Hence **Fle·ckless** *a.* without spot or blemish.

Fleck, *sb.*[2] Now *dial.* 1575. = FLARE *sb.*[2]

Fleck, (flek), *v.*[1] ME. [f. FLECK *sb.*[1]] To spot, streak, or stripe; to dapple, variegate.

Two Kids Both fleck'd with white DRYDEN.

Fleck, *v.*[2] Now *dial.* 1565. [? var. of FLAG *v.*[1]] *intr.* To fly low; to flit, flutter about. Also *transf.* and *fig.*

Flecker (fle·kəɹ), *v.* 1828. [f. FLECK *v.* + -ER[5].] To mark with flecks; to scatter like flakes.

†**Flect,** *v. rare.* 1548. [ad. L. *flectere.*] *trans.* To bend, *lit.* and *fig.* –1578.

Flection, -al, -less: see FLEX-.

Flector, (fle·ktǒɹ, -əɹ). 1666. [f. FLECT *v.* + -OR.] = FLEXOR.

Fled (fled), *ppl. a.* 1621. [f. FLEE *v.*] In senses of the vb.

Fledge, *a.* Now *dial.* [OE. **flycge*, :— WGer. *fluggjo-*, f. **flug-* root of **fleugan* to FLY.] **1.** Fit to fly; having the feathers developed, fledged ME. **2.** Furnished for flight. Const. *with.* Also *fig.* 1631.

2. All the fond hopes, which forward Youth and Vanitie are f. with MILT. Hence **Fle·dgeless** *a.*

Fledge (fledʒ), *v.* 1566. [f. prec.] **1.** *intr.* Of a young bird: To become fully plumed. Also *fig.* **2.** *trans.* To bring up (a young bird) until its feathers are grown. Also *fig.* 1589. **3.** To furnish or adorn with or as with feathers or down 1597. **4.** To feather (an arrow) 1766.

2. Shylocke..knew the bird was fledg'd *Merch. V.* III. i. 32. 3. The Iuuenall whose Chin is not yet fledg'd 2 *Hen. IV*, I. ii. 23. *fig.* Lightlier move The minutes fledged with music TENNYSON.

Fledgeling, fledgling (fle·dʒliŋ). 1830. [f. FLEDGE *a.* + -LING.] **1.** A young bird just fledged. Also *fig.* 1846. **2.** *attrib.*, as *f. poets.*

Fledgy (fle·dʒi), *a.* [f. as prec.] Covered with feathers. KEATS.

Flee (flī), *v.* *Pa. t.* and *pple.* **fled** (fled). [Com. Teut.: OE. *flēon* :— OTeut. **þleuhan.* Already in OE. confused with FLY.]

I. *intr.* **1.** To run away from or as from danger; to take flight. **2.** To withdraw hastily, take oneself off, go away. Const. *from, out of.* OE. **3.** To make one's escape ME. **4.** To disappear, vanish. Also with *away.* ME. **5.** Occas. used for FLY (= L. *volare*) OE.

1. The Rogue fled from me like Quick-siluer SHAKS. In vain for Life He to the Altar fled PRIOR. 2. Two years later he fled from society 1848. 4. As I approached, the morning's golden mist..fled SHELLEY. 5. Loues golden arrow at him should haue fled SHAKS.

II. *trans.* **1.** To run away from; to avoid, shun OE. **2.** To contrive to avoid, escape from, evade. Now *rare.* ME.

1. So fled his Enemies my Warlike Father SHAKS. F. fornication 1 *Cor.* vi. 18.

Fleece (flīs), *sb.* [Com. WGer.: OE. *flēos*; prob. conn. w. root of L. *pluma* feather, PLUME.] **1.** The woolly covering of a sheep or similar animal. **2.** The quantity of wool shorn from a sheep at one time 1460. **3.** Anything resembling a fleece 1513. **4.** *spec.* The thin sheet of cotton or wool fibre that is taken from the breaking-card 1853.

1. Its [the Alpaca's] f. is superior to that of the sheep in length and softness SIMMONDS. *Order of the Golden F.*: an order of knighthood instituted at Bruges in 1430 by Philip the Good, duke of Burgundy. 3. Witnesse this snow-white f. vpon my head 1600. Soft as the fleeces of descending snows POPE.

Comb. **f.-wool,** that shorn from the living animal.

Hence **Flee·ced** *ppl. a.* furnished with a f. **Flee·celess** *a.*

Fleece (flīs), *v.* 1537. [f. prec. sb.] **1.** *trans.* To strip of the fleece; to clip off the wool from. *lit.* and *fig.* 1628. **2.** To pluck or shear (the wool) *from* a sheep. Hence *fig.* Now *rare.* 1537. **3.** To strip completely of money, property, etc.; to exact money from; to rob heartlessly; to victimize 1577. **4.** To overspread as with a fleece or with fleeces 1730.

1. A Clergy, that shall more desire to f., Then feed the flock WITHER. 3. In bad inns you are fleeced and starved GOLDSM. 4. Stones..fleeced with moss WORDSW.

Fleecy (flī·si), *a.* 1567. [f. FLEECE *sb.* + -Y[1].] **1.** Fleeced, wool-bearing; having a fleece-like nap 1590. **2.** Consisting of or derived from fleeces; resembling a fleece; woolly 1567.

1. *F. star* = Aries; The fleecie Starr that bears Andromeda MILT. *P. L.* III. 558. 2. F. wealth MILT., skies, snows DRYDEN, waves LONGF.

Fleer (flī·əɹ), *sb.*[1] Now *rare.* ME. [f. FLEE *v.*] One who flees.

Fleer (flīəɹ), *sb.*[2] 1604. [f. FLEER *v.*] **1.** A mocking look or speech. †**2.** 'A deceitful grin of civility' (J.) –1727.

1. Marke the Fleeres, the Gybes *Oth.* IV. i. 83. 2. Such a sly, treacherous f. upon their face SOUTH.

Fleer (flīəɹ), *v.* ME. [? Scand.; cf. Norw. dial. *flira*, Da. dial. *flire* to grin, titter.] †**1.** *intr.* To make a wry face; to grin, grimace –1790. **2.** To laugh coarsely 1553. †**3.** To smile obsequiously *on, upon* –1673. **4.** To smile or grin contemptuously; hence, to gibe, jeer, sneer ME. **5.** *trans.* To laugh in derision at 1622.

1. Let her fleere, and looke a scew B. JONS. 2. He whispered to me..'This is a Tythe-goose'; and then fleer'd 1747. Hence **Flee·rer. Flee·ringly** *adv.*

Fleet (flīt), *sb.*[1] [OE. *flēot*, f. *flēotan* FLEET *v.*] **1.** A sea force, or naval armament; in mod. use, a number of ships under the orders of the admiral in chief, or of the flag-officer in command of a division. **b.** A number of ships or boats sailing in company 1697. **c.** *transf.* of persons, birds, or other objects (now *rare*) ME.; a number of vehicles or aircraft forming a definite group or unit 1889. **2.** *Fisheries.* A row of herring nets fastened together end to end 1879.

1. Phr. *To go round* or *through the f.*: to be flogged on board each vessel in the fleet.

Fleet (flīt), *sb.*[2] Now *local.* [OE. *flēot*, f. OTeut. *fleutan; see FLEET *v.*[1]] A place where water flows; a creek, inlet, run of water.

The Fleet: a run of water flowing into the Thames between Ludgate Hill and Fleet Street, now a covered sewer; hence, the prison which stood near it. attrib.: *F. books*, the records of Fleet marriages. *F. marriage*, one performed clandestinely by a Fleet parson in the Fleet; also *Fleet-Street marriage.* *F. parson*, one of the disreputable clergymen who were to be found about the Fleet ready to perform clandestine marriages. *F. register* = *Fleet book.*

Fleet (flīt), *a.*[1] 1529. [cogn. w. ON. *fliótr* swift; f. root of FLEET *v.*[1]] 1. Swift in onward movement; nimble. Said primarily of living beings, their movements, etc.; hence of things viewed as self-moving, thoughts, etc. Not in colloq. use. 2. Evanescent, shifting; not lasting. *poet.* 1812.

1. Their conceites haue winges, Fleeter then arrowes, bullets, wind *L. L. L.* v. ii. 261. Their horses..f. and strong MILT. *Comb.* **f.-foot** *a. poet.* f. of foot; also *fig.* Hence **Flee·tly** *adv.* **Flee·tness**, swiftness, transitoriness.

Fleet (flīt), *a.*[2] *dial.* and *Agric.* 1621. [Perh. (ult.) f. root of FLEET *v.*[1]] Shallow.

Fleet (flīt), *v.*[1] [Com. Teut.: OE. *flēotan* to float:— OTeut. *fleutan, f. pre-Teut. root *pleud-, ploud-, plud-, an extended form of OAryan *pleu-, plu- (cf. Gr. πλέειν, L. *pluere*, etc.).]

I. 1. *intr.* To float; †to sail. †2. To drift. Also *transf.* –1744. †3. To swim –1600. †4. Of a person: To be afloat; to travel by water; to sail –1725. †5. To fluctuate, waver –1638.

1. Oil doth naturally f. above FRENCH.

II. †1. To flow –1630. †2. To overflow, abound –1526. 3. †a. To waste *away*; to fall to pieces –1661. b. To fade or die out. *Obs.* or *arch.* 1576. 4. To glide away like a stream; to slip away; hence, to flit, migrate, remove, vanish ME. b. *trans.* To pass, while away (time). *rare.* 1600. 5. *intr.* To move swiftly, to flit, fly ME.

1. Still gliding forth, altho' it f. full slow 1630. 3. b. How all the other passions f. to ayre SHAKS. 4. Our souls are fleeting hence MARLOWE. b. Many yong Gentlemen .. f. the time carelessly SHAKS.

III. *Naut. trans.* To change the position of, shift (a block, rope, etc.). Also *absol.* 1769.

Fleet (flīt), *v.*[2] ME. [prob. f. OE. *flēt* cream, f. root of *flēotan* FLEET *v.*[1]; or ? a use of FLEET *v.*[1]] *trans.* To take off that which floats upon the surface of a liquid; *esp.* to skim (milk, the cream from milk). Also *transf.* and *fig.*

Flee·ten, *a.* 1618. [Altered f. FLOTTEN.] 1. (See FLOTTEN.) 2. Of the colour of skimmed milk 1618. 3. quasi-*sb.* Skimmed milk. WEBSTER.

Fleeting (flī·tiŋ), *vbl. sb.* Now *dial.* ME. [f. FLEET *v.*[2]] The action of skimming a liquid, *esp.* milk. b. *concr.* in *pl.* Skimmings, curds 1611. *Comb.* **f.-milk**, skim-milk.

Fleeting (flī·tiŋ), *ppl. a.* OE. [f. FLEET *v.*[1]] That fleets; †shifting, unstable; changeable, inconstant –1650; passing swiftly by 1600; gliding swiftly away 1697; transitory 1563.

The f. Moone No Planet is of mine *Ant. & Cl.* v. ii. 240. The f. yeare SHAKS. Pleasure, the most f. of all things JOWETT. Hence **Flee·ting-ly** *adv.*, **-ness.**

Flegm, Flegm-: see **Phlegm, Phlegm-.**

†**Fleme**, *v.* [OE. *flieman*, f. *flēam*:— OTeut. type *flauhmo-, f. *flauh-* ablaut-var. of *fleuh-* to FLEE.] 1. *trans.* To cause to flee; hence, to banish, exile –1814. 2. *intr.* To flee, run away. *rare.* ME. only.

1. Lawe is nye flemede out of this contree HOCCLEVE. Hence †**Fle·mer**, one who puts to flight.

Fleming (fle·miŋ). ME. [a. MDu. *Vlāming*, f. *Flām-* (whence *Flanders*) + -ING[3].] 1. A native or inhabitant of Flanders. †2. A Flemish vessel. DRAKE.

Flemish (fle·miʃ), *a.* 1488. [ad. MDu. *Vlaemisch*; see FLEMING and -ISH.] 1. Of or belonging to Flanders or the Flemings. *absol.* The Flemish language 1727. 2. Resembling a Fleming 1598.

2. This F. drunkard *Merry W.* II. i. 23.
Comb.: **F. account**, one showing a deficit; **F. bond** (see BOND *sb.*[1]); **F. brick**, a hard yellowish brick, used for paving; **F. eye** (*Naut.*), 'a kind of eye-splice in which the ends are scraped down, tapered, passed oppositely, marled, and served over with spun yarn' (Smyth); **F. horse** (*Naut.*), a foot-rope at the yard-arms of topsail yards; **F. point**, 'a Guipure Lace, also known as Point de Brabant' (Caulfield); **F. stitch**, 'one of the Fillings in Honiton Lace' (*Ibid.*).

Flench, flinch, flense (flenʃ, flinʃ, flens), *v.* 1814. [a. Du. *flense* of same meaning.] 1. *trans.* To cut up and slice the fat from (a whale or seal). 2. To flay or skin (a seal) 1874.

Flesh (fleʃ), *sb.* [Com. WGer. and Scand.: OE. *flǽsc*, corresp. to OS. *flêsk*, OHG. *fleisc* (Ger. *fleisch*), of the same meaning, SW. *fläsk*, Da. *flesk* bacon.]

I. 1. The soft substance, *esp.* the muscular parts, of an animal body; that which covers the framework of bones. 2. *transf.* The soft pulpy substance of fruit, or a plant; that part which encloses the core or kernel, *esp.* when eatable. So Gr. σάρξ, L. *caro*, F. *chair.* 1573. 3. Put for: Quantity or excess of flesh; hence, embonpoint 1548. 4. Animal food; in recent use, butcher's meat, to the exclusion of poultry, etc., as well as of *fish* (see FISH *sb.*[1]). Somewhat *arch.* OE. 5. The visible surface of the body 1606.

1. Phr. *Raw f.*: that exposed by removal of the skin. *F. and fell*: the whole substance of the body; hence, as quasi-*advb.* phr.: entirely. *Proud f.*: the overgrowth of the granulations which spring up on a wound; also *fig.* *To go after* or *follow strange f.*: a Biblical expression referring to unnatural crime. 3. A beautefull Prince, beginninge a littel to growe in f. HALL. 4. No maner of person shall eate any Fleshe on the same [Fishe] daye 1562. 5. Although my f. be tawny 1657.

II. Fig., etc. uses (chiefly Biblical). 1. That which has corporeal life OE. 2. The physical frame of man; the body OE. b. The body (of Christ), as spiritually eaten by believers; also, the bread in the sacrament of the Lord's Supper OE. 3. Human nature with its corporeal necessities and limitations OE. 4. The sensual appetites and inclinations. In theol. language, the depraved nature of man in its conflict with the promptings of the Spirit. ME.

1. What f., what person could be saued PRYNNE. Phr. *All f.* (*omnis caro*, Vulg. = Hebraistic Gr. πᾶσα σάρξ): all animals; in narrower sense, all mankind. 2. In my fleysch y schal se god ME. Phr. *In (the) f.*: in a bodily form; also, in life, living. *After the f.*: in bodily likeness. 3. The thousand Naturall shockes That F. is heyre too *Haml.* III. i. 63. 4. I know what F. will object FULLER. *Sins of the f.*: esp. those of unchastity.
Phr. *One's (own) f.*: one's near kindred or descendants. Now *rare* exc. in FLESH AND BLOOD. *One f.*: said (after *Gen.* ii. 24) of husband and wife to express the closeness of the marriage tie.
attrib. and *Comb.* 1. General: as *f.-diet*, †*-market*, *-tint*; *-eater*, *-former*; *-gorged*; *-pink*, *-red*; etc. 2. Special: **f.-bird**, a carnivorous bird; **-brush**, a brush used for rubbing the body, in order to excite the circulation; **-flea**, the chigoe, *Sarcopsylla penetrans*; **-glove**, a glove used to stimulate the circulation by rubbing the f.; **-hook**, a hook for removing meat from the pot; **-juice**, 'the reddish acid liquid which is contained in dead muscle' (*Syd. Soc. Lex.*); **-knife** = *fleshing-knife*; **-meat**, flesh as an article of food; **-quake** [after EARTHQUAKE], a trembling of the body; **f. side**, the side of a skin that was nearest the f., opp. to *grain side*; **-taster**, an officer who tests the wholesomeness of meat; **-traffic**, 'the slave trade' (Smyth); **-worm**, a worm that feeds on f.; also the *Trichina spiralis*; **-wound**, a wound that does not extend beyond the f.

Flesh (fleʃ), *v.* 1530. [f. prec. sb.] I. *trans.* To give a taste of the flesh of the game killed to (a hawk or hound), in order to incite it to the chase. Hence, to render (an animal) eager for prey by the taste of blood. 2. *transf.* and *fig.* To initiate in or inure to bloodshed or warfare; to render inveterate, harden 1530; to incite, animate (? *Obs.*) 1573. 3. To plunge (a weapon) in the flesh, esp. for the first time. Also *transf.* and *fig.* 1592. 4. To clothe with flesh (chiefly *fig.*) 1661; †to fatten –1682. 5. *Leather-manuf.* To remove the adhering flesh from (a skin or hide) 1777.

1. An old bitten cur..fleshed to the game T. ADAMS. 2. Flesht and blooded in the slaughter of many thousands of the English nation 1646. Fleshing men in leudness and wickedness H. MORE. 3. Impatient strait to f. his virgin-sword POPE.

Flesh and blood. OE. [See prec. and BLOOD.] 1. The body. b. Mankind, an individual man or men OE. c. Humanity 1450. 2. (One's) near kindred ME. 3. The plant *Potentilla Tormentilla* 1853.

1. *In flesh and blood*: in a bodily form. *To take flesh and blood*: to become incarnate. b. *To be flesh and blood*: to have human feelings and weaknesses. c. Things which flesh and blood cannot bear DICKENS.

Fle·sh-colour. 1611. [f. FLESH *sb.* + COLOUR.] The colour of the flesh (of a 'white' human being) as seen through the skin; 'a light pink with a little yellow' (O'Neill). Hence **Fle·sh-coloured** *a.*

Fleshed (fleʃt), *ppl. a.* ME. [f. FLESH *sb.* and *v.*] 1. Clothed or furnished with flesh. 2. [Cf. F. *acharné.*] Inured to bloodshed; initiated; animated by hatred 1591.

2. Flesht Villaines, bloody Dogges *Rich. III*, IV. iii. 6.

Flesher (fle·ʃəɹ). Chiefly *Sc.* ME. [f. FLESH *sb.* + -ER.] 1. A butcher. 2. *U.S.* A fleshing-knife 1885.

Fle·sh-fly. ME. [f. FLESH *sb.* + FLY.] 1. A fly which deposits its eggs (or larvæ) in dead flesh; a blow-fly. 2. *fig.* of persons 1532.

2. These flesh-flies of the land, Who fasten without mercy on the fair COWPER.

Fle·shhood. *arch.* ME. [f. FLESH *sb.* + -HOOD.] The condition of being in the flesh; incarnation.

God .. who hast thyself Endured this f. MRS. BROWNING.

Fleshiness (fle·ʃinės). ME. [f. FLESHY *a.* + -NESS.] The state of being fleshy; fullness of flesh; *concr.* a fleshy growth.

Fleshing (fle·ʃiŋ), *vbl. sb.* 1576. [f. FLESH *v.* and *sb.*] 1. The action of FLESH *v.* (sense 1). 2. *Leather-manuf.* The action of scraping off the adhering flesh from a skin; also *pl.* that which is scraped off 1777. 3. *pl.* Flesh-coloured tights, as worn upon the stage 1838.

Comb. **f.-knife**, a large two-handled implement with a blunt edge, used in fleshing skins.

Fleshless (fle·ʃlės), *a.* 1586. [-LESS.] Without flesh; lean.

Fleshliness (fle·ʃlinės). [OE. *flǽsclicness*; see FLESHLY and -NESS.] 1. †a. In OE.: Incarnate condition. b. Carnality ME. †2. Fleshiness –1611.

†**Fle·shling.** *rare.* 1548. [see -LING.] A fleshly-minded person.

Fleshly (fle·ʃli). [OE. *flǽsclic*, f. *flǽsc*, FLESH + -*lic*, -LY[1].]

A. *adj.* 1. Of or pertaining to the flesh, i. e. the body; = CARNAL. 2. = FLESHY 1, 2, ME. †3. Of a hound: Fond of flesh. *rare.* 1576.

1. The fleschely arm WYCLIF. F. fansey 1550, lethargie 1602, reasonings CROMWELL. 2. To fatt and fleshlye 1562. The f. heart of man MARLOWE. F. integuments KANE.

†B. *adv.* 1. Corporeally; materially as opp. to spiritually –1635. 2. Carnally, sensually –1612.

Fleshment (fle·ʃmėnt). [see -MENT.] The action of 'fleshing'; hence, the excitement resulting from a first success. *Lear*, II. ii. 130.

†**Fle·shmonger.** OE. [see MONGER.] 1. A butcher –1597. 2. A fornicator, a pander –1624.

Fle·sh-pot. 1535. A pot in which flesh is boiled. Hence *pl.* Luxuries or advantages regarded with regret or envy.

When we sat by y^e flesh pottes, and had bred ynough to eate COVERDALE *Ex.* xvi. 3.

Fleshy (fle·ʃi), *a.* ME. [f. FLESH *sb.* + -Y[1].] 1. Well furnished with flesh; fat, plump. 2. Of, pertaining to, or consisting of flesh; without bone ME. b. Of a plant, leaf, fruit, etc.: Pulpy, not fibrous 1577. †3. = CARNAL 1, 3. –1668. 4. Resembling flesh 1555.

1. A fine, f., comfortable dame W. IRVING. 2. F. morsels DRYDEN. The f. tabernacle HAWTHORNE. b. The whole body of the Figge is fleshie 1577. 3. F. desires 1668. 4. A fleshie taste 1665.

Fletch (fletʃ), *v.* 1635. [? corrupt f. FLEDGE *v.*] *trans.* To fit (an arrow) with a feather. Also *fig.*

He .. fletches them [his curses] with a prophane classical parody WARBURTON.

Fletcher (fle·tʃəɹ). ME. [ad. OF. *flecher*, *flechier*, f. *flèche*; see FLÈCHE.] 1. One who makes or deals in (bows and) arrows. *Obs.* exc. *Hist.* or *arch.* †2. A bowman MORE.

‖**Fleur** (flör). 1841. [F.] An ornamental flower. Hence **Fleured** *ppl. a.* adorned with a f. or fleurs.

Fleur-de-lis (flör də lī, līs), **flower-de-luce** (flauəɹ dĭ lū·s). *Pl.* **fleurs-de-lis, -luce, flower de luces.** [The F. form (= 'lily-flower') is scarcely found in Eng. before the 19th c. The form *flower-de-luce* now survives only as a poetical archaism and in *U.S.* It is prob. of fanciful origin.] 1. The flower of a plant of the genus *Iris* (esp. *I. pseudacorus*); also, the plant. 2. The heraldic lily; a device supposed by some to have represented an iris, by others the top of a sceptre, or that of a battle-axe, or other weapon ME. b. The royal arms of France; hence the French royal family, the French flag (before 1789), the French nation or government ME. 3. The representation of a heraldic fleur-de-lis on any article. Also (*Fr. Hist.*) a brand-mark on a criminal 1475.

Fleuret[1] (flūə·rėt), ‖**fleurette** (flöre·t). 1811. [ad. F. *fleurette*, dim. of *fleur*.] An ornament like a small flower.

Fleuret[2]. 1648. [a. F. *fleuret* = It. *fioretto*, dim. of *fiore* flower; so called from the button (cf. BUTTON 2) at the point.] *Fencing.* A fencing-foil.

‖**Fleuron** (flöroṅ). ME. [a. F., f. *fleur*.] 1. A flower-shaped ornament, used *esp.* in architecture or printing, on coins, etc. 2. Puffs of pastry-work for garnishing 1724. Hence **Fleuronée** *a.* = BOTONÉ.

Fleury (flūə·ri), **flory** (flōə·ri), *a.* ME. [ad. F. *fleuré*, *-ée*, OF. *floré*, f. *fleur*.] *Her.* Decorated with fleurs-de-lis; *esp.* of a cross: Having its arms tipped with fleurs-de-lis.

Flew (flū). 1575. [?] Usu. *pl.* The large chaps of a deep-mouthed hound (e. g. the blood-hound). Hence **Flewed** *ppl. a.* having flews (of a stated kind).

Flew, pa. t. of FLY *v.*

Flex (fleks), *sb.* 1907. [abbrev. of FLEXIBLE.] Flexible insulated wire.

Flex (fleks), *v.* 1521. [f. L. *flex-*, ppl. stem of *flectere*.] *trans.* To bend. Now *scientific*.

A single muscle..flexes the thigh 1845. Hence **Flexed** (flekst) *ppl. a.* bent; now only *Her.* and in scientific use.

Flex(e, obs. form of FLAX.

†**Flexa·nimous,** *a.* 1621. [f. L. *flexanimus*, f. *flex-* (see FLEX *v.*) + *animus* + -OUS.] Having power to bend or influence the mind –1672.

Flexibility (fleksibi·lĭti). 1616. [a. F. *flexibilité*, ad. L. *flexibilitatem*; see FLEXIBLE and -ITY.] 1. The quality of being flexible; pliancy 1616; adaptability; freedom from stiffness or rigidity 1783. 2. Of the voice or fingers: Capacity for rapid and varied execution or delivery. Also *pl.* 1795.

1. The f. and instability of that gentleman's nature CLARENDON. F. of limb 1859, of intelligence 1865. 2. F. of throat 1795.

Flexible (fle·ksib'l), *a.* ME. [a. F., ad. L. *flexibilis*, f. *flex-* ppl. stem of *flectere* to bend.] 1. Capable of being bent, admitting of change in figure without breaking; yielding to pressure, pliable, pliant 1548. 2. Willing or disposed to yield to influence or persuasion; easily led, tractable ME. 3. Capable of modification or adaptation; pliant, supple 1643.

1. When the splitting winde Makes f. the knees of knotted Oakes SHAKS. 2. Our judge, therefore, must not be partial, f., nor ignorant 1533. The tender and f. age of her son 1642. 3. A more f. rule of judgement MYERS. F. politics SYD. SMITH. Hence **Fle·xibleness,** flexibility. **Fle·xibly** *adv.*

Flexile (fle·ksil), *a.* Now *rare.* 1633. [ad. L. *flexilem*.] 1. Easily bending or bent, pliant, supple, flexible. Of the features: Mobile. 2. *transf.* and *fig.* a. Yielding, tractable 1651. b. Versatile 1744.

Flexion, flection (fle·kʃən). 1603. [ad. L. *flectionem*. Orig. spelt *flexion* in Eng.; *flection* (first in 18th c.) follows *direction*, etc.] 1. The action of bending, curvature; bent condition; an instance of this 1656. b. *esp.* The bending of a limb or joint by the action of the flexor muscles. Cf. EXTENSION. 1615. 2. †Alteration, change, modification –1655; inflexion 1758. 3. *concr.* A bend, curve. Also, a joint. 1670. 4. *Gram.* Modification of the form of a word; *esp.* inflexion 1605.

2. Flections and intonations of the voice GROTE. 4. The f. or conjugation of the verb DE FOE.

Hence **Fle·xional, flect-** *a.* of, pertaining to, or of the nature of f., *esp.* in *Grammar*. Also, of a language: Possessed of, or based upon flexions. **Fle·xionless, flect-** *a.* devoid of f. or flexions; only in grammatical sense.

†**Fle·xive,** *a.* 1629. [f. L. *flex-*, *flectere* + -IVE.] Tending to bend, flexible –1791.

Flexor (fle·ksəɪ). 1615. [a. mod. L. *flexor*.] A muscle whose function it is to produce flexion in any part of the body; as, the *flexors* of the abdomen. Opp. to *extensor*.

Flexuose (fleksiuˌōu·s), *a.* 1727. [ad. L. *flexuosus*, f. *flexus* sb. a bending.] *Bot.* Winding in and out, undulating, crooked. Hence **Flexuo·sity,** f. quality; a winding.

Flexuoso-, comb. f. form of FLEXUOSE or FLEXUOUS, indicating a flexuous form or arrangement.

Flexuous (fle·ksiuˌəs), *a.* 1605. [ad. L. *flexuosus*.] 1. Full of bends or curves; winding, sinuous. Now chiefly of animal and vegetable structures. 2. Moving in bends or waves. *rare.* 1626.

2. The F. Burning of Flames BACON.

Flexure (fle·ksiŭɪ). 1592. [ad. L. *flexura*; see -URE.] 1. The action of flexing or bending; curvature; an instance of this. 2. Flexed or bent condition; bent figure or posture; bending, or winding form 1628. 3. Flexibility 1651. 4. *concr.* Anything of bent shape; a bend, curve, turn, winding 1607. 5. *Math.* The bending or curving of a line, surface, or solid 1672. 6. *Geol.* A bending of strata under pressure 1833.

1. There's those are made For f., let them stoope 1592. 2. The details..of giving f. to the rivers, [etc.] 1826. 4. Now the last f. of our way we reach'd CARY. 5. *F. of a curve*: its bending towards or from a straight line. Hence **Fle·xural** *a.* of or relating to f.

Flibbertigibbet (fli·bəɪtiˌdʒi·bėt). 1549. [orig. *flibbergib*; prob. echoic of unmeaning chatter.] 1. A gossip; a flighty woman. 2. The name of a fiend (*Lear* III. iv. 120); applied in Scott's *Kenilworth* to a mischievous and flighty urchin 1603.

Flibustier, var. of FILIBUSTER *sb.*

‖**Flicflac.** [Fr.; echoic of a succession of sharp sounds.] A kind of step in dancing. THACKERAY.

Flick (flik), *sb.*[1] ME. [Echoic; cf. prec.] 1. A light blow, e.g. one given with a whip; also, a jerk. 2. The sound of this; hence, any slight, sharp sound 1844. 3. *concr.* Something thrown off with a jerk; a dash, splash 1848. 4. *pl.* The cinema (*slang*) 1926.

Flick, *sb.*[2] *dial.* = FLECK *sb.*[2]

Flick, (flik), *v.*[1] *Cant.* 1677. [? dial. var. of FLITCH *v.*] To cut.

Flick (flik), *v.*[2] 1816. [f. FLICK *sb.*[1]] 1. *trans.* To strike lightly with something flexible, as a whip 1838. 2. To remove with a smart stroke of something flexible 1847. b. To jerk (*off*, etc.) 1816. 3. *intr.* To move with quick vibrations; to flutter 1853. 4. *trans.* To move or shake with a flick 1844.

1. Flicking each other with our towels 1875. 2. b. Spots of ink flicked at random out of a pen T. L. PEACOCK. 4. I was afraid of flicking my line into my host's eye 1877.

Flicker (fli·kəɪ), *sb.*[1] 1849. [f. FLICKER *v.*] 1. A flickering movement 1857. 2. A wavering unsteady light or flame. Also *fig.*

2. The last cold f. of twilight 1862. *fig.* This little f. of enthusiasm KANE.

Flicker (fli·kəɪ), *sb.*[2] *U.S.* 1849. [Echoic of the bird's note.] A name of various species of woodpecker; *esp.* the yellow-shafted woodpecker (*Colaptes auratus*).

The flicker's cackle is heard in the clearing THOREAU.

Flicker (fli·kəɪ), *v.* [OE. *flicorian*, an onomatopœic formation expressing quick movement.] 1. *intr.* Of a bird: To flutter or hover; *occas.*, to flap the wings. †2. To caress; hence, to dally, hanker, look longingly (after) –1806. 3. To wave to and fro; to flutter; to quiver, vibrate, undulate 1450. 4. To flash up and die away by turns. Of a flame: To burn fitfully. (The prevailing sense.) Also *transf.* and *fig.* 1605.

1. Above hir heed her dowves flikeringe CHAUCER. 3. The high masts flicker d as they lay afloat TENNYSON. 4. Sheet lightning, flickering harmlessly in the distance FROUDE. The fire .. flickers low 1871. Hence **Fli·ckeringly** *adv.*

†**Fli·ckermouse.** 1630. [var. of FLITTERMOUSE.] A bat –1708.

Flidge, obs. f. FLEDGE.

Flier, alternative f. FLYER.

Flight (fləit), *sb.*[1] [OE. *flyht* :— OTeut. **fluhti-*, f. **flug-* root of **fleugan* to FLY.] 1. The action or manner of flying or moving through the air with or as with wings. b. *Falconry.* Pursuit of game, etc. by a hawk; also, the quarry flown at 1530. 2. Swift movement, e. g. of a projectile ME. 3. *fig.* A mounting or soaring; an excursion or sally (of the imagination, wit, ambition, caprice, etc.) 1668. 4. The flight feathers 1735. 5. The distance which a bird can or does fly; also *fig.* and *transf.* 1600. 6. The series of stairs between any two landings; also *transf.* of terraces, locks, etc. 1703. 7. A number of beings or things flying in or passing through the air together ME. 8. The young birds that take wing at one time 1577. 9. A flight-arrow (see *Comb.*) 1464; also = FLIGHT-SHOOTING 1557. 10. The husk or glume of oats 1831. 11. *Naut.* = FLY-BOAT. 1769. 12. *Angling.* The set of fish-hooks in a spinning-trace 1865.

1. c. A Royal Air Force unit consisting of about five or six machines 1914. 2. The f. of a Javelin POPE, of years YOUNG, of ships SHELLEY, of clouds RUSKIN. 3. Old Pindar's flights DENHAM. Speculative flights LAW. 5. Within an eagle's f. S. ROGERS. Phr. *F. of a shot*: 'the trajectory formed between the muzzle of a gun and the first graze' (Smyth). 7. A f. of flies 1556, of angels HAWTHORNE, of arrows TENNYSON. Phr. *In the first f.* (colloq.): in the van. 8. The March f. of pigeons (*mod.*). 9. *Much Ado* I. i. 40.

Comb.: In titles of officers of various ranks in the Royal Air Force, as *F. Commander*, *F. Lieutenant*; **f.-arrow,** a light and well-feathered arrow for long-distance shooting; **-feather,** one of the wing-feathers on which power of f. depends.

Flight (fləit), *sb.*[2] [OE. **flyht* :—OTeut. **pluhti-z*, f. root *pleuh-* to FLEE.] The action of fleeing or running away from or as from danger, etc.; hasty departure ME.

Pray ye that your f. be not in the winter *Matt.* xxiv. 20. To seek safety in f. 1760. Phr. *To put to f.*

†**Flight,** *a.* 1581. [f. FLIGHT *sb.*[1]] Swift, fleet –1642.

Flight (fləit), *v.* 1571. [f. FLIGHT *sb.*[1] and [2].] 1. *trans.* To put to flight; hence, to frighten. 2. †To migrate; = FLIT –1752; also, to fly in flights 1879. 3. To feather (an arrow) 1869.

Flighted (fləi·tėd), *ppl. a.* 1634. [f. FLIGHT *sb.*[1]] 1. Having a certain flight. Only in *drowsy-f.* MILT. 2. Feathered 1735.

Flighter (fləi·təɪ). 1825. [? f. FLIGHT + -ER[1]. ? Orig. = 'wing'.] *Brewing.* 'A horizontal vane revolving over the surface of wort in a cooler, to produce a circular current in the liquor' (Knight).

Fli·ght-shooting, *vbl. sb.* 1801. [f. FLIGHT *sb.*[1] + SHOOTING *vbl. sb.*] 1. *Archery.* Distance-shooting with flight-arrows. 2. Shooting wild-fowl as they fly over 1840.

Fli·ght-shot. 1455. [f. FLIGHT *sb.*[1] + SHOT *sb.*] 1. The distance to which a flight-arrow is shot, a bow-shot. 2. A shot taken at wildfowl in flight 1887.

1. Some two flight-shoot to th' Alehouse J. TAYLOR.

Flighty (fləi·ti), *a.* 1552. [f. FLIGHT *sb.*[1] + -Y[1].] 1. Swift, fleet. *rare.* 2. Given to flights of imagination, humour, caprice, etc.; guided by whim or fancy; fickle, frivolous. Of a horse: Skittish. 1768. 3. Light-headed. Also *absol.* 1802.

1. The f. purpose neuer is o're-tooke Vnlesse the deed go with it *Macb.* IV. i. 145. 2. A f. gossiping damsel 1878. Hence **Fli·ghtily** *adv.* **Fli·ghtiness.**

Flim-flam (fli·mflæm). 1538. [Echoic; expressive of contempt. Cf. *whimwham*, etc.]

A. *sb.* 1. A piece of nonsense 1546. 2. A paltry trick or pretence 1538. 3. *collect.* Nonsense; humbug, deception 1570.

3. I tell thee 'tis all flim-flam FIELDING.

B. *adj.* Frivolous, nonsensical; also deceptive, sham 1577.

Flimsy (fli·mzi). 1702. [? onomatopœic; suggested by *film*.]

A. *adj.* 1. Without strength or solidity; easily destroyed; slight, unsubstantial †Of persons, etc.: Frail, delicate –1753 2. Without solid value, slight, trivial; frivolous, trifling, superficial 1827.

1. As fine As bloated spiders draw the f. line COWPER. I have a very f. constitution H. WALPOLE. 2. A f. hypothesis learnt from Bolingbroke L. STEPHEN.

B. *sb.* 1. *slang.* A bank-note 1824. 2. Thin or transfer paper; hence, reporters' copy 1859. Hence **Fli·msily** *adv.* **Fli·msiness.**

Flinch (flinʃ), *v.* Also †**flench.** 1563. [app. a nasalized form of obs. *flecche* to bend, flinch. Cf. OF. *flenchir, flainchir*, vars. of *flechir.*] 1. *intr.* To give way, draw back, yield ground. In later use: To shrink *from* something as dangerous, painful, or difficult 1579. †2. To slink, sneak off –1622. 3. To shrink under pain; to wince 1677; to BLENCH 1883. 4. quasi-*trans.* To withdraw from, lose (one's ground) 1674.

1. The peasants withstood without flinching several attacks in front ALISON. 3. A child..may..be accustom'd to bear very..rough usage without flinching LOCKE. Hence **Flinch** *sb.* the action of flinching. **Fli·ncher,** one who flinches or shrinks *from* (an undertaking, etc.); one who passes the bottle. **Fli·nchingly** *adv.*

Flinder-mouse (fli·ndəɪ,maus). Now *dial.* 1481. [f. ME. *vlindre* (= mod. Du. *vlinder*, butterfly) + MOUSE.] A bat. Cf. FLITTER-MOUSE.

Flinders (fli·ndəɪz), *sb. pl.* rarely *sing.* 1450. [cf. Norw. *flindra* chip, splinter, Du. *flenter* fragment.] Fragments, pieces, splinters. Chiefly in phrases, as *to break* or *fly in*(*to flinders*.

Fling (fliŋ), *sb.* 1550. [f. next vb.] 1. An act of flinging; a cast, throw 1589. 2. *fig.* A passing attempt at or attack upon something; also, a gibe, scoff 1550. 3. A hasty, reckless, or wanton movement; a rush. *lit.* and *fig.* Now *rare.* 1556. 4. A flinging about of the body or limbs; *esp.* in the dance called *the Highland f.* 1806. b. A plunge; of a horse: A kicking out 1568. 5. A fit or spell of unrestrained indulgence of one's impulses 1827. †6. 'A thing of nought.' FULLER.

2. A f. at the Ægyptian crowne GREENE, at the clergy 1760. 4. Highlanders..dancing the f. to the music of the bagpipe 1806. 5. I should like to have my f. out before I marry THACKERAY.

Fling (fliŋ), *v.* *Pa. t.* and *pple.* **flung** (flʊŋ). ME. [app. related to ON. *flengja*, MDa. *flænge* to flog (mod. Icel. *flengja*, Da. *flenge*, also *intr.* to move impetuously).]

I. *intr.* 1. To move with haste or violence from or towards an object; to dash, rush. 2. Of a horse, etc.: To kick and plunge violently, to be unruly or restive ME. b. Similarly of persons. Also, *to f. out*: to break out into invective or complaint. 1531 3. *Sc.* To caper, dance 1528.

1. He flung from me like a whirlwind GALT. As sword that, after battle, flings to sheath MRS. BROWNING. 2. A Colt, giue him the bridle, he flinges about GOSSON.

II. *trans.* 1. To throw, cast, toss, hurl; *esp.* to throw with violence or hostile intent ME. Also *absol.* 2. *refl.* = sense I. 1. Also *fig.* 1700. 3. To extend (one's arms) with a sudden movement; *transf.* of a plant, etc. Also, to kick *up* (one's heels), etc. 1657. 4. To cast scornfully (one's eyes, etc.) in a certain direction 1654. 5. To emit, send forth, give out, diffuse 1632. 6. To throw down; *spec.* in wrestling. Of a horse: To throw off (his rider). Also *fig.* To give a fall to. 1790.

1. Who loues the King..F. vp his cap SHAKS. F. dirt enough and some will stick 1706. 3. The young colt..flung up her heels TENNYSON. 5. West winds ..About the cedarn allies f. Nard and casia's balmy smells MILT. *Comus* 989. 6. His horse started, flung him, and fell upon him H. WALPOLE.

Phrases. *To f. aside*, to disregard, reject. *To f. away*, to discard, dismiss; to throw away, squander. *To f. down*, to throw on the ground, overthrow, demolish. *To f. off*, to abandon, disown; to throw off the scent. *To f. up*, to throw up (an earthwork); to give up, abandon; also (*dial.*) to rake up and utter as a reproach. *To f. in one's teeth*: see CAST *v.* *To f. open*, to open suddenly and violently; similarly, *to f. to*, to shut suddenly or forcibly.

Comb. **f.-dust, -stink,** a street-walker, a harlot. Hence **Fli·nger,** one who flings; (*intr.*) a dancer; (of a horse) a kicker; (*trans.*) one who throws.

Flint (flint), *sb.* [OE. *flint* = MDu. *vlint*, Da. *flint*, Sw. *flinta*; ? cogn. w. Gr. πλίνθος tile.] 1. A hard stone, most commonly of a steely grey colour, found in roundish nodules, usually covered with a white incrustation. It is one of the purest native forms of silica. In early use, any hard stone. Also *transf.* OE. b. As a type of anything hard and unyielding ME. 2. A piece of this stone, as giving off sparks when struck with iron or steel OE. 3. A nodule or pebble of flint ME.

1. Arrow-heads of f. LONGF. b. Callum, f. to other considerations, was penetrable to superstition SCOTT. 2. Sparks struck from a Flint and a Steel 1665. The F. of the Pistol failed 1679.

Phr. *To skin a f.*, a hyperbolical exemplification of avarice.

Comb.: **f.-flake,** a flake or chip of f. used in prehistoric times as a cutting instrument; **-gravel,** gravel containing flints; **-gun,** a gun with a flint-lock; **-head,** an arrow-head made of f.; †**-heart** *a.* = next; **-hearted** *a.*, hard-hearted; **-mill,** (*a*) *Pottery*, a mill in which flints are ground to powder for mixing with clay; (*b*) *Mining*, 'a mode formerly adopted for lighting mines, in which flints studded on the surface of a wheel were made to strike against a steel and give a quick succession of sparks' (Knight); **-rope,** the stem of the sponge *Hyalonema Sieboldii* (Cass.); **-skinning,** *fig.* parsimonious saving; **-wall,** 'a wall made of broken flints set in mortar, and with quoins of masonry' (Knight); **-ware,** U.S. name for STONE-WARE, q.v.; **-wood,** a name in N.S. Wales for *Eucalyptus pilularis*; †**-wort,** a name for aconite, as growing on bare rocks (*nudis cautibus*), according to Pliny.

Flint (flint), *v.* 1803. [f. prec. sb.] To provide with a flint or flints; also, to pave with flints.

Flint-glass. 1675. 1. A pure lustrous glass, now made from a composition of lead oxide, sand, and alkali; originally made with ground flint or pebble as the siliceous ingredient 1683. †2. An article made of this glass –1766. 3. *attrib.* 1683.

1. A Pipe made of Chrystal, or Flint-Glass 1683.

Fli·nt-lock. 1683. [See LOCK.] a. A gunlock in which a flint, screwed to the cock, is struck against the hammer and produces sparks which ignite the priming. Also *attrib.* b. A gun fitted with this lock.

Fli·ntstone. ME. [f. FLINT *sb.* + STONE.] = FLINT *sb.*

Flinty (fli·nti), *a.* 1542. [f. FLINT *sb.* + -Y[1].] 1. Of, consisting of, or derived from flint; containing flint-stones 1591. 2. Resembling flint 1542. 3. *fig.* Obdurate, harsh 1536.

1. F. bulwarkes SHAKS., gravel BACON. 3. The f. heart..of base self-interest BURKE. Hence **Fli·ntily** *adv.* **Fli·ntiness.** **Fli·nty-hearted** *a.* having a hard heart or core.

Flip (flip), *sb.*[1] 1682. [?f. FLIP *v.*] †1. The slimy scum rising to the surface of salt-pans. 2. A mixture of beer and spirit sweetened with sugar and heated with a hot iron. (Cf. *egg-flip.*) 1695.

Comb. **f.-dog,** an iron heated to warm f.

Flip (flip), *sb.*[2] 1692. [f. FLIP *v.*] 1. A smart stroke or blow. Also *fig.* 2. A sudden jerk or movement 1821. 3. A trip by aircraft (*colloq.* or *slang*) 1914.

Flip (flip), *v.* 1594. [Prob. echoic; cf. FILLIP *v.*] 1. To put into motion with a flip; to toss (a coin) 1616. 2. To move with a flip or jerk. *trans.* and *intr.* 1712. 3. *trans.* and *intr.* To strike smartly and lightly (*at*) 1861.

1. Flipping the ash from his cigarette 1885.

Flipe (fləip), *v.* Chiefly *Sc.* ME. [Cf. MDa. *flippe* to skin.] 1. *trans.* To peel, flay. Now *dial.* †2. To turn up or down, fold back; also, to turn inside out –1788.

Flip-flap (fli·pflæp). 1529. [reduplication of FLAP.] A. *adv.* With a repeated flapping movement 1583.

B. *sb.* †1. Something that 'goes flip-flap', e.g. a hanging piece of cloth, a fan –1611. 2. *slang.* a. A kind of somersault; also, a costers' dance 1676. b. *Fireworks.* A cracker 1885. c. In a place of amusement, a machine with passenger cars hung at ends of horizontal rotating arms 1908. 3. *U.S.* A kind of tea-cake 1876.

3. Dough-nuts and flipflaps BESANT & RICE.

C. *adj.* That 'goes flip-flap' 1841.

Flippancy (fli·pănsi). 1746. [f. next; see -ANCY.] The quality of being FLIPPANT.

Flippant (fli·pănt), *a.* 1605. [app. f. FLIP *v.* (sense 2). Cf. ON. *fleipr* babble, *fleipa* to talk nonsense.] †1. Moving lightly or alertly; pliant, flexible, limber –1677. 2. Of the tongue: Nimble, voluble. Hence of persons and of conversation: Fluent, voluble –1794. †3. Sportive, playful –1784. 4. Displaying unbecoming levity 1724. 5. *absol.* A flippant person 1791.

1. A bird of the flippantst wing 1622. 2. She was wise, a most f. tongue she had CHAPMAN. 3. The squirrel, f., pert, and full of play COWPER. 4. Sherlock's f. but entertaining letters MAD. D'ARBLAY. Hence **Fli·ppant-ly** *adv.*, **-ness.**

Flipper (fli·pəɪ), *sb.* 1822. [f. FLIP *v.*] 1. A limb used to swim with; e.g. any limb in a turtle, a seal, or a walrus; the fore-limb of a cetacean; the wing of a penguin; the fin of a fish. 2. *transf.* The hand 1832. 3. *Theat.* 'Part of a scene, hinged and painted on both sides, used in trick changes' (Farmer).

Flirt (flɔ̄ɪt), *sb.* 1549. [f. next.] 1. A rap, fillip. Now *dial.* 1577. 2. A sudden jerk, a quick throw or cast, a darting motion 1590. †3. A jest; a gibe –1726. †4. 'A pert young hussey' (J.) –1774. 5. One who FLIRTS (sense 6); also, a person to flirt with 1732. 6. *Watch-making.* 'A lever or other device for causing sudden movement of mechanism' (Britten) 1786.

2. Hedge-sparrows have a remarkable f. with their wings G. WHITE. 4. My aunt told me she was a forward f. JOHNSON. 5. A f. too, in the worst and meanest degree of flirtation JANE AUSTEN. General Tufto is a great f. of mine THACKERAY.

Flirt (flɔ̄ɪt), *v.* 1553. [Onomatopœic; cf. *flick, spurt*, etc.] 1. *trans.* To throw or propel with a jerk or sudden movement. Cf. FILLIP *v.* 1583. †2. To rap, fillip –1631. 3. To give a brisk, sudden motion to; to flick 1665. †4. a. *intr.* To turn up one's nose; hence, to sneer, gibe, scoff *at* –1734. †Also *trans.* –1686. 5. *intr.* To move with a jerk or spring; to spring, dart 1583. †Also *fig.* 6. To play at courtship; to practise coquetry. Often *to f. with* (a person). 1777. b. To play, trifle *with* (something) 1859.

1. To f. inke in everie mans face DEKKER. 3. Those birds which have a habit of flirting up the tail 1834. *To f. a fan*: to open and shut it with a jerk, to wave it smartly. 6. Every man likes to f. with a pretty girl, and every pretty girl likes to be flirted with GEO. ELIOT. Hence **Fli·rter.** **Fli·rtingly** *adv.*

Flirtation (flɔ̄ɪtē[1]·ʃən). 1718. [f. prec.] †1. 'A quick, sprightly motion. A cant word among women.' (J.) 1737. 2. The action or behaviour of a flirt; †frivolity; playing at courtship. Also *transf.* and *fig.* 1718.

2. The great art of f. 1876. *transf.* The flirtations ..between Mr. Pitt and Ld. Loughborough 1792.

Flirtatious (flɔ̄ɪtē[1]·ʃəs), *a.* 1834. [f. prec.; see -OUS.] Given to flirtation; of the nature of flirtation.

Hence **Flirta·tious·ly** *adv.*, **-ness.**

†**Flirt-gill** (-dʒil). Also **-gillian.** 1592. [f. FLIRT *sb.* or *v.* + GILL nickname for *Juliana.*] A woman of light behaviour. Cf. GILL-FLIRT.

I am none of his flurt-gils *Rom. & Jul.* II. iv. 162.

Flirtigig, -gigs (flɔ̄·ɪtigig(z). *dial.* 1683. [f. FLIRT + GIG.] A giddy, flighty girl.

Flisk (flisk), *sb. dial.* 1818. [f. next.] 1. A whim, a freak. *Sc.* 2 A fillip with the finger 1891.

Flisk (flisk), *v.* Now *dial.* 1596. [Onomatopœic.] 1. To frisk, caper. 2. *trans.* To put out, displease 1792. 3. To flick 1847.

1. To flit away the flisking flies GOSSON. Hence **Fli·sky** *a.* frolicsome; skittish.

Flit (flit), *sb.* 1835. [f. next vb.] a. A removal. b. A flutter; a light touch 1873.

†**Flit,** *a. poet.* 1590. [var. of FLEET *a.*, influenced by FLIT *v.*] a. Swift, quickly-moving –1600. b. Fleeting; airy, unsubstantial –1633.

a. Now, like a stag; now, like a faulcon f. SPENSER.

Flit (flit), *v.* [ME. *flitten, flutten*, a. ON. *flytja*, f. **flut-* weak grade of the root of *fliôta*; see FLEET *v.*[1]] 1. *trans.* To remove to another place. †2. To get rid of; to drive *away* –1596. 3. *intr.* To shift one's position; to be gone, depart, pass away ME. 4. *intr.* To remove from one habitation to another. Chiefly *north.* or *Sc.* 1504. †5. To change; to alter, shift about, give way –1816. b. Of a flame: To die down 1839. 6. To move along, pass, proceed; to fly or pass lightly and swiftly. Also, to flutter. ME.

2. Fannes .. To f. away the flisking flies GOSSON. 3. To f. owt of this lyfe 1619. 5. God..that may not chaunge and flitte CHAUCER. b. Like a candle..flitting and flaring alternately MARRYAT. 6. Postmen.. f. to and fro DICKENS. A shadow flits before me TENNYSON. So smoothly o'er our heads th days did f. MORRIS.

Hence †**Flit, Fli·tted,** †**Fli·tten** *ppl. a.* that has gone away. **Fli·tting-ly** *adv.*

Flitch (flitʃ), *sb.* [OE. *flicce*:– OTeut. **flikkjo*[m], f. root **flĭk*, found in ON. *flik* rag, and perh. in FLECK *sb.*] 1. The side of an animal, now only of a hog, salted and cured; a 'side' of bacon. **2. a.** A square piece of blubber from a whale 1787. **b.** A steak cut from a halibut 1884. **3.** A slice, cut lengthways from the trunk of a tree 1823. **b.** One of several planks fastened side by side to form a compound beam 1874.

Comb. **f.-beam,** 'a beam made in layers of material pinned together' (Knight).

Flitch (flitʃ), *v.* 1875. [f. prec.] *trans.* To cut into flitches; to cut as a flitch is cut.

Flite, flyte (fləit), *v.* Now *dial.* [Com. WGer.: OE. *flītan* (cf. mod. Ger. *sich befleissen*, to busy oneself).] †**1.** *intr.* To contend, strive; to wrangle –1725. **2.** To scold. Const. *at.* 1500. Also *trans.* **3.** *intr.* To debate ME. †**4.** To complain –1585.

Flitter (fli·təɹ), *sb.*[1] 1820. [f. FLITTER *v.*] A flittering motion. *Comb.* **f.-winged** *a.* having wings that flutter.

Flitter (fli·təɹ), *sb.*[2] 18.. [a. Ger. *flitter.*] A minute square of thin metal, used in decoration. Also *collect.*

Flitter (fli·təɹ), *v.* 1542. [f. FLIT *v.* + -ER[5].] **1.** *intr.* Of birds, etc.: To flit about; to flutter 1563. †**2.** Of a flower: To fade, wither –1847. †**3.** To fly all about –1677. **4.** *trans.* To make to flit; to shuffle (cards). *rare.* 1864.

Flitter-mouse (fli·təɹmaus). 1547. [f. FLITTER *v.* + MOUSE, after Ger. *fledermaus.* Cf. FLICKER-, FLINDERMOUSE.] A bat.

Fli·ttern. 1682. A young oak tree; †also, a strip of its wood. *Comb.* **f.-bark,** the bark of young oak trees.

Fli·tters, *sb. pl.* Now *dial.* 1620. [Altered f. FITTERS.] Fragments; splinters, tatters.

Flitting (fli·tiŋ), *vbl. sb.* ME. [f. FLIT *v.*] **1.** The action of FLIT *v.* **2.** *esp.* A removal from one abode to another. Chiefly *north.* and *Sc.* ME.

2. Phr. *Moonlight f.*: removal by moonlight, i.e. by night or by stealth.

†**Fli·tty,** *a.* [f. FLIT *v.* + -Y[1].] Unstable, flighty. HENRY MORE.

Flivver (fli·vəɹ). orig. *U.S. slang.* 1920. [?] A cheap motor car or aeroplane.

Flix (fliks). 1666. [?] Fur; the down of a beaver.

Flix, obs. f. FLUX.

†**Flo.** *Pl.* **flon.** [OE. *flā.*] An arrow –1450.

Float (flōut), *sb.* [(1) OE. *flot* action or state of floating; (2) OE. *flota* ship; f. (ult.) Teut. root *fleut-, flaut-, flot-* (see FLEET *v.*).]

I. 1. The action or condition of floating; *esp.* in phr. *on* (rarely *at*) *f.* = AFLOAT. Now *rare.* †**2.** The flux of the tide. *lit.* and *fig.* –1797. †**3.** A wave, billow. *lit.* and *fig.* Also, the sea. –1655. †**4.** An overflow; a flood. *lit.* and *fig.* –1763.

1. And now the sharp keel of his little boat Comes up with ripple and with easy f. KEATS. **2.** Hee being now in F. (= at high water) for Treasure BACON. **3.** *Temp.* I. ii. 234.

II. A floating object. **1.** A mass of weeds, ice, etc. floating on the water 1600. **2.** A raft or raft-like construction 1535; a flat-bottomed boat 1557. **3.** Any floating appliance for supporting something in the water; e.g. the cork or quill attached to a fishing-line to show by its movement when a fish bites ME.; the cork used to support a fishing net, etc. in the water 1577; a hollow or inflated part or organ that supports an animal in the water 1832; an inflated bag or pillow to sustain a person in the water 1874; a structure fitted to a flying machine to enable it to float on water 1897. **4.** A hollow metallic ball, or the like, used to regulate the water-level in a boiler or tank 1752. **5.** *Theatr. pl.* The footlights; *sing.* a row of footlights 1862. **6.** A float-board (see *Comb.*) 1611.

III. 1. Something broad, level, and shallow; *esp.* a low-bodied cart for carrying heavy articles, live stock, etc. 1866. †**2.** A unit of measurement for embanking work 1707.

2. [Banks] are measured by the F. or Floor, which is eighteen foot square, and one deep MORTIMER.

IV. 1. A tool for floating or making level; e.g. in *Plastering*, a trowel or rule for giving a plane surface to the plaster 1703; a single-cut file 1750; a polishing-block used in marble-working; the serrated plate used by shoemakers for rasping off the ends of the pegs inside the boot or shoe 1874. **2.** A dock or place where vessels may float 1840. **3.** One of the trenches used in 'floating' land 1785. **4.** *Geol.* and *Mining.* Loose rock brought down by water from its original formation. Also short for *f.-ore* (see *Comb.*). Chiefly *U.S.* 1814. **5.** *Weaving.* The passing of weft-threads over a portion of the warp without being interwoven with it; also, the mass of thread so passed 1863.

Comb.: **f.-ball,** the ball of a ball-cock; **-board,** one of the boards of an undershot water-wheel, one of the paddles of a paddle-wheel; **-case,** a CAISSON or CAMEL; **-copper** (see *float-mineral*); **-file,** a single-cut file; **-gauge,** a water gauge, where the height of water in a steam-boiler is registered by means of a f.; **-gold** (see *float-mineral*); **-ironed** *a.*, ironed by a machine having springs and resilient padding to the rollers; **-mineral,** fragments of ore detached and carried away by the action of water or by erosion; also, fine particles of metal which are detached in the process of stamping and do not readily settle in water; **-ore, -quartz** (see prec.); **-valve,** a valve actuated by a f.

Float (flōut), *v.* *Pa. t.* and *pple.* **floated.** [OE. *flotian* :—OTeut. **flotōjan*, f. **flot-* root of **fleutan* to float or flow; see FLEET *v.*]

I. *intr.* **1.** To rest on the surface of any liquid; to be buoyed up; to be or become buoyant. **2.** To move quietly and gently on the surface of a liquid, participating in its motion ME. **3.** To be suspended *in* a liquid with freedom to move; to swim 1596. **4.** To move freely and gently in or through the air, as if buoyed up or carried along by it. Also *fig.* 1634. **5.** *Weaving.* Of a thread: To pass over or under several threads either of the warp or weft, instead of being interwoven with them 1878. **6.** *Comm.* Of an acceptance: To be in circulation 1778. **b.** Of a company, etc.: To get floated (see II. 3) 1884.

1. Her timbers yet are sound, And she may f. again COWPER. **2.** The boat floating near to him, he seized hold of it W. IRVING. *fig.* The vulgar f. as passion drives YOUNG. **4.** The clouds that flit, or slowly f. away COWPER. *fig.* Here floated the latest anecdote of Bolivar DISRAELI.

II. *trans.* **1.** To cover or flood with a liquid; also *transf.* and *fig.* 1586. **2.** To cause to float; to cause to rest or move on the surface of a fluid; also *fig.* 1606. **3.** To get (a company, scheme, etc.) afloat or fully started; to procure public support for 1883. **4.** To convey by or along the surface of water 1739. **5.** *techn.* **a.** To levigate (pigments) by causing them to float in a stream of water 1883. **b.** *Electrotyping* and *Stereotyping.* To cover (a forme, a page of type) with fluid plaster of Paris, either to fill up spaces, or to form a plaster mould 1880. **6.** To render smooth and level. **a.** *Plastering.* To level (the surface of plaster) with a float 1703. **b.** *Farriery.* To file the teeth of (a horse) 1886. **7.** *Weaving.* To form (a figure) with floating threads (see I. 5) 1894.

1. The field was floated with blood JAS. MILL. To f. meadows at five pounds an acre 1833. **2.** For want of water to f. them over some flats in the Lagunes DAMPIER. **3.** To f. loans 1872, rumours 1883. **4.** The treasures of Africa were floated on rafts to the mouth of the Euphrates GIBBON.

Hence **Floa·table** *a.* that can f., or (*U.S.*) be floated on; *absol.* something that floats.

Floatage (flōu·tėdʒ). 1626. [f. FLOAT *sb.* + -AGE. Cf. F. *flottage.*] **1.** The action or state of floating. **2.** *concr.* Anything that floats; e.g. FLOTSAM; also the right to flotsam 1672. **3.** Buoyancy 1877. **4.** The part of a ship above the water-line 1839.

Floatation, flotation (flotēi·ʃən). 1806. [f. FLOAT *v.* + -ATION = F. *flottaison.* The form *flotation*, though unjustifiable, is the more usual.] **1.** The action, fact, or process of floating; the condition of keeping afloat. **2.** The action of floating a company, etc. 1889.

1. *Centre of f.*: the centre of gravity in a floating body. *Plane* or *line of f.* = Fr. *flottaison, ligne de flottaison*, the plane or line in which the horizontal surface of a fluid cuts a body floating in it. *Stable f.*: the position of equilibrium in a floating body.

Floa·t-boat. ME. [f. FLOAT *sb.* or *v.* + BOAT; so called because it was towed astern.] †A ship's long-boat –1659. **b.** A raft 1600.

Floater (flōu·təɹ). 1717. [f. as prec.] **1.** One who or that which floats; *esp.* 'a contrivance indicating the height of level of a fluid in a vessel, whose depth we cannot at the time directly examine' (Nichol). **2.** *Stock-Exch.* A government stock certificate, a railway-bond, etc. accepted as a recognized security 1871. **3.** *U.S. Politics.* One who casts a vote at an election to which he is not entitled.

Floating (flōu·tiŋ), *vbl. sb.* 1562. [f. FLOAT *v.* + -ING[1].] **1.** The action of FLOAT *v.* **2.** *concr.* in *Plastering.* 'The second coat in three-coat work' (P. Nicholson) 1823.

Floating (flōu·tiŋ), *ppl. a.* 1578. [f. as prec. + -ING[2].] **1.** That floats (see the vb.). **2.** *Comm.* Of a cargo: At sea. Of trades, rates, etc.: Of or pertaining to cargoes at sea. 1848. **3.** Having less than the usual attachment 1806. **4.** Fluctuating 1594. **5.** *Finance.* Not fixed or permanently invested; unfunded 1816. **b.** Of an insurance policy: Variable 1839.

1. The sun-beams trembling on the f. tides POPE. **3.** *F. Ribs*, 'the last two of the false ribs, whose anterior extremities are not connected to the rest or to each other' MAYNE. F. kidney 1889. **4.** The f. population of the city 1876. **5.** Variations in the amount of f. capital McCULLOCH. The f. debt 1893.

Comb.: **f.-anchor,** 'a frame of spars and sails dragging overboard, to lessen the drift of a ship to leeward in a gale' (Knight); **f. battery,** a vessel fitted up and used as a battery; **f. dock,** a large (usually rectangular) vessel made with water-tight compartments, and used as a graving-dock; **f. harbour,** 'a breakwater composed of large masses of timber, anchored and chained together..which rise and fall with the tide' (Brees); **f. lever** (*Railway*), a name applied to the horizontal brake-levers beneath the car-body; **f. pier,** a landing-stage which rises and falls with the tide; **f. plate** (*Stereotyping*), a flat cast-iron plate, upon which the mould is laid, with the impression downwards.

Floating bridge. 1706. [f. FLOATING *ppl. a.*] **a.** A bridge in the form of a redoubt, consisting of two boats covered with planks. **b.** One made of two small bridges, laid one over the other in such a manner that the uppermost can be run out by the help of cords and pulleys placed along the sides of the under-bridge 1727. **c.** A collection of beams of timber, floating on the surface of a river, and reaching across it. **d.** A flat-bottomed ferry steamboat in harbours or rivers, running on chains laid across the bottom 1858. **e.** A passage formed across a river or creek by means of bridges of boats 1867.

Floating island. 1638. [f. as prec.] **1.** An island that floats. **2.** *Cookery.* (*U.S.*) A custard with floating masses of whipped cream or white of eggs 1771.

Floating light. 1793. [f. as prec.] **a.** A lightship. **b.** A life-buoy with a lantern, for use at night.

Floatingly (flōu·tiŋli), *adv.* 1660. [f. as prec.] In a floating manner.

Floa·t-stone. 1703. [f. FLOAT *v.* + STONE.] **1.** A rubbing-stone upon which bricks with curved surfaces are rubbed. **2.** A stone so light as to float upon water, e.g. a spongy variety of opal 1805.

Floaty (flōu·ti), *a.* ME. [f. FLOAT *sb.* or *v.* + -Y[1].] †**1.** Watery. ME. only. **2.** Capable of floating; hence, of a ship: Drawing little water 1608.

Floccillation (flǫksilēi·ʃən). 1842. [f. L. **floccillus* dim. of *floccus* + -ATION.] = CARPHOLOGY.

Flo·cci-nau·ci-ni·hili-pi·li-fica·tion. *joc.* 1741. [f. L. *flocci, nauci, nihili, pili* words signifying 'at little' or 'at nothing' (see Eton Latin Grammar) + -FICATION.] The action or habit of estimating as worthless.

Floccose (flǫ·kōus, flǫkōu·s), *a.* 1752. [ad. late L. *floccosus*; see -OSE.] **1.** Furnished with a tuft or tufts of woolly hair. **2.** *Bot.* Covered with or composed of flocci 1830.

Floccular (flǫ·kiŭlăɹ), *a.* 1870. [f. FLOCCULUS + -AR.] *Anat.* Of or pertaining to the flocculus of the cerebellum.

Flocculate (flǫ·kiŭlėt), *a.* 1826. [f. FLOCCULUS + -ATE[2].] *Entom.* Furnished with a curling lock of hair.

Flocculate (flǫ·kiŭleit), *v.* 1877. [f. as prec. + -ATE[3].] *trans.* To aggregate into flocculent masses. Hence **Floccula·tion,** the process of flocculating.

Flocculence (flǫ·kiŭlĕns). 1847. [f. FLOCCULENT; see -ENCE.] The condition of being flocculent. So **Flo·cculency.**

Flocculent (flǫ·kiŭlĕnt), *a.* 1800. [f. L. *floccus* + -ULENT.] 1. Resembling flocks or tufts of wool; woolly. 2. Of the atmosphere: Holding particles of aqueous vapour in suspension 1878. 3. Downy 1870.

‖**Flocculus** (flǫ·kiŭlŏs). *Pl.* -**li.** 1799. [mod. L., dim. of L. *floccus.*] A small flock or tuft. 1. A small quantity of loosely-aggregated matter resembling a flock of wool, held in suspension in, or precipitated from, a fluid. 2. *Anat.* A small lobe in the under surface of the cerebellum; the subpeduncular lobe 1840.

‖**Floccus** (flǫ·kŏs). *Pl.* -**i.** 1842. [L.] Something resembling a flock of wool. a. *Bot.* A tuft of woolly hairs; also *pl.* the *hyphæ*, or thread-like cells, which form the mycelium of a fungus. b. *Zool.* The tuft of hairs which terminate the tail in mammals 1842. c. 'A tuft of feathers on the head of young birds' (Webster). d. 'The down of unfledged birds' (Worcester).

Flock (flǫk), *sb.*[1] [OE. *flocc* = ON. *flokkr* (Sw. *flock*, Da. *flok*); ? a var. of FOLK. Not found in the other Teut. langs.] 1. A band, body, or company (of persons). Now only as *transf.* from 2 or 3. 2. A number of animals of one kind, feeding or travelling in company. Now chiefly of birds (*esp.* geese) or as in sense 3. Also *transf.* ME. 3. *esp.* A number of sheep or goats kept together under the charge of one or more persons. Also *transf.* and *fig.* ME. 4. *fig.* A body, or the whole body of Christians, in relation to Christ; a congregation in relation to its pastor ME.; a family of children in relation to their parents.

1. A flocke of men of armes LD. BERNERS. 2. Sixteene Elephants together in one flocke RALEIGH. 3. A goat, the patriarch of the f. SCOTT. 4. Feede the flocke of God which is among you 1 *Pet.* v. 2.

Comb. f.-**duck** (*U.S.*), a scaup-duck.

Flock (flǫk), *sb.*[2] ME. [prob. a. OF. *floc* lock of wool, etc. :—L. *floccus.*] 1. A lock, tuft, particle (of wool, cotton, etc.); †hence, anything of no account. 2. *pl.* A material consisting of the coarse tufts and refuse of wool or cotton, or of cloth torn to pieces by machinery, used for stuffing beds, cushions, mattresses, etc. ME. 3. *pl.* (later *collect. sing.*) Powdered wool or cloth, or cloth-shearing, used formerly for thickening cloth and now in making flock-paper 1483. 4. *pl.* Of chemical precipitates, etc.: Light and loose masses, resembling tufts of wool 1592.

1. I will never care three flocks for his ambition LYLY. 2. Their fleece [is] for flockes, not cloath 1589.

Comb.: f.-**bed**, one stuffed with f.; -**paper**, 'paper prepared for walls by being sized in the first instance ..and then powdering over it f...which has been previously dyed' (Brande); -**powder** = sense 3.

Flock (flǫk), *v.*[1] ME. [f. FLOCK *sb.*[1]] †1. *trans.* To gather together into a company -1586. †2. To lead *away* in a flock -1672. 3. *intr.* To gather in a company or crowd; to come or go in great numbers, to troop ME. †4. *trans.* To crowd upon 1609.

3. Many yong Gentlemen flocke to him euery day SHAKS. 4. Good fellowes trooping, flock'd me so 1609.

Flock (flǫk), *v.*[2] 1530. [f. FLOCK *sb.*[2]] 1. *trans.* a. To stuff with flocks. b. To cover with flock or wool-dust (see FLOCK *sb.*[2] 3) 18.. †2. To treat with contempt; also *absol.* -1575.

†**Flo·ckling.** [see -LING.] One of a flock. BROME.

†**Flo·ck-meal,** *adv.* [OE. *floccmǣlum*, f. *flocc* FLOCK *sb.*[1] + *mǣlum*, dat. pl. of *mǣl* measure; cf. *piecemeal.*] By companies, troops, or heaps -1611.

Flocky (flǫ·ki), *a.* 1597. [f. FLOCK *sb.*[2] + -Y[1].] a. Flock-like. b. Floccose.

Floe (flōu). 1817. [perh. a. Norse *flo* layer :—ON. *flo.*] A sheet of floating ice; a detached portion of a field of ice. Also *ice-f.*

Comb.: floeberg, a berg of f.-ice; f.-**flat**, a seal = *floe rat*; -**ice**, undulating ice forming a vast plain; f. **rat**, the small ringed seal (*Phoca hispida*).

Flog (flǫg), *v.* 1676. [? school abbrev. of *flagellate.*] 1. To beat, whip; to chastise with repeated blows of a rod or whip. 2. *gen.* To beat, lash, strike. *Fishing.* To cast the fly-line over (a stream) repeatedly. *Cricket.* To punish (bowling). 1801. b. *intr.* Of a sail: To flap heavily 1839.

2. A salmon bullied into rising by a customer who.. kept flogging on 1867. Hence **Flo·gger,** one who or that which flogs; also, a kind of tool, a bung-starter.

Flogging (flǫ·giŋ), *vbl. sb.* 1758. [f. prec.] The action of FLOG *v.*

Comb.: f.-**chisel,** a large cold chisel used in chipping castings; -**hammer,** a small sledge-hammer used for striking a f.-chisel.

Flon, flone, vars. of †*flane*, arrow.

Flong, obs. pa. t. and pple. of FLING *v.*

Flood (flʌd), *sb.* [Com. Teut.: OE. *flōd* :—OTeut. **flōđu(z* :—pre-Teut. *plotús*, f. Aryan vbl. stem **plō*, whence FLOW *v.* The primary sense is 'action of flowing'.] 1. The flowing in of the tide; as in *ebb and f.*, etc. Also *fig.* 2. A body of flowing water; a river, stream, usually a large river. Now only *poet.* OE. 3. Water as opp. to land, often contrasted with *field* and *fire*. Also *pl.* Now *poet.* or *rhet.* OE. 4. An overflowing or irruption of a great body of water over land not usually submerged; an inundation, a deluge OE. 5. A profuse and violent outpouring of water; a swollen stream; a violent downpour of rain. ME. Also *fig.* ME. b. *transf.* of tears, flame, light, lava, a concourse or influx of persons, etc. 1589. †6. *pl.* = FLOODING 2. (Dicts.)

1. *fig.* There is a Tide in the affayres of men, which taken at the F., leades on to Fortune SHAKS. 2. The water of the f. Iordan 1605. 3. Through f., through fire, I do wander euerie where SHAKS. The accidents of f. and field [cf. *Oth.* I. iii. 135] 1857. 4. *The F.*: the deluge in the time of Noah; hence often *Noah's f.* Shipwreck..fire, and f. COWPER. *transf.* His eyes in f. with laughter SHAKS.

Comb.: f.-**anchor,** 'that which the ship rides by during the flood-tide' (Smyth); -**flanking** (*Hydraulic Engin.*), a mode of embanking with stiff moist clay; -**light,** artificial light projected from different directions so that shadows are eliminated; hence as vb.; so f.-**lit** *a.*; -**loam** = ALLUVIUM; -**mark,** the high-water mark.

Flood (flʌd), *v.* ME. [f. prec. *sb.*] 1. *trans.* To cover with a flood; to inundate. 2. To cover or fill with water. Of rain, etc.: To fill (a river) to overflowing. 1881. 3. To pour in a flood. *rare.* 1829. 4. *intr.* To come in a flood or floods. *lit.* and *fig.* 1755. 5. To suffer from uterine hæmorrhage 1770.

1. The streets in Oxon were all flouded with water WOOD. 2. To f. grass lands LOUDON, a colliery 1883. 4. Far back, through creeks and inlets making, Comes silent, flooding in, the main CLOUGH. Hence **Floo·der.**

Floo·d-ga·te, floo·dgate. ME. [f. FLOOD *sb.* + GATE.] 1. *sing.* and *pl.* A gate or gates that may be opened or closed, to admit or exclude water, *esp.* the water of a flood; *spec.* the lower gates of a lock. b. *transf.* and *fig.* ME. 2. A sluice 1559. †3. The stream that is closed by or passes through a flood-gate; a strong stream, a torrent. Also *transf.* and *fig.* -1651.

1. b. The floodgates were opened, and mother and daughter wept THACKERAY. 3. Of her gored wound ..He..did the floudgate stop With his faire garment SPENSER.

Flood-hatch. 1587. [see HATCH.] A framework of boards sliding in grooves, to be raised in time of flood; a sluice, floodgate. *lit.* and *fig.*

Flooding (flʌ·diŋ), *vbl. sb.* 1674. [f. FLOOD *v.* + -ING[1].] 1. The action of FLOOD *v.*; *pl.* floods; *fig.* fullness. 2. Uterine hæmorrhage, *esp.* in connexion with parturition 1710.

Floo·d-ti·de. 1719. [f. FLOOD *sb.* + TIDE.] = FLOOD *sb.* 1.

Flook: see FLUKE.

Flookan, flooking (flu·kăn, -iŋ). 1728. [?] *Mining.* A cross-course or transverse vein composed of clay; also, a sort of clayey substance, often found against the walls of a quartz reef, and accompanying cross-spurs and slides.

Floor (flōᵊɹ), *sb.* [OE. *flōr*, corresp. to Du. *vloer*, MHG. *vluor* (mod. Ger. *flur*), ON. *flōr* :—OTeut. **flōru-s* :—pre-Teut. **plāru-s* or **plōru-s*. Cf. OIr. *lār*, Welsh *llawr.*]

I. 1. The layer of boards, brick, stone, etc. in an apartment, on which people tread; the under surface of the interior of a room. Hence, any analogous surface. 2. The structure of joists, etc. supporting the flooring of a room 1703. Hence, the ceiling of a room. Also *transf.* of the sky. 1596. 3. *Naut.* a. 'The bottom of a vessel on each side of the kelson' (Smyth). †b. The deck -1683. c. *pl.* = *floor-timbers* 1805. 4. In legislative assemblies, the part of the house where the members sit, and from which they speak. Hence *fig.* The right of speaking. 1774. 5. A set of rooms and landings in a house on the same level; a story. See FIRST-FLOOR. 1585.

2. The floore of heauen SHAKS. 4. Phr. *To take the f.*: to get up to address a meeting; to take part in a debate; said also of taking part in a dance. Chiefly *U.S.* 5. Old footsteps trod the upper floors TENNYSON.

II. 1. An artificial platform or levelled space, for the carrying on of some industry, *esp.* threshing OE. 2. A naturally level surface. Also = the ground (now *dial.*). ME.

2. Sunk though he be beneath the watery f. MILT.

III. 1. A foundation. ? *Obs.* 1556. 2. The stratum on which a seam of coal, etc. immediately lies 1869.

IV. 1. A layer, a stratum; a horizontal course 1692. 2. A unit of measurement used for embankment work (= 400 cubic feet) 1707. 3. = FLOAT *sb.* III. 2, q.v. 1707.

Comb.: f.-**arch,** an arch with a flat extrados; -**frame,** (*a*) the framework of the f. in a vessel; (*b*) *U.S.* the main frame of the body of a railway-carriage underneath the f.; -**head,** (*a*) the upper end of one of the f.-timbers in a vessel; (*b*) 'the third diagonal, terminating the length of the floors near the bilge of the ship' (Smyth); -**hollow,** 'the inflected curve that terminates the f. next the keel, and to which the f.-hollow mould is made'; -**light,** a frame with glass panes in a f.; -**plan,** (*a*) *Ship-building*, 'a longitudinal section, whereon are represented the water-lines and ribband-lines' (Smyth); (*b*) *Arch.*, a horizontal section, showing the thickness of the walls and partitions, the arrangement of the passages, apartments, and openings at the level of the principal f. of the house; -**riband,** the riband next below the f.-heads which supports the floors; -**timber(s,** those parts of the ship's timbers which are placed immediately across the keel; -**walker,** *U.S.* = SHOP-WALKER.

Floor (flōᵊɹ), *v.* ME. [f. prec.] 1. *trans.* To cover or furnish with a floor or floors; to form the floor of. 2. To bring to the floor or ground; to knock down 1642. 3. *fig.* (*colloq.*) a. To nonplus 1840. b. To overcome in any way 1827. c. To do thoroughly; to finish 1836. d. *intr.* ? To get a fall. J. H. NEWMAN. 4. To place *upon* (something) as a floor 1871.

1. Forests, floored with bright-green moss B. TAYLOR. 2. Crib .. floored him with a blow of great strength 1812. 3. b. I was the only man who could f. O'Connell LD. BEACONSFIELD. c. To f. a paper 1852, a bottle 1861.

Floorage (flōᵊ·rėdʒ). *rare.* 1734. [f. as prec. + -AGE.] Floors collectively, amount of flooring.

Floor-cloth, floo·rcloth. 1746. [f. as prec. + CLOTH.] 1. A fabric for covering floors; e.g. oilcloth, linoleum, etc. 2. A housemaid's cloth for washing floors 1851.

Floorer (flōᵊ·rəɹ). 1795. [f. FLOOR *v.*] One who or that which floors (*lit.* and *fig.*); e.g. a knock-down blow, a piece of bad news, a decisive argument or retort. Also in university slang, a question or paper too hard to be mastered.

Flooring (flōᵊ·riŋ), *vbl. sb.* 1624. [f. as prec.] 1. The action of FLOOR *v.* 1632. 2. *concr.* The floor of a room, etc.; also, the materials of which it is made 1624; a natural floor 1697. 3. *Malting.* The operation of spreading the grain on the malt-floor, and treating it 1839. *Comb.* f.-**clamp,** an implement for closing up the joints of flooring boards.

Floorless (flōᵊ·ɹlės), *a.* 1847. [see -LESS.] Having no floor.

Flop (flǫp), *sb.* *colloq.* and *dial.* 1662. [See the vb.] 1. An act of flopping; the resulting sound 1823. †2. = FLAP *sb.* 1 b. 1662.

Flop (flǫp), *adv.* and *interj.* *colloq.* 1728. [The vb. stem.] With a flop, or flopping noise.

Flop (flǫp), *v.* *colloq.* and *dial.* 1602. [var. of FLAP *v.*, indicating a heavier sound.] 1. *intr.* To swing or sway about heavily and loosely; to FLAP. 2. To move clumsily and heavily; to move with a sudden bump or thud 1692. 3. *trans.* To throw suddenly, usually with a flop 1823. 4. To move (wings) heavily and loosely up and down 1859.

2. A..grey sea flopping up on our weather bow 1887.

Floppy (flǫ·pi), *a. colloq.* 1858. [f. FLOP *v.* + -Y [1].] Having a tendency to flop about.

Flora (flōᵊ·ră). *Pl.* **-æ**; also **-as.** 1508. [a.L. *Flora* the goddess of flowers, f. *flor-, flos* flower.] **1.** In Latin mythology, the goddess of flowers; hence, the personification of nature's power in producing flowers. **2.** A descriptive catalogue of the plants of any area, period, etc. 1777. **3.** The plants or plant life of a region or epoch 1778.

1. With voice Milde, as when Zephyrus or F. breathes MILT.

Floral (flōᵊ·răl), *a.* 1647. [ad.L. *floralis* of or pertaining to *Flora*. Cf. F. *floral.*] **1.** *Hist.* Pertaining to or in honour of Flora. **2.** Pertaining to a flora or floras 1870. **3.** [f. L. *flos, flor-.*] Of or pertaining to a flower or flowers 1753.

1. Phr. *F. shows* = L. *Floralia.* 2. Phr. *F. zone*: one of the tracts into which the earth's surface may be divided with reference to vegetable life. 3. *F. Leaf* expresses one found near the flower, and which never appears but with the flower CHAMBERS. *F. envelope* (see ENVELOPE *sb.*). Hence **Flo·rally** *adv.* in the manner of a flower.

†**Flo·ramour.** Also **-amor.** 1548. [a.OF. **flor amour* lit. 'flower of love'.] A name given to various species of *Amaranthus* -1676.

‖**Floreal** (flōᵊ·rĭăl), *sb.* 1827. [F. *Floréal*, f. L. *flor-, flos* + -AL.] The eighth month of the year in the French Republican calendar, extending from April 20 to May 19.

Florence (flǫ·rěns). ME. [The chief city of Tuscany (early It. *Fiorenze*, now *Firenze*, F. *Florence*).] †**1.** A gold florin -1598. **2.** A woven fabric: **a.** of wool (*Obs.* exc. *Hist.*) 1483; **b.** of silk 1882. †**3.** A kind of wine brought from Florence -1757.

Comb.- **F.-flask** (see FLASK *sb.*); **-oil,** a superior kind of olive oil.

Florentine (flǫ·rěntəin). 1545. [ad. L. *Florentinus* of or pertaining to *Florentia* Florence.]

A. *adj.* Of or pertaining to Florence; *esp.* in **F. mosaic,** a kind of mosaic made by inlaying precious stones in marble or the like 1603.

B. *sb.* **1.** A native or inhabitant of Florence 1591. **2.** A textile fabric of silk or †wool 1545. 3. A kind of pie or tart; *esp.* a meat pie 1567. **4.** The Florentine dialect of Italian. MILMAN.

3. A Florendine of a kidney of Veal 1750.

‖**Flores** (flō·res). 1858. [Sp.; pl. of *flor* FLOWER.] The best quality of indigo dye.

Florescence (flore·sěns). 1793. [See next and -ENCE.] The process of bursting into flower; the period or state of flowering; *concr.* flowers collectively.

Florescent (flore·sěnt), *a.* 1821. [ad. L. *florescentem*, pr. pple. of *florescere*, inceptive of *florere*; see FLOURISH.] Bursting into flower, flowering. *lit.* and *fig.*

Floret (flōᵊ·rět). 1671. [ad. OF. *florete*, F. *fleurette*, dim. of *fleur* flower.] **1.** *Bot.* One of the little flowers that make up a composite flower or the spikelet in grasses. **2.** A floweret 1791.

1. The *florets of the disk*..occupy the centre of the head of a composite; while *florets of the ray* occupy the circumference 1866.

Floret, obs. var. of FLEURET [2].

†**Flo·riage.** [badly f. L. *flor-, flos*, after *foliage.*] **1.** Bloom, blossom. J. SCOTT. **2.** 'The leaves of flowers' (Webster).

Floriated (flōᵊ·riˌeɪtěd), *ppl. a.* [f. L. *flor(i)-, flos* + -ED [1].] Decorated with floral ornaments; as, a *floriated coronet.* var. **Flo·reated.**

Floricomous (flori·kǒməs), *a. rare.* 1727. [f. as prec. + *coma* hair + -OUS.] †**1.** Having the top adorned with flowers. **2.** *Zool.* Epithet of certain sponges, the rays of which end in a bunch of curved branches.

Floriculture (flǫ·-, flōᵊ·rikɒltiŭr). 1822. [f. as prec. + CULTURE.] The cultivation of flowering plants. Hence **Floricu·ltural** *a.* **Floricu·lturist,** one devoted to or skilled in f.

Florid (flǫ·rid), *a.* 1642. [ad. L. *floridus*, f. *flor-, flos* flower: see -ID.] †**1.** Abounding in or covered with flowers; flowery -1682. **2.** *fig.* Profusely adorned as with flowers; elaborately, or excessively ornate 1656. **3. a.** *Mus.* Running in rapid figures, divisions, or passages; also, = FIGURATE *a.* 4 a. 1879. **b.** *Arch.* Enriched with decorative details 1704. †**4.** Of blooming appearance; brilliant. Of colour: Bright. -1770. **5.** Of the complexion, etc.: Rosy, flushed with red 1650. †Of the blood: Bright red (i.e. arterial) -1797. **6.** In the bloom of health. Now *rare.* 1656.

1. This f. Earth MILT. The f. glories of the Spring VAUGHAN. 2. A f. speech 1658. In f. impotence he speaks POPE. A f. apparel THACKERAY. 3. A f. style of Jacobean architecture 1886. 5. A f. face 1865. 6. Vigorous and f. Health HUME.

Hence **Flori·dity,** f. quality or state. **Flo·rid·ly** *adv.*, **-ness.**

Florida (flǫ·ridă). The name of a State in the extreme south-east of the United States, used *attrib.*, as in **F.-water,** a perfume similar to eau-de-Cologne, largely used in the United States; etc.

Florideous (flori·dĭəs), *a.* 1884. [f. mod. L. *Florideæ* (f. L. *floridus* FLORID) + -OUS.] *Bot.* Belonging to the *Florideæ*, an order of Algæ, or having the characters of that group.

Floriferous (flori·fěrəs), *a.* 1656. [f. L. *florifer* + -OUS.] Producing flowers.

Florification (flōᵊːrifikēɪ·ʃən). 1796. [a. F.; see -FICATION.] The action or process of flowering.

Floriform (flōᵊ·rifǭɪm), *a.* 1805. [f. L. *flor(i)-, flos* + -FORM.] Having the form of a flower.

Florikan, floriken (flōᵊ·rikăn, -kěn). Also **-can, -kin.** 1780. [?] Either of two species of small bustard, the Bengal Florikan (*Sypheotides bengalensis*), or the Lesser Florikan (*S. auritus*).

†**Flo·rilege.** 1651. [a. F. *florilège*; see next.] = next. -1665.

Florilegium (flōᵊrilī·dʒiǒm). 1647. [mod. L., f. *florilegus* flower-cutting; Gr. ἀνθολόγιον ANTHOLOGY.] *lit.* A collection or selection of flowers; hence *transf.* an anthology.

Florin (flǫ·rin). ME. [a. F. *florin* = It. *fiorino*, f. *fiore*:—L. *florem, flos*; the coin orig. so called having the figure of a lily stamped upon it. Cf. FLORENCE 1.] **1.** The English name of a gold coin weighing about 54 grs., first issued at Florence in 1252. **2.** An English gold coin of the value of six shillings and eightpence, issued by Edward III. Now *Hist.* 1480. **3.** The English name of various continental coins 1611. **4.** An English silver coin of the value of two shillings, first minted in 1849.

Florist (flǫ·-, flōᵊ·rist). 1623. [f. L. *flor-, flos* + -IST.] One who cultivates flowers; one skilled in knowledge of flowering plants; also, one who deals in flowers.

Floroun, var. of FLEURON.

‖**Floruit** (flōᵊ·riuˌit). 1843. [L., 3rd sing. perf. indic. of *florere.* Cf. *habitat.*] Used for: The period during which a person 'flourished'.

Florula (flōᵊ·riŭlă). 1847. [as if dim. of L. *flora* (see FLORA).] A small flora or collection of plants.

Florulent (flōᵊ·-, flǫ·riŭlěnt), *a.* 1592. [ad. L. *florulentus.*] Abounding in flowers, flowery.

Flory, *a. Her.* = FLEURY.

Floscular (flǫ·skiŭlăɪ), *a.* 1793. [f. L. *flosculus* + -AR.] Composed of floscules or flowerets.

Floscule (flǫ·skiul). 1669. [a. F., ad. L. *flosculus*, dim. of *flos.*] *Bot.* A floret. Also *fig.*

†**Flo·sculet.** [f. as prec. + -ET.] A little flower. HERRICK.

Flosculous (flǫ·skiŭləs), *a.* 1646. [f. L. *flosculus* + -OUS.] †**1.** Of the nature, or having the savour, of flowers -1682. **2.** *Bot.* Composed of floscules or florets. Of a floret: Tubular. 1830. So **Flosculo·se** *a.* (Dicts.)

‖**Flos-ferri** (flǫ·sfe·rəi). 1748. [L.; = 'flower of iron'.] *Min.* A coralloid variety of aragonite, often found with iron ore.

Flosh (flǫʃ), *sb.* 1874. *Metallurgy.* 'A hopper-shaped box in which ore is placed for the action of the stamps' (Knight).

Floss [1] (flǫs). 1759. [? Cf. OF. *flosche* down, pile of velvet; also as adj. in *soye flosche* (mod. F. *soie floche*) floss-silk (= It. *seta floscia*).] **1.** The rough silk which envelops the cocoon of the silk-worm 1759; *transf.* the silk of maize and other plants 1846. **2.** = FLOSS-SILK. 1871. **3.** A flossy surface; also, fluff 1784. **4.** *attrib.*, as in *f. thread*, etc. 1864. Hence **Flo·ssy** *a.* floss-like.

Floss [2] (flǫs). 1839. [a. Ger. *floss*, cogn. w. FLOAT *sb.*] *Metallurgy.* **1.** The fluid glass floating upon the iron in the puddling furnace produced by the vitrification of the oxides and earths which are present. **2.** White cast iron, as employed for the manufacture of steel 1839.

Comb. **f.-hole,** (*a*) a hole at the back of a puddling furnace, at which the slags of the iron pass out; (*b*) 'the tap-hole of a melting-furnace' (Knight).

Floss [3] (flǫs). [Cf. Ger. *floss* in same sense. (In *The Mill on the Floss* the word *Floss* is a proper name.)] A stream. CARLYLE.

Floss-silk. Also **flox-, flosh-silk.** 1759. [f. FLOSS [1].] **a.** The rough silk broken off in the winding of cocoons. **b.** Untwisted filaments of silk used in embroidery and crewel-work 1863.

Flota (flōᵘ·tă). 1690. [a. Sp.; = 'fleet'.] The name given to the Spanish fleet which used to bring back to Spain the products of America and the W. Indies.

Flotage, Flotation, etc.: see FLOAT-.

Flotant (flōᵘ·tănt), *a.* 1610. [ad. Fr., f. *flotter* to float.] *Her.* A term applied to anything flying in the air, or displayed, or swimming.

†**Flote,** *sb.*[1] [OE. *flota*; see FLOAT *sb.*] **1.** A fleet or flotilla -1577. **2.** = FLOTA. 1673.

†**Flote,** *sb.*[2] ME. [a. OF. *flote* company, multitude:—pop. L. type **flotta*, prob. f. Teut. **flot-*, **fleutan* FLEET *v.* in sense 'to flow'.] A company, troop; also, a herd (of cattle), a shoal (of fish) -1647.

†**Flote,** *v.* 1573. [? back-formation f. *floten* FLOTTEN.] *trans.* = FLEET *v.*[2] 1. -1669.

Floter, obs. f. FLUTTER.

Flotilla (floti·lă). 1711. [a. Sp., dim. of *flota*; see FLOTA.] A small fleet; a fleet of boats or small vessels.

Flotsam (flǫ·tsăm). 1607. [ad. AF. *floteson* (= mod. F. *flottaison*):—late L. type **flottationem.*] **1.** *Law.* Wreckage found floating on the surface of the sea. Usually assoc. w. JETSAM. Also *transf.* and *fig.* **2.** Newly ejected oyster-spawn 1879.

†**Flo·tten,** *ppl. a.* Also *floten.* 1600. [pa. pple. of Fleet *v.*[1] and [2].] **1.** Flooded with water 1601. **2.** Skimmed. *F. milk*, skim-milk. -1661.

Flounce (flauns), *sb.*[1] 1583. [f. FLOUNCE *v.*[1]] The action of flouncing; a sudden fling or jerk; a plunging or flopping movement; occas. expressing impatience or disdain.

Flounce (flauns), *sb.*[2] 1713. [Later form of FROUNCE.] **1.** A strip gathered and sewed on by its upper edge around the skirt of a lady's dress, and left hanging and waving. **2.** *Mil.* The leather flap closing the holster-pipe 1833.

Flounce (flauns), *v.*[1] 1542. [Cf. Norw. *flunsa* to hurry, Sw. dial. *flunsa* to plunge.] **1.** *intr.* To dash, flop, plunge, rush. **2.** To make abrupt and jerky movements with the limbs or body; to throw the body about; to plunge, flounder, struggle. Usu. said of bulls, horses, or aquatic animals. 1609. †**3.** To express displeasure by agitated movements -1756. †**4.** *trans.* To dash or drive with violence -1794.

1. He flounced from the water like a carp 1784. 2. When one hath struck a great fish, he plungeth and flounceth 1641. 3. If you f., I fly FOOTE.

Flounce (flauns), *v.*[2] 1672. [Altered f. FROUNCE *v.*] †**1.** *trans.* To curl, frizz. **2.** To adorn or trim with a flounce or flounces, also *transf.* 1711.

2. Flounced and furbelowed from Head to Foot ADDISON.

Flouncing (flau·nsiŋ), *vbl. sb.* 1766. [f. FLOUNCE *v.*[2]] **a.** The action of the vb. **b.** *concr.* A flounce; also, material for flouncing.

Flounder (flau·ndəɪ), *sb.*[1] 1450. [Cf. ON. *flyðra*, Sw. *flundra*, Da. *flynder.*] **1.** A small flat-fish, *Pleuronectes Flesus.* In U.S. applied to other species of flat-fish. **2. a.** *dial.* = FLUKE 2. 1853. **b.** *Bootmaking.* A tool used 'to stretch leather for a boot front in a blocking or crimping board' (Knight) 1874.

Flounder (flau·ndəɹ), *sb.*2 1867. [f. next vb.] The action of FLOUNDER *v.*

Flounder (flau·ndəɹ), *v.* 1592. [? Nasalized form of Du. *flodderen* to splash through mire, to flop about.] **1.** *intr.* In early use, to stumble; later, to struggle violently and clumsily; to plunge, to roll and tumble about in or as in mire. Also with *on, along,* etc. Also *transf.* and *fig.* †**2.** *trans.* To cause to flounder; to confound -1685.

1. You f. in mud at every step THACKERAY. *fig.* They f. about between fustian in expression, and bathos in sentiment HAZLITT.

Flour (flauəɹ), *sb.* ME. [A specific use of FLOWER; cf. F. *fleur de farine* the 'flower' or finest part of the meal.] **1.** Orig., the finest quality of meal; hence, the finer portion of meal (wheat or other) which is separated by bolting. Also, in mod. use, the meal of wheat as opp. to that from other grain. **2.** Hence, the fine soft powder of any substance ME. **3.** *attrib.*, as *f.-dredge, -mill,* etc. 1806.

2. F. of mustard 1855, of sulphur 1894.

Comb.: **f.-beetle,** a beetle (*Tenebrio molitor*) which feeds on f.; **-bolt, -bolter,** a flour-sieve; **-dresser,** a cylinder for dressing f., instead of passing it through bolting cloths; **-emery,** emery reduced to a fine powder; **-gold,** the finest alluvial drift-gold; **-mite,** one of several acarids which are found in f.; **-moth,** a moth which feeds on f., esp. *Pyralis farinalis.*

Flour (flauəɹ), *v.* 1651. [f. prec. sb.] **1.** *trans.* To sprinkle with flour; to powder (a wig). **2.** *U.S.* To grind (grain) into flour 1828. **3.** *intr. Mining.* Of mercury: To break up into dull particles coated with some sulphide and incapable of coalescing with other metals 1882. Hence **Floured** *ppl. a.* (in senses 1, 3).

Flourish (flʊ·riʃ), *sb.* 1500. [f. next vb.] **1.** The blossom on a fruit-tree. *Sc.* and *n. dial.* **2.** †The condition of being in blossom -1818; *fig.* prosperity, vigour; perfection, prime (now *rare*) 1597. †**3.** Ostentatious embellishment; gloss -1632. **4.** *Penmanship.* A decoration executed with a sweep of the pen 1652. **5.** Literary or rhetorical embellishment; parade of fine words or phrases; a florid expression 1603. †**b.** A boast, brag -1706. **6.** An ostentatious waving about of a weapon or anything else; a showy movement 1601. **7.** *Mus.* **a.** A fanfare (of horns, trumpets, etc.) 1594. **b.** A florid passage; a florid style of composition; a decorative addition introduced by player or singer 1646.

2. *fig.* The *Court Circular* remains in full f. THACKERAY. 3. Time doth transfixe the florish set on youth SHAKS. 5. He commenced with a f. about his sufferings for the Plot SCOTT. 6. Like seeming Fencers we are meeter for a f., then defence 1601. 7. a. They..received him [Waverley] with a triumphant f. upon the bagpipes SCOTT.

Flourish (flʊ·riʃ), *v.* *Pa. t.* and *pple.* **flourished.** ME. [a. OF. *floriss-* lengthened stem of *florir* (mod. F. *fleurir*) :—vulgar L. **florire*, f. *flor-, flos* flower.]

I. *intr.* **1.** Of a plant or tree: †To blossom -1578; to grow vigorously and luxuriantly; to thrive ME. **2.** *gen.* To thrive ME. Of things: To attain full development; to be prosperous or successful, be in vogue ME. **3.** To be at the height of fame or excellence; to be in one's prime. Also used in pa. t. of a person to indicate the date of his activity (cf. FLORUIT). ME.

1. To smelle the sote savour of the vyne whanne it florissheth CHAUCER. I the Lord..have made the dry tree to f. *Ezek.* xvii. 24. 2. The poor law system ..has flourished for over three centuries 1885. 3. Spenser and Fairfax both flourished in the reign of Queen Elizabeth DRYDEN.

II. †**1.** *trans.* To adorn with flowers or verdure; to cause to thrive -1614. †**2.** *gen.* To adorn, embellish, ornament -1716; to embellish with flourishes (see FLOURISH *sb.* 4) -1660. **3.** †To embellish with flowers of speech -1691; *intr.* to use florid language 1700. †**4.** *trans.* To work up ornamentally. BACON.

3. You have..wanted no art to f. your warm passion SHIRLEY.

III. **1.** To brandish (a weapon, etc.); to wave about by way of show or triumph. Also *intr.* of the weapon, etc. ME. Also †*absol.* **2.** **a.** *trans.* To display ME. **b.** *intr.* 'To boast, brag' (J.); to 'show off' 1674. †**3.** To move with a flourish -1735. †**4.** *Mus.* and *Fencing.* To give a short fanciful exhibition by way of exercise before the real performance. To play, with a flourish. Of trumpets: To sound a flourish. -1810.

1. Old Mountague..flourishes his Blade in spight of me SHAKS. 2. a. He..florisht his colours in signe of victory 1638. 4. Why do the Emperors trumpets f. thus SHAKS.

Hence **Flou·risher,** one who or that which flourishes. **Flou·rishingly** *adv.* in a flourishing manner; †ostentatiously.

Floury (flauə·ri), *a.* 1591. [f. FLOUR *sb.* + -Y1.] Of or resembling flour; yielding flour; covered with flour or powder.

Flout (flaut), *sb.* 1570. [f. FLOUT *v.*] A mocking speech or action.

Flout (flaut), *v.* 1551. [? special use of *floute,* ME. form of FLUTE *v.* Cf. Du. *fluiten* to play the flute, also to mock.] **1.** *trans.* To mock, jeer, insult; to express contempt for. †**b.** To quote mockingly. *Much Ado* I. i. 290 **2.** *intr.* To behave with contumely, to mock, jeer, scoff; to express contempt by action or speech. Const. *at.* 1575.

1. Where the Norweyan Banners flowt the Skie *Macb.* I. ii. 49. Phillida flouts me WALTON. 2. Ah, you may f. and turn up your faces BROWNING.

Hence †**Flou·tage,** mockery B. JONS. **Flou·ter. Flou·tingly** *adv.* in a flouting manner. †**Flou·ting-stock,** (*a*) a butt for flouting; (*b*) = FLOUT *sb.* (*Merry W.* IV. v. 83.)

Flow (flōᵘ), *sb.*1 1450. [f. FLOW *v.*] **1.** The action or fact of flowing; an instance or mode of this. Orig. said of liquids, now of air, electricity, etc. Also 'The course or direction of running waters' (Smyth). **b.** The quantity that flows 1807. **c.** *concr.* That which flows 1802. **2.** *transf.* and *fig.* Any movement resembling the flow of a river and connoting a copious supply; an outpouring or stream; *esp.* of speech. Hence, of dress, outlines, etc. 1641. **3.** The incoming of the tide; opp. to *ebb* 1583. Also *fig.* **4.** †A deluge, flood -1579; an overflowing 1606. **5.** *Porcelain Manuf.* A flux for causing the colours to flow or blend in firing 1878. †**6.** A full-bottomed wig -1756.

1. The f. of a brook 1856, of a current of air TYNDALL. c. The f. Of Iser, rolling rapidly CAMPBELL. Flows of lava LYELL. 2. The Feast of Reason and the F. of Soul POPE. A f. of callers 1812, of talk 1873. Phr. *F. of spirits*: in early use, a sudden access of exhilaration; now, a state of habitual cheerfulness. 3. Ocean's ebb and ocean's f. BURNS.

Flow (flōᵘ), *sb.*2 Also **flo(w)e.** 16.. [? a. ON. **flówe* (Icel. *flói*) of same meaning.] **1.** 'A watery moss, a morass' (Jam.). Also, a low-lying piece of watery land. **2.** A quicksand 1818. **3.** *attrib.*, as in *f.-bog* or *f. moss,* a peat bog, the surface of which rises and falls with every increase or diminution of the water 1831.

Flow (flōᵘ), *v.* *Pa. t.* and *pple.* **flowed** (flōᵘd). [OE. *flówan,* a redupl. str. vb. occurring as such only in Eng., f. root **flō-*. Not connected with L. *fluere.* Cf. Gr. πλώειν to swim, L. *plorare* to weep. See also FLOOD *sb.*]

I. **1.** *intr.* Of fluids, a stream, etc.: To move with a continual change of place among the particles or parts; to move along in a current; to circulate. †**2.** To become liquid; to melt. *lit.* and *fig.* -1737. **b.** *Ceram.* To work or blend freely: said of a glaze (*Cent. Dict.*). **c.** Of a metal: To change its form under impact or tensile or compressive strain 1888. **3.** To come, go, move or pass as a stream ME. **4.** Of a garment, hair, etc.: To hang loose and waving 1606. **5.** *Math.* To increase or diminish continuously by infinitesimal quantities. See FLUENT. 1715. †**6.** *trans.* To make to flow -1579.

1. Siloa's Brook that flow'd Fast by the Oracle of God MILT. *P. L.* I. 11. Trade, which like blood should circularly f. DRYDEN. 2. Oh that..the mountains might f. down at thy presence *Isa.* lxiv. 1. 3. As fast years f. away SHELLEY. Conversation flowed freely 1870. 4. Her bright hayre loose flowing B. JONS.

II. **1.** To stream forth OE.; to issue or proceed *from, out of.* Also *transf.* and *fig.* ME. **2.** Of the menstrual discharge. Said also of the person. 1754.

1. Endless tears f. down in streams SWIFT. *fig.* This rule flows..from the nature of a remainder CRUISE.

III. **1.** Of the sea, etc.: To rise and advance. OE. †**2.** To rise and overflow. Also *fig.* -1625. (The obs. pa. pple. *flown* was orig. used in this sense.) †**3.** Of the eyes: To become overfull -1710. **4.** Of wine, etc.: To be poured out abundantly; also *fig.* OE. **5.** *trans.* To flood ME.; hence, to cover with varnish, glaze, or the like, by allowing it to flow over the surface 1864.

1. Thys yere the Thamys did flowe three times in one daye 1568. *fig.* Doth it [pride] not f. as hugely as the Sea SHAKS. 2. Let Nylus f. BEAUM. & FL. *fig.* The Sons of Belial, flown with insolence and wine MILT. *P. L.* I. 501.

Hence **Flow·age,** the act of flowing; flooded state.

Flowe(n, obs. pa. t. and pple. of FLY.

Flower (flauəɹ, flau·əɹ), *sb.* [ME. *flour, flur,* a. OF. (mod. F. *fleur*) :—L. *florem, flos,* f. Aryan root **bhlo-*: see BLOW *v.*2] **1.** A complex organ in phenogamous plants, comprising a group of reproductive organs and its envelopes. In pop. use, the characteristic feature of a *flower* is the coloured (not green) envelope; in botanical use, a flower consists normally of one or more stamens or pistils (or both), a corolla, and a calyx. **b.** In *Bryology,* the growth comprising the reproductive organs in mosses. **2.** *transf.* **a.** The down of the dandelion and thistle. ? *Obs.* 1530. †**b.** *pl.* = CATAMENIA. [After F. *fleurs.*] -1741. **c.** *Anc. Chem.* (*pl.*, earlier *sing.*): The pulverulent form of any substance, *esp.* as condensed after sublimation ME. **d.** Applied to various fungoid growths; a scum formed on wine, vinegar, etc. in fermentation 1548. **3.** A blossom considered independently of the plant; also *fig.* ME. **4.** A flowering plant 1500. **5.** The representation of a flower; *esp.* the FLEUR-DE-LIS (senses 2, 3) ME. **6.** An adornment or ornament; *esp.* an ornament of speech (*rare* in *sing.*) 1508. **7.** 'The pick' of a number of persons or things ME. **8.** The best, choicest, most attractive part of anything; also the gist (of a matter) 1568. **9.** The brightest example of any quality ME. **10.** The condition of being in bloom, 1697. **11.** The period or state of bloom, vigour, or prosperity ME.

1. *fig.* This bud of Loue..May proue a beautious F. when next we meete SHAKS. 3. *fig.* Nay hee's a f., in faith a very f. SHAKS. 5. Flowers were the first Ornaments that were used at the head of.. Pages LUCKOMBE. Phr. *F. of the winds* (Naut.): 'the mariner's compass on maps and charts' (Smyth). 6. That's Æneas..hee's one of the flowers of Troy SHAKS. 7. The flowre..of the Elect TOMSON. 8. Thrice-happy days! The f. of each, those moments when we met TENNYSON. 9. He is not the f. of curtesie SHAKS. 10. An Orchard in F. ADDISON. 11. A man in the f. of life, about thirty SCOTT.

Comb.: **f.-animals,** the Anthozoa; **-cup,** (*a*) the calyx; (*b*) the cup-shaped receptacle formed by a f.; **-fence,** the plant *Poinciana pulcherrima*; **-head,** an inflorescence consisting of a close cluster of sessile florets; **-pecker,** (*a*) any bird of the family *Dicæidæ*; (*b*) an American honey-creeper or guitguit; **-piece,** (*a*) a picture with flowers for its subject; (*b*) an arrangement of flowers; **-stalk,** the peduncle supporting the flower-head.

Flower (flau·əɹ), *v.* ME. [f. prec. sb.] **1.** *intr.* To bloom or blossom; to produce flowers. Of a flower: To expand. Also *fig.* **b.** *trans.* To bring into flower 1850. †**2.** *transf.* Of beer, etc.: To froth, mantle -1750. †**3.** *intr.* To FLOURISH -1531. †**4.** *trans.* To adorn or cover with or as with flowers or a flower -1791. **5.** To embellish with figures of flowers 16..

1. A rose, þat flowred and fayled ME *fig.* Whose drooping phansie never flowred out MORE. 2. It makes beer to mantle, f., and smile at you 1694. 5. The waistcoat I am flowering RICHARDSON.

Hence **Flow·ered** *ppl. a.* covered or adorned with flowers; bearing flowers (of a specified kind or number). **Flow·erer,** a person or thing that flowers.

Flowerage (flauə·rėdʒ). 1688. [f. FLOWER *sb.* and *v.* + -AGE1.] **a.** Flowers collectively, blossom; a display of flowers; floral decoration. *lit.* and *fig.* **b.** The process or result of flowering. *lit.* and *fig.*

Floweret (flauə·rėt). Chiefly *poet.* ME. [f. FLOWER *sb.* and -ET.] A small flower.

Flowerful (flauə·ɹfŭl), *a.* 1848. [See -FUL.] Abounding in or filled with flowers.

†**Flow·er-ge·ntle.** 1561. [f. FLOWER *sb.* + GENTLE *a.*; app. after F. *fleur noble.*] = FLORAMOUR. -1783.

Flow·ering, *vbl. sb.* ME. [f. FLOWER *v.* + -ING [1].] 1. The action of FLOWER *v.* in various senses. 2. In *pl.* Figures of flowers 1864.

Flowering (flau^ə·riŋ), *ppl. a.* ME. [f. as prec. + -ING [2].] 1. That flowers; often in plant-names, as *flowering ash, box, fern*, etc. (see the sbs.) 1592. †2. Flourishing –1621. 3. = FLOWERY. Also, pertaining to or issuing from flowers. 1593.

3. Groves of Myrrhe, And flouring Odours MILT.

Flowerless (flau^ə·ɹlės), *a.* 1500. [-LESS.] Without flower or bloom; *spec.* in *Bot., f. plant* = CRYPTOGAM. Hence **Flow·erlessness.**

Flower-pot, flowerpot (flau^ə·ɹpǫt). 1598. 1. A vessel, commonly of red earthenware, for soil in which flowers are grown. 2. A kind of fire-work 1842.

Flowery (flau^əri), *a.* ME. [See -Y [1].] 1. Abounding in, covered with, or producing flowers. 2. Composed of flowers; proceeding from or characteristic of flowers 1635. 3. Ornamented with flowers or figures of flowers 1667. 4. Abounding in flowers of speech; florid 1603. 5. *Her.* = FLEURY. 1681.

4. A man of f. tongue 1879.

Flowing (flōu·iŋ), *vbl. sb.* OE. [f. FLOW *v.* + -ING [1].] 1. The action of FLOW *v.* in various senses. 2. *concr.* That which flows, a stream, a wave (now *rare*) ME.; †an overflowing; a flood –1663.

Flowing (flōu·iŋ), *ppl. a.* OE. [f. as prec. + -ING [2].] 1. That flows (see FLOW *v.*). †b. *Math.* = FLUENT. –1842. 2. Of lines, curves, etc.: Smoothly continuous and free from stiffness 1709. 3. Of hair, garments, etc.: Waving, unconfined, streaming 1606. 4. Rising like the tide; brimming, copious 1526.

1. Phr. *F. Metals*: see FLOW *v.* I. 2 c. F. eloquence 1627, numbers COWPER, urbanity 1766. 2. Phr. *F. tracery* (Arch.): tracery where the lines branch out into leaves, arches, etc., 1812. 3. A ship is therefore said to have a *flowing sheet* when the wind crosses the line of her course nearly at right angles FALCONER. 4. Fat contentions and f. fees MILT.

Hence **Flow·ing-ly** *adv.*, **-ness.**

Flowk, obs. Sc. f. FLUKE.

Flown (flōun), *ppl. a.* [1] 1608. [pa. pple. of FLY *v.* [1]] Used adjectively in senses of FLY *v.* [1] Also with *out*, and as in *far-, new-flown.*

Floyt(e, var. of FLOTE, FLUTE.

Fluate (flū·eit), *sb.* 1794. [f. FLU(ORIC) + -ATE.] 1. *Chem.* Now called FLUORIDE, q.v. 2. A hydrofluosilicate applied to building-stone to harden it 1887.

Fluc(c)an: = FLOOKAN, q.v.

Flucti-, comb. f. L. *fluctus* wave, in **flucti·ferous** *a.*, bearing or producing waves; **flucti·sonous** *a.*, sounding with waves; etc. (Dicts.)

Fluctuable (flɒ·ktiuăb'l), *a. rare.* [as if ad. L. **fluctuabilis*; see -ABLE.] Capable of fluctuating. (Dicts.) Hence **Fluctuabi·lity**, the quality of being f. H. WALPOLE.

Fluctuant (flɒ·ktiuănt), *a.* 1560. [ad. L. *fluctuantem*; see FLUCTUATE *v.*] 1. Moving like the waves. Chiefly *fig.* 2. Floating on the waves 1605.

1. His genius is f. and moonstruck SWINBURNE. 2. Whether it be f. as the ark of Noah [etc.] BACON.

Fluctuate (flɒ·ktiu,eit), *v.* 1634. [f. L. *fluctuat-*, *fluctuare* to undulate, f. *fluctus*.] 1. *intr.* To move like a wave or waves, rise and fall in or as in waves; to be tossed up and down on the waves. Now *rare.* 2. *fig.* To vary irregularly, undergo alternating changes; to be unstable; to vacillate, waver, 1634. 3. *trans.* To unsettle 1788; to throw into a wave-like motion 1850.

1. So sounds, so fluctuates, the troubled sea 1711. 2. Fluctuating..betuix love and feare 1634. Money fluctuates in price CRUMP. 3. A breeze began to..f. all the still perfume TENNYSON.

Fluctuation (flɒktiu,ēi·ʃən). 1450. [ad. L. *fluctuationem*; see prec. and -ATION.] 1. A motion like that of the waves, an alternate rise and fall. Now *rare* in physical sense. 1646. b. *Path.* The undulation of a fluid in any cavity or tumour of the body 1620. 2. The action or condition of fluctuating; repeated variation, vicissitude. In *pl.* 'ups and downs'. 1609. 3. Vacillation, wavering 1450.

1. This f. of the sea GOLDSM. 2. Changes and fluctuations of government 1712. F. of temperature and season PALEY. 3. Fluctuations of the Mind 1717.

Flue, flew (flū), *sb.* [1] ME. [cf. MDu. *vluwe* fishing-net.] A fishing-net; a. a drag-net; b. a fixed net. Also *flue-net.*

Flue (flū), *sb.* [2] 1589. [? See FLUFF *sb.* [1]] Down, nap; fluff. Also *pl.* bits of down.

Flue (flū), *sb.* [3] 1582. [?] 1. In early use = CHIMNEY; subseq. a smoke-duct in a chimney. Hence applied to a hot-air passage in a wall; a pipe or tube for conveying heat to water in some steam-boilers; and the like. 2. *Organ-building.* The fissure or wind-way of mouth-pipes (hence also called flue-pipes) 1879. 3. *slang.* = SPOUT *sb.* 4. 1821.

3. *In f.*: in pawn. *Up the f.*: (*a*) pawned; (*b*) dead.

Comb.: **f.-boiler,** 'a steam-boiler whose water space is traversed by flues' (Knight); **-bridge,** a wall of fire-brick in a reverberatory furnace, between the hearth and the f.; **-pipe,** an organ-pipe with a f. (see 2), a mouth-pipe, as opp. to a reed-pipe; **-plate,** 'a plate into which the ends of the flue are set' (Knight); **-stop,** an organ-stop made up of f.-pipes, or for a f. opening; **-work,** the f.-stops of an organ collectively as dist. from the reed-stops.

Flue (flū), *sb.* [4] 1860. [?] *Naut.* The FLUKE of an anchor, or that of a harpoon.

Flue (flū), *sb.* [5] Also **flu.** *colloq.* 1839. Short for INFLUENZA.

†**Flu·ence.** 1607. [a. F., ad. L. *fluentia.*] 1. A flowing, a stream. CHAPMAN. 2. = FLUENCY 2. –1691.

Fluency (flū·ĕnsi). 1623. [ad. L. *fluentia*; see prec. and -ENCY.] †1. Affluence, copiousness –1726. 2. Readiness, smoothness; ease; used *esp.* of speech 1636.

1. All his f. of thought 1852. 2. He indulged his satirical f. on the scientific collectors 1814.

Fluent (flū·ĕnt). 1589. [ad. L. *fluentem*, *fluere*.]

A. *adj.* 1. That flows, flowing. Also *transf.* and *fig.* 1607. 2. Capable of flowing easily; fluid, liquid 1601. b. *fig.* Fluid, liable to change 1648. †3. Flowing freely or abundantly –1682. 4. Of speech, style, etc.: Flowing easily and readily 1625. b. Of a speaker, etc.: Ready in the use of words 1589. 5. *Math.* In the doctrine of fluxions: Continuously increasing or decreasing by an infinitesimal quantity 1734.

2. b. The general body of opinion is very f. HELPS. 4. Their f. praying and preaching WOOD. b. Fluent Shakespear scarce effac'd a line POPE.

Hence **Flu·ent-ly** *adv.*, †**-ness.**

B. *sb.* †1. A stream, a current of water –1705. 2. *Math.* The variable quantity in fluxions which is continually increasing or decreasing 1706. Hence †**Flue·ntial** *a.* of or pertaining to fluents.

Fluey (flū·i), *a.* 1861. [f. FLUE *sb.* [2] + -Y [1].] Covered with flue.

Fluff (flɒf), *sb.* [1] 1790. [? a modification of FLUE *sb.* [2]] 1. Anything light, feathery, and flocculent. 2. A soft, downy mass or bunch 1862. b. *Bit of fluff* (slang): a young woman 1903.

Fluff (flɒf), *sb.* [2] *Sc.* and *n. dial.* 1818. [see FLUFF *v.* [2]] A puff; a whiff; a slight explosion. *lit.* and *fig.*

Comb.: **f.-gib,** a squib. SCOTT.

Fluff (flɒf), *v.* 1859. [f. FLUFF *sb.* [1]] 1. *trans. Leather-manuf.* To whiten the flesh side of a skin 1882. 2. To pick into oakum 1892. 3. To shake *out* or *up* into a soft mass like fluff 1885. 4. *intr.* To move or float softly like fluff; to settle *down* like a ball of fluff 1872. 5. *slang.* In *Fluff it!* = 'take it away, I don't want it' 1859.

3. The 'Johnny Crows'..f. and plume and dust themselves without cessation LADY BRASSEY.

Fluffy (flɒ·fi), *a.* 1825. [f. FLUFF sb. [1] + -Y [1].] 1. Consisting of or resembling fluff; soft and downy. 2. Covered with fluff, down, fur, or the like; downy 1848.

1. F. whiskers THACKERAY. 2. The f. yellow chickens 1879.

Hence **Flu·ffiness,** f. quality.

Flugelman: see FUGLEMAN.

Fluid (flū·id). 1603. [a. F. *fluide*, ad. L. *fluidus*, f. *fluere*; see -ID.]

A. *adj.* 1. Having the property of flowing; consisting of particles that move freely among themselves, so as to give way before the slightest pressure. (A general term including both *gaseous* and *liquid* substances.) Also *fig.* and of non-physical things. 2. Flowing easily and clearly; fluent; as speech, etc. 1691.

1. The language of the Bible is f., passing, and literary, not rigid, fixed, and scientific M. ARNOLD.

B. *sb.* 1. A fluid substance 1661.

Fluids are divided into liquids, which are incompletely elastic, and gases, which are completely so.

2. One of several subtle, imponderable, all-pervading substances, whose existence has been assumed to account for the phenomena of heat, magnetism, and electricity 1750.

1. The air being a f. BOYLE. Moderate exercise will enrich the Fluids 1704. 2. The particles of the electrical f. FRANKLIN.

Comb.: **f.-compass,** 'that in which the card revolves in its bowl floated by alcohol' (Adm. Smyth); **-lens,** one in which a liquid is imprisoned between circular glass disks of the required curvature.

Hence **Flu·idal** *a.* (*Geol.*) of or resembling a f., as the *fluidal* structure of vitreous rocks. **Flui·dic** *a.* of the nature of a f.; in *Spiritualism*, of or belonging to a supposed inner 'double' (of fluid or ethereal consistence) possessed by every being. **Flui·dify** *v.* to make f. **Fluidifica·tion.**

Fluidism (flū·idiz'm). 1835. [f. prec. + -ISM.] 1. The theory which refers all diseases to the state of the fluids in the body. 2. *Spiritualism.* The hypothesis of the existence of supersensible fluidic bodies (see FLUIDIC). So **Flu·idist,** one who supports f. (in either sense).

Fluidity (flu,i·dĭti). 1603. [f. FLUID *a.* + -ITY. Cf. F. *fluidité.*] 1. The quality or condition of being FLUID 1605. 2. Of speech, etc.: The quality of flowing easily and clearly.

1. *fig.* The f. of Radicalism 1886. 2. There is the same comparative tenuity and f. of verse SWINBURNE.

†**Flu·idness.** 1626. [-NESS.] = FLUIDITY. –1670.

Fluke (flūk), *sb.* [1] [OE. *flóc*, cogn. w. ON. *flóke*; related by ablaut to Ger. *flach* flat.] 1. A flat fish, *esp.* the common flounder, *Pleuronectes Flesus.* 2. A parasitic trematoid worm, of several species, found *esp.* in the livers of sheep, so called from its shape 1668. 3. A variety of kidney potato 1868.

1. Wry-mouthed Flooke CAREW. Hence **Flu·ky** *a.* [1] infested with flukes.

Fluke (flūk), *sb.* [2] 1561. [? transf. use of FLUKE *sb.* [1], from the shape.] 1. One of the broad triangular plates of iron on each arm of the anchor, which enter the ground and hold the ship. b. Anything resembling the prec. in shape; esp. *U.S.* 'one of the barbs of a harpoon or toggle-iron; a flue' (*Cent. Dict.*) 1605. 2. *pl.* 'The two parts which constitute the large triangular tail of the whale' (Smyth) 1725.

1. Her owne anker, which by one of the floukes tooke fast hold HOLLAND. b. The f. of a lance 1613, of an arrow CATLIN. *Fluke*, in mining..an instrument used for cleansing the hole previous to blasting (Weale). 2. Phr. *To turn* or *peak the flukes*: of a whale, to go under; hence (*Naut. slang*) to go to bed.

Fluke (flūk), *sb.* [3] *colloq.* 1857. [?] In *Billiards*, A successful stroke made by accident or chance. Hence *gen.* an unexpected success; a piece of good luck. *A f. of wind*: a chance breeze. Hence **Flu·ky** *a.* [2] of the nature of a f.; uncertain. **Flu·kily** *adv.*

Fluke (flūk), *v.* [1] 1840. [f. FLUKE *sb.* [2]] 1. *intr.* Of a whale: To use the flukes in swimming 1840. 2. *trans.* a. To disable the flukes of (a whale) by spading. b. To fasten (a whale) by means of a chain or rope (*Cent. Dict.*).

Fluke (flūk), *v.* [2] 1881. [f. FLUKE *sb.* [3]] 1. *Billiards. trans.* To hit or pocket (a ball) by a fluke; to make (a stroke) by a fluke. 2. *transf.* To get (*in*) or obtain by a fluke 1885.

Flume (flūm), *sb.* [ME. *flum, flun*, a. OF.:— L. *flumen*, f. *fluere*.] †1. A stream, a river; also, water –1652. 2. A mill-tail 1855. 3. *U.S.*, etc. An artificial channel for a stream of water to be applied to some industrial use 1784. b. A deep narrow channel or ravine with a stream running through it 1792.

Flummery (flɒ·məri). 1623. [a. Welsh *llymru*, of unkn. etym.; the *fl-* is for Welsh *ll-*.] 1. 'A kind of food made by coagulation of wheatmeal or oatmeal (J.). In *Mod. Cookery*, any of various sweet dishes made with milk, flour, eggs, etc. 2. *fig.* Mere compliment; nonsense, humbug, empty trifling 1749. Also *attrib.*

2. A fine f. about the..eminent genius of the person whom they are addressing THACKERAY.
Hence †Flu·mmer *v.* to humbug.

Flummox (flɒ·məks), *v. colloq.* or *vulgar.* 1837. [prob. of Eng. dial. origin.] 1. *trans.* To bring to confusion; to 'do for'; to bewilder, nonplus. 2. *intr. U.S.* To give up, collapse 1847. Hence **Flu·mmox** *sb.* any failure.

Flump (flɒmp), *v. colloq.* 1790. [Echoic.] 1. *intr.* To fall or move heavily with a dull noise 1816. 2. *trans.* To set or throw *down* with a dump 1830. 3. Used advb. With a flump 1790. Hence **Flump** *sb.* the action or sound of flumping.

Flung (flɒŋ), pa. pple. of FLING *v.*

Flunk (flɒŋk), *v. U.S.* 1823. [Cf. FLINK, FUNK.] 1. *intr.* To give up, back out, fail utterly. Also quasi-*trans.* To shirk (a recitation). 2. *trans.* To cause to flunk; to pluck. Hence **Flunk** *sb.* a total failure, *esp.* in a college examination.

Flunkey (flɒ·ŋki), *sb.*[1] 1782. [? a dim. corruption of FLANKER. Orig. Sc.] 1. A male servant, usu. in livery, *esp.* a footman, lackey; often *contempt.* Hence 2. One who behaves obsequiously to his superiors in rank or position; a toady, snob 1855. Hence **Flu·nkeydom**, the domain of flunkeys; flunkeys collectively; the spirit of a f. **Flu·nkeyism**, the manners, speech, etc. of a f.

Flunkey (flɒ·ŋki), *sb.*[2] *U.S.* 1841. [f. FLUNK *v.* or *sb.* + -Y.] One who 'flunks' or fails; *esp.* an ignorant person who dabbles in financial speculation.

Fluo- (flū·o). *Chem.* and *Min.* Abbrev. of FLUOR, used as comb. form in compounds containing fluorine.
Flu·obo·rate, a salt of fluoboric acid. **Flu·o-bo·ric acid**, orig. the gas terfluoride of boron (BF_3), now applied to the compound ($H_2B_2O_4 . 6HF$) obtained by saturating water with this. **Flu·oce·rine, Flu·o-ce·rite**, a native fluoride of cerium and the allied metals. **Flu·o-hy·dric** (acid) = *Fluorhydric*. Also in the names of other acids of which fluorine is a component, and in the names of salts as **Flu·o-pho·sphate, -si·licate**, etc.

Fluor (flū·ǫɹ), *sb.* 1621. [a. L., f. *fluere.* Cf. OF. *flueur.*] †1. A flow or flowing; a flux, stream –1671. 2. *spec.* in *Path.* †a. *pl.* = FLOWERS. 1621. ‖b. **Fluor albus** = LEUCORRHŒA. 1754. †3. A fluid state; *concr.* a fluid mass; in *pl.* the humours (of the body) –1721. 4. *Min.* †a. A generic name for a class of minerals resembling gems, but readily fusible, and useful as fluxes in smelting 1661. b. Since 1771 applied *spec.* to such of these minerals as contain fluorine, chiefly (now only) to calcium fluoride or FLUOR-SPAR. 5. *attrib.* †f. acid, hydrofluoric acid 1791.

Fluor- (flū·or), comb. f. FLUORINE bef. vowels. **Fluorhydric** [+ HYDR(-OGEN) + -IC] acid, *Chem.* hydrofluoric acid (HF).

Fluorated (flū·ŏreɪtėd), *ppl. a.* 1796. [f. FLUOR- + -ATE + -ED[1].] Combined with hydrofluoric acid.

Fluorene (flū·ŏrīn). 1883. [f. FLUOR + -ENE.] *Chem.* A hydro-carbon extracted from coal-tar ($C_{13}H_{10}$); when impure it is fluorescent, whence the name.

Fluoresce (fluŏre·s), *v.* 1874. [f. FLUORESCENCE.] To be or become fluorescent.

Fluorescein (fluŏre·sɪ,in). 1876. [f. prec. + -IN.] *Chem.* A product fluorescent in solution obtained by heating phthalic anhydride with resorcin.

Fluorescence (fluŏre·sĕns). 1852. [f. FLUOR(-SPAR), after *opalescence.*] The coloured luminosity produced in some transparent bodies by the direct action of light, esp. of the violet and ultra-violet rays; the property, in certain substances, of rendering the ultra-violet rays visible, so as to produce this phenomenon.

Fluorescent (fluŏre·sĕnt), *a.* 1853. [f. FLUORESCE + -ENT.] Possessing or proceeding from fluorescence.

Fluoric (fluǫ·rik), *a.* 1790. [ad. F. *fluorique*; see FLUOR and -IC.] Pertaining to or obtained from fluor or fluor-spar.

Fluoride (flū·ŏrid, -əid). Also **-id.** 1826. [f. FLUOR-INE + -IDE.] *Chem.* A binary compound of fluorine with another element.

Fluorine (flū·ŏrin, -əin). 1813. [f. FLUOR + -INE, after BROMINE, etc.] *Chem.* A non-metallic element (symbol F), forming, with bromine, chlorine, and iodine, the halogen group.

Fluorite (flū·ŏrəit). 1868. [f. FLUOR + -ITE.] *Min.* = FLUOR-SPAR.

Fluoroid (flū·ŏroid). [f. FLUOR + -OID.] *Crystallogr.* A solid bounded by twenty-four triangular planes; occurring frequently in fluor-spar.

Fluor-spar (flū·ǫɹ,spāɹ). 1794. [f. FLUOR + SPAR.] *Min.* Native fluoride of calcium (CaF_2); found abundantly in Derbyshire, and often called *Derbyshire spar.*

Flurry (flɒ·ri), *sb.* 1698. [? echoic.] 1. A sudden agitation of the air, a gust or squall. b. Chiefly *U.S.* A sharp and sudden shower; a sudden rush (of birds) 1828. 2. A sudden commotion; nervous agitation, flutter, hurry 1710. b. The death-throes of a whale 1823.
1. Flurries from the Hills FRYER. b. Flurries of snow W. IRVING. 2. In a fright and a f. TUCKER.

Flurry (flɒ·ri), *v.* 1757. [f. prec. sb.] 1. *trans.* To agitate, 'put out'. 2. *intr.* To flutter down in sudden or gusty showers. ? *U.S.* 1883. Hence **Flu·rried** *ppl. a.*; **-ly** *adv.*

Flurt, obs. f. FLIRT.

Flush (flɒʃ), *sb.*[1] 1596. [f. FLUSH *v.*[1]] A flight of birds suddenly started up.

Flush (flɒʃ), *sb.*[2] ME. [f. FLUSH *v.*[2]] †1. A pool or puddle –1513. 2. A sudden flow; a rush of water coming or let down suddenly 1529. b. A sudden abundance of anything 1592. 3. A rush of emotion or passion; elation or excitement arising from this, or from success, etc. 1614. 4. A fresh growth (of grass, leaves, or flowers) 1773. 5. The act of cleansing a drain by flushing 1883. 6. A glow of light or colour, *esp* the reddening in the face caused by a rush of blood; the rush of blood itself 1630. 7. Glow, freshness, vigour (of beauty, health, life) 1735.
2. b. The great f. of gold BACON. 3. Unreasonable flushes of proud and vaine joy RALEIGH. Phr. *In the (first, full) f.* 4. The young shoots, now in full f. after a heavy shower 1893. 6. Hectic flushes 1803.

Flush (flɒʃ), *sb.*[3] 1529. [? f. (ult.) L. *fluxus* flow (cf. *run*); assoc. w. prec.] *Cards.* A hand consisting of cards all of one suit.

Flush (flɒʃ), *a.*[1] 1550. [? f. FLUSH *v.*[2]] 1. Abundantly full; in flood. 2. Full of life or spirit. Hence, Self-confident. Now *rare.* 1604. 3. Plentifully supplied (*esp.* with money). Const. *of.* Of money: Plentiful. 1603. 4. Of a high colour; blushing; flushed 1594. 5. Even, level, in the same plane (*with*) 1626; even or level with the adjacent surface 1823.
1. In the f. moment of joy DISRAELI. 2. F. youth reuolt SHAKS. 3. Tom..is always very f. or very hard up 1871. 4. Thy Cheeke, now f. with Roses DRAYTON. Hence **Flu·shness**, f. condition.

Flush (flɒʃ), *a.*[2] 1591. [f. FLUSH *sb.*[3]] *Cards.* †Holding a flush. Of a hand or sequence: Forming or including a flush.

Flush (flɒʃ), *v.*[1] ME. [perh. echoic; cf. *fly, flutter,* and *rush.*] 1. *intr.* To fly up quickly and suddenly; to take wing. †Also, to fly with a whirr. †Also *fig.* of persons –1642. 2. *trans.* To cause to fly or take wing; to put up 1450.
2. Lete the spanyell flusch up the covey 1450.

Flush (flaʃ), *v.*[2] 1548. [? same wd. as prec.; infl. by FLASH *v.*[2] and BLUSH *v.*]
I. Expressing sudden movement. 1. *intr.* To rush out suddenly and copiously; to flow with force. Also *fig.* 2. *trans.* To cause (water) to flow; to draw off water from 1815. 3. To cleanse (a drain, etc.) by means of a rush of water 1789; to inundate (a meadow) 1861. 4. *intr.* Of a plant: To shoot. Also *trans.* to cause to shoot. 1810. 5. *intr.* 'To become fluxed or fluid' (*Cent. Dict.*).
1. The..Well-head, whence first flushed forth this muddy Nylus 1624. 2. To f. a pond 1594. 3. Sewer pipes should be flushed from time to time 1871. *fig.* F. out your sins with tears 1884.
II. With reference to light or colour. 1. *intr.* To glow with sudden brilliance. Cf. FLASH *v.*[2] 1809. 2. Of the blood, etc.: To come with a rush, produce a heightened colour 1667. 3. Of the face, etc.: To become suddenly red or hot 1709. 4. *trans.* To make red or ruddy 1697; to suffuse or adorn with glowing colour 1746. 5. To animate 1633.
1. As I have seen the rosy red flushing in the northern night TENNYSON. 2. In her Cheek distemper flushing glowd MILT. *P. L.* IX. 886. 4. How faintly-flush'd, how phantom-fair Was Monte Rosa TENNYSON. 5. Armies flush'd with conquest ADDISON.

Flush (flɒʃ), *v.*[3] 1842. [f. FLUSH *a.*[1] 5.] 1. *trans.* To make flush; to fill in (a joint) level with the surface; to point. 2. *Weaving.* To throw (a thread) on the surface over several threads without intersection. Also *intr.* of the thread. 1878.

†**Flush** (flɒʃ), *adv.* [f. FLUSH *a.*[1]] Directly, straight. FARQUHAR.

Flusher (flɒ·ʃəɹ). *dial.* Also **flasher.** 1674. [Cf. FLUSH *v.*[2]] The Red-backed Shrike, *Lanius collurio.*

Flushing (flɒ·ʃiŋ), *sb.* 1833. [Name of a port in Holland (Du. *Vlissingen*).] A kind of rough and thick woollen cloth, first made at Flushing.

Flu·shing, *vbl. sb.* 1573. [f. FLUSH *v.*[2] + -ING.[1]] The action of FLUSH *v.*[2] in various senses; *esp.* the cleansing (of a sewer, etc.) by a rush of water.

Fluster (flɒ·stəɹ), *sb.* 1676. [see next vb.] 1. †a. Heat from drinking 1710. b. A confused or agitated state of mind; a flurry, flutter 1728. †2. ? Pomp, splendour –1716.

Fluster (flɒ·stəɹ), *v.* ME. [Cf. mod. Icel. *flaustr* hurry, bustle, *flaustra* to bustle. Cf. BLUSTER *v.*] †1. ? To excite, stimulate. ME. only. 2. *trans.* To flush or excite with drink 1604. 3. *intr.* To be excited or eager; to bustle 1613. 4. *trans.* To flurry, confuse 1724.
2. His head is flustered with burgundy THACKERAY. 3. The Dutch gunboat came flustering up KIPLING. Hence **Flu·stered** *ppl. a.* half-tipsy; confused, flurried.

Flustrate (flɒ·streɪt), *v. vulgar.* 1712. [f. FLUSTER *v.* + -ATE [3].] = FLUSTER *v.* 2 and 4. Hence **Flustra·tion**, fluster, agitation.

Flute (flūt), *sb.*[1] [ME. *flowte*, later *fluit(e,* a. OF. *fleüte, flaüte, flahute* (also written *flahuste*), mod. F. *flûte* = Pr. *flauta* fem., of unkn. origin.] 1. A musical wind instrument, consisting of a hollow cylinder or pipe, with holes along its length, stopped by the fingers, or by keys which are opened by the fingers.
The flute of the ancients was blown through a mouthpiece at the end. The modern flute, which is the *transverse* or *German flute*, is blown through an orifice at the side near the upper end.
2. A flute-player 1542. 3. An organ-stop having a flute-like tone; also *f.-stop* 1613. 4. Anything resembling a flute in shape; e.g. a long thin French breakfast-roll; †a tall, slender wine-glass; etc. 1649. 5. *Arch.* A channel or furrow in a pillar, resembling the half of a flute split lengthwise, with the concave side outwards 1660. 6. Hence any similar groove or channel 1727.
1. Indians met vs on the way, playing vpon Flutes; which is a token that they come in peace PURCHAS.
Comb.: **f.-bird** (*Australia*), the piping crow (*Gymnorhina tibicen*); **-bit**, a boring tool, used in boring hard woods; **-glass**, see 4 above; **-stop** = sense 3 above.

Flute (flūt), *sb.*[2] 1567. [perh. a transf. use of *fluit* = prec.] *Naut.* 1. 'A pink-rigged fly-boat, the after part of which is round-ribbed' (Smyth). 2. A vessel of war, carrying only part of her armament, to serve as a transport 1666. Hence *Armed en f.* (Fr. *armé en flûte*), said of such a vessel.

Flute (flūt), *v.* ME. [f. FLUTE *sb.*[1]] 1. *intr.* To play upon a flute or pipe; also, to whistle or sing in flute-like tones. 2. *trans.* To play (an air, etc.) on a flute; to sing in flute-like notes 1842. 3. To form flutes (see FLUTE *sb.*[1] 5, 6) in; to arrange a dress, etc. in flutes 1578.
1. quasi-*trans.* And f. his friend, like Orpheus, from the dead M. ARNOLD. 2. Some..swan..fluting a wild carol ere her death TENNYSON. The redwing flutes his o-ka-lee EMERSON.

Fluted (flū·tėd), *ppl. a.* 1611. [f. FLUTE *sb.*[1] and *v.*] 1. Having, furnished, or ornamented with flutes. 2. *Mus.* Of a thin and flute-like tone 1787.
1. *F. spectrum*, one in which the spectrum lines appear to be grouped in flutes. F. pillars BERKELEY. 2. A f. falsetto BECKFORD.

‖**Flute-douce** (flū̆tˌdus). 1676. [Fr. *flûte douce* lit. 'sweet flute'.] †1. The highest-pitched variety of the old flute with a mouth-piece –1747. 2. An organ-stop so named 1876.

Fluter (flū̆·tǝɹ). ME. [f. FLUTE *v.*] 1. A flute-player. Now *rare*; repl. by FLUTIST or FLAUTIST. 2. One who makes flutings 1858.

Fluting (flū̆·tiŋ), *vbl. sb.* 1481. [f. FLUTE *v.* + -ING[1].] 1. The action of FLUTE *v.*; *esp.* the action of making flutes in columns, frills, etc.; ornamentation with flutes; fluted work. Also *attrib.*, as *f.-lathe, -plane*, etc. 2. = FLUTE *sb.*[1] 5, 6. Also *collect.* 1611.

1. The earliest flutings of the lark 1874. 2. She ran her fingers through the flutings of her frills 1880.

Flutist (flū̆·tist). 1603. [f. FLUTE *sb.*[1] + -IST. Cf. F. *flûtiste*.] A player on the flute.

Flutter (flɒ·tǝɹ), *sb.* 1641. [f. next vb.] 1. A fluttering; the action or condition of fluttering. b. *colloq.* A run, a burst 1857. 2. An agitated or disordered condition 1748. †3. Ostentatious display, fuss, sensation, stir –1822. 4. *slang.* A venture, e.g. at betting, cards, etc. 1874.

1. The f. of a Fan ADDISON. 2. Phr. *To be in, fall, put*, etc., *into a f.* 3. All f., pride, and talk POPE.

Comb. **f.-wheel**, a water-wheel placed at the bottom of a chute so as to receive the impact of the water in the chute and penstock.

Flutter (flɒ·tǝɹ), *v.* [OE. *flotorian*, a freq. f. *flot-* weak-grade of root of *flēotan* FLEET *v.*] †1. *intr.* To float to and fro. Also *fig.* –1513. 2. Of birds: To move or flap the wings rapidly without flying or with short flights. Also *transf.* and *fig.* OE. 3. *transf.* To move about aimlessly, restlessly, sportively, or ostentatiously 1694. 4. To move with quick vibrations or undulations 1561. 5. To tremble with excitement; to be in agitation 1668. 6. *trans.* (*causatively*). To cause to flutter; to move (a thing) in quick irregular motions 1621; *fig.* to throw (a person) into confusion, agitation, or tremulous excitement 1664.

2. Like as byrdes flotre aboute their nestes COVERDALE *Isa.* xxxi. 5. 3. One flaunts in rags, one flutters in brocade POPE. 4. Teach..little hearts to f. at a Beau POPE. It [the pulse] paused—it fluttered SHELLEY. 5. Fluttering with her own audacity THACKERAY. 6. All unawares, Fluttering his pennons vain MILT. *fig.* Like an Eagle in a Dove-coat, I Flutter'd your Volcians in Coriolus *Cor.* (F. 3) v. vi. 116.

Hence **Flu·tterer**, one who or that which flutters (*lit.* and *fig.*). **Flu·tteringly** *adv.*

Fluty (flū̆·ti), *a.* 1823. [f. FLUTE *sb.*[1] + -Y[1].] Flute-like in tone, soft and clear.

Fluvial (flū̆·viăl), *a.* ME. [a. F., ad. L. *fluvialis*, f. *fluvius*.] Of or pertaining to a river or rivers; found or living in a river. Hence **Flu·vialist**, one who explains certain geological phenomena by the action of streams.

Fluviatile (flū̆·viătil), *a.* 1599. [a. F., ad. L. *fluviatilis*, f. *fluvius*.] Of or pertaining to a river or rivers; found, growing, or living in rivers; formed or produced by the action of rivers.

F. Fishes 1681, mud 1823, denudation HUXLEY.

†**Fluvia·tion.** [f. L. *fluviatus*.] The process of steeping (flax) in water. SIR T. BROWNE.

Fluvio- (flū̆·vio), comb. f. L. *fluvius* river, as in **flu·vio-marine** *a.*, an epithet of deposits formed by river-currents at the bottom of the sea; etc.

Flux (flɒks), *sb.* ME. [a. F.:— L. *fluxus*, f. *fluere* (Lat. root **flugv-*) to flow.]

I. *spec.* 1. An abnormally copious flowing of blood, excrement, etc. from the bowels or other organs. *spec.* An early name for dysentery. 2. A flowing out, issue, discharge (of humours, etc.) 1447; †also, that which flows or is discharged –1654.

1. Phr. *Bloody f.* (cf. BLOODY); Rendered unfit for action by a bloody f. WATSON. 2. *A. Y. L.* III. ii. 70.

II. *gen.* 1. The action of flowing. Now usu. *fig.* 1600. 2. The flowing in of the tide. Often in phr. *flux and reflux*. 1612. 3. A flowing stream, a flood. Also *transf.* and *fig.* 1600. 4. The passing away (of life, time, etc.) –1759. 5. A continuous succession of changes 1625. 6. *Math.* A continued motion (of a point) 1656. 7. *Physics.* The rate of flow of any fluid across a given area; the amount which crosses an area in a given time 1863.

1. Fire to subsist requires a F. of Air 1748. 2. A.. f. and reflux of hopes and fears DE FOE. 3. *transf.* The Fluxe of companie *A. Y. L.* II. i. 52. *fig.* This f. of guesses M. ARNOLD. 5. The bodies of all animals are in a constant f. BUTLER.

III. †1. Liquefaction or fusion –1799. 2. *Metall.* Any substance that is mixed with a metal, etc. to facilitate its fusion; also a substance used to render colours fusible in enamelling and the colouring of porcelain and glass 1704.

2. The *black f.* is formed, by setting fire to a mixture of one part of nitrate of potassa, and two of bi-tartrate of potassa.. *White f.* is obtained by projecting into a red-hot crucible equal parts of the same salts HENRY.

†**Flux** (flɒks), *a.* 1677. [ad. L. *fluxus, fluere*.] That is in a state of flux; fluctuating, ever-changing –1797.

Flux (flɒks), *v.* 1477. [f. FLUX *sb.*] †1. *trans.* To treat by subjecting to a flux; also, to produce a flux in (a person); †also *fig.* –1785. †b. *intr.* –1785. 2. *intr.* †a. To bleed copiously 1638. b. To flow copiously 1823. 3. *trans.* To make fluid, fuse 1477. 4. To treat with a flux (see FLUX *sb.* III. 2) 1781. 5. *intr.* To become fluid; to melt 1669.

1. *fig.* Praying for the Dead, which doth so f. the pocket 1660. 2. b. Once fix the seat of your disorder, and your fancies f. into it LAMB. Hence †**Fluxa·tion**, treatment by fluxing; flowing on.

Fluxible (flɒ·ksib'l), *a.* *Obs.* or *arch.* 1471. [a. OF., ad. L. *fluxibilis*, f. *flux-, fluere*.] 1. Apt to flow, fluid 1551. 2. Capable of being melted 1471. 3. Liable to flux or change 1561. Hence **Flu·xibly** *adv.* **Fluxibi·lity. Flu·xibleness**, f. quality.

Fluxile (flɒ·ksil), *a.* *Obs.* or *arch.* 1605. [ad. late L. *fluxilis*; see prec. and -ILE.] = FLUXIBLE 1, 3. Hence **Fluxi·lity**, f. quality.

Fluxion (flɒ·kʃǝn). 1541. [a. F., ad. L. *fluxionem*; see -ION.] 1. The action of flowing; a flowing forth. Also continuous or progressive change. Now *rare*. 1599. †b. = EFFLUVIUM 2 a. –1748. 2. An excessive flow of blood, serum, etc. to any organ or part of the body. Also *concr.*, that which flows. 1541. 3. = FLUX *sb.* I. 1563. 4. *Math.* In the Newtonian form of the infinitesimal calculus: 'The rate or proportion at which a flowing or varying quantity increases its magnitude' (Hutton). (But used by 18th c. writers for what Newton called the 'moment' of a fluent, and modern analysts call the 'differential'.) b. Hence *Fluxions* is used as a name for the Newtonian calculus 1702. ¶ c. *loosely.* An infinitesimal quantity. DE QUINCEY.

Comb. **f.-structure** (*Geol.*), an arrangement of the crystallites, crystals, or particles of a rock in streaky lines..indicative of the internal movement of the mass previous to its consolidation. Called also *flow-structure.*

Hence **Flu·xional** *a. Math.* of or pertaining to a f. or the method of fluxions; pertaining to flowing, flexible. **Flu·xionary** *a. Math.* fluxional; of the nature of, or subject to continuous change. **Flu·xionist**, one who uses or is skilled in mathematical fluxions.

†**Flu·xive**, *a.* 1597. [f. L. *flux-, fluere*; see -IVE.] Apt to flow, fluid (*lit.* and *fig.*). Also fluctuating, variable. –1716.

†**Flu·xure** (flɒ·ksiŭɹ). 1596. [ad. L. *fluxura*, f. as prec.] a. The quality of being fluid 1599. b. That which flows –1622.

Fly (flǝi). *sb.*[1] *Pl.* **flies** (flǝiz). [OE. *flēoge, flȳge* :— OTeut. **fleugôn-*, f. root of **fleugan* to fly.] 1. †Any winged insect; as the bee, gnat, locust, moth, etc.; cf. BUTTERFLY –1774. b. Any dipterous or two-winged insect OE. 2. In farmers' and gardeners' language, the insect parasite chiefly injurious to a particular crop or animal; hop-fly, potato-fly, sheep-fly. Hence *collect.* in *sing.* the corresponding disease. 1704. 3. *Angling.* a. An insect attached to a hook as a lure in fly-fishing 1653. b. An artificial fly, i.e. a fish-hook dressed to resemble some insect 1589. †4. a. A familiar demon. b. *transf.* A spy (cf. F. *mouche*). c. A parasite (cf. L. *musca*). –1649. 4. *Printing.* The person who takes the sheets from the press; also, that part of a printing machine which usually does this now. 1732.

1. Phr. *F. in amber*: see AMBER. *To break, crush, a f. upon the wheel* (fig.): to spend great energy and labour on something not worth it *A f. in the ointment* [after Eccl. x. 1]: a trifling circumstance which spoils the enjoyment of a thing. *There are no flies on*: there is no fault to be found with; there is nothing 'shady' about (orig. *Colonial* and *U.S. slang*). **Black f.**, *U.S.* any one of the species of the genus *Simulium*, some of which cause great suffering by their bites. **Hessian f., Spanish f., Tsetse -f.**, etc.: see HESSIAN, etc. 3. Or with a Flie, either a natural or an artificial Flie WALTON.

Combs.

1. General: as *f.-belt, -country, -maggot, -maker, -tackle, -taker*, etc.

2. Special: **f.-bird**, a humming-bird (cf. F. *oiseau-mouche*); **-blister**, a plaster made of *Cantharides*; **-book**, a case in the form of a book for artificial flies; †**-cap**, a kind of head-dress formerly worn by women; **-case**, the covering of an insect; *spec.* the elytron of beetles; **-hook**, a hook baited with a f.; **-line**, a line for f.-fishing; **-nut**, 'a nut with wings, to be twisted by the hand' (Knight); **-paper**, paper prepared to catch or poison flies; **-powder**, a powder used to kill flies; **-rod**, a rod for f.-fishing; **-snapper**, *U.S.*, a name of certain f.-catching birds, (*a*) the genus *Myiagra*; (*b*) *Phainopepla nitens*; **-speck, -spot**, a stain produced by the excrement of an insect; **-water**, a solution of arsenic, or decoction of quassia-bark, for killing flies; **-weevil**, *U.S.*, the common grain-moth (*Gelechia cerealella*); **-weight**, a boxer whose weight is 8 st.

b. In plant-names, as **f.-agaric**, *Agaricus muscarius*, called also FLY-BANE; **-honeysuckle**, (*a*) a variety of honeysuckle (*Lonicera Xylosteum*); (*b*) a species of Halleria; **-orchid, -orchis**, a name for *Ophrys muscifera.*

Fly (flǝi), *sb.*[2] *Pl.* **flies.** OE. [f. FLY *v.*[1]]

I. 1. †The action, or (*rec.*) an act of flying. 2. *On the f.*: orig. on the wing; hence, in motion; in *Baseball*, the course of a ball that has been struck, until it touches the ground. 1851.

II. 1. A quick-travelling carriage; *esp.* a light vehicle, introduced at Brighton in 1816, and originally drawn by men; subseq. extended to any one-horse covered carriage, as a cab or hansom, let out on hire. 2. Something attached by the edge (cf. FLAP *sb.*); as a. A strip or lap on a garment, to contain or cover the button-holes 1844; b. The sloping part of the canvas of a tent; also, the flap at the entrance, forming a door 1810; c. The breadth from the staff of a flag to the end; also, the part of a flag farthest from the staff 1864; d. *pl. Theatr.* The space over the proscenium 1805. 3. *techn.*

a. *Naut.* A compass card 1571. b. A speed-regulating device, usually consisting of vanes on a rotating shaft, used in the striking parts of clock-machinery, etc. 1599. c. A fly-wheel, a pair of weighted arms, or other similar device, used to regulate the speed of machinery 1599. d. = FANNER 2. 1807. e. One of the cylinders of a carding machine 1842. f. In *Knitting* (*machine*), another name for the Latch; in *Spinning*, the arms which revolve around the bobbin in a spinning-frame, to twist the yarn; in *Weaving*, a shuttle driven through the shed by a blow or jerk (Knight). Also in *Hand-spinning*: the spindle 1851. g. In the pianoforte, a hinged board which covers the keys when not in use.

4. Waste cotton 1879.

Comb.: **f.-ball** (*Base-ball*), a ball that may be caught 'on the f.'; **-bill**, a handbill to be scattered broadcast, also *attrib.*; **-block** (*Naut.*), 'the block spliced into the topsail-tye' (Smyth); **-bridge** = FLYING BRIDGE; **-coach** = FLY *sb.*[2] II. 1; **-governor** = FLY *sb.*[2] II. 3 c; **-press**, a screw press worked by a f. (see FLY *sb.*[2] II. 3 c); **-punching-press**, a press for cutting teeth on saws, and the like; **-rail**, that part of a table which turns out to support the leaf; **-table**, a table with flaps; **-title**, the half-title in front of the general title, or which divides sections of a work.

Fly (flǝi), *a.* *slang.* 1811. [? f. FLY *v.*[1]] 1. Knowing, wide-awake. 2. Of the fingers: Nimble, skilful 1834.

Fly (flǝi), *v.*[1] Pa. t. **flew** (flū̆); pa. pple. **flown** (flōun). [Com. Teut. str. vb.: OE. *flēogan, flīogan* :— OTeut. **fleugan* :— pre-Teut. **pleugh-, plough-, plugh-*. Not cogn. w. FLEE *v.* The origin of the form *flew(e* is not explained.]

I. 1. *intr.* To move through the air with wings. Also *fig.*; *esp.* of fame, a report, etc. ME. b. Occas. = 'fly away' 1480. c. *intr.* and *trans.* To travel or traverse by aircraft; to pilot aircraft 1884. 2. *trans.* (*causatively*). To set (birds) flying 1607. 3. *Hawking.* a. Of the hawk: To gain by flying a position of attack. Const. *at.* 1674. b. Of the falconer: To cause to attack by flying 1591. c. To chase with a hawk. Also of the hawk. 1590. 4. *intr.* To pass or rise quickly in or through the air OE. b. Of stairs: To descend or ascend without change of direction 1685. 5. *trans.* (*causatively*). To cause to fly 1739. 6. *intr.* To float loosely, to flutter, wave 1659. **b.** *trans.* To set flying; to carry at the mast-head; to hoist; occas. with *out* 1655. **7.** *intr.* To move or travel swiftly; *esp.* of time ME. **8.** To move with a start or rush 1590. **9.** Of things: To be forced or driven off suddenly or with a jerk ME. Of money: To 'go' rapidly 1632. **b.** To break up suddenly, shiver, split up 1470. **c.** *Naut.* Of the wind: To shift or veer suddenly 1699.

1. Phr. *As the crow flies*: see CROW *sb.*[1] *fig.* *To f. high, low*: to aim at, avoid, distinction, notoriety, etc. **b.** The black bat, night, has flown TENNYSON. **2.** Ile flie my Hawke with yours 1607. **4.** You leaden messengers..f. with false ayme SHAKS. To f. over a gate 1791. **5.** O Madam, You f. your thoughts like kites TENNYSON. *To f. a kite* (colloq. or slang): to raise money by an accommodation bill; hence *to f. a bill*. **6.** To..march with drums beating and colours flying 1659. **b.** The steamship .. flying signals of distress 1885. **7.** The velocity with which the earth flies through space TYNDALL. **8.** In a violent commotion, they had flown to arms 1847. She flew upstairs 1854. Phr. *To f. in the face of*: see FACE *sb.* *To f. at, on, upon*: to spring with violence upon, attack with fury, rush upon; *lit.* and *fig.* *To f. in* or *into* (a passion, etc.); to pass suddenly into. *To f. off*: *lit.* to start away; to revolt; *fig.* to take another course; to break away (from an agreement, etc.). *To f. out*: (*a*) to rush out; (*b*) to explode or burst out into violent action, language, or temper. **9.** From the could stone sparkes of fire doe flie SHAKS. I shall certainly make his money f. LADY C. BURY. Phr. *To f. open, to, up.* **b.** The crackling faggot flies GOLDSM. **c.** The Winds f. in a moment quite round the Compass DAMPIER. *To f. up in the wind*, is when a ship's head comes suddenly to windward, by carelessness of the helmsman SMYTH.

Phrase. *To let f.* **a.** To discharge (missiles); *absol.* to fire, shoot. Also *fig.* **b.** *Naut.* To allow (a sail or sheet) to f. loose; rarely to set (a sail), to carry, hoist (colours).

II. In senses of FLEE (exc. II. 2) OE.

I'll make him f. the land B. JONS. Unless..one f. into the Ports for shelter 1653. He [Hermes] grasps the wand that causes sleep to f. POPE. True pity.. flies the rich PRAED.

Fly (flai), *v.*[2] Pa. t. and pple. **flied, flyed.** 1836. [f. FLY *sb.*[1] and [2].] To travel by, or convey in, a fly.

Fly-away. 1775. [f. vbl. phr.]

A. *adj.* Ready or apt to fly away. Of articles of dress: Streaming, loose. Of persons: Flighty, extravagant.

Servants with flyaway caps on their heads 1871.

B. *sb.* One that flies away. Cf. *runaway.* 1838. **b.** *Naut.* A delusive appearance of land, a mirage. Also *quasi*-proper name, *Cape Flyaway.* 1867.

Truth is such a flyaway EMERSON.

Fly-bane. 1597. [f. FLY *sb.*[1] + BANE.] **1.** A pop. name of plants: (*a*) = CATCHFLY; (*b*) the ploughman's spikenard (*Inula Conyza*); (*c*) *Agaricus muscarius.* **2.** Poison for flies. SWIFT.

Fly·bi·tten, *ppl. a.* 1597. [f. as prec. + BITTEN.] Bitten by flies: †**a.** Fly-specked; †**b.** FLY-BLOWN 1598; **c.** Stung by flies 1884.

a. These Fly-bitten Tapistries 2 *Hen. IV*, II. i. 159.

Fly·-blow, *sb.* 1556. [f. FLY *sb.*[1] + BLOW *sb.*[2]] The egg or young larva of a blow-fly. Also *collect.*

Fly·-blow, *v.* 1603. [f. FLY *sb.*[1] + BLOW *v.*[1]] **1.** *trans.* Of the fly: To deposit eggs in (meat, etc.); hence, to corrupt secretly, taint. Chiefly *fig.* **2.** *intr.* Of flies: To deposit their eggs. POPE.

Fly-blown (flai·blōun), *ppl. a.* 1529. [f. as prec. + BLOWN *ppl. a.*] **1.** Full of fly-blows; tainted, putrid, impure. Also *fig.* **2.** *slang.* Drunk 1887.

Fly-boat (flai·bōut). 1577. [app. ad. Du. *vlieboot*, orig. one of the small boats used on the *Vlie*, afterwards applied in ridicule to the small war-vessels of the *Gueux de mer* (1572). In Eng. assoc. w. FLY *v.*[1]] **1.** A fast-sailing vessel used: **a.** *esp.* in the coasting trade (*Obs.* exc. *spec.* a Dutch flat-bottomed boat) -1577; **b.** for warlike purposes, voyages of discovery, etc. (*Obs.* exc. *Hist.*) 1590. †**2.** A small boat, *esp.* a ship's boat -1820. †**3.** A Shetland herring buss -1794. **4.** A swift passage boat used on canals 1841.

Fly·-catcher. 1600. [f. FLY *sb.*[1] + CATCHER.] **1.** One who, or that which, catches flies. **2.** A bird that catches flies; in England, esp. *Muscicapa grisola*; in America, esp. *Tyrannus Carolinensis* or *T. pipiri* 1678. **3. a.** A spider that catches flies 1750. **b.** = FLY-TRAP 2. 1863.

1. 'The fly-catcher', as he [Darwin] was known to the crew, was a prime favourite 1887.

Fly·-dung, *v.* 1860. [f. FLY *sb.*[1] + DUNG *v.*] *Dyeing.* In the process of dyeing with madder: To subject for the first time to the process of dunging (see DUNG *v.*).

Flyer, flier. ME. [f. FLY *v.*[1] + -ER [1]. Both forms are in good mod. use.] **1.** That which flies or is carried by the air. **b.** An airman. **2.** One who or that which moves with exceptional speed, e.g. a fish, horse, ship, etc. 1795. **3.** Applied to parts of a machine that have a quick revolution; e.g. an appliance for regulating the motion of a roasting-jack; a sail of a windmill; that part of a spinning machine which twists the thread as it conducts it to and winds it upon the bobbin; etc. 1674. **4. a.** *pl.* Steps forming a straight flight; opp. to *winders* 1667. **b.** *U.S.* A small handbill or fly-sheet 1889. **c.** *Printing.* 'A vibratory rod with fingers which take the sheet of paper from the tapes and carry it to the delivery table' (Knight). **5.** A flying jump or leap 1883. **b.** Hence, *U.S.*, A speculative purchase of stock by one not a regular buyer, in hope of immediate profit 1886. **6.** = FLEER *sb.*[1] 1460.

Fly·-fish, *v.* 1755. [f. FLY-FISHING *vbl. sb.*] *intr.* To fish with a fly as bait. Hence **Fly·-fisher.**

Fly·-fishing, *vbl. sb.* 1653. [f. FLY *sb.*[1]] Fishing with a fly.

Fly·-flap. ME. [f. FLY *sb.*[1] + FLAP *sb.*] **1.** An instrument for driving away flies. †**2.** A stroke with a fly-flap 1735. Hence **Fly·-flap** *v.* to strike with a fly-flap; to beat, whip. **Fly·-flapper,** one who drives away flies with a fly-flap; a FLY-FLAP (sense 1).

Flying (flai·iŋ), *vbl. sb.* 1548. [f. FLY *v.*[1] + -ING [1].] **1.** The action of FLY *v.*[1] **2.** *attrib.*, as *f.-machine*; also **f. country, county** (*Hunting*), one that affords long unbroken runs; **f. fence,** one to be taken at a flying leap; **f. time,** the time when a hawk is in condition to be flown.

Flying (flai·iŋ), *ppl. a.* OE. [f. FLY *v.*[1] + -ING [2].] **1.** That moves through the air with wings. **b.** In names of insects, as *f.-glow-worm.* Also of fish, reptiles, quadrupeds, etc., which by means of special appendages make movements resembling flight; as *f.-frog, -gurnard, -herring, -lemur, -lizard, -phalanger, -squid.* Also **f.-dog,** a kind of vampire-bat; **f. hart, stag** = F. *cerf-volant*, a stag-beetle. 1626. **2.** That passes (quickly) through the air 1535. **3.** Floating loosely, fluttering; hanging loose 1607. **4.** That passes or travels swiftly; rapid 1658. †**b.** *esp.* in *f. post*, a post travelling by relays of horses -1705. **c.** Passing; hasty, transient. Also, Rapidly constructed, temporary. 1763. **5.** That flies about; used *esp.* of a tale, rumour, etc. circulating without definite authority ME. **6.** That flees. 1594.

1. So seem'd Farr off the f. Fiend MILT. Phr. †*F. pension* (fig.): a pension to commence if the pensioner lost his place H. WALPOLE. **2.** A f., shuting, or falling star 1563. **3.** Phr. *F. jib*, 'a light sail set before the jib, on the *flying jib-boom*'. *With f. colours* (fig.): with outward signs of success. †*Under* or *with f. seal*: said of a letter with seal attached but not closed; I enclose the letter which I have written to the Prince Regent under a f. seal WELLINGTON. **4.** The f. Hours ROWE. Phr. *F. leap*: a running jump. *F. handicap, mile*: one in which the starting post is passed at full speed. **c.** A f. trip to London 1806. To lay down a f. line to Lucknow 1857. Phr. (*Mil.* and *Naval*) *F. brigade, column, hospital, party, squadron.* *F. artillery*: a corps trained to rapid evolutions. *F. camp*: see CAMP. *F. sap*: a sap formed by placing and filling several gabions at the same time. **5.** *F. sheet*: a leaflet printed for distribution broadcast. F. pains 1805. **6.** To persecute from far the f. Doe DRYDEN.

Fly·ing bri·dge. 1489. [f. FLYING *ppl. a.*] †**a.** As tr. F. *pont-levis* (drawbridge) CAXTON. †**b.** = FLOATING BRIDGE. -1726. **c.** A temporary bridge for military purposes 1876.

Fly·ing bu·ttress. 1669. A prop or stay (usually carried by a segment of an arch), springing from a pier or other support, and abutting against a structure, for the purpose of resisting thrust.

Fly·ing fish. 1511. [f. FLYING *ppl. a.* + FISH.] Either of two kinds of fish (*Dactylopterus* and *Exocœtus*), which are able to rise in the air by means of enlarged wing-like pectoral fins. **b.** A constellation 1868.

Fly·ing fo·x. 1759. [f. as prec. + FOX.] A family of fruit-eating bats (*Pteropidæ*), found in the tropical East and in Australia.

Fly·ing machi·ne. 1736. **1.** A kind of trapeze. **2.** A machine capable of being controlled in the air; usu. a heavier-than-air machine dependent on motor power 1848.

Fly·ing squi·rrel. 1613. [f. as prec. + SQUIRREL.] A name for two genera (*Pteromys* and *Sciuropterus*) of *Sciuridæ*, which can float through the air by means of an extension of the skin connecting their fore and hind limbs.

Fly·-leaf. 1850. [FLY *sb.*[2]] A blank leaf at the beginning or end, but *esp.* at the beginning, of a book; the blank leaf of a circular, etc.

Fly·man. 1845. [f. FLY *sb.*[2] + MAN *sb.*] **1.** One who drives a fly. **2.** *Theatr.* A man stationed in the flies, to work the ropes, etc.

Fly·-net. [f. FLY *sb.*[1] OE. *flēohnet.*] A net to keep away flies.

Flysch (fliʃ). 1853. [Swiss dial.] *Geol.* An Alpine series of tertiary strata, consisting of slates, marls, and fucoidal sandstones.

Fly·-sheet. 1875. [f. FLY *v.*[1]] = *flying sheet*: see FLYING *ppl. a.*

Fly·-trap. 1774. [f. FLY *sb.*[1] + TRAP.] **1.** A trap for flies 1855. **2.** A fly-catching plant, esp. *Apocynum androsæmifolium.* Venus's fly-trap = *Dionæa muscipula.*

Fly·-wheel. 1784. [f. FLY *sb.*[2] + WHEEL.] A wheel with a heavy rim, attached to a revolving shaft, in order either to regulate the motion of the machinery, or to accumulate power.

†**Fnese,** *v.* [OE. **fnēosan*, cogn. w. Du. *fniezen*, ON. *fnýsa.*] *intr.* To sneeze; also, to puff, snort -ME.

Foal (fōul), *sb.* [Com. Teut.: OE. *fola* :— OTeut. **folon-*, cogn. w. Gr. πῶλος, L. *pullus.*] **1.** The young of the equine genus of quadrupeds; *properly*, a colt; but also, a filly. **2.** *attrib.*, as **f.-teeth,** the first teeth of a horse 1696.

Phr. *In f., with f.*, (of a mare) pregnant.

Foal (fōul), *v.* ME. [f. prec. sb.] **1.** *trans.* To bring forth (a foal); said of a mare, she-ass, etc. **2.** *absol.* or *intr.* 1521.

Foalfoot (fōu·lfut). Also **foal's foot.** ME. [Named from the shape of the leaves.] = COLTSFOOT 1.

Foam (fōum), *sb.* [OE. *fām* :—WGer. **faimo-* :—pre-Teut. **poimo-* or **phoimo-.*] **1.** The aggregation of minute bubbles formed in water or other liquid by agitation, fermentation, effervescence, etc. **b.** *spec.* The foaming saliva issuing from the mouth in epilepsy, rabies, etc. OE. Also *fig.* **2.** Foaming water, the sea. *arch.* OE. **3.** *Min.* = APHRITE.

Comb.: **f.-bow,** a bow similar to a rainbow, formed by sunlight upon f.; **-cock** (*Steam-engine*), a cock at the water level, to blow off scum; **-spar, -stone,** see APHRITE and APHRODITE.

Foam (fōum), *v.* ME. [New formation on FOAM *sb.* superseding OE. *fǣman.*] **1.** *intr.* To emit foam; *esp.* to froth at the mouth. Often used hyperbolically. Of a horse, etc.: To be covered with foam. **2.** To froth, gather foam. Also fig. ME. **3. a.** *intr.* Of a goblet, etc.: To be filled with foaming liquor. **b.** *trans.* To fill or brim with foaming liquor 1725. **4.** *trans.* To send forth or emit in or like foam. Chiefly *fig.* ME. **5.** *nonce-use.* To draw (a chariot) *along* amid foam. KEATS.

1. He [Cæsar]..foam'd at mouth, and was speechlesse SHAKS. **2.** The anger'd Ocean fomes *Ant. & Cl.* II. vi. 21. **4.** Foaming out their own disgrace COWPER. Hence **Foa·mingly** *adv.*

Foamless (fōu·mlės), *a.* 1821. [See -LESS.] Free from foam.

Foamy (fōu·mi), *a.* [OE. *fāmig, fǣmig*, f. *fām*, FOAM.] **1.** Covered with foam, frothy. **2.** Consisting of, pertaining to, or resembling foam ME.

2. The f. surf COWPER. F. lilac-blossom MALLOCK.

Fob (fǫb), *sb.*[1] ME. [?] †**1.** A cheat, imposter. ME. only. **2.** A trick, an artifice. Now only *slang.* 1622.

Fob (fǫb), *sb.*[2] 1653. [?] **1.** A small pocket formerly made in the waistband of the breeches and used for carrying a watch, money, etc. **2.** U.S. = *fob-chain* 1889. **3.** *attrib.*, as **f.-chain**, the chain attached to a watch carried in the fob.

Fob (fǫb), *v.*[1] 1583. [Cogn. w. or f. Fob *sb.*[1] **1.** Cf. Ger. *foppen* to befool.] **1.** *trans.* To cheat, deceive, 'take in'. **2.** To procure, or promote by trickery. Also with *in, into, upon.* ? *Obs.* 1653. **3. Fob off.** To put off deceitfully; to baffle, cajole; to put off *with* something inferior 1597. †**b.** To put off or get rid of by a trick -1641.

1. While every one else he is fobbing, He still may be honest to me FIELDING.

Fob (fǫb), *v.*[2] 1818. [f. Fob *sb.*[2]] To put into one's fob, to pocket.

Focal (fōᵘ·kăl), *a.* 1693. [ad. mod. L. *focalis*, f. Focus; see -AL.] Of or pertaining to a focus; collected or situated at a focus. Also *fig.* 1713.

Phr. *F. distance* or *length* (of a lens or mirror): the distance between the centre and the focus. *F. plane*: the locus of the foci of different systems of parallel rays refracted through a lens. *F. plane shutter* (Photogr.): a blind with (usu. adjustable) slit that moves across the front of the plate or film. *F. point*: the intersection of a f. plane with the axis of the lens. Hence **Fo·cally** *adv.* at a focus.

Focalize (fōᵘ·kăləiz), *v.* 1845. [f. Focal *a.* + -IZE.] **1.** *trans.* To bring to a focal point; to focus. Also *fig.* **2.** To adjust the focus of (the eye); also *absol.* (of the eye) 1878.

1. Light is focalized in the eye, sound in the ear DE QUINCEY. Hence **Focaliza·tion.**

Focimeter (fosi·mɪ̄təɹ). Also **foco-.** 1853. [f. Focus + -METER.] *Photogr.* An instrument for finding the chemical focus of a lens which has not been properly achromatized.

Focimetry (fosi·mĕtri). Also **foco-.** 1881. [Gr. -μετρία.] Measurement of focal distance.

Fo'c'sle: see FORECASTLE.

Focus (fōᵘ·kǒs), *sb.* Pl. **foci**; also **focuses**, irreg. **focusses.** 1644. [a. L. *focus* hearth, fireplace.] **1.** *Geom.* **a.** In plane geometry: One of the points from which the distances to any point of a given curve are connected by a linear relation 1656. **b.** In solid geometry (see quot.) 1874. **2.** *Optics, Heat*, etc. The point at which rays meet after being reflected or refracted; also, the point from which the rays appear to proceed (= *virtual f.*) 1685. Also *transf.* and *fig.* **b.** That point or position at which an object must be situated, in order that the image produced by the lens may be clear and well-defined. Hence *in*, or *out of f.* (lit. and fig.). 1713. **c.** The focal length (of a lens); also, the adjustment (of the eye, or an eyeglass) necessary to produce a clear image 1693. **3.** *Acoustics.* The point or space towards which the sound waves converge 1644. **4.** Of a disease: The, or a, principal seat 1684. **5.** The centre of activity, or area of greatest energy, of a storm, eruption, etc. Also *fig.* 1796.

1. The ellipse and hyperbola have each two foci; but the parabola only one HUTTON. **b.** A point through which can be drawn two lines, each touching the surface and the imaginary circle at infinity and such that the tangent plane to the surface through either also touches the circle at infinity SALMON. **2.** *Conjugate foci*: see CONJUGATE *a.* *Principal f.*: the point at which parallel rays meet after passing through a convergent lens. *Solar f.* = prec. *Actinic* or *chemical f.* (of a lens), the point to which the actinic rays converge. **b.** *fig.* The bringing of all these scattered counsels into a f. FRANKLIN. **5.** The centre or f. of the West Indian hurricanes BEDFORD. *fig.* The principal f. of scientific activity HUXLEY.

Focus (fōᵘ·kǒs). *v.* Pples. **focused, -ing**; irreg. **focussed, -ing.** 1775. [f. prec. sb.] **1.** *trans.* To cause to converge to or as to a focus 1807. Also *intr.* for *refl.* **2.** To adjust the focus of (the eye, a lens, etc.) 1814. **3.** To bring into focus 1775.

3. The image..is focussed..by..adjusting the lens 1865.

Fodder (fǫ·dəɹ). *sb.* [OE. *fódor*, extended form of *fóda* FOOD, q. v.] †**1.** Food in general -1634. **2.** Food for cattle; now only dried food, as hay, straw, etc., for stall-feeding OE.

Fodder (fǫ·dəɹ), *v.* ME. [f. prec. sb.] *trans.* To give fodder to (cattle); to feed *with* (something) as fodder. Also *transf.* and *fig.* Hence **Fo·dderer**, one who fodders or feeds (cattle).

Fodient (fōᵘ·diĕnt). 1676. [ad. L. *fodientem*, *fodere.*]

A. *adj.* Digging; burrowing. **B.** *sb.* [*sc.* animal.] 1879.

Foe (fōᵘ), *a.* and *sb.* [repr.: (1) OE. *fáh*, *fág* adj. (:— OTeut. *faiho-); (2) the compound *gefá* sb., which lost the prefix *ge-*, *i-* in early ME. Alliance with FIEND is doubtful.]

†**A.** *adj.* **1.** At feud *with*; inimical (*to*) -1603. **2.** Hindering progress, rough. ME. only.

1. An enemie-country and f.-land FLORIO.

B. *sb.* (Now usu. repl. by ENEMY, exc. *rhet.*) **1.** In early use, an adversary in deadly feud or mortal combat; now, one who hates and seeks to injure another OE. Also *transf.* and *fig.* **2.** One belonging to a hostile army or nation, an enemy in battle or war ME. **3.** *collect.* A hostile force 1593.

1. He makes no friend who never made a f. TENNYSON. *transf.* and *fig.* A F. to th' publike Weale SHAKS. Grief is a f. CRABBE. **2.** Give thy brave foes their due ADDISON. **3.** Whispering with white lips—'The f.! they come! they come!' BYRON.

Hence †**Foe** *v.* to set at enmity; to make or treat as an enemy. †**Foe·hood**, enmity; a state of mutual hostility.

Fœderal, -ly, Fœdity: see FED-.

Foeman (fōᵘ·măn). *arch.* and *poet.* [OE. *fáhman*, f. *fah*, FOE *a.* + MAN.] An enemy in war.

Fœtal, fetal (fɪ̄·tăl), *a.* 1811. [f. Fœtus + -AL.] Of or pertaining to or of the nature of a fœtus; in the condition of a fœtus.

Fœta·tion, feta·tion. 1669. [f. L. *fetare* to produce offspring.] The formation of a fœtus or embryo.

Fœticide, feticide (fɪ̄·tisəid). 1844. [f. FŒTUS; see -CIDE 2.] The action of destroying a fœtus or causing abortion.

Hence **Fœtici·dal** *a.* of or pertaining to f.

Fœtid, Fœtor, var. ff. FETID, FETOR.

Fœtus, fetus (fɪ̄·tǒs). ME. [a. L. *fetus*, f. root *fe- to produce offspring :— Aryan *bhwe-, extension of *bheu-, bhu- to come into being; see BE *v.* The better form with *e* is almost unknown in use.] The young of viviparous animals in the womb, and of oviparous animals in the egg, when fully developed.

Fog (fǫg). *sb.*[1] ME. [of unkn. origin; Welsh *ffwg* 'dry grass' is from Eng.] **1. a.** The aftermath. **b.** The long grass left standing through the winter; rank grass. **2.** *Sc.* and *north.* = Moss 1450.

1. b. (*To leave*) *under f.*: with the long grass standing.

Fog (fǫg), *sb.*[2] 1544. [prob. from FOGGY *a.*]

†**I.** Flabby substance (in the body), unwholesome fat; waste flesh 1586.

II. 1. Thick mist or watery vapour suspended in the atmosphere at or near the earth's surface; an obscured condition of the atmosphere due to this 1544. **2.** *transf.* and *fig.* 1601. **3.** *Photogr.* A cloud or coating obscuring a developed plate 1858.

1. Drooping fogge as blacke as Acheron SHAKS. **2.** Phr. *In a f.*: at a loss to know what to do. More puzzel'd then the Ægyptians in their fogge SHAKS.

Combs. **1.** General: esp. in the names of instruments used for giving warning in foggy weather, as *f.-alarm, -bell, -gun, -horn, -trumpet, -whistle.* Also F.-SIGNAL. **2.** Special: **f.-bow**, a bow, similar to the rainbow, produced by the action of light on the particles of f.; **-circle** = prec.; **-ring**, a bank of f. arranged in a circular form.

Fog (fǫg), *v.*[1] 1715. [f. FOG *sb.*[1]] **1.** *intr.* To become overgrown with moss. *Sc.* **2.** *Agric. trans.* **a.** To leave land under fog (see FOG *sb.*[1] 1) 1814. **b.** To feed (cattle) on fog 1828.

Fog (fǫg), *v.*[2] 1599. [f. FOG *sb* [2]] **1.** *trans.* To envelop with or as with fog; to stifle with fog. Also *fig.* **2.** *intr.* To become covered or filled with fog. (Dicts.) **3.** *Photogr. trans.* To cloud or cover with an obscuring coating 1854.

Phr. *To f. off*: to perish from damp, as cuttings.

†**Fog**, *v.*[3] *rare.* 1588. [? f. FOGGER [1].] *intr.* To act in a pettifogging manner -1641.

Where would'st thou f. to get a fee 1628.

Fog-bank. 1659. [f. FOG *sb.*[2] + BANK *sb.*[1]] 'A dense haze, presenting the appearance of a thick cloud resting upon the horizon' (Smyth).

Foge (fōᵘdʒ). *Cornwall.* 1778. [? local pronunc. of FORGE.] *Min.* A forge or blowing-house for smelting tin.

Foggage (fǫ·gĕdʒ). *Sc.* 1500. [ad. Sc. Law-Lat. *fogagium* prob. f. FOG *sb.*[1]] **1.** *Law.* The pasturing of cattle on fog; the privilege of doing this. **2.** = FOG *sb.*[1] **2.** 1786.

Fogger [1] (fǫ·gəɹ). 1576. [prob. f. *Fugger*, surname of the Augsburg family of merchants and financiers.] †**1.** A person given to underhand practices for the sake of gain; *esp.* a low-class lawyer. Usually preceded by *petty.* -1600. **2.** *dial.* A huckster 1800. **3.** A middleman in the nail and chain trade 1868.

Fogger [2] (fǫ·gəɹ). *dial.* 1851. [? f. FOG *v.*[1] + -ER [1].] A farm-hand chiefly engaged in feeding cattle.

Foggy (fǫ·gi), *a.* 1529. [f. FOG *sb.*[1] + -Y[1].] **1.** Resembling, consisting of, or covered with fog 1635. †**2.** Boggy, marshy -1661. †**3.** Of flesh, etc.: Flabby or spongy in consistency; = BOGGY *a.* Hence of persons or animals: Unwholesomely bloated, puffy. -1828. **4.** [Cf. L. *pinguis aer.*] Of air, mist, cloud, etc.: Thick, murky. Hence (through FOG *sb.*[2]): Of the nature of, or resembling, fog or thick mist; full of fog. 1544. **b.** *fig.* Obscure, dull, bemuddled 1603. **5.** Beclouded, dim, indistinct 1840. **6.** *Photogr.* Fogged, indistinct 1859.

4. The..f. asthmatic town of Glasgow COL. HAWKER. Hence **Fo·ggily** *adv.* **Fo·gginess.**

Fogle (fōᵘ·g'l). *slang.* 1811. A (silk) handkerchief.

Fogless (fǫ·glĕs), *a.* 1853. [f. FOG *sb.*[2] + -LESS.] Without fog, clear.

Fog-signal. 1759. [f. FOG *sb.*[2] + SIGNAL *sb.*] **1.** *Naut.* Any sound made in fogs as a warning to other vessels. **2.** *Railways.* A detonator placed on the metals in foggy weather to guide drivers of trains 1856.

Fogy, fogey (fōᵘ·gi). 1780. [? FOGGY *a.* in sense 2, moss-grown, or in sense 3, bloated, used subst.] **1.** *Sc.* An invalid or garrison soldier 1785. **2.** (Orig. *Sc.*) A man advanced in life; *esp.* one with antiquated notions, an old-fashioned fellow. Usu. preceded by *old.* 1780.

2. The honest rosy old fogies THACKERAY.

Hence **Fo·gydom, fogeydom**, the state or condition of a f.; fogies as a class. **Fo·gyish** *a.* somewhat antiquated. **Fo·gyism**, the state of being a f.; the characteristic behaviour of fogies.

Foh, var. of FAUGH.

‖**Föhn** (fōn). 1865. [Ger.; acc. to Grimm a. Rumansch *favugh* :— L. *Favonius.*] A warm dry south wind which blows down the valleys on the north side of the Alps.

Foible (foi·b'l). 1648. [a. F. *foible*, obs. f. *faible*; see FEEBLE.]

†**A.** *adj.* Weak -1741.

B. *sb.* **1.** A weak point; a failing or moral weakness 1673. **2.** *Fencing.* The portion of a sword from the middle to the point. 1648.

1. A f. of Mr. Holt's..was omniscience THACKERAY.

‖**Foiblesse.** ? *Obs.* 1685. [a. F., obs. sp. of *faiblesse*, f. as prec.] A failing; a weakness *for* (something).

Foil (foil), *sb.*[1] ME. [a. OF. *foil* masc. (:— L. *folium* leaf, cogn. w. Gr. φύλλον), and OF *foille* fem. (mod. F. *feuille* :— L. *folia*, pl. of *folium*).] †**1.** A leaf -1450. **2.** The representation of a leaf: **a.** *Her.* 1562; **b.** *Arch.* One of the small arcs or spaces between the cusps of a window 1835. †**3.** Anything flat and thin; as a layer, a paring, a counterfoil -1738. **4.** Metal hammered or rolled into a thin sheet; as *gold-, silver-, tin-f.* ME. **b.** An amalgam of tinfoil and mercury placed behind the glass of a mirror, to produce a reflection 1583. **c.** A backing 1684. **5.** A thin leaf of some metal placed under a precious stone to increase its brilliancy or under some transparent substance to make it appear to be a precious stone 1592. †**b.** The setting (of a jewel) -1650. **6.** Anything that serves by contrast of colour or quality to adorn or set off another thing 1581.

5. b. A foyle wherein thou art to set The precious Iewell of thy home returne SHAKS. **6.** I need no

foile, nor shall I think I'me white only between two Moores 1639. *Comb.* **f.-stone**, an imitation jewel.

Foil (foil), *sb.*² 1478. [f. FOIL *v.*¹ II. 1.] †1. *Wrestling.* A throw which is almost a fall –1687. 2. A repulse, defeat; a baffling check. *arch.* 1478.

2. It may give a man many a..f. and many a disheartening blow SOUTH.

Foil (foil), *sb.*³ 1576. [f. FOIL *v.*¹ I. 2.] The track of a hunted animal. Also *transf.* and *fig.*

Phr. *To run (upon) the f.*: to run over the same track a second time (thus baffling the hounds).

Foil (foil), *sb.*⁴ 1594. [? altered form of FOIN *sb.*; or ? transf. use of FOIL *sb.*¹ a leaf (cf. F. *fleuret* fencing foil, lit. 'floweret').] 1. A light weapon used in fencing; a kind of small-sword with a blunt edge and a button at the point. 2. *pl.* The exercise of fencing with foils 1600.

1. They would have most willingly taken the buttons off the foils DRUMM. OF HAWTH.

Foil (foil), *v.*¹ ME. [irreg. repr. of OF. *fuler, foler, fouler*, to full cloth, to tread, trample down, etc. :—(ult.) L. *fullo* a fuller; cf. FULL *v.*]

I. In sense of F. *fouler.* †1. *trans.* To tread under foot, trample down –1603. 2. *Hunting.* Of animals: To run over or cross (the ground, scent, or track) with the effect of baffling the hounds 1651.

II. 1. To overthrow, defeat; to beat off, repulse, discomfit. †In *Wrestling*: To inflict a foil upon: see FOIL *sb.*² 1. Also *fig.* 1548. 2. To frustrate, render nugatory; to baulk; to baffle 1564.

1. The Wrastler That did but lately foile the synowie Charles SHAKS. Those Armies bright, which but th' Omnipotent none could have foyld MILT. 2. Faith shall be easily shaken, hope quickly foyled 1612.

III. Influenced by FOUL *a.* and *v.* 1. To foul, defile, pollute. Now *dial.* ME. †2. To dishonour; to violate –1592.

Hence **Foi·ler**, one who foils.

†**Foil**, *v.*² 1616. [perh. ad. F. *fouiller* to grub up.] *trans.* To subject (land) to the third ploughing in preparing it for sowing –1669.

Foil (foil), *v.*³ 1611. [f. FOIL *sb.*¹] *trans.* To apply foil or a foil to.

Foiling (foi·liŋ), *vbl. sb.*¹ 1533. [f. FOIL *v.*¹ + -ING¹.] The action of FOIL *v.*¹; *esp.* the treading of a deer or other animal. Hence the slot or trail 1576.

Foiling (foi·liŋ), *vbl. sb.*² 1583. [f. FOIL *v.*³ + -ING¹.] a. The action or process of backing (glass) with foil. b. *Arch.* Ornamentation by foils; a foil ornament 1849.

†**Foin**, *sb.*¹ ME. [a. OF. *foine* (F. *fouine*), altered f. *faïne* :—late L. *fagina*, f. *fagum* accus.] The beech-marten (*Mustela foina*), or its fur –1718.

Foin (foin), *sb.*² 1450. [f. FOIN *v.*] 1. A thrust or push with a pointed weapon. *Obs.* or *arch.* Also *fig.* †2. = FOIL *sb.*⁴. –1701.

Foin (foin), *v.* ME. [app. f. OFr. *foine, foisne, fouisne* (F. *fouine*), a three-pronged fish-spear :—L. *fuscina.*] 1. *intr.* To make a thrust with a pointed weapon; to lunge, push. Also *transf.* and *fig.* †2. *trans.* To thrust at, pierce, prick –1548.

1. Ye foine only at your owne shadow JEWEL. *transf.* The boare continually foining at him with his great tuskes 1562. Hence †**Foi·nery**, thrusting with the foin, fencing with the point. **Foi·ningly** *adv.*

Foison (foi·z'n), *sb.* ME. [a. OF. *foison, fuison* :—pop. L. **fūsionem*, for L. *fūsionem*, a pouring, f. *fundere.*] 1. Plenty; a great quantity or number. *arch.* b. Plentiful crop or harvest 1587. 2. Inherent vitality; power, strength, capacity. *pl.* Resources. Now chiefly *Sc.* ME.

1. b. Earths increase, foyzon plentie, Barnes and Garners neuer empty SHAKS. Hence **Foi·sonless** *a.* (chiefly *Sc.*), wanting substance, strength, or sap.

†**Foist, fust**, *sb.*¹ 1485. [a. OF. *fuste*, ad. It. *fusta*, f. L. *fustis* cudgel.] 1. A light galley propelled by oars and sails –1777. 2. A barge –1616.

Foist, *sb.*² 1533. [a. OF. *fust* (F. *fût*) cask :—L. *fustem, fustis* cudgel.] †1. A cask for wine. 2. Hence, fustiness 1819.

†**Foist**, *sb.*³ 1591. [f. FOIST *v.*¹] 1. A cheat, a rogue; a pickpocket –1700. 2. A piece of roguery –1677. 3. Something foisted in. NORTH.

Foist (foist), *v.*¹ 1545. [prob. ad. Du. dial. *vuisten* to take in the hand, f. *vuist* fist.] †1. *Dicing. trans.* To palm (a 'flat' or false die), so as to be able to introduce it when required. Also *intr.* to cheat by this means. –1565. †2. *intr.* To cheat. Cf. COG *v.*³ –1611. †3. To put forth fraudulently –1678. b. To introduce surreptitiously or unwarrantably *into*; also with *in* adv. 1563. c. To palm off; to fix stealthily or unwarrantably *on* or *upon* 1599.

1. Through Foisting and Cogging their Die, and other false play 1565. Phr. *To f. in*: to introduce (the flat) surreptitiously when palmed. 3. b. Interpolations..foisted into the Odyssey LYTTON. c. To attempt to f. himself upon a borough with which he had no connexion S. WARREN. Hence †**Foi·ster.**

Foist (foist), *v.*² 1563. *Obs.* exc. *dial.* [f. FOIST *sb.*²] *intr.* To smell or grow musty.

Foisty (foi·sti), *a.* See also FUSTY. 1519. [f. FOIST *sb.*² + -Y¹.] Fusty, musty, mouldy. *lit.* and *fig.* So **Foi·stied** *ppl. a.* become f. **Foi·stiness**, f. quality or condition.

Fokker (fǫ·kəɹ). 1913. [f. the name of A. H. G. *Fokker*, Dutch inventor.] A German tractor monoplane.

Fold (fōuld), *sb.*¹ [OE. *falæd, falod, falud, fald*; cf. EFris. *folt* enclosure, dunghill.] A pen or enclosure for domestic animals. b. The sheep in a fold 1669.

The lee-lang night we watch'd the fauld BURNS. *fig.* There shall be one f. and one shepherd *John* x. 16. b. The bleating f. DRYDEN.

Comb. **f.-garth, -yard**, farm-yard.

Fold (fōuld), *sb.*² [ME. *fald*, f. *falden* FOLD *v.*¹] 1. A bend or ply in or as in anything flexible; either, or both together, of the parts brought together in folding. Also *fig.* and *transf.* 2. Something that is or may be folded; e.g. one of the leaves of a folding door ME. 3. The action of folding; †a clasp 1606. 4. The mark made by folding 1840. 5. By an erron. analysis *manifold, threefold*, etc. (see -FOLD *suffix*): Times, repetitions ME.

1. The f. of a mantle SCOTT. *fig.* The folds and doubles of Sylla's disposition DRYDEN. *transf.* The folds (= coils) of an adder SHAKS., of the mountains W. IRVING, of the alimentary canal 1841.

Fold (fōuld), *v.*¹ Pa. t. and pple. **folded** (fōu·ldėd). [Com. Teut.: OE. *fealdan* :—OTeut. **falþan*, f. **falþ* :—pre-Teut. **plt-*, found in Gr. διπαλτος, also διπλάσιος double. Allied to Gr. πλέκειν, L. *plicare* to plait, fold.] 1. *trans.* To arrange (a piece of cloth, etc.) so that one part lies reversed over or alongside another; to bend over upon itself. Also with *in, over, together.* Also *intr.* for *refl.* 1857. 2. *trans.* To coil, wind (*about, round*, etc.). Also *intr.* for refl. 1579. †3. *intr.* To give way; to fail, falter –1596. 4. *trans.* To lay (the arms, etc.) together, so as to overlap; to clasp (the hands) together. Also *intr.* for *refl.* OE. 5. To enclose in or as in a fold or folds; to wrap up; to swathe, envelop. Now only with *in.* ME. 6. To clasp (*in one's arms, to one's breast*), embrace ME.

1. *fig.* When death hath foulded up thy dayes EARL MANCH. 2. When I feel about my feet The berried briony f. TENNYSON. 3. I..feele my wits to faile, and tongue to f. SPENSER. 4. Folde thine handes together yet a litle, that thou mayest slepe COVERDALE *Prov.* vi. 10. 6. The mountain isles..Folded in shadows gray B. TAYLOR.

Fold (fōuld), *v.*² OE. [f. FOLD *sb.*¹] 1. *trans.* To shut up (sheep, etc.) in a fold; also *absol.* Also *fig.* 2. To place sheep in a fold upon (ground) for the purpose of manuring it 1671.

1. The star that bids the shepherd f. MILT. *Comus* 93. Hence **fo·lder**, a shepherd.

-fold, *suffix* (OE. *-feald*, ME. *-fald, -fold*), cogn. w. FOLD *v.*¹, and with the Gr. -παλτος, -πλασιος, also with πλο- in ἁπλόος, and prob. with the L. (*sim-*)*plex.* Appended to cardinal numerals (and adjs. meaning 'many'), forming adjs. which serve chiefly as arithmetical multiplicatives. In educated use this multiplicative sense survives chiefly in the adv. and quasi-sb.; the adjs. express rather a plurality of things more or less different, as in 'a two-fold charm'.

†**Foldage** (fou·ldėdʒ). 1533. [f. FOLD *sb.*² + -AGE. Cf. FALDAGE.] a. = FALDAGE –1628. b. The practice of feeding sheep in movable folds –1657.

Folder (fōu·ldəɹ), *sb.* 1552. [f. FOLD *v.*¹ + -ER¹.] One who or that which folds; *esp.* an instrument for folding paper, etc.; *U.S.* a small folded but unstitched pamphlet.

Folderol, *v.* 1847. To sing folderol.

Folding (fōu·ldiŋ), *ppl. a.* 1611. [f. FOLD *v.*¹ + -ING².] That folds; that is or can be folded; as *f.-bed, -boat, -screen, -table*, etc.

Fo·lding doo·r. 1611. [f. prec. + DOOR.] A door consisting of two parts hung on opposite jambs, so that their edges come into contact when the door is closed. Now usu. *pl.*

Foldless (fōu·ldlės), *a.*¹ 1822. [f. FOLD *sb.*¹ + -LESS.] Having no fold or pen.

Foldless (fōu·ldlės), *a.*² 1845. [f. FOLD *sb.*² + -LESS.] Without a fold or crease.

†**Foleye·**, *v.* [ad. OF. *foleier*, f. *fol* foolish.] *intr.* To play the fool. CHAUCER.

‖**Folia** (fōu·liă), *sb. pl.* 1730. [L., pl. of *folium* leaf.] 1. *Bot.* Leaves (of a plant). 2. Laminæ 1796.

Foliaceous (fōuli,ē̆i·ʃəs), *a.* 1658. [f. L. *foliaceus* leafy, f. *folium*; see -ACEOUS.] 1. Having the appearance or nature of a leaf. Of cryptogamous plants: Having organs resembling leaves. b. Of or pertaining to a leaf or leaves 1816. 2. Consisting of or having the character of thin leaf-like plates or laminæ 1728. 3. *Zool.* & *Entom.* Shaped or arranged like leaves 1828.

1. Teeth of the calyx f. 1806. b. A f. or farinaceous diet 1816. 2. A..f. spar 1728. 3. Valves f. WOODWARD.

Foliage (fōu·li,ėdʒ), *sb.* 1598. [altered f. *foillage*, a. F. *feuillage* (earlier *foillage*), f. *feuille* leaf; see FOIL *sb.*¹ and -AGE.] 1. Leaves (of a plant or tree) collectively; leafage 1601. 2. In *Art*: The representation of leaves, or of a cluster of leaves, sprays, or branches, used for decoration or ornament.

1. These naked shoots..Shall put their graceful f. on again COWPER.

Comb.: **f. leaf**, a leaf in the restricted sense of the word, excluding petals and other modified leaves; **f. plant**, one cultivated for its f., and not for its blossom.

Hence **Fo·liage** *v.* to adorn with f. or with a representation of leaves and flowers.

Foliaged (fōu·li,ėdʒd), *ppl. a.* 1754. [f. FOLIAGE *sb.* and *v.*] 1. Decorated or ornamented with the representation of foliage. 2. Covered or furnished with (natural) foliage 1815.

1. F. velvet SHENSTONE. 2. A f. lattice SHELLEY.

Foliar (fōu·liăɹ), *a.* 1875. [ad. mod. L. *foliaris*, f. L. *folium.* Cf. F. *foliaire.*] Of, pertaining to, or of the nature of a leaf.

In many Ferns the original axile bundle widens out ..into a tube, which..has..a relatively small slit or *foliar gap*..from the margin of which one or several bundles pass into the leaf BOWER & SCOTT. So **Fo·lial** *a.* in same sense.

Foliate (fōu·li*ĕ*t), *a.* 1626. [ad. L. *foliatus* leaved; see -ATE.] †1. Beaten out into a thin sheet or foil –1819. 2. Leaf-like 1658. 3. *Bot.* a. Furnished with leaves 1677. b. Having (so many) leaflets 1840.

2. Phr. *F. curve* (Geom.): a curve of the second order..consisting of two infinite legs crossing each other, forming a kind of leaf HUTTON. 3. b. 10-f. 1840.

Foliate (fōu·li,*e*ⁱt), *v.* 1665. [f. L. *folium* + -ATE.] 1. †*trans.* To beat to a leaf or foil 1721; *intr.* to split into leaves or laminæ 1798. 2. *trans.* To foil (glass) 1665. 3. *intr.* To put forth leaves 1775. 4. *trans.* To decorate with foils (see FOIL *sb.*¹ 2 b) 1812. 5. *trans.* To mark the folios or leaves of (a volume, etc.) with consecutive numbers 1846.

4. The Arabs pointed and foliated the arch RUSKIN.

Foliated (fōu·li,*e*ⁱtėd), *ppl. a.* 1650. [f. prec. + -ED.] †1. = FOLIATE *a.* 1. BOYLE. b. Silvered 1665. 2. Composed of laminæ. Chiefly *Geol.* and *Min.* 1650. 3. Shaped like a leaf or leaves 1846. 4. *Arch.*, etc. a. Ornamented with foils 1840. b. Consisting of or ornamented with leaf-work 1849. 5. Furnished with or consisting of leaves 1721.

2. Mica schist and gneiss f. 1866. 4. a. *F. Arch*, an arch with a trefoil, cinquefoil, or multifoil under it PARKER.

Foliation (fōuli,ē̆i·ʃən). 1623. [f. FOLIATE *a.*; see -ATION.] 1. The leafing (of a plant); the state of being in leaf. †b. *concr.* Something resembling a leaf 1658. 2. *Bot.* †a. The assemblage of leaves or petals forming a corolla –1747. b. = VERNATION 1794. 3. The action of beating (metal) into foil 1755. 4. *Geol.* The process and the property of splitting up into leaf-like layers; also the laminæ or plates into which crystalline rocks are divided 1851. 5. *Arch.* Tracery consisting chiefly of small arcs or foils 1816. 6. The consecutive numbering of the folios (or leaves) of a book or MS. 1846. 7. The application of foil to glass. (Dicts.)

2. a. The f. of a tulip HERVEY. b. Flowers regular, with..gyrate f. LINDLEY. 5. Foliations hanging free like lace-work FREEMAN.

Folia·to-, comb. f. L. *foliatus*, in sense 'formed like a leaf'.

Fo·liator. 1848. [f. FOLIATE *v.* + -OR.] One who foliates the leaves of a book.

Foliature (fōu·liătiŭɹ). 1676. [ad. late L. *foliatura.*] 1. A cluster of leaves; also, leaf-ornamentation. 2. 'The state of being hammered into leaves' (J.).

Foliicolous (fōu:li,ikǒləs), *a.* 1874. [f. L. *folii-* comb. f. *folium* + *col-* (stem of *colere*) + -OUS.] Growing parasitically on leaves. So **Foli·i·ferous** *a.*, also *erron.* **foliferous**, bearing leaves. **Fo·liifo·rm** *a.* leaf-shaped. **Fo:lii·parous** *a.* 'producing leaves only' (*Treas. Bot.*).

Folily, cf. FOLIFUL, FOLLIFUL *a.*

Folio (fōu·lio). 1533. [a. L. *folio*, abl. of *folium* leaf, in L. phr. *in folio.*]

A. *sb.* I. With reference to pagination. 1. A leaf of paper, parchment, etc. which is numbered only on the front. 2. *Bookkeeping.* The two opposite pages of an account-book when used concurrently; also one page when used for both sides of an account 1588. 3. *Printing.* The page-number of a printed book 1683. 4. *Law.* A certain number of words (in England 72 or 90, in U.S. generally 100) taken as a unit in reckoning the length of a document 1836.

II. With reference to size. 1. *In folio*, i.e. 'in the form of a full-sized sheet folded once'. Also *transf.* and *fig.* 1582. 2. A sheet of paper when folded once 1616. 3. A volume made up of sheets of paper folded once; a volume of the largest size 1628. Also *attrib.*

1. I am for whole volumes in f. *L.L.L.* I. ii. 192. 2. Severall folios of dried plants EVELYN.

B. *adj.* Formed of sheets or a sheet folded once; folio-sized. Often following the sb. 1597.

A history in ten volumes f. (*mod.*).

Folio (fōu·lio), *v.* [f. prec. sb.] = FOLIATE *v.* 5.

Foliolate (fōu·liǒlėit), *a.* 1866. [See FOLIOLE and -ATE.] Of, pertaining to, or consisting of folios or leaflets; as in '3-foliolate,' etc.

Foliole (fōu·liǒul). 1794. [a. F., ad. L. *foliolum*, dim. of *folium.*] 1. *Bot.* One of the divisions of a compound leaf; a leaflet. 2. *Zool.* A small leaf-like appendage 1849.

Foliose (fouliōu·s), *a.* 1727. [ad. L. *foliosus*; see -OSE.] Having, or abounding in, leaves; leafy. Hence **Folio·sity**, f. condition.

Folious (fōu·liəs), *a.* 1658. [ad. L. *foliosus*, f. *folium*; see -OUS.] Abounding in, or of the nature of, leaves; foliose.

‖**Folium** (fōu·liǒm). 1848. [L.] 1. = FOLIO *sb.* II. 2. 1886. 2. *Geom.* a. A finite loop of a nodal curve terminated at both ends by the same node. b. *F. of Descartes*, a plane nodal cubic curve with real nodal tangents, and one real inflexion at infinity. 1848.

Folk (fōuk). [OE. *folc* = ON. *folk* people, army, detachment (Sw., Da. *folk*) :—OTeut. **folkom.*] 1. A people, nation, race, tribe. Now *arch.* b. *transf.* of animals. (After Heb.) ME. 2. An aggregation of people in relation to a superior, e.g. God, a king or priest; the mass; the people; the vulgar. *Obs.* exc. *arch.* OE. 3. Men, people indefinitely; often qualified by an adj. or phr. (Now chiefly *colloq.*) OE. 4. *pl.* The people of one's family, parents, children, relatives 1715.

1. b. The conies are but a feeble f. *Prov.* xxx. 26. 2. The said hoost of the Hebreux..were al folke of God CAXTON. 3. Upon the steedes..Ther seeten f. CHAUCER. I have heard wise folks say [etc.] SWIFT. Unkind to the poor f. 1845. 4. Your young folks are flourishing HT. MARTINEAU.

attrib. and *Comb.* 1. General: *esp.* with the sense 'of, pertaining to, current or existing among, the people'; as *f.-belief, -custom, -dance, -laws, -literature, -name, -play, -song, -speech, -tale*, etc.

2. Special: **f.-etymology**, usu. the popular perversion of the form of words in order to give it a meaning; **-free** *a.*, having the rights of a freeman; **-leasing** (OE. *Law*), public lying, slander.

Fo·lkland. *Obs.* exc. *Hist.* A term of OE. law, designating land held by a certain kind of tenure; opp. to BOOKLAND.

The prevailing view of the antithesis has been that *folkland* was land belonging to the state, which the king or the witan might grant to a person for his life, but which did not descend to heirs, while *bookland* was land held by charter or deed. Another view is that *folkland* was land heritable by *folkright* or common law, while the estate in *bookland* was conferred by deed, and could be alienated freely. See *Eng. Hist. Rev.* VIII. (1893).

Folk-lore (fōu·k,lōᵊɹ). 1846. [f. FOLK + LORE.] The beliefs, legends, and customs, current among the common people; the study of these.

Fo·lkmoot, folkmote. *Obs.* exc. *Hist.* [OE. *folc-mót, -gemót*, f. *folc* FOLK + *mót, gemót* meeting.] A general assembly of the people of a town, city, or shire. Hence †**Fo·lk-mooter**, ? a parochial politician. MILT.

Fo·lkright. *Obs.* exc. *Hist.* [OE. *folc-riht*, f. *folc* FOLK + *riht* RIGHT.] 'Common law, public right, the understood compact by which every freeman enjoys his rights as a freeman' (Bosw.).

Follicle (fǫ·lik'l). 1646. [ad. L. *folliculus* little bag, dim. of *follis* bellows.] 1. *Anat.* A small sac. Chiefly, 'a simple lymphatic gland, consisting of lymphoid tissue arranged in the form of a sac' (*Syd. Soc. Lex.*). 2. *Bot.* 'A kind of fruit, consisting of a single carpel, dehiscing by the ventral suture only' (Lindley); formerly, any capsular fruit 1706. b. A small bag or vesicle distended with air 1793. 3. *Entom.* A cocoon 1856.

Hence **Folli·cular** *a.* of the nature of, or resembling, a f.; composed or consisting of follicles; *Path.* affecting the follicles of a particular organ. **Folli·culated** *ppl. a.* provided with a f. or follicles; contained in a cocoon. **Folli:culi·tis**, *Path.* inflammation of a f. or follicles. **Folli:culo·se, Folli·culous** *adjs.* full of or containing follicles; of the nature or appearance of a f.

†**Fo·lliful**, *a.* Also **foliful**. 1549. [f. FOLLY *sb.* = + -FUL.] Full of foolishness –1763.

Follow (fǫ·lou), *sb.* 1870. [f. next vb.] 1. The action of FOLLOW *v.* 2. *Billiards.* A stroke which causes the player's ball to follow the object-ball after impact. Also, the impulse given to the ball by this stroke. 3. *Cricket* (also **follow-on**) 1881; *Golf*, etc. (**follow-through**) 1897: see FOLLOW *v.*

Follow (fǫ·lou), *v.* [Two types: (1) OE. *folgian* (*o-* stem); (2) OE. *fylgan* (*-jo-* stem); not recorded in Goth.]

I. *trans.* 1. To go or come after; to move behind in the same direction. b. To go forward along, keep in (a path, track, etc.). *lit.* and *fig.* ME. 2. *fig.* To come after in sequence or series, order of time, etc.; to succeed ME. 3. To go after as an attendant, or as an admirer, auditor, or the like OE. 4. *fig.* To go with; to be consequent upon OE. 5. To go in pursuit of, try to come up with; to pursue, chase OE. †b. *fig.* To follow up, prosecute; to enforce (law) –1693. 6. *fig.* (Cf. sense 3.) To treat or take as a guide, leader, or master; to accept the authority or example of; to espouse the opinions or cause of OE. 7. To act upon or in accordance with (advice, example, etc.); to take as a model, 'walk after' OE. 8. To walk in, pursue, or practise (a way of life, etc.); *esp.* to practise (a calling) for a livelihood OE. 9. To watch the progress or course of (a moving object, etc.); to keep up with (an argument, train of thought, etc.; also a person as he reasons or recounts) 1697.

1. As any kyde or calf folwynge his dame CHAUCER. b. To f. the turnpike road COBBETT. Phr. *To f. the drum*: to be a soldier. *To f. the hounds*: to hunt with dogs. 2. One misfortune followes another 1659. Punishment must f. conviction 1817. 3. Thou for wages followest thy master SHAKS. 4. Surely goodnes and mercie shall followe me all the daies of my life *Ps.* xxiii. 6. 5. To f. pleasure CHATHAM, knowledge TENNYSON. b. Since I haue euer followed thee with hate SHAKS. 6. With pure harte and mynde to folowe thee *Bk. Com. Prayer.* 7. Most men admire Virtue, who f. not her lore MILT. *P.R.* I. 483. 8. Phr. *To f. the sea*: to practise the calling of a sailor. 9. The argument is too difficult for them to f. JOWETT.

II. *intr.* 1. To go or come after a person or thing; also, to go as an attendant, etc. Const. *after.* Also *fig.* ME. 2. To result; to be, or occur as, a consequent. Const. *from.* ME. 3. To go in pursuit. Const. *after.* Also *fig.* of things. ME.

1. For still temptation follows where thou art SHAKS. Phr. *As follows*: a prefatory formula, *impers.* in const., and therefore to be always used in the sing. *F.-my-leader*, game in which each player must do as the leader does. 3. Vp, f. after the men *Gen.* xliv. 4. Phr. *To f. after*: to strive to compass; *Ps.* cxix. 150.

Combs. (with advbs.). **F. on.** a. *intr.* To continue following. b. *intr.* Of a side at *Cricket*: To go in again at once after the first innings, in consequence of having made a prescribed number of runs less than the other side in the first innings. **F. through** *Golf*, etc. (*intr.*): to carry the stroke through to the full extent after striking the ball; **F. up.** *trans.* a. To go after or pursue closely. b. To prosecute with energy.

Follower (fǫ·lou,əɹ). [OE. *folgere*, f. as prec. + -ER [1].] 1. One who follows; a pursuer 1593; an attendant or servant OE.; an adherent or disciple ME. b. *colloq.* One who courts a maidservant 1838. 2. Something that succeeds something else 1450. 3. *Sc.* and *n. dial.* The young of cattle 1584. 4. *Mech.*

a. In various kinds of presses: The plate or block by which the pressure is applied 1676. b. *Steam-engine.* The cover or plug of a stuffing-box, which rests upon and compresses the packing; a gland 1874. 5. *Stationery.* A sheet of parchment, which is added to the first or indenture, etc. sheet 1858.

Following (fǫ·lou,iŋ), *vbl. sb.* ME. [f. as prec. + -ING [1].] 1. The action of FOLLOW *v.* 2. *concr.* A body of followers; followers collectively 1450.

Fo·llowing, *ppl. a.* ME. [f. as prec. + -ING[2].] 1. That follows 1626. 2. That comes next or after; succeeding, ensuing ME. Also *absol.* (*the f.*). ME. 3. Of wind or tide: ? Moving in the direction of the ship's course 1807. 4. *Billiards*, etc. *F. stroke* = FOLLOW *sb.* 2. 1867.

Folly (fǫ·li), *sb.* Pl. **follies.** [ME. *foly(e*, a. OF. *folie*, f. *fol, fou* foolish, mad (see FOOL).] 1. The quality or state of being foolish; want of good sense, weakness or derangement of mind; also, unwise conduct. b. With *a* and *pl.* ME. †2. Wickedness, evils, michief, harm. Also with *a* and *pl.* –1535. †3. Lewdness, wantonness. Also with *a* and *pl.* –1634. †4. Madness, mania (= F. *folie*); hence, rage –1670. 5. A name given to any costly structure considered to have shown folly in the builder. (But cf. F. *folie*, 'delight', 'favourite abode'.) 1654.

1. Where ignorance is bliss, 'Tis f. to be wise GRAY. b. The follies of the town GOLDSM. 2. Because he hath..committed folye in Israel COVERDALE *Josh.* vii. 15. 3. *Oth.* v. ii. 132. Hence **Fo·lly** *v.* to commit f.

‖**Fomalhaut** (fōu·măl,hǫ:t). 1594. [Arab.; = 'mouth of the fish', Sp. *fomahant.*] *Astron.* A star of the first magnitude in the constellation Southern Fish (*Piscis Australis*).

Fo·ment, *sb.* Now *rare.* 1540. [ad. L. *fomentum*, contr. of **fovimentum*, f. *fovere* to cherish, warm.] 1. = FOMENTATION 1 b. †2. *fig.* Fomentation, encouragement; also, stimulus –1704.

Foment (fome·nt), *v.* 1611. [ad. F. *fomenter*, ad. late L. *fomentare*; see prec.] 1. *trans.* To bathe with warm or medicated lotions; to apply fomentations to. †2. 'To cherish with heat, to warm' (J.) –1667. †3. To rouse or stir up; to excite, irritate. Also *intr.* for *refl.* –1724. 4. To promote the growth or spread of; to cherish; to stimulate, encourage, instigate; *esp.* in a bad sense 1622.

2. All things..these soft fires..f. and warme MILT. *P.L.* iv. 669. 4. That humour which foments thy malady QUARLES. To..f. extravagance M. PATTISON. var. †**Fo·mentate** *v.* (in sense 1). Hence **Fome·nter.**

Fomentation (fōumĕntēi·ʃən). ME. [ad. late L. *fomentationem*; see prec.] 1. *Med.* The application to the surface of the body of flannels, etc. soaked in hot water, whether simple or medicated, or of any other warm, soft, medicinal substance. Also *concr.* that which is so applied. **2.** *fig.* Encouragement, instigation; a stimulus 1612.

2. The f. of Hungarian discontent 1861.

‖**Fomes** (fōᵘ·mīz). *Pl.* **fomites** (fōᵘ·mitīz). 1658. [L.; = 'tinder'.] †**a.** The morbific matter (of a disease). **b.** 'Any porous substance capable of absorbing and retaining contagious effluvia' (Mayne). Also *fig.* 1803.

The most important fomites are bed-clothes, bedding, woollen garments, carpets, curtains, letters, etc. 1882.

†**Fon.** ME. [Belongs to FON *v.*] **A.** *sb.* A fool -1595. **B.** *adj.* Foolish, silly -1538.

†**Fon,** *v.* ME. [prob. the source of prec. Cf. FUN *v.* (whence FUN *sb.*).] **1.** *intr.* To lose savour. Only in pa. pple.; see FOND *a.* **2.** To be or become foolish or infatuated -1570. **3.** *trans.* To befool -1460.

Fond, *sb.*[1] †Also **fonds.** Now only as F., pronounced (fon̄). 1664. [a. F. *fond, fonds* :— OF. *fonz, fons* :—(ult.) L. *fundus.* In 18th c. repl. by FUND, exc. as Fr.] **1.** Foundation, ground, groundwork. (In Fr. now *fond.*) **2.** A source of supply. (In Fr. now *fonds.*) 1685. †**3.** A stock of money; pecuniary means, revenues. (In Fr. now *fonds.*) -1691. †**4.** A sum of money, stock of goods, or the like, serving as a security for specified payments. (In Fr. now *fonds.*) 1677. †**5.** *Printing.* = FOUNT. 1678.

1. The present Prizes..being a better fond of credit 1665.

Fond (fǫnd), *a.* and *sb.*[2] [ME. *fonned,* f. FON *v.* + -ED[1].]

A. *adj.* **1.** That has lost its savour; insipid. *Obs.* exc. *dial.* **2.** Infatuated, foolish; now, foolishly credulous or sanguine ME. **3.** Idiotic, imbecile; also, dazed. Now *dial.* ME. †**4.** Of things: Valued only by fools -1645. **5. a.** Of persons, their actions, etc.: Foolishly tender; doting. Now in good sense: Affectionate, loving. Also with *of,* †*on.* 1579. **b.** Of opinions, etc.: Cherished with unreasoning affection 1635. **6.** †Eager for, desirous of (const. *of*) -1779; also with *to* and *inf.* 1546.

2. His own f. ineptitude CARLYLE. 4. Not with f. Sickles of the tested gold SHAKS. 5. a. I called up the many f. things I had to say GOLDSM. F. of the sports of the field STRUTT. b. Edward's..f. opinion of his own capacity CARTE.

†**B.** *absol.* and *sb.* A foolish person -1575.

†**Fond,** *v.*[1] [OE. *fandian.*] To attempt, try, endeavour, tempt.

†**Fond,** *v.*[2] 1530. [f. FOND *a.*] **1.** *intr.* To play the fool -1541. **2.** To dote. Const. *on, over, upon.* -1601. **3.** *trans.* To make a fool of -1567. **4.** To fondle; also, to beguile -1697.

4. The Tyrian hugs, and fonds thee on her breast DRYDEN.

Fond, obs. pa. t. FIND: obs. f. FOUND *v.*[1]

‖**Fondaco** (fǫ·ndakǫ). 1632. [It., ad. Arab.] An inn.

Fondant (fo·ndănt). 1877. [a. F., f. *fondre* to melt.] A name for sweetmeats that melt in the mouth.

Fondle (fǫ·nd'l), *v.* 1694. [freq. of FOND *v.*[2]] †**1.** *trans.* To cocker, pamper -1789. **2.** To handle or treat with fondness. Also, to press fondly *to* (the heart). 1796. **3.** *intr.* To behave fondly; to toy 1720.

2. The prince fondled it [the bird] to his heart W. IRVING. Hence **Fo·ndler,** one who fondles. **Fo·ndle** *sb.* an act of fondling.

Fondling (fǫ·ndliŋ), *vbl. sb.* 1714. [see -ING[1].] Affectionate handling; a fond gesture.

Fondling (fǫ·ndliŋ). ME. [f. FOND *a.* + -LING.] †**1.** A fond or foolish person. Also *transf.* of animals. -1781. **2.** One who is much fondled or caressed; a pet. Also *fig.* Now *rare.* 1640.

Fondly (fǫ·ndli), *adv.* ME. [f. FOND *a.* + -LY[2].] †**1.** Foolishly -1648. **2.** With fond credulity 1762. **3.** Affectionately, lovingly, tenderly. Also, caressingly. 1593.

2. You would f. persuade me that [etc.] GOLDSM. 3. My heart untravell'd f. turns to thee GOLDSM.

Fondness (fǫ·ndnės). ME. [f. FOND *a.* + -NESS.] **1.** Foolishness; 'weakness; want of sense or judgement' (J.). Now *dial.* **2.** Foolish affection; unreasoning tenderness 1579. **3.** Affectionateness, tenderness 1603. **4.** Instinctive liking 1654.

1. The fondnesse of this opinion 1609. 3. A mother's f. reigns without a rival HAN. MORE. 4. The f. of the negro races for fables 1885.

Fondon. 1881. *Mining.* A large copper vessel, in which amalgamation is practised. RAYMOND.

Fondu (fondü). Also **-us.** 1848. [a. F. *fondu* sing., *fondus* pl., f. *fondre* to melt.] That kind of painting on calico in which the colours melt into each other.

‖**Fondue** (fondü). 1878. [ad. F., f. as prec.] A dish of melted cheese with eggs, etc.

Fone, obs. pl. of FOE.

Fonly: see FON *sb.* and *a.*

Font (fǫnt), *sb.*[1] [OE. *font, fant,* ad. eccl. L. *fontem or fontes (baptismi).* In sense 3, a var. of FOUNT.] **1.** A receptacle, usu. of stone, for the water used in baptism. **2.** *transf.* **a.** A receptacle for holy water 1542. **b.** The reservoir for oil in a lamp 1891. **3.** = FOUNT. *poet.* 1611.

1. Crystnyd I was in a funt of stoon BOKENHAM. 3. Near f. or stream SHENSTONE.

Font (fǫnt), *sb.*[2] 1578. [ad. F. *fonte,* f. *fondre* to melt.] **1.** The process of casting or founding. *rare.* **2.** *Printing.* = FOUNT[2], q.v.

Fontal (fǫ·ntăl). 1656. [ad. med. L. *fontalis,* f. *font-, fons* FOUNT, FONT.]

A. *adj.* **1.** Of or pertaining to a fountain, spring, or source; original, primary. **2.** Baptismal 1797.

1. Godhead F. and Deriv'd KEN.

B. *sb.* †**1.** Source, well-spring (*fig.*) 1711. **2.** *Her.* A water-pot 'from whence issues water all proper' 1688.

Fontanelle, fontanel (fǫntăne·l). 1541. [a. F. *fontanelle,* dim. of *fontaine* FOUNTAIN.] **1.** *Anat.* †**a.** The hollow between two muscles. R. COPLAND. **b.** One of several membranous spaces in the head of an infant which lie at the adjacent angles of the parietal bones 1741. †**2.** *Med.* An artificial ulcer or a natural issue for the discharge of humours from the body -1779. **b.** Hence, Any outlet 1649.

2. b. This narrow fontanel of perforated rock 1848.

‖**Fontange** (fontanʒ). 1689. [Fr., f. *Fontanges* the territorial title of a mistress of Louis XIV.] A tall head-dress formerly worn.

Food (fūd), *sb.* [OE. *fōda,* f. (ult.) OAryan root **păt,* whence Gr. πατέεσθαι to feed. Cf. FODDER.] **1.** What one takes into the system to maintain life and growth, and to supply waste; aliment, nourishment, victuals. **b.** What one eats, as opp. to 'drink' 1610. **c.** An article, or kind of food ME. **2.** With ref. to plants: That which they absorb from the earth and air; nutriment 1759. **3.** *fig.*; *esp.* in sense: Matter to discuss or dwell upon OE.

1. Phr. *To be f. for fishes*: to be drowned. *F. for powder*: fit only to be shot at or to die in battle. 3. Chewing the f. of sweet and bitter fancie SHAKS. F. for thought SOUTHEY.

Comb.: **f.-rent,** rent in kind; **-yolk,** the non-germinative part of the yolk of an egg, which nourishes the embryo. Hence †**Food** *v.* to supply f. to; to feed, support.

Foodful (fū·dful), *a.* Chiefly *poet.* 1638. [see -FUL.] Abounding with or supplying food or nutriment.

The f. Earth 1638. *fig.* The f. nurse of ambition BURKE.

Foodless (fū·dlės), *a.* ME. [see -LESS.] Without food; (of a country, etc.) barren.

Foody (fū·di), *a.* [see -Y[1].] Full of, or supplying food. CHAPMAN.

Fool (fūl), *sb.*[1] and *a.* [ME. *fōl* sb. and adj., ad. OF. *fol* sb. and adj. (mod. F. *fou*) :— L. *follem, follis,* lit. 'bellows', hence, in late pop. L., 'wind-bag', 'fool'.]

A. *sb.* **1.** One deficient in judgement or sense, a silly person, a simpleton. (In Biblical use applied to vicious or impious persons.) **2.** One who professionally counterfeits folly for the entertainment of others, a jester, clown ME. **3.** One who is made to appear a fool; a dupe. Now somewhat *arch.* ME. **4.** One who has little or no reason or intellect; a weak-minded or idiotic person. *Obs.* exc. in *natural* or *born f.* 1540.

1. There ben more fooles than Wysemen CAXTON. The f. hath said in his heart, There is no God *Ps.* xiv. 1. Phr. *To be a f. to*: to be as nothing compared to. 2. Phr. *To play the f.*: to act the part of a jester; hence *gen.* to act like a f. (sense 1). 3. Phr. *To make a f. of. To be a f. for one's pains,* to have one's labour for nothing.

Comb.; **f.-begged** *a.,* ? foolish, idiotic (cf. BEG); **-born,** begotten by a f.; **-duck** (*U.S.*), the ruddy duck, *Erismatura rubida*; **-fish** (*U.S.*), a pop. name for *Manocanthus broccus,* also for *Pleuronectes glaber*; †**-happy** *a.,* lucky without contrivance; **-hen** (*U.S.*), grouse, *esp.* young grouse, in the early part of the season.

b. Comb. with genitive *fool's*: **fool's errand**: see ERRAND; †**fool's gold,** iron pyrites; **fool's paradise,** a state of illusory happiness or good fortune; **fool's parsley,** a poisonous weed, the Lesser Hemlock (*Æthusa Cynapium*); hence, a book name of the genus *Æthusa.*

B. *adj.* Foolish, silly. *Obs.* exc. *Sc.* and *dial.* and *vulgar*; frequent since *c* 1800 in U.S.

Fighting is a f. thing COLVIL.

Fool (fūl), *sb.*[2] 1598. [prob. a use of prec.; cf. *trifle* in quot.] †**1.** (See quot.) -1688. **2.** A dish of fruit stewed, crushed, and mixed with milk, cream, or custard 1747.

1. *Mantiglia,* a kinde of clouted creame called a foole or a trifle in English FLORIO.

Fool (fūl), *v.* ME. [f. FOOL *a.* or *sb.*[1]] †**1.** *intr.* To be or become foolish or insane -1489. **2.** To play the fool, trifle, idle 1593; †to play the buffoon -1641. Also quasi-*trans.* *Twel. N.* v. i. 44. **3.** *trans.* To make a fool of; to dupe. Also, to balk. 1596. †**4.** To make foolish; to infatuate -1641.

2. While I stand fooling heere SHAKS. 3. That you are fool'd, discarded, and shook off By him, for whom these shames ye underwent SHAKS. 4. *Lear* II. iv. 278. Phr. *To f. away* (also *simply*): to throw away or part with foolishly.

Foolery (fū·lėri). 1552. [f. FOOL *sb.*[1] + -ERY.] **1.** The practice of fooling or acting foolishly 1579. **2.** A ridiculous action, performance, or thing 1552. **3.** Fools as a class. SYD. SMITH.

1. But sike fansies weren foolerie SPENSER. 2. The pleasing levities, and agreeable fooleries of a girl 1772.

Foo·lha:rdiness. ME. [f. FOOLHARDY + -NESS.] The quality of being foolhardy. So †**Foolhardice,** †**Foo·lha:rdiment.**

Foolhardy (fū·lhā:ɹdi), *a.* ME. [a. OF. *fol hardi,* comb. of *fol* foolish with *hardi* bold.] Daring without judgement, foolishly adventurous or bold. Hence **Foo·lha:rdily** *adv.* Also **Foo·lha:rdihood,** foolhardiness.

†**Fool-hasty,** *a.* ME. [a. OF. *fol hastif,* comb. of *fol* FOOL *a.* and *hastif* HASTY.] Foolishly hasty, precipitate -1600.

†**Foo·lify,** *v.* 1581. [f. FOOL *sb.*[1] + -(I)FY.] To make a fool of, render foolish -1641.

Fooling (fū·liŋ), *vbl. sb.* 1601. [f. FOOL *v.* + -ING[1].] The action of FOOL *v.* 1609. **b.** Preceded by an adj. = Condition or humour for fooling.

b. Put me into good f. *Twel. N.* I. v. 36.

Foolish (fū·liʃ), *a.* ME. [f. FOOL *sb.*[1] + -ISH.] **1.** Fool-like, wanting in sense or judgement. **2.** Befitting a fool; proceeding from, or indicative of folly ME. **3.** Ridiculous 1514. **4.** Humble, paltry, poor, mean, trifling. *arch.* or *dial.* 1592.

1. Women are so very f., Mr. Squeers DICKENS. 2. Where Wits..wonder with a f. face of praise POPE. 3. A f. figure He must make PRIOR. 4. We haue a trifling f. Banquet towards SHAKS. Hence **Foo·lishly** *adv.*

Foolishness (fū·liʃnės). 1470. [f. prec. + -NESS.] **1.** The quality or condition of being foolish. **2.** A foolish act or thing.

2. They deuysed another foolishnes COVERDALE *Wisd.* xix. 3.

†**Fool-large.** ME. [a. OF. *follarge,* f. *fol-* FOOL *a.* + *large* liberal; see LARGE.] **A.** *adj.* Foolishly liberal, prodigal -1603. **B.** *sb.* **1.** A spendthrift -late ME. **2.** = next. CAXTON.

A. In spenynge he was fol large R. GLOUC.

Fool-proof (fū·lprūf), *a.* orig. *U.S.* 1902. [PROOF *a.* 1 b.] Proof against even the incompetence of a fool; safeguarded against all accidents.

Foo·l's-cap, foo·lscap. 1632. **1.** A cap, usually garnished with bells, formerly worn by fools or jesters. **2.** The device of a fool's cap used as a watermark for paper 1795. **3.** A long folio writing- or printing-paper, $16\frac{1}{2}$ to 17 inches by $13\frac{1}{2}$ inches in size 1700.

attrib., as **foolscap folio, octavo, quarto,** said of a volume consisting of sheets of foolscap size folded in the manner specified.

Fool's coat. 1589. 1. The motley coat of a buffoon. Also *transf.* and *fig.* 2. A name for the goldfinch 1682. 3. A bivalve mollusc, *Isocardia cor* (*Cent. Dict.*).

Foot (fut), *sb. Pl.* **feet** (fīt). [Com. Teut.: OE. *fōt*, pl. *fēt*. The OTeut. **fōt-* represents OAryan **pōd-*, **pĕd-*, *pŏd-*: cf. Skr. *pād* (gen. *padás*) foot, Gr. πούς, gen. ποδός; L. *pēs*, accus. *pĕdem*, etc. See also FETTER *sb.*, and perh. FET *v.*, FETCH *v.*, FETLOCK.]

I. 1. The lowest part of the leg beyond the ankle-joint. †b. The whole limb from the hip-joint to the toes. Also *great f.* -1661. 2. Viewed as the organ of locomotion OE. b. Hence, a person as walking. *Obs.* exc. *dial.* in *first f.* ME. 3. *ellipt.* Foot-soldiers 1568. 4. The end of a bed, a grave, etc. towards which the feet are placed. Formerly often *pl.* ME. b. The part of a stocking, etc. which covers the foot 1577.

1. The fote to go, and hand to hold and rech 1538. 2. Death, Which I did thinke, with slower f. came on SHAKS. *fig.* Unless..I lame the f. Of our design *Cor.* IV. vii. 7. 3. The Forty-Fourth Foot 1878. 4. In a cofre at my beddes feet HOCCLEVE.

II. *Pros.* [tr. of L. *pes*, Gr. πούς; said to be with reference to the movement of the foot in beating time.] A division of a verse, consisting of a number of syllables one of which has the ictus or principal stress OE.

III. 1. A lineal measure originally based on the length of a man's foot. (The English foot consists of 12 inches. Hence *square* or *cubic f.*, equal to the content respectively of a square and a cube the side of which measures one foot. Often in *sing.* when preceded by numerals. OE. 2. (See quot.) 1602.

1. A doore in brede iiij foote standard 1459. Ile starue ere I rob a foote further SHAKS. Phr. †*Every f.* (*and anon*): incessantly. 2. *Foot*, an ancient measure for black Tin, two gallons; now a nominal measure, but in weight 60 lb. PRYCE.

IV. Analogous uses. 1. The lower part, on which an object rests; the base ME. 2. a. *Zool.* Applied to various organs of locomotion or attachment in invertebrate animals 1835. b. *Bot.* The part (of a petal) by which it is attached; the part (of a hair) below the epidermis; etc. 1671. 3. The extremity of the leg (of a pair of compasses, a chair, etc.) 1551. 4. *pl.* The commercial name for the small plates of tortoise-shell which line the carapace.

1. A Lauer of brasse, and his foote also of brasse *Exod.* xxx. 18.

V. 1. The lowest part or bottom, as of an eminence, a wall, ladder, staircase, etc. ME. b. The beginning or end of the slope (of a bridge) 1450. 2. The lower end, bottom (of a page, a list, a table, etc.) 1669. †3. What is written at the foot; as, the sum (of an account) -1712; the refrain (of a song) -1621. 4. (Pl. *foots.*) Bottoms, dregs, as of oil, sugar, etc. 1560.

1. At þe f. of the hille Mount Olympus TREVISA. The F. of a Mast 1815. 2. *At f.*: at the bottom (of a page); Placing the correction at f. 1855.

Phr. *F. of a fine* (Law): that one of the parts of a tripartite indenture recording the particulars of a fine (see Fine *sb.*[1]), which remained with the court. It was actually at the foot of the undivided sheet, and had its indentation at the top.

VI. †1. Standing-ground -1662. †2. = FOOTING *vbl. sb.* 6-1827. †3. Standard rate of calculation or value -1734.

2. I wish all correspondence was on the f. of writing and answering when one can FRANKLIN. 3. †*Under f.*: below standard value; Not deem'd a pen'worth under f. QUARLES.

Phrases.

a. *To have one f. in the grave*: to be near death. b. *F. to f.*: in close combat. *Feet foremost*: lit., hence also 'as a corpse'. c. *To find* or *know the length of* (a person's) *f.*: to discover or know his weaknesses. d. *To set* (a person) *on his feet*: to make his position or means of living secure. *To drop* or *fall on one's feet*: see FALL *v.* *To keep one's feet*: to stand or walk upright. e. *To put one's f. down*: to take up a firm position. *To put one's f. in* or *into it*: to get into difficulties; to blunder (*colloq.*). f. *To take to one's feet*: to walk. g. *To put* (or *set*) *the* (or *one's*) *best f. foremost*: see BEST *a.* h. *At* (a person's) *feet*: low on the ground close to him; also, *fig.* in the attitude of supplication, homage, subjection, or discipleship. i. **On foot**: walking or running; astir; in active existence, employment, or operation. j. **Under foot**: beneath one's feet; *Naut.* 'Under the ship's bottom; said of an anchor which is dropped while she has headway' (Adm. Smyth); also of the movement of the tide, etc.

Combs.: 1. General: as *f.-gear*, etc.; *-party*, etc.; *-company*, *-drill*, etc.; *-passage*, *-road*, *-track*, etc.; *-bellows*, *-lathe*, *-press*, etc.; *-feathered*, *-gilt*, etc.

2. Special: †**f.-and-half-f.** *a.*, sesquipedalian; **-and-mouth-disease**, a febrile affection of horned cattle, etc., communicable also to man; **-bank** (*Fortif.*) = BANQUETTE; **-base** (*Arch.*) the moulding above a plinth; **-bath**, (*a*) the act of bathing the feet; (*b*) a vessel for this purpose; **-bone**, the tarsus; **-bridge**, (*a*) a bridge for f.-passengers only; (*b*) an arched bridge which carries a footstep bearing; **-cushion**, *spec.* (*Entom.*) a pulvillus; **-fault** (*Lawn Tennis*), a fault made by overstepping the base-line, or by failure to maintain contact with the ground, while serving; hence as vb.; **-halt**, a disease which attacks the feet of sheep; **-hill**, a hill lying at the base of a mountain; **-hole**, a hole in which to place the f. (in climbing); **-iron**, (*a*) an iron fastened to the f.; (*b*) a step for a carriage; **-jaw**, one of the anterior limbs of crustacea, etc., which are modified so as to assist in mastication; **-key**, an organ pedal; **-level**, an instrument which serves as a level, a square, and a foot-rule; **-licker**, a toady; **-line**, (*a*) *Printing*, the bottom line in a page; (*b*) *Fishing*, 'the lead-line or lower line of a net or seine' (*Cent. Dict.*); **-pad**, *spec.* (*Entom.*) = *f.-cushion*; **-page**, a boy attendant or servant; **-plate**, (*a*) a carriage step; (*b*) the platform on a locomotive engine for the driver and fireman; **-post**, a postman or messenger who travels on f.; postal delivery by their means; **-pound**, (*Mech.*), the quantity of energy required to raise a pound weight one foot; **-poundal**, a unit consisting of the energy of a pound weight moving at the rate of one foot per second; **-race**, a race run by persons on f.; **-rail**, (*a*) a rail (e.g. of a table or seat) upon which the feet are rested; (*b*) a railroad rail having wide-spreading foot flanges; (*c*) a narrow moulding raised on a vessel's stern; **-rope** (*Naut.*), (*a*) the bolt-rope to which the lower edge of a sail is sewed; (*b*) a rope extended beneath a yard upon which the sailors stand when furling or reefing; **-rot**, an inflammatory disease of the foot of cattle and sheep; whence *f.-rotting* (vbl. sb.), treating sheep that have the f.-rot; **-rule**, a measuring rule one foot long; **-screw**, a supporting foot, for giving a machine or table a level standing on an uneven floor; **-space-rail** (*Naut.*), the rail that terminates the foot of the balcony, and in which balusters step; **-stick** (*Printing*), a bevelled stick put at the bottom of a page or pages to quoin up against; **-stove**, a stove to warm the feet; **-sugar** = *foots*: see FOOT *sb.* V. 4; **-ton**, the amount of energy capable of raising a ton weight one foot; **-trench**, a shallow trench; **-tubercle**, one of the lateral processes on each segment of some of the Annelida; also called *Parapodia*; **-valve** (in a steam-engine), the valve between the air-pump and the condenser; **-waling** (*Naut.*), the inside planking or lining of a ship over the floor-timbers; **-wall** (*Mining*), the wall or side of rock which is under a vein or lode; **-washing**, the washing of another's feet, *esp.* as a religious observance; **-work**, (*a*) a work to protect the foot of a structure; (*b*) *Football*, dribbling, etc.; **-worn** *a.*, (*a*) worn by the feet; (*b*) footsore.

Foot (fut), *v.* ME. [f. prec. sb.] 1. *intr.* To step or tread to measure or music; to dance. Esp. in *to f. it.* Also quasi-*trans.* with cogn. object. 2. To move the feet as in walking; to go on foot. Now *rare.* 1570. 3. *trans.* To set foot on; to tread; to walk over 1557. 4. To settle, establish. Chiefly *refl.* and in *pass.* = to have or get a foothold *in.* 1599. †5. *trans.* To strike with the foot; to kick; *fig.* to spurn -1808. b. *intr.* or *absol.* To do foot-work. *colloq.* (*Football*). 1852. 6. *trans.* Of a hawk, etc.: To clutch with the talons. Also *fig.* 1575. 7. To make or add a foot to 1465. 8. To sum up at the foot of (a bill, etc.). Now usu. with *up.* Chiefly *colloq.* 1490. b. To pay (a bill). *colloq.* 1848. c. *intr.* To total *up* to. Const. with or without *to.* 1867.

1. F. it featly here and there SHAKS. To f. a hornpipe 1842. 2. Theeues doe f. by night SHAKS. 3. Lucil..vsed to fote the streates of Rome NORTH. 5. *Merch. V.* I. iii. 119. 6. The holy eagle Stoop'd, as to f. us SHAKS. 8. c. His total losses footed up to £5,000 (*mod.*).

Football, foot-ball (fu·tbǭl). ME. [f. FOOT *sb.* + BALL *sb.*]. 1. An inflated ball used in the game (see 2). It consists of an inflated bag or bladder enclosed in a leather case. 1486. 2. An open-air game played with this ball by two sides, each of which endeavours to kick or carry the ball to the goal of the other side ME. 3. *fig.* 1532.

2. Foote balle, wherin is nothinge but beastlie furie and exstreme violence ELYOT. 3. The..institutions of the mistress of the world had become the f. of ruffians FROUDE. Hence **Foo·tball** *v.* to kick like a f.; also *fig.*

Footboard (fu·tbōᵊɹd). 1766. [f. FOOT *sb.* + BOARD.] 1. A board to support the foot or feet; a board to stand on; e.g. a small platform at the back of a carriage on which the footman stands; the foot-rest of a driving-box; in *U.S.* the foot-plate of a locomotive engine. b. A treadle 1874. 2. An upright board set across the foot of a bedstead 1843.

Foo·tboy. 1590. †a. A boy-attendant. b. A page-boy.

Foo·t-breadth, †-brede. ME. [See BREADTH and BREDE *sb.*[2]] The breadth of a foot (as a measure).

No, not so much as a foot breadth [of their land] *Deut.* ii. 5.

Foo·t-cloth. 1480. †1. A large richly-ornamented cloth laid over the back of a horse and hanging down to the ground on either side -1805. 2. A cloth to set the feet upon, a carpet 1639.

2. A foot-cloth for your majesty's chief room of state SWIFT.

Footed (fu·tėd), *ppl. a.* 1453. [f. FOOT *sb.* and *v.* + -ED.] Furnished with or having feet (*rarely* a foot). 1. Furnished with feet; having feet *like* (a dog, etc.) 1529. 2. Having, or provided with, a foot or feet; also, mended with a (new) foot 1453. 3. *Archery.* Of an arrow: Having a different and harder wood dovetailed on at the pile end 1856.

1. An animal..f. like a goat 1727. *Brazen-*, *cat-*, *claw-f.*: see those words. 2. New-f. boots and shoes 1844.

Footer (fu·təɹ), *sb.*[1] 1608. [f. FOOT *sb.* or *v.* + -ER[1].] 1. One who goes on foot. *rare.* 2. *Falconry.* Of the hawk: One good at seizing the quarry with its talons 1879. 3. With a numeral prefixed: A person or thing of that number of feet in height or length; as *six-f.*, etc. 1844.

Footer (fū·təɹ), *sb.*[2] *dial.* or *slang.* 1753. [? var. of FOUTRE.] One who potters about.

Footer, *sb.*[3]: see -ER [6].

Foo·tfall, foot-fall. 1610. The fall of the foot on the ground in walking; a footstep, tread.

Her footfall was so light 1872.

Foo·t-guards, foo·tguards. 1675. A body of picked foot-soldiers for special service as a guard. Now the proper name of five infantry regiments, the Coldstream, Grenadier, Irish, Scots, and Welsh Fusilier Guards.

Foothold (fu·tˌhōᵘld). 1625. [See HOLD *sb.*] A hold or support for the feet; a surface (secure or otherwise) for standing or walking on; stable position of the feet. Also *transf.* and *fig.*

Foot-hook: see FUTTOCK.

Foo·t-ho·t, *adv.* ? *Obs.* ME. [f. FOOT *sb.* + HOT *a.* or *adv.*; cf. *footsore.*] a. In hot haste, without pause. b. Occas. = 'closely', as in *to follow foot-hot.*

Footing (fu·tiŋ), *vbl. sb.* ME. [f. FOOT *v.* + -ING[1].] 1. The act of walking; a step or tread. Now *rare.* 1583. b. Dancing 1561. 2. A footprint, or footprints collectively; a trace, trail. Also *fig.* Now *rare.* 1572. 3. The action of placing the feet securely; stable position of the feet, foothold ME. 4. Surface for walking or standing upon 1596. 5. *fig.* Firm or secure position; established place; foothold, establishment 1586. 6. The agreed or understood basis, conditions or arrangements on which a matter is established; the position assigned to a person, etc. in estimation or treatment 1657. b. Relative status (as an equal, etc.) 1742. 7. Entrance on a new position, etc.; hence, a fee demanded on the occasion of such entrance, etc. 1710. 8. The action of putting a foot to anything 1805; also *concr.* that with which something is footed 1591. 9. *Arch.* A projecting course or courses at the foundation of a wall, etc. 1703. 10. *Whale-fishing.* The refuse whale blubber, not wholly deprived of oil 1820.

3. Stande sure, and take good fotyng SKELTON. 4. Where scarce was f. for the goat SCOTT. 5. In former times, when England had a f. in France WALSINGHAM. 6. b. I was admitted to his table upon the f. of half friend, half underling GOLDSM. *Comb.*: **f. beam**, f. dormant, the tie-beam of a roof.

Footle (fū·t'l), *v. slang.* 1892. [?] *intr.* To talk or act foolishly. Hence **Foo·tle** *sb.*, twaddle, **Foo·tling** *ppl. a.*, 'drivelling', 'blithering'.

Footless (fu·tlės), *a.* ME. [-LESS.] Having no foot or feet. Also *transf.* and *fig.*

Footlights (fu·tləits), *sb, pl.* 1836. A row of lights placed in front of the stage of a theatre, on a level with the feet of the actors. Often *transf.* = 'the stage'.

Footman (fu·tmæ̆n). ME. [f. FOOT *sb.* + MAN.] **1.** One who goes on foot, a pedestrian. Now chiefly *dial.* †**b.** A footpad –1666. **2.** A foot-soldier. ME. †**3.** An attendant or foot-servant; formerly, a servant who ran before his master's carriage –1818. **4.** A man-servant in livery employed chiefly to attend the carriage and wait at table 1706. Also *fig.* **5.** A stand to support a kettle, etc. before the fire 1767. **6.** A moth of the family *Lithosiidæ* 1819.

4. *fig.* The Whigs, who..submitted to be the footmen of the Duke of Newcastle MACAULAY.

Footmanship (fu·tmæ̆nʃip). 1562. [f. prec. + -SHIP]. **1.** The action of, or skill in, running or walking. ? *Obs.* **2.** The office of a footman 1833.

†**Foo·t-mantle.** ME. **a.** ? An over-garment worn by women when riding. **b.** = FOOT-CLOTH 1. –1818.

Foot-mark, footmark (fu·tmāɹk). 1641. A mark on, or made by, the foot; a footprint.

Foo·t-note (fu·tˌnōᵘt). 1841. A note or comment added at the foot of the text.

Foot-pace (fu·tpēⁱs). 1538. [See PACE *sb.*] **1.** A walking-pace. **2.** Something on which to set the feet: †**a.** a carpet or mat –1653; **b.** a raised portion of a floor: e.g. the step on which an altar stands 1580; **c.** a hearth-stone 1652; **d.** a half-landing on a staircase, etc. 1703.

Footpad (fu·tpæd). *Obs.* exc. *Hist.* 1683. [See PAD]. A highwayman who robs on foot.

Foot-path, footpath (fu·tpaþ). 1526. **1.** A path for foot-passengers only. †**2.** ? A pedestal 1580. **3.** *attrib.* 1611.

1. Horseway, and foot-path *Lear* IV. i. 58. 3. Jog-on, Jog-on, the foot-path way *Wint. T.* IV. iii. 132.

Footprint (fu·tprint). 1552. The impression left by the foot; *spec.* in *Geol.* Also *fig.*

Certain fossil foot-prints of a reptile..found in strata of the ancient coal-formation LYELL.

Footrill (fu·tril). Also **footrail, futteril.** 1686. [?] *Coal-mining.* The entrance to a mine by means of a tunnel driven into a hill-side.

Foot-slog (fu·tslǫg), *v.* 1906. [SLOG *v.* 2.] *intr.* To tramp, march. Hence **Foo·t-slog** *sb.* **Foo·t-slo·gger,** an infantryman, a pedestrian.

Foo·t-sore. 1719. **A.** *adj.* Sore as to the feet. **B.** *sb.* A complaint of the foot 1874.

Footstalk (fu·tstǭk). 1562. [f. FOOT *sb.* + STALK.] A slender stem or support fitted into a foot or base. **a.** *Bot.* The stalk or petiole of a leaf; the peduncle of a flower. **b.** *Zool.* A process resembling a petiole; e.g. the muscular attachment of a barnacle, the stalk of a crinoid, etc. 1826. **c.** *gen.* 1831.

Footstall (fu·tˌstǭl). 1585. [f. FOOT *sb.* + STALL *sb.*]. **1.** The base or pedestal of a pillar, etc. **2.** 'A woman's stirrup' (J.).

Footstep (fu·tstep). ME. [See STEP.] **1.** A step of the foot; a footfall; also, the distance traversed by the foot in stepping 1535. **2.** A footprint ME. Also *fig.* †**3.** *fig.* A mark, token, or indication left by anything –1785. **4.** A step or raised structure on which to put the foot 1549. **b.** A bearing to sustain the foot of a vertical shaft or spindle 1683.

1. Hold up my goings in thy paths, that my footsteps slip not *Ps.* xvii. 5. 2. *fig.* Phr. *To follow* or *walk in a person's footsteps.* 4. At the footestep of the Altar SIR T. BROWNE.

Foo·tstool. 1530. **1.** A stool upon which to rest the foot or feet. **b.** *U.S.* The earth 1821. †**2.** A stool to step upon in mounting –1702.

1. *fig.* Sit thou at my right hand, until I make thine enemies thy f. *Ps.* cx. 1.

Footway (fu·twēⁱ). 1526. [f. FOOT *sb.* + WAY. **1.** = FOOT-PATH 1. **2.** *Mining.* 'The series of ladders and sollars by which men enter or leave a mine' (Raymond) 1778.

Footy (fū̆·ti), *a*[1]. 1752. Paltry, mean; insignificant. *dial.* and *colloq.*

Footy (fu·ti), *a.*[2] 1864. [f. FOOT *sb.* + -Y[1].] Having foots or dregs. (Dicts.)

Foozle (fū̆·z'l), *sb.* 1860. [Cf. next vb.] **1.** A fogy; (*U.S.*) a fool. **2.** *Golf.* A foozling stroke 1890.

Foozle (fū̆·z'l), *v.* 1857. [Cf. Ger. dial. *fuseln* to work badly.] **1.** *intr.* To fool. **2.** *trans.* To make a mess of, bungle. *Golf* and *slang.* Also *absol.* 1892.

2. To f. one's tee shot (*mod.*). Hence **Foo·zler.**

Fop (fǫp), *sb.* ME. [Conn. w. next. Cf. F. *fat*, orig. 'fool', now 'fop'.] †**1.** A fool –1716. **2.** One who is foolishly attentive to his appearance, dress, or manners; a dandy, an exquisite 1672.

2. His tightened waist, his stiff stock [etc.]..denoted the military f. DISRAELI. Hence **Fo·pling,** a petty f.

†**Fop,** *v.* 1529. [?] **1.** *intr.* To play the fool. **2.** *trans.* = FOB *v.*[1] –1694.

†**Fopdoodle.** 16.. [f. FOP *sb.* + DOODLE.] A fop, fool, or simpleton –1664.

Foppery (fǫ·pĕri). 1546. [f. FOP *sb.* and *v.* + -ERY.] †**1.** Foolishness, imbecility; a foolish action, etc.; something foolishly esteemed –1758. **2.** The characteristics of a fop; coxcombry, dandyism 1697. **b.** *concr.* Foppish finery 1711.

2. Modern politeness..runs often into affectation and f. HUME.

Foppish (fǫ·piʃ), *a.* 1605. [see -ISH.] †**1.** Foolish, silly –1720. **2.** Resembling or befitting a fop or dandy 1699.

1. Wisemen are growne f. SHAKS. 2. A vain, f. young man EVELYN. **Fo·ppish·ly** *adv.*, **-ness.**

For (fǭɹ, fǫɹ, fəɹ), *prep.* and *conj.* [OE. *for* prep.; prob. an apocopated form of OTeut. **fora* FORE *adv.* and *prep.* Not found as a conj. earlier than the 12th c.]

A. *prep.* †**I.** = BEFORE in various uses. **1. a.** In front of –1601. **b.** In asseveration. (Cf. Gr. πρός.) In later use repl. by FORE. -ME. **2.** Of time -ME. **3.** In preference to, above –1504.

1. a. F. whose throne 'tis needfull..to kneele SHAKS.

II. 1. Representing, as representative of OE. **2.** In place of, instead of OE. **3.** In exchange for; as the price of OE; in requital of OE.

1. Walker returned thanks f. his lady 1843. Phr. *Once f. all.* 2. Will he f. a fish giue him a serpent *Luke* xi. 11. They will employ somebody to do the business f. them 1895. 3. Men gaf fiueten schillynges f. a goos or a heen ME. Punishment f. his misdeeds 1818.

III. In defence or support of; in favour of, on the side of. Opp. to *against.* OE. **b.** In honour of. Also *To name a child for* (= after) a person (now *Sc.* and *U.S.*) 1800.

Take my Word f. it she is no Fool STEELE. You argue f. it in vain HELPS. Hence quasi-*sb. Fors and againsts*: 'pros and cons'.

IV. 1. With the object or purpose of OE. **b.** For the purpose of being or becoming 1489. **c.** Conducive to 1553. **2.** In order to obtain ME. **3.** Indicating the object to which the activity of the faculties or feelings is directed 1592. **4.** Before an *inf.*, usu. *for to* = 'in order (to)'. Hence *for to* merely for *to.* Now *arch.* or *vulgar.* ME. **5.** Indicating destination. **a.** With the purpose of going to. Now chiefly after *to depart, start, sail, leave, steer, make*; also after the pple. *bound.* 1489. **b.** *transf.* of time 1885. **c.** Introducing the intended recipient, or the thing to which something is intended to belong, or the like ME. **6. a.** Following a vb., adj., or noun of quality, denoting appointment, appropriation, fitness, etc. ME. **b.** Following a sb., or predicatively = Appointed, adapted, or suitable for ME. **7.** Of result or effect; used after *cause, ground, motive, reason*, etc. (See the sbs.) **8.** Designating an amount to be received or paid. Also in *Cricket*: With the result of (so many runs), at the cost of (so many wickets). 1776.

1. An order..f. the payment of the balance to the plaintiff 1891. To go out f. a walk (*mod.*). Phr. *For company*: see COMPANY. **b.** To go f. a soldier 1741. **c.** It is f. the general good 1664. 2. The drawers struck work f. an advance of wages 1883. Phr. *I would not f. anything, f. a great deal, f. the world*, etc. Hence also, *To play f. a certain stake. To try a man f. his life. F.* (*one's*) *life*: in order to save one's life; also hyperbolically, with one's utmost efforts. *To run f. it*: see IT. 3. O f. a Falkners voice To lure this Tassell gentle back again SHAKS. 4. What went ye out f. to see *Luke* vii. 25. 5. a. We sailed from hence directly f. Genoa ADDISON. b. It is getting on f. four (*mod.*). c. Madam, they are f. you SHAKS. A fireproof chamber f. the muniments M. PATTISON. 6. a. Very fit f. a wife JANE AUSTEN. Important enough f. separate treatment (*mod.*). b. By no means a match f. his enemies ADDISON. 8. The signature was good f. more than that STEVENSON. The score stood at 150 for 6 wickets (*mod.*).

V. 1. With the purpose or result of benefiting or gratifying; as a service to OE. Also *ironically.* **2.** As affecting the interests or condition of (a person or thing) 1537. **3.** Governing a sb. or pers. pron. followed by an inf., with sense '*that he*, etc. *may, might, should*', etc. 1508.

1. Dangers..Which he f. us did freely undergo MILT. To shift f. my selfe 1631. 2. This bodes ill f. the peace of Europe 1883. 3. What a condition f. me to come to 1843.

VI. Of attributed or assumed character; = as OE.

Know f. trouth that..god loueth fayth LD. BERNERS. I know f. a fact that [etc.] 1843. Phr. *To take f. granted, to leave f. dead*, etc. *F. certain, sure*, see these adjs. (*I*, etc.) *f. one. F. the first, second*, etc. *time. F. good* (*and all*): see GOOD.

VII. 1. By reason of (a feeling, etc.) OE. **2.** On account of OE. **b.** In adjurations = *for the sake of.* Also in exclams. OE. **3.** Of an operative cause: As the effect of. (Now chiefly after comparatives.) ME. **4.** Of a preventive cause or obstacle. **a.** In spite of, notwithstanding OE. **b.** Indicating the presence or operation of an obstacle. In neg. sentences; also after *if it were not, were it not*; occas. = for fear of. OE. †**c.** Against –1728.

1. Our men raised a shout f. joy DE FOE. Phr. *F. fear of, that*, etc.; see FEAR *sb.* 2. Notorious both f. covetousness and f. parsimony MACAULAY. Phr. *F. cause*: see CAUSE *sb.* **b.** Alas! f. my master 1460. F. shame! BYRON. †*For because*: see BECAUSE. 3. To die f. thirst standyng in the river HALL. The worse f. liquor (*mod.*). Phr. *F. want of*: see WANT *sb.* 4. a. This Alexander the Great f. all his greatness died H. MORE. F. all her feelings are so fine 1786. b. Uninhabitable f. heat RAY. Spare not f. spoiling of thy steed SCOTT.

VIII. Of correspondence or correlation. **1.** Prefixed to a number or quantity to which another corresponds in some different relation ME. **2.** Preceded and followed by the same sb. (without article or defining word), in idiomatic expressions indicating equality in number or quantity between objects compared or contrasted ME.

1. It contains..f. one inch of lean four or five of stringy fat 1806. 2. Bulk f. bulk heavier than a fluid BENTLEY.

IX. 1. As regards ME. **2.** In proportion to, considering; considering the nature or capacity of 1631.

1. The king's condition f. money PEPYS. Phr. †*F. me* = as f. me; *f. my, his*, etc. *part*: see PART; *f. the rest* (= F. *du reste*): see REST *sb. As f.*: see AS. *F. all* or *aught I know*, I know nothing to the contrary. (*He may do it*) *f. me*, i.e. with no opposition from me. *F. all the world*: used to emphasize assertions of likeness. 2. A man of an excellent character f. a Lawyer RICHARDSON.

X. 1. Marking actual or intended duration; e.g. *f. long, f. the time, f. life, f. ay, ever* 1450. *F. once, f. the nonce*: see ONCE, NONCE.

B. *conj.* **1.** Because. *Obs.* exc. *arch.* ME. **2.** Introducing the ground or reason for something previously said: Seeing that, since OE. †**3.** In order that –1593. †**4.** *F. and*: = 'and moreover' –1617.

1. They are..iealious for they are iealious SHAKS. 2. Nowe is good tyme F. al Englond praith f. vs CAXTON. 3. 3 *Hen. VI*, III. i. 9. 4. A Spade f. and a shrowding-Sheete *Haml.* V. i. 103.

For-, *pref.*[1] [OE. *for-, fær-*; app. repr. OTeut. **fer-, fra-, fur-*; see FOR and FORE. The primary notion of the prefix is that of 'forward, forth'.] A prefix used to form vbs. and adjs.; now entirely obsolete as a living formation.

I. Forming vbs. **1.** Prefixed to vbs. with sense 'away', 'off', as in FORCAST –ME. **2.** With sense of prohibition, exclusion, or warding off, as in FORBID; **forsay,** to renounce, exclude by command –1579. **3.** With the notion of passing by, abstaining from, or neglecting, as in FORBEAR, FORGO –ME. **4.** Implying destructive, painful, or prejudicial effect, as in FORDEEM, FORDO –1563. **b.** With sense of 'asunder, in pieces', as in **forhale,** *fig.* to distract. **5.** Expressing the notion of something done in excess, or so as to overwhelm or overpower; in pa. pples.; as **forfrighted,** greatly terrified; etc. –1598. **b.** Prefixed to intr. vbs., with sense 'to weary or exhaust (oneself) by' doing what the vb. denotes, as in FORWANDER, FORWEEP. Also in pa. pples. and ppl. adjs.: **forsung (-songen); forwake, -waked,** wearied with waking or watching. 6. With sense 'all over', 'through and through', as in **forcratch**, to scratch all over. 7. Prefixed to transitive vbs. with intensive force, or, occas., without modifying the sense, as in FORDREAD. 8. Forming factitive vbs. from adjs. or sbs. of quality; as in **formeagre**, to make lean; **forfatted** pa. pple., fattened.

II. In adjs. [Cf. L. *per-*, Gr. περι-.] Giving to an adj. the sense of an absolute superlative, 'very', 'extremely'; as *for-black, -dry, -hoar, -old, -weary.*

For-, *pref.*2, OE. *for-*; freq. in OE. and ME. as a var. of FORE-; cf. ME. *forganger* and FORE-GANGER.

For-, *pref.*3, occurring only in wds. adopted from Fr., as FORFEIT; repr. OF. *for-, fors-*, identical with *fors* adv. (mod. F. *hors*):—L. *foris, foras.*

Forage (fǫ·rėdʒ), *sb.* ME. [a. F. *fourrage*, f. OF. *feurre* fodder :—Com. Rom. **fodro*, of Teut. origin; see FODDER and -AGE.] 1. Food for horses and cattle; in early use, *esp.* dry winter food, as opp. to grass. Also *transf.* and *fig.* 2. The act of foraging or providing forage 1481. †3. In *pl.* Foragers –1603.

2. A detachment for f. LYTTON. *transf.* And he [the lion] from forrage will incline to play *L.L.L.* IV. i. 93. *Comb.* **f.-cap**, the undress Glengarry cap worn by infantry soldiers.

Forage (fǫ·rėdʒ), *v.* ME. [ad. F. *fourrager*; see prec.] 1. *trans.* To collect forage from; to overrun (a country) for the purpose of obtaining or destroying supplies. Also, to plunder, ravage. 2. *intr.* To rove in search of forage or provisions; also, to raid 1530. 3. To make a roving search *for*; to rummage 1768. †4. To raven. *lit.* and *fig.* –1698. 5. *trans.* To supply with forage or food 1552. 6. To obtain by foraging 1656.

1. To F. whole Countries 1700. 2. Oxen and bulls ..taken in foraginge ELYOT. 3. Foraging among the old manuscripts W. IRVING. 4. Whiles his..Father ..Stood smiling to behold his Lyons Whelpe F. in blood of French Nobilitie SHAKS.

Forager (fǫ·rėdʒəɹ). ME. [ad. OF. *forragier*; also a. OF. *forrageour*; see FORAGE *sb.* and *v.*] †1. A harbinger –1616. 2. One who forages 1489. b. A foraging ant (*Eciton*) 1863.

Foralite (fōᵊ·răləit). 1859. [f. L. *forare* to bore + -LITE.] *Geol.* A name for certain tube-like markings which occur in sandstones, etc.

‖**Foramen** (forē·mĕn). *Pl.* **foramina** (foræ·mină). 1671. [L., f. *forare* to bore.] An opening or orifice, a hole or short passage. Applied variously in *Anat., Zool.*, etc.

The *f. of an ovule* is an aperture through the integuments, allowing the passage of the pollen tubes to the nucleus *Treas. Bot.* s.v.

Foraminate (foræ·minėt), *a.* [ad. L. *foraminatus.*] = FORAMINATED.

Foraminate (foræ·mineit), *v.* 1599. [f. L. *foramin-*, FORAMEN + -ATE3.] To bore, pierce, perforate.

Foraminated (foræ·mineitėd), *ppl. a.* 1599. [f. L. *foraminatus* + -ED1.] Bored, pierced, perforated.

Foraminifer (forămi·nifəɹ). 1841. [f. L. *foramin-*, FORAMEN + *-fer* bearing.] A rhizopod of the order *Foraminifera.*

‖**Foraminifera** (foræmini·fĕră), *sb. pl.* 1835. [mod. L. neut. pl. of prec.] *Zool.* An order of *Rhizopoda*, furnished with a shell or test, usually perforated by pores (*foramina*). So **Fora:mini·feral** *a.* pertaining to the *Foraminifera*; consisting of or containing foraminifera. **Fora:mini·ferous** *a.* furnished with foramina; said of the *Foraminifera* and their shells; also (less correctly), consisting of or containing foraminifera. †**Fora·minous** *a.* full of holes, perforated, porous.

Forasmuch (fǫrăzmɒ·tʃ), *adv.* ME. [Orig. *for as much.*] Only in *Forasmuch as*: a. In consideration that, seeing that. Now *formal* or *arch.* †b. Occas.: So far as –1654.

Foray (fǫ·rei), *sb.* ME. [see next vb.] 1. A hostile or predatory incursion, a raid. Also *transf.* and *fig.* †2. Booty taken in a foray –1598. †3. The advance-guard of an army –1587.

1. Red hand in the f., How sound is thy slumber SCOTT.

Foray (fǫ·rei), *v.* ME. [? A back-formation from FORAYER, and source of prec.] 1. *trans.* To scour or ravage in search of forage or booty; to pillage. (Revived by Sir W. Scott.) 2. *intr.* To make a raid; to pillage ME.

1. When Roderick foray'd Devanside SCOTT.

Forayer (fǫ·reiəɹ). [Two forms: (1) ME. *forrier*, a. OF.:—med. L. type **fodrarius*, f. **fodro* fodder (see FORAGE, *sb.*); (2) ME. *forrour, forreour*, a. OF. *forreor*, agent-n. f. *forrer* to forage.] 1. One who forays; a forager, a raider. †2. A foregoer, harbinger, or courier –1549.

1. Sending with forreiars certaine guides HOLLAND.

†**Forba·r, foreba·r**, *v.* ME. [ad. AF. *forbarrer*, f. *for-*, FOR- *pref.*3 + *barrer* to bar.] 1. *trans.* To hinder –1450. 2. To shut out; to bar, deprive, or exclude (a person); *esp.* in *Law* –1671.

Forbear, forebear (foɹbēᵊɹ, fōᵊ·ɹbeᵊɹ), *sb.* Orig. *Sc.* 1470. [f. FOR- *pref.*2 or FORE- *pref.* + BEER *sb.*2, lit. one who exists before.] An ancestor, progenitor (usu. more remote than a grandfather).

Forbear (fǫɹbēᵊ·ɹ), *v.* Pa. t. **-bore** (-bōᵊ·ɹ), pa. pple. **-borne** (-bōᵊ·ɹn). [OE. *forberan*; see FOR *pref.*1 and BEAR *v.*] †1. *trans.* To bear; to tolerate, endure –1585. †2. To bear up against, control. Also *refl.* and *intr.* for *refl.* –ME. †3. To do without, spare –1667; †to part with or from –1590; †to avoid, shun; to leave alone –1673. 4. To abstain or desist from ME. 5. *absol.* and *intr.* To abstain, refrain. Const. *to* with *inf.*, also *from*. ME. 6. *trans.* To withhold, keep back ME.; *refl.* to refrain (*rare*) 1535. 7. To spare, show mercy or indulgence to. Now *rare*. OE. b. *intr.* To show forbearance. Const. *with*. 1591. 8. *trans.* To abstain from enforcing (what is due), *esp.* the payment of (a debt). Now *rare*. 1570.

3. MILT. *P. L.* ix. 747. 4. I forbore pressing them further 1655. 5. The lovers of Hampden cannot f. to extol him at Falkland's expense M. ARNOLD. 6. F. thy bloody hand MARLOWE. *refl.* Forbeare thee from medling with God. 2 *Chron.* xxxv. 21. 7. The quycke fire doth not forbeare the wod be it wette or drye LD. BERNERS. Phr. *To bear and f.* (now *intr.* but orig. *trans.*). 8. Money lent, or forborn HUTTON. Hence **Forbea·rant** *a.* forbearing. **Forbea·rer**, one who or that which forbears. **Forbea·ring-ly** *adv.*, **-ness.**

Forbearance (fǫɹbēᵊ·răns). 1576. [f. prec. + -ANCE.] 1. The action or habit of forbearing. Const. *to, from, to* with *inf.* 1591. 2. Forbearing conduct or spirit; long-suffering; lenity 1599. 3. Abstinence from enforcing what is due, *esp.* the payment of a debt 1576.

1. True Noblenesse would Learne him f. from so foul a wrong SHAKS. 2. The vertue of patience or f. 1599. 3. F. is no quittance *Provb.* He..soon shall find F. no acquittance MILT.

Forbecause: see BECAUSE A. 1 and B. 1.

†**Forbi·d**, *sb.* 1602. [f. next vb.] A forbidding –1740.

Forbid (fǫɹbi·d), *v.* Pa. t. **forbad, -bade** (-bæ·d); pa. pple. **forbidden** (-bi·d'n). [OE. *forbéodan*, f. FOR- *pref.*1 + *béodan* to BID; = Du. *verbieden*, Ger. *verbieten.*] 1. *trans.* To command not to; to prohibit. Also *absol.* 2. a. *fig.* To exclude, keep back, hinder, restrain. Now chiefly: To render impossible or undesirable. OE. †b. To defy, challenge. BP. ANDREWES. †c. To lay under a ban –1819.

1. Forbeed us thing, and that desire we CHAUCER. F. the Sea for to obey the Moone SHAKS. The governor of the Castle forbad the Church Service to be performed 1865. 2. For bede þi tonge fra ill HAMPOLE. Th' Applause of list'ning Senates to command..Their Lot forbad GRAY. *God, Heaven, the Lord f.*, a deprecatory phr.; also *absol.* as an exclam. c. He shall liue a man forbid *Macb.* I. iii. 21.

Hence †**Forbi·d** *ppl. a.* forbidden. **Forbi·ddance**, the action of forbidding; prohibition, interdiction. **Forbi·dder.**

Forbidden (fǫɹbi·d'n), *ppl. a.* ME. [pa. pple. of prec.] In senses of the vb.

Phr. *F. degrees*, certain degrees of relationship within which people are forbidden to marry. *F. fruit*, (*a*) that forbidden to Adam (*Gen.* ii. 17), also *fig.*; (*b*) hence, a name for varieties of *Citrus*, esp. *C. decumana.*

Hence **Forbi·dden-ly** *adv.*, **-ness.**

Forbidding (fǫɹbi·diŋ), *ppl. a.* 1573. [see -ING2.] 1. That forbids (see the vb.). 2. *esp.* Repellent, repulsive, uninviting 1712.

2. An elderly man of remarkably hard features and f. aspect DICKENS. The morning looked f. enough T. HARDY. Hence **Forbi·dding-ly** *adv.*, **-ness.**

Forblack: see FOR- *pref.*1 II.

†**Forbo·de**, *sb.* *Obs.* exc. *arch.* [OE. *forbod*; see FORBID.] A forbidding; a prohibition. Hence †**Forbo·de** *v.* to forbid.

†**Forbrui·se**, *v.* ME. [f. FOR- *pref.*1 + BRUISE.] To bruise severely; to break to pieces –1450.

Forby(e (fǫɹbəi·). ME. [f. FOR- *adv.* or *prep.* + BY. Cf. Ger. *vorbei.*]

A. *prep.* 1. Of position: Hard by. *Obs.* exc. *Sc.* 1596. 2. Of motion: Close by; past. *Obs.* exc. *arch.* ME. 3. Besides; not to mention. Only *north.* or *arch.* 1536.

2. They passed foreby the frenchmens busshment LD. BERNERS.

B. *adv.* 1. Of motion: Aside ME.; along, past (now *rare*) ME. 2. Besides, in addition 1590.

1. He salutyd them in passynge forby LD. BERNERS.

†**Forca·rve**, *v.* [OE. *forceorfan*, f. FOR- *pref.* + *ceorfan* to CARVE.] *trans.* To carve or cut asunder, down, out, through; to cut in two, to pieces –1460.

Force (fōᵊɹs), *sb.*1 ME. [a. F.:—pop. L. **fortia*, n. of quality f. L. *fortis* strong.]

I. †1. Physical strength. Rarely in *pl.* (= F. *forces*). –1816. 2. Strength, impetus, violence, or intensity of effect ME. 3. Power or might; *esp.* military power ME. b. In early use, the strength (of a defensive work, etc.). Subseq., the fighting strength (of a ship). 1577. 4. A body of armed men, an army. In *pl.* the troops or soldiers composing the fighting strength of a kingdom or of a commander ME. b. A body of police; often absol. *the force* = policemen collectively 1851. 5. Physical strength or power exerted upon an object; *esp.* violence or physical coercion ME. b. *spec.* in *Law*: Unlawful violence offered to persons or things 1480. 6. Mental or moral strength. Now only, power of effective action, or of overcoming resistance. ME. 7. Of things: Power to influence, affect, or control 1582; virtue, efficacy 1590. 8. Of a law, etc.: Binding power, validity 1594. 9. The real import or significance (of a document, word, sentence, symbol, etc.) 1555. 10. †a. (Without article prefixed): A large quantity or number; const. *of* –1570. b. *A force*: a large number or quantity. *The f.*: the majority. *Obs.* exc. *dial.* 1722. 11. *Physics*, etc. (Cf. mod. scientific uses of L. *vis.*) a. (= Newton's *vis impressa*: cf. sense 5). An influence operating on a body so as to produce an alteration or tendency to alteration in its state of rest or of uniform motion in a straight line; the intensity of such an influence as a measurable quantity. (Now merely the name for a measure of change of motion.) 1665. b. Formerly used for kinetic (often including potential) energy: see ENERGY. 1841. c. The cause of motion, heat, electricity, etc., conceived as consisting in principle or power inherent in, or coexisting with, matter; such principles or powers viewed generically. (This sense is no longer recognized. *Force* is now generic.) 1842. d. *transf.* and *fig.* An agency, influence, or source of power likened to a physical force 1785.

1. His eye was not dimme, nor his naturall f. abated *Deut.* xxxiv. 7. Phr. *With all one's f.* 2. They break the f. of the fall GOLDSM. 3. Inferior in fighting f. 1888. b. Ships of good f. DAMPIER. 4. The valour and atchievements of our forces by sea and land SWIFT. 5. F. can accomplish many things which would be beyond the reach of cunning BENTHAM. Phr. *By force* = by employing violence, also †under compulsion. b. *By f. and arms*: tr. Law L. *vi et armis*. It seems I broke a close with f. and arms TENNYSON. *A f.*: an act of unlawful violence. 6. A Task which is infinitely above his F. DENNIS. 7. It [learning] teacheth men the f. of circumstances BACON. Beauty loses its f., if not accompanied with modesty STEELE. In these two reasons there is f. GROTE. 8. Hath not his edict the f. of a law HOOKER. Phr. †*Of force*: of binding power; For a Testament is of f. after men are dead *Heb.* ix. 17. *In f.*: operative at the time. So *to put in f.*; *to come into f.* 9. The f. of a Sacrament BONNER, of the Particle *For* STEELE, of a fine BLACKSTONE. 10. a. With f. hawberks, swerdes and knyvys ME. 11. a. The f. of gravity 1871. b. Phr. *Conservation of f.*: see CONSERVATION. d. To be a f. in the Legal Profession 1891.

II. Senses derived from FORCE *v.*1 †1. The

plunger of a force-pump -1747. 2. The upper die in a metal-stamping machine 1879. 3. *Cards.* An act of forcing 1862. 4. *Billiards.* A screw-back. *U.S.* 1881.

Phrases. a. *By force of*: by dint of, by virtue of. Also (later), *by the f. of.* b. *Inf.*: (*a*) *Mil.* Of a host, enemy, etc.: (Collected) in numbers and strength; (*b*) of persons: In full command of one's powers, energies, or abilities. †c. *Of f.*: with *inf.*, powerful enough *to* do something. †d. *Of* (or *on*) *f.*: of necessity, perforce. †e. *It is f.*: it is of consequence; usu. neg. †f. *To hunt,* (etc.) *at f.* (also *of* or *by f.*): to run (the game) down with dogs.

Comb.: f.-bill, a bill of a coercive nature, esp. one authorizing the use of troops to secure its enforcement; -pipe, the pipe of a FORCE-PUMP in which the piston works.

Force (fōəɹs), *sb.*[2] *north.* Also **foss.** 1600. [a. ON. *fors* (Sw. *fors,* Da. *fos*).] A waterfall or cascade.

Force (fōəɹs), *v.*[1] ME. [a. F. *forcer*; see FORCE *sb.*[1]]

I. 1. *trans.* To use violence to; to violate (a woman). 2. To constrain by force (whether physical or moral); to compel ME.; to put a strained sense upon (words) 1662. b. *Whist.* To compel (a player) to trump a trick, by leading a suit of which he has none 1746. 3. To compel or constrain (a person, oneself, etc.) *to do* a thing (†occas. with *to* omitted) ME. 4. To urge, compel to violent effort; †to exert (one's strength) to the utmost. Also †*refl.* and *intr.* ME. 5. To overpower by force; to enter, take, or pass through, by force; to storm (a stronghold); to board (a ship) 1581. b. To break open (a gate, etc.); to break (a lock). Also *to f. open.* 1623. †c. To overpower (troops, a guard) -1781. 6. To drive by force, impel. Chiefly const. with prep., or with advbs. 1582. 7. *intr.* To make one's way by force. Now *rare.* 1653. †8. To lay stress upon, press home, urge. Also, To enforce (a law, etc.) -1607. 9. To bring about by force or effort; to effect. *lit.* and *fig.* 1551. 10. To obtain or take by force; to win by violence; to extort, elicit 1602. 11. To hasten by artificial means the maturity of. Also *intr.* for *refl.* 1719.

1. To f. a maide 1620. 2. Art thou King, and wilt be forc't SHAKS. Phr. *To f. one's hand*: to compel one to act prematurely or the like. 3. To f. a person to resign JUNIUS. 4. High on a Mounting Wave, my head I bore, Forcing my Strength, and gath'ring to the Shore DRYDEN. Phr. *To f. the pace* or *the running* (in a race). *To f. the bidding* (at a sale by auction). *To f. one's voice.* *To f. the game* in *Cricket*: to take risks in order to score rapidly. 5. At length the Citie..was forced by assault GOLDING. 6. We were forc'd by contrary Winds into St. Remo ADDISON. 7. We gradually f. ahead, breasting aside the floes KANE. 9. I don't f. my appetite CONGREVE. Phr. *To f. a passage, one's way.* 10. It stuck so fast .. That scarce the Victor forc'd the Steel away DRYDEN.

II. †1. To strengthen, reinforce; also, to garrison, to man -1810. †2. Chiefly in neg. sentences: To attach force to; to care for, regard -1614; with *inf.* as *obj.*: To care *to* -1591. †b. *intr.* To care. Const. *for, of,* occas. *on.* -1605. †3. *impers.* To be of force; to matter, signify -1603.

1. *Macb.* v. v. 5. 2. I f. not argument a straw SHAKS. *Lucr.* 1021. Your oath once broke, you f. not to forsweare *L. L. L.* v. ii. 440.

†**Force,** *v.*[2] ME. [altered f. FARCE, *v.*[1], by confusion with prec.] = FARCE *v.* 1, 2. Also *fig.* -1793.

fig. Wit..larded with malice and malice forced with wit *Tr. & Cr.* v. i. 64.

Forced (fōəɹst), *ppl. a.* 1576. [f. FORCE *v.*[1] + -ED[1].] 1. Subjected to violence 1621. 2. Enforced, compulsory; not spontaneous or optional 1576. 3. Produced or maintained with effort 1596. b. In literary use: Strained, distorted 1583. c. Artificial, constrained, unnatural 1621. †4. Artificially made; opp. to *natural.* Chiefly of soils. -1688. 5. Of plants, etc.: Made to bear, or produced, out of the proper season 1695. †6. Fortified -1602.

2. A f. peace 1734. Phr. *F. move* (in a game). 3. Phr. *F. march.* b. Forc'd interpretations A. COLLINS. c. Her forc'd civilities DRYDEN. Hence **Fo·rced·ly** *adv.*, -ness.

Forceful (fōə·ɹsˌful), *a.* 1571. [f. FORCE *sb.*[1] + -FUL.] 1. Full of force; powerful; cogent. 2. Acting with force or violence 1592. 3. quasi-*adv.* Forcefully 1718.

1. A f. minister BRYCE, argument 1870. 2. Against the Steed he threw His f. Spear DRYDEN. Hence **Fo·rceful·ly,** *adv.*, -ness.

Forceless (fōə·ɹslės), *a.* 1532. [f. as prec. + -LESS.] Without force; feeble.

Feeble heart and f. hand SCOTT.

Force-meat (fōə·ɹsˌmīt). 1688. [f. FORCE *v.*[2] + MEAT.] Meat chopped fine, spiced, and highly seasoned, chiefly used as stuffing or as a garnish. Also *attrib.*

Forcement (fōə·ɹsmĕnt). ME. [a. F.; see FORCE *v.*[1] and -MENT.] †1. Strengthening; a fortification -1533. †2. Compulsion -1634. 3. *Gunnery.* Excess of diameter of the projectile over that of the bore 1892.

Forceps (fǭ·ɹseps). *sing.* and *pl.* 1634. [a. L.] 1. An instrument of the pincers kind, used for seizing and holding objects, *esp.* in surgical and obstetric operations. 2. *Anat., Entom.,* and *Zool.* Some organ or part of the body that has the shape of, or may be used as, a forceps. †Also, one of the two branches of this. 1661. Also *attrib.*

Fo·rce-pump. 1659. [f. FORCE *sb.* or *v.* + PUMP.] 1. A pump employed to force water, etc. beyond the range of atmospheric pressure. 2. The plunger-pump for supplying the boiler of a locomotive engine 1858.

Forcer (fōə·ɹsəɹ). 1556. [f. FORCE *v.*[1] + -ER[1].] 1. One who or that which forces. 2. An instrument or means of forcing; e.g. the plunger or piston of a force-pump 1634; a force-pump 1731; †a contrivance for propelling water -1736.

Forcible (fōə·ɹsib'l), *a.* ME. [a. OF., f. *force* FORCE *sb.* Also †*forceable,* as if f. FORCE + -ABLE.] 1. Done by force; involving the use of force; *esp.* in Law, *Forcible detainer, entry.* 2. Possessing force; †strong, powerful -1802; telling; convincing 1570. †3. Unavoidable -1574. †4. 'Valid, binding, obligatory' (J.) 1584. 5. quasi-*adv.* Forcibly 1582.

1. A f. entry or detainer; which is committed by violently taking or keeping possession, with menaces, force, and arms, of lands and tenements, without the authority of the law BLACKSTONE. 2. He prepared a f. armie to attend him RALEIGH. A f. argument 1594. F. reasons BURKE. Hence **Fo·rcibleness. Fo·rcibly** *adv.*

Fo·rcible fee·ble. 1844. [after SHAKS. 2 *Hen. IV*, III. ii. 179.] A feeble person who makes great pretence of vigour. Also *attrib.* or as *adj.*

Italics, that last resource of the Forcible Feebles DISRAELI.

Forcing (fōə·ɹsiŋ), *vbl. sb.* ME. [see -ING[1].] 1. The action of FORCE *v.*[1] †2. *concr.* A material used in forcing wine -1743.

2. The Victualler puts..with it the usual Forcing or Fining 1743.

Comb.: f.-engine, a fire-engine; -hazard (*Billiards*), a stroke requiring more than usual force. Also in reference to the forcing of flowers, etc., as *f.-bed, -frame, -glass, -house, -pit,* etc.; and quasi-*adj.* with sense 'suitable for forcing', as in *f. rose, variety.*

Fo·rcing-pump. 1727. = FORCE-PUMP.

†**Fo·rcipal,** *a.* [f. L. *forcip-* FORCEPS + -AL.] Of the nature of a forceps. SIR T. BROWNE.

Forcipate (fǭ·ɹsipeᶦt), *a.* 1668. [f. as prec. + -ATE.[2]] *Bot.* and *Zool.* Formed like a forceps. So **Fo·rcipated** *a.*

Forcipa·tion. [f. as prec. + -ATION.] †1. Torture by nipping with forceps. BACON. 2. *Zool.* The state of being forcipated (*Cent. Dict.*).

Forcite (fōə·ɹsəit). Also **forsite.** 1883. [f. FORCE *sb.*[1] + -ITE.] A variety of dynamite.

Forclose: see FORECLOSE.

†**Forcu·t,** *v.* ME. [f. FOR- *pref.*[1] + CUT *v.*] To cut into, cut in pieces. CHAUCER.

Ford (fōəɹd), *sb.* [OE. *ford* = OS. *-ford* (in place-names), f. (ult.) Aryan root **per-*, Teut. **fer-, far-, fur-* to go, pass; see FARE *v.*] 1. A shallow place in a river or other water, where a man or beast may cross by wading. †2. a. A tract of shallow water. b. *poet.* A stream, current. -1780.

1. Drown'd in passing thro' the f. TENNYSON. 2. b. With water of the f. Or of the clouds, to moisten their roots dry SPENSER. Hence **Fo·rdless** *a.* without a f.; that cannot be forded.

Ford (fōəɹd), *v.* 1614. [f. prec. sb.] 1. *trans.* To cross (water) by means of a ford; to wade through. Also *fig.* and *causatively.* 2. *intr.* To cross (*over*) by means of a ford 1675.

1. *fig.* His last Section which is no deepe one, remains only to be foarded MILT. Hence **Fo·rdable** *a.* that may be forded. **Fo·rdableness.**

Fordo, foredo (fǭɹ-, foəɹdū·), *v.* Pa. t. -did (-di·d). Pa. pple. -done (-dʋ·n). [OE. *fordón,* f. FOR- *pref.*[1] + *dón* to DO. 1. *trans.* To put an end to. *Obs.* exc. *arch.* OE. 2. To destroy, ruin, lay waste. *arch.* OE. †3. To undo (a person) -1647. 4. To do away with ME. 5. Pa. pple. only: Exhausted, worn out. *arch.* 1547.

1. She for dispayr fordede hyre self CHAUCER. Its rites foredone, its guardians dead WHITTIER. 4. To wipe away and foredoe the shamefull blot HOLLAND. 5. With Indian heats at last fordone M. ARNOLD. Hence **Fordo·ne** *ppl. a.* exhausted, overcome, tired out.

†**Fordri·ve,** *v.* [OE. *fordrīfan,* f. FOR- *pref.*[1] + *drīfan* to DRIVE.] *trans.* To drive forth, drive about -1513.

†**Fordru·nken,** *ppl. a.* [OE. *fordruncen,* f. FOR- *pref.*[1] + DRUNKEN.] Drunk, overcome with drink -1513.

†**Fordry·,** *v.* [OE. *fordrūgian* (intr.), f. FOR- *pref.*[1] + *drūgian* to DRY.] *intr.* To dry up -1494.

†**Fordwi·ne,** *v.* OE. [f. FOR- *pref.*[1] + DWINE.] *intr.* To fade away, wither; to vanish -ME.

†**Fore,** *sb.* [OE. *fōr*:—OTeut. **fōrā-*, f. **fōr-*, ablaut-var. of **far-* to go; see FARE *v.*] 1. A journey, expedition. Also, an expeditionary force. -ME. 2. A track, trace -ME.

2. Who folweth Cristes gospel and his f. CHAUCER.

Fore (fōəɹ), *a.* 1490. [f. sbs. like *forepart,* etc., written as two words.]

I. As adj. *in concord.* 1. Situated or appearing in front, or in front of something else; usually opp. to *back, hind-* 1500. †2. Anterior, previous, former -1718.

1. The alimentary canal may therefore be distinguished into a f. and a hind gut HUXLEY.

II. quasi-*sb.* or *ellipt.* The fore part of anything, e.g. the bow of a ship 1888. b. *Naut.* (see quot.) 1860.

b. *At the f.,* means at the fore-royal mast-head W. C. RUSSELL.

Phr. **To the f.** a. Of a person: On the spot, within call. b. Alive. c. Of money, etc.: Forthcoming; available. d. In view, conspicuous. So *to come to the f.,* to come to the front, or into view.

Fore (fōəɹ), *adv.* and *prep.* [Com. Teut.: OE. *fore,* f. the same root as in L. *pro, præ, per,* Gr. πρό, παρά, παραί, περί, etc. Since 16th c. often written *'fore,* as if short for *before.*]

†A. *adv.* 1. Before, previously -1600. 2. In advance -1500.

1. The eyes (f. dutious) now .. looke an other way SHAKS.

B. *prep.* = FOR *prep.* in various uses OE.

F. these witnesses *Wint. T.* IV. iv. 401. F. God I thinke so SHAKS. Prizest him 'fore me SHAKS.

Fore (fōəɹ), *int.* 1878. [prob. short for BEFORE.] *Golf.* A warning cry to people in front of the stroke.

Fore-, *prefix.* In OE. used as a prefix (1) to verbs, adding the sense of 'before' (either in time, position, order, or rank), and (2) to sbs., either forming designations of objects or parts occupying a front position, or expressing anteriority of time. For occasional, or self-explanatory combinations see N.E.D.

Combs.

a. With reference to place: f.-action, the movement of a horse's front legs; †-beak, the prow of a vessel; †-buttock (joc.), the breast (of a woman) SWIFT; -flank, (*a*) the front part of the flank; (*b*) a projection of fat, upon the ribs, immediately behind the shoulder; -hearth, a projecting bay in the front of a blast-furnace hearth; -hooks (*Naut.*) = *breast-hooks*; -page, the first page (in a printed work); -piece (*Saddlery*), the flap attached to the fore-part of a side-saddle, to guard the rider's dress; -step, (*a*) a step forward; (*b*) *pl.* steps in front, tracks; -thwart, the seat of the bowman in a boat; -winning (*Mining*), advanced workings.

b. With reference to time: †f.-eatage, the opportunity of pasturing one's cattle before others; †-title, prescriptive title.

Forea·ct, *v.* 1618. [f. FORE- + ACT *v.*] *trans.* and *intr.* To act beforehand (see ACT *v.*).

Fore-adapt, -advise, etc.: see FORE- and the simple vbs.

†**Fo·re-alle·ged,** *ppl. a.* 1587. [see FORE-.] Previously alleged or quoted -1701.

Fore and aft. 1618. *Naut.*

A. *adv.* 1. Of position: In or at both bow

and stern; hence, along the length of or all over the ship 1627. **2.** Of motion or direction: Alternately towards the bow and stern, backwards and forwards 1726. **3.** From stem to stern 1618.

3. He..raked her fore and aft with his cannon 1709.

B. *adj.* (usu. with hyphens). Placed or directed in the line of the vessel's length. Of sails: Applied to all sails which are not set to yards. 1820.

Fo·re-appoi·nt, *v. arch.* 1561. [see FORE-.] To appoint beforehand. Hence **Fore-appoi·ntment**, previous appointment, preordination.

Forearm (fōᵊ·rˌāɹm), *sb.* 1741. [f. FORE- + ARM *sb.*] The part of the arm between the elbow and the wrist. Also *transf.*

Forearm [foᵊrā·ɹm), *v.* 1592. [f. as prec. + ARM *v.*] *trans.* To arm beforehand. *lit.* and *fig.*

Forewarned, forearmed GREENE.

Fore-axle, -beam: see FORE- and AXLE, BEAM.

Forebode (foᵊɹbōᵘ·d), *v.* 1603. [f. FORE- + BODE *v.*] **1.** *trans.* To announce beforehand 1664; of things, to betoken, portend 1656. **2.** To have a presentiment of (*usually* evil); to anticipate, to apprehend beforehand 1603. **b.** *intr.* or *absol.* To forecast 1711.

1. Old men foreboded evil days to come 1879. Long flights f. a fall COWPER. 2. I foreboded mischief the moment I heard [etc.] 1793. b. If I f. aright W. IRVING. Hence †**Forebode** *sb.*, **Forebo·dement,** a foreboding. **Forebo·der,** one who or that which forebodes. **Forebo·dingly** *adv.*

Foreboding (foᵊɹbōᵘ·diŋ), *vbl. sb.* ME. [f. prec. + -ING¹.] **1.** The action of FOREBODE *v.*; hence, a prediction, a presage. Now only of evil. **b.** A portent, omen ME. **2.** A presentiment of coming evil 1603.

Fore-body (fōᵊ·ɹbǫdi). 1830. [f. FORE-.] *Naut.* That part of a ship before the dead flat.

Fo·re-cabin. 1816. [f. FORE- + CABIN.] A cabin in the fore-part of the vessel; *spec.* one for second-class passengers with inferior accommodation.

Forecast (fōᵊ·ɹkɑst), *sb.* 1535. [f. next vb.] **1.** The action, habit, or faculty of forecasting; foresight of consequences and provision against them. Now *rare.* 1541. **b.** A forecasting or anticipation, *esp.* with regard to the weather 1673. †**2.** A plan, scheme, or device made beforehand –1754.

1. Evils which no f. could avert PRESCOTT. b. The 'wet or dry' part of our forecasts *Times.* 2. That f. or decree by the power of which the world was 1674.

Forecast (foᵊrkɑ·st), *v.* Pa. t. and pple. **-cast, -casted.** ME. [f. FORE- + CAST *v.*] **1.** *trans.* To contrive or plan beforehand; to foreordain, predestine. **b.** To consider of beforehand 1534. **2.** To estimate, or conjecture beforehand 1494. **3.** (? from the *sb.*) To take a forecast of; to foreshadow 1883.

1. At the first sight the thing which was forecast by good order, seemeth to happen by adventure GOLDING. 2. Quene Margaret..ever forcastyng and doubtyng, the chaunce that might happen HALL. *absol.* If it happen as I did f. MILT. Hence **Foreca·ster,** one who forecasts.

Fo·recastle. Also **fo'c'sle,** after sailors' pronunc. (fōᵘ·ks'l). ME. [f. FORE- + CASTLE.] **1.** *Naut.* A short raised deck forward; in early use raised like a castle to command the enemy's decks. Now *arch.* or *Hist.* **2.** The fore-part of a ship 1490. **3.** In merchant vessels, the forward part, under the deck, where the sailors live 1840. **4.** *attrib.*, as *f.-deck*, etc. 1726.

†**Forechoo·se,** *v.* ME. [see FORE-.] *trans.* To choose beforehand, pre-elect –1580. Hence **Forecho·sen** *ppl. a.*

Fo·re-ci·ted, *ppl. a.* 1576. [f. FORE- + CITED.] Previously cited.

Foreclose (foᵊɹklōᵘ·z), *v.* [ME. *forclose*, f. *forclos-*, stem of OF. *forclore*, f. *for-*, FOR- *pref.*³ + *clore* to CLOSE.] **1.** *trans.* To bar, shut out completely. †**2.** To close fast, stop up (an opening, way, etc.) –1751. **3.** To hinder the action, working, or activity of 1536. **4.** *Law of Mortgage.* To bar or exclude (the person entitled to redeem) upon non-payment of money due; to deprive of the equity of redemption. Const. *from.* 1728. **b.** To bar (a right of redemption); to take away the power of redeeming 1704. **5.** To close or settle by anticipation 1722. **6.** To establish an exclusive claim to 1599.

1. The Puritans being thus foreclosed and shut out of the Church NEAL. 3. The Imbargo with Spaine..foreclosed this trade CAREW. 4. To f. the mortgage W. IRVING. 6. Finding..even virtue and truth foreclosed and monopolized EMERSON.

Foreclosure (foᵊɹklōᵘ·ʒ'ɹ). 1728. [f. prec. + -URE.] The action of foreclosing (a mortgage); a proceeding to bar the right of redeeming mortgaged property.

†**Fo·reconcei·ve,** *v.* 1553. [f. FORE-.] *trans.* To conceive beforehand, to preconceive –1662.

Fore-court (fōᵊ·ɹkoᵊɹt). 1535. [f. FORE- + COURT *sb.*] The court or enclosed space in front of a building, the outer court.

Fore-dated, -day: see FORE- and the simple words.

†**Fo·re-deck.** 1565. [f. FORE- + DECK *sb.*] The deck at the fore-part of a ship; the forepart of the deck –1747.

†**Fo·redee·m,** *v.* 1542. [f. FORE- + DEEM.] **1.** *trans.* To judge beforehand; to forecast. Also *intr.* with *of.* –1660. **2.** To deem in advance 1612.

1. To foredeme the wurste UDALL.

Forede·stine, *v.* ME. [f. FORE- + DESTINE *v.*] To destine beforehand, predestine. So **Forede·stiny,** †prediction; destiny.

Foredoom (fōᵊ·ɹˌdūm), *sb.* 1563. [f. FORE- + DOOM *sb.*] A judgement pronounced beforehand; destiny.

Foredoom (foᵊɹˌdū·m), *v.* 1592. [f. FORE- + DOOM *v.*] **1.** *trans.* To doom beforehand (*to* or *to do*); to foreordain (a thing) 1608. **2.** To forecast, foreshadow 1592.

1. Efforts..foredoomed to failure 1878. Foredooming that which is to be N. FAIRFAX.

Fore-edge (fōᵊ·rˌedʒ). 1665. [f. as prec. + EDGE.] The front or outer edge; *esp.* of a book, or of a leaf in a book.

Fore-elders (fōᵊ·rˌeldəɹz), *pl.* Chiefly *north.* ME. [f. FORE- + ELDER(S.] Ancestors, progenitors.

Fore-end (fōᵊrˌend). ME. [f. as prec. + END.] **1.** Of place: The fore-part, front. Now chiefly *Naut.* **b.** The fore-part of the stock of a gun 1881. **2.** Of time: The beginning. Now *dial.*; chiefly = *spring* 1611.

In all The fore-end of my time *Cymb.* III. iii. 73.

Forefather (fōᵊ·ɹfāðəɹ). ME. [f. as prec. + FATHER.] An ancestor, a progenitor. Chiefly *pl.*

The rude Forefathers of the Hamlet GRAY. Phr. *Forefathers' day* (U.S.): the anniversary of the day on which the first settlers landed at Plymouth, Mass.

Forefeel (foᵊɹfī·l), *v.* 1580. [f. FORE- + FEEL *v.*] To feel beforehand, have a presentiment of.

With unwieldy waves the great sea forefeels winds That both ways murmur CHAPMAN. Hence **Fo·refeel** *sb.* **Fo·refeeling** *vbl. sb.* a presentiment.

†**Fo·refence,** *sb.* 1609. [f. as prec. + FENCE *sb.*] A first or front defence; a bulwark –1677.

Forefend: see FORFEND.

Forefield (fōᵊ·ɹfīld). 1681. [f. FORE- + FIELD *sb.*] *Mining.* The face of the workings.

Forefinger (fōᵊ·ɹfiŋgəɹ). 1450. [f. FORE- + FINGER.] The finger next the thumb; the *first* or *index finger.*

[**Foreflow** *v.*, 'to flow before', *Dryden*, in Dicts. is a mistake for *foreslow.*]

Fore-foot (fōᵊ·ɹfut), *sb.* 1481. [f. FORE- + FOOT.] **1.** One of the front feet of a quadruped. †**b.** *joc.* The hand. *Hen. V*, II. i. 71. **2.** *Naut.* 'A timber which terminates the keel at the forward extremity, and forms a rest for the stem's lower end' (Adm. Smyth) 1770.

Forefront (fōᵊ·ɹfrʋnt). 1470. [f. FORE- + FRONT.] **1.** The principal face or foremost part. Now *rare.* Now usually *fig.* **2.** The front of the body as opp. to the 'back' 1880.

1. Set ye Uriah in the f. of the hottest battle *2 Sam.* xi. 15. Hence **Fo·refront** *v.* to build a (*new*) f. to STERNE.

Fo·re-game. 1594. [f. FORE-.] A preliminary game.

Foreganger (foᵊ·ɹgæŋəɹ). ME. [f. FORE- + GANGER.] †**1.** A fore-runner; also, a predecessor –1460. **2.** *Naut.* 'A short piece of rope immediately connecting the line with the shank of the harpoon, when spanned for killing' (Adm. Smyth) 1794.

Foregate (fōᵊ·ɹgēⁱt). 1503. [f. FORE- + GATE.] The front gate or principal entrance.

Foregather: see FORGATHER.

Foregift (fōᵊ·ɹgift). 1744. [f. FORE- + GIFT.] *Law.* 'A premium for a lease' (Wharton).

Forego (foᵊɹgōᵘ·), *v.* Pa. t. **forewent;** pa. pple. foregone. [OE. *fore-gán*, f. FORE- + *gán* to GO.] *trans.* To go before, precede, in place or time. Also *intr.* Also quasi-*trans.* with cognate obj. OE. See also FORGO.

The cause doth alwayes his effect fore-goe 1619. *intr.* And now they bene to heauen forewent SPENSER. Hence **Forego·ing** *ppl. a.* preceding (in place or time); also *absol.* (quasi-*sb.*).

Foregoer (foᵊɹgōᵘ·əɹ). ME. [f. FORE- + GOER.] †**1.** A forerunner, a harbinger; *spec.* a purveyor –1745. **2.** One who or that which goes in front; a leader; hence, an example, pattern ME. **3.** A predecessor 1553. **4.** *Naut.* = FOREGANGER 2. 1694.

3. He..in knowledge clerely exceded all his foregoers 1553.

Foregone (foᵊɹgǭ·n), *ppl. a.* 1600. [pa. pple. of FOREGO *v.*] That has gone before or gone by; (of time) past.

Foregone conclusion: a Shakesperian phrase (see CONCLUSION). Now used for: A decision or opinion formed before the case is argued or the full evidence known; also, a result that might have been foreseen as inevitable.

Foreground (fōᵊ·ɹgraund). 1695. [f. FORE- + GROUND.] **1.** That part of a view which is in front and nearest the spectator; *esp.* as represented in a picture. **2.** *fig.* The most conspicuous position 1816. **3.** *attrib.* 1827.

1. White can subsist on the f. of the picture DRYDEN. 3. F. studies in colour RUSKIN.

Foreguess (fōᵊɹge·s), *v.* ME. [f. as prec. + GUESS.] *trans.* To forecast, conjecture.

Fo·re-ha·mmer. *Sc.* and *n. dial.* 1543. [f. as prec. + HAMMER.] The large hammer which strikes first; a sledge-hammer.

Forehand (fōᵊ·rˌhænd). 1545. [f. FORE- + HAND.]

A. *adj.* †**1.** *Archery. F.* (*shaft*): an arrow for shooting straight before one. Opp. to *underhand.* –1597. **2.** Done or given at some earlier time. Of payments, etc.: Made in advance. ? *Obs.* exc. *dial.* 1599. **3.** Foremost 1644. **4.** *Lawn Tennis.* Of a stroke or court: Not back-handed (cf. BACK-HAND *sb.* 1) 1889.

2. F. notice of a trial 1678. To pay a f. rent 1790. 3. Our auld f. ox SCOTT.

B. *sb.* **1.** The position in front or above 1557. **b.** That which holds the front position; the vanguard, hence the mainstay. *Tr. & Cr.* I. iii. 143. **2.** That part of a horse which is in front of the saddle 1617.

1. But for Ceremonie, such a Wretch..Had the f. and vantage of a King *Hen. V*, IV. i. 297.

Fo·re-ha·nded. 1591. [f. as prec. + -ED².] †**1.** Having a forehand; 'formed in the foreparts' (J.). Said of horses, and *transf.* –1680. **2.** Looking to the forehand; prudent, thrifty; hence, well-to-do. Now only *U.S.* 1650. **3.** *Lawn Tennis.* Played forehand 1889.

2. An early and f. care JER. TAYLOR. The wives of f. farmers..were apt to be somewhat exalted 1883.

Forehead (fǫ·rėd). [OE. *forhéafod*, f. FOR², FORE- + *héafod* HEAD.] **1.** That part of the face between the eyebrows and the natural line of the hair. Also *transf.* and *fig.* 1602. †**2.** (Cf. L. *frons.*) **a.** Capacity of blushing; modesty. **b.** Command of countenance; assurance. –1775. **3.** The front part, forefront; *spec.* in *Mining*, = FOREFIELD. 1525. †**4.** A leader –1641.

1. *fig.* The forhead of the morning *Cor.* II. i. 57. 2. b. With what f. Darest thou call me so DRYDEN. 4. Pretending to be a f. of Divinity SIR E. DERING. Hence **Fo·reheadless** *a.* †without sense of shame; destitute of confidence.

Forehea·r, *v.* 1599. [f. FORE- + HEAR *v.*] To hear beforehand. *trans.* and *intr.*

Fore-hearth, etc.: see FORE- *pref.*

†**Forehe·nt,** *v.* [f. FORE- + HENT.] *trans.* To seize beforehand, cut off (in flight). SPENSER.

†**Forehew,** *v.* erron. f. obs. *forhew*, to hew in pieces. (Dicts.)

Forehold (fōᵊ·rˌhōᵘld). 1641. [f. FORE- + HOLD *sb.*] †**1.** Advance. **2.** *Naut.* 'The part of the hold before the fore hatchway' (Adm. Smyth) 1790.

[**Foreholdings,** quoted by Johnson from L'Estrange, is a mistake for *Forebodings*.]

Fo·rehook. 1867. [f. FORE- + HOOK.] *Naut.* = *breast-hook*.

Fo·re-horse. 1483. [f. FORE- + HORSE.] The foremost horse in a team, leader. Also *transf.* and *fig.*

Foreign (fǫ·rėn). [ME. *forein(e, foreyn(e*, a. OF. *forain* :—pop. L. type **foranus*, f. *foras, foris*; see FOR- *pref.*[3]]

A. *adj.* †1. Out of doors; outside –1619. †b. ? Excluded (from court, etc.) 1613. 2. Not one's own; = L. *alienus*. Now *rare*. ME. 3. Proceeding from other persons or things ME. 4. Alien in character; irrelevant, dissimilar, inappropriate. Now only with *from, to*. ME. 5. Introduced from outside; *esp.* in surgical use, of substances embedded in tissues of the body 1621. 6. Situated outside an estate, district, province, etc. 1495; belonging to or coming from another district, society, etc. 1460. 7. Not in one's own land ME. 8. Not domestic nor native ME. 9. Carried on or taking place abroad, into or with other countries 1548. 10. Dealing with matters concerning other countries. Also, intended for use in transactions, etc. with other countries, as in *foreign bill*, etc. 1655. ¶11. Used as tr. L. *forensis*: Made in open court. CHAUCER.

1. [The steward] is to see into all offices, soe well foraine, as at home 1605. b. *Hen. VIII*, II. ii. 129. 3. Foreyne helpe CHAUCER. A f. impulse 1712, cause 1834. 4. F. to people's thoughts SWIFT, to the argument BERKELEY. A purpose f. from his pursuits HELPS. 7. Forain universities 1700. They [in U.S.] usually talk of corporations belonging to other States as 'foreign' BRYCE. 9. F. Missions 1796. F. trade 1840. 10. The f. policy of England EMERSON. *Foreign Office*: the department of the 'Secretary of State for F. Affairs'; also, the buildings.

Phrases *F. attachment*: see ATTACHMENT. †*F. intent*: a constructive sense not implied in the wording of the instrument; opp. to *common intent*.

Comb. Chiefly locative and parasynthetic, as *f.-built, -going, -looking, -made, -manned, -owned*, adjs.

B. *sb.* †1. = FOREIGNER 1. Also, a foreign vessel. –1643. †2. Short for *chambre foreine*, i.e. a privy. CHAUCER. 3. That part of a town which lies outside the parish proper. Now *local*. 1668. b. *pl.* The outer court of a monastery 1668.

Hence **Fo·reignism,** the imitation of what is foreign; a f. idiom, phrase, or term. **Fo·reignize** *v.* to become, or render, f. **Fo·reignness.**

Foreigner (fǫ·rėnəɹ). ME. [f. FOREIGN *a.* + -ER[1].] 1. A person born in another country; an alien. (Chiefly applied to those whose native language is a foreign one.) b. *transf.* Some thing produced or brought from abroad; *esp.* a foreign vessel 1677. 2. One of another country, parish, etc.; an outsider. Now *dial.* †Also *fig.* ME.

1. Horse and Foot..as well English as Foreigners 1703. 2. No F., as men of Bolton, Blackburne, or any other places 1565. *fig.* Joy is such a forainer, So meere a stranger to my thoughts DENHAM.

Fo:re-inte·nd, *v.* 1580. [f. FORE-.] To intend beforehand.

Fore-judge (fōəɹ,dʒɒ·dʒ), *v.* 1561. [f. FORE- + JUDGE *v.*] 1. *trans.* To determine beforehand or without a fair trial; to prejudge. Also *absol.* †2. To form an opinion of beforehand. Also *intr.* with *of*. –1792. So **Foreju·dgement,** judgement formed beforehand; †a judicial precedent.

Foreknow (foəɹnōu·), *v.* 1450. [f. FORE- + KNOW *v.*] 1. *trans.* To know beforehand, have previous knowledge of. 2. *intr.* To have previous knowledge *of* 1703.

1. St. Paul..fore-knew there would be Heresies among them 1680.

Hence **Foreknow·ingly** *adv.* Also †**Foreknow·able** *a.* that may be foreknown. †**Foreknow·er.**

Foreknowledge (foəɹnǫ·lėdʒ). 1535. [f. FORE-.] Knowledge of an event, etc. before it exists or happens; prescience.

If I foreknew, F. had no influence on their fault MILT. *P. L.* III. 118.

Forel, forrel (fǫ·rĕl). ME. [a. OF. *forel, fourrel* (F. *fourreau*), dim. f. *forre, feurre* case, sheath, etc. (see FUR *sb.*).] 1. †A sheath. ME. only. b. A case or covering for a book or manuscript. Now *dial.* ME. 2. A kind of parchment resembling vellum, used for covering (account-) books 1549. 3. A selvedge or border 1691. Hence †**Fo·rel, fo·rrel** *v.* to cover with f. or a f.

Foreland (fōə·ɹlănd). ME. [f. FORE- + LAND.] 1. A cape, headland, or promontory. 2. A strip of land in front of something; e.g. a space left between the base of a canal bank, and an adjacent drainage cut or river, so as to favour the stability of the bank 1867. b. *Fortif.* = BERM, q.v. 1704. 3. Land or territory lying in front 1851.

1. Unum foreland vocat. le Holyhede BOTONER.

Forelay (foəɹlē·), *v.* 1548. [f. FORE- + LAY *v.*] 1. *trans.* To lie in wait for, waylay. *Obs.* exc. *dial.* b. *fig.* To lay obstacles in the way of. Now *rare*. 1571. 2. To lay down or plan beforehand. *Obs.* exc. *dial.* 1605.

1. b. The Lord..forlayeth their craftynesse GOLDING. 2. I levell at no man with a forelayd designe 1640.

†**Foreleader.** ME. [f. FORE-.] One who leads the advance; a chief leader –1648.

Foreleg (fōə·ɹleg). 1483. [f. FORE- + LEG *sb.*] One of the front legs of a quadruped.

Fore-lie, -lift, etc.: see FORE- and LIE, LIFT, etc.

Forelive (foəɹli·v), *v.* 1599. [f. FORE-.] To live before another.

Forelock (fōə·ɹlǫk), *sb.*[1] 1467. [f. FORE- + LOCK *sb.*[1]] †1. a. ? Some piece of horse-harness. b. In mediæval armour, a clasp or catch to hold the helm (*Cent. Dict.*). 2. A wedge (usu. of iron) thrust through a hole in the end of a bolt in order to keep it in its place. Now chiefly *Naut.* 1514.

Comb.: f.-bolt, a bolt fitted to receive a f.; -hook (*Rope-making*), a winch in the tackle-block by which a bunch of three yarns is twisted into a strand.

Hence **Fo·relock** *v. trans.* to fasten with a f.

Forelock (fōə·ɹlǫk), *sb.*[2] OE. [f. FORE- + LOCK *sb.*[2]] 1. A lock of hair growing from the fore-part of the head. 2. *fig.* 1589.

2. Phr. *To take time, opportunity*, etc. *by the f.* (Suggested by Phædrus *Fab.* v. viii.) The occasion ..was bald behind, and must be grasped by the f. MOTLEY.

Forelook (fōə·ɹluk), *sb.* ME. [f. as prec. + LOOK *sb.*] a. A look forward (*Obs.* exc. *U.S.*). †b. Foresight, providence.

Forelook (foəɹlu·k), *v.* Also **for-.** ME. [f. as prec. + LOOK *v.*] 1. *trans.* To look at or see beforehand. 2. *intr.* To look ahead or forward 1494. †3. To bewitch –1611. Hence **Foreloo·ker.**

Forelouper, -loper (fōəɹlū·pəɹ, -lōu·pəɹ). *S. Afr.* 1863. [ad. Du. *voorlooper.*] A boy who walks with the foremost pair of a team of oxen.

Foreman (fōə·ɹmæ̆n). *Pl.* **foremen.** ME. [f. FORE- + MAN.] †1. One who goes in front –1674. 2. The principal juror who acts as spokesman of the jury, and communicates their verdict to the court 1538. 3. One who takes the most prominent part. *Obs.* exc. *locally* in municipal use. 1603. 4. The principal workman; *spec.* one who has charge of a department of work 1574. ¶5. As tr. Du. *voerman*, carrier 1641.

2. I will looke grauely..like the fore-man of a Jury DEKKER. 3. The f. of the Apostles, Peter PORSON. 4. *Working f.*: one who both supervises and works himself.

Foremast (fōə·ɹmast). 1582. [f. FORE- (and FORE *prep.*) + MAST.] 1. The forward lower-mast in all vessels. 2. ? The station of being 'before the mast'; hence, quasi-*adj.* characteristic of a foremast man 1626.

2. Foremast man, seaman, a sailor below the rank of petty officer. His f. air, and somewhat rolling gait BYRON.

Fore-mean: see FORE- and MEAN *v.*

Fo:re-me·ntion, *v.* 1587. [f. FORE- + MENTION.] To mention beforehand. Hence **Fo:re-me·ntioned** *ppl. a.*; also *ellipt.*

Foremost (fōə·ɹmoust, -məst). [OE. *formest, fyrmest*, f. OTeut. **formo-* (FORME *a.*) with additional superl. suffix (see -EST). Afterwards written as if f. FORE *a.* + MOST *adv.*]

A. *adj.* 1. First †in time –1587, †in serial order –1542, or position ME. 2. Most notable or prominent, best, chief OE.

1. Our formest fader Adam CAXTON. The f. fynger 1542. Formost to stand against the Thunderers aime MILT. *P. L.* II. 28. 2. Men ever famous, and formost in the achievements of liberty MILT.

B. *adv.* First in position or rank; †formerly also, in time, serial order, etc. Also in *first and f.* OE.

Hence †**Fo·remostly** *adv.* in front.

Foremother (fōə·ɹmɒðəɹ). 1582. [f. FORE-, after *forefather.*] A female ancestor.

Forename (fōə·ɹnē^i^m), *sb.* 1533. [f. FORE- + NAME *sb.*] First or Christian name; in *Rom. Antiq.* = PRÆNOMEN.

†**Fo·rename,** *v.* 1490. [f. FORE- + NAME *v.*] *trans.* To name beforehand –1655. Hence **Fo·renamed** *ppl. a.* named or mentioned before.

Forenight (fōə·ɹnəit). 1513. [f. FORE- and FORE *prep.*] †1. The previous night 1583. 2. *Sc.* The interval between twilight and bedtime.

Forenoon (fōə·ɹnū·n). 1506. [f. as prec. + NOON.] The part of the day before noon. Also *attrib.*

Fore-notice: see FORE- and NOTICE.

†**Fore·nsal,** *a.* [f. as next.] = next. H. MORE.

Forensic (fǫre·nsik). 1659. [f. L. *forensis* + -IC.]

A. *adj.* Pertaining to, connected with, or used in courts of law; suitable or analogous to pleadings in court.

A f. term LOCKE, manner DICKENS. *F. medicine*: medicine in its relation to law; medical jurisprudence.

B. *sb. U.S.* A speech or written thesis maintaining one side or the other of a given question. Hence †**Fore·nsical** *a.*, **-ly** *adv.*

Foreordain (foə:rǫ̆ɹdē^i^·n), *v.* ME. [f. FORE + ORDAIN.] *trans.* To ordain or appoint beforehand; to predestinate.

Fo:reo·rdinate, *v.* [f. FORE- + ORDINATE.] *trans.* To foreordain. Hence **Fo:reordina·tion,** previous ordination or appointment, predestination.

Fore-part, forepart (fōə·ɹpaɹt). ME. [f. FORE- + PART.] 1. The foremost, first, or most advanced part; the front. †2. A stomacher –1640. 3. The earlier part 1614.

Forepassed, -past (foəɹpɑ·st), *ppl. a.* 1557. [f. FORE- + PASSED, PAST.] That has previously passed, or been passed. Now only of time.

Fo·repeak. 1693. [f. FORE- + PEAK.] *Naut.* The extreme end of the forehold in the angle of the bows.

Fore-piece (fōə·ɹpīs). 1788. [f. FORE- + PIECE.] The foremost, first, or front piece. b. *Theatr.* A 'curtain-raiser' 1814. c. *Saddlery.* The flap attached to the fore-part of a side-saddle, to guard the rider's dress 1874.

†**Fo:re-posse·ss,** *v.* 1579. [f. FORE- + POSSESS.] *trans.* To possess beforehand *with* –1635.

†**Forepri·se, -prize,** *v.* 1577. [f. FORE- + PRISE, after *apprise*, etc.] *trans.* To take beforehand; to take for granted; to allow for; to forestall, anticipate –1693.

Fo·re-purpose, *sb.* 1551. [f. FORE- + PURPOSE.] A purpose settled beforehand. Hence **Forepu·rpose** *v.*

†**Fore-quo·te,** *v.* 1598. [f. FORE- + QUOTE.] *trans.* To quote or cite beforehand –1670.

Fore-rank, etc.: see FORE and RANK, etc.

Fo:re-rea·ch, *v.* 1644. [f. FORE- + REACH *v.*] Chiefly *Naut.* 1. *intr.* To shoot ahead. 2. *trans.* To reach beyond, pass. Also *fig.* 1803. 3. To anticipate. WHITTIER.

2. *fig.* The general, coming back by a different route, had fore-reached them in such a scheme NAPIER.

†**Fore-rea·d,** *v.* 1591. [f. FORE- + READ.] *trans.* To read beforehand 1620; to signify beforehand –1612; to predestine 1636.

Fore-recited, etc.: see FORE-.

Fore-rider (fōə·ɹ,rəidəɹ). 1470. [f. FORE + RIDER.] One who rides in front; *esp.* †a scout; an outrider; †a harbinger.

Foreright (fōə·ɹ,rəi·t), rarely **-rights.** ME. [f. FORE- + RIGHT *adv.* and *adj.*]

†A. *adv.* Directly forward, straight ahead –1796.

No less fore-right the rapid chace they held POPE.

B. *prep.* †1. Straight along. FULLER. 2. Opposite. *dial.* 1858.

C. *adj.* †1. Straight forward –1748. 2. Of a branch, etc.: Shooting straight out 1741. 3. *dial.* Of persons: Headstrong; straightforward; plain-spoken 1736.

1. His sayle Being fill'd and prosper'd with a fore-right Gale QUARLES.

D. *sb.* [The *adj.* used *absol.*] Something that is foreright 1754.

Fore-run (fōᵊɹ,rʊ·n), *v.* OE. [f. FORE- + RUN *v.*] **1.** *intr.* To run on in front. OE. only. **2.** *trans.* To outrun. *Obs.* exc. *fig.* 1513. †**3.** To run in front of; hence, to act as harbinger of. Also *transf.* to precede. –1750. **4.** To be the precursor of 1590. **5.** To forestall 1591.

4. These signes f. the death of Kings SHAKS. 5. By anticipating and forerunning false reports RALEIGH.

Forerunner (fōᵊ·ɹʊ:nəɹ). ME. [f. prec. + -ER¹.] **1.** One who runs before, *esp.* one sent to prepare the way and herald a great man's approach, a harbinger; also, a guide. Also *transf.* and *fig.* **2.** A predecessor; also, an ancestor 1595. **3.** A prognostic or sign of something to follow 1589. **4.** *Naut.* **a.** = FOREGANGER. 1694. **b.** A piece of rag, terminating the stray-line of the log-line 1815.

1. John the baptist, whych was the fore runner of.. Christ COVERDALE. Death our Fore-runner is, and guides to Sion KEN. 2. Arthur, that great fore-runner of thy bloud *John* II. i. 2.

Foresaid (fōᵊ·ɹsed), *a.* OE. [f. FORE- + SAID.] = AFORESAID.

Fore-sail (fōᵊ·ɹsᵊl). 1481. [f. FORE- + SAIL.] The principal sail set on the foremast; in square-rigged vessels, the lowest square sail on the foremast; in fore-and-aft rigged, the triangular sail before the mast.

Fore-say (fōᵊɹsē·), *v.* [OE. *foresęcgan*, f. FORE- + *sęcgan* to SAY.] *trans.* To foretell, predict. Now *rare.*

Foresee (foᵊɹsī·), *v.* [OE. *foresēon*, f. FORE- + *sēon* to SEE.] **1.** *trans.* To see beforehand, have prescience of. †**2.** To provide –1637; to see to beforehand –1626. †**3.** *intr.* To exercise foresight, make provision –1626.

1. A prudent man foreseeth the euil, and hideth himselfe *Prov.* xxvii. 12. 3. He plots, complots, forsees, prevents, directs QUARLES.

Phr. (*Alway*) *foreseen* or *foreseeing that*: provided that; Forseen alwey, that yf.. my doughtres dye [etc.] ME. Hence **Foresee·able** *a.*, **Foresee·r.** **Foresee·ingly** *adv.*

Foreshadow (fōᵊ·ɹʃæ:dou), *sb.* 1831. [f. FORE- + SHADOW *sb.*] *fig.* A shadow cast before; an indication of something to come.

Foreshadow (foᵊɹ,ʃæ·dou), *v.* 1577. [f. FORE- + SHADOW *v.*] *trans.* To serve as the shadow thrown before (an object); hence, to represent imperfectly beforehand, prefigure. Occas. (of a person), to have a foreboding of. Hence **Foresha·dower.**

Fore-sheet (fōᵊ·ɹʃīt). 1667. [f. FORE- + SHEET.] *Naut.* **1.** The rope by which the lee corner of the fore-sail is kept in place. **2.** *pl.* The inner part of the bows of a boat, fitted with gratings upon which the bow-man stands (Adm. Smyth) 1719.

Foreship (fōᵊ·ɹʃip). [OE. *forscip*, f. FOR- *pref.*², FORE- + *scip*, SHIP.] The fore-part of a ship; the prow.

Foreshore (fōᵊ·ɹʃōᵊɹ). 1764. [f. FORE- + SHORE.] **1.** The fore-part of the shore; that part which lies between the high- and low-water marks. Also *transf.* **2.** *Hydraulic Engin.* **a.** A bank a little distance from a sea-wall to break the force of the surf. **b.** The seaward projecting, slightly inclined portion of a breakwater. 1841.

Foreshorten (foᵊɹ,ʃǭ·ɹt'n), *v.* 1606. [f. FORE- + SHORTEN *v.*] *trans.* To cause to be apparently shortened in the directions not lying in a plane perpendicular to the line of sight. Also, to delineate so as to represent this effect. Also *transf.* and *fig.*

fig. Lives that lie Fore-shorten'd in the tract of time TENNYSON.

Foreshot (fōᵊ·ɹʃǫt). 1839. [f. FORE- + SHOT.] **1.** A projecting part of a building. **2.** In distilling: The spirits which first come over 1893.

Foreshow (foᵊɹʃōᵘ·), *v.* [OE. *foresc̄eawian*, f. FORE- + *scēawian* to SHOW.] †**1.** *trans.* To look out for; to provide. OE. and early ME. only.

2. To show beforehand; to foretell; to prefigure 1561. †**3.** To show forth –1608.

2. Astrologers, that future fates foreshew POPE. The falling of the mercury foreshews thunder IMISON. 3. Your lookes fore-shew You haue a gentle heart SHAKS. Hence †**Fo·reshow** *sb.* a manifestation beforehand. **Foresho·wer.**

Foreside (fōᵊ·ɹ,səid). ME. [f. FORE- + SIDE.] **1.** The fore-part; the front or upper side. Now *rare* exc. *techn.* **2.** The front side or edge 1703.

Foresight (fōᵊ·ɹsəit). ME. [f. FORE- + SIGHT.] **1.** The action or faculty of foreseeing; prevision. **2.** The action of looking forward (*lit.* and *fig.*) 1591; perception gained by looking forward; prospect ME. **3.** Care or provision for the future ME. **4.** *Surveying.* 'Any reading of the leveling-rod, after the first taken at a given station'. ? U.S. only. **5.** The muzzle-sight of a gun 1859.

1. Want of f. makes thee more merry BP. HALL. 2. Let Eve.. Here sleep below, while thou to f. wak'st MILT. 3. Shapd in the glass of the divine F. COWLEY. Hence **Fo·resighted** *ppl. a.* having f.; characterized or controlled by f. **Fo·resightful** *a.* full of f.

Foresignify (foᵊɹsi·gnifəi), *v.* 1565. [f. FORE- + SIGNIFY *v.*] *trans.* To signify beforehand; to prefigure; †to foretell. Hence **Fore·significa·tion**, a premonition (*rare*).

Foreskin (fōᵊ·ɹskin). 1535. [f. FORE- + SKIN *sb.*] The prepuce.

Fore-skirt: see FORE- and SKIRT.

Foreslack: see FORSLACK.

Foresleeve (fōᵊ·ɹ,slīv). ME. [f. FORE- + SLEEVE.] **a.** The fore part of a sleeve. **b.** That part of a dress-sleeve which covers the fore-arm.

Foreslow: see FORSLOW.

Forespeak (foᵊɹ,spī·k), *v.* Also **for-**. ME. [FORE- + SPEAK *v.*] **1.** *trans.* To speak or speak of beforehand; to foretell, predict. Now *rare.* †**2.** *intr.* To speak beforehand; to prophesy –1656. †**3.** *trans.* To speak forth or out –1547. **4.** To speak for in advance 1659.

1. To f. fair weather 1654. 2. These are the days fore-spoken of 1646. 4. To f. impunity for so strange boldness L'ESTRANGE. Hence **Forespea·king** *vbl. sb.* †a preface; †a prediction.

Forespeak: see FORSPEAK, to bewitch, etc.

†**Fo·respeech.** [f. FORE- + SPEECH; in OE. *foresprǣc*, *-spǣc*.] An introductory speech, a preface –1688.

†**Forespe·nt**, *ppl. a.* 1578. [f. FORE- + SPENT, SPEND.] Spent previously –1641.

Forest (fǫ·rėst), *sb.* ME. [a. OF. *forest* (F. *forêt*), ad. med. L. *forestem* (*silvam*) the outside wood (i.e. that not fenced in), f. *foris* out of doors.] **1.** An extensive tract of land covered with trees and undergrowth, sometimes intermingled with pasture. Also *transf.* and *fig.* **b.** In Great Britain, the name of districts formerly covered with trees, as *Ashtown*, *Ettrick*, *Sherwood*, *Wychwood F.* **2.** *Law.* A woodland district, usually belonging to the king, set apart for hunting wild beasts and game, etc., having its own laws and officers ME. †**3.** A wild, uncultivated waste –1659.

attrib. and *Comb.*

1. General: as *f.-alley*, etc.; and *esp.* with sense 'haunting or inhabiting a f.', as *f.-bear*, *-boar*, *-dove*.

2. Special: **f.-bed** (*Geol.*), a stratum originating from a primæval f.; **-fly**, a fly of the genus *Hippobosca*, esp. *H. equina*; **-laws**, laws relating to royal forests, enacted by the Norman kings; **-marble**, an argillaceous laminated shelly limestone, forming one of the upper portions of the Lower Oolite; **-tree**, any tree of large growth, fitted to belong to a f.; **-wards** *adv.* towards the f.

Hence **Fo·restage**, duty paid by foresters to the king; duty paid to the king's foresters; *collect.* tree-growth. **Fo·restal** *a.* of or pertaining to a f.

Forest (fǫ·rėst), *v.* 1818. [f. prec.] *trans.* **a.** To place in a forest. KEATS. **b.** To plant with trees 1865.

a. O Haunter.. of.. woods.. Where.. Art thou now forested KEATS.

†**Fo·re-staff.** 1669. [f. FORE- + STAFF.] *Naut.* = CROSS-STAFF 2. –1769.

†**Fo·re-stage.** ME. [f. FORE- + STAGE.] *Naut.* = FORECASTLE 1; hence a ship with a forecastle –1481.

Forestall (fōᵊ·ɹ,stǫl), *sb.* [In sense 1, OE. *for-*, *foresteall*, f. FORE- + *steall*, (app.) 'position taken up'. In sense 2, f. FORE- + STALL.] †**1.** In OE.: An ambush, plot. Hence in *Law*, 'waylaying' or 'intercepting in the highway'; also the jurisdiction in respect of this offence. –1610. **2.** Something situated in front; *esp.* the space in front of a farm-house, or the way leading to it. *dial.* 1661. **3.** A (horse's) frontlet. Cf. *headstall*. 1519.

Forestall (foᵊɹ,stǭ·l), *v.* [ME. f. OE. *foresteall*: see prec.] †**1.** To lie in wait for, intercept, cut off –1741. **2.** To intercept (goods, etc.) before they reach the public markets; to buy (them) up privately with a view to enhance the price. (Formerly an indictable offence.) ME. **b.** To anticipate or prevent sales at (a market, etc.) by buying up or selling goods beforehand or by dissuading persons from bringing them in ME. †**3.** To beset, obstruct by armed force (a way, etc.) –1611. **4.** Hence *gen.* To hinder, obstruct, or prevent by anticipation. Now *rare.* 1579. †**b.** To bar or deprive by previous action *from*, *of*, *out of* –1660. †**5.** To preoccupy, secure beforehand –1685. **6.** To be beforehand with in action; to anticipate. (The chief current sense.) 1585.

2. Suffer not these riche men to bie up al, to ingrosse and forstalle 1551. b. *fig.* To f. the market of honour FULLER. 4. b. May This night f. him of the comming day *Cymb.* III. v. 69. 6. What need a man f. his date of grief MILT. *Comus* 362. And this he did to forestal any tidings BUNYAN. Hence **Foresta·ller**, one who forestalls; *esp.* one who forestalls the market. **Foresta·lment.**

Forestalling (foᵊɹ,stǭ·liŋ), *vbl. sb.* ME. [f. prec. + -ING¹.] †**1.** The action of obstructing a person in the highway or a deer on its way back to the forest –1594. **2.** The buying up of goods beforehand, etc. 1548. **3.** The action of anticipating 1642. †**4.** The action of appropriating beforehand. FULLER.

2. Usury is.. a f. of money 1800.

Fore-stay (fōᵊ·ɹ,stē¹). ME. [f. FORE-.] **1.** *Naut.* A stay or strong rope reaching from the fore mast-head towards the bowsprit end; also, a sail hoisted on the fore-stay. **2.** *Printing. F. of press*, the leg which supports the frame or ribs of a hand-press. 1833.

Forester (fǫ·rėstəɹ). ME. [ad. OF. *forestier*, f. *forest* FOREST.] **1.** An officer having charge of a forest (see quot.); also, one who looks after the growing timber on an estate. Occas. (*poet.*), a huntsman. **2.** One who lives in a forest 1513. **b.** A bird or beast of the forest 1630. **c.** A name of some moths of the family *Zygænidæ* 1819. **d.** = *forest-tree* 1664. **4.** A member of the 'friendly society' called the 'Ancient Order of Foresters' 1851.

1. A Forester is an officier of a forest of the King (or of an other man) that is sworne to preserue the Vert and Venison of the same forest, and to attend vpon the wild beasts within his Bailiwick, and to attach offendors there.. and the same to present at the courts of the said forest MANWOOD. 2. Above the loftiest ridge.. Where foresters and shepherds dwell WORDSW. Hence **Fo·restership.**

Fore-stick (fōᵊ·ɹ,stik). *U.S.* 1872. [f. FORE-.] The front stick lying on the andirons in a wood fire.

Forestry (fǫ·rėstri). 1823. [f. FOREST *sb.* + -RY.] **1.** Wooded country; a vast extent of trees. **2.** The science and art of forming and cultivating forests, management of growing timber 1859.

1. *transf.* Lost amid the f. of masts BYRON.

Foret, obs. f. FERRET sb.¹ and ².

Fore-tack (fōᵊ·ɹtæk). 1669. [f. FORE- + TACK *sb.*] *Naut.* The rope by which the weather corner of the fore-sail is kept in place.

Foretaste (fōᵊ·ɹ,tē¹st), *sb.* ME. [f. FORE- + TASTE *sb.*] A taste beforehand; an anticipation, partial enjoyment in advance.

Foretaste (foᵊɹ,tē¹·st), *v.* 1450. [f. FORE- + TASTE *v.*] **1.** *trans.* To taste beforehand, have a foretaste of. **2.** 'To taste before another' (J.) 1667.

2. Foretasted Fruit Profan'd first by the Serpent MILT. *P. L.* IX. 929. Hence **Foreta·ster.**

†**Foretea·ch**, *v.* 1591. [f. FORE- + TEACH *v.*] *trans.* To teach beforehand –1661.

Foretell (foᵊɹte·l), *v.* ME. [f. FORE- + TELL *v.*] **1.** To tell of beforehand; to predict, prophesy; to foreshow. †**2.** To inform or enjoin beforehand –1679. †**3.** *intr.* To prophesy *of* –1667.

1. These Magi.. foretold things to come DE FOE. 3. One Greater, of whose day he shall f. MILT. *P. L.* XII. 242. Hence **Forete·ller.**

Forethink (fo°ɹþi·ŋk). [OE. *foreþęnc(e)an*, f. FORE- + *þęnc(e)an* to THINK.] †**1.** *trans.* To think out beforehand, contrive, plan -1715. **2.** To contemplate beforehand; to presage (evil). Now *rare.* 1547. †Also *intr.* with *of.* -1701.

2. Rather of a friend [to] hope the best, then forethinke the worst 1547.

Forethought (fō°ɹþǫt), *sb.* ME. [f. FORE- + THOUGHT *sb.*] **1.** A thinking out or contriving beforehand; previous consideration; anticipation. †**2.** A pre-conceived idea or design, an anticipation -1729. **3.** Thought for the future 1719.

1. (*Crime, evil,* etc.) *of f.*: premeditated; we urge no crimes, that were not crimes of f. BURKE. **3.** Just so much f. as is necessary to provide for the morrow JOWETT. Hence **Forethou·ghtful** *a.* having f.

Forethought (fō°·ɹþǫt), *ppl. a.* ME. [pa. pple. of FORETHINK *v.*] **1.** Thought out or contrived beforehand; premeditated. Cf. AFORETHOUGHT. †**2.** Anticipated 1666.

1. Slaine..with malice prepensed or f. COKE.

Foretime (fō°·ɹtəim), *sb.* 1540. [f. FORE- + TIME *sb.*] Former time; a former time; the past. Also *attrib.* and †as *adv.*

It was called in f. Norton Dany HOLLAND.

Foretoken (fō°·ɹtōuk'n), *sb.* [OE. *foretācn*, f. FORE- + *tācn* TOKEN.] A premonitory token; a prognostic.

Foretoken (foɹtō^u·k'n), *v.* ME. [f. prec. sb.] *trans.* To be a foretoken of; to betoken beforehand.

A dolefull chance, but yet..foretokening good luck 1598.

Fore-tooth (fō°·ɹ,tūþ). OE. [f. FORE- + TOOTH.] **1.** One of the front teeth. *rare* in *sing.* †**2.** *pl.* The first or milk-teeth -1651.

Foretop (fō°·ɹtǫp). ME. [f. FORE- + TOP.] †**1.** The fore-part of the crown of the head; *loosely,* the top of the head -1781. †**2.** The lock of hair upon the fore-part of the head; the similar part of a wig -1814. **3.** The tuft of hair hanging between the ears of a horse, etc. 1607. **4.** The TOP of a foremast 1509. **b.** Short for *fore-topgallant-masthead* 1800. **5.** *U.S.* The front seat on the top of a vehicle 1850.

4. *Military f.*: an armed f. of a war vessel.

Fore-topgallant (fō°ɹ,tǫpgæ·lănt), *a.* 1627. [f. FORE- + TOPGALLANT.] *Naut.* In **fore-topgallant-mast**, the mast above the fore-topmast; hence with sense 'of or belonging to the fore-topgallant-mast', as *f.-sail,* etc.

Fore-topmast (fō°ɹ,tǫ·pmɑst). 1626. [f. FORE- + TOPMAST.] *Naut.* The mast above the foremast; also *attrib.*

Fore-topsail (fō°ɹtǫ·psēil, -s'l). 1582. [f. FORE- + TOPSAIL.] *Naut.* The sail above the fore-sail; also *attrib.*

Forever (fǫre·vəɹ), *adv.* Now chiefly *U.S.* 1670. **1.** *For ever* (see EVER), written as one word. **2.** quasi-*sb.* Eternity 1858.

2. Life, death, and that vast for-ever KINGSLEY. So **Fore·vermore** *adv.*: see EVERMORE 1.

Fore-vouched: see FORE- and the second element.

†**Fo·reward.** ME. [f. FORE- + WARD *sb.*] **1.** The first line of an army, vanguard, front -1664. **2.** The command of, or a position in, the van -1576.

Forewarn (foɹwǭ·ɹn), *v.* ME. [f. FORE- + WARN *v.*] *trans.* To warn, caution, or admonish beforehand; also, to give previous notice to.

We were fore-warned of your comming SHAKS.

†**Fo·re-wind.** 1561. [f. FORE- + WIND *sb.*] A wind that blows a ship forward on her course -1682.

†**Fo·re-wit,** *sb.* ME. [f. FORE- + WIT.] **1.** Foresight, prudence -1631. **2.** A leading wit, a leader in matters of taste and literature. B. JONS.

1. Yet is one good f. woorth two after wits 1546.

†**Fore-wit,** *v.* Pres. 1st, 3rd sing. **-wot.** [OE. *forewitan*, f. FORE- + *witan*, WIT *v.*] *trans.* To know beforehand -ME. Hence **Fore·wi·tter.**

Forewoman (fō°·ɹwumăn), pl. **-women** (-wimėn). 1709. [f. FORE- + WOMAN.] A woman who acts as chief: **a.** in a jury of matrons; **b.** in a shop or department.

Foreword (fō°·ɹwɒ̄ɹd). 1842. [f. FORE- + WORD.] A word said before something else; hence, a preface.

Fore-yard[1] (fō°·ɹ,yaɹd). ME. [f. FORE- + YARD[1].] The yard or court in front of a building.

Fore-yard[2] (fō°·ɹ,yaɹd). 1627. [f. FORE- + YARD[2].] *Naut.* The lowest yard on the foremast.

Forfalt, -fault, -faute: see FORFEIT.

†**Forfa·re,** *v.*: see FOR- *pref.*[1] and FARE *v.*

†**Forfear,** *v.* ME. only. [f. FOR- pref.[1] + FEAR *v.*] To terrify. Only in pa. pple.

Forfeit (fǭ·ɹfit), *sb.* ME. [a. OF. *forfet, forfait* :—med. L. *foris factum* trespass, fine, neut. pa. pple. of *foris facere* to transgress, f. *foris* outside + *facere* to do.] †**1.** A misdeed, crime, transgression; hence, wilful injury. Also with *of*: Breach or violation *of.* -1668. **2.** Something to which the right is lost by the commission of a crime or fault; hence, a penal fine, a penalty 1450. **b.** *transf.* of a person. *Meas. for M.* IV. ii. 167. **3.** A trivial mulct or fine for breach of a rule or by-law, or the like. Also, in certain games, an article given up by a player for making some mistake, and afterwards redeemed by performing some ludicrous task. 1603. **4.** [f. the vb.] = FORFEITURE. ME.

1. The Censure..dayly toke hede to the forfaytes done 1533. **2.** I craue the Law, The penaltie, and forfeite of my bond SHAKS. **3.** And here I took pleasure to take forfeits of the ladies PEPYS. **4.** Debts they could clear no other way but by the f. of their honour 1716.

Forfeit (fǭ·ɹfit), *a.* ME. [ad. OF. *forfait* pa. pple.; see prec.] Lost or to be given up as the penalty of a crime or fault or breach of an engagement. Const. *to, unto.*

His braines are forfeite to the next tile that fals SHAKS. The wish To tread the f. Paradise EMERSON.

Forfeit (fǭ·ɹfit), *v.* ME. [f. prec. sb.] †**1.** *intr.* To do amiss, sin, transgress -1530. **2.** *trans.* To lose, lose the right to; to render oneself liable to be deprived of; also, to have to pay in consequence of a crime, offence, breach of duty, or engagement. Const. *to.* 1466. **b.** *gen.* To lose by misconduct ME. **c.** To lose or give up, as a necessary consequence ME. **d.** *absol.* 1727. **3.** To subject to forfeiture; to confiscate. *Obs.* exc. *Hist.* ME. †**4.** To exact a forfeit from -1736. †**5.** To cause the forfeiture, loss, or ruin of -1705.

2. My life and effects were all forfeited to the English Government DE FOE. **b.** He had done nothing to f. her love TROLLOPE. **c.** The moral sentiment..never forfeits its supremacy EMERSON. **3.** All his substance shall be forfeited *Ezra* x. 8. **5.** Such another forgetfulness Forfeits your life 1611. Hence **Fo·rfeitable** *a.* subject to forfeiture. **Fo·rfeiter,** †an evil-doer; one who forfeits or incurs forfeiture.

Forfeiture (fǭ·ɹfitiŭɹ). ME. [a. OF. *forfeture, forfaiture.*] †**1.** Transgression or violation of a law; crime, sin -1628. **2.** The fact of losing or becoming liable to lose (an estate, goods, life, an office, right, etc.) in consequence of a crime, offence, or breach of engagement. Const. *of,* †*on.* ME. †**b.** The penalty of the transgression -1667. **3.** *concr.* That which is forfeited; a penalty, a fine. ? *Obs.* ME.

2. Vppon peyne of forfetor of xl[s] 1467. **b.** MILT. *P. L.* III. 221. **3.** A f., part of which went to the informer COBBETT.

Forfend, forefend (fǭɹfe·nd, foɹfe·nd), *v.* ME. [f. FOR- *pref.*[1] + FEND *v.*] †**1.** *trans.* To forbid, prohibit -1823. **2.** To avert; *esp.* in *God* (etc.) *forfend*; also *absol.* as an exclam. *arch.* ME. **3.** To secure or protect by precautionary measures. Now chiefly *U.S.* 1592.

2. F. the sight FIELDING.

Forfex (fǭ·ɹfeks). 1712. [a. L.] **1.** A pair of scissors. **2.** *Entom.* A pair of anal organs, which open or shut transversely, and cross each other 1826. So **Fo·rficate** *a.* shaped like a pair of scissors.

Forficulate (fǫɹfi·kiŭlēⁱt), *v.* [f. mod. L. *forficula*, dim. of *forfex.*] *intr.* To 'creep', as if a *forficula* or earwig were crawling on one's skin. LYTTON.

Forfou·ghten, *pple.* and *ppl. a.* *Obs.* exc. *Sc.* ME. [f. FOR- *pref.*[1] + FOUGHTEN.] Worn-out with fighting. Also *transf.*

We are f., & moche blood haue we loste MALORY.

Forgather, foregather (fǭɹgæ·ðəɹ), *v.* Chiefly *Sc.* 1513. [f. FOR- *pref.*[1] + GATHER.] **1.** *intr.* To gather together. **2.** To encounter, meet (accidentally); *esp.* to meet *with* 1600. **b.** To associate *with* 1782.

1. The Scottis all forgadderit in Argyle 1535. **2.** Twa dogs..Forgather'd ance upon a time BURNS.

Forge (fō°ɹdʒ), *sb.* ME. [a. OF. *forge* :—Com. Rom. **faurga* :—L. *fabrica*; see FABRIC.] †**1.** Manufacture, construction; make, workmanship -1691. **2.** A smithy. Also *transf.* and *fig.* ME. **3.** An open hearth or fireplace with a bellows attached, used by blacksmiths for heating iron to render it malleable; a similar apparatus on wheels for military use. Also *transf.* and *fig.* 1481. **4.** A hearth or furnace for melting or refining metals. Also, the workshop, etc., where this work is carried on. 1601. **5.** *Comm.* Short for *forge iron* 1890.

1. In the greater Bodies the F. was easie, the matter being ductile and sequacious RAY. **2.** *fig.* The brain ..is the f. in which all the speculations of the understanding..are hammered-out COLLIER. **3.** *fig.* Come to the F. with it, then shape it: I would not haue things coole *Merry W.* IV. ii. 239.

Comb.: **f.-cart** (*Mil.*), a travelling f. for service in the field; **-cinder,** the slag from a f. or bloomary; **-fire,** (*a*) a smith's fire; (*b*) a puddling furnace; **-man,** a forger or smith; *spec.* a superior class of coachsmith, having a hammer-man under him; **-pig,** a pig of forge-iron, also *collect.*; **-rolls,** the train of rolls by which the slab or bloom is converted into puddled bars; **-wagon** = *forge-cart*; **-water,** water in which heated irons have been dipped, formerly in use as a medicine.

Forge (fō°ɹdʒ), *v.*[1] ME. [ad. OF. *forgier* (F. *forger*) :—L. *fabricare*; see FABRICATE.] **1.** *trans.* = FABRICATE *v.* 1. Now only as *transf.* use of 2. **2.** To shape by heating in a forge and hammering; to beat into shape; †to coin (money). Also fig. ME. **b.** *absol.* or *intr.* To work at the forge ME. †**3.** To frame or fashion -1562; †to coin (a word, etc.) -1690. **4.** *esp.* To fabricate, invent (a false story, lie, etc.); to devise (evil). Also, to fable. ME. **5.** To make (something) in fraudulent imitation of something else; to make or devise in order to pass off as genuine ME.; to counterfeit 1535. **6.** *intr.* To commit forgery 1591.

1. Of wexe he forged an ymage GOWER. **2.** Cursyd be he..that forgyd thy sword LD. BERNERS. Phr. †*To f. and file*: to fashion completely, make ready. **3.** To f. newe English wordes 1571. **4.** In which delit they wol f. a long tale CHAUCER. **5.** To f. a will 1605, the University Seal WOOD. **6.** But Pens can f., my Friend, that cannot write POPE.

Forge (fō°ɹdʒ), *v.*[2] 1796. [? transf. use of prec.] *intr.* Of a vessel: To make way, 'shoot ahead' (Adm. Smyth), *esp.* by mere momentum, or the pressure of tide.

She forged on without any sail FORREST.

Forger (fō°·ɹdʒəɹ). ME. [f. FORGE *v.*[1] + -ER[1].] **1.** One who forges, makes, or frames; now only, a fabricator (of false stories, etc.). **2.** One who forges (metal) or works at a forge; a smith; †a coiner of money ME. **3.** One who makes fraudulent imitations (of documents, coins, etc.) 1552.

Forgery (fō°·ɹdʒĕri). 1574. [f. FORGE *v.*[1] + -ERY.] †**1.** The action or craft of forging metal -1671. **2.** Invention; fictitious invention, fiction. Now only *poet.* 1583. **3.** The making of a thing in fraudulent imitation of something; *esp.* the forging, counterfeiting, or falsifying of a document 1593. **b.** The being forged. *rare.* 1665. **c.** *concr.* That which is forged, counterfeited, or fabricated 1574.

1. Useless the f. Of brazen shield and spear MILT. **2.** I in f. of shapes and tricks, Come short of what he did SHAKS. **3.** F. or the *crimen falsi*..'the fraudulent making or alteration of a writing to the prejudice of another man's right' BLACKSTONE. **c.** A manifest f. GIBBON.

Forget (fǭɹge·t), *v.* Pa. t. **forgot** (-gǫ·t), *arch.* **forgat** (-gæ·t). Pa. pple. **forgotten** (gǫ·t'n), *arch.* and *poet.* **forgot** (-gǫ·t). [OE. *forgietan*, f. OTeut. **getan* (see GET *v.*) in sense 'to hold, grasp' + FOR- *pref.*[1] 3.] **1.** *trans.* To lose remembrance of; to cease to retain in one's memory; to fail to recall to mind 1787. Also *absol.* **2.** To omit or neglect through inadvertence. Chiefly with *infinitive* as obj. In poetry occas. *fig.* of things. OE. **3.** To cease or omit to think of OE. **4.** To neglect wilfully, disregard, overlook, slight ME.

1. And a fourth whose name I have forgot 1676. *absol.* Hee hath said in his heart, God hath forgotten

Ps. x. 11. 2. The winds f. to roar POPE. 3. The world forgetting, by the world forgot POPE. 4. Men wallow in wealth, and f. God 1703.

Phr. *To f. oneself*: to omit care for oneself; to behave unbecomingly; to lose consciousness.

Hence **Forge·ttable** *a.* that may be forgotten. **Forge·tter,** one who forgets. **Forge·ttingly** *adv.* forgetfully.

Forgetful (fǫɹge·tfŭl), *a.* ME. [f. prec. + -FUL.] 1. Apt to forget; having a bad memory. Also, that forgets. 2. Heedless, neglectful 1526. 3. That causes to forget. Chiefly *poet.* 1557.

1. F. of the glory of the past TYNDALL. 2. Be not f. to entertain strangers *Heb.* xiii. 2. 3. The sound of that f. shore TENNYSON. Hence **Forge·tfully** *adv.*

Forgetfulness (fǫɹge·tfulnės). ME. [f. prec. + -NESS.] 1. The quality of being apt to forget, the state of forgetting 1477. 2. The condition of forgetting everything ME. 3. The state of being forgotten, oblivion. ? *Obs.* 1561. 4. Disregard, inattention, neglect 1576.

1. A sweet f. of human cares POPE. 2. Euer with deth cometh forgetfulnes ME. 4. F. of social duties 1757.

Forgetive (fōᵊ·ɹdʒėtiv), *a.* 1597. [? f. FORGE *v* 1+-TIVE.] Now used for: Apt at forging, inventive, creative. The orig. meaning is uncertain. See 2 *Hen. IV*, IV. iii. 107.

Forge·t-me-no·t. 1532. [In sense 1, = OF. *ne m'oubliez mye.* The flower was supposed to ensure that those wearing it should never be forgotten by their lovers.] 1. The name of various kinds of *Myosotis*, esp. *M. palustris*, a plant having bright blue flowers with a yellow eye. 2. The Germander Speedwell (*Veronica Chamædrys*) 1853. †3. The Ground Pine (*Ajuga Chamæpitys*) –1597.

1. Eyes..Blue as the blue forget-me-not TENNYSON.

Forging (fōᵊ·ɹdʒiŋ), *vbl. sb.* ME. [f. FORGE *v.*[1] + -ING[1].] 1. The action of FORGE *v.*[1]; an instance of the same. b. *concr.* A forged mass (of iron, etc.) 1858. 2. *attrib.*, as *f.-hammer*, etc. 1874.

Forgivable (fǫɹgi·văb'l), *a.* Also **-eable.** 1550. [f. next + -ABLE.] That may be forgiven, pardonable.

Forgive (fǫɹgi·v), *v.* Pa. t. **forgave** (fǫɹgēⁱ·v). Pa. pple. **forgiven** (fǫɹgi·v'n). [OE. *forgiefan*; see FOR- *pref.*[1] and GIVE *v.*] †1. *trans.* To give, grant –1483. †2. To give up, cease to harbour (resentment, etc.) –1533. 3. To remit (a debt); to give up claim to requital for, pardon (an offence). Const. with simple obj.; also with thing in the accus. and person in the dat. OE. 4. To give up resentment against, pardon (an offender). Also (now *rarely*) to abandon one's claim against a debtor. OE. 5. *absol.* (of 3 and 4) OE. 6. To make excuse for, regard indulgently. Now only in *imper.* as an entreaty. 1667. †7. = MISGIVE. Holland.

2. Oberon..forgaue all the yll wyll that he had to Huon LD. BERNERS. 3. Forgiue a moytie of the principall SHAKS. The people that dwel therein shalbe forgiuen their iniquitie *Isa.* xxxiii. 24. 4. F. me if I remind you, that [etc.] SCOTT. 5. To err is human, to f. divine POPE. 6. Thy frailtie and infirmer Sex forgiv'n MILT. *P. L.* x. 956. F. these wild and wandering cries TENNYSON.

Hence **Forgi·ver. Forgi·ving** *ppl. a.* that forgives; inclined to f.; indicating forgiveness. **Forgi·ving·ly** *adv.*, **-ness.**

Forgiveness (fǫɹgi·vnės). [OE. *forgifennys*, f. *forgifen* forgiven + -NESS.] 1. The action of forgiving; the condition or fact of being forgiven. 2. Disposition or willingness to forgive ME. b. in *pl.* (A Hebraism.) 1611.

1. In whom we have..the f. of sins *Eph.* i. 7. The f. of injuries BUTLER. 2. But there is f. with thee, that thou mayest be feared *Ps.* cxxx. 4. b. To the Lord our God belong mercies and forgiuenesses *Dan.* ix. 9.

Forgo, forego (fǫɹ-, fōᵊɹgōᵘ·), *v.* Pa. t. **for-, forewent.** Pa. pple. **for-, foregone.** [OE. *forgán, -gangan*; see FOR- *pref.*[1] and GO.] †1. *intr.* To go past, pass away –1563. †2. *trans.* To go by, pass over (*lit.* and *fig.*). Hence, to neglect, overlook, slight. *Obs.* exc. *arch.* OE. 3. To go from, forsake, leave. *Obs.* exc. *arch.* ME. 4. To abstain from; to let go or pass; to give up OE. †5. Only in pa. pple.: Exhausted with going, wearied; faint –1597.

3. Their altars they f., their homes they quit WORDSW. 4. I am vnarm'd, forgoe this vantage, Greeke *Tr. & Cr.* v. viii. 9. He had foregone to be a Christian HAWTHORNE. Hence **Forgo·er.**

Forgotten: see FORGET *v.*

Forhale: see FOR- *pref.*[1] 4.

†**Fori·nsecal,** *a.* 1539. [f. L. *forinsecus* (adv.) out of doors + -AL.] = FOREIGN *a.* in various senses –1732.

Forisfamiliate (foᵊ:ris₍fămi·li₍eⁱt), *v.* Pa. pple. *Sc.* **-at, -ate.** 1609. [f. ppl. stem of med. L. *forisfamiliare*, f. *foris* outside + *familia* family.] *Civil* and *Sc. Law.* To emancipate (a son) by assigning to him part of the heritage and giving him seisin thereof. Hence **Fo:risfami:lia·tion,** the action of forisfamiliating (a son); also *transf.*

Forjudge, forejudge (fǫɹdʒɒ·dʒ), *v.* ME. [ad. OF. *for-, fors-, fourjugier*, f. *for(s-*, FOR- *pref.*[3] + *jugier* JUDGE *v.* In sense 2 app. f. FOR-[1].] 1. To exclude, oust, or dispossess by a judgement. *Obs.* exc. in *Law.* 1470. †2. To condemn judicially (*to* a penalty) –1697.

1. To be forejudged of life and limb BLACKSTONE. Hence †**Forjudgement.**

Fork (fǫɹk), *sb.* [OE. *forca* masc., *force* fem., ad. L. *furca.*]

I. 1. An instrument consisting of a long straight handle, furnished at the end with two or more prongs or tines, and used for carrying, digging, lifting, or throwing; often specialized as *dung-, hay-,* etc. *f.* †b. The forked tongue of a snake. SHAKS. 2. An instrument with two, three, or four prongs, used at table, in cooking, etc. 1463. 3. *pl.* The prongs of a fork. Also *transf.* 1674. 4. A steel instrument with two prongs which, when set in vibration, gives a musical note; a *tuning-fork* 1799.

1. b. Thou dost feare the soft and tender forke Of a poore worme SHAKS. 3. *transf.* A thunderbolt with three forks ADDISON.

II. An object having two (or more) branches. †1. A gallows –1680. 2. A stake, staff, or stick with a forked end; used as a prop, a rest, or the like ME. b. A divining-rod 1886. †3. The barbed head of an arrow. *Lear* I. i. 146. 4. *techn.* a. A piece of steel fitting into the chuck of a lathe, used for carrying round the piece to be turned 1858. b. The front or back projection of a saddle 1833. 5. *Mining.* The bottom of the sump 1778. 6. [f. the vb.] A forking, bifurcation, or division into branches; the point at which anything forks. Hence, each of the branches. (See quots.) ME.

5. When a mine is *in fork* the bottom of the engine-shaft is clear of water 1869. 6. The thigh, and entire leg from the f. to the ankle BAKER. The f. of a road W. IRVING, of a plant or tree 1843, of flame 1871, of a river 1877.

Comb.: **f.-beam** (*Naut.*) 'a forked piece of timber, scarphed, tabled, and bolted, for additional security to the sides of beams athwart large openings in the decks' (Weale); **-beard,** any of various fishes of the genus *Phycis*; **-chuck** (*Wood-turning*), a chuck with two or more teeth; **-moss,** *Dicranum bryoïdes*; **-wrench,** a spanner with two jaws which embrace a nut or square on a coupling.

Fork (fǫɹk), *v.* ME. [f. prec.] 1. *intr.* To form a fork; to divide into branches. Of corn: To sprout 1707. †Also *fig.* 2. *trans.* To make fork-shaped 1640. 3. To raise or move with or as with a fork; to dig, take, or throw *in, out, up,* etc., with a fork 1802. 4. *Mining.* To pump (a mine) dry; to remove (water) by pumping 1702.

1. The lightning forked and flashed 1851. Here the road forked 1853. 3. To f. hay 1802. Phr. *To f. out, over,* or *up*: to give up, hand over, pay; F. out your balance in hand DICKENS. 4. The mine has been 'forked' 1893.

Forked (fǫɹkt), *ppl. a.* ME. [f. FORK *sb.* + -ED[2].] 1. Having a fork; shaped like a fork, bifurcate, branching. b. Having (so many) forks or prongs, as *three-f.* 1535. †c. Of an arrow: Barbed –1673. 2. Two-legged. *Lear* III. iv. 113. 3. Horned 1586. †4. Of an argument, etc.: That points more than one way; containing a dilemma; equivocal –1681. 5. *ellipt.* for *f.-headed* or *-tailed* 1674.

1. Like a f. Radish, with a Head fantastically caru'd vpon it SHAKS. F. Light'nings 1729. Yon f... hill SHELLEY. A three-f. flickering tongue BOWEN. 4. Giue f. counsel; take prouoking gold On eyther hand, and put it vp B. JONS. **Fo·rked-ly** *adv.*, **-ness.**

Fo·rk-head. 1590. †1. An arrow with barbed head. SPENSER. 2. *Mech.* 'The double head of a rod which divides in order to form a connection by means of a pin' (Knight) 1874. b. = CROSS-TAIL. 1839.

Fork-tail. 1611.

†A. *adj.* = *forked-tail(ed.*

B. *sb.* 1. A salmon in the fourth year of its growth 1753. 2. Formerly applied in England to the Kite; now in India to birds of the genus *Henicurus*. NEWTON. Hence **Fork-tailed** *a.* having a forked tail.

Forky (fǭ·ɹki), *a.* 1508. [f. FORK *sb.* + -Y[1].] Shaped like a fork, forked. Also *fig.* and *allusively.*

A meagre man with a..black f. beard SWIFT. Hence **Fo·rkiness,** the condition of being f.

Forlay: see FORELAY.

†**Forlea·ve,** *v.* ME. only. [f. FOR- *pref.*[1] + LEAVE *v.*] *trans.* To leave behind, give up, abandon.

†**Forle·se,** *v.* Pa. pple. **forloren, forlorn.** [OE. *forléosan*, f. FOR- *pref.*[1] + *-léosan*, ME. *lesen*; see LESE *v.* After 15th c. only in pa. pple.] 1. *trans.* To LOSE, in various senses –1663. 2. To destroy, cause to perish –1664. 3. To leave, forsake –1600.

†**Forle·t,** *v.* [OE. *forlǽtan*; see FOR- *pref.*[1] and LET *v.*[1]] 1. *trans.* To allow –ME. 2. To leave, forsake; to abandon –1610. 3. To omit; to cease from –ME. 4. To let go –ME.

Forlore: pa. t. and pple. of FORLESE.

Forlorn (fǫɹlǭ·ɹn). OE. [pa. pple. of FORLESE.]

A. *adj.* †1. Lost, not to be found 1577. †2. Morally lost; depraved –1683. 3. †Lost, doomed to destruction –1719; desperate, hopeless 1603. 4. Abandoned, forsaken; desolate 1535. 5. In pitiful condition, wretched 1582.

3. †*F. fort*: one held at extreme risk. [We] sit down in a f. Scepticism BERKELEY. 4. Yon dreary Plain, f. and wilde MILT. *P. L.* I. 180. Like one that..is of sense f. COLERIDGE. 5. His f. appearance GIBBON.

†B. *sb.* 1. A forlorn person –1814. 2. Short for FORLORN HOPE. Also *pl.*, the men forming a forlorn hope. Also *transf.* and *fig.* 1645.

1. Forc'd to liue in Scotland a Forlorne SHAKS. 2. Captain Ireton with a f. of Colonel Rich's regiment CROMWELL. *fig.* Criticks..Who..still charge first, the true f. of wit DRYDEN.

Hence **Forlo·rn-ly** *adv.*, **-ness.**

Forlo·rn ho·pe. 1539. [ad. Du. *verloren hoop*, lit. 'lost troop' (*hoop* = HEAP). Cf. F. *enfants perdus.*] 1. Orig., a picked body of men, detached to the front to begin the attack. Now usually, a storming-party. Also *transf.* and *fig.* 1572. b. *pl.* Reckless bravos 1539. c. A desperate enterprise 1768. 2. With word-play: A faint hope, a 'hope against hope' 1641.

1. c. The wary .. never went upon a forlorn hope JUNIUS. 2. She had had a forlorn hope of a letter 1885.

Form (fǭɹm), *sb.* ME. [a. OF. *fo(u)rme, furme*, ad. L. *forma* shape.] 1. The visible aspect of a thing; now usu., shape, configuration; *occas.*, the figure of the body as dist. from the face ME. b. *pl.* The shape of the different parts of the body 1837. c. *Crystallogr.* A set of faces symmetrically related 1878. †d. Beauty, comeliness –1632. †2. An image, likeness, or representation (of a body). Also *fig.* –1610. 3. A body considered in respect to its outward shape; *esp.* that of a person ME. 4. *Philos.* a. In the Scholastic philosophy: The essential determinant principle of a thing; that which makes anything (*matter*) a determinate species or kind of being; the essential creative quality ME. b. In Bacon's usage: The objective conditions on which a sensible quality or body depends for its existence 1605. c. In Kant: That (subjective) factor of knowledge which gives reality and objectivity to the thing known 1803. 5. The particular mode in which a thing exists or manifests itself ME.; a species, kind, variety 1542. b. *Gram.* (*a*) One of the various modes of pronunciation, spelling, or inflexion under which a word may appear. (*b*) The external characteristics of words, as dist. from their signification. 1861. 6. †a. *gen.* A grade or degree of rank, quality, excellence, or eminence –1710. b. *spec.* One of the numbered classes into which the pupils of a school are divided according to proficiency 1560. †7. A model, type, or pattern –1690. 8. Due shape; regularity, good order; also, military formation 1595. 9. Style of expressing the thoughts and ideas in composition, including the arrangement and order of the parts. Also, good or just order (of ideas, etc.); †logical sequence. 1551. †10. Manner, method, way (of doing anything) –1641. 11. Formal procedure (*e.g.* at law) ME. 12. A set or fixed order of words ME. 13. A set method of outward behaviour or procedure; a ceremony or formality. (Often *slightingly*.) 1612. †b. A way of behaving oneself; in *pl.* = manners –1639. 14. Observance of etiquette, ceremony, or decorum. Often *depreciatively*: Mere outward ceremony or formality. ME. 15. *Sporting.* Of a horse: Condition in regard to health and training; fitness; style and speed in running. Said also of athletes and players generally. 1760. b. *transf.* Liveliness, high spirits, conversational powers, or the like. *colloq.* 1877.

1. Her face was expressive: her f. wanted no feminine charm MACAULAY. In the f. of a globe (*mod.*). In painting, colour is subordinate to f. (*mod.*). d. Hee hath no forme nor comelinesse *Isa.* liii. 2. 3. To forget the f. I loved COLERIDGE. 5. For Forms of Government let fools contest POPE. A f. of cold BAIN. 6. a. A Physician of the first f. 1710. 8. In goodly f. comes on the enemy SHAKS. 9. *Haml.* III. i. 171. *spec.* (*Mus.*) the shape and order in which musical ideas are presented 1876. 10. Phr. *In like f.*: in like manner. 11. A paper..sent to me as a matter of f. 1787. Phr. *In f.* (now usu. *in due* or *proper f.*). 12. Any set f. of common prayer HOOKER. The f. of the fine is [etc.] CRUISE. 13. The Forms and Civilities of the last Age ETHEREDGE. It doth much adde to a Mans Reputation .. to have good Formes BACON. 14. The glass of fashion and the mould of f. SHAKS. Phr. *In (full, great) f. Good* (or *bad*) *f.*: (good or bad) manners. 15. Phr. *In f.*: in condition; so *out of f.*

II. 1. A long seat without a back. [So OF. *forme*, med. L. *forma*.] ME. 2. *Mech.* A mould, shape, or implement on which anything is fashioned 1653. 3. *Printing.* A body of type, secured in a chase, for printing at one impression. (Often *forme*.) 1481. 4. The nest or lair in which a hare crouches. Also *rarely*, of a deer. Also *transf.* ME.

4. *transf.* Some Fames are most difficult to trace home to their f. FULLER.

Comb. f.-word (*Gram.*), a word serving the function of an inflexion.

Form (fǭɹm), *v.*[1] ME. [a. OF. *fourmer* (F. *former*), ad. L. *formare*, f. *forma* FORM *sb.*] 1. *trans.* To give form or shape to; to fashion, mould ME. b. To give a specified form to; to mould or fashion *into*, *after*, *by*, *from*, *upon*; to conform *to* ME. 2. To mould by discipline or education; to train, instruct. Also *refl.* ME. 3. To place in order, arrange. Also, to embody, organize *into* ME. Also *intr.* for *refl.* 4. To construct, frame; to bring into existence, produce. Const. *from*, *of*, *out of*. Also, to articulate (a word, etc.). ME. b. To frame in the mind, conceive; †to imagine 1595. c. *refl.* and *intr.* for *refl.* 1801. 5. To develop in oneself (habits); to enter into, contract (an alliance, friendship, etc.) 1736. 6. To go to make up, to compose ME.; to serve for; to make *one* or *part of* ME. 7. *Gram.* To construct by derivation, composition, etc. 1824. 8. *Mil.* and *Naval.* To draw up (troops, etc.) in order ME. Also *refl.* and *intr.* 1722.

1. The Rib he formd and fashond with his hands MILT. b. A state formed after the model of Crete JOWETT. 2. Van Helmont..was formed in the school of Alchemy SIR H. DAVY. Men formed for command (*mod.*). 4. The sound of mans voice was not yet formed 2 *Esdras* vi. 39. b. To f. an estimate BURKE, a notion 1861, a judgment MARTINEAU. 5. Active habits are to be formed by exercise BUTLER. To f. a junction 1781, connexions COWPER. 6. Letters four do f. his name COLERIDGE. 8. *intr.* Riflemen f. TENNYSON. Phr. *To f. the siege* (*of* a place): to commence active siege-operations against it.

Form (fǭɹm), *v.*[2] 1575. [f. the sb.: see FORM *sb.* II. 4.] *intr.* Of a hare: To take to her form; to seat.

First think which way shee fourmeth, on what wind B. JONS.

Form- (fǭɹm), in *Chem.*, combining form of FORMIC or FORMYL, as in Fo·rmamide, the amide of formic acid. (Cf. the termination of *chloro-form*.)

-form (fǭɹm), repr. F. *-forme*, L. *-formis*, f. *forma* FORM *sb.*, a termination used to form adjs. (1) with the sense 'having the form of', as in *cruciform*, etc.; (2) referring to number of forms, as *uniform*, etc. The termination is always preceded by *-i-*.

Formal (fǭ·ɹmăl). ME. [ad. L. *formalis*; see -AL. Cf. F. *formel*.] A. *adj.* 1. Pertaining to FORM. a. *Metaph.* Pertaining to the constitutive essence of a thing. Opp. to *material*. So *formal cause* (see CAUSE *sb.*). ME. b. Pertaining to the visible form, arrangement, or external qualities of a thing 1639. c. *Logic.* Concerned with the form, as dist. from the matter, of reasoning 1856. d. Of or pertaining to conventionality. POPE. 2. That is (so and so) in respect of form 1563. 3. That is according to form or rule ME. †b. Of a story, etc.: Circumstantial –1708. †4. a. Regular, methodical –1701. b. Of feature, stature, etc.: Regular –1576. c. Normal in intellect, sane 1590. 5. Done or made with the forms that ensure validity; explicit and definite 1547. 6. Ceremonial, 'state' 1602. 7. That is merely matter of form 1648. 8. Of persons, their manners and actions: Rigorously observant of forms; precise; prim in attire; ceremonious. Usually *reproachful*. 1514. 9. Marked by excessive regularity or symmetry; wanting in ease or freedom 1597.

1. a. For deceit is the f., constituent reason of hypocrisy SOUTH. d. Still in constraint your suff'ring Sex remains, Or bound in f., or in real chains POPE. 2. *F. sin* (Theol.): one which is such not merely in the outward act, but in the constitutive circumstances, *e.g.* intention. So *f. schism*, *schismatic*, etc. †*F. Protestants*, i.e. those who are such merely in outward form. 3. A f. sylogysme MORE, siege DE FOE, courtship FIELDING. 4. c. With wholsome sirrups, drugges, and holy prayers To make of him a formall man againe *Com. Err.* v. i. 105. 5. A f. decision JUNIUS, inhibition FROUDE. 6. A f. call 1875. 7. A f. preachment MILTON, act CRUISE. 8. F. bows PRIOR. 9. The old f. school of gardening 1874.

B. *sb.* In *pl.* Things that are formal 1605.

Forma·ldehyde. 1873. Formic aldehyde, used in solution as a disinfectant. Hence Fo·rmalin [-IN[1]] 1893.

Formalism (fǭ·ɹmăliz'm). 1840. [f. FORMAL *a.* + -ISM.] 1. Strict or excessive adherence to prescribed forms; an instance of this. 2. The disposition to exalt what is formal or outward, *esp.* in matters of religion 1856.

1. The constitutional f. of three reigns STUBBS. 2. The family devotions were long, but there was no f. FROUDE.

Formalist (fǭ·ɹmălist). 1607. [f. as prec. + -IST.] †1. A solemn pretender to wisdom. BACON. †2. A time-server in religion –1632. 3. A stickler for forms, etiquette, routine, or ceremonial 1637.

3. Though the f. will say, what no decency in Gods worship MILTON. Hence **Formali·stic** *a.*

Formality (fǫɹmæ·lĭti). 1531. [ad. L. *formalitas*. Cf. F. *formalité*.] †1. Formal or essential nature –1737. †b. Formal aspect or category –1668. †2. That which pertains to outward form –1649. †3. Method, regularity; uniform practice –1655. †4. Literary or artistic form –1677. 5. Conformity to rule; customary propriety. Often *depreciatively*. 1597. 6. Ceremony, elaborate procedure 1666. 7. A ceremony; a formal act or observance 1674. 8. Something required to be done for form's sake (often *depreciatively*) 1647; †ceremonious attention –1726. 9. *pl.* or *collect. sing.* Robes or insignia of office or dignity. *Obs.* exc. *Hist.* 1575. 10. The attribute of being formal; precision; excessive regularity or stiffness 1599.

1. Motion is the f. of wind GOAD. 3. Such Judges (whose f. was first to Imprison, and after, at their leisure, to Examine) CLARENDON. 5. The attyre.. being a matter of meere formalitie HOOKER. 6. To Gresham College..where a great deal of do and f. in choosing of the Council PEPYS. 8. Fasts, vigils, formalities, and mass-work CARLYLE. 10. The frozen f. ..of Charles occasioned extreme disgust 1789.

Formalize (fǭ·ɹmăləiz), *v.* 1597. [f. FORMAL *a.* + -IZE.] †1. *trans.* To give formal being to; to 'inform' –1678. 2. To give definite shape to 1646. 3. To render formal 1855. 4. *intr.* To act with formality 1656. †5. To cavil at, or (*intr.*) to cavil; also (*intr.*) to affect scruples –1797. Hence **Fo·rmaliza·tion.**

Formally (fǭ·ɹmăli), *adv.* ME. [f. FORMAL *a.* + -LY[2].] 1. In formal respects 1570. †2. In good form –1548. †3. According to the principles of art or science –1597. †4. Regularly –1674. 5. Explicitly 1523. 6. In prescribed or customary form; statedly 1564. 7. Ceremoniously 1611. 8. As a matter of form 1870.

1. Hence what is f. correct may be materially false 1864. 5. You and your followers do stand f. divided against the authorised guides of the church HOOKER. 6. Waller..has f. refused H. WALPOLE.

‖**Format** (fǭ·ɹmæt, fǭ·ɹmā, ‖forma). 1840. [ad. F. (18th century); ad. G. *format* (17th century), ad. pa. pple. of L. *formare* FORM *v.*[1]; see -ATE *suffix*[2].] The shape and size of a book, e.g. folio, quarto, octavo.

Formate (fǭ·ɹmĕt), *sb.* Also (less well) formiate. 1807. [f. FORM(IC) + -ATE.] *Chem.* A salt of formic acid.

Formation (fǫɹmē¹·ʃən). 1450. [ad. L. *formationem*; see -ATION.] 1. A putting or coming into form; creation, production. 2. *concr.* The thing formed 1646. 3. The manner in which a thing is formed; formal structure, conformation 1774. 4. *Mil.* An arrangement or disposition of troops 1796. 5. *Geol.* 'Any assemblage of rocks, which have some character in common, whether of origin, age, or composition' (Lyell) 1815.

1. The F. of the Body in the Womb COWLEY. 3. Remarks..as to the f. of clouds 1808. 4. The usual Roman f. in battle was in triple line FROUDE.

Formative (fǭ·ɹmătiv), *a.* (*sb.*) 1490. [a. OF. *formatif*, *-ive*; see FORM *v.* and -IVE.] 1. Having the faculty of forming or fashioning. 2. Of or pertaining to formation or moulding 1850. 3. *Biol.* and *Path.* Producing, or attended with the production of, new tissue 1877. 4. *Gram.* Serving to form words 1711.

1. The f. Word of God GAUDEN. 4. To get at the root of a word we must remove all the f. elements 1872.

B. *sb. Gram.* a. A formative element (see A. 4) 1816. b. 'A word formed in accordance with some rule or usage, as from a root' (Webster).

Hence **Fo·rmative·ly** *adv.*, **-ness.**

†**Fo·rme,** *a.* [OE. *forme*:—OTeut. **formon-*, a superlative (with *-m-* suffix), f. root of FORE *adv.*] 1. First; also, former –1450. 2. Foremost –1523.

quasi-*Comb.*, in **f.-fader**, (*a*) (our) first father, Adam; (*b*) = FOREFATHER; **-moder**, (our) first mother, Eve; **-mete**, breakfast; **-ward**, vanguard.

Forme (*Printing*): see FORM *sb.* II. 3.

Formé, -ée (fǭ·ɹme), *a.* Also **Formy.** 1610. [a. F., f. *former*.] *Her.* = PATTÉE.

Formed (fǭɹmd), *ppl. a.* ME. [f. FORM *v.* + -ED[1].] 1. In senses of FORM *v.* 2. *esp.* †a. Drawn up according to rule; formal, set –1725. b. Decided, definite, settled 1605. c. Perfected by training or discipline; matured 1833. 3. *Her.* = FORMÉ, -ÉE. 1592.

2. b. Without any f. intention of mendacity JAS. MILL.

†**Formedon** (fǭ·ɹmĕdǫn). *Obs.* exc. *Hist.* 1485. [AF., f. Law L. phr. *forma doni* form of gift.] *Law.* A writ of right formerly used for claiming entailed property.

†**Fo·rmel, formal,** *sb.* ME. [a. F. *formel* adj. (see FORMAL), an epithet applied to hawks, perh. in the sense 'regular', 'proper', the female being the better for sport.] The female of the eagle or the hawk. Also *attrib.* –1688.

Formene (fǭ·ɹmīn). 1884. [f. FORM(IC) + -ENE.] Methane or marsh-gas.

Former (fǭ·ɹməɹ), *sb.*[1] ME. [f. FORM *v.* + -ER.[1]] 1. One who forms; a maker, creator, fashioner. 2. A tool or instrument used in forming articles; e.g. a templet, pattern, or gauge by which pottery, etc. is shaped; a cutter by which patterns, etc. are cut; etc. 1644.

†**Fo·rmer,** *sb.*[2] 1530. [ad. OF. *formoir* chisel, f. *former*; see also FIRMER.] A kind of chisel or gouge; said to be used before the paring chisel in all works –1751.

Former (fǭ·ɹməɹ), *a.* OE. [A comparative formed after *formest*, FOREMOST.] 1. Earlier in time. Now chiefly: Pertaining to the past, or to a period anterior to that in question. †b. *Occas.* = FORME, first, primeval –1529. c. Formerly possessed, occupied, etc. ME. 2. *The former* (often *absol.*): a. The first in order of two. †Also the (immediately) preceding. 1588. b. The first mentioned of two; opp. to *latter* 1597. †3. Front, fore –1678.

1. He shall come vnto vs..as the latter and f. raine *Hos.* vi. 3. More like her f. self 1852. b. A Blysful

lyf...Ledden the peoples in the f. age CHAUCER. **d.** *U.S.* Used to designate a former holder of an office ; = English *ex-* 1905.

Formeret (fǭ·ɹmĕrĕt). 1872. [a. F., app. f. *forme* FORM *sb.*] *Arch.* Rib moulding placed at the junction of a vault with the vertical wall.

Formerly (fǭ·ɹməɹli), *adv.* 1590. [f. FORMER *a.* + -LY².] †1. Before another or something else; first –1645. 2. At some past time 1599. †3. Just now –1766.

3. *Merch. V*, IV. i. 362. So †**Fo·rmerness.**

Formful (fǭ·ɹmfŭl), *a.* 1727. [f. FORM *sb.* + -FUL.] Full of form or forms; shapely; imaginative.

Formic (fǭ·ɹmik), *a.* 1791. [for **formicic*, f. L. *formica* ant + -IC.] 1. *Chem.* In *F. acid*: a colourless irritant volatile acid contained in a fluid emitted by ants. 2. Of or pertaining to ants. *rare.* 1816.

Phr. *F. ethers*, ethers obtained by substituting alcoholic radicals for the basic hydrogen of f. acid.

‖**Formica** (fǭɹməi·kă). ME. [L.; = 'ant'.] 1. *Entom.* The typical genus of the family *Formicidæ*, the ant 1865. 2. A kind of ulcer, abscess, or excrescence, occurring *esp.* in a hawk's bill or a dog's ears ME.

Formicarioid (fǭmikēᵊ·riˌoid), *a.* 1874. [f. L. **formicarius* (see next) + -OID.] Of or belonging to the *Formicarioideæ* or ant-thrushes. Also *sb.*, one of this family.

Formicary (fǭ·ɹmikări). 1816. [ad. med. L. *formicarium* (also used), neut. sing. of **formicarius* pertaining to ants, f. L. *formica.*] An ant's nest, ant-hill.

Formicate (fǭ·ɹmikeᵗt), *v.* 1684. [f. ppl. stem of L. *formicare.*] *intr.* To crawl like ants; *transf.* to swarm *with* moving beings.

Formication (fǭɹmikēᵗ·ʃən). 1707. [ad. L. *formicationem.*] *Path.* A sensation as of ants creeping over the skin.

Formicid (fǭ·ɹmisid). Also **-cide.** 1878. [ad. mod. L. *Formicidæ*; see -ID.]

A. *sb.* A member of the family *Formicidæ* or ants.

B. *adj.* Of or belonging to this family.

Formidable (fǭ·ɹmidăb'l), *a.* 1508. [a. F., ad. L. *formidabilem*, f. *formidare* to dread; see -ABLE.] That gives cause for fear or alarm; fit to inspire apprehension. Now usually: Likely to be difficult to deal with; giving cause for apprehension of defeat or failure. Often used playfully.

Barbarossa, that f. pirat 1678. Swords of f. dimensions 1834. Hence **Fo·rmidabi·lity, Fo·rmidableness,** the quality of being f. **Fo·rmidably** *adv.*

†**Formi·dolous,** *a.* 1656. [ad. L. *formidolosus*, f. *formido* dread.] Fearful, terrible; also, timorous –1773.

Forming (fǭ·ɹmiŋ), *vbl. sb.* ME. [f. FORM *v.*¹ + -ING¹.] The action of FORM *v.*¹; the fact or process of being formed.

The f. of mens wils to the observation of the Law HOBBES.

Formless (fǭ·ɹmlės), *a.* 1591. [f. FORM *sb.* + -LESS.] Devoid of, or wanting in, form; shapeless; having no determinate or regular form.

The rising world of waters..won from the void and f. infinite MILT. **Fo·rmless·ly** *adv.*, **-ness.**

Formo- (fǭ·ɹmo). 1834. *Chem.* Comb. f. FORMIC.

Formula (fǭ·ɹmiŭlă). *Pl.* **-æ, -as.** 1638. [a. L., dim. of *forma.* Cf. F. *formule.*] 1. A set form of words in which something is defined, stated, or declared, or which is prescribed by custom or authority for use on ceremonial occasions. In recent use, after Carlyle, often applied disparagingly. 2. A prescription or detailed statement of ingredients; a recipe 1706. 3. *Math.* A rule or principle expressed in algebraic symbols 1796. 4. *Chem.* An expression of the constituents of a compound by means of symbols and figures 1846. 5. In general scientific use, a group of symbols and figures condensing a set of facts 1855.

1. The excellent scholastic f. *Transeat*, meaning either 'Not proven', or 'Nothing to the purpose' 1892. Man lives not except with formulas; with customs, ways of doing and living CARLYLE. 5. *Dental f.*: see DENTAL.

Formular (fǭ·ɹmiŭlăɹ). 1563. [f. prec. As sb., a. F. *formulaire*; see -AR¹, ².]

A. *adj.* 1. Formal, correct in form 1773. 2. Pertaining to formulæ; formulary 1880.

B. *sb.* A prescribed or set form, formulary; hence, a pattern, type. ? *Obs.* 1563.

Hence **Fo·rmulari·stic** *a.* pertaining to or exhibiting formularization. **Fo·rmularize** *v.* to express in a formula; to formulate. **Fo:rmulariza·tion,** the action of formularizing.

Formulary (fǭ·ɹmiŭlări). 1541. [ad. F. *formulaire* sb. = collection of formulæ; see FORMULA and -ARY.]

A. *sb.* A collection or system of formulas; a statement drawn up in formulas; a document containing the set form or forms according to which something is to be done. b. ? A formula 1782.

A committee of council to settle the f. of the coronation NORTH.

B. *adj.* Of the nature of a formula; of or relating to formulas 1728. Of a person: Adhering to formulas. CARLYLE.

Formulate (fǭ·ɹmiŭleᵗt), *v.* 1860. [f. FORMULA + -ATE³.] To reduce to, or express in (or as in), a formula; to set forth in a definite and systematic statement.

Hence **Formula·tion.**

†**Fo·rmule,** *sb.* 1677. [a. F., ad. L. *formula.*] = FORMULA. –1773.

Formulism (fǭ·ɹmiŭliz'm). 1840. [f. FORMULA + -ISM.] Adherence to or dependence on formulas; also, a system of formulas. So **Fo·rmulist,** one fond of formulas. **Formuli·stic** *a.* displaying fondness for formulas.

Formulize (fǭ·ɹmiŭləiz), *v.* 1851. [f. FORMULA + -IZE.] To reduce to or express in a formula. Hence **Formuliza·tion.**

Formyl (fǭ·ɹmil). 1879. [f. FORM- + -YL.] *Chem.* The hypothetical radical (CHO) of formic acid.

Fornical (fǭ·ɹnikăl), *a.* [f. L. *fornicem* arch + -AL.] Pertaining to the fornix.

Fornicate (fǭ·ɹnikeᵗt), *v.* 1552. [f. L. *fornicat-, fornicari*, f. *fornic-, fornix* brothel, orig. arch, vaulted chamber.] *intr.* To commit fornication.

Fornicate (fǭ·ɹnikĕt), *a.* 1828. [ad. L. *fornicatus*, f. *fornix*; see -ATE².] = next.

Fornicated (fǭ·ɹnikeᵗtėd), *ppl. a.* [f. L. *fornicatus* (see prec.) + -ED¹.] Arched, bending over; *esp.* in *Bot.* of a leaf, etc.

Fornication¹ (fǭɹnikēᵗ·ʃən). ME. [a. OF., f. late L. *fornicationem*; see FORNICATE *v.* and -ATION.] Voluntary sexual intercourse between a man (strictly, an unmarried man) and an unmarried woman. In Scripture extended to adultery. b. *fig.* The forsaking of God for idols, idolatry ME.

Fornication² (fǭɹnikēᵗ·ʃən). 1703. [ad. L. *fornicationem*, f. *fornicatus* vaulted; see -ATION.] *Arch.* An arching or vaulting.

Fornicator (fǭ·ɹnikeᵗtəɹ). ME. [a. L.; see FORNICATE.] One who commits fornication. So **Fo·rnicatress,** a woman given to or guilty of fornication.

Fornix (fǭ·ɹniks). 1681. [a. L.] Something resembling an arch. a. *Anat.* An arched formation of the brain. b. *Bot.* A small elongation of the corolla 1823. c. *Conchol.* The excavated part of a shell, situated under the umbo 1848.

Forpa·ss, *v.* ME. [ad. OF. *for-, fourpasser*, f. *fors*, FOR- *pref.*³ + *passer* to PASS; in Spenser the prefix is app. taken as FORE-.] 1. *trans.* To go beyond –1579. 2. *intr.* To pass beyond. In Spenser: To go past. –1591.

As he forpassed by the plaine With weary pace SPENSER.

Forpi·ne, *v. Obs.* exc. *arch.* ME. [f. FOR- *pref.*¹ + PINE *v.*] *trans.* To cause to pine.

Pale as a for-pyned goost CHAUCER.

Forrader (fǫ·rədəɹ), *adv.* 1898. Colloq. pronunc. of *forwarder* 'more or further forward', as in *no f.*

Forra(y, obs. f. FORAY.

Forsake (fǫ̆ɹsēᵗ·k), *v.* Pa. t. **forsook** (fǫ̆ɹsu·k). Pa. pple. **forsaken** (fǫ̆ɹsēᵗ·k'n). [OE *forsacan*, f. FOR- *pref.*¹ + *sacan* to contend, dispute, deny.] †1. *trans.* To deny –1537. †2. To decline or refuse –1605. 3. To give up, surrender OE.; to break off from, renounce ME. 4. To abandon, leave entirely, withdraw from; to desert ME.

2. He..forsooke a right worshipful roome when it was offered to him CAMDEN. 3. Forsaking country, kindred, friends COWPER. To f. idolatry 1894. 4. Thou hast forsook Thy Juba's cause ADDISON. Larks ..f. that climate in winter GOLDSM. *absol.* He'll learn to flatter and f. PRAED.

Hence **Forsa·ken,** †**forsake** *ppl. a.* deserted, left solitary or desolate; †morally abandoned. **Forsa·ken·ly** *adv.*, **-ness. Forsa·ker** (now *rare*).

†**Forsay, Forseek,** etc.: see FOR- *pref.*¹

†**Forsha·pe,** *v.* [OE. *forsceppan*; see FOR- *pref.*¹ and SHAPE *v.*] *trans.* To metamorphose; to misshape, disfigure –1532.

†**Forsla·ck, foreslack,** *v.* ME. [f. FOR- *pref.*¹ + SLACK *v.*] 1. *intr.* To be or grow slack. *rare.* –1579. 2. *trans.* To neglect; to lose or spoil by slackness –1660.

†**Forslo·th,** *v.* ME. [f. FOR- *pref.*¹ + SLOTH *v.*] *trans.* To lose, neglect, spoil, or waste through sloth –1557.

Forslow·, foreslow·, *v.* [OE. *forslāwian*, f. FOR- *pref.*¹ + *slāwian* to be slow.] 1. *trans.* To be slow about; to lose or spoil by sloth; to put off. *Obs.* exc. *arch.* 2. *intr.* To make slow, hinder, obstruct. *Obs.* exc. *arch.* 1563. †3. *intr.* To be slow or dilatory –1593.

3. Foreslow no longer, make we hence amaine SHAKS.

Forsooth (fǫ̆ɹsū·þ), *adv.* [OE. *forsōð*; see FOR *prep.* and SOOTH *sb.*] 1. In truth, truly. Now only parenthetically with an ironical or derisive statement. 2. quasi-*sb.* 1712.

1. For sute, madam, I lost all that I payd for him 1481. She has no Secrets, f. STEELE. 2. Her innocent *forsooths* STEELE. Hence **Forsoo·th** *v.* to say f. to, treat ceremoniously PEPYS. **Forsoo·th** *sb.* one who says 'forsooth' freq., an affected speaker. B. JONS.

Forspeak (fǫ̆ɹspī·k), *v.* Also **fore-.** ME. [f. FOR- *pref.*¹ + SPEAK.] 1. To bewitch. Now *Sc.* †2. To forbid, renounce –1579. †3. To speak against –1611.

3. *Ant. & Cl.* III. vii. 3.

Forspend, forespend (fǫ̆ɹspe·nd), *v.* [OE. *forspendan*; see FOR- *pref.*¹ and SPEND *v.*] *trans.* To spend completely; to wear out; *rare* exc. in pa. pple. and ppl. adj. 1571.

Forstall: see FORESTALL.

†**Forstrau·ght,** *pa. pple.* ME. [f. FOR- *pref.*¹ + *straught* in DISTRAUGHT.] Distracted. CHAUCER.

†**Forswa·t,** *ppl. a.* ME. [pa. pple. of **forsweat*, f. FOR- *pref.*¹ + SWEAT *v.*] Covered with sweat –1580.

Forswear (fǫ̆ɹswēᵊ·ɹ), *v.* Pa. t. **forswore** (-swǭᵊ·ɹ). Pa. pple. **forsworn** (-swǭ·ɹn). [OE. *forswerian*; see FOR- *pref.*¹ and SWEAR *v.*] 1. *trans.* = ABJURE. 2. To deny or repudiate on oath or with strong asseveration ME. 3. *intr.* To swear falsely, commit perjury OE. Also *refl.*, Also *pass.* to be guilty of perjury. 4. *trans.* To swear (something) falsely; to break (an oath); to forsake (sworn allegiance) 1580.

1. I shall f. your company SHERIDAN. 2. If thou durst, [thou] would'st f. thy own hand and seal ARBUTHNOT. 3. Thou shalt not forswere WYCLIF *Matt.* v. 33. He sware by his fathers soule, wherby he was neuer forsworne LD. BERNERS. Hence **Forswea·rer,** a perjurer. **Forswo·rn,** †**forswore** *ppl. a.* perjured; falsely sworn. **Forswo·rnness,** perjury.

Forsythia (fǫɹsəi·þiă). 1814. [mod.L., f. the name of William *Forsyth* (1737–1804), English botanist: see -IA ¹.] Any plant of the genus of spring-flowering shrubs so named, having bright-yellow bell-shaped flowers.

Fort (fōᵊɹt), *sb.* 1557. [F. *fort* adj. used *absol.*] 1. *Mil.* A fortified place; a position fortified for defensive or protective purposes, usually surrounded with a ditch, rampart, and parapet, and garrisoned with troops; a fortress. b. In British N. Amer. and U.S.: A trading station (orig. fortified) 1776. 2. Now = FORTE, q.v.

1. *fig.* If there were sought in knowledge..a f. or commanding ground for strife BACON.

Fort (fōᵊɹt), *v.* ? *Obs.* 1559. [f. FORT *sb.*] *trans.* To defend or protect with a fort; to fortify; to enclose in a fort; also with *in.*

It deserues..A forted residence, 'gainst the tooth of time *Meas. for M.* v. i. 12.

Fortalice (fǭ·ɹtălis). †Also **fortilage, fortiless,** etc. ME. [ad. med. L. *fortalitia*, f.

fortis strong.] In early use = FORTRESS; now chiefly used for: A small fort. Also *transf.* and *fig.*

Nought feard their force, that fortilage to win SPENSER.

Forte (fōᵊɹt), *sb.* 1648. [a. F. *fort*: see FORT *a.* The fem. form of the Fr. adj. has been ignorantly substituted for the masc.; cf. *locale*, etc.] **1.** The strong point, that in which one excels 1682. **2.** *Fencing.* The strongest part of a sword-blade. Also *fig.* 1648.

1. Those things are not our f. at Covent Garden GOLDSM. 2. *fig.* Acquainted..with his 'forte' and his 'foible' DE QUINCEY.

‖**Forte** (fǭ·ɹte). 1724. [It. = 'strong, loud'.] *Mus.*

A. *adj.* (*adv.*) A direction: Strong, loud. Also *forte forte* very loud. (Abbrev. *f.*, *ff.*)

B. *sb.* 'Forte' tone; a 'forte' passage 1759.

Forte-piano (fǭ·ɹtepiā·no). 1769. [It.; see FORTE and PIANO.]

A. *adj.* (*adv.*) *Mus.* A direction: Loud, then suddenly soft. (Abbrev. *fp.*)

B. *sb.* The original name of the PIANOFORTE.

Forth (fōᵊɹþ). [OE. *forð*:— OTeut. **furþo*-:— pre-Teut. **pṛto*-, f. root of FORE *adv.* + suffix -*to*-.]

A. *adv.* **1.** Forwards; opp. to backwards. †Also with ellipsis of *go*. †**2.** Onwards from a specified point -1535. †**b.** In ME. *forth mid, with* = 'along with'. **3.** Onwards in time. Now only in *from this time* (*day*, etc.) *f.* (somewhat *arch.*) OE. †**b.** Joined to a vb., with sense 'to go on doing' what the vb. denotes. Cf. *on*. 1808. †**4.** At or to an advanced point -1485. **5.** Forward, into view. Only with *bring, come, show*, and the like. Now often repl. by *out*. OE. **6.** Away or out from a place of origin, residence, or sojourn. Also with ellipsis of *go* (now *arch.*). Now often repl. by *out*. OE. †**7.** Abroad -1607.

1. Then f., deare Countreymen *Hen. V*, II. ii. 189. 2. *Right f.* (see RIGHT *a.*). 5. Stretch f. your Hand 1692. 6. In form of Battel drawn, they issue f. DRYDEN. Maternity must f. to the streets CARLYLE. 7. Say he dines f. SHAKS.

Phrases. **F. of.** = *out of* in various senses. Now only *poet.* or *rhet.* **And so f.** †(*a*) And then in regular sequence. †(*b*) And similarly. (*c*) Now only (like *and so on*): And the like, etcetera. †**As** or **so f.**: as or so far (*as, that*).

B. *prep.* †**1.** Forward to, up to. Chiefly with *even*. Also in *F. that*: until. -1449. **2.** Forward, out or away from; out of, from out of. Now *rare.* 1566.

2. See 'em f. the gates OTWAY. Poor Troy..From f. her ashes shall advance her head 1592.

†**C.** *sb.* In *To have one's f.*: to have outlet; *fig.* to have free course, to have one's fling -1611.

D. Forth- in composition. In mod. Eng. *forth-* is often used as a prefix in the formation of nouns of agent and action, and ppl. adjs. corresponding to the verbal phrases in which the adv. follows the vb. Compound vbs. formed with *forth-* are rare. See Main Words.

Forth(e, obs. f. FORD.

For that, *conj.* ME. [See FOR *prep.* VII. 2.] **1.** For the reason that, because. *arch.* ¶Distinguish the mod. use of *for that* in reported speech (where both words are conjs.). †**2.** For the purpose that; in order that -1572.

1. For that I love your daughter..I must advance the colours of my love *Merry W.* III. iv. 82. ¶He had told them to go to supper..for that nothing more would be done that day MACAULAY.

†**Forthby**, *adv.* ME. = FORBY *adv.* 1. -1489.

Forthcome (fōᵊɹþkɒ·m), *v.* OE. [f. FORTH *adv.* + COME *v.*] *intr.* To come forth. Now only as a back-formation from the *ppl. a.*

Forthcoming (fōᵊɹþkɒ·miŋ), *ppl. a.* 1521. [f. FORTH *adv.* + COMING *ppl. a.*] **1.** About or likely to come forth; also *simply*, coming or approaching (in time); *esp.* ready to appear or be produced when required. **2.** Ready to make or meet advances 1835.

1. Possible but never f. claimants 1893.

†**Forthgo·**, *v.* [OE. *forþgān*; see FORTH *adv.* and GO.] **1.** *intr.* To go forth. Occas. w. cogn. obj. Of day, night, etc.: To pass away, pass. -1600. **2.** To come forth as from a source -ME.

Forthgoing (fōᵊɹþgōᵘ·iŋ), *vbl. sb.* ME. [f. FORTH *adv.* + GOING *vbl. sb.*] A going forth.

Forthgoing (fōᵊɹþgōᵘ·iŋ), *ppl. a. rare.* 1851. [f. as prec. + GOING *ppl. a.*] That goes forth; *esp.* disposed to make advances; enthusiastic.

†**Forthi·nk**, *v.* [Two words: **a.** OE. *forðencan* (f. FOR- *pref.*[1] + *ðencan* to THINK); **b.** f. FOR- *pref.*[1] + OE. *þyncan* to seem.]

I. f. OE. *þyncan*. **1.** *trans.* To displease -1535. **2.** *impers.* and quasi-*impers.* (*It*) *forthinks* (*me, him*, etc.): I, etc., feel regret, repent. Const. *of, for*, or *that*. -1588.

1. A thing that myght the forthenke CHAUCER. 2. It forthinkes me sore that I haue sinned 1588.

II. f. OE. *ðencan*. **1. a.** *trans.* To despise or neglect. OE. only. **b.** *intr.* To be reluctant -ME. **2.** *trans.* To think upon with pain; to regret -1704. **3.** *refl.* To change one's mind; to repent, be sorry. Also *intr.* for *refl.* -1599.

Forthputting (fōᵊɹþpu·tiŋ), *vbl. sb.* 1640. [f. FORTH *adv.* + PUTTING *vbl. sb.*] **1.** The action of putting forth. **2.** *U.S.* Obtrusive behaviour 1861.

Forthputting (fōᵊɹþpu·tiŋ), *ppl. a.* 1570. [f. FORTH *adv.* + PUTTING, pr. pple. of PUT *v.*] That puts forth; *esp.* that puts oneself forward; forward, obtrusive. (Now chiefly *U.S.*)

Forthright (fōᵊɹþˌrəi·t, fōᵊ·ɹþˌrəit), rarely **-rights.** OE. [f. FORTH *adv.* + RIGHT *a.* and *adv.*]

A. *adv.* **1.** Directly forward. **2.** Straightway ME.

2. F. upon his steed [he] Leapt SWINBURNE.

B. *adj.* **1.** Proceeding in a straight course, straight forward OE. **2.** *fig.* Going straight to the point; also, unhesitating 1855.

2. The home-thrust of a f. word LOWELL.

C. *sb.* A straight course or path (*lit.* and *fig.*). Chiefly after Shakespeare.

Here's a maze trod indeede Through fourth rights and meanders *Temp.* III. iii. 3.

Hence **Fo·rthrightness**, straightforwardness.

Fo·rthward, -wards. *Obs.* exc. *arch.* [OE. *forðweard*, f. FORTH *adv.* + -WARD.]

A. *adv.* **1.** Of place: Onward(s, forward ME. **2.** Of time: †**a.** Continually, prospectively. OE. only. **b.** For the future onwards OE.

B. *adj.* = FORWARD *a.* 1470.

Forthwith (fōᵊɹþwi·þ, -wi·ð), *adv.* 1450. [For *forth with* (prep.) = earlier *forth mid*, along with, see FORTH *adv.* 2 b.] Immediately, at once, without delay or interval.

When a defendant is ordered to plead f., he must plead within twenty-four hours WHARTON. So †**Fo·rthwithal** *adv.* (in same sense).

†**For-thy·**, *conj.* [OE. *forðī*, *forðȳ*, f. FOR *prep.* + *ðȳ*, instr. of THE.] For this reason, therefore -1647. Hence **F. that**, earlier **f. the**, because.

Fortieth (fǭ·ɹtiėþ), *a.* (*sb.*) [OE. *féowertigoða*, f. FORTY on the analogy of TENTH.] The ordinal numeral belonging to the cardinal forty.

Phr. *The f. man*: one man in forty. *F. part*: one of forty equal parts of anything. Also *absol.* and quasi-*sb.*

Fortifiable (fǭ·ɹtifəiăb'l), *a.* 1609. [f. FORTIFY *v.* + -ABLE; cf. F. *fortifiable*.] That may be fortified.

Fortification (fǭ·ɹtifikēⁱ·ʃən). 1489. [a. F., ad. L. *fortificationem*.] **1.** The action of fortifying in senses of the vb. 1530. **2.** *Mil.* A defensive work; a wall, earthwork, tower, etc. Chiefly *collect. pl.* 1489. **b.** *transf.* and *fig.* A means of defence 1586.

2. To make Bulwerkes, Brayes..and all other fortifications 1512. *Comb.* **f.-agate**, a variety of agate showing, when polished, markings well described by the name.

Fortifier (fǭ·ɹtifəiˌəɹ). 1552. [f. next + -ER[1].] One who or that which fortifies; one who constructs fortifications; a supporter, upholder.

Fortify (fǭ·ɹtifəi), *v.* ME. [ad. F. *fortifier*, ad. L. *fortificare*, f. *fortis* strong; see -FY.]

I. 1. *trans.* To strengthen structurally 1450; to impart strength or vigour to ME. †**2.** To render more powerful or effective -1725. **3.** To strengthen mentally or morally 1477; to confirm, add support to ME. †**4.** *intr.* To grow strong -1660.

1. To f. a Fabrick with Pitch 1697, a ship with additional timbers 1820. To f. the stomach 1849. 2. He fortified Burdeaux with Englishmen and victayle HALL. 3. Timidity was fortified by pride GIBBON. A charge..fortified by particulars HT. MARTINEAU.

II. To strengthen against attack. **1.** *trans.* To provide with defensive works ME. Also *transf.* **2.** To put in a position of defence 1548. **3.** *intr.* To establish a position of defence. Also *transf.* and *fig.* 1570.

1. The houses haue yee broken downe to fortifie the wall *Isa.* xxii. 10. 3. For such a time do I now fortifie Against confounding Ages cruell knife SHAKS.

Fortilage, fortiless, obs. ff. FORTALICE.

†**Fo·rtin.** 1706. [a. F., dim. of *fort*.] A small fort; a field-fort -1744.

‖**Forti·ssimo**, *adv.* 1724. [It., superl. of *forte*; see FORTE.] *Mus.* Very loud. (Abbrev. *ff.*, *ffor.*, or *fortiss.*) Also quasi-*adj.* and as *sb.*

[**Fortition**, a spurious word: see SORTITION.]

Fortitude (fǭ·ɹtitiūd). 1500. [a. F., ad. L. *fortitudo*; see FORT *a.*] †**1.** Physical or structural strength -1703. **2.** Moral strength or courage. Now only in passive sense: Firmness in the endurance of pain or adversity. (One of the cardinal virtues.) 1500.

1. The F. of the place is best knowne to you *Oth.* I. iii. 222. 2. She could bear the disappointments of other people with tolerable f. DICKENS. So **Forti·tu·dinous** *a.* endowed with or characterized by f.

Fortlet (fǭ·ɹtlėt). ME. [f. FORT *sb.* + -LET.] A small fort.

Fortnight (fǭ·ɹtnəit). [Contr. f. OE. *féowertyne niht* fourteen nights. Cf. SENNIGHT, and see Tacitus *Germania* xi for the ancient Germanic method of reckoning by nights.] A period of fourteen nights; two weeks.

Phr. *This day, Monday,* †*Monday was* (*a*), etc. *f.*: a fortnight from (this day, etc.).

Fortnightly (fǭ·ɹtnəitli). 1800. [f. prec. + -LY.]

A. *adj.* Happening or appearing once in a fortnight.

B. *adv.* Once in a fortnight.

†**Fortrea·d**, *v.* [OE. *fortredan*; see FOR- *pref.*[1] and TREAD *v.*] *trans.* To tread down; to destroy by trampling -1450.

In helle schulle þay be al fortrode of deueles CHAUCER.

Fortress (fǭ·ɹtrės), *sb.* ME. [a. OF. *forteresse* strength, a strong place, f. *fort* strong; a var. of FORTALICE.] A military stronghold, fortified place; now chiefly, one capable of receiving a large force; often applied to a strongly fortified town. Also *transf.* and *fig.*

Fortress (fǭ·ɹtrės), *v.* 1542. [f. prec. sb.] To furnish with a fortress or fortifications; to protect with or as with a fortress. Chiefly *transf.* and *fig.*

Fortuitous (fǫɹtiū·itəs), *a.* 1653. [f. L. *fortuitus*, f. *forte* by chance, f. *fors* + -OUS.] That happens or is produced by fortune or chance; accidental, casual.

A f. rencontre SCOTT. Phr. *F. concourse of atoms*: see CONCOURSE. *F. event* (Law): 'a term in the civil law applied to denote that which happens by a cause which cannot be resisted..Or it is that which neither of the parties has occasioned or could prevent' BOUVIER. Hence **Fortu·itous-ly** *adv.*, **-ness.**

Fortuity (fǫɹtiū·iti). 1747. [irreg. f. L. *fortuitus*; see prec. and -ITY.] Fortuitous character; accident, chance; an accidental occurrence.

Fortunate (fǭ·ɹtiŭnėt), *a.* (*sb.*) ME. [ad. L. *fortunatus*; see FORTUNE *v.*] **1.** Favoured by fortune; possessed of or receiving good fortune; lucky, prosperous. Const. *to* and *inf.* **2.** Bringing or presaging good fortune; auspicious, favourable, lucky ME. **3.** *absol.* or *sb.* A fortunate person or thing; *esp.* in *Astrol.* a fortunate planet, sign, etc. 1614.

1. Burleigh (f...to serve the best of Queens) 1705. *Fortunate Islands* (= L. *Fortunatæ Insulæ*), fabulous isles of the Western Ocean, the abode of the blessed dead. Also *fig.* 2. A f. omen 1741, day 1841, circumstance 1849. 3. The f. are satisfied with the possession of this world GIBBON. Hence **Fo·rtunate-ly** *adv.*, **-ness.**

†**Fo·rtunate**, *v.* ME. [f. L. *fortunat-*, *fortunare*; see FORTUNE *v.* and -ATE[3].] *trans.* To make fortunate, prosper. Also *absol.* -1792.

Fortune (fǭ·ɹtiŭn), *sb.* ME. [a. F., ad. L. *fortuna*, related to *forti-*, *fors* chance, and *ferre* to BEAR.] **1.** Chance, hap, or luck, regarded as a cause of events and changes in men's affairs. Often (after L.) personified as a goddess, having for emblem a wheel, betokening vicissitude. †2. A chance, hap, accident, an adventure -1726; a mishap, disaster -1627. 3. The chance or luck (good or bad) which falls or is to fall to any one. Also in *pl.* ME. b. Attributed to things, purposes, undertakings 1665. 4. *absol.* (= good fortune) ME. 5. One's condition or standing in life; often *absol.* a prosperous condition. Also *pl.* 1600. 6. Amount of wealth; *concr.* wealth, substance; †formerly also *pl.* Also (with *a* and *pl.*) an ample stock of wealth. 1596. †7. Short for: A woman of fortune; an heiress -1823. 8. *Astrol.* A name for the planets Jupiter and Venus 1671.

1. The chaunces of the worlde also, That we f. clepen so GOWER. You have f. on your side JUNIUS. Phr. *The f. of war. Soldier of f.*: one who fought for pay in any country or state that would employ him; also, one who has risen from the ranks by merit. 3. Chieflie the mould of a Mans f. is in himself BACON. Phr. *To try one's f. To tell a person his f. To tell fortunes.* 4. Your F., and Merit both, haue been Eminent BACON. 5. My pride fell with my fortunes *A.Y.L.* I. ii. 263. Phr. *To make one's f.* 6. He paid much too dear for his Wife's F., by taking her Person into the bargain CLARENDON. Phr. *To make a, one's f.* Men of rank and f. BERKELEY.

Comb.: **f.-book**, 'a book consulted to know f. or future events' (J.); **-hunter**, one who seeks to win a f., *esp.* by marriage; **-tell** *v.*, to tell fortunes; **-teller**, one who tells fortunes; **-telling** *vbl. sb.*, the practice of telling fortunes.

Fortune (fǭ·ɹtiŭn), *v.* ME. [a. OF. *fortuner*, ad. L. *fortunare* to make fortunate, f. *fortuna*; see prec.] †1. *trans.* To assign a (certain) fortune to -1606. 2. To endow with a fortune; to dower. *rare.* 1748. †3. *intr.* Of events, etc.: To happen, chance, occur -1739. b. *impers.* 1462. †4. With person or thing as subject: To happen or chance *to be* or *to do* (something) -1798.

3. b. It so fortuned, that he was taken by pirates at sea BACON. Hence †**Fo·rtune** *adv.* haply, perchance.

Fortuned (fǭ·ɹtiŭnd), *ppl. a.* Now *rare.* ME. [f. FORTUNE *sb.* and *v.* + -ED.] Having fortune (of a specified kind); also, possessed of a fortune.

The full-Fortun'd Cæsar *Ant. & Cl.* IV. xv. 24.

Fo·rtuneless, *a.* 1596. [See -LESS.] Without (good) fortune, luckless. Also, destitute of a fortune.

†**Fo·rtunize,** *v. rare.* 1596. [f. FORTUNE *sb.* + -IZE.] *trans.* To regulate the fortunes of; to make fortunate -1652.

†**Fortunous,** *a.* ME. [a. OF. *fortuneus*; see -OUS.] 1. Fortuitous. CHAUCER. 2. Successful 1470.

Forty (fǭ·ɹti). [OE. *féowertig*; see FOUR and -TY.]

A. *adj.* The cardinal number equal to four tens. Symbols 40, xl, or XL. Also used indefinitely to express a large number.

On fairie ground I could beat fortie of them SHAKS.

B. *sb.* 1. The age of 40 years 1732. 2. A yacht of forty tons burden 1894.

Phrases. *The forties*: the years between forty and fifty of a century or of one's life. *The forty*: a designation applied to certain bodies from the number of their members; e.g. to several courts of justice in the Venetian republic; to the French Academy, and (occas.) to the Royal Academy of Arts in London. *The roaring forties*: the part of the South Atlantic, Pacific, and Indian Oceans between 40° and 50° south latitude, characterized by exceptionally boisterous westerly winds.

Comb.: **f.-spot**, the Tasmanian name for a bird, *Pardalotus quadragintus* (Gould); **-tonner** = B. 2.

Forty-five. *The Forty-five*: the year 1745, and the Jacobite rebellion of that year.

Forum (fōə·rŏm). 1460. 1. The public place or market-place of a city. In ancient Rome the place of assembly for judicial and other public business. Also *fig.* 2. A court, tribunal 1848. Also *transf.* and *fig.* 1690.

1. Rienzi..The forum's champion, and the people's chief BYRON. 2. Phr. *Law of the f.*: the legal rules of a particular court or jurisdiction; Limitation and prescription are applied only according to the law of the f. PARSONS. *fig.* In the f. of conscience (= L. *in foro conscientiæ*) 1874.

Forwake(d: see FOR- *pref.*[1] 6 b.

Forwa·nder, *v.* Now *arch.* or *Sc.* ME. [f. FOR- *pref.*[1] + WANDER.] To weary oneself with wandering; to wander far and wide.

Forward (fǭ·ɹwəɹd). [OE. *for(e)weard* adj. and adv.; see FORE *adv.* and -WARD.]

A. *adj.* †1. In OE. The front, first, or earliest part of (anything). 2. Near, at, or belonging to the fore-part 1601; that lies in front 1643. 3. Onward; also 'outward' as opp. to 'return' 1603. 4. *Comm.* Prospective, relating to future produce 1883. 5. That is in an advanced state or condition; early. Chiefly *predicative.* 1526. 6. Ready, prompt, eager; *esp.* with const. *to* 1523. b. *transf.* and *fig.* of things. ? *Obs.* 1605. 7. Precocious 1591. 8. In bad sense: Presumptuous; bold, immodest 1561. 9. Of persons: Advanced, extreme; in mod. use, aggressive 1608.

2. Let 's take the instant by the f. top SHAKS. The f. horizon KINGLAKE. The f. sight of a gun 1876. 3. The f. path CARY. *F. play* (in *Cricket*): the method of playing f.: see the *adv.* 3 (quot.). 5. As the most f. Bud Is eaten by the Canker ere it blow SHAKS. 6. How fondly do'st thou spurre a f. Horse SHAKS. F. to give C. MATHER. A wood very f. to grow DE FOE. 7. It will be a f. cock that croweth in the shell LYLY. 8. A f. prating coxcomb T. BROWN. 9. Outrage and dynamite, and what are generally known as f. measures 1887.

B. *adv.* 1. Towards the future. Now only in phrases *from this day* (*time*, etc.) *f.* OE. b. *Comm.* For future delivery or payment 1882. †2. Onward or farther in a series -1663. 3. Towards the front 1513. 4. Towards what is in front; (moving) onwards, on. Also with ellipsis of some part of the vb. *go.* ME. b. Ahead 1838. 5. To the front or to a prominent position, into view 1611. 6. At a point or position which is beyond or farther than another 1523. Of time: In advance 1571. 7. *Naut.* At or towards the fore-part of a vessel 1630. 8. *fig.* Onward, so as to progress or advance 1513.

1. Phr. *To look f.* b. Maize still.. dear, but cheaper f. (*mod.*). 2. Phr. *And so f.* = and so forth, et cetera. 3. Phr. *To play f.* (in *Cricket*): to reach f. so as to play short-pitched balls. 5. Phr. *To bring f. To come f. To put f.* 8. Now f. with your tale *Temp.* III. ii. 91. Phr. *To go f.*: to be going on.

C. *sb.* [The *adj.* used *absol.*] †1. The fore, front, or first part -ME. †2. *Wrestling.* A throw which causes the opponent to fall forward -1612. 3. *Football, Hockey*, etc. One who plays in the front line; one of the 'forwards', as opp. to 'backs' (see BACK *sb.*) 1879.

Hence **Fo·rward·ly** *adv.* (and *a.*), **-ness.**

Forward (fǭ·ɹwəɹd), *v.* 1596. [f. FORWARD *adv.*] 1. *trans.* To help forward; to advance, hasten, promote, urge on. Also, †to set on foot (*rare*). 2. To accelerate the growth of (plants) 1626. 3. To send to an ulterior destination. In *Comm.* often loosely, to dispatch. 1757. 4. *Bookbinding.* To get (a sewed book) ready for the finisher by putting a plain cover on 1892.

1. To f. its interests FREEMAN. 2. Of Efficacy to f. the Flowers 1707. 3. Forwarded this day to your address per S.W.R. three boxes marked [etc.] (*mod.*). Hence **Fo·rwarder**, one who or that which forwards; *spec.* in sense 4.

Fo·rwarding, *vbl. sb.* 1635. [f. prec. + -ING[1].] 1. The action of FORWARD *v.* in various senses. 2. *Bookbinding.* The operation of putting a plain cover on a book previously sewn, and preparing it for the 'finisher' 1893. 3. *attrib.*, as *f. room*, etc.; **f. agent, merchant**, one whose business is the receiving and shipment or transmission of goods.

Forwards (fǭ·ɹwəɹdz). ME. [f. FORWARD; see -WARDS.]

A. *adv.* = FORWARD *adv.* (As dist. from *forward*, the form *forwards* expresses a definite direction in contrast with other directions. But in some contexts either form may be used.)

He was backwards and f. constantly DICKENS.

†B. *adj.* = FORWARD *a. rare.* -1626.

†**Forwa·rn, forewa·rn,** *v.* [OE. *forwiernan*; see FOR- *pref.*[1] and WARN *v.*] *trans.* To prohibit, forbid -1820.

He did not know that the thing had been forewarned LAMB.

†**Forwa·ste,** *v.* 1563. [f. FOR- *pref.*[1] + WASTE *v.*] = WASTE *v.* -1630.

Forweary (fǭɹwīə·ri), *v.* *Obs.* or *arch.* Also fore-. ME. [f. FOR-*pref.*[1] + WEARY *v.*] *trans.* To weary, tire out.

†**Forwee·p,** *v.* ME. [f. FOR- *pref.*[1] + WEEP *v.*] *intr.* To exhaust oneself with weeping. Of a vine: To bleed excessively. -1500.

†**Forwe·lk,** *v.* ME. [f. FOR- *pref.*[1] + WELK *v.*] *trans.* To wither -1616.

†**Forwhy·.** [OE. *for-hwí*, f. FOR *prep.* + *hwí*, WHY, instr. of *hwæt*, neut. of *hwá* WHO.]

A. *adv.* 1. For what reason, why. 2. With connective force: For which cause, wherefore ME.

B. *conj.* 1. Because; = FOR *conj.* 1. ME. 2. = FOR *conj.* 2. ME.

Forworn (fǭɹwǭ·ɹn), *ppl. a.* 1508. [f. FOR- pref.[1] + *worn* pa. pple. of WEAR *v.*] Worn out, decayed, grown old.

A silly man, in simple weedes forworne SPENSER.

†**Forwra·p,** *v.* ME. [f. FOR- *pref.*[1] + WRAP *v.*] *trans.* To wrap up. Also *fig.* -1571.

Al moot be seyd, and no thyng excused, ne forwrapped CHAUCER.

†**Foryie·ld,** *v.* OE. [f. FOR- *pref.*[1] + YIELD *v.*; = mod. Ger. *vergelten.*] *trans.* To repay, recompense, requite. Also *intr.* with *of.* Phr. *God*, etc. *foryield* (it.) -1560.

‖**Forzando** [fǫrtsa·ndo), *adv.* 1828. [It., f. *forzare* to force.] *Mus.* = SFORZANDO.

‖**Fossa** (fǫ·să). *Pl.* **fossæ.** 1830. [L. = 'ditch'; fem. pa. pple. (with *terra* understood) of *fodere* to dig.] *Anat.* A shallow depression, pit, or cavity.

Fossane (fǫ·sein). 1781. [a. F.; the native name is given as *foussa*] A species of weasel or genet, found in Madagascar, etc.

Fosse (fǫs). ME. [a. F., ad. L. *fossa* (see FOSSA).] 1. An excavation narrow in proportion to its length; a canal, ditch, or trench; in *Fortif.*, etc., a moat. †2. A pit -1855. 3. *Anat.* = FOSSA. 1730.

Hence **Fossed** *a.* encircled with or as with a f.

‖**Fossé** (fo·se). 1708. [F. :—late L. *fossatum*, neut. pa. pple. of *fossare*, freq. of *fodere.*] A fosse, ditch, or sunk fence.

Fosset, obs. f. FACET, FAUCET, FORCET.

Fossette (fǫse·t). 1848. [a. F. *fossette* dimple, dim. of *fosse*; see FOSSE.] A little hollow, depression, or dimple. a. *Zool.* 1856. b. *Path.* 'A small ulcer of the transparent cornea, the centre of which is deep' (Ogilvie).

Fossick (fǫ·sik), *v.* *Austral.* 1852. [Cf. '*Fossick*, a troublesome person, *fossicking*, troublesome. *Warw.*' (Halliwell).] 1. *intr.* in *Mining.* To search for gold by digging out crevices with knife or pick, or by working in washing-places and abandoned workings. 2. *gen.* To rummage or hunt about 1887. 3. *trans.* To dig *out*, to hunt *up* 1870. Hence **Fo·ssicker**, one who fossicks, *esp.* a pocket-miner or a prospector for gold.

Fossil (fǫ·sil). 1569. [a. F. *fossile*, ad. L. *fossilis* dug up, f. *fodere.*]

A. *adj.* 1. Obtained by digging; found buried in the earth 1654. 2. Now applied to the remains of animals and plants, belonging to past ages, and found embedded in the strata of the earth. (Commonly taken as the *sb.* used attrib.) Also *fig.* 1665. b. Used in names of certain mineral substances supposed to resemble organic products, as *f. copal, cork, farina* (see the sbs.); *f. flax, paper, wood, wool*, varieties of asbestos; etc. 3. Belonging to the past, out of date; 'petrified' 1859.

1. F. coal, and..bitumen 1816. 2. The fossill Bones of an Alligator found..near Whitby 1758. *fig.* Language is f. poetry EMERSON. 3. F. politicians 1894.

B. *sb.* †1. Any rock, mineral, or mineral substance dug out of the earth -1814. 2. Now only: The remains of a plant or animal of a former geological period found in the strata of the earth 1736. 3. *fig.* Something 'petrified', or incapable of growth or progress 1844.

3. When a man endures what ought to be unendurable, he is a f. C. BRONTË.

Comb. **f.-ore**, fossiliferous red hematite.

Hence **Fossili·ferous** *a.* bearing or containing fossils or organic remains. **Fo·ssilism**, the scientific study of fossils (*rare*); also, the state of being a f. **Fo·ssilist** (now *rare*), an authority on fossils, a palæontologist.

Fossilize (fǫ·siləiz), *v.* 1794. [f. FOSSIL *sb.* + -IZE.] 1. To turn into a fossil. *trans.* and *intr.* 2. *fig.* To cause to become antiquated, rigid, or fixed; *rarely*, to preserve as if in fossil form. Also *intr.* for *refl.* 1856. 3. *intr.* To search for fossils. LYELL.

1. 'Petrifying wells' do not..f. the things put into them 1854. 2. Ten layers of birthdays on a woman's head Are apt to f. her girlish mirth MRS. BROWNING. Hence **Fossiliza·tion.**

†**Fossi·logy.** 1776. [Incorrectly f. FOSSIL *sb.* + -LOGY.] That branch of science which treats of fossils; palæontology; also, a treatise on this -1812. So †**Fossi·logist,** one who studies f. vars. **Fossilo·logy** (*rare*), **Fossilo·logical** *a.*, **Fossilo·logist.**

‖**Fossor** (fǫ·sǭɹ). 1854. [L.] An officer of the early Church charged with the burial of the dead.

Fossorial (fǫsōə·riăl). 1836. [f. L. *fossorius*, f. *fossor*, *fodere* + -AL.]
A. *adj.* **1.** Having a faculty of digging, burrowing, fodient. **2.** Of or pertaining to fodient animals, adapted for burrowing 1845.
1. *F. Hymenoptera*, a family of insects called *Fossores*.
B. *sb.* A fossorial animal 1855.
var. **Fosso·rious** *a.*

‖**Fossula** (fǫ·siŭlă). 1843. [L., dim. of *fossa*; see FOSSA.] A small fossa; *spec.* in *Anat.* and *Zool.* (see next).

Fossulate (fǫ·siŭlět), *a.* 1839. [f. L. *fossula* (see prec.) + -ATE².] *Anat.* and *Zool.* Having one or more long narrow grooves or depressions.

Foster (fǫ·stəɹ), *sb.*¹ *Obs.* exc. in *Comb.* [OE. *fóstor*, f. (ult.) root **fōd-* (see FOOD) + instr. suffix *-tro-*.] **1.** Food, nourishment -1670. **2.** Guardianship, keeping. *At f.*, at nurse (with a foster-parent). -1861. **3.** Offspring -1513; also, a foster-child, nursling -1585. **4.** *attrib.* and *Comb.*, as F.-BROTHER, -SISTER; -CHILD, -SON. Also F.-FATHER, -MOTHER; hence, *f.-city*, *-earth*. 1582.

Fo·ster, *sb.*² *Obs.* exc. *arch.* [OE. (*cild-*)*fóstre* nurse; see prec.] A foster-parent, nurse.

†**Fo·ster,** *sb.*³ ME. [contr. f. FORESTER.] = FORESTER. -1607.

Foster (fǫ·stəɹ), *v.* [OE. *fóstrian*, f. *fostor*, FOSTER *sb.*¹] †**1.** *trans.* To supply with food; to nourish, feed, support -1719. Also *fig.* †**2.** To bring up with parental care; often, to be a foster-parent to -1697. **3.** To nurse, tend with care; to cherish ME. **4.** To encourage, help to grow; to promote the development of ME.
1. One, bred but of Almes, and foster'd with cold dishes *Cymb.* II. iii. 119. 2. Some say, that Rauens f. forlorne children SHAKS. 3. Hir olde poore fader fostred she CHAUCER. 4. To f. a system of concealment BURKE, an insurrection 1844, enmities DISRAELI, superstitions 1885.
Hence **Fo·sterage,** the action, also the office or charge, of fostering (another's child); the condition of being a foster-child; the custom of putting (a child) under a foster-mother; the action of encouraging. **Fo·sterer,** a nurse, foster-parent; one who cherishes, favours, or promotes the growth of (anything); in *Anglo-Irish*, a foster-brother. **Fo·steringly** *adv.* †**Fo·sterment,** food, nourishment, subsistence.

Fo·ster-brother. [OE. *fóster-bróðor*, f. FOSTER *sb.*¹] A male child nursed at the same breast as, or reared with, another of different parentage.

Foster-child. [OE. *fostercild*.] A nurseling.

Fo·ster-father. [OE. *fósterfæder*, f. FOSTER *sb.*¹] **a.** One who performs the duty of a father to another's child. **b.** The husband of a nurse.

Fosterling (fǫ·stəɹliŋ). [OE. *fóstorling*; see FOSTER *sb.*¹ and -LING.] A foster-child.

Fo·ster-mother. [OE. *fóster-*, *fóstormódor*, f. FOSTER *sb.*¹] A woman who nurses and brings up another's child, either as an adoptive mother or as a nurse.

Fo·ster-nurse. 1607. [f. FOSTER *sb.*¹] A nurse who brings up another's child as her own.

Fo·ster-sister. 1649. [f. as prec.] A female child nursed at the same breast as, or reared with, another of different parentage.

Fo·ster-son. 1450. [f. as prec.]. One brought up as a son though not a son by birth.

Fostress (fǫ·strės). 1603. [see -ESS.] A female who fosters (see FOSTER *v.*).

Fother (fǫ·ðəɹ), *sb.* [OE. *fóðer* :— WGer. **fōþr(o)*. The root is taken to be an ablaut var. of *faþ-* to stretch out; see FATHOM.] **1.** A load; a cart-load; hence, a mass, a lot. **2.** *spec.* A definite weight: a. of lead, = 19½ cwt. ME.; b. of coals, = 17⅞ cwt. 1607.

Fother (fǫ·ðəɹ), *v.* Also **fodder.** 1789. [prob. ad. Du. *voederen* (now *voeren*), or LG. *fodern* = Ger. *füttern* to line.] *Naut.* **1.** *trans.* To cover (a sail) thickly with oakum, rope yarn, or the like, with the view of getting some of it sucked into a leak, over which the sail is drawn. **2.** To stop a leak by this method 1800. Hence **Fo·ther (fodder)** *sb.* the material used for fothering.

†**Fo·tive** *a.* [f. L. *fot-*, ppl. stem of *fovere* + -IVE.] Cherishing, warming. T. CAREW.

†**Fo·tmal.** ME. only. [app. a use of OE. *fótmæl*, foot measure.] A weight used for lead, app. about 70 lb.

Fou (*fū*), *a.* *Sc.* 1535. [var. of FULL *a.*] Drunk.

Foudroyant (fudroi·ănt, Fr. fudrwayañ), *a.* 1840. [a. F., f. *foudroyer* to strike with or as with lightning.] **1.** Thundering, stunning; also, dazzling. **2.** *spec.* in *Path.* of a disease: Beginning suddenly in a very severe form.

†**Fouga·de.** 1643. [a. F., ad. It. *fugata*.] = FOUGASSE; also *fig.* -1827.

Fougasse (fuga·s). 1832. [a. F.] 'A small mine from 6 to 12 feet underground, charged either with powder or loaded shells' (Voyle).

Fought (fǫt), *ppl. a.* 1550. [pa. pple. of FIGHT *v.*] In senses of the vb. In attrib. use usually with advs., as *well-f.* var. **Fou·ghten.** *arch.*

†‖**Fougue** (fūg). Also †**fogue.** 1660. [a. F., ad. It. *foga*.] Fury; ardour, impetuosity -1683.

Foul (faul). [OE. *fúl* :—OTeut. **fūlo-*, f. root **fu-* :—Aryan **pu-* (in Skr. *pū* to stink, Gr. πύον, L. *pus*, etc.).]
A. *adj.* **I.** Grossly offensive to the senses, physically loathsome. **b.** Charged with offensive matter; (of a carcase) tainted with disease ME.
Thy..place of doom obscure and foule MILT.
†*The f. disease* or *evil*: (*a*) epilepsy, (*b*) syphilis.
II. Opp. to CLEAN *a.* II. **1.** Dirty, soiled; covered with or full of dirt or mire. Now chiefly: Disgustingly dirty, filthy. OE. **2.** †Of handwriting: Blotted, illegible. *F. copy*: a first copy, defaced by corrections (now *rare*). *F. proof*: one marked with many faults. 1467. **3.** Charged with defiling or noxious matter; discoloured 1535. **4.** Of food: Coarse, gross, rank; unclean, putrid. Hence applied to the eating, or the eaters, of such food. 1713. **5.** Clogged, choked, or encumbered with something foreign 1470. **b.** *Path.* Of the tongue: Furred 1800. **6.** Morally or spiritually polluted; abominable, wicked OE. **7.** Of speech: Obscene; also, disgustingly abusive OE. **8.** Applied to fish immediately after spawning (*mod.*).
1. Þe way was foule 1450. 2. By cause of the foule wrytyng and interlynyeng 1467. *F. bill of health*: see BILL *sb.*³ 3. The Seine is f. and turbid as the Avon 1756. Workings charged with f. gas 1885. 5. *F. bottom* (Naut.), the bottom of the sea if rocky, or unsafe from wrecks. Also of a ship: Having the bottom overgrown with seaweed, shell-fish, etc. *F. coast*, one beset by reefs and breakers. *F. ground*, synonymous with *f. bottom*. 6. Babylon the great.. is become .. the hold of every f. spirit *Rev.* xviii. 2. A court f. with all the vices of the Restoration MACAULAY. *F. fiend*, see FIEND. *F. thief*: the devil. 7. Foule speech deserues a double hate 1530. F. songs 1833. A f. mouth 1834, tongue 1852.
III. Opp. to FAIR *a.* **1.** Ugly. Now *rare* in literary use. ME. **2.** Disgraceful, ignominious, shameful ME. **3.** *Sporting* and *Games.* Contrary to rule, irregular, unfair; said also of the player. **4.** Of the weather, etc.: Unfavourable; wet and stormy ME. **5.** Of the wind: Contrary 1726. **6.** Of a means or procedure, language, etc.: Harsh, rough, violent ME. **7.** *Naut.* (opp. to *clear*): 'Entangled, embarrassed, or contrary to' (Adm. Smyth). Const. *of*, †*on*. 1627.
1. My face is fowle with weeping *Job* xvi. 16. A foule noyse HOLLAND. 2. A f. charge 1756, deed SCOTT. 3. A f. blow 1797. F. riding 1892. Phr. *F. ball* (Baseball): a ball that falls outside the lines drawn from the home base through the first and third bases. *F. play*: unfair conduct in a game; *transf.* unfair or treacherous (and often violent) dealing. 4. In foule wether at my booke to sit WYATT. 5. In the teeth of a f. wind 1883. 6. War is a f. game EMERSON. 7. Phr. *To fall, run f. of*: see the vbs. *F. berth*, 'when a ship anchors in the hawse of another she gives the latter a f. berth' SMYTH. *F. anchor*, the anchor when it hooks some other anchor, wreck, or cable, or when the slack cable is entangled about the upper fluke of it. Also, the badge of the British Admiralty.
B. *sb.* [The adj. used *absol.* or *ellipt.*] **1.** That which is foul; something foul OE. **2.** A disease in the feet of cattle and sheep. Also, in dogs. 1523. **3.** (Partly f. FOUL *v.*) A collision or entanglement, *esp.* in riding, rowing, running, etc. In *Baseball*: A foul hit. 1754.
1. *F. befall* (see FAIR *sb.*²). 3. *To claim a f.*: to allege unfair action on the part of an opponent, and claim the penalty.
C. *adv.* In a foul manner, in various senses (see the adj.) ME.

Foul (faul), *v.*¹ [In form repr. OE. *fúlian* intr. In the trans. use, prob. a new formation.] **1.** *intr.* To be or become foul. **2.** *trans.* To render filthy or dirty; to defile ME. **3.** *fig.* To pollute (with guilt); to dishonour, disgrace ME. **4.** To make ugly; to deface, disfigure ME. **5.** Chiefly *Naut.* To cause to become entangled. Also, to jam or block; to make (a sea bottom) foul or obstructed. 1726. **b.** *intr.* To get foul 1857. **c.** *trans.* To run foul of 1859. **6.** *Sporting* and *Games.* To handle or strike an opponent in a foul manner. *Baseball.* To hit a foul ball.
1. Prince's breech-loader fouls in the proportion [etc.] 1858. 2. To f. a smock SWIFT. 3. With hands not fouled with confiscation BURKE. 5. A ship.. fouled her propeller 1892. b. The chain fouled on the windlass 1860. c. She fouled the pier 1859.

†**Foul, fowle,** *v.*² ME. [a. F. *fouler* to tread.] *trans.* To trample, tread, tread down -1643.

Foulard (fular, fulā·ɹd). 1864. [a. F.] **1.** A thin flexible material of silk, or of silk and cotton. **2.** A handkerchief of this 1879.

†**Fou·lder,** *v.* 1559. [ad. OF. *fouldrer*, f. *fouldre*; see next.] *trans.* To flash or thunder forth. Also *absol.* -1594.

Foully (fau·l,li), *adv.* OE. [f. FOUL *a.* + -LY²; in OE. *fúllíce*.] In a foul manner; filthily ME.; hideously ME.; abominably, cruelly, treacherously ME.; obscenely OE.; insultingly ME.; †grievously -1655.
F. murdered Miss BRADDON, slandered MACAULAY.

Foul-mouthed (fau·l,mau·ðd), *a.* 1596. [f. Foul *a.* + MOUTH + -ED².] Using obscene, profane, or scurrilous language. Hence **Fou·l-mou:thedness.**

Foulness (fau·lnės). ME. [f. FOUL *a.* + -NESS.] The quality or condition of being foul (see FOUL *a.*). Also *concr.* Foul matter.
The f. of the linen PEPYS, of the Ways and Weather PENN. *concr.* Foulnesses without number 1790.

Foumart. [ME. *fulmard* :—OE. **fúl mearð* (*fúl*, FOUL *a.* + *mearð* marten).] **1.** The polecat (*Putorius fœtidus*) ME. **2.** *attrib.*, as *f.-skin*; **f.-dog,** a dog used for hunting the f.

Found (faund), *sb.* 1540. [f. FOUND *v.*²] The process of founding (metal, etc.).
†*Of f.* (Sc.) = of cast metal; Cross-bows, hagbuts of f. SCOTT.

Found: pa. pple. of FIND *v.*

Found (faund), *v.*¹ Pa. t. and pple. **founded.** ME. [a. F. *fonder* :—L. *fundare*, f. *fundus* bottom, foundation.] **1.** *trans.* To lay the base or substructure of; to set *on* a firm ground or base; to base, ground. Also *refl.* and *intr.* (for *refl.*) **b.** To serve as the base of 1690. **2.** To begin the building of, be the first builder of ME. **3.** *fig.* To originate, create, initiate ME. †**b.** To endow -1612. †**4.** To fasten or attach *to*. Also *fig.* -1641.
1. It fell not, for it was founded upon a rock *Matt.* vii. 25. Our understanding cannot in this body f. itself but on sensible things MILT. I f. upon the evidence of my senses 1882. b. A folio Common-place Founds the whole pile, of all his works the base POPE. 2. I founded palaces, and planted bowers PRIOR. 3. To f. a school of novelists L. STEPHEN.

Found (faund), *v.*² ME. [ad. F. *fondre* :— L. *fundere* to pour, melt, FUSE.] †**1.** *trans.* To mix *together*. **2.** To melt (metal) and run it into a mould; to form (an article) by running molten metal into a mould; to cast 1562. **b.** To melt or fuse (the materials for making glass); to make (glass) by melting the materials in a furnace 1782.
2. Veins..of mineral..Whereof to f...their balls Of missive ruin MILT. Hence **Fou·nding** *vbl. sb.*

Foundation (faundē¹·ʃən). ME. [ad. L. *fundationem*; see FOUND *v.*¹] **1.** The action of founding or building upon a firm substructure; the state or fact of being founded. Also *fig.* **2.** *esp.* The establishing of an institution, together with provision for its perpetual maintenance ME. †**b.** The charter of establishment or incorporation -1546. **3.** That which is founded or established by endowment; an endowed institution (e.g. a monastery, college, or hospital) 1513. **b.** The endowment ME. **4.** The solid ground, basis, or principle, on which anything (material or immaterial) is founded ME. **5.** *transf.* That upon which any structure is built up; e.g. in *Dress-making,* an underskirt over which the outer skirt is hung or draped; stiffening for a garment; etc. 1874.

1. The f. of the world *John* xvii. 24, of the Empire of Baghdad LANE. 2. The f. of religious houses 1859. 3. Corpus is a very small establishment,—twenty fellows and twenty scholars, with four exhibitioners, form the f. COLERIDGE. Phr. *On the f.:* said of the members of an endowed college, etc.

Comb.: **f. -school,** an endowed school; **-stone,** one of the stones forming the f. of a building; also, a stone laid to celebrate the founding of the edifice; also *fig.*; **f. stop,** (*a*) an organ-stop whose pipes are in unison with, or one or more octaves higher or lower than, the piano strings sounded by the corresponding keys: opp. to *mutation stop*; (*b*) any one of the fundamental flue stops, as contrasted with the reed stops, etc.

Hence **Founda·tional** *a.* of, pertaining to, or of the nature of a f.; fundamental. **Founda·tioner,** one who is on the f. of an endowed school or college. **Founda·tionless** *a.* without f., baseless.

Founded (fau·ndĕd), *ppl. a.* 1605. [f. FOUND *v.*[1]] Based, having a (specified) base (with qualifying adv.). †Also without adv. = 'well founded', etc.

Macb. III. iv. 22. Thy hopes are not ill founded MILT. *Sams.* 1504.

Founder (fau·ndəɹ), *sb.*[1] ME. [f. FOUND *v.*[1] + -ER[1].] **1.** 'One who raises an edifice; one who presides at the erection of a city' (J.). **2.** One who institutes for the first time; †an originator (of a custom, etc.) ME. **3.** One who founds and endows (an institution) ME. †**4.** One who maintains another -1613.

Phr. **Founders'-shares, (-parts)** *pl.,* shares issued to the so-called founders of a public company, as part of the consideration for the concession, scheme, etc., which is taken over, and not forming a part of the ordinary capital. Founders' shares are now somewhat discredited. Hence **Fou·ndress,** a female f.

Founder (fau·ndəɹ), *sb.*[2] ME. [f. FOUND *v.*[2]] **1.** One who casts metal, or makes articles of cast metal. Often specialized as *bell-, iron-, type-f.* **2.** One who founds glass 1853.

Comb.: **founder's dust,** charcoal powder and coke and coal dust ground fine and sifted for casting purposes; **founder's sand,** a species of sand obtained from Lewisham, Kent, and elsewhere, for making foundry moulds.

Founder (fau·ndəɹ), *sb.*[3] 1577. [app. f. *found,* pa. pple. of FIND *v.* + -ER[1].] †**1.** = FINDER. **2.** *Lead-mining.* (*Derbysh.*) The first finder of a vein; hence, a miner 1601. **3.** That portion of a lead-mine which is given to the first finder of a vein; hence, the part first worked 1653.

Founder (fau·ndəɹ), *sb.*[4] 1547. [f. FOUNDER *v.*] **1.** Inflammation of the laminar structures of a horse's foot, usually caused by overwork; a similar disease in dogs. **2.** A rheumatic affection of the muscles of the chest in horses. Called also *body-, chest-f.* 1737.

Founder (fau·ndəɹ), *v.* ME. [a. OF. *fondrer* to plunge to the bottom, f. L. *fundus.*] †**1.** *trans.* To burst or smash in. ME. only. †**2.** To send to the bottom -1490. **3.** *intr.* Of earth, a building, etc.: To fall down, give way 1489. †Also *causal.* -1656. **4.** *intr.* To stumble violently, collapse; to fall lame; *occas.*, to sink or stick fast (in mire or bog). (Chiefly of a horse or its rider.) ME. **5.** *trans.* To cause to break down or go lame; *esp.* to cause to have the founder; also *fig.* 1589. **6.** *intr.* Of a vessel: To fill with water and sink 1600. Also *fig.* **7.** *trans.* To cause to fill with water and sink 1659. ¶ **8.** *erron.* = F. *fondre*: To burst (into tears) 1477.

4. For which his hors for feere gan to turne, And leep asyde, and foundred as he leep CHAUCER. To f. in a quicksand 1875. 5. O stumbling Jade..Plague f. thee 1608. 6. *fig.* But in this point All his tricks f. SHAKS.

Founderous (fau·ndərəs), *a.* 1767. [f. FOUNDER *v.* + -OUS.] Causing or likely to cause to founder; full of ruts and holes.

Foundling (fau·ndliŋ). [ME. *fundeling,* f. *funden,* pa. pple. of FIND *v.* + -LING.] A deserted infant; a child whom there is no one to claim. Also *transf.* and *fig.*

Comb.: **f.-hospital, †-house,** an institution for the reception of foundlings; **-stone,** an erratic boulder.

Foundry (fau·ndri). 1601. [a. F. *fond(e)rie,* f. *fondre*; see FOUND *v.*[3]] **1.** The art or business of casting metal; *concr.* castings. **2.** An establishment in which founding of metal or glass is carried on. Also *fig.* 1645.

Comb.: **f.-iron,** iron containing sufficient carbon to make it suitable for castings; **-proof,** the final proof before stereotyping or electrotyping.

Fount[1] (faunt). Chiefly *poet.* 1593. [ad. F. *font* or L. *fontem* after *mount, fountain,* etc.] A spring, source, FOUNTAIN.

As cleere as Founts in Iuly SHAKS. Hence **Fou·nting** *ppl. a.* welling up like a spring. HOOD.

Fount[2] (faunt), **font** (fǫnt). Also **found**; cf. FUND 1683. [see FONT *sb.*[2]] *Printing.* A complete set of type of a particular face and size. Also fully, *f. of letter* or *type.*

Fountain (fau·ntĕn). [late ME. *fontayne,* a. OF. *fontaine*:—late L. *fontana,* fem. of L. *fontanus,* f. *font-, fons* FOUNT *sb.*[1]] **1.** A spring of water issuing from the earth; also, the head-spring or source *of* a stream or river. Now *arch.* or *poet.* 1450. **b.** *fig.* A spring, source, well. (Often in *pl.*) ME. **2.** A jet or stream of water made to rise or spout up artificially; the structure built for such a jet or stream to rise and fall in; also, an erection in a public place for a constant supply of water for drinking 1509. **b.** A metal vessel or box for aerated water (cf. *soda-f.*) 1873. **3.** *Her.* A roundel, barry wavy of six, argent and azure 1610. **4.** A reservoir or compartment for holding oil, ink, etc., in a printing press, an Argand lamp, etc. **5.** *attrib.*, as in *f. light,* etc. 1645.

1. Making Rivers to ascend to their Fountains RAY. b. The Crown is the f. of honour LD. BROUGHAM. 2. Like a Fountaine, with a hundred spouts SHAKS. Modern drinking fountains 1882.

Comb.: **f.-fish,** a ctenophoran; **-pen,** a pen furnished with an ink-reservoir; **-pipe,** one which supplies a f. with water; **-tree,** the deodar; also, 'a tree in the Canary Isles which distills water from its leaves' (W.); †**-water,** spring-water.

Hence **Fou·ntained** *ppl. a.* having a f. or fountains. **Fou·ntainless** *a.* without fountains. **Fou·ntainlet,** a little f. FULLER. **Fou·ntainous** *a.* of the nature of a f. (*lit.* and *fig.*); containing springs of water.

Fou·ntain-head. 1585. **1.** The head-spring or source of a stream. **2.** *fig.* The chief or prime source of anything; *esp.* of information, news, etc. 1606.

2. To trace an error to its fountain-head is to refute it BENTHAM.

Fountful (fau·ntful), *a. poet.* 1611. [f. FOUNT[1] + -FUL.] Full of founts or springs.

Four (fō͡əɹ). [Com. Teut. and Aryan: OE. *féower.* The OAryan type is *qetwer-, -wōr-, qetur-,* regularly represented by Skr. *catvār-, catur-,* Gr. τέσσαρες, L. *quatuor,* etc.] The cardinal number next after *three.* Symbols 4 iv, or IV.

A. as *adj.* **1.** In concord with the sb. expressed. **2.** With ellipsis of sb. ME.

1. Phr. *Within the f. seas*: within the boundaries of Great Britain. *The f. corners* (*of the earth,* etc.): the uttermost parts. 2. Be sure to come at f. (*sc.* hours of the clock) SWIFT. A barouche and f. (*sc.* horses) 1858. Phr. †*On* (*upon,* etc.) *all f.* (*sc.* feet); now *on* ALL-FOURS.

B. as *sb.* **1.** The abstract number four ME. **2.** A set of four persons or things; e. g. a four-oared boat or a crew of four oarsmen (whence *Fours,* races for four-oared boats); (*Cricket*) a hit for which four runs are scored; etc. 1599.

2. Phr. *In fours*: arranged in groups of f.; *spec.* in *Bibliography,* the number of leaves in a sheet or gathering.

Comb.: **f.-ale,** ale sold at fourpence a quart; **-centred arch** (*Arch.*), one described from f. centres; †**-corner, -cornered** *adjs.*, square; **-course** (*Agric.*), a f. years' series of crops in rotation; **-dimensional** *a.* (*Math.*), of or belonging to a fourth dimension; **-dimensioned** *a.*, having f. dimensions; **-field course** (*Agric.*), a series of crops grown in f. fields in rotation; **f. figures,** one thousand pounds or over; **-foot (way),** the space (really 4 ft. 8½ in.) between the rails on which the train runs; **f. hundred** (*U.S.*) the exclusive social set of any place; **f. -inch** *a.*, that measures f. inches, also *ellipt.* = four inch rope; **-oar,** a boat rowed with f. oars; **-oared** *a.*, propelled by f. oars or oarsmen; **-part** *a.* (*Mus.*), composed for f. parts or voices; **-post, -posted** *adjs.*, (of a bedstead) having f. posts (to support a canopy and curtains); **-poster,** a f.-posted bedstead; **-pounder,** (*a*) a gun to carry a four-pound shot; (*b*) something weighing f. pounds, as a loaf; **-stroke** *attrib.*, (of internal combustion engines) having a cycle of four strokes, intake, compression, combustion, and exhaust; **-way(s,** the place where two roads cross or f. roads meet; **-way** *a.* (in *four-way cock* or *valve*), having communication with four pipes.

†**Fourb(e,** *sb.* 1654. [a. F. *fourbe* masc. and fem., f. *fourbir* to FURBISH, taken *fig.*] **1.** A cheat, an impostor -1761. **2.** A trick, an imposture -1691.

Fourché(e (fuɹʃe), *a.* 1706. [a. F. *fourchée*] *Her.* Divided into two parts towards the extremity.

Fourchette (fuɹʃet). 1754. [a. F., dim. of *fourche*; see FORK *sb.*] A fork; something forked or fork-like. **a.** *Anat.* The thin commissure, by which the labia majora of the pudendum unite together. **b.** *Surg.* A forked instrument formerly used to divide the frænum of the tongue when short 1854. **c.** *Ornith.* The furcula of a bird 1854.

Fourfold (fō͡ə·ɹfōuld). OE. [f. FOUR + -FOLD.]

A. *adj.* **1.** Consisting of four things; made up of four parts ME. **2.** Quadruple OE.

1. A f. advantage BOYLE. *Comb. f.-visaged* adj.

B. *adv.* In fourfold proportion 1535.

And he shall restore the lamb f. 2 *Sam.* xii. 6.

C. *sb.* A fourfold amount ME.

I restore him foure fold *Luke* xix. 8. Hence **Fou·rfold** *v.* to assess in a f. ratio. *U.S.*

Four-foot, *a. Obs.* exc. *poet.* ME. [f. FOUR *a.* + FOOT *sb.*] = next.

Fou·r-foo·ted, *a.* ME. [f. as prec. + -ED[2].] Having four feet, quadruped; pertaining to quadrupeds.

Birds and four-footed beasts BERKELEY.

‖**Fourgon** (furgoṅ). 1848. [a. F.] A baggage-wagon, a van.

Four-handed, *a.* 1774. **1.** Having four feet which resemble hands; quadrumanous. **2.** Suitable for four persons 1824.

1. The fourhanded mole TENNYSON. 2. four-handed cribbage 1824.

Fourierism (fūᵊ·riĕriz'm). 1841. [f. the name *Fourier*; see -ISM.] A system invented by the French socialist Charles *Fourier* for the reorganization of society; phalansterianism. So **Fou·rierist, Fou·rierite,** an adherent of Fourierism; also *attrib.*

Four-in-hand. 1793. **1.** A vehicle with four horses driven by one person. **2.** quasi-*adv.* With a four-in-hand 1812. **3.** *attrib.*, as *four-in-hand club,* etc. 1849; quasi-*adj.* 1799.

1. The four-in-hands of the Yorkshire squires DISRAELI. 3. quasi-*adj.* The tobacco-smoking, four-in-hand Miss Coventry WHYTE MELVILLE.

Fou·r-leaved, *a.* 1450. [f. FOUR + LEAF + -ED[2].] Having four leaves.

Four-leaved grass: †**a.** a four-leaved variety of *Trifolium repens*; **b.** the plant *Paris quadrifolia.*

Fourling (fō͡ə·ɹliŋ). 1855. [f. FOUR *sb.* + -LING.] **1.** One of four children born at the same time. (Dicts.) **2.** *Min.* A twin crystal made up of four independent individuals (*Cent. Dict.*).

†**Fourneau.** 1678. [a. F., OF. *fornel*:—late L. type *furnellus,* dim. of *furnus* (F. *four*) oven.] *Mil.* A cavity in which powder is placed for blasting.

Four o'clock. 1756. **1.** (More fully *four o'clock flower.*) The plant *Mirabilis Jalapa* or Marvel of Peru. (Its flowers open in the afternoon; hence the name.) **2.** The Australian friar-bird, *Philemon corniculatus,* so called from its cry 1848. **3.** A seed-head of the dandelion 1883. **4.** A light meal taken by workmen about four o'clock in the afternoon 1825.

Fourpence (fō͡ə·ɹpĕns). 1722. [f. FOUR *a.* + PENCE.] A sum of money or coin equal to four pennies.

Fourpence-halfpenny: app. the Irish sixpence of Elizabeth; the Irish shilling of the same period was called and valued at ninepence. The [Spanish] half real..is called..in New England, f. ha'penny, or simply f. BARTLETT.

Fourpenny (fōᵊ·ɪpĕni), *a.* 1481. [f. FOUR *a.* + PENNY.] 1. That costs or is valued at fourpence; quasi-*sb.* a fourpenny piece. 2. *F. nail*: a nail 1¼ in. long, of which 4 lbs. go to the thousand (i. e. 10 nominal hundreds or 1120).

Fou·rrier. *Obs.* exc. *Hist.* 1481. [a. F., var. of OF. *forrier*; see FORAYER.] 1. = FORAYER. 2. A quartermaster 1678.

Fourscore (fōᵊ·ɪskōᵊɪ), *a.* ME. [f. FOUR *a.* + SCORE *sb.*] Four times twenty, eighty. Now *arch.* or *rhet.*

Foursome (fōᵊ·ɪsɒ̆m). 15.. [f. FOUR *a.* + -SOME.]

A. *adj.* 1. Four (together). Also *absol.* 2. Performed by four persons together 1814.

2. A Scotch f. reel SCOTT.

B. *sb.* *Golf.* A match in which four players take part, two against two, the partners on each side playing alternately 1867.

Four-square. ME. [f. FOUR *a.* + SQUARE.]

A. *adj.* Having four equal sides; square. Also *transf.* and *fig.* b. quasi-*adv.* In a square form or position ME.

b. That tower of strength which stood four-square to all the winds that blew TENNYSON.

B. *sb.* A figure having four equal sides 1587.

Fourteen (fōᵊɪtī·n, fōᵊ·ɪtīn). [OE. *féowerténe*; see FOUR and -TEEN.] The cardinal number composed of ten and four. Symbols 14, xiv, or XIV.

A. as *adj.* 1. In concord with the sb. expressed. 2. With ellipsis of sb. 1480. †3. = FOURTEENTH *a.* -1553.

1. †(*A*) *f. night*: a fortnight. 2. Thee 's not fourteene SHAKS. *Comb.* f.-gun *a.* (a vessel) carrying f. guns.

B. as *sb.* 1. The abstract number fourteen OE. 2. *pl.* Candles fourteen to the pound 1883.

Hence **Fourtee·ner**, a poem of f. lines; also, a line of f. syllables.

Fourteenth (fōᵊɪtī·nþ, fōᵊ·ɪtīnþ). [OE. *féowertéoða*, f. *féowerténe* FOURTEEN after *téoða* tenth. Cf. FIFTEENTH.] The ordinal numeral belonging to the cardinal fourteen.

A. *adj.* in concord with sb. expressed; also *ellipt.*

F.-part: one of 14 equal parts of any whole.

B. *sb.* A fourteenth part. b. *Mus.* The octave or replicate of the seventh 1597.

Hence **Fourteenthly** *adv.* in the f. place.

Fourth (fōᵊɪþ). [OE. *féorða*. The Com. Aryan type is **qeturto-* or *qetwrto-*, whence Skr. *caturtha*, Gr. τέταρτος, L. *quartus*.] The ordinal numeral belonging to the cardinal four.

A. *adj.* 1. In concord with sb. expressed. 2. With ellipsis of sb.; *esp.* of 'day' ME.

1. *F. estate*: see ESTATE *sb.* 2. *The f.* (*of July*) U.S., the anniversary of the Declaration of Independence; also *attrib.* Also quasi-*sb.* in *pl.*

Phr. *F. part*, †*deal*: one of four equal parts of any whole.

B. *sb.* 1. The fraction indicated by a unit in the fourth place in any system of notation having a constant modulus 1594. 2. = *F. part.* 1741. 3. *Mus.* A tone four diatonic degrees above or below any given tone; the interval between any tone and a tone four degrees distant from it; the harmonic combination of two such tones 1597. 4. *pl.* Articles of the fourth degree in quality 1832.

Hence **Fou·rthly** *adv.* in the f. place, †for the f. time.

Fou·r-wheeled, *a.* 1622. [f. FOUR *a.* + WHEEL *sb.* + -ED[2].] Having or running upon four wheels.

Four-whee·ler. 1846. [f. as prec. + -ER[1].] A vehicle with four wheels; *esp.* a four-wheeled hackney carriage.

Foutre, fouter (fū·tǝɪ). 1597. [a. OF. *foutre*:—L. *futuere* (the inf. used subst.).] A term of contempt.

A footra [Q. footre] for the World, and Worldlings base SHAKS. A cowardly *foutre* MARRYAT.

Fovea (fōᵘ·vĭă). 1849. [a. L.] *Anat.*, *Zool.*, *Bot.* A small depression or pit; *esp.* a depression of the retina of the eye. Hence **Fo·veal** *a.* of or pertaining to or situated in a f. (Dicts.) **Fo·veate, Fo·veated** *adjs.* marked with foveæ, pitted.

‖**Foveola** (fovī·ŏlă). 1849. [L., dim. of FOVEA.] A small fovea. Hence **Fo·veolate, Fo·veolated** *adjs.* marked with small foveæ; pitted. var. **Fo·veole.**

Fovilla (fovi·lă). 1793. [mod.L., used by Linnæus in 1766; ? an alteration of *favilla*.] *Bot.* The substance contained in the pollen-cells.

Fowage, var. of FEUAGE.

Fowl (faul), *sb.* [Com. Teut.: OE. *fugel, fugol, fugul*:—OTeut. **foglo-z, fuglo-z*; believed to be ultimately f. *flug-* to FLY.] 1. Any feathered vertebrate animal; = BIRD 2. Now *rare* exc. *collect.* †2. Winged creatures. Also *collect.* in pl. sense. -1648. 3. A barn-door fowl, a domestic cock or hen; a bird of the genus *Gallus.* Often specialized as *barn-door-, game-*, etc. *f.* In U.S. applied also to a domestic duck or turkey. (The prevailing sense.) 1580. 4. The flesh of birds used for food. Now only in *fish, flesh, fowl*, etc. In narrower sense: The flesh of the domestic fowl. 1673.

1. Behold the fowls of the air.. your heavenly Father feedeth them *Matt.* vi. 26. *collect.* All the f. of heaven were flocking to the feast KINGSLEY. 2. Battes, or Rear-mice and other fowle GAGE.

Comb.: f.-cholera = *chicken-cholera* (see CHOLERA); -foot, the plant *Ornithopus perpusillus*; -grass, -meadow-grass, *Poa trivialis*; -run, a place where fowls may run.

Fowl (faul), *v.* [OE. *fug(e)lian*, f. *fugel* FOWL.] *intr.* To catch, hunt, shoot, or snare wildfowl. †b. quasi-*trans.* To hunt over, beat (a bush). B. JONS.

Such persons as may lawfully hunt, fish, or f. BLACKSTONE.

Fowler (fau·lǝɪ). [OE. *fugelere*; see prec.] 1. One who hunts wild birds, whether for sport or food, *esp.* with nets. Now *rare.* †2. A kind of light cannon, *esp.* for use on board ship -1642.

Fowlerite (fau·lĕrǝit). 1832. [named after Dr. S. *Fowler*; see -ITE.] *Min.* A flesh-red variety of rhodonite containing zinc.

Fow·ling-piece. 1596. [f. FOWL *v.* + PIECE *sb.*] 1. A light gun for shooting wild fowl. 2. A picture of game 1888.

Fox (fǫks), *sb.* [Com. Teut.: OE. *fox*, f. (ult.) OTeut. **fuh-*:—pre-Teut. **puk-*, connected by some scholars with Skr. *puccha* tail.]

I. 1. An animal of the genus *Vulpes*, having an elongated pointed muzzle and long bushy tail. Usually *V. vulgaris*, preserved in England and elsewhere as a beast of the chase. 2. *fig.* A crafty man OE. 3. The fur of the fox 1591. 4. The constellation *Vulpecula* 1868. 5. Some beast or fish likened to a fox, *esp.* the gemmeous dragonet (*Callionymus lyra*), called also *f.-fish. Flying-fox, Sea-fox*: see those words. 1611.

1. The wily F. remain'd A subtle pilf'ring Foe SOMERVILLE. 2. Go ye, and tell that f. [Herod], Behold, I cast out devils *Luke* xiii. 32. 3. Furd with Foxe and Lamb-skins too *Meas. for M.* III. ii. 9.

II. Obscure senses. †1. A kind of sword; perhaps so called from the figure of a wolf, on certain sword-blades, being mistaken for a fox -1821. 2. *Naut.* A sort of strand, formed by twisting several rope-yarns together, and used as a seizing, or for mats, etc. 1769. 3. A wedge driven into a split in the end of a bolt called a *fox-bolt* 1874. 4. *In U.S. Colleges*: A freshman. Cf. Ger. *fuchs.* 1839.

1. Put up your f., and let us be jogging SCOTT.

attrib. and *Comb.* 1. General: as *f.-bitch, -burrow, -cover, -cub, -earth, -gin, trap*, etc.

2. Special: f.-beagle, a beagle used for f.-hunting; -bolt (see sense II. 3); -brush, the tail of a f.; -chase, = FOX-HUNT; -colour, a reddish-yellow colour, whence *f.-coloured* adj.; -evil, a disease in which the hair falls off, alopecia; -hound, a superior variety of hound trained and used for f.-hunting; -key, 'a splitcotter with a thin wedge of steel driven into the end to prevent its working back'; -sleep, a pretended sleep; -terrier, one of a breed of short-haired terriers, used for unearthing foxes, but kept chiefly as pets; -trot, a pace with short steps, as in changing from trotting to walking; also, an American dance; also as vb.; -wedge, a long wedge driven between two other wedges with their thick ends placed in the opposite direction; †-whelp, a cub of the f. (used also as a term of contempt); -wood, decayed wood, *esp.* such as emits a phosphorescent light (U.S.)

b. in names of animals, etc., more or less resembling the f.: f.-bat = FLYING-FOX; -fish, see FOX I. 5; -lynx, a variety of lynx; -moth, a greyish-brown European bombycid moth (*Lasiocampa rubi*); -shark, the sea-fox (*Alopias vulpes*); -snake, a large harmless snake of the United States (*Coluber vulpinus*); -sparrow, a N. Amer. sparrow (*Passerella iliaca*); -squirrel, a N. Amer. squirrel (*Sciurus cinereus, S. niger*, etc.).

c. in plant names: f.-bane, *Aconitum Vulparia*; -berry = BEARBERRY; -grape, a U.S. name for several species of wild grapes.

d. in names of games in which one of the players acts as a f.: f. and geese, a game played on a board with pegs, draughtsmen, or the like; f. and hounds, a boys' game in which the 'hounds' chase the 'fox'; †f. in or to the or thy hole, a boys' game in which they lift up one leg and hop on the other.

Fox (fǫks), *v.* 1567. [f. prec. sb.] 1. †*trans.* To play the fox for; *intr.* to play the fox, sham. Now *dial.* and *slang.* 1602. 2. *trans.* To intoxicate 1611. †Also *transf.* and *fig.* †3. *trans.* To pierce with a fox (see FOX *sb.* II. 1) -1589. 4. *trans.* To discolour (the leaves of a book) 1848. 5. *intr.* Of beer: To turn sour in fermenting; also *trans.* (causatively) 1744. 6. To repair (boots or shoes) by renewing the upper leather 1796. 7. *intr.* To hunt the fox. *U.S.* 1887.

2. The last of whom I did almost f. with Margate ale PEPYS. Hence **Foxed** *ppl. a.* intoxicated; repaired by foxing; discoloured by decay; stained with brownish-yellow spots; etc.

Foxery (fǫ·ksĕri). ME. [f. FOX *sb.* + -ERY.] The character or behaviour of a fox, wiliness, cunning.

Fox-fire. Now only *U.S.* 1483. The phosphorescent light emitted by decayed timber.

Fox-fu·r. 1599. The fur of the fox; a gown trimmed with fox-fur. Hence **Fo·x-furred** *a.* trimmed with fox-fur; wearing fox-fur, or a fox-furred gown.

Fox-glove (fǫ·ksˌglɒv). [OE. *foxes glófa*: see FOX *sb.* and GLOVE. ? Why assoc. w. the fox.] 1. The popular name of *Digitalis purpurea*, a common ornamental flowering plant. b. Used in medicine: see DIGITALIS. 1801. 2. Applied to plants of other genera; e.g. formerly to the Mullein 1587. 3. *attrib.* 1811.

1. Fox-glove and nightshade, side by side, Emblems of punishment and pride SCOTT.

Fo·x-hunt. 1816. The chase of a fox with hounds. So **Fo·x-hunting** *vbl. sb.* the sport of hunting the fox. **Fo·x-hunter, -huntsman**, etc.

†**Fo·xish**, *a.* ME. [see -ISH.] Fox-like; also *fig.* -1699.

Foxite (fǫ·kseit). 1782. [see -ITE.] A political follower of Charles James Fox. Also *attrib.*

Fox-like (fǫ·kslǝik), *a.* 1577. [f. FOX *sb.* + LIKE *a.*] Like a fox; esp. crafty.

†**Fo·xly.** ME. [f. as prec. + -LY[1] and [2].]

A. *adj.* Crafty, cunning -1594.

B. *adv.* Craftily.

Foxship (fǫ·ksˌʃip). [see -SHIP.] The character or qualities of a fox. *Cor.* IV. ii. 18.

Fo·xtail. ME. [f. FOX *sb.* + TAIL *sb.*] 1. The tail of a fox, a fox's brush. Formerly a jester's badge. 2. a. One of various species of grass with soft brush-like spikes of flowers, esp. *Alopecurus pratensis* 1552. b. A club-moss (*Lycopodium clavatum*) 1866. 3. *Metall.* The cinder obtained in the last stage of the charcoal-finery process 1873.

Comb.: f.-saw, a dovetail saw; -wedging, a method of fixing a tenon in a mortise by splitting the end of the tenon and inserting a projecting wedge, then entering the tenon into the mortise and driving it home.

Foxy (fǫ·ksi), *a.* 1528. [f. FOX *sb.* + -Y[1].] 1. Fox-like; crafty. 2. Fox-coloured, reddish brown or yellow 1850; in *Painting*, over-hot in colouring 1783. 3. Used to denote various defects of colour and quality resulting from age, damp, improper treatment, etc. 1805. 4. Of beer, wine, etc.: Turned sour, not properly fermented 1847. 5. Of grapes: Having the coarse flavour of the fox-grape (Webster).

1. Modred's narrow f. face TENNYSON. 2. In some of the England series there is a violent f. tone, very hot and oppressive THORNBURY *Turner* II. 342. Hence **Fo·xiness.**

†**Foy**, *sb.*[1] 1590. [a. F. *foi*, later form of *fei* FAY *sb.*[1]] Faith, allegiance, fealty. Also as an exclam. -1694.

Foy (foi), *sb.*[2] Now *dial.* 1496. [a. Du. *fooi*, prob. a. F. *voie* way, journey.] A parting entertainment, present, etc., given by or to one setting out on a journey.

He did at the Dog give me, and some other friends of his, his f., he being to set sail to-day PEPYS.

‖**Foyer** (fwaye). 1859. [F. *foyer*:—L. **focarium*, f. *focus*.] 1. = FOCUS 4. 1878. 2. Orig., the green-room in French theatres; now usually, a large room in a theatre, etc., to which the audience may retire during the intervals.

Foysen, -so(u)n, -zon, etc., obs. ff. FOISON.

Fozy (fōu·zi), *a.* *Sc.* and *dial.* 1821. [Cf. Du. *voos* spongy.] Spongy, loose-textured; also of flesh = FOGGY. Also *fig.* 'fat-witted'. Hence **Fo·ziness.**

Frab (fræb), *v. dial.* 1848. [Onomatopœic.] *trans.* To harass, worry.

Fracas (fraka; in U.S. frē¹·kăs). 1727. [a. F., ad. It. *fracasso*, vbl. sb. f. *fracassare* to make an uproar.] A disturbance, uproar, brawl.

Frache. ? *Obs.* 1662. A metal tray for holding glass-ware in the annealing process.

†**Fra·cid,** *a.* 1655. [ad. L. *fracidus*, f. *frac-, frax* lees of oil.] Rotten from over-ripeness.

Fra·cted, *ppl. a.* 1547. [f. L. *fract-, frangere* + -ED¹.] *Her.* Having a part displaced as if broken 1828.

Fraction (fræ·kʃən), *sb.* ME. [a. OF. *fraccion* (F. *fraction*), ad. eccl. L. *fractionem*, f. *frangere.*] 1. The action of breaking 1504. †2. The result of breaking; the state of being broken; a broken place, breach, fissure, rupture; *spec.* in *Surg.* a fracture -1798. †3. Discord, dissension; a rupture; brawling -1721. 4. Something broken off; a portion; a fragment 1606. 5. *Arith.* and *Alg.* One or more aliquot parts of a unit or whole number; an expression for a definite portion of a unit or magnitude ME.

1. Though it may be said..that he suffreth f. or breaking in the Sacrament when it is broken..yet [etc.] 1602. 4. Crumbling into Fractions and Factions 1657. 5. *Common* or *vulgar fractions*: those in which the numerator and denominator are represented by numbers placed the one above, the other below, a horizontal line. *Complex, compound, continued, decimal, proper, improper fractions*: see those words. Hence **Fra·ction** *v.* to break into fractions CARLYLE.

Fractional (fræ·kʃənăl), *a.* 1675. [f. prec. + -AL.] Of, pertaining to, or dealing with a fraction or fractions; comprising or constituting a fraction; of the nature of a fraction. Hence, Incomplete, partial, insignificant.

F. currency: small coin, or paper notes, in circulation, of less value than the monetary unit (Webster). *F. distillation*: see DISTILLATION. Hence **Fra·ctionally** *adv.*

Fractionary (fræ·kʃənări), *a.* 1674. [f. as prec. + -ARY.] a. = prec. b. Dealing with or carried on by fractions or fragments 1840. c. Tending to divide into fractions 1867.

Fractionate (fræ·kʃəneⁱt), *v.* 1867. [f. as prec. + -ATE ³.] *trans.* To separate (a mixture) by distillation or otherwise into portions of differing properties. Hence **Fractiona·tion,** the action of fractionating.

Fractionize (fræ·kʃənəiz), *v.* 1675. [f. FRACTION + -IZE.] *trans.* (and *absol.*) To break up into fractions.

Fractious (fræ·kʃəs), *a.* 1725. [f. FRACTION (sense 3), after *captious*, etc.] Refractory, unruly; now chiefly, cross, fretful; *esp.* of children.

A terribly peevish f. fellow W. IRVING. F. cows 1880. Hence **Fra·ctious-ly** *adv.*, **-ness.**

Fracture (fræ·ktiŭı), *sb.* 1525. [a. F., ad. L. *fractura*, f. *fract-, frangere.*] 1. The action of breaking or fact of being broken; breakage; *spec.* in *Surg.* the breaking of a bone, etc. 1541. 2. The result of breaking; a crack, division, split; †a *splinter* 1641. 3. The appearance of the fresh surface in a mineral, when broken irregularly by the blow of a hammer 1794. 4. *Phonology.* Diphthongization of a vowel before a consonant group 1891.

Fracture (fræ·ktiŭı), *v.* 1612. [f. prec. sb.] 1. *trans.* To cause a fracture in, *esp.* a bone, etc.; to break; to crack. 2. *intr.* for *refl.* To suffer fracture; to break 18...

1. To f. a rib 1803, parts of a machine 1858.

‖**Frænulum** (frī·niŭlŏm). 1706. [dim. of FRÆNUM.] *Anat.* A small frænum; a frænum.

‖**Frænum, frenum** (frī·nŏm). *Pl.* **-na.** 1741. [L.; = 'a bridle'.] 1. *Anat.* A small ligament or membranous fold which restrains the motion of the organ to which it is attached. 2. One of two minute folds of skin, in some cirripedes, which serve, through the means of a sticky solution, to retain the eggs until they are hatched. DARWIN.

Fragile (fræ·dʒil), *a.* 1513. [a. F., ad. L. *fragilis*, f. *frag-, frangere.*] 1. Liable to break or be broken; brittle; easily destroyed. Also *fig.* Of persons, etc. = FRAIL. 1607. †2. Liable to err or fall into sin; frail -1548.

1. Of Bodies, some are F.; and some are Tough, but not F. BACON. A single f. life FROUDE. Hence **Fra·gile·ly** *adv.*, **-ness.**

Fragility (frădʒi·lĭti). ME. [a. F., ad. L. *fragilitatem*; see FRAILTY.] 1. The quality of being fragile or easily broken; hence, weakness, delicacy 1474. Also *fig.* †2. Moral weakness, folly -1624.

1. An appearance of delicacy, and even of f., is almost essential to it [beauty] BURKE. *fig.* The f. of life, of beauty JOHNSON, of popular government MAINE. 2. The fragylyte [of Adam and Eue] LD. BERNERS.

Fragment (fræ·gmĕnt). 1531. [a. F., or ad. L. *fragmentum.*] 1. A piece broken off; a (comparatively) small portion of anything 1583. 2. *transf.* and *fig.* A detached, isolated, or incomplete part, e.g. of a writing or composition 1531.

1. *John* vi. 13. Fragments of old walles LITHGOW. 2. Howe fragmentes or partes of a Globe are measured 1571. He conuerses much in fragments and *Desunt multa*'s EARLE. The 'New Atlantis' is but a f. JOWETT.

Hence **Fragme·ntal, fra·gmental** *a.* fragmentary; *Geol.* consisting of the débris of older rocks, or of the aggregated remains of plants or animals. **Fra·gmentally** *adv.*

Fragmentary (fræ·gmĕntări), *a.* 1611. [f. FRAGMENT + -ARY. Cf. F. *fragmentaire.*] Of the nature of, or composed of, fragments; not complete or entire; disconnected; in *Geol.* composed of fragments of previously-existing rocks, etc. Hence **Fra·gmentarily** *adv.* **Fra·gmentariness.** var. **Fragmenti·tious** *a. rare.*

Fragmentation (frægmĕntē¹·ʃən). 1881. [f. as prec. + -ATION.] A breaking or separation into fragments; in *Biol.* separation into parts which form new individuals.

Fragmented (fræ·gmĕntėd), *pa. pple.* and *ppl. a.* 1830. [f. FRAGMENT + -ED². Cf. F. *fragmenté.*] Broken into fragments, made fragmentary.

Fragmentist (fræ·gmĕntist). 1874. [f. as prec. + -IST.] A writer of fragments or of works which survive only in fragments. So **Fra·gmentize** *v.* to break into fragments.

†**Fragor.** *rare.* 1605. [a. L., f. *frag-, frangere.*] A loud harsh noise, a crash, a din -1702.

Fragrance (frē¹·grăns). 1667. [a. OF., ad. L. *fragrantia*; see FRAGRANT.] Sweetness of smell; sweet or pleasing scent.

Eve separate he spies, Veiled in a cloud of f. MILT.

Fragrancy (frē¹·grănsi). Now *rare.* 1578. [see prec. and -ANCY.] The quality of being FRAGRANT. Also with *pl.*

The goblet crown'd Breath'd aromatic fragrancies around POPE.

Fragrant (frē¹·grănt), *a.* 1500. [a. F., or ad. L. *fragrantem*, f. *fragrare* to smell sweetly.] Emitting a pleasant odour; sweet-smelling.

F. the fertil earth After soft showers MILT. *P. L.* IV. 645. Hence **Fra·grant-ly** *adv.*, †**-ness.**

Frail (frē¹l), *sb.* ME. [a. OF. *frayel*, of unkn. origin.] 1. A basket made of rushes, used for packing figs, raisins, etc.; the quantity (30 to 75 lb.) contained in this. 2. 'A rush for weaving baskets' (J.) 1755.

Frail (frē¹l), *a.* ME. [ad. OF. *fraile, frele* (Fr. *frêle*):—L. *fragilis.*] 1. Liable to break or be broken; easily destroyed. Of immaterial things: Subject to casualties, transient. 2. Weak; easily overcome ME. 3. Morally weak; unable to resist temptation; *occas.*, that lives unchastely ME. †4. Tender. SPENSER.

1. In that f. bark the lovers sit 1812. A profounder but a frailer bliss J. MARTINEAU. 2. That I may know how fraile I am *Ps.* xxxix. 4. 3. Our most fraile affections HOOKER. Most likely a child of the f. Abbess of Leominster FREEMAN. Hence **Frai·lly** *adv.* **Frai·lness.**

Frailty (frē¹·lti). ME. [ad. OF. *frailete*:—L. *fragilitatem*; see FRAGILE.] 1. Liability to be crushed or to decay; perishableness, weakness; an instance of this; †also, a flaw. Now *rare.* 2. Moral weakness; instability of mind; liability to err or yield to temptation; also, a weakness ME.

1. The works of man inherit..Their author's f., and return to dust COWPER. 2. No farther seek..to..draw his frailties from their dread abode GRAY.

†‖**Fraischeur.** *rare.* 1599. [F. (now *fraîcheur*), f. *frais, fraîche* fresh.] Freshness. -1661.

Fraise (frē¹z), *sb.*¹ 1775. [a. F. *fraise* fem.; app. a transf. use of *fraise* mesentery of a calf.] 1. A ruff 1801. 2. *Fortif.* A palisade, made horizontal or slightly inclining to the horizon, placed for defence round a work near the berm.

Fraise (frē¹z), *sb.*² 1874. [a. F., f. *fraiser, fraser*, to enlarge a circular hole, f. *fraise* (see prec.).] A tool for enlarging a circular hole; also, in *Watchmaking*, for cutting teeth in a wheel.

Fraise (frē¹z), *v.* 1706. [ad. F. *fraiser* (see FRAISE *sb.*¹).] *trans.* To fence or defend with or as with a fraise.

Fraken(e, -yn(e, var. ff. FRECKEN.

Framable, frameable (frē¹·măb'l), *a.* 1577. [f. FRAME *v.* + -ABLE.] Capable of being framed; †conformable.

Frambœsia (fræmbī·ziă). 1803. [mod.L., f. F. *framboise*; see next.] *Path.* The yaws. Hence **Frambœ·sioid** *a.* like f.

†**Framboise.** 1578. [a. F., *framboise*, ? a corruption of Du. *braambezie*, lit. bramble-berry; see BRAMBLE, BROOM, BERRY.] The raspberry (*Rubus Idæus*).

Frame (frē¹m), *sb.* ME. [In sense I, perh. repr. OE. *fram* adj., forward (see FROM *prep.*); in other senses, f. the vb.]

†I. Advantage, benefit. ME. only.

II. †1. The action of framing, fashioning, or constructing; a contrivance -1645. 2. The manner or method of framing; construction, structure; constitution, nature 1590. 3. An established order, plan, scheme, system, *esp.* of government 1599. †b. A form of words; a formula; a type of syllogism -1739. †4. Adapted or adjusted condition; order, regularity, shape -1810. 5. Mental or emotional disposition or state (more explicitly *f. of mind, soul*, etc.) 1665. 6. *F.-up* (cf. FRAME *v.* 8e) 1907.

1. John the bastard, Whose spirits toile in f. of villanies SHAKS. 2. We have in our inward f. various affections BUTLER. 3. But let the f. of things disioynt, Both the worlds suffer SHAKS. 4. Put your discourse into some f. *Haml.* III. ii. 321. 5. I am a Fellow of a very odd F. of mind STEELE. In this thankful f. I continued DE FOE.

III. 1. A structure, fabric, or engine constructed of parts fitted together. Now *obs.* or *arch.* exc. as applied to the heaven, earth, etc., regarded as a structure, or to the animal, *esp.* the human body, with ref. to its build, etc. ME. 2. A structure of timber, joists, etc. forming the skeleton of a building ME.; a building; in later use, one composed chiefly or entirely of wood (*Obs.* exc. *U.S.*) ME. 3. A skeleton structure or support; e.g. the ribs or stretchers for an umbrella or parasol; (*Printing*) a desk containing type cases for the use of a compositor, or the stand supporting them; (*Naut.*) the bends of timbers, or the corresponding parts of an ironclad, constituting the shape of the ship's body; etc. 1536. 4. That in which something, *esp.* a picture, pane of glass, etc., is set or let in, as in a border or case 1600. 5. Hence applied to utensils of which the frame or border is an important part; as: a. (*Founding*) a kind of ledge enclosing a board, which being filled with sand, serves as a mould for castings 1724; b. (*Embroidery* and *Weaving*) †a loom; now short for *lace-, stocking-f.*, etc. 1523; c. (*Horticulture*) a glazed structure for protecting seeds and young plants from frost, etc. 1664.

1. The starry f. 1594. This goodly f. the Earth. SHAKS. 4. *fig.* A grass-plat..set in the heavy f. of the forest C. BRONTË.

Comb. (sense III. 2) as *f. building, cottage, house*; f. **-breaker,** one of those who resisted with violence the introduction of frames for weaving stockings, etc.; **-bridge,** a bridge constructed of pieces of timber framed together; **-dam,** a dam formed of balks of fir wood, placed endwise against the pressure; **-level,** a mason's level; **-saw,** a saw stretched in a f. to make it rigid; **-stud** (see STUD *sb.*¹ I. 1); **-tubbing,** solid wood tubbing.

Frame (frē¹m), *v.* [OE. *framian* to further, f. *fram* forward *adj.* and *adv.* (see FROM).] †1. *intr.* To profit, be of service -ME. †2.

To gain ground; to get on (*with*); to succeed -1669. †3. To make ready for use; also, to furnish *with*. ME. only. †4. To prepare (timber) for use in building; to perform the carpenter's work for (a building) ME. 5. To shape; to give shape, expression, or direction to 1543. b. *refl.* and *absol.* To shape one's course; to resort. *Obs.* exc. *dial.* = 'go'. 1576. c. *intr.* for *refl.*, now chiefly *dial.* 1602. 6. *trans.* To adapt, adjust, fit *to* or *into* 1550. †Also *intr.* for *refl.* To conform, fit -1642. 7. *trans.* To make, construct. Now always implying the combination and fitting together of parts, and adaptation to a design. 1555. 8. a. To contrive (a plot, etc.); to fabricate; to compose; to put into words 1514. b. To articulate 1609. c. To form in the mind 1597. †d. To bring to pass -1597. e. *To f. up* (orig. *U.S. slang*): to pre-arrange (an event) with sinister intent; to fake the result of (a race, etc.); also (*to f.*), to concoct a false charge against 1910. 9. [f. the sb.] To enclose in or as in a frame; to serve as a frame for 1705.

2. It framed not according to expectation WORLIDGE. 5. The Iron..is softned and framed 1678. Why I can ..f. my Face to all occasions SHAKS. God knows how, after that, my life was framed CARY. b. The beauty of this sinful dame Made many princes thither f. SHAKS. 6. Unto this he frames his song WORDSW. 7. The sovran Planter, when he fram'd All things to mans delightful use MILT. The fieldfare framed her lowly nest SCOTT. 8. a. This was a Story framed long after BURNET. d. Which Heauen so f. SHAKS.

Fra·me-house. 1817. [f. FRAME *sb.* and *v.* + HOUSE.] A house constructed with a wooden framework covered with boards.

Framer (frē¹·məɹ). 1561. [f. FRAME *v.* + -ER¹.] One who frames.

The f. of the government LOCKE, of an objection 1741, of a picture 1870.

Fra·mework. 1644. [f. FRAME *sb.* + WORK *sb.*] 1. A structure composed of parts framed together; a frame or skeleton. Also *transf.* and *fig.* 2. (As two words or hyphened.) Work done in or with a frame 1819.

1. The f. of vertebrate animals 1885. *fig.* The outward f. of law and government FREEMAN.

Framing (frē¹·miŋ), *vbl. sb.* ME. [f. FRAME *v.* + -ING.¹] 1. The action, method, or process of constructing, making, or shaping anything. 2. *concr.* Framed work; a frame or set or system of frames 1703.

Comb. **f.-chisel**, a heavy chisel for making mortises.

Frampold, *a.* Also *frample*, etc. *Obs.* exc. *dial.* 1598. [?] 1. Sour-tempered, disagreeable, peevish. 2. Of a horse: Fiery, mettlesome 1603.

1. She leads a very f. life with him *Merry W.* II. ii. 94. 2. Good phrampell iades MIDDLETON & DEKKER.

Franc (fræŋk). ME. [a. F. *franc*, said to be derived from the legend *Francorum rex* 'king of the Franks', on the first coins so called.] The name of a French coin or money of account. a. A gold coin, in the 14th c., weighing about 60 grs. b. A silver coin, first struck in 1575, valued in the 18th c. at 9*d.* or 10*d.* c. Since 1795, a silver coin, the monetary unit of the decimal system, worth nearly 10*d.*

‖**Franc-archer** (frankarʃe). Pl. **franc(s-)archers.** 1675. [Fr.; *franc* free + *archer* archer.] *Fr. Hist.* One of a body of archers established by Charles VII, and exempted from taxes in consideration of their service.

Franchise (fræ·ntʃiz, -tʃəiz), *sb.* ME. [a. OF. *franchise* freedom, frankness, f. *franc* free, FRANK *a.*²]

I. †1. Freedom; exemption from servitude or subjection -1648. 2. a. A legal immunity or exemption from a particular burden, or from the jurisdiction of a particular tribunal, granted to an individual, a corporation, etc. In early use also *collect.* or in generalized sense: The immunities, etc., belonging to a municipality, etc. ME. b. More widely: A privilege granted by the sovereign power to any person or body of persons. In England now chiefly *Hist.*; in U.S. applied *esp.* to the powers conferred on a company for some purpose of public utility. ME. †3. Freedom from arrest, secured to fugitives in certain privileged places; right of asylum or sanctuary. Hence *concr.* an asylum, sanctuary. -1601. 4. The freedom of a body corporate or politic; citizenship 1579. †5. The district over which a particular privilege extends -1774. 6. The right of voting at public elections, *esp.* for members of the legislative body. (The prevailing sense.) 1790. b. In recent use: One of the various qualifications for the elective franchise. *Fancy f.*: see FANCY. 1884.

2. a. All franchises and liberties of the bisshopperricks..deryvid from the crowne 1559. b. The f. of waife and stray COKE. Fairs, Markets, and other franchises 16.. The form which corruption takes in the populous cities [of the U.S.] is the sale of 'franchises' (especially monopolies in the use of public thoroughfares) BRYCE. 5. Phr. †*To go* or *ride the franchises*: to beat the bounds.

†II. 1. Nobility of mind; liberality, magnanimity -1658. 2. Freedom or licence of speech or manners 1567.

†**Fra·nchise**, *v.* ME. [a. OF. *franchiss-*, *franchir*, f. *franc* free; see FRANK *a.*²] = ENFRANCHISE *v.* Const. *from*, *of*. -1793. Hence †**Fra·nchisement** = ENFRANCHISEMENT.

Francic (fræ·nsik), *a.* ? *Obs.* 1698. [ad. med.L. *Francicus*, f. *Francus* FRANK *sb.*¹] = FRANKISH.

Francisc (fransi·sk). Also **-esque, -isque.** 1801. [ad. med.L. *francisca.*] A kind of battle-axe used by the Franks.

Franciscan (fransi·skăn). 1592. [f. med.L. *Franciscus* Francis + -AN.]

A. *adj.* Of or belonging to the order of St. Francis; pertaining to the Franciscans.

The long F. controversy about poverty PUSEY.

B. *sb.* A friar of the order founded by St. Francis of Assisi in 1209.

Francize (fræ·nsəiz), *v.* 1661. [ad. F. *franciser*, f. *français* French.] *trans.* To make French. Hence **Franciza·tion**, the making French; the status thus conferred.

Franco- (fræ·ŋko), orig. med.L., comb. f. *Franci* the Franks or French; chiefly in combs., as *F.-American*, etc.

Francolin (fræ·ŋkŏlin). 1653. [a. F., ad. It. *francolino.*] A bird of the genus *Francolinus* (sub-family *Perdicinæ* or Partridges), somewhat resembling a pheasant. Also *f. partridge.*

Francolite (fræ·ŋkŏləit). 1850. [f. *Franco* + -LITE.] *Min.* A variety of apatite found at Wheal *Franco* in Devonshire in stalactitic masses.

Francophil(e (fræ·ŋkŏfil). 1889. [f. FRANCO- + Gr. φίλος friend. A newspaper word.]

A. *adj.* Characterized by partiality to the French.

B. *sb.* One who is affected.

‖**Franc tireur** (frantīrör). 1870. [F.; f. *franc* free + *tireur* shooter.] One of a corps of light infantry, originating in the wars of the French Revolution, and having an organization distinct from that of the regular army.

Frangent (fræ·ndʒĕnt), *a.* [ad. L. *frangentem*, *frangere.*] Causing fractures. H. WALPOLE.

Frangible (fræ·ndʒib'l), *a.* 1440. [a. OF., f. L. *frangere.*] Capable of being broken. Hence **Frangibi·lity**, f. quality.

Frangipane (fræ·ndʒipē¹n). 1676. [a. F., said to be from *Frangipani*, name of the inventor.] 1. A perfume prepared from, or imitating the odour of, the flower of the red jasmine. 2. The red jasmine tree (*Plumiera rubra*) 1866. 3. A kind of pastry, containing cream, almonds, spice, etc. 1858. var. **Frangipan(n)i** (in sense 1).

Frangulin (fræ·ŋgiŭlin). 1864. [f. the name of the tree (*Rhamnus*) *Frangula* + -IN.] *Chem.* 'A yellow crystallisable colouring matter, contained in the bark of the berry-bearing alder' (Watts). Hence **Frangu·lic (acid)** *a.*

†**Fra·nion.** 1571. [?] A gallant, paramour. Also, in Spenser, a loose woman. -1810.

Frank (fræŋk), *sb.*¹ and *a.*¹ [ad. L. *Francus*, F. *Franc*; a name of Teut. origin, repr. OHG. *Franko* = OE. *Franca* :—prehistoric **Frankon-*. The Franks were supposed to be named from their national weapon, OE. *franca* javelin.]

A. *sb.* 1. A person belonging to the Germanic nation, or coalition of nations, that conquered Gaul in the 6th c., and from whom the country received the name of France. 2. A name given in the Levant to an individual of Western nationality. Cf. FERINGHEE. 1687. †3. With ellipsis of 'language'. A *lingua franca* or mixed tongue. NEVILE.

†B. *adj.* Belonging to, characteristic of, or customary among the Western nations of Europe -1688.

†**Frank**, *sb.*² ME. [a. OF. *franc.*] An enclosure, *esp.* a sty. Also, the process of fattening animals. -1736. Hence **f.-fed** *a.* fed in a f.; fatted.

†**Frank**, *sb.*³ 1578. [f. FRANK *v.*] A name given to the plant Spurry, from its property of fattening cattle; also *f. spurry* -1659.

Frank (fræŋk), *sb.*⁴ 1713. [f. FRANK *v.*²] 1. The signature of a person entitled to send letters post free. 2. A letter or envelope bearing such a signature 1755.

1. I must..send this scrawl into town to get a f...it is not worthy of postage SCOTT.

Frank (fræŋk), *sb.*⁵ *dial.* 1823. [from its note.] A heron.

Frank, *a.*¹: see after FRANK *sb.*¹

Frank (fræŋk), *a.*² ME. [a. OF. *franc* :— med.L. *francus* free; orig. identical with the ethnic name *Francus* (see FRANK *sb.*¹).] 1. = FREE in various applications (see quots.). 2. Liberal, bounteous, generous, lavish 1484. 3. Not practising concealment; ingenuous, open 1555; unreserved, outspoken 1548; avowed; downright 1752. †4. Of plants, trees, etc.: Of superior quality; producing good and abundant fruit or the like. Of drugs, etc.: Of high quality. Cf. FRANKINCENSE -1648. †5. Lusty, vigorous -1626.

1. F. and free borne in a free cytye 1470. He shulde goo f. and quite 1475. Desyrouse of f. lyberty 1538. Landes..franke and free simpliciter and wythout anye condicion MORE. It is of franke gift SPENSER. 2. In such f. style the people lived FROUDE. 3. In their conversation f. and open BURKE. To be f. with any-one 1870. 5. The Sap is not so f. as to rise all to the Boughs BACON.

†**Frank**, *v.*¹ ME. [f. FRANK *sb.*²] 1. *trans.* To shut up and feed in a frank -1600. 2. To feed high; to cram -1633. Also *fig.* Hence †**Franked** *ppl. a.* fattened in a frank or pen.

Frank (fræŋk), *v.*² 1708. [f. FRANK *a.*²] 1. *trans.* To sign (a letter, etc.), so as to ensure its being sent free of charge; to send or cause to be sent free of charge. *Obs.* exc. *Hist.* b. *fig.* To facilitate the coming and going of (a person) 1801. 2. To convey gratuitously 1809. 3. To exempt. Const. *against*, *from*. 1876.

2. He got an opportunity of being franked to Poland BURTON.

Frank-almoign, -almoin. [a. AF. *fraunke almoigne*; see FRANK *a.*² and ALMOIGN.] *Law.* See ALMOIGN 2.

Fra·nk chase. 1587. [f. FRANK *a.*² + CHASE *sb.*] *Law.* Free chase.

None but the King can have a forest; If he chance to passe one over to a Subject, 'tis no more Forest, but frank Chase HOWELL.

Fra·nk-fee. 1531. [f. FRANK *a.*² + FEE *sb.*] A tenure of lands in fee-simple, *esp.* as opp. to *ancient demesne*; also, land so held.

†**Frank-ferm.** [a. AF. *franke ferme*; see FRANK *a.*² and FARM *sb.*²] *Law.* Freehold tenure at a fixed rent. BLACKSTONE.

Fra·nkfold. 1609. [f. FRANK *a.*² + FOLD *v.*²] *Law.* = FALDAGE.

Frankfort (fræ·ŋkfɔ̆ɹt). 1823. The name of a German city. **Frankfort black,** a fine black pigment used in copper-plate engraving.

Frankincense (fræ·ŋkinsens), ME. [a. OF. *franc encens*; see FRANK *a.*² 4 and INCENSE.] 1. An aromatic gum resin, yielded by trees of the genus *Boswellia*, used for burning as incense: olibanum; *occas.*, the smoke from the same. 2. Resin resembling this, obtained from firs and pines. Also, the tree itself. 1577.

1. Curling f. ascends to Baal PRIOR.

Frankish (fræ·ŋkiʃ), *a.* (*sb.*) 1594. [f. FRANK *sb.*¹ + -ISH.] 1. Of or pertaining to the Franks 1802. 2. Of or pertaining to the Western nations 1594. 3. *sb.* The language of the Franks 1863.

†**Frank-law.** 1607. [f. FRANK *a.*² + LAW.] *Law.* The condition of a full freeman (*liber et legalis homo*), esp. the liberty of being sworn in courts, as a juror or witness -1641.

Franklin (fræ·ŋklin). ME. [First recorded as Anglo-L. *franc-colanus, francalanus, franchelanus*; f. (ult.) med.L. *francus*, OF. *franc* FRANK *a.*[2]; but the suffix is obscure.] †1. A freeman. ME. only. 2. A freeholder; in 14-15th c. the designation of a class of landowners ranking next below the gentry ME. †3. Applied to: A liberal host -1727.

2. Ful wel biloved and famulier was he With frankeleyns over al in his cuntre CHAUCER.

Franklinian (frænkli·niăn). 1767. [f. *Franklin* proper name + -IAN.]

A. *adj.* Of or pertaining to Benjamin Franklin; following Franklin (in politics).

B. *sb.* A follower of Franklin 1794.

So **Frankli·nic** *a.*, an epithet applied to electricity produced by friction; **Fra·nklinism**, frictional electricity; **Fra·nklinist**, one who follows Franklin in his theory of electricity.

Franklinite (fræ·nklinəit). 1820. [f. *Franklin*, New Jersey + -ITE.] *Min.* A compound of oxides of iron, manganese, and zinc, found in brilliant black crystals.

Frankly (fræ·ŋkli), *adv.* 1540. [f. FRANK *a.*[2] + -LY[2].] In a frank manner; freely.

Kindness so f. offered C. BRONTË.

†Fra·nk-ma·rriage. OE. [a. AF. *franc mariage*; see FRANK *a.*[2] and MARRIAGE.] *Law.* A tenure in virtue of which a man and his wife held lands granted to them by the father or other near relative of the wife, the estate being heritable to the fourth generation of heirs of their bodies, without any service other than fealty.

Frankness (fræ·nknės). 1553. [f. FRANK *a.*[2] + -NESS.] The quality of being FRANK; †liberality -1771; candour, ingenuousness, openness, *esp.* in speech 1553; freedom of artistic treatment 1784.

2. That happy union of f. and reserve HELPS. Military f. GIBBON.

Fra·nk-pledge. *Obs.* exc. *Hist.* 1502. [a. AF. *franc-plege*, f. *franc* FRANK *a.*[2] + *plege* PLEDGE; app. a Norman mistranslation of OE. *friþ-borh* (see FRITHBORH).] *OE. Law.* 1. The system by which every member of a tithing was answerable for the good conduct of, or the damage done by, any one of the other members 16.. 2. One of the mutually responsible members of a tithing, etc *Occas.*, the tithing itself.

1. *transf.* The servants of the Crown were not, as now, bound in f. for each other MACAULAY. Phr. †*View of frankpledge*: a court held periodically for the production of the members of a tithing, later of a hundred or manor. Cf. COURT-LEET. ME.

Fra·nk-te·nement. 1523. [a. AFr.; see FRANK *a.*[2] and TENEMENT.] *Law.* = FREEHOLD. So **Fra·nk-te·nure.**

Frantic (fræ·ntik). [ME. *frentik, frantik*, a. OF. *frenetique* (mod. *frénétique*), ad. late L. *phreneticus* delirious (see PHRENETIC). See FRENZY.]

A. *adj.* 1. Affected with mental disease, lunatic, insane; in later use, ragingly mad. Now *rare.* b. *transf.* and *fig.* 1547. 2. †Attended by frenzy -1594; delirious, wild, insanely foolish 1533. †3. quasi-*adv.* Frantically. *rare.* -1652.

1. I haue obserued .. in phrenticke persons the strength doubled vpon them 1586. b. *fig.* A heart.. Raging more wilde then is this franticke sea MARSTON. 2. She displayed a f. and impotent rage GIBBON. Hence **Fra·ntically, Fra·nticly** *advs.* in a f. manner. **Fra·nticness**, f. state or condition.

†B. *sb.* One who is frantic; a lunatic, a delirious patient -1758.

Frap (fræp), *v.* ME. [a. OF. *fraper* (mod. *frapper*); perh. f. the Teut. root *flap-*; see FLAP.] 1. *trans.* and †*intr.* To strike; to beat. 2. *Naut.* To bind tightly. [So in Fr.] 1548. b. To brace the cords of a drum by pulling them together 1874.

†Fra·pe. ME. [? a. OF. *frap*, f. *fraper*; see prec.] 1. A crowd; a mob, the rabble -1710. 2. ? Tumult. R. BRUNNE.

†Fra·ple, *v.* 1595. [Cf. FRAP *v.*] *intr.* To dispute, wrangle, bluster -1609. Hence **Fra·pler** *sb. arch.* a blusterer.

‖**Frappé** (frape), *a.* 1848. [Fr.; pa. pple. of *frapper.*] Iced, cooled.

Frass (fræs). 1854. [a. Ger. *frass*, f. root of *fressen* to devour.] The excrement of larvæ; also, the refuse left behind by boring insects.

‖**Frate** (frā·te). *Pl.* **-ti** (-tī). 1722. [It.; = 'brother'.] A friar.

Frater[1] (frē·tər). Now *Hist.* ME. [a. OF. *fraitur*, short for *refreitor*, repr. med.L. *refectorium* REFECTORY.] The eating room of a monastery; a refectory.

‖**Frater**[2] (frē·tər). 1561. [L.; = 'brother'.] †1. A friar -1639. †2. *Cant.* = ABRAM-MAN. -1673. 3. A brother, comrade. Also *attrib.* 1794.

Fraternal (frătō·ınăl), *a.* 1494. [f. L. *fraternus* + -AL. Cf. F. *fraternel.*] Of or pertaining to brothers or a brother; brotherly.

The old F. quarrel of thy Race COWLEY. A f. affection for Addison L. STEPHEN. **Frate·rnally** *adv.*

Fra·ternate, *v.* *U.S.* *rare.* 1846. [f. L. *fraternus* + -ATE.] To fraternize. Hence **Fraterna·tion** (*U.S. rare*), fraternization. So **Fra·ternism** (*U.S. rare*), in same sense.

Fraternity (frătō·ıniti). ME. [a. OF. *fraternité*, ad. L. *fraternitatem*; see FRATERNAL and -ITY.] 1. The relation of a brother or brothers; brotherhood. 2. The state or quality of being fraternal; brotherliness 1470. †3. A family of brothers. *rare.* 1635. 4. A body or order of men organized for religious or devout purposes ME. 5. A body of men associated by some common interest; a company, guild ME. 6. A body of men of the same class, occupation, pursuits, etc. 1561.

2. To substitute the principles of f. in the room of that salutary prejudice called our country BURKE. 5. I William Caxton..of the fraternyte and felauship of the mercerye CAXTON. 7. *U.S.* A literary or social association of the alumni of a college or university; a 'Greek-Letter' Society 1777.

Fraternization (fræ:təınəizē·ʃən). 1792. [a. F. *fraternisation*; see FRATERNIZE and -ATION.] The action of fraternizing or uniting as brothers, fraternal association.

They..give the kiss of f. to negroes 1792.

Fraternize (fræ·təınəiz, frē·tər-), *v.* 1611. [ad. F. *fraterniser*, ad. med. L. *fraternizare*, f. *fraternus*, f. *frater*; see -IZE.] 1. *intr.* To associate or sympathize *with* as a brother or as brothers; to form a fraternal friendship. 2. *trans.* To bring into fraternal association or sympathy. Now *rare.* 1656.

1. We fraternised on the spot BAKER. 2. A regular correspondence for fraternizing the two nations BURKE. Hence **Fraterni·zer**, one who fraternizes.

Fratriage (frē·tri,ėdʒ). Also **fratrage.** 1730. [ad. med.L. *fratriagium*, f. L. *fratr(i)-*; see -AGE.] *Law.* A younger brother's inheritance.

Fratricide[1] (frē·trisəid, fræ·tri-). 1450. [a. F., ad. L. *fratricida*, f. *frater* + *-cidere*; see -CIDE 1.] One who kills his (or her) brother. Hence **Fra·trici:dal** *a.* that kills or has killed his brother; concerned with the slaughter of brothers.

Fratricide[2] (frē·trisəid, fræ·tri-). 1568. [a. F., ad. L. *fratricidium*, f. *frater* + *-cidere*; see -CIDE[2].] The action of killing one's brother. (In *Law* also the killing of one's sister.)

Fratry[1], **fratery** (frē·tri, -těri). 1538. [app. f. FRATER[1] + -Y.] = FRATER[1].

Fra·try[2]. 1532. [ad. med.L. *fratria*, *fratreia*, f. *frater*; app. infl. by Gr. φρατρία. Cf. FRIARY.] a. A fraternity. b. A convent of friars.

Frau, var. of FROW.

Fraud (frǭd), *sb.* ME. [a. OF. *fraude*, ad. L. *fraudem.*] 1. The quality of being deceitful. Now *rare.* 2. Criminal deception; the using of false representations to obtain an unjust advantage or to injure the rights or interests of another ME. 3. An act or instance of deception, a dishonest trick ME. 4. A fraudulent contrivance; in mod. colloq. use, a spurious or deceptive thing 1658. b. *colloq.* of a person: An impostor, a humbug 1850. †5. State of being defrauded or deluded. MILT.

2. They look upon f. as a greater crime than theft SWIFT. *In fraud of, to the fraud of* (Law): so as to defraud; to the detriment or hindrance of. 3. *Statute of Frauds* (Law): the statute 29 Chas. II, c. 3, by which written memoranda were in many cases required to give validity to a contract. Phr. *Pious fraud*: a deceit practised for the advancement of religion, or the like. 6. *Comb.* f. order *U.S.*, an official order prohibiting the use of the mails to a person suspected of using them fraudently.

Hence **Frau·dful** *a.* full of f., treacherous; -ly *adv.* **Frau·dless** *a.* free from f.; -ly *adv.*, -ness.

Fraudulence (frǭ·diŭlĕns). 1610. [a. OF.; see FRAUDULENT and -ENCE.] The quality or fact of being fraudulent. So **Frau·dulency.**

Fraudulent (frǭ·diŭlĕnt), *a.* ME. [a. OF., ad. L. *fraudulentus*; see FRAUD *sb.* and -ULENT.] 1. Guilty of or addicted to fraud; deceitful, dishonest. 2. Characterized by, or of the nature of, fraud; serving the purpose of, or accomplished by means of, fraud ME. †3. *Path.* (After the L. transl. of Avicenna.) Deceptive -1615.

1. Agayne is the seruaunt fals and fraudelent BARCLAY. 2. A f. balance 1833, prospectus 1891. F. misrepresentation SIR J. W. CHITTY.

Hence **Frau·dulently** *adv.*

Fraught (frǭt), *sb.* *Obs.* exc. *Sc.* ME. [prob. a. MDu. or MLG. *vracht* (also *vrecht*: see FREIGHT *sb.*); origin uncertain.] = FREIGHT *sb.* 1, 2.

Fraught (frǭt), *v.* *Obs.* exc. in pa. pple. ME. [f. prec. sb.] = FREIGHT *v.* 1, 2.

Fraught (frǭt), *pple.* and *ppl. a.* ME. [pa. pple. of FRAUGHT *v.*] 1. Of a vessel: Laden. Also *full f.* 2. *transf.* Stored, furnished, filled, equipped *with* ME.

1. Ships..wyth riches full yfraught GASCOIGNE. 2. Wisedome (whereof I know you are f.) *Lear* I. iv. 241. Phr. *Fraught with*: a. attended with; b. destined to produce.

Fraughtage (frǭ·tėdʒ). *arch.* ME. [f. FRAUGHT *v.* + -AGE.] = FREIGHTAGE †1, 2.

Fraxin (fræ·ksin). 1864. [f. L. *frax(inus)* ash + -IN.] *Chem.* A substance, $C_{16}H_{18}O_{10}$, occurring in the bark of the common ash, and also, together with æsculin, in the bark of the horse-chestnut.

Fraxine·lla. 1664. [mod. L., dim. of L. *fraxinus* ash.] A name for cultivated species of dittany, esp. *Dictamnus Fraxinella.*

Fray (frē), *sb.*[1] ME. [aphetic f. AFFRAY.] 1. A feeling of fear; fright, terror. †2. An assault, attack -1575. 3. A disturbance; a brawl; a fight ME.

3. Fleete-street fraies, when Prentices with Clubs did knocke thee downe 1609.

Fray, *sb.*[2] 1630. [f. FRAY *v.*[2]] A frayed place.

Fray (frē), *v.*[1] ME. [aphet. f. AFFRAY, EFFRAY *v.*] 1. *trans.* To make afraid, frighten. 2. To frighten or drive away. *Obs.* exc. *arch.* 1526. †3. To assault, attack -1575. 4. *intr.* To quarrel or fight. *Obs.* exc. *arch.* 1460.

1. A Puritan is a Protestant fray'd out of his Wits 1604. 2. Can he f. off the vultur from his breast SOUTH.

Fray (frē), *v.*[2] 1450. [ad. F. *frayer*:— OF. *freiier*:—L. *fricare* to rub; see FRICTION.] 1. *intr.* Of deer: To rub (against trees). Also *trans.* in *to f. their heads.* 1576. 2. *trans.* To rub away; to ravel *out* the edge or end of; *occas.*, to chafe by friction 1710. b. *intr.* Of material: To become frayed, to ravel out 1721. †3. *trans.* To deflower 1565. †4. *intr.* To clash -1483. 5. [from Fr.] *trans.* To clear, force (a path, way) 1849.

2. The bell-rope..was frayed into a fringe DICKENS. A suit of fray'd magnificence TENNYSON. 5. Paths, frayed by the elephant and rhinoceros 1849. Hence **Fray·ing** *vbl. sb.*

†Fray, *v.*[3] *rare.* 1450. = DEFRAY *v.* -1631.

Frazzle (fræ·z'l), *v.* orig. *dial.* and *U.S.* 1825. [?] *trans.* To fray, wear out. Hence **Frazzle** *sb.*, esp. in phr. *to a f.*, to a condition of exhaustion 1865.

Freak (frīk), *sb.*[1] 1563. [? cogn. w. OE. *frician* to dance.] 1. A sudden causeless change or turn of the mind; a capricious humour, notion, whim, or vagary. 2. Capriciousness 1678. 3. A prank, a caper 1648. 4. A product of irregular fancy 1784. b. (more fully *f. of nature* = *lusus naturæ*): A monstrosity of any species; in recent use, a living curiosity exhibited in a show 1847. 5. quasi-*adj.* denoting something abnormal or capriciously irregular 1898.

Freak (frīk), *sb.*[2] 1870. [f. FREAK *v.*] A fleck or streak of colour.

Freak (frīk), *v.* 1637. [f. FREAK *sb.*[1]; app. coined by Milton.] 1. *trans.* To fleck or streak capriciously; to variegate, usu. in pa. pple. 2. *intr.* To practise freaks; to frolic 1663.

1. The pansy freaked with jet MILT. *Lycidas* 144.

Freakish (frī·kiʃ), *a.* 1653. [f. FREAK *sb.*[1] + -ISH.] 1. Full of, or characterized by freaks, capricious, whimsical. 2. Of the nature of a freak, curious 1805.

1. An ill-contrived, ugly, f. fool WYCHERLEY. Our f. climate LOWELL. **Frea·kish-ly** *adv.*, **-ness.**

Freck, frack (frek, fræk), *a.* *Obs.* exc. *Sc.* [Com. Teut.: OE. *frec, fric, fræc.*] 1. Desirous, eager, quick, ready. 2. Lusty, strong, vigorous 1500. Hence †**Fre·ckly, fra·ckly,** *adv.*

Freck (frek), *v.* 1621. [? var. of FREAK *v.*] *trans.* To mark with spots or freckles; to dimple.

Fre·cken. Now *dial.* ME. [a. ON. *freknur* pl.] A freckle.

A fewe freknes in his face y-spreynd CHAUCER.

Freckle (fre·k'l), *sb.* ME. [altered f. prec.] 1. A yellowish or lightish-brown spot in the skin. 2. Any small spot or discoloration 1547.

Freckle (fre·k'l), *v.* 1613. [f. the sb.] 1. *trans.* To cover with freckles or spots; *intr.* to appear in spots or patches. 2. *intr.* To become marked with freckles 1842. Hence **Fre·ckling** *vbl. sb.* a mark like a freckle; a marking with freckles.

Freckled (fre·k'ld), *ppl. a.* ME. [f. FRECKLE *sb.* + -ED[2].] 1. Marked with freckles. 2. Spotted ME. †3. Resembling a freckle. *Lev.* xiii. 39.

1. A f. face MARSTON. 2. F. trout 1614, cowslips 1821.

Fred-stole: see FRITH-STOOL.

Free (frī), *a.* [Com. Teut.: OE. *frēo, frīo, frīg*:—OTeut. **frijo* free:—OAryan **priyo-*, represented by Skr. *priyá* dear, f. root **pri* to love (OE. *frēon* to love, whence FRIEND).]

I. 1. Not subject as a slave is to his master; enjoying personal rights and liberty of action. Also *fig.* 2. Of a state, its citizens, institutions, etc.: Enjoying civil liberty; existing under a government which is not arbitrary or despotic, and does not encroach upon individual rights. Also, not subject to foreign dominion. ME. †3. Noble, honourable, of gentle birth and breeding. In ME. an epithet of courtesy. -1632. †4. Hence: Noble, honourable, generous, magnanimous -1604.

1. Delicate Ariel, I'll set thee f. for this SHAKS. 2. Till the iniurious Romans did extort This Tribute from vs, we were f. *Cymb.* III. i. 49. 3. Mirthe, that is so fair and f. CHAUCER. 4. *Oth.* III. iii. 199.

II. 1. At liberty; allowed to go anywhere; not kept in confinement. Also, liberated. 1483. 2. Released from ties, obligations, etc. 1596; exempt from work or duty 1697. 3. Guiltless, innocent, acquitted. Const. *from, of.* ? *Obs.* 1602. 4. Unimpeded, unrestricted, unhampered ME. b. with *to* and *inf.*: At liberty, †feeling it right, *to do* something ME. 5. Of composition, etc.: Not observing strict laws of form; (of a translation, etc.) not adhering strictly to the original 1813. 6. Allowable or allowed (*to* or *for* a person *to do*); open *to* 1576; open *for* all 1870. 7. Clear, unobstructed ME. 8. Clear *of* or *from* ME. 9. *Naut.* Of the wind: Not adverse 1840. 10. Not fixed or fastened 1590. 11. Disengaged from contact or connexion with anything else; relieved from the pressure of anything adjacent or superincumbent. In *Bot.* not adnate to other organs. 1715. 12. *Chem.*, etc. Uncombined 1800. 13. Of power or energy: Disengaged 1825. 14. Of a material: Easily worked, loose and soft in structure 1573.

1. We would let them go f. DE FOE. Deer, as f. as in an American forest MACAULAY. 2. A fortnight hence I shall be f. as air SIR R. PEEL. 3. My hands are guilty, but my heart is f. DRYDEN & LEE. 4. F. admission of the light of Heaven RUSKIN. Phr. (*To have* or *give*) *a f. hand*: complete liberty of action. b. I made him.. Sufficient to have stood, though f. to fall MILT. 5. The limits between f. translation and paraphrases 1813. 6. What God.. commands to some, leaves f. to all MILT. *A f. fight*: one in which all and sundry engage. 7. Are not the streets as f. For me as for you SHAKS. 8. Ice.. f. from air-bubbles TYNDALL. 10. Phr. *To get f.*: to get loose, to extricate.

III. 1. Acting of one's own will or choice; not determined from without. (See also FREE WILL.) OE. 2. Ready; acting willingly or spontaneously; (of an act) spontaneous; (of an offer, assent, etc.) readily given or made ME. Of a horse: willing 1477. 3. Ready in giving, liberal. Const. *of.* Said also of the gift. ME. 4. Acting without restriction or limitation 1578. b. Abundant, copious 1635. 5. Frank and open, ingenuous, unreserved; also, in bad sense = forward, ready to 'take liberties' 1635. 6. Of speech: Frank, plain-spoken 1611; licentious 1852.

1. A man is said to be f., so far forth as he can do what he will BERKELEY. F. choice FREEMAN. 2. His noble f. offers left us nothing to ask BACON. F. to confess BYRON. Horses that be f. Do need no spurs GREENE. 3. I was not very f. of it, for my Store was not great DE FOE. A f. gift 1791. 4. Too f. feeding hath occasioned you this dreame 1632. How f. the present age is in laying taxes on the next POPE. b. A f. bloomer 1887. 5. His Grace is very f. and open 1693. Not so f., fellow SHERIDAN. Phr. *To make* (or *be*) *f. with*: to treat unceremoniously: also *Naut.* to approach boldly. 6. Where she.. listened to much f. talk THACKERAY.

IV. 1. Exempt from, not subject or liable to OE. 2. a. Exempt from, or not subject to, some particular jurisdiction or lordship. b. Possessed of certain exclusive rights or privileges. ME. 3. Of land: Held without obligation of rent or service ME. 4. Invested with the rights or immunities *of*, admitted to the privileges *of* (a corporation, city, etc.). Used with *of*, also simply. 1496. b. Hence: Allowed the enjoyment *of* 1687. 5. Said of non-unionist workmen and their labour 1890. 6. Exempt from restrictions in regard to trade; open to all traders; also, not subject to tax, toll, or duty 1631. 7. Without payment, gratuitous 1585.

1. F. from all tax and imposition 1630, from pulmonary consumption 1885, from real difficulty 1895. 2. a. The f. towns of Lübeck, Bremen, and Hamburg M. PATTISON. b. *F. chapel* (see CHAPEL *sb.*). *F. chase* = FRANK CHASE. *F. fishery* (see FISHERY). *F. marriage* = FRANK-MARRIAGE. *F. warren* (see WARREN). 4. F. of the Grocers B. JONS., of the city ENTICK. b. F. of the house DICKENS. 6. F. markets 1631. A f.-port SHAFTESB. 7. F. tickets 1830, seats MACAULAY. A f. pass over a line of railway 1894. Phr. *Free school*: 'a school in which learning is given without pay' (J.). (This meaning has been denied, but on inconclusive grounds. See N.E.D.) 1494.

†B. *sb.* 1. The adj. used *absol.* ME. only. 2. A person of noble birth or breeding; a knight or lady -1549.

C. *adv.* In a free manner, freely. Now only *techn.* or *arch.* 1559. b. Without cost or payment. Often with *gratis*. *Scot free*: see SCOT. 1568. c. Naut. (*To sail, go,* etc.) *f.*: i. e. with bow-lines slackened and sheets eased; opp. to *close-hauled* 1812.

Comb. a. in derivative combs. based upon some phrase in which the adj. is used, as *f.-agency, -citizenship*, etc. (after *f. agent, citizen*, etc.).

b. in comb. with a verbal or agent noun (where *free* seems partly adverbial), as F.-LIVER, -THINKER, etc.

c. In spec. phrases, etc.: †**f. alms** = *frank-almoign* (see ALMOIGN); **f. companion,** a mercenary belonging to no particular nation, but attached for the time to any prince who paid him: so **f. company; f. grace,** the unmerited favour of God; **f. love,** the doctrine of the right of free choice in sexual relations without the restraint of marriage or other legal obligation; **f.-milling** *a.* (*Mining*), (of ores) easily reducible; **f.-stuff** (*Building*), timber which is quite clean or without knots; †**f. suitor,** one of the tenants entitled to attend a manorial court; †**f. ward,** detention not involving close or ignominious restraint; **f. wheel,** the driving-wheel of a bicycle able to rotate while the pedals are at rest; also as vb.

Free (frī), *v.* Pa. t. and pple. **freed.** [OE. *frēon, frēoȝ(e)an*:— OTeut. **frijējan*, f. **frijo-* FREE *a.*] 1. *trans.* To make free; to set at liberty; to release from bondage or constraint. 2. To relieve; to deliver, or exempt *from*, rid or ease *of*; to confer immunity upon OE. 3. To clear, disengage, or disentangle (a thing) from some obstruction or encumbrance. Const. *from, of.* 1613. Also *refl.* †b. To open so as to allow free passage -1700. †4. To remove so as to leave the place clear, get rid of -1638. †5. To frank (a letter) -1823. 6. *Lead-mining.* To register (a new mine, vein, etc.) by making the proper payment to the barmaster 1601.

1. They.. freed the citie, and vpheld the lawes 2 *Macc.* ii. 22. Freed from the restraints of fear BUTLER. 2. Freed from feudal services CRUISE, from stamp duty CRUMP. 3. *refl.* To f. oneself from one's difficulties 1852. 4. F. thine owne torment DANIEL.

Free and easy. 1699. A. *adjectival phr.* Unconstrained, natural; also, careless, slipshod. Also quasi-*adv.*

A free-and-easy way of carrying things on NEWMAN.

B. *sb.* A convivial gathering for singing, at which one may drink, smoke, etc. 1823.

Free bench. 1670. *Law.* 'That estate in Copyhold Lands which the Wife, being espoused a Virgin, hath, after the death of her Husband, for her Dower, according to the custom of the Mannor' (Blount, *Law Dict.*).

Free-board (frī·bōᵊɹd). 1676. [= AF. *franc bord*; see FREE *a.* and BOARD *sb.*] 1. *Law.* The right of claiming a certain quantity of land outside the fence of a park or forest; also, the land thus claimed. 2. *Naut.* The space between the plank-sheer and the line of flotation 1726.

Free-boot, *v.* 1592. [f. FREEBOOTER.] *intr.* To act as a freebooter, plunder. Hence **Free·-booting** *vbl. sb.* and *ppl. a.*

Freebooter (frī·bū:təɹ). 1570. [ad. Du. *vrijbuiter*, f. the equivalents of FREE *a.*, BOOTY or BOOT *sb.*[2], -ER[1]. See also FILIBUSTER.] One who goes about in search of plunder; *esp.* a pirate or piratical adventurer. Also *transf.* and *fig.*

The Danites were.. Free-booters.. and did all by force 1659. Hence **Free·-boo·tery,** the practice of freebooters.

†**Free·-booty.** 1623. [f. FREE *a.* + BOOTY, after prec.] Spoil (to be) taken by force -1749.

Free·-born, *a.* ME. [f. FREE *a.* + BORN *ppl. a.*] 1. Born free, born to the conditions and privileges of citizenship, inheriting liberty. 2. Of or befitting a free-born man 1510.

2. The f. and martial virtues of the desert GIBBON.

Free Church. 1843. 1. *gen.* A church free from state control. In *pl.* a Nonconformist name for the Congregationalists, Baptists, etc., as dist. from the Established Church. 1869. Hence **Freechu·rchman.** 2. *The Free Church of Scotland*: the organization formed by the ministers who seceded from the established Presbyterian Church in 1843.

†**Free cost.** 1563. In phr. *at, of, on, upon free cost* = cost-free, gratis -1764. Also as advb. phr. without prep. -1720.

Nothing comes free-cost here HERRICK.

†**Free-de·nizen,** *sb.* 1576. = DENIZEN 2. -1653. So †**Free-de·nizen** *v.* = DENIZEN *v.* 1.

Free·dman. 1601. [f. *freed* pa. pple. + MAN *sb.*] A man who has been a slave and is manumitted or emancipated.

Freedom (frī·dəm). [OE. *frēodōm*; see FREE *a.* and -DOM.] 1. Exemption or release from slavery or imprisonment; personal liberty ME. 2. Exemption from arbitrary control; independence; civil liberty ME. 3. The state of being FREE; †generosity, liberality -1530; liberty of action ME. 4. The quality of being free from the control of fate or necessity; the power of self-determination OE. †5. Readiness -1697. 6. Frankness, openness, familiarity; outspokenness 1699; undue familiarity 1618. 7. Ease, facility 1613. 8. Boldness of conception or execution 1643. 9. *Physics.* Capability of motion 1879. 10. An immunity, privilege ME.; a franchise (cf. FRANCHISE *sb.* 2 a) 1596. 11. The right of participating in the privileges of: a. membership *of* a company or trade 1744; b. citizenship *of* a town or city 1579; often conferred *honoris causa* upon eminent persons. Also the diploma conferring such freedom. c. The liberty or right to practise a trade; also, the 'fine' paid for this 1712. d. *transf.* Unrestricted use *of* 1652.

2. They died for the Libertie and Free-dome of their Cittie HOLLAND. F. of the press BYRON. 3. He was of Knyghthod and of fredam flour CHAUCER. F. of Thought is like F. in Actions 1718. 6. Those innocent Freedoms I allow her OTWAY. 10. F. from Tallage 1711, from arrest KEIGHTLEY. 11. b. They presented me with the f. of the city WESLEY. d. The f. of the library BURTON.

Comb. **f.-fine,** a payment made on being admitted to the f. of a city, guild, or corporation.

Freedstool: see FRITH-STOOL.

Free-hand (frī·hænd), *a.* 1862. Of drawing: Done with a free hand, i. e. without measurements or artificial aid. Also *absol.* or quasi-*sb.*

Free-ha·nded, *a.* 1656. [f. FREE *a.* + HAND *sb.* + -ED [2].] Open-handed, generous.

Free-hea·rted, *a.* ME. [f. FREE *a.* + HEART + -ED [2].] Having a free heart; frank, open, unreserved; impulsive; generous, liberal.
The bond of freeharted and willing love GOLDING. Hence **Free-hea·rted-ly** *adv.*, **-ness.**

Freehold (frī·hōuld). 1467. [= AF. *fraunc tenement*; f. FREE *a.* + HOLD *sb.*[1] II. 1.] **1.** A tenure by which an estate (or office or dignity) is held in fee-simple, fee-tail, or for term of life 1523. **2.** An estate or office held by this tenure 1467. **3.** *attrib.* or *adj.* Held by, relating to, or of the nature of, freehold 1527.

Freeholder (frī·hōuldəɹ). ME. [= AF. *fraunc tenaunt*; f. FREE *a.* + HOLDER.] One who possesses a freehold estate.

Free lance. 1820. A term used by recent writers to denote one of those military adventurers who in the Middle Ages offered their services as mercenaries, or with a view to plunder, to belligerent states; a condottiere, a free companion. Hence *fig.* of politicians, etc.

Free-liver. 1711. One who gives free indulgence to his appetites. So **Free-li·ving** *a.*

Freely (frī·li), *adv.* [OE. *frēolīce*, ME. *freoliche, freliche, frely*, f. FREE *a.* + -LY [2].] **1.** In a free manner; unreservedly; readily, spontaneously. **2.** Frankly, openly, plainly 1596. **3.** Without let, hindrance, or interference ME. **b.** Loosely 1869. **4.** Without stint ME. †**5.** In freedom; with absolute possession –1647. †**6.** Nobly; excellently. ME. only. †**7.** = FREE *adv.* –1759.
1. Graces.. gyuen to us frely 1526. F. we serve, Because we f. love, as in our will To love or not MILT. **2.** To speak one's mind f. BERKELEY. **3.** To breathe more f. 1695. **4.** Of euery tree of the garden thou mayest f. eate *Gen.* ii. 16.

Freeman (frī·măn). [OE. *frēoman*; see FREE *a.* and MAN *sb.*] **1.** One who is not a slave or serf; also later, one who is politically free. **2.** One who possesses the freedom of a city, borough, company, etc. ME.
1. A coloured free-man LYELL. **2.** The electors are citizens, burgesses, or freemen H. COX.

Freemartin (frī·mā:ɹtin). 1681. [?] An imperfect female of the ox kind, twin-born with a male.

Freemason (frī·mēˈs'n, -s'n). ME. [f. FREE *a.* + MASON.] †**1.** A member of a certain class of skilled workers in stone, who travelled from place to place, working wherever any great building was being erected, and recognizing each other by a system of secret signs and passwords. In later use (16–18th c.) a term used merely as a more complimentary synonym of 'mason'. –1723. **2.** A member of the fraternity called *Free and Accepted Masons* 1646.
Early in the 17th c., the societies of freemasons (sense 1) began to admit honorary members, who were instructed in the secret signs and in the legendary history of the craft. These were called *accepted masons*, and the distinction of being an 'accepted mason' became a fashionable object of ambition. In 1717 four of these societies or 'lodges' in London united to form a 'grand lodge', with a new constitution and ritual, and a system of secret signs; the object of the society as reconstituted being mutual help and the promotion of brotherly feeling among its members. The London 'grand lodge' has been the parent of other lodges in Great Britain and in most parts of the world.
3. *attrib.* (of or pertaining to freemasons, as *f. knock*, etc.) 1807.

Freemasonry (frī·mēˈs'nri). ME. [see -RY.] †**1.** The craft or occupation of a freemason. ME. only. **2.** The principles, practices, and institutions of freemasons 1802. **3.** *fig.* Secret or tacit brotherhood, instinctive sympathy 1810.
3. The wonderful f. of childhood 1886.

Freeness (frī·nės). Now *rare.* ME. [f. FREE *a.* + -NESS.] The quality or state of being FREE; freedom; readiness; liberality; openness, frankness.

Free-qua·rter. *Hist.* 1648. The obligation of having to provide free board and lodging for troops; also, the right to be billeted in free quarters.

Freer (frī·əɹ). 1610. [f. FREE *v.* + -ER[1].] One who frees or sets free.

Freesia (frī·ziă). 1882. [mod.L.] *Bot.* A genus of iridaceous bulbous plants of the Cape of Good Hope, allied to *Gladiolus*.

Free soil. *U.S.* 1848. **A.** *sb.* Territory in which slaveholding was prohibited 1850.
B. *adj.* Epithet of a political party in 1846–56, which opposed the extension of slavery into its territories; pertaining to this party or its principles.
I went to a free soil meetin' once LOWELL. Hence **Free-soiler, Free-soilism.**

Free-spoken, *a.* 1625. [cf. *plain-spoken.*] Accustomed to speak plainly and openly. Hence **Free-spokenness.**

Free state. 1646. **1.** Occas. = REPUBLIC. Now *rare.* **2.** *U.S.* Before the Civil War of 1861–5, a state of the Union in which slavery did not exist 1861. **3.** *Irish F. S.*, the part of Ireland separated from the U.K. and established as a Dominion 1922.

Free·-stone, freestone [1]. ME. [f. FREE *a.* + STONE *sb.*; = OF. *franche pere*, 'stone of excellent quality'.] Any fine-grained sandstone or limestone that can be cut or sawn easily; a slab of such stone. Also *attrib.*

Free·-stone [2]. 1866. A variety of the peach (or nectarine) in which the flesh parts freely from the stone when ripe. Also *f. peach.*

Free-thinker (frī·þi:ŋkəɹ). 1692. One who refuses to submit his reason to the control of authority in matters of religious belief; a designation claimed *esp.* by the deistic and other rejectors of Christianity in the early 18th c. Also *transf.* So **Free-thi·nking** *vbl. sb.* the principles or practice of a free-thinker; *ppl. a.* holding the principles of a free-thinker; pertaining to free-thinkers or free-thought. **Free-thought** = *Free-thinking* vbl. sb.

Free trade, free-trade. 1606. **1.** An open and unrestricted trade. **2.** Trade or commerce left to follow its natural course, i.e. without the interference of customs duties or of bounties. Also, the principles of those who advocate this state of things. Also *transf.* 1823. **3.** Smuggling 1824. **4.** *attrib.* 1829.
2. To 'inculcate in the mind of the Bourbons wise principles of free trade!' COBBETT.

Free-tra·der. 1698. **1.** One allowed to trade without restriction. **2.** A smuggler; also, a smuggling vessel 1815. **3.** An advocate of free trade 1849.

Free will, free:-wi·ll, free·wi·ll. ME. [See FREE *a.*] **1.** (Best as two words.) Spontaneous will, unconstrained choice (to do or act). **2.** 'The power of directing our actions without constraint by necessity or fate' (J.) ME. **3.** *attrib.* (in *free-will offering*) = given spontaneously 1535.
1. To wander at their own free will JOWETT. **2.** The third way of bringing things to pass, distinct from necessity and chance, namely, freewill HOBBES. Hence **Free-wi·ller,** a contemptuous term for one who believes in the doctrine of free will, an Arminian.

Freeze (frīz), *sb.* ME. [f. FREEZE *v.*] The action of FREEZE *v.* (*lit.* and *fig.*).

Freeze (frīz), *v.* Pa. t. **froze** (frōᵘz). Pa. pple. **frozen** (frōᵘ·z'n). [Com. Teut.: OE. *frēosan*, pa. pple. *froren* :—OTeut. **freusan*, f. root **freus-, fraus-, fruz-* :—pre-Teut. **preus-, prous-, prus-*, cf. L. *pruina*, Skr. *prusva* hoar-frost; also Skr. *plus* to burn.]
I. intr. uses. **1.** *impers.* *It freezes*: the cold is such that water becomes ice. **2.** To be converted into, or covered with, ice ME.; to become hard or rigid as the result of cold ME. **3.** To become fixed *to* (something) or *together* by the action of frost 1460. **4.** To feel very chill; to die by frost ME.; to be utterly devoid of heat 1613. Also *fig.*
1. Still it frised HALL. **2.** Port wine froze solid 1748. Our ropes were now froze 1748. *fig.* The smile on his lips froze C. BRONTË. **3.** Phr. *To f.* (*on*) *to* (U.S. and Austral.): to hold on *to*; also, to 'take to'. **4.** The north-west, where Davies freezed to his rest COLVIL. *fig.* To f. with fears POPE.
II. trans. uses. **1.** To change to a solid form by the action of cold; to congeal; to form ice on the surface of (a river, etc.). Also causatively. 1494. **b.** To congeal as if by frost ME. **c.** *fig.* To chill (feelings, etc.); to paralyse (powers, etc.) 1595. **2.** To affect with frost; to stiffen, harden, injure, kill, etc. by chilling 1596. **3.** *To f. out*: **a.** *lit.*: see FROZEN. **b.** *fig.* To exclude from business, society, etc. by chilling behaviour, severe competition, etc. (*U.S.*) 1890.
1. A froste that.. frose yᵉ Thamys FABYAN. Phr. *To f. over*: to cover with ice. *To f. in, up.* **b.** A Tale ..whose lightest word Would..f. thy young blood *Haml.* I. v. 16. **c.** Chill Penury..froze the genial current of the soul GRAY. Hence **Free·zer,** one who or that which freezes, or keeps extremely cold.

Freeze, obs. f. FRIEZE.

Freezing (frī·ziŋ), *vbl. sb.* ME. [f. prec. + -ING [1].] The action of FREEZE *v.* *At f.* = at *freezing-point.*
Comb.: **f.-mixture,** a mixture, e.g. of salt and snow, which, while remaining liquid, is cold enough to f. some other liquid within its influence; **-point,** the point on the thermometer, viz. 32° Fahrenheit, 0° Centigrade, marking the temperature at which a liquid, *esp.* water, freezes.

Freezing (frī·ziŋ), *ppl. a.* 1611. [f. as prec. + -ING [2].] **1.** That freezes (see the vb.). **2.** *fig.*; *esp.* of manners: Chilling 1813.
2. The f. reason's colder part TENNYSON. **Free·zingly,** *adv.*

Freiesle·benite. 1850. [f. *Freiesleben* proper name + -ITE.] *Min.* A sulph-antimonide of lead and silver, which crystallizes in striated prisms. Cf. DIAPHORITE.

Freight (frēˈt), *sb.* 1463. [prob. a. MDu. or MLG. *vrecht*, var. of *vracht*; see FRAUGHT *sb.* Cf. F. *fret* hire of a ship, Sp. *flete*, Pg. *frete.*] **1.** Hire of a vessel for the transport of goods; the service of transporting goods (orig., by water; now, esp. in *U.S.*, by land also); the sum paid for this. †Formerly also: Passage-money. **2.** The cargo or lading (of a ship); a ship-load. In *U.S.*: Anything carried by sea or land. Also *transf.* and *fig.* 1502.
1. Phr. †*To take f.*: to take passage DE FOE. **2.** A f. of sea-coals 1789. **b.** *U.S.* = *f. train* (see below). *attrib.* and *Comb.* (esp. *U.S.*), as *f. car* (= goods truck or van), *f. train* (= goods train); *f.-handler*, etc.

Freight (frēˈt), *v.* 1485. [f. prec. sb.; cf. FRAUGHT *v.*] **1.** *trans.* To furnish or load (a vessel) with a cargo; to hire or let out (a vessel) for the carriage of goods and passengers. Also *transf.* **2.** To carry as freight 1540.
1. Donco, where the marchauntes..fraight theyr shyppes 1555.

†**Freight,** *pple.* and *ppl. a.* 1494. [Contracted pa. pple. of prec.] **1.** Freighted, laden–1649. Also *transf.* and *fig.* –1711. **2.** Fraught, abounding *with* –1623.

Freightage (frēˈ·tėdʒ). 1694. [f. FREIGHT *v.* + -AGE.] **1.** Hire of a vessel for the transport of goods; cost of conveyance of goods. **2.** Freight, cargo; quantity of cargo conveyed; also *transf.* and *fig.* 1803. **3.** Transport of goods. *U.S.* 1886.

Freighter (frēˈ·təɹ). 1622. [f. as prec. + -ER [1].] **1.** 'One who loads a ship, or one who charters and loads a ship' (W.). **b.** One who consigns goods for carriage inland 1872. **2.** One whose business it is to receive and forward freight 1714. **3.** A cargo vessel 1878.

Freightless, *a. rare.* 1791. [see -LESS.] Without freight or load.

Fremd (fremd), *a.* *Obs.* exc. *Sc.* and *n.* [Com. Teut.: OE. *fręmede, fręmde, fręmþe*, f. (ult.) root **fram-*; see FROM.] **1.** Foreign. **2.** Strange OE; wild, as opp. to *tame* ME. **3.** Unfriendly OE. **4.** Not related; opp. to *sib* or *kin* ME.

Fremescent (frėme·sėnt), *a. rare.* 1837. [as if from L. **fremescere*, freq. of *fremere* to roar.] Murmuring, growing noisy. CARLYLE. Hence **Freme·scence** (*rare*), an incipient roaring.

‖**Fremitus** (fre·mitŭs). 1820. [f. L. *fremere.*] A dull roaring noise; in *Path.*, a palpable vibration, e.g. of the walls of the chest.

Fren: see FRENNE.

French (frenʃ). [OE. *fręncisc*, f. *franca* FRANK *sb.*[1] + *-isc*, -ISH; the suffix produces umlaut. Cf. *Scotch* from *Scottish.*]
A. *adj.* **1.** Of or pertaining to France or its inhabitants. **2.** French-like ME.
Phrases, etc. **a.** In names of things of (attributed) French origin, as **F. barley** (see BARLEY); **F.-blue,** artificial ultramarine; **F. bread,** a kind of fancy bread; **F. casements,** windows turning upon two vertical edges attached to the jambs; **F. chalk,** a variety of steatite, used for making marks on cloth, etc.; **F. drain,** a rubble drain; †**F. eaves,** eaves provided with a gutter to carry off the water; **F.**

fake, a variety of the Flemish fake; **F.-grey,** a tint composed of white with ivory black, Indian red and Chinese blue; **F. hem,** a kind of hem employed for the finishing of flounces; **F. horn,** a metal wind-instrument (see HORN); **F. paste,** a kind of glass into which a certain quantity of oxide of lead is introduced; **F. purple,** a beautiful dye prepared from lichens; **F. red** or **rouge,** genuine carmine; **F. rice** = AMELCORN; **F. roll** (see ROLL); **F.-roof,** a mansard roof; **F. tub,** a mixture used by dyers, of the protochloride of tin and logwood; **F. window,** a long window opening like a folding door, and serving for exit and entrance.

b. In names of trees and plants; as **F.-bean** (see BEAN); **F. berry** = AVIGNON BERRY; **F. cowslip** (see COWSLIP); **F. plum,** the fruit of a variety of *Prunus domestica*, dried and exported from France.

c. In names of venereal diseases; as *F. disease*, etc.

B. *absol.* and *sb.* 1. The French language ME. 2. *The French* (pl.): the French people. Also (rarely) without article = French persons 1595.

1. For Frensh of Paris was to hir unknowe CHAUCER. Phr. *Pedlar's F.*: cant, thieves' slang. 2. Phr. *F. and English*: a children's game.

French (frenʃ), *v. rare.* 1639. [f. prec. adj.] 1. *To French it*: to speak French. FULLER. 2. To render into French or give a French form to 1887.

†**French crown.** 1599. The English name for the French coin called ECU, ESCU –1608. b. *Punningly*, with reference to the baldness produced by the 'French disease'. *Mids. N.* I. ii. 99.

Frenchify (fre·nʃifəi), *v.* 1592. [f. FRENCH *a.* + -FY.] 1. *trans.* To make French, imbue with French qualities. 2. *intr.* To become French in ideas, manners, etc.; to have French sympathies 1775.

1. F. our English solidity into Froth and Whip-syllabub 1741. Hence **Fre·nchified** *ppl. a.* Frenchlike (*contemptuous*); having the 'French disease'.

Frenchism (fre·nʃiz'm). 1750. A French custom, idiom, or characteristic; a Gallicism.

French leave. 1771. Originally, the custom (in the 18th c. prevalent in France) of going away from a reception, etc. without taking leave of the host or hostess. Hence, joc., *to take French leave*: to go away, or do anything, without permission or notice.

French-like. 1550. [f. FRENCH *sb.* + -LIKE.]

A. *adv.* After the manner of the French; in French fashion.

B. *adj.* Like the French 1848.

Frenchman (fre·nʃmæ̆n). OE. [f. FRENCH *a.* + MAN; orig. two words.] 1. A man of French birth or nationality. 2. A (good, etc.) French scholar. *colloq.* 1670. 3. A French ship 1889. Hence **Fre·nchmanlike** *a.* and *adv.*

French polish. 1819. 1. A polish for wood-work; a solution of resin or gum resin in alcohol or wood naphtha. 2. The smooth glossy surface produced on wood-work by the application of this. Also *punningly*. Hence **French-polish** *v. trans.* to make smooth and glossy with French-polish (*lit.* and *fig.*). **French-polisher.**

Frenetic, etc.: see PHRENETIC, etc.

†**Frenne, fren.** 1553. [corrupt var. of *frend*, FREMD, infl. by *forenne*, FOREIGN.]

A. *adj.* Strange, not related. *rare.*

B. *sb.* A foreigner, stranger, enemy –1614.

Frenum: see FRÆNUM.

†**Fre·nzic, -al,** *a.* 1547. [f. FRENZY *sb.* + -IC, + -AL.] Affected with frenzy; crazy, mad; wildly enthusiastic –1748.

Frenzied (fre·nzid), *ppl. a.* 1796. [f. FRENZY *v.* + -ED[1].] Affected with frenzy; crazy; distracted, frantic; wildly enthusiastic.

F. dreams SCOTT, enthusiasts L. STEPHEN. Hence **Fre·nziedly** *adv.*

Frenzy, phrenzy (fre·nzi). [ME. *frenesie*, a.OF., f. late L. *phrenesis*, a pseudo-Gr. formation after *phreneticus*, corruption of Gr. φρενιτικός; see FRANTIC. The sp. *phrenzy* is now rare.]

A. *sb.* 1. Mental derangement; delirium, or temporary insanity; now chiefly, the rage or excitement of a paroxysm of mania. Now *rare* in lit. sense. Also *fig.* 2. A wild idea; also, a craze (*for* something) 1632.

1. Demoniac f., moping melancholy, And moon-struck madness MILT. *fig.* The Poets eye in a fine f. rolling SHAKS. 2. The Frensy of Travelling 1707.

B. *adj.* [? sb. used attrib.] †1. Mad, insane, crazy –1647. 2. *dial.* Angry; passionate 1859. Hence **Fre·nzy** *v.* to drive to f., infuriate.

Frequence (frī·kwĕns). 1535. [a.F. *fréquence*, ad. L. *frequentia*; see FREQUENT and -ENCE.] 1. An assembling in large numbers; a crowded state or condition; also *concr.* concourse, crowd. Now *arch.* †2. Constant use of (something); familiarity –1624. 3. Frequent occurrence or repetition 1603.

1. The Most High, who, in full f. bright Of angels ..spake MILT.

Frequency (frī·kwĕnsi). 1553. [see prec. and -ENCY.] †1. The state or condition of being crowded; also *concr.* a concourse –1723. †2. The constant use or repetition *of* –1785; familiarity *with* –1680. 3. The fact of occurring often or being repeated at short intervals 1641. b. *Physics*, etc. Rate of recurrence, e.g. of a vibration 1831; *Electr.* The number of complete cycles per second of an alternating current 1891. c. *Statistics.* The ratio of the actual to the number of possible occurrences of an event 1897.

3. The Strength and F. of the Pulse ARBUTHNOT. The diminished f. of wars 1836. b. Alternating currents of high f. 1893.

Frequent (frī·kwĕnt), *a.* 1531. [ad. L. *frequentem* pr. pple. of **frequere*; cogn. w. *farcire* to cram (see FARCE *v.*[1]).] †1. Crowded, full –1746. 2. Found at short distances apart; numerous. Somewhat *arch.* 1605. 3. Commonly used or practised, well known. Now *rare.* 1531. †Of a report, etc.: Widely current –1631. 4. Happening at short intervals; often recurring. Of the pulse: Faster than normal. (The prevailing sense.) 1604. 5. Addicted *to*; accustomed *to do*; given to repetition *in* 1560. 6. †a. That is often *at* or *in* (a place) –1624. b. Constant, habitual 1628. †c. That is often *with* (a person), familiar; conversant *in* (a subject) –1632. 7. quasi-*adv.* 1614.

1. In a ful and f. assemblie HOLLAND. 2. Populous cities..f. Hospitals [etc.] CAMDEN. 4. You may expect frequente letters MARVELL. F. forgeries 1750, blights 1795. 5. Lesse f. to his Princely exercises then formerly SHAKS. 6. a. In prisons more f.: in death oft 2 *Cor.* xi. 23. b. A f. Comunicant 1628.

Frequent (frĭkwe·nt), *v.* 1477. [ad. L. *frequentare*; see prec.] 1. *trans.* To visit often; to resort to habitually 1555. †2. To use habitually; to practise; to attend (a meeting) –1667; to honour with observances –1581. †3. *intr.* To resort *to* or *unto*; to associate *with*; to be often *in* or *about* –1810. †4. *trans.* To crowd, fill –1667.

1. A Coffee-house which I myself f. STEELE. To f. good company BERKELEY. 3. Far from all the ways where men f. POPE. 4. MILT. *P.L.* x. 1091.

Hence **Freque·ntable** *a.* that may be frequented, easily accessible. **Frequenta·tion,** the action or habit of frequenting or resorting to; habitual visiting. **Freque·nter,** one who frequents or resorts to.

Fre·quentage. 1814. *rare.* [f. prec. + -AGE.] The practice or habit of frequenting.

Frequentative (frĭkwe·ntătiv). 1530. [ad. L. *frequentativus*; see FREQUENT *v.* and -IVE. Cf. F. *fréquentatif, -ive*.] A. *adj.* †1. Versed *in. Obs. Sc.* ROLLAND. 2. *Gram.* Of a verb or verbal form: Expressive of the frequent repetition of an action 1533.

B. *sb.* A frequentative verb, verbal form, or conjugation 1530.

Frequently (frī·kwĕntli), *adv.* 1531. [f. FREQUENT *a.* + -LY[2].] At frequent or short intervals, often, repeatedly; †numerously –1638.

Frere, obs. f. FRIAR.

Frescade (freskā·d). 1656. [a. F., ad. It. *frescata*, f. *fresco* cool, FRESH.] A cool walk; a shady alley.

Fresco (fre·sko), *sb.* Pl. **frescos, -oes.** 1598. [ad. It. *fresco* cool, FRESH.] †1. Cool, fresh air; occas. a fresh breeze –1785. 2. A kind of painting executed in water-colour on mortar or plaster which is not quite dry; a painting so executed 1598. Also *attrib.*

2. The grand sibyls..painted in f. by Michel Angelo EMERSON. Hence **Fre·sco** *v.* to paint in f.

Fresh (freʃ). [OE. *fersc* (opp. to 'salt'), ME. *fresshe, freche, fressche*, etc. Ultimate etym. obscure.]

A. *adj.* I. 1. New, novel ME.; additional, other, further ME. 2. Recent; newly made, received, or taken in ME. 3. Raw, inexperienced; 'green' 1595. Also (*Univ. slang*) characteristic of a freshman. b. [cf. G. *frech* impudent]. Forward, impertinent, free in behaviour (orig. *U.S.*) 1848.

1. MILT. *Lycidas* 193. 3. SHAKS. *John* III. iv. 145.

II. 1. New; not artificially preserved; not salted, pickled, or smoked OE. 2. Of water: Not salt or bitter; †(of a marsh) containing fresh as opp. to salt water OE. b. Of or pertaining to such water ME. 3. Untainted, pure; hence, invigorating, refreshing. Said *esp.* of air and water. ME. †b. Cool (*rare*) –1697. 4. Retaining its original qualities; not stale, musty, or vapid. Also *transf.* of immaterial things. ME. 5. Not faded or worn ME. 6. Not sullied or tarnished; blooming ME.; †gaily attired –1587. 7. Not exhausted or fatigued ME. 8. Of the wind: Strong. Hence, of the way of a ship: Speedy, steady. 1533. 9. a. Sober. Now only *Sc.* ME. b. Partially intoxicated 1812.

1. F. meat 1648, butter 1864. 2. He always found the ice f. that floated up in the sea-water BOYLE. 3. F. dews and flowers MILT. The desire of f. air SCOTT. 4. F. egges 1632. Burton ale—f. or stale DIBDIN. News f. and f. ADDISON. 5. My glory was f. in mee *Job* xxix. 20. When the memory of things was f. BERKELEY. 6. The fresshe daysy CHAUCER. Hast thou beheld a fresher Gentlewoman SHAKS. 7. I never felt fresher in my life 1863. 8. If it comes on to blow f. I shall make the signal for Boats to repair on board NELSON. *Comb.* †**f.-new** *a.* unpractised.

B. *adv.* In a fresh manner, freshly (see A.) ME. *Comb.* **f.-run** *a.* (a salmon, etc.) that has freshly run up from the sea.

C. *sb.* [The adj. used *absol.*] 1. The fresh part or period 1715. 2. A freshet, flood 1538; also, a gust, squall 1719. 3. A pool, spring or stream of fresh water 1571. 4. The part of a tidal river next above the salt water; also, the lands adjoining this part. Freq. in *pl.* Now *U.S.* 1634.

1. The f. of the morning NORTH. 2. Sometimes there are great freshes in the River of Tyne 1682. 3. I'le not shew him Where the quicke Freshes are *Temp.* III. ii. 75.

Fresh, *v.* ME. [f. FRESH *a.*] To †make or become fresh or lively.

Freshen (fre·ʃən, fre·ʃ'n), *v.* 1697. [f. as prec. + -EN[5].] 1. *intr.* To become FRESH; to increase in strength; also with *up*. b. To become bright 1819. c. To lose salt or saltness (Webst.) 1864. 2. *trans.* To make FRESH; *esp.* to renew, revive, give freshness to; to remove salt or saltness from 1749. 3. *Naut.* 'To relieve (a rope) of its strain, or danger of chafing, by shifting or removing its place of nip' (Adm. Smyth) 1855.

1. The wind now freshened fast MARRYAT. To f. into smiles W. IRVING. 2. Air to f. the room 1801. To f. up my Italian LOWELL, their memory 1874. 3. *To f. hawse, the nip*: to pay out more cable so as to change the part exposed to friction. *To f. ballast*: to divide or separate it, so as to alter its position. *To f. way*: to increase the speed.

Hence **Fre·shener,** something that freshens; *spec.* a spell of exercise for freshening a horse.

Fresher (fre·ʃəɹ). 1882. [f. FRESH *a.* + -ER[1].] a. *Univ. slang*: = FRESHMAN. b. A fresh breeze.

Freshet (fre·ʃĕt). Also *erron.* **fresh shot.** 1596. [f. FRESH *sb.*[1] + -ET.] 1. A small stream of fresh water. *Obs.* exc. *poet.* 1598. 2. A stream or rush of fresh water flowing into the sea 1596. 3. A flood or overflowing of a river caused by heavy rains or melted snow 1654.

3. The f. in the river .. was so sudden that cattle .. were in danger of being drowned 1784. Hence **Fre·shet** *v.* to flood as with a f.

Freshly (fre·ʃli), *adv.* ME. [f. FRESH *a.* + -LY[2].] In a fresh manner; newly, recently; with renewed or unabated vigour; briskly; with undiminished strength, purity, distinctness, etc.; with fresh appearance, odour, etc.; †gaily –1523.

F. torn BYRON, pursued STOW. Looks he as f., as he did the day he wrastled *A.Y.L.* III. ii. 243.

Freshman (fre·ʃmæ̆n). 1550. [f. FRESH *a.* + MAN.] 1. A new-comer; a novice. 2. A student during his first year, *esp.* his first term, at a University (or *U.S.* a school) 1596.

2. He was but yet a f. in Cambridge NASHE.

Comb. f.-class *U.S.*, 'the lowest of the four classes in an American college' (Webst.). Hence **Fre·shmanship**, the condition of being a f.; the period during which it lasts; also *joc.*, the personality of a f.

†**Fre·shment.** [f. FRESH *v.* + -MENT.] Refreshing influence. J. CARTWRIGHT.

Freshness (fre·ʃnės). ME. [f. FRESH *a.* + -NESS.] The quality of being FRESH. Also *concr.* a fresh stream (KEATS).

Jollitie, pleasaunce, and freshnesse 1500. The f. of the Aire BACON, of Waters BOYLE, of the Evening 1712. The glory and the f. of a dream WORDSW.

Fre·shwater, *a.* 1528. [f. FRESH *a.* + WATER *sb.*] 1. Of or pertaining to, yielding, produced by, or living in water that is not salt. 2. Unaccustomed to salt water, new to the sea 1621; hence, unskilled, raw, insignificant.

1. F. fish 1765, lakes GOLDSM., flowers 1828, shells LYELL. 2. A f. sailor DE FOE. *fig.* Ignorant, unlearned, and f. critics FIELDING. Hence †**Fresh-watered** *a.* unskilled, raw.

Fresison (frĭsəi·sǫn). 1827. *Logic.* A mnemonic word designating the fifth mood of the fourth syllogistic figure, in which a universal negative major premiss and a particular affirmative minor yield a particular negative conclusion.

Fret (fret), *sb.*[1] ME. [app. a. OF. *frete* trellis-work.] 1. Ornamental interlaced work; a net; an ornament consisting of jewels or flowers in a network. 2. *Her.* Orig. a figure formed by two bendlets, dexter and sinister, intersecting; = F. *frette.* Later, 'a figure formed by two narrow bands in saltire, interlaced with a mascle' (Cussans). 1572. 3. †a. *Arch.* Carved ornament, *esp.* in ceilings, consisting of intersecting lines in relief –1664. b. An ornamental pattern composed of continuous combinations of straight lines, joined usually at right angles. Also *attrib.* 1664.

1. A frette of goold sche hadde next hyre her CHAUCER. 3. b. The f. or herring-bone is of common occurrence on vases of the oldest style BIRCH.

Comb.: f.-cutting *vbl. sb.*, the cutting of wood with a fret-saw into ornamental designs; also *attrib.*; -saw, a saw used for cutting frets, scrolls, etc.

Fret (fret), *sb.*[2] 1545. [f. FRET *v.*[1]] 1. A gnawing or wearing away, erosion. Now *rare.* Also *concr.* †a fretting sore; a decayed spot. 2. Pain in the bowels, grips, colic. Also *pl.* Now *dial.* 1600. 3. Agitation of mind; irritation, vexation; also, querulous utterance 1556. †4. A gust, squall (of wind) –1734. 5. Secondary fermentation in liquors 1664.

3. My lord was in as great a f. as I DE FOE. Phr. *F. and fever, f. and fume. On* or *upon the f.*: in a state of agitation, irritation, ill humour, or impatience.

Fret (fret), *sb.*[3] 1500. [?] In musical instruments like the guitar, formerly a ring of gut (Stainer), now a bar or ridge of wood, metal, etc. placed on the fingerboard, to regulate the fingering.

Fret, *sb.*[4] *rare.* 1587. [ad. OF. *frete, fraite, fraicte* breach.] A breach or passage made by the sea.

†**Fret,** *sb.*[5] 1576. [ad. L. *fretum.*] A strait –1661.

Fret (fret), *v.*[1] Pa. t. and pple. **fretted.** Pr. pple. **fretting.** [OE. *fretan*, f. OTeut. *fra-* (see FOR- *pref.*[1]) + **etan* to EAT.] †1. *trans.* To eat, devour –ME. 2. To gnaw; to consume, torture or wear away by gnawing. Now only of small animals. Also *intr.* ME. 3. *transf.* of slow and gradual destructive action, as of frost, rust, disease, corrosives, etc. Const. *into, to* (the result). Also *fig.* Also *absol.* ME. 4. To form or make by wearing away 1593. †5. *intr.* To make a way by gnawing or corrosion (*lit.* and *fig.*) –1676. †6. *intr.* for *refl.* To become eaten, corroded, or worn; to waste away; to decay –1804. 7. *trans.* To chafe, irritate ME. 8. *intr.* To distress oneself with constant regret or discontent; to chafe, worry. Often with additional notion of querulous utterances. 1551. Also quasi-*trans.* with *away, out* 1605. 9. *intr.* Of liquor: To undergo secondary fermentation. Now *dial.* 1664. b. *trans.* (*causatively*) 1742. 10. *intr.* Of a stream, etc.: To move in agitation or turmoil; to chafe 1727. 11. *trans.* (*causatively*). To cause to rise in waves; to ruffle 1794.

2. Like as it were a moth fretting a garment 1551. 3. The river frets away the rocks along its banks HUXLEY. Phr. *To f. the heart* (fig.). 4. With cadent Teares f. channels in her cheekes *Lear* I. iv. 308. 7. Horses..fretted into a foam W. IRVING. 8. He only frets to keep himself employed GOLDSM. quasi-*trans.* A poore Player, That struts and frets his houre vpon the Stage *Macb.* v. v. 25. Hence **Fre·tter. Fre·tting** *vbl. sb.* and *ppl. a.*

Fret (fret), *v.*[2] ME. [In part a. OF. *freter*, f. *frete*: see FRET *sb.*[1] In sense 2, the word agrees with FRETISH *v.*[2]; ? ad. OF. *fraitir.*] †1. *trans.* To adorn with interlaced work; to adorn richly with gold, silver, or jewels –1668. b. *transf.* To variegate 1601. 2. *Arch.* To adorn (*esp.* a ceiling) with carved or embossed work in patterns 1611. 3. *Her.* To interlace 1572.

1. Frenyeis of fyne silk, fretit ful fre 1450. b. Yon grey Lines That f. the Clouds SHAKS. 2. This Maiesticall Roofe, fretted with golden fire SHAKS.

†**Fret,** *v.*[3] ME. [?] 1. *trans.* To rub, chafe. Causatively: To make pass by rubbing. 2. *intr.* To rub, produce friction; to fray *out* 1643. (Merged in FRET *v.*[1])

Fret (fret), *v.*[4] 1600. [f. FRET *sb.*[3]] *trans.* To furnish (a guitar, etc.) with frets.

Fretful (fre·tfŭl), *a.* 1593. [f. FRET *v.*[1] + -FUL.] †1. Corrosive, irritating (*lit.* and *fig.*); also, inflamed –1804. 2. Disposed to fret, irritable, peevish; impatient 1602. 3. Of water, etc.: Agitated, broken into waves. Of the wind: Blowing in frets; gusty. 1613. 4. Characterized by or productive of fretting 1737.

1. 2 *Hen. VI*, III. ii. 403. 2. The fretfull Porpentine SHAKS. 4. The f. stir Unprofitable and the fever of the world WORDSW. **Fre·tful-ly** *adv.*, -**ness.**

†**Fre·tish, fre·tize,** *v.*[1] 1521. [f. *frediss-* lengthened stem of OF. *fredir* (F. *froidir*).] *trans.* To chill, benumb. Only in *pass.* –1639.

†**Fre·tish, Fre·tize,** *v.*[2] In 7 **frettish.** 1579. [? ad. OF. **fraitiss-*, **fraitir.* Cf. FRET *sb.*[1], *v.*[2]] = FRET *v.*[2] –1703.

Frette, var. of FRET *sb.*[1]

Fretted (fre·tėd), *ppl. a.*[1] 1545. [f. FRET *v.*[1] + -ED [1].] 1. Eaten or worn into holes, chafed. 2. Worried, vexed, distressed 1756.

Fretted (fre·tėd), *ppl. a.*[2] ME. [f. FRET *v.*[2] + -ED [1].] 1. Adorned with fretwork; carved or wrought into frets. Also *transf.* and *fig.* 1552. 2. *Her.* Interlaced 1586.

Fretty (fre·ti), *a.* 1562. [ad. OF. *fretté*, f. *frete*; see FRET *sb.*[1]] *Her.* 'Covered with a number of narrow bars or sticks, usually eight, lying in the directions of the bend and bend-sinister, interlacing each other' (Cussans). †Of a charge: Fretted or interlaced *with.*

†**Fre·twise, -ways,** *adv.* ME. [f. FRET *sb.*[1] + -WISE.] In the form of a fret; so as to interlace –1717.

Fre·twork. 1601. [f. FRET *sb.*[1] + WORK *sb.*] 1. *Arch.* Carved work in decorative patterns consisting largely of intersecting lines, *esp.* as used for ceilings. Also *attrib.* 2. Woodwork cut with a fret-saw into ornamental designs 1881. 3. The ornamental part of lead-light work 1859.

Freudian (froi·diăn), *a.* and *sb.* 1910. (A disciple) of Dr. Sigmund *Freud* or his doctrines of PSYCHOANALYSIS, q.v. Hence **Freu·dianism, Freu·dism.**

Friable (frəi·ăb'l), *a.* 1563. [a. F., ad. L. *friabilis*, f. *friare* to crumble into small pieces.] Capable of being easily crumbled or reduced to powder; pulverizable, crumbly.

A f. substance like rust of iron G. WHITE. Hence **Friabi·lity, Fri·ableness,** the quality of being f.

†**Fri·and.** 1598. [a. F., f. *friant*, pr. pple. of *frire.*] A. *adj.* Dainty; delicious to the palate; fond of delicate food –1818. B. *sb.* An epicure.

Friar (frəiər, frəi·əɪ), *sb.* [ME. *frere*, a. OF. *frere* (mod. *frère*), earlier *fredre* :—L. *fratrem* brother.] †1. = BROTHER, in fig. uses –1821. 2. In the *R. C. Ch.*: A brother or member of any religious order, but esp. of one of the four mendicant orders: the Franciscans (†*Friars minors, Minorites*, or *Grey Friars*); the Augustines (*Austin Friars*); the Dominicans (*Friars Preachers, Black Friars*); and the Carmelites (*White Friars*) ME. b. *pl.* The quarters or convent of a particular order; hence often a name for the part of a town where the convent was ME. 3. A name of various fishes; e. g. the silversides, a N. American fish 1603. 4. An Australian bird of the genus *Philemon*; now usu. *f.-bird* 1798. 5. *Print.* A white or light place on a printed page 1683. 6. *White friars*: 'a small flake of light-coloured sediment floating in wine' 1745.

Comb.: **friar's balsam,** tincture of benzoin compound used as an application for ulcers and wounds; **f.-bird**: see sense 4; **friar's cap(s,** the Monkshood, *Aconitum Napellus*; **friar's cowl,** the Cuckoo-pint or Wake Robin, *Arum maculatum*; **friar's crown,** *Carduus eriophorus*; **friar's lantern** = *Ignis fatuus*; **f.-skate,** the *Raia alba.*

Hence †**Friar** *v. intr.* to play the f. **Fri·arly** *a.* of or pertaining to friars; friar-like; *adv.* in friarly fashion.

†**Friar Rush.** 1603. The proper name (Ger. *Rausch*) of the hero of a popular story, which tells of the adventures of a demon disguised as a friar. ¶Confused by Scott with *Ignis fatuus.*

Friary (frəi·əri), *sb.* 1538. [f. FRIAR *sb.* + -Y[2].] 1. A convent of friars. 2. A fraternity of friars 1631. †3. The institution of friars –1661. 4. *attrib.* (of or pertaining to a friary or friaries) 1598.

†**Fri·ary** *a.* 1589. [f. FRIAR *sb.* + -Y [1].] Of or pertaining to friars –1605.

†**Fria·tion.** 1656. [f. L. *friare* to rub into small pieces.] The action of rubbing or crumbling into small pieces –1743.

Fribble (fri·b'l). 1664. [f. next vb.]

A. *sb.* 1. A trifler. 2. A trifling thing or idea 1832. 3. Frivolity 1881.

1. The fop, the f., and the beau 1771.

B. *adj.* Trifling, frivolous, ridiculous 1798.

Fribble (fri·b'l), *v.* 1627. [echoic; ? infl. by FRIVOL.] †1. *trans.* To falter, stammer; *intr.* to totter in walking –1709. 2. *intr.* In early use, to act aimlessly or feebly; to fiddle. Now only: To behave frivolously. 1640.

2. Not as you treat those fools that are fribbling round about you THACKERAY. Hence **Fri·bbler,** a trifler. **Fri·bbling** *vbl. sb.* **Fri·bblery,** frivolity.

Friborgh, -burgh: see FRITHBORH.

†**Fricace** *sb.* 1533. [ad. L. *fricatio.*] = FRICATION. –1643.

Fricandeau (frikændōu·). Pl. **-deaux.** 1706. [a. F.] A slice of veal or other meat dried or stewed and served with sauce; a fricassee of veal.

Fricandel, -elle (frikænde·l). 1872. [quasi-Fr. var. of prec.] Hashed meat made into balls and fried.

Fricassee (frikăsī·), *sb.* 1568. [a. F. *fricassée*, f. *fricasser* to mince and cook in sauce; of unkn. origin.] Meat sliced and fried or stewed and served with sauce. Now usually a ragout of small animals or birds cut in pieces. Also *fig.*

Fricassee (frikăsī·), *v.* 1657. [f. prec.] To make a fricassee of; to dress as a fricassee. Also *transf.*

†**Frica·tion.** 1533. [ad. L. *fricationem*, f. *fricare* to rub.] 1. The action of chafing or rubbing –1694. 2. Friction –1725.

Fricative (fri·kătiv). 1860. [ad. mod.L. *fricativus*; see -ATIVE.]

A. *adj.* 1. Of a consonant-sound: Produced by the friction of the breath through a narrow opening between two of the mouth-organs. 2. 'Sounded by friction, as certain musical instruments' (*Cent. Dict.*).

B. *sb.* A fricative consonant 1863.

Fricatrice (fri·kătris). 1605. [ad. L. **fricatricem*, f. *fricare.*] A lewd woman.

†**Frickle.** 1681. A basket (for fruit) that holds a bushel. (Dicts.)

Friction (fri·kʃən). 1581. [a. F., ad. L. *frictionem*, f. *fricare* to rub.] 1. The action of chafing or rubbing (the body or limbs). 2. The rubbing of one body against another; attrition 1704. 3. *Physics* and *Mech.* The resistance which any body meets with in moving over another body 1722. 4. *fig.*; *esp.* of opinions, temperaments, etc. 1761.

1. A cold bath, with f. and a little exercise HAMERTON. 3. Phr. *Angle of f.*, the maximum slope at which one body will rest upon another without sliding down. *F. at rest*, the amount of f. between two touching bodies that are relatively at rest. 4. The f. between parent and child 1884.

Comb., chiefly *Mech.*: **f.-ball,** one of the balls used to lessen the f. bearings, etc.; **-block,** a block which is pressed against a revolving body to arrest its motion by f.; **-brake,** a form of dynamometer in which a pair of f.-blocks are screwed to a journal rotating at a given speed; also, a brake which measures the amount of work performed by any prime mover, by allowing it during the time of trial to waste all its work on f.; a measurer of the lubricity of oils; a brake operating by means of f.; **-breccia** (*Geol.*) = *fault-rock* (see FAULT); **-clutch, -cone, -coupling, -disc,** contrivances for transmitting motion by frictional contact; **-fremitus** (*Path.*) = *f.-sound*; **-fuse** = *f.-tube*; **-gear, -gearing,** gear or gearing for transmitting motion by frictional contact; **-machine,** an electrical machine, generating electricity by contact with amalgamated silk; **-powder,** a composition of chlorate of potash and antimony, which readily ignites by f.; **-primer,** U.S. name for *f.-tube*; **-roller,** a roller placed so as to lessen the f. of anything passing over it; also, = *f.-wheel* (*b*); **-sound** (*Path.*), the auscultatory sound heard when the pleuræ or pericardium are roughened by inflammation and effused lymph; **-tube,** a tube used for firing cannon by means of ignition; **-wheel,** (*a*) see *friction-roller*; (*b*) one of the small rollers which revolve in bearings, and sustain an axle in the depression formed by the contiguity of the upper portion of their peripheries.

Hence **Fri·ction** *v. trans.* to chafe or rub (the body, etc.). **Fri·ctionless** *a.*, **-ly** *adv.*

Frictional (fri·kʃənăl), *a.* 1850. [f. prec. + -AL.] Of or pertaining to friction, moved or produced by friction.

Phr. *F. electricity*, electricity developed by friction. *F. gearing* (*-wheels*), wheels which transmit motion by friction instead of by teeth. Hence **Fri·ctionally** *adv.*

Friday (frəi·dẽ¹, -di). [OE. *frīgedæg* 'day of (the goddess) *Frīg*'; a Com. WGer. transl. of the late L. *dies Veneris*, day of (the planet) Venus. The OE. name *Frīg* corresponds to ON. *Frigg*, name of the wife of Odin (not to *Freyja*), and is the fem. of the OTeut. adj. **frijo-* 'beloved, loving'; see FREE.] **1.** The sixth day of the week. **2.** A reception or entertainment given on that day 1836. **3.** *attrib.* as *F. morning*. 1592.

1. *Black F.*: applied to various historic dates of disastrous events which took place on Friday, as May 11, 1866, when a panic ensued on the failure of Overend, Gurney, & Co.; etc. *Good F.*: the Friday before Easter Day, observed in commemoration of Christ's crucifixion.

Fridge (fridʒ), *v.* 1550. [app. echoic.] †**1.** *intr.* To fidget –1681. †**2.** To chafe, rub, scrape (*upon*, etc.) –1651. **3.** *trans.* To rub, fray, chafe. Now chiefly *dial.* 1617.

Fried (frəid), *ppl. a.* ME. [f. FRY *v.*] Cooked by frying.

Friend (frend). [Com. Teut.: OE. *frēond*, pr. pple. of OTeut. **frijōjan* to love (OE. *frēogan*), f. pre-Teut. **priyo-* dear: see FREE *a.*]

A. *sb.* **1.** 'One joined to another in mutual benevolence and intimacy' (J.). Not ordinarily used of lovers or relatives. **2.** Applied *loosely*, e.g. to a mere acquaintance, or to a stranger; also, used by members of the 'Society of Friends' as the ordinary mode of address. Also often *ironically*. ME. **3.** A kinsman or near relation. Now only in *pl.* OE. †**4.** A lover or paramour of either sex –1765. **5.** One who wishes (another, a cause, etc.) well; a sympathizer, patron, or supporter. Const. *of, to*. ME. **b.** *transf.* Anything helpful ME. **6.** One not an *enemy*; one who is on good terms with another, not hostile or at variance; one who is on the same side in warfare, politics, etc. OE. **7.** A Quaker 1679.

1. And night as welcome as a f. would fall M. ARNOLD. Phr. *F. of God*: one eminent for piety, and enjoying God's special favour. See *James* ii. 23. 2. Nay, keep it, f., keep it,' said Dinah Plait MAR. EDGEWORTH. My learned f. (*mod.*). 3. Friends agree best at a distance *Sc. Provb.* 4. *Meas. for M.* I. iv. 29. 5. Friends to marriage 1782, of order 1878. Phr. *F. in* or *at court*: one influential in high quarters who is disposed to help another.

Phr. *To be, keep, make friends with*: to be or get on good terms with; also absol. *to be friends*.

†**B.** *adj.* Well-disposed, friendly, not hostile. (Cf. ENEMY *a.*) –1690.

Friend (frend), *v.* ME. [f. FRIEND *sb.*] †**1.** *trans.* To make (persons) friends or friendly; to join in friendship –1604. **2.** To act as a friend to, befriend; to assist, help. *arch.* or *poet.* 1562. Also *fig.* of things.

2. Well, the Gods are aboue, time must f. or end SHAKS. Hence **Frie·nded** *ppl. a.* having a f. or friends; befriended (*rare*).

Friendless (fre·ndlės), *a.* OE. [f. FRIEND *sb.* + -LESS.] **1.** Destitute of friends. **2.** = Unfriendly. SHELLEY.

1. †*Friendless man*: in OE. law, an outlaw. Hence **Frie·ndlessness.**

Friendlike (fre·ndləik), *a.* 1559. [f. FRIEND + -LIKE.] Like a friend or friends, friendly.

Friendly (fre·ndli). [OE. *frēondlic* adj., *-lice* adv.; see -LY [1, 2].]

A. *adj.* **1.** Having the qualities or disposition of a friend, disposed to act as a friend kind. **2.** Characteristic of or befitting a friend or friends; manifesting friendship ME. **3.** Not hostile, on amicable terms. Const *to, with*. 1595. **4.** Well-wishing; disposed to help or support 1535. **5.** Kindly, propitious, favourable; convenient. Const. *to*, †*unto*. ME. †**6.** Of things: Not jarring or conflicting –1793.

2. A f. nod 1868. Phr. *F. lead*, an entertainment given, among the poorer classes in London, for the benefit of a friend in distress, etc. 3. The King's flag is insulted at every F. Port we look at NELSON. *A f. match* (at *Football*, etc.): one not played in competition for a cup, etc. 4. The Gods to day stand f. *Jul. C.* v. i. 94. 5. Trees with f. shade DRYDEN. 6. F. colours POPE.

Phr. **Friendly Society.** Orig., the name of a particular fire-insurance company. Later, one of various associations, the members of which pay fixed contributions to insure help in sickness and old age, and provision for their families in the event of death.

B. *sb.* A friendly native; also, a friendly match 1870.

C. *adv.* In a friendly manner or spirit OE.

Hence **Frie·ndlily** *adv.* in a f. manner. **Frie·ndliness,** the quality or condition of being f.; occas. *pl.* manifestations of friendliness.

Friendship (fre·ndʃip). [OE. *frēondscipe*; see -SHIP.] **1.** The state of being a friend; association of persons as friends; a friendly intimacy. **2.** Friendly feeling or disposition felt or shown; friendliness ME. †**3.** A friendly act; friendly aid –1613. †**4.** 'Conformity, affinity, correspondence, aptness to unite' (J.) 1695.

1. Without f., society is but meeting BACON. My college friendships TENNYSON. 2. Christ's f. to his disciples SOUTH. 3. *Lear* III ii. 62. 4. Colours which have a F. with each other DRYDEN.

†**Friese,** *a.* and *sb.* 1481. [The native name.] = FRISIAN, q.v. Hence **Frie·sic** *a.*, † **Frie·sish** *a.* = FRISIAN.

Frieze (frīz), *sb.*¹ ME. [a. F. *frise*, f. *friser* to curl; see FRIZZ *v.*¹] **1.** A kind of coarse woollen cloth, with a nap, usually on one side only; now *esp.* of Irish make. †**2.** The nap or down on a plant –1657. **3.** An abrasion of the grain in leather 1885.

1. An old calash..lined with green frize STERNE.

Frieze (frīz), *sb.*² 1563. [a. F. *frise* fem., prob. related to It. *fregio* masc. :—L. *Phrygium* (sc. *opus*) a Phrygian work (cf. *Phrygiæ vestes* embroidered garments).] *Arch.* **1.** That member in the entablature of an order which comes between the architrave and cornice. A band of painted or sculptured decoration 1847. **2.** In a column = HYPOTRACHELIUM. 1569. **3.** *attrib.*, as *f.-work*. Also **f.-panel,** one of the uppermost panels of a six-panelled door. 1678.

1. The..f. adorned in stucco with sea-monsters H. WALPOLE. 2. The freezes gold, and gold the capitals POPE.

Hence **Friezed** *ppl. a.* furnished with a f.

Frieze (frīz), *v.*¹ 1509. [ad. F. *friser* or Sp. *frisar*; see FRIZZ *v.*¹] **1.** *trans.* To cover with a nap. *Hist.* †**2.** = FRIZZ *v.*¹ Hence **Frie·zing** *vbl. sb.*; also *attrib.*

Frieze (frīz), *v.*² 1577. [ad. F. *friser*, related to *frise* FRIEZE *sb.*²] **1.** *trans.* To embroider with gold. Now *rare*. **2.** *Naut.* (See quot.) 1769. **3.** To cover (a silver plate) with chased patterns 1678.

2. **Friezing,** ornamental carving or painting above the drift-rails, and likewise round the stern or bow of a ship 1850.

Friezed (frīzd), *ppl. a.* Now *Hist.* 1509. [f. FRIEZE *v.*¹ and *sb.*¹] **1.** Of cloth: Having a nap. **2.** Of a plant: Downy 1578.

Friezer (frī·zəɪ). 1557. [f. FRIEZE *v.*¹ + -ER¹.] One who friezes cloth.

Frigate (fri·gĕt). 1585. [ad. F. *frégate*, ad. It. *fregata*. Etym. unkn.] **1.** A light and swift vessel, orig. built for rowing, afterwards for sailing. *Obs.* exc. *poet.* **2.** †**a.** A merchantman –1800. **b.** A war-vessel. In the Royal Navy, formerly a vessel of the class next in size and equipment to ships of the line, carrying from 28 to 60 guns on the main deck and a raised quarter-deck and forecastle. Not now applied to a distinct class of vessel. 1630. **3.** A large swift-flying raptorial bird (*Fregata aquila*), found near land in the tropical and warmer temperate seas. Also *f.-bird, -petrel*. 1738. **4.** *attrib.* 1657.

Comb.: **f.-built** *a.* having 'a descent of some steps from the quarter-deck and forecastle into the waist' (Adm. Smyth); **-bird, -petrel** (see 3).

Frigatoon (frigătū·n). 1721. [ad. It. *fregatone*, augm. of *fregata* FRIGATE.] A Venetian vessel, with a square stern, having only a mainmast, mizzen-mast, and bowsprit. 'Also applied to a ship sloop-of-war' (Adm. Smyth).

†**Fri·gefact,** *v. rare.* 1599. [ad. L. *frigefactare*, f. *frigere* to be cold + *fact-*, *facere*.] *trans.* To chill –1656. So †**Frigefa·ction,** the action or process of chilling. †**Frigefa·ctive** *a.* chilling.

Fright (frəit), *sb.* [OE. *fryhto*, a metathetic form of *fyrhto*, *-u* :—OTeut. **furhtīn*, f. **fuhrto-*, *forhto-* adj., afraid.] **1.** In OE.: Fear in general. *Obs.* In ME. and in mod. use: Sudden fear, violent terror, alarm. An instance of this. **2.** †Anything that causes terror. Hence (*colloq.*) a person or thing of a shocking, grotesque, or ridiculous appearance 1634.

1. Least by his clamour..The Towne might fall in f. SHAKS. Hence **Fri·ghtless** *a.* without fear.

Fright (frəit), *v.* [OE. **fryhtan*, metathetic var. of *fyrhtan* :—OTeut. **furhtjan* to fear, f. **furhto-* afraid.] †**1.** *intr.* To be afraid –ME. **2.** *trans.* To affect with fright; to scare, terrify. Repl. by *frighten*, exc. *poet.* OE.

2. Frighting the maids GOLDSM. Hence **Fri·ghted** *ppl. a.* affected with fright; pervaded with fear (MILT. *P. L.* II. 994). **Fri·ghtedly** *adv.* †**Fri·ghter,** one who or that which causes fright or scares away.

Frighten (frəi·t'n), *v.* 1666. [f. FRIGHT *sb.* + -EN 5. Replacing FRIGHT *v.*] = FRIGHT *v.* 2.

Frightened by a shadow FROUDE.

Frightful (frəi·tful), *a.* ME. [f. FRIGHT *sb.* + -FUL.] †**1.** Full of terror; timid; alarmed –1802. **2.** Alarming (const. *to*); shocking, dreadful, revolting 1700.

1. The wild and frightfull Heards DRAYTON. 2. The f. effects of jealousy HUME. A f. scandal FROUDE. Hence **Fri·ghtfully** *adv.* (often a mere intensive). **Fri·ghtfulness,** the quality or state of being f.; *esp.* terrorizing of non-combatants as a military resource.

Frightment (frəi·tmĕnt). *rare.* 1607. [f. FRIGHT *v.* + -MENT.] The state of being in a fright; something that causes fright.

Frigid (fri·dʒid), *a.* 1622. [ad. L. *frigidus*, f. *frigere*, f. *frigus*.] **1.** Intensely cold, devoid of heat or warmth, of a low temperature 1639. †**2.** *transf.* Wanting in sexual heat; impotent –1732. **3.** *fig.* Destitute of ardour or warmth of feeling, lacking enthusiasm or zeal; cold, apathetic; formal, stiff 1658. Of things: Chilling, depressing 1844. **b.** Dull, flat, insipid 1713; †lacking force or point –1699.

1. Nuns in f. cells LONGF. *Frigid zone*: each of the two regions which lie within the north and south polar circles respectively. 3. Our reception was f. JOHNSON. A f. adieu T. HARDY. b. F. splendours 1888. Hence **Fri·gid-ly** *adv.*, **-ness.**

‖**Frigidarium** (fridʒidēᵊ·riŏm). 1706. [L., f. *frigidus*.] The cooling-room in a Roman bath. Also *transf.*

Frigidity (fridʒi·dĭti). ME. [a. F. *frigidité*; see FRIGID and -ITY.] **1.** The state or quality of being frigid; intense coldness. **2.** *transf.* Want of generative heat; impotence 1586. **3.** *fig.* Want of warmth of feeling or zeal; apathy, coldness 1631; lack of fire or spirit; flatness, insipidity; also quasi-*concr.* 1642.

1. The benumming frigiditie of Groenland 1630. The f. of a decrepit Age GLANVILL. 3. To write with f. JOHNSON. The f. of the French drama 1763.

Frigoric (frigǫ·rik). 1812. [f. L. *frigor-*, *frigus* + -IC.]

†**A.** *sb.* An imagined imponderable cause of cold.

B. *adj.* 'Pertaining to or consisting in the application of cold' (*Cent. Dict.*). *rare.* 1887.

Frigorific (frigŏri·fik), *a.* 1667. [a. F. *frigorifique*, ad. L. *frigorificus* cooling; see prec. and -FIC.] Producing cold, freezing; cooling.

Frill (fril), *sb.*[1] 1591. [perh. from sense 3 (though not recorded till recently); cf. CHITTERLING and F. *fraise* (mesentery of a calf, ruff, frill, etc.); or ? a metathetic form of FURL.] 1. An ornamental edging of woven material, of which one edge is gathered and the other left loose so as to give it a wavy or fluted appearance. Also *transf.* b. Anything resembling this; e.g. a fringe of feathers round the neck of a bird, a tuft on the neck of a dog, etc. 1878. 2. A kind of scallop-shell 1803. 3. Used by butchers for: The mesentery of an animal 1879. 4. *Photogr.* [f. the vb.] The irregular rising of a gelatine film at the edges of a plate.

1. *fig.* (*pl.*) Showy or useless embellishments or accomplishments.

Comb.: f.-**back**, a variety of pigeon, having an extraordinary frill-like appendage encircling the neck; -**lizard**, an Australian lizard of the genus *Chlamydosaurus*, whose neck is encircled by a broad erectile membrane. Hence **Fri·lly** *a.*, full of or resembling frills; also as *sb. pl.* frilled undergarments.

Frill, *sb.*[2] [f. FRILL *v.*[3]; prob. an etymologizing figment to account for FRILL *sb.*[1]] The ruffling of a hawk's feathers when frilling with cold. WORCESTER.

Frill (fril), *v.*[1] 1574. [conn. w. FRILL *sb.*[1], q.v.] 1. *trans.* To furnish or decorate with a frill. †2. To furl *up.* 1603. 3. *Photogr.* To raise (a film) in flutes like a frill. Also *intr.* 1891.

†**Frill**, *v.*[2] *rare.* 1677. [prob. echoic.] Of the eagle: To scream –1688.

†**Frill**, *v.*[3] [ad. OF. *friller.*] To shiver with cold. (Dicts.)

Frilled (frild), *ppl. a.* 1825. [f. FRILL *sb.*[1] or *v.*[1] + -ED[1] or [2].] Having, wearing, or adorned with or as with a frill. Of a photographic plate: Raised in flutes at the edges.

F. lizard = *frill-lizard.* Hence **Fri·lledness.**

Frilling (fri·liŋ), *vbl. sb.* 1815. [f. FRILL *v.*[1] + -ING[1].] 1. The putting a frill to (a garment); *concr.* frilled edging; frills. 2. *Photogr.* The rising in flutes along the edge 1880.

Frim, *a.* Now *dial.* [OE. *freme* :—prehist. **frami-*, cogn. w. *fram* adj., forward, etc.] a. Vigorous, flourishing; plump. b. Abundant in sap, juicy; abundant. c. Soluble, fusible.

b. The f. sap..From the full root DRAYTON.

‖**Frimaire** (frimę·r). 1838. [F., f. *frimas* hoar-frost.] The third month of the French revolutionary calendar (Nov. 21 to Dec. 20).

Fringe (frindʒ), *sb.* [ME. *frenge*, a. OF. :—pop. L. **frimbia*, metathetic alteration of cl. L. *fimbria* border, fringe.] 1. An ornamental bordering, consisting of a narrow band to which are attached threads of silk, cotton, etc., either loose or formed into tassels, twists, etc. 2. Anything resembling this; a border or edging 1649; an outer edge or margin of any kind; an outer limit of a country, area, etc. 1898. b. *fig.* An appendage or sequel; also (*colloq.*) irrelevant matter 1642. c. A portion of the front hair brushed forward and cut short 1883. d. In plants and animals 1601. e. *Anat.* = FIMBRIA. 1857. f. *Optics.* One of the coloured spectra produced by diffraction 1704.

1. She had..made many yards of f. JANE AUSTEN. 2. The f. of the foam BYRON. b. In.. the confines of Grace and the fringes of Repentance JER. TAYLOR.

Comb.: f.-**net**, a net to confine a fringe of hair; -**pod**, the Californian name of *Thysanocarpus laciniatus*; -**tree**, *Chionanthus virginica*.

Hence **Fri·ngeless** *a.* having no f.

Fringe (frindʒ), *v.* 1480. [f. prec. sb.] 1. *trans.* To furnish, adorn, or encircle with or as with a fringe. 2. To serve as a fringe to 1794.

Fringent (fri·ndʒĕnt), *a. rare.* 1847. [? formed to correspond with *friction*; cf. *frangent.*] Exercising friction.

A shower of meteors..lit by f. air, Blaze EMERSON.

Fringilla·ceous, *a.* 1853. [f. L. *fringilla* finch + -ACEOUS.] Pertaining to the finches. **Fringi·llide** [anglicized f. mod. L. *fringillidæ*], a bird of the finch family. **Fringi·lline** *a.* of or pertaining to the finches.

Fringy (fri·ndʒi), *a.* 1750. [f. FRINGE *sb.* + -Y[1].] 1. Of the nature of or resembling a fringe. 2. Furnished with a fringe or fringes; covered with fringes 1831.

‖**Fripo·n(n)erie.** *rare.* 1708. [F., f. *fripon* a rogue.] Roguery.

†**Fri·pper.** 1598. [ad. F. *fripier*, f. (ult.) OF. *frepe* rag.] = next. –1697.

Fripperer (fri·pərəɹ). 1584. [see prec. and -ER.[1]] A dealer in cast-off clothing.

Frippery (fri·pĕri). 1568. [a. or ad. OF. *freperie*, f. *frepe* rag.] †1. Cast-off clothes –1824. 2. Finery in dress, *esp.* tawdry finery. Also *gen.* 1637. b. Trifles 1803. c. *fig.* Empty display, *esp.* in speech, etc.; showy talk 1727. †3. An old-clothes shop –1635. †4. Trade or traffic in old clothes –1606. 5. Tawdry style (*rare*) 1802.

1. I'll reduce him to f. and rags CONGREVE. 2. She is as fond of gauze and French f. as the best of them GOLDSM. b. Boxes, baskets, and other f. 1803. 3. *Temp.* IV. i. 225.

Frippery (fri·pĕri), *a.* 1625. [from the *sb.* used attrib.] Frivolous; contemptible; trumpery.

†**Fri·sco.** 1519. [? pseudo-It. form of FRISK *sb.*] A brisk movement in dancing; a caper –1675.

Frisette (frize·t). 1818. [F.] A cluster of small curls worn on the forehead.

‖**Friseur** (frizǒr). Now *rare.* 1750. [F., f. *friser* to FRIZZ.] A hairdresser.

Frisian (fri·ziăn). 1598. [f. L. *Frisii* pl. (ad. the native name: OFris. *Frise, Frese*) + -AN.] A. *adj.* Of or pertaining to the people of Friesland. B. *sb.* An inhabitant of Friesland; the language of Friesland. So †**Fri·sic** *a.* of or pertaining to Friesland.

Frisk (frisk), *sb.* 1525. [f. FRISK *v.*] †1. A brisk and lively movement in horsemanship or dancing; a caracole or curvet; a caper. 2. *transf.* and *fig.* A brisk sportive movement; a frolic; a freak 1665.

2. I'll have a f. with you JOHNSON.

†**Frisk**, *a.* 1528. [a. OF. *frisque*, perh. ad. Teut. **frisk-*, FRESH *a.*] Full of life and spirit; brisk, lively –1705.

Frisk (frisk), *v.* 1519. [f. prec. adj.] 1. *trans.* To move briskly and sportively; to dance, frolic, gambol. 2. *trans.* To move (*up, out*, etc.) in a sportive or lively manner 16..

1. As twyn'd Lambs, that did f. i' th' Sun SHAKS. Hence **Fri·sker**, one who or that which frisks. **Fri·skingly** *adv.*

Frisket (fri·skĕt). 1683. [ad. F. *frisquette*, of unkn. etym.] *Printing.* A thin iron frame hinged to the tympan, having tapes or paper strips stretched across it, for keeping the sheet in position while printing.

Friskful (fri·skfŭl), *a. rare.* 1728. [f. FRISK *sb.* or *v.* + -FUL.] Apt to frisk, frolicsome.

Frisky (fri·ski), *a.* 1500. [f. FRISK *sb.* + -Y[1].] Given to frisking; lively; playful.

Like so many f. buffalo calves 1861. Hence **Fri·skily** *adv.* **Fri·skiness.**

†**Fri·slet.** *rare.* 1607. [? f. OF. *fresel*, dim. of *fraise* ruff + -ET.] 'A kind of small ruffle' (Halliwell).

Frist, *sb. Obs.* exc. *arch.* [OE. *first, fryst, frist* masc.] 1. A space of time, time; a certain time. 2. Delay, respite; also, a truce ME. Hence †**Frist** *v. intr.* to delay, grant respite; *trans.* to lend or give on credit; to give credit or time for payment; to grant time for payment of (a debt).

†**Fri·sure.** 1755. [a. F., f. *friser.*] Fashion of curling the hair –1811.

Frit (frit), *sb.* 1662. [ad. It. *fritta*, fem. pa. pple. of *friggere* to FRY.] 1. *Glass-making.* A calcined mixture of sand and fluxes ready to be melted in a crucible to form glass. 2. *Ceramics.* The vitreous composition from which soft porcelain is made 1791. 3. *attrib.* and *Comb.*, as *f.-brick*, etc. 1853.

Frit (frit), *v.* 1805. [f. prec. sb.] *trans.* To make into frit; to fuse partially; to calcine.

Fri·t-fly. 1881. A small fly of the genus *Oscinis*, destructive to wheat.

Frith, *sb.*[1] *Obs.* exc. *Hist.* [Com. Teut.: OE. *friðu, frioðu, freoðu* str. masc. and fem., *frið* str. neut., f. OTeut. root **fri-* to love; see FRIEND.] 1. Peace; freedom from molestation; security. †2. A game-preserve, deer-park –ME.

Comb.: f.-**guild**, a guild for the maintenance of peace; also *attrib.*; frithsoken (*OE.* and *Hist.*), an asylum, a sanctuary.

Frith (friþ), *sb.*[2] [OE. (*ge*) *fyrhðe* str. neut. :—OTeut. type *(*ga*)*furhiþjom*, app. a collective f. **furhâ* FIR.] 1. A wood of some kind, or wooded country collectively. 2. A piece of land grown sparsely with trees or with underwood only. Also, a plain between woods; unused pasture land. Now only *dial.* 1538. 3. Brushwood, underwood; occas. hedgewood 1605. 4. A hedge; also, a hurdle 1511. †The same used as a fish-weir. CAREW.

Frith (friþ), *sb.*[3] 1600. [Metathetic form of FIRTH *sb.*[2]] = FIRTH[2].

†**Frith**, *v.*[1] [OE. *friðian, freoðian*, f. FRITH *sb.*[1]] 1. *trans.* To keep in peace, make peace with; to defend, help, preserve, protect –ME. 2. To free –1470.

Frith (friþ), *v.*[2] *Obs.* exc. *dial.* ME. [f. FRITH *sb.*[2]] 1. *trans.* To fence in. Also *fig.* 2. *intr.* To wattle; also, to cut underwood 1807.

†**Fri·thborh.** Only *OE.* and *Hist.* [OE. *friðborh* lit. 'peace-pledge'. A mistranslation of the corrupt form *friborg* gave the later name FRANKPLEDGE.] = FRANKPLEDGE.

†**Frith-stool.** *Hist.* [OE., f. *frið* FRITH *sb.*[1] + *stól* seat; see STOOL.] a. A refuge. OE. only. b. A seat, usu. of stone, formerly placed near the altar in some churches, which afforded privilege of sanctuary 1610.

‖**Fritillaria** (fritilēᵊ·riă). 1578. [mod.L., f. *fritillus* dice-box.] A genus of liliaceous plants, including the CROWN IMPERIAL (*F. imperialis*), and the Common Fritillary or Snakeshead (*F. Meleagris*) found locally in moist meadows.

Fritillary (friti·lări, tri·tilări). 1633. [Anglicized f. prec.] 1. Any plant of the genus *Fritillaria*, esp. *F. Meleagris.* 2. A name for species of butterfly, e.g. the Silver-washed Fritillary (*Argynnis paphia*) and the Queen of Spain Fritillary (*A. lathonia*) 1857.

1. I know what white, what purple fritillaries The grassy harvest of the river-fields Above by Ensham, down by Sandford yields M. ARNOLD.

†**Friti·niency.** [f. L. *fritinnire* to twitter. In mod. Dicts. spelt *fritinancy.*] Twittering. SIR T. BROWNE.

Fritter (fri·təɹ), *sb.*[1] ME. [a. F. *friture* :—L. type **frictura*, f. *frigere* to FRY.] 1. Usu. *pl.* A portion of batter, occas. containing slices of meat, apple, etc., fried in oil, lard, etc. Often qualified as *apple-, oyster-, rice-f.* 2. *pl.* = FENKS. 1631.

Fritter (fri·təɹ), *sb.*[2] 1686. [app. an altered form of FITTERS.] 1. *pl.* Minute pieces, fragments, shreds. Also, trifles. Now *rare.* Also *attrib.* 2. [from the vb.] Excessive breaking-up 1803.

Fritter (fri·təɹ), *v.* 1728. [f. prec.] 1. *trans.* To break or tear into pieces or fragments; to subdivide minutely. Now *rare.* Also *intr.* for *refl.* 2. With *away, down*: To do away with piecemeal; to attenuate, wear down; to waste on trifles 1728.

1. Frittering and crumbling down the attention by a blind unsystematick observance of every trifle BURKE. 2. To f. away money in paying debts 1868. Hence **Fri·tterer**, one who fritters or wastes (time).

Frivolity (frivǫ·lĭti). 1796. [ad. F. *frivolité.*] 1. The quality of being frivolous; disposition to trifle, levity. 2. A frivolous act or thing 1838. So †**Fri·volism.** PRIESTLEY.

Frivolous (fri·vŏləs). 1549. [f. L. *frivolus* + -OUS.] 1. Of little or no weight or importance; paltry, trumpery; not worth serious attention. b. *Law.* In pleading: Manifestly futile 1736. 2. Characterized by lack of seriousness, sense, or reverence; given to trifling, silly 1560.

1. F. information JUNIUS, ornaments 1776, complaints SCOTT. b. The appeal [was] adjudged f. 1736. 2. From reading f. Books, and keeping as f. Company STEELE. Hence **Fri·volous-ly** *adv.*, **-ness.**

Friz, var. of FRIZZ.

Frize, obs. f. FREEZE, FRIEZE.

Frizel, var. of FRIZZLE *sb.*[2]

Frizette, Frizeur, vars. of FRISETTE, FRISEUR.

Frizz, friz (friz), *sb.* 1646. [f. next vb.] The state of being frizzed or curled; frizzed hair; a row or wig of crisp curls. Also *attrib.* *fig.* A similar full-bottomed well-curled friz of words HARE.

Frizz, friz (friz), *v.*^{1} 1620. [ad. F. *friser* to curl, raise a nap on. Orig. pronounced (frīz).] **1.** *trans.* To curl or crisp (the hair); to form into small crisp curls. **2.** *intr.* Of hair: To stand up in short crisp curls. Also *trans.* To set up (hair) on end. 1696. **3.** *trans.* = FRIEZE *v.*^{1} 1806. **4.** In *Leather-dressing*: To rub (wash-leather, etc.) with pumice-stone or a blunt knife, so as to soften the surface, and make uniform in thickness 1697.

1. Dressing of herself with her hair frized short up to her eares PEPYS.

Frizz (friz), *v.*^{2} 1835. [f. FRY *v.*; echoic.] To make a sputtering noise in frying.

Frizzle (fri·z'l), *sb.*^{1} 1565. [See FRIZZLE *v.*^{1}] **1.** Frizzled hair; a short crisp curl 1613. **2.** [f. the vb.] The state of being frizzled 1850. **3.** *attrib.* 1565.

Frizzle (fri·z'l), *sb.*^{2} *dial.* 1629. [? corruption of FUSIL.] In flint and steel guns the piece of iron acted on by the flint to produce the explosion.

Frizzle (fri·z'l), *v.*^{1} 1565. [? freq. of FRIEZE *v.*^{1} Much earlier than FRIZZ *v.*] **1.** *trans.* To curl in small crisp curls. **2.** *intr.* for *refl.* To form into crisp curls; to curl or twist *up* 1607. †**3.** *trans.* To touch lightly –1652.

1. Lockes with bodkins frisled fine 1573. Hence **Fri·zzler**, one who frizzles.

Frizzle (fri·z'l), *v.*^{2} 1839. [f. FRIZZ *v.*^{2}; see -LE.] **a.** *intr.* = FRIZZ *v.*^{2} **b.** *trans.* To fry or grill (with a sputter) 1858. Hence **Fri·zzle** *sb.* the action of the vb.

Frizzly (fri·zli), *a.* 1707. [f. FRIZZLE *sb.*^{1} + -Y^1.] Full of frizzles or crisp curls.

Frizzy (fri·zi), *a.* 1870. [f. FRIZZ *sb.* + -Y^1.] Of, pertaining to, or resembling a frizz.

Fro (frōu), *Sc.* FRAE (frē). ME. [a. ON. *frá*, corresp. to OE. *fram*, FROM.]

A. *prep.* (Now only *Sc.* and *dial.*) = FROM in all its senses.

B. *adv.* In a direction or position that is remote or apart; away. Now only in *to and fro* (see TO). ME.

†**C.** *conj.* (Chiefly *north.*) **1.** From the time that; as soon as, when –1513. **2.** Since, seeing that –1609.

Frock (frǫk), *sb.* ME. [a. F. *froc.* Cf. Pr. *floc*, med.L. *froccus, floccus.* 'Prob. so called because woollen' (Skeat).] **1.** A long habit with large open sleeves; the outer dress of a monk. *Rarely*, a cassock. Hence, the priestly office. Cf. UNFROCK *v.* **2.** An upper garment worn chiefly by men; a long coat, tunic, or mantle ME. **3.** An overall; a *smock-frock* 1668. **b.** A woollen guernsey or jersey worn by sailors 1811. **4.** The outer garment, for indoor wear, of women and children, consisting of a bodice and skirt; a gown, dress 1538. **5.** A coat with long skirts; a FROCK-COAT 1719; a similar coat used as a military uniform 1753.

2. Phr. *F. of mail*: a defensive garment, armour (MILT. *Sams.* 133). 5. A light blue f. with silver frogs RICHARDSON. *Frock*, in the British service, the undress regimental coat of the guards, artillery, and royal marines WILHELM.

Frock (frǫk), *v.* 1828. [f. FROCK *sb.*] *trans.* To provide with or dress in a frock (*lit.* and *fig.*); to invest with priestly office or privilege.

Fro·ck-coa·t. 1823. A double-breasted coat with long skirts which are of the same length in front as behind.

Frocked (frǫkt), *pple.* and *ppl. a.* 1550. [f. FROCK *sb.* and *v.* + -ED.] Dressed in a frock.

Froe, frow (frōu). Now chiefly *U.S.* 1573. [Orig. *frower*, ? a subst. use of FROWARD *a.* 'turned away'.] A wedge-shaped tool used for cleaving and riving staves, shingles, etc. It has a handle in the plane of the blade, set at right angles to the back; hence the name.

Froe, obs. f. FROW, Dutchwoman.

Frog^1 (frǫg). [OE. *frogga* wk. masc.; a hypocoristic formation, peculiar to Eng. The root of the various Teut. synonyms is not settled.] **1.** A tailless amphibious animal of the genus *Rana*, or of the family *Ranidæ*. **2.** A name of frog-like animals, e.g. the FROG-FISH or ANGLER 2. 1769. **3.** A name given to certain diseases of the throat or mouth 1656. **4.** *attrib.* 1836.

1. The Pike will eat venemous things (as some kind of Frogs are) WALTON.

Comb.: **f.-crab**, a member of the crustacean genus *Ranina*; **-eater**, one who eats frogs, a term vulgarly applied to Frenchmen; **-hopper**, a group of homopterous insects of the family *Cercopidæ*, so called from their shape and leaping powers; **-pecker**, a heron; **-plate**, a plate for viewing the circulation of the blood in the web of a frog's foot; **-shell**, a name of various species of shells of the genus *Ranella*; **-spit, -spittle**, (*a*) = CUCKOO-SPIT^1; (*b*) = *frog-spawn*; **-tongue**, a tumour under the tongue. **b.** In plant-names: **f.-bit**, (*a*) *Hydrocharis Morsus-ranæ*, an aquatic plant; (*b*) *Limnobium Spongia*, a similar plant of America; **-cheese**, (*a*) one of the larger puff-balls when young; (*b*) *Malva sylvestris*; **frog('s-foot**, duckweed (*Lemna*); **-grass**, (*a*) = CRAB-GRASS 1; †(*b*) *Juncus bufonius*; **-stool** = TOADSTOOL; **-wort**, a name of species of *Orchis*.

Frog^2 (frǫg). 1610. [? a use of prec., infl. by *forchetta*, the It. name.] An elastic horny substance growing in the middle of the sole of a horse's hoof.

Frog^3 (frǫg). 1719. [? ad. Pg. *froco* (repr. L. *floccus* FLOCK *sb.*).] **1.** An attachment to the waistbelt for carrying a sword or bayonet or hatchet. **2.** A fastening for the front of a military coat or cloak, consisting of a button, covered with silk, etc., which passes through a corresponding loop on the opposite side of the front of a coat or cloak 1746.

Frog^4 (frǫg). 1860. *Railroads.* A grooved piece of iron placed at the junction of the rails where one track crosses another.

Frog-fish. 1646. A name of fishes; *esp.* of the Angler or Fishing-frog (*Lophius piscatorius*); also of varieties of the genera *Batrachus* and *Chironectes*.

Frogged (frǫgd), *ppl. a.* 1774. [f. FROG^3 + -ED^2.] Of a coat, etc.: Fastened or ornamented with frogs.

Froggy (frǫ·gi), *sb.* 1840. [f. FROG^1 + -Y^6.] **1.** A playful designation of a frog. **2.** *slang.* A vulgar term for a Frenchman, from their reputed habit of eating frogs 1872.

Froggy (frǫ·gi), *a.* 1611. [f. as prec. + -Y^1.] **1.** Having or abounding in frogs. **2.** Frog-like 1837.

Frogland (frǫ·glænd). 1721. [f. FROG^1 + LAND *sb.*] Marshy land in which frogs abound, as the Fens, Holland, etc. Also *attrib.* So **Fro·glander** (*slang*), a Dutchman.

Frog-march, frog's-march. *slang.* 1871. The method of carrying a drunken or refractory prisoner face downwards between four men, each holding a limb.

Frog-mouth, frog's mouth. 1851. **1.** The great Snapdragon (*Antirrhinum majus*). **2.** A bird of the family *Podargidæ* 1888.

Frog-spawn, frog's spawn. 1621. **1.** The ova, spawn, or young of frogs. **2.** Certain freshwater algæ, which form green and slimy masses on the surface of ponds and ditches 1864. **3.** *Sugar-manuf.* A fungus destructive to saccharine solutions 1887.

Froise, fraise (froiz, frēiz). ME. [? f. (ult.) pop. L. **frixum, -a*, var. of *frīxum, -a*, f. *frigere* to FRY.] A kind of pancake or omelette, often containing slices of bacon.

Frolic (frǫ·lik), sb. 1616. [f. FROLIC *v.* or *a.*] **1.** An outburst of fun, gaiety, or mirth; a prank 1635; fun, merriment 1676. **2.** A merry-making; a party 1645. †**3.** ? Humorous verses sent round at a feast –1631. †**4.** A toy. FULLER.

1. There 's mirth and frolick in 't D'URFEY.

Frolic (frǫ·lik), *a.* 1538. [a. Du. *vroolijk*, f. MDu. *vrô* glad, joyous.] **1.** In early use: Joyous, merry, mirthful. In later use: Frolicsome, sportive, full of pranks. †**b.** *transf.* of colours, wine, etc. –1648. †**2.** Free; liberal (*of*) 1593.

1. The f. wind that breathes the spring MILT. *absol.* Lamb, the f. and the gentle WORDSW. **b.** And yet, each Verse of thine Out-did the meat, out-did the frolick wine HERRICK. Hence †**Fro·licly, fro·lickly** *adv.*

Frolic (frǫ·lik), *v.* Inflected **frolicked, frolicking.** 1583. [f. the adj.] **1.** *intr.* To make merry; later, to play pranks, gambol, caper about. †**2.** *trans.* To make joyous or merry –1677.

1. 'Tis Whitsontyde, and we must frolick it MARSTON. Hence **Fro·licker**, one who frolics.

Frolicsome (frǫ·liksǒm), *a.* Also †**frolicksom(e.** 1699. [f. FROLIC *v.* or *sb.* + -SOME.] Full of frolic; gay, merry, mirthful.

In their frolicksome malice the Fates had ordered [etc.] W. IRVING. **Fro·licsome-ly** *adv.*, **-ness.**

From (frǫm). [OE. *fram, frǫm* (see FRO). The primary sense is 'forward'; hence 'onward', 'on the way', 'away', whence the transition to the prepositional use.]

A. *prep.* **1.** Denoting departure or moving away: indicating a starting-point **a.** in space; **b.** in defining an extent in space OE.; **c.** in a series or statement of limits OE.; **d.** in time OE. **2.** Indicating a place or object which is left at a distance, behind, or on one side, by an object which withdraws or turns away OE. **3.** Denoting (statically) distance, absence, remoteness OE.; also used *simply* = away from, apart from, absent from, etc. (now only in *from home*) ME. **4.** Denoting removal, abstraction, separation, expulsion, exclusion, or the like; also, privation, separation, abstention, freedom, deliverance, etc. (*from* a state, condition, action, etc.) OE. **5.** Indicating a state, condition, etc., which is abandoned or changed for another. Often as if with ellipsis of *being.* ME. **6.** Used after words which signify distinction, difference, unlikeness, etc. ME. †**b.** used *simply*: = away from, apart or aside from, out of, alien to –1637. **7.** Indicating the place, quarter, etc. whence something comes or is brought or fetched; often = out of; also after words denoting choice, etc. out of a number 1621. **b.** with ellipsis of vb. or pple. = coming from, taken from, etc. 1745. **8.** Indicating a place or position where action or motion is originated which goes thence, while the originator remains there. Similarly after words which express 'hanging', 'depending', etc. 1592. **9.** Indicating a person as a more or less distant source of action. In OE. = by. OE. **10.** Denoting derivation, descent, or the like; *esp.* 'noting progress from premisses to inferences' (J.) ME. **11.** Indicating a model, rule, copy; also, a person or thing after which another is named 1596. **12.** Denoting ground, reason, cause, or motive. Now repl. in some uses by *for.* 1611.

1. She leet no morsel f. her lippes falle CHAUCER. Phr. *F. post to pillar, f. door to door.* **b.** F. the uprising to the setting Sunne SPENSER. **c.** F. 16 to 20 or 24 Oars DAMPIER. **d.** I knew him f. a boy C. BRONTË. Phr. *F. time to time.* 2. We will not f. the Helme, to sit and weepe SHAKS. Why speak'st thou f. me BEAUM. & FL. 3. Phr. *Away, absent, apart f.* Far apart F. wicked men like thee KEATS. 4. Release me f. my bands *Temp.* Epil. 9. To refrain f. laughing BERKELEY. 5. F. a slave she became to be a Princesse 1641. Temples..which tremblingly grew blank F. bright BROWNING. 6. You can't tell one flower f. another L. CARROLL. **b.** Phr. †*F. oneself* = beside oneself, out of one's wits. 7. She drew a knife f. her bosom ARNOLD. He came f. Cambridge 1879. **b.** Cavaliers f. the country MACAULAY. 8. God f. the mount of Sinai..will himself..Ordain them laws MILT. *fig.* F. their point of view they are perfectly right L. CARROLL. 9. He bad me, f. him, call thee Thane of Cawdor SHAKS. You shall hear f. my attorney 1843. 10. Eve, who..anomalously proceeded f. Adam SIR T. BROWNE. Cuts f. a sabre 1870. To draw a conclusion f. premisses 1887. 11. Enos, nam'd f. me DRYDEN. To colour f. nature 1811. 12. To speak out and act f. principle 1796. Remarkable f. the neatness..of its architecture DISRAELI. F. your silence I fear [etc.] 1855.

Phrases. **a.** With obj. an adv., as *f. above, afar,* etc. Also, pleonastically, before *hence, thence,* etc.: see those words. **b.** *F. amidst, beneath,* etc., indicating a static condition. **c.** Followed, pleonastically, by *out, out of, forth, off,* where each prep. strengthens or supplements the sense of the other.

†**B.** quasi-*adv.* = away. Only in *to and f.*, *f. and back.* –1608.

†**C.** quasi-*conj.* = from the time when –1602.

†**Fro·mward.** OE. [f. FROM + -WARD.]

A. *adj.* = Turned from or away –1576.

B. *adv.* In a direction which leads from, or is turned from, a given place or object. Also, of time. –1711.

C. *prep.* Away from –1713.

So **Fro·mwards** *adv.* and *prep.*

Frond (frǫnd), *sb.* 1785. [ad. L. *frond-, frons* leaf, applied *spec.* by Linnæus.] **1.** *Bot.* The leaf-like organ formed by the union of stem and foliage in certain flowerless plants. Formerly (and still loosely) applied also to the large compound leaves, e.g. of the palm, banana, etc. **2.** *Zool.* A leaf-like expansion found in certain animal organisms 1846. Hence **Frond** *v. intr.* to wave with fronds. **Fro·ndage,** fronds collectively; also, erron., foliage.

†**Fronda·tion.** *rare.* [ad. late L. *frondationem.*] The act of stripping trees of some of the luxuriant branches and sprays. EVELYN.

‖**Fronde** (frōnd). 1798. [F.; = 'sling'.] *Fr. Hist.* The name given to the party which rose against Mazarin and the Court during the minority of Louis XIV; hence, a malcontent party; also, violent political opposition.

Was there ever a mixed constitution without a *f.* 1808.

†**Fro·nded,** *ppl. a.*[1] 1640. [ad. L. *frondatus.*] Having leaves or foliage. HOWELL.

Fronded (frǫ·ndėd), *ppl. a.*[2] 1882. [f. FROND *sb.*[1] + -ED [2].] Having fronds.

Frondent (frǫ·ndĕnt), *a.* 1677. [ad. L. *frondentem, frondere* to put forth leaves.] Full of fronds, leafy.

Frondesce (frǫnde·s), *v.* 1816. [ad. L. *frondescere,* freq. of *frondere.*] *intr.* To put forth leaves. So **Fronde·scent** *a.* springing into leaf; expanding into fronds. **Fronde·scently** *adv.*

Frondescence (frǫnde·sĕns). 1841. [ad. mod.L. *frondescentia,* f. *frondescentem*; see -ENCE.] The process or period of coming into leaf; the conversion of other organs into leaves; fronds or leaves collectively.

‖**Frondeur** (frōndör). 1798. [F., f. *fronde* (see FRONDE).] **1.** *Fr. Hist.* A member of the Fronde. **2.** *transf.* A malcontent, an irreconcilable 1847.

Frondiferous (frǫndi·fĕrəs), *a.* 1599. [f. L. *frondifer*; see -(I)FEROUS.] Bearing leaves or fronds.

Frondlet (frǫ·ndlėt). 1862. [f. FROND *sb.*[1] + -LET.] A little frond.

Frondose (frǫndōᵘ·s), *a.* 1721. [ad. L. *frondosus.*] Covered with fronds; resembling a frond. In early use, †Leafy, leaf-like.

Frondous (frǫ·ndəs), *a.* 1828. [ad. L. *frondosus*; see -OUS.] Leafy; having branches bearing both leaves and flowers.

‖**Frons** (frǫnz). 1856. [L.] *Entom.* The middle part of the face of insects, between the eyes.

Front (frɒnt), *sb.* (and *a.*) ME. [a. OF. and F. *front,* ad. L. *frontem, frons* the forehead.]

I. 1. = FOREHEAD **1.** Now only *poet.* or *rhet.* **2.** Hence: The whole face ME. **3.** †**a.** The face as expressive of emotion or character; expression of countenance. **b.** Bearing or demeanour in confronting anything. Also *transf.* ME. **4.** Effrontery, impudence. Now *rare.* 1653.

1. The f. of Ioue himselfe SHAKS. The mark of fool set on his f. MILT. *Sams.* 496. *fig* The verie head, and f. of my offending SHAKS. 2. F. to F., Bring thou this friend of Scotland and my selfe SHAKS. 3. b. Who, patient in adversity, still bear The firmest f. FALCONER. The..unclouded f. of an accomplished courtier SCOTT.

II. 1. *Mil.* **a.** The foremost line or part of an army or battalion. Also, in words of command; e.g. *files to the f.* ME. **b.** Line of battle ME. **c.** The foremost part of the ground occupied, or of the field of operations; the part next the enemy. Also, the foremost part of a position, as opposed to *rear.* 1665. **d.** The direction towards which the line faces when formed 1832. **2.** *Arch.* 'Any side or face of a building, but more commonly.. the entrance side' (Gwilt); occas. *collect.* in *sing.* and *pl.* = 'the four sides' (of a mansion) ME. **3.** *gen.* The part or side of an object which seems to look out or be presented to the eye; the foremost part of anything. Opp. to *back.* ME. **b.** *transf.* With reference to time: The first period; the beginning (*poet.*) 1600. **c.** A frontage 1766. **d.** *Theatr.* The audience 1810. †**4.** The first part or line of anything written or printed -1697. **5.** False hair, or false curls worn by women over the forehead 1687. **b.** That part of a man's shirt which covers the chest; a shirt-front; also, a 'dicky', or the like 1844. **6.** Forward position or situation 1609. †**7.** [f. the vb.] Encounter, onset. LD. BERNERS. **8.** *attrib.* 1600.

1. a. Both our powers, with smiling Fronts encountring SHAKS. b. Preserving an even and unbroken f. THIRLWALL. c. British Regiments were wanted..at the F. Kipling. d. Phr. *Change of f.*: see CHANGE *v.* *F. of fortification*: two half bastions, and a curtain. 3. Had he his hurts before? I, on the F. SHAKS. b. In summer's f. SHAKS. 4. Phr. *In the f.* (of a page, etc.): at the head. 6. *To come to the f.*: to emerge into publicity. 8. At the Play, in a F. Row 1718.

Comb., etc.: **f. bench,** the foremost bench on either side of the Houses of Lords and Commons, occupied by ministers and ex-ministers respectively; **f. door,** the principal entrance-door of a house; **f.-stall,** an appendage to the bridle covering the horse's forehead; **-ways, -wise** *advs.* in a position or direction facing to the front.

Front (frɒnt), *v.* 1523. [ad. OF. *fronter,* f. *front* FRONT *sb.*] **1.** *intr.* To have the front in a specified direction; to face, look. **2.** *trans.* To have the front towards; to face, stand opposite to 1606. **3.** To stand face to face with, face, confront, *esp.* in defiance or hostility. *lit.* and *fig.* Said also of things. 1583. **4.** To set face to face *with* 1617. **5.** To adorn in front; to furnish with a front. Also, to face (with some material). 1635. †**6.** To preface -1732. **7.** To be in front of, serve as a front to 1591. **8.** Chiefly *Mil.* **a.** To turn the front or face in a specified direction. Also, as a word of command. 1635. **b.** To form a front 1802. **c.** *trans.* (causatively, from *Front!*): To cause to form a front 1796.

1. Philip's dwelling fronted on the street TENNYSON. 2. Like a gate of steele, Fronting the Sunne SHAKS. The church..was to have fronted the Plaza 1847. 3. He dare now to fronte princes SPENSER. Those Warres Which fronted mine owne peace SHAKS. 5. To new front a house H. WALPOLE. 7. Yonder wals that pertly f. your Towne..Must kisse their owne feet SHAKS. 8. Phr. *To f. about*: to turn round so as to face in another direction. **Fro·ntingly** *adv.*

Frontage (frɒ·ntėdʒ). 1622. [f. FRONT *sb.* + -AGE.] **1.** Land which abuts on a river or piece of water, or on a road. **2.** Extent of front 1844. **3.** The front face or part of a building. Also *collect.* 1861. **4.** The action of fronting in a certain direction; exposure, outlook 1859.

Hence **Fro·ntager,** an owner of f. (sense 1).

Frontal (frɒ·ntăl), *sb.* [ME. *frountel,* a. OF. *frontel*:— late L. *frontale,* f. *front-, frons*; see FRONT *sb.* and -AL.] †**1.** Something applied to the forehead: **a.** A band or ornament -1611; **b.** *Med.* a medicament to cure headache -1753. **2.** A movable covering for the front of an altar, generally of embroidered cloth, silk, etc., but occas. of metal ME. **3.** The façade of a building 1784. †**4.** *Arch.* A little pediment occas. placed over a little door or window -1736.

Frontal (frɒ·ntăl), *a.* 1656. [ad. mod.L. *frontalis*; see FRONT and -AL.] **1.** Of or pertaining to the forehead, or to the corresponding part in the lower animals. **2.** Of or pertaining to the fore-part or foremost edge 1860. **b.** Of an attack, etc.: Directed against the front 1884. **3.** quasi-*sb.* = *f. bone* 1854.

1. Phr. *F. artery, bone, sinus, vein,* etc. 2. *F. hammer* or *F. helve,* a forge-hammer lifted by a cam, acting upon a tongue immediately in front of the hammer-head.

Frontate (frǫ·-, frɒ·nteᵗt), *a.* 1855. [ad. mod.L. *frontatus,* f. *front-, frons*; see FRONT and -ATE [2].] *Bot.* Of the leaf of a flower: Growing broader and broader, and at last terminating in a right line. So †**Fronta·ted** *a.*

Fronted (frɒ·ntėd), *ppl. a.* 1615. [f. FRONT *sb.* or *v.* + -ED.] Having, or formed with, a front. MILT. *P. L.* II. 532.

Frontier (frǫ·n-, frɒ·ntiəɹ). ME. [a. OF. *frontier* masc., *frontiere* fem. (mod. *frontière*), f. *front* FRONT *sb.*]

A. *sb.* †**1.** The front side; the fore-part -1551. †**2.** The front line or foremost part of an army. Hence, 'attack, resistance'. -1523. **3.** *sing.* and *pl.* The part of a country which fronts, faces, or borders on another country; the marches. Also *transf.* and *fig.* ME. **b.** *U.S.* 'That part of a country which forms the border of its settled or inhabited regions' (*Cent. Dict.*) 1870. †**4.** A fortress on the frontier; a frontier town -1796; a barrier against attack -1690.

4. His Navies do carry a moveable Frontire to all the habitable world MARVELL.

B. *adj.* **1.** Of, belonging to, or situated on the frontier; bordering 1523. †**2.** Fronting; opposite. HOLLAND.

Frontier (frǫ·n-, frɒ·ntiəɹ), *v.* 1579. [f. prec. sb.] †**1.** *intr.* To be a frontier, or as a frontier; to border *on* -1662. **2.** *trans.* To look upon the boundary or coast of; to face (now *rare*); †to stand in front of; to oppose 1579.

Fro·ntierman, fro·ntiersman. 1813. [f. FRONTIER *sb.* + MAN.] One who lives on the frontier, or on the outlying districts of civilization.

Frontignac (frǫntinyæ·k), *sb.* Often *attrib.* 1629. [erron. form of next.] **1.** A muscat wine made at Frontignan, France. **2.** The grape from which this is made 1641.

†**Frontignan.** 1756. = prec. -1777.

Frontispiece (frɒ·ntispīs), *sb.* 1597. [a. F. *frontispice,* ad. med.L. *frontispicium* lit. 'looking at the forehead', f. L. *front(i)-* + *spicium,* f. early L. *specere* to look.] **1.** The principal face or front of a building; more usually, the decorated entrance. **2.** The pediment over a door, gate, etc. Also, a decorated panel. 1601. †**3.** The first page of a book or pamphlet, or what is printed on it; the title-page including illustrations and table of contents; hence, an introduction or preface. Also *fig.* -1721. **4.** An illustration facing the title-page of a book or division of a book. (The current sense.) 1682. **5.** The front part of anything 1625.

2. A Kingly Palace Gate, With Frontispiece of Diamond and Gold Embellisht MILT. *P. L.* III. 506. Hence **Fro·ntispiece** *v. trans.* to furnish *with* as a f.; to represent on the f.; to put as a f.

Frontless (frɒ·ntlės), *a.* 1605. [f. FRONT *sb.* + -LESS.] Having no front; esp. *fig.* unblushing, shameless, audacious (now *rare*).

The..most frontlesse piece Of solid impudence B. JONS. Hence **Fro·ntless-ly** *adv.*, **-ness.**

Frontlet (frɒ·ntlėt). 1478. [a. OF. *frontelet,* dim. of *frontel, fronteau* FRONTAL *sb.*; see -LET.] **1.** Something worn on the forehead: **a.** an ornament or band; also *fig.*; **b.** = PHYLACTERY 1578; **c.** = *front-stall* 1805. **2.** = FOREHEAD **1.** Now only of animals. 1659. **b.** *Ornith.* The margin of the head, behind the bill, of birds, usu. clothed with rigid bristles 1874. **3.** = FRONT *sb.* II. 2; also *transf.* 1808. **4.** A superfrontal; also, an ornamental border to an altar-cloth 1536.

1. a. *fig.* What makes that F. on? You are too much of late i'th'frowne *Lear* I. iv. 208. b. It shalbe..as frontlets betwene thine eyes BIBLE (Genev.) *Ex.* xiii. 16.

Fronto- (frǫ·nto), used for *fronti-,* comb. f. L. *frontem, frons* FRONT, with sense 'pertaining to the front or forehead and to something else', as *f.-nasal, -occipital, -parietal,* etc.

Fronton (frɒ·ntǫn). 1698. [a. F., ad. It. *frontone,* f. *fronte* FRONT.] **1.** *Arch.* A pediment. **2.** = FRONTAL *sb.* 2. 1749. ‖**3.** A building where pelota is played. [Sp.] 1896.

Frontward, -wards (frɒ·ntwǫɹd, -z), *adv.* (*sb.*) 1553. [f. FRONT *sb.* + -WARD(S).] **1.** Towards the front; also with *of* 1865. †**b.** quasi-*sb.* The direction towards the front 1553. **2.** With the face in a specified direction. MRS. BROWNING.

†**Fro·ppish,** *a.* 1659. [? f. **frop,* var. of FRAP *v.* + -ISH.] Froward, fretful, peevish -1784. Hence †**Fro·ppishness.**

Frore (frōᵊɹ), †**froren,** †**frorn(e,** *pa. pple.* and *ppl. a.* ME. [pa. pple. of FREEZE *v.*] **1.** With ppl. sense: FROZEN. *Obs.* exc. *dial.* **2.** Intensely cold, frosty, frost-like. Now only *poet.* in form *frore* (after Milton) 1483.

2. The parching Air Burns frore, and cold performs th' effect of Fire MILT. Hence **Fro·ry** *a.* (in sense 2); also, †foamy.

Frost (frǫst), *sb.* [Com. Teut.: OE. *frost,* usu. *forst,* str. masc.:—OTeut. **frusto-,* f. **freusan* to FREEZE.] **1.** The act or state of freezing or becoming frozen; the temperature of the air when it is below the freezing-point of water; extreme cold. Also *personified* in *Jack Frost.* **2.** Frozen dew or vapour. More fully *hoar(y, rime,* or *white f.* OE. **3.** *fig.*; *esp.* of a person: Coldness of behaviour or temperament, frigidity; (*slang*) a 'coolness' 1635. **4.** *slang* (orig. *Theatr.*). A failure 1886. †**5.** A colour like that of hoar-frost; silver-grey; also, gold or silver frost-work -1702.

1. *Black f.*: frost unaccompanied by rime; opp. to *white f.* (see sense 2). When rigorous Winter binds you [river] up with F. COWLEY. F. will penetrate eight inches, sometimes more 1891. **2.** Seed-time and Harvest, Heat and hoary F., Shall hold their course MILT. *P.L.* 899. **3.** Renaissance frosts came, and all perished RUSKIN.

Comb.: **f.-bearer** = CRYOPHORUS; **-bird,** the American Golden Plover; **-blite,** the plant *Chenopodium album*; **-dew,** hoar-frost, rime; **-fern,** a fern-like figure produced by the freezing of a moist surface; **-fish,** (*a*) the Tomcod, *Microgadus tomcodus*, which appears on the coast of N. America as the frost sets in; (*b*) the scabbard-fish, *Lepidophus caudatus*; **-fog** = *f.-mist*; **-grape,** an American species of *Vitis cordifolia* or *riparia*; **-lamp,** an oil-lamp placed beneath the oil-tube of an Argand lamp to keep the oil in a flowing condition; **-mist,** mist caused by the freezing of vapour in the atmosphere; **-nail** *sb.*, a nail driven into the shoe to prevent slipping in frosty weather; so **-nail** *v.*; **-rime** = *f.-smoke*; **-smoke,** a thick mist in high latitudes, arising from the surface of the sea when exposed to a temperature much below freezing; **-valve,** a valve which opens to allow water to escape from the portion of the pipe or pump where it is liable to be frozen; **-weed, -wort,** the plant *Helianthemum canadense*; so called because, late in autumn, crystals of ice shoot from the cracked bark at the root.

Frost (frǫst), *v.* 1572. [f. prec. sb.] **1.** *trans.* To freeze, frost-bite, nip with frost 1807. **2.** To cover with or as with rime. Chiefly *fig.* 1635. **3.** To give a frosted surface to (glass or metal) 1832. **4.** To treat by the insertion of frost-nails, roughing, etc., as a protection against slipping in frosty weather; to shoe (a horse) in this way 1572.

2. The rising moon, While with a hoary light she frosts the ground WORDSW.

Fro·st-bi·t, *pple.* and *ppl. a. rare.* 1749. = FROST-BITTEN.

Fro·st-bi·te, *sb.* 1813. The inflamed or gangrenous condition of the skin and adjacent parts produced by exposure to severe cold.

Fro·st-bi·te, *v.* 1593. *trans.* †To injure with intense cold; also *fig.*; †to invigorate by exposure to the frost; to get (oneself or one's limbs) frost-bitten.

My wife up, and with Mrs. Pen to walk in the fields to f. themselves PEPYS.

Fro·st-bi·tten, *pple.* and *ppl. a.* 1593. Injured by exposure to frost.

Frosted (frǫ·stėd), *ppl. a.* 1645. [f. FROST *sb.* and *v.* + -ED.] **1.** Frozen, frost-bitten 1807. **2.** Covered with rime or hoar-frost 1720. **3.** Covered as with rime; hoary, white 1645. **4.** Of glass, silver, etc.: Having a surface made to resemble a coating of hoar-frost 1689. **5.** Made to resemble rough ice 1790.

3. *F. cake*: cake covered with 'icing'. When I, with f. hairs, Should look at what I was G. DANIEL. **4.** F. Buttons 1711, tumblers 1852.

Frosting (frǫ·stiŋ), *vbl. sb.* 1617. [f. FROST *v.*] **1.** The action of FROST *v.* **2.** *concr.* **a.** A substance powdered and used for frosting purposes; *esp.* pulverized white sugar used for icing cake 1756. **b.** A frosted surface 1892.

Fro·stless, *a.* 1711. [see -LESS.] Without frost.

Fro·st-ni·p, *v.* 1642. To nip or injure with frost. FULLER. Hence **Fro·st-ni·pped** *pple.* and *ppl. a.* = FROST-BITTEN.

Frost-work. 1648. **1.** Work produced by frost; *esp.* the tracery formed on the surface of glass, etc. by frost 1729. Also *attrib.* **2.** Ornamentation in imitation of this.

Frosty (frǫ·sti), *a.* [f. FROST *sb.* + -Y[1]; OE. had *fyrstig.*] **1.** Affected with or characterized by frost; at or below freezing-point; ice-cold OE.; †belonging to the season of frost ME. **2.** *transf.* and *fig.* Cold as frost; without ardour or warmth of feeling, frigid ME. **3.** Covered with hoar-frost 1577. **4.** Covered as with frost; of the hair: Hoary, white ME.; hence, Characteristic of old age 1588. **b.** *spec.* in *Entom.* Of a glistening white colour 1698.

1. The noise of f. woodlands TENNYSON. The f. feldefare CHAUCER. **2.** He red for shame, but f. in desire SHAKS. **4.** Blessings on your f. pow BURNS. Hence **Fro·stily** *adv.* **Fro·stiness.**

Frot (frǫt), *v.* Also †**frote,** etc. ME. [a. OF. *froter* (mod. *frotter*), of unkn. etym.] †**1.** *trans.* To rub, chafe; in early use, to stroke (an animal) -1688. **2.** *Tanning.* To work or render supple by rubbing 1853. Hence †**Fro·terer.**

Froth (frǫþ), *sb.* [ME. *frothe*, perh. a. ON. *froða* wk. fem., related to ON. *frauð* neut. Cf. OE. *á-fréoðan* to froth.] **1.** = FOAM *sb.* **1.** Also *transf.* and *fig.* **b.** *spec.* Foaming saliva issuing from the mouth ME. **c.** Scum 1533. **2.** Something unsubstantial or of little worth 1593. **3.** Applied contemptuously to persons. Cf. SCUM. 1598.

1. *fig.* Society is f. above and dregs below LANDOR. **2.** The thing I seeke..a f. of fleeting ioy SHAKS. **3.** F., and scum thou liest *Merry W.* I. i. 167.

Comb.: **f.-spit** = CUCKOO-SPIT 1; **-stick,** a stick for whipping cream, etc. Also in names given to the frog-hopper, as **f.-fly, -frog-hopper, -insect, -worm.**

Hence **Fro·thery** (*nonce-wd.*), mere f., triviality (CARLYLE). **Fro·thless** *a.* **Fro·thsome** *a.* frothy.

Frothy (frǫ·þi), *a.* 1533. [f. FROTH *sb.* + -Y[1].] **1.** Full of, covered with, or accompanied by froth or foam; foamy. **2.** Consisting of, or resembling, froth, spumous 1605; †soft, not firm or solid, flabby -1658. **3.** *fig.* Vain, empty, unsubstantial 1593.

3. A f. mob orator 1884. F. fine writing 1885. Hence **Fro·thily** *adv.* **Fro·thiness.**

‖**Frou-frou** (frū frū). 1870. [Fr.; echoic.] A rustling, *esp.* that of a dress.

Frounce (frauns), *sb.*[1] ME. [a. OF. *fronce*, *fronche.*] †**1.** A wrinkle -1721. †**2.** A fold, crease; a pleat; *fig.* duplicity. ME. only. †**3.** = FLOUNCE *sb.*[2] 1. 1619. **4.** A piece of foppish display. (Cf. MILT. *Pens.* 123.) 1881. Hence †**Frou·nceless** *a.* unwrinkled. CHAUCER.

†**Frounce,** *sb.*[2] 1450. [?] **1.** A canker or sore in the mouth of a hawk -1820. **2.** A disease in the mouth of a horse -1725.

Frounce (frauns), *v.* ME. [ad. OF. *froncier*, *froncir* (mod. *froncer*), f. *fronce* FROUNCE *sb.*[1]] †**1.** *trans.* To gather in folds or wrinkles; to knit, purse; occas. to knit the brows of -1628. †**b.** *intr.* To knit the brows; to look angry. Also of the face or forehead: To become wrinkled. -1600. **2.** *trans.* To fizz, curl; also, to curl the hair of 1526. †**3.** To gather into creases or pleats; to pleat -1805.

1. b. They frounced and tooke on most insolently HOLLAND. **2.** Not trick'd and frounc'd as she was wont MILT. **3.** Their shurts frounced LD. BERNERS.

Frouzy: see FROWZY.

Frow (frau), *sb.* ME. [ad. Du. *vrouw.*] **1.** A Dutchwoman. **2.** A woman, a lady, a wife. Chiefly with reference to Dutch or German women. 1587. †**3.** Applied to the Mænads or Bacchantes of paganism; also *transf.* -1616. **4.** *dial.* An idle, dirty woman 1781.

Frow: see FROE.

Froward (frōᵘ·wəɹd). [Early ME. f. *fra*, FRO + -WARD.]

A. *adj.* (Not now in colloq. use.) **1.** Disposed to go counter to what is demanded or is reasonable; perverse; refractory; also, †bad, evilly-disposed, 'naughty'. (The opposite of *toward.*) **2.** Of things: †**a.** Adverse, untoward; refractory. †Of shape: Ill-formed. **b.** In later use only as *fig.* of sense 1. ME.

1. A F. Retention of Custome BACON. A f. child 1848. **2. a.** The f. chaos of futurity WORDSW. **b.** To take his f. fortune..with..patience 1576.

†**B.** *adv.* **1.** = FROMWARD. -1596. **2.** *fig.* Untowardly, perversely -1580.

C. *prep.* = FROMWARD. *Obs.* (or *arch.*) ME. Hence **Fro·ward-ly** *adv.*, **-ness.**

Frower; see FROE *sb.*

Frown (fraun), *sb.* 1581. [f. next.] **1.** A wrinkled aspect of the brow, expressive of disapprobation or severity, occas. of deep thought or perplexity. Also, the habit of frowning. 1605. **2.** A manifestation of disapprobation.

1. You are too much of late i'th'frowne SHAKS. *fig.* The f. of angry Heav'n 1783. **2.** To this no answer was given, but frowns WODROW. Hence **Frow·nful** *a.* full of frowns. **Frow·ny** *a.* habitually frowning.

Frown (fraun), *v.* [ME. *froune*, ad. OF. *froignier*, *frongnier* (cf. mod. *refrogner*), of obscure origin.] **1.** *intr.* To knit the brows in displeasure or (less frequently) in concentration of thought; to look sternly. Said also of the brow. Of inanimate things: To look gloomy or threatening 1642. **2.** To express disapprobation or unfriendliness by a look. Const. *at*, *on, upon.* 1576. **3.** quasi-*trans.* To enforce, express, produce, etc. by a frown; also with *away, back, down, off,* etc. 1678.

1. He ended frowning, and his look denounc'd Desperate revenge MILT. They saw the times to frowne and trouble to come ROGERS. **2.** I frowne vpon him, yet he loues me still SHAKS. The heauens..are angry And frowne vpon 's SHAKS. **3.** She smiles preferment, or she frowns disgrace SHERIDAN. Hence **Frow·ner.** **Frow·ning-ly** *adv.*

Frowst (fraust), *sb. colloq.* 1880. Also froust. [?] Fusty heat in a room; hence as vb., to stay in or enjoy this. So **Frow·sty** *a.* 1865.

Frowzy (frau·zi), *a.* 1681. [? cogn. w. FROWSTY.] **1.** Ill-smelling, fusty, musty. **2.** Dingy, rusty, slatternly, unkempt. Of the complexion: Red and coarse, blowsy 1710.

1. My study was so f. I couldn't sit in it HUGHES. **2.** A f. dirty-colour'd red Sits on her cloudy wrinkled face SWIFT. *fig.* A drowsy f. poem BYRON. Hence **Frow·ziness.**

Frozen (frōᵘ·z'n), *ppl. a.* ME. [pa. pple. of FREEZE *v.*] **1.** Congealed by extreme cold; subjected to extreme cold. Also *fig.* and of immaterial things. **b.** Of credits, assets, etc.: Impossible to liquidate or realize at maturity or other given time (opp. to LIQUID *a.* II. 5) 1922. **2.** *F.-out, -up*: cut off, stopped, by frost 1885.

1. The nauigation by the frosen sea EDEN. F. limbs 1698, meat 1872. *fig.* A f. stare 1867.

Hence **Fro·zenly** *adv.* in a f. manner; with a cold look or action; (*U.S.*) stubbornly. **Fro·zenness,** f. condition.

†**Fru·bbish,** *v.* Also †**frobish.** 1570. [var. of FURBISH.] To furbish. †**Fru·bbisher.**

Fructed (frʊ·ktėd), *a.* 1610. [f. L. *fructus* + -ED[2].] *Her.* Of a tree or plant: Having fruit (of a specified tincture).

Fructescent (frʊkte·sĕnt), *a.* 1862. [ad. mod.L. *fructescentem*, *fructescere*, f. *fructus.*] Beginning to bear fruit. Hence **Fructe·scence,** the fruiting season, when vegetables scatter their seeds.

Fructiculose, a spurious wd.; see FRUTICULOSE.

‖**Fructidor** (frü̆ktidǫr). 1793. [Fr.; f. L. *fructus* + Gr. δῶρον.] The twelfth month of the French revolutionary calendar (Aug. 18 to Sept. 16); the revolution which took place on 18th Fructidor (Sept. 4), 1797.

Fructiferous (frʊkti·fĕrəs), *a.* 1632. [f. L. *fructifer* (f. *fructus* + *-fer* bearing) + -OUS.] Bearing or producing fruit. Hence **Fructi·ferously** *adv.*

Fructification (frʊ·ktifikēⁱ·ʃən). 1615. [ad. L. *fructificationem.*] **1.** The action or process of fructifying or producing fruit (now *rare* exc. *Bot.*). Also, fecundation. **2.** *concr.* in *Bot.* **a.** The fruit of a plant. **b.** *collect.* The organs of fruiting or reproduction, *esp.* the reproductive parts of ferns and mosses. 1764.

Fructify (frʊ·ktifəi), *v.* ME. [a. F. *fructifier*, ad. L. *fructificare*, f. *fructus*; see -FY.] **1.** *intr.* To bear fruit, become fruitful. Also *fig.* **2.** *trans.* To make fruitful; to fecundate 1583.

1. Hys land shall frutyfye 1538. **2.** To fructifie and increase the earth STUBBES. Hence †**Fru·ctifi·able** *a.* capable of bearing fruit. **Fru·ctifier.**

Fructose (frʊ·ktōᵘs). 1864. [f. L. *fructus* + -OSE.] *Chem.* 'Fruit sugar or lævulose. Also applied to the sugar found in fruit' (*Syd. Soc. Lex.*).

Fructuary (frʊ·ktiuări). 1643. [ad. L. *fructuarius*; see -ARY.]

A. *adj.* in *Rom. Law.* Of or belonging to usufruct. Only in *f. stipulation.* POSTE. †**B.** *sb.* **1.** A usufructuary -1687. **2.** Something enjoyed by usufruct 1651.

†**Fru·ctuate,** *v. rare.* 1663. [f. L. *fructus* + -ATE[3].] *intr.* To bear fruit; to fructify 1663. Hence **Fructua·tion,** the action of the vb.; †*concr.* a crop of fruit.

Fructuous (frʊ·ktiuəs), *a.* ME. [a. OF. *fructuous* (mod.F. *fructueux*), ad. L. *fructuosus*; see -OUS.] **1.** Full of, abounding with, or producing fruit. 2. *fig.* Productive of results; advantageous, profitable ME.

1. An olyue plenteous, fair, f. WYCLIF *Jer.* xi. 16. Hence **Fru·ctuous-ly** *adv.*, **-ness.**

†**Fru·cture.** [a. OF., ad. L. *fructura*, f. *frui* (*fruct-*) to enjoy.] The use or enjoyment (of something). COTGR.

Frugal (frū·găl), *a.* 1598. [ad. L. *frugalis*, f. *frugi* used as indecl. adj., orig. dat. of *frux* (chiefly in pl. *fruges* fruits); see -AL. Cf. F. *frugal.*] 1. Careful or sparing in the use of food, goods, etc.; economical. Const. *of.* 2. Of things: Sparingly supplied or used; of small cost; opp. to *luxurious* 1603.

1. 'Tis now the cheap and f. fashion, Rather to Hide than Pay the Obligation COWLEY. 2. A f. meal, which consisted of roots and tea GOLDSM. Hence **Fru·gally** *adv.*

Frugality (frugæ·lĭti). 1531. [a. F. *frugalité*, ad. L. *frugalitatem*; see prec. and -ITY.] 1. The quality of being frugal; moderate or sparing expenditure or use of provisions, goods, etc. 2. The product of frugality, wealth amassed by economy; also in *pl.* frugal ways of living, frugal fare 1725.

1. Riches are gotten with industry, and kept by f. HOBBES. 2. Wastes the wise f. of Kings POPE.

Frugiferous (frudʒi·fĕrəs), *a.* 1633. [f. L. *frugifer* (f. *frugi-*, *frux* fruit + *-fer* bearing) + -OUS.] Fruit-bearing, fruitful.

Frugivorous (frudʒi·vŏrəs). *a.* 1713. [f. L. *frugi* (see prec.) + *-vorus* devouring + -OUS.] Eating or feeding on fruit.

Fruit (frūt), *sb.* ME. [a. OF. *fruit* (later often *fruict*) :—L. *fructus*, f. **frugv-* root of *frui* to enjoy.] 1. Vegetable products in general, that are fit to be used as food by men and animals. Now usu. in *pl.* 2. The edible product of a plant or tree, consisting of the seed and its envelope, *esp.* the latter when juicy and pulpy, as in the apple, orange, plum, etc. ME. †3. A fruit-tree; also a food-plant. *rare.* –1767. †4. A course of fruit; the dessert –1602. 5. The seed of a plant or tree, regarded as the means of reproduction, together with its envelope; *spec.* in *Bot.* 'the ripe pistil containing the ovules, arrived at the state of seeds' (Lindley); also, the spores of cryptogams 1794. 6. Offspring, progeny. Also, an embryo, fœtus. Orig. a Hebraism. Now *rare.* ME. 7. Anything accruing, produced, or resulting from an action or fact, the operation of a cause, etc.: a. material produce, increase; *pl.* products, revenues ME.; b. a result, issue, consequence (*sing.* and *pl.*) ME.; c. advantage, enjoyment, profit ME.

1. To give and preserve to our use the kindly fruits of the earth *Bk. Com. Prayer.* *fig.* The only f. which he could reap from a victory 1783. 2. We take Branches from a Tree, to add to the F. POPE. The glow of ripe fruits 1795. 4. *Haml.* II. ii. 52. 6. Blessed shalbe the frute of thy body COVERDALE *Deut.* xxviii. 4. 7. a. Milke..which is the f. of the breasts 2 *Esdras* viii. 10. b. Riches and Plenty are the natural Fruits of Liberty ADDISON. c. She tooke the Fruites of my Aduice *Haml.* II. ii. 145.

Comb.: f.-bat (see FLYING-FOX); **-bud**, a bud containing a fruit germ, dist. from *leaf-bud*; **-dot** (Bot.), the sorus of ferns; **-fly**, a gardener's name for a sort of small black fly, found in numbers among fruit-trees in spring; **-frame**, a trellis or espalier; **-mill**, a mill for grinding grapes for must or apples for cider; **-piece**, 'a pictured or sculptured representation of fruit' (*Cent. Dict.*); **-pigeon**, a general name for pigeons of the genera *Carpophaga* and *Treron*; **-press**, an apparatus for extracting the juice from fruit by pressure; **-spur**, a small branch whose growth is stopped to ensure the development of fruit-buds; **-stalk**, a stalk that bears fruit; *spec.* = PEDUNCLE; also occas. = CARPOPHORE; **-sugar** = GLUCOSE or LÆVULOSE; **-tree**, a tree cultivated for its fruit; **-wall**, a wall against which fruit-trees are trained; †**-yard**, an orchard.

Fruit (frūt), *v.* ME. [f. prec. sb.] 1. *intr.* To bear fruit. 2. *trans.* (*causatively*) To make bear fruit; to cultivate to the point of bearing fruit. *lit.* and *fig.* 1640. Hence **Frui·ted** *ppl. a.* having fruit upon it; fruit-laden.

Fruitage (frū·tédʒ). 1578. [a. OF., f. *fruit* FRUIT.] 1. The process, season, or state of bearing fruit. 2. Fruit collectively; also *fig.* 1610. †3. A decorative arrangement of fruits; a representation of this –1719.

1. In full f. COLERIDGE. 2. Greedily they pluck'd The Frutage fair to sight MILT.

Fruitarian (frutẽə·riăn). 1893. [f. FRUIT *sb.* + -ARIAN, after *vegetarian.*] One who adopts a fruit diet. Also as adj.

Fruiter (frū·təɹ). 1483. [orig. a F. *fruitier*; later f. FRUIT *sb.* or *v.* + -ER[1].] A dealer in fruit; also, a vessel engaged in the fruit-trade; a tree that produces fruit; a fruit-grower.

Fruiterer (frū·tĕrəɹ). ME. [f. as prec. + -ER[1].] 1. A dealer in fruit. 2. A fruit-grower –1813. **Frui·teress**, a female f.

Fruitery (frū·tĕri). 1609. [ad. F. *fruiterie*, f. *fruit.*] †1. A place for growing or storing fruit –1816. 2. Fruit collectively *c* 1600.

†**Fruitester.** [f. FRUIT *sb.* + -STER.] = FRUITERESS. Chaucer.

Fruitful (frū·tfŭl), *a.* ME. [f. FRUIT *sb.* + -FUL.] 1. Productive of fruit; bearing fruit abundantly. Of soils, etc.: Fertile. Of rain, etc.: Causing fertility. 2. Productive of offspring; not barren; prolific 1520. †3. Abundant, copious. Chiefly in Shaks. –1697. 4. *transf.* and *fig.* 1535. 5. Productive of good results ME.

1. Your Summer Fields, and fruitfull Vines SHAKS. 2. God blessed them, saying, Be fruitfull and multiply *Gen.* i. 22. 3. One f. Meale SHAKS. 4. Golden days, f. of golden deeds MILT. 5. Fruytfull occupacyoun ME. Hence **Frui·tful-ly** *adv.*, **-ness.**

Fruition (frŭi·ʃən). ME. [a. OF. *fruission*, *fruition*, ad. L. *fruitionem*, f. *frui*; see FRUIT *sb.*] The action of enjoying; enjoyment, pleasurable possession, the pleasure arising from possession. ¶ Erron. assoc. w. FRUIT.

1. The f. of our bookes HAKLUYT. All desire is for f. A. SIDNEY. Repaid by such a..brief f. THACKERAY.

Fruitive (frū·itiv), *a.* 1635. [ad. med.L. *fruitivus*, f. L. *frui*; see prec.] Consisting of, arising from, or producing fruition; having the faculty or function of enjoying 1635.

Fruitless (frū·tlės), *a.* ME. [f. FRUIT *sb.* + -LESS.] 1. Not producing fruit; barren, sterile. †*Rarely*: Not producing offspring. 1513. 2. Yielding no profit or advantage; producing no result; ineffectual, unprofitable, useless; idle, vain ME. 3. Of persons: unsuccessful 1843.

1. Rotton and fruyteles trees 1546. 2. The..fruitlessest of al passions SIDNEY. A fruitlesse vision SHAKS. Our search was..f. DAMPIER. F. regrets JORTIN. Hence **Frui·tless-ly** *adv.*, **-ness.**

Fruitlet (frū·tlėt). 1882. [see -LET.] A little fruit; in *Bot.* a single member of an aggregate fruit (see AGGREGATE *a.*).

Fruity (frū·ti), *a.* 1657. [f. FRUIT *sb.* + -Y[1].] 1. Of, pertaining to, or resembling fruit. 2. Of wine: Tasting of the grape 1851. 3. *colloq.* Full of rough humour or (usu. scandalous) interest 1900. Hence **Frui·tiness.**

Frumentaceous (frūmĕntẽ·ʃəs), *a.* 1668. [f. late L. *frumentaceus* + -OUS.] Of the nature of or resembling wheat or other cereals.

Frumenta·rious, *a.* *rare.* 1670. [f. L. *frumentarius* + -OUS.] Of or pertaining to corn.

Frumentation (frūmĕntẽ·ʃən). 1623. [ad. L. *frumentationem.*] *Rom. Antiq.* A public largesse of corn.

Frumenty (frū·mĕnti), **Furmety** (fə̄·ɹmėti). [ME. *frumentee*, *furmente*, a. OF. *frumentée*, *fourmentee*, f. *frument*, *fourment* (mod. *froment*) :—late pop. L. **frūmentum* = late cl. L. *frūmentum* corn.] 1. A dish made of hulled wheat boiled in milk, and seasoned with cinnamon, sugar, etc. †2. A kind of wheat or spelt –1601.

Frump (frɒmp), *sb.* 1553. [?] †1. ? A derisive snort –1650. †2. A flout, jeer –1700. †3. A hoax –1791. 4. *pl.* Sulks, ill humour. Now *dial.* 1668. 5. A cross, old-fashioned, dowdily-dressed woman. Also, *rarely*, of a man. 1817.

5. They voted me a prig, a f., a fogram GODWIN. Hence †**Fru·mpery**, abuse; also, a flout, mock. **Fru·mpish** *a.* disposed to mock or flout; ill-tempered, cross. **Fru·mpy** *a.* cross-tempered; also, dowdy.

Frump (frɒmp), *v.* 1566. [Conn. w. prec.] 1. *trans.* To mock, flout, jeer; to taunt, insult, snub. *Obs.* or *arch.* 1577. †2. *intr.* To scoff, mock. Const. *at.* –1662. †3. To sulk 1693. Hence **Fru·mper**, one who frumps.

Frush (frɒʃ), *sb.*[1] *Obs.* exc. *Sc.* ME. [a. OF. *fruis*, *frois*, f. *fruissier*, *froissier*; see FRUSH *v.*] †1. A rush, charge, collision –1533. b. The noise of this ME. 2. *collect.* Fragments, splinters 1583.

Frush (frɒʃ), *sb.*[2] Now *dial.* 1607. [? short for F. *fourchette* (Topsell).] = FROG *sb.*[2] Also, thrush.

Frush (frɒʃ), *a.* *Sc.* and *n. dial.* 1802. [? f. FRUSH *v.*] 1. Liable to break; brittle, dry, fragile. 2. Soft, not firm in substance 1848.

Frush (frɒʃ), *v.* ME. [a. OF. *fruissier*, *froissier* (mod. *froisser*) :—pop. L. **frustiare* to shiver in pieces, f. L. *frustum*; see FRUSTUM.] †1. *trans.* To strike violently so as to crush, bruise, or smash; also *fig.* –1609. †2. *intr.* To rush violently –1450. †3. *trans.* The term of art for: a. To carve (a chicken) –1708; b. To dress (a chub) –1787. 4. To straighten (the feathers of an arrow). *Hist.* 1548.

1. High Cedars are frushed with tempests, when lowe shrubs are not toucht with the wind GREENE.

†**Frust** (frɒst). 1765. [ad. L. *frustum.*] A fragment. –1820.

†**Fru·strable**, *a.* *rare.* 1674. [ad. late L. *frustrabilis*; see FRUSTRATE *v.*] Capable of being frustrated –1677.

†**Frustra·neous**, *a.* 1643. [f. L. type **frustraneus* + -OUS.] Vain, ineffectual, unprofitable –1780.

Frustrate (frɒ·strėit), *pa. pple.* and *ppl. a.* *arch.* ME. [ad. L. *frustratus*, *frustrari*, *frustrare*; see next.]

†A. *pa. pple.* In senses of the vb. –1693.

Bid him yeeld, Being so f. *Ant. & Cl.* v. i. 2.

B. *ppl. a.* 1. Bereft or deprived *of*; destitute *of.* *Obs.* exc. *arch.* 1576. 2. Failing of effect 1529. †Of a legal document: Invalid, null –1664. 3. Of a hope, etc.: Balked, defeated, futile 1588. †4. Idle, purposeless –1535.

2. The f. dart POPE. 3. And multitude makes f. the design DRYDEN.

Frustrate (frɒ·strėit), *v.* Pa. pple. **frustrated**, †**frustrate.** ME. [f. L. *frustrat-*, *frustrari*, f. *frustra* in vain.] 1. *trans.* To balk, disappoint. Const. *of* (now *rare*). 2. To render ineffectual; to neutralize, counteract 1471; to make null and void; to do away with 1528. 3. To render vain; to baffle, defeat, foil. (The current use.) 1500.

1. They were frustrated in their designes WOOD. Frustrated of his end 1754. 2. To f. the opperacion [of poisons] EDEN. To f. the Laws and Statutes of this Realm R. COKE. 3. To f. a villany BLACKSTONE, a motion 1809, a negotiation 1844.

So **Fru·strative** *a.* tending to f., balk, or defeat; disappointing. †**Fru·stratory** *a.* Frustrative.

Frustration (frɒstrẽ·ʃən). 1555. [ad. L. *frustrationem.*] The action of frustrating; disappointment; defeat.

An entire f. of the main object of the deed 1884.

Frustule (frɒ·stiŭl). 1857. [a. F., ad. late L. *frustulum*, dim. of FRUSTUM.] The siliceous two-valved shell of a diatom, with its contents.

†‖**Fru·stulum.** *Pl.* **-la.** 1700. [L.] a. A fragment, an atom. b. *Math.* A small frustum. –1785. So **Fru:stulo·se** *a.* consisting of small fragments.

Frustum (frɒ·stɒ̆m). *Pl.* **-a, -ums.** 1658. [a. L.; = 'piece broken off'.] 1. *Math.* The portion of a regular solid left after cutting off the upper part by a plane parallel to the base; or the portion intercepted between two planes, either parallel or inclined to each other. b. Applied to the sections of the shaft of a column 1835. 2. *gen.* A portion or fragment. *rare.* 1721.

Frutage, obs. f. FRUITAGE.

Frutescent (frute·sĕnt), *a.* 1709. [Incorr. f. FRUT-EX + -ESCENT; better **fruticescent.*] *Bot.* Becoming shrubby; having the appearance or habit of a shrub. Hence **Frute·scence**, shrubbiness.

Frutex (frū·teks). 1664. [a. L.] *Bot.* A plant having a woody stem, but smaller than a tree; a shrub.

What is meant by trees, frutexes, etc. EVELYN.

†**Fru·ticant**, *a.* [ad. L. *fruticantem*, *fruticare* to sprout.] Putting forth shoots, sprouting. EVELYN.

†**Fruti·ceous**, *a.* [f. L. *frutic-* FRUTEX + -EOUS.] Shrubby, bushy. SIR T. BROWNE.

Fruticose (frū·tikōᵘs), *a.* 1668. [ad. L. *fruticosus*; see FRUTEX.] 1. Of the nature of a shrub; having woody stalks. 2. Shrublike; said *e.g.* of minerals, etc. 1805.

1. The f. Rubi HOOKER. 2. The F. Lichens VINES. var. **Fru·ticous.**

Fruticulose (fruti·kiŭlōᵘs), *a.* 1830. [as if ad. L. **fruticulosus*, f. **fruticulus*, dim. of FRUTEX.] Resembling a small shrub. Also in comb. form **Fruticulo·so-.**

Fru·tify, *v. nonce-wd.* A comic blunder put into the mouth of an illiterate person; *notify*, the word meant, is confused with *fructify*. *Merch. V.* II. ii. 142.

†**Fruz**, *sb.* [onomatopœic.] A collection of small branches, producing a frizzy appearance. EVELYN.

Fry (frəi), *sb.*[1] ME. [a. ON. *frió*, *freó*, *fræ* neut., seed.] 1. Offspring, young (of human beings); a man's children or family; *rarely*, a child. Now only as transf. from sense 3. ME. 2. The roe (of a female fish) ME. 3. Young fishes just produced from the spawn; *spec.* the young of salmon in the second year, more fully *salmon fry* ME. Also *transf.* and *fig.* 4. Hence, a collective term for: a. the smaller kinds of fish or other animals 1666; b. young or insignificant persons 1577; c. a heap of inanimate things 1587.

1. What you Egge? Yong f. of Treachery SHAKS. 4. a. Not onely Pike and Carp, but lesser F. N. COX. b. That indigested heap, and frie of Authors MILT. c. The smaller f. of Christmas Books 1861.

Fry (frəi), *sb.*[2] 1634. [f. FRY *v.*] †1. Excessive heat 1634. 2. Food cooked in a frying-pan 1639. b. Applied locally to internal parts of animals, usually eaten fried, as *lamb's f.*, etc. 1847.

Fry (frəi), *v.* Inflected **fried, frying.** ME. [a. F. *frire*:—L. *frigere* to roast, fry, cogn. w. Gr. φρύγειν, Skr. *bhrajj*, to fry.] 1. *trans.* To cook with fat in a shallow pan over the fire. †2. *transf.* and *fig.* To torture by fire; to burn or scorch -1697. 3. *intr.* To undergo the operation of cooking with fat in a pan (*rare* in lit. sense) ME. Also *transf.* and *fig.* †4. Of water: To be agitated, boil, seethe, foam -1697. b. To ferment; to seethe (in the stomach) -1647.

1. Phr. *To have other fish to f.* (see FISH *sb.*). 2. Raging Sirius fries the thirsty Land BLACKMORE. Phr. *To f. a faggot* (see FAGGOT *sb.*). 3. Phr. *To f. in one's own grease*: orig. *transf.* e.g. of persons burning alive, and *fig.*; now only, to suffer the consequences of one's own folly. In his owene grece I made him frye For angre, and for verray Ialousye CHAUCER. *fig.* What kindling motions in their breasts do f. FAIRFAX. 4. b. To keep the Oyle from frying in the Stomach BACON. Hence **Fry·er, fri·er,** one who fries (fish); a vessel for frying; *pl.* fish for frying. **Fry·ing** *vbl. sb.*

Fry·ing-pa·n. ME. [f. prec.] A shallow pan, usually of iron, with a long handle, in which food is fried.

Phr. (*To jump*, etc.) *out of the frying-pan into the fire*: to escape from one evil only to fall into a greater one.

Fuage, var., of FEUAGE, hearth-tax.

Fub, var. of FOB *v.*

†**Fub(b, fub(b)s.** 1614. [onomatopœic.] A small chubby person (a term of endearment) -1694.

†**Fu·bbery,** *rare.* [f. FUB *v.* + -ERY.] Cheating, deception. MARSTON.

Fubby (fv·bi), *a. rare.* 1790. [f. FUB *sb.* + -Y[1].] = next.

Fubsy (fv·bzi), *a.* 1780. [f. FUB(S + -Y[1].] Fat and squat.

Fat and f. fellows of colleges 1826.

Fucaceous (fiukē·ʃəs), *a.* 1891. [f. mod. L. *fucaceæ* (f. L. *fucus*: see FUCUS) + -OUS.] Of or belonging to the group *Fucaceæ* of seaweeds.

†**Fu·cate,** *a.* 1531. [ad. L. *fucatus*, *fucare* to paint, rouge, f. *fucus* FUCUS.] Artificially coloured; hence, falsified, disguised, counterfeit -1621. So †**Fucated** *ppl. a.* †**Fuca·tion,** the action of painting the face; counterfeiting.

Fuchsia (fiū·ʃiă). 1753. [mod.L., f. Leonhard *Fuchs* (16th c.).] A genus of ornamental shrubs (N.O. *Onagraceæ*) with drooping flowers; a plant of this genus. Also *attrib.*

Fuchsine (fū·ksin). 1865. [f. prec. + -INE. Named from its resemblance to the colour of the flower.] A salt of rosaniline, crystallizing in iridescent green tablets, soluble in water and forming a deep red liquid; used as a dye.

Fucivorous (fiusi·vŏrəs), *a.* 1860. [f. L. *fucus* + -*vorus* devouring + -OUS.] Eating, or subsisting on, seaweed.

Fucoid (fiū·koid). 1839. [f. FUCUS + -OID.]

A. *adj.* a. Resembling or belonging to seaweeds, *esp.* those of the group *Fucaceæ*. b. Characterized by impressions of such seaweeds or markings similar to them.

B. *sb.* a. A seaweed of the group *Fucaceæ* 1848. b. A fossil marine plant resembling these 1857.

So **Fucoi·dal** (in sense A. b).

‖**Fucus** (fiū·kŏs). *Pl.* ‖**fuci** (fiū·səi); also †**fucus(s)es,** †**fucus's,** †**fucos,** †**fucu's.** 1599. [a. L.; cf. Gr. φῦκος neut.] †1. Paint or cosmetic for beautifying the skin; a wash or colouring for the face -1757. †Also *fig.* -1742. 2. A genus of sea-weeds with flat leathery fronds. Formerly applied more widely. 1716.

Fud (fŏd). *Sc.* and *n. dial.* 1785. [?] 1. 'The backside or buttocks' (Jam.). 2. The tail or scut of a hare or rabbit 1787. 3. *Woollen-manuf.* Woollen waste 1873.

Fudder (fŏ·dəɹ). 1679. [ad. Ger. *fuder* (= FOTHER).] A tun (of wine).

Fudder, obs. f. FODDER, FOTHER.

Fuddle (fv·d'l), *sb. slang* or *colloq.* 1680. [f. next vb.] †1. Drink, liquor, 'booze' -1706. 2. A drinking bout 1813. 3. Intoxication; an intoxicated state 1764. 4. *transf.* The state of being muddled, or the like 1827.

Fuddle (fv·d'l), *v.* 1588. [?] 1. *intr.* To have a drinking bout; to tipple, booze. Also quasi-*trans.* with *away*. 2. *trans.* To confuse with or as with drink 1600. 3. *transf.* and *fig.* To stupefy, muddle, confuse. Formerly also of joy, etc.: To intoxicate. 1617.

2. A Cup of Ale .. under a Pint, yet it almost fuddled him 1706. 3. He is fuddled with animal spirits 1803. Hence **Fu·ddler,** a tippler.

Fudge (fvdʒ). 1766. [?] A. *interj.* Stuff and nonsense! Bosh! B. *sb.* 1. Contemptible nonsense, stuff, bosh 1791. 2. A made-up story, a deceit 1797. 3. A piece of stop-press news inserted in a newspaper page at the last minute 1899. 4. A soft-grained sweetmeat made from milk, sugar, chocolate, etc. 1897.

Fudge (fvdʒ), *v.* 1615. [app. an onomatopœic var. of FADGE *v.*] 1. *trans.* To put together clumsily or dishonestly; to patch or fake *up*; to cook accounts 1674; to foist *in* 1776. 2. *intr.* To fit in with what is anticipated, come off; also, to turn out 1615. 3. [f. prec. sb.] To talk nonsense, tell 'crams'. Also quasi-*trans.* 1834.

1. To f. accounts 1879. That last suppose is fudged in FOOTE. *To f. a day's work* (Naut.): to work a dead reckoning by 'rule of thumb' methods. 2. We will see how this will f. SCOTT.

Fuel (fiū·ĕl), *sb.* ME. [a. OF. *fowaille*, *feuaile*:—pop. L. *focalia*, neut. pl. of *focalis* adj., f. *focus*; see FOCUS.] 1. Material for burning, combustible matter for fires, etc.; *fig.* something that serves to feed or inflame passion, excitement, etc. 1580. 3. (With *a.* and *pl.*) A kind of fuel. †Also *pl.* articles serving as fuel. 1626.

1. *fig.* F. for Dissention STEELE. 2. Turf, and Peat, and Cow-sheards are cheap Fewels, and last long BACON.

Comb.: **f.-economizer,** a contrivance for saving fuel in an engine or furnace; **-gas,** gas for use as fuel.

Fuel (fiū·ĕl), *v.* 1592. [f. prec. sb.] *trans.* To feed or furnish with fuel. *lit.* and *fig.* 2. *intr.* To get fuel 1880.

1. Wealth fuel'd Sin KEN. 2. The right of fuelling in the park DIXON. Hence **Fu·eller** (now *rare*), one who or that which supplies fuel for fires; also *fig.*

Fuff (fvf), *sb.* Chiefly *Sc.* 1535. [f. next vb.] 1. A puff of wind; the 'spit' of a cat; a whiff. 2. A huff, fume 1834.

Fuff (fʌf), *v. Sc.* and *dial.* 1513. [echoic.] 1. *intr.* To puff. 2. Of a cat or tiger: To 'spit' 1693. 3. *trans.* To puff (a tobacco-pipe) 1787.

Fuffy (fv·fi), *a. Sc.* and *n. dial.* 1824. [f. FUFF *sb.* + -Y[1].] 1. Light and soft. 2. 'Huffy' 1858.

Fug (fvg), *sb. colloq.*, orig. *dial.* and *school slang.* 1888. [etym. obsc.] A close stuffy atmosphere. Hence **Fug** *v. intr.* to stay indoors in this. **Fu·ggy** *a.* close and stuffy.

Fugacious (fiugē·ʃəs), *a.* 1634. [f. L. *fugaci-*, *fugax* (f. *fugere* to flee) + -OUS.] 1. Apt to flee away or flit; evanescent, fugitive; volatile. 2. *Bot.* and *Zool.* Falling or fading early; soon cast off. Cf. CADUCOUS. 1750.

1. The f. nature of life and time HT. MARTINEAU. Hence **Fuga·cious·ly** *adv.*, **-ness.**

Fugacity (fiugæ·sĭti). 1656. [f. as prec.] The quality of being fugacious; instability; transitoriness; volatility.

The f. of pleasure, the fragility of beauty JOHNSON.

†**Fu·gacy.** 1600. [as if ad. L. **fugacia*, f. *fugax*.] Flight; also, the fact of being a fugitive slave -1661.

Fugal (fiū·găl), *a.* 1854. [f. FUGUE + -AL.] *Mus.* Of, pertaining to, or of the nature of fugues.

‖**Fugato** (fugā·to), *adv.* 1866. [It. *fugato* fugued, f. *fuga* FUGUE.] In the fugue style, but not in strict fugue form. Also *sb.* Music composed in this style.

-fuge (fiūdʒ), *suffix*, occurring in words (adj. and sb.) f. mod.L. types in -*fugus*. In the medical words *febrifugus*, etc., the ending takes its sense from L. *fugare* to put to flight, not from *fugere* to flee.

Fu·gie. *Sc.* Now *Hist.* 1777. [? f. *fugæ* in the Law L. phr. *in meditatione fugæ*.] A cock that will not fight; a runaway. Hence, a coward.

Comb. **f.-warrant,** a warrant granted against a debtor on sworn information that he intends to flee.

Fugitive (fiū·dʒitiv). ME. [a. F. *fugitif*, -*ive*, ad. L. *fugitivus*, f. *fugit-* ppl. stem of *fugere* to flee.]

A. *adj.* 1. Apt or tending to flee; given to, or in the act of running away; also *fig.* 1606, b. That has taken flight. †Also, of a debtor: Meditating flight. 1467. †2. Driven out, banished, exiled. Const. *from*, *of*. -1598. 3. Moving from place to place; vagabond; *fig.* fickle 1481. 4. Evanescent, fleeting 1510; quickly fading or becoming effaced; perishable 1678; volatile (*rare*) 1666. 5. Of compositions (occas. of writers): Ephemeral, occasional 1766.

1. The Fugitive Parthians SHAKS. *fig.* A f. and cloister'd vertue..that never sallies out and sees her adversary MILT. b. Felons fugitif 1495. A f. daughter RICHARDSON, slave 1880. 3. F. preachers make f. congregations 1883. F. securities 1893. 4. F. Follies 1635, flowers 1830, dyes 1842. 5. You're a f. writer, I think, sir, of rhymes BYRON.

B. *sb.* 1. One who flees from danger, an enemy, justice, or an owner ME.; †a deserter -1659; an exile, refugee 1591. 2. One who shifts about from place to place; a vagabond, wanderer. Also of the lower animals. 1563. 3. Something fleeting, or that eludes the grasp 1683.

1. Ranke me..A Master leauer and a fugitiue *Ant. & Cl.* IV. ix. 22. The fugitives from Rome MILMAN. 3. That airy f., called wit 1774.

Hence **Fu·gitiveness,** the quality or condition of being f. **Fu·gitivi·sm,** the condition of a f.

Fugle (fiū·g'l), *v.* 1837. [f. FUGLEMAN.] *intr.* To do the duty of a fugleman; to act as guide or director; to make signals. *lit.* and *fig.*

Wooden arms with elbow-joints are jerking and fugling in the air, in the most rapid mysterious manner CARLYLE.

Fugleman (fiū·g'lmæ̆n). 1804. [ad. Ger. *flügelmann* leader of the file, f. *flügel* wing + *mann* MAN.] A soldier especially expert and well-drilled, formerly placed in front of a regiment or company as an example and model to the others. Also *transf.* and *fig.*

This Hohman was now *Flügelmann* ('fugleman' as we have named it, leader of the file) CARLYLE.

Fugue (fiūg), *sb.* 1597. [a. F., ad. It. *fuga* lit. 'flight':—L. *fuga*.] *Mus.* 'A polyphonic composition constructed on one or more short subjects or themes, which are harmonized according to the laws of counterpoint, and introduced from time to time with various contrapuntal devices' (Stainer and Barrett).

Double f., a common term for a f. on two subjects, in which the two start together GROVE. Hence **Fugue** *v. intr.* to compose, or perform, a f. **Fu·guist,** a composer of fugues.

-ful, *suffix*, orig. identical with FULL *a.* **1.** Forming adjs., in composition with a preceding sb., orig. with sense 'having', 'characterized by' (the attribute denoted by the sb.). In the 14th c., in a few forms, the suffix had the force of 'possessing the qualities of'; e. g. in *masterful, manful*. In mod.Eng. adjs. in *-ful* are sometimes formed directly on verb-stems, the sense of the suffix being 'apt to', 'able or accustomed to', as in *distractful, mournful*. See also *bashful*.

2. Forming sbs., orig. not only with its proper sense, but in the transf. sense of 'quantity that fills or would fill' (a receptacle). In mod.Eng. *-ful* forms derivatives with the general sense 'quantity that fills or would fill' (something). The pl. forms *spoonsful, cupsful*, etc., though historically justifiable, are ambiguous, and contrary to good modern usage.

†**Fu·lciment.** 1648. [ad. late L. *fulcimentum*, f. *fulcire*.] A prop or support; usu. *spec.* a fulcrum -1796.

Fulcra, pl. of FULCRUM.

Fulcraceous (fvlkrē¹·ʃəs), *a.* 1866. [f. FULCRUM + -ACEOUS.] *Bot.* Of or pertaining to the fulcra of plants.

Fulcrate (fv·lkreʹt), *a.* 1760. [f. FULCRUM + -ATE ².] *Bot.* Supported by or provided with fulcra.

Fulcrum (fv·lkrŏm). *Pl.* **-ra.** 1674. [a. L. (in cl. L. 'the post or foot of a couch'), f. root of *fulcire* to prop.] **1.** A prop or support; now only *spec.* in *Mech.* the point on which a lever is placed to get purchase or upon which it turns. Also *fig.* **2.** (Chiefly *pl.*) **a.** *Bot.* Accessory organs or appendages of a plant; e. g. bracts, stipules, etc. 1785. **b.** *Ichth.* (*pl.*) The small osseous scales arranged in a row and situated on the anterior ray of the fins of many ganoid fishes 1880. var. Fu·lcre.

Fulfil (fulfi·l), *v.* Pa. t. and pple. **fulfilled** (fulfi·ld). [OE. *fullfyllan*, f. FULL *a.* + *fyllan* to FILL.] **1.** *trans.* To fill up, make full. Const. *of, with*. *arch.* †**2.** To satisfy the appetite or desire of -1601. **3.** To make complete; to supply what is lacking in. Also, to supply the place of (something); to compensate for. *Obs.* exc. *arch.* ME. **4.** To carry out (a prophecy, promise, etc.); to satisfy (a desire, prayer). Orig. a Hebraism. ME. **5.** To perform, execute, do; to obey or follow ME.; to answer (a purpose), comply with (conditions) 1784. **6.** To bring to an end, complete ME.

1. All Beastes I byd yow multeply..the earth to fulfill 1500. He..fulfilleth both heaven and earth with his presence 1563. 4. To fulfill the Prophecies 1633. Full of bright promise never fulfilled BRYCE. 5. The Law of God exact he shall f. MILT. Every stone fulfils its place inside and out SMEATON. 6. Whan thy tyme is fulfylled yᵗ thou shalt slepe with thy fathers COVERDALE 2 *Sam.* vii. 12. Hence **Fulfi·ller**, one who fulfils.

Fulfilment (fulfi·lmĕnt). 1775. [f. prec. + -MENT.] The action or an act or process of fulfilling; accomplishment, performance, completion.

The f. of a condition 1891.

Fulgent (fv·ldʒĕnt), *a.* ME. [ad. L. *fulgentem, fulgere*; see -ENT.] Shining brightly; brilliant, glittering, resplendent. Now *poet.* or *rhet.*

His f. head And shape Starre-bright MILT. Hence †**Fu·lgence**, †**Fu·lgency**, f. quality; brightness, splendour. **Fu·lgent-ly** *adv.*, **-ness.**

Fulgid (fv·ldʒid), *a.* 1656. [ad. L. *fulgidus*, f. *fulgere*.] **1.** Flashing, glittering, shining. **2.** *Nat. Hist.* A bright, fiery red. Hence **Fulgi·dity**, f. state or condition.

Fulgor, fulgour (fv·lgŏɪ, -əɪ). *arch.* 1602. [a. L. *fulgor*.] A brilliant or flashing light; dazzling brightness, splendour. Also *fig.* Hence **Fu·lgorous** *a. rare*, flashing, brilliant, lustrous (*lit.* and *fig.*).

Fulgurant (fv·lgiŭrănt), *a.* 1647. [ad. L. *fulgurantem, fulgurare*.] Flashing like lightning.

Fu·lgurate, *v.* 1677. [f. L. *fulgurat-* ppl. stem; see prec. and -ATE ³.] To emit flashes like lightning. Hence **Fu·lgurating** *ppl. a.*; also *transf.* (of pains) darting like lightning through the body.

Fulguration (fvlgiŭrē¹·ʃən). 1633. [ad. L. *fulgurationem*; see prec. and -ATION.] **1.** The action of lightening or flashing like lightning; chiefly in *pl.* flashes of lightning. Now usu. *fig.* **2.** *Assaying.* = BLICK, q. v. 1676.

Fulgurite (fv·lgiŭrəit). 1834. [L. *fulgur* + -ITE.] **1.** *Geol.* Any rocky substance that has been fused or vitrified by lightning. Also (less correctly) *fulgorite*. **2.** An explosive, consisting of nitro-glycerine mixed with some coarsely ground farinaceous substance 1882.

Fulgurous (fv·lgiŭrəs), *a.* 1616. [f. L. *fulgur* + -OUS.] Resembling, full of, or charged with lightning. Also *fig.*

Fulham (fu·lăm). *slang.* 1550. [? f. the place-name *Fulham*, once a haunt of gamesters.] A die loaded at the corner. (A *high f.* was loaded so as to ensure a throw of 4, 5, or 6; a *low f.* one of 1, 2, or 3.) See *Merry W.* I. iii. 94.

Fuliginosity (fiŭli:dʒinǫ·sĭti). 1758. [ad. F. *fuliginosité*, f. L. *fuliginosus* + -ITY.] The condition or quality of being fuliginous or sooty; sooty matter, soot. Also *fig.*

Fuliginous (fiŭli·dʒinəs), *a.* 1574. [ad. L. *fuliginosus*, f. *fuligo*; see -OUS. Cf. F. *fuligineux, -euse*.] **1.** Pertaining to, consisting of, containing, or resembling soot; sooty 1621; blackened with soot (*joc.*) 1763. †**2.** In old physiology applied to certain thick vapours or exhalations said to be formed by organic combustion, and noxious to the head and vital parts -1725. **3.** (Chiefly *Nat. Hist.*) Soot-coloured, dusky 1822.

2. It is not amiss to bore the scull with an instrument to let out the f. vapours BURTON. Hence **Fuli·ginous-ly** *adv.*, **-ness.**

‖**Fuligo** (fiŭləi·go). 1646. [L.] Soot.

Fulimart, obs. f. FOUMART.

Full (ful). [Com. Teut.: OE. *full*:—OTeut. **follo-, fullo-* :—OAryan **pḷ-nó*. Akin to Skr. *puru*, Gr. πολύς, πιμπλάναι, πλήρης, πλῆθος, L. *plenus, plus*, etc.]

A. *adj.* **1.** Having within its limits all it will hold; having no space empty; replete. Const. *of.* **b.** *fig.*; *esp.* of the heart: Overcharged with emotion ME. **2. a.** Containing abundance *of*; charged, crowded OE. †**b.** Of a surface: Covered (with) -1657. **c.** In non-material sense: Abounding (in). Const. *of*, occas. †*with*. OE. **3.** Engrossed with or absorbed in. Now only with *of* 1607. **4.** Having eaten or drunk to repletion. Now *arch.* (or *vulgar*). OE. **b.** Having had one's fill of anything. *Obs.* exc. in Hebraisms *f. of days, years, children.* ME. **c.** †Sated, weary *of.* Similarly in *full up* (colonial slang). ME. †**5.** Amply supplied with means -1683. **6.** Abundant, copious, satisfying, satisfactory OE.; complete or abundant in detail 1656. **7.** Complete, entire, perfect; answering in every respect to a description OE. **8.** Complete in number, quantity, magnitude, or extent. Of the moon: Having the disk completely illuminated. Of the face or front: Entirely visible to the spectator. OE. **b.** Of an assembly, etc.: One from which none or few are absent 1557. **9.** Possessed of, delivered with, or exerting the utmost force ME. **10.** Having a rounded outline; large, swelling, plump, protuberant OE. **b.** Of portions of dress: Containing plenty of material which is arranged in gathers or folds 1789. **11.** *Naut.* Of a sail: Filled. Of the ship: Having her sails filled with wind. 1627.

1. A f. stomach 1590. Phr. *F. as an egg, f. to the brim* (see BRIM *sb.*²), *f. to overflowing, f. up* (colloq.). **b.** Speake, for my heart is f. *Oth.* v. ii. 175. 2. As f. of spite and ill nature as a Spider with poyson 1621. **b.** The rind..f. of wrinkles 1657. **c.** O f. of all subtilty and all mischiefe *Acts* xiii. 10. Phr. *A f. man*: One whose mind is richly stored; Reading maketh a f. man BACON. 3. The king seemed mighty f. that we should have money to do all that we desired PEPYS. F. of business 1853. 4. The f. soule loatheth an honie combe *Prov.* xxvii. 7. **c.** I am f. of the burnt offerings of rammes *Isa.* i. 11. 5. I haue all, and abound. I am f. *Phil.* iv. 18. 6. A f. Repast DRYDEN. Experience 1707. The fullest report of a case 1866. 7. Phr. *F. point, stop* (see those words). When it was f. Day 1717. At f. liberty to speak his mind BERKELEY. In f. possession of his faculties MACAULAY. Phr. *F. brother, sister*: born of the same father and mother (opp. to HALF-BROTHER). The man commands Like a f. soldier *Oth.* II. i. 36. 8. The ful ordir of preesthod 1463. A f. yeere SHAKS., regiment PURCHAS, Age 1655. The head of a Roman Emperor drawn with a f. face ADDISON. **b.** *Oth.* IV. i. 275. Phr. *F. flood, sea, tide* (*lit.* and *fig.*), indicating the greatest height of the water, or the time when it is highest. 9. A f. gale of wind 1634, Huzza 1700, pulse 1783. Phr. *F. butt, cry, gallop, sail, speed*, etc. (see those words). 10. A f. black Eye 1688. F. round Faces..f. Lips, and short Chins DAMPIER. **b.** Sleeves full and high on the shoulders 1891. 11. Phr. *Keep her* (i. e. the ship) *f.* *F. and by*: see BY *adv.*

Comb. 1. General: as, *f.-draught, -power*, etc.; *f.-fed, -flowing*, etc.; *f.-banked, -blossomed, -fortuned, -rigged, -sized, -statured, -throated*, etc.

2. Special: **f.-back** (*Football*), position in the field behind the other backs; a player in this position; also *attrib.*; **-bodied** *a.*, having a f. body (*esp.* of wine: see BODY); also *fig.*; **-breasted** *a.*, having a f. breast: also *transf.*; **-brimmed** *a.*, f. to the brim; **-centre arch** [F. *arc à plein-cintre*], a semicircular arch; one describing the f. amount of 180°; **-circle** *adv.*, with the form of a f. circle or disc; **-eyed** *a.*, †(*a*) perfectly visible; seen in the front; (*b*) having f. eyes; **-flavoured** *a.*, having a f. or strong flavour (*esp.* of cigars); also *fig.*; **-front** *v.*, to present a f. front to; †**-mouth**, a chatterer; also *attrib.* = FULL-MOUTHED; **-orbed** *a. poet.* (of the moon), having its disk completely illuminated; also *fig.*

B. quasi-*sb.* and *sb.* **1.** The *adj.* used *absol.*, passing into *sb.* ME. **2.** = FILL *sb.*¹ 1. Now *rare.* ME. **3.** Complete scope; entire amount; completeness, fullness. Now *rare.* ME. **4.** The period, point, or state of the greatest fullness or strength ME.; of a month or season, the height, the middle 1658.

1. Phr. **At (the) f.**: †fully, completely; at the position or moment of fullness; in the state of fullness. **In (†the) f.**: at f. length, in extenso; to the f. amount. *In f. of*: in f. discharge or satisfaction of. **To the f.**: to the utmost extent, completely, fully. 3. With my opinions, to the f. of which I dare not confess J. H. NEWMAN. 4. June was not over Though past the f. BROWNING. Phr. *The f. of the moon* (also ellipt. *the f.* and in phr. *at f.*); the period or state of complete illumination of the moon's disk.

C. *adv.* **1.** Simply intensive: Very, exceedingly: **a.** with adjs. of quality (now only *poet.*) OE.; **b.** with adjs. of quantity or indef. numerals (now *arch.*) ME.; **c.** with advs. (now *arch.*) OE. **2.** Completely, entirely, fully, quite: **a.** with adjs., *esp.* numerals OE.; **b.** with advs. (now *rare*) ME.; **c.** with advb. phrases 1529. **3.** Of position or direction: Exactly, directly, straight 1582; due (? *Obs.*) 1559. †**4.** With vbs. or pples.: Fully, completely, quite, thoroughly -1807.

1. **a.** Anger is like A f. hot horse SHAKS. **b.** Fulle many a tere 1450. **c.** F. early lost WORDSW. 2. **a.** F. fadom fiue *Temp.* I. ii. 396. **c.** Butter..does f. as well MRS. GLASSE. 3. Winds..f. in our teeth 1698. The..Wind is..F. East 1708.

Comb.: with pres. and pa. pples., as *f.-acorned*; **f.-blown** ¹, filled with wind, puffed out (*lit.* and *fig.*); see BLOW *v.*¹; **-blown** ², in full bloom (*lit.* and *fig.*); see Blow *v.*²

Full (ful), *v.*¹ [ME. *fullen*, f. FULL *a.*] †**1.** *trans.* To make full -1647; *intr.* to be or become full (now only *dial.* and in U.S. of the moon) ME. †**2.** *trans.* To fulfil, complete -1640. **3.** *Dressmaking.* To make full; to gather or pleat 1831.

1. The moon fulls at midnight WEBSTER.

Full (ful), *v.*² ME. [ad. OF. *fuler* (mod. *fouler*); see FOIL *v.*¹] **1.** *trans.* To tread or beat (cloth) for the purpose of cleansing and thickening it; hence, to cleanse and thicken (cloth, etc.). †**2.** *gen.* To beat or trample down; also, to destroy -1641.

†**Fu·llage.** 1611. [a. OF. *foullage* (mod. *foulage*), f. *fouler* to FULL.] **1.** Money paid for the fulling of cloth. (Dicts.) **2.** Refuse, street-sweepings -1780.

Full age. 1622. Adult or mature age, *esp.* (as opp. to *nonage*) the age of 21 years. Hence †**Full-aged** *ppl. a.*; *spec.* of a horse: Exceeding the age of 6 years (now simply *aged*).

Full-blood, *a.* 1882. **a.** Of a brother or sister: Born of the same parents. **b.** Of pure or unmixed race. So **Full-bloo·ded** *a.* = FULL-BLOOD (*lit.* and *fig.*); also, having plenty of blood. Hence **Full-bloo·dedness.**

Fu·ll-bottom. 1713. [f. FULL *a.* + BOTTOM *sb.*] A full-bottomed wig.

Fu·ll-bottomed, *a.* 1711. [f. as prec. + -ED ².] **1.** Of a wig: Having a full or large bottom. **2.** *Naut.* Epithet of vessels designed to carry large cargoes. 1867.

Full dress. 1790. See DRESS *sb.* Also *fig.* Also *attrib.* as in *full-dress dinner, rehear-*

sal, etc.; also *fig.*, as in *full-dress debate*, a formal debate in which important speeches are delivered on both sides.

Fuller (fu·ləɹ), *sb.*[1] [OE. *fullęre*, ad. L. *fullo* (of unkn. origin).] One whose occupation is to full cloth.

Comb.: fuller's clay = FULLER'S EARTH: **fuller's grass, herb, weed,** *Saponaria officinalis*; **fuller's teazel, thistle,** *Dipsacus fullonum*; **fuller's thorn?** = prec.

Fu·ller, *sb.*[2] 1855. [?f. FULL. *v.*[1] 3 + -ER [1].] **1.** *Blacksmithing*, etc. A grooved tool on which iron is shaped by being driven into the grooves 1864. **2.** A groove made by a fuller 1855. Hence **Fu·ller** *v.* to stamp with a f.; to groove by stamping; *dial.* to goffer (linen).

Fu·ller's ea·rth. 1523. A hydrous silicate of alumina, used in cleansing cloth; also *Geol.* a group of strata containing this. Also *fig.*

Fu·ll-fa·ced, *a.* 1610. [f. FULL *a.* + FACE + -ED [2].] **1.** Having a full face; *esp.* of persons 1622. **2.** Having the face turned fully on the spectator or in some specified direction.

Fu·ll-gro·wn, *a.* 1667. [f. FULL *adv.* + GROWN.] Fully grown; having attained full size or maturity.

Fu·ll-hea·rted, *a.* 1611. [f. FULL *a.* + HEART + -ED [2].] **a.** Full of courage and confidence; hence of a work: Carried on with zeal. **b.** Full of feeling.

Fulling (fu·liŋ), *vbl. sb.* 1688. [f. FULL *v.*[2] + -ING [1].] The process of cleansing and thickening cloth by beating and washing; also called *milling*.

Comb. **f.-mill,** a mill in which cloth is fulled or milled (now) by being pressed between rollers and cleansed with soap or fuller's earth.

Full length. 1709. The entire length or extension of any object. **1.** In advb. phr. (*at*) *full length*. **2.** *attrib.*, as *full-length figure*, etc. Also ellipt. *a full-length*. 1850.

Full moon. OE. **1.** The moon with its entire disk illuminated. **2.** The period at which this occurs (L. *plenilunium*) ME. **3.** *attrib.* 1780.

Fu·ll-mou·thed, *a.* 1577. [f. FULL *a.* + MOUTH *sb.* + -ED.[2]] **1.** Of cattle: Having the full number of teeth. †**2.** Having the mouth filled with food; hence, festive. Also *transf.* and *fig.* -1701. **3. a.** Sounding or talking loud 1648. **b.** Produced or uttered with a loud voice or with violence 1605.

2. Full-mouth'd Easter's neare QUARLES.

Fullness, fulness (fu·lnės). ME. [f. FULL *a.* + -NESS. The spelling *fullness* is more in accordance with analogy.] **1.** The quality or condition of being FULL, in various senses. **2.** The condition of containing in abundance, or of abounding in; *concr.* all that is contained in (the world, etc.) ME.

1. Fulnesse of ioy *Ps.* xvi. 11. Phr. *The f. of time* (= Gr. πλήρωμα τοῦ χρόνου): in Bibl. language, the proper or destined time. F. of diet 1682, of Body 1698, of colour, sound, etc. 1851. 2. Þe world and þe fulnes of it is myn ME.

Full-summed, *a.* 1486. **1.** *Falconry.* In full plumage. **2.** *nonce-use.* Fully developed or accomplished. TENNYSON.

Fu·ll-ti·mer. 1870. [f. phr. *full time* + -ER [1].] A child that attends school during the full school hours; opp. to HALF-TIMER.

Fully (fu·li), *adv.* [OE. *fullīce*, f. FULL *a.* + *līce* -LY [2].] In a full manner or degree; completely, entirely; thoroughly, exactly, quite.

I satisfied him f. GOLDSM. Day had f. dawned C. BRONTË. †(*To eat, feed*) *f.* = to satiety. *Comb.* **f.-fashioned** *a.* (of women's stockings), fitting the shape of the leg.

Fullymart, obs. f. FOUMART.

Fulmar (fu·lmaɹ). 1698. [orig. Hebridean, and so prob. Norse; ?f. ON. *fúl-l* FOUL (in odour) + *má-r* MEW, gull.] A sea-bird of the petrel kind (*Fulmarus glacialis*).

Fulminant (fʊ·lminănt). 1602. [a. F., or ad. L. *fulminantem*; see FULMINATE *v.*]

A. *adj.* **1.** = FULMINATING. **2.** *Path.* Developing suddenly 1876.

1. This F. Gold 1693. 2. The f. forms of anthrax 1876.

B. *sb.* Something that fulminates; a thunderbolt; an explosive. *rare.* 1808.

Hence **Fu·lminancy,** f. character. CARLYLE.

Fulminate (fʊ·lminėᵗt), *sb.* 1826. [f. FULMIN(IC) + -ATE.] *Chem.* A compound of fulminic acid with a base, detonating by percussion, friction, or heat.

Fulminate (fʊ·lminėᵗt), *v.* Pa. pple. **fulminate.** 1450. [f. L. *fulminat-*, *fulminare* to lighten, strike with lightning, f. *fulmen*.]

I. **1.** *intr.* To thunder and lighten (*rare*) 1610. **2.** To issue as a thunderbolt 1861. †**3.** *Metall.* Of gold: To become suddenly bright and uniform in colour 1727. **4.** To flash forth like lightning 1630. **5.** †To cause to explode, or (*intr.*) to explode with a loud report 1667.

II. *fig.* [Orig. a rendering of med L. *fulminare* to issue eccl. censures, etc.; afterwards used more widely.] **1.** *trans.* To thunder forth; to utter or publish (a condemnation or censure) upon a person 1450. **2.** To strike with the thunderbolts of eccl. censure; hence *gen.* to condemn vehemently 1687. **3.** *intr.* Of the pope, etc.: To issue censures or condemnations (*against*); *gen.* to inveigh violently *against* 1639.

1. The pope fulminated a bull against him..for having hanged an archbishop 1832. 2. To f. such vain and impious wretches BURKE. 3. Pulpits fulminated, presses groaned SIR J. STEPHEN.

Fulminating (fʊ·lminėᵗtiŋ), *ppl. a.* 1626. [f. prec. + -ING [2].] That fulminates (*lit.* and *fig.*); *spec.* detonating, violently explosive.

F. gold, mercury, platinum, silver, various fulminates or salts of fulminic acid. *F. powder*, formerly, a mixture of nitre, potash, and sulphur; now occas. applied to other explosive powders, chiefly containing fulminate of mercury.

Fulmination (fʊlminēᵗ·ʃən). 1502. [ad. L. *fulminationem*; see FULMINATE *v.*] **1.** The bursting forth of thunder and lightning. Usu. *fig.* 1623. **2.** The action of fulminating or detonating; loud explosion 1667. †**3.** *Metall.* See FULMINATE *v.* I. 3. 1612. **4.** The formal emission of an ecclesiastical condemnation or censure. Subseq.: Violent denunciation or threatening; an instance of this. 1502.

1. The f. of divine Anger 1650. 4. These Fulminations from the Vatican were turn'd into Ridicule AYLIFFE.

Fulminatory (fʊ·lminătəri), *a.* 1611. [ad. F. *fulminatoire*; see FULMINATE *v.* and -ORY.] Sending forth fulminations, thundering.

Fulmine (fʊ·lmin), *v.* 1590. [ad. L. *fulminare*; see FULMINATE *v.*] **1.** *trans.* To send forth (lightning or thunder); *fig.* to flash *out* 1847. **2.** *intr.* To thunder, speak out fiercely or energetically. (Now chiefly after Milton.) 1623.

2. Whose resistless eloquence..Shook the Arsenal and fulmined over Greece MILT.

Fulmineous (fʊlmi·nĭəs), *a.* ? *Obs.* 1727. [f. L. *fulmineus.*] Pertaining to thunder or lightning.

Fulmi·nic (fʊlmi·nik), *a.* 1825. [f. L. *fulmin-* + -IC.] *Chem.* In *F. acid*: $C_2H_2N_2O_2$, nitro-acetonitril, an acid (not yet isolated) forming explosive salts with some metals.

Fulminous (fʊ·lminəs), *a.* 1635. [f. as prec. + -OUS.] Of or pertaining to thunder and lightning; fulminating.

Fulminurate (fʊlminiūᵒ·rėᵗt). 1864. [f. as next + -ATE; see URATE.] *Chem.* A salt of fulminuric acid.

Fulminuric (fʊlminiū·rik), *a.* 1864. [f. FULMIN(IC) + URIC.] *Chem.* Only in *F. acid*: '$C_3H_3N_3O_3$ Isocyanuric acid. An acid isomeric with cyanuric acid' (Watts).

Fulness: see FULLNESS.

†**Fulsa·mic,** *a.* [? corruptly f. next + -IC.] = FULSOME. Congreve.

Fulsome (fʊ·lsəm), *a.* ME. [f. FULL *a.* + -SOME.] †**1.** Abundant, plentiful, full -1583. †**2.** Full and plump, fat, well-grown; also, over-grown -1678. †**b.** App.: Lustful, rank. *Merch. V.* I. iii. 87. †**3.** Of food: Satiating, filling; also *fig.*; coarse, gross -1770; †sickly in taste -1743. †**4.** Strong- or foul-smelling -1725. †**5.** Offensive to the senses; disgusting, foul, or loathsome -1720. **6.** Offensive to normal sensibilities; repulsive, odious ME.; †morally foul, obscene -1726. **7.** Of language, style, behaviour, etc.: Offensive to good taste; *esp.* from excess or want of measure. Now chiefly of flattery, over-demonstrative affection, etc. 1663.

1. F. fieldes 1510. Suche f. pasture made him a double chin 1515. 3. I dined with the lord-mayor.. We had two turtles, and a f. great dinner WILKES. 4. A rank and f. smell BACON. 5. SHAKS. *John* III. iv. 32. 6. b. *Oth.* IV. i. 37. 7. This fawning and f. court-historian J. WARTON. F. publicity HELPS. Hence **Fu·lsome-ly** *adv.*, **-ness.**

Fulvid (fʊ·lvid), *a.* Now *rare.* 1599. [ad. med.L. *fulvidus*, f. L. *fulvus.*] = FULVOUS.

Fulvous (fʊ·lvəs), *a.* 1664. [f. L. *fulvus* reddish-yellow + -OUS.] Reddish-yellow, dull yellowish-brown or tawny.

‖**Fulwa** (fu·lwă). 1835. [corruptly ad. Bengali *phulwara*, the native name of *Bassia butyracea.*] A solid buttery oil obtained from *Bassia butyracea.*

†**Fum,** *v.* 1607. [echoic.] *intr.* To play (on a guitar) with the fingers -1672.

Follow me, and f. as you goe DEKKER & WEBSTER.

Fuma·cious, *a.* [f. L. *fumare*; see -ACIOUS.] Fond of smoking. (Dicts.)

Fumade (fiumēᵗ·d). Also †**fumado,** †**fumatho,** and, corruptly, FAIR MAID. 1599. [app. ad. Sp. *fumado* (fuma·ðo) pple., smoked.] A smoked pilchard.

Fu·mage. *Hist.* 1755. [ad. med.L. *fumagium*, f. *fumus.*] Hearth-money.

As early as the conquest mention is made in domesday book of f. or fuage, vulgarly called smoke farthings BLACKSTONE.

Fumant (fiū·mănt), *a.* 1828. [a. F., f. *fumer.*] *Her.* Emitting vapour or smoke.

Fumarin (fiū·mărin). 1864. [f. mod.L. *Fumaria* FUMITORY.] *Chem.* An organic base contained in fumitory. So **Fuma·ric acid,** $C_4H_4O_4$, an acid produced by the dehydration of malic acid. **Fu·marate,** a salt of this acid.

Fumarole (fiū·mărōᵘl). 1811. [ad. F. *fumerolle* (*fumarolle*); see FEMERELL.] A hole or vent through which vapour issues from a volcano; a smoke-hole.

Fumatory (fiū·mătəri). Also erron. **fumitory.** 1530. [ad. L. type **fumatorium*, f. *fumare*; see -ORY.] †**1.** A censer 1530. **2.** A place set apart for smoking or fumigating purposes 1704.

Fumble (fʊ·mb'l), *v.* 1508. [prob. onomatopœic. Perh. 'due to the sb. appearing as A.S. *folm*, the palm of the hand, L. *palma*' (Skeat).] **1.** *intr.* To use one's hands or fingers awkwardly or ineffectually; to grope about 1534. Also *transf.* and *fig.* **2.** *trans.* To handle awkwardly or nervously. Also with *on*, *out*, *over*. 1606. **3.** To wrap up clumsily, huddle together. Also with *up*. 1572. **4.** *slang.* (Cf. FUMBLING *ppl. a.* c.) Also *absol.* and *intr.* 1508. **5.** *intr.* To hesitate in speaking; to mumble, mutter. Also *trans.* 1563.

1. I saw him f. with the Sheets, and play with Flowers SHAKS. 2. Fumbling two large kid gloves THACKERAY. Phr. *To f. the ball* (e.g. in *Cricket*): to fail to take it cleanly. 3. So many f. this, last and next weeks devotion all in a prayer FULLER. 5. Never lose time fumbling and prating about it SCOTT. Hence **Fu·mble** *sb.* a piece of fumbling. **Fu·mbler.**

Fu·mbling, *ppl. a.* 1532. [f. FUMBLE *v.* + -ING [2].] **a.** That gropes about; characterized by fumbling 1847. **b.** *fig.* That does something clumsily or awkwardly; also, hesitating in speech 1532. **c.** Sexually impotent 1576. Hence **Fu·mblingly** *adv.*

Fume (fiūm), *sb.* ME. [a. OF. *fum* masc. :—L. *fumus* smoke; also OF. *fume* fem., f. *fumer*.]

I. **1.** The volatile matter produced by and usually accompanying combustion; smoke. Also with *a* and *pl.* *Obs.* or *arch.* †**b.** Something for producing aromatic vapour -1722. **2.** Odour or odorous exhalation (either fragrant or offensive) ME. **3.** Vapour or steam; *esp.* the vapour given off by acids and volatile substances ME. **4.** A vapour or exhalation produced as an excrement of the body; *esp.* a noxious vapour supposed formerly to rise to the brain from the stomach ME.

1. In fiery flames and f. 1549. The fumes of choice tobacco DICKENS. 2. Aromatyke lycoure, fragraunt of f. HAWES. The fumes of the table 1718. 3. The inhalation of acrid fumes 1834. 4. The wine..raise[d] disagreeable fumes from the stomach into the head DE FOE.

II. *fig.* **1.** Something unsubstantial, transient,

imaginary, etc. 1531. 2. Something which goes to the head and clouds the faculties 1574. 3. A fit of anger or irritation 1522.

1. Loue is a smoake made with the f. of sighes SHAKS. To smother him with fumes and eulogies BURTON. 2. Sometimes his head gets a little hot with the fumes of patriotism M. ARNOLD. 3. Phr. *In a f.* Hence **Fu·meless** *a.* free from fumes.

Fume (fiūm), *v.* ME. [a. F. *fumer* :—L. *fumare*, f. *fumus.*] **1.** *trans.* To apply smoke or fumes to; to fumigate; to perfume with incense 1641; †to perfume -1740; †to smoke-dry (provisions) -1661. **2.** *intr.* To emit fumes, smoke, or vapour; also *fig.* 1532. **3.** *intr.* Of smoke, etc.: To issue, rise, pass off 1593. Also with *away.* †**4.** *trans.* To send forth or emit as vapour, disperse in vapour. Also with *away, out*, etc. -1707. †**5.** *intr.* Of the brain: To be clouded with fumes (of liquor). *Ant. & Cl.* II. i. 24. **6.** *fig.* To give way to or exhibit anger or irritation 1522.

1. To f. a ship or house in time of infectious aires 1612. She fum'd the temples with an od'rous flame DRYDEN. *fig.* They demi-deify and f. him so COWPER. Lawne sheetes fum'd with Vyolets MARSTON. 2. A Censer..fuming all the day and night PURCHAS. 3. Incense Clouds Fuming from Golden Censers, hid the Mount MILT. 6. To fret and f. about trifles 1878.

‖**Fumé** (fümé), *a.* 1883. [F.] Of glass: Having a smoky tint. Of oak: Treated with fumes of ammonia.

Fumer (fiū·məɹ). 1611. [f. FUME *v.* + -ER[1].] †**1.** A perfumer 1611. **2.** One who fumes or gets into a fume 1894.

Fumerel(l, -ill, obs. ff. FEMERELL.

Fu·met[1]. *Obs.* or *arch.* ME. [app. a. AF. **fumets* (**fumez*) pl., f. *fumer* (repr. L. *fimare*).] The excrement (of a deer).

†**Fumet**[2], **fume·tte.** 1723. [a. F. *fumet*, f. *fumer.*] The scent or smell of game when high; game flavour -1796.

†**Fu·mid**, *a.* 1597. [ad. L. *fumidus.*] Fuming, vaporous -1797. Hence †**Fumi·dity**, †**Fu·midness**, f. condition or quality.

†**Fumi·ferous**, *a. rare.* 1656. [f. L. *fumifer* (f. *fumus* + *-fer* bearing) + -OUS.] Bearing or producing smoke -1742.

Fumify (fiū·mifəi), *v.* [ad. L. *fumificare.*] *trans.* (*joc.*) To fumigate. T. BROWN.

Fumigant (fiū·migănt). 1727. [ad. L. *fumigantem.*]

†**A.** *adj.* That fumes.

B. *sb.* That which fumigates (*rare*) 1890.

Fumigate (fiū·migeit), *v.* 1530. [f. L. *fumigat-*, *fumigare*, f. *fumus* FUME *sb.*] **1.** *trans.* To apply smoke or fumes to; *esp.* to disinfect or purify by exposure to smoke or fumes 1781. **b.** To perfume 1530. **2.** To darken (oak) by the process of fuming. See FUMING *vbl. sb.* 18.. Hence **Fu·migator.**

Fumigation (fiūmigēi·ʃən). ME. [ad. L. *fumigationem*; see prec.] **1.** The action of generating odorous smoke or flames, *esp.* in incantations; the action of perfuming with herbs, etc. Also *concr.* the preparation used to produce this, or the fumes resulting from it. **2.** The action or process of fumigating 1572. **3.** *Med.* Exposure to fumes, *esp.* in order to produce a therapeutic effect. Also *concr.* the fumes generated for this purpose. ME.

Fumigatory (fiū·migātəri). *rare.* 1799. [See FUMIGATE *v.* and -ORY.]

A. *adj.* Having the quality of fumigating.

B. *sb.* 'A room or an apparatus used for fumigation' (*Syd. Soc. Lex.*).

Fuming (fiū·miŋ), *vbl. sb.* 1529. [f. FUME *v.* + -ING[1].] **a.** The action of FUME *v.* **b.** The treatment of oak with fumes of ammonia to give it an antique appearance 1893. **c.** *Photogr.* The process of subjecting albuminized paper to the fumes of ammonia 1889.

Fuming (fiū·miŋ), *ppl. a.* 1575. [f. as prec. + -ING[2].] That fumes (see FUME *v.*).

F. liquor of Boyle: hydrogureted sulphuret of ammonia, first described by Boyle. **Fu·mingly** *adv.*

†**Fu·mish**, *a.* 1519. [f. FUME *sb.* + -ISH.] **1.** Emitting smoke or vapour; smoky; seething -1599. **2.** Of the nature of fumes; causing or emitting fumes -1693. **3.** *fig.* Inclined to fume; exhibiting anger or irascibility -1608. Hence **Fu·mish·ly** *adv.*, **-ness.**

†**Fu·mishing.** 1527. [app. f. OF. *femer, fumer* to dung.] = FUMET[1]. -1726.

Fumitory (fiū·mitəri). ME. [O.F. *a fumeterre*, ad. med.L. *fumus terræ* lit. 'smoke of the earth'.] A plant of the genus *Fumaria* (or the related *Corydalis*), usually *F. officinalis.*

Fumitory, incorrect f. FUMATORY.

Fummel: see FUNNEL[2], sort of mule.

Fumose (fiūmōu·s), *a.* ME. [ad. L. *fumosus*, f. *fumus.*] **1.** Full of fumes, vaporous, flatulent. **2.** Smoky, like smoke ME. **3.** *Bot.* Smoke-coloured 1866.

†**Fumo·sity.** ME. [ad. F. *fumosité*; see prec. and -ITY.] **1.** The quality of being full of fumes or vapours -1652. **2.** The flatulent quality of various foods; the heady quality of wine, etc. -1542. **3.** Vaporous humour rising into the head from the stomach -1678. **4.** The state of giving off fumes; *concr.* a fume; the volatile part given off from a mineral or the like -1750.

Fumous (fiū·məs), *a.* ME. [f. L. *fumosus* + -OUS. Cf. F. *fumeux.*] †**1.** Giving off fumes; *esp.* flatulent -1706. †**2.** Consisting of fumes; vaporous, windy -1678. **3.** Pertaining to smoke or smoking. Now *joc.* 1661. †**4.** Full of passion, angry, furious -1684. **5.** *Bot.* = FUMOSE 3. 1866.

1. Abstaine from Garlick, Onions..and such like f. things 1610. Hence **Fu·mously** *adv.*

Fumy (fiū·mi), *a.* 1570. [f. FUME *sb.* + -Y[1].] Composed of, or full of, fumes, vapours, or smoke; of the nature of fume or fumes.

This fumie Citie [London] SIR H. WOTTON. Hence **Fu·mingly** *adv.*

Fun (fʋn), *sb.* 1700. [prob. f. FUN *v.*] †**1.** A cheat or trick; a hoax -1719. **2.** Diversion, sport; also, boisterous gaiety, drollery 1727.

2. The mirth and f. grew fast and furious BURNS. Phr. *To make f. of, poke f. at*: to ridicule. *For* or *in f.*: as a joke, not seriously.

Fun (fʋn), *v.* 1685. [Perh. a dial. pronunc. of FON *v.*] **1.** *trans.* To cheat, hoax; also, to cajole. Const. *of, out of.* Now *dial.* **2.** [f. the sb.] *intr.* To make fun or sport; to fool, joke 1728.

†**Funa·mbulant.** 1606. [as if ad. L. **funambulantem*, f. (ult.) *funambulus* (see FUNAMBULE) or its elements.] A rope-walker, a funambulist. So **Funa·mbulate** *v.* to walk on a stretched rope (in Dicts.). **Funa·mbula·tion**, the action of walking on a rope. **Funa·mbulator**, a rope-walker. **Funa·mbulatory** *a.* pertaining to rope-walking; that walks on a rope.

†**Funa·mbule**, *sb.* [ad. L. *funambulus* (also used), f. *funis* rope + *ambulare* to walk. Cf. F. *funambule.*] A rope-walker. EVELYN.

Funambulist (fiunæ·mbiŭlist). 1793. [f. prec. + -IST.] A rope-walker, a rope-dancer. So **Funa·mbulism**, rope-walking.

‖**Funa·mbulo.** *arch.* 1605. [Sp. or It.] A funambulist.

Function (fʋ·ŋkʃen), *sb.* 1533. [a. OF. *function* (mod.F. *fonction*), ad. L. *functionem*, f. *fungi* (*fungor*) to perform.] †**1.** The action of performing; discharge or performance *of* -1701. †**2.** Activity; action in general, physical or mental; also, bearing -1605. **3.** The special kind of activity proper to anything; the mode of action by which it fulfils its purpose: **a.** of a physical organ (often specialized as *animal, organic, vital*, etc.) 1590; **b.** of the intellectual and moral powers, etc. 1604; **c.** of things in general 1541. **4.** The kind of action proper to a person as belonging to a class, *esp.* to the holder of any office; hence, the office itself, an employment, calling, trade 1533. †**b.** *collect.* The persons following a profession or trade; an order, class -1732. **c.** *pl.* Official duties 1550. **5.** A religious ceremony; orig. in the R. C. Ch. 1640. **b.** A public ceremony; a social or festive meeting conducted with ceremony 1864. **6.** *Math.* A variable quantity regarded in its relation to one or more other variables in terms of which it may be expressed, or on the value of which its own value depends 1779.

1. His hand, his eye, his wits all present, wrought The f. of the glorious Part he beares DANIEL. 2. *Haml.* II. ii. 582. 3. a. Dark night, that from the eye his f. takes SHAKS. b. The first f. of the conscience 1868. c. The f. of money ADAM SMITH. 4. The quill, which is the badge of the f. LAMB. Our f. as ministers 1878. 5. The Christmas functions here were showy MRS. PIOZZI. b. A F. of some kind—a Launch—a Reception—a Royal Visit 1878. 6. Let us take a f. a little more complicated, $u = ax^2$ BABBAGE. Hence **Fu·nctioned** *ppl. a.* furnished with a f.

Function (fʋ·ŋkʃən), *v.* 1856. [f. prec. sb. Cf. F. *fonctionner.*] *intr.* To fulfil a function; to perform one's part; to act.

Functional (fʋ·ŋkʃənăl), *a.* 1631. [f. FUNCTION *sb.* + -AL.] **1.** Of or pertaining to a function or office; official; formal. **2.** *Phys.* Of or pertaining to the functions of an organ; affecting the functions only, not structural; serving a function (opp. to *rudimentary*) 1843. **3.** *Math.* Of or pertaining to a FUNCTION (sense 6) 1806.

2. So-called f. diseases, such as epilepsy, chorea, neuralgia MAUDSLEY. Hence **Functiona·lity**, f. character; in *Math.* the condition of being a function. **Fu·nctionalize** *v.* to place or assign to some function or office (Webst.). **Fu·nctionally** *adv.* with respect to the functions; in the discharge of the functions.

Functionary (fʋ·ŋkʃənări), *sb.* 1791. [f. FUNCTION *sb.* + -ARY[1], after F. *fonctionnaire.*] One who has certain functions to perform; an official.

Their republic is to have a first f. (as they call him) under the name of king or not, as they think fit BURKE. Hence **Fu·nctionarism**, officialism.

Fu·nctionary, *a.* 1822. [f. as prec. + -ARY[2].] **1.** = FUNCTIONAL **2.** **2.** Official; = FUNCTIONAL 1. 1862.

Functionate (fʋ·ŋkʃəneit), *v. rare.* 1856. [f. as prec. + -ATE[3].] *intr.* To perform one's function; to work; to officiate.

Functionless (fʋ·ŋkʃənlės), *a.* 1836. [see -LESS.] Having no function; chiefly in physiological sense.

Fund (fʋnd), *sb.* 1677. [ad. L. *fundus* the bottom; also, a piece of land. Cf. FOND *sb.* The senses represent those of F. *fond, fonds*, rather than those of L. *fundus.*] †**1.** The bottom; in various applications; occas. *Phys.* = FUNDUS. -1761. †**2.** = FOND *sb.* 1. -1748. **3.** Source of supply; a permanent stock that can be drawn upon 1695. **4. a.** *sing.* A stock or sum of money, *esp.* one set apart for a particular purpose 1694. **b.** *pl.* Pecuniary resources 1728. **5.** †**a.** A portion of revenue set apart as a security for specified payments -1776. **b.** *The* (*public*) *funds*: the stock of the national debt, considered as a mode of investment 1713. **6.** *Printing.* = FOUNT[2]. Also *attrib.* 1683.

3. The..British product, being the f. of its inland trade DE FOE. 3. b. There is a f. of good sense in this country, which cannot be deceived JUNIUS. 4. a. Phr. *Sinking fund*: see SINKING *vbl. sb.* The f. for decayed musicians 1795. b. (*To be*) *in funds*: in possession of money; When he was in funds he preferred a hansom MISS BRADDON. 5. a. The 500,000*l*, lately proposed without F. or Period 1740. b. Look what the funds were on the 1st of March THACKERAY. *Comb.*: **f.-holder**, one who has money invested in the funds; **-lord** (coined by Cobbett after *landlord*), a magnate whose position is due to money in the funds; **-monger**, one who speculates in the public funds. Hence **Fu·ndless** *a.*, without funds.

Fund (fʋnd), *v.* 1776. [f. prec. sb.] **1.** *trans.* Orig., to provide a fund (see FUND *sb.* 5) for the regular payment of the interest on (a public debt); hence, to convert (a floating debt) into a more or less permanent debt at a fixed rate of interest. **2.** To put into a fund or store (see FUND *sb.* 3); to collect; to store 1806. **3.** To put (money) in the funds (see FUND *sb.* 5 b); to invest 1855.

1. Exchequer bills which he says he shall..f. ADDINGTON. Hence **Fu·ndable** *a.* capable of being funded.

Fundal (fʋ·ndăl), *a.* 1889. [f. FUNDUS + -AL.] Relating to the fundus or base of an organ.

Fundament (fʋ·ndămĕnt). Also †**found·ment.** [ME. *fondement*, a. OF. :—L. *fundamentum*, f. *fundare* (see FOUND *v.*[2]), f. *fundus* bottom; see FUND *sb.*] †**1.** = FOUNDATION **4.** **2.** The lower part of the body, on which one sits; the buttocks; also, the anus. In birds, the vent. ME.

Fundamental (fʋndăme·ntăl). ME. [See prec. and -AL.]

A. *adj.* **1.** Of or pertaining to the foundation, basis, or groundwork. **2.** Serving as the foundation or base. Now only in immaterial applications. Const. *to* (rarely *of*). 1601. **b.** Primary, original; from which others are derived ME. **3.** Of strata: lying at the bottom 1799. **4.** *Mus.* Applied to the lowest or root note of a chord; also to the tone produced by the vibration of the whole of a sonorous body, as dist. from the HARMONICS produced by that of its parts 1752.

1. The f. analogy of sound and light TYNDALL. 2. A f. truth 1835. 3. The f. rock..is a black slate LYELL. 4. *F. bass*, a low note, or series of notes, forming the root or roots of a chord or succession of chords. *F. chord*, an old name for the common chord; now, any chord formed of harmonics of the fundamental tone.

B. *sb.* **1.** A leading or primary principle, rule, law, or article, which serves as the groundwork of a system; an essential part. Chiefly in *pl.* 1637. **2.** *Mus.* Short for *f. tone* or *note*: see A. 4. (Formerly = *key-note.*) 1727.

1. There is an odd tenacity in the fundamentals of ..legends BURTON.

Hence **Fu·ndamenta·lity,** the quality or state of being f. **Fundame·ntally** *adv.*

Fundame·ntalism. 1923. [f. prec. + -ISM.] Strict adherence to traditional orthodox tenets (e.g. the literal inerrancy of Scripture) held to be fundamental to the Christian faith: opposed to *liberalism* and *modernism.* Hence **Fundame·ntalist,** an adherent of f.; also as adj.

Fundatorial (fɒndătōə·riăl), *a.* [f. L. type **fundatorius* (f. *fundare*) + -AL.] Pertaining to a founder. FREEMAN.

Funded (fɒ·ndėd), *ppl. a.* 1776. [f. FUND *v.* + -ED 1.] **1.** Made part of the permanent debt of the state (cf. FUND *v.* 1). **b.** Invested in the funds 1848. **2.** Stored up 1841.

1. The publick debts of Great Britain f. and unfunded ADAM SMITH. b. F. property MILL.

Funding (fɒ·ndiŋ), *vbl. sb.* 1776. [f. FUND *v.* + -ING 1.] Conversion of a floating debt into a permanent one. Also *attrib.*

The ruinous expedient of perpetual f. ADAM SMITH.

‖**Fundus** (fɒ·ndɒ̆s). 1754. [L.; = 'bottom'.] *Anat.* The base or bottom of an organ; the part remote from the external aperture.

F. of the eye: 'the back part of the globe of the eye behind the crystalline lens' (*Syd. Soc. Lex.*).

Funebrial (fiunī·briăl), *a.* Now *rare.* Also funebral. 1604. [f. L. *funebris* (f. *funus* funeral) + -AL.] = FUNEREAL. So †**Fune·brious.**

Funeral (fiū·nĕrăl). ME. [The adj. is a. OF. *funeral*, ad. med.L. *funeralis*, f. *funer-, funus*, funeral, death, dead body. The sb. is ad. OF. *funeraille*, collect. fem. sing., ad. med.L. *funeralia*, neut. pl. of the adj. Used in the pl. with the same sense as in the sing. till *c* 1700, after the F. usage.]

A. *adj.* **1.** Of or pertaining to the ceremonial burial (or cremation) of the dead; used etc. at a burial. Now felt as the sb. used *attrib.* **2.** = FUNEREAL. 1651.

1. Funerall griefe DEKKER. *F. pile, pyre*, the pile of wood, etc. on which a dead body is burned. The F. Pyre was out and the last Valediction over SIR T. BROWNE.

B. *sb.* **1.** The ceremonies connected with the burial (or cremation) of the body of a dead person; obsequies; a burial (or its equivalent) with the attendant observances 1512. Also *fig.* †**b.** pl. with sing. sense -1711. †**2.** *pl.* The expenses attending a funeral -1626. **3.** A funeral sermon or service (now *U.S.*) 1641. **4.** A burial procession 1745. **5.** Indefinitely: **a.** death; **b.** grave; **c.** monument 1575.

1. Went to Mr. Cowley's f., whose corpse..was conveyed to Westminster Abbey in a hearse with six horses EVELYN. 3. Mr. Giles Laurence preached his Funeralls FULLER. 4. There is no f. so sad to follow as the f. of our own youth LANDOR.

Hence †**Fu·nerally** *adv.* with f. ceremonies.

Funerary (fiū·nĕrări), *a.* 1693. [ad. late L. *funerarius*; see FUNERAL.] Of or pertaining to a funeral or burial.

†**Fu·nerate,** *v.* 1548. [f. L. *funerat-, funerare*; see FUNERAL.] To bury with funeral rites -1568. So **Funeration,** the performance of funeral rites.

Funereal (fiunīə·rĭăl), *a.* 1725. [f. L. *funereus* + -AL.] Of, pertaining to, or appropriate to, a funeral. Hence, dark, dismal, melancholy, mournful.

Near some lone fane, or yew's f. green SHENSTONE. Hence **Fune·really** *adv.*

Funest (fiune·st), *a.* Now *rare.* 1654. [ad. F. *funeste*, ad. L. *funestus*, f. *funus.*] Causing or portending death or evil; fatal, disastrous; deeply deplorable.

The execution was..one of the funeste effects of the war 1671.

Fungaceous (fɒŋgēⁱ·ʃəs), *a.* 1874. [f. L. *fungus* + -ACEOUS.] Of the nature of a fungus or fungi.

Fungal (fɒ·ŋgăl). 1835. [ad. mod.L. *fungalis*, f. L. *fungus.*]

A. *adj.* Of or pertaining to a fungus; of the nature of a fungus.

B. *sb.* A fungus 1845.

Fu·ngate, *sb.* 1821. [f. FUNGUS + -ATE 1. Cf. F. *fongate.*] *Chem.* A salt formed by the combination of fungic acid with a base.

Fungate (fɒ·ŋgēⁱt), *v.* 1847. [f. FUNGUS + -ATE 3.] *Path.* To grow up with a fungous appearance; to grow rapidly like a fungus. See FUNGUS *sb.* 2.

†**Funge.** ME. [a. OF. **funge, fonge*, ad. L. *fungus.*] **1.** A mushroom or fungus. ME. only. **2.** A soft-headed fellow. [After L. *fungus.*] 1621.

Fungible (fɒ·ndʒib'l). 1765. [ad. med.L. *fungibilis* ('*res fungibiles*' Du Cange) f. *fungi* (with sense as in *fungi vice* to fulfil the office of).] *Law.*

A. *adj.* Said of a thing which is the subject of an obligation when another thing of the same or another class may be delivered in lieu of it 1818.

B. *sb.* A fungible thing.

Fu·ngic, *a.* 1819. [f. FUNGUS + -IC. Cf. F. *fongique.*] Of or pertaining to fungi or mushrooms.

F. acid, 'a mixture of citric, malic, and phosphoric acids'.

Fungicide (fɒ·ndʒisəid). 1889. [f. *fungi-* FUNGUS + -CIDE 2.] Something used for destroying fungi.

Fungiform (fɒ·ndʒifǭɹm), *a* 1823. [f. *fungi-* FUNGUS + -FORM. Cf. F. *fongiforme.*] Having the form of a fungus or mushroom. Said esp. of papillæ on the tongue.

‖**Fungillus** (fɒndʒi·lɒ̆s). 1830. [mod.L., dim. of L. *fungus.*] A little fungus. Hence **Fungi·lliform** *a.* = FUNGIFORM.

Fungin (fɒ·ndʒin). (Erron. **fungine.**) 1819. [f. FUNGUS + -IN.] The substance which forms the cell-walls of a mushroom or fungus.

†**Fu·ngite.** 1691. [f. FUNGUS + -ITE.] A kind of fossil coral -1756.

Fungivorous (fɒndʒi·vŏrəs), *a.* 1826. [f. L. *fungi-, fungus* + *-vorus* devouring + -OUS.] Feeding on mushrooms or fungi.

Fungoid (fɒ·ŋgoid). 1836. [f. FUNGUS + -OID. Cf. F. *fongoïde.*]

A. *adj.* Resembling, or of the nature of, a fungus; *spec.* in *Path.* (see FUNGUS 2).

B. *sb.* A fungoid plant. Also *attrib.* 1861.

Fungology (fɒŋgǫ·lŏdʒi). 1860. [f. FUNGUS + -(O)LOGY.] The science or study of fungi. Hence **Fungolo·gical** *a.* **Fungo·logist.**

Fungo·se, *a.* 1713. [ad. L. *fungosus*, f. *fungus.*] = FUNGOUS 1. Hence **Fungo·sity,** the quality or condition of being fungous; *concr.* a fungous growth.

Fungous (fɒ·ŋgəs), *a.* ME. [ad. L. *fungosus*; see FUNGUS and -OUS. Cf. F. *fongueux.*] **1.** Of or pertaining to fungi; having the nature of a fungus; †spongy. *spec.* in *Path.* (see FUNGUS 2). **2.** Growing suddenly like a mushroom, not durable or substantial 1751.

Fungus (fɒ·ŋgɒ̆s), *sb.* Pl. **fungi** (fɒ·ndʒəi), funguses. 1527. [a. L. *fungus*, cogn. w. Gr. σφόγγος, σπόγγος SPONGE.] **1.** A mushroom, toadstool, or one of the allied plants, including the various forms of mould. In *Bot.*, a cryptogamous plant, characterized by the absence of chlorophyll, and deriving its sustenance from dead or living organic matter. Also *collect.* in *sing.* Also *transf.* and *fig.* **2.** *Path.* A spongy morbid growth or excrescence, such as exuberant granulation in a wound 1674. †**3.** An excrescence of lamp-black or charred fibre on the wick of a candle or lamp. Also *fig.* (So in L.) -1813. **4.** The vegetable growth employed as tinder 1831. **5.** *attrib.* 1880.

Funic (fiū·nik), *a.* 1857. [f. FUNIS + -IC.] Pertaining to the funis or umbilical cord.

Funicle (fiū·nik'l). 1664. [Anglicized f. FUNICULUS.] = FUNICULUS, *esp.* senses 2, 3.

Funicular (fiuni·kiŭlăɹ), *a.* 1664. [f. L. *funiculus* + -AR. Cf. F. *funiculaire.*] **1.** Of or pertaining to a FUNICULUS. **2.** Of or pertaining to a rope or its tension 1828. **3.** Resembling a cord; *spec.* in *Anat.* and *Bot.* 1835.

1. †*F. hypothesis*: see FUNICULUS 2. 2. *F. machine*: an arrangement of a cord, pulleys, and suspended weights, designed to illustrate statical principles. *F. polygon*: the figure assumed by a cord supported at its extremities, and having weights suspended from it at various points. *F. railway* (also simply *funicular*): a cable railway, esp. one for the ascent of a mountain; *spec.* one in which the weight of an ascending car is partly or wholly counterbalanced by the weight of a descending car.

Funiculate (fiuni·kiŭlēⁱt), *a.* 1826. [f. FUNICULUS + -ATE 2.] *Bot.* and *Zool.* Having a funiculus.

‖**Funiculus** (fiuni·kiŭlɒ̆s). 1662. (L., dim. of *funis* rope.] †**1.** A little rope (*rare*) 1706. †**2.** A hypothetical string or filament of extremely rarefied matter, imagined to be the agent in the Torricellian experiment 1662. **3.** The umbilical cord; = FUNIS. Hence *transf.* in *Bot.* A little stalk by which a seed or ovule is attached to the placenta 1830. **4.** *Entom.* 'A term for the part of the antenna which lies between the scape and the club in certain insects' (*Syd. Soc. Lex.*) 1877. **5.** *Anat.* 'Applied to the primitive cord or bundle of nerve fibres, bound together in a sheath of connective tissue, called the perineurium or neurilemma' (*Syd. Soc. Lex.*) 1877.

Funiform (fiū·nifǭɹm), *a.* 1865. [f. L. *funis* rope + -FORM.] Having the form of a cord or rope.

Funiliform (fiuni·lifǭɹm), *a.* 1856. [as if f. L. **funilis* adj. (f. *funis* rope) + -FORM.] *Bot.* 'Tough, cylindrical, and flexible, like a chord'. HENSLOW.

Funipendulous (fiū:nipe·ndiŭləs), *a.* 1706. [f. L. *funis* + *pendulus* hanging + -OUS.] Hanging from a rope; connected with a hanging rope.

‖**Funis** (fiū·nis). ME. [L.; = 'rope'.] *Anat.* †**a.** Short for *funis brachii*, 'an old name for the median vein' (*Syd. Soc. Lex.*). **b.** The umbilical cord.

†**Funk,** *sb.*1 ME. [? ad. MDu. *vonke* (Du. *vonk*), spark.] **1.** A spark. ME. only. **2.** Touch-wood -1825.

†**Funk,** *sb.*2 1623. [f. FUNK *v.*1] A strong smell or stink -1725.

Funk (fɒŋk), *sb.*3 *slang.* 1743. [First quoted as Oxford slang; ? a. Flemish *fonck.*] **1.** Cowering fear; a state of panic. *Blue f.*: see BLUE *a.* **2.** One who funks 1860.

1. *Comb.* **F.-hole** (*Mil. slang*), a trench dug-out; employment used as a pretext for evading military service. Hence **Fu·nky** *a.* in a state of f.

Funk (fɒŋk), *v.*1 *slang.* 1699. [? a. F. dial. *funkier*:—L. **fumicare, fumigare*, f. *fumus* smoke.] **1.** *trans.* To blow smoke upon (a person) 1699; to smoke (a pipe, tobacco) 1704; *intr.* to smoke 1829. **2.** To cause an offensive smell 1708.

Funk (fɒŋk), *v.*2 *slang.* 1737. [Conn. w. FUNK *sb.*3] **1.** *intr.* To flinch or shrink through fear; to try to back out of anything. **2.** *trans.* To fight shy of, wish or try to shirk or evade 1857. **3.** To be afraid of (a person) 1836. **4.** To scare 1819.

1. To F. right out o' p'lit'cal strife aint thought to be the thing LOWELL. 3. 'I rather f. the governor' 1849. 4. The jury, funked by the Anarchists, returned [etc.] 1892. Hence **Fu·nker.**

Funnel (fɒ·nĕl), *sb.*1 [ME. *fonel*, app. a. OF. **founil* (whence Breton *founil*). Mod. Pr. dialects have *founil, enfounilh*, prob. corrupted adoptions of L. *infundibulum*, f. *infundere* to pour in.] **1.** A cone-shaped vessel usually fitted at the apex with a short tube, by means of which a liquid, powder, etc. may be conducted through a small opening. **b.** *spec.* in *Casting.* The hole through which the metal is poured into the mould 1874. **c.** *Anat.* and *Zool.* A funnel-shaped organ or limb; an infundibulum 1712. **2.** A tube or shaft for lighting or ventilating purposes; also, the metal chimney of an engine, steamboat, etc. 1555. b. The flue of a chimney 1688. 3. Applied to a funnel-shaped opening, shaft, or channel in rocks, etc. 1774. 4. A cylindrical band of metal; *esp.* that fitted on to the head of a mast, to which the rigging is attached 1694.

Comb.: f.-form = *f.-shaped*; -shaped *a.* shaped like a funnel, infundibuliform, *esp.* in *Bot.*; -stays, ropes or chains leading from eye-plates near the top of the funnel to the ship's sides.

Hence Fu·nnelled *ppl. a.* funnel-shaped; also *fig.*; in *Bot.* infundibuliform.

Funnel (fʊ·nĕl), *sb.*[2] *dial.* 1835. [?] A mule whose sire is an ass.

Funny (fʊ·ni), *a.* 1756. [f. FUN *sb.* + -Y[1].] 1. Affording fun, comical, facetious. 2. Queer, odd, strange. *colloq.* 1806. †3. *slang.* Tipsy 1756. *Comb.* f.-bone, that part of the elbow over which the ulnar nerve passes, so called from the peculiar sensation experienced when it is struck. Hence Fu·nnily *adv.* in a f. manner. Fu·nniment *joc.*, drollery, humour; also, a joke. Fu·nniness, the quality or state of being f.; a f. saying or joke.

Fur (fɔ̃ɪ), *sb.* ME. [f. FUR *v.*] 1. A trimming or lining for a garment, made of the dressed coat of certain animals; *hence*, the coat of such animals as material for such use. Also, a garment made of, or trimmed or lined with, this material; now chiefly *pl.* 2. The short, fine, soft hair of the sable, ermine, beaver, otter, bear, etc. growing thick upon the skin, and dist. from the ordinary hair ME. 3. *pl.* Skins of such animals with the fur on them 1555. 4. *Her.* A tincture representing tufts upon a plain ground, or patches of different colours supposed to be sewn together. (The eight principal furs are ermine, ermines, erminois, pean, vair, countervair, potent, and counterpotent.) 1610. 5. *collect.* Furred animals 1827. 6. Anything resembling fur, or coating a surface like fur; e.g. a coat or crust of mould, of deposit from wine, etc. 1843. b. *esp.* A coating formed on the tongue in certain diseased conditions of the body 1693. c. A crust formed by the deposit of carbonate of lime on the interior surface of a kettle, boiler, etc. 1805. 7. *Carpentry.* A piece nailed upon a rafter to strengthen it when decayed 1703. 8. *attrib.* 1597.

1. Furred with no menivere, But with a furre rough of here, Of lambe-skinnes CHAUCER. 2. To want the strength of Bulls, the f. of Bears POPE. Phr. *To stroke the f. the wrong way* (fig.): to cause irritation. *To make the f. fly* (U.S. slang): to claw, scratch, wound severely. 3. Bargains for hides and furs SCOTT. 5. Phr. *F. and feather*: see FEATHER *sb.*

Comb. 1. General: as *f.-trader*; *f.-dressing*; *f.-clad*, *f.-collared*, etc.

2. Special: f.-puller, one who scrapes the loose down off rabbit and other skins; -seal, the seal which affords the fur known as seal-skin.

Fur (fɔ̃ɪ), *v.* ME. [a. OF. *forrer* (mod. *fourrer*) to line, encase, sheathe, a Com. Rom. vb. f. **fod(e)ro* case, a. Teut. **fôðro-* (OE. *fôdor*, mod.Ger. *futter*). Cf. FOTHER *v.* Usually felt as a derivative of FUR *sb.*] 1. *trans.* To line, or serve to line, trim, or cover with fur. 2. To clothe or adorn with fur ME. 3. To coat or cover with or as with fur or morbid matter 1593. 4. *intr.* To become furred or coated with morbid matter. Also, to collect as fur. 1550. 5. *trans.* To clean off the fur of (a boiler) 1867. 6. *Carpentry.* To fix strips of wood to (floor-timbers, rafters, etc.) in order to bring them to a level, or the like 1678. 7. (? after F. *fourrer*). To foist or thrust *in*. BACON.

1. A mantell furryd with ermyns LD. BERNERS. 3. It [the water]..furs everything in which it is kept 1839. 4. Teeth .. Which though they furre, will neither ake nor rot HERRICK.

Furacious (fiurē¹·ʃəs), *a.* Now *pedantic* or *joc.* 1676. [f. L. *furaci-* (nom. *furax*), f. *furari* to steal + -OUS.] Given to thieving, thievish. Hence Fura·city, the quality of being f.; tendency to steal.

Furbelow (fɔ̃·ɹbĭlo), *sb.* 1680. [altered f. FALBALA.] 1. A flounce; the pleated border of a petticoat or gown. Now often in *pl.* as a contemptuous term for showy ornaments or trimming. 1706. 2. Anything resembling a flounce 1742. 3. A name for *Laminaria bulbosa*, a seaweed with a large wrinkled frond 1846. 4. *attrib.* = 'having furbelows' 1680.

3. The dimpled flounce of the sea-f. TENNYSON.

Furbelow (fɔ̃·ɹbĭlo), *v.* 1701. [f. prec. sb.] To ornament with or as with a furbelow.

Furbish (fɔ̃·ɹbiʃ), *v.* ME. [ad. OF. *forbiss-* lengthened stem of *forbir*, ad. OHG. *furban* in same sense.] 1. *trans.* To remove rust from; to brighten by rubbing, burnish. Also *fig.* 2. To brush or clean up; to do up afresh, renovate, revive. Chiefly with *up*. 1587.

1. The swerd is whettid and furbishid WYCLIF *Ezek.* xxi. 9. *fig.* F. new the name of John a Gaunt SHAKS. 2. To f. up old baronies DISRAELI. Hence Fu·rbisher.

Furcate (fɔ̃·ɹkeᶦt, -ĕt), *a.* 1819. [ad. med.L. *furcatus* (of a hoof) cloven, f. L. *furca* fork.] Formed like a fork; forked and branched; as, a *furcate* tail. Hence Fu·rcately *adv.* Also Furca·to- = forkedly-. So Fu·rcated *ppl. a.*

Furcation (fɔɪkē¹·ʃən). 1646. [f. L. *furca* fork; see -ATION.] A forking; hence, a fork-like division or branch.

Furciferous (fɔɪsi·fĕrəs), *a.* 1823. [f. L. *furcifer* fork-bearer, hence (with ref. to the 'fork' or yoke placed on the necks of criminals) rascal, jail-bird + -OUS.] 1. *Entom.* Bearing a forked process; said of the larvæ of some butterflies. 2. Rascally. DE QUINCEY.

‖**Furcula** (fɔ̃·ɹkiŭlă). 1859. [L., dim. of *furca.*] *Ornith.* A forked bone below the neck of a bird, consisting of the two clavicles and an interclavicle; the merry-thought or wishbone. Hence Fu·rcular *a.* of or pertaining to the f.; in early use, to the collar-bone.

‖**Furculum** (fɔ̃·ɹkiŭlŏm). 1833. [mod.L., badly formed dim. of *furca.*] = FURCULA.

†**Fu·rdel, fu·rdle**, *v.* 1594. [var. of FARDEL *v.*] *trans.* To furl or fold. Also with *up.* –1682.

Furfur (fɔ̃·ɹfɔ̃ɪ). *Pl.* furfures. 1621. [a. L. *furfur* bran.] Dandriff, scurf; *pl.* particles of epidermis or scurf. Hence Furfura·ceous *a.* resembling bran; scurfy; in *Bot.* covered with bran-like scales. Furfura·tion (*rare*), 'the shedding of the skin in small branny particles' (*Syd. Soc. Lex.*).

Furfurine (fɔ̃·ɹfiŭrin). 1845. [f. L. *furfur* + -INE.] *Chem.* An organic base, isomeric with furfuramide, and produced therefrom under the influence of caustic potash, or of heat.

Furfurol (fɔ̃·ɹfiŭrǫl). 1845. [f. L. *furfur* + -OL.] A volatile oil obtained by distilling bran with dilute sulphuric acid.

Furfurous (fɔ̃·ɹfiŭrəs), *a.* 1547. [f. as prec. + -OUS.] Resembling or containing bran; made of bran.

†**Fu·rial**, *a.* ME. [a. OF., ad. L. *furialis*, f. *furia* FURY.] Furious, raging –1640.

Furibund (fiū·ribʊnd), *a.* 1490. [ad. L. *furibundus*, f. *furere* to rage.] Furious, raging, mad. So †Fu·ribundal.

Furiosity (fiuri,ǫ·sĭti). ME. [ad. L. *furiositatem*, f. *furiosus*; see -ITY.] 1. The quality or state of being FURIOUS; fury. Now *rare.* 1509. 2. Madness, *esp.* in *Sc. Law.*

‖**Furioso** (fūriō·so). 1670. [It.; = L. *furiosus*; see FURIOUS *a.*]

A. *adj.* (*Mus.*) A direction: With vehemence 1823.

B. *sb.* A furious person. (Also furiosa fem.)

Furious (fiū·riəs), *a.* ME. [a. OF. *furieus* (mod. *furieux*), ad. L. *furiosus*, f. *furia* FURY.] 1. Full of fury or fierce passion; proceeding from or exhibiting fury; fierce, raging, frantic. Also *transf.* of the elements; also of pains, diseases, etc. 2. *Hyperbolically* (after F. use): Excessive, extravagant. *rare.* 1668. 3. Mad, insane. *Obs.* exc. in *Sc. Law.* 1475.

1. Parties of religion are more f. HUME. *transf.* The f. Winters rages *Cymb.* IV. ii. 259. F. agues GERARDE. Hence Fu·rious-ly *adv.*, -ness.

Furl (fɔ̃ɪl), *sb.* 1643. [f. next vb.] 1. A roll, coil, or curl of any furled body. 2. The action of furling or state of being furled, the manner in which a sail is furled 1836.

Furl (fɔ̃ɪl), *v.* 1556. [prob. an alteration of FURDLE *v.*] 1. *trans.* 'To roll up and bind (a sail) neatly upon its respective yard or boom' (Adm. Smyth); to roll up (a flag) into small compass. Also *transf.* and *fig.* †2. To furrow, wrinkle (a surface) –1763. 3. *intr.* To become furled; to curl *up* 1676.

1. Till. .the battle-flags were furl'd TENNYSON.

Furlong (fɔ̃·ɹlǫŋ). [OE. *furlang* str. neut., f. *furh*, FURROW + *lang*, LONG *a.*] 1. Orig., the length of the furrow in the common field; usually understood to be equal to 40 poles (rods, perches). Early regarded as = the Roman *stadium*, which was ⅛ of a Roman mile; and hence always used as a name for the eighth part of an English mile. The present statute furlong is 220 yards, and is equal both to the eighth part of a statute mile, and to the side of a square of 10 statute acres. 2. An area of land a 'furlong' each way, containing ten acres 1819. 3. The headland of a common field. *Obs.* exc. *dial.* OE. 4. An indefinite division of an unenclosed field ME. 5. 'The line of direction of plowed lands' (Marshall) 1787.

1. †*F. way*: a short distance, hence a brief space; They sitten stille wel a f. way CHAUCER.

Furlough (fɔ̃·ɹlo^u), *sb.* 1625. [a. Du. *verlof*, app. formed after Ger. *verlaub*, f. *ver-* FOR- *pref.*[1] + root *laub-*; see LEAVE *sb.*] 1. Leave of absence, *esp.* a permit given to a soldier to be absent from duty for a stated time. Also *attrib.* †2. A passport; a licence, or permit –1826.

1. Like a Low-Countrey vorloffe, or Welsh-briefe B. JONS. Hence Fu·rlough *v.* (chiefly *U.S.*), to grant (a person) a f.; to give leave of absence to.

Furmente, -ty, furmety, -ity: vars. of FRUMENTY.

Furnace (fɔ̃·ɹnĕs), *sb.* [ME. *forneis*, a. OF. *fornais* masc., repr. L. *fornacem*, *fornax*, f. *fornus*, *furnus*, oven.] 1. An apparatus consisting essentially of a chamber to contain combustibles for the purpose of subjecting minerals, metals, etc. to the continuous action of intense heat. b. *transf.* A volcano 1660. c. *fig.*, esp. used to express any severe test or trial. Also, a place of excessive heat; a hot-bed ME. †2. Used of an incubating chamber –1585. 3. A closed fireplace for heating a building by means of hot-air or hot-water pipes; also, 'the fireplace of a marine boiler' (Smyth) 1691. 4. A boiler, cauldron, crucible. *Obs.* exc. *dial.* ME. 5. *attrib.*, as *f. air-pipe*, etc. 1664.

1. The Louer, Sighing like a F. SHAKS. c. I have chosen thee in the fornace of affliction *Isa.* xlviii. 10. The very f. of Mahometan bigotry KINGLAKE.

Comb.: f.-bar = *fire-bar* (see FIRE *sb.*); -bridge, 'a barrier of fire-bricks or of iron plates containing water thrown across the furnace at the extreme end of the fire-bars, to prevent the fuel being carried into the flues, and to quicken the draft' (Knight); f. cadmia or cadmium, the oxide of zinc which accumulates in the chimneys of furnaces smelting zinciferous ores; -tube, the tube within which the fuel is enclosed in an internally fired boiler.

Furnace (fɔ̃·ɹnĕs), *v.* 1598. [f. prec. sb.] 1. *trans.* To exhale like a furnace; *intr.* to issue as from a furnace. 2. *trans.* To subject to the heat of a furnace 1612.

1. He furnaces The thicke sighes from him SHAKS.

Fu·rnage. Now *Hist.* 1468. [a. OF. *furnage* (mod. *fournage*), f. OF. *forn* (mod. *four*) :—L. *furnus* oven.] The process of baking; the price paid for baking; in *Feudal Law*, the fee paid to the lord by tenants, bound to bake in the lord's oven, for permission to use their own.

†**Fu·rniment.** 1553. [ad. OF. *fourniment*, f. *fournir.*] The condition of being furnished; *pl.* accoutrements, decorations, fittings –1596.

Furnish (fɔ̃·ɹniʃ), *sb.* 1500. [f. next vb.] †A furnishing or providing; *concr.* a provision of anything; *colloq.* a setting off or embellishing.

Furnish (fɔ̃·ɹniʃ), *v.* 1477. [a. OF. *furniss-* lengthened stem of *furnir* = Pr. *fornir* (F. *fournir*), app. a Com. Rom. alteration of an earlier **formire*, *fromire* to further, f. **frum-* ablaut-var. of **fram-* forward; see FROM.] †1. *trans.* To accomplish; to ensure *that* –1551. †2. To fill, occupy –1692. †3. To supply, provide for (needs, etc.) –1666. 4. To provide or supply *with* (something necessary, useful, or desirable). †Also const. *in*, *of*. 1529. †5. *simply.* To supply with what is necessary –1743; to decorate, embellish –1690. 6. To fit up (an apartment, a house) with all that is requisite, including movable furniture (see FURNITURE), which is now the predominant notion 1650. 7. To provide, contribute, afford, supply, yield. (Perh. due to mod. Fr. influence.) 1754.

1. To f. a message LD. BERNERS. 3. To f. his Majestye's present occasions MARVELL. 4. Let your wiues.. furnishe them selues with al pointes of honest housewifery 1550. He [Plato] has furnished us with the instruments of thought JOWETT. 5. We haue two houres To f. vs SHAKS. Six led Horses, all..nobly furnish'd 1703. 6. He had taken more pains to f. his house, than his mind THIRLWALL. 7. The idea of inheritance furnishes a sure principle of conservation BURKE.

Comb. with advs. **F. forth.** Used by Shaks. with the sense = 5 above; by Scott in sense 7. **F. out.** (*a*) To supply what is lacking in; to complete. (*b*) To supply adequate provision for.

Hence **Fu·rnishable** *a.* **Fu·rnisher** *spec.* one who supplies furniture. **Fu·rnishing** *vbl. sb. spec. pl.* furniture, fixtures, apparatus, etc. **Fu·rnishment,** the action of furnishing; *spec. pl.* supplies; munitions of war (now *rare*).

Furniture (fɒ·ɹnitiŭɹ). 1529. [ad. F. *fourniture*, f. *fournir* to furnish.] †1. The action of furnishing (see FURNISH *v.* 1, 5, 7) –1699. 2. The condition of being equipped; preparedness for action; mental cultivation, culture. *Obs.* exc. *arch.* 1560. †3. That with which one is provided; a provision of anything (whether material or immaterial); stores in general; necessaries –1787. b. Something to fill or occupy (a receptacle, etc.), contents. Now *rare*. 1612. 4. Means of equipment; *esp.* the harness, housings, etc. of a horse or other draught animal (rarely in *pl.*) 1553. 5. Apparatus, appliances, or instruments for work: a. material (now chiefly *Naut.*) 1577; b. immaterial (now only with *mental* or the like) 1561. 6. Accessories, appendages (formerly also *pl.*). Now only *techn.*; used, e.g., for the finger-plates, handles, locks, etc. of a door; the plates and handles, etc. of a coffin, and the like 1568. †b. *pl.* Adjuncts of a salad –1727. c. *Printing.* 'The wooden inclosing strips and quoins which surround the matter in the chase' (Knight) 1683. 7. Movable articles in a dwelling-house, place of business, or a public building. (The prevailing sense.) 1573. 8. *Mus.* 'The name of one of the mixture stops in an organ' (Stainer and Barrett) 1690.

1. Exercises, apt to the f. of a gentilemannes personage ELYOT. They..stop all f. of food and victuals DRUMM. OF HAWTH. 2. Great defect of inward F. and Worth HALES. 3. A noble F. of Divine Learning 1683. 4. Rachel had taken the images, and put them in the camels f. *Gen.* xxxi. 34. The saddles and rich f. of the cavalry GIBBON. 5. a. Ladders, bridges, shot, powder, and other furnitures 1601. *Furniture*, the rigging, sails, spars, anchors, cables, boats, tackle, provisions, and every article with which a ship is fitted out SMYTH. b. The statesmanlike f. of his mind LOWELL.

Comb.: **f.-pad**, a piece of india-rubber or the like attached to a piece of furniture to prevent rubbing or striking against objects; **-picture**, one painted for the trade; a 'pot-boiler'; **-stop** (*Mus.*), see 8.

‖**Furor** (fiū·rǫɹ). 1477. [orig. a. F. *fureur*, ad. L. *furorem*; now only occas. as L.] 1. Fury, rage, mania. 2. The inspired frenzy of poets and prophets; an excited mood 1589. 3. A rage or craze 1704.

2. Rises into f. almost Pythic CARLYLE. 3. The athletic f. 1868.

‖**Furore** (fŭrǭre). 1851. [It. form of prec.] Enthusiastic popular admiration; a rage, craze.

Furred (fɒ̄ɹd), *ppl. a.* ME. [f. FUR *sb.* and *v.* + -ED.] 1. In the senses of FUR *v.*; *esp.* covered or coated with morbid matter, encrusted. 2. Of an animal: Provided with or having fur 1545.

1. Teeth f. and throat sore 1803. A f. tongue 1878. 2. Thou maist know a foxe by his f. tayle 1545.

†**Fu·rrier**[1]. See also FORAYER. 1525. [ad. F. *fourrier*, OF. *forier*, f. *feurre* FORAGE.] One who went in advance of an army, etc. to secure accommodation, etc.; hence also a courier, harbinger –1704.

Furrier (fɒ·riəɹ). ME. [f. FUR *sb.* + -IER; cf. *clothier*.] A dealer in or dresser of fur or furs. Hence **Fu·rriery,** †furs collectively; the business of a furrier.

Furring (fɒ̄·riŋ), *vbl. sb.* ME. [f. FUR *v.* + -ING[1].] 1. The action of clothing or adorning with fur; *concr.* a lining or trimming of fur. Also *collect.* 2. The process of becoming furred or encrusted; furred state; also, a coating of fur 1601. 3. a. *Shipbuilding.* The action or process of double planking a ship's side; also, a piece of timber used for this 1622. b. *Building.* The nailing on of thin strips of board in order to level or raise a surface for lathing, boarding, etc. Also, the strips laid on. 1678. c. *Building.* 'A lining of scantling and plasterwork on a brick wall, to prevent the dampness of the latter reaching the room' (*Cassell*).

Furrow (fɒ·rou), *sb.* [Com. Teut.: OE. *furh* str. fem. :—OTeut. **furh-* :—pre-Teut. **pr̥k-*; cf. L. *porca* ridge between furrows.] 1. A narrow trench made in the earth with a plough, esp. for the reception of seed. Also *transf.* and *fig.* b. *poet.* Used *loosely* for ploughed land, the cornfields ME. 2. A trench, drain; *spec.* a water-furrow. 3. Anything resembling a furrow; e.g. a rut or track, a groove, indentation, or depression narrow in proportion to its length ME.; a deep wrinkle 1589; etc.

1. *fig.* When in thee times forrwes I behould SHAKS. b. What time the laboured ox In his loose traces from the f. came MILT. 3. They make..furrows in the cheeks of the sufferers HELPS.

Comb.: f.-board = MOULD-BOARD; **-weed,** a weed that grows on the furrow or ploughed land.

Hence **Fu·rrowy** *a.*, full of furrows or wrinkles.

Furrow (fɒ·rou), *v.* ME. [f. prec. sb.] 1. *trans.* To make furrows in with a plough; to plough; also *transf.* 2. To make furrow-like depressions, channels, or wrinkles in 1593. 3. *intr.* To make furrows or grooves; to make wrinkles 1576. b. quasi-*trans.*, as in to *f.* (*out, up*) *one's way* 1613.

1. *transf.* To f. large space of stormy seas SURREY. 2. Thou canst helpe time to f. me with age SHAKS. Fair cheeks were furrowed with hot tears BYRON.

Furry (fɒ̄·ri), *a.* 1674. [f. FUR *sb.* + -Y[1].] 1. Consisting of fur; composed of furs. 2. Covered with fur; wearing fur 1687. 3. Made of fur, lined or trimmed with fur. Also *transf.* and *fig.* 1691. 4. Resembling fur 1876. 5. Of the nature of, or coated with, fur or morbid matter 1739.

1. F. spoils of beasts POPE. 2. His [the Czar's] F. Troops 1717. 4. A sort of f. moss T. HARDY.

Furry (fɒ·ri), *sb. dial.* 1790. [? conn. w. FAIR *sb.*, L. *feria*.] A festival observed at Helston, Cornwall, on the eighth of May; also, a dance used on that occasion. (Also called *Flora*.) Also *attrib.*

Further (fɒ̄·ɹðəɹ), *a.* [OE. *furðra* :—OTeut. **furþeron-* wk., f. **furthero-* str. (the acc. neut. of which appears in FURTHER *adv.*) :—pre-Teut. *pr̥-tero-*, f. root of FORE *adv.* + compar. suffix as in *af-ter, o-ther*. Cf. FARTHER B.] †1. That is before another in position, order, or rank; front –1609. 2. More extended, going beyond; additional, more ME. 3. More distant, remoter, esp. the remoter of two. Of a horse: The off (side). 1578.

2. Without f. ambiguity 1634, Preface ADDISON. 3. They would..goe into a f. countrey 2 *Esdras* xiii. 41.

Further (fɒ̄·ɹðəɹ), *adv.* [OE. *furðor*; see FURTHER *a.* For the senses cf. FARTHER A.] 1. To or at a more advanced point: a. of space (*lit.* and *fig.*); b. of time ME. 2. To a greater extent, more OE. 3. In addition; moreover ME. 4. At a greater distance in space ME.

1. a. Hitherto shalt thou come, but no f. *Job* xxxviii. 11. Proverb, *To go f. and fare worse*. 2. Men who pretend to believe no f. than they can see BERKELEY. 4. Your best Friends shall wish I had beene f. SHAKS.

Further (fɒ̄·ɹðəɹ), *v.* [OE. *fyrðr(i)an*, f. *furðor*, -*ðra* FURTHER *adv.* and *adj.*] 1. *trans.* To help forward, assist (usu. things); to promote, favour. †2. To honour. ME. only. 3. *intr.* To go on, continue; to make progress. *Obs.* exc. *Sc.* ME. †4. *trans.* To put further, defer. WOLSEY.

1. Ire..furthereth all euyl 1477. To f. a general system of school training 1869. Hence **Furtherer,** a promoter; an aid.

Furtherance (fɒ̄·ɹðərăns). ME. [f. FURTHER *v.* + -ANCE.] The fact or state of being helped forward; the action of helping forward; advancement, aid. Also *concr.* a means or source of help.

The pompes of the funeralls are rather solaces to the liuing then furtherances to the dead HEALEY. Some few furtherances have been shown HELPS.

Furthermore (fɒ̄·ɹðəɹmōəɹ), *adv.* See also FARTHERMORE. ME. [f. FURTHER *adv.* + MORE *adv.*] †1. Still further; = FURTHER *adv.* 1 a. –1552. †2. = FURTHER *adv.* 2. –1450. 3. = FURTHER *adv.* 3. ME.

Furthermost (fɒ̄·ɹðəɹmoust), *a.* ME. [f. FURTHER *a.* + -MOST.] †1. Foremost, first. ME. only. 2. Most distant 1765.

Furthersome (fɒ̄·ɹðəɹsɒ̆m), *a.* 1626. [f. FURTHER *v.* or *adv.* + -SOME.] Adapted to further or help forward, advantageous, helpful. Const. *to*.

F. to the interests of the drama 1880.

Furthest (fɒ̄·ɹðĕst). ME. [formed as superl. to FURTHER.]

A. *adj.* 1. Most advanced in any direction. Also as superl. of FAR *a.* (now usu. repl. by FARTHEST): Most remote (*lit.* and *fig.*). 2. Most remote in time; †earliest; latest. *Obs.* exc. *absol.* in *at* (*the*) *f.* 1552.

1. The f. corner of Naboth's vineyard SWIFT.

B. *adv.* To or at the greatest distance, farthest ME.

Furtive (fɒ̄·ɹtiv), *a.* 1490. [a. F. *furtif*, -*ive*, ad. L. *furtivus*, f. *fur* thief; cf. *furtim* by stealth.] 1. Done by stealth; clandestine, surreptitious, secret. 2. Of a person, etc.: Stealthy, sly 1858. 3. Stolen; also, taken by stealth or secretly 1718. 4. Thievish 1816.

1. A f. glance W. IRVING. 2. That f. mien M. ARNOLD. 3. Columba's f. copy from St. Finnian's psalter 1894. 4. The f. Indian 1816. Hence **Fu·rtive-ly** *adv.*, **-ness.**

Furuncle (fiūə·rɒŋk'l). 1676. [ad. L. *furunculus*, orig. 'little thief', dim. of *fur*. Cf. F. *furoncle*.] A boil or inflammatory tumour. Hence **Furu·ncular, Furu·nculous** *adjs.* of, pertaining to, or characterized by boils.

Fury (fiūə·ri), *sb.* ME. [a. F. *furie*, ad. L. *furia*, related to *furere* to rage, be mad.] 1. Fierce passion, disorder or tumult of mind approaching madness; *esp.* wild anger, frenzied rage. Also, a fit of this. 2. Fierce impetuosity or violence. †Rarely, fierce cruelty. 1534. b. Hist. *The* (*Spanish*) *Fury*: the massacre perpetrated by the Spaniards at Antwerp in Oct.–Nov. 1576. 3. *transf.* (e.g. of a tempest, a wind, etc.) 1585. 4. Inspired frenzy; esp. poetic 'rage'. Now *rare*. 1546. 5. One of the avenging deities (L. *Furiæ, Diræ*, Gr. Ἐρινύες, Εὐμενίδες), sent from Tartarus to avenge wrong and punish crime: in later accounts, three in number (Tisiphone, Megæra, Alecto). Hence *gen.* An avenging or tormenting infernal spirit. ME. b. One of the three 'Fates' or *Parcæ*. MILT. *Lycidas* 75. 6. *transf.* One like an infernal spirit; *esp.* a ferociously angry or malignant woman ME.

1. Suche folk as falle in furye LYDG. The vnreasonable Furie of a beast SHAKS. 2. The furies of the Border war SCOTT. 3. The F. of the Heats 1698, of the Storm 1726. 4. Whatsoeuer they write, proceeds of a diuine f. SIDNEY. 5. The furies three with alle hir mortel brond CHAUCER. 6. Remember, sir, your f. of a wife DRYDEN.

†**Fu·ry,** *v.* [f. prec.] *refl.* To drive oneself to fury. FELTHAM. So **Fu·rying** *ppl. a.* raging. CLOUGH.

Furze (fɒ̄ɹz). [OE. *fyrs* str. masc.; no connexions are known.] 1. The pop. name of *Ulex europæus*, a spiny evergreen shrub with yellow flowers, growing abundantly on waste lands throughout Europe. Also named *gorse*, *whin*. Also *transf.* and *fig.* 2. In pop. names of other plants, as **Dwarf furze** (*Ulex nanus*); etc. 1578. 3. *attrib.*, *esp.* in *f.-bush*, also (*obs.* and *dial.*) **furzen bush**; also in pop. names of birds, as **furze-chat**, the whinchat (*Pratincola rubetra*); **-chucker**, the mountain finch or brambling; **-lark**, the tit-lark; **-wren** = FURZELING.

Hence **Fu·rzeling**, the Dartford Warbler (*Melizophilus undatus*).

Furzy (fɒ̄·ɹzi), *a.* 1613. [f. FURZE *sb.* + -Y[1].] 1. Composed of furze; overgrown with furze; of or pertaining to furze. 2. Fuzzy 1719.

‖**Fusain** (fü·zæ̃n). 1870. [F.; = 'Spindle-tree'.] A charcoal crayon made of the wood of the Spindle Tree; also *attrib.* as *f. drawing*. b. A drawing executed with this.

Fusarole (fiū·zărōul). 1664. [a. F. *fusarolle*, ad. It. *fusaruola*, f. (ult.) L. *fusus* spindle.] *Arch.* 'A member whose section is that of a semicircle carved into beads. It is generally placed under the echinus..in the Doric, Ionic, and Corinthian orders' (Gwilt.)

Fuscin (fʊ·sin). Also **-ine.** 1864. [f. L. *fusc-us* (see FUSCOUS) + -IN.] *Chem.* A dark-coloured substance obtained from various animal oils when they are decomposed by heat.

Fusco- (fʊ·sko), comb. f. L. *fuscus* 'dusky', as in **fusco-ferruginous** *a.* dull rust-coloured; etc.

Fuscous (fʊ·skəs), *a.* 1662. [f. L. *fuscus* dark, dusky + -OUS.] Of a dark or sombre hue; dusky, swarthy. (Chiefly *Nat. Hist.*)

Fuse, *sb.*^{1} 1611. [perh. ad. OF. *fuies, pl.* of *fuie* :—L. *fuga.*] The track of an animal. Also *fig.*

Fuse, fuze (fiūz), *sb.*^{2} 1644. [ad. It. *fuso* (:—L. *fusus*) spindle, hence applied to a spindle-shaped tube. Cf. FUSEE ^{2}.] **1.** A tube, casing, cord, etc., filled or saturated with combustible material, by means of which a military shell, the blast of a mine, etc. is ignited and exploded. **2.** *attrib.*, as *f.-hole*, etc. 1692.

†**Fuse, fuze,** *sb.*^{3} *rare.* 1674. [var. of FUSEE^2, assim. to prec.] = FUSEE ^{2} 2. –1701.

Fuse, *sb.*^{4} 1884. [f. FUSE *v.*^{1}] *Electr.* A wire or strip of fusible metal inserted in an electric circuit; it melts when the current increases beyond a certain safe strength.

Fuse (fiūz), *v.*^{1} 1681. [f. L. *fus-* ppl. stem of *fundere* to pour, melt, FOUND *v.*] **1.** *trans.* To make fluid by means of intense heat; to liquefy, melt. Also *transf.* **b.** *fig.* Often with the sense: To blend, unite into one whole, as by melting together 1817. **2.** *intr.* To become fluid or liquefied with heat; to melt; also *fig.* 1800. **b.** Of an electric light: To be extinguished owing to the melting of a fuse (*colloq.*) 1930. **3.** *Anat.* Of contiguous vessels, bones, etc.: To coalesce 1870.

Fuse, fuze, *v.*^{2} 1802. [f. FUSE *sb.*^{2}] To furnish with a fuse.

Fusee, fuzee ^{1} (fiuzī·). Now *Hist.* 1661. [a. F. *fusil* (pronounced fūzi).] = FUSIL ^{2} 2.

Fusee, fuzee ^{2} (fiuzī·). 1589. [a. F. *fusée* spindleful of tow (:—med.L. *fusata*, f. L. *fusus* spindle).] †**1.** A spindle-shaped figure. PUTTENHAM. **2.** A conical pulley or wheel, *esp.* the wheel of a watch or clock upon which the chain is wound and by which the power of the mainspring is equalized 1622. **3.** = FUSE *sb.*^{2} 1. 1704. **4.** *Farriery.* An exostosis upon one of the cannon-bones 1720. **5.** A kind of match with a large head of combustible material; a lucifer, vesuvian 1832.

Fusel (fiū·zĕl). 1850. [a. Ger. *fusel* bad spirits.] *attrib.* in *Fusel oil*, an acrid oily liquid accompanying various alcoholic liquids, and consisting of several alcohols, chiefly amyl alcohol, to which the name is esp. applied.

Fuselage (fiū·zelāʒ, -édʒ). 1909. [Fr., f. *fuseler* to make spindle-shaped.] The body of an aeroplane, containing the cockpit, engine, etc.: so called from its shape.

Fusible (fiū·zib'l), *a.* ME. [a. F., f. L. *fus-*: see FUSE *v.*^{1}] Capable of being fused.

The *fusible metal* consisting of 8 parts of bismuth, 5 of lead, and 3 of tin..melts at the heat of boiling water or 212° Fahr. URE. *Fusible plug*, one placed in the skin of a steam-boiler, so as to be melted and allow the discharge of the contents when a dangerous heat is reached. Hence **Fusibi·lity. Fu·sibleness.**

Fusiform (fiū·zifǭɹm), *a.* 1746. [f. L. *fusus* spindle + -(I)FORM.] Spindle-shaped; esp. in *Bot.*, *Entom.*, and *Zool.*

Root caulescent, f. 1805. Shell f., elongated WOODWARD.

Fusil ^{1} (fiū·zil). 1486. [ad. OF. *fu(i)sel* (mod. *fuseau*) :—pop. L. *fusellus*, dim. of *fusus* spindle.] *Her.* A bearing in the form of an elongated lozenge; orig. a representation of a spindle covered with tow.

Fusil ^{2} (fiū·zil). 1580. [a. F. :—late L. **focile*, f. *focus* hearth (in pop. L. fire).] †**1.** A fire steel for a tinder-box. HOLLYBAND. **2.** A light musket or firelock 1680.

Fusile (fiū·zil), *a.* Also **fusil.** ME. [ad. L. *fusilis*; see FUSE *v.*^{1} and -ILE.] **1.** Capable of being melted. Now *rare.* 1605. **2.** Running or flowing by the force of heat. Now *rare.* 1631. **3.** Formed by melting or casting. Also *fig.* ME.

2. And o'er the silver pours the fusil gold POPE. **3.** What else might be wrought Fusil or grav'n in mettle MILTON.

Fusilier (fiūzilīə·ɹ). 1680. [a. F., f. *fusil* FUSIL ^{2}.] Orig., a soldier armed with a fusil (see FUSIL ^{2} 2). The designation 'Fusiliers' is still retained by certain regiments in the British army which are distinguished from other regiments of the line only by some small peculiarities of costume. Also *attrib.*

Fusillade (fiūzilē·d), *sb.* Also **fusilade.** 1801. [a. F., f. *fusiller* to shoot, f. *fusil* FUSIL^2.] A simultaneous discharge of fire-arms; a wholesale execution by this means. Also *transf.* and *fig.* Hence **Fusilla·de** *v.* to assault (a place), to shoot down (persons) by a simultaneous discharge of fire-arms.

Fusing (fiū·ziŋ), *vbl. sb.* 1832. [f. FUSE *v.*^{2} + -ING ^{1}.] The action or process of fusing (see FUSE *v.*^{2}).

Phr. *Fusing point* or *temperature*, the point or temperature at which fusion takes place.

Fusion (fiū·ʒən). 1555. [ad. L. *fusionem*, f. *fundere*. Cf. FOISON and F. *fusion.*] **1.** The action or operation of fusing or rendering fluid by heat; the state of flowing or fluidity in consequence of heat. †**2.** *Path.* and *Phys.* Thinning, attenuation of the blood –1725. **3.** The union or blending together of different things as if by melting; the result or state of being so blended. Const. *into*, *with.* 1776. **b.** *Politics.* The coalition of parties 1845. Also *attrib.*

1. †*Watery f.*: the melting of certain crystals by heat in their own water of crystallization. **3.** Everything English is a f. of distinct and antagonistic elements EMERSON. **b.** The f. of parties [became] the babble of the clubs DISRAELI.

Fusionless: see FOISONLESS.

Fusk, *a. rare.* Also **fusc.** 1599. [ad. L. *fuscus.*] Dark brown, fuscous.

Fusoid (fiū·zoid), *a.* 1889. [f. L. *fusus* + -OID.] = FUSIFORM.

Fuss (fʊs), *sb.* 1701. [Perh. echoic.] **1.** A bustle or commotion out of proportion to the occasion; ostentatious or officious activity. **2.** A state of (more or less ludicrous) consternation or anxiety 1705. **3.** [f. the vb.] One who fusses 1875.

1. She got under weigh with very little f. R. H. DANA. **2.** Madame Legoux..has been in a fine f. about us 1813.

Fuss (fʊs), *v.* 1792. [f. prec. sb.] **1.** *intr.* To make a fuss; to be in a bustle; to busy oneself restlessly about trifles. Also *transf.* **2.** *trans.* To put into a fuss; to worry; to bother about trifles 1816.

Fussy (fʊ·si), *a.* 1831. [f. FUSS *sb.* + -Y ^{1}.] **1.** Fond of fuss; habitually busy about trifles. **2.** Of places: Full of bustle. *dial.* and *U.S.* 1848. **3.** Of dress, etc.: Full of petty details 1858.

1. No f. visiting of the poor JESSOP. *transf.* The f. little Conservancy tug 1895. Hence **Fu·ssily** *adv.* in a f. manner. **Fu·ssiness,** f. quality or habit.

†**Fust,** *sb.*^{1} 1481. [a. OF. *fust* (mod. *fût*); see FOIST *sb.*^{2}] **1.** A wine-cask –1601. **2.** A strong, musty smell 1755. **3.** *Arch.* The shaft of a column, or trunk of a pilaster –1819.

Fust, *sb.*^{2} Now *dial.* 1703. [var. of FIRST *sb.*] The ridge of the roof of a house.

Fust (fʊst), *v.* 1592. [f. FUST *sb.*^{1} 1, 2.] *intr.* To become mouldy or stale-smelling; *esp.* Of wine: To taste of the cask; also *fig.*

Fustanella (fʊstăne·lă). 1849. [a. It. lingua franca *fustanella* dim.: mod. Gr. φουστάνι, Albanian *fustan*, perh. a. It. *fustagno* FUSTIAN.] A stiff full petticoat of white cotton or linen worn by men in Modern Greece.

Fusteric (fʊ·stĕrik). 1860. [f. FUST-ET; after *turmeric.*] The colouring matter of fustet.

Fustet (fʊ·stĕt). 1821. [a. F. *fustet*, ad. Pr. *fustet* = Sp. *fustete*, an etymologizing corruption (as if dim. of Pr. *fust*, Sp. *fuste* stick) of the Arab. source of FUSTIC.] A small European shrub (*Rhus cotinus*), from which a yellow dye is extracted; called also *young fustic.*

Fustian (fʊ·stiăn). ME. [a. OF. *fustaigne*, *-aine* (mod. *futaine* fem.), repr. med.L. (*pannus*) *fustaneus*, (*tela*) *fustanea*; derived from *Fostat*, a suburb of Cairo, whence the stuff first came.]

A. *sb.* **1.** Formerly, a coarse cloth made of cotton and flax. Now, a thick, twilled, cotton cloth with a short pile or nap, usually dyed of a dark colour. †Also, a blanket of this material. **2.** *fig.* Inflated, turgid, or inappropriately lofty language; bombast, rant; in early use also †jargon, gibberish 1590.

2. With humble service, and such other f. 1651. Between f. in expression, and bathos in sentiment HAZLITT.

B. *adj.* **1.** [The sb. used attrib.] Made of fustian 1537. Also *fig.* **2.** Of language: Ridiculously lofty in expression; bombastic, inflated, pompous 1592. †Hence of a writer or speaker –1782. **3.** Worthless, sorry, pretentious 1523; †imaginary B. JONS.

2. Then comes he out..with his f. eloquence GREENE. **3.** Such a F. Rascall 2 *Hen. IV*, II. iv. 203. Hence **Fu·stianist,** one who writes f.

Fustic (fʊ·stik). 1545. [a. F. *fustoc*, a. Sp., a. Arab. *fustuq*, ad. Gr. πιστάκη PISTACHIO.] **1.** The name of two kinds of wood, both used for dyeing yellow. **a.** The wood of the Venetian sumach (*Rhus Cotinus*). Now only as *young* or *Zante f.* **b.** The wood of the *Cladrastis* (*Chlorophora*, *Maclura*) *tinctoria* of America and the West Indies. Occas. called *old f.* **2.** A yellow dye extracted from the wood of these trees 1858. **3.** *attrib.*, as *f.-tree*, *-wood* 1630.

Fustigate (fʊ·stigeˈt), *v.* Now *joc.* 1658. [f. L. *fustigat-*, *fustigare* to cudgel to death, f. *fustis* stick.] *trans.* To cudgel, beat. Hence **Fustiga·tion,** the action of cudgelling or beating. **Fustiga·tor.**

†**Fustila·rian.** (? *nonce-wd.*) [? Comic formation on next.] ? = next. 2 *Hen. IV*, II. i. 66 (Qo. 1600).

Fustilugs (fʊ·stilʊgz). 1607. [? f. FUSTY *a.* + LUG something heavy or slow.] A person, esp. a woman, of gross or corpulent habit; a fat, frowzy woman.

Fusty (fʊ·sti), *a.* ME. [f. FUST *sb.*^{1} 2.] **1.** Stale-smelling, musty; smelling of mould or damp. **2.** *fig.* That has lost its freshness and interest; fogyish 1606; †peevish PEPYS.

1. As good cracke a fustie nut with no kernell SHAKS. **2.** F. Latin and Greek 1842. Hence **Fu·stily** *adv.* **Fu·stiness.**

†**Fut,** *interj.* An exclamation of surprise. MARSTON. Also, variant of PHUT.

Futchel(l (fʊ·tʃĕl). 1794. [?] One of the pieces of timber carrying or supporting the shafts, or pole, or splinter-bar of a carriage.

Futhorc (fū·þɒɹk). Also **-ark, -ork.** 1851. [Named from the first six letters, *f*, *u*, *þ*, *o* or *a*, *r*, *k*.] The Runic alphabet.

Futile (fiū·təll, -il), *a.* 1555. [a. F., or ad. L. *futilis* (for **fudtilis*), f. *fud-* stem of *fundere* to pour out.] **1.** Incapable of producing any result; useless, ineffectual, vain. **2.** Addicted to trifling; lacking in purpose. ? *Obs.* 1736. †**3.** Unable to hold one's tongue, loquacious. [From the etymological sense, 'leaky'.] BACON.

1. As f. in its effects, as it is feeble in its principle BURKE. **2.** 'Davy..'tis a f. fellow' BOSWELL. **3.** Talkers and F. Persons BACON. Hence **Fu·tile·ly** *adv.*, **-ness.** var. †**Futi·litous** *a.* [irreg. f. FUTILITY + -OUS]. STERNE.

Futility (fiuti·lĭti). 1623. [ad. F. *futilité*; see FUTILE and -ITY.] **1.** The quality of being futile; want of weight or importance; ineffectiveness, uselessness. **2.** Lack of purpose, frivolousness 1692. †**3.** Loquacity, inability to hold one's tongue –1692. **4.** Something that is futile 1667.

1. The f. of a reply 1777, of contending against the most rooted of prejudices M. ARNOLD. **4.** His mouth full of loud futilities CARLYLE. Hence **Futilita·rian** *a.* devoted to f.; *sb.* one who is devoted to f. (A humorous coinage.) SOUTHEY.

†**Fu·tilous.** 1607. [irreg. f. L. *futi-* FUTILE + -OUS.] = FUTILE. –1703.

Futtock (fʊ·tək). 1611. [prob. a pronunciation of *foot-hook.*] **1.** One of the middle timbers of the frame of a ship, between the floor and the top timbers.

Comb.: **f.-hoop,** a hoop encircling the mast at a point below the head, and serving for the attachment of the shackles of the f.-shrouds; **-plate,** one of the iron plates crossing the sides of the top-rim perpendicularly, to which the f.-shrouds are secured; **-shroud,** one of the small shrouds which secure the lower dead-eyes and f.-plates of topmast rigging to a band round a lower mast.

†**Fu·turable,** *a.* [f. FUTURE + -ABLE.] That may happen in the future. FULLER.

Future (fiū·tiŭı, fiū·tʃəı). ME. [a. OF. and F. *futur, future,* ad. L. *futurus,* fut. pple. of *esse,* f. stem *fu-* (see BE).]

A. *adj.* 1. That is to be, or will be, hereafter. Often qualifying a sb., with sense: The person or thing that is to be (what the sb. denotes). Also *absol.* or *ellipt.*; esp. in phr. *in future.* 2. Of or pertaining to time to come; esp. in *Gram.* of a tense: Relating to time to come; describing an event yet to happen. Also *ellipt.* (= *future tense*) 1530. ¶ 3. Loosely used for: Subsequent 1600.

1. I wish I were the f. Lady Vargrave LYTTON. Phr. *A f. state, life*: existence after death.

B. *sb.* †1. *pl.* Future events -1654. 2. *The future.* a. Time to come ME. b. What will happen in the future 1607. 3. a. A condition in time to come different from the present 1852. b. The prospective condition (of a person, country, etc.) 1858. 4. *Gram.* = *future tense*: see A. 2. 1881. 5. One's betrothed 1827. 6. *Comm.* in *pl.* Goods and stocks sold for future delivery. Also contracts to sell or buy on these terms. 1880.

2. b. The f. comes apace *Timon* II. i. 157. 6. American futures in better demand 1880.

Hence †**Fu·ture** *v.* to make f., put off to a f. day. **Fu·tureless** *a.* without a f. †**Fu·turely** *adv.* in f., at a f. time, hereafter. Also *loosely,* thereafter.

Futurism (fiū·tiŭriz'm, -tʃər-). 1909. [cf. It. *futurismo,* F. *futurisme.*] A movement in art, literature, etc., orig. in Italy, marked by violent departure from traditional forms and by the use of arbitrary symbols in the expression of emotion. So **Fu·turist** [cf. It. *futuristo,* F. *futuriste*]. a. *Theol.* one who believes that the Scripture prophecies are still to be fulfilled in the future; b. an adherent of futurism; also *attrib.* Hence **Futuri·stic** *a.*

Futurition (fiūtiuri·ʃən). 1641. [ad. med.L. *futuritionem,* irreg. f. *futurus* FUTURE.] *Philos.* 1. Existence or occurrence in the future. Now *rare.* b. A future event or existence 1668. 2. The quality or fact of being future; the fact that (something specified) will be 1666.

1. The f. of salvation PEARSON. b. Some mere f., as metaphysicians love to speak, some event in futurity 1840. So **Futuri·tial** *a.* relating to what is to come. (Dicts.)

Futurity (fiutiū°·rīti). 1604. [f. FUTURE + -ITY.] 1. = FUTURITION 2. *rare.* 1637. 2. Future time 1604. 3. Future condition; also, existence after death 1651.

2. Purpos'd merit in f. *Oth.* III. iv. 117. Futurity's blank page S. ROGERS. 3. A secret dread of f. BERKELEY. The f. of representative governments MILL.

Fuzil: see FUSIL.

Fuzz (fɒz), *sb.*¹ 1601. [Cf. FOZY.] 1. Loose volatile matter 1674. †2. = FUZZ-BALL. -1702. 3. *Photogr.* = FUZZINESS. 1889. *Comb.* f.-wig, a wig of crisp curls.

†**Fuzz,** *sb.*² [Cf. FUZZ *v.*¹] A fuddled or muddled state. SWIFT.

†**Fuzz,** *v.*¹ [Perh. conn. w. next through the notion of blurring or confusing.] *trans.* To make drunk, fuddle. WOOD.

Fuzz (fɒz), *v.*² 1702. [f. FUZZ *sb.*¹] 1. *intr.* To fly out in light particles. 2. *trans.* To cover with fine particles 1851.

Fuzz-ball (fɒ·zbǫl). 1597. [f. FUZZ *sb.*¹ + BALL.] A pop. name of the fungus *Lycoperdon Bovista,* puff-ball. Also *transf.* and *fig.*

†**Fuzzle** (fɒ·z'l), *v.* 1621. [Cf. FUZZ *v.*¹, FUDDLE.] *trans.* To make drunk, confuse, muddle; = FUZZ *v.*¹ -1632.

Fuzzy (fɒ·zi), *a.* 1616. [f. FUZZ *sb.*¹ + -Y¹. Cf. FOZY.] 1. Not firm or sound in substance; spongy. 2. Frayed into loose fibres; covered with fuzz; fluffy 1713. 3. Blurred 1778. 4. Of hair; Frizzy, fluffy 1825.

1. A f. sort of Earth, that we call Moss 1725. 3. It makes the picture more f. 1871. *Comb.* f.-wuzzy a nickname for the Soudanese warrior, from his method of dressing his hair. **Fu·zzily** *adv.* **Fu·zziness.**

Fy, obs. f. FIE. **Fy-**: see also FI-.

-fy, *suffix,* forming *verbs.* The older Eng. vbs. in *-fy* are adoptions from Fr. vbs. in *-fier* (:—L. *-ficare*). In med.L. *-ficare* was often substituted for *-facere* in L. vbs. so ending, and hence Fr. and Eng. vbs. in *-fier, -fy* sometimes correspond to L. vbs. in *-facere*; e.g. F. *liquéfier* liquefy, etc. Exc. in the case of these vbs. the ending has normally the form *-ify* (see -FIC).

Fyke (fəik). *U.S.* 1860. [a. Du. *fuik.*] A bag-net used for catching fish, esp. shad; called also *f.-net.*

Fylfot (fi·lfǫt). 1500. [Perh. simply *fill-foot,* a pattern for filling the foot of a painted window.] A name for the figure called also a cross cramponnee (see CRAMPONNEE), and identified with the SWASTIKA of India, the *gammadion* of Byzantine ornament. Also *f. cross.*

Fyrd (fə̄rd, fi°ıd). 1832. [OE. *fyrd*; see FERD.] The military array of the whole country before the Conquest; also the obligation to military service.

Fytte: see FIT *sb.*¹ *Obs.*

G

G (dʒī), the seventh letter of the Roman alphabet, was orig. a differentiated form of C, q. v. In Latin G represented the voiced guttural stop; but in the later period of the language it was probably pronounced before front vowels as a palatal.

In OE. the letter stood for four different sounds, viz. the voiced guttural and palatal stop (g, *g*), and the voiced guttural and palatal spirant (ʒ, *ʒ*). In early ME. the palatal stop developed into the complex sound (dʒ).

The form ȝ, here employed for ME. words, was commonly used in ME. for the sound of (y) initial and final, for the guttural and palatal unvoiced spirant final or before *t* (as in *inouȝ, auȝt, niȝt*), and, so long as the sound was in use, for the guttural voiced spirant. From the 13th c., however, the ȝ was by some scribes wholly or partly discarded for *y* or *gh*; a few texts have *yh.*

See also KEY TO THE PRONUNCIATION.

II. 1. G, g, *g* is used to denote anything occupying the seventh place in a series. 2. *Mus.* G is the name of the 5th note of the diatonic scale of C major; called *sol* in France and Italy. Also the scale or key which has that note for its tonic. *G clef*: the treble clef (see CLEF¹) placed on the line in the stave appropriated to the note G.

III. *Abbreviations.* 1. In *Physics* g is the symbol for acceleration by gravity = about 32 ft. per second. 2. *Math.* G.C.F. or G.C.M. = Greatest Common Factor or Measure. 3. In *Freemasonry,* G.M. = Grand Master. 4. G.B.E. = (Knight, or Dame) Grand (Cross of the Order of the) British Empire.

Gab (gæb), *sb.*¹ ME. [a. OF. *gab, gabe,* mockery; cf. It. *gabbo* jest, and ON. *gabb* mockery. See GAB *v.*¹] †1. Mockery, deception; a deceit. ME. only. 2. A piece of brag; a gasconade 1737.

Gab (gæb), *sb.*² *colloq.* or *vulgar.* 1681. [See GAB *v.*²] The action of gabbing; conversation, prattle, twaddle 1790.

Phr. *The gift of the g.*: a turn for speaking.

Gab, *sb.*³ *Sc.* 1724. Var. of GOB *sb.*²

Gab (gæb), *sb.*⁴ 1792. [Cf. Flem. *gabbe* notch, gash.] A hook, or open notch, in a rod or lever, which drops over a spindle, and forms a temporary connexion between valve or other motions. *Comb.* **g.-lever,** the lever which forms the connexion between the slide valve spindle and the eccentric rod in some forms of marine engine valve; also *gen.*

Gab (gæb), *v.*¹ ME. [app. a. OF. *gab-(b)er* to mock. Cf. GAB *sb.*¹] †1. *intr.* To speak mockingly -1573. †2. To tell lies -1475; †also (*trans.*) to deceive -1460. 3. *intr.* To brag (quasi-*arch.* and *Hist.*) 1825.

3. [He] gabbed; and his boast was [etc.] WRIGHT.

Gab (gæb), *v.*² 1786. [app. onomatopœic; cf. GABBLE.] *intr.* To talk much or glibly.

†**Gab,** *v.*³ [Cf. dial. *gobber-tooth*; also GAG-TOOTH.] *intr.* Of teeth: To project. HOLLAND.

Gabardine (gæbăıdīn). 1904. [Var. GABERDINE, q.v.] A dress material of cotton or silk with a wool lining.

Gabber (gæ·bəı), *sb.*¹ ME. [f. GAB *v.*¹ + -ER¹.] †1. A mocker; a deceiver -1450. 2. A vaunter 1869.

Gabber (gæ·bəı), *sb.*² 1793. [f. GAB *v.*² + -ER¹.] A chatterer.

†**Ga·bber,** *v.* 1706. [Cf. JABBER, GIBBER, GAB *sb.*² and *v.*²] *trans.* To talk volubly, to jabber -1808. Hence **Ga·bber** *sb.* jabber.

Gabble (gæ·b'l), *sb.* 1601. [f. the vb.] 1. Voluble, noisy, incoherent talk 1602. 2. Inarticulate noises made by animals.

1. MILT. *P. L.* XII. 56. 2. Choughs language, g. enough, and good enough *All's Well* IV. i. 22.

Gabble (gæ·b'l), *v.* 1577. [onomatopœic; cf. GABBER.] 1. *intr.* To talk volubly, inarticulately and incoherently; to chatter, jabber, prattle. 2. *trans.* To utter rapidly and unintelligibly 1758. 3. Of geese, etc.: To GAGGLE 1697.

1. To g. like Tinkers SHAKS. 3. I..g. like a Goose, amidst the Swan-like Quire DRYDEN. Hence **Ga·bblement. Ga·bbler,** one who gabbles.

Gabbro (gæ·brο). 1837. [a. It.] *Geol.* A name given by Italian artists to a rock essentially composed of felspar and diallage. Hence **Gabbro·ic** *a.*

Gabelle (gabe·l). Also †**gabel(l,** †**gable.** ME. [a. F. *gabelle,* ad. med.L. *gabella,* a deriv. from *gablum, gabulum,* a tax, impost; see GAVEL.] 1. A tax; *spec.* the salt-tax imposed in France before the Revolution. 2. *attrib.* as *g.-man,* etc. 1650.

The thre estates ordenid..that the gabell of salt shulde ron through the realme LD. BERNERS. Hence **Ga·belled** *ppl. a.* liable to a tax. †**Gabe·ller,** a tax-gatherer.

Gaberdine (gæ·bəıdīn). 1520. [orig. *gawbardyne,* a. OF. *gauvardine, galvardine, gallevardine,* perh. a deriv. of MHG. *wallevart* pilgrimage; hence Sp. *gabardina.*] 1. A loose upper garment or frock of coarse material, worn formerly by Jews, almsmen, and beggars. 2. *trans.* and *fig.* Dress, covering; also (see *Temp.* II. ii. 40), protection 1594.

1. You..spet vpon my Iewish g. *Merch. V.* I. iii. 113.

Gaberlunzie (gæ:bəılɒ·nzi, -yi). *Sc.* 1508. [Of unkn. origin; *-lunzie* = *-lunyie,* which would be pronounced (-lü·nyi).] A strolling beggar. Also, a BEADSMAN.

Barking at a g. SCOTT.

Gabion (gē^i·biən). 1579. [a. F., ad. It. *gabbione,* augm. of *gabbia* cage:—L. *cavea.* See CAGE.] 1. A wicker basket, of cylindrical form, usually open at both ends, to be filled with earth, for use in fortification and engineering. ¶ 2. Used *fig.* by Scott for a curiosity of small value 1832. 3. *attrib.* 1633.

Gabionade (gē^i·bionē^i·d). Also †**gabionnade.** 1706. [ad. F. *gabionnade*; see prec. and -ADE.] A work formed of gabions.

Gabionage (gē^i·bionēdʒ). 1864. [see GABION and -AGE.] Gabions collectively.

Gabioned (gē^i·biənd), *ppl. a.* 1589. [f. GABION + -ED².] Having gabions; protected with or as with gabions.

Gable (gē^i·b'l), *sb.*¹ ME. [a. OF. *gable, jable,* prob. a. ON. *gafl,* of the same meaning.] 1. The vertical triangular piece of wall at the end of a ridged roof, from the level of the eaves to the summit. b. Any architectural member having the form of a gable 1850. 2. The triangular-topped end wall of a building; a gable-end ME. 4. *attrib.* ME.

Comb.: *g.-roof* (hence *-roofed* adj.), *-wall*; **g.-window,** a window in the gable or gable-end of a building.

†**Ga·ble,** *sb.*² ME. Var. of CABLE *sb.*, frequent in the 15–16th c. Also *fig.* Also *attrib.* -1615.

Gable (gē^i·b'l), *v.* 1848. [f. GABLE *sb.*¹] *trans.* To make (a roof) end in a gable; *intr.* to form gables.

Gabled (gē^i·b'ld), *ppl. a.* 1849. [f. GABLE *sb.*¹ or *v.*] Furnished with a gable or gables.

Ga·ble-e·nd. ME. 1. An end-wall that is surmounted by a gable. †2. = GABLE *sb.*¹ 1, 1 b. -1703.

Gablet (gē^i·blėt). ME. [a. AF. *gablet*: see GABLE *sb.*¹ and -ET.] A little gable, esp. one constructed as an ornament over a tabernacle, niche, buttress, etc.

Gablock (gæ·blǫk). Now *dial.* 1688. [var. of GAVELOCK.] †1. An artificial metallic spur for a fighting cock (Dicts.). 2. *dial.* An iron crowbar 1746.

Gaby (gē·bi; *dial.* gǭ·bi). *colloq.* and *dial.* 1796. [?] A simpleton.

Gad (gæd), *sb.*[1] ME. [a. ON. *gaddr* spike, nail:—OTeut. **gazdo-z* (cf. L. *hasta*). Influenced by OE. *gād* GOAD.] 1. A sharp spike of metal. Now *Hist.* †b. Applied to a stylus –1588. 2. A bar of metal; also, an ingot. ? *Obs.* ME. b. *Mining.* A pointed tool of iron or steel; e.g. a wedge, or a small iron punch with a wooden handle 1671. 3. A spear. *Hist.* 1548. 4. A goad ME. 5. *dial.* A rod or wand, esp. a fishing rod. Also, a stake. 1535. 6. A measuring rod for land; hence, a measure of length ME. b. A division of an open pasture; = SWATH. 1593.

1. b. I will goe get a leafe of brasse, And with a G. of steele will write these words SHAKS. 2. Flemish-steel is made—some in Bars and some in Gads MOXON. 4. Phr. †*Upon the g.*: as if pricked with a g.; suddenly. *Lear* I. ii. 26.

Gad (gæd), *sb.*[2] 1815. [f. GAD *v.*[2]] The action of gadding. Only in phr. *On, upon the g.*

Gad (gæd), *sb.*[3] 1728. [a. Ir. and Gael. *gad.*] *Mil.*, etc. A band or rope made of twisted fibres of rough twigs.

Gad (gæd), *sb.*[4] Now *arch.* 1611. [Minced pronunc. of GOD. Cf. EGAD.] 1. Substituted for *God*; esp. in *By Gad!* 2. quasi-interj. (? 'by' omitted) 1608. 3. In *Gadswoons, Gadzooks*, etc. 1695.

1. Phr. *Gads me, Gads my life*: ? God save me, my life. 2. G., that's exceeding foolish DRYDEN.

Gad (gæd), *v.*[1] 18.. [f. GAD *sb.*[1]] a. *trans.* To furnish with a gad or gads. b. (*Mining.*) *intr.* To use a gad; *trans.* to break up (rock) by means of a gad. c. *trans.* To fasten with a gad-nail.

Gad (gæd), *v.*[2] 1460. [? from GADLING[2].] 1. *intr.* To go from one place to another, to wander about; †*rarely*, to rush madly about. 2. *fig.* To go wandering, in desire or thought. Now *rare.* 1579. 3. Of a plant, tree, etc.: To straggle in growth (*arch.*) 1637.

1. He was alwayes gadding up and downe the world CAMDEN. 2. Yet, idle eye, wilt thou be gadding still HEYWOOD. 3. Wild thyme and the gadding vine MILT. Hence **Ga·ddingly** *adv.*

Gadabout (gæ·dăbaut). 1817. [f. prec. + ABOUT.]

A. *adj.* Given to gadding, wandering.
B. *sb.* One who gads about 1837.

Ga·d-bee:. 1530. [f. GAD *sb.*[1]] = GADFLY 1.

Gadder[1] (gæ·dəɹ). 1887. [f. GAD *v.*[1] + -ER[1].] An instrument for splitting rock.

Gadder[2] (gæ·dəɹ). 1550. [f. GAD *v.*[2] + -ER[1].] One who gads.

Gadding (gæ·diŋ), *vbl. sb.* 1753. [f. GAD *v.*[1] + -ING[1].] The action or process of splitting rock with gads.

Comb. g.-car (*Quarrying*), one which carries a drilling machine so arranged as to drill a series of holes in line.

Gade (gēⁱd). 1836. [ad. mod.L. *gadus*, ad. Gr. γάδος codfish.] A fish of the genus *Gadus*; a codfish.

Gadean (gē·diăn). 1854. [f. mod.L. *gadus* (see prec.) + -(E)AN.] A fish of the family *Gadidæ*, of which the typical genus is *Gadus* (cod).

Gader, obs. f. GATHER.

Ga·d-fly:. 1591. [f. GAD *sb.*[1]] 1. The pop. name of a fly which bites and goads cattle, *esp.* a fly of the genus *Tabanus* or of the genus *Œstrus*; a bot-fly, breeze 1626. 2. *fig.* One who torments or worries another. Also (after L. *æstrus*), an irresistible impulse. 1649.

Gadget (gæ·dʒĕt). *colloq.* 1886. [Origin obsc.; orig. in nautical use.] A small tool or piece of mechanism. b. *gen.* An accessory or adjunct, esp. of a trivial character 1915.

Gadhelic (gădeˑlik), *a.* and *sb.* Cf. GOIDELIC. 1796. [Literary formation from Ir. *Gaedheal*, OIr. *Gáidel, Góidel*, the original form of GAEL.] Pertaining to the Gaels (in the widest sense).

Gadid (gē·did). 1889. [f. mod.L. *gadus* cod + -ID.] = GADOID *sb.* So **Ga·dine.**

Gadinic (gădi·nik), *a.* 1864. [f. as prec. + -INE + -IC.] *Chem.* In *Gadinic acid*: a crystalline fatty acid, obtained from cod-liver oil.

†**Gaditan.** 1607. [ad. L. *Gaditanus*, f. *Gades* Cadiz.]

A. *adj.* Of or belonging to Cadiz –1626.
B. *sb. pl.* The inhabitants of Cadiz. var. **Gadita·nian** *a.* and *sb.*

Gadite (gē·dəit), *a.* [f. L. *Gades* + -ITE.] Belonging to Cadiz. SCOTT.

Gadling[1] (gæ·dliŋ). 1592. [f. GAD *sb.*[1] + -LING.] One of the metal spikes on the knuckles of a gauntlet.

†**Gadling**[2]. [OE. *gædeling*:—OTeut. **gaduliŋgo-z*, f. root **gad-* (in OE. *gæd* fellowship) + -LING.] 1. Orig., a companion or fellow –ME. 2. In bad sense: A 'fellow' ME. 3. A vagabond –1565. 4. Hence *attrib.* (in sense of 'wandering'); also as *vbl. sb.* 1594.

†**Gadman.** Chiefly *Sc.* 1450. [f. GAD *sb.*[1]] A goadsman –1827.

Gadoid (gē·doid). 1842. [f. mod.L. *gadus* cod + -OID.] A. *sb.* A fish of the family *Gadidæ*, of which the cod is the type. B. *adj.* Of, belonging to, or resembling the *Gadidæ*.

Gadolinite (gæ·dǒlinəit). 1802. [Named from *Gadolin*, a mineralogist; see -ITE.] *Min.* Silicate of yttrium, found in black crystals. So **Gadoli·nic** *a.* derived from g.

Gadroon (gădrū·n). Also in mod. Dicts. *godroon.* 1723. [ad. F. *godron* (OF. *goderon, gauderon*), of unkn. origin.] One of a set of convex curves or arcs joined at their extremities to form a decorative pattern used in ornamenting plate, in architecture, costume, etc. Chiefly in *pl.* Also *attrib.* Hence **Gadroo·ned, godrooned** *ppl. a.* ornamented with gadroons.

Gadso (gæ·dsō), *interj.* 1687. [var. of CATSO, infl. by GAD.] An exclam. of asseveration.

Gaduin (gæ·diuin). 1861. [irreg. f. mod.L. *gadus* cod + -IN.] A fatty substance found in cod-liver oil.

Gadwall (gæ·dwǭl). 1666. A freshwater duck, *Anas strepera* or *Chaulelasmus streperus*, of the north of Europe and America; the grey duck or grey.

†**Gaedelian**, *a. rare.* [f. OIr. *Gaedel* + -IAN; see GAELIC.] Belonging to the Gaelic branch of the Celtic race. MORSE.

Gael (gēⁱl). 1810. [a. Sc. Gael. *Gaidheal*, a member of the Gaelic race = OIr. *Gaidel, Goidel.*] A Scottish Highlander or Celt; also, in more recent use, an Irish Celt.

Gaelic (gēⁱ·lik). 1774. [f. GAEL + -IC.]

A. *adj.* Of or pertaining to the Gaels or Celtic Highlanders of Scotland; occas. in wider sense, including the Irish and Manx.
B. *sb.* The Gaelic language 1775.

Gaff (gæf), *sb.*[1] ME. [a. F. *gaffe* boathook.] 1. a. An iron hook; a staff armed with this. Now *dial.* b. *spec.* A barbed fishing spear; also, a stick with an iron hook for landing salmon, etc. 1656. 2. *Naut.* 'A spar used in ships to extend the heads of fore-and-aft sails which are not set on stays' (Adm. Smyth) 1769. 3. a. = GABLOCK 1. 1688. b. The spike of a spur 1808.

Gaff (gæf), *sb.*[2] *slang.* 1812. [Cf. GAB *sb.*[1]] 1. Stuff and nonsense 1877. 2. In phr. *To blow the g.*: (*fig.*) to reveal a secret or a plot.

Gaff (gæf), *sb.*[3] *slang.* 1753. [?] 1. A fair. 2. Any public place of amusement. Hence, a low-class theatre or music hall. Also *penny-gaff.*

Gaff (gæf), *v.*[1] 1837. [f. GAFF *sb.*[1]] To strike or to draw *out* with a gaff.

Gaff (gæf), *v.*[2] *slang* and *colonial.* 1812. *intr.* To gamble; *esp.* to toss up.

Gaffe (gæf). 1909. Also **gaff.** [Fr.] A blunder, an indiscreet act or remark, a 'faux pas'.

Gaffer (gæ·fəɹ). 1575. [contr. f. *grandfather.*] 1. A term of respect prefixed to a proper name, the designation of a calling, office, etc. In 17–18th c. = GOODMAN. b. = *My good fellow* 1590. 2. An elderly rustic. Also, a fellow. 1589. 3. A master. Now *dial.* 1659. b. A foreman; a headman 1841.

1. G. Bishops 1635, Phoebus 1651, Homer 1806, Glover SCOTT. b. I pray your blessing, g. 1628. 2. Go to each g. and each goody 17..

†**Ga·ffle.** 1497. [prob. a. Du. *gaffel* = OE. *geafol* fork; see GABLE.] 1. A steel lever for bending the cross-bow –1672. 2. A steel spur for fighting cocks 1755.

Gaff-topsail. 1794. 1. 'A light triangular or quadrilateral sail, the head being extended on a small gaff which hoists on the topmast, and the foot on the lower gaff' (Smyth). Also *attrib.* 2. *U.S.* 'A kind of sea-catfish, *Ælurichthys marinus*' (Cent. Dict.).

Gag (gæg), *sb.*[1] 1553. [app. f. GAG *v.*[1]] 1. Something thrust into the mouth to keep it open and prevent speech or outcry. b. *fig.* (Now often applied to the 'closure' in parliamentary proceedings.) 1623. c. *School slang.* (See quot.) 1820. 2. *Theatr.* Matter interpolated in a written piece by the actor 1847.

1. c. The repugnance of the school to gags, or the fat of fresh beef boiled LAMB. 2. The performance consisted of all g. MAYHEW.

Comb.: **g.-bit**, a powerful bit, used for breaking horses, etc.; **-law** (*U.S.*), 'a law or regulation made or enforced for the purpose of preventing or restricting discussion (*Cent. Dict.*); **-rein** (*Saddlery*), a rein passing through a g.-runner, so as to draw the bit upward in the horse's mouth; **-runner**, a loop depending from the throat-latch, through which the g.-rein passes to the bit.

Gag (gæg), *sb.*[2] *slang.* 1805. [?fig. uses of prec.; or ? onomatopœic.] A made-up story; an imposture, a lie. b. *U.S.* A laughing-stock 1840.

Gag (gæg), *v.*[1] ME. [app. imitative of the sound made in choking.] †1. *trans.* To strangle. ME. only. b. *intr.* To choke (*lit.* and *fig.*). Also, to retch. Also *trans.* (*causatively*). Now *dial.* 1707. 2. *trans.* To stop up the mouth of (a person) with a gag in order to prevent speech or outcry; *spec.* in *Surg.* 1509. b. *transf.* and *fig.*, esp. to deprive of power or freedom of speech 1601. 3. To apply a gag-bit to (a horse); to obstruct the working of (a valve); to stop up the valves of (an engine) 1833. 4. *Theatr. intr.* To introduce gag into a piece 1852; *trans.* to fill *up* with gag 1861.

2. G. him, we may haue his silence B. JONS. b. The time was not yet come when eloquence was to be gagged, and reason to be hoodwinked MACAULAY.

Gag, *v.*[2] 1570. [? onomatopœic.] †1. *trans.* To jerk. Also, to toss *up* (the head). –1617. †2. *intr.* To make thrusts or pricks (*at*) 1622; *trans.* ? to prick 1570. 3. *intr.* To stick out. [Cf. GAG-TOOTH.] 1599.

Gag (gæg), *v.*[3] *slang.* 1777. [See GAG *sb.*[2]] *trans.* To impose upon (a person), to 'stuff'; *intr.* to practise imposture.

†**Gagate.** OE. [ad. L. *gagates*, Gr. γαγάτης, from *Gagæ* and *Gages* a town and river in Lycia. Hence (through OF.) JET.] 1. Jet –1708. 2. Occas. used for AGATE (*Achates*). FULLER.

Gage (gēⁱdʒ), *sb.*[1] ME. [a. OF. *g(u)age* (mod. *gage*):—Rom. **gwadjo*, a. Teut. **wadjo*m; see WED, and WAGE.] 1. Something deposited to ensure the performance of some action, and liable to forfeiture in case of non-performance; a pawn, pledge 1457. 2. *spec.* A pledge (usu. a glove thrown down) of a person's appearance to do battle in support of his assertions. Hence, a challenge. Also *g. of battle.* ME.

1. He also left Philip..for the g. of his promises to Pelopidas RALEIGH. 2. Caste downe your g. in that quarrell, and ye shall fynde him that shall take it vp 1523.

Gage, *sb.*[2] *slang.* ME. [? f. prec., or ? var. of GAUGE, a measure.] A quart pot; a quart pot full.

Gage (gēⁱdʒ), *sb.*[3] = GREENGAGE.

Gage (gēⁱdʒ), *v.* 1489. [ad. F. *gager*, or aphet. f. ENGAGE.] †1. *trans.* = ENGAGE *v.* 1. –1592. 2. To stake, wager; to risk or bet. *Obs.* or *arch.* 1599. Also *fig.* to pledge 1529. †3. To bind as by a formal promise –1606. 4. *intr.* for *refl.* To assert on one's own responsibility *that* 1811. †5. *trans.* To fix *in* or *upon.* MOXON. †6. To bind or entangle *in* 1596.

1. Phr. †*To g. battle*: to pledge oneself to judicial combat. 2. Against the which a Moity competent

Was gaged by our King *Haml.* I. i. 91. *fig.* To all which pointes I g. myne honour and faith ESSEX. 6. The great debts wherein my time something too prodigall Hath left me gag'd *Merch. V.* I. i. 130.

Gage, Gager, obs. ff. GAUGE, GAUGER.

Gagger [1] (gæ·gəɹ). 1621. [f. GAG *v.*[1] + -ER [1].] One who gags (see GAG *v.*[1]).

Ga·gger, *v.*[2] 1858. [? f. GAG *v.*[2] + -ER [1].] 'A lifter used by the founder, consisting of a light T-shaped piece of iron' (Simmonds).

Ga·gger. *slang.* 1781. [f. GAG *v.*[3] + -ER [1].] One who gags, cheats, or hoaxes.

Gaggle (gæ·g'l), *sb.* 1470. [f. the vb.] 1. A flock (of geese); also, a company (of women). 2. Chatter, gabble 1668.

Gaggle (gæ·g'l), *v.* ME. [Prob. f. the syllable *gag* (*gag-gag*), often used to imitate the cry of the goose. Cf. GABBLE, CACKLE.] 1. *intr.* Of geese: To cackle. †2. *transf.* and *fig.* To make a noise like geese; to gabble, chatter –1706. †3. *trans.* To express with gaggling or chattering; to babble. Also with *out.* –1650.

†**Gag-tooth.** 1585. [Cf. GAG *v.*[2] 3.] A projecting or prominent tooth –1680. Hence **Gag-toothed** *a.*

Gahnite (gā·nəit). 1808. [f. *Gahn*, a Swedish chemist + -ITE.] *Min.* An oxide of zinc and alumina, or zinc aluminate occurring in octahedrons; called also *zinc-spinel.*

Gaiety (gē̆·ĕti). Also, now *U.S.*, **gayety.** 1634. [ad. F. *gaieté, gaîté,* f. *gai* GAY.] 1. The quality or condition of being gay; cheerfulness, mirth 1647; †levity CLARENDON. 2. Merrymaking, festivity; a festive occasion; freq. in *pl.* 1634. 3. Bright appearance; showiness; showy dress; occas. *pl.* 1657.

1. Health and gayety of heart COWPER. 2. The gaieties of Paris 1791. 3. To lay aside all g. in dress 1866.

Gail(e, Gailer, -or, obs. ff. GAOL, GAOLER.

Gaillard, Gaillard-: see GALLI-.

‖**Gaillardia** (gēlā·ɹdiă). 1888. [mod.L.; after M. *Gaillard*, an amateur botanist.] *Bot.* A genus of composite plants, producing showy flowers, for the most part red with a border of yellow.

Gaily, gayly (gē·li), *adv.* ME. [f. GAY *a.* + -LY [2]. Usually spelt *gaily*; cf. *daily.*] In a gay manner. 1. Brightly, showily, smartly. 2. Cheerfully, joyously, festively; airily, jauntily ME.

1. Like some fair flow'r..That gayly blooms POPE. To dance and sing, be gaily drest TENNYSON. 2. Dr. Johnson was gaily sociable MAD. D'ARBLAY.

†**Gain,** *sb.*[1] ME. only. [ad. ON. *gagn, gegn,* adj. used subst. (see GAIN *a.*).] Advantage, use, avail; remedy, help.

Gain (gēn), *sb.*[2] 1473. [a. OF. *gain, gaain,* (mod. *gain*) masc., *gaigne, gaaigne* (mod. *gagne*) fem., f. *gaaigner* GAIN *v.*[2]] †1. Booty, prey, spoil –1490. 2. Increase, of possessions, resources, or advantages, consequent on some action or event; profit, emolument; opp. to *loss.* Also 'lucre', 'pelf', as an object of desire. 1496. b. In *pl.* Sums acquired by trade, etc.; emoluments, profits, etc. 1546. c. An increase in amount, magnitude, or degree. Opp. to *loss.* 1851. 3. The action of acquiring, winning, etc. (*rare*) 1576.

2. Wythout regard of pryuate gayne and profyt 1538. Greedy as they were of g., they seldom became rich MACAULAY. b. Their dubious gains 1893. c. I was weighed yesterday and found a g. of five pounds CARLYLE.

Gain (gēn), *sb.*[3] 1679. [? Perh. two wds.] 1. *Carpentry.* = TUSK, HORN. 2. a. *Carpentry,* etc. A notch, groove, niche (? *U.S.*) 1848. b. *Coal-mining.* A transverse cutting made in the sides of an underground roadway 1883.

Gain, *a.* Now *dial.* OE. [a. ON. *gegn* adj., straight, favourable, helpful:—OTeut. **gagino-, gagano-,* whence OE. **gegn*; see GAIN-.] 1. Of roads or directions: Near, straight; esp. in superl. 2. Of persons: Ready, well-disposed, kindly ME. 3. Of things: Available, handy, convenient ME.

1. Fur I wur a Baptis wonst..Till I fun that it warn't not the gaäinst waäy to the narra Gaäte TENNYSON.

†**Gain,** *v.*[1] ME. [a. ON. *gegna,* to meet, hence, to be meet, from the adj. and adv. *gegn* against, opposite to.] 1. *intr.* To be suitable, or useful; to avail, help; to serve, suffice (*for*). Const. *dat.* of person. –1724. 2. *trans.* a. To be an equipoise *to.* b. Of sleep: To come upon. c. To meet, encounter, oppose. –1500.

1. Us gayneth no raunsoun CHAUCER.

Gain (gēn), *v.*[2] 1530. [ad. F. *gagner*:—OF. *gaaignier*:—Com. Rom. **gwadaniare*, ad. OHG. **weidinjan* to pasture, also, to forage, f. *weida* (mod.Ger. *weide* pasture, pasturage):—OTeut. **waiþâ, -þjâ.*] 1. *trans.* To obtain (something desired or advantageous) 1570. 2. To obtain as profit; to earn, 'make' (a livelihood) 1530. Also, To obtain by way of increment or addition 1612. 3. *absol.* or *intr.* To make a gain or profit; to be advantaged 1572; also with *in* 1841. 4. *trans.* To acquire or reclaim (land) from the sea 1641. 5. To obtain or win as the result of a contest; †to capture in fight 1548. 6. To bring over to one's side, to persuade (often in bad sense, to bribe); also *to gain over* 1582. 7. To reach, arrive at 1605; to accomplish (now *rare*) 1733.

1. To gaine pardon of the sinne to Rosemond 1595. Sirs, ye should have hearkened unto me, and not have loosed from Crete, and to have gained (? = 'gotten', as in R.V., or = 'spared', as in De Wette, etc.) this harm and loss *Acts* xxvii. 21. Phr. *To g. time* [= F. *gagner du temps*]: to obtain a delay by pretexts, etc. *To g. the ear of*: see EAR *sb.* *To g. the wind* (Naut.): to arrive on the weather-side of some other vessel. 2. Lord, thy pound hath gained ten pounds *Luke* xix. 16. To g. a scanty sustenance TENNYSON. 3. To g. in moral height TENNYSON. 5. To g. the prize COWPER. He that gain'd a hundred fights TENNYSON. 6. I have gain'd the guard BYRON. 7. To gayne the timely inne *Macb.* III. iii. 7.

Phrases. 1. *To g. ground* [= F. *gagner du terrain*]; orig. *Mil.* to conquer ground from the enemy; hence a. To make progress; to acquire ascendency. b. *To g. ground on*: to make progress at the expense of. c. *To g. ground upon*: to get nearer to. 2. *To g. on* or *upon* [= F. *gagner sur*]: a. To encroach upon (now only of the sea encroaching on the land). b. To come closer to some object pursued. c. To win favour with.

Gain (gēn), *v.*[3] ? *U.S.* 1874. [f. GAIN *sb.*[3]] To mortise; to cut gains in (wood).

Gain-, *prefix*, in OE. *gegn-, géan-* (see GAIN *a.*). Its senses are chiefly those of opposition, return, or reversal, answering to L. *re-*. See GAINSAY, etc.

Gainable (gē·năb'l), *a.* 1611. [f. GAIN *v.*[2] + -ABLE.] Capable of being gained or won over.

†**Gainage.** ME. [ad. AF. *gaignage* (Anglo-L. *wainagium*), f. *gaigner.*] 1. Profit or produce from the tillage of land. ME. only. 2. Husbandry. MARKHAM. 3. In Law Dicts. of 17–18th c.: Implements of husbandry –1706.

Gained (gēnd), *ppl. a.* 1598. [f. GAIN *v.*[2] + -ED [1].] Acquired. Of time: Saved.

Gained day (Naut.): the twenty-four hours gained by circumnavigating the globe to the eastward. SMYTH.

Gainer (gē·nəɹ). 1538. [f. as prec. + -ER [1].] One who gains, or derives advantage.

Gainful (gē·nful), *a.* 1555. [f. GAIN *sb.*[2]] 1. Productive of gain or profit; *esp.* pecuniary gain. 2. Bent upon making gain; adapted to make gain (*rare*) 1870.

1. A g. undertaking 1791. A g. (= paid) occupation (chiefly *U.S.*). **Gain·ful-ly** *adv.*, **-ness.**

Gain-giving, *vbl. sb.* ME. [f. GAIN- *pref.* + GIVING *vbl. sb.*] †1. A giving in return. ME. only. 2. A misgiving (*arch.*) 1602.

Gaining (gē·niŋ), *vbl. sb.* 1874. [f. GAIN *v.*[3]] The cutting of gains (see GAIN *sb.*[3]) in wood. *Comb.* **g.-machine,** a machine for cutting gains in a beam.

Gai·ning, *ppl. a.* 1642. [f. GAIN *v.*[2] + -ING [2].] That gains. Phr. *Gaining-twist*: in rifled fire-arms, a twist of the grooves that increases regularly towards the muzzle.

Gainless (gē·nlĕs), *a.* 1640. [f. GAIN *sb.*[2] + -LESS.] Producing no gain; unprofitable. Hence **Gai·nlessness.**

Gainly (gē·nli), *a.* ME. [f. GAIN *a.* + -LY [1].] 1. Proper, becoming. *Obs.* exc. *Sc. dial.* 2. a. Tactful. b. The reverse of ungainly; graceful, shapely. 1855. Hence **Gai·nliness.**

†**Gai·npain.** ME. [a. OF. *gaignepain* (in 13th c. *wagnepain*) a sort of gauntlet. Commonly identified with the F. *gagnepain*, lit. 'bread-winner', but prob. much older.] 1. A sort of gauntlet –1500. ¶2. Explained after Fr. dicts., as 'The sword of a hired soldier'. Not in Eng. use. (Dicts.)

Gainsay (gē·nsē), *sb.* 1559. [f. next.] †a. A moot question 1559. b. Contradiction 1601.

Gainsay (gē·nsē, gēnsē·), *v.* Infl. **-say-ing, -said** (rarely **-sayed**). ME. [f. GAIN- *pref.* + SAY *v.* Now only literary. In *gainsaid* the last syllable is usually (-sĕ·d), not (-sed).] 1. *trans.* To deny. 2. To contradict ME. 3. To speak or act against, oppose, hinder ME. 4. To refuse (*rare*) ME.

1. Facts which cannot be gainsayed FREEMAN. 2. Evidence that can scarcely be gainsaid 1874. 3. Too facil then thou didst not much g., Nay, didst permit MILT. *P. L.* IX. 1158.

Gainsayer (gē·nsē¹,əɹ). ME. [f. prec. + -ER [1].] One who gainsays.

Such proofe..as may satisfie gaine-sayers HOOKER.

†**Gai·nsome,** *a.*[1] *rare.* 1569. [f. GAIN *sb.*[2] + -SOME.] Lucrative, advantageous –1646.

Gai·nsome, *a.*[2] Now *dial.* [f. GAIN *a.* + -SOME.] Ready, prompt, ? †willing to assist. MASSINGER.

Gainst, *prep.* Also **'gainst.** 1590. Aphet. f. AGAINST. *poet.*

Gainstand (gēnstæ·nd), *v.* *Obs.* or *arch.* ME. [f. GAIN- *pref.* + STAND *v.*] *trans.* To withstand, resist.

Vtterly to impugne & g. the scripture FOXE.

†**Gainstri·ve,** *v.* 1549. [f. GAIN- + STRIVE *v.*] *trans.* To strive against, oppose, –1590; *intr.* to make resistance –1596.

Gairfish, obs. f. GARFISH.

Gairfowl, Gairish: see GAREFOWL, GARISH.

Gait (gēt), *sb.* Also †**gate,** †**gaite.** 1509. [A spec. use of GATE *sb.*[2], q.v. The spelling *gait* was orig. Sc.] Manner of walking or stepping, carriage. b. *pl.*, esp. of a horse: Paces 1684. c. *U.S.* Rate of movement; pace.

Scarse thy legs uphold thy feeble gate SPENSER. Hence **Gai·ted** *ppl. a.* having a (specified) g., as *slow gated* (SHAKS.).

Gaiter (gē·təɹ), *sb.*[1] 1775. [a. F. *guêtre*, of unkn. origin.] 1. A covering of cloth, leather, etc. for the ankle, or ankle and lower leg. 2. *U.S.* A kind of shoe of similar form 1864. 3. *attrib.* 1862. Hence **Gai·ter** *v.* to dress or furnish with gaiters.

Gai·ter, *sb.*[2] Now *dial.* OE. [OE. *gâte tréow* = goat's tree, corrupted.] Prop. the Dogwood (*Cornus sanguinea*); also, the Spindletree (*Euonymus europæus*), etc. Also *attrib.*

Gala (gē·lă). 1625. [a. F. *gala*, a. It.] 1. Gala dress. Now only in phr. *in gala.* †2. Festivity, rejoicing –1809. 3. A festive occasion 1800.

Comb.: **g. day,** a day of festivity, finery and show; **g. dress,** a dress for a g.; fine or showy dress; **g. meet,** a (hunting) meet attended with festivities.

Galactic (gălæ·ktik), *a.* 1839. [ad. Gr. γαλακτικός, f. γαλακτ-, γάλα milk.] 1. Of or pertaining to milk; = LACTIC. 1844. 2. *Astron.* Of or pertaining to the Galaxy or Milky Way 1839.

2. *Galactic circle*, the mean or centre line of the Galaxy, or Milky Way zone. *G. poles*: the two opposite points of the heavens, situated at 90° from the g. circle.

Galactin (gălæ·ktin). 1838. [f. Gr. γαλακτ-, γάλα milk + -IN.] a. A vegetable substance, obtained from the sap of the Cow-tree (*Galactodendron utile*) of S. America, and used as cream. b. 'The coagulating principle of milk' (Mayne) 1854. c. A gelatin-yielding substance said to exist in milk (Watts) 1864. d. = LACTIN (*Syd. Soc. Lex.*) 1885.

Galacto- (gălækto), bef. a vowel *galact-*, comb. f. Gr. γάλα, γαλακτ-, milk.

gala·ctagogue [+ Gr. -αγωγός] *a.*, inducing a flow of milk; also *sb.* anything that does this; **galacto·meter** [Gr. μέτρον] = LACTOMETER; **galacto·phagist** [Gr. γαλακτοφάγος + -IST] *a.*, milk-fed; **galacto·phorous** [Gr. γαλακτοφόρος + -OUS] *a.*, conveying milk, as the excretory ducts of the mammary gland; **gala:ctopoe·tic, -poie·tic** [+ Gr. ποιητικός] *a.*, that tends to produce milk; also *sb.* anything that does this; **galactorrhœ·a** [+ Gr. ῥοία], an excessive flow of milk.

Galactose (gălæ·ktōus). 1869. [f. as prec. + -OSE [2]. Cf. DEXTROSE.] (See quot.)

Dilute acids convert lactose into a peculiar glucose, called g. ROSCOE.

Galago (găl$\bar{e}^i$·go). 1848. [a. mod.L.] A genus of *Lemuridæ*, of nocturnal habits, found in parts of Africa.

Galam butter. 1855. [f. *Galam*, on the Senegal.] A solid oil or fat which is expressed from the seeds of *Bassia butyracea*; much used as food.

Galanga (gălæ·ŋgă). 1485. [a. med.L. *galanga*; see GALINGALE.] = GALINGALE.

Galantine (gæ·läntin). ME. [a. F. *galantine*, altered f. *galatine* a sauce for fish; infl. by the adj. *galant*.] †1. A kind of sauce for fish or fowl –1658. 2. A dish of white meat, freed from bones, tied up, boiled, and served cold 1725.

1. Pyk walwed in galauntyne CHAUCER.

Galanty show (gălæ·nti,ʃōu) 1821. [? a. It. *galanti*, pl. of *galante*; see GALLANT.] A shadow pantomime produced by throwing shadows of miniature figures on a wall or screen.

‖**Galapee·**. 1756. A W. Indian tree, *Sciadophyllum Brownei*.

Galatea (gælătī·ă). 1882. [From H.M.S. *Galatea*; the material was used for children's sailor suits.] A cotton material striped in blue on a white ground.

Galaxy (gæ·lăksi), *sb.* ME. [ad. OF. and F. *galaxie*, ad. L. *galaxias*, Gr. γαλαξίας, f. γαλακτ-, γαλα.] 1. A luminous band or track, encircling the heavens irregularly, consisting of innumerable stars, perceptible only by the telescope; the Milky Way. Also extended to other groups of stars of similar extent. 2. *transf.* and *fig.*; now chiefly a brilliant crowd of beautiful women or distinguished persons 1590.

1. Lo, the Galaxyë Which men clepeth the Milky Wey, For hit is whyt CHAUCER. 2. Those beauties, who form a g. around the throne of England SCOTT. Hence **Ga·laxy** *v. trans.* to gather like a g. *into* (something). C. MATHER.

Galbanum (gæ·lbănŏm). ME. [a. L. *galbanum* = Gr. χαλβάνη, prob. the Hebr. *chelbenāh*.] 1. A gum resin obtained from certain Persian species of *Ferula*. 2. *fig.* after Fr. usage: Bosh, humbug 1764. var. †**Galbane**; also †**Galban**.

Galbulus (gæ·lbiŭlŏs). 1706. [a. L.; = 'the fruit of the cypress'.] *Bot.* 'A cone when spherical, and of thickened scales with narrow base, as that of Cypresses' (Gray).

Gale ($g\bar{e}^i$l), *sb.*[1] [OE. *gagel*, *gagol*.] The bog-myrtle, *Myrica Gale*; also *Sweet gale*.

†**Gale**, *sb.*[2] ME. only. [? repr. two wds.: (1) ME. *gal* (f. *galen*, OE. *galan* to sing); (2) OF. *gale* gaiety = It. *gala*.] 1. Singing, a song; mirth. 2. Speech, talk.

Gale ($g\bar{e}^i$l), *sb.*[3] 1547. [? ellipt. for *gale* (or *gall*) *wind*.] 1. a. A wind of considerable strength, implying, in naut. use, 'what on shore is called a storm' (Smyth); in pop. lit. use, 'a wind not tempestuous, but stronger than a breeze' (J.). b. *poet.* and *rhet.* A gentle breeze 1728. c. *transf.* and *fig.* 1623. 2. *fig.* A state of excitement or hilarity. *U.S.* 1838.

1. A calme, a brese, a fresh gaile, a pleasant gayle, and a stiffe gayle CAPT. SMITH. A common brisk g. is about 15 miles an hour 1772. *Equinoctial g.* (see EQUINOCTIAL). b. While every g. is peace, and every grove Is melody THOMSON. c. Some unexpected gaile of opportunity MARVELL. The music..Storm'd in orbs of song, a growing g. TENNYSON.

Gale ($g\bar{e}^i$l), *sb.*[4] 1640. [? contr. f. GAVEL[1].] 1. A periodical payment of rent, the amount paid periodically 1672. 2. An instalment (*rare* exc. *local U.S.*) 1789. 3. In the Forest of Dean: The royalty paid for a plot of land, with the right to dig for coal, iron, or stone; a licence or grant of land for this purpose; the area granted 1775. 4. *attrib.*, as (sense 1) *g.-day*; (sense 3) *g.-book*, *-fee* 1832.

Hence **Ga·leage** (sense 3), galiage, royalty paid for a g.

†**Gale**, *v.*[1] [OE. *galan*; cogn. w. GALE *sb.*[2], *-gale* (singer) in NIGHTINGALE.] 1. *intr.* and *trans.* To sing –1480. 2. *intr.* Of a dog: To bark, yelp. Of a bird: To utter its note. –1560. 3. *transf.* To make an outcry. ME. only.

1. '*Domine labia*' gan he crye and g. 1480. 3. Thogh that the Somnour g. CHAUCER.

Gale ($g\bar{e}^i$l), *v.*[2] 1692. [f. GALE *sb.*[3]] *Naut.* To sail *away* before a gale.

Gale ($g\bar{e}^i$l), *v.*[3] 1832. [f. GALE *sb.*[4]] To grant or take the gale of a mine.

Galea ($g\bar{e}^i$·lĭă). 1706. [a. L.; = 'helmet'.] 1. *Bot.*, *Zool.*, etc. Any structure resembling a helmet in shape, function, or position; e.g. the upper part of a labiate flower; the membrane covering the jaws of the Orthoptera and some other insects; etc. 1834. 2. *Med.* a. A headache which 'takes in the whole Head like a helmet' (Phillips) 1706. b. A kind of bandage for the head 1854.

Galeas(s(e, obs. ff. GALLIASS.

Galeate (gæ·lĭēt), *a.* 1706. [ad. L. *galeatus*, f. *galea*.] = GALEATED 1 and 2.

Galeated (gæ·lĭe^itėd), *ppl. a.* 1686. [f. as prec. + -ED[1].] 1. Shaped like a helmet. 2. *Zool.* Covered as with a helmet 1728. 3. Furnished with a helmet; wearing a helmet 1760. Also *fig.*

3. The g. head of Minerva 1879.

Galeeny (gălī·ni). 1796. [a. Sp. *gallina morisca*, lit. 'Moorish hen'.] A guinea-fowl.

Galeid ($g\bar{e}^i$·lĭid). [ad. mod. L. *Galeidæ*, f. *Galeus* = Gr. γαλεός, name of the typical genus.] A shark of the family *Galeidæ* (*Cent. Dict.*). Hence **Gale·idan** = prec.

Galen ($g\bar{e}^i$·lĕn). Also †**Galien.** 1598. [ad. L. *Galenus*, Gr. Γαληνός.] A celebrated physician of the 2nd century A.D., born at Pergamus in Asia Minor. Hence joc.: A physician.

What saies my Esculapius? my Galien *Merry W.* II. iii. 29. Hence **Gale·nian** *a.* = GALENIC *a.*[1] **Ga·lenism**, the medical principles or system of G.

Galena (gălī·nă). Also †**galæna.** 1671. [a. L. *galena*, dross that remains after melting lead; identified, perh. erron., with Gr. γαλήνη a calm.] *Min.* Native lead sulphide; the common lead ore. *False* or *pseudo-g.* = BLACK JACK 2. Also called *lead glance*.

Galenic (găle·nik), *a.*[1] 1668. [f. GALEN + -IC.] Of or pertaining to Galen, to his followers, to his principles and practice; *esp.* pertaining to vegetable preparations, as dist. from chemical remedies. Also *joc.*: Medical. *G. figure* (Logic): see GALENICAL.

Galenic (găle·nik), *a.*[2] 1828. [f. GALENA + -IC.] Pertaining to or containing galena. (Dicts.)

Galenical (găle·nikăl). 1652. [f. GALENIC *a.*[1] + -AL.]

A. *adj.* = GALENIC *a.*[1]

G. figure (Logic): the fourth syllogistic figure, added by Galen. Hence **Gale·nically** *adv.* with g. or vegetable remedies.

B. *sb.* A galenical or vegetable remedy, a simple 1768.

Galenist ($g\bar{e}^i$·lĕnist). 1594. [f. GALEN + -IST.] A follower of Galen. So †**Ga·lenite**[1].

Galenite[2] (gălī·nəit). 1868. [f. GALENA + -ITE.] *Min.* = GALENA.

Galenoid (gălī·noid). 1882. [f. GALENA + -OID.]

A. *adj.* Resembling galena 1884.

B. *sb. Crystall.* The Trigonal Trisoctahedron. (The form occurs most freq. in galena, hence the name.)

Galeod ($g\bar{e}^i$·lĭɒd). 1868. [ad. Gr. γαλεώδης; see next.] *Ichth.* A shark.

Galeoid ($g\bar{e}^i$·lĭoid), *a.* 1847. [ad. Gr. γαλεοειδής, f. γαλεός a kind of shark; see -OID.] a. *Ichth.* Resembling a shark or dogfish. b. *Entom.* Belonging to the arachnidans of the family *Galeodidæ*.

Galeopithecus ($g\bar{e}^i$:lĭopiþī·kŏs). 1835. [mod.L., f. Gr. γαλέη marten-cat + πίθηκος ape.] A flying lemur.

Galericulate (gæ:liəri·kiŭlĕt), *a.* 1706. [f. L. *galericulum* (dim. of *galerum* cap) + -ATE[2].] *Bot.* = GALEATE.

Galerite (gălīə·rəit). 1828. [ad. mod.L. *galerites*, f. *galerum* cap; see -ITE.] A fossil sea-urchin of the genus *Galerites*. (Dicts.)

†**Ga·lianes**, *sb. pl.* [f. *Galien* GALEN.] Drinks named after Galen. CHAUCER.

Galilean (gælilī·ăn), *a.*[1] and *sb.* 1611. [f. L. *Galilæa* + -AN.]

A. *adj.* Of or belonging to Galilee, in Palestine 1637.

The pilot of the G. lake MILT.

B. *sb.* A native or inhabitant of Galilee; used by pagans as a contemptuous designation of Christ, and hence as = 'Christian'. Also, a member of a fanatical sect which arose in Galilee in the 1st c.

Are not all these which speake, Galileans *Acts* ii. 7. And dying, *Thou hast conquered*, he said, *Galilean* SWINBURNE.

Galilean (gælilī·ăn), *a.*[2] 1727. [f. *Galileo* the astronomer + -AN.] Epithet of the form of telescope invented by Galileo.

Galilee (gæ·lilī). 1593. [a. OF. *galilée*, a. med.L. *galilæa*, a use of the proper name. Cf. 'Galilee of the Gentiles' (*Matt.* iv. 15).] A porch or chapel at the entrance of a church. Also *attrib.*

Galimatias (gælimæ·tiăs, gælim$\bar{e}^i$·ʃiăs). 1653. [a. F.; origin unkn.] Confused language, meaningless talk, gibberish. Also *transf.*

transf. Her dress, like her language, is a g. of several countries H. WALPOLE.

Galingale (gæ·liŋ$g\bar{e}^i$l). OE. [ad. OF. *galingal* (*garingal*), a. Arab. *khalanjān*, said to be a. (through Pers.) Chinese *Ko-liang-kiang*, lit. 'mild ginger from Ko'.] 1. The aromatic root of certain East Indian plants of the genera *Alpinia* and *Kæmpferia*, formerly used in medicine and cookery. Hence, †a dish seasoned with galingale. BEAUM. & FL. 2. An English species of sedge, *Cyperus longus*, sometimes dist. as 'English galingale', the root of which is also aromatic 1578.

2. Many a..meadow, set with slender g. TENNYSON.

Galiot: see GALLIOT.

Galipot (gæ·lipɒt). Also **gallipot.** 1791. [a. F. *galipot*, *galipo*. See Littré *Suppl.*] The turpentine or resin which exudes from, and hardens upon, the stem of certain pines.

Galipot, obs. f. GALLIPOT.

Galium ($g\bar{e}^i$·liŏm). 1548. [a. mod.L., ad. Gr. γάλιον.] *Bot.* = BEDSTRAW 2.

Gall (gǭl), *sb.*[1] [OE. *gealla* :—OTeut. types**gallo^m*, *gallon-*, *-ôn* :—pre-Teut. **gholno-*, represented in Gr. χολή, χόλος, and in L. *fel*.]

I. 1. The secretion of the liver, bile. Now applied only to that of the lower animals, esp. to *ox g.* (see OX). Used as the type of an intensely bitter substance. Also *fig.* 2. The gall-bladder and its contents ME. 3. Bitterness of spirit, asperity, rancour (supposed to have its seat in the gall) ME. †b. Spirit to resent injury or insult –1680. 4. *U.S. slang.* Assurance, impudence 1890.

1. *fig.* For I perceive that thou art in the g. of bitterness *Acts* viii. 23. 2. The drie coler with his hete, By wey of kinde his propre sete Hath in the galle, where he dwelleth GOWER. 3. Full of mirth without g. HOLINSHED. b. †*To break one's g.*: to break the spirit, cow.

II. *transf.* †1. Poison, venom –1450. 2. *G. of the earth* [L. *fel terræ*], the Lesser Centaury, from its bitterness 1567. 3. The scum of melted glass [F. *fiel de verre*]; see GLASS-GALL.

Comb.: **g.-bladder**, the vessel in the animal system which contains the g. or bile; **-duct**, **-pipe**, the tube through which the g. passes †**-sickness**, a form of intermittent fever, common in the Netherlands.

Gall (gǭl), *sb.*[2] [OE. *gealla* a sore on a horse; perh. identical with GALL *sb.*[1]] 1. Orig., A painful swelling, pustule, or blister, esp. in a horse (cf. WINDGALL). Later, a sore produced by rubbing or chafing. 2. *fig.* Something galling; a state of mental soreness or irritation 1591. †3. A person or thing that harasses. SPENSER. †b. Galling effect. HALL. 4. A place rubbed bare; an unsound spot, fault or flaw. Now only *techn.* 1545. 5. A bare spot in a field or coppice 1573. †6. Filth, impurity; *fig.* refuse. ME. only.

2. They did great hurt unto his title, and have left a perpetuall g. in the minds of that people SPENSER. 3. b. The smart, and gaules of the arrowes 1548.

Gall (gǭl), *sb.*[3] ME. [a. F. *galle* :—L. *galla* the oak-apple, gall-nut.] 1. An excrescence produced on trees, esp. the oak, by the action of insects, chiefly of the genus *Cynips*. Oak-galls are largely used in the manufacture of ink and tannin, as well as in dyeing and in medicine.

2. *attrib.* esp. in the names of insects producing galls, as *g.-beetle, -gnat, -insect*, etc. 1759.

Comb.: **g.-apple** = sense 1; **-leaf,** a leaf on which a g. is formed; **-oak, †-tree,** the oak (*Quercus infectoria*) upon which are produced the galls of commerce; **-steep,** 'a bath of nutgalls, for the process of galling in Turkey-red dyeing' (Cassell).

Gall (gǭl), *v.*[1] ME. [app. f. GALLED *ppl. a.*[2], q. v.] **1.** *trans.* To make sore by rubbing or chafing. **2.** To fret or injure (inanimate objects) by rubbing or contact 1600. **†3.** To break the surface of (ground, soil); to fret or wash *away* –1691. **4.** *fig.* To vex, harass, oppress 1614. **5.** To harass or annoy in warfare 1548. **6.** *intr.* To become sore or chafed 1614.

1. My Horse..gall'd under the Saddle-Bow 1696. 2. The Gabriell..had her Cable gauld asunder with a piece of driuing yce HAKLUYT. 4. Neckes..gawled with the yoke of forraine dominion RALEIGH. Galled by narrow circumstances BOSWELL. †*To g. at* (intr.): To scoff at *Hen. V*, v. i. 77. 5. With shot of the English archers were so curried and galled that they were driuen to retire HOLINSHED.

Gall (gǭl), *v.*[2] 1581. [f. GALL *sb.*[3]] *Dyeing.* To impregnate with a decoction of galls.

Gallant (gæ·lănt, gălæ·nt). ME. [a. F. *galant*, pr. pple. of OF. *galer* to make merry (conn. w. *gale* merrymaking; see GALE *sb.*[2] and GALA).]

A. *adj.* **1.** Showy in appearance, finely-dressed, smart (*arch.*). **†2.** Of women: Fine-looking –1650. **†3.** Suited to fashionable society; polished, courtier-like –1645. **4.** *loosely*: Excellent, splendid, fine, grand. Now *rare.* 1539. **b.** Of a ship: Noble, stately 1583. **5.** Chivalrously brave, nobly daring 1596. **b.** A conventional epithet of a military or naval officer 1875. **6.** (Usu. *galla·nt.*) Markedly polite and attentive to ladies 1680. **7.** (Usu. *galla·nt.*) Of or pertaining to love, amorous, amatory. Now *rare.* 1673.

1. Garments of Cotten exceeding g. 1578. 3. Such g. pastyme STUBBES. 4. A stable of g. horses DE FOE. b. Our royall, good, and g. Ship *Temp.* v. i. 237. 5. Our galant countryman, Sir Philip Sidney STEELE. b. The hon. and g. gentleman 1875. 6. Th' antique Sage, that was g. t' a Goose BUTLER. *Comb.* **†g.-springing** *a.*, 'growing up in beauty' (Schmidt).

B. *sb.* **1.** A man of fashion and pleasure; a fine gentleman. (Occas. with added notion of A. 5.) *arch.* ME. **†**Of a woman: A fashionably dressed beauty –1662. **†2.** As a courteous mode of address, *esp.* in pl.; = 'Gentlemen'. Also used playfully. –1810. **3.** (Occas. *galla·nt.*) A ladies' man (now *rare*). Also, a lover; (in bad sense) a paramour. 1450. **†4.** *Naut.* A name formerly applied to 'all flags borne on the mizen-mast' (Smyth).

1. She would fain be a g. PEPYS. 3. How few nowadays use the word 'gallant' to describe a lady's man M. ARNOLD.

Hence **Ga·llantness,** the state or quality of being g.

Gallant (gălæ·nt, gæ·lănt), *v.* 1608. [f. the adj.]

I. (? stressed *ga·llant.*) **1.** *intr.* To play the gallant, 'cut a dash'. **†2.** To make gallant or fine 1614.

II. (Usu. *galla·nt.*) **1.** *intr.* To play the gallant, flirt 1744. **2.** *trans.* To play the gallant to, flirt with 1672. **3.** *esp.* To act as cavalier or escort to (a lady) 1690; to conduct, escort, convey 1806. **†4.** *To g. a fan*: To handle or manipulate it 1711.

3. Young Ranter talks to her, gallants to her coach, and follows her home 1690. The little black steamer ..sometimes gallanting a tall ship in and out HAWTHORNE.

Gallantly (gæ·lăntli, gălæ·ntli), *adv.* 1552. [f. GALLANT *a.* + -LY [2].] In a gallant manner: showily 1552; splendidly, finely 1552; bravely, heroically 1590; with courtesy or politeness (now only as regards women) 1611.

Gallantry (gæ·lăntri). 1606. [ad. F. *galanterie*, f. *galant* GALLANT *a.*; see -ERY.] **†1.** Gallants collectively –1688. **†2.** Splendour, magnificence –1801. **†b.** An elegant practice or habit –1720. **†c.** *concr.* in *pl.* Knick-knacks –1720. **3.** Bravery, heroic bearing 1647. **†b.** A brave deed –1711. **†4.** Excellence –1657. **5.** Courtliness or polite attention to ladies 1675. **6.** A courtesy 1673. **7.** The occupation or behaviour of a gallant 1632. **8.** Amorous intercourse or intrigue 1678; **†**an intrigue –1750.

1. Hector..and all the g. of Troy. SHAKS. 2. The old men..who could call to minde the greatness and g. of the former [Temple] FULLER. 3. The unpremeditated g. of a soldier JUNIUS. 6. The prince..said a thousand gallantries DRYDEN. 8. She was not without a charge of g. T. HUTCHINSON.

Gallate (gæ·lĕt). 1794. [f. GALL-IC *a.*[2] + -ATE.] *Chem.* A salt of gallic acid.

†Ga·llature. [ad. It. *gallatura*, f. *gallare* to fecundate (an egg), f. *gallo* cock.] The germ in an egg. SIR T. BROWNE.

Galleass: see **Galliass.**

Galled, *ppl. a.*[1] *nonce-wd.* 1604. [f. GALL *sb.*[1] + -ED [2].] Mixed with gall, made bitter.

Galled (gǭld), *ppl. a.*[2] OE. [orig. f. GALL *sb.*[2] + -ED [2], but later as if f. GALL *v.*[1] + -ED [1].] **1. a.** Affected with galls or painful swellings. **b.** Sore from chafing. Often with defining word, as *saddle-g.*, etc. **2.** *fig.* Irritated, unquiet, distressed 1601. **3.** Of land: Having bare patches 1881.

Gallein (gæ·lĭ,in). 1885. [f. GALL-IC *a.*[2] + -(E)IN.] A brown-red powder, or small green crystals, obtained by heating pyrogallol and phthalic anhydride. Used as a dye.

Galleon (gæ·liŏn). 1529. [a. F. *galion*, and Sp. *galeon*, med.L. *galionem, galeonem*, from *galea* a galley.] A kind of vessel, shorter but higher than the galley; a ship of war, esp. Spanish; also, the large traders used by the Spaniards. **b.** *fig.* A great prize or catch 1706.

We took a Galloon, And the Crew touch'd the Agent for cash to some tune DIBDIN.

Gallery (gæ·lĕri), *sb.* 1500. [ad. F. *galerie* = med.L. *galeria*, of unkn. origin.] **1.** A covered space for walking in, partly open at the side, or having the roof supported by pillars; a piazza, portico, colonnade. **2.** A long, narrow platform or balcony, constructed on the outside of a building, at some elevation from the ground, and open in front except as having a balustrade 1509. **b.** A similar passage on the roof of a house 1535. **c.** *Arch.* A long narrow passage either made in the thickness of a wall, or supported on corbels, open towards the interior of a building 1756. **d.** *Naut.* A balcony built outside the body of a ship, at the stern (*stern-gallery*), or at the quarters (*quarter-gallery*) 1627. **3.** A platform, supported by columns or brackets, projecting from the interior wall of a building; *esp.* **a.** in churches 1630; **b.** in a theatre (now *spec.* of the highest of such platforms, containing the cheapest seats) 1690. **4.** *transf.* **a.** The occupants of the gallery portion of a theatre, the 'gods'; formerly often in *pl.* Hence *fig.* the less instructed portion of the public. 1649. **b.** The body of persons who occupy a public gallery in a senatorial chamber 1817. **5.** A long narrow corridor 1541. **6.** An apartment or building for the exhibition of works of art 1591. **7.** *Mil.* and *Mining.* An underground passage; a level or drift 1631. **b.** *Mil.* 'A covered walk, the sides whereof are musket-proof' 1704. **8. †**A passage made by a deer, etc. through brushwood 1674; also, a passage made by an animal underground, or through a rock 1849. **9.** *Tennis.* *Winning-gallery*, the opening most remote from the dedans 1699. **10.** An ornamental parapet or railing running along the edge of a table, shelf, or the like 1853. **11.** *attrib.* 1480.

2. Our old coaching inns, with their roomy yards and railed galleries 1894. 3. Phr. *Ladies'-, members'-, press-, strangers'-g.* (in a senatorial chamber). b. The people were cracking nuts in the g. DICKENS. 4. a. Phr. *To play to* (or *for*) *the gallery*: to address oneself to those in the g. (also *fig.*). 6. For in my G. thy Picture hangs 1 *Hen. VI*, II. iii. 37. 8. The.. galleries made by Crustaceans MURCHISON.

Comb.: **g.-hit,** a piece of showy play (primarily in *Cricket*) intended to gain applause from the uncritical; **-shot, -stroke** (cf. *g.-hit*).

Hence **Ga·llery** *v.* to furnish with a g. or balcony; *Mil.* to make an underground passage.

Galley (gæ·li), *sb.* [ME. *galei(e*, ad. OF. *galie, galee*, med.L. *galea, galeia*, late Gr. γαλαία, γαλέα. Ult. etym. unkn.] **1.** A low flat-built sea-going vessel with one deck, propelled by sails and oars, formerly in common use in the Mediterranean. Cf. GALLIASS. The rowers were mostly slaves or condemned criminals. **2.** Applied to the Greek or Roman warships, large vessels with one or more banks of oars 1513. **3.** A large open row-boat, e.g. one formerly used on the Thames by custom-house officers, and by the press-gang (Smyth); also, a large pleasure-boat 1570. **4.** The cooking-room or kitchen on a ship. Also, a ship's cooking-range. 1750. **5.** *Printing.* [F. *galée.*] An oblong tray of brass, wood, or zinc, to which the type is transferred from the composing-stick 1652. **6.** [= F. *galère.*] An oblong furnace, used to heat stone-ware bottles in the distillation of aqua fortis 1789. **7.** *attrib.* 1599.

1. Phr. *To condemn*, or *send, to the galleys*, also simply *the galleys*, the punishment of a galley-slave.

Comb.: **g.-arch,** a covered structure in Mediterranean ports for the reception of galleys; **-house** = *g.-arch*; **-packet,** a made-up story, lie, yarn; **-press,** 'a small hand-press for pulling proofs in slip form' (Jacobi); **-proof,** a proof in slip form so taken; **-slip** = *g.-proof*; **-stick,** one of the long side-sticks used for quoining up galleys.

Ga·lley-man. ME. [f. GALLEY *sb.* + MAN.] **1.** One who rows in a galley. **†2.** A name formerly given to traders, esp. Genoese, from beyond the sea, who 'usually arrived in galleys' –1706.

Galleypot, obs. f. GALLIPOT.

Ga·lley-slave. 1567. [f. GALLEY *sb.* + SLAVE *sb.*] **1.** One condemned to row in a galley. Often *fig.* **†2.** *Printing.* A nickname for a compositor 1683.

†Galley-tile. 1610. [f. GALLEY *sb.* + TILE *sb.*; see GALLIPOT.] A glazed tile used for wall-decoration. Also *collect.* the material of which these are made. –1768.

It is to be known of what stuff galletyle is made BACON.

Galleyworm, gallyworm (gæ·liwɒ̆ɹm). 1658. [f. GALLEY *sb.* + WORM *sb.*, from the resemblance to an oared galley.] An insect of the class *Myriapoda*; an iulus.

Gall-fly (gǭ·l,fləi). 1822. [f. GALL *sb.*[3]] An insect (esp. of the genus *Cynips*) which produces galls on trees.

Galliambic (gæliæ·mbik). 1846. [f. L. *galliambus* a song of the *Galli* or priests of Cybele (f. *Gallus* + IAMBUS) + -IC.]

A. *adj.* Epithet of a lyric metre (founded on the Ionic a minore tetrameter catalectic, with anaclasis), supposed to have been used by the priests of the Phrygian Cybele in their songs 1876.

B. *sb.* The galliambic metre; a verse written in this metre 1846.

The G. of Catullus may be a relic..of Phrygian poetry LANDOR.

†Gallian (gæ·liăn), *a.* 1591. [f. L. *Gallia* + -AN.] Gallic, French. Also as *sb. pl.* –1630.

Galliard (gæ·liăɹd), *a.* and *sb.*[1] ME. [ad. OF. and F. *gaillard, -art*, of unkn. origin; see -ARD for the suffix. The sb. B. 2, 3 is a. F. *gaillarde* adj. fem. used subst.]

A. *adj.* **1.** Valiant, 'stout', sturdy (*arch.*). **2.** Lively, brisk, gay (*arch.*) ME. **†3.** Spruce –1605.

2. There lives not .. a more frank, galiard, and supine people EVELYN *State France.* Hence **†Ga·lliardness.**

B. *sb.* **†**A man of courage and spirit –1658; a man of fashion (*arch.*) 1768. **2.** *Hist.* A quick and lively dance in triple time 1533. **†3.** The music for this dance –1674.

2. Why dost thou not goe to Church in a G. SHAKS. Never a hall such a g. did grace SCOTT.

Galliard (gæ·liăɹd), *sb.*[2] 1875. [?] *Geol.* A name for very siliceous sandstones with an even close grain.

Galliardise (gæ·liăɹdəi:z). Also **-ize.** *arch.* 1570. [ad. F. *gaillardise*; see GALLIARD *sb.*[1]] Gaiety, mirth, revelry; a merry trick.

No way..disposed for the mirth and g. of company 1643.

Galliass, galleas (gæ·liæ̆s). Now *Hist.* 1544. [ad. OF. *galeace, galeasse, galiasse*, also *gall-*, ad. It. *galeazza*, augm. of *galea* GALLEY *sb.*] A heavy, low-built vessel, larger than a galley, impelled both by sail and oars, chiefly employed in war.

A first-rate galley, otherwise called a galleasse FALCONER.

Gallic (gæ·lik), *a.*[1] and *sb.* 1672. [ad. L. *Gallicus* Gaulish (in mod.L. 'French'), f. *Gallus* GAUL.]

A. *adj.* **a.** Of or pertaining to the Gauls or Gaul; Gaulish 1796. **b.** Often used rhet. or joc. for 'French'.

B. *sb.* A Frenchman. J. ADAMS.

Gallic (gæ·lik), *a.*[2] 1791. [ad. F. *gallique*; see GALL *sb.*[3] and -IC.] *Chem.* In *g. acid*: a crystalline acid prepared from the oak-gall, etc.

Gallican (gæ·likăn). 1598. [ad. L. *Gallicanus*, f. *Gallicus* GALLIC *a.*[1] Cf. F. *gallican* in eccl. sense.]

A. *adj.* **a.** *gen.* = GALLIC *a.*[1] **b.** *Eccl.* (= med.L. *Gallicanus*), distinctive epithet of the ancient Church of Gaul or France, and of its characteristic usages, liturgies, etc. Hence applied to that school of French Roman Catholics which maintains the right of the French Church to be in certain respects free from papal control; opp. to *Ultramontane*. 1633.

b. This more correct Psalter .. obtained first in Gaul about 580.. From which circumstance it came to have the name of G., in contradistinction to the Roman WATERLAND.

B. *sb.* A member of the Gallican party in the French Church 1882.

Hence **Ga·llicanist**, one who favours Gallicanism. **Ga·llicanism**, the principles and practice of the G. party.

Gallicism (gæ·lisiz'm). 1656. [a. F. *gallicisme*; see GALLIC *a.*[1] and -ISM.] **1.** A French idiom or mode of expression, esp. one used by a speaker or writer in some other language; also, free use of French idiom. **2.** A French characteristic, custom, mode of thought, or the like 1715.

1. His [H. Walpole's] style is..deeply tainted with Gallicisms MACAULAY.

Gallicize (gæ·lisəiz), *v.* 1773. [f. L. *Gallicus* + -IZE.] **1.** *intr.* To become Gallic or French in habits, speech, etc. 1775. **2.** *trans.* To render French-like 1773.

Galliform (gæ·lifǫɹm), *a.* [ad. mod.L. *galliformis*, f. L. *gallus* cock + *forma* form.] *Ornith.* Belonging to the *Galliformes*, an order of birds, including ostriches, gallinaceous birds, rails, cuckoos, and parrots (*rec.*).

Galligaskin (gæligæ·skin). Now chiefly in *pl.* 1577. [app. a corruption of F. *garguesque*, a metathetic var. of *greguesque*, ad. It. *grechesca* sb., orig. fem. of *grechesco* Greek (this kind of hose being in 16th c. described as *alla grechesca* = Fr. *à la grecque* in the Greek fashion). Prob. in pop. etym. assoc. w. GALLEY.] **1.** A kind of wide hose or breeches worn in the 16th and 17th c.; later, a jocose term for loose breeches in general. Also *attrib.* **2.** Leggings, gaiters (*dial.*) 1859. **3.** A variety of the Cowslip (*Primula veris*) 1629.

Gallimatia(s, obs. f. GALIMATIAS.

Gallimaufry (gælimǭ·fri), *sb.* 1551. [ad. F. *galimafrée*, of unkn. origin.] **1.** A hash of odds and ends of food; a hodge-podge, a ragout (*rare* exc. *dial.*) 1591. **2.** *transf.* and *fig.* A ridiculous medley 1551. **3.** *attrib.* 1630.

1. Lattin whole-meats are nowe minc'd, and serude in for English Gallimafries DEKKER. **2.** That G. of Prophesies 1668. A compound of Player, Soldier, Stroller, Sailor, and Tinker! An odd g. 1781.

Gallinacean (gælinē^i·ʃiăn). 1842. [f. as next + -AN.]

A. *adj.* = next.

B. *sb.* A bird of the order *Gallinaceæ* or *Gallinæ*.

Gallinaceous (gælinē^i·ʃəs), *a.* 1783. [f. L. *gallinaceus* (f. *gallina*) + -OUS.] **1.** Of or belonging to the order *Gallinæ*, which comprises the ordinary domestic fowls, pheasants, partridges, etc. **2.** *joc.* 'Cocky' 1879; consisting of fowls 1885. So **Ga·lline** *a.* (*rare*).

Gallinaginous (gælinæ·dʒinəs), *a.* 1876. [f. mod.L. *gallinaginem*, *gallinago* woodcock (f. *gallina* hen) + -OUS.] Of or pertaining to a woodcock.

Gallinaginous crest, transl. of L. *caput gallinaginis*, lit. 'woodcock's head'; the prominent fold of the lining membrane in the prostatic portion of the urethra.

Gallinazo (gælinā·zo). 1760. [corruptly a. Sp. *gallinaza* a vulture, f. *gallina* hen + augm. suffix *-aza*.] An American vulture (*Cathartes aura* or *Catharista atrata*).

Galling (gǭ·liŋ), *ppl. a.* 1583. [f. GALL *v.*[1] + -ING[2].] Chafing, irritating, harassing (*lit.* and *fig.*).

Between two g. fires MCCARTHY. *fig.* G. mortifications 1820. Hence **Ga·lling·ly** *adv.*, **-ness.**

Ga·llini·pper. *U.S.* 1818. [?] A large mosquito.

Gallinule (gæ·liniul). 1776. [ad. mod.L. *gallinula*, the name of the genus, dim. of L. *gallina* hen.] Book-name for a genus of birds, typified by the moor-hen (*Gallinula chloropus*). Also used of allied genera.

Galliot (gæ·liŏt). Also †**galiot.** See also GALLIVAT. ME. [a. F. *galiote*, OF. *galiot*, dim. of Com. Rom. *galea* GALLEY *sb.*[1]] **1.** A small galley or boat, propelled by sails and oars, used for swift navigation; in Eng. applied specially to Mediterranean vessels. **2.** [Du. *galjoot*.] A Dutch cargo-boat or fishing-vessel 1794. **3.** Used of ancient Roman vessels (? *Obs.*) 1718.

Gallipot (gæ·lipǫt). 1465. [Cf. GALLEY-TILE, etc. The first part is perh. identical with GALLEY *sb.* Thus etymologically = pottery brought in *galleys*, i.e. from the Mediterranean. The Du. synonym *gleipot* is a century later, and by some *glei* is taken as a var. of *galei* GALLEY *sb.*] **1.** A small earthen glazed pot, *esp.* one used by apothecaries for ointments, etc. Also *transf.* and *fig.* **2.** Hence *joc.* An apothecary 1785.

Gallium (gæ·liŏm). 1875. [mod.L.; said to be f. L. *gallus* cock, a tr. of *Lecoq*.] *Min.* A soft, tough, bluish-white metal, easily melted, discovered by M. *Lecoq* de Boisbaudran in a zinc-blende from the Pyrenees.

Gallivant (gælivæ·nt), *v.* 1823. [? a jocose perversion of GALLANT *v.*] *intr.* To gad about, esp. with persons of the other sex. Also = FLIRT.

†**Gallivat.** 1613. [ad. Pg. *galeota*; cf. GALLIOT.] A large boat used in Eastern seas, having oars and a triangular sail –1862.

Galliwasp (gæ·liwǫsp). 1725 [?] A small W. Indian lizard (*Celestus occiduus*).

Gallize (gæ·ləiz), *v.* Also **gallisize.** 1888. [From Dr. L. *Gall* of Treves, who invented the process.] *trans.* To treat (unfermented grape-juice) with water and sugar, so as to increase the quantity of wine produced.

Gall-nut (gǭ·lˌnɒt). 1572. [f. GALL *sb.*[3]] = GALL *sb.*[3] 1.

Gallo- (gæ·lo), comb. f. L. *Gallus*, a Gaul. **1.** In cl. Latin only in *Gallo-græci*, Gauls who went east and settled in Asia Minor; also *Gallo-græcia*, Galatia. **2.** Used with the sense 'Gallic' (i.e. French); as in **Ga·llo-Celtic** *a.*, belonging to the Celts of France; also in **Ga·lloman** [ad. F. *Gallomane*] = *Gallomaniac*; **Galloma·nia** [Gr. -μανία], unreasoning attachment to France or to what is French; whence **Galloma·niac**; **Ga·llophil** [Gr. -φίλος], a friend of France and of what is French; **Gallo·philism**; **Gallopho·be** [Gr. -φόβος], one affected with Gallophobia; **Gallopho·bia** [Gr. -φοβία], morbid dread of the French, or of what is French.

Galloglass (gæ·lŏglas). Also †**gallow-.** Now *Hist.* 1515. [a. Ir. and Gael. *gallóglách*, f. *gall* foreigner, stranger + *óglách* youth, servant, warrior.] **1.** One of a particular class of soldiers or retainers formerly maintained by Irish chiefs. **2.** In the Highlands: = HENCHMAN 2. 1703.

Gallon (gæ·lən). [ME. *galun*, *galon*, a. ONF., app. cogn. w. F. *jale* bowl. Ult. origin unkn.] An English cubic measure of capacity. The imperial gallon contains 277¼ cubic inches; the wine-gallon of 231 inches is the standard in U.S. **b.** As a dry measure for corn, bread, etc. 1684.

Me were leuere slepe, Than the beste galon wyn in Chepe CHAUCER.

Galloon (gălū·n). 1604. [ad. F. *galon*, f. *galonner*. Of unkn. origin.] A kind of narrow, close-woven ribbon or braid, of gold, silver, or silk thread, used for trimming articles of apparel; a trimming of this.

A Negro Boy..with a broad brimm'd white Hat, edged with Silver G. 1681. Hence **Galloo·ned** *a.*

Gallop (gæ·ləp), *sb.* 1523. [a. OF. *galop* (app. f. *galoper* to GALLOP). See also WALLOP *sb.* and GALOP.] **1.** The most rapid movement of a horse, etc., in which in each stride the animal is entirely off the ground, with the legs flexed under the body. Hence, a ride at this pace. **2.** *transf.* and *fig.* 1651.

2. Horace is always on the amble, Juvenal on the g. DRYDEN. Phr. *False g.*: orig. a canter; now only *fig.* *Full g.*: the extreme pace of a horse; also used *advb.*; also *fig.*

Gallop (gæ·ləp), *v.* 1523. [a. F. *galoper*. Replacing *walope*, WALLOP.] **1.** *intr.* Of a horse, etc.: To go at a gallop (see GALLOP *sb.* 1) 1533. **2.** *intr.* Of a horseman: To ride at full speed 1523. **3.** *trans.* To make (a horse, etc.) go at full speed 1533. †**4.** To traverse (a space) rapidly by means of horses. *Tit. A.* II. i. 7. **5.** *transf.* and *fig.* (from senses 1, 2) 1583. †**6.** To dance a GALOP –1826. **7.** *trans.* To convey rapidly by means of galloping horses 1882.

2. Up the hill Gallopt the gallant three hundred TENNYSON. **3.** Never g. Pegasus to death POPE. **5.** They g. fast that deils and lasses drive RAMSAY. Phr. *To g. away*: to talk fast. *To g. over* or *through*: to hurry over, read cursorily. **7.** We galloped the left gun at it 1882.

Gallopade (gælŏpē^i·d), *sb.* Also **galopade.** 1753. [a. F. *galopade*, f. *galoper*; cf. GALOP.] **1.** A lively dance, of Hungarian origin. 1831. **2.** *Manège.* A sidelong or curveting kind of gallop. Hence **Gallopa·de** *v. rare*, to dance a g.

Galloper (gæ·ləpəɹ). 1576. [f. GALLOP *v.* + -ER[1].] **1.** One who, or that which, gallops, esp. a galloping horse. **2.** *Mil.* An aide-de-camp, or orderly officer 1871. **3.** *fig.* One who proceeds at great speed. Also, a gadabout. 1671. **4.** A light field-gun, formerly attached to regiments; also *attrib.* in *g. carriage*, *-gun* 1746.

Galloping (gæ·ləpiŋ), *ppl. a.* 1641. [f. GALLOP *v.* + -ING[2].] That gallops, in senses of the vb.

Phrases. *Galloping consumption*: a consumptive disease that makes rapid progress. *G. nun*: a temporal religious pensioner, without any vows. *G. carriage* (Mil.) = 'galloper carriage'; see GALLOPER 4.

Gallo-tannate (gæ:loˌtæ·nēt). 1864. [f. next + -ATE.] *Chem.* A compound of gallo-tannic acid with a base.

Gallo-tannic (gæ:loˌtæ·nik), *a.* 1858. [f. *gallo-*, taken as comb. f. L. *galla* GALL *sb.*[3] + TANNIC.] *Chem.* In *gallo-tannic acid*, tannic acid prepared from nut-galls.

Gallow, obs. f. GALLY *v.*, to frighten.

Galloway (gæ·lŏwē^i). 1597. [A district in the SW. of Scotland.] **1.** One of a small but strong breed of horses peculiar to Galloway. Also *g.-mare*, *-nag*. Also *attrib.* **2.** One of a breed of cattle peculiar to Galloway 1805.

Gallows (gæ·lo^uz). [OE. *galga*, *gealga* :– OTeut. **galgon-*.] **1.** An apparatus for execution by hanging, usually two uprights and a cross-piece, from which the criminal is suspended by the neck. (Orig. both sing. and pl. were used for 'a gallows'; later, the pl. *gallows* became the prevailing form, and is now used as a sing., with pl. *gallowses*.) OE. **2.** The punishment itself 1483. **3.** One deserving of the gallows 1588. **4.** Anything consisting of two or more supports and a cross-piece; e.g. in *Printing*, 'a frame used for supporting the tympans of the old wooden presses when turned up' (Jacobi) –1833. **5.** 'Suspenders' for trousers; braces. Now *dial.* 1730.

1. Let them make a galowe of fiftye cubites hie COVERDALE *Esther* v. 14. Who doth he [Time] gallop withal?..With a theefe to the gallowes SHAKS. Make bonfires of the gallowses 1673. **2.** Phr. *To have the gallows in one's face*: to have the look of one predestined to be hung. His complexion is perfect Gallowes. SHAKS. **3.** 'Now, young g.!' DICKENS.

Comb.: **g.-bitts**, a strong frame of oak about eight inches square, made in the form of a gallows, and fixed at the fore and main hatchway, to support spare top-masts, yards, etc.; also called *gallows*; †**-clapper** = G.-BIRD; **-foot**, the space immediately in front of the gallows; **-ripe** *a.*, ready to be hanged; **-top** = *gallows-bitts*.

Gallows (gæ·lo^uz, gæ·ləs), *a.* ME. [f. the sb. used attrib.] **1.** Fit for the gallows; villainous, wicked. Now only *dial.*: Impish, wild. **2.** *dial.* and *slang.* As an intensive: Very great, 'fine', etc. 1789.

1. *Gallows air* = *hangdog air*: see HANGDOG *a.*

Gallows (gæ·lo^uz, gæ·ləs), *adv. dial* and *slang.* 1823. [f. the sb.] Extremely, very.

Gallows-bird (gæ·ləzˌbɔ̄ɹd). 1785. [f. GALLOWS *sb.* + BIRD.] One who deserves to be hanged.

Ga·llows-tree. [OE. *galg-tréow*.] **1.** = GALLOWS *sb.* 1. OE. †**2.** An iron support for a pot over a kitchen fire 1590.

Gall-stone (gǭ·lˌstōun). 1758. [f. GALL *sb.*[1] + STONE.] A morbid calculous formation in the gall-bladder.

†**Ga·lly,** *a.*[1] or *sb.* used *attrib.* 1567. [? attrib. use of GALLEY *sb.*] In *g. breeches, hose, slops*, app. = GALLIGASKINS. –1622.

Gally (gǭ·li), *a.*[2] ? *Obs.* 1530. [f. GALL *sb.*[1] + -Y[1].] Gall-like, bitter. Chiefly *fig.*

Gally (gǭ·li), *a.*[3] Now *dial.* ME. [f. GALL *sb.*[2] + -Y[1].] **1.** Having galls or sores. ME. only. **2.** Full of bare or wet places 1602.

Gally (gæ·li), *v.* Also †**gallow.** 1605 [OE. *a-gælwan* to alarm.] *trans.* To frighten, daze, scare. Now only *dial.* and in the whale fishery. *Comb.* **g.-** (also **galli-**) **crow,** a scare-crow.

Galoch(e, obs. f. GALOSH.

Galoot (gălū·t). *slang.* 1812. **1.** *Naut.* 'A soubriquet for the young or "green" marine' (Smyth). **2.** *U.S.* An awkward or uncouth fellow: often used playfully 1866.

Galop (gæ·lǫ̆p). 1837. [a. F. *galop*; see GALLOP *sb.*] A lively dance in $\frac{2}{4}$ time.

†**Galopin.** Also **gall-.** 1567. [a. F., f. *galoper*.] A turnspit; an errand-boy; a page –1824.

Galore (gălōᵊ·ɹ). 1675. [ad. Ir. *go leór*, f. *go* to + *léor* sufficiency, sufficient.]
A. *adv.* In plenty.
B. *sb.* Abundance.

Galosh, golosh (gălǫ·ʃ, gǒlǫ·ʃ), *sb.* Also †**galoche.** ME. [a. F. *galoche*:—pop. L. **galopia*, f. **galopus*, a. Gr. καλόπους shoemaker's last, f. κᾶλον wood (only pl. logs) + πούς foot (Hatz.-Darm.).] **1. a.** In early use: A patten or clog. **b.** In later use: An over-shoe worn in wet or dirty weather. **2.** A piece of leather running round the lower part of a boot or shoe above the sole 1853.

1. a. Ne were worthy to unbokel his galoche CHAUCER. Hence **Galo·sh, golo·sh** *v.* to furnish with a g.

†**Galp,** *v.* ME. [Cogn. w. YELP; or ? an onomatopœic var. of GAPE.] **1.** *intr.* To gape, yawn –1532. Also *transf.* and *fig.* **2.** *trans.* To vomit *forth* –1558. ¶ **3.** Of an animal: To yelp. CAXTON.

Galt (*Geol.*): see GAULT.

Galumph (gălʋ·mf), *v.* 1872. [Coined by 'L. Carroll' (perh. a fusion of *gallop* and *triumph*). Cf. CHORTLE *v.*] *intr.* To march exultingly with irregular bounding movements. Hence **Galu·mphing** *ppl. a.* (*lit.* and *fig.*).

Galvanic (gælvæ·nik), *a.* 1797. [f. GALVANISM + -IC. Cf. F. *galvanique*.] Of, pertaining to, or produced by galvanism. Also *fig.* with allusion to the effects produced by galvanism.

fig. A sort of g. grin HAWTHORNE. Phr. *G. battery*, an apparatus for the production of galvanic electricity *G. belt*, a belt containing a galvanic apparatus to be worn round the body. *G. electricity* = GALVANISM. *G. pile*, a pile consisting of thirty pieces of silver, and as many of zinc, with pieces of cloth that were dipped in a saturated solution of common salt. Hence **Galva·nical,** *a.*, **-ly,** *adv.*

Galvanism (gæ·lvăniz'm). 1797. [a. F. *galvanisme*, after L. *Galvani* who first described it; see -ISM.] Electricity developed by chemical action. Also, the use of this therapeutically. Hence **Ga·lvanist,** one versed in g. **Ga:lvani·stical** *a.* of, pertaining to, or versed in g.

Galvanization (gælvănəizēⁱ·ʃən). 1860. [f. GALVANIZE *v.* + -ATION.] **1.** The process of applying galvanism to. **2.** The being galvanized. Also *fig.* 1875.

Galvanize (gæ·lvănəiz), *v.* Also **-ise.** 1802. [ad. F. *galvaniser*; see GALVANISM and -IZE.] **1.** *trans.* To apply galvanism to; to stimulate by means of a galvanic current. Also *fig.* **2.** To cover with a coating of metal by means of galvanic electricity. Commonly but incorrectly applied to the coating of iron with zinc. 1839.

1. *fig.* Her approach always galvanized him to new and spasmodic life C. BRONTË.
Phr. *Galvanized iron*, trade name of iron coated with zinc. Hence **Ga·lvanizer.**

Galvano- (gæ·lvăno), comb. f. GALVANIC or GALVANISM.

galvano-caustic *a.*, relating to the use of galvanic heat as a caustic; **-cauterization,** cauterization by means of the galvano-cautery; **-cautery,** a cautery heated by galvanism; **-magnetic** *a.*, pertaining to galvano-magnetism; **-magnetism,** magnetism produced by galvanic electricity; **-puncture,** the introduction into the tissues of fine needles, connected with the poles of a galvanic battery; **-therapeutics,** the use of galvanism for the treatment of disease; **-thermometer,** 'an instrument for measuring the heating effect of a galvanic current' (Cassell).

Galvanograph (gæ·lvănograf). [f. GALVANO- + -GRAPH.] 'A plate formed by the galvanographic process; an impression taken from such a plate' (Ogilvie). Hence **Ga:lvanogra·phic** *a.* pertaining to galvanography.

Galvanography (gælvănǫ·grăfi). 1854. [f. as prec. + Gr. -γραφία.] **a.** 'A method of producing plates for copperplate engraving by the galvanoplastic process without etching' (Ogilvie). **b.** A process by means of which plastic objects may be exactly copied in copper, and bronzed or gilt 1854.

Galvanology (gælvănǫ·lŏdʒi). 1848. [f. GALVANO- + LOGY.] A treatise on galvanism, or a description of its phenomena. So **Galvano·logist,** one who describes the phenomena of galvanism.

Galvanometer (gælvănǫ·mītəɹ). 1802. [f. as prec. + METER.] An apparatus for determining the direction and intensity of a galvanic current. Hence **Ga:lvanome·tric, -al** *a.* pertaining to the g., or to galvanometry. **Galvano·metry,** the measurement of galvanic currents.

Galvanoplasty (gæ:lvănoˌplæsti). 1870. [f. as prec. + Gr. -πλαστός moulded + -Y[3].] The process of coating any substance with metal by galvanism. Hence **Ga:lvanopla·stic** *a.* of or pertaining to g.

Galvanoscope (gæ·lvănoskōup). 1832. [f. GALVANO- + Gr. -σκόπος looker.] An instrument for ascertaining the presence of galvanic electricity. Hence **Ga:lvanosco·pic** *a.* pertaining to, or of the nature of, a g. **Galvano·scopy,** the employment of galvanism in physiological experiment. Also, the use of the g.

Galvano·tropism. 1885. [f. GALVANO- + Gr. τρόπος + -ISM.] *Bot.* The phenomenon of curvature produced in growing plant-organs by the passage of electric currents through them.

Galwegian (gælwī·dʒiăn). 1774. [f. *Galloway*; cf. *Norroway*, *Norwegian*.]
A. *adj.* Belonging to Galloway.
B. *sb.* An inhabitant or native of Galloway.

Gam (gæm), *sb.* 1850. [? dial. var. of GAME *sb.*] A herd or school of whales; also, a social meeting of whalers at sea.

Gam (gæm), *v.* 1851. [Cf. prec.] **1.** *intr.* Of whales: To gather together and form a school 1889. **2.** *trans.* Of whalers: To meet and gossip with (another ship). Also *intr.*

Gama grass (gā·măˌgrɑs). Also **gamma.** 1858. [? Altered f. GRAMA.] A tall and strong fodder grass, the *Tripsacum dactyloides* of Linnæus, native of the south-eastern coasts of N. America.

Gamash (gămæ·ʃ), *arch.* and *dial.*; chiefly in *pl.* 1596. [a. F. *gamache*; identified with Sp. *guadamaci* a kind of leather, perh. a. Arab. *ghadāmasī*, f. the name of Ghadāmas in Tripoli, where a special kind of leather was made.] A kind of leggings or gaiters, worn to protect the legs from mud and wet.

‖**Gamba**[1] (gæ·mbă). [L.; see JAMB.] *Anat.* The elongated metacarpus or metatarsus of the Ruminants or Solipeds. BRANDE.

Gamba[2] (gæ·mbă). 1598. [Short for VIOL DA GAMBA.] **1.** = VIOL DA GAMBA. Also *gamba viol.* **2.** An organ-stop, resembling a violoncello in tone 1869.

Gambade (gæmbēⁱ·d). 1821. [A readoption (by Scott) of F. *gambade*: see GAMBOL.] A leap or bound of a horse; also *fig.* a prank, frolic.

Gambado[1] (gæmbēⁱ·do). Chiefly in *pl.* **-oes, -os.** 1656. [f. It. *gamba* leg + -ADO[2].] A kind of large boot or gaiter, attached to the saddle, to protect the rider's legs and feet.

His thin legs tenanted a pair of gambadoes, fastened at the side with rusty clasps SCOTT.

Gambado[2] (gæmbēⁱ·do). Chiefly in *pl.* **-os, -oes.** Also more correctly **gambadas.** 1820. [a. Sp. *gambada* = F. *gambade*; see GAMBOL.] **1.** = GAMBADE. **2.** A fantastic movement; a caper 1859. **3.** *fig.* Any sudden or fantastic action 1857. Hence **Gamba·do** *v. intr.* to prance, caper.

Gambeson (gæ·mbĭsǫn). Now *Hist.* ME. [a. OF. *gambison*, *gambeison*, *wambizon*, etc.; prob. f. (ult.) OTeut. *wambâ* belly (see WOMB).] A military tunic of leather or thick cloth, sometimes padded; worn esp. in the 14th c., under the habergeon, but sometimes without other body-armour.

Gambet (gæ·mbĕt). 1776. Anglicized f. next.

‖**Gambetta** (gæmbe·tă). 1678. [mod.L., a. It., f. *gamba* leg.] *Ornith.* The name of a bird somewhat resembling the Redshank. Now used for the Ruff.

Gambier (gæ·mbiᵊɹ). Also **gambeer, gambir.** 1830. [Malay *gambīr*, the plant.] An astringent extract prepared from an Eastern plant (*Uncaria Gambir*), and largely used for tanning and dyeing.

Gambist (gæ·mbist). 1823. [f. GAMBA[2] + -IST.] *Mus.* A performer on the viola da gamba.

Gambit (gæ·mbit). 1656. [Ult. ad. It. *gambetto* (= OF. *gambet*, *jambet*) tripping up the heels (in wrestling), f. *gamba* leg.] *Chess.* A method of opening the game, in which a pawn or piece is sacrificed for position. Also *fig.*

fig. The widow's g. was played, and she had not won the game 1860.

Gamble (gæ·mb'l), *sb.* Chiefly *colloq.* 1823. [f. GAMBLE *v.*] **1.** An act of gambling 1879. **2.** Any course involving risk and uncertainty.

Gamble (gæ·mb'l), *v.* 1775. [Prob. a dial. survival of an altered form of ME. *gamene-n*, OE. *gamenian* to sport, play.] **1.** *intr.* To play games of chance for money; to stake money on some chance. Also *fig.* **b.** To speculate recklessly 1884. **2.** *trans.* To stake 1885; with *away*: To lose by gambling 1808.

1. *fig.* Gambling against the world for life or death CARLYLE. 2. Bankrupts and sots, who have gambled or slept away their estates 1808. Hence **Ga·mbler,** †a fraudulent gamester, a sharper; one who habitually plays for money.

Gamboge (gæmbōu·dʒ, -būdʒ). 1712. [ad. mod.L. *gambogium* (now in pharmacy *cambogia*), f. *Cambodia*, in Annam, whence obtained.] **1.** A gum-resin obtained from trees of the genus *Garcinia*, natives of Cambodia, Siam, etc. It is largely used as a pigment, giving a bright yellow colour, and also as a drastic purgative. **2.** *attrib.*, as *g.-yellow*, etc. 1837. Hence **Gambo·gian** *a.* g.-coloured.

Gambogic (gæmbōu·dʒik), *a.* Also **gambodic, cambogic.** 1839. [f. GAMBOGE + -IC.] Only in *gambogic acid*, a resin which is the chief constituent of gamboge.

Gambol (gæ·mbŏl), *sb.* 1503. [orig. *gambad*, *-baud(e*, *-bald(e*, a. F. *gambade* leap or spring, ad. It. *gambata*, f. *gamba* leg. Subseq. the *d* was dropped in *gambald*; cf. *curtal*.] †**1.** The bound or curvet of a horse (*rare*) –1533. **2.** A leap or spring in dancing or sporting; a caper, frisk. Now chiefly *pl.*, of the sportive movements of children or animals. 1513. **b.** *transf.* and *fig.* in *pl.* Frolicsome movements or proceedings. Rarely *sing.*, a frolic. 1596. †**3.** A plaything –1630. †**4.** *attrib.* Playful –1664.

2. b. Those crisped snakie golden locks Which makes such wanton gambols with the wind SHAKS.

Gambol (gæ·mbŏl), *v.* Infl. **gambolled** (-bŏld), **gambolling** (in U.S. often with single *l*). 1507. [ad. F. *gambader*; cf. prec.] †**1.** *intr.* Of a horse: To bound or curvet (*rare*) –1533. **2.** To leap or spring, in dancing or sporting; now chiefly of animals or children 1508. Also *transf.* and *fig.* 1508.

2. *fig.* A nation, gamboling in an ocean of superfluity BURKE.

Ga·mbrel. Now *dial.* See also CAMBREL. 1547. [perh. a. OF. (Norman) **gamberel* (=

sense 1).] 1547. 1. = CAMBREL 1. 2. = CAMBREL 2. 1601. 3. *U.S.* Short for *gambrel roof* 1859. *Comb.* **g. roof**, a curved or hipped roof, so called from its resemblance to the shape of a horse's hind leg; hence *g.-roofed* adj.

Gambroon (gæmbrū·n). 1831. [? after *Gambroon*, a town on the Persian Gulf.] 'A kind of twilled cloth for linings' (Simmonds).

Game (gēⁱm), *sb.* [Com. Teut.: OE. *gamen, gomen* str. neut., identified by some with Goth. *gaman* neut., f. *ga-* prefix, together, 'com-' (see Y- prefix) + root of MAN.] 1. Amusement, fun, sport. *Obs.* exc. *dial.* †2. Jest, as opp. to *earnest.* Also (with *a*), a jest. -1626. 3. An amusement, diversion. †Also *collect.*, play. ME. †b. *spec.* Amorous play. *Tr. & Cr.* IV. v. 63. c. *colloq.* A 'lark' 1838. 4. A diversion of the nature of a contest, played according to rules, and decided by superior skill, strength, or good fortune ME. b. *Gr.* and *Rom. Antiq.* Usu. *pl.* (= L. *ludi*): Athletic, dramatic, and musical contests; gladiatorial and other shows ME. c. *The game*: the proper method of play 1889. 5. *fig.* A proceeding, scheme, intrigue, undertaking, followed up like a game ME. b. A person's policy; also, the course best suited to one's interests 1698. c. *pl.* Tricks, dodges 1660. 6. A definite portion of play in any GAME (sense 4); 'a match at play' (J.) ME. b. Position or advantage in play 1677. c. The course or event of a game. Also *fig.* 1827. †7. The winning position, the victory, the mastery; also, the prize -1621. 8. a. A 'set' of players 1741. b. *pl.* In trade use: Apparatus for games 1895. c. The number of points required for winning. d. The state of the game (*mod.*). †9. Sport derived from the chase -1719. 10. The quarry ME. b. *transf.* and *fig.* An object of pursuit; an object in view 1573. 11. *collect.* Wild animals or birds such as are pursued, caught or killed in the chase ME. b. The flesh of such animals used for food 1848. 12. A flock or herd of animals kept for pleasure. *Obs.* exc. in *a g. of swans* 1482. 13. The characteristics of a game-fowl; spirit for fighting, pluck, endurance. Also predicatively of a person possessing these qualities. 1747. 14. Short for *game-fowl* 1867.

1. *L. L. L.* v. ii. 360. 2. *Mids. N.* I. 240. Phr. *To make* (†*a*) *g. of*: to make fun of, turn into ridicule. 3. A wilde pleiere of someres gamenes WYCLIF. c. 'Oh, here's a g.', whispered the rest of us HUGHES. 4. A g. in which there was an agreeable mingling of skill and chance GEO. ELIOT. Phr. *Round, square g.* (see ROUND, SQUARE). c. He..is not playing the g. 1889. 5. Alva..resolved to play his g. warily 1650. No man ever knew better how to play *a waiting g.* WOLSELEY. b. In the present state of things, it [a battle] is more Buonaparte's g. than mine SIR J. MOORE. Phr. *The same old g.* 6. A Rubber is two games won out of three 1862. Phr. *The game is up* = is lost. *To force the g.* (see FORCE *v.*[1]). *G. and g.*: one g. to each side. (*To play*) *a good, a poor,* etc. *g.*: to be a good, a poor, etc. player. c. France ..held the g. in her hands HALLAM. 9. 3 *Hen. VI*, IV. v. 11. 10. Hearke, the G. is rows'd..The G. is vp *Cymb.* III. iii. 98, 107. b. Phr. *Fair g.*: a legitimate object of pursuit, attack, etc.; also *forbidden g.* I fly at higher g. MARRYAT. 11. Sanguinary laws were enacted to preserve the g. GOLDSM. b. G. every day THACKERAY. 13. Phr. *Cock of the g.*: see COCK *sb.*[1] The fifth..died all g. and bottom BYRON.

Comb. 1. General: as *g.-bird, -pie,* etc.; *g.-preserver, -stealer,* etc.

2. Special: **g.-act**, an Act of Parliament regulating the killing of g.; **-bag**, a bag for holding the g. killed by a sportsman; **gameball** (Tennis), the position in which one side requires a single point to win; **g. bantam**, a bantam of a fighting breed; **-cast** (*Bowls*), a ball placed so as to make sure of the g.; **-certificate** = *game-licence*; **-hole**, the last hole on a cribbage-board; **-licence**, a licence to kill or deal in g.; **-tenant**, one who rents the shooting or fishing on an estate; **-trespass**, trespassing in pursuit of g.

Game (gēⁱm), *a.*[1] 1727. [f. the sb. (sense 13).] Having the spirit of a game-cock; full of pluck, showing fight; spirited. b. Having the spirit or will *for* or *to do* (something) 1856.

She [the mare] was evidently g. to the backbone MAYNE REID. Phr. *To die g.*: to meet death resolutely; *fig.* to maintain one's pluck to the last. The ruffian lay perfectly still and silent. 'He's gaun to die g., ony how', said Dinmont SCOTT.

Game (gēⁱm), *a.*[2] 1787. [?] Of a leg or arm: Lame. Also *transf.*

Game (gēⁱm), *v.* [OE. *gam(e)nian*, ME. *gam(m)en*, f. *gamen* GAME *sb.*[1]] 1. *intr.* To play, sport, jest; to amuse oneself; *occas.* to indulge in amorous play. Now *dial.* †2. *trans.* To amuse, please. ME. only. 3. *intr.* To play at games of chance for a prize, stake, or wager; to gamble 1510. b. With *away*, etc.: To get rid of (money, etc.) by gambling 1634.

3. 'Tis a great pity he..games so deep SHERIDAN.

Ga·me-cock. 1677. [f. GAME *sb.* + COCK *sb.*[1]] A cock of the breed used in cock-fighting.

Ga·me-fowl. 1784. [f. GAME *sb.* + FOWL *sb.*] a. A fowl of some species regarded as game. b. A domestic fowl of the species used in cock-fighting 1867.

†**Ga·meful**, *a.* ME. [f. GAME *sb.* + -FUL.] 1. Joyful, playful, sportive, jesting -1725. 2. Fond of field sports 1704. 3. Abounding in game -1704. Hence **Ga·mefully** *adv.*

Ga·mekee·per. 1670. [f. GAME *sb.* + KEEPER.] A servant employed to take care of game, prevent poaching, etc.

Ga·me-law. 1714. [f. GAME + LAW.] Usu. *pl.* Laws enacted for the preservation of game.

Gameless (gēⁱ·mlės), *a.* 1848. [see -LESS.] Destitute of game.

Gamely (gēⁱ·mli), *adv.* 1861. [f. GAME *a.*[1] + -LY[2].] With spirit, pluckily.

Gameness (gēⁱ·mnės). 1810. [f. GAME *a.*[1] + -NESS.] Game quality; endurance, pluck.

Gamesome (gēⁱ·msŏm), *a.* ME. [f. GAME *sb.* + -SOME.] Full of play; frolicsome, sportive.

The Shepherd..piping to his Flocks and g. Kids THOMSON. Hence **Ga·mesome-ly** *adv.*, **-ness.**

Gamester (gēⁱ·mstəɹ). 1553. [f. GAME *sb.* + -STER.] †1. A player at any game; also, an athlete -1775. b. *dial.* (Berks.) A player at backsword or wrestling 1857. 2. A gambler. Also *fig.* 1553. †3. A merry, frolicsome person -1613. †4. One addicted to amorous sport; a lewd person -1668. 5. The keeper of a 'game' of swans. *Hist.* 1880.

2. The G...Oft risks his fortune on one desperate throw GOLDSM. 3. *Hen. VIII*, I. iv. 45. 4. *All's Well*, v. iii. 188. Hence **Ga·mestress**, a female g.

Gamete (gæmī·t). 1886. [ad. mod.L. *gameta*, ad. Gr. γαμετή a wife, γαμέτης a husband, f. γαμεῖν, f. γάμος.] *Biol.* A sexual protoplasmic body which on conjugation with another gives rise to a body called zygote. Also in comb. f. **gameto-**, as **gametophyte**, the sexual form of a thallophyte, as dist. from the sporophyte, or asexual form.

Hence **Ga·metal** *a.* of or pertaining to a g.: conjugating, reproductive. **Ga·metange** [Gr. ἀγγεῖον vessel], the cell or organ in which gametes are produced.

Gamgee (gæ·mdʒi). 1895. The name of S. *Gamgee* (1828-86) used *attrib.* in *Gamgee tissue*, or *absol.*, to designate an absorbent cotton-wool for dressing wounds.

Gamic (gæ·mik), *a.* 1856. [ad. Gr. γαμικός, f. γάμος marriage.] 1. *Biol.* Having a sexual character; sexual 1864. 2. *Geom. G. edges*, corresponding edges of an autopolar polyhedron. Also as *sb.*

Gamin (gamæ̃n). 1840. [a. F. *gamin.*] A neglected boy, left to run about the streets; a street Arab.

There are the little gamins mocking him THACKERAY.

Gaming (gēⁱ·miŋ), *vbl. sb.* 1501. [f. GAME *v.* + -ING[1].] 1. Gambling. †2. *Gr.* and *Rom. Antiq.* The celebration of games (see GAME *sb.* 4 b) -1606. 3. *attrib.* 1589.

Gamma (gæ·mă). ME. [Gr. γάμμα.] 1. The third letter of the Greek alphabet, Γ, γ. †2. = GAMUT. -1825. 3. A common moth, *Plusia gamma.* In full *g. moth.* 1869. 4. *Comb.* **gamma rays** (or γ-rays), specially penetrating rays emitted by radioactive substances.

‖**Gammadion** (gămēⁱ·diŏn). Also **gammation.** 1848. [a. late Gr., f. γάμμα] = FYLFOT.

Gammarid (gæ·mărid). 1852. [ad. mod.L. *Gammaridæ*, f. L. *gammarus* (*cammarus*), a. Gr. κάμμαρος a sea-crab or lobster; see -ID.] *Zool.* An individual of the family *Gammaridæ* of amphipodous crustacea, of which the typical genus is *Gammarus.* So **Gamma·rolite**, a fossil crustacean of the genus *Gammarus* or some allied genus.

Gammer (gæ·məɹ), *sb.* 1575. [contr. f. *grandmother.*] A rustic title for an old woman, corresponding to GAFFER for a man.

Gammon (gæ·mən), *sb.*[1] 1486. [a. ONF. *gambon* (mod.F. *jambon*) ham, f. *gambe* (mod. F. *jambe*) leg.] †1. The ham or haunch of a swine. Also *transf.* -1613. 2. The bottom piece of a flitch of bacon; also, a smoked or cured ham 1529.

Gammon (gæ·mən), *sb.*[2] 1689. [?] *Naut.* The lashing of the bowsprit. Now usu. GAMMONING.

Gammon (gæ·mən), *sb.*[3] 1730. [app. a survival of ME. *gamen* GAME *sb.*[1]] 1. The game of backgammon. Now *rare.* 2. A term of backgammon, denoting a victory in which the winner removes all his men before the loser has removed any; it scores equal to two 'games' 1735.

Gammon (gæ·mən), *sb.*[4] *slang* or *colloq.* 1720. [app. orig. thieves' slang, ? with allusion to prec. or *sb.*[2]] 1. *Thieves' slang.* In phrases *To give g.*: 'to side, shoulder, or stand close to a man or a woman, whilst another picks his or her pocket.' *To keep in g.*: to engage (a person's) attention while a confederate is robbing him. 2. Talk, chatter 1781. 3. Humbug, rubbish; ridiculous nonsense 1805. 4. quasi-*interj.* 1825.

Gammon (gæ·mən), *v.*[1] 1694. [f. GAMMON *sb.*[3]] 1. *trans.* To beat at backgammon by a gammon. †2. *intr.* To cheat at play in some particular way 1700.

Gammon (gæ·mən), *v.*[2] [f. GAMMON *sb.*[1]] To cure (bacon) by salting and smoking.

Gammon (gæ·mən), *v.*[3] 1711. [f. GAMMON *sb.*[2]] To lash (the bowsprit) with ropes to the stem of a ship. Said also of the rope.

Gammon (gæ·mən), *v.*[4] *slang* or *colloq.* 1789. [f. GAMMON *sb.*[4]] 1. *intr.* To talk (plausibly). 2. To pretend 1812. 3. *trans.* To stuff with nonsense, to humbug, hoax. Const. *into, out of.* 1812. Hence **Ga·mmoner**, one who gammons; one who gives gammon to an accomplice.

Gammoning (gæ·məniŋ), *vbl. sb.* 1833. [f. GAMMON *v.*[3] + -ING[1].] The lashing of ropes by which the bowsprit is made fast to the stem or cutwater.

Gamo- (gæ·mŏ), comb. f. Gr. γάμος marriage.

gamoma·nia [MANIA], a form of insanity characterized by strange and extravagant proposals for marriage; **gamomo·rphism** [Gr. μορφή], that stage of development of organized beings in which the spermatic and germinal elements are formed, matured, and generated, in preparation for another act of fecundation. Chiefly in adjs. used in Botany, describing plants or organs in which certain specified parts are united together, as **gamoga·strous** [Gr. γαστήρ], having the ovaries united: said of the pistil; **gamope·talous** [PETAL], having the petals united; **gamophy·llous** [Gr. φύλλον], having the leaves united; **gamose·palous** [SEPAL], having the sepals united.

Gamogenesis (gæmŏdʒe·nėsis). 1861. [See GAMO- and GENESIS.] *Biol.* Generation by the conjunction of structures from different individuals; sexual reproduction. Hence **Gamoge·ne·tic** *a.* of or pertaining to g., producing or produced by g. **Gamogene·tically** *adv.* in a gamogenetic manner.

Gamp (gæmp). 1864. [after Mrs. Sarah *Gamp*, a monthly nurse in *Martin Chuzzlewit*, who carried a large cotton umbrella.] 1. A monthly nurse or sick nurse of a disreputable type. 2. An umbrella, esp. one tied up in a loose, bulgy fashion 1864. Hence **Ga·mpish** *a.* (in sense 2).

Gamut (gæ·mət). 1529. [Contr. of med.L. *gamma ut*; f. GAMMA the name of the symbol Γ (repr. in the Middle Ages a note one tone lower than A) + UT, q.v., first of the six notes forming a hexachord.] 1. The first or lowest note in the mediæval scale of music, answering to the modern G on the lowest line of the bass stave. Now *Hist.* 1530. 2. The 'Great Scale' (ascribed to Guido d'Arezzo). Now *Hist.* 1529. 3. Hence: The whole series of notes that are used by musicians. Occas. also: The major diatonic scale, or any specified scale. 1709. **b.** The full range of notes of a voice or instrument 1639. **4.** *transf.* and *fig.* The whole scale, range, or compass of a thing 1626.

3. b. The gammuth of every municipal fidler MILT. 4. The painter's g. HOGARTH. The whole g. of Crime DICKENS.

Gamy (gēⁱ·mi), *a.* Also †**gamey.** 1844. [f. GAME *sb.* + -Y¹.] **1.** Abounding in game; bent upon game 1848. **2.** Spirited, plucky; showing fight to the last 1844. **3.** Having the flavour of game, esp. when it is 'high' 1863.

1. Any gamey..district 1892. 2. The g. bass 1883.

Gan, pa. t. of GIN; obs. inf. of GO.

†**Ganch,** *sb.* Also †**gaunch.** 1625. [related to next.] **1.** The apparatus employed in execution by ganching; the punishment itself. **2.** A gash made by a wild boar's tusk 1818.

†**Ganch,** *v.* Also †**gaunch.** 1614. [ad. F. **gancher* (in pa. pple. *ganché*), ad. It. **ganciare,* f. *gancio* hook.] **1.** *trans.* To impale upon sharp hooks or stakes as a mode of execution –1783. **2.** Of a boar: To tear or gash with the tusk –1783.

1. G. him, impale him, rid the world of such a monster DRYDEN.

Gander (gæ·ndəɹ), *sb.* [OE. *gan(d)ra,* the *d* being excrescent as in *thunder.* Used as the masc. of GOOSE (OE. *gōs* :—OTeut. **gans*), but perh. not cogn. with it.] **1.** The male of the goose. **2.** *fig.* A dull or stupid person 1553. **b.** *slang.* 'A married man; in America one not living with his wife' (Farmer).

Comb. **g.-month, -moon,** the month after a wife's confinement.

†**Gane,** *v.* [OE. *gánian* :—OTeut. **gainōjan.*] *intr.* To open the mouth wide, to gape or yawn –1570.

See how he ganeth lo this dronken wight CHAUCER.

Gang (gæŋ), *sb.* [OE. *gang, gong* :—OTeut. **gaŋgo-z,* related to **gaŋgan* GANG *v.*¹ to GO.]

I. †**1.** *pl.* Steps, goings, journeyings. OE. only. †**2.** The power of going –ME.; gait or carriage –1626. †**3.** A journey –ME. **4.** A way, road, or passage. Now *dial.* OE. **b.** A walk or pasture for cattle. *Sc.* and *n. dial.* 1808.

II. 1. A set of articles ME.; *esp.* a set of tools so arranged as to work simultaneously 1806. **2.** A company of workmen 1627; a company of slaves or prisoners 1790. **3.** Any company of persons who go about together or act in concert (in mod. use mainly for criminal purposes) 1632.

1. A g. of extremely light harrows A. YOUNG. 2. A g. of coopers 1863. 3. Nutt the pirate..with all his g. of varlets 1632. This company, both the ladies and all, are of a g. PEPYS.

attrib. and *Comb.,* as (sense II. 1) *g.-cultivator, -drill, -plough, -press, -saw,* etc.; (senses II. 2, 3) *g.-driver, -master, -robber, -system, -work.* Also **g.-mill,** a saw-mill in which g.-saws are used; **-rider,** one who rides on mine-cars or trams; **-road** (*local*), a road between a harbour and the buildings.

Gang, *v.*¹ Now *Sc.* and *dial.* [Com. Teut.: OE. *gangan, gongan* :—OTeut. **gaŋgan.* See GO.] *intr.* To walk, go. Also quasi-*trans.*

False gelden, g. thy gait B. JONS.

Gang (gæŋ), *v.*² 1856. [f. GANG *sb.* II. 2.] **1.** *trans.* To arrange in a gang. **2.** *intr.* With *in*: to come in a gang 1891. **3.** *U.S.* To go in company *with* 1928.

Ga·ng-board. 1748. [f. GANG *sb.*] Chiefly *Naut.* **1.** A narrow platform on deep-waisted ships, leading from the quarter-deck to the forecastle. **2.** A plank, usu. with cleats or steps nailed on it, for walking upon, esp. into or out of a boat 1777.

Ga·ng-cask. 1779. [f. GANG *sb.* + CASK.] *Naut.* A water-cask used on board ships for bringing water on board in boats.

Ga·ng-days. *Obs.* exc. *Hist.* OE. [f. GANG *sb.* + DAY; so called from the processions held on these days.] The three days preceding Ascension-day or Holy Thursday; also called Rogation-days.

Gange (gændʒ), *v.* 1861. [?] **1.** *trans.* To protect (a fish-hook, etc.) with fine wire. Now *dial.* or *arch.* **2.** To fasten (a fish-hook) to the GANGING (*Cent. Dict.*).

Ganger (gæ·ŋəɹ), *sb.*¹ ME. [f. GANG *v.*¹ + -ER¹.] **1.** One who travels on foot. **2.** A fast-going horse 1818.

Ganger (gæ·ŋəɹ), *sb.*² 1849. [f. GANG *sb.* or *v.*² + -ER¹.] An overseer in charge of a gang of workmen.

Ganger (gæ·ŋəɹ), *sb.*³ 1860. [? Short f. FOREGANGER.] *Naut.* Two or more lengths of chain cable shackled to the sheet anchor.

Gangetic (gæn,dʒe·tik), *a.* 1677. [ad. L. *Gangeticus,* f. *Ganges,* a. Gr.] Belonging to the river Ganges. †Also *sb. pl.* Those who live on the banks of the Ganges.

†**Ga·ng-flower.** 1597. [f. GANG *sb.* + FLOWER.] The milkwort (*Polygala vulgaris*), so called because it blossoms in the Gang or Rogation week.

Ganging (gæ·ndʒiŋ), *vbl. sb.* 1883. [f. GANGE *v.* + -ING¹.] **a.** 'The act of fastening a fish-hook to the line'. **b.** 'A section or part of a fishing-line to the free end of which a hook is ganged' (*Cent. Dict.*).

Gangliac (gæ·ŋgliæk), *a.* 1848. [f. GANGLION + -AC.] Relating to a ganglion. So **Ga·nglial** *a.,* **Ga·ngliar** *a.* pertaining to, or resembling a ganglion.

Gangliated (gæ·ŋgliēⁱtėd), *ppl. a.* 1804. [f. GANGLION + -ATE³ + -ED¹.] Furnished with ganglia.

Gangliform (gæ·ŋglifǭɹm), *a.* Also **ganglioform.** 1681. [f. as prec. + -FORM.] Having the form of a ganglion.

Ganglion (gæ·ŋgliǫn, -ən). *Pl.* **ganglia**; also **-as, -ons.** 1681. [a. Gr. γάγγλιον a tumour under the skin, on or near tendons or sinews; used by Galen to denote the complex nerve-centres.] **1.** *Path.* A tumour or swelling of the sheath of a tendon. 'Also . . an enlarged bursa mucosa' (*Syd. Soc. Lex.*). **2.** *Phys.* An enlargement or knot on a nerve, forming a centre from which nerve-fibres radiate 1732. **b.** A collection of grey matter (neurine) in the central nervous system, forming a nerve nucleus 1855. **c.** *fig.* A centre of force, activity, or interest 1828. **3.** *Phys.* A lymphatic gland 1831. **4.** 'Applied to the class of organs to which the spleen, the thymus gland, the thyroid body, and the adrenals belong' (*Syd. Soc. Lex.*) 1885. **5.** *Bot.* A swelling on the mycelium of certain fungi 1866.

2. c. A little g., or nervous centre, in the great vital system of immensity CARLYLE.

Comb.: **g.-cell, -corpuscle, -globule,** a nerve-cell in the grey matter of the central nervous system.

Hence **Ga·nglionary** *a.* furnished with ganglia. **Ga·ngliona:ted** *ppl. a.* = GANGLIATED. **Ganglio·nic** *a.* relating to, composed of, or furnished with ganglia.

Ga·ng-plank. *U.S.* 1861. [f. GANG *sb.* + PLANK.] A landing-plank; a gang-board.

Gangrel (gæ·ŋgrėl). *dial.* and *arch.* 1530. [app. f. GANG *sb.* or *v.*¹; cf. *haverel, wastrel,* etc.] **1.** A vagabond; a wandering beggar. **b.** *attrib.* or *adj.* Vagabond, vagrant 1538. **2.** A lanky, loose-jointed person 1585. Also *attrib.* as *adj.* 1650.

Ga·ngrenate *v.* 1582. [f. GANGRENE *sb.* + -ATE³.] To make, or become, gangrenous –1758.

Gangrene (gæ·ŋgrīn), *sb.* 1543. [ad. L. *gangræna* (*-grena*), a. Gr. γάγγραινα an eating sore.] **1.** A necrosis of part of the body, extending over some considerable area in a visible mass. Occas., the first stage of mortification. **2.** *fig.* 1602.

2. To the community..corruption is a g. JOHNSON. Hence **Ga·ngrenous** *a.* having the nature of g., or affected with it.

Gangrene (gæ·ŋgrīn), *v.* 1607. [f. prec. sb.] To become or cause to become mortified. Also *fig.* Hence **Gangrene·scent** *a.* becoming gangrenous.

Gangsman (gæ·ŋzmăn). 1793. [f. GANG *sb.* + MAN.] **1.** A dock-porter. **2.** One who has charge of a gang of workmen 1863.

Gangster (gæ·ŋstəɹ). orig. *U.S.* 1896. [f. GANG *sb.* + -STER.] A member of a gang of criminals or toughs.

Gangue (gæŋ). Also **gang.** 1809. [a. F. *gangue,* ad. Ger. *gang* a vein or lode, f. as GANG *sb.*] The earth or stony matter in a mineral deposit; the matrix in which an ore is found.

Gangway (gæ·ŋweⁱ). [OE. *gangweg,* f. GANG *sb.* + *weg* WAY.] **1.** A road, thoroughfare, or passage of any kind. Now *dial.* **2.** A passage in a building; *esp.* one between rows of seats in a public edifice 1702. **b.** In the House of Commons, the cross-passage about half-way down the House, giving access to the rear-benches (rarely *pl.*) 1875. **3.** *Naut.* **a.** = GANG-BOARD 1. 1688. **b.** A narrow passage left in the hold of a laden ship 1780. **c.** The opening in the bulwarks by which persons enter or leave a vessel; now more commonly = GANG-BOARD 2. 1780. **4.** *Mining.* 'A main level, applied chiefly to coal mines' (Raymond) 1776.

Phr. *To bring to the g.*: 'to punish a seaman by seizing him up to a grating, there to undergo flogging' (Smyth).

Comb.: **g.-ladder,** a ladder over the side by which the ship is entered; **g. netting,** in war-ships, the netting with which the g. between quarter-deck and forecastle is fenced.

†**Ga·ng-week.** [OE. *gangwuce,* f. GANG *sb.* + *wuce* WEEK.] Rogation week, in which the GANG-DAYS fell –1607.

Ganister (gæ·nistəɹ). Also †**gann-.** 1811. [?] A close-grained siliceous stone from the lower coal-measures in Yorkshire, used to form furnace-hearths; also in lining Bessemer converters.

‖**Ganja** (gæ·ndʒă). 1800. [Hindi *gāṅjhā.*] A preparation of Indian hemp (*Cannabis sativa,* variety *indica*), strongly intoxicating and narcotic.

Gannet (gæ·nėt). [OE. *ganot,* f. (ult.) the same root as GANDER.] The Solan goose (*Sula bassana*).

Ganocephalan (gæ:nose·fălăn). 1865. [f. mod.L. *ganocephalus* (f. Gr. γάνος brightness + κεφαλή head) + -AN.] A fish of the extinct order *Ganocephala* (so called because their heads were covered with shining bony plates). So **Ganoce·phalous** *a.* belonging to this order.

Ganoid (gæ·noid). 1839. [a. F. *ganoïde,* f. Gr. γάνος + -ειδής; see -OID.]

A. *adj.* **1.** Of a fish-scale: Having a smooth shining surface, from being covered with a layer of enamel 1854. **2.** Covered with polished bony plates; distinctive epithet of an order of fishes (mod.L. *Ganoidei*) 1847.

B. *sb.* A ganoid fish 1839.

Hence **Ganoi·dal** *a.* = GANOID A. 2. **Ganoi·dean** *a.* and *sb.,* **Ganoi·dian** *a.* and *sb.* = GANOID A. 2 and B.

Ganoin (gæ·no,in). Also **-ine.** 1859. [f. Gr. γάνος + -IN.] The hard polished enamel which forms the superficial layer of ganoid scales.

Gansa, gansaw, obs. ff. GANZA.

Gantlet, obs. f. GAUNTLET.

Gantline, erron. f. GIRTLINE.

Gantlope (gæ·ntlōᵘp). Now *rare* exc. as GAUNTLET². 1646. [corruptly a. Sw. *gatlopp* (f. *gata* lane, GATE *sb.*² + *lopp* course).] A military punishment in which the culprit had to run stripped to the waist between two rows of men who struck at him with a stick or a knotted cord. *rare* exc. in *to run the g.* Also *transf.* and *fig.*

Gantry, gauntry (gæ·ntri, gǭ·ntri). 1574. [app. f. GAWN + TREE; or ? a perversion of OF. *gantier,* var. of *chantier* (:—med.L. *cantarium*) gantry.] **1.** A four-footed wooden stand for barrels. **2.** A frame or platform for carrying a crane or similar structure 1810.

Ganymede (gæ·nimīd). 1591. [ad. L. *Ganymedes,* a. Gr. Γανυμήδης, cupbearer to Zeus.] **1.** A cupbearer; *joc.* a pot-boy 1608. **2.** A catamite 1591. **3.** The largest satellite of the planet Jupiter 1868.

Ganza (gæ·nză). 1633. [Reading of the old edd. of Pliny *N.H.* x. xxii.] One of the birds (called elsewhere 'wild swans') which drew Domingo Gonsales to the moon in Bp. Godwin's romance.

Gaol (dʒēⁱl), **Gaoler** (dʒēⁱ·ləɹ), variant spellings of JAIL, JAILER. Both forms are correct, but recent Dictionaries prefer the J forms.

Gap (gæp), *sb.* ME. [a. ON. *gap*, chasm; sb. related to ON. and Sw. *gapa*, Da. *gabe* to GAPE.] 1. A breach in a wall or hedge; also *fig.* 2. A notch (now *rare*) 1530. 3. A mountain pass (common in U.S.) 1555. 4. An unfilled space or interval; a hiatus 1523.

1. A gappe in the churchyard wall 1584. Phr. *To stand in the g., to open a g.* 3. Two great Gaps that led thro' this Circuit of Mountains ADDISON. 4. *spec.* The distance between the upper and lower planes of a biplane, or between the spiral courses of the blades of an aeroplane propeller. b. *Electr.* = *spark-gap* (SPARK *sb.*[1]).

Comb.: **g.-bed-lathe, g.-lathe**, one with an opening in the bed or shears to allow a larger object to be turned; **-window**, a long and narrow window.

Gap (gæp), *v. rare.* 1847. [f. prec.] To become, or make, jagged or notched.

Gape (gēⁱp), *sb.* 1535. [f. GAPE *v.*] 1. The act of gaping; a yawn. 2. An open-mouthed stare; also *fig.* 1660. 3. The expanse of an open mouth or beak 1766; the part of the beak which can be opened 1833. 4. A rent or opening of any kind 1658.

Phr. *The gapes*: a. A disease in poultry, etc., of which frequent gaping is the symptom. b. A fit of yawning or staring (*joc.*).

Gape (gēⁱp), *v.* ME. [a. ON. *gapa* to open the mouth, gape, Sw. *gapa*, Da. *gabe*. Not found in Gothic. Cf. GALP *v.*] 1. *intr.* To open the mouth wide, esp. to bite or swallow anything. Said also of the mouth. Also *transf.* of earth, hell, etc. ME. 2. *intr.* To open as a mouth; to split, crack, part asunder 1577. 3. *absol.* To stare in wonder or admiration ME. 4. With *for, after,* †*at*: To be eager to obtain, to long for (something) ME. †5. To gasp from pain, heat, etc. –1572. 6. To yawn, esp. from weariness ME.

1. Opening their Mouths as wide as they could g. 1710. 2. When the ground gapes with the heate of the Sunne 1577. A wound that gapeth 1688. The seams g., or let in water SMYTH. 3. And ever he gaped upward into the eire CHAUCER. 4. A minde that gapeth for nothing but money 1638. 6. She stretches, gapes, unglues her eyes, And asks if it be time to rise SWIFT.

Comb. **g.-eyed** *a.*, in *Herpetology*, naked-eyed; having apparently no eyelids. Hence **Ga·pingly** *adv.*

Gaper (gēⁱ·pəɹ). 1559. [f. prec. + -ER [1].] 1. One that gapes 1637; †one who gapes for a thing –1628. 2. *Ornith.* a. The open-bill (*Anastomus oscitans*) 1871. b. One of the *Eurylæmidæ*; a broad-bill 1884. 3. A fish, the *Serranus Cabrilla*, also called *comber* 1828. 4. A bivalve mollusc of the family *Myidæ*: also *g.-shell* 1853.

Gape-seed (gēⁱ·psīd). 1600. [f. GAPE *sb.* or *v.* + SEED *sb.*] Something stared at by a gaping crowd; also, the act of staring.

Phr. *To seek, buy,* or *sow gape-seed*: to stare gapingly at a fair or market, instead of doing business.

Gaping (gēⁱ·piŋ), *vbl. sb.* ME. [f. GAPE *v.* + -ING [1].] 1. The action of GAPE *v.* 2. An opening or chasm in the earth. ? *Obs.* 1539. 3. *attrib.*, as **g.-stock**, an object of open-mouthed wonder 1817.

Gapped (gæpt), *ppl. a.* 1562. [f. GAP *sb.* or *v.* + -ED.] 1. Having the edge notched. 2. Full of holes or breaches 1854.

Gap-toothed (gæ·ptūþt), *a.* 1567. [f. GAP *sb.*[1] + TOOTHED.] Having the teeth set wide apart.

Gar (gāɹ), *sb.* Also **garr, guard.** 1765. [Short f. GARFISH.] a. A fish of the Pike or Esox family of the genus *Belone*, having long bill-like jaws; the gar-fish or gar-pike. b. A ganoid fish of the genus *Lepidosteus*, having rhombic scales. *Alligator-gar*, a gar (*L. tristœchus*) with a head like that of an alligator. 1843.

Gar (gāɹ), *v.* Chiefly *Sc.* and *n. dial.* ME. [a. ON. *ger(v)a* (Sw. *göra*, Da. *gjöre*) to make, do, etc. :—OTeut. **garwjan*, f. the adj. **garwu-* YARE.] †1. *trans.* To do, perform; to make. *rare.* –1662. 2. To make, to cause ME.

Garage (gæ·rāʒ, gæ·rėdʒ). 1902. [F., f. *garer* to shelter.] A building for the storage or refitting of motor vehicles. Also as vb.

Garancin (gæ·rănsin). Also **-ine.** 1843. [a. F. *-cine*, f. *garance* madder; see -IN.] *Chem.* A dyeing substance obtained from madder.

Garb (gāɹb), *sb.*[1] 1502. [a. ONF. *garbe*; of Teut. origin.] A wheat-sheaf. *Obs.* exc. *Her.*

Garb (gāɹb), *sb.*[2] 1591. [ad. It. *garbo* grace, elegance; of Teut. origin.] †1. Grace, elegance –1670. †2. A person's outward bearing –1703. †3. Style, manner, fashion –1694. 4. Fashion of dress, esp. official or other distinctive dress; hence *concr.* dress, costume. Also *transf.* and *fig.* 1622.

3. You thought, because he could not speake English in the natiue g., he could not therefore handle an English Cudgell *Hen. V*, v. i. 80. 4. Hose and doublet, The horse-boy's g. FLETCHER.

Garb (gāɹb), *v.* 1599. [f. prec. sb.] *trans.* To cover with a garb, to clothe, dress. Also *fig.*

These black dog-Dons G. themselves bravely TENNYSON.

Garbage (gā·ɹbėdʒ), *sb.* ME. [prob. adopted from AF. Cf. OF. *garbe* sheaf with sense 3.] 1. The offal of an animal used for food; esp. the entrails. 2. Refuse in general (in U.S. *esp.* kitchen, etc. refuse); filth. Also *fig.* of literary matter. 1583. †3. Wheat straw and the ears, chopped small as food for horses –1617.

†Garbage (gā·ɹbėdʒ), *v.* 1542. [f. prec. *sb.*] 1. *trans.* To remove the offal from; to gut (fish) –1672. 2. *intr.* To feed on offal 1650.

1. Pilchards .. are there taken, garbaged, salted, hanged in the smoke HOLLAND.

Garbell, obs. f. GARBOARD.

Garble (gā·ɹb'l), *sb.* 1502. [prob. ad. It. *garbello*, f. *garbellare* to GARBLE.] †1. Refuse (of spices); extraneous matter –1809. †2. Goods containing dross or waste –1638. 3. The process of garbling 1808.

Garble (gā·ɹb'l), *v.* Also **†garbel.** 1483. [App. ad. It. *garbellare*, ad. Arab. *gharbala* (also *karbala*) to sift, select; perh. f. late L. *cribellare*, f. *cribellum*, dim. of *cribrum* sieve.] †1. *trans.* To sift, cleanse (const. *of*); also with *out* –1812. 2. To select or sort out the best in. Now *rare.* Also with *out.* 1483. 3. To make selections from with a purpose; to mutilate with a view to misrepresentation 1689.

1. To g. red pepper 1657. 2. Phr. *To g. the coinage.* 3. To g. correspondence MILL, evidence PEEL.

Garbler (gā·ɹbləɹ). 1592. [f. prec. + -ER [1].] 1. An official who garbled spices, etc. *Obs.* exc. *Hist.* 2. One who garbles or mutilates (statements, etc.) 1693.

Garbling (gā·ɹbliŋ), *vbl. sb.* 1483. [f. GARBLE *v.* + -ING [1].] 1. The action of GARBLE *v.* 2. *concr. pl.* The refuse or remainder of a commodity after selection of the best 1881.

Garboard (gā·ɹbōᵊɹd). Also **†garbell, †-ble.** 1626. [app. a. Du. *gaarboord*, f. *garen* short for *gaderen* to GATHER + *boord* BOARD *sb.*] The first range of planks laid upon a ship's bottom, near the keel. Also *transf.* of iron vessels. Also *attrib.*, as **g.-strake** = garboard.

Garboil (gā·ɹboil), *sb. Obs.* exc. *arch.* 1548. [ad. OF. *garbouil, garbouille*, ad. It. *garbuglio*, conn. w. L. *bullire* to BOIL; the origin of *gar-* is disputed.] Confusion, disturbance, tumult; an instance of this. Hence **†Ga·rboil** *v.* to confuse, agitate, disturb. (Also erron. for GARBLE *v.*)

‖Garçon (garsoñ). 1839. [Fr.] A boy, serving-man, waiter; in Eng. use a waiter in a French hotel or restaurant.

Gard, gard-: see GUARD, GUARD-.

Gardant, obs. f. GUARDANT.

‖Garde-du-corps (gardədükor). 1651. [Fr.; lit. 'guard of the body'.] A body-guard; a member of a body-guard.

Garden (gā·ɹd'n), *sb.* ME. [a. ONF. *gardin* :—pop.L. **gardinum*, f. **gardum*, a. Teut. **gardo-z* (see GARTH and YARD).] 1. An enclosed piece of ground devoted to the cultivation of flowers, fruit, or vegetables; often with defining word, as *flower-, fruit-, kitchen-*, etc. *g.* b. *pl.* Ornamental grounds, used as a place of public resort 1838. c. *transf.* of a region of great fertility 1596. 2. a. Short for *Covent Garden, Hatton Garden*, localities in London 1763. b. *pl.* In names of squares and streets 1848. 3. A name for the school of Epicurus (who taught in a garden) 1867.

1. Ile fetch a turne about the G. *Cymb.* I. i. 81. c. Fruitful Lombardie, The pleasant g. of great Italy *Tam. Shr.* I. i. 4. *The G. of England*: a name assumed by various counties. 3. [Neither] the Porch, the G., nor the Academy M. PATTISON.

Comb. 1. General: a. with sense 'of or belonging to a garden', for use in a garden', as *g.-alley, -bed, -mould, walk, -wall*, etc. b. with sense 'cultivated or growing in a garden', as *g.-creeper, -flower*, etc.; *g.-honesty, -mint, -pea, -poppy*, etc.; **†g.-balsam,** *Trifolium odoratum.* c. with sense 'having the garden as its habitat', as *g.-ant, -ousel*, etc.; **-warbler,** the bird *Sylvia hortensis*; **-white,** a white cabbage butterfly of the genus *Pieris.* d. in the slang phr. *common or g.* = 'common', 'ordinary'.

2. Special: **g. city,** a real estate development combining the advantages of town and country life, as by providing open spaces and garden plots; so **g. suburb**; **-engine,** a portable force-pump used for watering gardens; **-frame** (see FRAME *sb.*); **-glass,** (*a*) a bell glass used for covering plants in a g.; (*b*) a round globe of dark-coloured glass, placed on a pedestal, in which the surrounding objects are reflected—much used as an ornament of gardens in Germany; **-party,** one held on a lawn or in a g.; **-plot,** a plot of land used as a g.: **-pot,** †a watering-pot; a flower-pot; **-roller,** a heavy cylinder fitted with a handle or shafts, for smoothing a lawn or path; **g. seat,** a seat for use in a g.; a similar seat fixed on the roof of an omnibus, etc.; hence **-seated** *a.*; **-stuff,** vegetables raised in a g.; **-wall-bond** (*Brick-laying*), a bond consisting of three stretchers and one header in nine-inch walls.

Garden (gā·ɹd'n), *v.* 1577. [f. the sb.] 1. *intr.* To cultivate a garden; to work as a gardener; †also, to lay out a garden. 2. *trans.* To cultivate as a garden 1862.

1. When Ages grow to Ciuility .. Men come to Build Stately, sooner then to G. Finely BACON.

Gardener (gā·ɹd'nəɹ). ME. [a. OF. **gardinier*, (mod. *jardinier*), f. *gardin*; see GARDEN *sb.* and -ER [2].] One who tends, lays out, or cultivates a garden; *spec.* a servant who does this.

Comb.: **gardener's delight, eye,** *Lychnis coronaria*; **gardener's garters,** the striped garden variety of *Phalaris arundinacea.* Hence **Ga·rdenership.**

Gardenesque (gā·ɹd'nˌesk), *a.* 1838. [f. GARDEN *sb.* + -ESQUE; after *picturesque.*] Partaking of the character of a garden.

Ga·rden-ga·te. ME. [f. as prec. + GATE *sb.*[1]] A gate leading into a garden. Also used *dial.* as a name for Herb Robert, the Pansy, and London Pride.

Ga·rdenhood. [f. as prec. + -HOOD.] Garden-like character. H. WALPOLE.

Ga·rden-house. 1603. [f. GARDEN *sb.* + HOUSE.] 1. Any small building in a garden. 2. A dwelling-house situated in a garden 1607. †b. A brothel –1625.

Gardenia (gaɹdī·niă). 1760. [mod.L., f. the name of Dr. Alex. *Garden* (died 1791).] A genus of trees and shrubs, often spiny (N.O. *Rubiaceæ*), natives of the Cape of Good Hope, etc.

Gardening (gā·ɹd'niŋ), *vbl. sb.* 1577. [f. GARDEN *v.* + -ING [1].] The action or occupation of laying out or cultivating a garden; horticulture. Also *attrib.*

Gardenless (gā·ɹd'nlės), *a.* 1834. [f. GARDEN *sb.* + -LESS.] Destitute of gardens or of a garden.

Gardenly (gā·ɹd'nli), *a. rare.* 1819. [f. as prec. + -LY [1].] Befitting a garden.

Garderobe (gā·ɹdrōᵘb). Now *Hist.* ME. [a. F., f. *garder* to keep + *robe* ROBE. See WARDROBE.] Prop., a store-room, armoury, wardrobe (occas. also the contents of this); by extension, a private room, a bedchamber.

†Gardon. 1611. [a. F.] A kind of roach (*Leuciscus idus*).

Gardyloo (gāɹdilū·). 1771. [app. f. *gare de l'eau*, pseudo-Fr. for *gare l'eau.*] An old Edinburgh cry before throwing slops, etc. from the windows into the street.

†Gare, *sb.* 1542. [a. AF. *gare* = OF. *gard, jart.*] Coarse wool such as grows about the shanks of a sheep –1607.

‖Gare (gāɹ), *v. imp.* 1653. [a. F.] A cry: Look out! Take care!

Gare-fowl (gēᵊ·ɹfaul). Also **†gairfowl.** 1698. [ad. ON. *geir-fugl.* The meaning of *geir-* is unkn.] The great auk (*Alca impennis*).

Garfish (gā·ɹfiʃ). ME. [app. f. OE. *gār* spear + FISH, in allusion to its long sharp nose.] A fish (*Belone vulgaris*) with a long spear-like snout, called also green-bone, horn-fish, sea-pike, etc. In America and Australia a name for other fishes of similar form, e. g. various species of *Lepidosteus* and *Hemirhamphus.*

†**Ga·rgalize**, *v. rare.* 1605. [var. of GARGARIZE, prob. affected by GARGLE.] To gargle -1611.

Garganey (gā·ɹgăni). 1668. [Given by Gesner as the It. name used about Bellinzona.] A species of teal (*Anas querquedula*).

Gargantua (gāɹgæ·ntyuă). 1571. Name of the large-mouthed voracious giant of Rabelais' work (1542); *gen.* a giant. Hence **Garga·ntuan** *a.* gigantic 1596.

You must borrow me Gargantuas mouth first SHAKS.

†**Gargarism** (gā·ɹgăriz'm). ? *Obs.* ME. [ad. L. *gargarisma*, a. Gr., f. γαργαρίζειν to gargle.] **1.** A gargle. **2.** A disease of the throat which attacks swine -1688. var. (sense 1) †**Gargarise.**

Gargarize (gā·ɹgărəiz), *v.* ? *Obs.* 1533. [ad. L. *gargarizare*, ad. Gr. γαργαρίζειν. Repl. by GARGLE.] **1.** *trans.* To wash or cleanse (the mouth or throat) with a gargle. **2.** To gargle (a liquid) 1578. **3.** *intr.* To gargle 1569.

†**Garget**[1]. *rare.* ME. only. [a. OF. *gargate, garguette*; see GARGIL[1], GARGOYLE.] The throat.

Garget[2] (gā·ɹgėt). 1587. [? spec. use of prec.] **1.** An inflamed condition of the head or throat in cattle and pigs. **2.** Inflammation in a cow's or ewe's udder 1725. **3.** *transf.* and *fig.* A distemper, plague 1615. **4.** Short for **g.-plant** (*U.S.*), the Virginian poke-weed 1788.

†**Gargil**[1]. *rare.* 1558. [ad. OF. *gargouille*, perh. conn. w. L. *gurgulio*.] The gullet -1632.

Gargil[2]. Now *dial.* 1601. [f. prec.] **1.** A disease in cattle and pigs, also in geese, attacking the head and throat. **2.** = GARGET[2] 2. 1760.

Gargil(l(e, obs. ff. GARGOYLE.

Gargle (gā·ɹg'l), *sb.* 1657. [f. GARGLE *v.*] Any liquid used for gargling.

Gargle (gā·ɹg'l), *v.* 1527. [ad. F. *gargouiller*, f. *gargouille* throat; cf. GARGIL[1].] **1.** *trans.* To hold (a liquid) suspended and rattling in the throat. ? *Obs.* **2.** To wash (the throat or mouth) with a liquid held suspended in the throat 1616. **3.** *fig.* To utter with a sound as of gargling 1635. **4.** *intr.* To perform the act of gargling 1601.

Gargol, obs. f. GARGIL[2], GARGLE.

Gargoyle (gā·ɹgoil). Also †**gurgoyle**, etc. ME. [a. OF. *gargouille, gargoule*; app. a spec. sense of *gargouille* throat. With *gurgoyle* cf. med.L. *gurgulio*.] A grotesque spout, representing some animal or human figure, projecting from the gutter of a building, in order to carry the rain-water clear of the walls. Also *attrib.*

Garibaldi (gæribæ·ldi). 1862. [Name of an Italian general (1807–82).] **1.** A kind of blouse worn by women, in imitation of the red shirt worn by Garibaldi and his followers. Orig. *attrib.* as *G. jacket.* **b.** *Garibaldi biscuit*, a sandwich biscuit containing a paste of currants 1898. **2.** A red pomacentroid fish (*Hypsypops rubicundus*) of the Californian coast 1885.

Garish (gē°riʃ), *a.* 1545. [Orig. *gaurish*, perh. f. GAURE *v.* to stare.] **1.** Obtrusively or vulgarly bright in colour, showy, gaudy. **2.** Of colour, light, etc.: Excessively bright, glaring 1568. **3.** †Wanting in self-restraint; flighty -1678.

1. The g. service of the Masse 1636. The g. scene W. IRVING. **2.** Som .. garment .. gaurish in colour ASCHAM. The G. Sun SHAKS. Day's g. eye MILT. The g. day NEWMAN. **3.** Fame and glory makes the mind loose and g. SOUTH. **Ga·rish-ly** *adv.*, **-ness.**

Garland (gā·ɹlănd), *sb.* ME. [a. OF. *garlande, gerlande.* Also found as F. *guirlande*, It. *ghirlanda.* Of unkn. origin.] **1.** A wreath made of flowers, leaves, etc., worn on the head like a crown, or hung about an object for decoration. Also *fig.* **2.** A wreath, chaplet, or coronet of gold or silver work, or the like ME. **3.** †**a.** A royal crown or diadem -1615. **b.** The wreath conferred upon the victor in the Greek and Roman games, etc. 1500. †**c.** *fig.* The principal ornament, 'glory' -1637. **4.** *fig.* An anthology, a miscellany 1612. **5.** *Her.* A wreath of laurel or of oak leaves, interspersed with acorns 1828. **6.** Something that resembles a garland: e. g. **a.** *Arch.* an ornamental band surrounding a spire, etc. 1490; †**b.** a ring-like marking or band -1673; **c.** the ring in a target in which the mark was set 1847. **7.** *Mining.* 'A spiral groove, made behind and in the stoning or ginging of a shaft, for collecting the water which oozes out of the different strata' (Rees) 1819. **8.** *Naut.* **a.** A band or collar of rope (or iron) used for various purposes; **b.** (also *Mil.*) a receptacle for shot; **c.** a kind of net used by sailors as a locker or cupboard for provisions 1769.

1. The horned Sacrifice, mantled with Ghirlonds 1652. **3. a.** *Rich. III*, III. ii. 40. **b.** *To gain, get, win*, etc. *the g.* **c.** You..call..Him vilde, that was your G. *Cor.* I. i. 188.

Comb. **g.-flower**, (*a*) a flower suited for making garlands; (*b*) a common name for *Hedychium*; also applied to *Daphne Cneorum*, etc.

Hence **Ga·rlandage** (*rare*), display of garlands. **Ga·rlandless** *a.* **Ga·rlandry**, garlands collectively.

Garland (gā·ɹlănd), *v.* ME. [f. prec. *sb.*] **1.** *trans.* To form (flowers) into a garland (*rare*). **2.** To deck with or as with a garland 1593.

2. Their hair..gyrlanded with sea grass B. JONS.

Garlic (gā·ɹlik). [OE. *gárléac* (f. *gár* spear + *léac* LEEK).] **1.** A plant of the genus *Allium* (usu. *A. sativum*) having a bulbous root, a very strong smell, and an acrid, pungent taste. †**2.** Name of a jig or farce -1630.

1. *Clove of g.* (see CLOVE *sb.*[1] 1). *Oil of g.*, an essential oil obtained from the bulb and stem of g.

Comb.: **g.-pear (tree**, the American plant *Cratæva gynandra*; **-shrub**, *Bignonia alliacea*; also *Petiveria alliacea*; **g. (treacle)-mustard**, †**g. treacle-wort**, *Sisymbrium Alliaria* (*Alliaria officinalis*); **-wort** = *g.-mustard.*

Hence **Ga·rlicky** *a.* savouring or smelling of g.

Garment (gā·ɹmĕnt), *sb.* ME. [a. OF. *garniment, garnement* (pl. *garnemens*) equipment, etc., f. Rom. **gwarnire*, OF. and mod. *garnir* to furnish; see GARNISH.] Any article of dress; in *sing.* esp. an outer vestment; in *pl.* = clothes. Now somewhat *rhet.* Also *fig.*

I do not like the fashion of your garments *Lear* III. vi. 84. Hence **Ga·rmentless** *a.* **Ga·rmenture**, array, attire.

Garment (gā·ɹmĕnt), *v.* 1547. [f. prec.] *trans.* To dress or clothe; chiefly in pa. pple. *garmented.* Also *transf.* and *fig.*

And thus were they garmented CAMDEN.

Garner (gā·ɹnəɹ), *sb.* [ME. *gerner*, a. OF. *gerner, gernier, grenier* :—L. *granarium*, f. *granum* grain. Now *granary* is usual, exc. *rhet.*] A storehouse for corn, granary. Also *attrib.* var. †**Ga·rnery.**

Garner (gā·ɹnəɹ), *v.* ME. [f. prec.] **1.** *trans.* To store or deposit in or as in a garner. **2.** *intr.* To accumulate. TENNYSON.

1. But there where I haue garnerd vp my heart *Oth.* IV. ii. 57.

Garnet[1] (gā·ɹnėt). ME. [a. OF. **gernat, grenat*, ad. med.L. *granatum*, ? transf. use of L. *granatum* POMEGRANATE (cf. next), so called from its resemblance in colour to the pulp of the fruit; or ? a deriv. of L. *granum, grana* GRAIN, cochineal. See also GRANATE[2].] A vitreous mineral, commonly found as a distinct crystal, and in the form of a rhomboidal dodecahedron, but also occurring in other shapes. The precious garnet is of a deep transparent red. Also *attrib.* as *g.-red* adj.

Comb.: **g.-berry**, the red currant, *Ribes rubrum*; **-blende**, a sulphide of zinc; **-rock**, a rock consisting mainly of g. Hence **Garneti·ferous** *a.* producing garnets.

†**Garnet**[2]. ME. [a. OF. (*pome*) *garnette, gernate* POMEGRANATE.] The pomegranate; also *g.-apple* -1673.

Garnet[3] (gā·ɹnėt). 1485. [cf. Du. *granaat, kranaat.*] *Naut.* A tackle for hoisting light goods into a ship. *Comb.* **clew-garnets**, 'a sort of tackle wove through a g.-block' (Smyth).

Garnierite (gā·ɹniĕrəit). 1875. [After Jules *Garnier*, its discoverer; see -ITE.] *Min.* A hydrous silicate of nickel and magnesium.

Garnish (gā·ɹniʃ), *sb.* ME. [f. GARNISH *v.*] †**1.** A set of vessels for table use, *esp.* of pewter -1674. †**2.** Dress. *Merch. V.* II. vi. 45. **3.** Embellishment, decoration. Also *concr.* an ornament. *lit.* and *fig.* ? *Obs.* 1615. **4.** Things added to a dish for ornament; also *fig.* of literary 'dishes' 1673. **5.** *slang.* Money extorted from a new prisoner as a jailer's fee, or as drink-money for other prisoners (abolished by 4 Geo. IV, c. 43, § 12) 1592. **b.** A similar payment among workmen; also *maiden-g.* 1759.

3. To put on some g. and dress of virtue to impose on the world CLARENDON. **5.** [Gaoler, to a prisoner] You know the custom, Sir. G., Captain, G. *Beggar's Opera* II. vii. (1728) 27.

Comb.: **g.-bolt**, a bolt having a chamfered or faceted head; **-money** = sense 5.

Garnish (gā·ɹniʃ), *v.* Pa. t. and pple. **garnished** (-niʃt). ME. [ad. OF. *garniss-, garnir, guarnir, warnir* to fortify, defend (oneself), provide (mod.F. *garnir*); ? ad. Teut. **warnjan*, represented by OE. *warnian* refl. to take warning, beware (ME. *wernen* trans. = WARN *v.*[1]).] †**1.** *trans.* To furnish with means of defence -1786. †**2.** To equip or arm (oneself) -1750. **3.** To fit out with anything that beautifies; to decorate, embellish (*with*, †*of*). Now somewhat *rhet.* ME. **4.** To decorate (a dish) for the table 1693. †**5.** Of trees: To cover (a wall, etc.). Also *absol.* -1712. **6.** *slang.* To fit with fetters (J.) 1755. **7.** *Law.* **a.** To serve notice on (a person), for the purpose of attaching money belonging to a debtor 1577. **b.** To serve (any one) with notice of payments to be made before he can be returned as an heir (abol. 6 Geo. IV, c. 105) 1585. **c.** To summon as party to a litigation already in process.

3. When he is come he findeth it [the house] empty, swept, and garnished *Matt.* xii. 44. **4.** G. the dish with lemon, and send it to table MRS. GLASSE.

Hence **Ga·rnished** *ppl. a.*; *spec.* in *Her.* provided with appendages of different (specified) tincture. **Ga·rnishry**, adornment. BROWNING.

Garnishee (gāɹniʃī·). 1627. [f. GARNISH *v.* 7 + -EE.] *Law.* One in whose hands money belonging to a debtor is attached at the suit of the creditor. Also *attrib.*, as *g.-order*, etc. Hence **Garnishee·** *v.* to attach a debtor's money thus.

Garnisher (gā·ɹniʃəɹ). 1515. [f. GARNISH *v.* + -ER[1].] One who garnishes (GARNISH *v.*).

Garnishment (gā·ɹniʃmĕnt). 1550. [f. GARNISH *v.* + -MENT.] **1.** Adornment. **2.** *Law.* A notice, either general, or for (*a*) summoning a third party to appear in a suit, (*b*) attaching money in the hands of a third person 1585.

†**Garnison**, *sb.* ME. [a. OF. *garnison* (ONF. *warnison*: see WARNISON), f. *garnir* to GARNISH. Repl. in 16th c. by GARRISON.] **1.** Defence; means of defence -1489. **2.** Provisions for an army, a besieged place, etc. -1500. **3.** A body of men stationed in a place for defence -1609. Hence †**Garnison** *v.* (*rare*), to garrison (a place).

Garniture (gā·ɹnitiŭɹ). 1532. [a. F., f. *garnir.*] **1.** Furniture, appurtenances. **2.** Ornament, added to dress 1667; or generally 1685. **3.** Apparel 1827. **4.** Dressing of a dish. Also *fig.* 1725.

2. A man of g. and feather DRYDEN. That train of female g. which passeth by the name of accomplishments LAMB.

‖**Garookuh, garrooka.** 1855. 'A fishing-craft of the Gulf of Persia' (Smyth).

Garotte: see GARROTTE.

†**Garous**, *a.* [f. L. *garum* + -OUS.] Of or resembling GARUM. Sir T. Browne.

Gar-pike (gā·ɹpəik). 1776. [see PIKE.] = GARFISH.

Garran: see GARRON.

Garret (gæ·rėt), *sb.* [ME. *garite*, a. OF. *garite, guerite* (mod. *guérite*) watch-tower; of Teut. origin, conn. w. OF. *guarir, warir* to preserve, ad. Teut. **warjan* to defend.] †**1.** A turret; a watch-tower -1598. **2.** A room within the roof of a house; an attic 1483. **3.** *slang.* The head 1796.

1. She putte her in a garet to see the Kinge Josue passe 1450. **2.** A dissertation upon the advantage of living in garrets L. STEPHEN.

Comb.: **g.-lock**, an inferior lock, made by men who work in a g.; **-master**, a cabinet-maker, locksmith, etc., who works on his own account, supplying both capital and labour.

Garret (gæ·rėt), *v.* 1845. [?] *Build.* To insert small pieces of stone into the joints of (coarse masonry).

Garreted (gæ·rėtėd), *ppl. a.* 1531. [f. GARRET *sb.* + -ED[2].] **1.** Provided with garrets (see GARRET *sb.* 1). **2.** Lodged in a garret (*rare*) 1837.

2. G., in his ancestral palace WORDSW.

Garreteer (gæ:rėtīᵊɹ). 1720. [f. GARRET *sb.* + -EER.] One who lives in a garret; *esp.* a literary hack.

Garrison (gæ·risən), *sb.* [ME. *garison*, a. OF. *garison, gareison, guerison* (ONF. *warison* WARISON), f. *garir, guerir*, ad. OHG. *warjan* to defend. In the later senses confused with F. *garnison* GARNISON.] †1. Store; gift. ME. only. †2. Protection; means of defence –1561. 3. †a. A fortress –1494. b. (from sense 4) A garrisoned place 1568. 4. †A troop –1535; hence, a body of soldiers stationed in a place for its defence. Also *fig.* 1542.

4. *fig.* A g. of empty..precepts MILT.
Phrases. *In g.* (*To go* or *be sent*) *into g.*
Comb.: *g.-artillery, -gun*, etc.; **g.-hack**, *slang*, a woman who flirts with the officers of a g.; **-hold**, occupation by means of a g.; **-town.**

Garrison (gæ·risən), *v.* 1569. [f. prec.] 1. To place troops in for defence. Also *fig.* 2. To occupy as a garrison. Also *transf.* and *fig.* 1645. 3. To put 'in garrison' or on garrison-duty. Also *fig.* 1596.

1. *fig.* Garrisoned against..fears GEO. ELIOT. 3. *fig.* Garrisoned round about him like a camp Of faithful souldiery MILT.

Garron, -an (gæ·rən). 1540. [a. Gael. *gearran*.] A small and inferior kind of Irish or Scotch horse.

Garrooka: see GAROOKUH.

Garrot[1] (gæ·rət). 1829. [a. F.] A sea-duck; esp. the Golden-eye (*Clangula glaucion*).

Garrot[2] (gæ·ret). 1824. [a. F.; see next.] 1. *Antiq.* A lever for winding a cross-bow. 2. *Surg.* A tourniquet 1845.

Garrotte, garotte (gărǫ·t), *sb.* 1622. [a. Sp. *garrote* = F. *garrot* stick. Cf. prec.] †1. A rackpin to tighten cords in packing (*rare*) 1629. 2. Execution by strangulation, as in Spain; the instrument of this 1622. 3. Highway-robbery by throttling 1852. Phr. *To tip the g.* (*slang*): to rob thus.

Garrotte, garotte (gărǫ·t), *v.* 1851. [ad. Sp. *garrotear*, f. *garrote*; see prec.] 1. *trans.* To execute by means of the garrotte. 2. To throttle in order to rob 1858. 3. *transf.* and *fig.* To strangle 1878. Hence **Garro·tter, garo·tter.**

Garrulity (gărū·līti). 1581. [a. F. *garrulité*, ad. L. *garrulitatem*.] The quality of being garrulous.

My crime, Shameful g. MILT.

Garrulous (gæ·rŭləs), *a.* 1611. [f. L. *garrulus* (f. *garrire* to chatter) + -OUS.] 1. Loquacious; *transf.* of birds, etc.: Chattering, babbling 1854. 2. Of speech: Wordy 1838.

1. Age..g., recounts The feats of youth THOMSON. *transf.* Birds grew g. PATMORE. 2. G. comments DISRAELI, history FREEMAN. Hence **Ga·rrulous-ly** *adv.*, **-ness.**

Garter (gā·ɹtəɹ), *sb.* *Sc.* **gartan, -en.** ME. [a. OF. *gartier, jartier*, f. OF. *garet, jaret* (mod. *jarret*) the bend of the knee. The *n* in the Sc. forms is obscure.] 1. A band worn round the leg to keep the stocking in place. b. *Naut. slang.* Fetters 1769. 2. *The Garter*, the badge of the highest order of English Knighthood, instituted *c* 1344; membership of this order; the order itself ME. 3. *Her.* a. = BENDLET. 1658. b. A strap or ribbon buckled in a circle, with the free end hanging down 1882. 4. *transf.* Anything resembling a garter in function or in shape; esp. a. *techn.* a semicircular plate, fitting into a groove in the screw of a bench-vice 1874; b. the band used in 'prick the g.'; whence, the game itself 1827; c. tapes for a circus-performer to leap over 1854. 5. Short for: a. *G. King of Arms* (see KING); b. *g.-snake* 1880.

2. Record the Garter's glory; A badge for heroes and for kings to bear DRYDEN. As well ask..for the next vacant g. THACKERAY. 4. Item, for a g. for the sydes [of cucking stool]..iijᵈ 1556. 5. b. The g. and the copperhead 1880.
Phrases. *To cast one's g.* (Sc.): to secure a husband. *In the catching up of a g.*: in a moment. *Pricking in the g.* (also *prick-the-g.*): a swindling game (see FAST-AND-LOOSE).
Comb.: **g.-blue**, dark blue, the colour of the G. ribbon; **-fish**, the scabbard-fish (*Lepidopus caudatus*); **-knee**, the left knee; **-robes**; **-snake** *U.S.*, a name of grass- or ribbon-snakes of the genus *Eutænia*; **-webbing**, elastic webbing for garters.

Garter (gā·ɹtəɹ), *v.* ME. [f. prec.] 1. *trans.* To tie with a garter. Also with *on, up*. Also *absol.* Also *transf.* 2. *Her.* To surround with a GARTER (sense 3b) 1864. Hence **Ga·rtered** *ppl. a.*; *spec.* wearing the Garter. **Ga·rtering** *vbl. sb.*; *spec.* the material of garters; in *pl.* = garters.

Garth[1] (gāɹþ). ME. [a. ON. *garð-r* = OE. *geard* YARD. Still dial.] 1. A piece of enclosed ground, usu. beside a building, a yard, garden, or paddock; freq. with defining word, as *cloister-, willow-g.*, etc. b. Short for: Cloister-g. (*rec.*). 2. = FISHGARTH. 1609.

1. A garden for potatoes..called a g. A YOUNG. b. The central grassplot of the cloisters—the g. 1890.

Garth[2] (gāɹþ). *n. dial.* ME. [North. form of *gerth* (see GIRTH).] 1. A saddle-girth. 2. A wooden hoop 1483. 3. Girth 1684.

‖**Garum** (gēᵊ·rǒm). 1587. [a. L., Gr. γάρον.] A Roman sauce made of fermented fish.

Garvie (gā·ɹvi). *Sc.* 1742. [?] A sprat.

Gas (gæs), *sb.*[1] Pl. **gases** (gæ·sėz). 1658. [A word invented by Van Helmont (1577–1644), modelled on Gr. χάος, Du. *g* representing Gr. χ.] †1. A supposed occult principle in all bodies, regarded as an ultra-rarefied condition of water –1743. 2. Any aeriform or completely elastic fluid 1779. *spec.* a. Gas for lighting or heating; orig. = COAL-GAS, now including *oil-gas*, etc. 1794. b. *Coal-mining.* Fire-damp mixed with air 1853. c. Coal-gas used to fill a balloon or airship 1792. d. = LAUGHING GAS 1894. e. Stomachic vapours 1882. f. = POISON-*gas* 1915. 3. A gas jet 1872. 4. *slang.* Empty talk; bombast 1847.

2. The three gases which compose the atmosphere HUXLEY. c. *fig.* Poltroons Swell'd by the g. of Courage to Balloons WOLCOTT.
Comb. 1. General: as *g.-globe* (GLOBE *sb.* 6), *-range* (RANGE *sb.*[1] III. 1), *-stove, -works* (WORK *sb.* II. 10), etc.
2. Special: **g.-alarm**, (*a*) one to warn of g.; (*b*) one to alarm by explosion of g.; **-bath**, a bath heated by g.; **-battery**, a voltaic battery operating by the generation of gases; **-bill**, (*a*) one granting powers to make and supply g.; (*b*) a bill for g. consumed; **-bleaching**, 'bleaching by means of sulphur dioxide' (*Cent. Dict.*); **-blower**, a stream of g. from a coal-seam; **-bottle**, (*a*) a retort; (*b*) *Med.* a vessel to hold compressed g.; **-buoy**, one with chambers filled with g. to supply the lamp; **-burner** (see BURNER); **-chandelier** = GASELIER; **-check**, a device in guns to prevent an escape of g. at the breach; **-coal**, bituminous coal used in making g.; **-cock**, a tap fitted to the g.-pipe; **-coke**, residuum of coal used in g.-making; **-condenser**, an apparatus for freeing coal-g. from its tar; **-drain** (*Coal-mining*), a heading for carrying off fire-damp; **-dregs**, the refuse of g.-making; **-engine**, one in which the power is obtained by the production or the rhythmical combustion and explosion of g. in a closed cylinder; **-firing**, firing a furnace so that the gaseous products of combustion are utilized as fuel; **-fixture**, a bracket or gaselier for g.; **-furnace**, (*a*) one for making g.; (*b*) one heated by g.; **-helmet** = *g.-mask*; **-holder**, a gasometer; **-indicator**, one for showing the pressure of g.; **-lime**, lime which has been used to purify coal-g.; **-mask**, a mask worn as a protection against poison-gas; **-microscope**, one lit by oxyhydrogen light; **-motor**, a g.-engine; **-pendant**, a g.-pipe hung from the ceiling and fitted with burners; **-pipe**, (*a*) one for conveying g.; (*b*) joc. term for an inferior gun; (*c*) = *gas-drain*; **-plate**, a steel disk, in Krupp guns, to receive the direct force of the powder-gases; **-retort**, a vessel for holding the material of which g. is to be made; **-ring**, (*a*) a thin perforated plate of metal used as a g.-check; (*b*) a hollow iron ring with jets burning g. for heating purposes; **-sand**, sandstone yielding g.; **-shell**, one charged with poison-gas; **-spectrum**, one formed from the rays of an incandescent g.; **-stoker**; **-stoking**, the heating of g.-retorts; **-tar**, COAL-TAR produced in the manufacture of coal-g.; **-tar** *v.*, to coat with g.-tar; **g. thermometer**, one in which g. is the expanding medium; **-washer**, one for removing the ammonia from g.; **-water**, water through which coal-g. has passed; **-well**, a boring in the earth, tapping natural g.

Gas, *sb.*[2] *U.S.* 1905. Colloq. abbrev. of GASOLENE b.

Phr. *To step* or *tread on the g.* (orig. *U.S.*): to accelerate a motor engine by pressing down the accelerator-pedal with the foot; *gen.* to put on speed.

Gas (gæs), *v.* Infl. **gassing, gassed.** 1847. [f. GAS *sb.*[1]] 1. To supply or light up with gas (*colloq.*) 1886. 2. To pass through a gas-flame, to remove fibres, as in gassing lace 1859. 3. To impregnate (slaked lime) with chlorine, in making bleaching-powder 1880. 4. To affect by or attack with (poison-) gas 1889. 5. *slang.* To deceive by talking gas (*U.S.*) 1847; *intr.* to vapour, talk idly 1875.

Gasalier, var. of GASELIER.

Ga·s-ba:g. 1827. 1. A bag in which gas is kept; *spec.* an airship's gas-container. 2. An inflated bag for plugging a gas-main during repairs 1884. 3. A 'windbag' 1889.

Gascoign, obs. f. GASKIN.

Gascon (gæ·skǫn), *sb.* ME. [a. F. *Gascon*.] 1. A native of Gascony. 2. Hence, a braggart 1771. 3. *attrib.* or *adj.* Pertaining to Gascony 1488. 4. *ellipt.* †a. Gascon wine 1630; b. Gascon dialect 1813.

2. They [the Irish] are the Gascons of Britain SCOTT.

Gasconade (gæskǫnē·ᵊd), *sb.* 1709. [See prec. and -ADE.] Extravagant boasting. Hence **Gascona·de** *v. intr.* to indulge in gasconades. **Gascona·der**, a braggart.

Gasconism (gæ·skǫniz'm). 1807. [See -ISM.] A spirit of vaunting.

Gascoyne, obs. f. GASKIN, GASCON.

Gaseity (gæsī·ĭti). 1852. [f. GASE-OUS + -ITY.] The state of being a gas.

Gaselier (gæsĕlīᵊ·ɹ). Also **gasalier.** 1849. [f. GAS *sb.*[1]] A frame to hold gas-burners.

Gaseous (gæ·sīəs, gē¹·sīəs), *a.* 1799. [f. GAS *sb.*[1] + -EOUS.] 1. Having the nature, or in the form, of gas. Also *fig.* 2. Relating to gases 1805.

1. *fig.* His g., illimitably expansive conceit GEO. ELIOT.

Ga·s-fi:tter. 1858. One who fits up buildings with gas-appliances.

Ga·s-fi:tting. 1865. 1. *pl.* Pipes, brackets, etc. for the use of gas. 2. Fixing gas-appliances. Also *attrib.*

Gash (gæʃ), *sb.* 1548. [(ult.) a. OF. **garse*, f. *garser*.] 1. A long and deep cut or slash, made in the flesh, or in any object. Also *fig.* b. The act of making such a cut 1829. 2. *U.S. slang.* The mouth 1852. 3. *attrib.*, as **g.-vein** (*Austral. Mining*), a V-shaped vein 1869.

1. He..received a mortal g. 1807. To heal..the sloe-tree's g. BROWNING.

Gash (gæʃ), *a.*[1] Now only *Sc.* 1589. [?] Dismal to look at.

His g. lookes and his abrupt answeres GREENE.

Gash (gæʃ) *a.*[2] *Sc.* 1706. [?] 1. Sagacious. 2. Wise-looking 1826. 3. Well-dressed 1785.

Gash (gæʃ), *v.* 1562. [For earlier *garsh*, f. ON. *garser, garsher* (Palsgr.).] 1. *trans.* To cut or slash; also *absol.* b. With *asunder* TENNYSON. 2. *intr.* To open in a gash (*rare*) 1750.

1. With barbarous blows they g. the dead BYRON.

Ga·shful, *a.* Now *dial.* 1620. [cf. GASHLY.] Ghastly.

Ga·shly, *a.* Now *dial.* 1633. [? altered f. GHASTLY.] Also *advb.* Hence **Ga·shliness.**

By all that is hirsute and g.! I cry STERNE.

Gasifica·tion. 1812. [f. GAS *sb.*[1] + -(I)FICATION.] The process of making into gas.

Gasiform (gæ·sifǭɹm), *a.* 1800. [f. GAS *sb.*[1] + -(I)FORM.] In a gaseous state.

Gasify (gæ·sifəi), *v.* 1828. [f. GAS *sb.*[1] + -(I)FY.] To make or become gaseous. Hence **Ga·sifi:able** *a.*

Gasket (gæ·skėt). 1622. [?] 1. A small rope for securing a furled sail to the yard. Chiefly in *pl.* 2. Tow, plaited hemp, etc. for packing a piston or caulking a joint 1829. Hence **Ga·sket** *v.* to tie with gaskets.

Gaskin[1] (gæ·skin). 1573. [? spec. use of GASCON.] †1. A kind of breech or hose. Chiefly *pl.* –1611. 2. The hinder thigh of a horse 1652.

Ga·skin[2]. *rare.* = GASKET.

Ga·s-light. 1808. a. The light of gas. b. A jet of lighted gas; chiefly *pl.* Also *attrib.* as *g.-l. paper, plate, print* (in Photography).

Ga·sma:n. 1821. 1. One who makes or supplies gas. b. A collector of gas-accounts. 2. One who attends to the gas-lights in a theatre 1865. 3. *Coal-mining.* (*U.S.*) One who examines the workings for fire-damp 1883.

Gasogene, var. of GAZOGENE.

Gasolene, gasoline (gæ·sǒlīn). 1871. [f. GAS *sb.*[1] + -OL + -ENE, -INE.] A volatile inflammable liquid, produced in distilling crude petroleum, and used for heating, etc. b. *U.S.* The petrol used for motor engines (cf. GAS *sb.*[2]) 1895.

Gasometer (gæsǫ·mĭtəɹ), **gazometer.** 1790. [ad. F. *gazomètre*, f. *gaz* GAS *sb.*[1] + *mètre*, ad.

Gr. μέτρον measure.] **1.** An apparatus for holding and measuring gas. **2.** A tank in which gas is stored for distribution 1808.

Gasometry (gæsǫ·mėtri). 1790. [f. GAS sb.[1]; see -METRY.] The science of measuring gases. Hence **Gasome·tric** a. relating to g.

Gasoscope (gæ·sǫskōup). 1858. [f. GAS sb.[1]; see -SCOPE.] An apparatus for indicating the presence of gas.

Gasp (gasp), sb. 1577. [f. GASP v.] A convulsive catching of the breath from exertion, the lessening of vital action, etc. Also *transf.*

Phr. *(One's) last g.*: the last attempt to breathe before death. *At the last g.*: at the point of death.

Gasp (gasp), v. ME. [a. ON. *geispa* to yawn (Sw. *gäspa*).] **1.** *intr.* To catch the breath with open mouth, as from exhaustion or astonishment. **2.** *trans.* To exhale (*occas.* to inhale) with convulsive breathings 1534.

1. Names..That would have made Quintilian stare and g. MILT. Phr. *To g. for* (occas. *after*); to pant for (air); also *fig.* The sick, for Air before the Portal g. DRYDEN. 2. He..lay gasping life away COWPER. Phr. *To g. one's last. To g. out*: to utter with gasps.

Gasper (ga·spəɹ). 1914. *colloq.* [f. prec.] A cheap cigarette.

Ga·s-pla:nt. 1. Bastard Dittany. (U.S. Dicts.) **2.** The apparatus in a gas-works 1889.

Gassendist (gæse·ndist). 1821. [f. *Gassendi* + -IST.] A follower of Gassendi.

Gasserian (gæsīə·riăn), a. Also **Casserian.** 1831. [f. Johann Laurentius *Gasser*; see -IAN.] Distinguishing epithet of the ganglion on the sensory trunk of the fifth cranial nerve.

Gassy (gæ·si), a. 1757. [f. GAS sb.[1] + -Y[1].] **1.** Full of gas; of the nature of gas. **2.** *slang.* Characterized by 'gas' (see GAS sb.[1] 4); given to 'gassing' 1863. Hence **Ga·ssiness.** *rare.*

†**Gast,** v. [OE. *gǽstan* :—OTeut. type **gaistjan.* See GHOST.] *trans.* To scare, terrify -1616.

Gasted by the noise I made *Lear* II. i. 57. Hence †**Gast** *ppl. a.* terrified.

†**Ga·ster,** v. 1593. [freq. of GAST v.; see -ER[5].] *trans.* To scare, terrify -1787.

Gasteromycetous (gæ:stėroməisī·təs), a. 1861. [f. Gr. γαστερ(ο)-, γαστήρ + μύκητες (pl. of μύκης fungus) + -OUS.] *Bot.* Of, belonging, or relating to the *Gasteromycetes*, one of the orders of Fungi.

Gasteropod, gastropod (gæ·stėrǫpǫd, gæ·strǫpǫd). Also †-pode. 1826. [ad. mod.L. *gasteropoda, gastropoda*; see next.]

A. *sb.* One of the Gasteropoda.

B. *adj.* Gasteropodous 1836.

‖**Gasteropoda, gastropoda** (gæstėrǫ·pǫdă, gæstrǫ·pǫdă), sb. pl. 1828. [mod.L., f. Gr. γαστερο-, γαστήρ stomach + ποδ-, πούς foot.] *Zool.* A class or group of molluscs (including the snails, limpets, etc.) so called from the ventral position of the locomotive organ. Hence **Gastero·podous, gastro·podous** a. belonging to the G.; pertaining to or marking a gasteropod.

Gastful: see GHASTFUL.

Gastly, obs. f. GHASTLY.

†**Ga·stness.** ME. [f. GAST *ppl. a.* + -NESS.] Terrified condition; terror, dread -1604.

Gastræa (gæstrī·ă). 1877. [mod.L., f. Gr. γαστερ-, γαστήρ.] **1.** = GASTRULA. Huxley. **2.** A primitive sac-like animal, whose existence Haeckel assumes, consisting of two layers of cells, an ectoderm and an endoderm.

Gastræa theory, the theory which makes this the ancestral form of the whole animal kingdom. So **Gastræ·ad,** one of the *Gastreades*, a division of sponges which does not develop beyond the gastrula stage.

‖**Gastralgia** (gæstræ·ldʒiă). 1822. [mod.L., f. as prec. + ἄλγος pain.] *Path.* Pain in the stomach. Hence **Gastra·lgic** a. and sb.

Gastric (gæ·strik), a. 1656. [f. as prec. + -IC.] Of or pertaining to the stomach; situated in the stomach; of the nature of a stomach.

The g. cavity 1830, artery 1842.

Phr. *Gastric fever*: now usually, enteric or typhoid fever. *G. juice* (formerly also *g. acid, liquor*): thin, clear, almost colourless fluid, of an acid nature, secreted by certain glands in the stomach, where it is the chief agent in digestion. Hence **Ga·stricism,** 'stomach diseases generally' (*Syd. Soc. Lex.*).

Gastriloquist (gæstri·lǫkwist). 1731. [f. *gastri-*, comb. f. Gr. γαστερ-, γαστήρ, after *ventriloquist.*] = VENTRILOQUIST. So **Gastri·loquous** a., **Gastri·loquy,** etc.

‖**Gastritis** (gæstrəi·tis). 1806. [mod.L., f. Gr. γαστερ-, γαστήρ + -ITIS.] *Med.* Inflammation of the coats of the stomach.

Gastro- (gæ·stro), occas. bef. a vowel **gastr-,** comb. f. Gr. γαστερ-, γαστήρ belly.

ga·stro-cata·rrhal a., connected with gastric catarrh; **ga·strocele** [Gr. κήλη tumour], hernia of the stomach; **gastro-co·lic** [Gr. κόλον the colon] a., pertaining to the stomach and the colon; **ga:stro-duode·nal** a., pertaining to the stomach and the duodenum; **-duodeni·tis,** inflammation of the stomach and the duodenum; **-ente·ric** a., pertaining to the stomach and intestines; **-enteri·tis,** inflammation of the stomach and intestines; hence **-enteri·tic** a.; **-epiplo·ic** a., pertaining to the stomach and the epiploon; **-hepa·tic** a., pertaining to the stomach and the liver; **-hystero·tomy,** the Cæsarean operation (see CÆSAREAN a.); **-intesti·nal** a. = *gastro-enteric*; **ga:stro-phre·nic** a., pertaining to the stomach and to the diaphragm; **ga:stro-pneumo·nic** a., pertaining to the stomach and to the lungs; **-pu·lmonary** a., **-pulmo·nic** a. = prec.; **-sple·nic** a., pertaining to the stomach and to the spleen; **-va·scular** a., pertaining jointly to the abdominal cavity and to a vessel.

‖**Gastrocnemius** (gæ:strǫˌknī·miǒs). *Pl.* **-cnemii** (knī·miəi). 1676. [mod.L., f. Gr. γαστροκνημία the calf of the leg.] The muscle which gives a 'bellying' form to the calf of the leg. Hence **Ga·strocne·mial, -ian** *adjs.* of or pertaining to the g.

Gastrodisc (gæ·strǒdisk). 1881. [See GASTRO- and DISK.] *Embryol.* The germinal area of a mammal.

Gastrolith (gæ·strǒliþ). 1854. [f. GASTRO- + Gr. λίθος.] A calculus in the stomach; *spec.* = CRAB'S-EYE 1.

Gastrology (gæstrǫ·lǒdʒi). 1810. [ad. Gr. γαστρολογία, f. γαστρο-, γαστήρ + λόγος.] The science of catering for the stomach; hence, cookery, good eating. So **Gastro·loger. Gastrolo·gical** a.

‖**Gastromalacia** (gæ:stromălē·ʃ[i]ă). 1855. [mod.L., f. GASTRO- + Gr. μαλακία softness.] *Path.* Softening of the coats of the stomach.

Gastromancy (gæ·stromænsi). Now *Hist.* 1610. [f. Gr. γαστρο-, γαστήρ + μαντεία.] Divination by the belly, i.e. either by figures seen in bellied glass vessels full of water, or by ventriloquism.

Gastronome (gæ·strǒnōum). 1823. [a. F., f. *gastronomie.*] One versed in good eating. So **Gastro·nomer. Gastro·nomist.**

Gastronomic, -al (gæstronǫ·mik, -ăl), a. 1828. [ad. F. *gastronomique*, f. as prec.] Of or pertaining to gastronomy. Hence **Gastrono·mically** *adv.*

Gastronomy (gæstrǫ·nŏmi). 1814. [ad. F. *gastronomie*, a. Gr. γαστρονομία, f. γαστρο-, γαστήρ, after ἀστρονομία.] The art and science of good eating.

Gastropod, Gastropodous: see GASTER-.

Gastrorrhaphy (gæstrǫ·răfi). Also **gastroraphy.** 1739. [ad. F. *gastroraphie*, ad. Gr. γαστρορραφία, f. Gr. γαστρο-, γαστήρ + root of ῥάπτειν to sew.] Suture of wounds in the abdomen.

Gastroscopy (gæstrǫ·skǒpi). 1855. [f. Gr. γαστρο-, γαστήρ + -σκοπία; see -SCOPY.] Examination of the abdomen for disease.

Gastrostomy (gæstrǫ·stŏmi). 1854. [f. GASTRO- + Gr. στόμα + -Y[3].] *Surg.* The operation of opening the stomach for the introduction of food.

Gastrotomy (gæstrǫ·tŏmi). 1656. [f. GASTRO- + Gr. -τομία.] The opening of the abdomen by incision, or of the stomach through the abdominal walls.

Gastrula (gæ·strulă). 1877. [mod.L. dim., f. Gr. γαστήρ.] *Embryol.* That form of the metazoic germ which consists of a cup with two layers of cells in the wall. Also *attrib.* Hence **Ga·strular** a. pertaining to a g., or to gastrulation. **Gastrula·tion,** the formation of a g.

Gastruran (gæstrū·răn). [f. mod.L. *Gastrura* neut. pl., f. Gr. γαστερ-, γαστήρ + οὐρά + -AN.]

A. *adj.* Of or pertaining to the *Gastrura* or stomatopodous crustaceans.

B. *sb.* [sc. *animal.*] In recent Dicts. So **Gastru·rous** a.

Gat (gæt). Also **gate.** 1723. [app. a. ON. *gat* opening, passage; see GATE sb.[1]] An opening between sandbanks; a channel, strait; in Kent, an opening in the cliffs.

Gat, pa. t. of GET v.

Gate (gēɪt), sb.[1] [OE. *geat* :—OTeut. type **gatom*. Perh. not allied either to GET or to GATE sb.[2]] **1.** An opening in a wall for entrance and exit, with a movable barrier for closing it; said with reference to a city or other enclosure, or the enclosure-wall of a large building. **2.** *ellipt.* for *gate(s of the city* as a place of judicial assembly. [A Hebraism.] OE. **3.** *trans.* A mountain-pass. Also *pl.* 1601. **4.** *fig.* A means of entrance or exit ME. **5.** The barrier itself; a framework of wood or iron, either of open-work or solid, turning on pivots or hinges, or sliding in a groove, and used either in a pair or singly OE. **b.** A contrivance for stopping or regulating the passage of water. (Cf. *flood-, lock-, sluice-g.*) 1496. **6.** *techn.* **a.** (*Locksmithing*) One of the apertures in the tumblers for the passage of the stub 1874. **b.** = SASH sb.[2] 2. 1874. **c.** An H-shaped arrangement of slots through which a gear-lever is pushed 1906. **7.** The number of persons who pay at the gates to see an athletic contest, etc.; also, the *gate-money* thus received 1888.

1. The Ladies Coach so stopt the G., that the Duke's could not possibly pass COTTON. Phr. *The gate(s of heaven, hell, paradise*, perhaps orig. apprehended in a material sense. Also *the gate(s of death*: a near approach to death. Most like the struggle at the g. of death KEATS. 2. Then went Boaz up to the g. and sat him down there *Ruth* iv. 1. 4. They [the senses] are the gates and windows of its [the soul's] knowledge DRUMM. OF HAWTH. Phr. *The ivory g., the g. of horn*: in Greek legend, those through which false and true dreams respectively come.

Comb.: **g.-bill** (at Oxford and Cambridge), a record of the times at which a man returns to college (or lodgings) after hours; also, the account of fines charged against a man for staying out late; **-boot,** the right of cutting wood for gates; **-chamber,** a recess in the side wall of a canal-lock, which receives the g.; **-crasher,** an uninvited intruder at a reception, etc. (*colloq.*, orig. *U.S.*); **-leg, -legged** a., designating a table with legs in a gate-like frame swinging back to allow the leaves to be shut down; **-money,** money paid at the gates for admission to an athletic meeting, etc.; **-saw,** a mill-saw which is strained in a g. or sash to prevent buckling; **-vein,** the *Vena portæ* (*Obs.* exc. *fig.*); **-works,** fortifications at the g. of a town, etc. Hence **Ga·ted** *ppl. a.* furnished with a g. or gates.

Gate (gēɪt), sb.[2] Now only *Sc.* and *n. dial.* ME. [a. ON. *gata.* See also GAIT sb.] **1.** A way, road, or path. **2.** A street, as in *Gallowgate*, etc. 1470. †**3.** A going, journey, course (*lit.* and *fig.*) -1677. **4.** Manner of going. *Obs.* exc. *spec.* (see GAIT sb.) 1637. **5.** Way, manner, or method of doing or behaving; a peculiar habit ME.

1. Phrases. *To come, go, ride a, the, his, her,* etc. *g. This (that) g.*: used advb. = this (that) way, in this (that) direction. *Some, any g.*: somewhere, anywhere.

Gate (gēɪt), sb.[3] 1677. [Cf. OE. *gyte* sb., pouring out.] *Founding.* **1.** †**a.** The little spout in the brim of casting ladles 1683. **b.** The opening or channel through which the molten metal flows into a mould 1677. **2.** The waste piece of metal cast in the gate 1839.

Gate (gēɪt), v. 1831. [f. GATE sb.[1]] *trans.* At Oxford and Cambridge: To confine (an undergraduate) to college.

Gate, obs. f. GOAT.

Gatehouse (gēɪ·tˌhaus). ME. [f. GATE sb.[1] + HOUSE sb.] **1.** A house (for a servant) at or over a gate. **2.** The apartment over the gate of a city or palace, often used as a prison; *spec.* that over the gate of the palace at Westminster 1587.

2. [The king's] messenger..was..committed to the G. 1647.

Ga·te-keeper. 1572. [f. GATE sb.[1] + KEEPER.] **1.** One who has charge of a gate. **2.** A species of butterfly 1819.

Gateless (gēɪ·tlės), a. 1608. [See -LESS.] Without a gate.

Ga·te-post. 1522. [f. GATE sb.[1] + POST sb.] A post belonging to a gate, either that on which it hangs, or that against which it shuts.

Ga·teway. 1707. [f. GATE *sb.*[1] + WAY.] 1. An opening through a fence or wall. ? *Obs.* 2. A frame or arch in which a gate is hung; a structure built at or over a gate, for ornament or defence. Also *attrib.* 1762. 3. *transf.* and *fig.* a. A means of egress or ingress 1842. b. = GATE *sb.*[1] 3. 1884.

3. a. At the gateways of the day TENNYSON.

Gather (gæ·ðəɹ), *sb.* 1555. [f. GATHER *v.*] 1. The amount gathered, crop. 2. *The gathers* (pl.), that part, *esp.* of a dress, which is gathered or drawn in 1663. 3. *techn.* 'The inclination forward of an axle journal, or spindle, usually one-tenth of its diameter' (Knight) 1874.

Gather (gæ·ðəɹ), *v.* [OE. *gad(e)rian* :—WGer. type *gadurðjan. The OTeut. root is *gad-.]

I. *trans.* †1. (Only with prefixed *ge-*.) To join; to put together. *Obs.* since early ME. 2. To bring together; to collect OE. 3. To collect (flowers, etc.) from the place of growth; to cull, pick, pluck; to collect as harvest (also *to g. in*) OE.; to pick up 1715. †4. To compile (literary matter) –1677. 5. To be the means of bringing together or accumulating ME. 6. To collect (contributions). Also *absol.* to make a collection. Now *rare.* ME. 7. To collect or acquire by way of increase; to gain 1590. 8. To collect (knowledge) by observation and reasoning; to infer, deduce, conclude. (= L. *colligere.*) 1535. 9. To draw into smaller compass, contract 1617; *spec.* to draw together or pucker (part of a dress) by means of a thread 1576. b. *Arch.* To contract or make narrower (a drain, chimney, etc.) 1703. 10. *techn.* a. *Glass-making.* To collect (melted glass) on the end of the blowing-tube 1839. b. To collect and place in order according to signatures (the printed sheets of a book). Also *absol.* 1683.

2. Up roos our host..And gadrede us togidre, alle in a flok CHAUCER. To g. the materials for nests GOLDSM. Phr. *To be gathered to one's fathers, to one's people*: to be buried with one's ancestors; hence, to die. 3. But they that have gathered it [the corn] shall eat it *Isa.* lxii. 9. A Rose just gather'd from the Stalk DRYDEN. 5. Standing streames geather filth GOSSON. To g. rust 1687. 7. Phr. *To g. breath*, etc.: to gain or recover breath. *To g. oneself (together).* †*To g. ground*: to gain ground. As Ev'ning Mist.. gathers ground fast at the Labourer's heel MILT. *To g. head*: to acquire strength; also to swell as a festering sore. *To g. way* (Naut.): 'to begin to feel the impulse of the wind on the sails, so as to obey the helm' (Smyth). 8. Pliny supposed amber to be a resin..which he gathered from its smell BERKELEY. 9. Golden the clasp that gathers her shining robe to her side BOWEN.

II. *intr.* (Chiefly = refl. uses of I). 1. To congregate, assemble OE. 2. Of things: To collect; to form or increase by the coming together of material ME. b. To accumulate and come to a head. Hence, of a sore, etc.: To develop a purulent swelling. OE. 3. To contract; to form folds or wrinkles (*rare*) 1577. 4. *Naut.* To make way (towards an object) 1577.

1. There gathered vnto him..a very great multitude 1 *Esdras* viii. 91. 2. One knows how a story gathers like a snowball MRS. CARLYLE. b. *fig.* Now do's my Proiect g. to a head SHAKS. 3. As fast years flow away, The smooth brow gathers SHELLEY. *To g. into the wind* (Naut.): to sail nearer to the wind.

Hence **Ga·therable** *a.* capable of being inferred.

Gatherer (gæ·ðərəɹ). ME. [f. prec. + -ER [1].] 1. One who gathers or collects (see GATHER *v.*); often with defining word, as *rent-, tax-g.* (now usu. *-collector*). 2. One of the front teeth of a horse 1696.

Ga·thering, *vbl. sb.* OE. [f. as prec. + -ING [1].] 1. The action of GATHER *v.*, in various transitive senses. Also with *in, out, up.* b. The action, also the result, of drawing in or contracting 1580. 2. The action of coming together; the result of this; union, accumulation OE. 3. *spec.* A suppurated swelling OE. 4. An assembly or meeting OE.; a signal (by beat of drum, etc.) 1653. 5. That which is gathered or brought together; *esp.* a collection in money (now *dial.*) ME. 6. *Bookbinding.* The arrangement of the loose sheets of a book in proper order 1683.

Comb.: **g.-board** (*Bookbinding*), a horseshoe-shaped table on which signatures are laid to be gathered; **-coal**, a large piece of coal, laid on the fire to keep it burning during the night; **-cry**, a summons to assemble for war; **-ground**, area from which the feeding waters of a river, etc., are collected; **-hoop**, one used by coopers to draw in the ends of the staves so as to allow the hoop to be slipped on them; **-peat**, a fiery peat which was sent round by the borderers to alarm the country in time of danger; also, a peat put into the kitchen-fire at night, to keep it alive till the morning.

Gatling (gæ·tliŋ). 1870. [The inventor's name, Dr. R. J. *Gatling.*] *attrib.* in *Gatling gun*, a form of machine gun, with a cluster of barrels into which the cartridges are automatically loaded at the breach. Also *Gatling* simply.

Gatten, var. of GAITER *sb.*[2]

†**Gat-toothed,** *a.* *rare.* [app. = GAP-TOOTHED, f. GAT *sb.* opening.] Having the teeth wide apart (pop. regarded as a sign of luck and of much travelling). CHAUCER.

‖**Gauche** (gōʃ), *a.* 1751. [F.] 1. Awkward, clumsy. 2. *Math.* Skew, not plane 1879.

2. If various points of the line do not lie in one plane, we have in one case..a curve of double curvature, in the other a g. polygon THOMSON & TAIT.

‖**Gaucherie** (gōʃəri). 1798. [F., f. prec.] Want of tact or manner, awkwardness; a gauche proceeding.

Gaucho (gau·tʃo, gō·tʃo). Also erron. Guacho. 1824. [Sp., prob. f. native S. Amer.] One of a mixed European and Indian race of equestrian herdsmen.

Gaud, *sb.*[1] Also **gaude.** *Obs.* exc. *Hist.* ME. [Prob. f. L. *gaudia.*] One of the larger beads placed between the decades of 'aves' in a rosary.

Gaud (gōd), *sb.*[2] [ME. *gaude*, f. (ult.) L. *gaudere* to rejoice.] †1. A trick, prank; often, a pretence; also a pastime –1796; a scoff, a laughing-stock –1650. 2. *concr.* A plaything, toy. Also, something gaudy; a gewgaw; a piece of finery. Now *rhet.* Also *fig.* ME. 3. *pl.* Fine doings, gaieties. Now *rhet.* 1650. 4. *sing.* Idle display 1800.

2. Solomon..giueth us gaudes to play withall 1591.

†**Gaud,** *v.*[1] ME. [f. GAUD *sb.*[1] and [2].] 1. *trans.* To furnish with gauds (see GAUD *sb.*[1]) –1552. 2. To ornament –1607.

2. Their nicely gawded Cheekes *Cor.* II. i. 233.

†**Gaud,** *v.*[2] 1532. [perh. f. GAUD *sb.*[2]] *intr.* To make merry; to jest; to scoff (*at*) –1580. He was sporting and gauding with his Familiars NORTH.

‖**Gaudeamus** (gōdi,ē·mŏs). 1823. [First word of a mod.L. students' song.] A college-students' merry-making.

Gaudery (gō·dĕri). 1597. [f. GAUD *sb.*[2] + -ERY.] Gaudy decoration; finery, fine clothes; a piece of finery.

Vice..trickt up with its alluring gauderies 1663.

†**Gau·dish,** *a.* 1538. [f. GAUD *sb.*[2] + -ISH.] Trivial; gaudy, showy –1587. Hence **Gau·dish-ly** *adv.*, **-ness.**

Gaudy (gō·di), *sb.* ME. [ad. L. *gaudium.*] †1. = GAUD *sb.*[1] –1560. †2. A taper (one of five, burnt to commemorate the Virgin's five joys) –1852. †3. = GAUD *sb.*[2] 2. 1555. †4. Rejoicing; a merry-making –1647. 5. A grand feast or entertainment; *esp.* an annual college dinner 1651. †Hence *pl.* 'Commons' for gaudy-days –1706.

†**Gau·dy,** *a.*[1] [ME. *gaude* app. a. OF. *gaude* weld + -Y [1].] Only in **gaudy-green,** green dyed with weld, yellowish green –1590.

Gaudy (gō·di), *a.*[2] 1529. [Cf. GAUDY *sb.* 4, also GAUD *sb.*[2], and -Y [1].] †1. Of fare: Luxurious –1601. 2. Brilliantly (now chiefly glaringly) fine or gay, showy 1583. b. *slang.* In neg. sentences: Very good 1884.

1. Where they make reuell and g. chere 1550. 2. Costly thy habit as thy purse can buy; But not exprest in fancy: rich, not gawdie *Haml.* I. iii. 71. A late notable gawdy Orator BAXTER. G. Dreams SEDLEY. b. Not a g. lot ASTLEY. Hence **Gau·dily** *adv.* **Gau·diness.**

Gau·dy, *v.* 1482. [f. GAUDY *sb.* and *a.*[2]] †1. *trans.* To furnish (a rosary) with gaudies –1542. 2. To make gaudy. SOUTHEY.

Gau·dy-day. 1567. [f. GAUDY *sb.* + DAY.] A day of rejoicing; *esp.* the day of a college gaudy. So **Gaudy-night** (*Ant. & Cl.* III. xiii. 183).

Gaudy-green: see GAUDY *a.*[1]

Gauffer, gauffre: see GOFFER.

Gauge, gage (gēdʒ), *sb.* Late ME. [a. ONF. *gauge* (mod. *jauge*), of unkn. origin. Not in other Rom. langs. The spelling *gauge* prevails in Eng., exc. in sense I. 5. American Dicts. prefer *gage.*]

I. 1. A standard measure or scale of measurement; *esp.* a measure of the capacity of a barrel, the diameter of a bullet, or the thickness of sheet iron. b. *transf.* and *fig.* Capacity, extent; dimensions, proportions 1655. †2. A limit of distance or extent. Also *fig.* HOLLAND. 3. *spec.* The distance between the rails of a railway, tramway, etc.; also, between the opposite wheels of a carriage 1841. 4. *techn.* a. The length of projection or *margin* of a slate or tile beyond that which overlaps it 1703. b. A measure of slate, one yard square 1847. 5. *Naut.* (Usually *gage.*) a. The position of one vessel with reference to another and the wind 1591. b. The depth to which a vesssel sinks in the water with a full cargo 1644. 6. *Plastering.* The greater or less quantity of plaster of Paris used with common plaster to accelerate its setting 1842.

1. The gadge of Hering 1595. A bullet of 50-gauge 1858. b. He [Howard] has visited all Europe..to take the gage and dimensions of misery, depression, and contempt BURKE. 3. *Mixed g.*: a broad and narrow g. laid down together. See also BROAD GAUGE, NARROW GAUGE. 5. Phr. *To have* or *keep the weather gage of*: to be to windward of; also *fig.* to get the better of. Also *lee gage.*

II. †1. A gauging-rod –1706. 2. A graduated instrument or vessel for gauging the force or quantity of a fluctuating object, as wind, etc. Also *rain-, wind-gauge*, etc.: see RAIN, etc. 1688. 3. A contrivance attached to a boiler, etc., to show the height or condition of its contents; more fully *g.-cock, -glass.* Of an air-pump: An instrument which indicates the degree of exhaustion in the receiver; usu. defined, as *barometer, siphon g.* (see those words) 1794. 4. An instrument for ascertaining and verifying dimensions 1677. 5. A carpenter's tool for marking lines parallel to the edge of a board 1678. 6. A contrivance to regulate the penetration of a cutting tool; as *auger-, boring-g.* 7. *fig.* A test 1691.

Comb.: **g.-cock,** one of two or three small cocks for ascertaining the height of the water in a steam boiler; **-concussion,** 'the lateral rocking of railway carriages against the rails' (Ogilvie); **-door,** a wooden door fixed in a mine airway for regulating the ventilation; **-glass,** a glass tube attached to a boiler to show the height of the water; **-knife,** a knife with a contrivance for regulating the amount cut off; **-ladder,** a horsing-block for raising the ends of wheeling planks in excavating; **-lathe,** a lathe for turning work to pattern or size; **-pin** (*Printing*), a small steel pin with teeth, for securing the lay on small platen machines; **-point,** a point marked to indicate the diameter of a cylinder one inch high containing a unit of a given liquid measure; **-rod,** a graduated rod for measuring with great accuracy the internal diameters of portions of work; **-saw,** a saw with a frame or clamp to determine the depth of kerf; **-stuff,** mortar containing three-fifths of fine-stuff and one of plaster of Paris; **-weir,** a weir fitted with movable shutters; **-wheel,** one attached to the forward end of a plough-beam, to gauge the depth of furrow.

Gauge, gage (gēdʒ), *v.* ME. [a. ONF. *gauger*, related to *gauge*; see prec.] †1. *trans.* To measure or measure off. ME. only. 2. To measure the dimensions, proportions, or amount of ME. 3. To ascertain the capacity or content of (a cask, etc.) by combined measurement and calculation 1483. 4. *fig.*; esp. to 'take the measure' of (a person, etc.) 1583. 5. To render conformable to a given standard; also *to g. up.* Hence *fig.* to limit. 1600. 6. To mark off (a measurement) 1678. 7. *Plastering.* To mix plaster in the right proportions for any purpose 1686. 8. *Dressmaking.* To draw up in parallel gatherings 1881.

2. To g. a foord NORTH, the mind CARLYLE, wire 1833, a river PHILLIPS. 3. To g. beer barrels MACAULAY. 4. You shall not gage me By what we doe to night *Merch. V.* II. ii. 208. 5. The stones are gauged and dressed by the hammer GWILT.

Gaugeable (gē·dʒăb'l), *a.* 1768. [f. prec. + -ABLE.] That may be gauged.

Gauged, gaged (gēdʒd), *ppl. a.* 1678. [f. GAUGE *v.* + -ED [1].] 1. Marked or measured with a gauge. 2. *Bricklaying.* Of bricks: Cut or rubbed accurately to size 1823. 3. *Plastering.* Mixed in the proper proportions for quick drying 1848.

3. *G. stuff* = gauge-stuff (see GAUGE *sb.*).

Gauger (gē¹·dʒəɹ). 1483. [a. AF. *gaugeour*, f. *gauger* GAUGE *v.*] 1. One who gauges (see the vb.); esp. an exciseman. 2. A gauging instrument 1580. Hence **Gau·gership.**

Gauging, gaging (gē¹·dʒiŋ), *vbl. sb.* ME. [f. GAUGE *v.* + -ING [1].] The action of GAUGE *v.*
Comb.: **g.-line**, a graduated line drawn on a gauging-rod or slide-rule; **-rod** = GAUGE-ROD.

Gauk, var. of GAWK.

Gaul (gǫl). 1601. [f. *Gaul*, a. F. *Gaule*, ad. L. *Gallia*, f. *Gallus* a Gaul.]
A. *sb.* a. An inhabitant of ancient Gaul 1630. b. *poet.* and *joc.* A Frenchman (*mod.*).
†B. *adj.* Gallic -1606.

Gaulish (gǫ·liʃ). 1659. [f. GAUL *sb.* + -ISH.]
A. *adj.* Of or pertaining to the ancient Gauls. Also (*poet.* or *joc.*): French.
B. *sb.* The language of the Gauls 1668.

Gault (gǭlt), *sb.* 1575. [?] *Geol.* Name of a series of beds of clay and marl, which appear between the upper and the lower greensand. Hence **Gault** *v. dial.* to dig g. **Gau·lter.**

Gaultheria (gǭlþī³·riă). 1848. [f. M. *Gaultier*, a Canadian botanist.] *Bot.* A genus of evergreen aromatic plants (N.O. *Ericaceæ*). The American Wintergreen, *G. procumbens*, yields a volatile oil called *g. oil*, used in the pharmacopœia.

Gaum (gǭm), *v.* 1796. [Cf. GOME *sb.*] *trans.* To smear with a sticky substance; to daub.

Gaunt (gǭnt, gānt), *a.* ME. [?] †1. Slim, slender, not fat -1736. 2. Abnormally lean, as from hunger; haggard-looking; tall, thin, and angular ME. 3. *transf.* Grim or desolate 1814.
2. G. am I for the graue, g. as the graue SHAKS. A tall g. woman 1882. 3. Like the g. echo of a hollow tomb 1814. Hence **Gau·ntly** *adv.*, **-ness.**

Gauntlet (gǭ·ntlėt), *sb.*[1] [ME. *gantelet*, a. F., dim. of *gant* glove (of Germ. origin); see -LET.] A glove worn as part of mediæval armour, usu. made of leather, covered with plates of steel. b. Used for CESTUS [2]. Dryden. 2. In rec. use: A stout glove, covering part of the arm as well as the hand, used in driving, wicket-keeping, etc. 1858. Also, the part covering the wrist 1882. †3. The plant *Campanula Trachelium*. LYTE. 4. *Naut.* 'A rope round the ship to the lower yard-arms, for drying scrubbed hammocks' (Smyth). [? A distinct wd.]
1. Phr. *To throw (down)*, etc., *the g.* (= F. *jeter le gant*): to give a challenge, from the mediæval custom of throwing down a glove or gauntlet on such occasions. *To take up*, etc., *the g.*: to accept a challenge (F. *relever le gant*). I cast them my G., take it vp who dares 1590. Hence **Gau·ntleted** *a.* covered or armed with a g. **Gau·ntlet** *v. trans.* to strike with a g. TENNYSON.

Gauntlet (gǭ·ntlėt, gā·ntlėt), *sb.*[2] 1661. [corrupted f. GANTLOPE, assim. to prec.] = GANTLOPE.

Gauntree, gauntrie, -y: see GANTRY.

Gaur (gauᵊɹ). Also **gour, gore.** 1806. [a. Hindustani.] A large species of ox, *Bos gaurus*, found wild in parts of India.

†**Gaure**, *v.* ME. [? freq. of GAW *v.*] *intr.* To stare, gape -1579.

Gauss (gaus). 1882. [f. Karl F. *Gauss*, the German mathematician (1777-1855).] *Physics.* A unit of intensity of a magnetic field. Hence **Gau·ssage**, the intensity of a magnetic field expressed in gausses. **Gau·ssian** *a.*, discovered or formulated by Gauss. **Gaussi·vity**, the intensity of magnetizing force expresssed in gausses.

Gauze (gǭz). 1561. [a. F. *gaze*, of unkn. origin. Identified with late L. *gazzatum* (Du Cange), and said to be named from Gaza in Palestine.] 1. A very thin, transparent fabric of silk, linen, or cotton; also, any similar fabric, as *wire-g.* 2. *transf.* A thin transparent haze 1842.
2. A blue g. of smoke T. HARDY. *Comb.* **g.-lamp**, a safety-lamp in which the flame is surrounded by wire-g.
Hence **Gau·zy** *a.* (whence **Gau·ziness**).

Gavel (gæ·vĕl), *sb.*[1] Now *Hist.* [OE. *gafol*, from the Teut. root **geb-* (OE. *giefan* GIVE).] 1. †Tribute. Only OE. and early ME. b. Rent OE. †2. Interest on money lent -1496. 3. *attrib.*, chiefly in legal terms relating to payments or services exacted from tenants OE.

Gavel (gæ·vĕl), *sb.*[2] Now *dial.* ME. [a. ONF. *gavel* masc., *gavelle* fem. (mod. *javelle*).] A quantity of corn cut and ready to be made into a sheaf.
Phr. *To lie on the g.*: to lie unbound.

Gavel (gæ·vĕl), *sb.*[3] *Pseudo-arch.* 1803. [f. GAVEL(KIND).] A partition of land among the whole tribe or sept at the death of the holder, with reference to Celtic practice. *Comb.*: **g.-act** or **g.-law**, a statute of Ireland (2 Anne) enforcing the principle of (English) gavelkind on Irish Catholics.

Gavel (gæ·vĕl), *sb.*[4] *U.S.* 1860. a. 'A mason's setting maul' (Knight). b. A president's mallet 1866.

Gavel (gæ·vĕl), *v.*[1] Now *dial.* ME. [f. GAVEL *sb.*[2]] *trans.* To collect mown corn into heaps, for loading.

Gavel (gæ·vĕl), *v.*[2] *Pseudo-arch.* 1828. [f. GAVEL *sb.*[3]] *trans.* To divide (land), according to the practice of gavelkind. Also *fig.*
They 'gavelled' the lands of Papists and made them descendible to all the children equally MAINE.

Gavel, north. var. of GABLE.

†**Gavelet.** ME. [f. GAVEL *sb.*[1] + ?] *Law.* A legal process against a tenant for non-payment of rent; chiefly relating to lands held in gavelkind -1741.

Gavelkind (gæ·vĕlkəind). [ME. *gavel(i)-kende* points to an OE. **gafol-ȝecynd*, sb. neut., f. *gafol* GAVEL *sb.*[1] + *ȝecynd* sort, condition, KIND. App. not of Celtic origin.] 1. The name of a land-tenure existing chiefly in Kent; orig. identical with SOCAGE, but quite early distinguished by the custom under which a tenant's land at his death was divided equally among his sons. 2. From the 16th c., often used to denote this custom generally 1531. Also *fig.* 3. *transf.* A similar Welsh custom of dividing property 1542. b. *Irish gavelkind*: a custom by which land, on the decease of its occupant, was thrown into the common stock, and the whole area redivided among the members of the sept 1612. 4. *attrib.* 1570.

Gaveller (gæ·vĕləɹ). ME. [f. GAVEL *sb.*[1] + -ER [1].] †1. A usurer. ME. only. 2. *Mining.* In the Forest of Dean: An officer of the Crown who grants gales to the miners 1692. 3. *Hist.* One who pays gavel for land rented 1862.

Gavelock (gæ·vĕlǫk). *Obs.* exc. *Hist.* and *dial.* [OE. *gafeluc*, in form a dim. of *gafel*, *ȝeafel* fork (see GABLE *sb.*).] 1. A spear or dart. †2. = GABLOCK 1. 1698. 3. An iron crowbar or lever 1497.

Ga·verick. *Cornwall.* 1846. The Red Gurnard.

Gavial (gē¹·viăl). Also **gar(rh)ial, etc.** 1825. [a. F., corruptly ad. Hindustani *ghariyāl.*] A saurian inhabiting the Ganges, dist. by its elongated muzzle from the American alligator and the African crocodile.

Gavotte (găvǫ·t). Also †**gavot(t.** 1696. [a. F., ad. mod. Pr. *gavoto*, dance of the Gavots, i. e. natives of the Alps.] a. A dance resembling the minuet, but more lively. b. The music for this dance; a piece of music in common time, moderately quick, and consisting of two parts, each of which is repeated.

†**Gaw**, *v.* ME. [cf. ON. *gá* to heed.] *intr.* To gape, stare -1825. Hence †**Gaw·ish** *a.* staring, gaping; gaudy.

Gawk (gǭk), *sb.* 1837. [? f. next; but see GAWK *v.*] An awkward person; a fool; a simpleton. (Confounded by Johnson and others with GOWK.) Hence **Gaw·kish** *a.*

Gawk (gǭk), *a.* Also **gauk.** 1703. [?] Left, as in *g.-handed.*

Gawk (gǭk), *v. dial. U.S.* Also **gauk.** 1785. [? f. the sb.; or ? an iterative form of GAW *v.*] *intr.* To stare or gape.

Gawky (gǭ·ki). 1724. [f. GAWK *sb.* (? or *v.*) + -Y [1].]
A. *adj.* Of persons: Awkward and stupid; ungainly. Also *transf.* of things. 1759.
A g. Country Boy 1759. A great g. ship L. HUNT.
B. *sb.* An awkward lout; a simpleton 1724.

Gawn (gǭn). Now *dial.* 1565. [contr. from GALLON.] 1. A gallon. 2. Any vessel for lading out liquids 1688.

Gay (gē¹). ME. [a. F. *gai*; of unkn. etym.]
A. *adj.* 1. Full of or disposed to joy and mirth; light-hearted, exuberantly cheerful, sportive, merry. b. Airy, off-hand. JOHNSON. †c. Applied to women, as a conventional epithet of praise -1802. 2. Addicted to social pleasures and dissipations; often *euphem.*: Of immoral life 1637. 3. Bright or lively-looking, esp. in colour; brilliant, showy ME. 4. Showily dressed. Now *rare.* ME. 5. Brilliant, attractive. †Formerly also of reasonings, etc.: Specious. 1529. †6. Excellent, fine -1593. 7. *dial.* In good health 1855.
1. This Absolon..jolif was and g. CHAUCER. b. G. indifference 1779. c. The learned man hath got the lady g. SHAKS. Phr. *The gay science* (= Pr. *gai saber*): the art of poetry. 2. Is this that Haughty, Gallant, G. Lothario ROWE. *Euphem.* Two sisters—both g. 1825. 3. Costumes g. with ribbons 1870. Dressed in his gayest 1842. 4. Women..sell their soules and bodyes to go g. BARCLAY. 7. I don't feel very g. (*mod.*).
B. *adv.* †1. = GAILY 1, 2. -1754. 2. Very; also 'pretty'. Freq. in *dial.* Often written GEY. 1686.
C. *sb.* [the adj. used *absol.*] †1. A gay lady. Also, rarely, a 'gallant'. -1475. 2. An ornament (now *dial.*) ME.; †*fig.* a childish amusement -1694. 3. A picture in a book (now *dial.*) 1646.

‖**Gayal** (gē¹·ăl, gayā·l). 1790. [Hindi.] A kind of ox (*Bibos frontalis*), common in Burma, Assam, and Bengal.

Gaydiang (gē¹·diæŋ). 1855. An Annamese vessel, somewhat resembling a Chinese junk.

Gayety: see GAIETY.

Gaylussite (gē¹·lū·səit). 1826. [f. *Gay-Lussac*, the French physicist + -ITE.] *Min.* A double carbonate of calcium and sodium, found in white or yellowish crystals.

Gayly, Gayn-: see GAILY, GAIN-.

Gayness (gē¹·nės). ME. [f. GAY *a.* + -NESS.] The quality, condition, or state of being GAY.

Gaysome (gē¹·sŏm), *a.* Now *rare.* 1610. [f. GAY *a.* + -SOME.] Full of gaiety; inspiring with gaiety.

Gaze (gē¹z), *sb.*[1] ME. [f. GAZE *v.*] †1. That which is gazed at -1797. 2. A steady or intent look ME. Also *fig.*
1. Made of my enemies the scorn and g. MILT. *Sams.* 34. 2. A Lover's ardent G. STEELE. Phr. *At g.*, †*at a* or *the g.*; said of a deer (now chiefly *Her.*), also of persons: in the attitude of gazing, esp. in wonder, expectancy, bewilderment, etc. So in *to stand at g.* *At g.*: by sight (said of a hunting-dog).

Gaze (gē¹z), *v.* ME. [? root of GAW *v.*, with an *-s-* suffix. Rietz gives a Sw. dial. *gasa* to gape.] †1. *intr.* Orig.: To look vacantly; also, to stare. In mod. use: To look fixedly, intently, or deliberately at something. Now chiefly *literary.* b. quasi-*trans.* with adv. or phrase 1713. 2. *trans.* To stare at, look fixedly at. *poet.* 1591.
1. I did make them all g. to see themselves served so nobly PEPYS. The mute rapture with which he would g. upon her in company W. IRVING. quasi-*trans.* So Scotia's Queen..Rose on her couch and gazed her soul away S. ROGERS. 2. To g. the Skie MILT.

Gazebo (găzī·bo). Also †**gazeebo(o, etc.** 1752. [Explained as f. GAZE *v.*, after L. *videbo* 'I shall see', or the like; but prob. a corruption of some oriental word.] 1. A turret or lantern on the roof of a house, commanding an extensive prospect; also, a similar erection in a garden, etc. 2. A projecting window or balcony 1843.

†**Ga·zeful**, *a.* [f. GAZE *sb.* + -FUL.] That gazes intently. SPENSER.

Ga·ze-hound. 1570. [f. GAZE *sb.* + HOUND *sb.*] A species of dog which hunts by sight. Now chiefly *Hist.*

Gazel, var. of GHAZAL.

Gazelle (găze·l). Also †**gazel** (erron. **gazhal**). 1600. [a. F., ad. Arab. *ghazāl*, prob. through Sp.] A small delicately-formed antelope, of which the typical species (*Gazella Dorcas*) is a native of Northern Africa; other varieties are found in parts of Africa and Asia. The gazelle is noted for the grace of its movements and the softness of its eyes. Also *attrib.*
The turtle-dove, the timid fawn, the soft-eyed g. W. IRVING.

Ga·zement. *rare.* 1596. [f. GAZE + -MENT.] Stare, observation.

Gazer (gē̆·zəɹ). 1548. [f. GAZE *v.* + -ER.[1]] **1.** One who gazes. **2.** A fish (*Polyprosopus macer*) 1861.

†**Gaze·t(t.** 1605. [a. F. *gazette*, a. It. *gazzetta.*] A Venetian coin –1682.

Gazette (găze·t), *sb.* 1605. [a. F., ad. It. *gazzetta*, pl. *gazzette*, app. from the coin of that name (see GAZET), paid for the paper or for a perusal of it; or ? from *gazzetta*, dim. of *gazza* magpie. At one time stressed on the first syllable.] **1.** A news-sheet; a periodical publication giving an account of current events. Now only *Hist.* 1605. **2.** *spec.* One of the three official journals entitled *The London G.*, *The Edinburgh G.*, and *The Belfast G.*, issued by authority twice a week, and containing legal and government notices. Hence *gen.* the official journal of any government. 1665.

2. Phr. *To be in the g.*: to be published a bankrupt. The first issues of the *London G.*, published at Oxford while the Court was resident there in 1665, were entitled *The Oxford G.* The official record of the acta and agenda of the university is entitled *The Oxford University G.* In recent times *Westminster G.*, *Pall Mall G.* are examples of the use for general newspapers.

Gazette (găze·t), *v.* 1678. [f. prec.] To publish in a gazette. Chiefly pass. *To be gazetted*: to be announced in the official gazette as appointed *to* a command, or the like.

Phr. *To be gazetted out*: said of an officer whose resignation is announced in the gazette.

Gazetteer (gæzĕtī³·ɹ). 1611. [a. F. *gazettier* (now *gazetier*); see GAZETTE and -EER.] **1.** One who writes in a gazette; a journalist; *spec.* one appointed and paid by Government. †**2.** A newspaper, gazette –1769. **3.** A geographical index or dictionary 1704.

1. *Gazetteer*, it was lately a term of the utmost infamy, being usually applied to wretches who were hired to vindicate the court JOHNSON.

Ga·zing-sto:ck. 1535. [f. GAZING *vbl. sb.* + STOCK.] One on whom others gaze or stare.

Gazogene (gæ·zŏdʒīn). Also **gaso-**. 1853. [a. F., f. *gaz* GAS *sb.*[1] + *-gène*; see -GEN.] A gas-producer; *spec.* an apparatus for the production of aerated waters.

Gazolyte (gæ·zŏləit). 1842. [a. F., f. *gaz* GAS + Gr. λυτός soluble.] **a.** A name given by Berzelius to such simple gases as are permanently elastic. These are oxygen, nitrogen, and hydrogen. **b.** Ampère's term for a body which is resolvable into a gas. 1885.

Gazometer, obs. f. GASOMETER.

†**Gazon.** 1704. [a. F. *gazon* grass; *pl.* pieces of turf; a. OHG. *waso* (G. *wasen*) sod, turf, etc.] A sod or piece of turf, cut wedge-shaped, used to line parapets, etc., in fortification –1768.

Geal (dʒīl), *v.* Now *dial.* ME. [a. F. *geler*:—L. *gelare.*] To congeal. *trans.* and *intr.*

Gean (gīn). Now chiefly *Sc.* 1533. [a. F. *guigne*; of unkn. origin.] The wild cherry (*Prunus avium*); also, its fruit.

Geanticlinal (dʒiˌæntikləi·năl). 1879. [f. Gr. γῆ earth + ANTICLINAL.] **A.** *adj.* Of the nature of a general upward flexure of the earth's crust. **B.** *sb.* The flexure itself.

Gear (gī³ɹ), *sb.* [ME. *gere*, ad. ON. *gervi* = OE. **gieru* (poet. in pl. *gearwe*) :—OTeut. **garwin-*, f. **garwu-* ready, YARE.] **I.** Equipment. **1.** *collect. sing.* Apparel, dress, vestments. Now *rare.* **2.** Armour, arms, accoutrements. Rarely *pl.* *Obs.* exc. *arch.* ME. **3. a.** Riding equipment. (Now always *riding-g.*) ME. **b.** Harness for draught animals. Till 19th c. chiefly *pl.* †Also *fig.* ME.

1. My Lady's geer alone..filld four portmantel trunks 1727.

II. Apparatus. **1.** Appliances, tackle, tools, ME. †**b.** *Weaving.* A leaf of heddles –1839. **2.** *Machinery.* **a.** A combination of wheels, levers, etc. for a given purpose. Often specialized as *expansion-*, *hand-*, *steering-*, *winding-g.* 1523. **b.** Wheels working one upon another, by means of teeth, or otherwise. Often specialized as *bevel-*, *crown-*, *spur-g.* 1829. **3.** *Machinery.* = GEARING. *vbl. sb.* 3. 1814. **b.** The relation of the diameter of a wheel of a cycle or motor vehicle to the gearing, indicative of speed capacity; hence *loosely*, speed 1897. **4.** *Naut.* Rigging 1669.

3. Phr. *In, out of g.*: in, out of connexion with the motor. So *to get* (*put, set, throw*) *in, into, out of g.* *High, low g.*; so *top, bottom g.* *fig.* The whole organization of labour was thrown out of g. GREEN.

III. Stuff. **1.** Goods, movable property, household necessaries ME. †**b.** *Sc.* and *n. dial.* Possessions 1535. †**2.** A material stuff; in depreciatory sense, rubbish –1805; †foul matter, pus –1653. **3.** *fig.* = MATTER, STUFF, in various uses (see quots.) ME.

1. Some harmelesse Villager, Whom Thrift keeps up about his Countrie Geare MILT. 3. Discourse, talk; stuff, nonsense: Priests with prayers and other godly g. DRYDEN. Doings (*arch.* or *dial.*): Our gambols, and our boyish geer K. WHITE. †A matter, business: Whilest this gere was a brewing NORTH.

attrib. and *Comb.*, as (sense II. 2 b) *g.-cutter*; **g.-box, -case,** the case enclosing the gearing of a bicycle, etc.; **-wheel,** (*a*) a cog-wheel; (*b*) in a bicycle, etc., the cog-wheel by means of which the motion of the pedals is transmitted to the axle.

Gear (gī³ɹ), *v.* [ME. *geren*, f. *gere* GEAR sb.] †**1.** *trans.* To array; to dress –1691. **2.** To equip (*arch.*) ME. **3.** To harness 1638. **4.** To put (machinery) into gear; to connect by gearing 1851. **b.** *intr.* Of a toothed wheel, or its teeth: To fit exactly *into*; to be in gear, so as to work smoothly *with* 1734.

4. Phr. *To g. up*: to make the driving wheels go round faster than the pedals. So *to g. down, level.*

Gearing (gī³·riŋ), *vbl. sb.* 1825. [f. GEAR *sb.* and *v.* + -ING[1].] **1.** Harness (*dial.*) 1863. **2.** 'Plant' 1825. **3.** The action of fitting a machine with gear; the manner in which a machine is geared; *concr.* apparatus for the transmission of motion or power, e.g. a train of toothed wheels = GEAR *sb.* II. 3. Often specialized, as *bevel-*, *spur-*, etc. *g.*; also with advs., as in *g.-down*, *-up.* 1833.

Comb., as *g.-chain*, an endless chain transmitting motion from one toothed wheel to another.

†**Gea·son.** [OE. *gǽsne*, *gésne* barren. Cf. OHG. *keisinî* barrenness.]

A. *adj.* **1.** Producing scantily –ME. **2.** Scantily produced; scarce –1674. **3.** Extraordinary –1583.

B. *sb.* Rarity, scarcity (*rare*) –1557.

Geat(e, obs. f. GATE, GET, JET.

Gebur (gĕbū³ɹ). [OE. *gebúr*; see NEIGHBOUR.] *Hist.* A tenant-farmer (in the early English community).

Gecarcinian (dʒīkarsi·niăn). 1838. [f. mod.L. *Gecarcinius* (Gr. γῆ earth + καρκίνος crab) + -IAN.] A land-crab.

Geck (gek), *sb.*[1] Now *dial.* 1515. [app. a. LG. *geck*; related to *gecken* GECK *v.*] A fool, simpleton; a dupe.

The most notorious gecke and gull *Twel. N.* v. i. 351.

Geck (gek), *sb.*[2] Chiefly *Sc.* 1500. [= Du. *gek*, G. *geck* vbl. sb.] A gesture of derision; an expression of scorn or contempt.

Geck (gek), *v.* *Sc.* and *n. dial.* 1583. [app. a. LG. *gecken.*] **1.** *trans.* To mock, cheat. **2.** intr. *To g. at*: to scoff at 1603. **3.** To toss the head, as in scorn 1724.

Gecko (ge·ko). *Pl.* **-os, -oes.** 1774. [a. Mal. *gēkoq*, echoing the animal's cry.] A house-lizard, found in the warmer regions of both hemispheres, remarkable for its cry, and for its power of climbing walls.

Ged (ged). *n.* and *Sc.* ME. [a. ON. *gedda*, app. f. ON. *gaddr* spike, GAD. (Cf. PIKE.)] The fish *Esox lucius*; the pike.

Gee (dʒī), *sb.* *colloq.* 1887. [f. GEE *interj.*] A horse (orig. a child's word).

Gee (dʒī), *v.* *slang.* 1700. [? f. next.] *intr.* To go; to fit, suit (only in neg. phrases). Of persons: To agree, get on well (*together*).

Gee (dʒī), *interj.* 1628. A word of command to a horse, variously used to bid it turn to the right, go forward, or move faster.

Geebung (dʒī·bvŋ). Also **gibong, jibbong.** 1827. [Native Austral.] The fruit of species of *Persoonia*, an Australian tree.

Gee-gee (dʒī·dʒī). *colloq.* 1869. [Redupl. of GEE *interj.*] A horse. Cf. GEE *sb.*

Geer, obs. f. GEAR.

Geese, pl. of GOOSE.

Geest (gīst). 1847. [a. Du. *geest* dry or sandy soil.] *Geol.* Old alluvial matter on the surface of land; coarse drift or gravel.

Geet, obs. f. JET.

Gee-up (dʒīˌv·p), *interj.* Also **gee-hup.** 1733. [f. GEE *interj.* + HUP *interj.* (confused with UP *adv.*)] = GEE *interj.* Hence **Gee-(h)up** *v.* to say 'gee-up' to; to obey this call.

‖**Gehenna** (gĭhe·nă). 1594. [a. eccl. L. *gehenna*, a. Hellenistic Gr. γέεννα, ad. post-Biblical Heb. *gēhinnōm* hell, place of fiery torment for the dead.] **1.** The place of future torment; hell. **2.** *transf.* A place of torture; a prison 1594.

1. [Moloch] made his Grove The pleasant Vally of Hinnom, Tophet thence And black G. call'd the Type of Hell MILT.

Geic (dʒī·ik), *a.* 1844. [f. Gr. γῆ earth + -IC.] In *g. acid*, a product of the conversion of wood into vegetable mould. Also called *humic* or *ulmic acid.*

Gein (dʒī·in). Also **geine.** 1844. [f. Gr. γῆ + IN.] *Chem.* A brown precipitate obtained by boiling mould or decayed vegetable matter with alkalies.

†**Geir.** Also **geier.** 1567. [a. Du. *gier.*] A vulture –1615.

Comb. **G.-eagle** (= G. *geier-adler*), used in A.V. to render Heb. *raḥam*, a species of vulture. See *Lev.* xi. 18.

‖**Geisha** (gē̆·ʃă). *Pl.* **geisha, -as.** 1891. [Japanese.] A Japanese dancing-girl.

Geitonogamy (gəitǫnǫ·gămi). 1880. [f. Gr. γειτονο-, γείτων neighbour + -γαμία marriage.] *Bot.* Fertilization by pollen of other flowers of the same plant.

‖**Geist.** 1871. [Ger.] Mind; reason; intelligence.

I do exhort..England to get..'Geist'; to search and not rest till it sees things more as they really are M. ARNOLD.

Gel (dʒel). 1904. [The first syllable of *gelatin.*] A jelly-like material formed by the coagulation of a colloidal liquid. Also as vb.

Gelastic (dʒelæ·stik), *a.* *rare.* 1704. [ad. Gr. γελαστικός, f. γελᾶν.] Serving the function of laughter, risible. Also (*nonce-use*) as *sb. pl.* remedies operating by causing laughter (SOUTHEY).

Gelatification (dʒe:lătifikē̆·ʃən). 1860. [f. GELATIN + -FICATION.] The production of, or conversion into, gelatin or jelly.

Gelatigenous (dʒe:lăti·dʒĕnəs), *a.* 1854. [f. GELATIN + -GEN + -OUS.] Producing or developing gelatin; as, *g. tissues.*

Gelatin, gelatine (dʒe·lătin). 1800. [a. F. *gélatine*, ad. It. *gelatina*, f. *gelata* jelly. In medical L. *gelatina* was orig. 'any sort of clear gummy juice'; its present use is due to scientific chemistry. The pop. spelling is *gelatine*, often pronounced (dʒelătī·n); the scientific form is *gelatin.*] **1.** The basis of the jellies into which certain animal tissues (skin, tendons, ligaments, etc.) are converted by prolonged boiling. It is amorphous, brittle, without taste or smell, transparent, and of a faint yellow tint; and is composed of carbon, hydrogen, nitrogen, oxygen, and sulphur. **b.** *Vegetable g.*: one of the constituents of gluten, identical with animal gelatin 1852. **2.** An explosive compound (more fully *blasting* or *explosive g.*), made by dissolving collodion-cotton in about nine times its weight of nitroglycerine 1878.

1. Soup..thickened by gelatine 1878.

attrib. and *Comb.*, as (sense 1) *g. capsule, pellicle*; *g.-coated* adj.; (sense 2) *g.-shell.* Also **g. dry-plate,** a plate, usually of glass coated with a film of g., containing sensitive silver bromide; **g. dynamite,** an explosive intermediate between blasting g. and dynamite; it consists of a thin blasting g. mixed with other substances; **g. emulsion,** 'an emulsion of g. containing a sensitive silver compound'; also *attrib.*; **g. paper** (*Photogr.*), paper coated with sensitized g.; **g. picture,** a photograph produced by the action of light on bichromated g.; **g. process,** any photographic process in which g. is employed; **g. sugar** = GLYCOCOLL. Hence **Ge·latined** *a.* coated with g.

Gelatinate (dʒelæ·tineʹt), *v.* 1796. [f. GELATIN + -ATE.] = GELATINIZE 1, 2. Hence **Gelatina·tion.**

†**Ge·latine.** 1713. [f. L. type **gelatinus.*] **A.** *adj.* Of the nature of jelly, gelatinous. DERHAM. **B.** *sb.* *Zool.* Kirby's name for the Acalephæ of Cuvier, from the gelatinous consistency of their bodies –1855.

Gelatiniferous (dʒelæ:tini·fĕrəs), *a.* 1878. [f. GELATIN + -(I)FEROUS.] Yielding gelatin.

Gelatiniform (dʒelăti·nifǭɹm), *a.* 1830. [f. as prec. + -(I)FORM.] Having the form of gelatin.

Gelatinize (dʒėlæ·tinəiz), *v.* 1809. [f. GELATIN + -IZE.] **1.** *intr.* To become gelatinous. **2.** To render gelatinous or jelly-like 1843. **3.** To coat with gelatin 1890. Hence **Gela:tiniza·tion,** conversion into a gelatinous state.

Gelatino- (dʒe·lătĭno), comb. f. GELATIN, in words denoting its association with other chemical substances, as *g.-albuminous*, etc.; also in *g.-bromide, -chloride*, etc. used *attrib.* to signify the use of gelatin as a vehicle.

Gelatinoid (dʒėlæ·tinoid). 1866. [f. GELATIN + -OID.]
A. *adj.* Resembling gelatin, gelatinous.
B. *sb.* [sc. *substance.*] 1882.

Gelatinous (dʒėlæ·tinəs), *a.* 1724. [ad. F. *gélatineux*, f. *gélatine*; see GELATIN.] **1.** Having the character or consistency of a jelly; jelly-like. Also *fig.* **2.** Of, pertaining to, or consisting of gelatin 1798.

Gelation (dʒėlē¹·ʃən). 1854. [ad. L. *gelationem*, f. *gelare* to freeze.] Solidification by cold, freezing.

Geld (geld), *sb.* Also *erron.* **gelt.** 1610. [ad. med.L. *geldum* (in Domesday Book), ad. OE. *ʒield, ʒeld, ʒyld* payment, tribute, also GUILD :—OTeut. **geldom*, f. root of **gelþan*; see YIELD *v.*] *Hist.* The tax paid to the crown by English landholders before the Conquest, and continued under the Norman kings.
Comb.: **g.-acre, -hide** (Domesday *acra, hida ad geldum*), an acre or a hide as reckoned for the purposes of g.

Geld (geld), *a.* Now *dial.* See also YELD. ME. [a. ON. *geldr* :—OTeut. **galdu-*.] Barren; †also, sexually impotent.

Geld (geld), *v.*¹ Infl. **gelt** and **gelded.** ME. [a. ON. *gelda*, f. *geldr* GELD *a.*] **1.** *trans.* To castrate or emasculate; also, to spay. †**2.** *transf.* and *fig.* To deprive *of* some essential part; to mutilate; to expurgate –1729. **3.** †**a.** To cut superfluous shoots, etc. from (a plant or tree) –1664. †**b.** To cut out the old comb from (a bee-hive) –1657.
2. Bereft and gelded of his patrimonie SHAKS. To g. the text [of a book] 1693. **3. a.** G. and prune Strawberries EVELYN. Hence **Ge·lder.**

Geld (geld), *v.*² Also *erron.* **gelt.** 1630. [f. GELD *sb.*] *Hist.* To charge with, or pay, geld. So **Ge·ldable** *a.* liable to pay geld.

Gelder(s rose, obs. f. GUELDER ROSE.

Gelding (ge·ldiŋ), *sb.* ME. [a. ON. *geldingr*, f. *geldr* GELD *a.*] †**1.** A gelded person, a eunuch –1785. **2.** A gelded animal, esp. a horse ME.
1. Putiphar, the geldyng of Pharao WYCLIF *Gen.* xxxvii. 36.

Gelding (ge·ldiŋ), *vbl. sb.* ME. [See -ING ¹.] The action of GELD *v.*¹

Gelid (dʒe·lid), *a.* 1606. [ad. L. *gelidus*, f. *gelum* (*gelus, gelu*) frost; see COLD *a.*] Extremely cold, ice-cold, frosty. Also *fig.*
The Brightness of the G. Moon 1695. G. founts THOMSON. Hence **Geli·dity** (? *Obs.*), extreme cold. **Ge·lid·ly** *adv.*, **-ness.**

Gelignite (dʒe·lignəit). 1889. [? f. GEL(ATIN + L. *ignis* + -ITE.] A variety of gelatin dynamite.

Gelly, obs. f. JELLY.

†**Gelo·scopy.** Better GELOTOSCOPY. 1730. [f. Gr. γέλως, γελωτ- + -σκοπια.] Divination by laughter.

Gelose (dʒĭlōᵘ·s). 1864. [f. GEL-ATIN + -OSE.] *Chem.* An amorphous gelatinous substance obtained from Japan moss and seaweeds.

Gelosie, obs. f. JEALOUSY.

†**Gelotoscopy.** Better form of GELOSCOPY. Evelyn.

‖**Gelsemium** (dʒelsī·miŏm). 1875. [mod.L., f. It. *gelsomino* JASMINE.] **a.** A genus of twining shrubs of the N.O. *Loganiaceæ*. **b.** The roots of a plant of this genus (*G. sempervirens*), or a preparation of them, used as a medicine; also called **gelseminum.** Hence **Ge·lsemine** (also **Gelse·minine**), a colourless, inodorous, bitter alkaloidal substance obtained from the root of *G. sempervirens.* **Gelse·mic acid,** a crystalline substance obtained from the root of *G. sempervirens.*

Gelt (gelt), *sb.*¹ *rare.* [a. Ir. *geilt* a frenzied person.] A lunatic. SPENSER.

Gelt (gelt), *sb.*² 1529. [a. Ger.; see also GELD *sb.*] Money; now only *dial.* ¶ In Spenser perh. = *gold.*
His whole army cryed out for g. USSHER.

Gelt (gelt), *ppl. a.* ME. [pa. pple. of GELD *v.*] Gelded. *lit.* and *fig.*

Gelt, obs. f. GELD *sb.*, GILT.

Gelt, var. GILT, young sow.

Gem (dʒem), *sb.* [OE. *ʒim*, a. L. *gemma* bud, hence jewel, f. root *gen-* to produce. In ME. refash. after F. *gemme.*] **1.** A precious stone of any kind, *esp.* when cut and polished; a jewel. **2.** *transf.* and *fig.*; *esp.* an object of rare beauty or worth; the choicest part of (anything). Now playfully: Something greatly prized, a 'treasure'. 1560. **3.** A precious stone, bearing an engraved design in relief or in intaglio 1791. †**4.** A bud, esp. a leaf-bud –1813. **5.** *Zool.* = GEMMA 2. 1832. **6.** *Printing.* A size of type intermediate between Brilliant and Diamond 1888. **7.** *U.S.* A light muffin.
2 Deliteful dames and gemmes of jolitie GASCOIGNE. A little cabinet picture..which will be quite a g. W. IRVING. **3.** Antique Gems, their Origin, Uses, and Value (*title*) C. W. KING.

Gem (dʒem), *v.* Infl. **gemmed, gemming.** OE. [f. prec.] †**1.** *intr.* To bud; *trans.* to put forth (a blossom, a fruit) –1747. **2.** To adorn with or as with gems 1610. **3.** *trans.* To excavate for gems 1889.
1. MILT. *P.L.* VII. 325. **2.** Gemmed with rubies 1877. A coppice gemm'd with green and red TENNYSON.

‖**Gemara** (gėmā·ră). 1613. [Aramaic; = 'completion'.] The later portion of the Talmud, consisting of a commentary on the older part (the Mishna). Hence **Gema·ric** *a.* pertaining to the G.

‖**Gematria** (gĭmē¹·triă). 1686. [Rabbinical Heb., a. Gr. γεωμετρία GEOMETRY.] A cabbalistic method of interpreting the Hebrew Scriptures by interchanging words whose letters have the same numerical value when added.

Gemel (dʒe·mĕl). ME. [a. OF. *gemel* (mod. *jumeau*) :—L. *gemellus*, dim. of *geminus* twin.] †**1.** *pl.* Twins; pairs –1603. †**b.** *attrib.* or *adj.* Twin –1657. **2.** *Her.* in *pl.* Bars, or barrulets, placed together as a couple 1592. **3.** A kind of double ring. Now *Hist.* Also *g.-ring.* Cf. GIMMAL. 1572. **4.** A hinge. Now only in *g.-hinge.* 1536.
Comb.: **g.-hinge** (*Locksmithing*), a hinge consisting of an eye or loop and a hook. var. (in all senses) †**Gemew, gemow.**

[**Geminal:** a spurious word.]

Geminate (dʒe·minĕt). 1598. [ad. L. *geminatus, geminare*, f. *geminus* twin.]
A. *adj.* Duplicated, combined in pairs, twin, binate; as, *g. leaves.* Hence **Ge·minately** *adv.*
B. *sb.* A doubled consonant (*rec.*).

Geminate (dʒe·mineᶦt), *v.* 1637. [f. L. *geminat-* ppl. stem; see prec.] *trans.* To double.

Gemination (dʒeminē¹·ʃən). 1597. [ad. L. *geminationem.*] **1.** A doubling, duplication, repetition. **b.** The union of contiguous teeth 1859. †**2.** *Rhet.* The repetition of a word, phrase, or the like, for effect –1666. **3.** *Gram.* **a.** The doubling of a consonant sound 1877. **b.** The doubling of a letter 1875.

Gemini (dʒe·minəi). ME. [a. L. *gemini* (pl. of *geminus*) twins.] **1.** *Astron.* A constellation, otherwise 'Castor and Pollux'; also the third sign of the zodiac, anciently identified with this. †**2.** A couple, a pair; *esp.* in pl. form, a pair of eyes –1700. **3.** A mild oath or exclam. *vulgar.* 1664.
1. When..the starry G. hang like glorious crowns Over Orion's grave TENNYSON. **2.** *Merry W.* II. ii. 8. Hence **Ge·minids** *pl.* the meteoric bodies forming the star-shower that has its radiant point in G. var. **Geminy.**

Geminiflorous (dʒe·mini͵flōᵒ·rəs), *a.* 1866. [f. L. *gemini-, geminus* + *flor-, flos* + -OUS.] Having flowers in pairs.

Geminous (dʒe·minəs), *a. rare.* 1646. [f. L. *geminus.*] Double; occurring in pairs.

‖**Gemma** (dʒe·mă). *Pl.* **gemmæ.** 1770. [L.; see GEM.] **1.** *Bot.* A leaf-bud, as dist. from a flower-bud. In mosses, etc.: A small cellular bulbel. 1830. **2.** *Zool.* A bud-like growth upon animals of low organization, which becomes detached and develops into a new individual 1841. Hence **Gemma·ceous** *a.* pertaining to, or of the nature of leaf-buds.

Gemman (dʒe·mæ̆n). Vulgar pronunc. of GENTLEMAN.

†**Ge·mmary.** ME. [ad. late L. *gemmarius*, f. *gemma* GEM.]
A. *adj.* Of, pertaining to, or concerned with gems –1682.
B. *sb.* An engraver of gems, a jeweller. ME. only.

Gemmary: see GEMMERY.

Gemmate (dʒe·mĕt), *a.* 1846. [ad. L. *gemmatus*; see next.] *Bot.* and *Zool.* Furnished with buds; reproducing by buds.

Gemmate (dʒe·mēᶦt), *v.* 1623. [f. L. *gemmat-, gemmare*, f. *gemma* GEM.] †**a.** *trans.* To deck with gems –1697. **b.** *intr.* To put forth buds; to propagate itself by buds 1846.

Gemmation (dʒemē¹·ʃən). 1760. [a. F., f. L. *gemmare*; see prec.] **1.** *Bot.* **a.** The action of budding. **b.** The time when leaf-buds are put forth. **c.** The arrangement of buds on the stalk; also, of leaves in the bud. **2.** *Zool.* Reproduction by gemmæ; the formation of a new individual by the protrusion and complete or partial separation of a part of the parent; budding 1836.

Gemmeous (dʒe·mĭəs), *a.* 1605. [f. L. *gemmeus* (f. *gemma* GEM) + -OUS.] Of or pertaining to, of the nature of, or resembling a gem. *G. Dragonet*: the fish *Callionymus Lyra.*

†**Gemmery** (dʒe·mĕri). Also **gemmary.** 1656. [f. GEM *sb.* + -ERY; see also -ARY.] A jewel-house –1721.

Gemmiferous (dʒemi·fĕrəs), *a.* 1656. [f. L. *gemmifer* + -OUS.] **1.** Producing gems. **2.** Producing a gemma or bud 1804.

Gemmiparous (dʒemi·părəs), *a.* 1793. [f. mod.L. *gemmiparus* + -OUS.] **a.** Producing offspring by gemmation. **b.** Of or pertaining to gemmation. Hence **Gemmi·parously** *adv.* Also **Gemmipa·rity,** the attribute of being g.

Gemmule (dʒe·miul). 1845. [a. F., ad. L. *gemmula*, dim. of *gemma* a bud, GEM.] **1.** *Bot.* **a.** = PLUMULE. 1844. **b.** One of the reproductive cells of cryptogams 1874. **2.** *Zool.* A small GEM (sense 5) or gemma; *spec.* a ciliated embryo of one of the *Cœlenterata*; an encysted mass of sponge-particles, from which new ones are produced 1845. Hence **Gemmuli·ferous** *a.* bearing gemmules.

Gemmy (dʒe·mi), *a.* ME. [f. GEM *sb.* + -Y ¹.] **1.** Abounding in gems, covered or set with or as with gems. **2.** Gem-like; glittering 1580.
1. The g. bridle glitter'd free TENNYSON. Hence **Ge·mmily** *adv.* **Ge·mminess.**

†**Ge·monies.** 1598. [ad. L. (*scalæ*) *Gemoniæ*; of unkn. origin.] *Rom. Antiq.* Steps on the Aventine Hill leading to the Tiber, to which the bodies of criminals were dragged to be thrown into the river. ¶ Misapplied *fig.* for 'tortures'. –1683.

Gemot(e (gėmōᵘ·t). [repr. OE. *gemót*, f. *ʒe-* together (see Y-) + *mót* MOOT.] *Eng. Hist.* A meeting; an assembly (in England before the Norman Conquest) for judicial or legislative purposes. See also WITENAGEMOT.

‖**Gemsbok** (ge·mzbǫk). 1777. [Du. *gemsbok* (prop. chamois), a. Ger. *gemsbock*, f. *gemse* fem., chamois + *bock* buck.] S. African name for a large antelope (*Oryx capensis*).

Gemshorn (ge·mz͵hǫɹn). 1825. [a. Ger.; = 'chamois horn'.] An organ stop with tapering metal pipes, yielding a tone like that of a horn in quality.

-gen (dʒen), *suffix*, forming *sbs.*; ad. F. *-gène*, repr. (ult.) Gr. -γενής (f. γεν- root of γίγνεσθαι to be born, become, γένος kind, etc.; see KIN) an adjective suffix meaning: (1) 'born in a certain place or condition', as in οἰκογενής born in the house; (2) 'of a (specified) kind', as in ὁμογενής of the same kind. The F. *gène* has two applications, both of which have been adopted in Eng.
1. *Chem.* In Lavoisier's *Traité de Chimie* 1789 the etymon of the suffix is said to be 'Gr.

γείνομαι, j'engendre'. Hence the sense 'that which produces'. In Eng. *-gène* became *-gene*, and later *-gen*, as in *nitrogen*, etc.

2. *Bot.* The botanical use of *-gène* is due to De Candolle, and is merely a different application of the *-gène* used in chemical terms, referred vaguely to a Gr. root meaning 'to produce, to grow'. The adjs. *endogène, exogène* (De Candolle) became in Eng. *endogenous, exogenous*; from these Lindley *c* 1845 formed the sbs. *endogen, exogen*; hence many analogous terms denoting classes of plants.

Genappe (dʒenæ·p). 1858. [f. *Genappe* in Belgium, where first made.] A worsted yarn or cord of exceptional smoothness, used in the manufacture of braids, fringes, etc.

‖**Gendarme** (ʒanda·rm, dʒendā·ɹm). *Pl.* †**gens d'armes,** †**gensdarmes, gendarmes.** 1550. [F. *gendarme*, a sing. formed from the pl. *gens d'armes* men of arms; hence a fresh pl. *gendarmes*. In mod. F. the form *gens d'armes* has only the historic sense.] **1.** (Chiefly *pl.*) In the older French army, a horseman in full armour, having others under him; later, a mounted trooper. Now *Hist.* **2.** A soldier, who is employed on police duties, esp. in France. Also *fig.* 1796. **3.** *attrib.*, in *g. blue* 1884.

2. *fig.* Projecting pieces of rock, which are called gendarmes; apparently from their..stopping travellers 1883. Hence **Genda·rmery, -erie,** gendarmes as a body; also *attrib.*

Gender (dʒe·ndəɹ), *sb.* [ME. *gendre*, a. OF. *gen(d)re* (mod. *genre*), ad. L. *gener-, genus* = Gr. γένος, f. root γεν- to produce; the *d* is excrescent; cf. KIN.] †**1.** Kind, sort -1784. **2.** *Gram.* Each of the three (or two) grammatical 'kinds', corresponding more or less to distinctions of sex (or absence of sex), into which sbs. are discriminated according to the nature of the modifications they require in words syntactically associated with them; the property (in a sb.) of belonging to, or (in other parts of speech) of having the form appropriate to concord with, a specified one of these kinds. Also, the distinction of words into 'genders'. ME.

Mod. Eng. has 'natural' as opposed to 'grammatical' gender; i.e. nouns are masculine, feminine, or neuter according as the objects they denote are male, female, or of neither sex. For *common, epicene g.*, see those wds.

3. *transf.* Sex. Now only *joc.* ME. †**4.** Offspring -1662.

Gender (dʒe·ndəɹ), *v.* [ME. *gendren*, a. OF. *gendrer, genrer*, ad. L. *generare* to beget, f. *gener-, genus*; see GENDER *sb.*] **1.** *trans.* To beget, engender (*arch.*) ME. †**2.** *intr.* To copulate -1634. **3.** *trans.* †To generate (heat, etc.) -1653; to engender (a feeling, etc.) (*arch.*) 1450.

Genderless (dʒe·ndəɹlės), *a.* 1887. [See -LESS.] Without distinction of gender.

Gene (dʒīn). 1913. Also **gen.** [irreg. f. Gr. γεν- to produce.] *Biol.* One of the factors or elements concerned with the development in the offspring of hereditary characters.

Genealogic, -al (dʒe:nɪ̆ălǫ·dʒik, -ăl, dʒī-), *a.* 1577. [ad. F. *généalogique*, ad. med.L. *genealogicus*, a. Gr., + -AL; see GENEALOGY.] That belongs to genealogy, or that traces family descent.

Genealogical tree: a table of family descent under the form of a tree with branches. Hence **Ge·nealo·gically** *adv.* Earlier **Ge·nealo·gical** *a.* 1447.

Genealogist (dʒenɪ̆æ·lŏdʒist, dʒī-). 1605. [f. as prec. + -IST.] One who traces genealogies, or one interested in the study of them.

Genealogize (dʒenɪ̆æ·lŏdʒəiz, dʒī-), *v.* 1602. [f. as prec. + -IZE.] *trans.* To draw up a genealogy of; *intr.* to make out genealogies.

Genealogy (dʒenɪ̆æ·lŏdʒi, dʒī-). ME. [a. OF. *gene(a)logie* (mod. *généalogie*), ad. late L. *genealogia*, a. Gr., f. γενεαλόγος, f. γενεά race + -λόγος; see -LOGY.] **1.** An account of a person's descent from an ancestor or ancestors, by enumeration of the intermediate ancestors; a pedigree. Also *transf.* †**2.** Lineage, pedigree, family stock -1549. †**3.** Progeny. STERNE. **4.** The investigation of pedigrees as a branch of study or knowledge. TUCKER.

Genera, pl. of GENUS.

Generable (dʒe·nĕrăb'l), *a.* 1450. [ad. L. *generabilis*; see -ABLE.] That may be generated or produced.

General (dʒe·nĕrăl). ME. [a. OF. *general* (mod. *général*), ad. L. *generalis*, f. *gener-* GENUS, class, kind, race.]

A. *adj.* **1.** Pertaining to all, or most, of the parts of a whole; completely or approximately universal within implied limits; opp. to *partial* or *particular*. †**b.** Pertaining in common to various persons or things -1667. **c.** With collect. or pl. sb. All, whole. *Obs.* exc. in *g. body*. 1591. **2.** Concerned with the whole; opp. to *local, sectional*, etc. ME. **3.** Catholic, addressed to all 1611. **4.** Prevalent, widespread, usual ME. **5.** Not specifically limited in application; applicable to a whole class of objects, cases, or occasions ME. **b.** True for a variety of cases; in later use, true in most instances, but not without exceptions (opp. to *universal*) ME. **c.** Of a word, name, etc.: Applicable to each member of a class or genus, COMMON. Of a concept, notion, etc.: Including only what is common to the individuals of a class. 1551. **6.** Not restricted to one department. †Also formerly: Widely accomplished. 1552. †**b.** Open, affable to all -1630. **7.** Not belonging to, or confined to, a class; miscellaneous 1639. **8.** Comprising, dealing with, or directed to the main elements, features, etc. 1563; hence, wanting in details; indefinite, vague (opp. to *precise*) 1601. **9.** *Mil.* Epithet indicating superior rank and extended command 1576. **b.** Applied also to civil and legal functionaries, as *attorney-, postmaster-g.*, etc. (see those wds.) 1591.

1. A g. Battel 1659, Request 1665, peace ADDISON. Phr. *G. average*: see AVERAGE *sb.*[2] *G. paralysis*: see PARALYSIS. **b.** So spake our g. Mother MILT. **c.** The gen'ral sex shall suffer in her shame POPE. **2.** Phr. *G. chapter, council* (see COUNCIL 2), *election* (opp. to *by-election*). *G. ticket* (U.S.): the system by which the whole list of candidates for the representation, e.g. of a state or city, is voted upon by the undivided body of electors (= F. *scrutin de liste*). *G. Post*: formerly, the post or mail that was sent from the G.P.O. in London on certain days (opp. to the local 'penny' or 'two-penny' post); hence the first delivery in the morning is still officially called the *G.P.* or *General Post delivery*. Also the name of a game. Also *attrib. G. orders*, the orders issued by the commander-in-chief. **3.** The Generall Epistle of Iames BIBLE 1611. **4.** The g. taste 1752. A g. opinion PALEY. The theme of g. remark 1885. **5.** After we had answered the g. questions, they began to be more particular DE FOE. The *g. costs* of the action BOWEN. Phr. *G. confession, pardon* (sometimes also in sense 1). *G. issue* (Law): a plea or pleas importing an absolute and general denial of what is alleged in the declaration. **b.** I guess you are right there, as a g. rule LYTTON. **c.** The g. term..Majolica FORTNUM. **6.** Phr. *G. dealer, merchant, agent*, etc. *G. practitioner. G. servant*: a maid-of-all-work. Taking away such a g. and onely man as Mr. Cheeke is ASCHAM. **7.** Not very intelligible to the g. reader 1862. The g. public TYNDALL. Phr. *General ship*, where persons unconnected with each other load goods on board SMYTH. **8.** A g. knowledge was all that could be expected 1860.

Phrases. **In g.**: †(*a*) collectively, universally; †(*b*) in all respects; (*c*) generally; opp. to *in special, in particular*; (*d*) as a general rule, usually. **In the g.**: generally; on a general view; in the main.

B. *sb.* **I.** †**1.** The adj. used *absol.*: The total, the whole, or in weaker sense, the most part -1771. **b.** The public; the multitude (*arch.*) 1601. **2.** Something that is general; chiefly *pl.* Now *rare* (chiefly in antithesis to *particulars*, etc.) 1566. †**b.** That which is common to all. *Tr. & Cr.* I. iii. 180. †**c.** *pl. Oxford Univ.* = Responsions -1841. †**3.** *Logic.* = GENUS. -1705. †**4.** *Painting.* Name of a neutral colour -1662. **5.** *Mil.* Also as F. *générale, generale.* The first beat of the drum for the assembly of all the troops 1706.

1. The g. of people at his time of life MAD. D'ARBLAY. **b.** The Play..pleased not the Million, 'twas Cauiarie to the Generall *Haml.* II. ii. 457. **2.** The deceitfull and wrangler walketh in generalles 1566. To whom I refer thee for generals and common news PENN. **5.** The generale was beat at half-past four, the assembly at half-past five WELLINGTON.

II. **1.** *Eccl.* The chief of a religious order 1561. **2.** *Mil.* A general officer (see A. 9); orig., the commander of the whole army, subseq. also any divisional commander. In mod. use, designating an officer as holding definite military rank (i.e. the rank next below that of a field-marshal; untechnically extended to those of LIEUTENANT-GENERAL and MAJOR-GENERAL) 1576. Also *transf.* and *fig.* **b.** A tactician, strategist 1615. **c.** The head of the Salvation Army 1882. †**3.** *Naut.* = ADMIRAL -1717. **4.** *colloq.* A maid-of-all-work 1884.

2. Successe vnto our valiant Generall SHAKS. [Waterloo] was perhaps on both sides rather a soldiers' than a general's battle SEELEY. *fig. Rom. & Jul.* V. iii. 219. **b.** Cortez was certainly a great g. PRESCOTT.

Generale: see GENERAL B. I. 5 *sb.*

‖**Generalia** (dʒenĕrē̆·liă), *sb. pl.* 1832. [L., neut. pl. of *generalis*.] General principles.

Generalism (dʒe·nĕrăliz'm). 1809. [f. GENERAL *sb.* + -ISM.] A general statement.

‖**Generalissimo** (dʒe:nĕrăli·simo). 1621. [a. It., superl. of *generale*.] The supreme commander of a combined naval and military force, or of several armies in the field. Also *transf.* and *fig.* Hence ‖**Ge:nerali·ssima,** a female g.

Generality (dʒe:nĕræ·lĭti). 1482. [ad. F. *généralité*, a. L. *generalitas*, f. *generalis*.]

I. **1.** The quality or fact of being general (see GENERAL *a.*); now chiefly, applicability to a whole class; also, vagueness. †Formerly also, prevalence. **2.** quasi-*concr.* Something that is general; †a general class; a general proposition or statement; a general point; chiefly in *pl.* 1551. **3.** The main body, the bulk of. (Now only with *sb. pl.* or *collect.*) †Also, people in general. 1563.

1. A method of great g. and power BREWSTER. The g. of a conclusion TYNDALL. **2.** Keep to your sounding generalities, your tinkling phrases HAZLITT. **3.** Some were good scholars, but the g. dunces WOOD.

II. Special senses. †**1.** The dignity or office of general 1686. †**2.** The general staff of an army -1676. **3.** *Fr. Hist.* A fiscal and administrative division of the kingdom of France, under an officer called *général des finances* or *intendant* 1630.

Generalization (dʒe:nĕrăləizē̆·ʃən). 1761. [f. next vb. + -ATION. Cf. F. *généralisation*.] **1.** The action or process of generalizing, i.e. of forming general notions or propositions from particulars. **2.** quasi-*concr.* A general inference 1794. **3.** The process of spreading over every part 1897.

1. Hasty g. is the bane of all science TAIT. **3.** The g. of an infective disease ALLBUTT.

Generalize (dʒe·nĕrăləiz), *v.* 1751. [f. GENERAL *a.* + -IZE. Cf. F. *généraliser*.] To make general. **1.** *trans.* To reduce to general laws; also, to form a general concept. **2.** *trans.* To infer inductively from particulars 1795. **3.** To draw general inferences from 1828. **b.** *Math.* and *Philos.* To throw (a proposition, etc.) into a general form, including the particular case 1812. **4.** *intr.* To form general notions by abstraction from particular instances; to arrive at general inferences 1785. **5.** *trans.* To render indefinite; to soften down the special features of 1809. **6.** To make general; to popularize. Also, to spread over a system or surface in general. 1818.

1. Generalizing those names, so as to make them represent a class JAS. MILL. Causes which do not admit of being generalized G. C. LEWIS. **2.** A mere conclusion generalized from a great multitude of facts COLERIDGE. **3.** Copernicus generalized the celestial motions..Newton generalized them still more 1828. Knowledge is experience generalized MILL. **5.** Travelling tends to generalise and rub off local habits, prejudices, [etc.] 1835. **6.** To g. the use of the potatoe 1824.

Hence **Ge·nerali:zable** *a.* capable of being generalized. **Ge·neralized** *ppl. a.*; *spec.* of a disease: That has extended itself to the system in general. **Ge·neralizer.**

Generally (dʒe·nĕrăli), *adv.* ME. [f. GENERAL *a.* + -LY[2].] †**1.** So as to include all; as a whole, collectively -1613. †**2.** Universally; with respect to all or nearly all. With neg. = *at all.* -1653. Hence **b.** For the most part, extensively ME. **3.** In a general sense or way; opp. to *specially* ME. **4.** As a general rule; commonly 1654.

1. *Tam. Shr.* I. ii. 274. **2.** Two [sacraments] onely, as g. necessarie to salvation *Bk. Com. Prayer.* **b.** A fact now g. received 1820. **3.** He gave all his lands to Richard, g. CRUISE. Phr. *G. speaking* = 'in general'. **4.** [Winds] from the land are g. dry GEIKIE.

Generalness (dʒe·nĕrălnės). 1561. [f. as prec. + -NESS.] The state, quality, or fact of being GENERAL. Now *rare.*

Generalship (dʒe·nĕrălʃip). 1591. [f. GENERAL *sb.* + -SHIP.] 1. †The functions of a general; also, conduct in command. 2. The office, or †tenure of the office, of general 1610. 3. Skill in the management of an army; strategy 1788; *transf.* skilful management 1768.
1. Cicero..laughs, indeed..at his g. BOLINGBROKE. 3. Hannibal gave great proofs of g. LANGHORNE. *transf.* An artful stroke of g. in Trim to raise a dust STERNE.

†**Ge·neralty.** ME. [a. OF. **generalté*, f. *general* GENERAL.] = GENERALITY, in all senses -1676.

Generant (dʒe·nĕrănt). 1665. [ad. L. *generantem*, *generare*.]
A. *sb.* That which generates; in *Math.* = GENERATRIX 1842.
B. *adj.* Productive (*rare*) 1875.

Generate (dʒe·nĕrĕt), *ppl. a.* 1509. [ad. L. *generatus*; see next.] Generated.

Generate (dʒe·nĕreit), *v.* 1509. [f. L. *generat-*, ppl. stem of *generare* to beget, etc., f. *gener-*, *genus*; cf. GENDER *sb.*, GENUS.] †1. *trans.* To beget, procreate, engender -1697. b. *absol.* or *intr.* To produce offspring. (Now *rare.*) 1626. 2. To bring into existence (substances, animals, etc.). Chiefly in *pass.* 1563. b. *esp.* To produce, evolve (steam, gas, etc.; also heat, friction, etc.) 1791. c. *Math.* To produce or evolve (a line or figure); said chiefly of a point, line, or surface doing this by its own motion 1698. 3. To bring about, give rise to, produce 1626.
1. b. Some Liuing Creatures g. but at certaine Seasons of the Yeare BACON. 2. A region where rain was generated TYNDALL. c. We know how a circle is generated BOWEN. 3. The love of killing game generates a sincere wish to preserve it KINGLAKE. Hence Ge·nerating *ppl. a.* that generates; esp. (in mod. use) of electrical apparatus.

Generation (dʒenĕrēi·ʃən). ME. [a. L. *generation-em*; cf. F. *génération*.]
I. 1. The act or process of generating or begetting; procreation; propagation of species. b. The fact or manner of being begotten ME. c. Manner of descent; genealogy (*rare*) ME. d. *Theol.* The origin of the Son from the Father 1659. 2. Production by natural or artificial processes; often opposed to corruption (Aristotle's φθορά) ME.
1. Phr. *Equivocal, spontaneous g.*, see the adjs. c. The book of the g. of Jesus Christ *Matt.* i. 1. d. Strange G. this? Father and Son Co-eval, two distinct and yet but one KEN. 2. Of the generacyon and cause of stone and metall, and of plantis and herbys 1519. The g. of happiness GODWIN, of heat 1863.
II. That which is generated. †1. Offspring -1674; descendants -1704; produce (of the vine) -1565. 2. Offspring of the same parent regarded as a step in a line of descent from an ancestor; = DEGREE. ME. 3. The whole body of individuals born about the same period; also, the time covered by the lives of these. (A generation is usually computed at thirty years.) ME. †4. Family, breed, race; class, kind, or set of persons -1727.
2. A family party, consisting of three generations 1834. 3. Why doth this g. seek after a sign *Mark* viii. 12. The hopes of the rising g. JOHNSON. 4. Thy Mothers of my g.: what's she, if I be a Dogge *Timon* I. i. 205. They could not brook the fighting in conjunction with this wicked g. [the Irish] DE FOE.

Generationism (dʒenĕrēi·ʃəniz'm). 1864. [f. prec. + -ISM.] The doctrine that not only the body but the soul comes from the parents; called also *traducianism*.

Generative (dʒe·nĕrĕtiv), *a.* ME. [f. GENERATE *v.* + -IVE. Cf. F. *génératif*.] Pertaining to generation; having the power or function of generating (see the *vb.*); productive.
Causes..generatiue of sedition SPEED.

Generator (dʒe·nĕrēitəɹ). 1646. [a. L.] 1. One who generates or begets. 2. That which generates or produces; *esp.* an apparatus for producing gases, steam, or electricity 1794. 3. *Mus.* The fundamental tone of a series of harmonics or of a chord 1825.

Generatrix (dʒenĕrēi·triks). 1657. [a. L., fem. of prec.] †1. A female parent -1813. 2. *Math.* A point, line, or surface conceived as producing by its motion a line, a superficial or a solid figure respectively 1840. 3. = GENERATOR 2.

Generic (dʒĕne·rik), *a.* 1676. [f. L. *gener-*, *genus* + -IC; cf. F. *générique*.] Belonging to a genus or class; applied to a large group or class of objects; general (opp. to SPECIAL or SPECIFIC); esp. in *g. character*, *name*, *term*. Also *absol.* So Gene·rical *a.* generic, general. Gene·rically *adv.* with reference to genus. Gene·ricalness (*rare*).

Generification (dʒene:rifikēi·ʃən). 1837. [f. as prec. + -ATION.] *Logic.* (See quot.)
The abstraction which carries up species into genera, is called..G., or, more loosely, Generalisation SIR W. HAMILTON.

Generosity (dʒenĕrǫ·sĭti). ME. [ad. L. *generositatem*.] 1. Nobility of birth or lineage. Now only *arch.* 2. †High spirit, nobility of conduct. Now only: Willingness to forgive injuries; magnanimity. 1623. 3. Liberality in giving; munificence 1677. 4. *pl.* Instances of generosity (senses 2, 3). *rare.* 1647.
1. The Virginians especially lay claim to this g. of lineage LOWELL. 2. G. is never a characteristic of political party warfare SIR T. MARTIN.

Generous (dʒe·nĕrəs), *a.* 1588. [ad. F. *généreux*, ad. L. *generosus*, f. *gener-*, *genus* stock, race; cf. It. *generoso*.] 1. Of noble lineage; high-born. Now only *arch.* †b. Of animals; Of good breed -1781. 2. Of actions, character, etc.: Appropriate or natural to one of noble birth or spirit; hence, †gallant; magnanimous 1588. b. Of persons: †High-spirited, gallant; magnanimous 1623. †c. Of animals: Spirited (*rare*) -1661. 3. Liberal in giving, munificent 1696; *transf.* of land: Rich 1853. 4. Furnished liberally; hence, abundant, ample 1615. b. Of diet: Ample and rich; strengthening. Also of colour: Rich, full. 1833. 5. Of wine, etc.: Rich and full of strength; invigorating 1630. †6. Of remedies: Vigorous -1677.
1. Most g. sir SHAKS. b. A g. race of horses GIBBON. 2. This is not g., not gentle SHAKS. This g. disposition to defy control SCOTT. b. So g. a conqueror GIBBON. c. A g. creature a horse is FULLER. 3. He was himself g. as a giver, parting, indeed, with that which did not altogether belong to himself 1882. 4. Strong liquors..in g. portions 1790. b. The glow of g. colour KINGLAKE. 5. It [metheglin] is a most g. liquor FULLER. Hence Ge·nerous-ly *adv.*, -ness.

Genesial (dʒĕnī·siăl), *a.* 1882. [f. GENESIS + -AL.] Pertaining to generation; as, *genesial cycle*. So Gene·siology, the science of generation.

Genesis (dʒe·nesis). OE. [a. L., a. Gr. γένεσις origin, creation, generation, f. *γεν- root of γίγνεσθαι to come into being.] 1. The first of the books of the Old Testament, containing the account of the creation of the world. (So named by the Gr. translators.) †2. *Astrol.* Nativity, horoscope -1652. †3. = SYNTHESIS (orig. with reference to geometry, opp. to *analysis*; see *Eth. Nic.* III. iii) -1674. 4. Origin, mode of formation or production (freq. in mod. usage) 1604. †b. *Math.* = GENERATION -1726.
4. The g. of our Clothes-Philosopher CARLYLE.

-ge·nesis, repr. Gr. γένεσις (see GENESIS), in compounds denoting modes of generation, as *abiogenesis*, *biogenesis*, *parthenogenesis*, etc.

Genet (dʒe·nĕt). ME. [a. OF. *gen(n)ete*, *-ette* (mod. *genette*), a. Arab. *jarnait*.] 1. A kind of civet-cat, a native of Southern Europe, Western Asia, and Africa. The common species (*Genetta vulgaris* or *Viverra Genetta*) is found in the south of France. 1481. †2. *pl.* Genet skins as fur for garments -1694. b. The fur of the genet; also, any imitation of this 1882.

Genet, obs. f. JENNET.

†**Gene·thliac.** 1584. [Ult. ad. Gr. γενεθλιακός belonging to one's birth or birthday (= γενέθλιος, f. γενέθλη, f. *γεν- to bear, bring forth).]
A. *adj.* Relating to the casting of nativities; also, to a birthday -1693.
B. *sb.* 1. One who calculates nativities (so in L. and Gr.) -1844. 2. *pl.* = GENETHLIALOGY; also, horoscopes -1755. 3. A birthday ode 1687.

Genethliacal (dʒenĕþləi·ăkăl), *a.* 1613. [f. as prec. + -AL.] = GENETHLIAC *a.* Hence Genethli·acally *adv.*

‖**Genethliacon** (dʒenĕþləi·ăkǫn). 1589. [L., f. Gr.] A birthday ode.

Genethlialogy (dʒenĕþliæ·lŏdʒi). Also -ology. 1656. [See GENETHLIAC and -LOGY.] The science of casting nativities.

†**Genethliatic.** [f. Gr. γενέθλια neut. pl.; see -ATIC.] = GENETHLIAC *sb.* 1. DRUMM. OF HAWTH.

Genetic (dʒĕne·tik), *a.* See also GENETICS. 1831. [f. GENESIS; cf. *antithesis*, *antithetic*, etc.] 1. Pertaining to, or having reference to, origin. ¶ 2. Occas. misused for: Generative, productive (= Gr. γεννητικός) 1838. 3. quasi-*sb.* (*pl.*) The principles or laws of origination 1872.
1. Phr. *G. affinity, connexion, relation(ship)* (Biol.): one that results from a common origin. *G. definition* (Logic): one which defines a thing 'as in the progress to be, as becoming'. var. Gene·tical *a.* (in senses 1, 2); †also = SYNTHETIC. Hence Gene·tically *adv.* with respect to genesis or origin.

-gene·tic (see prec.), *suffix* forming adjs. corresp. to sbs. in *-genesis* and *-geny*, as *biogenetic*, etc.

Genetics. [pl. of GENETIC used as sb., after *politics*, etc.; see -ICS.] That part of biological science which is concerned with the study of heredity and variation. BATESON.

Genetrix, genitrix (dʒe·nitriks). Now *rare.* 1500. [a. L. (cf. GENITOR).] A female parent, a mother. Also *fig.*

Geneva[1] (dʒĭnī·vă). 1706. [ad. Du. *genever*, *jenever*, ad. OF. *genevre* (mod. *genièvre*) :—L. *juniperus* juniper.] A spirit distilled from grain, and flavoured with juniper berries; made in Holland, and also called *Hollands*, formerly *Hollands Geneva*. (Often with capital G by confusion with next.)

Geneva[2] (dʒĭnī·vă). Name of a town in Switzerland, used *attrib.* or quasi-*adj.* with sense 'belonging to, made or originated at Geneva'; often with reference to Calvinism.
Geneva bands, clerical bands resembling those worn by the Swiss Calvinist clergy. **Geneva bible**, the Eng. translation of the Bible first printed at G. in 1560. **Geneva convention** (see CONVENTION). **Geneva cross**, a red Greek cross on a white ground, used in war time as a badge under the G. convention. **Geneva gown**, a black gown such as was worn by the Calvinist clergy when preaching. †**Geneva hat**, a hat of the style distinctive of the Puritan clergy.

Genevan (dʒĭnī·văn), †**Gene·vian.** 1564. [f. prec. + -AN, -IAN.]
A. *adj.* Of or pertaining to Geneva; esp. Calvinistic 1573.
B. *sb.* A native of Geneva; also, one who adheres to the doctrines of Geneva. Hence †Gene·vanism, Calvinism.

Genevese (dʒenĭvī·z). 1650. [f. as prec. + -ESE.]
A. *adj.* Pertaining to Geneva 1860.
B. *sb.* A native of Geneva. (Not now inflected in pl.) var. †Genevois *sb.*

Genial (dʒī·niăl), *a.*[1] 1566. [ad. L. *genialis*; see GENIUS. Cf. OF. *genial*.] 1. Of or pertaining to marriage, nuptial; also, generative. Now *rare.* 1566. †2. Of or pertaining to a feast; festive -1762. 3. Conducive to growth (const. *to*); now chiefly, pleasantly warm, mild 1647. Also *fig.* 4. Cheering 1746. 5. Sympathetically cheerful, jovial, kindly 1746. †6. Pertaining to 'genius' or natural disposition; natural -1850. 7. Of, pertaining to, or marked by genius (see GENIUS 5, and cf. Ger. *genial*, *genialisch*) 1827.
1. Phr. *G. bed* = L. *lectus genialis*. The bridale bowre and geniall bed SPENSER. The g. Angel (i.e. the angel presiding over marriage or generation) MILT. 2. G. cups MILT. 3. The Soil was not G. to the Seed 1705. To seek a more g. climate 1834. 5. A great broad-shoulder'd g. Englishman TENNYSON. 6. So much I feel my g. spirits droop MILT.

Genial (dʒĕnəi·ăl), *a.*[2] 1831. [f. Gr. γένειον chin (f. γένυς jaw = L. *gena*) + -AL.] *Anat.* Of or pertaining to the chin; = MENTAL *a.*[2]; as, *g. process*, *tubercle*.

Geniality (dʒīniæ·lĭti). 1609. [f. GENIAL *a.*[1] + -ITY.] The quality of being GENIAL; sympathetic cheerfulness, good-nature; mildness (of air, etc.).

Genialize (dʒī·niăləiz), *v.* 1849. [f. GENIAL *a.*[1] + -IZE.] *trans.* To impart geniality to.

Genially (dʒīˑniăli), *adv.* 1661. [f. as prec. + -LY [2].] †1. By genius or nature; naturally. GLANVILL. 2. In a genial manner; pleasantly; kindlily 1751.

2. This g. garrulous Fellow of Oriel LOWELL. So **Geˑnialness** = GENIALITY.

Genian (dʒĕnəiˑăn), *a.* 1885. [f. as GENIAL *a.*[2] + -AN.] *Anat.* = GENIAL *a.*[2]

Geniculate (dʒĕniˑkiŭlĕt), *a.* 1668. [ad. L. *geniculatus*, f. *geniculum* (see prec.).] *Nat. Hist.* Having knots or joints like a knee; bent like a knee; as, a *g. ganglion*.

Geniculate (dʒĕniˑkiŭleᵗt), *v.* 1623. [f. L. *geniculat-*, *geniculare* to bend the knee; see prec.] To bend like a knee; to form or be formed into joints. *trans.* and *intr.* Hence **Geni:culaˑtion**, †genuflexion; the state of being geniculated; *concr.* a kneed part or process.

Genie (dʒīˑni). 1655. [a. F. *génie*, ad. L. *genius.*] 1. †a. A tutelary spirit –1702. b. A JINNEE (see GENIUS 2) 1748. 2. a. Natural bent. (Common in A. Wood.) 1662. †b. A person of genius –1687.

2. a. But his g...led him in the pleasant paths of Poetry WOOD.

Genii, pl. of GENIUS.

†**Genio.** 1609. [a. It., ad. L. *genius.*] = GENIUS 2, 3, 4, and 6. –1710.

Genio- (dʒĕnəiˑo), comb. f. Gr. γένειον (see GENIAL *a.*[2]), with sense 'pertaining to the chin or lower jaw and —'.

geniˑo-glossal [see GLOSSAL] *a.* = next; **-hyˑo-glossal** *a.*, pertaining to the chin, the hyoid bone, and the tongue; **-hyˑoid** [see HYOID] *a.*, pertaining to the chin and to the hyoid bone; also *absol.* quasi-*sb.* = *genio-hyoid muscle*; **-meˑntal** [see MENTAL [2]] *a.*, pertaining to the lower jaw and the chin.

Genip (dʒeˑnip). *W. Indian.* 1756. [? short f. next.] *attrib.* in genip-tree, a name of *Genipa americana*, N.O. *Rubiaceæ*; also applied to similar trees of the N.O. *Sapindaceæ*, esp. *Melicocca bijuga* and *paniculata*.

Genipap (dʒeˑnipæp). 1613. [app. a native name.] The fruit of *Genipa americana*.

‖**Genista** (dʒĕniˑstă). 1625. [L.; = 'broom'.] *Bot.* A plant of the genus (N.O. *Leguminosæ*) represented by Dyer's Broom or Greenweed (*G. tinctoria*); including, according to some, the Common Broom (*Cytisus scoparia*).

Genital (dʒeˑnităl). ME. [ad. L. *genitalem*, f. *genit-*, ppl. stem of *gignere* to beget; see -AL. Cf. F. *génital.*]

A. *adj.* Pertaining to animal generation.

B. *sb.* The †organ or (*pl.*) organs of generation, usually of the male ME.

‖**Genitalia** (dʒenitēˑliă), *sb. pl.* 1876. [L.] = GENITALS (see prec. B).

Geniting, obs. f. JENNETING.

Genitival (dʒenitəiˑvăl), *a.* 1818. [f. next + -AL.] Belonging to the genitive case; as, a *g. termination*.

Genitive (dʒeˑnitiv). ME. [ad. L. *genetivum*, *genitivum* belonging to birth or generation (f. **gen-* root of *gignere* to beget); *genetivus* (*casus*) is a mistranslation of Gr. γενική (πτῶσις) = 'generic case'.]

A. *adj.* 1. *G. case*: a grammatical form of sbs., etc., used to denote that the person or thing signified by the word is related to another as source, possessor, or the like. †2. Pertaining to generation –1656.

1. There is no g. case in the Persian SIR W. JONES.

B. *sb.* = *genitive case*; also, a part of speech in this case 1620.

The Cumulative or Double G., a peculiarly English combination, where both the *of* and the *'s* are retained, as 'that boy of Norcott's' EARLE.

Genito- (dʒeˑnito), mod. comb. f. L. *genitalis* genital, used in terms which refer to the genital organs in conjunction with other parts of the body, as *g.-crural*, *-urinary*, etc.

†**Genitor** [1], **genitory.** Chiefly *pl.* ME. [a. OF. *genitoir*, app. f. L. type **genitorium.*] A testicle; *pl.* the testicles, but in later use = *genitals* –1708.

Genitor [2] (dʒeˑnitŏr). Now *rare.* 1447 [a. L., f. **gen-* root of *gignere* to beget, bear.] A male parent, father; in *pl.* = parents.

†**Geniture.** 1548. [ad. L. *genituram* begetting, etc. Cf. OF. *geniture.*] 1. Begetting, generation; birth –1759. 2. *Astrol.* Nativity, horoscope –1819. 3. Offspring, product –1698. 4. The generative seed of animals –1683. 5. *pl.* = Genitals 1548.

Genius (dʒīˑniŏs). *Pl.* **-ii** (-iˌəi), **-iuses.** 1513. [a. L., f. **gen-* root of *gignere*, Gr. γίγνεσθαι.] 1. The tutelary god or attendant spirit allotted to every person at his birth, to preside over his destiny in life; also, the tutelary spirit of a place, institution, etc. (Now only in *sing.*) †b. After L. use: This spirit as propitiated by festivities; hence, one's appetite –1693. c. The personification of something immaterial, e.g. of a virtue, a custom, etc. Hence *transf.* a person or thing fit to be this. 1597. 2. A demon or spirit in general. Now chiefly in pl. *genii*, as transl. Arab. *jinn* (see JINN). (In *sing.* repl. by GENIE.) 1590. 3. †a. Characteristic disposition; inclination; bent –1804. b. Prevailing character or spirit (of a nation, age, language, law, etc.) 1639. c. The associations or suggestions (of a place) 1823. †d. Of material things, diseases, etc.: The natural character, inherent tendency –1747. 4. Natural ability; quality of mind 1649; natural aptitude (and inclination) †*to*, *for* 1643. 5. (Only in *sing.*) Native intellectual power of an exalted type; extraordinary capacity for imaginative creation, original thought, invention, or discovery. Often contrasted with *talent.* 1749. 6. One who has *great*, *little*, etc. 'genius' (sense 4); one who has a 'genius' (sense 3); one endowed with 'genius' (sense 5) (now only *geniuses* in pl.) 1647.

1. Vnder him My G. is rebuk'd, as it is said Mark Anthonies was by Cæsar SHAKS. Phr. (*A person's*) *good*, *evil g.*: the two spirits (also *angels*), good and evil, attendant on every person throughout life. Hence *transf.* of a person who powerfully influences another for good or evil. c. He was the very G. of Famine SHAKS. 2. They mock even the G. of Socrates as a feigned thing STANLEY. 3. a. My g. is always in extremes JOHNSON. b. The G. of the Age BOYLE, of Tragedy BENTLEY, of the British Constitution ADAM SMITH. 4. The Squire whose active g. [etc.] LYTTON. Walton had a g. for friendships LOWELL. 5. G. always imports something inventive or creative BLAIR. G...means transcendent capacity for taking trouble, first of all CARLYLE. 6. That g. [Inigo Jones] H. WALPOLE. Phrase. ‖**genius loci** [L. = 'genius of the place'], the presiding deity or spirit (see sense 1); but often in sense 3 c.

Genoa (dʒeˑnoˌă). 1615. The name of a city of Italy. Used *attrib.* in **G. cake**, a rich currant cake with almonds on the top; **G. treacle** (see TREACLE). Also *absol.* = *G.-velvet.*

Genoblast (dʒeˑnoblɑst). 1877. [f. Gr. γένος offspring + -BLAST.] The bisexual nucleus of the impregnated ovum. Hence **Genoblaˑstic** *a.*

Genocide (dʒeˑnosəid). 1944. [irreg. f. Gr. γένος race + -CIDE [2].] Annihilation of a race.

Genoese (dʒenoˌīˑz). 1553. [f. GENOA + -ESE.] A. *adj.* Of or pertaining to Genoa 1756. †var. **Genoˑan.** B. *absol.* and *sb.* *The G.* (pl.): the Genoese people. var. **Geˑnovese** *a.* and *sb.*

Genouillere (ʒənuyḗr). ME. [a. F. *genouillère*, f. OF. *genouil* (mod. *genou*) knee:—pop. L. **genuclum*, f. *genu.*] 1. A flexible piece of armour for covering the knees. 2. *Fortif.* That part of the interior slope of the parapet immediately below the embrasures 1802.

‖**Genre** (ʒaṅr). 1816. [F.; see GENDER.] 1. Kind; sort; style. 2. A style of painting which depicts scenes and subjects of common life 1873. 3. *attrib.*, as *g.-piece*, etc. 1849.

Gens (dʒenz). *Pl.* **gentes** (dʒeˑntīz). 1847. [a. L., f. root **gen-* of *gignere*, Gr. γίγνεσθαι.] *Rom. Antiq.* A clan or sept; a number of families having a supposed common origin, a common name, and common religious rites. Hence as transl. Gr. γένος, and applied to any similar group of families.

Gens d'armerie, Gens d'armes, var. ff. GENDARMERY, GENDARMES.

Gent (dʒent), *sb.* 1564. [Short for GENTLEMAN.] = GENTLEMAN; now *vulgar*, exc. as applied derisively to men of the class who use the word; now frequent in tradesmen's notices.

London audiences of shop-boys and flashy gents 1878.

†**Gent** (dʒent), *a.* ME. [a. OF. *gent*:—pop. L. **gentum* for cl. L. *genitum* born, hence, well-born, noble, etc. Cf. GENTLE.] 1. Noble, high-born; having the qualities attaching to high birth –1672. 2. Graceful, elegant, shapely; neat –1824.

1. Jesu so gente ME. 2. He lov'd..a Lady g. SPENSER.

Genteel (dʒentīˑl). 1599. [A re-adoption of F. *gentil*, which had become GENTLE. In educated use, slightly sarcastic or playful.]

A. *adj.* 1. Belonging to the gentry. *Obs.* or *arch.* 1628. 2. Appropriate to persons of quality 1599; suited to the station of a gentleman or gentlewoman 1602. 3. Having the habits characteristic of superior station; in early use, †polished, well-bred. (Now chiefly touched with sarcasm.) 1648. †b. Of behaviour: Polite, obliging –1814. 4. Of persons: Gentlemanly or ladylike in appearance; well-dressed. (Now *vulgar*, exc. as depreciatory.) 1629. 5. Elegant, graceful. *Obs.* of immaterial things. 1678.

1. Thomas Wyatt..of an ancient and gentile family WOOD. 2. The genteelest dinner..I have seen PEPYS. G. Conversation 1766, accomplishments 1801. A g. maintenance V. KNOX. 3. Zimri and Cosbi.. g. Sinners M. HENRY. The straits of g. poverty 1885. 5. His countenance beautiful; his limbs g. and slender HUME.

B. *sb.* A genteel person; a gentleman. *Obs.* exc. *occas.* 1675. Hence **Genteeˑlish** *a.* somewhat g. **Genteeˑl-ly** *adv.*, **-ness.**

Gentian (dʒeˑnʃən). OE. [ad. L. *gentiana*, f. *Gentius*, king of Illyria (Pliny).] 1. Any plant belonging to the genus *Gentiana* (cf. FELWORT); esp. *G. lutea*, the officinal gentian which yields the gentian-root of the pharmacopœia. *Fringed g.* = *G. crinita.* Also *transf.* of other orders and genera. 2. *attrib.*, as in *g.-blue*, etc.; **g.-bitter**, the tonic principle extracted from g.-root; **g.-worts**, Lindley's name for N.O. *Gentianaceæ.*

Hence **Gentianaˑceous** *a.* of or belonging to the N.O. *Gentianaceæ*; **Gentiaˑnic** *a.* pertaining to or derived from the g., as *gentianic acid*; **Geˑntianin** (also †-ine) = *gentianic acid.*

Gentianal (dʒeˑnʃənăl), *a.* 1846. Of or pertaining to the gentians.

Gentianella (dʒeːnʃəneˑlă). 1658. [mod. L., dim. of L. *gentiana.*] A name for species of gentian, esp. *Gentiana acaulis*, bearing flowers of an intense blue colour.

Gentil, obs. f. GENTEEL, GENTLE.

Gentile (dʒeˑntəil, -til). ME. [a. or ad. F. *gentil*, ad. L. *gentilis*, f. *gent-*, *gens* nation, GENS.]

A. *adj.* I. Senses derived from the Vulgate (dʒeˑntəil). Usu. with capital G. 1. Of or pertaining to any or all of the non-Jewish nations. †2. Heathen, pagan –1789.

II. Senses derived from cl. L. (Usu. dʒeˑntil.) 1. Pertaining to or indicating a nation or tribe. Now *rare.* 1513. 2. Of or pertaining to a gens or to gentes 1846.

2. There were in every gens or family special g. deities GROTE.

B. *sb.* I. From A. I. (dʒeˑntəil). (Usu. with capital G.) 1. One of any non-Jewish nation ME. (Similarly by Mormons opposed to 'Saint'.) 2. A heathen, a pagan. Now *rare.* ME. †b. *spec.* Of a Hindoo, as dist. from a Mohammedan –1727.

1. No more shalt thou by oracling abuse The Gentiles MILT.

II. From A. II. (dʒeˑntil). 1. *Gram.* A part of speech indicating the locality or nation to which anything belongs 1612. 2. *Rom. Law.* A member of the same gens 1875.

1. The words Italian, American..are gentiles 1889.

Gentilesse (dʒeːntileˑs). Now *arch.* ME. [ad. F. *gentillesse*, f. *gentil*; see GENTLE.] 1. Courtesy, politeness, good breeding. 2. Elegance. CHAUCER.

Gentilic (dʒentiˑlik), *a.* 1604. [f. L. *gentilis* + -IC.] †a. Heathen; var. †**Gentiˑlical.** b. Tribal, national.

†**Geˑntilish,** *a.* 1550. [f. GENTILE + -ISH.] Of Gentile nature, origin, or character; heathenish –1651.

Gentilism (dʒeˑntiliz'm). 1577. [f. as prec. + -ISM.] 1. Heathenism, paganism; a heathen belief or practice. Now only *occas.*, as opp. to *Judaism.* †b. *concr.* Heathendom –1654. 2. The bond uniting the members of a gens (*rare*) 1847.

Gentilitial (dʒentili·ʃăl), *a.* 1611. [f. L. *gentilitius* (f. *gentilis*) + -AL.] 1. Peculiar to a nation; national 1650. 2. Of or pertaining to a gens or family 1611. 3. Of or pertaining to gentle birth. [? f. med.L. *gentilitia* = GENTILESSE.] 1816. var. **Gentili·tian** (in sense 1).

Gentilitious (dʒentili·ʃəs), *a.* 1613. [f. as prec. + -OUS.] †1. Pagan (*rare*) 1613. 2. = GENTILITIAL 1. 1646. 3. = GENTILITIAL 2; hence, hereditary (? *Obs.*) 1646.

Gentility (dʒenti·lĭti). ME. [ad. OF. and F. *gentilité*, ad. L. *gentilitas*; see GENTILE, GENTLE, GENTEEL.]

I. In relation to GENTLE, GENTEEL. 1. Gentle birth; honourable extraction. Also quasi-*personified*. †b. *concr.* Gentlefolks. Also *The g.* –1622. c. The heraldic status of a gentleman 1642. 2. The quality of being gentle (in manners, status, etc.) or genteel 1588. b. quasi-*personified*. Also in *pl.* Genteel people; also, marks of gentility. 1840.

1. G. has long since confuted Job's Aphorism, Man is born to labour 1659. 2. There is nothing so vulgar as g. 1872. b. Shabby g. O. W. HOLMES.

II. In relation to GENTILE. †1. Heathenism, paganism –1650; †*concr.* heathendom, heathen people –1582. 2. Relationship between members of the same gens; †the gens itself 1577.

Gentilize (dʒe·ntiləiz), *v.*[1] *arch.* 1581. [f. F. *gentil* GENTLE + -IZE.] 1. *trans.* To make gentle or gentlemanly. †b. *intr. To g. it*: to act the gentleman –1613. †2. *trans.* To lenify 1679.

Gentilize (dʒe·ntiləiz, dʒe·ntəiləiz), *v.*[2] 1593. [f. GENTILE + -IZE.] 1. *intr.* To live like a Gentile or heathen. 2. *trans.* To make gentile, paganize 1827.

Gentill-: see GENTEEL, GENTIL-, GENTLE, etc.

Gentiopicrin (dʒentiəpi·krin). 1875. [f. *gentio-* comb. f. GENTIAN + Gr. πικρός + -IN.] *Chem.* 'The bitter principle of gentian, a colourless crystalline glycoside' (*Syd. Soc. Lex.*).

Gentisic (dʒenti·sik), *a.* 1838. [irreg. f. GENTIAN; see -IC.] *Chem.* In *g. acid* = gentianic acid. So **Ge·ntisate** [-ATE], a salt of this acid. **Ge·ntisin** [-IN], a synonym of g. or gentianic acid.

Gentle (dʒe·nt'l). [ME. *gentil(l, -yl*, a. OF. :—L. *gentilis* of the same gens or race, f. *genti-, gens*. The sense 'of a good family' is Rom., not L. See also GENTILE.]

A. *adj.* 1. Well-born; belonging to a family of position; orig. = *noble*, but afterwards designating a lower degree of rank. Also in *Her.*: Having the rank of 'gentleman', and therefore entitled to bear arms. *Obs.* exc. in *gentle and simple*, and in Comb. b. Of excellent breed or spirit; now only in *gentle* (also *gentil*) *falcon* ME. †c. Of things: Noble, excellent (*rare*) –1556. 2. Of birth, etc.: Honourable, belonging to the class of 'gentlemen' ME. b. Of occupations, etc.: Suitable for one of gentle birth 1592. 3. Noble, generous, courteous, polite. Now only *arch.* ME. b. Used in polite or conciliatory address, or in compliment. *Obs.* exc. *arch.* in 'Gentle Reader'. 1500. 4. Of a tree, etc.: Cultivated (opp. to *wild*). Now *rare*. ME. Of an animal: Tame, easily managed 1532. †5. Not harsh or irritating to the touch; soft, tender; pliant, supple –1769. 6. Not violent or severe 1563; not rough 1593; not harsh 1605; mild 1576. 7. Of a slope: Gradual; not steep 1697. 8. Used advb. = GENTLY (esp. in *compar.*) 1601.

1. Noble men and gentile ne bereð nout packes ME. G. and Simple, Squire and Groom BARHAM. b. A Lion saw I late..Vpon the g. beast to gaze it pleased me SURREY. c. That gentil text CHAUCER. 2. His birth being admitted as g., gave him access to the best society in the county SCOTT. b. *The g. craft* (joc.): †(*a*) shoemaking; (*b*) angling; similarly *the g. art*, now often used transf. 3. [Robin Hood] The gentlest thief that ever was FULLER. b. You g. Romans SHAKS. 4. We marry A gentler sien to the wildest stock SHAKS. 6. As when the Woods by g. Winds are stirr'd DRYDEN. The g. voice of Peace COLLINS. A g. River 1791. A g. heat 1816. G. methods SCOTT. A g. aperient 1835. You have grown g. to me and have left off scolding JOWETT. 8. Hee put it by thrice, everie time gentler then other *Jul. C.* I. ii. 231.

B. *sb.* 1. One who is of gentle birth or rank (*rare* in *sing.*; *Obs.* in *pl.* exc. *arch.*) ME. †b. Used in polite address –1641. 2. = FALCON-GENTLE. 1776. 3. A maggot, the larva of the flesh-fly or blue-bottle, used as bait by anglers 1578.

1. b. Gentles I would entreat you a courtesie MARMION.

Gentle (dʒe·nt'l), *v.* ME. [f. prec.] †1. *trans.* To ennoble –1630. 2. To render mild or pleasant (*rare*) 1651; to break in (a horse, etc.) 1735; to mollify (a person) 1795.

1. Be he ne're so vile, This day shall g. his Condition SHAKS.

Gentlefolk, -folks (dʒe·nt'lfōuk, -fōuks). 1594. [f. as GENTLE *a.* + FOLK. The sing. is recent.] Persons of good position and family.

The Queene's Kindred are made gentle Folkes SHAKS.

Gentlehood (dʒe·nt'lhud). 1860. [See -HOOD.] Position or character attaching to gentle birth.

Gentleman (dʒe·nt'lmăn). ME. [f. GENTLE + MAN, after OF. *gentilz hom* (mod. *gentilhomme*).] 1. A man of gentle birth; prop., one entitled to bear arms, though not noble, but also applied to any person of distinction. Now chiefly *Hist.* b. Used as a complimentary designation of a member of certain societies or professions 1537. 2. *spec.* A man of gentle birth attached to the household of the sovereign or of a person of rank 1463. 3. A man of chivalrous instincts and fine feelings ME. 4. A man of superior position in society; often, a man of money and leisure. In recent use often a courteous synonym for 'man'. 1583. b. In *pl.* (†also in *sing.*) a polite term of address without reference to rank 1579. c. In legal documents, a person who has no occupation 1862. 5. In contemptuous or joc. uses; esp. *old g.* = old fellow, *spec.* the devil; *my g.* = 'the fellow' 1622.

1. Early in the 11th century the order of 'gentlemen' as a separate class seems to be forming as something new FREEMAN. b. A gentellman of the Inner Temple 1537. Gentlemen of the faculty 1768. 2. The gentylmen of the kynges housholde and the gentylmen of the Erles housholde 1520. †*G.-pensioner*, now *G.-at-arms*: one of forty gentlemen who act as guards or attendants to the sovereign on state occasions. *G. at large*, †a g. attached to the court but without specific duties; hence *joc.* one who is out of work. 3. Who so is vertuous..he is gentil, bycause he doth As longeth to a gentilman ME. 4. The rich Tradesman .. laid the Tradesman down and commenc'd G. DE FOE. b. Your name, honest G. SHAKS. 5. But afterwards..the copy of my Gentlemans countenance was quickly altered MABBE. You *gentlemen's gentlemen* (= valets) are so hasty SHERIDAN.

Phrases. *The g. in black velvet*: a mole (a Jacobite phrase, referring to the belief that the death of William III was caused by his horse's stumbling over a mole-hill). *G. of fortune*: a pirate. *Gentleman's (-men's) agreement*: an agreement binding in honour, but not enforceable at law (orig. *U.S.*).

Hence **Ge·ntlemanhood**, the position or character of a g. **Ge·ntlemanism**, the state of being a g., the affectation of gentlemanliness. **Ge·ntlemani·ze** *v.* to make into a g. **Ge·ntlemanship**, gentlemanhood; the office of a g. (-in-waiting, etc.).

Ge·ntleman-co·mmoner. 1687. [See COMMONER.] One of a privileged class of undergraduates formerly recognized in the Universities of Oxford and Cambridge.

Ge·ntleman-fa·rmer. 1749. A country gentleman engaged in farming, usually on his own estate.

Gentlemanlike (dʒe·nt'lmănləik). 1542. [f. GENTLEMAN + LIKE.]

A. *adj.* Appropriate or natural to a gentleman 1557; resembling a gentleman 1581.

†B. *adv.* After the fashion of a gentleman –1606.

Ge·ntlemanly. ME. [See -LY.] A. *adj.* 1. Having the character, behaviour, or appearance of a gentleman 1454. 2. Natural or appropriate to a gentleman 1581.

B. *adv.* As befits a gentleman. Now *rare*. ME. Hence **Ge·ntlemanliness**, the attribute of being g.

Ge·ntleman-u·sher. 1485. A gentleman acting as usher to a person of superior rank. *G.-usher of the Black Rod* (see BLACK ROD).

Gentleness (dʒe·nt'lnĕs). ME. [f. GENTLE + -NESS.] †1. The condition of being GENTLE *a.* (sense 1) –1671. 2. †Good breeding, courtesy, affability; kindliness, mildness ME. 3. The condition of being gentle (in other senses of the adj.); freedom from harshness or violence, etc. 1614.

Gentleship (dʒe·nt'lʃip). [-SHIP.] The condition or quality of being a gentleman. ASCHAM.

Gentlewoman (dʒe·nt'lwumăn). ME. [f. GENTLE *a.* + WOMAN.] 1. A woman of good birth or breeding. 2. A female attendant (orig. a gentlewoman by birth) upon a lady of rank. Now only *Hist.* ME.

Gently (dʒe·ntli), *adv.* ME. [f. GENTLE *a.* + -LY[2].] In a gentle manner (see GENTLE *a.*); also used as an expression of remonstrance.

G. born and bred TENNYSON. G., Mr. Testy 1806.

Gentoo (dʒentū·), *sb.*[1] and *a.* 1638. [Anglo-Indian ad. Pg. *gentio* GENTILE.]

A. *sb.* 1. A Hindoo, opp. to a Mohammedan. 2. The language of the Gentoos 1698.

B. *attrib.* (*adj.*) Of or pertaining to the Gentoos 1686.

Gentoo (dʒentū·), *sb.*[2] 1860. [? a use of prec.] A kind of penguin frequenting the Falkland Islands. Also *G. Penguin*.

Gentrice. *Obs.* exc. *arch.* (*Sc.*) ME. [ad. OF. *genterise*, var. of *gentelise*, f. *gentil*.] 1. Gentle birth. 2. Gentle or honourable feeling ME. 3. Gentility. SCOTT.

Gentry (dʒe·ntri). ME. [app. an altered form of prec., taken as pl.] 1. Rank by birth (usu., high birth). *Obs.* exc. *arch.* b. The quality or rank of gentleman (*arch.*) 1447. †c. Good breeding; also, courtesy, generosity –1595. 2. People of gentle birth and breeding; the class to which they belong; now *spec.* the class immediately below the nobility 1585. 3. Playfully or contemptuously: People, folks 1717.

1. To presume..upon..birth and G. 1647. b. His g. sits as ill upon him, as if he had bought it with his penny OVERBURY. c. True gentrie they have put to flight 1595. 2. Grave g. of estate and name WORDSW. 3. These crusty g. W. IRVING.

Genty (dʒe·nti), *a.* *Obs.* exc. *Sc.* 1721. [var. of GENTEE.] Neat; graceful; genteel.

‖**Genu** (dʒī·niu). 1854. [L.; = 'knee'.] *Anat.* Name for a knee-like bend in various organs of the body. Hence **Ge·nual** *a.* of or pertaining to the g. **Ge·nuant** *a.* (*Her.*) kneeling. **Ge·nuclast** (*Surg.*), an instrument for breaking down adhesions in the knee-joint.

Genuflect (dʒe·niuflekt), *v.* 1630. [f. med. L. *genuflectere*, f. L. *genu* + *flectere* to bend.] *intr.* To bend the knee, esp. in worship. Hence **Genufle·ctory** *a.* of or pertaining to genuflexion or kneeling. var. **Genufle·x**.

Genuflexion, genuflection (dʒeniufle·kʃən). 1526. [ad. med.L. *genuflexionem*; see prec.] The act of kneeling or bending the knee, esp. in worship; also *Surg.* as a curative measure in popliteal aneurism.

Genuine (dʒe·niu,in), *a.* 1596. [ad. L. *genuinus*, f. pre-L. *genwo-, f. Aryan root *gen- to beget, be born, etc.; see KIN.] †1. Natural, not acquired, native –1712. 2. Pertaining to the original stock, pure-bred 1728. 3. Not spurious; AUTHENTIC. (The 18th c. distinction between *genuine* and *authentic* is not well founded.) 1661. 4. Being as represented; real, true, not counterfeit, †unadulterated 1639. b. Properly so called 1682.

1. This g. blemish 1644. 2. [A bull-dog] of a pure and g. breed T. MEDWIN. 3. Two volumes more.. indubitably g. JOHNSON. 4. Natural Religion in its g. simplicity BUTLER. b. A g. son of the sea SCORESBY. Hence **Ge·nuine-ly** *adv.*, **-ness**.

‖**Genus** (dʒī·nəs). *Pl.* ‖**genera** (dʒe·nĕră). 1551. [L. = Gr. γένος, f. Aryan root *gen- to beget, be born, etc.; see KIN.] 1. *Logic.* A class or kind of things which includes subordinate kinds (called SPECIES) as having certain attributes in common; a general concept. (One of the five PREDICABLES, q.v.) 2. *Zool.* and *Bot.* A classificatory group comprehending (one or) a number of species possessing certain common structural characters distinct from those of any other group. Also *transf.* 1608.

The genus ranks next under the family or sub-family, and above the species; it is sometimes divided into sub-genera. The generic and specific names (always in Latin or considered as Latin) together form the scientific proper name of an animal or plant, the generic name standing first and being written with an initial capital.

3. *Mus.* Each of the three scales in ancient Greek music 1763. 4. *gen.* A kind, class, order, tribe, etc. 1649.

1. *Highest g.* (L. *summum genus*), one which does not become a species of a higher g.; opp. to *subaltern g.* The Highest G. in any special science is the general class, comprehending all the objects whose properties that science investigates MANSEL.

-geny, *suffix* = mod. F. *-génie*, added to Gr stems to form sbs. with sense 'mode of production (of something specified)' as in *anthropogeny*, etc.

Genyplasty (dʒe·niplæsti). 1857. [f. Gr. γένυς jaw, cheek + πλαστός moulded + -Y [3].] *Med.* An operation for restoring the cheek.

Geo- (dʒī·o-, dʒiˌǫ·-), repr. Gr. γεω-, comb. f. Gr. γῆ earth. **ge·oblast** [-BLAST], 'a plumule which in germination rises from underground, such as that of the Pea' (GRAY); **ge:obota·nical** *a.*, of or pertaining to geographical botany; **ge:ochro·nic** *a.*, of or pertaining to geological time; **ge:ocy·clic** *a.*, of or pertaining to the revolutions of the earth; also, circling the earth periodically; **ge:odyna·mic, -al** *a.*, of or pertaining to the (latent) forces of the earth; **ge:oi·sotherm**, an underground isotherm; **ge:onaviga·tion**, navigation by dead reckoning —opp. to *Cælo-navigation*; **geo·nomy**, the science of the physical laws relating to the earth; **ge:ophy·sical** *a.*, relating to the physics of the earth; **ge:ophy·sics** *pl.*, the physics of the earth; **ge:osele·nic** *a.*, relating to the earth and the moon; **ge:osta·tic** [Gr. στατικός] *a.*, suited to bear the pressure of earth, as a *geostatic arch*; **ge:osta·tics** *pl.*, 'the statics of rigid bodies' (*Cent. Dict.*); **ge:otecto·nic, -al** *a.*, of or pertaining to the structure of the earth; structural; **ge:othe·rmal** *a.*, of or pertaining to the internal heat of the earth; so **ge:othe·rmic** *a.*; **ge:othermo·meter**, an instrument for measuring terrestrial heat, esp. in mines and artesian wells.

Geocentric (dʒīˌose·ntrik), *a.* (*sb.*) 1667. [f. GEO-; see CENTRIC. Cf. F. *géocentrique*. Opp. to HELIOCENTRIC.] 1. Referred to the earth as a centre; considered as viewed from the centre of the earth; as, the *g. latitude, longitude, place*, etc. of a planet 1686. 2. Having, or representing, the earth as centre; also *fig.* 1696. 3. *sb.* An adherent of the geocentric theory 1667.

2. In the universe of being the difference between a heliocentric and a g. theory is of..small moment M. PATTISON. Hence **Geoce·ntrically** *adv.* **Geoce·ntricism**, the g. theory.

Geocronite (dʒīˌǫ·krǫnəit). 1844. [f. GEO- + Gr. Κρόνος Saturn (in alchemy assoc. with lead) + -ITE.] *Min.* A sulphide of lead and antimony.

Geodæsia: see GEODESY.

Geode (dʒī·oᵘd). 1676. [a. F. *géode*, ad. L. *geodes* = Gr. γεώδης earthy, f. γῆ.] A nodular stone, containing a cavity usually lined with crystals or mineral matter. b. The cavity itself; also, any similar formation 1849. Hence **Geo·dic** *a.* of, pertaining to, or resembling a g. **Geodi·ferous** *a.*

Geodesy (dʒiˌǫ·dėsi). 1570. [ad. F. *géodésie*, ad. mod.L. *geodæsia* (also used), Gr. γεωδαισία, f. γεω-, γῆ earth + δαίειν to divide.] †a. Land surveying –1855. b. In mod. use: That branch of applied mathematics which determines the figures and areas of large portions of the earth's surface, and the figure of the earth as a whole 1853. So †**Geodesian**, a land-surveyor. Hence **Geode·sic** *a.* of or pertaining to g.; *sb.* a geodesic line. **Geode·sical** *a.* = prec. adj. **Geo·desist**, one versed in g.

Geodetic (dʒīˌode·tik). 1674. [as if ad. L. *geodæticus*, a. Gr., f. γῆ + δαίειν.]

A. *adj.* Of or pertaining to geodesy 1834.

Phr. *Geodetic line*: the shortest possible line that can be drawn from one point of a surface to another, the plane of curvature of which will be everywhere perpendicular to the surface.

B. *sb.* 1. A geodetic line (see A. quot.) 1879. 2. in pl. form **Geodetics** = GEODESY. (Dicts.)

Hence **Geode·tical** a. of or pertaining to geodesy. †**Geode·tically** *adv.*

Geoduck (dʒī·odʌk). 1883. [? Amer. Indian.] A large edible clam (*Glycineris generosa*) from the Pacific coast of the U.S.

Geogeny (dʒiˌǫ·dʒėni). 1855. [See GEO- and -GENY.] That branch of geology which treats of the formation of the earth's crust. Hence **Geoge·nic** *a.* pertaining to g.; earth-forming.

Geognost (dʒī·ǫgnǫst). 1804. [ad. F. *géognoste*, f. Gr. γεω- + γνώστης one who knows.] One versed in geognosy. Hence **Geogno·stic, -al** *a.* of or pertaining to geognosy. **Geogno·stically** *adv.*

Geognosy (dʒiˌǫ·gnǒsi). 1791. [ad. F. *géognosie*, f. as prec. + γνῶσις.] 1. A knowledge of the structure of the earth, its strata, and their relative position. Often = GEOLOGY. 2. a. A knowledge of the natural position of minerals in particular rocks, and of the grouping, distribution, and relations of those rocks 1811. b. Local geology 1839. var. **Geo·gnosis.**

Geogony (dʒiˌǫ·gǒni). 1828. [f. Gr. γεω- GEO- + -γονία production.] The theory of the formation of the earth. Also, an account of this. Hence **Geogo·nic, -al** *a.* of or pertaining to g.

Geographer (dʒiˌǫ·grăfəɹ). 1542. [f. med. L. *geographus*; see -ER *suffix* [1] 4.] One who is versed in, or writes upon, geography. var. †**Ge·ograph.**

Geographic (dʒīˌogræ·fik). 1610. [ad. Gr. γεωγραφικός, f. γεωγράφος. Cf. F. *géographique.*]

A. *adj.* Of or pertaining to geography; of the nature of geography. Now *rare.*

Phr. *Geographic latitude*: the angle made with the plane of the equator by a perpendicular to the surface of the earth at any point.

B. *sb.* pl. **Geographics** (*rare*), geographical science; †a treatise on this 1610.

Geographical (dʒīˌogræ·fikăl), *a.* 1559. [f. as prec. + -AL.] = GEOGRAPHIC *a.*

Geographical mile: a measure of length = 1′ of longitude on the equator. Hence **Geogra·phically** *adv.*

Geography (dʒiˌǫ·grăfi). 1542. [a. F. *géographie*, ad. L., a. Gr. γεωγραφία, f. γεω- GEO- + -γραφία writing.] 1. The science that describes the earth's surface, its form and physical features, its natural and political divisions, its climates, productions, etc. Also *transf.* b. The subject-matter of geography; the range or extent of what is known geographically 1737. 2. A treatise on this science 1559.

1. Phr. *Mathematical, physical, political g.* †*Subterranean g.* = GEOLOGY. *transf.* The g. of Mars (*mod.*). b. The islands..added to the g. of the globe COOK.

Geoid (dʒī·oid). 1881. [ad. Gr. γεοειδής adj., earth-like; see -OID.] A geometrical solid, nearly identical with the terrestrial spheroid, but having the surface at every point perpendicular to the direction of gravity. Hence **Geoi·dal** *a.*

Geolatry (dʒiˌǫ·lătri). *rare.* 1860. [f. GEO- + -LATRY.] Earth-worship.

Geologic (dʒīˌolǫ·dʒik), *a.* 1799. [f. GEOLOGY + -IC.] Of, pertaining to, or derived from geology (now used mainly as an epithet of things forming part of the subject-matter of the science, e. g. a *geologic epoch*, as dist. from *geological*). Also *transf.* So **Geolo·gical** *a.* Hence **Geolo·gically** *adv.*

Geologist (dʒiˌǫ·lŏdʒist). 1795. [f. GEOLOGY + -IST.] One versed in geology. vars. **Geo·loger** (now *rare*), **Geolo·gian** (now *rare*).

Geologize (dʒiˌǫ·lŏdʒəiz), *v.* 1831. [f. GEOLOGY + -IZE.] 1. *intr.* To make geological researches. 2. *trans.* To examine geologically 1834.

1. During Midsummer geologized a little in Shropshire DARWIN.

Geology (dʒiˌǫ·lŏdʒi). 1735. [ad. med.L. *geologia*, orig. 'science of earthly things', as law, etc., f. Gr. γεω- GEO- + -λογία; see -LOGY.] †1. The science which treats of the earth in general –1755. 2. The science which investigates the earth's crust, the strata which compose it, with their mutual relations, and the successive changes to which their present condition and positions are due 1795. b. The geological features of a district 1816.

Geomalism (dʒiˌǫ·măliz'm). 1884. [f. Gr. γεω-, γῆ + ὁμαλός level + -IC.] *Biol.* The tendency of an organism to grow symmetrically in a horizontal plane. So **Geo·maly.**

Geomancy (dʒī·omæ:nsi). ME. [a. F. *géomancie*, ad. L. *geomantia*, a. late Gr., f. γεω-, comb. f. γῆ + μαντεία.] The art of divination by means of lines and figures, formed orig. by throwing earth on some surface, and later by jotting down on paper dots at random. Hence **Ge·oma:ncer**, also **Ge·omant** (*rare*), one who practises g.

Geomantic (dʒīˌomæ·ntik). 1590. [ad. med.L. *geomanticus*, f. *geomantia*; see prec. Cf. F. *géomantique.*]

A. *adj.* Belonging to geomancy; var. **Geoma·ntical.**

†B. *sb.* A geomancer –1652. Hence **Geoma·ntically** *adv.*

Geometer (dʒiˌǫ·mĭtəɹ). 1483. [ad. L. *geometra, -metres*, a. Gr., f. γεω- GEO- + -μέτρης measurer. Cf. F. *géomètre.*] 1. One who studies, or is skilled in, geometry. 2. The name of a class of caterpillars (so called from their walk) 1816.

Geometric, -al (dʒīˌome·trik, -ăl), *a.* 1552. [ad. L. *geometricus*, a. Gr., f. γεωμέτρης GEOMETER, + -AL.] 1. Belonging to geometry; determined or constructed according to the methods of geometry. 2. That works by the methods of geometry (*rare*) 1682.

1. †*Geometrical cubit, foot, mile, pace*: measures of length, some of which are app. fixed by geographical computation (1 degree = 60 miles, 1 mile = 1,000 paces, 1 pace = 5 feet). *Geometrical figures*, formerly restricted to those whose construction involved only the straight line and circle, all other curves being called mechanical. *Geometrical ratio* (now usually *ratio* simply): that kind of relation between two quantities which is expressed by dividing the first by the second; the quotient expressing this. *G proportion*: a proportion which involves an equality of geometrical ratio in its two parts, as 1 : 3 :: 4 : 12. *G. progression*: a series in which the ratio between the successive quantities is constant, as 1 : 3 : 9 : 27 : 81, etc. *Geometric(al spider*, a spider which constructs a web of a geometrical form. *Geometrical staircase*, 'one whose opening is down its centre..in which each step is supported by one end being fixed in the wall or partition' (Gwilt). *Geometrical tracery*, tracery in which the openings are of geometrical form (circles, trefoils, etc.). 2. The g. artist of Laputa KANE. Hence **Geome·trically** *adv.* vars. †**Geometral**, †**Geometrial.**

Geometrician (dʒiˌǫ:mėtri·ʃăn). 1483. [f. L. *geometricus* + -AN.] 1. One who studies geometry. Now *rare.* †2. One who measures the earth or land –1676. var. †**Geometrian** (*rare*).

Geometrid (dʒiˌǫ·mėtrid). 1865. [f. L. *Geometra* mod. name for a genus of moths + -ID.]

A. *adj.* Belonging to the family of moths of which *Geometra* is the typical genus; see GEOMETER.

B. *sb.* A moth of this family. So **Geome·triform** *a.* 'resembling in form a moth of the family *Geometridæ*' (*Cent. Dict.*).

Geometrize (dʒiˌǫ·mėtrəiz), *v.* 1658. [f. GEOMETRY + -IZE.] *intr.* To work by geometrical methods; *trans.* to form geometrically. (Cf. Plato's phrase ἀεὶ γεωμετρεῖν τὸν θεόν.)

Knowing that God geometrizes eternally DE QUINCEY.

Geometry (dʒiˌǫ·mėtri). ME. [a. F. *géométrie*, a. L. *geometria*, a. Gr., f. γεω- comb. f. γῆ earth + -μετρία measuring.] 1. The science which investigates the properties and relations of magnitudes in space, as lines, surfaces, and solids. (At first regarded as a practical art, and mainly assoc. with Architecture.) †2. The art of measuring ground –1621.

Geophagy (dʒiˌǫ·fădʒi). 1850. [ad. Gr. *γεωφαγία the eating of earth, f. γεω- comb. f. γῆ + φαγεῖν.] The practice of eating earth; also **Geo·phagism.** So **Geo·phagist**, one that eats earth.

Geophilous (dʒiˌǫ·filəs), *a.* 1854. [f. mod. L. *Geophilus* + -OUS.] *Zool.* and *Bot.* Belonging to one of the genera named *Geophilus* or *Geophila.*

Geoponic (dʒiˌopǫ·nik). 1608. [ad. Gr. γεωπονικός, f. γεωπόνος husbandman, f. γεω-, γῆ + πον-, πένεσθαι to labour. Cf. F. *géoponique.*]

A. *adj.* Relating to the cultivation of the ground. Also *joc.* countrified. 1663.

B. *sb.* †**1.** A writer on agriculture. SELDEN. **2.** *pl.* The science of agriculture or husbandry; a treatise on this 1608.

Hence **Geopo·nical** *a.* So **Geo·pony,** agriculture.

Georama (dʒiˌorā·mă). ? *Obs.* 1847. [a. F., f. Gr. γῆ + ὅραμα.] A French invention, in the shape of a hollow sphere, exhibiting a complete view of the seas, lakes, rivers, and mountains on the earth's surface.

Geordie (dʒǭ·ɹdi). *Sc.* and *n. dial.* 1786. [dim. of GEORGE.] †**1.** (*Yellow*) *G.*: a guinea –1893. **2. a.** A coal-pitman 1876. **b.** A collier-boat 1884. **c.** Miner's name for George Stephenson's safety-lamp 1881.

George (dʒǭɹdʒ). [ad. L. *Georgius*, a. Gr. Γεώργιος, a saint who suffered martyrdom in the reign of Diocletian. Adopted as patron of the Order of the Garter, and recognized as patron saint of England from the time of Edward III.]

I. Saint George. 1. A cry formerly used by English soldiery 1594. **2.** *St. George's day*: April 23. *St. George's Cross*: an upright and a horizontal bar of red, crossing each other in the centre. 1611.

1. God, and Saint George, Richmond and Victory SHAKS.

II. George. 1. The jewel of the Order of the Garter, with a figure of St. George armed, on horseback, encountering the dragon 1506. †**2.** *slang.* A coin bearing the image of St. George; a half-crown; also, (*yellow*) *G.*, a guinea –1812. **3.** A brown loaf. ? *Obs.* 1755. **4.** *By George* (†*before, for, fore G.*): an exclam. or mild oath 1598.

Comb. †**George-noble,** a gold coin worth 6*s.* 8*d.*

Georgette (dʒǫɹdʒe·t). 1920. [Fr., f. the name of Mme. *Georgette*, a French modiste.] A thin silk dress-material. Also *g. crêpe.*

Georgian (dʒǭ·ɹdʒiăn), *a.*[1] 1787. [f. *George* + -IAN.] **1.** Belonging to the time of the four Georges, Kings of Great Britain 1855. †**2.** *G. planet* = GEORGIUM SIDUS. –1812.

Georgian (dʒǭ·ɹdʒiăn), *a.*[2] and *sb.* ME. [f. *Georgia* + -AN.]

A. *adj.* **1.** Belonging to Georgia, in the Caucasus, its inhabitants, or their language 1607. **2.** Belonging to Georgia, one of the United States of America 1762.

B. *sb.* **1.** A native, or the language, of Georgia in Asia ME. **2.** An inhabitant of the State of Georgia 1741.

Georgic (dʒǭ·ɹdʒik). 1513. [ad. L. *georgicus*, a. Gr., f. γεωργός husbandman, f. γεω-, γῆ + root ἐργ- of ἔργον work. Cf. F. *géorgique.*]

A. *adj.* Relating to agriculture. *Obs.* exc. semi-*joc.* 1711.

B. *sb.* †**1.** A husbandman (*rare*) 1703. **2.** *pl.* **a.** The science of land-culture 1802. **b.** The title of Virgil's poem on husbandry, in four books; hence occas. in *sing.* a poem dealing with rural occupations 1513. So **Geo·rgical** *a.* (now *rare*), agricultural.

‖**Georgium Sidus** (dʒǭ·ɹˌdʒiŏm səi·dŏs). 1783. [mod.L.] One of the greater planets (now called Uranus), so named by its discoverer, Sir W. Herschel, in honour of George III.

Geoselenic, -static, etc.: see GEO-.

Geosynclinal (dʒīˌosinkləi·nal). 1873. [f. GEO- + SYNCLINAL.] *Geol.*

A. *adj.* Forming a large depression in the surface of the earth, from the lowest point of which there is a gradual rise to either side. The opposite is *geanticlinal.* 1879.

B. *sb.* A geosynclinal depression.

Geotic: see GOETIC; a *Spurious Word.*

Geotropic (dʒīˌotrǫ·pik), *a.* 1875. [f. Gr. γεω- GEO- + τροπικός, f. τροπή turning.] *Bot.* Pertaining to, marked by, or of the nature of, geotropism. Hence **Geotro·pically** *adv.*

Geotropism (dʒiˌo·trǫpiz'm). 1875. [f. as prec. + -ISM.] *Bot.* A term for the phenomena of irritability shown by various parts of plants in relation to the action of gravity.

Positive g.: the tendency (of roots, etc.) to grow towards the centre of the earth. *Negative g.*: the tendency (of stems, etc.) to grow away from the centre of the earth. So also **Geo·tropy.**

Gephyrean (dʒefirī·ăn). 1881. [f. mod.L. *Gephyrea* sb. pl. (f. Gr. γέφυρα bridge) + -AN.]

A. *adj.* Of or pertaining to the *Gephyrea*, a class or group of the *Vermes* or worms.

B. *sb.* A worm of this class.

†**Gepoun,** var. of †GIPON.

Gerah (gīᵊ·ră). 1534. [a. Heb.] *Heb. Antiq.* A Hebrew coin and weight, the twentieth part of a shekel. *Exod.* xxx. 13.

Geranin (dʒĕrīᵊ·nin). Also **-iin.** 1864. [f. next + -IN.] An astringent principle obtained from *Geranium maculatum.*

Geranium (dʒĕrēᵊ·niŏm). 1548. [a. L., a. Gr. γεράνιον, f. γέρανος crane.] **1.** A genus of herbaceous plants (N. O. *Geraniaceæ*), growing wild in temperate regions, and bearing a fruit similar in shape to the bill of a crane; a plant of this genus or its flower. **2.** A plant of the genus Pelargonium (N.O. *Geraniaceæ*), natives of S. Africa, of which many varieties are cultivated in Great Britain 1760. **3.** *U.S. Pharm.* The rhizome of *G. maculatum* used as an astringent 1854.

Geratology (dʒerătǫ·lŏdʒi). 1884. [f. Gr. γηρατ-, γῆρας old age; see -LOGY.] The science of the phenomena of decadence, esp. in a species of animals approaching extinction.

Gerbe (dʒōɹb). 1698. [a. F. *gerbe.*] †**1.** A wheat-sheaf 1808. **2.** Something resembling a sheaf of wheat; esp. a kind of firework. Also *transf.*

Gerbille (dʒō·ɹbil). Also **gerbil.** 1849. [a. F., ad. mod.L. *gerbillus*, dim. of *gerbo* JERBOA.] Any animal belonging to the genus *Gerbillus.*

Gerbo, obs. f. JERBOA.

†**Gere.** See also GARE *sb.*[1] ME. [?] A transient fit of passion, feeling, fancy, or the like –1609.

These loveres in hir queynte geres CHAUCER.

Gere, obs. f. GEAR.

Gerent (dʒīᵊ·rĕnt). *rare.* 1576. [ad. L. *gerentem, gerere.*]

A. *sb.* A manager, ruler. Also *attrib.*

B. *adj.* Bearing, carrying. (Dicts.)

Gerfalcon (dʒō·ɹfǭ:lkŏn, -fǭ:k'n). Also †**jer-,** †**gyr-,** †**gierfalcon,** etc. ME. [a. OF. *gerfaucon*, also *gerfauc* (mod. *gerfaut*), f. (ult.) the root **gîr* in OHG. *giri, gîri* greedy; see FALCON. Others derive from L. *gyrus*, with the sense 'a bird that circles in its flight'.] Orig., a large falcon, esp. one used to fly at herons; now, any large falcon of the northern regions; esp. the white gerfalcon of Iceland (*Falco islandus*).

†**Ge·rful,** *a.* [f. GERE + -FUL.] Changeful, fitful; wayward. CHAUCER. So †**Ge·rish.**

Gerland, Gerlond, obs. ff. GARLAND.

Germ (dʒōɹm), *sb.* 1644. [a. F. *germe*:–L. *germen* sprout; ? f. root **gen-* of *gignere*, or root *ges-* of *gerere.*] **1.** That portion of an organic being which is capable of development into a new individual; a rudiment of a new organism. (In mod. use, *germ-* often signifies the female reproductive element, as opp. to *sperm-.*) **2.** †**a.** The ovary –1829. **b.** The seed (*lit.* and *fig.*) 1823. **3.** In early use, vaguely, the 'seed' of a disease. In mod. use, a micro-organism or microbe, esp. one which causes disease 1803. **4.** *fig.* That from which anything springs or may spring. *In g.*: in a rudimentary form. 1777.

1. Mr. Bonnet supposes..that all the germs of future plants..were really contained in the first g. PRIESTLEY. The germes of existence contained in the earth MALTHUS. 4. Thereby to eradicate every germe of liberty 1777.

Comb.: **g.-cell,** the first nucleated cell that appears in the impregnated ovum, after the reception of the spermatozoon and the disappearance of the germinal vesicle; also *g.-cellule*; **-cup,** a gastrula; **-gland,** one that produces germs; **-layer** = *germinal layer*; **-membrane** = BLASTODERM; **-plasm,** the protoplasm peculiar to a g. or ovum; **-polyp,** a polyp produced by germination; **-pore,** the place of exit for the tubular outgrowths from the spore at the time of germination; **-shield,** the shield-shaped spot which is the first rudiment of the dorsal portion of the embryo; called by Haeckel the *notaspis*; **-stock,** the part of the body from which budding takes place in certain animals; **-theory,** 'the theory of the origin of many diseases in the morbific influence of certain fungi, which are introduced into the organism by means of their germs or spores' (*Syd. Soc. Lex.*); **-tube,** the tube-like growth emitted from a spore in germination; **-vesicle** = *germinal vesicle.*

Germ (dʒōɹm), *v.* 1483. [orig., ad. F. *germer*, f. *germe*; now, f. GERM *sb.*] *intr.* To put forth germs or buds. Now only *fig.*

Germain(e, obs. f. GERMAN *a.*

German (dʒō·ɹmăn), **germane** (dʒəɹmēᵊ·n, dʒō·ɹmeᵊn), *a.*[1] and *sb.*[1] ME. [a. OF. *germain*, ad. L. *germanus* (sense I. 1, also 'genuine, real').]

A. *adj.* **I.** Closely akin. **1.** 'Own' (brother or sister). *Obs.* exc. in BROTHER-, SISTER-GERMAN. **2.** = 'First' or 'own' (cousin). *Obs.* exc. in COUSIN-GERMAN. ME. †**3.** Closely related; akin –1657. **4.** Closely connected; relevant 1602.

3. *Timon* IV. iii. 344. 4. The phrase would be more Germaine to the matter: If we could carry Cannon by our sides *Haml.* V. ii. 165.

II. Genuine, true, thorough. *Obs.* or *arch.* ME.

Sincere, germane and true learning 1542. Hence **Germa·nely** *adv.*

†**B.** *sb.* One sprung from the same stock; a brother, a near relative –1604.

Coursers for Cozens: and Gennets for Germaines SHAKS.

German (dʒō·ɹmăn), *a.*[2] and *sb.*[2] 1552. [ad. L. *Germanus*, said to be of Celtic origin. Formerly pronounced (dʒā·ɹmăn).]

A. *adj.* **1.** Of or pertaining to Germany or its inhabitants. **2.** *transf.* German-like 1861. **3.** Belonging to, written or spoken in, the German language 1748.

Combs., etc. **a.** In names of things of attributed German origin (sometimes hyphened), as **G. bit,** a wood-boring tool for use in a brace; **G. clock,** in 16–17th c. chiefly one of elaborate construction, often containing automatic figures, etc.; †**G. devil,** ? a sort of screw-jack; **G. flute** (see FLUTE *sb.*[1]); **G. mile,** a distance of between 4 and 5 English miles; **G. paste,** a food for cage birds, made of pea-meal, hemp-seed, lard, etc.; **G. process,** in copper smelting, the process of reduction in a shaft-furnace after roasting, if necessary; **G. sarsaparilla,** a substitute for sarsaparilla; **G.-sausage,** a polony, a cleaned gut stuffed with meat partly cooked; **G. sixth** (*Mus.*), a chord consisting of a note with its major third, fifth, and augmented sixth; **G. steel,** a metal made of charcoal-iron obtained from bog-iron or the sparry carbonate; **G. text,** a black letter resembling Old English or modern G.; also *attrib.*; **G. tinder** = AMADOU; **G. wool** = *Berlin wool* (see BERLIN). **b.** In names of plants, as **G. millet,** *Sitaria germanica*, orig. imported from India; **G. wallflower** (see WALLFLOWER); etc. **c. G. measles,** an infectious disease of a mild type resembling measles and scarlatina; rubella.

B. *sb.* **1.** A native of Germany 1530. **2.** The German language 1748. **3. a.** Short for *G. cotillon* (see COTILLION); also, a party for dancing this 1879. **b.** = *G. sausage* 1883. **c.** *Coal-mining.* A straw filled with gunpowder to act as a fuse in blasting operations 1883.

2. *High G.*: the variety, orig. confined to 'High' or southern Germany, but now the accepted literary language of Germany. *Low G.*: prop. = 'Plattdeutsch', i.e. all dialects of Germany which are not High G.; applied by philologists to all West Germanic dialects except High G.; and formerly including Gothic and Scandinavian.

Germander (dʒəɹmæ·ndəɹ). ME. [ad. med.L. *germandra, -drea* (F. *germandrée*,) altered f. *gamandrea, -ia*, corruptly ad. late Gr. χαμανδρυά, itself a corruption of Gr. χαμαίδρυς, lit. 'ground-oak', f. χαμαί + δρῦς.] The name of plants of the genus *Teucrium*, esp. *T. Chamædrys*, the Common or Wall Germander. Also *attrib.*

Garlic or Water G. = *T. Scordium.* Wood G. = *T. Scorodinia.* In the U.S. applied to *T. Canadense.* G. Chickweed, *Veronica agrestis.* G. Speedwell or Wild G., *Veronica Chamædrys.*

Germane: see GERMAN *a.*[1]

Germanic (dʒəɹmæ·nik). 1633. [ad. L. *Germanicus*, f. *Germanus* German. Cf. F. *germanique.*]

A. *adj.* **1.** Of or pertaining to Germany or to the Germans. Now chiefly *Hist.* in *G. Confederation, Empire.* **2.** Of or pertaining to the Teutonic race, or any of the Teutonic peoples 1841.

2. *East G.*: designation of the group of langs. including Gothic, Burgundian, Vandal, etc. *North G.* = 'Scandinavian'. *West G.*, epithet of the group including High and Low German, English, Frisian, Dutch, etc.

B. *sb.* The language of the Germanic people; Teutonic; see A. 2. 1892.

Germanism (dʒɔ̄·ɹmăniz'm). 1611. [f. GERMAN *a.*² + -ISM.] 1. A German idiom; esp. one used in a non-German language. 2. German ideas; German modes of thought or action 1841; attachment to these 1864. 3. Affectation of what is German 1807.

Germanist (dʒɔ̄·ɹmănist). 1831. [f. GERMAN *a.*² + -IST.] One versed in the German language, or in Teutonic philology; one influenced by German thought.

Germanium (dʒəɹmē̆·niŏm). 1886. [mod. L., f. *Germanus* GERMAN *a.*²] *Chem.* An element, found in a mineral named Argyrodite, app. intermediate between antimony and bismuth.

Germanize (dʒɔ̄·ɹmănəiz), *v.* 1598. [f. GERMAN *a.*² + -IZE.] 1. *trans.* To translate into German. 2. To make German in character, etc. 1609. 3. *intr.* To become German (in style, tastes, habits, sympathies, etc.) 1665. Hence **Ge:rmaniza·tion**, the action of Germanizing.

Germano-, comb. f. 'German', as in **Ge:rmano·ma·nia**, a mania for things German; **Ge:rmanopho·bia**, a morbid dread of Germany and things German; etc.

Ge·rman si·lver. 1830. A white alloy consisting of nickel, zinc, and copper, orig. obtained from an ore found at Hildburghausen. Also *attrib.*

Germen (dʒɔ̄·ɹmen). Also †**germain(e**, †**germin.** 1605. [a. L.; see GERM *sb.*] 1. A germ. Now only *fig.* †2. A shoot or sprout –1786. 3. *Bot.* The rudiment of a seed-vessel, an ovary 1759.

1. Cracke Natures moulds, all germaines spill at once That makes ingratefull Man *Lear* III. ii. 8.

Germicide (dʒɔ̄·ɹmisəid), *sb.* (*a.*) 1880. [f. GERM *sb.* + -CIDE 1.] 1. That which kills germs; *spec.* an agent used to destroy disease-germs 1881. 2. quasi-*adj.* Destructive to germs. So **Ge·rmici·dal** *a.* (in sense 2).

Germiculture (dʒɔ̄·ɹmikɒltiŭɹ). 18.. [f. GERM *sb.* + CULTURE; after *horticulture*, etc.] The artificial cultivation of the bacteria connected with certain diseases. Hence **Germicu·lturist**, a bacteriologist.

Germigene (dʒɔ̄·ɹmi,dʒīn). 1859. [f. GERM *sb.* + -*gene*, -GEN.] *Biol.* 'The gland of the female generative apparatus of cestoid and Trematode worms in which the germinal vesicles are formed' (*Syd. Soc. Lex.*).

Germin (dʒɔ̄·ɹmin), *v.* ME. [ad. L. *germinare*; see GERMINATE *v.*] *intr.* To put forth shoots; also, to begin to produce vegetation. Also *trans.* To bud or shoot forth into.

Germin, var. of GERMEN.

‖**Germinal** (ʒɛrmīnal, dʒɔ̄·ɹminăl), *sb.* 1833. [F., f. L. *germen*; see GERM *sb.*] The seventh month of the French Revolutionary calendar (Mar. 21–Apr. 19).

Germinal (dʒɔ̄·ɹminăl), *a.* 1808. [ad. mod.L. *germinalis*; see GERM *sb.*] Of or belonging to a germ or to germs; of the nature of a germ; *transf.* that is in the germ.

G. cell = *germ cell*. *G. layer*, each of the three layers of cells into which the blastoderm divides. *G. matter*, Beale's term for vitally active matter. *G. membrane* = BLASTODERM. *G. pole*, 'the part or pole of the egg where lies the germinal spot' (*Syd. Soc. Lex.*). *G. spot*, the nucleolus of the permanent ovum, situated in the g. vesicle. *G. vesicle*, the nucleus of the permanent ovum of animals.

Germinant (dʒɔ̄·ɹminănt), *a.* 1605. [ad. L. *germinantem*; see next.] That develops like a germ; germinating, sprouting (*rare* in lit. sense). Also *fig.* of the ground.

Germinate (dʒɔ̄·ɹmineⁱt), *v.* 1610. [f. ppl. stem of L. *germinare*, f. *germin-*, *germen*; see GERM *sb.*] 1. *intr.* To sprout, put forth shoots, begin to vegetate. Of a plant: To bud and develop shoots and branches. Also *fig.* 1647. 2. *trans.* To cause to shoot or sprout. Also *fig.* 1610. 3. *intr.* Of a salt, etc.: To effloresce. ? *Obs.* 1626.

Germination (dʒɔ̄ɹminē̆·ʃən). 1594. [ad. L. *germinationem*; cf. F. *germination.*] 1. The action or process of germinating, sprouting, or putting forth shoots. Used properly of seeds; hence of plants, and of spores in cryptogams. Also *fig.* 2. *transf.* Efflorescence, ebullition 1665.

1. *fig.* A time of g. in religious history STUBBS.

Germinative (dʒɔ̄·ɹmineⁱtiv), *a.* 1707. [See GERMINATE *v.* and -IVE.] Of or belonging to germination; also, having power to bud or sprout, or to develop.

fig. Any vital or g. truth 1865.

Germini·parous, *a.* [f. GERMEN + L. *parere* + -OUS.] Producing offspring through seeds. H. T. COLEBROOKE.

Germless (dʒɔ̄·ɹmlės), *a.* 1833. [See -LESS.] Containing no germs (see GERM *sb.* 3).

†**Gernative**, *a.* [? f. *gern* GIRN *v.* + -ATIVE.] ? Addicted to grumbling. MIDDLETON.

Gerocomy (dʒiɒrǫ·kŏmi). *rare.* 1818. [ad. Gr. γηροκομία, f. γηρο-, γῆρας + -κομία tending.] The science of the treatment of the aged. Hence †**Geroco·mical** *a.*

Geronomite (dʒĕrǫ·nŏməit). 1754. [a. Sp. or It. *geronomita.*] = HIERONYMITE.

Gerontic (dʒĕrǫ·ntik, gĕr-), *a.* 1885. [f. Gr. γεροντ-, γέρων + -IC.] Of or pertaining to old age, senile. *sb. pl.* = *GERIATRICS.

Gerontocracy (dʒe:rǫntǫ·krăsi, ger-). 1830. [f. as prec. + -κρατία government.] Government by old men; a governing body of old men.

‖**Geropiga** (dʒerǫpī·gă). Also **jeru-** and (in Dicts.) **gero-**, **jerupigia.** 1858. [a. Pg. *geropiga* = HIERAPICRA.] A mixture of grape-juice, brandy, sugar, and red colouring-matter, used to adulterate port-wine.

-gerous, in use always **-igerous** (i·dʒerəs), an adjectival suffix f. L. *-ger* bearing (f. root of *gerere*) + -OUS. In mod. scientific language added freely to L. stems, as in *frondigerous*, etc.

Gerrymander (gerimæ·ndəɹ), *sb.* *U.S.* 1868. [f. the surname *Gerry.*] A method of arranging electoral districts so that one party will be enabled to elect more representatives than they could on a fair system. This was done in Massachusetts, in 1812, while Elbridge Gerry was Governor; hence the name.

Gerrymander (gerimæ·ndəɹ), *v.* Also *erron.* (in England) **jerry-**. 1859. [f. the sb.] *trans.* To subject (a state, a constituency) to a gerrymander. Also *transf.* to manipulate in order to gain an unfair advantage.

To g. a bench of magistrates 1893.

Gerund (dʒe·rɒnd). 1513. [ad. L. *gerundium*, app. f. *gerundum* = *gerendum*, gerund of *gerere* to carry on.] A form of the Latin vb. capable of being construed as a sb., but retaining the regimen of the vb. Hence applied to equivalent forms in other langs., e.g. to the Eng. verbal noun in *-ing*.

Comb.: **g.-grinder**, derisive name for one who instructs in Latin grammar; a pedantic teacher.

Gerundial (dʒĕrɒ·ndiăl), *a.* 1846. [f. L. *gerundium* (see prec.) + -AL.] Pertaining to or of the nature of a gerund. Also *ellipt.* = *g. infinitive.*

Gerundival (dʒerɒndəi·văl), *a.* 1884. [f. L. *gerundivus* (see next) + -AL.] Of, pertaining to, or of the nature of a gerundive.

Gerundive (dʒĕrɒ·ndiv). 1483. [ad. late L. *gerundivus* (*modus*), f. *gerundium* GERUND.]

A. *adj.* 1. Pertaining to, akin to, or of the nature of, a gerund 1612. 2. *joc.* Crammed with gerunds 1616.

2. That G. maw of yours, that without *Do* will end in *Di* and *Dum* instantly BEAUM & FL.

B. *sb.* 1. = GERUND. 1483. 2. In Latin grammar, a verbal adj., of the nature of a passive pple., expressing the idea of necessity or fitness; its suffix is the same as that of the gerund. Hence *transf.*

Hence **Geru·ndively** *adv.* as, or in place of, a gerund.

Gerusia (gerū·ziă). 1838. [a. L., Gr. γερουσία, f. γέρων.] An assembly of elders, *spec.* the senate in Dorian cities.

†**Ge·ry**, *a.* ME. [f. GERE + -Y¹.] Changeable, fitful –1529.

Gesling, -lyng, obs. ff. GOSLING.

Gess(e, obs. f. GUESS, and of *guests* pl. of GUEST.

‖**Gesso** (dʒe·so). 1596. [a. It.:—L. *gypsum*; see GYPSUM.] 1. Plaster of Paris; gypsum. b. A prepared surface of plaster as a ground for painting 1860. †2. A work of art in plaster 1758. 3. *attrib.*, as *g. work* 1745.

1. No colour is so noble as the colour of a good painting on canvas or g. RUSKIN.

Gest (dʒest), *sb.*¹ ME. [a. OF. *geste*, *jeste* (fem.), action, exploit (chiefly *pl.*), romance; ad. L. *gesta*, neut. pl. of pa. pple. of *gerere* to carry on.] 1. *pl.* Notable deeds, exploits (later also *sing.*); esp. the deeds *of* a person or people as narrated, history. *Obs.* exc. *arch.* 2. A romance in verse; also simply, a story, tale. *Obs.* exc. *Hist.* ME. †3. a. A lampoon. b. An idle tale; now JEST. –1470.

1. The Gestes of the great Charles FABYAN. 2. Phr. *In g.* = in verse. *The English g.*, *the French g.*: metrical chronicles of England, of France.

Gest (dʒest), *sb.*² *Obs.* exc. *arch.* 1509. [ad. F. *geste*, ad. L. *gestus* (masc.), gesture, bearing, f. *gerere.*] 1. Bearing, carriage, mien. 2. A gesture 1521.

1. Look and geste Of buried saint, in risen rest MRS. BROWNING.

†**Gest**, *sb.*³ *pl.* **Gesses.** 1550. [Later form of GIST ¹.] The various stages of a journey, esp. of a royal progress; the route planned and followed. b. *sing.* The time allotted for a halt. *Wint. T.* I. ii. 41.

†**Gest**, *v.*¹ ME. [f. GEST *sb.*¹] *intr.* To tell a tale –1508.

†**Gest**, *v.*² 1523. [f. L. *gest-*, *gerere.*] To perform; only in phr. *gested and done* –1541.

Gest(e, obs. f. GUEST, JEST.

Gestant (dʒe·stănt), *a.* *rare.* 1851. [ad. L. *gestantem*, *gestare* to go with young.] Pregnant (*fig.*).

Storm-clouds g. with the heat Of undeveloped lightnings MRS. BROWNING.

Gestation (dʒestē̆·ʃən). 1533. [ad. L. *gestationem* (f. *gestare* to carry), found esp. in sense 1. Cf. F. *gestation.*] 1. A carrying or being carried, e.g. on horseback, or in a carriage, by way of exercise. Now *rare.* †2. The wearing (of rings). SIR T. BROWNE. 3. The action or process of carrying young; the condition of being carried in the womb from conception to birth. Also *fig.* 1615.

Gestatorial (dʒe:stătōᵊ·riăl), *a.* 1864. [f. as next + -AL.] *G. chair*: a chair in which the Pope is carried on certain occasions.

Gestatory (dʒe·stătəri), *a.* *rare.* 1682. [ad. L. *gestatorius*, f. (ult.) *gestare* to carry.] †a. Adapted for carrying or wearing. SIR T. BROWNE. b. Of or pertaining to carrying as a form of exercise 1804.

†**Ge·ster.** ME. [f. GEST *v.*¹ + -ER ¹.] A professional reciter of romances –1496.

Gestic (dʒe·stik), *a.* 1764. [f. GEST *sb.*² + -IC.] Of or pertaining to bodily movement, esp. dancing.

The gay grandsire, skilled in g. lore GOLDSM.

Gesticulant (dʒesti·kiŭlănt), *a.* *rare.* 1877. [ad. L. *gesticulantem*, *gesticulari.*] Exhibiting gestures.

The poor g. orator RUSKIN.

Gesticulate (dʒesti·kiŭleⁱt), *v.* 1601. [f. L. *gesticulat-*, *gesticulari*, f. *gesticulus*, dim. of *gestus* (see GEST *sb.*²).] 1. *intr.* To make lively or energetic motions with the limbs or body; *esp.* in speaking or in lieu of speech 1613. 2. *trans.* To convey by gestures 1601.

1. A Frenchman .. gesticulates while he speaks, much more than an Englishman BLAIR. Hence **Gesti·culative** *a.* given to gesticulation. **Gesti·culator.** **Gesti·culatory** *a.* full of, consisting in, or of the nature of, gesticulation.

Gesticulation (dʒe:stikiŭlē̆·ʃən). 1603. [ad. L. *gesticulationem*; see prec.] The action or process of gesticulating. Also, an instance of this (chiefly in *pl.*).

Persons skilled in g. can communicate by it a long series of facts and even complicated trains of thought 1876.

Gestion (dʒe·stiən, dʒe·stʃən). 1599. [ad. L. *gestionem*, f. *gerere.*] Conduct, management.

Gestor, -our(e, var. of GESTER.

Gesture (dʒeˑstiŭɹ), *sb.* ME. [ad. med.L. *gestura*, f. *gerere*.] †1. Bearing, carriage, deportment (rarely in *pl.*) -1810. †2. Posture, attitude, *esp.* in prayer or worship -1729. 3. †a. In early use: The employment of bodily movements, attitudes, looks, etc., as a means of giving effect to oratory -1791. b. Now only: Movement of the body or limbs as an expression of feeling 1804. 4. A movement of the body or any part of it; now only as expressive of thought or feeling 1551. b. *transf.* A (friendly) move or course of action 1916.

1. *A. Y. L.* v. ii. 69. 2. As for their g. or position, the men lay downe leaning on their left elbow SIR T. BROWNE. 3. To put life into words by countenance, voice, and g. HOOKER. G. is the imitation of words JOWETT. 4. The Shaking of the Head..is a G. of slight refusal BACON. Hence **Geˑstural** *a.* of or pertaining to g.; consisting of gestures. **Geˑstureless** *a.*

Gesture (dʒeˑstiŭɹ), *v.* 1542. [f. the sb.] 1. *intr.* To make gestures, to gesticulate. 2. *trans.* To express by gestures 1589.

1. The Mayor speaking and gesturing his persuasivest CARLYLE. 2. It is not orderly read nor gestured as beseemeth HOOKER. Hence †**Geˑsturement** = GESTURE *sb.* 3 b.

Get (get), *sb.* ME. [f. GET *v.*] 1. What is got or begotten; gain, earnings (now *dial.*); an offspring; *collect.* progeny. 2. Begetting. Now only in sporting use. ME.

Get (get), *v.* Pa. t. **got** (arch. **gat**). Pa. pple. **got** (**gotten**). Pres. pple. **getting**. [ME. *geten*, a. ON. *geta* = OE. *-ʒietan* (only in Comb.: see BEGET, FORGET):—OTeut. **getan*, *gat-*, etc. The OAryan root **ghed*, **ghod* 'to seize', 'take hold of' is found also in L. *præda* (:—**præ-hĕda*) booty, *prædium* an estate, *prehendere* to lay hold of, Gr. χανδάνειν (aor. ἔχαδον) to hold, contain, be able.]

I. *trans.* 1. To obtain possession of; *absol.* to acquire wealth or property. 2. To earn ME. 3. To obtain by way of profit 1490. †Also *absol.* †4. To capture (a fortress, etc.) -1676. 5. To gain (a victory, etc.) ME. 6. To win, acquire ME. 7. To learn, commit to memory 1582. 8. To find out, obtain as a result, by calculation or experiment 1559. 9. To become possessed of; to receive ME. 10. To obtain, come to have, attain ME. 11. To catch, contract (an illness) 1610. 12. To receive, meet with, suffer ME. 13. To procure or obtain in any way ME. 14. To get hold of, capture (a person); also *colloq.* to 'corner' 1596. 15. The perfect tense is used familiarly as = the present tense of *have* or *possess* 1607.

1. Get Money POPE. 2. I.. get that I weare SHAKS. *absol.* Getting and spending WORDSW. Phr. *To g. a living.* 3. Alas, he gets nothing by that SHAKS. 5. Phr. *To g. the upper hand* (*of*); *to g. the start, the advantage*, etc. (*of*); *to g. the wind of*; *to g. the better of.* 6. *Tam. Shr.* II. i. 120. Reason is not..gotten by Experience onely HOBBES. Phr. *To g. wind of*: to hear of. 7. Phr. *To g. by heart* (see HEART *sb.*); *to g. by rote.* 8. Dividing nine by three we g. three (*mod.*). 9. As to salaries, an officer..usually gets sixty pounds 1892. Phr. *To g. the name of*: to have the reputation of (being so-and-so). *To g. mercy, forgiveness, leave*, etc.; *to g. an answer, information*, etc. 10. When I had gotten my libertye RALEIGH. Phr. *To g. one's own way.* *To g.* (*a*) *sight*, etc. *of*, *to g.* (*a*) *hold of.* *To g. religion* (U.S. vulgar): to be converted. 11. To g. a Cold STEELE. 12. To g. a Fall SWIFT. Phr. *To g. the worst of it* (cf. 5). To g. six months 1889. *To g. it* (colloq. or slang): to 'catch it'. 15. The thing has got to be fought out 1889.

†II. To gain, reach, arrive at (a place) -1712.

III. To beget, procreate; now only of animals, *esp.* horses ME.

IV. With complement, indicating some change effected in the position or state of the object. 1. With prep. or adv. of place; as, *to, from, into, out of, through, over*, etc. 1450. Also *refl.* 2. With pa. pple. as compl. (see quots.) 1500. 3. With adj.; esp. in *to g. ready* 1590. 4. With an infinitive 1460.

1. To g. luggage through the custom-house 1859. Phr. *To g. with child.* *To g.* (a person) *upon* (a subject). 2. Difficulty..in getting laws obeyed 1877. I got my right wrist dislocated T. JEFFERSON. 4. To g. them to listen to reason 1771.

V. *intr.* 1. To succeed in coming or going *to, from, into, out of*, etc.; also, to come in the course or at the end of a journey *to*. Formerly conjugated with *be*. ME. b. To come *to* an end aimed at, a condition, a state 1626. 2. With infinitive: To come (to be or do); to acquire a habit of (doing) 1583. b. With pr. pple.: To come to be (doing something) 1727. 3. With adj., etc. as compl.: To make oneself; to become; to grow (with comparatives) 1596. 4. a. With pa. pple.: To complete an action. Now only *colloq.* (*rare*). 1716. b. With passive pple.: To cause oneself to be treated in a certain way or to undergo a certain action; also, to come to be the object of a certain action. Often = *be* as an auxiliary. 1652.

1. Hercules that year got into Italy NEWTON. b. Phr. *To g. to blows.* *To g. there* (U.S. slang): to succeed. *To g.*, also *git* (U.S. colloq. or slang): to 'clear out'. 2. To g. to be friends 1891. b. Phr. *To g. better, well.* *To g. drunk.* *To g. clear, quit of, rid of, shut of.* 4. b. I got caught in the storm 1887. Phr. *To g. done with* = to have done with.

VI. *intr.* With preps., in specialized senses. **G. at —.** a. To come at, reach. b. To find out. c. *colloq.* and *slang.* To tamper with (a horse); to bribe. d. *slang.* To assail; also, to make game of. **G. off —.** a. To dismount from (a horse). b. To obtain release from (a contract). **G. on —.** a. To mount (a horse). b. To enter upon (a subject), esp. by chance. **G. over —.** a. To overcome (a difficulty); to evade the force of (evidence); to cease to be surprised or troubled by. b. To recover from (a shock, etc.). c. To cover (a distance). d. To finish (an action). e. To circumvent. **G. round —.** To circumvent, cajole. **G. through —.** a. To reach the end of. b. To be passed by (Parliament, etc.). c. To find occupation for (a period of time).

VII. With adverbs. **G.** (**it**) **across** or **over**: to reach the audience or the public. **G. along** = *get on.* **G. away.** a. *intr.* To escape. Also, in *Hunting*, etc.: To start. b. *imper.* = Be off. c. *To g. away with it*: to succeed in what one tries; to escape punishment or retribution. **G. back.** a. *intr.* To return. b. *trans.* To recover. **G. in.** a. *intr.* To be elected to represent a constituency in Parliament. b. *trans.* To gather in (harvest produce). c. To collect (contributions of money, esp. sums due). d. To sow (seed). e. To succeed in planting (a blow). **G. in with.** a. *intr.* To become familiar with. b. *Naut.* To come close up to. **G. off.** a. *intr.* To escape; to start. b. To escape from punishment or defeat; to be acquitted. c. *trans.* To deliver from punishment. d. To commit to memory. **G. on.** a. *intr.* To advance; to make haste. b. To prosper, succeed. Also, to fare. c. To manage (*without, with*). d. To agree *with, together.* **G. out.** a. *imper.* = 'Go away' (*colloq.*). b. *Stock Exchange.* To get rid of one's shares. c. To elicit by inquiry. **G. out of.** a. *intr.* To succeed in issuing from; to escape from; to quit. b. To get beyond. c. To evade, avoid. d. To elicit; also, to succeed in obtaining. **G. round.** *intr.* To recover from illness. **G. through.** a. *intr.* To reach a destination. b. Of a bill: To pass in Parliament. c. To pass in an examination. **G. under.** *trans.* To subdue, esp. a fire. **G. up.** a. To rise; esp. to rise from bed or to one's feet. b. To mount; esp. to mount on horseback; also *fig.* c. To come close to. d. Of fire, wind, the sea: To increase in force or violence. e. *Cricket.* Of the ball: To rise off the pitch higher than usual. f. To organize, set on foot, make ready. g. To dress (linen). h. To dress or 'turn out' in a (specified) way. Chiefly in pa. pple. *got up.* Also *intr.* for *refl.* 1782. i. To cause to rise; also, to improve (one's health). j. To work up.

Get-a·t-able, *a.* 1799. Reachable, accessible.

Ge·t-away. 1852. a. Breaking cover (of a fox). b. Escape (as of a thief with booty) 1890.

Ge·ttable, *a.* 1555. That can be got.

Getter (geˑtəɹ). ME. [f. GET *v.* + -ER [1].] 1. One who gets, obtains, acquires, begets, or procreates. 2. With advs., as with *g.-up* 1820.

Getting (geˑtiŋ), *vbl. sb.* ME. [f. GET *v.* + -ING [1].] 1. The action of GET *v.*, in various senses. 2. *concr.* (usually in *pl.*) That which is got; gains, earnings. Now *arch.* ME.

1. He had not the genius for g. THACKERAY.

Get-up. 1847. [See GET *v.*] 1. Style of equipment or costume. 2. Style of production or finish, esp. of a book 1865.

‖**Geum** (dʒīˑŏm). 1548. [mod.L. use of L. *geum.*] A genus of rosaceous plants, including *G. urbanum*, Avens or Herb Bennet, and *G. rivale*, Water Avens.

Gewgaw, gew-gaw (giūˑgǫ). ME. [A reduplicated formation. Commonly referred to the root of GIVE *v.*, but see N.E.D.] 1. A gaudy trifle, a toy or bauble. Also *fig.* In *pl.* also, 'vanities'. ME. 2. *attrib.* Of the nature of a gewgaw; hence *fig.* 'splendidly trifling, showy without value' (J.) 1631.

1. A heavy Gugaw, (call'd a Crown) DRYDEN. 2. Seeing his g. Castle shine New as his title TENNYSON. Hence **Gewˑgawed** *ppl. a.* dressed out with gewgaws.

Gey (gē̆ⁱ), *a.* and *adv.* *Sc.* 1725. [var. of GAY.] 1. *adj.* Considerable 1815. b. quasi-*advb.* in *g. and* — 1725. 2. *adv.* Very; pretty 1816.

Geyser (gēˑsəɹ, gəiˑsəɹ, gəiˑzəɹ). 1780. [a. Icel. *Geysir* (also used), proper name of a hot spring in Iceland; lit. 'gusher'; akin to *geysa* to gush.] 1. An intermittent hot spring, throwing up water, etc. in a column. Also *fig.* 2. An apparatus for rapidly heating water for a bath 1891.

1. The Azores..abound in geysers LADY BRASSEY. Hence **Geyˑseric** *a.* pertaining to or of the nature of a g. **Geyˑserite** (*Min.*), a concretionary variety of opal, found deposited about the orifices of geysers.

‖**Gharry** (gæˑri, gɒˑri). *Anglo-Ind.* 1810. [Hindi *gāṛī.*] A horsed vehicle resembling a bathing-machine.

Ghast (gast), *a.* *arch.* or *poet.* 1622. [? f. GHASTLY.] = GHASTLY *a.*

Ghast, var. of GAST *v.*

Ghastful, gastful (gaˑstfŭl), *a.* *Obs.* or *arch.* ME. [f. GAST *v.* + -FUL.] 1. Full of fear. 2. Dreadful, frightful ME.

2. Here will I dwell apart In gastfull groue SPENSER. Hence †**G(h)aˑstfully** *adv.*, †**-ness.**

Ghastly, †gastly (gaˑstli), *a.* ME. [f. GAST *v.* + *-lich*, -LY [1].] 1. †Orig.: Causing terror. Now (cf. 2): Affecting like the sight of death or carnage; horrible, frightful, shocking. Also used *hyperbolically*. 2. (Influenced by GHOST.) Spectre-like, death-like, wan. Of light: Lurid. 1581. †3. Full of fear -1634.

1. The g. dreams, That haunt the parting soul 1812. A g. failure (*colloq.*). 2. G. with wounds PRIOR. A g. grin LYTTON. 3. *Temp.* II. i. 309. Hence **Ghaˑstily** (*rare*), **Ghaˑstlily, Ghastly** *advs.* in a g. manner; fearfully.

‖**Ghaut, ghat** (gǫt). *Anglo-Ind.* 1603. [Hindi *ghāṭ*. Sense 3 is the primary sense.] 1. *The Ghauts*: the name given by Europeans to the mountain ranges parallel to the east and west coasts of India. 2. A mountain pass or defile 1698. 3. A passage or steps leading down to a river; hence, a landing-place, the place of a ford or ferry 1783.

‖**Ghazal** (gæˑzæl). Also **gazel, ghazel**, etc. 1800. [Pers., Arab.] A species of Oriental lyric poetry, usually erotic, having a limited number of verses and a recurrent rhyme.

‖**Ghazi** (gāˑzī). 1753. [Arab., f. *ghazā* to fight.] A champion, *esp.* against infidels; also as a title of honour. Now used chiefly of Mohammedan fanatics who devote themselves to the destruction of infidels.

Gheber, -bre, vars. of GUEBRE.

‖**Ghee** (gī). 1665. [Hindi *ghī*, f. *ghr* to sprinkle.] Butter made from buffalo's milk, clarified by boiling, so as to resemble oil in consistency. Also *attrib.*

Gherkin (gɔ̄ˑɹkin). 1661. [a. early mod. Du. **gurkkijn*, **agurkkijn* (now *gurkje, augurkje*), dim. of *agurk*, *augurk* (also *gurk*) cucumber; prob. of Slav. origin. The primary form appears in late Gr. ἀγγούριον; see ANGURIA.] A young green cucumber, or one of a small kind, used for pickling.

Ghess(e, Ghest, obs. ff. GUESS, GHOST.

‖**Ghetto** (geˑto). 1611. [It., ? abbrev. of *borghetto*, dim. of *borgo* BOROUGH.] The quarter in a city, chiefly in Italy, to which the Jews were restricted.

The place where the whole fraternity of the Iews dwelleth together, which is called the G. CORYAT.

Ghibelline (giˑbĕlin, -əin). 1573. [ad. It. *Ghibellino*, corrupt f. Ger. *Waiblingen*, a Hohenstaufen estate in Germany.]

A. *sb.* One of the Emperor's faction in the Italian states; opp. to GUELPH.

B. *adj.* Of or adhering to the Ghibellines 1826. Hence **Ghiˑbellinism.**

Ghole, var. of GHOUL. *Obs.*

Ghost (gōˑst), *sb.* [Common WGer.: OE. *gāst, gǽst*, ME. *gost(e, goost(e* = OHG. *geist* :—OTeut. type **gaisto-z.* Prob. of pre-Teut. formation, meaning 'fury, anger'. The *gh*-form appears first in Caxton.] 1. The soul or spirit. †2. Breath, a blast -1625. †3. A person -1590. †4. An incorporeal being -1618;

a good spirit -1485; an evil spirit -1529. 5. Formerly used in the sense of SPIRIT (of God). Now only in HOLY GHOST, the Third Person of the Trinity. OE. †6. The soul of a deceased person, spoken of as inhabiting the unseen world. Later only = MANES; sometimes *pl.* -1674. 7. The soul of a deceased person, spoken of as appearing to the living. (The prevailing sense.) ME. Also *transf.* and *fig.* b. An apparition; a spectre 1592. †8. A corpse. 2 *Hen. VI*, III. ii. 161. 9. An unsubstantial image; hence, a slight trace or vestige 1590. 10. *Optics*, etc. a. A bright spot or secondary image appearing in the field of a telescope, produced by a defect in a lens 1867. b. *Photogr.* = FLARE *sb.*[1] 3. 1864. 11. One who secretly does artistic or literary work of which his employer takes the credit 1884.

1. He gasped thryse, and gaue away the g. 1574. Whose faire immortall beame Hath darted fyre into my feeble g. SPENSER. 6. Rainsborough, to whose G. he design'd an ample sacrifice CLARENDON. 7. There needs no G...come from the Graue, to tell vs this SHAKS. Phr. *To lay a g.*: to cause it to cease appearing. *To raise a g.*: to cause it to appear. b. Death—'Grim-grinning g.' SHAKS. 9. Pitiful ghosts, or rather shadowes of men 1590. Not the g. of a chance (*mod.*).

Comb.: **g.-bird** (*U.S. local*), 'the American yellow-breasted chat (*Icteria virens*); **-candle,** one of several kept burning round a corpse to scare away ghosts; **-dance,** a fanatical observance among the N. American Indians; **-moth,** a nocturnal moth (*Hepialus humuli*); **-plant,** the tumble-weed (*Amarantus albus*); **-word,** a word which does not really exist.

Ghost (gōᵘst), *v.* 1586. [f. prec. sb.] †1. *intr.* To give up the ghost, expire -1689. 2. *trans.* To haunt as an apparition 1606. 3. To prowl as a ghost 1833.

†Ghostless (gōᵘ·stlės), *a.* OE. [See -LESS.] Without life or spirit; without strength or virtue -1651.

Ghostlike (gōᵘ·stləik). 1611. [See -LIKE.] 1. *adj.* Like a ghost or a place haunted by ghosts. 2. *adv.* In the manner of a ghost 1859.

Ghostly (gōᵘ·stli), *a.* [OE. *gástlic*, f. *gást* GHOST + *-lic*, -LY[2].] 1. Pertaining to the spirit or soul; spiritual. Opp. to *bodily* or *fleshly*; occas. to *natural*. Now *lit.* and *arch.* †2. Of persons, etc.: Spiritual, devout -1483. 3. Concerned with sacred things, or with the church; *spiritual* as opp. to *lay*, *secular*, or *temporal*. Now *arch.* OE. 4. Of, pertaining to, or issuing from a ghost; resembling a ghost; *occas.* haunted by ghosts OE.

1. Both worldly and g. comfort SCOTT. Phr. *G. enemy*: the Devil. *G. father*: a father confessor. 3. His chrism and his rood, his g. weapons FREEMAN. 4. G. legends LONGF. Hence **Gho·stliness,** the condition or quality of being g.

Ghostly (gōᵘ·stli), *adv.* Now *rare.* [OE. *gástlíce*; see -LY[2].] †In a spiritual manner or sense; opp. to *bodily* or *carnally*; in spirit, as a spirit -1642. Now *rarely*: As a ghost.

Ghostology (gōᵘstǫ·lŏdʒi). 1824. [badly f. GHOST *sb.* + -(O)LOGY.] Ghost-lore.

Ghoul (gūl). 1786. [a. Arab. *ghūl*, from a root meaning 'to seize'.] An evil spirit supposed (in Mohammedan countries) to rob graves and prey on human corpses.

fig. Ghouls feasting on the fresh corpse of a reputation THACKERAY. Hence **Ghou·lish** *a.* resembling, or characteristic of ghouls.

Ghyll: see GILL *sb.*[2]

‖**Giallo antico** (dʒaˌlˌlo antīˑko). 1741. [It.; = 'ancient yellow'.] A rich yellow marble found among ruins in Italy; identified by some with the *marmor Numidicum*. Also *attrib.* or *adj.*

‖**Giallolino** (dʒalˌlolīˑno). ? *Obs.* 1728. [It., old dim. of *giallo* yellow.] A fine yellow pigment, much used as Naples yellow.

Giambeux, Spenser's sp. of JAMBEUX.

Giant (dʒəi·ănt). [ME. *geant*, ad. OF. *geant* (mod. *géant*) :—pop. L. **gagantem*, corrupted f. cl. L. *gigantem* (nom. *gigas*), a. Gr. γιγαντ-, γίγας, of unkn. etym.]

A. *sb.* 1. A supposed being of human form but superhuman stature. In Gr. mythology, used *spec.* (chiefly in *pl.*, with initial capital) as = Gr. γίγας, one of *the Giants*, a savage race of men who were destroyed by the Gods. b. *fig.* Applied to an agency of enormous power, and prefixed as a title to names of personified qualities 1631. 2. A human being of abnormally high stature; often *hyperbolical* 1559. Also *transf.* 3. A person of extraordinary powers, mental or bodily 1535.

1. The Gyaunte Atlas beareth the worlde on hys shoulders 1553. 3. The schoolmen were mental giants 1868. Giants of Faith 1871.

Comb.: **Giant's causeway,** a collection of basaltic columns in County Antrim, Ireland; **g.-cell,** (*a*) one of the large protoplasmic masses, without cell wall, and containing many roundish nuclei, found in tubercle; (*b*) one of certain large gangliónic cells found in the frontal and the ascending parietal convolutions of the brain; hence **-celled** *a.*; **giant's kettle,** one of the very large pot-holes (moulins) on the coast of Norway; **g.-powder,** also simply *giant*, a form of dynamite, consisting of infusorial earth saturated with nitroglycerine.

B. *adj.* [the sb. used attrib., or appositively.] Of extraordinary size, extent, or force; gigantic, huge, monstrous 1480. b. In the names of plants and animals 1578.

Hence **Gi·antess,** a she-giant. **Gi·antize** *v.* (*rare*), to give the appearance of a g. to. **Gi·antlike** *a.* resembling a g. or what belongs to a g. **Gi·antly** *a.* giantlike (now *rare*); †*adv.* in a giantlike manner. **Gi·antry** (*rare*), giants collectively; g.-mythology. **Gi·antship,** the state of being a g.; the personality of a g.

‖**Giaour** (dʒaur). 1564. [Pers. *gaur*, *gōr*, pronounced by the Turks (gyaur), var. *gebr*; see GUEBRE.] A term of reproach applied by Turks to non-Mussulmans, esp. Christians.

Gib (gib), *sb.*[1] ME. [Short for *Gilbert.*] 1. A familiar name for a cat. 2. A cat, *esp.* a male cat; later, a castrated cat (*dial.*) 1561. 3. A term of reproach, esp. for an old woman 1529. 4. *Gib-cat* = sense 2. 1596.

Gib (gib), *sb.*[2] 1564. [?] 1. †A hook 1567; a hooked stick 1788. 2. The hooked gristle which grows at the end of the lower jaw of a male salmon after spawning. Also *g.-fish*, a salmon with a g. 1818. *Comb.* **g.-staff,** a staff to gauge water, or to push a boat.

Gib (dʒib, gib), *sb.*[3] 1794. [?] A piece of wood or metal used to keep some part of a machine, etc. in place. Also as vb.

†**Gib,** *v.*[1] [f. GIB *sb.*[1]] *intr.* To behave like a cat. BEAUM. & FL.

Gib (gib), *v.*[2] 1883. [var. of GIP.] = GIP. Hence **Gi·bber,** one who disembowels fish.

Gib, var. of JIB *sb.* and *v.*

Gibbed cat. 1633. [orig. var. of *gib-cat* (GIB *sb.*[1] 4); later taken as f. an assumed vb. **gib* to geld.] = *Gib-cat*.

Gibber (dʒi·bəɹ, gi·bəɹ), *sb.*[1] 1832. [f. GIBBER *v.*[1]] Rapid inarticulate utterance.

‖**Gibber** (gi·bəɹ), *sb.*[2] 1857. [L.] *Bot.* A pouch-like swelling at the base of a calyx, corolla, etc.; *gen.* a hump.

Gibber (dʒi·bəɹ, gi·bəɹ), *v.* Occas. **jibber.** 1604. [Echoic.] *intr.* To speak rapidly and inarticulately; to chatter. Said also of an ape. *Haml.* I. i. 116.

Gibberish (gi·bəriʃ). 1554. [? f. GIBBER *v.* + -ISH.] A. *sb.* Unintelligible speech; inarticulate chatter, jargon.

He repeated some g., which by the sound seemed to be Irish SMOLLETT.

†B. *adj.* Of or pertaining to gibberish, expressed in gibberish; unintelligible -1821.

That old entanglement of iniquity, their gibrish Lawes MILTON.

Gibbet (dʒi·bėt), *sb.* [ME. *gibet(t*, a. OF. *gibet* gallows, in early use, cudgel, dim. of *gibe* staff; see JIB.] 1. Orig. = GALLOWS; later, an upright post with projecting arm from which the bodies of criminals were hung in chains after execution. Also *fig.* ME. 2. The punishment of death by hanging 1751. 3. The projecting arm of a crane; also called JIB 1729. †4. A cudgel -1691.

Gibbet (dʒi·bėt), *v.* 1646. [f. GIBBET *sb.*[1]] †1. *intr.* To hang as on a gibbet. SHAKS. 2. *trans.* To put to death by hanging 1726; to hang on a gibbet by way of exposure. Also with *up.* 1752. 3. *transf.* and *fig.* 1646.

3. *fig.* I mean to hang and g. up thy Name OLDHAM.

Gibbier, var. of GIBIER.

Gibble-gabble (gi·b'lˌgæ·b'l). 1600. [Redupl. of GABBLE.] Senseless chatter. †Also as *vb.*

Gibbon (gi·bən). 1774. [a. F. *gibbon* (Buffon).] *Nat. Hist.* Any long-armed ape of the genus *Hylobates*, esp. one of the species *Hylobates lar* which inhabits the islands of the Indian Archipelago.

Gibbose (gibōᵘ·s), *a.* 1674. [ad. L. *gibbosus*, f. *gibbus* hump.] 1. = GIBBOUS *a.* 1. 2. = GIBBOUS *a.* 2. 1721.

Gibbosity (gibǫ·sĭti). ME. [ad. F. *gibbosité*; see prec.] 1. The state or quality of being gibbose or gibbous 1547. 2. A swelling; a protuberance.

Gibboso- (gibōᵘ·so), comb. f. L. *gibbosus* GIBBOUS, with sense 'gibbous and —'.

Gibbous (gi·bəs), *a.* ME. [f. L. *gibbus* hump + -OUS.] 1. Convex, rounded, protuberant. b. *Astron.* Said of the moon or a planet when the illuminated portion is more than a semicircle, but less than a circle 1690. 2. Hunch-backed; having a hump; hump-shaped. 1646.

2. He [William de Longchamp] had a g. chest 1879. Hence **Gi·bbous-ly** *adv.*, **-ness.**

Gibbsite (gi·bzəit). 1822. [f. George *Gibbs*, American mineralogist; see -ITE.] *Min.* Aluminium hydrate found in stalactitic forms, often as an incrustation.

Gibe, jibe (dʒəib), *sb.* 1573. [f. the vb.] A sneering speech; a taunt, flout, or jeer.

A great master of gibes, and flouts, and jeers DISRAELI.

Gibe, jibe (dʒəib), *v.* 1567. [? ad. OF. *giber*, app. meaning 'to handle roughly in sport'. Cf. JIB *v.*] 1. *intr.* To speak sneeringly; to utter taunts; to jeer, flout, scoff. Const. *at*, †*with.* 2. *trans.* To address with scoffs and sneers 1582.

1. Richardson .. is always gibing at Fielding L. STEPHEN. 2. The deane..would be alwaie gibing him at meales WOOD. Hence **Gi·bingly** *adv.*

Gibel (gi·bĕl). 1841. [a. Ger. *gibel*, *giebel.*] The Prussian or Crucian Carp, *Carassius* (formerly *Cyprinus*) *gibelio* (see CARP *sb.*[1]). Also *g. carp*.

Gibeonite (gi·bĭənəit). 1798. [f. *Gibeon* + -ITE.] A menial, a drudge (see *Josh.* ix. 27).

Giber, jiber (dʒəi·bəɹ). 1563. [f. GIBE *v.* + -ER[1].] One who utters gibes and taunts.

‖**Gibier** (ʒibie). Also †**gibbier.** Now *rare.* 1514. [Fr.] Game; wild-fowl.

Giblet (dʒi·blėt). [ME. *gibelet(te*, a. OF. *gibelet*, app. a stew of game; cf. mod.F. *gibelotte* rabbit-stew.] 1. †a. Entrails. ME. only. b. *pl.* rarely *sing.* The portions of a goose that are separated before cooking, the liver, gizzard, etc., with the pinions and feet 1539. c. *fig.* Odds and ends. Now chiefly *dial.* 1638. 2. *attrib.*, as *g.-pie* 1693.

Gibraltar (dʒibrǫ·ltăɹ). 1592. 1. A fortified town on the south coast of Spain, since 1704 a British possession. *fig.* An impregnable stronghold. 1856. †2. ? A Gibraltar monkey -1608. 3. A sweetmeat; a piece of this. Also *G. rock.* 1831. 4. *attrib.* 1707.

Gibus (dʒəi·bɒ̆s). 1848. [Name of the first maker.] An opera or crush hat. Also *g.-hat.*

Gid[1] (gid). 1601. [short f. GIDDY *sb.*] Giddiness; *spec.* a brain-disease of sheep, caused by the hydatid *Cœnurus cerebralis.* Also GIDDY.

Gid[2]. ? *Obs.* 1674. Local name for the Jack Snipe.

Gid(d, obs. f. GED.

Giddy (gi·di), *a.* [OE. *gidig* insane, var. of **gydig* :—prehistoric **gudigo-*, app. f. OTeut. **gudo^m* GOD. Thus primarily 'god-possessed, ἔνθεος'.] †1. Insane, stupid -ME. 2. Having a sensation of swimming or whirling in the head, with proneness to fall; affected with vertigo, dizzy ME. †b. *transf.* Of a ship: Staggering as if giddy -1725. c. Rendering dizzy 1585. d. Whirling or circling round with bewildering rapidity 1593. 3. Mentally intoxicated, 'elated to thoughtlessness' (J.); light-headed, frivolous, flighty, inconstant 1547. 4. *Comb.*, as *g.-head*, *-headed*, *-paced* 1652.

2. His brains having been a little g. (like one looking from a great height) DRUMM. OF HAWTH. c. The g. footing of the Hatches *Rich. III*, I. iv. 17. d. The strong tempestuous treble .. Ran into its giddiest whirl of sound TENNYSON. 3. She said twenty g. things that looked like joy GOLDSM. Hence **Gi·ddily** *adv.* **Gi·ddiness.** **Gi·ddyish** *a.* somewhat g.

Giddy (gi·di), *v.* 1602. [f. the adj.] To make or become giddy.

Gier-eagle: see GEIER-.

Gierfalcon, obs. f. GERFALCON.

Gieseckite (gī·sĕkəit). 1821. [f. Sir Charles *Giesecke*, who brought it from Greenland; see -ITE.] *Min.* A variety of pinite, believed to be a pseudomorph after nephelite.

Gif (gif), *conj. Sc.* and *n. dial.* [An alteration of ME. *ȝif*, IF.] 1. = IF. Also *gif that*. Now *rare*. ME. †2. = WHETHER. Also *gif that*. –1567.

Giff-gaff (gi·f-gæf). *Sc.* and *n. dial.* 1549. [redupl. of GIVE *v.*] 1. Give and take. 2. Interchange of remarks 1787.

Gift (gift), *sb.* [Com. Teut.: OE. *gift* :— OTeut. **gifti-z*, f. root **geƀ-* GIVE *v.*]

I. Giving. 1. The action of giving; a giving. Also, the power or right of giving. 2. *Law.* a. A transfer of property in a thing, voluntarily and without any valuable consideration 1471. b. The conveyance of an estate tail 1818.

1. The rich living was in the g. of the Herberts DISRAELI. *At a g.* (colloq.): for nothing. 2. a. To complete a g. of goods and chattels delivery is absolutely necessary 1838.

II. The thing given. 1. Something, the property in which is voluntarily transferred to another without the expectation or receipt of an equivalent ME. Also *transf.* 2. An offering to God or to a heathen deity ME. 3. Something given to corrupt; a bribe ME. 4. A faculty, power, or quality miraculously bestowed; occas. in sense of inspiration OE. b. A natural endowment, faculty, ability, or talent ME. 5. A white speck on the finger-nails, supposed to portend a gift 1708.

1. When we seek, as now, thy g. of sleep MILT. 3. For giftes the wysest will deceave 1594. 4. Phr. *The g. of tongues*: see TONGUE. We have not the g. of miracles BERKELEY. The g. of holiness NEWMAN. Faith is..an excellent g. MOZLEY. b. Endowed with highest gifts, The vision and the faculty divine WORDSW. The gifts of the wise lawgiver and firm administrator FREEMAN.

Comb.: **g.-book**; **-horse**, a horse given as a present; see also HORSE *sb.* Hence **Gi·ftling**, a small g.

Gift (gift), *v.* 15.. [f. GIFT *sb.*] 1. *trans.* To endow with gifts (see esp. GIFT *sb.* II. 4); to endow or present *with*. 2. To make a present of. Chiefly *Sc.* 1619.

1. See how the Lord gifted him above his brethren 1608. Hence **Gi·fted** *ppl. a.* endowed with gifts; †given (MILT.). **Gi·ftedness**, the quality of being gifted; also, a gift.

Giftless (gi·ftlės), *a.* ME. [see -LESS.] 1. That has no gift to offer. 2. That receives no gift ME. 3. Untalented 1894.

1. *G. gifts* = gifts that are no gifts (after Gr. ἄδωρα δῶρα).

†**Gi·ft-rope.** 1704. [? a spurious word.] *Naut.* = GUEST-ROPE.

Gig (gig), *sb.*^{1} ME. [Perh. onomatopœic.]

I. Something that whirls. †1. A whipping-top –1793. 2. = GIG-MILL. 1842.

1. Thou disputes like an Infant: goe whip thy Gigge *L. L. L.* v. i. 70.

II. †1. A flighty, giddy girl –1780. 2. An oddity; *dial.* a fool. Chiefly *Eton slang.* 1777.

1. The little g. told all the quarrels..she led in her family MAD. D'ARBLAY. 2. What Mr. Daly..called uncommon gigs HOOK.

III. †A joke –1821; fun, glee 1777.

Phr. *On the (high) g.*: in a state of hilarity; *dial.* eager.

Gig (gig), *sb.*^{2} 1790. [Transf. sense of GIG *sb.*^{1} I.] 1. A light two-wheeled one-horse carriage 1791. 2. *Naut.* A light, narrow, clinker-built ship's boat. Also *cutter-*, *whale-g.* 1790. b. A form of this, used as a rowing boat, for racing purposes 1865. 3. A wooden box, with two compartments, one above the other, used by miners in ascending and descending a pit-shaft. Also = KIBBLE. 1881.

Comb.: **gigsman** (also simply **gig**), one of the crew of a ship's g.; **g.-pair**, a g. for two rowers; **-work**, practice in rowing in a g.

Gig (gig), *sb.*^{3} 1722. [Short for FISHGIG or FIZGIG.] A kind of fish-spear.

†**Gig** (gig), *v.*^{1} 1651. [f. GIG *sb.*^{1} I. 1.] To throw out (a smaller gig); app. referring to a whipping-top of peculiar construction which does this. Hence *fig.* (*trans.* and *intr.*) –1690. Dicts. derive from L. *gignere*, with sense 'to engender'. See DRYDEN *Amphitryon* Prol. 21.

Gig (gig), *v.*^{2} 1693. [perh. onomatopœic.] †1. *intr.* ? To move to and fro. DRYDEN. 2. *trans.* To move backwards and forwards. Chiefly *U.S.* 1875.

Comb. **g.-saw**, 'a thin saw to which a rapid vertical reciprocation is imparted' (Knight).

Gig (gig), *v.*^{3} 1789. [? f. GIG-MILL.] *trans.* To raise the nap of (cloth) with a gig. Also in *Comb.*, as *g.-machine*, 'a machine for dressing woolen cloth by subjecting it to the action of teasels' (Knight). Hence **Gi·gger**, one who works a g.-machine.

Gig (gig), *v.*^{4} 1816. [f. GIG *sb.*^{3}] To fish, also to spear (fish), with a gig.

Gig, *v.*^{5} 1807. [f. GIG *sb.*^{2}] *intr.* To travel in a gig.

Gig: see JIG.

Gigantean (dʒəigæntī·ăn), *a.* 1611. [f. L. *giganteus* + -AN.] = GIGANTIC *a.*

Gigantesque (dʒəigænte·sk), *a.* 1821. [a. F., ad. It. *gigantesco*, f. *gigante*, ad. L. *gigantem* GIANT.] Having the characteristics of a giant; befitting a giant.

How g. the campanile is in its mass and height HAWTHORNE.

Gigantic (dʒəigæ·ntik), *a.* 1612. [f. L. *gigant-*, *gigas* (see GIANT) + -IC.] †1. Of, pertaining to, or characteristic of, a giant or giants –1774. 2. Having the proportions of a giant 1651. 3. Hence: Extraordinary; huge, enormous 1797.

1. On each hand slaughter and g. deeds MILT. 3. This g. telescope 1812. var. †**Gigantal**. Hence †**Gigantical** *a.* = GIGANTIC. **Giga·ntically** *adv.*

Giganticide^1. (dʒəigæ·ntisəid). 1806. [f. L. *gigant(i)-* + -CIDE^1.] A giant-killer.

Giga·nticide^2. 1860. [f. as prec. + -CIDE^2.] The killing of giants.

†**Gigantine**, *a.* 1605. [a. F. *gigantin*, f. L. *gigant-*, *gigas*.] = Gigantic. –1696. So †**Gigantive**.

Gigantology (dʒəigæntǫ·lŏdʒi). 1773. [a. F. *gigantologie*, f. Gr. γίγαντ(ο)-, γίγας; see -LOGY.] Discussions or treatises about giants.

Gigantomachy (dʒəigæntǫ·măki). Also in Gr. form **-machia**. 1606. [a. and ad. Gr. γιγαντομαχία, f. as prec. + μάχη battle.] The war of the giants against the gods; hence, any similar contest.

†**Gigge**, *v.* [f. *gigge*, GUIGE.] *trans.* To fit the GUIGE or arm-strap to (a shield). CHAUCER.

Gigget(t, giggot, obs. ff. GIGOT.

Giggish (gi·giʃ), *a.* 1523. [f. GIG *sb.*^{1} III. + -ISH.] Lively, flighty, wanton. Hence **Gi·ggishness.**

Giggle (gi·g'l), *sb.* 1611. [f. the vb.] 1. A minx, a GIGLET. 2. A giggling laugh 1677.

Giggle (gi·g'l), *v.* 1509. [Echoic; cf. *gaggle*, *cackle*.] *intr.* To laugh continuously in a manner suggestive of foolish levity or of uncontrollable amusement. Also quasi-*trans.* to utter with a giggle.

A quiet day..giggling and making g. among the kind and frank-hearted young people SCOTT. Hence **Gi·ggler**. **Gi·ggly** *a.* addicted to giggling.

Gi·g-lamp. 1853. [f. GIG *sb.*^{2} + LAMP.] 1. One of the lamps at either side of a gig 1888. 2. *pl.* Spectacles (*slang*) 1853.

Giglet, giglot (gi·glėt, -ət). ME. [? conn. w. GIG *sb.*^{1} II. 1, and later assoc. w. GIGGLE *v.*] †a. A wanton woman -1632. b. A giddy, romping girl 1725.

attrib. and *Comb.*, as in *g.-fortune*, *-wench*. Also **g.-fair**, a statute fair for hiring servant-girls.

Gigman^1 (gi·gmæ̆n). 1830. [f. GIG *sb.*^{2} + MAN.] One who keeps a gig: used by Carlyle as one whose respectability is measured by his keeping a gig; a 'Philistine'.

Gi·gman^2. *U.S.* 1889. [f. GIG *sb.*^{3}] One who fishes with a gig.

Gig-mill. 1551. [f. GIG *sb.*^{1} + MILL.] A machine for raising a nap on cloth by the use of teazles; also, a building in which these machines are used.

Gigolo (dʒi·gǒlo). 1927. [Fr., masc. correl. of *gigole* tall thin woman, etc.] A professional male dancing-partner.

Gigot (dʒi·gǒt). 1526. [a. F., of unkn. origin.] 1. A leg or haunch of mutton, veal, etc. Now *Sc.* †2. A slice –1626.

Comb. **g.-sleeve** = 'leg of mutton sleeve'. Also *gigot*.

Gilbertian (gilbə̄·ɹtiăn), *a.* 1887. [f. the name of W. S. *Gilbert* (1836-1911), librettist + -IAN.] Of the ludicrously incongruous kind characteristic of Gilbert and Sullivan opera.

Gilbertine (gi·lbəɹtin, -əin). Only *Hist.* 1540. [ad. med.L. *Gilbertinus*, f. *Gilbertus*; see -INE.] A. *adj.* Of or belonging to Gilbert of Sempringham in Lincolnshire, or to the religious order founded by him (*c* 1140). B. *sb* A canon or nun of this order.

Gild (gild), *sb. Hist.* Also **guild.** 1656. [ad. med.L. *gildum*; cf. GELD *sb.*^{1}] A payment or tax.

Gild (gild), *v.*^{1} Infl. **gilt** and **gilded.** ME. [repr. OE. *gyldan* = ON. *gylla* :—OTeut. **gulþjan*, f. **gulþo*^{m} GOLD.] 1. *trans.* To cover in whole or part with a thin layer of gold. b. *transf.* To smear (with blood) 1595. 2. *Alch.* To impregnate (a liquid) with gold. Also *intr.* (for *refl.*) –1685. 3. *fig.* To supply with gold or money; *esp.* to make attractive by this means 1584. 4. To cover or adorn with a golden colour 1588. 5. *fig.* To adorn with a fair appearance; to give a specious lustre to 1596. †6. To impart a flush to (the face) –1683.

1. To guild a Crown of Silver 1684. b. *John* II. i. 316. 3. I will .. guild my selfe With some more ducats SHAKS. 4. Eternal summer gilds them [the Isles of Greece] yet BYRON. 5. To colour and g. black Designes 1660. 6. This grand Liquor that hath gilded 'em SHAKS.

†**Gild**, *v.*^{2} Also **guild.** 1645. [var. of GELD *v.*^{2}] *intr.* To pay taxes. *Hist. rare.* –1746.

Gi·lded, *ppl. a.* OE. [f. GILD *v.*^{1} + -ED^1. See also GILT *ppl. a.*] In senses of GILD *v.*^{1}

Phr. *G. Chamber*: the House of Lords. *G. spurs*: an emblem of knighthood. *G. youth* (= F. *jeunesse dorée*): fashionable young men of wealthy families.

†**Gi·lden**, *a.* [OE. *gylden*, f. (ult.) OTeut. **gulþo*^{m} GOLD; see -EN^4.] 1. Golden –1591. ¶ 2. Occas. used instead of GILDED 1530.

Gilder (gi·ldəɹ), *sb.* 1550. [f. GILD *v.*^{1} + -ER^1.] One who gilds; one whose occupation is gilding.

Gilder, obs. f. GUILDER, GUELDER(-ROSE).

Gilding (gi·ldiŋ), *vbl. sb.* ME. [f. GILD *v.*^{1} + -ING^1.] 1. The action of GILD *v.*^{1} 2. The golden surface produced by gilding. Also *transf.* and *fig.* 1634.

2. It was a spacious building Full of barbaric carving, painting, g. BYRON. *Comb.* **g.-metal**, 'an alloy composed of 4 parts of copper, 1 part of Bristol old brass, and 14 ounces of tin, to every pound of copper' (Francis).

Gile, obs. f. GUILE *sb.* and *v.*

Gill (gil), *sb.*^{1} Chiefly *pl.* ME. [Of obscure origin; Sw. *gäl*, Da. *gjælle*, account for the meaning, but not for the form.] 1. The organ of respiration in water-breathing animals, which is so arranged that the venous blood is exposed to the aerating influence of the water. In fishes, the gills are on each side of the neck; in other aquatic animals their position and structure is varied. 2. Applied to organs, etc. resembling the gills of a fish. a. The wattles or dewlap of a fowl 1626. b. The radiating plates arranged vertically in the under side of the cap or pileus of fungi 1715. 3. Attributed to persons: The flesh under the jaws and ears 1626. 4. *slang.* Only in *pl.* The corners of a stand-up collar 1826.

1. The gills or *branchiæ*. These are delicate processes of skin richly supplied with blood, and capable of absorbing oxygen MIVART. 3. Phr. *To be rosy, white, blue, yellow about the gills*: to look well, dejected, ill.

Comb.: **g.-arch, -bar**, one of the cartilaginous arches to which the gills of fishes are attached; **-cavity, chamber**, the cavity or compartment in which the g. is contained; **-cleft** = *gill-opening* **-comb** = CTENIDIUM; **-cover**, the bony case covering the gills of fish; **-footed** *a.* = BRANCHIOPODOUS; **-lamella, -leaf, -leaflet** = *gill-plate*; **-lid**, the covering of the gills; **-net**, a fishing-net so constructed that the fish are caught by the gills; **-opening**, the aperture by which water is admitted to the gills; **-plate**, one of the vascular lamellæ forming part of the gills of fishes, molluscs, etc.; **-plume** = *gill-comb*; **-raker**, one of a line of cartilaginous or bony projections on the inner side of a g.-arch.

Gill (gil), *sb.*[2] Also †**ghyll.** ME. [a. ON. *gil* a deep glen. The sp. *ghyll* is app. due to Wordsworth.] **1.** A deep rocky cleft or ravine, usually wooded and forming the course of a stream. **2.** A brook or rivulet 1625.

Gill (dʒil), *sb.*[3] ME. [a. OF. *gille, gelle,* a vessel or measure used for wine.] **1.** A measure for liquids, containing one-fourth (or locally, one-half) of a standard pint. **2.** A vessel holding a gill ME. **3.** *attrib.*, as *g.-house* 1673.

Gill, jill (dʒil), *sb.*[4] 1460. [Abbrev. of GILLIAN.] †**1.** A lass, wench –1665. **2.** *dial.* Short for *Gill-go-by-ground* (see *Comb.*). ? *Obs.* 1727. **b.** Short for *g.-ale* or *g.-beer* 1755.

1. Phr. *Jack and G.* = lad and lass. Our woing doth not end like an old Play: Iacke hath not G. SHAKS.

Comb.: *G.-creep-* (or *go-*) *by-ground*, dial. name for Ground Ivy (*Nepeta Glechoma*); †*attrib.* (sense 2) *g.-ale, -beer, -tea.*

Gill (gil), *sb.*[5] 1839. [? transf. use of GILL *sb.*[1]] A flax-comb, used for preparing, drawing, and roving flax and hemp, and for combing and spinning long wool. Also *attrib.*

Gill (gil), *v.*[1] ME. [f. GILL *sb.*[1]] **1.** *trans.* To gut or clean (fish). **2.** To cut away the gills of a mushroom 1728. **3.** To catch (fish) by the gills in a gill-net. Said also of the net. 1884.

Gill (gil), *v.*[2] 1882. [f. GILL *sb.*[5]] *trans.* To dress (flax or wool) by means of a gill.

Gill-flirt (dʒi·lflɜ̄rt). Also **Jil(l)-.** 1632. [f. GILL *sb.*[4] + FLIRT *sb.*] A wanton; a giddy young woman or girl. Now only *arch.*

†**Gillian.** 1573. [a. F. *Juliane*, a. L. *Juliana*, f. *Julius*, a Roman gentile name.] A girl, wench –1685.

Comb. G.-flirt = prec. *G.-spend-all*: an unthrifty woman.

Gillie (gi·li). Also †**gilly.** 1681. [a. Gael. *gille* lad, servant.] **1.** *Hist.* An attendant on a Highland chief. †*G.-wetfoot* = Gael. *gille-casfliuch*): Lowlanders' name for a Highland chief's follower; spec. the servant who carried the chief across streams. **2.** One who attends a sportsman in the Scottish Highlands 1848.

Gilling (gi·liŋ). *dial.* 1640. [? var. of GIRLING.] A salmon on his second return from the sea.

Gillyflower (dʒi·liflauəɹ). Also †**gilli-,** †**July-.** ME. [a. OF. *girofle, gilofre* clove; see CLOVE-GILLYFLOWER.] †**1.** A clove –1513. **2.** Applied to native plants having clove-scented flowers, esp. to the clove-scented pink (*Dianthus Caryophyllus*), and *dial.* to the wallflower (see *Wall-gillyflower*) or to the white stock (see *Stock-gillyflower*) ME. **3.** A variety of apple; also *g.-apple* 1657. **4.** *attrib.*, as †*g.-grass* –1685.

Comb.: **dame's g.** (see DAME'S-VIOLET); **English g.**, the carnation; **feathered g.**, *Dianthus plumarius*; **mock-g.**, soap-wort (*Saponaria officinalis*); **single g.**, *Dianthus plumarius*; **striped g.**, a variety of *Dianthus Caryophyllus*; **yellow g.**, wall-flower. See also *water-, winter-*, etc. *g.*

Gilour(e, var. of GUILER.

Gilra·vage, *v. north.* and *Sc.* 1818. [?] *intr.* To feast or make merry in an excessive or riotous manner. Hence **Gilra·vager.**

Gils(e, var. of GRILSE.

Gilt (gilt), *sb.*[1] 1492. [f. GILT *ppl. a.* in *silver and gilt*, etc.] †**1.** Gilt plate 1492. **2.** Gilding. Also *fig.* 1593. **3.** Gold, money (cf. GELD, GELT *sbs.*). Now only *slang.* 1598.

2. Phr. *to take the g. off the gingerbread* (see GINGERBREAD). 3. So that some guilt may grease his greedy fist MIDDLETON.

Gilt (gilt), *sb.*[2] Now *dial.* Late ME. [a. ON. *gylt-r* young sow :—OTeut. type **gultjâ*, related to ON. *gǫlt-r* boar.] A young sow or female pig.

Gilt (gilt), *ppl. a.* ME. [f. GILD *v.*[1]] **1.** = GILDED *ppl. a.* **2.** *G. youth* (fig.): a transl. of F. *jeunesse dorée*, applied first to the dandies who assisted in the downfall of Robespierre in 1794.

1. As a parrot turns Up thro' g. wires a crafty loving eye TENNYSON. *Comb.* **g.-edged**, *lit.* of writing paper or books; applied *fig.* (also **g.-edge**) in commercial slang to 'paper' (i.e. bills) of the best quality; also *absol.* a g.-e. security.

†**Gilt**, *v.* ME. [By extension from prec.] = GILD *v.*[1] –1641. Hence **Gi·lted** *ppl. a.*

Gi·lt-head. ? *Obs.* 1555. [f. GILT *ppl. a.* + HEAD.] A name of fishes which have the head marked with golden spots or lines: The striped tunny or bonito; the dorado or dolphin (*Coryphæna hippuris*); the cunner or golden wrasse (*Crenilabrus melops* or *tinca*).

Gi·lt-tail. 1651. [f. GILT *ppl. a.* + TAIL.] A little short worm.

Gilty(e, obs. f. GUILTY.

Gim (dʒim), *a.* Now *dial.* 1513. [? var. of JIMP *a.*] Smart, spruce.

Gimbal (dʒi·mbăl). 1577. [altered f. GIMMAL.] †**1.** = GIMMAL 1. –1711. †**2.** *pl.* = GIMMAL 2. –1652. **3.** *pl.* A contrivance by means of which articles for use at sea (e.g. the compass, the chronometer) are suspended so as to keep a horizontal position. It usually consists of a pair of rings moving on pivots in such a way as to have a free motion in two directions at right angles, so as to counteract the motion of the vessel. **4.** *attrib.*, as *g.-joint.* Also **g.-ring**, a single g. by which the cock-eye of the upper mill-stone is supported on the spindle to permit vibration. Hence **Gi·mballed** *ppl. a.* fitted with a g.

Gimcrack (dʒi·mkræk). [ME. *gibecrake*, perh. conn. w. OF. *giber* to shake (see JIB *v.*), and in some way with CRACK *sb.* or *v.* Sense 3 is perh. infl. by GIM *a.*]

A. *sb.* †**1.** App. some kind of inlaid work in wood. ME. only. **2.** †**a.** A fanciful notion; also, a 'dodge' –1639. **b.** A mechanical contrivance; also *pl.* scientific apparatus 1712. **c.** Now usually applied to anything showy and useless, a trumpery article, a knick-knack 1676. †**3.** A fop; in later use applied to women. A term of contempt. –1785. **4.** A 'Jack of all trades'. Now only *dial.* 1766.

B. *adj.* Trivial; showy but worthless; trumpery 1750. Hence **Gi·mcrackery**, gimcracks collectively.

Gimlet (gi·mlėt), *sb.* ME. [a. OF. *guinbelet, guimbelet*, a dim. of the word which appears in Eng. as WIMPLE.] A kind of boring-tool; it has a grooved steel body, a cross handle at one end, and a worm or screw at the other.

Comb.: **g.-eye**, (*a*) a squint-eye, (*b*) a piercing eye; hence **-eyed** *a.*; **-hole**, a hole made by a g.

Gimlet (gi·mlėt), *v.* 1828. [f. prec. sb.] **1.** *trans.* To pierce with or as with a gimlet 1840. **2.** *Naut.* To turn round (an anchor) by the stock, with a motion like turning a gimlet (Webst.).

Gimmal (dʒi·məl). 1596. [altered f. GEMEL.] **1.** *Antiq.* A finger-ring so made as to divide into two (or three) rings. Also *g.-ring.* 1607. †**2.** *pl.* Joints, links, connecting parts (in machinery) –1867. †**3.** *pl.* The voussoirs of an arch (*rare*) 1639. †**4.** = GIMBAL 3. –1793. †**5.** ? A hinge; = GIMMER[1] 2. 1605. Hence †**Gi·mmaled** *ppl. a.* made with gimmals.

Gimmer[1] (dʒi·məɹ). Now *dial.* 1520. [Corrupt f. GIMMAL, GEMEW.] †**1.** = GIMMAL 1. *rare.* 1570. **2.** A hinge. *Obs.* exc. *dial.* 1520. †**3.** = GIMMAL 2. (Rare in *sing.*) –1668.

Gimmer[2] (gi·məɹ). *Sc.* and *n. dial.* ME. [a. ON. *gymbr* a ewe lamb one year old. Ult. connexions unkn.] **1.** A ewe between the first and second shearing. **2.** 'A contemptuous term for a woman' (Jam.) 1774. **3.** *attrib.* 1546.

Gimp, gymp (gimp), *sb.*[1] 1664. [Du. *gimp* in the same sense is earlier than the Eng. word. Cf. F. *guipure*, f. *guiper* to 'whip' or wrap (a cord, etc.) with thread or silk. Recent Fr. has *guimpe.*] **1.** Silk, worsted, or cotton twist with a cord or wire running through it. Now chiefly, a kind of trimming made of this. **2.** A fishing-line composed of silk, etc., similarly strengthened 1827. **3.** In *Lace-making*: The coarser thread which forms the outline of the design 1839. **4.** *attrib.*, as *g.-nail* –1661.

Gimp (gimp), *sb.*[2] 1747. [a. F. *guimpe*, repr. OF. *guimple*, WIMPLE.] A neckerchief (worn by a nun).

Gimp (dʒimp), *v.*[1] *rare* in lit. use. 1697. [?] *trans.* To give a scalloped or indented outline to.

Gimp (gimp), *v.*[2] 1755. [f. GIMP *sb.*[1]] **1.** *trans.* To trim with gimp. **2.** To 'whip' or twine (wire, etc.) into a plait or twist of something softer. **3.** To give a ribbed surface to 1902.

Gimp: see JIMP *a.*

Gin (dʒin), *sb.*[1] ME. [Aphetic f. OF. *engin*, ENGINE, q.v.] †**1.** Skill, ingenuity. Also, in bad sense, craft –1470. †**2.** A scheme, device. Also, an artifice, trick. –1723. **3.** A mechanical contrivance; a machine; †a tool; †a spring ME. **4.** *spec.* A snare, net, trap, or the like. Also *fig.* ME. †**5.** An engine of torture; the rack –1592. †**6.** A machine used in warfare for casting missiles –1650. †**7.** A bolt, bar, or the like –1710. **8. a.** An apparatus for hoisting heavy weights; now usually a tripod, with a winch or drum round which the rope is wound ME. **b.** *Mining.* A drum or windlass for hoisting, pumping, etc. 1686. **9.** A machine for driving piles 1682. **10.** A machine for separating cotton from its seeds; also *cotton-g.* 1796. **11.** *Naut.* A small iron frame, having a swivel-hook, furnished with an iron sheave, to serve as a pulley for the use of chain in discharging cargo, etc. 1860. **12.** *attrib.*, as *g.-block, -tackle*, etc. 1497.

Comb.: **g.-horse**, a horse that works a g. (sense 8 b); **-house**, a house where cotton is ginned; **-pit**, a shallow mine- or pit-shaft, worked by a g.; **-race**, **-ring**, the circle or track in which a g.-horse moves; **-saw**, one used in a cotton-g. for drawing the fibres through the grid, leaving the seed in the hopper; **-wheel**, (*a*) the wheel or drum of a g. for hoisting, etc.; (*b*) a wheel in a cotton g.

Gin (dʒin), *sb.*[2] 1714. [Abbrev. of GENEVA[1].] An ardent spirit distilled from grain or malt; see GENEVA[1]. Also *attrib.*

In the form GIN, the name chiefly denotes a spirit of British manufacture, usually flavoured not with juniper but with some substitute; but sometimes GIN and GENEVA are used indiscriminately.

Comb.: **g.-drinker's liver**, 'atrophic cirrhosis of the liver', frequently caused by g.; also **-liver**; **-trap** (*slang*), the mouth.

Gin (gin), *v.*[1] *Obs.* exc. *arch.* ME. [Aphetic f. BEGIN (or ONGIN); in ME. chiefly in the pa. t. *gan.* Now sometimes written *'gin.*] **1.** *intr.* To begin. In ME. poetry *gan* is usually a mere auxiliary (= mod. *did*), and periphrastic. **2.** *absol.* To begin, commence ME. **3.** *trans.* To begin (something) ME.

1. Phœbus gins arise *Cymb.* II. iii. 23. 3. Whence the Sunne ginns his reflection *Macb.* I. ii. 25.

Gin (dʒin), *v.*[2] 1625. [f. GIN *sb.*[1]; cf. ENGINE *v.*] **1.** *trans.* To catch in a gin or trap. **2.** To remove the seeds of (cotton) with a gin 1789.

Gin (gin), *prep. Sc.* 17.. [= GAIN *prep.* 3.] Against or by (a certain time).

Gin (gin), *conj. Sc.* and *dial.* 1674. [App. in some way related to GIF.] If; whether.

†**Ging**, *sb.* [OE. *gęnge* troop, company; f. root of GANG *v.*] **1.** A company or host of armed men. ME. only. **2.** A family, household, train of servants. Also *pl.* One's 'people'; people in general. –1626. **3.** *gen.* A gang, pack, train –1653. **b.** *spec.* The crew of a ship or boat –1670. **c.** A crew, rabble; rout –1659.

3. *transf.* A whole g. of words and phrases MILT.

Gingall, jingall (dʒi·ngǭl). 1818. [ad. Hindi *janjāl.*] A heavy musket fired from a rest; a light swivel-gun. Used in China and India. Also *attrib.*

Ginger (dʒi·ndʒəɹ), *sb.* and *a.*[1] [OE. *gingiber, gingifer(e*, a. late L. *gingiber* = *zingiber(i*, a. Gr. *ζιγγίβερις*, app. a. Prakrit :—Skr. *çṛṅgavēra*, a compound of *çṛṅga* horn and *vera* body. Yule thinks the Skr. word a perversion of the Malayalam synonym *inchi-ver* (f. *inchi* root).]

A. *sb.* The rhizome of the tropical plant *Zingiber officinale*, characterized by its hot spicy taste; used in cookery and medicine, and as a sweetmeat. **2.** The plant *Zingiber officinale* ME.; also similar plants 1838. **3.** *slang.* Mettle, spirit (*fig.*) 1843. **4.** *dial.* and *slang.* A light sandy colour 1865; also, a sandy-haired person 1885.

Comb.: **g.-ale**, an effervescing drink flavoured with g.; **-cordial**, a liqueur made from raisins, lemon-rind, g. and water, occas. strengthened with brandy or whisky; **-grass**, (*a*) *Andropogon Nardus*, an East Indian grass, yielding an essential oil with a strong smell of g.; (*b*) *Panicum glutinosum*, a coarse grass of Jamaica; **-nut** = GINGERBREAD-NUT; **-snap,** (*a*) a thin brittle cake flavoured with g.; (*b*) a hot-tempered person (*U.S.*); **-spice** = GINGER *sb.* 1; **-wine,** a wine made by the fermentation of sugar, water, and bruised g.; **-wort,** Lindley's name for the order *Zingiberaceæ*.

B. *adj. dial.* Of the colour of ginger. Of a person: Sandy-haired. Of a cock: Having red plumage. 1825.

Gi·nger, *a.*[2] Now *dial.* 1600. [f. GINGERLY.] = GINGERLY *a.*

Ginger (dʒi·ndʒəɹ), *v.* 1823. [f. the sb.] 1. *trans.* To put ginger into (a drink) 1825. 2. To treat (a horse) with ginger; *fig.* to put mettle into, spirit *up*.

Gi·nger-bee·r. 1809. [f. GINGER + BEER.] An aerated drink, flavoured with ginger. Also *attrib.*

Gingerbread (dʒi·ndʒəɹbred). [ME. *gingembras, gingimbrat* preserved ginger, ad. med. L. **gingi(m)bratum*, neut. ppl. a., f. med.L. *gingiber* GINGER. The 3rd syllable was early confounded with *bread*.] 1. †a. Orig.: Preserved ginger. b. Later: A kind of plain cake, highly flavoured with ginger, and formerly made into fanciful shapes, which were often gilded. 2. *fig.* Anything showy and unsubstantial 1605. 3. *slang.* Money 1700. 4. *attrib.* 1748.

1. Roial spicerye and Gyngebreed CHAUCER. 2. *To take the gilt off the g.*: to strip something of its attractive qualities. 4. *G. work*, gaudy and tasteless decorations, orig. of a ship.

Comb.: **g.-nut,** a small round button-like cake of g.; **-tree,** (*a*) = DOUM-PALM; (*b*) *Parinarium macrophyllum*, a West African fruit-tree with a farinaceous fruit; **-plum,** the fruit of *Parinarium macrophyllum*.

Gingerly (dʒi·ndʒəɹli). 1519. [f. **ginger* (of unkn. origin) + -LY[2].]

A. *adv.* †a. Orig.: Elegantly, daintily; later, mincingly -1607. b. Cautiously; also, timidly, fastidiously 1607.

b. But Lord! How g. he answered it PEPYS.

B. *adj.* †a. Dainty, delicate. b. Extremely cautious or wary. 1533.

Hence **Gi·ngerliness,** the quality of being g.

Gi·nger-po·p. 1827. [f. GINGER + POP *v.*] 1. *colloq.* = GINGER-BEER. 2. *slang.* A policeman 1887.

Gingery (dʒi·ndʒəri), *a.* 1852. [See -Y[1].] Ginger-coloured, sandy; also spiced with or as with ginger.

Gingham (gi·ŋăm). 1615. [a. F. *guingan, guingamp*, ult. a. Malay *ginggang*, 'striped', used subst.] 1. A kind of cotton or linen cloth, woven of dyed yarn, often in stripes or checks. In *pl.* fabrics of this kind. 2. *colloq.* An umbrella (prop. of gingham) 1861. 3. *attrib.* 1793.

Gingival (dʒindʒəi·văl), *a.* 1669. [f. L. *gingiva* gum; see -AL.] 1. Of or pertaining to the gums. 2. quasi-*sb.* Sounds, in uttering which the tongue is pressed against the gums 1874. So **Gi·ngivi·tis,** inflammation of the gums.

Gingle, obs. f. JINGLE.

Gingles, var. of SHINGLES. Fuller.

Ginglyform (gi·ŋ-, dʒi·ŋglifǭɹm), *a.* 1847. [f. GINGLYMUS + -FORM.] *Anat.* Hinge-shaped. So **Gi·nglymate** *v. intr.* to form a hinge. **Gi·nglimoid, Ginglymoi·dal** *adjs.* resembling a hinge; hinge-like.

Ginglymus (gi·ŋ-, dʒi·ŋglimǒs). 1657. [mod.L., a. Gr. γίγγλυμος hinge.] *Anat.* 'A diarthrodial joint having some likeness to a hinge, in that its motion is only in two directions, as the elbow-joint' (*Syd. Soc. Lex.*).

Ginkgo (gi·ŋkgo). Also **†gingo, †ginko, gingko.** 1808. A Japanese tree (*Ginkgo biloba* or *Salisburia adiantifolia*) cultivated for its handsome foliage. Also *attrib.*

Ginn, var. of JINN.

Ginnet, obs. f. JENNET.

Ginney, ginnie, obs. ff. GUINEA.

†**Gi·nning,** *vbl. sb.* ME. [f. GIN *v.*[1] + -ING[1].] = BEGINNING -1463.

Ginny-carriage (dʒi·ni,kæ̆rėdʒ). *dial.* 1824. A stout carriage for conveying materials along a railroad.

Gi·n-pa·lace. 1834. [f. GIN *sb.*[2]] A gaudily decorated public-house.

Ginseng (dʒi·nseŋ). 1654. [a. Chinese.] 1. A plant of two species of the genus *Aralia* or *Panax*, found in Northern China, the eastern United States, and elsewhere 1691. 2. The root of the plant; a preparation of this as a medicine 1654. 3. *attrib.*, as *g.-farm*, etc. 1758.

Gi·n-shop. 1714. [f. GIN *sb.*[2]] A dram-shop where gin is retailed.

Gin-sling. 1839. [f. GIN *sb.*[2] + SLING *sb.*[2]] A U.S. cold drink, made of gin, etc. flavoured and sweetened.

Giottesque (dʒǫte·sk). 1854. [f. *Giotto* + -ESQUE.] A. *adj.* Resembling the style of Giotto (13–14th c.). B. *sb.* The style founded by Giotto; also, an artist of the school, or imitating the style, of Giotto.

Gip, *sb.*: see GYP.

Gip (gip), *v.* 1603. [?] To clean (fish) for curing.

†**Gip,** *interj.* 1530. [Prob. an involuntary exclam.; cf. GEE-(H)UP and GUP.] a. An exclam. of anger or remonstrance addressed to a horse. b. Addressed to a person = 'get out' -1660.

Gipon. *Obs.* exc. *arch.* ME. [a. OF. *gip(p)on, jup(p)on*, f. *gipe, jupe*.] A tunic, frequently worn under the hauberk.

Gippo (dʒi·po). *Army slang.* 1914. [Alteration of dial. *jipper*.] Gravy, soup, stew.

Gipser (dʒi·psəɹ). Also **gipsire (gyp-).** *Obs.* exc. *arch.* ME. [ad. OF. *gibecier(e, gibessiere*, etc. purse, pouch (mod.F. *gibecière* game-bag), of unkn. origin.] A purse, pouch, or wallet, hung from a belt or girdle.

Gipsies, †gips, *sb. pl.* 1644. [Proper name of springs near Bridlington, now called the *Gipsy race*.] Intermitting springs.

Gipsy, gypsy (dʒi·psi), *sb.* Pl. **gipsies, gypsies.** 1537. [Early form *gipcyan*, aphet. for EGYPTIAN (B. 2). Skelton has 'By Mary Gipcy', by St. Mary of Egypt. The form *gypsy* in the sing. is rarer than *gypsies* in the pl.] 1. A member of a wandering race (by themselves called *Romany*), of Hindu origin, formerly believed to have come from Egypt. b. Gipsy language, Romany. (Recent Dicts.) 2. *transf.* †a. A cunning rogue -1635. b. Applied to a woman, as being cunning, deceitful, fickle, or the like. Now merely playful, and applied esp. to a brunette. 1632. 3. Short for *g.-bonnet, -hat, -moth, -winch* 1808. 4. *attrib.* or *adj.* Resembling what is customary among gipsies 1630.

1. Both in a tune like two gipsies on a horse *A.Y.L.* v. iii. 16. *Ant. & Cl.* IV. xii. 28. More ignorant in his art of divining then any G. MILT. 2. b. Cursing her [his mother-in-law] for a dissembling hypocritical Gypsie 1673. 4. A g. tent 1849, breakfast 1850.

Comb.: **g.-bonnet,** one with large side-flaps; so **-hat;** **-herring,** the pilchard; **-moth,** *Ocneria dispar*; **-ring,** a flat gold ring, with stones (orig. Egyptian pebbles) let into it, at given distances; **-rose,** the wild and garden scabious; **-winch,** a small winch having a drum, ratchet, and pawl, and attachable to a post; **-wort,** *Lycopus europæus*.

Hence **Gi·psydom,** gipsies collectively; also, their way of life (*rare*). **Gi·psyfy, gi·psify** *v.* to make or (*rarely*) become g.-like. **Gi·psyism,** the life and pursuits of gipsies, or what resembles this.

Gipsy (dʒi·psi), *v.* 1627. [f. the sb.] *intr.* To live or act like gipsies; esp. to camp out, picnic, etc.

Giraffe (dʒĭra·f). 1594. [Ult. ad. Arab. *zarāfah*, through F. *girafe*.] 1. A ruminant quadruped found in Africa, remarkable for its long neck and legs, and for its skin, which is spotted like a panther's; also called CAMELOPARD. 2. *Astron.* The constellation CAMELOPARD 2. 1836. 3. *Mining.* A form of cage or truck used on inclines 1881. †4. A kind of upright spinet. STAINER & BARRETT. Hence **Gira·ffid,** one of the *Giraffidæ*, the animal family of which the g. is the only living representative.

‖**Girandola** (dʒiræ·ndǒlă). 1644. [a. It., f. (ult.) L. *gyrare*, f. *gyrus*, a. Gr. γῦρος a circle.] 1. A kind of revolving firework 1670. 2. A revolving fountain-jet.

Girandole (dʒi·răndǭl). 1634. [a. F., ad. It.; see prec.] 1. = GIRANDOLA 1. 2. = GIRANDOLA 2. 1813. 3. A branched support for candles or lights 1769. 4. An ear-ring or pendant, esp. one with a central stone surrounded by smaller stones 1825. 5. *attrib.* 1799.

Girasol(e (dʒi·răsǫl, -sǭl). 1586. [a. It. *girasole*, f. *girare* to turn + *sole* the sun. Cf. HELIOTROPE.] †1. A sunflower. SIDNEY. 2. A variety of opal which reflects a reddish glow in a bright light; a *fire-opal* 1588.

Gird (gɔ̄ɹd), *sb.* ME. [f. GIRD *v.*[2]] †1. A sharp stroke or blow (*rare*) -1579. 2. A sudden movement or jerk, a spurt of action. *Obs.* exc. *dial.* 1545. 3. A spasm of pain. Now *dial.* 1614. 4. A sharp or biting remark; a gibe, 'dig'. Somewhat *arch.* 1566.

3. My heart relented, and gave me several Girds and Twitches STEELE. 4. For his girds were oblique, and touched to the quick NORTH.

Gird (gɔ̄ɹd), *v.*[1] Infl. **girded** and **girt.** [OE. *gyrdan*:—OTeut. **gurdjan*. See GIRTH, GARTH[2].] 1. *trans.* To surround, encircle with a belt or girdle. Chiefly *refl.* or *pass.* b. *fig.* To prepare (oneself) for action 1450. †c. To bind (a horse) with a saddle-girth -1677. 2. *fig.* To invest or endue *with* attributes OE. 3. To equip *with* a sword suspended from a belt fastened round the body OE. 4. To fasten by means of a belt, a girdle, etc. OE.; to put (a cord, etc.) *round* something (*rare*) 1726. 5. *transf.* and *fig.* †a. To tie firmly or confine -1674. b. To besiege, blockade 1548. 6. Said of that which surrounds: To encircle, enclose, confine ME.

1. Let your loins be girded about *Luke* xii. 35. Leaves..To g. thir waste MILT. b. To g. oneself for one's life's work MOTLEY. 2. The Son..Girt with Omnipotence MILT. 3. Upon Easter day..he was gyrde with the sworde of the Duke of Briteyn R. GRAFTON. 4. He dyd on his helme and gyrte on his sword LD. BERNERS. So they girded sackcloth on their loynes 1 *Kings* xx. 32. 5. Sommers greene all girded up in sheaues SHAKS. 6. Girt with the iron ring of Fate CARLYLE. Boadicea..Girt by half the tribes of Britain TENNYSON.

Gird (gɔ̄ɹd), *v.*[2] ME. [?] †1. *trans.* To strike, smite. Also of pain: To touch sharply (*rare*). -1618. †2. To impel or move hastily or rudely -1650. 3. *intr.* To move suddenly or rapidly; to rush, start, spring. *Obs.* exc. *dial.* ME. 4. *fig.* a. *absol.* To jest or gibe *at* (rarely *against, upon*). The current sense. 1546. b. *trans.* To sneer or scoff at. ? *Obs.* 1573.

4. a. I wonder why many men g. so at the law MIDDLETON. b. Hee is still girding the ages vanity EARLE.

Girder[1] (gɔ̄·ɹdəɹ). 1611. [f. GIRD *v.*[1] + -ER[1].] 1. a. A main beam in a framed floor, supporting the system of joisting that carries the flooring. b. An iron or steel longitudinal beam used for the same purpose; esp., a latticed plate, or other compound structure used to form the span of a bridge 1853. †2. In masonry. a. A bond-stone. b. A bonding-course. LEONI. 3. *attrib.*, as **g.-bridge,** a bridge whose superstructure consists of longitudinal girders carrying the platform or roadway; **-rail,** a form of tramway rail, resembling in its section that of the ordinary iron girder used in construction. 1854. Hence **Gi·rderage,** girders collectively.

†**Gi·rder**[2]. *rare.* 1584. [f. GIRD *v.*[2] + -ER[1].] One who sneers or cavils -1611.

Girding (gɔ̄·ɹdiŋ), *vbl. sb.* ME. [f. GIRD *v.*[1] + -ING[1].] 1. The action of GIRD *v.*[1] and [2]. 2. That which girds; esp. †a girdle ME.

2. Instead of a stomacher a g. of sackcloth *Isa.* iii. 24.

Girdle (gɔ̄·ɹd'l), *sb.*[1] [OE. *gyrdel*, f. *gyrdan* to GIRD; see -LE.] 1. A belt worn round the waist to secure or confine the garments; also used to carry a weapon, a purse, etc. †2. The part of the body round which the girdle is worn -1732. Also *transf.* and *fig.* 3. *transf.* uses of 1. a. That which surrounds as a girdle; †a zone OE. b. That which confines; a restraint, limit 1616. 4. *spec.* a. *Anat.* In mod. use applied chiefly to the bony supports for the upper and lower limbs, the *shoulder* (or *pectoral*) and *pelvic* (or *hip*) g. 1601. b. The line or rim dividing the two faces of a brilliant 1819. c. *Arch.* A small circular band round the shaft of a column 1727. d. A belt or ring made round the trunk of a tree by the removal of the bark 1896. e. *Mining.* A term applied locally to very thin beds of stone 1819.

1. By hire girdel heeng a purs of lether CHAUCER. Phr. (*To have, hold*) *under one's g.*: in subjection,

under one's control. 3. a. †*The g. of the world*: the ecliptic, the equator. The billows roll, From the world's g. to the frozen pole COWPER. †*To put (make, cast) a g. (round) about*: to go round, make the circuit of. He put a g. about the earth, in forty minutes SHAKS. b. The iron g. of a solemn..oath 1833.

Comb.: **g.-beds**, alternations of thin sandstones and sandy shales; **-bone**, the sphenethmoid bone; **-wheel**, a spinning wheel small enough to be hung at the g.

Girdle (gɔ̄·ɹd'l), *sb.*[2] *north* and *Sc.* ME. [var. of GRIDDLE by metathesis of *r*.] A circular plate of iron which is suspended over a fire and upon which cakes are baked.

Girdle (gɔ̄·ɹd'l), *v.* 1582. [f. GIRDLE *sb.*[1]] 1. *trans.* To surround with a girdle. Also with *about, in, round.* (Chiefly *transf.* and *fig.*) 2. To cut through or remove the bark of a tree in a circle extending round the trunk, either to kill it, or to render it more fruitful. Also with *round*, 1662.

1. The Noble Talbot, Who now is girdled with a waste of Iron, And hem'd about with grim destruction 1 *Hen. VI*, IV. iii. 20.

Girdler (gɔ̄·ɹdləɹ). ME. [f. GIRDLE *sb.*[1] + -ER[1].] 1. A maker of girdles. 2. One that encompasses 1879.

Girdlestead (gɔ̄·ɹd'lste·d). *arch.* ME. [f. as prec. + STEAD *sb.*] That part round which the girdle passes; the waist. b. Used for 'lap' 1882.

Smalish in the girdilstede CHAUCER.

Gire, var. of GYRE.

Girkin, obs. f. GHERKIN.

Girl (gɔ̄ɹl), *sb.* [ME. *gurle, gerl(e, girle*; of obscure etym.; see N.E.D.] †1. A child or young person of either sex. Chiefly in *pl.* ME. only. 2. A female child; applied to all young unmarried women 1530. b. A maid-servant 1668. c. A sweetheart. Also (*U.S. colloq.*) *best g.* 1791. †3. A roebuck in its second year –1726. 4. *attrib.* 1589.

1. *Knave g.*: a boy. 2. *G. Guide*: see GUIDE *sb.* 2 d. *Old g.*: applied *colloq.* to a woman of any age, either disrespectfully or by way of endearment; also to a mare.

Girland, -ond, obs. f. GARLAND.

Gi·rlery. [See -ERY.] Girls collectively. LAMB.

Girlhood (gɔ̄·ɹlhud). 1785. [f. GIRL *sb.* + -HOOD.] The state or time of being a girl; *concr.* girls collectively.

Girlie (gɔ̄·ɹli). 1860. [See -IE, -Y[4].] A little girl.

Girlish (gɔ̄·ɹliʃ), *a.* 1565. [See -ISH[1].] Of or pertaining to a girl or to girlhood; characteristic of or like a girl.

G. laughter DRAYTON. **Gi·rlish-ly** *adv.*, **-ness.**

Girn (gɔ̄ɹn), *v.* ME. [var. of GRIN *v.* with metathesis of *r*.] 1. *intr.* To show the teeth in rage, pain, disappointment, etc.; to be fretful or peevish. Now only *north.* and *Sc.* †2. To show the teeth in laughing; to grin –1711. Hence **Girn** *sb.* a snarl; †also (*rare*) = GRIN *sb.*[2]

‖**Giro** (dʒī·ro). 1607. [It.; = a circuit :—L. *gyrus*, a. Gr γῦρος circle.] A tour, circuit; a 'turn'.

Gironde (ʒirǭ·nd, dʒirǭ·nd). 1876. [see next.] The Girondist party.

Girondist (dʒirǭ·ndist), *sb.* (*a.*) 1801. [ad. F. *Girondiste* (now *Girondin*), f. *Gironde* + *-iste, -ist.*] A member of the moderate republican party (in the French assembly 1791–1793); its leaders were the deputies from the department of the Gironde. Also *attrib.* or *adj.*

‖**Girouette** (ʒiruę·t). 1822. [Fr.] A weathercock. Also *fig.*

Girrock. ?*Obs.* A sea-fish, *Acus major.* RAY.

Girt (gɔ̄ɹt), *sb.* 1563. [var. of GIRTH *sb.*[1]] = GIRTH *sb.*[1] 1, 2, 6. Also *attrib.*

Girt (gɔ̄ɹt), *v.* Now *rare.* ME. [Two formations: (1) Altered f. GIRD *v.*[1] (2) f. GIRT *sb.*] 1. *trans.* = GIRD *v.*[1] 2. To measure the girth of; also *intr.* 1663. 3. Of trees, etc.: To measure (so much) in girth or girt 1750.

1. The .. Ceremony .. consisted .. in Girting the Grand Signior with a Sword 1688. 3. The tree 'girts' eighteen and a half feet, and spreads over a hundred O. W. HOLMES. Phr. *To g. against*: to press against (said of a ship's cable).

Girt (gɔ̄ɹt), *ppl. a.* 1627. [pa. pple. of GIRD *v.*[1]] 1. In senses of GIRD *v.*[1] 1791. 2. *Naut.* Said of a ship which is moored so rigidly by her cables, extending from the hawse to two distant anchors, as to be prevented from swinging or turning about.

Girth (gɔ̄ɹþ), *sb.* [ME. *gerth(e*, a. ON. *gjǫrð* girdle, girth, hoop :—OTeut. **gerdâ.* Cf. GARTH[1], GIRD *v.*[1], GIRDLE *sb.*] 1. A belt or band of leather or cloth, placed round the body of a horse, etc. and drawn tight, so as to secure a saddle, pack, etc. upon its back. 2. Measurement round the human body, the trunk of a tree, or any object which is more or less circular 1664. 3. *Mining.* 'A horizontal brace in the direction of the drift' (Raymond) 1881. 4. *transf.* That part of a horse where the girth is fastened 1846. 5. *fig.* Something that encircles 1871. 6. *U.S.* 'A small horizontal beam or girder' (Webst.) 1864.

2. A leafy olive .. pillar-like in g. COWPER. 5. Girdled about with the round sea's g. As a town with its wall SWINBURNE.

Girth (gɔ̄ɹþ), *v.* 1450. [f. GIRTH *sb.*] 1. *trans.* To gird, surround, encompass. 2. To fit or bind with a girth 1580. 3. To secure by means of a girth 1819. 4. To draw (a string) close round a surface which is being measured. Also *absol.* 1825. 5. *intr.* To measure in girth 1858.

Gi·rth-we·b. ME. [f. GIRTH *sb.* + WEB *sb.*] Woven material of which girths are made; a band made of this.

Gi·rt-li·ne. 1769. *Naut.* A rope taken up to the mast-head from which the stay leads, and rove through a block, to hoist up the rigging. Also (erron.) **Ga·ntline.**

Girtonian (gəɹtōu·niăn). 1887. [f. *Girton* + -IAN.] One who is, or has been, a student at Girton, a Cambridge college for women.

†**Gis, jis.** 1528. [Minced f. *Jesus.*] An oath or exclam.: *By Gis!* see *Haml.* IV. v. 58.

Gisarme (gizā·ɹm). *Obs.* exc. *Hist.* ME. [a. OF. *g(u)isarme*, of unkn. origin.] A kind of battle-ax, bill, or halberd, having a long blade in line with the shaft, sharpened on both sides and ending in a point.

Gise (dʒəis), *v. dial.* 1695. [var. of GIST *v.*] To put cattle out to grass at so much per head.

Gise, obs. f. GUISE.

†**Gi·sel.** ME. only. [a. ON. *gísl* = OE. *gīs(e)l.*] A hostage.

Gisement (dʒəi·zmĕnt). 1695. [var. of GISTMENT.] Cattle taken in to graze at a certain price; also, the money received for this.

Gismondine, gismondite (gizmǭ·ndin, -əit). 1823. [f. Prof. *Gismondi*, who first described it; see -INE, -ITE.] *Min.* A hydrous silicate of aluminium and calcium, found near Rome.

†**Gist**, *sb.*[1] ME. [a. OF. *giste* (mod. *gîte*) resting-place, etc., related to *gis-, gésir* to lie. Cf. GEST *sb.*[3]] A halting-place or lodging. Also *pl.* a list of stages in a royal progress –1706.

These Quailes have their set gists, to wit, ordinarie resting and baiting places HOLLAND.

†**Gist**, *sb.*[2] 1493. [f. GIST *v.*] = AGISTMENT. –1641.

Gist (dʒist), *sb.*[3] Also (sense 1 only) in later F. form †**gît**, corruptly **gite**, †**gîte**, †**jet.** 1726. [a. OF. *gist* (mod. *gît*), 3 sing. pres. ind. of *gésir* to lie, *gésir en* to consist in, depend on.] 1. *Law.* The real ground or point (of an action, etc.). 2. The substance or pith of a matter, the essence 1823.

2. This is the g. Here lies the whole of it COBBETT.

Gist (dʒəist), *v.* Now *dial.* 1483. [Aphet. f. AGIST; cf. also GISE *v.*] = AGIST *v.* 1, †2.

Git, var. of GATE *sb.*[3]

‖**Gitano** (dʒitāno; in Sp. χitā·no). 1834. [Sp. repr. pop. L. **Ægyptianus* Egyptian.] A male (Spanish) gipsy. So **Gita·na**, a female gipsy.

†**Gite**[1], **gide.** ME. [app. a. OF. *guite.*] A dress or gown –1614. ¶ Used by Peele for: Splendour.

She cam after in a gyte of reed CHAUCER.

‖**Gite**[2] (ʒīt). Also **gite.** *rare.* 1798. [F.; see GIST *sb.*[1]] A halting-place, lodging.

Gite, gite: see GIST *sb.*[3]

Gith (giþ). ME. [a. L.] Any plant of the genus *Nigella*, esp. *N. sativa.* b. The Corncockle, *Lychnis Githago* 1597.

Gitter (gi·təɹ). 1876. [Ger.; = lattice, grating.] *Optics.* A diffraction grating.

Gittern (gi·təɹn), *sb. arch.* ME. [a. OF. *guiterne*, ult. f. Gr. κιθάρα CITHARA. Cf. GUITAR, CITHERN.] A cithern.

Of harpis, luttis, and getarnys ME. Hence †**Gi·ttern** *v.* to play on the g.

‖**Giunta** (dʒu·nta). *Hist.* See also JUNTA. [It., f. *giugnere* to JOIN.] In the Venetian republic, a number of patricians chosen to act as assessors to the Council of Ten in emergencies; later, the name of the 60 co-opted members of the council of *pregadi*, by whom the affairs of the state were administered.

†**Giust**, Spenser's quasi-It. sp. of JOUST.

Give (giv), *sb.* 1887. [f. GIVE *v.*] A yielding, giving way.

The apparent 'give' in the weather 1893.

Give (giv), *v.* Infl. **gave** (gēⁱv), **given** (gi·v'n), **giving** (gi·viŋ). [Com. Teut. str. vb.: OE. *ʒiefan* (:—OTeut. **ʒeƀan*), whence ME. *yeve, yive*, which was superseded by *geve, give*, under Scand. influence.]

I. *trans.* To bestow gratuitously. 1. To hand over as a present; to confer gratuitously the ownership of on another person. b. To render (a service) without payment 1719. 2. To confer, grant, or bestow OE. 3. To bequeath or devise ME. 4. To sanction the marriage of (a daughter or female ward) OE.

1. Good sir, this ring was giuen me by my wife SHAKS. *absol.* When Maidens sue Men giue like gods SHAKS. b. We gave him his passage, that is to say, bore his charges DE FOE. 2. To g. a Lordship 1584, one's heart (see HEART *sb.*), true love TENNYSON. Hee takes pleasure in those gifts, hee gave QUARLES. Phr. *God, Christ g.*, etc. *Give me*: = 'what I would have is —'. G. me the good old times LYTTON. 4. Take not a wife of another Law nor g. your daughters to men of another Law PURCHAS.

II. To deliver, hand over. 1. To deliver or hand (something) to a person; to put (food and drink) before a person ME.; to deliver (a message, etc.) 1611. 2. To commit, consign, entrust OE. 3. To hand over as a pledge. Also *fig.* to pledge (one's word, etc.). ME.

1. Giue me some Sack SHAKS. *To g. to eat, drink*, etc. (now only *literary*). G. my love to Clive THACKERAY. 2. We gaf hem the sovrante LYDG. Phr. *To g. into custody*: in recent use, to direct a policeman to take as a prisoner. 3. I gave them the word of a sailor DOYLE.

III. 1. To make over to another in exchange for something else; to pay (a sum of money); to sell for a price ME. 2. To hand over to a superior; to pay (taxes, tithes, etc.). *Obs.* exc. with Biblical reference. OE.

1. For as much money as it is worth he shall g. it me *Gen.* xxiii. 9. Phr. *To g. (one) as good as he brings, to g. (one) his due* (see DUE *sb.*), *a Roland for an Oliver. To g. the world*, etc., *one's ears* (see EAR). 2. Is it lawful to g. tribute unto Cæsar *Matt.* xxii. 17.

IV. 1. To sacrifice for some object. Also *refl.* ME. 2. To devote, dedicate. Also to consign *to*, to commend *to* ME. 3. To addict, devote oneself *to* ME.

1. The Abbots of Peterborough..had given their lives in the cause of England FREEMAN. 2. Thus I let you go, And giue you to the Gods *Ant. & Cl.* III. ii. 64. 3. To my great task..I gave me wholly CARY.

V. 1. To put forth from oneself ME. b. *absol.* or *intr.* To deal a blow, make an attack or charge (*at, on, upon*). *Obs.* exc. in *Pugilism.* ME. 2. To make, esp. suddenly; to put forth, emit ME. 3. To put forth in words; to address (words) *to*; to impose and make known; to pronounce (a blessing, curse) ME. 4. To deliver authoritatively; to award (costs, etc.) *to, against* ME. 5. *pa. pple.* (cf. DATE *sb.*[2]): Dated ME. 6. To provide as host 1523.

1. Phr. *To g. a kiss, a blow, look, push*, etc.; also *a scolding*, etc. *To g. the point* (Sword exercise): to make a direct thrust. *To g. a broadside, a volley, a shot* (see the sbs.). *To g. fire* (see FIRE *sb.*). 2. They..gave three cheers 1822. Some bitter notes my harp would g. TENNYSON. 3. G. them good words DE FOE. To g. the word of command 1890. Phr. *To g.* (= to wish) *good day, a merry Christmas*, etc. (now *obsolescent*). Hence (now *dial.*) *To g. the (time of) day (to)*: to salute with 'good morning', 'good evening', etc. (as the case may be). 4. Judgment had been given against him MACAULAY. Phr. *To g. the case* (idiomatically *to g. it*): to declare *for* or *against.* The umpire gave (= declared) it out 1891. 6. To g. a ball POPE, a dinner TENNYSON, a treat 1892.

VI. 1. To present; to hold out to be taken OE. †2. Of one's heart, mind, conscience, etc: To suggest (to one) *that*; also, to misgive. Also, to prompt (one) *to* do something. –1820. 3. To expose or offer to view or observation; to mention, include in a list, etc. ME. b. To indicate; to state *at* 1665. †4. To display as an armorial bearing; to bear –1640. 5. To represent. †Also *refl.*: To present itself as. 1607. 6. To read, recite, sing, act in the presence of auditors or spectators 1460. 7. To offer as a sentiment or toast 1728.

1. To g. the breast to a child PURCHAS, sails to the wind ROGERS. He holds out his hand; she gives her own HAWTHORNE. 3. So can I giue no reason SHAKS. The far-off farms..gave no sign of life 1889. b. He gives the average..at 0·81 lbs. 1856. 4. Teare the Lyons out of England's Coat;..giue Sheepe in Lyons stead SHAKS. 6. Who will g. us a song THACKERAY.

VII. To communicate, impart 1470; to supply 1639.

The broom which gives their title to the Plantagenets M. PATTISON. Phr. *To g.* (a person) *a piece of one's mind* (colloq.): usually, to express emphatically one's disapprobation. *To g. to the world, to the public*: to publish. *To g.* (a person) *to believe, understand*, etc.: to impart to him that which will lead him to believe, etc.

VIII. 1. To allot, apportion OE.; to assign (a name) ME. 2. To ascribe, assign 1559. 3. In pa. pple. (cf. GIVEN *ppl. a.*): Posited as a basis of calculation or reasoning 1667.

1. He was given the contract 1891. To give a child a name PURCHAS. 2. They gave it [a pamphlet] to Lord Camden BURKE. †*To g. for*: to set down as. All gave her for a Papist MARVELL.

IX. 1. To yield as a product or result ME. †2. To fetch (a price) –1799. †3. Of experience, reasoning, etc.: To yield the conclusion *that*. Of a name: To import. –1677.

1. The lamps gave an uncertain light 1891. [His] name in Hebrew characters gives us 666—the mystic number of the Antichrist 1890.

X. 1. To cause to have; to produce in a person or thing. Said both of persons and things. ME. ¶ 2. *To give to reflect, think*: to supply material for reflection or thought. (A Gallicism.) 1890.

1. Finding the Army a meere Chaos, he had given it forme MORYSON. *refl.* We ought not to g. ourselves airs JOWETT.

XI. 1. To concede, yield 1548. 2. *intr.* To yield, give way. a. To yield to pressure or strain 1577. b. Of a joint, the nerves, etc.: To lose tension, become relaxed, fail 1892. c. (Of persons): To accommodate one's attitude *to*; (of a dress) to adjust itself *to*. Also, to allow free play *to*. Also, to give ground. 1823. d. To be affected by atmospheric influences; (*a*) of colours, to fade 1546; (*b*) to deliquesce, effloresce, soften, etc. from damp 1677; (*c*) to become damp, exude moisture 1590; (*d*) of timber, to shrink from dryness 1627. e. Of frosty weather: To become mild, to thaw 1678.

1. They never gave their enemies one daye to repose HALL. She said she would never g. the *pas* to a tradesman's daughter THACKERAY. 2. a. My boots had begun to g. 1872. b. Rendered..useless by his knee giving 1892. c. Dare we to this fancy g. TENNYSON. d. *fig.* Flinty mankinde: whose eyes do neuer giue But thorow Lust and Laughter SHAKS.

XII. *intr.* †1. Of the sun: To direct its rays 1616. 2. To look, open, lead. (A Gallicism.) 1840.

2. No window giving on to the Street 1885.

XIII. Phrases.

1. G. birth to. a. To bear; bring forth. b. *fig.* To produce; result in. 2. G. ground. a. To retire before a superior force. b. *fig.* To yield; to relax effort. 3. G. it. a. With *dat.* or *to*: To make an attack. Also colloq., *to g. it hot.* †b. = *to g. tongue* (see TONGUE). 4. G. place (const. *to*). †a. To give ground. b. To yield precedence. †c. To defer (to advice). d. To be succeeded or superseded (by another person or thing). 5. G. rise to. To be the origin of; to produce. 6. G. way. a. Of fighting men: = *g. ground*. Also *transf.* and *fig.* Const. *to*. †b. To make way. c. To be superseded by. Const. *to*. †d. To allow free scope or liberty of action *to*. e. Of things: To yield, break down, fail. f. Of persons: To make concessions; to defer to the will of another. Const. *to*. g. To abandon oneself *to*. h. To allow one's self-control or fortitude to be broken down. i. Of stocks and shares: To fall in price. j. *Naut.* The order to renew rowing, or to row harder.

XIV. Used *intr.* with preps. in specialized senses.

†1. G. against —. To impinge against; to attack, run counter to. †2. G. into —. [After F. *donner dans.*] To enter into, fall in with; to engage deeply in; to fall into. Now repl. by *g. in to*.

XV. Idiomatically combined with adverbs.

1. G. about. †a. *trans.* To encompass (L. *circumdare*). b. To distribute; to spread (a rumour). 2. G. again. a. *trans.* To g. back or in return. b. *intr.* To soften; to yield. *lit.* and *fig.* 3. G. away. a. *trans.* To alienate from oneself by gift; to dispose of gratuitously. b. To hand (a bride) to the bridegroom at a marriage. †c. To sacrifice (another's interests or rights). d. *slang.* To betray, expose to detection or ridicule; to let slip (a secret). e. To distribute. f. = *g. way* (now *U.S.*). 4. G. back. a. *trans.* To restore; to surrender again; to reciprocate; to reflect, to echo, etc. †b. *intr.* To retreat. †c. To yield to pressure. 5. G. forth. †a. *trans.* To hold out. b. To emit. c. To spread abroad; to report, rumour. 6. G. in. a. *intr.* To yield; to acknowledge oneself beaten. b. To yield *to* (a habit, opinion, etc.). [Prob. due to a false analysis of *give into* (see XIV. 2).] †c. To intervene. Also, to rush into conflict. d. *trans.* To hand in, deliver to the proper person. *To g. in one's adhesion to*: to notify formally one's acceptance of. e. To bestow in addition. 7. G. off. †a. *trans.* To relinquish; to leave off. †b. *intr.* To cease; to withdraw. c. *trans.* To emit. d. To send off as a branch. †8. G. on. *intr.* To make an assault. 9. G. out. a. *trans.* To utter, publish; to report, proclaim. b. To announce (a hymn) to be sung; to read out for the congregation to sing. c. To emit. †Also, to put forth, utter (prayers). d. To issue; to distribute. e. *intr.* Of persons: To desist (now, to desist through exhaustion of strength or patience). Of a limb, a machine, etc.: To break down, fail. Of a supply: To fail. 10. G. over. a. *trans.* To leave off, finish; to give up. b. *absol.* or *intr.* To cease; desist. †c. *trans.* To abandon, desert. d. To devote, resign, surrender, hand over. e. To pronounce incurable so far as concerns the speaker. f. To abandon the hope of seeing, finding, overtaking, etc. Also, *To g. over for* (*dead, lost*): see FOR. 11. G. up. a. *trans.* To resign, surrender; to hand over. †Also *ellipt.*, to yield (precedence) to. b. To forsake, relinquish, desist from, relinquish the prospect of; to cease to have to do with (a person); to sacrifice (one's life). c. *intr.* To leave off; to cease from effort; to stop. Also, to succumb. d. *trans.* To devote entirely *to*; to abandon, addict *to*. †e. To give in (an account, etc.); to present (a petition, etc.). f. To emit; to utter (a cry). *Obs.* exc. in *To g. up the ghost.* g. To divulge. h. (*a*) To pronounce incurable, insoluble as far as concerns the speaker. (*b*) To renounce the hope of seeing. *To g. up for* (*lost*): see FOR.

Give and take, *sb.* 1769. [See GIVE *v.*] 1. *Sporting.* a. In *give and take plate*, a prize for a race in which horses above a standard height carry more, and those under it less, than the standard weight. b. Implying the alternation of favourable and unfavourable conditions 1769. 2. Compromise, exchange of equivalents. Also *attrib.* 1816. 3. Exchange of talk, esp. of repartee, jest, or raillery 1870.

Give, obs. f. GYVE.

Given (giv'n), *ppl. a.* ME. [pa. pple. of GIVE *v.*] 1. Bestowed as a gift. 2. Used predicatively: Inclined, addicted, prone. Const. *to*. ME. 3. Granted as a basis of calculation, reasoning, etc.; definitely stated, fixed, specified 1570.

1. G. goods never prosper 1892. Phr. *Given name*: the name given at baptism, the Christian name. ?Chiefly *Sc.* and *U.S.* 2. I'm not g. that way myself 1885.

Giver (gi·vəɹ). ME. [f. GIVE *v.* + -ER [1].] One who gives. Often specialized as *alms-*, *law-*, etc. *g.*

Giving (gi·viŋ), *vbl. sb.* ME. [f. GIVE *v.* and -ING [1].] The action of GIVE *v.* 1. In trans. senses. Occas. *pl.* 2. In intr. senses 1710. 3. With adverbs, as *giving in, over, out*, etc. Also *giving way.* 1530. †4. *concr.* That which is given; a gift –1667.

1. His gains were sure; his givings rare POPE. 2. Upon the first G. of the Weather ADDISON. 4. MILT. *P.L.* VI. 730.

Gizzard (gi·zăɹd). [ME. *giser*, a. OF. *giser*, etc., also *guiser* (mod. *gésier*) gizzard, explained as :—pop. L. **gicerium* = L. *gigeria* neut. pl., cooked entrails of a fowl. The *d* is added.] 1. The second or muscular stomach of birds, in which the food is ground, after being mixed with gastric juice in the proventriculus or first stomach. b. The stomach of the red Irish trout 1776. c. *Entom.* The proventriculus of certain insects 1826. d. *Zool.* The thickened muscular stomach of certain molluscs 1841. 2. Attributed joc. to persons 1668. ¶3. Used to translate L. *jecur*, liver. CHAUCER. 4. *attrib.*, as *g.-trout*; etc. 1765.

2. Phr. *To fret one's g.*: to worry oneself. *To stick in one's g.*: to remain as something unpleasant or distasteful. Don't let that stick in your g. SWIFT.

‖**Glabella** (glăbe·lă), **glabellum** (glăbe·lŏm). 1823. [mod.L.; orig., fem. and neut. of L. *glabellus* adj., dim. of *glaber*. Cf. F. *glabelle.*] 1. *Anat.* The space between the eyebrows and immediately above a line from one to the other. 2. 'The smooth median portion of the cephalic shield of a Trilobite' (*Syd. Soc. Lex.*) 1849. Hence **Glabe·llar** *a.* pertaining to the g. **Glabello-**, comb. f. GLABELLA, 'pertaining to the g. and —'.

Glabrate (glē·brĕt), *ppl. a.* 1857. [ad. L. *glabratus*, *glabrare* to make bald or smooth, f. *glaber* GLABROUS.] *Bot.* and *Zool.* Smooth; bald; glabrous; having no hair or other appendages.

Glabreity (gleⁱbrī·ĭti). 1885. [ad. F. *glabréité.*] Smoothness; baldness. var. †**Gla·brity.** (Dicts.)

Glabrescent (gleⁱbre·sĕnt), *a.* 1857. [ad. L. *glabrescentem*, *glabrescere* to grow smooth.] *Bot.* Used of a surface, hairy when young, but smooth when mature.

Glabrous (glē·brəs), *a.* 1640. [f. L. *glaber* (see GLAD) + -OUS.] Free from hair, down, or the like; smooth. Now only as a scientific term.

‖**Glacé** (glase), *a.* 1850. [Fr., pa. pple. of *glacer*, f. *glace* ice.] 1. Having a smooth surface with a high polish. Also *absol.* = *g. silk*, and *attrib.* as *g. finish.* 2. Of fruits: Covered with icing 1882.

†**Gla·ciable.** [f. L. *glaciare* + -BLE.] That may be frozen. SIR T. BROWNE.

Glacial (glē·ʃiăl, -ʃăl), *a.* 1656. [a. F., ad. L. *glacialis*, f. *glacies* ice.] 1. Full of, or having the nature of, ice; icy. *rare.* b. Consisting of ice 1794. 2. Glass-like; crystallized. (*Obs.* exc. as in quots.) 1681. 3. *Geol.* Characterized by the presence of ice 1846. b. Produced by glacier-ice, or by its action; pertaining to glaciers or ice-sheets 1858.

1. *fig.* His manner..g. and sepulchral MOTLEY. b. Enormous g. masses 1794. 2. *G. acetic acid*, pure acetic acid in crystals; *g. phosphoric acid*, metaphosphoric acid (HPO_3); *g. sulphuric acid*, †*g. oil of vitriol*, pure sulphuric acid in crystals. 3. *G. epoch, era, period* (called also in U.S. *drift epoch, ice-age*, etc.), a geological period during which the northern hemisphere was largely covered by an ice-sheet. *G. sea*: the sea of the g. epoch. b. G. denudation HUXLEY.

Hence **Gla·cialism**, the theory of the action of ice upon the earth's surface. **Gla·cialist**, a student of g. phenomena; one who explains certain geological phenomena as due to g. action. **Gla·cially** *adv.* by means of g. action; icily (*lit.* and *fig.*).

Glaciate (glē·ʃiˌeⁱt), *v.* 1623. [f. L. *glaciat-*, *glaciare*, f. *glacies* ice.] 1. To freeze. *trans.* and †*intr.* 2. *Geol.* In pass. pple. *glaciated.* a. Rubbed or polished by glacial action 1865. b. Furnished with glaciers 1880. 3. *techn.* 'To give an ice-like or frosted appearance to' 1887. Hence **Glacia·tion**, †freezing; †a result of this; *Geol.* the condition of being covered by an ice-sheet or by glaciers; glacial action or its result.

Glacier (glæ·siəɹ, glē·ʃiəɹ). 1744. [a. F. *glacier* (earlier *glacière*), f. *glace*; a Savoyard wd. Cf. GLETSCHER.] An immense mass or river of ice in a high mountain valley, formed by the descent and consolidation of the snow that falls on the higher ground. Also *attrib.*, as *g.-drift, -moraine, -water*, etc.

Comb.: **g.-mill** = MOULIN; **-mud**, an unstratified mass of coarse gritty mud, containing pebbles, boulder, and stony particles, found resting on the surface of ice-worn rocks; **-silt** = *glacier-mud*; **-snow**, the snow at the upper end of a g., not yet hardened into ice by pressure; **-table**, a flat mass of rock, raised high upon a column of ice.

Hence **Gla·ciered** *ppl. a.* covered with glaciers. **Gla·cierist**, one who studies glaciers. WHEWELL.

†**Gla·cious**, *a.* [ad. F. *glacieux* (obs.).] Resembling ice. SIR T. BROWNE.

Glacis (glē·sis, glasi). 1672. [a. F. *glacis*, orig. 'a place made slippery by frozen rain'.] 1. A gently sloping bank. 2. *Fortif.* 'The parapet of the covered way extended in a long slope to meet the natural surface of the ground, so that every part of it shall be swept by the fire of the ramparts' (Voyle) 1688.

†**Glad**, *sb.* OE. [f. the adj.] Gladness, joy –1608.

Glad (glæd), *a.* [OE. *glæd*. The orig. sense of the word is found in OHG. *glat* smooth. The OTeut. type **glađo-* is cogn. w. L. *glaber* smooth.] †1. Bright, shining, beautiful –1500. 2. †Cheerful in disposition; joyful, happy (*arch.*) OE. 3. = FAIN *a.*; pleased. Now only *predicative*. OE. 4. Of feelings, looks, etc.: Filled with, marked by, or expressive of joy or delight OE. †b. Acceptable –1690. 5. Full of brightness or beauty; suggesting feelings of delight 1667. 6. quasi-*adv.* = GLADLY *adv.* (*poet.*) ME.

2. Be mirry and glaid, honest and vertewous DUNBAR. Often, g. no more, We wear a face of joy, because We have been g. of yore WORDSW. 3. A wise son maketh a g. father *Prov.* x. 1. Phr. *G. of*: †(*a*) made happy, pleased with (a thing possessed); (*b*) = g. to have or get; (*c*) joyful on account of (an event, etc.). Also const. *at, for,* †*in,* †*with*. When his heart is g. Of the full harvest TENNYSON. I am g. I came 1855. I was g. to see the mangrove-belt 1897. 4. So yong so lusty with hire eyen glade CHAUCER. *Luke* viii. 1. c. *G. eye*: see EYE *sb.*[1] I. 4. *G. rags* (U.S. slang), (one's) best or ceremonial clothes; esp. evening dress 1903. 5. G. Eevning and g. Morn crownd the fourth day MILT.

Glad (glæd), *v.* Pa. t. and pple. **gladded.** [OE. *gladian* :—OTeut. **glađōjan*, f. **glađo* GLAD. The intr. sense 'to be glad' is the orig. one.] †1. *intr.* To become or to be glad –1622. 2. *trans.* To make glad OE. Also *transf.* and *refl.* (now *arch.*).

2. They were greatly gladded thereat BUNYAN. *transf.* Now bright Arcturus glads the teeming grain POPE.

Gladden (glæ·d'n), *v.* ME. [f. GLAD *a.*; see -EN [5].] 1. *intr.* To be glad; to rejoice; ? *Obs.* 2. *trans.* To make glad, joyous, or bright 1558.

1. As we climb Hills and g., as we climb BLOOMFIELD. 2. [An orchard] gladdened..by flushes of almond and double peach blossom RUSKIN.

†**Gladder.** ME. [f. GLAD *v.* + -ER [1].] 1. One who rejoices. ME. only. 2. One who makes glad –1700.

Gladdon (glæ·d'n). Now chiefly *dial.* OE. [? a. pop. L. **gladina*, altered f. L. *gladiolus* 'sword-lily', dim. of *gladius*.] Pop. name of the iris (*Iris Pseudacorus* and *Iris fœtidissima*). *Corn-g.* = CORN-FLAG. Also *attrib.*

†**Glade**, *sb.*[1] ME. [Perh. Scandinavian.] *To go to g.*: to set, sink to rest (said of the sun) –1788.

Glade (glēd), *sb.*[2] 1529. [? conn. w. GLAD *a.* (sense 1).] 1. A clear open space or passage in a wood or forest. 2. *U.S.* a. An everglade 1644. b. An opening in the ice of rivers or lakes, or a place left unfrozen. (*Local, U.S.*) 1698. †3. A clear or bright space in the sky; a flash –1741.

Comb.: **g.-net**, a net hung across an opening in a wood, for the purpose of snaring birds.

Gladen(e, var. of GLADDON.

Gladful (glæ·dful), *a.* ME. [f. GLAD *sb.* + -FUL.] Full of gladness or joy. Now only *arch.* Hence **Gla·dful-ly** *adv.*, **-ness.**

Gladiate (glē·diět), *a.* 1793. [f. L. *gladius* + -ATE [2].] *Bot.* Sword-shaped, as the leaves of an iris.

Gladiator (glæ·diēʹtəɹ). 1541. [a. L., f. *gladius*.] 1. *Roman Hist.* One who fought with a sword or other weapon at public shows. Also *fig.* †2. A professional swordsman or fencer –1769.

1. *fig.* The gladiators in the lists of power feel..the presence of worth EMERSON. Hence **Gla:diato·rial, Gladiato·rian** *adjs.* of or pertaining to gladiators; also *fig.* **Gla·diatorism**, the practice of fighting after the fashion of gladiators; also *fig.* **Gla·diatorship**, the occupation or skill of a g. So †**Gla·diature**, gladiatorship.

†**Gla·diatory.** 1602. [ad. L. *gladiatorius*.]
A. *adj.* Gladiatorial –1730.
B. *sb.* Gladiatorial art or practice. Also *fig.* 1653.

Gladiole (glæ·diōul). ME. [ad. L. *gladiolus*; see next.] = next.

‖**Gladiolus** (glædəɪ·ŏləs, glædiōu·ləs). *Pl.* **-i, -uses.** OE. [L., dim. of *gladius*. Cf. F. *glaïeul*.] 1. †a. The corn-flag or GLADDON. b. An iridaceous plant having sword-shaped leaves and spikes of brilliant flowers. 2. *Anat.* 'The second piece or body of the sternum' (*Syd. Soc. Lex.*) 1885.

‖**Gladius** (glē·diŏs). 1520. [L.] 1. A sword (*nonce-use*) 1873. 2. The sword-fish. 3. *Anat.* 'The horny endoskeleton or pen of cuttle-fishes' (*Syd. Soc. Lex.*) 1872.

Gladless (glæ·dlės), *a. rare.* 1590. [f. GLAD *sb.* + -LESS.] Devoid of gladness or joy.

Gladly (glæ·dli), *a. Obs.* exc. *arch.* OE. [f. as prec. + -LY [1].] †a. Bright, beautiful, precious. OE. only. b. Glad, joyous.

Gladly (glæ·dli), *adv.* Compared **gla·dlier, gla·dliest**; also (now usually) with *more, most*. OE. [f. GLAD *a.* + -LY [2].] 1. With gladness or joy. Also, willingly, with alacrity. †2. Aptly, naturally –1483.

1. Will you doe this g. and willingly *Bk. Com. Prayer.* So **Gla·dness**, joy, rejoicing; †also, alacrity (in action). †**Gla·dship**, gladness.

Gladsome (glæ·dsŏm), *a.* ME. [f. GLAD *sb.* + -SOME.] 1. Productive of gladness; cheering, pleasant. 2. Expressive of, or characterized by, gladness. Also *transf.* of nature, etc. ME. 3. Having a glad or joyous nature or mood; filled with gladness ME.

1. G. tidings SPEED. 2. G. countenances 1832. The g. sunshine 1868. 3. Like g. birds in May WORDSW. Hence **Gla·dsome-ly** *adv.*, **-ness.**

Gladstone (glæ·dstən). 1864. [f. W. E. *Gladstone* (1808–98).] a. *Gladstone* (*claret*): a jocular name for the light French wines which Gladstone sought to popularize by a reduction of the Customs duty in 1860. b. *G.* (*bag*): a light kind of travelling-bag 1882. c. 'A roomy four-wheeled pleasure carriage with two inside seats, calash top, and seats for driver and footman' (Webster) 1864.

Gladstonian (glædstōu·niăn). 1847. [f. prec. + -IAN.]

A. *adj.* Belonging to or characteristic of W. E. Gladstone; *spec.* (since 1886) the designation of the party which supported Gladstone's proposals for establishing Home Rule in Ireland 1861.

B. *sb.* 1. A supporter of Gladstone; a member of the Gladstonian party 1847. 2. = GLADSTONE a. 1864.

Gladwin(e, -wyn, vars. of GLADDON.

Gla·dy, *a. rare.* 1837. [f. GLADE *sb.*[2] + -Y [1].] Glade-like; full of glades.

Glair (glēᵊɹ), *sb.*[1] ME. [a. F. *glaire*, f. L. *clara*, fem. of *clarus* bright, clear.] 1. The white of an egg. Also a technical term for preparations made from the whites of eggs. 2. *transf.* Anything viscid or slimy 1529. Hence **Glai·reous** *a.* glairy. **Glairi·genous** *a.* producing slime, mucus, or glairin.

†**Glair**, *sb.*[2] [a. OF. *glaire* :—L. *glarea*.] Gravel. CAXTON.

Glair (glēᵊɹ), *v.* 1563. [f. GLAIR *sb.*[1]] *trans.* To smear with glair; †also *gen.* to daub.

Glairin (glēᵊ·rin). Also **-ine.** 1838. [f. GLAIR *sb.*[1] + -IN.] A glairy organic substance found in many mineral waters after exposure to the air.

Glairy (glēᵊ·ri), *a.* 1662. [f. GLAIR *sb.*[1] + -Y [1].] Of the nature of glair; viscid, slimy. Chiefly *Path.* Hence **Glai·riness**, viscidity.

Glaive (glēⁱv), *sb.* ME. [a. OF. *glaive, gleive* lance (mod.F. *glaive* poet. = sword).] †1. A lance or spear –1592. †b. A lance set up as winning-post in a race, and given as a prize to the winner; hence, a prize –1555. †2. A weapon consisting of a blade fastened to a long handle; a soldier armed with a glaive –1678. 3. A sword; *esp.* a broadsword. *arch.* and *poet.* –1470.

3. The g. and brown-bill, the good old weapons of his country SCOTT.

Glamour (glæ·məɹ), *sb.* Also †**glamer.** 1720. [Corrupt f. GRAMMAR. Orig. *Sc.*; introduced by Scott.] 1. Magic, enchantment, spell. 2. A magical or fictitious beauty attaching to any person or object; a delusive or alluring charm 1840. 3. *attrib.*, as *g.-gift, -might* 1805.

1. When devils, wizards or jugglers deceive the sight, they are said to cast g. o'er the eyes of the spectator RAMSAY. 2. That scene of g. HOOD. Hence **Gla·morous** *a.* full of g. **Gla·morously** *adv.* **Gla·mour** *v.* to affect with g. var. **Gla·moury, -ie.**

Glance (glɑns), *sb.*[1] 1503. [f. GLANCE *v.*] 1. A swift oblique movement or impact. Also *fig.* ? *Obs.* 1570. †2. *fig.* a. A satirical hit, a jest *at* (or *upon*) something 1602. b. Allusion, reference 1665. 3. A sudden movement producing a flash or gleam; also, the flash or gleam 1503. 4. A brief or hurried look 1591.

1. The stroke (in *Cricket*)..best described as the leg g. 1892. 2. a. This was but the glaunce of Diogenes, who made more accompt of his scoffe then his state FULBECKE. 3. The ruby g. DUNBAR. Fish..sporting with quick g. MILT. 4. G. or toy Of amorous intent MILT.

Comb.: **g.-pitch**, a substance of the nature of petroleum in a bituminous form; **-wood**, a hard wood grown in Cuba, and used for carpenters' rules, etc.

Glance (glɑns), *sb.*[2] 1828. [ad. Ger. *glanz* lustre, also glance-ore.] A variety of ore having a lustre which indicates its metallic nature. *Obs.* exc. in *antimony-, bismuth-, copper-, iron-, lead-, silver-g.*, q. v.

Comb. **g.-coal**, a variety of anthracite.

Glance (glɑns), *v.*[1] 1450. [? a nasalized form of OF. *glaichier* to slip, slide.] 1. *intr.* To strike and glide off an object. †2. To move rapidly, esp. in an oblique or transverse direction; to dart, shoot; to spring *aside* –1786. 3. With reference to discourse: To pass quickly *over*, glide *from, off* 1570. 4. To cause a flash of light by rapid movement. Of light: To dart, flash, gleam. 1568. 5. Of the eye: To move quickly, to cast a momentary look, to flash 1583. 6. *trans.* a. To catch a glimpse of 1635. b. To convey with a glance (of the eye) 1717. †7. To touch obliquely; to graze; also *fig.* –1651. 8. a. To direct obliquely (*lit.* and *fig.*) 1656. b. To emit with a flash or gleam 1746.

1. The blow only glanced on the bone, and scarce drew blood SCOTT. 2. The warre..glanced into Asia BOLTON. 3. Verses..wherein he glanced at a certain reverend doctor SWIFT. 4. In thee [Sion] fresh brooks and soft streams g. MILT. 5. Phr. *To g. one's eye, look*: †(*a*) to turn aside one's gaze; (*b*) to give a quick look; also, to look quickly *at* or *upon*. 7. In company I often glanced it *Com. Err.* v. i. 66. 8. a. To g. an Innuendo SWIFT, a censure at the General CARLYLE. b. The..pewter and earthenware..glanced back the flame of the lamp merrily SCOTT. Hence **Gla·ncer** (*nonce-wd.*). **Gla·ncingly** *adv.* in a glancing fashion.

Glance, *v.*[2] *U.S.* 1894. [? ad. Du. *glanzen*, f. *glans* lustre.] To planish (metals).

Gland [1] (glænd). 1631. [ad. L. *glandem*, *glans* acorn.] 1. An acorn. *Obs.* exc. (occas.) *Bot.* = GLANS 2. 2. = GLANS 1. 1854.

Gland [2] (glænd). 1692. [ad. F. *glande*, altered f. OF. *glandre* (see GLANDER).] 1. *Phys.* An organ, composed of nucleated cells, and either simple or complex in structure, which separates from the blood certain constituents for use in the body, or for ejection from it.

Certain organs, such as the spleen, thymus, thyroid, and adrenals, which perform the function of glands but have no excretory duct, are known as DUCTLESS (also *aporic*) glands.

2. *Bot.* A secreting cell or group of cells on the surface of a plant-structure 1785. 3. *attrib.*, as *g.-cell, -cyst*, etc. 1849. Hence **Gla·ndless** *a.*

Gland [3] (glænd). 1825. [Cf. Sc. *Glaun(d* 'a clamp of iron or wood'.] *Mech.* 1. A sleeve employed to press a packing tight on a piston-rod (cf. FOLLOWER) 1839. 2. A cross-piece or clutch made fast to a shaft, and communicating motion to a machine by engaging with part of the gearing 1825. 3. *Founding.* a. A hooked bar for clamping together the parts of a moulder's flask. b. A clip-plate. 1875.

Glander (glæ·ndəɹ). 1483. [a. OF. *glandre*, **glandle* GLAND [2], ad. L. *glandula* GLANDULE.] †1. A glandular swelling about the neck –1523. 2. *pl.* (const. as *sing.*) (*The*) *glanders*: a contagious disease in horses, marked by swellings beneath the jaw and discharge of mucous matter from the nostrils 1523. b. The same disease given to man 1871. Hence **Gla·ndered** *ppl. a.* affected with glanders. **Gla·nderous** *a.* affected with, or of the nature of, glanders.

Glandiferous (glændi·fĕrəs), *a.* 1647. [f. L. *glandifer* acorn-bearing + -OUS.] Bearing acorns or similar fruit.

Glandiform (glæ·ndifǭɹm), *a.* 1822. [f. L. *glandi-, glans* + -FORM.] Acorn-shaped; also, resembling a gland.

Glandular (glæ·ndiŭlăɪ), *a.* 1740. [ad. F. *glandulaire*; see GLANDULE and -AR.] Of or pertaining to a gland; of the nature of a gland; containing, bearing, or consisting of, a gland or glands.

Glandulation (glændiŭlēⁱ·ʃən). 1760. [f. as prec. + -ATION.] 'The mode of occurrence or presence of glands in plants' (*Syd. Soc. Lex.*) 1760.

Glandule (glæ·ndiŭl). Chiefly *pl.* ME. [a. F., ad. L. *glandula*, dim. of *gland-*, *glans* acorn; cf. GLAND [1].] †1. A gland -1748. **b.** A small gland 1751. †2. *pl.* A swelling of the glands in the throat or neck (so L. *glandulæ*). *rare.* -1616. 3. A morbid swelling or growth in the body 1656. So **Glanduli·ferous** *a.* bearing glands or glandules. **Gla·nduliform** *a.* having the appearance of a gland or g.

Glandulous (glæ·ndiŭləs), *a.* ? *Obs.* ME. [ad. F. *glanduleux*, ad. L. *glandulosus*, f. *glandula.*] Of or pertaining to a gland or glandule; having the nature of a gland; containing, or consisting of, glands. So **Gla·ndulose** *a.* †**Glandulo·sity** (*rare*), a gland-like formation.

‖**Glans** (glænz). 1650. [L. *glans* acorn.] 1. *Anat.* The *glans penis.* 2. *Bot.* A name for nuts enclosed or surrounded by a cupule, as the acorn, etc. 1704.

Glare (glēⁱɹ), *sb.*[1] ME. [f. GLARE *v.*] 1. Dazzling brilliance (of a light, etc.); a strong fierce light. Also *absol.* dazzling or oppressive sunshine, esp. when reflected and unrelieved. **b.** The glistening of some surface 1658. 2. *fig.* 1706. 3. A fierce or piercing look 1667.

1. The naked negro, panting at the line..Basks in the g. GOLDSM. 2. The pomp and g. of rhetoric 1856. 3. About them round A Lion now he [Satan] stalkes with fierie g. MILT.

Glare (glēⁱɹ), *sb.*[2] 1567. [?] †Frost, icy condition; also *U.S.* a sheet of ice.

Glare (glēⁱɹ), *a.* *U.S.* Also **glair.** 1856. [? prec. used attrib.] Smooth and translucent, glassy. Chiefly of ice.

Glare (glēⁱɹ), *v.* [ME. *glaren* = MDu., MLG. *glaren* to gleam, glare. Prob. conn. w. GLASS.] 1. *intr.* To shine with a brilliant or dazzling light. Also of the light. Also *fig.* 2. To look fixedly and fiercely (*at, on, upon*) 1609. Also *fig.* 3. *trans.* To give out or reflect with a glare 1667.

1. Hyt is not al golde that glareth CHAUCER. The morning light glared strangely TYNDALL. *fig.* She glares in Balls, front Boxes, and the Ring POPE. 2. And each upon his rival glared SCOTT. 3. Every eye Glar'd lightning MILT.

Glareous (glēⁱ·rĭəs), *a.*[1] ME. [ad. L. *glareosus*, f. *glarea* gravel.] †a. Of soil: Gravelly -1675. **b.** *Bot.* Growing in gravel 1880. var. **Gla·reose.**

Glareous, *a.*[2]: cf. GLAIRY.

Gla·ring (glēⁱ·riŋ), *vbl. sb.* ME. [see -ING [2].] 1. Of the eyes: Staring fiercely and wildly. 2. That gives out or reflects a dazzling light; excessively bright 1515. 3. Obtrusively conspicuous. Now chiefly with sbs. like *fault, falsehood*, etc. 1706.

3. This g. absurdity 1812. Hence **Gla·ring-ly** *adv.*, **-ness.**

Glary (glēⁱ·ri), *a.* 1632. [f. GLARE *sb.*[1] + -Y [1].] Full of glare; dazzling, glaring. Hence **Gla·riness.**

Glass (glɑs), *sb.* [OE. *glæs*:—OTeut. **glăsom.*]

I. As a substance. 1. A substance, in its ordinary forms transparent, lustrous, hard, and brittle, produced by fusing sand (silica) with soda or potash (or both), usually with the addition of lime, alumina, or lead oxide. 2. Applied to similar substances 1579. 3. The substance as made into things. Hence as collect. sing = things made of glass; e.g. vessels of glass, window-panes, etc. 1625. **b.** *esp.* as used for greenhouses, frames, etc. Hence, greenhouses, etc., collectively. 1838.

1. CROWN-, FLINT-, PLATE-, WATER-G.; also *bottle-, crystal-, cut-g.*, etc. (see the different words). 2. *G. of Antimony*, a vitreous oxy-sulphide fused. *G. of Borax*, a vitreous transparent substance obtained by exposing to heat the crystals of sodium biborate. *G. of lead*, a g. made with the addition of a large quantity of lead, and used in making counterfeit gems. *G. of phosphorus*, a transparent substance consisting of phosphoric acid, with phosphate, and a little sulphate of lime. 3. The g. blew in TENNYSON. **b.** Fruit Culture under g. (*title*) 1873.

II. Something made of glass. 1. A glass vessel or receptacle. (Now usu. *spec.* as in 2.) Also, its contents. ME. 2. *spec.* A drinking-vessel made of glass; hence, its contents, and *fig.* drink ME. 3. A SAND-GLASS for measuring time; *esp.* an HOUR-GLASS, and *Naut.* the half-hour glass, the half-minute and quarter-minute glasses 1557. **b.** The time taken by the sand of these to run out. *Naut.* Usually said of the half-hour glass; hence, a glass = half an hour. 1599. **c.** *fig.* 1638. 4. A pane of glass, esp. the window of a coach; a glazed frame or case (e.g. for protecting plants) ME. 5. A glass mirror. Also *transf.* and *fig.* ME. **b.** A magic mirror, a crystal, etc. 1566. 6. A piece of glass shaped for a purpose, a lens, a watch-glass, a burning-glass 1545. 7. An optical instrument used as an aid to sight; a telescope (more explicitly SPY-, FIELD-, OPERA-GLASS) 1613; a microscope or *magnifying-g.* 1646; an EYE-GLASS; also in *pl.* spectacles 1660. †8. *transf.* The eye-ball, the eye (*poet.*) -1621. 9. A WEATHER-GLASS, a barometer 1688.

2. A deepe g. of Reinish wine SHAKS. 3. The g. that bids man mark the fleeting hour COWPER. **b.** Our Ship, which but three glasses since, we gaue out split Is tyte SHAKS. 4. Bang went the door, up went the g. T. HOOK. 5. A Fop who admires his Person in a G. ADDISON. *poet.* The clear Sun on his wide watrie G. Gaz'd hot MILT. **b.** *Macb.* IV. i. 119. 7. My eyes were so dim that no glasses would help me WESLEY. 8. Euen in the glasses of thine eyes I see thy greeued heart. SHAKS.

†III. [?another word.] = GLOSS *sb.*[2] 1. -1622.

attrib. and *Comb.* 1. *simple attrib.* **a.** Made of glass; as a *g. vessel, g.-bead factory*, etc. **b.** Glazed, having pieces of glass set in a frame; as G.-CASE, -COACH, -HOUSE, etc.

2. Special comb.: **g.-artist**, one who designs coloured or stained g. windows; **-bell** = BELL-GLASS; **-blower**, one who blows and fashions g.; **-crab**, the larva of a palinuroid or scyllaroid shrimp; **-culture**, culture of fruit, etc. under g.; **-dust**, powdered g.; **-enamel**, an opaque g., which owes its milkiness to the addition of binoxide of tin; **-faced** *a.*, reflecting, like a mirror, the looks of another; **-furnace**; **-gall**, a whitish salt scum cast up from g. in a state of fusion; **-gazing** *a.*, given to contemplating oneself in a mirror; **-glazed** *a.*, (of pottery) having a glaze of substantial thickness; **-grenade**, one made with a case of g.; **-height-gauge**, an instrument for measuring the height of watch-glasses; **-metal**, g. in a state of fusion; **-mosaic**, a mosaic formed of small squares of coloured g.; **-mould**, a metallic shaping-box in which g. is pressed or blown to form; **-oven**, a heated chamber for cooling gradually new-made articles of g.; **-paper**, paper covered with finely powdered g. for polishing bone, etc.; so **-paper** *v.*; **-pock**, **-pox**, an eruptive disease, *Varicella coniformis*; **-pot**, a pot or crucible used for fusing the materials of g. in a g.-furnace; **-press**, a device to apply pressure to g. in a mould while plastic; **-rope (sponge)**, the genus HYALONEMA; **-sand**, sand used in making g.; **-shell**, a name of certain molluscs, species of *Hyalea*, whose shells look like the thinnest g.; **-shrimp**, a larval form of stomatopodous crustaceans; **-slag**, refuse of g.-manufacture; **-snail**, one of the genus *Vitrina*, having a translucent shell; **-snake**, (*a*) a lizard, *Ophiosaurus ventralis*, with a very brittle tail; (*b*) a lizard of the genus *Pseudopus*; **-sponge** = *glass-ropesponge*; **-tinner**, the workman who applies tin-foil to g.; **-ware**, articles made of g.; **-wool**, g. spun out to a very fine fibre; used in the filtration of acids; **-worm**, the glow-worm.

Glass (glɑs), *v.* 1540. [f. GLASS *sb.*; cf. GLAZE *v.*[1]] 1. *trans.* = GLAZE *v.*[1] Now *rare.* 2. To protect by a covering of glass, to enclose in glass 1588. †3. = GLAZE *v.*[1] 2. -1661. 4. To set (an object, oneself) before a mirror; also to see as in a mirror 1586; (of a mirror), to reflect 1628. 5. *techn.* To dress (leather) with a glassing-machine 1885.

4. Thou glorious mirror, where the Almighty's form Glasses itself in tempests BYRON. Never more Shall the lake g. her, flying over it M. ARNOLD.

Gla·ss-cloth. 1851. 1. A linen cloth used for drying glass-ware, etc. 2. A woven fabric made of fine-spun glass thread. (Only as two wds.) 1875. 3. Cloth covered with powdered glass, used like sand-paper 1873.

†**Glass-coach.** 1667. Original name of a coach with glass windows; esp. applied to a 'private' coach let out for hire, as dist. from those on public stands.

Gla·ss-cu·tter. 1703. 1. One whose occupation is to cut glass (e.g. to sizes), or to ornament glass-ware by grinding. 2. A glazier's diamond 1881.

Gla·ssen, gla·zen, *a.* Now *dial.* or *arch.* [OE. *glæsen*, f. *glæs* GLASS *sb.*[1] + -EN.] 1. Made of glass. Also *fig.* 2. Resembling glass. Of eyes: Glassy, glazed. ME.

2. [The palsied gamester] pursues The Dice with glassen eyes B. JONS.

Glass eye. 1605. †1. An eye-glass; usu. *pl.* -1721. 2. A false eye made of glass 1687. 3. *Farriery.* A species of blindness in horses 1831. 4. **a.** A Jamaican thrush (*Turdus jamaicensis*), so called from its glass-like iris 1847. **b.** *U.S.* The wall-eyed pike (*Stizostedion vitreum*) 1884.

1. Get thee glasse-eyes, and like a scuruy Politician, seeme to see the things thou dost not *Lear* IV. vi. 174.

Glassful (glɑ·sful), *sb.* Pl. **-fuls.** 1663. [f. GLASS *sb.*[1] + -FUL 2.] As much as fills a glass.

†**Gla·ssful,** *a.* *rare.* [f. GLASS *sb.*[1] + -FUL 1.] ? Mirror-like. MARSTON.

Glass-house. ME. 1. The building where glass is made. 2. A building made chiefly of glass, *esp.* a greenhouse 1838.

Glassing (glɑ·siŋ), *vbl. sb.* 1544. The action of GLASS *v.* 1617. **b.** *attrib.* and *Comb.*, as *g. effect*; **g.-jack, -machine,** machines used in dressing leather.

Glassite (glɑ·səit). 1772. [f. the name *Glass* + -ITE.] A member of the religious sect founded by the Rev. John Glass, a minister of the Established Church of Scotland (deposed in 1728). The Glassites are also called *Sandemanians.*

Gla·ss-man. 1597. 1. A dealer in glass-ware. 2. A man engaged in glass-making 1610.

Gla·ss-work. 1611. 1. *pl.* (rarely *sing.*) The works where glass is made 1626. 2. The manufacture of glass and glass-ware. Also, glazing. 3. Articles made of glass; glass as manufactured 1725. Hence **Gla·ss-wo·rker,** one who works in glass.

Glasswort (glɑ·swɒɹt). 1597. A name for plants containing much alkali, and on that account formerly used in glass-making. **a.** A plant of the genus *Salicornia*, esp. *S. herbacea*; called also *jointed glasswort.* **b.** *Salsola Kali;* called also *prickly glasswort.*

Glassy (glɑ·si), *a.* ME. [f. GLASS *sb.*[1] + -Y [1].] 1. Having the nature or properties of glass, vitreous; resembling glass in its properties; appearing as if made of glass. †**b.** *fig.* Brittle and frail as glass -1785. 2. Of the eye: Lacking fire or life, dull ME. †3. Of glass; made of glass -1807.

1. *G.* (now usu. VITREOUS) *humour* (of the eye): so called as resembling melted glass. The clear hyaline, the g. sea MILT. A g. calm 1871. **b.** G. and slippery youth 1637. 2. His eyes have an odd g. stare MACAULAY. 3. The g. globe that Merlin made SPENSER. Hence **Gla·ssily** *adv.* **Gla·ssiness.**

Glastonbury (glɑ·stənbəri). 1691. [A town in Somersetshire, famous for its abbey.] Used *attrib.* in **Glastonbury chair,** a kind of arm-chair, designed after that of 'the Abbot of Glastonbury'; **G. thorn,** a variety of hawthorn.

Glau·ber. 1799. Short for GLAUBER'S SALT(S.

Glauberite (glǭ·-, glau·bərəit). 1809. [f. *Glauber* (see next) + -ITE.] *Min.* Sulphate of calcium and sodium.

Glauber's salt, -s. Also **Glauber salt, -s.** 1736. [f. Johann Rudolf *Glauber*, German chemist (1604–1668).] Sulphate of sodium (first artificially made by Glauber).

Glaucescent (glǭse·sĕnt), *a.* 1829. [f. L. *glaucus* + -ESCENT.] Somewhat glaucous. Hence **Glauce·scence,** g. condition. var. **Glau·cine.**

Glaucic (glǭ·sik), *a.* 1844. [f. mod.L. *Glaucium* a genus of papaveraceous plants + -IC.] *Chem.* In *Glaucic acid*, 'an acid obtained from *Glaucium luteum*, identical with *Fumaric acid*' (*Syd. Soc. Lex.*).

Glaucodot (glǭ·kŏdǫt). Also **-dote, glaukodot.** 1850. [Said to be f. Gr. γλαυκός (see GLAUCOUS) + δοτήρ giver, the mineral being used in making smalt.] *Min.* A sulph-arsenide of cobalt and iron, occurring in tin-white, orthorhombic crystals.

Glaucoma (glǭkōu·mă). 1643. [a. Gr. γλαύκωμα; see GLAUCOUS.] A disease of the eye, characterized by increased tension of the globe and gradual impairment or loss of sight. Formerly used for cataract. Hence **Glaucomatic** *a.* of or pertaining to g. **Glaucomatous, Glaucomatose** *adjs.* glaucomatic; affected with g.

Glauconite (glǭ·kŏnəit). 1836. [f. Gr. γλαυκόν adj. neut. + -ITE.] *Min.* Hydrous silicate of iron, potassium, and other bases, commonly called green earth. Hence **Glauconitic** *a.* containing or resembling g.

Glaucophane (glǭ·kŏfēⁱn). 1849. [f. Gr. γλαυκός + -φανής shining.] *Min.* A mineral closely resembling Amphibole.

Glaucosis (glǭkōu·sis). 1706. [a. Gr., f. γλαυκός; see next and -OSIS.] 'The origination of *Glaucoma.* Also, blindness from *Glaucoma.*'

Glaucous (glǭ·kəs), *a.* 1671. [f. L. *glaucus* bluish-green or grey + -OUS.] Of a dull green colour passing into greyish blue; *spec.* in *Bot.* covered with 'bloom'.

‖**Glaucus** (glǭ·kŏs). 1520. [mod.L.; prob. subst. use of *glaucus* adj. (see prec.).] †1. Some kind of fish -1706. 2. The burgomaster gull (*Larus glaucus*) 1785. 3. A genus of nudibranchiate molluscs, found in the warmer seas, beautifully coloured with blue 1847.

Glaum (glǭm), *v.* *Sc.* Also **glam.** 1715. *intr.* To snatch *at.* Also, to make threatening movements.

†**Glave**, var. of GLAIVE.

†**Gla·ver**, *v.* ME. [?] 1. *trans.* To flatter, deceive with flattery -1594. 2. *intr.* To talk plausibly and deceitfully; to flatter -1681. Hence †**Gla·verer.**

Glaymore, var. of CLAYMORE.

Glaze (glēⁱz), *sb.* 1700. [f. GLAZE *v.*¹ Not in J.] 1. The vitreous composition used for glazing pottery, etc. 1807. 2. *gen.* Any coating used to produce a glazed or lustrous surface; *spec.* in *Cookery.* 1784. 3. A smooth and glossy surface 1791. 4. *U.S.* A coating of ice; also, a stretch of ice 1752. 5. *Painting.* A thin coat of transparent colour laid over another colour 1860. 6. *slang.* A window 1700.

2. *Glaze* is made from clear stock, boiled down until it forms a sort of meat varnish or strong jelly CASSELL.

Comb.: **g.-kiln**, a kiln in which glazed ware is placed for firing; **-wheel**, a wooden wheel used by cutlers for polishing knives, etc.; **-worm**, a glow-worm.

Glaze (glēⁱz), *v.*¹ [ME. *glasen*, f. *glas* GLASS *sb.*¹] 1. *trans.* To furnish or fill in with glass or windows of glass, to cover with glass. 2. To cover (pottery, etc.) with a vitreous substance which is fixed by fusion. Also, to vitrify the surface of. ME. b. *fig.* To gloss *over* 1605. 3. To overlay or cover with a smooth and lustrous coating. Also, to cover (the eyes) with a film. 1593. 4. *Painting.* To cover (a painted surface) with a thin coat of a different transparent colour. Also, to lay (a transparent colour) *over* another. 1622. 5. To make to shine like glass; to polish, render brilliant ME. 6. *intr.* To become glazed 1747.

1. A portrait framed and glazed 1878. 3. Sorrowes eye, glazed with blinding teares SHAKS. Where winter ..doth g. the Scythian seas 1627.

Glaze, *v.*² Now *dial.* [cf. GAZE, GLARE.] *intr.* To stare. *Jul. C.* I. iii. 21.

Glazen, var. of GLASSEN.

Glazer (glēⁱ·zəɹ), *sb.* ME. [f. GLAZE *v.*¹ + -ER¹.] †1. = GLAZIER. -1466. 2. A polisher or burnisher; one who applies glaze to pottery, etc. 1586. 3. An implement for glazing; *esp.* a wheel used in roughly polishing knives, etc. 1812.

Glazier (glēⁱ·ziəɹ, glēⁱ·ʒiəɹ). ME. [f. GLASS *sb.* + -ER¹, after wds. in -IER, q.v.] †1. A glass-maker -1477. 2. One whose trade is to glaze windows, etc. ME. 3. = GLAZER 3. 1688. †4. *old slang. pl.* The eyes -1785. Hence **Gla·ziery**, glazier's work; also *attrib.*

Glazing (glēⁱ·ziŋ), *vbl. sb.* ME. [f. GLAZE *v.*¹ + -ER¹.] 1. The action of furnishing a building with windows or filling windows with glass; the trade of a glazier. *concr.* Glazier's work. 2. The action of polishing or burnishing ME. 3. The action of coating with a glaze 1677. b. *concr.* = GLAZE *sb.* 2, 3. 1694. 4. *Painting.* The application of a thin coat of transparent colour over another colour in order to modify the tone; the colour thus applied 1706.

Comb.: **g.-wheel**, a wooden wheel charged with emery and used for polishing.

Glazy (glēⁱ·zi), *a.* 1724. [f. GLAZE *sb.* or *v.* + -Y¹.] 1. a. Glass-like, glassy. b. Having the appearance of a glaze or glazed surface 1768. 2. Of the eye, etc.: = GLASSY *a.* 2. 1838. Hence **Gla·zily** *adv.* **Gla·ziness.**

Glead, obs. f. GLEED *sb.*

Gleam (glīm), *sb.* [OE. *glǣm*, f. (ult.) root *glim-; see GLIM, GLIMMER, GLIMPSE.] 1. Orig., a brilliant light (e.g. of the sun). Now, a subdued or transient appearance of light. b. *fig.* ME. †2. *transf.* Brightness, radiance; radiant beauty -1683. b. A bright look 1769.

1. The dying lamp feebly emits a yellow g. GOLDSM. b. A g. of hope MACAULAY, of good fortune L. STEPHEN. 2. b. His black visage lighted up with a curious, mischievous g. 1852.

Gleam (glīm), *v.*¹ ME. [f. prec.] I. *intr.* To emit gleams; in mod. use chiefly, to shine with a subdued brightness. Also *fig.* Also quasi-*trans.* 1593. †2. To glance, look (*rare*) -1508.

1. The palace gleams with shining swords DRYDEN. There g. the columns of Capua LYTTON. quasi-*trans.* Dying eyes gleem'd forth their ashie lights SHAKS. Hence **Glea·mingly** *adv.*

Gleam, *v.*² ? *Obs.* 1575. [Later f. obs. *gleim* *v.*] *Falconry.* Of a hawk: To cast filth from her gorge.

Gleamy (glī·mi), *a.* 1593. [f. GLEAM *sb.* + -Y¹.] 1. That gleams or sends forth gleams (of light). 2. That is lighted up by gleams, e.g. of intermittent sunshine. Now *rare.* 1681. 3. Of light or colour: Having the nature of a gleam 1700.

1. Fish, g. with prismatic hues DISRAELI. 2. Antique castles seen through g. showers WORDSW.

Glean (glīn), *sb.*¹ Now *dial.* ME. [a. OF. *glene, glane* = med.L. *glena, glana*, sb. related to late L. *glenare* to GLEAN.] Something gleaned or gathered; e.g. a handful of corn, a sheaf of hemp, etc.

transf. The Gleans of yellow Thime distend his Thighs DRYDEN.

†**Glean**, *sb.*² 1601. [? var. of *clean* (? f. CLEAN *v.*).] The placenta or after-birth, esp. of a cow -1750.

Glean (glīn), *v.* [ME. *glenen*, a. OF. *glener, glainer* (mod. *glaner*) = late L. *glenare*, of unkn. origin.] 1. *intr.* To gather ears of corn left by the reapers. 2. *trans.* To pick up (ears of corn, etc.) after the reapers, etc. ME. b. To strip (a field, vineyard, etc.) of what is left 1533. 3. *transf.* and *fig.* To gather or pick up in small quantities. Now chiefly with immaterial object. ME. †b. To cut off (a remnant or stragglers) in warfare -1726.

1. I pray you, let mee gleane and gather after the reapers amongst the sheaues *Ruth* ii. 7. 2. To gleane the broken eares after the man That the maine haruest reapes SHAKS. b. *Lev.* xix. 10. 3. To g. materials for history 1759, a joy BYRON. b. *Judges* xx. 45. Hence **Glea·nable** *a.* **Glea·ner**, one that gleans.

†**Glean**, var. of GLEEN.

Gleaning (glī·niŋ), *vbl. sb.* ME. [f. prec. + -ING¹.] The action of GLEAN *v.*; also (chiefly *pl.*) that which is or may be gleaned.

Humble gleanings in Divinity B. JONS.

Glebe (glīb), *sb.* ME. [ad. L. *gleba, glæba* clod; land, soil.] 1. The soil of the earth, as the source of vegetable products; land. Now only *poet.* or *rhet.* 2. A piece of cultivated land; a field. Now *poet.* ME. b. *spec.* A portion of land assigned to a clergyman as part of his benefice ME. †3. a. A clod or piece of earth, ore, etc. -1766. b. A small grain or speck -1765. †4. An earth, earthy mineral -1723.

1. Howses..he raseth, To make the common gleabe, his priuate land 1598. 2. b. This parish is a rectory; it has a g., and a good solid house COBBETT.

Comb.: **g.-house**, a parsonage, manse (now only in Ireland); **-land(s** = 2 b. above.

Hence **Glebe** *v.* (*rare*) to furnish with a g. **Gle·beless** *a.*

Glebous (glī·bəs), *a. rare.* 1671. [ad. L. *glebosus*, f. *gleba.*] Earthy; abounding in clods.

Gleby (glī·bi), *a.* ? *Obs.* 1566. [f. GLEBE *sb.* + -Y¹.] Of soil: Full of clods; rich, fertile.

Glede, gled (glīd, gled). [OE. *glida*, f. (ult.) root *glid-* of *glīdan to GLIDE.] The kite (*Milvus regalis*). Now chiefly *north.* and *Sc.* (in form *gled*). Also applied locally to the buzzard, osprey, and peregrine falcon.

Glede, obs. f. GLEED.

†**Gle·dy**, *a.* [f. *glede* GLEED + -Y¹.] Glowing hot. CHAUCER.

Glee (glī), *sb.* [OE. *glīw, glēo* neut. = ON. *glý* (*rare*).] †1. Entertainment, play; *occas.* scornful jesting -1607. †2. Musical entertainment; music, melody. Also *fig.* of other sounds. -1523. b. A musical composition, grave or gay, for three or more voices (one voice to each part), (in strict use) without accompaniment 1659. 3. Mirth, joy, rejoicing; in mod. use, a lively feeling of delight caused by special circumstances ME. †b. A state of exaltation -1588. †4. Bright colour, beauty -1580. *Comb.* **g.-club.**

Glee *v.*, var. of GLEY.

Gleed (glīd), *sb.* [Com. Teut.: OE. *glēd, glēd* :—OTeut. *glōdi-z, related to GLOW *v.*] 1. A live coal; an ember. Now only *dial.* exc. *arch.* Also *fig.* †2. A fire -1755. †3. A beam (of light) -1566. 4. *local. pl.* Cinders, coke used as fuel 1853.

Gleeful (glī·ful), *a.* 1586. [f. GLEE *sb.* + -FUL.] Full of glee; feeling or showing glee. Hence **Glee·fully** *adv.*

Gleek (glīk), *sb.*¹ 1533. [a. OF. *glic*, earlier *ghelicque*, perh. ad. MDu. *ghelic* (Du. *gelijk*, Ger. *gleich*) LIKE (see sense 2).] 1. A game at cards, played by three persons. *Hist.* †2. A set of three court cards of the same rank in one hand, in this game -1670; hence, three of anything, a trio -1710.

†**Gleek**, *sb.*² 1550. [?] 1. A gibe, jest, gird -1819. 2. A coquettish glance (*rare*) -1623.

2. A pretty g. coming from Pallas' eye 1623.

†**Gleek**, *v.* 1534. [f. prec.] 1. *trans.* To trick, circumvent -1653. 2. *intr.* To make a jest or gibe (*at* a person) -1687.

2. Nay, I can gleeke vpon occasion SHAKS.

Gleeman (glī·mæ̆n). *Obs.* exc. *Hist.* OE. [f. GLEE *sb.* + MAN.] A professional entertainer; esp. a singer, musician, or minstrel.

Gleen (glīn), *sb.* Also **glean.** *Obs.* exc. *arch.* 1656. [Cf. Sw. (dial.) *glena*, Du. (dial.) *glene* a clear strip of sky.] A gleam of light; a warm blaze of sunlight.

†**Gleen**, *v. rare.* 1547. [See prec.] = GLEAM *v.*¹ -1709.

Gleesome (glī·sŏm), *a.* 1603. [f. GLEE *sb.* + -SOME.] = GLEEFUL. Hence **Glee·some·ly** *adv.*, **-ness.**

Gleet (glīt), *sb.* [ME. *glette*, a. OF. *glette* slime, filth, etc.] 1. Slimy matter. Also *fig.* *Obs.* exc. *Sc.* 2. Phlegm collected in the stomach, esp. of a hawk. *Obs.* exc. *Sc.* ME. 3. A morbid discharge of thin liquid from a wound, ulcer, etc. Now *rare.* 1535. b. *spec.* A morbid discharge from the urethra 1718. Hence **Glee·tous** *a.* (of a hawk), afflicted with phlegm. **Glee·ty** *a.* slimy (now *Sc.* and *north.*); of the nature of g.

Gleet, *v.* 1527. [f. prec.] †1. *intr.* Of a morbid discharge, also of water: To ooze, flow slowly -1725. 2. To discharge a thin purulent matter. Also quasi-*trans.* 1676.

Gleg (gleg), *a. north.* and *Sc.* ME. [a. ON. *gleggr* clear, clear-sighted :—OTeut. *glawwu-.] 1. Quick in perception by the senses; esp. sharp-sighted. 2. Quick in action; sharp, smart 1755. 3. Sprightly 1818.

2. Phr. *G. at the uptake*, quick in understanding a thing. Hence **Gle·gly** *adv.* **Gle·gness.**

Gleir(e, obs. f. GLAIR *sb.*¹

Glen (glen). 1489. [a. Gael. *gleann*, earlier *glenn*, mountain-valley.] A mountain-valley, usually narrow, and forming the course of a stream.

Your lowly glens o'erhung with spreading broom COLLINS.

Glendoveer (glendŏvīᵊ·ɹ). 1810. [Altered f. *grandouver* in Sonnerat *Voy. aux Indes*

(1782); app. repr. Skr. *gandharva*, a kind of semi-divine spiritual being.] One of a race of beautiful sprites in Southey's quasi-Hindu mythology.

‖**Glene** (glīˑnī). 1706. [mod.L., a. Gr. γλήνη ball or pupil of the eye; used by Galen for a shallow joint-socket.] *Anat.* **a.** The ball or socket of the eye. **b.** A glenoid cavity. (Dicts.)

Glengarry (glengæˑri). 1858. [f. *Glengarry* in Inverness-shire.] A kind of man's cap, higher in front than at back, of Highland origin.

Glenlivet (glenliˑvĕt, Sc. -līˑvĕt). 1822. [f. *Glenlivet* in Banffshire, where made.] A variety of Scotch whisky.

Gleno-, comb. f. GLENE, as in *g.-humeral*, belonging to the glenoid cavity and the humerus; etc.

Glenoid (glīˑnoid), *a.* 1709. [ad. Gr. γληνοειδής, f. γλήνη (see GLENE) + εἶδος; cf. F. *glénoïde*.] *G. cavity, fossa, surface*, a shallow cavity on a bone (esp. the scapula) which receives a projection of another bone to form a joint. So **Glenoiˑdal** *a.*

Glent, *sb.* and *v.* ME. [Prob. Scandinavian.] = GLINT.

‖**Gleˑtscher.** *rare.* 1762. [Ger. = F. *glacier*.] A glacier.

Glew, obs. f. GLUE.

Gley (gləi), *v.* *Obs.* exc. *north.* and *Sc.* Also glee. ME. [Normal vars. of an orig. ME. *gleȝen*. Of obscure origin.] *intr.* To squint; to look obliquely.

Gliadin (gləiˑădin). 1830. [a. F. *gliadine*, f. Gr. γλία glue.] *Chem.* The viscid portion of gluten. Called also *glutin*.

Glib (glib), *sb.* 1537. [a. Irish *glib*.] A thick mass of matted hair hanging over the eyes, formerly worn by the Irish. Also, a man who wears this. Now *Hist.*

Glib (glib). 1594. [See GLIBBERY *a.*]

A. *adj.* **1.** Smooth and slippery; easy, unimpeded. Now *rare* exc. *dial.* 1599. **2.** Of an action, method, etc.: easy; off-hand 1598. **3.** Of speech, etc.: Ready and fluent. Chiefly *contemptuous.* 1602.

1. The snow lies g. as glass and hard as steel BROWNING. 3. That g. and oylie Art, To speak and purpose not SHAKS. Hence **Gliˑb-ly** *adv.*, **-ness.**

B. *adv.* **1.** Smoothly, easily. Now *rare.* 1594. **2.** Volubly, fluently 1628.

1. The Bill did not pass g. NORTH.

Glib (glib), *v.*[1] 1598. [f. the adj.] **1.** *trans.* To render glib (see GLIB *a.*). **2.** *intr.* To talk volubly. Now *dial.* 1602.

†**Glib**, *v.*[2] *rare.* 1611. [app. a corruption of LIB *v.*] *trans.* To castrate; to geld –1640. *Wint. T.* II. i. 149.

†**Gliˑbbery**, *a.* 1601. [? in ablaut-relation to OHG. *gleif* sloping; or ? onomatopœic.] Slippery (*lit.* and *fig.*) –1646.

The g. ice Of vulgar favour MARSTON.

Glick(e, obs. f. GLEEK *sb.*[1]; var. of GLEEK *sb.*[2] and *v.*

Glidder (gliˑdəɹ), *a.* *Obs.* exc. *dial.* [OE. *glidder*, f. *glid-*, root of *glīdan* GLIDE *v.*] Slippery. Hence **Gliˑdder** *v. dial.* to glaze over; to cover with ice. **Gliˑddery** *a. dial.* slippery.

Glide (gləid), *sb.* 1590. [f. next.] **1.** The action of gliding (see GLIDE *v.*) 1596. **2.** *concr.* †A stream; also, the part of a stream which glides, a shallow. **3.** *Mus.* and *Phonetics.* (See quots.) 1835.

1. [The snake] with indented glides, did slip away Into a bush SHAKS. 2. Eurotas silver g. GREENE. 3. *Glide*, the slur, to join two successive sounds without articulation, also the unaccented notes or anticipations in a *portamento* passage WILSON *Dict. Mus.* 1835. A series of semi-consonant, semi-vowel sounds..which we call 'Glides' A. MELVILLE-BELL. The 'glide', or sound produced in passing from the one position [of the organs of speech] to the other SWEET. *Comb.* **g.-vowel**, a vowel which cannot form a syllable by itself.

Glide (gləid), *v.* Pa. t. and pple. **glided.** [A Com. WGer. str. vb.: OE. *glīdan*, ME. *gliden*. The OTeut. type is **glīđan*. The Eng. vb. remained strong until last century. Cf. GLAD *a.*] **1.** *intr.* To pass along by a smooth and continuous movement, without effort or difficulty. **b.** *Aeronautics.* To fly without motor power 1894. **2.** To go unperceived, quietly, or stealthily ME. †**3.** *poet.* To go or come –1596. **4.** To slide. Also †to slip, lose one's footing on ice, etc. ME. **b.** To slip *away*, like something greasy 1510. **5. a.** Of time, one's life, etc.: To pass gently and imperceptibly ME. **b.** *To g. into*: to pass by imperceptible degrees into 1800. **c.** Phonetics. *To g. on to*: (of a consonant or vowel) to be uttered continuously with 1800. **6.** *trans.* = to cause to glide 1650.

1. The river glideth at his own sweet will WORDSW. 3. Like sparke of fire that from the andvile glode SPENSER. 5. b. To g. hopelessly into debt LECKY. Hence **Gliˑder** *spec.* an engineless aeroplane 1897.

Gliff (glif), *sb.* Now *Sc.* or *north.* 1570. [f. next.] **1.** A passing sight; a glance, glimpse. **2.** A moment 1816. **3.** A sudden fright; a scare 1732.

2. Bide a g. SCOTT.

Gliff (glif), *v.* Now *Sc.* or *north.* ME. [?] †**1.** To slip (*lit.* and *fig.*). ME. only. †**2.** To look quickly; also quasi-*trans.* *to g. one's eyes* –1570. **3.** *trans.* To frighten 1823.

†**Glike**, var. of GLEEK *sb.*[2] and *v.*

Glim (glim), *sb.* ME. [Ult. f. the weak-grade of the Teut. root **glīm-*, *glaim-* (see GLEAM).] †**1.** ? Brightness. ME. only. **2.** *Sc.* †A passing look. Hence, a scrap. 1620. **3.** *slang.* **a.** A light; a candle, a lantern. 1700. **b.** An eye 1820.

3. a. Phr. *Douse the g.* (see DOUSE *v.*). Sure enough, they left their g. here STEVENSON.

Glimmer (gliˑməɹ), *sb.*[1] 1567. [f. the vb.] **1.** A feeble or wavering light; a sheen, shimmer 1590. **2.** *fig.* A faint gleam (of knowledge, hope, etc.) 1837. **3.** *slang.* †**a.** A fire –1665. **b.** *pl.* The eyes 1814.

1. In gloss of satin and g. of pearls TENNYSON.

Glimmer (gliˑməɹ), *sb.*[2] 1683. [a. Ger., f. *glimmen*.] Mica.

Glimmer (gliˑməɹ), *v.* [OE. **glimorian*, a frequentative f. the root *glim-*; see GLIM *sb.*, GLEAM.] †**1.** *intr.* To glitter; to flash –1530. **2.** To give a faint or intermittent light; to shine faintly. Also *transf.* and *fig.* 1483. **3.** To look or glance with half-closed eyes (*rare*) 1579.

2. The West yet glimmers with some streakes of Day SHAKS. *transf.* The voice came glimmering and bubbling up a flight of stone steps HAWTHORNE. *Comb.* **g.-gowk** (*dial.*), an owl.

Glimmering (gliˑməriŋ), *vbl. sb.* ME. [See -ING[1].] **1.** The shining of a faint or wavering light. **2.** A partial view; a glimpse, an inkling; a faint notion ME.

1. Shadows and sunny glimmerings WORDSW. 2. Syre Percyuale hadde a glemerynge of the vessel and of the mayden that bare hit MALORY.

Glimpse (glimps), *sb.* 1540. [f. the vb.] **1.** A momentary shining, a flash (*lit.* and *fig.*) 1602. **2.** A faint and transient appearance. †Also, a tinge or trace. 1540. **3.** A momentary and imperfect view (*of*), a passing sight. (The current sense.) Also *fig.* 1570.

1. *The glimpses of the moon*: the earth by night; often quoted as = sublunary scenes. *Haml.* I. iv. 53. 2. In his face The glimpses of his Father's glory shine MILT. 3. A g. of the whole of Coniston Lake 1872, of the inner history of an English town 1874.

Glimpse (glimps), *v.* [ME. *glymsen* = MHG. *glimsen*, f. root of GLIM *sb.* and *v.*] **1.** *intr.* To shine faintly or intermittently (*lit.* and *fig.*). **b.** To appear faintly; to dawn. Now only *poet.* or *arch.* 1603. **2.** *trans.* To give a glimpse of (*rare*) 1663. **3.** To catch a glimpse of; to see by glimpses 1779. **4.** *intr.* To cast a passing glance. Const. *at*, *upon*, etc. 1833.

1. Little glow-worms glimpsing in the dark 1601. Yet sometimes glimpses on my sight, Through present wrong, the eternal right WHITTIER.

Glint (glint), *sb.* ? 1541. [f. the vb.] **1.** A gleam. **2.** A passing look; a glance; a glimpse. Chiefly *Sc.* or *north.* 1832.

1. The earliest g. o' morn 1826.

Glint (glint), *v.* ME. [Prob. altered f. GLENT *v.* Orig. Sc.; adopted into Eng. literary use in the last century.] **1.** *intr.* To move quickly, esp. obliquely; to glance aside. **2.** To shine with a flashing light; to gleam, glitter ME. Also *causative* (trans.). 1844. **3.** *intr.* To peep 1888.

2. The specks of sail that glinted in the sunlight far at sea DICKENS.

Glioma (gləiˌōuˑmă). *Pl.* **-mata.** 1870. [mod.L., f. Gr. γλία glue.] *Path.* 'A tumour originating from, and largely consisting of, the neuroglia cells of the central nervous system, esp. of the brain' (*Syd. Soc. Lex.*). Hence **Glioˑmatous** *a.* of the nature of g.

Glirine (gləiˑrin), *a.* 1836. [f. L. *glir-*, *glis* dormouse + -INE.] Pertaining to the order *Glires* of mammals. So **Gliˑriform** *a.* resembling the *Glires* in form or character.

Glissade (glisāˑd, -ēˑd), *sb.* 1843. [a. F., f. *glisser* to slide.] **1.** *Mountaineering.* The action of sliding down a snow slope or the like 1862. Also *fig.* **2.** *Dancing.* A step consisting of a glide to right or left 1843. Hence **Glissaˑde** *v. intr.* to perform a g. **Glissaˑder.**

Glissette (gliseˑt). 1870. [f. F. *glisser* (after *roulette*).] *Math.* (See quot.).

Glissettes are the curves traced out by points, or enveloped by curves, carried by a curve, which is made to slide between given points or given curves W. H. BESANT.

Glist (glist), *sb. rare.* 1715. [See GLISTEN *v.*] **1.** A gleam, glistening 1864. **2.** = MICA. 1715.

Glisten (gliˑs'n), *sb.* 1840. [f. the vb.] Glitter; sparkle.

Glisten (gliˑs'n), *v.* [OE. *glisnian*, f. OTeut. root **glis-*; see -EN[5].] *intr.* To shine with a twinkling light; to glitter; to sparkle (*lit.* and *fig.*).

The ladies eyes glistened with pleasure RICHARDSON. A mass glistens white as if it were snow GEIKIE. Hence **Gliˑsteningly** *adv.*

Glister (gliˑstəɹ), *sb.* 1535. [f. the vb.] **1.** A glistering; brilliance, lustre. Also *fig.* **2.** *Min.* = GLIST *sb.* 2. 1722.

Glister (gliˑstəɹ), *v.* *arch.* and *dial.* ME. [f. root **glīs-* + *-t-* + -ER[5].] *intr.* To sparkle; to glitter; to be brilliant. †**b.** quasi-*trans.* SIDNEY.

All that glisters is not gold SHAKS. Hence †**Gliˑsterer**, a showy person (EARLE). **Gliˑsteringly** *adv.*

Glister, obs. or dial. f. CLYSTER.

Glitter (gliˑtəɹ), *sb.* 1602. [f. the vb.] **1.** Brilliant or sparkling light; lustre, splendour. Also *fig.* **2.** Erron. for GUTTER (Goldsm. *Nat. Hist.* III. v. 114.).

1. Tinsill g. MARSTON. False g. MILT. The g. of gold 1788, (*fig.*) of Junius L. STEPHEN.

Glitter (gliˑtəɹ), *v.* [ME. *gliteren*, prob. a. ON. *glitra*, a frequentative f. the Teut. root **glīt-* in OS. *glītan* to shine.] **1.** *intr.* To shine with a brilliant but broken and tremulous light; to emit bright fitful flashes of light; to gleam, sparkle. **2.** *fig.* To be showy or splendid (in dress, etc.) 1548.

1. Many helmes gletred agaynst the sonne LD. BERNERS. All is not gold that glitters *Provb.* 2. I saw her [the queen of France] glittering like the morning star BURKE. Hence **Gliˑtterance** (*rare*), glittering appearance. **Gliˑtteringly** *adv.*

Gloam (glōᵘm), *sb. rare.* 1821. [f. GLOAMING.] Twilight.

Gloam (glōᵘm), *v.* *Sc.* 1819. [f. as prec.] *intr.* To darken, become dusk.

Gloaming (glōᵘˑmiŋ). [repr. OE. *glōmung*, f. *glōm* twilight, prob. f. the Teut. root **glō-* (see GLOW). In literary language a recent adoption from Sc.] **1.** Evening twilight. Also *fig.* 1785. **2.** *attrib.* (occas. *adj.*), as **g.-shot**, (*a*) a shot in the twilight; (*b*) the beginning of twilight; etc. 1788.

1. 'Tween the g. and the mirk HOGG.

Gloat (glōᵘt), *v.* 1575. [? = MHG. and mod.G. *glotzen* to stare, ON. *glotta* to grin, Sw. (dial.) *glotta* to peep.] †**1.** *intr.* To look askance –1727. †**2.** To cast amorous or admiring glances. Const. *on*, *upon*. –1727. **3.** To gaze with intense or passionate (usu. lustful, avaricious, or malignant) satisfaction 1748.

3. Phr. *To gloat on, upon*, or *over*: to feast one's eyes upon, to dwell upon with fierce or unholy joy. Never did miser g. on his money with more delight W. IRVING. To g. over the mysteries of iniquity L. STEPHEN. Hence **Gloat** *sb.* **Gloaˑtingly** *adv.*

Global (glōᵘˑbăl), *a.* 1676. [f. GLOBE *a.* + -AL 1.] **1.** Globular. *rare.* **2.** [after Fr.] Pertaining to or embracing the totality of a group of items, categories, or the like 1892.

Globate (glōᵘˑbeit, -ĕt), *a. rare.* 1847. [ad. L. *globatus*, *globare*, f. *globus* GLOBE *sb.*] Having the form of a globe. So **Gloˑbated** *a.* formed into or as into a globe.

Globe (glōᵘb), *sb.* 1551. [a. F., ad. L. *globus*.] 1. A body having a spherical form. b. *fig.* A complete or perfect body, a 'full-orbed' combination 1607. 2. *The* (or *this*) *globe*: the earth 1553. b. Any planetary or celestial body 1566. 3. A spherical structure showing the geographical configuration of the earth (*terrestrial globe*), or the arrangement of the stars (*celestial globe*) 1553. 4. The golden ball borne along with the sceptre as an emblem of sovereignty (cf. BALL *sb.*) 1614. 5. *Globe of the eye*, the eye-ball 1774. 6. A glass vessel of approximately spherical shape; esp. a lamp-shade 1665. 7. A compact body (of persons). After L. use. 1610.

1. b. In the discharge of thie place, sett before thee the best Exemples; For Imitacion is a G. of Preceptes BACON. 2. We the G. can compasse soone SHAKS. 4. With crown, with sceptre, and with g., Emblems of empery SCOTT. 7. Him round A G. of fierie Seraphim inclos'd MILT. Phrase. *G. of compression* (= F. *globe de compression*): an overcharged mine, the explosion of which produces a crater of greater radius than depth.

Comb.: **g.-amaranth(us** (see AMARANTH); †**-animal**, **-animalcule**, a minute globular locomotive organism (*Volvox globator*); **-artichoke** = ARTICHOKE 1; **-crowfoot** = *globe-flower*; **-daisy**, *Globularia vulgaris*; **-fish**, a fish of globular form, esp. one of the *Tetrodontidæ* or *Diodontidæ*, which assume this form by inflation; **-flower**, *Trollius europæus*, a ranunculaceous plant with yellow flowers; **-ranunculus** = *globe-flower*; **-sight**, a sight for a rifle, etc., consisting of a ball or disk; **-slater**, a sessile-eyed crustacean of the genus *Sphæroma*; **-thistle**, a name for species of the genus *Echinops*; **-trotter**; **-trotting**, extensive and hurried travelling over the g.; **-valve**, (*a*) a ball-valve; (*b*) a valve enclosed in a spherical chamber.

Globe (glōᵘb), *v.* 1641. [f. prec.] To form into, or have the form of, a globe. Hence **Globed** *ppl. a.*; *spec.* furnished with a globe.

Globical (glǫ·bikăl, glōᵘ·bikăl), *a.* 1612. [f. GLOBE *sb.* + -IC + -AL.] †1. Globular –1698. 2. *Her.* Having the general outline circular 1688.

Globiferous (glōᵘbi·fĕrəs), *a.* 1826. [f. L. *globi-* GLOBE *sb.* + -FEROUS.] *Entom.* Having a globe or bulb at the end of the antennæ.

‖**Globigerina** (glōᵘbiˌdʒĕrəi·nă). *Pl.* **-næ.** 1847. [mod.L., f. L. *globi-* GLOBE *sb.* + *-ger* carrying + *-ina* -INE.] A foraminiferous rhizopod, found in numbers in deep parts of the ocean. Also *attrib.*, as *g.-mud*, *-ooze*, deep-sea mud or chalky ooze, consisting of decayed globigerinæ. Hence **Globi·gerine** *a.*

Globin (glōᵘ·bin). 1877. [f. L. *globus* + -IN.] The proteid which is precipitated when a solution of hæmoglobin is exposed to the air.

Globoid (glōᵘ·boid). 1875. [f. GLOBE *sb.* + -OID.]

A. *adj.* Somewhat globular in form 1887.

B. *sb.* Non-crystalline, roundish, or clustered granules, consisting of a double calcium and magnesium phosphate, the latter base greatly in excess.

Globose (gloᵘbōᵘ·s), *a.* 1475. [ad. L. *globosus*, f. *globus*.] Having the form of a globe; spherical, or nearly so. Now only in scientific use. Hence **Globo·se·ly** *adv.*, **-ness.**

Globosity (gloᵘbǫ·sĭti). 1657. [See GLOBOSE and -ITY.] The condition of being globose; roundness. Also a rounded part.

Globous (glōᵘ·bəs), *a.* 1610. [ad. L. *globosus*.] = GLOBOSE. Now *rare*.

Globular (glǫ·biŭlăɪ), *a.* 1656. [f. L. *globulus* GLOBULE. Commonly used in senses corresp. to those of GLOBE.] 1. Having the form of a globe; spherical, round. 2. Composed of globules 1733.

1. In this station two g. hills appeared COOK. Phr. *Globular projection*, that method of map-making in which the sphere is represented as it would appear if viewed from a distance = half the chord of 90°. *G. chart*, a chart on this projection. *G. sailing*, sailing over an arc of a great circle, or the shortest distance between two places. Hence **Globula·rity**, **Glo·bularness**, the property of being g. **Glo·bularly** *adv.*

Globule (glǫ·biŭl). 1664. [a. F., ad. L. *globulus*, dim. of *globus*.] 1. A small globe; a round drop (of water, oil, etc.). b. *Biol.* Applied to various minute spherical structures. 2. *Bot.* The antheridium of *Characeæ* 1830. 3. A small pill or pilule, such as homœopathists use 1849.

1. Exceedingly minute globules of water BREWSTER. 3. Prescribe sometimes for myself the globules 1876. Hence **Glo·bulet** (*rare*), a minute g. **Glo·buli·ferous** *a.* that bears or produces globules. **Globuli·meter** = HÆMATOMETER b. **Glo·bulism**, occas. term for homœopathy.

Globulin (glǫ·biŭlin). Also **-ine.** 1845. [f. prec. + -IN, -INE.] *Biochem.* Any of a group of proteins, as fibrinogen, etc., insoluble in pure water, but soluble in dilute solutions of neutral salts.

Globulite (glǫ·biŭləit). 1879. [f. GLOBULE + -ITE.] *Min.* (*pl.*) Minute rounded bodies developed in the process of devitrification. Hence **Globuli·tic** *a.*

Globulous (glǫ·biŭləs), *a.* Now *rare*. 1668. [a. F. *globuleux*.] Globular in form; consisting of globules. var. **Glo·bulose.** Hence †**Glo·bulousness.**

‖**Globus** (glōᵘ·bǫ̆s). 1794. [L.] *Path.* Short for *globus hystericus*, a choking sensation, as of a lump in the throat, to which hysterical persons are subject.

Glo·by, *a.* 1600. [-Y¹.] Globular.

Glochidiate (glōᵘki·diĕt), *a.* Also **-date.** 1829. [ad. mod.L. *glochidium* barbed hair of a plant (a. Gr. *γλωχίδιον, dim. of γλωχίς point of an arrow) + -ATE.] *Bot.* Barbed at the tip.

Glockenspiel (glǫ·kenʃpīl,-spīl). 1876. [G., lit. bell-play.] 1. = CARILLON 1. 2. A musical instrument consisting of a series of metal bars which are struck with two hammers. b. A similar instrument with tubes or bells instead of bars. 3. An organ stop 1898.

Glod, glode, obs. str. pa. t. of GLIDE.

Glome (glōᵘm). 1643. [ad. L. *glomus* ball, clue.] †1. A ball or clue of yarn, etc. –1656. 2. *Bot.* = GLOMERULE 1. 1793.

Glome of frog: name for the two rounded, elastic eminences, separated by a cleft, which form the posterior extremity of the frog of the horse's foot.

Glomerate (glǫ·mərĕt), *a.* 1793. [ad. L. *glomeratus*; see next.] Compactly clustered, having the form of a rounded mass or cluster. Chiefly *Bot.*; also *Anat.*

†**Glo·merate,** *v.* 1634. [f. L. *glomerat-*, *glomerare*, f. *glomer-*, *glomus*.] a. *trans.* To roll or wind up into a ball; to gather into a rounded mass. b. *intr.* To wind or twist about. –1798.

Glomeration (glǫmĕrē¹·ʃən). *rare.* 1626. [ad. L. *glomerationem*; see prec.] The process of forming into a ball or rounded mass; more widely, a heaping together, agglomeration; also quasi-*concr.*

Glomerule (glǫ·mĕrŭl). 1793. [a. F. *glomérule*, ad. mod.L. *glomerulus* (also used), dim. of *glomer-*, *glomus*.] 1. *Bot.* a. A cluster or head of flowers. b. A soredium 1855. 2. A compact cluster of small organisms, animal tissues, etc.; esp. a plexus of capillary blood-vessels, as those in the Malpighian corpuscles of the kidney 1856. Hence **Glome:ruli·tis**, inflammation of the glomerules of Malpighi and their capsule. **Glome·rulose** *a.* gathered in small clusters.

Glonoin(e (glǫ·noˌin). 1860. [app. f. GL(YCERINE + O (oxygen) + NO_3 (nitric anhydride) + -IN.] A name for nitroglycerine, esp. as used in medicine.

Glood(e, obs. pa. t. of GLIDE.

Gloom (glūm), *sb.*¹ 1596. [In sense 1 f. GLOOM *v.*; in senses 2–3 f. GLOOMY; app. not conn. w. OE. *glóm* twilight.] 1. (Only *Sc.*) A sullen look, frown, scowl. ? *Obs.* 2. An indefinite degree of darkness or obscurity. In recent use: A painful or depressing darkness. Sometimes *pl.* 1629. b. A deeply shaded or darkened place 1706. 3. A state of melancholy or depression; a despondent look. Also in *pl.* fits of melancholy. 1744.

2. This mournful g. For that celestial light MILT. A g. unbroken, except by a lamp burning feebly GEO. ELIOT. b. Through glades and glooms the mingled measure stole COLLINS. 3. A comet.. aggravated the general g. 1786. A fit of the glooms MARY LAMB. Hence **Gloo·mful** *a.*

†**Gloom,** *sb.*² 1577. [? repr. OE. *glóm*; see GLOAMING.] *Hot gloom*, excessive heat (of the sun). *Comb.* **g.-stove** (also **gloom** simply), a drying-oven used in the manufacture of gunpowder.

Gloom (glūm), *v.* [ME. *gloum(b)e* (**glumen* :—OE. *glūmian*) = MG. *glūmen*, ? to be savage. See also GLUM *v.* App. not cogn. w. OE. *glóm* twilight.] 1. *intr.* To look sullen or displeased; to frown, scowl, lower. In recent use (infl. by GLOOMY): To look dismal or dejected. 2. Of the sky, etc.: To lower, look dark or threatening; to be or become dull and cloudy. Also *fig.* ME. b. = GLOAM *v.* 1595. 3. To have a dark or sombre appearance 1770. 4. *trans.* To make dark or sombre 1576; *fig.* to make dark, dismal, or melancholy 1745.

1. He gloomed from beneath his Eyes, bit his Lips [etc.] 1720. Her father, sitting glooming in his place at the other end of the table THACKERAY. 2. The sky gloomed through the dusky garret windows HAWTHORNE. b. This long weary day..at last I see it gloome SPENSER. 3. The black gibbet glooms beside the way GOLDSM. 4. A black yew gloom'd the stagnant air TENNYSON. *fig.* Such a mood as that, which lately gloom'd Your fancy TENNYSON. Hence **Gloo·mingly** *adv.*

Glooming (glū·miŋ), *vbl. sb.* 1572. [f. prec. + -ING¹.] 1. Frowning, etc.; a frown, scowl; a fit of sullenness. 2. *poet.* Twilight, gloaming; also, early dawn 1842.

2. Or while the balmy g., crescent-lit, Spread the light haze along the river-shores TENNYSON.

†**Gloo·mth.** [See -TH.] Gloom. H. WALPOLE.

Gloomy (glū·mi), *a.* 1588. [f. GLOOM *sb.*¹ + -Y¹.] 1. Full of gloom; dark, shaded, obscure. 2. Affected with gloom or depression of spirits; having dark or sullen looks 1590. 3. Causing gloom; dismal, disheartening 1710.

2. The ruthlesse, vast, and g. woods *Tit. A.* IV. i. 53. Gloomie clouds MARSTON. 2. His countenance being dark, bilious, and g. EARL ORRERY. 3. G. apprehensions GIBBON, reflections THIRLWALL. The gloomiest view of the position 1873. Hence **Gloo·mily** *adv.* **Gloo·miness.**

Gloppen (glǫp'n), *v.* Now *dial.* [ME. *glopnen*, *glopen*, a. ON. *glúpna* to be downcast.] †1. *intr.* a. To be downcast. b. To be startled or frightened. ME. only. 2. *trans.* To startle, frighten, astound ME.

Glore, *v.* Now *dial.* [ME. *gloren* to glow, stare; app. f. the root *glo-*; see GLOW *v.*¹] †1. *intr.* = GLARE *v.* 1. –1540. 2. = GLARE *v.* 2, GLOWER *v.* ME.

‖**Gloria** (glōᵊ·riă). Pl. *occas.* **glorias.** ME. [L.] 1. a. A name for: (*a*) *Gloria Patri*, the doxology beginning 'Glory be to the Father', which follows the recitation of the psalms, etc. (*b*) *Gloria tibi*, the response 'Glory be to Thee, O Lord', which follows the announcement of the gospel in the communion mass or service. (*c*) *Gloria in excelsis*, the hymn 'Glory be to God on high' (*Luke* ii. 14), forming part of the communion service or mass. b. The music to which the last-mentioned is set. 2. An aureole or nimbus 1784.

Gloriation (glōᵊriē¹·ʃən). 1504. [ad. L. *gloriationem*, f. *gloriari*.] The action of glorying; boasting; triumphing.

But al this g. is vain GALE.

Glorification (glōᵊ:rifikē¹·ʃən). 1460. [ad. late L. *glorificationem*, f. *glorificare*.] †1. *Alch.* The action of refining; the state of being refined –1470. 2. The action of glorifying; the condition of being glorified 1549. b. *esp.* The exaltation (of Christ) to the glory of heaven 1502. c. *joc.* A festive occasion 1843. 3. The ascription of glory to 1850; a doxology 1660.

3. The g. of Labour 1862, of 'science' HUXLEY.

Glorify (glōᵊ·rifəi), *v.* ME. [ad. F. *glorifier*, ad. late L. *glorificare*, f. *glorificus*, f. *gloria* + *facere* to make.] 1. *trans.* To render glorious; to invest with glory or radiance. 2. a. To advance the glory of (God, His name) by faithful action or suffering. b. To ascribe glory in adoration to (God). ME. 3. To extol, honour, magnify with praise 1557. 4. *refl.* To make one's boast, exult. Now *rare*. ME. 5. *Alch.* To sublime 1657.

1. Jesus was not yet glorified *John* vii. 39. As the bright sunne glorifies the skie SHAKS. To g. common life 1880. 2. b. I bless and glorifie thy name JER. TAYLOR. Hence **Glo·rified** *ppl. a.* in senses of the vb.; *colloq.* transformed into something glorious (often used sarcastically). **Glo·rifier.**

Gloriole (glōᵊ·rioul). 1813. [a. F., ad. L. *gloriola*, dim. of *gloria*.] †A scrap of glory; an aureole, a halo.

†Glorio·so. 1589. [a. It., ad. L. *gloriosus*.] A boaster –1661. Hence †**Glorio·ser.**

Glorious (glōᵊ·riəs), *a.* ME. [a. AF. *glorious* = OF. *glorieus*, ad. L. *gloriosus*; see -OUS.] †1. Boastful; ostentatious; haughty; vainglorious –1734. †2. Eager for glory –1704. 3. a. Possessing glory; illustrious. (Now somewhat *rare*.) ME. b. Of an action, state of things, etc.: Conferring glory; entitling to brilliant and lofty renown. Const. *to*. 1548. 4. Splendid in beauty or adornment. Now only with emotional connotation. †Formerly also: Brilliant, shining, lustrous. ME. 5. Vaguely: Splendid, magnificent, intensely delightful. Often with jocular hyperbole. 1623. 6. *joc.* Ecstatically drunk 1790.

3. a. Her late g. majesty SWIFT. By nothing is England so g. as by her poetry M. ARNOLD. b. The g. Battel (but with small fruit) of Lepanto 1659. 4. The sunshine is a g. birth WORDSW. 5. G. John (i. e. Dryden) touches them off a little sharply SCOTT. The g. uncertainty of the law 1759, of cricket (*mod.*). 6. Kings may be blest, but Tam was g. BURNS. Hence **Glo·rious-ly** *adv.*, **-ness.**

Glory (glōᵊ·ri). [ME. *glorie*, a. OF. *glorie* (also in semi-pop. form *glo(i)re*), ad. L. *gloria*.] 1. Boastful spirit. *Obs.* exc. in VAINGLORY. 2. Exalted (and, in mod. use, merited) praise, honour, or admiration accorded by common consent to a person or thing; honourable fame, renown ME. 3. Something that brings honour or renown; a subject for boasting; a distinguished ornament; a special distinction; a 'boast and pride'. Also *pl.* ME. 4. Praise, honour, and thanksgiving offered in adoration ME. 5. *The glory of God*: the majesty and splendour attendant upon a manifestation of God ME. 6. Resplendent beauty or magnificence (now often with a tinge of sense 5 or 7). Also *pl.* splendours. ME. 7. The splendour and bliss of heaven ME. 8. A state of exaltation and splendour 1613. 9. The circle of light represented as surrounding the head, or the whole figure, of the Saviour, the Virgin, or Saints; an AUREOLE or NIMBUS 1646. b. *transf.* Any circle or ring of light 1693. 10. In names of insects and plants 1819.

1. G., or internal gloriation or triumph of the minde HOBBES. 2. What..abatynge of the glorie of a kynge FORTESCUE. The g. of Malebranche HUME. Phr. *The g. of God*: the honour of God, considered as the final cause of creation, and as the highest moral aim of intelligent creatures. 3. Are all thy Conquests, Glories, Triumphes, Spoiles, Shrunke to this little Measure *Jul. C.* III. i. 149. The glories of Mr. Pitt's administration 1792. 4. G. to God in the highest *Luke* ii. 14. 6. There hath past away a g. from the earth WORDSW. *pl.* I have seen The glories of the world 1693. 7. Thou, bright Saint, high sit'st in g. MILT. *To go to g.* (colloq.): to die. 8. Phr. *In one's g.*: in one's highest state; also *colloq.* in a state of unbounded gratification.

Comb.: **g.-pea**, a name for the Australasian genus *Clianthus*; **-tree**, a shrub of the genus *Clerodendron*.

Glory (glōᵊ·ri), *v.* ME. [ad. L. *gloriari*, f. *gloria*.] 1. *intr.* To exult with triumph, rejoice proudly. †2. To boast –1673. †3. *trans.* To give glory to; also, to make glorious, adorn –1661. †4. *intr.* Of light: To spread like a 'glory'. N. BACON.

1. Let 'em looke they g. not in mischiefe SHAKS. 2. *Gal.* vi. 14. 3. The troop That gloried Venus at her wedding-day 1594.

Glo·ry-hole. 1845. [Cf. Sc. *glaury* adj.] 1. *dial.* A receptacle (as a drawer, room, etc.) in which things are heaped together without order or tidiness. 2. *Glass-making.* An opening in the wall of a blast-furnace, disclosing the white light of the interior 1849.

Glos(e, Glos-: see GLOZE, GLOZ-.

Gloss (glɒs), *sb.*¹ 1548. [var. of *glose*, GLOZE *sb.*, refash. after L. *glossa*, Gr. γλῶσσα.] 1. A word inserted between the lines or in the margin as an explanatory rendering of a word in the text; hence, a similar rendering in a glossary or dictionary. Also, a comment, explanation, interpretation. Often in bad sense: A sophistical or disingenuous interpretation. (Cf. GLOZE *sb.* 1.) b. A collection of such explanations, a glossary; also, an interlinear translation or explanation of a text 1579. ¶c. In sense of Gr. γλῶσσα: A foreign or obscure word, requiring explanation *Obs.* 1603. 2. *attrib.* 1624.

1. Malicious Glosses made upon all he had said CLARENDON. A parenthesis or g. slipt into the text COLERIDGE. b. Mostly obscure words, only found in glosses 1894.

Gloss (glɒs), *sb.*² 1538. [Cf. Du. (obs.) *gloos* a glowing, gleaming, Sw. (dial.) *glossa*, *glåsa* to gleam, glow (of coals). Icel. *glossi* a blaze.] 1. Superficial lustre. Also *pl.* b. *fig.* A deceptive appearance, fair semblance, plausible pretext 1548. 2. A layer of glowing matter (*rare*) 1762. †3. = GLAZE *sb.* 1. 1835.

1. G. of satin TENNYSON. b. Yet all his vertues.. Doe in our eyes, begin to loose their glosse SHAKS. Art, that sets a G. on what's amiss BUTLER. The g. of novelty GOLDSM.

Gloss (glɒs), *v.*¹ 1579. [f. GLOSS *sb.*¹] 1. *trans.* = GLOZE *v.* 1. 1603. 2. *trans.* To veil with glosses; to explain away; to read a different sense into 1638.

1. The Celts seem to have had a special habit of glossing MAINE. 2. Who have gloss'd and warp'd all the severe Rules of the Gospel about Chastity BENTLEY.

Gloss (glɒs), *v.*² 1656. [f. GLOSS *sb.*²] *trans.* To put a gloss upon. a. To veil in specious language. b. To render bright and glossy; to glaze 1762.

a. His friends..g. over his foible, by calling him an agreeable novelist FOOTE. b. Back black, glossed with blue BEWICK.

Glossal (glɒ·săl), *a.* 1860. [f. Gr. γλῶσσα + -AL.] Of or pertaining to the tongue.

Glossanthrax (glɒs,æ·nþræks). 1849. [f. Gr. γλῶσσα + ANTHRAX.] A disease of the tongue and mouth in horses and cattle, attended by ulceration.

Glossary (glɒ·sări). 1483. [ad. L. *glossarium*, f. *glossa* GLOSS *sb.*¹; see -ARY.] A collection of glosses; a list with explanations of abstruse, antiquated, dialectal, or technical terms; a partial dictionary. Hence **Glossa·rial** *a.* of, pertaining to, or of the nature of, a g. **Glossa·rian, Glo·ssarist,** one who writes a gloss or commentary; one who compiles a g.

Glossator (glɒsē·təɹ). ME. [a. med.L. *glossator*, f. *glossare*, f. *glossa* GLOSS *sb.*¹] A writer of glosses; a commentator, esp. on the texts of Civil and Canon Law.

†Glo·ssem. [ad. Gr. γλώσσημα, f. γλῶσσα GLOSS *sb.*¹] A gloss, comment. BP. HALL.

Glosser¹ (glɒ·səɹ). 1603. [f. GLOSS *v.*¹ + -ER¹.] = GLOSSATOR.

Glosser² (glɒ·səɹ). 1828. [f. GLOSS *v.*² + -ER¹.] One who puts on a gloss.

Glossic (glɒ·sik), *a.* and *sb.* 1871. [f. Gr. γλῶσσα + -IC.] Applied by A. J. Ellis to a phonetic system of spelling in which each letter or digraph represents the sound it most commonly expresses in English. Usu. *absol.* as *sb.*

Glossist (glɒ·sist). 1641. [f. GLOSS *sb.*¹ + -IST.] A commentator.

Glossitis (glɒsəi·tis). Also **Glottitis.** 1822. [f. Gr. γλῶσσα + -ITIS.] *Path.* Inflammation of the tongue. Hence **Glossi·tic** *a.* pertaining to, or affected with g.

Glosso- (glɒ·so), rarely **glotto-** (glɒ·to), occas. **gloss-** bef. vowels, comb. f. Gr. γλῶσσα, γλῶττα tongue. **Glo:ss(o)-epiglo·ttic** (also glo:tto-), **-epiglo·ttid, -epiglotti·dean** *adjs.*, pertaining to the tongue and to the epiglottis. **Glo:ssohy·al** [HY(OID) + -AL] *a.* pertaining to the tongue and to the hyoid bone; *sb.* a bone or cartilage extending forward from the basihyal, and constituting the hard basis of the tongue. **Glo:sso-lary·ngeal** *a.*, pertaining to the tongue and to the larynx. **Glo:sso-phary·ngeal** *a.*, pertaining to the tongue and to the pharynx or gullet.

†‖Glo:ssoco·mium. 1676. [mod.L., ad. Gr. γλωσσοκομεῖον a case for the reeds or tongues of musical instruments, f. γλῶσσα + κομέειν.] A case or frame for reducing a fractured or dislocated limb.

Glossograph (glɒ·sŏgraf). 1883. [(1) f. GLOSSO- + -GRAPH; (2) ad. Gr. γλωσσογράφος.] 1. A contrivance for reproducing speech automatically by electric action. 2. = next. 1885.

Glossographer (glɒsɒ·grăfəɹ). Also **glottographer.** 1607. [f. Gr. γλωσσογράφος (f. γλωσσο- + -γράφος): see GLOSSO-, -GRAPHER.] A writer of glosses or commentaries.

Glossography (glɒsɒ·grăfi). 1623. [ad. F. *glossographie*, f. GLOSSO- + Gr. -γραφία.] 1. The writing of glosses or commentaries; the compiling of glossaries. 2. A description of the tongue 1842. 3. A description or grouping of languages 1889. Hence **Glo:ssogra·phical** *a.*

‖Glossolalia (glɒ:solæ·liă). Also **-laly.** 1879. [f. Gr. γλωσσο- + -λαλιά.] The gift of speaking with tongues.

Glossology (glɒsɒ·lŏdʒi). 1716. [f GLOSSO- + Gr. -λογία; see -LOGY.] 1. †a. The study of a language or languages –1857. b. The science of language (= GLOTTOLOGY) 1874. 2. = TERMINOLOGY 1832. 3. *Med.* The study of the tongue (*rare*) 1844. Hence **Glossolo·gical** *a.* of or pertaining to g. **Glosso·logist,** one who defines and explains terms; one versed in g.

Glossotomy (glɒsɒ·tŏmi). 1842. [f. GLOSSO- + -τομία.] Dissection, amputation, or excision of the tongue.

Glossotype, earlier f. GLOSSIC, q. v.

Glossy (glɒ·si), *a.* 1556. [f. GLOSS *sb.*² + -Y¹.] Having a gloss; smooth and shining; polished; lustrous; *spec.* in *Path.*, designating morbid symptoms, as *g. skin, tongue.* Also *fig.*

fig. He [Ld. Chesterfield], however, with that g. duplicity which was his constant study, affected to be quite unconcerned BOSWELL. Hence **Glo·ssily** *adv.* **Glo·ssiness.**

Glost (glɒst). 1875. [app. a dial. alteration of GLOSS *sb.*² 3.] *Ceramics.* The lead glaze used for pottery. In **g.-fireman,** the man who attends to a g.-oven; **-oven,** the oven in which glazed ware is fired.

Glottal (glɒ·tăl), *a.* 1846. [f. GLOTTIS + -AL.] Pertaining to, or produced in, the glottis.

The most familiar example of this 'glottal catch' is an ordinary cough SWEET.

Glottic (glɒ·tik), *a.*¹ 1802. [ad. Gr. γλωττικός.] Linguistic.

Glottic (glɒ·tik), *a.*² 1839. [f. GLOTTIS + -IC.] Of or pertaining to the glottis. So **Glotti·dean** *a.*

Glottid (glɒ·tid). 1880. [a. Gr. γλωττιδ-, γλωττίς.] A vocal sound produced by the glottis.

Glottis (glɒ·tis). 1578. [a. mod.L. *glottis*, a. Gr., f. γλῶττα var. of γλῶσσα.] The opening at the upper part of the trachea, or windpipe, and between the vocal chords.

Glotti·tis. *Path.* = GLOSSITIS.

Glotto-: see GLOSSO-.

Glottology (glɒtɒ·lŏdʒi). 1841. [f. GLOTTO- (see GLOSSO-) + -LOGY.] The science of language. Hence **Glottolo·gic, -al** *a.* **Glotto·logist.**

Gloucester (glɒ·stəɹ). 1802. Name of an English county; hence *single-, double-G.*, the name of a cheese made there, seldom in full *Gloucester cheese.*

Glout (glaut), *v.* Now *rare.* ME. [? ablaut var. of GLOAT *v.*] *intr.* To look sullen, frown. Also *transf.*

transf. Heavy clouds that hung glouting H. WALPOLE. Hence **Glout** *sb.* (*rare*), a frown; a sullen look.

Glove (glɒv), *sb.* [OE. *glōf* = ON. *glōfe*; ? f. *ga-* prefix (see Y-) + *lōf-* root of Goth. *lōfa*, ON. *lófe*, hand (see LOOF *Sc.*).] 1. A covering for the hand, usu. one with a separate sheath for each finger. 2. = *Boxing-glove* 1725. 3. In *Hat-making*, a smooth piece of wood, fastened to the hand by a string, employed in rubbing the sheets of felt at the 'battery' 1875.

1. Phr. *To take up, throw (down) the g.* (as a pledge or challenge to battle). Heere's my Gloue: Giue mee another of thine SHAKS. *To fit like a g.*: to fit perfectly. *To handle without gloves*: to treat without mercy. Also HAND AND GLOVE.

Comb.: **g.-finger** (see FINGER *sb.*); **-money,** (*a*) a gratuity given to servants ostensibly to buy gloves with; (*b*) *Law*, extraordinary rewards formerly given to officers of English courts, etc.; *esp.* money given by the sheriff of a county, in which no offenders were left for execution, to the clerk of assize and the judges' officers; **-sponge**, a kind of sponge in the shape of a g.; **-stretcher.**

Glove (glɒv), *v.* 1573. [f. prec.] *trans.* To cover with, or as with, a glove; to provide with gloves.

Glover (glɒ·vəɹ). ME. [f. GLOVE *sb.* + -ER [1].] One who makes or sells gloves.

Comb.: **glover's stitch,** (*a*) the stitch used in sewing the seams of gloves; (*b*) a stitch resembling this, used in sewing up wounds; **glover's suture,** a suture made with the *glover's stitch.*

Glow (glōu), *sb.* 1600. [f. next vb.] **1.** The state or condition of glowing with heat 1793. **2.** Brightness and warmth of colour; a flush. Applied esp. to the warm red of the cheeks in youth or health. 1600. **3.** Warmth of feeling or passion; ardour 1748.

2. The red glowe of scorne SHAKS. The transmutation—Jura's black to one gold g. BROWNING. **3.** The g. of self-approbation J. H. NEWMAN.

Comb.: **g.-beetle** = GLOW-WORM, **-fly** = FIRE-FLY; **-lamp,** a lamp in which the light results from the incandescence of a resisting substance, e.g. carbon, produced by the passage of an electric current; **-lighting,** lighting by g.-lamps.

Glow (glōu), *v.*[1] Pa. t. and pple. **glowed.** [OE. *glōwan.* The Teut. root **glô-* appears also in GLEED.] **1.** *intr.* To be incandescent; to emit bright light and heat without flame. Said also of a fire. **2.** To shine, emit light, appear suffused with radiance, like something intensely heated ME.; to gaze with glowing eyes (MRS. BROWNING). **3.** To be brilliant and warm in colouring ME. **4.** To be excessively hot; to be on fire, to burn (*lit.* and *fig.*) ME. **5.** To burn with bodily heat; usually with the accompaniment of a heightened colour ME. **6.** To burn with the fervour of emotion or passion. Said of persons and their feelings. 1649. †**7.** *trans.* To make hot; to heat -1683.

1. I..found it [Newgate] in ruins, the fire yet glowing JOHNSON. **2.** Now glow'd the Firmament With living Saphirs MILT. The eye [of Burns]..glowed (I say literally glowed) when he spoke with feeling or interest SCOTT. **3.** A gown that glows with Tyrian rays DRYDEN. **4.** The rapid axles g. 1789. **5.** Girls, all glowing with the flush of life 1884. **6.** The courage of the first ages of the republic glowed in his breast GIBBON. The Tories, glowing with resentment [etc.] MACAULAY. **7.** *Ant. & Cl.* II. ii. 209. Hence **Glo·wingly** *adv.*

Glow, *v.*[2] *Obs.* exc. *dial.* ME. [? a use of prec.] *intr.* To stare

†**Glowbard.** 1475. [f. GLOW *v.* + BIRD.] A glow-worm -1607.

Glower (glauəɹ, glau·əɹ), *v.* 1500. [? f. GLOW *v.*[2] + -ER [5].] **1.** *intr. Sc.* To stare with wide-open eyes; to gaze intently. **2.** To look crossly; to scowl. Also *dial.* of the weather: To be gloomy. 1775. Hence **Glower** *sb.* (chiefly *Sc.*), the action of glowering.

Glow-worm (glōu·wɜɹm). ME. [f. GLOW *v.* + WORM.] A coleopterous insect (*Lampyris noctiluca* Linn.), the female of which emits a shining green light from the extremity of the abdomen. The female is wingless; the male is winged, but non-luminous. Also *fig.* Also *attrib.*

The Glowworme..gins to pale his vneffectuall Fire SHAKS. *attrib.* My..Glow-worme Muse 1630.

Gloxinia (glǫksi·niă). 1816. [mod.L., f. B. P. *Gloxin.*] An American tropical plant (N.O. *Gesneraceæ*) with large bell-shaped flowers.

Gloze (glōuz), *sb.* ME. [a. OF. *glose*, ad. med.L. *glosa*, L. *glossa*, a word needing explanation, hence later the explanation itself, a. Gr. γλῶσσα.] **1.** = GLOSS *sb.*[1] **1.** *arch.* **2.** Flattery, deceit; a flattering speech, etc. Now *rare.* ME. **b.** A pretence, specious show; also, a disguise. Now *rare.* ME. **3.** = GLOSS *sb.*[1] **2.** ROSCOE.

2. This is a verray sooth with outen glose CHAUCER. **b.** Gloses, and goodly shews of words HOLLAND.

Gloze (glōuz), *v.* ME. [a. F. *gloser*, f. *glose* GLOZE *sb.*] †**1.** *trans.* To make glozes or glosses upon; to comment upon, interpret. Also *absol.* or *intr.*-1872. **2.** *trans.* To veil with specious comments; to palliate; to explain away. Freq. with *over.* ME. **3.** *intr.* To talk smoothly and speciously; to fawn ME. **4.** *trans.* To flatter; to coax, wheedle ME.

1. *Hen. V*, I. ii. 40. **3.** I kan nat glose, I am a rude man CHAUCER. **4.** The parasite glozes his master with sweet speeches CARLYLE. Hence †**Glo·zer,** one who writes glosses; a flatterer, sycophant. **Glo·zing** *vbl. sb.* the action of glossing; flattery, specious talk.

Glucate (gl¹ū·kėt). 1840. [f. GLUC(IC + -ATE [4].] *Chem.* A salt of glucic acid.

Glucic (gl¹ū·sik), *a.* 1840. [a. F. *glucique*, f. Gr. γλυκύς sweet; see -IC.] *Chem.* In *glucic acid*, an acid obtained by the action of alkalis or acids on glucose.

Glucina (gl¹usəi·nă). Formerly also **glucine, glycine.** 1800. [mod.L. f. Fr. *glucine*, f. Gr. γλυκύς sweet (some of the salts of glucina tasting sweet). For the ending *-a* cf. *soda*, etc.] *Chem.* The oxide of glucinum or beryllium.

Glucinum (gl¹usəi·nɒm). Also **glucinium.** 1812. [quasi-L. f. GLUCINA.] *Chem.* A white metal obtained from beryl. Also called BERYLLIUM. Symbol Be or Gl.

Glucogene, -genic: see GLYCOGEN, -GENIC.

Glucose (gl¹ū·kōus). Also **glycose.** 1840. [f. Gr. γλυκύς sweet + -OSE [2].] *Chem.* **a.** = DEXTROSE or grape-sugar; now chiefly a trade name for dextrose obtained from starch by the action of sulphuric acid. **b.** Any member of the group of sugars having the common formula $C_6H_{12}O_6$, and including dextrose, levulose, mannitose, galactose, etc. Hence **Gluco·sic** *a* of or pertaining to g.

Glucoside (gl¹ū·kǒsəid). 1866. [f. GLUCOSE + -IDE.] *Chem.* One of a class of vegetable substances which being treated with dilute acids or alkalis, or subjected to the action of ferments, are resolved into glucose and some other substance.

Glue (gl¹ū, glū), *sb.* ME. [ad. OF. *glu* (sense 1):—late L. *glutem, glus* glue.] †**1.** Bird-lime. Also *fig.* -1704. **2.** A hard, brittle, brownish gelatin, obtained by boiling the hides and hoofs of animals to a jelly; when gently heated with water, it is used as a cement for uniting substances ME. **3.** Used loosely for any substance that serves as a cement ME. Also *fig.* **4.** *Soap-making.* A name for the condition of soap at an early stage of its manufacture 1885. **5.** *attrib.* 1755.

2. *Fish-g.* (see FISH *sb.*[1]). *Dutch* or *Flanders g.*: a very fine kind of g. **3.** *Marine g.*: a solution of caoutchouc in naphtha, to which a proportion of shellac is added. *Comb.* **g.-plant,** a sea-weed, *Plocaria tenax.*

Glue (gl¹ū, glū), *v.* ME. [f. the sb.] **1.** *trans.* To join or fasten with glue or other viscous substance. **2.** *transf.* and *fig.* To fix or attach firmly (as if by gluing). Formerly often: To attach in sympathy or friendship. ME. †**3.** *intr.* **a.** To stick together. Also *fig.* **b.** To admit of being fastened by glue. -1701. †**4.** *trans.* To smear with glue or other viscous substance -1808.

1. Two boards glued up edge to edge GWILT. Phr. *To g. up*: to seal up as with glue. **2.** My Loue and Feare, glew'd many Friends to thee SHAKS. He glued the huge flagon to his lips SCOTT. Hence **Glu·er.**

Glue·-pot. 1483. A pot in which glue is melted by the heat of water in an outer vessel.

Gluey (gl¹ū·i, glū·i), *a.* ME. [f. GLUE *sb.* + -Y [1].] Resembling, or of the nature of, glue; viscous, glutinous, sticky. In early use: †Bituminous. Hence **Glu·eyness.**

Gluish (gl¹ū·iʃ, glū·iʃ), *a.* ME. [See -ISH.] Somewhat gluey.

Glum (glɒm), *sb. rare.* 1523. [f. GLUM *v.* or *a.*] †**1.** A sullen look -1530. **2.** Glumness. LOCKHART.

Glum (glɒm), *a.* 1547. [Related to GLUM *v.*] **1.** Sullen, frowning. **2.** Gloomy, dark; dismal. Now only *fig.* from sense 1. 1557.

1. [He] sat g. BESANT. **2.** The g. old bridge THACKERAY. Hence **Glu·mly** *adv.* †**Glu·mmish** *a.* somewhat g. **Glu·mmy** *a.* †gloomy; glum. **Glu·mness,** the condition of being g.

Glum, *v. Obs.* exc. *dial.* 1460. [var. of *glo(u)mbe*, GLOOM *v.*] *intr.* To look sullen; to scowl.

Glumaceous (gl¹u-, glumē¹·ʃəs), *a.* 1828. [f. GLUME + -ACEOUS.] Of the nature of glumes; bearing glumes. Also, belonging to the N.O. *Glumaceæ* of plants, which includes the grasses and sedges.

Glumal (gl¹ū-, glū·măl), *a.* 1846. [f. GLUME + -AL.] = prec.: Lindley's name for an alliance of glume-bearing endogens. Also **Glu·mal** *sb.* a member of this alliance.

Glume (gl¹ūm, glūm). 1789. [ad. L. *gluma* (rare) hull, husk (of grain).] *Bot.* One of the chaff-like bracts which form the calyx or outer envelope in the inflorescence of grasses and sedges; the husk of corn or other grain.

‖**Glumella** (gl¹u-, glume·lă). 1861. [mod.L., dim. of L. *gluma.*] *Bot.* An inner glume or palea. So **Glume·lle** (*rare*). Hence **Glume·llule,** one of the scales frequently found at the base of the ovary in grasses; a lodicule.

Glumose (gl¹u-, glumōu·s), *a.* 1793. [ad. mod.L. *glumosus*, f. *gluma* GLUME.] Furnished with a glume or husk. var. **Glu·mous.**

Glump (glɒmp), *v. dial.* 1746. [Cf. GLUM, DUMP, etc.] *intr.* To sulk, be glum or sullen. Hence **Glump** *sb.* a sulky person; (*pl.*) the sulks. **Glu·mpish, Glu·mpy** *adjs.* glum, sullen, sulky.

Glunch (glɒnʃ), *v. Sc.* 1719. [Cf. GLUM *a.* and CLUNCH *a.* 2.] *intr.* To look sour or glum. Hence **Glunch** *sb.* a sour look; *a.* sulky.

†**Glunimie.** *Sc.* Also **glune-amie.** 1745. [? corruption of Gael.] Lowland name for a Highlander -1828.

Glut, *sb.*[1] *Obs.* exc. *dial.* 1533. [a. OF. *glout* gulp; see GLUT *v.*[2]] A gulp; the amount swallowed at a gulp.

Glut (glɒt), *sb.*[2] 1579. [f. GLUT *v.*[1]] **1.** The act of glutting or condition of being glutted with food, etc.; indulgence to satiety or disgust; one's fill; a surfeit 1594. **2.** *Comm.* A supply of a commodity which greatly exceeds the demand 1594. **3.** An excessive number or quantity. Now *rare.* 1653. †**4.** An excessive flow of saliva, bile, etc. -1719. †**5.** That which gluts or chokes up -1704.

1. This g. of wealth, and a full satiety of all pleasure 1659. **2.** Phr. *A g. in the market.* **3.** Extream gluts of rain 1661.

†**Glut,** *sb.*[3] 1611. [Altered f. *glit* GLEET *sb.*] = GLEET *sb.* 2. -1615.

Glut (glɒt), *sb.*[4] *techn.* or *dial.* 1790. [? altered f. *clut*, dial. var. of CLEAT.] †**1.** A wedge of wood or iron. **2.** 'A small brick or block introduced into a course to complete it' (Knight) 1875. **3.** *Naut.* 'A piece of canvas sewed into a sail, near the head' (Dana) 1841.

Glut, *sb.*[5] A kind of eel.

Glut (glɒt), *v.*[1] ME. [Prob. f. OF. *glut*, *glout* greedy, gluttonous.] **1.** *trans.* To feed to repletion; to gorge. Chiefly *refl.* and *pass.* Const. *with.* **2.** *fig.* To gratify to the full (esp. a ferocious or lustful desire) 1549. **b.** *intr.* To take one's fill of thinking, gazing, etc. *on*; to gloat *on.* Also to long greedily *for* (*rare*). 1632. **3.** To surfeit with food; hence, to surfeit, cloy, or sicken with excess of anything ME. **4.** To fill to excess; to choke up; to saturate, impregnate thoroughly *with* some substance. Now *rare.* 1471. **5.** To overstock with mercantile goods 1624.

1. Grim Slaughter strides along Glutting her greedy Jaws SOMERVILLE. **b.** Horses that have broken fence, And glutted all night long breast-deep in corn TENNYSON. **b.** Love doth with an hungry eye G. on Beauty CAREW. **3.** I found The fickle ear soon glutted with the sound PRIOR. **5.** Phr. *To g. the market.*

Glut (glɒt), *v.*[2] Now *rare.* 1600. [ad. F. *glotir, gloutir* (obs.) to swallow :—L. *gluttire.* Cf. ENGLUT.] *trans.* To swallow greedily, gulp down.

Hee'l be hanged yet, Though euery drop of water sweare against it, And Gape at widst to g. him SHAKS.

Glut-, abbreviated comb. f. GLUTEN, as in **Glutaco·nic** *a.*, derived from gluten and aconitine; *g. acid*, $C_5H_6O_4$. **Gluta·mic** or **Glutami·nic** *a.*, derived from gluten and amidogen; *g. acid*, $C_5H_9NO_4$. **Gluta·mine** = *glutamic acid.* **Gluta·ric** *a.*, derived from gluten and tartaric acid $(CO_2H)_2\ (CH_2)_3$. **Glu·tazine,** $C_5H_6N_2O_2$, a white crystalline compound derived from pyridine.

Glutæal, gluteal (gl¹ū-, glutī·ăl), *a.* 1804. [f. next + -AL.] Of or belonging to the glutæi. So **Glute·an** *a.*

‖**Glutæus, gluteus** (glu-, glutī·ŏs). *Pl.* **-tæi, -tei** (-tī·əi). 1681. [mod.L., f. Gr. γλουτός rump, buttock.] One of the three large muscles (dist. as *g. maximus, medius, minimus*) which form the buttock, and serve to move the thigh in man; occas. the analogous muscle in the lower animals. Also *attrib.*, in *g. muscle, glutæi muscles.*

Gluten (glū-, glū·ten). 1597. [a. L., perh. through F.] 1. Any sticky substance (*rare*) 1639. †2. The albuminous element of animal tissues, now called FIBRIN -1834. 3. The nitrogenous part of the flour of wheat or other grain, which remains behind as a viscid substance when the starch is removed by kneading the flour in a current of water 1803.

Comb.: **g.-bread**, bread containing a large proportion of g., prescribed in cases of diabetes; **-casein, -fibrin**, the vegetable casein and fibrin which form constituents of g.

Glutin (glū-, glū·tin). Also **-ine.** 1825. [a. F. *glutine* (obs.), prob. f. L. *gluten* + *-ine*; see -IN.] †1. = GLUTEN 1 and 3. 2. = GLIADIN 1838. 3. A distinct form of gelatin obtained from skin, hoof, bone, etc. 1845.

†**Glu·tinate,** *v.* 1564. [f. L. *glutinat-, glutinare*, f. *gluten* glue.] 1. *trans. Med.* To close up, heal (a wound); to constipate (the bowels, veins, etc.). Also *absol.* -1748. 2. To glue together. (Dicts.) Hence †**Glutina·tion.** †**Glu·tinative** *a.* constrictive; *sb. pl.* medical preparations which serve to close up or bind together.

Glutinosity (glū-, glūtinǫ·sĭti). ME. [f. L. *glutinosus* + -ITY.] The quality of being glutinous.

Glutinous (glū-, glū·tinəs), *a.* 1576. [ad. L. *glutinosus*, f. *glutin-* GLUTEN. Cf. F. *glutineux.*] Of the nature of glue or gluten; viscid, sticky, gluey. var. **Glu·tinose.** Hence **Glu·tinous-ly** *adv.*, **-ness.**

Glutton (glʊ·t'n). [ME. *glutun, gloton, -oun*, a. OF. *glutun, gluton* (mod. *glouton*):— L. *glutonem, gluttonem*, sb. related to *glutire* to swallow.]

A. *sb.* 1. One who eats to excess; a gormandizer. Also of animals. 2. *fig.* One who is inordinately fond of some specified object or pursuit, esp. *a g. of books*, L. *helluo librorum* 1704. b. *Sporting slang.* 'One who takes a deal of punishment before he is satisfied' 1809. †3. As a general term of reproach or contempt -1523. 4. A voracious animal, *Gulo luscus* or *arcticus*, belonging to the *Mustelidæ* or weasels and martens, but much larger than other members of that family. The American variety is called WOLVERENE or CARCAJOU. 1674.

1. *fig.* Suche a gredie glotton is avarice HALL. 2. Foes alike to Good, Gluttons in Murder, wanton to destroy GRANVILLE.

B. *adj.* = GLUTTONOUS; also (see A. 3) †villainous ME.

In pleasure some their g. souls would steep DRYDEN.

†**Glu·tton,** *v.* 1600. [f. the sb.] *intr.* To feed voraciously or to excess -1781.

Glutton'd at last, [you] return at home to pine LOVELACE.

Gluttonish (glʊ·tənɪʃ), *a. rare.* 1586. [f. GLUTTON *sb.* + -ISH.] Glutton-like, voracious.

Gluttonize (glʊ·tənəiz), *v.* 1656. [f. as prec. + -IZE.] *intr.* To feast gluttonously.

Gluttonous (glʊ·tənəs), *a.* ME. [f. GLUTTON *sb.* + -OUS.] Given to excess in eating; characterized by, or of the nature of, gluttony. Also *transf.* Hence **Glu·ttonously** *adv.*

Gluttony (glʊ·təni). [ME. *glutunie, glotonie*, a. OF. *glutunie, glutonie*, etc., abstr. sb. related to GLUTTON, in mod.F. repl. by *gloutonnerie.*] The vice of excessive eating. (One of the seven deadly sins.) Also *personified.*

Their sumptuous gluttonies MILT. Swinishg. MILT.

Glyceral (gli·seræl). 1872. [f. GLYCER(INE + -AL(DEHYDE.] *Chem.* A compound obtained by heating glycerine with an aldehyde.

Glycerate (gli·sĕrĕt). 1864. [f. GLYCER(IC + -ATE [4].] 1. *Chem.* A salt of glyceric acid. 2. 'A solution of some substance in glycerin' (*Syd. Soc. Lex.*) 1885.

Glyceric (glise·rik, gli·sĕrik), *a.* 1864. [f. GLYCER(INE + -IC.] *Chem.* Of, derived from, or relating to glycerine.

G. acid, an acid obtained by the action of nitric acid on glycerine.

Glyceride (gli·sĕrəid). 1864. [f. GLYCERINE + -IDE.] *Chem.* A compound ether of glycerine.

Glycerine, glycerin (gli·sĕrin). 1838. [f. Gr. γλυκερός sweet + -IN, -INE.] 1. A colourless, sweet, syrupy liquid obtained from animal and vegetable oils and fats by saponification. Chemically it is a triatomic alcohol, the hydrate of glyceryl. The name GLYCEROL is now preferred. 2. Formerly a general name for the group of alcohols of which glycerine is a member 1866. 3. *Pharm.* Any preparation consisting of a specified substance dissolved or suspended in glycerine 1879.

Glycerite (gli·sĕrəit). 1875. [f. GLYCER(INE + -ITE.] *Pharm.* A preparation dissolved or suspended in glycerine.

Glycero- (gli·sĕro), comb. f. GLYCERINE. **Gly:ceropho·sphate**, a salt of glycerophosphoric acid. **Gly:cerophospho·ric acid**, an acid produced by the action of phosphoric acid or phosphoric anhydride on glycerine.

Glycerol (gli·sĕrǫl). 1884. [f. GLYCER(INE + -OL.] *Chem.* = GLYCERINE 1.

Glycerole (gli·sĕroul). 1861. [f. GLYCERINE + *-ole* (used arbitrarily).] *Pharm.* A preparation in which glycerine is the vehicle.

Glyceryl (gli·sĕril). Also **-yle.** 1845. [f. GLYCER(INE + -YL.] *Chem.* The triatomic radical of glycerine and the glycerides.

Glycic (gli·sik), *a. Chem.* Corrected form of GLUCIC (acid).

Glycide (gli·səid). 1864. [f. GLYC(ERINE + -IDE.] *Chem.* $C_3H_6O_2$, the hypothetical radical corresponding to the glycidic ethers. Hence **Glyci·dic** *a.* pertaining to, or derived from g. *Glycidic ethers*, a class of diatomic ethers, produced from the glycerides by the action of alkalis.

Glycin (gli·sin). Also **-ine.** 1881. [f. Gr. γλυκύς + -IN.] *Chem.* = GLYCOCOLL.

Glyco- (glə·i·ko, gli·ko), irregularly used (instead of *glycy-*) as comb. f. Gr. γλυκύς sweet, and in names of chemical compounds to indicate the presence of *glycerol* or some other substance with a name beginning with *glyc-*, as in **Glycogelatin**, a combination of glycerine and gelatin used in the making of lozenges and pastilles.

Glycocholate (gləikokǫ·lĕt, glik-). 1872. [f. as next + -ATE [1].] *Chem.* A salt of glycocholic acid.

Glycocholic (gləikokǫ·lik, gliko-), *a.* 1864. [f. GLYCO- + CHOLIC *a.*] *Chem. Glycocholic acid*, the principal acid in ox-gall.

Glycocin (gləi·kŏsin, gli·-). 1852. [app. after prec.; see -IN.] *Chem.* = GLYCOCOLL. Now little used.

Glycocoll (gləi·kŏkǫl, gli·-). 1840. [f. GLYCO- + Gr. κόλλα glue.] *Chem.* A crystalline substance contained in bile and formed when glycocholic acid and hydrochloric acid are boiled together. Also called *gelatin-sugar.*

Glycogen (gləi·kŏdʒən, gli·kŏ-). Also **glu-.** 1860. [f. GLYCO- + -GEN; the substance being the source of the sugar in animal tissues.] *Chem.* A white, amorphous, tasteless, inodorous, starch-like substance found in animal tissues, esp. the liver; it is converted into dextrose by boiling in dilute acid.

Glycogenic (gləikodʒe·nik, gliko-), *a.* Also **glu-.** 1859. [f. as prec. + -IC.] Of or pertaining to the formation of sugar, esp. in the animal body. So **Glycoge·nesis**, the formation of sugar, esp. in the animal body. **Glyco·gene·tic, Glyco·genous** *adjs.* ? = GLYCOGENIC. **Glyco·geny** = *glycogenesis.*

Glycol (gləi·kǫl, gli-). 1858. [f. GLYC(ERINE + -OL; orig. meant as a name for a substance intermediate between glycerine and alcohol.] *Chem.* a. Formerly applied to the compound now called *ethyl glycol* or *ethylene alcohol* $C_2H_4(OH)_2$, a sweetish, colourless, inodorous viscid liquid obtained from the decomposition of ethylene dibromide. b. A general name for the group of fatty diatomic alcohols of which this is the type, having the general structure $C_nH_{2n}(OH)_2$. Hence **Glyco·llate**, a salt of glycollic acid.

Glycollic, glycolic (gləikǫ·lik, gli-), *a.* 1852. [f. GLYCOL + -IC.] Of or containing glycol. *Glycollic acid*, an acid obtained by the oxidation of glycol.

Glycollide. [f. GLYCOL + -IDE.] *Chem.* $C_2H_2O_2$, a compound isomeric with glyoxal, and differing from glycollic acid by 1 at. water. WATTS.

Glycolytic (gləikoli·tik, gliko-), *a.* 1897. [f. GLYKO- + Gr. λυτικός, f. λύειν.] Having the property of decomposing sugar.

Glycone·an, glyco·nian, *a. rare.* 1727. [f. L. *Glyconius, -eus*, Gr. Γλυκώνειος (see next) + -AN.] = next.

Glyconic (gləikǫ·nik). 1670. [f. Γλύκον, Greek lyric poet + -IC.]

A. *adj.* Epithet of a lyric metre or verse, essentially a logaœdic tetrapody consisting of three trochees and a dactyl; also, composed or consisting of such verses 1779.

B. *sb.* A glyconic verse.

‖**Glycosuria** (gləi:kosiūə·riă, gliko-). 1860. [quasi-L., f. F. *glycose* GLUCOSE + Gr. οὖρον urine + L. suffix *-ia.*] *Path.* A condition in which sugar appears in the urine. Hence **Glycosu·ric** *a.* relating to or affected with g.

†**Gly·cyrize.** 1599. [ad. L. *glycyrrhiza* (see next).] Liquorice -1661.

Glycyrrhizin (glisirəi·zin). 1838. [f. Gr. γλυκύρριζα LIQUORICE + -IN.] *Chem.* The glucoside contained in the root of liquorice (*Glycyrrhiza glabra*).

Glyn(n, obs. f. GLEN.

Glyoxal (gləi,ǫ·ksæl). 1858. [f. GLY(COL + OX(ALIC + *-al* (in CHLORAL, etc.).] *Chem.* A white amorphous solid, called also *oxalic aldehyde.* Hence **Gloxa·lic** *a.*, in *glyoxalic acid*, an acid obtained by treating ethylic alcohol with nitric acid.

Glyoxilin (gləiǫ·ksilin). Also **-yline.** 1875. [? after *glyoxalic* (see prec.).] An explosive, gun-cotton saturated with nitroglycerine.

Glyph (glif). 1775. [ad. Gr. γλυφή carving, f. γλύφειν.] 1. A sculptured mark or symbol (*rare*) 1825. 2. *Arch.* A groove or channel, usually vertical, used esp. in the Doric frieze. Cf. TRIGLYPH. Hence **Gly·phic** *a.* carved, sculptured; *sb.* = GLYPH 1.

Glyphograph (gli·fŏgraf), *sb.* 1855. [f. next.] A plate made by glyphography, or an impression taken from such a plate. So **Glypho·grapher**, one who practises glyphography. **Glyphogra·phic** *a.* relating to or produced by glyphography.

Glyphography (glifǫ·grăfi). 1843. [f. Gr. γλυφο-, γλυφή carving + -γραφία, f. γράφειν to write.] An electrotype process by which a copy of an engraved plate is obtained with a raised surface, suited for letter-press printing.

Glyptic (gli·ptik). 1818. [ad. Gr. γλυπτικός, f. γλύφειν to carve. Cf. F. *glyptique.*]

A. *adj.* 1. Of or pertaining to carving or engraving, esp. on gems. 1847. 2. *Min.* Figured (Webster) 1864.

B. *sb.* The art of carving or engraving, esp. on gems. Also *pl.* Hence **Gly·ptical** *a.* = prec. A. 1.

Glyptodon (gli·ptŏdǫn). Also **-dont.** 1838. [mod.L., f. Gr. γλυπτός + -όδοντ-, ὀδούς.] An extinct S. American quadruped allied to the armadillos, of the size of an ox, covered with a solid carapace, and having fluted teeth. Hence **Glyptodo·ntoid** *a.* resembling (that of) a g.

Glyptography (gliptǫ·grăfi). 1797. [f. Gr. γλυπτός + -γραφία; cf. F. *glyptographie.*] The art of engraving upon gems; the descriptive science of engraved gems. So **Gly·ptograph**, an engraving on a gem. **Glypto·grapher. Glyptogra·phic** *a.* pertaining to g.

Glyster(e: see CLYSTER.

Gmelinite (gme·linəit). 1825. [f. Prof. C. A. *Gmelin*; see -ITE.] *Min.* Hydrous silicate of aluminium, calcium, and sodium, found in colourless, yellow, and flesh-coloured crystals.

Gnapweed, Gnar, var. ff. KNAPWEED, KNAR.

Gnar (nāɹ), *v.* Also **Gnarr.** 1496. [Echoic; cf. MLG. *gnarren*, etc.] *intr.* To snarl, growl. *fig.* A thousand wants Gnarr at the heels of men TENNYSON.

Gnarl (nāɹl), *sb.*[1] 1824. [f. GNARLED.] A contorted knotty protuberance, esp. on a tree. Hence **Gna·rly** *a.*

Gnarl, *sb.*[2] [f. GNARL *v.*[1]] A snarl. E. BRONTË.

†**Gnarl** (nāɹl), *v.*[1] 1593. [freq. of GNAR *v.*] *intr.* To snarl –1814.

Wolues are gnarling, who shall gnaw thee first SHAKS.

Gnarl (nāɹl), *v.*[2] Chiefly in pa. pple. 1814. [f. GNARLED.] *trans.* To contort, twist, make knotted and rugged like an old tree. Also *transf.* and *fig.*

Her lean large hands, So gnarl'd with bone 1814.

Gnarled (nāɹld), *ppl. a.* 1603. [var. of KNURLED; occurs first in Shaks.] Of a tree: Covered with protuberances; distorted, twisted; rugged, knotted.

The vn-wedgable and g. Oke *Meas. for M.* II. ii. 116.

Gnash (næʃ), *sb. rare.* 1804. [f. GNASH *v.*] A gnashing or snap of the teeth.

Gnash (næʃ), *v.* 1496. [app. a var. of GNAST *v.*] 1. *intr.* To strike together or grind the teeth, esp. from rage or anguish. Also said of the teeth. 2. *trans.* To strike (the teeth) together, as in rage or anguish 1590. 3. To bite upon, grind the teeth upon 1812.

1. There they him laid, Gnashing for anguish and despite and shame MILT. 3. I strove..To rend and g. my bonds in vain BYRON.

†**Gnast,** *v.* [ME. *gnaist(e*, ? ad. ON. **gneista*, ablaut-var. of *gnista* to gnash the teeth. Prob. (ult.) echoic.] 1. *intr.* = GNASH *v.* 1. –1530. 2. *trans.* = GNASH *v.* 2. –1460.

Gnat[1] (næt). [OE. *gnæt(t*, cogn. w. Ger. dial. *gnatze.*] 1. A small two-winged fly of the genus *Culex*, esp. *Culex pipiens*, the female of which has a sharp pointed proboscis, by means of which it punctures the skins of animals and sucks their blood. In U.S., the common mosquito, *Culex mosquito.* 2. Applied to insects resembling this; in U.S., to a small stinging fly of the genus *Simulium* 1787.

1. Her waggoner, a small gray-coated G. SHAKS.

Comb.: **g.-catcher,** an American bird of the genus *Polioptila*, esp. *P. cærulea*; **-flower,** *Ophrys apifera*; **-snap, -snapper,** a name of various small birds; see also GNAT[2]; also *fig.*, as a term of contempt; **-strainer,** one who places too much importance on little things (after Matt. xxiii. 24); **-worm,** the larva of a g.

Gnat[2] (næt). *Obs.* exc. *dial.* 1616. [Corruption of KNOT *sb.*[2]] A kind of Sandpiper (*Tringa canutus*); also, local name for the Lesser Tern (*Sterna minuta*).

Gnathic (næ·þik, nē·þik), *a.* 1882. [f. Gr. γνάθος jaw + -IC.] Of or pertaining to the jaws; *spec.* alveolar.

Skulls with a g. index below 98 are orthognathous 1882. So **Gna·thal** *a.*

Gnathite (nē·þəit). 1870. [f. as prec. + -ITE.] *Zool.* One of the mouth-appendages of Arthropoda.

‖**Gnathitis** (neiþəi·tis). 1847. [mod.L., f. as prec. + -ITIS.] *Med.* Inflammation of the cheek or upper jaw.

†**Gna·tho.** 1533. [a. L. *Gnatho*, ad. Gr. γνάθων, used as the proper name of a parasite, (f. γνάθος jaw).] A person resembling the Gnatho of Terence; a parasite, sycophant –1704. Hence **Gnatho·nic,** †**-al** *a.* parasitical, toad-eating. **Gna·thonism,** sycophancy (COLERIDGE). †**Gna·thonize** *v. rare*, to behave as a sycophant.

Gnathopod (nē·þǒpǫd). 1887. [f. Gr. γνάθος + ποδ-, πούς foot.] *Zool.* = next.

Gnathopodite (neiþǫ·pǒdəit). 1882. [f. as prec. + -ITE.] *Zool.* 'One of those limbs which, in crustaceans, have been modified into accessory organs of mastication' (Ogilvie).

Gnathostegite (neiþǫ·stėdʒəit). 1877. [f. as prec. + στέγειν to cover + -ITE.] *Zool.* (See quot.)

A broad plate, which, with its fellow, covers over the other organs, and hence receives the name of the g. HUXLEY.

Gnatling (næ·tliŋ). 1614. [See -LING.] A small gnat; also *fig.*

‖**Gnatoo** (nătu·; prop. ŋa·tu). 1817. [Polynesian; now spelt *gatu* (g = ŋ).] The substance prepared from the bark of the Chinese paper mulberry tree; used for clothing.

Gnaw (nǭ). Pa. t. **gnawed.** Pa. pple. **gnawed, gnawn.** [OE. *gnagan* (ME. *gnawen*, pa. t. *gnew, gnow*); corresp. to OHG. *gnagan*, ON. *gnaga.*] 1. *trans.* To bite persistently so as to injure or remove portions; to wear away by a continued biting or nibbling. Also *absol.* or *intr.* ME. 2. To corrode, waste away, consume 1530. 3. *fig.* Said esp. of passion, remorse, etc. ME. Also *absol.* and *intr.* 1598.

1. They gnawed their tongues for pain *Rev.* xvi. 10. [He] gnaw'd his pen, then dash'd it on the ground POPE. 2. When eating Time shall g. the proudest towers P. FLETCHER. 3. As the flower is gnawed by frost, so every human heart is gnawed by faithlessness RUSKIN. Hence **Gnawed** *ppl. a.*; *spec.* in *Bot.* having the margin irregularly toothed, as if bitten by some animal. **Gna·wer,** one that gnaws; a rodent. Chiefly *Zool.* **Gnaw·ing** *vbl. sb.* a persistent fretting pain (in the bowels); *pl.* pangs of hunger. **Gnaw·ingly** *adv.* **Gnawn** *ppl. a.* bitten away, corroded.

Gneiss (nəis, gnəis). 1757. [a. Ger.] *Geol.* A metamorphic rock, composed, like granite, of quartz, feldspar or orthoclase, and mica, but dist. from it by its foliated or laminated structure. Hence **Gnei·ssic** *a.* of the nature of g. So **Gneissi·tic** *a.* **Gnei·ssoid** *a.* resembling g.; imperfectly gneissic. **Gnei·ssose** *a.* = *gneissic*; also quasi-*sb.* = gneissic rock. **Gnei·ssy** *a.* = *gneissic.*

Gneu, gnew(e, obs. pa. t. of GNAW *v.*

†**Gnide,** *v.* [OE. *gnīdan* = OHG. *gnītan, knītan*, etc.] *trans.* To rub with or between the hands; to bruise, crush. Also *intr.* to crumble away. –ME.

†**Gnoff.** Also **gnof.** ME. [Cf. East Fris. *knufe* lump.] A churl, boor, lout –1610.

Gnome[1] (nōum, nōu·mi). 1577. [a. Gr. γνώμη; pl. γνῶμαι sayings, maxims, f. γνω- root of γιγνώσκειν.] A general maxim; proverb, aphorism, or apophthegm.

Gnome[2] (nōum). 1712. [a. F., ad. mod.L. *gnomus*, used by Paracelsus as a synonym of *Pygmæus.*] 1. One of a race of diminutive spirits fabled to inhabit the interior of the earth and to be the guardians of its treasures; a goblin, dwarf. 2. *U.S.* A name of humming-birds, as the Giant Gnome (*Patagona gigas*) 1889. *Comb.* **g.-owl** *U.S.*, a small owl of the genus *Glaucidium.* Hence **Gnomed** *ppl. a.* inhabited by gnomes.

Gnomic (nōu·mik). 1815. [ad. Gr. γνωμικός, f. γνώμη GNOME[1]; cf. F. *gnomique.*]

A. *adj.* Of the nature of, or consisting of, gnomes or general maxims.

In Euripides [the poetical faculty developed itself] in g. wisdom 1838. *G. poet*, a composer of verses. *G. aorist* (Gram.), the aorist used in proverbs, etc. to express what *once happened* FARRAR. So **Gno·mical** *a.*

B. *sb. pl. The gnomics* (= F. *les gnomiques*), the older Greek g. poets 1821. So **Gno·mist** (*rare*), a g. poet or writer.

Gnomology (nōumǫ·lŏdʒi). 1645. [ad. Gr. γνωμολογία, f. γνώμη GNOME[1]; see -LOGY.] 1. A collection of general maxims or precepts. 2. GNOMIC discourse; the sententious element in writing 1806.

1. Gnomologies, or collections of moral sentences from the poets HALLAM. Hence **Gnomolo·gic, -al** *a.* of the nature of general maxims; sententious. **Gnomo·logist** (*rare*), a gnomic writer.

Gnomon (nōu·mǫn). 1546. [a. Gr. γνώμων inspector, indicator (*spec.* the gnomon of a dial, a carpenter's square), f. γνω-, γιγνώσκειν to perceive, judge, KNOW.] 1. A pillar, rod, etc. which by its shadow indicates the time of day; esp. the pin or triangular plate in an ordinary sun-dial. b. A column or style employed in observing the meridian altitude of the sun 1625. †c. *joc.* The nose –1803. †2. A rule, canon of belief or action –1698. 3. *Geom.* That part of a parallelogram which remains after a similar parallelogram is taken away from one of its corners. (So Gr. γνώμων, from the resemblance to a carpenter's square.) 1570. †4. Something shaped like a carpenter's square; an L-shaped bar, etc. –1777.

Gnomonic (nōumǫ·nik). 1601. [ad. L. *gnomonicus*, a. Gr., f. γνώμων GNOMON.]

A. *adj.* 1. Of or pertaining to the gnomon or sun-dial, or to the measuring of time, etc. by means of this. 2. *transf.* That indicates like a gnomon. COLERIDGE.

1. *G. column*: a cylinder, on which the hour of the day is represented by the shadow of a style. *G. projection*: a projection in which the point of sight is the centre of a sphere. So called from its relation to the art of dialling. So **Gnomo·nical** *a.* Hence **Gnomo·nically** *adv.*

B. *sb.* Pl. *Gnomonics* (rarely sing. *gnomonic*): the art of dialling. *Obs.* exc. *Hist.* 1656.

Hence †**Gno·monist,** one skilled in gnomonics.

‖**Gnosis** (nōu·sis). *Pl.* (rare) **gnoses** (nōu·siz). 1703. [a. Gr. γνῶσις, f. γνω-, γιγνώσκειν to KNOW.] A special knowledge of spiritual mysteries. Often: Gnostic philosophy, Gnosticism.

Gnostic (nǫ·stik). 1585. [ad. Gr. γνωστικός pertaining to knowledge, f. γνω-; see prec.]

A. *adj.* 1. Relating to knowledge; cognitive; intellectual 1656. b. Possessing esoteric spiritual knowledge 1800. c. *joc.* Clever, knowing 1819. 2. Pertaining to the Gnostics; occult 1838.

1. c. I said you were a d—d g. fellow SCOTT.

B. *sb.* 1. *Hist.* Chiefly *pl.* The name of certain heretical sects among the early Christians who claimed to have superior knowledge of spiritual things, and interpreted the sacred writings by a mystic philosophy (cf. GNOSIS) 1585. 2. †One skilled or learned in any subject 1641; 'a knowing one', an adept in dishonest acts 1819.

1. The ghastly dream of G. and Manichæan TRENCH. Hence **Gno·stical** *a.* = GNOSTIC *a.* **Gno·stically** *adv.* **Gno·sticism,** the system or principles professed by the Gnostics. **Gno·sticize** *v. intr.* to adopt or expand G. views; *trans.* to interpret on G. principles.

Gnow(ȝ)e, obs. pa. t. of GNAW *v.*

Gnu (nū). 1777. [Hottentot wd.] A S. African quadruped (*Catoblepas gnu*) belonging to the antelope family, but resembling an ox or buffalo in shape; also known as *wildebeest.* The brindled gnu (*C. gorgon*) is a distinct species.

Go (gōu), *sb.* Pl. **goes.** 1680. [f. the vb.] 1. The action of going, in various senses. Also, gait (*rare*). 1727. 2. *colloq.* Orig. of a horse: Power of going, mettle. Hence: Dash, energy; animation, 'swing'. 1825. 3. *colloq.* or *vulgar.* A proceeding; an (awkward) turn of affairs 1796. 4. *colloq.* A turn (at doing something); an attempt *at* 1835. 5. A quantity of anything supplied at one time 1799. 6. *Cribbage.* A cry uttered by the player if he cannot play a card in his turn; the position thus disclosed (for which the adversary scores one point) 1821. 7. *colloq.* Something that 'goes'; a success. *U.S.* 1877.

1. Phr. *Come and go*: see COME *sb.*[1] 2. A queer man..full of 'go', but never getting on 1864. The 'swing' and 'go' of ballads 1884. 3. It must have been a *pretty go* 1833. 4. I..sat down, and they had a go 1889. 5. The goes of stout..passed round merrily THACKERAY.

Phrases. (*It's*) *no go* (colloq.): the attempt is hopeless. *The go* (now only *all* or *quite the go*): the height of fashion; the 'correct thing'; the 'rage' (*colloq.*). *Near go*: a 'close shave'. *On the go*: in constant motion, in a restless state. *Great go, Little go*, see the adjs.

Go (gōu), *v.* Pa. t. **went** (went); pa. pple. gone (gǫn). [Com. Teut. defective vb.: OE. inf. *gān*; pa. t. *ēode*, ME. *gede, yede, yode*, superseded in the 15th c. by *went*, pa. t. of WEND, in the south, and by *gaed*, formed on the present-stem *gæ-, gai-*, in Sc. and n. dial.]

gen. Intransitive verb of motion, expressing a movement (I) irrespective of the point of departure or destination; (II) *away from* the position occupied by the speaker; and (III) *to* or *towards* a point not occupied by the speaker either in fact or in thought. *spec.* In addition, it had formerly the special sense of *walking.* The movement may be either self-originated or impressed.

I. Of movement, irrespective of the point of departure or destination.

†1. = To walk (opp. to *creep, ride*, etc.); to walk at an ordinary pace (opp. to *run*, etc.) –1836. b. *To go upon the earth* (also simply): to live and move –1579. c. To walk or step in a certain manner; *esp.* of a horse: *to go narrow, wide* (see adjs.); *to go above his ground* = to step high –1838. 2. To move along, travel.

Of persons and things. OE. **b.** with *adj.* or *adv.*: *lit.* and *fig.* *Go bet* (see BET, *adv.*[2]). *To go like blazes* (see BLAZE *sb.* 2 b), *even* (see EVEN *adv.* I. 2), *full drive, tilt* (see sbs.). ME. **c.** with advb. acc. of the way pursued, distance, speed ME. **d.** with cognate obj., *to go (the) circuit, a cruise*, etc. 1526. †**e.** Hence occas. *trans.*: To go through, over –1683. **3.** *spec.* In *Hunting* = to ride (to hounds) 1841. **4.** To take a specified course (physical or moral), often with adv. acc. Of persons and things. OE. **b.** *Naut. As you go! As she goes* = on the same tack 1692. **c.** Of a line, etc.: To 'run' (in a certain direction) 1889. **d.** with various advs., as *amiss, aside, counter*, etc.: see advs. ME. **5. a.** Of persons: To be guided *by*. *To go with the tide* or *the times*. 1485. **b.** Of things: To be regulated *by*; to proceed *upon* (an idea, etc.) 1590. **6.** with adj. or phr.: To be habitually, *esp.* as to attire or circumstances. Cf. *to go without* (see VI), *short* (see SHORT *a*). OE. **7.** Of a female: To pass (a period) in gestation. In full, *to go with calf, child*, etc. ME. **8.** To be moving. **a.** Of persons, *esp.* in *Who goes? Who goes there?* 1593. **b.** Of the sea (with defining word) 1611. **c.** Of a piece of mechanism: to act, work 1680. *transf.* and *fig.* 1565. **d.** *esp.* Of a watch, etc. (with defining word or phr.): To keep (good or bad) time 1588. **9.** with reference to sound. **a.** Of a musical instrument: To sound. Of a gun: To be fired. 1503. **b.** Of a clock: To strike (the hour) 1709. **10.** In senses 8 and 9, with imitative additions, e.g. *to go bang, crash, smash, snap*, etc. 1791. **11.** Of time: To pass ME. **12.** Of coin, etc.: To circulate; to pass current *at* a certain value ME. **13.** Of a report, etc.: To pass from mouth to mouth. Const. *of*, †*on*, †*upon*. 1542. **14.** *To go by or under the name or title of*: to be known as; to be ascribed to 1599. **15.** To be ordinarily. *As men, things*, etc. *go*. 1545. **16.** Of a document, etc.: To run 1605. **17.** Of verses: To glide along. Of a song: To admit of being sung; to follow the measure of (a tune). 1589. **18.** Of a series of events, etc.: To turn out (well or ill). Const. *with*, (†*for*). 1489. **b.** Of a war, etc., a vote, an election; To result in a specified manner. Also of a constituency or a politician; *colloq.* with adj. 1597. **c.** To take its course; *esp.* in phr. *to let (judgement, etc.) go by default* 1820. **d.** *What has gone of—? What is gone with—?* = 'What has become of—?' or 'What ails—?' 1771. **19.** Of a performance, etc.: To proceed *well, badly*, etc. 1665. **b.** To succeed 1742. ¶ **20.** *That goes without saying* = 'that is a matter of course'; tr. F. *cela va sans dire*. 1878.

1. I have resolved to run when I can, to go when I cannot run, and to creep when I cannot go BUNYAN. **2.** And so she went, and she went, and never rested the evening, where she went in the morning, till [etc.] SIDNEY. **b.** The Government..are going very strong, as the rowing-man says 1893. **c.** To go three miles in an hour MIEGE. **e.** I went the wasteful woodes and forest wyde SPENSER. **4.** They didna gang the road by the turnpike,..they gaed by the sands SCOTT. **d.** There are more ways of going wrong than of going right H. SPENCER. **5. a.** Had he gone on the chances, he would have won 'CAVENDISH'. **b.** Promotion goes solely by length of service 1892. **6.** Why, he us'd to go very fine, when he was here in town SWIFT. **7.** The mother of man is said to *go* nine months in producing him 1841. **8. b.** The sea went very high DE FOE. **c.** [The] church clock has not gone for twenty years 1890. *transf.* Those who believe that democracy ..will go of itself LOWELL. **9. b.** The clock on the mantel-piece went eight WESTALL. **10.** Clatter, clatter, went the horses' hoofs BARING-GOULD. **12.** Bank-notes, she supposes, will go everywhere 1872. **13.** Now the story goes that he [the young Pretender] is in the Highlands W. HARRIS. **14.** Shakespeare did not write that play, though it generally goes under his name M. J. GUEST. **16.** You shall be King. And Thane of Cawdor too: went it not so? SHAKS. **17.** This is a passing merry one, and goes to the tune of two maids wooing a man SHAKS. **18.** All went merry as a wedding-bell MRS. LYNN LYNTON. **b.** A general election went decidedly against him T. F. TOUT. **d.** What's gone with that boy? DICKENS. **19.** The annual dinner..never goes better than when he is in the chair 1892. **b.** It became evident from an early point in the play that it would 'go' 1893.

II. Uses in which movement *from* a place is the primary notion.

1. To depart. Const. *from*, †*of*. Cf. *go away* (VII below) OE. **b.** with cognate acc. *To go one's way*, etc. ME. **c.** *fig.* e.g. *to go from one's word*, etc. 1530. †**d.** In *imp.* as a rebuke. SHAKS. **e.** *To let go* (see LET *v.*). **2.** To begin to move from a given point or state; *esp.* in *go!* said by the starter in a race, etc. Of an explosive = *to go off* (see VII); also *fig.* HERE *goes*, THERE *goes*, TOUCH *and go*. *From the word Go*: from the start (*U.S. colloq.*). ME. **3.** with adjs. like *quit, unpunished*, etc.: orig. to leave court, now to continue 'quit', etc. ME. *To go free* (see FREE *a.*) ME. **4.** To pass by sale. Const. *at, for*; also *to go cheap*. So *Going!* = on the point of being sold! *Gone!* = sold! ME. **5.** Of money: To be parted with, spent. Const. *in*. ME. **6.** To be given up, sacrificed 1715. **7.** To cease to exist; to be taken away; to come to an end ME. **b.** *Cricket.* Of a wicket: To be 'lost' 1890. **8.** To 'depart this life', die ME. **b.** In phrases, e.g. *to go the way of all the earth* (1 *Kings* ii. 2), *to a better world*, etc.; also joc. and slang, *to go aloft, off the hooks, to (the) pot*, etc. **9.** To fail, give way. **a.** Of a material object: To break, to crack; to wear 1798. **b.** To faint 1768. **c.** Of a crop, etc. 1735. **d.** Of living beings, their organs, or faculties 1809.

1. Go, baffled coward, lest I run upon thee MILT. **d.** Go, go, you are a counterfeit cowardly knaue SHAKS. **2.** On the word 'to go' being given Oxford started well 1892. **3.** Such forays usually went unpunished MISS YONGE. **4.** I'll knock 'em down at forty pounds. Going—going—gone SHERIDAN. **6.** The house must go, the carriage must go, the horses must go, and yet [etc.] FR. A. KEMBLE. **7.** One of the results of using those..drugs is, that the will entirely goes BLACK. **8.** Thy neighbour's wife..dyeth. Every one can say, Why! wee are all mortall;..but when his owne goes, then [etc.] HEALEY. **9. a.** About half-past three the foremast went in three places NELSON. **d.** Omnibus-horses generally go first in the loins 1892.

III. Of movement *not* towards the speaker or the position occupied by him in thought.

**of self-originated movement or action.*

1. To move, or proceed to or towards a place, into the presence of a person, or in a specified direction Const. *to, towards, into*, or with any prep. or adv. of motion whither. OE. **b.** *To go to Jericho, Bath, Hong Kong, Putney*, etc.: used in imper. etc. to imply that one desires to see no more of a person. So *to go to Halifax* (see GIBBET). 1648. **c.** *transf.* Of a road, passage, etc. To 'lead' *to, into*, etc. ME. **2.** With an additional meaning implied. **a.** The destination implies what is done there, as in *to go to the* BALL, *to* BED, CHURCH, PRESS, SCHOOL, etc. **b.** Of female animals: *To go to (the) bull, cow*, etc. = to copulate with 1577. **c.** As in *to go to college, the university*, etc.: to enter on the mode of life associated with college, etc. So *to go to the bar*, †*on the highway* (or †*the road*), *the stage, the streets*: to become a barrister, a highwayman, an actor, a prostitute. 1727. **d.** *To go to sea*: to go a voyage; usu. to become a sailor. Of rigging: To be carried adrift. 1599. **3.** The motive of going is often indicated: e.g. **a.** by the simple *inf.* (*arch.* and *dial.*) OE. **b.** by the *inf.* with *to* ME. **c.** by *and* with a verb, where the force of *go* tends to disappear. *To go and* (do something) = to be so foolish, unreasonable, or unlucky as to —. OE. **d.** by a sb. (governed by *to*) denoting an action, a ceremony, etc. ME. **e.** by the vbl. sb. governed by *a* (= *on*; now often omitted); also by ordinary sbs. denoting an action, governed by †*in, on, upon*. *Go a begging*. ME. **f.** by a sb., denoting function or capacity. *Obs.* exc. in *to go apprentice*, and *to go bail*, now usu. *fig.* = 'I will be bound', I am certain. 1665. **4.** To have recourse, appeal *to* (an authority, etc.); to carry one's case *to* or *before* (a tribunal, etc.). *To go to the country* (see COUNTRY, 6). ME. **5.** To turn *to* (an occupation, etc.); to resort to a specified course of action. *To go to law, war, work*, etc. ME. **b.** *To go (for) to* (do something); *vulg.* = 'To be so foolish, bold, or severe as to —' 1752. **6.** To carry one's action so far as, etc. Const. *to*; also with adv. or advb. phr., or cognate or advb. acc., e.g. *to go the* LENGTH *of*. For phrases see FAR, NEAR, NIGH. 1577. **b.** *esp.* of offers or abatements in negotiations. †*To go less*: to offer or accept less. 1626. **c.** 'To share equally in', as in *to go halves (with), to go shares, snacks*, etc.; or *to go sharer, mates, partners* (see sbs.). **d.** To put oneself *to* (trouble, etc.) 1842. **e.** *trans.* (as with cognate accs.). To go to the extent of. *To go the whole hog* (see HOG). 1855. **7.** *trans.* To risk, stake. Also *absol.* *To go better*, at cards, to stake more. Also *to go one better*: hence *fig.* to outbid or outdo. 1605.

1. That he do appoint a fleet to go to the Northward PEPYS. **b.** 'She may go to Tunbridge, or she may go to Bath, or she may go to Jericho for me' THACKERAY. **2. c.** I..advise you to go upon the road..the only post of honour left you SWIFT. **d.** I should like to go to sea with Uncle Maurice NELSON. **3. a.** Your Streatham and my Bookham may go hang JANE AUSTEN. **c.** Would'st thou haue me go and beg my food SHAKS. **d.** When they were all gone one day to dinner SIDNEY. **e.** I was resolved not to go sneaking to the lower professors GOLDSM. **f.** He won't marry her now, I'll go bail RIDER HAGGARD. **4.** You must go to Aristotle for that BLACKIE. **5.** He that..goes to Law to be relieved Is sillier than a sottish chews BUTLER. **6.** The generality..want either force or inclination to go to the bottom and try the merits COLLIER. **b.** Lewis consented to go as high as twenty-five thousand crowns MACAULAY. **7.** Men that would go forty guineas on a game of cribbage GOLDSM.

***of passive movement, change of state*, etc.

8. To be carried, moved, etc. *to, towards, into*, etc. (*lit.* and *fig.*) OE. *To go to the bottom* (see BOTTOM *sb.*). **b.** fig. *To go to one's heart*: to cause one great sorrow. 1481. **9. a.** To be capable of passing *into, through*, etc. Of a number, to be contained *in*; also *impers.* ('won't go') in division or subtraction. 1686. **b.** To be usually or properly placed 1729. **10.** To pass *to*; to be allotted to 1607. **b.** To pass by inheritance, or succession 1818. **11.** To be applied or appropriated to. Const. *to, towards, to* with *inf.* ME. **12.** To contribute to a result. Const. *to, towards, to* with *inf.* 1607. **b.** To amount *to* 1841. **13.** To conduce, tend *to*; with *sb.* or *v.* in *inf.* †To have a result amounting *to*. 1781. **14.** To reach, extend; with advb. phr. 1586. **b.** *As* (or *so*) *far as it goes*: a phrase of limitation ME. **c.** *To go a good, great, short way (to* or *towards)*: to have a great, little effect; to have great influence *with* 1697. **d.** With *far, as* or *so far, further, a long way*, etc. Of provisions, etc.: To hold out. Of clothing: To last. Of money: To have purchasing power. ME. **15.** To pass into a condition. **a.** With adj.: To become, get to be. (Cf. COME, III. 5.) 1583. **b.** To turn *to*; to be reduced *to*. 1591. **c.** Const. *to* with *sb.* in phr. *to go to pieces, to rack, ruin, smash*, etc. (see *sbs.*).

8. I am further of opinion..that there was evidence of negligence to go to the jury LD. SHAND. **9. a.** Elzevirs..go readily into the pocket A. LANG. Four from three won't go—borrow one 1890. **10.** American ships..divide the freights which formerly went to the British..shipowner 1849. **11.** All the Revenue goes to the keeping up of the Magnificence of the Court 1688. **12.** Whole gardens of roses go to one drop of the attar 1890. **13.** The bill, therefore, went to the confiscation of the whole of the Company's property JAS. MILL. It goes to show that the Dutch are not the equals of the English 1889. **14.** But the difference goes still further DEUTSCH. **b.** The poor law system ..is, so far as it goes, Socialism pure and simple 1885. **d.** £4 a year..in those days would go as far as forty would do now M. J. GUEST. **15. a.** He went bankrupt 1861. **b.** The devil's corn all goes to bran MRS. BARR.

IV. Quasi-*trans.* with pronoun as obj.

1. With pleonastic refl. pron. *arch.* [Cf. F. *s'en aller.*] ME. **2. Go it.** †**a.** To direct one's course. 1689. †**b.** *imp.* = Be off! 1797. **c.** *colloq.* and *slang.* To go along at great speed; to engage recklessly in dissipation. *To go it blind*: without regarding the consequences. 1821.

V. Special uses of the pples.

Of going. a. *Going in*, or *of —*: about to attain (a specified age); also without prep. **b.** *Going to* (with inf.): on the way to, preparing to. Now = *about to*. Cf. F. *je vais*. (*To be) just going to.* **Of gone. a.** *To be gone*: to take oneself off. Cf. BEGONE. So *to get oneself gone* (see GET *v.*). **b.** In *Archery*, beyond the mark. In *Bowls*, beyond the jack (*transf.* of the player). **c.** Dead. *Dead and gone* (see DEAD). **d.** In a swoon. Dead drunk. **e.** Infatuated. *Gone on* (colloq. or vulg.): infatuated about. **f.** *Far gone*: in disease; deeply entangled; exhausted, etc. **g.** Lost, ruined, undone. Of a battle, game, etc. †**h.** = AGO, SINCE. **i.** = reckoned from a past date. **j.** = over the age mentioned.

VI. With preposition, in specialized uses.

Go about —. †**a.** To encompass. **b.** To busy oneself about; also †to seek after. (Cf. *to be* ABOUT.) **Go after —.** To pursue; to visit as a wooer, or a disciple. **Go against, †again —.** †**a.** To go to meet. **b.** Of an enterprise, etc.: To result unfavourably to. **c.** To run counter to. **d.** *To go against the* GRAIN, HAIR, †*heart* (also *against me* = against my feelings): to be uncongenial (see AGAINST). **Go at —.** To attack; take in hand vigorously. *To go at it*: to enter upon with energy. **Go before —. a.** To precede in time or order. †**b.** To take precedence of. **Go behind —.** To reopen a question previously closed. **Go by —.** †**a.** To pass without notice. (Cf. GO-BY *sb.*) †**b.** *To go by the worse, worst*: to be worsted. **Go for —.** †**a.** To start for. **b.** To go to fetch. **c.** To pass as; to be valued as. Now *to go for nothing, little, something*. **d.** To have for one's aim; †also = *to go in for*; to exert oneself to attain. **e.** *colloq.* To assail, attack. **Go into —. a.** See simple senses and INTO. †*To go into the field*: i.e. to fight a duel. *To go into* (*a cabinet, Parliament*). *To go into society*. **b.** To take part in. †**c.** To accede to. **d.** To enter upon a state, condition, or process; to take up an attitude. **e.** To pass *into* (ecstasies, hysterics, etc.). **f.** To enter as a profession, etc. **g.** To adopt as a style of dress, to dress in (*esp.* mourning). **h.** *To go into* (†*a*, †*the*) *committee* (see COMMITTEE). Said also of a bill. **i.** To examine minutely. *To go into detail(s* (see DETAIL *sb.*). **Go off —. a.** See simple senses and OFF. *To go off one's head* or *chump* (see HEAD *sb.*, CHUMP *sb.*). *To go off milk*: (of a cow) to cease to yield. **b.** To fail to fulfil. **Go on —. a.** See simple senses and ON. *To go on a wind*: to avail oneself of it for sailing. *To go on board* (see BOARD *sb.*). *To go on one's knees* (see KNEE). †**b.** To approach (a point of time). †**c.** *U.S. colloq.*: To care for. **d.** To become chargeable to (the PARISH, etc.). **Go over —. a.** To cross. **b.** To visit and inspect. **c.** To admit of being laid over. **d.** To consider seriatim. **e.** To rehearse. **f.** To repeat. **g.** To examine in detail; to revise and retouch throughout. **Go through —. a.** To deal in succession with all the stages of (a business, etc.). **b.** To examine seriatim. **c.** To declaim, recite, etc. at length; to perform in detail. **d.** To experience, undergo. **e.** Of a book: To have all the copies sold of (an edition); now, to be published successively in (so many editions). (Cf. *pass, press through*.) **Go upon —.** (See simple senses and UPON.) **a.** To take in hand. **b.** To proceed upon as a foundation. **Go with —. a.** To accompany; to 'keep company with' (vulg.). **b.** To be associated with. **c.** To side with. **d.** To match. **e.** To follow intelligently. **Go without —.** Not to have; put up with the want of. Also *absol.* or *ellipt.*

VII. Combined with adverbs.

Go about. a. To go to and fro, travel; to be current; also †to complete a cycle. **b.** *Mil.* To turn round. †**c.** To use circumlocution. **d.** *Naut.* (See ABOUT A). **e.** *To go about to* (see ABOUT A). **Go abroad.** (See simple senses and ABROAD.) **a.** Of a report, etc.: To circulate (*arch.*). **b.** To go out of doors (*obs.* exc. *dial.*). **c.** To go to a foreign country. **Go ahead.** (See AHEAD.) To make one's way to the front in a race, etc. Also (chiefly U.S.), to make rapid progress. **Go along. a.** See simple senses and ALONG *adv.* In imp. *Go along! Go along with you!* = 'Be off'; also = *Go on*. **b.** *To go along with*: to proceed in company with; †to follow intelligently; to approve of (up to a point); to attend upon; to be the regular concomitant of; †to be classed with. **Go away.** (See simple senses and AWAY.) **a.** To depart *from*. †Of time: To pass. **b.** *To go away with*: to carry off. **c.** To go freely. **Go back.** (See simple senses and BACK *adv.*) **a.** To return; *fig.* to revert to a former state or mode of action; †to lose ground. **b.** To carry one's view backward in time. **c.** *To go back from* (colloq. *of, on, upon*): to withdraw from (an engagement, etc.). **d.** *To go back on*: to betray (*colloq.*); orig. U.S. **e.** To extend backwards (in space or time). **Go backward(s. a.** See simple senses and BACKWARD, BACKWARDS. †To change for the worse. **Go before.** (See simple senses and BEFORE.) **a.** *lit.* To go in advance. **b.** To precede in time or order. **Go by. a.** To go past (see BY *adv.*). †**b.** To go unregarded, etc. **Go down.** (See simple senses and DOWN *adv.*) **a.** To proceed to a lower place or condition; to descend (*from*, †*of*); *transf.* (of a road, etc.) to lead downwards. Of a vessel: to sink. *To go down on one's knees* (see KNEE). **b.** To be continued down *to*. **c.** To be overthrown. **d.** To be set down in writing. **e.** Of waves, wind, etc.: To subside. **f.** To be swallowed. **g.** *fig.* To find acceptance *with*. **Go forth.** (Now *arch.* or *rhet.*) **a.** See simple senses and FORTH. (Cf. FORTHGO.) **b.** Of a decree, etc.: To be issued. **Go forward**: see FORWARD *adv.* **Go in. a.** See simple senses and IN. **b.** To enter as a competitor. Phr. *go in and win*. In *Poker* = to play for the pool. **c.** *Cricket.* To take the batting. Also *to go in to bat*. **d.** Of the sun, etc.: To be obscured. **e.** *To go into* or *unto* (O. T. after Heb.): To have carnal knowledge of. **f.** *To go in at*: To assail vigorously (*colloq.*). **Go in for.** (*Rec.* and *colloq.*) **a.** To make one's object; select as one's 'line', style, or fashion; commit oneself to (a principle, etc.); to venture on acquiring or wearing; to indulge in. **b.** To offer oneself for examination in; as a candidate *for*. (Cf. *to be* IN *for*.) **Go in with.** †**a.** To agree with. **b.** To join. **Go off.** (See simple senses and OFF.) **a.** To depart (suddenly); to set out. Of an actor: To leave the stage. At cards: to lead. *To go off at score* (see SCORE). *To go off at a tangent* (see TANGENT). **b.** To be taken off (esp. quickly). **c.** Of firearms, etc.: To be discharged, explode. **d.** To pass away, die. **e.** Of a sensation: To pass away. **f.** To deteriorate. **g.** To start into sudden action; to break *into* a fit of laughter, etc. **h.** To pass into unconsciousness; *to go off to sleep, in* or *into a fit*, etc. **i.** To fall through. **j.** To be disposed of by sale. Of daughters, to be married (*colloq.*). **k.** Of a performance, etc.: To succeed. **Go on.** (See simple senses and ON.) **a.** To continue a journey. **b.** To continue in a course of action; in speech. Const. *in, with*, †*to* with inf.; also *simply*. Also with pr. pple. **c.** To proceed *to*, as the next step. **d.** To get on; to 'manage'. **e.** To continue further; also, to be in progress. Of time: To pass. **f.** To behave (reprehensibly). **g.** *colloq.* To talk volubly; to rail *at*. **h.** Of dress: To admit of being put on. **i.** *Cricket.* To take up the bowling. *Theatr.* To appear in a part. **j.** *imper.* (*int.*) = Go your ways (*colloq.*). **k.** *Going on for*: approaching (an age or period). Also = 'nearly'. †**l.** To make an attack. **Go out. a.** *lit.* To go from within; *esp.* from one's house. (See simple senses and OUT.) **b.** To take the field (chiefly *Hist.* with reference to 1715 and 1745); to fight a duel. *To go out to fight*. **c.** Of a fire, etc.: To be extinguished. Also *transf.* and *fig.* **d.** In University use. †(*a*) To take the degree of (doctor, etc.). (*b*) At Cambridge: To take the degree of B.A. *in* a subject, or *in* honours. **e.** To die. *To go out of the world*. **f.** Of the tide: To recede. **g.** To retire from office. **h.** *ellipt.* for *to go out of date, fashion*, etc. **i.** Of a year: To terminate. **j.** To go *to* another country as a colonist, ambassador, etc. **k.** Chiefly of girls and women: To find work away from home. Const. *to*. **l.** To mix in general society. **m.** To be published. **n.** To abandon work. In full, *to go out on strike*. **o.** To be drawn *to*, by affection or sympathy. Also of the feeling: To go forth *to*. **Go out of.** See simple senses and OUT. *To go out of the stable*: to be entered for a race. *To go out of hand* (see HAND). **b.** *To go out of cultivation, fashion*, etc.: to cease to be cultivated, fashionable. *To go out of print*: Of a book, etc., when all the printed copies are sold off. *To go out of gear* or *order*: to become disarranged. *To go out of one's mind* or *senses*: to become deranged. **Go over.** See simple senses and OVER; often, to cross a piece of water, a hill, etc. **b.** To pay a visit at some distance. **c.** To pass *to* another owner. **d.** To change one's party. *To go over* (*to Rome*): to become Roman Catholic. *To go over to the majority* (= L. *abire ad plures*): to die (see MAJORITY). **e.** Of a vehicle. To be upset. So of driver, or passengers. **Go round. a.** To rotate. Of the head: To 'swim'. **b.** To complete a revolution. **c.** To make a circuit; to visit various places in succession. **d.** To pass from one to another in a company. **e.** To make a detour. Also *colloq.* to visit informally. **f.** To be long enough to encompass. **g.** Of food, etc.: To be sufficient to supply every one. In *cards*, when all the players can follow suit. **Go through. a.** See simple senses and THROUGH. †**b.** To complete what is begun. **c.** Of a proposition: To be carried. **Go through** *with*. **a.** To carry to completion. **Go to, †go till.** †**a.** To set to work. In *imp.* = Come on! L. *age*. **b.** In *imp.*, to express disapprobation or the like = Come, come! **Go together. a.** See simple senses and TOGETHER. *To go together by the ears* (see EAR *sb.*[1]). **b.** To be mutually concomitant. **Go under.** Of persons: To fail; to disappear from society; in *U.S. slang*, to die. Of a literary work: To drop out of sight. **Go up. a.** To pass to a higher place or position; to rise. †Of a sword: To be put *up* (into the sheath). **b.** Chiefly *U.S.* To go to ruin; become bankrupt. **c.** Of a cry, etc. = ASCEND I. **c. d.** To be put up. **e.** To increase in number, price, or value. **f.** *To go up and down* (see UP).

VIII. Phraseological combs. (*colloq.* or *techn.*) serving as sb. or adj.

Go-ashore (*a*) *adj.*, characteristic of a sailor when ashore; (*b*) *sb. pl.*, clothes worn by him when ashore; (*c*) *New Zealand*, an iron cauldron with three feet and attachments for hanging it over a fire; **go-as-you-please** *a.*, unfettered by regulations; **go-getter** (*U.S. colloq.*), an enterprising, pushing person; so **-getting** *ppl. a.*; **go-no-further**, a kind of apple; **go-out**, a sluice for allowing water to escape from tidal lands; **go-slow** *a.* (cf. CA'CANNY); **go-to-bed**, one who is sleepy; **go-to-bed-at-noon** = GOAT'S-BEARD 2; **go-to-meeting** *a.*; **go-within-each-other** *a.*, of boxes.

Goa (gōᵘ·ă). 1846. [Corruptly a. Tibetan *dgoba*.] A Tibetan antelope, *Procapra picticauda*.

Goad (gōᵘd). [OE. *gád*, corresp. to Lombard *gaida* arrow-head:—OTeut. type **gaidâ*.] **1.** A stick, pointed at one end, for driving cattle, esp. oxen used in ploughing. **2.** *fig.* Anything that pricks or wounds like a goad 1561. **3.** †**a.** A cloth-measure = 4½ feet -1727. **b.** A land-measure = 15, or (locally) 9, feet 1587. **4.** = GAD *sb.*[1] **1.** 1855.

Goad (gōᵘd), *v.* 1579. [f. prec.] **1.** *trans.* To prick with a goad; to drive or urge on *to* something by such means 1619. **2.** *fig.* To assail or prick as with a goad; to instigate or impel by mental pain or annoyance 1579.

2. This [mutiny] shall seeme..their owne, Which we haue goaded on-ward *Cor.* II. iii. 271. Hence **Goa·dster**, a driver who uses a goad. CARLYLE.

Goaf (gōᵘf). Also **goave**. 1839. [? Cf. GOB *sb.*[4]] *Coal-mining.* The empty space from which the coal has been extracted. Hence **Goa·fing** (in same sense); also, the refuse left behind in working coal.

Go-ahead (gōᵘ·ăˌhe:d), *a. colloq.* (orig. *U.S.*) 1834. [orig. phr. *go ahead*.] Forward and energetic; pushing, enterprising.

What a go-ahead place France is C. KINGSLEY.

Goal (gōᵘl), *sb.* [ME. *gol*, of difficult etym. Usually taken as ad. F. *gaule* pole, stick; but see N.E.D.] †**1.** A boundary, limit. SHOREHAM. **2.** The terminal point of a race; any object by which this is marked; a winning-post, or the like 1531. Also *fig.* of the object of effort or ambition, or the destination of a (difficult) journey 1608. **3.** In football, and similar games, the posts between which the ball is driven to win a point in the game. Also, the winning of a goal, the point scored for this. 1548. **4. a.** *Rom. Antiq.* As tr. L. *meta*, the conical column marking each of the two turning-points in a chariot-race. Also *fig.* 1634. ¶ **b.** The starting-point of a race. Also *fig. rare.* 1697.

2. *fig.* Then Honour be but a Goale to my Will, This day Ile rise SHAKS. **3.** Phr. *To get, take, win a g.* (often *fig.*). *To make, score a g.* *To drop a g.*: see DROP *v.* **4. a.** Part curb thir fierie Steeds, or shun the G. With rapid wheels MILT. **b.** Hast thou beheld, when from the G. they start DRYDEN.

Comb.: **g.-keeper**, a player whose special duty is to protect the g.; **-line**, the line which bounds each end of the field of play, and in the centre of which the g. is placed; **-post**.

Goar, obs. f. GORE.

Goat (gōᵘt). *Pl.* **goats**. [Com. Teut.: OE. *gát* fem.:—OTeut. **gait-*, cogn. w. L. *hædus* kid:—Aryan **ghaidos-*. In ME., north. dialects have *gāt, gait*, pl. *gait* (= ON. *geitr*), southern *goot* (pl. *geet*). OE. *gát* denoted only the female goat; the male was called *bucca* BUCK *sb.*[1] The terms *he-goat* and *she-goat* appear about the end of the 14th c.] **1.** A ruminant quadruped of the genus *Capra*. Occas. used with reference to *Matt.* xxv. 32, 33. **b.** Used *Zool.* in *pl.* = mod.L. *Caprinæ*, the name of the sub-family to which the genus *Capra* belongs. Also applied to certain antelopes. 1731. **2.** *transf.* **a.** The zodiacal sign Capricorn ME. †**b.** The star Capella (Alpha Aurigæ) -1674. †**c.** [tr. Gr. *αἶξ*.] A fiery meteor. STANLEY. **3.** *fig.* A licentious man 1675. **4.** *To play* or *act the* (*giddy*) *g.*: To play the fool 1879. **5.** *To get* (*a person's*) *g.*, to annoy him 1912.

1. A jet-black g. white-horned, white-hooved TENNYSON. **b.** †**Blue g.** = BLAUWBOK. **Rocky Mountain g.**, *Haplocerus montanus*. **Yellow g.** = DZEREN.

Combs.: **a. g.-antelope**, an antelope of the genus *Nemorhædus*; **-chafer**, a capricorn beetle; **-fig** (= L. *caprificus*), the fig-tree in its wild state; **-fish**, the *Balistes capriscus* and the *Phycis furcatus* of Europe, the *Upeneus maculatus* of America, etc.; **-leap** = *goat's-leap*; **-moth**, *Cossus ligniperda*; **-owl** = GOAT-SUCKER; **-root**, the plant *Ononis Natrix*; **-rue** = *goat's rue*; **-singing, -song**, renderings of Gr. *τραγῳδία* TRAGEDY; **-star** = GOAT 2 b; **-weed**, a name for the W. Indian plants *Capraria biflora* and *Stemodia durantifolia*; **-willow**, *Salix capræa*.

b. Comb. with *goat's*: **goat's bane**, *Aconitum tragoctonum*; **goat's foot**, a name for the S. African plant *Oxalis caprina*; **goat's leaf**, the foliage of the Woodbine; †**goat's leap** = CAPRIOLE; **goat's-rue**, *Galega officinalis*; **goat's thorn**, a name for *Astragalus Tragacanthus* and other species; **goat's-wheat**, the genus *Tragopyrum*, allied to the buckwheat; **goat's-wool**, (*a*) something non-existent; (*b*) the fine wool mingled with the hair of some species of goats.

Goatee (gōᵘtī·). 1844 (*-y*). [See -EE [2].] A beard trimmed in the form of a tuft hanging from the chin, resembling that of a he-goat.

Goat-herd, goatherd (gōᵘ·tˌhəɹd). OE. [f. GOAT + HERD *sb.*[2]] One who tends goats.

Goatish (gōᵘ·tiʃ), *a.* 1529. [See -ISH.] Characteristic of, or resembling, a goat; *spec.* lascivious.

A g., ram-faced rascal SMOLLETT. Hence **Goa·tishly** *adv.*, **-ness**.

Goatling (gōᵘ·tliŋ). 1870. [See -LING.] A goat above 12 months and under 2 years old.

Goa·t's-bea:rd. 1548. A name of plants. 1. *Spiræa Ulmaria*, meadow-sweet 1578. 2. *Tragopogon pratensis*; also *T. porrifolius*, salsify. 3. Some species of mushroom. ? *Obs.* 1688.

Goatskin (gōu·tˌskin). ME. The skin of a goat, esp. one used for a garment, a wine-bottle, etc. Also *attrib.*

Goa·tsu:cker. 1611. [transl. of L. *caprimulgus* (f. *capra* + *mulgere* to milk), Gr. *αἰγοθήλας* (f. *αἰγο-*, *αἴξ* + *θηλάζειν* to suck).] The bird *Caprimulgus europæus*, supposed to suck the udders of goats. Also applied to other birds of the same genus, or of the family *Caprimulgidæ*.

Goaty (gōu·ti), *a.* 1600. [See -Y 1.] Goat-like; goatish.

Gob (gǫb), *sb.*1 ME. [App. a. OF. *gobe*, *goube* (mod. *gobbe*), a mouthful, lump, conn. w. *gober* to swallow; see GOBBET.] A mass or lump (now *dial.*); a lump, clot of some slimy substance (now *dial.* or *vulgar*) 1555.

Gob (gǫb), *sb.*2 *n. dial.* and *slang.* 1550. [? a. Gael. and Ir. *gob* beak, mouth.] The mouth.

Gob (gǫb), *sb.*3 *dial.* 1695. [= GAB *sb.*2] Talk, language.

Gob (gǫb), *sb.*4 1839. [? altered f. GOAF, infl. by GOB *sb.*1] *Coal-mining.* The empty space from which the coal has been extracted in the 'long-wall' system of mining (cf. GOAF); also, the rubbish used for packing such a space. Also *attrib.*

Gob (gǫb), *v.* 1863. [? f. GOB *sb.*1] *trans.* To choke up (a furnace). *intr.* Of a furnace: To become choked.

Gobang (gōubæ·ŋ). 1886. [Corruptly a. Jap. *goban*, said to be ad. Chinese *k'i pan* chess-board.] A game played on a chequer-board, each player endeavouring to be the first to get five pieces into line.

Gobbet (gǫ·bėt). Now *rare* or *arch.* ME. [a. OF. *gobet*, dim. of *gobe* GOB *sb.*1] 1. †A piece or fragment of anything that is divided, cut, or broken –1878; *spec.* a piece of raw flesh ME. Also *fig.* †2. A lump or mass –1712. †3. A large lump or mouthful of food; *spec.* a ball of flour, etc. used in feeding poultry [= F. *gobbe*] –1862. b. A lump of half-digested food. Also *fig.* 1553.

1. Gobbettes of wodde vnder ye name of percelles of the holy crosse 1538. *spec.* an extract from a text set for translation or comment. 3. b. Belching raw gobbets from his maw, o'ercharged ADDISON. Hence †**Go·bbetmeal** *adv.*, in gobbets; piecemeal.

†**Gobbet**, *v.* 1450. [a. OF. *gobeter*, or f. GOBBET *sb.*] 1. *trans.* To swallow as a gobbet or in gobbets –1692. 2. To divide into portions or gobbets –1726.

Gobbing (gǫ·biŋ), *vbl. sb.* 1839. [f. GOB *sb.*4] *Coal-mining.* Packing with waste rock; the material used for this. var. (dial.) **Go·bbin.**

Gobble (gǫ·b'l), *sb.* 1878. [prob. f. next.] *Golf.* A rapid straight putt into the hole.

Gobble (gǫ·b'l), *v.*1 1601. [prob. f. GOB *sb.*1 or 2, and partly echoic.] 1. *trans.* To swallow hurriedly in large mouthfuls, esp. in a noisy fashion. 2. *U.S. slang.* To snatch up, lay hold of, 'collar' 1825.

1. The Supper gobbled up in haste SWIFT.

Gobble (gǫ·b'l), *v.*2 1680. [Imitative.] *intr.* Of a turkey-cock: To make its characteristic noise in the throat; also (rarely) *transf.*

transf. A tiny geyser gobbled R. KIPLING. Hence **Gobble** *sb.* the noise made by a turkey-cock. **Go·bbler**, a turkey-cock.

Gobelin (gobəlæ̃n, gǫ·bəlin). Also **Gobelins.** 1823. [f. *Gobelins*, the state-factory of tapestry in Paris, so named after its founders.] 1. Used *attrib.*, as in *G. tapestry*, a tapestry made at Gobelins, and imitations of this. 2. *absol.* 'A variety of damask used for upholstery, made of silk and wool or silk and cotton' (*Cent. Dict.*).

‖**Gobemouche** (gobəmuʃ). 1818. [a. F. *gobe-mouches* (sing. and pl.).] One who credulously accepts all news. Also *attrib.*

The g. expression of countenance with which he is swallowing an article in the National KINGLAKE.

Gobet, obs. f. GOBBET.

Go·-betwee:n. 1598. [f. GO *v.* + BETWEEN.] 1. One who passes to and fro between parties, with messages, proposals, etc.; an intermediary. 2. Anything that goes between or connects two other things. Also *attrib.* 1862.

Gobiid (gōu·biˌid). 1884. [f. L. *gobius* GOBY + -ID.]

A. *adj.* Belonging to the *Gobiidæ* or gobies proper.

B. *sb.* One of these; a goby.

Gobioid (gōu·biˌoid). 1854. [f. as prec. + -OID.]

A. *adj.* Belonging to the family *Gobioides* of Cuvier or to the *Gobioidea*, comprising fishes allied to the goby.

B. *sb.* A fish of this kind.

Goblet 1 (gǫ·blėt). [ME. *gobelet*, a. OF., f. *gobel*, *gobeau* cup, of unkn. origin.] 1. A drinking-cup, properly bowl-shaped and without handles, sometimes mounted on a foot and fitted with a cover. Later, a wine-cup. Now only *arch.* b. A glass with a foot and stem, as dist. from a tumbler. †2. A conical cup or thimble used by conjurers –1692.

1. I doe thinke him as concaue as a couered g., or a Worme-eaten nut SHAKS.

†**Goblet** 2. 1530. = GOBBET *sb.* –1742.

Goblin (gǫ·blin). [ME. *gobelin*, a. F.; perh. f. med.L. *cobalus*, *covalus*, a. Gr. *κόβαλος* a rogue, goblin.] 1. A mischievous and ugly demon. 2. *attrib.* (or *adj.*) 1649.

1. To whom the G. [Death] full of wrath replied MILT. 2. The affrightment of this G. word, *Demagogue* MILT. Hence **Go·blinize** *v.* to convert into a g. **Go·blinry**, the acts or practices of goblins.

Gob-line. 1841. *Naut.* A rope leading from the martingale inboard (R. H. Dana).

Goby (gōu·bi). 1769. [ad. L. *gobius*, *cobius*, a. Gr. *κωβιός* (usually rendered GUDGEON).] One of a genus (*Gobius*) of small acanthopterygian fishes having the ventral fins joined into a disk or sucker. Also, a member of the family *Gobiidæ*.

Go-by (gōu·bəi). 1611. [f. GO *v.* + BY *adv.*] 1. The action of going by. *Obs.* exc. in *nonce-uses*. 1673. 2. *Racing*, etc. The action of getting in front of another dog or horse 1611.

1. Phr. *To give the go-by to*: a. To outstrip. †Also, to leave. b. To give the slip to, elude. c. To pass without notice; to 'cut'; to evade.

Go·-cart. 1676. [f. GO *v.* + CART.] 1. A light framework, moving on castors, in which a child may learn to walk without falling. Also *fig.* 1689. b. A child's carriage drawn by hand 1854. 2. A litter, palankeen, or the like 1676. 3. A hand-cart 1759. 4. A kind of light open carriage 1828.

Goclenian (gǫklī·niăn), *a.* Epithet of a variety of the sorites due to Rudolf *Goclenius* (1547–1628). See SORITES.

God (gǫd). [Com. Teut.: OE. *god*:— OTeut. type **guđom*. The primary meaning has been given as 'what is invoked' and as 'what is worshipped by sacrifice'.]

I. Pre-Christian senses. 1. A superhuman person (regarded as masc.: see GODDESS) who is worshipped as having power over nature and the fortunes of mankind; a deity. (Chiefly of heathen divinities, but often with a Christian colouring.) 2. An image or other object which is worshipped; an idol OE. 3. *transf.* of persons OE.; of things 1586. 4. *Theat. pl.* The occupants of the gallery, so called because seated on high. Also *rarely* in *sing.* 1752.

1. They conteyne the wicked actes and whoredomes of the goddes 1577. Come, let us go—to a land wherein gods of the old time wandered CLOUGH. Phr. *The g. of day*: the Sun. *The g. of war*: Mars (Ares). *The g. of love, the blind g.*: Amor (Eros), or Cupid. *The g. of wine*: Bacchus. *A feast, sight*, etc. *fit for the gods*. 2. Thou shalt make thee no molten gods *Exod.* xxiv. 17. 3. Sweare by thy gratious selfe, Which is the G. of my Idolatry SHAKS. The old mans g., his gold, has wonne upon her FLETCHER.

II. In the Christian and monotheistic sense. The One object of supreme adoration; the Creator and Ruler of the Universe. (Now always with capital G.) OE. †b. In ME. often used for Christ. So, in 16th c., *in the year of G.* = Anno Domini. (Cf. *Mother of God*: see MOTHER.) –1565.

Phrases. *With G.*, in heaven. *Act of God* (Law): see ACT *sb.* *God's truth*: the absolute truth. *On God's earth*: emphatic for 'on earth'. *God eyld (ild, dild) you* = God yield you (see YIELD). *God wot* (arch.), *God knows.* b. By god that for us deyde CHAUCER.

Comb. a. **g.-bote**, a fine for crimes and offences against God; also an eccl. fine; **-home** *nonce-wd.*, the home of God, heaven; also as transl. of ON. *Goðheimr*, the abode of the gods (W. MORRIS).

b. possessive, as †**God's body**, the sacramental bread; **God's book**, the Bible; †**God's house**, (*a*) ? a pyx, (*b*) an almshouse [cf. F. *maison Dieu*]; **God's image**, the human body (*Gen.* i. 27); **God's service** = worship, an act of worship; **God's Sunday**, Easter day.

God (gǫd), *v.* Now *rare.* 1576. [f. the sb.] a. *trans.* To deify. b. quasi-*trans.* *To god it*: to play the god. 1595.

God-almighty (gǫdǭlməi·ti). Also (*colloq.* and *dial.*) **God-a-mighty.** OE. a. = GOD *sb.* II. b. In derisive use (with *a* and in *pl.*): One who poses, or is regarded, as omnipotent 1682.

†**God-a-me·rcy**, *int. phr.* ME. [= *God have mercy*, i. e. 'God reward you' (see MERCY); hence used as an expression of thanks.] 1. An exclam. of applause or thanks. Const. *of*. –1828. 2. quasi-*sb.* = 'thank you' –1692.

2. It would not be worth God-ha-mercy 1626.

Go·d-chi:ld. ME. [f. GOD *sb.* + CHILD (see GODFATHER).] A person considered in relation to his or her god-parent or god-parents; a godson or god-daughter.

God-da·mn(-me). ME. [f. GOD *sb.* and DAMN *v.*] 1. The utterance of this as a profane oath. Also *attrib.* 1640. †2. One who is addicted to swearing. Also *attrib.* –1713. ‖3. (After F. *goddam.*) An Englishman ME.

Go·d-dau:ghter. OE. [See GODFATHER.] A female considered in relation to her sponsors.

Goddess (gǫ·dės). ME. [f. GOD *sb.* + -ESS.] 1. A female deity. 2. Applied to a woman 1579.

1. A Goddesse that was clept Deane ME. Phr. *G. of love, night*, etc. 2. He call'd her his G., she call'd him an Ass 1729.

Gode, obs. f. GOOD.

Godelich, godely, obs. ff. GODLY, GOODLY.

Godet (gode·t, ‖gode). 1580. [a. F. *godet.*] †1. A drinking-cup –1629. 2. A triangular piece of stuff inserted in a dress, glove, etc. 1923.

Go·dfa:ther, *sb.* OE. [f. GOD *sb.* + FATHER *sb.*] 1. A male sponsor considered in relation to his god-child.

The sponsors, in making profession of the Christian faith on behalf of the person baptized, and guaranteeing his or her religious education, were held to enter into a spiritual relationship with the person baptized and with each other, and were in OE. denoted by designations formed by prefixing *god-* to the words expressing natural relationship, as *godfæder*, *godmódor*, *godbearn*, etc.

b. A male sponsor at Confirmation 1549. c. A sponsor at the consecration of a bell 1498. 2. *transf.* and *fig.* 1588. †b. *pl.* (*joc.*) Jurymen –1634.

1. Right so as he that engendreth a child is his flesshly fader right so is his g. his fadere spiritueel CHAUCER. 2. These earthly Godfathers of heauens lights, That giue a name to euery fixed Starre SHAKS. b. *Merch. V.* IV. i. 398.

Go·dfather, *v.* 1780. [f. prec.] *trans.* To act as godfather to; to take under one's care; to give a name to.

Go·d-fea:ring, *ppl. a.* 1835. That fears God, deeply religious.

A grave and staid God-fearing man TENNYSON.

Godhead (gǫ·dhed). ME. [f. GOD *sb.*; see -HEAD.] 1. The quality of being God or a god; divine nature or essence; deity. 2. a. *The Godhead* = GOD *sb.* II. ME. b. A deity (now *rare*) 1586.

1. Man .. sinns Against the high Supremacie of Heav'n, Affecting God-head MILT. 2. a. 'Tis true I am alone; so was the G., ere he made the world DRYDEN.

Godhood (gǫ·dhud). ME. [See -HOOD.] 1. = GODHEAD 1. †2. = GODHEAD 2 b. 1602.

Go·dkin. 1802. [See -KIN.] = GODLING.

Godless (gǫ·dlės), *a.* 1528. [f. GOD *sb.* + -LESS.] Without God or a god; irreligious, ungodly; impious, wicked. **Go·dlessness.**

Godlike (gǫ·dləik), *a.* 1513. [See -LIKE.] 1. Resembling God (or a god); divine. b. quasi-*adv.* After the fashion of a god 1667. 2. Appropriate to a god; resembling (that of) God or a god 1555. b. *absol.* CARLYLE.

1. The G. Angel MILT. 2. The God-like faculty of reason COLERIDGE. Hence **Go·dlikeness.**

Godling (gǫ·dliŋ). 1500. [See -LING.] A little god. (Chiefly joc.)

Godly (gǫ·dli), *a.* ME. [f. GOD *sb.* + -LY¹.] 1. Of or pertaining to God; coming from God; divine; spiritual. *Obs.* exc. *arch.* 2. Observant of the laws of God; religious, pious. Also *absol.* 1526.

2. For g. sorowe causeth repentaunce TINDALE 2 *Cor.* vii. 9. *absol.* The g. are not better than other men MACAULAY. Hence **Go·dlily** *adv.* **Go·dliness.**

Godly (gǫ·dli), *adv.* Now *rare.* 1530. [See prec. and -LY².] In a godly fashion. *Comb.*: †**g.-learned** *a.*, learned in divinity; †**-wise** *a.* wise in divine things.

Go·d-mamma·. 1828. Childish or fam. for GODMOTHER.

Go·d-ma·n. 1559. [tr. Gr. θεάνδρος, θεάνθρωπος.] One who is both God and man; said of Christ.

Go·dmo:ther. OE. [Cf. GODFATHER.] A female sponsor in relation to her god-child.

Go-dow·n. 1641. [f. phr. *go down*; see GO *v.*] 1. A draught, gulp. ? *Obs.* 2. *Sc.* A drinking match. SCOTT. 3. *U.S.* (Western). 'A cutting in the bank of a stream for enabling cattle to.. get to the water' (*Cent. Dict.*).

Godown (gōᵘdaun). *Anglo-Ind.* 1588. [ad. Malay *gadong, godong.*] A warehouse or store for goods in the East.

Go·d-papa:. 1826. Childish or fam. for GODFATHER.

Go·d-pa:rent. 1865. A godfather or godmother.

†**Go·d-phere.** [? for rustic *godfer.*] A godfather. B. JONS.

Godroon, mod. var. of GADROON.

God's acre. 1617. [ad. Ger. *Gottesacker.* Properly, 'God's seed-field', in which the bodies of the departed are 'sown' (1 *Cor.* xv. 36-44).] A churchyard.

Godsend (gǫ·dsend). 1814. [Altered f. *God's send.*] 1. Something sent by God, esp. something unexpected of which the recipient is greatly in want. b. *spec.* A wreck (*dial.*) 1814. 2. A welcome event; a happy chance 1831.

1. Mr. Telford..has left me £500..This is truly a G. SOUTHEY.

Godship (gǫ·dʃip). 1553. [f. GOD *sb.* + -SHIP.] The position or personality of a god: esp. as a joc. title.

I..beg his British godship's humble pardon BYRON.

Godsib, -sip, obs. ff. GOSSIP *sb.*

Godson (gǫ·dsʊn). OE. [Cf. GODFATHER.] A male god-child.

Go·d-spee·d. 1526. [See GOD *sb.* and SPEED *v.*] 1. *To bid* (*wish*) *one God-speed*, to utter the words 'God speed (you)'; *esp.* to wish one success in an enterprise, etc. 2. In subst. use, *a God-speed*, a parting wish for one's success 1856. Also *attrib.* 3. *fig.* 1606.

1. A brace of Draymen bid God speed him well SHAKS. 2. *attrib.* A Godspeed dinner 1867. 3. †*The Godspeed* (of a thing), the finish.

Go·d's-pe·nny. ME. [Cf. *God's earth* (see GOD *sb.*). Cf. F. *denier à Dieu.*] 1. A small sum paid as earnest-money on striking a bargain (cf. ARLES-, EARNEST-PENNY). Now only *dial.* †2. A penny given in charity 1550.

Godward (gǫ·dwǝɹd). ME. [f. GOD *sb.* + -WARD.]

A. *adv.* 1. Towards God; in the direction of God. 2. In relation or with reference to God ME. So **Go·dwards** *adv.*

B. *adj.* Tending or directed towards God 1861.

Godwit (gǫ·dwit). 1552. [?] A marsh-bird (genus *Limosa*) resembling a curlew, but having the bill slightly curled upwards. The black-tailed godwit (*L. ægocephala* or *melanura*) and the bar-tailed godwit (*L. lapponica* or *rufa*) are British species; others are natives of northern Europe and America. Formerly in great repute for the table.

Godwyts..accounted the daintiest dish in England; and I think, for the bigness, of the biggest price SIR T. BROWNE.

Goen, obs. f. *gone*: see GO *v.*

Goer (gōᵘ·ǝɹ). ME. [f. GO *v.* + -ER¹.] 1. One who or that which goes (see GO *v.*). †2. A foot. CHAPMAN.

1. A g. to tauernes LANGL. Goers betweene SHAKS. A light grey Nag..a very good G. 1697.

Goethian (gö·tiǎn). Also **-ean.** 1840. [f. Johann Wolfgang von *Goethe* (1749-1832) + -IAN.]

A. *adj.* Of, pertaining to, or characteristic of Goethe, his writings, opinions, etc.

The G. paganism 1856.

B. *sb.* An admirer or follower of Goethe 1850.

Goety (gōᵘ·ĭti). *Obs.* exc. *arch.* 1569. [ad. Gr. γοητεία, f. γοητ-, γόης sorcerer, through F. *goétie.*] Witchcraft or magic performed by the invocation and employment of evil spirits; necromancy. Hence **Goe·tic** *a.* of or pertaining to g.; *sb.* a magician, sorcerer.

Goff (gǫf). *Obs.* exc. *dial.* 1570. [app. a. F. *goffe*, ad. It. *goffo* (of unkn. origin).] A dolt, a stupid fellow.

Goff, var. of GOLF.

Goffer (gǫ·fǝɹ), *sb.* 1865. [ad. F. *gaufre.*] 1. A goffering-tool. 2. 'An ornamental plaiting used for the frills and borders of women's caps, etc.' (Ogilvie).

Goffer (gǫ·fǝɹ, gōᵘ·fǝɹ), **gauffer** (gǭ·fǝɹ), *v.* 1706. [ad. F. *gaufrer*, f. *gaufre* honeycomb.] *trans.* To make wavy by means of heated goffering-irons; to flute or crimp (lace, etc.). Hence **Go·fferer.**

Goffered (gǫ·fǝɹd), *ppl. a.* 1706. [f. prec. + -ED¹.] 1. Of frills, etc.: Fluted, crimped. 2. *Bookbinding* and *Printing.* Embossed or impressed with ornamental figures, esp. *goffered edges* 1866. 3. *Entom.* Of the elytra of certain beetles: Having very prominent longitudinal lines or carinæ, which in many cases diverge from the base and converge towards the tip (*Cent. Dict.*).

Goffering (gǫ·fǝriŋ), *vbl. sb.* 1848. [f. as prec. + -ING¹.] The action of GOFFER *v.*; also its result; goffered lace, frills, etc.

Comb.: **g.-iron, -tongs,** an iron tool used for goffering lace, frills, etc.; **-press,** a press for crimping the material used in making artificial flowers.

†**Gog¹.** ME. Corrupt f. GOD in oaths, etc. -1602.

†**Gog².** 1573. [app. f. *on gog*, substituted for earlier AGOG (q.v.).] *To set on g.*, to excite, make eager -1673.

Goggle (gǫ·g'l), *sb.* 1616. [f. the vb.] 1. One who goggles (*rare*). †2. A goggling look; a squint, leer, stare -1688. 3. *slang.* In *pl.*: The eyes 1710. 4. *pl.* (rarely *sing.*) A kind of spectacles, having glasses (usually coloured) or fine wire-netting, fixed in short tubes, and worn to protect the eyes from dust, excess of light, etc.; formerly also to correct squinting. Also (*colloq.* and *joc.*) Spectacles with round glasses. 1715. b. Blinds for horses 1808.

Phr. *The goggles*, a disease of sheep; the staggers 1793.

Goggle (gǫ·g'l), *a.* 1540. [Prop. the vb.-stem in comb.] Of the eye: Protuberant, full and rolling; also, †squinting.

His g. eyes were always rolling about wildly THACKERAY.

Goggle (gǫ·g'l), *v.* ME. [? freq. of *gog, expressing oscillating movement (cf. *jog, joggle*).] 1. *intr.* To turn the eyes to one side or other, to look obliquely, to squint. In later use, to roll the eyes about. Now *rare.* b. Of the eyes: To squint. In mod. use, to project and move unsteadily, to roll. 1540. 2. *trans.* To turn (one's eye) to one side, or (now) from side to side with an unsteady motion 1583. 3. *intr.* To sway or roll about ME.

1. b. The frog's hideous large eyes were goggling out of his head THACKERAY. Hence **Go·ggled** *ppl. a.* (now *rare*) = GOGGLE *a.*

Goggle-eye (gǫ·g'l₁əi:). ME. [See GOGGLE *a.* and *v.*] †a. One who squints. †b. Squinting. c. *U.S.* = GOGGLER 2. d. 'One of two or more species of American fresh-water fishes of the family *Centrarchidæ*' (Webster).

Goggle-eyed (gǫ·g'l₁əid), *a.* ME. [f. *goggle eye* (see GOGGLE *a.*) + -ED².] Having prominent, staring or rolling eyes; also, †squint-eyed.

Goggler (gǫ·glǝɹ). 1821. [f. GOGGLE *v.* + -ER¹.] 1. *slang.* An eye. 2. *U.S.* The big-eyed scad, *Trachurops crumenophthalmus* 1884.

Goglet (gǫ·glėt), **gugglet** (gʊ·glėt). *Anglo-Ind.* Also †**gurglet.** 1698. [ad. Pg. *gorgoleta.*] A long-necked vessel of porous earthenware for keeping water cool by evaporation.

†**Go·gmago·g.** ME. [f. *Goemagot*, a British giant; altered after the names *Gog* and *Magog* (Ezek. xxxviii-xxxix).] A giant, a man of immense stature and strength -1630.

Goidel (goi·dėl). *Hist.* 1882. [a. OIr. *Góidel* (pl. *Góidil*), a GAEL. See GADHELIC.] A GAEL in the widest sense, including the Irish and the Highlanders of Scotland. Hence **Goide·lic** *a.* of or pertaining to the Goidels; *sb.* the language of the Goidels.

Going (gōᵘ·iŋ), *vbl. sb.* ME. [f. GO *v.* + -ING¹.] 1. The action of GO *v.*; *esp.* departure ME.; †the faculty of walking -1635. †2. Manner of going; gait -1805. 3. *Building.* Width of passage (of a stair) 1712. 4. Condition of the ground for walking, driving, hunting, etc. 1859.

1. Stand not vpon the order of your g. SHAKS. The day is placid in its g. WORDSW. 4. The fences are fair, and the g. pretty good 1887.

Phrases. *Going down*: setting (of the sun). *Goings-on*: proceedings, actions, doings (usu. with implied censure). †*Goings-out*: expenses, outgoings. *To set g.* (or *a-going*): to set in motion.

Comb.: **g.-barrel,** the barrel of a watch or clock round which are teeth for driving the train direct without the intervention of a fusee; also *attrib.*; **in g. order** (primarily of a clock), in a condition for going properly; **-train,** a train of wheels in a clock, answering the same purpose as the g.-barrel in a watch; **-wheel,** an arrangement for keeping a clock in motion while it is being wound up.

Going (gōᵘ·iŋ), *ppl. a.* ME. [-ING².] That goes; departing; current; working.

Phr. *A g. concern*: one in actual operation.

Goitre (goi·tǝɹ). Also **goître,** *U.S.* **goiter.** 1625. [a. F. *goitre, goître*, f. *goitreux*, ad. Prov. *goitros*:—pop. L. *gutturiosum*, f. *guttur* throat.] *Path.* A morbid (often enormous) enlargement of the thyroid gland of the neck; bronchocele. 2. A swelling of the neck in some lizards 1834. **Goi·tral, Goi·tred** *adjs.* = next.

Goitrous (goi·trǝs), *a.* 1796. [ad. F. *goitreux*; see prec. and -OUS.] Affected with, like, or pertaining to, goitre. Of a locality: Characterized by the prevalence of goitre.

Golconda (gǫlkǫ·ndă). 1780. Old name of Hyderabad, formerly celebrated for its diamonds, used as = 'a mine of wealth'.

Gold (gōᵘld). [Com. Teut.: OE. *gold*:—OTeut. *gulþom :—pre-Teut. *ghlto-, app. f. root *ghel- yellow (see GALL *sb.*¹), with suffix -*to*-.] 1. The most precious metal; characterized by its yellow colour, non-liability to rust, high specific gravity, and great malleability and ductility. Chemical symbol Au. 2. The metal as a valuable possession or as a medium of exchange; hence, gold coin; also, in rhet. use, wealth OE. 3. *fig.* Something brilliant, beautiful, or precious 1553. b. Gilding. *Merch. V.* II. vii. 36. c. *pl.* Kinds of gold (*rare*) 1683. †4. The metal as used to ornament textile fabrics; gold thread; as in *g. of Venice*, etc. Hence textile materials embroidered with or partly made of this. ME. 5. Used with defining words in the names of kinds of gold, alloys, imitations of gold, etc. 1839. 6. The colour of the metal ME. 7. *Archery.* The gilt centre or bull's-eye of a target 1876. 8. *attrib.* or *adj.* a. Made or consisting of gold ME. b. Gold-coloured, golden yellow 1590. c. With reference to the use of gold for coinage and as a standard of value, as *g. standard*; also, of sums in depreciated currencies: reckoned at par 1776.

1. The roof was fretted g. MILT. 2. Where g. makes way Ther is no interruption 1616. 3. *Heart of g.*: a noble-hearted person (= F. *un cœur d'or*). The King's..a Heart of G. SHAKS. Time will run back and fetch the Age of G. MILT. 4. Vallens of Venice g., in needle worke SHAKS. 5. ANGEL, DUTCH, FULMINATING, etc. G.: see these words. *Dead g.*, unburnished or g. without lustre; *jeweller's g.*, 'an alloy containing three parts of g. to one of copper' (Webster); *red g.*, g. alloyed with copper. *Fairy g.* = fairy money (see FAIRY). 6. Many a colourd plume sprinkl'd with G. MILT. 7. *To make a g.*: to hit the bull's-eye. 8. a. That Booke..That in G. claspes, Lockes in the Golden storie SHAKS. b. *Old g.*, of a dulled golden yellow with a brownish tinge. Gowns of old g. sateen 1882.

Combs. 1. General: as *g.-coast, -ore, -vein*, etc.; *-bearing, -broker*, etc.; *-embroidered, -inlaid, -mounted*, etc.; *-red*, etc.; *-hilted, -striped*, etc.

2. Special: **g.-amalgam,** g. combined with mercury in a soft or plastic state (found native in 1848); †**-beat,** †**-beaten** *ppl. adjs.*, adorned with beaten g.; **-beating,** the process of beating out g. into a leaf; **g.**

beetle *U.S.*, any of various beetles of the family Chrysomelidæ and Cassididæ; **g. beryl** = CHRYSOBERYL; **-bug** *U.S.*, (*a*) = *gold-beetle*; (*b*) a plutocrat; also, an advocate of a single (gold) standard; **-carp** = GOLDFISH; **-cloth**, cloth of g. (see CLOTH *sb.*); **-digging**, (*a*) digging for g.; (*b*) *pl.* the place where g.-digging is carried on; **-driver** = GOLD-BEATER 1; **†-end-man**, one who buys up broken pieces of g.; **-fever**, the rage for going in search of g.; **goldfinny**, a fish of the wrasse family; **†-flint**, flint containing g.; **-flux** = AVENTURINE 1; **-fringe**, a moth, *Pyralis costalis*; **-mill**, a mill in which g. ore is crushed; also *fig.*; **-mouthed** *a.*, whose speech is golden; **-note** *U.S.*, one payable only in g.; **g. plate**, vessels made of g.; **-plating**, g. in thin sheets; **-purple**, the compound oxide which is precipitated upon mixing the solutions of g. and tin; **-rush**, a rush to the gold-fields; **-sand**, sand containing particles of g.; also *fig.*; **-shell**, a shell on which powdered g. mixed with gum water is spread for painters' use; **goldsinny** = *goldfinny*; **-size**, a size laid on as a surface on which to apply g.-leaf; **-solder**, †(*a*) = CHRYSOCOLLA 1; (*b*) an alloy for soldering g.; **-spangle**, a moth, *Noctua bractea*; **-spot**, a moth, *Noctua festucæ*; **-stone**, †(*a*) the yellow topaz; (*b*) a piece of g. ore; (*c*) pop. name of breccia; (*d*) = AVENTURINE 1; **g. swift**, a moth, *Hepialus hectus*; **-tail** (moth), *Porthesia chrysorrhœa*; **-thread**, spun g., a flatted g. wrapped or laid over a thread of silk, by twisting it with a wheel, etc.; **-web**, †(*a*) cloth of g.; a covering for sweetmeats made of melted sugar, spun with a knife; **†-worm**, a glow-worm.

b. in names of plants, as **g.-balls**, old name for buttercups; **-bloom**, the marigold; **-flower**, †(*a*) *Helichrysum Stœchas*; (*b*) the S. African genus *Gorteria*; **g. of pleasure**, *Camelina sativa*; **-shrub**, *Palicourea speciosa*; **-thread**, *Coptis trifolia*, so called from its fibrous yellow roots.

c. in names of birds, as **g.-breasted trumpeter**, *Psophia crepitans*; **-capped weaver bird**, *Ploceus icterocephalus*; **goldcrest** = *golden-crested wren* (see WREN); **-hammer**, the yellow-hammer; **-head**, the pochard, *Fuligula ferina*; **g. robin**, the Baltimore oriole.

Go·ld-bea·ter. ME. **1.** One who beats out gold into gold leaf. **2.** *pl.* A genus of Coleopterous insects remarkable for their golden-green and copper colours.

1. *Goldbeater's skin*, a prepared animal membrane used to separate the leaves of gold-foil during the process of beating; also, occas., to cover wounds.

Gold dust, go·ld-dust. 1703. **1.** Gold in very fine particles, as commonly obtained in a natural state. **2.** *Bot.* A pop. name of *Alyssum saxatile*. Also of *Sedum acre*. 1866.

Golden (gōᵘ·ld'n), *a.* ME. [f. GOLD + -EN 4, repl. GILDEN (q. v.).] **1.** Made of, consisting of, gold. **2.** Containing gold; auriferous. Of a district: Abounding in gold. ME. **3.** Of the colour of gold. Also *fig.* ME. **4.** Most excellent, important, or precious 1498. **5.** Of rules, precepts, etc.: Of inestimable utility; often *spec.* with reference to Matt. vii. 12. 1542. **6.** Of a time or epoch: Flourishing, joyous 1530. **†7.** Pertaining to gold (as the object of desire, pursuit, etc.) –1720.

1. *The g. fleece*, the fabulous fleece of gold in search of which Jason went to Colchis; (*Order of the*) *G. Fleece* (see FLEECE *sb.*). *G. ball*, the apple of discord (see APPLE). *G. gates*, the gates of Heaven. **2** Some bound for Guinea, g. Sand to find DRYDEN. **3** G. corn POPE, (*fig.*) promises SHAKS. **4** I haue bought G. Opinions from all sorts of people SHAKS. **5** *The g. mean*, the avoidance of excess and defect [tr. L. *aurea mediocritas*]. *G. number* [tr. med.L. *aureus numerus*; so called from its importance in calculating the date of Easter]: the number of any year in the Metonic lunar cycle of 19 years. The number for a year *n* of the Christian era is the remainder of the operation $(n+1)\div 19$.

Combs., etc.: **g. book**, a register of the nobility of the state of Venice; **g. ear**, a moth, *Hydrœcia nictitans*; **g. earth**, yellow arsenic or orpiment; **g. maid**, the fish *Crenilabrus melops* or *tinca*; **-mouth**, used to render the name *Chrysostom* (see GILDEN *a.*); **-mouthed** *a.*, whose speech is g. (used chiefly as prec.); **g. perch**, 'a fresh-water fish of Australia, *Ctenolates ambiguus*' (Morris); **g. rain**, a kind of firework; **-ring**, a worm that gnaws the vine and wraps itself up in its leaves; **g. spur**, a papal order, the order of St. Sylvester; **g. star**, 'a kind of monstrance or ciborium used at Rome in the Papal High Mass on Easter-day' (Lee); **g. sulphide, sulphuret**, persulphide of antimony or antimony pentasulphide, Sb_2S_5 (Watts); **g. syrup** (see SYRUP); **-wasp**, a brightly-coloured hymenopterous insect of the family *Chrysididæ*, esp. *Chrysis ignita*; **g. wedding** (see WEDDING); **g. wrasse** = *golden maid*.

b. in names of plants, as **†g. apple**, the tomato; **-club**, the American plant *Orontium aquaticum*; **-crown**, the American genus *Chrysostemma*; **g. cudweed**, *Helichrysum orientale*; also *Pterocaulon virgatum*; **-cup**, pop. name of species of *Ranunculus*, *Caltha*, *Trollius*; **g. feather**, the common g.-leaved *Pyrethrum*; **g. flower**, the corn marigold; **g. flower of Peru**, the sunflower; **-hair**, *Chrysocoma comaurea*; **g. herb**, the orach; **-locks**, the fern *Polypodium vulgare*; also *Pterocaulon virgatum*; **g. moss**, †(*a*) the moss *Polytrichum commune*; (*b*) the Stonecrop, *Sedum acre*; **g. nugget**, *Balsamita grandiflora*; **g. oat**, the yellow oat-grass; **g. osier**, (*a*) *Salix vitellina*; (*b*) *Myrica Gale*; **g. samphire**, *Inula crithmoides*; **g. saxifrage**, the genus *Chrysosplenium*; **-seal**, *Hydrastis Canadensis* of N. America; **g. spur**, a variety of daffodil; **g. thistle**, the composite genus *Scolymus*, esp. *S. hispanicus*; **g. trefoil**, *Hepatica triloba*; **g. tuft**, *Pterocaulon virgatum*; **-withy**, *Myrica Gale*.

c. in names of birds, as **g. back**, 'the American golden plover, *Charadrius dominicus*' (*Cent. Dict.*); **-wing**, the g.-winged woodpecker (*Colaptes auratus*); etc.

Golden (gōᵘ·ld'n), *v. rare.* 1850. [f. the adj.] To make or become golden.

Golden age. 1555. [tr. L. *aurea ætas*; see GOLDEN *a.* 6 and AGE *sb.*] The first and best age of the world, in which, according to the Greek and Roman poets, mankind lived in a state of ideal prosperity and happiness, free from all trouble or crime. Hence, the period in which a nation, literature, etc., is at its acme.

With Ovid ended the g. age of the Roman tongue DRYDEN. The g. age of Roman law LECKY.

†Go·ldeney. 1552. [? f. GOLDEN *a.* + -Y 4.] The name of some fish, perh. the golden wrasse, but commonly = L. *aurata* or *scarus* –1661.

Go·lden-eye. 1678. **1. a.** A sea-duck of the genus *Clangula*, esp. *C. glaucion*. **b.** 'The bird *Melithreptus lunulatus*' (Morris) 1827. **c.** The Tufted Duck, *Fuligula cristata* (Newton). **2.** A fish, *Hyodon chrysopsis* (*Cent. Dict.*). **3.** A neuropterous insect of the genus *Chrysopa* 1753.

Goldenly (gōᵘ·ld'nli), *adv.* 1600. [f. GOLDEN *a.* + -LY 2.] **1.** Excellently, splendidly. **2.** Like gold 1827. **3.** As with gold 1825.

Go·lden-ro·d. 1568. A plant of the genus *Solidago*, esp. *S. Virgaurea*, having a rod-like stem and a spike of bright yellow flowers. **b.** Goldenrod-tree, a shrub (*Bosea Yervamora*), a native of the Canary Isles 1829.

Go·ld-field. 1852. A district in which gold is found. Also *attrib.*

Goldfinch (gōᵘ·ldfinʃ). [OE. *goldfinc*; f. GOLD + FINCH.] **1.** A bright-coloured singing-bird (*Carduelis elegans*) of the family *Fringillidæ*, with a patch of yellow on its wings. **b.** *U.S.* Applied to other yellow finches, esp. *Spinus tristis*, the thistle-bird 1858. **2.** A kind of artificial salmon-fly 1867. **3.** *slang.* **†a.** One who has gold –1700. **b.** A guinea or sovereign 1602.

Go·ld-fi·nder. 1611. **1.** One whose occupation is to find gold 1631. **†2.** A scavenger –1755.

Go·ld-fish. 1698. **†a.** A fish with gold markings found in the South Seas. **b.** A small golden-red fish (*Cyprinus auratus*) of the carp family, a native of China, commonly bred and kept for ornament in tanks, glasses, etc. **c.** = GARIBALDI 2.

Go·ld-foil. ME. Gold beaten out into a thin sheet. (Techn. *gold leaf* is thinner than *gold-foil*.)

Goldilocks (gōᵘ·ldilǫks). 1550. [f. GOLDY *a.* + LOCK *sb.*] **†1.** Golden hair; woman's hair in general –1596. **†2.** One who has golden hair –1687. **3.** A name of plants, esp. **a.** *Ranunculus auricomus*, a kind of buttercup; **b.** *Chrysocoma Linosyris*; **c.** *Helichrysum Stœchas*; **d.** *Trollius europæus*.

†Go·lding. 1580. [f. GOLD + -ING 3. Still used locally as a name of the marigold, and in Kent of the ladybird.] **1.** A gold coin. **2.** A kind of apple –1660.

Go·ldish, *a.* ME. [See -ISH.] Somewhat golden.

Go·ld-laced, *a.* 1630. Ornamented with gold lace.

Gold leaf. (Often *hyphened.*) 1727. **a.** (with *pl.*) A minute quantity of gold, beaten out into an extremely thin sheet, from 3 to 3½ inches square. **b.** (*sing.* only.) Gold in this form for gilding, etc.

Gold leaf electrometer, electroscope, galvanoscope, appliances in which gold leaf is used as a detector.

Go·ldless, *a. rare.* ME. [See -LESS.] Without gold.

Gold-mine. 1483. A mine from which gold is obtained. Also *fig.* a source of wealth.

Goldney, -nie, -ny: var. ff. GOLDENEY.

Goldsmith (gōᵘ·ldsmiþ). OE. **1.** One who fashions gold into jewels, ornaments, etc. ¶Down to the 18th c. goldsmiths acted as bankers. **2.** Short for *goldsmith-beetle* 1863. *Comb.* **g.-beetle**, a large scarabæid beetle (*Cotalpa lanigera*) having wing-covers of golden lustre; also *Cetonia aurata* or other species. Hence **Go·ldsmi·th(e)ry**, the art or trade of a g.; goldsmith's work; articles made by a g.

Gold stick, go·ld-stick. 1804. **a.** The gilt rod carried on occasions of state by the colonel of the Life-guards or the captain of the Gentlemen-at-arms. **b.** The bearer of this; also *gold-stick in waiting.*

Go·ld-wa·sher. 1515. **†a.** One who sweats gold coins. **b.** One who washes auriferous soil to separate the gold. **c.** An appliance for gold-washing. So **Go·ld-wash**, a place where gold-washing is carried on. **Go·ld-washing**, (*a*) the process of obtaining gold by washing; (*b*) = *gold-wash* (chiefly in *pl.*).

†Gold-weight. 1500. **a.** *pl.* Scales for weighing gold –1683. **b.** *sing.* Exact weight, such as is sought in weighing gold –1727.

Go·ld-work, -works. 1683. **a.** *sing.* The art or process of working in gold. **b.** Goldsmith's work. **c.** *pl.* A place where gold is washed, mined, or smelted. So **Go·ld-worker**, one engaged in the obtaining or working of gold. **Go·ld-workings**, a place or places where gold is mined or washed.

Go·ldy, *sb. dial.* 1802. [f. GOLD 1 + -Y 4.] **a.** The goldfinch. **b.** The yellow-hammer.

Goldy (gōᵘ·ldi), *a.* 1605. [f. GOLD + -Y 1.] Gold-like, resembling gold in colour and sheen. *Comb.* **g.-stone** = AVENTURINE.

Goldylocks: see GOLDILOCKS.

†Golee. *rare.* Also **gole.** ME. only. [a. OF. *golee*, *gulee*, etc., f. (ult.) L. *gula* mouth, throat + *-ata*; see -ADE.] A mouthful, throatful (of words). CHAUCER.

Golet(te, obs. f. GULLET.

Golf (gǫlf, gǫf), *sb.* 1457. [Said to be ad. Du. *kolf*, *kolv-* 'club', but golf is mentioned earlier than any of the Du. sports. See N.E.D.] A game in which a small hard ball is struck with various clubs into a series of small cylindrical holes made at intervals on the surface of a moor, field, etc.

Comb.: **g.-club** (see CLUB *sb.* I. 2); **-links**, the ground on which g. is played. Hence **Golf** *v.* **Go·lfer.**

Golgotha (gǫ·lgǒþă). 1593. [a. L. (Vulg.) *golgotha*, Gr. γολγοθά, ad. *gogolþā*, Aramaic form of Heb. *gulgoleþ* skull; see CALVARY.] **1.** A place of interment; a graveyard, a charnel-house. **†2.** *Univ. slang.* (See quot.) –1803.

2. Golgotha, that is, the place of sculls or heads of colleges and halls, where they meet and debate AMHERST.

Goliard (gōᵘ·liaɹd). Now *Hist.* 1483. [a. OF. *goliard*, *-art*, *-ar* glutton, f. *gole* (mod. *gueule*):—L. *gula* gluttony.] One of the class of educated jesters, buffoons, and authors of ribald Latin verse, who flourished chiefly in the 12th and 13th c. Hence **Goliardery**, the practices of a g.

†Goliardeys. ME. [ad. OF. *goliardois*; see prec.] = GOLIARD –1643.

Goliath (gǒləi·ăþ). Often erron. **Goliah.** 1591. [a. L. (Vulg.) *Goliath*, Heb. *golyath* the giant slain by David, 1 Sam. xvii.] **1.** A giant; often allusively. **2.** A very large lamellicorn beetle of the genus *Goliathus* 1826. **3.** (Also *g. crane*) A powerful travelling crane 1888.

1. The G. of English literature 1846.

†Goll. 1586. [?] A hand –1690.

Golly (gǫ·li), *interj.* 1848. Substituted for *God* in oaths, etc.

Gollywog (gǫ·liwǫg). 1895. Also **golliwog**(g. A black (male) grotesque doll, with staring eyes and fuzzy hair.

Golosh, goloshe, etc.: see GALOSH.

Goluptious (gǒlɒ·pʃəs), *a. joc.* 1856. [Arbitrary, perh. after VOLUPTUOUS.] Luscious, delightful.

Gomarist (gōu·mărist). 1674. [f. *Gomar* + -IST.] A follower of Francis *Gomar* (1563–1641), Professor of Divinity at Leyden, who defended Calvinism as against Arminianism. So **Goma·rian.**

Gombeen (gǫmbī·n). *Anglo-Ir.* 1862. [a. mod. Ir. *gaimbín*, conn. w. med.L. *cambium*; see CHANGE.] Usury. Chiefly *attrib.*, as **g.-man**, a usurer. Hence **Gombee·nism**, borrowing or lending at usury.

Gombroon, gomroon (gǫmbrū·n, gǫmrū·n). 1698. [Name of a town on the Persian Gulf. Cf. GAMBROON.] A kind of Persian pottery, imitated in Chelsea ware.

†**Gome** 1. [Com. Teut.: OE. *guma* :—pre-Teut. **ghəmon-* cogn. w. L. *homo, hominis*. Cf. BRIDEGROOM.] A man –1515.

Gome 2. 1611. [Cf. COOM *sb.*1] The black and oily grease on the axle of a cart wheel.

†**Gomer** 1. OE. [a. L. *gomor*, Gr. γομόρ, transliteration of Heb.; see OMER.] A Heb. measure; = OMER –1631.

Gomer 2 (gōu·məɹ). 1828. [f. the inventor's name.] *Gomer chamber*, a conical chamber with spherical bottom used in smooth-bore guns and mortars.

Gomerel (gǫ·mərĕl), *sb. Sc.* and *north.* 1814. [See -REL.] A fool, a simpleton.

†**Gomorr(h)ean.** 1522. [f. *Gomorrah, Gomorrha*, after names in *-ean.*]

A. Of or pertaining to Gomorrah (see *Gen.* xviii, xix) –1593.

B. *sb.* An inhabitant of Gomorrah; hence, one who follows the practices of its inhabitants –1613.

Gomphiasis (gǫmfəi·ăsis). 1706. [a. Gr., f. γομφίος molar tooth.] *Path.* Disease of the (molar) teeth, causing them to become loose in their sockets.

Gomphodont (gǫ·mfŏdǫnt), *a.* 1889. [f. Gr. γόμφος bolt + ὀδοντ- (ὀδούς) tooth.] *Path.* Having the teeth inserted by gomphosis.

‖**Gomphosis** (gǫmfōu·sis). 1578. [mod.L., a. Gr., f. γομφόειν to bolt together, f. γόμφος.] *Anat.* A form of immovable articulation, in which one hard part (e.g. a tooth) is received into the cavity of another.

Gon, obs. inf. (etc.) of Go *v.*

-gon (gǫn), *suffix.* The second element (repr. Gr. -γων-ος, -ον, -angled) of HEPTAGON, etc., sometimes used with algebraic symbols (as *m*-gon, *n*-gon).

Gonad (gǫ·næd). 1880. [f. Gr. γονή, γόνος generation, seed, etc. + -AD, after mod.L. *gonas*, pl. *gonades.*] *Biol.* An undifferentiated germ-gland, serving both as ovary and spermary. Hence **Go·naduct** (for *gonad-duct*).

‖**Gonangium** (gǫnæ·ndʒiǫ̆m). *Pl.* **-ia.** 1871. [mod.L., f. Gr. γόνος generation + ἀγγεῖον vessel.] *Zool.* An external chitinous receptacle within which, in the calyptoblastic genera of Hydrozoa, the sporosacs or planoblasts are developed. Hence **Gona·ngial** *a.*

Gondola (gǫ·ndŏlă). 1549. [ad. It. *gondola* of obscure origin; see Diez, Körting, etc.] **1.** A light flat-bottomed boat in use on the Venetian canals, having a cabin amidships and rising to a sharp point at either end; it is usually propelled by one man at the stern with a single oar. Also *transf.* †**2.** A ship's boat 1626. **3.** *U.S.* A large flat-bottomed river boat for freight; used also as a gun-boat 1774. **4.** = *gondola car* 1875. **b.** [cf. G., Du. *gondel*] A car attached to the under side of a dirigible balloon or airship 1914.

1. The far lights of skimming gondolas BYRON. *transf.* In cabs, those gondolas on wheels 1827. *Comb.* **g.-car** *U.S.*, a railway car having a platform body with low sides.

Gondolet (gǫndŏle·t). 1602. [ad. It. *gondoletta*, dim. of *gondola.*] A small gondola.

Gondolier (gǫndŏlīᵊ·ɹ). 1603. [a. F., ad. It. *gondoliere.*] One who rows a gondola.

And silent rows the songless g. BYRON.

Gone (gǫn), *ppl. a.* 1598. [pa. pple. of Go *v.*] **1.** Lost, ruined, undone. **2.** That has departed or passed away 1820.

1. *A g. case*, a hopeless case. *A g. sensation* (*feeling*), a feeling of faintness or exhaustion. *G. coon* (U.S.): see COON. **2.** *Past and g. Dead and g.* (see DEAD *a.*). Hence **Go·ner** (*slang*), one who is dead or undone.

Goneness (gǫ̆·nnĕs). 1853. [f. prec. + -NESS.] Faintness; lassitude; exhaustion.

Gonfalon (gǫ·nfălǫn). 1595. [ad. It. *gonfalone* (also used), later form of GONFANON.] A banner or ensign, frequently with tails or streamers, suspended from a cross-bar instead of being fastened to the pole, esp. as used by the Italian republics or in eccl. processions.

Gonfalonier (gǫ:nfălŏnīᵊ·ɹ). 1586. [a. F., or ad. It. *gonfaloniere* (also used), f. prec.] The bearer of a gonfalon, a standard-bearer; *spec.* (*a*) the title of the chief magistrate in several Italian republics; (*b*) the Pope's standard-bearer, an office claimed as hereditary by the Dukes of Parma. Hence **Go:nfalonie·rship.**

Gonfanon (gǫ·nfănǫ̆n). Now *Hist.* ME. [a. OF. *gunfanun, gonfanon*, etc., f. **gund-* (OE. *gūþ*) :—OTeut. **gunþjā* war + *fano* banner, FANON.] **1.** = GONFALON. In the middle ages chiefly applied to the small pennon immediately beneath the steel head of a knight's lance. Also *fig.* †**2.** A lance carrying a gonfanon. CAXTON.

†**Gong** 1. [Special use of OE. *gang, gǫng*; see GANG *sb.*1] A privy –1576.

Gong 2 (gǫŋ). 1600. [a. Malay *gŏng*; echoic.] A metallic disk with upturned rim (usu. made of an alloy of four parts copper to one of tin) which produces resonant musical notes when suspended and struck with a soft mallet. **b.** A saucer-shaped bell, struck by a hammer or tongue moved by some mechanical device; used chiefly as an alarm or a call-bell 1864. *Comb.* **g.-bell** = **b.** Hence **Go·ng-go·ng**, a name given to various analogous instruments in use among barbarous peoples. ? *Obs.*

Gongorism (gǫ·ŋgŏriz'm). 1813. [f. *Gongora* + -ISM.] An affected type of diction and style introduced into Spanish literature by the poet Gongora y Argote (1561–1627). So **Go·ngorist.** Also **Go·ngoresque.**

Goniatite (gōu·niătəit). 1838. [ad. mod.L. *goniatites*, f. Gr. γωνία angle.] *Palæont.* A genus of fossil cephalopods with angular markings.

‖**Gonidium** (goni·diǫ̆m). *Pl.* **-ia.** 1845. [mod.L., dim. on Gr. type of γόνος child, produce.] *Bot.* **1.** One of the cells filled with chlorophyll which are formed beneath the cortical layer in the thallus of lichens; now known to be imprisoned algæ. **2. a.** A reproductive cell produced asexually in algæ. **b.** The conidium in fungi. 1882. Hence **Goni·dial, Goni·dic** *adjs.* of, or pertaining to gonidia. **Gonidio·genous** *a.* producing or having the power to produce gonidia. **Goni·dioid** *a.* resembling the gonidia of lichens. **Goni·diose** *a.* containing or provided with gonidia. Also **Goni·diophore** = CONIDIOPHORE.

Gonimic (goni·mik), *a.* 1857. [f. mod.L. *gonimon* adj. neut. producing offspring + -IC.] In *g. layer, stratum*, orig. = 'gonidial layer'. The adj. is now taken to mean: Relating to gonimia; containing gonimia. var. **Go·nimous** *a.* (in the orig. sense).

‖**Gonimium** (goni·miǫ̆m). *Pl.* **-ia.** 1882. [mod.L., f. *gonimon* (see prec.).] *Bot.* A gonidium which is not of an absolutely green (grass-green) colour.

B. *sb.* A fish of this family.

Goniometer (gōuniǫ·mɪ̆təɹ). 1766. [ad. F. *goniomètre*, f. Gr. γωνία + μέτρον.] An instrument used for measuring angles. (In measuring the angles of crystals two kinds are used, the old *contact-* or *hand-goniometer*, and the more accurate *reflecting goniometer* invented by Wollaston.) So **Gonio·metry**, measurement of angles. Hence **Go:niome·tric, -al** *a.* of or pertaining to goniometry.

Gono- (gǫ·no), *prefix*, bef. a vowel **gon-**, repr. Gr. γονο-, comb. f. γόνος, γονή generation, offspring, semen, etc.

Go·noblast [see -BLAST], *Biol.* a cell which takes part in reproduction; hence **Gonobla·stic** *a.* ‖**Go:noblasti·dium** (pl. *-idia*) [f. GONOBLAST + Gr. -ίδιον dim. suffix], *Zool.* = BLASTOSTYLE; hence **Go:noblasti·dial** *a.* ‖**Go·nocalyx** [see CALYX 2], *Zool.* the bell-shaped disk forming the swimming organ of a medusiform gonophore; hence **Gono-ca·lycine** *a.* **Go·nocheme** [Gr. ὄχημα vehicle], *Zool.* a medusiform planoblast which gives origin directly to the generative elements. **Gonoco·ccus** [see COCCUS], *Path.* the micrococcus found in the discharge of gonorrhœa. **Go·nosome** [Gr. σῶμα], *Zool.* name for the collective body of reproductive zooids of a hydrozoan; hence **Go:noso·mal** *a.* **Go·nosphere** [SPHERE], *Bot.* the irregular globule formed by the condensation of the protoplasm of the oogonium in certain fungi; also ‖**Gonosphæ·rium** (pl. *-ia*). ‖**Gonothe·ca** [Gr. θήκη case], *Zool.* = GONANGIUM; hence **Gonothe·cal** *a.* **Gonozo·oid** [ZOOID], *Zool.* one of the sexual zooids enclosed in certain of the gonophores of the *Hydrozoa*; also *attrib.*

Gonoph (gǫ·nǫf). *slang.* 1852. [a. Heb. *gannābh* thief.] A pickpocket.

Gonophore (gǫ·nŏfoᵊɹ). 1835. [f. Gr. γόνο- GONO- + -φορος. Cf. F. *gonophore.*] **1.** *Bot.* The short stalk which bears the stamens and carpels in *Anonaceæ*, etc., due to the elongation of the receptacle above the corolla. **2.** One of the medusoid buds which contain the reproductive elements in *Hydrozoa* 1859.

Gonorrhœa (gǫnŏrī·ă). Also †**-rhea**, etc. 1547 [med.L., ad. Gr. γονόρροια, f. γόνος seed + ῥοία flux; so called because it was supposed to be a discharge of semen.] An inflammatory discharge of mucus from the membrane of the urethra or vagina. Hence **Gonorrhœ·al, -e·al,** †**Gonorrhœ·an** *adjs.* of, pertaining to, or affected with g.

Gonosome, -sphere, etc. : see GONO-.

Gonys (gǫ·nis). 1836. [app. a mistake for *genys* = Gr. γένυς under-jaw.] *Ornith.* The keel of a bird's bill; the inferior margin of the symphysis of the lower jaw. Hence **Gony·deal** *a.* of or pertaining to the g.

Goober (gū·bəɹ). *U.S.* 1885. The peanut, *Arachis hypogæa.*

Good (gud), *a.*, *adv.*, and *sb.* [Com. Teut.: OE. *gōd*, root *gōð-*, *gað-* (see GATHER *v.*), hence orig. = fitting, suitable. Compared BETTER, BEST; *goodest* (sense II. 3) is playful. *Adv.* WELL.]

A. *adj.* **I.** A term of general or indefinite commendation. **1.** Of things: Being what they are called or ought to be. **2.** Of persons: (originally) Of high rank or valour OE. **3.** Of personal qualities: Commendable in the person OE. **4.** Of a state of things, a purpose, etc.: Right, sound OE. Chiefly *predicative.* Also *absol.* as an exclam., expressing satisfaction.

1. Plates of silver god (= 'pure' *obs.*) ME. A ryght g. dyuer CAXTON. To g. wine they do vse g. bushes SHAKS. Phr. *That's a good 'un*: used ironically to characterize a statement that is incredibly mendacious or absurdly exaggerated (*slang*). G. townes, G. shyppes ME. (now conventional, as in 'the g. ship A—'; 'the g. town of B—'). **2.** Rare in orig. sense, exc. in phr. *g. men and true, as g. as.* †In forms of address, or courtesy, as, Gode sirs 1420. She's my g. Lady SHAKS. G. your Ladyship 1742. (*Obs.* exc. in jocular use) 'My g. friend', 'the g. woman of the house'; and euphemistically in 'the g. people' = fairies. **3.** An..emulator of euery mans g. parts SHAKS. G. qualities (*mod.*). Of a g. family DE FOE. Of g. birth (*mod.*). Take g. herte CHAUCER. *G. cheer* (see CHEER *sb.*). G. name in man and woman SHAKS. G. fame, A g. face SHAKS. A g. leg THACKERAY. **4.** Hell is full of g. meanings HERBERT. It was.. g. that they should be respected MACAULAY. *absol.* It is a promise, g. DISRAELI. Very g., my lord 1829. Phr. *It is* (*seems*) *g. to, to think g. to.*

II. 1. Morally excellent: **a.** of persons. ME. **b.** of conduct. OE. **2.** Applied to God, and in exclams. *G. God! gracious!* etc. OE. **3.** Kind. OE. Constr. *to.* OE. **4.** Pious, holy OE.

1. **a.** The hand that hath made you faire hath made you g. SHAKS. **b.** Gode dæda, *opp. to* misdæda *O. E. Chron.* A..g. conscience CLARENDON. Be g., sweet girl, and let who will be clever KINGSLEY. Be a g. girl (= well-behaved) 1695. **2.** It was a wicked woman's curse—God's g., and what care I COLERIDGE. 'G. Lord! What Fools!' said the Physician 1890. **3.** Be g. to Rome SHAKS. G. to me (*mod.*). It is the gooddest soule B. JONS. *To be g. enough* (or *so g. as*) *to* (do something) 1652. *G. offices, turn* (see TURN). †*G. words* (= *bona verba*) –1592. G. words are worth much and cost little HERBERT. To say a g. word for (*mod.*). Good (= simple) easie Man SHAKS. **4.** Reading g. books and drinking tea (*mod.*). GOOD FRIDAY.

III. 1. Agreeable OE. **2.** Amusing 1530. **3.** Salutary, wholesome OE. **4.** Favourable, laudatory 1601.

1. Give us alle god endyng ME. G. fortune 1481, newes 1573. G. wynd and whedyr ME. Wine, and g. fare 1755. So in *g. morning*, etc. with ellipse of

to you ME.; *to have a good time of it* (now an Americanism); had as g. a time as heart could wish PEPYS; *to have a g. night* 1701. A g. smell 1684. **2.** *G. Company* (see COMPANY) 1530. *As g. as a play.* **3.** Godne mete OE. G. for the short winded 1599, for a cold STEELE; also †*g. against.* **4.** Purchase vs a g. opinion *Jul. C.* II. i. 145. God is in a g. sence..jelous 1617. The Apostles were Fishers of men in a g. sense 1665. *To take in g. part* (see PART *sb.*).

IV. Useful, reliable for a purpose, or efficient in a function, pursuit, creed, etc. (either specified or understood) OE. Const. *for*, †*to*, *to* with *inf.*

Which of the Goods d'ye mean, g. for something, or g. for nothing SWIFT. He was not now g. for much CARLYLE. *In g. time* (see TIME). G. fightyng men 1548. G. Saracens PURCHAS. G. Shepherds after Sheering drench their Sheep DRYDEN. G. Latin scholars MACAULAY. A g. writer, hater, shot (*mod.*). †*G. under sail* –1561. Good *at*, e.g. the needle 1617, descriptions THACKERAY. G. men of their hands MACAULAY. He is called a G. Man upon the exchange who hath a responsible estate FULLER (cf. SHAKS. *Merch. V.* I. iii. 15). A g. life (for purposes of insurance) 1828. G. debts (= debts good as assets); hence **Good-for** *sb.* S. Afr. = IOU. G. for twenty years, for a ten miles walk (*mod.*). We had seven minutes g. (= available) 1711.

V. 1. Adequate ME., effectual, thorough; valid (esp. in *Law*) OE. **2.** Used as an intensive, before another adj. or with statements of quantity, etc. OE.

1. *G. heed, g. speed* (see sbs.). *In g. earnest, faith, sooth* (see sbs.). [He] made a very g. stand 1617. My Lord..will give a very g. accompt of them 1617. I gave him a g. blow SWIFT. Administering a g. beating to his wife S. WALPOLE. I have taken g. care That shall not be SHELLEY. Licenses g. only for one year 1562. It is g. in Law too MASSINGER. G. claim, prize, reason, cause, excuse (*mod.*). *To have a g. mind to* (see MIND). **2.** A g. smart cut 1787. He writes a g. bold hand (*mod.*). *A g. deal, few, many* (see those wds.). Gode hand fulle OE. Geve to everyone three spoonefulles g. 1570. We have three quarters g. to a voyage of half an hour, a g. two miles off, he played a g. hour on the violoncello (*mod.*).

VI. Phrases.

1. As good. Orig. *adj.* Me had been as g. to goo ME. To be as g. as one's word 1577. Later, *semi-adv.*: I were as g. (= I might as well); or *adv.*: We had as g. make tracks (*mod.*). *As g. as*: advb. phr. = Practically. As g. as gone ME. **2. Make good.** To make up for (a deficiency) ME. To perform (a promise); to effect (a purpose) 1535. To substantiate (a charge), esp. make g. *on any one, on his person* 1523. To make secure (a kingdom, walls, prisoners) 1606. To repair (a building) 1568. To succeed (orig. *U.S.*) 1901.

B. *adv.* **a.** qualifying a vb.: Well. Now *vulgar* or *slang*. Also in †*as good as* = 'as well as'. †**b.** qualifying an adj. or adv., with intensive force: In a high degree. **c.** In *as good* (see A. VI) the adj. occas. becomes an adv.

C. quasi-*sb.* and *sb.* **1.** The adj. used *absol.* as *pl.* Good persons. Now only with *the* (exc. in *good and bad*) ME. **2.** The neut. adj. used *absol.* That which is good: **a.** *gen.* OE. **b.** The good portion, side, or aspect 1670. **c.** Well-being, profit, benefit, advantage OE. **3.** A particular thing that is good: **a.** That which it is good to attain or possess OE.; †**b.** *occas.* A good quality, virtue, grace –1563; **c.** *pl.* Property; now movable property; also *sing.* (*obs.* exc. *arch.*) OE.; †**d.** *sing.* Money –1548; **e.** *pl.* Live stock (now *dial.*) 1485. **4.** *spec.* (Now only *pl.*) Merchandise, wares (now chiefly manufactured articles) 1460. Also *attrib.* as *goods agent, engine, train*, etc. 1858.

2. a. To know G. from Evil 1688. **b.** The g. and bad of an affair 1670. **c.** Zeale to promote the common g. BIBLE *Transl. Pref.* To drink..for the g. of the house GOLDSM. As much as he can see the g. of E. IRVING. Phr. *To do g., much g. may it do you, to do any g.* *To the g.*: as a balance on the right side. *To come to g.*: orig. of a dream, †to come true; later, to yield a g. result. *For g.* (*and all*): as a valid conclusion; hence, finally. *To be any, some, no g.* (colloq.). **3. a.** The goods of the mind SIR T. BROWNE, of fortune BURKE. Life..is a doubtful g. to many GEO. ELIOT. **b.** The goods and graces wherewith they were indued *Homilies*. **c.** Misers will as easily part with their blood, as with their g. TRAPP. **d.** (*A*) *great g.*: a great sum of money. *Marriage g.*: a marriage portion. **4.** Phr. *To deliver the goods*: to supply the objects contracted for; to carry out one's part of the agreement; to come up to expectations (chiefly *U.S.*). *The goods*: what is supplied or provided; what is expected or required; the real thing; the genuine article (chiefly *U.S.*).

Comb. **1.** †**a.** denoting a grandparent, as *good-dame, -sire*; **b.** denoting a relation by marriage, = -in-law, or step-, as GOOD-FATHER, -MOTHER, *-brother*, -SISTER, -SON, -DAUGHTER.

2. Special: as †**g.-deed** *adv.*, in very deed; **-enough** *a.*, that has a quality in a sufficient degree; **-face**, one that carries a fair or smooth face; **-for-little** *a.*, of little use, insignificant; **-for-something**, one who is of some use; cf. GOOD-FOR-NOTHING; **-woolled** *a.*, (of a sheep) having a g. fleece; (of persons) having plenty of pluck and go (*dial.* or *slang*).

†**Good**, *v.* OE. [f. the adj.] **1.** *intr.* To improve –ME. **2.** *trans.* To endow (a church, etc.). OE. only. **3.** To improve; to manure (land) –18.. **4.** To benefit (a person). Also *absol.* –1620.

Good-bye (gudbəi·). 1573. [A contr. of *God be with you* (or *ye*); perh. affected by *good morning*, etc.] **1.** As an exclam.: Farewell. **2.** *sb.* A saying 'good-bye' 1573. Also *attrib.*

2. He hurried through his good-byes 1879.

Good-daughter. *Sc.* and *north.* 1513. [See Good.] A daughter-in-law.

Good day. ME. [See GOOD *a.* III. 1.] **1.** A phrase of salutation at meeting or parting. **2.** The salutation expressed by this phrase ME.

1. God so ȝeve ȝou god day CHAUCER. A good day, thou, and thou 1460. **2.** *To bid, give* (a person) *good day.*

Good-den: see GOOD EVEN.

Goo·d-do·er. ME. [f. GOOD *sb.* + DOER.] **1.** Now commonly *a doer of good*; a benefactor. **2.** *dial.* An animal or plant that thrives well 1877.

Good even. *Obs.* exc. *dial.* ME. [See GOOD *a.* III. 1.] A form of salutation; = Good evening (but used at any time after noon: see *Rom. & Jul.* II. iv. 116 ff.) 1481.

Oh, 'giue ye-good-e'vn *Two Gent.* II. i. 104. Godden to your Worships *Cor.* II. i. 103.

Good-father. *Sc.* 1533. [See GOOD.] A father-in-law; also, a step-father.

Good-fellow, *sb.* ME. [See FELLOW *sb.*] **1.** An agreeable companion; *esp.* a boon companion, a convivial person. †**2.** A thief or robber –1633. Hence †**Goodfellow** *v.* (*rare*), to call (a person) a good fellow. **Good-fe·llowship**, the spirit or habits of a good fellow, conviviality; now also, the spirit of true friendship or companionship.

Goo·d-for-no·thing. 1711. [The phr. *good for nothing* used *attrib.* or as *sb.*: see GOOD *a.* IV.]

A. *adj.* Of no service or use; worthless.

We reckon him here a good-for-nothing fellow SWIFT

B. *sb.* One who is good for nothing; a worthless person (†or thing). So **Goo·d-for-nou·ght** *a.* and *sb.*

Good Friday. ME. [See GOOD *a.* II. 4.] The Friday before Easter-day, observed as the anniversary of the death of Christ.

Goodhap (gu·dˌhæp). *arch.* 1557. [See GOOD *a.* and HAP *sb.* 1; = *good hap.*] Good fortune.

Good humour. 1616. The condition of being in a cheerful and amiable mood; also, the disposition or habit of amiable cheerfulness.

Her good humour made her willing to divert me 1718. Hence **Good-humoured** *a.* possessed of or characterized by good humour; indicative of good humour. **Goodhu·mouredly** *adv.*

Goodish (gu·diʃ), *a.* 1756. [See -ISH.] Somewhat good.

A g. sort of woman MRS. DELANY. A g. sum 1894.

†**Goo·dless**, *a.* OE. [See -LESS.] Devoid of good or of goods –1581.

Goo·dlihead. ME. [f. GOODLY *a.* + -HEAD.] **1.** Comeliness (*arch.*). †**2.** Excellence, goodness –1503. †**3.** The personality of one who is goodly. SPENSER.

Goo·dlike, *a.* Now *dial.* 1572. [f. GOOD *a.* + -LIKE.] **a.** Goodly; good-looking. **b.** Resembling what is good.

Good-liking. ? *Obs.* 1583. [See GOOD *a.* I. 4 and LIKING *vbl. sb.*] **1.** Kindly feeling towards a person 1586. **2.** Good-will; satisfaction 1583. †**3.** Personal fancy. LOCKE. †**4.** Good condition, embonpoint –1656.

1. A match of prudence and common good-liking SWIFT. **4.** Their yong ones are in good liking *Job* xxxix. 4.

Goodliness (gu·dlinės). ME. [f. GOODLY *a.* + -NESS.] The quality or condition of being goodly; comeliness; †kindness –1555; excellence, value (*rare*) 1832.

Her goodlinesse was full of harmony to his eyes SIDNEY.

Good-looking, *a.* 1780. Having a good appearance; *esp.* with reference to beauty of countenance. So **Goo·d-loo·ker** (chiefly *U.S.*).

Goodly (gu·dli), *a.* [OE. *gōdlic*; see GOOD and -LY[1].] **1.** Of good appearance; well-favoured or proportioned; comely, fair, handsome. **2.** Considerable in size, quantity, or number (freq. with mixture of sense 1) ME. **3.** Of good quality. Also, good for a purpose, proper, convenient (often with mixture of sense 1). Often *ironical.* ME. †**4.** Gracious, kind. ME. only.

1. Þe goodlieste mayde..in al þe toun CHAUCER. **2.** Surely a g. stature is most majestical FULLER. **3.** G. Corne B. GOOGE. Heere's a g. Watch indeed SHAKS. Phrase. *G. and gracious!* (see GRACIOUS).

Goodly (gu·dli), *adv.* [ME. *godliche.*] †**1.** Beautifully, gracefully –1556. †**2.** Graciously, kindly; courteously –1677. **3.** In a goodly fashion; excellently. Also *ironical.* Now *rare.* ME. †**4.** Conveniently –1513. †**5.** In neg. clauses: Easily, readily –1652.

Goodman (gu·dmæ̆n). ME. [GOOD *a.* + MAN.] †**1.** = *Good man.* Perh. really two wds. ME. only. **2.** The male head of a household; †the host (of an inn), †the keeper (of a prison) ME. **b.** Hence, a husband (now only *Sc.* or *arch.*) 1513. †**3.** Prefixed to designations of occupation –1638. **4.** A man of substance, not of gentle birth; a yeoman, etc. *Obs.* exc. *Hist.* or *poet.* 1587. †**b.** *Sc.* The laird or tenant *of* a specified estate or farm –1824.

2. When the g. mends his armour MACAULAY. **3.** Nay, but heare you, g. deluer *Haml.* v. i. 13. **4.** He is called a Good Man in common discourse, who is not dignified with Gentilitie FULLER. **b.** The G. of Primrose Knowe SCOTT.

Good morrow, good-mo·rrow. ME. **1.** A salutation equiv. to the later *good morning* (see GOOD *a.* III. 1). Now *arch.* †**2.** Something as empty as 'good-morrow'; a trivial saying or matter –1704.

1. Giue you good-morrow, sir SHAKS.

Good-mother. *Sc.* 1536. [see GOOD.] A mother-in-law; also, a step-mother.

Good nature, good-na·ture. 1450. **1.** Pleasant or kindly disposition; chiefly denoting undue easiness of disposition. †**2.** Natural goodness of character; virtue (*rare*) –1677.

Good-natured. (The stress varies.) 1577. [f. prec. + -ED[2].] Characterized by good nature (see prec.).

If it is abuse—why, one is always sure to hear of it from one damn'd good natur'd friend or another SHERIDAN. Hence **Good-natured-ly** *adv.*, **-ness.**

Goo·d-nei·ghbourhood. 1817. [f. *good neighbour* + -HOOD.] The disposition and behaviour characteristic of a good neighbour; friendly feeling and intercourse. So **Goo·d-neighbourliness.**

Goodness (gu·dnės). [OE. *gōdnes.*] **1.** The quality or condition of being good, in various senses; esp. moral excellence; benevolence; also beneficence OE.; kindly feeling OE. †**2.** Advantage, profit –1583. †**3.** quasi-*concr.* A good act or deed –1568. **4.** In exclams., orig. with reference to the goodness of God 1613.

1. Vertue is bold, and goodnes neuer fearefull SHAKS. The g. of the Lord WESLEY, of a custom STEPHEN, of a cause 1870. Phr. *Have the g. to..*: a form of polite request. **4.** *G. gracious! G.* (*only*) *knows! For goodness' sake! I wish to g.! Surely to g.! Thank g.! Goodness!*

Good night. (Also *hyphened.*) ME. [See GOOD *a.* III. 1.] **1.** A customary phrase used at parting at night or going to sleep; †orig. *have good night,* (*God*) *give you good night*, etc. Also *fig.* Also *attrib.* **2.** *transf.* Any parting salutation at night 1597.

1. *fig.* When our beauty fades, godnight with vs MARSTON. *attrib.* One good-night carol more BYRON.

Good now, goo·d-now·. *Obs.* exc. *dial.* 1579. [See GOOD *a.* I. 4 and NOW.] An exclam. of acquiescence, entreaty, expostulation, or surprise.

Goods. See GOOD C. quasi-*sb.* and *sb.*

Good sense. 1688. [Cf. F. *bon sens.*] Native soundness of judgement.

†**Goo·dship.** OE. [See -SHIP.] Goodness. *pl.* Kindnesses –ME.

Good-sister. *Sc.* 1666. [See GOOD.] A sister-in-law. So **Good-son** (*Sc.*), a son-in-law.

Good-tempered, *a.* (The stress varies.) 1768. [f. *good temper* (see TEMPER *sb.*) + -ED[2].] Having a good temper; not easily vexed.

Good Templar. 1874. One of an order of total abstainers established in the U.S. in 1851, and introduced into England in 1868.

Good thing. 1694. [See GOOD *a.*] A successful act or speculation; a witty saying; *pl.* dainties.

Goodwife (gu·dwəif). ME. [Cf. GOODMAN.] **1.** The mistress of a house, etc. Now chiefly *Sc.* **†2.** = Mrs. Also, a civil form of address. -1824.

Goodwill (gudwi·l). OE. [Orig. two wds. (still often so written exc. in sense 4): see GOOD *a.* II. 1, 2.] **†1.** Virtuous, pious, upright disposition or intention. (In *Luke* ii. 14, *good will* has this sense in the pre-Reformation versions, in 16th c. versions and in A.V. it has sense 2, while R.V. renders 'On earth peace among men in whom he is well pleased'.) -1602. **2.** The state of wishing well to a person, a cause, etc. OE. **3.** Cheerful acquiescence or consent; readiness, zeal ME. **4.** *Comm.* The privilege, granted by the seller of a business to the purchaser, of trading as his recognized successor; the possession of a ready-formed connexion of customers, considered as a separate element in the saleable value of a business 1571.

2. Peace vpon earth, and vnto men a good wyll COVERDALE. 3. And, though my portion is but scant, I give it with good will GOLDSM.

Goody (gu·di), *sb.*[1] 1559. [Short for GOODWIFE; cf. *hussy*.] A term of civility formerly applied to a (married) woman in humble life. Hence such a woman. **b.** *U.S.* A woman who looks after students' rooms 1827.

G. Blake and Harry Gill WORDSW.

Goody (gu·di), *sb.*[2]. 1745. [f. GOOD *a.* + -Y.[6]] A sweetmeat.

Goo·dy, *sb.*[3] 1859. *U.S.* = LAFAYETTE 1.

Goo·dy, *a.* and *sb.*[4] 1810. [-Y [6].]

A. *adj.* **1.** ?Cosy. T. MOORE. **2.** Weakly or sentimentally good. Also, *to talk g.* 1830.

B. *sb. U.S.* A goody person 1878. Hence **Goo·dyness, goo·diness,** the quality of being g.

†Goodyear. Also in pseudo-etym. form **goujeres, goujeers.** 1555. [GOOD *a.* + YEAR. Perh. elliptical = 'as I hope for a good year'.] **a.** A meaningless expletive, chiefly in *What a* (or *the*) *good year.* **b.** Some malefic power or agency (app. from its equivalence with *what the plague, what the pox,* etc.) 1591.

b. The good yeares shall deuoure them, flesh and fell *Lear* v. iii. 24.

Goo·dy-goo·dy, *a.* (and *sb.*) 1871. Reduplic. GOODY *a.* and *sb.*[4] **Goo·dy-goo·d** *a.* 1851.

Goof (gūf). *slang.* [cf. dial. *goof,* GOFF.] A silly stupid person. Hence **Goo·fy** *a.*, silly.

Go-o·ff. *colloq.* 1851. [f. phr. *go off*; see GO *v.*] **1.** The action or time of going off; commencement. **2.** *Banking.* The amount of loans falling due (and therefore going off the books) in a certain period 1900.

Googly (gū·gli). 1904. [?] *Cricket.* An off-break ball bowled with leg-break action. Hence **Goo·gle** *v.* of the ball or the bowler. **Goo·gler.**

Gooroo, guru (gu·ru, gurū·). 1613. [a. Hindi *guru* teacher, priest.] A Hindu spiritual teacher or head of a sect. Hence **Guruship.**

Goosander (gusæ·ndəɹ). 1622. [? f. GOOSE; for *-ander* cf. BERGANDER and ON. *ǫnd* (pl. *ander*).] The bird *Mergus merganser,* allied to the ducks but having a sharply serrated bill.

Goose (gūs), *sb.* Pl. **geese** (gīs). [Com. Teut.: OE. *gōs* (pl. *gēs*) :—OTeut. **gans-* :— OAryan **ghans-*, whence L. *anser* (for **hanser*), Gr. χήν, etc.] **1.** Any large web-footed bird of the sub-family *Anserinæ* (family *Anatidæ*), including *Anser* and allied genera.

The word is applied without addition to the common tame goose (*Anser domesticus*), which is descended from the wild or greylag goose (*A. ferus* or *cinereus*). The other species are dist. by adjuncts, as *black, blue,* etc. *g.*; *fen-, -marsh-g.*; *American (wild),* etc. *g.*

b. *spec.* The female bird; the male being the GANDER, the young GOSLINGS ME. **c.** *fig.* A simpleton 1547. **d.** Hissing; sibilation; esp. *Theatr. slang.* 1805. **2.** Applied to other birds of the same or a related family, or resembling the true goose, as **Cape Barren g.** (*Coreopsis novæ-hollandiæ*), **Egyptian** or **Nile g.** (*Chenalopex ægyptiaca*), **Spur-winged g.** (the African genus *Plectropterus*), etc.; also the SOLAN GOOSE 1772. **†3.** *Winchester goose*: a venereal disorder; also, a prostitute -1778. **†4.** (*Game of*) *goose*: A game played with counters on a board divided into compartments, in some of which a goose was depicted -1801. **5.** A tailor's smoothing-iron. Pl. *gooses.* [The handle resembles in shape a goose's neck.] 1605.

1. Phr. *All (his) geese are swans*: he always over-estimates. *To cook one's g.*: to do for a person or thing; to ruin or kill (*slang*). *To kill the g. that laid* or *lays the golden eggs*: to sacrifice future advantage to present necessities. *To say bo to a g.* (see BO *interj.*). 5. Come in Taylor, here you may rost your G. SHAKS.

Comb.: **g.-barnacle** = BARNACLE *sb.*[2] 2; **-bone,** a bone of a g., esp. one used as a weather-guide; **-chase** (see WILD-GOOSE-CHASE); **-club; -dung-ore,** *Min.* an impure iron sinter containing silver; **-file** = single or *Indian file*; **-fish** *U.S.*, the fishing-frog, *Lophius piscatorius*; **-pen,** (*a*) a pen or enclosure for geese: †(*b*) a quill-pen; **-silver-ore** = *goose-dung-ore* (above); **-teal,** 'the English name for a very small goose of the genus *Nettopus*' (Morris); **†-trap,** a trap for a g., a quibble, sophism; **Mother Carey's g.,** the largest of the petrels.

Goose (gūs), *v.* 1808. [f. the sb.] **1.** *trans.* To press or iron with a tailor's goose. **2.** *Theatr. slang.* To hiss, to express disapproval of by hissing 1853.

Gooseberry (gū·zbĕri). 1532. [Prob. f. GOOSE *sb.* + BERRY *sb.*] **1.** The edible berry of any of the thorny species of the genus *Ribes*; also the shrub itself. **2.** Applied to shrubs resembling the gooseberry in some way 1847. **3.** Short for *gooseberry-wine* 1766. **4.** A chaperon, esp. in *to play g.* 1837.

1. Not worth a Goose berry SHAKS. 2. **Barbados g.,** *Pereskia aculeata*; **Cape g.,** *Physalis edulis* or *P. peruviana*; **Coromandel g.,** *Averrhoa Carambola.* Phr. *Old g.* (slang) = the deuce (see DEUCE [2]); esp. *to play old g.*, to make havoc.

Comb.: **g.-caterpillar,** the caterpillar of the g.-moth; **-louse** = HARVEST-BUG; **-moth,** the magpie-moth (*Abraxas grossulariata*); **-season,** the time when gooseberries are ripe, *esp.* in *big g. season,* the time of year when the newspapers record marvels.

Goo·seberry foo·l. 1719. [FOOL *sb.*[2]] **1.** A dish made of gooseberries stewed or scalded and pounded with cream. **2.** A plant-name: **a.** Willow-herb (*Epilobium hirsutum*), also called *gooseberry-pie*; **b.** Lungwort (*Pulmonaria officinalis*) 1794.

Goo·se-bill. 1597. [From the resemblance.] **1.** The plant *Galium Aparine*; = GOOSE-GRASS 2. **†2.** A kind of forceps for extracting bullets, etc. -1823.

Goo·se-egg. ME. The egg of a goose; hence *U.S.* the score zero or 'O'. (Cf. DUCK'S EGG.)

Goo·se-flesh, goo·seflesh. ME. **1.** The flesh of a goose. **2.** A rough pimply condition of the skin, produced by cold, fear, etc.; horripilation. (Cf. GOOSE-SKIN.) 1810.

Goo·se-foot. 1516. [From the resemblance.] **1.** A plant of any of various species of the genus *Chenopodium*; so called from the shape of the leaves. Pl. *goosefoots.* 1548. **2.** Anything suggesting the shape of a goose's foot; *e.g.* a three-branched hinge, or roads diverging from a common point. Pl. *goose-feet.*

Goo·se-grass. Also *erron.* **goose-grease.** ME. [See GOOSE and GRASS.] A name of plants, mostly used at some time as food for geese. **1.** Silver-weed (*Potentilla anserina*). **2.** Cleavers (*Galium Aparine*) 1530. **†3.** **Purple goose-grass,** field-madder or spur-wort (*Sherardia arvensis*) 1548. **4.** The wild grass, *Bromus mollis* 1853. **5.** *U.S.* **a.** *Polygonum aviculare.* **b.** *Poa annua.*

Goo·se-grease. ME. The melted fat of the goose.

Goo·se-neck. 1688. Anything shaped like the neck of a goose; e.g. *Mech.* a pipe or piece of iron; *Naut.* a curved iron, fitted outside the after-chains, to receive a spare spar; etc.

Goo·se-quill. 1552. One of the wing-feathers of a goose; hence, a pen made of this.

Goosery (gū·sĕri). 1642. [f. GOOSE *sb.* + -ERY.] **1.** Silliness as attributed to the goose (*rare*). **2.** A place in which geese are kept; a collection of geese 1828.

1. The finicall g. of your neat Sermon-actor MILTON.

Goo·se-skin. 1700. **1.** The skin of a goose. FLOYER. **2.** = GOOSE-FLESH 2. 1785. **3.** A thin soft kind of leather. Also *attrib.* 1826. **4.** The impression made upon copal by sand 1859.

Goo·se-step. 1806. *Mil.* An elementary drill in which the recruit balances his body on either leg alternately, and swings the other; also, the German stiff-legged parade step. Also as *v. intr.*, to perform this step.

Goo·se-wing. ME. **1.** The wing of a goose. **2.** *Naut.* One of the clues or lower corners of a ship's main-sail or fore-sail, when the middle part is furled or tied up to the yard 1626. Hence **Goo·se-winged** *a.*

Goo·sish, *a.* ME. [See -ISH.] Goose-like, silly. So **Goo·sy** *a.*; also, like 'goose-flesh' (1857).

Gopher (gōu·fəɹ), *sb.*[1] *U.S.* Also **†gophir.** 1791. [? ad. colonial F. *gaufre,* transf. use of *gaufre* honeycomb (see GOFFER).] **1.** A burrowing rodent of the genera *Geomys* and *Thomomys*; a pocket gopher or pouched rat 1812. **2.** A burrowing or ground squirrel of the genus *Spermophilinæ*; a spermophile 1874. **3.** A burrowing land-tortoise (*Testudo carolina*), of nocturnal habits 1791. **4.** A large burrowing snake of the southern U.S. Also *g.-snake.* 1884. **5.** *Mining.* A *gopher-drift,* q.v. 1881.

Comb.: **g.-drift,** an irregular prospecting drift, following the ore without regard to maintenance of a regular grade or section; **-hole,** (*a*) the opening of a gopher's burrow; (*b*) a mine-opening begun without any reference to future permanent development; **-plum,** the Ogeechee lime (*Nyssa capitata*).

Gopher (gōu·fəɹ), *sb.*[2] 1611. [a. Heb.] The tree of the wood of which the ark was made. Chiefly in comb. **g.-wood:** applied in U.S. to the yellow-wood (*Cladrastis tinctoria*).

Make thee an Arke of Gopher-wood *Gen.* vi. 14.

Gopher (gōu·fəɹ), *v. U.S.* 1893. [f. GOPHER *sb.*[1]] **1.** *intr.* To burrow. **2.** *Mining.* To mine without any reference to future permanent development (*mod.*).

‖**Goral** (gō·răl). Also **gooral.** 1834. *Zool.* An Indian antelope (*Cemas goral*).

Go·rbelly, *sb.* (and *a.*) *Obs.* exc. *dial.* 1519. [? f. *gor,* GORE *sb.*[1] (sense 1) + BELLY.] **†1.** A protuberant belly -1790. **2.** A person with a protuberant belly 1530. **†3.** *attrib.* -1603. Hence **†Go·rbellied** *a.* corpulent.

†Gorce. 1480. [f. AF. *gortz,* pl. of *gort* (OF. *gord, gourt*) :—L. *gurgitem, gurges* whirlpool.] **a.** A whirlpool. **b.** Any stop in a river, such as weirs, mills, stakes -1741.

Gorcock (gǫ·ɹkǫk). *Sc.* and *n. dial.* 1620. [f. *gor* of obscure origin + COCK.] The male of the Red Grouse.

Gorcrow (gǫ·ɹkrōu). 1605. [f. *gor,* GORE *sb.*[1] + CROW.] The Carrion Crow.

Gordian (gǭ·ɹdiăn). 1561. [f. L. *Gordius* or *Gordium* (see sense 1) + -AN.]

A. *adj.* **1.** **Gordian knot:** an intricate knot tied by Gordius, king of Gordium in Phrygia. The oracle declared that whoever should loosen it should rule Asia, and Alexander the Great cut it through with his sword 1611. Also *fig.* or allusively 1579. **2.** Resembling the Gordian knot; intricate, involved 1606.

1. *fig.* Turne him to any Cause of Pollicy, The Gordian Knot of it he will vnloose SHAKS. 2. Tedious and G. difficulties MILTON.

†B. *sb.* **1.** = *Gordian knot* -1709. **2.** An inhabitant of Gordium; one who ties intricate knots 1606.

Hence **†Go·rdian** *v. trans.* to tie in a Gordian knot. KEATS.

Gore (gōəɹ), *sb.*[1] [OE. *gor* dung, dirt; cf. Sw. *gorr* dirt, etc.] **1.** Dung, fæces; filth of any kind. *Obs.* exc. *dial.* **2.** Blood in the thickened state that follows effusion. Often *poet.* Blood shed in carnage. 1563.

2. Phr. †(*All*) (*in*) *a g. of blood*: bathed in or besmeared with blood. PEPYS.

Gore (gōəɹ), *sb.*[2] [OE. *gāra,* app. related to OE. *gār* spear, the reference being to the shape of the spear-head.] **1.** A triangular piece of land. **†2.** *poet.* The front section of a skirt, wider at the bottom than at the top; the lap of a gown, an apron. Hence, a skirt, petticoat, or gown. -1570. **3.** Any wedge-shaped or triangular piece of cloth forming part of a garment, sail, etc., and serving to produce difference of width at different points ME. 4. *Her.* A charge formed by two curved lines meeting in the fesse-point, the one drawn from the sinister or dexter chief and the other from the lowest angle of the base 1562. 5. Any triangular or lune-shaped piece forming part of the surface of a globe, a balloon, the covering of an umbrella, a dome, etc. 1796.

Gore (gōᵊɹ), *v.*[1] ME. [?] 1. *trans.* To pierce or stab deeply, with a sharp weapon, spike, spur, or the like. *Obs.* exc. as in sense 2. 2. *spec.* To pierce, or wound, as with horns, or (*rarely*) the tusk. Also *transf.* and *fig.* Also *absol.* 1523.

2. It is the nature of bulls to g. each other 1865. *fig.* Aquinas..was called bos mutus, a dumbe Oxe; and..with two hornes..gored all unbeleevers 1641.

†**Gore**, *v.*[2] Only in **Gored, Goring.** 1566. 1. *trans.* To cover with or as with gore. Only in pa. pple. -1655. 2. *intr.* To lie soaking *in* blood. STANYHURST.

Gore (gōᵊɹ), *v.*[3] 1548. [f. GORE *sb.*[2]] 1. *trans.* To cut into a gore or gores; to furnish with gores. †2. *Naut. intr.* To swell or jut *out* 1627.

Go·rebill. *local.* 1862. [? f. *gore*, GARE *sb.*[1] + BILL *sb.*[1]] The garfish.

Gore-fish. 1839. [? f. obs. *gore*, a spear or javelin.] ? = GARFISH.

Gorge (gǭɹdʒ), *sb.*[1] ME. [a. OF. and F. *gorge* :—pop. L. **gorga*, of unkn. origin.]

I. 1. The external throat; the front of the neck. *Obs.* exc. *arch.* 2. The internal throat. Now only *rhet.* ME. 3. *Falconry.* The crop of a hawk. Hence, opprobriously, of the maw, devouring capacity, of a monster, a person, etc. *Obs.* exc. *arch.* Also *fig.* 1450. †4. A meal for a hawk -1677. 5. What has been swallowed; in phrases (primarily of *Falconry*) †*to cast up, heave*, etc. *one's g.* Freq. used *fig.* to express disgust or violent resentment. 1532.

3. *fig.* The first are in destruction's g. SCOTT. Phr. *A full g.* (often taken erron. in sense 4). 5. How abhorred my Imagination is, my g. rises at it SHAKS.

II. 1. *Fortif.* The neck of a bastion or other outwork; the entrance from the rear to the platform or body of a work 1669. 2. A narrow opening between hills; a ravine, *esp.* one that gives passage to a stream 1769. 3. *Arch.* The neck of a column; also, a kind of moulding, hollow on the inside 1706. 4. *Mech.* The groove of a pulley 1812. 5. *Angling.* A solid object, intended to be swallowed by the fish 1883. 6. *U.S.* A mass choking up a narrow passage; esp. in *ice-g.* (see ICE *sb.*) 1884. †7. *Pottery. pl.* Pitchers. [? a distinct wd.; cf. BROWN GEORGE.] 1684.

2. Through the g. of this glen they found access to a black bog SCOTT.

Comb., as (sense II. 5) *g.-hook*; also **g.-circle**, in gearing, 'the outline of the smallest cross-section of a hyperboloid of revolution' (Webster).

Gorge (gǭɹdʒ), *sb.*[2] 1854. [f. next vb.] An act of gorging oneself; a glut (of food, etc.).

Gorge (gǭɹdʒ), *v.* ME. [ad. OF. and F. *gorger*, f. *gorge* GORGE *sb.*[1]] 1. *intr.* To fill the gorge; to feed greedily. Const. *on, upon.* 2. *trans.* To fill the gorge of; to glut, satiate. Also *transf.* and *fig.* 1486. 3. To swallow; to devour greedily 1614. 4. To fill full, distend; to choke, choke up. Chiefly in *pa. pple.* 1508.

1. To..g. upon the Church MILT. 2. Messes To g. his appetite *Lear* I. i. 120. *fig.* Gorged with wealth 1639. 3. You must..let him have time to g. your hook WALTON. 4. During excessive laughter..the head and face become gorged with blood DARWIN.

Gorged (gǭɹdʒd), *ppl. a.* 1610. [f. GORGE *sb.*[1] + -ED[2].] *Her.* Having the gorge or neck encircled (with a coronet, etc.).

Gorgelet (gǭ·ɹdʒlėt). 1872. [f. as prec. + -LET.] A patch of colour on the throat of a bird.

Gorgeous (gǭ·ɹdʒəs), *a.* 1495. [ad. OF. *gorgias* elegantly or finely dressed; of uncertain origin.] 1. Adorned with rich or brilliant colours; showy, magnificent. b. *transf.* of literary phraseology, etc.: Dazzling 1561. 2. *colloq.* As an epithet of approbation. (Cf. *splendid.*) 1883.

1. I am not gorgious in attire DEKKER. The land of g. sunsets BLACK. *transf.* G. and fine woordes 1561. 2. A g. time 1883. Hence **Go·rgeous-ly** *adv.*, **-ness.**

Go·rgeret. 1758. [a. F., f. *gorge* throat, from its tubular shape.] *Surg.* = GORGET[2].

Gorgerin (gǭ·ɹdʒĕrin). 1664. [a. F., f. *gorge* throat.] 1. *Arch.* = HYPOTRACHELIUM. 2. = GORGET[1] I. 1849.

Gorget[1] (gǭ·ɹdʒėt). 1470. [a. OF. *gorgete* (mod. dial. *gorgette* a collar), dim. of *gorge* throat.] 1. A piece of armour for the throat. Now *Hist.* b. *transf.* A collar 1629. 2. An article of female dress, covering the neck and breast; a wimple. Now *Hist.* 1575. 3. An ornament for the neck; a necklace 1570. 4. *Mil.* A gilt crescent-shaped badge suspended from the neck, formerly worn by officers on duty 1786. 5. *Zool.* A patch of colour on the throat of a bird, etc. 1801.

1. Cavaliers with ruff, rapier, buff-coat, and g. THACKERAY. 2. Goodly dames in ruff and g. SCOTT.

Gorget[2] (gǭ·ɹdʒėt). 1740. [Corruption of GORGERET.] *Surg.* A steel instrument having the form of a channel, used in operations for the stone, etc.

‖**Gorgio** (gǭ·ɹdʒio). 1851. [Romany.] Gipsy term for a non-gipsy.

Gorgon (gǭ·ɹgǫn), *sb.* (and *a.*) 1529. [ad. L. *Gorgonem, Gorgo*, a. Gr. Γοργώ (pl. Γοργόνες), f. γοργός terrible.] 1. *Gr. Myth.* One of three mythical sisters, with snakes for hair, whose look turned the beholder into stone. Medusa, the only one mortal, was slain by Perseus, and her head fixed on Athene's shield. 1614. b. Short for *Gorgon's head.* BURKE. †2. An African quadruped; ? the gnu. TOPSELL. 3. A very terrible or very ugly person 1529. 4. *attrib.* Petrifying, terrible 1575.

1. Gorgons and Hydra's, and Chimera's dire MILT. 4. Your G. looks Turn me to stone MASSINGER. *Comb.* **Gorgon's head**, (*a*) the head of Medusa; (*b*) 'a kind of basket-fish' (*Cent. Dict.*).

Gorgoneion (gǭɹgonəi·ǫn). 1842. [a. Gr., neut. of γοργόνειος, of or pertaining to a GORGON.] A representation of a Gorgon's head.

Gorgonia (gǫɹgōᵘ·niă). Pl. **-iæ, -ias.** 1767. [a. mod.L., fem. of *gorgonius*, f. *gorgonem* GORGON. The name refers to its petrified character.] *Zool.* A genus of polyps (family *Gorgoniaceæ*); one of these; a sea-fan, sea-plume. Hence **Gorgo·nian** *a.*[1] pertaining to the gorgonias or their family; *sb.* a polyp of the family.

Gorgonian (gǫɹgōᵘ·niăn), *a.*[2] 1616. [f. GORGON + -IAN; cf. L. *gorgoneus.*] Of or pertaining to the Gorgon; Gorgon-like, terrible. Of a shield: Bearing the Gorgon's head.

The rest his look Bound with G. rigor not to move MILT.

Gorgonize (gǭ·ɹgǫnəiz), *v.* 1609. [f. GORGON + -IZE.] *trans.* To petrify as by the glance of a Gorgon; to render hard or stony.

Gorgonzola (gǭɹgənzōᵘ·lă). 1885. A ewe-milk cheese made at Gorgonzola, near Milan, Italy. *G.-Hall* (joc.), the Stock Exchange.

Gorilla (gŏri·lă). 1853. [An alleged African word, found (in acc. pl. γορίλλας) in the Greek account of the voyage of the Carthaginian Hanno, adopted as the specific name of the ape *Troglodytes gorilla* by Dr. Savage in 1847.] The largest of anthropoid apes, a native of western equatorial Africa; it closely resembles man in its structure, is very powerful and ferocious, and arboreal in its habits.

Goring (gōᵊ·riŋ), *vbl. sb.* 1626. [f. GORE *v.*[3] + -ING[1].] a. The action of GORE *v.*[3]; the act of cutting out, or fitting with, gores. b. A piece of cloth used as a gore; esp. *Naut.* Also *g.-cloth.*

Gorman, gormand(e: see GOURMAND.

Gormandize (gǭ·ɹmăndəiz), *sb.* 1450. [ad. F. *gourmandise.*] †a. Gluttony. b. Indulgence or connoisseurship in good eating. Now chiefly as F. (spelt *gourmandise*).

Gormandize (gǭ·ɹmăndəiz), *v.* 1548. [f. prec. sb.] 1. *intr.* To eat like a glutton. 2. *trans.* To devour greedily, gobble up (*lit.* and *fig.*) 1603. Hence **Go·rmandizer**, a glutton.

Gorse (gǭɹs). [OE. *gorst* :—Indogermanic type **ghrzdo-*, whence L. *hordeum* barley.] 1. Common furze or whin. 2. = JUNIPER. OE.

Comb.: **g.-bird, -linnet**, the common linnet; **-chat, -hatch, -hatcher, -thatcher**, local names for the whinchat, stonechat, wheatear, and linnet; **-duck**, the landrail; **-kid**, a bundle of g. Hence **Go·rsy** *a.* abounding in g.; of or pertaining to g.

Gory (gōᵊ·ri), *a.* 1480. [f. GORE *sb.*[1] + -Y[1].] †1. Of blood: Gore-like, clotted -1590. 2. Covered with gore 1480. 3. = BLOODY 4. 1586. 4. Blood-red (*rare*) 1822.

2. Neuer shake Thy goary lockes at me SHAKS. 3. Goarie blowes 1586. 4. *G. dew*: a minute freshwater alga, *Palmella cruenta.*

Gos, short for GOSHAWK. Burns.

Gosh (gǫʃ). 1757. [Minced f. GOD.] An exclam., (*By*) *g.!*

Goshawk (gǫ·shǭk). [OE. *gós-hafoc*, f. *gós* GOOSE + *hafoc* HAWK; cf. ON. *gáshaukr.*] A large short-winged hawk (*Astur palumbarius*, and other species).

Shrill As goss-hawk's whistle on the hill SCOTT.

Goshen (gōᵘ·ʃĕn). 1611. [Heb., the fertile land allotted to the Israelites in Egypt, in which there was light during the plague of darkness.] Allusively: A place of plenty or of light.

Go·slet. *U.S.* 1884. [f. GOOSE + -LET.] One of a few diminutive species of geese, of the genus *Nettepus.*

Gos-lettuce, var. of *Cos lettuce*; see COS.

Gosling (gǫ·zliŋ). [ME. *geslyng*, a. ON. *gæsling-r*, f. *gás* GOOSE *sb.*; see -LING.] 1. A young goose. 2. *fig.* One who is young and 'green' 1607. 3. A catkin 1706.

Comb.: **g.-colour, -green**, a pale yellowish green; **-grass, -weed**, local names for GOOSE-GRASS 2.

Gospel (gǫ·spĕl), *sb.* [OE. *godspel*, = *gōd spel* (GOOD *a.*, SPELL *sb.*) good tidings, transl. med.L. *bonus nuntius*, Gr. εὐαγγέλιον EVANGEL; later assoc. w. *God.*] 1. 'The glad tidings (of the kingdom of God)'; see Matt. iv. 23. Hence, the Christian revelation, religion, or dispensation. Often contrasted with the *Law*, i.e. the O.T. dispensation. b. *gen.* Any revelation from heaven 1481. 2. The record of Christ's life and teaching, contained in the books written by the four evangelists OE. b. One of these books. Also applied to certain *apocryphal* lives of Christ, as the *G. of Nicodemus*, etc. ME. 3. Eccl. *The g.* (*for* or *of the day*): the portion from one of the four Gospels read at the Communion Service OE. 4. Something as 'true as the gospel' ME. 5. a. Something that serves as a guide to human action 1652. b. A doctrine preached with fervour as a means of social or political salvation 1790. 6. *attrib.* 1538.

1. The Jews saw Christ in the law; the Christians see Christ in the g. JEWEL. 2. b. The four gospels are particularly mentioned by Julian PRIESTLEY. 4. Phr. *To take for g.* And all was g. that a monk could dream CRABBE. 5. a. Hireling wolves, whose G. is their maw MILT. b. The g. of the intellect in the kitchen HAMERTON.

Comb.: **g.-oath**, an oath sworn upon the Gospels, or one equally binding; **-shop**, derisive name for a Methodist chapel; **-side**, the side of the altar at which the g. is read, the north side; **-true** *a.*; **-truth.** Hence **Go·spelless** *a.*

Go·spel, *v.* [f. prec.; in OE. *godspellian.*] †a. *trans.* = EVANGELIZE *v.* 3. -1659. b. *intr.* To preach the gospel (*rare*) 1565.

Gospelize (gǫ·spĕləiz), *v.* 1643. [f. GOSPEL *sb.* + -IZE.] †1. *trans.* To modify according to the spirit of the gospel -1658. 2. = EVANGELIZE 3. Now *rare.* 1646.

1. This command thus Gospelliz'd to us MILT. 2. To fetch the Jew to Gospellize his child 1704.

Gospeller (gǫ·spĕləɹ). Also †**gospeler.** OE. [f. GOSPEL *sb.* and *v.* + -ER[1].] †1. One of the four evangelists -1674. 2. A missionary (*rare*) 1673. 3. One who reads the Gospel in the Communion Service 1506. †4. A book containing the Gospels (see GOSPEL *sb.* 3). 5. One who identifies the gospel with himself and his party 1533.

1. Marke the G., who followed Peter for instruction 1623. 3. I was g. at my Ordination S. MOSTYN. Phr. *Hot g.*: a zealous Protestant or Puritan.

Goss (gǫs). 1906. A kind of crest china invented by W. H. Goss of Stoke-on-Trent.

Goss, var. of GORCE, GORSE.

Gossamer (gǫ·sămǝɹ). [ME. *gos(e)somer(e*, app. f. GOOSE *sb.* + SUMMER *sb.* Perh. primarily 'St. Martin's summer', when geese are in season; hence, gossamer, which is then chiefly observed. Cf. G. *mädchensommer, altweibersommer*, which also have these meanings.]

A. *sb.* A fine filmy substance, consisting of

cobwebs, spun by small spiders, which is seen floating in the air, esp. in autumn, or spread over a grassy surface. Occas. with *a* and *pl.*, a thread or web of gossamer. Also *transf.* and *fig.* 2. A very delicate kind of gauze 1872. 3. a. In England: A very light silk hat (so named by a hatter) 1837. b. *U.S.* A very light kind of waterproof 1888. 4. *attrib.* 1802.

1. All the silvery gossamers That twinkle into green and gold TENNYSON. *fig.* A decent g. of conventional phraseology MOTLEY.

B. *adj.* Light, flimsy; (of persons) frivolous, volatile 1806. Hence **Go·ssamered** *ppl. a.* coated with g., g.-like. **Go·ssamery** *a.* = GOSSAMER *a.*

Gossan (gǫ·zăn). 1776. [Cornish dial.] *Min.* Decomposed rock, of a reddish or ferruginous colour (due to oxidized iron pyrites), forming a part of the outcrop of a metallic vein. Also *transf.* of a rusty wig. Hence **Gossani·ferous** *a.* producing g.

Gossep(pe, obs. forms of GOSSIP.

Gossip (gǫ·sip), *sb.* [OE. *godsibb* (f. *god* GOD + *sib(b* adj. related: see SIB *a.*).] 1. A godfather or godmother; a sponsor. Now only *arch.* and *dial.* 2. A familiar acquaintance, friend, chum. Now only (somewhat *arch.*) of women. ME. 3. A person, mostly a woman, who delights in idle talk; a tattler 1566. 4. The tattle of such a person; idle talk; trifling or groundless rumour 1811. 5. Some kind of game. THACKERAY.

1. Fully designed to come and stand g. in person to Dr. Hudson's child HEARNE. 2. She is to her Gossypes gone to make mery 1560. All the gossips present at their mothers labours FULLER. 3. A negligent, busy, prating G. HEARNE. 4. All this g. about their neighbours HT. MARTINEAU.

Gossip (gǫ·sip), *v.* 1590. [f. prec.] †1. *trans.* To give a name to –1716. †2. *intr.* To act as a gossip; to take part; to make oneself at home –1645. 3. To talk idly, mostly about other people's affairs; to go about tattling 1627. Also *transf.* and *fig.* 1627. 4. *trans.* To tell like a gossip 1611.

1. *All's Well* I. i. 189. 2. Ile G. at this feast SHAKS. 3. You g. everywhere, of every thing 1846. 4. It is so Gossipt in the Queenes chamber HEYWOOD. Hence **Go·ssiper.**

Gossipred (gǫ·sipred). ME. [f. GOSSIP *sb.* + -RED.] 1. The relation of gossips (see GOSSIP *sb.* 1, 2); spiritual affinity. Now only *Hist.* ¶2. In some mod. writers = GOSSIP *sb.* 4. 1828.

Gossipry (gǫ·sipri). 1550. [f. GOSSIP *sb.* + -RY.] 1. = GOSSIPRED 1. b. *concr.* A relative in general. BROWNING. 2. Small talk, gossip; also, a gossiping conversation 1818. b. *concr.* A body of gossips 1853.

Gossipy (gǫ·sipi), *a.* 1818. [See -Y[1].] Full of, or devoted to, gossip.

Gossoon (gǫsū·n). Chiefly *Anglo-Ir.* 1684. [Altered f. *garsoon*, GARCON.] A boy; a servant-boy, lackey.

Gossypine (gǫ·sipəin), *a.* [f. mod.L. *Gossypium* the generic cotton-plant + -INE.] Cottony, flocculent.

Got (gǫt), *ppl. a.* 1593. [Shortened pa. pple. of GET *v.*] Gained, acquired; gathered as a crop. Now only with adv., as *ill got*, etc.

Gote (gōut). Chiefly *n. dial.* ME. [f. *got-*, wk. root of OE. *ȝéotan* to pour (see YETE *v.*).] 1. A channel for water; a stream. 2. A sluice 1531.

Goter(e, obs. f. GUTTER.

Goth (gǫþ). [OE. *Gothan* pl. (*Gota* sing.), ad. late L. *Gothi*, Gr. Γότθοι pl., ad. Goth. **Gutôs* or **Gutans* pl.] 1. One of a Germanic tribe, who in the third, fourth, and fifth centuries, invaded both the Eastern and Western empires, and founded kingdoms in Italy, France, and Spain. 2. *transf.* One who behaves like a barbarian; a rude, uncivilized, or ignorant person. Often with *Vandal.* 1663.

1. Till Goths and Vandals, a rude northern race, Did all the matchless monuments deface DRYDEN.

Gotha (gōu·tă). 1919. [A town in Germany.] A large German aeroplane.

Gotham (gǫ·tăm; often erron. gōu·þăm). 1460. 1. The name of a village, proverbial for the folly of its inhabitants ('wise men of Gotham'). (There is a village so named in Notts.) †2. A 'man of Gotham', a simpleton. CROWNE. †3. *attrib.* (or *adj.*): Of or pertaining to Gotham; foolish, stupid –1694. Hence †**Go·thamist**, a blunderer, a simpleton. **Go·thamite**, (*a*) = *Gothamist*; (*b*) a New-Yorker.

Gothic (gǫ·þik). 1611. [ad. L. *gothicus*, f. *Gothi*; see GOTH.]

A. *adj.* 1. Of, pertaining to, or concerned with the Goths or their language. †2. = TEUTONIC or GERMANIC –1685. 3. †a. Mediæval, romantic, as opp. to classical. In early use: Belonging to the dark ages. –1782. b. Applied to the style of architecture prevalent in Western Europe from the 12th to the 15th c., of which the chief characteristic is the pointed arch. Applied also to buildings, architectural details, and ornamentation. 1641. 4. Barbarous, rude, uncouth, in bad taste. Of temper: Savage. 1695. 5. *Writing* and *Printing.* a. In England, the name of the type used for printing German, as dist. from roman and italic characters. (Formerly = *black letter.*) 1781. b. In U.S., applied to the type called in English GROTESQUE (formerly *stone letter*).

1. Vlpilas is reported..to haue translated the Scriptures into the Gothicke tongue BIBLE *Transl. Pref.* 2. He raised up the G. or Teutonic race MAURICE. 3. a. The Castle of Otranto, a G. story H. WALPOLE (*title*). b. The Gothick manner of Architecture (so the Italians called what was not after the Roman style) WREN. 4. The G. crime of duelling BERKELEY. Hence **Go·thically** *a.* in a g. manner.

B. quasi-*sb.* or *sb.* a. The Gothic language. b. Gothic architecture or ornamentation. 1644.

Gothicism (gǫ·þisiz'm). 1710. [f. GOTHIC *a.* + -ISM.] 1. Rudeness, barbarism; absence of polish. 2. Conformity to the Gothic style of architecture 1754. 3. a. Conformity to Teutonic notions 1847. b. A Gothic idiom 1818. So **Go·thicist**, one who affects what is Gothic, esp. in architecture.

Gothicize (gǫ·þisəiz), *v.* 1750. [f. GOTHIC *a.* + -IZE.] †1. *intr.* To indulge one's taste for what is Gothic or mediæval. H. WALPOLE. 2. *trans.* a. To render mediæval 1808. b. To give an architecturally Gothic character to 1798.

2. b. Arabic forms of parapet, more or less Gothicised RUSKIN.

Gothish (gǫ·þiʃ), *a.* 1602. [f. GOTH + -ISH.] 1. †a. = Gothic *a.* 1. b. Looking Gothic, or like a Goth. 1605. 2. Goth-like, barbarous, tasteless 1602. †3. = GOTHIC *a.* 3. –1663.

Gotten (gǫ·t'n), *ppl. a.* ME. [pa. pple. of GET *v.*] 1. Obtained, acquired, won (usu. with adv.). Now *rare*, exc. in ILL-GOTTEN. †2. = BEGOTTEN –1637.

Gou-: see GOV-.

‖**Gouache** (guaʃ). 1882. [F., ad. It. *guazzo.*] A method of painting with opaque colours ground in water, and mixed with gum and honey. Also, a painting thus executed, and the pigment itself.

Gouge (gaudʒ, gūdʒ), *sb.*[1] 1495. [a. F. :—late L. *gubia, gulbia* (Isidore). Prob. of Celtic origin.] 1. A chisel with a concave blade for cutting rounded grooves or holes in wood. In *Surgery*, a similarly-shaped tool for removing portions of bone, etc. b. A stamping tool for cutting out forms in leather, paper, etc. 1875. c. *Book-binding.* An instrument for impressing curved lines or segments of a circle upon leather 1885. 2. *Mining.* A layer of soft material along the wall of a vein, which the miner can gouge out with a pick 1877. 3. *U.S. colloq.* a. A scooping out. b. A swindle. Also, an impostor. 1845.

Comb. **g.-bit**, a bit shaped at the end like a g.

†**Gouge**, *sb.*[2] [a. OF.] A wench. SCOTT.

Gouge (gaudʒ, gūdʒ), *v.* 1570. [f. GOUGE *sb.*[1]] 1. *trans.* To make or cut holes in, with or as with a gouge. Also *intr.* 2. *trans.* To cut *out*, hollow or scoop *out*, with or as with a gouge. Also, to hollow *into* (a certain form). 1616. 3. To cut or force out with or as with a gouge; to push out (a person's eye) with the thumb. 1800. b. To force out the eye of (a person). Also *absol.* 1785. 4. *U.S.* To cheat, impose upon. Also *absol.* 1875.

3. b. When they had gotten him on his back, one gouged him like a Yankee 1827. 4. He's regularly gouged me in that ere horsehair spekilation B. HARTE. Hence **Gou·ger**, one who gouges (senses 3, 4).

‖**Goujat** (guʒa). 1776. [F.] A soldier's boy.

[**Goujeers, goujeres**: see GOODYEAR.]

Goulan(d: var. *gollan(d)*: see GOWAN.

Goulard (gulā·ɹd). 1806. [f. Thomas *Goulard*, a French surgeon.] In full, *Goulard's extract* or *G. water*: a solution of subacetate of lead, used as a lotion in cases of inflammation.

Goulash (gū·laʃ). 1900. [Magyar *gulyás* (*hús*), f. *gulyás* herdsman + *hús* meat.] 1. A highly-seasoned stew of beef or veal and vegetables. 2. *Contract Bridge.* A re-deal before which each player arranges his cards in suits and order of value 1927.

Gour, var. of GAUR; obs. f. GIAOUR.

‖**Goura** (gūə·ră). 1855. [Native name.] A genus of large crested pigeons inhabiting New Guinea and adjacent islands; one of these.

Gourd (gōəɹd, guəɹd). ME. [ad. F. *gourde*, repr. L. *cucurbita.*] 1. The large fleshy fruit of the trailing or climbing plants of the N.O. *Cucurbitaceæ*; *spec.* the fruit of *Lagenaria vulgaris*, used as a vessel when dried and hollowed out. †b. *Wild g.* = COLOCYNTH –1560. 2. A plant of this order; esp. *Lagenaria vulgaris*, the bottle-gourd. *Bitter g.* = COLOCYNTH. ME. Also *transf.* 3. The shell of the fruit dried and excavated, used as a water-bottle, float, rattle, etc. 1624. 4. *transf.* †a. A bottle or cup –1583. b. = CUCURBIT[1] 1. –1683.

2. And the Lord God prepared a gourde, and made it to come vp ouer Ionah BIBLE (Genev.) *Jonah* iv. 6. 4. b. Distill this liquor in a glasse g. FRENCH.

Comb.: **g.-pear**, a pear shaped like a g. (L. *pirum cucurbitinum*); **-shell** = sense 3; **-tree**, the calabash-tree (see CALABASH); **-worm**, a name for the fluke, and for the segments of the tapeworm, from the likeness to the seeds of the g.

†**Gourd**[2]. 1545. [Cf. OF. *gourd* a swindle.] A kind of false dice –1610.

Gou·rdy, *a.* 1540. [? a. OF. *gourdi*, pa. pple. of *gourdir* to swell, benumb.] †1. Stuffed out. PALSGR. 2. *Farriery.* Swollen in the legs. ? *Obs.* 1704. Hence **Gou·rdiness.**

Gourmand (gūə·ɹmănd, ‖gurmaṅ). 1491. [a. F., of unkn. origin.]

A. *adj.* Gluttonous; fond of eating 1530. The insatiable and gurmand throate NORTH.

B. *sb.* †1. A glutton; also *fig.* –1692. 2. A judge or devotee of good eating. In this sense often as Fr. 1758.

1. That great gourmond, fat Apicivs B. JONS. 2. Their table is always good, for the Landgrave is a *G.* CHESTERF. So †**Gourmand** *v.* to eat greedily. **Gou·rmandism**, love of good fare.

‖**Gourmet** (gurme). 1820. [Fr., repr. of OF. *gourmet, groumet*, a wine-taster's assistant.] A connoisseur in eating and drinking.

Gournard, gournit, obs. ff. GURNARD.

Gout (gaut), *sb.*[1] ME. [a. OF. *goute* (mod. *goutte*) drop, gout :—L. *gutta* drop, in med.L. applied to diseases attributed to a defluxion of humours.]

I. 1. A constitutional disease occurring in paroxysms, usually hereditary and in male subjects; characterized by painful inflammation of the smaller joints, esp. that of the great toe, and the deposition of sodium urate in the form of chalk-stones; it often spreads to the larger joints and the internal organs. a. With *a* and *pl.*: orig. perh. an affection of a particular joint; later = a fit of the disease, or simply, the disease itself. b. *sing.* only (often *the g.*) ME. †2. A disease in hawks, etc.; esp. a hard swelling on the feet –1600. 3. A disease in wheat, caused by the larva of the gout-fly (see *g.-fly*) 1828.

1. a. In foote and hand A grievous g. tormented him full sore SPENSER.

II. 1. A drop, esp. of blood. Later, usually: A large splash or clot. 1503. 2. A spot of colour resembling a drop. (Cf. GOUTTE *Her.*) R. MUDIE.

1. On thy Blade, and Dudgeon, Gouts of Blood SHAKS. *Comb.*: **g.-fly**, the fly (*Chlorops tæniopus* or *lineata*) whose larva causes the g. in wheat; **-stone** = CHALK-STONE; **-weed, -wort**, the plant *Ægopodium Podagraria.*

Gout (gaut), *sb.*[2] ME. [? var. of GOTE; but cf. F. *égout.*] †1. ? A flow of water. Only ME. 2. A channel for water; a sluice; a culvert 1598.

‖**Goût** (gū). 1586. [F., earlier *goust* :—L. *gustus* taste. Cf. GUST, GUSTO.] = TASTE, in various senses.

Goutify (gau·tifəi), *v.* 1749. [f. GOUT *sb.*[1] + -(I)FY.] To make gouty, afflict with gout.

Goutish (gau·tiʃ), *a.* ME. [f. GOUT *sb.*[1] + -ISH.] **a.** Somewhat gouty; predisposed to gout. **b.** Pertaining to, or of the nature of, gout 1700.

‖**Goutte** (gūt). ME. [Fr.] *Her.* A small drop-shaped figure (of specified tincture), used as a charge.

Goutté, goutty, *Her.*: see GUTTÉ.

Gouty (gau·ti), *a.* ME. [f. GOUT *sb.*[1] + -Y[1].] **1.** Affected with, or subject to, gout. Also *fig.* †**b.** Of a horse's legs: Swollen –1577. **2.** Of, pertaining to, or of the nature of, gout 1615. **b.** Used during a fit of gout 1733. **c.** Having a tendency to produce gout 1802. **3.** *transf.* and *fig.* Swollen or bulging; †knotty 1595. †**4.** Of land: Boggy –1790.

1. A man aged and gowtie 1581. 2. G. Matter 1724, concretions 1846. A g. diathesis M. PATTISON. b. My g. shoes BERKELEY. c. G. wines 1897. *Comb.* **g.-stem** (tree), the Australian baobab (*Adansonia Gregorii*). Hence **Gou·tily** *adv.* **Gou·tiness,** tendency to gout (*lit.* and *fig.*). **Gou·tyish** *a.* somewhat g.

Gouv-: see GOV-.

‖**Gouvernante** (guvɛrnānt). 1716. [Fr., fem. pr. pple. of *gouverner*.] †**1.** A female ruler –1772. **2. a.** A housekeeper (*rare*) 1772. **b.** A chaperon or duenna 1716. **c.** A governess 1781.

2. a. Rousseau..crossed the country with his g. H. WALPOLE.

Govern (gɒ·vəɹn), *v.* ME. [a. OF. *governer* (mod. *gouverner*) :—L. *gubernare* to steer, ad. Gr. κυβερνᾶν.] **1.** *trans.* To rule with authority, esp. with that of a sovereign; to direct and control the actions and affairs of (a people, etc.), whether despotically or constitutionally; to regulate the affairs of (a body of men). Also *absol.* **2.** To sway, influence; to direct, guide, or regulate ME. †**b.** To prevail over. SHAKS. **3.** *intr.* To hold sway, prevail, have decisive influence 1596. †**4.** *trans.* To administer, manage, order –1741. †**5.** To attend to; *esp.* to tend in respect to health –1680. †**6.** To work or manage (a ship, etc.) –1697. †**7.** To control the working of; to regulate –1807. **8.** To hold in check, curb, bridle 1513. **9.** To constitute a law or rule for; *esp.* in *Law*, to serve in determining or deciding (a case) 1818. **10.** *Grammar.* To require (a noun or pronoun) to be *in* a particular case, or a verb to be *in* a certain mood; to be necessarily followed by (a particular case or mood) 1530.

1. She must..gouerne the maides, and keepe them at their woorke B. GOOGE. Those that think must g. those that toil GOLDSM. *absol.* The king reigned, but his ministers governed MAY. 2. Ordinary Minds are wholly governed by their Eyes and Ears STEELE. He really helped to g. the events KINGLAKE. 3. Let it be as humors and conceits shall gouerne SHAKS. Fooles that want wit to gouerne themselves well 1608. 8. To g. the tongue SHAKS., the temper DICKENS. 9. The law there stated clearly governs this case SIR H. C. LOPES. 10. Prepositions governing the dative 1881.

Hence **Go·vernable** *a.* capable of being governed (in various senses). **Go·vernabi·lity, Go·vernableness,** the state or quality of being governable. **Go·vernably** *adv.* in a governable manner.

†**Governail.** ME. [a. OF. *governail* (mod. *gouvernail*) :—L. *gubernaculum*, pl. *gubernacula* rudder, f. *gubernare*; see prec.] **1.** A rudder; also, steering –1561. **2.** Government; authority. (In early use often *pl.*) –1597. **b.** Management; also, tending (of plants, wounds) –1590. **c.** Behaviour; rule of conduct –1598.

Governance (gɒ·vəɹnăns). ME. [a. OF. *gouvernance*; see GOVERN and -ANCE.] **1.** The action or manner of governing (see the vb.); the fact that (a person, etc.) governs. **b.** Control ME. †**c.** The state of being governed –1590. **2.** The office, function, or power of governing ME.; †governing person or body –1643. †**3.** Method of management, system of regulations –1660. †**4.** Mode of living, behaviour, demeanour. †**b.** Wise self-command –1600.

1. Goddes gouvernaunce UDALL. b. An irascible spirit under no gre[illegible] g. BURNEY. 2. To han the gouernance of hous and lond CHAUCER. 3. Of the Foundation, Erection, and G. of Hospitals R. COKE. 4. b. In him is bountee, wisdom, governaunce CHAUCER. So †**Go·vernancy** (in sense 2).

†**Go·vernante.** 1639. Anglicized f. GOUVERNANTE, q.v. –1823.

†**Governeress.** ME. [ad. OF. *gouverneresse*.] A female governor; = GOVERNESS, in various senses –1652.

Governess (gɒ·vəɹnĕs), *sb.* 1483. [shortened f. prec.] **1.** A woman who governs; a female ruler. *Obs.* exc. as *nonce-use.* †Also *fig.* –1706. **2.** †A woman who has charge of a person, esp. of a child –1771; a female teacher; now chiefly, one so employed in a private household. (The current use.) 1712. **3.** The wife of a Governor. *Obs.* exc. *joc.* 1697. *Comb.* **g.-car, -cart,** a light two-wheeled vehicle with seats at the sides only. Hence **Go·verness** *v.* to earn one's living as a g.

Governing (gɒ·vəɹniŋ), *ppl. a.* 1635. [See -ING[2].] That governs, in senses of the vb.

G. body: the body of managers of a hospital, public school, etc. Hence **Go·verningly** *adv.*

†**Go·vernless,** *a.* 1621. [See -LESS.] Without government –1679.

The sad ends of many dissolute and g. persons SIR T. BROWNE.

Government (gɒ·vəɹnmĕnt). 1483. [a. OF.; see GOVERN *v.* and -MENT. Repl. GOVERNANCE.] **1.** The action of governing (see the vb.); *spec.* the action of ruling and directing the affairs of a state 1566. †**2.** The manner in which one's action is governed; movements, demeanour; regimen –1612; conduct; discretion –1639. **3.** The office or function of governing; authority to govern 1584; †an appointment as governor –1769. †**4.** Period of rule, tenure of office –1664. **5.** The portion of country ruled over by a governor. Also, *occas.*, the territory united under a common rule, as a kingdom, etc. 1603. **6.** Form or kind of polity 1553. **7.** The governing power in a state; the body of persons charged with the duty of governing; in England esp. the *ministry* or *administration* 1702. **8.** *Grammar.* The influence of one word over another in determining the case of a noun or pronoun or the mood of a verb 1755.

1. The g. of the tongue BUTLER. The business of g. is to promote the happiness of the society by punishing and rewarding BENTHAM. 3. The G. I cast vpon my brother SHAKS. 6. Phr. *Civil* or *political, church* or *ecclesiastical g.*; *monarchical, oligarchical, republican g.*; *episcopal, presbyterian g.* 7. The Liberal G. G. DUFF. The United States g. JEVONS. In America people usually speak of the President and his ministers as the 'administration', not as the 'government' BRYCE. 8. Adverbs have no g. 1762.

Comb.: †**g.-general,** the territory under a governor-general; **-house,** a governor's official residence; **-man,** (*a*) a man connected with the g.; (*b*) *Austral.* a convict; **-paper,** bonds, exchequer bills, etc. issued by a g.; **-securities,** (*a*) = prec.; (*b*) *slang*, fetters; **-valve** = SAFETY-VALVE.

Hence **Governme·ntal** *a.* of or pertaining to g., or to the g. of a country, etc. **Governme·ntally** *adv.*

Governor (gɒ·vəɹnəɹ). ME. [ad. OF. *governeür* (mod. *gouverneur*) :—L. *gubernatorem.*] †**1.** A steersman, pilot, captain –1611. **2.** One who governs ME. **3.** An official appointed to govern a province, country, town, etc. Now the official title of the representative of the Crown in a colony or dependency; also of the executive head of each of the United States. ME. **b.** The commander of a fortress or garrison 1647. **4.** One who bears rule in an establishment, institution, society, etc. Now chiefly as an official title. ME. †**5.** The commander of a company, esp. an armed force –1625. †**6.** A tutor, esp. of a prince or young noble –1788. **7.** *colloq.* or *slang.* **a.** An employer 1802. **b.** Applied by sons to their fathers 1827. **c.** A vulgar form of address to a man 1866. **8.** *Machinery.* A self-acting contrivance for regulating the passage of gas, steam, water, etc., esp. in order to ensure an even and regular motion in a machine 1819. **9.** *Angling.* A particular fly 1867.

1. *Jas.* iii. 4. 2. History is full, down to this day, of the imbecility of kings and governors EMERSON. The..moral G. of the world BONAR. 3. Wm. Penn.. Governer of Pensilvania 1683. b. The g. of Portsmouth CLARENDON. 5. My hopes do shape him for the Gouernor *Oth.* II. i. 55.

Go·vernor-ge·neral. 1586. A governor who has under him deputy- or lieutenant-governors, as, the *Governor-General of India.* Hence **Go·vernor-ge·neralship.**

Governorship (gɒ·vəɹnəɹʃip). 1644. [See -SHIP.] **1.** The office of a governor 1658. **2.** The exercise or tenure of this office.

Gowan (gau·ăn). *Sc.* and *n. dial.* 1570. [app. a var. of obs. *gollan(d*, related to GOLD.] A name for various yellow or white field flowers, esp. the Common Daisy (*Bellis perennis*).

Whare gowans grew, Sae white and bonie BURNS. Hence **Go·waned** *ppl. a.*, **Go·wany** *a.* covered with gowans.

Gow·die. *Sc. dial.* 1810. [Local pronunc. of GOLDY.] The fish *Callionymus Lyra.*

Gowk (gauk), *sb.* Orig. *Sc.* and *n. dial.* ME. [a. ON. *gaukr* = OE. *géac* :—OTeut. **gauko-z.*] **1.** The cuckoo. **2.** A half-witted person; a fool 1605.

Gowk, *v. rare.* 1513. [? f. prec.] *intr.* To stare foolishly.

Gowl (gaul), *v.* Chiefly *Sc.* and *n. dial.* ME. [a. ON. *gaula*, perh. f. root **gau-* to bark. But cf. YOWL.] *intr.* To howl, yell; also, to whine. Also *transf.* of the wind. Hence **Gowl** *sb.* a howl, a yell, a loud cry.

Gown (gaun), *sb.* [ME. *goun(e*, a. OF. *goune, gon, gonne* fem., a Com. Rom. wd. :—med.L. *gunna*, a garment of fur for infirm monks. The Rom. wd. is prob. not of Celtic origin.] **1.** A loose flowing upper garment; esp., in mod. use, a woman's garment fitting close to the upper part of the body with flowing skirts; a FROCK ME. †**2.** = DRESSING GOWN, NIGHTGOWN –1778. **3.** Used as the name of the Roman toga. Hence: 'The dress of peace' (J.). ME. **4.** A more or less flowing robe as worn: **a.** by an alderman, a judge or magistrate; also *collect.* the magistracy ME.; **b.** by members of the legal or clerical profession; hence the profession itself, and *collect.* the members of it 1564; **c.** by members of a University 1665. **5.** *collect. sing.* The resident members of a University; opp. to *town* (now only without article) 1659.

1. The Queene..hath bespoke herself a new gowne PEPYS. 2. I came down..in my g. and slippers DE FOE. 3. He Mars deposed, and arms to gowns made yield DRYDEN. 4. a. The Maire and Aldermen, cled in long gownys of skarlet 1486. b. The Cut-throat Sword and clamorous G. shall jar DRYDEN. I have now taken the g. [i.e. holy orders] 1784. *Comb.* **g.-boy,** a boy belonging to a scholastic foundation, e.g. that of the Charterhouse. Hence **Gown** *v. trans.* to dress in a g.; *intr.* (for *refl.*) to put on a g. **Gowned** *ppl. a.* dressed in a g.; in *g. war*, warfare waged in the law-courts (COWLEY).

Gownsman (gau·nzmăn). Also **gownman.** 1579. [f. GOWN *sb.* + MAN; cf. *craft(s)-man*, etc.] †**1.** An adult Roman. NORTH. **2.** One wearing the gown, or 'dress of peace'; a civilian 1607. **3.** One who wears a gown: **a.** as a lawyer, barrister, or judge 1627; **b.** as a clergyman (now *rare*) 1641; **c.** as a member of a University (often opp. to *townsman*) 1665.

2. It was rather a military spirit than that of the gownman BURKE. 3. a. A gownman's lie 1735.

Gozzard (gǫ·zăɹd). ME. [repr. OE. **goshierde.*] One who takes care of geese.

Graafian (grā·fiăn), *a.* 1841. [f. R. de *Graaf*, a Dutch anatomist (1641–73) + -IAN.] *Anat.* In *G. follicle, vesicle*, one of the small sacs in the ovary of mammals in which the ova are matured.

Grab (græb), *sb.*[1] *Anglo-Ind.* 1680. [a. Arab. *ghurāb*, lit. 'raven'.] A large coasting-vessel, built with a prow and usually two-masted; used in the East.

Grab (græb), *sb.*[2] 1777. [f. GRAB *v.*] **1.** A quick sudden clutch, grasp, or attempt to seize 1824. **b.** The action or practice of grabbing 1883. **2.** The thing grabbed. *Sc.* 1777. **3.** One who grabs; a resurrectionist, a catchpoll, etc. ? *Obs.* 1823. **4.** A mechanical device for clutching or gripping objects; *esp.* one for withdrawing drills, etc. from artesian and other wells 1875. **5.** A children's game at cards.

Comb.: **g.-bag** (*U.S.* at fancy fairs), a bag containing various articles, into which one may dip on payment of a certain sum; also *fig.*; **-game,** a mode of stealing, in which one of several confederates grabs the money at stake in a dispute and runs off.

Grab (græb), *v.* 1589. [Cf. MDu., MLG. *grabben*, mod. Sw. *grabba*; perh. a modification of the root of GRIP.] 1. *trans.* To grasp or seize suddenly and eagerly; hence, to appropriate unscrupulously. 2. To capture or arrest 1800. 3. *intr.* To make a grab *at* (U.S. *for*) 1852. Hence **Gra·bber**, one who or that which grabs; *esp.* in (or short for) **land-grabber**, used chiefly in Ireland for one who takes a holding from which another has been evicted.

Grabble (græ·b'l), *v.* 1579. [Corresp. to Du. *grabbelen*, freq. of *grabben* GRAB *v.*] 1. *intr.* To feel or search with the hands, to grope about. Also *trans.* 2. *intr.* To sprawl or tumble about on all-fours 1736. †3. *trans.* To handle rudely or roughly –1790. 4. To seize 1796.

1. Thou must stoop..And g. for't [gold] in ground SHIRLEY.

Gra·bby. *slang.* 1868. An infantryman.

Grace (grēⁱs), *sb.* ME. [a. F. *grâce*, a. L. *gratia*, f. *gratus* pleasing, GRATEFUL.]

I. 1. Attractiveness, charm; now usually, the charm belonging to elegance of proportions, or (esp.) ease and refinement of movement, action, or expression. b. Becomingness, creditable aspect. Hence, *a bad, an ill g.*, an unbecoming appearance. 1586. c. Hence, *with a good g.*, with a show of willingness; *with a bad or ill g.*, ungraciously 1754. 2. An attractive or pleasing quality or feature ME. †b. An ornament –1700. c. An attitude, etc. adopted with a view to grace 1607. 3. *Mus.* An embellishment consisting of additional notes introduced into vocal or instrumental music, not essential to the harmony or melody 1657. 4. *Myth.* One of the sister goddesses (= L. *Gratiæ*, Gr. Χάριτες) regarded as the bestowers of beauty and charm, and portrayed as women of exquisite beauty. Usually spoken of (after Hesiod) as three in number, Aglaia, Thalia, and Euphrosyne. 1579. 5. *The graces*: a game played with hoops and pairs of slender rods 1842.

1. G., indeed, is beauty in action DISRAELI. b. Henry..retired with a good g. from an impossible position FROUDE. 2. Graces of Mind and Person RICHARDSON. c. Old Sir Pitt..chuckled at her *airs and graces* THACKERAY. 4. Euphrosyne..Whom lovely Venus, at a birth, With two sister Graces more, To ivy-crowned Bacchus bore MILT.

II. Favour. 1. Favour or its manifestation (now only on the part of a superior); favour or goodwill, as dist. from right or obligation, as the ground of a concession. Rather *arch.* ME. 2. The condition or fact of being favoured 1463. 3. An instance of favour; an exceptional favour, a privilege, a dispensation (now only *Hist.*) ME. 4. In University use. a. †Orig., a dispensation from some of the statutable conditions required for a degree. Hence b. Leave of Congregation to take a degree. c. Other decrees of the Governing Body, being very often dispensations from the permanent statutes. d. In mod. use, the permission which a candidate for a degree is required to obtain from his College or Hall. ME. †5. Hap, luck, or fortune (good or bad) –1591. 6. *Theol.*, etc. a. The free and unmerited favour of God ME. Hence, The source of grace, God. *All's Well* I. iii. 226. b. The divine influence which operates in men to regenerate and sanctify, and to impart strength to endure trial and resist temptation ME. c. The condition of one who is under such influence ME. d. An individual virtue or excellence, divine in its origin ME. Also *transf.* 7. Favour shown by granting a delay, or immunity from penalty during a specified period 1711. b. Comm. *Days of grace*, the period (in England 3 days) allowed by law for the payment of a bill of exchange, after the expiration of the term for which it is drawn. Similarly, the period allowed for payment of a premium of insurance or the like, after the date at which it is said to be due. 1731. 8. Mercy, clemency; hence, pardon. Now *rare* or *arch.* ME. 9. A courtesy-title now given only to a duke, a duchess, or an archbishop. Formerly used in addressing a king or queen. (Usu. written with capital.) 1500.

1. The marks of g. which Elizabeth..shewed to young Raleigh SCOTT. Phr. *By the g. of God* (tr. L. *Dei gratiâ*), appended to the formal statement of the titles of sovereigns, etc. †*Save your g.*: = 'by your leave'. †*Hard g.*: displeasure, ill will (CHAUCER) 2. Till all graces be in one woman, one woman shall not come in my g. SHAKS. Phr. *A person's good graces*: his favour and good opinion. 3. But, to return and view the chearful Skies,..To few great Jupiter imparts this G. DRYDEN. *Expectative g.* (see EXPECTATIVE *a.*). 5. *Two Gent.* III. i. 146. 6. a. *Doctrines of g.*: by Calvinists applied esp. to the doctrines of election, predestination, etc. b. *Prevenient g.*: that which produces the repentance and faith without which the *g. of justification* cannot be received. *Sufficient g.*: that which (merely) renders the soul capable of performing a supernatural act, as dist. from *efficacious g.*, that which really effects the end for which it is given. c. Phr. *To fall from g.* (see FALL *v.*). *transf.* I think the Boy hath g. in him, he blushes SHAKS. The powerfull g. that lies In Plants SHAKS. Phr. *transf. To have the g.* (to do something). 7. Phr. *Year of G.*: orig., a year as reckoned from the birth of Christ (*arch.*); (at the Universities), a year allowed to the person chosen to succeed to a college living, at the end of which he must resign either his living or his fellowship. *Time of g.*, a close time (for beasts of the chase). *Day of g.* (Theol.): the time allowed for repentance. 8. [Thou] Stand'st at our g., a captiue HEYWOOD. Phr. *Act of g.*: a formal pardon, *spec.* a free and general pardon, granted by Act of Parliament.

III. †1. *pl.* Thanks, thanksgiving –1533. 2. (Till 16th c. usu. *pl.* in sing. sense; now only *sing.*) A short prayer either asking a blessing before, or rendering thanks after, a meal ME.

2. A youth came forward..and pronounced the ancient form of g. before meals EMERSON.

Comb.: **g.-hoop**, 'a hoop used in playing the game called *graces*'; **-note** = sense I. 3; †**-term**, a term of the period required for a degree, in which residence was customarily dispensed with.

Grace (grēⁱs), *v.* ME. [In sense 1, a. OF. *gracier*; in other senses, f. prec.] †1. *trans.* To thank. ME. only. †2. To show favour to; to countenance –1626. †3. To endow with (heavenly) grace –1701. 4. To adorn, embellish, set off 1586; *Mus.* to add grace-notes, cadenzas, etc., to 1659. 5. To confer honour or dignity upon; also, to do honour or credit to 1585. †b. To name honourably. MILT. †6. To gratify, delight –1703. 7. To address by the title 'your Grace' 1610.

4. He left nothing unassayed..to g. his friend SIDNEY. 5. Pleas't your Highnesse, To g. vs with your Royall Company SHAKS.

Gra·ce-cup. 1593. The cup of liquor passed round after grace is said; the last cup drunk before retiring, a parting draught. Also *fig.*

Graced (grēⁱst), *ppl. a.* 1593. [f. GRACE *sb.* or *v.* + -ED.] Endowed with grace; favoured; having a grace or graces; embellished, etc.

A well grac'd Actor SHAKS. Their well g. fourmes of speech BACON.

Graceful (grēⁱ·sfŭl), *a.* ME. [See -FUL.] †1. Full of divine grace –1611. †2. Favourable. *Ant. & Cl.* II. ii. 60. 3. Possessed of pleasing or attractive qualities; now usually, elegant in form, proportions, action, etc. (see GRACE *sb.* I) 1586.

1. *Wint. T.* V. i. 171. 3. A fine queint gracefull and excellent fashion SHAKS. A g. speaker on any subject CLARENDON. A g. dome STANLEY. Hence **Grace·ful-ly** *adv.*, **-ness.**

Graceless (grēⁱ·slės), *a.* ME. [See -LESS.] 1. Not in a state of grace, unregenerate; hence depraved, wicked ME.; wanting sense of propriety 1508. Also *absol.* †2. Lacking favour –1579. †3. Merciless, unfeeling –1658. 4. Wanting grace, charm, or elegance, unlovely 1638.

1. G. zealots POPE. The g. Youth ADDISON. 3. Asking grace of a graceles face 1658. 4. The composition is g. 1884. **Graceless-ly** *adv.*, **-ness.**

Gracile (græ·sil), *a.* 1623. [ad. L. *gracilis* slender.] Slender, thin, lean. ¶ Recently misused (through association w. *grace*) for: Gracefully slender. Hence **Graci·lity, g.** state; slenderness, leanness.

Graciosity (greⁱʃiǫ·sĭti). 1477. [Late ME. *graciousete*, ad. F. *gracieuseté*; subseq. refash. after L.] Graciousness.

‖**Gracioso** (greⁱʃiōᵘ·so; in Sp. graþiō·so). 1650. [Sp.; = GRACIOUS *a.*] †1. A court favourite –1670. 2. The buffoon of Sp. comedy 1749.

Gracious (grēⁱ·ʃəs), *a.* ME. [a. OF. *gracious* (mod. *gracieux*), ad. L. *gratiosus*, f. *gratia.*] †1. Enjoying favour; acceptable, popular. Const. *to, with.* –1821. 2. Having pleasing qualities. Somewhat *arch.* or *poet.* ME. †b. Attractive; also, graceful, elegant –1649. 3. Characterized by or exhibiting kindness or courtesy. Now *rare* (chiefly *poet.*). ME. 4. Condescendingly kind, indulgent and beneficent to inferiors. Now only of exalted personages, or playful or sarcastic. ME. 5. Of the Deity, Christ, the Virgin Mary: Disposed to show grace, merciful, benignant ME. b. *ellipt.* for God (in exclams.) 1713. †6. Godly, pious, regenerate –1757. †7. Happy, fortunate –1611. †8. Given by way of indulgence or mercy –1726.

2. A Citie, to the sight most gratious 1601. G. herbs HAWTHORNE. 3. Sir Lancelot..Was g. to all ladies TENNYSON. 4. The g. intentions of his sovereign BURKE. A g. master MACAULAY. 5. Under the shadow of Thy gratious Wing 1635. b. *Gracious! Good gracious! Gracious me!* 7. Goe: fresh Horses, And g. be the issue SHAKS. Hence **Gra·cious-ly** *adv.*, **-ness.**

Grackle (græ·k'l). 1772. [Anglicized f. *Gracula* generic name, a mod.L. fem. corresp. to L. *graculus* jackdaw.] 1. A name for various birds included in the genus *Gracula*. 2. *Angling.* Name of an artificial fly 1894.

1. *Grackle*..a word..restricted to members of the families *Sturnidæ* (starling) belonging to the Old World, and *Icteridæ* belonging to the New..In the New World the name G. has been applied to several species of the genera *Scolecophagus* and *Quiscalus*.. The best known are the Rusty G., *S. ferrugineus*.. and *Q. purpureus*, the Purple G. or Crow-Blackbird NEWTON.

Gradate (grădēⁱ·t), *v.* 1753. [f. GRADATION.] 1. To pass or cause to pass by imperceptible grades from one tone or shade to another; to shade off. Also *absol.* 2. *trans.* To arrange in steps or grades. ? Only in *pass.* 1869. 3. *Chem.* (? *U.S.* only.) 'To bring to a certain strength or grade of concentration' (Webster); 'to concentrate as by evaporation' (Funk).

1. Retiring shades, which g. or go off by degrees HOGARTH.

‖**Gradatim** (grădēⁱ·tim), *adv.* 1583. [L.] Step by step, gradually.

Gradation (grădēⁱ·ʃən). 1538. [ad. L. *gradationem*; see GRADE *sb.* and -ATION.] †1. The process of advancing step by step –1750. 2. A series of successive stages in a process or course. ? *Obs.* 1549. 3. *pl.* Steps, progressive movements; stages of transition 1599. †4. *pl.* Arrangements resembling a flight of steps –1802. 5. A scale or series of degrees; the fact or condition of including or being arranged in a series of degrees 1677. 6. *pl.* Degrees of rank, merit, intensity, etc. 1605. 7. The action of arranging in steps or grades. WHEWELL. 8. a. *Rhet.* = CLIMAX 1. ? *Obs.* 1538. †b. *Logic.* = SORITES (*rare*) 1727. †9. *Alch.* Exaltation –1641. 10. *Fine Arts.* a. *Painting.* An insensible passing from one colour or shade to another 1727. b. *Mus.* 'A diatonic ascending or descending succession of chords' (Brande) 1842. 11. *Philol.* = ABLAUT; also, a modification resulting from ablaut 1870.

2. The regular g. of civil honours GIBBON. 5. A g. of ranks in society HT. MARTINEAU. 6. Who shall enumerate the gradations between insect and man 1793. 10. a. What curvature is to lines, g. is to shades and colours RUSKIN. Hence **Grada·tional** *a.* pertaining to, or characterized by, g.

Gradatory (grēⁱ·dătəri), *sb.* 1670. [as if ad. L. **gradatorium.*] A flight of steps, esp. from the cloisters to the choir of a church.

Gradatory (grēⁱ·dătəri), *a.* 1793. [as if ad. L. **gradatorius.*] 1. Proceeding by steps or grades (*rare*). 2. Adapted for stepping; said of the extremities of a quadruped which are adapted for ordinary progression on dry land 1842.

Grade (grēⁱd), *sb.* 1511. [a. F., ad. L. *gradus*. See also GREE *sb.*[1]] †1. *Math.* A degree; the 90th part of a right angle or quadrant –1593. 2. A step or stage in a process; rarely *spec.* a step in preferment 1796. 3. A degree in the scale of rank, dignity, proficiency, etc. 1808; a number of persons holding the same position in the scale; a class 1827. 4. A degree of comparative quality or value; a class of things of the same quality or value 1833. 5. *Path.* Degree or intensity (of a disease) 1803. 6. A result of cross-breeding, a hybrid. Also *attrib.* 1796. 7. *Zool.* A group of animals presumed to have branched from the common stem at about the same point of its development 1877. 8. *Philol.* The position occupied in an ablaut-series by a particular vowel or form of a root 1891. 9. *U.S.* = GRADIENT *sb.* 1835. b. An inclined portion of a railway or road. Also DOWN G., UP G. 1883. c. *U.S. local.* In mining districts: A portion of road 1877. 11. Of a surface: Degree of altitude; level (*rare*) 1851.

2. Grades of depreciation 1796. 3. Teachers of every grade BUCKLE. All grades of railway employés 1897. 4. Low grades of cotton 1880. Ore of low g. SELOUS. b. (*U.S.*) A class at school in relation to advancement 1852.

Comb.: g.-crossing (U.S.), a place where a road and a railway, or two railways cross each other at the same level; g. school = *graded school* (see GRADED *ppl. a.*).

Grade (grēˈd), *v.* 1563. [f. GRADE *sb.*] †1. *trans.* To admit to a (specified) degree. FOXE. 2. To arrange in grades or classes; to class; to sort; to determine the grades or degrees of 1659. b. To blend so as to affect the grade of 1889. 3. *trans.* To reduce (the line of a road, railway, or canal) to levels or practicable gradients 1835. 4. *Stock-breeding.* To cross with some better breed 1887. 5. *Philol.* In *pass.*: To be altered by gradation or ablaut 1887. 6. To cut (steps) at regular intervals 1896. 7. *intr.* To pass imperceptibly from one grade *into* another. Also *down, up, off.* 1903.

Graded (grēˑdĕd), *ppl. a.* 1840. [f. GRADE *sb.* and *v.* + -ED.] 1. Formed like a flight of steps 1850. 2. Divided according to grades of rank, quality, etc. 1859. 3. Of a road, etc.: See GRADE *v.* 3. 4. Of cattle: Improved by crossing 1887.

2. *Graded school* (chiefly U.S.): 'a school divided into departments..in which the children pass from the lower departments to the higher as they advance in education' (*Cent. Dict.*).

Gradely (grēˑdli), *a.* Now only *dial.* [ME. *greiðlic*, a. ON. *greiðlig-r*, f. *greið-r* GRAITH *a.* + *-lig-r* -LY [1].] 1. Of persons, their actions, etc.: Decent, respectable, worthy; *occas.* of a girl, comely. Also 'regular', thorough (*dial.*) 1746. b. *predicatively.* Well in health 1851. 2. Of things: Excellent, suitable, handsome ME.; real proper (*dial.*) 18.. So Graˑdely *adv.* †promptly; carefully, exactly; properly; really; well

Grader (grēˑdəɹ). 1868. [f. GRADE *v.* + -ER [1].] 1. One who grades 1870. 2. A machine for grading 1868.

Gradient (grēˑdiĕnt). 1641. [ad. L. *gradientem* pr. pple. of *gradi.*]

A. *adj.* 1. Of animals: Walking, ambulant. 2. Of a railway line: Rising or descending by regular degrees of inclination. (Only in Dicts.)

B. *sb.* Of a road or railway: Amount of inclination to the horizontal 1835. b. A portion of a way not level (Webster). 2. *transf.* The proportional amount of rise or fall of the barometer or thermometer in passing from one region to another 1870. 3. *Math.* A rational integral function of a number of quantics of assigned weights, which is of one degree and one weight throughout (Prof. Elliott) 1887.

2. A g. of 4 means that over a distance of 60 nautical miles, the barometer rises $\frac{4}{100}$ or $\frac{1}{25}$ of an inch HUXLEY.

Gradin, gradine [1] (grēˑdin, grădīˑn). 1834. [a. or ad. F. *gradin*, ad. It. *gradino*, f. *grado* GRADE *sb.*] 1. One of a series of low steps or seats raised one above the other. 2. A shelf or ledge at the back of an altar 1877.

Gradine [2] (gradīˑn). 1860. [a. F.] A toothed chisel used by sculptors.

Grading (grēˑdiŋ), *vbl. sb.* 1835. [f. GRADE *v.* + -ING [1].] The action of GRADE *v.*; *spec.* the action or process of reducing a road to practicable gradients.

‖**Gradino** (gradīˑno). 1883. [It.; see GRADIN.] a. = GRADIN 2. b. A work of painting or sculpture to ornament the gradin of an altar.

Gradual (græˑdiuăl), *sb.* 1563. [ad. med.L. *graduale* sb., orig. adj. neut.; see next.] 1. An antiphon sung between the Epistle and the Gospel at the Eucharist; it was sung at the steps of the altar or while the deacon was ascending the steps of the ambo. 2. A book of such antiphons; = GRAIL [1] 1619. †3. The steps of an altar. DRYDEN.

Gradual (græˑdiuăl), *a.* 1541. [ad. med.L. *gradualis*, f. *gradus* step.] †1. Of or pertaining to degree; only in *g. difference* = difference in degree -1658. †2. Arranged in, or admitting of, degrees or gradation -1712. 3. Of a process: Taking place by degrees; advancing step by step. Of a slope: Gentle. 1692. b. *poet.* Tapering; sloping gradually; moving or changing gradually 1739. c. quasi-*adv.* (*poet.*) 1736.

3. Isabel By g. decay from beauty fell KEATS. b. Thy dewy fingers draw The g. dusky veil COLLINS. c. The distant view, That g. fades GILB. WHITE. Phr. *G. psalms*: fifteen psalms (cxx–cxxxiv) each of which is entitled in the A.V. 'Song of Degrees', in R.V. 'Song of Ascents', in the Vulgate *Canticum graduum*, in LXX ᾠδὴ ἀναβαθμῶν. The sense of the Heb. is disputed. Hence Graˑdualness.

Gradualism (græˑdiuăliz'm). 1835. [f. prec. + -ISM.] The principle or method of gradual as opp. to immediate change, e.g. in the abolition of slavery.

Graduality (grædiu,aˑlĭti). 1646. [f. as prec. + -ITY.] The quality or condition of being gradual.

Gradually (græˑdiuăli, græˑdʒuăli), *adv.* 1646. [f. GRADUAL *a.* + -LY [2].] †1. In respect of degree -1701. †2. In a graduated scale; by degrees of rank, etc. -1755. 3. Little by little 1646.

3. You must understand it g...a little at a time DE FOE.

Graduate (græˑdiu,ĕt). 1479. [ad. med.L. *graduatus*, pa. pple. of *graduare* to GRADUATE.]

A. *pa. pple.* and *ppl. a.* 1. Admitted to or holding a University degree. *Obs.* exc. as attrib. use of the sb. 1494. 2. Arranged by steps or degrees (now *rare*) 1628.

2. The starry ranks..In g. scale of might 1855.

B. *sb.* 1. One who has obtained a degree from a University, college, etc. In U.S. occas.: A pupil who has completed a school course. 1479. 2. *transf.* A proficient in an art, etc. (now *rare*) 1582. 3. A graduated cup, tube, or flask; a measuring glass used by apothecaries and chemists; the quantity this holds 1883. 4. *attrib.* 1895.

2. Your gradiate in the schoole of warre 1642. 4. G. members of the University (*mod.*).

Graduate (græˑdiu,eˑt), *v.* 1588. [f. med.L. *graduat-* ppl. stem; see prec.]

I. 1. *trans.* To admit to a University degree. Now *rare* exc. *U.S.* Also *fig.* †2. Of an acquirement, etc.: To qualify (a person) for a degree or as a proficient in an art, etc. -1829. 3. *intr.* To take a University degree 1807; also *transf.* to qualify (*as*); also, to train in order to qualify 1829.

1. Thence to Oxford, to be graduated HOWELL. 3. He (Mandeville) graduated at Leyden 1808. *transf.* To g. as a saint SOUTHEY.

II. *gen.* 1. *trans.* To divide into degrees 1594. b. To arrange in gradations; to adapt *to* by graduating. Also *intr.* for *refl.* 1610. †2. To improve the scale or quality of; *spec.* in *Alch.* to transmute (a metal, an essence) into one of a higher grade -1669. b. To concentrate (a solution) by evaporation. So F. *graduer* (Littré). 1828. 3. *intr.* To pass by degrees or gradations; to change gradually; *spec.* in *Geol.*, *Bot.*, and *Zool.* 1786.

1. The thermometer..graduated according to the scale of Fahrenheit 1748. b. The proposal to g. the Income-tax FAWCETT. 2. Dyars..advance and g. their colours with Salts SIR T. BROWNE. 3. This sandstone graduates into the inferior conglomerates DE LA BECHE. Carriers..g...into the rock-pigeon DARWIN.

Graduated (græˑdiu,eˑtĕd), *ppl. a.* 1655. [f. prec. + -ED.] In senses of the vb.; esp.: a. Qualified 1828. b. Marked with lines to indicate degrees, grades, or quantities 1762. c. Arranged in grades or gradations; advancing or proceeding by degrees 1678.

b. A g. measure 1806. c. G. taxation MILL, privilege 1896. *Graduated*, in Ornithology, when the quill-feathers of the tail increase in length by regular gradations BRANDE.

Graduateship (græˑdiu,ĕt,ʃip). 1644. [f. GRADUATE *sb.* + -SHIP.] The period during which one is a graduate; the condition of being a graduate.

A topic folio, the gatherings and savings of a sober graduatship MILTON.

Graduation (grædiu,ēˑʃən). 1477. [f. GRADUATE *v.*; see -ATION.] The action of graduating. 1. a. The action of dividing into degrees, etc. on a graduated scale 1833. b. *pl.* Lines to indicate degrees of latitude and longitude, quantity, etc. 1594. c. The manner in which something is graduated 1653. 2. Arrangement in degrees or gradations; 'regular progression by succession of degrees' (J.) 1658. b. An elevation by degrees into a higher condition; also quasi-*concr.* a degree 1643. †3. *Alch., Chem.*, etc. The process of tempering the composition of a substance, or of refining an element, a metal -1683. b. Concentration by evaporation. Also *attrib.* 1839. †4. *U.S. Railways.* Formerly used for GRADIENT. 5. The action of receiving or conferring a University degree, or the like. Also, the ceremony of conferring degrees. Chiefly *Sc.* and *U.S.* 1639.

2. b. [Justice] Silence [in 2 *Hen. IV*] is an embryo of a man..a g. from nonentity towards intellectual being MRS. C. CLARKE.

Graduator (græˑdiu,eˑtəɹ). 1828. [f. GRADUATE *v.* + -OR.] One who or that which graduates. a. One who graduates glasses, instruments, etc. b. An instrument for dividing any line, straight or curved, into small regular portions. c. A contrivance for concentrating a solution by rapid evaporation.

‖**Gradus** (grēˑdŏs). 1764. Short for *Gradus ad Parnassum* 'a step to Parnassus', the L. title of a dictionary of prosody until recently used in public schools as an aid in writing Latin verses. Hence applied to other similar works.

attrib. A commonplace or g. epithet 1887.

Græcian, obs. f. GRECIAN.

Græcism, Grecism (grīˑsiz'm). 1450. [ad. F. *grécisme*, ad. med.L. *Græcismus*, f. *Græcus.*] †1. The *Græcismus*, a 12th c. grammatical treatise (*rare*). 2. An idiom, or other feature, belonging to the Greek language; esp. as used by a speaker or writer in another language 1570. 2. The Greek spirit or style in art, mode of thought, etc.; adoption or imitation of these 1609.

1. Milton..has infused a great many..Græcisms..into the language of his poem ADDISON. 2. The singular Grecism in Shakespeare's mind RUSKIN.

Græcize, Grecize (grīˑsəiz), *v.* 1692. [ad. L. *Græcizare*; see -IZE.] 1. *trans.* To give a Greek cast, character, or form to. 2. *intr.* To become Greek-like; to adopt Greek expressions, idioms, modes of life, etc. 1840.

Græco-, Greco- (grīˑko), comb. f. L. *Græcus* GREEK, with sense 'relating to the Greek settlements or states established in certain regions abroad', as in *Græco-Asiatic*, etc., or 'partly Greek and partly —', as in *Græco-Latin*, etc.

Græcomania (grīkomēˑniă). 1800. [f. GRÆCO- + Gr. μανία.] A mania for things Greek. Hence Græcomaˑniac.

Græcophil (grīˑkŏfil). 1889. [f. as prec. + Gr. φίλος. A newspaper wd.] A lover of Greece or of what is Greek.

‖**Graf** (grăf). 1630. [Ger.; see GRAVE *sb.*[3]] German equivalent of COUNT and EARL.

Graff (graf), *sb.*[1] *arch.* ME. [a. OF. *grafe*, *greffe* (mod. *greffe*), ad. late L. *graphium*, ad. Gr. γραφίον, γραφεῖον stylus, f. γράφειν. The sense 'graft' was suggested by the similarity of shape.] = (and repl. by) GRAFT *sb.*[1] 1, 2.

Graff (graf), *sb.*[2] Now *Hist.* 1637. [prob. ad. MDu. *grave* = GRAVE *sb.*[1]] A trench serving as a fortification; a foss or moat; *rarely*, a canal (in Holland).

Graff (graf), *sb.*[3] 1523. [? var. of GRAFT *sb.*[2]] 1. = GRAFT *sb.*[2] 1. 2. *dial.* = GRAFT *sb.*[2] 2. 1875.

Graff (graf), *v. arch.* ME. [f. GRAFF *sb.*[1]] Superseded by GRAFT *v.*[1], q. v.

Graffage (graˑfĕdʒ). *dial.* 1798. [? f. GRAFF *sb.*[2] + HEDGE.] A railed fence at the junction of two ditches, or where a ditch abuts on a road at right angles.

†**Graffer.** 1513. [ad. F. *greffier.*] A notary -1615.

‖**Graffito** (grafˌfī·to). *Pl.* **-ti.** 1851. [It., f. *graffio* a scratch.] A drawing or writing scratched on a wall or other surface, as at Pompeii and Rome. Also, a method of decoration by scratches through a superficial layer of plaster, glazing, etc. on a ground of different colour; chiefly *attrib.*, as in *g.-pottery*, etc.

Graft (graft), *sb.*[1] 1483. [A modification of GRAFF *sb.*[1] The nature of the *-t* is uncertain.] **1.** A shoot or scion inserted in a groove or slit made in another stock, so as to allow the sap of the latter to circulate through the former. †**2.** A twig fit for use in grafting; a scion, a sucker; hence *gen.* a branch, plant. Also *fig.* -1624. **3.** *Surg.* 'A portion of living tissue transplanted from one place to another on the same or another organism, with a view to its adhesion or growth' (Billings); also, the operation or its result 1886. **4.** [f. the vb.] **a.** The process or product of grafting. **b.** The place where the scion is inserted in the stock. 1802.

Comb.: **g.-hybrid,** a plant produced by the union of the cellular tissue of two distinct species, bearing leaves and sterile flowers intermediate in character between the scion and the stock; **-hybridism, -hybridization,** hybridizing by means of a g.

Graft (graft), *sb.*[2] 1620. [? a. ON. *grøft-r* action of digging, f. (ult.) **grab-* GRAVE *v.* to dig.] **1.** A 'spit' of earth. Often *spade('s) g.* **2.** A kind of spade for digging drains 1894.

Graft (graft), *sb.*[3] orig. *U.S. slang.* 1889. [Origin uncertain.] A means of making illicit profit; dishonest gains or illicit profits, esp. in connexion with political or municipal business.

Graft (graft), *v.*[1] 1483. [var. of GRAFF *v.*] **1.** *trans.* To insert (a shoot from one tree) as a graft into another tree. Const. *in, into, on, upon.* Also *transf.* and *fig.* **2.** *absol.* and *intr.* To insert a graft or grafts 1626. **3.** *trans.* To fix a graft or grafts upon (a stock). Also *vaguely*, to perform the operation of grafting on (a tree), to produce (fruits) by grafting 1624. **4.** *transf.* To plant, implant 1562. **5.** *Naut.* To cover (a ring-bolt, block-strop, etc.) with a weaving of small cord or rope-yarns 1860. **6.** *Surg.* To transplant (skin, tissue, etc.): cf. GRAFT *sb.*[1] 3. 1868.

1. *fig.* No Art can be grafted with success on another art SIR J. REYNOLDS. **3.** G. thy pears, O Daphnis, the fruit thy sons shall enjoy BOWEN.

Graft (graft), *v.*[2] orig. *U.S. slang.* 1903. [f. GRAFT *sb.*[3]] *intr.* To practise or make 'graft'. Hence **Gra·fter.** **Gra·fting** *vbl. sb.* and *ppl. a.*

Grafter (gra·ftəɹ). 1599. [f. GRAFT *v.*[1] + -ER [1].] **1.** One who grafts trees 1616. †**2.** The original tree from which a scion has been taken for grafting on another -1770. **3.** A kind of hand-saw used in grafting 1884.

2. *Hen. V*, III. v. 9.

Grafting (gra·ftiŋ), *vbl. sb.* 1483. [f. GRAFT *v.*[1] + -ING [1].] **1.** The action of GRAFT *v.*[1] **2.** In techn. senses: **a.** *Naut.* 'An ornamental weaving of fine yarns, etc., over the strop of a block; or applied to the tapered ends of the ropes, and termed pointing' (Smyth). **b.** *Surg.* The transference of a portion of skin, etc. to another part of the body or to another body 1896. **c.** *Carpentry.* 'A scarfing or endwise attachment of one timber to another' (Knight). **d.** Knitting new feet to stockings 1858.

1. *Cleft-, crown-, saddle-, tongue-, whip-*, etc. *g.*, see the sbs. CLEFT, etc. *Comb.*: **g. clay, wax,** a mixture of clay or wax and other ingredients, forming a composition with which to cover the united parts of a scion and stock in grafting.

Grahamism (grē¹·ămiz'm). *U.S.* 1845. [f. *Graham* + -ISM.] The vegetarian principles advocated by Sylvester Graham (1794–1851). So **Gra·hamite,** a follower of Graham.

Grail[1] (grē¹l). [ME. *graell*, ad. OF. *grael* :—Eccl. L. *gradale*, var. of *graduale* GRADUAL.] = GRADUAL *sb.* 1, 2.

Grail[2] (grē¹l). Also †**greal,** †**graal.** ME. [ad. OF. *graal, grael*, etc. :—med.L. *gradalis* a cup or platter, of uncertain origin; commonly referred (ult.) to L. *crater* cup.] *The (Holy) Grail, the Saint Grail* or SANGREAL: in mediæval legend, the platter used by our Saviour at the Last Supper, in which Joseph of Arimathea received the Saviour's blood at the cross. According to one story it was brought by Joseph of Arimathea to Glastonbury. ¶Sometimes supposed erron. to be the cup or chalice used at the Last Supper.

Three angels bear the Holy Grail TENNYSON.

Grail[3] (grē¹l). *poet.* 1590. [? short for GRAVEL.]

Grail[4] (grē¹l). Also †**graille.** 1688. [a. F. *grêle*, f. *grêler* to make slender, *spec.* to taper and smooth (the teeth of a comb).] A comb-maker's file.

Grain (grē¹n), *sb.*[1] ME. [(1) a. OF. *grain, grein* (mod. *grain*) :—L. *granum* a grain, seed; (2) a. OF. *grain(n)e* (mod. *graine*) :—pop. L. *grana* fem., orig. pl. of *granum.*]

I. Seed; corn. †**1.** A single seed, esp. one which is small, hard, and roundish. (After 15th c. usually: The stone or pip of a fruit.) -1823. Also *fig.* **2.** *spec.* A seed or corn of a cereal plant ME. **3.** *collect. sing.* The fruit or seed of wheat and the allied fruit-plants or grasses (†*rarely* of beans, etc.); the plants themselves ME. **b.** A particular species of corn. †Also *pl.* Crops of grain. ME. **4.** Spec. uses of the *pl.* **a.** (in full *grains of Paradise*): The capsules of *Amomum Meleguetta*; called also *Guinea grains* (see GUINEA) ME. **b.** Refuse malt after brewing or distilling 1583. †**c.** = DUCKWEED -1597. **5.** †**a.** A berry, grape -1693. **b.** One part of a collective fruit 1674. **c.** *Bot.* A tubercle (see GRAINED *ppl. a.*[2]) 1829.

1. The G. of a Grape 1684. *fig.* No greine of pite GOWER. Phr. †*In the g.*: in the stage of forming seed. **2.** A Caryopsis or G. GRAY. **3.** The lab'ring Swain Scratch'd with a Rake, a Furrow for his G. DRYDEN. **b.** Barley is a summer g. 1704.

II. Senses orig. transf. from 1 and 2. †**1.** A bead, esp. a bead of a rosary; also, a pearl -1662. **2.** A small, round, usually hardish particle (e.g. of sand, salt, etc.) ME. **b.** *spec.* Of gunpowder: A particle of definite size. Also *attrib.* in *large, small*, etc. *g. powder.* 1667. **3.** The smallest English and U.S. unit of weight (orig. the weight of a grain of wheat taken out of the middle of the ear); now = $\frac{1}{5760}$ of a lb. Troy, $\frac{1}{7000}$ of a lb. avoirdupois 1542. **4.** *fig.* (from 2 prec. senses): The smallest possible quantity; esp. in neg. contexts ME.

2. A g. of Mustard-seed HOBBES. *With a g. of salt* (see SALT). **3.** From eight to twelve Grains of Calomel WESLEY. A *diamond g.* is but ·7925 of a true g. A. H. CHURCH. *Fine g.* (see FINE *a.*). **4.** A.. stupid Blockhead, without one G. of Learning HEARNE.

III. With reference to dyeing. [OF. *graine.*] **1. a.** *Hist.* The Kermes or Scarlet Grain (see ALKERMES); later also Cochineal. Also the dye from either of these. ME. **2.** Dye in general, esp. a fast dye; colour, hue. Now only *poet.* ME.

1. The chief reds were scarlet and g. 1883. Phr. *To dye in g.*: orig. to dye in scarlet g.; subseq., to dye in any fast colour, to dye in the fibre, or thoroughly. *In g.* [short for *dyed in g.*], adjectival phr. = dyed scarlet or crimson, fast dyed; hence in fig. use, esp. with *ass, fool*, etc.: Downright, by nature, thorough. Also as *predicate*, ineradicable, INGRAINED. ME. **2.** All in a robe of darkest g. MILT. *fig.* Sins of so deep a graine 1660.

IV. 1. Granular texture; hence in an engraving, etc. a granular appearance produced by dots or lines ME. **2.** *spec.* Of leather: **a.** The rough surface resulting from the growth of papillæ 1607. Also *transf.* **b.** = *grain-side* 1851. **3.** The arrangement and size of the constituent particles of any substance, determining its texture 1600. **b.** *concr.* Internal substance 1579. **4.** The longitudinal arrangement of fibres or particles in wood 1565; the plane of cleavage in coal, stone, etc. 1664. **5.** *fig.* (from 2 prec. senses): Quality, nature, temper; inclination, tendency 1641. **6.** *pl.* A preparation used in graining leather. (Recent Dicts.)

3. Coarse complexions, And cheeks of sorry g. MILT. The clouded olive's easy g. POPE. A.. stone, of a close g. SMEATON. **b.** The graine of the bone is somewhat more yellow than the Ivorie HAKLUYT. **4.** *Tr. & Cr.* I. iii. 8. As the gun-flint makers observe, 'flint has no g.'. It has not in fact the slightest cleavage. J. PRESTWICH. **5.** Crossing the G. of our Nature and Desires BARROW. Phr. *Against* (also, *contrary to*) *the g.* Cut Prejudice against the g. TENNYSON.

V. *attrib.* and *Comb.* **1.** General: as *g.-farm, -merchant*, etc.; *g.-weight*; *g.-dyer*; *g.-eating*, etc.; *g.-fed* adj.

2. General: **g.-colour,** (*a*) scarlet dye; (*b*) a fast colour; also a cloth dyed with this; **-cut,** *a.* (*Shipbuilding*), of timber, cut athwart the g.; **-founder** = *grain-sick*; **-gold,** gold formed into grains by heat after parting; **-intoxication,** that arising from the use of musty g.; **-leather,** leather dressed with the g.-side outwards; **-moth,** a moth (esp. *Tinea granella*) whose larvæ devour g. in storehouses; **-poisoning,** see *grain-intoxication*; **-process** (*Photogr.*), a process in which a granular texture is given to the plate; **-sick,** a disease in cattle, consisting of an excessive distension of the rumen with food; **-side,** the side of a skin on which the hair grew, opp. to *flesh-side*; **-soap,** in soap-making, soap that has become solid; **g. tin** (see TIN); **-tree** (*Her.*), an imaginary plant bearing kermes grains; **-weevil,** a small weevil which injures stored g.; **-whisky,** whisky made of barley in the g. stage.

Grain (grē¹n), *sb.*[2] [ME. *greyn(e*, ad. ON. *grein* division, branch.] †**1.** *pl.* The fork of the body -1612. **2.** A bough or branch. *Obs.* exc. *dial.* 1501. **3.** †**a.** An arm (of the sea); a branch (of a stream) -1533. **b.** A valley branching out of another (*dial.*) 1542. **4.** A prong of a fork. *Obs.* exc. *dial.* 1486. *pl.* (formerly also *grainse* constr. as *sing.*): A fish-spear or harpoon with two or more prongs 1815.

Grain (grē¹n), *v.*[1] ME. [f. GRAIN *sb.*[1]] †**1.** *intr.* To yield grain. Of corn: To form its grains. -1604. **2. a.** *trans.* To cause to deposit grains; to form into grains. **b.** *intr.* for *refl.* Of salt, etc.: To form into grains. 1706. **3.** *Brewing.* To free from grain 1882. **4.** To dye in grain (see GRAIN *sb.*[1]) 1530. **5.** To give a granular surface to 1888. **6.** *Leather-dressing.* **a.** To remove the hair from (skins). **b.** To soften or raise the grain of (leather, etc.). 1530. **7.** To paint in imitation of the grain of woods or of marble. Also *absol.* 1798.

†**Grain,** *v.*[2] *rare.* [f. GRAIN *sb.*[2]] To divide. POWER.

Grainage (grē¹·nėdʒ). 1610. [f. GRAIN *sb.*[1] + -AGE.] †**1.** Crop of grain. W. FOLKINGHAM. **2.** *Farriery.* Mangy tumours on the legs of horses 1847.

Grained (grē¹nd), *ppl. a.*[1] ME. [f. GRAIN *v.*[1] + -ED [1].] **1.** Dyed in grain. Also *fig.* **2.** Formed into grains 1800. **3.** Of leather (see GRAIN *v.*[1] 6) 1714. **4.** Painted to imitate the grain of woods or of marble 1798.

1. *fig.* Thou turn'st mine eyes into my very soule, And there I see such blacke and g. spots, As will not leaue their Tinct SHAKS.

Grained (grē¹nd), *ppl. a.*[2] 1529. [f. GRAIN *sb.*[1] + -ED [2].] **1.** Having grains, seeds, or particles. *Obs.* exc. in *large-, small-g.*, etc. 1611. **2.** Of wood, stone, leather, flesh, etc.: Having a grain, or granular structure or surface (see GRAIN *sb.*[1] IV. 1–4) 1529. **3.** *Bot.* Having tubercles, as the segments of the flowers of the *Rumex* 1818.

Grained (grē¹nd), *ppl. a.*[3] 1513. [f. GRAIN *sb.*[2] + -ED [2].] Having tines or prongs; forked.

Grainer (grē¹·nəɹ). 1813. [f. GRAIN *v.*[1] + -ER [1].] One who or that which grains. **1.** *Leather-dressing.* **a.** An alkaline lye consisting of water impregnated with pigeon's or hen's dung; also, the pit or vessel containing it. Cf. BATE *sb.*[4] **b.** A tool for graining skins 1839. **2.** A house-painter's graining-tool 1858. **3.** One who paints in imitation of the grain of woods or of marble 1837.

Graining (grē¹·niŋ), *vbl. sb.* 1664. [f. GRAIN *v.*[1] + -ING [1].] **1.** The action of GRAIN *v.*[1] 1823; quasi-*concr.* the result of this action, *esp.* in house-painting 1834. **2.** *Coinage.* †**a.** A ring of grain-like protuberances on the face of a coin, close to its edge (= F. *grènetis*) EVELYN. **b.** = MILLING 1691. *Comb.* **g.-comb,** a tool resembling a comb, used by house-painters in graining.

Graining (grē¹·niŋ), *sb.* 1772. [?] A small freshwater fish, *Leuciscus Lancastrensis.*

Grainy (grē¹·ni), *a.* 1611. [f. GRAIN *sb.*[1] + -Y [1].] **1.** Granular; grain-like. **2.** Full of grain or corn 1755.

Graip (grē¹p). *Sc.* and *n. dial.* 1459. [a. ON. *greip* corresp. to OE. *grāp* grasp; see GRIP, GROPE.] A three- or four-pronged fork used as a dungfork, etc.

Graith (grē¹þ), *sb.* In later use only *Sc.* ME. [a. ON. *greiðe*, f. (ult.) OTeut. **ga-* pref. (see Y-) + **raið-*; see READY.] †**1.** A state of preparation -1460. **2.** Equipment; dress, articles of dress; armour ME.; harness

1663. 3. Apparatus, gear, tackle; a contrivance ME. †4. Wealth, money -1786. 5. Material, stuff (for a purpose) 1513.

1. *In g.*: in proper order; also, without delay. *Out of g.*: out of order. 2. I will sleep like a sentinel, with my g. about me SCOTT.

†**Graith**, *a.* and *adv.* ME. [a. ON. *greið-r* = OE. *gerǽde*; see READY.]

A. *adj.* 1. Ready -1475. 2. Of a road: Direct. Of a measure: Exact. Of a sign, truth, etc.: Plain. ME. only.

B. *adv.* Readily; clearly, plainly -1450.

Graith (grēⁱþ), *v. Obs.* exc. *dial.* ME. [a. ON. *greiða*, f. *greið-r* ready; see prec.] 1. *trans.* To make ready; also, to procure. 2. To equip, furnish; to array; to bedeck ME. †3. = MAKE in various senses. ME. only. Hence **Grai·thing** *vbl. sb.* (now *dial.*), preparation; furnishing; furniture, attire.

Grakle, var. of GRACKLE.

Grallatorial (grælătōᵊ·riăl), *a.* 1835. [f. mod.L. *grallatorius* (f. L. *grallator* one who walks on stilts) + -AL.] *Ornith.* Pertaining to the order *Grallatores*, which consists of long-legged wading birds, such as the crane, heron, etc. So **Gra·llatory** *a.*

Grallic (græ·lik), *a. rare.* 1828. [f. L. *grallæ* stilts + -IC.] *Ornith.* Of or pertaining to the *Grallæ* or wading birds. So **Gra·lline** *a.*

Gralloch (græ·lǫχ), *sb.* 1882. [a. Gael. *grealach* intestines.] The viscera of a dead deer. Hence **Gra·lloch** *v.* to disembowel (prop. a deer).

Gram[1] (græm). 1702. [ad. Pg. *grão*:—L. *granum* grain.] The chick-pea, *Cicer arietinum*. Hence, any kind of pulse used as food for horses. Also *attrib.*

Gram[2]: see GRAMME.

-gram (græm), repr. (chiefly) Gr. γράμμα something written, letter (of the alphabet). The older Eng. sbs. with this ending are: (1) adaptations of Gr. sbs. in -γραμμα, derived from vbs. f. prep. + γράφειν, as *anagram*, *diagram*, etc.; (2) compounds of a Gr. sb. with γράμμα, as *chronogram*, etc.; (3) compounds of a numeral with γράμμα, or γραμμή line, of which the Gr. type is a neut. adj. in -γραμμον, as *monogram*, *hexagram*, etc. In 1857 *telegram*, which violates Gr. analogy, was introduced as a shorter term for 'telegraphic message'. Similar formations are *cablegram* for 'cable telegram', *pistolgram* for an instantaneous photograph.

Grama, gramma (grā·mă, græ·mă). See GAMA GRASS. 1851. [a. Sp. *grama* a sort of grass.] A name for several low pasture grasses found in the western U.S., esp. *Bouteloua oligostachya*.

Gramarye (græ·mări). *Obs.* exc. *arch.* ME. [a. OF. **gramarye*; see GRAMMAR.] †1. Grammar; learning -1483. 2. Occult learning, magic, necromancy. (Revived by Scott.) 1470.

Gramash (grămæ·ʃ). 1681. [Sc. var. of GAMASH.] = GAMASH.

Grame (grēⁱm), *sb. Obs.* exc. *arch.* [OE. *grama*, related to *gram* GRAME *a.*] †1. Anger, wrath, ire -1621. 2. Grief, sorrow; harm. In *pl.* Troubles. OE. So †**Grame** *a.* angry; vexed; furious; of heat, fierce. †**Grame** *v.* to be vexed or displeased; also *trans.* to vex.

Gramercy (grămɔ̄·ɹsi), *interj. phr. Obs.* exc. *arch.* ME. [a. OF. *grant merci*; *grant* great + *merci*; see MERCY. Primarily = 'God reward you greatly'.] 1. = Thanks; thank you. †b. with *dat.* or *to*: = Thanks *to*; by the instrumentality of -1734. 2. ? As an exclam. of surprise, etc. = 'mercy on us!' 1607. †3. quasi-*sb.* The salutation 'thanks' or 'thank you' -1670.

1. G. for thy caution SCOTT. b. Gremercy God, and that good Man 1450. 2. G.! they for joy did grin COLERIDGE. 3. *Worth g.*, worth a 'thank you', of some value. What g. (= what special merit) to be sober, just, or continent MILTON.

Gramineous (grēⁱmi·nīəs), *a.* 1658. [ad. L. *gramineus* (f. *gramin-*, *gramen*) + -OUS.] Of, pertaining to, or resembling grass; grassy; *spec.* belonging to the N.O. *Gramineæ*. So **Gramina·ceous**, **Grami·neal** *adjs.* (in same sense). var. **Gra·minous.** ? *Obs.*

Graminiferous (græmini·fĕrəs), *a.* 1834. [f. L. *gramin-*, *gramen* + -*fer* bearing + -OUS.] Producing grass.

Graminivorous (grămini·vŏrəs), *a.* 1739. [f. as prec. + -(*i*)*vorus* devouring + -OUS.] Eating or feeding on grass.

Grammalogue (græ·mălǫg). 1845. [f. Gr. γράμμα + λόγος word.] *Shorthand.* A letter-word; a word represented by a single sign; also, a letter or character representing a word (more correctly LOGOGRAM).

Grammar (græ·məɹ), *sb.* [ME. *gram*(*m*)*ere*, ad. OF. *gramaire* (mod. *grammaire*), an irregular semi-pop. adoption of L. *grammatica*, ad. Gr. γραμματική (sc. τέχνη), f. (ult.) root of γράφειν to write.] 1. That department of the study of a language which deals with its inflexional forms or their equivalents, and with the rules for employing these correctly; usually treating also of the phonetic system of the language and its representation in writing. (Till the 16th c. *grammar* in Eng. use meant mainly Latin grammar.) 2. A treatise or book on grammar 1530. 3. An individual's manner of using grammatical forms; speech or writing as it conforms to or violates grammatical rules; also speech or writing that is correct according to these rules 1586. 4. The system of inflexions and syntactical usages characteristic of a language 1846. †5. Used for LATIN, or the Latin language. *By g.*: in Latin. (Cf. GRAMMAR-SCHOOL.) -1576. 6. *transf.* a. The fundamental principles or rules of an art or science. b. A book presenting these methodically (now *rare*). 1642.

1. Concerning speech and words, the consideration of them hath produced the science of G. BACON. *Historical G.*: the study of the historical development of the inflexional forms and syntactical usages of a language. *Comparative G.*: the comparative treatment of the phenomena of two or more related languages, with reference to the nature and degree of their relationship. *General*, *Philosophical* or *Universal G.*: the science concerned with the general principles which underlie the grammatical phenomena of all languages. 2. I read it in the Grammer long ago SHAKS. 3. He had German enough to scold his servants..but his g. and pronunciation were very bad MACAULAY. 6. a. Manly sports are the Grammer of Military performance FULLER.

Grammar (græ·məɹ), *v. rare.* 1593. [f. the sb.] †a. *intr.* To discuss grammar. BEAUM. & FL. b. To ground *in* something, as in the rudiments of grammar. BUNYAN. c. To classify, as the parts of speech in grammar 1883.

Grammarian (grămēᵊ·riăn). [ME. *gramarien*, a. OF., f. *gramaire* GRAMMAR; see -IAN.] 1. One versed in the knowledge of grammar, or of language; a philologist; a writer upon, or teacher of grammar. †2. A grammar-school boy -1607.

1. I have seene a G. toure, and plume himselfe over a single line in Horace SIR T. BROWNE. Hence **Gramma·rianism**, the principles or practice of a g.

Grammarless (græ·məɹlės), *a.* 1823. [See -LESS.] Having no grammar; said of a language, also of persons, speech, etc.

Gra·mmar-school. ME. A school for teaching grammar. 1. In England a class of schools founded in the 16th c. or earlier for the teaching of Latin grammar. They are now secondary schools of various degrees of importance. Also *attrib.* 2. *U.S.* In the system of graded common schools in the United States, the grade or department in which English grammar is taught 1860.

1. Thou hast most traiterously corrupted the youth of the Realme, in erecting a Grammar Schoole SHAKS.

†**Grammates**, *sb. pl.* [? ad. Gr. γράμματα.] Rudiments. FORD.

Grammatic (grămæ·tik), *a.* 1599. [ad. L. *grammaticus*; see -IC.] = GRAMMATICAL *a.* 1.

Grammatical (grămæ·tikăl), *a.* 1526. [f. as prec. + -IC.] 1. Of or pertaining to grammar 1530. 2. Conforming to the rules of grammar 1752. 3. *transf.* of the grammar of an art 1846. †4. *absol.* as *sb. pl.* The subjects taught in a grammar-school -1716.

1. *Grammatical gender*: gender which is not determined by the real or attributed sex; opp. to *natural gender*. *G. sense*: the sense obtained by the simple application of the rules of grammar to a text. So *g. meaning*, *interpretation*, †*translation*. 3. The ..g. accuracy of the tones of Turner RUSKIN. *G. accent* (Mus.): the accent regularly occurring at the beats of a bar; opp. to *oratorical accent*. Hence **Gramma·tically** *adv.*

Grammaticaster (græmæ·tikæstəɹ). 1601. [med.L.; see GRAMMATIC and -ASTER.] A petty grammarian. (Contemptuous.)

†**Grammatication.** 1582. [f. GRAMMATIC + -ATION.] A discussion of points in grammar -1680.

Gramma·ticism. Now *rare.* 1610. [f. as prec. + -ISM.] A point or principle of grammar; a grammatical definition.

Grammaticize (grămæ·tisəiz), *v.* 1673. [f. as prec. + -IZE.] 1. *trans.* To render grammatical 1780. 2. *intr.* To discuss grammatical points. BP. WARD.

Grammatist (græ·mătist). 1589. [ad. F. *grammatiste*, ad. med.L. *grammatista*, ad. Gr. γραμματιστής, f. γράμμα.] a. A grammarian. (Usu. disparaging.) b. A teacher of letters 1849. Hence **Grammati·stical** *a.* befitting a g.

Grammatolatry (græmătǫ·lătri). 1847. [f. Gr. γραμματο- comb. form + λατρεία; see -LATRY.] The worship of letters; adherence to the letter (of Scripture).

Gramme, gram[2] (græm). 1797. [a. F. *gramme*, ad. late L. *gramma*, Gr. γράμμα a small weight.] In the Metric system, the unit of weight; the weight of a cubic centimetre of distilled water at the maximum density, weighed *in vacuo*; = 15.432 Troy grains. Also *attrib.*

Comb.: **g.-centimetre**, a unit equivalent to the work done in raising one gramme vertically one centimetre; **-degree**, the quantity of heat required to raise a gramme of water 1° (Centigrade); **-equivalent** (*Electrolysis*), that quantity of the metal which will replace one gramme of hydrogen.

Gramophone (græ·mŏfōun). Also **grammophone.** 1888. [app. formed by inversion of PHONOGRAM. The sp. *grammo-* is an attempt to correct the formation.] An instrument for recording and reproducing vocal, instrumental, and other sounds; *esp.* a reproducing instrument consisting essentially of a revolving turn-table capable of carrying disks on which are impressed, in a spiral track, wave-forms corresp. to sound vibrations, to reproduce which a stylus, attached to an acoustic device or electric system, travels along the track.

Grampus (græ·mpŭs). 1529. [Early 16th c. *graundepose*, app. an etymologizing alteration (after GRAND *a.*) of GRAPEYS.] One of various kinds of blowing, spouting, blunt-headed delphinoid cetaceans. b. *transf.* A person who breathes loud 1836.

1. Coughing like a g. DICKENS. b. The blustering old g. of a governor 1851.

Granada, -ade, obs. ff. GRENADO, -ADE.

Granadilla, grenadilla (grænă-, grenădi·lă). 1613. [a. Sp., dim. of *granada* pomegranate.] A name of tropical species of the Passion-flower; esp. of *Passiflora quadrangularis* or its fruit, which is esteemed as a dessert fruit. Also *attrib.*

†**Grana·do.** 1582. [app. a corrupt var. of *Granada*; cf. -ADO.] Only in *G. silk*, *silk of G.* -1618.

†**Gra·nage.** In mod. Dicts. **grainage.** 1582. [AF., f. F. *grain*; see GRAIN *sb.*[1] and -AGE.] A duty in London on salt imported by an alien -1820.

Granary (græ·nări). 1570. [ad. L. *granarium*, f. *granum*.] A storehouse for grain after it is threshed. b. *transf.* and *fig.* 1570. Also *attrib.*

b. Sicily..when 'twas styled the G. of Great Rome 1632.

†**Gra·nat.** [a. Du. *granaat*.] = GRENADE. B. JONS.

†**Gra·nate**, *sb.*[1] ME. [ad. med.L. *granatum*.] = GARNET[1].

†**Gra·nate**, *sb.*[2] 1568. [a. L. (*pomum*) *granatum*; see POMEGRANATE. Cf. GRENADE[1].] 1. The pomegranate -1698. 2. Short for 'granate-colour' -1805.

Granatite (*Min.*), var. of GRENATITE.

Grand (grænd). ME. [a. OF. *grand*:—L. *grandem* great.]

A. *adj.* †1. *The Grand*: = 'the Great' -1529. 2. In titles: Chief, highest in rank or office. Now chiefly *Hist.* or with reference to foreign countries. 1609. 3. [Orig. transf. of 2; cf. ARCH- *pref.* 2.] Pre-eminent, chief; most properly so called. ? *Obs.* 1584. 4. *Law.* Great; principal, chief; opp. to *petty* or *common* 1562. 5. Of things, events, etc.: Specially great or important; chief, main 1597. b. With *a*, or with sb. in pl.: Of first-rate magnitude, scale, or importance 1611. 6. Used to designate a comprehensive unity in relation to its constituent portions. Now only in *grand total.* 1576. 7. Main, principal 1601. 8. = GREAT in various senses 1660. 9. Characterized by great solemnity, splendour, or display; conducted with great form and on a great scale 1735. b. Of persons, their belongings, etc.: Fine, splendid, gorgeously arrayed. Also more widely: Giving evidence of wealth or high social position. 1766. 10. a. Of natural objects, architecture, etc.: Imposing by reason of beauty coupled with magnitude 1712. b. Of ideas, style, design, etc.: Lofty and dignified in conception, treatment, or expression 1755. c. Of persons: Imposing morally or intellectually; also, stately, noble, dignified 1832. d. In recent use, coupled with sbs. qualified by *old* 1833. 11. As a general term of admiration (*colloq.*) 1816.

2. *G. Almoner, Falconer* (see the sbs.). *G. Pensionary, Pensioner*, the prime minister or president of the Council of Holland, when a republic. *G. Vizier*, the chief minister of the Turkish empire. *G. Turk*, the Sultan of Turkey. 3. Sin and Death, the two g. foes MILT. 4. *G. assize, compounder, distress, larceny*, etc. (see the sbs.). *Grand* (or *Gaudy*) *days*: Ascension day, St. John Baptist's day, All Saints' day, and Candlemas, four days, one in every term, which are observed as holidays in the Inns of Court and Chancery. 'And these are no days in Court.' 5. The g. rebellion SWIFT. The g. article of my expense is food WESLEY. b. A g. imposture 1842. 7. The g. entrance 1855, staircase 1860. 8. A g. sonata or a g. concerto meant one in complete classical form 1879. *G. Opera*, a French term, denoting a lyric drama in which spoken dialogue is excluded 1879. 9. G. wedding festivities 1893. G. company 1860. A very g. lady on state occasions THACKERAY. 10. b. *G. style*: a style fitted to the expression of lofty ideas and great subjects in literature and art. In what used to be called the g. style, at once noble and natural LOWELL. d. Since, 'gainst the classes, He heard, of late, the Grand Old Man (= W. E. Gladstone) Incite the masses M. ARNOLD.

Comb.: **g. action**, the action of a g. pianoforte; **g. committee** (*Parliament*), (*a*) *Hist.* each of the four committees (for religion, for grievances, for courts of justice, and for trade) annually appointed by the House of Commons until 1832; †also, in 17th c., 'committee of the whole house'; (*b*) now, applied to the two 'standing committees' (each of 60 to 80 members) since 1882 appointed every session to consider bills relating to matters of Law and Trade; **G. Fleet**, the main part of the British fleet in the war of 1914–18; **g. lodge** (see LODGE); **g. pianoforte, piano**, a large pianoforte, usually harp-shaped and horizontal, whose size admits of the most effective arrangement of the mechanism (see also UPRIGHT *a.*); **g. stand**, the principal stand for spectators at a race-course, etc.; also *fig.* and *attrib.* (U.S.).

b. used (after F.) to denote the second degree removed in ascent or descent of relationship, as GRANDFATHER, GRANDSON, etc.

B. quasi-*sb.* and *sb.* 1. quasi-*sb. The grand*: that which is grand 1742. †2. *sb.* = GRANDEE –1669. 3. a. Among Freemasons, any officer whose title contains the adj. b. In some clubs, the title of the chairman. Also *Noble Grand, Vice Grand*, the chairman and vice-chairman of a lodge of Odd Fellows. 1747. 4. A grand pianoforte 1840. 5. *Sugar Manuf.* The largest evaporating pan of a battery 1839. 6. *U.S.* A thousand dollars 1930.

Grand air. 1775. [prop. Fr., but pronounced as Eng.] An air of distinction; also (in bad sense) an affected loftiness of manner.

Grandam, grandame (græ·ndăm, -dēⁱm). ME. [a. AF. *graund dame*; see GRAND *a.* and DAME.] 1. = GRANDMOTHER 1, 2. 2. An old woman; a gossip 1550. 3. *fig.* 1602. 4. *attrib.* (quasi-*adj.*) 1598.

Gra·nd-aunt. 18.. [See GRAND *a.*] One's father's or mother's aunt; a great-aunt.

Grandchild (græ·nd-, græ·nˌtʃəild). 1587. [See GRAND *a.*] The child of one's son or daughter. Also *fig.*

Grand-dad, grandad (græ·ndˌdæd, græ·ndæd). 1819. [See GRAND *a.*] Childish or affectionate for GRANDFATHER.

Gra·nd-daughter. 1611. [See GRAND *a.*] The daughter of one's son or daughter.

Grand duchess. 1757. a. The wife or widow of a Grand Duke. b. A lady holding in her own right the sovereignty of a duchy. c. A daughter of the Czar of Russia. So **Grand duchy**, the territory ruled by a Grand Duke or Duchess.

Grand duke. 1693. [a. F. *grand-duc*; see DUKE.] 1. a. The title of the sovereigns of Grand Duchies, who rank one degree below kings. b. In Russia, any son of an emperor. 2. The Great Eagle Owl (*Bubo ignavus*) 1855. Hence **Grand-du·cal** *a.* of or belonging to a Grand Duke. **Grand-du·kedom.**

Grandee (grændī·). 1598. [a. Sp., Pg. *grande* great (person), see GRAND *a.*] A Sp. or Pg. nobleman of the highest rank. Also *transf.* and *gen.* Hence **Grandee·ship**, the position or dignity of a g.

Grandeur (græ·ndiŭ). 1500. [a. F., f. *grand* great; see GRAND *a.*] †1. a. Height; tall stature. b. Greatness (in amount or degree). –1658. 2. Greatness of power or rank. Now somewhat *rare.* 1616. 3. Transcendent greatness or nobility of intrinsic character 1669. 4. The quality of being GRAND; sublimity, majesty. Also an instance of this. 1662. 5. Conscious greatness, lofty dignity. †Also, arrogance. 1644. 6. Magnificence of appearance, style of living, trappings, etc. Also *pl.* 1652.

4. The Majesty and Grandure of Tragedy BENTLEY. 5. The English go to their estates for g. The French live at court, and exile themselves to their estates for economy EMERSON.

Grandeval (grændī·văl), *a. rare.* 1650. [f. L. *grandævus* + -AL.] Of a great age, old, ancient.

†**Grande·vity.** 1623. [ad. L. *grandævitas*; see next and -ITY.] Great or old age –1688.

†**Grande·vous,** *a.* [f. L. *grandævus*, f. *grandis* great + *ævum* age; see -OUS.] Aged, old. H. MORE.

†‖**Grande·zza, grande·za.** 1642. [It. *grandezza*, Sp. *grandeza*:—pop. L. type *granditia*, f. *grandis*; see GRAND *a.*] Grandeur, greatness, magnificence; also, an instance of this –1675.

Grandfather (græ·nd-, græ·nfāðəɹ). ME. [f. GRAND *a.* + FATHER; after F. *grand-père.*] 1. The father of one's father or mother. Also *fig.* 2. A male ancestor 1613.

1. Who begot thee? Marry, the son of my G. SHAKS. 2. Our g. Adam HIERON. *Comb.*: **g.-long-legs** = DADDY-LONG-LEGS; **grandfather's clock** [suggested by a popular song about 1880], the weight-and-pendulum eight-day clock in a tall case formerly in common use. Hence **Gra·ndfatherly** *a.* of, befitting, or resembling a g.

Gra·ndfather, *v. rare.* 1748. [f. the sb.] *To g.* (a thing) *on*: *fig.* [after FATHER *v.*] to impute to (a person) as its mediate originator.

Grand Guignol (grañ ginʸol). 1920. [Fr.] A dramatic entertainment consisting of a succession of short sensational pieces.

Grandiloquent (grændi·lŏkwĕnt), *a.* 1593. [f. L. *grandiloquus*, f. *grandis* + *-loquus*, f. *loqui* to speak; after *eloquent*, etc.] Characterized by swelling or pompous expression. Hence **Grandi·loquence**, the quality of being g. **Grandi·loquently** *adv.* So **Grandi·loquous** *a.*

Grandiose (græ·ndiōus), *a.* 1840. [a. F. *grandiose*, ad. It. *grandioso*, f. L. *grandis*; see -OSE, -OUS.] 1. Producing an effect of grandeur; characterized by largeness of plan or nobility of design 1843. 2. Of speech, style, etc.: Characterized by formal stateliness; in bad sense, pompous.

1. Things painted by a Rubens..all more g. than the life BROWNING. 2. With a strut more than usually g. 1847. Hence **Gra·ndiosely** *adv.* **Grandio·sity,** g. quality.

Grandisonant (grændi·sŏnănt), *a. rare.* 1684. [f. L. *grandis* + *sonantem.*] Stately-sounding. So **Grandi·sonous** *a.*

Grandisonian (grændi·sōuniăn), *a.* 1829. [f. *Grandison* (see below) + -IAN.] Of deportment, manner, etc.: Of or resembling that of Sir Charles Grandison in Richardson's novel of that name.

†**Gra·ndity.** 1589. [ad. L. *granditas*; see GRAND and -ITY.] Grandeur, stateliness. Also, a mark of greatness. –1839.

Grandly (græ·ndli), *adv.* 1654. [f. GRAND *a.* + -LY [2].] In a grand manner; magnificently, grandiosely, etc.

A mind that is g. simple EMERSON.

Grandmamma (græ·nd-, græ·nmămā). 1763. [See GRAND *a.*] = GRANDMOTHER. *colloq.*

Grand master. 1549. †1. The chief officer of a royal household –1748. 2. The head of one of the military orders of knighthood, *e.g.* the Hospitallers, Templars, etc. 1553. b. The head of the order of Freemasons, or of the Odd Fellows, etc. 1724. Hence **Grandma·stership.**

Grandmaternal (grændmătə·ɹnăl), *a.* 1790. [f. GRAND *a.* + MATERNAL *a.*] = GRANDMOTHERLY. Somewhat *joc.*

Grandmother (græ·nd-, græ·nmɒðəɹ). ME. [See GRAND *a.*] 1. The mother of one's father or mother. Also *fig.* 2. A female ancestor 1526. 3. *attrib.* 1649. Also as vb.

Grandmotherly (græ·nd-, græ·nmɒðəli), *a.* 1842. [f. prec. + -LY [1].] Pertaining to or befitting a grandmother. Now often *fig.* of government, legislation, etc.

Grand-nephew. 1639. [See GRAND *a.*] The son of a nephew or niece.

Grandness (græ·ndnės). 1722. [See -NESS.] The state or quality of being grand. Also, a grand action (BROWNING).

Grand-niece. 1830. [See GRAND *a.*] The daughter of a nephew or niece.

Grandpapa (græ·nd-, græ·npăpā). 1753. [See GRAND *a.*] = GRANDFATHER. *colloq.* Also **Grandpa.**

Grandparent (græ·ndpēərĕnt). 1830. [See GRAND *a.*] The parent of a parent. So **Grandparentage.**

Grandpaternal (græ·ndpătə·ɹnăl), *a.* 1844. [f. GRAND *a.* + PATERNAL *a.*] = GRANDFATHERLY. Somewhat *joc.*

Grand signior. 1592. [ad. It. *gran signore* 'great lord'.] 1. *The Grand Signior*: the Sultan of Turkey. †2. A great noble. HOLLAND.

Grandsire (græ·nd-, græ·nsəiəɹ). ME. [a. AF. *graunt sire*; see GRAND *a.* and SIRE.] 1. = GRANDFATHER 1 (*arch.* and *dial.*). Also *transf.* of a horse, etc. 1881. 2. A forefather (*arch.*) ME. 3. An old man (*arch.*) 1596. 4. *attrib.* 1592. 5. *Bell-ringing.* A particular method of ringing the changes on a peal of bells 1671.

1. By Woden wild, (my grandsire's oath) SCOTT. 2. Our Grand-sire Adam 1599. 3. *Tam. Shr.* IV. v. 50. 4. I am prouerb'd with a Grandsier Phrase SHAKS.

Grandson (græ·nd-, græ·nsɒn). 1586. [See GRAND *a.*] A son's or daughter's son. Also *transf.* of a horse.

Grand tour. 1748. [Orig. Fr. = 'great circuit'.] A tour of the principal cities and places of Europe, formerly supposed to be necessary to complete the education of young men of position.

Gra·nd-uncle. 1475. [See GRAND *a.*] One's father's or mother's uncle.

Grane, north. f. GROAN.

Grange (grēⁱndʒ), *sb.* ME. [a. AF. *graunge* (mod. *grange*):—med.L. *granea, granica*, f. *granum.*] 1. A repository for grain; a granary. 2. An establishment where farming is carried on. Now, A country house with farm buildings attached, usually the residence of a gentleman-farmer. ME. b. *esp.* An outlying farm-house with barns, etc. belonging to a monastery or a feudal lord, for storing tithes in kind, etc. ME. †3. A country house –1633. 4. *U.S.* A lodge of the order of 'Patrons of Husbandry'; an association for promoting the interests of agriculture 1875.

2. The thousand waves of wheat, That ripple round the lonely g. TENNYSON. b. A g. of the monks of Abingdon GREEN.

Granger (grēⁱ·ndʒəɹ). ME. [a. AF. *graunger* (F. *grangier*), f. *grange* GRANGE *sb.*] 1. A farm-bailiff. 2. *U.S.* a. A member of a grange (see GRANGE 4) 1875. b. A farmer 1887.

c. *pl.* Short for *granger shares* 1885. **3.** *attrib.* (sense 2), as **g. road** (*U.S.*), one of the railways which convey grain from the Western States; **g. shares,** shares in the g. roads 1892.

Grangerize (grēⁱ·ndʒərəiz), *v.* 1882. [f. James *Granger* who in 1769 published a 'Biographical History of England', with blank leaves for engraved portraits, etc.] To illustrate (a book) by the addition of prints, engravings, etc., usually cut out of other books. Hence **Gra·ngerism,** the practice of grangerizing. **Gra·ngerite,** one who grangerizes.

Graniferous (grăni·fĕrəs), *a.* 1656. [f. L. *granifer* (f. *grani-*, *granum* + *-fer* bearing) + -OUS.] Bearing grain or seed like grain.

Graniform (græ·nifǭɹm), *a.* 1778. [f. L. *granum* + -(I)FORM.] Formed like grains of corn; *spec.* in *Anat.* and *Bot.*

‖**Granilla** (grăni·lă). 1812. [Sp., dim. of *grana*; see GRAIN *sb.*[1]] The refuse of cochineal, consisting of the dried bodies of small or half-grown cochineal-insects.

Granite (græ·nit). 1646. [ad. It. *granito* (orig. a ppl. adj. = 'grained'), f. *grano.*] **1.** A granular crystalline rock, consisting essentially of quartz, orthoclase-feldspar, and mica, and usually light grey, white, or light red in colour. **2.** *attrib.* Consisting or made of granite 1703.

1. The tremendous granites of the Grimsel RUSKIN. 2. *The g. City*, Aberdeen. *The g. State*, New Hampshire, U.S. *Comb.*: **g.-quartzy** *a.*, intermediate between g. and quartz; **g. ware,** (*a*) pottery with a colouring imitating that of g.; (*b*) a kind of enamelled ironware. Hence **Grani·tic, -al** *a.* pertaining to, or of the nature of g.; composed of, or containing g.; (of water) obtained from g. soils; also *fig.* **Grani·ticoline** *a.* growing upon g., as a lichen. **Grani·tiferous** *a.* g.-bearing. **Grani·tiform** *a.* resembling g. **Gra·nitoid** *a.* resembling, or having the structure of g.; *sb.* [sc. *rock*].

Granivorous (grani·vŏrəs), *a.* 1646. [f. mod.L. *granivorus* (f. L. *grani-* comb. form + *vorare*) + -OUS.] That feeds on grain.

Grannam (græ·nəm). 1597. Colloq. pronunc. of GRANDAM.

Granny, grannie (græ·ni). 1663. [See -IE, -Y[4] and prec.] A grandmother; also, an old woman, a gossip.

Comb.: **granny's bend** (*Naut.*), a slippery hitch made by a lubber; **granny's knot** (*Naut.*), a reef-knot crossed the wrong way, which cannot be untied when it is jammed.

Granolithic (grænoli·þic), *a.* 1883. [f. L. *grano-* irreg. comb. form of L. *granum* + Gr. λίθος stone + -IC.] A kind of concrete. Hence, of buildings, etc.: Made of granolithic concrete.

Granose (grēⁱnōᵘ·s), *a. rare.* 1889. [ad. L. *granosus*; see -OSE.] *Entom.* Having the form of a string of grains, as the antennæ of many insects.

Grant (grɑnt), *sb.* ME. [f. the vb.] The action of granting; the thing granted. †**1. a.** Consent –1648. **b.** Promise –1575. **c.** Admission –1700. Also, what is agreed to, promised, etc. **2.** The action of according (a request, etc.) ME. **3.** An authoritative bestowal or conferring of a right, etc.; a gift or assignment of money, etc. out of a fund ME. **b.** The thing which is the subject of the grant 1815. **4.** *Law.* **a.** A conveyance by deed. †**b.** Formerly: A conveyance of such property (viz. incorporeal hereditaments) as can pass only by deed. 1596. **5.** Chiefly *U.S.* The name given to a portion of land in the occupation of specified persons. *The Hampshire Grants*: now the State of Vermont. 1719.

3. The g. of a patent 1824, of certain Customs duties 1874. b. I am an enemy of the present system of what are called *grants in aid* GLADSTONE. *Capitation-grant* (see CAPITATION). 4. b. A thing is said *to lie in graunte* which cannot be assigned with out deed COWELL.

Grant (grɑnt), *v.* Pa. t. and pple. **granted.** ME. [a. AF. *graunter*, *granter*, OF. *graanter*, *greanter*, altered f. *craanter*, *creanter* :—pop. L. type **credentare*, f. *credentem*, *credere.*] †**1.** *intr.* To agree, consent –1593. **2.** *trans.* To agree to, promise, undertake. *Obs.* exc. in legal documents. ME. **3.** To accede to, consent to fulfil ME. **4.** To allow as an indulgence; to bestow as a favour, or in answer to a request ME. †**b.** To permit (an action). CHAUCER. **5.** To bestow by a formal act. Also in *Law*, to transfer (property), esp. by deed. ME. †**6.** To give up –1613. **7.** To admit, confess, acknowledge. Now only of conceding a proposition to be used as a basis of argument. ME.

2. A. covenanted, granted, and agreed that [etc.] CRUISE. 3. Iesus g. him his praier ME. 4. To g. better conditions to a garrison 1711. 5. They granted charters to the towns and privileges to the inhabitants BUCKLE. 7. If thus much be granted..how is not our principle conceded KEBLE. I g. him brave, But wild SCOTT. Phr. *To take for granted*: to regard as not requiring proof, or as likely to be generally admitted. Hence **Gra·ntable** *a.* capable of being granted.

Grantee (grɑntī·). 1491. [f. prec. + -EE.] *Law.* The person to whom a grant or conveyance is made.

Grantor (grɑntǭ·ɹ). 1626. [a. AF. *grantor*; see -OR.] *Law.* One who makes a conveyance in legal form.

‖**Granula** (græ·niŭlă). *Pl.* **-læ**; also †**-laes.** 1658. [mod.L., irreg. dim. of *granum* = late L. *granulum.*] = GRANULE.

Granular (græ·niŭlăɹ), *a.* 1794. [f. late L. *granulum* (see prec.) + -AR.] **1.** Consisting of grains or granules. **2.** Having a granulated surface or structure 1833. **3.** Of the nature of a granule or granules 1834.

1. Dynamite is a solid g. explosive 1868. Hence **Gra·nularly** *adv.* So **Gra·nulary** *a.*

Granulate (græ·niŭlĕt), *a.* 1793. [f. as prec. + -ATE[2] 2.] = GRANULATED *ppl. a.* 2. ¶ Also in pseudo-L. comb. form *granulato-*.

Granulate (græ·niŭleⁱt), *v.* 1666. [f. as prec. + -ATE[3].] **1.** *trans.* To form into granules or grains; *intr.* for *refl.* to become granular. **2.** *trans.* To raise in granules or small asperities; to roughen the surface of 1691. **3.** *intr.* in *Path.* Of a wound, etc.: To develop small prominences, producing a roughened surface, as if sprinkled with granules 1737.

Granulated (græ·niŭleⁱtĕd), *ppl. a.* 1677. [f. GRANULATE *v.* + -ED[1].] **1.** Formed into, or consisting of, granules, or grain-like bodies 1694. **2.** Having the surface raised in granules or small prominences. **3.** *Path.* = GRANULAR *a.* 2. 1835.

2. *G. glass*, a kind of roughened glass used in stained windows.

Granulation (græniŭlēⁱ·ʃən). 1612. [f. as prec.; see -ATION.] **1.** *gen.* The act or process of forming into granules or grains; the being so formed; *concr.* a granular formation. **2.** *Path.* The formation of grain-like prominences on sores when healing 1786; *concr.* in *pl.* the grain-like bodies so formed 1739. **3.** *Bot.* and *Zool.* **a.** The formation of granular bodies on the surface of a plant, a crustacean, etc. **b.** *concr.* The granular structure, or (*pl.*) the granules, so formed. 1796. **4.** *attrib.*, as *g.-tissue*, etc. 1873.

2. b. Granulations formed, and a cicatrix took place ABERNETHY.

Granulator (græ·niŭleⁱtəɹ). 1839. [See -OR.] One who or that which granulates; *spec.* a granulating-machine.

Granule (græ·niŭl). 1652. [ad. late L. *granulum*, perh. through F.] A small grain; a small compact particle; a pellet. Also *attrib.*

G. is the best word to describe the luminous particles on the Sun's surface G. F. CHAMBERS.

Granuliferous (græniŭli·fĕrəs), *a.* 1840. [f. late L. *granulum* + -(*i*)*fer* + -OUS.] Bearing granules or granulations.

Granuliform (grĕniŭ·lifǭɹm), *a.* 1847. [f. as prec. + -(I)FORM.] Having a granular structure.

Granulite (græ·niŭləit). 1849. [f. GRANULE + -ITE.] *Geol.* A rock consisting of feldspar and quartz intimately mixed. Hence **Granuli·tic** *a.*

Granulo- (græ·niŭlo), comb. f. L. *granulum* GRANULE, with sense 'granular and —', as in *g.-adipose*, etc.

Granulose (græniŭlōᵘ·s). 1852. [f. as prec. + -OSE.]

A. *sb.* The main constituent (the other being cellulose) of the starch granule, which gives a blue colour with iodine, and is converted into sugar by the saliva 1875.

B. *adj.* = GRANULAR.

Granulous (græ·niŭləs), *a.* 1547. [f. GRANULE + -OUS.] = GRANULAR, in various senses.

Grape (grēⁱp), *sb.* ME. [a. OF. *grape*, *grappe* bunch of grapes (mod. *grappe*), prob. a vbl. sb. f. *graper* to gather grapes with a vine-hook, f. *grape* hook.] **1.** One of the berries, growing in clusters on a vine, from the juice of which wine is made. Chiefly *pl.* **b.** Put for wine 1636. †**2.** *transf.* The berry of other plants –1601. **3.** The plant that produces grapes; the vine; chiefly with some word prefixed, as *Frontignac*, *Muscatel*, etc. *g.* ME. **4.** *Mil.* = GRAPE-SHOT. Now only *collect. sing.* 1687. **5.** *Farriery. pl.* A diseased growth resembling a bunch of grapes on the pastern of a horse, mule, etc.; also on the pleura 1600. **6.** The knob or pommel at the rear end of a cannon; formerly called the CASCABEL 1864.

1. Do men gather grapes of thorns *Matt.* vii. 16. **b.** He had me taste of it; and 'twas—the Grape FITZGERALD. 3. *Seaside g.* = *g.-tree* (q. v.).

Comb.: **g.-berry-moth** (*U.S.*) = *grape-moth*; **-cure,** treatment by a diet of grapes; **-eater,** the Australian bird *Zosterops chloronotus*; **-fern,** a plant of the genus *Botrychium*, from the appearance of its fructification; †**-flower** = *grape-hyacinth*; **-fruit** (*U.S.*), the pomelo; **-fungus,** a mould (*Oidium Tuckeri*) on vines, vine-mildew; **g. hop,** a variety of hop, so called because the cones hang in clusters like bunches of grapes; **-hopper** (*U.S.*), an insect destructive to vine-leaves; **-hyacinth** (see HYACINTH); **-louse** (*U.S.*), the phylloxera; **-moth** (*U.S.*), *Eudemis botrana*, the larva of which devours grapes; **-pear,** *Amelanchier Botryapium*; **-sugar** = DEXTROSE or GLUCOSE; **-tree,** (*a*) in W. Indies, a tree of the genus *Coccoloba*; (*b*) a grape-vine; **-weevil** (*U.S.*), a weevil (*Cœliodes* or *Craponius inæqualis*) which destroys green grapes; **-worm** (*U.S.*), the larva of the g.-moth. Hence **Gra·peless** *a.* having no grapes; wanting the flavour of grapes. **Gra·pelet,** †**Gra·peling** a small g.; also *transf.*

Grapery (grēⁱ·pĕri). 1812. [f. GRAPE *sb.*] A building in which grapes are grown; a plantation of vines; a vinery.

Gra·pe-shot. 1747. [f. as prec.] Small cast-iron balls, strongly connected together, so as to form a charge for cannon.

Gra·pe-stone. 1589. [f. GRAPE *sb.* + STONE.] **1.** The seed of a grape. **2.** *Min.* Occas. used for BOTRYOLITE 1860.

Gra·pe-vine. Now chiefly *U.S.* and *Austral.* 1736. **1.** The vine which bears grapes; any species of the genus *Vitis*, esp. *V. vinifera.* **2. a.** A canard: current during the American Civil War, and short for 'a despatch by grape-vine telegraph' 1867. **b.** A figure in skating 1868.

Grapeys. ME. [a. OF. *grapois*, *graspeis* (also *craspois*) :—med.L. *crassum piscem* fat fish. Hence GRAMPUS.] The flesh of the grampus.

Graph (grɑf), *sb.* 1878. [Orig. short for 'graphic formula'; see GRAPHIC.] **1.** A symbolic diagram expressing a system of chemical or mathematical connexions. **2.** *Alg.* A graphical representation of the locus of a function; the traced curve of an equation 1886. **3.** A line or system of lines symbolizing variations of occurrence or intensity.

Graph (grɑf), *v.* 1898. [ad. Gr. γράφειν.] *Math.* To trace (a curve) from its equation; to trace the curve corresponding to (a given equation).

-graph (grɑf), repr. F. *-graphe*, L. *-graphus*, Gr. -γραφος. The Greek termination was chiefly used in the sense 'written', whence *autograph*, *holograph*, *photograph*, etc.; sometimes in the active sense 'that writes'. In many of the words in *-graph* this element expresses the meaning of 'instrument that marks, portrays, or records', as *heliograph*, *seismograph*; the earliest of these is *telegraph* (1794), from French.

-grapher (grăfəɹ), an ending first found early in the 16th c. The normal mode of anglicizing a real or assumed Gr. word in -γραφος denoting a personal agent, and of providing a personal designation correlative to sb. in -GRAPHY denoting an art or science.

Graphic (græ·fik), *a.* 1637. [ad. L. *graphicus*, Gr. γραφικός, f. γραφή drawing or writing.] †**1.** Drawn with a pencil or pen. B. JONS. **2.** Of or pertaining to drawing or painting 1756. **3.** Vividly descriptive, life-like 1669. **4.** Of or pertaining to writing 1774. **b.** Of a mineral: Presenting an appearance of written or printed characters 1814. **5.** Pertaining to the use of diagrams, linear figures, or symbolic curves 1866. **b.** Concerned with position and form; opp. to *metric*. CLIFFORD. **6.** quasi-*sb.* in **Graphics**: the use of diagrams as a means of calculation 1889.

2. *G. arts*: drawing, painting, engraving, etching, etc. G. representations LAMB. **4. b.** *G. granite*..a binary compound of felspar and quartz—the quartz being disposed through the felspar matrix like lines of Arabic writing PAGE. *G. gold, ore,* or *tellurium*: = SYLVANITE. **5.** *G. formula*: in *Chem.*, a formula in which lines are employed to indicate the connexions of the elements represented by the symbols. *G. method, solution*: a method of solving problems (e.g. in *Statics*) by the construction of a diagram from which the result is obtained by direct measurement instead of calculation. *G. method*: the method of recording movements of a part of the body by some automatic instrument, e.g. those of the pulse by the sphygmograph. Hence **Gra·phicness**, vividness of description.

-graphic (græ·fik), repr. Gr. -γραφικός, as in *historiographic*. In Eng. adjs. prob. formed on sbs. in *-graphy* (or *-graph*) + -IC. The prevailing sense is 'of or pertaining to ——graphy.'

Graphical (græ·fikăl), *a.* 1610. [f. GRAPHIC *a.* + -AL.] = GRAPHIC *a.* 1–5. Hence **Gra·phically** *adv.*, **-ness.**

Graphiology (græfiǫ·lŏdʒi). 1854. [irreg. f. Gr. γράφειν + -(O)LOGY.] = GRAPHOLOGY 2.

-graphist, sometimes used instead of -GRAPHER in anglicizing Gr. wds. in -γράφος or forming derivs. from sbs. in *-graphy*; as in *telegraphist*, etc.

Graphite (græ·fəit). 1796. [Ger. *graphit*, f. Gr. γράφειν + -ITE.] A crystalline allotropic form of carbon (see CARBON), called also BLACK LEAD and PLUMBAGO. Hence **Gra·phitoid, Graphitoi·dal** *adjs.* having the appearance of g.

Graphitic (grafi·tik), *a.* 1864. [f. prec. + -IC.] Of, pertaining to, or of the nature of graphite.

Graphitic acid, an acid produced from graphite by the repeated action of chlorate of potassium and nitric acid. *G. carbon*, that portion of the carbon in iron and steel which is present as graphite.

Graphitoid (græ·fitoid), *a.* 1858. (f. GRAPHITE + -OID.] Having the appearance of graphite. Also **Graphitoi·dal** *a.*

Grapholite (græ·fŏləit). 1796. [f. Gr. γραφο-, comb. f. γραφή + -LITE] Any species of slate suitable for writing on.

Graphology (grăfǫ·lŏdʒi). 1878. [f. as prec. + -λογία; see -LOGY.] **1.** The study of handwriting 1882. **2.** *esp.* The art or science of inferring character, disposition, and aptitudes from handwriting 1886. **3.** The system of graphic formulæ 1878. Hence **Graphólo·gic, -al** *a.* of or pertaining to g.

Graphometer (grăfǫ·mĭtəɹ). 1696. [ad. F. *graphomètre*, f. as prec. + μέτρον.] A semicircle, used for measuring angles in surveying. †Also, a goniometer used in crystallography.

Graphoscope (græ·fŏskōᵘp). 1879. [f. Gr. γραφο-, γραφή + -σκοπος; see -SCOPE.] An apparatus containing a magnifying lens arranged for viewing engravings, photographs, etc.

Graphotype (græ·fŏtəip), *sb.* 1866. [f. as prec. + TYPE.] A process for producing a design in relief for surface-printing; also, the block or plate so produced. Hence **Gra·photype** *v. trans.* to print by means of the g.

-graphy (grăfi) = F., G. *-graphie*, L. *-graphia*, repr. Gr. -γραφία in Gr. or quasi-Gr. sbs. Some of the sbs. with this ending denote processes or styles of writing, drawing, or graphic representation, as *stenography, lithography, photography*, etc. More commonly they are names of descriptive sciences, as *geography, bibliography*, etc.

Grapnel (græ·pnĕl), *sb.* ME. [a. AF. *grapenel, dim. of *grapon*, of the same meaning; cf. F. *grapin, grappin*.] **1.** An instrument with iron claws for throwing in order to seize and hold an object, esp. an enemy's ship. **2.** A small anchor with three or more flukes, used esp. for boats, and for securing a balloon on its descent ME. **3.** Any of various instruments for grasping or clutching 1875. Hence **Gra·pnel** *v.* to catch or seize with a g.

Grapple (græ·p'l), *sb.* 1530. [In I, prob. a. OF. **grapelle*, dim. of *grape* hook; in II, f. the vb.]

I. 1. = GRAPNEL 1. Also *transf.* and *fig.* †**2.** = GRAPNEL 2. –1807. **3.** = GRAPNEL 3. 1593.

1. The end of the lever, with an iron g. affixed to it, was lowered upon the Roman ships ARNOLD.

II. [f. the vb.] The action of grappling, or grappling *with*; the state of being grappled; the grip of a wrestler; a contest in which the combatants grip one another. Said also of immaterial contests. 1601.

In the G., I boorded them *Haml.* IV. vi. 18.

Comb.: **g.-plant**, a S. Afr. herb, *Uncaria procumbens*, the fruit of which has many projecting claw-like hooks; **-shot**, a projectile attached to a cable, with hinged flukes which catch in the rigging of a ship in distress.

Grapple (græ·p'l), *v.* 1530. [f. the sb.; infl. by GROPE, GRIP, GRASP.] **1.** *trans.* To seize or hold (a ship, etc.) with a grapnel; to fasten *to* something with grappling-irons. Also *fig.* **2.** *intr.* for *refl.* To fasten oneself firmly (*to* an object) by means of a grapple. Also *fig.* 1563. **3.** *trans.* To take hold of with the hands; to seize; to grip firmly; *hence*, to come to close quarters with 1583. **4.** *intr.* To take a firm hold, as with a grapple, esp. in wrestling; to get a tight grip; to contend in close fight. Also with *together*. 1583. **5.** To grope (*rare*). ? *Obs.* 1596.

1. *fig.* The friends thou hast, and their adoption tride, G. them to thy Soule, with hoopes of Steele *Haml.* I. iii. 62. **3.** Man grapples man COWPER. **4.** To tug or g., and to close MILT.

Phr. **To g. with —. a.** To make fast one's ship to (an enemy) with grappling-irons; to come to close quarters with. **b.** To grip as in wrestling; to close with bodily. **c.** To encounter hand to hand; also *fig.* **d.** *esp.* To try to overcome (a difficulty); to take in hand (a task, etc.).

†**Gra·pplement.** *rare.* [See -MENT.] A grappling. SPENSER.

Grappler (græ·pləɹ). 1628. [f. GRAPPLE *v.* + -ER [1].] One who or that which grapples; a grappling-iron, a grapnel; *slang*, a hand.

Grappling (græ·pliŋ), *vbl. sb.* 1598. [f. as prec. + -ING [1].] **1.** The action of GRAPPLE *v.* 1601. †**2.** A place where one may grapple a vessel –1784. **3.** *concr.* = GRAPPLE *sb.* I. 1, 2. 1598.

2. *To come, bring to a g.*: to come to anchor. **3.** The crooked Grappling's steely Hold they cast ROWE. *Comb.* **g.-hook, -iron** = GRAPNEL.

Grapsoid (græ·psoid), *a.* 1852. [f. mod.L. *grapsus* + -OID.] Of or pertaining to the genus *Grapsus* of crabs, or the family *Grapsidæ*.

Graptolite (græ·ptŏləit). 1838. [f. Gr. γραπτός painted or marked with letters + -LITE; in 1, ad. mod.L. *graptolithus* (Linn.).] †**1.** Any stone showing a resemblance to a drawing –1847. **2.** A fossil zoophyte of the genus *Graptolites* (or *Graptolithus*), or of the family of which this genus is the type 1841. Hence **Graptoli·tic** *a.* of, pertaining to, or containing graptolites.

Grapy (grēᵊ·pi), *a.* ME. [f. GRAPE *sb.* + -Y [1].] **1.** Of or pertaining to grapes or to the vine; composed or savouring of grapes 1594. †**2.** Epithet of the CHOROID coat of the eye. (Cf. UVEA.) –1696.

1. His soul quite sousèd lay in g. blood P. FLETCHER.

Grasp (grɑsp), *sb.* 1561. [f. the vb.] **1.** That which grasps or is grasped; the fluke of an anchor, a handle. Now only *Naut.* the handle of an oar. **2.** The action of grasping; the grip of the hand; †an embrace 1606. **3.** *fig.* **a.** Firm hold or control; mastery 1605. **b.** Intellectual hold; *esp.* mastery of the whole of a subject; hence, mental comprehensiveness 1683.

2. Beshrew the witch!..she..flies the grasps of loue SHAKS. Phr. *Within, beyond (one's) g.* **3. a.** To rescue liberty from the g. of executive power WEBSTER. **b.** Men of immense mental g. RUSKIN.

Grasp (grɑsp), *v.* [ME. *graspen*, metathesis of *grapsen*, perh. repr. OE. **græpsan*, f. (ult.) **graip*- GROPE *v.*] †**1.** *intr.* To make clutches with the hand; often = GROPE. *Obs.* exc. in *to grasp at*. †**b.** To grapple *with* –1766. **2.** To clutch at; to seize greedily 1642. **3.** To seize and hold firmly (*lit.* and *fig.*) 1586. †**4.** To clasp in the arms, embrace –1766. **5.** To grip 1774. **6.** To lay hold of with the mind; to become completely cognizant of or acquainted with; to comprehend 1680.

1. 2 *Hen. VI*, III. ii. 172. Like quicksilver [which] grasped at, slips away COWPER. To g. at a proposal W. IRVING. **2.** *Prov.* G. all, lose all. **3.** Thy Hand is made to graspe a Palmers staffe SHAKS. *To g. the nettle*: *fig.* to attack a difficulty boldly. To g. an argument JOWETT. **6.** To g. the eternal and unchangeable JOWETT. Hence **Gra·spable** *a.* that may be grasped. **Gra·sper**, one who or that which grasps; esp. a grasping person.

Grasping (grɑ·spiŋ), *ppl. a.* 1577. [-ING [2].] **1.** That grasps; tenacious. **2.** *fig.* Eager for gain, greedy, avaricious 1748.

2. The corrupt, g. and ambitious part of human nature MACAULAY. Hence **Gra·spingly** *adv.*, **-ness.**

Graspless (grɑ·splės), *a.* 1794. [See -LESS.] Without grip; relaxed.

In its g. hold her hand Felt that the sceptre shivered 1886.

Grass (grɑs), *sb.* [Com. Teut.: OE. *græs, gærs* :—OTeut. **grasom*, f. root **gra*-: *grō*-:—OAryan **ghrā*- to grow, whence L. *gramen*.] **1.** Herbage in general, the blades or leaves and stalks of which are eaten by horses, cattle, etc. Also, in a narrower sense = **2 b.** Now only *collect. sing.* **2.** A kind of grass. †**a.** A (medicinal) herb –1587. **b.** One of the non-cereal *Gramineæ*, or other similar plants. Often defined as *blue-, bunch-, dog-*, etc. *g.* (see those wds.). *Grass of the Andes*: an oat-grass, *Arrhenatherum avenaceum*. *G. of Parnassus*: a name for *Parnassia palustris*. 1548. **c.** Any species of plants grown for pasture 1677. **d.** *Bot.* Any plant belonging to the order *Gramineæ* (*Graminaceæ*), which includes grass (sense 1) together with the cereals (barley, oats, rye, wheat, etc.), the reeds, bamboos, etc. 1611. **3.** An individual plant of grass or †corn; a blade or spire of grass. Now only in *pl.*, and *rare*. ME. †**4.** The blade stage of growth; corn in the blade –1733. **5.** Pasture; the condition of an animal at pasture 1471. **b.** *fig.* of persons rusticated, or going away for a holiday, etc. 1589. **6.** Grazing OE. **7.** Pasture-land 1609. **8.** The yearly growth of grass; hence, spring and early summer, when the grass grows 1485. **9.** Grass-covered ground ME.; the earth's surface above a mine 1776; *slang*, the ground 1625. **10.** Short for *sparrow-grass*, corrupt f. ASPARAGUS. Now *vulgar*. 1747.

1. Her treading would not bend a blade of grasse B. JONS. *fig* All flesh is grasse *Isa.* xl. 6. Phr. *To cut the g. from under a person's feet*: to thwart, trip him up. *To let no g. grow under one's feet*: to make the most of one's time. **3.** Strange grasses were sometimes perceived in her hair DICKENS. **4.** *fig.* Our faith is yet in the grasse 1579. **5.** In Cheapside shall my Palfrey go to grasse SHAKS. *fig.* If to g. sent from Oxon or Granta 1801. **6.** Not as much as the g. of a goat 1880. **7.** Half the lands of a farm ..ought to be g. A. YOUNG. **8.** Six years old last G. 1685. **9.** About 70 tons [of quartz] are now at g. awaiting crushing 1890.

Comb.: **g.-bass**, a freshwater edible fish (*Pomoxys sparoides*) of the U.S.; **-beef**, the flesh of g.-fed oxen; **-bird**, (*a*) a name for *Tringa maculata*, and other American sandpipers; (*b*) in Australasia, one or more species of *Sphenœacus*; **-bleached** *ppl. a.*, bleached by exposure on g.; so *g.-bleaching* vbl. sb.; **-butter**, that made from the milk of cows at g.; **-chat** = WHINCHAT; **-comber**, a sailor's term for one who has been a farm-labourer; **-drake** = CORN-CRAKE; **-finch**, (*a*) a common American sparrow (*Poœcetes gramineus*); (*b*) any Australian finch of the genus *Poëphila*; **-flesh**, the flesh gained by an animal at g.; **-hand**, (*a*) a compositor temporarily engaged; (*b*) an irregular cursive hand used by the Chinese and Japanese in business and private writing; **-ill**, a disease of lambs; **-lamb**, (*a*) a lamb suckled by a dam which is running on pasture land; (*b*) the flesh of the same; **-lawn**, a fine gauze-like material, the colour of unbleached linen; **-moth**, one of many small moths of the genus *Crambus* or family *Crambidæ*, found in dry meadows; **-oil**, one of several fragrant essential oils, obtained in India by distillation from grasses (*Andropogon* and other genera); **-parakeet**, an Australian parakeet of the genus *Euphema* or *Melopsittacus*; †**-poly**, *Lythrum Hyssopifolia*; **-quit**, one of several finches of tropical America, esp. species of *Phonipara*; **-rope** (*Naut.*), a rope made of coir; **-snake**, (*a*) the common ringed snake (*Tropidonotus natrix*); (*b*) the common green snake of U.S.; **-snipe** *U.S.* = *grass-bird* (*a*); **-sparrow** = *grass-bird* (*a*); **-sponge**, an inferior kind of sponge from Florida and the Bahamas; **-table** (*Arch.*) = EARTH-TABLE; **-warbler** *Austral.*, a bird of the genus *Cisticola*; **-wrack**, a seaweed (*Zostera marina*), with g.-like leaves.

Grass (gras), *v.* 1460. [f. prec. sb.] †1. *trans.* To plunge or sink in grass –1670. 2. *trans.* †a. To GRAZE (cattle). b. To supply (cattle) with grass. 1500. 3. To cover, or (*intr.*) become covered, with grass or turf 1573. 4. To lay or stretch on the grass or on the ground (see quots.) 1765. 5. *intr. Printing.* To do casual or jobbing work 1894. 6. *Mining.* To bring to the surface 1890.

3. The graves being levelled and grassed over J. BROWN. 4. To g. flax for bleaching 1765. A blow.. which floored or grassed him 1814. To g. a fish 1856. 6. Stone grassed from the 50 foot shaft 1890.

†**Grassant,** *a.* 1659. [ad. L. *grassantem*, *grassari.*] Roaming about, or lying in wait, with evil intent –1734.

†**Grassation.** 1610. [ad. L. *grassationem*; see prec.] The action of making violent assaults; also, lying in wait to attack –1680. So †**Grassator,** a footpad, violent assailant.

Gra·ss-cloth. 1857. a. A fine light cloth, resembling linen, woven from the fibres of the inner bark of the grass-cloth plant (*Bœhmeria nivea*). b. A thick fabric made in the Canary Islands from vegetable fibre.

Grassed (grast), *ppl. a.* 1731. [f. Grass *sb.* and *v.* + -ED.] 1. Grown or covered with grass. 2. *Golf.* Of a driver, etc.: Having a slightly filed-back face 1878.

Grass-green, *a.* (Stress variable.) OE. 1. Of the colour of grass. Also *absol.* 2. Green with grass 1602.

2. At his head a grasse-greene Turfe *Haml.* IV. v. 31.

†**Grasshop.** [OE. *gærs-hoppe*, *-hoppa*, f. *gærs* GRASS *sb.* + *hoppa*, related to *hoppian* HOP *v.*[1]] A grasshopper, locust –1607.

Grasshopper (gra·shǫpəɹ). ME. [f. GRASS *sb.* + HOPPER[1].] 1. Any orthopterous insect of the families *Acridiidæ* and *Locustidæ*, remarkable for their powers of leaping, and the chirping sound produced by the males. 2. In a pianoforte: = HOPPER. 1807. 3. An artificial bait for fish 1867.

1. The grashopper shall be a burden *Eccl.* xii. 5. *Comb.*: **g.-beam,** a form of working-beam in steam-engines, pivoted at one end instead of in the centre (hence *g.-engine*, *-principle*); **-lark** = *grass-warbler*; **-sparrow,** a small U.S. sparrow of the genus *Coterniculus*, named from its note; **-warbler,** a small warbler, *Locustella nævia*, named from its note.

Grass land. 1689. Pasture or grazing land.

Gra·ssless, *a.* 1591. Without grass.

Gra·ss-plat, -plot. 1610. [f. GRASS *sb.*[1] + PLAT, PLOT. *Grass-plot* is the older form.] A piece of ground covered with turf, sometimes ornamented with flower-beds.

Here on this grasse-plot..To come and sport SHAKS.

Gra·ss-tree. 1802. A name of several Australasian trees. The liliaceous genus *Xanthorrhœa*; *Richea dracophylla* and *R. pandanifolia* of Tasmania; the *Pseudopanax crassifolium* of N. Zealand; the cabbage-tree of N. Zealand, *Cordyline australis*; the juncaceous plant *Kingia australis*.

Grass widow. 1528. [f. GRASS + WIDOW; cf. G. *strohwittwe* (lit. 'straw-widow').] 1. An unmarried woman who has cohabited with one or more men. ? *Obs.* 2. A married woman whose husband is absent from her 1859.

1. I have made more matches in my time than a grass widow GOLDSM. Hence **Grass-wi·dowhood.** So **Grass-widower,** a man living apart from his wife.

Grassy (gra·si), *a.* 1513. [f. GRASS *sb.* + -Y[1].] 1. Covered with or abounding in grass. 2. Pertaining to, consisting of, or containing grass 1697. 3. Resembling grass 1567.

1. The grassye ground with daintye Daysies dight SPENSER. 2. G. Fare DRYDEN. 3. Grassie colour 1567. Hence **Gra·ssiness** (*rare*).

Grate (grēⁱt), *sb.* ME. [app. a. med.L. *grata*, ad. It. *grata* grate, gridiron, hurdle, altered f. *grate* :—L. *cratem*, *cratis* hurdle.] 1. A framework of bars or laths, parallel to or crossing each other, fixed in a door, etc., to permit communication while preventing ingress. Now somewhat *rare.* 2. A similar framework for other purposes; *rarely*, †a gridiron ME. †3. The railing round a monument, building, etc. –1645. 4. A frame of metal bars for holding the fuel in a fireplace or furnace. Hence, the fireplace itself. 1605. 5. *Mining.* A screen used when stamping ores 1776. †6. A barred place of confinement, a prison or cage –1777. †7. One of the spaces between the bars of a grate (*rare*) –1649.

1. But in the same [doore] a little g. was pight, Through which he sent his voyce SPENSER. 4. An old-fashioned G. consumes Coals, but gives no Heat STEELE. 6. Else had you look'd through the g., like a Geminy of Baboones SHAKS. *Comb.* **g.-area, -surface,** the area in square feet covered by the fire-bars of a furnace or boiler.

†**Grate,** *a.* 1523. [ad. L. *gratus.*] 1. Pleasing, acceptable –1665. 2. Grateful –1596. Hence †**Gra·tely** *adv.*

Grate (grēⁱt), *v.*[1] ME. [a. OF. *grater* (mod. *gratter*); Com. Rom. ad. Teut. **krattōjan.*] †1. *trans.* To scrape, file, abrade; to rub harshly –1660. 2. To reduce to small particles by rasping or rubbing against a rough or indented surface. Often with *in, into, over.* ME. 3. *fig.* To fret, harass, irritate. Now *rare.* 1555. 4. *intr. To grate on* or *upon*: †a. To oppress with exactions or importunities –1705. b. To have an irritating effect *on* or *upon* 1635. †5. *trans.* To obtain by oppression or importunity –1542. †6. *trans.* To make (a weapon) strike or bite. *intr.* Of a weapon: To strike or bite. –1700. 7. *trans.* To rub harshly against (something) 1555. 8. *intr.* To rub *against* with a harsh, grinding noise; to sound harshly; to move creakingly 1596. b. *trans.* To produce by jarring movement. MILT. †9. *intr.* To dwell querulously *upon* a subject –1698.

1. *Tr. & Cr.* III. ii. 195. 2. To g. a Nutmeg 1732. 3. This outrageous merriment grated my spirits 1826. 4. a. *Merry W.* II. ii. 6. b. To choose What grates upon the sense GEO. ELIOT. 7. His galley now Grated the quay-stones KEATS. 8. Their lean and flashy songs G. on their scrannel pipes of wretched straw MILT. A key grated in the lock 1797. b. Th' infernal dores..on thir hinges g. Harsh Thunder MILT.

Grate (grēⁱt), *v.*[2] 1528. [f. GRATE *sb.*] †1. *trans.* To confine within grates or bars. MORE. 2. To fit or furnish with a grate or grating 1547.

2. The windows grated with iron MASSINGER.

Grateful (grēⁱ·tfŭl), *a.* 1552. [f. GRATE *a.* + -FUL (q.v.).] 1. Pleasing to the mind or the senses, agreeable, acceptable. Now only of things. 1553. 2. Of persons, their actions, etc.: Feeling gratitude; actuated by or manifesting gratitude; thankful 1552. b. Of land: Responsive to labour, fertile 1832.

1. The g. and cooling shade SCOTT. 2. I cannot giue thee lesse to be cal'd gratefull SHAKS. A g. Sacrifice WESLEY. **Gra·teful-ly** *adv.*, **-ness.**

Grater (grēⁱ·təɹ). ME. [a. OF. *grateor*, *gratour*, f. *grater* to GRATE *v.*[1]] 1. An instrument with a rough indented surface used for grating or rasping; *esp.* a kitchen utensil for grating ginger, nutmegs, etc. †2. One who or that which grates; chiefly *fig.* –1628.

2. He is no base G. of his Tythes, and will not wrangle for the odde Egge EARLE.

‖**Gratia Dei** (grēⁱ·ʃiă dīᵊi). ME. [L.; = 'grace of God'.] The Hedge Hyssop (*Gratiola officinalis*); formerly also the Lesser Centaury (*Erythræa Centaureum*) and *Geranium pratense.*

Graticulation (grătikiŭlēⁱ·ʃən). 1724. [ad. F., f. *graticuler*, f. *graticule* (see next).] The division of a design or plan into squares with the object of reproducing it accurately on a different scale; *concr.* a surface so divided.

Graticule (græ·tikiŭl). 1887. [a. F., ad. med.L. *graticula* for *craticula* gridiron, dim. of *cratis* hurdle.] A design or plan divided into squares to facilitate its reproduction on other scales; the style or pattern of such division.

Gratification (grætifikēⁱ·ʃən). 1576. [ad. L. *gratificationem*, f. *gratificari* to GRATIFY.] 1. The act of gratifying 1598. 2. The state or fact of being gratified or pleased; enjoyment, satisfaction 1712. b. with *a.* and *pl.* An instance of this; a thing that gratifies or pleases 1711. 3. A reward, recompense, gratuity; a bribe 1576.

1. The g. of his love of domineering MILL. 2. G. is of the mind when receiving wisdom and knowledge JOWETT. 3. Giveing the g. of twoe thousand poundes 1624.

Gratify (græ·tifəi), *v.* 1540. [ad. F. *gratifier*, or L. *gratificari*, f. *gratus*; see -FY.] †1. *trans.* To show gratitude to; to reward, requite –1655. 2. To make a present (usually of money) or give a gratuity to, esp. as a recompense, or as a bribe. Now *arch.* 1590. †3. To express pleasure at –1612. 4. To give pleasure to; to please, oblige; to do a favour to 1568. 5. To please by compliance; to humour, indulge 1665; †to comply with; to concede (an objection) –1855. †6. To render acceptable –1698.

1. It remaines..To gratifie his Noble seruice SHAKS. 2. The Messenger he richly gratifies 1613. 4. Pilate himself (to gratifie the Jews) delivered him to be crucified HOBBES. 5. Mankind have ungoverned passions which they will g. at any rate BUTLER. 6. *L. L. L.* IV. ii. 161. Hence **Gra·tifiedly** *adv.* with pleasure or satisfaction. **Gra·tifier. Gra·tifying** *ppl. a.*; affording pleasure. **Gra·tifyingly** *adv.*

Gratility (grăti·lĭti). Joc. perversion of *gratuity* in *Twel. N.* II. iii. 27.

‖**Gratin** (gratæ̃n). 1846. [F., f. *gratter*, earlier *grater* GRATE *v.*[1]] *Cookery.* A manner of preparing viands by treating them with raspings of bread and cooking them between two fires so as to produce a light crust; hence, the dish so cooked.

Grating (grēⁱ·tiŋ), *vbl. sb.*[1] ME. [f. GRATE *v.*[1] + -ING[1].] 1. The action of GRATE *v.*[1] 2. The discordant sound made by rubbing harshly against something 1611. 3. *fig.* Irritation, fretting. SOUTH.

Grating (grēⁱ·tiŋ), *vbl. sb.*[2] 1597. [f. GRATE *sb.* and *v.*[2] + -ING[1].] 1. The action of GRATE *v.*[2] (*rare*). 2. = GRATE *sb.* 1, 2 1739; *esp. Naut.* the open wood-work cover for the hatchway 1626. 3. *Optics.* An arrangement of parallel wires in a plane, or a surface of glass or polished metal ruled with a series of very close fine parallel lines, designed to produce spectra by diffraction 1877. *Comb.* **g. spectrum,** a diffraction spectrum produced by a g.

Grating (grēⁱ·tiŋ), *ppl. a.* 1563. [f. GRATE *v.*[1] + -ING[2].] 1. That grates, in senses of the vb. 2. That makes a grinding or creaking sound; hence, sounding harsh or discordant 1718. Hence **Gra·tingly** *adv.*

‖**Gratiola** (grĕtəi·ŏlă). 1579. [mod.L., f. *gratia* grace; so called from its supposed medicinal virtues.] *Bot.* A genus of scrophulariaceous plants, of which the best known species is *G. officinalis*, the Hedge Hyssop.

Gratiolin (grĕtəi·ŏlin). 1886. [f. prec. + -IN.] *Chem.* A bitter resinous principle obtained from *Gratiola officinalis.*

Gratis (grēⁱ·tis). 1477. [L. *gratis*, contr. f. *gratiis* lit. out of favour or kindness, abl. pl. of *gratia.*]

A. *adv.* 1. For nothing; without charge, cost, or pay; gratuitously. †2. Without a reason or due cause –1818.

B. *adj.* Given or done for nothing; free, gratuitous 1659.

No Chinke no Drink; Nothing is G. now 1659.

Gratitude (græ·titiŭd). 1500. [a. F., or ad. late L. *gratitudo*, *-inem*, f. *gratus.*] 1. The quality or condition of being grateful; a warm feeling of goodwill towards a benefactor; gratefulness. Also with *a.* and *pl.* 1565. †2. Grace, favour; a favour. Chiefly *Sc.* –1557. †3. A free gift; a gratuity, reward –1699.

1. Which g. Through flintic Tartars bosome would peepe forth, And answer thankes SHAKS.

Gratuitous (grătiū·itəs), *a.* 1656. [f. L. *gratuitus* (cogn. w. *gratia*, *gratus*) + -OUS.] 1. Freely bestowed or obtained; granted without claim or merit; costing nothing to the recipient; free. 2. Done, made, adopted, or assumed without any good ground or reason; uncalled-for; unjustifiable 1691. b. Of the agent: Acting without reason or justification 1864. †3. Requiring no proof. JOHNSON.

1. We..Mistake the G. Blessings of Heaven, for the Fruits of our Own Industry L'ESTRANGE. 2. A g. interference with private rights 1844, supposition LINGARD. b. A g. liar SALA. Hence **Gratu·itously** *adv.*, **-ness.**

Gratuity (grătiū·ĭti). 1523. [ad. F. *gratuité*, or med.L. *gratuitas*, f. *gratia*, *gratus.*] †1. Graciousness, favour; a favour, a kindness –1646. 2. A gift or present (usu. of money), often in return for favours or services, the amount depending on the inclination of the giver; in bad sense, a bribe. Now, a 'tip'. 1540. †b. Payment, wages –1832. 3. *spec.* A bounty, esp. that given to soldiers on re-enlistment, retirement, or discharge 1804. †4. = GRATITUDE 1. –1660. 5. Gratuitousness (*rare*) 1858.

1. I..had a small g. above my wages JOHNSON. b. A large hundred marks annuitie, To be given me in gratuitie For done service and to come B. JONS.

Gratulant (græ·tiŭlănt), *a.* 1471. [ad. L. *gratulantem, gratulari.*] Expressing joy or satisfaction; congratulatory.

†Gra·tulate, *a.* [ad. L. *gratulatus.*] To be rejoiced at. SHAKS.

There's more behinde that is more g. *Meas. for M.* v. i. 535.

Gratulate (græ·tiŭleit), *v.* Now *arch.* and *poet.* 1556. [f. L. *gratulat-, gratulari,* f. *gratus* pleasing, thankful.] 1. *trans.* To express joy at the appearance of; to welcome; to greet. 2. = CONGRATULATE 2. 1584. 3. = CONGRATULATE 4. Const. *on, upon,* †*in.* 1598. Also *absol.* †4. To be grateful or show gratitude for; to thank –1673. †5. To recompense (a service, etc.) –1633. †6. To gratify, please –1809.

1. To g. the sweet return of morn MILT. 2. I g. the newes B. JONS.

Gratulation (grætiŭlēⁱ·ʃən). 1482. [ad. L. *gratulationem*; see prec.] 1. A feeling of gratification, joy, or exultation. (Now only with mixture of sense 3.) 2. Manifestation, or a manifestation, of joy 1549. 3. The expression of pleasure at a person's success, good fortune, or the like; compliment, congratulation 1542; a complimentary or congratulatory speech 1614. †4. A welcome –1638. †5. Thanksgiving; also, an instance of this –1677. †6. = GRATIFICATION 3. –1628.

1. With great ioie of hart and godlie g. 1577. 3. After this Complement, and some g. for the Kings victorie BACON.

Gratulatory (græ·tiŭlĕtəri), *a.* (*sb.*) 1555. [f. L. *gratulari*; see -ORY.] 1. Expressing joy for the good fortune, etc. of another; congratulatory, complimentary. †2. Expressing gratitude or thanks –1739. †3. *sb.* A congratulatory speech. NORTH.

1. G. poems 1763, cries 1867. 2. No propiciatorie sacrifice but a gratulatorie sacrifice 1555. Hence **Gra·tulatorily** *adv.*

Graunt, obs. f. GRANT.

‖**Grauwacke** (grau·vakə). 1794. [Ger., f. *grau* GREY + *wacke* WACKE.] *Geol.* = GREYWACKE.

Gravamen (grăvēⁱ·men). *Pl.* **gravamina** (grăvēⁱ·mină). 1602. [a. late L. *gravamen,* f. *gravare* to load, f. *gravis.*] 1. A grievance 1647. 2. †a. A formal complaint or accusation –1880. b. *Eccl.* A memorial presented by the Lower House of Convocation to the Upper representing the existence of disorders or grievances in the church 1602. 3. The part of an accusation that bears most heavily on the person or thing accused 1832.

3. The g. of the charge against the principle of utility MILL. So **†Gravament** (in sense 1).

Grave (grēⁱv), *sb.*[1] [OE. *græf,* f. root of OE. *grafan* to dig, GRAVE *v.*[1]] 1. A place of burial; an excavation in the earth for the reception of a corpse; formerly, †a mausoleum or the like. b. A grave-mound 1868. 2. *occas.*, The condition or state of being buried, death ME. 3. *rhet.* Anything that is, or may become, the receptacle of what is dead 1559. 4. A pit or trench. *Obs.* exc. in sense of a trench for earthing up potatoes, etc. 1526.

1. Phr. *Secret as the g. Enough to make a person turn in his g.*: said hyperbolically of something which was abhorrent to the person in his lifetime. 2. Both Rich and Poor are equal'd in the g. QUARLES. The path of glory leads but to the g. GRAY. 3. His vast and wandering g. TENNYSON. *Comb.*: **g.-mound,** a hillock, or a barrow or tumulus, indicating the site of an interment; **-plant,** *Datura sanguinea*; **†-wax** = ADIPOCERE.

Grave (grēⁱv), *sb.*[2] *local.* ME. [a. ON. *greife,* of obscure origin; prob. = G. *graf* GRAVE *sb.*[3]] †a. A steward, a person placed in charge of property. b. In parts of Yorkshire and Lincolnshire, each of a number of administrative officials formerly elected by the inhabitants of a township.

†Grave, *sb.*[3] 1605. [ad. MDu. *grave* (mod. *graaf*) = GRAF. Now only as in *landgrave,* etc.] A foreign title = COUNT 1; chiefly used of the counts of Nassau –1718.

Grave (grēⁱv), *a.*[1] (*sb.*) 1541. [a. F. *grave,* ad. L. *gravem, gravis* heavy, important.]

A. *adj.* †1. Of persons: Having weight or importance; influential; authoritative –1749. 2. Of works, employments, etc.: Weighty, important; requiring serious thought 1592. b. Now *esp.* of faults, evils, difficulties, etc.: Highly serious. Of diseases or symptoms: Threatening a fatal result, serious. 1824. 3. Marked by dignity and weight; in later use, serious, not mirthful or jocular; opp. to *gay* 1549. 4. Of colour, dress, etc.: Dull, sombre, not gay or showy 1611. 5. Physically ponderous, heavy. *Obs.* or *arch.* 1570. 6. Of sounds: Low in pitch, deep in tone; opp. to *acute* 1609.

1. Most reuerend and graue Elders SHAKS. 2. When our council is assembled, we will treat of graver matters SCOTT. b. G. errors 1858, doubts 1866, news from the front (*mod.*). 3. With g. Aspect he rose, and in his rising seem'd A Pillar of State MILT. 6. *G. accent* (see ACCENT 1, 2). *G. harmonic* (see HARMONIC B. 2).

B. *sb.* A grave accent; †a grave note. 1609.

‖**Grave** (grāv, grā·ve), *a.*[2] 1683. [F. or It. *grave* = GRAVE *a.*[1]] *Mus.* A term indicating a slow and solemn movement.

Grave (grēⁱv), *v.*[1] [Com. Teut. str. vb.: OE. *grafan* to dig, to engrave, f. OTeut. root **grab-, grōb-* (whence GRAVE *sb.*[1], GROOVE *sb.*) :—pre-Teut. **ghrăbh-*. Not conn. w. Gr. γράφειν to write. The str. pa. t. *grove* is obs.; the str. pa. pple. *graven* is still usual.]

I. 1. *intr.* To dig. *Obs.* exc. *dial.* 2. *trans.* To dig, form by digging; to excavate. Also with *out, up.* Now *rare* exc. *dial.* OE.

2. And next the shryne a pit thaun doth she g. CHAUCER.

II. To deposit (a corpse) in the ground, in a tomb; to bury ME.; †to hide under ground (ME. only); †to swallow up in or as in a grave –1611.

Ditches graue you all *Timon* IV. iii. 116.

III. 1. To form by carving, to carve, sculpture (*lit.* and *fig.*); also *absol.* *Obs.* exc. *poet.* OE. †2. a. To cut into (a hard material). b. = ENGRAVE *v.*[2] –1677. 3. To engrave (letters, etc.) upon a surface, (a surface) *with* letters. Hence, to record by engraved or incised letters. *arch.* ME. b. *fig.* = ENGRAVE *v.* 3. ME. †4. = ENGRAVE *v.* 4. –1818.

1. Ymages..craftely grauen ME. 2. Hard was it youre herte for to graue CHAUCER. 3. There..graving our names in the trees CAPT. SMITH. b. His wrinkles and furrows were inscriptions that Time had graved HAWTHORNE.

Grave (grēⁱv), *v.*[2] 1461. [? f. F. *grave* = *grève* shore.] *trans.* To clean (a ship's bottom) by burning off the accretions, and paying it over with tar, while aground on a beach, or placed in a dock.

Grave-clothes, *sb. pl.* 1535. The clothes or wrappings in which a corpse is laid out for burial.

Grave-digger (grēⁱ·vˌdigəɹ). 1593. [f. GRAVE *sb.*[1]] 1. One who digs graves. 2. A name given to insects that bury the bodies of small animals and insects, for the use of their larvæ on quitting the egg; *esp.* a beetle of the genus *Necrophorus*; also, a digger-wasp, e.g. one of the genus *Sphex.*

‖**Gravedo** (grăvī·do). 1706. [L.; = heaviness (in the limbs or head).] A cold in the head; coryza.

Gravel (græ·vĕl), *sb.* ME. [a. or ad. OF. *gravele, gravelle* (in sense 4 mod.F. *gravelle*), dim. of OF. *grave* (mod. *grève*) coarse sand, also, sea-shore; of Celtic origin.] †1. Sand –1712. 2. Coarse sand and water-worn stones, often slightly intermixed with clay, much used for laying roads and paths ME. Also *fig.* b. *Geol.* and *Mining.* A stratum of this material, *esp.* one that contains gold 1849. 3. *U.S.* Ballast 1868. 4. *Path.* An aggregation of urinary crystals which can be recognized as masses (as dist. from *sand*); also, the disease of which these are characteristic. Also, pop., pain or difficulty in passing urine with or without any deposit. ME. 5. *Financial slang.* A term used when the supply of money in the market is growing bare 1884. 6. *attrib.* 1603.

1. *Quick g.*: quicksand. *Golden g.* (see GOLDEN). 2. Proofes as cleere as Founts in July, when Wee see each graine of grauell SHAKS. b. *Pay g.*: g. containing gold enough to yield a profit. *Comb.*: **g.-grass,** *Galium verum*; **-plant,** *Epigæa repens*; **-powder,** coarse gunpowder, pebble-powder; **-root,** *Eupatorium purpureum.*

Gravel (græ·vĕl), *v.* 1543. [f. prec. sb.] 1. *trans.* To cover (a path, etc.) with gravel or sand. †Also with *up.* †2. To bury in gravel or sand; to overwhelm with gravel; hence *fig.* to suppress, stifle –1686. †3. To run (a ship) aground on the gravel or beach, mud, etc. Also in *pass.*, of a person. Also *fig.* –1682. 4. *fig.* a. To set fast, non-plus, perplex 1548. b. Of a question, etc.: To confound, perplex, puzzle. Also *U.S.* To go against the grain with. 1601. 5. *Farriery.* in *pass.* and *intr.* Of a horse or its feet: To be injured by gravel lodged between the shoe and the hoof 1593.

3. When we were fallen into a place betwene two seas, they graveled the ship N.T. (Rhem.) *Acts* xxvii. 41. *fig.* I was gravell'd, like a ship that's grounded WITHER. 4. a. When you were grauel'd for lacke of matter SHAKS. b. It will perhaps g. even a philosopher to comprehend it BERKELEY.

Gravel-blind, *a.* 1596. Orig. *high-gravel-blind,* in *Merch. V.* II. ii. 38, an intensive synonym for SAND-BLIND. Hence, in later writers, 'nearly stone-blind'. Also *fig.*

Graveless (grēⁱ·vlĕs), *a.* 1606. [See -LESS.] Having no grave or graves.

Graveling (græ·vĕliŋ). Also **gravelling.** 1587. [?] The parr or young salmon.

Gravelling (græ·vĕliŋ), *vbl. sb.* 1523. [f. GRAVEL *v.* + -ING[1].] 1. The action of laying down gravel. Also, a gravelled surface. 1577. †2. *Farriery.* A disease in a horse's foot (see GRAVEL *v.* 5) –1639.

Gravelly (græ·vĕli), *a.* ME. [f. GRAVEL *sb.* + -Y[1].] 1. †Sandy; full of or abounding in gravel; consisting of gravel; strewn with gravel. Also, resembling gravel. 2. *Path.* Of the nature of gravel (see GRAVEL *sb.* 4); characterized by, or arising from, the presence of gravel 1607. †3. Containing gritty particles –1727.

†Gra·velous, *a.* ME. [a. F. *graveleux*; see GRAVEL *sb.* and -OUS.] a. Gravelly. b. Granular –1758.

Gra·vel-pit. ME. An excavation from which gravel (or †sand) is or has been obtained.

Gra·vel-stone. ME. [f. GRAVEL *sb.* and STONE *sb.*] 1. A pebble. Also *fig.* †2. = CALCULUS 1. Holland.

Gravel-walk. 1663. An alley or path laid with gravel.

Gravely (grēⁱ·vli), *adv.* 1553. [f. GRAVE *a.*[1] + -LY[2].] In a grave manner (see GRAVE *a.*[1]).

Graven (grēⁱ·v'n), *ppl. a.* ME. [pa. pple. of GRAVE *v.*[1]] 1. Sculptured, hewn. b. quasi-*sb.* A graven image. BIBLE (Douay) *Ps.* lxxvii. 58. 2. Carved on a surface, engraved 1821.

1. Thou shalt not make unto thee any g. image *Exod.* xx. 4.

Graveness (grēⁱ·vnĕs). 1577. [f. GRAVE *a.*[1] + -NESS.] The quality or state of being grave (see GRAVE *a.*[1]).

Had put off levity and put g. on TENNYSON.

Graveolent (grăvī·ŏlĕnt), *a.* 1657. [ad. L. *graveolentem,* f. *grave* advb. neut. + *olentem, olere* to smell.] Having a rank smell; fetid. So **Graveolence, -ency,** a rank offensive smell. (Dicts.)

Graver (grēⁱ·vəɹ). ME. [f. GRAVE *v.*[1] + -ER[1]. Cf. F. *graveur.*] 1. One who carves or engraves: †a sculptor –1628; an ENGRAVER (sense 1) (now *rare*) ME. 2. A cutting or shaving tool; an engraver's tool, a burin (now the principal use) 1548.

†Gra·very. 1601. [f. GRAVE *v.*[1] + -ERY.] The employment of an engraver; engraving –1695.

Graves, obs. f. GREAVES.

Graves's disease. 1868. [f. Dr. R. J. *Graves* of Dublin.] *Med.* Exophthalmic goitre; also called Basedow's disease.

Gravestone, grave-stone (grēⁱ·vˌstōun). ME. [f. GRAVE *sb.*[1] + STONE *sb.*] A stone placed over or at the head or foot of a grave, or at the entrance of a tomb.

Graveyard (grēⁱ·vˌyaɹd). 1825. [f. GRAVE *sb.*[1] + YARD.] A burial-ground.

The..desolate g. of Donore MACAULAY.

Gra·vic, *a.* 1864. [irreg. f. L. *gravis* + -IC.] Pertaining to or causing gravitation. (Dicts.)

Gravid (græ·vid), *a.* 1597. [f. L. *gravidus*, f. *gravis*.] Pregnant, heavy with young. Also *fig.*

A carefull husband [*sc.* a dolphin] over his g. associate 1638.

†**Gra·vidate**, *v. rare.* 1623. [f. L. *gravidat-*, *gravidare* to burden; see prec. and -ATE³.] *intr.* To be gravid or pregnant; *trans.* to make heavy or gravid. Hence **Gra·vidated** *ppl. a.* pregnant. †**Gravida·tion**, pregnancy.

Gravidity (grăvi·dĭti). 1651. [f. L. *graviditas*, *-tatem*, f. *gravidus* GRAVID.] The state of being gravid; pregnancy.

Gravific (grăvi·fik), *a.* 1807. [f. L. *gravis* + -FIC.] That makes heavy or produces weight.

Gravigrade (græ·vigrēᵉd). 1847. [f. mod.L. *Gravigrada* (see below) f. *gravis* heavy + *gradi* to walk.] *Zool.*

A. *adj.* 'Walking heavily'; of or belonging to the extinct edentate group *Gravigrada*, which includes the Megatherium and the Mylodon 1884.

B. *sb.* Formerly, a heavy-paced animal, e.g. an elephant; now, one of the *Gravigrada* (see A).

Gravimeter (grăvi·mĭtəɹ). 1797. [ad. F. *gravimètre*, f. L. *gravis* heavy; see -METER.] *Physics.* A kind of hydrometer for determining the specific gravity of bodies, whether liquid or solid. Hence **Gravime·tric**, **-al** *a.* pertaining to the g., or to gravimetry. **Gravime·trically** *adv.* in respect of measurement by weight. **Gravi·metry**, measurement of weight.

Graving (grēᵉ·viŋ), *vbl. sb.*¹ ME. [f. GRAVE *v.*¹ + -ING¹.] †1. Digging –1486. †2. Carving, sculpturing; incision of lines, etc. in stone, metal, and the like –1727; *concr.* a carving, sculpture; an inscription –1801. 3. The engraving (of a design, etc.) on metal or wood; an engraved plate, or an impression from it. *Obs.* or *arch.* 1646. 4. *attrib.*, as *g. tool*, etc. ME.

2. *concr.* The g. of palme-trees in the front therof 1609.

Graving (grēᵉ·viŋ), *vbl. sb.*² 1626. [f. GRAVE *v.*² + -ING¹.] The cleaning of a ship's bottom by scraping or burning, and coating with tar. *Comb.* **g.-dock**, a dock into which vessels are floated to be graved; = DRY DOCK.

Gra·vitate, *a.* [f. L. *gravitas* + -ATE.] Endowed with gravity. COLERIDGE.

Gravitate (græ·vitēᵉt), *v.* 1644. [f. mod.L. *gravitat-*, *gravitare*, f. *gravis*, *gravitas*.] †1. *intr.* To exert weight or pressure; to move or tend to move downward –1808. 2. *intr.* To be affected by gravitation; to move or tend to move by the force of gravity *towards* a body 1692. b. To sink or fall by, or as by, gravitation (*lit.* and *fig.*) 1823. c. *trans.* To cause to descend or sink by gravitation 1894. 3. *transf.* and *fig.* (*intr.*) To move or tend to move towards (some centre of influence) 1673.

2. Systems of bodies which g. round a central body LOCKYER. 3. The market price..is continually gravitating towards the natural price ADAM SMITH.

Gravitation (grævitēᵉ·ʃən). 1644. [ad. mod.L. *gravitationem*; see prec.] 1. *Physics.* The action or process of gravitating; now in wide sense, the moving or tending to a centre of attraction 1645. b. The degree of such attraction 1812. 2. The attraction of one body for another; the tendency of every particle of matter towards every other particle 1646. 3. *transf.* and *fig.* Natural tendency (*to* or *towards*); in bad sense, tendency to sink to a low level 1644. 4. *attrib.* 1850.

1. The mutual g. of bodies BERKELEY. 2. Phr. *The law of gravitation*, the law according to which the attractive force of bodies varies directly as their masses and inversely as the square of the distance between them. 3. That strong g. towards evil 1876.

Gravitational (grævitēᵉ·ʃənăl), *a.* 1855. [f. GRAVITATION + -AL.] Of, pertaining to, or caused by gravitation.

Gravitational astronomy: a system based, as by Sir Isaac Newton, on the theory of gravitation.

Gravitative (græ·vitēᵉtiv), *a.* 1799. [f. GRAVITATE *v.* + -IVE.] Of, pertaining to, or produced by gravitation.

Gravity (græ·vĭti). 1509. [ad. F. *gravité*, or L. *gravitatem*; see GRAVE *a.*¹ First used in Eng. in fig. senses.]

I. 1. †Weight, influence –1741; solemnity 1647; a grave subject, speech, or remark (now *arch.*) 1609. 2. Grave character or nature; importance, seriousness 1519. 3. Weighty dignity of conduct or demeanour; staidness. In later use opp. to *levity* and *gaiety*. 1509.

1. The g. of that supreme court CLARENDON. 2. The g. of the offence SIR T. MORE, of the occasion 1878. 3. A man of his place, grauity, and learning SHAKS. The settled g. of his face 1894.

II. In physical senses. 1. †a. The quality of having weight, ponderability; tendency to downward motion (opp. to *levity*, or upward tendency, as e.g. of fire) –1678. b. Weight, heaviness; chiefly = *specific gravity*. Now mainly in *centre of g.* (see CENTRE *sb.*). 1641. c. **Specific gravity.** The degree of relative heaviness characteristic of any kind or portion of matter; expressed by the ratio of the weight of a given volume to that of an equal volume of some substance taken as a standard (viz. usually water for liquids and solids, air for gases). Now sometimes called *density*. Abbrev. *sp. gr.* 1666. 2. The attractive force by which all bodies tend to move towards the centre of the earth. Also often more widely, the degree of intensity with which one body is affected by the attraction of gravitation exercised by another body. 1692. 3. Of sounds: Lowness of pitch 1669.

Comb.: g. **battery**, **cell**, a galvanic battery or cell in which the liquids are kept apart by the force of g. alone; **-railroad**, a railroad in which the cars descend under the action of g. alone.

Gravo-, bad comb. form of GRAVE *a.*

Gravure (gravü·r, græ·viuᵊɹ). 1893. [Short for PHOTOGRAVURE.] Engraving by means of photography; a print thus produced. Also *attrib.*

Gravy (grēᵉ·vi). ME. [? a misreading of ON. *grané*, cogn. w. *grain*, 'anything used in cooking' (Godef.), and w. GRENADE², GRENADINE¹.] †1. A dressing of some sort used for white meats, fish, and vegetables –1513. 2. The fat and juices which exude from flesh in cooking; a dressing for meat and vegetables made from these 1591. 3. *attrib.* 1694.

Gray, etc.: see GREY.

Graybeard: see GREYBEARD.

Graylag: see GREY LAG.

Grayling (grēᵉ·liŋ). 1450. [f. *gray* GREY *a.*; see -LING.] 1. A freshwater fish of the genus *Thymallus* (family *Salmonidæ*), of a silvery-grey colour and characterized by a long and high dorsal fin. The European grayling is *Thymallus vulgaris*; other species are *T. signifer*, the American or Alaskan grayling, and *T. ontariensis*, the Michigan grayling. 2. A common butterfly (*Hipparchia Semele*), so called from the grey under-side of the wings 1819.

1. In this riuer [Wie] be vmbers, otherwise called graylings 1577.

Graymalkin, var. of GRIMALKIN.

Graze (grēᵉz), *sb.* 1692. [f. GRAZE *v.*²] 1. An act or instance of grazing; said esp. of shot. 2. A superficial wound or abrasion, caused by an object rubbing against the skin 1847.

Graze (grēᵉz), *v.*¹ [OE. *grasian*, f. *gras-*, *græs* GRASS *sb.*] 1. *intr.* To feed on grass or growing herbage. 2. *transf.* and *fig.* a. 'To move on devouring' (J.). ?*Obs.* b. *joc.* of persons: To feed. 1579. 3. *trans.* To feed on, eat (growing herbage). Chiefly *poet.* 1667. †Also said of fish (DRYDEN). 4. *causal.* To put (cattle) to feed on pasture 1564. 5. *intr.* (or *absol.*) To pasture cattle 1645. 6. *trans.* To put cattle to feed on (grass, land, etc.); also, to tend while feeding 1601. 7. *intr.* Of land: To produce grass. *Obs.* exc. *dial.* 1625.

1. The..horses were turned out to g. W. IRVING. 2. b. *To send to g.*: to send packing. Will you..Send the clergy all to g. SWIFT. 4. When Iacob graz'd his Vncle Labans sheepe SHAKS. 7. The Quarters to G., being kept Shorne BACON. Hence **Gra·zer**, an animal that grazes.

Graze (grēᵉz), *v.*² 1604. [? Transf. use of prec. (Skeat).] 1. *trans.* To touch lightly (a surface) in passing; *esp.* to roughen or abrade (the skin, etc.) in brushing past. Also *fig.* b. Said of a ray of light 1839. 2. *intr.* To move so as to touch lightly in passing, or so as to produce slight abrasion. †Also, of a bullet: To ricochet. 1632.

1. Our little canoe grazed the steps 1863. b. The sun's..rays..grazing the summit of the mountain TYNDALL. 2. Points Of slander, glancing here and grazing there TENNYSON.

Grazier (grēᵉ·ziəɹ). 1502. [f. GRASS *sb.*; see -IER.] †1. = VERDERER. 2. One who feeds cattle for the market 1523.

2. The savage..chooses to be a g. rather than to till the ground 1853.

Graziery (grēᵉ·ziəri). 1731. [f. prec.; see -ERY.] a. The business of a grazier. b. Grazing-ground, pasture (*rare*).

Grazing (grēᵉ·ziŋ), *vbl. sb.* ME. [f. GRAZE *v.*¹ + -ING¹.] 1. The action of GRAZE *v.*¹; pasturing. Also *fig.* 2. Grazing-ground, pasture-land, pasture 1517. 3. *attrib.*, as g. **guard**, a guard placed over the cattle of an army whilst grazing 1626.

Gre, var. of GREE.

Grease (grīs), *sb.* [ME. *grece*, *grees(s)e*, a. OF. *gresse* (mod. *graisse*) :—pop.L. **crassia*, f. *crassus* (F. *gras*) adj., fat.] †1. The fat part of the body of an animal; also, fatness, corpulence –1672. 2. Melted or rendered fat of animals, esp. when in a soft state. Hence, oily or fatty matter in general, esp. such as is used as a lubricant. ME. 3. A disease which attacks the heels of a horse (see quot.) 1674. 4. The oily matter in wool; also, wool before it has been cleansed of this 1835.

3. *Grease* is a specific inflammation of the sebaceous follicles of the skin of the heels, followed by an increased morbid secretion YOUATT.

Comb.: **g.-band**, a band coated with cart-grease mixed with tar fastened round a tree-trunk to prevent the ascent of flightless moths; hence as vb.; **bird**, the Canada Jay; **g.-bush** = *grease-wood*; **-season**, **-time**, the period when the deer are fat and fit for killing; **-trap**, an appliance for catching g. in a drain; **-wood**, a name for various stunted and prickly chenopodiaceous shrubs of the genera *Sarcobatus*, *Atriplex*, etc., which contain oil and are found in dry alkaline valleys of the western U.S.

Grease (grīz, grīs), *v.* ME. [f. prec. Cf. F. *graisser*.] 1. *trans.* To smear, anoint, or lubricate with grease; to make greasy 1613. 2. To apply a salve of tallow and tar to (sheep). Also *absol.* ME. 3. *fig* a. Phr. *To g. the wheels*: to make things run smoothly; to pay the expenses ME. b. To ply with money, to bribe 1526. †c. To gull, cheat –1634. 4. To cause (a horse) to become affected with grease. Also *intr.* of a horse. 1737.

3. b. While pluralities greas'd them thick and deepe MILT. Phr. *To g. a person's hand, palm.*

Greaser (grī·zəɹ, -səɹ). 1641. [f. prec. + -ER¹.] 1. †One who greases (sheep); one who cleans and lubricates machinery, etc. with grease; *U.S.* the head fireman on a steamer. 2. *U.S. slang.* A nickname for a native Mexican or a native Spanish American 1849.

Greasy (grī·zi, -si), *a.* 1514. [f. GREASE *sb.* + -Y¹.] 1. Smeared, covered, or soiled with grease. †2. Anointed or smeared with grease or chrism. (Applied contemptuously to R. C. priests in reference to unction.) –1583. 3. Composed of or containing grease; of the nature of grease. Of food: Containing too much grease. 1592. 4. Of wool: Containing a natural grease; used *spec.* of wool not cleansed of this. Also of flannel. 1600. 5. Of a horse: Affected with the grease 1701. 6. Having the feel of grease 1703; (of a road) slimy with mud or moisture 1801. 7. Filthy, obscene, low 1588. 8. Of manners, voice, etc.: 'Unctuous', oily 1848.

1. Greasie Napkins SHAKS. Sweepe on you fat and greazie Citizens SHAKS. G. sophisters MILT. 3. When a German dish is not sour it is sure to be g. HOOD. 4. *A. Y. L.* III. ii. 55. 7. His g. Jest 1687. 8. A g. simper THACKERAY.

Comb.: g. **fritillary**, a species of butterfly, *Melitæa Artemis*; g. **pole**, a pole rubbed with g. to make it harder to climb or walk upon (used at fairs or village sports); g. **steam**, steam which becomes its own lubricant by a mechanical admixture of g. with it.

Great (grēᵉt). [Com. WGer.: OE. *grēat* :—OTeut. **grauto-* :—pre-Teut. **ghroudo-*.]

A. *adj.*

I. 1. Coarse of grain or texture. Of diet: Coarse, not delicate. *Obs.* exc. *Sc.* 2. Thick, stout, massive, bulky, big. (Opp. to *small* in sense of 'slender'.) OE. 3. Pregnant.

far advanced in pregnancy. Chiefly with *with* (*child*, etc.). *arch.* and *dial.* ME. †Also *fig.* –1654. †4. Full or big with courage, emotion, etc.; angry, grieved; proud, arrogant –1832. 5. Of the sea, a river: In high flood 1670.

3. Hyr body is grete, and she with childe 1460. *fig.* I am g. with woe, and shall deliver weeping SHAKS. 4. My harte is g.: but it must break with silence SHAKS.

II. Having a high position in a scale of measurement. (Opp. to *small, little.*) 1. Of material objects, with reference to size (see quots.) ME. †2. Grown up; full-grown. Chiefly in *Hunting* language. –1774. 3. Of collective unities, numbers, quantities, dimensions, etc. OE. 4. Of qualities, emotions, conditions, actions, or occurrences; with reference to degree or extent ME.

1. The g. Globe it selfe SHAKS. A g. big Man 1766. A g. oak stump SHELLEY. Of letters: = CAPITAL, as *g. A*, capital A. Thus makes she her g. P's SHAKS. Of animal and vegetable species of larger size than others so named: The g. Horn-Owl RAY. The black or g. ostrich 1802. In names of constellations, as *G.* (formerly *Greater*) *Bear, G. Dog*; of anatomical structures, as *G. artery, pelvis*, etc. (See the sbs.) G. Malvern (opp. to *Little* Malvern), G. Ouse, G. Portland Street, etc. = Main, principal; William Rufus builded the g. hall there [Westminster] about..1097 STOW. 2. ij hennes, or a grete ghoos CAXTON. 3. *G. deal, many* (see those words). Grete possessions 1460. G. Dust they raised HOBBES. *G. gross*, twelve gross, 1728. *G. hundred*, a long hundred, 120. 4. The g. heates are abated 1573. I will take g. care of them HEARNE. G. agitation 1849, ignorance, poverty BUCKLE.

III. In fig. extensions of II. 1. Important, elevated, distinguished ME. 2. Of persons: Eminent by reason of birth, rank, wealth, power, or position. b. Applied (more or less conventionally) to the Deity, or deities; also to saints ME. c. = GRAND *a.* 2. 1532. 3. Of things: Pertaining to or occupied by persons of high place or rank ME. †4. 'Of elevated mien' (J.) –1697. 5. (usually qualifying *man*) Eminent in point of attainments or achievement; exhibiting signal excellence in some important work. In recent use, often with an implication of more or less loftiness and integrity of character. 1709. b. Lofty, magnanimous, noble 1726. 6. Hence: a. *predicatively.* Having considerable knowledge (of a subject) or skill (in doing something); const. *at*, †*in* 1784. b. Of surpassing excellence; hence, Magnificent, splendid, grand, immense. *U.S.* and *colloq.* 1809. 7. Qualifying a descriptive sb. (see quots.) ME. 8. Favourite; high in favour *with* ME. 9. Intimate, familiar, friendly; 'thick' *with* 1483.

1. G. matters..could not but be full of g. difficulties 1655. A name g. in story BYRON. The g. day of the Exclusion Bill MACAULAY. The g. attraction was [etc.] DICKENS. The g. sin of g. cities HELPS. 2. The g. man, at whose frown, a few days before, the whole kingdom had trembled MACAULAY. *The g. world* [= F. *le grand monde*]: aristocratic society. *The Great* (following a proper name): (*a*) as merely honorific (*obs.* or *arch.*); (*b*) implying both that the person so designated is the most famous person of the name, and that he ranks among the great men of history. *The G. King*: in *Gr. Hist.*, the King of Persia. *The G. Cham, Mogul, Turk*, see CHAM, etc. c. *The Lord Great Chamberlain* 1727. 3. Of G. Place BACON (*title*). 4. Dido.. Amidst the Crowd, she walks serenely g. DRYDEN. 5. He is a g. man, eloquent in conception and in language BURKE. b. Nothing can be g. which is not right JOHNSON. 6. a. He is very 'great' on dogs JEFFERIES. b. Phr. *To run a g. filly, dog*, etc.: said of one that runs a fine race. 7. With sense: Eminently entitled to the designation; A g. scoundrel 1828. With sense: That is much in the habit of performing the action; also, that is on a large scale. I am a g. eater of beefe SHAKS. The g. Dealers in Wit POPE. 9. The Duchess of York and the Duke of York are mighty g. with her PEPYS.

Combs. 1. With sbs., and normally preceded by the definite article. **Great Bible**, usually applied to the version by Coverdale in 1539; occas. also to revised versions of this, esp. to Cranmer's Bible of 1540. **G. day**, (*a*) the Day of Judgement; (*b*) Easter Day; (*c*) a feast- or fast-day of high importance. **G. fast**, the season of Lent. **G. organ**, one of the divisions of a large organ, having the pipes of largest scale and loudest tone; **G. week** = HOLY WEEK. See also *Great* ASSIZE, etc.

2. Prefixed to terms denoting kinship, to form designations for persons one degree further removed in ascending or descending relationship. [After F. *grand*, which follows L. *avunculus magnus*, etc.] **a. Great-uncle, -aunt**, a father's or mother's uncle, aunt; **-nephew, -niece**, a son's or daughter's nephew, niece; etc. **b. Great-grandfather, -grandmother**, a grandfather's or grandmother's father, mother (also *transf.* a remote male or female ancestor); **-grandchild**, grandchild's child; **-grandson, -granddaughter**, a grandson's or granddaughter's son, daughter; etc. Similarly with repetition of *great.*

3. In parasynthetic adjs., as **g.-bellied**, having a big belly, pregnant; *fig.* big with events, etc.; **-eyed**, *lit.* having large or prominent eyes; *fig.* far-seeing, taking a large view; **-mouthed**, *fig.* loud-voiced, boastful, bragging; **†-stomached**, high-spirited.

B. *adv.* In a great degree; to a great extent; greatly, exceedingly, highly; much; very. *Obs.* exc. *dial.* ME.

Say that he thriue, as 'tis g. like he will SHAKS.

C. as quasi-*sb.* and *sb.*

I. The adj. used *absol.* 1. a. As *pl.*: Great persons; freq. in *g. and small.* Now usually *the g.* ME. b. (With *the.*) That which is great; great things, aspects, qualities, etc. collectively 1557. 2. **By the g., †by g.** a. Of work done: At a fixed price for the whole amount; by task; by the piece. Now *dial.* 1523. †b. In gross, wholesale –1640. †c. *transf.* and *fig.* In the mass; by wholesale –1755. †3. **In g.** [Cf. F. *en grand, en gros.*] a. In the mass, in the bulk; in the gross, wholesale; by the piece ME. b. On a large scale 1652.

II. As *sb.* †1. A great person –1649. †2. The chief part; the main point; the sum and substance; the general drift or gist. ME. only. †3. a. Thickness. b. Greatness, magnitude (*rare*) –1629. 4. **Greats** (*Oxford Univ. colloq.*). The final examination for the degree of B.A.; *esp.* the examination for Honours in Literæ Humaniores. Formerly GREAT GO, 1853.

Great-coat, greatcoat (grēⁱ·tkōᵘ·t). 1661. A large heavy overcoat, a top-coat. Hence **Great-coated** *a.* dressed in or wearing a g.

Greaten (grēⁱ·t'n), *v.* Now *arch.* ME. [f. GREAT *a.*; see -EN [5].] †1. *intr.* To become pregnant. ME. only. 2. *trans.* To render great or greater in size or amount 1626. 3. To render eminent, prominent, distinguished, or important; to exalt, aggrandize. Also *absol.* 1614. b. To exalt mentally or spiritually; chiefly in good sense 1647. 4. *intr.* To become great or greater 1716.

2. Everything concurred to g. the fire PEPYS. 3. So much doth the means of facilitating carriage g. a city PETTY. 4. My blue eyes greatening in the looking-glass MRS. BROWNING.

Greater (grēⁱ·təɪ). [OE. *grýttra* :—OTeut. **grautizon-*, comp. of **grauto-* GREAT *a.*; but now mostly refash. on the positive; see -ER [3].]

A. *adj.* 1. The comparative of GREAT. †2. Older, elder. [A Latinism.] –1535. 3. In special or technical use, opp. to *lesser* 1551.

1. Lesser then Macbeth, and g. SHAKS. 3. In names of constellations, as *the G. Dog*, etc. Also †*g. circle* = 'great circle': see CIRCLE. *Mus.* Applied to intervals now usu. called MAJOR. In names of plants, as *G. Knapweed*, of birds, etc., and in *Anat.*

†B. *adv.* In a greater degree 1496.

C. quasi-*sb.* and *sb.* The adj. used *absol.* and *ellipt.*

The g. scornes the lesser SHAKS. Thou Sun, of this great World both Eye and Soule, Acknowledge him thy G. MILT.

Greatest (grēⁱ·tėst). ME. [f. GREAT *a.* + -EST.]

A. *adj.* The superlative of GREAT. †2. Eldest 1535. 3. *absol.* and *ellipt.* (quasi-*sb.*) ME.

1. The world knows nothing of its g. men SIR H. TAYLOR. *G. happiness of the g. number* (see HAPPINESS). *G. common measure* (see MEASURE). 3. Our g. yet with least pretence TENNYSON.

†B. *adv.* Most greatly or highly; most 1553.

Great go. 1820. [See GREAT *a.* and GO *sb.*] *Univ. slang.* The final examination for the degree of B.A. (At Oxford now called *Greats.*)

Great-grandfather, etc.: see GREAT *a.*

Great-great-: see GREAT *a.*

Great-head (grēⁱ·thed). *U.S.* 1844. [f. GREAT *a.* + HEAD *sb.*] U.S. name for the golden-eye, *Clangula glaucion.*

Great-hearted, *a.* (Stress variable.) ME. [f. GREAT *a.*; see HEARTED.] †a. High-spirited; proud –1647. b. Having a noble or generous heart or spirit; magnanimous. Hence **Greathea·rtedness.**

Greatly (grēⁱ·tli), *adv.* ME. [f. GREAT *a.* + -LY [2].] 1. To a great extent, in a great degree; much, very. 2. Largely 1670; mainly, chiefly (*rare*) 1742. 3. In a great manner; magnanimously, nobly; †illustriously; with brilliant success ME. 4. In or to a high rank or position (*rare*) 1800.

1. To heare Musicke, the Generall do's not g. care *Oth.* III. i. 18. It is g. probable H. WALPOLE. 3. Small time: but in that small, most g. liued This Starre of England SHAKS. 4. G. born 1800. To expect to marry g. JANE AUSTEN.

Greatness (grēⁱ·tnės). [f. GREAT *a.* + -NESS; in OE. *grétnys.*] †1. Thickness, coarseness; stoutness –1536; pregnancy –1634. 2. The attribute of being great in size, extent, or degree ME. †3. Magnitude –1765. 4. Eminence, distinction, importance. *Occas.* in *pl.* ME. 5. Inherent nobility or dignity; grandeur 1597. 6. Intimacy *with*. *Obs.* or *arch.* 1625.

3. An Elephant excedeth in greatnes thre wilde oxen EDEN. 4. Some atcheeues greatnesse SHAKS. 5. This Language..has a Natural G. in it DRYDEN.

†Greave [1]. [OE. *grǽfa* :—prehist. **graiƀjon-*, f. **graiƀo-* GROVE.] 1. a. Brushwood. (OE. only.) b. *pl.* Branches, twigs –1612. 2. A thicket –1609.

Greave [2] (grīv). Chiefly *pl.* ME. [a. OF. *greve* shin, armour for the legs, of unkn. origin.] 1. Armour for the leg below the knee. †2. The shin 1600. Hence **Greaved** *ppl. a.* furnished with greaves.

Greaves, graves (grīvz, grēⁱvz), *sb. pl.* 1614. [app. orig. a term of the whale fisheries; ad. LG. *greven* pl.; cf. OE. *gréoua* (= **gréofa*) 'olla'.] The fibrous matter or skin found in animal fat, which forms a sediment on melting and is pressed into cakes for dogs'-food, fish-bait, etc.; the refuse of tallow; cracklings.

Grebe (grīb). 1766. [a. F. *grèbe*, of unkn. origin.] 1. The name for the diving birds of the genus *Podiceps* or family *Podicipedidæ*, characterized by a short body, flattened and lobed feet set far behind, and the virtual absence of tail. 2. The plumage of the grebe 1859. *Comb.* **g.-cloth**, a cotton cloth with a downy surface on one side.

Grece (grīs). *Obs.* exc. *dial.* [ME. *grese*, a. OF. *grez, greyz, greis*, pl. of *gré* GREE *sb.*[1]; deduced from a double pl. *greces, greeses* with the meaning 'flight of steps' and 'steps in a flight'.] 1. A flight of stairs or steps; a stairway ME. 2. a. *pl.* Steps or stairs collectively; = sense 1. ME. b. *pl.* Steps or stairs (in a flight); *spec.* in *Her.* with spelling **grieces** (whence GRIECED *a.*) ME. c. *sing.* A single step or stair 1448.

Grecian (grī·ʃăn). 1547. [f. L. *Græcia* + -AN.]

A. *adj.* Of or pertaining to Greece or the Greeks; Greek. Now *rare* exc. with reference to architecture and facial outline. 1577.

Comb.: **G. bend**, an affected carriage of the body, in which it is bent forward from the hips; **†G. calends** (see CALENDS); **G. fire**, (*a*) = Greek fire (see FIRE *sb.*); (*b*) a kind of firework; **G. horse**, the wooden horse by means of which Troy was captured.

B. *sb.* 1. A Greek. *Obs.* or *arch.* 1547. b [tr. Gr. Ἑλλανιστής.] = HELLENIST 1. 1611. 2. One learned in the Greek language; a Greek scholar 1557. b. A boy in the highest class at Christ's Hospital 1820. †3. A member of the Greek Church –1766. 4. *slang.* An Irishman 1853.

1. Was this faire face the cause, quoth she, Why the Grecians sacked Troy SHAKS. b. There arose a murmuring of the Grecians [*R.V.* Grecian Jews] against the Hebrewes *Acts* vi. 1.

Grecing (grī·siŋ). *Obs.* exc. *dial.* ME. [f. GRECE *sb.* + -ING [1].] Chiefly *pl.* Steps in a flight; flights of steps; stairs. Rarely *sing.* A step.

Grecism, Grecize, Greco-: see GRÆC-.

‖**Grecque** (grek, as Fr. grek). 1836. [Fr., fem. of *grec* GREEK.] *Arch.* A Greek fret.

Gree (grī), *sb.*[1] *Obs.* exc. *Sc.* ME. [a. OF. *gré* (see GRECE) :—L. *gradum* step.] †1. = DEGREE 1. –1693. †2. *fig.* = DEGREE 2. –1589 †3. = DEGREE 3. –1617. †4. = DEGREE 4. –1590. 5. Pre-eminence; superiority; mastery; victory in battle; hence, the prize for a victory. Now *Sc.* ME. †6. = DEGREE 6, 7, 9. –1563.

Gree (grī), *sb.*² Now *arch.* ME. [a. OF. *gré, gred, gret* (mod. *gré*) pleasure, goodwill, will :—L. *grātum* adj. neut. used subst.] †1. Favour, goodwill -1590. 2. *To do* or *make gree*: to give satisfaction for an injury ME. †3. (One's) good pleasure; will, desire; consent -1734.

1. In gree: with goodwill or favour, in good part. Accept in g...the words I spoke FAIRFAX.

Gree, *v.* *Obs.* exc. *dial.* ME. [aphet. f. AGREE *v.*, or f. GREE *sb.*² Cf., however, OF. *greer.*] = AGREE *v.*

Greed (grīd), *sb.* Orig. *Sc.* 1609. [f. GREEDY.] Inordinate or insatiate longing, esp. for wealth; covetous desire. Const. *of.*

Greedily (grī·dili), *adv.* [Coalescence of: (1) OE. *grǣdelīce*, f. **grǣd* (*u*-stem, = ON. *grāð-r*) + *-līce* -LY²; (2) OE. *grǣdi(ȝ)līce*, f. *grǣdiȝ* GREEDY + *-līce* -LY².] In a greedy manner; hungrily; rapaciously OE.; eagerly, zealously ME.

Greediness (grī·dinės). OE. [f. GREEDY + -NESS.] The attribute of being greedy; gluttony ME.; avarice, rapacity OE.; excessive longing or desire in general 1553.

The greedinesse of the Wolfe 1641. The g. and extortion of the Court of Rome 1661. A G. of Knowledge, that is impatient of being confin'd BOYLE.

Greedy (grī·di), *a.* [OE. *grǣdiȝ* :—OTeut. **grǣdago-, -ugo-*, f. **grǣdu-z*, cogn. w. Skr. *grdh* to be greedy.] 1. Having an intense desire or inordinate appetite for food or drink; ravenous, voracious, gluttonous. †In early use: Hungry. Const. *of* (OE. *genitive*). Also *transf.* and *fig.* 2. Eager for gain, wealth, and the like; avaricious, covetous, rapacious OE. 3. Eager, keen; †zealous ME. †4. *transf.* Of spoil, prey: Greedily pursued -1648.

1. Two gredy sowes LANGL. *fig.* The..noise of g. Acheron CARLYLE. *transf.* Air..g. of moisture 1800. 2. A wolvish, g., and covetous heart GAGE. 3. With g. hope to find His wish MILT. G. of novelty 1734. 4. Running headlong after g. spoils MARLOWE.

Gree·dy-gut(s. Now *dial.* and *vulgar.* 1550. [See GUT.] A voracious eater; a glutton.

Greegree (grī·grī). Also †**griggory**, †**grigri.** 1698. [? of African origin; in F. *grisgris* (Littré).] 1. An African charm, amulet, or fetish. 2. The ordeal tree of Guinea, *Erythrophleum guineense* 1847. 3. *attrib.*, as greegree man, a 'medicine-man' 1788.

Greek (grīk), *sb.* [In I: OE. *Crecas* pl. :—**Krēko-z*, early Teut. ad. L. *Græcus*, pl. *Græci*, the Roman name for the Ἕλληνες. Ult. refash. after L. In II the sb. is an absol. use of GREEK *a.* The L. *Græci* is ad. Gr. Γραικοί (see Aristotle *Meteor.* I. xiv), app. an adjectival deriv. of *Graius*, a poet. synonym of *Græcus.*]

I. 1. A native of Greece; a member of the Greek race OE. 2. A member or adherent of the Greek Church ME. †3. A Hellenized Jew -1685. 4. A cheat, sharper, esp. one who cheats at cards. (Cf. F. *grec.*) 1528. 5. Qualified by *merry, mad, gay*: A merry fellow; a roysterer; a person of loose habits 1536. 6. *slang.* An Irishman 1823.

1. Come worthy Greeke, Ulisses, come DANIEL. When Greeks joyn'd Greeks, then was the tug of War LEE. 4. In carde playinge he is a goode greke 1528.

II. [the adj. used *absol.*] 1. The Greek language ME. 2. Unintelligible speech, gibberish 1600.

1. Though thou hadst small Latine, and lesse Greeke B. JONS. in *Shaks. Wks.* Pref. verses. 2. I knew this was heathen G. to them WESLEY. *St. Giles's G.*: slang.

Greek (grīk), *a.* ME. [f. GREEK *sb.*, infl. by L. *Græcus* and F. *grec* adjs.] 1. Of or pertaining to Greece or its people; Hellenic; Grecian. 2. As the designation of a language (see GREEK *sb.* II. 1). Hence: Belonging to, or written in, the Greek language. 1548. 3. Distinctive epithet of the *Eastern* or (*Holy*) *Orthodox Church*, now representing the Christianity of Greece, Russia, and the Turkish Empire, which acknowledges the primacy of the Patriarch of Constantinople and which formally renounced communion with the Roman see in the ninth century A.D. Also applied to its clergy, rites, buildings, etc. 1560.

1. Thise noble clerkes grekes CHAUCER. The straight G. nose 1888. 2. This small packet of Greeke and Latine bookes SHAKS. *G. fathers*: those early Christian fathers (see FATHER *sb.*) who wrote in G. 3. The Romanists called the G. church the G. schism CHAMBERS.

Comb., etc.: **G. braid** (*ornament*), ornament arranged in the pattern of a fret (see FRET *sb.*¹); **G. Calends** (see CALENDS); **G. cross** (see CROSS *sb.*); **G. gift**, a gift covering some act of treachery (see Virgil *Æn.* II. 49); **G. masonry**, that in which every alternate stone is made of the whole thickness of the wall; †**G. pitch** (L. *pix Græca*) = COLOPHONY; **G. point**, a kind of needle-made lace; **G. rose** [tr. L. *rosa græca*], a book-name for the Campion.

†**Greek**, *v.* 1615. [f. GREEK *sb.* Cf. L. *Græcari.*] 1. *To Greek it*: to follow the practice of the Greeks; to play the Greek scholar -1799. 2. Only in *Greeking*: To cheat at cards -1825. So **Gree·kery**, card-sharping.

Greekish (grī·kiʃ), *a.* [In I, repr. OE. *crēcisc, grēcisc*, f. *Crēcas, Grēcas* (see GREEK *sb.*) + *-isc*, -ISH. In II, f. GREEK *sb.* or *a.* + -ISH.]

I. 1. Of or pertaining to Greece or the Greeks; Greek, Grecian (*arch.*) ME. †2. = GREEK *a.* 2. -1647. †3. = GREEK *a.* 3. -1639.

1. The..famous light of all the G. hosts SPENSER.

II. Somewhat Greek; resembling Greek persons or things; characteristic of a Greek or Greeks 1568. b. Pagan. CARLYLE. Hence **Gree·kishly** *adv.* after the Greek fashion.

Greekize (grī·kəiz), *v.* *rare.* 1796. [see -IZE.] = GRÆCIZE 1. So **Gree·kism** = GRÆCISM 2. **Gree·kist**, a student of Greek.

Greekling (grī·kliŋ). 1636. [f. GREEK *sb.* + -LING, after L. *Græculus.*] A little Greek; a degenerate, contemptible Greek.

Green (grīn). [OE. *grēne* :—OTeut. **grōnjo-*, f. OTeut. root **grō-*, whence GROW *v.* Cf. GRASS.]

A. *adj.*

I. 1. Of the colour which in the spectrum is intermediate between blue and yellow; in nature chiefly conspicuous as the colour of growing herbage and leaves. 2. Covered with a growth of herbage or foliage; verdant; (of trees) in leaf OE. b. Of a season of the year: Characterized by verdure; hence, of a winter or Christmas: Mild, temperate ME. 3. Of the complexion: Having a pale, sickly, or bilious hue, indicative of fear, jealousy, ill-humour, or sickness. (Cf. Gr. χλωρός green, pale.) ME. 4. Consisting of green herbs, plants, or vegetables 1460. 5. When applied to fruits or plants, often implying some additional sense: (*a*) Unripe; (*b*) young and tender; (*c*) vigorous, flourishing; (*d*) retaining the natural moisture, not dried OE.

1. How lush and lusty the grasse lookes? How greene SHAKS. The g. Wave MILT. Wing-coverts g. STARK. Meat g. (i.e. putrid from long keeping) before cooking (*mod.*). Phr. †*To give a woman a g. gown*: to roll her, in sport, on the grass so that her dress is stained with g.; hence *euphem.* to deflower her. 2. Yonder Allies g. MILT. The broad way and the g. (cf. *primrose path*) MILT. b. A g. Christmas is neither handsome nor healthfull FULLER. 3. The duke..waxed pale and grene as a lefe LD. BERNERS. 4. G. food for cattle 1804. 5. Hurte the grene blade, & you shall haue no whete there 1526. *Green corn* (U.S.), the unripe and tender ears of maize, commonly cooked as a table vegetable.

II. *transf.* and *fig.* 1. Full of vitality; not withered or worn out OE. †2. Of tender age, youthful -1818. 3. Unripe, immature, undeveloped. Often with mixture of sense 4 below. ME. b. Raw, untrained, inexperienced 1548. c. Simple, gullible 1605. 4. That has not been prepared by drying; hence, not ready for use or consumption 1460. 5. Unaltered by time or natural processes; fresh, new ME.

1. The example is fresh and greene FENTON. He is yet in g. and vigorous senility LAMB. *In the g. tree* (after Luke xxiii. 31): under conditions not involving pressure or hardship. 2. In that new world and greene age of the Church A.V. *Transl. Pref.* 4. 3. The Regency..was still g. and raw BURKE. G. probationers in mischief LAMB. Another young fellow almost as g. as myself 1871. *G. hand* (cf. HAND). 4. Like greene timber SHAKS. Fish-Cod dry ..*Ditto* G. 1714. A g. ham wants no soaking MRS. GLASSE. The g. hide of an eland bull SELOUS. *G. sand*: 'sand used for moulds without previous drying or mixture' (Raymond). 5. A Man that studieth Revenge, keepes his owne Wounds greene BACON. G. Mortar 1776. It [Port] strengthens Digestion..which g. Wines of any kind can't do STEELE. Phr. *G. in earth*: just buried (*Rom. & Jul.* IV. iii. 42).

Comb. 1. General: as *g.-backed, -curtained*, etc.; *g.-dropping, -glimmering*, etc.; *g.-black, -blue, -yellow* adjs. (occas. sbs.).

2. Special: **g.-book**, a book with a g. cover, *spec.* an official publication of the Indian Government; **-charge**, gunpowder of which the ingredients have been mixed but have not yet undergone the incorporating process; **g. crop**, a crop used for food while in an unripe state, as opp. to a grain crop, hay crop, etc.; **g. ebony**, the wood of the W. Indian tree *Jacaranda ovalifolia*; also of *Excœcaria glandulosa*; **g. fat**, the g. gelatinous portion of the turtle, highly esteemed by epicures; **g. fire**, a pyrotechnical composition, consisting of sulphur, potassium chlorate, and a salt of barium, which burns with a g. flame; **g. gill** (*U.S.*), the condition of oysters when tinged g. by feeding on confervæ; so **g.-gill, -gilled** *adjs.*, affected with g. gill; **g. gland**, 'one of a pair of large glands in Crustacea, supposed to serve as kidneys' (Webster); **g. glass**, bottle-glass; **g. goods** *pl.*, counterfeit greenbacks (see GREENBACK *sb.* 1); also *attrib.*; **-jerkin**, one who wears a g. jerkin, a forester; **g. manure**, a mass of growing plants ploughed while g. into the soil, to enrich it; **g. oak**, the wood of oak branches stained g. by a parasitic fungus (used in making Tunbridge ware); **g. oyster**, an oyster coloured g. (see GREEN *v.*), formerly regarded as a delicacy; **g. ribbon**, a ribbon of g. colour worn (*a*) as the badge of the King's Head Club, consisting of supporters of the Duke of Monmouth (1679–85); (*b*) as part of the insignia of the Order of the Thistle; †**g. rushes**, fresh rushes spread on the floor of a house in honour of a guest who is a great stranger; hence used as an exclam. of surprise or welcome; **-salted** *a.*, salted down without tanning; **-soil**, soil in which g. crops are raised; hence **-soil** *v.*, to provide with such a soil; **-stick** *Path.*, a form of fracture of a long bone in which whilst one side of the bone is broken the other is only bent; **-stuff**, vegetation, herbage; *pl.* a commercial term for g. vegetables; **g. syrup** (*Sugar-making*), the syrup which flows off from the loaves; **g. table**, a table covered with g. cloth; hence (*a*) *Hist.* the board of Covenanting notables which ruled Scotland in 1638–41; (*b*) a gaming-table; **-ware**, †(*a*) = *greenstuffs*; (*b*) *Ceramics*, articles just moulded or otherwise shaped, before drying and baking; **g. water**, †(*a*) some remedy for venereal disease; (*b*) *Med.* a name for lochia in the later stage; (*c*) the condition of the Nile when the water is low and unwholesome. For *g. apron, ginger*, etc., see the sbs.

b. In names of animals: **g. bass**, the black bass (see BASS *sb.*¹); **g. blights**, plant-lice, aphides; **g. bone**, (*a*) the garfish; (*b*) the viviparous blenny; **-bottle**, a fly, *Musca Cæsar*; **-cod**, (*a*) = GREENFISH 1; (*b*) the Coal-fish, *Gadus virens*; (*c*) the Cultus Cod, *Ophiodon elongatus*; **g. cormorant**, the shag, *Phalacrocorax graculus*; **g. crab**, the common shore crab, *Carcinus mænas*; **g. drake**, the common May-fly, *Ephemera vulgata*; **g. grosbeak** = GREENFINCH 1; **-leek**, an Australian parrakeet, *Polytelis Barrabandi*; **g. linnet** = GREENFINCH 1; **-louse**, a plant-louse or aphis; **g. plover**, the lapwing; **-pollack**, the coal-fish; **-tail** (*fly*), the grannom fly; **-wing**, the green-winged teal, *Querquedula crecca* of Europe, *Q. carolinensis* of America. For *g. grasshopper, turtle*, etc., see the sbs.

c. In names of plants and fruits: **g. ash**, a variety of the ash tree, so called from the colour of the young shoots; **g. brier**, American name for *Smilax*; **g. broom**, the common broom, *Sarothamnus* or *Cytisus scoparius*; **g. dragon**, (*a*) the plant *Dracunculus vulgaris* (formerly *Arum D.*); (*b*) the U.S. plant *Arisæma Dracontium*, dragon-root (Webster); **g. laver**, an edible seaweed, *Ulva lactuca* and *U. latissima*, also called locally *g. oyster*; **-wort**, sneezewort, *Achillea Ptarmica*. For *g. hellebore, rose*, etc., see the sbs.

d. In names of mineral and chemical substances: †**g. brass** = VERDIGRIS; **g. diallage**, (*a*) DIALLAGE, a variety of pyroxene; (*b*) = SMARAGDITE, a variety of amphibole; **g. earth** = GLAUCONITE; **g. gold** ? *Obs.*, an alloy of gold and silver; **g. iron ore** = DUFRENITE; **g. lead ore** = PYROMORPHITE; **g. marble** = SERPENTINE; **g. mineral** = MALACHITE. For *g. bice, copperas*, etc., see the sbs.

B. *sb.* 1. The adj. used *absol.* That which is green; the green part of anything OE. 2. Green colour. In *pl.* = different tints of green ME. 3. A green dye or pigment; usu. defined as *Brunswick, emerald*, etc. 1611. 4. Green clothing or dress (*lit.* and *fig.*) ME. 5. *Antiq.* As the distinctive colour of one of the factions in the circus. Also *pl.* the adherents of this faction. 1693. 6. The emblematic colour of Ireland; hence adopted as the colour of the 'nationalist' party 1797. 7. Greenness, as indicative of vigour, youthfulness, virility 1586. 8. Verdure, vegetation, greenery ME. †9. A tree, herb, or plant. (Mostly in pl.) -1719. 10. *pl.* a. Freshly cut greenery used for decoration. Now *U.S.* 1697. b. Green vegetables such as are boiled for the table (*colloq.*) 1725. 11. Grassy ground; a grassy spot. Now *rare.* ME. b. A piece of grassy land situated in or near a town or village 1477. **c.** A piece of grassy land used for some particular purpose, as BOWLING-GREEN. In *Golf*, the putting-ground; sometimes = the whole links. 1646. **12.** *attrib.* Of or pertaining to a bowling-green or golf-links, as *g.-keeper* 1705.

4. A hunter all in grene ME. 6. They are hanging men and women for the wearing of the green 1798. 7. Phr. *In the g.*: in the period of youthful vigour. Thy leaf has perish'd in the g. TENNYSON. 10. b. Bacon and Greens WESLEY. 11. Goodly gardens and pleasant greenes KNOLLES. b. Every Holiday, she danced upon the g. 1718.

Green (grīn), *v.* [OE. *grénian*, f. *gréne* (see prec.).] **1.** *intr.* To become green, as growing herbage; *occas.* to appear or look green. **2.** *trans.* To impart a green colour to; to clothe with green 1570. **b.** *Oyster-culture.* To turn oysters green in the gills by putting them in pits. Also *absol.* 16.. **3.** *slang.* To make to appear green; to hoax, take in 1884.

2. Have not rains Green'd over April's lap KEATS. 3. To g. a visitor 1884.

Greenback (grī·nbæk), *sb.* 1778. [f. GREEN *a.* + BACK *sb.*[1]] **1.** One of the legal-tender notes of the U.S., first issued in 1862 and so called from the devices printed in green ink on the back. Hence, 'any note issued by a national bank in the U.S.' (Funk). Also *attrib.*, as in **Greenback party**, a party in U.S. politics, which advocated that greenbacks should be made the sole currency of the country. **2. a.** The garfish, *Belone vulgaris.* **b.** The American golden plover, *Charadrius dominicus.* **c.** *slang.* A frog. 1778. Hence **Gree·nbacker**, a member of the g. party.

Green bag, green-bag. 1677. A bag made of green material used formerly by barristers and lawyers for documents and papers. Also *attrib.*

Gree·n-blind, *a.* 1881. Suffering from colour-blindness in respect of green light-rays. Hence **Green-blindness.**

Green cheese. ME. **a.** New or fresh cheese. **b.** An inferior kind of cheese made from skim milk or whey. **c.** Cheese coloured green with sage; also called *sage cheese.*

Green cloth, greencloth. 1536. **1.** In full, *Board of Green Cloth*: A department of the Royal Household, consisting of the Lord Steward and his subordinates, which has control of various matters of expenditure, and legal and judicial authority within the sovereign's court-royal, with power to correct offenders, and to maintain the peace of the verge of the court-royal, which extends every way two hundred yards from the gate of the palace. (So called from the green-coloured table at which its business was originally transacted.) Also *attrib.* **2.** *colloq.* The green baize covering of a billiard, etc. table; hence, the table itself 1871.

Greenery (grī·nəri). 1797. [f. GREEN *a.* or *sb.* + -ERY.] **1.** Green foliage or vegetation; verdure. **2.** Green branches or leaves for decoration. (Rarely *pl.*) 1867. **3.** A place where plants are reared or kept 1847.

Green-eyed (grī·n,əid), *a.* (Stress variable.) 1596. [f. GREEN *a.* + EYE *sb.* + -ED[2].] Having green eyes. *The green-eyed monster* (Shaks.): jealousy. Hence *fig.* Viewing everything with jealousy.

Oh, beware my Lord, of ielousie, It is the greene-ey'd Monster *Oth.* III. iii. 166.

Greenfinch (grī·nfinʃ). 1532. [See GREEN *a.*[1] and FINCH.] **1.** A common European bird of the family *Fringillidæ*, *Coccothraustes* or *Ligurinus chloris*, so called from its green and gold plumage. Called also *green linnet.* **2.** The Texas sparrow (*Embernagra rufivirgata*) 1883. **3.** *slang.* One of the Pope's Irish guard 1865.

Green-fish (grī·nfiʃ). 1460. [See GREEN *a.* II. 4.] †**1.** Fresh, unsalted fish; *spec.* applied to cod –1867. **2. a.** *local.* The coal-fish 1880. **b.** *U.S.* The blue-fish (*Pomatomus saltatrix*) 1884.

Gree·n-fly. 1686. **1.** *Angling.* A particular kind of artificial fly. **2.** An aphis or plant-louse, from its colour. Usually *collect. sing.* 1744.

Greengage (grī·ngē·dʒ). 1759. [f. GREEN *a.* and the surname of Sir William *Gage.*] A variety of plum of roundish shape, green colour, and fine flavour. Also *attrib.*

Green goose. 1564. [See GREEN *a.* or *sb.*] **1.** A young goose, a gosling. ? Now *dial.* (See also quot.) **2.** A simpleton (*rare*) 1768.

1. The greene goose is better than the stubble goose COGAN.

Greengrocer (grī·ngrōᵘ:səɹ). 1723. [See GREEN and GROCER.] A retail dealer in vegetables and fruit. Hence **Gree·ngro:cery**, the business of a g.; the articles retailed by a g.; also *attrib.*

Green head, gree·nhead. 1569. [f. GREEN *a.* + HEAD *sb.*] †**1.** A young, immature, or untrained intellect –1694. **2.** A simpleton, an ignoramus. ? *Obs.* 1589. †**3.** One entitled to wear the green turban, a descendant of Mahomet –1625. Hence †**Green-headed** *a.* raw.

Greenheart (grī·nhāɹt). 1756. [See GREEN *a.* and HEART *sb.*] **1.** The name of several W. Indian trees. **a.** A large lauraceous tree of Guiana, *Nectandra Rodiæi*, which furnishes very hard timber. **b.** The cog-wood tree, *Ceanothus Chloroxylon.* **c.** A small rhamnaceous tree, the *Colubrina ferruginosa* of Jamaica. **d.** *Bastard* or *False Greenheart*, a small myrtaceous tree, *Calyptranthes Chytraculia.* **2.** The timber of 1. a, used in shipbuilding, for fishing-rods, etc. Also *attrib.* 1794. **b.** A fishing-rod of this wood 1884.

Gree·nhew. *Obs.* exc. *Hist.* 1598. [? f. GREEN *a.* + HEW *v.*] **1.** = VERT. Also *attrib.* **2.** The right to cut greenery for fodder; payment for this right 1869.

Greenhorn (grī·nhǭɹn). 1650. [GREEN *a.*] **1.** A raw recruit –1682. **2.** A raw, inexperienced person; an ignoramus; hence, a simpleton 1682. Hence **Gree·nhornism**, inexperience.

Green-house, greenhouse (grī·nhaus). 1664. **1.** [f. GREEN *sb.*] A glass-house in which delicate and tender plants are reared and preserved. Also *attrib.* **2.** *Pottery.* A house in which 'green ware' (see GREEN *a.*) is left to dry, before being placed in the kiln 1875.

Greening (grī·niŋ), *sb.* 1600. [f. GREEN *a.* + -ING[3].] **1.** †**a.** A variety of pear –1632. **b.** An apple, which is green when ripe 1664.

Greenish (grī·niʃ), *a.* ME. [See -ISH.] Somewhat green. **b.** Qualifying adjs. or sbs. of colour, as *g.-blue* 1644.

Greenland (grī·nlănd). 1678. [f. GREEN *a.* + LAND *sb.*, ult. after ON. *Grœnland.* So named by its discoverer, 'because it would induce settlers to go there, if the land had a good name'.] **1.** A large island or small continent to the north-east of N. America. Also *attrib.* **2.** *slang.* The country of greenhorns. DICKENS. Hence **Gree·nlander**, a native or inhabitant of G. **Greenla·ndic** *a.* of or pertaining to G., its language and its inhabitants; *sb.* the language of G.

Greenless (grī·nlės), *a.* 1618. [f. GREEN *sb.* + -LESS.] Without greenness or verdure.

Greenlet (grī·nlėt). 1831. [f. GREEN *a.* + -LET; app. = L. *vireo.*] A name for the numerous species of small greenish American singing-birds of the genus *Vireo* or family *Vireonidæ.*

Greenling (grī·nliŋ). *rare.* 1440. [f. GREEN *a.* + -LING.] = GREEN-FISH 1 and 2.

Greenly (grī·nli), *adv.* 1583. [See -LY[2].] **1.** With a green colour; with green vegetation. **2.** *fig.* Freshly, vigorously, youthfully 1633. **3.** In an inexperienced or unskilful manner (*arch.*) 1599.

3. We haue done but g. SHAKS.

Green man, greenman. 1638. †**1.** A man dressed up with greenery to represent a wild man of the woods; a Jack-in-the-green –1810. **2.** A fresh, raw, or inexperienced man; *spec.* in whale-fishing, one who had not been to sea before. *Obs.* exc. *Hist.* 1682. **3.** A name for *Aceras anthropophora* 1829.

Greenness (grī·n,nės). [OE. *grénnes*, f. *gréne* GREEN; see -NESS.] **1.** The quality or condition of being green; *concr.* or semi-*concr.* verdure. **2.** Unripeness; immaturity; crudity; inexperience; gullibility ME. **3.** The vigour or freshness of growth; vitality 1649. **4.** Freshness, newness. ? *Obs.* 1553.

1. The g. of fields LAMB, of the sea TYNDALL. 2. The g. of his yeares FENTON, of his troops 1875.

Greenockite (grī·nəkəit). 1844. [Named after Lord *Greenock*; see -ITE.] *Min.* Native sulphide of cadmium, found usually in yellow coatings, rarely in crystals.

Green-peak (grī·n,pīk). Also **-peek.** 1598. [tr. It. *picchio verde* or F. **pic-vert* (now *pivert*).] The Green Woodpecker, *Gecinus viridis.*

Gree·n-room. 1701. **1.** A room in a theatre for actors and actresses when not required on the stage, perh. orig. painted green. *transf.* The players who frequent the green-room. **2.** A room in a warehouse or factory for the reception of goods in a 'green' state, such as fresh cloth, undried pottery, etc. (Recent Dicts.)

Gree·n-sand, gree·nsand. 1796. **1.** *Min.* and *Geol.* **a.** = GLAUCONITE. **b.** A variety of sandstone, usually imperfectly consolidated, consisting largely of glauconite. **c.** A formation consisting largely of this sandstone; denominated *Upper* or *Lower Greensand* from the position of the stratum relatively to the gault. **2.** See GREEN *a.* II. 4.

Greenshank (grī·nʃæŋk). 1766. A large sandpiper, *Totanus glottis*; prob. so called from its olive-coloured legs.

Green sickness, green-sickness (grī·n-si·knės). 1583. [See GREEN *a.* I. 3.] An anæmic disease which mostly affects young women about the age of puberty and gives a pale or greenish tinge to the complexion; chlorosis. Also *transf.* and *fig.* (often with reference to the morbid appetite which characterizes chlorosis). Also *attrib.*

attrib. Out you greene sicknesse carrion, out you baggage, You tallow face SHAKS.

Green-sleeves. 1580. A woman wearing green sleeves; the name given to an inconstant lady-love in a ballad published in 1580; hence, the ballad and the tune themselves.

Let it thunder to the tune of Greene-sleeues SHAKS.

Green snake. *U.S.* 1791. **1.** One of two green harmless snakes of the U.S. **2.** An air-plant resembling the snake 1883.

Green-stone, gree·nstone. 1772. [f. GREEN *a.* + STONE *sb.*] **1.** *Geol.* A wide term, usually comprising the greenish-coloured eruptive rocks containing feldspar and hornblende (or augite), such as diorite, melaphyre, etc. 1805. Also *attrib.* **2.** *Min.* = NEPHRITE, a variety of jade 1772. **3.** A hard and close-textured stone used for putting the last edge on delicate surgical instruments (*Cent. Dict.*).

Greensward (grī·nswǭɹd). 1600. Turf on which grass is growing. Also *attrib.*

Greenth (grīnþ). 1753. [f. GREEN *a.* + -TH; coined by H. Walpole.] Verdure.

Green wax, gree·nwax. *Obs.* exc. *Hist.* ME. Sealing-wax of a green colour; hence **b.** A seal of green wax, as affixed to documents delivered by the Exchequer to sheriffs. **c.** An estreat, etc. bearing this seal; also *process of green wax.* **d.** The fines or amercements exacted in accordance with such a document.

Greenweed (grī·nwīd). 1599. [f. GREEN *a.* + WEED.] **1.** The plant *Genista tinctoria*; used for dyeing. **2.** A green sea-weed 1856.

Greenwich (gri·nidʒ). A town on the south bank of the Thames adjoining London on the east, famous for its astronomical observatory and its hospital; used *attrib.* in **G. stars,** 'those used for lunar computations in the nautical ephemeris' (Smyth); **Greenwich time,** mean time for the meridian of Greenwich, the standard time for English astronomers.

Greenwood (grī·nwud). ME. [See GREEN *a.* I. 2.] A wood or forest when in leaf. Also *attrib.*

Phr. *To go to the g.*: to become an outlaw. I muste too The grene wode goo Alone a bannysshed man 1500.

Greeny (grī·ni), *a.* 1593. [See -Y[1].] †**1.** Green, verdant. Also *fig.* Vigorous. –1674. **2.** = GREENISH *a.* 1826.

Green-yard, greenyard (grī·nyāɹd). 1578. An enclosure covered with grass or turf (not paved); *spec.* a pound for stray animals, etc.; also, a grass yard for hounds to take exercise in.

†**Greet**, *sb.*[1] 1591. [f. GREET *v.*[1]] A greeting –1634.

Greet (grīt), *sb.*[2] *Obs.* exc. *Sc.* ME. [f. GREET *v.*[2]] Weeping, lamentation; a cry of sorrow.

Greet (grīt), *v.*[1] [Com. WGer.: OE. *grǣtan*, of uncertain etym.] †1. *trans.* To approach, come up to; to begin upon. OE. only. †2. To assail, attack –ME. 3. To address with expressions of goodwill or courtesy; to offer in speech or writing to (a person) the expression of one's own or another's friendly or polite regard. Now only *literary*. Also *absol.* OE. b. To salute *with* words or gestures; also *transf.* OE. †c. In Spenser: to offer congratulations on (an achievement, etc.); const. *unto* or *dative*. †d. To gratify. *Per.* IV. iii. 38. 4. To receive or meet with demonstrations of welcome 1605. 5. Of a thing (now only of sights or sounds): To meet 1698.

3. There's others of our friends Will g. vs heere anon SHAKS. *absol.* There greete in silence as the dead are wont SHAKS. b. To g. the strangers with a nod DICKENS. 4. We will g. the time SHAKS. 5. A wide extent of sea greets the eye 1872.

Greet (grīt), *v.*[2] Now *Sc.* and *n. dial.* [Coalescence of (1) OE. *grǣtan* to weep, etc. :—OTeut. **grǣtan*, f. OAryan root **ghrēd-* : *ghrod-* found also in Skr. *hrād* to resound; (2) OE. *grēotan*, of conjectural etym.] 1. *intr.* To weep, cry, lament, grieve. †2. To cry or call out in supplication or in anger –1513.

Greet(e, obs. f. GREAT *a.*

Greeter[1] (grī·təɹ). 1552. [f. GREET *v.*[1] + -ER[1].] One who greets or salutes.

Greeter[2] (grī·təɹ). *Sc.* 17.. [f. GREET *v.*[2] + -ER[1].] One who greets or cries.

Greeting (grī·tiŋ), *vbl. sb.* OE. [f. GREET *v.*[1] + -ING[1].] The action of GREET *v.*[1]; a salutation.

Health, and faire g. from our Generall SHAKS. Phr. *Sendeth g.*: a transl. (now *arch.*) of L. *salutem (dicit)*, Gr. χαίρειν; also with ellipsis of the vb.

Greeve, obs. f. GRIEVE.

Greffier (gre·fiəɹ, F. grefye). 1590. [a. F., f. *greffe*; see GRAFF *sb.*[1]] 1. A registrar, clerk, or notary. 2. A white hunting dog. TURBERV.

Gregal (grī·găl), *a.* 1540. [ad. L. *gregalis*, f. *greg-*, *grex*.] 1. Pertaining to a flock, or to the multitude (*rare*). †2. = GREGARIOUS –1658.

‖**Gregale** (gregā·le). Also **grigale, grecale.** 1804. [It.; app. repr. a late L. **græcalem*, f. L. *Græcus*.] The north-east wind in the Mediterranean.

Gregarian (grĕgēə·riăn), *a. rare.* 1632. [f. L. *gregarius* (see GREGARIOUS) + -AN.] Belonging to the herd or common sort. Of a soldier: Common, private.

Gregarine (gre·gărin). 1867. [f. mod.L. *Gregarina* (f. L. *gregarius*: see next), the typical genus of the *Gregarinidæ*.]

A. *adj.* Of or pertaining to the genus *Gregarina* or class *Gregarinida* of protozoans, parasitic chiefly in insects, molluscs, and crustacea. (Rec. Dicts.)

B. *sb.* One of the *Gregarinida*.

Gregarious (grĕgēə·riəs), *a.* 1668. [f. L. *gregarius* (f. *greg-*, *grex* flock, herd) + -OUS.] 1. *Nat. Hist.* Of animals: Living in flocks or communities, given to association with others of the same species. b. *transf.* of persons 1789. 2. *Bot.* Growing in open clusters 1829. 3. *Path.* Clustered 1822. 4. Of or pertaining to a flock or community; characteristic of persons gathered together in crowds 1833.

1. Stares are g. birds, living and flying together in great flocks RAY. 4. Mere religious zeal is a g. thing MOZLEY. Hence **Grega·rious-ly** *adv.*, **-ness.**

‖**Grège** (grēʒ). Also **greige.** 1927. [ad. F. *grège* raw (silk).] (Of) a colour between beige and grey.

†**Greg(g)e**, *v.* ME. = *agregge*, AGGREGE.

‖**Grego** (grī·go). Also †**greiko.** 1747. [a. some Rom. form of L. *Græcus* GREEK *a.*] A coarse jacket with a hood, worn in the Levant. Also *slang*, a rough great-coat.

Gregorian (grĭgōə·riăn). 1641. [ad. mod.L. *gregorianus*, f. late L. *Gregorius* (a. Gr. Γρηγόριος), a man's name; in some senses used with reference to the Eng. surname Gregory; see -AN, -IAN.]

A. *adj.* 1. Of or pertaining to Pope Gregory I (who reigned 590–600); chiefly applied to the ancient system of ritual music, also known as *plain-chant* or *plain-song* (characterized by free rhythm, a limited scale, etc.), which is founded on the *Antiphonarium* ascribed to Pope Gregory. So *G. chant, music, tones*, etc. 1653. 2. Of, pertaining to, or established by Pope Gregory XIII. 3. Distinctive epithet of the reflecting telescope invented by J. Gregory (died 1675) 1761. †4. *G. tree*, the gallows, so named from Gregory Brandon, a hangman –1785.

2. *G. calendar*: see CALENDAR 1; so *G. style* = 'new style'. *G. epoch*, the time from which the G. calendar dates (1582).

B. *sb.* 1. A variety of wig, named after one Gregory, a Strand barber 1598. 2. A member of an 18th c. society (often classed with the Freemasons) 1742. 3. A Gregorian chant; †also, one versed in Gregorian music 1609.

1. A quaint G. to thy head to binde HARINGTON. Hence **Grego·rianist**, one who advocates the use of G. chants.

Gregory-powder. Also **gregory.** 1886. [f. James *Gregory*, a Scottish physician (1758–1822).] The 'compound powder of rhubarb' (*Pulvis rhei composita*) of the British Pharmacopœia. Usually called *Gregory's powder*.

Greisen (grəi·z'n). 1878. [Ger.; a dial. var. of *greiss*, f. *greissen* to split.] *Min.* A granitic rock with crystalline granular texture, consisting chiefly of quartz and mica.

Greit, obs. f. GREET *sb.*[2], *v.*[2]

Greith(e, obs. form of GRAITH.

Gremial (grī·miăl). 1563. [ad. late L. *gremialis*, f. *gremium* lap, bosom.]

A. *adj.* 1. Of or pertaining to the bosom or lap. Of a friend: Intimate (cf. *bosom-friend*). *Obs.* exc. in *g. veil* = B. 2. 1631. 2. Dwelling within the bosom of a University or society, resident. Also opp. to *honorary*. *Obs.* exc. *Hist.* 1730.

B. *sb.* 1. A resident member (of a University, etc.). *Obs.* exc. *Hist.* 1563. 2. *Eccl.* A silken apron placed on the bishop's lap when celebrating Mass or conferring orders 1811.

Grenade[1] (grĕnē^i·d). 1532. [a. F. *grenade*, a. Sp. *granada* pomegranate (see GARNET); hence transf. See also GRENADO.] †1. A pomegranate –1664. 2. A small explosive shell, usually of metal, thrown or shot into the trenches or among clusters of the enemy 1591. See HAND-GRENADE, RIFLE-*grenade*. b. A glass receptacle to be thrown in order to burst and disperse its contents 1891.

2. b. *Drain g.*, one filled with a strong-smelling fluid, to be used in detecting a leakage in a drain. *Fire-g.* = HAND-GRENADE 2.

Grenade[2] (grĕnē^i·d). 1706. [Alleged to be Fr.; perh. f. *grain* GRAIN *sb.*[1], with sense 'something spiced'. Cf. GRENADINE[1].] *Cookery.* A dish of larded veal-collops, with six pigeons and a ragout in the middle, and covered above and below with thin slices of bacon.

Grenadier (grenădī·əɹ). 1676. [a. F., f. *grenade* GRENADE *sb.*[1] 2.] 1. Orig., a soldier who threw grenades. At first four or five were attached to each company, but, later, each battalion or regiment had a company of them. When grenades went out of general use, the name of 'grenadiers' was retained for a company of the finest and tallest men in the regiment. Now, in the British army, the word is retained only in the name of the Grenadier Guards (*colloq.* Grenadiers), the first regiment of household infantry. Also *attrib.* 2. a. A S. African weaver-bird, *Pyromelana* (or *Ploceus*) *oryx*, with vivid red and black plumage. Also *g. grosbeak*, *g. waxbill*. 1751. b. The fish *Macrurus fabricii* or *M. rupestris* 1889.

1. Now were brought into service a new sort of soldiers call'd *Granadiers*, who were dextrous in flinging hand granados EVELYN.

Grenadilla: see GRANADILLA.

Grenadine[1] (gre·nădīn). 1706. [a. F. *grenadin*; cf. GRENADE[2].] *Cookery.* A dish of veal or of fillets of poultry, etc., smoothly trimmed, larded, and brightly glazed.

Grenadine[2] (gre·nădīn). 1865. [a. F.; ? f. *Granada* in Spain.] An open silk or silk and wool textile used for dresses.

Grenado (grĕnē^i·do). *arch.* 1611. [ad. Sp. *granada*: see GRENADE[1] and -ADO.] = GRENADE[1] 2. Also *attrib.*

Grenatite (gre·nătəit). Also **granatite.** 1804. [f. F. *grenat* garnet + -ITE.] *Min.* = STAUROLITE.

Grene, obs. f. GRAIN, GREEN.

Gres, obs. f. GRASS, GREASE.

†**Gre·ssible**, *a.* 1600. [f. L. *gress-*, *gradi*; see -BLE.] Able to walk –1610.

A two legd liuing creature, g., vnfeathered *Timon* v. iv. 86. So †**Gre·ssile** *a.* (*rare*).

Gressorial (gresōə·riăl), *a.* 1842. [f. mod. L. *gressorius* (f. *gressor*, f. L. *gradi*) + -IAL.] Adapted for stepping or walking, ambulatory.

Gressorial, in Ornithology, is applied to the feet of birds which have three toes forward, two of which are connected, and one behind BRANDE. So **Gresso·rious** *a.*

Gret, obs. f. GREAT, GREET *sb.*[2]; obs. pa. t. of GREET *v.*[1] and [2].

Grete, obs. f. GREAT, GREET.

Grew, pa. t. of GROW, *v.*

Grewsome, obs. f. GRUESOME.

Grey, gray (grē^i). [OE. *grǣg*, repr. two OTeut. types **grǣgo-* and **grǣwo-*, with variable accent. Not conn. w. OHG. *grîs* (Ger. *greis*), whence F. *gris*. In Great Britain the form *grey* is the more frequent.]

A. *adj.* 1. Of the colour intermediate between black and white, or composed of a mixture of black and white with little or no positive hue; ash-coloured, lead-coloured. Also *fig.* ¶ b. (See quot.) 1885. 2. Epithet of (*a*) the Cistercian monks, (*b*) the Franciscan friars, (*c*) the sisters of the third order of St. Francis, on account of the colour of their habits. See also GREY FRIAR. ME. 3. Of the eyes: Having a grey iris ME. 4. Of a horse: Having a grey coat ME. 5. Of the hair or beard: That is turning white (with age or grief) ME. b. Of a person: Grey-haired 1483. c. *fig.* Ancient, old 1662. d. Belonging to old age; hence (of experience, etc.), mature 1602.

1. The night is chill, the cloud is gray COLERIDGE. The grass path grey with dew BROWNING. b. Grey is composed only of black and white; the term gray is applied to any broken colour of a cool hue, and therefore belongs to the class of chromatic colours FIELD. 2. It was the Friar of Orders gray SHAKS. 3. With kamuse nose and eyen greye as glas CHAUCER. 4. My horse, gray Capilet SHAKS. Proverb. *The grey mare is the better horse*: the wife rules the husband. 5. I..with grey haires and bruise of many daies, Do challenge thee SHAKS. c. Mac-Kinnon's chief, in warfare grey SCOTT. d. Type of grey honour, and sweet rest RUSKIN.

Comb.: 1. General: as *grey-black, -blue*, etc.; *grey-eyed, -haired*, etc.

2. Special: as **grey band**, a grey laminated quartzose sandstone; **grey groat**, emphatic for *groat*; also a type of something of little value; **grey matter**, the grey-coloured matter of which the active part of the brain is composed; also *fig.*; **grey millet** = GROMWELL, q.v.; **grey powder**, a powder consisting of mercury and chalk; **grey russet**, coarse cloth of a dull grey colour; **grey wethers**, detached oolitic sandstones of various sizes; applied also in Devonshire to two circles of stones which nearly touch each other, and look like sheep, when seen from a distance.

b. In names of animals, as **grey bass**, a sea-fish of the perch family, but resembling the mullet in taste; **grey crow**, the Hooded Crow, *Corvus cornix*; **grey duck**, the gadwall; **grey falcon**, (*a*) the hen-harrier; (*b*) the common or Peregrine Falcon; **grey fly**, perh. a dor-beetle; **grey fowl**, grouse in winter plumage; **grey mullet** (see MULLET); **grey owl, parrot** (see the sbs.); **grey pike** = HORN-FISH 2; **grey plover, sandpiper**, etc. (see the sbs.); **grey snipe**, 'the dowitcher in winter plumage' (Webster); **grey trout** (see TROUT); **grey whale**, *Rhachianectes glaucus*.

c. In names of minerals, as **grey antimony, cobalt** (see the sbs.); **grey copper** (ore), tetrahedrite; **grey ore**, chalcocite.

B. *sb.* 1. Grey material or clothing ME.; *techn.* unbleached material 1884. †2. *spec.* Grey fur; usu. of badger skin –1702. 3. A grey or subdued light; esp. in phr. *the g. of the morning* 1592. 4. Grey colour. In *pl.* = shades of this 1825. b. *Gunmaking.* A grey spot indicating a flaw 1881. c. A grey-coloured pigment 1888. †5. A grey-haired person –1513. †6. A badger –1686. 7. A grey horse. Chiefly *pl.* 1760. 8. *pl.* (in full *Scots Greys*). A regiment of dragoons, now the 2nd Dragoons 1751. 9. A kind of fish; ? a GRILSE 1686.

1. A Gown of gray 1640. 3. Yon gray is not the mornings eye SHAKS. 7. Mrs. Mantrap..drives her greys in the Park THACKERAY.

Grey (grēⁱ), *v.* Also **gray.** ME. [f. GREY *a.*] 1. *intr.* To become or grow grey. 2. *trans.* To make grey 1879.

Grey-back, greyback (grēⁱ·bæk). 1864. 1. *U.S. colloq.* A Confederate soldier in the American civil war. 2. *dial.* and *U.S. colloq.* A louse 1864. 3. A name of birds. a. The Hooded Crow, *Corvus cornix.* Also *g. crow.* b. *U.S.* The N. American Knot, *Trigla canutus.* c. *dial.* and *U.S.* The scaup duck, *Fuligula marila.* 1888. 4. *U.S.* The grey whale 1884.

Greybeard (grēⁱ·bīᵊɹd). Also **graybeard.** 1579. 1. A man with a grey beard; hence, an old man. 2. A large earthenware or stoneware jug or jar, used for holding spirits 1788. 3. A hydroid polyp which infests oyster-beds, *Sertularia argentea.* (Rec. Dicts.) 4. *attrib.* **Greybeard lichen,** *Usnea barbata.* Hence **Greybearded** *a.*

Grey·-coat. 1644. One who wears grey clothing; *spec.* a Cumberland yeoman. b. *attrib.*: **Grey-coat Hospital,** a charity school, where the scholars were clothed in grey; **grey-coat parson,** an impropriator; a holder of lay tithes. Hence **Grey-coated** *a.*

Grey friar. ME. [See GREY *a.*]. A member of the order of Franciscan or Minor friars, founded by St. Francis of Assisi in 1210. *Grey Friars,* a convent of this order.

Grey goose. OE. The greylag goose.

Grey-hen (grēⁱ·hen). late ME. Female of the black grouse (*Tetrao tetrix*), the heath-hen. (The male is called the BLACKCOCK.)

Greyhound (grēⁱ·haund). [OE. *grighund,* **grieghund,* f. **grieg* (of unkn. etym.) + *hund* dog, HOUND.] 1. A variety of dog used in the chase, characterized by its long slender body and long legs, its keenness of sight, and its great speed in running. 2. *transf.* An ocean steamship specially built for speed. Also *ocean g.* 1887. *Comb.* **g. fox,** a name given to the largest and boldest variety of the fox kind; **g. racing** (contr. **greycing**), a sport in which a mechanical hare is coursed by greyhounds.

Greyish (grēⁱ·iʃ), *a.* Also **grayish.** 1508. [See -ISH.] Somewhat grey.

Grey lag goose, grey·lag (goose). 1713. [Orig. three words. The bird remains longer in England than the other migratory species; hence the use of LAG *a.*] The common wild goose of Europe, *Anser cinereus* or *ferus.*

Greyling, obs. f. GRAYLING.

Greyness, grayness (grēⁱ·nės). 1483. [See -NESS.] The state or quality of being grey; grey colour. Also *fig.*

Greystone, graystone (grēⁱ·stōᵘn). 1815. [f. GREY *a.* + STONE *sb.*] *Min.* A grey volcanic rock, composed of feldspar (sometimes replaced by leucite or melilite), augite, or hornblende, and iron.

Greywacke (grēⁱ·wækə). Also **graywacke, greywack.** 1811. [Anglicized f. GRAUWACKE.] *Geol.* A conglomerate or grit rock consisting of rounded pebbles and sand firmly united together; orig. applied to various strata of the Silurian series· now little used Rarely *pl.*

Gribble (gri·b'l). 1838. [? cogn. w. GRUB *v.*] A small marine boring crustacean, *Limnoria terebrans,* resembling a wood-louse.

Grice (grəis). *Obs.* exc. *Sc.* and *arch.* ME. [a. ON. *gríss* young pig, pig.] A pig, *esp.* a young pig, a sucking pig; †*occas.* and *spec.* in *Her.*, a wild boar.

Prov. Bring the head of the sow to the tail of the *g.*: balance your loss with your gain.

Grice, obs. f. GRECE, steps.

Grid (grid). 1839. [f. GRIDIRON.] 1. A grating. 2. = GRIDIRON 1. 1875. 3. = GRIDIRON 3. *Naut.* 1867. 4. The wire spiral between the filament and the plate of a wireless valve 1922. 5. A network of lines on a map 1918. 6. A network of electric lines, etc. 1926.

Griddle (gri·d'l), *sb.* [ME. *gredil(e,* app. a. early OF. **gredil* = *greil* (mod. *gril*) or **gredille* (mod. *grille*); see GRILL *sb.*[1]] †1. = GRIDIRON 1. –1746. 2. = GIRDLE *sb.*[2] ME. 3. *Mining.* A wire-bottomed sieve 1776.

Comb.: **g.-bread, -cake,** bread or cake baked on a g.; †**-iron** = sense 2.

Griddle (gri·d'l), *v.* ME. [f. the sb.] 1. *trans.* To cook on a griddle. 2. *Mining.* To *g. out*: to screen ore with a griddle 1776.

Gride (grəid), *sb.* 1830. [f. GRIDE *v.*] A strident or grating sound.

Gride (grəid), *v.* Chiefly *poet.* ME. [metathetic f. GIRD *v.*[2], adopted by Spenser from Lydgate.] 1. *trans.* To pierce with a weapon; to wound; †also, to inflict (a wound) by piercing. Also *fig.* 2. *intr.* To pierce *through.* Now usually, To cut, scrape, or graze *along,* etc., with a strident, grating, or whizzing sound, or so as to cause rasping pain 1590. 3. *trans.* To clash or graze against with a strident sound; to cause to grate 1821.

2. Through his thigh the mortall steele did gryde SPENSER. 3. The wood which grides and clangs Its leafless ribs and iron horns Together TENNYSON.

Gridelin (gri·dĕlin). Also †**gridaline,** †**grizelin.** 1640. [ad. F. *gridelin, gris-de-lin* 'grey of flax', flax-grey.]

A. *sb.* The name of a colour, a pale purple or grey violet; occas., a pale red.

B. *adj.* Having this colour.

Gridiron (gri·dəiᵊɹn), *sb.* [ME. *gredire,* appearing in the same text with *gredile* GRIDDLE. The *-ire* was early identified with ME. *ire* = *iren* IRON. See also ANDIRON.] 1. A framework of parallel metal bars, used for broiling flesh or fish over a fire. †Also formerly, a griddle. b. A similar structure used in torture by fire. (The first sense in Eng.) ME. 2. *fig.* 1590. 3. Any object resembling or likened to a gridiron; esp. *Naut.* a heavy framework of beams in parallel open order used to support a ship in dock. (So F. *gril.*) 1846.

3. b. A football field (*U.S.*) 1896. *Comb.*: **g. pendulum,** a compensation pendulum composed of parallel rods of different metals; **g. valve,** a sliding valve in which the cover and seat are both composed of parallel bars with spaces between them.

Gri·diron, *v.* 1857. [f. the sb.] *trans.* To mark with parallel lines suggesting the form of a gridiron; said *esp.* of railways as they appear on a map.

Grieced (grīst), *a.* [f. *griece,* var of GRECE + -ED[2].] *Her.* = DEGRADED *a.*

Grief (grīf), *sb.* Pl. **griefs.** [ME. *gref, greve,* a. OF. *grief, gref,* vbl. sb. f. *grever* to GRIEVE.] †1. Hardship, suffering; a kind, or cause, of these –1722. †2. Hurt, harm, mischief inflicted or suffered; molestation, trouble, offence –1584. †b. A wrong or injury which is the subject of formal complaint or demand for redress. Also, a document stating the grievance. –1651. †3. Feeling of offence; displeasure, anger –1573. †4. A sore, wound; a blemish of the skin; a disease, sickness –1727. b. The seat of this –1624. †5. Physical pain or discomfort –1621. 6. Mental pain, distress, or sorrow. In mod. use: Deep or violent sorrow caused by loss or trouble; keen or bitter regret or remorse ME. b. A cause or subject of grief 1535.

6. Griefe of my Sonnes exile hath stopt her breath SHAKS. Their father died of g. for his eldest son 1883. b. The one g. of having no children RUSKIN.

Phr. *To come to g.*: to meet with disaster; (*Sporting*) to have a fall; to fail. So *to bring to g.* Chiefly *colloq.*

Comb. **g.-muscles,** Darwin's name for certain muscles concerned in the facial expression of g.

Hence **Grie·fful** *a.* painful, sorrowful; †grievous. **Grie·fless,** *a.* free from g. **Grie·flessness,** griefless condition.

Grieko, var. of GREGO.

†**Grie·vable,** *a.* ME. [a. OF. *grevable,* f. *grever* to GRIEVE.] Causing grief or pain –1500

Grievance (grī·văns). [ME. *grevance,* a. OF. *grevance, grievance,* f. *grever* to harm, GRIEVE; see -ANCE.] †1. The infliction of wrong or hardship on a person; injury, oppression; a cause or source of injury –1768. b. = GRIEF 2 b. †2. The state or fact of being oppressed, injured, or distressed; distress; suffering, pain –1592. 3. A circumstance or state of things felt to be oppressive. In mod. use, something (real or supposed) which is considered a legitimate ground of complaint. 1481. †4. A disease, ailment, hurt –1761. †5. Displeasure, indignation, offence –1523.

3. Irregular and grinding courts, the maine grievances MILT. The length of Chancery suits was a real public g. 1882. Hence †**Grie·vancer,** one who gives ground for complaint FULLER.

Grieve (grīv), *sb.* [OE. *grǣfa* = WS. *geréfa* (see REEVE).] 1. A governor of a province, town, etc. Now only *Hist.* = SHERIFF. 2. *Sc.* and *north.* The overseer, manager, or head-workman on a farm; a farm-bailiff 1480.

2. He has got a ploughman from Scotland who acts as g. SCOTT *Diary.* Hence **Grie·veship,** a district under charge of a g.

Grieve (grīv), *v.* [ME. *greve,* a. F. *grever* :—pop. L. **grevare* = cl. L. *gravare,* f. *gravis* heavy, GRAVE *a.*] †1. *trans.* To press heavily upon. Only in *pass.* ME. only. †2. To harass, trouble; to oppress –1651; to cause damage to –1574. †3. To hurt, injure –1810. †Also *absol.* †4. To affect with pain or disease –1592. 5. To affect with grief or deep sorrow. †Formerly, To cause pain, anxiety, or vexation to; to annoy. ME. †6. To make angry; to incense, offend –1535. 7. *intr.* To feel grief; to sorrow deeply. Const. *at, for, over,* or *to* with *inf.* ME. b. *trans.* To feel or show grief at or for; to regret deeply (*poet.*) 1598.

2. The whiche garyson hadde greuyd sore the towne of Cambray LD. BERNERS. 5. It greveth me to se hym in this case PALSGR. Griev'd at his heart, when looking down he saw The whole Earth fill'd with violence MILT. 6. How oft did they..grieue him in the desert *Ps.* lxxviii. 40. 7. Grieving, if aught inanimate e'er grieves, Over the unreturning brave BYRON. b. Sorrow doth utter what it still doth g. DRAYTON. Hence **Grie·vedly** *adv.* †**Grie·vement,** a hurt, injury.

Griever (grī·vəɹ). 1598. [See -ER[1].] †1. One who molests or troubles another –1660. 2. A person or thing that grieves or distresses 1641. 3. One who feels or shows grief 1819.

Grieving (grī·viŋ), *ppl. a.* 1450. [f. GRIEVE *v.* + -ING[2].] a. That causes grief, pain, or annoyance. b. That feels or expresses grief. Hence **Grie·vingly** *adv.*

Grievous (grī·vəs), *a.* [ME. *grevous,* a. OF. *grevos, -(o)us,* f. *grever* to GRIEVE.] †1. Burdensome, oppressive; in later use only of public grievances –1765. †b. Of penalties, etc.: Heavy, severe –1659. 2. Bringing serious trouble or discomfort; having injurious effects; †causing hurt or pain. (Now only with mixture of sense 5—'grievous to think of'.) ME. 3. Of a disease, wound, or pain: Acute, severe. Now *rare.* ME. 4. Of a fault, crime, etc.: Deserving heavy penalties. Later: Atrocious, flagrant, heinous. Now only *arch.* ME. 5. Causing mental pain or distress. Now less widely: Exciting grief or intense sorrow. ME. 6. Full of grief (*rare*) ME.

1. Thy father made our yoke grieuous 1 *Kings* xii. 4. 2. A g. delusion 1864. 4. A Haynous and Grevious Crime 1683. 5. The Loss [of Sight] must be very g. STEELE. 6. A deep g. expression of countenance HAWTHORNE. Hence **Grie·vous·ly** *adv.*, **-ness.**

Griff (grif), *sb.*[1] *Anglo-Ind.* 1829. [app. short f. GRIFFIN, q.v.] = GRIFFIN [2]. Hence **Griff** *v.* to take in (anyone).

Griff (grif), *sb.*[2] *rare.* 1820. [a. F. *griffe* (also used).] A claw.

Griff (grif), *sb.*[3] Also **Griffe, griffo(n,** etc. 1850. [?] The offspring of a mulatto and a negro, three parts black.

Griff (grif), *sb.*[4] 1860. [?] *Weaving.* A frame composed of horizontal bars employed in pattern-weaving. Also *g.-frame.*

Griffe, obs. f. GRAFF *sb.*[1], *sb.*[3], *v.*[1]

Griffin[1] (gri·fin), **griffon, gryphon** (gri·fən). ME. [a. OF. *grifoun* (mod. *griffon*), f. L. *gryphus* = *gryps* (gen. *gryphis*), a. Gr. γρύψ (gen. γρυπός). Now usually spelt *griffin* exc. in sense 2; *gryphon* is supposed to be dignified.] 1. A fabulous animal having the head and wings of an eagle and the body and hind quarters of a lion. (Believed by the Greeks to inhabit Scythia and to guard its gold.) b. A representation or figure of a griffin ME. 2. A vulture; now = griffon-vulture (see 3) ME. 3. *attrib.*, as **griffin's foot,** a surgical instrument, so called from its shape; **griffon-vulture,** a vulture of the genus *Gyps,* esp. *G. fulvus* 1641.

1. As when a Gryphon through the Wilderness.. Pursues the Arimaspian, who by stealth Had from his wakeful custody purloind The guarded Gold MILT. b. Grim stone griffins surmount the terrace-steps 1863.

Griffin [2] (gri·fin). *Anglo-Ind.* 1793. [?] A European newly arrived in India, and unaccustomed to Indian ways; a novice, newcomer, greenhorn. Hence **Gri·ffinage**, the state of being a g.; one's first year in India.

Griffin [3]. *U.S.* A mulatto: see GRIFF *sb.*[3]

Griffon (gri·fən). 1882. [a. F. *griffon* 'chien anglais'.] A species of coarse-haired dog, resembling a terrier.

Griffon-vulture: see GRIFFIN [1] 3.

Grig (grig), *sb.*[1] ME. [?] †1. A dwarf –1629. 2. A short-legged hen. *Obs.* exc. *dial.* 1589. 3. A species of eel; a small or young eel. Also *g.-eel.* 1611. 4. A *merry* (or †*mad*) *g.*: an extravagantly lively person. Also in phr. *as merry as a g.* [? from sense 3 or 2.] 1566. 5. *slang.* A farthing; *pl.* cash, 'dibs' 1656.

Grig (grig), *sb.*[2] *dial.* 1674. [a. W. *grug*, Cornish *grig.*] The common heath or heather, *Calluna vulgaris*; also, cross-leaved heath, *Erica Tetralix.*

†**Grill**, *sb.*[1] *rare.* 1597. [After Spenser's *Gryll*, which is ad. Gr. γρύλλος a pig.] Quasi-proper name for a low or lazy person –1644.

Grains are fitter for G., then Pearles QUARLES.

Grill (gril), *sb.*[2] 1766. [f. GRILL *v.*] 1. Meat, fish, etc. broiled on a gridiron. Also *fig.* 2. Short for *g.-room* 1896. 3. A spell of grilling 1842. 4. *attrib.*, as **grill-room**, a room in a restaurant, etc., in which grills are served 1883.

Grill (gril), *sb.*[3] 1685. [a. F. *gril*, perh. :—pop.L. **graticulum.*] A gridiron.

Grill, *sb.*[4]: see GRILLE *sb.*

†**Grill**, *a.* ME. [Cf. Du. *gril* (*grel*) angry, rough, etc., LG. *grel, grell.*] 1. Of persons: Fierce, harsh, cruel –1529. 2. Of things, etc.: Cruel, painful, bitter, severe, terrible –1570.

Grill (gril), *v.* 1668. [a. F. *griller*, f. *gril* (*grille*) GRILL *sb.*[3]] 1. *trans.* To broil on a gridiron or the like over or before a fire. b. To scallop (oysters or shrimps) 1727. c. *transf.* To torment with heat 1825. d. To subject to severe questioning (*U.S.*) 1928. 2. *intr.* To undergo broiling. Chiefly *fig.* 1842.

1. c. Oh, Barton man! but I am grilled here FITZ-GERALD. 2. The spleen which was..grilling within him 1883.

†**Grilla·de**, *sb.* 1656. [a. F.] 1. Something grilled, a broiled dish –1727. 2. *Cookery.* The browning of any dish with a hot iron. CHAMBERS. Hence †**Grilla·de** *v. trans.* to grill.

Grillage (gri·lėdʒ). 1776. [a. F., f. *grille* GRILLE *sb.*] *Engineering.* A heavy framework of cross-timbering, sometimes resting on piles, serving as a foundation on treacherous soil.

Grille, grill (gril), *sb.* 1661. [a. F. *grille*, OF. *greille*:—pop.L. **graticula*, cl. L. *craticula*, f. *cratis* a hurdle; cf. GRIDDLE.] 1. A grating; an arrangement of parallel or cross bars, or structure of open metal-work, used to close an opening or separate one part of a room, etc. from another 1686. †2. One of the bars in the visor of a helmet 1661. 3. *Tennis.* The square opening in the end wall on the hazard side of the court, adjacent to the main wall 1727. 4. *Pisciculture.* A wooden frame fitted with glass tubes, between which the fish-eggs lie during incubation 1883. 5. A rectangular pattern of small dots impressed on postage stamps 1898. Hence **Grille** *v.* to fit or impress with a g.

†**Gri·lly**, *v. rare.* [a. F. *griller.*] = GRILL *v.* BUTLER *Hud.*

Grilse (grils). ME. [?] The name given to a young salmon on its first return to the river from the sea and retained for the year.

Grim (grim). [OE. *grim*(*m*. The OTeut. root **grem-* is an ablaut-var. of **gram-*; see GRAME *a.*]

A. *adj.* 1. Of persons and animals: Fierce, cruel, savage, or harsh. Also, daring, determined, bold. (Now merged in sense 4.) 2. Of actions, character, feelings, etc. a. Fierce, furious, cruel. (*Obs.* or *arch.*) b. In mod. use: Stern, merciless; resolute, uncompromising. OE. 3. Of pain, wounds, conditions, etc.: Cruel, terribly severe OE. †b. Of weapons, etc.: Cruel, formidable –1485. 4. Of stern, forbidding, or harsh aspect. †Also, hard-featured, ugly. ME. 5. *transf.* Of things, scenes, etc.: Harsh or repellent of aspect; uninviting 1820. 6. Of laughter, jests, etc.: Stern, implying no softening. In recent use often: Dealing with ghastly or painful subjects. 1641.

1. The g. Woolf with privy paw MILT. 2. The ridges of g. Warr MILT. G. earnestness 1853. 3. Wind and weather wax'd so g. SCOTT. 4. The g. face of law DENHAM. Phr. *To hold on, cling*, etc. *like g. death.* A g. and crabbed look EVELYN. 6. One of those g. pleasantries in which Oliver took delight MILMAN.

B. *adv.* (OE. *grimme*) or quasi-*adv.* In a grim manner or mood; fiercely, savagely, horribly.

Thus chides she Death, Grim-grinning ghost SHAKS.

Grim (grim), *v.* ME. [In 1, ad. Du. *grimmen*, f. *grim*(*m* adj. GRIM. In 2, f. GRIM *a.*] †1. *intr.* To be angry, look fierce –1848. 2. *trans.* To make grim or fierce; to give a grim look to 1710.

2. The sculptured effigies That g. the silence of chivalric aisles GALT.

Grimace (grimē·s), *sb.* 1651. [a. F. *grimace*, of uncertain origin.] 1. A distortion of the countenance whether spontaneous or involuntary, expressive of some feeling or tending to excite laughter; a wry face. 2. An affected look or †gesture 1678. 3. *fig.* Affectation, pretence, sham. ? Now *rare.* 1655.

1. I tried to laugh, but could only make a g. W. IRVING. 2. Our conferences go no further than a Bow and a G. ADDISON. 3. All this my parade and g. of philosophy CIBBER. Hence **Grima·ce** *v. intr.* to distort the countenance; to make a wry face; †to put on an affected air. **Grima·ced** *ppl. a.* affected (*rare*). **Grima·cer.**

Grimalkin (grimæ·lkin, -mǭ·lkin). 1630. [prob. f. GREY *a.* + MALKIN.] A name given to a cat; hence, a cat, *esp.* an old she-cat; *contemptuously* applied to a jealous or imperious old woman.

Grime (grəim), *sb.* 1590. [= mod. Flemish *grijm*; cf. GRIME *v.*] Soot, smut, coal-dust, or other black particles, deposited upon or ingrained in some surface.

fig. The dirt and g. of human affairs DE FOE.

Grime (grəim), *v.* 1470. [Cf. mod. Flemish *grijmen*, Fris. *griemjen*, LG. *gremen* to blacken, dirty.] *trans.* To cover with grime, to blacken, befoul. Also *fig.*

Grimgribber (gri·mgri:bəɹ). 1786. In Steele the name of an imaginary estate, extemporized in a discussion between two sham counsel respecting a marriage settlement. Hence: Legal or other technical jargon, learned gibberish. Also *attrib.*

Griminess (grəi·minės). 1650. [f. GRIMY *a.* + -NESS.] The quality or state of being grimy.

Grimly (gri·mli), *a.* *Obs.* or *arch.* [OE. *grimlic*; see GRIM *a.* and -LY [1].] Grim-looking; grim in nature. Hence **Gri·mliness**, the state of being g.

Grimly (gri·mly), *adv.* [OE. *grimlīce*; see GRIM *a.* and -LY [2].] 1. In a grim fashion; fiercely, cruelly; also, in mod. use, austerely, rigidly. †2. Dreadfully –1470 3. With a grim look or air ME.

3. The Auguries..looke g. SHAKS.

Grimm(**e** (grim). 1834. [a. F. *grimme* (Buffon), ad. mod.L. (*Capra*) *grimmia*, the name given by Linnæus to a S. African antelope described by Herm. Nic. Grimm (1641–1711).] A West African antelope, the coquetoon.

Grimness (gri·mnės). OE. [f. GRIM *a.* + -NESS.] The quality or condition of being grim; fierceness; sternness; formidable aspect.

†**Gri·msir**(**e.** 1450. [f. GRIM *a.* + -SIR, SIRE.] An austere, stern, morose, or overbearing person –1621.

Grimy (grəi·mi), *a.* 1612. [f. GRIME *sb.* + -Y [1].] Covered with grime; begrimed, dirty. Also, swarthy.

Grin, *sb.*[1] [OE. *grin, gryn.*] 1. A snare for catching birds or animals, made of cord, etc., with a running noose. *Obs.* exc. *dial.* or *arch.* Also *fig.* †2. A noose; also, a halter –1591.

Grin (grin), *sb.*[2] 1635. [f. GRIN *v.*[2]] An act of grinning.

On the (*broad* or †*high*) *g.*: grinning (openly).

Grin, *v.*[1] *Obs.* exc. *dial.* OE. [f. GRIN *sb.*[1]] *trans.* To catch in a noose; to snare, ensnare; to choke, strangle.

Grin (grin), *v.*[2] [OE. *grennian* (:—OTeut. type **granjōjan*), cogn. w. OHG. *grennan* to mutter :—OTeut. **granjan*; possibly related to *granā* moustache.] 1. *intr.* Of persons and animals: To draw back the lips and show the teeth: a. generally, or as an indication of pain or †anger; b. by way of a forced or unnatural smile, or of a broad smile 1480. 2. a. *trans.* To express by grinning 1681. b. *intr.* Of a feeling: To find expression by grinning. FIELDING.

1. a. As the wolfe doth g. before he barketh SHAKS. b. They often grinned and capered with heavy hearts W. IRVING. 2. a. The surgeon grinned approbation SMOLLETT.

Phr. *To g. and bear it*: to submit with no other sign of impatience than a grin. *To g. like a Cheshire cat* (see CAT *sb.*[1]).

Grind (grəind), *sb.* ME. [f. GRIND *v.*[1]] 1. The action of grinding (*lit.* and *fig.*). 2. *colloq.* Steady hard work; *esp.* close and hard study; a dull and laborious task 1851. 3. *Univ. slang.* a. A steeplechase; also, a 'constitutional' 1857. b. *U.S.* A hard student 1896.

Grind (grəind), *v.* Pa. t. and pple. **ground.** [OE. *grindan*, f. pre-Teut. root **ghrendh-*, perh. represented in L. *frendere* to gnash the teeth, to bruise, pound.] 1. *trans.* To reduce to small particles or powder by crushing between two hard surfaces; *esp.* to make (grain) into meal or flour in a mill. b. Denoting the action of teeth; = to masticate ME. c. *transf.* and *fig.* 1535. d. *intr.* To admit of being ground (fine, etc.). 2. *fig.* To crush, to oppress; to harass with exactions 1626. 3. *fig.* To torment. Also *absol.* Now only *U.S.* to annoy, vex. ME. 4. To produce by grinding ME. 5. To wear down by friction so as to make sharp or smooth (a tool, a weapon, glass, etc.) ME. 6. *intr.* or *absol.* To perform the operation of grinding OE. 7. a. *intr.* To work as if grinding with a hand-mill 1840. b. quasi-*trans.* To produce (music) on a barrel-organ, etc. 1784. 8. *intr.* To work laboriously and steadily; *esp.* to study hard. Const. *at.* Also with *away, on.* 1855. b. *trans.* To teach (a subject) in a steady laborious manner; also, to prepare (a pupil) in a subject 1815. 9. *intr.* To scrape or rub *on* or *against* something; to make a grating noise OE. b. *trans.* To rub gratingly *against* or *upon*; to force *into* by grinding; also quasi-*trans.* to make (one's way) by grinding 1644. 10. †a. *intr.* To gnash *with the teeth.* Const. *at.* –1581. b. *trans.* To rub the teeth together with a grating sound. Const. *at.* ME.

1. Any corne or meale, ground or to be grynded 1568. b. *Ant. & Cl.* III. v. 16. c. He grinds divinity of other days Down into modern use COWPER. 2. Laws g. the poor, and rich men rule the law GOLDSM. Phr. *To g. the faces* (or *face*) *of* (a Hebraism). 5. The bristled Boar..New grinds his arming Tusks DRYDEN. 6. Though the mills of God g. slowly, yet they g. exceeding small LONGF. 8. So..Ground he at grammar BROWNING. 9. The villainous centre-bits G. on the wakeful ear TENNYSON.

Grinded (grəi·ndėd), *ppl. a.* 1613. [f. GRIND *v.* + -ED [1].] = GROUND *ppl. a.*

Grinder (grəi·ndəɹ). ME. [f. GRIND *v.* + -ER [1].]

I. 1. That which grinds; e.g. a molar tooth; hence *joc.* in *pl.*, the teeth generally. 2. The upper millstone or runner; †a muller or pestle 1688.

II. 1. A person who grinds 1483. 2. A crammer 1813. 3. One who sweats workmen 1851. 4. A bird that makes a grinding noise: a. The flycatcher (*Sisura inquieta*) of Australia 1848. b. The night-jar or goat-sucker.

Comb. **grinder's asthma, phthisis, rot** (*Path.*), 'a lung disease produced by the mechanical irritation of the particles of steel and stone given off in the operation of grinding' (Webster).

Grindery (grəi·ndəri). 1805. [f. GRIND *v.* + -ERY.] 1. Materials, tools, etc. used by shoemakers and other workers in leather. (Orig. applied only to the whetstone.) Also *attrib.* 2. A place for grinding tools, weapons, etc. 1884.

Grinding (grəi·ndiŋ), *vbl. sb.* ME. [f. GRIND *v.* + -ING [1].] 1. The action of GRIND *v.* 2. *attrib.* a. Adapted for, or connected with, grinding, as *g.-clamp, -machine*, etc. b.

Suitable for being ground, as *g.-barley*, etc. *Comb.* **g.-wheel**, (*a*) a wheel for grinding or polishing; (*b*) a building fitted up with water or steam power for grinding cutlery or tools.

Gri·nding, *ppl. a.* OE. [f. GRIND *v.*[1] + -ING [2].] That grinds. Hence **Gri·ndingly** *adv.* in a g. manner.

Grindle (gri·nd'l). *U.S.* 1884. [a. G. *gründel*, f. *grund* GROUND, bottom.] The mud-fish, called also 'John A. Grindle', or lawyer.

Grindle stone. *Obs.* exc. *dial.* ME. [prob. repr. OE. **grindelstán*, f. **grindel* (instrumental n., f. *grindan* to grind) + *stán* STONE.] A grindstone; = †also, a piece, or kind, of stone suitable for making grindstones.

Grindstone (grəi·ndstōun). ME. [f. GRIND *v.* + STONE.] **1.** A millstone. *Obs.* exc. in *nonce-use*. **2.** A disk of stone revolving on an axle, and used for grinding, sharpening, and polishing ME. **3.** A kind of stone suitable for making grindstones. Also *g. grit*. 1703.

2. Phr. *To hold* (*keep, bring, put*) *one's nose to the g.*: to grind down or oppress; also, in mod. use, to keep continually engaged in hard and monotonous labour.

‖**Gringo** (gri·ŋgo). 1884. [Mexican Sp.] Among Spanish Americans, a contemptuous name for an Englishman or an Anglo-American.

Grinner (gri·nəɹ). 1440. [f. GRIN *v.*[2] + -ER [1].] One who grins.

Grinning (gri·niŋ), *ppl. a.* ME. [f. as prec. + -ING [2].] That grins. Hence **Gri·nningly** *adv.* in a g. manner.

†**Grint,** *v.* ME. [app. onomatopœic, after GRIND, GRUNT, etc.] *intr.* To grind or gnash the teeth. Said also of the teeth –1491.

He grynte with his teeth, so was he wrooth CHAUCER.

Grip (grip), *sb.*[1] [Two formations: (1) OE. *gripe* grasp, clutch, corresp. to OHG. *griff*; (2) OE. *gripa* handful; both f. root of GRIPE.] **1.** Firm hold or grasp; the action of gripping, grasping, or clutching; also, grasping power. **b.** Sometimes used with reference to the mode of grasping the hand by which members of a secret society, e.g. Freemasons, recognize one another 1785. **2.** *fig.* Firm or tenacious hold, grasp, or control; power, mastery (esp. now assoc. with the idea of irresistible force) 1450. **b.** Power to apprehend or master a subject 1861. **3.** A seizure or twinge of pain; a spasm ME. **4.** A handful OE. **5.** Something which grips or clips 1800. **6.** That which is gripped or clasped; e.g. the handle of a sword, a golf-club, etc. 1867. **7.** *U.S.* = GRIPSACK 1883.

1. The horrors of the bear's g. 1885. **b.** Masons' mystic word and g. BURNS. Phr. *At grips*: in close combat. **2.** The g. of poverty 1894, of malarial fever 1897. **b.** A g. of the essential facts 1894. **4.** Phr. *To lie in g.*: (of corn) to lie as left by the reapers (*dial.*). *Comb.*: **g.-brake**, a brake worked by gripping with the hand; **-car** (*U.S.*), a tramcar worked on an endless cable to which the car is attached by a g. (sense 5), a cable-car; **-man**, the man who manipulates the g. of a cable-car.

Grip (grip), *sb.*[2] Now only *Hunting* or *dial.* [ME. *grip*, OE. *gryp-e* (or *-a*), cogn. w. *greóp* burrow.] **1.** A small open furrow or ditch; a trench, drain. **2.** The gutter in a cowhouse 1825.

Grip (grip), *v.*[1] OE. [ONorthumb. *grippa* :—WGer. type **grippjan*, f. **gripi-z* GRIP *sb.*[1]] **1.** *trans.* To grasp or seize firmly or tightly with the hand; to seize with the mouth, claw, beak, etc. Also *transf.* of a disease. **2.** *absol.* and *intr.* To take firm hold; to get a grip (*lit.* and *fig.*) ME. **3.** *trans.* To join firmly *to* something, as with a grip, etc. 1886. **4.** *fig.* To take hold upon (the mind, the emotions) 1891.

1. The gout.. grips him by both legs DICKENS. **2.** *Grip*..to hold, as 'the anchor grips' SMYTH.

Grip (grip), *v.*[2] Now *dial.* 1597. [f. GRIP *sb.*[2]] *trans.* To make grips in; to ditch, trench.

Gripe (grəip), *sb.*[1] ME. [f. GRIPE *v.*[1]] **1.** The action of griping, clutching, or seizing tenaciously, *esp.* with the hands, arms, claws, and the like. **b.** *fig.* Grasp, hold, control, grip ME. **c.** *Surg.* An act of compressing (e.g. an artery) with the fingers 1676. **2.** *transf.* and *fig.* **a.** The clutch or pinch of something painful. Formerly often in *pl.*: Spasms, pangs. ?*Obs.* 1547. **b.** An intermittent spasmodic pain in the bowels. Usu. *pl.*, colic pains. 1601. †**3.** The hand held in the position for grasping or clutching –1791. **4.** A handful 1570. **5.** = GRIP *sb.*[1] 6. 1610. †**6.** *slang.* A covetous person, a usurer. Also *Gripes* (as quasi-proper name). –1700. **7.** Something which gripes or clutches; *esp.* a BRAKE 1578. **8.** *Naut. pl.* Lashings formed by an assemblage of ropes, etc., to secure a boat in its place on the deck; also, two broad bands passed respectively round the stem and stern of a boat hung in davits, to prevent swinging 1762. **9.** *attrib.* as *g. mixture* 1891.

1. All the Locks and Gripes of Wrestling MILT. **b.** I take my cause Out of the gripes of cruell men SHAKS. **2. a.** Heart-strook with chilling g. of sorrow MILT.

Gripe (grəip), *sb.*[2] 1674. Dial. var. of GRIP *sb.*[2]

†**Gripe,** *sb.*[3] ME. [ad. L. *grypem*, *gryphem*, *gryps* GRIFFIN, in med.L. also 'vulture'.] **1.** A griffin –1592. **2.** A vulture –1767.

2. Like a white hind under the gripe's sharp claws SHAKS. *Comb.* **g.-shell** = GRIPE'S-EGG.

†**Gripe,** *sb.*[4] Also †**grype.** 1506. [ad. obs. F. *grip* a pirate ship (Diez).] A vessel used in the Levant –1599.

Gripe (grəip), *sb.*[5] 1580. [Orig. *greepe*, ad. Du. *greep*, but later assim. to GRIPE *sb.*[1]] *Naut.* The piece of timber terminating the keel at the forward extremity; occas. taken as = FOREFOOT 2.

Gripe (grəip), *v.*[1] [Com. Teut.: OE. *grípan* :—pre-Teut. **ghreib-*: *ghroib-* (see GROPE *v.*).] †**1.** *intr.* To make a grasp or clutch, to seek to get a hold (*lit.* and *fig.*) –1820. **2.** *trans.* To lay hold of, seize; to get into one's power or possession. *Obs.* exc. *arch.* OE. **3.** To grip ME. †**b.** To encircle tightly –1758. **c.** *absol.* 1597. †**4.** To clench (the fist, etc.) (*rare*) –1728. †**5.** *fig.* To apprehend; to comprehend (*rare*) –1742. **6.** To pinch, squeeze. (Said also of poverty.) 1645. **7.** To grieve, afflict, distress. Now *rare*. 1559. **8.** To affect with gripes. Now chiefly in pa. pple. 1611. **b.** *absol.* To produce pain in the bowels as if by constriction or contraction; to cause gripes 1702. **9.** *Naut.* **a.** *trans.* To secure (a boat) with gripes. (In *pa. pple.* only.) 1840. **b.** *intr.* Said of a ship which has a tendency to come up into the wind in spite of the helm 1627.

1. Upon whose heart may all the Furies g. MARLOWE. **2.** Woldest thou g. both gaine and pleasure 1551. **3.** Let each..g. fast his orbed Shield MILT. **6.** For this, he grip'd the Poor, and Alms denied SAVAGE. **7.** How inly Sorrow gripes his Soule SHAKS. *Comb.*: **g.-all**, a grasping, avaricious person; †**-money**, **-penny**, a miser, niggard. Hence **Gri·ping-ly** *adv.*, **-ness.**

Gripe, *v.*[2] 1597. Dial. var. of GRIP *v.*[2]

Gripeful (grəi·pful), *sb.* *rare.* 1727. [f. GRIPE *sb.*[1] + -FUL.] As much as can be grasped in the hand.

Gripeful (grəi·pfŭl), *a.* *rare.* 1864. [f. GRIPE *v.*[1] + -FUL.] Apt to gripe; gripy.

Griper (grəi·pəɹ). 1573. [f. GRIPE *v.*[1] + -ER [1].] One who, or that which, gripes; an extortioner (now *rare*); †an instrument of torture.

Gripe's egg. ME. [GRIPE *sb.*[3]] A large egg supposed to be that of a gripe; a vessel shaped like this; an oval-shaped cup.

†**Griph.** 1652. [ad. L. *griphus* (also used), a. Gr. γρῖφος creel; an enigma.] A puzzling question; a riddle, enigma –1796.

‖**Grippe** (grip). Also (anglicized) **grip.** 1776. [Fr., vbl. sb. f. *gripper* to seize.] = INFLUENZA.

Grippe, obs. f. GRIP.

Gripper (gri·pəɹ). 1570. [f. GRIP *v.*[1] + -ER [1].] †**1.** = GRIPER 1. **2.** *spec.* **a.** 'In Ireland, a sheriff's officer; a bailiff' (Cassell) 1884. **b.** *Austral. slang.* One who catches sheep for the shearers 1886. **3.** Any contrivance for gripping, clutching, or grasping tightly 1857. **4.** *attrib.*, as *g. mechanism* 1871.

†**Gri·pple,** *sb.* *rare.* 1530. [f. root of GRIP, GRIPE; cf. GRAPPLE.] **1.** A hook to seize things with. **2.** Grasp. SPENSER.

Gri·pple, *a.* Now only *dial.* or *arch.* [OE. *gripul*, f. *grip-*, wk. root of *grípan* GRIPE *v.*[1]] **1.** Griping, niggardly, usurious. **2.** Gripping; tenacious 1513.

1. While g. owners still refuse To others what they cannot use SCOTT.

†**Gri·pple,** *v.* 1591. Altered f. GRAPPLE *v.* –1630.

Gripsack (gri·pˌsæk). *U.S. colloq.* 1883. [f. GRIP *v.*[1] + SACK.] A traveller's handbag.

†**Gris,** *sb.* ME. [a. OF. *gris* adj. used subst. (see next).] A kind of grey fur –1575.

†**Gris,** *a.* *rare.* ME. [a. F. *gris*, a. OHG. *gris* (mod. *greis*), of unkn. origin.] Grey –1513.

Grisaille (grizē¹·l, as F. grizay). 1848. [a. F., f. *gris* grey (see prec.).] *Painting.* Decorative painting in grey monotone to represent objects in relief. **b.** *attrib.* or *adj.* Executed in grisaille 1860.

Gris-amber: see AMBERGRIS.

Grisard (gri·săɹd). *rare.* 1607. [ad. F. *grisard*, f. *gris*; see -ARD.]

†**A.** *adj.* Greyish. TOPSELL.

B. *sb.* A grey-haired man. BROWNING.

Grise, var. of GRIS *Obs.*; obs. f. GRECE.

Griseous (gri·zīəs), *a.* 1819. [f. med.L. *griseus* + -OUS.] Grey; *spec.* in *Zool.* and *Bot.*, bluish grey, pearl-grey.

‖**Grisette** (grize·t). 1700. [a. F., f. *gris* grey; see -ETTE.] **1.** A cheap grey dress fabric, formerly worn by working girls in France. **2.** A French girl or young woman of the working class, e.g. a shop assistant or a seamstress 1723. **3.** A noctuid moth, *Acronycta strigosa* 1869.

Griskin (gri·skin). 1700. [? f. *gris*, GRICE a pig + -KIN.] The lean part of the loin of a bacon pig.

Grisled, var. of GRIZZLED *a.*

Grisly (gri·zli), *a.* Now *arch.* or *literary.* [Late OE. *grislic*; ult. f. root *gris-* + *-lic*, -LY [1]; of unkn. history.] **1.** Causing horror, terror, or extreme fear; horrible to behold or hear. Now: Causing uncanny or unpleasant feelings; grim, ghastly. **2.** Ugly (*dial.*) 1674. †**3.** Inspired by fear –1698.

1. A man of grislie and sterne grauitie 1551. Grieslie ghostes, night SPENSER. G. Grones SIDNEY, oaths SCOTT. **3.** G. drede CHAUCER. Hence **Gri·sliness**, g. quality or condition. **Gri·sly** *adv.* (*Obs.* exc. *arch.*)

Grisly, obs. f. GRIZZLY *a.* and *sb.*[1]

Grison (gri·zən), *sb.* 1796. [a. F.; app. the same word as next. (Both animals are grey.)] **1.** A carnivorous quadruped of S. America, of the family *Mustelidæ*, allied to the glutton and marten. **2.** A S. American monkey (*Lagothrix canus*), said to be a remarkable glutton 1840.

†**Grison,** *a.* 1438. [a. F., f. *gris* grey.] Grey.

Grist (grist), *sb.*[1] [OE. *grist* :—OTeut. type **grinstu-*, f. *grind-* GRIND *v.*] †**1.** The action or an act of grinding –1676. **2.** Corn to be ground; also (with *pl.*) a batch of this ME. Also *fig.* **b.** *U.S.* A lot, number, quantity (*of*) 1840. **3.** Corn that has been ground 1566. **4.** Malt crushed or ground for brewing 1822. **5.** *attrib.*, as *g.-cart* 1602.

1. Phr. *To bring g. to the* (*one's*) *mill*: to bring one business or advantage. *All is g. that comes to his mill*: he turns everything to account. **b.** There's an onaccountable g. on 'em [bees] J. F. COOPER. *Comb.* **g.-mill**, a mill for grinding corn.

Grist (grist), *sb.*[2] 1733. [? conn. w. GIRD *v.*[1]] The size or thickness of yarn or rope.

Common g. is a rope 3 inches in circumference, with twenty yarns in each of the three strands KNIGHT.

Grist, *v.* 1825. [f. GRIST *sb.*[1]] *trans.* To grind (corn). Hence **Gri·sting** *vbl. sb.* the action of grinding corn, or its result.

Gristle (gri·s'l), *sb.* [OE. *gristle*; cogn. w. OE. *grost* gristle. Of obscure etym.] **1.** = CARTILAGE 1. Also *fig.* and †*transf.* †**2.** *fig.* A tender or delicate person –1652. **3.** *attrib.* ME.

1. *fig. In the g.*: in an initiatory, or unformed stage of existence. BURKE.

Gristly (gri·sli), *a.* ME. [f. GRISTLE *sb.* + -Y [1].] **1.** Pertaining to, or of the nature of gristle; consisting or full of gristle; cartilaginous. **2.** Having a texture resembling that of gristle, in toughness, etc. 1601.

Grit (grit), *sb.*[1] [OE. *gréot* :—OTeut. **greuto*m; perh. assim. to GRIT *sb.*[2], q. v.] **1.**

collect. sing. Formerly: Sand, gravel. Now: Minute particles of stone or sand, as produced by attrition or disintegration. **b.** A particle of sand (*rare*) 1601. **2.** Coarse sandstone, esp. of the kinds used for millstones and grindstones; gritstone ME. **3.** Earth, soil, mould; †the ground. *Obs.* exc. *dial.* ME. **4.** The grain or texture of a stone 1529. **5.** *colloq.*; orig. *U.S. slang.* Firmness or solidity of character; indomitable pluck or spirit; stamina 1825. **b.** In Canadian politics, a Radical or Liberal. Formerly *clear g.* 1884.

4. These stonis at Stonehenge be all of one gryt, without chaunge of colour, or vayne 1529. 5. If you were a chip of the old block you would be just what he called 'the grit' (= the right sort) THACKERAY.

Comb.: g.-**berry**, the genus *Comarostaphylis*; -**board**, the earth-board of a plough; -**emery**, coarse emery; -**rock** = GRITSTONE.

Grit (grit), *sb.*[2] Now only *pl.* and *dial.* [OE. *grytt(e*, usu. in pl. *grytta(n*, f. (ult.) Teut. root **greut-*, *graut-*, *grūt-*, whence also GROATS, and GRIT *sb.*[1]] †**1.** Bran, chaff, mill-dust -ME. **2.** Oats husked but not ground (or only coarsely); coarse oatmeal 1579.

Grit (grit), *v.* 1762. [f. GRIT *sb.*[1]] **1.** *intr.* To produce a grating sound, as of the crushing of grit; to move with such a sound. **2.** *trans.* To cover with grit or sand 1842. **3.** To grind or grate (the teeth) 1848.

1. The sanded floor that grits beneath the tread GOLDSM.

Grith (griþ). Now *Hist.* [OE. *gri*, a. ON. *grið* neut., orig. domicile, home; in pl., truce, peace, pardon.] †**1.** Protection, defence; safe conduct -1650. **2.** *spec.* in *OE. Law.* Security, peace, or protection guaranteed under limitations OE. **3.** *concr.* A sanctuary, asylum ME. †**4.** Peace -1460. †**5.** Quarter (in battle) -1475. **6.** *attrib.* ME.

2. *Church-g.* (OE. *ciric-grið*), security within the precincts of a church. To ask the privilege of g. and sanctuary SCOTT. Hence **Grithbreach**, breach of the peace, or its penalty.

Gritstone (gri·stōun). 1555. [f. GRIT *sb.*[1] + STONE *sb.*] = GRIT *sb.*[1] 2.

Gritty (gri·ti), *a.* 1598. [f. GRIT *sb.*[1] + -Y.] **1.** Of the nature of or resembling grit; containing, consisting of, or full of grit; sandy. **2.** Full of or containing minute hard particles; also *fig.* of literary style, with allusion to the quality of gritty bread 1882. **3.** *U.S. colloq.* Having grit (see GRIT *sb.*[1] 5) 1847.

Grivet (gri·vėt). 1859. [Of unkn. origin.] A small greenish-grey monkey of north-east Africa (*Circopithecus griseiviridis*); the tota.

Grise, rare obs. form of GRECE, stairs.

Grizel (gri·zĕl). 1565. Later form of *Grisilde* (= *Griseldis*, *Griselda*) in Chaucer's *Clerk's Tale*, the proverbial type of a meek, patient wife.

For patience shee will proue a second Grissell *Tam. Shr.* II. i. 297.

Grizelin, obs. f. GRIDELIN.

Grizzle (gri·z'l). [ME. *grisel*, a. OF. *grisel*, f. *gris*; see GRIS *a.*]

A. *adj.* Of grey colour, grey, grizzled. †Of a horse: Roan.

B. *sb.* †**1.** A grey-haired old man. ME. only. **2.** A grey horse or other animal 1620. **3.** Grey hair; a sprinkling of grey hair 1601; a grey wig 1755. **4.** Grey colour; the colour grey; †light roan 1611. **5.** A second-class stock brick, so called from its colour 1843.

3. O thou dissembling Cub: what wilt thou be When time hath sow'd a g. on thy case SHAKS.

Grizzle (gri·z'l), *v.* 1740. [f. GRIZZLE *a.*] **1.** *trans.* To render grey or grey-haired. **2.** *intr.* To become grey, etc. 1875.

Grizzled (gri·z'ld), *a.* 1458. [f. GRIZZLE *a.* + -ED[2].] **1.** Grey, grizzly; roan-coloured (*dial.*). **2.** Having grey hair 1606.

2. To the Boy Cæsar send this grizled head SHAKS.

Grizzly (gri·zli), *a.* and *sb.*[1] 1594. [f. GRIZZLE *a.* + -Y.]

A. *adj.* Grey; greyish; grey-haired; grizzled. Old Squirrels, that turne Grisly BACON. **Grizzly bear**: a large and ferocious bear, *Ursus horribilis*, peculiar to the mountainous districts of western North America 1791.

B. *sb.* The grizzly bear 1808.

Grizzly (gri·zli), *sb.*[2] 1877. *Mining. U.S.* A grating of parallel iron bars with interstices between to allow the finer material to fall into the sluices below while the larger stones are screened off.

Grizzly, var. of GRISLY *a.*

Groan (grōun), *sb.* ME. [f. GROAN *v.*] An act of groaning; a low vocal murmur emitted involuntarily in pain or great distress; *occas.*, an expression of strong disapprobation. **b.** attributed to inanimate things 1605.

b. Such groanes of roaring Winde *Lear* III. ii. 47.

Groan (grōun), *v.* [OE. *grānian*, f. (ult.) Teut. root **grai-*, *grī-*, whence OHG. *grīnan* to distort the countenance, etc.] **1.** *intr.* To breathe with a deep-toned murmur; to utter a low deep sound expressive of grief or pain. Also quasi-*trans.* Also *fig.* 1642. **b.** attributed to inanimate things 1602. †**2.** *spec.* Of the buck: To utter its cry at rutting-time -1686. **3.** *trans.* To utter with groans 1606; †to bewail (*rare*) -1766. **4.** *intr.* To be oppressed to the point of groaning. Const. *beneath*, *under*, *with*. 1613. Also *fig.* and *transf.* 1513. **5.** To express earnest longing by groans; to yearn, as if with groans; hence *fig.* of things. Const. *for*, *to* with inf. 1560. **6.** *trans.* To express disapproval by means of groans 1799.

1. *fig.* Beshrew that heart that makes my heart to groane SHAKS. quasi-*trans.* He fell, and deadly pale, Groand out his Soul MILT. 3. 'No trifle', groan'd the husband TENNYSON. 4. Modest merit..Is left in poverty to g. CHURCHILL. The press groans with productions JEFFERSON. The door upon its hinges groans KEATS. 5. *Jul. C.* III. i. 275. Hence **Groa·ner**, one who groans; also *slang*, a thief who attends funerals, etc. **Groa·ningly**, in a groaning manner.

Groanful (grōu·nfŭl), *a. rare.* 1590. [f. GROAN *sb.* + -FUL.] Full of groans or groaning; lugubrious.

Groat (grōut, grǫt). [ME. *groot*, a. MDu. *groot*, prop. an ellipt. use of the adj. = *great* (in the sense 'thick'). The pronunc. (grǫt) is now old-fashioned.] **1.** *Hist.* A denomination of coin (med.L. *grossus*, F. *gros*, It. *grosso*, MDu. *groot*), recognized from the 13th c. in various countries of Europe. Its standard was theoretically one-eighth of an ounce of silver. **2.** The English groat coined in 1351-2 was made equal to four pence. The groat ceased to be issued for circulation in 1662. **3.** *attrib.*, as **g.-silver**, a customary gratuity of a g. ME.

1. A Pin a Day, says our frugal Proverb, is a G. a Year ADDISON. I do not care a g. what it is CHESTERF. *A cracked* or *slit g.*: a type of something worthless.

Groats (grōuts, grǫts), *sb. pl.* [OE. **grotan* wk. pl., cogn. w. *grot* neut., fragment, particle, and with GRIT *sb.*[2], q. v.] **1.** Hulled, or hulled and crushed grain, chiefly oats, but also wheat, barley, and †maize. *Embden groats*: crushed barley or oats. †**2.** Naked oats -1725. *Comb.* †**g.-sugar**, coarse sugar.

†**Groa·tsworth.** 1562. [f. *groat's*, genitive of GROAT *sb.* + WORTH.] As much as a groat will buy; *fig.* a small amount -1678.

Grobian (grōu·biăn). 1609. [a. Ger., ad. med.L. *Grobianus*, name for a typical boor, f. G. *grob* coarse, rude; see GRUFF.] A clownish slovenly person. Also as *adj.*

Grobians and sluts, if once they be in loue, they will be most neat and spruce BURTON.

Grocer (grōu·səɹ). [ME. *grosser*, ad. OF. *grossier*:—med.L. *grossarius*, f. *grossus* GROSS.] †**1.** One who buys and sells in the gross, a wholesale dealer or merchant. (The company of Grocers consisted of wholesale dealers in spices and foreign produce; hence prob. sense 2.) 1689. **2.** A trader who deals in spices, dried fruits, sugar, etc. 1465.

2. What should an Irenmonger meddle with Grocer's ware BARCLAY. *Grocer's itch*, eczema caused by handling sugar.

Grocery (grōu·səri). ME. [f. prec. + -Y.] **1.** *collect. sing.* The goods sold by a grocer; *pl.* various sorts of such goods. **2.** The trade of a grocer 1689. **3.** *U.S.* A grocer's shop 1828; a dram-shop 1846. **4.** *attrib.*, as *g.-warehouse* 1554.

1. A deal box..to bring home groceries in GOLDSM. A parcel of g. 1865. *Comb.* **g.-captain**, the captain of an East Indiaman.

Grog (grǫg), *sb.* 1770. [Said to be short for GROGRAM; applied first as a nickname to Admiral Vernon, who wore a grogram cloak, and afterwards to the mixture which he ordered to be served out instead of neat spirit.] A drink consisting of spirits (orig. rum) and water. *Seven-water g.*, a sailor's term for very weak grog.

Comb.: g.-**blossom**, a redness or pimple on the nose caused by excessive drinking; -**shop**, a dram-shop; also (*pugilistic slang*) the mouth.

Grog (grǫg), *v.* 1833. [f. the sb.] **1.** *intr.* To drink grog. **2.** *trans.* To extract spirit from (an empty cask) by pouring hot water into it, and letting it stand 1878.

Groggery (grǫ·gəri). *U.S.* 1855. [f. GROG *sb.* + -ERY.] A grog-shop.

Groggy (grǫ·gi), *a.* 1770. [f. GROG *sb.* + -Y[1].] **1.** Intoxicated; also, bibulous. **2.** *Farriery.* Of a horse: Having a weakness in the forelegs, which causes a hobbling or tottering movement 1828. **3.** *slang.* Weakened in a fight, so as to stagger; hence *gen.* shaky 1832. Hence **Gro·gginess**, g. condition or state.

Grogram (grǫ·grăm). 1562. [Earlier *grogran(e*, ad. F. *gros grain* large or coarse grain.] **1.** A coarse fabric of silk, of mohair and wool, or of these mixed with silk; often stiffened with gum. **2.** A garment made of grogram 1633. **3.** *attrib.*, as *g.-cloak*, etc. 1582.

Groin (groin), *sb.*[1] *Obs.* exc. *dial.* ME. [ad. OF. *groign* (mod. *groin*):—pop. L. **grunnium* f. L. *grunnire* to grunt like a swine.] †**1.** A grunting, grumble. CHAUCER. **2.** The snout, *esp.* of a swine ME. †**3.** *Naut. The groin* (*of Spain*) [an etymological perversion of Sp. *Coruña*]: a sailor's name for Corunna -1719.

Groin (groin), *sb.*[2] ME. [orig. *grynde*, *grinde*, of uncertain origin. Not conn. w. GRAIN *sb.*[2]] **1.** The fold or depression on either side of the body between the abdomen and the upper thigh. †*fig.* The seat of lust. B. JONS. †**2.** A deep trench -1587. **3.** *Arch.* The edge formed by the intersection of two vaults. Also, the rib or fillet of stone or wood with which this is usually covered. 1725.

1. *fig.* To see The fury of mens gullets, and their groines B. JONS.

†**Groin**, *v.*[1] ME. [ad. OF. *grognir* (also *grogner*):—L. *grunnire.*] **1.** *intr.* Of animals: To grunt; to growl -1596; *esp.* of the buck: To utter its cry at rutting-time (cf. GROAN *v.*) -1711. **2.** *transf.* Of persons: To grumble, murmur -1583.

Groin (groin), *v.*[2] 1805. [f. GROIN *sb.*[2]] *Arch.* **1.** To form into or furnish with groins; to build with groins 1812. **2.** *intr.* Of an arch, etc.: To spring as a groin.

Groin: see GROYNE *sb.* and *v.*

Groined (groind), *ppl. a.* 1789. [f. GROIN *sb.*[2] and *v.*[2] + -ED.] Built or furnished with groins.

Grom(m)et, -it: see GRUMMET.

Gromil, -ill, -ille, obs. ff. GROMWELL.

Gromwell (grǫ·mwĕl). [ME. *gromylle*, *-ille*, a. OF. *gromil*, *gremil* (mod. *grémil*), of doubtful origin. Affected by *speedwell.*] Any of the plants of the genus *Lithospermum* (N.O. *Boraginaceæ*), characterized by hard stony seeds; formerly used in the cure of gravel. Also *attrib.*

Grond, obs. pa. t. of GRIND *v.*[1]

Gront(e: see GRUNT.

Groof, grufe (grūf), *adv.* ME. [a. ON. *grúfa*, in phr. *á grúfu* face downwards.] On the face, on the belly; prone -1567.

She on here armes two Fil gruf, and gan to wepe CHAUCER.

Groo-groo, gru-gru (grū·grū). 1796. [? Native name.] **1.** In the W. Indies and S. America, a name for two species of palm, *Astrocaryum aculeatum* and *Acrocomia sclerocarpa*. **2.** Usu. *groo-groo worm*: The grub of the coleopterous insect *Calandra palmarum* 1796.

Groom (grūm), *sb.* ME. [Of unkn. etym. 'Boy, male child' seems to be the orig. sense.] †**1.** A man-child, boy -1675. **2.** A man, male person. Sometimes *contemptuous* = 'fellow'. *Obs.* exc. *arch.* ME. **3.** A man-servant; a male attendant. *Obs.* exc. *arch.* ME. **4.** The specific designation of several officers of the English Royal Household, chiefly in the Lord Chamberlain's department; as *Groom of the Chamber, of the Stole, in waiting*, etc. 1464. 5. A servant who attends to horses. (Orig. a contextual use of 3; now the current sense.) 1667. 6. Short for BRIDEGROOM. (Usu. in context with *bride*.) 1604. 7. *attrib.* 1483.

2. *Tit. A.* IV. ii. 164. 3. You logger-headed and vnpollisht groomes, What, no attendance SHAKS. 5. Horses led, and Grooms besmeared with Gold MILT. 6. Drinking health to bride and g. TENNYSON.

Groom (grūm), *v.* 1809. [f. GROOM *sb.*] 1. *trans.* To curry, feed, and generally attend to (a horse); to 'fettle'. 2. *transf.* To tend or attend to carefully; to give a smart appearance to 1843. 3. *pass.* To be made a bridegroom. BYRON. 4. *U.S.* To prepare as a political candidate 1889.

Groo·mer. 1884. [f. prec. + -ER [1].] A brush rotated by a flexible or jointed revolving shaft, for the mechanical grooming of horses.

Groom-porter. *Obs.* exc. *Hist.* 1502. An officer of the English Royal Household, abolished under George III, whose principal functions were to regulate gaming within the precincts of the court, to furnish cards and dice, and to decide disputes arising at play.

Groomsman (grū·mzmæ̆n). 1698. [f. *groom's* + MAN, after BRIDESMAID, q.v.] A young man acting as friend or attendant on the bridegroom at a marriage, either alone (as 'best man') or as one of a company.

Grooper, obs. f. GROUPER.

Groove (grūv), *sb.* ME. [ad. early mod. Du. *groeve* 'sulcus, fossa, scrobs', Du. *groef*, f. OTeut. root **grōƀ-*, *graƀ-* (see GRAVE *sb.*[1] and *v.*[1]).] 1. A mining shaft; a mine, pit. Now *dial.* 2. A channel or hollow, cut by artificial means, in metal, wood, etc. 1659. 3. A channel or furrow of natural formation; *spec.* in *Anat.* and *Zool.* 1787. 4. *transf.* and *fig.* A channel or routine of action or life. Often, in bad sense: A rut. 1842. †5. A gardener's transplanting tool –1726.

4. His ideas were wont to travel rather in a g. HELPS. *Comb.* **g.-board** (in an organ), a second upper board in which grooves are cut to supply room for the larger pipes, etc.

Groove (grūv), *v.* 1483. [f. GROOVE *sb.*] 1. *intr.* To sink a mining shaft; to mine (*dial.*). 2. *trans.* To cut a groove or grooves in; to provide with grooves 1686. 3. To cut in the form of a groove or channel; to excavate (a channel) 1866. 4. *pass.* and *intr.* To fit or be fitted as *into* a groove (*rare*) 1854.

Groover (grū·vəɹ). 1610. [f. GROOVE *v.* + -ER [1].] One who or that which grooves; a miner (now *dial.*); a gouge (*rare*) 1865.

Grooving (grū·viŋ), *vbl. sb.* 1678. [f. GROOVE *v.* + -ING [1].] 1. The action of GROOVE *v.*; mining (*dial.*) 1892. 2. The making or forming of grooves or channels; a groove or set of grooves. Also *fig.* 1728. 3. *attrib.*, as *g.-plane*, etc. 1678.

Grope (grōup), *sb.* 1500. [f. GROPE *v.*] The action or an act of groping (*lit.* and *fig.*).

Grope (grōup), *v.* [OE. *grāpian*, f. (ult.) OTeut. root **graip-*, ablaut-var. of **grīp-*, whence GRIP *sb.*[1] and *v.*[1]] †1. *intr.* To use the hands in feeling, touching, or grasping; to handle or feel something –1568. 2. To attempt to find something by feeling about as in the dark or as a blind person; to feel about in order to find one's way OE. Also *fig.* †3. *trans.* To touch with the hands; to handle, feel; to probe (a wound). Also, to take hold of, grasp, seize. –1738. b. To search, rummage. *Obs.* exc. *Sc.* 1526. †4. *fig.* a. To apprehend as something palpable –1642. †b. To examine, sound, probe; to investigate –1651.

2. She gropeth alwey forther with hir hond And foond the bed CHAUCER. Fish must be grop't for, and be tickled too BUNYAN. *fig.* As blindly groped they for a future state DRYDEN. Phr. *To g. one's way*: to find one's way by groping (*lit.* and *fig.*). 4. b. Felix gropeth him, thinking to haue a bribe N.T. (Genev.) *Acts* xxiv. *Contents.* Hence **Gro·pingly** *adv.* in a groping manner.

Groroilite (grorǫi·ləit). 1844. [f. *Groroi* in France + -LITE.] *Min.* Earthy manganese, occurring in roundish masses, of a brownish-black colour with reddish-brown streaks.

Grosbeak (grōu·sbīk). Also †**gross-beak.** 1678. [ad. F. *gros-bec*, f. *gros* + *bec*.] Any of various small birds having a large stout bill, chiefly of the families *Fringillidæ* and *Ploceidæ*. The common grosbeak is the hawfinch (*Coccothraustes vulgaris*). Other species are: green g. = GREENFINCH 1; pine g., *Pinicola enucleator*; cardinal g. (see CARDINAL *sb.*); grenadier g. (see GRENADIER [2]); also (in U.S.) blue g. (*Guiraca cærulea*), evening g. (*Hesperophona vespertina*), rose-breasted g. (*Hedymeles ludovicianus*).

‖**Groschen** (grōu·ʃĕn). 1617. [Ger., altered form (not dim.) of MHG. *gros*, *grosse* = F. *gros*; see GROSS *sb.*[2]] A small silver coin and money of account variously = $\frac{1}{24}$, $\frac{1}{30}$, or $\frac{1}{36}$ of a thaler. Not a part of the present German monetary system.

‖**Gros de Naples** (gro də nap'l). 1799. [F. *gros* GROSS *a.*, used subst.] A heavy silk fabric, made originally at Naples. Also *attrib.* So ‖**Gros de Tours.**

‖**Gros grain.** [See GROGRAM.] Commercial name of a strong corded silk fabric. (Recent.)

†**Gross,** *sb.*[1] 1638. [repr. F. *gros*, It. *grosso*.] A name for various foreign coins; e.g. the German GROSCHEN, and the Italian *grosso*, worth about 3*d.* Cf. GROAT. –1705.

Gross (grōus), *sb.*[2] ME. [a. F. *grosse*, orig. the fem. of *gros* big, GROSS *a.*] Twelve dozen. Not found in *pl.* Also *small g.*, in opposition to *great g.* = 12 gross.

Bowe stringes, xl gros 1549.

Gross (grōus), *a.* and *sb.*[3] ME. [a. F. *gros*, fem. *grosse*:—late L. *grossus* thick (freq. in the Vulgate).]

A. *adj.*

I. †1. Thick, stout, massive, big –1794. 2. Big-bodied, corpulent, burly. (Now only *dial.*) Hence, Overfed, unwholesomely fat and corpulent. Hence said also of the habit of body. 1577. †3. Of conspicuous magnitude; palpable, striking; plain, evident –1793. 4. Glaring, flagrant, monstrous 1581.

1. The Foe Approaching g. and huge MILT. In a strong g. hand BLACKSTONE. Phr. †*To fly g.* (Hawking), i.e. at great birds. 2. One of them is wellknowne..a grosse fat man SHAKS. A full g. Habit of Body ARBUTHNOT. 3. Lyes..grosse as a Mountaine, open, palpable SHAKS. 4. G. Folly and Stupidity BENTLEY, sophistry 1781, impostors 1817, perfidy GROTE, credulity CHURCH.

II. †1. Of a denomination of value or weight: Relatively large; containing lower denominations –1801. 2. Entire, total, whole. Now only as opp. to *net*. 1523. †b. Main, the great majority of –1793. 3. Concerned with large masses or outlines; general, opp. to *particular* ME.

1. Phr. *A hundred g.* = 112 lb. or 1 cwt. 2. The g. personal estate is sworn at £37,405..the net at £29,389. 3. †*G. average* = general average (see AVERAGE).

III. 1. Dense, thick 1460. †2. Solid; having three dimensions. DIGGES. †3. Of a body of armed men: Compact, solid –1670.

1. Darkness..so g. that it might be felt 1592. Spirits of purest light, Purest at first, now g. by sinning grown MILT.

IV. †1. Consisting of comparatively large parts or particles. Hence, Wanting in fineness or delicacy. –1793. 2. †Of commodities, etc.: Coarse, inferior, common –1763. b. Of diet: †(*a*) In early use, plain, not delicate; (*b*) in recent use, repulsive in quality. *G. feeder*, one who feeds grossly; said *transf.* of plants. 1599. 3. Lacking in delicacy of perception; dull, stupid. *Obs.* of persons, their opinions, etc.; *arch.* of faculties, after Matt. xiii. 15. 1526. †b. Rough, rough and ready, clumsy –1675; approximate, general, indefinite –1818. 4. Rude, uninstructed (now *rare*) 1561; †uncultivated; †unlearned, untechnical –1781. 5. Extremely coarse in behaviour or morals 1532.

2. Fish and oil, and such g. commodities DE FOE. 3. Men..g. of ear, of vision dim WHITTIER. G. and confus'd Conceptions LOCKE. 4. Peter and John..grosse vnlerned men 1561. The vulgar dialect of the city was g. and barbarous GIBBON. 5. Agamemnon's Wife was a g. Butcher DRYDEN. Terms of the grossest abuse 1850.

B. quasi-*sb.* (the adj. used *absol.*) and *sb.* †1. **By gross**: in large quantities, wholesale –1660. 2. **In gross, in the gross.** [F. *en gros*.] a. In a general way, generally; in the main (now *rare*) ME. †b. 'En masse' –1647. †c. In bulk, wholesale; opp. to *by retail* –1818. †d. Nothing being omitted or withheld –1774. e. *Law.* [med.L. *in grosso*.] Said of that which is absolute and independent, belonging to the person, and not to a manor; esp. in *advowson*, *villain in g.* 1626. 3. †The greater part; the majority, the bulk –1766; *esp.* of an army, etc.: The main body (now *arch.*) 1600; †the sum; the whole –1728. †4. Chiefly *Mil.* A large body; a mass –1700.

2. a. You cannot refuse in the g., what you have so often acknowledged in detail BURKE. 3. The g. of an audience STEELE, of Mankind BUTLER.

Gross-beak, obs f. GROSBEAK.

†**Gro·sshead.** 1580. [f. GROSS *a.* + HEAD.] A thick-headed person, a dullard –1606.

Grossification (grōu:sifikēⁱ·ʃən). 1835. [f. GROSS *a.* + -(I)FICATION.] *Bot.* The swelling of the ovary after fertilization.

Grossly (grōu·sli), *adv.* 1526. [f. GROSS *a.* + -LY [2].] In a gross manner; †plainly –1771; excessively, flagrantly 1594; †coarsely –1823; †materially –1601; †stupidly, †awkwardly, roughly 1526; indelicately, indecently 1547.

Grossness (grōu·snės). 1494. [See -NESS.] The quality or condition of being gross (see GROSS *a.*).

The G. of a City Feast DRYDEN. That chastity of honour..under which vice itself lost half its evil, by losing all its g. BURKE. The very g. of this flattery DICKENS.

Grossular (grǫ·siŭlăɹ). Also **-are.** 1819. [ad. mod.L. *grossularia*, an application of the specific name of the gooseberry.] *Min.* A pale-green variety of garnet from Siberia, often called the gooseberry garnet. So **Grossula·rious, Gro·ssularite** *adjs.* of the nature of, or resembling, the gooseberry.

†**Grot** [1]. [OE. *grot*, related to GRIT *sb.*[1], GRIT *sb.*[2], GROUT; see also GROATS.] A fragment, particle, atom –ME.

Grot [2] (grǫt). Now only *poet.* 1506. [ad. F. *grotte*; see GROTTO.] = GROTTO.

Grote, obs. f. GROAT, GROATS.

Grotesque (grote·sk). 1561. [Earlier *crotesque*, a. early mod.F. *crotesque*, ad. It. *grottesca* (= *opera* or *pittura grottesca*) adj. fem. used ellipt., f. *grotta*; see GROTTO and -ESQUE.]

A. *sb.* 1. A kind of decorative painting or sculpture, in which portions of human and animal forms are fantastically interwoven with foliage and flowers. b. A work of art in this style. Chiefly *pl.*; in pop. use, figures or designs comically distorted or exaggerated. 1643. 2. A clown, buffoon, or merry-andrew 1864. 3. *Printing.* A square-cut letter without ceriph, THUS; formerly called *stone-letter* 1875.

B. *adj.* 1. *Arch.* Having the character of the work described in A. 1. 1603. 2. More widely: Characterized by distortion or unnatural combinations; fantastically extravagant; bizarre, †quaint. Also *transf.* of literary style, etc. 1653. †b. Of landscape: Romantic, picturesquely irregular –1764. 3. Ludicrous from incongruity 1747.

2. Those G. monsters..with which the spouts..of ancient buildings are decorated H. WALPOLE. b. MILT. *P. L.* IV. 136. 3. But what added most to the g. expression of his face, was a ghastly smile DICKENS. Hence **Grote·sque** *v.* to caricature, travesty. **Grotesque·ly** *adv.*, **-ness.** **Grote·squerie,** g. objects collectively; g. quality; a piece of grotesqueness.

Grotto (grǫ·to). *Pl.* **-os, -oes.** 1617. [ad. It. *grotta*:—pop. L. *crupta*, *grupta* (= literary L. *crypta*), ad. Gr. κρύπτη vault, f. κρύπτειν.] 1. A cave or cavern, esp. one which is picturesque or an agreeable retreat. 2. An excavation or structure made to imitate a rocky cave, often adorned with shell-work, etc. 1625. *Comb.* **g.-work** = sense 2.

Grouch (grautʃ), *sb.* *U.S.* 1903. [Var. GRUTCH *sb.*] Grumbling; a fit of the sulks; a grumbler. Hence **Grouch** *v.* **Grou·chy** *a.*

Ground (graund), *sb.* [Com. Teut.: OE. *grund*:— OTeut. **grundu-z*:— pre-Teut. **ghrn̥tú-s*. No cognates outside Teut.]

I. †1. The bottom; the lowest part or downward limit of anything –1824. 2. The solid bottom or earth underlying the sea (†or other water). Now only *Naut.* OE. 3. *pl.* The particles deposited by a liquid in the bottom of a vessel; dregs, lees. †Also *sing.* a sediment. ME. Also *fig.* b. Refuse (of meal, wool, etc.) (*rare*) 1629.

1. A customer..that's near the grund of the purse SCOTT. *fig.* Let vs rather blesse God from the g. of our heart BIBLE *Transl. Pref.* 2. The bottome of the deepe, Where Fadome-line could neuer touch the g. SHAKS. *To break g.* (Naut.): to heave the anchor clear of the bottom. *To strike g.*: to obtain soundings. *To take the g.*: to run ashore, strand. 3. Smoking black coffee (half grounds) 1860.

II. †1. The solid base or foundation on which a structure is raised. In early use also *pl.* (cf. *foundations*). –1715. 2. In immaterial applications: a. The basis, foundation ME. †b. A fundamental principle; also *pl.* rudiments –1762. c. A reason, motive; often, a valid reason, etc. ME. 3. The foundation on which other parts are overlaid, or on which they rest for support or display: a. in a composite textile fabric ME. b. Any material surface which is taken as a basis to work upon; *esp.* in painting and decorative art, a main surface or first coating of colour serving as a support for other colours or as a background for designs; the prevailing colour of any object, picture, etc.; the portion of a surface which is not operated upon. Also *pl.* ME. †c. *Mus.* The plain-song or melody on which a descant is raised. Also = *ground-bass.* –1811. d. *Etching.* (See quot.) Also *etching-ground.* 1727. e. *Carpentry.* (See quot.) Usu. *pl.* 1823. †4. The main constituent or the essential part of anything –1737.

1. Salomon..buylded the walles..from the grounde of y^e house vnto the rofe COVERDALE 1 *Kings* vi. 15. 2. a. Which of all goodly manners is the g. SPENSER. b. There is a g. in the law, that inheritance may.. not lyneally ascend *Littleton's Tenures.* c. Hee refus'd; his grounds I know not P. HENRY. What grounds for apprehension SHERIDAN. 3. a. To weave coarse work upon a precious g. DRYDEN. b. Mosaick work of Green, upon a G. of fine Gold 1687. c. SHAKS. *Rich. III*, III. vii. 49. d. Ground in etching denotes a gummous composition, smeared over the surface of the metal to be etched; to prevent the aqua fortis from eating, or having effect, except in places where this *ground* is cut through, or pared off CHAMBERS. e. *Grounds.*—Pieces of wood concealed in a wall, to which the facings or finishings are attached P. NICHOLSON.

III. The surface of the earth or a part of it. 1. The earth as the surface upon which man and his surroundings rest or move. Also *fig.* OE. b. The portion of the earth's surface on which a person or thing stands or moves; often *fig.* 1530. c. The bare floor (= pit) of a theatre. B. JONS. d. *Fox-hunting.* (*To run*) *to g.*: into a burrow or hole, 'to earth' 1797. †2. The earth as contrasted with (*a*) heaven –1742, (*b*) the sea –1697. 3. With *a* and *pl.* †a. A region, land, country (*rare*) –1609. †b. A piece or parcel of land –1733. c. *pl.* Enclosed land surrounding or attached to a dwelling-house or other building, serving chiefly for ornament or recreation. †Formerly = lands, fields 1460. 4. Area or distance on the face of the earth. (Usu. without article.) ME. b. *fig.* Subject-matter; things that may be the object of study or discourse 1796. 5. Area or space having a specified extent or character, or adapted for a specific purpose ME. 6. With reference to possessor or occupier, denoted by a genitive, etc. ME. 7. The space or area under consideration, or one used for some special purpose, *esp.* the scene of any contest or meeting ME. 8. *Telegraphy.* The contact of the conductor of an electric circuit with the earth; the escape of current resulting from this 1870.

1. The grassye g. with daintye Daysies dight SPENSER. *fig.* Phr. †*To bring to the g.*: To cast down, overthrow, overcome. *To fall to the g.*: (of schemes) to come to nothing; so *to be dashed to the g.* (of hopes). *Down to the g.*: completely (*colloq.*). *Above g.*: unburied, alive. b. *To cut the g. from under one* or *one's feet.* 2. 'Twixt sky and g. SHAKS. 3. c. Like a Theefe to come to rob my grounds; Climbing my walles inspight of me the Owner SHAKS. 4. Phr. *To gain, gather, get g.*: to advance, make progress (*lit.* and *fig.*). *To give g.*: to recede, retire. *To lose g.*: to fall back, decline. *To take g.*: to take up, or move into, a certain position. b. *fig.* The learned Dr. Robertson has travelled partly over the same g. 1804. 5. From a g. of advantage 1618. On some spot of English g. SHELLEY. 6. A fair house, built on another mans g. SHAKS. Phr. *To hold, keep, maintain, stand shift one's g.* (now usu. *fig.*). 7. *On the g.*: engaged, in a duel. He has been 'on the ground' I don't know how many times THACKERAY. *The g.* (Cricket): (*a*) The space on which the game is played; (*b*) the space within which a player may lawfully stand, e. g. while batting; (*c*) the paid staff of players attached to a club (also *g.-staff*).

IV. The soil of the earth. Also without article: Soil, earth, mould; now only in *Mining.* With *a.* and *pl.* A kind or variety of soil. ? *Obs.* ME.

There be many maner of groundes and soyles FITZHERB.

Comb. 1. General: a. *g.-level, -pipe, -sward,* etc.; b. with sense 'fundamental', †'deep-seated', etc.: *g.-idea, -principle, -root, -thought, -tint, -tone,* etc. (mostly recent imitations of German compounds); †c. with sense 'to the bottom', hence 'completely, thoroughly, extremely': *g.-hot, -stalwart,* etc.

2. Special: **g.-air**, the air contained in the soil, which contains a large portion of carbonic acid gas, due to the disintegration of organic substances; **-angling**, fishing with a weighted line, without a float; **-bailiff**, a superintendent of mines; **-bass** (*Mus.*), a bass-passage of four or eight bars in length, constantly repeated with a varied melody and harmony (Stainer & Barrett); **-bundle** (*Anat.*), one of the bundles of nerve-fibres lying on either side of the grey matter of the spinal cord; **-cable**, that part of a mooring-cable which lies on the sea-bottom; **-chamber**, one on the ground-floor; **-colour**, (*a*) a first coating of paint; (*b*) the prevailing colour of an object having markings of other colours; **-crab**, a kind of hoisting apparatus used in mining; **†-ebb**, low water; also as *adj.*, at low water; **-fast** *a.*, firmly fixed in the g.; **-fish**, a fish which lives at the bottom of the water; **-fishery, -fishing**, fishing with the bait at or near the bottom of the water; **-game**, game which lives on the g., as hares and rabbits; **†-hold**, the anchors of a vessel; **-joint**, the joining of one stone or course in masonry with the g. or course immediately below; **-joist**, a joist supporting the ground floor of a building; **-landlord**, the owner of land which is leased for building on; **-mail** *Sc.*, payment for burying-ground; **-mass**, the compact basal part of an igneous rock, in which the distinctive crystals are embedded; **-moraine**, subglacial till, boulder-clay; also *attrib.*; **-net**, a trawl or drag-net; **-note** (*Mus.*), the note on which a common chord is built, called also the *fundamental bass*; also *fig.*; **-officer**, one who has charge of the grounds and lands of an estate; **-plane**, the horizontal plane of projection in perspective drawing; **-rope**, a rope by which the lower edge of a trawl is kept on the g.; **-row**, a row of gas-jets on the floor of a theatre-stage; **-seine**, a form of seine or drag-net; **-sluice** *sb.* (*Mining*), a channel cut in the bottom or bed-rock, into which the earth is conveyed by a stream of water; **-story** = GROUND-FLOOR; **-substance** (*Phys.*), the homogeneous matrix in which the structural elements of a tissue are embedded; **-sype**, water filtering through from the surface, opp. to *spring water*; **-table** (*Arch.*), the plinth or projecting course resting on the foundation of a wall; an earth-table; **-tier**, (*a*) the lowest tier of goods in a vessel's hold; (*b*) the lowest range of boxes in a theatre; **-timbers**, the main timbers laid on the keel of a ship, floor-timbers; **-tissue** (*Bot.*), the mass of cells separating the vascular bundles from each other and from the epidermis; **-torpedo**, a torpedo fixed to the g. or bottom of the sea; **-tow**, the loose hemp that comes from the sides of the hatchellers and spinners; **-water**, all water found in the surface soil of the crust of the earth, except such as may be in combination with the materials of the crust of the earth; **-ways**, the large blocks and thick planks which support the cradle on which a ship is launched; **-wire** (*Telegraphy*), a metaphorical term applied to the earth when used as a return circuit; **-worm**, an earth-worm. See also Main Words.

b. In names of animals (esp. birds of terrestrial habits, and animals that burrow, or lie in holes or on the ground); as **g.-bear**, the common brown bear, *Ursus arctos*; **-beetle**, a general name for all beetles of the family *Carabidæ*; **-cuckoo**, a member of one of the four genera of *Neomorphinæ*, a sub-family of the *Cuculidæ*; **-dove**, a dove or pigeon of terrestrial habits, esp. of the genera *Chamæpelia* and *Geopelia*; **-finch**, (*a*) a bird of Swainson's sub-family *Fringillinæ* or true finches; (*b*) an American finch of the genus *Pipilo*; **-gudgeon**, the loach; **-hornbill**, the African genus *Bucorvus* (or *Bucorax*) of hornbills; **-hornet**, a hornet that has its nest on the g.; **-lackey**, *Bombyx castrensis*; **-lark**, the tree pipit; also the bunting; **-lizard**, *Ameiva dorsalis*; **-parrakeet**, any bird of the genera *Geopsittacus* and *Pezoporus*; **-parrot**, (*a*) = prec.; (*b*) the Kakapo of New Zealand; **-pearl**, an insect which lives beneath the soil in crevices frequented by ants, and acquires a shell-like calcareous scaly covering; **-pig**, the ground-rat (*Aulacodus Swinderianus*); **-pigeon**, a pigeon which passes most of its time on the ground; esp. one of the family *Gouridæ*; also = *ground-dove*; **-puppy** = HELL-BENDER; **-rat** (see *ground-pig*); **-scratcher**, a name for the *Rasores* or gallinaceous birds; **-shark**, any species of shark that rarely comes to the surface, *esp.* the spinous shark (*Echinorrhinus spinosus*); **-sloth**, one of an extinct group intermediate between the existing sloths and ant-eaters; **-snake**, *Coronella australis*; **-sparrow** *U.S.*, one of several sparrows of terrestrial habits, e.g. the grass-finch and savannah-sparrow; **-spearing**, a fish, *Trachinocephalus myops*; **-spider**, any kind of spider that burrows or lives under stones; **-thrush**, (*a*) a thrush of the genus *Geocichla*; (*b*) a bird of the Australian genus *Cinclosoma*; (*c*) the pitta or ant-thrush; **-tit**, a small Californian bird (*Chamæa fasciata*), allied to the wrens and titmice; **-wasp**, a wasp that has its nest on the g.; **-wren**, (*a*) the willow wren, *Sylvia trochilis*; (*b*) = *ground-tit.* See also Main Words.

c. In names of plants, generally denoting dwarfish plants and sometimes those of a trailing habit; as **g.-archil**, *Lecanora parella*, a lichen used in dyeing; **-berry**, (*a*) *U.S.* = CHECKER-BERRY; (*b*) *Austral.* a name for *Astroloma humifusium* and *A. pinifolium*; **-box**, *Buxus sempervirens*, the small variety used for edgings; **-cedar**, a cedar-like trailing plant; **-cherry**, (*a*) the Dwarf Cherry, *Cerasus Chamæcerasus*; (*b*) an American plant of the genus *Physalis*; **-cistus**, *Rhododendron Chamæcistus*; **-cypress**, *Santolina Chamæcyparissus*; **-elder**, a name for *Sambucus Ebulus, Angelica sylvestris, Ægopodium Podagraria*, and *Mercurialis perennis*; **-fir** = GROUND-PINE; **-flax**, the genus *Camelina*; **-hemlock**, an American variety of the common yew, *Taxus baccata*; **-holly** = CHECKER-BERRY; **-jasmine**, *Passerina Stelleri*; **-laurel**, the Trailing Arbutus (*Epigæa repens*) of N. America; **†-myrtle**, Butcher's Broom (*Ruscus aculeatus*); **-oak**, (*a*) an oak-sapling; (*b*) a species of dwarf-oak; **-pea** = GROUND-NUT 2; **-plum**, *Astragalus caryocarpus*, the fruit of which, a pod, closely resembles a plum; **-thistle**, the cardoon (*Cynara Cardunculus*); **-willow**, a dwarf willow; **-yew** = CROWBERRY 1. See also Main Words.

Ground (graund), *v.* ME. [f. GROUND *sb.*] †1. *trans.* To lay the foundations of (a house); to found; to fix or establish firmly. Also *fig.* –1684. 2. To set on a firm basis, to establish. Const. *on*, also *in* (now only in *pass.*). ME. †3. To establish, settle (a person in respect of his position, beliefs, etc.). Const. *in, of.* –1657. †4. *refl.* To rest or rely *upon* –1812. †Also *intr.* for *refl.* –1682. 5. *trans.* To instruct *in* main or elementary principles ME. 6. To form or supply a basis, ground, or reason for (*rare*) 1667. 7. To furnish with a ground (see GROUND *sb.* II. 3) ME. 8. To knock down ME.; †*fig.* to 'floor', 'gravel' (*rare*) –1598. 9. To set on the ground; to cause to touch the ground; to lay down 1650. b. *Electr.* To connect with the earth as a conductor 1883. c. *intr.* To come to or strike the ground 1751. 10. *intr.* Of a vessel: To run ashore or aground; to strand. Const. *on.* c 1430. b. *trans.* To cause to run ashore. Also *fig.* 1658.

1. That house..was grounded vpon ye rocke COVERDALE *Luke* vi. 48. 2. Moral vertue grounded vpon trouþe CHAUCER. Their suspicions and fears were not ill grounded THIRLWALL. 5. He came young and not well grounded from Oxford University 1617. 7. Whether he grounds a head..or whether he grounds the whole picture RUSKIN. 9. To g. one's bat STRUTT. Phr. *To g. arms* (Mil.): to lay one's arms upon the ground, *esp.* as an act of surrender. 10. Three of our ships seemed to be grounded 1806. Hence **Grou·nd·ed·ly** *adv.*, †**-ness** (*rare*).

Ground (graund), *ppl. a.* 1765. [pa. pple. of GRIND *v.*] 1. Reduced to fine particles by grinding or crushing. 2. Having the surface abraded or fashioned by grinding, esp. of joints, stoppers, etc. intended to fit closely 1807. 3. *Ground glass.* †a. Plate glass –1823. b. Glass made opaque by grinding, etc.; also *attrib.* 1848.

Groundage (grau·ndédʒ). 1440. [f. GROUND *sb.* + -AGE.] 1. †a. Some kind of toll or tax. ME. only. b. A duty levied on vessels lying upon a shore or beach, or entering a port 1567. b. *Mining.* = ROYALTY. 1852.

Ground-ash. 1664. 1. A young ash-plant; an ash sapling. Also *attrib.* 2. *dial.* The gout-weed, *Ægopodium Podagraria* 1796; also, *Angelica sylvestris* 1853.

Grou·nd-bait. 1651. 1. †a. A bait used in bottom-fishing (*rare*). T. BARKER. b. A bait thrown to the bottom of the water, in order to lure the fish. Also *fig.* 1655. 2. *Northumb.* The loach or groundling 1867.

Ground-bird. 1560. †1. One, or perh. more than one, swan out of a 'game', ? as the due of the owner of the land –1887. 2. Any columbine, gallinaceous, grallatorial, or struthious bird 1840. 3. *U.S.* The grass-finch or ground-sparrow 1856.

Grou·nden, obs. pa. pple. of GRIND *v.*

Grounder (grau·ndəɹ). ME. [f. GROUND *v.* + -ER [1].] 1. One who, or that which, grounds (see GROUND *v.*). 2. *colloq.* a. A catching the ground (in angling) 1847. b. A knock-down blow 1889. c. In *Cricket*, etc.: A ball sent along the ground.

Grou·nd-floor. 1601. The floor in a building which is more or less on a level with the ground outside. Also *attrib.*

Phr. *To get* (or *be let*) *in on the ground-floor* (U.S.): to be allowed to share in a speculation on the same terms as the original promoters.

Ground-hog. 1840. 1. = AARD-VARK. 2. The American marmot (*Arctomys*) 1843.

Ground-ice. 1694. [Du. *grondijs*, Ger. *grundeis*.] Ice formed at the bottom of the water; *anchor-ice*.

Grounding (grau·ndiŋ), *vbl. sb.* ME. [f. GROUND *v.* and *sb.* + -ING [1].] 1. The action of founding or establishing; chiefly in immaterial sense. Also quasi-*concr.* That on which something is grounded (now *rare*). 2. Elementary instruction 1644. 3. The preparation or laying of a ground in arts and manufactures. Also *grounding-in*, the application of the secondary colours in calico-printing. 1466. 4. The action of laying, or of running, a ship aground 1691. 5. *attrib.* 1790.

Comb.: g.-**machine**, a machine for grounding in the manufacture of wall-paper; -**tool**, in mezzotint engraving, the tool with which the plate is roughened.

Ground-ivy. ME. 1. a. The herb ale-hoof, *Nepeta Glechoma* or *Glechoma hederacea*, a common labiate plant having bluish-purple flowers and kidney-shaped leaves. †b. The periwinkle, *Vinca minor* (*rare*). (These plants were classed as *hedera* solely on account of their creeping stems.) †2. The barren trailing ivy (*Hedera Helix*). GERARD. †3. The ground-pine (*Ajuga Chamæpitys*). PARKINSON.

Groundless (grau·ndlės), *a.* [OE. *grundléas*, f. *grund* GROUND *sb.* + -*léas* -LESS.] †1. Bottomless, unfathomable (*lit.* and *fig.*) -1605. 2. Destitute of foundation, authority, or support; having no real cause or reason; unfounded 1620.

1. Ground-less gulfs SYLVESTER. 2. A g. fiction that cannot be proved BAXTER. Hence **Grou·nd-less·ly** *adv.*, -**ness.**

Ground-line. 1450. [Cf. Du. *grondlijn*, G. and Sw. *grundlinie* (in senses 2 and 3).] 1. A line used for bottom-fishing. 2. *Geom.* †a. The base upon which a diagram is constructed -1659. b. The intersecting line of the vertical and horizontal planes of projection 1857. 3. *pl.* Outlines (*lit.* and *fig.*) 1624.

Groundling (grau·ndliŋ). 1601. [f. GROUND *sb.* + -LING.] 1. A name for various small fishes which live at the bottom of the water, *esp.* a gudgeon or loach. 2. A creeping plant, or one of low growth 1822. 3. A frequenter of the ground or pit of a theatre; hence, an uncritical or unrefined person. (Only in literary use, after *Haml.* III. ii. 12.) 1602. †4. One of humble rank (*rare*) -1630. 5. *attrib.* or *adj.* 1825.

3. But how do you like sharing the mirth of the groundlings LYTTON.

†**Grou·ndly,** *adv.* ME. [f. GROUND *sb.* + -LY [2].] Firmly established; in relation to the ground or root; profoundly -1602. †Also as *adj.*

Ground-man. Also **groundsman.** 1785. a. A labourer employed to dig or work on the ground. b. (Now always *groundsman*) One who is employed to keep a cricket, etc. ground in order 1886.

Ground-nut. 1636. [With 1, cf. Du. *grondnoot.*] 1. One of the small farinaceous edible tubers of the wild bean (*Apios tuberosa*), a climbing plant of N. America; also, the plant. 2. The pea-nut or ground-pea (*Arachis hypogæa*), the fruit of which is a pod ripening under ground 1769. Also *attrib.* 3. The earth-nut (*Bunium flexuosum*) 1653.

Ground-pine. 1551. 1. The plant *Ajuga Chamæpitys*, said to be named from its resinous smell. 2. The club moss (*Lycopodium clavatum*), or other species of *Lycopodium* 1847.

Ground-plan. 1731. [Cf. Du. *grondplan.*] 1. The representation on a plane of the arrangements, divisions, etc. of a building or other structure, at the ground-level. 2. *fig.* The outline, general plan or basis upon which any work is constructed or composed 1831.

Ground-plate. 1663. [Cf. Du. *grondplaat.*] 1. The lowest horizontal timber in a framing; a ground-sill. 2. a. A bed-plate carrying railway sleepers or ties (Knight) 1875. b. A piece of flattened metal on which anything is fixed 1871. c. *Electr.* A metal plate sunk in the ground and connecting an electric current with the earth 1875.

Ground-plot. 1563. 1. The portion of ground covered by a building, etc.; foundation. ? *Obs.* †2. = GROUND-PLAN 1, 2. -1794.

Ground-rent. 1667. [Cf. Du. *grondrente.*] The rent paid to the owner of land which is let for building upon.

Ground-sea. 1642. A heavy sea in which large waves rise and dash upon the coast without apparent cause.

Groundsel (grau·ndsĕl), *sb.*[1] [OE. *gundæswelg(i)æ*, *grundeswylige*; of difficult etym.] Any plant belonging to the genus *Senecio* (N.O. *Compositæ*), esp. *S. vulgaris* ('common groundsel'), given as food to cage-birds and formerly largely used for medical purposes.

Comb. g.-**tree**, a N. American shrub, *Baccharis halimifolia*.

Groundsel (grau·ndsĕl), *sb.*[2], **ground-sill** (-sil). ME. [app. f. GROUND *sb.* + SILL, but the second element early became a mere termination.] 1. A timber serving as a foundation to carry a superstructure, esp. a wooden building; the lowest member of a wooden framework; a ground-plate; hence, the foundation of any structure. Now chiefly *techn.* b. *fig.* An underlying principle 1604. 2. The lower framing-timber of a door; a door-sill, threshold. †Also, a window-sill. 1523. 3. *attrib.* 1625. Hence †**Grou·ndsel, grou·ndsill** *v. trans.* to lay the foundation or threshold of.

Groundsman: see **Ground-man.**

Ground-squirrel. 1772. 1. A terrestrial squirrel-like rodent: a. of the genus *Tamias*; esp. the chipmuck (*T. striatus*) of the *U.S.*; b. = GOPHER *sb.*[1] 2. 2. An African squirrel of the genus *Xerus* 1867.

Ground-swell. 1818. A deep swell or heavy rolling of the sea, the result of a distant storm or seismic disturbance. Also *fig.*

fig. The deep-raking, g. of passion, as we see it in the sarcasm of Lear LOWELL.

Ground-tackle. 1556. [Cf. Du. *grondtakel.*] A general name for all tackle made use of in anchoring, mooring, or kedging a vessel.

Grou·ndward. 1562. [See -WARD.]

A. *adv.* Towards the ground. Now *rare*.

B. *adj.* Turned or inclined towards the ground 1878.

Groundwork (grau·ndwɔːk). 1550. [Cf. MDu. *gront-werck* (mod. *grondwerk*).] 1. The solid base on which a structure is built; foundation. Now *rare*. Also *fig.* 2. The body or foundation on which other parts are overlaid, or on which they rest for display, as in painting, etc. 1655. b. The principal ingredient (*rare*) 1822.

1. *fig.* No Thought can be valuable, of which good Sense is not the G. ADDISON. 2. Cushions of flower'd Satin, the g. thereof Gold and Silver 1662.

Group (grūp), *sb.* Also †**groupe.** 1686. [ad. F. *groupe*, ad. It. *gruppo* group; prob. adapted from Teut. **kroppo-*: see CROP. The etymological sense is app. 'lump' or 'mass'.] 1. *spec.* a. *Fine Art.* An assemblage of figures or objects forming together either a complete design, or a distinct portion of one. b. *Mus.* (*a*) A series of notes, of small time-value, grouped together; a division or run. (*b*) The method of setting out band parts in score. 1727. 2. *gen.* An assemblage of objects standing near together, and forming a collective unity; a knot (of people), a cluster (of things). In early use there is often a notion of confused aggregation. 1736. 3. A number of persons or things in a certain relation, or having a certain degree of similarity 1729. 4. *esp.* in scientific classification. Chiefly used as an indefinite term for any classificatory division whatever its relative rank (so, e.g., in *Zoology*) 1826. 5. *Math.* A set or system of operations so constituted that the product of any number of these operations is always itself a member of the group 1854.

1. The beautiful Grouppe of Figures in the Corner of the Temple STEELE. 2. They stood, clustered in a dark and savage g. J. F. COOPER. A fine groupe of crystals HERSCHEL. 3. Man can only make progress in co-operative groups BAGEHOT. Natural groups of languages 1892. (*Oxford*) *g. movement*: a movement characterized by the 'sharing' of religious experiences by groups of persons. 4. The forms of life..become divided into groups subordinate to groups DARWIN. *attrib.* g. **captain**, a rank in the Royal Air Force equivalent to colonel in the army.

Group (grūp), *v.* 1718. [f. the sb. Cf. F. *grouper.*] 1. *trans.* To make a group of, to form into a group; to place in a group *with* 1754. b. *intr.* for *refl.* To form a group or part of a group; to gather in a group or groups 1801. 2. *trans.* To dispose (colours, figures, etc.) so as to form a harmonious whole. Also with *about*, *together*. 1718. Also *intr.* for *refl.* 3. *trans.* To arrange in groups with reference to some common feature or property 1862.

1. Scattered huts or cells grouped around a church or oratory 1894. 2. Six figures will form too many for a sculptor to g. to advantage LOCKHART. Hence **Grou·page**, arrangement in a g. or groups.

Grouped (grūpt), *ppl. a.* 1702. [f. prec. + -ED [1].] Arranged or forming a group or groups.

Grouped columns: three, four, or more columns placed upon the same pedestal.

Grouper (grū·pəɪ). 1687. [ad. Pg. *garupa*, ? repr. some S. American name.] 1. One of several species of the genus *Epinephelus* of serranoid fishes, inhabiting W. Indian waters and the Mexican gulf. The chief species are the Red G. (*E. morio*) and Black G. (*E. nigritus*). In California, a name of the rock-fish (*Sebastichthys*). 2. *Austral.* A percoid fish of the genus *Oligorus* 1865. *Blue groper*: a labroid fish, *Cossyphus gouldii* 1880.

Grouping (grū·piŋ), *vbl. sb.* 1748. [f. GROUP *v.* + -ING [1].] The action of placing in groups, a manner in which things are grouped.

Grouse (graus), *sb.* 1531. [?] 1. a. Any of the gallinaceous birds having feathered feet (the family *Tetraonidæ* of many naturalists, of which the largest genera are *Tetrao* and *Lagopus*). b. In pop. use, restricted to *Lagopus* (formerly *Tetrao*) *scoticus*, more particularly called **Red Grouse**, and also Moor Fowl or Moor Game. c. Applied to birds of the genera *Syrrhaptes* and *Pterocles*, the SAND-GROUSE, q. v. 1772. d. The flesh of the bird 1786. †2. As a term of contempt. B. JONS. 3. *attrib.*, as *g.-drive*, etc. 1814.

1. a. Besides the Red Grouse, the most important British varieties are: **Black G.**, *Tetrao tetrix*, Black Game or Heath Fowl, the male being called BLACK COCK and the female GREY HEN. **Wood** or **Great G.**, the capercailye, *Tetrao urogallus*. **White G.**, *Lagopus mutus*, the ptarmigan, locally called also Rock Grouse. Other varieties are: **Canada G.**, *Canace* or *Dendragapus canadensis*, called also Spotted Grouse. **Dusky G.**, *Canace* or *Dendragapus obscurus*. **Pinnated G.**, *Cupidonia cupido*. **Ruffed G.**, *Bonasa umbellus*; another species is the HAZEL-GROUSE, *B. silvestris*. **Sage G.**, *Centrocircus urophasianus*. **Sharp-tailed G.**, a g. of the genus *Pediœcetes*. *Comb.* g.-**pigeon**, the sand-grouse.

Grouse (graus), *v.*[1] 1798. [f. prec.] *intr.* To shoot grouse. Also *transf.* (cf. *snipe* v.).

Grouse (graus, grūs), *v.*[2] orig. *Army slang.* 1892. [?] *intr.* To grumble. Also as sb.

Grouser (grau·səɪ). 1876. [?] *Hydraulics.* An iron-pointed pile or timber attached to a boat, etc. as a means of anchorage or of keeping it in position.

Grout (graut), *sb.*[1] [OE. *grút*; related to GRIT *sb.*[1], GRIT *sb.*[2], GROATS.] 1. Coarse meal, peeled grain. In *pl.* = GROATS. Now *rare*. 2. The infusion of malt before and during fermentation. Also, small beer. *Obs.* exc. *dial.* OE. †b. (= Du. *grute*) app. some plant formerly used for flavouring beer -1671. 3. Whole meal porridge. ? *Obs.* 1587. 4. Sediment; dregs; lees; grounds 1697.

4. Wherefore should we turn the g. In a drained cup ROSSETTI.

Grout (graut), *sb.*[2] 1638. [? a use of prec.] Thin fluid mortar, which is poured into the interstices of masonry and wood-work. Also *attrib.*

Grout (graut), *v.* 1838. [f. prec.] *trans.* To fill up or finish with grout or liquid mortar; to cement. Also with *in*. Hence **Grou·ting** *vbl. sb.* filling of chinks, etc. with grout; chiefly *concr.* the material used in this operation.

†Grout-head. Also **growthed.** 1550. [f. GROUT *sb.*[1]; in 2 confused with *great*. Cf. *pudding-head*.] **1.** A blockhead, thickhead, dunce –1649. **2.** A big head; a person with a big head –1706. So **Grout-headed** *a.* thick-headed, stupid (now *dial.*).

†Groutnoll. 1578. [f. GROUT *sb.*[1] + NOLL.] = prec. –1658.

Grouty (grau·ti), *a. U.S.* 1836. [See -Y[1].] Sulky, cross, ill-tempered. Hence **Grou·tiness.**

Grove (grōuv). [OE. *grāf* :—prehistoric **graibo-*. Cf. GREAVE *sb.*[1]] **1.** A small wood; a group of trees affording shade or forming avenues or walks. Also *transf.* and *fig.* ¶**2.** In Eng. versions of the Bible, an erron. rendering: **a.** of Heb. *Ashērāh*, now understood as the name of a goddess or of a pillar serving as an idol 1535; **b.** of Heb. *ēshel* (R.V. 'tamarisk tree') 1535. **3.** *attrib.* 1535.

1. I..like a Forrester, the groues may tread SHAKS. *transf.* Through Groves Of Coral MILT. *Comb.* **g.-dock,** *Rumex Nemolapathum*; **-snail,** *Helix Sylvatica*. Hence †**Grovet,** a little g.

Grovel (grǫ·v'l), *v.* 1593. [f. GROVELLING *adv.*, apprehended as a pr. pple.] *intr.* To lie prone or with the face downwards; to move with the body prostrate upon the ground 1593. Also *fig.*

Gaze on, and grouell on thy face SHAKS. *fig.* The vindictive Laud grovelled in a meaner..victory D'ISRAELI. Hence **Grovel** *sb.* the action of grovelling. **Gro·veller, gro·veler,** one who grovels, chiefly *fig.*

Grovelling, groveling (grǫ·v'liŋ), *a.* (*ppl. a.*) 1538. [Orig. an attrib. use of GROVELLING *adv.*; subseq. taken as pr. pple. of GROVEL *v.*] **1.** Having the face or belly towards or on the ground; prone. Applied also to a low-growing plant. **2.** *transf.* and *fig.* Of persons, qualities, etc.: Abject, base, low, mean, sordid 1608.

1. Circe..Whose charmed cup Whoever tasted, lost his upright shape, And downward fell into a groveling Swine MILT. 2. Our groueling earth-desires SYLVESTER. Hence **Gro·vellingly** *adv.*

Grovelling, groveling (grǫ·v'liŋ), *adv.* [ME. *grovelynge*, f. GROOF + -LING[2].] Face downward; in or to a prone or prostrate position.

Sir launcelot..pulled hym grouelyng doune MALORY. So **Gro·vellings** *adv.* (*Obs.* exc. *dial.*)

Grovy (grōu·vi), *a.* Also †**grovey.** 1594. [f. GROVE + -Y.] Of, pertaining to, or resembling a grove; abounding in groves; situated in a grove.

Grow (grōu), *v.* Pa. t. **grew** (grū, grĭū). Pa. pple. **grown** (grōun). [OE. *grōwan*, pa. t. *grēow*, pa. pple. *grōwen*, f. OTeut. root *grō-* (see GRASS).]

I. Intr. senses. (In early use always with *be*, and still when a state or result is implied.) †**1.** Of a plant: To manifest vigorous life; to put forth foliage, flourish, be green –ME. **2.** In weaker sense: To have vegetative life. Hence also, to exist as a living plant in a specified habitat, or with specified characteristics. OE. **b.** *transf.* †(*a*) Of minerals: To be native in a certain situation; (*b*) *joc.*, of other things ME. **c.** *Naut.* Of a cable: To stretch out forward towards the starboard side 1780. **3.** With advs. or preps. forming phrases chiefly used *transf.* or *fig.* 1593. **4.** With especial reference to the beginning of vegetable, or (*transf.*) animal life OE. **5.** *fig.* Of immaterial things: To spring up; to arise, originate, be developed as from a germ; to spring naturally as from a stock OE. **6.** To increase gradually in size by natural development. (Cf. WAX *v.*) OE. **7.** To increase gradually in magnitude, quantity, or degree ME. **8.** To increase in some specified quality or property. Const. *in*, †*of*. ME. **9.** To advance in age (now *arch.*) 1477. **10.** To come or pass by degrees *into* some state or condition. Also const. *to* with *inf.* Now *rare*. 1450. **11.** To become or come to be by degrees, sometimes with inclusion of the literal sense ME.

2. [They] show you slips of all that grows From England to Van Diemen TENNYSON. b. There groweth Yron, Steele and Copper, and what not LYLY. 3. For euer may my knees g. to the earth,..Vnlesse [etc.]. SHAKS. †*To g. to*: to be an organic or integral part of. 2 *Hen. IV*, I. ii. 100. 4. Sugar-canes g. without planting 1660. Here grows..this Fruit Divine MILT. *transf.* Horns only g. upon the Male N. COX. 5. Rumour of battle grew TENNYSON. [The States] g. out of human characters JOWETT. Phr. †*To g. to*: to arise or come into existence to the benefit or injury of (a person, etc.). Also *absol.* without *to*. *The law of growing-to*: reversion, escheat. 6. Great Weeds do g. apace SHAKS. She plumes her feathers, and lets g. her wings MILT. 7. New moons may g. or wane, may set or rise PRIOR. 8. Growe in grace TINDALE. He grew to no place of more honour FULLER. Phr. *To g. on* or *upon* (a person, etc.): (*a*) To increase so as to be more troublesome to. (*b*) To acquire more and more influence over. Hence: To gain more and more of (a person's) liking or admiration. 9. *To g. on*: to advance, make progress. My houre grows on a pace BEAUM. & FL. 10. To g. into a Consumption 1616, into gentility LAMB. 11. To g. old with a good Grace STEELE. The soldiers grew..out of all discipline DE FOE.

Comb. **Grow up.** **a.** To advance to or towards maturity. **b.** Of plants: To emerge from the soil, spring up; also, to g. to full size. **c.** Of a custom, state of things, etc.: To arise gradually.

II. Trans. senses. **1.** *causative.* To cause to grow 1774; to produce, *esp.* by cultivation 1847; to let grow on the body 1819. **2.** *pass.* Of land, etc.: To be covered with a growth of something. Also with *over*. 1470.

1. Wool, grown in Norfolk 1842. To g. potatoes 1847. To g. quills SOUTHEY, a beard 1860. 2. It was all growen over with thornes *Prov.* xxiv. 31.

Hence **Grow·able** *a.* capable of being grown or cultivated. **Grow·ingly** *adv.*

Growan (grōu·ăn). *Cornish dial.* Also **grouan.** 1753. [f. Cornish *grou*; see GRAVEL *sb.* Cf. Bret. *grouan* gravel.] A soft decomposed granite, overlying the veins of tin in Cornwall. *Hard g.*: granite or moorstone.

Grower (grōu·əɹ). 1562. [f. GROW *v.* + -ER[1].] **1.** Of a plant: One that grows (in a specified way). **b.** 'A thick limb of a thorn hedge' (*E. Dial. Dict.*) 1829. **2.** One who grows (produce) 1687.

Growing (grou·iŋ), *vbl. sb.* ME. [f. GROW *v.* + -ING[1].] **1.** The action of GROW *v.*: **a.** in intr. senses; **b.** in trans. senses 1889. †**2.** Growth; the faculty, period, or process of growth. Rarely *pl.* –1561. †*concr.* A growth, a crop –1722. †**3.** Advance, progress. *Wint. T.* IV. i. 16. **4.** *attrib.* ME.

Comb.: **g.-cell,** a microscope-slide on which minute objects are kept growing in water; **-pains,** the neuralgic pains common in young persons during the period of growth; **-point** (*Bot.*), the terminal portion of an organ with permanent apical growth, consisting entirely of primary meristem; **-slide** = *growing-cell*; **g. weather,** weather conducive to the growth of plants.

Growl (graul), *sb.* 1727. [f. GROWL *v.*] **1.** An act of growling; a low angry guttural sound uttered by an animal. Also *transf.* of cannon, earthquake, thunder, etc. 1833. **2.** An expression of anger or dissatisfaction uttered by human beings 1821.

Growl (graul), *v.* ME. [Prob. echoic.] **1.** *intr.* †**a.** Of the bowels: To rumble. ME. only. **b.** Of an animal: To utter a low guttural sound, expressive of rising anger 1719. **c.** *transf.* Of thunder: To rumble 1727. **2.** Of persons: **a.** *intr.* To murmur angrily 1707. **b.** To utter or express with a growl. Also with *out*. 1758.

2. a. He Growls, he Rages, he Swears 1707. b. To g. out criticisms L. STEPHEN. **Grow·lingly** *adv.*

Growler (grau·ləɹ). 1753. [f. GROWL *v.* + -ER[1].] **1.** One who or something which growls. **2.** *colloq.* A four-wheeled cab 1865. **3.** *U.S.* A species of black-bass (*Grystes salmonoides*) 1880. Also, the grunt or pig-fish (*Cent. Dict.*).

Growlery (grau·ləri). 1852. [f. GROWL *v.* + -ERY.] A place to growl in; applied joc. to a person's private sitting-room.

'This, you must know, is the G. When I am out of humour I come and growl here' DICKENS.

Grown (grōun), pa. pple. of GROW *v.*

Grown up. 1633. [See GROW *v.*] *ppl. a.* Having reached the age of maturity; adult. *sb.* An adult 1813.

sb. No children for me. Give me grown-ups DICKENS.

Growth (grōuþ). 1557. [f. GROW *v.* + -TH.] **1.** The action, process, or manner of growing; vegetative development; increase 1587. **2.** Stage in the process of growing; size or stature attained by growing. *Obs.* exc. in *full growth*. 1557. **3.** Production by cultivation 1663. **4.** *concr.* Produce, product 1580. In *Path.* often *spec.* a morbid formation 1847.

1. When I haue pluck'd thy Rose, I cannot giue it vitall g. againe *Oth.* v. ii. 14. The g. of Anabaptism *Bk. Com. Prayer* Pref. Of foreign g. 1879. 2. Men are but Children of a larger g. DRYDEN. 4. Hogsheads of Claret, the best Growths of France 1715. *Comb.* **g.-line** (*Phys.*), a line indicating a stage of g. Hence **Grow·thful** *a.* full of g.; capable of growing.

Groyne (groin), *sb.* Also †**groin,** †**groyn.** 1582. [perh. identical with GROIN *sb.*[1]; cf. OF. *groin* (lit. 'snout') promontory.] A framework of timber, or now sometimes a low broad wall of concrete or masonry run out into the sea, to arrest and retain the washed-up sand and shingle.

Groyne (groin), *v.* 1872. [f. prec.] *trans.* **a.** To build groynes or breakwaters against the sea. **b.** To furnish with groynes or breakwaters. Hence **Groy·ning** *vbl. sb.* the building of groynes; a system of groynes.

Grozing-iron (grōu·ziŋ əi·əɹn). Also **grosing-.** 1688. [After Du. *gruisijzer*, f. *gruis-* stem of *gruizen* to trim glass, to crush.] †**1.** A tool in the form of nippers formerly used by glaziers in cutting glass –1847. **2.** An iron tool terminating in a bulb, used, when heated, for smoothing the solder joints of lead pipes 1825.

Grub (grɒb), *sb.* ME. [?f. GRUB *v.*] **1.** The larva of an insect, esp. of a beetle; a caterpillar, maggot; also (now *dial.*) a worm. **2.** *contemptuous.* †**a.** A short, dwarfish fellow –1706. **b.** A dull industrious drudge, a literary hack; in recent use, an ill-dressed, unpleasant fellow 1653. **c.** *U.S.* A hard-reading student 1847. **3.** *Cricket.* A ball bowled along the ground 1894. **4.** *slang.* Food or provender 1659. **5.** *U.S.* A root left in the ground after clearing 1875.

2. b. Mr. Nahum Tate:—this poor g. of literature DE QUINCEY. 4. How you'll relish your g. MARRYAT. *Comb.* **g.-stake** *U.S.*, 'the outfit, provisions, etc. furnished to a prospector on condition of participating in the profits of any find he may make, a lay-out (*Cent. Dict.*); **-worm** = sense 1, also *contemptuous*.

Grub (grɒb), *v.* [Perh. repr. OE. **grybban*, f. (ult.) OTeut. **grub-* ablaut-var. of **grab-* to dig, GRAVE *v.*[1]] **1.** *trans.* To dig superficially; to clear (ground) of roots and stumps. Said *occas.* of animals. **2.** To dig up by the roots; to root up, uproot; *esp.* with *up*. Also *transf.* and *fig.* 1555. **3.** With *up*, *out*: To extract by digging. Also *transf.* and *fig.* ME. **4.** *intr.* To dig. In recent use, connoting the idea of mean and laborious occupation. ME. Also *transf.* of animals 1647. **5.** *transf.* and *fig.* To rummage 1800. **6.** To lead a grovelling existence; to toil, 'fag' 1735. **7.** [?f. the sb.] *slang.* **a.** To take grub; to feed 1725. **b.** *trans.* To provide with food 1812.

1. To manure grounds that are newly grubb'd 1653. Like the swine That grubb'd the turf 1827. 2. *fig.* To g. up morality 1807. 4. I met plenty of people, grubbing in miserable little fields STEVENSON. 5. Grubbing among Roman remains and relics A. LANG. *Comb.*: **g.-ax** (corruptly †*grubbage*), **-hoe, -hook,** implements used in grubbing up roots, stumps, etc.; **-fell** *v. trans.*, to bring down (a tree) by cutting at the root; **-saw,** a hand-saw used for sawing marble.

Grub- (in *Grub-Pegasus*), = GRUB-STREET (sense 2). SWIFT.

Grubber (grɒ·bəɹ). ME. [f. GRUB *v.* + -ER[1].] **1.** One who grubs (*lit.* and *fig.*). **2.** An implement for grubbing up roots, stumps, etc. (*local*) 1598. **3.** An eater, a feeder 1861.

Grubble (grɒ·b'l), *v.* 1690. [var. of GRABBLE *v.*, infl. by GRUB *v.*] †**1.** *intr.* and *trans.* To grope –1719. **2.** *intr.* To root (*rare*) 1867.

Grubby (grɒ·bi), *a.* 1611. [f. GRUB *sb.* + -Y.] **1.** Infested with grubs; also, grub-like 1725. **2.** Stunted, dwarfish. Now *dial.* 1611. **3.** Dirty, grimy; also, underbred 1845.

3. A g. lot Of sooty sweeps HOOD. Hence **Gru·bbiness.**

Grub-street (grɒ·bstrīt). 1630. **1.** *orig.* The name of a street near Moorfields in London (now Milton Street), 'much inhabited by writers of small histories, dictionaries, and temporary poems' (J.); hence, the tribe of literary hacks. **2.** *attrib.* or as *adj.* Pertaining to, emanating from, or characteristic of Grub-street; of the nature of literary hack-work 1648.

1. The very Spirit of Grubstreet Reigns in you SHADWELL. 2. Grubstreet and Polemical Divinity MARVELL. Hence †**Grubean** *a.* (*joc.*) of or belonging to Grub-street. SWIFT.

Grucche, obs. f. GRUTCH.

Grudge (grɒdʒ), *sb.* 1477. [f. GRUDGE *v.*, or var. of GRUTCH *sb.*] †1. Murmur, grumbling; discontent; reluctance –1611. †2. Murmuring of the conscience; scruple, doubt, misgiving –1598. 3. Ill will or resentment due to some special cause. (*Obs.* exc. as in b.) 1477. b. An instance of this: const. *against* (a person) 1531. †4. = GRUDGING *vbl. sb.* 2. –1678. †5. Injury (*rare*) –1641.

3. Queen Elizabeth bare..secret g. against her 1635. b. Public affairs were mingled with private grudges SIDNEY. Phr. *To have a g. against, to bear, owe* (a person) *a g.*, etc. 5. Struggling against the grudges of more dreadfull Calamities MILTON. Hence **Gru·dgeful** *a.* resentful; **-ly** *adv.*

Grudge (grɒdʒ), *v.* 1450. [Altered f. GRUTCH *v.*] †1. *intr.* To murmur; to grumble, complain; to be discontented –1632. 2. *trans.* To be unwilling to give, grant, or allow; to begrudge 1500. †3. *trans.* To envy (a person); *intr.* to be envious (*rare*) –1661. 4. *trans.* To trouble or vex mentally. Also *impers.* –1558. †5. *pass.* and *intr.* To be seized *with* a disease; to have the first touch or access of a fever –1549. †6. To cram [? for *gregge*]. ROGERS.

1. To g. or complain of injustice HOOKER. Phr. †*To g. a thought*: to think an envious thought. 1 *Hen. VI*, III. i. 176. 2. The English are very good Sea-men..never grudging their labour 1687. Long the Gods..Have grudg'd thee, Cæsar, to the World below DRYDEN. Hence **Gru·dger**, one who grudges. **Gru·dging-ly** *adv.*, **-ness.**

Grudgeons, obs. f. GURGEONS.

Grudging (grɒ·dʒiŋ), *vbl. sb.* ME. [See -ING [1].] 1. The action of GRUDGE *v.* †2. A slight symptom or trace of an illness; a touch –1796. †3. A secret longing or inclination –1694.

2. The g. of my ague yet remains DRYDEN.

Gruel (grū·ĕl), *sb.* ME. [a. OF. *gruel* (mod. *gruau*) ground grain, flour, gruel, for **grueau, gruyau*:—med.L. **grutellum*, dim. of *grutum* of Teut. origin; cf. OE. *grūt* GROUT.] 1. Fine flour, meal, or the like. *Obs.* or *dial.* 2. A light, liquid food made by boiling oatmeal or other farinaceous substance in water or milk ME. †3. Broth or pottage of oatmeal in which chopped meat has been boiled –1601.

Phr. *To have* or *get one's g.*: to receive one's punishment. Hence **Gru·el** *v. trans.* to exhaust or disable; to punish; also (*nonce-use*) to feed with g. **Gru·elly** *a.* of the nature of or resembling g.

Grueller (grū·ĕləɹ). 1691. [See -ER [1].] †1. One who feeds on gruel; a name given to a set of Oxford students in the 17th c. –1708. 2. *colloq.* A poser, settler. KINGSLEY.

Gruesome (grū·sɒ̆m), *a. dial.* Also †**grewsome.** 1570. [= Da. *grusom* cruel, = f. *gru* horror + *-som* -SOME (Skeat). App. brought into literary use by Scott.] 1. Inspiring fear, awe, or horror; fearful, horrible; grisly. 2. Full of or inspired by fear (*rare*) 1869.

1. As grave and grewsome an auld Dutchman as e'er I saw SCOTT. **Grue·some·ly** *adv.*, **-ness.**

Gruf, obs. f. GROOF.

Gruff (grɒf). 1533. [app. a. Du. or LG. **grof* = mod.G. *grob*, of uncertain origin.]

A. *adj.* 1. Coarse, coarse-grained (now only *techn.*); of immaterial things, rude, gross, unpolished 1681. 2. Rough of aspect, voice, or manner, surly, sour 1690.

1. The..purchase of sugar and other g. goods WELLESLEY. 2. A g. religionist 1862. Hence **Gru·ffish** *a.* somewhat g. **Gru·ffly** *adv.* in a g. manner, with a g. voice. **Gru·ffness**, g. condition or quality.

B. *sb.* 1. *Pharmacy.* The coarse residue, which will not pass through the sieve in pulverization 1853. 2. A quarrel, tiff. ? *local U.S.* 1857.

Gruft (grɒft). *local.* 1803. Particles of soil which are washed up by rain among the grass. Hence **Gru·fted** *ppl. a.* begrimed, dirty. TENNYSON.

Gru-gru: see GROO-GROO.

Grum (grɒm), *a.* 1640. [Cf. *grim, glum, gruff*, etc.; also Da. *grum* cruel.] = GLUM *a.* 1. †b. *dial.* Of the voice: Gruff, harsh, and deep in tone. ALMOND.

The King replyed nothing but Look'd very g. 1640. Hence **Gru·mness**, g. quality.

Grumble (grɒ·mb'l), *sb.* 1623. [f. GRUMBLE *v.*] 1. An act of grumbling; a subdued utterance of complaint. 2. *The grumbles* (*joc.* as if a malady): ill humour, vented in grumbling 1861.

Grumble (grɒ·mb'l), *v.* 1586. [Cf. F. *grommeler*, Du. (*g*)*rommelen*, G. (*g*)*rummeln*, etc.] 1. *intr.* To utter dull inarticulate sounds; to mutter, mumble; to growl faintly 1596. Of thunder, a drum, etc.: To rumble, esp. faintly 1621. 2. To utter murmurs of discontent; hence *gen.* to complain 1586. 3. *trans.* To express or utter with mumbling, muttering, or complaining 1824.

1. Who art thou that dost g. there i' th' straw SHAKS. The Lion..with sullen pleasure, grumbles o'er his prey DRYDEN. 2. He was always grumbling about his food TROLLOPE. **Gru·mbler**, one who grumbles; a name for the GURNARD. **Gru·mblingly** *adv.*

Grumbletonian (grɒmb'ltōu·niăn). 1690. [f. GRUMBLE *v.*, after *Muggletonian*, etc.] †1. A nickname for the members of the 'Country Party' in English politics after the Revolution, who were accused by the 'Court Party' of being actuated by dissatisfied personal ambition. Also *attrib.* –1855. 2. A grumbler. GOLDSM.

1. No more of your g. morals, brother; there's preferment coming DRYDEN.

Grume (grūm). 1555. [ad. late L. *grumus* little heap, hillock; cf. obs. F. *grume*, mod.F. *grumeau* clot, It. *grumo.*] †1. A lump. EDEN. 2. *Med.* A clot of blood; blood in a viscous condition. Also, any viscous fluid. 1619.

Grummet, grommet (grɒ·met). 1626. [ad. F. *gromette*, now *gourmette* curb of a bridle, f. *gourmer* to curb, of unkn. origin.] A ring or wreath of rope, *spec.* one consisting of a single strand laid three times round. a. One of those used to secure the upper edge of a sail to its stay. b. A ring of rope or an eyelet of metal used for a rowlock. 1802. c. A wad for keeping the shot steady in the bore when firing at a depression 1828.

Grumose (grumōu·s), *a. rare.* 1753. [See next and -OSE.] = GRUMOUS 3.

Grumous (grū·məs), *a.* 1665. [ad. mod.L. **grumosus*, f. *grumus* GRUME; see -OUS.] 1. Containing, consisting of, or resembling grume; clotted; thick, viscid. 2. *transf.* Of diseases, etc.: Characterized or caused by grume 1779. 3. *Bot.* Of roots, etc.: Consisting or formed of clustered grains 1688.

2. A small g. tumour PALEY. **Gru·mousness.**

Grump (grɒmp), *sb.* 1727. [? Suggested by GRUNT.] †1. *Humps and grumps*: slights and snubs –1760. 2. *pl.* The sulks. W. CORY. Hence **Gru·mpish, Gru·mpy** *adjs.* surly, ill-tempered.

Grundel (grɒ·ndĕl). ME. [f. *grund* GROUND *sb.* + -EL [1].] A fish; = GROUNDLING 1.

Grundsil(l, obs. f. GROUNDSEL *sb.*[2]

Grundy (grɒ·ndi). 1798. The surname of an imaginary personage (*Mrs. Grundy*), proverbially referred to as a personification of the tyranny of social opinion in matters of conventional propriety.

'If shame should come to the poor child—I say, Tummas, what would Mrs. Grundy say then' T. MORTON.

Grunswel(l, obs. f. GROUNDSEL *sb.*[1]

Grunt (grɒnt), *sb.* 1553. [f. GRUNT *v.*] 1. The characteristic low gruff sound made by a hog; a similar sound made by other animals 1615. 2. A similar sound made by a man. In early use, a groan. 1553. 3. A name for American fishes of the genus *Hæmulon* and allied species (as *Orthopristis chrysopterus*). So called from the noise they make when taken. 1713. b. An Eng. fish, ? the perch 1851.

Grunt (grɒnt), *v.* [OE. *grunnettan*, freq. of *grunian* to grunt (echoic).] 1. *intr.* Of a hog: To utter its characteristic low gruff sound. Also of other animals and of persons: To utter a sound like this. †b. To groan –1602. 2. To grumble, murmur ME.; *trans.* to utter or express with a grunt 1613. †3. *trans.* To grind (the teeth) –1483.

1. Sneak with the scoundrel fox, or g. with glutton swine BEATTIE. b. *Haml.* III. i. 77. Hence **Gru·ntingly** *adv.*

Grunter [1] (grɒ·ntəɹ). ME. [f. GRUNT *v.* + -ER [1].] 1. An animal or person that grunts; *esp.* a pig. 2. A name for fishes making a grunting noise (cf. GRUNT *sb.* 3) 1726.

1. Jerome has no name for him but the 'grunter' FARRAR.

Grunter [2] (grɒ·ntəɹ). 1858. An iron rod bent like a hook, used by mechanics.

Gru·nting, *ppl. a.* 1567. [-ING [2].] That grunts.

Comb.: **g.-ox**, the yak, *Poëphagus grunniens* (*Cent. Dict.*); **-peck** *slang*, pork.

Gruntle (grɒ·nt'l), *v.* ME. [f. GRUNT *v.* + -LE (dim. or freq.).] 1. *intr.* To utter a little or low grunt. *Rarely* of persons. *Obs.* exc. *dial.* 2. To grumble, murmur, complain 1589.

Gruntling (grɒ·ntliŋ), *sb.* 1686. [f. GRUNT *v.* + -LING.] A young pig.

†**Grutch,** *sb.* ME. [f. GRUTCH *v.*] = GRUDGE *sb.* 1–3. –1687.

Grutch (grɒtʃ), *v.* Now *dial.* or *arch.* [ME. *gruce, gruchche*, etc., a. OF. *groucier, groucher*, etc., to murmur, grumble (whence med.L. *groussare*) of unkn. origin.] 1. = GRUDGE *v.* 1, 2. †2. To make a jarring or grating sound –1509.

‖**Gruyère** (gruyēəɹ; Fr. grüyęr). 1826. [Name of a town in Switzerland, used *attrib.* in 'Gruyère cheese', also with 'cheese' omitted.] A cheese made of cow's milk, of firm consistence, containing numerous cavities.

†**Gry.** 1679. [a. L. *gry* (in Plautus *Most.* I. iii. 67), a. Gr. γρῦ in the phr. οὐδὲ γρῦ, and explained as meaning (1) the grunt of a pig, (2) the dirt under the nail; hence the veriest trifle.] The smallest unit in Locke's proposed decimal system of linear measurement, being the tenth of a line –1813.

Gry-: see GRI-.

†**Grylle.** *rare.* [ad. L. *gryllus*, a. Gr. γρύλλος.] A cricket. EDEN.

Gryllotalpa (gri:lotæ·lpă). 1791. [f. L. *gryllo-*, comb. f. *gryllus* + *talpa.*] The mole-cricket.

Grype: see GRIPE.

†**Gryph(e.** ME. [A perversion of GRIPE, after L. *gryphus*; see GRIFFIN.] 1. A griffin –1579. 2. A vulture. Also *fig.* –1586.

Gryphite (gri·fəit). 1796. [f. L. *gryphus*; see GRIFFIN and -ITE.] *Min.* A fossil oyster-shell of the genus *Gryphæa*. (Cf. CROWSTONE.)

Gryphon: see GRIFFIN.

Grysbok (grəi·sbǫk). Also †**greisbok.** 1786. [ad. Du. *grijsbok*, f. *grijs* GREY + *bok* BUCK.] A small grey S. African antelope (*Antilope melanotis*).

‖**Guacharo** (gwa·tʃărο). 1830. [Sp., of S. Amer. origin.] A nocturnal bird, *Steatornis caripensis*, of S. America and Trinidad, valued for its oil; the oil-bird. Also *attrib.*

Guacho, erron. sp. of GAUCHO.

‖**Guaco** (gwā·ko). 1822. [Sp.-Amer.] The name given to *Mikania Guaco, Aristolochia anguicida*, and other plants used as an antidote to snake-bites. Also, the substance obtained from these. Hence **Gua·conize** *v. trans.* to treat with g.

Guaiac (gwai·ăk). 1558. [ad. mod.L. *guaiacum.*] = GUAIACUM 2, 3. Also *attrib.*, as *g.-resin*, etc.

‖**Guaiacum** (gwai·ăkɒ̆m). 1533. [mod.L., ad. Sp. *guayaco, guayacan*, of native Haytian origin.] 1. A genus of trees and shrubs (N.O. *Zygophallaceæ*), native to the W. Indies and tropical America; a tree of this genus, esp. *Guaiacum officinale* and *G. sanctum* 1553. 2. The hard and heavy brownish-green wood of *G. officinale* and *G. sanctum*, used in medicine; lignum vitæ 1533. 3. A resin obtained from the tree; also, the drug made from it. Also *gum g.* 1553. 4. *attrib.* 1596.

Hence **Guai·acene**, *Chem.* a light colourless oil, obtained by the dry distillation of g. resin. **Guaia·cic** *a.*, in *Guaiacic acid* $C_6H_8O_3$, a substance obtained from g. resin and wood. **Guai·acin, -ine**, *Chem.* a non-nitrogenous vegetable principle discovered in the wood and bark of *G. officinale*, having a sharp acrid taste.

Guan (gwān). 1743. [? a native name.] One of a family or subfamily (*Pelopinæ*, Newton) of gallinaceous birds of S. America, allied to the curassows.

Guana (gwā·nă). Also *Austral.* †**go(h)anna.** 1607. [var. of IGUANA.] **1.** The IGUANA, a large arboreal lizard of the W. Indies and S. America. **2.** *Colonial.* Any large lizard, e.g. *Sphenodon punctatum* of New Zealand 1802.

Guana, var. of GUANO.

‖**Guanaco** (gwănā·ko). 1604. [Quichua *huanaco, huanacu.*] A S. Amer. mammal, *Auchenia huanaco,* a kind of wild llama producing a reddish brown wool.

Guanamine (gwæ·nămein). Also **-in.** 1881. [f. GUAN(O + AMINE.] *Chem.* One of a series of bases formed by the action of heat on the guanidine salts of the fatty acids.

Guanidine (gwæ·nidin). Also **-in.** 1864. [Modified from GUANIN.] *Chem.* A strongly alkaline base CN_3H_5, formed by the oxidation of guanin. Hence **Gua·nidinic** *a.*

Guaniferous (gwăni·fĕrəs), *a.* 1844. [f. GUAN(O + -(I)FEROUS.] Producing guano.

Guanin (gwā·nin). Also **-ine.** 1850. [f. GUAN(O + -IN.] *Chem.* A white amorphous substance obtained from guano, forming a constituent of the excrement of birds, and found in the liver, pancreas, etc. of animals.

Guano (gwā·no, giu,æ·no), *sb.* Also †**guana.** 1604. [Sp. *guano,* S. Amer. Sp. *huano,* ad. Quichua *huanu* dung.] **1.** A natural manure found in great abundance on some sea-coasts, esp. on the islands about Peru, consisting of the excrement of sea-fowl. Also *fig.* **2.** *transf.* Artificial manure, esp. that called *fish-manure* or *fish-g.* 1844. **3.** A general name for sea-birds which produce guano. ? *Obs.* 1697. **4.** *attrib.* 1844. Hence **Gua·nize, Gua·no** *vbs.* to treat with g.

‖**Guara** [1] (gwā·ră). 1678. [mod.L., a. Tupi *guará* 'bird'.] The Scarlet Ibis, *Eudocimus ruber.*

‖**Guara** [2] (gwā·ră). Also **aguara.** 1884. [Tupi *jagoára* 'dog, ounce' (Dias); cf. JAGUAR.] A large-maned wild dog of S. America, *Canis jubatus.*

‖**Guaracha** (gwara·tʃa). Also *erron.* **guaracia.** 1828. [Sp.] 'A lively Spanish dance in $\frac{3}{8}$ or $\frac{3}{4}$ time, usually accompanied on the guitar by the dancer himself' (Stainer and Barrett).

‖**Guarana** (gwărā·nă). 1838. [Tupi *guaraná.*] A Brazilian shrub, *Paullinia sorbilis*; a paste prepared from its seeds (*g. bread, paste*).

Guarani (gwarā·ni). [Name of a S. American tribe.] The unit of currency in Paraguay since November 1943, superseding the peso.

Guaranin (gwără·nin). Also †**-ina, -ine.** 1838. [f. GUARANA + -IN.] *Chem.* A crystalline principle (? = caffeine) contained in guarana.

Guarantee (gærăntī·), *sb.* 1679. [Earlier *garanté,* perh. a. Sp. *garante* = F. *garant,* OF. *guarant, warant* (whence WARRANT *sb.*). The form *guarantee* was subseq. misused for GUARANTY, perh. after F. *garantie.*] **1.** A person or party that makes a guaranty or gives a security. **2.** = GUARANTY *sb.* 1. 1786. **3.** = GUARANTY *sb.* 3. 1832. **4.** A person to whom a guaranty is given: the correl. of *guarantor* 1853. **5.** *attrib.*: **guarantee fund,** a sum of money pledged as a contingent indemnity for possible loss; **g. society,** a joint-stock company, which, for a premium, guarantees to an employer the honesty of a person employed, and undertakes to make good any defalcations in his accounts.

1. That promise, of which our King was the Garante 1683. 2. This I relate as I heard it, without g. STEVENSON. 3. This announcement was received as a g. of their personal safety KANE. Hence **Guarantee·ship.**

Guarantee (gærăntī·), *v.* 1791. [f. prec. sb.] **1.** *trans.* To be a guarantee, warrant, or surety for; *spec.* to undertake with respect to (a contract, the performance of a legal act, etc.) that it shall be duly carried out; to make oneself responsible for the genuineness of (an article); *hence,* to assure the existence or persistence of. **b.** with *inf.* or *obj. cl.*: To engage to do something; to warrant that something will happen or has happened 1820. **2.** To secure the possession of (something) *to* a person, etc. 1838. **3.** To secure (a person) *against* or *from* (risk, etc.); to secure *in* (the possession of anything) 1804.

1. By the treaty of alliance she guaranteed the Polish constitution in a secret article LD. BROUGHAM. b. I'll g. that he'll never return 1884. 2. Liberty to follow the Confession of Augsburg..was guaranteed to the city S. AUSTIN. 3. To g. them against all exactions WELLESLEY.

Guarantor (gærăntǭ·ɹ). 1853. [f. as prec., by substituting -OR for its correl. -EE [1].] One who makes or gives a guaranty or security. Hence **Guaranto·rship.**

Guaranty (gæ·rănti), *sb.* 1592. [ad. AF. *guarantie* (also *warantie,* WARRANTY), f. *guarant, warant* (see WARRANT).] **1.** The action or an act of securing, warranting, or guaranteeing; security, warranty; *spec.* a written undertaking made by a *guarantor* to be answerable for the payment of a debt or the performance of an obligation by another person who is in the first instance liable to such payment or obligation. †**2.** A person who gives a guaranty (sense 1) –1692. **3.** Something which guarantees the existence or persistence of a thing 1697.

1. Our g. of the pragmatic sanction 1792. 3. The best G. of a Peace, is a good Force to maintain it 1697.

Guaranty (gæ·rănti), *v.* 1732. [f. the sb. Now repl. by GUARANTEE *v.*] = GUARANTEE *v.*

Guard (gāɹd), *sb.* [ME. *garde,* a. or ad. F. *garde,* earlier also *guarde* :—Rom. **guarda,* a. OTeut. **wardâ.* Cf. WARD.] †**1.** Keeping, guardianship, custody, ward; used *spec.* in *Law.* –1711. **2.** Protection, defence. (*Obs.* or *arch.*) 1576. **3.** *Sword-exercise, Boxing,* etc. A posture of defence; hence, the weapons or arms in such a posture 1596. **4.** The condition or fact of guarding, protecting, or standing on the defensive; watch; *esp.* in *to keep g.* 1596. **5.** †**a.** Caution, precaution. **b.** (with *pl.*) A precaution (now *rare*) 1597. **6.** One who keeps, protects, or defends; *spec.* one of a guard (sense 8), a sentry, sentinel ME. **b.** The man who has general charge of a stage-coach or a railway train. (Orig. an armed man to protect a mail-coach against robbery; hence the name.) 1788. **7.** *pl.* The household troops of the English army, consisting of the FOOT-GUARDS, the HORSE-GUARDS, and the LIFE-GUARDS. Also applied to the Dragoon Guards. 1661. **8.** A body of persons, esp. soldiers (†also *occas.* ships), engaged to protect or control a person or position. Also *transf.* and *fig.* 1494. **9.** A protection, defence (*lit.* and *fig.*) 1606. **10.** An ornamental border or trimming on a garment. *Obs.* exc. *Hist.* or *arch.* Also *fig.* 1529. †**b.** *transf.* A stripe, band of colour –1613. †**11.** *Astr. pl.* The stars Beta and Gamma of the Lesser Bear; also *guards of the pole.* Also, the two 'pointers' of the Great Bear. –1819. **12.** A contrivance of metal, wood, etc. made to protect an object from injury, prevent accidents by falling, etc.; often in comb., as *fire-g.* etc.

a. *gen.* 1774. **b.** That part of the hilt of a sword that protects the hand 1596. **c.** Protections to a book 1892. **d.** A piece of metal to protect the trigger of a gun 1687. **e.** *pl.* The wards of a lock 1677. **f.** = *fire-guard* (see FIRE *sb.*) 1845. **g.** *Archery* = BRACER [2]. 1853. **h.** *Railway.* An iron placed in front of a locomotive engine to catch and remove obstacles; *U.S.* a cow-catcher 1838. **i.** A lateral extension of the deck of a steamboat beyond the lines of the hull so as to overhang the water 1850. **j.** *Conch.* In cephalopods, a calcareous structure enveloping the apex of the phragmacone; the rostrum. **k.** A light frame in which the nuts of bolts fit to prevent their unscrewing by the vibration of the engine (Knight) 1875. **l.** A welt inserted between the leaves of a scrap-book, etc. for the attachment of additional leaves 1708. **m.** *Electr.* A device for protecting electrical apparatus from leakage currents, or for rearranging the magnetic or electric field (cf. *g.-ring*).

†**13.** Short for *g.-room* or *g.-house.* PURCHAS.

1. He broke from those that had the g. of him SHAKS. 3. Phr. *At open g.*: a position which leaves the swordsman open to attack. 4. Haue you had quiet G. SHAKS. 6. Thy cries will wake the guards, and they will seize thee B. TAYLOR. b. In the winter [*c* 1820] the g. carried a blunderbuss for protection in a box near him PEEL. 8. Phr. *To mount, relieve* (†*the*) *g. G. of honour*: a body of soldiers, sailors, policemen, etc. appointed to receive a person of distinction and to attend at state ceremonials. *Yeoman of the G.*: see YEOMAN. 9. His greatnesse was no gard To barre heauens shaft SHAKS.

Phrases. **On** or **upon one's g., on g.**: in a position of defence, on the defensive (*orig.* with reference to fencing and sentry duty). **Off one's g.**: in or into a defenceless condition; unsuspicious of danger. †**Out of (one's) g.**: = *off (one's) g. Twel. N.* I. v. 93.

Comb.: **g.-bolt,** a flat-headed screw-bolt, fully counter-sunk, for fastening the guards of mowing machines to the bars; **-brush,** on an electric railway, a metallic brush by means of which the current is conveyed to the motor; **-cell** (*Bot.*), one of the two cells that embrace the stomata of plants; **-chamber** = GUARD-ROOM; **-detail,** 'men from a company, regiment, etc. detailed from g. duty' (Webst.); **-duty,** the duty of watching, patrolling, etc.; **-finger,** 'one of the teeth projecting forward from the cutter-bar of a harvester and through which the knife plays' (Knight); **-book,** a blank book, furnished with guards (sense 12 l); **-iron,** (*a*) *Naut.* one of certain curved or arched bars of iron placed over the ornamental figures on a ship's head or quarter, to protect them from injury; (*b*) = 12 h; **-lock,** a *tide-lock,* forming a communication between a basin and tide-water; **-pin,** (*a*) *Horol.* a pin in the lever escapement that prevents the pallets leaving the escape wheel when the hands of the watch are turned back; (*b*) in a rifle, the pin by which the guard (sense 12 d) is attached; **-plate,** (*a*) in an electrometer = *guard-ring*; (*b*) 'the plate which closes the opening in front of a cupola furnace, to whose iron casing it is attached by staples' (Knight); **-polyp** (*Zool.*), a zooid modified to serve a defensive function, as in the nematophore of a cœlenterate, a macho-polyp; **-ring,** (*a*) a keeper; (*b*) *Electr.* an annular horizontal surface surrounding the balanced disk in the absolute electrometer; **-stops,** the two points placed one on each side of a numeral, letter, figure, etc.; **-tube** (*Electr.*), a metal tube surrounding a dry pile used with a quadrant electrometer, or its like.

Guard (gāɹd), *v.* 1500. [f. GUARD *sb.,* or ad. F. *garder*; see WARD, GUARD *sbs.*] **1.** *trans.* To keep in safety from injury or attack; to stand guard over; to take care of, protect, defend 1583. **b.** To accompany as a guard (*arch.*) 1597. **2.** To provide with safeguards, or (*Med.*) correctives 1726. **3.** To keep watch over; to keep in check, control (thoughts, etc.) 1742. †**4.** To parry (a blow) –1695. **5.** To ornament with guards; to trim; also *transf.* to stripe 1500. Also *fig.* **6.** *intr.* To be on one's guard; to stand as a sentinel; to take up or maintain a position of defence 1590. **7.** *Curling.* **a.** *trans.* To cover a stone by planting one in a line between it and oneself. Also *absol.* **b.** *intr.* Said of a stone so planted. Similarly in *Bowls.* 1685. **8.** *Chess. trans.* To support a piece or pawn with another 1761. **9.** *Bookbinding.* To supply (a guard book) with guards.

1. Draw not thy sword to gard iniquitie SHAKS. Guarding realms and kings from shame TENNYSON. b. My blessing..like a beacon, guards thee home TENNYSON. 2. To g. oneself from being supposed [etc.] 1891. 3. He that guardeth his mouth keepeth his life R.V. *Prov.* xiii. 3. 5. *fig.* To g. a Title, that was rich before; to gilde refined Golde *John* IV. ii. 10. Also *Much Ado* I. i. 288. Hence **Gua·rdable** *a.*

‖**Guarda-costa** (gā·ɹdă kǫ·stă, Sp. gwa·rda-). 1731. [Sp.; f. prec. + Sp. *costa* COAST.] A Spanish vessel used for the protection of the coast; a custom-house cutter.

†**Gua·rdage.** *rare.* 1604. [f. GUARD *v.* + -AGE.] Keeping, guardianship –1621.

Guardant (gā·ɹdănt). 1572. [a. F. *gardant,* pr. pple. of *garder.*]

A. *adj.* **1.** Guarding, watching; on guard 1574. **2.** *Her.* Of a beast: Having the full face towards the spectator. (Cf. AFFRONTÉ and GAZE *sb.*) Also *fig.* 1572.

B. *sb.* A keeper, guardian, protector 1591.

Guard-boat (gā·ɹdbōᵘt). 1696. **a.** A boat appointed to row the rounds among the ships of war in a harbour, to observe that a good look-out is kept. **b.** A boat employed to enforce custom-house or quarantine regulations.

Guarded (gā·ɹdèd), *ppl. a.* 1509. [f. GUARD *v.* or *sb.* + -ED.] **1.** Protected, watched; having a guard or sentinel 1570. **2.** Reserved, restrained; on one's guard; hence: Careful; prudent; cautious 1709. **3.** Ornamented, as with lace, etc.; tricked out; having guards. *Obs.* exc. *Hist.* and *spec.* in *Her.* of a garment: Trimmed or turned up with some material 1509. **4.** Of a book: Having guards (see GUARD *sb.* 12 l) 1888.

1. The g. mount, gold MILT., pass SCOTT. 2. Learn to be more g. GAY. **Gua·rded-ly** *adv.,* **-ness. Gua·rder,** one who or that which guards (*lit.* and *fig.*).

Guard-fish, var. of GARFISH.

Guardful (gā·ɹdfŭl), *a.* Now *rare.* 1611. [f. GUARD *sb.* + -FUL.] Watchful, careful. Hence **Gua·rdfully** *adv.*

Guard-house (gā·ɹdhaus). 1592. **a.** A building to accommodate a (military) guard. **b.** A building in which prisoners are kept under guard.

Guardian (gā·ɹdiăn). [ME. *gardein*, a. AF. *gardein*, OF. *g(u)arden*, f. *garde* GUARD *sb.*, q.v. See also WARDEN.] **1.** One who guards, protects, or preserves; 'one to whom the care or preservation of any thing is committed' (J.); occas. = *guardian angel* 1477. Also *occas.* used of things. **2.** *spec.* in *Law.* One who has or is entitled to the custody of the person or property (or both) of an infant, an idiot, or other person legally incapable of managing his own affairs; a tutor. (Correl. of *ward.*) 1513. †**3.** In official titles; now more commonly WARDEN. -1632. **4.** The superior of a Franciscan convent. (L. *custos.*) 1466. **5.** *attrib.*, as **g.-cell** = *guard-cell* 1880; also as *adj.* with sense 'protecting, tutelary', in **g.-angel.**

1. The attorney-general is *ex officio* the g. of liberty JUNIUS. The Sacred Store-house of his Predecessors, and G. of their Bones SHAKS. *G. of the Poor* (often simply *G.*): one of a board elected to administer the poor laws in a parish or district. 2. A wastefull Prince, that had neede of a G., or ouerseer A. V. *Transl. Pref.* Phr. *G. in chivalry*: the g. of a minor holding by knight service. *G. in socage*: the g. of a tenant in socage. *G. by nature*: the father. *G. by nurture*: the father, and, after his death, the mother, until the minor is 14. (These four are guardians *by the common law.*) *G. ad litem*: one appointed by the courts, to defend a prosecution or suit instituted by or against an infant.

Hence †**Gua·rdianage** (*rare*), †**Gua·rdiance, Gua·rdiancy** (*rare*), = GUARDIANSHIP. **Gua·rdianess**, a female g. **Gua·rdianless** *a.* having no g.

Guardianship (gā·ɹdiănʃip). 1553. [f. GUARDIAN + -SHIP.] The condition or fact of being a guardian; the office or position of a guardian; used *spec.* in *Law.*

Guardless (gā·ɹdlĕs), *a.* 1611. [f. GUARD *sb.* + -LESS.] **1.** Without a guard; without safeguards; unprotected. **2.** Off one's guard 1654. **3.** Of a sword: Having no guard 1882.

Guard-rail (gā·ɹd₁rēl). 1860. **1.** A hand- or other rail to guard against accidents. **2.** *Railway.* A short rail placed on the inside of a main rail, so as to keep a wheel on the track; used in switches, crossings, etc. 1875.

Guard-room (gā·ɹd₁rūm). 1762. = GUARD-HOUSE.

Guardship[1] (gā·ɹdʃip). *rare.* 1624. [f. GUARD *sb.* + -SHIP.] The condition or position of a guard or guardian.

Guard-ship, guardship[2] (gā·ɹdʃip). 1689. **a.** A vessel of war appointed to protect and regulate a harbour, and to receive seamen until they can join their ships. **b.** 'The ship (of the squadron) having guard-duty for the day' (Funk).

Guardsman (gā·ɹdzmæ̆n). 1817. [In 1, f. *guard's*; in 2, f. *Guards* pl.] **1.** A man who acts as a guard; a member of a guard 1854. **2.** A soldier, usu. an officer, of the household guards.

‖**Guariba** (gwarī·bă). 1753. [Native Brazilian.] The Howling Monkey.

†**Gua·rish,** *v.* 1474. [a. OF. *g(u)ariss-*, stem of *g(u)arir*, mod. *guérir* :—OTeut. **warjan* to protect, defend. See also WARISH.] **1.** *trans.* To cure, heal -1596. **2.** *intr.* for *pass.* To recover. Const. *of.* CAXTON.

‖**Guava** (gwā·vă). 1555. [Sp. *guayaba*, *-abo*, app. a. S. Amer.] **1.** A tree of the myrtaceous genus *Psidium* of tropical America, esp. *P. Guayava*, which yields a fruit of an acid flavour, used to make jelly, etc. **2.** This fruit 1555. **3.** *attrib.* 1630.

1. White G., *Psidium pyriferum.* **Red G.,** *P. pomiferum.*

‖**Guazzo.** 1722. [It.] = GOUACHE.

Gubernaculum (giūbəɹnæ·kiŭlŏm). Pl. **-la.** 1661. [L., f. *gubernare.*] Applied to several animal and vegetable structures which are used for steering (e.g. in flight), or for regulating the (embryonic) development or course of an organ. Hence **Guberna·cular** *a.*

†**Gubernance.** 1455. [f. L. *gubernantem*, after GOVERNANCE.] Governance, government -1550.

Gubernation (giūbəɹnē¹·ʃən). Now *rare.* ME. [ad. L. *gubernationem.*] The act or fact of governing; government.

Gubernative (giū·bəɹnĕtiv), *a.* Now *rare.* ME. [ad. L. **gubernativus*, f. *gubernare.*] Of or pertaining to government; governing.

Gubernator (giū·bəɹneⁱtǫɹ). *rare.* 1522. [a. L., f. *gubernat-*, *gubernare.*] A ruler, governor. Hence **Gu·bernato·rial** *a.* (chiefly *U. S.*), of or pertaining to a governor or government, or to 'the governor', i.e. one's father. So ‖**Guberna·trix,** she that rules or governs.

Gudgeon (gʊ·dʒən), *sb.*[1] [ME. *gojon*, *gogen*, a. F. *goujon* :—L. *gobionem*, *gobio*, by-form of *gobius* GOBY.] **1.** A small European freshwater fish (*Gobio fluviatilis*), much used for bait. †**b.** Applied to fishes of the genus *Gobius* or family *Gobiidæ*; see GOBY -1774. **2.** *fig.* **a.** One that will swallow anything; a gullible person 1584. **b.** A bait 1579. **3.** *attrib.* 1599.

1. The Gudgion is an excellent fish to eat WALTON. 2. a. In vain at glory g. Boswell snaps WOLCOT. b. The Gullings and Gudgeons that he had given him 1620. Hence **Gu·dgeon** *v.* to play the g.; also *trans.* to cheat.

Gudgeon (gʊ·dʒən), *sb.*[2] ME. [a. OF. *gojon*, *goujon*, etc.; perh. an application of prec.] **1.** A pivot, usually of metal, fixed on or let into the end of a beam, spindle, axle, etc., and on which a wheel turns, a bell swings, or the like; now used more widely of various kinds of journals, etc. **2.** The ring or eye in the heel of a gate which turns on the hook or pintle in the gate-post 1496. **3.** *Naut.* A metal socket in which the pintle of a rudder turns 1558. **4.** A metallic pin used for securing together two blocks of stone, etc. SPON. **5.** *attrib.*, as *g.-pin*, etc. 1839.

†**Gue.** [ad. F. *gueux* beggar.] A rogue. J. WEBSTER.

Guebre (gī·bəɹ, gē¹·bəɹ). 1687. [a. F. *guèbre*, ad. Pers. *gabr.* Cf. GIAOUR.] A Zoroastrian, fire-worshipper, Parsee.

Guelder rose (ge·ldəɹ₁rōuz). 1597. [Named from *Guelders* (in Prussia) or *Guelderland* (a province of Holland).] The plant *Viburnum Opulus*, esp. the cultivated form; the snowball-tree. Also, the flower of this plant.

Guelph (gwelf). Also †**Guelf.** 1579. [ad. It. *Guelfo*, med.L. *Guelphus*, ad. MHG. *Welf*, name of the founder and of many chiefs of the family now represented by the ducal house of Brunswick and the present dynasty of Great Britain and Ireland. A member of one of the two great parties in mediæval Italian politics, characterized chiefly by supporting the popes against the emperors. (Cf. GHIBELLINE.)

Guelphic (gwe·lfik), *a.* Also †**Guelfic.** 1823. [f. GUELPH + -IC.] **1.** Of or pertaining to the family or the faction of the Guelphs.

‖**Guenon** (gənoṅ). 1838. [Fr.; of unkn. origin.] Name for a group of monkeys belonging to the ancient continent and its islands, of which the Green Monkey, *Cercocebus sabæus*, is typical.

Guepard (ge·păɹd). Also **gepard.** 1882. [a. F. *guépard* (Buffon); ? corrupt f. Eng. *leopard.*] **a.** = CHEETAH. **b.** A kind of leopard, *Cynailurus guttata.*

Guerdon (gɔ̄·ɹdən), *sb.* Now *poet.* and *rhet.* ME. [a. OF. *guerdon* :—med.L. *widerdonum*, repr. OHG. *widarlôn* = OE. *wiðerléan*, f. *wiðer* again + *léan* payment.] A reward, requital, or recompense.

Death in g. of her wrong Giues her fame *Much Ado* v. iii 5. The g. of our wicked works H. COGAN. Hence **Gue·rdonless** *a.* without g.

Guerdon (gɔ̄·ɹdən), *v.* Now *poet.* and *rhet.* ME. [a. OF. *guerdoner*; see prec.] *trans.* To reward, recompense. Also *absol.*

She may right wel g. hym for hys seruice LD. BERNERS. Confusion g. his base villainie HEYWOOD. Hence **Gue·rdonable** *a.* that may be guerdoned.

‖**Guereza** (ge·rīză). 1859. [? African.] An Abyssinian monkey (*Colobus guereza*) with long hair and a bushy tail.

Guerilla: see GUERRILLA.

Guérite (gerī·t). 1706. [a. F.; see GARRET *sb.*] A turret or box of wood or stone for a sentry.

Guernsey (gɔ̄·ɹnzi). The name of one of the Channel Islands. **1.** Used *attrib.* in †**G. flower, lily,** a ? Japanese or S. African plant (*Nerine Sarniensis*), with handsome lily-like flowers, naturalized in Guernsey 1578. **2.** (orig. *ellipt.*) A thick, knitted, closely-fitting vest or shirt, usu. made of blue wool, worn by seamen 1851. **b.** One of a breed of cattle of the Channel Islands 1834.

Guerrilla, guerilla (geri·lă, gĕri·lă). 1809. [a. Sp. *guerrilla*, dim. of *guerra* war.] **1.** An irregular war carried on by small bodies of men acting independently 1819. **2.** One engaged in such warfare 1809. **3.** *attrib.* (or *adj.*), esp. in *g. war* (= sense 1) 1811. Also *fig.*

1. Arkansas is now the theatre of a large g. 1862. So ‖**Guerrillero, guerillero** (= sense 2).

Guess (ges), *sb.* ME. [f. GUESS *v.*] **1.** The action or an act of guessing; a conjecture, rough estimate; a supposition based on uncertain grounds. **2.** *attrib.* 1863.

1. *By g.*: at haphazard, by rough estimation; by conjecture. By my g. we should come upon Crackskull common GOLDSM.

Guess (ges), *v.* [ME. *gessen*, f. (ult.) the root of GET *v.* In the 14th c. the usual rendering of L. *æstimare.*] **1.** *trans.* To form an approximate judgement of without actual measurement or calculation; to estimate. Also *absol.* †**2.** *intr.* To take aim (const. *to*) -1530. †**3.** *trans.* To esteem, account, reckon. ME. only. †**4.** To think, judge, suppose. ME. only. **5.** To form an opinion or hypothesis respecting (some unknown state of facts), either at random or from uncertain indications; to conjecture. Const. *by*, *from.* Also *absol.* and *ellipt.* ME. **6.** *I guess*: sometimes used playfully in reference to a fact or secure inference. Hence *colloq.* in U. S. = 'I am pretty sure'. 1692. **7.** *intr.* To form conjectures ME. **b.** *To keep* (a person) *guessing*: to keep in a state of uncertainty (*colloq.*, orig. *U.S.*) 1905. **8.** *trans.* 'To conjecture rightly' (J.); to divine 1548.

1. Mo than a thousand stories as I gesse Koude I now telle CHAUCER. To g. Time 1726. 5. I g. it to have been a Piece of the Chapell HEARNE. I..little guessed the end MRS. BROWNING. He went Alone, as you may g., to banishment SHELLEY. 6. I g... you winna be the waur o' a glass of the right Rosa Solis SCOTT. Hence **Gue·ssable** *a.* **Gue·sser. Gue·ssingly** *adv.* by guess-work.

†**Gue·ssive,** *a.* [See -IVE.] Conjectural. FELTHAM.

Guess-rope: see GUEST-ROPE.

Guess-warp (ge·s₁wǭɹp). 1495. [See GUEST-ROPE (GUESS-ROPE) and WARP *sb.*] *Naut.* **1.** 'A rope carried to a distant object, in order to warp a vessel round it, or to make fast a boat' (Smyth). By some used of any rope attaching a boat astern of a vessel. **2.** = GUEST-ROPE 2. Also *attrib.* 1833.

Gue·ss-work. 1725. [f. GUESS *sb.*] Procedure consisting in or based on guessing.

Guest (gest), *sb.* [Com. Teut.: OE. *giest*, *gæst* :—OTeut. **gasti-z* :—WAryan **ghosti-s*, represented also by L. *hostis*, orig. 'stranger', in classical use 'enemy'.] **1.** One who is entertained at the house or table of another. Also *transf.* and *fig.* †**2.** A stranger -1578. **3.** A temporary inmate of an hotel, inn, or boarding-house ME. **4.** A man, 'fellow'. *Obs.* exc. *dial.* ME. **5.** A parasite animal or vegetable. Also *g.-fly.* 1864.

1. The sacred name of g. SCOTT. *fig.* I thought of times when Pain might be thy g., Lord of thy house and hospitality, And Grief WORDSW. 3. If our landlord supplies us with beef and with fish Let each g. bring himself GOLDSM.

Comb.: **g.- (gall-) fly** (see INQUILINE 2); **-moth,** an inquiline moth; **-night,** the night on which guests are entertained at a club, college, etc.; **-room** = GUEST-CHAMBER.

Guest (gest), *v.* ME. [f. GUEST *sb.*] **1.** *trans.* To make a guest of; to entertain, lodge, put up. **2.** *intr.* To be or become a guest; to lodge (*rare*) 1615.

2. Tell me..who he was That guested here so late CHAPMAN.

Gue·st-cha·mber. 1526. A room used for the lodging or entertainment of a guest.

Guest house. [OE. *giest-hús* = G. *gasthaus*; see GUEST *sb.* and HOUSE.] †**1.** An inn

-ME. 2. A house or apartment for the reception of strangers or guests. Also *attrib.* OE. †b. A hospital –1641.

Guestless (ge·stlės), *a.* 1598. [See -LESS.] Having no guests; also *occas.*, as tr. Gr. ἄξενος, inhospitable.

Gue·st-rope, gue·ss-rope. 1623. [Referred to GUEST *sb.* ('a rope to assist guests in coming on board'; but this suits sense 2 only), and to GUESS *sb.* (cf. GUESS-WARP).] 1. A second rope, fastened to a boat in tow, to keep it steady. 2. A stout rope slung outside a vessel fore and aft, formerly also fastened to the end of a boom, to give a hold for boats coming alongside.

Gue·stwise. 1548. [See -WISE.]
†A. *sb. In, on, a g.*: as a guest –1641.
B. *adv.* After the manner of a guest or stranger *Mids. N.* III. ii. 171.

Guffaw (gɒfǭ·), *sb.* Orig. *Sc.* 1720. [Echoic.] A burst of coarse laughter. So **Guffaw·** *v. intr.* to laugh coarsely or harshly; *trans.* to say with a g.

Guffer (gɒ·fəɹ). *Sc.* 1684. The Viviparous Blenny (*Zoarces viviparus*). Also *g.-eel.*

Guggle (gɒ·g'l), *sb.* 1680. [f. GUGGLE *v.*] 1. a. *slang.* The windpipe. 2. A guggling sound 1821.

Guggle (gɒ·g'l), *v.* 1611. [Echoic.] 1. *intr.* = GURGLE *v.* 2, 2 b. 2. *trans.* To bring *up* or pour *forth* with a guggling sound 1731.

‖**Guglio** (gū·lyo). *Pl.* **guglio(e)s.** 1644. [It. *guglia*, aphet. var. of *aguglia* needle.] An obelisk, needle.

‖**Guhr** (gūr). 1686. [Ger. dial.; lit. 'ferment'; see YEAST.] *Min.* A loose earthy deposit from water found in the cavities of rocks.

Guiac, -an, -ol, -um, obs. ff. GUAIAC, etc.

Guib (gwib). Also †**guiba.** 1774. The harnessed Antelope of W. Africa, *Tragelaphus scriptus.*

Guidage (gəi·dėdʒ). 1440. [a. OF. *guidage*; in 2, f. GUIDE *v.* + -AGE.] †1. *Old Law.* A fee or tax paid for guidance or safe conduct –1800. 2. Guidance. SOUTHEY.

Guidance (gəi·dăns). 1538. [f. GUIDE *v.* + -ANCE.] 1. The action of guiding; directing agency; leadership, direction. 2. Something which guides or leads 1712.

1. They steered by the g. of the stars GIBBON. Instructions..for the g. of his son MACAULAY.

Guide (gəid), *sb.* ME. [a. F. *guide*, orig. fem., now masc., altered f. OF. *guie* (see GUY *sb.*[1]):—Com. Rom. **guida*, f. *guidare*; see GUY *v.*[1] The *d* of the Fr. word is due to the influence of Pr. forms.]

I. 1. One who leads or shows the way, esp. to a traveller in a strange country; *spec.* one who is hired to conduct a traveller or tourist, and to point out objects of interest. Also *transf.* and *fig.* 2. *Mil.* One employed or forced to accompany an invading army, in order to show the way, etc. 1540. b. *pl.* Men formed into corps for this service 1802. c. One of the two officers of a company, called respectively the *right* and *left guide*, superintending and acting as pivots, etc. in evolutions. Also a vessel which guides the others in the manœuvres of a fleet. 1870. d. (In full *Girl Guide*) A member of an organization of girls corresp. to the Boy Scouts 1908. 3. One who directs another in his ways or conduct; †a ruler. Also *transf.* of things ME. 4. In the titles of books: a. A book of elementary instruction or information 1617. b. A guide-book 1759.

1. He which is the g. goeth before mounted on a cammel 1585. *transf.* The World was all before them ..and Providence thir g. MILT. 3. Now God be his gide for his grete pite 1450. *transf.* They were dangerous guides, the feelings TENNYSON.

II. 1. *gen.* Something that guides 1700. 2. *Mech.* Something which serves to steady or direct the motion of a thing, and upon, through, or against which it moves, slides, or is conducted in the required direction; *esp.* a bar, rod, etc. which guides or 'bears' machinery having reciprocating motion; often in *pl.* 1763. b. Something which guides a tool or the work operated upon; *spec.* in *Surgery*, a director 1680. 3. Something which marks a position or serves to guide the eye 1875. 4. *Mus.* = DUX 2. 1753. 5. *Mining.* A cross-course or -vein 1874.

III. The action of GUIDE *v.*; direction; conduct; guidance. Now *rare.* 1500.

Goats, which now he had in g. CHAPMAN.

Combs. 1. General: as *g.-bar, -chain, -curve*, etc.
2. Special: **g.-block,** a block or piece of metal which slides between or upon guides or guide-bars; **-board,** a board erected at a fork in a road, for the direction of travellers; **-pulley,** (*a*) *Oval-turning*, a pulley by means of which motion is communicated to the guide (sense II. 2 b); (*b*) a pulley over which a band or cord is passed, where its course is altered or where it needs support; **-screw,** a screw-thread in a screw-cutting lathe which regulates the thread of the screw being cut; **-tackle,** a rope secured to the top of a pole, etc., to steady it; **guideway,** a groove, track, or way along which a thing is moved or run in the required direction.

Guide (gəid), *v.* ME. [a. F. *guider*, altered form (infl. by Pr. *guidar*) of the older *guier*, whence GUY *v.*[1]] 1. *trans.* To act as guide to; to go with or before for the purpose of leading the way. b. To direct the course of (a vehicle, tool, etc.) 1460. 2. *fig.* and in immaterial senses: To lead or direct in a course of action, etc.; to determine the course of (events, etc.) ME. †3. To lead or command (an army, etc.) –1548; to lead and tend (a flock) –1615. 4. To conduct the affairs of (a household, state, etc.) ME.; to manage (money, etc.); also *absol.*; now *Sc.* 1465. 5. *trans.* To use (a person) in a specified manner. *Sc.* and *n. dial.* 1768.

1. Some heauenly power g. vs Out of this fearefull Country *Temp.* v. i. 105. The stars will g. us back 1868. b. Men Who g. the plough CRABBE. 2. The spirit of trueth..will g. you into all trueth *John* xvi. 13. Guided by the reports of a board 1863. 3. [He] guided them in the wildernesse like a flocke *Ps.* lxxviii. 52. Hence **Gui·der,** one who, or something which, guides.

Gui·de-book. 1823. A book for the guidance of visitors or strangers in a district, town, building, etc.

Guideless (gəi·dlės), *a.* 1557. [See -LESS.] 1. Without a guide or †steersman. 2. Without a director or ruler 1561.

Gui·de-post. 1774. A post with a direction-board affixed, set up for the guidance of travellers, *e.g.* at a fork of a road. Also *transf.* and *fig.*

Great men are the guide-posts and land-marks in the state BURKE.

†**Gui·deress.** ME. [See -ESS.] A female who guides –1650.

Guidon (gəi·dən, -dǫ̃n). 1548. [a. F., ad. It. *guidone*, perh. conn. w. *guida* GUIDE *sb.*] 1. A flag or pennant, broad at the end next the staff and forked or pointed at the other. It is the standard now used by dragoon regiments. 2. An officer who carries such a standard 1591. †3. A troop –1610. 4. *Mus.* A direct. 1811.

2. The Cornet or Guydon is the same that the Ensigne on foot is F. MARKHAM.

Guidonian (gwidō̆u·niăn), *a.* 1721. [f. *Guidon-*, stem of *Guido* + -IAN.] *Mus.* Of or pertaining to the Italian musician *Guido* d'Arezzo (11th c.), reputed the inventor of the system of hexachords.

‖**Guige** (gīʒ). [ME. *gyge*, a. OF. *guige*, recently re-adopted.] *Hist.* An extra strap, forming an additional support for the shield.

Guild, gild (gild). [A coalescence of several forms: (1) OE. *gild, gyld* (*ʒield*), recorded only twice in this sense; (2) OE. *gegyld* (see Y- *prefix*); both :—OTeut. **geldom*. (3) The pronunc. with (g) must be due to adoption of, or influence from, the ON. *gildi* guild, guild-feast, also payment, value, from the same Teut. root, which is prob. to be taken in these derivs. in the sense 'to pay, contribute'.] 1. A confraternity or association formed for the mutual aid and protection of its members, or for the furtherance of some common purpose. The term is *primarily* applied to associations of mediæval origin, but is also used in the names of various modern associations, more or less imitating these. b. *transf.* Any company or fellowship 1630. †2. The place of meeting of a guild; the home of a religious guild –1644.

1. The *g. of merchants, merchant g.* (or *g. merchant*, late OE. *cēapmanna ʒild*) was an incorporated society of the merchants of a town or city, having exclusive rights of trading within the town. It often became the governing body of the town. (Cf. *Dean of Guild* s.v. DEAN.) The *trade guilds* were associations of persons exercising the same craft, formed to protect and promote their common interests. They are historically represented in London by the Livery Companies. St. George's G. RUSKIN. The Church and Stage G. 1900. b. Names..enrolled in the guilds of the learned COLERIDGE.

Comb.: **g.-rent,** rent payable to the Crown by a g.; **g. socialism,** a system by which an industry is to be controlled by a council of its members; **-wite,** a fine levied by a g.

Guild-brother. ME. A member of a guild.

Guilder (gi·ldəɹ). 1481. [Corrupt. of GULDEN.] a. A gold coin formerly current in the Netherlands and parts of Germany. b. A Du. silver coin, worth about 1*s.* 8*d.* English.

Guild-hall. (Stress level or variable.) OE. [See GUILD and HALL.] The hall in which a guild met. Often synon. with 'town-hall.' *spec.* (*the Guildhall*) the hall of the Corporation of the City of London, used for meetings, etc.

Guildship (gi·ldʃip). [OE. *gieldscipe*; see GUILD and -SHIP.] 1. = GUILD 1. 2. Membership of a guild 1844. So **Gui·ldsman,** a member of a guild.

Guile (gəil), *sb.* ME. [a. OF. *guile*; prob. of Teut. origin. See WILE *sb.*] 1. Insidious cunning, deceit, treachery. †2. A deceit, stratagem, wile, trick –1767.

1. Behold an Israelite indeed, in whom is no g. *John* i. 47. Jael, who with inhospitable g. Smote Sisera sleeping MILT. 2. I count thy specious gifts no gifts but guiles MILT. Hence †**Guiled** *ppl. a.* full of g.; treacherous SHAKS.

Guile (gəil), *v. Obs.* or *arch.* ME. [a. OF. *guiler*, f. *guile*; see prec. Cf. WILE *v.*] *trans.* To beguile; to deceive.

Guileful (gəi·lfŭl), *a.* Now only *literary.* ME. [See -FUL.] Full of guile; deceitful, treacherous.

Gylefull wyles of women CAXTON. Hence **Gui·lefully** *adv.*, **-ness.**

Guileless (gəi·l,lės), *a.* 1728. [See -LESS.] Devoid of guile.

G. youth 1844. Hence **Gui·leless-ly** *adv.*, **-ness.**

†**Gui·ler.** [ME. *guilour*, ad. OF. *guilleor*, *gileor, gyllour*, f. *guil(l)er, giler*; see GUILE *v.*] A beguiler; a deceiver –1590.

To beguile the Guyler of his pray SPENSER. So **Gui·lery** (now *dial.*), deception, deceit, trickery; also with *a* and *pl.* a trick, etc.

Guilfat: see GYLE-FAT.

Guillem (gi·lĕm). 1603. [app. a. Welsh *Gwilym* = William.] = GUILLEMOT.

Guillemot (gi·lĭmǫt). 1678. [a. F. *guillemot*, app. a deriv. of *Guillaume* = William.] A name of species of sea-birds of the genus *Alca* or *Uria*; esp. *Uria* or *Alca troile*, the Common or Foolish Guillemot, and *Uria grylle*, the Black Guillemot.

Guillevat, var. (in Dicts.) of GYLE-FAT.

Guilloche (gilō̆u·ʃ, Fr. gīyoʃ), *sb.* 1842. [a. or ad. F. *guillochis* the ornament itself or *guilloche* the tool for making it.] *Arch.* 'An ornament in the form of two or more bands or strings twisting over each other, so as to repeat the same figure, in a continued series, by the spiral returning of the bands' (Gwilt). So **Guillo·che, Guillochee·** *vbs., trans.* to decorate with guilloches.

Guillotinade (gi:lŏtinē̆·d). 1835. [ad. F.; see next and -ADE.] An execution by means of the guillotine.

Guillotine (gilŏtī·n), *sb.* 1793. [a. F. *guillotine*, f. *Guillotin*, a physician at whose suggestion it was employed in 1789.] 1. An instrument for beheading, consisting of a heavy knife-blade sliding between grooved posts. Also, execution by means of this. 2. The name of instruments of similar action; *esp.* a. *Surg.*, an instrument for excising the tonsil or uvula, etc. 1866. b. A machine for cutting the edges of books, paper, straw, etc. 1883. 3. a. *U.S.* The dismissal of Government officials on the coming in of a new President 1883. b. The method of closure by compartments, applied to shorten or prevent discussion of a bill in Parliament 1893.

1. One makes new noses, one a g. BYRON.

Comb.: **g.-cravat,** a fashion of cravat current during the French Revolution; **-window** [F. *fenêtre à guillotine*], an ordinary sash window, the sashes of which slide in grooves.

Guillotine (gilǒtīˑn), *v.* 1794. [ad. F. *guillotiner*; see prec.] **1.** *trans.* To behead by the guillotine. Also *transf.* and *fig.* **2.** To cut (the edges of a book) with a guillotine; to cut short discussion upon (a bill, a clause); etc. 1893.

Guilt (gilt), *sb.* [OE. *gylt* :—prehistoric type **gulti-z*, related to next vb. No cognate word is known.] †**1.** A failure of duty, delinquency; offence, crime, sin –ME. †**2.** The fault of (some person) –1671. †**3.** Desert (*of* a penalty) –1625. **4.** The fact of having committed, or of being guilty of, some specified or implied offence; guiltiness ME. **5.** The state of having wilfully committed crime or heinous moral offence; criminality, great culpability 1510. **b.** An instance, kind, or degree of guilt (*rare*) 1500. **c.** Conduct involving guilt; heinous sin or crime 1729. ¶**d.** Misused for 'sense of guilt'. TILLOTSON. **6.** In legal use: The state of being justly liable to penalty 1765.

3. Phr. *Without g.*: innocently. 4. The g. of blood is at your door TENNYSON. 5. G. resides in the intention BURKE. b. Close pent-vp guilts *Lear* III. ii. 57. c. One chain of g. from the cradle to the gallows 1780. 6. A ship contracts g. by a breach of blockade KENT. *Comb.*: *g.-sick* adj.; †**guiltwite**, penalty for commission of crime.

†**Guilt,** *v.* [OE. *gyltan* :—prehistoric type **gultjan*; related to prec. sb.] **1.** *intr.* To commit an offence or trespass, to sin –1530. **2.** [f. the sb.] *trans.* To render guilty 1553.

Guiltless (giˑltlės), *a.* [Late OE. *gyltléas*, f. *gylt* GUILT + *léas* -LESS.] **1.** Free from guilt; innocent. †**b.** *transf.* Of things, places, etc.: Free from the stain of crime –1784. **2.** Having no acquaintance, dealings, or familiarity with, no experience or use of (something) 1667.

1. Some Cromwell, g. of his country's blood GRAY. 2. The teeming earth, yet g. of the plough DRYDEN. Hence **Guiˑltless-ly** *adv.*, **-ness.**

Guilty (giˑlti), *a.* [OE. *gyltig*; see GUILT *sb.* and -Y [1].] **1.** That has been in fault; delinquent, criminal. Now: That has incurred guilt; deserving punishment and moral reprobation; culpable. Often *absol.* **b.** *transf.* of the instrument, the scene of crime, etc. 1588. **2.** That has committed, or is justly chargeable with, a particular offence or fault. Const. *of.* ME. †**3.** *Guilty of*: culpably responsible for; to blame for the loss or destruction of –1715. †**4.** Deserving *of*, liable *to* (a penalty). Also bound to the performance *of* (a vow) = L. *reus voti.* –1700. **5.** Of actions, etc.: Involving guilt 1591. **6.** Of the conscience, etc.: Laden with guilt. Of feelings, etc.: Prompted by sense of guilt. 1593. †**7.** Conscious, cognizant, privy –1691.

1. The guiltiest still are ever least ashamed COWPER. b. Vpon me the guiltie doores were shut SHAKS. 2. You must plead to the Court, G. or not G. 1681. He finds his fellow g. of a skin Not coloured like his own COWPER. 3. Severn swift, g. of Maiden's death MILT. 5. His Trespas yet liues guiltie in thy blood. SHAKS. 6. Naked left To g. Shame MILT. *Comb. g.-like* adv. SHAKS. Hence **Guiˑltily** *adv.* **Guiˑltiness.**

Guinea (giˑni). 1598. [Occurs first in Pg. as *Guiné*; of unkn. origin.]

I. 1. The European name of a portion of the West Coast of Africa, extending from Sierra Leone to Benin, used *attrib.* and *Comb.* in the following:

G. bird, a G.-hen or G.-fowl (also *fig.*); **G. corn** (also with small *g*), DURRA or Indian millet, *Sorghum vulgare*; **G. cubebs,** *Piper Afzelii*; **G. deer,** the CHEVROTAIN; **G. goose,** the Chinese goose or swan-goose, *Anser* or *Cygnopsis cygnoides*; **G. grains,** grains of Paradise; **G. grass** (also with small *g*), *Panicum maximum*; **G. hog,** the river-pig of G., *Potamochœrus pictus*; **G. merchant,** one who trades with G.; hence, a slave-dealer; **G. (oil) palm,** *Elais guineensis*; **G. peach,** a strong climbing shrub of western tropical Africa, *Sarcocephalus esculentus* (N.O. *Rubiaceæ*), yielding a peach-like fruit; **G. plum,** the plum-like fruit of a large W. African tree, *Parinarium excelsum*; **G. pods,** the fruit of *Capsicum frutescens*; **G. ship,** a ship trading to G., a slave-ship; **G. sorrel,** *Hibiscus sabdariffa*; **G. trader** = *Guinea merchant*; **G. weed,** *Petiveria alliacea*; †**G. wheat,** Indian corn; †**G. wood** = RED-WOOD.

†**2.** Short for GUINEA-FOWL, GUINEA-HEN –1661.

II. The coin so called. **1.** An English gold coin, not coined since 1813, first struck in 1663 with the nominal value of 20*s.*, but from 1717 current as legal tender at the rate of 21*s.* **2.** A name for the sum of 21*s.* 1688.

When first coined, 'in the name and for the use of the Company of Royal Adventurers of England trading with Africa', these pieces were to bear for distinction the figure of a little elephant, and were made of gold from Guinea. They received the popular name of *guineas* almost at once.

1. *Double g.*: a coin of the value of two guineas. *Spade g.*: a g. of the pattern of 1787–1800, so called from the form of the escutcheon on the reverse. 2. Such substitutes..shall be paid at the rate of seven guineas per day 1885. *Comb.* **g.-gold,** †(*a*) *collect.* guineas; (*b*) gold of which guineas were coined, gold of 22 carats.

†**Guinea-cock.** 1577. **1.** An early name for the Turkey-cock –1601. **2.** = GUINEA-FOWL. H. BUTTES.

Guiˑnea-fowl. 1788. [Imported from Guinea in 16th c.] A gallinaceous bird of the genus *Numida*, esp. *N. Meleagris*, a common domestic fowl in Europe. It has slate-coloured plumage with white spots.

Guiˑnea-hen. 1578. †**1.** The Turkey-hen or Turkey –1698. **2.** The Guinea-fowl, or the female of this 1599. †**b.** *slang.* A prostitute –1708.

2. b. *Oth.* I. iii. 317. *Comb.*: **guinea-hen flower,** the fritillary, *Fritillaria Meleagris*; **guinea-hen weed,** a W. Indian herb, *Petiveria alliacea.*

Guinea-man (giˑnimæ̆n). 1695. **1.** = *Guinea ship. Obs.* exc. *Hist.* †**2.** A Guinea merchant (*rare*) 1756. **3.** A native of Guinea 1830.

Guinea pepper. 1597. †**a.** Cayenne pepper. **b.** The seeds of two species of *Amomum*, found on the west coast of Africa, within the tropics; they are aromatic, stimulant, and cordial.

Guinea-pig (giˑnipig). 1664. [Confusion with *Guiana* seems unlikely.] **1.** A rodent mammal (*Cavia Cobaya*) of the genus *Cavia*, originating in S. America, but now widely distributed. **2.** *Naut.* A midshipman in the E. Indian service 1747. **3.** *joc.* or *contempt.* One who receives a fee of a guinea; e.g. a clergyman performing temporary duty, a director of a company 1821.

Guinea trade. 1673. †**1.** Trade with Guinea. **2.** *joc.* Taking of guinea fees 1808.

Guinea worm. 1699. A parasitic nematoid worm (*Filaria medinensis*) frequent in Guinea, whence its name; it is long and thread-like, of a white colour, inhabiting the human skin, where its presence causes painful suppuration. Also, the disease occasioned by this.

Guinness (giˑnės). 1842. (A bottle or glass of) stout made by the firm of Guinness of Dublin.

‖**Guipure** (gipür). 1843. [F., f. *guiper* to cover with silk, etc.] **1.** A kind of lace 'where the flowers are either joined by . . large coarse stitches, or lace that has no ground at all' (Mrs. Palliser). **2.** A kind of gimp 1864.

Guirlande, obs. f. GARLAND.

†**Guiˑsard,** *sb.*[1] 1607. [a. F., f. (*duc de*) *Guise.*] A partisan of the Guise faction in France in the 16th c. –1683.

Guisard (gəiˑsăɹd), *sb.*[2] Chiefly *Sc.* 1626. [f. GUISE *v.* + -ARD.] A masquerader, a mummer.

Guise (gəiz), *sb.* ME. [a. OF. and F. *guise*, of Teut. origin; cf. WISE *sb.*] †**1.** Manner, method, way; fashion, style. Rarely *pl.* –1782. †**2.** Usual manner; custom, habit, practice; the 'ways' (of a country) –1725. †**3.** Manner of carrying oneself; behaviour, conduct, course of life –1813. **4.** Attire, costume, garb. Now only *arch.*, as in *in the g. of...*, *in lowly*, etc. *g.* ME. **5.** External appearance, aspect, semblance. Also *fig.* and in immaterial sense. ME. **b.** In bad sense: Assumed appearance, pretence 1662. †**6.** *Sc.* A disguise, a mask. Also, a masquerade, show –1801.

1. He began in artful g. to sound the Marquis H. WALPOLE. 2. It never was our g. To slight the poor POPE. 3. By thir g. Just men they seemd MILT. 5. A fox in the g. of a priest M. CONWAY. *fig.* He will put on the g. of benevolence 1773.

Guise (gəiz), *v.* ME. [f. GUISE *sb.*] **1.** *trans.* To attire, attire fantastically; dress, 'get up' (*arch.*). **2.** *intr.* To go about in disguise, or in masquerade dress. Chiefly *Sc.* and *north.* 1876. Hence **Guiˑser,** a masquerader, a mummer.

Guisian (gīˑziăn). 1562. [f. F. (*duc de*) *Guise* + -IAN.]

A. *adj.* Of or pertaining to the duke of Guise, or his family or faction 1579.

B. *sb.* = GUISARD [1].

B. To give the watch-word like a G. of Paris to a mutiny or massacre MILTON.

Guitar (gitāˑɹ), *sb.* 1621. [a. Sp. *guitarra* (also used), and F. *guitare*, a. Gr. κιθάρα. See also CITHER, CITOLE, GITTERN.] A musical instrument of the lute class, with six strings, and a handle or finger-board provided with frets for stopping the notes—played upon with the fingers. Hence **Guitaˑr** *v.* to serenade with a g. **Guitaˑrist,** one who plays the g.

Guit-guit (gwit gwit). 1893. [Echoic.] A name used for any species of the Neotropical genera *Cœreba, Dacnis*, and their allies.

‖**Gul** (gul). 1813. [Pers.] The Pers. word for 'rose'.

Where the light wings of Zephyr..Wax faint o'er the gardens of Gúl in her bloom BYRON.

‖**Gula** (giūˑlă). ME. [L.; = 'throat', 'appetite'.] †**1. a.** The external throat. ME. only. **b.** The gullet, or its analogues 1661. **2.** *Entom.* 'The chitinous plate which supports the submentum in many Insecta' (*Syd. Soc. Lex.*) 1826. **3.** = CYMA I. 1664.

Gular (giūˑlăɹ), *a.* (*sb.*). 1828. [f. GULA (L. *gula*) + -AR.] **1.** Of, pertaining to, or situated upon the gula. **2.** Devoted to good eating (*nonce-use*) 1854. **3.** *sb.* A gular plate beneath the throat of a serpent or a fish 1884.

Gulaund. 1784. [Icel. *gulönd*, f. *gulr* yellow + *önd* (formerly *aund*) duck.] The Icelandic name of the Goosander. (Dicts.)

†**Gulch,** *sb.*[1] 1601. [f. GULCH *v.*] A glutton or drunkard –1611.

Gulch (gvlʃ), *sb.*[2] *U.S.* 1850. [? Conn. w. GULCH *v.*] A narrow and deep ravine, with steep sides, marking the course of a torrent; esp. one containing gold.

Gulch, *v. Obs.* exc. *dial.* ME. [Echoic.] **1.** *trans.* To swallow or devour greedily. †**2.** *To g. out*: to vomit. ME. only.

Guld = *Gold-bloom*, marigold.

‖**Gulden** (guˑldĕn). 15.. [Ger., Du. *gulden*, strictly an adj. = of gold, golden.] †**a.** A gold coin, *spec.* one of various obs. gold coins of Germany and the Netherlands. **b.** A silver coin, which survives with the value of about 1*s.* 8*d.* in Holland (see GUILDER) and Austria-Hungary.

†**Gule,** *sb.*[1] ME. [ad. L. *gula.*] **1.** The gullet –1750; in *Arch.*, the neck of a column 1706. **2.** Gluttony –1535.

Gule (giūl), *sb.*[2] 1543. [a. OF. *gule, goule*, med.L. *gula Augusti*, of unkn. etym.] *The Gule of August*: Lammas Day, Aug. 1.

†**Gule,** *v. rare.* 1609. [f. *gule* GULES.] *trans.* To stain or dye gules –1632.

Gules (giūlz). ME. [ad. OF. *goules, gueules* (mod. *gueules*) = med.L. *gulæ* pl., ermine dyed red. The ult. etym. is uncertain.] Chiefly *Her.*

A. *sb.* Red, as one of the heraldic colours; in engraving represented by vertical lines. Hence *poet.* and *rhet.*, red generally.

The wintry moon..threw warm g. on Madeline's fair breast KEATS.

B. quasi-*adj.* and *adj.* Red in colour 1503.

Follow thy Drumme, With mans blood paint the ground Gules, Gules *Timon* IV. iii. 59.

Gulf (gvlf), *sb.* [ME. *golf*, ad. OF. and F. *golfe* (in sense 1), ad. Pr., It., etc. *golfo*, ad. late Gr. κόλφος, from cl. Gr. κόλπος, lit. 'bosom', hence, 'bay, gulf' (= L. *sinus*), etc.] **1.** *Geog.* A portion of the sea partially enclosed by a sweep of the coast. (Not always clearly dist. from a *bay.*) **2.** A profound depth (in a river, the ocean); the deep (*poet.*) ME. Also *transf.* **3.** An absorbing eddy; a whirlpool. In later use chiefly *fig.* 1538. **b.** A voracious appetite 1566. **4.** A yawning chasm or abyss; a vast ravine or gorge 1533. Also *fig.* **b.** (After Luke xvi. 26.) An impassable gap 1557. **5.** *Univ. slang.* The position of candidates for honours who fail, but are allowed (at Oxford) to take a pass, or are allowed (at Cambridge) the ordinary degree 1827. †6. [f. GULF *v.*] = GULP *sb.* -1771. 7. *Mining.* A large deposit of ore in a lode 1778.

1. The Goulf of Venyse MANDEV. 2. Slippery cliffs arise Close to deep gulfs BRYANT. *transf.* Gulphs of air BLACKMORE. 3. England his approaches makes as fierce, As Waters to the sucking of a Gulfe SHAKS. b. Maw and Gulfe Of the rauin'd salt Sea sharke SHAKS. 4. Phr. *A fiery g., g. of fire*: an abyss full of flame. *fig.* The g. of his debts 1894. b. Betwene you and vs there is a great gulfe [χάσμα] set N.T. (Genev.) *Luke* xvi. 26.

Comb.: **g.-dream**, a dream of drowning in, or falling into, a g.; **G. State**, any State on the G. of Mexico.

Gulf (gɒlf), *v.* 1538. [f. GULF *sb.*] †1. *intr.* To rush along like a gulf; to eddy, swirl -1658. 2. *trans.* To swallow like, or as in, a gulf; to engulf (*lit.* and *fig.*) 1807. 3. *Univ. slang.* To place the name of (an undergraduate) in the gulf (see GULF *sb.* 5) 1831. ¶4. Used for GULP *v.* 1650.

2. *fig.* A yawning valley, gulfed in blackness STEVENSON.

Gulf Stream, Gulf-stream. 1775. *Geog.* A great oceanic current of warm water that issues from the Gulf of Mexico and runs parallel to the American coast as far as Newfoundland, and thence in the direction of Europe. Occas. also applied to a similar current along the shore of Japan.

Gulf-weed. 1674. A species of sea-weed (*Sargassum bacciferum* of the sub-order *Fucaceæ*) found in the Gulf Stream, the Sargasso Sea, and elsewhere; it has a number of berry-like air-vessels.

Gulfy (gɒ·lfi), *a. poet.* 1594. [f. GULF *sb.* + -Y[1].] Full of eddies or whirlpools; *fig.* full of hollows or depths.

†**Gulist.** 1632. [f. L. *gula* + -IST.] A glutton.

Gull (gɒl), *sb.*[1] ME. [? a. Welsh *gŵylan*, Cornish *guilan* :—OCeltic *voilenno-; cf. Breton *goelaff* to weep. The probable sense was 'wailer' from its cry.] Any long-winged, web-footed bird of the family *Laridæ* and sub-family *Larinæ*, which contains several genera, *Larus* being the largest. In pop. use the name includes the Terns and Skuas.

The **Common Gull** is *Larus canus.* Other species are the **Greater Black-backed G.,** *Larus marinus*; the **Lesser Black-backed G.,** *Larus fuscus*; **Glaucous G.,** *Larus glaucus*, the BURGOMASTER; **Herring G.,** *Larus argentatus*; etc.

Comb.: **g.-billed tern,** *Sterna anglica*; **-teaser,** a bird that torments gulls, as a tern or jäger.

Gull (gɒl), *sb.*[2] Now *dial.* ME. [Prob. GULL *a.* yellow used subst.] An unfledged bird, *esp.* a gosling.

Gull (gɒl), *sb.*[3] 1594. [Of doubtful origin; cf. GULL *sb.*[2] and GULL *v.*[3]] 1. A credulous person; a dupe, simpleton, fool. †2. [f. the vb.] A trick, deception, fraud; a false report -1668. 3. *slang.* A trickster, cheat 1700.

2. I shoulde thinke this a g., but that the white-bearded fellow speakes it SHAKS.

Gull (gɒl), *sb.*[4] ME. [? var. of GOLE] †1. The gullet -1663; *transf.* an orifice (RAYNOLD). 2. A breach or fissure made by a torrent; a chasm, gully; a channel made by a stream. *Obs.* exc. *dial.* 1553.

†**Gull,** *a.* ME. [a. ON. *gulr* yellow.] Yellow, pale -1600.

†**Gull,** *v.*[1] 1530. [? f. GULL *sb.*[4]] 1. *trans.* To swallow, guzzle; also *transf.* and *fig.* Also *absol.* -1674. 2. *trans.* To gorge -1604.

Gull (gɒl), *v.*[2] Now *dial.* and *techn.* 1577. [f. GULL *sb.*[4]] 1. *transf.* Of water: To make channels or ruts in; to hollow out; to sweep *away*, wear *down*. Also *absol.* 2. *intr.* To become worn away or hollowed out 1763.

Gull (gɒl), *v.*[3] 1550. [Related to GULL *sb.*[3]] 1. *trans.* To make a gull of; to dupe, take in, deceive. Also *absol.* †2. To cheat *out of*, deprive *of* by trickery -1783.

1. Nothing is so easy as to g. the public W. IRVING. 2. To g. people of their money DE FOE. Hence **Gu·llable** *a.* gullible. †**Gu·llage,** deception, cajolery. †**Gu·ller,** one who dupes; a cheat. **Gu·llery** (now *arch.*), deception, trickery; a deception, trick.

Gullet (gɒ·lèt), *sb.* [ME. *golet*, a. OF. *golet, goulet*, dim. of *gole, goule* (mod. *gueule*) :—L. *gula* throat. Cf. GULL *sb.*[4]] 1. The passage by which food and drink pass from the mouth to the stomach; the œsophagus; also, *loosely*, the throat, neck. 2. †A piece of armour for the neck. ME. only. b. The lower end of a horse-collar 1875. 3. A water channel; a strait, estuary, river mouth, etc. Now *local.* 1515. 4. A defile; a gully or ravine; a narrow passage. ? *Obs.* or *dial.* 1600. †5. The flue of a chimney -1672. 6. A concave cut made in the teeth of some saw-blades (Webst.) 1864.

Gulleting (gɒ·lètiŋ), *vbl. sb.* 1869. [f. GULLET *sb.* or *v.* + -ING[1].] 1. Making gullets in saws 1875. 2. *Shipbuilding.* The groove to receive the rudder.

Gullible (gɒ·lĭb'l), *a.* 1825. [f. GULL *v.*[3] + -IBLE.] Capable of being gulled; easily duped. Also *absol.* So **Gullibi·lity** 1763. (Cf. CULLIBILITY, CULLIBLE.)

Gullish (gɒ·liʃ), *a.* 1598. [f. GULL *sb.*[3] + -ISH.] Of the nature of a gull; foolish, simple.

Gully (gɒ·li), *sb.*[1] 1538. [Prob. an alteration of GULLET.] †1. The gullet -1552. 2. A channel or ravine worn in the earth by the action of water, esp. in a mountain or hill side 1657. b. *Cricket.* The part of the field lying behind the slips 1920. 3. A deep gutter, sink, or drain 1789.

Comb.: **g.-drain,** a drain, generally of earthenware piping, which is the means of communication between the sewer and the g.-hole; **-hole,** the opening from the street into a drain or sewer; **-squall** (*Naut.*), a violent gust of wind from a mountain ravine.

Gully (gɒ·li), *sb.*[2] *Sc.* and *north.* 1582. [?] A large knife. Also *attrib.*, as in *g.-knife.*

Gully (gɒ·li), *sb.*[3] Also **gulley.** An iron tram-plate or -rail.

Gully (gɒ·li), *v.* 1775. [f. GULLY *sb.*[1]] *trans.* To make gullies or deep channels in; to form (channels) by the action of water. Also with *out.*

‖**Gulo** (giū·lo). 1607. [L.; = 'glutton', f. *gula.*] Formerly, the glutton, *Gulo luscus*; now, the name of its genus.

Gulosity (giulǫ·sĭti). Now *rare.* 1500. [ad. late L. *gulositatem*, f. *gulosus* gluttonous.] Gluttony, greediness, voracity.

Gulp (gɒlp), *sb.* 1568. [f. GULP *v.*] 1. The action or an act of gulping. Also *transf.* and *fig.* b. Capacity for gulping, swallow. CARLYLE. c. An effort to swallow 1873. 2. A mouthful 1611.

Gulp (gɒlp), *v.* ME. [Echoic; cf. Du. *gulpen.*] 1. *trans.* To swallow in large draughts or morsels hastily or with greediness. Chiefly with *down.* Also *absol.* Also *transf.* and *fig.* 2. *intr.* To gasp or choke when or as when drinking large draughts 1530.

1. *fig.* The worthy knight fairly gulped down the oaths SCOTT. [She] had gulped down her sobs TROLLOPE. Hence **Gu·lpin,** one who will swallow anything; *Naut.* a marine.

Gulph, obs. f. GULF, GULP.

Gult, obs. f. GILT *ppl. a.*

Gult(e, Gulti(f, -y, obs. ff. GUILT, GUILTY.

†**Gu·ly,** *a.* 1592. [f. GULE-S + -Y.] *Her.* Of the colour gules -1641.

Those fatall g. Dragons MILT.

Gum (gɒm), *sb.*[1] [OE. *gōma*; perh. belonging to the OAryan root **ghĕu-, ghŏu-* to yawn, whence Gr. χάος χαῦνος.] †1. *sing.* or *pl.* The inside of the mouth or throat -ME. 2. *pl. collect.* The firm fleshy integument of the jaws and bases of the teeth. Also *sing.* the portion of this attached to a single tooth. ME. 3. *slang.* 'Jaw'. SMOLLETT.

Comb.: **g.-rubber,** something for a child to rub its gums on; **-stick** = prec.; **-tickler** *U.S.*, the first stage in dram-drinking; **-tooth,** a molar tooth.

Gum (gɒm), *sb.*[2] [ME. *gomme*, a. OF. *gomme* :—pop. L. *gumma* = cl. L. *gummi, cummi*, a. Gr. κόμμι.] 1. A viscid secretion of many trees and shrubs, which hardens in drying, but is usually soluble in water, unlike resin. Occas. including resins (cf. 2). Also with *a* and *pl.* b. *British gum* (see BRITISH). †2. Chiefly *pl.* Products of this kind employed as drugs or perfumes, or for burning as incense -1780. Often qualified (see quots.). 3. The sticky secretion that collects in the corner of the eye 1599. 4. Short for GUM-TREE. Also specialized as *black, blue, white, mountain, spotted*, etc. *g.* 1802. b. *U.S.* A log cut from a gum-tree, hollowed out for a bee-hive, a water-trough, or a well-curb 1817. 5. *U.S. colloq.* Short for *elastic gum*, i.e. india-rubber; *occas.* an india-rubber garment. Also *pl.* Galoshes. 1859. 6. A disease in fruit-trees consisting in a morbid secretion of gum 1721. 7. A hard transparent sweetmeat made of gelatine, etc. 1921.

1. As for to speke of gomme or erbe or tre CHAUCER. 2. Altars I would reare .. and thereon Offer sweet smelling Gumms MILT. *G. acacia, ammoniac, copal, elemi, guaiacum, lac, ladanum, olibanum, sandarac, tragacanth* (see the second member); **g.-arabic** (see ARABIC); **-dragon** = TRAGACANTH; **-juniper** = SANDARAC; **-senegal** or †**-senega,** a variety of gum-arabic, obtained from Senegal. **G. elastic** [after F. *gomme élastique*], india-rubber, caoutchouc (also *elastic-gum*; see ELASTIC); rarely applied to gutta-percha. **G. ivy,** †**g. of ivy**: the inspissated juice of the stem of the ivy. 3. *Hen. V*, IV. ii. 48.

Comb.: **g.-animal,** the Senegal galago, which feeds much on gums; **-boots** *U.S.*, boots made of g. or india-rubber; **-flowers** *Sc.*, artificial flowers; **-shoe** *U.S.*, a galosh; also *attrib.* and *fig.* and as vb.; **-sucker** *Austral.*, a native Australian (esp. a Victorian) or Tasmanian; †**-taffeta** = *gummed taffeta*; **-water,** a solution of gum-arabic in water; **-wood,** the wood of the gum-tree; the tree itself; also *attrib.* b. In names of plants yielding g.; **g.-cistus,** one of the shrubs of the genus *Cistus* which yield ladanum; **-plant,** a plant of the genus *Grindelia*, which is covered with a viscid secretion; **-succory,** (*a*) *Chondrilla juncea*; also, the g. from this; (*b*) *Lactuca perennis*; **-thistle,** *Onopordium acanthium.*

Gum, *sb.*[3] See RED-GUM[1].

Gum (gɒm), *sb.*[4] *dial.* and *vulgar.* 1832. Deformation of *God*: in phr. *by* (or *my*) *g.*

Gum (gɒm), *v.*[1] ME. [f. GUM *sb.*[2]] †1. *trans.* To treat with aromatic gums -1485. 2. To stiffen with gum; to coat or smear with or as with gum 1610. 3. To fasten, or fix in position with gum or the like 1592. 4. *intr.* To exude gum as a morbid secretion 1794. 5. To become gummous 1874. 6. *trans.* To cheat, delude, humbug. *U.S. slang.* 1848.

6. You can't g. me, I tell ye now LOWELL.

Gum (gɒm), *v.*[2] 1859. [f. GUM *sb.*[1]] *trans.* To deepen and enlarge the spaces between the teeth of (a worn saw). See GUMMER.

Gumbo (gɒ·mbo). *U.S.* Also **gombo.** 1859. [Negro patois.] 1. a. The okra plant or its pods (*Hibiscus esculentus*). Also *attrib.* b. A soup thickened with the mucilaginous pods of this plant. Also *g. soup.* 2. a. *Geol.* 'The stratified portion of the lower till of the Mississippi valley' (Funk). b. *Colloq. Western U.S.* The mud of the prairies. Also *g. mud.* 1881. 3. A Creole patois in New Orleans, etc. Also *attrib.* 1882.

Gumboil (gɒ·mboil). 1753. [f. GUM *sb.*[1] + BOIL *sb.*[1]] An inflammatory swelling or small abscess on the gum.

Gum-gum (gɒ·mˌgɒm). 1700. [Prob. Malay.] A hollow iron bowl, which is struck with an iron or wooden stick; a series of these.

'What is a gum-gum?' eagerly enquired several young ladies DICKENS.

‖**Gumma** (gɒ·mă). *Pl.* **-as, -ata.** 1722. [mod.L. (neut.), f. L. *gummi* GUM *sb.*[2]] *Path.* A tumour usually of syphilitic origin, so called from the gummy nature of its contents. Hence **Gu·mmatous** *a.* of the nature of or resembling a g., as *gummatous tumour.*

Gummer (gɒ·məɹ). *U.S.* 1859. [f. GUM *v.*[2] + -ER[1].] A workman who enlarges the spaces between the teeth of a saw; a machine for this purpose.

Gummic (gɒ·mik), *a.* 1838. [f. L. *gummi* GUM *sb.*[2] + -IC.] In *G. acid*: an acid obtained from gum = *Arabic acid* (see ARABIC *a.*). So **Gummi·ferous** *a.* producing gum.

Gumminess (gɒ·minės). 1600. [See -NESS.] The quality or condition of being gummy. Also quasi-*concr.*, a gummy concretion, etc.

Gummite (gɒ·məit). 1868. [f. L. *gummi* + -ITE.] *Min.* A hydrate of uranium of reddish-yellow colour, which looks like gum.

Gummosity (gɒmǫ·sĭti). ME. [ad. L. *gummositatem*, f. *gummosus* GUMMOUS.] The quality of being gummous; †*concr.* a gummy substance, deposit, concretion, etc. -1683.

Gummous (gv·məs), *a.*[1] 1669. [ad. L. *gummosus*, f. *gummi* GUM *sb.*[2]; see -OUS. Cf. F. *gommeux.*] **1.** Of the nature of gum; gum-like. †**2.** = GUMMY 2. 1693. var. **Gummo·se.**

Gummous (gv·məs), *a.*[2] 1588. [f. mod.L. GUMMA + -OUS.] = GUMMATOUS.

Gummy (gv·mi), *a.*[1] ME. [f. GUM *sb.*[2] + -Y[1].] **1.** Of the nature of gum; viscid, sticky. **2.** Abounding in gum ME. **3.** Suffused with or exuding gum, or its like 1580; †*transf.* sticky, dirty -1720. **4.** Of the ankles, legs, etc.: Puffy, swollen 1737.

1. The gummie fatte of a fygge 1575. **3.** Foul teeth, and g. eyes SWIFT. G. chestnutbuds TENNYSON.

Gummy (gv·mi), *a.*[2] 1861. [f. GUMMA + -Y.] = GUMMATOUS.

Gump (gvmp), *sb. dial.* and *U.S.* 1825. A foolish person, a dolt.

Gumption (gv·mpʃən). *colloq.* 1719. [Orig. Sc.] **1.** Common sense, mother wit, shrewdness. **2.** *Painting.* **a.** The art of preparing colours. SIR W. SCOTT. **b.** A vehicle for colour 1854.

Gum resin, gum-re·sin. 1712. [f. GUM *sb.*[2] + RESIN.] A vegetable secretion consisting of resin mixed with gum or mucilage; e.g. ammoniac, euphorbium, gamboge.

Gu·m-tree. 1676. [f. GUM *sb.*[2] + TREE.] Any tree that exudes gum: *spec.* **a.** Any tree of the genus *Eucalyptus*; **b.** Various species of the N. American genus *Nyssa*; **c.** *Sweet gum tree* of the U.S., *Liquidambar styraciflua*.

Phr. (*U.S.*) *To be up a gum-tree*: to be on one's last legs. (*Austral.*) *He has seen his last gum-tree* = it is all up with him.

Gun (gvn), *sb.* [ME. *gunne, gonne*; ? shortened from Icel. *Gunnhildr*, a fem. proper name. An account of munitions at Windsor Castle in 1330-1 mentions 'una magna balista de cornu quæ vocatur Domina Gunilda'. (Skeat.) Or *gunne* might be echoic.]

I. 1. A weapon consisting essentially of a metal tube from which heavy missiles are thrown by the force of gunpowder, or (in later use) by explosive force of any kind; a piece of ordnance, cannon, great gun. Also *fig.* †**2.** In 15th c. used vaguely for a large engine of war -1534. **3.** (Orig. HAND-GUN.) Any portable firearm (in U.S., a pistol or revolver); a musket, fowling-piece, rifle, etc. ME. †**4.** A missile hurled from an engine of war. CHAUCER. **5.** *transf.* One of a shooting party 1870; an artilleryman 1896.

1. Bowes of brake and brasene gonnes LANGL. The guns of the British nation may be divided into four classes—Park, or Field artillery, Siege guns,..garrison guns, and marine artillery GREENER. *Morning* and *evening g.* (in the navy), 'warning-pieces' fired at morning and evening respectively; hence, the times at which these guns are fired. [I slept] till the morning g. 1899. **2.** The gones [L. *aries*] beare downe the walls 1534. **5.** Five guns went before breakfast 1870.

Phrases. *As a g.* = perfectly, absolutely, *esp.* in (*as*) *sure as a g.*: to a dead certainty. *To stand* or *stick to one's gun(s*: to maintain one's position. *Son of a g.*, depreciatory for 'man, fellow'. **Great gun,** a fire-arm of the larger kind which requires to be mounted for firing; hence, a person of distinction or importance. *To blow great guns*: to blow a violent gale.

II. Transf. uses. **1.** *Mining.* A hollow cylinder or plug used in cleaving rocks with gunpowder. **2.** *slang* and *dial.* A flagon (of ale) 1645. **3.** *joc.* A tobacco pipe 1708. **4.** *slang.* A thief; also 'rascal', 'beggar' 1858. **5.** *attrib.*, esp. with a prefixed numeral, qualifying *ship, frigate*, etc. 1485.

Comb.: g. **apron,** a cover for the protection of the vent and tangent blocks of guns against rain and dirt; g. **barrel** (see BARREL *sb.*); **-brig,** a two-masted ship of war, now obsolete; **-brush,** a brush for cleaning the bore of a g.; **-carriage** (see CARRIAGE); **-fire,** the firing of a g. or guns; *Naut.* and *Mil.* the time at which the morning or evening g. is fired; **g. flint** (see FLINT *sb.*); **-harpoon,** a harpoon which is fired from a g.; **g. hoop,** one of the coiled or forged steel envelopes shrunk on the central tube of a modern cannon; **-iron,** (*a*) the iron used in making guns; (*b*) a gun-harpoon; **-money,** (*a*) = GUNNAGE; (*b*) money coined (by James II in Ireland) from the metal of old guns; **-pendulum,** 'a device employed to determine the initial velocity of projectiles by means of the recoil of the gun' (Hamersly); **-pit,** (*a*) *Fortif.* an excavation made to receive guns for protection from the enemy's fire; (*b*) 'a pit for receiving the mold used in casting a gun, or for receiving the tube or jacket in assembling a built-up gun' (*Cent. Dict.*); **-port,** a port-hole for a g.; **-runner** *colloq.*, one engaged in **g.-running,** i.e. illegally conveying firearms and ammunition into a country; **-searcher,** an iron instrument used to find whether the bore of a g. is honey-combed; **-slide,** in naval guns, 'the chassis on which the top-carriage carrying the gun slides in recoiling' (*Cent. Dict.*); **-sling,** long rope grommets used for hoisting in and mounting guns; **-stick,** a ramrod, rammer; **-tackle,** (*a*) *Naut.* in full *gun-tackle-purchase*, 'a tackle composed of a rope rove through two single blocks' (Smyth); also *attrib.*; (*b*) an arrangement of blocks and ropes for moving guns; **-work,** (*a*) any labour performed in connexion with ordnance; (*b*) shooting with a g. or rifle.

Gun (gvn), *v.* Infl. **gunned, gunning.** 1622. [f. prec.] †**1.** To provide with guns; to assail with guns -1698. **2.** *intr.* To shoot with a gun; hence, to make war. Chiefly *to go gunning* (= *a-gunning*). 1622.

‖**Guna** (gu·nă), *sb.* 1804. [Skr. *guṇa.*] In *Skr. Grammar*, the middle grade of an ablaut-series of vowels; the process of raising a vowel to the middle grade by prefixing *ă*. Hence sometimes used in Indo-germanic comparative grammar for the *ĕ* grade of the o : *ĕ* : *ŏ* series. Also *attrib.* Hence **Gu·na** *v. trans.* to GUNATE.

Gunarchy, obs. f. GYNARCHY.

Gunate (gu·neɪt), *v.* 1864. [f. GUNA + -ATE[3].] *trans.* In *Skr. Grammar*, to subject to the change known as guna. Hence **Guna·tion.**

Gun-boat, gunboat (gv·nbōut). 1793. A boat or small vessel of light draught carrying one or more large guns. Also *attrib.*

Gun-cotton (gv·nkǫ:t'n). 1846. A highly explosive compound prepared by steeping cotton in nitric and sulphuric acids, now almost superseded by dynamite. Chemically, it is one of a series of nitrates of cellulose, from other members of which are obtained celluloid and collodion. See also PYROXYLIN.

Gun-deck. 1677. *Naut.* A deck which carries guns; *esp.* in an old-fashioned ship of the line, the lowest of the decks on which guns are placed. Also *attrib.*

Gundelet, -olet, obs. ff. GONDOLA.

‖**Gunge, gunj** (gvndʒ). Also †**gunja.** 1776. [a. Pers. *ganj* magazine, granary.] A market.

Gunja, var. of GANJA; obs. f. GUNGE.

Gun-lock (gv·nlǫk). 1731. That part of the mechanism of a gun by which the charge is exploded. (See LOCK *sb.*) Also *attrib.*

Gunmaker (gv·nmēɪkəɹ). ME. One who manufactures guns.

Gun-man, gunman (gv·nmæ̆n). 1624. **1.** One who is armed, or who shoots, with a gun. Now (esp. from *U.S.* use 1903) a lawless man who uses fire-arms, an armed robber. **2.** One who has to do with guns or their making 1881.

Gu·n-metal. 1541. A bronze formerly much used for cannon; now, a name for alloys of copper and tin, or zinc.

Gunnage (gv·nědʒ). 1703. [f. GUN *sb.* + -AGE.] The money distributed among the captors of a ship, assigned in proportion to the number of guns on the captured ship. ? *Obs.*

Gunnel (gv·něl). 1686. [?] A small, eel-shaped marine fish, *Centronotus* or *Murænoides gunnellus*; the butter-fish. Also *spotted g.*

Gunnel: see GUNWALE.

Gunner (gv·nəɹ). [ME. *gonner, gunner*, f. *gunne* GUN, after AF. analogies; see -ER[2].] **1.** One whose office it is to work a cannon. In the British army, now applied to all privates of artillery except the drivers. **b.** In the navy, a warrant officer who has special charge of the battery, small arms, ordnance stores, etc. 1495. **c.** *fig.* 1657. **3.** A gun-maker, gunsmith. *Obs.* exc. *dial.* 1463. **4.** One who goes shooting game 1753. **5.** With number prefixed: A vessel carrying (so many) guns 1829. **6.** *dial.* **a.** The Sea Bream 1859. **b.** The Great Northern Diver, *Colymbus glacialis* 1837. **7.** *attrib.* 1628.

1. The nimble g. with lynstock now the devilish cannon touches SHAKS. †*Master g.*: the chief g. in charge of ordnance. Phr. *Gunner's daughter*: joc. name for the gun to which sailors were 'married', i.e. lashed, to receive punishment. *Gunner's quadrant* (see QUADRANT).

Gunnery (gv·nəri). 1497. [f. GUN + -ERY.] **1.** The science and art of constructing and managing guns 1605. **2.** The firing of guns; the use of guns for sporting purposes 1816. **3.** *concr.* Guns collectively 1497. **4.** *attrib.*, as **g.-lieutenant,** 'one who, having obtained a warrant from a g.-ship, is eligible to large ships to assist specially in supervising the g. duties' (Smyth); **-ship,** a ship for training men in g.

Gunnies (gv·nis). *Cornwall.* Also (in Dicts.) **gunnis(s.** 1778. A crevice in a mine or lode; 'the vacant space left where the lode has been removed' (Raymond); hence (app.) taken as a measure of breadth or width. (By some writers used as *pl.*)

Gunning (gv·niŋ), *vbl. sb.* 1562. [f. GUN *sb.* and *v.* + -ING[1].] **1.** Gunnery 1570. **2.** Shooting with a gun; esp. the act or practice of hunting game with guns 1624. †**3.** Provision of guns. MARVELL. **4.** *attrib.* 1562.

Gunny (gv·ni). 1711. [a. Hindi *gōn, gōnī* :—Skr. *gōṇī* sack.] A coarse material used chiefly for sacking and made from the fibres of jute or from sunn-hemp; a sack made of this. Also *attrib.*

Gunpowder (gv·npaudəɹ). ME. [f. GUN *sb.* + POWDER *sb.*] **1.** An explosive mixture of saltpetre, sulphur, and charcoal, used chiefly in gunnery and blasting. Also *fig.* **2.** (In full, *g. tea.*) A fine kind of green tea, each leaf of which is rolled up into a pellet 1771. **3.** *attrib.* Explosive; also *fig.* 1550.

1. The best g...is composed of 70 parts (in weight) of nitre, 18 parts of sulphur, and 16 parts of charcoal 1797. *White g.*: **a.** a tri-nitro-cellulose, prepared from sawdust; **b.** a blasting mixture made of chlorate of potash, potassium ferrocyanide, and sugar. **3.** Such Gunne-powder Oathes 1604.

Comb.: **g.-cake,** g. in a cake, i.e. before it is corned; **-engine,** a gas-engine in which the movement of the piston is produced by the evolution of gas resulting from the combustion of g. (Knight); **-hammer,** a pile-driving machine worked by the explosion of g.; **-press,** a press for compacting mill-cake into hard cake for granulation; **g. tea** (see 2). **b. Gunpowder plot:** the plot to blow up the Houses of Parliament on Nov. 5, 1605, while the King, Lords, and Commons were assembled. (So *g. treason, traitor*, etc.)

Hence **Gu·npowderous** *a.* pertaining to or characteristic of g.; of the bluish colour of g.; also *fig.*

Gun-room (gv·nrum). 1626. **1.** In large ships of war, a compartment orig. occupied by the gunner and his mates, but now by the junior officers; in smaller vessels, the lieutenants' mess-room. Also *attrib.* **2.** A room in which guns are kept 1773.

2. The story of Ould Grouse in the gun-room GOLDSM.

Gun-shot (gv·nʃǫt). 1471. [Orig. *gonnes shott.*] **1.** Shot fired from a gun or cannon; †also the shooting of guns. Now *rare.* Also *fig.* **2.** The range of a gun; the distance to which a shot can be effectively thrown from a gun 1532. †Also *transf.* and *fig.* -1687. ¶**3.** A pistol. BUTLER *Hud.* **4.** *attrib.*, as in *g. fracture* 1672.

2. They [mallards] were always out of g. JEFFERIES. *fig.* Not yet out of the gun-shot of the Devil BUNYAN.

Gun-shy (gv·nʃəi), *a.* 1884. Frightened at the report of a gun; said *esp.* of a sporting dog.

Gunsmith (gv·nsmiþ). 1588. **1.** One who makes and repairs small fire-arms. **2.** *slang.* A thief 1869. Hence **Gu·nsmithery,** the trade of a g.; also, the place where the work is carried on.

†**Gu·nster.** *slang.* 1709. [f. GUN *sb.* + -STER.] 'A Cracker, or bouncing Fellow' (*un Bavard*) BOYER. See STEELE *Tatler* No. 88 ¶ 2. -1727.

Gun-stock (gv·nstǫk). 1495. The wooden stock or support to which the barrel of a gun is attached; †a support on which to place a cannon on board ship.

†**Gu·nstone.** ME. [f. GUN *sb.* + STONE *sb.*] **1.** A stone used for the shot of a cannon or gun; a cannon-ball -1808. **2.** *Her.* = PELLET, OGRESS. -1847.

Gunter (gv·ntəɹ). 1679. [The name of a distinguished mathematician, Edmund *Gunter* (1581-1626).] **1.** In *Gunter's chain*: the chain of 4 poles' length now in general use for land-surveying (see CHAIN *sb.*). *Gunter's line*: a logarithmic line on Gunter's scale used for multiplying and dividing mechanically; also called *Gunter's proportion. Gunter's quadrant*: an apparatus for finding the hour of the day, the azimuth, etc. **b.** Short for *Gunter's scale*: A flat rule, two feet long, marked on one side with scales of equal parts, of chords, sines, tangents, etc., and on the other with scales of the logarithms of those parts; much used in surveying and navigation 1706. **2.** *Naut.* Applied to a method of rigging in which the topmast slides up and down the lower mast on rings or hoops; a mast so rigged or a sail attached to such a mast (more fully *sliding-g.*) 1794.

Gunwale, gunnel (gʌ·nĕl). 1466. [f. GUN *sb.* + WALE, the gunwale having formerly served to support the guns. The usual spelling is *gunwale*, but the pronunc. (gʌ·nwēl) is not favoured.] The upper edge of a ship's side; in large vessels, the uppermost planking, which covers the timber-heads and reaches from the quarter-deck to the forecastle on either side; in small craft, a piece of timber extending round the top side of the hull.

†**Gup,** *interj.* 1529. [Contr. f. *go up.*] **a.** A cry of anger or chiding addressed to a horse. **b.** An exclam. of derision, remonstrance, or surprise; often with *marry*. –1682.

Gurge (gɔ̄ɹdʒ), *sb. rare.* 1667. [ad. L. *gurges.*] A whirlpool (*lit.* and *fig.*).

MILT. *P.L.* XII. 41.

Gurge (gɔ̄ɹdʒ), *v.* 1523. [f. L. *gurges.*] †**1.** *trans.* To turn into a whirlpool. LD. BERNERS. **2.** *intr.* To swirl, surge 1578.

Gurgeons (gɔ̄·ɹdʒənz), *sb. pl.* Now *dial.* 1483. [Cf. F. *grugeons*; conn. w. *gruger* to crunch.] Coarse meal; the coarse refuse from flour; pollards.

Gurgitation (gɔ̄ɹdʒitē·ʃən). 1542. [ad. late L. **gurgitationem*, f. (ult.) *gurgit-, gurges.*] †**1.** = INGURGITATION –1658. **2.** Surging or whirling up and down 1864.

Gurgle (gɔ̄·ɹg'l), *sb.* 1562. [f. the vb.] †**1.** = GARGLE *sb.*[1] **2.** The action or an act of gurgling; the noise of a stream flowing over a stony bed, or the like 1757. **b.** A guttural sound produced by gargling, etc. 1862.

2. A g. of innumerable emptying bumpers CARLYLE.

Gurgle (gɔ̄·ɹg'l), *v.* 1562. [? echoic; cf. L. **gurguliare*, f. *gurgulio* gullet. See also GARGLE, GUGGLE.] †**1.** *intr.* = GARGLE *v.* –1611. **2.** Of water, etc.: To flow in a broken irregular current, with intermittent low noises 1713. **b.** *transf.* To utter intermittent guttural sounds 1779. **3.** *trans.* To utter with gurgling sounds 1814.

2. Ayr gurgling kiss'd his pebbled shore BURNS. 3. He gurgled-out his pursy chuckle of a cough-laugh CARLYLE. Hence **Gu·rglingly** *adv.* with a gurgle.

Gurglet, obs. f. GOGLET.

Gurgoyl(e, var. of GARGOYLE.

Gurjun (gɔ̄·ɹdʒən). Also **gurjon.** 1858. Native name for a large E. Indian tree, *Dipterocarpus alatus*, from which and other species a viscid balsamic liquid is obtained, called *g. balsam* or *g. oil*, used as a varnish and medicinally. Hence **Gurju·nic** *a.* in *gurjunic acid*, $C_{34}H_{14}O_{51} + 3H_2O$.

Gurle, obs. f. GIRL.

‖**Gurlet** (gɔ̄·ɹlĕt). 1875. [F. *grelet.*] 'A pickaxe with one sharp point and one cutting-edge' (Knight).

[**Gurmie,** spurious wd. in Dicts.: see GUNNIES.]

Gurnard (gɔ̄·ɹnăɹd), **gurnet** (gɔ̄·ɹnĕt). ME. [Prob. a. some var. of F. *grognard*, f. *grogner* to grunt. Cf. F. *grondin* gurnard, f. *gronder* to grunt.] One of the marine fishes of the genus *Trigla* or family *Triglidæ*, characterized by a large spiny head with mailed cheeks and three free pectoral rays. Applied also to allied genera 1704.

†*Soused g.*: a term of opprobrium. *Hen. IV*, IV. ii. 12. *Flying g.*, a flying fish of the family *Cephalacanthidæ* or *Dactylopteridæ*.

Gurry[1] (gʌ·ri). Now *dial.* 1523. Diarrhœa.

‖**Gurry**[2] (gʌ·ri). *Anglo-Ind.* 1786. [Hindustani *garhī*, *garh* a hill fort.] A small native Indian fort.

Gurry[3] (gʌ·ri). Chiefly *U.S.* 1850. *Whale-fishing.* The refuse from cutting-in and boiling out a whale. Also, fish-offal.

Gurt (gɔ̄ɹt). *dial.* 1633. [? a. AF. *gort*: see GORCE.] A trench or gutter, *esp.* in *Mining*.

Gurts, obs. dial. pl. of GRIT *sb.*[2]

Gush (gʌʃ), *sb.* 1682. [f. GUSH *v.*] **1.** The action or an act of gushing; a copious or sudden emission of fluid; a rush; also *concr.* a quantity of fluid so emitted. **2.** *transf.* and *fig.* A sudden and violent outbreak; a burst 1704. **3.** *colloq.* Objectionably effusive or sentimental display of feeling 1866.

1. One G. of Tears STEELE. A red g. spurted over the garments of the Indian MAYNE REID. 2. A g. of wind 1704, of light DICKENS, of violets RUSKIN, of rhetoric L. STEPHEN. 3. G. and twaddle 1869.

Gush (gʌʃ), *v.* [ME. *gosshe, gusche*; perh. onomatopœic.] **1.** *intr.* 'To flow or rush out with violence' (J.); to issue suddenly or copiously, as water when released from confinement. Freq. with *down, in, forth, out, up.* Also *transf.* and *fig.* **2.** Of a person, parts of the body, etc.: To have a copious flow of blood, tears, etc. 1530. **3.** *trans.* 'To emit in a copious effusion' (J.) 1553. **4.** *intr.* (*colloq.*) To act or speak in an over-effusive, exaggerated, or sentimental fashion. Also *trans.* 1864.

1. He brought waters out of the stony rocke, so that they gusshed out like the ryuers COVERDALE *Ps.* lxxvii[i]. Then gush'd the tears POPE. 2. Myne eyes gusshe out with water COVERDALE *Ps.* cxviii [cxix]. 3. Davids eyes gusht out rivers of waters BP. HALL.

Gusher (gʌ·ʃəɹ). 1864. [f. GUSH *v.* + -ER[1].] One who or that which gushes; *spec.* in *U.S.*, a gas-well or oil-well from which the material flows profusely without pumping.

Gushing (gʌ·ʃiŋ), *ppl. a.* 1583. [-ING[2].] That gushes. **1.** Flowing or issuing with violence or in copious streams. **2.** Emitting fluid copiously; also *transf.* 1717. **3.** *fig.* Effusive, overflowing, displaying itself impulsively 1807. **b.** Given to or characterized by gush (*colloq.*) 1864.

1. G. fountains W. IRVING. 2. My g. eyes o'erflow POPE. 3. A g. affluence of imagery MRS. CARLYLE. b. A g. speech 1878. Hence **Gu·shing-ly** *adv.*, **-ness.**

Gusset (gʌ·sĕt). ME. [a OF. *gouchet, gousset*, app. f. *gousse* shell of nuts, etc.] **1.** In a suit of mail, a piece of chain-mail protecting a joint. **2** A triangular piece of material let into a garment to strengthen or to enlarge some part 1570. **b.** *pl.* The flexible sides of a pair of bellows 1861. **c.** An elastic insertion in the side of a boot 1881. **3.** *transf.* A triangular piece of land 1650. **4.** *Her.* An abatement formed by a line drawn from the dexter or sinister chief to a central point and continued perpendicularly to the base of the escutcheon. (Cf. GORE *sb.*[2]) 1562. **5.** *techn.* A bracket or angular piece of iron fixed at the angles of a structure to give strength or firmness 18 . .

2. The gussets of his waistcoat 1878. 3. Which gore, or gusset of ground, was called Apherema FULLER. *Comb.* **g. needle** (*Knitting*), one of the two side needles used in knitting the foot of a stocking. Hence **Gu·sseted** *a.* having a g. or gussets. **Gu·sseting** *vbl. sb.* insertion or making of gussets; *concr.* a g.

Gust (gʌst), *sb.*[1] 1588. [app. a. ON. *gustr*, related to *giósa* to gush or *gióta* to pour.] **1.** A sudden violent rush or blast of wind; †formerly often, a whirlwind. Also *transf.* **2.** *fig.*; also *gen.*, a burst, outbreak, outburst 1611.

1. The stormy gusts of winters day SHAKS. 2. The first little sudden g. of passion against these gentlemen BURKE.

Gust (gʌst), *sb.*[2] Now *arch.* ME. [ad. L. *gustus*; cf. GOUT, GUSTO.] = TASTE, in various senses. **1.** The sense or faculty of taste. †**2.** Individual taste or liking –1732. †**3.** Æsthetic or artistic taste (*rare*) –1716. **4.** Keen relish, appreciation, or enjoyment 1635. **5.** Savour or flavour (of food, etc.) 1536. **b.** Pleasing taste or flavour; relish 1649. †**6.** A taste of something; also, a foretaste –1698.

1. I am for a Set-meal, where I may enjoy my full G. DRYDEN. 4. He drinks his simple beverage with a g. COWPER. I had no g. to antiquities DE FOE. 5. The whole vegetable tribe have lost their g. with me LAMB. b. The g. of novelty D'ISRAELI.

Gust (gʌst), *v.* Now only *Sc.* ME. [? f. GUST *sb.*[2], or ad. L. *gustare.*] *trans.* To taste, to relish. Also *absol.*

Gustable (gʌ·stăb'l). Now *rare.* 1480. [ad. late L. *gustabilis*; see prec. and -ABLE.] **A.** *adj.* **1.** That can be tasted; also, having a pleasant taste, appetizing. **2.** Of qualities: Perceptible by the sense of taste. Of perceptions: Gustatory. 1657.

1. Mylk, hony & herbes g. CAXTON. 2. G. and olefactible perceptions BP. BERKELEY.

B. A thing that can be tasted; an article of food 1642.

†**Gustard.** *Sc.* 1536. [f. GOOSE + (BUS)-TARD.] A bustard –1655.

Gustation (gʌstē·ʃən). 1599. [ad. L. *gustationem*, f. *gustare.*] The action or faculty of tasting, taste.

Gustative (gʌ·stătiv), *a.* 1620. [f. L. *gustare*: see -ATIVE.] Having the function of tasting; also, concerned with tasting.

Gustatory (gʌ·stătəri), *a.* 1684. [f. L. *gustat-, gustare* + -ORY.] Pertaining to or concerned with tasting or the sense of taste. *G. nerve* (Anat.): the lingual nerve upon which the sense of taste depends.

Gustful (gʌ·stfŭl), *a.*[1] *Obs.* exc. *arch.* 1645. [f. GUST *sb.*[2] + -FUL.] **1.** Full of gust or flavour; tasty. **2.** *fig.* Pleasant to the mind or feelings 1645. Hence **Gu·stful-ly** *adv.*, **-ness.**

Gustful (gʌ·stfŭl), *a.*[2] *rare.* [f. GUST *sb.*[1] + -FUL.] Gusty.

†**Gu·stless,** *a.* 1597. [f. GUST *sb.*[2] + -LESS.] Tasteless, insipid –1695.

‖**Gusto** (gʌ·sto). 1629. [It. = Fr. GOÛT:— L. *gustus* taste. Cf. GUST *sb.*[2]] **1.** Particular liking, relish, or fondness 1647. **2.** Zest 1629. **3.** Artistic style; *occas.* fashionable style in matters of taste. Often qualified as *great* (= It. *gran gusto*), *high, noble.* 1662. †**4.** Æsthetic perception –1711. †**5.** Flavour or savour (of food). DERHAM.

2. He read me, though with too much g., some little poems of his own PEPYS.

Gusty (gʌ·sti), *a.*[1] 1600. [f. GUST *sb.*[1] + -Y.] **1.** Characterized by gusts; blown upon, tossed, or disturbed by gusts of wind 1725. **2.** *fig.* Given to or marked by fits or bursts 1690.

1. Great store of snowe, with some gustie weather HAKLUYT. The long carpets rose along the g. floor KEATS. Hence **Gu·stily** *adv.*

Gusty (gʌ·sti), *a.*[2] Chiefly *Sc.* 1721. [f. GUST *sb.*[2] + -Y.] Tasty, savoury, appetizing.

Gut (gʌt), *sb.* [OE. *guttas* str. masc. pl.; perh. (ult.) from the root of OE. *ġéotan* to pour.] **1.** *collect. pl.* The contents of the abdominal cavity; the bowels, entrails. Formerly in dignified use with regard to man. In the Bible occas. *fig.* = 'inward parts'. **b.** *transf.* The inside, contents of anything 1663. **c.** Spirit; force of character (*slang*) 1893. **2.** = INTESTINE. ME. **b.** Hence, the whole of the alimentary canal or its lower portion 1460. **3.** *sing.* The belly or stomach, *esp.* as the seat of appetite or gluttony. Now *dial.* and *vulgar.* ME. **b.** *pl.* A corpulent or gluttonous person. Now *rare* or *dial.* 1550. **4.** The intestines of animals employed for various purposes (see quots.) 1602. **5. a.** A narrow passage of water 1538. **b.** On land: A narrow passage between two declivities; hence, any narrow passage 1615.

1. Falstaffe, you caried your Guts away..nimbly SHAKS. b. Phr. †*To have guts* (= 'something') *in one's brains.* 2. BLIND GUT, the cæcum; *transf.* a cul-de-sac. 3. b. Thou Clay-brayn'd Guts SHAKS. 4. a. *pl.* = OFFAL 1602. b. For making violin strings; now *sing.* as the name of a material; Seven strings of very fine g. GOLDSM. c. *sing.* The silken fibre obtained from the intestine of the silkworm; Silkworm g. for angling URE. 5. a. The G. of Gibraltar 1829. *The Gut* (Oxford and Cambridge): a bend of the river in the racing-course. b. The signal-box in this narrow g. of traffic 1896.

Comb.: **g.-bread,** sweetbread, pancreas; **-scraper** (*joc.*), a violin-player; **-weed,** *Sonchus arvensis.*

Gut (gʌt), *v.* ME. [f. GUT *sb.*] **1.** *trans.* To take out the guts of; to eviscerate. **2.** *transf.* To clear out the contents or inside of; *esp.* to remove or destroy the internal fittings of (a building). Const. *of.* 1688. Also *fig.* **3.** *intr.* To cram the guts (*vulgar*) 1616.

2. We took an Arabian junk..We gutted him of the pearl DE FOE. *fig.* T-m Br-wn, of facetious Memory..having gutted a proper Name of all its intermediate Vowels, used to..make as free with it as he pleased ADDISON. To g. a book (*mod.*).

‖**Gutta**[1] (gʌ·tă). *Pl.* **guttæ** (gʌ·tī). ME. [L.; = 'a drop'. Cf. GOUT *sb.*[1]] **1. a.** *Pharmacy* and *Path.* A drop. In prescriptions *gt,* pl. *gtt.* 1652. **b.** *Arch.* = DROP. 1563. **c.** *Her.* = GOUTTE. 1868. †**2.** A kind of gum. In 18th c. = GAMBOGE. -1712.

1. b. **Guttæ band** (*Arch.*), the listel from which the guttæ seem to hang. *Comb.*: **gutta opaca**, cataract; **g. serena** = AMAUROSIS; also *fig.*

Gutta [2] (gʊ·tă). 1852. [ad. Malay *getah* gum, whence mod.L. *gutta*, assim. to prec.] **1.** Short for GUTTA-PERCHA. **2.** *Chem.* A white amorphous substance $C_{10}H_{16}$, the principal constituent of gutta-percha. WATTS.

Gutta-percha (gʊ·tă,pə·ɹtʃă). 1845. [ad. Malay *getah percha*, lit. 'the gum of percha' (the name of the tree).] **1.** The inspissated juice of various trees found chiefly in the Malayan archipelago (see sense 2), now much used in the arts. **2.** (Short for *gutta-percha tree.*) One of the trees that yield this juice, esp. *Isonandra* (or *Dichopsia*) *Gutta* (N.O. *Euphorbiaceæ*) 1860.

Comb.: **gutta-percha-tissue,** 'gutta-percha in a very thin leaf, used as a waterproof covering to dressings to prevent evaporation' (*Syd. Soc. Lex.*); **gutta-percha-wire** (*Telegraphy*), wire covered with gutta-percha.

Guttate (gʊ·tēᵗt), *a.* 1826. [ad. L. *guttatus* speckled, spotted, f. *gutta* drop.] In the form of drops; furnished with drops, spotted as if by drops. So **Gutta·ted** *a.* spread about as if in drops or spots.

‖**Guttatim** (gʊtē·tim). 1694. [L.; = 'by drops', f. *gutta.*] Drop by drop.

‖**Gutté** (gute), *a.* 1572. [AF. *gutté* (= F. *goutté*) :—L. *guttatus.*] *Her.* Besprinkled with drops; as in *gutté de sang*, etc. *Gutté reversed*: charged with drops having the bulb or globe upwards. vars. †**Gu·tted** *a.*, **Guttee.**

Gutter (gʊ·təɹ), *sb.* ME. [a. OF. *gutiere, goutiere* (mod. *gouttière*), f. *goutte* drop (see GOUT *sb.*[1]).] †**1.** A watercourse; later, a small brook or channel -1797. **b.** A furrow or track made by running water 1586. **c.** *Austral. gold-mining.* The lower part of the channel of an old river of the Tertiary period containing auriferous deposits 1864. **2.** A shallow trough fixed under the eaves of a roof, etc., to carry off the rain-water ME. **3.** A hollowed channel at the side of a road or elsewhere, to carry away the surface water ME. Also *fig.* as the haunt of children, etc., of low birth or breeding 1846. **b.** A sink (*lit.* and *fig.*). Now *dial.* 1440. **c.** Mud, filth. Chiefly *Sc.* (only *pl.*). 1785. **4.** A shallow trough or open conduit or pipe for the outflow of fluid 1657. †**5.** A groove in an animal or vegetable body. *Obs.* in gen. sense. -1712. **6.** An artificial groove or channel. Now only *techn.* 1555. **7.** In *Printing* = *gutter-stick* (see Comb.). Also in *Bookbinding*, 'the white space between the pages of a book' 1841.

3. The gutters run blood ZANGWILL. *fig.* To die in the g. HALL CAINE.

Comb.: **g.-bird,** the sparrow, hence *fig.* a disreputable person; **-board,** a board forming the foundation on which is laid the lining-material forming the g. itself; **-child,** a child such as haunts the gutters; **-drift** = sense 1 c; **-flag** *Austral.*, a flag fixed on the surface to denote where the course of a g. has been discovered; **-member** (*Arch.*), a member made by decorating the outside face of a g. with regularly spaced ornaments; **g. plane,** a moulding plane with a semi-cylindrical sole for planing gutters; **-snippet,** app. a dim. of GUTTER-SNIPE (Kipling); **-stick** (*Printing*), one of the pieces of furniture which separate pages in a forme; **-tree,** the Wild Cornel or Dogwood, *Cornus sanguinea* (*Syd. Soc. Lex.*).

b. *attrib.* (or *adj.*) Brought up in or appropriate to the g.; low, disreputable; as the *gutter Press*, *g. journalism* 1851.

Gutter (gʊ·təɹ), *v.* ME. [f. prec.] **1.** *trans.* To make gutters in; to furnish with gutters; to furrow with streams, tears, etc. **2.** *intr.* Of water: To form gutters or gullies 1632. **3.** To flow in streams, to stream *down* 1583. **4.** Of a candle: To melt away rapidly by becoming channelled on one side; to sweal. (The chief current sense.) 1706.

Gutter-blood (gʊ·təɹblʊd). *Sc.* One of the rabble. SCOTT.

Gutter-snipe (gʊ·təɹsnəip). 1869. **1. a.** *dial.* The common snipe, *Gallinago cælestis* 1893. **b.** The common American snipe, *Gallinago wilsoni* or *delicata* 1874. **2. a.** A gatherer of refuse from the gutter 1869. **b.** A street arab 1882. **3.** *Printing.* (*U.S.*) A small and narrow poster for pasting on curbstones 1871.

Guttifer (gʊ·tifəɹ). 1846. [ad. mod.L. *guttifera* (sc. *planta*); see GUTTA and -IFEROUS.] *Bot.* A plant that exudes gum or resin; a plant of the order *Guttiferæ*.

Guttiferous (gʊti·fĕrəs), *a.* 1847. [f. as prec.] Yielding gum or resinous substances; pertaining to N.O. *Guttiferæ*, of trees and shrubs remarkable for their abounding in a resinous sap. So **Gutti·feral** *a.* epithet of an alliance including the order *Guttiferæ*; *sb.* a plant belonging to this alliance. LINDLEY.

Guttiform (gʊ·tifǭɹm), *a.* 1874. [f. L. *gutta* + -(I)FORM.] Drop-shaped.

Guttle (gʊ·t'l), *v.* 1654. [? f. GUT *sb.*, after *guzzle.*] **1.** *intr.* To eat voraciously; to gormandize. **2.** *trans.* To devour or swallow greedily 1685. Hence **Gu·ttler,** a glutton; a gormandizer.

‖**Guttula** (gʊ·tiŭlă). 1887. [L., dim. of *gutta.*] A small drop or drop-like spot. Hence **Gu·ttular** *a.* spotted. **Gu·ttulate** *a.* (*Nat. Hist.*), having drops or spots, as *3-guttulate.* †**Gu·ttulous** *a.* in drop-like form.

‖**Guttur** (gʊ·tʊ̆ɹ). 1562. [L.; = 'throat'.] The throat; used rarely in techn. applications.

Guttural (gʊ·tʊ̆ral). 1594. [ad. mod.L. *gutturalis*; see prec. and -AL.]

A. *adj.* Of or pertaining to the throat 1625; (of sounds) produced in the throat.

The g. orifice of the Eustachian tube 1836. The g. nasal seems to have been the regular pronunciation of *ng* in English A. J. ELLIS.

B. *sb.* [*sc.* sound; *occas.* utterance.] 1696.

His speech was..all gutturals DE FOE.

Hence **Gu·tturalism,** g. quality or characteristics. **Guttura·lity,** g. nature, character, or condition. **Gu·tturalize** *v. trans.* to pronounce or utter gutturally; to render g. in character. **Gutturaliza·tion. Gu·ttural-ly** *adv.* in a g. manner; **-ness,** gutturality.

†**Gutturine,** *a.* [f. GUTTUR + -INE.] Pertaining to the throat. RAY.

Gutturize (gʊ·tʊ̆rəiz), *v.* [f. as prec. + -IZE.] *trans.* To enunciate gutturally. COLERIDGE.

Gutturo- (gʊ·tʊ̆ro), taken as comb. f. L. *guttur* throat; as in *g.-maxillary*, relating to the throat and the jaw; *g.-nasal*, guttural and nasal; etc.

Gutty (gʊ·ti), *sb.* *Golfers' slang.* 1890. [f. GUTTA [2] + -Y.] A gutta-percha ball.

Gutty (gʊ·ti), *a.* Chiefly *Sc.* 1785. [f. GUT *sb.*[1] + -Y [1].] Pot-bellied.

Gutwort (gʊ·twɒ̄ɹt). ? *Obs.* 1597. [f. GUT *sb.*[1] + WORT.] The plant *Globularia Alypum*, a violent purgative, of S. Europe and Africa.

Guy (gəi), *sb.*[1] ME. [a. OF. *gui-s*, also *guie* = It. *guida* (see GUIDE *sb.*).] †**1.** A guide; a conductor or leader (*rare*) -1520. **2.** Chiefly *Naut.* A rope used to guide and steady a thing which is being hoisted or lowered; a rope, chain, rod, etc. to secure and steady anything likely to shift its position or to be carried away, as the mast, funnel, etc. of a vessel, a derrick, a suspension-bridge, etc. 1623. **3.** *attrib.*, as in **guy rein,** a guiding or leading rein 1793.

Guy (gəi), *sb.*[2] *Pl.* **guys.** 1806. **1.** An effigy of Guy Fawkes carried about in the streets on the anniversary of Gunpowder Plot (Nov. 5), and burnt in the evening. **2.** A person of grotesque looks or dress; a fright 1836. **3.** A man, fellow (*U.S. slang*) 1896.

1. Dressed up..like a g. TROLLOPE. 2. Grisly guys some of them turn out 1836.

†**Guy,** *v.*[1] ME. [a. OF. *guier* (later *guider*: see GUIDE); prob. f. some form of the root of Goth. and OE. *witan* to know (see WIT *v.*).] = GUIDE *v.* 1-4. -1600.

Guy (gəi), *v.*[2] 1712. [f. GUY *sb.*[1] 2.] *trans.* To fasten or secure with a guy or with guys. Chiefly *Naut.* Also *transf.*

Guy (gəi), *v.*[3] 1851. [f. GUY *sb.*[2]] **1.** *intr.* To carry an effigy of Guy Fawkes about the streets on Nov. 5. **b.** *trans.* To exhibit a person in effigy 1894. **2.** *trans.* (Orig. *Theatr. slang.*) To make an object of ridicule 1872.

Guze (giūz). 1562. [?] *Her.* A roundle of a sanguine tint.

Guzzle (gʊ·z'l), *sb.* 1598. [? f. the vb.] **1.** A gutter, drain. Also *fig.* Now *dial.* **2.** Drink, liquor 1704. **3.** A debauch 1836.

1. That sinke of filth, that g. most impure MARSTON.

Guzzle (gʊ·z'l), *v.* 1576. [Earlier *gussel*, ? a. OF. *gosiller*, conn. w. *gosier* throat.] **1.** *trans.* To swallow (liquor, *rarely* food) greedily or to excess 1583. **2.** To consume (time, money, etc.) in guzzling 1653. **3.** *intr.* To drink largely or greedily, to swill 1579.

1. How it annoyed me to behold Belvidera [Mrs. Siddons] g. boiled beef and mustard C. K. SHARPE. 2. To g. away money 1797. 3. To shoot and g. at his country seat MACAULAY. Hence **Gu·zzler,** one who guzzles.

Gwyniad (gwi·niæ̆d). Also †**guiniad,** †**gwiniad,** †**gwinead.** 1611. [a. Welsh *gwyniad*, f. *gwyn* white.] A fish of the salmon or trout kind (*Coregonus Pennantii*) with white flesh, found in lakes, esp. Bala.

Gy-, in wds. of Gr. etym., is herein marked to be pronounced with (dʒ), but with regard to the less common words there are many, esp. among scholars, who prefer the 'hard *g*'.

Gyal, obs. f. GAYAL.

Gybe, *sb.*[1] *Thieves' slang.* ? *Obs.* 1561. [?] A counterfeit pass or licence.

Gybe (dʒəib), *sb.*[2] 1880. [f. next.] *Naut.* An act of gybing.

Gybe (dʒəib), *v.* 1693. [app. a. Du. *gijben*; but the initial (dʒ) is obscure.] **1.** *intr.* Of a fore-and-aft sail and its boom: To swing from one side of the vessel to the other. Also *trans.* **2.** *intr.* To put about or alter the course of a boat so that her boom-sails gybe. Said also of the boat. Also *trans.* with the boat as object; also, to sail round by gybing. 1693.

Gye, obs. f. GUY *sb.*[1]; obs. var. of GUY *v.*[1]

Gyle (gəil). 1440. [a. Du. *gijl*, earlier *ghijl*, conn. w. *gijlen* to ferment. Of unkn. origin.] *Brewing.* **1.** A brewing; the quantity brewed at one time 1594. **2.** Wort in process of fermentation 1440. **3.** A gyle-tun 1836. **4.** *attrib.*, as **gyle-tun** = GYLE-FAT; etc. 1498.

Gyle-fat. *Obs.* exc. *dial.* ME. [FAT *sb.*[1]] The vat in which the wort is left to ferment.

Gym (dʒim). 1889. Colloq. abbrev. of GYMNASIUM.

Gymkhana (dʒimkā·nă). Orig. *Anglo-Ind.* 1861. [app. a refash. of Hindustani *gend-khāna* 'ball-house', i.e. racket-court, after *gymnastics.*] 'A place of public resort at a station where the needful facilities for athletics and games . . are provided' (Yule). Hence, an athletic sports display. Also *attrib.*

Gymmal(l, obs. ff. GIMMAL.

Gymnasial (dʒimnē·ziăl), *a.* 1852. [f. GYMNASIUM + -AL.] Of or pertaining to the Continental gymnasia or similar educational establishments.

Gymnasiarch (dʒimnē·ziaɹk). 1658. [ad. L. *gymnasiarchus* and *gymnasiarcha*, a. Gr., f. γυμνάσιον + -αρχος, -αρχης ruling.] **1.** *Gr. Antiq.* An Athenian official who superintended athletic schools and games. **b.** *transf.* A leader among athletes 1825. **2.** A governor of a school or college; a head instructor 1682. So **Gymna·siarchy,** the office or function of g.

Gymnasiast (dʒimnē·ziæst). 1828. [f. Gr. γυμνάσιον; in sense 2, after Ger.] **1.** A student in a (Continental) gymnasium. **2.** A gymnast 1857.

Gymnasium (dʒimnē·ziŏm). *Pl.* **-ia, -iums.** 1598. [L., a. Gr. γυμνάσιον, f. γυμνάζειν to train, exercise, lit. to train naked, f. γυμνός (γυμνάς).] **1.** A place or building for practice of or instruction in athletic exercises; a gymnastic school. Also *transf.* Also *attrib.* **2.** †A high school, college, or academy; *spec.* in Germany and elsewhere, a school of the highest grade preparatory for the universities. Now often as Ger. (gimnā·zium). 1691.

1. Galen..inveighs against the..violent Practices of the G. 1704. 2. Cambridge and Oxford..surpass..the gymnasia of foreign countries JOHNSON. Hence **Gymna·sic** *a.* pertaining to the g. (sense 2). CARLYLE.

Gymnast (dʒi·mnæst). 1594. [ad. Gr. γυμναστής trainer of athletes, f. γυμνάζειν (see prec.).] One skilled in gymnastic exercises; a gymnastic expert.

Gymnastic (dʒimnæ·stik). 1574. [ad. L. *gymnasticus*, a. Gr. (subst. ἡ γυμναστική gymnastics); see GYMNASIUM.]

A. *adj.* 1. Pertaining to or connected with athletic exercises of the body; concerned with gymnastics (see B. 2). b. Physically active (*rare*) 1784. 2. *fig.* 'Pertaining to disciplinary exercises for the intellect' (Webster) 1710.

1. b. A form not now g. as of yore COWPER. 2. The difference of the g. and dogmatic styles GIBBON.

B. *sb.* 1. *sing.* [= Gr. ἡ (τέχνη) γυμναστική.] = 2. 1598. Also *fig.* 2. *pl.* **Gymnastics** [see -ICS, -IC 2]. a. The practice of athletic exercises for the development of the body, now esp. of such as are performed in a gymnasium (sense 1) 1652. Also *fig.* †b. A treatise on athletic exercises. SIR T. BROWNE.

1. Good gymnastic will give health to the body JOWETT. 2. a. Gymnastics..have not until lately been practised HONE. *fig.* I think Hindoo books the best gymnastics for the mind EMERSON. Hence **Gymna·stical** *a.* = A. **Gymna·stically** *adv.* (*rare*), in a g. manner; in respect of gymnastics.

Gymnic (dʒi·mnik). Now *rare.* 1601. [ad. L. *gymnicus*, a. Gr., f. γυμνός naked; see -IC.]

A. *adj.* = GYMNASTIC *a.* 1.

Have they not Sword-players, and ev'ry sort of G. Artists, Wrestlers, Riders, Runners, Juglers and Dancers MILT.

B. *sb. pl.* **Gymnics**: = *gymnastics* (see GYMNASTIC *sb.* 2) 1621. Hence †**Gy·mnical** *a.* = A.

Gymnite (dʒi·mnəit). 1843. [f. Gr. γυμνός naked, in allusion to Bare Hills, Maryland, where found; see -ITE.] *Min.* A hydrated silicate of magnesium.

Gymno- (dʒimnǒ), bef. a vowel **gymn-**, comb. f. Gr. γυμνός naked, bare.

Gymnobla·stic [Gr. βλαστός (see -BLAST)] *a.*, *Zool.* having the nutritive or generative buds unprotected by an external receptacle (hydrotheca or gonangium); so **Gymnobla·stous** *a.* **Gymnobra·nchiate** [Gr. βράγχια *pl.*, gills] *a.*, belonging to the *Gymnobranchiata*, a group of gastropods having naked gills; *sb.* an animal of this group. **Gymnoce·ratous** [Gr. κερατ-, κέρας horn] *a.*, *Entom.* belonging to the *Gymnocerata*, a group of heteropterous insects having exposed antennæ. ||**Gymnocyta, -cyte** [Gr. κύτος cell], *Biol.* 'Haeckel's term for a naked or wall-less cytode having a nucleus' (*Syd. Soc. Lex.*). **Gy·mnodont** [Gr. ὀδοντ-, ὀδούς], *Ichthyol.*, *a.* belonging to the *Gymnodontes*, a group of plectognath fishes having the jaw prolonged into a beak covered with a dental plate; *sb.* a fish of this group. **Gy·mnogen** [see -GEN], *Bot.* = GYMNOSPERM. **Gymno·genous** [see -GENOUS] *a.*, *Bot.* = GYMNOSPERMOUS. **Gy·mnogram** [Gr. γραμμή line, mark], *Bot.* a fern of the genus *Gymnogramme* or *-gramma*, having the lines of spore-cases on the lower side of the frond uncovered. **Gymno·gynous** [see -GYNOUS] *a.*, *Bot.* having a naked ovary. **Gymnolæ·matous** [Gr. λαιμός throat, gullet] *a.*, *Zool.* belonging to the *Gymnolæmata*, a division of Polyzoa having no epistome or valve to close down upon the mouth. **Gymno·merous** [Gr. μηρός thigh] *a.*, *Zool.* pertaining to the *Gymnomera*, a division of cladocerous crustaceans. **Gymnomy·xine** [Gr. μύξα slime] *a.*, *Zool.* pertaining to the *Gymnomyxa*, a low grade of Polyzoa which are naked or not corticate. **Gymnophtha·lmate, -ophtha·lmatous, -ophtha·lmic, -ophtha·lmous** [Gr. ὀφθαλμός] *adjs.*, *Zool.* belonging to the *Gymnophthalmata* or naked-eyed medusæ. **Gymno·pterous** [Gr. πτέρον] *a.*, *Entom.* having naked wings, without hairs or scales; having sheathless wings. **Gymnorhi·nal** [Gr. ῥῖν-, ῥίς nostril] *a.*, *Ornith.* having naked or unfeathered nostrils. **Gymnoso·mate, -so·matous, -so·mous** [Gr. σωματ-, σῶμα] *adjs.*, *Zool.* pertaining to the *Gymnosomata*, an order of pteropods having a naked body. **Gy·mnospore** [SPORE], *Bot.* a naked spore; so **Gymno·sporous** *a.*, having uncovered spores. **Gymnotetraspe·rmous** [Gr. τετρα- four, σπέρμα seed] *a.*, *Bot.* having such a four-lobed ovary as is found in labiates, which was formerly thought to consist of four naked seeds. **Gymno·tocous** [Gr. τόκος] *a.*, *Zool.* having the genital products uncovered, as certain hydroids. **Gymnozo·idal** [Gr. ζῷον: see -ID³] *a.*, *Zool.* pertaining to the *Gymnozoida*, a section of Infusoria in Saville Kent's classification.

Gymnocarpous (dʒimnǒkā·ɹpəs), *a.* 1856. [f. Gr. γυμνόκαρπος + -OUS.] *Bot.* Having a naked fruit; applied to lichens with open or expanded apothecia, or to a fructification of this character.

Gymnogene (dʒi·mnǒdʒīn). 1875. [ad. mod.L. *Gymnogenys*, lit. naked-chinned.] A book-name for an African hawk, *Polyboroides typicus* or *P. capensis.*

Gymnopædic (dʒimnǒpī·dik), *a.* 1850. [ad. Gr. γυμνοπαιδικός, f. γυμνός + παιδ-, παῖς.] *Gr. Antiq.* Distinctive epithet of the dances, etc. performed by naked boys at public festivals.

Gymnosophist (dʒimnǫ·sǒfist). ME. [ad. L. (pl.) *gymnosophistæ*, ad. Gr., f. γυμνός naked + σοφιστής SOPHIST.] One of a sect of ancient Hindu philosophers of ascetic habits, who wore little or no clothing, denied themselves flesh meat, and gave themselves up to mystical contemplation. They were known to the Greeks through the reports of the companions of Alexander. Also *occas.*, an ascetic or mystic. So **Gymno·sophy**, the doctrine or system of gymnosophists. var. **Gy·mnosoph** (*rare*). COLERIDGE.

Gymnosperm (dʒi·mnǒspɔ̄ɹm). 1838. [ad. mod.L. *gymnospermus*, ad. Gr., f. γυμνός + σπέρμα.] *Bot.* A plant which has naked seeds, as the pine, hemlock fir, etc.; one of the *Gymnospermæ*, a class of exogenous plants so characterized.

Gymnospermous (dʒimnǒspɔ̄·ɹməs), *a.* 1727. [f. mod.L. *gymnospermus* (see prec.) + -OUS.] *Bot.* Naked-seeded, i.e. not provided with a seed-vessel; belonging to the class *Gymnospermæ*. So **Gymnospe·rmal, -spe·rmic** *adjs.* in same sense.

Gymnostomous (dʒimnǫ·stǒməs), *a.* 1861. [f. Gr. γυμνός + στόμα.] *Bot.* Naked-mouthed; applied to mosses in which the mouth of the sporangium has no peristome. So **Gymnosto·matous** *a.* in same sense.

Gymnotus (dʒimnōu·tǒs). *Pl.* **-ti** (-təi). 1775. [mod.L. (Linn.) for **gymnonotus*, f. Gr. γυμνός naked + νῶτον back, with allusion to the absence of dorsal fins.] A freshwater eel-like fish of S. America, *Electrophorus* (formerly *Gymnotus*) *electricus*, capable of giving an electric shock; an electric eel.

Gyn, obs. f. GIN *sb.*¹

||**Gynæceum** (dʒəi-, dʒinīsī·ǒm). 1610. [L., a. Gr. γυναικεῖον, f. γυναικ-, γυνή.] 1. *Gr. and Rom. Antiq.* 1. The women's apartments in a house; any building set apart for women 1723. †b. Under the Roman empire: A textile manufactory -1781. 2. *Bot.* The female organs of a flower. Now usually spelt gynœcium, as if from Gr. οἰκίον house, with correl. ANDRŒCIUM.

Gynæcian, *a. rare.* Also **gynecian** (in Dicts.) 1640. [f. Gr. γυναικ-, γυνή + -IAN.] Pertaining or relating to women.

Gynæcic (dʒəinī·sik), *a.* Also **gynecic.** 1878. [ad. Gr. γυναικικός.] Relating to diseases peculiar to women.

Gynæco- (dʒəi-, dʒinī·kǒ), also (esp. *U.S.*) gyneco-, repr. Gr. γυναικο-, comb. f. γυνή woman, female.

gynæco-cœ·nic [Gr. κοινός] *a.*, having women in common; **-phore** [Gr. -φορος bearing], *Zool.* in certain invertebrate animals, as some trematodes, a receptacle in the male in which the female is borne; hence **-phoric** *a.*; **-physiology,** the PHYSIOLOGY of the female generative organs.

Gynæcocracy (dʒəi-, dʒinīkǫ·krăsi). 1612. [ad. Gr. γυναικοκρατία, f. γυναικο-, γυνή + -κρατία -CRACY. Cf. F. *gynécocratie.*] Government by a woman or women; female rule; petticoat government. Hence **Gynæcocra·tic, -al** *a.* pertaining to g.

Gynæcology (dʒəi-, dʒinīkǫ·lǒdʒi). Also gynecology. 1847. [f. GYNÆCO- + -LOGY.] That branch of medical science which treats of the functions and diseases peculiar to women. Also *loosely*, the science of womankind. Hence **Gynæcolo·gical** *a.* pertaining to or relating to g. **Gynæco·logist**, an expert in g.

Gynander (dʒəinæ·ndəɹ). 1828. [ad. Gr. γύνανδρος (see GYNANDROUS).] A plant of the class *Gynandria.*

Gynandrian (dʒəi-, dʒinæ·ndriăn), *a.* 1828. [f. mod.L. *Gynandria* (Linn.), f. Gr. γυνή + ἀνδρ-, ἀνήρ (see GYNANDROUS) + -IAN.] Pertaining to the class *Gynandria* of plants having gynandrous flowers.

Gynandro- (dʒəi-, dʒinæ·ndro), comb. f. Gr. γύνανδρος (see GYNANDROUS).

Gynandromo·rphism, *Entom.* the condition of being gynandromorphous. **Gynandromo·rphous** [Gr. μορφή] *a.*, having both male and female characters; applied to some insects. **Gyna·ndrophore,** *Bot.* a gonophore which bears both the stamens and the pistil.

Gynandrous (dʒəi-, dʒinæ·ndrəs), *a.* 1807. [f. Gr. γύνανδρος 'of doubtful sex' + -OUS; cf. GYNO- and -ANDROUS.] *Bot.* Applied to those flowers and plants in which the stamens and pistil are united in one column, as in orchids; said also of the stamens.

Gynantherous: see GYNO-.

Gynarchy (dʒəi·naɹki). 1577. [f. Gr. γυνή + -αρχία, ἀρχή.] Government by a woman or women.

Gyneocracy (dʒəi-, dʒinīǫ·krăsi). *rare.* 1611. [f. as prec. + -(O)CRACY.] Incorrect f. GYNÆCOCRACY.

Gyniolatry (dʒəi-, dʒiniǫ·lătri). 1876. [Badly f. Gr. γυνή + -(O)LATRY.] Adoration or worship of women. LOWELL.

Gyno- (dʒəino, dʒinǒ), bef. a vowel **gyn-** (dʒəin, dʒin), reduced form of GYNÆCO-, used chiefly in *Bot.* with the meaning 'pistil', 'ovary'.

Gyna·ntherous [ANTHER] *a.*, *Bot.* pertaining to an abnormal condition of the flower in which the stamens are converted into pistils. **Gynodiœ·cious** [DIŒCIOUS] *a.*, *Bot.* having perfect and female flowers on different plants; so **Gynodiœ·cism,** the condition of being gynodiœcious. **Gynomonœ·cious** [MONŒCIOUS] *a.*, *Bot.* having both perfect and female flowers on the same plant. ||**Gynoste·gium** [Gr. στέγη roof], *Bot.* the sheath of a gynæceum. ||**Gynoste·mium** [Gr. στήμων thread, stamen], *Bot.* the column consisting of the united stamens and pistil, as in the orchis.

Gynobase (dʒəi·n-, dʒi·nǒbēˡs). Also in mod.L. form **gynobasis.** 1830. [f. GYNO- + BASE.] *Bot.* The flat or conical enlargement of the receptacle of a flower supporting the gynæceum. Hence **Gynoba·sic** *a.* pertaining to or having a g.; *gynobasic style*, one rising from the base of the ovary.

Gynocracy (dʒəi-, dʒinǫ·krăsi). 1728. [f. GYNO- + -CRACY.] = GYNÆCOCRACY; also quasi-*concr.*

||**Gynœcium**: see GYNÆCEUM.

Gynophore (dʒəi·n-, dʒi·nǒfōᵊɹ). 1821. [f. GYNO- + Gr. -φορος bearing. Cf. F. *gynophore.*] 1. *Bot.* The pedicel or stalk which in some flowers supports the ovary. 2. *Zool.* One of the branches bearing the female gonophores in certain Hydrozoa 1861.

-gynous (dʒinəs), *Bot. suffix* forming adjs., f. mod.L. *-gynus* (a. Gr. -γυνος, f. γυνή) + -OUS; used as = 'having . . . female organs or pistils', as in *monogynous* having one pistil, etc.

Gyp¹ (dʒip). Also †**gip.** 1750. [perh. short for GIPSY.] 1. At Cambridge and Durham, a college servant or bed-maker. 2. *U.S. slang.* A thief 1889.

Gyp². *dial.* or *colloq.* 1898. [app. contr. of GEE-UP.] *To give* (a person or thing) *gyp*: to punish, thrash, treat roughly.

Gyps (dʒips). ME. Anglicized f. GYPSUM.

Gypseous (dʒi·psǐəs), *a.* 1661. [f. late L. *gypseus* (f. *gypsum*) + -OUS.] 1. Like or having the nature of gypsum. 2. Containing or consisting mainly of gypsum 1771. var. **Gy·psous.**

Gypsi·ferous, *a.* 1847. [f. GYPSUM + -(I)FEROUS.] Yielding or containing gypsum.

†**Gy·psine,** *a. rare.* 1695 [See -INE.] = GYPSEOUS. -1753.

Gypsography (dʒipsǫ·grăfi). *rare.* 1840. [f. Gr. γύψος gypsum + -GRAPHY.] The art or practice of engraving on gypsum, or on plaster of Paris.

Gypsum (dʒi·psǒm), *sb.* *Pl.* **-sa, -sums.** 1646. [a. L. *gypsum*, ad. Gr. γύψος.] *Min.* Hydrous calcium sulphate, the mineral from which plaster of Paris is made. Hence **Gy·psum** *v.* to dress (land or a crop) with g.

Gypsy, alternative form of GIPSY.

Gyral (dʒəi·răl), *a.* 1750. [f. GYRE or GYRUS *sb.* + -AL.] a. Moving in a circle or spiral; whirling, gyratory. b. Pertaining to a gyrus or giri (see GYRUS). Hence **Gy·rally** *adv.*

Gy·rant, *a.* Also †**girant.** [ad. L. *gyrantem.*] Moving in a circle or spiral. MRS. BROWNING.

Gyrate (dʒəiə·rɛ̆t), *a.* 1830. [ad. L. *gyratus* rounded; see GYRE *v.*] Arranged in rings or convolutions. *Bot.* = CIRCINATE; also, surrounded by an elastic ring, as the theca of ferns.

Gyrate (dʒəiə·reɪt), *v.* 1822. [f. L. *gyrat-*, *gyrare*; see GYRE *v.*] *intr.* To move in a circle or spiral; to revolve round a fixed point or axis; to rotate, whirl. Also *fig.* Hence **Gyra·tor.**

Gyration (dʒeiərēɪ·ʃən). 1615. [f. L. *gyrare*; see GYRE *v.*] 1. The action or process of gyrating; motion in a circle or spiral; revolution round a fixed centre or axis, wheeling, whirling; an instance of any of these. Also *fig.* 2. *concr.* in *Conch.* One of the whorls of a spiral univalve shell 1889.

1. If a burning Coal be nimbly moved round in a Circle with Gyrations continually repeated NEWTON. In the gyrations of the storm MAURY. *fig.* His life was a g. of energetic curiosity DISRAELI.

Gyratory (dʒəiə·rătəri), *a.* 1816. [f. L. *gyrare* to GYRATE.] Moving in a circle or spiral; revolving, whirling.

Gyre (dʒəiə·ɪ), *sb.* 1556. *poet.* and *literary.* Also †**gire.** [ad. L. *gyrus*, ad. Gr. γῦρος ring, circle. Cf. GIRO.] 1. A turning round, revolution, whirl; a circular or spiral turn. 2. *concr.* A ring, circle, spiral; also, a vortex 1590.

1. Be thy wheeling gyres Of ample circuit, easy thy descent CARY. 2. Others run still in the same g., to wearinesse BP. HALL. Hence †**Gy·reful** *a.* circling, whirling.

Gyre (dʒəiəɪ), *v. poet.* Also †**gire.** ME. [ad. L. *gyrare*, f. *gyrus* (see prec.).] To turn or whirl round (*rare*). *trans.* and *intr.* Hence **Gy·ringly** *adv.* with revolving motion.

Gyrencephalate (dʒəiərĕnse·fălĕt), *a.* 1859. [f. mod.L. *Gyrencephala*, f. GYRUS + Gr. ἐγκέφαλος brain.] *Zool.* Of or pertaining to the *Gyrencephala*, in which the cerebrum is convoluted. Also **-ous** *a.*

Gyrfalcon, obs. f. GERFALCON.

Gyro- (dʒəiə·rŏ), comb. f. Gr. γῦρος ring, circle, spiral: **Gy·ro-co·mpass**, a form of gyroscope used as a compass, being continuously driven and thus retaining a fixed direction 1913.

Gyrogonite (dʒəiərǫ·gŏnəit). 1832. [f. GYRO- + Gr. γόνος seed + -ITE.] *Geol.* A petrified seed-vessel of plants of the genus *Chara*, spiral in form, and formerly supposed to be a shell.

Gyroidal (dʒəiəroi·dăl), *a.* 1864. [f. GYRE or GYRUS + -OID + -AL.] 1. *Crystall.* Having a spiral arrangement, as certain planes, etc. in some crystalline forms. 2. *Optics.* Turning the plane of polarization to the right or left; rotatory in respect to polarized light 1864. Hence **Gyroi·dally** *adv.*

Gyromancy (dʒəiə·rŏmænsi). 1557. [a. med.L. **gyromantia*, f. Gr. γῦρος + μαντεία.] A mode of divination by walking in a circle till the person fell down from dizziness, the inference being drawn from the place in the circle at which he fell.

Gyron (dʒəiə·rɒn). 1572. [a. F. *giron*, ad. OHG. *gêro* triangular piece, gusset; see GORE *sb.*[1]] *Her.* An ordinary of triangular form made by two lines drawn from the edge of the escutcheon to meet in the fesse-point and occupying half of the quarter. Also *attrib.*

Gyronny (dʒəiərǫ·ni), *a.* ME. [a. F. *gironné*; see prec. and -Y.] *Her.* Of an escutcheon: Divided into or having gyrons; *g. of eight*, having eight gyrons.

Gyroscope (dʒəiə·rŏskōᵘp). 1856. [ad. F. *gyroscope*; see GYRO- and -SCOPE.] *Dynamics.* A solid rotating wheel mounted in a ring, and having its axis free to turn in any direction; designed to illustrate the dynamics of rotating bodies. Foucault's gyroscope is contrived so as to render evident the rotation of the earth, through the tendency of the wheel to maintain its rotation in a fixed plane independently of the earth's motion. Hence **Gyrosco·pic** *a.* pertaining to or of the nature of the g.; rotatory.

Gyrose (dʒəiə·rōᵘs), *a.* 1836. [f. GYRUS; see -OSE.] *Bot.* Folded and waved, marked with wavy lines.

Gyrostat (dʒəiə·rŏstæt). 1879. [f. GYRO- + Gr. στατός standing.] *Dynamics.* An instrument used to illustrate the dynamics of rotating bodies: a rapidly rotating fly-wheel pivoted as finely as possible within a rigid case, having a convex curvilinear polygonal border, in the plane perpendicular to the axis through the centre of gravity of the whole. Hence **Gyrosta·tic** *a.* pertaining to the g. or to gyrostatics; connected with the theory that a rotating body tends to maintain its plane of rotation. **Gyrosta·tically** *adv.* **Gyrosta·tics** *sb. pl.* that part of physical science which deals with the rotation of solid bodies.

‖**Gyrus** (dʒəiə·rɒs). *Pl.* **gyri** (-rəi). 1846. [L., a. Gr. γῦρος ring, circle.] *Anat.* A convoluted ridge between grooves or sulci; *esp.* a convolution of the brain.

Gyse, obs. f. GUISE.

Gyte (gəit), *a. Sc.* 1725. [?] Out of one's senses.

Gyve (dʒəiv), *sb.* Usu. *pl.* Now *arch.* or *poet.* [ME. *give*, of obscure origin. Orig. pronounced (gəiv).] A shackle, esp. for the leg; a fetter. Also *transf.* and *fig.*

Eugene Aram walked between With gyves upon his wrist HOOD.

Gyve (dʒəiv), *v.* ME. [f. GYVE *sb.*] *trans.* To fasten with, or as with gyves; to fetter, shackle. Also *fig.*

fig. Oth. II. i. 171.

H

H (ēɪtʃ), the eighth letter of the Roman alphabet, repr. historically Semitic 𐤇, *Hheth* or *Kheth*, through Gr. Η, *Heta, Eta.* The Semitic letter represented a laryngal or guttural spirant, or a rough aspirate, and it was with the aspirate value that the letter was orig. used in Gr. and passed thence into Roman use. In OE., *h* occurred not only bef. the vowels, but also bef. the consonants *l, n, r, w*, as in *hláf* loaf, *hræfn* raven, etc.; it now stands initially only bef. vowels. Its power is that of a simple aspiration or breathing, with just sufficient narrowing of the glottis to be heard bef. a vowel. It is also used to form consonantal digraphs (*sh, th*, etc.) with simple sounds; and it is often silent, or merely lengthens a preceding vowel.

The name *aitch* goes back through ME. *ache* to OF. *ache*, pointing to a late L. **accha*, **ahha*, or **aha*, exemplifying the sound. (The earlier L. name was *ha.*) Pl. *aitches, aches, hs, h's.*

Comb. H-piece, in a force-pump, a piece standing on the wind-bore, under the door-piece, by which the water is forced through the door-piece into the stand-pipe.

II. Besides serial order, *H* or *h* signifies *spec.* 1. *Mus.* The note B natural in the German system of nomenclature (the letter B being used only for B flat). 2. *Math.* In the differential calculus, *h* denotes a small increment. 3. In *Cryst.*, *h, k, l* are used for the quantities which determine the position of a plane.

III. Abbreviations. H. = *Henry, Helen*, etc. H (*Chem.*) = Hydrogen. H. in the Shipping Register = *Hoy*. h. (in a ship's log) = hail. H or h. = hour. H or h (*Physics*) = horizontal force. H (on lead pencils) = hard; the various degrees of hardness being denoted by HH, HHH, etc. H (*Mus.*), as a direction = horns. HB (on lead pencils) = hard black (i.e. of a medium hardness). H.B.C. = Hudson's Bay Company. H.B.M. = His (or Her) Britannic Majesty. H.C. = Heralds' College, House of Commons. H.C.F. (*Math.*) = Highest Common Factor. H.E.I.C. = Honourable East India Company. H.G. = Horse Guards. H.H. = His (or Her) Highness, or His Holiness. H.I.M. = His (or Her) Imperial Majesty. H.M. = His (or Her) Majesty. H.M.C. = His (or Her) Majesty's Customs. H.M.S. = His (or Her) Majesty's Ship or Service. H.P. = horse-power, half-pay. H.R.H. = His (or Her) Royal Highness. †H.q. = L. *hoc quære*, seek this, q.v. H.T., h.t., high tension.

H', formerly used for *he* bef. a vowel or *h*: see HE.

Ha (hā), *int.* (*sb.*) ME. [Not in OE., exc. in the *ha ha* of laughter.] 1. An exclam. of surprise, wonder, joy, suspicion, indignation, etc., according to the intonation. b. Repeated, *ha ha!* it represents laughter: see HA-HA. 2. esp. after a question; = EH 2. (Chiefly in SHAKS.) 1594. 3. Expressing hesitation or interruption in speech (hō or ə). Often with *hum.* 1606. 4. *sb.* The interjection as a name for itself; see HUM, also HAW 1610.

1. Ha? Let me see: I, giue it me, it's mine SHAKS. 2. What saies that foole of Hagars offspring? ha SHAKS. Hence **Ha** *v.*, also **hah**, to utter 'ha!' in hesitation.

Ha, pron., ME. form of HE, HEO she, HI they.

Ha, ha', worn-down form of HAVE *v.*

Ha' (hā), Sc. form of HALL. *Comb.*: **ha'-Bible**, the great Bible that lay in the *ha'* or principal apartment; **ha' house**, the manor-house.

Haaf (hāf, haf). 1809. [a. ON. *haf* sea, high sea, ocean.] In Shetland and Orkney: The deep or main sea: now used only in connexion with deep-sea fishing; hence, deep-sea fishing ground or station. Also *attrib.*

Haak, dial. f. HAKE.

Haar (hāɪ). *local.* 1671. [? a. ON. *hárr* hoar, hoary; cf. *hoar-frost.*] A wet mist or fog; esp. a cold sea-fog.

Hab (hæb), *adv.* (*sb.*) *Obs.* exc. *dial.* 1530. [? repr. OE. *hæbbe*, early south. ME. *habbe*, pres. subj. of HAVE *v.*, in conjunction with the corresp. neg. form OE. *næbbe*, ME. *nabbe.*] 1. In the phrases *hab or nab, hab nab* (*habs-nabs*), get or lose, hit or miss; anyhow; at a venture 1542. 2. quasi-*sb.* In phr. *at* (*by*) *hab or nab* = prec. So †**Hab** *v.* in *hab or nab*, have or not have.

‖**Habeas corpus** (hēɪ·bi,ĕ̄s kǭ·ɪpɒs). 1465. [L.; = thou (shalt) have the body (*sc.* in court).] A writ requiring the body of a person to be brought before a judge or into court for the purpose specified in the writ; *spec.* the prerogative writ *habeas corpus ad subiiciendum*, requiring the body of a person restrained of liberty to be brought before the judge or into court, that the lawfulness of the restraint may be investigated and determined. Also *fig.*

Habeas Corpus Act: the Act 31 Chas. II. c. 2 (1679), facilitating the granting and enforcing of the prerogative writ.

‖**Habendum** (hăbe·ndɒm). 1607. [L. = 'to be had' or 'to be possessed'.] *Law.* That part of a deed (beginning in Law with the words *habendum et tenendum*, and in Eng. deeds 'to have and to hold') which defines what estate or interest is thereby granted.

†**Ha·berdash**, *v.* [f. HABERDASHER.] *intr.* To deal in haberdashery. QUARLES.

Haberdasher (hæ·bərdæʃəɪ). ME. [? f. AF. *hapertas*, of unkn. origin.] Formerly, a dealer in a variety of articles, including caps, and probably hats. In the 16th c.: **a.** A dealer in, or maker of, hats and caps, a hatter -1711; in *U.S.*, a dealer in men's hats, collars, cuffs, and underwear. **b.** A dealer in thread, tape, ribbons, and the like 1611. Also *fig.*

a. The H. heapeth wealth by hattes GASCOIGNE.

Haberdashery (hæ·bəɪdæ:ʃəri). ME. [f. prec.] 1. The goods and wares sold by a haberdasher. 2. The shop of a haberdasher 1813. 3. *attrib.*, as *h.-ware*, etc. 1547.

†**Haberdine** (hæ·bəɪdīn, -din). ME. [repr. MDu. *abberdaen* (Du. *abberdaan*), var. of *labberdaen*, connected by De Vries with the name of a Basque district, *le Labourd*, or from *Lapurdum* ancient name of Bayonne.] The name of a large sort of cod, used esp. for salting; salt or sun-dried cod -1708. Also *attrib.*

Habergeon (hæ·bəɪdʒən, hăbə̄·ɪdʒən), **haubergeon** (hǭ·bəɪdʒən). [ME. a. F. *haubergeon*, deriv. (dim.) of OF. *hauberc*, now *haubert*; see HAUBERK and -ON. Since 16th c. only historical.] A sleeveless coat or jacket of mail or scale armour, orig. smaller than a HAUBERK, but sometimes app. the same as that.

Habilatory (hăbi·lătəri), *a. rare.* 1827. [Arbitrary f. F. *habiller*, after adjs. in *-atory.*] Having reference to dressing.

Habile (hæ·bil), *a.* ME. [var. of ABLE (formerly *hable, abil*, etc.), conformed to mod. F. *habile* or L. *habilis.*] †1. Suited; suitable; competent. Chiefly *Sc.* -1795. †2. Manageable 1741. †3. Having the capacity or power (*to do* a thing) -1678. 4. Handy; skilful, adroit, dexterous 1485.

Habiliment (hăbi·limĕnt). [ME. *abilyment*, etc., a. OF. *habillement, abillement*, f.

habiller to render fit, fit out, f. *habile* fit; see ABLE.] 1. (without *pl.*) Outfit, array, attire. (Now only of personal attire.) 1470. †2. *pl.* Munitions, or apparatus of war. (In this sense usually spelt without *h*, quasi 'things making *able* for war'.) –1686. †b. *esp.* Armour, warlike apparel; trappings (of a horse) –1816. 3. *pl.* The vestments appropriate to any office or occasion. Also *joc.* Ordinary clothes. (The chief extant sense.) Also *fig.* 1491. †4. = BILIMENT –1621. †5. *fig.* Mental equipment; *pl.* abilities, faculties, powers –1640.

3. My riches, are these poore habiliments SHAKS. Hence **Habi·limented** *ppl. a.* equipped, apparelled, dressed.

†**Habi·litate,** *ppl. a.* [ad. med.L. *habilitatus*; see next.] Endowed with ability; capacitated, qualified. BACON.

Habilitate (habi·līteit), *v.* Also **abilitate.** 1604. [f. L. *habilitat-*, *habilitare*, f. *habilitas* ABILITY.] †1. *trans.* To capacitate, qualify –1819. 2. *intr.* for *refl.* To qualify oneself for office. [After Ger. *habilitiren.*] 1881. 3. *trans.* To clothe, dress (*rare*) 1885. Hence **Habi·lita·tion,** also *abilitation*, the action of enabling; capacitation, qualification; *spec.* in *U.S.*, the furnishing of means to the owner of a mine, to enable him to work it. **Habi·litator** [Sp. *habilitador*], one who furnishes means for the working of a mine under contract with the owner.

Hability (hăbi·līti). ME. Early ABILITY, after OF. *habilete*; in 19th c. sometimes restored with the mod.F. sense of *habilité*, the quality of being habile.

Habit (hæ·bit), *sb.* [ME. *abit*, *habite*, a. OF. *habit*, *abit*; ad.L. *habitus*, f. *habere* to have, *refl.* to be. In mod.F. the word is narrowed down to branch I below, other senses being supplied by *habitude.*]

I. Dress. 1. Bodily apparel or attire; dress (*arch.*). b. with *a.* and *pl.* A set or suit of clothes, a dress (of a specified kind) (*arch.*) ME. c. *pl.* Clothes, garments 1477; hence in *sing.* A garment (*arch.*) 1714. d. *transf.* and *fig.* 1549. 2. *spec.* The dress of a particular rank, degree, profession, or function; *esp.* the dress of a religious order ME. 3. = RIDING-HABIT. 1798.

1. It is her habite onely, that is honest SHAKS. c. MILT. *Comus* 157. d. Tory to-day, and Whig to-morrow, All habits and all shapes he wore PRAED. 2. *The habit*, the monastic order or profession (cf. 'the cowl').

II. †1. Bearing, deportment, behaviour; posture –1687. 2. Bodily condition or constitution 1576; †the bodily system –1733; †the outer part, surface, or external appearance of the body –1725. 3. *Zool.* and *Bot.* The characteristic mode of growth and appearance of an animal or plant. Hence *transf.*, e.g. in *Crystall.* 1691. †4. Habitation (*rare*). FLORIO.

2. Originally..of a spare h., but now..inclined to corpulency DISRAELI. 3. Plants..of a tufted h. HOOKER.

III. 1. Mental constitution, disposition, character ME. 2. A settled disposition or tendency to act in a certain way, esp. one acquired by frequent repetition of the same act; a settled practice, custom, usage; a customary manner of acting. (The chief sense.) Said occas. of inanimate things. 1581. b. without *a* or *pl.*: Custom, use, wont 1605. c. (Usu. in *pl.*) Applied *transf.* to animals and plants 1774. †3. The condition of being accustomed to something; familiarity –1859.

1. If we respect more the outward shape, then the inward habit LYLY. 2. How vse doth breed a h. in a man SHAKS. *Disposition* properly denotes a natural tendency [to action], *habit* an acquired tendency SIR W. HAMILTON. c. The h. of cotyledons rising vertically at night DARWIN. 3. The h. of affairs BURKE.

†IV. *Logic.* The eighth of the categories or predicaments of Aristotle: Having or possession: in Gr. ἔχειν, L. *habitus.* (See CATEGORY 1.) –1837.

Habit (hæ·bit), *v.* ME. [a. F. *habiter*, ad. L. *habitare*, f. *habit-*, *habere*; see the *sb.*] †1. *intr.* To dwell, abide –1649. 2. *trans.* To dwell in 1598. 3. To attire. (Usu. in *pa. pple.*) 1588. †4. To habituate –1814; to render habitual –1660.

1. Although he h. on the earth GREENE. 3. Or is it Dian habited like her SHAKS. 4. Men..habited in falsehood FELTHAM.

Habitable (hæ·bităb'l), *a.* Also †**abitable.** ME. [a. F., ad. L. *habitābilis*, f. *habitare*; see -ABLE.] Suitable for habitation; fit to live in, inhabitable; also *absol.* the habitable globe (MILT. *P.L.* VIII. 157). Hence **Ha·bitabi·lity, Ha·bitableness. Ha·bitably** *adv.*

Ha·bitacle. *Obs.* exc. *Hist.* ME. [a. F., ad. L. *habitaculum*, dwelling-place.] 1. A dwelling-place. Also *transf.* and *fig.* 2. A canopied niche in the wall of a building ME. var. †**Habita·cule** (in sense 1).

Ha·bitance. [a. OF., f. *habiter*; see -ANCE.] A habitation. SPENSER.

Habitancy (hæ·bitănsi). 1792. [f. next; see -ANCY.] 1. Residence as an inhabitant. 2. Inhabitants collectively 1832.

Habitant (hæ·bitănt). 1490. [a. F., ad. L. *habitantem* pr. pple.]

A. *adj.* Indwelling. R. A. VAUGHAN.

B. *sb.* 1. One who dwells in a place; an inhabitant 1490. ‖2. (pronounced abitañ; pl. often *habitans*). A native of Canada (also of Louisiana) of French descent; one of the race of original French colonists, chiefly small farmers.

1. *fig.* O Love! no h. of earth thou art BYRON. 2. To ascertain the feelings of the *habitans*, or French yeomanry W. IRVING.

Habitat (hæ·bitæt). 1796. [a. L. *habitat*, *lit.* 'it inhabits', in Floras and Faunas, written in Latin.] *Nat. Hist.* The locality in which a plant or animal naturally grows or lives; habitation. Applied (*a*) to the *geographical area* over which it extends; (*b*) to the particular *station* in which a specimen is found; (*c*) but chiefly used to indicate the kind of locality, as the sea-shore, chalk hills, or the like. Hence *gen.* Habitation 1854.

The Black Spleenwort..occurs on rocks as a native h. E. NEWMAN. *gen.* Brook Street, the favourite h. of physicians 1869.

Habitation (hæbitēi·ʃən). [ME. *habitacioun*, a. F., ad. L. *habitationem.*] 1. The action of dwelling in or inhabiting; occupancy by inhabitants. 2. *concr.* A place of abode or residence ME. Also *fig.* 3. The name adopted for local branches of the 'Primrose League' in 1883. 4. A settlement. [After Fr.] 1555.

1. Every Starr perhaps a World Of destin'd h. MILT. 2. They had no Cities, nor setled Habitations 1662. *fig.* The Sonne and Mone remayned still in their habitacion COVERDALE *Hab.* iii. 11.

†**Ha·bitator.** [a. L., f. *habitare.*] A dweller, inhabiter. SIR T. BROWNE.

Habited (hæ·bitĕd), *ppl. a.* 1605. [f. HABIT *v.*] 1. Inhabited 1866. 2. Clothed, dressed 1807. †3. That has become habitual; accustomed –1651.

2. Statues of the Habited Graces 1807.

Habitual (hăbi·tiuăl). 1526. [ad. med.L. *habitualis*, f. *habitus* HABIT.]

A. *adj.* †1. Belonging to the habit or inward disposition (see HABIT *sb.* III. 1); inherent or latent in the mental constitution. 2. Of the nature of a habit; fixed by habit; constantly repeated; customary 1611. Hence *transf.* of an agent 1825. 3. Constantly used; usual 1654.

1. I distinguish between habituall and actuall Jurisdiction BRAMHALL. 2. H. dissoluteness of manners BURKE, diffidence and awkwardness of address W. IRVING, actions DARWIN. *transf.* A h. drunkard MACAULAY, volcano LYELL, tea-drinker 1875. 3. Romola's h. seat GEO. ELIOT.

B. *ellipt.* as *sb.* A habitual criminal, drunkard, etc. (*colloq.*) 1884.

Hence **Habi·tualize** *v. trans.* to render h. **Habi·tual-ly** *adv.*, **-ness.**

†**Habituate** (hăbi·tiu,ĕt), *ppl. a.* 1526. [ad. L. *habituatus*; see next.] 1. Made or become habitual –1720. 2. Of a person: Grown accustomed (*to* a thing); established in a habit –1679.

Habituate (hăbi·tiu,eit), *v.* 1530. [f. L. *habituat-*, *habituare*, f. *habitus* condition, HABIT. Cf. F. *habituer.*] †1. *trans.* To form (anything) into a habit –1649. 2. To fix (any one) in a habit; to accustom *to.* *Pa. pple.* Used, accustomed. 1530. †3. To settle as an inhabitant (*in* a place). [After Fr.] –1695. 4. To frequent. *U.S.* 1872.

2. Minds not habituated to accurate thinking 1864.

Habituation (hăbitiu,ēi·ʃən). 1449. [ad. med.L. *habituationem.*] †1. The action of rendering or becoming habitual –1673. 2. The action of habituating or accustoming, or the being habituated (*to* something) 1816.

Habitude (hæ·bitiud). ME. [a. F., ad. L. *habitudo* condition, plight, etc., f. *habit-*, *habere.*] 1. = HABIT *sb.* II. 2, III. 1. †2. Relation, respect (to something else) –1732. †3. Familiar relation or acquaintance; familiarity, intimacy; intercourse –1796. 4. = HABIT *sb.* III. 2. 1603. †5. *Chem.* (*pl.*) Behaviour of one substance *with* another; reaction –1832.

1. Helth is a temperat habytude of the bodye 1540. 2. The h. (which we call proportion) of one sound to another MORLEY. †*In full h.*: entirely. 4. Many habitudes of life, not given by nature BUTLER. The fetters of h. 1889.

Habitué (abitüe). 1818. [Fr. (fem. *-ée*), pa. pple. of *habituer.*] One who has the habit of frequenting a place.

Old *habitués* of the boxes THACKERAY.

†**Ha·biture.** [f. L. *habit-*; see HABIT.] = HABITUDE. Marston.

‖**Habitus** (hæ·bitŏs). 1886. [L.] = HABIT *sb.* II. 2, 3.

Hable, early f. ABLE; see also HABILE.

Hab-nab, Hab or nab: see HAB.

‖**Hachure** (haʃü·r), *sb.* 1858. [mod.F., f. *hacher*; see HATCH *v.* and -URE.] *pl.* The lines used in hill-shading to indicate the more or less steep slope of the surface. Also *attrib.*, as *hachure lines.* Hence **Ha·chure** *v.* to shade (a map) with hachures.

‖**Hacienda** (asi,e·ndă). 1760. [Sp. (aþye·nda) :–L. *facienda* things to be done, f. *facere.*] In Spain, and Sp. colonies, etc.: An estate or plantation with a dwelling-house upon it; a farming, mining, or manufacturing establishment in the country; *occas.*, a country-house. ‖**Haciendado** (a:siendā·do), the owner of an h.

Hack (hæk), *sb.*[1] ME. [In sense 1, app. cogn. w. MHG. and Ger. *hacke*, Da. *hakke* pick-ax, mattock, hoe; related to HACK *v.*[1] In other senses, prob. f. the vb.] 1. A tool or implement for breaking or chopping up: a. Any tool of the mattock, hoe, and pick-ax type. b. A two-pronged tool like a mattock, for dragging dung, etc. 1797. c. A miner's pick for breaking stone 1681. d. A bill for cutting wood 1875. 2. A gash or wound made by a cutting blow; *spec.* a notch made in a tree to serve as a guide; a 'blaze' (*U.S.*); a chap in the skin 1575. b. *Football.* A cut or gash in the skin caused by a kick 1857. 3. A ridge of earth thrown up by ploughing or hoeing. *Obs.* exc. *dial.* 1744. 4. Hesitation in speech 1660. 5. A short dry hard cough 1885.

Hack, *sb.*[2] 1575. [In sense 2, a fusion of HATCH and HECK.] 1. *Falconry.* The board on which a hawk's meat is laid. Hence applied to the state of partial liberty in which eyas hawks are kept before being trained. 2. A rack to hold fodder for cattle. ? *Obs.* exc. *dial.* 1674. 3. A frame on which bricks are laid to dry before burning; a row of bricks laid out to dry 1703. 4. = HAKE *sb.*[3] 1. 1808.

2. Phr. *To live at h. and manger*, i. e. in plenty. *Comb.* **h.-board** = sense 1.

Hack, *sb.*[3] (*a.*) 1687. [An abbrev. of HACKNEY, mostly familiar or contemptuous.] 1. A hackney horse. a. A horse let out for hire; hence, a sorry jade 1721. b. *spec.* A horse for ordinary riding; a saddle-horse for the road. (Technically a half-bred horse with more bone and substance than a thorough-bred.) 1798. 2. = HACKNEY 5. Now only *U.S.* 1704. †3. The driver of a hackney carriage –1713. 4. A common drudge; *esp.* a literary drudge; hence, a poor writer, a mere scribbler 1700. b. *slang.* A prostitute; a bawd 1730. †5. Anything that is hackneyed; a hackneyed sermon, book, quotation, etc. –1805. b. Applied to persons; as, a *garrison hack* 1876. 6. *Naut.* A watch used, in taking observations, to obviate the necessity of moving the standard chronometer. Also *hack-*, *job-watch* 1851.

1. a. Butcher's hacks that 'shambled' to and fro HOOD. b. *Covert-hack*, a horse for riding to the meet, or to the cover, as dist. from the hunter. 4. Here lies poor Ned Purdon..Who long was a bookseller's h. GOLDSM.

attrib. and *Comb.* **1.** In apposition or *attrib.*, as *h.-horse* (= sense 1); *-cab*, etc.; also *h.-attorney, -author, -moralist*; *h.-rider, -stand*, etc. **2.** *attrib.* or *adj.* **a.** Hackneyed; trite, commonplace, as a *hack speech*. **b.** Of a hired sort, as HACK-WORK.

Hack (hæk), *v.*¹ [Early ME. *hacken*, repr. OE. **haccian* :—Com. WGer. **hakkōn*.]

I. Trans. senses. **1.** To cut with heavy blows irregularly or at random; to notch; to mangle by jagged cuts. In earlier use chiefly, To chop *up* or into pieces, to chop *off*. **2. a.** Of frost: To chap or crack the skin (*dial.*) 1673. **b.** *Football.* To kick the shin of (an opponent) 1866. **3.** *Agric.* Applied to various operations involving cutting and chopping 1620. **4.** To hoe or plough up (the soil) into ridges; to rake (hay) into rows (*dial.*) 1744. †**5.** *Mus.* To break (a note) –1496. †**6.** *fig.* To mangle (words) in utterance. Also *absol.* –1676.

1. My Sword hackt like a Hand-saw SHAKS. **6.** Let them keepe their limbs whole, and h. our English SHAKS.

II. Intr. senses. **1.** To make rough cuts, to deal cutting blows 1450. **2.** Of the teeth: To chatter. *Obs.* exc. *dial.* ME. **3.** To hesitate in speech; to stammer. *Obs.* exc. *dial.* 1553. †**4.** To haggle –1613. **5.** To cough with short, dry, oft-repeated cough 1802.

5. *Hacking cough*, a short, dry, frequently repeated cough.

Hack, *v.*² 1875. [f. HACK *sb.*²] **1.** *trans.* To place (bricks) in rows upon hacks. **2.** *Falconry.* To keep (young hawks) 'at hack' or in a state of partial liberty 1883.

Hack, *v.*³ 1745. [f. HACK *sb.*³] **1.** *trans.* To put to indiscriminate or promiscuous use; to make common by such treatment; to hackney. **2.** To employ as a literary hack 1813. **3. a.** *trans.* To employ (a horse) as a hack. **b.** *intr.* To ride on the road; dist. from *cross-country* or *military* riding. 1857. **4.** *intr.* To ride in a cab. *U.S.* 1879.

1. If ever tale was hackt about, Grown obsolete, [etc.] 1762. ¶ The sense of *hack* in *Merry W.* II. i. 52, 'These knights will hack', is doubtful. The history and chronology of the vb. are against the senses suggested in Johnson and Nares.

Hack-, stem of HACK *v.*¹ in Comb., in sense 'hacking, chopping'. Hence **h.-saw**, a saw used in metal-cutting; etc.

Hackamore (hæ·kămoəɹ). *U.S.* 1889. [? corruption of Sp. *jaquima*, formerly *xaquima*, halter.] A halter of horse-hair or raw hide having a nose-piece fitted to serve as the head-piece of a bridle.

Hackberry (hæ·kberi). 1796. [var. of HAGBERRY, q.v.] **1.** = HAGBERRY. **2.** In N. America, the fruit of the tree *Celtis occidentalis*, which resembles the bird-cherry in size; also the tree itself 1796.

Hackbolt (hæ·kbōult). Also **hagbolt.** 1843. The greater Shearwater, *Puffinus major*.

†**Ha·ckbush, ha·gbush.** Also †**hackbus.** 1484. [a. rare OF. *haquebusche*, a. MFl. *haec-, haegbusse*, f. *haken, hake*, etc. hook + *bühse, busse* gun; lit. 'hook-gun', so called from the hook orig. used to attach the gun to a point of support.] = HACKBUT.

Hackbut, hagbut (hæ·k-, hæ·gbɒt). *arch.* and *Hist.* 1541. [a. F. *haquebut, -bute*; see prec. Cf. HARQUEBUS.] An early form of portable fire-arm; = prec.

†**Hackbut à croc**: see HARQUEBUS 2.

Hackbutter, hagbutter (hæ·kbɒtəɹ, hæ·g-). *arch.* and *Hist.* 1544. [f. prec. + -ER.] A soldier armed with a hackbut; a harquebusier. vars. **Hackbuteer, -ier.**

Hacked (hækt), *ppl. a.* ME. [f. HACK *v.*¹ + -ED¹.] In the senses of the vb.; *spec.* in *Her.*, indented, with the notches curved on both sides, as a bend, etc.

Hackee (hæ·kī). 1860. [After the animal's cry.] A species of ground squirrel, the Striped Squirrel, or Chipmuck, of N. America.

Hacker (hæ·kəɹ), *sb.* 1481. [f. HACK *v.*¹ + -ER¹.] **1.** One who hacks, in various senses 1581. **2.** That which hacks; *spec.* in *U.S.*, a tool for making an oblique incision in a tree, as a channel for the passage of sap, gum, or resin 1875.

Hackery (hæ·kəri). *Anglo-Ind.* 1698. [? corrupt f. Hindī *chhakṛā* a two-wheeled bullock-cart.] A bullock-cart for the transport of goods; also, locally, a lighter carriage (drawn sometimes by horses) for the conveyance of persons.

Hackle (hæ·k'l), *sb.*¹ [OE. *hacele* and *hæcele*, wk. fem., 'cloak, mantle, cassock', corresp. to OHG. *hachul*, MHG. *hachel*, etc., also to ON. *heckla* str. f. 'cowled or hooded frock'.] †**1.** A cloak, outer garment; a chasuble –ME. **2.** A covering of any kind, as a bird's feathers, a serpent's skin, etc. *Obs.* exc. *dial.* ME. **3.** The straw roofing of a bee-hive; the straw covering of the apex of a rick; the case of a Florence flask 1609.

Hackle (hæ·k'l), *sb.*² ME. [prob. from the root *hak-* of OHG. **hakjan*, *hęcchen*, *hęcken* to prick, pierce, stab, and of HOOK, q.v.] **1.** A comb for splitting and combing out the fibres of flax or hemp; = HECKLE, HATCHEL. 1485. **2.** Local name of the stickleback 1655. **3.** The long shining feathers on the neck of the domestic cock, peacock, pigeon, etc. ME. **4.** *Angling.* An artificial fly, dressed with a hackle-feather, or something like this; a 'palmer'. Also *h.-fly*. 1676. **5.** *attrib.* 1681.

3. Phr. *To show h.*, to be willing to fight (*slang*). *With the hackles up*, as in a cock when he is angry; said also of a dog on the point of fighting, also *transf.* of a man. The 42nd [1st Batt. Royal Highlanders]..received the red h. as an honourable distinction 1884. Hence *hackles* is sometimes put for hair, whiskers, etc.

Hackle, *v.*¹ 1579. [dim. and freq. of HACK *v.*¹ Cf. HAGGLE *v.*] **1.** *trans.* To cut roughly, hack, mangle by cutting. †**2.** *intr.* To make a hacking. NASHE.

Hackle, *v.*² 1616. [f. HACKLE *sb.*² 1; cf. HECKLE *v.*] *trans.* To dress (flax or hemp) with a hackle; also *fig.* = HECKLE. Hence **Ha·ckler**, a flax-dresser, heckler.

Hackle, *v.*³ 1867. [f. HACKLE *sb.*² 3.] *trans.* To dress (a fly) with a hackle-feather.

Hackly (hæ·kli), *a.* 1796. [f. HACKLE *v.*¹ + -Y.] Rough or jagged, as though hacked; *esp.* of metals, etc.: Having the surface rough with short sharp points.

Hackman (hæ·kmăn). 1850. *U. S.* [f. HACK *sb.*³ 2.] The driver of a hack or hackney-carriage; a cab-driver.

Hackmatack (hæ·kmătæk). 1792. [Amer. Indian.] The American Larch or Tamarack (*Larix Americana*). Also *attrib.*

Hackney (hæ·kni), *sb.* (*a.*) [ME. *hakenai, -nei, -ney*, a. OF. *haquenée* fem. 'an ambling horse or mare, especially for ladies to ride on', (in 1373 latinized in England as *hakeneius*: see DU CANGE). Ult. deriv. unkn.]

A. *sb.* **1.** A horse of middle size and quality, used for ordinary riding; now techn. = HACK *sb.*³ 1. **b.** †**2.** Often taken as, A horse kept for hire 1614. Also *fig.* †**3.** One who does mean work for hire; a common drudge. Also *fig.* –1784. †**4.** A prostitute –1679. **5.** A HACKNEY-COACH. 1664.

1. He rode..a strong h. for the road, to save his gallant warhorse SCOTT. **2.** *fig.* Hector of Troy was an h. to him DEKKER. **3.** Public hacknies in the schooling trade COWPER.

attrib. and *Comb.* **1. a.** In apposition, as **hackney horse** = senses 1, 2. **b.** *attrib.* Of or pertaining to a hackney (horse), as *h. hire, stable, stud*, etc. **c.** Plying for hire, as HACKNEY-CARRIAGE, -CHAIR, -COACH, etc. †**2. a.** in apposition, or as *adj.* Hireling (also *fig.*), as *h. author, pen, tongue, writer*, etc. **b.** *attrib.* or *adj.* Done by a hackney or for hire, as *h. job, writing*. †**c.** Prostitute, as *h.-wench*.

†**B.** as *adj.* Worn out, like a hired horse, by indiscriminate use; trite, commonplace; hackneyed –1792.

Ha·ckney, *v.* Now *rare* exc. in *ppl. a.* HACKNEYED. 1577. [f. HACKNEY *sb.*] **1.** *trans.* = HACK *v.*³ 3. a. Also *fig.* †**2.** To convey in a hackney-carriage. COWPER. †**3.** *fig.* To drive hard; to post; to hurry. Also *intr.* (for *refl.*) –1798. †**4.** To let *out* for hire. Also *intr.* for *pass.* –1736. **5.** To make common by indiscriminate everyday usage; to render vulgar, trite, or commonplace 1596; †to undo the freshness or delicacy of –1808. **6.** To render habituated, practised, or experienced *in*. Often dyslogistic. 1751.

3. How are thy Angels hackney'd up and down To visit man QUARLES. **5.** So common hackney'd in the eyes of men SHAKS. **6.** Persons a little hackneyed in the world LYTTON.

Ha·ckney-ca·rriage. 1831. [f. HACKNEY *sb.* + CARRIAGE.] Any vehicle standing or publicly plying for hire.

Ha·ckney-chai·r. 1710. Formerly, a sedan chair, now a bath chair or the like, plying publicly for hire. Hence **Hackney-chairman.**

Ha·ckney-coa·ch. 1610. [f. HACKNEY *sb.* + COACH.] A four-wheeled coach, drawn by two horses, and seated for six persons, kept for hire. Hence **Ha·ckney-coa·chman.**

Hackneyed (hæ·knid), *ppl. a.* 1749. [f. HACKNEY *v.*] †**1.** Hired; kept for hire –1818. **2.** Made trite and commonplace; stale 1749. **3.** Experienced, *occas.*, to disgust or weariness 1760.

2. A h. expression HURD, objection BOSWELL, subject 1887. **3.** Hacknied statesmen D'ISRAELI.

Hackney-man (hæ·knimæn). ME. [f. HACKNEY *sb.* + MAN.] A man who keeps hacks or hackney-carriages for hire.

Hackster. *Obs.* exc. *dial.* 1581. [f. HACK *v.*¹ + -STER.] **1.** *lit.* One who hacks; a cut-throat; a swashbuckler. **2.** A prostitute 1594.

Hackthorn (hæ·kþǭɹn). 1863. [ad. Du. *haakedorn*, hook-thorn.] A S. African thorny shrub (*Acacia detinens*), also termed 'Wait-a-bit thorn'.

Hack-work (hæ·kˌwɒ̄ɹk). 1851. [HACK *sb.*³] Work (esp. literary work) done by a hack or hired drudge.

Hacqueton, hacton, vars. of HAQUETON, ACTON.

Had, pa. t. and pple. of HAVE *v.*

Hadder, obs. Sc. f. HEATHER.

Haddie (hæ·di). 1816. A Sc. dial. var. of *haddo'* = HADDOCK.

Haddock (hæ·dǒk). ME. [Origin unkn. The suffix *-ock* is app. dim., as in *bullock*, etc. The Gael. *adag* is from Eng.] A fish (*Gadus æglefinus*) allied to the cod, but smaller, abundant in the North Atlantic and the British seas, and much used for food. Also applied to allied fishes, as the *Norway* or *Norwegian h.*, the Bergylt or Sea Perch; etc. Hence **Ha·ddocker**, a person or vessel employed in fishing for h.

Hade (hēɪd), *sb.* 1789. [Goes with HADE *v.*] *Mining* and *Geol.* The inclination of a mineral vein or fault from the vertical; the complement of the *dip*. Also called *underlay* or *underlie*.

Hade (hēɪd), *v.* 1681. [? dial. form of *head*; cf. *tread, trade*.] *Mining*, etc. *intr.* To incline or slope from the vertical, as a shaft, a vein, a fault.

‖**Hades** (hēɪ·dīz). Also formerly **Ades.** 1597. [a. Gr. ᾅδης (orig. αἴδης, or ἀΐδης) of unkn. origin; in LXX and N.T. Greek, used as tr. Heb. *sheʾōl*, the abode of departed spirits.] **1.** *Gr. Myth.* Oldest name of the god of the dead, also called Pluto; hence, the kingdom of Hades, the lower world, the abode of shades 1599. **2.** In N.T. (R.V.): The state or abode of the dead, or of departed spirits after this life; = Heb. *Sheol* 1597.

1. Orcus and Ades, and the dreaded name Of Demogorgon MILT. The enthroned Persephone in Hades TENNYSON. **2.** Neither was he left in Hades, nor did his flesh see corruption R.V. *Acts* ii. 31.

‖**Hadj** (hæ·dʒ). 1704. [Arab. *ḥajj*.] A pilgrimage to Mecca.

‖**Hadji, hajji** (hæ·dʒī). 1612. [ad. Arab. *ḥājī*, f. *ḥājj*; see prec.] A title given to one who has made the greater pilgrimage (on 8th to 10th day of the 12th month) to the tomb of Mohammed at Mecca. **b.** An Oriental Christian who has visited the Holy Sepulchre at Jerusalem 1835.

Hadrosaur (hæ·drosǭɹ). 1877. [ad. mod.L. *Hadrosaurus* (name of the genus), f. Gr. ἁδρός thick, stout + σαῦρος (= σαύρα) lizard.] A genus of gigantic fossil saurian reptiles found in N. America.

Hæcceity (heksī·iti, hīk-). 1647. [ad. med.L. *hæcceitatem* 'thisness' (Duns Scotus), f. *hæc*, fem. of *hic* this.] *Scholastic Philos.* The quality implied in the use of *this*, as *this man*; 'thisness', 'hereness and nowness'; individuality.

Hæma-, hema-, repr. Gr. αἷμα blood, sometimes improp. used for HÆMATO- or

HÆMO-. For words in *hæma-* see HÆMO-. The sp. *he-* in words from Gr. *αἷμα* is favoured in U.S., but is rare in Gt. Britain.

Hæmad (hī·mæd), *sb.* 1891. [f. Gr. *αἷμα* + -AD, after *monad*, etc.] A blood-corpuscle.

Hæmal, hemal (hī·măl), *a.* 1839. [f. Gr. *αἷμα* + -AL.] *Anat.* Of or belonging to the blood or blood-vascular system; belonging to or situated on or towards that side or region of the body which contains the heart and great blood-vessels: opp. to *neural*; in the case of the Vertebrata and Tunicata, synonymous with *ventral*.

Hæmal arch, Owen's term for the inferior arch of a typical vertebra. *H. cavity*, the cavity formed by a series of h. arches (constituted by the ribs, costal cartilages, and breast-bone). *H. spine*, the ventral element of a h. arch.

Hæmapophysis (hīmăpǫ·fisis). 1849. [mod.L.; see HÆMO- and APOPHYSIS. (So called as situated towards the hæmal aspect of the body.)] *Anat.* Owen's term for that portion of the hæmal arch of a typical vertebra situated between the pleurapophysis and the hæmal spine. Hence **Hæ:mapophy·sial** *a.*

‖**Hæmatemesis** (hīmăte·mĭsis). 1800. [mod. L., f. Gr. *αἱματ-* + *ἔμεσις*.] *Path.* Vomiting of blood.

Hæmatic, hem- (hĭmæ·tik). 1854. [ad. Gr. *αἱματικός*, f. *αἷμα*.]

A. *adj.* Pertaining to blood; containing blood, sanguineous; acting upon the blood; of the colour of blood.

B. *sb.* **1.** A medicine that acts upon the blood 1854. **2. Hæmatics:** that branch of physiology or medicine which treats of the blood 1854.

Hæmatin, hem- (hī·mătin, he·m-). 1819. [mod. f. Gr. *αἱματ-* + -IN.] *Chem.* **1.** Earlier name of HÆMATOXYLIN. **2.** A bluish-black amorphous substance with metallic lustre, obtained from red blood-corpuscles, in which it exists as a constituent of hæmoglobin 1845. Hence **Hæmati·nic** *a.* of or relating to h. (sense 2); *sb.* a medicine which increases the h. in the blood. **Hæ:matino·meter**, an instrument for measuring the h. in the blood; **Hæ:matino·me·tric** *a.* relating to such measurement. ‖**Hæ:matinu·ria**, the passing of urine containing the colouring matter of the blood without the corpuscles (now called *hæmoglobinuria*).

Hæmatite, hem- (he·mătəit, hī·m-). 1543. [ad. L. *hæmatites* (formerly also used), Gr. *αἱματίτης* (sc. *λίθος*) *lit.* blood-like stone; see -ITE. The commercial and economic sp. is *hem-*.] *Min.* Native sesquioxide of iron (Fe_2O_3), a widely distributed iron ore, occurring in crystalline, massive, or granular forms; in colour, red, reddish-brown, or blackish with a red streak. Also *attrib.*

Brown hæmatite: a brown or brownish yellow mineral, consisting of hydrated sesquioxide of iron; also called *limonite*. Hence **Hæmati·tic** *a.*, also **hem-**, pertaining to, consisting of, or resembling h.

Hæmato-, hemato- (hīmăto, hemăto), bef. a vowel **Hæmat-, hemat-**, = Gr. *αἱματ-*, comb. f. *αἷμα* blood. See also HÆMO- for some shorter forms. The spelling *hemato-* is chiefly U.S.

hæ·matochro:me [Gr. *χρῶμα*], a red colouring matter developed in some Protozoa at a certain stage of existence: **hæ:matocry·al** [Gr. *κρύος* cold, frost] *a.*, belonging to the *Hæmatocrya* or cold-blooded Vertebrata; **hæ·matocy:st, -cy·stis**, a cyst containing blood; **hæ:matodyna·mics, -dynamo·meter** (see HÆMO-); **hæ:matoge·nesis** [see GENESIS], the formation of blood; **hæ:matoge·nic** *a.*, relating to hæmatogenesis; also = next; **hæmato·genous** *a.*, originating in the blood; **hæmato·phagous** [Gr. *-φαγος*] *a.*, feeding upon, or living in, the blood; **hæ·matophy:te** [Gr. *φυτόν*], a vegetable parasite inhabiting the blood; ‖**hæ:matopoie·sis** [Gr. *ποίησις*], the formation of blood; whence **hæ:matopoie·tic** *a.*; **hæ·matosco:pe, hæ:mato-spe·ctroscope**, an instrument for the determination of the quantity of oxyhæmoglobin in the blood; **hæmato·scopy**, a (spectroscopic) method of examining the blood; **hæ:matothe·rmal** *a.*, warm-blooded; **hæmatotho·rax**, hæmorrhage into the pleural cavities; **hæ:matozo·on** (pl. *-zo·a*) [Gr. *ζῷον*], an animal parasite inhabiting the blood; hence **hæ:matozo·an** = prec.; **hæ:matozo·ic** *a.*, of or pertaining to a hæmatozoon.

Hæmatoblast (hī·matoblɑ:st). 1876. [See HÆMATO- and -BLAST.] **a.** *Phys.* Name given to certain yellowish or greenish disks, smaller than the ordinary blood-corpuscles, found in the blood of viviparous Vertebrata; also called *blood-plates*. **b.** *Embryol.* Name given to cells of the mesoderm from which the first blood-corpuscles and blood-vessels originate. Hence **Hæmatobla·stic** *a.*

Hæ·mato-cry·stallin. 1863. [f. as prec. + CRYSTALLIN.] **a.** The special form of CRYSTALLIN or GLOBULIN found in the blood-corpuscles. **b.** Hæmoglobin when obtained in a crystalline condition.

Hæ:mato-glo·bulin. 1845. [for *hæmatino-globulin*, f. HÆMATIN + GLOBULIN, as composed of the two.] *Chem.* The colouring matter of the red corpuscles of the blood; also called **Hæmatoglo·bin**; now usu. shortened to HÆMOGLOBIN.

Hæmatoid, hem- (hī·mătoid, he·m-), *a.* 1840. [ad. Gr. *αἱματοειδής*; see -OID.] **a.** Resembling or containing blood. **b.** Consisting of hæmatoidin.

Hæmatoi·din, hem-. 1855. [f. prec. + -IN.] *Chem.* A yellow or yellowish-red crystalline substance found in extravasated blood; by some identified with bilirubin.

Hæmatoin (hīmătōᵘ·in). 1876. [Differentiated from *hæmatin*.] *Chem.* A derivative of hæmoglobin containing no iron.

Hæmatology (hīmătǫ·lŏdʒi). 1811. [f. HÆMATO- + -LOGY.] That branch of animal physiology which relates to the blood.

Hæmatometer, hem- (hīmătǫ·mĭtəɹ). 1854. [See HÆMATO- and -METER.] **a.** = *hæmodynamometer* (see HÆMO-). **b.** An instrument for numbering the blood-corpuscles.

Hæmatosin, hem- (he·m-, hī·mătəsin). 1834. [a. F. *hématosine*, irreg. f. Gr. *αἵματος* gen. + -IN.] = HÆMATIN 2.

‖**Hæmatosis** (hīmătōᵘ·sis). 1696. [med. or mod.L., a. Gr. *αἱμάτωσις* (Galen).] **a.** The formation of blood, esp. of blood-corpuscles; sanguification. **b.** Old name for hæmorrhage. **c.** The oxygenation of the blood in the lungs.

Hæmatoxylin, hem- (hīmătǫ·ksilin). 1874. [f. mod. Bot. L. *hæmatoxylon, -um* logwood (f. HÆMATO- + Gr. *ξύλον*) + -IN.] *Chem.* A crystalline substance $(C_{16}H_{14}O)_6$ obtained from logwood; colourless when pure, but affording fine red, blue, and purple dyes by the action of alkalis and oxygen. Hence **Hæmatoxy·lic** *a.* derived from h.

‖**Hæmaturia** (hīmătiūᵊ·riă). 1811. [f. HÆMATO- + URIA.] *Path.* The presence of blood in the urine. Hence **Hæmatu·ric** *a.*

Hæmic (hī·mik), *a.* 1857. [Arbitrary f. Gr. *αἷμα* + -IC; prop. HÆMATIC.] Pertaining or relating to the blood, as *hæmic asthma*.

Hæmin (hī·min). 1857. [f. Gr. *αἷμα* + -IN; cf. *hæmatin*.] *Chem.* A deep red crystalline substance obtained from blood, containing hæmatin and hydrochloric acid.

Hæmo-, hemo- (hīmo, hemo), bef. a vowel **hæm-, hem-** (hīm, hem), repr. Gr. *αἱμο-*, shortened f. *αἱματο-* HÆMATO-, comb. f. *αἷμα* blood.

hæ·mochrome (erron. *hæma-*) [Gr. *χρῶμα*] = HÆMOGLOBIN; hence **hæ:mochromo·meter**, 'an apparatus for calculating the amount of hæmoglobin in a liquid by comparison with a standard solution of normal colour' (*Syd. Soc. Lex.*); **hæ·mocœle** [Gr. *κοῖλος, κοιλία*], the body-cavity of an arthropod or mollusc, analogous to the cœlome of a vertebrate; **hæ:mocyto·meter** (erron. *hæma-*), an instrument for ascertaining the number of blood-corpuscles; **hæ:modromo·meter** (also **-dro·meter**), **-dro·mograph** [Gr. *-δρομος*: see -METER, -GRAPH], instruments for measuring and registering the velocity of the blood-current; **hæ:modyna·mics** [see DYNAMICS], 'the science of the forces connected with the circulation of the blood' (*Syd. Soc. Lex.*); **hæ:modynamo·meter** (erron. *hæma-*), an instrument for measuring the pressure of the blood; **hæmoglo·bulin** = HÆMOGLOBIN; **hæmoly·tic** [Gr. *λυτικός*] *a.*, destructive of the blood or of the blood-corpuscles; **hæ:mopatho·logy**, the pathology of the blood; **hæmopoie·tic** (see HÆMATO-); **hæ·moscope**, an apparatus for examining the blood; so **hæmo·scopy** (erron. *hæma-*), examination of the blood: see HÆMATO-; **hæ:motacho·meter** (erron. *hæma-*) [Gr. *τάχος*: see -METER], an instrument for measuring the velocity of the blood-current; so **hæ:motacho·metry**; **hæmotho·rax** (see HÆMATO-).

Hæmocyanin, hemo- (hīmo͵səi·ănin). Also erron. *hæma-*. 1845. [See HÆMO- and CYANIN.] **a.** A blue colouring matter which has been found in human blood. **b.** A substance containing copper, blue when oxidized and colourless when deoxidized, found normally in the blood of some invertebrates.

Hæmoglobin, hemo- (hīmoglōᵘ·bin). 1869. [Shortened f. HÆMATO-GLOBULIN.] *Chem.* The colouring matter of the red corpuscles of the blood, which serves to convey oxygen to the tissues in the circulation; it occurs in reduced form (*reduced h.*) in the blood of the veins, and, combined with oxygen (*oxyhæmoglobin*), in that of the arteries. Formerly called *cruorin, hæmatoglobulin, hæmoglobulin, hæmatoglobin.* Hence ‖**Hæ:moglobinæ·mia**, *Path.* the presence of free h. in the fluid part of the blood. **Hæ:moglobini·ferous** *a.* containing h. **Hæ:moglobino·meter**, an instrument for measuring the h. in blood; whence **Hæ:moglobino·metry.** ‖**Hæ:moglobinu·ria**, *Path.* the presence of free h. in the urine; whence **Hæ:moglobinu·ric** *a.* characterized by h.

Hæmometer (hīmǫ·mĭtəɹ). 1872. [See HÆMO- and -METER.] An instrument for measuring (*a*) the quantity of blood passing through a vessel in a given time; (*b*) the pressure of the blood (= *hæmodynamometer*); or (*c*) the amount of hæmoglobin in the blood (= *hæmoglobinometer*).

†**Hæmony** (hī·mŏni). [? f. Gr. *αἵμων* skilful, or *αἱμώνιος* blood-red.] An imaginary plant having supernatural virtues. MILT. *Comus* 638.

‖**Hæmophilia** (hīmofi·liă, hemo-). Also hæmo·phily (*rare*). 1854. [mod.L., f. HÆMO- + Gr. *φιλία*.] *Path.* A tendency to bleeding, either spontaneously, or from very slight injuries; hæmorrhagic diathesis. Hence **Hæmophi·lic** *a.*

‖**Hæmoptysis** (hīmǫ·ptisis). 1646. [mod.L., f. HÆMO- + *πτύσις* spitting.] *Path.* Spitting of blood; expectoration of blood, or of bloody mucus, etc., from the lungs or bronchi. Hence **Hæmopty·sic, -al** *a.* relating to or affected with h.

Hæmorrhage, hemo- (he·mŏredʒ). 1671. [f. as HÆMORRHAGY.] An escape of blood due to rupture of a blood-vessel; bleeding, esp. when profuse or dangerous. Also *fig.*

Hæmorrhagic, hemo- (hemŏræ·dʒik), *a.* 1804. [ad. Gr. *αἱμορραγικός*; see HÆMORRHAGY and -IC.] Belonging to, of the nature of, accompanied with, or produced by hæmorrhage.

†**Hæ·morrhagy, hemo-.** 1541. [Earlier *emorogie*, a. F., ad. L. *hæmorrhagia* (also used), a. Gr. *αἱμορραγία*, f. *αἷμα* + *-ραγια*, f. stem *ῥαγ-* of *ῥηγνύναι* to break, burst.] = HÆMORRHAGE. -1838.

Hæmorrhoid [1], **hemo-** (he·mŏroid); usu. in pl. [ME. *emeraudes, emeroudis*, a. OF. *emoroyde*, in 16th c. *hemorrhoides*, ad. L. *hæmorrhoida*, ad. Gr. *αἱμορροΐς* discharging blood, pl. *αἱμορροΐδες* (sc. *φλέβες*) veins liable to discharge blood; deriv. of *αἱμόρροος*.] **1.** *pl.* A disease characterized by tumours of the veins about the anus; = PILES, q.v. Rarely *sing.* †**2.** *pl.* Hæmorrhoidal veins -1541.

†**Hæmorrhoid** [2]. Also **hæmorrhe**, and in L. form **hæmorrhoïs, -rhus.** ME. [ad. L. *hæmorrhoïs, -idem*, a. Gr.; etym. as in prec.] A serpent whose bite was fabled to cause unstanchable bleeding -1774.

Hæmorrhoidal, hemo- (hemŏroi·dăl), *a.* (*sb.*) 1541. [f. HÆMORRHOID [1] + -AL.] **1.** *Path.* Of or pertaining to hæmorrhoids 1651. **2.** *Anat.* Applied to those arteries, veins, and nerves which are distributed to the rectum and adjacent parts 1671. **3.** *sb.* (in sense 2) 1541.

Hæmostatic, hemo- (hīmostæ·tik, hem-). Also erron. **hæma-, hema-**. 1706. [mod. f. HÆMO- + Gr. *στατικός* stopping.] **A.** *adj.* Having the property of stopping hæmorrhage; styptic 1854. **B.** *sb.* A styptic.

Haf, obs. pa. t. of HEAVE.

Hafnium (hæ·fniŏm). 1923. [f. Da. Kjöbn-*hafn* Copenhagen + -IUM.] *Chem.* A metallic element: symbol Hf, atomic number 72.

Haft (haft), *sb.*[1] Also **heft.** [OE. *hæft(e* neut., handle, f. (ult.) OTeut. root *haf-* HEAVE, or *hab-* HAVE; app. that which is taken hold of.] A handle; esp. that of a cutting or piercing instrument, as a dagger, knife, sickle, etc.

The h. of a razor GOLDSM. Hilt and heft BROWNING.

Haft, *sb.*[2] *Sc.* and *n. dial.* Also **heft.** 1785. [Goes app. w. HAFT *v.*[3]] **1.** Fixed place of abode. **2.** Accustomed pasture-ground 1800.

Haft, *v.*[1] Also **heft.** ME. [f. HAFT *sb.*[1]] **1.** *trans.* To fit with, or fix in, a haft or handle. †**2.** To drive *in* up to the haft. STANYHURST.

†**Haft,** *v.*[2] 1519. [? repr. an OE. type **hæftian* to stick.] *intr.* To use subtilty or deceit, to use shifts or dodges; to haggle, cavil; to hold off, hang back -1644. Hence †**Ha·fter** *sb.* a caviller, wrangler, haggler, dodger.

Haft, *v.*[3] *Sc.* and *n. dial.* Also **heft.** 1725. [Goes app. with HAFT *sb.*[2]; origin uncertain.] **1.** *trans.* To establish in a situation or place of residence; *spec.* to accustom (sheep, cattle) to a pasturage. Also *intr.* for *refl.* 1725. **2.** *transf.* and *fig.* To set or plant firmly, fix, root, settle 1755.

Hag (hæg), *sb.*[1] [ME. *hegge, hagge*; a shortened form of OE. *hægtesse, hæhtisse, hægtes, -tis* 'fury, witch, hag'; ? f. OE. *haga* (Ger. *hag*) a bush + *-tesse* fem. ending, witches being supposed to be seen in bushes at night.] **1.** An evil spirit, dæmon, or infernal being, in female form; applied to the Græco-Latin Furies, Harpies, etc.; also to the Teut. 'fairies' 1552. †**b.** Applied to ghosts, hobgoblins, and other terrors of the night -1634. **2.** A witch; sometimes an infernally wicked woman. Now assoc. w. 3. 1587. **3.** An ugly, repulsive old woman; often with implication of viciousness or maliciousness ME. Also *fig.* and †*transf.* of a man. **4.** †**a.** A kind of light said to appear at night on horses' manes and men's hair -1656. **b.** *dial.* A white mist usu. accompanying frost 1825. **5.** A cyclostomous fish (*Myxine glutinosa*) allied to the lamprey, eel-like in form, and living parasitically upon other fishes. Also *h.-fish.* 1611.

1. Noontide h. or goblin grim SCOTT. **b.** Blue meagre h., or stubborn unlaid ghost MILT. **2.** How now you secret, black, and midnight Hags SHAKS. **3.** *fig.* The h. Evil TENNYSON. *transf.* That old h. [Silenus] GOLDING.

Comb., as *h.-seed* (from 2); also **h.-fish** (see 5); **hag's teeth,** irregularities in a matting or pointing such as to spoil the uniformity; **-track** = FAIRY-RING.

Hag, *sb.*[2] *n. dial.* 1470. [perh. a. ON. *hagi*, Sw. *hage* enclosed field, pasture; cogn. w. OE. *haga* enclosure.] †**1.** ? A hedge. **2.** A wooded enclosure; a coppice or copse 1589.

2. He led me ouer holts and hags FAIRFAX.

Hag, *sb.*[3] *Sc.* and *n. dial.* 1615. [Of Norse origin; cf. ON. *hǫgg* cutting blow or stroke, also a hewing down of trees, f. *hǫggva* to hew, HAG *v.*[1]] **1.** A cutting, hewing, or felling 1808. **2.** The stump of a tree left after felling. Also *hagsnare.* 1615. **3.** A portion of a wood marked for cutting; hence, a lot of felled wood 1796.

3. Edward learned from her that the *dark hag*..was simply a portion of oak copse..to be felled that day SCOTT.

Hag, *sb.*[4] *Sc.* and *n. dial.* ME. [Cf. ON. *hǫgg*, in the sense 'cut-like gap or ravine in a mountain'; see prec.] †**1.** A break, gap, or chasm (in a crag or cliff). ME. only. **2.** 'Moss-ground that has formerly been broken up; a pit or break in a moss', i.e. marsh or bog (Jam.) 1662. **3.** The vertical margin of a peat-cutting; the shelving margin of a stream 1893.

Hag, *v.*[1] *n. dial.* ME. [a. ON. *hǫggva* (:—**haggwan* :—OTeut. **hauwan*) to hack, = OE. *héawan* to HEW.] *trans.* = HACK *v.*[1] **1.** Also *absol.* or *intr.*

Hag, *v.*[2] *Obs.* exc. *dial.* 1587. [In 1, f. HAG *sb.*[1]; in 2, 3 ?] †**1.** *trans.* To torment or terrify as a hag; to trouble as the nightmare -1700. **2.** To urge; to egg *on.* Now *dial.* 1587. **3.** To tire out, fag. Now *dial.* 1674.

Hagarene (hægărīn). 1535. [ad. L. *Agarenus*, f. *Agar*, Hagar.] A reputed descendant of Hagar the concubine of Abraham and mother of Ishmael; an Arab, a Saracen. Also *transf.*

transf. Hagarenes, sons of fornication and wrath MILMAN.

Hagberry (hæ·gberi). Also **hack-, heck-, heg·berry.** 1597. [Of Norse origin: Dan. *hæggebær*, Norw. *hagge-bär*, etc.] A northern name of the bird-cherry, *Prunus Padus.*

Hag-boat. Rarely **hag.** 1700. [?] A kind of vessel formerly used both as a man-of-war, and in the timber and coal trade; latterly, 'a clincher-built boat with covered foresheets and one mast with a trysail' (Smyth).

Hagbolt: see HACKBOLT.

Hagbush, -but(t, obs. ff. HACKBUSH, HACKBUT.

‖**Haggadah** (hăgā·dă). Also **Hagada(h, Agadah.** 1856. [Rabbinical Heb.; = 'tale', esp. 'edifying tale', f. *higgīd* to declare, tell. Heb. pl. *hagga·doth*, occas. used.] A legend, anecdote, parable, or the like, introduced in the Talmud to illustrate a point of the Law; hence, the legendary element of the Talmud, as dist. from the *Halachah.* Hence **Hagga·dic** *a.* of, pertaining to, or of the nature of H. **Hagga·dist,** a writer of H. **Haggadi·stic** *a.*

Haggard (hæ·gărd), *sb.*[1] 1586. [cf. ON. *heygarðr*, f. *hey* hay and *garðr* GARTH.] In Ireland and Isle of Man: A stackyard.

Haggard (hæ·gărd), *sb.*[2] 1567. [HAGGARD *a.* 1, used absol.] **1.** A wild (female) hawk caught when in her adult plumage. (With some, in 17-18th c. = peregrine falcon.) †**2.** *fig.* A wild and intractable person (at first, a female); one not to be captured -1680.

2. *Tam. Shr.* IV. ii. 39.

†**Haggard,** *sb.*[3] 1658. [? after HAG *sb.*[1]; cf. *dotard*, etc.] A hag -1715.

Haggard (hæ·gărd), *a.* 1567. [Cf. F. *hagard*, wild, froward, unsociable, orig. said of a falcon 'that preyed for her selfe long before she was taken' (Cotgr.). Others make it Norman-Picard for *haiard*, deriv. of *haie* 'hedge', i.e. living in a hedge, wild. But ?.] **1.** Of a hawk: Caught after having assumed the adult plumage; hence, wild, untamed. †**2.** *transf.* and *fig.* **a.** Wild, unreclaimed, untrained. **b.** 'Froward, contrarie, crosse, vnsociable' (Cotgr.) -1695. †**3.** In ragged plumage -1798. †**4.** Half-starved; gaunt, lean -1796. **5.** Of a person: Wild-looking; in early use applied esp. to the wild expression of the eyes, afterwards to the expression induced by privation, want of rest, anxiety, terror, or worry. Also *transf.* and *fig* 1697. **b.** Gaunt or scraggy-looking, from the loss of flesh with age 1807.

1. In time all haggred Haukes will stoope the Lures T. WATSON. **4.** The gaunt hagard forms of famine and nakedness BURKE. **5.** Staring his eyes, and h. was his look DRYDEN. **b.** H. beyond the power of rouge CARLYLE. Hence **Ha·ggardly** *a.* and *adv.* **Ha·ggardness.**

Hagged (hægd, hæ·gèd), *a.* Now *dial.* 1694. [f. HAG *sb.*[1]; prob. infl. by HAGGARD.] **1.** Bewitched; also, hag-like. ? *Obs.* 1700. **2.** Lean, gaunt; haggard; worn-out.

Haggis (hæ·gis). ME. [?] A dish consisting of the heart, lungs, and liver of a sheep, calf, etc. (or sometimes of the tripe and chitterlings), minced with suet and oatmeal, seasoned with salt, pepper, onions, etc., and boiled like a large sausage in the maw of the animal. (A popular English dish till 18th c., but now considered specially Scotch.)

Antinous a haggas brought, fill'd up With fat and blood CHAPMAN.

Haggish (hæ·giʃ), *a.* 1583. [See -ISH.] Like, resembling, or of the nature of a hag. Hence **Ha·ggish·ly** *adv.*, **-ness.**

Haggle (hæ·g'l), *v.* 1583. [In 1, freq. of HAG *v.*[1] (cf. HACKLE *v.*[1]).] **1.** *trans.* To mangle with repeated irregular cuts; to cut clumsily; to hack, mangle, mutilate 1599; *intr.* to hack 1768. **2.** *intr.* To cavil, wrangle, dispute as to terms; *esp.* to make difficulties in settling a bargain 1602; *trans.* to harass with haggling 1648. **3.** *intr.* To advance with difficulty 1583.

1. Suffolke first dyed, and Yorke all hagled ouer Comes to him, where in gore he lay *Hen. V*, IV. vi. 11. **2.** There were two points on which he haggled SCOTT. Hence **Ha·ggle** *sb.* wrangling about terms. **Ha·ggler,** a bungler (now *dial.*); one who haggles in making a bargain; also, a huckster, a CADGER.

Hagio-, hagi-, comb. ff. Gr. ἅγιος holy, saintly; as in **Ha·giarchy** [Gr. ἀρχή], the rule or order of saints; etc.

Hagiocracy (hægiǫ·krăsi). 1846. [f. Gr. ἅγιος + -CRACY.] A government or sovereignty of persons esteemed holy.

‖**Hagiographa** (hægiǫ·grăfă), *sb. pl.* 1583. [late L., a. Gr., f. ἅγιος + γραφή, -γραφος.] The Greek name (lit. 'sacred writings') of the last of the three divisions of the Hebrew scriptures (called in Heb. *k'thūbīm* writings) comprising all the books not included under 'the Law' and 'the Prophets'. (These are Psalms, Proverbs, Job; Canticles, Ruth, Lamentations, Ecclesiastes, Esther; Daniel, Ezra, Nehemiah, Chronicles.) Hence **Hagio·graphal** *a.* of or pertaining to the H.

Hagiographer (hægiǫ·grăfəɹ). 1656. [f. med.L. *hagiographus* + -ER[1]; cf. prec.] **1.** A sacred writer; *esp.* one of the writers of the Hagiographa. **2.** A writer of saints' lives; a hagiologist 1849. So **Hagiogra·phic, -al** *a.* of or pertaining to sacred writings or the sacred Scriptures; of or relating to the Hagiographa; pertaining to the writing of saints' lives. **Hagio·graphy,** the writing of the lives of saints; also = HAGIOGRAPHA.

Hagiolatry (hægiǫ·lătri). 1808. [f. Gr. ἅγιος + λατρεία.] The worship of saints.

Hagiology (hægiǫ·lŏdʒi). 1807. [f. Gr. ἅγιος; see -LOGY.] The literature that treats of the lives and legends of saints; also, of great men or heroes; a work on the lives and legends of the saints. Hence **Hagiolo·gic, -al** *a.* **Hagio·logist,** a writer of h.; one versed in h.

Hagioscope (hæ·giǫskōup). Also **agioscope.** 1839. [f. Gr. ἅγιος; see -SCOPE.] A small opening, cut through a chancel arch or wall, to enable worshippers in an aisle or side chapel to see the elevation of the host; a squint; also, a kind of chancel window. Hence **Hagio·sco·pic** *a.*

Hag-ridden (hæ·gridʼn), *ppl. a.* 1684. [f. HAG *sb.*[1] + RIDDEN *ppl. a.*] **1.** Ridden by a hag; *esp.* afflicted by nightmare. **2.** Oppressed in mind 1702. So **Ha·g-ride** *v.* to ride as a hag.

Hagseed: see HAG *sb.*[1]

Hagship (hæ·gʃip). 1604. [See -SHIP.] The personality of a hag; used as a mock title.

Hag-taper (hæ·gtēpəɹ). 1548. [f. ? + TAPER *sb.*] A plant, the Great Mullein (*Verbascum Thapsus*).

Hah, var. of HA *interj.* and *vb.*

Ha ha (hā hā·), *interj.* and *sb.*[1] OE. [A natural utterance.]

A. *interj.* The ordinary representation of laughter.

B. *sb.* A loud or open laugh 1806. Hence **Ha ha** *v.* to utter *ha ha* in laughter, to laugh aloud.

Ha-ha (hahā), *sb.*[2] Also **haw-haw.** 1712. [a. F. *haha*; according to Fr. etymologists, from *ha!* exclam. of surprise.] A boundary to a garden, pleasure-ground, or park, of such a kind as not to interrupt the view from within, and not to be seen till closely approached; a sunk fence. Also *attrib.*

Haidingerite (hai·diŋərəit). 1827. [f. von *Haidinger*, Austrian mineralogist.] *Min.* **1.** A hydrated arsenate of calcium, occurring in minute white crystals. †**2.** = BERTHIERITE -1868.

Haiduck, obs. f. HEYDUCK.

‖**Haik, haick** (haik, həik). Also †**hyke,** etc. 1713. [Arab. *ḥayk*, f. *ḥāk* to weave.] An oblong piece of cloth which Arabs wrap round the head and body, as an outer garment.

Hail (hēl), *sb.*[1] [Com. Teut.: OE. *hagol* (*-al, -el*), and *hægl* (*hægel*) :—WGer. **hagal, *hagl* :—OTeut. **hag(a)lo-*; perh. cogn. w. Gr. καχλ- in κάχληξ pebble; cf. *hailstone.*] **1.** Ice (frozen raindrops) falling in pellets or masses in a shower from the atmosphere. (In spring and summer usu. accompanying a thunderstorm.) **2.** With *a* and *pl.* A shower or storm of hail. Now usu. only *transf.* or *fig.* **3.** *attrib.*, as *hail-shower* (OE. *hæglscūr*), *-storm.*

1. Down comes a deluge of sonorous h. THOMSON. 2. *All's Well* v. iii. 33. *transf.* A perfect h. of roundshot assailed us 1893.

†**Hail,** *sb.*² Chiefly *north.* ME. [a. ON. *heill* health, cogn. w. OE. *hǣl*; see HEAL *sb.*] Health, safety, welfare –1549.

Phr. *To drink h.*, to drink wishing health, etc. to another.

Hail, *sb.*³ 1500. [HAIL *interj.* used subst., and n. of action f. HAIL *v.*²] 1. An exclam. of 'hail'; a (respectful) salutation. 2. The act of hailing some one; a shout of welcome; a call to attract attention 1811.

1. The Angel Haile Bestow'd, the holy salutation MILT. 2. Phr. *Within h.*: within call; so *out of h.*, beyond call. Orig. *Naut.*

†**Hail,** *a.* [ME. *heil*, a. ON. *heill* hale, sound, whole = OE. *hāl*; see HALE and WHOLE.] = HALE, WHOLE. Also *fig.* –1725.

Phr. *Hail be thou*, etc., an exclam. of well-wishing or reverence.

Hail (hēᵊl), *v.*¹ [OE. *hagalian* :—OTeut. **hag(a)lōjan.* See HAIL *sb.*¹] 1. *intr.* a. In *it hails* = hail falls. b. with subject: To pour or send down hail ME. 2. *trans.* To pour, throw, or send down with force like hail in a storm 1570.

2. He hail'd downe oathes that he was onely mine SHAKS.

Hail (hēᵊl), *v.*² ME. [f. HAIL *sb.*² and *interj.*] 1. *trans.* To salute with 'hail'; to salute, greet; to welcome. 2. To call to (a ship, a person, etc.) from a distance, in order to attract attention. (Orig. and chiefly *Naut.*) 1563. 3. *intr.* or *absol.* To call out in order to attract attention. (Formerly with *to*; now only *absol.*) 1582.

1. Such a Son as all Men hail'd me happy MILT. The restoration of the Stuarts had been hailed with delight MACAULAY. 2. To h. a cab (*mod.*). 3. Phr. *To h. from*: said of a vessel in reference to the port from which she has sailed; hence *transf.* of a person, to come from.

Hail (hēᵊl), *interj.* ME. [Orig. *be hail*, or the like (see HAIL *a.*; cf. OE. *hāl* similarly used).] An exclam. of greeting or salutation; now *poet.* and *rhet.*, and usually implying respectful or reverential salutation; = L. *ave, salve.*

H. holy Light, ofspring of Heav'n first-born MILT. H. to thee, blithe spirit SHELLEY.

Hail-fellow. 1580. [The greeting 'Hail, fellow!' (now *obs.* or *arch.*), used variously.]

A. *adj.* On a most intimate footing; over familiar. So *Hail fellow well met.*

All's hail-fellow, here SCOTT.

B. *adv.* On most intimate terms 1670.

†C. *sb.* The state or footing of intimate friends –1687.

This Youth hail Fellow with me made COTTON.

Hail Mary, *phr.* and *sb.* ME. 1. The angelic salutation (cf. Luke i. 58) = L. *Ave Maria.* 2. As a devotional recitation = AVE MARY. ME.

†**Hailse,** *v.* ME. [a. ON. *heilsa* to say hail (*to* a person); cf. HALSE *v.*] *trans.* To greet, salute –1596.

†**Ha·il-shot.** 1485. [f. HAIL *sb.*¹ + SHOT *sb.*] 1. Small shot which scatters like hail. Also *fig.* –1830. 2. The discharge of such shot. Also *fig.* –1696.

Hailstone (hēᵊ·lstōᵘn). [f. HAIL *sb.*¹ + STONE *sb.* OE. *hagolstān.*] A pellet of hail.

Hai·lstorm, hail-storm. 1697. [f. HAIL *sb.*¹ + STORM *sb.*] A violent fall or storm of hail. Also *fig.*

Haily (hēᵊ·li), *a.* 1552. [f. HAIL *sb.*¹ + -Y¹.] Consisting of or characterized by hail or hailstorms.

Hain (hēᵊn), *v.* Now *Sc.* and *dial.* ME. [a. ON. *hegna* to hedge, deriv. of OTeut. *hag-* fence, hedge.] 1. *trans.* To enclose or protect with a fence or hedge; *esp.* to preserve (grass) from cattle. 2. To spare, save. *Sc.* 1508. Also *absol.* or *intr.*

1. The uplands are usually 'hayned' or laid up at Candlemas 1834.

Hain't, haint, vulgar contr. of *have not.*

Hair (hēᵊɹ), *sb.* [Com. Teut.: OE. *hǣr*, *hēr* :—OTeut. **hǣrom*; not known in Gothic.] 1. One of the filaments that grow from the skin or integument of animals, esp. of most mammals, of which they form the characteristic coat; applied also to similar-looking filamentous outgrowths from the body of insects and other invertebrates, although these are generally of different structure. b. *pl. Hairs* = collective sense 2. [Cf. L. *crines*, F. *les cheveux*, etc.] Now *obs.* or *arch.* as in *grey hairs.* OE. 2. *collect.* The aggregate of hairs growing on the skin of an animal; also, hairs collectively, as used in manufactures, etc. OE. b. *fig.* 1594. 3. In plants: An outgrowth of the epidermis, consisting of an elongated cell, or a row of cells, usually soft and flexible like the hair of animals. In *Bot.* sometimes extended to prickles, spore-capsules, etc.: = TRICHOME. 4. *transf.* as in MAIDENHAIR, *Venus' hair*, etc. 1551. b. A spring mechanism which is freed by the HAIR-TRIGGER, q.v. 1864. 5. A jot or tittle; an iota; the slightest thing; the least degree ME. †6. *Of one hair*: of one colour and external quality; hence = sort; stamp, character –1625. 7. A haircloth 1485. 8. *attrib.*, as *h.-cell*, etc. 1565.

1. A sword..hanging by a haire over his head 1581. b. He rends his hairs in sacrifice to Jove POPE. 2. My h. is grey, but not with years BYRON. *fig.* Like a Comet..That..from his horrid h. Shakes Pestilence and Warr MILT. 6. Two notable knaues, both of a haire GREENE.

Phr. *Against the h.*: contrary to the direction in which an animal's h. naturally lies; against the grain, inclination, or sentiment. *To a h.*: to a nicety, with complete exactness. *A h. of the dog that bit you, of the same dog* (or *wolf*): see DOG *sb.* *To split hairs*: to make cavilling distinctions. *To keep one's h. on* (slang): to keep cool. *To put up her hair*: said of a girl when she passes into womanhood. *Not to turn a h.*: *lit.* of a horse, not to show sweat by the roughening of his hair; *fig.* not to show any sign of being ruffled, or affected by exertion.

Comb.: **h.-ball,** one of the masses of hair of different shapes and sizes found in the stomachs of cows, deer, etc.; **-bracket,** the moulding at the back of a ship's figure-head; **-compasses,** compasses which can be regulated to the breadth of a h.; **-drawn** *a.*, drawn out as fine as a hair; **-eel,** a kind of filiform worm inhabiting stagnant water; **-follicle,** the cylindrical depression in the skin from which a h. grows, extending through the corium to the subcutaneous connective tissue; **-hygrometer,** a hygrometer depending upon the expansion of hair when exposed to damp; **-kiln,** a hop-kiln covered with a haircloth on which the hops are spread out to dry; **-lead,** a very thin lead used for spacing in printing; **-lichen,** an eruption attacking the roots of the hair; **-mole** (†**-mold**), a mole on the skin having a h. or hairs on it; **-moss,** a moss of the genus *Polytrichum*; **-pencil,** a painter's brush made of camel's hair or the like; **-plate,** the plate at the back of a bloomery; **-pyrites** = MILLERITE; **-sac** = *hair-follicle*; **-salt** [Ger. *haarsalz*], alunogen; **-seal,** an eared seal of the family *Otariidæ*, sub-family *Tricophocinæ*; **-space,** a very thin space used in printing; **-spring,** the fine hair-like spring in a watch which regulates the movement of the balance-wheel; **-stone** [Ger. *haarstein*] = SAGENITE; †**-tail,** a name of fishes of the family *Trichiuridæ*; **-tail worm** = *hair-eel*; **-trunk,** a trunk covered with skin retaining the h.; †**-weed,** a conferva.

Hair, *v.* 1802. [f. prec.] 1. *trans.* To free from hair; to depilate. 2. *intr.* 'To produce or grow hair' (*Cent. Dict.*).

Hairbell, -brain, etc.: see HARE-.

Hairbreadth (hēᵊ·ɹbredþ). 1561. 1. The breadth or diameter of a hair; an infinitesimally small space or distance. 2. *attrib.* or as *adj.*: Very narrow or close, as *h. difference, escape*; hence, *h. adventure* 1604.

2. Haire-breadth scapes i' th' imminent deadly breach SHAKS.

Hairbrush (hēᵊ·ɹbrɒʃ). 1599. A toilet-brush for the hair.

Haircloth (hēᵊ·ɹklǫþ). 1500. [Cf. HAIRE.] 1. Cloth or fabric made of hair, used for tents, towels, shirts of penitents or ascetics; also in drying malt, hops, etc. Also *attrib.* 2. An article made of this fabric 1548.

Hai·rdresser. 1771. One whose business is to dress and cut the hair. So **Hai·rdressing,** the business of a h.

†**Haire.** [Two types: 1. ME. *hēre, heare, heere, heer*; 2. ME. *haire*, through OF. *haire*; both f. (ult.) WGer. **hārjā* deriv. of *hār* hair. The form from French, which survived longest, is now merged in HAIR *sb.* (sense 7).] Cloth made of hair, haircloth; *esp.* a hair shirt worn by penitents and ascetics; extended later to sackcloth or the like –1601.

Haired (hēᵊɹd), *a.* ME. [f. HAIR *sb.* + -ED².] Having hair. Often with adj. prefixed, as *black-haired*, etc.

He that hath not his Browes heyred is not seemely 1548.

Hai·ren, *a.* *Obs.* exc. *dial.* [OE. *hǣren*, **hēren*; see HAIR and -EN⁴.] Made or consisting of hair; hair-.

More..afflictive than his h. shirt JER. TAYLOR.

Hai·r-grass. 1759. [After L. generic name *Aira*, with reference to the slender hair-like branches.] A name for grasses of the Linnæan genus *Aira*.

Hairiness (hēᵊ·rinės). ME. [f. HAIRY + -NESS.] The quality or state of being hairy; hirsuteness.

†**Hair-lace.** ME. [f. HAIR *sb.* + LACE.] A string or tie for binding the hair; a fillet; also, a fillet in *Archit.* –1738.

Hai·rless, *a.* 1552. [See -LESS.] Destitute of hair.

Hai·r-line. 1731. 1. A rope or line made of hair. 2. A very thin line, as the up-stroke of a written letter 1846. 3. *Printing. Hair-line letter*: A very thin-faced type, generally used for lettering of mounts 1888.

Hair-lip, erron. f. HARE-LIP.

Hai·rpin, hai·r-pin. 1818. A kind of pin used in dressing and fastening up the hair, etc. b. In full *hairpin bend*: A sharp bend in a road likened to a hairpin in form 1923.

Hair-powder. 1663. A scented powder for the hair; now chiefly used by men-servants.

Hair's-breadth, hair's breadth (hēᵊ·ɹz-bredþ). 1584. = HAIRBREADTH. Also *attrib.* or as *adj.* b. *Bot.* The twelfth part of a line. LINDLEY.

Hair-shirt. 1737. A shirt made of haircloth, worn by ascetics and penitents. (Cf. HAIRE.)

Hair-sieve (hēᵊ·ɹ,si·v). ME. A sieve with the bottom made of hair finely woven; usu. for straining liquid.

Hai·r-splitter. 1849. One who 'splits hairs', or makes minute or cavilling distinctions. So **Hai·r-splitting** *vbl. sb.* the splitting of hairs; *ppl. a.* that splits hairs.

Hai·r-streak. 1816. In full, *hair-streak butterfly*: A butterfly of the genus *Thecla*; so called from the markings on the wings of some species.

Hai·r-stroke. 1634. 1. A very fine line made in writing or drawing; *esp.* a fine up-stroke in penmanship. 2. *Printing.* A CERIPH. 1875.

Hai·r-trigger. 1830. A secondary trigger in a firearm, which acts by setting free a spring mechanism called the *hair*, and, being delicately adjusted, releases the main trigger by very slight pressure. Also *attrib.* Hence **Hai·r-triggered** *a.* having a hair-trigger.

Hair-worm (hēᵊ·ɹwɒ̄ɹm). 1658. A nematoid worm of the genus *Gordius*; spec. *G. aquaticus.* (Sometimes applied to the Guinea-worm, *Dracunculus medinensis.*)

Hairy (hēᵊ·ri), *a.* ME. [f. HAIR *sb.* + -Y¹.] 1. Having much hair; hirsute. Also *transf.* 2. Consisting of hair; hair-like (now *rare*); made of hair 1535. 3. *Bot.* Covered with short weak thin pubescence 1597.

1. Esau my brother is an heeri man WYCLIF *Gen.* xxvii. 11. *transf.* Comets or hairie starres HOLLAND. 2. The h. gown and mossy cell MILT. *Comb.*: **h.-back,** a fish of the family *Trichonotidæ*; **h.-crown, -head,** species of Merganser.

Hait, heit (hēᵊt), *interj.* ME. [Cf. Ger. *hott!*] A word of encouragement or command given to horses to urge them forward.

Hake (hēᵊk), *sb.*¹ ME. [?] A gadoid fish, *Merlucius vulgaris*, resembling the cod. Applied also to the genus *Merlucius*, and to other gadoid fish, esp. to species of the genus *Phycis* found on the coast of N. America, and to the New Zealand *Lotella rhacinus.* Also *attrib.*

Hake, haik, *sb.*² 1768. [? f. the root *hak-* of HATCH and HECK.] 1. A wooden frame suspended from the roof for drying cheeses, etc.; a wooden frame for holding plates. *Sc.* 2. = HACK *sb.*² 3. 1840. 3. = HECK. 1863.

†**Hake**, *sb.*[3] Also **hack(e, hag(g, haque.** 1538. [app. an abbrev. of *haquebut, hagbut.*] A short 16th c. fire-arm –1656.

Hake, haik (hēik), *v. Sc.* and *n. dial.* 1450. [Cf. Du. *haken* to long, to hanker.] **1.** *intr.* 'To go about idly from place to place'. **2.** To go, advance; 'to tramp, trudge, or wend one's way' (Jam.) 1450. **3.** *trans.* To urge, to pester 1855.

‖**Hakeem, hakim** (hăkī·m). *Oriental.* 1638. [Arab. *ḥakīm* wise, learned, philosopher, physician.] A physician or doctor, in Mohammedan countries and in India.

‖**Hakim** (hā·kim). *Oriental.* 1615. [Arab. *ḥākim* governor.] A judge, ruler, or governor in Mohammedan countries and in India.

‖**Halachah, halakah** (hălā·kă). 1856. [Heb., f. *hālak* to walk.] A legal decision regarding a matter or case for which there is no direct enactment in the Mosaic law, deduced by analogy, and included as a binding precept in the Mishna. Hence **Hala·chist**, one who deduces laws from the Bible.

‖**Hala·lcor.** *E. Indies.* Also †**halichore.** 1662. [Pers. (Urdū), f. Arab.] One of the lowest and vilest class in Persia, India, etc., to whom everything is lawful food.

He is wholly driven from all honest society..He becomes an Halichore BURKE.

Halation (hălēⁱ·ʃən). 1859. [irreg. f. HALO + -ATION.] *Photogr.* The term for the spreading of light beyond its proper boundary in the negative image upon the plate, producing local fog around the high lights, etc.

Halberd, halbert (hæ·lbərd, -əɹt), *sb.* 1495. [a. OF. *hale-, hallebard*, ad. MHG. *helmbarde*, mod.G. *hellebarde*, Du. *hellebaard*, of which the second element is OHG. *barta*, OLG. *barda* broad-ax, deriv. of Teut. **bardo-z* beard. The first element is either (1) the very rare OHG. *helm, halm* handle, as if 'handled broad-ax', or more prob. (2) *helm* helmet, with sense 'ax for smashing helmets'. Formerly pronounced hǭl-.] **1.** A military weapon; a kind of combination of spear and battle-ax, consisting of a sharp-edged blade ending in a point, and a spear-head, mounted on a handle five to seven feet long. †**2.** *transf.* A soldier armed with a halbert –1603.

Comb.: **halberd-headed, -shaped,** *adjs. Bot.* (of leaves) shaped like the ax of a halberd; **-weed,** the W. Indian shrub *Neurolæna lobata*.

Halberdier (hælbəɹdī·ɹ). 1548. [a. OF. *hale-, hallebardier*; see prec. and -IER.] A soldier armed with a halberd; *spec.* a member of certain civic guards carrying a halberd as a badge of office. So **Ha·lberdman.**

Halcyon (hæ·lsiən, hæ·lʃiən). ME. [a. L. *halcyon*, more prop. *alcyon*, a. Gr. ἀλκυών kingfisher. The spelling ἁλ- *hal-* is prob. due to the fancy that the word was f. ἅλς sea + κύων conceiving.]

A. *sb.* **1.** A bird anciently fabled to breed about the time of the winter solstice in a nest floating on the sea, and to charm the wind and waves so that the sea was then specially calm; usu. identified with a species of kingfisher, hence a poetic name of this bird. Also *fig.* **b.** In *Zool.* a kingfisher of the Australasian genus *Halcyon*, or of the sub-family *Halcyoninæ* 1772. †**2.** Calm, quietude, halcyon days –1797.

1. There came the h., whom the sea obeys, When she her nest upon the water lays SHENSTONE. var. †**Ha·lcydon.**

B. *attrib.* or *adj.* **1.** Of, or pertaining to, the halcyon or kingfisher 1601. **2.** Calm, quiet, peaceful, undisturbed. (Usu. qualifying *days.*) 1578.

1. Phr. *Halcyon days* [Gr. ἀλκυονίδες ἡμέραι, L. *alcyonei dies, alcyonides, alcedonia*]: fourteen days of calm weather, anciently believed to occur about the winter solstice when the h. was brooding.

Hence †**Halcyo·nian** *a.* = B.

Halcyonic, -ite, -oid, vars. of ALCYONIC, etc.

Ha·lcyonine, *a. Ornith.* Of or pertaining to the sub-family of kingfishers (*Halcyoninæ*) of which the genus *Halcyon* is the type.

†**Hale,** *sb.*[1] ME. [A parallel form to HEAL *sb.*, ME. *hele*, and HAIL *sb.*[2], after the adj., OE. *hāl.*] = HAIL *sb.*[2], HEAL *sb.* –1795.

†**Hale,** *sb.*[2] ME. [app. a. OF. *hale* (mod. *halle*), a. OS. and OHG. *halla*, an area covered over. Thus a doublet of HALL.] A place roofed over, but usually open at the sides; a pavilion; a tent; a booth, etc. –1606.

Hale (hēl), *sb.*[3] Now *rare* or *Obs.* 1470. [f. HALE *v.*[1] See also HAUL *sb.*] In *hoise and h., h. and how*, exclams. of sailors in hauling; also, the act of haling or hauling.

Hale (hēl), *a.* (*adv.*) [The n. dial. repr. of OE. *hāl*, which became in s. and midl. dial. *hōl, hool, hole*, WHOLE.]

I. 1. Free from injury; safe, sound. Now only *Sc.* and *n. dial.* **2.** Free from disease, well; 'whole'. Now *Sc.* and *n. dial.* OE. **3.** Free from infirmity; sound, vigorous. (The current literary sense; usu. of old persons.) 1734.

3. Finding my old friend..so h. at 83-4 JARVIS.

II. = WHOLE, in its current senses ME.

Hale (hēl), *v.*[1] ME. [a. OF. *haler*, in sense 1 (12th c.), a. OFrankish *hâlon* = OHG. *halôn, holôn*, mod.G. *holen*, to fetch, etc.] **1.** *trans.* To draw or pull. †**a.** = DRAW *v.* in various senses –1842. **b.** Now repl. by HAUL. ME. **2.** *fig.* ME. †**b.** To harry, molest –1641. **3.** *absol.* or *intr.* To pull, tug ME. †**4.** *intr.* To move along as if drawn or pulled; to move with force; *spec.* of a ship, to proceed before the wind with sails set, to sail. Also *fig.* –1727. **b.** To flow, run down in a stream. *Obs.* exc. *Sc.* and *n. dial.* (Later, written *hail.*) ME.

1. a. The rope that hal'd the buckets from the well TENNYSON. **b.** As one hal'd to execution JER. TAYLOR. **2.** Texts..haled to their purposes by force of wit HOBBES. **b.** To let them still h. and worrey us with their band-dogs MILT.

†**Hale,** *v.*[2] ME. [? f. HALE *a.*, or var. of HEAL *v.*] *trans.* To make hale or whole; to heal –1530.

‖**Halesia** (hēlī·siă). 1760. [f. Stephen *Hales*, an English botanist (1677–1761).] *Bot.* A genus of plants (N.O. *Styraceæ*), containing the Snowdrop or Silver-bell tree of the southern U.S., *Halesia tetraptera*, and other species.

Half (hāf), *sb.* Pl. **halves** (hāvz); †**halfs.** [Com. Teut.: OE. *healf* fem.; see HALF *a.* The oldest sense is 'side'.]

I. †**1.** Side; one of the (two) sides; the right or left side (of any one); the direction indicated by the side or hand –1532. †**2.** *fig.* One of the opposite sides in a conflict, sexes in descent, etc. –1563. †**b.** Side, part (as of one of the parties to a transaction) –1526.

1. On this halfe the fest of Ester 1495. **2.** He was, in hys moder alf, Seynt Edwardes broþer R. GLOUC. **b.** It shal not lakke, certeyn, on myn halve CHAUCER. Phr. †*On God's h.*: in God's name, for God's sake.

II. 1. One of two opposite, corresponding, or equal parts into which a thing is or may be divided OE. **2.** More vaguely: One of two (†or more) divisions more or less approaching equality; esp. with comparatives ME. †**3.** One of two partners or co-sharers –1596. **4.** In various ellipt. uses of HALF *a.*, some sb. being omitted (*colloq.*). See quots. 1659.

1. The two Sides, or Halves of the Float 1717. One-half or three-fourths of an inch thick SCORESBY. Phr. *One and a h.* (see HALF *a.*). **2.** Swear..it broke into three halves SWIFT. Phr. *Better half*, a wife (or †husband). **3.** *Tam. Shr.* v. ii. 78. Phr. *To go halves.* **4. a.** = Half-year, or -term. It..has..stopped the boats for this h. 1820. **b.** = Half-boot; There's two pair of halves in the commercial DICKENS. **c.** = Half-pint, half-gill of spirits; Two halves of ale and a cigar 1891. **d.** = Half-back (at Football). **e.** = Half-mile (race); etc.

Phrases. *To (the) halves* (now *U.S.*) = so as to have a half-share in the profits (in letting or hiring a house, a piece of land, etc.). *By halves*: to the extent of a h. only; half-heartedly; imperfectly. *By h.*: by a great deal. *To go halves* (cf. II. 3): to share equally (with a person). *To cry halves*: to claim a half-share in what is found by another.

Comb. **a.** *attrib.*, as *h.-share.* **b.** quasi-*adv.*, as *h.-partner*, etc.

Half (hāf), *a.* [Com. Teut.: OE. *healf, half*; not known outside Teut.] **1.** Forming a half or moiety (see quots.). **2.** Half the length (or breadth) of. Now *rare* or *Obs.* 1481. **3.** As a measure of degree: Attaining only half-way to completeness; partial, imperfect. (In this use now usu. hyphened: see HALF-.) ME.

1. A h. length, share (*mod.*). *H. the length* (in mod. use occas. viewed as a *sb.* with *of* suppressed). The..wind blew h. a gale BYRON. *H. a crown* (= the equivalent of *a half-crown*, e.g. five sixpences; see HALF-). **2.** Within h. Pistol shot 1681. **3.** A h. toleration, known by the name of the Indulgence MACAULAY.

Phr. †OE. *þridda healf*, †ME. *thridde half* or *half thrid* = two and half, i.e. a half-unit less than the corresponding cardinal number. Cf. Ger. *dritte-halb*, etc.

Half, *v.* Obs. and dial. f. HALVE *v.* (q.v.); also *mod. colloq.* in sense To 'be half', go halves.

Half (hāf), *adv.* [OE. *half, healf*, in composition; written separate or hyphened, with no difference of sense; see HALF- 1.] **1.** To the extent of half. Hence loosely: In part, partially; in some degree. **2.** Used correlatively: *Half ... half ...* OE. **3.** Idiomatic uses, in which *half* may have been orig. the adj. or sb. (see quots.) 1726.

1. She ran..Like one h. mad FAIRFAX. In her halfe ruin'd cell 1615. The lily was not h. so fair ADDISON. **2.** He was h. man and h. beste GOWER. **3.** *Half past* (or *after*) *one* or *one o'clock*, etc. = half an hour past the time named. *Half* (Naut.) = half a point (i.e. 5⅝°) from the first towards the second of two points (of the compass) mentioned. *Half four* (in soundings) = 4½ fathoms.

Phr. *Not half*: a long way from the due amount; in mod. *slang* and *colloq.* use = not at all, as 'not half bad'.

Half- in *comb.* [OE. *half-, healf-* was regularly combined with an adj. or pple., or with a sb. In OTeut. *halƀ-* was app. a later substitute for the original *sāmi-*, OE. *sam-*, = L. *semi-*, Gr. ἡμι-, Skr. *sāmi-*, etc.]

I. In advb. relation. **1.** With adjs. and pa. pples. The two elements are often written separately when the adj. is in the predicate; when it is attributive the hyphen is regularly used as implying a feeling of closer unity of notion in the compound attribute, as in *h.-thought-out recollections* OE. **2.** With advs., as *h.-angrily, -questioningly*, etc. 1700. **3.** With vbs., as *h.-murder*, etc. 1674.

Comb.: **h.-equitant** *a. Bot.* = OBVOLUTE; **-imperial** *a.*, half imperial-folio size; **-large** *a.*, (a card) 3×2¼ inches (Jacobi *Printer's Vocab.*); **-saved** *a.*, half-witted (*dial.*).

II. In attrib. relation to a sb. The number of these has latterly become enormous, esp. through the practice of hyphening an adj. and sb. when these have a special or individualized application.

a. In names of *Coins, Weights, Measures, h.-barrel, -farthing, -florin, -inch*, etc. Also HALF-CROWN, -DOLLAR, -HOUR, -MINUTE, etc. **b.** In *Her.* = DEMI-B 1, as *h.-belt*, etc. **c.** In *Artillery*, etc., *h.-cannon, -lance*, etc. (cf. DEMI-). Also HALF-PIKE, -SWORD, etc. **d.** In Mil., *h.-squadron, -turn, -wheel*, etc.; **h.-battery** = three subdivisions; **-company**, same as subdivision; **-distance**, the regular interval or space between troops drawn up in ranks, or standing in column; **-file**, half the given number of any body of men drawn up two deep. Also HALF-FACE, etc. **e.** In *Fortif.*, **h.-bastion, -caponier, -sap** (see DEMI-BASTION, etc.); **h.-merlon**, that solid portion of a parapet which is at the right or left extremity of a battery. Also HALF-*circle*, -MOON. **f.** *Naut.* and *Shipbuilding*: **h.-beam**, a short beam introduced to support the deck where there is no framing; **-breadth staff**, a rod having marked upon it half the length of each beam in the ship; †**-wind**, a side-wind. **g.** In *Mus.*, **h.-cadence, -close**, an imperfect cadence; **-demisemiquaver**; **-rest** (*U.S.*), a minim rest; **-shift**, a position of the hand in violin playing; it lies between the open position and the first shift. Cf. DEMI-. Also HALF-NOTE, -TONE. **h.** Applied to a stuff which is half of inferior material, as *h.-silk, -yarn*, etc. **i.** In *Games*, **h.-back** (*Football*), a position immediately behind the 'forwards'; a player in this position; **-ball** (*Billiards*), a contact in which the half of one ball is covered by half of the other; **-hit** (*Cricket*), a mistimed hit that sends the ball into the air; **-volley** (*Cricket, Football*, etc.), a ball which pitches so that it can be hit or kicked as soon as it rises from the ground. Also *half-bowl*, etc. **j.** In *Bookbinding*, 'half' signifies that only the back and corners of the binding are of the materials specified; e.g. *h.-calf*, etc. **k.** In various connexions; as *h.-door, -honesty, -knowledge, -quotation, -reasoning, -whisper*, etc.

Special combs.: **h.-arm**, half arm's length; **-barrel** *a.*, semicylindrical (vaulting); **-bend**, a half fillet for the head; **-bent**, (*a*) the condition of being half-bent; (*b*) the catch by which the hammer of a gun is placed at half-cock; **-boarder**, one who has half his board, a day-boarder; **-box**, a box open at one side; **-chronometer**, *orig.*, a watch having an escapement compounded of the lever and chronometer; *now*, a fine lever watch which has been adjusted for temperature; **-column**, a column or pilaster half projecting from a flat surface; **-communion**, communion in one kind, as practised in the R. C. Ch.; †**-compass**, hemisphere; **-course** (*Mining*), half on the level and half on the dip; **-dike**, a sunk fence; **-hatchet**, 'a hatchet with one straight line, all the projection of the bit being on the side towards the hand' (Knight); **-header**, a half-brick used to close the work at the end of a course; **-house**, a shed open at the side; **-margin**, applied to paper folded in the centre, lengthways; **-plate**, a watch in which the top pivot of the fourth wheel pinion is carried in a cock so as to allow the use of a larger balance; **-plate paper**, machine-made paper of fine and soft quality used for woodcuts; **-press**, the work done by one man at a printing-press; **-principal** (*Carpentry*), 'a rafter which does not extend to the crown of the roof' (Knight); **-relief** = *demi-relief* (see DEMI-); **-royal**, a kind of millboard or pasteboard; **-shade** (*Painting*), a shade of half the extreme depth; **-sheet** (*Printing*), the off-cut portion of a duodecimo (Knight); **-space** = HALF-PACE 2; **-stitch**, a loose open stitch in braid work or pillow-lace making (Caulfield); **-story**, an upper story half the height of which is in the walls and half in the roof; **-stuff** (*Paper-making*), partly prepared pulp; **-swing plough**, a plough in which the mould-board is a fixture; **-text**, a size of hand-writing half the size of 'text' or large hand; **-throw**, **-travel**, half the full movement of a piston, valve, etc.; **-tint**, in a monochrome, all gradations between white and black; **-title**, the short title of a book; **-tongue** (*Law*), a jury of which one half were foreigners, formerly allowed to a foreigner tried on a criminal charge; **-trap**, a semicircular depression in a sewer pipe; **-uncial** = SEMI-UNCIAL; **-water** = HALF-TIDE; **h. wave**, one-half of a complete wave of electricity, light, or sound; chiefly *attrib.*; **h.-world**, hemisphere; the demi-monde.

Halfa (hæ·lfă). Also **alfa, alpha, halfeh**, etc. 1857. [Arab. *halfah*, or *halfā*.] The N. African name of Esparto (*Stipa tenacissima*) used in paper-making, etc.

Half-and-half, *phrase*. 1715. **1.** A mixture of ale and porter, or the like 1756. **2.** Something that is half one thing and half another, or half this and half that 1814. Also *attrib.* or *adj.* **3.** as *adv.* In two equal parts; half... and half not 1818. **4.** Half-intoxicated 1715.

Ha·lf-ape. 1883. A lemur.

Half-baked (hā·fbē·ikt), *a.* 1621. **1.** *lit.* See HALF *adv.* and BAKED; hence, underdone, not earnest; raw; incomplete, rude. **2.** Silly, half-witted (*dial.*) 1855.

Ha·lf-bapti·ze, *v.* 1836. To baptize privately or without full rites, as a child in danger of death.

Ha·lf-beak. 1880. A fish of the genus *Hemirhamphus*, having the lower jaw long and ensiform, and the upper short.

Ha·lf-bi·nding. 1864. A style of binding of books in which the back and corners are of leather, the sides being of cloth or paper.

Ha·lf-blood. 1553. **1.** The relation between persons having only one parent in common. **2.** A person or group of persons related in this way 1848. **3.** A half-breed 1826.

1. What, is a brother by the half bloud no kinne FULLER. Hence **Half-blooded** *a.* born of different races.

Ha·lf-boot. 1787. [HALF II.] A boot reaching half-way to the knee, or well above the ankle.

Ha·lf-bound, *ppl. a.* 1775. Of a book: Having a leather back and corners, with cloth or paper sides; cf. HALF-BINDING.

Ha·lf-bred, *a.* (*sb.*) 1701. [See BREED *v.*, BRED.] **1.** Of mixed breed; mongrel. Also *fig.* †**2.** Imperfectly acquainted with the rules of good-breeding; under-bred. ATTERBURY. **3.** *sb.* A half-bred horse, pigeon, etc. 1856.

Half-breed (hā·fbrīd). 1791. [See BREED *sb.*, and cf. HALF-CASTE.] **1.** One who is sprung from parents of two races; esp., in U. S., the offspring of whites or negroes and American Indians. **2.** *attrib.*, as *half-breed boys* 1837.

Half-brother. ME. [Cf. Ger. *halbbruder*, etc.] A brother by one parent only.

Ha·lf-cap. 1607. A half-courteous salute, shown by a slight movement only of the cap.

1. With certaine halfe-caps, and cold mouing nods, They froze me into Silence SHAKS.

Half-caste. Also **half-cast.** 1789. †**1.** A mixed caste; a race sprung from the union of two castes or races. WELLESLEY. **2.** A half-breed; *esp.*, in India, one born or descended from a European father and native mother 1789. **3.** *attrib.* (from 1), as, a *half-caste merchant* 1793.

Half-cheek. 1588. †**1.** A face in profile. **2.** *Naut.*: see CHEEK. 1860.

1. S. Georges halfe cheeke in a brooch SHAKS.

Half-cock, *sb.* 1701. †**1.** Part of a watch; cf. COCK *sb.*[1] **2.** Of a fire-arm: The position of the cock or hammer when raised only half-way and held by the catch, from which it cannot be moved by pulling the trigger. Hence *To go off* (*at*) *half-cock*, to go off prematurely, to speak or act without due forethought or preparation, and thereby to fail. So **Half-cock** *v. trans.* to put (a gun) at half-cock.

Half-cousin. 1871. The child of one's father's or mother's cousin; a second cousin. Occas. applied to the child of one's own cousin, or to the cousin of one's father or mother.

Half-crown. 1542. A coin of Great Britain, of the value of two shillings and six-pence; sometimes used for **Half a crown**, the equivalent sum.

Half-dead, *a.* OE. [See HALF *adv.*] In a state in which death seems as likely as recovery.

Ha·lf-deck. 1626. [See DECK *sb.*] **1.** *lit.* A deck covering half the length of a ship or boat, fore and aft. *spec.* **a.** In old ships of war: A deck extending from the mainmast aftward, situated between the then smaller 'quarter-deck' and the upper or main deck. These two were later reduced to one, and called 'quarter-deck'. †**b.** In colliers: A deck under the main deck, containing berths, etc. for the crew. **c.** In merchantmen: Accommodation for cadets and apprentices. **2.** *U.S. local.* The Slipper-limpet, *Crepidula fornicata*, which has an under half-shell (*Cent. Dict.*). Hence **Ha·lf-decked** *a.* that is about half covered in or decked. **Half-de·cker**, a half-decked boat.

Half-dime. 1796. A U. S. coin, value 5 cents, orig. of silver, but now of copper and nickel; pop. called a *nickel*.

Ha·lf-do·llar. 1786. A silver coin of the U. S. and other countries, equal to 50 cents.

Half-dozen, half a dozen. ME. The half of a dozen; six (or about six). See DOZEN.

Half-eagle. 1824. A gold coin of the U. S., value 5 dollars.

Half-ebb. ME. The state or time of the tide when its reflux is half completed.

†**Halfen**, *a.* [pseudo-arch., perh. taken from next.] Half. SPENSER.

Ha·lfendeal, ha·lven-. *Obs.* exc. *dial.* [OE. *þone healfan dǽl*, accus. case of *se healfa dǽl*, the half part, mechanically retained after the sense of inflexion was lost.]

A. *sb.* 'Half part'; a half, a moiety.
†B. *adj.* Half -ME.
†C. *adv.* Half, by half -1590.

Halfer: see HALVER.

Half-face, *sb.* 1542. **1.** Half of a face; a profile. Also *attrib.* **2.** *Mil.* The action or position of facing half-way to the right or left, i.e. at an angle of 45 degrees 1833. So **Half-face** *v.* (*Mil.*), *intr.* to make a half-face.

Ha·lf-faced, *a.* 1592. [f. prec. sb.] **1.** Presenting a half-face or profile. Of a coin: Having a profile stamped upon it; hence, of persons, having a thin, pinched face. So *half-faced groat*, applied contemptuously to a thin-faced man (*John* I. i. 94). **2.** With only half of the face visible 1593. **3.** Half-and-half, incomplete 1592.

Ha·lf-fish. 1677. A half-grown salmon, usually about twenty or twenty-two inches.

Half-flood. ME. The state or time of the flowing tide halfway between low and high water.

Ha·lf-gui·nea. 1696. An English gold coin worth (in 19th c.) 10*s.* 6*d.*, coined from Charles II to 1813.

Ha·lf-headed, *a.* 1621. Half-intelligent; stupid.

Ha·lf-hearted, *a.* 1611. Not having one's whole heart in a matter; wanting in courage, earnestness, or zeal. †**b.** Illiberal, ungenerous, unkind (Webster, citing Ben Jonson) 1864. Hence **Half-hea·rted·ly** *adv.*, **-ness.**

Half-hitch. 1769. [See HITCH *sb.*] *Naut.* A hitch formed by passing the end of a rope round its standing part, and then through the bight; the simplest form of hitch.

Half-ho·liday. Also †**-holyday.** 1552. †**1.** A day which is considered only half a holy day; a saint's day or holy day other than Sunday -1631. **2.** †**a.** The half of a holy day (used for recreation). **b.** The (latter) half of a working day, given up to recreation. **c.** A day of which the latter half is taken as a holiday. 1631.

†**Ha·lf-horse.** 1588. A centaur -1621.

Half-hour. ME. The half of an hour; thirty minutes. Also **b. Half an hour** (not used with a defining word) ME. Hence **Half-hou·rly** *adj.* occurring every half-hour; lasting half an hour; *adv.* every half-hour.

Half-impe·rial, *sb.* 1839. **1.** A gold coin of Russia valued orig. at 5 and later at $7\frac{1}{2}$ silver roubles. **2.** A size of mill-board 1858.

Half-island, half-isle. *Obs.* or *arch.* 1600. A peninsula.

Ha·lf-length. 1699. A portrait of half the full length. Also *attrib.* or *adj.*

Half-light. 1625. A light of half the full intensity; a dim, imperfect light. Also *fig. At half lights*: vaguely, dimly.

Half-mast. 1627. The half of a mast, half the height of a mast; in *at half-mast, half-mast* (*high*); said esp. of the position of a flag lowered to half the height of the staff as a mark of respect for the dead. Hence **Half-mast** *v. trans.* to hang half-mast high.

Half-measure. 1798. [See HALF *a.*] A measure, plan, effort, etc. wanting in thoroughness or energy; procedure marked by compromise.

Half-minute. 1798. [See HALF *a.*] The half of a minute; thirty seconds; also **Half a minute. b.** *attrib.* and *Comb.*, as *half-minute gun*; **half-minute glass** (*Naut.*), a sand-glass which marks the time for the running out of the log-line.

Half-moon, *sb.* 1530. **1.** The moon, when only half its disk appears illuminated; *loosely*, a crescent. Also *transf.* of things in the shape of a half-moon or crescent. **2.** *Fortif.* = DEMILUNE 2. 1642. †**3.** A cuckold (in allusion to his horns). SHIRLEY. **4.** *Mining.* Scaffolding filling up one half the sectional area of a *pit-shaft*, on which repairs are done (Gresley). **5.** *attrib.* Shaped like a half-moon, as *half-moon battery*, etc.; **half-moon knife**, a double-handed knife used by the dresser of skins for parchment (Knight).

1. *transf.* And cuts me from the best of all my Land, A huge halfe Moone, a monstrous Cantle out SHAKS. Hence **Half-moon** *v. trans.* to surround like a half-moon; *intr.* to move in a half-moon formation.

Half-mou·rning. 1820. **1.** The second stage or period of mourning, after full mourning. **b.** Attire in which black is relieved or replaced by white, or by such colours as grey, lavender, or purple. **2.** The Marbled White Butterfly; also called *half-mourner*.

Half-nephew. 1824. The son of one's half-brother or -sister.

Halfness (hā·fnės). 1530. [-NESS.] The condition or quality of being half or incomplete, or of being half one thing and half another.

Such H., such halting between two opinions 1831.

Half-niece. 1824. The daughter of one's half-brother or -sister.

Half-noble. 1480. A gold coin issued from Edw. III to Edw. IV.

Ha·lf-note. 1597. **1.** *Mus.* †**a.** A half-tone; a semitone -1763. **b.** A minim 1847. **2.** The half of a bank-note, cut in two for safe transmission by post 1882.

Half-pace. 1569. [prob. a corruption of earlier *haultpace, haltpace*, HALPACE, q.v.] **1.** A step, raised floor, or platform on which a throne, a dais, etc. is to be placed or erected. **b.** The platform at the top of steps on which an altar stands. **2.** A broad step or landing between two half flights in a staircase 1611. Hence **Ha·lf-paced** *a.* having a half-pace.

Half-pay. 1664. **1.** Half the usual or full wages or salary; a reduced allowance to an officer when not in actual service, or after retirement at a stated time. **2.** An officer in receipt of half-pay 1826. **3.** *attrib.*, as *half-pay officer*, etc. 1715.

Halfpenny (hē¹·pĕni, *dial.* hā·fpĕni, hā·pĕni, ha·pĕni, ha·pni.) *Pl.* **Halfpennies** (hē¹·pĕniz), **halfpence** (hē¹·pĕns). ME. [f. HALF *a.* + PENNY. The pl. *halfpennies* means the individual coins only; *halfpence*, usually, the sum.] **1.** A coin (formerly of copper, now of bronze) of half the value of a penny; a sum = two farthings. †**2.** A small fragment. *Much Ado* II. iii. 147. **3.** *attrib.* That costs a halfpenny, as *h. ballad*, etc.; of contemptible value (also *twopenny-halfpenny*) ME.

1. *H. under the hat*, a low game of chance. THACKERAY. *More kicks than halfpence*: see KICK *sb.*

Halfpennyworth (hē¹·pĕniwɒɹþ), *sb.*, contracted **ha'porth, ha'p'orth** (hē¹·pəɹþ). OE. [See WORTH.] As much as a halfpenny will purchase; a very small quantity.

Phr. *To lose the ship* (orig. and prop. *sheep, ewe, hog*) *for a h. of tar*: to lose an object by trying to save in a small detail. (*Sheep* is dialectally pronounced *ship* in many parts of England, and the tar was used to protect sore places on sheep from the attacks of flies.) Rather..to lose ten sheepe, than be at the charge of a halfe penny worth of Tarre 1631. Hence †**Ha·lfpennyworth** *v. intr.* to haggle about minute expenses (RALEIGH); *trans.* to deal *out* by halfpennyworths (MARVELL).

Half-pike. Now *Hist.* 1599. A short pike. There were two kinds; one, also called a *spontoon*, formerly carried by infantry officers; the other, used in ships for repelling boarders, a *boarding pike*.

Half-price. 1720. **1.** Half the usual or full price. Also, the time at which people are admitted to an entertainment or the like at half-price. Also *attrib.* or quasi-*adj.*

Half-round. 1662.

A. *adj.* Semicircular, in shape or section; semicylindrical, as *half-round bit*, etc.

B. *sb.* A semicircle; a hemispherical figure 1718. **b.** *Arch.* 'A semicircular moulding which may be a bead or torus' (Gwilt) 1842. Hence †**Half-rounding** *a.* forming a semicircle (MILT.).

†**Half-seal.** 1509. The impression of the reverse side or foot of the Great Seal, with which certain documents used to be sealed. Abolished in 1833.

Half-seas-over. 1551. [*Seas* was prob. a genitive case; *half sea's* = half of the sea.] **1.** Halfway across the sea. **b.** *transf.* and *fig.* Half through with a matter; halfway between one state and another 1697. **2.** Half-drunk (*joc.*) 1700.

1. About half Seas over, we discovered the Dutch Fleet 1688. b. I am half-seas over to death DRYDEN.

Half-sister. ME. **1.** A sister by one parent only. Also *fig.* †**2.** A lay sister in a convent 1482.

1. *fig.* Raw Haste, half-sister to Delay TENNYSON.

Ha·lf-snipe. 1766. The jack snipe or lesser snipe.

Ha·lf-so·vereign. 1503. **1.** An English gold coin, worth 10*s.* The sum, as dist. from the coin, is also expressed by *half a sovereign.* **2.** A pavior's name for a 6-in. Purbeck stone pitcher; also for a granite pitching 1851.

†**Half-strain.** 1673. The quality of being half of a good strain or stock and half of an inferior one; half-breed. Also *attrib.* DRYDEN. Hence †**Ha·lf-strained** *a.*

†**Ha·lf-sword.** 1552. **1.** A small-sized sword –1611. **2.** Half a sword's length –1616.

2. Phr. *To be at half-sword*, to be at close quarters with swords.

Ha·lf-tide. 1669. **1.** The state of the tide half-way between flood and ebb. **2.** *attrib.* and *Comb.* Left dry or accessible at half-tide, as *half-tide cavern*; half-tide basin or dock, one fitted with gates which are closed at half-ebb.

Ha·lf-ti·mber. 1842.

A. *sb. Shipbuilding.* (See quot.)

Half-timbers .. those timbers in the cant bodies which are answerable to the lower futtocks in the square body WEALE.

B. *adj.* **1.** Built half of timber 1842. **2.** Made of timber split in half 1874.

1. *Half-timber building*, a structure formed of studding, with sills, lintels, struts, and braces, sometimes filled in with brickwork and plastered over on both sides GWILT.

Hence **Half-timbered** *a.* = B. 1.

Half-time. 1645. **1.** Half of a (particular) period of time; *esp.* half the usual or full time during which work is carried on. (Occas. as *adv.*) 1861. **2.** *Football*, etc. The time at which the first half of the game is completed 1871. **3.** *attrib.* 1861.

3. *Half-time system*, the system by which children are allowed to attend school for half the usual time and spend the other half in earning money; so *half-time register*, a register of half-time scholars.

Half-timer. 1865. One who spends half the usual or full time at anything; *esp.* a half-time scholar (see prec.).

Half-tone, *sb.* 1875. **1.** *Mus.* = SEMITONE. 1880. **2.** *Art.* A tone intermediate between the extreme lights and extreme shades. Also *attrib.*

Half-truth. 1658. A proposition which is or conveys only one half or a part of the truth.

A half-truth is often a falsehood J. H. NEWMAN.

Half-way, halfway (hāfwē¹: see below). ME. [f. HALF *a.* + WAY *sb.*]

A. *adj.* (Stressed *ha·lfway* before, *ha:lf-way·* when following, the word it qualifies.) At or to half the distance. *To meet half-way*: see MEET *v.*

B. *adj.* (Usu. *ha·lfway.*) **1.** Midway or equidistant between two points 1711. **2.** *fig.* Half one thing and half another 169..

1. *Half-way house*, a house (often an inn) situated midway between two towns or stages of a journey, and therefore a convenient halting-place. Also *fig.* 2. Half-way measures PRESCOTT.

C. *sb.* A half-way place or house 1634.

Ha·lf-wit. 1678. [See WIT *sb.*] †**1.** One who is only half a wit –1720. **2.** One who has not all his wits 1755. So **Ha·lf-wi·tted** *a.* †simple, senseless; imbecile.

Ha·lf-word. ME. A word or speech which insinuates something, instead of fully asserting it; a hint, suggestion.

Half-year. OE. The half of a year; six months. As a space of time, expressed by *half a year.* In Schools, etc. = HALF *sb.* II. 4 **a.** Hence **Half-yearly** *a.* and *adv.*

Halibut (hæ·libɒt), **holibut** (hǫ·libɒt). [ME. *halybutte*, app. f. *haly*, HOLY + BUTT *sb.*¹ flat fish; cf. the similarly formed Du. *heilbot* flounder, G. *heilbutt* halibut.] A large flat fish (*Hippoglossus vulgaris*), abundant in the northern seas, and much used for food. (Pl. *halibuts*, also collect. *halibut.*) Also applied to other flat fish of the family *Pleuronectidæ*.

Halichondroid (hælikǫ·ndroid), *a.* 1887. [f. mod.L. *Halichondria*, name of a genus of sponges (f. Gr. ἅλς, ἁλι- sea + χόνδρος cartilage) + -OID.] *Zool.* Related to a group of sponges including *Halichondria palmata*, the largest British sponge.

‖**Halicore** (hăli·kŏrī). 1828. [f. Gr. ἅλς, ἁλι- sea + κόρη maiden, lit. 'mermaid'.] *Zool.* Name of the group of Sirenians, found in the Red Sea and Indian Ocean, to which the Dugong belongs.

Halidom (hæ·lidəm), **-dome** (dōᵘm). *Obs.* or *arch.* [OE. *háliᵹdóm*, f. OTeut. *hailag-, OE. *hálig*, HOLY; see -DOM.] †**1.** Holiness, sanctity –1626. **2.** A holy place, chapel, sanctuary (*arch.*) OE. **3.** A holy relic; anything regarded as sacred. Formerly much used in oaths and adjurations. OE.

2. The men of the Halidome, as it was called, of St. Mary's SCOTT. 3. As help me God and halidome MORE. By my hallidome, I was fast asleepe SHAKS.

Halieutic (hæliyū·tik). 1646. [ad. L. *halieuticus*, a. Gr., f. ἁλιευτής fisher, f. ἁλιεύειν, f. ἅλς sea.]

A. *adj.* Of or belonging to fishing 1854.

B. *sb. pl.* **Halieutics**: The art or practice of fishing; a treatise on fishing.

†**Halio·graphy.** 1656. [f. Gr. ἅλς, ἁλι- + -γραφία.] A description of the sea. So †**Halio·grapher.**

‖**Haliotis** (hæli,ōᵘ·tis). 1752. [f. as prec. + οὖς, ὠτ- the ear; so named from their resemblance to the ear.] *Zool.* A genus of univalve shells, the Ear-shells. Hence **Halio·toid** *a.* akin to the Ear-shell.

Halitosis (hælitōᵘ·sis). [mod.L., f. as next + -OSIS.] *Med.* Abnormally foul breath.

Halituous (hăli·tiuəs), *a.* 1616. [f. L. *halitus*; see next.] Of the nature of breath; vaporous.

‖**Halitus** (hæ·litɒs). 1661. [L.; = 'breath'.] A vapour, exhalation.

†**Halke.** ME. only. [? dim. of OE. *halh*, *healh* a corner; see HALE *sb.*²] A corner, recess, hiding-place.

Hall (hǭl), *sb.* [Com. Teut.: OE. *heall* str. f. :—OTeut. **hallā-* :—**halnā-*, deriv. of ablaut series *hel-*, *hal-*, *hul-* to cover, conceal.] †**1.** A large place covered by a roof; a temple, palace, court, royal residence. *Obs.* in gen. sense. **2.** The large public room in a mansion, palace, etc., used for receptions, banquets, etc., which till 1600 greatly surpassed in size the private rooms or 'bowers' (see BOWER *sb.*¹); a large or stately room in a house ME. **3.** The residence of a territorial proprietor, a baronial or squire's hall OE. **4.** A term applied, esp. in the English universities, to buildings set apart for the residence or instruction of students, and, hence, to the body of students occupying them. **a.** Orig. applied at Oxford and Cambridge to all residences of students, including the Colleges. Now only *Hist.*, *arch.*, or *poet.* for 'academic buildings'. ME. **b.** Later, halls were distinguished from colleges, as being governed by a head only, and having their property held in trust for them, they not being bodies corporate 1535. **c.** In recent times applied variously: e.g. at Oxford, to private halls for the residence of undergraduates, under the charge of a member of Convocation; to theological halls (e.g. Wycliffe Hall), halls for women students (e.g. Lady Margaret Hall), etc. 1879. **5.** In English colleges, etc.: The large room in which the members and students dine in common 1577; *transf.* dinner in hall 1859. **6.** A house or building belonging to a guild or fraternity of merchants or tradesmen ME. **7.** A large room or building for the transaction of public business, the holding of public meetings, or the like ME. †**b.** *The Hall*, Westminster Hall, formerly the seat of the High Court of Justice in England; hence, the administration of justice –1738. †**c.** A formal assembly held by the sovereign, or by the mayor, etc. of a town; usu. in phr. *to keep h.*, *call a h.* –1684. **8.** The entrance-room or vestibule of a house; hence, the lobby or entrance passage 1663. †**9.** *A hall! a hall!* a cry or exclam. to clear the way or make room, esp. for a dance; also to call people together –1808. **10.** *attrib.*, as *h.-bible*, etc. 1460.

2. In halle & i bure ME. *Servants' hall*: see SERVANT *sb.* 6. At Stationers H. 1654. 7. b. *Hen. VIII*, II. i. 2. 9. *Rom. & Jul.* I. v. 28. 10. **h. bedroom** *U.S.*, a small bedroom over the entrance hall; **hallway** *U.S.*, = sense 8; also, a corridor or passage on other floors.

†**Hallage** (hǭ·lėdʒ). 1607. [a. F., f. *halle* + -AGE.] A fee or toll paid for goods sold in a hall or market –1720.

Hall-door. ME. **a.** The door of a hall or mansion. **b.** The door leading into the hall; the front door.

‖**Hallel** (hæ·lē¹l, hæ·lel). 1702. [Heb., inf. and imper. 'praise, celebrate', the first word of Ps. cxiii.] A hymn of praise, consisting of Psalms cxiii to cxviii inclusive, sung at the four great Jewish feasts. Also *attrib.*

Hallelujah, -iah (hælĭlū·yă), *interj.* and *sb.*¹ 1535. [a. Heb. *hallělū-yāh* 'praise (ye) Jah (= Jehovah)'; see prec.] The exclam. 'Praise (ye) the Lord (Jah, or Jehovah)', which occurs in many psalms and anthems; hence, a song of praise to God; = ALLELUIA *interj.* and *sb.*¹

And the Empyrean rung with Halleluiahs MILT. *Comb.*: **H. Chorus**, a musical composition based on the word 'hallelujah'; **h.-lass**, a female member of the Salvation Army.

Hence **Ha:lleluja·tic, -iatic** *a.* of or pertaining to the h. So †**Hallelu·jous, -u·ious** *a.* QUARLES.

Hallelu·jah, *sb.*² = ALLELUIA *sb.*²

Hallidome: see HALI-.

†**Hallier.** 1479. [f. HALE *v.*¹] **1.** A hauler. –1642. **2.** A kind of net for catching birds. BRADLEY. **3.** Earlier form of HALYARD, q.v.

Ha·ll-mark, *sb.* 1721. [f. HALL *sb.* 6.] The official mark or stamp of the Goldsmiths' Company, used in marking the standard of gold and silver articles assayed by them; hence, generally, a mark used by Government assay offices for the same purpose. Also *fig.*

fig. The hall-mark of real military genius WOLSELEY. Hence **Hall-mark** *v.* to stamp with a hall-mark (*lit.* and *fig.*).

Hallo, halloa (hălōu·), *interj.* and *sb.* 1840. [A later form of HOLLO, q. v.] A shout or exclam. to call attention or to express surprise (e.g. on meeting some one unexpectedly). Cf. HALLOO.

Halloo (hălū·), *interj.* and *sb.* 1700. [Goes with HALLOO *v.*; perh. a var. of HOLLO *interj.*, suited to a prolonged cry.] An exclam. to incite dogs to the chase, to call attention at a distance, to express surprise, etc.

To horse! halloo! halloo! SCOTT. The far h. 1810.

Halloo (hălū·), *v.* 1568. [? f. prec., or var. of HALLOW *v.*[2]] **1.** *intr.* To shout 'halloo' to dogs in order to urge them on; *trans.* to urge on with shouts 1606. **2.** *intr.* To shout in order to attract attention 1722. **3.** *trans.* To shout (something) aloud 1602.

1. Old John halloos his hounds again PRIOR. 2. Phr. *Not to h. until one is out of the wood*, not to shout till one is safe from robbers in the forest; esp. *fig.* not to exult till danger or difficulty is past.

Hallow (hæ·lo^u), *sb.*[1]; usu. in pl. **hallows.** [OE. *hālga*, definite form of *hālig* adj. holy, used at length as an ordinary wk. sb.] **1.** A holy personage, a SAINT. (Now preserved only in ALL-HALLOWS and its combs., q. v.) **2.** In *pl.*, the shrines or relics of saints; the gods of the heathen or their shrines ME. **3.** HALLOW- in *Comb.* (chiefly in *Sc.*) is used for ALL-HALLOW- = All Saints'-, in HALLOW-E'EN, etc. 1795.

Hallow (hæ·lo^u), *sb.*[2] 1440. [f. HALLOW *v.*[2] Often identified in spelling with HALLOO, although differently stressed.] A loud shout or cry, to incite dogs in the chase, to assist combined effort, or to attract attention.

Hallow (hæ·lo^u), *v.*[1] [OE. *hālgian, -ode*, Com. Teut. deriv. of *heilag-* HOLY.] **1.** *trans.* To make holy; to sanctify. **2.** To consecrate, set apart (a person or thing) as sacred to God; to dedicate to some sacred or religious use or office; to bless a thing OE. †**b.** To consecrate (a person) to an office, as bishop, king, etc. –ME. **3.** To honour as holy (esp. God or his name) OE. **4.** *trans.* To keep (a day, festival, etc.) holy; to observe solemnly OE.

1. Those women whose teares Antiquitie hath hallowed 1638. 2. Leo..entered France..to h. the newly built church of his monastery FREEMAN. 3. Our father..hallowed be thy name *Matt.* vi. 9. 4. To h. the Sabboth day ABP. HAMILTON.

Hallow (hæ·lo^u), *v.*[2] [ME. *halowen*, prob. f. OF. *halloer* to pursue crying or shouting.] **1.** *trans.* To pursue with shouts; to urge on with shouts; to call or summon *in, back*, etc. with shouting. **2.** *intr.* To shout, in order to urge on dogs to the chase, attract attention, etc. ME. **3.** *trans.* To shout (something) aloud ME.

1. They [fox hounds] were then halloed back 1812. 2. The shepherd him pursues, and to his dog doth halow DRAYTON. 3. H. your name to the reuerberate hilles SHAKS.

Hallow-e'en. *Sc.* 1556. [Shortened from *All-hallow-even*; see ALL-HALLOW.] The eve of All Hallows' or All Saints'; the last night of October. Also *attrib.*

In the Old Celtic calendar the last night of October was 'old year's night', the night of all the witches, which the Church transformed into the Eve of All Saints.

Hallowmas (hæ·lomæ̆s). ME. [Shortened from *All-hallow-mass*; see ALL-HALLOW.] The feast of All Hallows or All Saints. Also *attrib.*

She came adorned hither like sweet May; Sent back like H., or short'st of day SHAKS.

†**Ha·llow-tide.** 1450. [Shortened from *All-hallow-tide*; see ALL-HALLOW.] The season of All Saints; the first week of November –1609.

Halloysite (hăloi·zəit). 1827. [f. *d'Halloy*, a Belgian geologist; see -ITE.] *Min.* A clay-like earthy mineral, a hydrated aluminium silicate, resulting from the decomposition of felspar.

Hallucal (hæ·liukăl), *a.* 1889. [f. HALLUX (*halluc-*) + -AL.] *Anat.* Of or belonging to the hallux or great toe. So **Ha·llucar** *a.* in same sense.

Hallucinate (hălˈiū·sineˈt), *v.* 1604. [f. pa. ppl. stem of L. (*h*)*allucinari* to wander in mind, talk idly. Cf. F. *halluciner.*] †**1.** *trans.* To deceive (*rare*) –1623. **2.** *intr.* To be deceived, entertain false notions, blunder, mistake. *Obs.* or *arch.* 1652. **3.** *trans.* To affect with hallucination 1822.

Hallucination (hălˈiūsinēˈ·ʃən). 1646. [ad. late L. *alucinationem* (*all-, hall-*); see prec. Cf. F. *hallucination.*] **1.** The condition of being deceived or mistaken, or of entertaining unfounded notions; with *a.* and *pl.*, an illusion 1652. **2.** *Path.* and *Psych.* The apparent perception of an external object when no such object is present. (Dist. from *illusion*, as not necessarily involving a false belief.)

1. Reason..swept away by the hallucinations of sentiment 1856. 2. The most celebrated men have been liable to hallucinations, without their conduct offering any sign of mental alienation 1859. So **Hallu·cinative** *a.* productive of h. **Hallu·cinator,** one who hallucinates. **Hallu·cinatory** *a.* characterized by, pertaining to, or of the nature of h.

‖**Hallux** (hæ·lŏks). *Pl.* **halluces** (hæ·liŭsīz). 1831. [mod.L., corrupted from *allex* (*allic-*) the great toe.] *Anat.* The innermost of the digits (normally five) of the hind foot of an air-breathing vertebrate; the great toe; in birds (when present) usually either the inner or the hind toe.

Halm: see HAULM.

‖**Halma** (hæ·lmă). 1890. [a. Gr. ἅλμα leap.] A game played on a checker-board of 256 squares, by two persons with 19 men each, or four persons with 13 each, the characteristic move consisting of a leap over any man in an adjacent square into a vacant square beyond, or of a series of such leaps. Named also *hoppity.*

Halo (hēˈ·lo), *sb.* *Pl.* **haloes, halos** (also **halones**). 1563. [= F. *halo*, ad. L. *halos*, a. Gr. ἅλως threshing-floor, disk of the sun, moon, or a shield.] **1.** A circle of light, either white or prismatically coloured, seen round a luminous body and caused by the refraction of light through vapour; *spec.* that seen round the sun or moon. **b.** Applied to other circular luminous appearances; hence, to other things in the form of a circle or a ring 1813. **c.** = AREOLA 3. 1706. **2.** The circle or disk of light with which the head is surrounded in representations of Christ and the Saints; a nimbus 1646. **3.** *fig.* The ideal glory with which a person or thing is invested by feeling or sentiment 1813.

3. A gilded h. hovering round decay BYRON. Hence **Ha·lo** *v.* to surround, encompass, or invest with a h. **Ha·loed** *ppl. a.* surrounded or invested with a h.

Halogen (hæ·loˌdʒen). 1842. [mod. f. Gr. ἅλς, ἁλο- salt + -GEN; cf. F. *halogène.*] *Chem.* An element or substance which forms a salt by direct union with a metal. The halogens are chlorine, fluorine, bromine, iodine, and the compound cyanogen. Hence **Halo·genated** *a.* combined with a h. **Halo·genous** *a.* of the nature of a h.

Haloid (hæ·loid, hæ·loˌid). 1841. [f. Gr. ἅλς salt + -OID.] *Chem.*

A. *adj.* Having a composition like that of common salt (sodium chloride, Na Cl); applied to all salts formed by the simple union of a halogen with a metal, as potassium iodide, KI.

B. *sb.* A salt of this nature 1846.

Ha·lomancy. 1864. [f. Gr. ἁλο- salt + μαντεία, -MANCY.] Divination by means of salt.

Halometer (hălǫ·mĭtəɹ). 1854. [f. as prec. + -METER.] An instrument for measuring the external form, angles, and planes of the crystals of salts.

Halotrichite (hælǫ·trikəit). 1849. [f. as prec. + -ITE.] *Min.* Iron alum, occurring in yellowish-white, fibrous masses.

Haloxylin, -ine (hælǫ·ksilin). 1883. [f. Gr. ἁλο- salt + ξύλον wood + -IN.] An explosive, in which a powdered cellulose substance and a rapid explosive are added to charcoal and saltpetre.

Halp, obs. pa. t. of HELP.

†**Halpace, haltpace.** 1507. [a. 16th c. Fr. *hault pas, haut pas*, lit. 'high step'.] = HAUT-PAS; HALF-PACE 1. –1587.

Halse, hals, *sb.* Now *Sc.* and *n. dial.* [Com. Teut.: OE. *hals, heals* :—OTeut. **hol-so-z* :—pre-Teut. **kolsos*; cf. L. *collum*, from **colsus.*] **1.** The neck. **2.** The throat, gullet 1440. †**3.** *transf.* A narrow neck of land or channel of water –1536.

†**Halse,** *v.*[1] [OE. *halsian, healsian* :—OTeut. **hailosōjan*, f. **hailos* weal, well-being; see HEAL *sb.*] **1.** *intr.* To augur, divine, soothsay. OE. only. **2.** *trans.* To call upon in the name of something divine or holy; to exorcize, adjure, conjure; to beseech –1553. **3.** To hail, salute, greet –1596.

Halse, *v.*[2] *Obs.* exc. *Sc.* (hās, hǫs). ME. [?f. *hals*, HALSE, neck, or f. prec., influenced by HALSE *sb.*] *trans.* To embrace. Also *transf.* and *fig.*

Halser, obs. f. HAWSER.

Halt (hǫlt), *sb.*[1] Also †**alt.** 1591. [Orig. in phr. *to make halt* = Ger. *halt machen*, f. *halt* 'hold', holding, stoppage, stand.] A temporary stoppage on a march or journey. **b.** A railway stopping-place for local services only and without regular station buildings, etc. 1910. Hence **Ha·ltless** *a.*

The distant foe..In motion or in alt MILT.

Halt, *sb.*[2] 1599. [f. HALT *v.*[1] and *a.*] **1.** A halting or limping, a limp (*arch.*). **2.** The disease foot-rot in sheep 1750.

Halt (hǫlt), *a.* *arch.* and *literary.* [Com. Teut.: OE. *halt, healt* :—OTeut. **halt-oz.*] Lame; crippled; limping.

Halt (hǫlt), *v.*[1] [OE. *haltian, healtian*, f. HALT *a.*] **1.** *intr.* To be lame, walk lame, limp (*arch.*). †**2.** To cease haltingly *from* (a way or course); to fall away –1613. **3.** To walk unsteadily or hesitatingly; to waver; to remain in doubt ME. **4.** *fig.* To proceed 'lamely'; to be at fault; to be defective, as a syllogism, metaphor, verse; not to go 'on all fours' ME. †**5.** To play false –1600.

1. I am ready to h. *Ps.* xxxviii. 17. 3. How long h. ye between two opinions 1 *Kings* xviii. 21. 4. The Lady shall say her minde freely; or the blanke Verse shall h. for it SHAKS.

Halt (hǫlt), *v.*[2] Also †**alt.** 1656. [f. HALT *sb.*[1]] **1.** *intr.* To make a halt. (At first a military term only, but occas. in later use = 'stop'.) **b.** *Mil.* In the imperative 1796. **2.** *trans.* To cause to halt 1805.

Halter (hǫ·ltəɹ), *sb.*[1] [OE. *hælftre* :-WGer. **halftra-*, f. root **halƀ-*, whence OE. *helfe*; see HELVE. Primarily 'that by which anything is held'.] **1.** A rope, cord, or strap with a noose or headstall, by which horses or cattle are led or fastened up. **2.** A rope with a noose for hanging malefactors 1460. Also *fig.* **b.** Used typically for death by hanging 1533.

2. A h. gratis, nothing else for Gods sake SHAKS. b. Threats of jail and h. TENNYSON.

Ha·lter, *sb.*[2] 1440. [f. HALT *v.*[1] + -ER [1].] One who halts or limps; a waverer 1611.

Ha·lter, *v.* 1440. [f. HALTER *sb.*[1]] **1.** *trans.* To put a halter upon; to fasten *up* with a halter. Also *fig.* **2.** To catch or entrap with a noose or lasso 1573. **3.** To put a halter about the neck of (a person); to hang with a halter. Also *fig.* 1616.

3. *fig.* Suffered to have rope enough, till they had haltered themselves in a Præmunire FULLER.

‖**Halteres** (hæltī^ə·rīz), *sb. pl.* Also **alteres.** 1533. [Gr. ἁλτῆρες (in sense 1), f. ἅλλεσθαι to leap.] **1.** Weights held in the hand to give an impetus in leaping. **2.** *Entom.* The pair of knobbed filaments, also called *balancers* and *poisers*, which in dipterous insects take the place of a pair of posterior wings 1823.

†**Halter-sack.** 1598. [f. HALTER *sb.*[1] + SACK.] A 'gallows-bird'; a term of obloquy –1616.

Ha·lting, *ppl. a.* ME. [f. HALT *v.*[1] + -ING [2].] **1.** That halts or limps; *fig.* maimed; defective 1533. **2.** Wavering 1585.

1. That h. slave, who in Nicopolis Taught Arrian M. ARNOLD. Hence **Ha·ltingly** *adv.*, -**ness.**

Ha·lvans, *sb. pl.* 1849. [Deriv. of *half, halve.*] Refuse ore.

Halve (hāv), *v.* [ME. *halfen, halven*, f. HALF *sb.*] **1.** *trans.* To divide into two equal parts; to share equally; to deal *out*, take, or complete the half of; to reduce to half. Also *fig.* **2.** *Carpentry.* To fit (timbers) together by HALVING, q.v. Also *intr.* for *pass.* 1804. †**3.** *intr.* To render half service –1680.

1. The fervid Sun had more than halved the day COLERIDGE. *To h. a hole, a round, a match* (Golf). Hence **Halved** (hāvd), **Ha·lving** *ppl. adjs.*

Halver (hā·vəɹ). 1517. [f. prec. + -ER [1].] **1.** One who halves or has a half-share 1625. **2.** (usu. *pl.*) A half-share (*Sc.* and *dial.*).

Halving (hā·viŋ), *vbl. sb.* ME. [f. HALVE *v.*] **1.** The action of HALVE *v.* **2.** *Carpentry,* A method of fitting two pieces of timber together by cutting out half the thickness of each, so as to let them into each other 1842.

Halwe, obs. f. HALLOW.

Halyard, halliard, haulyard (hæ·lyăɹd, hǭ·l-). ME. [orig. *halier, hallyer*, same as HALLIER, f. HALE *v.*; perverted by association with *yard.*] *Naut.* A rope or tackle used for raising or lowering a sail, yard, etc.

Ham (hæm), *sb.*[1] [OE. *ham(m, hom(m*, str. f.; app. f. an OTeut. **ham-, *hamm-* to be crooked.] **1.** That part of the leg at the back of the knee; hence **b.** the back of the thigh; the thigh and buttock collectively (usu. in *pl.*) 1552; **c.** in quadrupeds, the back of the hough; the hough 1607. **2.** The thigh of a slaughtered animal, used for food; *spec.* that of a hog salted and dried; also, the meat so prepared 1637.

1. With supple h. and pliant knee 1679. **b.** Squatting on their hams 1875. **2.** *attrib.*, as *h.-pie*, etc.

Ham, *sb.*[2] The OE. *hām* HOME, as in *Hampstead, Hampton* (:—*Hāmtūn*), *Oakham*, etc., and, in the shortened form *ham*, sometimes used by historical writers in the sense 'town, village, or manor' of the OE. period.

Hamadryad (hæmădrəi·ăd). *Pl.* **-ads**; also in L. form **-ades** (-ădīz). ME. [ad. L. *Hamadryas*, a. Gr. Ἁμαδρυάς, chiefly in pl. *Hamadryades*, Ἁμαδρυάδες wood-nymphs, f. ἅμα together + δρῦς tree.] **1.** *Gr.* and *L. Mythol.* A wood-nymph fabled to live and die with the tree which she inhabited. **2.** *Zool.* **a.** A large, very venomous, hooded serpent of India (*Naja hamadryas*, or *Hamadryas* (*Ophiophagus*) *elaps*), allied to the cobra 1863. **b.** A large baboon of Abyssinia (*Cynocephalus hamadryas*) 1894.

Hamate (hē¹·mĕ¹t), *a.* 1744. [ad. L. *hamatus*, f. *hamus* hook; see -ATE [2].] Furnished with hooks, or hook-shaped; hooked. (Chiefly in *Nat. Hist.*) So **Ha·mated** *a.*

Hamber-line (hæ·mbəɹ ləin). 1853. [corruption of *Hamburgh.*] *Naut.* Small line for seizings, lashings, etc.

Hamble, *v. Obs.* exc. *dial.* [OE. *hamelian* to mutilate, f. (ult.) an adj. appearing in OHG. as *hamal* maimed.] **1.** *trans.* To mutilate, maim; to dock; *spec.* to cut off the balls of the feet of (dogs) so as to render them unfit for hunting. (Erron. taken in 17–18th c. as = *Hamstring.*) **2.** *intr.* To walk lame (*dial.*) 1828.

Hamburg, -burgh (hæ·mbɒɪg, -bɒ̈ɹō). 1838. [*Hamburg*, a city of North Germany.] **1.** (Also *Hamburg grape*) A black variety of grape which is specially adapted to hothouse cultivation. **2.** Name of a small variety of the domestic fowl 1857.

Hame (hē¹m). ME. [Perh. f. an OTeut. root **ham-* to hold against, hinder.] Each of two curved pieces of wood or metal placed over, fastened to, or forming, the collar of a draught horse.

Hame, obs. and Sc. f. HOME.

Hamel. *Obs.* exc. *dial.* 1514. [a. OF. *hamel* (mod. *hameau*), dim. of **ham*, a. WGer. *haim* village, dwelling, HOME.] = HAMLET.

Hamel, var. of HAMBLE.

Hamesucken, †-soken (hē¹·msɒk'n). [OE., f. *hām* home, dwelling + *sōcn* fem., seeking, visiting, attack, assault.] *O.E.* and *Sc. Law.* **1.** The crime of assaulting a person in his own house or dwelling-place. Now only in Sc. Law. **2.** A franchise of holding pleas of this offence and receiving the penalties imposed on the offender; also the penalty itself. (Variously misunderstood.) OE. So †**Ha·mfare** [f. OE. *hām* + *faru* going] = sense 1.

Hamiform (hē¹·mifǭɹm), *a.* 1849. [f. L. *hamus*; see -FORM.] Hook-shaped.

Hamiltonian (hæmiltōu·niăn), *a.* (*sb.*) 1826. [f. the surname *Hamilton* + -IAN.] **1. a.** Pertaining to James Hamilton (1769–1831), or to his system of teaching languages. **b.** Pertaining to the Scottish philosopher and logician, Sir William Hamilton (1788–1856). **c.** Pertaining to or invented by the Irish mathematician, Sir William Rowan Hamilton (1805–65), as *Hamiltonian equation, function*, etc. **d.** Pertaining to or holding the doctrines of the American statesman, Alexander Hamilton, a leader of the Federalist party (1757–1804). **2.** *sb.* A follower of any of these.

Hamite (hæ·məit), *sb.*[1] and *a.* Also †**Chamite,** †**Khamite.** 1645. [f. *Ham* (formerly spelt *Cham*, Gr. Χάμ, L. *Cham*), name of the second son of Noah (Gen. vi. 10) + -ITE.]

A. *sb.* †**1.** A follower of Ham; a term of obloquy. (Cf. Gen. ix. 22–5.) PAGITT. **2.** A descendant of Ham (cf. Gen. ix. 18, 19); an Egyptian, or an African negro 1854.

B. *adj.* = Hamitic (see below) 1842.

Hence **Hamitic** (hæmi·tik) *a.* belonging to the Hamites; esp. applied to a group comprising the ancient Egyptian, and the Berber, Galla, and allied extant languages.

Hamite (hē¹·məit), *sb.*[2] 1832. [ad. mod.L. generic name *Hamites*, f. *hamus* hook; see -ITE.] A fossil cephalopod having a shell of a hooked shape.

Hamlet (hæ·mlĕt). [ME. *hamelet*, a. OF. *hamelet*, secondary dim. of *hamel*; see HAMEL.] A group of houses or small village in the country; *esp.* a village without a church. **b.** *transf.* The people of a hamlet (*poet.*) 1726.

A small village or h., where..some thirty or forty families dwelt together SCOTT. Hence **Ha·mleted** *a.* located in a h.

‖**Hammam, hummaum** (hɒmā·m). 1625. [Arab.] An Oriental bathing establishment, a Turkish bath.

Hammer (hæ·məɹ), *sb.* [Com. Teut.: OE. *hamor, -er, hǫmer* = ON. *hamarr*, etc. The Norse sense 'crag', and possible relationship to Slav. *kamy*, Russ. *kamenĭ* stone, point to an orig. meaning 'stone hammer'.] **1.** An instrument having a hard solid head, usu. of metal, set transversely to the handle, used for beating, breaking, driving nails, etc. Hence, a machine in which a heavy block of metal is used for the same purpose (see STEAM-HAMMER, etc.). **b.** *fig.* A person or agency that smites, beats down, or crushes, as with blows of a hammer. Cf. L. *malleus.* ME. **2.** *spec.* Anything in form or action resembling a hammer. **a.** A lever with a hard head arranged so as to strike a bell, as in a clock 1546. †**b.** The knocker of a door –1627. **c.** *Fire-arms.* (*a*) In a flint-lock, a piece of steel covering the flash-pan and struck by the flint; (*b*) in a percussion-lock, a spring lever which strikes the percussion-cap on the nipple; (*c*) applied to analogous contrivances in modern guns. 1590. **d.** A small bone of the ear; the malleus 1615. **e.** A small hammer or mallet used by auctioneers to indicate by a rap the sale of an article 1717. †**3.** A disease in cattle –1688. **4.** A match at throwing the hammer (*mod.*).

1. Mechanicke Slaues With greazie Aprons, Rules, and Hammers SHAKS. Phr. *Throwing the h.*, an athletic contest, consisting in throwing a heavy h. as far as possible. **b.** Saladinus..þe strong hamer of Cristen men TREVISA. The h. of affliction 1679. **2. e.** Phr. *To bring* (*send, put up*) *to the h.*; *to go* or *come to* or *under the h.*, to be sold by auction.

Phrases. *H. and tongs* (colloq.): with might and main (like a blacksmith smiting the iron taken with the tongs from the forge-fire). *Thor's h., h. of Thor*: (*a*) the h. carried by the god Thor in Norse mythology; (*b*) = FYLFOT; (*c*) a prehistoric ornament resembling a h.

Comb.: **h.-fish,** the h.-headed shark; **-harden** *v.*, to harden (metals) by hammering; **-mill,** a mill driving a h. in a small forge; **-oyster** = *hammer-shell*; **-scale,** the coating of oxide which forms on red-hot iron and can be separated by hammering (also called *forge-scale*); **-sedge,** *Carex hirta*; **-shark,** the h. headed shark; **-shell,** the h.-shaped shell of a bivalve mollusc of the genus *Malleus* (also called *hammer-oyster*); **-slag, -slough** = *hammer-scale*; **-stone,** a prehistoric stone implement resembling, or used as, a h.; **-toe,** persistent angular flexion of a toe; **-work,** (*a*) work performed with a h.; (*b*) something constructed or shaped with the h.; **-wrought** *a.*

Hammer, *v.* ME. [f. prec. sb.]

I. *trans.* **1.** To strike, beat, or drive with or as with a hammer; to fasten with or as with a hammer 1450; to beat out or shape with a hammer 1522. **2.** *fig.* **a.** To put into shape with much intellectual effort. Often with *out.* ('Used commonly in contempt' J.) 1583. †**b.** To debate. CAREW. **c.** To drive by dint of repetition (as an idea, etc. into a person's head) 1646. **d.** *Stock Exchange slang.* (*a*) To declare (a person) a defaulter 1887. (*b*) To depress (prices, a market) 1865.

1. Armillæ of pure gold, hammered into rounded bars 1851. **2. a.** To h. out an excuse 1751. **c.** Hammering common sense into his head 1866. **d.** The head Stock Exchange waiter strikes three strokes with a mallet..before making formal declaration of default of a member. Thus, to be 'hammered' is to be pronounced a defaulter. 1887.

II. *intr.* **1.** To deal blows with or as with a hammer; to thump ME. **2.** *fig.* †**a.** To devise plans laboriously, 'cudgel one's brains' (*upon, on, at, of*); with *upon*, sometimes, To reiterate, insist upon –1777. †**b.** Of an idea: To be in agitation –1667. **c.** To work hard, toil. Const. *at.* 1755. **3.** To stammer. Now only *dial.* 1619.

1. Hammering away with a geologist's hammer 1886. **2. a.** That Whereon, this month I haue bin hamering SHAKS. **b.** Blood, and reuenge, are Hammering in my head SHAKS.

Hence **Ha·mmerable** *a.* (*rare*), malleable.

Ha·mmer-beam. 1823. *Arch.* A short beam projecting from the wall at the foot of a principal rafter in a roof, in place of a tie-beam.

Hammer-cloth. 1465. A cloth covering the driver's seat or box in a state or family coach.

Hammerer (hæ·mərəɹ). 1611. [f. HAMMER *v.* + -ER [1].] **1.** One who hammers or wields a hammer; often, a geologist. **2.** 'The three-wattled bell-bird of Costa Rica, *Chasmorhynchus tricarunculatus*' (Cent. Dict.).

Ha·mmer-head. 1532. **1.** The striking part of a hammer 1562. †**2.** A blockhead. (Cf. *beetle-head.*) –1628. **3. a.** A hammer-headed shark; so called from the great lateral expansions of the head 1880. **b.** An American fish, *Hypentelium nigricans*, having a hammer-shaped head 1861. **4.** An African bird, the shadow-bird or umber-bird (*Scopus umbretta*); from the shape of the head 1890. Hence **Ha·mmer-hea:ded** *a.* having a hammer-shaped head; *fig.* stupid.

Ha·mmerless, *a.* 1875. [f. HAMMER *sb.* + -LESS.] Without a hammer; *esp.* of a gun.

Hammerman (hæ·məɹmæ̆n). 1483. A man who works with a hammer; *esp.* a smith or worker in metal; also, a blacksmith's striker. So **Ha·mmersmith.**

‖**Hammochrysos** (hæmǫkrəi·sǫs). 1706. [L. (Pliny), a. Gr., f. ἄμμος sand + χρυσός gold.] *Min.* A sparkling stone mentioned by the ancients; perhaps yellow micaceous schist, or the sand from it.

Hammock (hæ·mək). 1555. [Earlier *hamaca*, a. Sp. *hamaca*, of Carib origin; cf. F. *hamac.*] **1.** A hanging bed, consisting of a large piece of canvas, netting, etc. suspended by cords at both ends; used esp. on board ship, also in hot seasons on land. **2.** *transf.* Applied to the suspended case made by the caterpillars of certain moths, etc. 1859. †**3.** A cloth for the back of a horse. 1690.

1. Theyr hangynge beddes whiche they caule Hamacas EDEN.

Comb.: **h.-chair,** a folding reclining-chair with canvas support for the body; **-nettings,** *orig.* rope nettings in which the hammocks were stowed away on board ship, these being lashed or hung to the **h.-rails** above the bulwarks; hence, the long troughs afterwards constructed for this purpose on the top of the bulwarks of the spar-deck in a man-of-war; **-shroud,** a h. used as a shroud in which to bury a corpse at sea.

Hamose (hēⁱmōᵘ·s), *a.* 1709. [ad. L. type **hamosus*, f. *hamus.*] Having hooks, hooked. So **Ha·mous** *a.* ? *Obs.*

Hamper (hæ·mpəɹ), *sb.*[1] ME. [A phonetic reduction of HANAPER; cf. *ampersand.*] **1.** A large basket, with a cover, generally used as a packing-case. In earlier use a case or casket generally; but from 1500 usu. of wickerwork. **b.** *U. S.* In New York, an oyster-basket holding two bushels; in Virginia, a measure of small fish holding about a bushel (*Cent. Dict.*). †**2.** = HANAPER 3. -1714.

2. An annuity of 180 Marks out of the H. 1714.

Ha·mper, *sb.*[2] 1613. [f. HAMPER *v.*[1]] †**1.** Something that hampers; a shackle -1624. **2.** *Naut.* Things which form a necessary part of the equipment of a vessel, but are in the way at times. (See TOP-HAMPER.) 1835.

Hamper (hæ·mpəɹ), *v.*[1] ME. [? from a radical *ham-* (? *hamm-*); cf. Ger. *hemmen*, etc., to restrain, clog. The ending is freq. or dim.] **1.** *trans.* To obstruct the free movement of by fastening something on, or by obstacles or entanglements; to fasten, bind, fetter, shackle, clog; to entangle, catch (*in* something). **b.** To derange (a lock, etc.) so as to impede its working 1804. **2.** *fig.* and *gen.* To obstruct or impede in action; †to fetter; to entangle, encumber, or embarrass. (Now the common use.) ME. **3.** To pack up ME.

1. Such a novice, as to be still hamper'd in his owne hempe MILT. **2.** I believe no officer at the head of the army was ever so hampered WELLINGTON. The builder was hampered by the existence of aisles FREEMAN. Hence **Ha·mperer.**

Ha·mper, *v.*[2] 1603. [f. HAMPER *sb.*[1]] **1.** *trans.* To load or present with a hamper or hampers (*joc.*). **2.** To pack in a hamper 1775.

Hamshackle (hæ·mʃæk'l), *v.* 1802. [perh. f. radical *ham-*, as in HAMPER *v.*[1] + SHACKLE *v.*; but ?] *trans.* To shackle (a horse or cow) by a rope or strap connecting the head with one of the forelegs; hence *fig.* to fetter, curb, restrain.

Hamster (hæ·mstəɹ). 1607. [a. Ger. *hamster.*] A species of rodent (*Cricetus frumentarius*) allied to the mouse and rat, found in parts of Europe and Asia; it is of a stout form, about 10 inches long, and has cheek-pouches for carrying grain to its burrows; it hibernates during the winter. **b.** The fur of the hamster 1895.

Hamstring (hæ·mstriŋ), *sb.* 1565. [f. HAM *sb.*[1] + STRING *sb.*] **a.** In human anatomy, one of the tendons which form the sides of the ham or space at the back of the knee; they are the tendons of the muscles of the thigh. **b.** In quadrupeds, the great tendon at the back of the hough in the hind leg; it is the *tendo Achillis*, corresponding to that of the heel in man.

Hamstring (hæ·mstriŋ), *v.* Pa. t. and pple. **-stringed** (-striŋd), **-strung** (-strʊŋ). 1641. [f. prec. sb.] **1.** *trans.* To cut the hamstrings of, so as to lame or disable 1675. **2.** *transf.* and *fig.* To cripple, destroy the activity or efficiency of 1641.

2. So they have hamstrung the valour of the subject by seeking to effeminate us all at home MILTON.

Hamular (hæ·miŭlăɹ), *a.* 1839. [f. L. *hamulus* small hook + -AR.] Of the form of a small hook, hooked; applied *spec.* in *Anat.* to processes of certain bones.

Hamulate (hæ·miŭlĕt), *a.* 1886. [f. as prec. + -ATE.] **a.** *Bot.* Having a small hook at the tip (*Syd. Soc. Lex.*); also = HAMULOSE a. **b.** *Anat.* = HAMULAR.

Hamulose (hæmiŭlōᵘ·s), *a.* 1860. [f. L. *hamulus* + -OSE.] **a.** Covered with little hooked hairs or bristles. **b.** Having a small hook, hamulate. var. **Ha·mulous.**

‖**Hamulus** (hæ·miŭlŏs). *Pl.* **-li** (-ləi). 1727. [L., dim. of *hamus.*] **a.** *Anat.*, *Zool.*, and *Bot.* A small hook or hook-like process, as in certain bones, in feathers, etc.; in *Bot.* a hooked bristle. **b.** *Obstetrics.* A hook-shaped instrument for extracting the fœtus. var. **Ha·mule** (in sense a).

Han = *haven*, obs. inf. and pres. t. pl. of HAVE *v.*

Hanap (hæ·næp). *Obs.* exc. *Hist.* 1494. [a. OF. *hanap* cup, ciborium :—OFrankish **hnapp-*.] A drinking-vessel, a wine-cup or goblet; now, a mediæval goblet of an ornate character.

Hanaper (hæ·năpəɹ). *Obs.* exc. *Hist.* 1440. [a. OF. *hanapier* case to hold a hanap; see prec. and HAMPER *sb.*[1]] †**1.** A case for a hanap or hanaps; a plate-basket; a repository for treasure or money -1576. **2.** A round wicker case or small basket in which documents were kept 1768. **3.** The department of the Chancery, into which fees were paid for the sealing and enrolment of charters and other documents. (? So called because documents that had passed the Great Seal were here kept in a hanaper (sense 2); or with reference to the hanaper (sense 1) in which the fees were kept.) 1455.

†**Ha·naster, ha·nster.** [ME. *hauncer, hanster*, perh. f. *hansa* or *hanse*; see HANSE.] The name given (in the city of Oxford) to persons paying the entrance-fee of the guild-merchant (see HANSE 2), and admitted as Freemen of the City -1608.

Hance (hans), *sb.* 1534. [perh. a. AF. **haunce* = OF. *hauce, haulce*, later *hausse*, rise, raised part, f. *hausser*; see HANCE *v.*] †**1.** The lintel of a door or window -1618. **2.** *Naut.* **a.** A curved rise, as of the fife-rails or bulwarks from the waist to the quarter-deck. Also erron. *hanch* or *haunch*. **b.** = HAUNCH. 1637. **3.** *Arch.* The arc of smaller radius at the springing of an elliptical or many-centred arch. Now usu. viewed as the HAUNCH of the arch, and so spelt. 1703.

†**Hance,** *v.* [ME. *haunce*, app. a. AF. **hauncer* for OF. *haucer, haulcer* (mod. *hausser*) to raise. Cf. ENHANCE.] *trans.* = ENHANCE 1, 2. -1583.

Hand (hænd), *sb.* [Com. Teut.: OE. *hand, hǫnd*, fem. *u*-stem. Some connect it with Goth. *-hinþan* to seize; but this is doubtful.]

I. 1. The terminal part of the arm below the wrist, consisting of the palm and five digits, forming the organ of prehension characteristic of man. Also applied to the terminal members of all four limbs in the quadrumanous animals or monkeys. **b.** The terminal part of the fore-limb in quadrupeds, esp. when prehensile, or of any limb of an animal when prehensile. In *Anat.* and *Zool.*, the terminal part of the 'arm' or fore-limb in all vertebrates above fishes; also, the prehensile claw or chela in crustaceans. ME. †**c.** *transf.* The whole arm -1751. †**d.** The trunk of an elephant -1859. **e.** *fig.* 1592. **2.** Used to denote possession, custody, charge, authority, power, disposal OE. **b.** *Roman Law.* The power of the husband over his wife (tr. L. *manus*) 1875. **3.** = Agency, instrumentality OE. **b.** Part or share in the doing of something 1597. **4.** Side (right or left); hence *gen.*, side, direction, quarter. Also *fig.* (*arch.* or *dial.*) OE. **5.** As used in making a promise or oath; *spec.* as the symbol of troth-plight in marriage; pledge of marriage; bestowal in marriage ME. †**6.** Hence in oaths and asseverations -1636.

1. Moyses helde up his hond ME. The Gorilla's h. is clumsier..than that of a man; but no one has ever doubted its being a true h. HUXLEY. **d.** The brutes of mountain back..with their serpent hands TENNYSON. **e.** The griping Hands of the Law 1724. **2.** Phr. *In* (*into, to*, etc.) *the hands of, in other hands.* **3.** To suffer *by the hands of* the hangman 1639. **b.** Phr. *To have a h. in.* **4.** The mountains on either h. 1884. Phr. *On* (*upon, in, of*) *the mending h.* (fig.), i.e. in the way to mend or recover, getting better. **5.** Have here min honde, I shal the wedde GOWER. **6.** Tarry good Beatrice, by this h. I loue thee SHAKS.

II. As repr. the person. **1.** Often denoting the person in relation to his action 1590; hence *spec.* the person himself, *esp.* an artist, musician, writer, etc. 1644. **2.** One employed to do any manual work 1655; *spec.* each of the sailors belonging to a ship's crew 1669. **3.** *colloq.* Used (with defining adj.) of a person with reference to his ability or skill in doing something. (See also OLD *hand.*) Usu. with *at.* 1792. **b.** Used similarly in reference to a person's action or character. (*colloq.* or *slang.*) 1798. †**4.** Used of or in reference to a person as the source from which something is obtained (see quots.) -1811. **b.** With ordinal numerals, indicating a series of so many persons through whom something passes ME.

1. Except some charitable h. reclaimes him 1615. Paintings, by the most celebrated Hands 1696. **2.** All hands on board perished SCORESBY. **3.** I am a bad h. at criticising men J. H. NEWMAN. **b.** A cool h. 1860. **4.** I have heard it..from good hands 1614. †*At the best h.*, most profitably or cheaply. **b.** I had it [the tale] at the second h. 1589.

III. As put for its capacity or performance. **1.** Skill in doing with the hand, and hence in doing generally; ability, knack ME. **2.** *Horsemanship.* Skill in handling the reins, etc. ME. **b.** Used for a division of the horse into two parts (see quot.) 1727. **3.** The performance of an artist, etc.; handiwork; style of execution, 'touch'. †Also *concr.* Handiwork. 1667. **b.** Touch, stroke (in phr. *last h.*, etc.) 1648. **4.** *Games.* A turn, innings, etc. 17.. **5.** Handwriting; style of writing ME. **6.** Signature. *Obs.* or *arch.*, exc. in phrases in which *hand* is now understood more literally. 1534.

1. The 'hand for crust' which is denied to many cooks 1881. **2.** A jockey must therefore..have a h. for all sorts of horses 1881. **b.** The *fore-hand* includes the head, neck, and fore-quarters. The *hind-hand* is all the rest of the horse CHAMBERS. **3.** Carved work, the h. of famed artificers MILT. **b.** The compiler did not put his last h. to the work M. ARNOLD. **5.** A running h. 1576. He will recognize my h. LYTTON. **6.** In witness whereof, we have hereunto set our hands and seals 1726.

IV. Something like or of the size of a hand. **1.** An image or figure of a hand; *esp.* a conventional hand (☞) for drawing attention to something OE. **2.** The pointer or index on a dial, esp. that of a clock or watch 1575. **3.** A lineal measure, formerly three inches, now four; a palm, a HANDBREADTH. Now used only in giving the height of horses, etc. 1561. **4.** As a measure of various commodities; e.g. a bundle of tobacco leaves tied together; a cluster of bananas; etc. 1726. **5.** *Cookery.* A shoulder of pork 1825.

2. *Rom. & Jul.* II. iv. 119.

V. That which is held in the hand. **1.** *Cards.* The cards dealt to each player 1630. **b.** The person holding the cards 1589. **c.** A single round in a game 1622. **d.** *fig.* 1600. †**2.** A handle -1764; the part of a gun grasped by the hand 1881.

1. d. To PLAY *into the hands of another*, to FORCE *the h. of*, to SHOW *one's h.*, etc. (see the vbs.).

Phrases. * *With governing prep.* **At hand. a.** Near, close by. **b.** Near in time. †**c.** At the start (*Jul. C.* IV. ii. 23). †**d.** = By hand (*John* V. ii. 75). †**e.** *At* (*on, upon*) *any h.*: on any account, in any case. So *at no h.*: on no account. †**f.** *At every h.*: on all hands. **g.** *At the hand(s of*: from the hands of; from. **By hand. a.** With the hand or hands; by manual action. **b.** *By the h.*: expeditiously. **For one's own hand.** For one's own benefit. **In hand. a.** *lit.* (Held or carried) in the hand. †**b.** *In h., in one's h.*: (led) by the hand, or by a string, etc. **c.** In actual possession, at one's disposal; †in early use, Subject to one; in one's charge; in custody. (Also *in hands.*) †**d.** In suspense (with *hold, keep*). **e.** In process; being actually dealt with. **f.** *In h.*: under control, subject to discipline. **g.** Preceded by a numeral: see FOUR-IN-HAND. †**h.** *In any h.*: in any case. **Of..hands. a.** *Of one's hands* (rarely *hand*): in respect of one's actions, of action, of valour in fight. †**b.** *Of all hands*: on all hands, on all sides; also, in any case (*L. L. L.* IV. iii. 219). **Off hand. a.** See OFF-HAND. **b.** *Off one's hand(s*: out of one's charge or control. **On hand, upon hand. a.** In one's possession, charge, or keeping. *To have on h.*: to have with one; to be charged with; to have in order to deal with or dispose of; to be engaged on. **b.** At hand; in attendance (*U. S.*). **c.** *On, upon one's hands* (rarely *hand*): resting upon one as a charge, burden, or responsibility, or as a thing to be dealt with or attended to. **d.** *On all hands, on every h.*: on all sides, from all quarters. **e.** *On* (*the*) *one h., on the other h.*: used to indicate two contrasted sides of a subject, circumstances, points of view, etc. **f.** *On any h.*: on any account, in any case. **Out of hand. a.** Straight off; extempore. **b.** The opposite of *in h.* (in various senses). **To hand. a.** Within reach, accessible; †near; into one's possession or presence. **b.** *To h., to one's h.*: into subjection, under control. **c.** *To* (*unto*) *one's hand(s*: ready for one. **Under hand. a.** Secretly; see UNDERHAND. **b.** *Under one's hand(s*: under one's action, charge, care, or treatment. **c.** *Under the h. of*: with the signature of.

** *With verb and preposition.* (See also *bear in h.* (BEAR *v.*), etc.) **Come to hand. a.** To come to one; to be received or obtained. **b.** *Come to* (*one's*) *hands*: to come to close quarters. **Take in hand,** †**on hand.** To undertake; occas. *spec.* to undertake the discipline, care, or cure of (a person).

*** *With verb governing* hand. (For BEAR *a h.*,

FORCE (*a person's*) *h.*, HOLD (*one's*) *h.*, JOIN *hands*, KISS *the h.*, LAY *hands on*, LEND *a h.*, SET *h.* (*to, on*), SHAKE *hands*, STRIKE *hands*, TRY *one's h.*, WASH *one's hands of*, etc., see the vbs.) **Change hands.** To substitute one hand for the other; to pass from one person's h. or possession to another's. **Give** (one's) **hand.** To hold out the h. to be grasped, in token of salutation, bargaining, etc.; †also *fig.* **Make a hand. a.** To make one's profit; to make a success *of*. Freq. with *fair, fine* (often ironical), *good*, etc. **b.** *To make a hand of* (*with*): to 'do for'. *Obs.* or *dial.* **Put** (one's) **hand.** To exert oneself; now always with *to*: to undertake (a piece of work).

**** *With adj. qualifying* hand. (For BLOODY *h.*, EVEN *h.*, FREE *h.*, HIGH *h.*, etc., see the adjs.) **Better hand.** †The 'upper hand'; precedence. **Clean hands.** *fig.* Freedom from wrongdoing.

***** *With an adverb.* **Hand in, out.** *To have one's h. in*: to be actively engaged; to be in practice. **Hands off!** *colloq.* Keep off! A peremptory order. **Hands up!** A direction to people to hold up their hands to signify assent, etc.; also, a robber's, policeman's, etc., order to preclude resistance. Also as vb.

****** *With another noun.* (See also HAND AND GLOVE, etc.) **Hand . . fist. a.** *H. over fist* (colloq.) = HAND OVER HAND. **b.** *H. to fist* (colloq.) = HAND TO HAND. **Hand and foot.** Usually (now always) in adverbial construction; esp. in phr. *to bind h. and foot* (also *fig.*). *To wait upon h. and foot*: to wait upon or serve assiduously. **Hand . . hand. a.** *From h. to h.*: from one person to another. **b.** *H. under h.*: the opposite of HAND OVER HAND. **Hand's turn.** A stroke of work.

******* Phr. **a.** *As bare, flat, as one's h.* **b.** *To have one's hands full*: to be fully occupied. **c.** *In the turn*(*ing of a h.*: in a moment. **d.** (*To win*) *hands down* (orig. in Racing): with little or no effort.

Combs. 1. *attrib.* **a.** Of or belonging to the hand, as *h.-clasp*, etc. **b.** Worn on the hand, as *h.-ruffle*, etc. **c.** Portable, as *h.-anvil, -camera, -lamp*, etc. **d.** Managed or worked by the hand (occas. *spec.* with one hand); driven or operated by manual power, as *h.-bellows, -brake, -pump*, etc. **e.** Made or done by hand, as *h.-embroidery*.

2. Special Combs.: **h.-alphabet**, an alphabet of signs made by the hands; **handbell**, a small bell rung by being swung by hand; **-car** (*U.S.*), a light car propelled by cranks or levers worked by hand, used in the inspection, etc. of a railway line; **-drop**, a name for the paralysis of the h., induced by the action of lead; **-fish**, a pediculate fish, having the pectoral fin articulated; **-flower**, the flower of the *hand-plant* (q.v.); **-gear**, the starting-gear of an engine; **-language**, the art of conversing by signs made with the hands; **-lead** (*Naut.*), a small lead used in taking soundings less than 20 fathoms; **-light** (*Gardening*), a bell-glass; **-mast**, a round spar, of at least 24, and not more than 72 inches in circumference; also *attrib.*; **-mule** (MULE[1] 4 a); **h. orchis**, a name for *Orchis maculata*, from the finger-like lobes of the tubers; **-pick** *v. trans.*, to pick by hand; also *fig.*; **-plant**, a Mexican tree (*Cheirostemon platanoides*, N.O. *Sterculiaceæ*), having large flowers with bright red stamens, which are united at the base and then spread in five finger-like bundles; **-post**, a guide-post at the parting of roads; a FINGER-POST; **-promise**, a solemn form of betrothal among the Irish peasantry; **-reading** = PALMISTRY; **-screw**, a jack; also *attrib.*; **-spring**, a somersault; **-swipe**, a shadoof worked by h. for raising water; **-tree** = *hand-plant*; **-wave** *v.*, to smooth the surface of (a measure of corn) with the h., instead of using a strike.

Hand (hænd), *v.* 1610. [f. prec. sb.] **1.** *trans.* To touch or grasp with the hand; to manipulate, handle; also *fig.* to treat of. *Obs.* exc. *techn.* **2.** *Naut.* To take in, furl (a sail) 1634. **3.** To lead or conduct by the hand; to assist with the hand 1631. **4.** To deliver or pass with the hand or hands 1650. **b.** *transf.* and *fig.* To deliver, pass, transfer, transmit. Now only with adverbs, as *down, on, over*. 1642. **5.** To join the hands of (*rare*) 1643. †**6.** *intr.* To go hand in hand. MASSINGER.

1. *Temp.* I. i. 25. 3. He hands her o'er the stile CLARE. 4. To h. over money 1816. **b.** A story handed by Tradition 1698. The father handed on the work KINGSLEY.

Hand and glove, (also with - -), *pred.* or *adj. phr.* Also (later) **hand in glove.** 1680. In constant close relations; on very intimate terms.

Ha·nd-ax, -axe. ME. An ax to be wielded with one hand; anciently a battle-ax.

Hand-ball. ME. **1.** A ball for throwing with the hand. **2.** A game played with such a ball in a space between two distant goals 1581. **3.** A hollow ball of india-rubber punctured so as to emit a spray when pressed in the hand 1888.

Hand-barrow. ME. [BARROW *sb.*[3]] A flat rectangular frame of transverse bars, having shafts before and behind, by which it is carried.

Handbi·ll[1]. 1523. [BILL *sb.*[1]] A light bill or pruning knife.

Ha·ndbill[2]. 1753. [BILL *sb.*[3]] A printed notice on a single page, to be delivered or circulated by hand.

Handbook (hæ·ndbuk). [OE. *handbōc, -bōk*, as tr. L. *manualis* and Gr.-L. *enchiridion*. The current wd. is after Ger. *handbuch*.] A small book or treatise, such as may be held in the hand: †**a.** in OE. The MANUAL of eccl. offices and ritual; **b.** *spec.* A book containing concise information for the tourist 1836. **c.** *U.S.* A betting book 1903.

Ha·ndbreadth. 1535. A unit of lineal measure, a PALM; formerly taken as three inches, but now as four. So **Ha·ndbrede.** (*Obs.* exc. *n. dial.*)

Ha·nd-ca·nter. 1836. [CANTER *sb.*[3]] A gentle, easy canter.

Ha·nd-cart. 1810. A small cart drawn or pushed by hand.

†**Ha·ndcraft.** OE. = HANDICRAFT 1. –1599. †**Ha·ndcraftman**, †**Ha·ndcraftsman.**

Handcuff (hæ·nd,kʊf), *sb.* Also *dial.* handy-. 1775. [HAND *sb.* + CUFF *sb.*[1]] A manacle, consisting of a divided metal ring which is locked round the wrist. Handcuffs are used in pairs, connected by a short chain or jointed bar. So **Ha·ndcuff** *v. trans.* to put handcuffs on; to manacle.

Handed (hæ·ndėd), *a.* 1526. [f. HAND + -ED.] **1.** Having hands; esp. as specified 1552. **2.** = PALMATE 1854. **3.** Joined hand in hand 1643.

1. H. moles 1791. [An] open-handed master 1894. 3. Into the inmost bower H. they went MILT.

Hander[1] (hæ·ndəɹ). 1678. [f. HAND *v.* + -ER[1].] One who hands, delivers, or passes. Also with *down, in, out*, etc.

Ha·nder[2]. 1868. [f. HAND *sb.* + -ER[1] 1.] **1.** A blow on the hand. **2.** *-hander* in comb., **a.** as BACK-HANDER, a back-handed blow; **b.** as *left-hander*, a left-handed man 1882.

†**Ha·ndfast,** *sb.* 1545. [app. f. HAND *sb.* + FAST *a.* Senses 3, 4, go with HANDFAST *v.*] **1.** Firm hold or grip with the hands; also *fig.* –1656. *In h.*, in hold, held fast. **2.** A handle, e.g. of a flail (*local*). BARING-GOULD. **3.** The joining of hands in making a bargain. MIDDLETON. **4.** A covenant; *spec.* a betrothal or marriage-contract –1884.

Ha·ndfast, *a.* ME. [orig. pa. pple. of HANDFAST *v.*] †**1.** Contracted by the joining of hands; espoused. Also 'betrothed by joining of hands in order to cohabitation before marriage'. –1610. †**2.** Bound; manacled –1632. **3.** Tight-fisted, close-fisted (*lit.* and *fig.*) 1603.

3. Ludlow, a common, h., honest..wooden man CARLYLE.

Handfast (hæ·ndfast), *v.* Pa. pple. **-ed**; in earlier use **handfast.** *Obs.* exc. *Hist.* [In sense 1, early ME. a. ON. *hand-festa*, f. *hand-* + *festa* to fasten, make fast, etc. In other senses f. *hand* and *fast*.] **1.** *trans.* To make a contract of marriage between (parties) by joining of hands; to betroth. Also *fig.* †**2.** To grasp, seize with the hand; to take fast hold of. Also *fig.* –1662. †**3.** To manacle –1611.

Ha·ndfasting, *vbl. sb.* *Obs.* exc. *Hist.* 1530. [f. prec. + -ING[1].] Betrothal. **b.** Formerly treated as an uncanonical, private, or even probationary form of marriage. See Jamieson s.v. 1541.

†**Ha·ndfastly,** *adv.* [-LY[2].] By solemn engagement made by joining hands; firmly. HOLINSHED.

Handful (hæ·ndful), *sb.* [OE. *handfull* str. fem.; in OE. and ME. a true sb.; hence in pl. *handfuls*, not *handsful*.] **1.** A quantity that fills the hand; as many as the hand can grasp or contain. **2.** A small company or number; a small amount. (Usu. *depreciative*.) 1525. †**3.** = HAND *sb.* IV. 3. –1737. **4.** *fig.* As much as one can manage 1755.

1. A handfull or two of dried pease SHAKS. 2. His Page at other side, that handfull of wit SHAKS. 3. A bay Gelding 14 h. high 1676. 4. The boy was a h. 1887.

Ha·nd-ga·llop. 1675. An easy gallop, in which the horse is kept well in hand. Also *fig.*

Han·d-glass. 1822. **1.** A magnifying glass held in the hand. **2.** *Hort.* A portable glass shade used for protecting or forcing a plant 1828. **3.** A small mirror with a handle 1882. **4.** A half-minute or quarter-minute sand-glass used for measuring the time in running out the log-line 1875.

Hand-grenade (hæ·nd,grėnē·d). 1661. **1.** An explosive missile, smaller than a bombshell, thrown by hand. Now usually spherical, and made of cast-iron. **2.** A glass bottle containing a chemical, to be broken in order to extinguish a fire 1895.

Handgrip. Also **-gripe, handy-, handi-grip**(e. [OE. *handgripe*, f. *gripan* to gripe, grip.] **1.** Grasp, seizure with the hand. **2.** Grip or firm pressure of the hand in greeting 1884.

†**Hand-habend,** *a.* (*sb.*) [Early ME. form of OE. **hand-hæbbend* 'hand-having'.] *O. E. Law.* Of a thief: Having (the thing stolen) in hand. Applied as *sb.* to the offence, and to the franchise of holding plea thereof. –1828.

Handhold (hæ·nd,hōuld). 1643. [See HOLD *sb.*] **1.** Hold for the hand; that by which one can hold on in climbing. Also *fig.* **2.** That part of an implement, e.g. a fishing-rod, that is grasped by the hand 1833.

Handicap (hæ·ndikæp), *sb.* 1653. [app. from the phrase 'hand i' cap', or 'hand in the cap'. Formerly the name of a sport, described under the name of *Newe Faire* in *Piers Plowman*, B. v. 328, where it appears that it was a custom to barter articles, and to give 'boot' or odds, as settled by an umpire, with the inferior article. All the parties, including the umpire, deposited forfeit-money in a cap. The name refers to the drawing out of full or empty hands, to settle whether the match was accepted or not; see N.E.D.] **1.** The name of a kind of sport having an element of chance in it, in which one person challenged some article belonging to another, for which he offered something of his own in exchange. Also *fig.* **2.** *Horse-racing.* (orig. *attrib.*) †**a.** *Handicap match*: a match between two horses, the umpire decreeing the weight to be carried by the superior horse, and the parties drawing to declare whether the match should be 'on' or 'off'. If the two agree, the forfeit-money is taken by the umpire; but if not, by the party who is willing that the match should stand. 1754. **b.** *Handicap race* (shortened *handicap*): a horse-race in which an umpire (the handicapper) decrees what weights have to be carried by the various horses entered, according to his judgement of their merits, in order to equalize their chances. So *h. plate, sweepstakes*, etc. 1786. **3.** Any analogous race or competition 1875. **4.** The extra weight or other condition imposed in equalizing the chances; hence, any encumbrance or disability that weighs upon effort 1813. **5.** *attrib.*, as *h. match*, etc. 1754.

Ha·ndicap, *v.* 1649. [f., or f. as prec.] †**1.** *trans.* To draw or gain as in a game of chance. **2.** *intr.* To engage or take part in a handicap match 1839. **3.** *trans.* To equalize the parties to a handicap, by decreeing the odds to be given; also *fig.* 1852. **4.** *trans.* To weight race-horses in proportion to their known or assumed powers, in order to equalize their chances 1856. **5.** *trans.* To penalize a superior competitor in any match or contest, so as to equalize his chances with those of inferior competitors. More generally, To weight any one unduly. 1864. Hence **Ha·ndicapper**, one who handicaps; *spec.* the public official who decrees what weights the different horses are to carry in a handicap.

Handicraft (hæ·ndikraft). Also formerly handycraft. ME. [For *handcraft*, after *handwork, handiwork*.] **1.** Manual skill; skilled work with the hands. **2.** A manual art, trade, or occupation 1548. †**3.** A handicraftsman –1821. **4.** *attrib.*, passing into *adj.* = 'manual, practical' 1662.

Ha·ndicra·ftsman. Formerly also as 2 words or hyphened. 1551. [lit. *handicraft's man*, man of handicraft; cf. CRAFTSMAN.] A man who exercises a handicraft; one employed in manual occupation.

The best wit of any handicraft man in Athens SHAKS.

Handicuff. Also **handy-.** 1701. [f. HAND *sb.* or HANDY *a.* + CUFF *sb.*²; app. after *fisticuff.*] *pl.* Blows with the hands; fighting hand to hand. Also *fig.*

Ha·ndily, *adv.* 1611. [f. HANDY *a.* + -LY².] In a handy manner; expertly; †manually.

Ha·ndiness. 1647. [See -NESS.] **1.** The quality of being handy or expert. **2.** Manageableness, convenience 1877.

Hand in glove: see HAND AND GLOVE.

Hand in hand (also with - -), *adv. phr.* (*a., sb.*). 1500. [HAND *sb.*] **1.** *adv. phr.* With hands mutually clasped; also *fig.* **2.** *attrib.* or *adj.* Going hand in hand or side by side; well-matched 1611. **b.** Name given to a Fire Insurance Office; implying the mutual sharing of risks 1781. **3.** *sb.* **a.** A representation of two hands mutually clasped. STEELE. **b.** Mutual clasping of hands. TENNYSON. **c.** A company of persons hand in hand. G. MEREDITH.

1. They hand in hand, with wandring steps and slow, Through Eden took thir solitarie way MILTON. 2. A kind of hand in hand comparison *Cymb.* I. iv. 75.

Handiron, obs. form of ANDIRON.

Handiwork (hæ·ndi,wɒɹk). Also **handy-** and as 2 words. [OE. *hand-ȝeweorc*, f. *hand* + *ȝeweorc* work (a collective form). See HANDY.] **1.** A thing or collection of things made by the hands of any one. **2.** Work done by direct personal agency. Sometimes, the work of man's hands as opp. to nature. OE. **b.** Doing, performance 1838. **4.** Manual employment; practical work. [Cf. HANDY.] 1565.

1. The firmament sheweth his handywork *Ps.* xix. 1.

Handkerchief (hæ·ŋkəɹtʃif), *sb.* 1530. [f. HAND *sb.* + KERCHIEF, q.v. also for *handkercher* (now dial. and vulgar).] A small square of linen, silk, or other fabric, carried in the hand or pocket (*pocket-h.*), for wiping the face, hands, or nose, or used as a kerchief to cover the head, or worn about the neck (*neck h.* or *neckerchief*).

Ha·nd-labour. 1549. Manual labour; †'art' as opp. to nature; now, usually, manual as opp. to machine work.

Handle (hæ·nd'l), *sb.* [OE., deriv. of HAND.] **1.** That part of a thing which is grasped by the hand in using or moving it. **2.** *transf.* Something resembling a handle; in *Bot.* = MANUBRIUM. 1639. **3.** *fig.* That by which something is or may be taken hold of, or taken advantage of for some purpose; an occasion, excuse, pretext 1535. **4.** *attrib.* 1532. **Handle-bar,** the steering-bar of a bicycle, etc., with a handle at each end.

3. I would not give this h. to calumny 1732. Phr. *A h. to one's name* (colloq.): a title of rank, honour, or courtesy attached to the name.

Handle (hæ·nd'l), *v.*¹ [OE. *handlian*, deriv. of HAND *sb.*]

I. 1. *trans.* To subject to the action of the hand or hands: earlier, to touch or feel with the hands; later, to take hold of, turn over, etc., in the hand, to employ the hands on or about. Also *absol.* **b.** *intr.* (for *refl.*) To have a (specified) feel, behaviour, action, etc. when handled 1727. **2.** *trans.* To ply or wield with the hand ME.; *spec.* in *Mil.* 1684. **3.** To manage, direct, conduct, control (sometimes = carry out, perform). †Also *refl.* 1523. **4.** To use; to make due use of 1647.

1. I have handled and felt it 1717. To h. a book BURGON. *absol.* They haue handes and h. not COVERDALE *Ps.* cxiii. 15 [cxv. 7]. Phr. *To h. a horse*, to get him accustomed to the hand. 2. Iubal..was the father of all such as h. the harpe and organ *Gen.* iv. 21. 3. A smarter officer never handled a regiment 1874. 4. To h. one's fists GROSE.

II. 1. To deal with, treat 1542. †Also *intr.* -1581. **2.** To treat of, discuss OE. †Also *intr.* or *absol.* -1673. **3.** To treat artistically 1553. **4.** To have in hand or pass through one's hands in the way of business; to deal in; to buy and sell. *U. S.* 1888.

1. I wil h. him, euen as he hath dealte with me COVERDALE *Prov.* xxiv. 29. 2. The Preacher handeled his matter learnedly 1551. 4. Export houses which h. steel rails 1897. Hence **Handlable, -eable** *a.* **Ha·ndler**¹.

Handle, *v.*² 1600. [f. HANDLE *sb.*] *trans* To furnish with a handle. Hence **Ha·ndler**².

Handled (hæ·nd'ld), *a.* 1785. [f. HANDLE *sb.* and *v.*² + -ED.] Furnished with or having a handle. Used in *Her.* when the handle of a tool or weapon is figured of a different tincture from the blade, as 'a sickle or, handled gules'.

Handless (hæ·ndlės), *a.* ME. [See -LESS.] Without hands; *fig.* incapable in action (now only *dial.*).

Ha·nd-line. 1674. A line to be worked by hand; *esp.* a fishing-line worked without a rod.

Handling (hæ·ndliŋ), *vbl. sb.* OE. [f. HANDLE *v.* + -ING¹.] **1.** The action of HANDLE *v.* **2.** Treatment; management 1530. **3.** Artistic manipulation 1771. **4.** *attrib.* 1866.

1. Satire is one of those edged tools which require careful h. 1795. 3. H., that is, a lightness of pencil that implies great practice SIR J. REYNOLDS.

Ha·nd-list, *sb.* 1859. [Cf. *hand-book.*] A list of books, etc. in a form handy for reference. Handlist *v.* to enter (books, etc.) in such a list.

†**Ha·ndlock.** 1532. [See LOCK *sb.*] A handcuff -1633. Hence **Ha·ndlock** *v.* to handcuff. Also *transf.*

Ha·nd-loom. 1833. A weaver's loom worked by hand as dist. from a power-loom.

Ha·nd-made, *a.* 1613. Made by hand. Now usually dist. from the work of machinery.

Handmaid (hæ·ndmē͡ɪd), *sb.* ME. [f. HAND *sb.* + MAID.] **1.** A female attendant or servant. **b.** *fig.* (in common use) 1592. †**c.** A tender. HAKLUYT. **2.** A moth, *Datana ministra*, of the family *Bombycidæ* 1869. **3.** *attrib.* 1629.

1. I am the handmayde of the lorde TREVISA. 3. Her sleeping Lord with h. lamp attending MILTON. So **Ha·ndmai·den** = 1, 1 b. ME.

Ha·nd-me-down. *dial.* and *U.S.* 1888. = REACH-ME-DOWN.

Ha·nd-mill. 1563. A grinding mill consisting of one millstone turned upon another by hand, a quern. Now also applied to a form of coffee-mill, etc.

Hand of glory. 1707. [tr. F. *main de gloire*, a deformation of *mandegloire*, etc., orig. *mandragore* mandrake.] Orig., in French, a charm formed of the root of a mandrake; later, one made of the hand of an executed criminal.

Hand over hand, *adv. phr.* 1736. Chiefly *Naut.* **a.** With each hand brought successively over the other, as in climbing up or down a rope, or rapidly hauling it in. **b.** *fig.* With continuous advances; said of a vessel, etc. approaching another 1830. **c.** *attrib.* 1859.

Hand over head, *adv. phr.* Now *rare* or *Obs.* 1440. **1.** Precipitately, recklessly, without deliberation; †indiscriminately. **2.** *attrib.* or *adj.* (with - -). Precipitate, rash, reckless; †indiscriminate 1693.

Ha·nd-play. *arch.* OE. Interchange of blows in a hand-to-hand encounter. (Recently revived.)

Ha·nd-rail. 1793. A rail or railing supported on balusters, as a guard or support to the hand at the edge of a platform, stairs, etc.

Ha·nd-saw. ME. A saw managed by one hand. **b.** In *Haml.* II. ii. 367, generally explained as a corruption of *heronshaw* or *hernsew*, heron.

Handsel, hansel (hæ·ndsĕl, hæ·nsĕl), *sb.* ME. [Cf. Da. *handsel* 'handsel, earnest-money', also Ger. *handgeld, handgift, handkauf*, and esp. F. *étrenne*, OF. *estreine*, with senses 2, 3, 4.] †**1.** Lucky prognostic, omen, presage; token or omen of good luck -1681. **2.** A gift or present (expressive of good wishes) at the beginning of a new year, or on other occasions; orig., deemed to ensure good luck. [= L. *strena*, F. *étrenne.*] ME. **3.** A first instalment of payment; earnest money; the first money taken by a trader in the morning, a luck-penny; anything given or taken as an omen, earnest, or pledge of what is to follow 1569. **4.** The first use, trial, proof, or specimen of anything; often with the notion of its being auspicious of what is to follow 1573. **5.** *attrib.* 1585.

3. Take this..but for hansell, the gaine is to come CAMPION. They say, a fooles hansell is lucky B. JONS. 4. Such was the handsel, for Scott protested against its being considered as the house heating of the new Abbotsford LOCKHART. *Comb.* **H. Monday,** the first Monday of the year (usu. O.S.), on which New Year's h. is given. (*Sc.*)

Handsel, *v.* ME. [f. prec.] **1.** *trans.* To give handsel to (a person). **2.** To inaugurate with some ceremony or observance of an auspicious nature; to auspicate. Also *fig.* (*ironical*). 1583. **3.** To use for the first time; to be the first to test, try, prove, taste 1605.

3. Haman shall hansell his owne gallowes 1612.

Handsome (hæ·nᵈsɒ̆m), *a.* (*adv.*) ME. [f. HAND *sb.* + -SOME.] †**1.** Easy to handle, or to use in any way -1598. **b.** Handy, ready at hand, suitable. (*Obs.* or *dial.*) 1530. **2.** Of action, speech, etc.: Apt, dexterous, clever, happy. ? *Obs.* exc. *U.S.* 1563. **b.** Of an agent: Apt, skilled, clever. ? *Obs.* exc. *U. S.* 1547. †**3.** Proper, seemly, decent -1654. **4.** Of fair size or amount; 'decent', moderately large. Now *unusual.* 1577. **b.** Of a fortune, a gift, etc.: Considerable. Now (by association with 5): Generous, liberal, munificent. 1577. **5.** Of conduct, etc.: Fitting, seemly; courteous, polite. Now: Generous, magnanimous. 1621. **6.** Having a fine form or figure (usually in conjunction with full size or stateliness); 'beautiful with dignity' (J.), 'fine'. (The prevailing current sense.) 1590.

2. Mr. Recorder in a h. speech [etc.] LUTTRELL. 4. Pretty h. quantities of pickled salmon 1730. b. To get h. fortunes by small profits, and large dealings PRIESTLEY. 5. Through this h. conduct of the dean the dispute was amicably settled 1830. 6. This Ludouico is a proper man..A very h. man *Oth.* IV. iii. 37. A large and h. room 1849.

B. *adv.* = HANDSOMELY. Now only in vulgar use, exc. in *H. is that h. does.* ME.

†**Ha·ndsome,** *v.* 1555. [f. prec. adj.] *trans.* To make handsome (in various senses) -1657.

Handsomely (hæ·nsɒ̆mli), *adv.* 1547. [f. as prec. + -LY².] **1.** In a handsome manner. **2.** Carefully; without haste, gently, gradually. Now only *Naut.* 1550.

2. Ease off the main sheet, h. my lad—not too much 1832.

Handsomeness (hæ·nsɒ̆mnės). 1530. [f. as prec. + -NESS.] The quality of being handsome.

H. is the more animal excellence, beauty the more imaginative HARE.

Handspike (hæ·nd,spəik), *sb.* 1615. [Earlier *handspeck*, ad. early mod.Du. *handspaecke*, mod.Du. *handspaak*, (f. *spaak* pole, rod). In Eng. app. assim. to SPIKE.] **1.** A wooden bar, used as a lever or crow, chiefly on shipboard and in artillery-service. **2.** Incorrectly for Sc. *handspake*, HANDSPOKE.

Comb. h.-ring (*Artill.*), the thimble on the trail transom of a gun, for the h. by which it is manœuvred.

Ha·ndspoke. In Sc. also **-spake, spaik, spike.** 1727. [See SPOKE.] A spoke or bar of wood carried in the hand, e.g. in carrying the coffin at a funeral in Scotland.

Ha·nd-staff. ME. **1.** A staff-like handle; *spec.* that part of a flail by which it is held. †**2.** A staff carried as a weapon [tr. Heb.]. *Ezek.* xxxix. 9.

Ha·ndstroke. Also **handi-, handy-stroke.** 1523. [f. HAND *sb.* + STROKE.] †**1.** A stroke or blow with the hand -1840. **2.** *attrib.*, as *h. pull* (in *Bell-ringing*) 1880.

Hand to hand, *adv. phr.* (*a.*). ME. With close approach of hand; at close quarters; man to man. **b.** *attrib.* or *adj.*, as in *hand-to-hand valour* 1836.

Hand to mouth, *phr.* (*a., sb.*). 1509. **1.** *From hand to mouth*: by consuming food as soon as it is obtained; improvidently, thriftlessly. **2.** *attrib.* or *adj.* (with - -). Involving consumption (or *transf.* disposal of goods) as soon as obtained; improvident 1748. **3.** *sb.* Lack of provision for the future. TENNYSON.

Hand-vice. 1611. A vice that can be held in one hand; a small movable vice.

Handwork (hæ·nd,wɒɹk). [OE. *handweorc.*] †**1.** = HANDIWORK 1. -1594. **2.** Work done with the hands; manual operation or labour; now esp. as dist. from work done by or with machinery OE. So **Ha·nd-worked** *ppl. a.*, **-wo·rker, -working.**

Ha·nd-wrist. *Obs.* exc. *dial.* [OE. *handwrist, -wyrst*, f. HAND + WRIST.] The wrist or joint of the hand. Now *dial.*

Colonel Whalley only cut in the handwrist CROMWELL.

Handwriting (hæ·nd,rəitiŋ). 1500. [Cf. L. *manuscriptum.*] **1.** Writing with the hand; manuscript; the writing peculiar to a hand or person, time or nation. **2.** That which is written by hand; manuscript; a written document or note. *Obs.* or *arch.* 1534. Also *fig.*

1. A paper in his own h. BURKE. The study of handwritings 1891.

Handy (hæ·ndi), *a.* 1535. [In sense 1, app. f. HANDI(WORK, q.v.; in the later senses, f. HAND *sb.* + -Y.] †**1.** Of, or done by, the hand; manual –1713. **2.** Ready to hand; near at hand; conveniently ready for use 1650. **3.** Convenient to handle; easy to be manipulated or managed 1694. **4.** Able to turn the hand to anything 1662. **5. Handy-** in *comb.*, as **Handy-craft** (see HANDICRAFT); †**-fight**, a hand to hand fight; **-grip(e** (see HANDGRIP); **-stroke** (see HANDSTROKE); **-work** (see HANDIWORK); **-man**, a man useful for all sorts of odd jobs; etc. 1592.

1. H. Artificers 1576, labour 1631. 2. I happen to have it h. 1894. 3. The volume is delightfully h. 1897. 4. Two smart h. boys or girls 1790.

Ha·ndy-da·ndy, *sb.* or *adv. phr.* ME. [A riming jingle on *hand*, or its childish dim. *handy.*] **1.** A children's game in which a small object is shaken between the hands of one player, and, the hands being suddenly closed, the other player has to guess in which hand the object is 1585. **b.** The words as used in the game; = 'Choose which you please' 1598. †**2.** Something held in the closed hand; a covert bribe. ME. only.

Hang (hæŋ), *v.* Pa. t. and pple. **hung** (hɒŋ), **hanged** (hæŋd). [The OE. weak *hangian, hangode, -od*, (also *hong-*), intr., is derived from the base of the OE. str. *hón* (:—*hâhan*), *heng, hangen* (*hongen*), trans.; cogn. w. the ON. causal vb. *hengja* trans., which came into northern England as *heng(e*, also *hing*. For the history of the word see N.E.D.]

I. *trans.* **1.** To place (a thing) so that it is supported from above; to fasten or attach to an object above; to suspend. Also *fig.* †**b.** To hook (a fish) –1787. **c.** To suspend floating without attachment in the air, or in space ME. **2.** *spec.* To attach or suspend in such a way as to allow of free movement about or on the point of attachment; e.g. to hang a door (on its hinges), a coach (on springs), etc. Also, to attach in a well-balanced position, as to hang a scythe (on its 'snead'). 1535. **3.** To fasten up or suspend on a cross or gibbet; †**a.** formerly, *spec.* to crucify; **b.** now, *spec.* to put to death by suspension by the neck. (In this sense, *hanged* is now the spec. form of the pa. t. and pa. pple.) OE. **b.** *refl.* To commit suicide by hanging ME. **c.** Used as an imprecation, etc. ME. **4.** To let droop or bend downward; to cause to lean or slope over 1593. **5.** To furnish or decorate *with* things suspended about or around; *esp.* to deck or ornament (a place) with tapestry or hangings 1451. **6.** *To hang fire*: (of a fire-arm) to be slow in communicating the fire through the vent to the charge; hence *fig.* to hesitate, be slow in acting (Cf. II. 10.) 1781.

1. It were better for him that a millstone were hanged about his neck *Matt.* xviii. 6. H. it [venison] where the air comes MRS. GLASSE. **c.** He..hangeth the earth upon nothing *Job* xxvi. 7. 2. This Rogue's Tongue is well hung SWIFT. 3. To be hanged by the neck, till he was dead—that was the end DICKENS. 'Beef, sir, is hung, men are hanged' 18... **c.** *Tam. Shr.* II. i. 301. 4. Phr. *To h. the head (down)*: i.e. as a sign of shame, contrition, despondency, or sheepishness. *To h. the groin, a leg*: to hold back; to be reluctant or tardy 6. **b.** *To hang a jury (U.S.)*: to prevent a jury from reaching a verdict; also *intr.* of a jury: to fail to agree; so HUNG *ppl. a.* 1850.

II. *intr.* **1.** To remain fastened or suspended from above; to depend, dangle, swing loose OE. **b.** To be furnished or adorned with things suspended or attached ME. **2.** To be supported or suspended at the side, as on a hinge or pivot ME. **3.** *spec.* Of a person: To be suspended *on* or *upon* a cross, gibbet, gallows, etc.; to suffer death in this way; esp. as a form of punishment. Also as an imprecation (*arch.*). OE. **4.** To bend forward or downward; to lean over; also, to incline steeply OE. **5.** To rest, float (in the air, etc.) ME. Also *fig.* of an evil or doubt 1548. **6.** To rest *on, upon* for support or authority; to depend *upon*; to be dependent *on* OE. **b.** To remain in consideration or attention ME. **7.** To attach oneself for support; to cling, hold fast, adhere ME. **b.** To stick close, so as not to leave or let go 1508. **c.** Of the wind: To remain persistently in a certain point of the compass 1671. **d.** To be a hanger-on 1535. **8.** To cling or adhere as an encumbrance or drag; to be a depressing weight 1450. **9.** *fig.* To be attached as an adjunct 1596. **10.** To be or remain in dubious suspense. Also *to h. in the wind.* ME. **11.** Of a note in music: To be prolonged 1597. **12.** To remain with motion suspended 1667. **13.** To remain as unwilling to depart or move on; to loiter, linger, as with expectation or interest 1842. †**14.** To hanker *after* or *for* –1684.

3. If I h., Ile make a fat payre of Gallowes SHAKS. Wretches h. that jurymen may dine POPE. 4. The high hils which hanged ouer them 1598. 5. Yon hard crescent, as she hangs Above the wood TENNYSON. *fig.* Uncertainty hung over their movements 1865. 6. One upon whose hand and heart and brain Once the..fate of Europe hung TENNYSON. **b.** Enoch hung a moment on her words TENNYSON. 7. Shee hung about my necke SHAKS. **b.** The patient Pack H. on the Scent unweary'd SOMERVILLE. 8. Contempt and beggery hangs vpon thy backe SHAKS. Time hanging heavy on our hands 1768. 9. Wel, thereby hangs a tale SHAKS. 10. To h. betwixt life and death CARLYLE. 12. A noble stroke he lifted high, Which hung not MILT. 13. The witnesses were kept hanging about (*mod.*).

III. In comb. with advs. **Hang back.** *intr.* To resist advance by one's weight or inertia; *fig.* to be backward. **Hang off. a.** *intr.* To leave hold. *Mids. N.* III. ii. 260. **b.** To hang back, demur. **Hang on.** To continue to adhere; usually implying expectation, or the like. **Hang out. a.** *intr.* To protrude with downward direction. **b.** *trans.* To display as a sign or signal. **c.** *intr.* To lodge, live (*colloq.* or *slang*). **Hang together. a.** *intr.* To adhere together loosely. **b.** To be coherent or consistent. **c.** To hold together; *spec.* (of a person) to keep body and soul together. **Hang up. a.** *trans.* To fasten so as to be supported only from above; to suspend on a hook, peg, or the like. **b.** Phr. *To h. up (one's sword, gun,* etc.): to give up using. *To h. up one's hat*: said of a man who marries and goes home to the wife's house to live. †**c.** To hang on a gibbet; hence as an imprecation *L.L.L.* IV. iii. 54. *Rom. & Jul.* III. iii. 57. **d.** To put 'on the shelf' or into abeyance; to keep back indefinitely.

Hang (hæŋ), *sb.* 1797. [f. prec. vb.] **1.** The action of hanging; also, a downward slope or bend; a declivity 1807. **b.** A suspension of motion 1866. **2.** The mode in which a thing hangs or is poised 1797. **3.** *concr.* (*dial.*) Something that hangs; a hanging mass or clump; a crop of fruit; a hang-net 1825.

1. The south-east h. of a hill 1807. **b.** The h. and eddy of a stream 1867. 2. The h. of a discourse 1864, of a skirt 1885. Phr. *To get the h. of*: to become familiar with the proper wielding of a tool; *fig.* to get to understand, master; to acquire the knack of (*U.S. colloq.*) *Not..a h.* (usu. with *care*): = 'not a bit'.

Hang-, the vb.-stem used in comb.: **hang-bench** (dial. **hing-**), in *Lead-mining*, a piece of timber forming part of a stow, which is pinned to the sole-tree by wooden pins; **-choice**, a choice between two evils; **-nest**, a bird that constructs a pensile nest, a HANGBIRD; **-net**, a kind of net which is set vertically.

Hangar (hangār). 1852. [Fr.] A covered space, shed, or shelter. **b.** (hæ·ŋəɹ). A shed for accommodating aircraft 1902.

Hangbird (hæ·ŋbəɹd). 1856. [f. HANG *v.* + BIRD.] A bird that builds a hanging nest; *esp.* an American oriole of the genus *Icteridæ.*

Ha·ng-by. *Obs.* exc. *dial.* 1579. [f. HANG- + BY *adv.* and *prep.*] **1.** A contemptuous term for a dependant or hanger-on. **2.** An appendage, an adjunct 1585. Also *attrib.*

Ha·ng-dog. 1677. [f. HANG *v.* + DOG; cf. *cut-throat.*]

A. *sb.* A despicable fellow fit only to hang a dog, or to be hanged like a dog. Also *attrib.* in *apposition.* 1687.

Paws off..You young hang-dog THACKERAY.

B. *adj.* Of, befitting, or characteristic of a hang-dog; low, degraded; sneaking 1677.

A squinting, meager, hang-dog countenance OTWAY.

Hanged (hæŋd), *ppl. a.* 1451. [f. HANG *v.* + -ED [1].] **1.** Now *Obs.* in the general sense; the form in use being HUNG. **2.** Put to death by hanging by the neck 1470. **b.** As an expletive (also *advb.*): 'Confounded' 1887.

Hanger [1] (hæ·ŋəɹ). [OE. *hangra*, deriv. of HANG *v.* Now identified with the next.] A wood on the side of a steep hill or bank.

Hanger [2] (hæ·ŋəɹ). ME. [f. HANG *v.* + -ER [1].] **1.** One who suspends a thing from above; often in *comb.*, as *paper-h.*, etc. *spec.* One of those who select and hang the pictures for an exhibition. 1791. **b.** One who puts a person to death by hanging, or causes him to be hanged ME. **2.** Something that hangs down or is suspended; e.g. †a bell-rope; a pendent catkin, etc. 1483. **3.** Something that overhangs; in *Mining*, The rock over the vein or lode; the 'roof' 1631. **4.** That by which anything is hung; a rope, chain, or hook used to suspend something; a support for a journal-box, etc. of a shafting. Also *attrib.* 1864. †**b.** A loop or strap on a sword-belt from which the sword was hung –1676. **c.** A chain or iron rod to which a pot or kettle is hung by means of a pot-hook. Hence *transf.* A nursery name for the stroke with a double curve (*ɩ*); usually in the phr. *pot-hooks and hangers* 1599. **5. Hanger-on. a.** A follower or dependant (often *disparagingly*) 1549. †**b.** An appendage, an adjunct –1674.

Hanger [3] (hæ·ŋəɹ). 1481. [app. the same as HANGER [2].] A kind of short sword, orig. hung from the belt.

Hanging (hæ·ŋiŋ), *vbl. sb.* ME. [f. HANG *v.* + -ING [1].] **1.** The action of HANG *v.*; suspension. **2.** The action of putting to death on the gallows, etc.; the being so put to death ME. **3.** A downward slope or curve; esp. in *Ship-building* 1684. **4.** *concr.* Something that hangs or is suspended; something attached; also *fig.* (Usu. in *pl.*) 1549. **5.** *spec.* A piece of drapery with which a bedstead, the walls of a room, etc. are hung; also the material for this ME. **b.** *pl.* The pieces, folds, or masses of tapestry, etc., with which a room or bed is hung; also extended to wall-paper (*paper-hangings*) 1485. **6.** A steep slope or declivity of a hill. Now *local.* ME.

2. Many a good h. preuents a bad marriage SHAKS. 4. *Cymb.* III. iii. 63. 5. **b.** No more than a picture in the hangings DRYDEN.

Comb.: **h.-committee,** the committee who decide the hanging of pictures in an Exhibition (e.g. that of the Royal Academy); **-head, -post, -stile,** the post or upright which bears the hinges of a door or gate.

Hanging (hæ·ŋiŋ), *ppl. a.* (*prep.*) ME. [f. as prec. + -ING [2].] That hangs. **1.** Supported above, and not below; suspended, pendulous; hanging downwards 1483. **2.** Overhanging; steep ME.; situated on a steep slope, top of a wall, etc., so as to appear to hang over ME. †**3.** Remaining in suspense –1590. †**b.** Pending, during; orig. with a sb. in absolute construction; hence, occas. treated as a prep. –1628. **4.** Having a downward cast of countenance. (Often with play on HANG *v.* I. 3.) 1603. **5.** In trans. sense: Addicted to hanging; as, a *h. judge* 1848.

1. Phr. *H. sleeve*, a loose open sleeve hanging down from the arm. 2. A man with a heavy h. brow 1847. Phr. *H. Gardens* (of Babylon), a transl. of L. *pensiles horti* (Q. Curtius). 3. **b.** This matter thus hangyng, the king [etc.] GRAFTON. 4. A good fauor you haue, but that you haue a h. look SHAKS.

Comb.: **h. ball** (Golf), a ball lying on a downward slope; **h. buttress,** 'a buttress supported on a corbel, and not standing solid on the foundation' (Webster); **h.-coal, -side, -wall** (*Mining*), that which hangs or leans over the working; **h. gale,** the rent due at the previous gale-day (GALE *sb.*[4]); **-moss,** a lichen or moss that hangs in long fringes from the limbs of a tree; **h. valve,** a hinged valve which falls open by the action of gravity.

Hangman (hæ·ŋmăn). ME. [f. HANG *v.* + MAN.] A man whose office it is to hang condemned criminals; also, an executioner, a torturer, racker. **b.** *transf.* A term of reprobation; also used playfully 1553. Also *attrib.* **Ha·ngmanship,** the office or function of h.

Ha·ng-nail. 1678. [f. HANG *v.* + NAIL; cf. AGNAIL.] A small piece of epidermis hanging by one end, near to a nail.

Ha·ng-o·ver. *U.S.* 1894. Something remaining or left over; a remainder or survival.

Hank (hæŋk), *sb.* ME. [app. from Norse; cf. ON. *hǫnk* fem. (:—**hanku*) hank. coil, skein, clasp; Sw. *hank* m., string, etc.; Da. *hank* handle, etc.] **1.** A circular coil or loop of anything flexible 1483. **2.** A skein or coil of thread, yarn, etc.; a definite length of yarn or thread in a coil 1560. **3.** *Naut.* A hoop or ring of rope, wood, or iron, fixed upon the stays, to seize the luff of the fore-and-aft sails, and to confine the staysails thereto, at different distances (Smyth) 1711. **4.** *fig.* A hold; a power of restraint (now *rare* or *dial.*) 1613.

4. 'Twill give me such a h. upon her pride FARQUHAR.

Hank (hæŋk), *v.* ME. [prob. from Norse; cf. ON. *hanka* to coil, f. *hǫnk, hank* sb.; see prec.] **1.** *trans.* To fasten by a loop or noose; to entangle (now *dial.*). **2.** *intr.* To hang or remain fastened; to 'catch' 1547. **3.** *trans.* To make up (thread) in hanks 1818. †**4.** *intr.* = HANKER *v.* 1. –1716.

Ha·nker, *sb.* 1827. [f. HANKER *v.*] A longing after something.

Hanker (hæ·ŋkəɹ), *v.* 1601. [? freq. and intensive of HANG *v.*, but cf. HANK *v.* 4.] **1.** *intr.* To 'hang about', to linger *about* with longing or expectation. Now *dial.* **2.** To have a longing or craving. Const. *after*; occas. with *for* or *infin.* 1642.

2. The mind..always hankering after what she has not TUCKER. Hence **Ha·nkerer.** **Ha·nkering** *vbl. sb.* a mental craving or longing; **-ly** *adv.*

Hanky-panky (hæ·ŋki,pæ·ŋki). *slang.* 1841. [Arbitrary; cf. *hoky-poky.*] Jugglery, legerdemain; trickery, double dealing, underhand dealing. Also *attrib.*

Hanover (hæ·novəɹ, orig. as in Ger. hanō·vər). [Ger. *Hannover.*] A North German town, capital of Hanover, formerly an Electorate of the Empire, now a province of Prussia; in 1714 the Elector of Hanover became king of England. Hence **Hanove·rian** *a.* of or pertaining to H. or the House of H.; *sb.* an inhabitant of H.; also an adherent of the House of H. †**Hanoverianize** *v.* to make, or become, Hanoverian.

Hans (hans). 1569. Abbrev. in Ger. and Du. of *Johannes*, John; hence, a German or Dutchman.

Hans, obs. f. HANSE.

Hansard[1] (hæ·nsăɹd). *Hist.* 1832. [f. HANSE + -ARD.] A member of one of the establishments of the German Hanse.

Hansard[2] (hæ·nsăɹd). 1876. The official report of the proceedings and debates of the Houses of Parliament; long compiled by Messrs. Hansard (*colloq.*). Also *transf.* Hence **Ha·nsardize** *v.* to confront (a member of Parliament) with his former utterances as recorded in 'Hansard'. Also *absol.*

Hanse (hæns, ‖ha·nzə). *Hist.* ME. [a. OF. *hanse*, med.L. *hansa*, a. OHG. *hansa* (= OE. *hōs*) military troop, band, company, MHG. *hanse* fellowship, merchants' guild.] **1.** A company or guild of merchants in former times; also, the privileges and monopolies possessed by it; *occas.*, the guild-hall or hanse-house. **b.** *spec.* A famous political and commercial league of Germanic towns, which had also a house in London. *pl.* The Hanse towns or their citizens. ME. **2.** The entrance-fee of a mediæval trading guild; also, a toll levied on traders not of the guild ME.

Comb.: **H. city, H. town,** one of the towns of the German H. or Hanseatic League; so *H. association, league, merchant*, etc.; **h.-house,** a guild-hall.

Hanseatic (hænsi,æ·tik), *a.* 1614. [ad. med.L. *hanseaticus*, f. MHG. *hanse*; see prec.] Of or pertaining to the German Hanse.

Hansel: see HANDSEL.

†**Hanselin.** [a. OF. *hainselin, hamselin.*] A kind of jacket or slop. CHAUCER.

Hansom cab; also **hansom** (hæ·nsŏm). 1847. [f. *Hansom*, surname of an architect.] A low-hung two-wheeled cabriolet holding two persons inside, the driver being mounted on a dickey behind, and the reins going over the roof. Also *attrib.*

He hailed a cruising hansom..'Tis the gondola of London', said Lothair DISRAELI.

Han't, ha'n't, vulgar contr. of *have not.*

Hantle (hɑ·nt'l). *Sc.* and *n. dial.* 1692. [?] A (considerable) number or quantity.

Hap (hæp), *sb.*[1] *arch.* [Early ME., a. ON. *happ* neut., chance, good luck.] **1.** Chance or fortune (good or bad); luck, lot. **2.** (with *pl.*) A chance, accident, occurrence; often, an unfortunate event, mishap ME. †**3.** Good luck; success, prosperity –1813. **4.** Fortuity. (*Occas.* personified.) ME.

1. He sought them both, but wish'd his h. might find Eve separate MILT. Good h. and evil h. 1884. 3. Be it h., or be it harm SCOTT. 4. H. helpeth hardy man alday CHAUCER.

Hap, *sb.*[2] *n. dial.* 1724. [f. HAP *v.*[2]] A covering.

Hap (hæp), *v.*[1] *arch.* [ME. *happe(n*, f. HAP *sb.*[1]; cf. ODan. *happe* to chance.] **1.** *intr.* To come about by hap or chance; to happen, chance. **2.** To have the hap, fortune, or luck (*to do*, or with cl.) ME. **3.** To come or go by chance; to chance *on* or *upon* ME.

1. Happe how happe may, Al sholde I deye CHAUCER. 2. If the Skie fal, we may happe to catche Larkes 1566.

Hap, *v.*[2] Now only *Sc.* and *dial.* ME. [? Of Norse origin.] **1.** *trans.* To cover up or over. †Also *transf.* and *fig.* –1576. **2.** To cover for warmth; to wrap; to 'tuck *up*' (in bed) ME.

2. His chaplain hapt him up in bed KINGSLEY.

Haphazard (hæ·phæ:zăɹd). 1575. [f. HAP *sb.*[1] + HAZARD; lit. 'hazard of chance'.]

A. *sb.* Mere chance or accident; fortuity. Chiefly with *at, by,* †*in.*

It is hap hazard, if you escape undamnified 1576.

B. *adj.* Characterized by haphazard; random 1671.

C. *adv.* In a haphazard manner; casually 1857.

Hapless (hæ·plĕs), *a.* 1568. [f. HAP *sb.*[1] + -LESS.] Destitute of hap or good fortune; luckless.

An..haplesse love 1635. Hence **Ha·pless-ly** *adv.*, **-ness** (*rare*).

Haplo-, comb. f. Gr. ἁπλόος, ἁπλοῦς single, simple:

haplo·ca·rdiac [Gr. καρδία] *a.*, having a heart of simple structure; belonging to the *Haplocardia* or *Brachiopoda*; ‖**-cerus** [Gr. κέρας], generic name of Rocky Mountain sheep; hence **-cerine** *a.*; **-ste·monous** [Gr. στήμων] *a.*, *Bot.* having a single circle [Gr. ἁπλοτομία], a simple cutting or incision.

Haply (hæ·pli), *adv.* Now *arch.* or *poet.* ME. [f. HAP *sb.*[1] + -LY[2].] By hap; by chance or accident; perhaps.

Lest h. ye be found even to fight against God *Acts* v. 39.

Ha'p'orth: see HALFPENNYWORTH.

Happen (hæ·p'n), *v.* [ME. f. HAP *sb.*[1] + -EN[5] 2, or extended f. HAP *v*[1].] **1.** *intr.* To come to pass (*orig.* by hap or chance); to take place; to occur. The most general verb to express the simple occurrence of an event. †**2.** With *to, unto*: To fall to the lot of; to come in the way of –1764. **3.** To have the hap or fortune (*to do* something) ME. **4.** To chance to be or to come; to 'turn up', occur ME.; also with *on, upon*, occas. *of* 1533.

1. The greatest evill that can h. in this life HOBBES. As it happens JANE AUSTEN. No harm shall h. to you 1815. 3. I h. to know [etc.] DICKENS. 4. Phr. *Happen in*: to go or come in casually: *esp.* to drop in (at a house). *U.S.* **Ha·ppening** *vbl. sb.*, the action of the vb.; also (with *pl.*), an event, occurrence 1581.

Happily (hæ·pili), *adv.* Also †**happely.** ME. [f. HAPPY *a.* + -LY[2].] In a happy manner. **1.** = HAPLY (*arch.*). **2.** With or by good fortune; luckily, successfully. (Now often expressing only that it is well that things are so.) ME. **3.** Aptly, fitly, appropriately; felicitously 1577. **4.** With mental pleasure or content 1513.

2. The case h. stands alone in his biography MORLEY. 3. Minds..h. constituted for the cultivation of science MACAULAY. 4. He writes How h. he liues SHAKS.

Happiness (hæ·pinĕs). 1530. [f. as prec. + -NESS.] The quality or condition of being happy. **1.** Good fortune or luck; success, prosperity. **2.** The state of pleasurable content of mind, which results from success or the attainment of what is considered good 1591. **3.** Successful or felicitous aptitude, fitness, or appropriateness; felicity 1599.

1. Wish me partaker in thy happinesse, When thou do'st meet good hap SHAKS. 2. Oh H.! our being's end and aim! Good, Pleasure, Ease, Content! whate'er thy name POPE. Phr. *Greatest h. of the greatest number*: a principle of moral and political action, first enunciated by Hutcheson, 1725; shortened, later, to 'greatest h. principle', 'rule of greatest h.' 3. How pregnant (sometimes) his Replies are? A happinesse That often Madnesse hits on SHAKS.

Happy (hæ·pi), *a.* ME. [f. HAP *sb.*[1] + -Y.] †**1.** Fortuitous; chance (*rare*) –1677. **2.** Having good hap or fortune; lucky, fortunate; favoured by circumstance ME. †**b.** Blessed, beatified –1700. **3.** Characterized by or involving good fortune. (Now used only in association with senses 4 and 5.) ME. **4.** Having the feeling arising from satisfaction with one's circumstances or condition; also: Glad, pleased 1525. **5.** Apt, dexterous; felicitous ME. **6.** *colloq.* (*joc.*) Slightly drunk 1770.

1. Any h. concourse of atoms HALE. 2. The h. seat of liberty 1741. **b.** If yee know these things, h. are ye if ye doe them *John* xiii. 17. Phr. *Of h. memory.* 3. Many h. returns DICKENS. 4. Better be h. then wise 1562. H. as a king GAY. 5. He was apt and happie in armes LD. BERNERS. A most h. thought SHERIDAN, reply (*mod.*). Phr. *Happy dispatch*: see DISPATCH, HARA-KIRI.

†**Happy,** *v.* 1600. [f. prec.] To render happy –1632.

Ha·ppy-go-lu·cky. 1672.

A. *adv.* Just as it may happen; haphazard.

B. *adj.* Of persons, etc.: Easy-going 1856.

C. *sb.* A happy-go-lucky person, quality, or character 1851.

Haquebut, var. of HACKBUT.

Haqueton (hæ·ktŏn). *Obs.* exc. *Hist.* ME. [A later var. of ME. *aketoun*, ACTON (q.v.)] = ACTON.

‖**Hara-kiri** (hā:rakı·ri). Also corruptly hari-kari. 1856. [Japanese (colloq. and vulgar), f. *hara* belly + *kiri* cut.] Suicide by disembowelment, as formerly practised by the higher classes in Japan, when in disgrace, or under sentence of death. Also called (by Englishmen) *happy dispatch*: see DISPATCH *sb.* Also *fig.*

Harangue (hăræ·ŋ), *sb.* 1450. [Earlier *arang*, a. OF. *arenge, harangue*, ad. med.L. *harenga* in same sense. Referred by Diez to OHG. *hring*, MHG. *ring*, ring, circle of spectators, etc., arena.] A speech addressed to an assembly; a loud or vehement address, a tirade; occas., †a formal or pompous speech.

His grave H. 1610. Telemachus, intemp'rate in h. COWPER.

Harangue, *v.* 1660. [a. F. *haranguer.*] **1.** *intr.* To deliver a harangue; to declaim. **2.** *trans.* To address in a harangue; to make a formal speech to 1682.

1. My wife..undertook to h. for the family GOLDSM. 2. He often harangued the troops GIBBON. Hence **Hara·nguer.**

Haras (hæ·răs, ‖arā). Now treated as Fr. ME. [a. OF. *haraz*, later *haras* 'horses and mares kept only for breed'; of uncertain origin.] An enclosure or establishment in which horses are kept for breeding; hence, †a stud.

Harass (hæ·răs), *v.* 1618. [a. F. *harasser*; perh. a deriv. form of OF. *harer* to set a dog on.] **1.** *trans.* To wear *out*, or exhaust with fatigue, care, trouble, etc. *Obs.* or *dial.* †**2.** To harry, lay waste –1710. **3.** To trouble or vex by repeated attacks 1622. **4.** To worry, distress with annoying labour, care, importunity, misfortune, etc. 1656.

1. Troops..harassed with a long and wearisome march BACON (J.). 3. The Indians unceasingly harassed their march 1865. 4. Vext with lawyers and harass'd with debt TENNYSON. Hence **Ha·rass** *sb.* harassment. **Ha·rassedly, Ha·rassingly** *advs.* **Ha·rasser.**

Harassment (hæ·răsmĕnt). 1753. [f. HARASS *v.* + -MENT.] The action of harassing; the being harassed; vexation, worry.

The h. of these applications 1806.

†**Harbergage.** ME. [OF.; cf. next.] Lodging.

Harbinge (hā·ɹbindʒ), *v.* 1475. [ME. *herberge, herbige*, a. OF. *herbergier, herbigier*; see next.] †**1.** *trans.* To lodge. Also *intr.* (for *refl.*, as in OF.). –1603. **2.** [*nonce-use* from next.] *trans.* To be a harbinger of. WHITMAN.

Harbinger (hā·ɹbindʒəɹ), *sb.* [Early ME. *herbergere* and *herbergeour*, a. OF. *herbergere*, in obl. case *herbergeor* (*-geour*) one who provides shelter or lodgings, f. *herbergier* vb., f. *herberge* lodging, quarters (for an army, etc.), a. OHG. *heriberga*, f. *hari, heri*, host, army + *-berga* (= OE. *-berg, -beorg*) protection, shelter, f. *bergan* to protect. Cf. *passenger, messenger*, etc.] †**1.** One who provides lodgings; a host; a HARBOURER –1502. **2.** One sent on before to purvey lodgings for an army, a royal train, etc.;

a purveyor of lodgings; in *pl.* an advance company of an army sent to prepare a camping-ground; a pioneer ME. 3. A forerunner. Mostly in *transf.* and *fig.* senses, and in literary language. 1550.

3. The bright morning star, day's h. MILTON. The prophet and h. of better days STUBBS. **Harbinger of spring**: a small umbelliferous herb of N. America, *Erigenia bulbosa*, closely resembling the Earth-nut.

Ha·rbinger, *v.* 1646. [f. prec. (sense 3).] *trans.* To act as a harbinger to; to announce, presage.

To H. his learned name G. DANIEL.

Harbor, var. sp. of HARBOUR.

†Harborough, -borow, etc. ME. ff. HARBOUR *sb.* and *v.*

†Ha·rborous, *a.* 1526. [f. HARBOUR *sb.*[1], after *humorous*, etc.] 1. Affording harbour; given to hospitality –1632. 2. Furnished with harbours or havens for ships –1702.

2. A well known sea, called Euxine, or h. C. MATHER.

Harbour, also (now *U.S.*) **harbor** (hā·ɹbəɹ), *sb.*[1] [Late OE. *herebeorg*, f. *here* army, HERE *sb.* + *beorg* protection, ME. *her(e)berȝe*, *her(e)berwe*, with cognates in OHG. and ON. The late ME. form remains in *Market Harborough*, etc.] 1. Shelter, lodging, entertainment; sojourn, abode. 2. A place of shelter or sojourn; lodgings; inn; asylum. *Obs.* exc. *dial.* ME. †b. The 'house' of the sun or a planet in the zodiac. CHAUCER. c. The covert of wild animals 1576. d. *fig.* 1548. 3. A place of shelter for ships; *spec.* where they may lie sheltered by the shore or by works extended from it; a haven, a port ME. 4. *Glass-making.* A trough-like box for holding the mixed ingredients and conveying them to the pot for fusion 1891.

1. Our great Want..was Harbor and good Company BUNYAN. 2. Fair h. that them seems: so in they entred are SPENSER. 3. A Station safe for Ships, when Tempests roar, A silent H. and a cover'd Shoar DRYDEN.

Comb.: **h.-due**, a charge for the use of a h. (usually in *pl.*); **-master**, an officer who has charge of a h., and of the mooring of ships, etc. therein; **-watch**, a division or subdivision of the watch kept on night-duty, when the ship rides at single anchor.

†Harbour, *sb.*[2] 1505. [A form of ARBOUR *sb.*[1], intermediate between it and the earlier *herber*, *erber*.] a. = ARBOUR 1. –1820. b. A bower covered with climbing plants –1790.

Harbour, also (now *U.S.*) **harbor** (hā·ɹbəɹ), *v.* [Late OE. *herebeorgian*, f. *herebeorg* HARBOUR *sb.*[1]]

I. *trans.* †1. To provide a lodging for; to shelter; to lodge, entertain. Also *fig.* –1671. †2. To quarter (soldiers or retainers); to billet; *refl.* to encamp. Also *absol.* –1648. 3. To give shelter to, to shelter. Now mostly dyslogistic. Also *fig.* ME. †b. Of a place, etc.: To afford room for; to contain, hold –1680. 4. *fig.* To entertain; to cherish privately; to indulge (esp. evil thoughts or designs) ME. 5. To shelter in a haven or harbour 1555. 6. To trace (a stag) to his lair. Also *transf.* 1531.

1. She harbours you as her kinsman SHAKS. *fig.* The anguish of my soul, that suffers not Mine eye to h. sleep MILT. 3. To h. rebels 1849, vermin 1851, smuggled tobacco (*mod.*). 4. To h. suspicions 1766, the worst designs MACAULAY, resentment 1850.

II. *intr.* 1. To lodge, take shelter; to encamp; later, often with some notion of lurking or concealment. (*arch.* or *Obs.*) Also *fig.* ME. 2. Of a stag, etc.: To have its retreat or resort 1599. 3. To take shelter or cast anchor in a haven or harbour. Also *fig.* 1583.

1. For this Night, lets harbor here in Yorke SHAKS. 2. The place where the turtle were known to h. COOK. Hence **Ha·rbourer, -orer**, one who harbours (now usu. dyslogistic); one whose office it is to trace a deer to its covert.

Harbourage, -orage (hā·ɹbərėdʒ). 1570. [f. HARBOUR *sb.*[1] + -AGE.] 1. = HARBOUR 1. Also *transf.* and *fig.* 2. = HARBOUR 2. 1651. 3. Shelter for ships, shelter in a haven 1850.

1. Where can I get me h. for the night TENNYSON.

Harbourless (hā·ɹbəɹlės), *a.* ME. [See -LESS.] 1. Destitute of shelter, houseless. †2. Of a place: That affords no shelter –1589. 3. Without harbours for ships 1600.

Harbrough(e, Harburrow, obs. ff. HARBOUR *sb.* and *v.*

Hard (hāɹd), *a.* (*sb.*) [Com. Teut.: OE. *heard*:—OTeut. **hardús*, corresp. to pre-Teut. **kartús* = Gr. κρατύς strong.]

I. Passively hard. 1. That does not yield to blows or pressure; not easily penetrated or separated into particles; firm and resisting to the touch; solid, compact in substance and texture. Opp. to *soft*. 2. Of money: In specie as opp. to paper currency 1706. 3. Said of the pulse when the blood-tension is high 1727. 4. Not easy to wear out or cause to give way; formerly, *esp.*, hardy and bold in fight OE. †b. Inured, hardened. SHAKS. 5. Difficult to do or accomplish ME. b. Of the subject of an action: Having difficulty in doing something. *Obs.* exc. in *hard of hearing*. ME. 6. Difficult to understand or explain 1450. 7. Difficult to deal with, manage, control, or resist 1588. 8. Obdurate; callous; hard-hearted OE. 9. Not easily moved to part with money; niggardly, 'close' ME. 10. Not easily moved by sentiment; practical, shrewdly intelligent 1747.

1. H. stone 1568, egs SIR T. HERBERT. Harder than adamant PUSEY. *H. iron*, iron which retains its magnetic properties when removed from the magnetic field. *H. lead*, lead containing certain impurities, principally antimony. 2. H. cash to meet a run GALT. 4. The men..look as h. as nails 1885. b. *Ant. & Cl.* III. xiii. 111. 5. So h. a thing it is to please all BIBLE *Transl. Pref.* A h. thing to manage 1833. 6. To ask h. questions BURGON. 7. Phr. *H. case*, a difficult case to treat or deal with; a person that cannot be reclaimed; a 'bad lot'. *U.S.* 8. With his h. eye, casting envious looks at them LAMB. †*To die h.*: to die obdurate or impenitent. (See also HARD *adv.*, DIE *v.*[1]). 10. We Americans have got h. heads 1824.

II. Actively hard. 1. Difficult to bear or endure; severe, rigorous, oppressive, cruel OE. 2. Of persons: Harsh or severe in dealing with any one OE.; of things, actions, etc.: Unfeeling, cruel, harsh, rough OE.; strict, without concession 1612.

1. Phr. *H. lines*: see LINE. It was his h. lucke 1576. Money..a very necessary Commodity in H. times 1705. A 'hard' winter 1884. 2. Colonel, why so h. upon poor Miss SWIFT. H. words BUTLER, fare COWPER. A h. view of persons and things CARLYLE. To drive a h. bargain 1870.

III. In transf. senses. 1. Harsh or unpleasant to the eye or ear, or to the æsthetic faculty 1513. 2. a. Applied to water holding in solution mineral, esp. calcareous salts, which decompose soap and render the water unfit for washing purposes 1660. b. Of liquor: Harsh to the taste; acid; sour from being stale. (Now *dial.* or *slang.*) 1581. c. Intoxicating, strong (*colloq. U.S.*) 1879. 3. *Comm.* Of prices: High and unyielding; stiff. Said also of the market, etc. 1882. 4. *Phonetics.* Applied: a. to the letters *c*, *g*, when they have their original guttural sounds (k, g), as dist. from the palatal and sibilant sounds (tʃ, ts, s, dʒ, etc.); b. to the breath consonants (k, t, p, and sometimes χ, ʃ, s, þ, f) as opp. to the corresponding voiced consonants (g, d, b; γ, ʒ, z, ð, v) 1775. 5. *Electr.* Of or pertaining to an electron tube having a relatively high vacuum.

1. A h. rime SHAKS., face 1622, outline 1854, negative 1894. A Virgin h. of Feature POPE.

IV. †1. Intense in force or degree –1807. 2. Carried on unremittingly; (of study) close; involving great labour or effort; vehement, vigorous, violent OE. 3. Unremitting, persistent. Qualifying an agent-noun. 1663.

2. H. drinking 1714, study SWIFT. **Hard labour**: hard bodily labour of certain kinds imposed upon certain classes of criminals during their term of imprisonment. *H. swearing*, swearing (as a witness) to one effect regardless of perjury; hence, perjury. 3. A h. rider KINGSLEY.

Phrases and Combs. a. In names of trees and plants: **h.-corn**, a general name for wheat and rye; **-grass**, a name given locally to various coarse dry grasses, e.g. *Dactylis glomerata*, species of *Rottbœllia*, etc.; **-rush**, *Juncus effusus*; **-tinder fungus**, *Boletus igniarius*. b. Chiefly techn.: **h. bargain**, a thing or person not worth its cost; **-bread**, a kind of hard-baked cake or biscuit; **h. finish, -ing**, in *Plastering*, the third and last coat, consisting of fine stuff laid on to the depth of about an eighth of an inch; **h. fish**, cod, ling, etc., salted and dried.

B. *sb.* (the adj. used ellipt.) †1. That which is hard, something hard; hardship. ME. only. b. *In hard*, in hard cash, down. †2. Hard or firm ground –1629. 3. A firm beach or foreshore; also, a sloping stone roadway or jetty at the water's edge for landing, etc. (Hence, at Portsmouth, a street which adjoins the landing.) 1838. 4. *slang.* = *hard labour* 1890.

Phr. *When h. comes to h.*: when the worst comes to the worst.

Hard, *adv.* [OE. *hearde*, f. HARD *a.*] In a hard manner. 1. With effort or violence; strenuously, earnestly, vigorously; fiercely. In early use, occas. = exceedingly. 2. So as to bring or involve pain or hardship; severely; cruelly, harshly ME. †b. With an uneasy pace –1824. 3. With difficulty, hardly; scarcely ME. 4. Firmly, securely; tightly; fast. Now *rare.* ME. 5. So as to be hard ME.; on a hard ground, floor, etc. 1577. 6. Close, of time or place ME. b. *Naut.* Expressing the carrying of an action to its extreme limits, as in *hard-a-lee*, *-a-port*, etc.: see the second elements 1549. †7. Parsimoniously. STEELE.

1. Strangers..Who hunt me h. 1586. His majesty looked at me very h. FOOTE. Last night it froze h. (*mod.*). 2. H. put to it to veil their feelings 1885. b. He [Time] trots h. with a yong maid, between the contract of her marriage [etc.] *A. Y. L.* III. ii. 331. Phr. *To go h. with* (a person): to fare ill with him; with *but*, introducing a statement of what will happen unless prevented by overpowering difficulties. 3. Phr. *To die h.*: see DIE *v.*[1] 4. Bound h. and fast 1833. 5. Lakes..h. frozen 1632. The harder they lie, the sooner they fatte B. GOOGE. 6. *H. upon* sixty FOOTE. Phr. *To run* (a person) *h.* In *Comb.*, qualifying ppl. adjs., to which *hard* is always united by a hyphen, when they are used attrib., and generally when they are used predicatively: a. With effort, strenuously, violently, etc., as *h.-drinking*, *-fought*, *-hitting*, etc. b. With hardship, severely, etc., as *h.-faring*, *-living*, etc. c. With difficulty, as *h.-bought*, *-earned*, etc. d. So as to be hard, tight, etc., as *h.-baked*, *-pressed*, etc. e. **h.-boiled** of an egg: boiled till the white and yolk are solid; *fig.* (orig. *U.S.*) callous, hard-headed, shrewd; **-bound**, slow in action; costive; **-drawn**, drawn when cold, as wire; **-spun**, tightly twisted in spinning; etc.

†Hard, *v.* [OE. *heardian*, orig. intrans., f. *hard-* adj. HARD.] To make, be, or become hard (*lit.* and *fig.*) –1620.

Hard and fast, *a.* 1867. 1. *Naut.* Said of a ship on shore. 2. Rigidly laid down and adhered to 1867.

Hard-bake (hā·ɹdbēˈk). 1825. [f. HARD *a.* + BAKE *v.* and *sb.*] A sweetmeat made of boiled sugar or treacle with blanched almonds; almond toffee.

Hardbeam (hā·ɹdbīm). ? *Obs.* OE. [f. HARD *a.* + BEAM tree.] The HORNBEAM, *Carpinus Betulus.*

Hard-bitten, *a.* 1784. [f. HARD *a.* + BITTEN *pa. pple.* (here used actively; cf. *ill-spoken*).] Given to hard biting; tough in fight.

They will be hard-bitten terriers will worry Dandie SCOTT.

Hard by. *arch.* 1526. [f. HARD *adv.* 6 + BY *prep.* and *adv.*] A. *prep.* Close by; close to, very near to. (Now only of place.) B. *adv.* Close by; very near; †also *transf.* close at hand in time 1535.

Harden, hurden (hā·ɹd'n, hō·ɹd'n). late ME. [f. HARDS.] Coarse fabric made from hards.

Harden (hā·ɹd'n), *v.* ME. [f. HARD *a.* + -EN [5]; repl. OE. *heardian*, to HARD.]

I. *trans.* 1. To render or make hard; to indurate. Also *transf.* and *fig.* †2. To embolden, confirm; to incite to action –1658. 3. To make callous or unfeeling ME. 4. To make persistent or obdurate in a course of action or state of mind ME. 5. To make firm and tight 1523. 6. To render hardy, robust, or capable of endurance 1577. 7. *Phonetics.* To make a sound hard. See HARD *a.* 1871.

1. Snow hardened by frost TYNDALL. *fig.* Hardening customary into written rights 1874. 3. He hath blinded their eyes, and hardened their heart *John* xii. 40. 4. Harden'd in Impenitence DRYDEN. 6. It is not true..that cold hardens children 1793.

II. *intr.* 1. To become hard. Also *fig.* ME. 2. To become hard in feeling, constitution, etc. 1667. 3. *Comm.* Of prices: To rise; to stiffen. Cf. HARD *a.* 1674.

1. *fig.* This natural sequence hardened first into custom and then into law 1891. 2. Now his heart..hardning in his strength Glories MILT.

Hence **Ha·rdened** *ppl. a.* made hard, indurated; rendered callous; hard-hearted; obdurately determined in a course. **Ha·rdener**, one who hardens; *spec.* one who hardens metals; one who case-hardens guns.

Harderian (haɹdīᵊriăn), *a.* 1835. [f. J. J. *Harder*, Swiss anatomist (1656–1711) + -IAN.]

Anat. In *Harderian gland*: the lubricating gland of the nictitating membrane or 'third eyelid' in the inner angle of the eye of birds and some mammals.

Ha·rd-favoured, *a. arch.* 1513. [See HARD *a.* III. 1 and FAVOUR *sb.*] Having a hard or unpleasing 'favour', appearance, or look; ugly.

The Corsicans are in general..rather hard-favoured BOSWELL. Hence **Hardfa·vouredness.**

Ha·rd-featured, *a.* 1748. [See HARD *a.* III. 1.] Having hard, harsh, or unpleasing features.

Hard fern. 1828. Any fern of the genus *Lomaria*, as the Northern Hard Fern, *Lomaria* (*Blechnum*) *Spicant*, of Europe.

Ha·rd-fisted, *a.* 1656. Stingy, niggardly.

Ha·rdhack. *U.S.* 1851. [f. HARD *a.* + (?) HACK *v.*] A low shrub, *Spiræa tomentosa*, common in New England.

Ha·rd-handed, *a.* 1590. **1.** Having hard hands, from manual labour. †**2.** Niggardly, close-fisted. NORDEN. **3.** Ruling with a cruel hand; severe 1641.

1. Hard handed men..Which neuer labour'd in their mindes till now SHAKS.

Ha·rdhead, hard-head. 1519. **1.** A hard-headed person; one not easily moved; a blockhead. †**2.** A contest of butting with the head. Also *hard-heads*. DRYDEN. **3.** A name of fishes: **a.** The sea scorpion, *Cottus Scorpius* 1803. **b.** The grey gurnard, *Trigla gurnardus* 1810. **c.** The menhaden (*New England*) 1837. **4.** The Californian grey whale, *Rhachianectes glaucus*: so named from its habit of butting boats 1860. **5.** The plant Knapweed. Also *hard-heads*. 1794. **6.** A variety of sponge 1883. **7.** A residual alloy of tin, iron, and arsenic, produced in the refining of tin (Raymond).

Ha·rd-headed, *a.* 1583 **1.** *lit.* Having a hard head. †**2.** Not easily turned, as a horse; *fig.* stubborn –1642. **3.** Not moved by sophistry or sentiment; matter-of-fact, logical, practical 1779. Hence **Hardhea·ded·ly** *adv.*, **-ness.**

Ha·rd-hearted, *a.* ME. [f. *hard heart* + -ED [2].] Having a hard heart; unfeeling; unmerciful. Hence **Hardhea·rted·ly** *adv.*, **-ness.**

‖**Hardiesse** (hardiẹ·s). ME. [a. F., f. *hardi* HARDY. Adopted anew as Fr. in 18th c.] Hardihood, boldness.

Hardihood (hā·ɹdihud). 1634. [f. HARDY *a.* + -HOOD.] **1.** Boldness, hardiness; audacity. **2.** Robustness (of body or constitution) (*rare*) 1794.

1. With dauntless h., And brandish'd blade, rush on him MILT. Phr. *To have the h. to deny*, etc. So **Ha·rdihead** (*arch.*).

Hardily (hā·ɹdili), *adv.* ME. [f. HARDY *a.* + -LY [2].] **1.** Boldly. †**2.** Robustly; not tenderly (*rare*) –1793. †**3.** *Parenthetically.* = It may be boldly said; freely, assuredly, by all means. Changed later through *hardely* to *hardly*. –1600.

1. H. I make the assertion [etc.] 1799. **2.** Among those h. brought up BEDDOES.

Hardiment (hā·ɹdimĕnt). *arch.* ME. [a. OF., f. *hardi*; see -MENT.] Boldness, hardihood; †a bold exploit.

Now is the time to prove your h. WORDSW.

Hardiness (hā·ɹdinės). ME. [f. HARDY *a.* + -NESS.] **1.** Boldness; audacity; hardihood. Now *rare*. **2.** Capability of endurance. Now chiefly, Physical robustness. 1642. **3.** Catachr. for *hardness* 1539.

1. There being none that had the h. yet to declare ..for the King CLARENDON. **2.** The extreme h. of the race 1879.

Ha·rdish, *a.* 1580. [See -ISH.] Somewhat hard.

Hardly (hā·ɹdli), *adv.* ME. [f. HARD *a.* + -LY [2].] In a hard manner. †**1.** With energy; vigorously, forcibly, violently –1818. †**2.** Hardily –1622. **3.** With hard pressure; with severity or rigour; harshly 1523. **4.** With hardship; uneasily, painfully 1535. **5.** Not easily. *Obs.* exc. as in 6. 1535. **6.** Barely, only just; not quite; scarcely. (Formerly with superfluous negative.) 1553. **7.** Closely 1584. †**8.** *Parenthetically.* Certainly, assuredly, by all means.

3. The Sea used us h. BP. HALL. The rule worked h. 1886. **4.** The husbandmen live h. 1630. **5.** Easily provoked and h. pacified FORDYCE. **6.** When Day broke, I could h. believe my Eyes 1698. **7.** They were so h. pursued KNOLLES.

Hard-mouthed (hā·ɹdmauðd, -mauþt), *a.* 1617. **1.** Having a hard mouth: said of a horse not easily controlled by the bit. **2.** *fig.* Self-willed 1686.

Hardness (hā·ɹdnės). OE. [f. HARD *a.* + -NESS.] The quality or condition of being hard; difficulty of penetration, solution, apprehension, performance, endurance; inflexibility, stiffness, harshness; rigour, severity, cruelty; obduracy, obstinacy; hardiness, etc.; see HARD *a.* Also with *a.* and *pl.*

†**Ha·rdock.** [app. f. OE. *hār*, ME. *hôr*, HOAR + DOCK.] Some coarse weed; prob. burdock. *Lear.* IV. iv. 4 (Fol. 2).

Ha·rd-pan. *U.S.* 1828. [See PAN.] **1.** A firm subsoil of clayey, gravelly, or sandy detritus; also, hard unbroken ground. **2.** *fig.* Bottom; 'bed-rock' 1852.

Hards, hurds (hāɹdz, hɒ̄ɹdz), *sb. pl.* Now *local.* [OE. *heordan* fem. pl. Sometimes construed as sing.] The coarser parts of flax or hemp; tow.

Hard-set, *a.* ME. [f. SET *pa. pple.*] **1.** In a difficult position; beset by trouble. **2.** Set so as to be hard or firm 1813. **3.** Obstinate. SCOTT.

Ha·rdshell, ha·rd-shell. 1848. **A.** *adj.* **1.** Having a hard shell; as crabs, clams, etc. **2.** *fig.* Rigid in religious orthodoxy 1857. **B.** *sb.* A hard-shelled crab or clam (*U.S.*). So **Hard-shelled** *a.* = above; also, hardened, callous.

Hardship (hā·ɹdʃip). ME. [f. HARD *a.* + -SHIP.] †**1.** The quality of being hard to bear; hardness; severity –1676. **2.** Hardness of fate or circumstance; severe toil or suffering; extreme privation. Also with *a.* and *pl.* ME. †**b.** A piece of harsh treatment –1780.

2. Men to much misery and h. born MILT. **b.** To offer a h. or affront to religious prejudices BURKE.

Hard-tack. 1841. [f. HARD *a.* + TACK *sb.* (fig.).] Ship-biscuit; hence, ordinary sea fare in general.

Hard u·p, *advb.* and *adj. phr.* 1612. **1.** *adv. Naut.* Said of the tiller when it is put as far as possible to windward, so as to turn the ship's head away from the wind. (Usu. as a command.) **2.** *adj.* Hard put to it; in want, *esp.* of money. *Hard up for*, sorely at a loss for. *colloq.* (of slang origin). 1821.

Hardware (hā·ɹdˌwēəɹ). 1515. [See WARE.] Small ware or goods of metal; ironmongery. Also *attrib.* Hence **Ha·rdware-man.**

Ha·rdwood, *sb.* 1568. **1.** The wood or timber of deciduous trees, as dist. from that of pines or firs; *locally*, that of oak and ash. Mostly *attrib.* Chiefly *Sc.* and *U.S.* **2. a.** In Australia, any timber resembling teak, esp. *Backhousia Bancroftii*. **b.** A W. Indian shrub, *Ixora ferrea*. 1888.

Hardy (hā·ɹdi), *a.* ME. [a. OF. *hardi*, nom. sing. *hardiz*, pa. pple. of OF. *hardir* to harden, etc., a. WGer. **hardjan* to make hard, f. *hard* HARD.] **1.** Bold, courageous, daring. **2.** *opprobriously.* Presumptuously bold; showing temerity. Cf. FOOLHARDY. ME. **3.** Capable of enduring fatigue, hardship, rigour of the weather, etc.; robust, vigorous 1548. **b.** *Hort.* Able to grow in the open air throughout the year 1852.

1. A good Knight and hardie of his handes GRAFTON. A h. denial of facts JOHNSON. **3.** [Art] Thou then they Less hardie to endure MILT. The h. pine 1783. **b.** Phr. *Half h.*, able to grow in the open air except in winter. *H. annual*, an annual plant that ripens its seed and sows itself year after year. Also *fig.*, a subject that comes up year after year in Parliament, or in the newspapers.

Ha·rdy, *sb.* 1870. [prob. f. HARD, or HARDY *a.*] A movable piece, called also 'fuller', fitting into a socket in an anvil, used by blacksmiths.

Hare (hēəɹ), *sb.* [Com. Teut.: OE. *hara* :—OTeut. **hason-*, **hazon-*.] **1.** A rodent quadruped of the genus *Lepus*, having long ears and hind legs, a short tail, and a divided upper lip. The common hare of Great Britain and Europe is *L. timidus*. **b.** The buck is sometimes called *Jack hare*. During March (the breeding season) hares are unusually wild; hence the saying *As mad as a March h.* 1529. **2. a.** *fig.* Applied to persons, allusively ME. **b.** He who lays the 'scent' in the sport *hare and hounds*, also called 'paper-chase' 1845. **3.** A southern constellation, *Lepus* 1551. **4.** = SEA-HARE, a molluscous animal, *Aplysia depilans* 1591.

Phrases. *To hold* (*or run*) *with the h. and run* (*or hunt*) *with the hounds*; *to run with h. and hounds*: to try to keep in with both sides. *First catch your h.* (i.e. as the first step to cooking him): a direction jestingly ascribed to Mrs. Glasse, but much more recent.

Comb.: **h.-eyed** *a.*, having eyes that look all round, or that are never closed; **-hearted** *a.*, timid; **-kangaroo**, a small kangaroo of the genus *Lagorchestes*, so called from its resemblance to a h. in size and colour; **hare's eye** = lagophthalmia, a disease arising from the contraction of the upper eyelid, so that the patient is obliged to sleep with the eye half-open; **-sighted** *a.*, short-sighted; †**-sleep**, a very light sleep.

b. In names of plants: **hare's-bane**, *Aconitum Lagoctonum*; **hare's-beard**, the Great Mullein; **hare's colewort, house, lettuce, palace, thistle** (also *h.-thistle*), names for the Sow-thistle, *Sonchus oleraceus*; **hare's eye**, the Red Campion; **hare's-meat**, Wood-sorrel; **h.-parsley**, Wild Chervil; **hare's-tail (grass)**, *Lagurus ovatus*; **hare's-tail rush**, Single-headed Cotton-grass.

†**Hare,** *v.* 1523. [Origin not clear.] **1.** *trans.* To harry; to worry; to harass –1674. **2.** To scare –1750.

2. To h. and rate them thus at every turn, is not to teach them LOCKE.

Harebell, hare-bell (hēə·ɹbel). Also **hair-bell.** ME. [f. HARE *sb.* + BELL; perh. as growing where hares frequent.] **1.** = BLUE-BELL 2. **2.** = BLUEBELL 1. 1765.

2. E'en the slight hare-bell raised its head Elastic from her airy tread SCOTT.

Ha·re-brain. Also **hair-.** 1550. [f. HARE *sb.* + BRAIN. The sp. *hair-brain* is later.] †**1.** A person who has a brain like a hare's; a giddy or reckless person –1670. **2.** *attrib.* or *adj.* = HARE-BRAINED. 1566.

Ha·re-brained, *a.* Also **hair-.** 1548. [f. *hare brain* + -ED [2]. For *hair-* see prec.] Having no more brains or sense than a hare; heedless; rash, wild, mad.

They, out of a hare-brained lunacie, desire battaile 1615.

Ha·re-finder. A man whose business is to find or espy a hare in form. *Much Ado* I. i. 186.

Harefoot, hare-foot. ? *Obs.* ME. **1.** A foot resembling a hare's; *spec.* a long narrow foot found in some dogs 1748. **2.** A nickname for a fleet-footed person ME. **3.** A plant; = HARE'S-FOOT 1. ME.

Hareld (hæ·rĕld). 1841. [ad. mod.L. *Harelda*, altered from *Havelda*, f. Icel. name *havelle*.] A species of sea-duck, *Harelda glacialis*.

Hare-lip (hēə·ɹˌli·p). Also †**hair-.** 1567. [f. HARE *sb.* + LIP.] Fissure of the upper lip, caused by arrest of development; so called from resemblance to the cleft lip of a hare. Hence **Hare-lipped** *a.*

Harem, haram (hēə·rĕm). Also **hareem, harīm** (harī·m). 1634. [a. Arab. *ḥaram*, and *ḥarīm* lit. (that which is) prohibited or unlawful, a sacred place, sanctuary, enclosure; the women's part of the house; wives, women.] **1.** The part of a Mohammedan dwelling-house appropriated to the women; called also *seraglio*, and in Persia and India *zenana*. Also *transf.* and *fig.* **2.** The occupants of a harem collectively; *esp.* the wives and concubines collectively of a Turk, Persian, or Indian Mussulman 1781. Also *transf.* and *fig.* **3.** A Mohammedan sacred place or area. More usually *harām*, forbidden, sacred place 1855.

Hare·ngiform, *a.* 1828. [f. mod. Zool. L. *harengus* + -FORM.] Having the form of a herring. (Dicts.)

Hare's-ear (hēə·ɹzˌiəɹ). 1597. [From the shape of the leaves.] The name given to species of *Bupleurum* (N.O. *Umbelliferæ*), and *Erysimum* (N.O. *Cruciferæ*), having auricled leaves.

Hare's-foot. 1562. **1.** A species of clover (*Trifolium arvense*), with soft hair about the flowers. Also called *hare's-foot trefoil.* **2.** The Corkwood tree (*Ochroma Lagopus*) of the W. Indies and Central America; so called from the dehiscent ripe fruit with the cotton of the seeds protruding from it 1866.

Comb.: **Hare's-foot Fern,** a name of *Davallia canariensis*; also of other species, as *D. pyxidata.* **Hare's-foot Sedge,** *Carex lagopina.*

‖**Harfang** (hā·ɹfæŋ). 1774. [a. F., a. Sw. *harfång*, f. *har(e* hare + *fånga* to catch.] The Great Snowy Owl.

Haricot (hæ·riko, -kǫt), *sb.* 1653. [a. F. *haricot*; of uncertain origin. See Littré.] **1.** A ragout (orig. of mutton, now occas. of other meat). Also *attrib.* 1706. **2.** A leguminous plant of the genus *Phaseolus*, esp. *P. vulgaris*, the common Kidney-bean or French-bean; also *Haricot bean.* Applied both to the plant and to the beans. Hence **Haricot, Harico** *v. trans.* to make into a h. (sense 1).

Harier, obs. f. HARRIER.

Hari-kari, erron. f. HARA-KIRI.

†**Ha·riolate,** *v.* 1656. [f. L. *hariolat-*, *hariolari*, f. *hariolus* soothsayer.] *intr.* To soothsay; also, in 17th c., to practise ventriloquism –1677. Hence †**Hariola·tion.**

†**Harish** (hēᵊ·riʃ), *a.* 1552. [f. HARE *sb.* + -ISH.] Of the nature of a hare; mad, foolish –1581.

Hark (hāɹk), *v.* Early ME. *herkien* :— OE. type **heorcian*; in ablaut relation with MDu. *horken, horcken*, etc.] **1.** *trans.* To give ear or listen to. **2.** *intr.* To give ear, hearken, listen. Also *absol.* (chiefly in *imperative.*) ME. **3.** *intr.* Used in hunting, etc., as a call of attention and incitement 1610.

1. H. what he himself here saith 1680. 2. Just Lord, to my suit h. SIDNEY. *absol.* Harke, they rore *Temp.* IV. i. 262. *Hark'ee, harkee*: = hark ye (in the imperative); so, less commonly, *hark you*, and by confusion *hark thee.* 3. *Hark away, forward, in, off*: to proceed or go away, forward, in, draw off. *H. back*: (of hounds) to return along the course taken, till the lost scent is found again; hence *fig.* to retrace one's course or steps. *H. on, forwards* (trans.): to urge on with encouraging cries. *H. back*: to recall.

Hark, *sb.* 1737. [f. HARK *v.*] **a.** An act of harking. **b.** A shout starting or urging on the hounds in the chase; also *hark away.* **c.** *Hark back*: a backward move.

Harken, *v.* etc.: see HEARKEN, etc.

Harl, harle, *sb.* See also HERL. 1450. [app. = MLG. *herle, harle*, etc., LG. *harl* fibre of flax or hemp.] **1.** A filament or fibre (of flax or hemp) 1649. **2.** A barb or fibre of a feather 1450.

Harleian (haɹlī·ăn, hā·ɹliăn), *a.* 1744. [ad. mod.L. *Harleianus*, f. surname *Harley.*] Of or belonging to Robert Harley Earl of Oxford (1661–1724), and his son Edward Harley; esp. in reference to the library of books and MSS. collected by them, of which the MSS. were purchased in 1753 and deposited in the British Museum.

Harlequin (hā·ɹlĭkwin, -kin), *sb.* 1590. [a. F. *harlequin, arlequin*, ad. It. *arlecchino*; ? of Teut. origin.] **1.** A character in Italian and French light comedy; in English pantomime a mute character supposed to be invisible to the clown and pantaloon; he has many attributes of the clown (his rival in the affections of Columbine) with the addition of mischievous intrigue; he usually wears particoloured bespangled tights and a visor, and carries a light bat of lath as a magic wand. Also *transf.* **2.** A small breed of spotted dogs 1774. **3.** A northern species of duck, *Histrionicus minutus*, with variegated plumage; also *Harlequin duck* 1772.

1. A piece of patch-work, a mere harlequin's coat FOOTE. In the same manner as dumb h. is represented on our theatres JOHNSON.

II. *attrib.* or as *adj.* Resembling a harlequin or his dress; burlesque, ludicrous; particoloured 1779.

Comb.: **h.-bat,** an Indian species, *Scotophilus ornatus*, of pale tawny-brown, with white spots; **h. beetle,** a S. American longicorn beetle, *Acrocinus longimanus*, with particoloured elytra; **h. brant,** the American white-fronted goose, *Anser albifrons gambeli*, also called *pied* or *speckled brant*; **h. cabbage-bug,** an American hemipterous insect, *Murgantia histrionica*, having brilliant markings; **h. duck**: see 3; **h.-flower,** a name of the S. African genus *Sparaxis*, N.O. *Iridaceæ*, with great variety of colouring; **h. garrot,** the golden-eye duck or pied widgeon, a species of *Clangula*; **h. moth,** the magpie moth, *Abraxas grossulariata*; **h. pigeon,** an Australian Bronze-wing pigeon; **h. ring,** a ring so called because set round with variously-coloured stones; **h. rose,** a variety of rose with striped petals; **h. snake,** the coral-snake and other species of *Elaps*, so called from their variegated colouring of orange and black.

Harlequin, *v. rare.* 1737. [f. prec. sb.] **a.** *trans.* To conjure *away*, like harlequin. **b.** *intr.* To play the harlequin 1828.

Harlequinade (hāɹlĭk(w)inē¹·d), *sb.* 1780. [a. F. *arlequinade*; see prec. and -ADE.] A kind of pantomime; that part of a pantomime in which the harlequin and clown play the principal parts. Also *transf.* Hence **Harlequina·de** *v.* to play the harlequin; to act fantastically.

†**Ha·rlock.** 1631. Some flower not identified. It cannot well be either *hardock* or *charlock.* DRAYTON.

Harlot (hā·ɹlət, -ǫt), *sb.* ME. [Found first as masc., early in 13th c.; a. OF. *herlot, harlot, arlot* masc., lad, young fellow, base fellow, knave, vagabond. A Rom. word, of uncertain history and origin.] †**1.** A vagabond, beggar, rogue, villain, low fellow, knave. In 16–17th c., sometimes a man of loose life; also, often, a term of insult. –1699. †**2.** An itinerant jester or juggler –1483. †**3.** A male servant; a menial; cf. KNAVE –1536. †**4.** = 'Fellow' –1634. **5.** Applied to a woman. **a.** As a general term of execration (*rare*) 1485. **b.** *spec.* An unchaste woman; a strumpet ME. Also *fig.* **6.** *attrib.* That is a harlot; of or pertaining to a harlot ME.

4. He [Somonour] was a gentil h. and a kynde A bettre felawe sholde men noght fynde CHAUCER. 6. And teare the stain'd skin of my H. brow SHAKS.

Phr. *To play the h.* (Of both sexes, but chiefly of women.) Hence **Ha·rlot** *v.* to play the h.

Harlotry (hā·ɹlǫtri), *sb.* (*a.*) ME. [f. HARLOT *sb.* + -RY.] †**1.** Buffoonery; ribaldry; obscene talk or behaviour –1809. **2.** Unchastity; the conduct of a harlot; dealing with harlots; the practice or trade of prostitution ME. **3.** *concr.* A harlot; a term of opprobrium for a woman 1584. **4.** *fig.* Meretriciousness 1768. †**5.** *attrib.* or as *adj.* Base, filthy, trashy –1663.

3. A peeuish selfe-will'd h. SHAKS. 4. Ev'n as the virgin blush of innocence [eclips'd] The h. of art G. MASON.

Harm (hāɹm), *sb.* [Com. Teut.: OE. *hearm* :—OTeut. **harmo-z*; perh. cogn. w. Skr. *śrama* labour, toil.] **1.** Evil (physical or otherwise) as done or suffered; hurt, injury, damage, mischief. Also with *a.* and *pl.* †**2.** Grief, pain, trouble, affliction. Also with *a.* and *pl.* –1627.

1. Thou shalt have no harme truely CHAUCER. Of ij harmys the leste is to be taken 1461. Phr. *Out of harm's way*: out of the way of doing or of suffering injury.

Harm, *v.* [OE. *hearmian*, f. *hearm* HARM *sb.*] To do harm (to); to injure; to hurt, damage. Orig. *intr.* To be hurtful, with dative, which ult. became a simple object, making the vb. *trans.* Also *absol.*

An High Elme..in the midst of a Garden..harms all round about it 1659. When a man has no sense he is harmed by courage JOWETT.

‖**Harmala** (hā·ɹmălă), **harmel** (hā·ɹmel). OE. [Late L., = Gr. ἅρμαλα, from Semitic.] Wild rue, *Peganum Harmala*, a plant native to Southern Europe and Asia Minor. Hence **Harmaline** (hā·ɹmăləin), *Chem.*, a white crystalline alkaloid ($C_{13}H_{14}N_2O$) obtained from the seeds of wild rue.

†**Ha·rman.** *Thieves' Cant.* 1567. [f. ? + *-man(s* as in *darkmans*, etc.] **1.** pl. *Harmans*, the stocks –1609. **2.** Short for *Harman-beck*: A constable –1829. Hence †**Ha·rman-beck** [*beck*, BEAK *sb.*³], a constable.

‖**Harmattan** (haɹmæ·tăn, in 18th c. hā·ɹmătæn). 1671. [From *haramata*, the name in the Fanti lang. of W. Africa.] A dry parching land-wind, which blows during December, January, and February, on the coast of Upper Guinea; it obscures the air with a red dust-fog. Also *attrib.*

Harmel: see HARMALA.

Harmful (hā·ɹmfŭl), *a.* ME. [See -FUL.] Fraught with harm; injurious. **Ha·rmful-ly** *adv.*, **-ness.**

Harmine (hā·ɹməin). 1864. [f. HARMA(LA + -INE.] *Chem.* An alkaloid ($C_{13}H_{12}N_2O$) contained in the seeds of HARMALA, or obtained by oxidation of harmaline. **Harmi·nic** *acid*, an acid ($C_{10}H_8N_2O_4$) obtained by oxidation of h.

Harmless (hā·ɹmlės), *a.* ME. [-LESS.] **1.** Free from harm; unhurt, uninjured. Now *rare.* **2.** Free from loss, free from liability to punishment, or to pay for loss ME. **3.** Innocent (*arch.*) ME. **4.** Inoffensive, innocuous 1533.

2. *To save* the lessee *h.* from any claiming by, from, or under the covenantor 1818. 3. To follow h. Nature FELTHAM. **Ha·rmless-ly** *adv.*, **-ness.**

Harmonic (haɹmǫ·nik). 1570. [ad. L. *harmonicus*, a. Gr. ἁρμονικός, in neut. pl. ἁρμονικά as sb., theory of music, f. ἁρμονία HARMONY; see -IC.]

A. *adj.* **1.** Relating to music, musical; in reference to ancient music, Relating to melody as dist. from rhythm. *Obs.* exc. in spec. uses. **2.** Harmonious, in harmony, concordant 1667. **3.** *Mus.* Relating to harmony (as dist. from melody and rhythm); belonging to the combination of musical notes in chords 1661. **4.** *Acoustics* and *Mus.* Applied to the tones produced by the vibration of a sonorous body in aliquot parts of its length (see B. 2); relating to such tones 1831. **5.** *Math.* **a.** Applied to the relation of quantities whose reciprocals are in arithmetical progression (e.g. $1, \frac{1}{2}, \frac{1}{3}, \frac{1}{4}, \ldots$); or to points, lines, functions, etc., involving such a relation 1706. **b.** **Harmonic motion,** a periodic motion, which in its simplest form (*simple h. motion*) is like that of a point in a vibrating string, and is identical with the resolved part, parallel to a diameter, of uniform motion in a circle 1867. **6.** Relating to or marked by harmony, agreement, or concord; harmonizing in aspect or artistic effect; harmonious in feeling, etc. 1756. **7.** *Anat.* Belonging to or of the nature of a false suture 1826.

2. With Heav'nly touch of instrumental sounds In full h. number joind MILT. 4. *Harmonic scale*: the scale formed by the series of harmonics of a fundamental note. 5. a. *H. progression*, the relation of a series of quantities whose reciprocals are in arithmetical progression, or such a series itself. *H. proportion*, the relation of three quantities in h. progression; the second is said to be a *h. mean* between the first and third. b. *H. function*, a function consisting of a series of terms, each of which expresses a harmonic motion; in a wider sense, any function that satisfies a differential equation of a class of which that expressing a simple harmonic motion is the first example. *H. analysis*, the calculus of h. functions, an important part of modern mathematical analysis. *H. current* (*Electr.*), an alternating current the variations of which follow the law of a harmionc curve.

B. *sb.* **1.** *pl.* A theory or system of musical sounds or intervals; that part of acoustics which relates to music. (Rarely in *sing.*) *Obs.* exc. in reference to ancient systems 1709. **2.** (Short for *h. tone.*) One of the secondary tones produced by vibration of the aliquot parts of a sonorous body (as a string, reed, column of air in a pipe, etc.); usually accompanying the primary tone produced by the vibration of the body as a whole. Also called *overtones* or *upper partials.* 1777. **3.** *Math.* = *H. function* (A. 5 b), in the wider sense. *Spherical h.*, a h. function having a relation to Spherical Geometry akin to that which functions expressing harmonic motion have to Plane Geometry 1867. **4.** *Electr.* In an alternating circuit, a component current whose frequency is a multiple of the fundamental 1894.

Harmonica (haɹmǫ·nikă). 1762. [fem. of L. *harmonicus*, used subst.] **1. a.** An instrument consisting of a row of hemispherical glasses fitted on an axis turned by a treadle and dipping into a trough of water, played by the application of the finger. **b.** An instrument consisting of a row of glass plates mounted on a resonance box and struck with hammers. **c.** A kind of mouth organ. **2.** Name given to different organ-stops 1840.

Harmonical (haɹmǫ·nikăl), *a.* 1531. [f. as HARMONIC + -AL.] **1.** = HARMONIC *a.* 6. Now *rare.* **2.** Relating to collation of parallel passages in different books 1612. †3. = HARMONIC *a.* 1. –1837. †4. = HARMONIC *a.* 2. –1774. 5. = HARMONIC *a.* 3. ? *Obs.* 1727. †6. = HARMONIC *a.* 4. 1727. 7. *Math.* = HARMONIC *a.* 5. 1569. †b. as *sb.* (*pl.*) Quantities in harmonical progression –1796. †8. *Anat.* = HARMONIC *a.* 7. 1578.

Harmonically (haɹmǫ·nikăli), *adv.* 1589. [f. prec. + -LY [2].] †1. Harmoniously, agreeingly. (Sometimes *fig.* from 2.) –1681. †2. With harmony or concord of sounds –1751. 3. *Mus.* In relation to harmony 1775. 4. *Math.* In a harmonic relation or proportion 1597.

Harmonicon (haɹmǫ·nikǫ̆n). 1825. [a. Gr. ἁρμονικόν adj. neut. sing.] a. = HARMONICA 1 a, b. b. A mouth-organ consisting of a row of free reeds arranged in case so as to give different notes by expiration and inspiration.

Harmonious (haɹmōu·niəs), *a.* 1530. [ad. F. *harmonieux*, f. *harmonie*; see -OUS.] 1. Marked by harmony, agreement, or concord 1638. b. Marked by agreement of feeling or sentiment; consentient, unanimous 1724. 2. Characterized by harmony of sounds; concordant; tuneful; full of harmony 1549. b. *transf.* Of persons: Singing, playing, or speaking tunefully or agreeably 1530.

1. A .h. order of architecture in all its parts HOGARTH. 2. H. bells G. HERBERT. b. The popular air known as 'The Harmonious Blacksmith' GROVE. Hence **Harmo·nious-ly** *adv.*, **-ness.**

Harmoniphon, -phone (haɹmǫ·nifǫ̆n, -fōun). 1839. [f. Gr. ἁρμονία + -φωνος -sounding.] A musical instrument consisting of a tube like that of a clarinet, enclosing a set of free reeds governed by a keyboard. Also applied to a musical box with a combination of reeds and pipes.

Harmonist (hā·ɹmŏnist). 1570. [f. HARMONIZE *v.*; see -IST.] 1. One skilled in musical harmony. a. A musician. Also *fig.* A poet (cf. *singer*). 1742. b. A composer skilled in harmony (as dist. from melody, etc.); one versed in the theory of harmony 1790. c. One of a school of ancient Greek musical theorists who founded the rules of music on the subjective effects of tones, not on their mathematical relations, as the *canonists* did 1570. 2. One who collates and harmonizes parallel narratives, or the like; *esp.* one who makes a harmony of the Gospels 1713. 3. A harmonizer 1809. 4. (with capital *H.*) One of a communistic religious body in the United States, founded by Geo. Rapp of Würtemberg in 1803; they settled in Pennsylvania, and founded a town called Harmony (whence their name) 1824. Hence **Harmoni·stic** *a.* belonging to the work of a h. (sense 2); *sb.* (also in *pl.*) harmonistic studies. **Harmoni·stically** *adv.* in the manner of a h.; in relation to a harmony of writings.

Harmonium (haɹmōu·niǒm). 1847. [a. F. *harmonium*, deriv. of Gr.-L. *harmonia* or Gr. ἁρμονιός; cf. *melodium.*] A keyboard instrument, the tones of which are produced by free metal reeds, tongues, or vibrators, actuated by a current of air from bellows, usually worked by treadles; a kind of reed-organ.

Harmonization (hā·ɹmŏnəizēi·ʃən). 1837. [f. next + -ATION.] The action or process of harmonizing.

Harmonize (hā·ɹmŏnəiz), *v.* 1483. [a. F. *harmoniser*, f. *harmonie*; see -IZE.] †1. *intr.* To sing or play in harmony. CAXTON. 2. To be in harmony (*with*); to accord, agree 1629; to form a concord 1855. 3. *trans.* To bring into harmony, agreement, or accord 1700. Also *absol.* b. To reconcile 1767. 4. *Mus.* To add notes, usually of lower pitch, to the notes of (a melody) so as to form chords; to add harmony to. Also *absol.* 1790.

2. The colours do not h. (*mod.*). 3. A music harmonizing our wild cries TENNYSON. When social laws first harmonized the world JOHNSON. Hence **Ha·rmonizer,** one who harmonizes.

Harmonometer (hāɹmŏnǫ·mĭtəɹ). 1823. [ad. F. *harmonomètre*, irreg. f. *harmonie* + *-mètre* (see -METER).] An instrument for measuring the harmonic relations of musical notes.

Harmony (hā·ɹmŏni). ME. [a. F. *harmonie*, ad. L. *harmonia*, a. Gr., f. stem ἁρμο- of ἁρμόζειν to fit together, arrange.] 1. Combination or adaptation of parts, elements, or related things, so as to form a consistent and orderly whole; agreement, congruity 1532. 2. Agreement of feeling or sentiment; peaceableness, concord. (Sometimes as *fig.* from 4.) 1588. 3. Combination of parts or details with each other, so as to produce an æsthetically pleasing effect; agreeable aspect thus arising 1650. 4. The combination of musical notes, so as to produce a pleasing effect; melody; music. (The earliest sense in English.) ME. b. *gen.* Pleasing combination of sounds 1529. 5. *Mus.* The combination of (simultaneous) notes so as to form chords (dist. from *melody*, which is the succession of notes forming an air or tune); that part of musical art or science which deals with chords; the structure of a piece in relation to its chords 1526. 6. A collation of passages on the same subject from different writings, arranged so as to exhibit their consistency; as, a *harmony* of the Gospels 1588. 6. *Anat.* False suture or union by mere apposition. 1615.

1. *Pre-established harmony* (Leibnitz): a harmony between mind and matter established before their creation, whereby their actions correspond though no communication exists between them. 2. Harmonie to behold in wedded pair MILT. 3. The h. of a face 1650. 4. Songes ful of Armonye CHAUCER. Ten thousand Harpes that tun'd Angelic harmonies MILT. *H. of the spheres*: see SPHERE. b. O mighty-mouthed inventor of harmonies TENNYSON.

Harmost (hā·ɹmǫst). 1775. [ad. Gr. ἁρμοστής, f. ἁρμόζειν to fit, regulate.] One of the governors sent out by the Spartans during their supremacy to control the subject cities and islands.

Harmotome (hā·ɹmǒtoum). 1804. [a. F. *harmotome* (Haüy), f. Gr. ἁρμός joint + -τομος cutting.] *Min.* A hydrous silicate of aluminium and barium, commonly occurring in cruciform twin crystals of various colours. Also called *cross-stone*.

Harness (hā·ɹnės), *sb.* [ME. *harneis*, *harneys*, a. OF. *harneis*, *-ois* (mod. *harnais*). Ult. origin unkn.] †1. Tackle, gear, furniture, armament; e.g. of a ship, a fishing-rod, etc. –1632. 2. Body-armour; all the defensive equipment of an armed horseman, for both man and horse; military equipment or accoutrement. *Hist.* or *arch.* ME. Also *fig.* b. with *a*: A suit of mail 1489. 3. The trappings of a horse; now confined to the gear or tackle of a draught horse or other animal ME. b. *fig.* Working equipments; the routine of daily work 1841. †4. Furniture; apparel –1601. 5. The apparatus in a loom by which the sets of warp-threads are shifted alternately to form the shed; the mounting 1572. †6. Ware, gear; *fig.* affairs, matters. CHAUCER.

2. At least wee'l dye with Harnesse on our backe SHAKS. *fig.* Men who win power, easily put on its h., dignity LYTTON. 3. Wild horses..which had never before been in h. 1834. b. *In h.*, in the routine of daily work; *to die in h.*, i.e. in the midst of work.

Ha·rness, *v.* ME. [In form *harnesche*, a. OF. *harneschier*, f. *harnesc-*, OF. *harneis* HARNESS.] †1. To furnish, equip, accoutre; esp. to ornament with fittings of price –1534. 2. To equip in harness or armour; to arm (*arch.*) ME.; †to fortify (*Macc.* iv. 7). Also *fig.* 3. To put harness on (a horse, etc.); now only on draught animals, *esp.* carriage-horses ME. Also *fig.* 4. To dress, apparel, array. *Obs.* or *arch.* ME.

1. A gay daggere, Harneised wel and sharpe as point of spere CHAUCER. 2. H. yourselves for the war BUNYAN. 3. *fig.* Harnessed together in matrimony SHERIDAN. Hence **Ha·rnesser.**

†**Ha·rness-bearer.** 1563. An armour-bearer –1611.

Ha·rness-cask. 1818. *Naut.* A cask or tub with a rimmed cover used on board ship for keeping the salt meats for present consumption. Also *harness-tub*.

Harns, *sb. pl.*, brains.

Harp (hāɹp), *sb.* [Com. Teut.: OE. *hearpe* :—OTeut. **harpôn-*. Thence late L. *harpa.*] 1. A musical instrument consisting of a framework, now usually triangular in form, furnished with strings (and now with pedals), and played with the fingers. Also *fig.* 2. The northern constellation Lyra 1551. †3. a. = *harp-groat* (see *Comb.*). b. Short for *harp-shilling* (see *Comb.*). –1606. 4. A screen or sieve. *Sc.* 1768. 5. Also *harp-shell*: A mollusc of the genus *Harpa* of family *Buccinidæ*, and its shell 1751. 6. Also *harp-seal*: The Greenland seal: so named from the harp-shaped dark marking on the back 1784.

1. Our pleasures are the feast, the h., the dance COWPER. *Double harp*: one with two sets of strings differently tuned. *Æolian h.*: see ÆOLIAN.

Comb.: **h.-file,** a wire hook for filing papers, attached to a harp-shaped piece of iron; **-fish,** a fish of the genus *Lyra*, the Piper; **†-groat,** an Irish coin bearing the figure of a h. on the reverse; **-lute,** an instrument having twelve strings and resembling the guitar; **-seal,** see 6; **†-shilling**: see HARPER[1] 2; **†-star,** Vega, the chief star in Lyra.

Harp, *v.* [OE. *hearpian*, f. prec. sb.] 1. *intr.* To play on a harp. †2. *trans.* To play (notes, etc.) upon a harp –1777. †3. *trans.* To play upon, twang 1628. 4. *intr.* To make a sound like that of the harp 1657. 5. *trans.* To give voice to, to guess 1605. †b. *intr. To h. at*: To guess at. MILT.

1. Sworded seraphim..Harping in loud and solemn quire MILTON. *fig. To h. upon, on, a, one, the same* (etc.) *string*: to dwell on a subject to a wearisome or tedious length. *To h. on, upon*: to dwell wearisomely upon in speech or writing; Still harping on my daughter SHAKS. 5. Thou hast harp'd my feare aright SHAKS.

†**Harpagon.** 1553. [ad. L. *harpago*, *-onem*, f. Gr. ἁρπάγη.] A grappling-hook –1600.

Harper [1] (hā·ɹpəɹ). [OE. *hearpere*; see HARP *sb.* and -ER [1].] 1. One who harps or plays upon a harp. 2. Applied to Irish coins, bearing the figure of a harp; *esp.* the *harp-shilling*, worth 9*d.* English. *Obs.* exc. *Hist.* 1598. 3. The harp-seal (*Cent. Dict.*).

Harper [2] (also *harpier*), app. error for HARPY. *Macb.* IV. i. 3.

Ha·rping, *ppl. a.* 1641. [See -ING [2].] That harps or plays on a harp. Also *transf.*

†**Harping-iron** (hā·ɹpiŋ,əi·əɹn). 1596. [Related to F. *harper* to grapple, etc.] A barbed spear used for spearing whales and large fish; a harpoon –1814.

Harpings (hā·ɹpinz), *sb. pl.* Also †**harpins,** †**harpens.** 1658. [? f. HARP *sb.*] 1. a. The fore-parts of the wales which encompass the bow of a ship and are fastened to the stem. b. Pieces of oak, forming an extension of the ribbands, for holding the cant-frames of a vessel in place until the outside planking is worked. 2. *Cat-harpings*: the ropes or (now oftener) iron cramps that serve to brace in the shrouds of the lower-masts behind their respective yards. Also *cat-harping legs*. 1626.

Harpist (hā·ɹpist). 1613. [-IST.] A (professional) harper.

Harpoon (haɹpū·n), *sb.* 1625. [ad. F. *harpon*, deriv. of *harpe* dog's claw, cramp, cramp-iron, etc., ad. L. *harpe* (*harpa*) = Gr. ἅρπη sickle, scimitar.] †1. A barbed dart or spear –1697. 2. A barbed spear-like missile, to the shank of which a long line of rope is attached; it is used for capturing whales or large fish, being either hurled by the hand or fired from a gun 1694.

Comb.: **h.-fork,** a kind of hay-fork worked by tackle in loading or unloading hay; **-gun,** a gun for firing harpoons; **-rocket,** a bomb-lance for killing whales.

Harpoo·n, *v.* 1774. [f. prec.] *trans.* To strike or spear with a harpoon. Also *transf.* and *fig.*

Harpooneer (hāɹpūnī·ɹ). Now *rare.* Also †-ier. 1613. [f. HARPOON *sb.* + -EER, -IER.] = next.

Harpooner (hāɹpū·nəɹ). 1726. [f. HARPOON *v.* + -ER [1].] One who hurls or fires a harpoon.

Ha·rpress. [f. HARPER + -ESS.] A female harper. SCOTT.

†**Ha·rpsical** (also **-secol, -sicol,** vulg. **haspicols**). 1616. Corrupt ff. HARPSICHORD, prop. after *virginal* –1773.

Harpsichord (hā·ɹpsikǭɹd). 1611. [ad. obs. F. *harpechorde* (Cotgr.), f. L. *harpa* + *chorda* string. The *s* is intrusive.] A keyboard instrument of music (resembling in appearance the grand piano), in which the strings were plucked or set in vibration by quill or leather points set in jacks connected by levers with the keys. (In use from 16–18th c.) Also *attrib.*

Harpy (hā·ɹpi). 1540. [ad. L. *harpyia*, usu. in pl. *harpyiæ* = Gr. ἅρπυιαι 'snatchers'. Perh. immed. a. F. *harpie.*] **1.** *Gr.* and *L. Myth.* A fabulous monster, rapacious and filthy, having a woman's face and body and a bird's wings and claws, and supposed to act as a minister of divine vengeance. **2.** *transf.* and *fig.* A rapacious, plundering, or grasping person 1589. **3.** The HARPY-EAGLE 1838. **4.** The moor-buzzard, *Circus æruginosus* 1838. **5.** The HARPY-BAT, q.v.

1. Both table and provisions vanished quite With sound of harpies' wings, and talons heard MILT. **2.** The insolent carriage of Prince Rupert, and his Harpyes 1643. The harpies of taxation JOHNSON. Hence **Harpyian** (erron. **-peian, -pyan**) *a.*

Ha·rpy-ba·t. 1883. A name of two or more species of bat found in the East Indies.

Ha·rpy-ea·gle. 1830. A large and powerful bird of prey (*Thrasyaëtus harpyia*, or *Harpyia destructor*) with crested head and fan-shaped tail, a native of S. America.

Harquebus, arquebus (hā·ɹkwɪ̆bɒ̆s, ā·ɹk-), *sb.* 1532. [a. 16th c. F. (*h*)*arquebuse*, a corruption, through It., of MHG. *hake*(*n*)*bühse* lit. 'hook-gun'; see HACKBUSH, HACKBUT.] **1.** The early type of portable gun, varying in size, and, when used in the field, supported upon a tripod, trestle, or other 'carriage', or upon a forked rest. The name in German meant literally 'hook-gun', from the hook, cast along with it, by which it was attached to the carriage; but the meaning was forgotten, and the name became generic for portable fire-arms in the 16th c.; see 2. 1520. **†2. Harquebus à croc** (corruptly *of crock*): 'An arquebus supported on a rest by a hook of iron fastened to the barrel. From the size of its calibre it was used to fire through loopholes' (Meyrick) –1693. **3.** *collect.* Soldiers armed with harquebuses 1594.

So **Ha·rquebusa·de, a·rq-**, †a shot from a h.; a continuous discharge of such shots. **Ha·rquebusie·r, a·rq-**, a soldier armed with a h.; vars. **†Ha·rquebusher, -butter.**

†Harrage. A form used by Fuller, app. as = HARRY or HARASS (cf. *ravage*).

Harre, har. *Obs.* exc. *dial.* [OE. *heorr* (*hior*) fem. and m., and *heorra* m. :—OTeut. types **herra-* and **herron-*.] **1.** The hinge of a door or gate. **2.** *fig.* A cardinal point OE.

Harridan (hæ·ridæ̆n). 1700. [? altered f. F. *haridelle* an old jade of a horse.] A haggard old woman; a vixen; 'a decayed strumpet' (J.); usu. a term of abuse.

attrib. The old h. landlady MOORE.

Harrier[1] (hæ·riəɹ). 1556. [f. HARRY *v.* + -ER[1].] **1.** One who harries, ravages, or lays waste 1596. **†2.** A drover –1598. **3.** (Also †*harrower.*) A name for falcons of the genus *Circus*, and their allies; cf. MARSH-HARRIER, etc. 1556.

Comb.: **H. eagle**, *Circaetus gallicus*; **H.-hawk**, a hawk of the American genus *Micrastur.*

Harrier[2] (hæ·riəɹ). 1542. [app. f. HARE *sb.* + -IER.] **1.** A kind of hound, smaller than the fox-hound, used for hunting the hare. **b.** In *pl.* A pack of harriers; including the persons following the chase 1877. **2.** One of a 'hare-and-hounds' team 1891.

Harrovian (hǣrōᵘ·viăn). 1864. [f. mod.L. *Harrovia* + -AN.] *adj.* Of or pertaining to Harrow school. *sb.* One educated at Harrow.

Harrow (hæ·roᵘ), *sb.* [ME. *harwe*, answering to an OE. **hearwe* or **hearȝe*; ult. origin uncertain.] **1.** A heavy frame of timber (or iron) set with iron teeth or tines, which is dragged over ploughed land to break clods, pulverize and stir the soil, root up weeds, or cover in the seed. **2.** *transf.* A similar contrivance used for other purposes 1548. **b.** *Fortif.* A gate made of timber, well fastened to three or four cross bars, and secured with iron 1788. **3.** A diagonal arrangement of soldiers; also of wild geese in the air 1876.

1. *fig.* Under the h. of affliction LANDOR. *Comb.*: **revolving h.**, a h. of which the teeth are fixed on radiating arms, so as to revolve horizontally; *brake* (or *break*) *h.* (see BRAKE *sb.*[3]); BUSH-HARROW; *chain-h.* (see CHAIN *sb.*), etc.

Harrow (hæ·roᵘ), *v.*[1] ME. [f. prec.] **1.** *trans.* To draw a harrow over; to break up, crush, or pulverize with a harrow. Also *absol.* **†2.** *transf.* To cut through as a harrow; to plough (the sea, etc.). STANYHURST. **3.** To tear, lacerate, wound (*lit.* and *fig.*) 1602.

1. Canst thou binde the Vnicorne with his band in the furrow? or will he h. the valleyes after thee *Job* xxxix. 10. **3.** The thorns harrowing his sacred head T. ADAMS. *fig.* I could a Tale vnfold, whose lightest word Would h. vp thy soule SHAKS. Hence **Ha·rrower. Ha·rrowing-ly** *adv.*, **-ness.**

Harrow (hæ·roᵘ), *v.*[2] [A by-form of HARRY *v.*, OE. *herȝian*, of which the pa. t., pa. pple., and vbl. sb. regularly became in ME. *herwede, herwed, herwyng*, whence, by change of *-er* bef. a cons. to *-ar*, and levelling, came ME. *harwe, harowe, harrow.*] *trans.* To harry, rob, spoil.

By him [Christ] that harwed helle CHAUCER. These Picts..did oft-times h. the borders 1606.

†Harrow, haro (hæ·roᵘ), *interj.* ME. [a. OF. *haro, harou*, etc., of obscure origin.] **1.** A cry of distress or alarm; a call for succour. ‖**2.** In Law of Normandy and Channel Isles, in form *haro!*: A cry repeated thrice, and followed by action in the court, in cases of trespass or encroachment 1682.

To cry h. (on any one): to denounce (a person's) doings. Iohn..gan to crie h. and weylaway Our hors is lorn CHAUCER.

Harry (hæ·ri), *sb.* [ME. *Herry*, from *Henry*, *-er* subseq. becoming *-ar*, as in HARRY *v.*] Familiar for Henry. **1.** The proper name. **2.** A generic name for a young Englishman of a low-class type 1874. **3.** *Harrys* or *King Harrys*: playing-cards of the second quality 1842.

Phrases, etc.: **Old Harry**: A familiar name for the Devil. *To play Old H. with*: to play the devil with; to work mischief upon; to ruin. *By the Lord H.*: a form of swearing; of doubtful origin.

Comb.: **H.-bird**, the Greater Shearwater (*Puffinus major*). **H. Denchman, H. Dutchman**, local names of the hooded or Danish Crow. **H. groat**, a groat coined by Henry VIII. **H. noble**, a gold coin of Henry VI. **H. sovereign**, a sovereign of Henry VII or Henry VIII.

Harry (hæ·ri), *v.* [OE. *hęrȝian, hęrian* :—OTeut. type **harjôjan*, f. **harjo-* host, army, HERE *sb.* In this word OE. *ȝ* from *j* gave *w* in ME.] **1.** *intr.* To make predatory raids; to commit ravages. **2.** *trans.* To overrun with an army; to lay waste, sack, pillage, spoil ME. **†b.** *spec.* To despoil *hell*; as said of Christ after his death –1450. **3.** To worry, goad, harass; to maltreat ME. **4.** To carry off in a marauding raid. Now *Sc.* 1579. **5.** To drag. *Obs.* or *dial.* ME.

1. Harrie and make havock of all HOLLAND. **2.** Italie he harried as a conquered countrey SAVILE. **3.** That your mind should be harried it is no wonder JOHNSON. **5.** Þe holy mayde was haryed forth to turment CHAUCER.

Harsh (hāɹʃ), *a.* [ME. *harsk*, a northern word, found from *c.* 1300, agrees in form and sense with MLG. and mod.G *harsch*, harsh, rough. ? A deriv. in *-sk, -sh*, of *hard*, or of the root *har-* in *harm.*] **1.** Disagreeably hard and rough: **a.** to the touch; **b.** to the taste 1440; **c.** to the ear 1530. **2.** Of rough aspect; forbidding 1774; forbidding in general physical effect; rough, rude 1613. **3.** Repugnant to the feelings; severe, rigorous, cruel, rude, unfeeling 1579. **4.** Repugnant to the understanding or taste; strained, lacking smoothness, unpleasing 1594.

1. a. H. haire like goates 1600. **b.** Berries h. and crude MILT. **c.** And with h. din Broke the fair music MILT. **2.** Wild groups and h. faces GOLDSM. A picture without half tones is h. 1894. H. remedies DRYDEN. **3.** A h. sentence 1659, censure 1709, master JOWETT. The h. administration of Laud MACAULAY. **4.** H. transitions 1841. Hence **Ha·rshen** *v.* to render h. **Ha·rshly** *adv.* in a h. manner. **Ha·rshness**, the quality of being h.

Harslet: see HASLET.

Hart (hāɹt). [ME. *hert*, OE. *heort, heorot* :—OTeut. **herut-*; perh. related to Gr. κεραт- horn, as if 'the horned'.] The male of the deer, esp. of the red deer; a stag; *spec.* a male deer after its fifth year.

As the H. panteth after the water brookes *Ps.* xlii. 1. †*Hart of grease*, a fat h. *H. of ten*, a h. with ten branches on his horns. *H. royal*, a h. that has been chased by royalty.

Comb.: **h.-berry**, the Bilberry; **-clover, hart's clover**, Melilot; **hart's-balls** = *hart's truffles*; **†hart's eye**, wild dittany; **hart's-trefoil** = *hart-clover*; **hart's-truffle**, a kind of underground fungus (*Elaphomyces*); **†h.-wolf**, a fabulous animal, a hybrid between a deer and a wolf.

‖**Hartal** (hā·ɹtæl). 1920. *India.* [Hindi, for *hattāl* 'locking of shops'.] A day of national mourning when business is suspended, used as a form of boycott.

Hart(e)beest (hā·ɹtĕbīst, hă·ɹtbīst). 1786. [S. Afr. Du., f. Du. *hert* hart + *beest* beast.] A S. Afr. Antelope (*Alcephalus caama*).

Hartleian (hāɹtlī·ăn, hā·ɹtli,ăn). 1803. **A.** *adj.* Of or pertaining to the doctrines of David Hartley (1705–57), regarded as the founder of the English associationist school of psychologists. **B.** *sb.* One of the H. school.

Hartshorn (hā·ɹts,hǭɹn). OE. [f. *hart's* + HORN.] **1.** The horn or antler of a hart; the substance obtained by rasping, slicing, or calcining the horns of harts, formerly the chief source of ammonia. **†2. a.** Buck's-horn Plantain, *Plantago Coronopus* (also **H. Plantain**); **b.** Swine's Cress, *Senebiera Coronopus*. –1674.

1. *Spirit of h.*, also simply *h.*: the aqueous solution of ammonia (from any source). *Salt of h.*: carbonate of ammonia; smelling salts.

Comb.: **†h. beetle**, the stag-beetle; **h. jelly**, a jelly made formerly from the shavings of harts' horns, now from those of calves' bones; **h. plantain** (see 2).

Hart's-tongue. ME. [tr. med.L. *lingua cervi*; so named from the shape of the fronds.] The common name of *Scolopendrium vulgare*; also given to other species of the genus; occas. also to some other polypodiaceous ferns, as *Olfersia cervina*, etc. So **Hart's-tongue fern.**

Hartwort (hā·ɹtwɒɹt). 1562. [var. of HEARTWORT, q.v.] *Herb.* **1.** Formerly applied to the genus *Seseli*. **2.** A book-name for *Tordylium maximum*, one of the plants formerly included in the genus *Seseli* 1787.

Harum-scarum (hēᵊ·rəm,skēᵊ·rəm). *colloq.* 1674. [A riming comb., app. f. HARE *v.* + SCARE *v.*] **A.** *adv.* Recklessly, wildly. ? *Obs.* **B.** *adj.* Reckless, heedless; wild, rash 1751. **C.** *sb.* A reckless person; reckless action or behaviour 1784.

B. A dissolute, harum-scarum fellow..always in debt LYTTON.

‖**Haruspex** (hărɒ·speks). *Pl.* **-spices** (-isīz). Also **†aruspex.** 1584. [L., f. a root appearing in Skr. *hirā* entrails + L. *-spic-* beholding.] One of the ancient Roman soothsayers, of Etruscan origin, who performed divination by inspection of entrails, etc. Hence **Haru·spical** (**ar-**) *a.* belonging to, or having the function of, a h. So **†Haru·spicate** (**ar-**) *a.* in same sense. **Haruspica·tion**, divination by inspection of entrails.

Haruspicy (hărɒ·spisi). Also **†ar-.** 1569. [ad. L. *haruspicium*, f. *haruspicem*; see HARUSPEX.] The practice or function of a haruspex.

Harvest (hā·ɹvĕst), *sb.* [OE. *hærfest, hęrfest* :—OTeut. **harƀisto-z, -usto-z*, perh. f. a root **harƀ-* = L. *carpere* to crop, cf. Gr. καρπός.] **1.** The third season of the year, autumn. *Obs.* exc. *dial.* **2.** The season for reaping and gathering in the ripened grain. Also *transf.* and *fig.* ME. **3.** The reaping and gathering in of ripened grain; also *transf.* 1526. **4.** The ripened grain or fruit 1526; the season's yield of any natural product 1607. **5.** *fig.* The product of any action or effort; a 'crop' 1576. **6.** *attrib.* Of or pertaining to the autumn or harvest ME., or to the harvest-home 1602.

2. Seed time and H., Heat and hoary Frost Shall hold thir course MILT. *fig.* It is needfull that you frame the season for your owne haruest SHAKS. **3.** A field Of Ceres ripe for h. MILT. Phr. *Lord of the h.*, (*a*) the farmer to whom the crops belong, hence applied to God (*Matt.* ix. 8); (*b*) the head reaper. **4.** Along the furrow here, the h. fell COWPER. The grouse h. 1881. **5.** To reape the Haruest of perpetuall peace SHAKS.

Comb.: **h.-bell**, a flower, the Autumn bell, *Gentiana Pneumonanthe*; **h. festival, thanksgiving**, a service for the ingathering of the h., at which the church is usually decorated with fruit, grain, etc.; **-fish**, the butter- or dollar-fish of N. America, a species of *Stromateus*; **-fly**, a name in U.S. for species of *Cicada*, which appear during h. time; **-louse, -mite** = HARVEST-BUG; **-spider**, a long-legged spider, *Phalangium*, common in harvest-fields;

-tick, (*a*) = HARVEST-BUG; (*b*) any small spider of the genus *Leptidæ*; **-work,** the work of reaping and gathering in the h.

Harvest (hā·ɹvėst), *v.* ME. [f. prec. sb.] **1.** *trans.* To reap and gather in (the corn, hence, any ripe crop). Also *intr.* **2.** *transf.* To gather and lay up in store; to husband 1888.

Harvest-bug. 1768. A minute mite or acarid troublesome during harvest; also called *harvester, harvest-louse, -mite, -tick.*

Harvester (hā·ɹvestəɹ). 1589. [f. HARVEST *v.*] **1.** A reaper. **2.** Applied to various insects: **a.** = *harvesting ant* 1882. **b.** A harvest-bug. **3.** A reaping-machine, *esp.* one which also binds up the sheaves 1875.

Harvest-field. 1730. A field in which the corn is being reaped; a corn-field in harvest. Also *transf.* and *fig.*

Harvest home, harvest-home. 1573. **1.** The fact, occasion, or time of bringing home the last of the harvest; the close of the harvesting. Also *fig.* 1596. **2.** The festival to celebrate the successful homing of the corn. (Now rarely held.) 1573.

1. Like a stubble Land at Haruest-home SHAKS. *Comb.* **harvest-home goose,** one killed and eaten at the harvest-home feast; also called *harvest-goose.*

Ha·rvesting, *ppl. a.* 1873. [-ING [2].] That reaps or gathers in and stores up grain, etc.

Harvesting ant, a kind of ant which gathers and stores up the seeds of grasses; *h. mouse* = HARVEST MOUSE.

Ha·rvestless, *a.* 1868. [-LESS.] Devoid of harvests; sterile.

H. autumn, horrible agues, plague TENNYSON.

Ha·rvestman. 1552. **1.** A reaper; *esp.* one who leaves home to obtain harvest work. **2.** A name given to insects common in harvest-time; *esp.* a long-legged spider, *Phalangium.*

Harvest month. OE. The month (orig. September, but in Robert of Gloucester, August) during which the harvest is gathered in.

Harvest moon. 1706. The moon which is full within a fortnight of the autumnal equinox (22 or 23 Sept.), and which rises for several nights nearly at the same hour, at points successively farther north on the eastern horizon.

Harvest mouse. 1812. A very small species of mouse (*Mus messorius,* or *Micromys minutus*), which builds its nest in the stalks of growing grain.

Harvest queen. 1579. A name given **a.** to Ceres, the goddess of agriculture and crops; **b.** to a young woman chosen from the reapers, to whom was given a post of honour at the harvest home.

Ha·rvey, *v.* 1894. [f. the inventor's name.] **a.** To harden (steel) by a process invented by H. A. Harvey of New Jersey. **b.** To fit or supply (a ship) with armour plates so treated. Also **Ha·rveyize** *v.*

Has, 3rd sing. pres. ind. of HAVE *v.*

Hasard, Hase, obs. ff. HAZARD, HAZE.

Has-been (hæ·z,bīn), *sb.* (*a.*) 1606. One that *has been* but is no longer; a person or thing whose career or efficiency belongs to the past; a back number.

Hash (hæʃ), *v.* 1653. [Earlier *hache,* a. F. *hacher,* f. *hache* hatchet.] **1.** *trans.* To cut (meat) into small pieces for cooking; to make into a hash. Also *fig.* **2.** To cut up or hack about; to mangle. Now *Sc.* and *dial.* Also *intr.* 1663. Hence **Ha·sher.**

Hash (hæʃ), *sb.* 1662. [f. HASH *v.,* replacing *haché, hachee, hachey,* etc., from French.] **1.** Something cut up into small pieces; *spec.* a dish of meat which has been previously cooked, cut small, and warmed up with gravy and sauce. **2.** *transf.* and *fig.* Old matter served up in a fresh form 1672. **3.** A medley; a spoiled mixture; a mess, jumble 1735.

1. I had..at first course, a h. of rabbits, a lamb PEPYS. **2.** Chiefly a well-done h. of my own words DARWIN. Phr. *To make a h. of:* to mangle and spoil in dealing with. *To settle* (a person's) *h.:* to silence, subdue; to 'do for' (*slang* or *colloq.*).

‖**Hashish, hasheesh** (hæ·ʃiʃ, haʃī·ʃ). 1598. [Arab.] The top leaves and tender parts of the Indian hemp (which in warm countries develop intoxicating properties) dried for smoking or chewing, in Arabia, Egypt, Turkey, etc. Cf. BHANG. Also *fig.*

†**Hask, haske,** *sb.* 1579. 'A wicker pad, wherein they vse to cary fish' (SPENSER) –1611.

Haslet (hē¹·slėt), **harslet** (hā·ɹslėt). [ME. *hastelet, hastlet,* a. OF. *hastelet,* dim. of *haste* a spit, a piece of roasted meat :—L. *hasta* spear.] A piece of meat to be roasted, *esp.* part of the entrails of a hog; pig's fry.

Hasp (hɑsp), *sb.* [OE. *hæpse* (:—**hæspe*) wk. fem. 'fastening, clasp, hasp'. Cf. HANK.] **1.** A contrivance for fastening a door or lid; now chiefly, a hinged clasp of metal which passes over a staple and is secured by a pin or padlock. **b.** A latch for a sash window 1772. **2.** A clasp or catch for fastening two parts of a garment, the covers of a book, etc. ME. **3.** A hank or skein of yarn, thread, or silk; a definite quantity of yarn, the fourth part of a spindle ME. **4.** 'An instrument for cutting the surface of grass-land; a scarifier' (Webster) 1864.

Hasp, *v.* [OE. *hæpsian,* f. *hæpse* HASP *sb.*] **1.** *trans.* To fasten with, or as with, a hasp. †**2.** To confine or fasten in a tight place; to lock *up* –1711.

2. Being hasped up with thee in this publick Vehicle STEELE.

Hassock (hæ·sək), *sb.* [OE. *hassuc,* of unkn. etym.] **1.** A firm tuft or clump of matted vegetation; *esp.* of coarse boggy grass or sedge; a tussock. **b.** *transf.* A shock of hair 1785. **2.** A thick firm cushion or bass, used to rest the feet on, and *esp.* in church to kneel on 1516. **3.** The soft calcareous sandstone which separates the beds of ragstone in Kent. (? A different wd.) 1706.

2. Knees and hassocks are well-nigh divorc'd COWPER. Hence **Ha·ssocky** *a.* abounding in hassocks or clumps; consisting of calcareous h.

Hast, 2nd pers. sing. pres. ind. of HAVE.

Hastate (hæ·stē¹t), *a.* 1788. [ad. L. *hastatus,* f. *hasta;* see -ATE [2] 2.] Formed like a spear or spear-head 1854. **b.** *Bot.* Of leaves: Narrowly triangular nearly to the base, where two lateral lobes project at right angles to the midrib 1788. So †**Hasta·ted** *a.*

Ha·stately, *adv.* 1831. [-LY [2].] In a hastate fashion; chiefly in comb. with adjs., as *h.-lanceolate,* etc.

Hasta·to-, comb. f. L. *hastatus,* used like prec.

Haste (hē¹st), *sb.* ME. [a. OF. *haste* (mod. *hâte*) :—WGer. **haisti-,* in OE. *hǽst, hést* fem., violence, fury.] **1.** Urgency or impetuosity of movement tending to swiftness or rapidity; quickness, speed, expedition (properly of voluntary action). **2.** Such quickness of action as excludes due consideration; hurry, precipitancy, rashness ME. **3.** The condition of being obliged to act quickly on account of having little time; hurry ME.

1. This asketh h. CHAUCER. **2.** I said in my h., All men are liars *Ps.* cxvi. 11. Raw H., half-sister to Delay TENNYSON. **3.** The h. to get rich 1872.

Phr. *To make h.:* to put forth energy producing speed; to use expedition, to hasten. (Often with *inf.*)

Haste (hē¹st), *v.* ME. [a. OF. *haster* (mod. *hâter*), f. *haste, hâte,* HASTE *sb.*] **1.** *trans.* To cause to move quickly; to urge, drive, or press on; to hurry. **2.** *refl.* = 3. *arch.* ME. **3.** *intr.* To make haste; to come or go quickly; to act with expedition; (of time or events) to come on rapidly. (Often with *to* and *inf.*) ME.

1. They were so hastyd and pursewyd LD. BERNERS. **2.** Lorde, I call vpon the; haist the vnto me COVERDALE *Ps.* cxl. [cxli.] 1. **3.** If the reward were good, he would hast to gaine more 1581.

Hasteful (hē¹·stfŭl), *a. rare.* 1610. [-FUL.] Full of haste; hurrying, hurried. Hence **Ha·stefully** *adv.*

Hasteless (hē¹·stlės), *a.* 1873. [-LESS.] Without haste. Hence **Ha·stelessness.**

Hasten (hē¹·s'n), *v.* 1565. [Extended form of HASTE *v.*; see -EN [5].] **1.** *trans.* = HASTE *v.* 1. †**b.** To dispatch in haste –1748. **2.** *intr.* = HASTE *v.* 3. 1568.

1. Sorrowe ne neede be hastened on SPENSER. **2.** So do our minutes h. to their end SHAKS. Hence **Ha·stener,** one who or that which hastens; *esp.* a stand or screen for concentrating the heat of the fire on a roasting joint of meat (*dial.*); also **Haster.**

Hastif, -ly, -ness: see HASTIVE, -LY, -NESS.

Hastifoliate (hæstifōu·liět), *a.* 1886. [f. L. *hasta* + *folium;* see -ATE [2].] *Bot.* Having spear-shaped leaves. So **Hastifo·lious** *a.*

Hastiform (hæ·stifǭɹm), *a.* 1886. [f. L. *hasta;* see -FORM.] Spear-shaped.

Hastile (hæ·stəil), *a.* 1864. [f. as prec.; see -ILE.] *Bot.* = HASTATE.

Hastily (hē¹·stili), *adv.* ME. [f. HASTY *a.* + -LY [2].] In haste. **1.** Quickly, expeditiously; †soon, without delay, suddenly; rapidly. Now usu.: Hurriedly. **2.** With undue haste excluding consideration; precipitately, rashly 1586. **3.** In sudden anger 1573.

1. Over-hastily blooming Trees EVELYN. The Northern nobles marched h. to join their comrades GREEN. **2.** She had married h., and as h. grown weary of her choice FROUDE.

Hastiness (hē¹·stinės). ME. [f. as prec. + -NESS.] The quality or condition of being hasty; †swiftness –1591; precipitancy ME.; quickness of temper; passion ME.

Hasting, *ppl. a.* and *sb.* 1546. [f. HASTE *v.* + -ING [2].]

A. *ppl. a.* **1.** That hastes 1632. †**2.** That ripens early –1753.

B. *sb.* [the adj. used ellipt.] **1.** An early-ripening fruit or vegetable; *spec.* a kind of early pea. *Obs.* or *local.* 1573. †**2.** Hence applied to persons who hasten or make haste. Only in *pl.* –1700.

1. A day or two ago I heard the cry 'Green Hastings!'..fifty years ago, it was the usual cry for green peas 1878.

†**Ha·stive, ha·stif,** *a.* ME. [a. OF. *hastif, -ive,* f. *haste* (mod. *hâte*) HASTE *sb.* + -IVE. See also HASTY.] **1.** Speedy, swift (ME. only); (of fruit, etc.) maturing early –1751. **2.** Precipitate, rash. ME. only. **3.** Quick-tempered; angry –1489. Hence †**Ha·stive-, hastif-ly** *adv.,* †**-ness.**

Hasty (hē¹·sti), *a.* ME. [a. OF. *hasti* for *hastif;* see prec. The termination was doubtless identified with native *-i, -y* from OE. *-iᵹ,* cf. Du. *haastig,* Ger., Da., Sw. *hastig.*] Marked by haste. **1.** Speedy, expeditious; swift, rapid; sudden. *arch.* exc. as in b. **b.** Hurried 1590. **c.** Requiring speed; made in haste. *spec.* in *Cookery.* ME. †**d.** Early, forward [L. *præcox*] –1693. †**2.** In a hurry. Usu. with *inf.* –1754. **3.** Unduly quick of action; precipitate, rash, inconsiderate ME. **4.** Of persons, etc.: Quick-tempered, irritable. Of words or actions: Uttered or done in sudden anger or irritation. 1526.

1. We wish h. ruin to all tyrants MILTON. **b.** A h. sketch 1834, glance 1844, reader 1874. **d.** As the hastie fruit before the summer *Isa.* xxviii. 4. **2.** 2 *Hen. IV,* IV. v. 61. **3.** Hastie and furious of heart, and unware of perilles GRAFTON. **4.** Hee that is h. of spirit, exalteth folly *Prov.* xiv. 29.

Hasty pudding. 1599. A pudding made of flour stirred in milk or water to the consistency of a thick batter; in some parts applied to oatmeal porridge; in U.S. made with Indian meal and water.

Hat (hæt), *sb.* [OE. *hæt*:—OTeut. **hattuz,* later nom. *hattr,* hood, cowl, turban. The OTeut. **hattuz* goes back to earlier **hadnús,* from ablaut-series *had-, hôd-,* whence OE. *hód* HOOD.] **1.** A covering for the head; in recent use, one having a more or less horizontal brim all round the hemispherical, conical, or cylindrical part which covers the head. Worn by men and women. **2.** A head-dress showing the rank or dignity of the wearer; *esp.* a cardinal's hat (see CARDINAL *sb.*); whence *transf.* the office or dignity of a cardinal; called also *red hat* ME. **3.** *attrib.* 'Forming part of a hat', as *h.-brim,* etc.; 'for supporting or holding hats', as *h.-peg,* etc. 1794.

1. *Beaver, felt, silk, straw h.; high, tall (chimney-pot, stove-pipe, top) h.,* the ordinary cylindrical silk h. of the 19th c.; *opera, tennis h.; Rubens, Gainsborough h.:* see these words. **2.** †*H. of Maintenance:* see MAINTENANCE.

Phrases. *H. in hand,* with the head uncovered in respect; obsequiously, servilely. (*His*) *h. covers* (*his*) *family,* he is alone in the world. *To send round the h., go round with the h.,* etc.: applied to the collection of money by personal solicitation for charitable or benevolent purposes. *To hang up one's h.:* see HANG *v.* *To talk through one's h.:* see TALK *v.*

Comb.: **h.-block,** a form or mould upon which a man's h. is shaped; **-body,** the unshaped piece of felt from which a h. is formed; **-box,** a box for holding a hat; **-brush**; **-case** = *hat-box*; **-die** = *hat-mould*; **-homage, †-honour,** reverence shown by removing the h., an early Quaker phrase; **-mould,** the die on which a h. or bonnet is formed or shaped by pressing; **-piece,** a metal skull-cap worn under the h. as defensive armour; **-stand**; **-tree,** a hat-stand with projecting arms for hats and coats; **†-worship** = *hat-homage*.

Hat, *v.* ME. [f. prec.] *trans.* To cover, furnish, or provide with a hat. Also, to bestow the cardinal's hat upon.

Hatable, obs. var. of HATEABLE.

Ha·tband, hat-band. ME. **1.** A band or narrow ribbon, put round a hat above the brim. **2.** A band of crape, etc. worn round the hat as a sign of mourning 1598.

1. †*Gold h.*: a nobleman at the University; a 'tuft'.

Hatch (hætʃ), *sb.*[1] [OE. *hæc* :—WGer. **hakjā*. History and ult. signification obscure. Cf. HECK, and HACK *sb.*[2]] **1.** A half-door, gate, or wicket with an open space above; the lower half of a divided door. Also formerly, and still dial., any small gate or wicket. **2.** *Naut.* †**a.** Formerly (usu. in *pl.*), A movable planking forming a kind of deck in ships; hence, also, the permanent deck. **b.** Now: A trap-door or grated framework covering the openings in the deck called hatchways. ME. **c.** A square or oblong opening in the deck, by which cargo is lowered; a hatchway 1793. **3.** *transf.* **a.** An opening in the floor of a timber-shed or other building, which is covered by a trap-door; also, the trap-door itself 1888. †**b.** *Mining.* An opening made in the ground –1753. **4.** A flood-gate or sluice 1531. **5.** 'A contrivance for trapping salmon' (Smyth) 1826. **6.** A wooden bed-frame. ? *Obs.* 1832.

1. In at the window, or else ore the h. SHAKS. Phr. †*To keep a h. before the door* (fig.): to keep silence. 2. *Under hatches*: *orig.* = below deck, but now assoc. with sense 2 b. *Under (the) hatches* (fig.): down in position or circumstances; down out of sight. *Comb.* **h.-gate,** (*a*) a wicket; (*b*) = sense 4.

Hatch, *sb.*[2] 1629. [f. HATCH *v.*[1]] The action of hatching; that which is hatched; a brood (of young).

Hatch, *sb.*[3] Also **†hache.** 1658. [f. HATCH *v.*[2]] An engraved line or stroke; esp. for shading in an engraving

†Hatch, *sb.*[4] 1704. [a. F. *hache*.] A hatchet –1810.

Hatch, *v.*[1] [Early ME. *hacche(n*, prob. :—OE. **hæccean* (not found). Ult. etym. unkn.] **1.** *intr.* To bring forth young birds from the egg by incubation. **2.** *trans.* To bring forth from the egg either by natural or artificial heat ME. **3.** *intr.* for *pass.* **a.** Of the young: To come forth from the egg. **b.** Said of the egg. 1593. **4.** *transf.* (*trans.*) To bring forth, bring into existence, breed ME. **5.** *fig.* To bring to full development, esp. by a covert process; to contrive, devise 1549. Also *intr.* for *pass.*

2. In this fortress the male and female h. and bring up their brood in security GOLDSM. No Reptile hatches its eggs 1834. 3. Why should..hateful cuckoos h. in sparrows' nests SHAKS. 5. The Gunpowder Treason was hatched here in England 1678. *intr.* Treason hatching in his heart TRAPP.

Hatch, *v.*[2] 1480. [Earlier *hach(e*, a. F. *hacher*, f. *hache*; cf. CROSS-HATCH.] **1.** *trans.* To cut, engrave, or draw a series of lines, generally parallel, on; chiefly for shading in engraving or drawing 1598. **2.** To inlay with narrow strips or lines of a different substance. Also *transf* and *fig.* 1480.

1. Having heated the steel..they h. it over and across with the knife 1833. 2. The handle or pummell hatcht or inameld HAKEWILL. *fig.* His Sword.. Hatch't in Blood Royall G. DANIEL.

Phr. *Hatched moulding*: a kind of moulding used in Norman architecture, formed with two series of oblique parallel incisions crossing each other.

†Hatch, *v.*[3] 1581. [f. HATCH *sb.*[1]] To close (a door) with a hatch; to close –1608.

When sleepe begins with heauy wings To h. mine eyes SIDNEY.

Ha·tch-boat. 1858. [f. HATCH *sb.*[1] + BOAT.] **a.** 'A sort of small vessel known as a pilot boat, having a deck composed almost entirely of hatches' (Smyth). **b.** 'A kind of half-decked fishing-boat; one which has a hatch or well for keeping fish' (Simmonds).

Hatchel (hæ·tʃ'l), *sb.* ME. [A parallel form to HACKLE *sb.*[2], q.v.] An instrument for combing flax or hemp; = HECKLE.

Hatchel, *v.* ME. [f. prec.; cf. HACKLE, HECKLE.] **1.** *trans.* To dress (flax or hemp) with a hatchel; to heckle. **2.** *fig.* To harass, worry (*rare*) 1833.

2. Fleeced, hatchelled, bewildered and bedevilled CARLYLE. Hence **Ha·tcheller,** a flax-dresser, heckler.

Hatcher (hæ·tʃəɹ). 1581. [f. HATCH *v.*[1] + -ER[1].] **1.** One who or that which hatches (eggs) 1632; *spec.* an incubator 1884. **2.** *fig.* A contriver, designer, plotter 1581.

2. A great h. and breeder of business SWIFT.

Hatchery (hæ·tʃəri). 1880. [f. HATCH *v.*[1] + -ERY.] A hatching establishment; *spec.* one for hatching the ova of fish by artificial means.

Hatchet (hæ·tʃėt), *sb.* ME. [a. F. *hachette*, also in 15th c. *hachet*, dim. of *hache* ax.] A smaller or lighter ax with a short handle, for use with one hand.

Phrases. *To take* or *dig up the h.*: to commence hostilities. *To bury the h.*: to cease from hostilities (Derived from the customs of the N. Amer. Indians.) *Comb.*: **h.-face,** a narrow and very sharp face; so **-fist, -jaw**; **-faced** *a.*, having a h.-face. Hence **Ha·tchety** *a.* (said of the face).

Hatchettin (hæ·tʃėtin). Also **-ettine, -etin(e.** 1821. [f. C. *Hatchett*, the discoverer of columbium and tantalium; see -IN.] *Min.* **1.** = next. **2.** = CHRISMATITE. 1868.

Hatchettite (hæ·tʃėtəit). 1868. [f. as prec. + -ITE.] *Min.* A yellowish-white subtransparent fossil resin or wax-like hydrocarbon found in the coal-measures of South Wales.

Hatching, *vbl. sb.* 1662. [f. HATCH *v.*[2] + -ING[1].] The action of HATCH *v.*[2]; the drawing of parallel lines so as to produce the effect of shading; chiefly *concr.*, the series of lines so drawn; hatches.

Hatchment[1] (hæ·tʃmĕnt). 1548. [Altered f. ACHIEVEMENT (q.v.), through *atcheament*, *atchement*, *atch'ment*.] An escutcheon or ensign armorial; = ACHIEVEMENT 3; *esp.* a square or lozenge-shaped tablet exhibiting the armorial bearings of a deceased person, which is affixed to the front of his dwelling-place. Also *transf.*

No Trophee, Sword, nor H. o're his bones SHAKS.

†Hatchment[2]. 1616. [f. HATCH *v.*[2] + -MENT.] The hatching with which the hilt of the sword is ornamented –1649.

Five Marks in hatchments to adorn this thigh BEAUM. & FL.

Hatchway (hæ·tʃweⁱ). 1626. [f. HATCH *sb.*[1] + WAY.] **1.** *Naut.* A square or oblong opening in the deck of a ship down which cargo is lowered into the hold; also forming a passage from one deck to another. Qualified, as *after-*, *fore-*, *main-h.* **2.** An opening in a floor, etc. which may be closed by a hatch or trap-door. (Applied by Scott to the sliding-door of a box-bed.) 1814.

Hate (hēⁱt), *sb.*[1] [OE. *hęte* masc., with Teut. cognates, pointing to an OTeut. **hatoz*, *-izos* (:—pre-Teut. **kodos*, *kodesos*). In ME. changed into *hate*, after the vb.] An emotion of extreme dislike or aversion; detestation, abhorrence, hatred. Now chiefly *poet.* **b.** The object of hatred (*poet.*) 1592.

Unimaginable as h. in Heav'n MILT. **b.** My onely Loue sprung from my onely h. SHAKS.

Hate, haet (hēt), *sb.*[2] *Sc.* 1590. *orig.* The words *hae't* in *Deil hae't*, 'Devil have it!' This deprecatory expression became a strong negative, and thus = 'Devil a bit', i.e. not a whit. Hence *haet*, in *not a haet*, or the like, was taken as = 'whit, atom'.

Deil haet do I expect SCOTT.

Hate (hēⁱt), *v.* [OE. *hatian*, from root *hat-* (:—*kod-*), whence also HATE *sb.*[1]] **1.** *trans.* To hold in very strong dislike; to detest; to bear malice to. The opposite of *to love*. Also *absol.* **2.** To dislike greatly, be extremely averse (*to do* something). Also constr. with *vbl. sb.* ME.

1. Her presence, hated both of Gods and men TENNYSON. *absol.* She hated easily; she hated heartily; and she hated implacably MACAULAY. 2. I h. to promise much, and fail WALTON. To h. being bothered 1891.

Hateable (hēⁱ·tăb'l), *a.* Also **†hatable.** 1611. [-ABLE.] Deserving of being hated; odious.

Hateful (hēⁱ·tfŭl), *a.* ME. [f. HATE *sb.*[1] + -FUL.] **1.** Full of hate, cherishing hatred, malignant. **2.** Exciting hate; odious, repulsive ME.

1. Hide thee from their hatefull lookes SHAKS. 2. These Acts of h. strife, h. to all MILT. Hence **Ha·teful-ly** *adv.*, **-ness.**

†Hatel, *a.* [OE. *hatol*, *hętel* :—OTeut. **hatulo-*, *hatilo-*, cogn. with HATE *sb.*[1]; see -LE.] Full of hatred; malignant, hostile; severe, cruel; bitter –ME.

Hater (hēⁱ·təɹ). ME. [f. HATE *v.* + -ER[1].] One who hates.

Haters have I, more than haires C'TESS PEMBROKE.

Hath, arch. 3rd pers. sing. pres. ind. of HAVE

Ha·tless, *a.* 1450. [-LESS.] Having no hat.

Ha·t-money. 1676. [In F. *chapeau*, Sp. *sombrero*, app. because dropped in a hat.] (See quot.)

The word *primage* denotes a small payment to the master for his care and trouble..It is sometimes called the master's hat-money C. ABBOTT *Law Merch Ships.*

Hatred (hēⁱ·trėd). [Early ME., f. HATE *sb.*[1] (or *v.*) + -RED, OE. *rǣden* condition.] The condition or state of relations in which one person hates another; the emotion of hate; active dislike, detestation; enmity, ill-will, malevolence.

Dislike easily rises into h. DARWIN.

Hatte, obs. f. HATE *v.*, HOT *a.*

Hatte, obs. pa. t. of HEAT *v.*, HIGHT *v.*

Hatted, *ppl. a.* 1552. [f. HAT *v.* or *sb.* + -ED.] Wearing a hat, having a hat on.

Hatter (hæ·təɹ), *sb.* ME. [f. HAT *sb.* + -ER[1].] **1.** A maker of or dealer in hats. **2.** *Austral. Mining.* One who works alone. [Cf. *Hat covers his family* in HAT *sb.*] 1864.

1. *As mad as a h.*: see MAD.

Hatter, *v.* Now *Sc.* and *n. dial.* 1450. [? Onomatopœic with freq. ending; cf. *batter*, etc.] **1.** *trans.* To bruise with blows; to erode. ? *Obs.* **2.** To harass; to wear *out* 1687.

2. He's hattered out with penance DRYDEN.

‖**Hatti.** In full, *a.* **hatti-sherif** (ha:ti,ʃėrī·f). *β.* **hatti-humayun** (ha:ti,hŭmā·yūn). 1688. [Pers.] A decree or edict issued by the government of Turkey bearing the Sultan's special mark, and therefore irrevocable.

Ha·tting, *vbl. sb.* 1796. [f. HAT *v.* and *sb.* + -ING[1].] The trade of making hats; material for hats; also, the covering of a tan-pit with its hat of bark.

Hat trick. 1882. **1.** Any trick with a hat 1886. **2.** *Cricket.* The feat of a bowler who takes three wickets by three successive balls; entitling him to a new hat from his club.

Haubergeon, obs. f. HABERGEON.

Hauberk (hǭ·bəɹk). ME. [a. OF. *hauberc*, earlier *holberc*, later (and mod F.) *haubert*, a Com. Rom. deriv. of OHG. *halsberg* masc., f. *hals* neck + *-bergan* to cover, protect. See also HABERGEON.] A piece of defensive armour, orig. for the neck and shoulders; but early developed into a long military tunic, usually of ring or chain mail.

H. woven of polished chain BOWEN.

Hauerite (hau·ėrəit). 1847. [f. von *Hauer*, Austrian geologist.] *Min.* Native disulphide of manganese, occurring in reddish-brown crystals, usually octahedral.

Haugh (hāχ, hāχʷ, hāf). *Sc.* and *n. dial.* Also in north. Engl. **halgh** as in *Greenhalgh.* ME. [app. :—OE. *healh*, *halh* 'corner, nook'.] A piece of flat alluvial land by the side of a river, forming part of the floor of the river valley. Also *attrib.*

Haught (hǭt), *a. arch.* ME. [orig. *haut*, *hault* from French; see HAUT *a.*] **1.** High in one's own estimation; haughty (*arch.*). †**2.** High-minded; lofty –1577. †**3.** High-born –1627. †**4.** High, in other senses –1587. Hence **†Hau·ght-ly** *adv.*, **†-ness.**

Haughty (hǭ·ti), *a.* 1530. [An extension of *haut*, HAUGHT *a.*, as in *dusk-y*, etc., or after *doughty*, etc.] **1.** High in one's own estimation; proud, arrogant, supercilious. **b.** *fig.* Imposing in aspect; often with a mixture of sense 3. 1585. **2.** Of exalted character, style, or rank; eminent; high-minded, aspiring; of exalted courage (*arch.*) 1563. †3. High (in literal sense) –1621.

1. The Fiend..like a proud Steed reind, went hautie on MILT. b. His h. crest DRYDEN. 2. The hawtye verse, that Maro wrote B. GOOGE. No h. feat of arms I tell SCOTT. 3. From the toppes of hawtie towres B. GOOGE. Hence **Hau·ghti·ly** *adv.*, **-ness.**

Haul (hǭl), *v.* 1557. [var. of HALE *v.*¹, in 16th c. also *haul.*] 1. *trans.* To pull or draw with force; to drag, tug 1581. b. To transport by cart or other conveyance 1787. 2. *intr.* To pull, tug (*at* or *upon* something) 1743. Also *intr.* for *refl.* in passive sense 1797. 3. *Naut.* (*intr.*) To trim the sails, etc. of a ship so as to sail nearer to the wind (also *to h. up*); hence, to change the ship's course; to sail in a certain course. (Also *trans.* with the ship as object; also, to sail along *a coast.*) 1557. b. *transf.* and *fig.* To change one's course of action; to withdraw; to make one's way, to come or go 1802. 4. Of the wind: To shift, veer 1769.

1. We hauled anchor, and passed gently up the river COLERIDGE. Phr. *To h. up*: to bring up for a reprimand. Also, *to h. over the coals* (see COAL *sb.*). 2. I..pull'd, and haul'd, to try to turn him [a horse] 'G. GAMBADO'. 3. The enemy..hauled up on the Terpsichore's weather-beam A. DUNCAN. Phr. *To h. upon* or *to the wind*, also trans. *to h.* (a ship) *on a wind*, and *to h. the* (*her, our*, etc.) *wind*: to bring the ship round so as to sail closer to the wind. 4. The wind hauled to the southward R. H. DANA. *H. round*, said when the wind is gradually shifting towards any point of the compass.

Haul (hǭl), *sb.* 1670. [f. prec. vb.] 1. The act of hauling; a pull, a tug; *spec.* the draught of a fishing-net. 2. *concr.* a. A draught of fish 1854. b. *Haul of yarn* in *Rope-making*: about four hundred threads, when ready to be tarred 1794. 3. *fig.* The act of drawing or making a large profit or gain of any kind; *concr.* the amount thus gained 1776.

1. We caught..at one H...seven Hundred 1670. 3. A fine h. of prizes A. ADAMS. *Comb.*: **h.-rope**, a rope for hauling something; **-seine**, a drag-seine.

Haulage (hǭ·lėdʒ). 1826. [f. prec. + -AGE.] 1. The action or process of hauling; the traction of a load in a wagon or the like; the amount of force expended in hauling. 2. The expense of hauling 1864. 3. 'A traction-way' (Smyth).

Hauler (hǭ·ləɹ). 1674. [f. HAUL *v.* + -ER¹.] One who or that which hauls; a HAULIER.

Haulier (hǭ·liəɹ). 1577. [f. HAUL *v.* + -IER; cf. *collier*, etc.] A man employed in hauling something, e.g. coal in a mine.

Haulm, halm (hǭm, hām), *sb.* [OE. *healm* :—OTeut. **halmo-z*, repr. a pre-Teut. **kalmos*: cf. Gr. κάλαμος, L. *calamus* reed.] a. *collect. sing.* The stems or stalks of such plants as peas, beans, vetches, hops, potatoes, etc., now less commonly of corn or grass; *esp.* as used for litter and thatching; straw. b. with *a.* and *pl.* A stalk or stem (of a bean, potato, grass, etc.) OE. Hence **Haulm** *v.* to lay (straw or haulm) straight for thatching. **Hau·lmy** *a.* having (long or large) haulms.

Haulse, obs. f. HALSE *v.*²

Hault, haultie, obs. ff. HALT, HAUGHT, HAUT, HAUGHTY.

Haum(e, obs. f. HAULM.

Haunce, var. of HANCE *sb.* and *v.*

Haunch (hǭnʃ, hānʃ), *sb.* ME. [a. OF. *hanche* (ONF. *hanke*) = Pr., Sp., It., Pg. *anca* hip, buttock of the horse, prob. of German origin. Till 18th c. usu. spelt *hanch.*] 1. The part of the body lying between the last ribs and the thigh; the lateral expansions of the pelvis. b. The leg and loin of a deer, sheep, etc., prepared for table 1481. c. *fig.* The latter end. SHAKS. 2. The coxa or basal joint of the leg in insects, spiders, and crustaceans 1828. 3. *Arch.* = HANCE *sb.* 3, q.v. Hence, the corresponding part of any arched figure. 1793. 4. *Naut.* a. A sudden decrease in the size of a piece of timber 1823. b. = HANCE *sb.* 2 a. 1867.

1. c. A Summer Bird, which euer in the hanch of Winter sings The lifting vp of day 2 *Hen. IV*, IV. iv. 92.

†**Haunch,** *v.*¹ [f. HAUNCH *sb.*] *trans.* To bring down a deer upon its haunches. CAMDEN.

Haunch, *v.*² 1794. [f. HAUNCH *sb.* 4.] *trans.* To reduce in thickness. *intr.* Of a piece of timber: To decrease suddenly in thickness.

Hau·nch-bone. ME. The bone of the haunch; occas. the *os innominatum* as a whole, but usu. the *os ilium*.

Haunched, *a.* 1611. [f. HAUNCH *sb.* + -ED².] Having haunches; usu. in comb.

Haunt (hǭnt, hānt), *v.* ME. [a. F. *hanter*; origin uncertain.]

I. *trans.* †1. To practise habitually –1573. †2. To use or employ habitually or frequently; *refl.* to accustom *oneself* –1588. 3. To resort to frequently or habitually; to frequent (a place) ME. 4. To frequent the company of (a person); to 'run after' 1477. 5. *transf.* and *fig.* Of unseen or immaterial visitants: To visit frequently or habitually; *esp.*, as ghosts, etc., with manifestations of a molesting kind. *To be haunted*: to be subject to the visits and molestation of disembodied spirits. 1576.

2. *refl.* Haunte [*exerce*] thi silf to pite WYCLIF 1 *Tim.* iv. 7. 3. To h. the bathes 1585, the Mountains and the Plains DRYDEN. 4. To h. a minister of state SWIFT, rich men 1890. 5. Your beauty..did h. me in my sleepe SHAKS. Spirits haunted this dungeon, and walked there 1722.

II. *intr.* 1. To resort habitually; to stay or remain usually (in a place); to associate (with a person). Now usu. said of the lower animals. ME. †2. To have resort, go *to* –1632.

1. I haue charg'd thee not to h. about my doores SHAKS. Hence **Hau·nted** *ppl. a.* practised; frequented; *esp.* much visited by apparitions, etc. **Hau·nter,** one who or that which haunts.

Haunt (hǭnt, hānt), *sb.* ME. [f. HAUNT *v.*] 1. Habit, wont (now *dial.*); †habitual practice or use (of anything) –1585. †2. The act or practice of frequenting a place, etc.; resort –1712. 3. *concr.* A place of frequent resort or usual abode; the usual feeding-place of deer, game, fowls, etc.; often, a place frequented by the lower animals or by criminals. Also *fig.* ME. †4. ? A topic –1658. 5. A ghost that haunts a place. *local U.S.* and *Eng.* 1878.

3. We talke here in the publike h. of men SHAKS. Haunts of the buccaneers 1748, of coot and hern TENNYSON.

Haurient (hǭ·riĕnt), *a.* 1572. [ad. L. *haurientem, haurire* to draw (water, etc.).] *Her.* Of a fish borne as a charge: Placed palewise or upright with the head in chief, as if raising it above the water to draw in the air.

Hause, hawse (hǭs). *Sc.* and *n. dial.* 1781. [mod. north f. HALSE neck, used in a special sense.] A narrower and lower neck between two heights; a *col*; the name in the English Lake district and on the Scottish Border.

‖**Hausen** (hauz'n, hǭ·z'n). 1745. [Ger.] The largest species of sturgeon, *Acipenser huso*.

‖**Hausse** (hōs). 1787. [F., f. *hausser* to raise.] A kind of breech-sight for a cannon.

Haussmannize (hau·smănəiz). 1865. [f. Baron *Haussmann*, who, when prefect of the Seine (1853–70), remodelled Paris.] *trans.* To open out, widen, and straighten streets, and generally rebuild.

Haustellate (hǭ·stĕlĕt). 1835. [ad. mod.L. *haustellatus*, f. *haustellum*; see -ATE² 2.]

A. *adj.* 1. Provided with a haustellum; of or pertaining to the *Haustellata* or suctorial insects. 2. Adapted for sucking, suctorial 1835.

B. *sb.* A member of the *Haustellata* 1842.

‖**Haustellum** (hǭste·lŏm). *Pl.* **-a.** 1816. [mod.L. dim. of *haustrum* a machine for drawing water, f. *haurire, haust-.*] *Zool.* The sucking organ or proboscis of an insect or a crustacean.

‖**Haustorium** (hǭstōə·riŏm). *Pl.* **-ia.** 1875. [mod.L., f. L. *haustor*; see -ORIUM.] *Bot.* A small sucker of a parasitic plant, which penetrates the tissues of the host.

†**Haut.** See also HAUGHT. ME. [a. F. *haut, haute*, in OF. *halt* :—L. *altum* high. The *h* in OF. is after Ger. = *hoh, hoch.*]

A. *adj.* High, lofty, haughty; see HAUGHT. –1648.

B. *sb.* Height, a height –1686.

†**Hau·tain, -tein,** *a.* ME. [a. F. *hautain*, OF. (*h*)*altain, haultain*, f. *haut* high; see HAUT.] 1. = HAUGHTY 1. –1549. 2. Of the voice: Raised –1475. 3. High-flying. CHAUCER. 4. = HAUGHTY 2. –1485.

Hautboy, hoboy (hōu·boi). 1575. [a. F. *hautbois*, f. *haut* high + *bois* wood.] 1. A wooden double-reed wind instrument of high pitch, having a compass of about 2½ octaves, forming a treble to the bassoon. (Now usu. OBOE.) b. *transf.* One who plays a hautboy 1633. Also *attrib.* †2. *Forestry.* Lofty trees, as dist. from shrubs, etc. –1700. 3. A species of strawberry (*Fragaria elatior*). Also *hautboy strawberry*. 1731. Hence **Hau·tboyist** = OBOIST.

Hautein, -en, -eyn, vars. of HAUTAIN *Obs.*

‖**Hauteur** (hotör). 1628. [F., f. *haut.*] 1. Loftiness of manner or bearing; haughtiness. †2. A height (*rare*) 1711.

‖**Haut-goût** (ho₁gu). 1645. [F.; lit. 'high flavour', f. *haut* + *goût* (formerly *goust*) taste, etc.] †1. A high or piquant flavour; a strong relish; seasoning –1752. b. *fig.* 'Flavour', 'spice'. [So in F.] 1650. 2. In later use: A high flavour; a taint 1693. †3. A highly-seasoned dish –1817.

1. [Garlick] giving a delicious Hault-gust to most meats they eat FULLER.

‖**Haut-pas.** Now only as Fr. (ho₁pa). 1460. [F.; lit. 'high step'; anglicized as HALPACE, whence HALF-PACE, etc.] = HALF-PACE 1.

‖**Haut-relief** (ho·rĭlī·f). 1850. [F. (ho rəlyef).] High relief, ALTO-RELIEVO; opp. to *bas-relief*.

‖**Haut ton** (ho₁toṅ). 1801. [F.; = high tone. (Now little used.)] High fashion; *ellipt.* people of high fashion.

Haüyne (hā·win). 1814. [a. F.; named after *Haüy*, the French mineralogist.] *Min.* A silicate of aluminium and sodium with calcium sulphate, occurring in certain igneous rocks in crystals or grains of various shades of blue or green. Hence **Haüynite** (in same sense).

Havana (hăvæ·nă). Also **Havanna(h.** 1826. [Name of the Cuban capital, now in Sp. *Habana.*] (In full, *Havana cigar*): A cigar of the kind made at Havana or in Cuba. (Also applied to the tobacco of which these are made.)

A grilled bone, Havannahs, and Regents punch DISRAELI.

Have (hæv), *v.* [Com. Teut.: OE. *habban, hæfde, hæfed* :—OTeut. stem **habē-*. In ME. the *habb-* forms were reduced by levelling to *hav-* (*have(n, I have, they haven, having*); while the original *haf-* (= *hav-*) forms at length lost their *f* (*v*), before the following consonant (*ha-st, ha-th, ha-s, ha-d*).]

A. As a main verb (*trans.* or *intr.*).

I. 1. *trans.* To hold in hand, or in possession; to hold or possess as property, or as something at one's disposal. Also *absol.* 2. To hold or possess, in a relation other than that of property or tenancy OE. 3. To possess, bear, contain, as an appendage, organ, subordinate part, or adjunct; to contain as parts of itself OE. 4. To possess as an attribute, function, right, etc.; to be characterized by; to hold; to be charged with OE. 5. To be possessed or affected with (something physical or mental); to experience OE. 6. To possess as an intellectual acquirement, to know; to understand 1591. 7. To possess as a duty or thing to be done OE.

1. Having an axe in his hand 1483. To h. shares in a company (*mod.*). Phr. *To have and to hold* (cf. law L. *habendum et tenendum*): to have (or receive) and keep or retain, indicating continuance of possession. 2. Let me haue men about me, that are fat SHAKS. We had fifty-two fathom of water 1748. He having no son at the time CRUISE. They had him to dine with them at the inn THACKERAY. 3. The sea hath bounds SHAKS. Riches have wings to fly away from their owner LOWELL. The year has twelve calendar months (*mod.*). 4. They h. a Fashion to cut holes in the Lips DAMPIER. [They] had reason to regret his departure 1795. Their policy had the desired effect 1882. 5. Such as have the collicque 1599. I have had a real good time 1890. He has bad health (*mod.*). 6. He hath neither Latine, French, nor Italian SHAKS. You haue me, haue you not SHAKS. 'Ah! I have it!' he added 1839. 7. He had much to see MILT. *To h. to do* (see DO *v.*). The firm had to suspend payment 1883.

II. 1. To hold, keep, retain (*in* some relation to oneself) OE. 2. To hold or entertain in the mind (a feeling, etc.); to cherish OE.; hence, to show (such sentiment, etc.) in action ME. 3. To hold in (some specified) estimation; to account or regard as (*arch.*) OE. 4. To hold, keep up, carry on (some proceeding or performance); to engage in, maintain, or perform, as a chief actor; to engage in and perform some action OE. †5. *refl.* To comport oneself –1556. 6. To assert, maintain; to put it 1449.

1. The Government hath had some things in desire CROMWELL. 2. Let me see..what you h. against it 1656. Sir, haue pacience with me, and I will paye the all BIBLE (Great) *Matt.* xviii. 26. 3. They were then had in great reverence HANMER. 4. She and I had some Words last Sunday at Church SWIFT. You will then h. a good shot at him MARRYAT. 6. All the Town has it, that [etc.] SWIFT. Some will h. it, that I often write to my self ADDISON.

III. 1. To possess by obtaining or receiving; hence, to come into possession of; to obtain, get, gain, accept, to have learned (*from* some source); to take (food, drink) OE. 2. To get or have got into one's power, or at a disadvantage; to have caught (*fig.*), to have hold upon 1596. b. To get the better of, take in, 'do' (*slang*) 1805. 3. To get into a place or state; to bring, lead, convey, take, put (*arch.*) ME. †4. *intr.* (for *refl.*) or *absol.* To betake oneself, go –1849. 5. *intr.* or *absol.* *Have at*: To go at or get at, esp. in a hostile way; to have a stroke at, make an attempt at. Chiefly in imperative; app. 1st pers. pl., but often singular in sense, announcing the speaker's intention to get at or attack. So with other preps., as *after, with*, etc. ME.

1. [She] had two children at a birth 1583. They h. it..from his own mouth 1680. There is nothing to be had here (*mod.*). Phr. *To have it*: (*a*) to gain the victory or advantage; to win the match; (*b*) to receive (or have received) a drubbing, punishment, reprimand; *to let one h. it*, to 'give it' one (*colloq.*). 2. Now infidell I haue thee on the hip SHAKS. I admit that you h. me there 1890. b. If you've advanced money on 'em [diamonds], you've been had 1879. 3. He was had before the Juge CAXTON. Phr. *Have up*: to take up or cause to go before a court of justice in answer to a charge; to call to account. *H. out*: to cause to come out to a duel. To h. their Fortunes told them DE FOE. They are having the pavement up for the electric light (*mod.*). Phr. *To h. something done to one*: to receive, experience, or suffer it as the action of others or of fate. So *To h. some one do something, to have something happen to one.* 5. Well, sith here is no company, h. with ye to Jericho 1575.

Phrases. *To h.* ADO, *h. at* AVAIL, *h.* BUSINESS, *h. in* CHARGE, *h.* DONE, *h. a* HAND *in*, *h. in* HAND, *h. on* HAND, etc.: see the distinctive words.

Idiomatic uses. The past Subjunctive *had* = would have, is used with adjs. (or advs.) in the comparative, as *better, liefer, rather*, etc.; in the superlative, as *best*; or in the positive with 'as', *as soon, as well*, etc., to express preference or comparative desirability. In OE. the adjs. *léofre, betre* were construed with *be* and the dative, e.g. *him wǽre betere* = it would be better for him. In ME., side by side with this, appears *have* and the nominative, in the sense 'he (I, etc.) would hold or find it better or preferable'. The use of *as soon, sooner, well*, is recent, since *liefer* and *better* began to be felt as advs.

b. The two forms of expression are confused in *he* (*I*, etc.) *were better* (see BE *v.*), and *him* (*me*, etc.) *had liefer, rather*. c. *Had like* (*liked, likely*) *to*: see LIKE. *Had need to*: see NEED.

B. As an auxiliary verb. 1. The present tense of *have* forms a present of completed action, or 'present perfect'. a. To a trans. vb. with object OE. b. Extended to vbs. of action without object ME. c. Extended to intr. vbs. generally. Used early with *been*, and hence with the passive voice. With vbs. of motion later, partly displacing *be* as an auxiliary. ME. 2. The past of *have* forms a past tense of completed action or 'pluperfect'. a. With trans. vb. and object OE. b. With active vbs. without object, and with intr. and passive vbs. ME. 3. The compound tenses (*shall have*, etc.) are similarly employed ME. ¶4. In 15th and 16th c. occur many instances of redundant *have* in the compound tenses 1442.

1. a. Hauing burnt Holyhed POWEL. Phr. *I have got*, colloquially used for *I have*: see GET *v.* I've got a great deal on my hands MARRYAT. b. Every age hath abounded in instances WORDSW. c. Why haven't you been to see me 1882. 2. a. Thou hadest chosen me for thy wife 1582. b. They had sojourned there in great ease LD. BERNERS. He had been taught to dislike politeness MAR. EDGEWORTH. 3. I should haue lost the worth of it in Gold SHAKS.

Have (hæv), *sb.* ME. [f. prec. vb.] 1. Having, possession. *Obs.* exc. as *nonce-wd.* 2. *colloq.* One who *has* or possesses. (Usu. in *pl.*; and in conjunction with *have-not*.) 1836. 3. *slang.* 'A swindle; a *take-in*; a *do*' (Farmer).

Haveless, †havenless, *a. Obs.* exc. *dial.* [OE. *hafenléas*, f. *hæfene*, f. *haf-*, *hæf-* stem of *habban* to HAVE + -LESS.] †1. Without possessions, indigent. ME. only. 2. Without resource, shiftless; slovenly. *Sc.* and *dial.* 1868.

Havelock (hæ·vlǫk). *U.S.* 1861. [f. Gen. Henry *Havelock*, distinguished in the Indian Mutiny 1857.] A white cloth covering for the cap, with a flap hanging over the neck, worn by soldiers as a protection from the sun's heat.

Haven (hē¹·v'n), *sb.* [OE. *hæfen* str. fem. and *hæfne* wk. fem.; usu. taken as f. root either of HAVE *v.* or HEAVE *v.*, though possibly of ON. *haf*, Da. *hav*, OE. *hæf* sea.] 1. A recess or inlet of the sea, or the mouth of a river, affording good anchorage and a safe station for ships; a harbour, port. 2. *fig.* A refuge; an asylum ME.

1. Weymouth, a very convenient Harbour and H. CLARENDON. 2. My sole refuge and only h...is in the arms of death CARLYLE. Hence **Ha·venless** *a.*

Ha·ven, *v.* ME. [f. prec. sb.] †1. *intr.* To put into a haven –1621. 2. *trans.* To put (a ship, etc.) into a haven 1601.

2. *fig.* Blissfully haven'd both from joy and pain KEATS.

Ha·venage. 1864. [-AGE.] Harbour-dues.

Ha·vener, -or. 1495. [f. HAVEN *sb.* + -ER¹, -OR.] Harbour-master. Hence **Ha·venership,** the office of h.

Haver (hæ·vəɹ), *sb.*¹ ME. [f. HAVE *v.* + -ER¹.] A possessor, owner.

Haver (hæ·vəɹ), *sb.*² *dial.* [ME. *haver* (*hafyr*), corresp. to ON. *hafre* :—OTeut. **habron-* wk. masc. In Eng. only north.] Oats. Also *attrib.*, as *h.-meal*. *Comb.*: **h.-cake,** oatcake; **-grass,** 'oatgrass'; species of *Avena* and *Bromus*.

Haver, *sb.*³, usu. in pl. **havers** (hē¹·vəɹz). *Sc.* and *n. dial.* 1787. [?] Foolish talk; nonsense. So **Ha·ver** *v.* to talk foolishly; to talk nonsense. **Ha·verel,** one who havers; also *attrib.* or *adj.*

Haversack (hæ·vəɹsæk). 1749. [a. F. *havresac* (also used), ad. Ger. *habersack*, lit. 'oat-sack' (cf. HAVER *sb.*²), orig. the bag in which cavalry, etc. carried oats for their horses.] A bag of stout canvas, worn with a strap over the shoulder, in which a soldier carries his day's rations. Also, any similar bag used by travellers, etc. †b. 'A gunner's case for ordnance, being a leather bag used to carry cartridges from the ammunition-chest to the piece in loading' (Simmonds) 1858.

Haversian (hăvə̄·ɹsiăn), *a.* 1836. [f. Clopton *Havers*, an English anatomist (*c.* 1690).] *Anat.* Applied to certain structures in bone discovered by Havers, as in *H. canal*, one of the minute cylindrical passages in bone which form the channels for blood-vessels and medullary matter; *H. system*, 'the H. canal, its concentric lamellæ of bone, and the lacunæ with their canaliculi' (*Syd. Soc. Lex.*).

Haversine (hæ·vəɹsəin). 1875. [Abbrev. of *ha*(*lf*) *versine* (versed sine).] *Trigonometry.* A nautical term: Half the versed sine.

‖**Havildar** (hæ·vildāɹ). *E. Ind.* 1698. [Pers. *ḥawāl-dār*, f. Arab. *ḥawālah* charge + Per. *dār* holding.] 'A sepoy non-commissioned officer, corresponding to a sergeant' (Yule).

Having (hæ·viŋ), *vbl. sb.* ME. [-ING¹.] 1. Possession. 2. *concr.* (often in *pl.*) That which one has; possession, property, wealth, belongings ME. 3. (Often in *pl.*) Behaviour, manners. (Chiefly *Sc.*) ME.

2. Look to my house and havings; keepe all safe BROME. 3. By and attour her gentle havings SCOTT.

Having, *ppl. a.* ME. [-ING².] 1. That has; possessing property. (Now *rare* exc. as pple.) 2. Desirous of having; grasping. Now only *dial.* 1591.

2. She's as jealous and h. as can be GEO. ELIOT.

Haviour (hē¹·viəɹ), **†havour.** ME. [Orig. a. F. *aveir*, *avoir*, subst. use of *avoir*, OF. *aveir* to have. In 14–15th c. assoc. w. Engl. *have*, whence the *h*, and the vars. *haver*, *havoir*, *havour* (and subseq. *-eour*, *-iour*). Cf. AVER *sb.*] †1. The fact of having; possession; a possession; estate, substance –1616. 2. The action of bearing oneself; deportment, behaviour. Also *pl.* manners. *arch.* or *dial.* 1503.

2. A courteous haviour, gent and debonair 1756.

Havoc (hæ·vǫk), *sb.* ME. [a. AF. *havok*, altered f. OF. *havot*, used in same sense. Prob. of Teut. origin.] 1. In the phr. *cry havoc*, orig. to give to an army the order *havoc!*, as the signal for the seizure of spoil, and pillage. In later use (usually after Shaks.) *fig.* 2. Devastation, destruction; esp. in phr. *to make h., play h.* 1480.

1. Cæsars Spirit..Shall..Cry hauocke, and let slip the Dogges of Warre *Jul. C.* III. i. 273. 2. What havock the floud had made 1635. Hence **Ha·voc** *v.* (infl. **-ocked, -ocking**), to make h. of; to lay waste; also *absol.* and *intr.* **Ha·vocker.**

Haw (hǭ), *sb.*¹ *Obs.* exc. *Hist.* [OE. *haga*, corresp. to MDu. *hage*, *haghe* (whence *'s Graven hage*, the Count's Haw, The Hague) :—OTeut. **hagon-*; cf. HAY *sb.*², and HEDGE.] A hedge or encompassing fence (OE.); hence, an enclosed piece of ground; a messuage (OE.); generally, a yard, close, or enclosure.

Haw (hǭ), *sb.*² [app. the same wd. as prec.; ? short for **hæ̆gberie*.] 1. The fruit of the hawthorn. 2. The hawthorn, *Cratægus Oxyacantha* 1821. †3. A head or ear of grass. [Perh. a different wd.] –1825.

1. Stores of Haws and Heps do commonly portend cold Winters BACON.

Haw, *sb.*³ 1523. [?] The nictitating membrane of a horse, dog, etc. †b. *transf.* An excrescence in the human eye –1684.

Haw, *interj.* and *sb.*⁴ 1679. [Echoic.] An utterance marking hesitation. Usually with *hum*. See also HAW-HAW.

Haw, *v.* 1632. [f. HAW *interj.*] *intr.* To utter 'haw!' as an expression of hesitation. Usually in *to hum* (*hem*) *and h.*; see HUM *v.*

Hawbuck (hǭ·bɒk). 1805. [perh. f. HAW *sb.*¹ or ² + BUCK *sb.*¹ 2.] A country bumpkin.

Hawcubite (hǭ·kəbəit). 1712. One of a band of dissolute young men who infested the streets of London *c.* 1700; a street bully, a ruffian.

†Hawe-bake. Usu. taken as = 'haw(s) baken', baked haws, i.e. 'plain fare'; but qy. CHAUCER *Man of Law's Prol.* 95.

Hawfinch (hǭ·finʃ). 1674. [f. HAW *sb.*² + FINCH.] The common grosbeak, *Coccothraustes vulgaris*.

Haw-haw (hǭ·hǭ·). 1834. [Echoic; cf. HA HA.]

A. *interj.* An expression of hesitation uttered repeatedly in an affected tone. Also, the representation of loud laughter.

B. *sb.* The utterance of *haw haw*; a guffaw 1834.

C. *attrib.* or *adj.* Characterized by the utterance of *haw haw* 1841. Hence **Haw-haw** *v.* to utter *haw haw*; to laugh boisterously.

Haw-haw, var. of HA-HA *sb.*²

Hawk (hǭk), *sb.*¹ [Com. Teut.: OE. *hab̄uc*, *heafoc* :—OTeut. **hab̄uko-z*; generally referred to root *hab̄-*, *haf-* to seize, as L. *accipiter* to *capere*.] 1. Any diurnal bird of prey used in Falconry; any bird of the family *Falconidæ*. In *Nat. Hist.*, restricted to a bird of the subfamily *Accipitrinæ*, with rounded and shortish wings, which chases its prey near the ground. 2. *fig.* Applied to a person, in various senses: e.g. one who preys on others, a sharper or cheat; one who is keen and grasping; an officer of the law who pounces on criminals 1548.

1. *H. of the fist*, 'one that flies direct off the fist without mounting or waiting-on'. **Black Hawk,** the American rough-legged buzzard; **Musket-, Small-bird-,** or **Spar-h.,** the Sparrow-h.; **Ringtail H.** (*Falco Hudsonius*). *Night-h., dor-h., screech-h.*, applied to the goatsucker. (See these Words.) 2. Phr. *Ware h.*: see WARE *v.*¹ 2b.

Comb.: **H. eagle,** an eagle of the genus *Nisaetus*; **h.-eye** (*U.S.*), colloq. appellation of a native or inhabitant of Iowa, pop. called the 'Hawk-eye State'; **-eyed** *a.*, very keen-sighted; **-fly,** a fly of the family *Asilidæ*, also called hornet-flies, which prey on other insects.

Hawk (hǭk), *sb.*² 1700. [?] 'A small quadrangular tool with a handle, used by a plasterer, on which the stuff required by him is served' (Gwilt.) Hence **Hawk-boy**, the boy who brings him the material.

Hawk, *sb.*³ 1604. [f. HAWK *v.*³] An effort made to clear the throat; the noise thus made.

Hawk (hǭk), *v.*¹ ME. [f. HAWK *sb.*¹] **1.** *intr.* To chase or hunt game with a trained hawk; to practise falconry. **2.** *intr.* Of birds and insects: To hunt on the wing ME.; *trans.* to pursue or attack on the wing 1825.

1. Thei hauke, thei hunt, thei card, thei dyce LATIMER. 2. The bird [a martin] was hawking briskly after the flies G. WHITE. Phr. *To h. at*: to fly at or attack on the wing, as a hawk does; (of a person) to fly a hawk at. Who does h. at eagles with a dove G. HERBERT. †*To h. after* (*for*): to hunt after.

Hawk (hǭk), *v.*² 1542. [app. f. HAWKER *sb.*²] **1.** *intr.* To practise the trade of a hawker. **2.** *trans.* To carry *about* from place to place and offer for sale; to cry in the street. Also *transf.* and *fig.* 1713. **3.** To traverse with something in hand to dispose of 1865.

2. His works were hawk'd in every street SWIFT. 3. Hawking the world, Pragmatic Sanction in hand CARLYLE.

Hawk (hǭk), *v.*³ 1581. [prob. echoic.] **1.** *intr.* To make an effort to clear the throat of phlegm; to clear the throat noisily 1583. **2.** *trans.* To bring *up* by such an effort.

Haw·kbill. 1782. **1.** = HAWK'S-BILL 1. **2.** An instrument, such as 'a pliers with curved nose', etc. 1875. So **Hawk-billed** *a.* having a mouth like a hawk's beak, as the *hawk-billed turtle*.

Hawkbit (hǭ·kbit). 1713. [f. HAWK(WEED) + (Devil's) BIT.] A book-name for the genus *Apargia* of composite plants, resembling hawkweeds.

Hawked (hǭkt), *a.* 1577. [f. HAWK *sb.*¹ + -ED; cf. *hooked*.] Curved like a hawk's beak; aquiline.

Hawker (hǭ·kəɹ), *sb.*¹ [OE. *hafocere*; see HAWK *sb.*¹ and -ER ¹.] A falconer.

Hawker (hǭ·kəɹ), *sb.*² 1510. [app. a. MLG. *hoker* huckster, costermonger.] A man who goes from place to place selling his wares, or who cries them in the street. Now technically dist. from *pedlar*, as having a horse and cart, or van.

fig. This broad-brim'd h. of holy things TENNYSON.

Haw·k-moth. 1785. A moth of the family *Sphingidæ* or *Sphingina*; a sphinx-moth; so called from their manner of flight, which resembles the hovering and darting of a hawk. There are many genera and species, as DEATH'S-HEAD *h.*, ELEPHANT *h.*, etc.

Hawk-nose. 1533. A nose curved like a hawk's beak. Hence **Haw·k-nosed** *a.*

Hawk-owl. 1743. **a.** The Short-eared Owl, *Asio brachyotus.* **b.** The Day-owl, *Surnia ulula* or *funerea*. Both so called from their smaller heads, and habit of hunting in the day.

Hawk's-bell, hawk-bell. 1483. A small spherical bell, for fastening on the leg of a hawk.

Hawk's-bill. 1657. **1.** (Also *hawk's-bill turtle*.) A species of turtle, *Chelone imbricata*, having a mouth resembling the beak of a hawk, and furnishing the tortoise-shell of commerce. **2.** Part of the striking action of a clock 1875.

Hawkweed (hǭ·kˌwīd). 1562. [tr. L. *hieraceum* = Gr. ἱεράκιον, f. ἱέραξ hawk, falcon.] The common name for plants of the large genus *Hieracium* (N.O. *Compositæ*). Also applied to other yellow-flowered composites, as *Senecio hieracioides*, etc.

Hawm (hǭm), *v. dial.* 1847. [?] To move about awkwardly; to lounge.

Hawse (hǭz), *sb.*¹ 1497. [A phonetic spelling of *halse, haulse*, app. a. ON. *hals* neck, also *fig.*] *Naut.* **1.** That part of a ship's bows in which the hawse-holes are cut for the cables to pass through; hence, occas., in *pl.*, the hawse-holes themselves. †**2.** A cable, a hawser -1642. **3.** The space between the head of a vessel at anchor and the anchors, or a little beyond the anchors. Also *fig.* 1630. **4.** 'The situation of the cables before the ship's stem, when she is moored with two anchors out from forward, one on the starboard, and the other on the port bow' (Smyth) 1597.

1. We cut our cable at the h. 1567. 3. Phr. *Athwart* (†*thwart*) *the h.*, (cf. *athwart-hawses* v. ATHWART), *to cross the h.* 4. *Clear h.*, *open h.*, when both cables lead directly (without crossing) to their respective anchors. *Foul h.*, when the cables lie across the stem, or bear upon each other. *To clear the h.*, to untwist two cables, which being let out at two several hawses, are wound about one another. *To fresh* (*freshen*) *the h.*, to veer out a little more cable so as to let another part endure the stress.

Comb.: **h.-block**, a block of wood made to fit over the h.-holes when at sea; **-hole**, a cylindrical hole, of which there are two in the bows of a vessel, for the cable to run through; **-piece**, one of the timbers in the bow of a ship through which a h.-hole is cut; **-pipe**, a cast-iron pipe fitted into a h.-hole to protect the wood; **-plug**, a plug made to fit into the h.-pipe to prevent water from entering.

Hawse, *sb.*², var. of HAUSE.

†**Hawse**, *v.* 1500. [a. F. *hausser*, in 16th c. *haulser*:—late L. type **altiare*, f. *altus*.] *trans.* To raise, exalt, hoist -1600.

Hawser (hǭ·zəɹ). ME. [app. AF. *hauceour*, f. OF. *haucier* to HAWSE, hoist. Early associated with HAWSE *sb.*¹] **1.** A large rope or small cable, between 5 and 10 inches in circumference; used in warping and mooring; in large ships now made of steel. **2.** Used by confusion for HAWSE *sb.*¹ 3. 1684.

Comb.: **h.-bend**, a kind of hitch or knot; **-laid** *a.*, made of three or four strands laid into one.

Hawthorn (hǭ·þǭɹn). [OE. *haga-, hægu-, hægþorn*, f. *haga* HAW *sb.*¹ + *þorn* THORN.] **1.** A thorny shrub or small tree, *Cratægus Oxyacantha*, N. O. *Rosaceæ*, much used for forming hedges; the White-thorn. It bears white, and, in some varieties, red or pink blossom (called 'may'); its fruit, the haw, is a small round dark red berry. (Also extended to other species of *Cratægus*.) **2.** *Angling.* Short for *h.-fly* 1884.

1. A bussh..of white h. full of floures 1450.

Comb.: **h. china**, a kind of Oriental porcelain, in which the decoration represents branches of the Japanese plum-tree in white on a dark blue ground; **-fly**, a small black fly appearing on h.-bushes when the leaves first come out; an imitation of this for angling; **-grosbeak**, the hawfinch. Also **Hawthorn-tree**, †**Haw-tree**, in sense 1.

Hay (hēⁱ), *sb.*¹ [Com. Teut.: OE. *hieg, hīg, heg*:—OTeut. **haujom*, app. an adj. used subst. = (that) which can be mowed, f. stem of vb. **hauw-*, OE. *heaw-* to HEW, cut down.] **1.** Grass cut or mown, and dried for use as fodder; occas. including grass fit for mowing. **2.** *Burgundian* or *Burgundy h.*, Lucerne or Sainfoin.

Phrases. *To carry h. in one's horns*: to be ill-tempered or dangerous (L. *fænum habet in cornu*, Horace). *To look for a needle in a bundle of h.*: see NEEDLE. *To make h.*: (*a*) *lit.*, to mow grass and dry it by spreading it about; (*b*) *fig.* to make confusion. *To make h. of*: to turn topsy-turvy. *To make h. while the sun shines*: to lose no time, to profit by opportunities.

Comb.: **h.-box**, a box stuffed with hay in which heated food is left to continue cooking; **-plant**, an umbelliferous plant of Tibet, *Prangos pabularia*.

Hay, *sb.*² Now *arch.* or dial. [OE. *hege*, a deriv. of the same root as *haga* HAW *sb.*¹, HAG *sb.*², and HEDGE. In ME. assoc. w. F. *haie*.] **1.** A hedge, fence. **2.** An enclosure; a park 1630. †**3.** *Mil.* An extended line of men 1753.

†**Hay**, *sb.*³ ME. [AF. *haie*; origin uncertain.] A net used for catching wild animals, *esp.* rabbits, being stretched in front of their holes, or round their haunts -1821.

Hay, hey, *sb.*⁴ 1529. [?] **1.** A country dance having a serpentine movement. †**2.** Hay-de-guy, -guise. A kind of hay or dance -1694.

To dance the hay or *hays*: to go through varied evolutions like those of a dance.

Hay, *v.*¹ 1556. [f. HAY *sb.*¹] **1.** *trans.* To furnish with hay; to put (land) under hay 1708. **2.** *intr.* To make hay 1556. **3.** *trans.* To make into hay 1884.

†**Hay**, *v.*² [OE. *hegian*; see HAY *sb.*²] *trans.* To enclose by a hedge; to hedge -1610.

†**Hay**, *v.*³ 1440. [f. HAY *sb.*³] *intr.* To set hays or nets for rabbits, etc. -1613.

†**Hay**, *v.*⁴ 1768. [f. HAY *sb.*⁴] *intr.* To dance the hay -1777.

†**Hay**, *interj.* and *sb.*⁵ 1592. [a. It. *hai* (pron. *ai*) thou hast (it). Cf. L. *habet*.]

A. *int.* An exclam. on hitting an opponent. B. JONS.

B. *sb.* A home-thrust. *Rom. & Jul.* II. iv. 27.

Hay-a·sthma. 1827. [In F. *asthme de foin*.] = HAY-FEVER.

Hay·-bird. **1.** Any bird that builds its nest with hay, *esp.* the Blackcap, Garden Warbler, and Willow-wren. **2.** The Pectoral Sandpiper or Grass-snipe, *Tringa maculata* (U.S.).

Hay·bote. ME. [f. HAY *sb.*² + BOTE, BOOT *sb.*¹] Wood or thorns for the repair of fences; the right to take this from the landlord's estate or from the common; = HEDGE-BOTE.

Haycock (hēⁱ·kǫk). 1470. [f. HAY *sb.*¹ + COCK *sb.*²] A conical heap of hay in the field.

To the tanned h. in the mead MILT. *L'Allegro* 90.

Hay-de-guy, -guise. See HAY *sb.*⁴

Hay-fever. 1829. [f. HAY *sb.*¹] A catarrhal condition of the ocular, nasal, and respiratory mucous membranes, accompanied generally by asthmatic symptoms; a disorder of the early summer, usually caused by the pollen of grasses and some flowers, sometimes also by dust, etc.

Hay·field. 1784. [f. HAY *sb.*¹] A field in which grass has been cut or is standing to be cut for hay.

Hay-fork. 1552. [f. HAY *sb.*¹] A long-handled fork used for turning over hay to dry, or in pitching and loading it. **b.** A large fork elevated by a horse and pulley in unloading hay from a wagon to a mow; or *vice versa* (Knight) 1875.

Hayloft (hēⁱ·lǫft). 1573. [f. HAY *sb.*¹] A loft for hay over a stable or barn.

Hay·maker. ME. [f. HAY *sb.*¹] **1.** A man or woman employed in making hay, *esp.* after it is mown. **2.** An apparatus for shaking up and drying hay 1853. **3.** *pl.* The name of a country dance. Also *haymakers' jig*.

Hay·making, *vbl. sb.* 1588. [f. as prec.] The process of cutting and drying grass for hay. Also *attrib.*, as **h. machine**, an apparatus for drying grass for hay.

Hay-mow (hēⁱ·mau). 1483. [f. HAY *sb.*¹] A rick or stack of hay; in some places applied to the pile of hay stored in a barn, or to the compartment of a barn in which hay is stored.

†**Hayne.** ME. [?] A mean wretch, a niggard. CHAUCER.

Hay·-rack. 1825. [f. HAY *sb.*¹] **1.** A rack for holding hay for cattle. **2.** A light framework projecting from the sides of a wagon to increase its carrying capacity for hay, etc. *U.S.*

Hay·-rake. 1725. **1.** A hand-rake used in hay-making. **2.** An implement drawn by a horse for raking hay into windrows (Knight) 1875.

Hayrick (hēⁱ·rik). ME. [f. HAY *sb.*¹ + RICK.] A haystack.

Hay·-seed, hay·seed. 1577. [f. HAY *sb.*¹] **1.** The grass seed shaken out of hay. **2.** The redseed, brit, etc., on which mackerel largely feed (*U.S.*). **3.** Joc. name for a rustic (*U.S.*) 1889.

Haystack (hēⁱ·stæk). ME. [f. HAY *sb.*¹] A stack of hay built in the open air, of regular form.

Haythorn, obs. f. HAWTHORN.

Hayward (hēⁱ·wǫɹd). ME. [f. HAY *sb.*² + WARD, OE. *weard* guardian.] An officer having charge of the fences and enclosures, *esp.* to keep cattle from breaking through from the common into enclosed fields; sometimes, the herdsman of the cattle feeding on the common.

Hazard (hæ·zǎɹd), *sb.* ME. [a. OF. *hasard, -art*; prob. of Arabic origin.] **1.** A game at dice in which the chances are complicated by a number of arbitrary rules. **2.** Chance, venture; a chance 1583. **3.** Risk of loss or harm; peril, jeopardy 1548. †**4.** That which is staked. *Merch. V.* I. i. 151. **5.** *Tennis.* Each of the winning openings in a tennis-court 1599. †**6.** *Billiards.* One of the pockets in the sides of a billiard table -1751. **b.** Hence, A stroke by which one of the balls is driven into a pocket 1778. **7.** *Golf.* A general term for bunkers, furze, water, sand, loose earth, or any kind of bad ground 1857. **8.** A cab-stand (in Ireland) 1882. **9.** *attrib.* 1570.

1. Who will go to H. with me for twentie Prisoners SHAKS. 2. I will stand the h. of the Dye SHAKS. 3. Profits proportionable to their..h. HUME. 5. We will ..play a set, Shall strike his fathers Crowne into the h. SHAKS. *H. side*, the side of the tennis-court into which the ball is served. 6. b. *Winning h.*, a stroke in which the object ball is struck with the player's ball and pocketed. *Losing h.*, one in which the striker's ball is pocketed after contact with another.

Ha·zard, *v.* 1530. [a. F. *hasarder*, f. *hasard*; see prec.] **1.** *trans.* To put to the risk of being lost in a game of chance; to stake; to expose to hazard or risk. **b.** *refl.* To run or incur risks. †Also *intr.* 1549. **2.** *trans.* To run or take the risk of (a penalty, etc.) 1559. †**3.** To endanger (any person or thing) –1786. †**4.** To get by chance –1664. **5.** To take the chance or risk of; to venture upon; to venture (*to do*) 1581. †**6.** *Billiards.* To pocket (a ball). EVELYN.

1. To h. a prize by clutching it too soon FREEMAN. 2. Ready to h. all consequences 1827. 5. To h. a battle STEELE, a conjecture 1758, an assertion COLERIDGE. Hence **Ha·zardable** *a.* hazardous, risky; that may be risked. **Ha·zarder,** a player at hazard; a gamester; 'he who hazards' (J.). (Now *rare.*)

†**Ha·zardize,** *v. rare.* 1628. [f. HAZARD *sb.* + -IZE.] To put in hazard, jeopardize, risk –1631.

†**Ha·zardize,** *sb.* [For *hazardise*, after *merchandise.*] A condition of peril or risk. SPENSER.

Hazardous (hæ·zăɹdəs), *a.* 1580. [f. HAZARD *sb.* + -OUS.] **1.** Of the nature of the game of hazard; casual, fortuitous 1585. †**2.** Venturesome –1651. **3.** Fraught with hazard or risk; perilous 1618.

1. H. contracts, in which the performance depends upon some uncertain future event 1880. 3. The enterprize so h. and high MILT. Hence **Ha·zardous-ly** *adv.*, **-ness.**

†**Ha·zardry.** ME. [f. OF. type *hasarderie; see -ERY.] **1.** The playing at hazard; gambling –1590. **2.** The incurring of risk. SPENSER.

Haze (hēⁱz), *sb.* 1706. [? f. HAZY *a.*] An obscuration of the atmosphere near the earth's surface, caused by an infinite number of minute particles of vapour, etc. in the air. In 18th c. applied to a thick fog or hoar-frost; but now usually to a thin misty appearance, which makes distant objects indistinct, and often arises from heat. Also *transf.* and *fig.*

Till he disappeared in the silvery night h. 1833. A h. of sunshine 1891. *fig.* In the fog and h. of confusion all is enlarged BURKE. Hence **Ha·zeless** *a.*

Haze (hēⁱz), *v.*¹ 1678. [Cf. OF. *haser* (1450 in Godef.).] **1.** *trans.* To affright, scare; to scold; also, to punish by blows (*dial.*). **2.** *Naut.* To punish by keeping at disagreeable and unnecessary hard work; to harass by overwork 1840. **3.** To subject to cruel horse-play (as practised by American students); to bully (*U.S.*) 1850. **4.** *intr.* To frolic, lark (*U.S.*) 1848. **5.** *H. about*, to roam about aimlessly; cf. HAZY *a.* 2 b. 1841.

3. 'Tis the Sophomores rushing the Freshmen to h. 1850.

Haze, *v.*² 1674. [Cf. HAZE *sb.*, HAZY *a.*] **1.** *intr.* To drizzle (*dial.*) **2.** *trans.* To make hazy 1801.

Haze, *v.*³ *dial.* 1825. *trans.* To dry.

Hazel¹ (hēⁱ·z'l). [OE. *hæsel* :—OTeut. **hasalo-z* :—pre-Teut. **kósolos* = L. *corulus, corylus.*] **1.** A bush or small tree of the genus *Corylus*, having as its fruit a nut. The European species, *C. avellana*, grows to a small tree; the N. American species are *C. Americana*, a shrub forming dense thickets, and *C. rostrata.* **b.** The wood of this tree 1480. **c.** A stick of this wood 1603. **2.** Applied to other plants; *esp.* WITCH or WYCH HAZEL, q.v. **3.** The reddish brown colour of the nut when ripe 1774. **b.** *adj.* Of this colour; used esp. of the nut when ripe 1774. **b.** *adj.* Of this colour; used esp. of the eyes 1592. **4.** *attrib.* ME.

1. *Oil of h.*, a joc. name for an oil alleged to be contained in a green hazel rod, and to be the efficacious element in a sound drubbing; *to anoint with oil of h.*, to drub with a h. rod. 3. b. Her full dark eye of h. hue SCOTT.

Hence **Ha·zelly** *a.*¹

Ha·zel², **hazle.** 1613. [?] **1.** A kind of freestone (*local*) 1855. **2.** *attrib.* Consisting of a mixture of sand or gravel, clay, and earth, as *h. earth, ground, loam*, etc. So **Ha·zelly** *a.*²

Hazel grouse. 1783. = next.

Hazel-hen. 1661. [tr. mod.Ger. *haselhuhn*, f. *hasel* HAZEL + *huhn* HEN.] The European ruffled grouse, *Bonasia sylvestris.*

Hazeline (hēⁱ·zĕlīn). 1881. [-INE.] An alcoholic distillate from the Witch Hazel, *Hamamelis virginica.*

Hazel-nut (hēⁱ·z'lˌnʋt). [OE. *hæsselhnutu.*] The nut of the hazel. Also *attrib.*

Hazel-wood. ME. **1.** A wood or thicket of hazel bushes. **2.** The wood of the hazel 1573.

Phr. †*Hazelwoods shake*, or merely *hazelwood!* (in Chaucer) app. = Of course.

Ha·zelwort. 1578. [ad. OHG. *haselwurz*, f. *wurz* herb, WORT.] *Herb.* A book-name for Asarabacca.

Hazily (hēⁱ·zĭli), *adv.* 1833. [-LY 2.] In a hazy manner; dimly, indistinctly. Also *fig.*

Haziness (hēⁱ·zinės). 1709. [-NESS.] **1.** The quality of being hazy; mistiness, fogginess. **2.** The quality of being intellectually indistinct; vagueness 1872.

Hazle, hazzle (hæ·z'l), *v. dial.* 1642. [freq. of HAZE *v.*³; see -LE.] To dry on the surface. *trans.* and *intr.*

Hazy (hēⁱ·zi), *a.* 1625. [A century earlier than HAZE *sb.*; origin obscure.] **1.** Of the atmosphere, etc.: Characterized by the presence of haze; misty. (orig. *Naut.*) In 17–18th c. = foggy. **2.** *fig.* Lacking intellectual distinctness; vague, uncertain 1831. **b.** Somewhat confused with drink 1824.

1. A diffused light, which made the air seem h. 1799. 2. Some h. idea DICKENS.

He (hī, hĭ), *pers. pron., 3rd sing. masc. nom.* [The simplest form of the (orig. demonstr.) base *hi-*. OE. *he, hē*. In OE. the base *he* supplied all parts of the third personal pronoun, singular and plural. Subseq. some parts were lost; thus the fem. *hio, heo* became supplanted by SHE, q.v.; the pl. by a pl. of the demonstrative *that*; and in the neuter the acc. *hit* lost its initial *h* in all constructions. The present inflexion is therefore:

SING.	MASC.	FEM.	NEUT.	PLURAL.
Nom.	he	[she]	it	[they]
Acc. } *Dat.* }	him	her	it	[them]
Possess. *adj.*	his	her	its	[their]
absol.	his	hers	its	[theirs]

See the other inflexional parts in their alphabetical places.]

I. As proper masculine pronoun of the third person, nominative case. **1.** The male being in question, or the last mentioned. Used of persons and animals of the male sex. **2.** Of things not sexually distinguished ME. **3.** Used pleonastically along with its noun. Common in ballad style, and now in illiterate speech. OE.

1. He first, and close behind him follow'd she DRYDEN. 2. The Philosophres stoon Elixer clept..With al oure sleighte he wol nat come vs to CHAUCER. 3. 'Fair and softly', John he cried COWPER. The skipper he stood beside the helm LONGF.

II. As Antecedent pronoun, followed by relative, etc. (The neut. is *that*, the pl. *they* or *those.*) **1.** The or that man, or person of the male sex (*that* or *who*...). Hence *Indefinitely*, Any man, any one, a person (*that* or *who*). ME. **2.** Followed by a prepositional phrase (*arch.*) 1598.

1. He that hath ears to hear, let him hear *Matt.* xi. 15. 2. If he of the bottomlesse pit had not..broke prison MILT.

III. As demonstrative pronoun. *He and he*: this and that, the one and the other, both ME.

He snapped me on this hand and he on that 1620.

IV. As *sb.* (not changing in the objective). **1.** Man, person, personage (*arch.* and *poet.*) ME. **2.** Opp. to *she*: Male OE. **b.** A male. (With pl. *hes, he's*, †*hees.*) 1575.

1. The best he in the kingdom FIELDING. 2. Any one not a poet, whether he or she, might toil [etc.] 1888. b. Do we divide dogs into hes and shes JOWETT.

V. *attrib.* (Now usu. hyphened to following noun.) Male. (Now confined to the lower animals, as *he-goat*; in 16–18th c. with nouns denoting persons; this is now contemptuous.) ME. **b.** Occas. with names of plants 1626.

Pope Joan..this He-she FULLER. My he-cosen Harman PEPYS. *spec.* **he-man** (*U.S.*), a masterful or virile man. b. **He-oak,** an Australian tree, *Casuarina stricta*; also *C. suberosa.*

He *v. trans.* to speak to or of (a person) as 'he'.

He (hī), *interj.* OE. [A natural exclam.] Repeated, as *he, he*, or in comb. with *ha, ha*, etc.: A representation of laughter, usu. affected or derisive.

Head (hed), *sb.* [Com. Teut.: OE. *héafod* :—OTeut. **hauƀuđ-, -ido* (with suffix ablaut). The difference of the root vowel is against identification with L. *caput, capit-.*]

I. 1. The anterior part of the body of an animal, when distinguished from the rest of the body; it contains the mouth and special sense-organs and the brain. **2. a.** As the seat of mind, thought, intellect, memory, or imagination; cf. BRAIN *sb.* Often contrasted with *heart*, as the seat of the emotions. ME. **b.** As a part essential to life; hence = life OE. **3.** A representation, figure, or image of a head ME. **b.** The obverse side of a coin, when bearing the figure of a head; the reverse being called the *tail* 1684. **4.** The hair on the head ME. †**5.** The hair as dressed in some particular manner; hence, a head-dress –18... **6.** *Venery.* The 'attire' or antlers of a deer, etc. ME. **7.** Put for the person himself 1535. **b.** As a unit in numbering cattle, game, etc. (Pl., after a numeral, *head.*) 1513. **c.** An indefinite number of animals, esp. of game 1601.

1. The h. of John the Baptist *Mark* vi. 24, of a stag 1735. Phr. *Taller by a h.*; *to make shorter by the h.*, i.e. to behead. b. A headache or disordered head 1889. 2. They remembred, or it came into their heads 1573. Accounts..which he kept in his h. 1802. b. Proofs enough..to cost him his h. 1887. 3. b. Phr. *Head(s) or tail(s)*, used in tossing a coin to decide a chance. 5. At my toilette, try'd a new h. ADDISON. 6. Phr. *Of the first h.*: said of a deer, etc. at the age when the antlers are first developed; hence *fig.* of a man newly ennobled. 7. Different crowned heads DE QUINCEY. An anna a h. for each boy 1847. See also HOT-HEAD. b. Thirteen Head of Neat Cattel 1677. c. The possible h. of pheasants to be bagged next Christmas 1862.

II. A thing or part resembling a head in form or position. **1.** The upper or principal extremity of various things, esp. when rounded, projecting, or of some special shape ME. **2. a.** Any rounded or compact part of a plant, usually at the top of the stem OE. **b.** The rounded leafy top of a tree or shrub 1523. **3.** A collection of foam or froth on the top of liquor, esp. ale or beer 1545; a collection of cream on the surface of milk 1848. **4.** Techn. uses (see quots.) 1703. **5.** The top, summit, upper end ME. **6.** The top of a page or writing; hence, Something, as a title, written at the top; a heading 1586. **7.** The maturated part of a boil, abscess, etc. 1611. **8.** The upper end of something on a slope or so regarded OE. **9.** *spec.* The source of a river or stream. Also *fig.* ME. **10.** A body of water kept at a height for supplying a mill, etc.; the height of such a body of water, or the force of its fall (estimated in terms of the pressure on a unit of area). Sometimes, the bank or dam by which such water is kept up. 1480. **b.** *transf.* The difference of pressure (per unit of area) of two columns of fluid (liquid or gaseous) of different densities communicating at the base; the pressure (per unit of area) of a confined body of gas or vapour 1862. **c.** = BORE *sb.*³ 2, EAGRE. 1570. **11.** The foremost part or end; the front ME. †**12.** The beginning (of a word, writing, etc.). **b.** *Astrol.* The commencement of a zodiacal sign, i.e. the point where the sun enters it. –1816. **13.** The thick end of a chisel or wedge 1793. **14.** The fore-part of a ship, boat, etc.; the bows 1485. **15.** A cape, headland, promontory ME.; a projecting point of a rock or sandbank 1775. **16.** *Coal-mining.* = HEADING. 1664. **17.** An end, extremity (of anything of greater length than breadth). *Obs.* exc. in special uses (cf. HEADER 5). ME.

1. The h. of a spere, an arowe ME., of a golf-club PARK, of a pin, a nail, a screw (*mod.*), of a rib J. BELL, of a muscle 1877, of a comet 1878, of a gate 1854, of a cask MARRYAT, of an alembic 1800, of a carriage 1868, of an anchor 1706, (*Mus.*) of a note 1727, of a lute, violin, etc. 1611, of a violin-bow 1836. 2. a. A h. of

asparagus (*mod.*). **b.** Oaks..that had once a h. COWPER. **4.** A h. (= a bundle) of flax 1704, of silk 1876. *Head* in *Bricklaying*, a tile of half the usual length, used at the eaves of a roof. *Head* in *Gold-mining*, a rammer for crushing quartz. *Heads* (pl.) in *Tin Washing*, the purest ore, which collects at the h. of the table. **5.** The skyish h. of blew Olympus SHAKS. The h. of the stairs 1797. **6.** The heads of chapters 1854. **7.** Phr. *To come to a h.*, to suppurate. **8.** The h. of a bedde 1548, of the table 1786, of the Gulf 1862. **9.** 'Thames H.', or 'the very h. of Isis' PHILLIPS. *fig.* Acquiring facts at the fountain h. COLERIDGE. **10.** The h. of water is 132 feet 1861. **b.** Under a full h. of steam 1862. **11.** The h. of the vast column of troops KINGLAKE, of the pier BORLASE, of a plough 1842. **14.** They were moored by anchors h. and stern GROTE. Phr. *By* (*down by*) *the h.*, with the head lower in the water than the stern. *H. on*, with the head directly pointing at something. **15.** It shone on Beachy H. MACAULAY. **17.** The bridge's h. 1843.

III. Fig. uses. **1.** A person to whom others are subordinate; a chief, captain, ruler, principal person, head man OE. **b.** *spec.* The master or principal of a college in a university; also short for HEAD MASTER 1565. **c.** The chief city, capital; the chief part OE. **2.** Position of leadership, chief command, or greatest importance ME. **3.** One of the chief points of a discourse; the section of it pertaining to any such point; hence, a point, topic; a main division, section, chapter of a writing; a division of a subject, class, category 1500. **4.** Advance against opposing force; resistance; insurrection 1597. †**5.** A force raised, esp. in insurrection –1661. **6.** Issue, result; summing up; culmination, crisis; maturity; height; strength, force, power (gradually attained) ME.

1. The heed of the vnyuersall chirche is the pope FISHER. **c.** The h. of Syria is Damascus *Isa.* vii. 8. **2.** Men..who thought it better to be at the H. of a Sect, than at the Tail of an Establishment BOLINGBROKE. Phr. *H. of the river* (in Bumping races): the position of being first boat; also the boat, crew, or college which holds this position. **3.** Quarrelling Vpon the h. of Valour SHAKS. **4.** Phr. *To make* or *gain h.*; *to bear* or *keep h. against*, to hold one's own against. **5.** The Gothes have gather'd h. SHAKS. **6.** Phr. *To come, grow, gather to a h.*; *to bring, draw to a h.*; *to gather h.* It might bring things to a h., one way or the other T. HARDY.

Phrases.

* *With a preposition.* **Off** one's **h.** Crazy (*colloq.*). **On** or **upon . . h. a.** *On one's h.*: said of evil, vengeance, etc., or of blessing, etc. figured as descending upon a person; also of guilt, 'blood', etc., as resting upon him. †**b.** *On* (*upon*) *h.* (*a, the h.*): Headlong, rashly, inconsiderately. **Out** of one's **own h.** From one's own mind or invention. (Somewhat *colloq.*) **Over . . h. a.** Overhead, up aloft. **b.** *Over* (one's) *h.*: *lit.* above one, e.g. in the sky or air, or affording shelter; also of something rising and overwhelming one; hence *fig.* of danger or evil impending, etc. **c.** *Over* (some one's) *head*: passing over (a person) who has a prior right, claim, etc. **d.** *Over* (one's) *head*: (of time) past, over. **e.** *Over* (one's) *head*: beyond one's comprehension or mental capacity; without considering or consulting one. **To** (one's) **head.** To one's face. *Obs.* or *dial.*

** *With another sb.* **H. and ears. a.** *By the h. and ears*: violently, as one drags a beast. **b.** *Over h. and ears*: completely immersed; also *fig.* **H. . . foot.** *From h. to foot*: all over the person; *fig.* completely. **H. and front.** Orig. app. = 'summit, height, highest extent or pitch' (*Oth.* I. iii. 80); occas. used by mod. writers in other senses. **H. of hair.** The covering of hair on the head, esp. when copious. **H. . . heel**(**s. a.** *From h. to heel*: = from h. to foot (see above). **b.** *H. over heels*: a common corruption of *heels over head* (see HEEL *sb.*[1]). **H. and shoulders. a.** *By h. and shoulders* (*by* occas. omitted): by force, violently; *fig.* of something violently introduced into a speech or writing. **b.** (with *taller*, etc.) By the measure of the h. and shoulders; hence *fig.* considerably, by far. **H. or tail. a.** Either one thing or another; anything intelligible. (With neg.) Now always *to make h. or tail of.* **b.** *Head*(*s or tail*(*s*: see sense I. 3 b.

*** *With a verb.* (*To* BEAT *one's h.*, BREAK *Priscian's h.*, EAT *one's h. off*, KNOCK *on the h.*, etc.: see the verbs.) **Keep one's h.** To keep one's wits about one, keep calm: the opposite of *lose one's h.* **b.** *To keep one's h. above water*: to keep oneself in life; also *fig.* = out of debt. **Lose** one's **h. a.** *lit.* To be beheaded. **b.** *fig.* To lose self-possession or presence of mind. **Make h. a.** To advance, press forward, esp. in opposition to some person or thing; †also *to make a h.* Usually, *To make h. against*: to advance against; to rise in insurrection against; to resist successfully, advance in spite of. †**b.** *To make a h.*: to raise a body of troops. **Put** (a thing) **in** or **into** (a person's) **h.**: to suggest it to his mind; formerly also, to remind him of it. So *to put out of one's h.*, to cause one to forget. †**b.** Hence, by corruption, *to put* (a person) *in the h. of* (a thing): to put him in mind of it. **Take . . h.** †**a.** *To take* (one) *in the h.*: to occur to one. **b.** *To take into* (*in*) *one's h.*: to conceive the idea or notion of.

**** *With adverb.* **H. first, h. foremost**: with the head first or foremost; hence *fig.* precipitately. (Also with hyphen or as one word.)

***** *Fig. and proverbial phrases.* **To give** (a horse) **the h.**, also *to let him have the h.* not to check him with the bridle; to let him go freely. Hence *fig.* of persons. **To lay their heads together**: to consult together. **In spite of** or **maugre his h.**: notwithstanding all he can do. **To talk** (etc.) a person's **h. off** (joc.): i.e. until he is too weary to reply, or *ad nauseam.* So *to beat his h. off*, i.e. to beat him out and out. Provb. *Two heads are better than one* (cf. sense I. 2 a. and *Eccl.* iv. 9).

Attrib. uses. **1.** At the head (sense III. 2); in the position of command; chief, principal, capital OE. **2.** Situated at the head, top, or front; coming from the front, as *a head wind* ME.

Combs. **1.** General: as *h.-affection, -brush, -rest*, etc.; *h.-breaking, -breaker*, etc.; *h.-felt* adj.; *h.-lugged* adj.; *h.-high, -like* adjs.

2. Special: **h.** †**-bone**, the skull; **-boom** (*Naut.*), a boom at the ship's head; a jib-boom; **-cap** (*Bookbinding*), the leather cap over the head-band; **h. centre**: see CENTRE *sb.*; **-cheese** (*U.S.*), pork-cheese, brawn; **-chute** (*Naut.*), a tube leading from the ship's head down to the water, for conveying refuse overboard; **-coal**, the upper portion of a thick seam of coal which is worked in two or more lifts (Gresley); **-cringle** (*Naut.*), a cringle at the upper corner of a sail (Smyth); **-earing** (*Naut.*), an earing attached to a head-cringle (*ibid.*); **-fish** (*U.S.*), the sun-fish (Webst.); †**-fountain** = FOUNTAIN-HEAD; **-gate**, (*a*) one of the upper pair of gates of a canal lock; (*b*) a crown-gate, flood-gate, water-gate; **-hunter**, one who practises head-hunting; **-hunting**, the practice, among some savages, of making incursions for the purpose of procuring human heads as trophies, etc.; **-kidney**, foremost of the three parts of the elementary kidney in a vertebrate embryo, the pronephros; **-lease** (*Law*), a lease granted directly by the freeholder; **-lessee** (*Law*), a person to whom a head-lease is granted; **-light**, a light carried on the front of a locomotive, or on the mast-head of a steamer; *spec.* each of two powerful lamps carried on the front of a motor-vehicle; **-louse**, *Pediculus capitis*; **-netting** (*Naut.*), 'an ornamental netting used in merchant ships instead of the fayed planking to the head-rails' (Smyth); **-page**, a page on which the beginning of a book, chapter, etc. is printed; **-phone**, a telephone or wireless receiver attachable to a listener's ears; **-pump** (*Naut.*), a small pump at the h. of a ship, communicating with the sea, and used for washing the decks; **-rent** (*Law*), rent payable to the freeholder; **-sill**, the upper frame of a door or window; **-timber** (*Shipbuilding*), one of the upright pieces of timber which support the frame of the head-rails; **-tone** = HEAD-NOTE 2; **-valve**, in a steam-engine, 'the delivering valve, the upper air-pump valve' (Knight); †**-well** = HEADSPRING, FOUNTAIN-HEAD; **-word**, a word forming a heading; **-yard** (*Naut.*), one of the yards on the foremast.

Head (hed), *v.* ME. [f. HEAD *sb.* In sense 1, OE. had *behéafdian.*]

I. 1. *trans.* To cut off the head of; to behead. **2.** To top, poll (a tree or plant). Also *to h. down.* 1523.

2. The Willow is headed every three or four Years 1712.

II. 1. *trans.* To furnish or fit with a head 1530; to form the head or top of 1637. **2.** To furnish with a heading or head-line 1877; to stand at the head of (a page, list, etc.) 1832. **3.** *intr.* To form a head; to come or grow to a head ME. **4.** Of a stream: To have its head or source; to rise. Chiefly *U.S.* 1762. **5.** *trans.* (with *up*): To collect (water) so as to form a head. Also *fig.* 1829.

1. To h. a pin 1854. *To h. up* (a cask), to close it up by fitting a head on. **2.** Heaven heads the count of crimes With that wild oath TENNYSON. To h. the poll 1885. Phr. *To h. a trick* (at cards): to play a card of higher value. **3.** Cabbages would not h. O. W. HOLMES.

III. 1. *trans.* To be or put oneself at the head of ME. **2.** To go in front of; to lead; to precede; *fig.* to surpass, excel 1711.

1. I in person will my people h. POPE. **2.** The old Dogs..now headed the Pack 1711.

IV. 1. *intr.* To face 1610; to have an upward slope; opp. to *dip* 1802; *trans.* to cause to face 1610. **2.** *intr.* To shape one's course towards; to make *for.* (Esp. of a ship.) 1835. **b.** *trans.* To direct the course of 1885. **3.** *trans.* To move forward so as to meet; to face, front, oppose; to attack in front 1681. **b.** To get ahead of so as to turn back or aside; now often with *back, off*; also *fig.* 1716. **4.** To go round the head of (a stream or lake) 1657.

1. Two strong veins, heading in the direction of the main lode 1880. **2.** We h. for Venice 1835. **3.** Heading danger in the wars of Tyre 1681. **b.** The Bavarian General..tried to h. back Bony in his retreat from Leipsic SCOTT.

V. *trans.* To strike or drive with the head, e.g. in football 1784.

-head (hed), *suffix*, ME. **hēde, hēd,** not known in OE. Now repl. by *-hood*, exc. in one or two special forms, e.g. *godhead, maidenhead* See -HOOD.

Headache (he·dˌēɪk). OE. [See HEAD *sb.* and ACHE *sb.*] **1.** A continuous pain in the cranial region of the head. **2.** The wild poppy (*Papaver Rhœas*), so named from the effect of its odour (*local*) 1825.

Comb.: H.-tree, a verbenaceous shrub, *Premna integrifolia*, the leaves of which are used to cure h.; **-weed**, a shrub, *Hedyosmum nutans* (N.O. *Chloranthaceæ*), found in the W. Indies.

Hence **Hea·dachy** *a.* suffering from or subject to h.; accompanied with or producing h. **Hea·dachiness.**

Headband (he·dbænd). 1535. **1.** A band worn round the head, a fillet. **2.** A band round the top of trousers, etc. 1818. **3.** *Bookbinding.* A band (usually of silk or cotton) fastened to the inner back of a bound book at the head and tail 1611. **4.** *Arch.* = ARCHIVOLT. **5.** *Printing.* A thin slip of iron forming the top of the tympan of a printing-press 1841. Hence **Hea·dbander. Hea·dbanding.**

Head-block (he·dˌblǫk). 1642. †**1.** A block put at the back of the chimney to keep the fire in by night. FULLER. **2.** In a saw-mill: The device for holding the log upon the carriage, while it is sawn 1864. **3.** The piece which connects the wheel-plate or fifth wheel of a carriage with the fore-body 1875.

Head-board (he·dbōᵊɹd). 1730. **1.** A board at the upper end of anything, as a bedstead, etc. **2.** *Naut.* (*pl.*) 'The berthing or close-boarding between the head-rails' (Smyth).

Headborough (he·dbvːrǒ). 1440. Orig., the head of a *friðborh*, tithing, or frankpledge (see BORROW *sb.*); afterwards a petty constable; = BORSHOLDER, TITHINGMAN. Also *transf.*

Head-cloth (he·dˌklǫþ). OE. [See CLOTH *sb.* 1.] **1.** A covering for the head; in *pl.* the pieces composing a head-dress. **2.** A piece of cloth at the head of a bed 1730.

Head-court. *Hist.* 1545. A chief court (of justice); for some time used as a court for the registration of county voters.

Head-dress (he·dˌdres). 1703. Any dress or covering for the head; *esp.* an ornamental one worn by women.

Headed (he·dėd), *a.* and *ppl. a.* ME. [f. HEAD *sb.* and *v.* + -ED.] **1.** Having a head (of a specified kind). Freq. in comb., as *clear-h.*, etc. **2.** Of things: Furnished with a head; tipped, as an arrow, etc. 1450. **3.** Of a plant: Grown to a head 1577. **4.** That has come to a head, as a boil. *A.Y.L.* II. vii. 67. †**5.** Of flints: Faced (see FACE *v.*) –1717. **6.** Furnished with a heading 1838.

6. A five-lined whip, h. 'most important' 1884.

Header (he·dəɹ). ME. [f. HEAD *v.* and *sb.* + -ER[1].] **1.** One who or that which removes the head; *spec.* a reaping-machine which cuts off only the heads of the grain 1883. **2.** One who puts a head on something, e.g. casks, nails, pins, etc. 1755. **3.** One who heads or leads a party, etc.; a leader (*rare*) 1818. **4.** *Building.* A brick, or stone, laid with its head or end in the face of the wall; opp. to *stretcher.* Also applied to sods, etc. in fortification. 1688. **5.** *Pugilism.* A blow on the head 1818. **6.** A plunge or dive head foremost (*colloq.*) 1849. **7.** One who dives head foremost. CLOUGH. **8.** A collier or coal-cutter who drives a head 1883.

6. Four blacks..took a h. into the boiling current 1859.

Headfast (he·dfɑst), *sb.* 1569. [f. HEAD *sb.* + FAST *sb.*[2]] *Naut.* A rope or chain at the head of a vessel, to make her fast to a wharf, buoy, etc. Hence **Hea·dfast** *v. trans.* to make fast with a h.

Head-foremost, headforemost, *adv. phr.* and *a.* 1871. **a.** *adv. phr.* See *head foremost*, s.v. HEAD *sb.* **b.** *adj.* Headlong, precipitate (*rare*).

Head-gear (he·dˌgīəɹ). 1539. **1.** That which is worn on the head; a head-dress of any kind. **2.** The parts of the harness about a horse's head 1875. **3.** *Mining.* Apparatus at the head of a shaft 1841. **4.** The rigging on the fore-part of a vessel.

Headily (he·dili), *adv.* 1450. [f. HEADY + -LY[2].] In a heady manner; hastily, rashly; violently, impetuously; †eagerly. So **Hea·diness**, the quality or condition of being heady.

Heading (he·diŋ), *vbl. sb.* ME. [-ING[1].] **1.** The action of HEAD *v.*, in various senses. **2.** *concr.* A distinct part forming the head, top, or front of a thing; that which is at the top 1676. **3.** Material for the heads of casks 1772. **4.** The title or inscription at the head of a page, chapter, etc. 1849; *fig.* a division, section of a subject of discourse, etc. 1859. **5.** A gallery or adit in a mine; a drift; also, the end of a drift or gallery 1819. **6.** A top layer or covering, e.g. foam on beer 1777. **7.** *attrib.* 1513.

Comb.: **h.-course**, a course of bricks consisting of headers; **-joint** (*Carp.*), the joint of two or more boards at right angles to the fibres; **†-stone**, a faced or pitched stone.

Heading-machine. 1875. **a.** A kind of harvester (see HEADER 1). **b.** A machine for forming heads, as for casks, pins, bolts, etc. 1884.

Headland (he·dlǣnd). OE. [f. HEAD *sb.* + LAND *sb.*] **1.** A strip of land left for convenience in turning the plough at the end of the furrows, or near a fence; in old times used as a boundary. **2.** A point of land projecting into the sea or other expanse of water; a cape or promontory; now usu., a bold or lofty promontory 1527.

2. The Cape or Head-land of St. Bees 1769.

Headless (he·dlės), *a.* OE. [-LESS.] **1.** Without a head; beheaded. **b.** = ACEPHALOUS 3. 1880. **2.** Having no chief or leader ME. **3.** Wanting in brains or intellect 1526; (of actions) senseless, stupid 1586.

1. H. figures 1862, casks 1884. 3. Headlesse Captaines CHEKE. Headlesse Old-wiues Tales 1619.

Hea·d-line. 1626. **1.** *Naut.* **a.** One of the ropes that make a sail fast to the yard. **b.** The line sewed along the upper edge of flags to strengthen them 1794. **2.** *Printing.* **†a.** The upper line that bounds the short letter. MOXON. **†b.** The line which is drawn across the head of a page. CRABB. **c.** The line at the top of a page in which the running title, pagination, etc. are given; a title or sub-title in a book, etc. 1824. **3.** A rope attached to the head of a bullock, etc. Hence **Hea·d-line** *v.* to furnish with a head-line. **Hea·d-liner**, one who writes head-lines; also (*U.S.*), one whose name appears in a h.-l.; a chief person or performer.

Headlong (he·dlǫŋ). 1482. [Earlier *headling*, erron. assim. to -LONG; cf. *sidelong*.]

A. *adv.* **1.** Head foremost; head downmost. Also *fig.* **2.** With ungoverned speed; with blind impetuosity 1576; *fig.* without regard to where one is going; precipitately 1530.

1. *fig.* He casts him selfe head-long to hel 1602.

B. *adj.* **1.** Of heights, etc.: Precipitous. Now *rare.* 1550. **2.** Plunging downwards head foremost, as when one falls or dives: **a.** of actions 1586; **b.** *poet.* of a person 1663. **c.** Hanging head downmost. POPE. **3.** Wildly impetuous. Of actions and agents. 1590. **4.** *fig.* Precipitate; rash, reckless 1566.

1. You tumble down a h. Precipice 1692. 2. **a.** H. leaps of waters MRS. BROWNING. 3. H. torrents MACAULAY. 4. H. orator COWPER, ire SCOTT. Hence **†Hea·dlong** *v. trans.* to cast h.; *intr.* to proceed in a h. fashion. Also **Hea·dlongs** *adv.* (now *dial.*) = A.

Head-man, headman, head man. [OE. *hēafodman.*] **1.** Chief man, chief, leader. **†2.** = HEADSMAN. -1816.

Head Master, hea·d-ma·ster. 1576. The principal master of a school, having assistant masters under him. Hence **Head-ma·stership.**

Head Mistress, hea·d-mi·stress. 1872. The principal mistress of a school, having assistant mistresses under her. Hence **Head-mistress-ship.**

Hea·d-money. 1530. **1.** A fee, tax, etc. paid per head. **2.** A sum paid for each prisoner taken at sea, for each slave recovered, or for each person brought in certain circumstances 1713.

Hea·dmost, *a.* 1628. [f. HEAD *sb.* + -MOST.] **1.** Most forward in order or progression; said *esp.* of the foremost ship of a line. **2.** Topmost (*dial.*) 1798.

Hea·d-note. 1855. **1.** *Law.* A summary prefixed to the report of a decided case, stating the principle of the decision, with, latterly, an outline of the facts. **2.** *Mus.* A note produced in the second or third register of the voice; cf. HEAD-VOICE. 1869.

†Hea·d-pan. [OE. *hēafodpanne.*] Skull, brain-pan -ME.

Hea·d-penny. *Obs.* exc. *Hist.* ME. **1.** A capitation fee. **2.** A personal or individual eccl. payment or offering 1550.

Hea·d-piece. 1530. The piece that covers or forms the head. **1.** A helmet 1535. **2.** A cap 1552. **3.** The head, skull (*arch.*) 1576. **4.** The head, as the seat of intellect; brain 1588. **5.** **†a.** The protective covering of the forehead of a barded horse 1611. **b.** A halter, a head-stall 1530. **6.** The top piece or part 1611. **7.** *Printing.* A decorative engraving placed at the head of a volume, of chapters, etc.

3. In his headpeace he felt a sore payne SPENSER. 4. The hurt..had somewhat crazed his h. 1613. Is not this Steward of mine..a rare h. GAY.

Hea·d-plate. 1794. **1.** An ornament made to fix on the upper quarters of a coach or chariot. **2.** *Artillery.* 'The plate which covers the breast of the cheeks of a gun-carriage' (Knight) 1875. **3.** *Saddlery.* 'The plate strengthening the . . cantle of a saddle-tree' (Knight) 1874.

Hea·d-qua·rters, *sb. pl.* (Rarely *sing.*) 1647. **1.** *Mil.* The residence of the commander-in-chief of an army; the place whence a commander's orders are issued; also, the officers belonging to head-quarters 1812. **b.** The transport which carries the staff of an expedition (Smyth). **2.** A chief place of residence, meeting, or business; a centre of operations 1851. **3.** *attrib.*, usually in form *head-quarter* 1879.

1. On the way to report himself at head-quarters W. IRVING. 2. A strong continuous impulse from head-quarters BURGON.

Hea·d-race. 1846. The race or flume which brings water to a mill-wheel. Cf. *tail-race.*

Hea·d-rail[1]. 1823. **1.** One of the rails at the head of a ship. **2.** The upper horizontal piece of a door-frame 1874.

Hea·d-rail[2]. *Obs.* exc. *Hist.* [OE. *hēafodhrægl*, f. *hēafod* head + *hrægl* garment.] The kerchief or head-dress of women in OE. times.

Hea·d-rope. ME. **†1.** One of the stays of a mast -1475. **2.** That part of a bolt-rope which is sewed on the upper edge of any sail. Also, the small rope to which a flag is fastened, to hoist it to the mast-head, etc. 1627. **3.** A rope along the top of a fishing-net 1883. **4.** A rope for leading or tying up a horse 1854.

Head-sail. 1627. *Naut.* Any foremast or bowsprit sail.

Headship (he·dʃip). 1582. [-SHIP.] The position or office of head; leadership; supremacy, primacy.

Hea·dsman. ME. [f. *head's* gen. + MAN; cf. *draughtsman.*] **1.** A chief, head man. Now *rare.* **2.** One who beheads; an executioner 1601. **3.** *Mining.* A labourer in a colliery who pushes coal from the workings to the tramway; a 'putter' 1841.

Hea·dspring. ME. Fountain-head, source.

Head-stall, headstall (he·dˌstǭl), *sb.* ME. [f. HEAD *sb.* + STALL, OE. *steall* position, standing-place, etc.] The part of a bridle or halter that fits round the head 1480. Hence **Head-stall** *v.* (*rare*), to put a h. on (a horse).

Headstock. 1731. Name applied to the bearings or supports of revolving parts in various machines; as: **a.** That part of a lathe which carries the mandrel or live stock; **b.** The head which supports the cutters in a planing machine; etc.

Hea·dstone, head stone. 1535. **1.** (*head stone*) The chief stone in a foundation; the cornerstone. Also *fig.* **2.** (*hea·dstone*) An upright stone at the head of a grave 1775.

Headstrong (he·dstrǫŋ), *a.* ME. [f. HEAD *sb.* + STRONG *a.*; *lit.* strong of or in head.] **1.** Determined to pursue one's own course; wilful, obstinate. **2.** Of things, etc.: Characterized by or proceeding from wilfulness or obstinacy 1586.

1. To tie a h. girle from loue GREENE. 2. Dangerous and h. passions 1796. Hence **Hea·dstrongness.**

Head-tire (he·dˌtəiəɹ). Now *arch.* or *dial.* 1560. Attire for the head; a head-dress.

An head tyre of fine linnen BIBLE (Genev.) 1 *Esdras* iii. 6.

Hea·d-voice. 1849. One of the highest registers of the voice in singing or speaking; applied both to the second register, and to the third register or falsetto.

Headward (he·dwǭɹd). ME. [-WARD.] **†A.** *orig.* in *To the h.*, in the direction of the head. **b.** Of a ship: Ahead. -1674. **B.** *adv.* Towards or in the direction of the head 1798. **C.** *adj.* Being in the region or direction of the head 1667.

Head water, head-water. 1535. **1.** *pl.* *Head waters*: The streams from the sources of a river. **2.** *H.-w.-mark*, a mark showing the 'head' to be allowed above a weir, etc. 1894.

Headway (he·dweⁱ). 1708. [In I, short for *aheadway*; in II, f. HEAD *sb.* + WAY *sb.*]

I. 1. Of a ship: Motion ahead or forward; rate of progress 1748. **2.** *transf.* and *fig.* Advance, progress (in general) 1775.

1. The head-way..is feeble 1769.

II. 1. *Arch.* Room overhead; the clear height of a doorway, arch, tunnel, etc. 1775. **2.** *Mining.* (Also *headways.*) A narrow passage or 'gallery', connecting the broad parallel passages or 'boards' in a coal mine 1708. **3.** The interval of time or the distance between two trains, trams, etc., running on the same route and in the same direction (orig. *U.S.*) 1895.

Hea·d-work. 1843. [f. HEAD *sb.* + WORK *sb.*] **1.** Mental work. **2.** An ornament for the keystone of an arch 1864. **Hea·d-wo·rker.**

Heady (he·di), *a.* ME. [f. HEAD *sb.* + -Y.] **1.** Headlong, precipitate, impetuous, violent; headstrong; 'hurried on with passion' (J.). **2.** Apt to affect or 'go to' the head; intoxicating, stupefying 1577. **†3.** Of a tenure: In chief (*in capite*) MARSTON.

1. H. judgements 1545. A Flood With such a h. currance SHAKS. When a h. Prince comes to the Throne LOCKE. 2. There is such headie ale 1577.

†Heal, hele, *sb.* *Obs.* exc. *Sc.* [OE. *hǣlu, hǣlo, hǣl*, f. *hāl* adj. HALE, WHOLE.] **1.** Health; cure -1795. **2.** Well-being, safety; prosperity -1605.

Heal (hīl), *v.*[1] [Com. Teut.: OE. *hǣlan*, deriv. of *hail-s*, OTeut. **hailo-z*, OS. *hāl* HALE, WHOLE.] **1.** *trans.* To make whole or sound; to cure (*of* a disease or wound). Also *absol.* **2.** To cure (a disease); to restore to soundness (a wound); also to *h. up, over.* Also *absol.* OE. **3.** *fig.* To save, purify, cleanse, repair, amend OE. **4.** *intr.* (for *refl.*) To become whole or sound; to recover from sickness or a wound; to get well ME.

1. Physician, h. thyself *Luke* iv. 23. *absol.* I wound, and I heale *Deut.* xxxii. 39. 2. O foolish physick.. That heales up one, and makes another wound SPENSER. 3. So the waters were healed 2 *Kings* ii. 22. The breach in our ranks might be healed tomorrow 1887. 4. Those wounds heale ill, that men doe giue themselues SHAKS. Hence **Hea·lable** *a.* (*rare*), that may be healed.

Heal, *v.*[2], to cover; see HELE *v.*[2]

Heal-all (hī·lˌǭl). 1577. [f. HEAL *v.*[1] + ALL.] **1.** A universal remedy; a panacea. Also *fig.* **2.** *Herb.* A pop. name of plants, e.g. *Rhodiola rosea, Prunella vulgaris*, etc. 1853.

Heald (hīld). [app. = OE. *hęfeld, hefeld.*] *Weaving.* = HEDDLE.

Healer (hī·ləɹ). ME. [f. HEAL *v.*[1] + -ER[1].] **1.** One who heals or saves; in early use, Saviour. **2.** That which heals; a remedy 1523.

†Healful, *a.* ME. [f. HEAL *sb.* + -FUL.] Fraught with health; wholesome, salutary -1563.

Hea·ling, *vbl. sb.* OE. [f. HEAL *v.*[1] + -ING[1].] The action of HEAL *v.*[1]; *spec.* the touching by English sovereigns for the king's evil 1676. Also *transf.* and *fig.* ME.

Hea·ling, *ppl. a.* ME. [f. as prec. + -ING [2].] **1.** That heals or cures. Also *transf.* and *fig.* **2.** Of a wound: That cicatrizes or closes 1857.

1. The h. waters SCOTT. *fig.* To whom with h. words Adam reply'd MILT. Hence **Hea·lingly** *adv.*

†Healless, *a.* [f. HEAL *sb.* + -LESS.] Deprived of health or well-being. CHAUCER.

Health (helþ), *sb.* [OE. *hǽlþ*, f. (ult.) *hail-s* WHOLE, HALE; see -TH.] **1.** Soundness of body; that condition in which its functions are duly discharged. **2.** Hence, The general condition of the body; usually qualified as *good, bad, delicate,* etc. 1509. **†3.** Healing, cure -1555. **4.** Spiritual, moral, or mental soundness; salvation (*arch.*) OE. **†5.** Well-being, safety; deliverance -1611. **6.** A wish expressed for a person's welfare; a toast drunk in a person's honour 1596.

1. With a..Flush of H. in his Aspect ADDISON. 2. She enjoyed very tolerable h. 1802. Phr. *Bill of Health*: see BILL *sb.*[3] *Board of H.*, a Government Board which existed 1848–1858 for the control of matters affecting the public health. 4. There is no health in vs *Bk. Com. Prayer.* 5. Be thou a Spirit of h., or Goblin damn'd SHAKS.

Comb.: **-guard,** an officer appointed to enforce quarantine regulations (Smyth); **-officer,** an officer charged with the administration of the health laws and sanitary inspection; so **visitor; -resort; -roll,** a list showing the state of health of a company of people, as of a ship's crew.

Healthful (he·lþfŭl), *a.* ME. [f. HEALTH *sb.* + -FUL.] **1.** Promoting bodily or spiritual health; health-giving, salubrious; salutary. **2.** Of persons, etc.: Full of or characterized by health; healthy (now *rare*) 1550; marked by intellectual or moral soundness 1601.

1. Much subject to Earthquakes, else very h. 1694. H. elements of European civilization 1862. 2. He was generally h., and capable of much labour JOHNSON. The h. progress of the world 1884. Hence **Hea·lthful-ly** *adv.*, **-ness.**

Healthless (he·lþlės), *a.* Now *rare.* 1568. [-LESS.] **1.** Destitute of bodily, mental, or spiritual health; unhealthy. **2.** Not conducive to health; unwholesome 1650. Hence **Hea·lthlessness.**

Healthsome (he·lþsŏm), *a.* Now *rare.* 1538. [-SOME.] **†1.** Full of health; healthy -1635. **2.** Bestowing health; wholesome; salutary 1538. Hence **Hea·lthsome·ly** *adv.*, **-ness.**

Hea·lthward, *a.* 1884. [-WARD.] Tending towards health.

Healthy (he·lþi), *a.* 1552. [f. HEALTH *sb.* + -Y.] **1.** Possessing good health; hale or sound (in body) **2.** Conducive to health; wholesome, salubrious; salutary. Also *fig.* 1552. **3.** Denoting health or sound condition (*lit.* and *fig.*); opp. to *morbid* 1597.

1. My abstinence keeps me quite h 1815. 2. H. dwelling-houses 1871. *fig.* A h. influence upon society 1884. 3. The h. habit of the British constitution BURKE. Hence **Hea·lthily** *adv.* **Hea·lthiness.**

Heap (hīp), *sb.* [OE. *héap* :—OTeut. **haupo-z* In ablaut relation to Ger. *haufe*, etc. :—**hûpon*; from stem **hup-*, pre-Teut. **kub-*; cf. L. *cumbere, cubare.*] **1.** A collection of things lying one upon another so as to form an elevated mass roughly conical in form. **†b.** Mass, main body -1709. **2. a.** A heaped measure of capacity. **b.** A pile or mass of definite size, varying with the commodity. 1674. **3.** A great company (esp. of persons); a multitude, a host. Now only as in 4. OE. **4.** Hence, colloq.: A large number or quantity; a (great) deal; a lot. Also *pl.* in same sense. 1547. Also *absol* and as *adv.* (colloq.) 1834.

1. They haue..made Ierusalem an heape of stones COVERDALE *Ps.* lxxviii[i]. *Fallacy of the heap*: the fallacy which plays upon the difficulty of saying precisely when a number of things make a h. 4. She.. has a h. of servants TROLLOPE. *pl.* In heaps of time 1856. *absol.* It's nature I should think a h. of him MRS. STOWE. Phrases. *All of a h.*: all in a mass falling or fallen. *To strike all of a h.* (colloq.): to paralyse, cause to collapse. *Comb.*: **h.-cloud** = CUMULUS 2; **-flood,** a heavy sea.

Heap (hīp), *v.* [OE. *héapian*, deriv. of prec.] **1.** *trans.* To make, form, gather, or cast into a heap Often with *up, together, on.* **2.** *transf.* and *fig.* To amass, accumulate; to add many things together. Also *absol.* OE. **3.** *trans.* To fill, load, cumber with a heap or heaps. Also with *up.* 1526. **4.** To bestow in heaps. *Const.* upon. 1573. **5.** To load (a person) *with* (something in large quantities) 1583.

1. Though he heape vp siluer as the dust *Job* xxvii. 16. 2. Generations of antiquaries have heaped to gether vast piles of facts M. PATTISON. 3. The field is heaped with bleeding steeds, and flags, and cloven mail MACAULAY. 4. To h. insults on his memory BRIGHT. Phr. *Heaped measure*, a dry measure used for certain commodities which are heaped up in a cone above the brim of the measure.

Hence **Hea·per,** one who heaps up or accumulates.

Heapy (hī·pi), *a.* 1552. [f. HEAP *sb.* + -Y.] Full or consisting of heaps.

Hear (hīᵊɹ), *v.* Pa. t. and pple. **heard** (hɜɹd). [Com. Teut.: OE., early WS. *hieran*, late WS. *hýran*, Anglian *héran* (:— **héarjan*) :—OTeut. **hauzjan*. Relationship to the root *auz-* EAR, to L. *audire*, and Gr. ἀκούειν is unlikely.] **1.** *intr.* To perceive, or have the sensation of, sound; to possess or exercise the faculty of audition, of which the organ is the ear. The proper verb to express this faculty or function. **2.** *trans.* To perceive (sound or something that causes sound); to have cognizance of by means of the ear OE. **3.** To exercise the auditory function intentionally; to give ear, hearken, listen. **a.** *intr.* ME. **b.** *trans.* To listen to; to give ear to, hearken to; to give audience to. Orig. with dative of the person or thing. OE. **4.** *trans.* To attend and listen to (a lecture, sermon, etc.); to form one of the audience at ME. **5.** *trans.* To listen to judicially in a court of law; to give (one) a hearing; to try (a person or case) OE. **6.** To listen to with compliance; to accede to, grant OE. **7.** To obey. (Only OE., ME., and *arch.*) **8.** To learn by hearing; to be informed of OE. **9.** *absol.* or *intr.* To be informed, learn; to receive tidings *of*, a message or letter *from* ME. *To h. from*: also, to receive a reprimand from 1907. **†10.** To be spoken (well or ill) of. [After Gr. εὖ, κακῶς ἀκούειν, L. *bene, male audire.*] -1706. **b.** *To h. rather*: to prefer to be called. (A Latinism.) 1667.

1. He that hath eares to heare, let him here TINDALE *Matt.* xi. 15. To heare with eies belongs to loves fine wit SHAKS. 2. Lay thine eare close to the ground, and list if thou can heare the tread of Trauellers SHAKS. Eye hath not seen, nor ear heard..the things which God hath prepared for them that love him 1 *Cor.* ii. 9. Phr. *To h. say, h. tell*, etc., with ellipsis of *people, persons, some one*, before *say, tell*, etc. 3. a. Speak, Lord, for thy servant heareth 1 *Sam.* iii. 9. b. Wherfore hearest thou mens words 1 *Sam.* xxiv. 9. 4. To h. a play SHAKS. 5. To heare The cause SHAKS. 6. The prayer is heard KEBLE. Phr. *To h. of* (in U.S. also *to*) (with *will*, etc. and neg.): to refuse to listen to, entertain the notion of, permit. 8. Adam, soon as he heard The fatal Trespass don by Eve MILT. I h. there are no lodgings to be had 1808. 9. I too had been looking to h. from you SOUTHEY. Phr. *To h. of it*: to be called to account for it (*colloq.*). 10. Or hear'st thou rather pure Ethereal stream Whose Fountain who shall tell MILT.

Phr. **Hear!** (imper.), now usu. **Hear! Hear!** (formerly *Hear him! Hear him!*): an exclam. to call attention to a speaker's words, and hence a regular form of cheering (CHEER *sb.* 8). Hence also as *sb.* and *v.*

Hence **Hea·rable** *a.* that can be heard.

Hearer (hīᵊ·rəɹ). ME. [f. HEAR *v.* + -ER.[1]] **1.** One who hears: an auditor. **2.** One who attends lectures or sermons; a disciple 1686. **3.** *Eccl. Hist.* One admitted to hear the Scriptures read, but not to the common worship of the church 1697.

Hea·ring, *vbl. sb.* ME. [-ING [1].] **1.** The action of HEAR *v.*; the faculty or sense by which sound is perceived; audition. **2.** The action of listening (e.g. to a lecture, sermon, play, etc.); *spec.* attendance at preaching (*dial.*); audience. Also *fig.* ME. **3.** The listening to evidence and pleadings in a court of law; the trial of a cause; *spec.* a trial before a judge without a jury 1576. **4.** Knowledge by hearing or being told 1450. **5.** Something heard; report, rumour, news (*dial.*) ME.

1. Captivating..at the first h. PRIESTLEY. The organ of h. is not manifest in insects STARK. Phr *In ones h.* *Within h., out of h.*: within, or out of, hearing distance. 2. We begge your h. Patientlie SHAKS. 3. I'll..leaue to you the h. of the cause SHAKS. 4. Phr. *To come to one's h.* 5. Tis..a harsh h., when women are froward SHAKS.

Hearken, harken (hā·ɹk'n), *v.* [OE. *hercnian, heorcnian, hyrcnian*, formed with suffix *-n-* from **heorcian*, the OE. type of HARK *v.* The form *hearken* is usual in current English, *harken* in American Diets.] **1.** *intr.* To apply the ears to hear; to listen, give ear Const. *to*, in OE. and ME. with dative. **†2.** *intr.* To listen privily -1588. **3.** *intr.* To apply the mind to what is said; to have regard. Const. *to.* ME. **4** *trans.* To hear with attention, give ear to; to have regard to; to learn by hearing; to perceive by the ear. Now only *poet.* OE. **†5.** *intr. Hearken to*: Listen, give ear. [As if from *to-hearken*; cf. *Go to*, from vb. TO-GO.] -1535. **†6.** *intr.* To seek to hear tidings; to inquire *after*, ask *for* -1830. **†7.** *intr.* To lie in wait; to wait -1633. **†8.** *trans.* To get to hear of; to search *out* -1637. **†9.** To have regard or relation (*rare*). POPE.

1. She hearkens for his hounds and for his horn SHAKS. 3. No man wyll herken to it LATIMER. 4. This King of Naples..hearkens my Brothers suit SHAKS. 6. *Much Ado* v. i. 216. 7. *Tam. Shr.* I. ii. 260. 8. He has imploied a fellow..to harken him out a dumbe woman B. JONS. Hence **Hea·rkener, Hark-.**

Hearsay (hīᵊ·ɹsēˡ). 1532. [subst. use of phr. *to hear say.*] **1.** That which one hears or has heard some one say; report, tradition, rumour, common talk, gossip. With *a.* and *pl.* A rumour, a piece of gossip 1642. **2.** *attrib.* becoming an *adj.*, etc.: (*a*) Of the nature of hearsay; (*b*) founded upon what one has heard said, but not within one's direct knowledge; (*c*) of hearsay, speaking from hearsay. 1580.

1. Thou speakest by hearesaye, rather then by anye experience 1577. 2. An h. account by Bellonius SIR T. BROWNE. The report of h. witnesses CHALMERS. *Hearsay evidence*: evidence consisting in what the witness has heard others say or what is commonly said. H.-evidence is..rejected in law 1753. Yet.. (as in proof of any general customs, or matters of common tradition or repute), the courts admit of h. evidence BLACKSTONE.

Hearse (hɜɹs), *sb.* ME. [Formerly *herse.* a. F. *herse* = It. *erpice* :—L. *hirpicem* (*hirpex*) large rake used as a harrow; ? cf. Gr. ἅρπαξ. See HERSE.] **†1.** A harrow-shaped triangular frame, designed to carry candles, and used at the service of *Tenebræ* in Holy Week. **2. a.** A framework orig. for carrying lighted tapers, etc. over the bier or coffin while placed in the church at the funerals of distinguished persons; also called *castrum doloris, chapelle ardente,* or *catafalco* ME. **b.** A permanent framework of iron or metal, fixed over a tomb to support rich coverings or palls, etc. 1552. **c.** A temple-shaped structure of wood used in royal and noble funerals. It was decorated with banners, lighted tapers, etc., and often had short poems or epitaphs pinned upon it 1575. **3.** A light framework of wood used to support the pall over the body at funerals 1566. **†4.** A funeral pall -1603. **5.** A bier; a coffin; vaguely, a tomb, grave. *Obs.* or *arch.* 1601. **†6.** A dead body -1633. **7.** A carriage or car constructed for carrying the coffin at a funeral. (The current use.) 1650.

2. c. Underneath this sable herse Lyes the subject of all verse B. JONS. Be this my latest verse With which I now adorn his Herse COWLEY. 5. As thou my cradle wert, so wilt thou be my herse LISLE. 7. A h. too, with plenty of plumes MRS. CARLYLE.

Comb.: **h.-cloth,** a black cloth to cover a bier or coffin; a funeral pall; **-like** *a.*, like a h.; mournful.

Hearse, *v.* 1592. [f. the sb.] *trans.* To lay on a bier or in a coffin; to bury with funeral rites. **b.** (in recent use) To carry to the grave in a hearse. **c.** To enclose as in a bier 1608.

1. Would she were hearsed at my foote SHAKS. c. Worth may be hears'd but Envy cannot die CHURCHILL. Hence **Hearsed** *ppl. a.* placed on, in, or under a hearse (*Haml.* I. iv. 47).

Hearst. Also **†hearse.** 1674. *Hunting.* A hind of the second or third year.

Heart (hāɹt), *sb.* [Com. Teut.: OE. *heorte* :—OTeut. **herton-*. Radically related to L. *cor, cord-*, Gr. καρδία (also κῆρ from κηρδ-); root *kerd-, krd-*.]

I. *The bodily organ*, etc. **1.** The hollow muscular or otherwise contractile organ which, by its dilatation and contraction, keeps up the circulation of the blood. **b.** A diseased or disordered heart, as FATTY *h.*, *smoker's h.* 1871. **2.** The seat of life; the vital part or principle; hence occas. = life. *Obs.* or *arch.* OE. **3.** *transf.* The region of the heart; breast, bosom 1450. **4.** The stomach. *Obs.* or *dial.* 1542.

1. Why doe's my bloud thus muster to my h. SHAKS. *fig.* Nature's mighty h. SHELLEY. 2. Bread which strengtheneth man's h. *Ps.* civ. 15. 3. Lay hand on

h., aduise SHAKS. *fig.* He hugged his old conviction to his h. 1887. 4. Phr. *Next the h.*: on an empty stomach. (*Obs.* or *dial.*).

II. *As the seat of feeling, understanding, and thought.* 1. = MIND, in the widest sense OE. 2. The seat of one's inmost thoughts and secret feelings; one's inmost being; the soul, the spirit OE. 3. Intent, will, purpose, inclination, desire. Now only in phr. *after one's own h.* OE. †4. Disposition, temperament, character –1611. 5. The seat of the emotions generally; the emotional nature; opp. to *head* OE. †b. The sentiment one has in regard to a thing –1603. 6. *esp.* The seat of love or affection; hence, Affection, love, devotion. ME. b. Kindly feeling (*rare*) 1656. c. Sensibility; feeling 1735. 7. The seat of courage; hence, Courage, spirit OE. 8. The seat of the intellectual faculties. Often = understanding, intellect, mind, and (less often) memory. *arch.* exc. in phr. *by h.* OE. 9. The moral sense, conscience. Now only in *my*, etc. *h. smote me*, etc. ME.

1. His Heart's his mouth; What his Brest forges, that his Tongue must vent SHAKS. Behould the eares of my hart, are set before thee; open thou them 1620. 2. Great searchings of h. *Judg.* v. 16. 4. Not changing h. with habit SHAKS. 5. Her h. was too full to speak TROLLOPE. 6. Phr. *To give, lose one's h.* (*to*), *to have, obtain, gain a person's h.* *Near, nearest, one's h.*, close or closest to one's affection. She..won all hearts 1887. 7. Thy dauntless h...will urge thee to thy fate DRYDEN. Phr. *To pluck up, gather, keep* (*up*), *lose h.* *To have the h., take h.* *To have one's h. in, put one's h. into.* 8. Ephraim is like a silly dove without h. *Hosea* vii. 11.

III. *Put for the person.* 1. Used as a term of endearment ME. 2. = Man of spirit. Often in nautical use. 1500. †3. As a term of compassion: *Poor h.!* 1599.

1. Alas whan shall I mete yow, herte dere CHAUCER. 2. Heigh my hearts, cheerely, cheerely my harts SHAKS.

IV. *Something having a central position.* 1. The central part of anything; the middle ME. 2. *esp.* A central part of distinct conformation or character (see quots.) 1578. 3. *spec.* The solid central part of a tree without sap or alburnum ME. Hence fig. *Heart of oak*: a stout courageous spirit; a man of courage or endurance. Also *attrib.* 1609.

1. The H. of England 1658, of the City DE FOE, of the London season DISRAELI. 2. A goodly apple rotten at the h. SHAKS. The h. of a tree 1681, of a Flower 1707, of a rope 1841, of a cabbage 1866. 2. He was..a h. of oke, and a pillar of the Land WOOD.

V. *The vital part or principle.* 1. The vital part; essence 1533. 2. Of land, etc.: Strength, fertility; capacity to produce; 'proof' (of grass, etc.) 1573. 3. The best or most important part 1589.

1. Now (Sir John) here is the h. of my purpose SHAKS. 2. Phr. *In* (*good, strong*, etc.) *h.*: in prime condition. *Out of h.*: in poor condition, unproducive. *In h.*: in good condition.

VI. *Something of the shape of a heart.* 1. A figure of the human heart; esp. a symmetrical figure formed of two similar curves meeting in a point at one end and a cusp at the other. Also, an ornament in the shape of a heart. 1463. 2. A playing card marked with one or more figures of a heart; one of the suit so marked; *pl.* the suit of such cards 1529. 3. *Naut.* A kind of dead-eye, in shape resembling a heart, with one large hole in the middle 1769. 4. A heart-shaped wheel or cam (Knight) 1875.

1. A costly Iewell..A Hart it was bound in with Diamonds SHAKS.

Phrases.

* *With prep.* **At heart.** Inwardly, secretly; at bottom; in reality. **By heart.** In the memory; from memory; by rote. **From** one's **heart.** With the deepest feeling. **In..heart. a.** *In* (one's) *h.*: inwardly; secretly; at h. **b.** *In h.*: in good spirits. So *to put in* (or *into*) *h.* **c.** In good condition. **Out of heart. a.** In low spirits. **b.** In poor condition. **With..heart. a.** *With* (OE. *mid*) *all one's h.*, *With one's whole h.*: with great sincerity, or devotion; now, with the utmost goodwill. **b.** *With a h. and a half*: willingly. *With half a h.*: half-heartedly.

** *With verb and prep.* **Find** in one's **heart.** To feel willing; to prevail upon oneself (to do something): now chiefly in neg. and interrog. sentences. **Have at heart.** To have as an object in which one is deeply interested. **Lay to heart.** To think seriously about; to be deeply concerned about (a thing). **Take to heart.** To take seriously; to grieve over; †to be solicitous about.

*** *With governing verb.* **Break the heart of. a.** To crush with sorrow. **b.** To 'break the back of'. **Cry** (*plague, tease, weary*, etc.) one's **heart out**: to cry (etc.) violently or exhaustingly: see the vbs. **Eat** one's **heart.** To suffer or pine away from vexation or longing. See EAT *v.* **Have..heart.** *To have the h.*: to be courageous, spirited, or (in mod. use, with negs.) hard-hearted enough (to do something). **Take heart.** To pluck up courage. *To take h. of grace*, etc.: see HEART OF GRACE.

**** *With another noun.* **Heart and hand.** With will and execution; readily. **Heart..heart. a.** *H. of hearts* (orig. *h. of h.*, *heart's h.*): the heart's core; one's inmost h. or feelings. Usu. *in one's h. of hearts.* **b.** *A h. and a h.*, a Hebraism = duplicity. **c.** *H.-to-h.*: used to denote conversation, etc., of great intimacy and/or frankness and sincerity. **Heart and soul. a.** The whole of one's affections and energies. **b.** *advb.* With all one's energy and devotion.

***** *In ejaculations and invocations.* The commonest expressions now are: *Lord* (*God*) *bless my* (*your*, etc.) *h.!* elliptically *Bless my* (etc.) *h.!*

****** *Proverbial phrases*, etc. *One's h. sinks in one's shoes*, etc.: hyperbolical for 'one's h. sinks', connoting extreme fear or dejection. *To have one's h. in one's mouth*, etc., referring to the apparent leaping of the h. under the influence of a sudden start. *One's h. is in its right place*: one's sympathies are rightly placed. *To wear one's h. upon one's sleeve*: to expose one's feelings, etc. to every one. *To do one's h. good*: to make one feel gladdened, strengthened, etc.

Comb.: **h.-cam**, a form of cam used for converting a rotary into a reciprocating motion; **-clot**, a clot of blood or fibrin formed in the h., usually after death; **-cockle**, a bivalve mollusc, *Isocordia cor*, so called from its shape; **-moth**, *Dicycla Oo*; **-motion**, the motion generated by a heart-cam; **-sac**, the pericardium; **-shake**, a split or cleft in the centre of a tree; **-shell** = *heart-cockle*; **-strand**, the central strand of a rope; **-stroke**, (*a*) the impulse of the contraction of the h., apex-beat; (*b*) = Angina pectoris; **-trace**, 'the record on smoked paper made by the needle of a cardiograph' (*Syd. Soc. Lex.*); **-urchin**, a sea-urchin of the genus *Spatangus*, being heart-shaped; a spatangoid; **-wheel** = *heart-cam*.

b. In names of trees and plants: **h.-cherry**, a heart-shaped variety of the cultivated cherry; **-clover**, *Medicago maculata*; **-liver** = prec.; **-pea, -seed**, a name for plants of the genus *Cardiospermum*, from the heart-shaped scar which marks the attachment of the seed.

Heart (hāɹt), *v.* [OE. *hiertan, hyrtan*, f. (ult.) *hert, heort*, HEART *sb.*] 1. *trans.* = HEARTEN 1. *arch.* †2. To supply with physical strength or stimulus; to put (land) into good heart. TUSSER. 3. To take to heart, fix in the heart 1604. 4. *Building.* To fill up the central space within (a piece of masonry) with rubble, etc. Also with *in.* 1776. 5. *intr.* Of a cabbage, lettuce, etc.: To form a heart or close compact head 1866.

1. A grief..Hearted with hope TENNYSON. 3. I hate the Moore. My cause is hearted; thine hath no lesse reason SHAKS.

Heart-ache (hāɹt₁ēᵉk). OE. [f. HEART *sb.* + ACHE.] 1. Pain in the heart; formerly = HEARTBURN 2. 2. Pain or anguish of mind 1602.

Hea·rt-blood, heart's-blood. ME. Blood from the heart; life-blood; hence, vital energy, life. Also *fig.*

Hea·rt-bond. 1823. [See BOND *sb.*[1]] **a.** A union of hearts, betrothal. **b.** *Arch.* 'The construction of walling in which two stones side by side form the width of the wall, and a third stone of an equal breadth is put over the joint in the course above' 1851.

Hea·rt-break, *sb.* 1583. [See BREAK *sb.*[1]] A breaking of the heart; great and overwhelming sorrow or distress of mind. So **Hea·rt-breaking** *ppl. a.* causing intense sorrow or crushing grief. **Hea·rt-breakingly** *adv.*

Hea·rt-broken, *a.* 1586. [f. HEART *sb.* + BROKEN.] Having a broken heart; overwhelmed with grief or anguish. Also *transf.* of feelings, acts, etc. var. **Hea·rt-broke** (*arch.*). **Hea·rt-bro·ken-ly** *adv.*, **-ness.**

Heartburn (hāɹtbɒ̄n), *sb.* ME. [f. HEART *sb.* + BURN *sb.*[3]] †1. Burning of heart; fire of passion. ME. only. 2. = CARDIALGY. 1597. 3. = HEART-BURNING *sb.* 1. 1621.

†**Hea·rt-burn,** *v.* 1540. [f. HEART *sb.* + BURN *v.*; cf. next.] 1. *trans.* To affect with heart-burning. 2. To regard or treat with jealous enmity 1612.

Heart-burning (hāɹtbɒ̄miŋ), *sb.* 1513. [f. HEART *sb.* + BURNING *vbl. sb.*] 1. A heated and embittered state of mind, which is not openly expressed; jealousy or discontent; grudge. **b.** *pl.* Grudges 1605. †2. = HEARTBURN *sb.* 2. Also *attrib.* –1747.

1. A long continued grudge and hearte brennyng betwene the Quenes kinred and the kinges blood MORE.

Hea·rt-burning, *ppl. a.* 1588. [f. HEART *sb.* + BURNING *ppl. a.*] That kindles or consumes the heart; distressing the heart.

Hearted (hā·ɹtéd), *ppl. a.* ME. [f. HEART *sb.* and *v.*; see -ED [1], [2].] 1. Having a heart; *esp.* in comb., as FAINT-HEARTED, etc. †2. Full of heart; spirited –1595. 3. Having the shape of a heart; cordate 1834. 4. Fixed in the heart 1604.

4. *Oth.* III. iii. 448. Hence **-hearted-ly** *adv.*, **-ness** in comb.

Hearten (hā·ɹt'n), *v.* 1526. [Extended f. HEART *v.*; see -EN [5] 2.] 1. *trans.* To put heart into; to embolden; to inspirit, animate, cheer. †2. To give physical strength or stimulus to –1792. 3. *transf.* in weaker sense: To strengthen, help on, further, promote 1615.

1. Where God..heartened his own people..by drying up the waters of Jordan FULLER. 2. Good Ale, which inwardly must h. him 1586. To h. the ground with dung MAY, Punch with Brandy DAMPIER. Hence **Hea·rtener**, one who heartens, encourages, or cheers.

Hea·rt-felt, *a.* 1734. [f. HEART *sb.* + *felt*, pa. pple. of FEEL *v.*] Felt in the heart; hence, sincere, genuine, real.

Hea·rtful (hā·ɹtfŭl), *a.* ME. [f. HEART *sb.* + -FUL.] Full of heart, feeling, or affection; hearty. Hence **Hea·rtfully** *adv.* cordially, heartily; earnestly. **Hea·rtfulness**, h. quality.

Hearth (hāɹþ). [OE. *heorð* str. masc. :— WGer. **herþoz.*] 1. That part of the floor of a room on which the fire is made; the floor of a fireplace. **b.** 'Applied to the ship's fire-place, coppers, and galley generally' (Smyth) 1867. 2. Hence, the home, fireside OE. 3. Techn. **a.** The fireplace of a smith's forge. **b.** The floor in a furnace on which the ore or metal is exposed to the flame. **c.** The hollow at the bottom of a blast-furnace through which the molten metal descends to the crucible. **d.** A portable brazier used in soldering. ME.

1. A pile of blazing logs on the h. 1849. 2. Now this extremity, Hath brought me to thy h. SHAKS. Puissant defenders of the *h. and home* MAYNE REID.

Comb.: **h.-book**, a book containing a list of hearths for the purpose of the HEARTH-TAX; **-cinder**, the slag formed on the refinery-hearth; **-cricket**, the common house-cricket; **-fly**, an artificial fly used in angling; †**-yeld** = HEARTH-PENNY.

Hea·rth-money. *Hist.* 1660. †1. = CHURCH-SCOT. (Coke.) 2. A tax upon hearths or fireplaces; *esp.* a tax of two shillings per annum formerly levied on every fire-hearth in England and Wales; = CHIMNEY-MONEY. 1663.

Hearth-penny. *Hist.* OE. [So called because chargeable on every dwelling-house.] The payment also called Peter's pence and Rome-scot, formerly made to the Pope.

Hea·rth-rug. 1824. A rug laid before the fireplace.

Hea·rth-stead. 1475. [f. STEAD place.] The place of a hearth; fireside; hence = homestead.

Hearthstone (hā·ɹþstōᵘn), *sb.* ME. 1. The flat stone forming the hearth. Hence, the fireside or home. 2. A soft kind of stone used to whiten hearths, door-steps, etc.; a composition used for this purpose 1851.

1. Whate'er of peace about our h. clings BYRON. Hence **Hea·rthstone** *v.* to whiten with h.; also *absol.*

Hea·rth-tax. 1689. = HEARTH-MONEY.

Heartily (hā·ɹtĭli), *adv.* ME. [f. HEARTY *a.* + -LY [2].] 1. In a hearty manner; earnestly, sincerely; with goodwill. 2. Spiritedly, zealously ME. 3. With good appetite; abundantly, amply 1613. 4. Plenteously; to the full, thoroughly; exceedingly, very 1686.

1. Myn lady quod he thanke I hertyly CHAUCER. 2. To fight h. JOWETT. 3. To feed h. DE FOE. 4. They..were..h. beaten DE FOE.

Heartiness (hā·ɹtinės). 1530. [f. as prec. + -NESS.] The quality of being hearty.

The duke with a seeming h. gave his consent BURNET.

Heartless (hā·ɹtlės), *a.* ME. [-LESS.] **1.** *lit.* Without a heart 1586. **2.** Spiritless; out of heart, disheartened, dejected ME.; without warmth or zeal 1658. **3.** Destitute of feeling or affection; callous, unkind, cruel. (The current sense.) 1816. **4.** Of land: Without fertility 1594. **5.** Of food or drink: Without sustaining or stimulating power 1657. **6.** Of plants or trees: **a.** Without core. **b.** Not forming a heart. 1731.

2. In a h. mood Of solitude WORDSW. **3.** H. things Are done and said i' the world SHELLEY. **5.** H. Slops 1674. Bread, black and h. BURNET. Hence **Hea·rtless-ly** *adv.*, **-ness.**

Heartlet (hā·ɹtlėt). 1826. [-LET.] A little heart or core; a nucleus.

Hea·rtlike. 1616. *adj.* Like or having the appearance of a heart. *adv.* Like or after the manner of a heart 1844.

†**Hea·rtling.** [-LING.] Little or dear heart. SHAKS.

Ods heartlings!: a minced oath (= God's heart!).

†**Hea·rtly,** *a.* Also **hertely.** ME. [f. HEART *sb.* + -LY [1].] = HEARTY 3, 4. -1600. So †**Hea·rtly** *adv.* = HEARTILY 1–3.

Heart of grace, *phr.* 1530. [Origin and early form uncertain.] **a.** in phr. *to take h. of gr., h. a gr.*, to pluck up courage. **b.** Hence, *to get, give, keep, gather h. of gr.* 1587. †**c.** Also 16–17th c. *to take heart (hart) at grass, to grass.*

Hea·rt-piercing, *a.* 1590. [See PIERCE *v.*] That pierces, or is fitted to pierce, the heart; *fig.* that appeals keenly to the emotions. Hence **Hea·rt-piercingly** *adv.*

Hea·rt-quake. 1561. [See QUAKE, and cf. *earthquake.*] Palpitation of the heart; *fig.* sudden and violent terror, delight, etc.

Heartquakes shook the joints Of all the Trojans CHAPMAN. So **Hea·rt-qualm,** in same senses.

Hea·rt-rending, *a.* 1687. [See REND *v.*] That rends the heart; terribly distressing. So **Hea·rt-rendingly** *adv.*

Hea·rt-searching, *a.* 1647. [SEARCH *v.*] That rigorously examines the heart or feelings. So **Hea·rt-searching** *sb.*

Heartsease, heart's-ease (hā·ɹts,īz). ME. [See HEART *sb.* and EASE.] **1.** (prop. as two words.) Ease of heart; tranquillity or peace of mind; freedom from care. **2.** The Pansy (*Viola tricolor*). Also formerly the Wallflower. 1530.

Hea·rt-shaped, *a.* 1776. Having the shape of a (conventional) heart; cordate.

Hea·rt-sick, *a.* 1526. [f. HEART *sb.* + SICK *a.*] **1.** Sick at heart; *fig.* depressed or despondent. **2.** Pertaining to or characterized by heart-sickness 1591.

1. Chatham, heart-sick of his country's shame COWPER. Hence **Hea·rt-sickness.**

Heartsome (hā·ɹtsǝm), *a.* Chiefly *Sc.* 1567. [-SOME.] †**1.** Spirited. **2.** That gives heart; animating 1596. **3.** Cheerful, blithe 1724. Hence **Hea·rtsomely** *adv.*

Hea·rt-sore, *sb.* ME. [SORE *sb.*] **1.** Pain or grief of heart; a cause of this. †**2.** A disease of horses, etc. (obs. F. *encœur*) 1616.

Heart-sore, *a.* 1591. [SORE *a.*] Sore at heart; characterized by grief. *Two Gent.* I. i. 30.

Hea·rt-spoon. *Obs.* or *dial.* ME. [See SPOON *sb.*] **a.** The depression at the end of the breast-bone. **b.** The pit of the stomach; the navel or midriff.

Hea·rt-strike, *v. rare.* 1637. [See STRIKE *v.*] *trans.* To strike to the heart, deeply affect the feelings of. So **Hea·rt-stricken** *ppl. a.*, **-ly** *adv.*

Heart-strings (hā·ɹt,striŋz), *sb. pl.* 1483. [f. HEART *sb.* + STRING 'sinew, tendon'.] **1.** In old Anatomy, the tendons or nerves supposed to brace and sustain the heart. Also *transf.* and *fig.* **2.** *esp.* The most intense feelings; the deepest affections; the heart 1596.

2. The falsest woman, That ever broke man's heart-strings FLETCHER. To play upon the heart-strings 1887.

Hea·rt-struck, *ppl. a.* 1605. Struck to the heart: †**a.** Keenly distressing the heart; **b.** Smitten with mental anguish or dismay.

a. His heart-strooke injuries SHAKS.

Hea·rt-whole, *a.* 1470. [See WHOLE.] **1.** Having the spirits or courage unimpaired; undismayed. **2.** Having the affections unengaged 1600. **3.** Whole-hearted; free from hypocrisy or affectation; sincere, genuine 1684; unmitigated 1811.

2. Cupid hath clapt him oth' shoulder, but Ile warrant him heart hole SHAKS. **3.** A heart-whole laugh 1886, traitor LAMB. Hence **Hea·rtwholeness.**

Hea·rt-wise, *adv.* 1727. [-WISE.] After the manner or shape of a heart.

Hea·rt-wood. 1801. A name for the central part of the timber of exogenous trees, hardened and matured by age; duramen.

Ebony..is the heart-wood of the date-tree 1876.

Heartwort (hā·ɹtwɒɹt). ME. [From form of leaves (or ? seeds).] **1.** The plant *Aristolochia Clematitis*, also called Birthwort. †**2.** = HARTWORT, q. v. †**3.** A species of Mint. GERARDE.

Hearty (hā·ɹti), *a.* (*adv.*) and *sb.* ME. [f. HEART *sb.* + -Y [1].] Full of heart. **1.** †Full of courage. In later use: Zealous; energetic or thorough in one's support or action. †**2.** Possessed of understanding. WYCLIF. **3.** Full of kindly sentiment or goodwill; cordial, kind-hearted, genial, cheery 1440. **4.** Heartfelt, genuine, sincere 1479. **5.** Giving unrestrained expression to the feelings; vehement, vigorous 1661. **6.** In sound health, having good appetite and spirits; vigorous, hale 1552. **7.** Of food or drink: Strengthening, invigorating 1617. **8.** Of a meal, etc.: Satisfying; abundant, ample, full 1593. **9.** Of soil, etc.: In good heart, well fitted to bear crops 1573. **10.** Of timber: Consisting of heart-wood; strong, durable 1624.

1. H. for the government SWIFT, in the common cause MACAULAY. **3.** H. Salutations ADDISON. **4.** With herty thankes 1526. **5.** A h. curse SCOTT, slap on the back DICKENS. **8.** A h. and prolonged repast W. IRVING.

B. *adv.* or quasi-*adv.* = HEARTILY. 1753.

C. *sb.* A hearty fellow; a brave, vigorous man; *esp.* in nautical use. Hence, a sailor, a jack-tar 1839.

Heat (hīt), *sb.* [OE. *hǣtu, hǣto* str. fem., also *hǣte* wk. fem.; the former :—OTeut. **haitīn-*, f. **haito-* HOT; *hǣte* corresponds to a type **haitjôn-*.] **1.** The quality of being hot; often regarded as a substance or thing contained in or issuing from bodies; *esp.* In ordinary use, A high or sensible degree of this quality; high temperature; warmth. **b.** The sensation or perception of this quality or condition; one of the primary sensations, produced by contact with or nearness to fire or any body at a high temperature, by any agency that quickens the circulation of the blood, etc. 1704. **c.** With adjs. of colour, used in reference to the appearance of metals, etc. when at certain high temperatures, as BLUE *h.*, etc.; also with other defining words, as BLOOD-HEAT, etc.: see the defining words 1703. **2.** In *Physics*, formerly supposed to be an elastic material fluid (CALORIC), of extreme subtility, attracted and absorbed by all bodies; now held to be a form of ENERGY, viz. the kinetic and potential energy of the invisible molecules of bodies 1626. **3.** *spec.* A hot condition of the atmosphere or physical environment; hot weather or climate: often spoken of as an agent perceptible by its effects OE. **b.** (with *pl.*) A hot period or season ME. **c.** A fire. *Acts* xxviii. 3. **d.** High temperature produced by fermentation or putrefaction, as in a hotbed; hence *concr.* a hotbed, esp. in phr. *in h.* ME. **4.** As a quality or condition of animal bodies (see quots.) OE. †**5.** In mediæval physiology, as a quality of 'elements', 'humours', and bodies in general: see HOT *a.* -1626. **6.** The quality of being hot in taste 1586. **7.** A redness or eruption on the skin, accompanied by a sensation of heat, or indicating inflammation 1597. **8.** A heating; *esp.* a single operation of heating, as of iron in a furnace; hence *concr.* the quantity of metal heated at one operation 1594. †**b.** A run given to a race-horse in preparation for a race -1751. **9.** *fig.* A single bout of action; a stroke, a 'go'. Chiefly in phr. *at a h.* ME. **10.** A single course in a race, etc. (See also DEAD HEAT.) Also *transf.* and *fig.* 1663. **11.** Intensity or warmth of feeling OE. **b.** (with *pl.*) An access of feeling or intensity ME. **c.** (with *pl.*) A fit of passion or anger; †a quarrel 1549. †**d.** Passionateness, excitability -1718. **12.** The intense or violent stage of any action; height, stress (e.g. of conflict, etc.) 1588. **13.** Sexual excitement in animals during the breeding season 1768.

1. c. Several degrees of Heats Smiths take of their Iron..At first, a Blood-red H. Secondly, a White Flame H. Thirdly, a Sparkling, or Welding H. MOXON. **2.** *Radiant heat*: not properly h. at all, but the energy of vibration of the intervening ether when heat is transmitted from one body to another body not in contact; it is identical, within a certain range of wave-length, with light. *Latent h.* (Physics): the h. required to convert a solid into a liquid or vapour, or a liquid into vapour: formerly regarded as being absorbed and remaining latent in the resulting liquid or vapour; now viewed as the energy absorbed during the change of state. *Specific h.* (Physics): the h. required to raise the temperature of a given substance to a given extent (usually one degree). *Atomic, molecular h.* (Chem.): the product of the specific h. of a substance into its atomic or molecular weight. **3.** That knows not parching h. nor freezing cold SHAKS. **b.** The great heates are abated BARET. **4.** *Natural h., vital h.*: the warmth characteristic of a living body. The vital h. Forsakes her limbs DRYDEN. The burning h. of his skin 1782. **6.** The h. of the Ginger SHAKS. **7.** *Prickly h.*: a skin disease (*Lichen tropicus*), characterized by minute papulæ formed by the hyperæmia of the sweat follicles. **9.** Neither can a true just play, which is to bear the test of ages, be produced at a h. DRYDEN. **11.** In suddain h. and passion 1694. **c.** To keep alive heats and animosities WELLINGTON. **12.** To com vpon them, in the heate of their diuision SHAKS.

Comb.: **h.-apoplexy, -asphyxia** = *heat-stroke*; **-engine,** one in which the motive power is produced by h.; **-factor** = ENTROPY; **-spectrum,** the spectrum of heat-rays, visible and invisible; **-stroke,** an affection of the nervous system, often fatal, caused by exposure to excessive h.; **-unit,** a unit quantity of h.; usually reckoned as the amount of h. required to raise the temperature of a unit weight (pound, gramme, etc.) of water one degree.

Heat (hīt), *v.* Pa. t. and pple. **heated,** †**heate** (SHAKS.). [Com. Teut.: OE. *hǣtan* :—OTeut. **haitjan*, f. **hait-oz* HOT.]

I. *trans.* **1.** To communicate heat to; to make hot, to warm; to raise the temperature of. **2.** To cause to feel hot or warm; to bring into a condition of bodily heat, to inflame. Also *absol.* 1601. **3.** *fig.* To rouse to intense emotion; to excite in mind or feeling; to inspire with ardour; to inflame ME.

1. When I am cold, he heates me with beating SHAKS. **2.** Men heated with wine WARBURTON. **3.** He hath..cooled my friends, heated mine enemies SHAKS.

II. *intr.* **1.** To contract heat, become hot or warm, rise in temperature OE. **b.** To grow hot; to become inflamed physically ME. **2.** *fig.* To become inflamed or excited in mind or feeling; to wax warm ME.

1. Green hay heats in a mow, and green corn in a bin WEBSTER s.v. **b.** Let my Liuer rather heate with wine SHAKS. **2.** As I heated, so did she 1880. Hence **Hea·tedly** *adv.* with warmth of temper.

Hea·t-drop. 1615. Usu. in *pl.*: **a.** A few drops of rain ushering in a hot day. Also *fig.*, e.g. of tears. **b.** Drops of sweat.

Heater (hī·tǝɹ). 1500. [f. HEAT *v.* + -ER [1].] **1.** A person or thing that heats. **2.** *spec.* Any of various contrivances for imparting heat; e.g. an iron made hot, and put into a box-iron, smoothing-iron, tea-urn, etc.; a stove for heating a room, etc.; a vessel in which something is placed to be heated 1755. **3.** *attrib.*, as **h. shield,** a shield shaped like a flat-iron heater 1821.

Heath (hīþ), *sb.* [OE. *hǣð* (:—**haiþi-*), from pre-Teut. root **kait-*; cf. L. *bu-cetum* cow-pasture.] **1.** Open uncultivated ground; a bare, more or less flat, tract of land, naturally covered with low herbage and dwarf shrubs, esp. with heath, heather, or ling. †**b.** *transf.* Part of a garden left more or less wild. BACON. **2.** A name of plants and shrubs found upon heaths or in waste places. **a.** The ordinary name for species of *Erica*, esp. *E.* (now *Calluna*) *vulgaris*, common heath, heather, or ling, *E. cinerea*, and *E. tetralix* OE. **b.** With distinctive additions, applied to other species of *Erica*, and allied genera; and pop. to some other plants 1617. **c.** In Coverdale's and later versions of *Jer.* xvii. 6, xlviii. 6, applied to some desert plant, identified variously with Tamarisk, or with Savin, *Juniperus Sabina.*

3. Short for *heath butterfly, moth* 1827. 4. *attrib.* OE.

1. On holte and hethe the merye somers daye LYDG. An uninteresting flat, with many heaths of ling A. YOUNG. 2. a. Now would I giue a thousand furlongs of Sea, for an Acre of barren ground: Long heath [= *Erica vulgaris*], Brown Firrs, anything SHAKS.

Comb.: **h.-ale, -beer,** a traditional beverage anciently brewed from the flowers of heather; **-cropper,** *lit.* one that crops or feeds on h.; a sheep or pony living on open h.; hence, a person who inhabits a h.; **-fowl** = HEATH-BIRD; **-game,** grouse or moor-fowl; **-tax,** a tax to defray the expenses of repairing the course at Newmarket; **-throstle, -thrush,** the Ring-blackbird or Ring-ouzel, *Turdus torquatus*.

b. In names of trees and plants: applied to any species which grow on heaths, as *h. bedstraw*, etc.; **h.-fern,** the Sweet Mountain Fern, *Lastrea Oreopteris*; **-grass,** *Triodia decumbens*; **†-rose,** the rose of Jericho, *Anastatica Hierochuntina*.

Hea·th-bell. 1804. 1. The bell-shaped flower of the Heath; cf. HEATHER-BELL. 1808. 2. Any bell-shaped flower growing on heaths, esp. the Blue-bell.

Hea·th-berry. OE. A name of various berries growing on heaths, esp. the Bilberry and Crowberry.

Hea·th-bird. 1683. A bird which lives on heaths; *spec.* the Black Grouse, of which the male is the HEATH-COCK and the female the HEATH-HEN.

Hea·th-cock. 1590. The male of the HEATH-BIRD or Black Grouse (*Tetrao tetrix*), the Blackcock; in N. America, the Canada grouse.

Heathen (hī·ðĕn, -ð'n). [OE. *hǣðen*; cf. Goth. *haiþnô* Gentile or heathen woman. Orig. 'dweller on the heath', a loose rendering of L. *paganus*.]

A. *adj.* 1. Applied to persons or races whose religion is neither Christian, Jewish, nor Mohammedan; pagan; Gentile. In earlier times applied also to Mohammedans; now mostly restricted to those holding polytheistic beliefs. 2. Pertaining to such persons or races, or to their religion and customs OE. Also *transf.*

1. The h. priests SWIFT, Soldan SCOTT. 2. In al places crysten and hethen CAXTON. *transf.* Bishops of Durham and naked h. colliers EMERSON.

B. *sb.* (or *adj.* used *subst.*) 1. One who holds a religious belief which is neither Christian, Jewish, nor Mohammedan; a pagan OE. (The adj. pl., *the heathen*, is now collective; in O.T. = the Gentiles; the sb. pl. *heathens* is mostly individual.) 2. *transf.* One who is no better than a heathen 1818.

1. I was sorry to find more mercy in an h. than in a brother Christian SWIFT. 2. Puir frightened heathens that they are SCOTT.

Heathendom (hī·ðĕndəm). [OE. *hǣðendōm*; f. HEATHEN + -DOM. In mod. use app. formed anew after *Christendom*.] 1. = HEATHENISM. 2. The domain or realm of the heathen; the heathen world 1860.

Heathenesse (hī·ðĕnes). *arch.* [OE. *hǣðennes, -nys*; see HEATHEN and -NESS.] 1. Heathenism. 2. = HEATHENDOM 2. ME.

Heathenish (hī·ðĕniʃ), *a.* [OE. *hǣðenisc*. In mod. use prob. a new formation; see -ISH.] 1. Of or pertaining to the heathen (now *rare*). †2. = HEATHEN *a.* 1. -1718. 3. *transf.* and *fig.* a. Heathen-like; unworthy of a Christian. b. *colloq.* Abominable, 'beastly' 1593.

1. The h. temples BRYANT. 2. The h. philosopher Plutarch 1652. 3. Most H., and most grosse SHAKS. Hence **Hea·thenish-ly** *adv.*, **-ness.**

Heathenism (hī·ðĕniz'm). 1605. [-ISM.] 1. Heathen practice or belief; paganism. Also with *a* and *pl.* 2. *transf.* Unchristian state of things; unchristian degradation or barbarism 1742.

2. The practical h. of our great cities (*mod.*).

Hea·thenize, *v.* 1681. [-IZE.] 1. *trans.* To render heathen or heathenish. 2. *intr.* To become heathen or heathenish 1769.

Hea·thenly, *adv.* ME. [-LY [2].] After the manner of the heathen; barbarously.

Heathenness, var. HEATHENESSE.

Heathenry (hī·ðĕnri). 1577. [-RY.] 1. Heathen belief, practice, custom, character, or quality; heathenism. 2. Heathen people. R. F. BURTON.

1. In conuerting the Iland from heathenrie to christianitie 1577.

Heather (he·ðəɹ). ME. [Commonly referred to *heath*; but the earlier form *hadder* is against this.] 1. The Scotch name, now in general use, for the native species of *Erica*, called in the north of England LING; esp. *E.* (now *Calluna*) *vulgaris*, Common H., and *E. cinerea*, Fine-leaved Heath or Lesser Bell-h. Also *transf.* 2. *attrib.* Of, pertaining to, consisting of, or made from heather, as *h.-ale*, etc.; of the colour or appearance of heather, as *h.-mixture*, etc. 1819.

1. In the Northerne..places of this Island..They dry their malt with ling, or heath, called there h. 1633. Phr. *To set the h. on fire*: to make a disturbance. *To take to the h.*: to become an outlaw.

Comb.: **h.-cat,** a cat living wild among the h.; hence *fig.* of a person; **-grass** = *heath-grass*, *Triodia decumbens*; **-owl,** the Short-eared Owl, *Asio accipitrinus*.

Heather-bell. 1725. A name of: a. *Erica tetralix* (or its blossom); b. *E. cinerea*.

Hea·ther-blea·t(er. *Sc.* [Perversion of OE. *hæferblǣte*.] A snipe.

Heathery (he·ðəri), *a.* 1535. [f. HEATHER + -Y.] Covered with or abounding in heather; of the nature of heather.

Hea·th-hen. 1591. The female of the HEATH-COCK; applied in N. America to species of grouse.

Heath-pea (hī·þpī). Also **†-pease.** 1633. A tuberous-rooted leguminous plant, *Lathyrus macrorrhizus* (*Orobus tuberosus*), also called *Carmele*.

Heathy (hī·þi), *a.* 1450. [f. HEATH + -Y.] Abounding in or covered with heath; of the nature of heath; heathery.

Heating (hī·tiŋ), *vbl. sb.* ME. [f. HEAT *v.* + -ING [1].] The action of HEAT *v.*; imparting of heat or warmth; becoming hot; *techn.* 'getting the steel hot for rolling'.

Hea·ting, *ppl. a.* 1591. [-ING [2].] That heats or makes hot; making the blood too 'hot', as *h. diet*.

Heating surface, the total surface of a steam boiler, exposed on one side to the fire, on the other to water; the fire-surface. Hence **Hea·tingly** *adv.*

Hea·tless, *a. rare.* 1596. [-LESS.] Destitute of heat.

Heat-spot. 1822. a. A freckle. b. *Physiol.* A spot or point of the skin at which heat can be produced.

Heat-wave. 1878. a. A wave of radiant heat; one of those vibrations of ether that produce heating effects. b. A wave or access of excessive heat in the atmosphere, esp. when regarded as passing from one place to another.

Heaume (hōᵘm). *Obs.* or *arch.* 1572. [a. F. :—OF. *helme*; see HELM *sb.*[1]] A massive helmet, reaching down to the shoulders.

Heauto- (hiǫto), bef. vowel **heaut-,** comb. f. Gr. ἑαυτοῦ of oneself, used occas. for AUTO-: as **Heau·tomo·rphism** [Gr. μορφή], ascription of one's own characteristics to another.

Heave (hīv), *v.* Pa. t. and pple. **heaved** (hīvd), **hove** (hōᵘv). [Com. Teut. str. vb.: OE. *hębban, hōf, hafen* :—OTeut. *hafjan, hôf, haƀano-, corresp. to L. *capere, capio*, to take. The orig. sense was 'take', whence, through 'take up', came that of 'lift, raise'.]

I. *trans.* 1. To lift, raise, bear up. (Often with *up*.) In mod. use: To raise with effort or force; to hoist 1715. Also *absol.* 2. *transf.* and *fig.* To raise OE.; †to exalt; to extol -1641. †3. *spec.* To lift (a child) from the font; to stand sponsor to; hence *transf.* to baptize, christen -1571. †4. To lift and take away, carry off, remove -1649. †b. *Thieves' Cant.* To 'lift', to rob -1700. c. *Mining* and *Geol.* To move away or displace (a vein or stratum): said of another intersecting it 1728. 5. To cause to swell up or bulge out 1573. 6. To cause to rise in repeated efforts 1612. 7. To utter (a groan, sigh, sob; *rarely*, words) with effort; to fetch 1600. 8. To throw, cast, fling, toss, hurl (esp. with effort). Now only *Naut.* and *colloq.* 1592. 9. *Naut.* To haul up or raise by means of a rope; to haul, pull, draw with a rope or cable; to haul a cable; to weigh (anchor); to unfurl (a flag or sail; also, *to h. out*); to cause (a ship) to move in some direction, as by hauling at a rope. Also *absol.* 1626.

1. How could I once look up, or h. the head MILT. To h. a boat into a sloop SMEATON. 2. For the prevention of growing schisme the Bishop was heav'd above the Presbyter MILT. 6. The water was observed ..to be heaved up and agitated DE LA BECHE. 7. The wretched annimall heau'd forth such groanes SHAKS. 8. The Pirats had heaued me ouer boord GREENE. 9. We heau'd home our Anker 1633. *Heaving astern*, causing a ship to go backwards, by heaving on a cable fastened to some fixed point behind her.

II. *intr.* 1. To rise, mount, come up, spring up. *Obs.* exc. in spec. uses. ME. 2. To swell up, bulge out 1629. 3. To rise with alternate falling, as waves, etc. Also *fig.* 1618. 4. To draw in the breath with effort; to pant, gasp 1678. 5. To make an effort to vomit; to retch; also *fig.* 1601. †6. To make an effort to lift or move something; to push or press with force; to endeavour, labour, strive -1742. 7. To pull or haul (*at* a rope, etc.); to push (*at* the capstan so as to haul in the cable); to move the ship in some direction by such means; of the ship, to move or turn in some direction 1626.

1. Phr. *H. and set*: to rise and fall, as a floating object upon the waves. 2. Their Petticoats, which began to h. and swell before you left us ADDISON. 3. When heaved the long and sullen sea 1827. 4. He heaves for Breath DRYDEN. 5. (*trans.*) To heaue the gorge SHAKS. 6. Phr. †*H. at*: to aim at, strive after. †*H. at* (*fig.*): to meditate or threaten an attack upon; to oppose; to aim at with hostile intent. His adversaries heaved at him, to cast him out of his Bishoprick FULLER. 7. Phr. *Heaving ahead*, is the act of advancing or drawing a ship forward by heaving on a cable or rope made fast to some fixed point before her SMYTH.

Phrases. *To h. a-peak*: to bring (a ship) into the position in which the cable hangs perpendicularly between the hawse and the anchor; see A-PEAK. *To h.* (the ship) *in stays*: to bring her head to the wind in tacking; also *intr.* of the ship. *To h. short*: to h. in on the cable until the vessel is nearly over her anchor. *To h. taut*: to h. at the capstan until the cable is taut. *H. down*: to turn (a ship) over on one side by means of purchases attached to the masts; to careen. (Also *intr.* of the ship.) *H. to*: to bring the ship to a standstill by setting the sails so as to counteract each other; to make her lie to. *H. in sight*: to rise into view, become visible; hence (*colloq.*) *transf.* in general sense.

Heave (hīv), *sb.* 1571. [f. prec. vb.] 1. An act of heaving, in various senses (see quots.). 2. *Mining* and *Geol.* A horizontal displacement or dislocation of a vein or stratum, at a fault 1801. 3. *pl.* A disease of horses, broken wind 1828.

1. When his heaves renew..his heart panteth JEWEL. Divers heaves were made at the Duke of Lauderdale NORTH. *Heave*..3. Effort to vomit JOHNSON. The h. of the sea 1834. A h. of surprise STEVENSON.

Heave ho, *interj.* and *sb.* ME. [app. HEAVE (imper.), with HO *int.*] A cry of sailors in heaving the anchor up, etc.; also, the burden of a song. Also as *vb.* (with *vbl. sb.*)

Heaven (he·v'n), *sb.* [OE. *heƀen, hefen, -on, heofon, -un*, str. masc.; in late OE. also *heofone* wk. fem. Ult. etym. unkn.; not conn. w. *hafjan to HEAVE, the *e* being radical.] 1. The expanse in which the sun, moon, and stars are seen, which resembles a vast vault or canopy overarching the earth, on the 'face' or surface of which the clouds seem to float. Since 17th c. chiefly *poet.* in the sing. b. The pl. *heavens* was formerly used, esp. in O.T., in the same sense as the sing.; it is now the prose form for the visible sky. Hence *maps of the heavens*, etc. OE. 2. = Climate 1581. 3. The 'realm' or region of space beyond the clouds, of which the visible sky is poetically viewed as the 'floor' OE. †Also *transf.* b. In *pl.*: occas. = the regions of space in which the heavenly bodies move 1678. 4. Each of the 'spheres' or spherical shells, lying above or outside of each other, into which the realms of space outside the earth were formerly divided. Their number varied from seven to eleven. ME. 5. The celestial abode of immortal beings; the habitation of God and his angels, and of beatified spirits; the state of the blessed hereafter. Opp. to *hell*. OE. Also in *pl.* b. By the Jews seven heavens were recognized; the highest, the 'heaven of heavens', being the abode of God and the most exalted angels. Thence also the seven heavens of Mohammed. OE. c. The seat of the celestial deities of heathen mythology ME. 6. The power or majesty of heaven; Providence, God. (With capital H.) OE. Also in *pl.* The gods; God 1579. b. In asseverations and exclams. ME. 7. *fig.* a. A place of supreme bliss ME. **b.** A state of bliss ME. **8.** *transf.* [from 1]. The covering over an Elizabethan stage. [F. *ciel*, Ger. *himmel.*] 1611. **9. a.** simple attrib.: 'of heaven', etc. OE.; *h.-bliss* ME.–1583. **b.** objective, as *h.-kissing* SHAKS. **c.** advb. 'to or towards heaven', etc. 1591.

1. All that is vnder the heauen COVERDALE *Eccl.* iii. 1. Heaven's high canopy, that covers all DRYDEN. Trees, as high as h. TENNYSON. **b.** The heauens shal geue their dew COVERDALE *Zech.* viii. 12. **2.** Flowers of all heavens..Grew side by side TENNYSON. **3.** Looke how the floore of heauen Is thicke inlayed with pattens of bright gold SHAKS. **b.** Far above the starry heavens CUDWORTH. **4.** Deepening thro' the silent spheres H. over H. rose the night TENNYSON. *fig. Hen. V*, Prol. 2. **5.** H. lies about us in our infancy WORDSW. *pl.* Wee haue a great high Priest, that is passed into the heauens *Heb.* iv. 14. **b.** The heauen and heauen of heauens cannot conteine Thee 1 *Kings* viii. 27. **6.** The will And high permission of all-ruling H. MILT. **b.** By heav'n the story 's true ADDISON. Gracious H.! who are you 1801. Heavens..what an idea MRS. MARCET. **7.** I follow thee, and make a heauen of hell SHAKS. **b.** O what a h. is loue! O what a hell MIDDLETON & DEKKER. In the *seventh h.* (cf. 4) of delight SCOTT. **9. a.** Ere the Tower Obstruct Heav'n Towrs MILT. **b.** This h.-aspiring tower HAWTHORNE.

Hea·ven, *v.* 1627. [f. prec. sb.] *trans.* To make heavenly in character; also, to bless with heaven, beatify.

Hea·ven-born, *a.* 1595. **1.** Of celestial birth. **2.** Specially prepared or designed by Heaven for the work. Now often *sarcastic.* 1789.

1. The Heaven-born child MILT. **2.** A heaven-born teacher SCOTT; heaven-born amateur 1858.

Heaven-gate. ME. The gate or portal of heaven.

Heaven-high, *a.* and *adv.* OE. As high as heaven.

†Hea·venish, *a.* ME. [-ISH.] Of or pertaining to heaven –1577. Hence **†Hea·venishly** *adv.* CHAUCER.

Hea·venize, *v.* To render heavenly. BP. HALL.

Hea·venlike. 1548. [-LIKE.] **1.** *adj.* Heavenly. **2.** *adv.* After the manner of heaven. SWINBURNE.

Heavenly (he·v'nli), *a.* (*sb.*) [OE. *heofonlic*; see -LY[1].] **1.** Of, in, or belonging to heaven; celestial. **2.** Of or belonging to the natural heaven or sky; as *h. bodies*, i.e. the stars, planets, comets, etc. Formerly also, Coming from the clouds or atmosphere; as *h. dew.* ME. **3.** Having relation to heaven and divine things; divine ME. **4.** Of more than earthly excellence; 'divine' 1425. **5.** *absol.* in pl. *The heavenlies*: tr. Gr. (ἐν) τοῖς ἐπουρανίοις (Eph. i. 3, iii. 10), variously translated '(in) heavenly places' or 'things' 1844.

1. A showr of heauenly bread BIBLE *Transl. Pref.* **3.** A breaking..Of heauenly oaths SHAKS. **4.** The h. Rosaline SHAKS. A H. Voice STEELE, day 1779. Hence **Hea·venliness,** h. state or quality.

Hea·venly, *adv.* [OE. *heofonlice*; see -LY[2].] **1.** From or by heaven; in a heavenly manner or degree. **2.** To the extent of heaven, as in *h. wide* 1674.

1. Oh she was heauenly true *Oth.* v. ii. 135. Our h.-guided soul MILT.

Hea·venly-mi·nded, *a.* 1656. Having the thoughts and affections set on things above; holy, devout. Hence **Hea·venly-mi·ndedness.**

Hea·ven-sent, *a.* 1649. Sent from heaven.

Heavenward (he·v'nwǭɹd). ME. [f. HEAVEN *sb.* + -WARD.]

A. *adv.* Towards, or in the direction of, heaven. Orig. *to heaven-ward.*

B. *adj.* Directed towards heaven 1795.

So **Hea·venwards** *adv.*

Hea·ve-o·ffering. 1530. In the Levitical law: An offering which was heaved or elevated by the priest when offered; also used of other offerings. *Exod.* xxix. 27.

Heaver (hī·vəɹ). 1586. [f. HEAVE *v.* + -ER[1].] **1.** A person who heaves; *spec.* a dock-labourer employed in landing goods. **2.** Something that heaves; *spec.* (*Naut.*) a bar used as a lever or purchase 1598.

Heaves, a disease of horses; see HEAVE *sb.* 3.

Heave shoulder. 1530. In the Levitical law: The shoulder of an animal heaved or elevated in sacrifice. Also *transf.* and *fig.*

Hea·vier-than-ai·r, designating a flying machine whose weight is greater than the weight of the air which it displaces 1888.

Heavily (he·vili), *adv.* [OE. *hefiglice* adv., from *hefig* HEAVY; see -LY[2].] **1.** In a heavy manner; with or as with weight (*lit.* and *fig.*); ponderously; burdensomely ME. **2.** With heavy movement; laboriously, sluggishly OE. **3.** With sorrow, grief, or displeasure. *Obs.* or *arch.* OE. **4.** Forcibly, violently; intensely; severely OE. **5.** To a large or heavy amount 1819.

1. A Gentleman leaning upon me, and very h. STEELE. Time hangs h. on her hands (*mod.*). **2.** And broke off their charet wheeles, that they draue them heauily *Exod.* xiv. 25. **3.** Berkley..took this refusal very h. CLARENDON. **4.** Thou shalt be heauily punished SHAKS. **5.** H. wooded 1864.

Heaviness (he·vinės). [OE. *hefignes*; see -NESS.] The state or quality of being heavy; ponderousness; gravity; weight of impact ME.; burdensomeness OE.; †anger –1590; torpor; dullness; want of animation OE.; dejectedness of mind; †grief ME.

Heaving (hī·viŋ), *vbl. sb.* ME. [f. HEAVE *v.* + -ING[1].] The action of HEAVE *v.*, in various senses.

Comb.: **h.-line** (*Naut.*), a line, usually from 5 to 10 fathoms long, used for casting from a vessel to enable a hawser to be hauled ashore or to another vessel; **-net,** a net that is heaved or hauled up.

Hea·visome, *a.* *Obs.* or *dial.* ME. [f. HEAVY *a.* + -SOME.] Of heavy mood, doleful; dull.

Heavy (he·vi), *a.*[1] (*sb.*) [OE. *hęfig*:– OTeut. *haƀigo-, *haƀugo-, f. *hafi-z, OE. *hęfe* weight, f. *hafjan to HEAVE.]

I. 1. Of great weight; ponderous. **b.** Hence, in large quantity or amount, abundant 1728. **c.** *techn.* Possessing (non-negligible) weight 1871. **2.** Of great weight in proportion to bulk OE. **3.** Great with young. Also *fig.* 1622. **4.** Laden *with* (something) 1622. **5.** Applied to classes of goods, animals, etc. of more than a defined or usual weight 1617. Hence **b.** *transf.* Connected or concerned with the manufacture, carriage, etc. of such articles 1888. **6.** *Mil.* Carrying heavy arms or equipments: said chiefly of soldiers 1836.

1. [A coate] too heavie and hote for summer 1592. Phr. *To lie, sit h. upon,* or *at* (chiefly *fig.*). **b.** H. harvests POPE. **2.** Platinum, the heaviest metal LOCKYER. The pasty is h. 1887. **4.** His men h. and laden with booty BACON. **5.** H. artillery 1727. Phr. *H. metal*: guns or shot of large size; hence *fig.* ability; power; also, a person or persons of great ability or power. **b.** A curate in the H. Woollen District of Yorkshire 1888. **6.** Phr. *H. order* or *h. marching order*, that of a soldier equipped and carrying, besides his arms and ammunition, complete kit and great-coat.

II. 1. Having great momentum; that falls or strikes with force ME. **2.** Of ground, a road, etc.: That clings or hangs heavily to the spade, feet, wheels, etc. Also *transf.* 1577. **3.** That weighs upon the stomach; difficult of digestion 1574.

1. A h. sea SOUTHEY.. **2.** The h. state of the roads 1837. *transf.* H. walking THOREAU. **3.** Bacon is a coarse and h. food 1842.

III. 1. Of great import; weighty; grave. Now *rare* or *Obs.* OE. **2.** Grave, severe, profound, intense OE,

1. Trust him not in matter of heauie consequence SHAKS. **2.** H. complaints 1801, frost DICKENS.

IV. 1. Of the sky, clouds, etc.: Dark with clouds; lowering, gloomy 1583. **2.** Thick, coarse; also, massive; wanting in lightness or delicacy 1818. **3.** Having a sound like that made by a heavy object; loud and deep 1810.

2. H. features SCOTT, renaissance porch 1886, handwriting (*mod.*). **3.** A deep and h. bell SHELLEY.

V. 1. Ponderous and slow mentally ME. **2.** Acting or moving slowly, clumsily, or with difficulty; sluggish; unwieldy ME. **3.** Of things: Wanting in vivacity; tedious, uninteresting 1601. **4.** *Theatr.* Serious; relating to the representation of sombre or tragic parts 1826.

1. The heaviest man in the country PEPYS. **2.** His heels too h., and his head too light DRYDEN. Sleepless nights and h. days BYRON. If Time be h. on your hands TENNYSON. **3.** So h. a book SWIFT. **4.** As the h. villain at the Surrey Theatre would say HELPS.

VI. †1. Of persons: Oppressive; annoying; angry; violent –1703. **2.** Hard to bear; grievous, sore; distressful OE. **3.** Hard to perform; laborious, toilsome ME. **4.** Causing or occasioning sorrow ME. **5.** Oppressive to the bodily sense ME.

1. †*H. friend*: a troublesome or evil friend; an enemy. So *h. father.* **2.** Ile..endure Your heauiest Censure SHAKS. A h. calamity 1844. **4.** A heavie Christmasse GRAFTON. H. news CARLYLE. †*H. hill*: the ascent to Tyburn; the way to the gallows.

VII. 1. Weighed down with sorrow or grief; sorrowful ME. **2.** Weighed down by sleep, weariness, etc.; hence *esp.* weary from sleep, drowsy ME.

2. With eyelids h. and red HOOD.

VIII. That does what is expressed heavily, as in *a h. drinker* 1816.

Comb.: **h. drift-ice, h. ice,** that which has a great depth in proportion, and not in a state of decay; **-earth** = BARYTA; **h. pine,** the *Pinus ponderosa*; **h. swell** (*colloq.*), a man of showy and impressive appearance (with pun on sense II. 1).

B. *sb.* [the adj. used absol.] **1.** *pl.* *Heavies*: heavy cavalry; the Dragoon Guards. Rarely in *sing.* 1841. Also, heavy artillery. **2.** A stage wagon for the conveyance of goods. DE QUINCEY. **3.** = HEAVY WET.

Heavy (hī·vi), *a.*[2] 1864. [-Y[1].] Suffering from the heaves.

Heavy (he·vi), *adv.* [OE. *hefige*, f. *hefig* HEAVY *a.*] = HEAVILY. Now chiefly hyphened to pples. which it qualifies.

†Heavy, *v.* [OE. *hefigian*:—OTeut. *hebigôjan.] To make or become heavy, in various senses –1581.

Heavy-armed (he·vi,ɑɹmd), *a.* 1836. Bearing heavy armour or arms.

Hea·vy-ha·nded, *a.* 1633. **1. a.** Having the hands heavy from weariness. **b.** Clumsy 1647. **2.** Full-handed 1864. **3.** Overbearing 1883.

Hea·vy-hea·ded, *a.* 1552. **1.** Having a heavy or large head 1684. **2.** Dull, stupid 1590. **3.** Drowsy 1552.

3. This heavy-headed revel..Makes us traduced SHAKS.

Hea·vy-hea·rted, *a.* ME. **1.** Having a heavy heart; sad. **2.** Caused by a heavy heart; doleful 1562.

Hea·vy-la·den, *a.* 1440. **1.** Loaded heavily. Also *fig.* **2.** Oppressed; weighed down with trouble, etc. 1611.

2. Come vnto mee all ye that labour, and are heauie laden *Matt.* xi. 23. Also **h.-loaden** *Isa.* xlvi. 1.

Heavy spar. 1789. [tr. Ger. *Schwerspat.*] The native sulphate of barium, barytes; also improp. applied to barium carbonate, etc.

Heavy-weight. 1857. A person or animal of more than the average weight; *spec.* a jockey, etc., of more than the average weight; a boxer over 12 st. 7; *transf.* a horse that carries more than the average weight. Also *fig.*

Heavy wet. *slang.* 1821. [WET *sb.*] Malt liquor.

Hebdomad, -ade (he·bdŏmæd, -ēɪd). 1545. [ad. L. *hebdomas, hebdomad-*, a. Gr. ἑβδομάς (-αδ-).] **†1.** The number seven; a group of seven –1837. **2.** The space of seven days, a week 1600. **3.** In some Gnostic systems, a group of seven superhuman beings; also a title of the Demiurge 1837.

Hebdomadal (hebdǫ·mădăl), *a.* (*sb.*) 1613. [ad. L. *hebdomadalis*; see prec. and -AL.] **†1.** Consisting of or lasting seven days –1651; changing every week 1796. **2.** Meeting, taking place, or appearing once a week; weekly 1711.

1. H. politicians, who run away from their opinions without giving us a month's warning BURKE. **2.** *H. Council*: the representative board of the University of Oxford, which meets weekly. Hence **Hebdo·madally** *adv.*

B. *sb.* (*ellipt.*) A 'weekly' (*joc.*) 1835.

Hebdomadary (hebdǫ·mădări). ME. (*Sc.* -dar 1549.) [ad. eccl. L. *hebdomadarius*, f. *hebdomas* HEBDOMAD.]

A. *sb.* *R.C. Ch.* A member of a chapter or convent, who takes his (or her) weekly turn in the performance of the sacred offices of the Church. var. **He·bdomary, -arian.**

B. *adj.* Weekly; doing duty for a week 1625. var. **†Hebdoma·tical** *a. rare.*

‖Hebe (hī·bi). 1606. [a. Gr. ἥβη youthful prime; the daughter of Zeus and Hera.] **1.**

The goddess of youth and spring, the cup-bearer of Olympus; hence *fig.* **a.** A waitress; **b.** A woman in her early youth. **2.** *Astron.* The sixth of the asteroids 1858. **3.** *attrib.*, as *Hebe bloom*, etc. 1838.

Hebe- (hī·bi-), comb. f. Gr. ἥβη youth, also puberty, down of puberty, taken in senses **a.** Pubescence (in botanical terms), as in **Hebea·nthous** [Gr. ἄνθος] *a.*, having the corolla of the flower pubescent; etc. **b.** Puberty, as in **Hebephre·nia** [Gr. φρήν], a form of insanity incident to puberty.

Heben, Hebeny, -yf, obs. ff. EBON, EBONY.

†**He·benon, Hebon, Hebona.** 1592. In Shakspere and Marlowe: Some substance having a poisonous juice. Variously identified with *ebon, henbane*, and Ger. *eibe, eibenbaum* the yew.

Hebetate (he·bĭte'it), *v.* 1574. [f. L. *hebetat-, hebetare*, f. *hebes, hebet-* blunt, dull. Cf. F. *hébéter*.] To make, or become, dull or inert. So **He·betant** *a.* making dull. LAMB. Hence **Hebeta·tion.**

He·betate, *a.* [ad. L. *hebetatus*; see prec.] *Bot.* Having a dull or blunt and soft point.

Hebete (he·bīt), *a. rare.* 1743. [ad. L. *hebes, hebet-*.] Dull, stupid, obtuse.

Hebetude (he·bĭtiud). 1621. [ad. L. *hebetudo.*] The condition or state of being blunt or dull.

Hebræan (hĭbrī·ăn). 1509. [f. L. *Hebræus*; see HEBREW and -AN.] †**1.** A Jew. BARCLAY. †**2.** A Hebrew scholar –1801. **3.** One of a school in Holland, whose system rested upon the interpretation of certain hidden truths in the Hebrew language. SCHAFF.

Hebraic (hĭbrē·ik), *a.* ME. [ad. late L. *Hebraicus*, a. Gr., f. a stem Ἑβρα-; see HEBREW.] Pertaining or relating to the Hebrews or to their language; Hebrew. So **Hebra·ical** *a. rare.* Hence **Hebra·ically** *adv.* in Hebrew fashion; after the manner of the Hebrews or the Hebrew language (e.g. as written from left to right or 'backwards').

Hebraism (hī·bre,iz'm). 1570. [a. F. *hébraïsme*, or ad. mod.L. *Hebraismus*; see HEBREW and -ISM.] **1.** A Hebrew idiom or expression. **2.** A quality or attribute of the Hebrew people; Hebrew character or nature; Judaism 1847. **b.** Applied by M. Arnold to the moral, as opp. to the intellectual, theory of life; cf. *Hellenism* 1869.

2. b. Self-conquest, self-devotion..*obedience*, is the fundamental idea of..the discipline to which we have attached the general name of H. M. ARNOLD.

Hebraist (hī·bre,ist). 1753. [f. stem *Hebra-* in HEBRAIC; see -IST.] **1.** A Hebrew scholar. **2.** One who has the qualities of the Hebrew people 1879. **3.** A Jew of Palestine, who used the Hebrew Scriptures, as opp. to a Hellenistic Jew 1892. Hence **Hebrai·stic, -al** *a.* of or pertaining to Hebraists; marked by Hebraism; Hebraic. **Hebrai·stically** *adv.* var. †**Hebrai·cian** (in sense 1).

Hebraize (hī·bre,əiz), *v.* 1645. [ad. Gr. Ἑβραΐζειν to imitate Jews, f. stem Ἑβρα-; see HEBREW.] **1.** *intr.* To use a Hebrew idiom or manner of speech. **b.** To follow Hebraism as an ideal. M. ARNOLD. **2.** *trans.* To make Hebrew 1816.

Hebrew (hī·bru). [ME. *Ebreu*, a. OF. *Ebreu, Ebrieu* (nom. *Ebreus*), ad. med.L. *Ebreus* for cl.L. *Hebræus*, a. Gr. Ἑβραῖος, f. Aramaic. The ultimate meaning is 'one from the other side (of the river)'. Cf. the LXX, Gen. xiv. 13, Ἀβρὰμ ὁ περάτης, 'Abram the passer-over' or 'immigrant'. Initial *H* after cl.L.]

A. *sb.* **1.** A person belonging to the Semitic tribe or nation descended from Abraham, Isaac, and Jacob; an Israelite, a Jew. (In mod. use the term avoids the associations often attaching to *Jew*.) **2.** The Semitic language spoken by the Hebrews, and in which most of the books of the O.T. were written ME. **b.** *colloq.* Unintelligible speech; cf. *Greek* 1705

1. Thou knowst I am an Ebrew MILT.

B. *adj.* Belonging to the Hebrews; Israelitish, Jewish. Of H. extraction 1851. A *Hebrew scholar*, one learned in H. (In the N.T. = Aramaic or Syriac.)

Hence **He·brew-wise** *adv.* in H. fashion; in the manner of H. writing, from left to right, backwards. **He·brewess,** a Jewess. **He·brewism** = HEBRAISM.

Hebrician (hĭbri·ʃăn). Now *rare* or *Obs.* 1542. [var. of *Hebraician.*] †**1.** A Hebrew –1570. **2.** A Hebrew scholar 1565.

Hebridean (hebridī·ăn, -i·dĭăn), *a.* and *sb.* 1600. Also **-ian.** Belonging to, a native of, the Hebrides, islands off the west coast of Scotland.

An oarsong used by the Hebrideans JOHNSON.

‖**Hecate** (he·kătī). ME. [a. Gr. Ἑκάτη, fem. of ἕκατος far-darting, an epithet of Apollo. (Always disyllabic, like Fr. Hécate, in Shaks., exc. once.)] **1.** *Gr. myth.* A goddess, said to be of Thracian origin, daughter of Perses and Asteria; in later times identified esp. with Artemis, and thus (**b.**) with the moon; also with Persephone, and hence (**c.**) regarded as presiding over witchcraft, etc. **d.** *transf.* Hag, witch 1591. **2.** *Astr.* Name of the 100th asteroid, discovered in 1868.

1. c. Stay thy cloudy ebon chair, Wherein thou ridest with Hecat', and befriend Us thy vowed priests MILT. d. 1 *Hen. VI*, III. ii. 64. Hence **Hecatæ·an** *a.*

Hecatomb (he·kătǫm, -tūm), *sb.* 1592. [ad. L. *hecatombe*, a. Gr., ἑκατόν + βοῦς. The first pronunc. is now usual.] **1.** A great public sacrifice (prop. of a hundred oxen); a large number of animals offered or set apart for sacrifice. **2.** *transf.* and *fig.* A sacrifice of many victims; *loosely*, a large number or quantity 1598.

2. Whole Hecatombes of Tribute Rhimes G. DANIEL. A h. of reputations 1713. Hence **He·catomb** *v.* to furnish with a h.

Hecatomped (hekăt[?]·mpĕd), *a.* 1703. [ad. Gr. ἑκατόμπεδος, f. ἑκατόν + πεδ- ablaut-grade of πούς, ποδ-.] Measuring a hundred feet in length and breadth; a hundred feet square. So **Hecato·mpedon,** a temple of these dimensions, as the Parthenon at Athens.

Hecatontarchy (hekăt[?]·ntɑ̈ki). 1660. [ad. Gr. ἑκατονταρχία, f. ἑκατοντ(α)- comb. f. ἑκατόν + -αρχία, ἀρχή rule.] Government by a hundred rulers.

†**He·catontome.** [f. Gr. ἑκατόν + τόμος.] A collection of 100 volumes. MILT.

†**He·cco** = HICKWALL. Drayton.

Heck (hek). Chiefly *Sc.* and *n. dial.* [prob. a. MLG. *heck* enclosure, gate (LG. *hek* palisade, cheese-drying frame).] **1.** = HATCH *sb.*[1] **1.** *n. dial.* **2.** A grating or frame of parallel bars in a river to obstruct the passage of fish, or solid bodies, without obstructing the flow of the water ME. **3.** A rack made with parallel spars to hold fodder. *Sc.* and *n. dial.* ME. **4.** A loose board placed at the back part of a cart (*local*) 1825. **5.** A 'shuttle' or sluice in a drain (*local*) 1877. **6.** A contrivance in a spinning-wheel or warping-mill, by which the yarn or thread is guided to the reel or reels 1824.

Comb.: **h.-door** (see sense 1); **-board** (see sense 4); **-box,** a box used to divide the warp threads into two alternate sets, one for each heddle or heald.

Heck, Heckle = HACK, HACKLE *sb.*[2], q.v.

Heckle (he·k'l), *v.* 1325. [f. HECKLE *sb.*] **1.** *trans.* = HACKLE *v.*[2] **2.** To catechize severely, with a view to the discovery of weak points; *spec.* of the public questioning of parliamentary candidates 1808. Hence **He·ckler.**

‖**Hectare** (he·ktēəɹ), or as F. (h)ektā·ɹ). 1810. [F., irreg. f. Gr. ἑκατόν (see HECTO-) + ARE *sb.*[2]] In the Metric system, a superficial measure containing 100 ares, or 2·471 acres.

Hectic (he·ktik). ME. (**etik**). [ad. (through F.) late L. *hecticus*, a. Gr. ἑκτικός habitual, hectic, consumptive, f. ἕξις habit.]

A. *adj.* **1.** Belonging to or symptomatic of the bodily condition or habit: applied to that kind of fever which accompanies consumption or other wasting diseases, and is attended with flushed cheeks and a hot dry skin. **b.** Belonging to or symptomatic of this fever 1642. **c.** Affected with hectic fever 1664. **2.** *fig.* 1603. †**3.** Habitual, constitutional –1654. **4.** Stirring, exciting, disturbing (*colloq.*) 1904.

1. H. fever is more or less remittent 1807. **b.** A h. cough 1831. **c.** Young people with h. cheeks 1860. 2. Leaves..pale, and h. red SHELLEY. Thrill with.. h. feeling 1886.

B. *sb.* [the adj. used ellipt.] **1.** A hectic fever. Also *fig.* ME. **2.** A consumptive person 1653. **3.** A hectic flush. Also *transf.* and *fig.* 1768.

1. *fig.* Wishing, that constant h. of a fool YOUNG. 3. One man's cheek kindled with the h. of sudden joy DE QUINCEY.

So **He·ctical** *a.* = **A.** Hence **He·ctically** *adv.*

Hecto-, hect-, a non-etymological contr. of Gr. ἑκατόν hundred, used esp. in the Metric system to express a hundred times the unit.

Hectocotyl, -e (hecktǫkǫ·til). 1854. [ad. mod.L. *Hectocotylus* (also used), f. HECTO- + Gr. κοτύλη cup, hollow thing (cf. COTYLE).] *Zool.* A modified arm in male dibranchiate Cephalopods, which serves as a generative organ, and in some species is detached and remains in the pallial cavity of the female; in this position mistaken by Cuvier for a parasite, which he named *Hectocotylus octopodis.* Hence **Hectoco·tylize** *v. trans.*, (*a*) to convert into a h.; (*b*) to impregnate with a h. **Hectoco·tylism,** the formation of a h.

Hectogramme, -gram (he·ktǫgræm). 1810. [ad. F.; see HECTO- and GRAMME, GRAM.] In the Metric system, a weight containing 100 grammes, or 3·52 oz. avoirdupois.

Hectograph (he·ktǫgrɑf), *sb.* 1880. [f. HECTO- + Gr. -γραφος writing.] An apparatus for multiplying copies of writing; = CHROMOGRAPH 2. Also, the process of taking copies by means of this. Also as *vb.*

Hectolitre, -liter (he·ktǫlītəɹ). 1810. [F.; see HECTO- and LITRE.] In the Metric system, a measure of capacity containing 100 litres, or 3·531 cubic feet, or about 2¾ bushels.

Hectometre, -meter (he·ktǫmītəɹ). 1810. [F. *hectomètre*; see HECTO- and METRE.] In the Metric system, a measure of length containing 100 metres, or 328·089 feet.

Hector (he·ktǫ̆ɹ), *sb.* ME. [L. *Hector*, Gr. Ἕκτωρ, son of Priam and Hecuba, husband of Andromache, 'the prop or stay of Troy'; in origin, as adj. ἕκτωρ = holding fast, f. ἔχειν.] **1.** Name of a Trojan hero celebrated in the Iliad; hence *transf.* A warrior like Hector. **2.** A swaggering fellow; a swash-buckler; a blusterer, bully 1655. **3.** A species of butterfly, *Papilio Hector* 1863.

2. Muns and Tityre Tus had given place to the Hectors MACAULAY. Hence **He·ctorism,** the quality or practice of a h. or bully. **He·ctorly** *a.* blustering, insolent.

Hector (he·ktǫ̆ɹ), *v.* 1660. [f. prec. sb. (sense 2).] **1.** *intr.* To play the hector or bully; to brag, bluster, domineer. **2.** *trans.* To intimidate by bluster or threats; to domineer over; to bully 1664.

1. She does now and then h. a little FOOTE. Hence **He·ctorer.**

Hectostere (he·ktǫstīəɹ, Fr. ektostēr). 1864. [F. *hectostère*; see HECTO- and STERE.] In the Metric system, a measure of capacity containing 100 steres.

Heddle (he·d'l), *sb.* 1513. [app. :—OE. *hefeld*, earlier f. *hefeld*; see HEALD.] In *pl.*, The small cords (or wires) through which the warp is passed in a loom after going through the reed, and by means of which the warp threads are separated into two sets so as to allow the passage of the shuttle bearing the weft.

Comb.: **h.-eye,** the eye or loop formed in each h. to receive a warp-thread. Hence **He·ddle** *v.* to draw (warp-threads) through the eyes of a h.

†**Hede.** Also **hed.** [ME. *hede* :—OE. type **hǣdu* (accus. *hǣde*) fem., beside *hād* masc. See HAD *sb.*, -HEAD *suffix.*] **1.** Rank, order, condition, quality. ME. only. **2.** = mod.Eng. *-head*; see -HEAD –1585.

Heder (hī·dəɹ), *dial.* 1532. [f. HE + (?) DEER; cf. SHEDER.] A male sheep; *spec.* one from eight or nine months old till its first shearing.

Hederaceous (hedĕrē·ʃəs), *a.* 1727. [f. L. *hederaceus*, f. *hedera.*] Pertaining or allied to ivy.

Hederal (he·dĕrăl), *a.* 1656. [f. L. *hedera* + -AL.] Of or pertaining to ivy.

Hederated (he·dĕre'tĕd), *a.* [f. L. *hederatus* + -ED.] Adorned or crowned with ivy. FULLER.

Hederic (hīde·rik), *a.* 1865. [f. L. *hedera* + -IC.] *Chem.* Of or pertaining to ivy; as in *hederic acid.*

Hedge (hedʒ), *sb.* [OE. **hęcg, hęgg* str. fem.:—OTeut. **hagjā-*; from the same root as OE. *haga* HAW *sb.*[1] and *hęge* HAY *sb.*[2]] **1.** A row of bushes or low trees (e.g. hawthorn, or privet) planted closely to form a boundary between pieces of land or at the sides of a road. **b.** Locally or spec. applied to other fences 1850. **2.** A fishing weir of faggots or of wattle-work 1653. **3.** *transf.* Any line of objects forming a barrier, boundary, or partition 1523. **4.** *transf.* and *fig.* A barrier, limit, defence; a means of protection ME. **5.** *spec.* (*Betting.*) The act of hedging; a means of hedging; see HEDGE *v.* 6. 1736. **6.** *attrib.* **a.** 'Of or for a hedge', as *h.-shears*, etc. ME. **b.** Born, brought up, sheltering, plying their trade, etc. under hedges, or by the roadside (hence as an attribute expressing contempt), as *h.-bantling, -lawyer, -parson, -wench*, etc. 1530. **c.** Done, performed, etc. under a hedge, or clandestinely, as *h.-marriage, -press*, etc. 1667. **d.** Of mean, common, third-rate quality, as *h.-alehouse, -inn, -wine*, etc. 1594. Hence **e.** Mean, third-rate, paltry, despicable, rascally 1596.

1. *Quickset h., dead h.*: see the adjs. H. and ditch is the most common mode of fencing property FORSYTH. 3. Hedges of police from our little street to [etc.] H. MARTINEAU.

Phrases, etc. *To be on the right* (*better, safer*) or *wrong side of the h.*: to be in a right or wrong position. *To take a sheet off a h.*: to steal openly. *To be on the h.* = to sit on the fence.

Combs.: **h.-born** *ppl. a.*, born under a h., of low or mean birth; **-chafer,** the cockchafer; **-chanter, -chat,** the hedge-sparrow; **-green,** the green headland in a ploughed field; **-hook,** a bill-hook for trimming hedges; **-rustic,** the moth *Luperina Cespitis*; **-warbler,** the hedge-sparrow.

b. In names of plants and fruits growing on hedges, as **h.-bedstraw,** the white-flowered species, *Galium Mollugo*; **-bell(s, -bindweed,** the Greater Bindweed, *Convolvulus* (or *Calystegia*) *sepium*; also erron. *C. arvensis*; **-garlic,** *Sisymbrium Alliaria* (*Alliaria officinalis*), also called garlic mustard, a cruciferous weed with an odour like garlic; **-mushroom,** *Agaricus arvensis*; **-mustard,** the cruciferous plant *Sisymbrium officinale*; also applied to plants of the genus *Erysimum*; **-nettle,** any labiate plant of the genus *Stachys*, esp. *S. sylvatica*, also called *hedge woundwort*; **-parsley,** common name of the genus *Torilis*, esp. *T. Anthriscus*; also applied to species of *Caucalis*; **-taper** = HAG-TAPER; **h. violet,** *Viola sylvatica*; **h. woundwort,** *Stachys sylvatica.*

Hedge, *v.* ME. [f. HEDGE *sb.*] **1.** *trans.* To surround with a hedge or fence as a boundary, or for purposes of defence. **2.** *intr.* or *absol.* To construct hedges or fences ME. **3.** *trans.* To arrange so as to form a barrier 1812. **4.** To surround as with a hedge or fence. Also with *in, about, around.* 1500. **b.** To hem *in*; to restrict 1549. **5.** To obstruct as with a hedge 1535. **6.** *trans.* To secure oneself against loss on (a bet, etc.) by betting, etc. on the other side. Also *fig.* 1672. Also *absol.* or *intr.* 1676. **b.** To insure against risk of loss by entering into contracts which balance one another 1909. **7.** *intr.* To go aside from the straight way; to shift, shuffle, dodge; to leave open a way of retreat or escape 1598.

1. Plauntide a vynȝerd, and heggide it aboute WYCLIF. 4. England hedg'd in with the maine SHAKS. There's such Diuinity doth h. a King SHAKS. 5. †*H. in*, to secure (a debt), app. by including it in a larger one which is better secured; to include within the limits of something else. 6. I kept hedging my bets as I laid them 1813. *intr.* No man should venture to bet, who could not h. well 1819. 7. Prophesy as much as you like, but always h. O. W. HOLMES.

He·dge-bird. **1.** Any bird that lives in or frequents hedges 1884. **2.** *transf.* A vagrant; a footpad 1614.

2. Out, you rogue, you hedge-bird, you pimp B. JONS.

Hedgebote (he·dʒ₁bōut). 1565. [See BOOT *sb.*[1]] *Law.* = HAYBOTE.

†He·dge-creeper. 1548. 'One that skulks or creeps under hedges for bad purposes' (J.); a hedge-bird; a sneaking rogue –1708. So **†He·dge-creeping** *a.* clandestine, base.

Hedgehog (he·dʒ₁hǫg). 1450. [f. HEDGE *sb.* + HOG; named from its frequenting hedges and from its pig-like snout.] **1.** An insectivorous quadruped of the genus *Erinaceus*, armed with innumerable spines, and able to roll itself up into a ball with these bristling in every direction; an urchin. Also *fig.* **2.** Applied to other animals armed with spines; as, the Porcupine Ant-eater of Australia; the Tenrec of Madagascar; etc. 1598. **3.** A name for prickly seed-vessels or burs borne by plants, and for the plants which bear them, e.g. *Ranunculus arvensis, Medicago Echinus*, etc. 1711. †**4.** Applied to a person who is regardless of others' feelings; often as a term of obloquy –1660. **5.** *attrib.* (or *adj.*): Of, belonging to, or resembling a hedgehog 1610.

1. The h. underneath the plantain bores TENNYSON. 4. *Rich. III*, I. ii. 102.

Comb.: **h. cactus,** a plant of the genus *Echinocactus*, globular and spiny; **h. caterpillar** (*U.S.*), the larva of an insect, *Arctia Isabella*, which is thickly covered with stiff black hairs on each end and with reddish hairs on the middle of the body; **h. fruit,** the prickly fruit of an Australian tree, *Echinocarpus Australis*; **h. grass** †(*a*) a kind of sedge (*Carex flava*) having prickly fruit; (*b*) name of various grasses of which the spikelets form burs, esp. *Cenchrus tribuloides* of N. America; **h. mushroom,** an edible fungus of the genus *Hydnum*, having prickly hymenium; **h. parsley,** a name for bur-parsley, *Caucalis daucoides*; **h. rat,** a rodent of the subfamily *Echinomyinæ*, the coat of which is usually harsh, or bristly, or even mixed with spines; **h. thistle** = *hedgehog cactus.*

Hence **He·dgehoggy** *a.* difficult to get on with.

Hedge-hyssop. 1578. *Gratiola officinalis*, a scrophulariaceous plant of Central Europe, formerly noted for its medicinal properties. Applied also to similar British plants, e.g. *Scutellaria, Lythrum hyssopifolium.*

He·dgeless, *a.* 1802. [-LESS.] Destitute of hedges.

Hedge-pig. = HEDGEHOG. *Macb.* IV. i. 2.

He·dge-priest. 1550. An illiterate priest of inferior status.

Hedger (he·dʒəɹ). 1515. [f. HEDGE *sb.* or *v.* + -ER [1].] **1.** One who makes, repairs, or trims hedges. **2.** One who hedges in betting, etc. 1803.

Hedgerow (he·dʒ₁rōu). [f. HEDGE *sb.* + ROW *sb.* Cf. OE. *heggerǣw.*] A row of bushes forming a hedge, with the trees, etc. growing in it; a line of hedge. Also *attrib.*

attrib. By hedge-row elms, on hillocks green MILT.

He·dge-school. 1807. A school held by a hedge-side or in the open air, as formerly in Ireland; hence, a poor, low-class school. Hence **Hedge-schoo·lmaster.**

He·dge-sparrow. 1530. A common European bird, *Accentor modularis*, belonging to the *Sylviidæ* or Warblers.

Hedging (he·dʒiŋ), *vbl. sb.* ME. [-ING [1].] **1.** The action of HEDGE *v.* Also *concr.* Matter forming or made into a hedge. **2.** *attrib.*, as *h.-bill*, a bill with a long handle for cutting and trimming hedges 1497.

Hedonic (hidǫ·nik). 1656. [ad. Gr. ἡδονικός pleasurable, f. ἡδονή.]

A. *adj.* Of or relating to pleasure.

Mill's H. philosophy 1880.

B. *sb.* †**1.** One who maintains that pleasure is the proper end of action; applied to the Cyrenaics 1678. **2.** *pl.* **Hedonics:** The doctrine of pleasure; the part of ethics which treats of pleasure 1865.

2. Hedonics, or the science of human pleasure J. GROTE.

Hedonism (hī·dǒniz'm). 1856. [f. Gr. ἡδονή + -ISM.] The doctrine or theory of ethics in which pleasure is regarded as the chief good, or the proper end of action.

Hedonist (hī·dǒnist). 1856. [f. as prec. + -IST.] One who maintains the doctrine of hedonism.

(*Note*) Professor Wilson coined the English word *Hedonist* DE QUINCEY. Hence **Hedoni·stic** *a.* pertaining to hedonists, or of the nature of hedonism. **Hedoni·stically** *adv.*

Heed (hīd), *v.* [OE. *hēdan* :—WGer. **hōdjan*, deriv. of **hōda* sb., str. fem., heed, guard, care, keeping.] †**1.** *intr.* To take charge, take. OE. only. **2.** *intr.* To have a care, take notice (*arch.* and *dial.*) OE. **3.** *trans.* To care for, concern oneself about; to give attention to; to regard. (In Engl. now chiefly literary.) ME. †**4.** To observe, see, take note of. Also *intr.* To look. ME. only.

3. Not perceived, or not heeded, by other men HURD.

Heed, *sb.* ME. [app. f. HEED *v.*] **1.** Careful attention, observation, regard. (Now chiefly literary.) †**2.** That which one heeds. SHAKS.

1. I will..teach your eares to list me with more heede SHAKS. Phr. *To give, pay h.* (*to*). *To take* (†*nim*) *h.* 2. *L. L. L.* I. i. 82.

Heedful (hī·dfŭl), *a.* 1548. [-FUL.] Full of heed; careful, attentive, watchful, mindful. Hence **Hee·dful-ly** *adv.*, **-ness.**

Heedless (hī·dlės), *a.* 1579. [-LESS.] Without heed; paying no attention; careless, regardless.

There in the ruin, h. of the dead, The shelter-seeking peasant builds his shed GOLDSM. Hence **Hee·dless-ly** *adv.*, **-ness.**

†Heedy, *a.* 1548. [f. HEED *sb.* + -Y.] Heedful, careful, cautious –1645. Hence **†Hee·dily** *adv.*† **Hee·diness.**

Hee-haw (hī·hǭ), *sb.* 1815. [Echoic.] **1.** An imitation of the bray of a jackass; a name for this. **2.** A loud coarse laugh 1843. Hence **Hee-haw** *v. intr.* to bray, as an ass.

Heel (hīl), *sb.*[1] [OE. *hēla, hǣla* wk. masc., deriv. of **hanh-*, in OE. *hōh* hough, heel.] **1.** In man, the hinder part of the foot; the spurred heel, the spur ME.; the whole foot ME. **2.** The analogous part. **a.** In quadrupeds: the hinder part of the hoof 1674; the hind feet OE.; the hoof OE. **b.** In birds: the spur 1611. **c.** In insects (*rec.*). **3.** Pregnant uses: **a.** *To raise* or *lift the h. against, to make a h.*: to kick OE. **b.** *To set the h. on*: to trample down 1601. **c.** *To have* or *get the heels of*: to outrun 1523. **4.** A stocking or shoe heel 1577. **5.** A part of a thing resembling the human heel in position or shape, esp. *the heel of Italy* 1717; the h. of a golf-club, a ship, a rudder, a mast, a gate, a gun-stock, etc.; a cyma reversa. Also, the bottom (or top) crust of a loaf; the rind of a cheese ME. **6.** The end-part of a period; of a book, etc.; *Astrol.*, of a zodiacal sign 1584.

1. His Stockings are about his Heels BUDGELL. Then ply'd, With iron h., his courser's side BUTLER. Fauns with cloven h. MILTON. *Two for his heels*, in *Cribbage* (opp. to *One for his nob*) = two points for turning up a knave. 2. a. [Horses] fighting with heels and mouth 1658. b. A cock which has a dull h. MARKHAM. 3. He that etith my breed, schal reyse his heele aȝens me WYCLIF. Friday..had..the heels of the bear DE FOE. 4. *Mod.* She wears high heels. Slippers have no heels. 5. The h. of a Dutch cheese DICKENS. 6. The corps..in a close pursuit at the h. of the day, lost many men WELLINGTON.

Phrases.

At, on, upon, †in (one's) **heel(s.** Close behind ME. Also *fig.* **Down at heel** (*adv.* and *adj.*). **a.** In destitution: cf. next. **b.** Of shoes, etc.; and *fig.* slovenly 1732. **Out at heels** (*adv.* and *adj.*). With shoe or stocking heels worn through 1553; *fig.* in decayed circumstances. **To heel.** Of a dog: close behind; under rule (*mod.*). 1810. Also *fig.* **Heel and toe.** **a.** *adv.* Walking fairly, not running; also as *adj.* and *sb.* (*mod.*). **b.** Of dancing (also *heel over toe*). **Heels over head.** Upside down ME.; *to turn h. o. h.*, to turn a somersault. Also *attrib.* So (*Sc.*) *heels over gowdy.* **Kick** one's **heels.** To wait idly or impatiently 1760. Cf. *to cool one's heels*, COOL *v.* **Lay, set, clap by the heels.** To put in the stocks; to arrest; *fig.* to overthrow 1510. So *to have by the h.*; *to lie* or *be tied by the h.* **Take** to one's **heels.** To run away 1542. **Trip** (*kick, strike, throw*) **up** a person's **heels.** To trip (him) up 1600; also *fig.* **Turn on** (*upon*) one's **heel.** To turn sharply round 1757. **Turn** (*kick, tumble*) **up** a person's **heels.** To knock (him) down; to kill 1500. So *to turn* (*kick, lay, tip, topple*) *up one's heels*, to die. Also: †**a.** *To run* or *hunt heel, take it heel*, to run back on the scent, hunt counter 1674. **b.** *With the heels foremost* or *forward*, as a corpse is carried 1670.

Combs.

1. General: as *h.-leather, -sliding, -hurt* and the like. 2. Special: **a.** in *Shoemaking*, as **h.-blank,** a set of 'lifts' built up into a heel; **-block,** a block used in heeling a shoe; **-cutter; -fastener; -iron** = HEEL-PLATE; **-lift,** one thickness of material in a shoe heel; **-maker; -quarters,** the counter; **-seat,** the part to which the heel is attached; **-shave,** a tool for shaping the heel; **-tip** = HEEL-PLATE; **-trimmer.** **b.** *Naut.* (see sense 5), as **h.-brace,** a piece of iron-work to brace the lower part of a rudder; **-chain,** a chain for holding out the jib-boom; **-jigger,** a light tackle fastened to the heel of a spar; **-knee,** the knee that joins the keel and the stern-post. **c.** Other uses: **h.-cap,** a cap for the heel of a shoe or stocking; whence **-cap** *v. trans.*; **-dog,** esp. a retriever; **-fly,** a fly, *Hypoderma lineata*, that attacks the heels of cattle; **-pad,** a pad in a boot heel; **-ring,** the ring securing the blade of a plough, or scythe; **-string,**

the *Tendo Achillis*; -**tool**, a tool used by turners for roughing out iron; -**tree**, the swingle-tree of a harrow; -**way** *adv.*, backward on the scent; -**wedge**, (*a*) a wedge to fasten the coulter, (*b*) a wedge to tighten the heel-ring of a scythe.

Heel (hīl), *sb.*² 1698. [A form of HIELD, after HEEL *v.*²] *Naut.* Inclination of a ship to one side.

Heel (hīl), *v.*¹ 1605. [f. HEEL *sb.*¹] **1.** *intr.* To move the heel rhythmically in dancing; also *trans.* Also *to h. it.* 1606. **2.** *trans.* To add a heel to 1605; esp. to arm (a game-cock) with a spur 1755; hence (*U.S. slang*), to furnish (a person) with something, esp. with a revolver 1755. **3.** To catch by the heel (*nonce-use*); to fasten by the heels 1638. **4.** To follow at the heels of; also *absol.* 18.. **5. a.** *Football.* (*intr.* or *absol.*) To pass the ball *out* with the heels (*mod.*). **b.** *Golf.* To strike (the ball) with the heel of the club 1857. **6.** *Ship-building.* To rest with the heel *on* something 1850.

1. I cannot sing, Nor heele the high Lauolt SHAKS. 4. *absol.* See that he [the collie] heels properly 18.. 5. a. Oxford..heeled out quickly 1893.

Heel (hīl), *v.*² 1575. [A corruption of *heeld*, HIELD *v.*; cf. Du. *hellen* for **helden.*] Chiefly *Naut.* **1.** *intr.* Of a ship, etc.: To lean to one side. Also *fig.* 1575. **2.** *trans.* To lay (a ship) on her side. Also *absol.* 1667.

1. Eight hundred of the brave..Had made the vessel h. COWPER. Phr. *Heeling error*: the error of the compass caused by the heeling of the vessel. 2. The Dutch did heele 'the Charles' to get her down PEPYS.

Hee·l-ball, *sb.* 1822. A ball of wax and lamp-black, used **a.** for polishing the sole-edges of new shoes; **b.** for taking rubbings of brasses, etc. Hence **Heel-ball** *v. trans.*

Hee·l-bone. 1598. The bone of the heel; the *calcaneum.*

Heeled (hīld), *ppl. a.* 1562. [f. HEEL *sb.*¹, *v.*¹ + -ED.] **1.** Having a heel; esp. in comb., as *high-heeled.* **2.** Provided; esp. with a revolver (*U.S. slang*) 1883. **3.** *Golf.* Struck or made with the heel of a club 1890.

Heeler (hī·ləɹ). 1638. [f. as prec. + -ER¹.] **1.** One who puts heels on 1665. **2.** A cock that uses his heels 1688. **3.** A supplanter (see HEEL *v.*¹ 3) 1638. **4.** A disreputable follower of a political 'boss'. *U.S.* 1877.

Hee·ling, *vbl. sb.* 1591. [f. HEEL *v.*¹ + -ING¹.] **1.** The action of HEEL *v.*¹ 1859. **2.** *concr.* The heel of a stocking 1591, of a mast or spar 1794.

Hee·lless, *a.* 1841. [f. HEEL *sb.*¹ + -LESS.] Having no heel.

Hee·l-piece, *sb.* 1709. **1. a.** The piece forming, or added to, the heel of a shoe. **b.** Armour for the heel 1828. **c.** The heel of a mast, etc. 1794. **2.** *fig.* The end-piece of a book or play 1761. Hence **Heel-piece** *v. trans.* to put a heel-piece on.

Heel-plate. 1847. A plate on the butt-end of a gun-stock, or the heel of a shoe.

Heel-post. 1846. **a.** The post to which a door or gate is hung 1875. **b.** *Ship-building.* The post supporting the outer end of a propeller shaft 1864. **c.** The outer post which supports a stall-partition in a stable 1846.

Heel-rope, *sb.* 1794. A rope attached to the heel of anything, e.g. of a spar or rudder, or to the heels of a horse. Hence **Heel-rope** *v.*

Hee·l-tap, *sb.* 1688. **1.** A thickness or 'lift' of leather, etc. in a shoe-heel. **2.** The liquor left at the bottom of a glass after drinking 1780. Also *fig.*

1. Ivory heel-taps 1850. 2. 'Toss it off, don't leave any heeltap' DICKENS. *Heel-tap glass* (attrib.): one without shank or foot.

Heel-way. Longfellow's erron. rendering of *hele-wages*; see HELEWOU.

Heep, obs. f. HIP.

Heer (hīᵊɹ). *Sc.* 1777. [?] A measure of yarn; = 2 cuts.

Heer, obs. f. HAIR.

Heeze, heize (hīz), *v.* *Sc.* and *north.* 1513. [Cf. HOISE *v.*] *trans.* To hoist. Also *fig.* Hence **Heeze, heize** *sb.*, also **Hee·zy**, a lift.

Heft (heft), *sb.* 1555. [f. HEAVE *v.*; cf. *weave, weft*, etc.] **1.** Weight (*dial.* and *U.S.*). **2.** The bulk (*U.S. colloq.*) 1816. **3.** †A strain; a heaving effort (SHAKS.); a lift (*dial.*) 1881.

1. *A dead h.*: a weight that cannot be moved (*local*). 2. The h. of it [the crop] was bad 1816. 3. He cracks his gorge, his sides, With violent Hefts SHAKS.

Heft, *v.* *dial.* and *U.S.* 1661. [f. HEFT *sb.*] **1.** To lift, lift up. **2.** To lift to judge the weight 1816. **3.** *intr.* To weigh 1851.

Hefty, *a.* 1867. [f. HEFT *sb.* + -Y.¹] Weighty, heavy (*dial.*); big and strong (*colloq.*).

Hegelian (hĭgī·liăn, hegē·liăn). 1838. [f. G. W. F. *Hegel* (1770–1831).]

A. *adj.* Pertaining to Hegel or his philosophy. **B.** *sb.* A follower of Hegel 1860.

Hence **Hege·lianism**, also **He·gelism**, the H. system. **Hege·lianize** *v. trans.* to render H. So **He·gelize** *v. intr.* to do like Hegel.

Hegemonic (hedʒĭmǫ·nik, hīg-). 1656. [ad. Gr. ἡγεμονικός.] **1.** *adj.* Ruling. **2.** *sb.* The ruling part, the master-principle 1678. So **Hegemo·nical** *a.*

Hegemony (hĭdʒe·mǒni, he·dʒĭməni, hī-; or *with* g *hard.*) 1567. [ad. Gr. ἡγεμονία.] Leadership, predominance of one state of a confederacy, *orig.* in ancient Greece, whence *transf.*

The headship, or h., was in the hands of Athens GROTE.

‖**Hegira, hejira** (he·dʒĭră, *erron.* hĭdʒəi·ră). 1590. [a. med.L. *hegira*, ad. Arab. *hijrah* flight. The better form is HIJRAH.] **1.** The flight of Mohammed from Mecca to Medina in A.D. 622; hence, the Mohammedan era, which is reckoned from that date. **2.** *transf.* Any exodus 1753.

1. The 38th year of the Hejira 1800. 2. The London hegira H. WALPOLE. Hence **Hegiric, hejiric** *a.*

Hegumen (hĭgiū·mĕn). 1591. [ad. med.L. *hegumenus*, a. Gr., f. ἡγεῖσθαι.] In the Gr. Ch.: The head of a religious community; *spec.* = abbot; also, prior.

Heh (hē), *interj.* Also **hegh** (DE FOE). 1475. [Cf. F. *hé.*] An exclam. used to express sorrow or surprise, or to attract attention.

Heifer (he·fəɹ). [OE. *heahfore* (prob. *héahfore*), ME. *hayfare, hekfere*, etc.; not found outside English.] A young cow that has not had a calf; *fig.* wife.

To plough with one's h. (see *Judges* xiv. 18). Hence **Hei·ferhood**, the state or age of a h.

Heigh (hēⁱ, hē), *interj.* (*sb.*) 1573. **1.** A call of encouragement 1599; an expression of inquiry 1848. **2.** *sb.* A name for the exclam. 1573.

1. H. my hearts, cheerely, cheerely my harts SHAKS. 2. With fishes, and heighs 1595.

Heigh-ho (hēⁱ·ho), *interj.* (*sb.*, *v.*) 1553. [f. prec. + HO.] **1.** An exclam. to express yawning, sighing, languor, weariness, disappointment. **2.** *sb.* An utterance of *heigh-ho!*; an audible sigh 1600. **3.** *vb.* To utter *heigh-ho!* 1824.

1. Heigh ho for a husband SHAKS.

Height (həit), *sb.* [OE. *híehþo* = Goth. *hauhiþa*, f. *hauh-* HIGH + *-iþa*; see -TH. The current spelling *height* dates from 14th c. The form *highth* (still dial.) occurs in 19th c. after Milton; *height-th* is common dial.]

I. 1. Measurement from the base upwards; stature; elevation above a recognized level (e.g. the sea). Also *fig.* (see Eph. iii. 18.) ME. **2.** Great comparative altitude ME. **3.** = ALTITUDE 4. 1551. †**4.** *Geog.* = LATITUDE (cf. *high latitude*) –1694; position (at sea) = alongside of, and, hence, *off* some place –1753. †**5.** High pitch (of a note, etc.) –1697. †**6.** High rank, estate, etc. –1718. **7.** High degree of a quality (*arch.*) 1601. **8.** †Haughtiness; *hauteur.* Orig. *Sc.* Also, magnanimity (*arch.*). 1450.

1. Fiftene [elne] on..heit ME. About my height SHAKS. *fig.* The highth..of thy Eternal wayes MILT. 2. Bodies..named of their height *Meteors* 1563. 3. A Table of the sonnes height 1559. 4. Spain lyeth.. in the same h. and parallel with the Azores Islands 1622. 6. Exceeded by the hight of happier men SHAKS. 7. To such a heighth is licentiousness risen 1762. 8. A very resolute answer, and full of height CROMWELL. Something of the old Roman height LAMB.

II. Semi-concrete senses. **1.** A high point 1563. **2.** The top *of* anything OE. **3.** The utmost degree (of something immaterial) OE.

1. From what highth fal'n MILT. 2. From heav'ns highth MILT. *fig.* Scipio the highth of Rome MILT. 3. Ceasing to be the Height of Folly, it became the Height of Wickedness 1718.

III. Concrete senses. †**1.** The heavens –1615. **2.** An eminence ME. **3.** *Her.* (See quot.)

1. So is God in the height, and in the earth 1615. 2. The Heights of Abraham close to Quebec 1887. 3. *A plume of feathers* strictly consists of three..If there be more rows than one they are termed *heights* 1847.

Phrases.

At..height. *At the h.* (arch.), †*At h.*: at the highest point. Now usu. *at its h.* †**In..height.** *In h.*: on high. *In the h.*: in the highest degree. *In h., in the* (*its*, etc.) *h.* = *At height, at the height.* †**On** or **upon height**: **a.** Aloft. **b.** Aloud. **To the height.** *arch.* To the utmost.

Height, *v.* *Obs.* or *arch.* 1495. [f. HEIGHT *sb.*] **1.** To heighten, raise on high (*arch.*) 1515. **2.** To raise in amount, quality, etc. (*arch.*) 1528. Hence **Heighting** *vbl. sb.*, increase.

Heighted (həi·tĕd), *a.* 1892. [f. HEIGHT *sb.* + -ED².] Having a (certain) height.

Heighten (həi·t'n), *v.* 1523. [f. HEIGHT *sb.* or *v.*; see -EN⁵.] **1.** *trans.* To make high or higher 1530. **2.** To make high or higher in amount or degree 1523; to augment in description 1731. **3.** *spec.* To render (a colour) more luminous, or, *occas.*, more intense 1622. †**4.** To elate, excite –1692. **5.** *intr.* To become high or higher 1567; to rise in amount or degree 1803.

2. To h. the price ADAM SMITH, the flavour 1853. 4. Satiate at length, And hight'nd as with Wine MILT. 5. The Rock seemed to h. marvellously J. H. NEWMAN. Hence **Hei·ghtened** *ppl. a.*; *spec.* in *Her.* having another charge placed higher in the field. **Hei·ghtener.**

†**Heild**, *v.* *Sc.* 1508. Var. of HELE, to cover.

†**Heily**, *a.* *Sc.* 1470. Haughty.

Heinous (hē·nəs), *a.* ME. [a. F. *haineux*, in OF. *haïneus*, f. *haine*, hatred, *hair* to hate.] **1.** Odious; highly criminal; infamous; chiefly of offences, and offenders. **b.** Hence, of the accusation or charge 1548. †**2.** Grievous, severe –1675. †**3.** Full of hate –1580.

1. The hainous..act Of Satan done in Paradise MILT. H. offenders 1845. **b.** H. charges STUBBS. 3. To wreke Their hainous wrath SURREY. Hence **Hei·nous·ly** *adv.*, -**ness.**

Heir (ēᵊɹ), *sb.* [ME. *eir, eyr*, etc.; a. OF. *eir, heir*:—late L. *herem*, f. *heres* heir.] **1.** One who on the death of another becomes entitled by law to succeed him in the enjoyment of property or rank; one who so succeeds; pop., one who receives or is entitled to receive property of any kind as the legal representative of a former owner. **2.** *transf.* One who succeeds, or should succeed, to any gift, endowment, or quality of another. Often one to whom something (*e.g.* joy, punishment) is morally due. ME. †**3.** *fig.* Offspring –1593.

1. The onely haire Of a most mighty king SPENSER. *Heir-at-law*: one who succeeds another by right of blood in the enjoyment of his property; in English law confined to one who has such a right in real property. *H. general* = *Heir-at-law*: used to include heirs female. *H. male*: an h. who is a male, and who derives from the ancestor through males only. *H. presumptive*: he who, if the ancestor should die immediately, would be his h., but whose right may be defeated by the birth of a nearer h., or the like. *Right h.* = *heir-at-law.* 2. The thousand Naturall shockes That Flesh is heyre too SHAKS. 3. The first heire of my inuention SHAKS.

Heir, *v.* ME. [f. prec. sb.] *trans.* To inherit; to be heir to. Also *fig.*

Not one son more To h. his goods CHAPMAN.

Heir apparent. [See APPARENT *a.* 3.] Formerly also **apparent heir.** ME. The heir whose right is indefeasible, provided he outlives his ancestor.

Heirdom (ēᵊ·ɹdəm). 1597. [-DOM.] Succession by right of blood; the state of an heir; an inheritance.

Heiress (ēᵊ·rĕs). 1659. [-ESS.] A female heir. Also *fig.*

Heirless (ēᵊ·ɹlĕs), *a.* ME. [-LESS.] Without an heir.

The h. Duke 1892, sceptre PALGRAVE.

Heirloom (ēᵊ·ɹlūm). 1472. [f. HEIR *sb.* + LOOM tool, utensil.] A chattel that, under a will, settlement, or custom, follows the devolution of real estate. Hence, Any piece of personal property that has been in a family for several generations. Also *fig.*

A glass cup, called..'The Luck of Muncaster'..is carefully preserved as a precious h. 1872. *fig.* Political wisdom is the h. of no one class of society STUBBS.

Heirship (ē°·ɹʃip). 1478. [-SHIP.] The state, condition, or rights of an heir; right of inheritance. Also *fig.*

†*H. movables, goods* (*Sc. Law*), the best of certain kinds of movable goods, which the heir was entitled to take besides the heritable estate. (The right was abolished in 1868.)

Hejira, var. of HEGIRA.

†**Helas**, *interj.* 1484. [a. F. *hélas.*] An exclam. of grief, sorrow, etc.; alas! -1753.

Helco-, comb. f. Gr. ἕλκος 'festering wound, ulcer', used with sense 'ulcer'; as in **Helco·logy**, the branch of pathology that treats of ulcers; **He·lcoplasty** [Gr. πλαστός], the operation of grafting on an ulcer a piece of healthy skin from another part or person; etc.

Held (held), *ppl. a.* 1820. [pa. pple. of HOLD *v.*] Kept in, restrained.

Hele, heal (hīl), *v.* [OE. *helian.* f. (ult.) ablaut stem *hal-* of *helan.*] †1. *trans.* To hide. 2. To cover; to roof ME. b. To set (a plant) in the ground and cover it *in*.

1. But the preest alwey heled his synne CAXTON.

Hele, obs. f. HALE *a.*, HEAL *sb.* and *v.*

†**Helena** (he·līnă). 1563. [a. L. *Helena*, a. Gr. Ἑλένη proper name. Cf. also Gr. ἑλένη torch.] A meteoric light seen about the masts of ships; cf. CORPOSANT. -1601.

Helenin (he·līnin). 1838. [f. botanical name *Helenium* + -IN.] *Chem.* A colourless crystalline substance, C_6H_8O, obtained from the root of elecampane (*Inula Helenium*). Hence **He·lenene**, a yellow oily hydrocarbon obtained by distilling h. with phosphoric anhydride.

†**Helewou.** ME. [f. HELE + WOUGH.] End-wall.

Heliac (hī·li,æk), *a.* 1565. [ad. late L. *heliacus*, a. Gr., f. ἥλιος.] = next.

Heliacal (hĭləi·ăkăl), *a.* 1607. [f. as prec. + -AL.] 1. *Astron.* Said of the rising of a star when it first emerges from the sun's rays and becomes visible before sunrise, or of its setting when it is last visible after sunset before being lost in the sun's rays. 2. Solar 1801.

1. *Heliacal year*, the year reckoned from the h. rising of Sirius, the canicular year: see CANICULAR. Hence **Heli·acally** *adv.*

‖**Helianthus** (hīli,æ·nþŏs). 1776. [mod.L., f. Gr. ἥλιος + ἄνθος.] *Bot.* The genus including the common sunflower (N.O. *Compositæ*).

Hence **Heliantha·ceous** *a.* allied to the genus *H.* of composite plants. **Helia·nthic** *a.* of or belonging to H. **Helia·nthin**, an aniline dye of orange yellow colour. **Helia·nthoid** *a.* belonging to the *Helianthoidea*, an order of *Actinozoa*, comprising the sea anemones; *sb.* one of these. Also **Helianthoi·dean** *a.* and *sb.*

Helical (he·likăl), *a.* 1613. [f. L. *helix*, *helic-*; see HELIX.] Belonging to or having the form of a helix; spiral; as, a *helical spring.* Hence **He·lically** *adv.* spirally.

Helices (he·lisīz), pl. of HELIX.

‖**Helichrysum** (helikrəi·sŏm). Also -**os**, -**on**. 1551. [L., = Gr. ἑλίχρυσος, f. ἕλιξ spiral + χρυσός gold.] 1. A creeping plant with yellow flowers, so called by the ancients. 2. *Bot.* A large genus of composite plants, having mostly yellow flowers, called also *Everlastings* or *Immortelles* 1664.

Heliciform (he·lisifǭɹm), *a.* 1854. [ad. mod.L. *heliciformis*, f. *helix*; see -FORM.] Having the form of a helix; spirally wound.

Helicin (he·lisin). 1854. [f. L. *helix* + -IN.] *Chem.* 1. The glycoside of salicylic acid 1859. 2. An oily substance extracted from snails.

Helicine (he·lisəin, -in), *a.* 1833. [f. as prec. + -INE.] *Anat.* a. Spiral, coiled; applied to certain arteries of the penis and clitoris. b. Pertaining to the helix of the ear.

Helicograph (he·likograf). 1851. [f. *helico-*, comb. f. Gr. ἕλιξ HELIX + -GRAPH.] An instrument for describing the volutes and scroll-work found in Gr. architecture.

Helicoid (he·likoid). 1699. [ad. Gr. ἑλικοειδής; see HELIX and -OID. Cf. F. *hélicoïde.*] A. *adj.* 1. Having the form of a helix; screw-shaped; spiral 1704. 2. *Zool.* Belonging to or resembling the *Helicidæ*, gastropodous molluscs including the snail 1876.

1. *Helicoid parabola* (Geom.): the parabolic spiral.

B. *sb.* †1. Something of a spiral form (*rare*) 1699. 2. *Geom.* †a. = Helicoid parabola; see A. 1. b. A warped surface generated by a moving straight line which always passes through or touches a fixed helix 1855.

So **Helicoi·dal** *a.* = HELICOID A. 1. Hence **He·licoidly** *adv.* spirally.

Helicon (he·likǫn). 1529. [L. *Helicon* = Gr. Ἑλικών. See also HELIX.] 1. (With capital H.) A mountain in Bœotia, sacred to the Muses, in which rose the fountains of Aganippe and Hippocrene; in 16-17th c. often confused with these. 2. A large brass wind-instrument of a spiral form 1875.

Heliconian (helikǭᵘ·niăn), *a.* 1557. [In 1, f. L. *Heliconius* (see prec.). In 2, f. mod.L. *Heliconia*, a genus of butterflies.] 1. Pertaining to Helicon, or to the Muses. 2. *Entom.* Belonging to the genus *Heliconia*, or family *Heliconidæ* of butterflies. Also **Heliconi·deous**, **He·liconine**, **He·liconoid**, *adjs.*

Helicopter (he·likǫptəɹ). 1872. Also in Fr. form. [ad. F. *hélicoptère* (Gr. ἕλιξ spiral, πτέρον wing).] A flying machine designed to rise vertically by one or more lifting screws revolving horizontally.

He·lio, colloq. abbrev. of HELIOGRAPH.

Helio-, comb. f. Gr. ἥλιος sun:

helio-engra·ving = HELIOGRAVURE; **-·later** [Gr. -λάτρης worshipping], a worshipper of the sun; so **-·latrous** *a.*; **-·latry** [Gr. λατρεία], sun-worship; **-·logist**, one versed in heliology; **-·logy**, the science of the sun's energy and action; **-pho·bia** [Gr. -φοβία], dread of or shrinking from sunlight; so **-phobe** [Gr. -φοβος], one affected with heliophobia; **-pho·bic** *a.*

Heliocentric, -al (hīliose·ntrik, -ăl) *a.* (*sb.*) 1667. [f. HELIO-; see CENTRIC. Opp. to GEOCENTRIC.] 1. Referred to the sun as centre 1685. 2. Having, or taking, the sun as centre 1834. Also *fig.* †3. *sb.* One who takes the sun as a centre 1667.

1. *H. latitude, longitude, place*, etc. of a planet: that in which it would appear to an observer placed at the centre of the sun. Hence **Helioce·ntrically** *adv.* as viewed from the centre of the sun.

Heliochrome (hī·liokrōᵘm). 1853. [f. HELIO- + Gr. χρῶμα colour.] A photograph representing an object in its natural colours. So **Heliochro·mic** *a.* pertaining to *heliochromy.* **Heliochro·motype** = HELIOCHROME. **He·liochromy**, the production of heliochromes.

Heliograph (hī·liograf), *sb.* 1848. [f. HELIO- + -GRAPH.] 1. An engraving obtained by HELIOGRAPHY (sense 3). Also *attrib.* 1853. 2. An apparatus for taking photographs of the sun 1848. 3. An instrument for measuring the intensity of sunlight 1851. 4. An instrument for signalling by means of flashes of sunlight. Cf. HELIOTROPE 4. Also *attrib.* 1877. Hence **He·liograph** *v.* to communicate by h.; to photograph by h. **Helio·grapher.**

Heliographic, -al (hīliogræ·fik, -ăl), *a.* 1706. [f. HELIO- + -GRAPHIC.] 1. Pertaining to the description of the sun. 2. †Photographic -1855; belonging to photographic engraving 1851. 3. Pertaining to or obtained by a heliograph (see HELIOGRAPH 4) 1880.

1. *H. charts*: descriptions of the sun's body, and of its *maculæ* or spots. Hence **Heliogra·phically** *adv.* by means of a heliograph.

Heliography (hīli·ǫ·grăfi). 1730. [f. HELIO- + -GRAPHY.] 1. The description of the sun. (Cf. *geography.*) †2. Photography -1840. 3. A process of engraving in which a specially prepared plate is acted upon chemically by exposure to light 1845. 4. The system of signalling by the HELIOGRAPH (sense 4) 1887.

Heliogravure (hīliogrăviūᵊɹ). 1879. [a. F. *héliogravure*, f. HELIO- + *gravure* engraving.] A process of engraving by means of the action of light on a sensitized surface; an engraved plate, or an engraving, thus obtained; photogravure. Also *attrib.*

Heliometer (hīli·ǫ·mĭtəɹ). 1753. [ad. F. *héliomètre*, f. HELIO- + Gr. μέτρον.] 1. An astronomical instrument originally devised for measuring the diameter of the sun; now much used in determining the angular distance between two stars. †2. A complex form of portable sun-dial, used for ascertaining solar time, latitude, and the like (Knight) 1875. Hence **Heliome·tric, -al** *a.* pertaining to, or obtained by, the h.; relating to measurement of the sun.

Heliopore (hī·liopōᵊɹ). [ad. mod.L. *Heliopora*, f. Gr. ἥλιος + πόρος pore; cf. MADREPORE.] A coral of the genus *Heliopora*; a sun coral.

Helioscope (hī·lioskoᵘp). 1675. [a. F. *hélioscope*, f. HELIO- + -SCOPE.] An apparatus for observing the sun without injury to the eye, as through smoked or coloured glass, by reflectors, etc.; a telescope fitted with such an apparatus. So **Heliosco·pic** *a.* **Helio·scopy.**

Heliostat (hī·liostæt). Also **-stata, -state.** 1747. [a. mod.L. *heliostata*, F. *héliostat*, f. HELIO- + Gr. στατός standing.] An apparatus consisting of a mirror turned by clockwork so as to reflect the light of the sun in a fixed direction. (Also applied to an apparatus worked by hand, a *porte-lumière.*) Hence **Heliosta·tic** *a.*

Heliotrope (hī·liotroᵘp). OE. [ad. L. *heliotropium* (also used), a. Gr. ἡλιοτρόπιον (also ἡλιότροπος); f. ἥλιος + -τροπος turning, τρέπειν to turn. In current form, a. F. *héliotrope.*] 1. A name given orig. to plants of which the flowers turn so as to follow the sun; as the sunflower, marigold, etc.; now, a plant of the genus *Heliotropium*; esp. *H. Peruvianum*, commonly cultivated for its fragrance. Also *fig.* b. The shade of purple of the flowers of the heliotrope. Also *attrib.* 1882. 2. *Min.* = BLOODSTONE, q.v. ME. 3. An ancient kind of sun-dial 1669. 4. An instrument with a movable mirror for reflecting the sun's rays, used for signalling, etc., esp. in geodesy; cf. HELIOGRAPH (sense 4) 1822.

2. The pretious stone Heliotropium..is a deepe green in maner of a leeke..garnished with veins of bloud HOLLAND. Hence **He·liotroper**, one who manages a HELIOTROPE (sense 4). **Heliotro·pian** *a.* (*rare*), pertaining to or of the nature of the h. (1 and 2); †*sb.* = HELIOTROPE 2. **Heliotro·pic** *a. Bot.* bending or turning under the influence of light; pertaining to or marked by heliotropism; *gen.* 1657.

Heliotropism (hīli·ǫ·tropiz'm). 1854. [f. Gr. ἥλιος + -τροπος + -ISM.] *Bot.* The property of bending or turning in a particular manner under the influence of light. Some restrict the term to the case of bending towards the light (*positive h.*).

Heliotype (hī·liotəip). 1870. [f. HELIO- + Gr. τύπος impression, TYPE.] A picture obtained by printing from a film of gelatine which has been sensitized with bichromate of potash and exposed to light under a negative; also, this process. Also *attrib.* So **He·liotyped** *ppl. a.* produced by *heliotypy.* **Helioty·pic** *a.* of or belonging to *heliotypy.* **He·liotypy**, the heliotype process.

Heliozoan (hīlio,zōᵘ·ăn). [f. mod.L. *Heliozoa* sb. pl., f. Gr. ἥλιος + ζῷον.] 1. *adj.* Belonging to the *Heliozoa* or sun-animalcules, a group of marine Radiolarians. 2. *sb.* One of the *Heliozoa.* So **Heliozo·ic** *a.*

Helispherical (helisfe·rikăl), *a.* 1646. [irreg. f. HELIX + SPHERICAL.] Winding spirally upon a sphere.

H. line: the rhumb-line in Navigation (HUTTON).

Helium (hī·liŏm). 1878. [mod.L., f. Gr. ἥλιος sun, after *selenium*, etc.] *Chem.* One of the chemical elements, a transparent gas, first obtained by Prof. Ramsay in 1895, but previously inferred to exist from a line (D_3) in the solar spectrum. (Cf. CORONIUM.) Symbol He.

Helix (he·liks, hī·liks). Pl. **helices** (he·lisīz). 1563. [a. L., a. Gr. ἕλιξ anything of spiral form.] 1. Anything of a spiral or coiled form, whether in one plane (as a watch-spring), or advancing round an axis (like a corkscrew), but usually the latter; a coil, a spiral, as an electro-magnetic coil of wire, the thread of a screw, a tendril, etc. In *Geom.*, a curve on any developable surface (e.g. a cone) which becomes a straight line when the surface is unrolled into a plane; dist. from a *spiral*, which is applied only to plane curves 1643. **2.** *Arch.*, etc. A spiral ornament, a volute; *spec.* applied to the eight smaller volutes under the abacus of the Corinthian capital 1563. **3.** *Anat.* The curved fold which forms the rim of the external ear 1693. **4.** *Zool.* A genus of molluscs with spiral shells, of which the common snail is typical 1820.

Hell (hel), *sb.* [OE. *hel(l*, obl. cases *helle*, str. fem. :—OTeut. **haljâ* str. fem., lit. 'the coverer up or hider', f. *hel-*, *hal-*, *hul-* to hide, HELE.] **1.** The abode of the dead; the place of departed spirits; the infernal regions regarded as a place of existence after death; the grave; HADES. (In N.T. (R.V.) *hell* is everywhere reserved for γέεννα.) **2.** The abode of devils and condemned spirits; the place or state of punishment of the wicked after death OE. **3.** The powers or inhabitants of hell; also, the kingdom or power of hell ME. **4. a.** A place or state of wickedness, suffering, or misery ME. **b.** A place of turmoil and discord 1818. **c.** *A hell of a* — 1778. †**5.** A part of a building, etc. compared to hell 1310; the name of a part of the old law courts at Westminster, app. used as a record office; also, a place of confinement for debtors –1661. **6.** The 'den' to which captives are carried in Prisoner's Base, etc. 1557. **7.** A place into which a tailor throws his shreds, or a printer his refuse type, etc. 1592. **8.** A gambling-house 1794. **9.** In imprecations, etc., used like *devil* 1596.

1. His soul was not left in h. [*R.V.* Hades] *Acts* ii. 31. **2.** *P.L.* x. 230. **3.** H. heard th' unsufferable noise MILT. A H. of ougly Deuills SHAKS. **4. a.** The prisons were hells upon earth MACAULAY. **5.** One that before the Iudgment carries poore soules to hel SHAKS. **8.** The proprietor of a h. STEVENSON.

Phr. *Hell-for-leather*: at breakneck speed, orig. with reference to riding on horseback.

Comb.: **h.-bent** *a. U.S.*, 'fiendishly', doggedly, or recklessly determined; also as *adv.*; **-box**, a box for holding refuse type; **-broth**, a decoction of infernal character, or prepared for an infernal purpose; **-diver** *U.S.*, a grebe; **-driver** *U.S.*, the hellgrammite; **-hag**, a hell-cat; **-kite**, a kite of h., a person of hellish cruelty.

Hell, *v.* 1799. [a. Ger. *hellen*, f. *hell* clear.] *trans.* To burnish (gold or silver).

Hellbender (he·lbendəɹ). *U.S.* 1812. [f. HELL *sb.* + BENDER, one who or that which bends.] **1.** The menopome or American salamander, a repulsive amphibian, from one to two feet in length, of which two species (*Menopoma alleghaniensis*, *M. horrida*) are found in the Ohio and Mississippi valleys. **2.** A protracted and reckless debauch (Farmer).

He·ll-born, *a.* 1593. Born of or in hell.

He·ll-bred, *a.* 1590. Bred or engendered in hell.

He·ll-cat. 1605. [perh. suggested by *Heccat*, HECATE.] A furious vixen; a witch. Also applied to a man.

Hellebore (he·lĭboəɹ). [ME. *el(l)ebre*, ad. L. *elleborus*, a. Gr. ἐλλέβορος, occas. ἐλλ-. Refash. after the prevailing Gr. form.] **1.** A name anciently given to species of *Helleborus* and *Veratrum*, reputed as specifics for mental disease; now, in *Bot.*, applied to the species of *Helleborus* (N.O. *Ranunculaceæ*), including the Christmas Rose and its congeners: **a.** the plant; **b.** the drug. ME. **2.** *attrib.*, as *h.-root* 1792.

1. b. Wretches fitter for a course of h. than for the stake SCOTT. *Comb.*: **Black H.**, (*a*) of the ancients, *Helleborus officinalis*; (*b*) of some moderns, the Christmas Rose, *H. niger*; **White H.** (of the ancients), *Veratrum album*; **Swamp H.**, *V. viride*, also called *American* or *Green H.*

Hence **Hellebore·in, Hellebo·resin, Hellebore·tin,** and **Helle·borin,** chemical principles derived from h.

Helleborine (he·lĭborəin). 1597. [ad. Gr. ἑλλεβορίνη a plant like hellebore; see -INE.] *Bot.* An orchidaceous plant of the genus *Epipactis* (formerly called *Serapias*), or of the closely-allied genus *Cephalanthera*.

Helleborism (he·lĭboriz'm). 1621. [ad. Gr. ἑλλεβορισμός a curing by hellebore.] **a.** The treatment of diseases by hellebore. **b.** The symptoms of hellebore administered in excess. **c.** A purgative made from hellebore. So **He·lleborize** *v. trans.* to treat with hellebore, as for madness.

Hellene (helīn, he·līn). 1662. [a. Gr. Ἕλλην a Greek.] A Greek, ancient or modern.

Hellenian (helī·niăn), *a.* 1611. [f. Gr. Ἑλλήνιος HELLENIC + -AN.] Grecian; HELLENIC 1813.

Hellenic (helī·nik, -e·nik), *a.* (*sb.*) 1644. [ad. L. *Hellenicus*, a. Gr.; see HELLENE and -IC.] **1.** Of or pertaining to the Hellenes or Greeks, ancient or modern; Greek, Grecian. **2.** *sb.* **a.** The Greek language 1870. **b.** *pl.* Writings on Greek subjects 1847.

1. H. grace 1879. **2.** Hellenics LANDOR (*title*).

Hellenism (he·lěniz'm). 1609. [a. Gr. Ἑλληνισμός, f. Ἑλληνίζειν to HELLENIZE; see -ISM.] **1.** A phrase, idiom, or construction used or formed in the Greek manner. **2.** Conformity to Hellenic speech and ideas; imitation of Greek characteristics, e.g. by the Jews of the Dispersion, the later Romans, etc.; the principle of hellenizing 1862. **3.** The national character or spirit of the Greeks; Grecian culture 1865. **b.** Applied by M. Arnold to that form of culture, or ideal of life, of which the ancient Greek is taken as the type. (Cf. HEBRAISM.) 1869. **4.** Greek nationality; the Hellenic 'world' as a political entity 1883.

3. b. The great movement which goes by the name of the Renascence, was an up-rising and re-instatement of man's intellectual impulses and of H. M. ARNOLD.

Hellenist (he·lěnist). 1613. [ad. Gr. Ἑλληνιστής, f. Ἑλληνίζειν; see -IST.] **1.** One who used the Greek language, though not a native Greek. Applied *esp.* to the Jews of the Dispersion. Also *attrib.* **2.** One skilled in the Greek language and literature; a Greek scholar 1680. **3.** One of the Byzantine Greeks who contributed to the revival of classical learning in Europe in the 15th c. (Mod. Dicts.)

1. There arose a murmuring of the Grecian Jews [*marg.* Hellenists] against the Hebrews R. V. *Acts* vi. 1.

Hellenistic, -al (helěni·stik, -ăl), *a.* 1706. [f. prec. + -IC.] Of or pertaining to the Hellenists.

The term H. was coined to denote the language of Greek-speaking Jews WESTCOTT & HORT. Hence **Helleni·sticism,** the H. condition or stage of history. **Helleni·stically** *adv.*

Hellenize (he·lěnize), *v.* 1613. [ad. Gr. Ἑλληνίζειν to speak Greek, to make Greek, f. Ἕλλην.] **1.** *intr.* To use the Greek language; to become a Greek or Hellenist. **b.** To adopt Hellenism (sense 3 b.) M. ARNOLD. **2.** *trans.* To make Greek or Hellenistic in form or character 1799. Hence **He:lleniza·tion,** the action of hellenizing or condition of being hellenized. **He·llenizer.**

Hellespont (he·lěspǫnt). 1591. [ad. Gr. Ἑλλήσποντος; explained as sea (πόντος) of Helle (Ἕλλη), daughter of Athamas, said to have been drowned in it.] Ancient name for the Strait of the Dardanelles; hence *fig.* something that separates lovers. *Two Gent.* I. i. 22 & 26. Hence **Hellespo·ntine** *a.*

Hell-fire, hell fire. OE. [Orig. two wds., *helle* being genitive case; now usu. hyphened. In N.T. rendering Gr. γέεννα τοῦ πυρός, fiery hell.] **1.** The fire of hell. **2.** A member of a Hell-fire club 1720.

attrib. **Hell-fire club,** name given to clubs of reckless young men, early in the 18th c. So **Hell-fired** *a.* 'set on fire of hell' (*Jas.* iii. 6); 'damned'.

Hell-gate, *pl.* **hell-gates.** OE. [Orig. two wds.] The portal or entrance of hell. MILT. *P.L.* II. 246.

He·llgrammite, he·lgramite. *U.S.* 1877. The larva of a neuropterous insect, *Corydalus cornutus*, the hellgrammite fly, much used as a bait for the black bass.

He·ll-hound. OE. [Orig. two wds., *helle* in genitive case.] **1.** Hound or dog of hell; esp. Cerberus. **2.** A fiend; a fiendish person ME. **3.** *attrib.* 1719.

2. Tyrone with his Hell-hounds being not farre from Corke 1633.

He·llicat. *Sc.* 1815. [Coined by Scott; perh. with some notion of *hell-cat.*] **1.** *adj.* Light-headed, giddy. **2.** *sb.* A wicked creature 1816.

Hellier (he·lyəɹ). Now *dial.* [ME. *helyer*, f. HELE *v.*; cf. *sawyer.*] A slater or tiler.

Hellish (he·liʃ), *a.* (*adv.*) 1530. [-ISH.] **1.** Of or pertaining to hell; infernal. **2.** Of the nature of hell; worthy of hell; diabolical, fiendish 1549; as an intensive 1798. **3.** *adv.* Infernally, devilishly; execrably 1613.

1. Diabolical and h. magic DE FOE. **2.** H. noises SCOTT. Hence **He·llish·ly** *adv.*, **-ness.**

Hello (hĕlōu·), *interj.* and *sb.* 1854. Var. of HALLO, q.v. Hence **Hello** *v.* to shout *hello!*

‖**Helluo** (he·liu͵o). 1583. [L.] **1.** A glutton; Also *transf.* and *fig.* **2.** *Zool.* A genus of beetles belonging to the family *Carybidæ*.

1. *transf.* To let an H. loose upon the Revenue NORTH.

Hellward (he·lwǫɹd). ME. [See -WARD; orig. *to hellward.*] **1.** *adv.* Towards hell. **2.** *adj.* Directed or conducting to hell 1829.

†**He·lly,** *a.* (*adv.*) 1532. [See -Y (or ? -LY).] **1.** Hellish –1613. **2.** *adv.* Hellishly –1762.

Helm (helm), *sb.*[1] [Com. Teut.: OE. *helm* str. masc. :—OTeut. **helmo-z* :—pre-Teut. **kelmo-s*, f. root *kel-* to cover, conceal (see HELE *v.*).] **1.** A helmet. Now *poet.* and *arch.* **2.** The crown or top of anything (*Obs.* exc. *dial.*) OE. †**3.** The head of an alembic or retort –1718. **4.** (Also *helm-cloud.*) The local name in the Lake District of a cloud which forms over a mountain top before and during a storm; esp. that which accompanies the *helm-wind*, a kind of cyclone, revolving on a horizontal axis parallel to the escarpment of the Pennines near Cross Fell 1696.

Helm (helm), *sb.*[2] [OE. *helma* wk. masc., corresp. in stem to ON. *hjálm* str. fem.] **1.** The handle or tiller, in large ships the wheel, by which the rudder is managed; occas., the whole steering gear. **2. a.** *fig.* That by which affairs, etc. are guided OE. **b.** *transf.* Any part which is used like a helm 1660. †**3.** A handle, helve –1615.

1. Many times the ships will feele no helme SIR T. HERBERT. Phr. *Down with the helm*, *Down h.*, the order to place the h. so as to bring the rudder to windward. *Up with the h.*, *Up h.*, the order to place the h. so as to bring the rudder to leeward. See also ALEE, AMIDSHIPS, BEAR *v.*, EASE *v.*, FEEL *v.*, OVER, PORT, STARBOARD, WEATHER. **2. a.** You slander The Helmes o' th' State SHAKS. *Comb.*: **h. circle**, the smallest circle in which a ship can be turned; **h.-port**, 'that hole in the counter through which the head of the rudder passes'.

Helm, *sb.*[3] *dial.* ME. [? a development of OE. *healm* HAULM.] The stalk of corn; the stalks collectively, straw; *esp.* as made up for thatching. *Comb.* **h.-bote,** the right of cutting h. in a common field for thatching.

Helm, *v.*[1] [OE. *helmian*, f. HELM *sb.*[1]] *trans.* To furnish or cover with a helm. Chiefly *poet.*

Helm, *v.*[2] 1603. [f. HELM *sb.*[2]] *trans.* To guide with or as with a helm; to steer. Chiefly *fig.*

The businesse he hath helmed, must..giue him a better proclamation SHAKS.

He·lmage. *rare.* 1864. [f. HELM *sb.*[2] + -AGE.] Guidance, direction.

Helmed (helmd), *ppl. a.* ME. [f. HELM *v.*[1] or *sb.*[1] + -ED.] Wearing a helm; helmeted. The h. Cherubim, And sworded Seraphim MILT.

Helmet (he·lmět), *sb.* 1470. [a. obs. F. *healmet*, *helmet*, dim. of *helme* (see HEAUME and HELM *sb.*[1]).] **1.** A defensive cover for the head; a piece of armour, usually made of, or strengthened with, metal, which covers the head wholly or in part. **b.** Extended to other defensive or protective head-gear, e.g. that worn by policemen, firemen, and divers, and the felt or pith hat worn in hot climates 1842. **2.** *Her.* The figure of a helmet placed above the escutcheon in an achievement and supporting the crest 1610. **3.** = HELM *sb.*[1] 3. 1599. **4.** A kind of fancy pigeon; so named from the appearance of the head 1668. **5.** (in full *helmet-shell.*) The shell of a mollusc of the genus *Cassis* 1753. **6.** A fossil echinoderm, *Galerites albogalerus* 1887. **7.** *Bot.* The arched upper part of the corolla (or calyx) in labiates, orchids, etc. 1793. **8.** An appendage of the stipes of the maxilla of some insects, as the cockroach 1828.

Comb.: **h.-beetle,** a beetle of the family *Cassididæ*, having a dilated thorax forming a kind of h. covering the head; -bird, a turakoo; -cockatoo, *Callocephalon galeatum*, 'an iron-grey bird with a bright red head' (Newton); -crab, a species of King-crab, *Limulus longispinus*; -flower, a name for Monkshood or Aconite, and for orchids of the genus *Coryanthes*; -hornbill, *Buceros galeatus*; -quail, a quail of the American genus *Lophortyx*, having an elegant curled crest; -shell = sense 5; -stone (1681) = sense 6. Hence He·lmet *v.* to furnish with a h. He·lmeted *ppl. a.* wearing a h.; in *Bot.* h.-shaped, galeate. †Helmetie·r, Helmettier, a soldier wearing a h.

Helmet-crest. 1509. 1. (Also *helmet crest.*) The crest of a helmet. 2. A crested humming-bird of the genus *Oxypogon* 1863.

Helminth (he·lminþ). 1852. [ad. Gr. ἕλμινς, ἑλμινθ- (comb. form ἑλμινθο-) maw-worm.] 1. A worm, esp. an intestinal worm. 2. *Min.* A variety of chlorite occurring in felspar and quartz 1861.

Helminthagogue (helmi·nþăgǫg). 1704. [f. Gr. ἑλμινθ- (see prec.) + ἀγωγός drawing forth.] 1. *adj.* 'Having power to expel intestinal worms' (*Syd. Soc. Lex.*); anthelmintic 1854. 2. *sb.* [sc. *medicine.*]

Helminthiasis (helminþəi·ăsis). 1811. [mod.L., f. Gr. ἑλμινθιᾶν to suffer from worms; see HELMINTH and -ASIS.] *Path.* A diseased condition characterized by the presence of worms in the body.

Helminthic (helmi·nþik). 1704. [f. HELMINTH + -IC.] 1. *adj.* Pertaining to a helminth or intestinal worm 1755. 2. *sb.* = HELMINTHAGOGUE 2.

Helmi·nthite. 1859. [f. as prec. + -ITE.] *Geol.* One of the long sinuous tracks on the surfaces of many sandstones, usually considered as worm-trails.

Helmi·nthoid, *a.* 1854. [f. as prec. + -OID.] Resembling a helminth; vermiform.

Helminthology (helminþǫ·lŏdʒi). 1819. [f. as prec. + -LOGY.] That branch of zoology, or of medical science, which treats of helminths. Hence **Helmintholo·gic, -al** *a.* pertaining to h. **Helmintho·logist,** one versed in h.

Helmless (he·lmlės), *a.*[1] 1600. [f. HELM *sb.*[1] + -LESS.] Without a helm or helmet.

He·lmless, *a.*[2] 1824. [f. HELM *sb.*[2] + -LESS.] Without steering gear; rudderless. Also *fig.*

He·lmsman. 1622. [f. as prec. + MAN.] A steersman.

Helm-wind: see HELM *sb.*[1] 4.

Helot (he·lǫ̆t, hī·lǫ̆t). 1579. [ad. L. *Helotes*, a. Gr. Εἵλωτες (pl. of Εἵλως), also *Hilotæ*, a. Gr. Εἱλῶται (pl. of Εἱλώτης); usu. derived from Ἕλος Helos, a town in Laconia whose inhabitants were enslaved. (With capital H now only in the historical sense.)] *Gr. Antiq.* (*Helot*) One of a class of serfs in ancient Sparta intermediate in status between the ordinary slaves and the free Spartan citizens. b. *transf.* (*helot*) A serf, a bondsman 1823.

Drunken H.: in allusion to Plutarch's statement that Helots were, on certain occasions, compelled to appear in a state of intoxication, as a lesson to the Spartan youth. Hence He·lotage, He·lotism, the condition of a H. or h.; the Spartan system of serfage; a system under which a class of the community are treated as a permanently inferior order. He·lotize *v.* to reduce to the condition of a H. He·lotry, helots or serfs collectively; the condition of Helots; serfdom.

Help (help), *v.* Pa. t. **helped** (helpt), *arch.* **holp** (hōulp); pa. pple. **helped,** *arch.* **holpen** (hōu·lpĕn, -p'n). [Com. Teut. str. vb.: OE. *helpan, healp, holpen*; OTeut. ablaut series *help-, halp-, hulp-* (*holp-*). The pre-Teut. form should be **kelb-*: cf. Lith. *szẽlpti* to help. The weak inflexion *helped* appears *c.* 1300, and is now usual.] 1. *trans.* To furnish (a person, etc.) with what is serviceable to his efforts or his needs; to aid, assist. b. *absol.* or *intr.* To afford aid or assistance; often in *imper.* as a cry for assistance ME. †2. *trans.* To be of use or service to, to profit -1648. †b. *absol.* or *intr.* To be of use or service; to avail -1756. 3. *trans.* To make more effectual; to further, promote 1559. 4. With *infin.* or *clause* ME. 5. Ellipt. with advs. and preps. = to help to proceed, go, come, get (*away, down, forward*, etc.; *to, into, out of*, etc.) ME. b. With adv., etc. followed by *with*: esp. in reference to clothing, e.g. *to help* a person *on* (or *off*) *with* his coat = to help him to get it on or off ME. c. *To h. out* or *through*: to assist in completing something; to eke out, supplement. Also *absol.* 6. To serve (a person) with food at a meal. Const. *to.* 1688. b. *transf.* To distribute (food) at a meal 1805. 7. To succour in some distress or misfortune; hence, to deliver, save, relieve (*from, of*); *spec.* to cure of a disease, or the like. *Obs.* or *arch.* ME. 8. To relieve or cure (a malady); to remedy, amend. *Obs.* or *arch.* OE. 9. To remedy, obviate, prevent, cause to be otherwise. (With *can, cannot*, etc.) 1589. b. To avoid, refrain from, forbear; to do otherwise than. (With *can, cannot.*) Usu. with *vbl. sb.* (occas. *infin.*), or *it* = doing it. 1697. c. Idiomatically with *can* instead of *cannot* after a negative expressed or implied 1804.

1. Fortune helpeth bothe the good and euylle folke CAXTON. Helpe me Cassius, or I sinke SHAKS. Phr. *So help me God*, the formula in a solemn oath. *God h. him* (*them*, etc.), a parenthetical exclam. of pity. b. Helpe, O king 2 *Sam.* xiv. 4. 3. The troubles of the time helped..the progress of the town GREEN. 4. He help'd to bury whom he help'd to starve POPE. I would fain stay and h. thee tend him M. ARNOLD. 5. A Hangman to helpe him to bed SHAKS. To h. on a work 1886. b. H. me up the hill with this load (*mod.*). c. To h. out a bad cause WOLLASTON. Phr. *H.* (a person) *to*: to aid in obtaining; to provide with. Helpe me to a Candle SHAKS. *H. oneself to*: to take for oneself; *euphem.* to steal. Also without *to.* 6. He did not h. himself to any food SCOTT. b. A spoon to h. the gravy with 1889. 7. H. us from famine TENNYSON. 8. The jingling of the guinea helps the hurt that Honour feels TENNYSON. 9. One thing there is..which I fear will touch me; but I shall h. it, I hope PEPYS. b. Not one of us could h. laughing CARLYLE. c. I did not trouble myself more than I could h. SPURGEON.

Help (help), *sb.* [OE. *help* :—OTeut. **helpâ* str. fem.; f. stem of *helpan* to help.] 1. The action of helping; the supplementing of action or resources by what makes them more efficient; aid, assistance, succour. Also with *a.* and *pl.* (now *rare*). 2. *transf.* Any thing or person that affords help; an aid OE. 3. A person, or company of persons, whose office it is to render help ME. b. A person employed to give assistance in manual work; in *U.S.*, a hired labourer or servant, esp. a domestic servant 1645. c. The labour of hired persons; *collect.* the body of servants belonging to a farm or household (*U.S.*) 1817. 4. Relief, cure, remedy; now only, means of obviating or avoiding something OE. 5. A portion of food helped; a helping 1809.

1. Calling out for helpe SIR T. HERBERT. I am perfectly sensible of..the weakness and fewness of the helps BURKE. †*At h.*: in (our) favour. *Haml.* IV. iii. 46. 2. God is..a very present helpe in trouble *Ps.* xlvi. 1. Books are..helps to knowledge BLACKIE. 3. b. *Lady h.*, a lady engaged to assist and h. the mistress of a house. *Mother's h.*, a superior kind of nurse-maid. 4. What's past helpe Should be past greefe SHAKS. It is their way and there is no h. for it MRS. CARLYLE.

Helper (he·lpəɹ). ME. [f. HELP *v.* + -ER[1].] 1. One who (or that which) helps or assists; an auxiliary. 2. An assistant in some kind of work; *spec.* a groom's assistant in a stable 1686.

1. My..h. to a husband SHAKS. 2. Two sleepy helpers put the wrong harness on the wrong horses DICKENS.

Helpful (he·lpfŭl), *a.* ME. [f. HELP *sb.* + -FUL.] Full of help; rendering help; useful, serviceable, profitable.

Heauens make our presence and our practises Pleasant and helpfull to him SHAKS. Hence **He·lpful·ly** *adv.*, **-ness.** So †**Helply** *a.* ME.

Helping (he·lpiŋ), *vbl. sb.* ME. [-ING[1].] 1. The action of HELP *v.*; aid; †an aid; †an ally. 2. *concr.* A portion of food served at one time; = HELP *sb.* 5. 1824.

Helping, *ppl. a.* ME. (*h. hand* 1440.)

Helpless (he·lplės), *a.* ME. [f. HELP *sb.* + -LESS.] 1. Destitute of help; needy. 2. Unable to help oneself; shiftless. (The current sense.) 1620. 3. Affording no help; unavailing, unprofitable. Now *rare.* 1590. †4. That cannot be helped. SPENSER.

1. Helper of the H...be thou my Fortress 1694. H. of all that human wants require DRYDEN. 2. H. infants CRABBE. 3. A sharp accuser, but a h. friend POPE. Hence **He·lpless·ly** *adv.*, **-ness.**

Helpmate (he·lpmēⁱt). 1715. [f. HELP *sb.* or *v.* + MATE; prob. suggested by next.] A companion who is a help, or who renders help. Chiefly applied to a wife or husband.

In Minorca the ass and the hog are helpmates, and are yoked together in order to turn up the land PENNANT.

Helpmeet (he·lpmīt). 1673. [The two wds. *help meet* in Gen. ii. 18, 20 ('an help meet for him'), first improp. hyphened, and then taken as one word.] A suitable helper; a helpmate; usu. of a wife or husband.

More passed..between Selwyn and his h. 1805.

Helter-skelter (he·ltəɹ,ske·ltəɹ). 1593. [A jingling expression founded on *helter*, which is unexplained.]

A. *adv.* In disordered haste; pell-mell.

Helter-skelter haue I rode to thee SHAKS.

B. *attrib.* or *adj.* Characterized by disorderly haste or headlong confusion 1730.

C. *sb.* A helter-skelter run or flight 1713. b. A lighthouse-shaped structure down the outside of which pleasure-seekers slide seated on a mat 1906.

Such a helter-skelter of prayers and sins LONGF.

Helve (helv), *sb.* [OE. *hielfe, helfe* masc. or neut. :—**halƀjo-* :—OTeut. type **halƀinеut.*, from same root as HALTER.] 1. A handle of an ax, chisel, hammer, etc. *To throw h. after hatchet*: to risk everything. 2. (Also *helve-hammer.*) A tilt-hammer, the helve of which oscillates on bearings, so that it is raised by a cam carried by a revolving shaft, and falls by its own weight 1858. Hence **Helve** *v.* (ME., now *rare*), to furnish with a h.

Helvetian (helvī·ʃiăn). 1559. [f. *Helvetia* (sc. *terra*), f. L. *Helvetius.*] A. *adj.* a. Pertaining to the ancient Helvetii, a people of Gallia Lugdunensis. b. Swiss. B. *sb.* a. One of the ancient Helvetii. b. A Swiss. 1593.

Helvetic (helve·tik). 1708. [ad. L. *Helveticus*, f. *Helvetia*; see prec.]

A. *adj.* Helvetian, Swiss.

B. *sb.* A Swiss Protestant; a Zwinglian.

Helvin, -ine (he·lvin). 1818. [f. L. *helvus* light bay + -IN. *Min.* A honey-yellow or greenish silicate of glucinum and manganese, occurring in regular tetrahedral crystals. var. **He·lvite.**

Hem (hem), *sb.*[1] [OE. *hem(m.* App. from same root as OE. *hamm*, and NorthGer. *hamm* enclosure; the radical sense being 'border'.] 1. The border or edging of a piece of cloth or a garment. 2. *spec.* (in current use). A border made on a piece of cloth by doubling the edge itself, and sewing it down, to strengthen it and prevent ravelling 1665. †3. The edge, border, rim, margin of anything -1674. Also *fig.* 4. a. The partition which divides the hearth from the fireplace in a reverberatory furnace; the fire-bridge 1693. b. *Arch.* The projecting and spiral parts of the Ionic capital 1823.

3. Entomb'd vpon the very hemme o' th' Sea SHAKS.

Hem (h'm, hem), *interj.* and *sb.*[2] 1526. [A vocalized representation of the sound made in clearing the throat with a slight effort; more closely *hm* or *h'm.*]

A. *int.* An utterance like a slight half cough, used to attract attention, give warning, or express doubt or hesitation.

H., syr, yet beware of Had I wyste SKELTON.

B. *sb.* The utterance of this sound; the sound itself 1547.

After every sygh make an h., or cough after it 1547.

†**Hem, 'em** (ĕm), *pers. pron.*, 3rd *pl.*, *dat.-acc.* [Orig. OE. *him, hiom, heom*, dat. pl. in all genders of HE; subseq. supplanting the accus. *hi*; and finally itself displaced by *them*, exc. colloq. or dial.] 1. *Dative.* (To) them -1599. b. Governed by *prep.* Them -1750. 2. *Accusative.* Them -1868. 3. *Refl.* and *Reciprocal Pron.* (*dat.* and *acc.*) Themselves, to themselves; (to) each other -1579.

Hem, *v.*[1] 1440. [f. HEM *sb.*[1]] 1. *trans.* To edge or border; to decorate with a border, fringe, etc. 2. To turn in and sew down the edge of. *intr.* To do the particular kind of sewing used in this operation. 1530. 3. To confine or bound; to enclose, limit, restrain, imprison. Now usu. with *in*, also *about, round, up*; *hem out*, to shut out. 1538.

1. All the skirt about Was hemd with golden fringe SPENSER. 3. Hemm'd with warlike Foes DRYDEN.

Hem, *v.*² 1470. [f. HEM *interj.*] 1. *intr.* To utter the sound described under HEM *int.*; to stammer or hesitate in speaking. 2. *trans.* To remove, clear *away* with a hem or cough. Also *fig.* 1600.

1. She speaks much of her father..and hems and beats her heart SHAKS. 2. *A. Y. L.* I. iii. 19.

Hema-, Hemato-, var. sp. of HÆMA-, etc.

He-man: see HE *pron.* V.

Hemelytrum: see HEMI-ELYTRUM.

‖**Hemeralopia** (he:mĕrălǭu·piă). 1706. [mod.L., f. Gr. ἡμεράλωψ, f. ἡμέρα day + ἀλαός blind + ὤψ eye; cf. NYCTALOPIA.] *Path.* 'Day-blindness'; a usual defect in which the eyes see indistinctly, or not at all, by daylight, but fairly well by night or artificial light. (But others make the word = 'night-blindness', NYCTALOPIA.) Hence **Hemeralo·pic** *a.*

Hemerobian (hemĕrǭu·biăn). 1842. [f. mod.L. *Hemerobius*, a. Gr., f. ἡμέρα + -βιος living.] 1. *adj.* Pertaining to the genus *Hemerobius* or the family *Hemerobiidæ* of neuropterous insects. 2. *sb.* One of these; a day-fly.

‖**Hemeroca·llis.** 1656. [Gr. ἡμεροκαλλίς a kind of lily that blooms but for a day, f. ἡμέρα + κάλλος beauty.] The Day Lily, a genus of Liliaceous plants chiefly natives of temperate Asia and Eastern Europe.

Hemi- (he·mi, hī·mi), *prefix.* [a. Gr. ἡμι-, comb. element, = L. *sēmi-* (see SEMI-), Skr. *sami-*, OTeut. **sǣmi-*, OE. *sam-*, all meaning 'half-'.] Half-; one half, the half, pertaining to or affecting one half.

Hemialbu·min, *Chem.* a substance thought to be one of the two original constituents of ordinary albumin; it is converted on digestion into **Hemia·lbumose,** which is prob. an antecedent of *hemipeptone.* **Hemia·mb, -iambus,** *Pros.* an iambic dimeter catalectic. ‖**Hemianæsthe·sia,** *Path.* loss of sensation in one side of the body; hence **Hemianæsthe·sic** *a.* **Hemiana·tropous** *a.*, *Bot.* half-anatropous; = HEMITROPOUS. **Hemice·rebral** *a.*, *Anat.* of or pertaining to either of the two CEREBRAL hemispheres. **Hemico·llin** [COLLIN], *Chem.* a peptone-like body formed along with semi-glutin, when a solution of gelatin is boiled a long time. **He·mi-de:mise·miqua:ver,** *Mus.* a note of half the length of a demisemiquaver, also its symbol. **Hemidia·pe·nte,** *Anc. Mus.* a diminished or imperfect fifth. **Hemidi·tone** [DITONE], *Anc. Mus.* a minor third. **He:mi-encepha·lic** *a.*, *Anat.* of or pertaining to a *hemiencephalon*, or lateral half of the ENCEPHALON or brain. **Hemi·gamous** [Gr. γάμος] *a.*, *Bot.* said of grasses having one of the two florets of a spicule neuter, and the other unisexual. **Hemigeo·meter,** *Entom.* a caterpillar of the *Noctuidæ*, which in its mode of progression resembles the true geometer caterpillars. **He·miglyph,** *Arch.* the half-glyph or -groove at the edge of the triglyph in the Doric entablature. **Hemiholohe·dral** *a.*, *Cryst.* having half the number of planes in all the octants. **Hemimelli·tic,** *Chem.* a crystalline tribasic acid $C_9H_6O_6$. **Hemioctahe·dron,** *Cryst.* a tetrahedron; hence **Hemioctahe·dral** *a.* **He·mione** [Gr. ἡμίονος, f. ὄνος ass], *Zool.* the dziggetai. **Hemio·rthotype** [ORTHOTYPE] *a.*, *Cryst.* = monoclinic. ‖**Hemipara·ple·gia** [Gr. παραπληγία stroke on one side], paralysis of one lower limb. **Hemipe·ptone,** *Chem.* a variety of peptone derived from hemialbumose by a continuance of the digestive process; see *Hemialbumin.* **Hemipro·tein,** *Chem.* a kind of syntonin, obtained by boiling albumin with dilute sulphuric acid for a few hours. **Hemirha·mphine** *a.*, *Ichth.* (a fish) having the upper jaw very short in comparison with the lower, as in the genus *Hemirhamphus* or half-bills.

Hemiano·psia. 1885. [mod.L., f. HEMI- + Gr. ἀν- priv. + ὄψις.] *Path.* Half-blindness, being a loss of perception of one half the field of vision. Also **He:miano·pia, -o·psy.**

Hemibranch (he·mibræŋk). 1880. [f. HEMI- + Gr. βράγχια.] An incomplete gill; a fish of the order *Hemibranchii*, having the branchial apparatus incomplete. Hence **Hemibra·nchiate** *a.* half-gilled; *sb.* a h.

He·micarp. 1854. [f. HEMI- + Gr. καρπός fruit.] *Bot.* A half-fruit; one of the two carpels which constitute the fruit of the *Umbelliferæ.*

‖**Hemicrania** (hemikrēⁱ·niă). 1597. [L., a. Gr. ἡμικρανία, f. ἡμι- HEMI- + κρανίον skull.] *Path.* Headache confined to one side of the head, megrim. So †**Hemicrane.** Hence **Hemicra·nic** *a.* pertaining or subject to h.

Hemicycle (he·misəik'l). 1603. [a. F. *hémicycle*, ad. L. *hemicyclium*, a. Gr., f. ἡμι- + κύκλος.] A half-circle; a semicircular structure, as an apse-like recess, etc.

Forming themselves into a h. or half moon figure COWPER. Hence **Hemicy·clic** *a. Bot.* half-cyclic: said of flowers which have some parts arranged spirally (*acyclic*) and others in whorls (*cyclic*).

Hemida·ctyl. 1863. [f. HEMI- + Gr. δάκτυλος.] *Zool.* 1. *adj.* Having an oval disk at the base of the toes, as in the saurian genus *Hemidactylus* (Webster). 2. *sb.* A saurian of this genus; a gecko. Hence **Hemida·ctylous** *a.*

Hemidome (he·midǭum). 1868. [f. HEMI- + DOME *sb.*] *Cryst.* A pair of parallel and equal faces, parallel to the orthodiagonal in the monoclinic system (in which two such pairs constitute a dome). Hence **Hemidoma·tic** *a.* of or pertaining to a h.

‖**Hemi-elytrum** (hemi,e·litrŏm). *Pl.* **-a.** Also *erron.* **hemelytrum.** 1826. [mod.L., f. Gr. ἡμι- + ἔλυτρον ELYTRUM, sheath.] *Zool.* The fore wing of an insect, which is coriaceous at the base and membranous at the end, as in the *Hemiptera* and *Heteroptera.* Hence **Hemi-e·lytral** *a.*

Hemihedral (hemihī·drăl, -he·drăl), *a.* Also **hemiedral.** 1837. [f. HEMI- + Gr. ἕδρα seat, base + -AL.] Of a crystal: Having half the number of planes required by the highest degree of symmetry belonging to its system; thus, a tetrahedron is the hemihedral form corresponding to the holohedral octahedron. Hence **Hemihe·drally** *adv.*

Hemihedron (hemihī·drǭn, -he·drǭn). 1837. [f. as prec. after *hexahedron*, etc.] *Cryst.* A form or crystal of a hemihedral type. So **Hemihe·drism, Hemihe·dry,** the property of crystallization in hemihedral forms.

‖**Hemimetabola** (he:mi,mĭtæ·bŏlă), *sb. pl.* 1870. [mod.L. neut. pl. (sc. *insecta*), f. Gr. ἡμι- HEMI- + μετάβολος changeable.] *Entom.* A division of insects comprising those which undergo incomplete metamorphosis. Hence **Hemimeta·bolic, Hemimeta·bolous** *adjs.* of the nature of *Hemimetabola*; undergoing incomplete metamorphosis.

Hemimorphic (hemi,mǭ·ɹfik), *a.* 1864. [f. HEMI- + Gr. μορφή + -IC.] *Cryst.* Of a crystal: Having unlike planes or modifications at the ends of the same axis. So **Hemimo·rphism,** the property of being h. **Hemimo·rphous** *a.* = HEMIMORPHIC.

‖**Hemina** (hĭməi·nă). Also **hemine.** 1601. [L., a. Gr. ἡμίνα, f. ἡμι- half.] A liquid measure (orig. ancient Sicilian) of about half a pint; also, a measure for corn, variously computed.

‖**Hemio·pia, Hemio·psia.** Also **-opy, -opsy.** 1811. [mod.L., f. HEMI- + Gr. ὤψ, ὠπ- eye, ὄψις sight.] *Path.* = HEMIANOPSIA.

‖**Hemiplegia** (hemiplī·dʒiă). 1600. [Late L., a. Gr., f. ἡμι- HEMI- + πληγή stroke.] *Path.* Paralysis of one side of the body. Hence **Hemiple·giac** *a.* affected with or subject to h.; *sb.* one so affected. **Hemiple·gian** *a.* **Hemiple·gic** *a.* pertaining to or characterized by h.; affected with or subject to h. vars. **He·miplegy,** †**He·miplexy.**

Hemipod, -pode (he·mipǭd, -pǭud). 1862. [ad. mod.L. *hemipodius* (generic name), f. Gr. ἡμι- HEMI- + πούς, ποδός foot.] A member of the genus *Hemipodius*, or *Turnix*, of three-toed quail-like birds; a bush-quail, ortygan.

Hemiprism (he·mipriz'm). 1864. [HEMI-.] *Cryst.* A pair of parallel faces, parallel to the vertical axis of the crystal in the triclinic system (in which two such pairs constitute a prism). Hence **Hemiprisma·tic** *a.*

Hemipter (hĭmi·ptəɹ). 1828. [ad. F. *hémiptère*, f. L. *hemiptera*; see next.] One of the *Hemiptera.*

‖**Hemiptera** (hĭmi·ptĕră), *sb. pl.* Rarely in *sing.* **Hemipteron.** 1816. [mod.L., neut. pl. of *hemipterus*, f. *hemi-* HEMI- + Gr. πτερόν wing, in reference to the structure of the wings.] *Entom.* A large order of Insects, characterized by a suctorial mouth, and in the HETEROPTERA by wings coriaceous at the base and membranous at the tip. Also called *Rhyncota.* Examples are bugs, lice, and plant-lice. Hence **Hemi·pteral** *a.* hemipterous. **Hemi·pteran** *a.* hemipterous; *sb.* one of the *Hemiptera.* **Hemi·pterist,** a student or collector of *H.*

Hemipterous (hĭmi·ptĕrəs), *a.* 1816. [f. prec. + -OUS.] *Entom.* Pertaining to or characteristic of the *Hemiptera.*

Hemisect, *v.* 1878. [f. HEMI- + L. *sect-*, *secare.*] *trans.* To bisect, esp. longitudinally. So **Hemise·ction.**

Hemisphere (he·misfīᵊɹ). ME. [In form *hemispherie*, etc., ad. late L. *hemisphærium*, a. Gr. ἡμισφαίριον, f. ἡμι- HEMI- + σφαῖρα SPHERE; in form *hemisphere*, through OF.] 1. *gen.* A half-sphere; one of the halves formed by a plane passing through the centre of a sphere 1585. 2. *spec.* Half of the celestial sphere; in early use, esp. the sky above us; in *Astron.*, usually, one of the halves into which the celestial globe is divided by the equinoctial or by the ecliptic. (The earliest sense in Eng.) ME. 3. One of the halves of the terrestrial globe 1551. 4. A map or projection of half the (terrestrial or celestial) globe 1706. 5. *Anat.* See CEREBRAL. 1804. 6. *transf.* and *fig.* = 'sphere' of action, life, or thought 1503.

1. *Magdeburg hemispheres*, a contrivance invented by Otto von Guericke of Magdeburg to demonstrate the pressure of the air. It consists of two hemispheres, forming when fitted together a cavity from which the air can be withdrawn by an air-pump. When this has been done great force is required to separate the two parts. 6. Beyond the h. of my knowledge 1856. Hence **He·misphered** *a.* (*rare*), formed as a h.; having a cerebral h. (of such a kind). **Hemisphe·ric, -al** *a.* of, pertaining to, or resembling a h.; extending over a h. **Hemisphe·rically** *adv.* **Hemisphe·rico-,** comb. f. *Hemispheric.*

Hemispheroid (hemisfīᵊ·roid). 1727. [f. HEMI- + SPHEROID.] The half of a spheroid. Hence **Hemispheroi·dal** *a.* having the form of a h.

†**Hemisphe·rule.** 1696. A half-spherule; a small hemispherical lens –1756.

Hemistich (he·mistik). 1575. [ad. late L. *hemistichium* (also used), ad. Gr., f. ἡμι- HEMI- + στίχος row, line, verse.] *Pros.* The half or section of a line of verse; also, a line of less than the usual length. Hence **He·mistichal** *a.* pertaining to a h.

Hemisy·mmetry. 1881. [HEMI-.] *Cryst.* Same as HEMIHEDRISM. Hence **Hemisymme·trical** *a.* hemihedral.

Hemisystema·tic, *a.* 1878. [HEMI-.] *Cryst.* (See quot.)

A *hemi-systematic form* is a form in which only half the origin-planes or normals are extant STORY-MASKELYNE.

†**He·mitone.** 1603. [ad. L. *hemitonium*, ad. Gr., f. HEMI- + τόνος.] = SEMITONE –1760.

Hemi·tropal, *a.* 1864. [f. as next + -AL.] = HEMITROPOUS 2.

Hemitrope (he·mitrǭup). 1805. [ad. F. *hémitrope*, f. HEMI- + Gr. -τροπος turning.] *Cryst.* 1. *adj.* = HEMITROPIC. 2. *sb.* A hemitropic crystal 1805. So **Hemi·tropism, Hemi·tropy,** hemitropic crystallization.

Hemitropic (hemitrǭ·pik), *a.* 1886. [f. as prec. + -IC.] *Cryst.* Said of composite or twin crystals, which are united together in such a way that, if we conceive one of them as being turned through half a revolution round a particular axis, corresponding faces and edges in the two crystals would become parallel.

Hemi·tropous, *a.* 1860. [f. as prec. + -OUS.] 1. *Cryst.* = prec. 2. *Bot.* Said of an ovule so formed that the hilum lies half-way between the base and the apex.

Hemlock (he·mlǫk). [OE. *hymlice* wk. fem., *hymlic*, *hemlic*, str. masc.; of obscure origin.] 1. The common name of *Conium maculatum*, a poisonous umbelliferous plant, having finely divided leaves, and small white flowers; used as a powerful sedative. Also in rural use applied to the large *Umbelliferæ* generally. 2. A North Amer. tree, *Abies Canadensis*, more fully *Hemlock Fir, H. Spruce* 1729. b. *Ground H.*: a Canadian species or variety of Yew 1886. 3. A poisonous potion obtained from the Common Hemlock. (Believed to have been the poison administered to Socrates.) 1601.

2. The murmuring pines and the hemlocks, Bearded with moss LONGF. 3. A drowsy numbness pains My sense, as though of h. I had drunk KEATS.

Comb.: **h. dropwort**, *Œnanthe crocata*; **h. parsley**, a N. Amer. umbelliferous plant resembling h., but not poisonous; there are two species, *Conioselinum Canadense* and *C. Fischeri*.

Hemmel. *dial.* 1717. [var. HELM *sb.*[1]] Cow-shed.

Hemmer (he·məɹ). 1483. [f. HEM *v.*[1] + -ER[1].] One who hems. **b.** An 'attachment' to a sewing machine for doing hemming (Knight) 1875.

Hemo-, var. spelling of HÆMO-, usual in U.S., and occasional in Great Britain, as in *hemorrhage*, etc.

Hemp (hemp), *sb.* [OE. *hęnep, hænep* :— OTeut. **hanpi-z*, **hanapi-z*, cogn. w. Gr. κάνναβις, L. *cannabis*. The wd. is perhaps not Aryan.] 1. An annual herbaceous plant, *Cannabis sativa*, N.O. *Urticaceæ*, cultivated for its valuable fibre. 2. The cortical fibre of this plant, used for making cordage, and woven into stout fabrics ME. 3. In allusion to a rope for hanging 1532. 4. A narcotic drug obtained from the Indian hemp; bhang; hashish 1870. 5. Applied to other plants yielding a useful fibre, or otherwise resembling hemp 1597.

3. Let not Hempe his Wind-pipe suffocate SHAKS.

5. **African H.**, (*a*) = *bowstring hemp* (*a*); (*b*) *Sparmannia africana*. **Bastard H.**, Hemp-nettle and H.-agrimony. **Bowstring H.**, (*a*) a plant of the genus *Sanseviera*, esp. *S. guineensis*, a liliaceous plant of tropical Africa, the leaf-fibres of which are used for bowstrings and for making ropes; (*b*) in India, *S. Roxburghiana*; also *Calatropis gigantea* (N.O. *Asclepiadaceæ*). **Canada** or **Indian H.**, *Apocynum cannabinum*, a N. Amer. perennial. **Indian H.**, a tropical variety of common h., *Cannabis Indica*. **Manilla H.**, the fibre of *Musa textilis*. **Sisal H.**, the fibre of species of *Agave*, esp. *A. Sisalana*. **Water H.**, a name for *Eupatorium cannabinum* and *Bidens tripartita*, in U.S. for *Acnida cannabina*.

Comb.: **h.-cake**, the residue of crushed hempseed, after extraction of the oil; **-oil**, the oil pressed out of hempseed; **-palm**, a palm, *Chamærops excelsa*, of China and Japan, the fibres of which are made into cordage.

Hemp-agrimony. 1760. *Herb.* A book-name for *Eupatorium cannabinum*; also for other species. **b.** *Water Hemp-agrimony*, Bur-Marigold or *Bidens*.

Hempen (he·mpĕn), *a.* (*sb.*) ME. [f. HEMP *sb.* + -EN[4].] 1. Made of hemp; of or pertaining to hemp. 2. Resembling hemp 1651. 3. *sb.* Hempen cloth 1777.

1. *H. homespun*, homespun cloth made of hemp; hence, one clad in this, one of rustic manners. What h. home-spuns haue we swaggering here SHAKS.

He·mp-nettle. 1801. The genus *Galeopsis*.

Hempseed (he·mpsīd). ME. The seed of hemp. **b.** A gallows-bird. SHAKS. Also *attrib.*, as in **hempseed calculus** (*Path.*), a variety of the mulberry-calculus.

He·mpstring. 1566. *lit.* String made of hemp. Hence *transf.*, one who deserves the halter.

He·mpweed. 1796. A name of species of *Eupatorium*.

Hempy (he·mpi), *a.* 1440. [f. HEMP *sb.* + -Y.] Made of, like, or of the nature of hemp; producing hemp.

Hemself(e, -selve(n, themselves: see SELF.

He·m-stitch, *v.* 1839. [f. HEM *sb.*[1] + STITCH *v.*] *trans.* To hem with an ornamental stitch of a particular kind, giving the effect of a row of stitching; to ornament with this stitch. Hence **He·m-stitch** *sb.* ornamental needlework of this kind.

†**Hemule, hemuse.** 1486. [?] *Venery.* A roebuck of the third year -1660.

Hen (hen), *sb.* [OE. *hęnn* str. fem. :— WGer. **hannja*, deriv. of *hano*, OE. *hana* cock.] 1. The female of the common domestic fowl. (occas. = 'domestic fowls', including the males.) 2. The female of various other birds; also, = *hen-bird* ME. 3. A female fish or crustacean 1810. 4. *fig.* Of persons 1626. 5. A kind of bivalve shell-fish, *Venus mercenaria*. Also *locally*, A freshwater mussel. 1603. 6. *attrib.* in sense 'female' OE.

Comb.: **h.-blindness**, nyctalopia; **-driver**, the hen-harrier; †**-harm**, the hen-harrier; **-plant**, a name for *Plantago lanceolata* and *P. major*.

†**Hen, henne,** *adv.* [OE. **hionane, hionan*, f. root *hi-* 'this' of HE pron.] = HENCE: of time, place, or inference. OE. and ME. only.

†**He·nad.** 1678. [ad. Gr. ἑνάς, ἑνάδ- unit.] A unit, monad (in the Platonic philosophy).

Hen and chickens. †1. The Pleiades 1613. 2. A compound daisy 1794; London Pride, etc. 3. A children's game 1894.

Henbane (he·nbēⁱn). ME. [f. HEN *sb.* + BANE.] 1. Name of the annual plant *Hyoscyamus niger*, a viscid weed, growing on waste ground, having dull yellow flowers streaked with purple, and narcotic and poisonous properties; also, the genus as a whole. 2. The drug extracted from this 1840. 3. *attrib.* ME.

Henbit (he·nbit). 1578. [f. HEN *sb.* + BIT *sb.*[2]] Name of †**a.** Ivy-leaved Speedwell (*Veronica hederifolia*); also called *Small H.*; **b.** A species of Dead-nettle (*Lamium amplexicaule*); formerly known as *Greater H.* Also *H. Nettle, H. Dead-nettle*. 1597.

Hence (hens), *adv.* [ME. *hennes*, etc., f. *henne*, HEN *adv.*, with suffix *-es, -s*, as in *-ward, -wards*, etc. The spelling *hence* is phonetic.]

I. Of place. 1. (Away) from here; to or at a distance; away. Also with redundant *from*. 2. *ellipt.* Chiefly as a command: *Hence!* go hence. *H. with*: go away with, take away 1573. 3. *spec.* From this world ME.; †in the next world (SHAKS.).

1. High you hense 1440. Not past three quarters of a mile h. SHAKS. 2. H. with her, out o' dore SHAKS. 3. Before I go h., and be no more *Ps.* xxxix. 13.

II. Of time. From this time onward ME.; from now ME. Also with *from*.

Fro hennes in to domes day CHAUCER. Some houre h. SHAKS.

III. Of issue, etc. 1. From this, as a source or origin 1597. 2. (As a result) from this. Also with *from*. 1608. 3. (As an inference) from this; therefore 1586.

1. My Flora was my Sun.. All other faces borrowed h. Their light and grace SUCKLING. 2. Learn courage h. POPE. 3. It is so with men generally, and h. we assume it to be so with you (*mod.*).

†**Hence,** *v. rare.* 1580. [f. prec.] *trans.* To order hence; *intr.* to go hence, depart -1614.

Henceforth (he·ns,fōᵊɹþ, hensfōᵊ·ɹþ), *adv.* ME. [f. as prec. + FORTH *adv.*] From this time forth. Also with *from* (arch.).

A power.. with which the Monarchy was h. to reckon GREEN.

Hencefo·rward, *adv.* ME. [f. HENCE *adv.* + FORWARD.] From this time forward; henceforth. Also with *from* (*arch.*). So †**Hencefo·rwards** *adv.*

†**Hench-boy.** 1512. [f. *hench-* in HENCHMAN + BOY.] A page of honour, a boy attendant -1683.

Henchman (he·nʃmæ̆n). Also †**henxman.** *Pl.* **-men.** ME. [f. OE. *hęngest, hęngst* (see HENGEST) + MAN; perh. orig. 'attendant on a horse'.] 1. **a.** ? A groom. **b.** A squire, or page of honour to a prince or great man. In later 16th c. use, app. = HENCH-BOY. *Obs.* (exc. *Hist.*) since 17th c. 2. The chief gillie of a Highland chief; hence, generally, a trusty follower or attendant 1730. **b.** A stout political partisan; *esp.* in U.S. 'A mercenary adherent' (*Cent. Dict.*) 1839.

Hen-coop (he·n,kūp). 1697. A coop in which poultry are kept.

†**Hend, hende,** *a.* (*adv.*) [aphet. f. OE. *ʒehęnde* adj. (and adv.), near, convenient, lit. at hand, handy.] 1. Near, at hand -ME. 2. Convenient, handy (*rare*) -1513. 3. Ready with the hand, dexterous; skilful -1550. 4. Courteous; kind, 'nice' -1765. 5. Comely, fair -1450. 6. *absol.* or as *sb.* Gentle, courteous, or gracious one or ones (see 4) -1549. 7. *adv.* Near, at hand -1507; courteously, kindly, gently -1450.

Hendeca-, bef. a vowel **hendec-**; erron. **endeca-**. Comb. form of Gr. ἕνδεκα eleven, as in **Hende·cachord**, *Mus.* a series or scale of eleven notes; hence **Hendecacho·rdal** *a.*, relating to such a scale.

Hendecagon (hende·kăgǫn). Also erron. **en-**. 1704. [f. Gr. ἕνδεκα- (see prec.) + -γωνον, γωνία angle.] **a.** *Geom.* A plane figure having eleven sides and eleven angles. †**b.** *Fortif.* A fort with eleven bastions.

Hendecasyllabic (he:ndĕ-, hende:kăsilæ·bik). Also erron. **en-**. 1727. [f. as next; see also SYLLABIC.] *Pros.* 1. *adj.* Of a verse: Consisting of eleven syllables. 2. *sb.* A hendecasyllabic verse. (Usu. in *pl.*) 1836.

Hendecasyllable (he:ndĕ-, hende:kăsi·lă·b'l). Also erron. **en-**. 1603. [f. L. *hendecasyllabus*, a. Gr. ἑνδεκασύλλαβος, after SYLLABLE.] *Pros.* A verse or line of eleven syllables.

‖**Hendiadys** (hendəi·ădis). 1586. [Late or med.L., f. Gr. phr. ἓν διὰ δυοῖν 'one by means of two'.] *Gram.* A figure of speech in which a single idea is expressed by two words connected by a conjunction; e. g. by two sbs. with *and* instead of an adj. and sb.

Law and heraldry, a kind of h., meaning 'heraldic law' 1887.

†**Hendy,** *a.* ME. only. [f. HEND *a.* + -Y.] = HEND *a.*

Hen-egg. [In OE. two wds., with *henne* in genitive; now usually *hen's egg*.] The egg of a hen.

Henen, obs. var. of HEN, hence.

Henequen (he·nīken). Also **-quin, hennequen.** 1880. [ad. Sp. *jeniquen, geniquen*, from native name.] The fibrous product known as *Sisal hemp*, obtained from the leaves of species of *Agave*; also, the plant itself.

Heng, ME. inflexion of HANG *v.*

†**He·ngest.** [OE. *hęngest, hęngst*. (See also HENCHMAN.)] A male horse; usually a gelding -ME. (Also a proper name, and in various place-names.)

He·n-ha:rrier. 1565. [f. HEN *sb.* + HARRIER; in reference to its preying upon poultry.] *Ornith.* A European bird of prey, *Circus cyaneus*, also called Blue Hawk, Blue Kite.

He·n-hawk. 1855. *Ornith.* U.S. name for various species of Hawks and Buzzards, esp. *Buteo borealis* and *B. lineatus*. *Blue hen-hawk*, the adult Amer. goshawk.

He·n-hea:rted, *a.* 1522. Timorous; chicken-hearted.

He·n-house. 1512. A small house or shed in which poultry are shut up for the night.

He·nism. [f. Gr. εἷς, ἑν- one + -ISM.] = MONISM. Max Müller.

Henna (he·nă). 1600. [a. Arab. See also ALCANNA.] The Egyptian Privet, *Lawsonia inermis* (N.O. *Lythraceæ*); the shoots and leaves of this plant used, esp. in the East, as a dye for parts of the body, or made into a cosmetic with catechu. Also *attrib.*

He·nnery, 1859. [-ERY.] A place for rearing poultry.

Hennes, obs. f. HENCE.

Henny (he·ni). 1854. [f. HEN *sb.* + -Y.] 1. *adj.* Of or pertaining to a hen; hen-like: said of some male fowls; so *h.-feathered* 1855. 2. *sb.* A hen-like male fowl. 1854.

Henotheism (he·noþi,iz'm). 1860. [f. Gr. εἷς, ἑνό-ς + θεός + -ISM.] The belief in a single god without asserting that he is the only God: a stage of belief between polytheism and monotheism. So **He·notheist, Henothei·stic** *a.*

Henotic (henǫ·tik), *a.* 1878. [a. Gr. ἑνωτικός serving to unite, f. (ult.) ἕν one.] Unifying; reconciling. GLADSTONE.

He·n-peck, *v. colloq.* 1688. [f. HENPECKED.] *trans.* Of a wife: To domineer over or rule (the husband).

But—oh! ye lords of ladies intellectual.. have they not hen-peck'd you all BYRON.

Hen-pecked (he·n,pekt), *ppl. a. colloq.* 1680. [lit. pecked by a hen or hens: alluding to the plucking of the domestic cock by his hens.] Domineered over or ruled by a wife.

A Step-dame.. rules my hen-peck'd Sire DRYDEN.

Hen-roost. OE. [f. HEN *sb.* + ROOST *sb.*] A place where domestic fowls roost at night. **b.** *fig.* A source of plunder 1909.

Hen's-foot. 1578. [From the resemblance of the leaves to a hen's claws.] Name of: †**a.** [tr. L. *pes gallinaceus* (Pliny).] The Climbing Fumitory, *Corydalis claviculata* -1601. **b.** [L. *pes pulli*.] Bur-parsley, *Caucalis daucoides* 1597.

Hent, *v. Obs.* exc. *arch.* or *dial.* [OE. *hentan* (also *gehentan*), prob. related to Goth. *hinþan* to seize.] **1.** *trans.* To lay hold of, seize; to take or hold in one's hand; to catch (*arch.*). **2.** To get; to 'catch' (harm, etc.); to apprehend ME. Hence **Hent** *sb.* the act of seizing; *fig.* conception, intention, design. †**Henter**, one who seizes.

Henware (he·nwēᵊɹ). *Sc.* 1808. [app. f. HEN *sb.* + WARE *sb.*] The edible seaweed *Alaria esculenta*, also called *badderlocks*.

Heo, *dial.* **hoo**, *pers. pron.*, *3rd sing. fem.*, *nom. Obs.* exc. *dial.* [OE. *hiu, hio, héo*, fem. of HE. Later, the north. and e. midl. dialects exchanged *hio, heo, hyo, ȝho, ȝhe* for the forms, north. *sco, scho, sho*, e. midl. *scæ, sȝe, sche*, SHE.] The original fem. pron. corresponding to *he*; now repl. by SHE. Used of women, and of things grammatically feminine.

Heortology (hiǫɹtǫ·lŏdʒi). 1900. [ad. F. *héortologie*, G. *heortologie* (Gr. ἑορτή festival, -LOGY).] The department of ecclesiology which deals with festivals. Hence **-o·logist**.

Hep, var. form of HIP *sb.*[2]

‖**Hepar** (hī·paɹ). 1693. [med.L., a. Gr. ἧπαρ liver, in reference to its colour.] *Chem.* and *Med.* **1.** An old name for a metallic sulphide, having a reddish brown or liver colour. Also, for compounds of sulphur with other substances. 1796. **2.** Also more fully, *hepar sulphuris* or *hepar sulphur*: **a.** (*H. s. kalinum*) Old name for *potassa sulphurata* 1693. **b.** (*H. s. calcareum*) Homœopathic name for calcium sulphide 1866.

Hepat-, bef. a vowel = HEPATO-, comb. f. Gr. ἧπαρ, ἡπατ- liver: as in **Hepata·lgia**, neuralgia of the liver; hence **Hepata·lgic** *a.* **Hepatemphra·xis** [Gr. ἔμφραξις], obstruction of the liver; hence **Hepatemphra·ctic** *a.*

Hepatic (hĭpæ·tik). ME. [ad. L. *hepaticus*, a. Gr. ἡπατικός.]

A. *adj.* **1.** Of or pertaining to the liver 1599. **2.** Acting on the liver 1671. **3.** Liver-coloured, dark brownish-red; as in *H. aloes* ME. **4.** Pertaining to a hepar; sulphurous 1651. †**5.** *H. moss*, a liverwort (see HEPATICA 2) 1824.

1. Phr. *H. artery, ducts*; *h. apoplexy, disease.* 3. *H. pyrites*, decomposed liver-brown tessular crystals of iron pyrites. 4 †*H. air* or *gas*, sulphuretted hydrogen 1786. So †**Hepa·tical** *a.* (in sense 1).

B. *sb.* A medicine that acts on the liver and increases the secretion of bile 1486.

‖**Hepatica** (hĭpæ·tikă). 1548. [med.L., fem. (quasi *herba hepatica*) of *hepaticus*; see prec.] *Bot.* **1.** A subgenus or section of the genus *Anemone*; esp. *Anemone* (*Hepatica*) *triloba*, the three-lobed leaves of which were fancied to resemble the liver 1578. **2.** An old name for Common Liverwort, *Marchantia polymorpha*, a lichen-like plant which creeps over wet rocks and damp ground, rooting from the lower surface of the thallus. *Hepaticæ*, a group of Cryptogams allied to the Mosses, containing plants which have no operculum, and as a rule possess elaters; e.g. the Common Liverwort.

†**Hepatite**[1] (he·pătəit). ME. [ad. L. *hepatitis*, a. Gr.] A precious stone (*hepatitis gemma* Pliny) said to resemble the liver -1706.

Hepatite[2]. 1802. [Named by Karsten (*Hepatit*), from the older name *lapis hepaticus*.] *Min.* A name of varieties of Barytes emitting a fetid, sulphurous, or hepatic odour when rubbed or heated; liver-stone.

‖**Hepatitis** (hepătəi·tis). 1727. [a. Gr. ἡπατῖτις adj.; see -ITIS.] *Path.* Inflammation of the substance of the liver.

Hepatization (hepătəizēⁱ·ʃən). 1796. [f. next.] †**1.** *Chem.* Impregnation with sulphuretted hydrogen. KIRWAN. **2.** *Path.* Consolidation of the lung tissue, so that it becomes solid and friable somewhat like liver, being first of a red and afterwards of a grey colour 1822.

Hepatize (he·pătəiz), *v.* 1786. [f. Gr. ἧπαρ, ἡπατ- liver + -IZE.] *trans.* †**a.** *Chem.* To impregnate with sulphuretted hydrogen. **b.** *Path.* To convert (the lungs) by engorgement and effusion into a substance resembling liver.

a. Hepatized water 1786, ammonia 1834.

Hepato-, repr. Gr. ἡπατο-, comb. f. ἧπαρ liver; as in

He·patocele [Gr. κήλη tumour], hernia of the liver. **Hepatocy·stic** [CYST] *a.*, pertaining to the liver and the gall-bladder, or uniting the two. **Hepato-ga·stric** *a.*, pertaining to both the liver and the stomach. **Hepatoge·nic, Hepato·genous** *adjs.*, originating from the liver. **He·patolith** [Gr. λίθος], a gall-stone; hence **Hepatoli·thic** *a.* **Hepato·logy** [-LOGY], that part of medical science which treats of the liver; hence **Hepato·logist; Hepatolo·gical** *a.* **He·patopa·ncreas**, *Biol.* name for the glandular organ, called the liver in Invertebrates, in reference to its twofold function of secretion and digestion. **Hepato-re·nal** *a.*, relating to the liver and the kidneys. **Hepato·scopy** [Gr. -σκοπία], inspection of the liver; divination by means of this.

‖**Hephæstus** (hĭfī·stŏs). 1658. = Gr. Ἥφαιστος god of fire, identified by the Romans with Vulcan. Hence **Hephæ·stian** *a.* of, belonging to, or made by H. **Hephæ·stic** *a.* relating to fire, the forge, or use of the smith's hammer.

Hephthemimer (hefþĭmi·məɹ). Occas. **hephthemim.** 1706. [ad. late L. *hephthemimeres* (*-is*), a. Gr. ἑφθημιμερής 'containing seven halves', f. ἑπτ(ά + ἡμι- + μέρος, -μερης. Also used in L. form.] *Anc. Pros.* A group or catalectic colon of seven half-feet; the part of a hexameter preceding the cæsura when this divides the fourth foot, as in

'Inferretque deos Latio • genus unde Latinum •. Hence **Hephthemi·meral** *a.*, as in *h. cæsura.*

Hepper. 1861. Local name of a smolt, or young salmon of the second year.

Hepta-, bef. a vowel HEPT-, comb. f. Gr. ἑπτά seven. In *Chem.* it indicates the presence of seven atoms of an element, as *heptacarbon*, etc.

Heptaco·lic [Gr. κῶλον] *a.*, in ancient prosody: of seven cola or members, as 'a heptacolic period'. ‖**Hepta·meron** [Gr. ἡμέρα], a seven days' work; title of a collection of stories made by Queen Margaret of Navarre, *a* 1549 (cf. DECAMERON). **Heptaphy·llous** *a.*, *Bot.* having seven leaves or calyx sepals. **Heptase·mic** [late L. *heptasemos*, a. Gr.] *a.*, in ancient prosody: containing seven units of time or moræ. **Heptaspe·rmous** [Gr. σπέρμα] *a.*, *Bot.* bearing seven seeds. **He·ptastich** [Gr. στίχος], *sb.*, a group of seven lines of verse; *a.*, seven lines long. **Hepta·valent** [L. *valentem*] *a.*, *Chem.* combining with or capable of replacing seven atoms of hydrogen or other univalent element or radical.

Heptachord (he·ptăkǭɹd). 1694. [ad. Gr. ἑπτάχορδος, f. ἑπτά seven + χορδή string, CHORD.] *Mus.* †**1.** *adj.* Seven-stringed. **2.** *sb.* **a.** A musical instrument of seven strings 1765. **b.** A series of seven notes, formed of two conjunct tetrachords 1774. **c.** The interval of a seventh 1694.

Heptad (he·ptæd). 1660. [ad. Gr. ἑπτάς, ἑπταδ-, seven collectively.] **1.** The sum or number of seven; a group of seven; *spec.* = HEBDOMAD 1876. **2.** *Chem.* An atom or molecule whose equivalence is seven atoms of hydrogen. Hence **Hepta·dic** *a.*

He·ptaglot, *a.* and *sb.* 1684. [f. Gr. ἑπτά + γλῶττα tongue, -γλωττος -tongued.] **a.** *adj.* Using or written in seven languages. **b.** *sb.* A book in seven languages.

Heptagon (he·ptăgǫn). 1570. [ad. Gr. ἑπτάγωνον adj. neut., seven-cornered.] **1.** *Geom.* A plane figure having seven angles and seven sides. **2.** *attrib.* or *adj.* 1775. Hence **Hepta·gonal** *a.* having seven angles and seven sides. *Heptagonal numbers*, the series of POLYGONAL numbers 1, 7, 18, 34, 55, 81, etc. formed by continuous summation of the arithmetical series 1, 6, 11, 16, 21, 26, etc.

‖**Heptagynia** (heptădʒi·niă). 1760. [mod. L., f. HEPTA- + Gr. γυνή, taken in the sense of female organ, pistil.] *Bot.* An order in the Linnæan Sexual System, comprising plants having seven pistils. So **He·ptagyn**, a plant of this order. **Heptagy·nian, Heptagy·nious** *adjs.* of or pertaining to this order. **Hepta·gynous** *a.* having seven pistils.

Heptahedron (-hī·drǫn, -he·drǫn). 1658 [f. HEPTA- + Gr. ἕδρα base.] A solid figure having seven faces. So **Heptahe·dral** *a.* seven-sided, seven-faced.

Heptamerous (heptæ·mĕrəs), *a.* 1790. [f. HEPTA- + Gr. μέρος + -OUS.] Consisting of seven members or parts.

‖**Hepta·ndria.** 1753. [mod.L., f. (ult.) HEPTA- + ἀνδρ- stem of Gr. ἀνήρ man, male; cf. DIANDRIA.] *Bot.* The seventh class in the Sexual System of Linnæus, containing plants having seven stamens. So **Hepta·nder**, a member of this class. **Hepta·ndrian** *a.* of or belonging to H. **Hepta·ndrous** *a.* having seven stamens.

Heptane (he·ptēⁱn). 1877. [f. HEPT(A- + -ANE, formative of the names of paraffins.] *Chem.* The paraffin of the heptacarbon series, having the formula C_7H_{16}. 'Of these hydrocarbons nine are possible and four are known' (*Fownes' Chem.*). So **Heptene** (he·ptīn) [see -ENE], the olefine of the heptacarbon series (C_7H_{14}) also called **He·ptylene**, homologous and polymeric with ethene (C_2H_4); it is known to exist in three isomeric forms. **Heptine** (he·ptəin) [see -INE], the hydrocarbon of the same series (C_7H_{12}), homologous with acetyline or ethine. **Hepto·ic** *a.*, applied to fatty acids, aldehydes, etc. belonging to the heptacarbon series, as *heptoic acid*, $C_7H_{14}O_2$. **He·ptil** (he·ptil) [see -YL], the hydrocarbon radical (C_7H_{15}) of heptylic or oenanthylic alcohol and its derivatives; hence **Hepty·lic** *a.*; **He·ptylami·ne** (see AMINE).

Heptarch (he·ptaɹk). 1679. [f. HEPTA- + Gr. -αρχος; cf. next and *tetrarch.*] A ruler of one division of a heptarchy 1822. †**b.** A seventh king (see Rev. xvii. 9-11).

B. *adj. Bot.* Arising from seven distinct points of origin 1884.

So **Hepta·rchal, Hepta·rchic, -al** *adjs.* of or pertaining to a heptarchy.

Heptarchy (he·ptaɹki). 1576. [ad. mod.L. *heptarchia*, f. Gr. ἑπτά HEPTA- + -αρχία, after *tetrarchy.*] A government by seven rulers; an aggregate of seven petty kingdoms, each under its own ruler; *spec.* the seven kingdoms established by the Angles and Saxons. Also †**Heptarchate** 1650.

In that Heptarchie of our Saxons, vsually six of the Kings were but as subiects to the supreme SELDEN.

Heptasyllabic (heptăsilæ·bik), *a.* (*sb.*) 1771. [f. Gr. ἑπτά + συλλαβή + -IC.] (A verse) consisting of seven syllables.

Heptateuch (he·ptătiūk). 1678. [ad. Gr. ἑπτάτευχος, f. ἑπτά + τεῦχος a book.] A volume consisting of seven books; *occas.*, the first seven books of the Bible, after *Pentateuch.*

Her (hǝɹ, hĕɹ), *pers. pron.*, *3rd sing. fem.*, *dat.-accus.* [OE. *hire*, dative case of *hío*, HEO 'she', used in 10th c. instead of the original accus. *híe, hí, hig, hý*, and now repr. both cases, as in 'we met *her* and gave *her* the book to take with *her*'.] **1.** The female being in question: the objective case of SHE. **2.** For names of things feminine grammatically, or (later) by personification OE. **b.** Represented as used by Welsh or Gaelic speakers for *he, him*, or for the speaker himself 1526. **3.** *refl.* = herself; to herself. (Now *poetic.*) OE. **4.** Erron. for the *nominative* 1698.

Her (hǝɹ, həɹ), *poss. pron.*, *3rd sing. fem.* [OE. *hiere, hire*, gen. of *hío*, HEO 'she'. In OE. used both as an objective and possessive genitive; later as a possessive genitive only, with an absolute form HERS[1], also in later ME. HERN[1] (still *dial.*).] **1.** as *gen. case* of *pers. pron.*: Of her. OE. and ME. only. **2.** *Poss. adj. pron.* (orig. *poss. gen.*): Of or belonging to her; that female's; also *refl.* her own OE. **b.** Used of things feminine †grammatically, or by personification OE. **c.** Of animals regarded as feminine, irrespectively of sex ME. **3.** After a *sb.*, a substitute for the gender inflexion OE.

2. Her hopes, her fears, her joys, were all Bounded within the cloister wall SCOTT. **b.** The prestes broughte the Arke .. vnto hir place COVERDALE 2 *Chron.* v. 7. The Shippe boaring the Moone with her maine Mast SHAKS. **c.** Go to the Emmet (thou slogarde) considre hir wayes COVERDALE *Prov.* vi. 6. 3. The wyf of bathe hire tale ME.

†**Her**, *poss. pron.*, *3rd pl.* [OE. *hiera, hira*; *hyra, hiora, hiara, heora*, gen. pl., in all genders, of HE. In ME. treated as a possessive adj. Early encroached upon by *þeȝȝre* from Old Norse, which, in the form *their*, prevailed before 1500. The form *her* has long disappeared.]

Heraclean (herăklī·ăn), *a.* 1883. [f. L. *Heracleus*, also *-clius*, a. Gr., f. Ἡρακλῆς (see HERCULES); see -AN.] Pertaining to Heracles.

H. stone (*lapis Heracleus*, λίθος Ἡρακλεία): the magnet, so called from its great attractive power.

Heracleid, -id (he·răklǝid, -id). 1835. [ad. Gr. Ἡρακλείδης (pl. -αι), L. *Heracleides* (pl. -æ), a descendant of Ἡρακλῆς or Hercules.] One of the descendants of Heracles from whom the Dorian aristocracy of the Peloponnesus claimed descent. (Usu. in *pl.*) Hence **Heraclei·dan** *a.* pertaining to a H.

Heracleonite (heræ·kliŏnǝit). 1555. [f. name *Heracleon* + -ITE.] *Eccl. Hist.* One of a sect of Gnostics founded by Heracleon in the 2nd c.

Heraclitean (he·răklǝitī·ăn), *a.* (*sb.*) 1864. [f. L. *Heracliteus*, Gr. Ἡρακλείτειος + -AN.] 1. Of, pertaining to, or of the style of Heraclitus of Ephesus, of the 5th c. B.C. (called the 'weeping philosopher'), or his theories. 2. *sb.* A disciple of Heraclitus 1882. So **Heracli·tic** *a.* and *sb.*

Herald (he·răld), *sb.* [ME. *heraud*, *herault*, etc., repr. OF. *heraut*, *herault*, med.L. *haraldus*, *heraldus*; perh. from Teut.] 1. An officer having the duty of making royal or state proclamations, and of bearing ceremonial messages between princes or sovereign powers. Also, b., employed in the tourney to make proclamations, convey challenges, and marshal the combatants ME. Hence, c., having the function of arranging public processions, funerals, etc.; of regulating the use of armorial bearings (cf. DISCLAIM *v.*); of settling questions of precedence; and, later, of recording proved pedigrees ME. 2. *transf.* and *fig.* a. A messenger, envoy. Hence, a title of newspapers. ME. b. A forerunner, precursor 1592. 3. One skilled in heraldry 1821. 4. (In full, *Herald-moth.*) One of the noctuid moths, *Gonoptera libatrix* 1832.

1. †*Herald of arms* ME., †*h. at arms* 1646. †*King h.*, *Lyon h.*: ancient names of Garter king-of-arms and Lyon king-of-arms; see KING-OF-ARMS. *Heralds' College*, or *College of Arms*: a royal corporation, founded 1483, consisting of the Earl Marshal, kings-of-arms, heralds, and pursuivants, exercising jurisdiction in matters armorial, and now recording proved pedigrees and granting armorial bearings. *Heralds' Office*, the office of this corporation. 2. a. His tongue, the H. of his imagination, is a busie Officer 1615. b. It was the Larke the Herauld of the Morne SHAKS. *Comb.*: **h.-crab** = *heraldic crab*; **-moth**: see sense 4. Hence †**He·raldize** *v.* to emblazon. **He·raldship**, the office or dignity of a h.

He·rald, *v.* ME. [a. OF. *herauder*, *heraulder*, etc., f. prec.] *trans.* To proclaim, to announce, as at hand or drawing nigh; to usher *in*.

Heraldic, -al (hĕræ·ldik, -ăl), *a.* 1772. [f. HERALD *sb.*, prob. after Fr.] Of or pertaining to heraldry. Also *fig.*

Heraldic crab: a Japanese crab, *Huenia heraldica*, one of the *Maiadæ*; so called because the shape of its carapace suggests the shield and mantle of coat armour. Hence **Hera·ldically** *adv.*

Heraldry (he·răldri). 1572. [f. HERALD *sb.* + -RY; cf. *poetry*.] 1. The art or science of a herald; now esp. the art or science of blazoning armorial bearings, of tracing and recording pedigrees, and of deciding questions of precedence. †b. Heraldic practice. *Haml.* I. i. 87. †c. Heraldic title, rank, or precedence. *All's Well* II. iii. 280. 2. A heraldic emblazonment or device; also *collect.*; armorial bearings; heraldic symbolism. Also *fig.* 1593. 3. The office of herald 1594. 4. Heraldic pomp 1630.

2. This Heraudry in Lucrece face was seene, Argued by Beauties red and Vertues white SHAKS. So †**He·raldy** (in senses 1, 2).

Heraud, -aut, etc., obs. ff. HERALD.

Herb (hǝ̄ɹb), *sb.* [In ME. usually *erbe*, a. OF. *erbe* (mod. *herbe*) :—L. *herba*. Refash. after L.; but with *h* mute until 19th c.] 1. A plant of which the stem does not become woody and persistent, but dies down to the ground (or entirely) after flowering. 2. Applied to plants of which the leaves, or stem and leaves, are used for food or medicine, or for their scent or flavour ME. 3. *collect.* Herbage. Also *fig.* ME. 4. The leafy part of a plant, as dist. from the root 1662.

2. Erbis of vertue þat growen in them WYCLIF. *Comb.*: **h. beer**, a beverage prepared from herbs; **-tea, -water**, a medicinal infusion of herbs. b. In names of plants, as **h. Gerard**, Goutweed, *Ægopodium Podagraria*; **h. Margaret**, 'the daisy, *Bellis perennis*' (Prior); **h.-royal** [F. *herbe royale*] southernwood. See also *H.* ALOE, *H.* BENNET, *H.* CHRISTOPHER, *H.* TRINITY; also HERB-GRACE, H. PARIS, H. ROBERT, etc.

†‖**Herba**. 1585. [It.] A sort of grass-cloth imported formerly from India –1813.

Herbaceous (hǝɹbē̆ⁱ·ʃǝs), *a.* 1646. [f. L. *herbaceus* grassy, f. *herba*; see -ACEOUS.] 1. Of the nature of a herb; *esp.* not forming wood, but dying down every year; consisting of such plants, as *h. border*. b. Of the texture and colour of an ordinary leaf 1794. †2. Herbivorous. DERHAM.

1. Ginger is the root of neither tree nor shrub, but of an h. plant SIR T. BROWNE. b. Flowers..only green, or what botanists call h. MARTYN. **Herba·ceously** *adv.*

Herbage (hǝ̄·ɹbėdʒ). [ME. *erbage*, a. F., ad. med.L. *herbaticum*, f. *herba*: see -AGE.] 1. Herbs collectively; herbaceous growth or vegetation; esp. grass, etc., as used for pasture. 1390. 2. = HERB 4. 1701. 3. *Law.* The natural herbage of any land as a distinct species of property; hence 'a liberty that a man hath to feede his catell in another mans ground, as in the forest' (Cowell) 1450.

1. Chalk hills, covered with a scanty h. SIR B. BRODIE. Hence **He·rbaged** *a.* covered with h.

Herbal (hǝ̄·ɹbăl), *sb.* 1516. [f. L. *herbalis* adj. (in med.L.); cf. med.L. *manuale* handbook, etc.] 1. A book containing the names and descriptions of herbs, or of plants in general. *Obs.* exc. *Hist.* †2. = HERBARIUM. –1847.

Herbal (hǝ̄ɹbăl), *a.* 1612. [f. as prec.] 1. Belonging to, consisting of, or made from herbs. †2. Herbaceous 1682.

Herbalist (hǝ̄·ɹbălist). 1592. [f. HERBAL *sb.* + -IST.] 1. One versed in the knowledge of herbs or plants; a botanist. Now used of the early botanical writers. 1594. 2. A dealer in medicinal herbs or simples 1592. So †**He·rbalism** (*rare*), also †**He·rbarism**, the science of herbs or plants. **He·rbalize** *v.* (*arch.*), to collect (medicinal) herbs.

Herbar(e, obs. var. of ARBOUR.

†**Herba·rian**. 1577. [f. as next + -AN.] A herbalist –1578.

†**Herbarist**. 1577. [f. L. *herbaria* (sc. *ars*) botany + -IST.] A herbalist –1794.

Herbarium (hǝɹbē̆ᵊ·riŏm). 1776. [Late L.; adj. neut. f. *herba*; see -ARIUM.] A collection of dried plants systematically arranged; a *hortus siccus*. Also, a book or case for such a collection.

He·rbarize, *v. arch.* 1670. [f. as HERBARIST + -IZE.] = HERBORIZE.

Herbary (hǝ̄·ɹbări), *sb.* 1548. [Three wds.: ad. L. *herbarius* herbalist; *herbarium* 'collection of dried plants', etc.; L. *herbaria* botany.] †1. A herbalist –1568. 2. A herbarium 1591. 3. A garden of herbs or vegetables 1634. †4. The science of herbs. HAKEWILL.

Herbergage: see HARBERGAGE.

Herberger(e, -geour, -jour, etc., obs. ff. HARBINGER.

Herbescent (hǝɹbe·sĕnt), *a.* 1727. [f. L. *herba* + -ESCENT.] Growing like a herb; becoming herbaceous.

Herb-grace, herb of grace. 1548. [app. of English origin; perh. due to the coincidence of the name *Rue* with RUE *v.* and *sb.* repent, repentance.] 1 The herb Rue, *Ruta graveolens*. Now *Obs.* or *dial.* 2. A herb of virtue 1866. Also *fig.*

1. Ther's Rew for you, and heere's some for me. Wee may call it Herbe-Grace a Sundaies SHAKS.

Herbid (hǝ̄·ɹbid), *a.* ? *Obs.* 1657. [ad. L. *herbidus*, f. *herba*; see -ID.] Grassy, grass-like.

Herbiferous (hǝɹbi·fĕrǝs), *a.* 1656. [f. L. *herbifer* + -OUS.] Bearing herbs.

†**Herbist**. 1611. [f. HERB + -IST.] = HERBALIST. –1656.

‖**Herbivora** (hǝɹbi·vŏră), *sb. pl.* 1830. [neut. pl. (sc. *animalia*) of L. *herbivorus*.] *Zool.* A general name for animals, esp. Mammals, that feed on herbage or plants. *spec.* A division of Marsupials, including the kangaroos; also a division of Cetacea. So **He·rbivore**, one of the H. **Herbi·vorous** *a.* herb-eating; of or pertaining to the H.

†**Herb John**. 1440. [tr. OF. *herbe Johan*, med.L. *herba Johannis*, in sense 1.] 1. St. John's-wort, *Hypericum perforatum* –1460. 2. App. some tasteless neutral herb; hence, something inert or indifferent –1679.

2. Like Herb-John in the pot, that does neither much good nor hurt GURNALL.

He·rbless, *a.* 1682. [-LESS.] Destitute of herbs or herbage.

He·rblet. [-LET.] A little herb. SHAKS.

Herborist (hǝ̄·ɹbŏrist). 1578. [a. F. *herboriste*, 'from *herbe* by confusion with the radical of L. *arbor*' (Darmesteter).] A herbalist.

Herborize (hǝ̄·ɹbŏrǝiz), *v.* 1664. [a. F. *herboriser*; see prec.] 1. *intr.* To garden (*rare*). 2. To gather herbs; to botanize 1749. Hence **He:rboriza·tion**, the action of herborizing; also, by confusion, for ARBORIZATION.

Herborized, *ppl. a.* 1788. Used by confusion for *arborized*.

H. stones contain very fine mosses *tr. Fourcroy*.

Herbose (hǝɹbōᵘ·s), *a.* 1721. [ad. L. *herbosus*; see -OSE.] Abounding in herbs or herbage.

Herbous (hǝ̄·ɹbǝs), *a.* 1712. [ad. L. *herbosus*; see prec.] Of the nature of a herb; herbaceous.

Herb Paris. 1578. [ad. med.L. *herba paris*; ? gen. of *par*; or the Trojan *Paris*.] A book-name for *Paris quadrifolia* (N.O. *Trilliaceæ*), also called True-love, a dictyogenous plant, bearing a single greenish flower at the top of the stem, and just beneath it four large ovate leaves in the form of a cross.

Herb Robert. ME. [ad. med.L. *herba Roberti*. Variously referred to Robert Duke of Normandy, to St. Robert, and to St. Rupert.] A common wild species of Crane's-bill or Geranium (*G. Robertianum*).

Herbrough, obs. f. HARBOUR, *sb.* and *v.*

He·rb-woman. 1608. A woman who sells herbs.

Herby (hǝ̄·ɹbi), *a.* 1552. [-Y.] 1. Full of herbs; grassy. 2. Herbaceous; pertaining to herbs 1552.

1. An h. seat on broad Scamander's shore CHAPMAN.

Hercogamy (hǝɹkǫ·gămi). Also **herk-**. 1880. [f. Gr. ἕρκος fence + γάμος, -γαμια.] *Bot.* The prevention of self-fertilization in flowers by means of structural obstacles. Hence **Hercoga·mic, -o·gamous** *adjs.* unable to be self-fertilized.

Herculanean (hǝ̄ɹkiulē̆ⁱ·niăn), *a.* 1780. [f. L. *Herculaneus* + -AN.] Of or pertaining to Herculaneum, a town in Campania, which was buried with Pompeii in the eruption of Vesuvius 79 A.D.

Herculean (hǝɹkiū·liăn), *a.* 1596. [f. L. *Herculeus*, (f. *Hercules*) + -AN.] 1. Of or pertaining to Hercules 1610. 2. Like Hercules, esp. in strength, courage, or labours 1596. b. *transf.* Of things: Strong, powerful, violent 1602. 3. Requiring the strength of a Hercules; difficult to accomplish; excessive, immense 1617.

1. *H. pillars, straits*: see HERCULES. 2. The Danite strong, H. Samson MILT. 3. An h. task 1875.

Hercules (hǝ̄·ɹkiulīz). ME. [L., ad. Gr. Ἡρακλῆς, f. Ἥρα, Hera, wife of Zeus + κλέος glory, lit. 'having or showing the glory of Hera'.] 1. A hero of Greek and Roman mythology, celebrated for his great strength, and for the accomplishment of the twelve extraordinary tasks or 'labours' imposed upon him by Hera. After death he was ranked among the gods. b. A representation of Hercules 1638. 2. One who resembles Hercules in strength; a strong man 1567. 3. A name given to powerful machines; esp. a machine for cleansing the streets 1890. 4. *Entom.* (In full, *H. Beetle.*) A gigantic lamellicorn beetle, *Dynastes* (or *Megasoma*) *Hercules* 1816. 5. *Astron.* One of the northern constellations 1551.

1. 'Not H. against two' the proverb is GREENE. *Pillars of H.*, *Hercules' Pillars*: the rocks Calpé (now Gibraltar) and Abyla (Ceuta), on either side of the Strait of Gibraltar, fabled to have been set up by H.; so *Straits of H.* Hence *fig.* an ultimate limit.

Comb.: **H. braid**, a thick corded worsted braid; **H. knot**, a kind of knot very difficult to undo; **H. powder**, a powerful explosive used in mining operations.

Hercules' club. [From the club which Hercules bore.] **a.** A big and formidable stick 1657. **b.** A kind of firework 1688. **c.** A plant, *Xanthoxylon Clava-Herculis*; also, *Aralia spinosa* 1882.

Hercynian (həɹsi·niăn), *a.* 1598. [f. L. *Hercynia* (sc. *silva*); = Gr. Ἑρκύνιος δρυμός see -AN.] Applied to the wooded mountain-system of Middle Germany, or to portions of it; esp. to the Erzgebirge, whence *H. gneiss.*

Herd (hǝ̄ɹd), *sb.*[1] [Com.Teut.: OE. *heord* str. fem.:—OTeut. **herdâ-*=pre-Teut. **kerdhâ*; cf. Skr. *çardha-s* troop.] **1.** A company of domestic animals of one kind, kept together by a keeper. (The notion of a keeper is now little present.) **b.** As contrasted with *flock*, *herd* is restricted to bovine domestic animals 1587. **2.** A company of animals of any kind feeding or travelling together; a school (of whales, etc.) ME. **3.** A multitude of people. (Now always disparaging.) ME. **b.** Of things: A great number 1618.

1. The lowing h. winds slowly o'er the lea GRAY. **b.** *Lev.* xxvii. 32. **2.** The grisly Boar is singled from his H. SOMERVILLE. **3.** A h. of parasites JAS. MILL. Phr. *The herd*: the multitude, the rabble.

Herd, *sb.*[2] [Com. Teut.: OE. *hirde, hierde*, etc.:—OTeut. **herdjo-z*, f. **herdâ-* HERD *sb.*[1]] **1.** A keeper of a herd or flock of domestic animals; a herdsman. Now usu. in comb., but in the north a common word for *shepherd*. †**2.** *fig.* A pastor –1562.

Herd (hǝ̄ɹd), *v.*[1] ME. [f. HERD *sb.*[1]] **1.** *intr.* To go in a herd; to form a herd or herds. Said also contemptuously of men. **b.** Of things: To come together 1704. **2.** To join oneself to any band or company, faction or party; to go in company *with* ME. **3.** *trans.* To place in or among a herd. Also *fig.* 1592. **4.** To collect into a herd. Also *fig.* To amass. 1615.

1. They are but sheep which alwaies heard together SIDNEY. **3.** The rest, However great we are, honest, and valiant, Are hearded with the vulgar B. JONS.

Herd, *v.*[2] ME. [f. HERD *sb.*[2]] **1.** *trans.* To tend (sheep or cattle). Also *fig.* Also *intr.* †**2.** *fig.* (*trans.*) To keep safe –1560.

1. *fig.* God, who herds the stars of heaven As sheep within his sheepfold SWINBURNE.

He·rd-book. 1822. [f. HERD *sb.*[1] + BOOK.] A book containing the pedigree, etc. of a breed of cattle or pigs.

Herd-boy. 1637. [orig. f. HERD *sb.*[2] + BOY; but later erron. referred to HERD *sb.*[1], whence *herd's-boy*. See HERDSMAN.] **1.** A boy who acts as a herd or assists a herd. **2.** A cow-boy. *U.S.* and *colonial Eng.* 1878.

Herder (hǝ̄·ɹdəɹ). Chiefly *U.S.* 1635. [f. HERD *v.*[2] + -ER[1].] A herdsman. Also *fig.*

Herderite (hǝ̄·ɹdərəit). 1828. [f. Baron S. A. W. von *Herder*.] *Min.* A fluo-phosphate of glucinum and calcium, found in brilliant transparent crystals.

He·rdess. ME. [f. HERD *sb.*[2] + -ESS.] A shepherdess.

Herd-grass, herd's-grass. *U.S.* 1747. [f. HERD *sb.*[1] + GRASS.] Any grass grown for hay or pasture; esp. Timothy, *Phleum pratense*, and Redtop, *Agrostis vulgaris*.

†**Herd-groom.** ME. [f. HERD *sb.*[2] + GROOM.] A shepherd-lad –1633.

Herdic (hǝ̄·ɹdik). *U.S.* 1882. [f. Peter *Herdic*, the inventor.] A cab with a low-hung body, entered at the back.

†**He·rdman.** OE. [f. HERD *sb.*[2] + MAN.] A herdsman; *fig.* and *transf.* esp. a spiritual pastor –1656.

Herdsman (hǝ̄·ɹdzˌmæ̆n). 1603. [Altered f. HERDMAN (after *craftsman*, etc.), introduced when HERD *sb.*[2] went out of English use; thus = man of a herd. In the north HERD *sb.*[2] remains in use.] **1.** A keeper of domestic animals which go in herds. **2.** *Orkney*. The Common Skua 1885. So **He·rdswoman**, a woman who tends cattle SCOTT.

Herdwick (hǝ̄·ɹdwik). OE. [f. HERD *sb.*[2] + WICK; cf. *bailiwick*.] †**1.** The tract of land under the charge of a 'herd' employed by the owner; a pasture-ground –1564. **2.** (In full *H. sheep*): A hardy breed of mountain sheep, supposed to have originated on the herdwicks of the Abbey of Furness 1837.

†**Here**, *sb.* [Com.Teut.: OE. *here* masc. App. a deriv. (adj.) from a radical *har-*, pre-Teut. *kar-, kor-* in sense 'war'. Hence HARRY *v.*, HARBOUR, HERIOT *sbs.*] An armed host, an army. Also: A host; a great company –1470.

Here (hīᵊɹ), *adv.* [Com. Teut.: OE. *hēr*; app. from the pronominal stem *hi-* 'this' (see HE).] **1.** In this place; in the place where the speaker is, or places himself. **b.** *ellipt.* = Present, *adsum* OE. **c.** = Whom or which you see here 1596. **d.** Used for emphasis 1460. **2.** *Here is* = there is here, see or behold here. (F. *voici*.) 1460. **b.** *Here's to*: ellipt. for *Here's a health to* 1592. **3.** In this world; in this life; on earth OE. **4.** At this point in action, speech, or thought; in this passage OE. **5.** In this matter; in this case; in this particular ME. **6.** In ordinary use, taking the place of HITHER OE. **7.** Used ellipt. in calling an attendant, etc. Hence, to call attention to or introduce a command. 1632.

1. He is not h.: for he is risen *Matt.* xxviii. 6. **b.** *Mids. N.* I. ii. 45. **c.** My brother, h., is ready to give information (*mod.*). **2.** Heere's a change indeed in the Commonwealth SHAKS. **b.** Heere's to my Loue SHAKS. **3.** Man wants but little h. below GOLDSM. **4.** H. followeth the Anthem *Bk. Com. Prayer*. **5.** H. was his sin; An over-reaching of his commission BP. HALL. **6.** Call Pedro h. BYRON. **7.** H., take away the Tea-table SWIFT.

Phrases. **Here and there. a.** In this place and in that; at intervals of space (or time). **b.** To this place and to that; to and fro. **Here, there, and everywhere.** In every place, indicated or not. **Neither here nor there.** Of no account either one way or the other. **Here below.** On this earth, in this world. **Here goes!** An exclam. declaring one's resolution or resignation to perform some (bold or rash) act. **Here we (you) are.** Here is what we (you) want, *colloq.* **Here-** in comb. with adverbs and preps. These originated in the juxtaposition of *here* and another adv. qualifying the same vb., but later the adv. came to be felt as a prep., governing *here*.

B. as *sb.*: = This place; also, the present; the present life (*Lear* I. i. 264).

Hereabout (hīᵊrăbau·t), *adv.* ME. [f. HERE *adv.* + ABOUT.] †**1.** About or concerning this –1644. **2.** About or near this place ME. So **Hereabou·ts** *adv.*

Hereafter (hīᵊra·ftəɹ), *adv.* (*a., sb.*) [OE. *hēræfter*, f. *hēr* HERE *adv.* + AFTER.] **1.** After, in this writing, book, or place; occas. = immediately after. **2.** After this in time; in time to come OE. **3.** In a future state 1618. **4.** *adj.* To come, future (now *rare*) 1591.

2. More of this h. SHAKS. **4.** H. Ages SHAKS.

B. *sb.* **1.** Time to come; the future 1546. **2.** A future life; the world to come 1702.

2. What, if there be an h., a judgment to come? WESLEY.

†**Herea·fterward**, *adv.* Also **-wards.** ME. [f. HERE *adv.* + AFTERWARD.] = prec. adv. –1674.

Hereane·nt, *adv.* ME. Concerning this.

Hereat (hīᵊræ·t), *adv.* ME. [f. HERE *adv.* + AT.] †**1.** At this place; here –1650. **2.** At this; as a result of this 1557.

2. All admired h. FULLER.

Hereaway (hīᵊ·răwē¹), *adv.* Now *dial.* and *U.S.* ME. [f. as prec. + AWAY *adv.*] **1.** Away in this direction; hereabouts. **2.** Hither 1549.

Hereby (hīᵊɹbəi·, hīᵊ·ɹbəi), *adv.* ME. [f. HERE *adv.* + BY *prep.*] †**1.** (*hereby·*) By or near this place; close by –1655. **2.** By, through, or from this ME.

1. *L.L.L.* IV. i. 9. **2.** And h. wee doe knowe that we know him, if wee keepe his commandements 1 *John* ii. 3.

Hereditable (hĭre·dităb'l), *a.* 1494. [ad. L. type **hereditabilis*, f. *heres, heredem*.] **1.** Of things: That may be inherited; heritable. †**2.** Of persons: Capable of inheriting; having a right of inheritance –1655. **Here·ditabi·lity** = *Heritability*. **Here·ditably** *adv.* by way of inheritance.

Hereditament (herĭdi·tămĕnt, hĭre·dită-). 1475. [ad. med.L. *hereditamentum*, f. late L. *hereditare*, f. *heredem*.] **1.** *Law.* Any property that can be inherited; any thing, corporeal or incorporeal, that in the absence of a will descended to the heir at common law, and now to the 'real representative'; real property. **2.** Heirship, inheritance 1509.

Here·ditarily, *adv.* 1603. [f. HEREDITARY *a.* + -LY[2].] In a hereditary manner; by way of (an) inheritance.

Here·ditariness. 1640. [f. as prec. + -NESS.] The quality of being hereditary.

Hereditary (hĭre·ditări), *a.* 1577. [ad. L. *hereditarius*, f. *hereditas*. The L. *heres* and its derivs. were till recently often written *hær-*, whence also in Eng.] **1.** *Law* and *Hist.* Descending by inheritance from generation to generation; that has been or may be transmitted according to definite rules of descent; legally vesting, upon the death of the holder, in his heir 1601. **2.** Transmitted in a line of progeny; passing naturally from parents to offspring 1577. **3.** Of persons: Holding their position by inheritance 1651. **4.** Of or pertaining to inheritance 1790.

1. A h. priesthood..in the family of Aaron STANLEY. **2.** An h. gout 1699. The h. instincts of forest life 1862. **3.** H. bondsmen BYRON. **4.** H. transmission 1879.

Heredity (hĭre·diti). 1540. [a. F. *hérédité*, ad. L. *hereditatem*, f. *heres*; see -ITY.] †**1.** Hereditary succession; inheritance; an inheritance. **2.** *Law.* Hereditary character, quality, or condition; the fact of being hereditary or heritable 1784. **3.** *Biol.* The property in virtue of which offspring inherit the nature and characteristics of parents and ancestors; the tendency of like to beget like. (Often called a law of nature.) 1863.

Heregeld (he·rĕgeld). *Obs.* exc. *Hist.* [OE. *heregield*, f. *here* host, the (Danish) army + *gield*, etc. payment.] *O.E. Hist.* The tribute paid to the Danish host; Danegeld.

Here-hence, *adv.* *Obs.* or *dial.* 1526. [f. HERE *adv.* + HENCE.] **1.** As a result of this –1695. **2.** From henceforth –1616. **3.** From here.

Herein (hīᵊri·n), *adv.* OE. [orig. *hēr inne*, f. *hēr* HERE *adv.* + *innan, inne*, adv., subseq. IN, *adv.* and *prep.*] **1.** Here within, in here; in, also into, this place. **2.** In this ME.

2. Heare in is my father glorified TINDALE *John* xv. 8. **Herein above, h. after, h. before** = above, after, before, in this document, etc., are often written as one word.

Heremeit, -mit, -myt(e, obs. ff. HERMIT.

Hereness (hīᵊ·ɹnės). 1674. [-NESS.] The being here.

Hereof (hīᵊrǫ·v), *adv.* OE. [f. HERE *adv.* + OF *prep.*] **1.** Of this; concerning this. †**2.** From this; from here –1587.

1. Upon the Receipt h. STEELE. **2.** H...began [etc.] 1568.

Hereon (hīᵊrǫ·n), *adv.* Now *rare.* OE. [f. HERE *adv.* + ON *prep.*] †**1.** Herein –1573. **2.** On this subject, matter, etc.; on this basis ME. **3.** = HEREUPON 2. 1602.

Hereout (hīᵊrau·t), *adv.* ME. [f. as prec. + OUT *adv.*] Out of this place; †from this source –1568.

Hereri·ght. *s.w. dial.* ME. Straightway.

Heresiarch (he·rėsiˌāɹk, hĭrī·siˌaɹk). Also *hær-*. 1624. [ad. late L. *hæresiarcha*, ad. Gr., f. αἵρεσις HERESY + -αρχης ruler.] A leader or founder of a heresy. Also *transf.* Hence †**Heresiarchy**, the founding of a heresy; *erron.*, an arch-heresy (SIR T. HERBERT).

Heresiography (he·rėsiǫ·grăfi). 1645. [f. Gr. αἵρεσις + -(O)GRAPHY.] A treatise on heresy or heresies. So **Heresio·grapher**, one who treats of heresies.

Heresiologist (he·rėsiˌǫ·lŏdʒist). 1710. [f. as prec. + -(O)LOGIST.] One who treats of heresy or heresies. So **Heresio·loger. Heresio·logy.**

Heresy (he·rėsi). [ME. *eresie, heresie*, a. OF. *eresie, heresie* (mod. *hérésie*), ad. L. type **heresia*, for L. *hæresis*, a. Gr. αἵρεσις, f. αἱρεῖν to take, middle voice αἱρεῖσθαι to take for oneself, choose.] **1.** Theological opinion or doctrine held in opposition to the 'catholic' or orthodox doctrine of the Christian Church. Also *transf.* **b.** with *a* and *pl.* A heretical opinion or doctrine ME. **2.** Hence, Opinion or doctrine in philosophy, politics, science, art, etc. at variance with what is orthodox. Also with *a* and *pl.* ME. **3.** In sense of Gr. αἵρεσις: A school of thought; a sect ME.

1. Deluded people! that do not consider that the greatest heresie in the world is a wicked life TILLOTSON. b. False teachers..shal brynge in damnable heresies N.T. (Genev.) 2 *Pet.* ii. 1. 2. The doctrine of Evolution..which it is intellectual h...to question 1877. 3. It bihoueth heresies for to be WYCLIF 1 *Cor.* xi. 19. *Comb.* **h.-hunt, -hunter** (1765), **-ing.**

Heretic (he·rĕtik), *sb.* (*a.*) ME. [a. F. *hérétique*, ad. eccl. L. *hæreticus*, a. Gr., f. αἱρέεσθαι to choose; in eccl. writers (after αἵρεσις) heretical, heretic. The position of the stress is due to French derivation.] 1. One who maintains a heresy or heresies (see HERESY 1). 2. Hence, One who maintains opinions on any subject at variance with those generally received 1599. 3. *adj.* = next (*rare*) ME.

1. When a papist uses the word heretics, he generally means the protestants WATTS. 2. Thou wast euer an obstinate heretique in the despight of Beautie SHAKS. 3. Obedience to an h. prince DRYDEN.

Heretical (hĭre·tikăl), *a.* 1532. [ad. med.L. *hæreticalis*; see -AL.] Of or pertaining to heresy or heretics; of the nature of heresy. Hence **Here·tical-ly** *adv.*, **-ness.**

Hereticate (hĭre·tikeɪt), *v.* 1629. [f. med. L. *hæreticat-*, *hæreticare*.] 1. *trans.* To pronounce heretical. 2. To make a heretic of 1731.

1. Arbitrary and hereticating anathemas C. MATHER. 2. Could Peter Auterius really believe that he saved the souls of those whom he hereticated? S. R. MAITLAND. Hence **Heretica·tion.**

Here·ticide. [erron. f. HERETIC + -CIDE 2.] The putting of a heretic to death. C. MATHER.

Hereto (hīəɹtū·), *adv.* ME. [f. HERE *adv.* + TO *prep.*] †1. To this place -1598. 2. To this; with reference to this ME. 3. (Annexed) to this 1559. †4. Hitherto -1607.

Heretofore (hīəɹtŭfōə·ɹ), *adv.* (*a.*, *sb.*) ME. [f. HERE *adv.* + TOFORE, OE. *tóforan*.] 1. Before this; formerly. 2. *adj.* Former 1491. 3. *sb.* Time past 1824.

Heretoga (he·rĕtōugă), **heretoch, -togh.** [OE. *heretoga*, f. *heri*, *here* HERE *sb.* army + OE. *-toga*, f. *teohan, *téon* to lead; see TEE *v.* (cogn. w. L. *ducere*, *dux*).] *O. E. Hist.* The leader of an army; the commander of the militia of a shire. Taken in 17th and 18th c. as = DUKE.

Hereunder (hīərʊ·ndəɹ), *adv.* ME. [f. HERE *adv.* + UNDER *prep.*] Under this.

Hereunto (hīərʊntū·, -ʊ·ntu), *adv.* 1509. [f. as prec. + UNTO *prep.*] Unto or to this; to this document.

Hereupon (hīərŏpǫ·n), *adv.* ME. [f. as prec. + UPON *prep.*] 1. Upon this matter, etc. 2. Immediately following upon this (in time or consequence) ME.

Herewith (hīəɹwi·ð), *adv.* OE. [f. as prec. + WITH *prep.*] With this; †at the same time with this -1546. So **Herewitha·l** *adv.* (*arch.*).

†Herigaut. ME. [a. OF. *herigaut*.] An upper garment or cloak of 13th and 14th c.

Heriot (he·riǫt). [OE. *heregeatwa*, *-we*, f. *here* HERE *sb.* army, host + *geatwa*, *-we*, equipments, ornaments, armour.] 1. *Eng. Law.* A feudal service, orig. consisting of weapons, horses, or other military equipments, restored to a lord on the death of his tenant; afterwards a render of the best live beast or dead chattel of a deceased tenant due by legal custom to the lord of whom he held. Now an incident of manorial tenures only. Also *transf.* and *fig.* OE. 2. *attrib.*, as *h.-land* OE.

Comb.: **h. custom,** a h. depending merely upon immemorial usage; **h. service,** one due upon a special reservation in a grant or lease of lands. BLACKSTONE.

Hence **He·riotable** *a.* subject to the payment of heriots.

Herisson (he·risən). 1594. [a. F. *hérisson* :—late L. **hericionem* URCHIN, augm. of (*h*)*ericius*.] †1. A hedgehog -1600. ‖2. *Fortif.* A barrier, consisting of a revolving beam, armed with spikes 1704.

Heritable (he·rităb'l), *a.* (*sb.*) ME. [a. F. *héritable*, f. *hériter* :—L. *hereditare*.] 1. Capable of being inherited, inheritable. 2. Naturally transmissible from parent to offspring; hereditary 1570. 3. Of persons: Capable of inheriting; succeeding by right of inheritance 1575. 4. *sb. pl.* (*Sc. Law.*) Heritable possessions; lands and other property that passes to the heir-at-law 1801.

2. No h. disease in the family 1879. Hence **He·ritably** *adv.* by way or right of inheritance *c* 1440. **Heritabi·lity,** h. quality.

Heritage (he·ritėdʒ). ME. [a. OF. *eritage*, *heritage*, f. *hériter*; see -AGE.] 1. That which has been or may be inherited. b. *transf.* and *fig.* The 'portion' allotted to or reserved for any one ME. †2. The fact of inheriting; hereditary succession -1556. 3. Anything given or received to be a proper possession ME. b. The ancient Israelites, as the peculiar possession of God; the Church of God ME. 4. An inherited lot or portion 1621.

1. It was..part of my h., Which my dead father did bequeath to me SHAKS. b. Which hath his h. in helle GOWER. 3. Loe, children are an h. of the Lord *Ps.* cxxvii. 3. b. O Lorde..blesse thyne h. *Bk. Com. Prayer.* 4. Lord of himself;—that h. of woe BYRON.

Heritance (he·rităns). *arch.* ME. [a. OF., f. *hériter*.] Inheritance; heirship. Also *fig.*

Heritor (he·ritǫɹ). 1422. [a. AF. *heriter* :—late L. *hereditarium*, repl. *heredem* heir. See -OR.] 1. An heir or heiress. 2. *Sc. Law.* The proprietor of a heritable subject 1597. Hence **He·ritress, †-trice, -trix.**

Herl, *sb.* ME. [See HARL.] = HARL *sb.*

Herling, hirling. *Sc.* 1684. The name, on the Solway Firth, for the fish *Salmo albus.*

†Herm, ‖**Herma** (hō·ɹmă). 1579. [L. *Herma*, pl. *-æ*, a latinized form of *Hermes*, a. Gr. Ἑρμῆς Mercury.] A statue, consisting of a four-cornered pillar surmounted by a head or bust, usually that of Hermes. Such statues were numerous in ancient Athens, and were used as boundary-marks, mile-stones, sign-posts, etc. So **Hermæ·an** *a.* of Hermes.

Hermaic (həɹmē·ik), *a.* (*sb.*) 1678. [ad. Gr. Ἑρμαϊκός of or like Hermes.] 1. = HERMETIC *a.* 1. b. as *sb.* (*pl.*) The writings attributed to Hermes Trismegistus 1678. 2. = HERMÆAN. 1820.

‖**Hermanda·d.** 1760. [Sp. = brotherhood.] In Spain, orig. a league against the oppression of the nobles; a voluntary organization becoming afterwards regular national police.

†Hermaphrode·ity. [irreg. f. HERMAPHRODITE.] The state of being hermaphrodite. B. JONS.

Herma·phrodism. 1828. [a. F. *hermaphrodisme*.] *Biol.* = HERMAPHRODITISM.

Hermaphrodite (həɹmæ·frŏdəit). ME. [ad. L. *hermaphroditus*, a. Gr. ἑρμαφρόδιτος, orig. proper name of the son of Hermes and Aphrodite, who, according to the myth, grew together with the nymph Salmacis.]

A. *sb.* 1. A human being, or animal, in which parts characteristic of both sexes are combined. b. A catamite. ADDISON. 2. *Zool.* An animal in which the male and female organs are (normally) present in the same individual, as in some molluscs and worms 1727. 3. *Bot.* A plant or flower in which the stamens and pistils are present in the same flower 1727. 4. *fig.* A person or thing in which two opposites are combined 1659.

1. The monstrosity known as h. does exist, but is excessively rare VAN BUREN. 4. Henry the Eighth, was a kind of H. in Religion 1687. A very taught-rigged h., or brig forward and schooner aft 1833.

B. *adj.* 1. Having parts belonging to both sexes combined in the same individual. Also applied to organs which combine the characters of both sexes. 1607. 2. *transf.* and *fig.* Combining two opposites 1593.

1. Nero did shew certain H. Mares TOPSELL. This worm is h. 1797. This plant is occasionally h. in Sikkim HOOKER. 2. H. Convents, wherein Monks and Nuns lived together FULLER. A small h. brig R. H. DANA. Hence **Hermaphrodi·tic, -al** *a.* belonging to or of the nature of a h. (*lit.* and *fig.*); combining two opposites. **Hermaphrodi·tically** *adv.* **Herma·phroditism,** the condition of a h.

Hermeneut (hō·ɹmĭniūt). *rare.* [mod. f. Gr. ἑρμηνευτής, f. ἑρμηνεύειν, f. Ἑρμῆς messenger of the gods.] An interpreter, esp. in the early church.

Hermeneutic, -al (hōɹmĭniū·tik, -ăl), *a.* 1798. [ad. Gr. ἑρμηνευτικός; see prec. and -AL.] Pertaining to interpretation; esp. as dist. from exegesis. **Hermeneu·tically** *adv.*

Hermeneu·tics. 1737. [f. HERMENEUTIC *a.*; see -ICS.] The art or science of interpretation, esp. of Scripture. Commonly dist. from *exegesis* or practical exposition.

Hermes (hō·ɹmīz). 1605. [L., Gr. Ἑρμῆς.] 1. *Gr. Myth.* A deity, the son of Zeus and Maia, the messenger of the gods, the god of science, commerce, eloquence, and many of the arts of life; commonly figured as a youth, with the *caduceus* or rod, *petasus* or brimmed hat, and *talaria* or winged shoes. Identified with Mercury. Hence b. = HERMA. 1727. †2. The metal Mercury. MILT. *P. L.* III. 603. 3. *Hermes Trismegistus* (Gr. Ἑρμῆς τρὶς μέγιστος, Hermes thrice-greatest) the Egyptian god Thoth, as identified with the Grecian Hermes, and as the founder of occult science, esp. alchemy 1605.

3. Phr. †*Hermes' seal*: = Hermetic seal (see HERMETIC A). †*Hermes' fire*: = CORPOSANT; also, a will-o'-the-wisp.

Hermetic (həɹme·tik). 1637. [ad. med.L. *hermeticus*, irreg. f. *Hermes* (*Trismegistus*): see prec. Cf. *magnes*, *magneticus*.]

A. *adj.* 1. Pertaining to Hermes Trismegistus, and the writings ascribed to him 1676. 2. Hence, Relating to or dealing with occult science, esp. alchemy; magical; alchemical 1637. 3. Pertaining to the god Hermes, or to a HERMA (*mod.*).

2. Phr. *H. art*, *philosophy*, *science*: names for alchemy or chemistry. *H. seal*, *sealing*: air-tight closure of a vessel by fusion, soldering, or welding; also *Surg.* a method of dressing wounds by closing them externally. Also *fig.* Hence *hermetic* = 'hermetically sealed'.

B. *sb.* An alchemist or chemist 1684. 2. *pl.* Alchemy 1865. So **Herme·tical** *a.* = HERMETIC *a.* 1, 2. **He·rmetist,** a H. philosopher.

Hermetically (həɹme·tikăli), *adv.* 1605. [f. as prec. + -LY [2].] 1. By fusion; hence, by any mode which forms an air-tight closure. b. *Surg.* See HERMETIC *a.* 2 (quots.) 1870. c. *fig.* Tightly; absolutely (closed) 1698. †2. By alchemy 1664.

Hermit (hō·ɹmit), *sb.* See also EREMITE. [ME. *hermite*, *ermite*, a. OF. (*h*)*ermite*, L. *eremita*, ad. Gr. ἐρημίτης, f. ἐρημία desert.] 1. = EREMITE 1. Hence, A person living in solitude 1799. Hence, 2. A vagabond 1495; †a beadsman (also *fig.*) -1688.

1. A withered Hermite, fiuescore winters worne SHAKS. 2. For those [honours] of old..we rest your Ermites SHAKS.

Comb.: **h.-bird,** (*a*) a humming-bird of genus *Phaëthornis*; (*b*) a nun-bird; **-crab, †-fish, -lobster,** a crab of the family *Paguridæ*, which usually occupies a cast-off molluscan shell; **-crow,** the chough; **-thrush,** a N. American thrush, *Turdus solitarius*, celebrated for its song; **-warbler,** the western warbler, *Dendrœca occidentalis*, of the Pacific slope of N. America.

Hermitage (hō·ɹmitėdʒ). ME. [a. OF.; see prec. and -AGE.] 1. The habitation of a hermit; a solitary dwelling-place 1648. 2. A French wine produced from vineyards on a hill near Valence 1680.

1. The peaceful h., The hairy gown and mossy cell MILT.

Hermitary. *rare.* 1754. [ad. med.L. *heremitarium*: see -ARY [1] B. 2.] A hermit's cell; a hermitage. Also **Hermitory** ME.

He·rmitess. 1633. A female hermit. So †**Hermitress.**

Hermitic, -al (həɹmi·tik, -ăl), *a.* 1586. [Altered, after *hermit*, from (*h*)*eremitic*, *-al*; see -AL.] Of or pertaining to a hermit.

Hermo-, comb. f. HERMES, as in **Hermokopid,** a mutilator of Hermæ; etc.

Hermodactyl (hōɹmodæ·ktil). *Obs.* exc. *Hist.* ME. [ad. med.L. *hermodactylus*, a. Gr., lit. Hermes' finger.] 1. A bulbous root, prob. of a species of *Colchicum*, brought from the East, and formerly used in medicine. Also, the plant. 2. Applied by Lyte to the Meadow Saffron, *Colchicum autumnale*; and later to the Snake's-head Iris, *Hermodactylus tuberosus* 1578.

Hern, hirn (hōɹn), *sb. dial.* [OE. *hyrne* wk. fem., f. (ult.) stem of HORN *sb.*] A corner.

Lurkynge in hernes and in lanes blynde CHAUCER.

Hern, herne, *arch.* and *dial.* ff. HERON, freq. in lit. use.

Hern, *poss. pron.* ME. [f. HER *poss. pron.* [1]] *Obs.* exc. *s.* and *midl. dial.* = HERS.

‖**Hernia** (hǝ̄·ɹniă). *Pl.* **-æ, -as.** ME. [L., = rupture.] *Path.* A tumour formed by the displacement and resulting protrusion of a part of an organ through an aperture, natural or accidental, in the walls of its containing cavity; a rupture. Also *attrib.*, as *h. truss*, etc. Hence **He·rnial** *a.* of or pertaining to h.; chiefly in *hernial sac.* **He·rniary** *a.* of or pertaining to h. or its surgical treatment. **He·rniated,** †**He·rnious** *adjs.* affected with h.

Hernio-, comb. f. HERNIA, as in **Hernio·logy,** that part of pathology which treats of hernia, a treatise on hernia; etc.

Herniotomy (hǝ̄ɹniǫ·tŏmi). 1811. [f. HERNIO- + Gr. -τομία.] *Surg.* The operation of cutting for strangulated hernia. So **Hernio·tomist,** one who practises h.

Hernsew, -shaw, -shew: see HERONSEW.

Hero (hīᵊ·rǫ). Pl. **heroes** (hīᵊ·rouz). ME. [Ult ad.L *heros*, pl. *heroes*, a. Gr. ἥρως, pl. ἥρωες. In early use, beside the sing. *heros* is found a sing. *he·ro-ë*; this became later *he-roe*, and finally *hero.*] **1.** *Antiq.* A name given to men of superhuman strength, courage, or ability, favoured by the gods; regarded later as demigods, and immortal. **2.** One who does brave or noble deeds; an illustrious warrior 1586. **3.** A man who exhibits extraordinary bravery, firmness, or greatness of soul, in connexion with any pursuit, work, or enterprise; a man admired and venerated for his achievements and noble qualities 1661. **4.** The man who forms the subject of an epic; the chief male personage in a poem, play, or story 1697. **5.** *attrib.* 1670.

1. My young Ulyssean heroë CHAPMAN. A Chief sings some great Action of a God or Heroe 1763. **2.** See, the conquering h. comes MORELL. **3.** Who would not be the h. of an age? DRYDEN. No man is a h. to his *valet de chambre* FOOTE. *Comb.* **h.-worship,** the worship of heroes, and of great men generally.

Hence **Heroo·logist,** one who discourses on heroes. **He·roship,** the state, position, or character of a h.

Herodian (hĭrōu·diăn), *a.* and *sb.*¹ ME. [ad. L. *Herodianus*, a. Gr.; see -IAN.]

A. *adj.* **1.** Of or pertaining to Herod, king of Judæa (B.C. 38–4), or to members of his family of the same name; built by Herod 1633. **2.** Blustering, magniloquent 1886.

1. *Herodian disease*: phthiriasis or some like disease (see *Acts* xii. 23).

B. *sb. pl.* A Jewish party, mainly political, who were partisans of the H. dynasty, and lax in their Judaism. Hence, a term of reproach. ME.

They jumpe with Caesar, like the Herodians 1592.

Herodian (hĭrōu·diăn), *sb.*² 1609. [In 1, irreg. f. Gr. ἐρωδιός heron + -AN. In 2, f. mod.L. *herodius.*] †**1.** A heron. **2.** *Ornith.* One of an order of birds, *Herodii* or *Herodiones*, comprising the herons, storks, ibises, and spoonbills.

†**He·roess.** 1612. [f. HERO + -ESS.] = HEROINE. –1715.

Heroic (hĭrōu·ik). 1549. [ad. L. *heroicus*, Gr. ἡρωϊκός, f. ἥρως HERO.]

A. *adj.* **1.** Of or pertaining to a hero or heroes; characteristic of a hero; of the nature of a hero. **2.** Of or pertaining to the heroes of antiquity 1667. **3.** Relating to the deeds of heroes; epic 1581; (of verse) used in heroic poetry 1617; (of language) magniloquent; hence, high-flown 1591. **4.** Having recourse to bold, daring, or extreme measures; attempting great things 1664. **5.** In statuary: Of a size between life and colossal 1794.

1. A life h. MILT. Their heroick deliverer BURKE. The choir..rich in h. dust 1834. **2.** Th' H. Race.. That fought at Theb's and Ilium MILT. **3.** This Subject for H. Song MILT. The English Verse, which we call Heroique, consists of no more than Ten Syllables DRYDEN. (So in German and Italian; in Gr. and L. poetry it was the hexameter; in French, the Alexandrine of twelve syllables.) **4.** Commonplace reforms, which h. legislation has overlooked GOLDW. SMITH.

B. *sb.* †**1.** A hero; *esp.* a personage of the heroic age –1667. **2.** Heroic verse: chiefly in pl. 1596. **b.** *pl.* High-flown or bombastic language or sentiments 1700. †**3.** A heroic poet. BUTLER.

2. b. He [Cæsar] had..no Byronic mock heroics FROUDE. Hence **Hero·icness,** h. character or quality = HEROISM.

Heroical (hĭrōu·ikăl), *a.* 1513. [as prec. + -AL.] = HEROIC *a.* Hence **Hero·ically** *adv.*, **-ness.**

Heroi-co·mic, -al, *a.* 1712. [See HERO and COMIC.] That combines the heroic with the comic; of the nature of a burlesque on the heroic.

The Rape of the Lock. An Heroi-comical Poem. POPE.

Heroin (hĭrōu·in). *Chem.* 1899. [German.] A drug derived from morphine used as an anodyne and sedative.

Heroine (he·ro₁in), *sb.* (*a.*) 1659. [ad. L. *heroina, -ine*, a. Gr.; see -INE. Also used in L. form in 17th c.] **1.** A female hero; a demi-goddess. **2.** A woman of exalted spirit or achievements 1662. **3.** The principal female character in a poem, story, or play 1715.

1. He sees the shades of the ancient heroines POPE. **2.** That famous H. [Queen Elizabeth] EVELYN.

Heroism (he·ro₁iz'm). 1717. [ad. F. *héroïsme*, f. *héros.*] The action and qualities of a hero; exalted courage or boldness; heroic conduct; (with *pl.*) a heroic action or trait.

No way has been found for making h. easy EMERSON.

Heroize (hīᵊ·rouəiz), *v.* 1738. [f. HERO + -IZE.] To make a hero of; to play the hero BROWNING.

Heron (he·rən). Also *arch.*, *poet.*, *dial.* **hern** (hǝ̄ɹn). [ME. *heiroun, heyron*, a. OF. *hairon* (mod. *héron*):—late pop.L. **hagironem*, deriv. of **hagirus*, ad. OHG. **haiger, heiger* a heron.] **1.** A large natural group of long-necked long-legged wading birds, belonging to the genus *Ardea* or family *Ardeidæ*; esp. the Common or Grey Heron of Europe, *A. cinerea.* **b.** With defining epithet, applied to other species of *Ardea*, etc. 1577. **2.** *attrib.*, as *h.-hawking* 1709, *h.-plume* SCOTT.

1. I come from haunts of coot and hern TENNYSON. **b.** Night H., *Nycticorax Gardeni* RAY. The Great White H. (*Ardea alba*) YARRELL. The Great Blue H. of America, *Ardea herodias*, The Purple H., *A. purpurea* NEWTON.

†**He·roner.** ME. [a. F. *héronnier* adj., in *faucon héronnier.*] A falcon trained to fly at the heron; also, *falcon heroner* –1611.

Heronry, hernery (he·rənri, hǝ̄·ɹnəri). 1603. [-RY.] A place where herons breed.

Heron's-bill. ? *Obs.* 1578. A book-name for the British species of *Erodium* and *Geranium*; usu. called Stork's-bill and Crane's-bill.

He·ronsew, -shew, -shaw. Now somewhat *arch.* or *dial.* [ME. *heronsew*, etc., a. OF. *heronceau*, earlier *heroncel*, pl. *-çaux*, dim. of *heron.*] *lit.* A little or young heron; but in use = HERON.

Phr. *To know a hawk from a heronshaw*, conjectural emendation of 'I know a Hawke from a Handsaw' (Shaks.); see HANDSAW.

‖**Herpes** (hǝ̄·ɹpīz). ME. [L., a. Gr. ἕρπης (ἑρπητ-) shingles, lit. a creeping, f. ἕρπειν.] **1.** A disease of the skin (or occas. of a mucous membrane) characterized by the appearance of patches of distinct vesicles. (Applied to many cutaneous affections.) **2.** *Entom.* A genus of Coleoptera of the family *Curculionidæ* (weevils). Hence **Herpe·tic** *a.* pertaining to or of the nature of h.; affected with h. **Herpe·tiform** *a.* presenting the form of h. **He·rpetism,** a constitutional tendency to h., or the like.

Herpetology¹ (hǝ̄ɹpėtǫ·lŏdʒi). 1824. [f. Gr. ἑρπετόν creeping thing + -LOGY.] That part of zoology which treats of reptiles. Hence **He·rpetolo·gic, -al** *a.* pertaining to h. **He·rpetolo·gically** *adv.* **Herpeto·logist.**

Herpeto·logy². 1857. [f. Gr. ἑρπητ-HERPES + -LOGY.] That part of pathology which treats of herpes; a description of herpes.

Herpeto·tomy. [f. Gr. ἑρπετόν reptile + -τομία.] The dissection or anatomy of reptiles. So **Herpeto·tomist,** a dissector of reptiles.

Herring (he·riŋ). [OE. *hǽring, héring.* Ult. derivation uncertain.] A sea-fish, *Clupea harengus*, inhabiting the North Atlantic Ocean, and coming near the coast at certain seasons in vast shoals to spawn. Also other species of *Clupea*.

Comb.: **h.-drift**: see DRIFT *sb.* II. 5 b; **-gull,** a species of gull, *Larus argentatus*, which follows herring-shoals and preys upon them; **-hog** (*dial.*), the grampus; **-king,** also **King of the h–s,** *Chimæra monstrosa*; also a species of ribbon-fish, *Regalecus glesne.*

Herring-bone, *sb.* (*a.*) 1652. **1.** The bone of a herring. **2.** *attrib.* or *adj.* Resembling in appearance the bones of a herring; applied *spec.* in *Arch.* to a kind of masonry and of paving in which the stones or tiles are set obliquely in alternate rows so as to form a zigzag pattern; as *herring-bone ashlar, balk, bond, work*, etc. 1659.

2. Herring-bone stitch (*Sewing*), a kind of cross-stitch, chiefly used in flannel; hence *herring-bone seam, thread*, etc. **Herring-bone bridging** (*Carpentry*), strutting pieces between thin joists, laid diagonally, to prevent lateral deflexion. Hence **Herring-bone** *v. trans.* to work with a herring-bone stitch or pattern. Also *absol.* or *intr.*

Herring-pond. 1686. The sea, esp. the N. Atlantic Ocean (*joc.*).

‖**Herrnhuter** (he·rnhūtər). 1748. [f. *Herrnhut* (lit. the Lord's keeping), the name of their first German settlement on the estate of Count von Zinzendorf in Saxony.] One of the sect of 'United Brethren' or Moravians.

Hers (hǝ̄ɹz), *poss. pron.* ME. [A double possessive, f. poss. pron. *hire*, HER, thus *hires, her's, hers.* Of northern origin.] The absol. form of HER, used when no noun follows: = Her one, her ones; that or those pertaining to her. **b.** *Of hers* = belonging to her 1478.

As mine on hers, so hers is set on mine *Rom. & Jul.* II. iii. 59. Hers and mine Adultery *Cymb.* v. v. 186.

†**Hersall.** Short for REHEARSAL. Spenser.

Herschel (hǝ̄·ɹʃĕl). 1819. *Astron.* A name proposed for the planet Uranus, discovered by Sir W. Herschel in 1781.

Herschelian (həɹʃe·liăn), *a.* (*sb.*) 1792. [f. *Herschel* + -IAN.] Of or pertaining to Sir W. Herschel (1738–1822), or Sir John Herschel (1792–1871). *Herschelian* (*telescope*), a form of reflecting telescope with a concave mirror slightly inclined to the axis.

Herse (hǝ̄ɹs). 1480. [a. F. *herse* harrow:—L. *hirpex, hirpicem.* See also HEARSE.] †**1.** A harrow. **b.** A portcullis grated and spiked. *Hist.* 1704. **c.** *Her.* A charge representing a portcullis or a harrow 1525. **2.** *Mil.* A form of battle array. *Hist.* 1523. **3.** A frame on which skins are dried 1839. Hence **Hersed** *a.* drawn up in a h. (sense 2).

Herself (həɹse·lf), *pron.* [OE. *hire self, selfre*, f. *hire* HER *dat.-acc. pers. pron.* + SELF. *Self* was in OE. an adj., the dat. form of which is the source of the modern use.] **1.** Emphatic use. Very her, very she, that very woman, etc. = L. *ipsa* ME. **2.** Reflexive use. OE. **3.** From the 14th c., *her* has often been treated as the possessive pron., and *self* as sb., whence *her sweet self*, and the like.

1. Seke Vertu for hir selfe 1559. Iulia her selfe did giue it me SHAKS. The..Widdow, and her selfe..Are mighty Gossips SHAKS. *To be herself*: to be in her normal condition. Also used alone in predicate after *be, become*, etc. = by herself, alone. Also as HER *pers. pron.* 2 b. **2.** To talk to her self 1690. To forget herself TENNYSON.

Hership (hǝ̄·ɹʃip). *Sc. arch.* or *Hist.* ME. [f. HERE army, host, or stem of OE. *hergan* to HARRY + -SHIP.] **1.** Harrying; a foray. **2.** A harried condition; hence, ruin, distress, famine, caused by a foray, etc. 1536. **3.** Cattle, etc. forcibly driven off 1535.

Hert(e, obs. ff. HART, HEART, HURT.

Hertfordshire (hā·ɹfǭɹdʃəɹ). 1661. [Name of an Eng. county.] In phr. *H. kindness*: drinking to the person who immediately before drank to one.

Hertzian (hǝ̄·ɹtsiăn), *a.* 1890. [f. the name H. R. *Hertz* (1857–94), German physicist + -IAN.] Of or pertaining to Hertz or to the type of experiments, apparatus, etc., used by him. Also **Hertz** (hǝ̄ɹts, ‖hęrts) used attrib.

H. telegraphy: wireless telegraphy. *H. waves*: see WAVE *sb.* I. 5 a.

†**Hery,** *v.* [OE. *hęrian*:—Ger. **harjan.* In ME. app. sometimes confused with HEAR.] *trans.* To praise, exalt, worship –1622.

Hesitancy (he·zitănsi). 1617. [ad. L. *hæsitantia*, f. pres. pple. of *hæsitare*; see -ANCY.] The quality or condition of hesitating; indecision, vacillation. So **He·sitance.**

Hesitant (he·zitănt), *a.* 1647. [ad. L. *hæsitantem.*] Hesitating; undecided; stammering. Hence **He·sitantly** *adv.*

Hesitate (he·zite^i^t), *v.* 1623. [f. L. *hæsitat-*, *hæsitare*, freq. of *hærere* (pa. pple. *hæsum*) to stick.] 1. *intr.* To hold back in doubt; to show, or speak with, indecision; to find difficulty in deciding; to scruple. 2. To stammer 1706. 3. *trans.* To express or say with hesitation 1735.

1. He may pause, but he must not h. RUSKIN. 3. Just hint a fault, and h. dislike POPE. Hence **He·sitater, -or. He·sitating·ly** *adv.*, **-ness.**

Hesitation (hezitēⁱ·ʃən). 1622. [ad. L. *hæsitationem.*] 1. The action of hesitating; a pausing or delaying due to irresolution; the condition of doubt in relation to action. Also with *pl.* 2. Stammering 1709.

Hesitative (he·zitēⁱtiv), *a.* 1795. [f. as HESITATE; see -IVE.] Showing, or given to, hesitation.

His h. manner of speaking MOZLEY. So **He·sitatory** *a.* R. NORTH.

Hesper (he·spəɹ). *poet.* 1623. [ad. L. HESPERUS.] = HESPERUS.

A Phospher 'mongst the Living, late wert thou, But Shin'st among the Dead a H. now 1656.

Hesper-, stem of HESPERUS, used in the same sense as HESPERID-, as in **Hespe·ric, Hespere·tic, Hesperi·nic, Hesperi·sic** *adjs.*, denominating acids.

Hesperian (hespī^ə^·riăn). 1547. [f. L. *Hesperius*, Gr. ἑσπέριος of or situated towards the west, western, f. HESPERUS; see -AN.]

A. *adj.* 1. Western, of or pertaining to the land where the sun sets (*poet.*). 2. Of or pertaining to the HESPERIDES (*poet.*) 1622. 3. *Entom.* Of or pertaining to the family of butterflies called *Hesperidæ* or Skippers 1840.

2. Happy Iles, Like those H. Gardens fam'd of old MILT.

B. *sb.* 1. An inhabitant of a western land 1601. 2. A Hesperian butterfly; a Skipper.

Hesperid-, Gr. ἑσπεριδ- stem of Ἑσπερίδες Hesperides, with sense 'of or derived from the orange or its congeners'; see HESPERIDES 2.

Hence a. *Bot.* **Hespe·ridate, Hesperi·deous** *adjs.*, of the orange structure or kind. ||**Hesperi·dium**, a fruit of the structure of the orange, pulpy within and covered by a separable rind. b. *Chem.* **Hespe·ridene, Hespe·ridin, Hespe·ridine**, chemical products obtained from the hesperideous fruits.

||**Hesperides** (hespe·ridīz), *sb. pl.* 1590. [L., a. Gr. Ἑσπερίδες, pl. of ἑσπερίς 'western', 'a daughter of the west', 'land of the sunset', f. ἕσπερος; see HESPERUS.] 1. *Gr. Myth.* The nymphs, daughters of Hesperus, who were fabled to guard, with the aid of a dragon, the garden in which the golden apples grew in the Isles of the Blest, at the western extremity of the earth 1656. Also *transf.* b. Hence, the garden itself; also, the 'Fortunate Islands' or 'Isles of the Blest' (αἱ Μακάρων νῆσοι), in which the garden was situated 1590. 2. *Bot.* Name for a class of plants, containing the orange family (*Aurantiaceæ*) and related orders 1857.

Hence **Hesperi·dian, -ean** *a.* of or pertaining to the gardens of the Hesperides.

||**Hesperornis** (hespĕrǭ·ɹnis). 1871. [f. Gr. ἕσπερος western + ὄρνις bird.] *Palæont.* A genus of fossil birds of the western hemisphere.

||**Hesperus** (he·spĕrŏs). ME. [L., a. Gr. ἕσπερος adj. western; sb. the evening star.] The evening star.

Þe eue sterre hesperus CHAUCER.

Hessian (he·siăn), *a.* and *sb.*[1] 1677. [f. *Hesse* + -IAN.]

A. *adj.* Of or pertaining to Hesse in Germany. **Hessian boot**, a kind of high boot, with tassels in front at the top, first worn by the H. troops. **H. crucible**, a crucible made of the best fire-clay and coarse sand: used in U.S. in all experiments where fluxes are needed. **H. fly**, a fly or midge (*Cecidomyia destructor*), of which the larva is very destructive to wheat; so named, because erron. supposed to have been carried into America by the H. troops, during the War of Independence.

B. *sb.* 1. A native of Hesse; a soldier of or from Hesse 1742. 2. In U.S., A mercenary 1877. 3. (*hessians.*) Short for *Hessian boots* (see A) 1801. 4. A strong coarse cloth, used for packing bales 1881.

Hessian (he·siăn), *sb.*[2] 1856. [f. Dr. Otto *Hesse* of Königsberg.] *Math.* The Jacobian of the first derivatives of a function.

Hessite (he·səit). 1849. [f. G. H. *Hess* of St. Petersburg; see -ITE.] *Min.* Telluride of silver, occurring in grey, sectile masses.

Hest (hest), *sb. arch.* [OE. *hǽs* fem., repr. OTeut. **hait-ti-*, abstr. sb. from **haitan* to call upon by name; see HIGHT *v.* In ME. *heste, hest*, by assimilation to sbs. in *-te* :—OE. *-t.*] 1. Bidding, command, injunction, behest (*arch.*). †2. Vow, promise. Cf. BEHEST. -1599. †3. Will, determination -1845.

1. O my Father, I haue broke your h. to say so SHAKS. Hence †**Hest** *v.* to promise; to command.

†**He·stern,** *a.* 1577. [ad. L. *hesternus.*] Yester-. -1708.

Hesternal (hestə̄·ɹnăl), *a.* 1649. [f. L. *hesternus* + -AL.] Of yesterday.

Hesychast (he·sikæst). 1797. [ad. med.L. *hesychasta*, ad. eccl. Gr. ἡσυχαστής quietist, f. (ult.) ἥσυχος.] *Eccl. Hist.* One of a school of quietists which arose among the monks of Mt. Athos in the 14th c. Also *attrib.* Hence **Hesycha·stic** *a.* appeasing; in *Eccl. Hist.* pertaining to the Hesychasts.

||**Hetæra** (hĭtī^ə^·ră), **hetaira** (hĭtai·ră). Pl. **hetæræ** (-rī), **hetairai** (-rai). 1820. [Gr., fem. of ἑταῖρος.] (In ancient Greece, and hence *transf.*) A female companion; a mistress, concubine; a courtesan.

Hetærism (hĭtī·riz'm), **hetairism** (hĭtai·riz'm). 1860. [a. Gr. ἑταιρισμός; see HETÆRA and -ISM.] 1. Open concubinage. 2. *Anthropol.* Name for a supposed primitive form of the sexual relations: communal marriage in a tribe 1870. Hence **Hetairist, -istic** *a.*

Hetchel, early form of HATCHEL.

Hete: see HIGHT *v.*[1]

Hetero- (hetĕro), bef. a vowel **heter-**, comb. f. Gr. ἕτερος the other of two, other, different; often opp. to *homo-*, sometimes to *auto-, homœo-, iso-, ortho-, syn-*.

He·teracanth [Gr. ἄκανθα] *a.*, *Ichth.* having the spines of the dorsal and anal fins alternately broader on one side than the other; opp. to *homacanth.* †**He·terarchy**, the rule of an alien. **Heteroca·rpian, -ca·rpous** [Gr. καρπός] *adjs.*, *Bot.* producing fruit of different kinds; so **Heteroca·rpism. Heteroce·phalous** [Gr. κεφαλή] *a.*, *Bot.* applied to a composite plant producing flower-heads of different kinds, male and female. **Heterochi·ral** [Gr. χείρ] *a.*, of identical form but with lateral inversion, as the right and left hands; opp. to *homochiral*; hence **Heterochi·rally** *adv.* **Heterochro·mous** [Gr. χρῶμα colour] *a.*, of different colours, as the flowers of some *Compositæ*, e. g. the daisy and asters. **He·terocyst** [Gr. κύστις bladder], *Biol.* a cell of exceptional structure or form found in certain algæ and fungi. **Heteroda·ctyl, -da·ctylous** [Gr. δάκτυλος] *adjs.*, *Zool.* having the toes, or one of them, irregular or abnormal, as certain families of birds. **Hetero·ga·ngliate** *a.*, *Zool.* having the ganglia of the nervous system unsymmetrically arranged, as most molluscs; opp. to *homogangliate.* **Hetero·gynal, Hetero·gynous** [Gr. γυνή female] *adjs.*, *Zool.* applied to species of animals in which the females are of two kinds, fertile and neuter, as in bees, ants, etc. **Hetero·lobous** [Gr. λοβός lobe] *a.*, having unequal lobes. **Heteropo·lar** *a.*, having polar correspondence to something different from itself; having dissimilar poles. **Hetero·ptics** *nonce-wd.*, irregularity in vision. **Heteroso·matous** [Gr. σῶμα] *a.*, *Zool.* having a body deviating from the normal type; said esp. of flat fishes; so **He·terosome; Heteroso·mous** *a.* **Hetero·sporous** [Gr. σπόρος seed] *a.*, *Bot.* producing two different kinds of spores; opp. to *homosporous* or *isosporous.* **Heterothe·rmal** [Gr. θερμός hot] *a.*, *Biol.* having a temperature other than that of the surroundings, as plants and cold-blooded animals; opp. to *homothermal* or *homothermous.* **Hetero·trichal, Hetero·trichous** [Gr. θρίξ, τριχ- hair] *adjs.*, *Biol.* belonging to the order *Heterotricha* of ciliate infusorians, in which the cilia of the oral region differ in size and arrangement from those of the rest of the body; also said of the cilia. **Heterozo·nal** *a.*, *Cryst.* said of faces (or poles) of a crystallographic system which lie in different zones (or zone-systems); opp. to *tautozonal.*

Heterocercal (hetĕrosə̄·ɹkăl), *a.* 1838. [f. HETERO- + Gr. κέρκος tail + -AL.] Having the lobes of the tail unequal. Opp. to *homocercal.* Hence **Heterocerca·lity, He·terocercy**, the condition of being h.

Heterocerous (hetĕrǫ·sĕrəs), *a.* 1881. [f. mod.L. *Heterocera* neut. pl., f. HETERO- + Gr. κέρας.] *Entom.* Belonging to the sub-order of lepidopterous insects *Heterocera* (Moths); so called from the diversified forms of the antennæ.

Heterochronic (-krǫ·nik), *a.* 1854. [f. HETERO- + Gr. χρόνος, χρονικός.] *Biol.* and *Path.* a. Occurring at irregular times; intermittent: applied to the pulse. b. Occurring or developed at an abnormal time 1876. So ||**Heterochro·nia, Hetero·chronism, Hetero·chrony**, occurrence or development at an abnormal time.

Heteroclite (he·tĕrǫkləit). 1580. [a. F. *hétéroclite*, a. L. *heteroclitus*, a. Gr., f. ἑτερο- + -κλιτος, vbl. adj. from κλίνειν to bend.]

A. *adj.* 1. *Gram.* Irregularly or anomalously declined or inflected: chiefly of nouns 1656. 2. *fig.* Irregular, abnormal, eccentric. Said of persons and things. Now *rare.* 1598.

2. This h. animal [the bat] BOYLE. So †**Hetero·clital,** †**Heterocli·tic, -al,** †**Hetero·clitous** *adjs.*

B. *sb.* 1. *Gram.* A word irregularly inflected; *esp.* a noun which deviates from the regular declension 1580. 2. *fig.* A person or thing that deviates from the ordinary rule; an anomaly. Now *rare* or *Obs.* 1605.

2. Ther are strange Heteroclites in Religion now adaies HOWELL.

He·terodont. 1877. [f. HETER- + Gr. ὀδούς, ὀδοντ-.] A. *adj.* Having teeth of different kinds (incisors, canines, and molars), as most mammals. B. *sb.* A h. animal.

Heterodox (he·tĕrŏdǫks). 1619. [ad. Gr. ἑτερόδοξος of another opinion, f. ἑτερο- + δόξα.]

A. *adj.* 1. Of doctrines, opinions, etc.: Not in accordance with established doctrines or opinions, or those generally recognized as orthodox. Orig. in religion and theology. 1637. 2. Of persons: Holding unorthodox opinions 1657.

1. Some of the h. opinions which he avows..particularly his Arianism MACAULAY. So †**He·terodoxal** *a.*

†B. *sb.* A heterodox opinion or person -1691.

Heterodoxy (he·tĕrŏdǫksi). 1652. [ad. Gr. ἑτεροδοξία (see prec.).] 1. The quality or character of being heterodox; deviation from orthodoxy 1659. 2. with *a* and *pl.* A heterodox opinion 1652.

Heterodromous (hetĕrǫ·drŏməs), *a.* 1710. [f. mod.L. *heterodromus*, f. Gr. ἑτερο- + -δρομος running + -OUS.] Running in different directions; opp. to *homodromous.* †a. *Mech.* Applied to levers of the first order, in which the power and the weight move in opposite directions -1751. b. *Bot.* Turning in opposite directions on the main stem and on a branch, as the generating spiral of a phyllotaxis 1870. So **He·terodrome** 1849; **Hetero·dromy**, h. condition.

Heterodyne (he·tĕrŏdəin). 1908. [f. HETERO- + DYNE.] *Wireless Telegr.* and *Telephony.* A method by which incoming oscillations are combined with other oscillations of a slightly different frequency, so that a 'beat' is set up. Also = *h. receiver*, etc. Also as vb.

Heterogamous (hetĕrǫ·gāməs), *a.* 1842. [f. Gr. ἑτερο- + γάμος + -OUS.] 1. *Bot.* Applied to conditions in which stamens and pistils are not regularly present in each flower or floret. 2. *Biol.* Characterized by the alternation of differently organized generations, as of a parthenogenetic and a sexual generation 1897. 3. Pertaining to irregular marriage 1862.

Heterogamy (hetĕrǫ·gămi). 1874. [f. as prec. + -Y.] 1. *Bot.* Mediate or indirect fertilization of plants. 2. *Biol.* The quality of being HETEROGAMOUS (sense 2) 1884.

Heterogene (he·tĕrŏdʒīn), *a.* ? *Obs.* 1541. [ad. Gr. ἑτερογενής, f. ἑτερο- + γένος, γενε-.] = HETEROGENEOUS.

Heterogeneal (he:tĕrŏdʒī·niăl). 1602. [f. Scholastic L. *heterogeneus* (f. Gr. ἑτερογενής: see prec.) + -AL.] 1. *adj.* = HETEROGENEOUS. 2. *sb.* A heterogeneous person or thing 1602. So †**Heteroge·nean** *a.* = sense 1.

Heterogeneity (he:tĕro,dʒĭnī·ĭti). 1641. [ad. med.L. *heterogeneitas*, f. as prec.; see -ITY.] The quality or condition of being heterogeneous. b. with *a* and *pl.* A heterogeneous element or constituent 1651.

Heterogeneous (hetĕrŏdʒī·niəs), *a.* 1624. [f. as HETEROGENEAL + -OUS.] The opposite of *homogeneous.* 1. Diverse in kind or nature;

of completely different characters; incongruous; foreign. **2.** Composed of diverse elements or constituents; not homogeneous 1630. **3.** *Math.* **a.** Of different kinds, so as to be incommensurable. **b.** Non-homogeneous. *H. Surds*: such as have different radical signs. 1656.

Phr. *H. nouns*, nouns of different genders in the singular and plural. *H. numbers*, mixed numbers consisting of integers and fractions.

Hence **Heteroge·neous-ly** *adv.*, **-ness.**

Heterogenesis (he:tĕro₍dʒe·nĭ́sis). 1854. [f. Gr. ἑτερο- + γένεσις.] *Biol.* †**1.** Abnormal organic development. †**2.** Sexual reproduction from two different germs, male and female. CARPENTER. **3.** The origination of a living being otherwise than from a parent of the same kind 1864. **b.** *esp.* Abiogenesis; spontaneous generation 1878. **c.** Alternation of generations 1863. Hence **Heterogene·tic** *a.* of, pertaining to, or characterized by h. **Hetero·genist**, an upholder of the doctrine of spontaneous generation.

†**Hetero·genous,** *a.* Inferior f. HETEROGENEOUS.

Heterogeny (hetĕrǫ·dʒĭ́ni). 1647. [f. Gr. ἑτερογενής; or, in 3, f. HETERO- + -γενεια.] †**1.** Heterogeneousness. **2.** *concr.* A heterogeneous collection. HAWTHORNE. **3.** *Biol.* Spontaneous generation 1863. Hence **-genist.**

Heterogonous (hetĕrǫ·gŏnəs), *a.* 1877. [f. Gr. ἑτερο- + γόνος, -γονος + -OUS.] **1.** *Bot.* Having incongruous reproductive organs; applied to flowers in which cross-fertilization is secured by the stamens and pistils being dimorphic or trimorphic. Also **He·terogone** *a.* 1877. **2.** *Biol.* Producing offspring dissimilar to the parent 1883. So **Hetero·gonism, Hetero·gony,** the condition of being h.

Heterography (-ǫ·grăfi). 1783. [f. Gr. ἑτερο- + -γραφία. Opp. to *orthography.*] **1.** Incorrect spelling. **2.** Inconsistent spelling (as the current spelling of English). DE QUINCEY. So **Hetero·grapher,** one who practises h. **Heterogra·phic** *a.* pertaining to or characterized by h.

Heterologous (-ǫ·lŏgəs), *a.* 1822. [f. Gr. ἑτερο- + λόγος ratio, etc. + -OUS.] Having a different relation, or consisting of different elements; not corresponding. Opp. to HOMOLOGOUS. **a.** *Path.* Of a different formation from that of the normal tissue of the part. **b.** *Chem.* Gerhardt's term for bodies derived from each other by definite chemical metamorphoses 1880.

Heterology (-ǫ·lŏdʒi). 1854. [f. as prec. + -Y.] The condition of being heterologous; opp. to HOMOLOGY.

Hetero·meran. 1842. [f. mod.L. *Heteromera* neut pl., f. Gr. ἑτερο- + μέρος.] *Entom.* A beetle belonging to the *Heteromera*, a division of *Coleoptera* in which the two anterior pairs of legs have five tarsal joints, but the third pair only four.

Heteromerous (hetĕrǫ·mĕrəs), *a.* 1826. [f. Gr. ἑτερο- + μέρος + -OUS.] **1.** *Entom.* Having legs differing in the number of their tarsal joints; *spec.* belonging to the division *Heteromera* of coleopterous insects (see prec.). **2.** *Bot.* Having parts differing in arrangement, or in number 1875. **3.** *Chem.* Unrelated as to chemical composition, as in certain cases of isomorphism 1864.

Heteromorphic (hetĕromǭ·ɪfik), *a.* 1864. [f. Gr. ἑτερο- + μορφή + -IC.] **1.** Of different or dissimilar forms. **a.** *Entom.* Existing in different forms at different stages of life: said of insects which undergo complete metamorphosis (*Heteromorpha*). **b.** *Bot.* Applied to flowers or plants differing in the relative length of the stamens and pistils (including *dimorphic* and *trimorphic*) 1874. **2.** Of abnormal form (*mod.*). So **Heteromo·rphism, Heteromo·rphy,** h. condition or property.

Heteromorphous (hetĕromǭ·ɪfəs), *a.* 1826. [As prec. + -OUS.] **1.** Of abnormal or irregular form. **2.** *Entom.* = HETEROMORPHIC 1 a.

Heteronomic (-nǫ·mik), *a.* 1864. [f. Gr. ἑτερο- + νόμος + -IC.] Showing a different mode of operation or arrangement.

Heteronomous (-ǫ·nŏməs), *a.* 1824. [f. as prec. + -OUS.] **1.** Subject to different laws. **2.** *Biol.* Having different laws or modes of growth; applied to parts differentiated from the same primitive type 1870. **3.** Subject to an external law; opp. to *autonomous* 1894.

Heteronomy (-ǫ·nŏmi). 1824. [f. as prec. + -Y.] **1.** Presence of a different law. **2.** *Moral Phil.* Subjection to the rule of another being or power (e.g. of the will to the passions); subjection to external law. Opp. to *autonomy.* 1855. **3.** *Biol.* Heteronomous condition; differentiation from a common primitive type 1870.

Heteronym (he·tĕrŏnim). 1697. [f. as next, after *synonym.*] †**1.** One or other of two heteronymous terms. **2.** A word spelt like another, but having a different sound and meaning; opp. to *homonym* and *synonym* 1889. **3.** A name of a thing in one language which is a translation of the name in another language 1885.

Heteronymous (hetĕrǫ·niməs), *a.* 1697. [f. Gr. ἑτερώνυμος + -OUS.] **1.** Having different names, as two correlatives, e.g. *husband, wife*; opp. to *synonymous.* **2.** *Optics.* Applied to the two images of one object seen in looking at a point beyond it, when the left image is that seen by the right eye and *vice versa*; opp. to *homonymous* 1881. **3.** Pertaining to, of the nature of, or having a heteronym. Hence **Hetero·nymously** *adv.*

Heteroousian, heterousian (he:tĕro₍ū·siăn, hetĕrū·siăn, -ū·siăn). 1678. [f. Gr. ἑτεροούσιος, ἑτερούσιος, f. ἑτερο- + οὐσία. Opp. to *homoousian* and *homoiousian.*] *Theol.* **1.** *adj.* Of different essence or substance. **2.** *sb.* One who held the Father and the Son to be different in essence or substance; an Arian 1874. Hence **Heteroou·sious** *a.* = **1.**

Heteropathic (-pæ·þik), *a.* 1830. [f. as next + -IC.] **1.** *Med.* = ALLOPATHIC. **2.** Differing in their effect 1843.

Heteropathy (-ǫ·păþi). 1847. [f. Gr. ἑτερο- + -παθεια, f. πάθος suffering.] **1.** *Med.* = ALLOPATHY; opp. to *homœopathy.* **2.** *Path.* A state of abnormal organic susceptibility in the presence of any irritation 1886. **3.** Antipathy excited by suffering; opp. to *sympathy* 1874.

‖**Heterophasia** (-fē¹·ziă). 1877. [f. Gr. ἑτερο- + -φασια, φάσις speech.] *Path.* = HETEROPHEMY (as a result of mental disease).

He·terophemy (-fĭ́mi). 1875. [f. as prec. + -φημια, φήμη, φῆμις voice, speech.] The saying or writing of one word or phrase when another is meant. Hence **Heterophe·mism,** an instance of h. **Heterophe·mist,** one who says something else than he means to say.

Heterophyllous (-fi·ləs), *a.* 1828. [f. Gr. ἑτερο- + φύλλον + -OUS.] **1.** *Bot.* Bearing leaves of different form. **2.** *Zool.* Belonging to the group *Heterophylli* of cephalopods. So **He·terophy:lly,** the condition of being h.

He·teroplasm. 1878. [f. as prec. + Gr. πλάσμα anything moulded.] *Path.* A tissue formed in a part where it does not normally occur. So **Heteropla·stic** *a.* of or belonging to the formation of a h.; of the nature of a h.; in *Biol.* dissimilar in formation or structure, as the different tissues of the body.

Heteroplasty (he·tĕroplæsti). *Surg.* 1874. [f. Gr. ἑτερο- + πλάσσειν to mould.] Removal or grafting of tissue from an individual.

Heteropod (he·tĕrŏpǫd). 1835. [f. next.] *Zool.* **1.** *adj.* Of or belonging to the *Heteropoda* 1882. **2.** *sb.* One of the *Heteropoda.*

‖**Heteropoda** (hetĕrǫ·pŏdă), *sb. pl.* 1835. [mod.L., f. Gr. ἑτερο- + πούς, ποδ- foot.] **a.** A group of Crustacea including forms with 14 feet, some adapted for swimming. **b.** An order or subclass of Gastropods, having the feet modified into a swimming organ. **c.** A group of Echinoderms. Hence **Hetero·podan** = HETEROPOD *sb.* **Hetero·podous** *a.* = HETEROPOD *a.*

Hetero·pter. *Entom.* 1864. One of the *Heteroptera.*

‖**Heteroptera** (hetĕrǫ·ptĕră), *sb. pl.* 1826. [mod.L., f. Gr. ἑτερο- + πτερόν wing.] *Entom.* A suborder of HEMIPTERA, comprising those insects whose wings are coriaceous at the base and membranous at the tip; the true bugs. Opp. to HOMOPTERA. Hence **Hetero·pteran** = HETEROPTER. **Hetero·pterous** *a.* belonging to or like the *H.*

Heteroscian (hetĕrǫ·ʃiăn). 1616. [f. med.L. *heteroscius*, a. Gr. ἑτερόσκιος diversely-shadowed (f. ἑτερο- + σκιά) + -AN.] **1.** *sb.* A name applied to people of the two temperate zones in reference to the fact that, in the two zones, noon-shadows always fall in opposite directions. (Cf. *Amphiscian.*) Usu. in *pl.*; the L. pl. heteroscii is also used. **2.** *adj.* Of, pertaining to, or of the nature of noon-shadows in the temperate zones 1646.

Heterostatic (-stæ·tik), *a.* 1867. [f. HETERO- + STATIC.] *Electr.* Applied to electrostatic instruments in which there is electrification independent of that to be tested.

Heterostrophic (-strǫ·fik), *a.* [f. Gr. ἑτερο- + -στροφος + -IC.] Turning or winding in another direction; in *Conch.* applied *spec.* to certain univalve shells. So **Hetero·strophe, Hetero·strophy,** the condition of being h.

Heterostyled (he·tĕro₍staild), *a.* 1876. [f. HETERO- + STYLE + -ED².] *Bot.* = HETEROMORPHIC 1 b. So **Heterosty·lism, He·terostyly,** heteromorphism. **Heterosty·lous** *a.* = HETEROSTYLED.

He·terotaxy (-tæksi). 1854. [f. Gr. ἑτερο- + -ταξια, f. τάξις arrangement.] **1.** *Anat.* and *Bot.* Aberrant or abnormal disposition of organs or parts. **2.** *Geol.* Want of regularity in stratification 1889. So **Heterota·ctous** *a.* characterized by h.

Heterotopy (hetĕrǫ·tŏpi). 1876. [ad. mod L. *heterotopia* (also used), f. Gr. ἑτερο- + -τοπια, τόπος place.] Displacement in position, misplacement: **a.** *Path.* The occurrence of a tumour in a part where its elements do not normally exist. **b.** *Biol.* Gradual displacement of cells or parts by adaptation to the changed conditions of embryonic existence 1879. Hence **Heteroto·pic, Hetero·topous** *adjs.* of, pertaining to, or of the nature of h. **Hetero·topism** = HETEROTOPY.

Heterotropic (-trǫ·pik), *a.* 1885. [f. Gr. ἑτερο- + -τροπος turning + -IC.] *Physics.* = ÆOLOTROPIC, ANISOTROPIC.

Heterotropous (-ǫ·trŏpəs), *a.* 1819. [f. as prec. + -OUS.] = HEMITROPOUS 2. So **Hetero·tropal** *a.*

Heterozygote (he:tĕrozəi·gout). 1902. [f. HETERO- + ZYGOTE.] *Biol.* A zygote formed by the union of two unlike gametes. **Heterozygo·sis, -zygo·sity, -zy·goted** *a.*, **-zy·gous** *a.*

†**Hething,** *vbl. sb.* ME. [a. ON. *hǽðing* scoffing, derision, f. *hǽða* vb.] Derision; scorn, contempt; dishonour –1540.

‖**Hetman** (he·tmăn). Also **attaman.** 1710. [Polish *hetman* captain, app. ad. Ger. *hauptmann.*] A Polish captain or military commander.

Heugh, heuch (hiuχ). *Sc.* and *n. dial.* ME. [repr. of ME. *hogh*, OE. *hōh*, f. ablaut grade *hanh-* of HANG *v.*] **1.** A hanging descent; a precipice, cliff, or scaur; usu., one overhanging a river or the sea. **2.** A glen with steep overhanging sides 1450. **3.** The steep face of a quarry or the like (*quarry h.*); a coal-pit; *fig.* a pit 1592.

Heuk, var. of HUKE *Obs.*

Heulandite (hiū·lĕndəit). 1822. [f. H. *Heuland*, English mineralogist; see -ITE.] *Min.* A mineral of the Zeolite group; a hydrated silicate of aluminium and calcium, found in crystals of various colours with pearly lustre.

Heureka, the proper sp. of EUREKA, q. v.

Heuretic (hiure·tik), *sb. rare.* [ad. Gr. εὑρετικός inventive.] The branch of logic which treats of the art of discovery or invention. SIR W. HAMILTON.

Heuristic (hiuri·stik), *a.* (*sb.*) 1860. [irreg. f. Gr. εὑρίσκειν, app. after words in *-istic* from vbs. in -ιζειν -IZE.] **1.** Serving to find out; *spec.* applied to a system of education under which the pupil is trained to find out things for himself. **2.** *sb.* = prec. ABP. THOMSON.

Heved, obs. f. HEAD.

Hew (hiū), *v.* Pa. t. **hewed** (hiūd); pa. pple. **hewn** (hiūn), **hewed.** [A Com. Teut. vb.; orig. reduplicated. OE. *héawan*; OTeut. type **hauw-* :—pre-Teut. **kou-*, **kow-*. The strong pa. pple *hewen*, *hewn* has always been the more common. Cf. HAY *sb.*¹] **1.** *intr.* To deal blows with a cutting weapon. **2.** *trans.* To strike forcibly with a cutting instrument; to chop, hack, gash OE. **3.** To shape with cutting blows OE. **4.** To cut with an ax or the like so as to fell or bring down; *esp.* with *down*, etc. OE. **5.** To sever by a cutting blow; now with *away*, *off*, *out*, *from*, etc. OE. **6.** To chop into pieces; esp. with *asunder*, *to pieces*, etc. ME. **7.** To make, form, or produce by hewing OE.

1. Hewe not to hye, lest the chips fall in thine iye J. HEYWOOD. 3. When a rude and Unpolish'd Stone is hewen into a beautiful Statue CUDWORTH. *Rough hew*: see ROUGH-HEW *v.* 4. Command thou, that they h. me Cedar trees out of Lebanon 1 *Kings* v. 6. 5. The fragment of rock left when the rest is hewn away FREEMAN. 6. He tooke a yoke of oxen, and hewed them in pieces 1 *Sam.* xi. 7. 7. Phr. *To h. one's way.* Their Canoes..are hued out of one tree SIR T. HERBERT.

†**Hew,** *sb.* 1596. [f. HEW *v.*] An act of hewing; hacking, slaughter; a cut or gash produced by hewing –1618.

Hew, obs. f. EWE, HUE, YEW.

†**Hewe.** [OE. *hīwan* pl. (of **hīwa*), domestics, ME. *hiwen*, *heowen*, *hewen*, *heowes* and *hewes* pl.; also (later) *hewe* sing.; deriv. of root of Goth. *heiwa-* household. Cf. HIND *sb.*²] A domestic, a servant. OE. and ME. only.

Hewer (hiū·əɹ). ME. [f. HEW *v.* + -ER¹.] One who hews; in a colliery, the man who cuts coal from the seam 1708.

H. of wood and drawer of water (*Joshua* ix. 21), a labourer of the lowest kind, drudge.

Hewgh, *int.* = HEUGH, WHEW. *Lear* IV. vi. 93.

Hew-hole, var. of HICKWALL.

Hewn (hiūn), *ppl. a.* ME. [pa. pple. of HEW *v.*] **1.** Fashioned by hewing with a chisel, ax, etc.; made by or resulting from hewing. **2.** Excavated or hollowed out by hewing ME.

†**Hewt.** 1575. [prob. :—OE. *hiewet* hewing; cf. OF. *copeiz* COPSE.] ? A copse; a grove –1688.

Hex- (heks), Gr. ἕξ six, a comb. form, used chiefly in *Chem.*, in sense 'containing six atoms or molecules of the radical or substance'; as *hexdecyl* (= HEXADECYL), etc.

Hexa- (heksă), bef. a vowel **hex-**, comb. f. Gr. ἕξ six. In *Chem.* it indicates the presence of six atoms of some element, as in *hexacarbon*.

Hexaba·sic *a.*, *Chem.* having six atoms of a base, or of replaceable hydrogen. **Hexaca·psular** *a.*, *Bot.* having six capsules. **He·xace** (he·ksăsi) [Gr. ἀκή point], *Cryst.* the summit of a polyhedron formed by the concurrence of six faces. **Hexaco·lic** [Gr. κῶλον] *a.*, *Pros.* consisting of six cola. **Hexacora·llan, -co·ralline** [CORAL] *Zool.*, *adjs.* pertaining to the *Hexacoralla*, a chief division of the *Coralligena* or corals in which the fundamental number of intermesenteric chambers of the body cavity and of the tentacles is six; *sb.* one of these corals. **Hexa·ctine, Hexa·ctinal, -acti·nal** [Gr. ἀκτίς, ἀκτῖνος ray] *adjs.*, *Zool.* having six rays, as a sponge spicule. **Hexacti·nian** *a.*, *Zool.* pertaining to the *Hexactiniæ*, a group of *Actiniaria* having septa in pairs, in number six or a multiple of six. **Hexadacty·lic, Hexada·ctylous** [Gr. δάκτυλος] *adjs.*, *Anat.* having six fingers or six toes; so **Hexada·ctylism,** hexadactylous condition. **He·xaglot** [Gr. γλῶττα] *a.*, written or composed in six languages. **Hexape·talous** *a.*, *Bot.* having six petals. **Hexaphy·llous** [Gr. φύλλον] *a.*, *Bot.* applied to a calyx having six sepals or to a leaf consisting of six leaflets. **Hexapro·style** [PROSTYLE] *a.*, *Arch.* having a portico of six columns in front. **Hexa·pterous** [Gr. πτερόν] *a.*, provided with six wings or wing-like appendages. **He·xarchy** [Gr. -αρχία], a group of six states. **Hexase·mic** [Gr. ἑξάσημος] *a.*, *Pros.* containing six units of time or moræ. **Hexa·stichous** *a.*, *Bot.* arranged in six rows. **Hexastigm** [Gr. στίγμα], a figure determined by six points.

Hexachord (he·ksăkǭɹd). 1694. [ad. late Gr. ἑξάχορδος, f. ἑξα- + χορδή.] *Mus.* A diatonic series or scale of six notes, having a semitone between the third and fourth. See GAMUT. 1730. †**2.** The interval of a sixth –1741. **3.** A musical instrument with six strings 1858.

Hexactinellid (he:ksæktine·lid). 1865. [f. mod.L. *Hexactinellidæ*, (f. Gr. ἕξ + ἀκτίς (ἀκτῖν-) + L. dim. *-ell-*); see -ID.] **1.** *adj.* Of or belonging to the *Hexactinellidæ*, a family of siliceous sponges. **2.** *sb.* A sponge of this family 1879.

Hexad (he·ksæd). 1660. [ad. Gr. ἑξάς, -αδ- a group of six.] **1.** The number six (in the Pythagorean System); a series of six numbers. **2.** A group of six 1879. **3.** *Chem.* An element or radical that has the combining power of six units, i.e. of six atoms of hydrogen. Chiefly *attrib.* 1869. Hence **Hexa·dic** *a.* of the nature of a h. (sense 3).

Hexadecane (he·ksădīkēⁱn). 1872. [f. Gr. ἑξα- + δέκα ten (for ἑκκαίδεκα sixteen) + -ANE.] *Chem.* The paraffin of the 16-carbon series, also called CETANE. So **Hexadeco·ic** *a.* **Hexade·cyl,** the radical $C_{16}H_{33}$, also called CETYL.

‖**Hexaëmeron** (heksă,ī·mĕrǫn). Also **hexameron.** 1593. [Late L. = Gr. ἑξαήμερον adj. neut., f. ἕξ + ἡμέρα.] The six days of the creation; a history of the creation as contained in Genesis; or a treatise thereon.

Hexagon (he·ksăgǫ̆n). 1570. [ad. late L. *hexagonum*, a. Gr. ἑξάγωνον adj. neut., f. ἕξ + -γωνος, γωνία angle.] **1.** *Geom.* A plane figure having six sides and six angles. Also *attrib.* **2.** *Fortif.* A fort with six bastions 1669.

1. Bees..make their cells regular hexagons REID.

Hexagonal (heksæ·gŏnăl), *a.* (*sb.*) 1571. [f. prec. + -AL.] **1.** Of or pertaining to a hexagon; having six sides and six angles. **2.** Of solids: Whose section or base is a hexagon 1646. **3.** *Cryst.* Denominating a system of crystallization, which is referred to three lateral axes, normally inclined to each other at 60°, and a vertical axis at right angles to these and differing from them in length. Also, Of or belonging to this system. 1837. **4.** *Geom.* and *Cryst.* Having a relation to six angles, as *h. symmetry* 1878. **5.** *sb.* A hexagonal number 1796.

1. Phr. *Hexagonal numbers*, the series of POLYGONAL numbers 1, 6, 15, 28, 45, etc., formed by continuous summation of the arithmetical series 1, 5, 9, 13, 17, etc. Hence **Hexa·gonally** *adv.* **Hexa·gonalize** *v. trans.* to form into hexagons. vars. †**Hexago·nial,** †**Hexago·nical.**

Hexagonous (heksæ·gŏnəs), *a.* 1870. [f. HEXAGON + -OUS.] *Bot.* Having six edges; hexagonal in section. (Often written 6-*gonous*.)

Hexagram (he·ksăgræm). 1863. [f. HEXA- + Gr. γράμμα.] **1.** A figure formed by two intersecting equilateral triangles, each side of the one being parallel to a side of the other, and the six angular points coinciding with those of a hexagon 1871. **2.** *Geom.* A figure of six lines 1863.

‖**Hexagynia** (heksădʒi·niă). 1778. [Bot. L., f. HEXA- + Gr. γυνή in sense 'female organ, pistil'.] *Bot.* A Linnæan order of plants having six pistils. Hence **He·xagyn,** a plant of this order. **Hexagy·nian, Hexagy·nious** *adjs.* belonging to this order. **Hexa·gynous** *a.* having six pistils.

Hexahedral (heksăhī·drăl, -he·drăl), *a.* 1800. [f. next + -AL.] Of the form of a hexahedron; having six sides or faces. So †**Hexahe·drical** *a.* BOYLE.

Hexahedron (heksăhī·drǫ̆n, -he·drǫ̆n). 1571. [neut. sing. of Gr. ἑξάεδρος, f. ἕξ + ἕδρα.] *Geom.*, etc. A solid figure having six faces; *esp.* the *regular hexahedron* or cube.

Hexakis-, Gr. ἑξάκις six times, comb. form. **He:xakisoctahe·dron,** a solid figure contained by forty-eight scalene triangles. **He:xakistetrahe·dron,** a solid figure contained by twenty-four scalene triangles, being the hemihedral form of the hexakisoctahedron.

Hexamerous (heksæ·mĕrəs), *a.* 1857. [f. HEXA- + Gr. μέρος + -OUS.] Having the parts six in number. (In *Bot.* often written 6-*merous*.)

Hexameter (heksæ·mĭtəɹ). ME. [a. L., ad. Gr. ἑξάμετρος, f. ἑξα- + μέτρον.]

A. *adj.* (Now only sb. used attrib.) *Pros.* Consisting of six metrical feet; *esp.* dactyls and spondees 1546.

B. *sb.* A verse or line of six metrical feet; *esp.* the *dactylic hexameter* (*catalectic*), consisting of five dactyls and a trochee, or (in Latin poets) oftener a spondee; for any or all of the first four dactyls a spondee may be substituted, but in the fifth foot a spondee is admitted only for special effect ME.

These lame Hexameters the strong-wing'd music of Homer! No—but a most burlesque, barbarous experiment TENNYSON. Hence **Hexa·metral** *a.* of or pertaining to the h. **Hexame·tric, -al** *a.* of or pertaining to a h.; consisting of six metrical feet; composed in hexameters. **Hexa·metrist,** one who writes hexameters. **Hexa·metrize** *v. intr.* to write hexameters; *trans.* to celebrate in hexameters.

‖**Hexandria** (heksæ·ndriă). 1753. [mod.L. (Linn.), f. Gr. ἕξ + ανδρ-, ἀνήρ, in sense 'male organ, stamen'.] *Bot.* A Linnæan class of plants having six (equal) stamens. Hence **Hexa·nder,** a plant of this class. **Hexa·ndrian, -ious** *adjs.* of or pertaining to this class. **Hexa·ndric, Hexa·ndrous** *adjs.* having six (equal) stamens.

Hexane (he·ksēⁱn). 1877. [f. Gr. ἕξ + -ANE.] *Chem.* The paraffin of the hexacarbon series, C_6H_{14}; of this there are five forms. So **He·xene,** the olefine of the hexacarbon series (C_6H_{12}), also called *hexylene*, homologous and polymeric with ethene; it exists in many metameric forms. **He·xine,** the hydrocarbon C_6H_{10} of the same series. **Hexoic acid,** $C_6H_{12}O_2$, the same as caproic acid. **Hexo·ylene,** one of the isomeric forms of hexine.

†**He·xangle.** 1657. [A hybrid form, f. HEX(A- + ANGLE.] = HEXAGON.

Hexangular (heksæ·ŋgiŭlăɹ), *a.* 1665. [f. prec.] Having six angles; hexagonal.

‖**Hexapla** (he·ksăplă). Also **hexaple.** 1613. [a. Gr. (τὰ) ἑξαπλᾶ (title of Origen's work), neut. pl. of ἑξαπλοῦς sixfold.] A sixfold text in parallel arrangement, as that made by Origen of the O.T. Hence **He·xaplar, Hexapla·rian** *adjs.* of the form or character of a h.

Hexapod (he·ksăpǫ̆d), *sb.* (*a.*) 1668. [ad. Gr. ἑξαποδ- six-footed.] **1.** An animal having six feet, an insect. **2.** *adj.* Having six feet; belonging to the class *Hexapoda* or *Insecta*, hexapodous 1815. Hence **Hexa·podal, Hexa·podous** *adjs.* having six feet, belonging to this class. **Hexa·podan** *a.* and *sb.* = HEXAPOD *a.* and *sb.*

Hexapody (heksæ·pǒdi). 1844. [f. Gr. ἑξαποδ- of six feet.] *Pros.* A line or verse consisting of six feet.

Hexastich (he·ksăstik). 1577. [ad. mod.L. *hexastichon*, a. Gr., f. ἑξα- + στίχος row.] A group of six lines of verse.

Hexastyle (he·ksăstəil), *a.* (*sb.*) 1704. [ad. Gr. ἑξάστυλος, f. ἕξ (HEXA-) + στῦλος pillar. Cf. F. *hexastyle*.] **1.** Having six columns; applied to a portico or temple 1748. **2.** *sb.* A portico or temple having six columns.

Hexateuch (he·ksătiūk). 1878. [f. Gr. ἕξ (HEXA-) + τεῦχος, after *pentateuch*.] The first six books of the O.T.

Hexatomic (heksătǫ·mik), *a.* 1873. [f. HEXA- + ATOMIC.] *Chem.* Containing or consisting of six atoms; having six replaceable hydrogen atoms; also = next.

Hexavalent (heksæ·vălĕnt), *a.* 1886. [f. HEXA- + L. *valentem*.] *Chem.* Combining with or capable of replacing six atoms of hydrogen or other univalent element or radical.

Hexene, Hexine: see under HEXANE.

Hexoctahe·dron. 1570. [f. HEX(A)- + OCTAHEDRON.] *Geom.* etc. †**a.** The critical form of the CUBO-*octahedron*. DANA. **b.** = HEXAKISOCTAHEDRON.

Hexode (he·ksoud), *a.* 1894. [f. Gr. ἕξ + ὁδός.] *Electr. Telegr. lit.* Of six ways: applied to a mode of multiplex telegraphy, whereby six messages can be transmitted simultaneously.

Hexoic acid, Hexoylene: see under HEXANE.

Hexpa·rtite, *a.* 1842. [A hybrid form, f. Gr. ἕξ + L. *partitus*.] Sexpartite, sextipartite.

Hexyl (he·ksil). 1869. [f. Gr. ἕξ + ὕλη, -YL.] *Chem.* The hydrocarbon radical C_6H_{13}.

It may exist in various forms. Also *attrib.*, as in *h. alcohol*, etc. Hence **He·xylene** = HEXENE. **Hexy·lic** *a.* of or pertaining to h., as *hexylic acid*, etc.

Hey (hē̆ⁱ, hē), *int.* (*sb.*) [ME. *hei.* Cf. HEIGH.] A call to attract attention; also, an exclam. of exultation, incitement, surprise, etc.; sometimes an interrogative (= *eh ?*). As *sb.* A cry of 'hey!' ME.

Phr. *Hey for* —: an utterance of applause or exultant appreciation of some person or thing, or of some place which one resolves to reach 1661. **Hey-go-mad** (*dial.*), as *adj.* = boisterously excited. **Hey-pass, Hey presto**: exclams. of command by conjurors and jugglers; also as *sbs.*

Hey-day (hē̆ⁱ·dēⁱ·), *int. arch.* 1526. [earlier *heyda*, f. prec. Cf. G. *heida*, *-di.*] An exclamation of gaiety or surprise.

Hey-day, heyday (hē̆ⁱ·dēⁱ), *sb.* 1590. [? conn. w. prec. The second element was prob. not in its origin the word *day.*] **1.** State of exaltation or excitement. **2.** The stage or period when excited feeling is at its height. Often associated with *day*, and taken as the most flourishing or exalted time 1751. Also *attrib.*

1. At your age, The hey-day in the blood is tame *Haml.* III. iv. 69. **2.** In the hey-day of youth 1807, of his powers 1877.

Hey-day guise, -de-gay: see HAY *sb.*[4]

‖**Heyduck** (hai·duk, hē̆ⁱ·dɒk). 1615. [a. Boh., Pol., Serb., Roman. *hajduk*, Magyar *hajdú* pl. *hajdúk*, Turk. *haidūd*, etc., robber, brigand.] A term, app. meaning orig. 'robber, brigand' (as still in Serbia, etc.), which in Hungary became the name of a special body of foot-soldiers, and in Poland of the liveried personal followers and attendants of the nobles.

Heygh, obs. f. HIGH.

Hey-ho, hey ho (hē̆ⁱ·hōᵘ·), *int.* 1471. An utterance marking the rhythm of movement in heaving and hauling (cf. HEAVE HO); often used in the burdens of songs, etc.

Heynne, var. of HYNE *adv.*, hence.

Heyþen, obs. f. HEATHEN.

†**Hi**, *pron.*[1] OE., ME. Her.

†**Hi**, *pron.*[2] OE., ME. They; them.

Hi (həi), *int.* 1475. [Cf. HEY.] An exclam. used to call attention.

Hiant (həi·ănt), *a.* 1800. [ad. L. *hiantem*, *hiare* to gape.] Gaping.

Hiate (həi·eⁱt), *v. rare.* 1646. [f. L. *hiat-*, *hiare.*] *intr.* To gape; to cause a hiatus. **Hia·tion**, gaping.

Hiatus (həi,ēⁱ·tɒs). *Pl.* **hiatus, hiatuses.** 1563. [a. L.; see prec.] **1.** A break in continuity; a gaping chasm; an opening or aperture. Now *rare.* ‖**b.** *Anat.* A foramen 1886. **2.** A gap in a series; a lacuna in a writing, etc.; a missing link in a chain of events, etc. 1613. **3.** *Gram.* and *Pros.* The break between two vowels coming together without an intervening consonant in successive words or syllables 1706.

Hibernacle (həi·bəɹnă̆k'l). Also **hy-.** 1708. [ad. L. *hibernaculum.*] A winter retreat; a hibernaculum.

‖**Hibernaculum** (həibəɹnæ·kiulɒm). Also **hy-.** Pl. **-a.** 1699. [L., usu. in pl., f. *hibernus* wintry; see -CULE.] †**1.** A greenhouse for wintering plants. EVELYN. **2.** *Zool.* The winter quarters of a hibernating animal 1789. **3.** *Bot.* A part of a plant that protects the embryo during the winter, as a bulb or bud 1760. **4.** *Zool.* **a.** An encysted winter-bud of a polyzoan 1885. **b.** The false operculum of a snail 1888. Hence **Hiberna·cular** *a.*

Hibernal (həibə̄·ɹnăl), *a.* Also **hy-.** 1626. [ad. L. *hibernalis*, f. *hibernus* wintry.] Of, pertaining to, or proper to winter; appearing in winter. Also *fig.*

Hibernate (həi·bəɹneⁱt), *v.* Also **hy-.** 1802. [f. L. *hibernat-*, *hibernare* to winter.] *intr.* To winter; to spend the winter in some special state suited to resist it; said esp. of animals that pass the winter in a state of torpor. Also *transf.* of persons. Also *fig.*

fig. Inclination would lead me to h. during half the year SOUTHEY. Hence **Hi·berna·tor**, an animal that hibernates. **Hiberna·tion**, the action, condition, or period of hibernating; also *fig.*

Hibernian (həibə̄·ɹniăn), *a.* (*sb.*) Also **hy-.** 1632. [f. L. *Hibernia*, a corrupted form of *Iverna* = OCelt. **Iveriu*, whence Ir. *Eriu*, acc. *Eirinn*, *Erinn* Erin.] **1.** Of or belonging to Ireland; Irish. **2.** *sb.* A native of Ireland; an Irishman 1709.

1. The truly H. predicament of being notoriously unknown F. HALL. Hence **Hibe·rnianism**, Irish character or nationality; an Irish characteristic, trait, or idiom.

Hibernicism (həibə̄·ɹnisiz'm). 1758. [f. mod.L. *Hibernicus* Irish + -ISM; cf. *Scotticism.*] **1.** An idiom or expression characteristic of Irish speech; esp. an Irish bull (see BULL *sb.*[4]). **2.** Irish nationality 1807. So **Hibe·rnicize** *v.* to make Irish in form or character.

Hiberno-, formative element f. L. type **Hibernus*, as in **Hiberno-Celtic**, Celtic of Ireland.

‖**Hibiscus** (hibi·skɒs). 1706. [L., a. Gr. ἰβίσκος some malvaceous plant.] *Bot.* A large genus of malvaceous plants (herbs, shrubs, and trees), mostly from tropical countries; the Rose-mallows.

Hiccius doccius (hi·kʃiɒs dǫ·kʃiɒs). 1676. [A corruption of L. *hicce est doctus* 'here is the learned man', or ? nonsense.] A formula used by jugglers; hence, 'a cant word for a juggler; one that plays fast and loose' (J.). Also *attrib.*

Hiccup (hi·kɒp), *sb.* Also **hiccough.** 1580. [In form *hickop*, *hiccup*, a var. of *hickock*, HICKET, q.v. *Hiccough* is a mere error, due to the impression that the second element was *cough.*] An involuntary spasm of the respiratory organs, consisting in a quick inspiratory movement of the diaphragm checked suddenly by closure of the glottis, and accompanied by a characteristic sound. Also, a succession of such spasms. *fig.* 1669. Hence **Hi·ccup** *v. intr.* to make the sound of a h.; *trans.* to utter with hiccups, as a drunken person.

‖**Hic jacet** (hik dʒē̆ⁱ·set). 1601. [L. = 'here lies'.] The first two words of a Latin epitaph; hence, an epitaph.

The cold Hic Jacets of the dead TENNYSON.

Hick, *sb.*[1] 1565. [A by-form of *Richard.*] An ignorant countryman; a booby (now *U.S.*).

Hick, *sb.*[2] *rare.* Also **hic.** 1607. [See next.] A hiccup; a hesitation in speech. Hence **Hick** *v. intr.* to hiccup.

†**Hicket**, *sb.* 1544. [One of the earlier forms of *hiccup*, the other being *hickock*, both with a dim. formative *-et*, *-ock.* The stem *hick* is echoic.] Early form of HICCUP *sb.* –1684. So †**Hicket** *v.* Also †**Hickock** *sb.* and *v.*

Hickory (hi·kəri). 1676. [Short for Virginian *pawcohicora* oily liquor pressed from hickory kernels.] **1.** A N. American tree of the genus *Carya*, with tough heavy wood, and bearing drupes enclosing nuts, the kernels of which in several species are edible. Also **h.-tree.** 1682.

There are about a dozen species, all natives of N. America, the commonest being the Shell-bark, Scaly-bark, or Shag-bark H. (*C. alba*); others are the Bitter-nut or Swamp H. (*C. amara*), and the Pig-nut, Hog-nut, or Broom H. (*C. porcina*).

2. The wood of the American hickory, or a stick, or the like, made of it 1676. **3.** The nut of the American hickory 1866. **4.** *attrib.* 1741.

2. *Old Hickory*, a nickname of Andrew Jackson, President of U.S. 1829–1837.

Comb.: **h.-elm**, an American elm (*Ulmus racemosa*); **-eucalyptus**, an Australian tree, *Eucalyptus punctata*, with very hard tough wood; **-girdler**, a longicorn beetle, *Oncideres cingulatus*, of U.S.; **-horned** *a.*, having very tough or hard horns; **-pine**, N. American species of pine, *Pinus Balfouriana*, var. *aristata*, and *P. pungens*; **-shirt** (*U.S.*), a coarse and durable shirt, made of heavy twilled cotton with a narrow blue stripe or a check; **-tree** (see 1).

†**Hickscorner.** 1530. [See HICK *sb.*[1]] A character in an interlude of the same name repr. a travelled libertine who scoffs at religion; hence, a scoffer –1622. Hence **-scorning** *a.* 1601.

Hicksite (hi·ksəit). 1839. [f. the name *Hicks* + -ITE.] A member of a seceding body of American Quakers, founded by Elias Hicks in 1827, and holding Socinian doctrines.

Hickwall (hi·kwǫl). *local.* Also **hyghwhele, highaw(e, hickle,** etc. 14.. [Prob. echoic, in the early form *hyghwhele*, whence other forms modified by popular etymology. Cf. HECCO, HIGH-HOLE, WITWALL, YAFFLE, YUCKLE.] The Green Woodpecker.

Hid (hid), *ppl. a.* ME. [pa. pple. of HIDE *v.*[1]] Hidden, concealed, secret.

Hidage (həi·dedʒ). *Obs.* exc. *Hist.* ME. See HIDE *sb.*[2] and -AGE.] **1.** A tax payable to the royal exchequer for each hide of land. **2.** The assessed value or measurement of lands, on which the tax was levied 1862.

‖**Hidalgo** (hidæ·lgo). 1594. [Sp., formerly also *hijo dalgo*, i.e. *hijo* (*filho*) *de algo*, son of something. Cf. FIDALGO.] In Spain: One of the lower nobility; a gentleman by birth. Also *transf.*

Hidden (hi·d'n), *ppl. a.* 1547. [See HIDE *v.*[1]] **1.** Concealed, secret, occult, etc.; see HIDE *v.*[1] **2.** *Mus.* Applied to the consecutive fifths or octaves suggested between two parts when they move in similar motion to the interval of a fifth or octave 1869.

1. Who..wil lighten the hidden things of darkenes N.T. (Rhem.) 1 *Cor.* iv. 5.

Hi·ddenly, *adv.* 1580. [-LY[2].] In a hidden manner.

Hide (həid), *sb.*[1] [OE. *hȳd* str. fem. :— OTeut. **hūðiz* :— pre-Teut. **kūtis*: cf. L. *cutis*, Gr. κύτος.] **1.** The skin of an animal, raw or dressed; esp. applied to the skins of the larger beasts and such as may be tanned into leather. **2.** The human skin. (Now contemptuous or joc.) OE. **3.** A whip made of hide 1851.

1. Phr. (*In*) *hide and hair*: wholly, entirely. **2.** Who could have beleevd so much insolence durst vent it self out from the h. of a varlet? MILT.

Comb.: **h.-drogher**, a coasting vessel trading in hides; the master of such a vessel; **-money** [tr. Gr. δερματικόν], the money arising from the hides of the victims sacrificed at Athens; **-scraper, -stretcher, -worker.**

Hide, *sb.*[2] *Obs.* exc. *Hist.* [OE. *hīd* str. fem., earlier *hīgid*, app. from **hīwid*, deriv. of *hīw-*, *hīg-*, household, family. The suffix is obscure.] **1.** A measure of land in O.E. times, and later; primarily, the amount required by one free family with its dependants; defined as being as much land as could be tilled with one plough in a year. See CARUCATE. The *hide* was normally = 100 acres, but the size of the acre itself varied. **2.** *nonce-use.* (Assoc. with HIDE *sb.*[1]) As much land as could be measured by a thong cut out of a hide. MARLOWE & NASHE.

1. Phr. *Hide and gaine* [OF. *gaigne*], orig. synonyms of arable land; later, taken as a phrase.

Hide, *sb.*[3] ME. [f. HIDE *v.*[1]] †**1.** Concealment. ME. only. **2.** A cache 1649.

Hide (həid), *v.*[1] Pa. t. **hid**; pa. pple. **hid, hidden** (hi·d'n). [OE. *hȳdan* :—OTeut. **hūdjan*, f. root of OE. *hȳd*, HIDE *sb.*[1], or perh. :—pre-Teut. **keudh-*, *kudh-*, seen in Gr. κεύθειν.] **1.** *trans.* To put or keep out of sight; to conceal from the notice of others; to secrete. **2. a.** *refl.* To put or keep oneself out of sight OE. **b.** *intr.* To conceal oneself ME. **3.** *trans.* To keep from the knowledge of others; to keep secret ME. **4.** To prevent from being seen to obstruct the view of; to cover up ME.

1. She hidded the swerde CAXTON. Phr. *To h. one's face*: (*a*) to turn away one's eyes, take no heed (Biblical); (*b*) to keep out of sight. Thou didst h. thy face, and I was troubled *Ps.* xxx. 7. *To h. one's head*: (*a*) to take shelter; (*b*) to keep out of sight. †*All hid*: the cry in hide-and-seek; hence, the game itself. *L. L. L.* IV. iii. 78. **2. b.** *Hide fox and all after*: an old cry in hide-and seek. *Haml.* IV. ii. 32. **3.** He that has a secret should not only h. it, but h. that he has it to h. CARLYLE. **4.** A few seconds before the sun was totally hid 1810.

Hide, *v.*[2] 1757. [f. HIDE *sb.*[1]] **1.** *trans* To remove the hide from; to flay. **2.** To beat the hide of; to thrash (*slang* or *colloq.*) 1825.

Hide-and-seek. 1672. A children's game, in which one or more hide, and the rest, at a given signal, try to find them. Also *transf.*

The ragged boys..played hide-and-seek among the tombstones DICKENS. Also **Hide-and-go-seek.**

Hidebound (həi·dbaund), *a.* (*sb.*) 1559. [f. HIDE *sb.*[1] + *bound* ppl. a.; cf. *tongue-tied.*] **1.** Of cattle: Having the skin clinging closely to the back and ribs so that it cannot be loosened or raised with the fingers, as a result of bad feeding and emaciation. Also *transf.* and *fig.* **2.** Of trees: Having the bark so close and unyielding as to impede growth 1626; (of soil) starved and unproductive 1778. 3. *transf.* and *fig.* Of persons, etc.: Restricted in view or scope; hence, bigoted 1603. †b. Close-fisted –1683. 4. Bound with or in leather 1858.

3. The h. humor which he calls his judgement MILT.

†B. *sb.* The diseases affecting cattle and trees described above in 1, 2. –1778.

Hence **Hi·debind** *v.* to render h.; to confine, constrict 1642.

Hided (həi·dėd), *a.* ME. [f. HIDE *sb.*[1] + -ED[2].] 1. Having a hide (esp. of a specified kind). 2. Made of hide 1798.

†**Hidegeld, -gild.** [OE. *hidȝield, -ȝeld.*] *O. E. Law.* = HIDAGE. –1706.

Hi·deland. *Hist.* 1577. [f. HIDE *sb.*[2] + LAND.] = HIDE *sb.*[2] 1.

†**Hi·del(s.** [OE. *hȳdels*, f. HIDE *v.*[1] and -ELS. Cf. *riddle.*] Hiding-place.

Hideous (hi·diəs), *a.* (*adv.*) [ME. *hidous*, a. AF. *hidous* = OF. *hidos, -eus*, f. *hisde, hide* horror, fear.] 1. Frightful, dreadful, horrible; hence, horribly ugly or unpleasing, revolting. †b. Terrific on account of size; huge, immense. ME. 2. Revolting to the moral sense; abominable; odious ME. †3. *adv.* Hideously. MILT. *P.L.* vi. 206.

1. Hurld headlong..With h. ruine and combustion down To bottomless perdition MILT. *P. L.* I. 46. H. alleys KINGSLEY, noises 1896. b. Of stature huge and h. he was SPENSER. 2. This h. rashnesse SHAKS. Hence **Hi·deous·ly** *adv.* ME., **-ness** ME., **Hide·o·sity** 1856.

Hider (həi·dəɹ). ME. [f. HIDE *v.*[1] + -ER[1].] One who hides.

Hiding (həi·diŋ), *vbl. sb.*[1] ME. [f. HIDE *v.*[1] + -ING[1].] 1. The action of HIDE *v.*[1] (*lit.* and *fig.*); the condition of being hidden. 2. Something that hides; a hiding-place ME.

1. A gentleman who was 'in h.' after..Culloden SCOTT.

Hi·ding, *vbl. sb.*[2] *slang* or *colloq.* 1809. [f. HIDE *v.*[2]] A thrashing.

Hi·dlings, *adv.*, *sb.*, and *a. dial.* ME. [f. HID + -LINGS.] 1. *In h.*, secretly. 2. *sb.* (*pl.*) Hiding-places. 3. *adj.* Secret, clandestine.

Hidro-: see HYDRO-.

Hidrotic (hidrǫ·tik). 1705. [ad. med.L. *hidroticus*, a. Gr., f. ἱδρώς, -ῶτος.] *Med.* 1. *adj.* Of or pertaining to sweat; sudorific; diaphoretic 1727. 2. *sb.* A medicinal agent causing sweat.

Hie (həi), *v.* Now *arch.* or *poet.* [OE. *hīȝian* to strive, be eager, pant.] †1. *intr.* To strive, pant –ME. 2. To hasten, go quickly ME. †b. To hasten on; to make progress; to speed –1608. 3. *refl.* = sense 2. ME. 4. *trans.* To cause to hasten. Now U.S., of urging *on* a hound. 5. with advb. accus.; usu. *to hie one's way* ME.

2. Thither..Accurst..he [Satan] hies MILT. *P. L.* II. 1055. b. The night higheth fast SPENSER. 3. The Bees..high them home as fast as they can 1713. Hence †**Hie, hy** *sb.* haste, speed.

Hieland, obs. and Sc. var. of HIGHLAND.

Hield, heald, *v. Obs.* exc. *dial.* [OE. *hieldan* :—**halþjan*, f. *halþo-* inclined.] *trans.* and *intr.* To bend, incline. So †**Hield** *sb.*

Hiemal (həi·ĭmăl), *a.* Now *rare.* Also **hy-**. 1560. [ad. L. *hiemalis*, f. *hiems.*] Of or belonging to winter; winter-.

Hiemate (həi·ĭmēt), *v. rare.* 1623. [f. L. *hiemat-*, *hiemare.*] *intr.* To winter. Hence †**Hiema·tion.**

‖**Hiems** (həi·emz). 1450. [L. = winter.] Winter.

Hieracite (həi·ĕrăsəit). 1585. [ad. med.L. *Hieracitæ* (see below).] *Eccl. Hist.* A follower of Hierax, an Egyptian ascetic (*c* 300 A.D.), who denied the resurrection of the body, and taught celibacy, etc.

‖**Hieracium** (həiĕrē·ʃiǒm). 1565. [L., a. Gr. ἱεράκιον, f. ἱέραξ hawk.] *Bot.* A large genus of Composite plants, mostly with yellow flowers; Hawkweed.

Hieracosphinx (həiĕrē·kosfiŋks). *Egypt. Antiq.* A hawk-headed sphinx.

‖**Hiera picra** (həi·ĕră pi·kră). ME. [med.L., f. Gr. ἱερά (fem. of ἱερός sacred), a name of many medicines + πικρά, fem. of πικρός bitter.] *Pharmacy.* A purgative drug composed of aloes and canella bark, sometimes mixed with honey, etc. Also corruptly *hickery-pickery*, etc.

Hierarch (həi·ĕrāɹk). 1574. [ad. med.L. *hierarcha*, a. Gr. ἱεράρχης high priest, f. ἱερός + -αρχης, -αρχος, ruling, ruler.] 1. One who has rule or authority in holy things; an ecclesiastical potentate; a chief priest; an archbishop. 2. Applied to an archangel 1667.

1. Their great H. the Pope MILT. 2. The winged H. [Raphael] MILT. *P. L.* v. 468. Hence **Hiera·rchal, Hiera·rchic** *adjs.* of or belonging to a h. or a hierarchy.

Hiera·rchical, *a.* 1561. [as prec. + -ICAL.] †1. Belonging to a priestly hierarchy. 2. Belonging to a regular gradation of orders, classes, or ranks (see HIERARCHY 4) 1832. Hence **Hiera·rchically** *adv.*

Hi·erarchism. 1846. [f. HIERARCH (or HIERARCHY) + -ISM.] Hierarchical practice and principles. So **Hi·erarchist,** an adherent of a hierarchy.

Hierarchy (həi·ĕrāɹki). [ME., a. OF. *ier-, jerarchie*, ad. late L. *ierarchia*, for *hierarchia*, a. Gr. ἱεραρχία the power or rule of a ἱεράρχης (HIERARCH), episcopate.] 1. Each of the three divisions of angels, every one comprising three orders, in the system of Dionysius the Areopagite; see CHERUB. Also, the angelic host. b. *transf.* of other beings ME. 2. Rule or dominion in holy things; priestly government 1563. 3. *concr.* An organized body of priests or clergy in successive orders or grades 1619. 4. A body of persons or things ranked in grades, orders, or classes, one above another; *spec.* in *Nat. Science* and *Logic* 1643.

1. So sang the Hierarchies MILT. *P. L.* VII. 192. b. Olympus' faded h. KEATS. 4. A h. of Concepts 1864.

Hieratic, -al (həiĕræ·tik, -ăl), *a.* 1656. [ad. L. *hieraticus*, a. Gr. ἱερατικός priestly, f. (ult.) ἱεράομαι to be a priest.] 1. Pertaining to or used by the priestly class; used in connexion with sacred subjects. *spec.* a. Applied to a style of ancient Egyptian writing, which consisted of abridged forms of hieroglyphics 1669. b. *Hieratic paper* = next. 1656. c. Applied to a style of art (esp. Egyptian or Greek), in which earlier types or methods, fixed by religious tradition, are conventionally adhered to. Also *fig.* 1841. 2. *gen.* Priestly, sacerdotal 1859.

1. a. This mode of writing..has been called without much reason 'the hieratic' RAWLINSON. 2. The Law and the Prophets..constituted..the h. Hebrew books 1893.

Hieratica (həiĕræ·tikă). 1832. [L. (sc. *charta* or *papyrus*); see prec.] Papyrus of the finest quality, anciently appropriated to sacred writings. (Now, a trade name of a special quality of paper.)

Hiero-, bef. a vowel **hier-**, comb. f. Gr. ἱερός sacred, holy.

Hierocracy (həiĕrǫ·krăsi). 1794. [-CRACY.] 1. = HIERARCHY 2. 2. = HIERARCHY 3. SOUTHEY. Hence **Hierocra·tic, -al** *a.* of or pertaining to a h.

Hierodule (həi·ĕrodiūl). 1835. [ad. late L. *hierodulus*, a. Gr., f. ἱερόν (adj. neut. used subst.) temple + δοῦλος.] A slave (of either sex) dwelling in a temple, and dedicated to the service of a god.

Hieroglyph (həi·ĕroglif), *sb.* 1598. [f. HIEROGLYPHIC; cf. F. *hiéroglyphe.* The Gr. ἱερογλύφος meant 'a carver of hieroglyphics'.] 1. A hieroglyphic character; a figure of a tree, animal, etc., standing for a word, syllable, or sound, and forming an element of a species of writing found on ancient Egyptian monuments or records; thence extended to the like in the writing of other races. Also, a writing of this kind. 2. *transf.* and *fig.* A secret or enigmatical figure; an emblem 1646. Also *joc.* 3. One who makes hieroglyphic inscriptions (*rare*) 1863.

2. On your brows..An h. of sorrow, a fiery sign SWINBURNE. So **Hi·eroglyph** *v.* to represent by a h.; to write in hieroglyphs. **Hiero·glypher** (*rare*).

Hieroglyphic (həiĕro͵gli·fik). Also 7 **gie-**. 1585. [ad. F. *hiéroglyphique*, or late L. *hieroglyphicus*, a. Gr., f. ἱερός sacred + γλυφή carving. The adj. was used subst. by Plutarch, τὰ ἱερογλυφικά (sc. γράμματα), whence *hieroglyphics.*]

A. *adj.* 1. Of the nature of a hieroglyph (sense 1); written in or consisting of hieroglyphics. 2. *transf.* and *fig.* Having a hidden meaning; symbolical, emblematic 1647. 3. Containing or inscribed with hieroglyphs 1663. 4. *joc.* Difficult to decipher 1856.

1. The Chinese..was in its origin a h. system MAX MÜLLER. 2. So that all fair Species be Hieroglyphick marks of Thee COWLEY. 4. A h. scrawl 1856.

B. *sb.* 1. *orig.* in *pl.* = Gr. τὰ ἱερογλυφικά. The character or mode of writing used by the ancient Egyptians (or others), consisting of figures of objects directly or figuratively representing words (*picture-writing*), or, in certain cases, syllables or letters. The sing. is rarely used. 1586. 2. A picture standing for a word or notion; hence, a figure, device, or sign, having some hidden meaning; an enigmatical symbol, an emblem; a hieroglyph 1596. b. pl. *joc.* Characters difficult to make out 1734.

2. A silken string circles both their bodies as the Hyeroglyphic or bond of Wedlock SIR T. HERBERT. b. The hieroglyphics of Bradshaw 1862.

Hence †**Hierogly·phic** *v.* to represent by, or as by, a h.; to interpret or express, as a h. **Hierogly·phical** *a.* = HIEROGLYPHIC *a.* **Hierogly·phically** *adv.*

Hiero·glyphist. 1829. [? f. Gr. ἱερογλύφος + -IST.] A writer of hieroglyphs; one versed in hieroglyphs. So **Hiero·glyphize** *v.* to write or express by hieroglyphics.

Hierogram (həi·ĕrogræm). 1656. [f. HIERO- + -GRAM.] A sacred symbol; a hieroglyph (*lit.* and *fig.*).

Hierogra·mmate, -at. 1864. [f. Gr. ἱερογραμματεύς.] A writer of sacred records, *spec.* of hieroglyphics.

Hierogramma·tic, *a.* 1641. [f. HIEROGRAM.] Of the nature of a hierogram, relating to or consisting of hierograms. So **Hierogramma·tical** *a.* **Hierogra·mmatist** = prec.

Hierograph (həi·ĕrograf). 1835. [f. Gr. ἱερός sacred + -γραφος (see -GRAPH).] A sacred inscription or symbol; a hieroglyph. So **Hiero·grapher,** a sacred scribe. **Hierogra·phic, -al** *a.* of the nature of, or relating to, sacred writing or symbols. **Hiero·graphy,** a description of sacred things; †writing by hierograms.

Hiero·latry. 1814. [See HIERO- and -LATRY.] Worship of saints; hagiolatry. COLERIDGE.

Hierology (həiĕrǫ·lŏdʒi). 1828. [f. HIERO- + -LOGY.] †1. 'A discourse on sacred things' (Webster). †2. Hieroglyphic lore –1859. 3. Sacred literature or lore; e.g. that of the Egyptians, Greeks, Jews, etc. 1854. 4. = HAGIOLOGY. 1890. So **Hierolo·gic, -al** *a.* belonging to h. **Hiero·logist,** one versed in h.

Hi·eromancy. 1775. [See HIERO- and -MANCY.] Divination from observation of objects offered in sacrifice, or from sacred things.

Hieroma·rtyr. 1864. [f. HIERO- + MARTYR.] *Gr. Ch.* A martyr who was in holy orders.

‖**Hieromnemon** (həiĕrǫmnī·mǫn). 1727. [Gr. ἱερομνήμων adj. and sb., f. ἱερός + μνήμων.] A sacred recorder. 1. *Gr. Antiq.* The title of one of the two deputies sent by each tribe to the Amphictyonic council, whose office was concerned with religious matters 1753. 2. *Gr. Ch.* An officer who stood behind the patriarch, and showed him the prayers, psalms, etc. he was to rehearse.

Hieromonach (həiĕromǫ·năk). 1882. [ad. Gr. ἱερομόναχος (see HIERO- and MONK).] *Gr. Ch.* A monk who is also a priest; opp. to a 'secular' cleric.

Hieronymian (həiĕroni·miăn). 1656. [f. *Hieronymus* Jerome, a 5th c. father of the Church; see -IAN.] 1. *adj.* Of or belonging to St. Jerome, the author of the Latin Vulgate translation of the Bible 1884. 2. *sb.* = HIERONYMITE *sb.* So **Hierony·mic** *a.* = 1.

Hieronymite (həiĕrǫ·nimait). 1550. [f. as prec. + -ITE.] 1. *sb.* A hermit of any of the orders of St. Jerome. 2. *adj.* Belonging to any of these orders 1843.

Hierophant (həi·ĕrofænt). 1677. [ad. late L. *hierophantes, -phanta*, a. Gr., f. ἱερός sacred + φαίνειν bring to light. Cf. F. *hiérophante.*] 1. *Antiq.* An official expounder of sacred mysteries or ceremonies, esp. in ancient Greece; an initiating or presiding priest. **2.** *gen.* The minister of any 'revelation'; the interpreter of any esoteric principle 1822. So **Hi·erophancy,** the function of a h. **Hieropha·ntic** *a.* of or belonging to a h. or hierophants; resembling a h.

Hieroscopy (həiĕrǫ·skǒpi). 1727. [ad. Gr. ἱεροσκοπία.] = HIEROMANCY.

Hierosolymitan (həiĕrosǫ·limə̆ităn). 1538. [ad. late L. *Hierosolymitanus*, f. *Hierosolyma* = Gr. Ἱεροσόλυμα.] **1.** *adj.* Belonging to Jerusalem 1721. **2.** *sb.* A native or inhabitant of Jerusalem. So **Hieroso·lymite** *sb.* and *a.*

Hierurgy (həi·ĕrvɪdʒi). Also 8 **-ourgy.** 1678. [ad. Gr. ἱερουργία; see -URGY.] A sacred work; a religious observance or rite.

Hifalutin, var. of HIGHFALUTIN.

Higgle (hi·g'l), *v.* 1633. [app. related to HAGGLE, with vowel-modification.] **1.** *intr.* To cavil as to terms; *esp.* to stickle for petty advantages in bargaining; to chaffer. **2.** 'To go selling provisions from door to door' (J.) 1790.

1. We will not h. with so frank a chapman for a few months under or over FULLER. To h. over an argument JOWETT. Also **Higgle-haggle** CARLYLE.

Higgledy-piggledy (hi·g'ldi pi·g'ldi), *adv., sb., a.* 1598. [?] **1.** *adv.* Without any order of position or direction; in jumbled confusion. Usu. *contemptuous.* **2.** *sb.* A confusion; a disorderly jumble 1659. **3.** *adj.* Confused; topsy-turvy 1832.

Higgler (hi·glər). 1637. [f. HIGGLE *v.* + -ER [1].] **1.** One who higgles in bargaining. **2.** An itinerant dealer; esp. a carrier or huckster who buys up poultry and dairy produce, and supplies in exchange petty commodities from the shops in town 1637.

High (həi), *a.* [Com. Teut.: OE. *hēah, hēa-, hēaʒ-* :—OTeut. **hauho-z* :—pre-Teut. **koukos.* OE. *hēah, hēh,* gave ME. *hegh, heygh* (hēχ), whence, in 14th c., *hiȝ, high* (hīχ), and, later, *hie, hy.* Mod. Eng. retains the late ME. spelling *high,* with the pronunc. (həi).]

I. 1. Of considerable upward extent or magnitude; 'long upwards' (J.); lofty, tall. *High relief*: see RELIEF. **2.** Having a (specified) upward extent OE. **3.** Situated far above the ground or some base. Formerly, as in *High Asia,* etc. denoting the upper (or inland) part. OE. **4.** Of physical actions: Extending to or from a height; performed at a height 1596. **b.** Of a vowel-sound: Produced with the tongue or part of it in a raised position. SWEET.

1. The trees so straight and hy SPENSER. 2. The snow was..halfe legge h. 1633. 3. Up above the world so h. 1836. She lay in the Garret four Story h. DE FOE. 4. The bound and h. curuet Of Marses fierie steed *All's Well* II. iii. 299.

II. Fig. senses. **1.** Of exalted rank, station, dignity, position, or estimation OE. **2.** Of exalted quality, character, or style; high-class OE.; weighty, grave, serious ME.; advanced, abstruse ME. **3.** Chief, principal, main; special. Now only in certain collocations. ME. **4.** Rich in flavour or quality; luxurious ME. **5.** Of meat, esp. game: Slightly tainted; usu. as a desirable condition 1816. **6.** Of qualities, conditions, and actions: Of great amount, degree, force, or value ME. †**b.** Of the voice: Raised, loud -1776. **c.** *Geog.* Of latitude: At a great distance from the equator 1748. **d.** High-priced 1727. **e.** Played for high stakes 1828. **7.** Of a time or season: Well-advanced; fully come. (In *high noon, high day,* often with the notion that the sun is high in the heavens.) ME. **8.** 'Far advanced into antiquity' (J.); ancient 1601. **9.** Of or in reference to musical sounds: Acute in pitch; shrill ME. **10.** Showing pride, self-exaltation, resentment, or the like; haughty, pretentious, overbearing; wrathful ME. †**b.** Eager, keen -1709. **11.** Extreme in opinion (esp. political or religious); carrying an opinion or doctrine to an extreme 1675. **12.** Emotionally exalted; hilarious; chiefly in *high spirits* 1738; intoxicated (*slang*) 1627.

1. Princes and lordes of hie estate CAXTON. Phr. *High God, h. heaven*: emphatic for *God, heaven. The Most High*: the Supreme Being; God. How doth God know? and is there knowledge in the most H.? *Ps.* lxxiii. 11. 2. A man of hye merite CAXTON. H. resolves POPE, thinking WORDSW., crimes and misdemeanours H. COX. H. Mathematics (*mod.*). 3. A place..where the hie market is holden 1553. H. altar, HIGH ROAD, etc. 4. Like a Horse Full of h. Feeding SHAKS. 6. An heigh folye CHAUCER. H. speed SHAKS. The Exchange is H. LOCKE. H. Duties 1714, temperature SCORESBY, explosives (see below) 1897. d. I suppose now stocks are h. SWIFT. e. H. play 1889. 7. Tyle it was past hye none LD. BERNERS. H. summer 1860. 8. Poems of h. antiquity WARTON. 10. H. words 1592. Indeed the Bishops are so h., that very few do love them PEPYS. 11. H. and Low, Watchwords of Party, on all tongues are rife. WORDSW. 12. A h. old time 1897.

Phrases. *H. and dry*: said of a vessel on shore out of the water; hence *fig.* out of the current of events or progress, 'stranded'. *With a h. hand*: imperiously. *On the h. horse*: see HORSE. *H. and low*: (people) of all conditions. *H. and mighty*: (*a*) formerly an epithet of dignity; (*b*) *colloq.* Imperious, arrogant. *High priori*: a burlesque alteration of A PRIORI. *On the h. ropes* (colloq.): in an elated, disdainful or enraged mood. **On h.** (rarely *upon, of h.*) [orig. *an high*; see AN *prep.*]. **a.** In or to a height, above, aloft; *spec.* up to or in heaven. †**b.** Aloud. **c.** *From on h.* (rarely *from h.*): from a h. place or position; *spec.* from heaven.

Combs., etc. 1. In OE. *hēah* was often combined with a sb.; in ME. these combs. were often written *divisim,* and, when adjective inflexions were lost, they were indistinguishable from the ordinary use of the adj. bef. a sb. Thus: **a.** in lit. sense 'lofty', as *hēah-lond* HIGHLAND. **b.** High in degree, rank, or dignity, as *hēah-mæsse* high MASS; *hēah-strǣt* HIGH STREET; *hēah-tīd* HIGH TIDE. **c.** *esp.* in names of offices and dignities, with sense 'chief, principal, head, arch-', sometimes 'exalted, lofty': e.g. *hēah-diacon* archdeacon; *hēah-gerēfa* high REEVE; *hēah-god* high God, the Most High; etc. **d.** On the analogy of these, frequently used with later official titles, implying the supreme officer or dignitary, or the like; e.g. *High Admiral, Bailiff, Master* (of St. Paul's School, etc.), *Sheriff, Steward,* etc. See these wds.

2. Special combs.: **h. Change,** the time of greatest activity on 'Change, or the Exchange at such a time (cf. II. 7); **h. cross,** a cross set on a pedestal in a market-place, or in the centre of a town or village; **h. explosive,** an explosive, such as dynamite, which is more rapid and powerful than gunpowder; †**h. Mall,** the time of greatest resort in the Mall (cf. II. 7); **h. place,** in Scripture, a place of worship or sacrifice (usually idolatrous) on a hill or high ground; **h. table,** a table raised above the rest at a public dinner; *spec.* in colleges, the table at which the head and the fellows sit; **h. tea,** a tea at which meat or fish is served. **b.** With agent-noun, denoting a high degree of performance; as *h.-bidder, -jumper, -liver,* etc.

3. **a.** With nouns forming *attrib.* phrases: as *h.-action, -speed, -pressure,* etc. **b.** Parasynthetic combs.: as *h.-angled, -arched, -coloured,* etc.; **h.-blooded,** of high blood, race, or descent, **-kilted,** wearing the kilt or petticoat high, or tucked up; *fig.* indecorous; **-necked.** See also Main Words.

B. *sb.* [The adj. used absol.] **1.** A high place or region; a height. *Obs.* exc. *Sc.* ME. **b.** A high level or figure. †**2.** Height, altitude; *fig.* acme -1557. **3.** *Cards.* The ace or highest trump out. Also, the highest card in cutting for deal. See also ALL FOURS 1. 1680.

High (həi), *adv.* Compared HIGHER, HIGHEST. [OE. *hēah,* later *hēaʒe*; thence early ME. *hēʒe, heȝ,* blending in form with the adj.] **1.** At or to a great distance upward; far up; aloft. **b.** *Horsemanship.* With high action 1686. **2.** *fig.* In or to a high position, degree, estimation, amount, price, etc. ME.; †loudly -1648; richly; to excess 1628. **3.** In or into a high latitude 1662. **4.** †**a.** Far on, late (in time). **b.** Far back, early. 1523. **5.** At or to a high pitch, shrilly 1601. †**6.** In a high manner (see HIGH *a.* II. 10) -1844.

1. Such as clymbe to hye 1559. 2. Where it seems people do drink h. PEPYS. 5. *Twel. N.* II. iii. 42. 6. Others..reason'd high Of Providence MILT. *P.L.* II. 558.

Phrases. *H. and low*: †Wholly, entirely; up and down; in every place or part (1698). *To play h.*: to play for h. stakes; to play a h. card. *To run h.*: *lit.* said of the sea when there is a strong current with a h. tide, or with h. waves; hence *fig.* of feelings or conditions 1711.

Combs. **a.** In syntactic comb. with pres. or pa. pple. of any vb. which can be qualified in the active or passive by *high* or *highly*: e.g. *to aim h.,* hence *h.-aiming, h.-aimed*; †**h.-cargued, -carved** *Naut.* (see CARGUED, CARVED); **h.-descended,** of lofty descent; **-finished,** of high finish; highly accomplished; **-grown,** grown to a height; overgrown with tall vegetation; **-strung,** strung to a high tension or pitch; *fig.* in a h. state of vigour or sensitiveness. **b.** With an adj. = Highly as *h. fantasticall* 1601. **c.** Occas. hyphened to a vb. 1632.

†**High,** *v.* [OE. *hēan,* f. *hēah* HIGH *a.*] To make, or become, high or higher (*lit.* and *fig.*) -1633.

The tydes doe h. about some 6 Foot 1633.

Highball. **1.** A species of poker played with numbered balls. **2.** *slang.* A drink of whisky in a tall glass 1899.

Hi·gh-bi·nder. *U.S. slang.* 1806. [f. HIGH *a.* II. 10; cf. HELLBENDER.] **1.** A rough. **2.** One of a secret society of blackmailers said to exist among the Chinese in California and other parts 1887.

Hi·gh-blow:er. 1831. A horse that makes a blowing noise by flapping the nostrils at each expiration in galloping; a roarer.

Hi·gh-born, *a.* ME. Of noble birth.

High-bred, *a.* 1674. **1.** Of high breed, stock, or descent. **2.** Of, pertaining to, or characteristic of high breeding 1796.

Hi·gh-browed, *a.* 1875. [f. HIGH *a.* + BROW *sb.*[1] + -ED [2].] **1.** Lofty-browed. **2.** Intellectually superior. orig. *U.S.* 1908. So **Hi·gh-brow,** *a.*; *sb.* a person so characterized 1911.

High Church. 1702. [app. from *High-Churchman,* and used attrib. as in *High Church party,* and then subst.]

A. *adj.* or *attrib. phr.* Of, belonging to, or characteristic of High-Churchmen, or their principles and practices 1704.

B. *sb.* [orig. short for *H. C. party, H. C. principles.*] The party or principles of the High-Churchmen (see next). Hence **High-Chu·rchism,** High Church principles, doctrine, or practice. **High-Chu·rchist, -ite,** an adherent to High Church principles.

High-Chu·rchman. 1687. [orig. *high Churchman*; cf. *good Churchman,* etc.] A member of the Church of England holding opinions which give a high place to the authority and claims of the Episcopate and the priesthood, the saving grace of the sacraments, and, generally, to those points of doctrine, discipline, and ritual by which the Anglican Church is distinguished from the Calvinistic and the Protestant Nonconformist churches. Hence **High-Chu·rchmanship,** the doctrine or practice of High-Churchmen; adherence to the High Church party.

High court. 1450. A supreme court. Without qualification *High Court* now means 'High Court of Justice'. Also *attrib.*

High day, hi·gh-day, hi·ghday. ME. [f. HIGH *a.*; in 3, for *hey-day.*] **1.** A day of high celebration. †**2.** Full day, when the sun is high -1647. **3.** Perversion of HEY-DAY *sb.* 2. 1771. **4.** *attrib.* 1596.

4. Thou spend'st such high-day wit in praising him SHAKS.

Higher (həi·ər), *a.* (*sb.*) and *adv.* [OE.; see HIGH.] **A.** *adj.* **1.** The comparative of HIGH *a.,* q.v. **2.** *spec.* Superior to the common sort; passing or lying beyond the ordinary limits 1836. **3.** quasi-*sb.* One higher; a superior ME.

2. Phr. *The h. classes, the h. education of women, h. mathematics. H. criticism*: see CRITICISM.

B. *adv.* Comparative of HIGH *adv.,* q.v. OE.

Higher, *v. rare.* 1715. [f. prec. adj.; cf. *lower* vb.] **1.** *trans.* To make higher, raise. **2.** *intr.* To become higher, mount 1872.

2. In ever-highering eagle-circles up To the great Sun of Glory TENNYSON.

Highermost (həi·əɹmōust), *a.* (*adv.*) *rare.* 1629. [-MOST.] = HIGHEST.

Highest (həi·ėst), *a.* (*sb.*) and *adv.* [OE. *hīehst, hȳhst, hēhst,* and *hēahst, hēagost,* ME. *heʒest.*] **A.** *adj.* The superlative of HIGH *a.,* q.v. **B.** *absol.* or as *sb.* **1.** *absol. The Highest* (also *the most Highest*): the Supreme Being, God OE. †**2.** The highest part -1634. **3.** Highest position or pitch; usu. with *at* ME. **4.** That which is highest (in *fig.* sense) 1861. **b.** *In the highest* (Biblical): tr. L. *in excelsis,* Gr. ἐν ὑψίστοις = in the loftiest places, in the heavens; now *occas.,* 'in the highest degree' 1526.

3. Whan the sonne is in the hyest 1526. 4. We needs must love the h. when we see it TENNYSON. b. Glory to God in the h. *Luke* ii. 14.

C. *adv.* The superlative of HIGH *adv.,* q.v.

Highfalutin, -ing (həifălū·tin). orig. *U.S. slang.* 1848. [f. HIGH *a.* + ?] **1.** *sb.* Absurdly pompous speech or writing; bombast. **2.** *adj.* Absurdly pompous or bombastic in style 1857.

Hi·gh-flown, *a.* 1647. [f. HIGH *adv.* + FLOWN *pa. pple.* of FLY *v.*] †**1.** Soaring high; elevated; elated -1842. **2.** Extravagant, hyperbolical; bombastic 1665. †**3.** Of persons: Extreme in opinion or party feeling. Cf. *High-flyer* 3. -1705.

2. Such are the high-flown expressions of Prudentius GIBBON. **3.** He was a high-flone Cavalier WOOD.

Hi·gh-flyer, -flier. 1589. [f. HIGH *adv.* + FLYER.] **1.** *lit.* One who or that which flies high. **b.** Pop. name of the Purple Emperor butterfly, and of the genus *Ypsipetes* of moths 1773. **2.** One who soars high in his ambitions, notions, etc. 1663. **3.** One who has lofty or high-flown notions on some question of polity, esp. ecclesiastical; *spec.* in 17-18th c. a High-Churchman; a Tory 1680. †**4.** A fast stage-coach -1868. **5.** *slang.* A fashionable strumpet; a 'swell' beggar; a begging-letter writer 1700.

Hi·gh-flying, *a.* 1622. **1.** *lit.* That flies high, as a bird. **2.** Soaring high in notions, aims, etc. 1581. **3.** Holding the principles of the HIGH-FLYERS; extreme 1695.

3. A high-flying monarchy man 1792.

Hi·gh-ha·nded, *a.* 1631. Acting or done with a high hand, or in an overbearing or arbitrary manner. **High-ha·ndedly, -ness.**

Hi·gh(-)hat. *U.S.* 1899. A tall hat; *fig.* a person of affected superiority. Also *attrib.* or as *adj.*, and as *vb. intr.*

Hi·gh-hea·rted, *a.* ME. Courageous, high-spirited; in early use occas., Haughty. Hence **High-hea·rtedness.**

High-hoe. = HICKWALL.

Hi·gh-hole. *U.S.* 1860. [Etymologizing var. of *hyghwhele, highwale, hewhole,* early ff. HICKWALL.] The Flicker, *Colaptes auratus.* So **High-holder.**

Highland (həi·lĕnd). OE. **A.** *sb.* **1.** High or elevated land; a lofty headland or cliff. **2.** *spec.* (Now always *pl.*, Sc. pronunc. hī·lănts.) A mountainous district; *spec.* The territory in Scotland formerly occupied by the Celtic clans ME.

1. Off the h. of Valparaiso 1748.

B. *attrib.* or *adj.* **1.** Of, pertaining to, or inhabiting high land or a mountainous district 1595. **2.** *spec.* Of, belonging to, or characteristic of the Highlands of Scotland ME.

1. Merely the h. clouds over the mountains KANE. **2.** *H. dress,* the kilt, etc., worn by the H. clansmen and soldiers. A generation of H. Thieves and Red-shanks MILT.

Highlander (həi·lĕndəɹ). 1632. [f. prec. + -ER [1] **1.**] **1.** An inhabitant of high land. **2.** *spec.* A native of the Highlands of Scotland. Also, a soldier of a Highland regiment. 1642. **b.** Highland cattle 1787. **Hi·ghlandman** 1425.

High light, hi·gh-light. 1658. [HIGH *a.* II. 6, LIGHT *sb.* 12.] **1.** In painting, photography, and cinematography, any of the brightest parts of a subject or a representation of it; often *pl.* Also *transf.* and *fig.* **2.** A moment or detail of vivid interest. Chiefly *pl.* 1905.

†**High-lone,** *adv.* 1597. [Corruption of *alone.*] Quite alone, without support -1760.

High-low (həi·lōᵘ). 1801. [f. HIGH *a.* + LOW *a.*; in contrast with 'top' boots and 'low' shoes.] (Usu. *pl.*) A laced boot reaching up over the ankle.

Highly (həi·li), *adv.* [OE. *hēalice,* f. *hēah* HIGH + *-līce* -LY [2].] **1.** *lit.* In a high place or situation; aloft. **2.** In or to a high position or rank OE. **3.** In or to a high degree; very, much OE. **4.** With honour, appreciation, or praise ME. **5.** Proudly, arrogantly; ambitiously; with indignation or anger. *Obs.* or *arch.* ME. **6.** Hyphened to a ppl. adj., when this is used *attrib.* 1711.

Hi·ghman, high-man. 1592. [f. HIGH *a.* + MAN.] Usu. *pl.* Dice loaded so as to turn up high numbers.

Hi·gh-me·ttled, *a.* 1626. Of high mettle; high-spirited, high-couraged.

A military and high-mettled nation BACON.

Hi·gh-mi·nded, *a.* 1503. **1.** Haughty, proud, or arrogant in spirit (*arch.*) **2.** Having a morally lofty character; magnanimous 1556.

1. Lord, I am not hye mynded, I haue no proude lokes COVERDALE *Ps.* cxxx[i]. 1. **2.** Well-bred, and high-minded youths W. IRVING. Hence **High-mi·nded-ly** *adv.*, **-ness.**

Hi·ghmost, *a. Obs.* or *dial.* 1592. [-MOST.] = HIGHEST.

Highness (həi·nĕs), *sb.* [OE. *hēanes, -nis,* later *hēahnes,* f. *hēah* HIGH; see -NESS.] **1.** The quality or condition of being high; loftiness, tallness. In *lit.* sense now usu. HEIGHT. †**b.** *concr.* A height; top, summit -1491. **2.** With possessive (e.g. the King's Highness; His, Her, Your Highness), as a title of honour given to princes ME. †**3.** Haughtiness; overbearingness -1658. **4.** Greatness of degree, amount, force, etc. 1659.

4. The h. of the wind 1659, of the rates 1884.

Hi·gh-pitched, *a.* 1593. **1.** Of high pitch acoustically 1748. **2.** Of lofty tone or character 1593. **3.** Steep 1615.

2. High-pitch'd thoughts SHAKS., language 1875.

High priest, hi·gh-priest. ME. [See HIGH *a.* II. 3.] **1.** A chief priest; esp. the Jewish chief priest. Applied to Christ (*Heb.* iv. 14). **2.** *transf.* The head of any 'cult' 1767.

2. Ricardo, the high-priest of the bullionists 1878. So **High-prie·stess. High-prie·sthood,** the office of high priest (also *fig.*). **High-prie·stly** *a.*

Hi·gh-rea·ching, *a.* 1594. *lit.* That reaches high; *fig.* aspiring.

H. Buckingham growes circumspect SHAKS.

High road, hi·gh-roa·d. 1709. [After HIGHWAY.] A highway. Also *fig.*

†**Hi·gh-ru·nner.** 1670. A false die loaded so as to run on the high numbers; cf. HIGHMAN. -1721.

High school: see SCHOOL *sb.* I. 1 g.

Hi·gh-se·t, *a.* ME. **1.** Set in a high position. **2.** High-pitched 1631.

†**Hi·gh-shoe.** 1650. **1.** One who wears high shoes, as rustics did in the 17th c.; hence, a rustic, plain man -1695. **2.** *pl.* **High shoon** used *attrib.* = Rustic, boorish -1676. Hence †**Hi·gh-shod, -shoed** *a.*

Hi·gh-sou·nding, *a.* 1560. **1.** Highly sonorous. **2.** Having an imposing or pretentious sound 1784.

1. Tinkling cymbal and high-sounding brass COWPER.

Hi·gh-spi·rited, *a.* 1631. Possessing or marked by a lofty, courageous, or bold spirit; mettlesome.

Hi·gh-ste·pper. 1860. A horse which lifts its feet high from the ground in moving; *transf.* a person of stately walk or bearing. So **Hi·gh-ste·pping** *a.* 1855.

Hi·gh-sto·mached, *a. Obs.* or *arch.* 1548. [See STOMACH.] Of high courage or spirit; haughty.

High stomack'd are they both, and full of ire *Rich. II,* I. i. 18.

High street. OE. [See STREET.] Often down to 17th c., A highway, a main road, in country or town; now, usually, the proper name (*Hi·gh Street*) of that street of a town which is built upon a great highway, and is (or was orig.) the principal one in the town.

In OE. times often applied to one of the Roman Roads or 'Streets'; it remains as the name of one of these in Westmorland.

Hight, *v.*[1] *arch.* [Com. Teut. vb.; orig. reduplicated: OE. *hātan,* pa. t. *heht,* contr. *hēt,* pa. pple. *hāten* = Goth. *haitan,* pa. t. *haihait,* to call by name, to name, bid, command. In ME. the passive *form* had been lost, so that the active *hoten, hight,* came to be both 'to call' and 'to be called', the latter being the chief use in later times. The only parts still in literary use are the pa. pple. *hight* 'called', and the kindred pa. t. *hight* 'was called', both conscious archaisms.]

I. *trans.* †**1.** To command, bid; to order, ordain; to bid come (*arch.* in Spenser) -1591. **2.** To promise, to vow. *Obs* exc. *Sc.* OE. †**3.** *parenthetical.* To assure (one that it is as one says) -1515. **4.** To call, to name. (Now only in *pa. pple.*) OE.

2. Oon auow to grete god I heete CHAUCER. **4.** A little pest, hight Tommy Moore W. IRVING.

II. *intr.*; in origin *medio-passive.* To call oneself, be called, have or bear the name. (Now only in the archaic pa. t. *hight.*) OE.

Already in OE. the passive infinitive had to be supplied by the active **hātan,** ME. **hōten,** *north.* **hāte**; and from an early date in ME., the passive forms began to yield to the corresponding active ones: (*a*) in Pres. t. **hātan, hōte(n.** (By Spenser also erron. in pa. t.) (*b*) in Pa. t. **het, hete** · later also in pres. t. (*c*) in Pa. t. **highte** (etc.), later **hight.** (*d*) From 14th c. to 18th c. *hight* was extended to the pres. t., and to the infinitive.

This gentil hostelrye That highte the Tabard CHAUCER. Lowder (for so his dog hote) SPENSER. It rightly hot The well of life — *F. Q.* I. xi. 29.

¶**III.** Used by Spenser as a *pseudo-archaism* in senses: **a.** to direct; **b.** to commit; **c.** to name, designate, mention; **d.** to mean.

Hence †**Hi·ghting (heting, hetting, hoting)** *vbl. sb.* bidding or promising; *concr.* a promise, a vow.

†**Hight,** *v.*[2] [Early ME. *huihten, hihten,* of doubtful origin.] *trans.* To adorn, embellish, set off -1633.

Hight(h, obs. ff. or varr. of HEIGHT.

High-tide. [OE. *hēahtīd,* f. HIGH *a.* + TIDE. In mod. Eng. ad. Ger. *hochzeit.*] A high time, high day, festival.

High tide: see TIDE.

Hi·gh-toned, *a.* 1779. [f. *high tone* + -ED [2].] **1.** High in pitch (vocal or musical). **2.** High-strung, tense 1804. **3.** High-principled; expressing lofty sentiments; having dignified manners 1814. **b.** *U.S. colloq.* Excellent, tasteful.

2. His temper was naturally irritable and high-toned 1814. **3.** In whose high-toned impartial mind Degrees of mortal rank and state Seem objects of indifferent weight SCOTT.

Highty-tighty, var. of HOITY-TOITY, q. v.

High water. 1626. The state of the tide when the water is highest; the time when the tide is at the full.

High-water mark. a. *lit.* The mark left by the tide at high water; esp. the highest line ever so reached 1553. Also, the highest line touched by a flooded river or lake. **b.** *fig.* The highest point of intensity, excellence, prosperity, etc. attained 1750.

Highway (həi·wēⁱ). [From HIGH *a.* II. 3 + WAY. In OE. a true compound; but in 15-17th c. often two wds. Freq. antithetic to BY-WAY.] **1.** A public road open to all passengers, a high road; esp. a main or principal road. **2.** *transf.* **a.** The ordinary or main route by land or water ME. **b.** Any well-beaten track 1579. **3.** *fig.* A course of conduct leading directly to some end or result 1598; the ordinary or direct course (of conduct, thought, speech, etc.) 1637. **4.** *attrib.* 1600.

1. Phr. *The King's Highway*: an expression dating from the time when the king's h. was in a special manner under his protection. *To take* (*to*) *the h.*, to become a highwayman, footpad, etc. **2.** The Platte has become a h. for the fur traders W. IRVING. **3.** On the h. to ruin JOWETT. *Comb.* **h. rate, tax,** one imposed for the maintenance of highways.

Highwayman (həi·wēⁱmæn). 1649. [f. prec.] **1.** One who frequents the highway for the purpose of robbing passengers; esp. one who is mounted, as dist. from a *foot-pad.* **2.** *local.* A surveyor of highways 1888.

Hi·gh-wrought, *a.* 1604. **1.** Agitated to a high degree. **2.** Wrought with great art or skill; accurately finished 1728.

1. It is a high wrought Flood *Oth.* II. i. 2.

Higra, higre, obs. ff. EAGRE.

Hijacker (həi·dʒæ:kəɹ). *U.S. slang.* 1924. [?] An armed person who preys on bootleggers.

‖**Hijra(h).** See HEGIRA. Hence ‖**Hijri** *a.*

Hike (həik), *v. colloq.* orig. *dial.* 1809. [Obscure.] **1.** *intr.* To tramp (now esp. for pleasure). **2.** *trans.* To pull, drag 1867.

Hilar (həi·lăɹ), *a.* 1864. [f. HILUM + -AR [1].] Of or pertaining to a HILUM.

Hilarious (hilēᵉ·riəs), *a.* 1823. [f. L. *hilaris* + -OUS; cf. *atrocious,* etc.] **1.** Cheerful, cheery. **2.** Boisterously merry; rollicking 1835. Hence **Hila·rious-ly** *adv.*, **-ness.**

Hilarity (hilæ·rĭti). 1500. [ad. F. *hilarité,* ad. L. *hilaritatem,* f. *hilaris, -us* = Gr. ἱλαρός cheerful; see -ITY.] **1.** Cheerfulness, gladsomeness. **2.** Boisterous merriment 1840.

1. No, Sir; wine gives not light, gay, ideal h.; but tumultuous, noisy, clamorous merriment JOHNSON.

Hilary (hi·lări). 1577. [f. *Hilarius,* bishop of Poitiers (died 367), whose festival is on Jan. 13.] Name of a term or session of the High Court of Justice in England; also of one of the University terms at Oxford and Dublin. (At Oxford now usu. called *Lent term.*)

Hildebra·ndic, *a.* 1837. [f. *Hildebrand* + -IC.] Of, pertaining to, or resembling the policy of Hildebrand, who as Gregory VII was Pope 1073–85, and was distinguished by his unbending assertion of the power of the papacy and hierarchy, and of the celibacy of the clergy. So **Hi·ldebra:ndine** *a.*, **Hi·ldebrandism, -ist.**

Hilding (hi·ldiŋ). *Obs.* or *arch.* 1582. [?] †1. A worthless or vicious beast, esp. a horse –1719. 2. A good-for-nothing (man or woman) 1592. 3. *attrib.* (in apposition) 1582.

Hile: see HILL *v.*[1], HILUM.

Hill (hil), *sb.* [OE. *hyll* str. masc. and fem. :—OTeut. **hulni-z*, pre-Teut. **kulni-s*; cf. L. *collis*, *celsus*, *culmen*, etc.] 1. A natural elevation of the earth's surface rising more or less steeply above the level of the surrounding land. Formerly the general term, including mountains; but now restricted; e.g. in Great Britain, confined to heights under 2,000 feet. b. After *up*, *down*, used without the article 1667. 2. *fig.* Something not easily mounted or overcome 1440. 3. A heap or mound of earth, sand, etc., raised or formed by human or other agency. Cf. ANT-HILL, etc. ME. b. A heap formed round a plant by banking up or hoeing 1572. 4. *attrib.*, as *h.-country*, etc. ME.

1. Fast besyde salysbury upon an hull CAXTON. b. Up h. and down dale 1879. *The Hills*: in India, mountain districts of less altitude than the Himalayas, favoured as health resorts. 2. Those..That labour up the h. of heavenly Truth MILT.

Comb.: **h.-ant,** a species that forms ant-hills; **-bird,** (*a*) the fieldfare; (*b*) the upland plover or Bartramian sandpiper of N. America; **-fever,** a kind of remittent fever prevalent in the h. country of India; **-folk, -people,** hillmen; *spec.* (*a*) the Cameronians; (*b*) the elves or fairies of the hills; **-fox,** the Indian *Canis Himalaicus*; **-oat,** *Avena strigosa*; **-partridge,** a gallinaceous bird of India, *Galloperdix lunulatus*; **-tit,** a bird of the family *Liotrichidæ*; **-wren,** a bird of the genus *Pnoepyga*.

Hill, *v.*[1] *Obs.* exc. *dial.* [ME. *hulen* (*ü*), *hilen*, *hyllen*, *hillen*, prob. from Norse. See HELE *v.*] 1. *trans.* To cover, cover up, protect. Now *dial.* †2. To cover from sight; to hide, conceal. ME. only.

Hill, *v.*[2] 1577. [f. HILL *sb.*] 1. *trans.* To form into a hill or heap; to heap up; also *fig.* 1581. 2. *Agric.* To earth up the roots of (growing plants). Also *absol.* [App. a use of HILL *v.*[1] to cover, assoc. with HILL *sb.* 3 b.] 1577. †3. *intr.* To rise in or on a slope. LELAND. 4. To assemble on rising ground, as ruffs 1768.

1. Mr. Lloyd is much against hilling of manure A. YOUNG. 2. At Midsummer they h. them [hops] A. YOUNG. 4. During spring, when the ruffs h. FOLKARD.

Hill-altar. 1539. An altar on a hill or height.

Hi·llet. *rare.* 1538. [-ET.] A hillock.

Hill-fort. 1833. A fort constructed on a hill; *esp.* a hill-top fortification of prehistoric age.

That class of towns which, out of Gaulish hill-forts, grew into Roman and mediæval cities FREEMAN.

Hilliness (hi·linės). 1629. [f. HILLY *a.* + -NESS.] The quality or state of being hilly.

Hi·lling, *vbl. sb.*[1] Now *dial.* ME. [f. HILL *v.*[1] + -ING[1].] 1. Covering, hiding, protection. 2. *concr.* A covering; e.g. clothing, a bed-quilt, a roof, etc. ME.

Hi·lling, *vbl. sb.*[2] 1627. [f. HILL *v.*[2] + -ING[1].] The action of forming hills or heaps; *esp.* the earthing-up of plants.

Hill-man, hillman. 1830. 1. One who frequents the hills; *spec.* applied to the Scottish Covenanters. b. An inhabitant of a hill-country: applied to the hill-tribes of India (*mod.*). 2. An elf or troll 1882. 3. *spec.* A miner, a slate quarryman 1865; a hill-climber 1885.

1. a. The religious sect called Hill-men, or Cameronians 1830.

Hillo, hilloa (hi·lo, hilōu·), *interj.* (*sb.*) 1602. 1. A call used to hail a distant or occupied person, or, now, to express surprise at an unexpected meeting. 2. *sb.* A name for this call 1823.

Hillock (hi·lək), *sb.* ME. 1. A little HILL (senses 1, 3). †2. A protuberance or prominence on any surface –1668. Hence **Hi·llocky** *a.*

Hill-side. ME. The slope of a hill. Also *attrib.*

Hill-top. 1530. The top of a hill. Also *attrib.*

Hilly (hi·li), *a.* ME. [f. HILL *sb.* + -Y.] 1. Characterized by or abounding in hills. 2. Elevated, steep ME.; hill-like 1658. †3. Hill-dwelling –1698.

1. The hillier regions 1872. 2. A bay formed by h. promontories 1768. A h. Heap of Stones DRYDEN.

Hilt (hilt), *sb.* [OE. *hilt* str. n. and m. Of uncertain origin; not conn. w. *hold* vb.] 1. The handle of a sword or dagger. Formerly often in *pl.* with same sense. 2. The handle or haft of any other weapon or tool 1573.

2. The h. of his pistol KINGLAKE. Phr. *Up to the h.* (†*hilts*): completely. Hence **Hilt** *v.* to furnish or fit with a h.

Hi·lted, *a.* OE. [f. HILT *sb.* and *v.* + -ED.] Furnished with a hilt; in *Her.*, having a hilt of a different tincture from the blade.

‖**Hilum** (həi·lə̆m). 1659. [L. *hilum* little thing, trifle; orig. 'that which adheres to a bean' (Festus); hence in Bot. use.] †1. Something very minute. D. PELL. 2. *Bot.* The point of attachment of a seed to its seed-vessel; the scar on the ripe seed 1753. (Anglicized **hile** 1857.) 3. *Anat.* = HILUS 2. 'Applied also to certain small apertures and depressions' (*Syd. Soc. Lex.*).

‖**Hilus** (həi·lə̆s). 1700. [mod.L., altered from prec.] †1. = HILUM 2. 2. *Anat.* The point at which any one of the viscera has its junction with the vascular system; a notch or fissure where a vessel enters an organ 1840.

Him (him, *enclitic* -im), *pers. pron.*, *3rd sing. masc.* (and †*neut.*), *dat.-accus.* [OE. *him*, dat. sing., masc. and neut., of HE, IT. Subseq., in the neut. the accus. *hit*, *it* prevailed, so that *him* is now dat. and accus. masc. only.] 1. As proper masc. pron. of the 3rd pers. sing., dat. and accus. (objective indirect and direct) of HE. Also as antecedent pron. Used of persons and animals of male sex. 2. Formerly put also for other than male beings (see quots.) OE. 3. For the *nominative*; esp. after *than*, *as*, and in predicate after *be* ME. 4. *refl.* = himself, to himself. (= L. *sibi*, *se*, Ger. *sich.*) OE. 5. quasi-*sb.* Male person, man 1880.

1. Wel is hym that wyth pacience can indure BARCLAY. H. did you leaue..vn-seconded by you 2 *Hen. IV*, II. iii. 32. For Ialousie and fere of hym Arcite CHAUCER. 2. The Fire conteyneth in him the Aëre 1559. The Sun was sunk, and after h. the Starr Of Hesperus MILT. (*personif.*) Winter had wrapped his mantle about h. (*mod.*). 3. But sure it can't be h. VANBRUGH. Is it h.? BURKE. 4. He put the thought from h. (*mod.*). Then lies h. meekly down MILT. He who hath bent him o'er the dead BYRON.

Himalayan (himā·lăyăn, *erron.* himălē·ăn), *a.* 1866. [f. *Himālaya* (Skr. f. *hima* snow + *ālaya* abode) + -AN. The erron. pronunc. is still frequent.] Of or pertaining to the Himālayas, the mountain chain forming the northern boundary of India; *fig.* enormous.

‖**Hima·ntopus.** 1753. [L., a. Gr., f. ἱμάς, ἱμαντ- thong, strap + πούς.] *Ornith.* A genus of wading-birds; the stilts.

‖**Himation** (himæ·tiǫn). 1850. [Gr. ἱμάτιον.] The outer garment worn by the ancient Greeks; 'an oblong piece of cloth thrown over the left shoulder, and fastened either over or under the right' (Liddell & Scott).

Himne, obs. f. HYMN.

Himself (himse·lf), *pron.* OE. [f. HIM *dat.-acc. pers. pron.* + SELF. *Self* was orig. an adj.] 1. Emphatic use. = Very him, very he, that very man, etc. = L. *ipse*. 2. Reflexive use. = L. *sibi*, *se*; Ger. *sich* OE. 3. quasi-*sb.* 1622. 4. With *self* treated as a sb. (= person, personality), and the possessive *his* substituted for *him*. Prevalent in the dialects, but in standard English used only where an adj., etc. intervenes, as *his own*, *true*, etc. *self*. ME.

1. They toke him self alyue COVERDALE 1 *Macc.* viii. 7. (*In apposition*) Sanctified by saint Peter himselfe MORE. (*In substitution* for the nom. pron.) The dagger which h. Gave Edith TENNYSON. Phr. *To be himself*: to be in his normal condition (see SELF). 2. Euery man for him self, and god for vs all HEYWOOD. [He] bad him with good heart sustain h. TENNYSON.

Himyarite (hi·myărəit), *sb.* 1842. [f. *Himyar*, name of a traditional king of Yemen in Southern Arabia + -ITE.] One of an ancient people of Southern Arabia (formerly called HOMERITE). Also *attrib.* = **Himyari·tic** *a.* of or pertaining to the Himyarites, their civilization, etc.; commonly applied to their language (a distinct dialect of Arabic akin to Ethiopic), and to its alphabet, and the inscriptions preserved in it. So **Himya·ric** *a.*

‖**Hin** (hin), *sb.* ME. [ad. Heb. *hīn*.] A Hebrew measure for liquids, containing a little over a gallon.

Hin, hine, *pers. pron.*, *3rd sing. masc.*, *accus.* *Obs.* exc. *dial.* [OE. *hine*, *hiene*, accus. of HE; superseded by the dative *him*. In the reduced form *ĕn*, *ŭn*, *'n* (ən, 'n), still the ordinary accus. in s.w. dialects.] = HIM, *direct objective*. Also *reflexive*.

Hind (həind), *sb.*[1] [OE. *hind* str. fem., referred variously to Goth. *hinþan* to catch, or to Gr. κεμάς young deer, pricket.] 1. The female of the (red) deer; *spec.* a female deer in and after its third year. 2. (In full *h.-fish.*) One of various fishes of the family *Serranidæ* and genus *Epinephalus* 1734.

Comb. **hind's foot** (tr. F. *pied de biche*), a kind of crossbow.

Hind (həind), *sb.*[2] [Early ME. *hine* sing., from earlier OE. and ME. *hīne* pl.; app. developed from *hīna*, *hīgna* gen. pl. of *hīgan*, *hīwan*, 'members of a family or household' (see HEWE).] 1. A (farm) servant ME.; *Sc.* and *north. dial.* a married farm-servant, for whom a cottage is provided. b. A bailiff or steward on a farm (*local*) 1495. 2. *transf.* A rustic, a boor 1570. †3. A lad; hence, Person, fellow, chap –1550.

1. Laborious hinds That had survived the father, served the son COWPER.

Hind (həind), *a.* ME. [perh. shortened from ME. *be-hind*, orig. *be-hind-an*. See N.E.D.] Situated behind, in the rear, or at the back; posterior. Usu. opp. to *fore*, and often hyphened to its sb. b. Hence applied to the back part of (anything) 1870.

The fore-hoofs were upright and shapely, the h. flat and splayed G. WHITE. The hind-spring of your carriage MARRYAT.

Hi·ndberry. *Obs.* exc. *n. dial.* [OE. *hindbęrie*; see HIND *sb.*[1] and BERRY *sb.*[1] So called as supposed to be eaten by hinds.] The raspberry.

Hind-calf. [OE. *hindcealf*; see HIND *sb.*[1] and CALF.] The young of a hind; a fawn.

Hinder (həi·ndəɹ), *a.* ME. [Conn. w. HIND *a.*, as source, or (more prob.) as deriv.] 1. Situated behind, at the back, or in the rear; posterior. (More frequently used than *hind*.) Last. †2. Latter (as opp. to *former*) –1669.

1. As I was standing in the h. Part of the Box ADDISON. Hence †**Hi·nderest, Hi·ndermost** *adjs.* hindmost. So **Hinderland** = HINTERLAND.

Hinder (hi·ndəɹ), *v.* [OE. *hindrian* :— OTeut. **hindarōjan*, f. **hindar* adv., on that side of, beyond, behind. *lit.* To put or keep back; cf. FURTHER *v.*] †1. *trans.* To do harm to –1639; to speak to the injury of –1580. 2. To keep back; to impede, deter, obstruct, prevent. Often with *from* or *in*. ME. 3. *absol.* or *intr.* To delay or frustrate action; to be an obstacle or impediment ME.

1. To hindre and empaire the name, and memorialle of the dead 1555. 2. Not able..to helpe hym..in this his iourney..but rather to hynder and let hym 1526. These pleasures do h. me in my business PEPYS. That hinders not but that they are generally less doubtful LOCKE. 3. It is not the dark place that hinders, but the dim eye CARLYLE. Hence **Hi·nderer,** one who (or that which) hinders.

Hi·nd-head. *Obs.* or *arch.* 1666. [f. HIND *a.* + HEAD.] The back of the head; the occiput.

‖**Hindi** (hi·ndī). 1800. [a. Urdū *hindī*, f. *hind*, India.]

A. *adj.* Of or belonging to Northern India or its language 1825.

B. *sb.* The great Aryan vernacular language of Northern India, spoken from the frontiers of Bengal to those of the Punjāb and Sindh, and from the Himālaya Mountains to the Nerbudda.

Hindmost (həi·ndmoust, -məst), *a.* ME. [app. f. HIND *a.* + -MOST.] Furthest behind; last come to; most remote.

The hynmost of them were slayne COVERDALE 1 *Macc.* IV. 15.

Hindoo: see HINDU.

Hindrance (hi·ndrăns), *sb.* ME. [f. HINDER *v.* + -ANCE.] †1. Injury, hurt, disadvantage –1597. 2. Obstruction; an obstruction 1526.

2. Full liberty to speak without hinderance BAXTER. They become..hindrances rather than helps 1877. Hence †**Hi·ndrance** *v. trans.* to hinder.

Hind-sight, hi·ndsight. 1851. 1. (*hind-sight*) The backsight of a rifle. 2. (*hi·ndsight*) Perception after the event; opp. to *foresight* 1883. Hence **Hi·ndsighted** *a.* 1885.

Hindu, Hindoo (hi·ndu, hindū·). 1662. [a. Pers. *hindu*, Urdū *hindū*, adj. and sb., Indian; f. Pers. *hind* India = Skr. *sindhu* river, *spec.* the Indus, hence, the region of the Indus, Sindh; gradually extended to northern India as a whole.]

A. *sb.* An Aryan of Northern India (Hindustan), who retains the native religion (Hinduism); hence, any one who professes Hinduism.

B. *adj.* Of, pertaining to, or characteristic of the Hindus or their religion; Indian 1698.

Hence **Hi·nduism, Hindooism**, the polytheistic religion of the Hindus, a development of Brahmanism. **Hi·nduize, Hindooize** *v.* to render H.

Hindustani, Hindoostanee (hindustā·nī). 1800. [a. Urdū *hindūstānī*, Pers. *hindustānī* adj., of or pertaining to Hindustān, lit. 'the country of the Hindus'; see HINDU.]

A. *adj.* Of or pertaining to Hindustan (in the stricter sense, i.e. 'India north of the Nerbudda, exclusive of Bengal and Behar'), or its people or language (see B. 2).

B. *sb.* A native of Hindustan; a Hindu or Mohammedan of Upper India 1829. 2. The language of the Mohammedan conquerors of Hindustan, being Hindi with a large admixture of Arabic, Persian, etc.; also called *Urdū*, i.e. *zabān-i-urdū* language of the camp. It is now a kind of *lingua franca* over all India. 1808.

Hine, obs. or dial. f. HIND *sb.*¹ and ².

||**Hing** (hiŋ). 1586. [Hindī.] The drug asafœtida.

Hinge (hindʒ), *sb.* [ME. *heng, heeng*, a deriv. of HANG *v.*] 1. The joint or mechanism by which a gate or door is hung upon the side-post, so as to be opened or shut by being turned upon it. b. The similar mechanism of a lid, valve, etc. 1562. 2. A natural movable joint; e.g. that of a bivalve shell 1702. 3. *transf.* The axis of the earth; the two poles, and, by extension, the four cardinal points ME. 4. *fig.* That on which something hangs or turns; a pivot, prop 1604; the cardinal point 1638; a turning-point, crisis 1727.

1. The door upon its hinges groans KEATS. 3. The winds..rushed abroad From the four hinges of the world MILT. *P. R.* IV. 413. 4. Say, on what h. does his obedience move COWPER. Phr. *Off the hinges*: unhinged; out of order; in (or into) disorder, physical or moral.

Comb.: **h.-joint** (*Anat.*), a joint whose movement can only be in one plane (e.g. that of the elbow or knee); a GINGLYMUS; **-pin**, a pin which fastens together the parts of a h.

Hinge, *v.* 1607. [f. HINGE *sb.*] 1. *trans.* To bend (anything) as a hinge. 2. To hang with or as with a hinge 1758. 3. *intr.* To hang and turn *on*, as a door on its post 1719.

1. Be thou a Flatterer now..hindge thy knee *Timon* IV. iii. 211. 3. The point on which the decision must h. THIRLWALL.

Hinged (hindʒd), *a.* 1672. [f. HINGE *sb.* + -ED².] Having a hinge or hinges. So **Hi·ngeless** *a.* without a hinge 1614.

Hinnible (hi·nib'l), *a.* 1656. [f. late L. *hinnibilis*, f. *hinnire.*] Able to neigh or whinny.

Hinny (hi·ni), *sb.* 1688. [f. L. *hinnus*; cf. Gr. ἴννος.] The offspring of a she-ass by a stallion.

Hinny (hi·ni), *v.* ME. [Earlier *henny*, ad. F. *hennir*; now conformed to L. *hinnire.*] *intr.* To neigh as a horse, to whinny.

Hinny, hinnie, Sc. and north. f. of HONEY.

Hint (hint), *sb.* 1604. [app. f. HENT *v.*, with sense 'something that may be laid hold of'.] †1. An occasion; an opportunity –1818. 2. A slight indication; a suggestion or implication conveyed covertly but intelligibly 1604.

1. It is my h. to speak SCOTT. 2. A sharp girl that can take a h. JOHNSON.

Hint (hint), *v.* 1648. [f. HINT *sb.*, sense 2.] 1. *trans.* To give a hint of; to suggest or indicate slightly but intelligibly; †to give a hint to (a person) SIR T. BROWNE. 2. *intr. Hint at*: to make a slight, but intelligible suggestion of 1697.

1. Just h. a fault, and hesitate dislike POPE. 2. The spectator's imagination completes what the artist merely hints at HAWTHORNE. Hence **Hi·ntedly** *adv.* **Hi·nter. Hi·ntingly** *adv.*

||**Hinterland** (hi·ntəɹlænd). 1890. [a. Ger., f. *hinter-* behind + *land* land.] The district behind that lying along the coast (or along the shore of a river); the back country.

Hip (hip), *sb.*¹ [OE. *hype* masc.:—OTeut. **hupi-z*, pre-Teut. **kubis.*] 1. The projecting part of the body on each side formed by the lateral expansions of the pelvis and upper part of the thigh-bone; the haunch. Also used for the hip-joint. b. *Zool.* = COXA 2. 1834. 2. *Arch.* a. A projecting inclined edge on a roof, extending from the ridge or apex to the eaves, and having a slope on each side; the rafter at this edge 1690. b. A spandrel 1726.

1. Phr. *Down in the hip(s*: said of a horse when the haunch-bone is injured; hence *fig.*, out of spirits. *On* or *upon the h.* (usu. *to take, get, have* one on the h., phrases taken from wrestling): at a disadvantage. *H. and thigh*: with overwhelming blows; unsparingly. Usu. with *smite*, etc. (Biblical.)

a. *Comb.* in sense 1, as **h.-bath**, a bath in which a person can sit immersed up to the hips; **-belt**, a belt worn diagonally about the left h. and right side of the waist, a part of mediæval armour; **-disease**, a disease of the h.-joint, characterized by inflammation, fungous growth, and caries of the bones; **-pocket**, a pocket in a pair of trousers, just behind the h.; **-revolver**, one carried in the h.-pocket.

b. *Comb.* in sense 2, as **h.-knob**, a knob or ornament surmounting the h. of a roof; **-mould, -moulding**, (*a*) the mould or templet by which the h. of a roof is set out; (*b*) the 'back' or outer angle of the h.; **-pole**, a pole supporting the h.-rafter; **-rafter**, the rafter extending along the h. of a roof; **-tile**, a tile of special shape used at the h. of a roof; **-truss**, a combination of timbers supporting the h.-rafter.

Hip (hip), **hep** (hep), *sb.*² [OE. *héope, hīope* wk. fem.:— OTeut. types **heupôn-, *heupon-.*] The fruit of the wild rose, or of roses in general.

I fed on scarlet hips and stony haws COWPER.

Hip (hip), *sb.*³ Also *pl.* **hipps.** 1710. [var. of HYP, abbrev. of *hypochondria.* Usu. spelt with *y* in the sb., but with *i* in the vb., etc.] Morbid depression of spirits; the 'blues'.

Hip *v.*¹ [OE.**hyppan*; cf. G. *hüpfen.*] To hop.

Hip, *v.*² 1610. [f. HIP *sb.*¹] 1. *trans.* To dislocate or injure the hip of; to lame in the hip. 2. To give a cross-buttock in wrestling; to throw over the hip 1675. 3. To form with a hip, as a roof 1669.

Hip, *v.*³ *colloq.* 1842. [f. HIP *sb.*³, or HIPPED *a.*²] *trans.* To affect with hypochondria.

Hip, *interj.* (*sb.*⁴) Also **hep.** 1752. 1. 'An exclamation or calling to one' (J.). 2. An exclam. used to introduce a united cheer; hence as *sb.* 1827.

2. To..huzza after the 'hip! hip! hip!' of the toast giver HONE.

Hip-bone. ME. [HIP *sb.*¹] The bone of the hip; i.e. either the *ilium*, or the *ischium*, or the *os innominatum* as a whole, or the upper part of the thigh-bone.

Hipe (həip), *v.* 18.. [? f. HIP *sb.*¹] *Wrestling.* To throw (an antagonist) by lifting him from the ground, and rapidly placing one of the knees between his thighs.

Hip-girdle. [HIP *sb.*¹] 1. *Anat.* The pelvic girdle or arch, consisting of the ilium, ischium, and pubis. 2. = *Hip-belt*: see HIP *sb.*¹

Hip-gout. 1598. [f. HIP *sb.*¹ + GOUT.] = SCIATICA.

Hip-joint. 1794. [HIP *sb.*¹] The joint of the hip, the articulation of the head of the thigh-bone with the ilium.

Hip-joint disease = *hip-disease* (HIP *sb.*¹).

Hipo-: obs. spelling of HYPO-.

Hipparch (hi·pāɹk). 1656. [ad. Gr. ἵππαρχος, f. ἵππος + -αρχος.] *Gr. Antiq.* Commander of the horse.

||**Hipparion** (hipēə·riǫn). 1859. [mod.L., ad. Gr. ἱππάριον pony.] *Palæont.* An extinct genus of small quadrupeds, of Miocene and Pliocene age, regarded as ancestrally related to the horse.

Hipped, hipt (hipt), *a.*¹ 1508. [f. HIP *sb.*¹ and *v.*² + -ED.] 1. Having hips, as *large-hipped.* 2. *Arch.* Of a roof: Having hips (see HIP *sb.*¹ 2) 1805. 3. Having the hip injured or dislocated 1565.

Hipped (hipt), *a.*² *colloq.* 1710. [var. of HYPT, *hypp'd*, f. HIP *sb.*³] Morbidly depressed.

Hippiatric (hipiæ·trik). *rare.* 1646. [ad. Gr. ἱππιατρικός, f. (ult.) ἵππος + ἰατρός.]

A. *adj.* Relating to the treatment of diseases of horses 1674.

B. *sb.* One who treats diseases of horses. *pl.* Farriery; a treatise on this. So **Hippia·trical** *a.* **Hippia·trist. Hippia·try.**

Hippic (hi·pik), *a. rare.* 1846. [ad. Gr. ἱππικός.] Pertaining to horses, esp. to horse-racing.

Hippish (hi·piʃ), *a. colloq.* 1706. [var. of HYPPISH, q. v.] Low-spirited.

Hippo (hi·po). Colloq. abbrev. of HIPPOPOTAMUS.

Hippo- (hipo), bef. a vowel **hipp-**, comb. f. Gr. ἵππος horse; as in: **Hippo·machy** [Gr. -μαχία], a fight on horseback. **Hipponoso·logy, Hippopatho·logy**, 'the doctrine of the diseases of the horse' (*Syd. Soc. Lex.*).

Hippocamp (hi·pokæmp). 1613. = HIPPOCAMPUS 1.

Hippocampus (hipokæ·mpŏs). *Pl.* **-i.** 1576. [a. late L. *hippocampus*, a. Gr., f. ἵππος + κάμπος sea-monster.] 1. *Myth.* A sea-horse, having two fore-feet, and the tail of a dolphin or fish, represented as drawing the car of Neptune 1606. 2. *Ichth.* A genus of small fishes, having a head suggesting that of a horse; the sea-horse 1576. 3. *Anat.* Each of two elongated eminences (*h. major* and *minor*) on the floor of each lateral ventricle of the brain; so called from their supposed resemblance to the fish (sense 2) 1706.

Hippocentaur (hipose·ntǫɹ). 1533. [ad. L. *hippocentaurus* horse-centaur, opp. to ἰχθυοκένταυρος fish-centaur.] A fabulous creature, half man, half horse; a centaur. Hence **Hippocentau·ric** *a.* of the nature of a h.

Hippocras (hi·pokræs). *Obs.* exc. *Hist.* [ME. *ypocras*, a. OF. *ipocras, ypocras*, forms of *Hippocrates*; in sense 1, after the med.L. name *vinum Hippocraticum*, i.e. wine filtered through 'Hippocrates' sleeve' or 'bag'; see next.] 1. A cordial drink made of wine flavoured with spices, formerly much in vogue. †2. **Hippocras bag.** A conical bag of cotton, linen, or flannel, used as a filter –1674.

1. He drynketh Ypocras Clarree and Vernage Of spices hoote tencreessen his corage CHAUCER.

Hippocrates (hipǫ·krătīz). 1626. A famous ancient Greek physician born about 460 B.C.

†**Hippocrates' bag, sleeve** [tr. L. *manica Hippocratis*] = prec. 2.

Hippocratic (hipokræ·tik), *a.* 1620. [ad. med.L. *Hippocraticus*; see prec.] 1. Of or belonging to Hippocrates. 2. Applied to the shrunken and livid aspect of the countenance immediately before death; so called because described by Hippocrates. Also *fig.* 1713.

1. †*H. wine*, spiced wine, hippocras. 2. Succeeded by..Lethargy, a dismal H. Face, staring Eyes 1713. So **Hippocra·tian, Hippocra·tical** *adjs.* = prec. **Hippo·cratism**, the doctrine of Hippocrates.

Hippocrene (hi·pokrīn). 1634. [ad. L. *Hippocrēnē*, Gr. Ἱπποκρήνη or Ἵππου κρήνη 'fountain of the horse', fabled to have been produced by a stroke of Pegasus' hoof.] A fountain on Mount Helicon, sacred to the Muses; hence used allusively in reference to poetic inspiration.

O for a beaker..Full of the true, the blushful H. KEATS.

Hippocrepian (hipokrī·piăn), *a.* (*sb.*) 1877. [f. HIPPO- + Gr. κρηπίς shoe + -(I)AN.] *Zool.* and *Bot.* 1. Resembling a horseshoe: *spec.* applied to the lophophore of certain polyzoans, and so to these polyzoans themselves. 2. *sb.* A hippocrepian polyzoan. So **Hippocre·piform** *a. Bot.* shaped like a horseshoe.

†**Hippodame.** 1590. [ad. Gr. ἱππόδαμος horse-tamer, but in 1 app. confused with *hippotame*, HIPPOPOTAMUS.] 1. *erron.* for HIPPOCAMP. SPENSER *F. Q.* III. xi. 40. 2. A horse-tamer 1623.

Hippodrome (hi·pŏdrōᵘm), *sb.* 1585. [a. F., or ad. L. *hippodromos*, a. Gr., f. ἵππος + δρόμος.] 1. *Gr.* and *Rom. Antiq.* A course or circus for horse-races and chariot-races. Sometimes a name for a modern circus. 2. *U.S. Sporting slang.* A race, etc., in which the result is fraudulently prearranged.

Hippogriff, -gryph (hi·pogrif). 1656. [a. F. *hippogriffe*, ad. It. *ippogrifo*, f. Gr. ἵππος + It. *grifo*, late L. *gryphus* GRIFFIN.] A fabulous creature, like a griffin with the body and hind-quarters of a horse. Also *fig.*

Tell us no more of Icarus, Of Hypogryph, or Pegasus 1659.

Hippoid (hi·poid). 1880. [f. Gr. ἵππος + -OID.] *Zool.* An animal resembling, or allied to, the horse.

Hippolith (hi·polip). 1828. [ad. med.L. *hippolithus*, f. Gr. ἵππος + λίθος.] A concretion or calculus found in the intestines of a horse.

‖**Hippomanes** (hipǫ·mănīz). 1601. [Gr. ἱππομανές adj. neut., f. ἵππος + μαν-, μαίνεσθαι to be mad.] a. 'A small black fleshy substance said to occur on the forehead of a new-born foal.' b. 'A mucous humour that runs from mares a-horsing' (Liddell & Scott). Both reputed aphrodisiacs.

Hippophagy (hipǫ·fădʒi). 1828. [f. Gr. ἵππος + -φαγία.] The practice of eating horseflesh. So **Hippo·phagism** = prec. **Hippo·phagist**, an eater of horseflesh. **Hippo·phagous** *a.* eating horseflesh.

Hippopotamus (hipopǫ·tămŏs). *Pl.* **-muses, -mi.** [ME. *ypotame*, *-amos*, a. OF., med.L.; in 16th c. *hippopotame*, 17th c. *-amus*, a. late L. *hippopotamus*, a. late Gr., f. ἵππος horse + ποταμός river.] A pachydermatous quadruped, the African river-horse, *Hippopotamus amphibius*, a very large beast with a thick heavy hairless body, large muzzle and tusks, and short legs, inhabiting the African rivers, etc. Hence **Hi:ppopo·tamic** *a.* belonging to or like a h.; huge, unwieldy. **Hippopo·tamid** (*Zool.*), an animal of the family *Hippopotamidæ*.

Hippotomy (hipǫ·tŏmi), *rare.* 1854. [f. HIPPO- + Gr. -τομία.] The anatomy or dissection of the horse. So **Hippo·tomist** 1737.

Hippurate (hipiūᵊ·rĕt). 1854. [f. HIPPURIC + -ATE [4].] *Chem.* A salt of hippuric acid.

‖**Hippuria** (hipiūᵊ·riă). 1857. [mod.L., f. prec. and next.] *Path.* 'Bouchardat's term for the presence in excess of hippuric acid or hippurates in the urine' (*Syd. Soc. Lex.*).

Hippuric (hipiūᵊ·rik), *a.* 1838. [f. Gr. ἵππος + οὖρον urine + -IC.] *Chem.* In *Hippuric acid*, an acid ($C_9H_9NO_3$) found in the urine of horses and other herbivora.

Hippurite (hi·piurəit). 1842. [ad. mod.L. *Hippurites*, f. Gr. ἵππουρος horse-tailed.] 1. A fossil bivalve mollusc of the genus *Hippurites* or family *Hippuritidæ*. Also *attrib.* 2. 'A kind of fossil cup-coral, *Cyathophyllum ceratites* of Goldfuss' (*Cent. Dict.*). Hence **Hippuri·tic** *a.* pertaining to, or containing, hippurites (sense 1).

Hip-roof. 1727. [f. HIP *sb.*[1] 2.] A roof having hips or sloping edges, the ends being inclined as well as the sides; a hipped roof. Hence **Hip-roofed** *a.*

Hip-shot, *a.* (*sb.*) Also **-shotten.** 1639. [f. HIP *sb.*[1] + *shot* pa. pple.] 1. Having a dislocated hip-joint. 2. *fig.* Lame, clumsy; disabled 1642. 3. *sb.* Dislocation of the hip-joint 1720.

2. This hipshot grammarian MILT.

Hir, obs. ME. form of HER *pron.*

‖**Hircarra, -ah, hurcaru** (hɒɪkā·ră). *E. Ind.* 1747. [Hindī, Urdū, etc. *harkāra* messenger.] An E. Indian spy, messenger, or courier.

Hircic (hǭ·ɪsik), *a.* 1836. [f. L. *hircus* he-goat + -IC.] *Chem.* Of or pertaining to a goat. *Hircic acid*, a liquid fatty substance believed by Chevreul to be the odorous principle of mutton suet; now held to be a mixture of fatty acids.

Hircin (hǭ·ɪsin). 1836. [f. as prec. + -IN.] *Chem.* A substance existing in the fat of the goat (and sheep), on which its strong odour depends.

Hircine (hǭ·ɪsəin). 1656. [ad. L. *hircinus* (*hirquinus*) of a goat.]

A. *adj.* Of, belonging to, or resembling a goat; *spec.* Having a goatish smell. So **Hi·rcinous** *a.*

B. *sb.* A fossil amorphous resin which burns with a strong animal odour. Also called **Hircite.**

‖**Hircocervus** (hǭɪkosǭ·ɪvŏs). ME. [med.L. (f. *hircus* + *cervus*) transl. Gr. τραγέλαφος.] A fabulous creature, half goat, half stag.

Hire (həiᵊɪ), *sb.* [OE. *hȳr* str. fem. :— OTeut. type **hūrjā-*, not known in OHG., ON., or Goth.] 1. Payment contracted to be made for the temporary use of anything. (In OE., *esp.* usury, interest.) 2. Payment contracted to be made for personal service; wages ME. Also *fig.* 3. The action of hiring or fact of being hired 1615.

1. Bote hyre from Lambeth 1587. Bicycles on h. (*mod.*). 2. Their testimony against preaching for h. MORSE. *fig.* Treuli the hyris of synne, deeth WYCLIF *Rom.* vi. 22. 3. The h. of a horse (*mod.*). *Comb.* **h.-system**, a system by which a hired article becomes the property of the hirer after a stipulated number of payments; so **h.-purchase.**

Hire (həiᵊɪ), *v.* [OE. *hȳrian*, f. the sb.; see HIRE *sb.*] 1. *trans.* To engage the services of (a person) for a stipulated reward; to employ for wages. b. *transf.* To engage to do something by a payment or reward; to bribe ME. 2. To procure the temporary use of (any thing) for stipulated payment ME. 3. To grant the temporary use of for stipulated payment; to let *out* on hire; to lease ME.

1. He hir'd the workers by the day COWLEY. b. Cullin ..was hired..to kill the Queene 1631. 2. I hired an ass LADY M. W. MONTAGU. 3. They that were full, haue hired out themselues for bread 1 *Sam.* ii. 5. Phr. *To h. out* (*intr.* for *refl.*), to engage oneself as a servant for payment. *U.S.* and *Colonial.* Hence **Hi·reable, hirable** *a.* capable of being hired. **Hired** *ppl. a.*, applied *spec.* in U.S. to free men or women engaged as servants.

Hi·reless, *a.* 1651. [-LESS.] Without hire or pay.

Hireling (həiᵊ·ɪliŋ). [OE. *hȳrling* (rare), f. *hȳr* HIRE + -LING. App. formed anew in 16th c.]

A. *sb.* 1. One who serves for hire or wages. 2. One who makes material gain the motive of his actions; a mercenary. (Opprobrious.) 1574.

2. As an h., that loves the work for the wages BACON.

B. *adj.* Characteristic of or pertaining to a hireling; serving for hire or wages; mercenary. (Usu. opprobrious.) 1587.

The plot by h. witnesses improv'd DRYDEN.

†**Hiren** (həiᵊ·rĕn). 1597. [Corruption of *Irene*, F. *Irène*.] Name of a character in Peele's play of 'The Turkish Mahamet and Hyrin the fair Greek'; used subseq. as meaning 'a seductive woman', a harlot. 2 *Hen. IV*, II. iv. 173.

Hiren, obs. f. HERN, hers.

Hirer (həiᵊ·rəɪ). 1500. [f. HIRE *v.* + -ER [1].] 1. One who hires. 2. One who lets out something on hire. *Obs.* or *Sc.* 1591.

Hirondelle. *Obs.* exc. *Her.* 1600. [a. F.] A swallow.

The Swallow, or h., forms the very early coat of the Arundells 1880.

Hi·rple, *v.* *Sc.* and *north. dial.* 1450. [Orig. unkn.] To move with a gait between walking and crawling; to walk lame.

Hirrient (hi·riĕnt), *a.* (*sb.*) *rare.* 1832. [f. L. *hirrientem*, *hirrire* to snarl.] 1. Snarling; trilled. 2. *sb.* A trilled sound. (Cf. *litera canina*, Latin name for *r.*) 1860.

Hirsute (hǭ·ɪsiūt), *a.* 1621. [ad. L. *hirsutus*, f. **hirsus*, by-form of *hirtus*.] 1. Having rough hair; hairy, shaggy. 2. *Bot.* and *Zool.* Covered with long and stiffish hairs 1626. 3. Of or pertaining to hair; consisting of hair 1823. Also *transf.* and *fig.* 1621.

1. A rugged attire, h. head, horrid beard BURTON. Hence **Hi·rsuteness**, h. quality or condition. **Hirsuto-**, comb. f. L. *hirsutus*, HIRSUTE, as *hirsuto-atrous*, with black hairs.

†**Hirudinal** (hirū·dinăl), *a.* 1651. [f. L. *hirudo*, *hirudinem* leech + -AL.] Of or pertaining to a leech. So **Hiru·dinid**, a member of the *Hirudinidæ* or Leech family. **Hirudi·nean**, a member of the *Hirudinea* or order of annelids containing the leeches.

His (hiz, -iz), *poss. pron.*, *3rd sing. masc.* and †*neut.* [OE. *his* (*hys*), genitive of HE and *hit*, IT. About the 11th c., the genitive *his* began to be treated as an adj. (with pl. *hise*, occurring till the 15th c.).] †1. as *gen. case* of *pers. pron.*: a. *masc.* Of him; of the male being or thing in question, L. *ejus*; b. *neut.* of it; c. *refl.* of himself, of itself, L. *sui* –ME. 2. *Poss. adj. pron. masc.* (orig. *poss. gen.*, and then, like L. *ejus*, following its sb.). a. Of or belonging to him, that man's, the male being's; also *refl.* his own (L. *suus*) OE. b. Also used with objects which one ought to have, or has specially to deal with (e.g. to kill *his man*, to gain *his blue*), or in which every one is assumed to have his share (e.g. he knows *his Bible*, *his arithmetic*, etc.) 1709. c. In reference to inferior animals *his* (or *her*) varies with *its*; see HE, IT. OE. 3. Referring to neuter nouns or things inanimate. (Now superseded by ITS, exc. where personification is implied.) OE. 4. After a sb., used instead of the genitive inflexion. Chiefly with proper nouns. Archaically retained in Book-keeping and for some technical purposes. OE.

2. a. His bold defence of me ROWE. His friends retained his panoply GROTE. c. The owl, for all his feathers, was a-cold KEATS. 3. And thou hearest his sounde TINDALE *John* iii. 8 [(Great Bible) the sounde therof]. The Sun Had first his precept so to move MILT. *P. L.* x. 652. 4. King Edward the Fourth his death H. WALPOLE. Phr. *His own*: see OWN. *His self*: see HIMSELF 4 and SELF.

His (hiz), *absol. poss. pron.* OE. In ME. a form HISIS was tried for the absolute pron., but did not take root. Thus HIS remains for the absol. as well as for the simple possessive. See HISIS, HISN.] The absolute form of prec., used when no noun follows: = His one, his ones.

My beloued is mine, and I am his *Song Sol.* ii. 16.

His, obs. spelling of *is*.

Hish, *v.* ME. By-form of HISS.

†**Hi·sis**, *absolute poss. pron.* [f. HIS *poss. pron.*, after *hir-is*, *hir-es*, *hers*, etc., from *her*, etc. As the simple possessive itself ended in *s*, this form did not take root.] = next. WYCLIF.

Hisn, his'n (hi·z'n), *absol. poss. pron. dial.* Late ME. [f. HIS; cf. *hern*, etc. App. due to form-association with *my*, *mine*, etc., in which the *-n* distinguishes the absolute from the adjective form.] = HIS *absol. poss. pron.*

Hispanic (hispæ·nik), *a. rare.* [f. L. *Hispanicus*; see -IC.] Pertaining to Spain or its people. So †**Hispa·nian** *a.* 1550, †**Hispa·nical** *a.* 1584, **Hispa·nically** *adv.* **Hispa·nicism**, a Spanish idiom or mode of speech. **Hispa·nicize** *v.* to render Spanish.

Hispaniolate (hispæniōᵘlĕˈt), *v. rare.* 1860. [f. Sp. *españolar* to make Spanish, f. (ult.) L. *Hispania* Spain; see -ATE [3].] *trans.* To make Spanish. So **Hispa·niolize** 1583, **Hi·spanize** 1600 *vbs.*

Hispa·no-, comb. f. L. *Hispanus* Spanish; as in **H.-Gallican**, belonging in common to Spain and Gaul.

Hispid (hi·spid), *a.* 1646. [ad. L. *hispidus*.] Rough with stiff hairs or bristles; shaggy; bristly: in *Bot.* and *Zool.* Clothed with short stiff hairs or bristles; rough with minute spines. So **Hispi·dulous** *a.* slightly h.

Hiss (his), *sb.* 1513. [f. HISS *v.*] 1. A sharp continuous spirant sound such as is emitted by geese and serpents, and in the pronunciation of 's'. b. *Phonetics.* A consonant produced with a hiss; a sibilant. Also *attrib.* 1890. 2. This sound uttered in disapproval or scorn 1602.

1. The h. of russling wings MILT. *P. L.* I. 768. 2. A dismal universal h., the sound Of public scorn — x. 508.

Hiss (his), *v.* ME. [Echoic. (An alleged OE. *hysian* is an error.)] 1. *intr.* To make the sharp spirant sound emitted by geese, serpents, etc., or caused (e.g.) by the escape of steam through a narrow aperture, or uttered in the pronunciation of 's'. (L. *sibilare.*) ME. **2.** To make this sound by way of disapproval or derision. (Usu. with *at.*) ME. **3.** *trans.* To express disapproval of by making this sound 1599. **4.** To utter or express by hissing or with a hiss 1775.

1. But þei hissen, as serpentes don MAUNDEV. 2. Thou art disgraced and hissed at JER. TAYLOR. 3. They have hissed me LAMB. Phr. *To h. out, away, down.* 4. One of the threats hissed out by the Congress JOHNSON. Hence **Hi·sser.**

Hissing (hi·siŋ), *vbl. sb.* ME. [-ING [1].] **1.** The action of HISS *v.* **2.** *concr.* An occasion or object of expressed opprobrium (*arch.*) ME.

2. I will make this citie desolate and an h. *Jer.* xix. 8. So **Hi·ssingly** *adv.*

Hist (hist), *interj.* SHAKS. [A natural exclam. Cf. ST, WHISHT.] A sibilant exclam. used to enjoin silence, attract attention, or call on people to listen.

Hist (hist), *v.* Now *poet.* 1604. [f. prec.] †**1.** *trans.* To summon with the exclam. 'hist!'; to summon without noise -1778. **2.** To incite. MIDDLETON.

1. And the mute Silence h. along MILT. *Pens.* 35.

Histioid (hi·stioid), *a.* 1854. [f. Gr. ἱστίον, dim. of ἱστός web, tissue + -OID.] *Phys.* and *Path.* = HISTOID. So **Histio·logy** = HISTOLOGY.

Histo-, comb. f. Gr. ἱστός, with sense 'tissue'.

Hi·stoblast [Gr. βλαστός], the primary element or unit of a tissue. **Histoche·mical** *a.*, relating to **Histoche·mistry**, the chemistry of organic tissues. **Histogra·phic, -al** *a.*, belonging to **Histo·graphy**, description of the tissues. **Histo·lysis** [Gr. λύσις], disintegration or dissolution of organic tissue; hence **Histoly·tic** *a.*, belonging to histolysis. **Histo·phyly** [Gr. φυλή], the history of tissues within a particular tribe of organisms. **Histo·tomy** [Gr. -τομία], 'the dissection of the organic tissues' (Mayne). **Hi·stozyme** [Gr. ζύμη], Schmiedeberg's term for a substance that causes fermentation in the tissues.

Histogenesis (histo,dʒe·nėsis). 1854. [f. HISTO- + Gr. γένεσις.] *Biol.* The production or development of organic tissues. So **Histogene·tic** *a.* having the quality of producing tissue; relating to the formation of tissues. **Histogene·tically** *adv.* in relation to h. **Histo·geny**, in same sense.

Histoid (hi·stoid), *a.* 1872. [f. Gr. ἱστός web + -OID.] *Phys.* and *Path.* Like or of the nature of tissue, esp. connective tissue; spec. said of tumours.

Histology (histǫ·lŏdʒi). 1847. [f. Gr. ἱστός web + -LOGY.] The science of organic tissues; that branch of anatomy, or of biology, which is concerned with the minute structure of the tissues of animals and plants. Hence **Histolo·gic, -al** *a.* belonging to h.; relating to organic tissues. **Histolo·gically** *adv.* **Histo·logist**, one versed in h.

†**Histo·rial**, *a.* (*sb.*) ME. [a. F., ad. late L. *historialis*, f. *historia.*] **1.** Historical -1649. **2.** *sb.* History 1595. Hence †**Histo·rially** *adv.*

Historian (histōᵊ·riăn). 1531. [a. F. *historien*, f. L. *historia*; see -AN.] **1.** A writer or author of a history; esp. as dist. from the simple annalist or compiler. †**2.** A story-teller -1667. **3.** One versed in history (*rare*) 1645.

1. The H. [sayth] what men haue done SIDNEY. 3. Great captains should be good historians SOUTH. Hence **Histo·rianess** SCOTT.

Historiated (histōᵊ·rieɪtėd), *ppl. a.* 1886. [f. med.L. *historiatus* (f. *historia*) + -ED.] Decorated (as illuminated capitals) with figures of men or animals.

Historic (histǫ·rik), *a.* (*sb.*) 1669. [ad. L. *historicus*, a. Gr., f. ἱστορία HISTORY.] **1.** Of or belonging to history; of the nature of history as opp. to fiction or legend; historical. **2.** Dealing with or treating of history; = HISTORICAL 3. 1675. **3.** *esp.* Noted or celebrated in history. (The prevailing current sense.) 1794. **4.** Applied, in L. and Gr. Grammar, to those tenses of the vb. which are used in narration of past events; also, in L., to the infinitive mood when used instead of the indicative; and, generally, to the present tense, when used instead of the past in vivid narration 1845.

2. John Freeman, an h. painter H. WALPOLE. 3. My first introduction to the h. scenes, which have since engaged so many years of my life GIBBON.

B. *sb. rare.* A historic work, picture, subject, etc. 1830.

Historical (histǫ·rikăl), *a.* late ME. [f. L. *historicus* (see prec.) + -AL.] **1.** = HISTORIC 1. 1561. **2.** Relating to or concerned with history or historical events 1513. **3.** Dealing with history, treating of history, as a *h. treatise* or *writer*; based upon history, as a *h. play, novel*, etc. 1590; representing history, as a *h. painting* 1658. **4.** = HISTORIC 3 (now the usual word) 1834. **5.** *Gram.* = HISTORIC *a.* 4. 1867.

2. *H. Method*, a method of investigation in which the history of the object is studied. 4. This h. and gallant little ship [the May Flower] LONGF. Hence **Histo·rical-ly** *adv.*, **-ness.**

Historicity (histori·sĭti). 1880. [f. HISTORIC + -ITY.] Historical quality or character.

Historicize (histǫ·risəiz), *v.* 1846. [f. as prec. + -IZE.] **1.** *trans.* To make, or represent as, historic. **2.** *intr.* To recount historical events (*nonce-use*) 1887.

Historico-, comb. f. Gr. ἱστορικός: = historically..., historical and..., as in *h.-critical, -geographical*, etc.

Historied (hi·stŏrid), *a.* *rare.* 1818. [f. HISTORY *sb.* and *v.* + -ED.] **1.** Adorned with historical scenes. **2.** Having a history; storied 1818.

2. He sees, in some great-historied land [etc.] M. ARNOLD.

†**Histo·rier.** 1449. [ad. OF. *historieur*, f. *historier.*] A historian -1581.

‖**Historiette** (histōᵊri,e·t). 1704. [F., f. *histoire* + *-ette* dim. suffix (after L. *historia*).] A short history or story.

Historify (histǫ·rifəi), *v.* 1586. [f. L. *historia* + -FY.] **1.** *trans.* To relate the history of; to record in history. **2.** *absol.* To write history; to narrate 1614.

1. That Church which you have so worthily historified LAMB.

Historiographer (histōᵊriǫ·grăfəɹ). 1494. [f. late L. *historiographus* + -ER.] **1.** A chronicler or historian. **2.** *esp.* An official historian appointed in connexion with a court 1555. Also *transf.* **3.** A writer of natural history (see HISTORY *sb.* 4) 1579.

2. *transf.* Scott became the h. royal of feudalism M. ARNOLD. So †**Histo·riograph**, in same sense. Hence **Historio·graphership.**

Historiography (histōᵊriǫ·grăfi). 1569. [ad. Gr. ἱστοριογραφία, f. ἱστορία + -γραφία.] The writing of history; written history. Hence **Histo:riogra·phic, -al** *a.* pertaining to h.

Historiology (histōᵊriǫ·lŏdʒi). 1616. [f. as prec. + -LOGY.] The knowledge or study of history. Hence **Historiolo·gical** *a.* pertaining to h.

Historio·nomer. *nonce-wd.* [f. Gr. ἱστορία, after *astronomer.*] One versed in the laws which regulate the course of history. LOWELL.

Historize (hi·stŏrəiz), *v.* ? *Obs.* 1599. [f. HISTORY *sb.* + -IZE; cf. *botanize*, etc.] **1.** *trans.* To tell the history of; to narrate as history. †**2.** To represent EVELYN. **3.** *intr.* or *absol.* To act the historian 1632.

History (hi·stŏri), *sb.* ME. [ad. L. *historia*, a. Gr., f. ἵστωρ, ἱστορ- knowing, learned, wise man, judge, f. ϝιδ-, ἰδ- to know. Cf. STORY.] †**1.** A relation of incidents (in later use, only of those professedly true); a narrative, tale, story -1834. **2.** *spec.* A written narrative constituting a continuous methodical record, in order of time, of important or public events, esp. those connected with a particular country, people, individual, etc. 1485. **3.** (Without *a* or *pl.*) The formal record of the past, esp. of human affairs or actions 1482. Also *transf.*; esp. in pregnant sense, A career worthy of record 1654. **4.** A systematic account (without reference to time) of a set of natural phenomena. Now *rare*, exc. in NATURAL HISTORY. [Cf. the use of ἱστορία by Aristotle.] 1567. **5.** †A drama; *spec.* a historical play 1596. †**6.** A picture of an event or series of incidents -1776. ¶**7.** *Eccl.* = L. *historia*, liturgically applied (*a*) to a series of lessons from Scripture, named from the first words of the Respond to the first lesson; (*b*) to the general order of a particular Office.

1. A Mountebank on the Stage..gave them a H. of his Cures T. BROWN. 2. *Chronicles, Annals*, are simpler forms of h., in which the year or period is the primary division; whereas in a *history*, each movement, action, or chain of events is dealt with as a whole. (See N.E.D.) How can there be a true H., when we see no Man living is able to write truly the H. of the last Week? SHADWELL. 3. Phr. *Ancient H.*, history down to the fall of the Western Roman Empire in A.D. 476; also used *joc.* of 'matters which are out of date'. If fame were not an accident, and H. a distillation of Rumour CARLYLE. *transf.* The happiest women, like the happiest nations, have no h. GEO. ELIOT. 4. H. of British Birds (*title*) 1797. 5. The H. of Henrie the Fovrth (*title*) 1598. Last Scene of all, That ends this strange euentfull historie *A.Y.L.* II. vii. 164.

Comb.: **h.-maker,** (*a*) a writer of a h.; (*b*) one who 'makes history', i.e. performs actions which shape the course of h.; **-painter,** one who paints 'histories' (sense 6); so **-painting, -piece.**

†**History,** *v.* 1475. [ad. F. *historier*, ad. med.L. *historiare*, f. *historia.*] **1.** *trans.* To relate in a history; to recount -1597. **2.** To inscribe or adorn with 'histories' (sense 6) -1698.

‖**Histrio** (hi·striọ). 1658. [a. L.] = next.

Histrion (hi·striọ̆n). 1566. [a. F., ad. L. *histrionem.*] A stage-player. (Now usu. contemptuous.)

Histrionic (histriǫ·nik). 1648. [ad. late L. *histrionicus* (see prec.).]

A. *adj.* **1.** Of or relating to stage-players, or to play-acting; theatrical 1759. **2.** 'Stagey'; also *fig.* 'acting a part', hypocritical 1648.

2. H. mumm'ry, that let down The pulpit to the level of the stage COWPER. Phr. *H. paralysis* (Path.), facial palsy. *H. spasm*, spasm of the facial muscles.

B. *sb.* **1.** A stage-player. Also *fig.* 1859. **2.** *pl.* Theatricals; theatrical arts; acting, pretence 1864.

Hence **Histrio·nical** *a.* = HISTRIONIC *a.* 1, 2. **Histrio·nically** *adv.* **Histrio·nicism,** h. action.

Histrionism (hi·striŏniz'm). 1682. [f. HISTRION + -ISM.] Theatrical practice, action, or style; 'acting'.

Hit, *sb.* 1450. [f. HIT *v.*] **1.** A blow given to something aimed at; a stroke (at cricket, etc.); the collision of one body with another. **2.** A stroke of sarcasm, censure, etc. 1668. **3.** A fortunate chance 1666. **4.** A successful stroke of any kind 1815. **b.** A saying that goes to the point; a telling phrase 1836. **5.** *Backgammon.* **a.** A game won by a player after the opponent has removed one or more men from the board, as dist. from a *gammon* or a *backgammon.* **b.** The act of hitting a 'blot': see HIT *v.* I. 8. 1766.

1. A h., a very palpable h. *Haml.* v. ii. 292. 4. The noble speaker had made the h. of the evening 1884.

Hit (hit), *v.* Pa. t. and pple. **hit.** [Late OE. *hyttan* = ON. *hitta* to hit upon, meet with. App. from Norse; but the senses under I are Eng., from the notion 'get at, reach'.]

I. 1. To reach or get at with a blow or a missile; to strike ME. **b.** *Cricket.* To strike (the ball) with the bat: hence with the bowler as object 1857. **2.** *absol.* or *intr.* To give a blow or blows ME. **3.** Of a missile, etc.: To come upon with force; to strike ME. **4.** *absol.* or *intr.* To come with forcible impact (*against, upon*, etc.) ME. **5.** *trans.* To deliver (a blow, stroke, etc.) ME. **6.** *trans.* To knock (a part of the body) *against* or *on* something 1639. **7.** *fig.* To smite, wound, hurt ME. **8.** *Backgammon.* To 'take up' (a man) 1599.

1. *Twel. N.* II. v. 51. b. Dr. Grace hit Hill square for 4 1883. 3. *fig.* The sun, that now..hit the Northern hills TENNYSON. 4. b. To strike exactly or at the proper point; usu. in phr. *to be hitting on all four* or *six cylinders*: (of an internal-combustion engine) to be running or working perfectly; also *fig.* 5. Phr. *To h. any one a blow*: to strike him with a blow. 6. He hit his foot against the step (*mod.*). 7. Phr. *To h. home*: cf. HOME *adv. To be hard hit*: to be severely or deeply affected by something. This Objection hitteth not us at all 1678. 8. Phr. *To h. a blot*: to throw a number which enables a player to take up an unguarded man. Hence *fig.* to discover a weak point.

II. 1. *trans.* To come upon, light upon, get at, reach, find, esp. something aimed at OE. Also *intr.* with *upon, on,* †*of*, in same sense. **2.** *intr.* To attain the object aimed at; to succeed; to come off as intended. *Obs.* or *dial.* ME. **3.** *trans.* To imitate to a nicety 1602. **4.** To fall in with exactly 1580. †**5.** To fall in suitably or exactly; to square *with*, agree *with* -1722. **6.** *intr.* To agree together. *Obs.* or *dial.* 1605.

1. You have hit my meaning right 1581. Egad, I can't h. the Joint SWIFT. *intr.* To h. upon the right hypothesis SAYCE. 3. O, could he but haue drawne his wit As well in brasse, as he hath hit His face B. JONS. 4. [I] sought with deedes thy will to hitt SIDNEY. 5. The Scheme hit so exactly with my Temper DE FOE.

III. *intr.* To direct one's course; to pass, turn; to strike *out*, *in*, in a particular direction. ? Now *dial.* ME.

Phrases. *To h. it.* **a.** To guess the right thing. **b.** (Now usu. *to h. it off.*) To agree. **c.** To attain exactly to the point wanted; to strike the scent in hunting. *To h. the mark, the nail upon the head*, etc., usu. *fig.* *H. or miss*: Whether one hits or misses; happy-go-lucky. Also *attrib.* and *subst.*

Comb. with advs. **H. off. a.** To produce with success. **b.** To succeed in getting at or upon (e.g. the scent in hunting). **c.** To reproduce to a nicety. **H. out.** †**a.** *trans.* To knock out. **b.** To strike out, elicit. **c.** *intr.* To strike out with the fist. Also *fig.* **H. up** (*Cricket*): to make or score (runs).

Hit, obs. f. HIGHT *v.*, HEIGHT; obs. and dial. f. IT.

Hitch (hitʃ), *sb.* 1664. [f. HITCH *v.*] **1.** A short abrupt movement, pull, or push; a jerk 1674. **2.** *Mining.* A slight fault or dislocation of strata 1708. **3.** A limp, a hobble; an interference in a horse's pace 1664. **4.** The action of catching, as on a hook, etc. WEBSTER. **5.** Chiefly *Naut.* A noose or knot by which a rope is caught round or temporarily made fast to some object 1769. **6.** *fig.* An accidental or temporary stoppage; an impediment, obstruction 1748.

1. Ben..gives his trousers one h., and calls for a quartern MARRYAT. 5. CLOVE-HITCH, HALF-HITCH, etc. (see these wds.). 6. There was some h. in the execution of our treaty LD. MALMESBURY.

Hitch (hitʃ), *v.* 1440. [In *Promp. Parv.*, 1440, *hytchen*; also, later, without *h*, see ITCH *v.*[2] Of obscure origin. Cf. Sc. and north. *hotch.*] **1.** *trans.* To move as with a jerk; to shift a little away or aside; *esp.* to raise or lift with a jerk (orig. *Naut.*) 1833. Also *fig.* Also *intr.* for *pass.* **2.** *intr.* To shift one's position a little; to move with a jerk or succession of jerks 1629. **3.** To hobble; also (*dial.*) to hop 1513. **4.** *trans.* To catch as with a loop, noose, or hook; to fasten, esp. in a temporary way. Also *fig.* **b.** with *up*: To harness, yoke 1870. *To hitch horses together* (U.S.); to get on well, in harmony 1837; *pass.* (U.S.), to be married 1857. **5.** *intr.* To become fastened or caught, esp. by hooking on; to catch on something. Also *fig.* 1578. **6.** Of a horse: To strike the feet together in going; to interfere 1686.

1. Hitching his chair nearer the fire C. BRONTË. And then he hitch'd his trousers up BARHAM. *fig.* Now we must appear..affectionate, or Sneer will h. us into a story SHERIDAN. *intr.* for *pass.* Whoe'er offends, at some unlucky time Slides into verse, and hitches in a rhyme POPE. 4. Hitching our shawls in a bramble MISS MITFORD. **b.** Now that is the wisdom of a man..to h. his waggon to a star EMERSON. 5. The lariat hitched on one of his ears W. IRVING.

Hitchel, obs. and dial. f. HATCHEL.

Hithe, hythe (haið). [OE. *hȳð* fem.:—OTeut. type **hûþjâ-*.] A port or haven; *esp.* a small landing-place on a river. Now *Obs.* exc. *Hist.*, and in place-names, as *Hythe*, *Lambeth* (orig. *Lamb-hithe*), etc.

Hither (hi·ðəɹ). [OE. *hider*, f. demonstr. stem *hi-* (see HE, HERE) + same suffix as in L. *citra*. Not known in WGer. exc. in OE.]

A. *adv.* **1.** With vbs. of motion, etc.: To or towards this place. (Now only literary; see HERE.) †**2.** Up to this point (of time, etc.) -1607. †**3.** To this end or aim; to this subject or category; hereto -1694.

1. Come h. unto me 1550. 3. Hyther tendyth al prudence and pollycy 1538. Phr. **Hither and thither**: to this place and that; to and fro; in various directions.

B. *adj.* Situated on this side, or in this direction; the nearer. Also *fig.* of time. ME.

On this h. side of the riuer HOLINSHED.

Hence **Hi·thermost** *a.* most in this direction; nearest.

Hitherto (hiðəɹtū·, hi·ðəɹtu), *adv.* (*a.*) ME. [f. HITHER *adv.* + TO *prep.*] **1.** Up to this time, until now, as yet. †**2.** Up to this point (in writing, etc.) -1762. **3.** To this place; thus far (*arch.*) 1535. †**4.** = HITHER 3. -1656. **5.** quasi-*adj.* [attrib. use of adv.] 1787.

1. The Lord hath blessed me h. *Josh.* xvii. 14. 3. H. shalt thou come, but no further *Job* xxxviii. 11. 5. All his h. offences MME. D'ARBLAY. So †**Hither-toward(s**, †**Hitherunto·**, **-u·nto**, *advs.*

Hitherward (hi·ðəɹwǫ̈ɹd), *adv. arch.* [OE. *hiderweard*, f. *hider* HITHER + *-weard* -WARD. (In OE. also adj.)] **1.** Towards this place; hither. **2.** On this side (*of*). Also *fig.* 1864. †**3.** Until now; hitherto -1513.

1. Marching h. SHAKS. 2. H. of Sohr CARLYLE. So **Hi·therwards** *adv.*

Hitter (hi·təɹ). 1813. [f. HIT *v.* + -ER [1].] One who hits or strikes, as a *hard hitter*.

Hitty-missy (hi·ti mi·si), *adv.* (*a.*) 1553. [app. from *hit I, miss I.*] **1.** Hit or miss; at random, at haphazard. **2.** *adj.* Random, haphazard 1885.

Hive (həiv), *sb.* [OE. *hȳf*:—OTeut. type **hûfi-z*; prob. related to L. *cupa* tub, cask.] **1.** An artificial receptacle for the habitation of a swarm of bees; a beehive. Also *fig.* **2.** *transf.* **a.** A place swarming with busy occupants 1634. **b.** A place whence swarms of people issue 1788. **3.** A hiveful of bees, a hived swarm ME.; *transf.* a teeming multitude 1832. **4.** Anything of the shape or structure of a beehive 1597.

2. **a.** This great H., the City COWLEY. **b.** The h. whence the Pelasgian people issued 1835. 3. *transf.* There the h. of Roman liars worship a gluttonous emperor idiot TENNYSON. *Comb.* **h.-bee**, the common honey-bee. Hence **Hi·veless** *a.* destitute of a h.

Hive (həiv), *v.* late ME. [f. HIVE *sb.*] **1.** *trans.* To gather (bees) into a hive; to locate (a swarm) in a hive. Also *transf.* and *fig.* **2.** To hoard, as honey, in the hive 1580. **3.** *intr.* To take to the hive, as bees. **b.** To live together as bees in a hive; also *transf.* 1577.

1. Your Gardner must..watch his Bees, and h. them 1615. 2. Hiving wisdom with each studious year BYRON. 3. Drones hiue not with me, Therefore I part with him *Merch. V.* II. v. 48. Hence **Hiver**, one who hives bees.

Hives (həivz), *sb. pl.* 1500. [?] 'Any eruption on the skin, when the disorder is supposed to proceed from an internal cause' (Jamieson); applied to chicken-pox; also, croup.

Hizz (hiz), *v.* Now *rare.* 1583. [Echoic.] *intr.* To hiss.

H'm, h'm, *int.* See HEM *int.*, HUM *int.*

Ho (hōu), *int.*[1] (and *sb.*[1]) ME. [A natural exclam.] **1.** An exclam. of surprise, admiration, exultation (often ironical), triumph, taunting. **2.** An exclam. to attract attention; often after the name of a thing or place ME. **3.** *sb.* A cry of 'ho' ME.

1. Phr. *ho! ho! ho!*, an expression of derision or derisive laughter. 2. Then Westward-hoe *Twel. N.* III. i. 146. 3. With a hey, and a ho, and a hey nonino *A.Y.L.* v. iii. 18.

Ho, *int.*[2] (and *sb.*[2]) Also †**hoa**, †**hoe**. ME. [a. OF. *ho* halt! stop!] **1.** †A cry to stop or to cease what one is doing -1631. **b.** A call to an animal to stop or stand still 1828. **2.** *sb.* Cessation, halt, intermission; limit. *Obs.* or *dial.* ME.

2. *Withouten ho, Out of all ho*, without stopping, unceasingly. *No ho*, no limit.

Ho, *int.*[3] A sailor's cry in heaving or hauling.

Ho, obs. f. HE, HEO, HI *prons.*, HOW, WHO; var. of O *adv.*

‖**Hoactzin, hoatzin** (hōu,æ·ktsin, hōu,æ·t-sin). Also **hoazin.** 1661. [Native name, derived from the bird's 'harsh grating hiss'.] A bird, *Opisthocomus hoazin*, or *O. cristatus*, native of tropical America, type and sole member of a group named by Huxley *Heteromorphæ*.

Hoaming, *ppl. a.* *Obs.* or *dial.* 1670. ? = HUMMING *ppl. a.* 2.

What a Sea comes in. A h. Sea! we shall have foul weather DRYDEN & DAVENANT. [*Cf.* A great huminge sea NARBROUGH 1672.]

Hoar (hōəɹ). [OE. *hār* = OHG. *hêr* 'old', hence 'venerable, august'; usu. referred to an OTeut. **hai-*, pre-Teut. **koi-* to shine.]

A. *adj.* **1.** Grey-haired with age; venerable. **2.** Of colour: Grey, greyish white OE. †**3.** Used as an attribute of stones, etc. marking a boundary line. Hence in place-names. -ME. **4.** Mouldy, musty. Also *fig.* *Obs.* exc. *dial.* 1483.

1. Youth and h. age POPE. 2. Hoare haires *Isa.* xlvi. 4. Haire frost 1644. Some h. hill MILT. H. cliffs THOMSON. 4. An old Hare hoare is very good meat in Lent *Rom. & Jul.* II. iv. 141.

Comb.: **h.-leprosy**, elephantiasis; **-rime** = HOAR-FROST; **h. withy**, the White-beam, *Pyrus Aria.*

B. *sb.* **1.** Hoariness from age 1500. **2.** A hoary coating or appearance; esp. hoar-frost, rime 1567; †mould -1686.

2. The candy'd rhime and scattered h. 1731.

†**Hoar**, *v.* [OE. *hárian*, f. *hár* HOAR *a.*] To make or become hoary or musty -1750.

Hoard (hōəɹd), *sb.* [OE. *hord* = OS. *hord* treasure:—OTeut. **hozdo*[m], pre-Teut. **kuzdhó-*. The spelling *hoard* is rare bef. 18th c.] **1.** A stock, store, esp. of money, hidden away or laid by; a treasure. Also *fig.* †**2.** A repository; a hiding-place, store; a treasury. Also *fig.* -1663. †**3.** Hoarding up. CHAUCER.

1. The Squirrels h. *Mids. N.* IV. i. 40. A..h. of coins 1851.

Hoard (hōəɹd), *v.* [OE. *hordian*, f. *hord* HOARD *sb.*] *trans.* To amass and put away for preservation or future use; to treasure *up*: esp. money or wealth. Also *absol.* Also *fig.* and *transf.*

The Granaries of Joseph: wherein he hoorded corne 1615. *absol.* A savage race, That h., and sleep, and feed TENNYSON. *fig.* Revenge will be smothered and hoarded BURKE. Hence **Hoa·rder**, †a steward; one who hoards up.

Hoarding (hōə·ɹdiŋ), *sb.* 1823. [Cf. obs. F. *hourd* scaffold (Cotgr.), in OF. *hurt*, *hourt*, *hourd* palisade.] **1.** A temporary fence of boards enclosing a building while in course of erection or repair; hence, any hoarding on which bills are posted. **2.** *Mil.* An overhanging gallery, protected by boarding in front, thrown out from the surface of a wall, to enable the defenders to protect the foot of the wall 1865.

†**Hoared** (hōəɹd), *ppl. a.* 1496. [f. HOAR *v.*] Made or grown hoary or mouldy -1643.

Hoa·r-frost. ME. [Often two wds. See HOAR *a.* and FROST *sb.*] The white deposit formed by the freezing of dew, white frost.

He..scatereth y[e] horefrost like ashes COVERDALE *Ps.* cxlvii. 16.

Hoa·rhead. ME. [f. HOAR *a.* + HEAD *sb.*] A hoary head; an old grey-haired man. Also *attrib.* Hence **Hoar-headed** *a.*

Hoarhound, var. of HOREHOUND.

Hoariness (hōə·rinės). 1573. [f. HOARY *a.* + -NESS.] The quality or state of being hoary. So †**Hoa·rness.**

Hoarse (hōəɹs), *a.* [OE. *hás*, **hárs* (ME. *hōs*, *hōrs*, *hoors*, now *hoarse*):—OTeut. **haiso-*, or (more prob.) **hairso-*.] **1.** Rough and deep-sounding, as the voice when affected with a cold, or the voice of a raven or frog; husky, croaking, raucous. **2.** *transf.* Having a hoarse voice or sound OE. **3.** quasi-*adv.* 1709.

1. His voice was h. and lowe 1584. The Tides with their h. Murmurs DRYDEN. 2. The h. Raven.. croaking DRYDEN. The h. storm 1765. Hence **Hoa·rsely** *adv.* with a h. voice or sound. **Hoa·rsen** *v.* to make or become h. **Hoa·rseness**, the quality or condition of being h.

Hoar-stone. [In OE. two wds.: see HOAR *a.* and STONE.] **1.** *lit.* A hoar, i.e. grey or ancient stone. OE. only. **2.** *spec.* **a.** An ancient boundary stone OE. **b.** A stone of memorial; a standing stone 1666.

Hoary (hōə·ri), *a.* 1530. [f. HOAR *a.* or *sb.* + -Y.] **1.** Grey or white with age; grey-haired 1573; ancient 1609. **2.** Grey, greyish white 1573. †**3.** Mouldy, musty; corrupt -1693. **4.** *Bot.* and *Entom.* Covered with short dense white or whitish hairs; canescent 1597.

1. Thou shalt rise vp before the h. head *Lev.* xix. 32. The h. sinner FREEMAN. Windsor's h. towers COWPER. 2. The h. poplars HEBER.

Hoast (hōust), *sb.* Chiefly *n. dial.* [ME. *host*, = ON. *hóste* cough, f. (ult.) a root **hwōs-*, pre-Teut. **kwōs-*, *kās-*; cf. Skr. *kās* to cough.] A cough. So **Hoast** *v.* to cough.

Hoatzin: see HOACTZIN.

Hoax (hōᵘks), *v.* 1796. [Said to be contr. f. HOCUS.] *trans.* To deceive by an amusing or mischievous fabrication or fiction; to play upon the credulity of. Also *absol.* Hence **Hoax** *sb.* an act of hoaxing; a humorous or mischievous deception with which the credulity of the victim is imposed upon. **Hoa·xer,** one who hoaxes.

Hoazin: see HOACTZIN.

Hob (hǫb), *sb.*[1] ME. [A familiar form of *Rob* = Robin, Robert.] **1.** Formerly a generic name for: A rustic, a clown. **2.** = Robin Goodfellow or Puck; a hobgoblin, sprite, elf 1460.

2. From elves, hobs, and fairies..Defend us, good Heaven FLETCHER.

Hob, *sb.*[2] 1511. [? Cf. HUB.] **1.** In a fire-place, the part of the casing having a surface level with the top of the grate. Formerly also *hub.* **2.** A (rounded) peg or pin used as a mark in games, *esp.* in quoits 1589. **3.** (Also *hub.*) 'A hardened, threaded spindle, by which a comb or chasing-tool may be cut' (Knight) 1873. **4.** Short for HOBNAIL. 1828.

Hob, in *hob a nob, hob and nob, hob or nob*: see HOB-NOB.

Hobbesian (hǫ·bziăn), *a.* 1776. [f. Thomas *Hobbes* (1588–1679); see -IAN.] Of or relating to Hobbes or his philosophy. Hence **Ho·bbesianism** = HOBBISM.

†**Hobbinoll, hobinoll.** 1579. [app. f. *Hob, Hobby,* or *Hobbin* = 'rustic' + NOLL noddle.] The name of a shepherd in Spenser's *Shepherd's Calendar*; hence, A countryman, rustic, boor –1652.

Hobbism (hǫ·biz'm). 1691. [f. *Hobb(es* (see HOBBESIAN) + -ISM.] The philosophy or principles of Thomas Hobbes. So **Ho·bbist,** an advocate of H., a disciple of Hobbes 1681.

Hobble (hǫ·b'l), *sb.* 1727. [f. HOBBLE *v.*] **1.** The action of hobbling; an uneven, clumsy, infirm gait. Also *fig.* of utterance. **2.** An awkward or perplexing situation (*dial.* and *colloq.*) 1775. **3.** Anything used for hobbling horses, etc.; *transf.* a fetter 1831. **4.** (In full *h.-skirt*) A close-fitting skirt so narrow at the bottom as to impede the wearer in walking 1911.

Hobble (hǫ·b'l), *v.* ME. [app. cogn. w. Du. *hobbelen,* said to be a dim. of *hobben* to toss or rock (as a boat on the billows).] **1.** *intr.* To move unsteadily up and down in riding, floating, etc. **2.** To walk lamely and with difficulty; to limp ME. **3.** *fig.* To proceed irregularly and haltingly in action or speech; (of verse) to 'limp' 1522. **4.** To cause to limp (*lit.* and *fig.*) 1870. **5.** *trans.* To nonplus 1762. **6.** = HOPPLE *v.* 1831.

2. I now h. about the garden with a stick MME. D'ARBLAY. 3. She hobbles in alternate verse PRIOR. 6. The horses were hobbled, by a cord from the fore to the hind foot 1835. Hence **Ho·bblingly** *adv.* lamely.

Ho·bble-bush. 1842. The N. American Wayfaring-tree, *Viburnum lantanoides,* a small shrub with cymes of white flowers and purple berries.

Hobbledehoy (hǫ·b'ldihoi), **hobbadehoy** (hǫ·bă-), **hobbedehoy** (hǫ·bi-). *colloq.* 1540. [Of unkn. origin. Usu. associated with *hobble.*] A youth between boyhood and manhood, a stripling; *esp.* a clumsy or awkward youth. Also *transf.* Also *attrib.*

Why he's a mere hobbledehoy, neither a man nor a boy SWIFT. Hence **Hobbledehoy·dom, Hobbledehoy·hood,** the age or condition of a h. var. **Hob(b)letehoy.**

Hobbler[1] (hǫ·blər). *Obs.* exc. *Hist.* ME. [In AF. *hobeleor, -lour,* a deriv. of *hobi, hobin,* HOBBY *sb.*[1]] A retainer bound to maintain a hobby for military service; a soldier who rode a hobby, a light horseman. ¶Erron. used by Scott for *hobby.*

Hobbler[2] (hǫ·blər). 1594. [f. HOBBLE *v.* + -ER[1].] **1.** A person that hobbles in his gait 1665. †**2.** A child's top that spins unsteadily. **3.** An unlicensed pilot; also, a man on land employed in towing vessels by a rope 1800.

Hobby (hǫ·bi), *sb.*[1] [ME. *hobyn, hoby*; prob. the by-name *Hobin, Hobby,* var. of *Robin, Robbie.* Cf. DOBBIN.] **1.** A small or middle-sized horse; an ambling or pacing horse; a pony. Now *Hist., arch.,* or *dial.* †**2.** = HOBBY-HORSE 2. –1820. **3.** = HOBBY-HORSE 4. 1689. **4.** A favourite occupation or topic, pursued for amusement, and which is compared to the riding of a toy horse (sense 3); an individual pursuit to which a person is unduly devoted. Formerly HOBBY-HORSE (sense 5). 1816.

4. I quarrel with no man's h. SCOTT.

Hobby (hǫ·bi), *sb.*[2] 1440. [a. OF. *hobé, hobet,* dim. of *hobe* the same bird; perh. f. OF. *hober* to stir (Darmesteter).] A small species of falcon, *Falco subbuteo,* formerly flown at larks and other small birds. Hence †**Hobby** *v.* to hawk with a h. SKELTON.

Hobby-horse. 1557. [f. HOBBY *sb.*[1] + HORSE.] †**1.** = HOBBY *sb.*[1] 1. –1614. **2.** A figure of a horse, made of wickerwork, or the like, fastened about the waist of one of the performers in a morris-dance, or on the stage, who executed various antics in the character of a horse; also, the name of this performer. †**3.** *transf.* **a.** A foolish person, jester, buffoon. **b.** A lustful person; a prostitute. –1616. **4.** A stick with a horse's head which children bestride as a horse 1589; a wooden horse 1741. **5.** A favourite pursuit or pastime; = HOBBY *sb.*[1] 4. Now *rare.* 1676.

1. Prov. *The hobby-horse is forgot*: app. a phrase from some old ballad. *L. L. L.* III. i. 30. 3. *L. L. L.* III. i. 31. 5. Almost every person hath some hobby horse or other HALE. Hence **Hobby-ho·rsical** *a.* (*joc.*), belonging or devoted to a hobby, crotchety, whimsical.

Hobgoblin (hǫ·bgǫblin), *sb.* (*a.*) 1530. [f. HOB *sb.*[1] 2 + GOBLIN.] **1.** A mischievous, tricksy imp or sprite; another name for Robin Goodfellow; hence, a terrifying apparition, a bogy 1530. **2.** *fig.* A bugbear 1709. **3.** *attrib.* and *adj.* 1622.

2. A foolish consistency is the h. of little minds EMERSON. 3. H. terrors 1628.

Hobiler, var. of HOBBLER [1].

Hobits, Hobitzer, vars. of HOWITZ, HOWITZER.

Hobnail (hǫ·bnēl), *sb.* 1594. [f. HOB *sb.*[2] + NAIL.] **1.** A nail with a massive head and short tang, used for protecting the soles of heavy boots and shoes. **2.** *transf.* A man who wears hobnailed boots; a rustic, clodhopper 1645. **3.** *attrib.* or *adj.* Clownish, boorish 1624.

Comb. **h. liver,** a cirrhotic liver, studded with small prominences resembling hobnails. Hence **Ho·bnail** *v.* to set with hobnails; to trample down, as with hobnailed shoes. **Ho·bnailed** *a.* set with hobnails; *transf.* rustic, boorish.

Ho·b-nob, *phr.* and *adv.* 1601. [Orig. a var. of *hab nab*; see HAB *adv.*] **1.** phr. *Hob, nob*: have or have not; in Shaks., app. = 'give or take'. **2.** *adv.* = *Hab nab* (HAB *adv.* 1); hit or miss; at random 1660. **3. Hob or nob, hob a nob, hob and nob** (prob. = give or (and) take): used by two persons drinking to each other 1756. **b.** quasi-*adj.* On terms of good-fellowship 1851.

1. Hob, nob, is his word: giu't or take't *Twel. N.* III. iv. 262.

Ho·b-nob, *v.* 1763. [From the adv. phr.; see prec. 3.] **1.** *intr.* To drink to each other, drink together. **2.** To hold familiar intercourse, be on familiar terms *with* 1828.

Ho·b-nob, *sb.* 1761. [f. as prec.] †**1.** A 'sentiment' used in hob-nobbing –1770. **2.** A drinking to each other or together 1825.

Hobo (hōᵘ·bo). *U.S.* 1891. [?] A tramp.

Hoboe, hoboy, vars. of HAUTBOY.

Hobson's choice: see CHOICE *sb.*

Hob-thrush, Hob-thrust. *Obs.* exc. *dial.* 1590. [f. HOB *sb.*[1] + OE. *þyrs,* ON. *þurs* giant, goblin.] **1.** A goblin. **2.** (In full *h.-t. louse.*) A wood-louse (*dial.*) 1828.

‖**Hocco** (hǫ·ko). 1834. [Native name in Guiana.] A bird of the family *Cracidæ* (Curassows).

Hochheimer: see HOCKAMORE.

†**Hock** (hǫk), *sb.*[1] *Obs.* [OE. *hoc.*] A name for malvaceous plants, esp. the Common and Marsh Mallow and the Hollyhock –1611.

Hock (hǫk), *sb.*[2] 1540. [A by-form of *hoȝ, hoch,* HOUGH.] **1.** The joint in the hinder leg of a quadruped between the true knee and the fetlock, the angle of which points backward. **2.** The knuckle end of a gammon of bacon 1706. **3.** *attrib.,* as *h. action,* etc. 1641.

Hock (hǫk), *sb.*[3] 1625. [Shortened f. HOCKAMORE.] The wine called in German *Hochheimer,* produced at Hochheim on the Main; hence, any White German wine. Also *attrib.*

Hock, *sb.*[4] 1530. [? shortened from *hōk,* HOOK.] A rod, stick, or chain, with a hook at the end. EVELYN.

Hock, *v.* 1563. [f. HOCK *sb.*[2]; cf. HOUGH *v.*] *trans.* To disable by cutting the tendons of the hock; to hough, hamstring.

†**Hockamore** (hǫ·kămōᵊr). 1673. [Anglicized f. *Hochheimer.*] = HOCK *sb.*[3] –1747.

Hock-cart. Now only *Hist.* 1648. [Cf. HOCKEY [1].] The cart which carried home the last load of the harvest.

Hock-day. Now only *Hist.* ME. [?] The second Tuesday after Easter Sunday (or, according to some, Easter week): an important term-day, and, from the 14th c., a popular festival; also *pl.* including the preceding Monday.

†**Hocket.** 1601. [a. F. *hoquet.*] **1.** = HICKET, HICCUP –1617. **2.** *Mediæval Mus.* An interruption of a voice-part by rests, so as to produce a broken or spasmodic effect. Now *Hist.* 1776.

Hockey[1] (hǫ·ki), **hawkey** (hǭ·ki), **horkey.** 1555. [?] The feast at harvest-home (*local*). Also *attrib.*

Hockey[2] (hǫ·ki). 1527. [? conn. w. OF. *hoquet* 'crook'.] **1.** An outdoor game of ball played with sticks hooked or curved at one end, with which the players of each side drive the ball towards their opponents' goal. **2.** (*U.S.*) The stick used in this game 1839. **3.** *attrib.* (*h.-stick* 1527).

†**Hockle,** *v.*[1] 1668. [app. f. HOCK *sb.*[2]] To hough, to hamstring.

Hockle, *v.*[2] *local.* ? *Obs.* 1746. To cut up (stubble).

Hockmoney. Also *hocking-.* 1480–5. The money collected at hocktide.

Hocktide. *Obs.* exc. *Hist.* 1484. [f. *hock-* in HOCK-DAY + TIDE.] The season of the hock days: Hock Monday and Tuesday (the second Monday and Tuesday after Easter-day), long kept as a festival with various traditional customs.

Hocus (hōᵘ·kəs), *sb.* 1640. [Short for *Hocus Pocus,* HOCUS-POCUS.] †**1.** A conjuror –1699; †*transf.* an impostor (SOUTH). **2.** Jugglery, deception. *Obs.* or *arch.* 1652. **3.** Drugged liquor (*mod.*).

Hocus (hōᵘ·kəs), *v.* 1675. [f. prec.] **1.** *trans.* To 'hoax'. **2.** To stupefy with drugs, esp. for a criminal purpose; hence, to drug (liquor) 1831.

Hocus-pocus (hōᵘ·kəs pōᵘ·kəs), *sb.* (*a.*) 1624. [Name of or for a conjuror, being the first words of a sham Latin formula used by one.] †**1.** A conjuror, juggler. Also *transf.* a trickster. –17.. **2.** Used as a formula (sometimes with allusion to an assumed derivation from *hoc est corpus*) 1632. **3.** A juggler's trick; jugglery; sleight of hand; trickery, deception 1647. **4.** *attrib.* or *adj.* Juggling; cheating, tricky 1668.

1. He opens as Hokus Pocus do's his fists H. MORE. 2. The *hocus pocus* of a popish priest cannot turn bread into flesh FLETCHER. Hence **Hocus-pocus** *v. intr.* to juggle; to practise deception; *trans.* to play tricks upon.

Hod (hǫd), *sb.* 1481. [app. a var. of HOT *sb.*[1] in same sense.] **1.** An open receptacle for carrying mortar, bricks, etc.; also the quantity carried in it. **2.** A receptacle for carrying or holding coal. Orig. *dial.* and *U.S.* 1825.

Comb. **h.-bearer, -carrier** = HODMAN, q. v.

Hod, early ME. f. HAD, -HOOD, condition, etc.

Hodden (hǫ·d'n). *Sc.* 1591. [?] **1.** Coarse woollen cloth, as made formerly by country weavers on their hand-looms. Also *attrib.* **2. Hodden grey.** Grey hodden, made without dyeing, by a mixture of fleeces. Applied to cloth having the natural colour of the wool. Hence typical of rusticity 1724.

Hoddy-doddy. *Obs.* exc. *dial.* 1553. [? a nursery reduplication; f. *dod* in DODMAN a shell-snail. The element *hoddy-* also seems to mean 'snail' (or ? horned).]

A. *sb.* 1. A small shell-snail (*dial.*). †2. A short dumpy person –1723. †3. A cuckold, with ref. to the 'horns' (cf. sense 1) –1656.

B. *adj.* 1. Short and dumpy 1824. 2. *dial.* Confused, in a whirl 1809.

†**Ho·ddypeak.** 1500. [f. *hoddy* (see prec.) + PEAK *sb.* or *v.*] A fool, noodle, blockhead –1589.

Hodge (hǫdʒ). ME. [Abbrev. and altered from *Roger*.] 1. As a typical name for the English rustic. 2. *Jolly Hodge* (also *Jolly Roger*), the pirate's flag bearing the Death's Head and Cross-bones 1822.

Comb. **H.-razor**, a razor made to sell to Hodge; hence, in Carlyle, a sham.

Hodge-podge (hǫ·dʒipǫdʒ), *sb.* ME. [A corruption of HOTCHPOTCH, prob. assim. to prec.] 1. = HOTCHPOTCH 1. 1622. 2. *contemptuous.* A clumsy mixture of ingredients 1615. 3. = HOTCHPOTCH 2. ME. 4. *attrib.*, as **hodge-podge act**, a legislative act embracing incongruous matters 1602. Hence **Hodge-podge** *v. trans.* to make a hodge-podge of; also *intr.* So †**Ho·dgepot** = HODGE-PODGE 1.

Hodgkin's disease. 1877. [f. Dr. Thomas *Hodgkin* (1798–1866), who first described it.] A disease marked by enlargement of the lymphatic glands and spleen, with progressive anæmia; also called *lymphadenoma*.

Hodiernal (hōudiə·ɹnăl), *a.* 1656. [f. L. *hodiernus*, f. *hodie* to-day + -AL.] Of or belonging to the present day. So †**Ho·diern** *a.*

Hodman (hǫ·dmæ̆n). 1587. [f. HOD *sb.*[1] 1 + MAN.] 1. A man who carries the hod; a bricklayer's labourer. Also *fig.* 2. A term of contempt applied by undergraduates of Christ Church, Oxford, who were King's Scholars of Westminster School, to those who were not, and hence to other undergraduates 1677.

Hodmandod (hǫ·dmæ̆ndǫd), *sb.* (*a.*) 1626. [Redupl. var. of DODMAN; cf. HODDY-DODDY.] 1. A shell-snail, a dodman. Also *fig.* †2. Corrupt for HOTTENTOT –1729. 3. *adj.* Short and clumsy 1825.

Hodograph (hǫ·dograf). 1846. [f. Gr. ὁδός way + -γραφος.] 1. *Math.* A curve, of which the radius vector represents in magnitude and direction the velocity of a moving particle. Also *attrib.* 2. A machine for registering the paces of a horse, etc. (Commonly, but erron., spelt *odograph.*) 1883. Hence **Hodogra·phic** *a.* **Hodogra·phically** *adv.* by means of a h.

Hodometer (hodǫ·mĭtəɹ), **odometer.** 1791. [f. Gr. ὁδός way + μέτρον; cf. F. *odomètre*, whence the more frequent spelling without *h.*] An instrument attached to the wheel of a vehicle, which records the distance traversed; also a wheel used by surveyors, having a recording apparatus in the centre, and trundled along by a handle. Also applied to a pedometer. So **Hodome·trical** *a.* relating to the measurement of a ship's way, or to a h. **Hodo·metry, odo·metry**, measurement, as by a h., of distances traversed.

Hoe (hōu), *sb.*[1] *Obs.* exc. *dial.* [OE. *hôh*, *hô*, str. masc. :—OTeut. **hanho-*, from ablaut stem of HANG *v.* Cf. HEUGH.] 'A projecting ridge of land, a promontory' (Sweet); a height ending abruptly or steeply. Now only in place-names, etc.

That loftie place at Plimmouth call'd the Hoe DRAYTON.

Hoe (hōu), *sb.*[2] ME. [a. F. *houe* :—OHG. *houwâ* (mod.G. *haue*), hoe, mattock, pickax, f. *houwan* to HEW.] 1. A tool used chiefly for breaking up or loosening the surface of the ground, hoeing up weeds, covering plants with soil, etc. It consists of a thin iron blade fixed transversely at the end of a long handle. 2. A dentist's excavating instrument, shaped like a hoe 1875.

Dutch h., Scuffle h., kinds of *thrust-hoes*, as dist. from *draw-hoes* (the original type).

Hoe, *sb.*[3] *local.* 1804. [a. ON. *há-r* (Da. *haa*) dog-fish, shark.] In Orkney and Shetland the Picked Dog-fish, *Squalus acanthias*. Comb. **h.-mother** (contracted *homer*), the Basking Shark, *Selachus maximus*.

Hoe, *v.* ME. [f. HOE *sb.*[2]] 1. *intr.* To use a hoe; to work with a hoe. 2. *trans.* To weed (crops), thin *out* (plants), 'cultivate', with a hoe 1693. 3. To break or stir up (the ground) with a hoe 1712. 4. with adv. To dig *up*, raise *up*, take *away*, cut *down*, cover *in*, with a hoe 1699.

Hoe-cake (hōu·kēɪk). *U.S.* 1793. [Orig. cake baked on the broad thin blade of a cotton-field hoe (*Cent. Dict.*).] Coarse bread, made of Indian meal, water, and salt, usu. in the form of a thin cake.

Hoe·-plough, *sb.* ? *Obs.* 1733. = HORSE-HOE. Hence as *v.*

‖**Hoey.** 1865. [Chinese *hūy* (hŭi), society, club, guild.] A society of Chinese; esp. a secret society.

Hog (hǫg), *sb.*[1] ME. [late OE. *hogg.*] 1. A swine reared for slaughter; *spec.* a castrated male swine; hence, a swine generally. b. *U.S.* Pork 1860. 2. Used as the name of the species: = SWINE. b. Formerly spec. a wild boar of the second year. 1483. 3. Applied to different species of the family *Suidæ* 1732. 4. A young sheep that has not yet been shorn 1296. b. Specialized as *chilver-* or *ewe-h.*, *tup-h.*, etc. 1607. c. Short for *h.-fleece*, *-wool* 1854. d. Applied to domestic animals of a year old 1775. 5. *fig.* A coarse, self-indulgent, gluttonous, or filthy person ME. b. *spec.* A road hog (ROAD *sb.*) 1906. 6. *slang.* A shilling 1673. 7. a. A sort of broom or brush for cleaning a ship's bottom 1769. b. *Paper-making.* A device for agitating the pulp so as to keep it of uniform consistence 1807.

Phrase. *To go the whole h.*: to go all the way, to do the thing thoroughly (*slang*); hence, in derivative uses.

attrib. and *Comb.* a. **h.-cholera**, the swine-fever; **-constable** = HOG-REEVE; **hog('s)-flesh**, pork; **hog('s)-grease**, the lard or fat of a h.; **h.-pen, -pound**, a pigsty; **-ring**, a ring put into the snout of a pig to prevent grubbing; **-wallow**, a hollow in which pigs wallow; also, *spec.* in U.S., a natural depression having this appearance; **-ward**, a swine-herd; **hog('s)-yoke**, a frame of wood put round a hog's neck to prevent its getting through hedges.

b. From sense 4: **h.-bull**, a yearling bull; **-colt**, a yearling colt; **-fence**, pasture fenced off for feeding young sheep or 'hogs' during the winter; **-fleece**, the fleece obtained from a 'hog'; **-lamb**, a castrated wether lamb; **-sheep** = sense 4; **-wool** = sense 4 c.

c. In names of animals resembling the hog, or infesting swine, as **h.-ape**, the mandrill baboon, *Simia porcaria*; **-beetle**, a beetle of the family *Curculionidæ*; **-caterpillar**, 'the larva of a Sphinx-moth, *Darapsa myron*, so called from the swollen thoracic joints' (*Cent. Dict.*); **-choke, -choker** (*U.S.*), an American sole, *Achirus lineatus*, of no market value; **-mouse**, the shrew-mouse; **-sucker**, a N. American fish, the Hammer-head, *Hypentelium nigricans*; **-tapir**, the Mexican tapir; **-tick**, a tick parasitic on swine, *Hæmatopinus suis*.

d. In names of plants devoured by, fit for, or left to hogs or swine, as **hog('s)-grass**, Swine's Cress, *Senebiera Coronopus*; **hog('s)-meat**, (*a*) *Aristolochia grandiflora*, (*b*) *Boerhaavia decumbens* of Jamaica; **h.-peanut**, a twining plant of U.S., *Amphicarpæa monoica* (N.O. *Leguminosæ*), having purplish flowers and fleshy pea-shaped fruits; **hog's bane**, Goosefoot or Sowbane; **hog's bread**, Sowbread, *Cyclamen*; also = *hog-meat* b; **hog's garlic**, *Allium ursinum*; **hog's madder**, Ragwort, *Senecio Jacobæa*; **h.-wort**, *Heptalon graveolens* (N.O. *Euphorbiaceæ*) of U.S.

Hog, *sb.*[2] *local.* 1790. [?] A heap of potatoes or turnips covered with straw and soil; a 'pit'.

Hog (hǫg), *v.*[1] 1769. [f. HOG *sb.*[1]] 1. *trans.* a. To arch (the back) upward like that of a hog. b. To cause (a ship, her keel, etc.) to arch upwards in the centre, as the result of a strain 1798. 2. *intr.* To rise arch-wise in the centre, as a ship when the ends droop 1818. 3. *trans.* To cut (a horse's mane) short, so that it stands up like a hog's bristles 1769. 4. To make a 'hog' of (a lamb) 1853. 5. To appropriate greedily (*U.S. slang*) 1887. b. *intr.* To behave as a road hog 1925. 6. To clean a ship's bottom with a 'hog' 1651.

Hog, *v.*[2] 1730. [f. HOG.[2]] To store (potatoes, etc.) in a hog (see HOG *sb.*[2]).

Hogarthian (hogā·ɹþiăn), *a.* 1798. [f. William *Hogarth*, satirical painter and caricaturist + -IAN.] Of or pertaining to Hogarth, or like his style of painting.

Ho·gback, hog-back. Also **hog's back.** 1661. 1. A back like that of a hog. 2. Anything shaped like a hog's back; *esp.* a sharply crested hill-ridge, steep on each side and sloping gradually at each end; a steep ridge of upheaval 1834. 3. = HOG-FRAME 1886. Hence **Ho·g-backed** *a.* having a back like a hog's; having a rise in the middle like a hog's back.

Hog-brace: = HOG-FRAME.

†**Ho·g-cote.** Also **hog's-cote.** ME. A pigsty –1707.

Ho·g-deer. 1771. 1. Name of two small Indian deer, *Axis porcinus* and *A. maculatus*. 2. The Babiroussa or Indian hog 1777.

†**Hogen, hogan** (hōu·gĕn). 1657. [Abbrev. of next.]

A. *adj.* 1. High and mighty; superlatively fine –1733. 2. Dutch 1710. B. *sb.* 1. A Dutchman; *pl.* the Dutch, the States-General –1672. 2. Strong drink –1737.

Hogen Mogen (hōu·gĕn mōu·gĕn). Also **Hogan Mogan.** 1638. [Perversion of Du. *Hoogmogendheiden*, 'High Mightinesses', the title of the States-General. In transf. senses occ. with small initial letters.]

A. *sb.* †1. 'Their High Mightinesses', the States-General of the United Provinces of the Netherlands –1685. 2. Hence, the Dutch; a Dutchman: contemptuous 1672. †3. *transf.* Any high and mighty person. (*joc.* or *contemptuous.*) –1713.

3. White-hall..where our Hogens Mogens or Council of State sit 1649.

B. *attrib.* and *adj.* 1. Dutch. (*contemptuous.*) 1658. †2. High and mighty. (Often *contemptuous.*) –1705. †3. Strong, heady (of drink) –1663.

Hog-fish. 1597. [f. HOG *sb.*[1] + FISH. Cf. OF. *porpeis* (:—L. *porcum piscem*), PORPOISE.] †1. The Porpoise or Sea-hog –1686. †2. The West African Manatee –1613. 3. A fish of the genus *Scorpæna*, having bristles on the head 1608. 4. Also applied to the W. Indian *Lachnolæmus maximus* or *suillus*, having 14 dorsal spines, and the log-perch, *Percina caprodes*, of N. American rivers 1734.

Hog-frame. 1864. *Shipbuilding*, etc. A fore-and-aft frame, usually above deck and forming together with the frame of the vessel a truss to prevent hogging. Also called *hog-brace*, *hogging-frame*.

†**Ho·ggaster.** ME. [med.L. *hogaster*, dim. from Eng. *hog.*] 1. A boar in its third year –1831. 2. A young sheep, a hog or hogget –1706.

Hogged (hǫgd), *ppl. a.* 1764. [f. HOG *v.*[1] + -ED[1].] 1. a. Of a ship: Drooping at stem and stern; hog-backed. b. Of a road: Raised in the centre. 1769. 2. Of a horse's mane: Cut off short 1764.

Hogger (hǫ·gəɹ). *Sc.* and *n. dial.* 1681. [?] 1. A stocking without a foot used as a gaiter. 2. A short piece of pipe used as a connexion. Hence *h.-pipe*, *-pump*. 1851.

Hoggerel, hogrel (hǫ·gərĕl, hǫ·grĕl). 1530. [dim. of HOG *sb.*[1]] 1. A young sheep of the second year. †2. = HOGGET 1. 1786.

Hoggery (hǫ·gəri). 1819. [f. HOG *sb.*[1] + -ERY.] 1. A hog-yard. 2. Hogs or swine collectively 1856. 3. Hoggishness (*rare*) 1864.

2. Crime and shame And all their h. trample your smooth world MRS. BROWNING.

Hogget (hǫ·gĕt). Also **-it.** 1538. [f. HOG *sb.*[1] + -ET.] 1. A young boar of the second year. ? *Obs.* 1786. 2. A yearling sheep 1538. 3. A year-old colt (*dial.*) 1787. 4. *attrib.* 1841.

Ho·ggin. 1852. [? same as *hogging*, f. HOG *v.*[1]] Screened or sifted gravel.

Hogging-frame: = HOG-FRAME.

Hoggish (hǫ·giʃ), *a.* 1548. [f. HOG *sb.*[1] + -ISH.] Of, belonging to, or characteristic of a hog; swinish, piggish; gluttonous; filthy; mean, selfish.

Is not a h. Life the height of some Mens Wishes SHAFTESB. Hence **Ho·ggish-ly** *adv.*, **-ness.**

Hog gum. 1756. [f. HOG *sb.*[1] + GUM *sb.*] A kind of gum or resin obtained from various trees in the W. Indies, etc. Hence **Hog-gum tree.**

†Ho·gherd. ME. [f. HOG *sb.*[1] + HERD *sb.*[2]] A swineherd –1704.

Hog in armour. 1660. **1.** An awkward or clumsy person, stiff and ill at ease in his attire. (Hence Thackeray's 'Count Hogginarmo'.) **2.** The nine-banded armadillo, *Dasypus* or *Tatusia novemcinctus* 1729.

Ho·g-louse. 1587. [f. HOG *sb.*[1] + LOUSE.] The woodlouse.

Hogmanay (hǫ·gmănē', -nē'). *Sc.* and *n.* 1680. [App. of French origin. See N.E.D.] The name given, in Scotland, etc., to the last day of the year, also called 'Cake-day'; the gift of an oatmeal cake, or the like, expected by children on that day; the word shouted by children calling at friends' houses and soliciting this customary gift. Also *attrib.*

Hog mane. 1804. [See HOG *v.*[1] 3.] The mane of a horse when cut short. Hence **Ho·g-maned** *a.*

Ho·g-nose. 1736. A name given to some N. American species of ugly but harmless snakes of the genus *Heterodon*. More fully *Hog-nose snake*.

Ho·g-nut. 1771. **1.** *U.S.* The Broom Hickory, *Carya porcina*; also its fruit 1829. **2.** The Earth-nut or Pig-nut, *Bunium flexuosum*.

†Hogo (hōu·go). See also HAUT-GOÛT. 1649. [prop. *hogoo*, anglicized sp. of F. *haut goût* high flavour.] **1.** = HAUT-GOÛT **1.** –1688. **b.** A high or putrescent flavour; a taint; a stench, stink. Also *fig.* –1852. **3.** = HAUT-GOÛT 3. –1736. Hence †Hogo'd *a.* 1663.

Ho·g-plum. 1697. **1.** The fruit of the species *Spondias*, esp. *S. lutea*, a common food for hogs in the W. Indies, etc. Also the tree, more fully called *Hog-plum tree*. **b.** In N. America applied to the wild-lime of Florida (*Ximenia*), the Chickasaw plum (*Prunus angustifolia*), etc. 1889.

Ho·g-reeve. *U.S.* 1689. [f. HOG *sb.*[1] + REEVE.] An officer charged with the prevention or appraising of damages by stray swine. Formerly a town officer in New England.

Ho·g's bean, ho·g-bean. 1866. *Herb.* A transl. of the word *Hyoscyamus*.

Ho·g-score. Also **hog's score.** 1787. *Curling.* A distance-line drawn across the rink at about one-sixth of the rink's length from the tee, which a stone must cross in order to count. Also *fig.*

Hog's fennel. 1585. A name for some weeds with fennel-like leaves: **a.** Sow-fennel, *Peucedanum officinale*; **b.** Mayweed, *Anthemis Cotula*.

Hogshead (hǫ·gzhed). ME. [f. *hog's* poss. of HOG *sb.*[1] + HEAD.] **1.** A large cask for liquids, etc.; *spec.* one of a definite capacity, which varied for different liquids and commodities. **2.** Hence, Such a caskful of liquor; a liquid measure containing 63 old wine-gallons (= 52½ imperial gallons). Abbrev. hhd. 1483. **b.** Of other commodities: A cask of varying capacity, in later use holding from 100 to 140 gallons 1491. **3.** Applied allusively to a person 1515.

3. His jabberment in Law, the flashiest and the fustiest that ever corrupted in such an unswill'd h. MILT.

Ho·g-skin, ho·gskin. 1700. **1.** The skin of a hog; leather made of this, pigskin; chiefly *attrib.* 1705. **2.** The skin of a hog used as a wine-bottle.

Hog's pudding. 1614. The entrail of a hog, variously stuffed with oatmeal, suet, tripe, etc., or with flour, currants, and spice.

Ho·gsty. Also **hog's sty.** 1475. A pigsty.

Ho·g-tie, *v.* *U.S.* 1894. [f. HOG *sb.*[1] 1.] *trans.* To secure by tying the four feet, or the hands and feet, together.

Hog-trough (hǫ·gtrǫf). Also **hog's trough.** 1530. A trough for hogs to feed out of. **b.** = *hog-wallow* (see HOG *sb.*[1]) 1807.

Ho·g-wash. Also **hog's wash.** 1440. [See WASH *sb.*] Swill given to pigs.

Ho·gweed. 1707. A name given to herbs pleasing to, or fit only for, hogs; e.g. in England, to Cow-parsnip, *Heracleum Sphondylium*; in *U.S.*, to *Ambrosia artemisiæfolia*.

Hohl-flute (hōu·lflūt). 1660. [ad. Ger. *hohlflöte*, lit. hollow flute.] An open 8-ft. flute-stop on an organ, having a soft hollow tone.

Hoi, *int.* **Hoiden:** see HOY, HOYDEN.

Hoick (hoik), *v.* *slang* or *colloq.* 1907. [Perh. var. HIKE *v.* (sense 2).] **1.** *trans.* To lift up or hoist, esp. with a jerk. **2.** To force (an aeroplane) to climb up steeply 1918.

Hoicks (hoiks), **hoick** (hoik), *interj.* 1607. [Earlier *hoika, hoic a* (with the hound's name), app. var. of *hyke a* (Turbervile). Cf. YOICKS.] A call used in hunting to incite the hounds. Also *transf.* Hence **Hoicks** (**hoick**) *v. trans.* to incite with 'hoicks!'; *intr.* to 'hark *back*'.

‖**Hoi polloi** (hoi pǫ·loi). 1837. [Gr. οἱ πολλοί the many.] The masses, the rabble.

Hoise (hoiz), *v.* *Obs.* exc. *dial.* [In 15–16th c. *hysse, hyce*, corresp. w. Icel. *hísa*, Norw., Sw. *hissa*, LG. *hiesen, hissen*; also F. *hisser*, etc. The English examples are app. the earliest.] **1.** *trans.* To raise by means of tackle or other mechanical appliance. Orig. *nautical*; often with *up*. 1490. **2.** To raise aloft, lift up; cf. HEEZE *v.* 1548. †**3.** To exalt, elevate; to raise in amount or price –1730. †**4.** To lift and remove –1750. †**5.** *intr.* (for *pass.*) To rise –1570.

1. We..hoissed sailes for Sidon 1615. The kettle to the top was hoist SWIFT. 2. Phr. *Hoist with his own petard* (Shaks.): blown into the air with his own bomb; hence, injured or destroyed by his own device for the ruin of others. Hence **Hoi·ser**, one who or that which hoises. **Hoise** *sb.* a lift.

Hoist, *sb.* 1654. [f. HOIST *v.*] **1.** An act of hoisting; a lift. **2.** Something hoisted; *Naut.* a number of flags hoisted together as a signal 1805. **3.** An elevator, a lift, etc. 1835. **4.** *Naut.* **a.** The middle part of a mast. **b.** The perpendicular height of a sail or a flag. **c.** The fore edge of a staysail. 1764.

2. As the last h. was handed down Nelson turned to Captain Blackwood..with 'Now I can do no more' 1805.

Hoist (hoist), *v.* 1548. [orig. a corruption of *hoiss*, HOISE *v.*; cf. *graff, graft*.] **1.** *trans.* To raise aloft; to set or put up. (Also with *up*.) **b.** *spec.* To lift up on the back of another in order to receive a flogging 1719. **2.** = HOISE *v.* 1. †**3.** = HOISE *v.* 4. –1762. †**4.** To overtax –1611. **5.** = HOISE *v.* 5. 1647.

1. *Ant. & Cl.* IV. xii. 34. We saw the two forts h. their colours 1748. 2. Phr. *To h. down*: to lower.

Hoist-, in comb.: **hoistaway** (*U.S.*), a mechanical lift or elevator; **h.-bridge,** a form of drawbridge, in which the leaf or platform is raised; **-hole,** an opening through which things are hoisted; **-rope; -way** (*U.S.*) = *hoist-hole*, the shaft of a lift or elevator.

Hoit, *v.* *Obs.* or *dial.* Also **hoyt.** 1594. [? Cf. HOYDEN.] **1.** *intr.* 'To indulge in riotous and noisy mirth' (Nares); to act the hoyden. **2.** To limp. *Sc.* 1693.

Hoity-toity (hoi·ti toi·ti), *sb.*, *adj.*, *adv.*, *interj.* 1657. [app. a deriv. of prec., with reduplication.] **A.** *sb.* **1.** Riotous or giddy behaviour; disturbance; flightiness. Also **b.** Huffiness. **2.** A hoyden, romp (*dial.*) 1719. **B.** *adj.* Frolicsome, giddy. Also **b.** Assuming, petulant, huffy. 1690. †**C.** *adv.* In a frolicsome or giddy manner –1763. **D.** *interj.* An exclam. of surprise or contempt, esp. at flighty or unduly assuming speech or action 1695.

†Hoker, *sb.* [OE. *hocor*; perh. related to OE. *hux, husc* 'mockery', root *huc-, hoc-*.] Mockery, derision; scorn; abuse –ME. Hence †**Hoker** *v*, to mock, scorn, revile. †**Ho·kerful** *a.*, scornful. †**Ho·kerly** *adv.* scornfully, mockingly, contemptuously.

Hoker moker, obs. f. HUGGER-MUGGER.

Hokum (hōu·kəm). orig. *U.S. Theatrical slang.* 1922. [? A blending of HOCUS-POCUS and BUNKUM.] Theatrical speech, action, etc., designed to make a sentimental or melodramatic appeal to an audience; hence, bunkum.

Hol: see WHOLE.

Holarctic (holā·ɹktik), *a.* 1883. [f. Gr. ὅλος whole (HOLO-) + ARCTIC.] In the Geographical Distribution of Animals: Of or pertaining to the entire northern or arctic region, as the H. region, or H. family of birds.

Hold, *sb.*[1] OE. [f. HOLD *v.*] **I. 1.** The action or an act of holding, keeping in hand, or grasping; grasp. Also, an opportunity of holding, occas. almost *concr.*, something to hold by. (The main current sense.) **2.** *fig.* A grasp which is not physical ME. **3.** Confinement, custody, imprisonment (*arch.*) ME. †**4.** Contention, struggle; resistance –1654.

1. Phr. *To catch, get, lay, lose, take h.* *In holds* (Wrestling, etc.), at grips. Let go thy h. *Lear* II. iv. 73. 2. Tarry Iew, The Law hath yet another h. on you *Merch. V.* IV. i. 347. Phr. *Keep a good h. of the land*, i.e. keep as near it as can be done with safety.

II. *concr.* †**1.** Property held; a holding; *spec.* a tenement. Cf. COPYHOLD, etc. –1590. **2.** A place of refuge or shelter; a lurking-place ME. **3.** A fort or fortress; a STRONGHOLD (*arch.*) ME. **4.** Something which is laid hold of, or by or with which anything is laid hold of 1578; a thing that holds something 1517. †**5.** *Mus.* The sign now called a pause 1674. **6.** A prison-cell 1717.

2. *Cymb.* III. iii. 20. 3. Some greater Roman h. LYTTON. 4. *John* III. iv. 138. Locks, or Holds for water PLOT.

Hold (hōuld), *sb.*[2] 1591. [Corruption of HOLL, HOLE, prob. by association w. prec.] The interior cavity in a ship or vessel below the deck (or lower deck), where the cargo is stored.

Sixe foote water in h. RALEIGH.

Hold, *sb.*[3] Now only *Hist.* [a. ON. *hǫldr*, identified with OE. *hæleð*, Ger. *held*, in Norse law 'a kind of higher yeoman, the owner of allodial land', *poet.* a 'man'.] In OE. times, an officer of rank in the Danelaw, corresponding to the High Reeve among the English.

Hold (hōuld), *v.* Pa. t. **held;** pa. pple. **held,** *arch.* **holden** (hōu·ld'n). [A Com. Teut. redupl. str. vb. OE. *haldan, healdan*, pa. t. *heold*, pple. *halden, healden*. The pa. pple. became *holden*; in 16th c. this began to be replaced by *held*, and is now arch., but preserved by its use in legal and formal language.]

I. *trans.* †**1.** To keep watch over, keep in charge, herd, 'keep' (sheep, etc.); to rule (men). Only in OE. and early ME. **2.** To keep from getting away; to keep fast, grasp OE. **3.** To keep from falling, to sustain or support OE. **b.** In pregnant sense: To hold so as to keep in position, guide, control, or manage 1577. †**c.** To endure, 'stand' –1664. **4.** To carry, sustain, bear (the body, or a member) ME. **5.** To have or keep within it; to retain (fluid, etc.); *esp.* to contain (so much); to have capacity for OE. **6.** To have or keep as one's own; to own, as property; to be in possession or enjoyment of OE. **b.** To occupy (a position, office, quality, etc.) ME. **c.** *Mil.* To keep forcibly against an adversary, defend; to occupy OE. **d.** To occupy, be in (a place); to retain possession or occupation of ME. **e.** *fig.* Of disease, error, etc.: To possess, affect, occupy ME. **7.** To keep, preserve, retain; not to let go; to rivet the attention of. Also with complement. OE. †**b.** To continue to occupy; to 'keep' –1795. **8.** To keep together, to carry on; to perform (any function); to keep (company, silence, etc.); to use (language) habitually and constantly OE. †**9.** To keep unbroken or inviolate; to observe, abide by; the opposite of *to break* or *violate* –1625. **10.** To oblige, bind, constrain. *Obs.* or *arch.* ME. **11.** To keep back from action, hinder, prevent, restrain. *Obs.* or *arch.* exc. in special phrases. OE. **12.** To have or keep in the mind, entertain OE. **b.** With objective clause: To think, consider, believe (*that*) ME. **c.** To think, consider, esteem. Const. with simple compl. or (*arch.*) with *as, for*, or with infin. ME. **d.** Of a judge or court of law: To decide 1642. **e.** To have in a specified relation to the mind or thought; e.g. *to hold in esteem* ME. †**13.** To offer as a wager; to 'lay' –1768. †**b.** To accept as a wager –1626. ¶ **14.** *Billiards.* = HOLE *v.* II. 2. [A corruption of *hole*, by association of *holed* and *hold*.] 1869.

2. *Tr. & Cr.* V. iii. 59. A..boy rushed up..to h. the rector's horse 1892. b. *U.S.* To keep back, detain (in custody), keep under arrest 1891. 3. Ten brode arowis hilde he there CHAUCER. To h. good trumps 1879, the baby 1898. b. To h. the Plow B. GOOGE, a musket 1631. c. To h. compare WALLER. 5.

More diuels then vaste hell can h. *Mids. N.* v. i. 9. This jug holds two pints (*mod.*). 6. Phr. *To have and to h.*: see HAVE *v.* Farms are held on a variety of tenure 1844. b. To h. a place during good behaviour 1809, land of a superior lord CRUISE, a title by diploma SCOTT. 7. To h. the breath PURCHAS. She..found herself held by his eyes 1885. To h. to a Promise SHAKS., at bay 1892. b. She halt hire chambre CHAUCER. 8. To h. converse CARY, a meeting 1840. 10. So we..turned back, being holden (= BEHOLDEN) to the gentleman PEPYS. 11. Phr. *To h.* one's TONGUE. 12. The Church of England holds the three creeds as well as we 1667. d. The Court..held that the plea to its jurisdiction was insufficient 1863.

II. *intr.* and *absol.* 1. To do the act of holding; to keep hold; to cling ME. †b. In the imper., used in offering; = Here! take it! [= F. *tiens.*] -1605. c. *Comm.* To retain goods, etc.; not to sell 1890. d. Of a female animal: To retain the seed; to conceive. Also *to h. to* (the male). 1614. 2. Of things: To maintain connexion; not to give way or become loose ME. 3. To remain attached; to adhere, keep, 'stick' *to*; to abide *by* ME. 4. To have capacity or contents; *spec.* Of a covert: To contain game 1581. 5. To derive title to something (*of* or *from*) ME. †b. To be held (*of* or *from*) -1665. 6. To depend; to belong or pertain. Now only as *fig.* from prec. ME. 7. To maintain one's position; of a place, to be held or occupied; to hold out OE. 8. To continue in a state or course; to last, endure ME.; to be or remain valid; to subsist; to apply ME. 9. To continue to go, keep going, go on, or make one's way 1450. 10. To take place, be held; to occur, prevail 1461. 11. (for *refl.*) To restrain oneself, refrain (*from*); to stop. Often in *imper.* as an exclam.: = Stop! *arch.* 1589. 12. In shooting: To aim 1881.

1. There was no anchor, none, To h. by TENNYSON. b. Hold, there's money for thee SHAKS. 2. The lashings held bravely 1891. 3. Hee will holde to the one, and despise the other *Matt.* vi. 24. 5. As thou doest h. of thy kyng, so doth thy tenaunt holde of the 1550. b. My crown is absolute, and holds of none DRYDEN. 7. Our force by Land Hath Nobly held *Ant. & Cl.* III. xiii. 170. Phr. *To h. with* (arch. *of*, †*on*, *for*): to maintain allegiance to; to side with; *mod. colloq.* to agree with or approve of. 8. The frost still held 1888. Phr. *To h. good, true.* 9. Phr. *To h. on one's way, course.* 10. Stormy weather again holds in north of Scotland 1892. 11. Hold..a thought has struck me! SHERIDAN.

Phrases. *To h. at* BAY (*sb.*[4] 4), *to h. one's* BREATH, *to h. a* CANDLE *to*, *to* HAVE *and to h.*, *to h. the* FIELD, *to h. one's* GROUND, *to h. with the* HARE *and run with the hounds*, *to h. one's* JAW, *to h. one's* NOSE, *to h. one's* PEACE, *to h.* (*in*) PLAY, *to h.* SHORT, *to h.* TACK, *to h. one's* TONGUE, etc.: see these words.

Hold..hand. a. *To h. one's hand*: to stay one's hand in the act of doing something; hence *gen.* to refrain. †b. *To h. hand*: (*a*) to bear a hand, cooperate; (*b*) to be on an equality *with*, to match. †c. *To h. in hand*: to assure (one); to pay attention to; to keep in suspense. **Hold..head.** a. *To h. one's head high*: to behave proudly or arrogantly. b. *To h. up one's head* (fig.): to maintain one's dignity, self-respect, or cheerfulness. **Hold one's own.** To maintain one's position, stand one's ground. **Hold water.** a. To stop a boat by holding the blades of the oars flat against the boat's way. b. *fig.* To be sound, valid, or tenable; to hold good when put to the test. **Hold wind.** *Naut.* To keep near the wind without making lee-way; to keep well to windward: usu. *to hold a good wind.*

With adverbs. **Hold back.** a. *trans.* To keep back. b. *intr.* To refrain; to hesitate. **Hold down.** *trans.* to keep down (*lit.* and *fig.*) to keep under, repress, oppress. **Hold forth.** †a. *trans.* To offer, propound, set forth, exhibit. ? *Obs.* b. *intr.* [from *Phil.* ii. 16.] To preach; to discourse, harangue. (Usu. somewhat contemptuous.) **Hold hard.** *intr.* (orig. a sporting phrase): To pull hard at the reins in order to stop the horse; hence *gen.* to 'pull up', halt, stop. Usu. in *imper.* (*colloq.*). **Hold in.** a. *trans.* To keep in, confine; to keep in check. b. *intr.* To 'keep in'; to restrain oneself, refrain, keep silence; to 'keep in' *with.* **Hold off.** a. *trans.* To keep off, away, or at a distance: to put off. b. *intr.* To keep oneself off, away, or at a distance; to refrain from action; to delay. **Hold on.** a. *trans.* To keep (something) on; to retain in its place on something. b. *intr.* To keep one's hold on something; to cling on; also *fig.* c. To keep on, continue, go on (rarely *refl.*). d. *imper.* Stop! wait! (*colloq.*). e. In shooting: To aim directly at. **Hold out.** a. *trans.* To extend (the hand, etc.). †b. To exhibit. c. *fig.* To proffer. d. To represent. e. To keep out. Now *rare.* f. To keep up. †g. To bear to the end. h. To occupy or defend to the end. i. To maintain resistance; to continue, endure, persist, last. **Hold over.** a. *intr.* (*Law*) To remain in occupation or in office beyond the regular term. b. *trans.* To reserve till a later time; to postpone. **Hold together.** a. *trans.* To keep together. *lit.* and *fig.* b. *intr.* To continue in union or connexion; to remain entire; to cohere. *lit.* and *fig.* **Hold up.** a. *trans.* To keep raised or erect, support, sustain. b. *fig.* To support, sustain, keep up. c. To offer or present to notice; to exhibit; to present in a particular aspect. d. To keep back; in *Cards*, to keep in one's hand. e. (orig. *U.S.*) To stop by force and rob on the highway. (From the robbers' 'Hands up or I'll shoot!'). Also, to arrest the progress of (*lit.* and *fig.*). f. *intr.* (for *refl.*) To keep up, not to fall: usu. addressed to a horse. g. To endure, hold out; in *Hunting*, to keep up the pace. h. †To give in; to 'pull up' (*U.S. colloq.*). i. To keep from raining; rarely, to cease from raining. (Of the weather, the day, etc.).

Ho·ld-all. 1851. [f. HOLD *v.* + ALL.] A portable case for holding clothes and other articles required by soldiers, travellers, etc.

Ho·ld-back. 1581. [f. *hold back.*] 1. Something that holds one back; a hindrance. 2. The iron or strap on the shaft of a vehicle to which the breeching of the harness is attached. Also *hold-back hook.* 1864.

Holder[1] (hōᵘ·ldəɹ). ME. [f. HOLD *v.* + -ER[1].] 1. One who holds or grasps. 2. A tenant, occupier, possessor, owner. Often in comb., as *freeholder*, etc. ME. 3. A contrivance for holding 1833. 4. a. A canine tooth 1672. b. A prehensile organ in some animals 1774. 5. With adverbs, as **holder-forth**, a preacher, orator (somewhat *contemptuous*); **holder-up**, a supporter; *spec.* a workman who supports a rivet with a hand-anvil or sledge-hammer in riveting 1661. 6. That of which hold is taken; e.g. the strap by which a carriage window is drawn up 1794.

Holder[2]. 1495. [f. HOLD *sb.*[2] + -ER[1].] A workman employed in a ship's hold.

Holdfast (hōᵘ·ldfɑst). 1560. [f. *hold fast*: see HOLD *v.* I. 2 + FAST *adv.*]

A. *adj.* 1. That holds fast (*lit.* and *fig.*) 1567. †2. Tenacious of what one has 1560.

B. *sb.* 1. The action or fact of holding fast (*lit.* and *fig.*) 1578. 2. Something to which one may hold fast 1566. 3. One that holds fast: †a. A miser -1706; b. As name for a dog 1599. 4. Something that holds fast; *spec.* a staple, hook, clamp, or bolt 1576.

Holding (hōᵘ·ldiŋ), *vbl. sb.* ME. [f. HOLD *v.*]

I. 1. The action of HOLD *v.* b. *spec.* The tenure of land ME. †c. Consistency. SHAKS. 2. That which holds or lays hold 1770.

II. 1. That which is held: a tenement 1640; property, esp. stocks or shares 1573. †2. A tenet -1851. †3. The burden of a song -1606.

attrib. and *Comb.* Of or for holding; as **holding-ground**, a bottom in which an anchor will hold, anchorage; also *fig.*; **-note** (*Mus.*), a note sustained in one part while the others are in motion 1752.

H. company, a trading company having the whole of, or a controlling interest in, the share capital of one or more other companies 1912.

Holding, *ppl. a.* ME. [f. as prec. + -ING[2].] 1. That holds; retentive; grasping; tenacious. 2. Applied to animals kept for breeding 1547.

Hold-up. orig. *U.S.* 1837. [See *hold up*, HOLD *v.*] a. A check in the progress of a person or thing; a temporary stoppage of traffic. b. Detention by force for robbery. Also (for *h. man*), one who robs by 'holding up'. 1885.

Hole (hōᵘl), *sb.* [OE. *hol* neut., a hollow place, orig. neut. of *hol*, HOLL *a.*, hollow.]

I. 1. A hollow place or cavity in a solid body; a pit; an excavation made in the ground for an animal to live in; a hollow in the surface of the body, as *arm-hole.* 2. *transf.* †a. A secret place -1688. b. A dungeon or prison-cell. Cf. BLACK-HOLE. 1535. c. A small dingy lodging or abode; a dirty, untidy, or shabby place 1616. 3. *fig.* A scrape, 'mess' 1760. 4. A cavity or receptacle into which a ball or marbles are to be got in various games; hence, in *Golf*, a point scored by the player who holes his ball in the fewest strokes from the tee 1583. 5. = HOLL, HOLD (*sb.*[2]) of a ship 1483.

1. Hoole, or pyt yn an hylle, or other lyke ME. The foxes have holes *Luke* ix. 58. 2. b. He was clapped up in the H. PEPYS. 3. I'm in a h., no end of a h. OUIDA. 4. *Golf.* Also, the distance between the teeing-ground and the hole to be played 1891.

II. 1. An aperture passing through anything; a perforation, opening, orifice OE. 2. *fig.* A flaw, fault, ground for blame 1553.

1. Holes to look out to see thy enemyes 1529. 2. If I finde a h. in his Coat, I will tell him my minde SHAKS. Phr. *To pick a h.* or *holes in* something.

Phrases. *To make a h.* (*in* anything): to use it up largely. *To make a h.* or *holes in*: to shoot. *To make a h. in the water*: see WATER *sb.* 6. *A round peg* (or *man*) *in a square h.*: see PEG *sb.*[1]

Hole (hōᵘl), *v.* [OE. *holian* to hollow out, excavate, f. *hol-*, HOLL *a.*]

I. 1. *trans.* To make a hole or cavity in; to perforate, pierce. 2. To sink (a shaft), drive (a tunnel) through 1708. 3. *Mining.* To undercut (the coal) in a seam so as to release it from the other strata 1829. 4. *intr.* To make a hole or holes; to dig ME.

1. She [the ship] has holed her bottom 1864.

II. 1. *trans.* To put into or plant in a hole or holes; to put in prison 1608. 2. *spec.* in *Golf*, etc. To drive (the ball) into a hole or pocket. Also *to h. out.* 1803. 3. *intr.* To go into a hole 1614.

1. So their prodigal sons are holed in some loathsome jail 1618. 2. The..accuracy with which they..'h. out' 1867. 3. The fox has run to earth, or, as we have it, 'has holed' 1878. Hence **Ho·leable** *a.* (*Golf*).

Hole, -ful, -ly, -some, etc., the early (and etym.) spelling of WHOLE, etc.

Hole: see HOLL *a.*, HULL *sb.*[1]

Ho·le-and-co·rner, *adj. phr.* 1835. Done or happening in a 'hole and corner', or place which is not public; secret, clandestine, underhand. (*Contemptuous.*)

Holed (hōᵘld), *ppl. a.* ME. [f. HOLE *v.* or *sb.* + -ED.] Having a hole or holes.

H. stone, a perforated stone considered to be a monument of prehistoric times 1769.

Holer (hōᵘ·ləɹ). 1829. [f. HOLE *v.* + -ER[1].] *spec.* The collier who holes or undercuts a coal-seam.

Holethnic: see HOLO-.

Holey (hōᵘ·li), *a.* ME. [f. HOLE *sb.* + -Y.] Full of holes.

H. dollar, a Spanish dollar out of which a 'dump' had been cut, formerly current in Australia.

Holibut: = HALIBUT.

Holidam(e, early f. HALIDOM.

Holiday (hǫ·lidėⁱ), *sb.* [OE. *háligdæȝ*, found beside *hálig dæȝ* in two wds. The uncombined forms are treated under HOLY-DAY.] 1. A consecrated day, a religious festival. Now usu. HOLY-DAY, q.v. 2. A day on which work is suspended; a day of recreation or amusement. (In early use not separable from 1.) ME. b. *collect. pl.* or *sing.* A vacation ME. c. Cessation from work; recreation 1526. 3. *colloq. Naut.* A spot carelessly left uncoated in tarring or painting 1785. 4. *attrib.* or as *adj.* Of, belonging to, or used on a holiday; festive; superior to the workaday sort, as *h. clothes, terms, English.* Sometimes: Suited only for a holiday; dainty, idle, trifling. 1440.

2. It is holliday, a day to dance in, and make mery at the Ale house 1577. b. At home for the holidays 1806. c. Phr. *To make h.*, to cease from work. †*To speak h.*, to use choice language. 4. A Holy-day Wife, all play and no work 1695.

Holily (hōᵘ·lili), *adv.* [OE. *háliglíce*, f. HOLY *a.* + -LY[2].] 1. In a holy manner; with sanctity or devoutness. 2. Sacredly, scrupulously; solemnly. Now *rare* or *Obs.* ME.

Holiness (hōᵘ·linės). [OE. *hálignes, -nys*, f. *hálig* HOLY + -NESS.] 1. The quality of being holy; spiritual perfection or purity; sanctity; saintliness; sacredness. 2. *His Holiness*: a title of the Pope, given orig. to all bishops 1450.

1. Hir herte is verray chambre of hoolynesse CHAUCER. 2. His H. [Pope Leo] 1858.

Holing (hōᵘ·liŋ), *vbl. sb.* ME. See HOLE *v.*

Holinight (hǫ·linəit). [*nonce-use*, after HOLIDAY 2.] A night of pleasure. KEATS.

Holism (hǫ·liz'm, hōᵘ·liz'm). 1926 (J. C. Smuts). [f. Gr. ὅλος whole + -ISM.] The tendency in nature to produce wholes from the ordered grouping of units.

Holk, howk (hōᵘk, hauk), *v.* Now *dial.* [Northern ME. *holk*, f. root of HOLL *a.*] 1. *trans.* To excavate; to dig out or up. 2. *intr.* To dig, turn things up 1513.

Holl, *sb. Obs.* exc. *dial.* [OE. *hol*, late OE. and ME. *holl*, neut. of prec. adj. used subst.; retained chiefly in the north (*pronounced* hǫᵘl, houl).] †1. A HOLE OE.; an excavation; a ditch 1701. †2. The HOLD of a ship -1627.

Holl (hǫul), *a. Obs.* or *dial.* [OE. *hol* hollow; cf. OTeut. stem **hulo-*, pre-Teut. **kulo-*; perh. related to *helan* to cover; or with suffixal *-l*, from root **ku-*, **kaw-*, of L. *cavus* hollow.] 1. Hollow, concave; empty. 2. Deeply excavated or depressed; lying in a hollow OE.

Holla (hǫ·lă, *rarely* hǫlā·), *interj.* (*sb.*) 1523. [a. F. *holà* (15th c. in Littré).] †1. An exclam. meaning Stop! 2. A shout to excite attention 1588. 3. A shout of exultation 1727. 4. Also *holla ho!* [F. *holà ho!*] 1596. 5. *sb.* A shout of *holla!* 1592.

1. Phr. *To cry h.* 2. H., approach *L. L. L.* v. ii. 900. 4. H. hoa, Curtis *Tam. Shr.* IV. i. 12. 5. I thought I heard a h. M. SCOTT.

Holla *v.*: see HOLLO *v.*

Holland (hǫ·lănd). ME. [Du. *Holland*, in earliest sources *Holtlant*, f. *holt* wood + *-lant* land, describing the district about Dordrecht, the nucleus of Holland.] 1. The name of a province of the Northern Netherlands, now usually extended by foreigners to the kingdom of the Netherlands. 2. A linen fabric, originally called, from the province of Holland in the Netherlands, *H. cloth.* When unbleached called *Brown H.* ME. 3. *attrib.* or in *Comb.*: of holland 1554. Hence **Ho·llander**, a Dutchman 1547; also a Dutch ship. **Ho·llandish** *a.* (now *rare*), of or belonging to Holland (province or country); Dutch 1611.

Hollands (hǫ·lăndz), *sb.* 1788. [ad. Du. *hollandsch* (*ch* mute), in *hollandsch genever*, Hollands gin.] A grain spirit manufactured in Holland: more fully *Hollands gin*, formerly *Hollands geneva.*

Ho·llantide, short for *All-hollantide*, All-hallowtide. 1560.

Holler, dial. and U.S. var. HOLLO.

Hollin, hollen (hǫ·lin, -ĕn). Now *arch.* or *dial.* [OE. *holen*, *holegn*, cogn. w. Welsh *celyn* holly.] = HOLLY.

Hollo, hollow (hǫ·lǒ). 1588. [Akin to *holla* and *hallo.*] A. *interj.* = HOLLA 2, 3. B. *sb.* A shout of *hollo! esp.* in hunting 1598.

Hollo, hollow (hǫ·lǒ), **holla** (hǫ·lă), *v.* 1542. [Conn. w. HOLLA *int.*, HOLLO *int.*; also w. HALLO *int.* and HALLOW *v.*[2]] 1. *intr.* To shout; to halloo; to call to the hounds in hunting. 2. *trans.* a. With the thing shouted as object 1593. b. To call after (in hunting); to shout to 1605.

Phr. *Hollo away*, to drive away by holloing; *h. in*, *off*, to call in or off (dogs, etc.) by shouting; *h. out*, to shout out.

Holloa (hǫlō·), *interj.*, *sb.*, *v.* 1666. A form of HOLLO leading on to HALLOA, q. v.

Hollow (hǫ·lou), *sb.* [OE. *holh*:—OTeut. **holhwo-*, app. radically related to OE. *hol*, HOLL *a.*, and HOLE *sb.* App. the sb. was formed anew from the adj. *c* 1550.] 1. A hollow or concave formation or place, which is, or might have been, dug out; †a hole; †a bore; an excavation; an internal cavity; a void space. 2. *spec.* A depression on the earth's surface; a valley, a basin 1553. 3. The middle or depth (of night or of winter) 1865. 4. Short for *h. moulding, h. plane, h. square*: see HOLLOW *a.* 1726.

1. The h. of a Tree SHAKS., of a Rock 1687. Who hath measured the waters in the h. of his hand? *Isa.* xl. 12. 2. Within the inner compasse and h. of Africke HOLLAND.

Hollow (hǫ·lou), *a.* and *adv.* [ME. *holȝ*, *holeh*, also *holu*; see prec. Cf. *follow, hallow.*]

A. *adj.* 1. Having a hole or cavity inside; empty in the interior; opp. to *solid.* 2. Having a hole, depression, or groove on the surface; sunken, indented; excavated, concave ME. b. Of the sea: Having the troughs between the crests of the waves very deep 1726. 3. Empty, vacant, void; hence, hungry; lean ME. 4. *transf.* Of sound: Wanting body; sepulchral 1563. 5. *fig.* Wanting soundness, solidity, or substance; empty; insincere, false 1529. 6. [f. the adv.] Complete, thorough, out-and-out (*colloq.*) 1750.

1. A h. tooth 1577, tree 1817. 2. Our way to it was up a h. lane HAWTHORNE. H. and haggard faces LONGF. 3. H. Pouerty, and Emptinesse 2 *Hen. IV*, I. iii. 75. 4. My voice as h. as a ghost's 1798. 5. Flattering and h. words GIBBON. A h. truce MOTLEY. Hence **Ho·llow-ly** *adv.*, **-ness.**

Comb., etc.: **h.-adz, -auger**, tools with concave face, for curved work; **-bastion**, that which has only a rampart and a parapet, ranging about its flanks and faces, leaving a void space towards the centre; **h. fowl**, 'poultry, rabbits, etc., any meat not sold by butchers' (Halliwell); **h.-ground** *a.*, ground so as to have a concave surface, as a *h.-g. razor*; **h. spar** [tr. Ger. *hohlspat*], CHIASTOLITE; †**h. vein**, the *vena cava*; **h.-way**, a way, road, or path, through a defile or cutting. Also *Hollow* SQUARE, HOLLOW-WARE.

B. *adv.* 1. In a hollow manner; with a hollow sound. *Obs.* exc. in comb. LYDGATE. 2. Thoroughly, completely, out-and-out; also (*U.S.*) *all h.* (*colloq.*) 1668.

2. Local opinion would carry it h. J. H. NEWMAN.

Hollow (hǫ·lou), *v.*[1] 1398. [f. HOLLOW *a.*] 1. *trans.* To render hollow or concave. Also with *out.* 2. To form by making a hollow (*in* something); to excavate. Often with *out.* 1648. 3. *intr.* To become hollow or concave 1860.

1. A rock hollowed out like the entrance to a church 1727. Hollowing one hand against his ear TENNYSON. 2. A Grotto hollowed in the Rock 1687.

Hollow, *v.*[2]: see HOLLO *v.*

Ho·llow-ey·ed, *a.* 1529. Having the eyes deep sunk in their orbits.

Ho·llow-hea·rted, *a.* 1549. Insincere, false. Hence **Ho·llow-hea·rtedness.**

Ho·llow-root. 1578. [tr. Ger. *holwurtz*, *hohlwurtz*: see Grimm.] a. A name for *Corydalis tuberosa* (*C. cava*); also for other species of *Corydalis.* b. *erron.* A name for *Adoxa Moschatellina.*

Ho·llow-ware. 1416. Bowl- or tube-shaped ware of earthenware, wood, or (now esp.) metal. Also *attrib.*

Holly (hǫ·li). [Shortened f. OE. *holegn*, *holen*; see HOLLIN.] A plant of the genus *Ilex*; *orig.* and *esp.* the common European holly, *I. Aquifolium*, an evergreen shrub or small tree with dark-green tough glossy leaves, having indented edges set with sharp stiff prickles at the points, and bearing clusters of small green flowers succeeded by red berries; much used for Christmas decorations. The American holly, *I. opaca*, is found in the United States from Massachusetts southwards. Also *attrib.*

Comb.: **h.-fern**, *Aspidium* (or *Polystichum*) *Lonchitis*, so named from its stiff prickly fronds; **-laurel**, 'the islay, *Prunus ilicifolia*, of California' (*Cent. Dict.*); **-oak**, the holm oak, *Quercus Ilex*; **-rose**, †(*a*) an old name for species of *Cistus*; (*b*) *Turnera ulmifolia*, a W. Indian shrub with yellow flowers.

Holly, obs. f. WHOLLY.

Hollyhock (hǫ·lihǫk). ME. [f. HOLY *a.* + HOCK *sb.*[1] mallow; cf. the Welsh name *hocys bendigaid*, app. a transl. of a med.L. **malva benedicta.*] †1. *orig.* The Marsh Mallow, *Althæa officinalis* -1614. 2. Now, The plant *Althæa rosea*, of the same genus as the prec., a native of China and southern Europe; many varieties, with flowers of different tints of red, purple, yellow, and white, are cultivated in gardens 1548. *Comb.* **h.-rose**, an American species of club-moss, *Selaginella lepidophylla*, also called *resurrection-plant.*

Holm[1], **holme** (hōum). [In sense 1, OE. *holm* sea, ocean, wave; in sense 2, a. ON. *holmr* islet in a bay, etc., meadow on the shore; corresp. to OS., LG. *holm* hill.] †1. The sea, the wave. OE. only. 2. An islet; esp. in a river. Freq. in place-names. OE. 3. A piece of flat low-lying ground by a river or stream ME.

3. 'Oh! green', said I, 'are Yarrow's holms' WORDSW.

Holm[2] (hōum). ME. [A corruption of *holn* from OE. *holen*, HOLLIN, holly.] 1. The common holly. Now only *dial.* 2. The HOLM-OAK 1552.

Comb., as **h.-cock, -screech, -thrush**, local names of the missel-thrush, which feeds on holly-berries.

‖**Ho·lmgang.** 1847. [ad. ON. *holmganga*, 'going to the holm' (or islet) on which a duel was fought.] A duel to the death.

Holm-oak (hōu·m,ōuk). 1597. [f. HOLM[2] + OAK.] The evergreen oak (*Quercus Ilex*); its foliage resembles that of the holly.

Holm-tree. ME. [f. HOLM[2].] = HOLM[2].

Holo- (hǫlo), bef. a vowel **hol-**, comb. f. Gr. ὅλος 'whole, entire'; sometimes opp. to *hemi-* or *mero-*. In *Cryst.*, denoting that a crystal or crystalline form has the full number of faces (HOLOHEDRAL, HOLOSYMMETRICAL), or the full number of normals (HOLOSYSTEMATIC), belonging to its system.

‖**Hole·thnos** [Gr. ἔθνος], an undivided primitive stock or race; hence **Hole·thnic** *a.* (less correctly *holo-ethnic*), pertaining or relating to a holethnos. **Holobra·nchiate, -ious** *adjs.*, *Ichthyol.* having complete branchial apparatus: opp. to *hemibranchiate.* **Holoce·phalous** [Gr. κεφαλή] *a.*, having an entire or undivided skull, as the group *Holocephali* of fishes, in which the hyomandibular bone is continuous with the cranium; so **Holoce·phal**, a fish belonging to this group. **Holocry·ptic** *a.*, wholly hidden; *spec.* of a cipher incapable of being read except by those who have the key. **Holocry·stalline** *a.*, wholly crystalline in structure; opp. to *hemicrystalline.* **Holohemihe·dral** *a.*, *Cryst.* having the full number of planes in half the octants. **Holophanerous** (-fæ·nĕrəs) [Gr. φανερός] *a.*, *Entom.* wholly discernible; applied to the metamorphosis of insects when complete. **Holophy·tic** [Gr. φυτόν] *a.*, *Biol.* wholly plant-like; used in reference to the nutrition of certain Protozoa. **Holorhi·nal** [Gr. ῥιν- nose] *a.*, *Ornith.* having the nasal bones slightly or not at all cleft. **Holosiderite** (-si·dĕrəit) [Gr. σίδηρος: see -ITE], a meteorite consisting wholly or almost wholly of iron. **Holo·stean** [Gr. ὀστέον] *a.*, entirely bony; having a wholly osseous skeleton, as the group *Holostei* of ganoid fishes; *sb.* a fish of this group; so **Holo·steous** *a.* = prec. **Holoste·ric** [irreg. f. Gr. στερεός] *a.*, wholly solid; applied to a barometric instrument in which no liquid is employed, as an aneroid. **Holothe·cal** [Gr. θήκη case] *a.*, *Ornith.* having the tarsal envelope entire or undivided. **Holo·trichous** [Gr. θρίξ, τριχ-] *a.*, *Biol.* belonging to the order *Holotricha* of infusorians, which have similar cilia all over the body. **Holozo·ic** [Gr. ζῷον] *a.*, *Biol.* wholly like an animal in mode of nutrition; said of certain Protozoa, in opposition to *holophytic.*

Holoblastic (hǫloblæ·stik), *a.* 1872. [f. HOLO- + Gr. βλαστός germ, -BLAST + -IC.] *Biol.* Of an ovum: Wholly germinal; undergoing total segmentation. Opp. to *meroblastic.* So **Ho·loblast**, a h. ovum.

Holocaust (hǫ·lokǭst). ME. [a. F. *holocauste*, ad. late L. *holocaustum*, a. Gr. ὁλόκαυστον adj. neut., f. ὅλος whole + καυστός burnt.] 1. A sacrifice wholly consumed by fire; a whole burnt offering. 2. *transf.* and *fig.* a. A complete sacrifice or offering. b. A sacrifice on a large scale. 1497. c. Complete destruction by fire, or that which is so consumed; complete destruction, esp. of a large number of persons; a great slaughter or massacre 1671.

2. c. Like that self-begotten bird..That..lay erewhile a Holocaust MILT. *Sams.* 1702. Louis VII. ..once made a h. of thirteen hundred persons in a church 1833.

Holograph (hǫ·lograf). 1623. [a. F. *holographe*, or ad. late L. *holographus*, a. Gr., f. ὅλος + -γραφος.]

A. *adj.* Of a document: Wholly written by the person in whose name it appears 1669.

B. *sb.* 1. A letter or other document written wholly by the person in whose name it appears 1623. 2. *In h.*: wholly in the author's handwriting 1817.

2. Bequeathed.. by testament In h. BROWNING. Hence **Hologra·phic, -al** *a.* = A. **Holo·graphy**, writing wholly by one's own hand.

Holohedral (hǫlohī·drăl, -he·drăl), *a.* 1837. [f. HOLO- + Gr. ἕδρα + -AL.] *Cryst.* Having the full number of planes required by the highest degree of symmetry belonging to its system. So **Holohe·drism**, the quality of being h. **Holohe·dron**, a h. crystal or form.

‖**Holometabola** (hǫlomĭtæ·bŏlă), *sb. pl.* [mod.L., neut. pl. (sc. *insecta*), f. Gr. ὁλο- + μεταβόλος changeable.] *Entom.* The insects which undergo complete metamorphosis. (Usu. called *Metabola.*) Hence **Holometa·bolic**, **Holometa·bolous** *adjs.*

Holometer (hǫlǫ·mĭtəɹ). 1696. [f. HOLO- + -METER.] A mathematical instrument for making all kinds of measurements.

Holomorphic (hǫlomǭ·ɹfik), *a.* 1880. [f. HOLO- + Gr. μορφή + -IC.] 1. *Cryst.* = HOLOHEDRAL. 2. *Math.* Said of a function which is monogenic, uniform, and continuous 1880.

Holophote (hǫ·lofōut). 1859. [f. HOLO- + Gr. φῶς, φωτός. (The adj. *holophotal* was earlier.)] An optical apparatus, used in lighthouses, etc., by which practically the whole of the light from a lamp or other source is collected and made available for illumination. So **Holopho·tal** *a.* reflecting or refracting all, or nearly all, the light 1850. Hence **Holopho·tally** *adv.* **Holophoto·meter**, an apparatus for measuring the whole light emitted from a source.

Holophrastic (hǫlofræ·stik), *a.* 1860. [f. HOLO- + Gr. φραστικός, f. φράζειν to tell.] Expressing a whole phrase or combination of ideas by a single word.

Holostomatous (hǫlǫstǫ·mătəs), *a.* 1855. [f. HOLO- + Gr. στόμα, στοματ- + -OUS.] *Zool.* Having the mouth entire; as the division *Holostomata* of gastropod molluscs, having shells of which the mouth is not notched or prolonged into a siphon; or the group *Holostomi* of eel-like fishes, which have all the bones of the mouth fully developed. So **Holo·stomate, Holo·stomous** *adjs.* = prec. **Ho·lostome**, one of the *Holostomata* or *Holostomi* (see above).

Holosy·mmetry. 1895. *Cryst.* = HOLOHEDRISM. Also **-ic(al** *adjs.*

Ho:losystema·tic, *a.* 1878. *Cryst.* Having the full number of normals required by the complete symmetry of its system.

Holothurian (hǫloþiū·riăn). 1842. [f. mod.L. generic name *Holothuria*, f. *holothuria* (Pliny), a. neut. pl. of Gr. ὁλοθούριον, a kind of zoophyte.] **A.** *adj.* Of or pertaining to the genus *Holothuria* or division *Holothurioidea* of Echinoderms: see B. 1878.

B. *sb.* An animal belonging to the division of Echinoderms, of which *Holothuria* is the typical genus; they have an elongated form, a tough leathery integument, and a ring of tentacles around the mouth; a sea-slug, sea-cucumber, or trepang. So **Ho·lothure**, a holothurian. **Holothu·rid, Holothu·rioid** *adjs.* holothurian; *sbs.* a holothurian.

†**Holour.** ME. [a. OF. *holier, holer, huler*, var. of *horier, hourier, hurier*, ad. OHG. *huorari, huareri* whorer, fornicator.] A fornicator; a debauchee –1460.

Holp(e, holpen: see HELP *v.*

Hols (hǫlz), *sb. pl.* 1906. Colloq. (esp. school-children's) abbrev. of *holidays.*

Holsom(e, obs. f. WHOLESOME.

Holster (hōu·lstəɹ). 1663. [Corresponds to mod.Du. *holster* in same sense; also OE. *heolster* hiding-place; from ablaut stem *hel-, hul-* to cover.] A leather case for a pistol fixed to the pommel of a horseman's saddle or worn on the belt. Hence **Ho·lstered** *a.* bearing holsters BYRON.

Holt[1] (hōult). [OE. *holt* wood, etc. :— OTeut. **hulto-* :—pre-Teut. **kldó-*; cf. Gr. κλάδος twig, etc.] †1. Wood, timber. OE. only. 2. A wood; a copse. Now *poet.* and *dial.* (In many place-names.) OE. 3. A wooded hill 1567.

2. These holtes and these hayes That han in wynter ded ben and dreye CHAUCER. Wither'd h. or tilth or pasturage TENNYSON.

Holt[2]. ME. [Unexplained var. of HOLD *sb.*[1]] 1. Hold, grasp, grip; support. †2. A stronghold –1600. 3. A place of refuge or abode; an animal's lair or den, esp. that of an otter 1590.

3. An old otter going for a strong h. 1885.

Holus-bolus (hōu·lŏs bōu·lŏs). 1847. [Of dial. origin: app. mock-Latin.] All in a lump: all at once.

Holw(e, obs. ff. HOLLOW.

Holy (hōu·li), *a.* (*sb.*) [OE. *hālig, -eg* :— OTeut. type **hailag-oz.* A deriv. of the adj. **hailo-*, OE. *hāl*, whole, hale; see -Y.] 1. Kept or regarded as inviolate from ordinary use, and set apart for religious use or observance; consecrated, dedicated, sacred. b. Dedicated or devoted *to.* 2. Free from sin and evil, morally and spiritually perfect and unsullied OE. 3. Hence, a. Of persons: Specially belonging to, commissioned by, or devoted to God OE. b. Of things: Pertaining to God or the Divine Persons; having their origin or sanction from God, or partaking of a Divine quality or character OE. 4. Conformed to the will of God, entirely devoted to God; of godly character and life; sanctified, saintly; sinless OE.

1. Giue not that which is h. vnto the dogs *Matt.* vii. 6. All is h. where devotion kneels O. W. HOLMES. b. [The Nazarite] is h. vnto the Lord *Num.* vi. 8. H. to your businesse *Meas. for M.* v. i. 388. 2. For I the Lord am h. *Lev.* xx. 26. 3. a. A h. Prophetesse SHAKS. The holly Bishops 1626. Matthew and Mark and Luke and h. John CLOUGH. b. H. scripture ELYOT. 4. H., faire, and wise is she *Two Gent.* IV. ii. 41. So h., and so perfect is my loue *A. Y. L.* III. v. 99.

Combs., etc.: **H. Alliance:** an alliance formed in 1815, after the fall of Napoleon, between the sovereigns of Russia, Austria, and Prussia, with the professed object of uniting their respective governments in Christian brotherhood 1821. †**H. bone** [tr. L. *os sacrum*]: the SACRUM. **H. brotherhood** [tr. Sp. *Santa Hermandad*]: = HERMANDAD. **H. doors:** in the Greek Church, the doors in the screen which separates the altar and sanctuary from the main body of the church. †**H. oak:** an oak marking a parish boundary, at which a stoppage was made for the reading of the gospel in the 'beating of the bounds' during the Rogation days; called also *gospel-oak, gospel-tree* HERRICK. **H. One:** a holy person; a title of God or Christ; one dedicated to or consecrated by God COVERDALE. **Holy souls:** the souls of the faithful departed, the blessed dead OE. Also *Holy* CHURCH, *H.* CITY, *H.* FAMILY, *H.* FATHER, *H.* GRAIL, *H.* INQUISITION, *H.* LEAGUE, *H.* OFFICE, *H.* OIL, *H.* ORDER, *H.* PASSION, *H.* SATURDAY, *H.* SEE, *H.* SEPULCHRE, *H.* SPIRIT, *H.* SYNOD, *H.* TABLE, *H.* THURSDAY, *H.* WAR: see these words.

b. In names of plants: **h. grass,** a grass of genus *Hierochloe*, esp. *Northern H. g.*, *H. borealis*, which is strewn about Catholic churches on festival days; **h. hay,** Sainfoin; **h. tree,** an Indian tree, *Melia Azedarach*, also called Pride of India; †**h. wood,** the W. Indian *Guaiacum sanctum.* See also Main Words.

B. *absol.* or as *sb.* 1. That which is holy OE. †2. A holy person: = HALLOW *sb.* –1648. †3. *pl.* Devotions. PURCHAS. 4. **Holy of holies.** [A Hebraism, rendered in Exod. xxvi. 34 'most holy place', but literally reproduced in LXX and Vulgate, whence in Wyclif, etc.] The 'most holy place', the inner chamber of the sanctuary in the Jewish tabernacle and temple. Also *transf.* and *fig.* 5. superl. *Holiest*, used *absol.* a. As a title of God or Christ ME. b. = Holy of holies: see 4. *Heb.* x. 19.

6. a. Praise to the Holiest in the height J. H. NEWMAN.

†**Ho·ly,** *v.* 1578. [f. HOLY *a.*, instead of HALLOW *v.*] To sanctify, consecrate; to canonize –1622.

Holy bread. ME. The (ordinary leavened) bread which was blessed after the Eucharist and distributed to those who had not communicated (F. *pain bénit*). In post-Reformation times, The bread provided for the Eucharist.

Holy cross. ME. The cross upon which Jesus Christ suffered death (see CROSS *sb.*). Hence in the titles of certain religious societies. **b.** *attrib.* **Holy Cross day,** the festival of the Exaltation of the Cross, September 14th.

Holy-day (hōu·li,dē¹). [OE. *hālig dæg*, two wds. See also HOLIDAY, now usu. restricted to the sense 'day of recreation'.] A day set apart for religious observance, usually in commemoration of some sacred person or event; a religious festival. Also *attrib.*

Holy fire. *arch.* ME. [tr. L. *sacer ignis* (Celsus, Vergil).] Erysipelas, St. Anthony's fire; see FIRE *sb.*

Holy Ghost (hōu·li gōu·st). [Prop. two words; in OE. *se hālga gāst, hālig gāst*, in ME. often as comb. *haligast, holigost.*] 1. The Divine Spirit; the Third Person of the Godhead, the Holy Spirit. 2. a. The figure of a dove as a symbol of the Holy Spirit. b. The Cross of the Order of the Holy Ghost. 1520. 3. (Also *Holy Ghost's Root.*) The plant Angelica, *Archangelica officinalis* 1585. 4. *attrib.*, as in **Holy Ghost flower, plant,** an orchid, *Peristeria elata*, also called *dove-plant*, from the resemblance of part of the flower to a dove 1866.

1. *Order of the Holy Ghost*, a French order of Knighthood (*ordre du Saint-Esprit*), instituted by Henry III in 1578. *Cross of the Holy Ghost*, a cross worn by the knights of this order, having a circle in the middle and on it the Holy Ghost in the form of a dove.

Holy Land. ME. [tr. med.L. *terra sancta*, F. *la Terre Sainte.*] (with *the*) Western Palestine, or, more particularly, Judæa; so called as being the scene of the life and death of Jesus Christ, and as containing the Holy Sepulchre.

Holy place. 1526. A place that is holy; a sanctuary. *spec.* a. The outer chamber of the sanctuary in the Jewish tabernacle and temple. b. *pl.* Localities which are objects of pilgrimage in the Greek or Latin Church.

Holy rood (day). *arch.* [OE. *sēo hālige rōd.*] = HOLY CROSS (DAY).

Holy stone, holy-stone, *sb.* 1777. [?] 1. A soft sandstone used for scouring the decks of ships 1823. 2. [? for *holey stone.*] A stone with a natural hole in it, used as a charm. Hence **Ho·lystone** *v.* to scour with a h.

Holy tide, holy-tide. OE. A day or season of religious observance.

Holy water. [OE. *hāligwæter*, a true compound: subseq. analysed as two wds.] 1. Water blessed by a priest and used in various rites. 2. *attrib.* ME.

1. Provb. *As the devil loves holy water*, i.e. not at all. 2. **Holy water sprinkle,** †**springle,** (*a*) an aspergillum, (*b*) a club armed with spikes, (*c*) a fox's brush. **Holy water** †**stick,** †**stock,** †**stop,** mod. (1793) **stoup,** a stoup or basin for holding holy water, placed near the entrance of a church.

Holy Week. 1710. [after F. *la semaine sainte*, etc.] The week immediately preceding Easter Sunday.

Holy well. OE. [A combined form occurs in the proper names *Holywell, Hollywell, Halliwell.*] A well or spring reputed to possess miraculous healing properties.

Holy Writ. OE. See WRIT 1 c.

‖**Hom** (hōum). Also **homa.** 1855. [Pers. = Skr. *sōma.*] The sacred plant of the ancient Persians and Parsees; also its juice; orig. the same as the SOMA of the Vedas.

Homacanth: see HOMO-.

Homage (hǫ·mėdʒ), *sb.* ME. [a. OF. *ommage, homage, humage*, mod. *hommage* :— late L. *hominaticum*, f. *homo, homin-*; see -AGE. Cf. MANRED.] 1. In *Feudal Law*, Formal and public acknowledgement of allegiance, wherein a tenant or vassal declared himself the man of the king or the lord of whom he held, and bound himself to his service. b. An act of homage; a render or money payment made as an acknowledgement of vassalage 1599. 2. A body of persons owning allegiance; *spec.* in *Eng. Law*, the body of tenants attending a manorial court, or the jury at such a court ME. 3. *fig.* Acknowledgement of superiority; dutiful respect or honour shown ME.

1. Phr. *To do* (†*make*), *render h.*; *to resign h.*, formally to renounce allegiance. *Feudal h.*, h. paid to the lord. *Liege h.*, h. paid to the king. 2. With the consent of the 'homage', i.e. of his copyholders 1865. 3. To do h. and honour to almyghty god 1526. A reluctant h. to the justice of English principles MACKINTOSH. Hence †**Ho·mageable** *a.* bound to render h.

Ho·mage, *v.* 1592. [f. prec. sb.] †1. *trans.* To render or pay as a token of homage –1662. †2. *intr.* To pay homage –1636. 3. *trans.* To do homage or allegiance to 1632.

Homager (hǫ·mėdʒəɹ). ME. [a. OF. *hommager, -ier*, f. *hommage* HOMAGE; see -ER[2].] One who owes homage or fealty; one who holds lands by homage. Also *fig.* b. *spec.* in *Eng. Law*, A manorial tenant 1598.

Thou blushest Anthony, and that blood of thine Is Cæsars h. *Ant. & Cl.* I. i. 31.

Homalographic (hǫ·mălo,græ·fik), *a.* (*erron.* **homolo-**.) 1864. [f. Gr. ὁμαλός even, level + GRAPHIC.] *Geog.* Delineating in equal proportion; applied to a method of projection in which equal areas on the earth's surface are represented by equal areas on the map.

Homaloid (hǫ·măloid). 1876. [f. Gr. ὁμαλός + -OID.] *Geom.* A homaloidal space of any number of dimensions; a flat. So **Homaloi·dal** *a.* of the nature of a plane; flat.

Homarine (hǫ·mărəin). 1880. [f. mod.L. *Homarus*, generic name of the lobster, f. F. *homard* (formerly *homar*, a. ON. *humarr*, Da. *hummer*) lobster.] 1. *adj.* Related to or having the characteristics of a lobster. 2. *sb.* A crustacean of the genus *Homarus*; a lobster.

Homaxonial: see HOMO-.

Homburg (hǫ·mbɒɹg). 1901. [Name of a town in Prussia, where first worn.] In full *Homburg hat*: A man's soft felt hat with narrow brim and dented crown.

Home (hōum), *sb.*[1] and *a.* [Com. Teut.: OE. *hām*.]

A. *sb.* †1. A village or town; a vill with its cottages. OE. and early ME. 2. A dwelling-place, house, abode; the fixed residence of a family or household; one's own house; the dwelling in which one habitually lives, or which one regards as one's proper abode. Occas., the home-circle or household. Also *transf.* OE. 3. (Without qualifying word or pl.) The place of one's dwelling and nurturing, with its associations 1460. 4. *fig.* With reference to the grave, or future state ME. 5. A place, region, or state to which one properly belongs, in which one's affections centre, or where one finds rest, refuge, or satisfaction 1548. 6. One's own country, one's native land; the place where one's ancestors dwelt 1595. 7. The seat, centre, or native habitat 1706. 8. An institution providing refuge or rest 1851. 9. In games: The place in which one is free from attack; the goal 1855. 10. *attrib.* and *Comb.*

3. *A h. from h.*, a place away from home which provides home-like accommodation or amenities. 4. Man goeth to his longe h. *Eccl.* xii. 5. 5. Wherever woman has a tongue, there Mrs. Grundy has a h. LYTTON. 6. Till then.. Will I not think of h., but follow Armes *John* II. i. 31. H. always means England; nobody calls India h. 1837. 7. Sicily.. was the real h. of bucolic poetry 1886. 8. The H. for Confirmed Invalids 1863. 9. Not till the line for h. did he let the great horse [Persimmon] go 1897. 10. (Freq. in comb. from 16th c.) *h.-ache*, home-sickness 1762.

Phrases. **At home.** a. At or in one's own house. Also *fig.* b. In one's own neighbourhood; in one's native land. (Opp. to *abroad*.) In the mother-country. c. At one's ease, as if in one's own h.; in one's element. Hence, Unconstrained; familiar *with*, well versed *in*. d. = Accessible to visitors. Hence, a formula inviting company to an informal reception. Hence '*not-at-home*'. **From home.** Not at home; abroad. †**Nearer home.** a. *lit.* Nearer one's own dwelling-place or country. b. *fig.* In or into closer relation or connexion with oneself.

B. *attrib.* or *adj.* 1. Of, relating to, or connected with, home or one's home; reared, fostered, or carried on at home; proceeding from home; domestic, family 1552. 2. Near, or surrounding one's home, or the mansion on an estate. Hence, belonging to head-quarters, principal; as *h. station*. 1662. b. Belonging to a locality in which a sporting contest or match takes place 1886. 3. Domestic; opp. to *foreign* 1591. b. Treating of domestic affairs 1797. 4. In games: Of, pertaining to, or situated at or near home (see A. 9); reaching or enabling a player to reach home. (Also hyphened.) 1857. 5. That strikes home; searching, poignant, pointed; effective; to the point, close, direct. Now chiefly in *h. question*, *h. truth*. (Orig. adverbial (*h.-speaking = speaking h.*): see HOME *adv.* 4, 5; separation from the vbl. sb. caused it to be treated as an adj.; hence its extension to other sbs. as in *h. truth*.) 1625.

1. A h. pastime THACKERAY. Family or h. life SMILES. 2. The h. covers were shot on Friday 1886. Phr. *H. Counties*, the counties nearest London, sometimes including Hertford and Sussex. *H. Circuit*: the assize circuit which has London as its centre; its area has been often changed. b. Phr. *H.-and-h. matches*: applied to two matches, one of which is played at the h. or locality of each side. 3. The h. market 1794, trade 1842. H. politics 1885. b. *H. Office*: in Great Britain, the department of the 'Secretary of State for Home Affairs' (abbrev. *H. Secretary*); the building in which its business is carried on. 4. *The last or h. hole* (Golf). 5. People who pique themselves on telling h. truths 1843.

Home, *sb.*[2] *rare.* 1836. = HOMELYN.

Home (hōum), *adv.* OE. [Orig. accus. of HOME *sb.*[1], as the case of destination after a vb. of motion; cf. L. *ire domum* to go home.] 1. To one's home (see HOME, *sb.*[1] 2–6, 9). 2. = Come home, at home after absence 1587. 3. *Naut.* Towards or into the ship. Hence, of an anchor, away from its hold. 1603. 4. To the point aimed at; as far as it will go; into or in close contact; closely, directly 1548. b. *Naut.* Full in (from the sea), full to the shore 1793. 5. *fig.* To the very heart or root of a matter; closely, directly, thoroughly 1542. 6. To 'oneself'; hence, †to one's normal condition 1526.

1. I lugged the money h. DE FOE. The Regent Bedford.. wrote h. to the government in England 1874. 2. My son will be h. soon 1870. 3. A sudden gust of wind brought h. our anchor 1748. 4. Time is precious.. strike quick and h. NELSON. †*To come short h.*: to come to grief. 5. The charge is.. not brought h. to William FREEMAN. Phr. *To come (go) h. to*: to touch intimately. †*To speak h.*, i.e. plainly and to the point. b. *To bring oneself h., to be brought, come, get h.*: to recover oneself (financially), regain one's position. c. *Nothing to write h. about*: nothing to boast of.

Comb., as *h.-going*, etc.; *h.-driven*; *h.-push*, etc.

Home (hōum), *v.* 1765. [f. HOME *sb.*[1]] 1. *intr.* To go home. 2. To have one's home, dwell 1832. 3. *trans.* To establish in a home 1802.

1. One bird [swallow] homed from Paris in ninety minutes 1889.

Home-born, *a.* 1587. Born or produced at home; native.

Home-bred, *a.* 1587. 1. Bred or reared at home; native, indigenous; domestic. 2. Of homely breeding 1602.

1. Foreign invaders or home-bred rebels FREEMAN.

Home-brew. 1853. [f. HOME *sb.*[1] + BREW *sb.*] Home-brewed ale, beer, or other beverage. Also *fig.*

Home-brewed, *a.* 1754. Brewed at home or for home consumption. *absol.* = prec. Also *fig.*

Ho·me-coming, *sb.* ME. [f. HOME *adv.* (Replacing ME. *home come*.)] A coming home, arrival at home. So **Ho·me-comer.**

At myn homcomyng CHAUCER.

Home-felt, *a.* 1634. [f. as prec.] Felt 'at home', intimately or in one's heart.

A sacred and home-felt delight MILT.

Ho·me-keeping, *a.* 1591. That keeps or takes care of a home; that remains at home.

Home-keeping youth, haue euer homely wits SHAKS. So **Ho·me-keeping** *sb.*

Homeland (hōu·mlænd). 1670. The land which is one's home or where one's home is. Orig. *attrib.* b. = HOME *sb.*[1] 6. 1892.

Homeless (hōu·mlės), *a.* 1615. [See -LESS.] 1. Having no home or permanent abode. Usu. of persons; hence *transf.* of their condition, etc. 2. Affording no home 1797. Hence **Ho·meless-ly** *adv.*, **-ness.**

Ho·melike, *a.* 1817. [LIKE *a.*] Like home; suggestive of home; homely.

†**Ho·meling.** 1577. [-LING.] A home-born inhabitant; a native. Also *attrib.* or *adj.* –1649.

Homely (hōu·mli), *a.* ME. [-LY[1].] †1. Of or belonging to the home; domestic, family –1577. 2. Familiar, intimate; at home *with*. Now *rare* or *arch.* ME. 3. Such as belongs to home or is produced or practised at home (esp. a humble home); simple; plain; everyday; unpolished, rough, rude. (Sometimes approbative; but often apologetic, depreciative, or euphemistic for 'wanting refinement, or polish'.) ME. 4. Of persons, their features, etc.: Plain, uncomely 1590.

2. This goode emperoure was.. h. with euery man LD. BERNERS. 3. Plain h. terms ADDISON. The garden's homeliest roots BYRON. A dear little h. woman 1863. 4. Some parts of Man be.. comely, some h. 1619. Hence **Ho·melily** *adv.* **Ho·meliness.**

†**Homely**, *adv.* ME. [-LY[2].] 1. Familiarly –1650. 2. Kindly –1596. 3. Plainly, simply; without adornment; rudely, roughly –1697. 4. Directly home; straight to the point; plainly –1688.

Homelyn (hōu·mlin). 1666. [?] A fish, the Spotted Ray, *Raia maculata*.

Home-made, *a.* 1659. Made at home or for home consumption; of domestic manufacture. Also *absol.*

Homeo-: see HOMŒO-.

Homer[1] (hōu·məɹ). 1880. [f. HOME *v.* + -ER[1].] A homing pigeon.

‖**Homer**[2] (hōu·məɹ). Also **chomer.** 1535. [ad. Heb. *χōmer*, lit. 'heap'.] A Hebrew measure of capacity, containing 10 ephahs, or 10 baths (liquid measure). Its content was prob. about 80 gallons. ¶ Also erron. used for OMER, q.v.

Homer, contr. of *hoe-mother*; see HOE *sb.*[3]

Homeric (home·rik), *a.* 1771. [ad. L. *Homericus*, a. Gr. Ὁμηρικός, f. Ὅμηρος Homer.] Of, pertaining to, or characteristic of Homer, his poems, or the age with which they deal; like, or of the style of, Homer.

Phr. *The H. question*: the question of the authorship, date, and construction of the *Iliad* and the *Odyssey*. So †**Home·rical** *a.*, **-ly** *adv.* †**Home·rican** *a.*

Homerid (hōu·mĕrid). 1846. [ad. Gr. Ὁμηρίδης, usu. in pl. Ὁμηρίδαι, Lat. *Homeridæ*, a guild of poets in Chios who claimed descent from Homer and a hereditary property in the Homeric poems, which they recited publicly.] 1. One of the *Homeridæ* (see above). 2. A Homeric scholar. BLACKIE.

Homerite (hōu·mĕrəit). 1613. [a. Gr. Ὁμηρῖται *pl.*] = HIMYARITE.

Homerology (hōumĕrǫ·lŏdʒi). 1876. [f. *Homer* + -(O)LOGY.] The study of Homer and of the Homeric poems, their authorship, date, etc. Hence **Homero·logist.**

Home Rule. 1860 (but not in general use before 1871). [HOME *sb.* B. 3.] Government of a country, colony, province, etc., by its own citizens; the political principle or theory, according to which a country or province manages its own affairs; used *spec.* in British politics with reference to the movement, begun about 1870, to obtain for Ireland self-government through the agency of a national parliament. Also *attrib.* (also home-rule). Hence **Home-ru·ler**, one who advocates or practises Home Rule.

Home-sick, homesick (hōu·msik), *a.* 1798. [SICK *a.*] Affected with home-sickness.

Ho·me-sickness, homesickness. 1756. [f. HOME *sb.* + SICKNESS; app. a rendering of Ger. *heimweh*.] A depressed state of mind and body caused by a longing for home when away from it; nostalgia.

Homespun (hōu·mspʌn). 1590. [HOME *sb.*, in sense 'at home'.]

A. *adj.* 1. Spun at home; of home manufacture; made of the material mentioned in B. 1. 1591. 2. *fig.* Simple, unsophisticated; plain, homely; unpolished, rude 1600.

1. Plain, decent, h. cloth 1796. 2. The plainest h. morality 1874. Simple, h. characters L. STEPHEN.

B. *sb.* 1. Cloth made of yarn spun at home; hodden; also, a material made in imitation of this 1607. Also *fig.* 2. *transf.* One who wears homespun; hence, a rustic, a clown 1590.

1. Homespuns are still much worn 1883. 2. What hempen home-spuns haue we swaggering here? SHAKS.

Homestall (hōu·mstǫl). [OE. *hāmsteall*, f. *hām* HOME + *steall* position, place.] †1. = HOMESTEAD –1814. 2. A farm-yard (*dial.*) 1661.

Homestead (hōu·msted). [OE. *hāmstede*, f. *hām* HOME + *stede* place, STEAD.] 1. *gen.* The place of one's home: †a. The town, village, etc. in which one's dwelling is. b. A dwelling. 2. A house with its dependent buildings and offices; esp. a farm-stead 1700. 3. *U.S.* A farm occupied by the owner and his family; esp. the lot of 160 acres granted to a settler by the Homestead Act of Congress, 1862. Also *attrib.*

2. Twilight.. Brought back.. the herds to the h. LONGF. 3. *H. exemption*, in U.S., the exemption of a h. from forced sale under execution for general debts. Hence **Ho·mestea·der**, the holder of a h.; *spec.* in *U.S.*, one who holds lands acquired under the Homestead Act of Congress.

Ho·mester. 1847. [See -STER.] 1. A stay-at-home (*rare*). 2. *pl.* The home team in a sporting match 1891.

Ho·me-thrust. 1622. [f. HOME *adv.*] A thrust which goes home to the party aimed at.

Homeward (hōu·mwǫɹd). [OE. *hāmweard*, f. *hām* HOME + *-weard* -WARD.] A. *adv.* Towards one's home, dwelling-place, or native land. B. *adj.* Directed or going homeward; leading home.

Homeward-bound, *a.* 1602. [BOUND *ppl. a.*[1]] Bound homeward; esp. of a ship.

Homewards (hōu·mwǫɹdz), *adv.* [OE. *hāmweardes*: see -WARDS.] = HOMEWARD *adv.*

Ho·me-work. 1856. [HOME *sb.*[1] B. 1.] a. Work done at home, esp. as dist. from work done in a shop or factory. b. Lessons to be done by a school-child at home 1889.

Hom(e)y (hōu·mi), *a.* 1856. [f. HOME *sb.* + -Y[1].] Resembling or having a feeling of home.

Homicidal (hǫmisəi·dăl), *a.* 1725. [f. next + -AL.] Of, pertaining to, or characterized by homicide; tending to homicide; murderous.

H. mania: a state of partial insanity, accompanied by an impulse to the perpetration of murder. Hence **Homici·dally** *adv.*

Homicide (hǫ·misəid), *sb.*¹ ME. [a. F., ad. L. *homicida*, f. *homo, hominis*; see -CIDE 1.] A man-slayer; in earlier use often = murderer. Also *attrib.*

attrib. This regicide and h. government BURKE.

Ho·micide, *sb.*² ME. [a. F., ad. L. *homicidium*; see prec. and -CIDE 2.] The action, by a human being, of killing a human being.

In *Law*, usually classed as *justifiable, excusable*, or *felonious*. *Justifiable h.*, the killing of a man in obedience to law, or by unavoidable necessity, or for the prevention of an atrocious crime. *Excusable h.*, h. committed by misadventure, also in cases of self-defence, where the assailant did not originally intend murder, rape, or robbery. *Felonious h.* comprehends the wilful killing of a man through malice aforethought (murder); the unlawful killing of a man without such malice, either in a sudden heat, or involuntarily while committing an unlawful action not amounting to felony; also self-murder, suicide. Hence **Ho·micide** *v.* to kill or murder. var. †**Homicidy, -ie** (Chaucer).

Homiform, erron. f. HOMINIFORM.

Homilete (hǫ·milīt). *U.S.* 1875. [ad. Gr. ὁμιλητής disciple, scholar.] A HOMILIST.

Homiletic (hǫmile·tik). 1644. [ad. Gr. ὁμιλητικός affable, conversable, f. ὁμιλητός, vbl. adj. of ὁμιλέειν, f. ὅμιλος crowd.]

A. *adj.* Of the nature of or characteristic of a homily; by way of a homily.

H. divinity or *theology* = Homiletics: see B. 1.

B. *sb.* usu. in pl. **Homiletics** [see -ICS]. **1.** The art of preaching; sacred rhetoric 1830. **2.** *pl.* Homilies. CARLYLE.

1. If..the teaching of H. were confined to the multiplication of methods for laying out a discourse [etc.] PUSEY.

So **Homile·tical** *a.* †conversable, sociable; homiletic. **Homile·tically** *adv.* after the manner of a homily.

Homiliary (hǫmi·liări). 1844. [ad. med.L. *homiliarium, homiliarius* (*liber*), f. *homilia* HOMILY; see -ARY.] A book of homilies.

Homilist (hǫ·milist). 1616. [f. HOMILY + -IST.] One who writes or delivers homilies. Hence **Homili·stical** *a.* characteristic of a h.

Homilize (hǫ·miləiz), *v.* 1624. [f. HOMILY + -IZE.] *intr.* To discourse, preach, sermonize.

Homily (hǫ·mĭli). ME. [a. OF. *omelie*, mod. F. *homélie*, ad. eccl.L. *homilia*, a. Gr. ὁμιλία converse, discourse, f. ὅμιλος crowd, f. ὁμοῦ together + ἴλη troop.] A religious discourse addressed to a congregation; esp. a practical discourse with a view to spiritual edification. Applied *spec.* to the discourses contained in the *Books of Homilies* published in 1547 and 1563 for use in parish churches. **b.** *transf.* A serious admonition; a lecture; a tedious moralizing discourse 1600.

b. What tedious homilie of Loue haue you wearied your parishioners withall *A. Y. L.* III. ii. 164.

Hominal (hǫ·minăl), *a.* 1861. [a. F., f. L. *homo, hominem*: see -AL.] Of or relating to man (in Nat. Hist.).

Homing (hōᵘ·miŋ), *vbl. sb.* 1622. [f. HOME *v.*] †**1.** *Naut.* (with *in*) The curving inwards of the sides of a vessel above its extreme breadth; 'falling' or 'tumbling' home. **2.** The action of going home; return home; the faculty of returning home from a distance. Also *attrib.*, esp. in reference to pigeons. 1765. So **Ho·ming** *ppl. a.* that goes home; as *homing pigeon*.

Hominid (hǫ·minid). 1889. [ad. mod.L. *Hominidæ*, a family of mammals represented by the single genus *Homo*, f. L. *homo, hominis*; see -ID.] A member of the *Hominidæ*; a man (zoologically considered).

†**Ho·miniform,** *a.* [f. L. *hominem* + -FORM.] Of human shape. CUDWORTH.

Ho·minify, *v.* 1579. [f. as prec. + -FY.] To make human.

Hominivorous (hǫmini·vŏrəs), *a.* 1859. [f. as prec. + *-vorus* devouring + -OUS.] Man-eating.

Hominy (hǫ·mĭni). 1629. [Of American Indian origin.] Maize hulled and ground coarsely and prepared for food by being boiled with water or milk. Also *attrib.*

Homish (hōᵘ·miʃ), *a.* Also **homeish.** 1561. [See -ISH.] †**1.** Belonging to home; domestic–1577. **2.** Suggestive of home; homelike 1789. Hence **Ho·mishness.**

Hommack, var. of HUMMOCK.

‖**Homo** (hōᵘ·mo). 1596. The Latin word for *man*. **a.** = 'human being'. **b.** *Zool.* The genus of which Man is the single species. **Homo sapiens** (sē·pienz): the human species.

Homo is a common name to all men SHAKS.

Homo-, bef. a vowel **hom-,** comb. f. Gr. ὁμός same; often in opposition to *hetero-*.

Ho·macanth [Gr. ἄκανθα spine] *a.*, *Ichth.* having the spines of the dorsal and anal fins symmetrical; opp. to *heteracanth*. **Homaxo·nial, Homaxo·nic** *adjs.*, in *Morphology*, having all the axes equal. **Ho·mocatego·ric** [CATEGORIC] *a.*, belonging to the same category. **Homochiral** [Gr. χείρ], of identical form and turned in the same direction, as two right or two left hands. **Homochro·mic, -chro·mous** [Gr. χρῶμα] *adjs.*, of the same colour, as the florets of most *Compositæ*; opp. to *heterochromous*. **Homode·mic** [Gr. δῆμος] *a.* = *homophylic*. **Homode·rmic** *a.*, *Biol.* derived from, or relating to derivation from, the same primary blastoderm of the embryo. **Homody·namous** [Gr. δύναμις] *a.*, *Comp. Anat.* having the same force or value; applied to parts serially homologous; so **Homody·namy,** the condition of being homodynamous. **Homoga·ngliate** *a.*, *Zool.* having the ganglia of the nervous system symmetrically arranged, as in the *Articulata*; opp. to heterogangliate. **Homo·malous** [Gr. ὁμαλός even] *a.*, *Bot.* applied to leaves or branches (esp. of mosses) which turn in the same direction; opp. to *heteromalous*. **Homo-organ,** *Biol.* = HOMOPLAST 2. **Homophy·lic** *a.*, *Biol.* belonging to the same race; relating to homophyly. **Homo·phyly** [Gr. ὁμοφυλία], the condition of being of the same race. **Homopo·lar, -po·lic** *adjs.*, having equal poles; opp. to *heteropolar*. **Homo·rgan** *Biol.* = *homo-organ*. **Homorga·nic** *a.*, 'having the same, or a uniform, organization; applied to plants' (*Syd. Soc. Lex.*); in *Phonetics*, produced by the same vocal organ. **Homosyste·mic** *a.*, belonging to the same system. **Homothe·rmous** [Gr. θερμός] *a.*, *Biol.* having a uniform temperature, as warm-blooded animals; opp. to *heterothermal*. **Homo·tonous** [Gr. τόνος] *a.*, having the same tone or sound.

b. In *Chemistry*, denoting a compound homologous with that whose name follows, as in *homatropine, homocuminic*, etc.

Homocentric (hǫmose·ntrik). 1621. [ad. mod.L. *homocentricus*, f. Gr. ὁμο- HOMO- + κεντρικός CENTRIC.] **1.** *adj.* Having the same centre 1696. †**2.** *sb.* (In old Astronomy.) A sphere or circle concentric with another or with the earth; opp. to ECCENTRIC *sb.* BURTON.

Homocercal (hǫmosə·ɹkăl), *a.* 1838. [f. HOMO- + Gr. κέρκος tail + -AL.] *Ichthyol.* Having the lobes of the tail equal, having a symmetrical tail. Also said of the tail. Opp. to *heterocercal*. So **Ho·mocercy,** h. condition.

Homodont (hǫ·modǫnt). 1877. [f. HOM(O- + Gr. ὀδούς, ὀδοντ-.] **1.** *adj.* Having teeth all of the same kind. Also said of the teeth. Opp. to *heterodont*. 1888. **2.** *sb.* A homodont animal.

Homodromous (hǫmǫ·drŏməs), *a.* 1710. [f. mod.L. *homodromus*, f. Gr. ὁμο- HOMO- + -δρομος running + -OUS.] Running in the same direction; opp. to *heterodromous*. †**a.** *Mech.* Applied to levers of the second and third orders, in which the power and the weight run in the same direction. **b.** *Bot.* Turning in the same direction, as two generating spirals of a phyllotaxis (e.g. on the main stem and on a branch). So **Homo·dromal, Ho·modrome** *adjs.* = prec. b.; **Homo·dromy,** h. condition.

Homœo-, comb. f. Gr. ὅμοιος like, similar (also occas. written **homoio-**, in fully anglicized words, **homeo-**); sometimes opposed to *hetero-*.

Homœothe·rmal [Gr. θερμός] *a.*, *Biol.* = *Homothermous* (see HOMO-). **Homœo·topy** [Gr. τόπος], similarity of words or parts of words, as a cause of mistakes in copying. **Ho·mœozo·ic** [Gr. ζωή] *a.*, containing similar forms of life.

Homœoid (hǫ·mi,oid). 1883. [f. Gr. ὅμοιος + -OID.] *Math.* A shell bounded by two surfaces similar and similarly situated with regard to each other; sometimes restricted to a shell bounded by concentric ellipsoids. Hence **Homœoi·dal** *a.*

Homœomeral (hǫmiǫ·mĕrăl), *a.* [f. HOMŒO- + Gr. μέρος + -AL.] *Pros.* Consisting of (metrically) similar parts.

Homœomeric (hǫmiome·rik), *a.* 1836. [f. HOMŒO- + Gr. μέρος + -IC.] **a.** Relating to homœomery; of the nature of homœomeries. **b.** Homogeneous 1865. So **Homœome·rical** *a.* = prec. a.

Homœomerous (hǫmiǫ·mĕrəs), *a.* 1875. [f. Gr. ὅμοιος + μέρος + -OUS.] Having or consisting of similar parts. **1.** *Bot.* Applied to lichens in which the gonidia and hyphæ are distributed uniformly through the thallus; opp. to *heteromerous*. **2.** = HOMŒOMERIC a.

Homœomery (hǫmiǫ·mĕri). Also **homoio-,** and in L. form **homœomeria.** 1660. [ad. L. *homœomeria* (Lucr.), ad. Gr. ὁμοιομέρεια, f. ὁμοιομερής, f. ὅμοιος + μέρος.] **a.** The theory (propounded by Anaxagoras) that the ultimate particles of matter are homogeneous. **b.** *pl.* The ultimate particles of matter, regarded as homogeneous.

Homœomorphous (hǫmiomǭ·ɹfəs), *a.* 1832. [f. HOMŒO- + Gr. μορφή + -OUS.] Of similar form or structure. *spec.* in *Cryst.* Having similar crystalline forms; said esp. of substances differing in chemical composition or atomic proportions. Hence **Homœomo·rphism,** h. condition.

Homœopath (hǫ·m-, hōᵘ·miopæþ). Also **homeo-.** 1830. [Mod., f. HOMŒOPATHY.] One who practises or advocates homœopathy. So **Homœo·pathist.**

Homœopathic (hǫm-, hōᵘmiopæ·þik), *a.* 1830. [f. HOMŒOPATHY + -IC.] **1.** Of or pertaining to homœopathy; practising or advocating homœopathy. **2.** *fig.* Very small or minute, like the doses in homœopathy. (Often *joc.*) 1838.

2. The chapel was h. in its dimensions 1876. Hence **Homœopa·thically** *adv.*

Homœopathy (hǫm-, hōᵘmiǫ·păþi). Also **homeo-,** and formerly erron. **homöo-.** 1826. [Mod. (first used in Ger. *homöopathie* by Hahnemann), f. Gr. ὅμοιος like + -πάθεια, f. πάθος suffering. Cf. ALLOPATHY.] A system of medical practice founded by Hahnemann of Leipsic about 1796, according to which diseases are treated by the administration (usu. in very small doses) of drugs which would produce in a healthy person symptoms like those of the disease treated. The principle is expressed in the Latin adage 'Similia similibus curantur'.

‖**Homœoteleuton** (homī:o,tǐlʼū·tǫn). Also **homoio-.** 1586. [Late L., a. Gr. ὁμοιοτέλευτον (sc. ῥῆμα), f. ὅμοιος like + τελευτή ending.] **1.** *Rhet.* A figure consisting of a series of words with the same or similar endings. **2.** The occurrence of similar endings in two neighbouring words, clauses, or lines of writing, as a source of error in copying 1861. So **Homœo·teleu·tic** *a.* having similar endings.

Homogamous (hǫmǫ·găməs), *a.* 1842. [f. Gr. ὁμο- HOMO- + -γαμος married + -OUS.] *Bot.* **a.** Having all the florets hermaphrodite, or all of the same sex: said of certain grasses and composites. **b.** Applied to flowers in which the stamens and pistils ripen together 1854. **c.** *Evolution.* Of or pertaining to assortative mating 1903. So **Homo·gamy,** h. condition.

Homogen (hǫ·mŏdʒen). 1870. [f. HOMO- + -GEN.] *Biol.* A part or organ homogenetic with another; see HOMOGENETIC 1.

Homogene (hǫ·mŏdʒīn). Now *rare* or *Obs.* 1607. [ad. Gr. ὁμογενής, ὁμογενε-, of the same kind, f. ὁμο- HOMO- + γένος, γενε(σ)-.] **1.** *adj.* = HOMOGENEOUS. **2.** *sb.* That which is homogeneous 1725.

2. Cold and rain congregate homogenes; for they gather together you [Sheridan] and your crew, at whist, punch, and claret SWIFT.

Homogeneal (hǫmo,dʒī·niăl). Now *rare.* Also *erron.* **-ial.** 1603. [f. Scholastic L. *homogeneus* + -AL.] **1.** *adj.* = HOMOGENEOUS. **2.** *sb.* A homogeneous substance or person 1651. Hence **Homoge·nealness,** homogeneity.

Homoge·neate, *v. rare.* 1648. [f. as prec. + -ATE³.] *trans.* To make homogeneous.

Homogeneity (hǫmo,dʒĭnī·ĭti). 1625. [ad. Scholastic L. *homogeneitas*; see next and -ITY.] The quality or condition of being homogeneous: **a.** Identity of kind with something else; **b.**

Uniformity of composition or nature. **c.** *concr.* Something homogeneous 1638.

Homogeneous (hǫmo₍dʒī·niəs), *a.* 1641. [f. Scholastic L. *homogeneus* (f. Gr. ὁμογενε-: see HOMOGENE) + -OUS.] **1.** Of the same kind or nature; alike, similar, congruous. **2.** Of uniform nature or character throughout 1645. **3.** *Math.* **a.** Of the same kind, so as to be commensurable. **b.** Consisting of terms of the same dimensions. 1695.

1. The world and mind..are not h. BAIN. 2. Ice is a..h. concretion SIR T. BROWNE. Hence **Homoge·neous·ly** *adv.*, **-ness.**

Homogenesis (hǫmo₍dʒe·nĕsis). 1858. [f. HOMO- + -GENESIS.] *Biol.* †**1.** Applied to asexual reproduction. CARPENTER. **2.** The ordinary form of sexual reproduction, in which the offspring resembles the parent and passes through the same course of development.

Homogenetic (-dʒĭne·tik), *a.* 1870. [f. HOMO- + GENETIC.] *Biol.* **1.** Having a common descent or origin; applied to organs or parts of different organisms which show a correspondence of structure due to derivation from a common ancestor. **2.** Relating to HOMOGENESIS (sense 2) 1889. So **Homogene·tical** *a.* of, relating to, or having reference to, homogeny or community of descent.

Homogenous (hǫmǫ·dʒĭnəs), *a.* 1870. [f. HOMO- + Gr. γένος + -OUS.] *Biol.* = HOMOGENETIC 1.

Homogeny (hǫmǫ·dʒĭni). 1626. [Ult., ad. Gr. ὁμογένεια, f. ὁμογεν-; see HOMOGENE.] †**1.** Homogeneity. BACON. **2.** *Biol.* The quality of being homogenous; correspondence of structure due to common descent 1870.

Homogonous (hǫmǫ·gŏnəs), *a.* 1877. [f. HOMO- + Gr. -γονος + -OUS.] **1.** *Bot.* Having similar reproductive organs; applied to flowers in which there is no difference in length in the stamens and pistils of different individuals; opp. to HETEROGONOUS 1. **2.** *Biol.* Producing offspring similar to the parent; opp. to HETEROGONOUS 2. 1883.

Homograph (hǫ·mŏgraf). 1873. [f. HOMO- + Gr. -γραφος, -GRAPH.] *Philol.* A word of the same spelling as another, but of different origin and meaning.

Homographic (hǫmogræ·fik), *a.* 1859. [f. Gr. ὁμο- HOMO- + γραφικός GRAPHIC.] **1.** *Geom.* Having the same anharmonic ratio or system of anharmonic ratios, as two figures of the same thing in different perspective; belonging or relating to such figures. **2.** *Gram.* Said of spelling in which each sound is always represented by the same character, which stands for that sound and no other; strictly phonetic; opp. to *heterographic* 1864. **3.** *Philol.* Of, belonging to, or consisting of homographs 1880.

Homography (hǫmǫ·grăfi). 1859. [f. HOMO- + Gr. -γραφια, -GRAPHY.] **1.** *Geom.* = HOMOLOGY 4. **2.** *Gram.* Homographic spelling; see prec. (sense 2) 1864.

Homoio-: see HOMŒO-.

Homoiousian (hǫmoi₍au·siăn, -ū·siăn). 1732. [f. Gr. ὁμοιούσιος (f. ὅμοιος like + οὐσία essence) + -AN.]

A. *adj.* **a.** Of like essence or substance. **b.** Relating to or maintaining likeness (as dist. from *identity* and from *difference*) of substance between the Father and the Son; see B. (Dist. from *heteroousian* and *homoousian.*) 1854.

B. *sb.* One who held the Father and the Son, in the Godhead, to be of like, but not the same, essence or substance; a Semi-Arian.

†**Homo·logal**, *a.* 1570. = HOMOLOGOUS.

Homologate (hǫmǫ·lŏgeⁱt), *v.* Chiefly *Sc.* 1644. [f. med.L. *homologare*, after Gr. ὁμολογεῖν + -ATE ³.] **1.** *trans.* To express agreement with; to assent to; to countenance; to confirm, ratify. **2.** *intr.* or *absol.* To agree; to express assent 1649. **3.** *trans.* To identify (*with* something else). HUTTON. Hence **Homologa·tion,** the action of homologating; *spec.* in *Sc. Law*, the action of confirming or ratifying (a defective or informal deed) by some subsequent act.

Homological (hǫmŏlǫ·dʒikăl), *a.* 1849. [f. as HOMOLOGY + -ICAL.] Involving or characterized by, or relating to, homology; homologous.

Homologize (hǫmǫ·lŏdʒəiz), *v.* 1733. [f. as prec. + -IZE.] **1.** *intr.* To be homologous, to correspond. **2.** *trans.* To make, or show to be, homologous 1811. Hence **Homo·logizer** 1716.

‖**Homologon** (hǫmǫ·lŏgǫn). 1871. [Gr. ὁμόλογον adj. neut., f. ὁμός same + λόγος ratio, etc.] A homologue.

Homologous (hǫmǫ·lŏgəs), *a.* 1660. [f. Gr. ὁμόλογος agreeing + -OUS.] Having the same relation, proportion, relative position, etc.; corresponding. **1.** *Math.* Having the same ratio or relative value as the two antecedents or the two consequents in a proportion, or the corresponding sides in similar figures. **b.** *Mod. Geom.* Having a relation of homology, as two plane figures; homological 1879. **2.** *Biol.* Having the same relation to a fundamental type; corresponding in type of structure. (Dist. from *analogous.*) 1846. **b.** *Path.* Of the same formation as the normal tissue of the part; said of morbid growths. (Opp. to HETEROLOGOUS.) 1871. **3.** *Chem.* Applied to series of compounds differing in composition successively by a constant amount of certain constituents, and showing a gradation of chemical and physical properties 1850.

2. In the vertebrata the front and hind limbs are h. DARWIN. 3. Four classes of h. bodies..namely alcohols, ethers, aldehydes, and acids DAUBENY.

Homologue (hǫ·mŏlǫg). 1848. [a. F., ad. Gr. ὁμόλογον.] That which is homologous; a homologous organ, etc.: see above.

Homology (hǫmǫ·lŏdʒi). 1656. [ad. late L. *homologia*, a. Gr. ὁμολογία, f. ὁμόλογος HOMOLOGOUS.] **1.** Homologous quality or condition; sameness of relation; correspondence. **2.** *Biol.* Correspondence in type of structure; see HOMOLOGOUS 2. Also that branch of Biology or Comparative Anatomy which deals with such correspondences. 1835. **3.** *Chem.* The relation of the compounds forming a homologous series; see HOMOLOGOUS 3. 1876. **4.** *Mod. Geom.* The relation of two figures, such that every point in each corresponds to a point in the other, and collinear points in one correspond to collinear points in the other; every straight line joining a pair of corresponding points passes through a fixed point called the *centre of h.*, and every pair of corresponding straight lines in the two figures intersect on a fixed straight line called the *axis of h.* 1879.

2. *General h.*, the relation of an organ or organism to the general type. *Serial h.*, the relation of corresponding parts forming a series in the same organism (e.g. legs, vertebræ, leaves). *Special h.*, the correspondence of a part or organ in one organism with a homologous part in another (e.g. of a horse's knee with a man's wrist).

Homomorph (hǫ·momǭɹf). 1886. [f. Gr. ὁμο- HOMO- + μορφή.] A thing of the same form as another; applied to letters having the same form and to different words having the same spelling.

Homomorphic (hǫmomǭ·ɹfik), *a.* 1872. [f. as prec. + -IC.] Of the same or similar form. *spec.* **a.** *Entom.* Said of insects in which the larva more or less resembles the imago (*Homomorpha*); hemimetabolous or ametabolous. **b.** *Bot.* Applied to flowers or plants in which the relative length of the stamens and pistils does not differ; also to the self-fertilization of such flowers. **c.** *Biol.* Applied to organs or organisms showing an external resemblance, but not really related in structure or origin. So **Homomo·rphism, Ho·momo·rphy,** h. condition; resemblance of form, *esp.* without structural affinity. **Homomo·rphous** *a.* of the same form.

Homonomous (hǫmǫ·nŏməs), *a.* 1854. [f. Gr. ὁμόνομος (f. ὁμός same + νόμος law) + -OUS.] Subject to the same or a constant law; *spec.* in *Biol.* Having the same law or mode of growth.

Homonomy (-ǫ·nŏmi). 1643. [f. as prec. + -Y.] Homonomous condition (see prec.).

Homonym (hǫ·mŏnim). 1697. [ad. late L. *homonymum*, a. Gr. ὁμώνυμον adj. neut., HOMONYMOUS.] **1. a.** The same word used to denote different things. **b.** *Philol.* Applied to words having the same sound, but different meanings. **2.** A namesake 1851.

Homonymous (hǫmǫ·niməs), *a.* 1621. [f. late L. *homonymus*, a. Gr. ὁμώνυμος; f. ὁμός same + ὄνομα (Æol. ὄνυμα) name; see -OUS.] †**1.** Denoting different things by the same name; equivocal, ambiguous -1801. **2.** Having, or called by, the same name 1658. Hence **Homo·nymously** *adv.* So **Homony·mic** *a.* relating to homonyms or homonymy 1862. **Homo·nymy,** the quality of being h. 1597.

Homoousian, homousian (hǫ·mo₍au·siăn, hǫmau·siăn, -ū·siăn). 1565. [ad. med.L. *homousianus*, f. *homousius*, a. Gr. ὁμοούσιος, ὁμούσιος, f. ὁμός same + οὐσία essence, substance; see -AN. Opp. to *heteroousian* and *homoiousian.*]

Theol. **A.** *adj.* **a.** Of the same essence or substance. **b.** Relating to or maintaining the consubstantiality of the persons of the Trinity; see B. 1678.

The council of Nice established the homousian or consubstantial doctrine LARDNER.

B. *sb.* *Eccl. Hist.* One who holds the three persons of the Trinity to be of the same essence or substance 1565.

The Arrians called the Catholikes Homoousians 1565.

Homophene (hǫ·mofīn). 1883. [irreg. f. HOMO- + Gr. φαίνειν to show, to appear. (The regular form would be *homophane.*)] A word having the same form to the eye as another; used esp. in reference to the reading of deaf-mutes.

Homophone (hǫ·mofōᵘn). 1623. [ad. Gr. ὁμόφωνος, f. ὁμο- HOMO- + φωνή sound.]

A. *adj.* Having the same sound (*rare*).

B. *sb.* *Philol.* (Usu. in *pl.*) Applied to words having the same sound, but differing in meaning or derivation; also to different symbols denoting the same group of sounds 1843.

Homophonic (hǫmofǫ·nik), *a.* 1879. [f. as prec. + -IC.] *Mus.* **1.** Producing, or consisting of, sounds of the same pitch; unisonous. Opp. to *antiphonic.* 1881. **2.** *loosely.* Said of music characterized by the predominance of one part or melody, to which the rest merely furnish harmonies; more correctly called *monophonic* or *monodic.* Opp. to *polyphonic.* 1879.

Homophonous (hǫmǫ·fŏnəs), *a.* 1753. [f. as prec. + -OUS.] **1.** *Mus.* = HOMOPHONIC 1. **2.** Of the character of homophones 1820.

Homophony (hǫmǫ·fŏni). 1776. [ad. Gr. ὁμοφωνία, f. ὁμόφωνος; see HOMOPHONE.] **1.** *Mus.* Homophonic music or style. **a.** Unison, or music performed in unison; opp. to *antiphony.* **b.** Monophony, monody; opp. to *polyphony.* **2.** *Philol.* Homophonous quality; identity of sound (of words) 1842.

Homoplast (hǫ·moplæst). 1870. [f. Gr. ὁμο- HOMO- + πλαστός moulded; cf. *bioplast.*] *Biol.* **1.** An organ or part homoplastic with another; opp. to HOMOGEN. **2.** An aggregate or fusion of plastids all of the same structure; opp. to *alloplast* 1883.

Homoplastic (-plæ·stik), *a.* 1870. [f. as prec. + Gr. πλαστικός fit for moulding.] *Biol.* Having a similarity of structure without community of origin. Opp. to HOMOGENETIC.

Homoplasy (hǫmǫ·plăsi). 1870. [f. as prec. + Gr. -πλασια, f. πλάσις moulding.] *Biol.* Homoplastic condition; similarity of structure produced independently by similar external circumstances. Opp. to HOMOGENY 2.

‖**Homoptera** (hǫmǫ·ptĕră), *sb. pl.* 1826. [mod.L., f. Gr. ὁμο- HOMO- + πτερόν wing.] *Entom.* A suborder of HEMIPTERA, comprising insects of various forms, with wings of uniform texture; contrasted with HETEROPTERA. Hence **Homo·pter, Homo·pteran,** a member of the *H.* **Homo·pterous** *a.*

Homosexual (hǫmo₍se·ksiuăl), *a.* (*sb.*). 1897. [irreg. f. HOMO- + SEXUAL.] Having a sexual propensity for persons of one's own sex. Also as *sb.* Hence **Ho·mose·xualism, -se·xualist, -sexua·lity, -se·xualize** *v.*

Homostyled (hǫ·mo₍stəild), *a.* 1877. [f. HOMO- + STYLE + -ED ².] *Bot.* = HOMOGONOUS 1; opp. to *heterostyled.* Also **Homosty·lic, -sty·lous** *adjs.* **Homosty·ly.**

Homotaxial (-tæ·ksiăl), *a.* 1870. [f. HOMO- + Gr. -ταξια (f. τάξις) + -AL.] *Geol.* Applied to strata in different regions, having the same relative position with respect to those underlying and overlying them, but not necessarily contemporaneous; also to the fossil remains found in such strata. **Homota·xially** *adv.* **Homota·xeous, Homota·xic** *adjs.* = HOMOTAXIAL. **Ho·motaxy.**

Homo·tropal, *a.* 1844. *Bot.* = next.

Homotropous (-ǫ·trŏpəs), *a.* 1819. [f. Gr. ὁμο- HOMO- + -τροπος turning + -OUS.] *Bot.* Of the embryo of a seed: Having the radicle directed towards the hilum. Opp. to *antitropous* or *heterotropous.* Also **-trope** *a.* 1831.

Homotype (hǫ·motəip). 1840. [f. Gr. ὁμο- + τύπος TYPE.] *Biol.* A part or organ having the same type of structure as another, a homologue.

The femur, the h. of the humerus OWEN. Hence **Ho·motypal, Homoty·pic, -al** *adjs.* of the character of, or relating to, a h.; homologous. **Homotypy** (hǫ·motəipi, homǫ·tipi), relation of homotypes; homology.

Homousian: see HOMOOUSIAN.

Homozygote (hǫmozəi·gout). 1902. [f. HOMO- + ZYGOTE.] A zygote formed by the union of two like gametes. Hence **Ho·mozygo·sis, -zygo·sity, -zy·gous** *a.*

‖**Homuncio** (homʊ·nsio). 1643. [L., dim. of *homo.*] = HOMUNCULE.

Homuncule, -uncle (homʊ·ŋkiul, -ʊ·ŋk'l). 1656. [ad. L. *homunculus* (also used), dim. of *homo.*] A diminutive man; a manikin. Hence **Homu·ncular** *a.* pigmy.

Homy: see HOMEY.

Hond, obs. f. HAND.

Hone (hōun), *sb.*[1] [OE. *hān* str. fem. = ON. *hein* str. fem.] †**1.** A stone, a rock. OE. only. **2.** A whetstone used for giving a fine edge to cutting tools, esp. razors ME. **3.** Stone of which whetstones are made. (Various kinds of stone are used for this purpose.) 1793. *Comb.* **h.-stone** = senses 2 and 3; *spec.* a very siliceous clay slate having a conchoidal fracture across the grain of the rock; also called *novaculite.*

†**Hone,** *sb.*[2] 1633. A swelling or tumour.

Hone, *v.*[1] *dial.* and *U.S.* 1600. [a. OF. *hogner, hoigner,* Norman dial. *honer* to grumble, whine; app. f. *hon,* a cry of discontent.] *intr.* To grumble, murmur, whine, moan. Also with *for, after.*

He lies..honing and moaning to himself LAMB.

Hone, *v.*[2] 1788. [f. HONE *sb.*[1]] *trans.* To sharpen on a hone. Hence **Honer.**

On beuks to h. my rhymin' razor PICKEN.

Hone: see OHONE. Hence as *vb.* BORROW.

Honest (ǫ·nėst), *a.* ME. [a. OF. *honeste,* mod. *honnête,* ad. L. *honestus,* f. *honos, -or, honor-.*] †**1.** Of persons: Holding an honourable position; respectable –1692. **b.** As a vague epithet of appreciation. (Cf. *worthy.*) 1551. †**2.** Honourable; creditable –1720; respectable, decent, befitting –1674; decent in appearance; comely; neat, tidy –1566. **3.** Of persons: †Of good moral character, virtuous, upright –1702; *spec.* chaste, 'virtuous'; usu. of a woman (*arch.*) ME. **b.** Sincere, truthful, candid; that will not lie, cheat, or steal. (The prevailing modern sense.) ME. **c.** Ingenuous; open, frank 1634. **4.** Of actions, feelings, etc.: Fair, straightforward; free from fraud ME. **b.** Of money, gain, etc.: Legitimate 1700. **c.** Of a thing: Genuine 1598. **5.** *adv.* = Honestly; or (*poet.*) in comb. with another adj. = 'honest and ——' 1592.

1. Houses, wherein liue the honester sort of people, as Farmers in England 1624. Phr. *To make an h. woman of:* to marry (a woman) after seduction (*dial.* or *vulgar*) 1562. **b.** Your name h. Gentleman? *Mids. N.* III. i. 187. **2.** Many a manly wound All h., all before DRYDEN. H. mirth 1674. **3.** Wives may be merry, and yet h. too *Merry W.* IV. ii. 103. **b.** An h. man's the noblest work of God POPE. **4.** Their h. and reasonable excuses could not be heard GRAFTON. **b.** He turns an h. penny JESSOPP. **c.** *Merry W.* IV. ii. 126. **5.** As I have euer found thee h. true SHAKS.

So †**Honest** *v.* to honour; to justify, defend, excuse; to 'make an honest woman of'.

†**Hone·stete.** ME. only. [a. OF. :—Com. Rom. type *honestitatem, for L. *honestatem.*] = HONESTY.

Honestly (ǫ·nėstli), *adv.* ME. [f. HONEST *a.* + -LY[2].] †**1.** In a respectful manner; decently –1645. **2.** With upright conduct; esp. without fraud or falsehood; sincerely, fairly, frankly ME. †**3.** Chastely –1691.

2. I can h. say [etc.] BERKELEY. I came h. by it SWIFT. **3.** The married Women live h. PURCHAS.

Honesty (ǫ·nėsti). ME. [a. OF. (*h*)*oneste,* earlier (*h*)*onestet,* ad. L. *honestas, -atem.*]

I. †**1.** Honourable position or estate; respectability –1520; respect –1613; reputation, credit –1548. †**2.** Decency, decorum; comeliness –1652. †**3.** Honourable character (in a wide sense) –1611; *spec.* chastity –1634; liberality –1607. **4.** Uprightness of disposition and conduct; straightforwardness; the quality opposed to lying, cheating, or stealing. (The prevailing modern sense.) 1579. Also *transf.* of things.

3. Let not..wicked friendship force What h. and vertue cannot work B. JONS. A Venus (like in honestie, though not in beautie) SIR T. HERBERT. **4.** What other Oath, Then H. to H. ingag'd *Jul. C.* II. i. 127.

II. a. Pop. name of *Lunaria biennis,* a cruciferous plant with large purple (or occas. white) flowers and flat round semi-transparent pods (whence the name); also other species of *Lunaria.* 1597. **b.** (In full, *Maiden's H.*) A local name of wild Clematis (*C. Vitalba*) 1640.

Honewort (hōu·nwɒɹt). 1633. [f. HONE *sb.*[2] + WORT.] A name for Corn Parsley (*Petroselinum segetum*); also extended to *Sison Amomum,* and other umbelliferous plants.

Honey (hʊ·ni), *sb.* (*a.*) [OE. *hunig* :—OTeut. *huna(n)gom neut. In ME. *u* bef. *n* was usually written *o*; hence *honey.*] **1.** A sweet viscid fluid, being the nectar of flowers collected and worked up for food by certain insects, esp. the honey-bee. **2.** Applied to products of the nature of, or resembling honey; esp. the nectar of flowers 1732. **3.** *fig.* Sweetness 1592. **4.** A term of endearment: Sweet one. (Now chiefly Irish, and, in form *hinnie, hinny,* Sc. and North.) ME. **5.** *attrib.* Of, for, pertaining to, or connected with honey 1460.

1. A lande flowing with milke and hony *Exod.* iii. 8. **2.** The h. of poison-flowers TENNYSON. **3.** Death that hath suckt the h. of thy breath *Rom. & Jul.* v. iii. 92.

Comb.: **h.-ant,** an ant of the genus *Myrmecocystus,* the workers of which in summer have the abdomen distended with h., which the others feed upon when food becomes scarce; **-badger,** the ratel; **-bag,** the enlargement of the alimentary canal in which the bee carries h.; †**-beer,** ?mead; **-creeper,** a bird of the neo-tropical family *Cœrebidæ* or *Dacnididæ*; **-fall** = HONEY-DEW 1; also *fig.* good luck; **-gland,** a nectary; **-kite** = HONEY-BUZZARD; **-moth,** the honeycomb moth; **-tube,** one of the two setiform tubes on the upper side of the abdomen of an aphis, which secrete a sweet fluid; **-words,** words of sweetness.

b. In names of plants and fruits: **h.-balm,** a labiate plant, *Melittis Melissophyllum*; **-berry,** the sweet berry of a W. Indian tree, *Melicocca bijuga*; **-blob** *Sc.,* a sweet yellow gooseberry; **-bottle** (*local*), the bloom of *Erica Tetralix*; **-bread,** the Carob (*Ceratonia Siliqua*); **-garlic,** *Allium siculum*; **-locust,** the N. Amer. genus *Gleditschia*; **-stalks** *sb. pl.,* the stalks or flowers of clover (Shaks.); **-wood,** the Tasmanian tree *Bedfordia salicina.*

B. *adj.* Resembling, or of the nature of, honey; sweet, honeyed LYDGATE.

A thousand honie secrets shalt thou know SHAKS.

Honey, *v. arch.* ME. [f. prec. sb.] †**1.** *trans.* To make sweet with or as with honey –1645. †**2.** To use endearing terms to –1631. **b.** *absol.* or *intr.* To talk fondly or sweetly. *arch.* and *U.S.* 1602. †**3.** *trans.* To coax, flatter –1622.

2. b. The king came honeying about her TENNYSON.

Ho·ney-bear. 1838. **1.** The potto or kinkajou, *Cercoleptes caudivolvulus,* a native of tropical America. **2.** The sloth-bear, *Melursus labiatus,* of India 1875.

Ho·ney-bee. 1566. A bee that gathers and stores honey, esp. the common hive-bee.

Ho·ney-bird. 1605. †**1.** Fanciful name for a bee. **2.** A bird that feeds on honey or the nectar of flowers. Cf. HONEY-EATER, -SUCKER 1870. **3.** = HONEY-GUIDE 1. 1850.

Ho·ney-bu:zzard. 1674. A bird of prey of the genus *Pernis,* esp. the European species *P. apivorus,* which feeds chiefly on the larvæ of bees and wasps.

Honeycomb (hʊ·nikōum), *sb.* [OE. *hunigcamb,* f. *hunig* + *camb* COMB *sb.*[1]] **1.** A structure of wax containing two series of hexagonal cells separated by thin partitions, formed by bees for the reception of honey and their eggs. Also *fig.* †**2.** A term of endearment –1552. **3.** A cavernous flaw in metal work, esp. in guns 1530. **4.** The reticulum or second stomach of ruminants, so called from its appearance 1658. **5.** Honeycomb work 1838. **6.** *attrib.* Of or pertaining to a honeycomb; like a honeycomb; having a surface hexagonally marked; as *h. cell, coil* (Wireless), *decoration, work,* etc. 1721.

1. Swetter abouen huny and huny kambe HAMPOLE. **5.** A large white quilt, real h. 1882.

Comb.: **h. bag** = sense 4; **h. coral,** a coral of the genus FAVOSITES; **h. moth,** a tineid moth of the genus *Galleria* which infests beehives; **h. ringworm, scall,** species of the disease FAVUS; **h. stitch,** a stitch used to draw together the gathers upon the neck and sleeves of smock-frocks, etc.; **h. stomach** = sense 4; so **h. tripe.**

Hence **Honeycomb** *v.,* to fill with cavities, undermine (*lit.* and *fig.*); to mark with honeycomb pattern 1768.

Honeycombed (hʊ·nikoumd), *a.* 1627. [f. prec. + -ED.] Formed or perforated like a honeycomb; as *h. lava,* etc.

Ho·ney-dew. 1577. **1.** A sweet sticky substance found on the leaves and stems of trees and plants, held to be excreted by aphides; formerly imagined to be in origin akin to dew. **2.** An ideally sweet or luscious substance 1608. **3.** A kind of tobacco sweetened with molasses 1857.

2. Sweet, as the Hony-deaw, which Hybla hath G. DANIEL.

Ho·ney-drop. ME. A drop of honey; occas. taken as a type of what is sweet and delicious.

Ho·ney-ea:ter. 1731. An animal that feeds on honey; *spec.* = HONEYSUCKER.

Honeyed, honied (hʊ·nid), *a.* ME. [f. HONEY *sb.* + -ED[2].] **1.** Abounding in or laden with honey; sweetened as with honey; consisting of or containing honey. **2.** *fig.* Sweet ME.

1. Wyne lyke vnto honyed wyne TURNER. **2.** H. nothings 1852.

Ho·ney-flower. 1712. **1.** A flowering shrub of the Cape of Good Hope, of the genus *Melianthus.* **2.** An Australian flower, *Lambertia formosa* 1802.

Ho·ney-guide. 1786. **1.** A small African bird of the genus *Indicator* which guides men and animals to the nests of bees. **2.** A marking in a flower, which serves to insects as a guide to the honey 1879.

Ho·neyless, *a.* 1601. Destitute of honey. *Jul. C.* v. i. 35.

†**Honey-month.** 1696. [After next.] The first month after marriage –1710.

Honeymoon (hʊ·nimūn), *sb.* 1546. The first month after marriage. Now, usually, the holiday spent together by a newly-married couple, before settling down at home. Also *transf.*

And now their honey-moon, that late was clear, Doth pale, obscure, and tenebrous appear BRETON. *transf.* In the Honey-moon of his Accession BOLINGB. Hence **Ho·neymoon** *v. intr.* to spend the h.

Ho·ney-mouthed, *a.* 1539. Sweet or soft in speech; often implying insincerity.

If I proue hony-mouth'd, let my tongue blister SHAKS.

Ho·ney-pot. ME. **1.** A pot in which honey is stored. **2.** *pl.* A children's game. Also *attrib.* in reference to the posture 1821.

2. To squat low down on its haunches, like a political 'honey-pot' 1886.

Ho·ney-stone. 1795. = MELLITE.

Ho·neysu:cker. 1772. An animal that feeds on honey; *spec.* applied to various small birds, esp. the *Meliphagidæ, Cærebidæ,* etc.; a nectar-bird; a HONEY-EATER.

Honeysuckle (hʊ·nisʊk'l). [ME. *hunisuccle, -soukil,* app. extended from OE. *hunisuce,* ME. *honysouke.*] **1.** A name for the flowers of clover, and other flowers yielding honey. *Obs.* exc. *dial.* **2.** The common name of *Lonicera Periclymenum,* also called Woodbine, a climbing shrub with fragrant yellowish trumpet-shaped flowers; thence extended to the whole genus. *Fly-honeysuckle,* the species *L. Xylosteum* and *L. ciliata.* *Trumpet* or *Coral H.,* a N. American species, *L. sempervirens,* with evergreen foliage and scarlet flowers. 1548. **3.** Applied to shrubs or plants of other genera, in some way resembling the common honeysuckle; e.g. in Australia to species of *Banksia* 1592. **4.** A figure or ornament somewhat resembling a sprig or flower of honeysuckle; *esp.* in *Arch.* 1548.

1. As Honey-Suckles (both the Woodbine and the Trifoile) BACON. 2. *Mids. N.* IV. i. 47. 3. **False H.**, 'the genus *Azalea*' (Miller). **French H.**, name given to *Hedysarum coronarium*, a native of Italy, a leguminous plant, with flowers resembling those of the red clover. **White H.**, *Rhododendron viscosum* (*Azalea viscosa*); also white clover (see 1).

Comb.: **h.-grass** (*dial.*), **-trefoil**, clover.

Ho·neysuckled *a.* overgrown, or scented, with h.

Ho·ney-swee:t, *a.* OE. Sweet as honey, often a term of endearment.

Ho·ney-tongued, *a.* 1588. Speaking sweetly or winningly; using honeyed words.

Honeywort (hʊ·niwɒ̄ɪt). 1597. [See WORT.] A plant of the genus *Cerinthe* of boraginaceous plants, much frequented by bees.

‖**Hong** (hǫŋ) 1726. [ad. Chinese *hang* row, rank.] In China, a series of rooms used as a warehouse, factory, etc.; *spec.* (*a*) one of the foreign factories formerly maintained at Canton; (*b*) the corporation of Chinese merchants at Canton, who before 1842 had the monopoly of trade with Europeans; (*c*) a foreign trading establishment in China or Japan.

Hong(e, obs. inf., pa. t., etc. of HANG *v.*

Honied: see HONEYED.

Honiton (hǫ·nitən). 1851. The name of a town in Devonshire used attrib. to designate kinds of bobbin-lace.

Honk (hǫŋk), *sb.* 1843. [Echoic.] The snort of a pig; *U.S.* and *Canada*, the cry of the wild goose or swan. **b.** The harsh hoot of a motor-horn 1906. Hence **Honk** *v.*

Honor, Honorable: see HONOUR, etc.

†**Honorance.** ME. [a. OF., f. *honorer*; see -ANCE.] The action of honouring or doing homage; honour -1716.

Honorarium (hǫn-, ǫnǒrēᵊ·riǒm). *Pl.* -ums, -a. 1658. [Late L. *honorarium*, adj. neut. sing. used subst.] An honorary reward; a fee for (professional) services rendered.

The emoluments and honoraria of physicians 1895. So **Ho·norary** *sb.* (now *rare* or *Obs.*).

Honorary (ǫ·nŏrări), *a.* 1614. [ad. L. *honorarius*, f. *honor*; see -ARY.] **1.** Denoting or bringing honour; conferred or rendered in honour. **2.** *spec.* Conferred or rendered merely for the sake of honour, without the usual adjuncts 1661. **3.** Holding a title or position conferred as an honour, without emolument, or without the usual duties, privileges, etc.; titulary. Also, giving services (as secretary, treasurer, etc.) without emolument. 1705. **4.** Depending on honour; said of an obligation which cannot be legally enforced 1794.

1. The simple crown of olive, an h. reward GROTE. 2. H. titles or degrees 1813. *H. monument*, a cenotaph. 3. H. colonel of the 13th Infantry Regiment 1873. Phr. *H. feud* (Law): a title of nobility descendible to the eldest son.

Honorific (ǫnŏri·fik), *a.* (*sb.*) 1650. [ad. L. *honorificus*, f. *honor* + *-ficus* making, -FIC.] **1.** Doing or conferring honour; importing honour or respect; *spec.* applied to phrases, words, forms of speech, used, esp. in certain Oriental languages, to express respect. **2.** *sb.* An honorific word or phrase 1879.

1. The epithet Abu, father, is h. KEATINGE.

Honour, honor (ǫ·nəɪ), *sb.* ME. [a. OF. *onor, -ur, honor, -ur* (mod. *honneur*):—L. *honorem.* *Honor* and *honour* were equally frequent down to the 17th c. In England *honour* is now generally accepted, *honor* in U.S.] **1.** High respect, esteem, or reverence, accorded to exalted worth or rank; deferential admiration or approbation; as felt, rendered, or received. **2.** Personal title to high respect or esteem; honourableness; elevation of character; a fine sense of and strict allegiance to what is due or right 1548. **b.** Word of honour (*arch.*) 1658. **3.** (Of a woman) Chastity, purity; good name ME. **4.** Exalted rank or position; dignity, distinction ME. **b.** With possess. pron., = 'honourable personality': now a formal title, esp. for County Court judges 1553. **5.** (Usu. in *pl.*) Something conferred or done as a token of respect or distinction; a mark of high regard; *esp.* a position or title of rank, a dignity ME. †**b.** A bow or curtsy -1805. **c.** *pl.* Courtesies rendered, as at an entertainment 1659. **d.** *pl.* Special distinction gained, in an examination, for proficiency beyond that required for a pass 1782. **6.** A source or cause of honour; one who or that which does credit (*to*) 1568. **b.** (Usu. in *pl.*) A decoration, adornment, ornament (*poet.*) 1613. **7.** *Law.* A seigniory of several manors held under one baron or lord paramount ME. **8. a.** *Cards.* (Chiefly *pl.*) *Whist.* The ace, king, queen, and knave of trumps (*Bridge*, the ten also). *Ombre* and *Quadrille.* The aces of spades and clubs, and the lowest card of the trump suit. 1674. **b.** *Golf.* The privilege of playing first from the tee 1896.

1. To shew my h. for them STEELE. Deie we raþer wiþ onour R. GLOUC. 2. I could not love thee, dear, so much, Lov'd I not H. more LOVELACE. Say, what is H.? 'Tis the finest sense Of justice which the human mind can frame WORDSW. 3. So she may ..Her h. and her name save GOWER. 4. The king is likewise the fountain of h. BLACKSTONE. 5. Weare it for an Honor in thy Cappe SHAKS. Papists were admitted in crowds to offices and honors MACAULAY. c. Phr. *To do the honours.* *Honours of war*: the privileges granted to a capitulating force, as of marching out under arms with colours flying and drums beating. 6. Erasmus the honor of learning of all oure time ASCHAM. b. He..beares his blushing Honors thicke vpon him *Hen. VIII*, III. ii. 354.

Phrases. **a.** *Comm. For* (*the*) *h.* (*of..*): said of the acceptance or payment of a bill of exchange (which has been refused by the drawee and duly protested) by a third party to protect the credit of the drawer or indorser. **b.** *In h.*: as a moral duty: sometimes implying that there is no legal obligation. **c.** *On* or *upon one's h.*: a phrase staking the personal credit of the speaker on the truth of his statement; used formally by members of the House of Lords in their judicial capacity; hence, an expression of strong assurance. **d.** *To do h. to*: to treat with h., confer h. upon; to do credit to. **e.** *H. bright* (colloq.): a protestation of (or interrog. an appeal to) one's h. or sincerity 1819. **f.** *Code* or *law of h.*: the set of rules or customs which regulate the conduct of a class of persons according to a conventional standard of h. **g.** *Court of h.*: a court or tribunal for determining questions concerning the laws or principles of h., as the courts of chivalry in former days. See also AFFAIR, DEBT, LEGION, MAID, POINT, WORD *of h.*

Comb.: **h.-court**, a court held within an h. or seigniory (sense 7); **-man** (also *honours-man*), one who has taken, or studies for, academical honours (sense 5 d); so **honours degree, honour(s) school; -point** (*Her.*), the point just above the fess-point of an escutcheon; **-policy**, a policy wherein it is stipulated that the policy should be deemed sufficient proof of interest.

Honour, honor (ǫ·nəɪ), *v.* ME. [a. OF. (*h*)*onorer, -urer, -ourer*, etc. (mod. *honorer*):—L. *honorare*, f. *honorem.*] †**1.** *trans.* To do honour to, pay worthy respect to; to worship, perform one's devotions to; to do obeisance or homage to; to venerate -1697. **2.** To hold in honour, respect highly; to reverence, worship; to regard or treat with honour ME. **3.** To confer honour or dignity upon; to do honour or credit to; to grace ME. **4.** *Comm.* To accept or pay (a bill of exchange, etc.) when due. Also *fig.* 1706.

1. They..h. with full Bowls their friendly Guest DRYDEN. 2. H. thy father and thy mother *Exod.* XX. 12. 3. Thus shal ben honoured, whom euere the king wile honoure WYCLIF *Esther* vi. 9. A Custome More honour'd in the breach, then the obseruance *Haml.* I. iv. 16. 4. Nature has written a letter of credit upon some men's faces, which is honoured almost wherever presented THACKERAY.

Honourable, honor- (ǫ·nərăb'l), *a.* (*sb.*) ME. [a. OF. *honorable, honurable*; ad. L. *honorabilis*, f. *honorare*; see -BLE.] **1.** Worthy of being honoured; entitled to respect, esteem, reverence. †**b.** Respectable in quality or amount; decent -1666. **2.** Of distinguished rank; noble, illustrious ME. **b.** Applied as an official or courtesy title 1450. **3.** Characterized by or accompanied with honour ME.; consistent with honour or reputation 1548. **4.** Showing or doing honour ME. **5.** Upright, honest; the reverse of base 1592.

1. He [Crist] is honurabile till all HAMPOLE. Marriage is h., but House-keeping is a Shrew SWIFT. b. Dined with Lord Cornbury. who kept a very honorable table EVELYN. 2. Descended from an honorable family MACAULAY. b. The prefix 'Honourable' (Hon.) is given to younger sons of Earls and sons and daughters of peers below the rank of Marquess, to all present or past Maids of Honour, all Justices of the High Court (not being Lords Justices nor Lords of Appeal), to Lords of Session, the Lord Provost of Glasgow (during office), and especially to members of Governments or of Executive Councils in India and the Colonies. In the U.S. it is given to members of both Houses of Congress, and of State Legislatures, to judges, justices, etc. *Honourable* is also applied to the House of Commons collectively; 'honourable member' or 'gentleman' is applied to members individually; also formerly to members of the East India Company, etc. *Most Honourable* is applied to Marquesses; also to the Order of the Bath and H.M. Privy Council (collectively). *Right Honourable* is applied to peers below the rank of Marquess, to Privy Councillors, and to certain civil functionaries, as the Lord Mayors of London, York, and Belfast, and the Lord Provosts of Edinburgh and Glasgow; sometimes, also, in courtesy, to the sons and daughters of persons holding courtesy titles. 3. Sure the Match Were rich and h. *Two Gent.* III. i. 64. To effect an h. peace LYTTON. 4. An h. monument to his memory BOSWELL. 5. For Brutus is an H. man *Jul. C.* III. ii. 87–8. The best and most h. course RALEIGH.

B. *sb.* **a.** An honourable or distinguished person. **b.** One who has the title of Honourable. So *right h.* (colloq.) ME.

Six bear courtesy titles or are Honourables WARREN. Hence **Ho·nourableness, honor-. Ho·nourably, honor-** *adv.* in an h. manner.

Honourer, honorer (ǫ·nərəɪ). ME. [-ER[1].] One who honours; †a worshipper.

Ho·nourless, *a.* 1560. [-LESS.] Destitute of honour; unhonoured, or unworthy of honour.

Hont, etc., obs. f. HUNT, etc.

Hoo (hū), *int.* and *sb.* 1606. A natural exclam., used as a call to attract attention, etc. Also imitative of the sound of an owl, the wind, etc. (Cf. WHOO.) So **Hoo·oo.** Hence **Hoo** *v. intr.* to make the sound 'hoo!'.

Hoo, ME. sp. of Ho *int.* and *v.*

Hooch (hūtʃ). *U.S. slang.* 1903. Also **hootch.** [Abbrev. Alaskan *hoochinoo*, a powerful alcoholic drink.] Alcoholic liquor, spirits.

Hood (hud), *sb.* [OE. *hōd* str. masc. :— OTeut. **hōdo-z*, f. *hōd-*, in ablaut relation with **hattuz* HAT, q.v.] **1.** A covering for the head and neck (and sometimes the shoulders), either forming part of a larger garment (as the hood of a cowl or cloak) or separate; in the latter sense applied in 14–16th c. to a soft covering for the head worn under the hat. **b.** A soft covering for the head worn by women; also, the close-fitting head-covering of an infant ME. **c.** *fig.* A cap of foam, mist, or cloud 1814. **2.** As a mark of official, or professional dignity; now *spec.* the badge worn over the gown (or surplice) by university graduates as indicating their degrees ME. †**3.** The part of a suit of armour that covers the head -1874. **4.** A covering put over the head of a hawk to keep her quiet 1575. **5.** Anything serving for a covering, capping, or protection, or resembling a hood in shape or use:

a. The straw covering of a beehive. b. The head or cover of a carriage; the cover of a pump; *Naut.* 'a covering for a companion-hatch, skylight, etc.' (Smyth). c. A dome-shaped projection over a fire-place, chimney, or ventilator; the 'cowl' of a chimney. d. The leathern shield in front of a wooden stirrup. e. *Shipbuilding* (*pl.*) The foremost and aftermost planks, within and without, of a ship's bottom. f. In plants, any hood-like part serving as a covering, esp. the vaulted upper part of the corolla or calyx in some flowers. g. In animals (e.g. the cobra and the hooded seal), a conformation of parts, or an arrangement of colour, suggesting a hood. h. The waterproof folding top or cover of a perambulator, motor car, etc.; (*U.S.*) = BONNET *sb.* 5 f.

6. The hooded seal; = HOOD-CAP 2. 1854.

Comb.: **h.-end** (*Shipbuilding*), the end of any of the planks which fit into the rabbets of the stem and stern posts: **-gastrula**, a form of secondary gastrula resulting from unequal segmentation, an amphigastrula; **-sheaf**, each of two sheaves placed slantwise on the top of a shock of corn so as to carry off the rain. Hence **Hood** *v. trans.* to cover with or as with a h.; sometimes for protection or concealment.

-hood (hud), *suffix.* [ME. *-hod* (*-hode*) :—OE. *-hād* = OHG. *-heit.*] Orig. a distinct sb., meaning 'person, personality, sex, condition, quality, rank', which ultimately survived as a mere suffix. Cf. -HEAD.

Hood-cap (hu·d,kæp). 1842. [f. HOOD *sb.* + CAP *sb.*] **1.** A close cap or bonnet covering the sides of the face, formerly worn by women. **2.** The hooded or bladder-nosed seal, *Cystophora cristata*; so called from having a piece of loose skin over its head, which it inflates when menaced 1864.

Hooded (hu·dėd), *a.* 1440. [f. HOOD *sb.* and *v.*] **1.** Wearing or covered with a hood. **b.** Of a garment: Having a hood attached to it 1590. **2.** Of animals: Having a conformation of parts or an arrangement of colour suggesting a hood 1500. **3.** *Bot.* Hood-shaped, cucullate 1597. **4.** Having a protective covering 1847. **5.** *transf.* and *fig.* Covered; blindfolded; concealed 1652.

1. A h. hawk 1621. †*H. man*: (*a*) a Lollard; (*b*) a native Irishman. 2. **Hooded crow,** *Corvus Cornix.* **H. seal:** see HOOD-CAP 2. **H. serpent** or **snake,** a snake of the family *Elapidæ* or *Najidæ*, having the skin of the neck distensible, so as to resemble a hood; esp. the Indian cobra, *Naja tripudians.*

Hoodie, hoody (hu·di). 1789. [f. as prec. (sense 2) + *-ie*, -Y.] The Hooded or Royston Crow, *Corvus Cornix.* Also **hoodie-crow.**

Hoo·dless, *a.* ME. [-LESS.] Without a hood.

Hoodlum (hu·dlə̆m). *U.S. slang.* 1872. [?] A youthful street rowdy; a dangerous rough.

†Hoo·dman. 1565. A hooded man; the blindfolded player in BLIND-MAN'S-BUFF -1601. So **†Hoo·dman-bli·nd,** blind-man's-buff.

Hoo·d-mould. 1840. A moulding over the head of a window, door, etc.; a label or dripstone. So **Hoo·d-moulding** 1838.

Hoodoo (hū̆·dū̆), *sb.* (*a.*) *U.S.* 1885. [Altered f. VOODOO.] **1.** = VOODOO. **2.** A person or thing whose presence causes bad luck 1889. **B.** *adj.* Unlucky, bringing bad luck 1889.

Hoodwink (hu·dwiŋk), *v.* 1562. [f. HOOD *sb.* + WINK *v.*] **1.** *trans.* To cover the eyes with a hood or the like; to blindfold. **2.** *fig.* To cover up from sight 1600. **3.** *fig.* To blindfold mentally; to 'throw dust in the eyes of', humbug 1610. **†4.** *intr.* To wink. MILT.

1. Hawthorne's face was hoodwinked with a cloake 1631. 2. *Temp.* IV. i. 206. 3. The public..is easily hoodwinked 1756. Hence **Hoo·dwink** *sb.* †the act of hoodwinking; †the game of blind-man's-buff; a blind. **†Hoo·dwink** *a.* blindfold.

Hoodwort (hu·dwɒɹt). [f. HOOD *sb.* + WORT.] An American species of *Scutellaria* or Skull-cap, *S. laterifolia.*

Hoody: see HOODIE.

Hoof (hūt), *sb.* Pl. **hoofs,** occas. **hooves.** [Com. Teut.; OE. *hōf*:—OTeut. type **hōfo-z*:—pre-Teut. **kō-pos.*] **1.** The horny sheath which encases the ends of the digits or the foot of quadrupeds forming the order *Ungulata*, primarily that of the horse and other equine animals. Also *fig.* **2.** A hoofed animal, as the smallest unit of a herd or drove 1535; hence, †a fragment, particle 1655. **3.** The human foot (*joc.* or *derogative*) 1598.

1. Clattering flints batter'd with clanging hoofs TENNYSON. Phr. *To show the cloven h.* (see CLOVEN). 2. There shal not one hooffe be left behynde COVERDALE *Exod.* x. 26. 3. Phr. *To beat, pad, be upon the h.*: to be on the move. *To see a person's h. in anything*, to detect his influence in it. *Under the h.*: downtrodden.

Comb.: **h.-cushion, -pad,** a pad or cushion to prevent a horse's foot or shoe from striking or cutting the fellow foot; **-pick.**

Hence **Hoof** *v. intr.* to go on foot; *trans.* to strike with the h. **Hoo·fy** *a.* having a h. or hoofs.

Hoo·f-bound, *a.* (*sb.*) 1598. *Farriery.* Affected with a painful dryness and contraction of the hoof; lamed by having the shoe put on too tight. *sb.* A name for this affection.

Hoofed (hūft, hū·fėd), *a.* and *ppl. a.* Also **hooved** (hūvd). 1513. [f. HOOF *sb.* and *v.* + -ED.] **1.** Having hoofs, ungulate; as *broad-h.* **2.** Beaten with hoofs 1860.

Hooflet (hū·flėt). 1834. [-LET.] One of the divisions of a cloven hoof.

Hook (huk), *sb.* [OE. *hōc.* See also HAKE *sb.*[2]] **1.** A length of metal, or piece of other material, bent back, or fashioned with a sharp angle, adapted for catching hold, dragging, sustaining suspended objects, or the like. (Often qualified to indicate shape or use, as *boat-*, *chain-*, *chimney-h.*, etc.) **b.** *Zool.* and *Bot.* A recurved and pointed organ or appendage of an animal or plant 1666. **2.** A slender bent piece of wire, usually armed with a barb, which is attached to a fishing-line and carries the bait; an angle; *fig.* a snare, a catch ME. **3.** A curved instrument with a cutting edge, as a *weed-hook*, a *reaping-hook* OE. **4.** The crook or pin on which a door or gate is hung; forming the fixed part of the hinge ME. **†5.** A shepherd's crook -1697. **6.** *Shipbuilding.* A bent piece of timber used to strengthen an angular framework. Cf. FUTTOCK. 1611. **7.** A sharp bend or angle, esp. in a river (now in proper names) 1563. **8. a.** A hook-shaped character or symbol; a 'pothook' 1668. **†b.** *pl.* Brackets (in printing); also, inverted commas 1680-1806. **c.** *Mus.* One of the lines or marks at the end of the stem of a quaver (♪), etc. 1782. **9.** A projecting corner, point, or spit of land. [app. a. Du. *hoek.*] 1855. **10.** *Cricket*, etc. The act of hooking 1897.

2. Farewell, Loue..Thy bayted hokes shall tangle me no more WYATT. 3. *Prov.* Ill shearer ne'er a good h. had. 7. The very straight way that hath neither h. ne crook FOXE.

Phrases. *By h. and* (*or*) *by crook*: by any means, fair or foul. *Off the hooks*: †out of order; †to excess; †out of humour or spirits; at once, summarily. *To drop* (etc.) *off the hooks*, to die (*slang*). *On one's own h.*: on one's own account, at one's own risk (*colloq.*). *To sling* or *take one's hook*: to make off, decamp (*colloq.*).

Comb.: **h. and butt, h.-butt,** 'a mode of scarfing timber so that the parts resist tensile strain to part them' (Knight); **-climber,** a plant that climbs by means of its own hooklets, as members of the genera *Galium* and *Rubus*; **-pin,** a draw-pin; **-scarf, -scarf-joint** = *hook-butt*; **-squid,** a decapodous cephalopod of the family *Onychoteuthididæ*, having long tentacles armed with hooks, the bases of which are furnished with suckers; **-tip,** a moth of the genus *Platypteryx*, having the tips of the wings hook-shaped; **-wrench,** a spanner with a bent end adapted to grasp and turn a nut or coupling piece.

Hook (huk), *v.* ME. [f. prec. sb.] **1.** *trans.* To make hook-like or hooked (*rare*). **2.** *intr.* To bend as a hook ME. **3.** *intr.* To move with a sudden twist or jerk. Now *slang* or *dial.* To make off. Also *hook it.* ME. **4.** *trans.* To lay hold of with a hook; to make fast, attach, or secure with or as with a hook or hooks; to fasten together with hooks, or hooks and eyes 1611. **5.** *intr.* (for *refl.*) To attach oneself or be attached with or as with a hook. *H. on* (fig.): to join on. 1597. **6.** *trans.* To snatch with a hook; to steal 1615. **7.** To catch (a fish) with a hook 1771. Also *fig.* **8.** *transf.* and *fig.* **a.** To drag. **b.** To attach as with a hook. 1577. **c.** *Golf.* To drive (the ball) widely to the left hand. *Cricket.* = DRAW *v.* I. 12. 1857. **d.** *Boxing.* To strike (one's opponent) a swinging blow with the elbow bent 1898. **e.** *Rugby Football.* To secure and pass (the ball) backward with the foot in a scrummage 1906. **9.** To link by a hook or bent part 1823. **10.** To catch with the horns, attack with the horns, as a cow. Also *absol.* *U.S.* 1837.

3. He slipped from her and hooked it MAYHEW. 4. *To h. on, in, up*, to attach by means of a hook. 5. Go with her, with her: hooke-on, hooke-on SHAKS. 6. To h. the money and hide it MARK TWAIN. 7. *fig.* The first woman who fishes for him, hooks him THACKERAY. 9. He hooked his arm into Tom's HUGHES.

‖Hookah (hu·kă). 1763. [a. Arab. *ḥuqqah* casket, vase, cup, etc.] A pipe for smoking, of Eastern origin, having a long flexible tube, the smoke being drawn through water contained in a vase; the narghile of India.

Hook and eye, hook-and-eye. 1578. A metallic fastening, esp. for a dress, consisting of a hook of flattened wire, and an eye or wire loop on which the hook catches. Also *fig.*

Hook-bill. 1613. [See BILL *sb.*[1] and [2].] **1.** A billhook. **2.** 'The curved beak of a bird' (Ogilvie). **Hoo·k-billed** *a.* having a curved bill.

Hooked (hukt, hu·kėd), *a.* OE. [f. HOOK *sb.* or *v.*] **1.** Hook-shaped; hamate. **2.** Having a hook or hooks ME.

Hooker[1] (hu·kəɹ). 1567. [f. HOOK *v.* + -ER [1].] One who or that which hooks.

Hooker[2] (hu·kəɹ). 1641. [a. Du. *hoeker.*] **1.** A two-masted Dutch coasting or fishing vessel. **2.** A one-masted fishing smack on the Irish coast, similar to a hoy in build. Also *attrib.* **3.** Applied depreciatively or fondly to a ship 1823.

Hooklet (hu·klėt). 1816. [-LET.] A minute hook; esp. in *Nat. Hist.*

Hook-nose. 1681. A nose of a hooked shape with a downward curve; an aquiline nose. So **Hook-nosed** *a.*

Hooky (hu·ki), *a.* 1552. [f. HOOK *sb.* + -Y.] Hook-shaped; hooked.

Hool, obs. f. WHOLE.

‖Hoolee, holi (hū·lī, hōu·lī). *E. Indies.* 1687. [Hindī *hōlī.*] The great carnival of the Hindoos, held at the approach of the vernal equinox, in honour of Krishna and the Gopīs or milkmaids.

Hooligan (hū·ligăn). *slang.* 1898. [app. orig. the name of an Irish family in S.E. London conspicuous for ruffianism.] A (young) street rowdy or ruffian.

It is no wonder..that H. gangs are bred in these vile. byways *Daily News*, 26 July 1898. Hence **Hoo·liganism.**

‖Hoolock (hū·lǫk). 1809. [a. *hulluk*, native name.] The Black Gibbon, *Hylobates Hoolock*, native of Assam.

Hoom(e, obs. ff. HOME.

Hoop (hūp), *sb.*[1] [Late OE. *hōp*:—OTeut. type **hōpo-z.*] **1.** A circular band or ring of metal, wood, etc.; esp. a circle of wood or flattened metal for binding together the staves of casks, tubs, etc. Also *fig.* **2.** Applied to rings, bands, or loops, having similar uses 1867. **3.** A circle of wood or iron (orig. a barrel-hoop) which is trundled along by children 1792. **†4.** One of the bands at equal intervals on a quart pot; hence, the quantity of liquor contained between two of these -1609. **5.** A measure of corn, etc. of varying capacity. Now *local.* ME. **6.** A circle of whalebone, steel, or other elastic material, used to expand the skirt of a woman's dress; hence, a hoop-petticoat or -skirt 1548. **7.** A finger-ring 1500. **8.** Any hoop-like structure or figure; a circle, ring, arc 1530. **9.** One of the iron arches used in croquet 1872.

1. *fig.* The friends thou hast, and their adoption tride, Grapple them to thy Soule, with hoopes of Steele *Haml.* I. iii. 63. 4. 2 *Hen. VI*, IV. ii. 72. 6. The swelling h. sustains The rich brocade PRIOR. 7. A hoope of Gold, a paltry Ring *Merch. V.* v. i. 147.

Comb.: **h.-ash,** *Fraxinus sambucifolia*; also, the American Hackberry, *Celtis occidentalis*; **-bee,** a burrowing bee of the genus *Eucera*; **-cramp,** 'a ring-clutch for holding the ends of a hoop which are lapped over each other' (Knight); **-iron,** (*a*) thin flat bar-iron of which hoops are made; (*b*) the iron rod with which a child's h. is trundled; **-net,** a fishing-net, butterfly-net, etc. held open by a ring at its mouth; **-ring,** a ring consisting of a plain band; also, a finger-ring encircled with stones in a cut-down setting; **-shell,** a shell of the genus *Trochus*, a top-shell; **-skirt** = HOOP-PETTICOAT; **-snake,** a snake fabled to take its tail in its mouth and roll along like a h., *spec.* the harmless *Abastor erythrogrammus* of U.S.; **-tree,** *Melia sempervirens*; **-wood,** a tree yielding wood for hoops; in Jamaica *Calliandra latifolia*; in U.S. the Hoop-ash.

Hoop, *sb.*[2] ME. [f. HOOP *v.*[2] Cf. WHOOP *sb.* and *int.*, F. *houp* int.] **1.** A cry or call of 'hoop'. **2.** The sound attending hooping-cough 1811.

Hoop, *sb.*[3] 1481. [a. F. *huppe*:—pop.L. *ūpupa*, for *upupa* HOOPOE.] **†1.** The HOOPOE -1708. **2.** A local name for the Bullfinch. [? a different wd.] 1798.

Hoop, *v.*[1] 1440. [f. HOOP *sb.*[1]] **1.** To bind or fasten round with a hoop or hoops. **2.** *transf.* and *fig.* To encircle; to bind together, as the staves of a tub 1541.

Hoop, *v.*[2] ME. [a. F. *houper*, f. *houp*, imitative of the cry; see HOOP *sb.*[2]] **1.** *intr.* To utter a hoop. **†2.** To shout with astonishment. SHAKS. **3.** To make the sound characteristic of hooping-cough 1822.

1. Ther-with-al they shriked and they howped CHAUCER. 2. *A. Y. L.* III. ii. 203.

Hoop, *int.* = WHOOP.

Hooper[1] (hū·pəɹ). ME. [f. HOOP *v.*[1] + -ER [1].] One who fits hoops on casks, barrels, etc.; a cooper.

Hoo·per[2]. 1556. [f. HOOP *v.*[2] + -ER [1].] **1.** One who hoops or cries 'hoop'; only in *hoopers hide* = hide-and-seek 1719. **2.** The Whooping, Whistling, or Wild Swan, *Cygnus musicus* (*ferus*); so called from its cry.

Hoo·ping-cough. 1747. A contagious disease chiefly affecting children, and characterized by short, violent, and convulsive coughs followed by a long sonorous inspiration called the hoop (whoop); the chin-cough. Also WHOOPING-COUGH.

Hoop-la (hū·plā). 1909. [f. HOOP *sb.*[1] + LA *int.*] A game in which rings are thrown at objects that are won if encircled.

Hoopoe (hū·pū). 1668. [Alteration of HOOP *sb.*[3], after L. *upupa*, f. the cry (*up, up*) of the bird.] A bird of the family *Upupidæ*, esp. the typical *Upupa epops*, conspicuous by its variegated plumage and large erectile crest.

Hoo:p-pe·tticoat. 1711. **1.** A petticoat or skirt stiffened and expanded by hoops. **2.** A name for plants of the genus *Corbularia*; from the shape of the flower 1840.

Hoo·p-stick. 1703. **1.** A thin pliable stick or sapling suitable for making cask-hoops. **2.** One of the arched rails forming the framework of a carriage-head. W. FELTON.

Hoosh (hūʃ). *slang.* 1905. [?] Thick soup.

Hoosier (hū·ʒəɹ). *U.S.* 1833. [?] A nickname for a native of Indiana.

Hoot (hūt), *sb.* 1600. [f. HOOT *v.*] **1.** A loud inarticulate shout, outcry; *spec.* a shout of disapprobation or obloquy; the sound of a motor-horn. **2.** The cry of an owl 1795. **3.** Hoot owl, the Tawny Owl, *Syrnium aluco* 1885.

Phr. *Not to care a hoot* or *two hoots* (orig. U.S.).

Hoot (hūt), *v.* [ME. *hūten*, perh. echoic, gave later *hout, howt*, altered in 17th c. to *hoot.*] **1.** *intr.* To shout, call out, make an inarticulate vocal noise; now, esp., to utter loud sounds of disapproval or obloquy. Also with *at* or *after*. **2.** *trans.* To assail with shouts of disapproval or contempt ME. **3.** *intr.* Applied to the cry of some birds, esp. the owl 1500; also to the sounds produced by a siren, fog-signal, etc. 1883.

Hoot (hut), *int.* *Sc.* and *n. dial.* 1681. A natural exclam. of objection or repulsion; nearly synonymous with *tut!* with which it is combined in the more emphatic *hoot toot.* So **Hoots** *int.* [with advb. *-s.*] 1824.

Hooter (hū·təɹ). 1674. [-ER[1].] One who or that which hoots; e.g. an owl; a steam whistle or siren 1878; a motor-horn 1908.

Hoove (hūv). 1840. [f. OE. *hōf-*, ablaut-stem of HEAVE *v.*] A disease of cattle, characterized by inflation of the stomach, usually due to eating too much green fodder.

Hop (hǫp), *sb.*[1] [In 15th c. *hoppe*, a. MDu. *hoppe*, Du. *hop*; ult. origin unkn.] **1.** (Usu. in *pl.*) The ripened cones of the female hop-plant, used for giving a bitter flavour to malt liquors, etc. **2.** A climbing perennial diœcious plant (*Humulus Lupulus*, N.O. *Urticaceæ*, suborder *Cannabineæ*), with rough lobed leaves like those of the vine. Much cultivated for the green cones of the female plant. 1538.

Comb.: **h.-back**, a vessel with a perforated bottom for straining off the hops from the liquor in making beer; **-bind, -bine**, the climbing stem of the hop-plant; **-clover** = *hop-trefoil*; **-flea**, a very small beetle (*Phyllotreta* or *Haltica concinna*), destructive to the hop-plant; **-fly**, a species of aphis (*Phorodon humuli*), destructive to the hop-plant; **h. frog-fly, h. froth-fly**, a species of froth-fly (*Aphrophora interrupta* or *Amblycephalus interruptus*), destructive to the hop-plant; **h. hornbeam** (see HORNBEAM); **-jack** = *hop-back*; **-mildew**, a parasitic fungus of genus *Sphærotheca*, infesting the h.; **-oast**, a kiln for drying hops; **-pillow**, a pillow stuffed with hops to produce sleep; **-pocket** (see POCKET); **-pole**, a tall pole on which h.-plants are trained; **-tree**, a N. Amer. shrub, *Ptelea trifoliata*, N.O. *Rutaceæ*, with bitter fruit which has been used as a substitute for hops; **-trefoil**, a name for yellow clover (*Trifolium procumbens*); also applied to the hop medick, *Medicago lupulina*; **-vine**, the trailing stem or bine of the hop-plant, or the whole plant. See also Main Words.

Hop (hǫp), *sb.*[2] 1508. [f. HOP *v.*[1]] **1.** An act, or the action, of hopping; a short spring, esp. on one foot. **b.** One stage of a long-distance flight in a flying machine 1909. **2.** *slang* or *colloq.* An informal dance 1731.

1. To take the ball on the h. 1888. Phr. **Hop, step, and jump** (also *h., skip, and jump*, etc.): the action of making these three movements in succession; an athletic exercise in which the players try who can cover most ground with these movements. Also *transf.* and *fig.* Also *attrib.*, and as *vb. intr.*

Hop (hǫp), *v.*[1] Pa. t. and pple. **hopped, hopt** (hǫpt). [OE. *hoppian* :—OTeut. **huppōjan*, co-radicate with **huppjan* (see HIP *v.*[1]). The OTeut. stem *hupp-* prob. represented a pre-Teut. *kupn-*, f. root *kup-*.] **1.** *intr.* To spring a short way with a leap, or a succession of leaps; said of persons, animals, and things. Now implying a short or undignified leap. **b.** *spec.* Of animals: To move by leaps with both or all the feet at once 1440. **c.** Of a person: To leap on one foot, or move onwards by a succession of such leaps 1700. **2.** To dance (only playful) ME. **3.** To limp 1700. **4.** *trans.* To hop or jump on to or over 1900.

1. Why hoppe ye so, ye greate hilles? COVERDALE *Ps.* lxvii[i]. 16. **b.** H. as light as bird from brier SHAKS. **3.** Away he hops with his crutch DE FOE.

Hop the twig, hop it (*slang*): to go away quickly, 'be off'.

Hop (hǫp), *v.*[2] 1572. [f. HOP *sb.*[1]] **1.** *trans.* To impregnate or flavour with hops. (Chiefly in *pass.*) **2.** *intr.* Of the plant: To produce hops 1848. **3.** To gather or pick hops 1717.

Hope (hōᵘp), *sb.*[1] [Late OE. *hopa*, earlier *tō-hopa*, wk. masc. First found in LG. areas, whence in HG. and Scand.] **1.** Expectation of something desired; desire combined with expectation. Also in pl., in sing. sense. **b.** Personified; esp. as one of the three heavenly graces. (1 *Cor.* xiii. 13.) ME. †**2.** Expectation, prospect ME. **3.** *transf.* Ground of hope; promise; a person or thing that gives hope for the future; that which is hoped for ME. ¶See also FORLORN HOPE.

1. H. springs eternal in the human breast POPE. Great hopes were entertained at Whitehall that [etc.] MACAULAY. **b.** Fair H., with smiling face but ling'ring foot HAN. MORE. **3.** A Child of great hopes 1676. Ihesu Crist oure h. WYCLIF 1 *Tim.* i. 1. Their brave h. SHAKS. Staking his very life on some dark h. SHELLEY.

Hope (hōᵘp), *sb.*[2] [OE. *hop*, app. only in comb.] **1.** A piece of enclosed land, e. g. in the midst of fens or marshes. **2.** A small enclosed valley, esp. the upland part of a mountain valley ME. **3.** An inlet, small bay, haven ME.

Hope (hōᵘp), *v.* [OE. *hopian*, ME. *hopien, hopen.* Like HOPE *sb.*[1], first found in LG. areas.] **1.** *intr.* To entertain expectation of something desired; to look (mentally) with expectation. **2.** *intr.* To trust, have confidence. (Now only a strong case of sense 1.) OE. **3.** *trans.* To expect with desire, or to desire with expectation; to look forward to OE. †**4.** To anticipate; to suppose, think, expect –1632.

1. H. for the best 1726. I hoped for better things from him (*mod.*). **3.** None would live past years again; Yet all h. pleasure in what yet remain DRYDEN. When may we h. to see you SWIFT. **4.** Our Manciple I h. he wil be deed CHAUCER.

Hopeful (hōᵘ·pfŭl), *a.* (*sb.*) 1568. [f. HOPE *sb.*[1] + -FUL.] **1.** Full of hope; feeling hope; expectant of that which is desired 1594; expressive of hope 1607. **2.** Causing or inspiring hope; promising; sometimes ironical 1568. **3.** *sb.* A 'hopeful' boy or girl; chiefly ironical 1720.

1. H. of some reward 1665. **2.** Money to maintain h. students at the University WOOD. Here comes his h. nephew GOLDSM. **3.** Hoards diminish'd by young Hopeful's debts BYRON. Hence **Ho·peful-ly** *adv.*, **-ness.**

Hopeless (hōᵘ·plės), *a.* 1566. [-LESS.] **1.** Destitute of hope; having no hope; despairing 1590. **2.** Of or concerning which there is no hope; despaired of, desperate 1566. †**3.** Unexpected –1624.

1. On this [ice-floe] they spent a dismal and h. night SCORESBY. **2.** H. depravity JOHNSON, maladies MACAULAY. Hence **Ho·peless-ly** *adv.*, **-ness.**

Ho·per. ME. [f. HOPE *v.* + -ER[1].] One who hopes.

Ho·p-ga:rden. 1573. A piece of land devoted to the cultivation of hops.

Hoplite (hǫ·plait). 1727. [ad. Gr. ὁπλίτης, f. ὅπλον weapon, ὅπλα arms; see -ITE.] A heavy-armed foot-soldier of ancient Greece.

Hoplo- (hǫplo), bef. a vowel **hopl-**, comb. f. Gr. ὅπλον weapon, piece of armour, or of ὁπλή hoof, as in **Hoplognathous** (-ǫ·gnăþəs) [Gr. γνάθος] *a.*, 'having the jaw armed' (*Syd. Soc. Lex.*). **Hoplo·podous** [Gr. ὁπλή hoof, πούς, ποδ- foot] *a.*, *Zool.* having the feet protected by hoofs.

Hop-o'-my-thumb (hǫ·pŏmiþv:m). Also **Hopthumb.** 1530. [Orig. *hop on my thombe*, from HOP *v.*[1] (in imperative mood), applied hyperbolically to a very small person.] A dwarf, a pygmy. Cf. *Tom Thumb.*

Hopped (hǫpt), *a.* 1669. [f. HOP *sb.*[1] or *v.*[2] + -ED.] Furnished, mixed, or flavoured with hops.

Hopper[1] (hǫ·pəɹ). ME. [f. HOP *v.*[1] + -ER[1]. The origin of sense 5 is not clear.] **1.** One who hops; in *pl.* a kind of game: see HOPSCOTCH. **2.** That which hops, esp. an insect or insect-larva that hops. Applied to a grasshopper, a froth-hopper, a cheese-hopper, etc. ME. **3.** A receiver like an inverted pyramid or cone, through which grain or anything to be ground passes into the mill; so called because it had originally a hopping or shaking motion ME. **4.** Any article resembling a mill hopper in shape or use 1763. **5.** A basket; *esp.* that in which the sower carries his seed. Now *dial.* ME. **6.** A barge in attendance on a dredging machine, which carries the mud or gravel out to sea and discharges it through an opening in its bottom. Also *h.-barge.* 1759. **7.** *Pianoforte.* A piece attached at the back part of a key to raise the hammer and regulate the distance to which it falls back from the string after striking it. Also called *grasshopper.* 1840. **8.** *attrib.*, as *hopper feed*, etc. 1500.

Comb.: **h.-boy**, 'a name given in mills to a rake which moves in a circle, drawing the meal over an opening through which it falls' (Craig); **-car**, a kind of truck for carrying coal, gravel, etc., shaped like a h., and emptying through an opening at the bottom; **-cock**, a valve for water-closets, etc.; **-hood**, a hooded seal in its second year. Hence **Ho·pperings** *sb. pl.*, gravel retained in the hopper of a gold-washing cradle 1893.

Hopper[2] (hǫ·pəɹ). 1719. [f. HOP *v.*[2] + -ER[1].] **1.** A hop-picker. **2.** A brewer's vat in which the infusion of hops is prepared to be added to the wort (*Cent. Dict.*). **3.** *attrib.*, as *h.-house* 1883.

†**Hoppestere.** [OE. *hoppystre*, f. *hoppian* to hop; see -STER.] A female dancer. In Chaucer used attrib. = 'dancing'. -ME.

Hoppet (hǫ·pėt). Chiefly *n. dial.* 1671. [?dim. f. HOPPER[1].] **1.** A basket, esp. a small hand-basket. **2.** A large bucket, for lowering and raising men and materials in a mine shaft, etc. 1865. **3.** A beehive. *dial.*

Hop-picker. 1760. A labourer who picks the ripe hops from the bines; also, a machine for picking, cleaning, and sorting hops.

Hopping (hǫ·piŋ), *vbl. sb.*[1] ME. [f. HOP *v.*[1] + -ING[1].] **1.** The action of HOP *v.*[1] **2.** A dance; a rural festival ME.

Hopping, *vbl. sb.*[2] 1717. [f. HOP *sb.*[1] or *v.*[2] + -ING[1].] **1.** Hop-picking. **2.** The flavouring of malt liquor with hops 1816.

Hopping, *ppl. a.* 1785. [f. HOP *v.*[1] + -ING[2].] That hops (see HOP *v.*[1]). **Hopping-dick**, name for a species of thrush (*Merula leucogenys*) common in Jamaica, resembling the blackbird. Hence **Ho·ppingly** *adv.*

Hopple (hǫ·p'l), *v.* 1586. [?] *trans.* To fasten together the legs of (a horse, etc.) to prevent it from straying; also *transf.* to fetter (a human being); cf. HOBBLE *v.* 6. Hence **Ho·pple** *sb.* an apparatus for hoppling horses, etc.; *transf.* a fetter.

‖**Hoppo** (hǫ·po). 1711. [Chinese *hoopoo.*] In China: The board of revenue or customs. Also (short for **h.-man**) an officer of the customs.

Hop-sack, hopsack (hǫ·psæk). 1481. [f. HOP *sb.*[1]] **1.** A sack in which hops are packed. **2.** = next, b. 1892.

Hop-sacking. 1884. **a.** A coarse fabric of hemp and jute, of which hop-sacks are made. **b.** Applied to a woollen dress-fabric made with a roughened surface.

Hopscotch (hǫ·pskǫtʃ). 1801. [f. HOP *sb.*[1] + SCOTCH *sb.* a line or scratch.] A children's game, consisting in hopping on one foot and driving forward with it a flat stone from one compartment to another of an oblong figure traced out on the ground, so as always to clear each scotch or line. Also *Hop-score, Hop-scot*, and (earlier) *Scotch-hoppers.*

Hopthumb: see HOP-O'-MY-THUMB.

Ho·p-yard. 1533. = HOP-GARDEN.

Horal (hōᵊ·răl), *a.* 1717. [f. L. *hora* + -AL.] Of or pertaining to an hour or hours. Hence **Ho·rally** *adv.* hourly.

Horary, *sb. rare.* 1631. [ad. late L. *horarium* adj. neut. sing., used subst.] †1. *Eccl.* A book of offices for the canonical hours –1789. 2. An hourly narrative 1864.

Horary (hōᵊ·rări), *a.* 1620. [ad. med.L. *horarius*, f. *hora* HOUR; see -ARY and cf. F. *horaire.*] 1. Of, relating to, or indicating the hours 1664. 2. Occurring every hour 1632. †3. Lasting only for an hour, or a short time.

1. *H. angle* = HOUR-ANGLE. *H. circle*: see CIRCLE *sb.*; also, the circle of hours on a dial-plate. 2. H. shifts Of shirts and waste-coats B. JONS. 3. Melons, Cucumbers, and other H. Fruits FRYER. *H. question* (Astrol.): a question the answer to which is obtained by erecting a figure of the heavens for the moment at which it is propounded 1647.

Horatian (horē¹·ʃiăn), *a.* (*sb.*) 1851. [ad. L. *Horatianus.*] 1. Belonging to or characteristic of the Latin poet Horace, or his poetry. 2. *sb.* The language of Horace.

Horde (hōᵊɹd), *sb.* 1555. [Ult. ad. Turkī *ordā*, also *ordī*, *ordū*, *urdū* camp (see URDU). The initial *h* appears first in Polish.] 1. A tribe or troop of nomads, dwelling in tents or wagons, and migrating from place to place for pasturage, or for war or plunder. 2. *transf.* A great company, esp. of the savage, uncivilized, or uncultivated 1613. b. Of animals: A moving swarm or pack 1834.

1. *Golden H.*, a tribe who possessed the khanate of Kiptchak, in Eastern Russia and western and central Asia, from the 13th c. till 1480. 2. The h. of regicides BURKE. Hence **Horde** *v. intr.* to form a h.; to live as in a h.

Hordein (hǭ·ɹdᵢ̄in). 1826. [f. L. *hordeum* + -IN.] *Chem.* A pulverulent substance obtained from barley-meal; a mixture of starch, cellular tissue, and an azotized body.

Hore, obs. f. HOAR.

Horehound, hoarhound (hōᵊ·rhaund). [OE. *hāre hūne*, f. *hār* hoar, hoary + *hūne* name of some plant; thence ME. *hōrhowne*, altered by pop. etym. to *horehound.* The usual spelling in England, *hore-*, is non-analogical.] 1. A labiate herb, *Marrubium vulgare*, having stem and leaves covered with white cottony pubescence; its aromatic bitter juice is much used as a remedy for coughs, etc. Hence extended to allied herbs, horehound proper being then distinguished as *Common* or *White H.* 2. An extract of the plant *Marrubium vulgare*, used as a remedy for coughs 1562. 3. *attrib.* 1855.

1. **Black, Fetid,** or **Stinking H.,** *Ballota nigra*, a common weed with dull purple flowers; **Water H.,** species of *Lycopus*.

Horizon (horəi·zən, -z'n), *sb.* [ME. *orizont* (Chaucer), *-oun*, a. OF. *orizonte*, *orizon* (mod. *horizon*), ad. late L. *horizontem* (*horizōn*), a. Gr. ὁρίζων (sc. κύκλος) the bounding circle, f. (ult.) ὅρος limit. At first stressed *ho·rizon.*] 1. The boundary-line of that part of the earth's surface visible from a given point; the line at which earth and sky appear to meet. In strict use, the circle bounding that part of the earth's surface which would be visible if no irregularities or obstructions were present (called the *apparent*, *natural*, *sensible*, *physical* or *visible h.*, as dist. from 3), being the circle of contact with the earth's surface of a cone whose vertex is at the observer's eye. On the open sea or a great plain these coincide. 2. *fig.* The boundary or limit of any circle or sphere of view, thought, action, etc.; limit or range of one's knowledge, experience, or interest; occas. = the region so bounded 1607. 3. *Astron.* A great circle of the celestial sphere, the plane of which passes through the centre of the earth and is parallel to that of the sensible horizon of a given place; dist. as the *astronomical*, *celestial*, *mathematical*, *rational*, *real*, or *true h.* ME. b. *transf.* The celestial hemisphere within the horizon of any place 1577. 4. a. The broad ring (usu. of wood) in which an artificial globe is fixed, the upper surface of which represents the plane of the rational horizon 1592. b. *Artificial* or *false h.*: a level reflecting surface, usu. of mercury, used in taking altitudes 1812. 5. *Geol.* A plane of stratification assumed to have been once horizontal and continuous; a stratum characterized by particular fossils 1856. 6. *Zool.* and *Anat.* A level line or surface, as the horizon of the teeth, that of the diaphragm. 7. *attrib.* 1774.

1. And whiten gan the Orisonte shene CHAUCER. Nights Hemisphere had veild the H. round MILT. *P. L.* IX. 52. 2. The Minister, who then began to climb the H. of favour 1659. 3. b. When the Morning Sunne shall rayse his Carre Aboue the Border of this Ho·rizon 3 *Hen. VI*, IV. vii. 81. Hence **Hori·zon** *v.* to furnish with a h.; chiefly in *pa. pple.*; **Hori·zonless** *a.*, visually boundless.

Horizontal (hǫrizǫ·ntăl), *a.* (*sb.*) 1555. [f. L. *horizon*, *horizont-* (see prec.).] 1. Of or belonging to the horizon; on or occurring at the horizon. 2. Parallel to the plane of the horizon; level, flat; measured in a line or plane parallel to the horizon 1638. b. *Bot.* Applied to parts or organs having a position at right angles to the stem or axis 1753. c. *Zool.* and *Anat.* Applied to parts, organs, or markings parallel to a plane supposed to extend from end to end and from side to side of the body 1881.

1. *H. parallax*, the geocentric parallax of a heavenly body when on the horizon. 2. *H. plane* in *Perspective*, a plane at the level of the eye, intersecting the perspective plane at right angles, the line of intersection being the *h. line*. *H.* (*steam*) *engine*, one in which the piston moves horizontally. *H. wheel*, a wheel the plane of which is h., the axis being vertical; in a carriage, the wheel-plate or 'fifth wheel'.

B. *sb.* (the adj. used *ellipt.*) †1. = HORIZON 1555. 2. *ellipt.* A horizontal line, bar, member, etc. 1674.

Hence **Horizo·ntalism,** the quality of being, or of having some part, h. **Ho:rizonta·lity,** h. condition, quality, or position. **Horizo·ntalize** *v.* to place in a h. position; whence **Horizo:ntaliza·tion,** the action of making h.; in *Craniometry*, the placing of the skull with the datum-plane truly h. **Horizo·ntally** *adv.*

†**Horme·tic,** *a. rare.* 1666. [ad. Gr. ὁρμητικός, f. ὁρμᾶν to urge on; see -IC.] Having the property of urging on or impelling –1678.

Hormone (hǭ·ɹmoᵘn). *Physiol. Chem.* 1906. [f. Gr. ὁρμῶν, pres. part. of ὁρμᾶν to urge on.] A substance formed in an organ and serving to excite some vital process, as secretion. Hence **Hormo·nic** *a.*

Horn (hǭɹn), *sb.* [Com. Teut.: OE. *horn* masc. :—OTeut. **horno-*, cogn. w. L. *cornu*; in ablaut relation with Gr. κέρας.]

I. 1. A non-deciduous excrescence, often curved and pointed, consisting of an epidermal sheath growing about a bony core, on the head of certain mammals, as cattle, sheep, goats, antelopes, etc. Also *fig.* b. That borne by the Ram (Aries) and Bull (Taurus) as figured among the constellations, etc.; the stars situated in those parts of the constellations ME. c. Put for 'horned animal' 1588. 2. Each of the two branched appendages on the head of a deer. (These are osseous, deciduous, and (usually) borne only by the male.) OE. 3. †The tusk of an elephant; the tusk of a narwhal 1607. 4. A projection or process on the head of other animals; e.g. the excrescence on the beak of the HORNBILL, the antennæ or feelers of insects and crustaceans, the tentacles of gastropods, esp. of the snail and slug; also, loosely, a crest of feathers, a plumicorn, as in the horned owl, etc. ME. 5. Horns have been attributed to deities, demons, to Moses, etc., and are represented in images, pictures, etc. ME. †6. Cuckolds were said to wear horns on the brow –1822. 7. In Biblical uses: An emblem of power; a means of defence or resistance; hence *h. of salvation* used of God or Christ.

1. c. My Lady goes to kill hornes *L.L.L.* IV. i. 113. 3. Hornes of Iuorie, and Ebenie *Ezek.* xxvii. 15. 4. Phr. *To draw in* (*pull in*, etc.) *one's horns*: to lower one's pretensions: in allusion to the snail's habit of drawing in its retractile tentacles (which bear the eyes), when disturbed. 6. *Much Ado*, II. i. 28. 7. Phr. *To lift up the h.*: to exalt oneself; to show fight.

II. 1. The substance of which the horns of animals are made, as a material for manufacturing purposes, etc. 1545. 2. A structure of the nature of horn; the epidermis or cuticle of which hoofs, nails, corns, the callosities on the camel's legs, etc. consist ME. 3. An article made of horn; the side of a lantern; a horn spoon or scoop, a SHOE-HORN 1483.

1. H. is a still more powerful manure than bone 1843.

III. 1. A vessel formed from, or shaped after, the horn of a cow or other beast, for holding liquid, powder, etc.; a drinking-horn; a powder-flask; etc. Hence a hornful. OE. 2. A wind instrument more or less resembling a horn in shape. Often qualified, as *bugle h.*, *hunting-h.*, etc. OE. b. (More fully *French h.*) An orchestral wind instrument of the trumpet class, developed from the hunting-horn, and consisting of a continuous tube some 17 feet in length, curved for convenience in holding, and having a wide bell and a conoidal mouthpiece 1742. c. An 8-foot reed-stop on an organ 1722. d. An instrument on motor vehicles, etc., sounded as a warning signal 1901. 3. The wind instrument as used in legal process ME.

1. A penne and ink-horne 1583. Phr. *H. of plenty* or *abundance* = CORNUCOPIA. 2. Ther's a Post come from my Master, with his horne full of good newes *Merch. V.* v. i. 47. Phr. *To wind the h.*, to sound the h.; also *fig.* of insects piping or humming. What time the grey-fly winds her sultry h. MILT. *Lycidas* 28. b. The voice was drown'd By the French h. POPE. *English h.* (Fr. *cor anglais*), a wind instrument of the oboe kind, the tenor oboe in F. 3. Phr. *To put* (*denounce*) *to the h.*, to proclaim an outlaw.

IV. 1. A horn-like appendage or ornament worn on the head. (Cf. sense I. 5.) ME. 2. A horn-like projection at each corner of the altar in the Jewish temple; one of the two outer corners of the altar in some churches OE. 3. Each end of a crescent; each extremity of the moon in her first and last quarters; a cusp OE. b. Each tip or end of a bow 1611. 4. Each of the two wings of an army (L. *cornu*) 1533. 5. Each of two (or more) lateral projections, arms, or branches ME. 6. a. The awns of barley (*dial.*) 1825. b. *fig.* Rigid branches of leafless trees 1850. 7. A pointed or tapering projection (see below) ME. 8. *Arch.* Each of the Ionic volutes (likened to rams' horns); the projections of an abacus, etc. OE. 9. *Naut.* One of the jaws, or semicircular ends of booms and gaffs; also, the outer end of a cross-tree 1794. 10. *Fortif.* = HORNWORK 1709. 11. Each of the alternatives of a dilemma (schol. L. *argumentum cornutum*), on which one is figured as liable to be impaled 1548.

1. High head attire piked with horns CAMDEN. 2. *Exod.* xxvii. 2. 3. The Idol Isis, bearing two hornes of the Moone MORYSON. 5. Within the long horns of a sandy bay MORRIS. 7. a. The beak of an anvil. b. Each of the crutches on a side-saddle; also the high pommel of a Spanish saddle. c. A promontory. d. A mountain peak (occas. *fig.*, or = Swiss-Ger. *horn*). e. A part of a plant shaped like a horn, beak, or spur. f. The minute apex of a Hebrew letter. 11. Both the Horns of Fates Dilemma wound COWLEY.

attrib. and *Comb.* 1. General: as *h.-blower*; *h. bow*, *cup*, *lantern*; *h. measurement*, *shavings*, etc. 2. Special: †**h. ABC** = HORN-BOOK; †**-beast,** a horned beast; **-beech** = HORNBEAM; †**-coot** = HORN-OWL; **-core,** the central bony part of the h. of quadrupeds, a process of the frontal bone; **-distemper,** a disease of cattle, affecting the internal substance of the horn; **-drum** (*Hydraulics*), a water-raising wheel divided into sections by curved partitions (Knight); **-eyed** *a.*, having a horny film over the eye, dull-eyed; **-fly,** a dipterous insect, *Hæmatobia serrata*, which clusters on the horns of cattle; **-frog,** the horned frog; **h. grass,** a grass of the genus *Ceratochloa*; **-lead,** chloride of lead, which assumes a horny appearance on fusing; **-maker,** †one who cuckolds; **-mercury,** chloride of mercury; **-nose,** a rhinoceros; †**-penny** = HORNGELD; **-pike,** the garfish; **-pith,** the soft porous bone which fills the cavity of a h.; **-plant,** a seaweed, *Ecklonia buccinalis*; **-pock, -pox,** a mild form of small-pox or chicken-pox; **-poppy,** the Horned Poppy, *Glaucium luteum*; **-pout** (*U.S.*), a name of fishes of the genus *Amiurus*, esp. *A. catus*; **-quicksilver,** = *horn-mercury*; **-rimmed** *a.*, (wearing spectacles) having rims made of horn; **-snake,** the Pine Snake or Bull Snake, *Coluber melanoleucus*; **-tail,** an insect of the family *Uroceridæ*, having a prominent h. on the abdomen of the male; **-weed,** (*a*) = HORNWORT; (*b*) = *horn-plant*.

Horn (hǭɹn), *v.* ME. [f. prec.] 1. To furnish with horns or horn. †2. To cuckold 1550–1823. 3. To butt or gore with the horns 1599. b. *To h. in*: to 'butt in' (*U.S.*) 1912. 4. To adjust (the frame of a ship) so as to be at right angles to the line of the keel 1850. †5. *Sc. Law.* To 'put to the horn' –1705.

Hornbeak (hǭ·ɹnbīk). Now *dial.* 1565. = HORN-FISH 1.

Hornbeam (hǭ·ɹnbīm). 1568. [f. HORN *sb.* + BEAM.] A tree, *Carpinus Betulus*, indigenous in England; so called from its hard, tough, close-grained wood. Also *C. americana*, the Blue Beech. (Earlier called *hard-beam*.)

Hop Hornbeam, the genus *Ostrya*, so called from the hop-like appearance of the ripe catkins; it has two species, *O. vulgaris* of Southern Europe, and *O. virginica* of America.

Hornbill (hǭ·ɹnbil). 1773. [f. HORN *sb.* + BILL *sb.*[2]] A bird of the family *Bucerotidæ*, so called from the horn-like excrescence surmounting the bill.

H. Cuckoo, the keel-billed Cuckoo, *Crotophaga*, of N. America.

Hornblende (hǭ·ɹnblend). Also **-blend.** 1770. [a. Ger. *hornblende*, f. *horn* horn + BLENDE.] *Min.* A mineral closely allied to augite, and composed chiefly of silica, magnesia, and lime. It is a constituent of many rocks, as granite, syenite, etc., and has numerous varieties, which are sometimes all included under the name AMPHIBOLE. It is usually of a dark brown, black, or greenish-black colour. Also *attrib.*, as in **hornblende schist, slate,** hornblende rock of a schistose nature. Hence **Hornble·ndic** *a.* of the nature of, or containing h.

Horn-book (hǭ·ɹnbuk). 1588. A leaf of paper containing the alphabet (often, also, the ten digits, some elements of spelling, and the Lord's Prayer) protected by a thin plate of translucent horn, and mounted on a tablet of wood with a handle. See also BATTLEDORE 3. Also *transf.* a primer.

Yes, yes, he teaches boyes the Horne-booke *L. L. L.* v. i. 49.

Horned (hǭ·ɹnėd, hǭɹnd), *a.* ME. [f. HORN *sb.* + -ED[2].] **1.** Having horns. **2.** Having, bearing, or wearing an appendage, ornament, etc., called a horn; having horn-like projections or excrescences ME. †**3.** Applied to bishops with reference to the shape of the mitre –1651. **4.** Furnished or fitted with horn 1590.

1. Cerastes hornd, Hydrus, and Ellops drear MILT. *P. L.* x. 525. *H. syllogism* (*argument*, etc.): the dilemma 1548. **2.** One side of a Silver Medal we find Moses h. SIR T. BROWNE. **Horned crow** or **pie**, old name of the Hornbill. **H. frog, toad,** a lizard of the genus *Phrynosoma*, having the head and back covered with spikes (*U.S.*). **H. hog,** (*a*) the Babiroussa; †(*b*) a kind of fish with a horn on its head. **H. horse,** the Gnu. †**H.-snout,** the rhinoceros. Also *Horned* LARK, OWL, POPPY, etc. Hence **Ho·rnedness.**

Horner (hǭ·ɹnəɹ). ME. [f. HORN *sb.* or *v.* + -ER[1].] **1.** A worker in horn. **2.** One who blows or winds a horn ME. †**3.** One who cuckolds –1717. †**4.** *Sc. Law.* One who has been 'put to the horn' 1568.

Hornet (hǭ·ɹnėt). [OE. *hyrnetu*, *hyrnet* fem.; either a deriv. of, or associated with, *horn.*] **1.** An insect of the wasp family, esp. the European *Vespa Crabro* and the American *V. maculata*, much larger and stronger than other wasps, and inflicting a more serious sting. Also *transf.* and *fig.* †**2.** The horned beetle or stag-beetle –1598. **3.** An artificial fly for salmon-fishing 1867.

1. Phr. *To bring a hornets' nest about one's ears, arouse a nest of hornets*: to stir up a host of virulent enemies around one. *Comb.*: **h.-clearwing, -hawk, -moth,** names for certain moths of the genus *Sesia*; **-fly,** a dipterous insect of the family *Asilidæ*, a hawk-fly or robber-fly.

Horn-fish. OE. **1.** The garfish, *Belone vulgaris*, so called from its long projecting beak. **2.** The sauger or sand-pike, *Stizostedium canadense* 1885. **3.** A fish of the family *Syngnathidæ*; a pipe-fish.

†**Horngeld.** 12th c. [f. HORN *sb.* + GELD *sb.*] *Old Law.* = CORNAGE –1628.

Hornify (hǭ·ɹnifəi), *v.* 1607. [f. HORNY *a.* + -FY.] **1.** *trans.* To make horny or horn-like 1670. †**2.** To cuckold –1769.

Horning (hǭ·ɹniŋ), *vbl. sb.* ME. [f. HORN *sb.* or *v.*] †**1.** Covering or furnishing with horn. †**2.** Cuckolding, cuckoldry –1762. **3.** *Sc. Law.* 'Putting to the horn'; proclaiming an outlaw 1536. **4.** The fact of becoming a crescent 1646. **5.** *Shipbuilding*: see HORN *v.* 4. 1879.

3. *Letters of h.*: a process of execution issued under the signet directing a messenger to charge a debtor to pay or perform in terms of the letters, under pain of being 'put to the horn', i.e. declared rebel. (Not quite obsolete.)

Hornish (hǭ·ɹniʃ), *a.* 1634. [-ISH.] Of or pertaining to a horn; of the nature of horn.

‖**Hornito** (hornī·to). 1830. [Sp., dim. of *horno* (:—L. *furnus*) oven, furnace.] A low oven-shaped mound of volcanic origin, usually emitting smoke and vapour.

Hornless (hǭ·ɹnlės), *a.* ME. [-LESS.] Without horns.

Horn-mad, *a. arch.* 1579. App. orig. of horned beasts: Enraged so as to be ready to horn any one. Hence of persons: Stark mad; furious. †**b.** Sometimes by word-play: Furious because cuckolded –1822.

b. Why Mistresse, sure my Master is horne mad.. I meane not Cuckold mad, But sure he is starke mad *Com. Err.* II. i. 57.

Horn-owl. 1601. A horned owl, or one having plumicorns on the head, as some species of *Asio* and *Otus*; †a name for the Eagle-owl.

Hornpipe (hǭ·ɹnpəip). ME. **1.** An obsolete wind instrument. So called from having the bell and mouthpiece made of horn. **2.** A lively dance, usually performed by a single person, orig. to the accompaniment of the wind instrument, and associated with the merrymaking of sailors 1485. **3.** A piece of music for such a dance 1789. **4.** *attrib.* 1797.

A..Tabrere That..a Horne pype playd SPENSER.

Horn-plate. 1856. An iron frame attached to the lower part of a carriage or truck and having two guides in which the journal-box of the axle moves; an axle-guard, pedestal.

Horn-silver. 1770. [Ger. *hornsilber.*] *Min.* Native chloride of silver; cerargyrite.

†**Hornslate.** 1791. [Cf. Ger. *hornschiefer.*] *Min.* A schistous form of hornstone.

Hornstone (hǭ·ɹn,stōun). 1668. [tr. Ger. *hornstein*; so named from its appearance.] *Min.* Chert.

Ho·rnswo·ggle, *v. U.S. slang.* 1829. [?] *trans.* To best, swindle, humbug, bamboozle.

†**Horn-wood,** *a.* 1500. [+ WOOD *a.* mad.] = HORN-MAD –1600.

Hornwork (hǭ·ɹnwɒɹk). 1641. [f. HORN *sb.* + WORK.] **1.** *Fortif.* An outwork, consisting of two demi-bastions connected by a curtain and joined to the main work by two parallel wings. **2.** Work done in horn 1642. †**3.** Cuckoldry –1813.

Hornwort (hǭ·ɹnwɒɹt). 1805. [f. HORN *sb.* + WORT, after Gr. κερατόφυλλον, i.e. horn-leaf.] An aquatic plant, *Ceratophyllum demersum*, with dense whorls of finely divided leaves; also called *Horned Pondweed.*

Hornwrack (hǭ·ɹnræk). 1819. [f. as prec. + WRACK.] A polyzoon of the genus *Flustra*, resembling a seaweed, and of somewhat horny consistency.

Horny (hǭ·ɹni), *a.* ME. [f. HORN *sb.* + -Y.] **1.** Consisting of horn; resembling horn; corneous. **2.** *transf.* Callous and hardened so as to be horn-like in texture 1693; hence *h.-handed* 1859. **3.** Semi-opaque 1652. **4.** Having or abounding in horns or horn-like projections 1530.

1. The Ravens with their h. beaks Food to Elijah bringing MILT. *P. R.* II. 267. **2.** Till his hard h. Fingers ake with Pain DRYDEN. **3.** The dim and h. spectacle of senses BP. HALL.

Horography (horǫ·grăfi). 1727. [a. F. *horographie*, f. Gr. ὥρα + -γραφία.] **1.** The art of making or constructing dials. **2.** 'An account of the hours' (J.) 1755. So **Horo·grapher.**

Horologe (hǫ·rǒlǫdʒ). [ME. *orloge*, a. OF. *orloge* (mod. *horloge*) :—L. *horologium*, a. Gr. ὡρολόγιον, dim. of ὡρολόγος, f. ὥρα + -λογος telling. Refash. later after L.] An instrument for telling the hour; a timepiece; a dial, hour-glass, or clock. Also *transf.* and *fig.* (see quot.).

A Clokke or an abbey Orlogge CHAUCER. Many other flowers close and open their petals at certain hours of the day; and thus constitute, what Linneus calls the H., or Watch of Flora E. DARWIN. So **Horo·loger,** a clock- or watch-maker; a proclaimer of the hours. **Horo·logist,** a horologer.

Horologic (hǫrolǫ·dʒik), *a.* 1665. [ad. L. *horologicus*, a. Gr., f. ὥρα + -λογος telling; see -IC.] Of or pertaining to horology. So **Horolo·gical** *a.* of or pertaining to a horologe or to horology; measuring time.

†**Horologiography** (hǫ:rolǫdʒiǫ·grăfi). 1639. [f. Gr. ὡρολόγιον HOROLOGE + -GRAPHY.] **a.** A description of horologes or timepieces. **b.** The art of constructing them. –1696. Hence †**Horologio·grapher,** a maker of timepieces. †**Horologiogra·phic** *a.* relating to dialling.

‖**Horologium** (hǫrolǭ·dʒiǒm, -lōu·dʒiǒm). 1661. [L., a. Gr.; see HOROLOGE.] **1.** = HOROLOGE. **2.** *Astrol.* A southern constellation 1819. **3.** *Gr. Ch.* A book containing the offices for the canonical hours 1724.

Horology[1] (horǫ·lŏdʒi). ME. [ad. L. *horologium.*] †**1.** = HOROLOGE –1836. **2.** = HOROLOGIUM 3. 1890.

Horo·logy[2]. 1819. [f. Gr. ὥρα + -(O)LOGY.] The art or science of measuring time; the construction of horologes. So **Horo·logist** 1798.

Horometer (horǫ·mĭtəɹ). 1775. [f. Gr. ὥρα + -METER.] An instrument for measuring the time. Hence **Horome·trical** *a.* of or pertaining to the measurement of time.

Horometry (horǫ·mĭtri). 1570. [f. Gr. ὥρα + -METRY.] The measurement of time; also, 'the determination of the exact error of a time-piece by observation'.

Account of the Hindustanee H. 1798.

Horopter (horǫ·ptəɹ). 1704. [f. Gr. ὅρος limit + ὀπτήρ one who looks.] *Optics.* A line or surface containing all those points in space, of which images fall on corresponding points of the two retinæ; the aggregate of points which are seen single in any given position of the eyes. Hence **Horopte·ric, Horo·ptery** *adjs.* pertaining to or forming a h.; *horopteric circle*, the h.

Horoscopal (horǫ·skŏpăl), *a.* 1649. [f. L. *horoscopus* + -AL.] Of or pertaining to a horoscope.

Horoscope (hǫ·rŏskoup), *sb.* OE. [a. F *horoscope*, ad. L. *horoscopus* (also used), a. Gr. ὡροσκόπος nativity, horoscope, etc., f. ὥρα + σκοπός watcher.] **1.** *Astrol.* An observation of the sky and of the configuration of the planets at a certain moment, e.g. the instant of a person's birth; hence, a plan of the twelve houses or twelve signs of the zodiac, showing the disposition of the heavens at a particular moment. In early use, spec. = ASCENDANT, or *house of the ascendant.* Also *fig.* †**2.** A figure or table on which the hours are marked: **a.** a dial; **b.** a table showing the length of the days and nights at different places and seasons; **c.** the planisphere invented by John of Padua. –1696.

1. Phr. *To cast a h.* (see CAST *v.*), to calculate the degree of the ecliptic which is on the eastern horizon at a given moment, e.g. at the birth of a child, and thence to erect an astrological figure of the heavens, so as to discover the influence of the planets upon hi life and fortunes. *fig.* The h. of the Church MILT., of nations LONGF. Hence **Ho·roscope** *v. intr.* to form a h.; *trans.* to cast the nativity of. **Ho·roscoper,** one who casts horoscopes. **Horosco·pic, -al,** *adjs.* of or pertaining to a h.

Horoscopy (horǫ·skŏpi). 1651. [f. HOROSCOPE + -Y.] **a.** The casting of horoscopes. **b.** The aspect of the heavens at a given moment, esp. that of a nativity.

Horrendous (hǫre·ndəs), *a. rare.* 1659. [f. L. *horrendus*, *horrere* + -OUS; cf. *tremendous*, etc.] Fitted to excite horror; frightful, horrible.

Horrent (hǫ·rĕnt), *a.* Chiefly *poet.* 1667. [ad. L. *horrentem*, *horrere.*] **1.** Bristling; standing up as bristles; rough with bristling points. **2.** Shuddering 1721.

1. Inclos'd With bright imblazonrie, and h. Arms MILT. *P. L.* II. 513. **2.** H. they heard SOUTHEY.

Horribility (hǫrĭbi·lĭti). Now *rare.* [ME. (*h*)*orriblete*, etc., a. OF. *horribleté*, f. *horrible*; in mod. use f. HORRIBLE.] The quality of being horrible; †something horrible.

The h. of 'committing' puns DISRAELI.

Horrible (hǫ·rĭb'l), *a.* (*sb.*, *adv.*) ME. [a. OF. (*h*)*orrible*, ad. L. *horribilis*, f. *horrere*; see -BLE.] Exciting or fitted to excite horror; tending to make one shudder; extremely repulsive; dreadful, hideous, shocking, frightful, awful. **b.** as a strong intensive (now *colloq.*): Excessive, immoderate 1460.

A Dungeon h., on all sides round As one great Furnace flam'd MILT. *P. L.* I. 61. A h. monster DE FOE. **b.** [Solomon] multiplying wiues to an h. number SIR T. MORE. My h. cold LADY CHAWORTH.

B. as *sb.* A horrible person or thing ME.; a story of horrible crime or the like.

'Penny-dreadfuls' and 'halfpenny horribles' 1890.

C. as *adv.* Horribly, terribly; as an intensive, Exceedingly ME.

Hence **Ho·rribleness. Ho·rribly** *adv.*

Horrid (hǫ·rid), *a.* (*adv.*) 1590. [ad. L. *horridus*, f. *horrere*.] **1.** Bristling, shaggy, rough. (Chiefly *poet.*) **2.** Causing horror or aversion; revolting; dreadful, frightful; abominable, detestable. (In mod. use, somewhat less strong than *horrible.*) 1601. **3.** *colloq.* Offensive, disagreeable, detested; very bad or objectionable. (Often a feminine term of strong aversion.) 1666. **4.** *adv.* Horridly, abominably, very objectionably (*colloq.* or *vulgar*) 1615.

1. A rugged attire, hirsute head, h. beard BURTON. This h. Alp EVELYN. 2. They set up the horridest yell DE FOE. 3. A h. shame PEPYS. I should not wear those h. dresses LYTTON. H. weather 1864. 4. Went to bed h. soon 1753. Hence **Ho·rrid-ly** *adv.*, **-ness.**

Horrific (hǫri·fik), *a.* 1653. [a. F. *horrifique*, or ad. L. *horrificus*, f. stem of *horrere*; see -FIC.] Causing horror, horrifying. Hence **Horri·fically** *adv.*

Horrification (hǫrifikēⁱ·ʃən). 1800. [f. L. *horrificare*; see -ATION.] The action of horrifying; the being horrified; *concr.* something horrifying.

Horrify (hǫ·rifəi), *v.* 1791. [ad. L. *horrificare*; see -FY.] *trans.* To cause or excite horror in; to move to horror.

In a way horrifying to Quakers 1866.

Horripilation (hǫripilēⁱ·ʃən). 1656. [ad. late L. *horripilatio*, f. *horripilare*, f. stem of *horrere* to bristle + *pilus* hair.] Erection of the hairs on the skin by contraction of the cutaneous muscles (caused by cold, fear, etc.); creeping of the flesh. So **Horri·pilant** *a.* causing h.

Horrisonant (hǫri·sǒnănt), *a.* 1656. [f. stem of L. *horrere* + *sonantem*, *sonare*.] Sounding horribly. So †**Horri·sonous** *a.* = prec.

Horror (hǫ·rəɹ), *sb.* [ME. *orrour*, a. OF. *orror*, (*h*)*orrour* (mod. *horreur*):—L. *horrorem*.] **1.** Roughness, ruggedness. (Now *poet.* or *rhet.*) **2.** A shuddering or shivering; now *esp.* (*Med.*) as a symptom of disease 1533. †**b.** Ruffling of surface –1765. **3.** A painful emotion compounded of loathing and fear; a shuddering with terror and repugnance; the feeling excited by something shocking or frightful. Also in weaker sense, Intense dislike or repugnance. (The prevalent use always) ME. †**4.** A feeling of awe or reverent fear; a thrill of awe, or of imaginative fear –1720. **5.** *transf.* The quality of exciting repugnance and dread; horribleness; something horrifying ME.

1. Which thick with Shades, and a brown H., stood DRYDEN. 2. b. Such fresh h. as you see driven through the wrinkled waves CHAPMAN. 3. Ther shal horrour and grisly drede dwellen with-outen ende CHAUCER. Nature's h. of a vacuum N. ARNOTT. Phr. *The horrors* (colloq.): a fit of horror; *spec.* such as occurs in delirium tremens. 4. A reverend h. silenced all the sky POPE. 5. *Chamber of Horrors*, the name of a room in Madame Tussaud's waxwork exhibition, containing effigies of noted criminals and the like; hence *transf.* a place full of horrors. *Comb.*, as *h.-stricken*, *-struck* adjs.

‖**Hors,** *adv.* and *prep.* 1714. [Fr., doublet of *fors*:—L. *foris* out of doors, abroad.] Out, out of: in the following phrases:

‖**Hors de combat** (hordəkoṅba), *adv.*, out of fight, disabled from fighting; also *transf.* and *fig.* 1745.

‖**Hors d'œuvre** (hordövr), *adv.* and *sb.*

A. *adv.* Out of the ordinary course of things. ADDISON.

B. *sb.* [The Eng. pl. usually has *-s*.] **1.** Something out of the ordinary course. H. WALPOLE. **2.** An extra dish served as a relish at the beginning or between the courses of a meal. Also *fig.* 1742.

Horse (hǭɹs), *sb.* [Com. Teut.: OE. *hors*. Orig. neut., applicable to the male and female alike.]

I. The animal, etc. **1.** A solid-hoofed perissodactyl quadruped (*Equus caballus*), having a flowing mane and tail; its voice is a neigh. In the domestic state used as a beast of burden and draught, and esp. for riding upon. (The pl. was in OE. the same as the sing.; *horses* appears *c* 1205, and is now usual in literary language, though *horse* sometimes appears as the collective pl.) **b.** *spec.* The stallion or gelding, as dist. from a mare or colt 1485. **c.** In *Zool.* sometimes extended to all species of the genus *Equus*, or even of the family *Equidæ*. **2.** A representation, figure, or model of a horse ME. **3.** *Mil.* A horse and its rider; hence a cavalry soldier 1548. **4.** *fig.* Applied contemptuously or playfully to a man, with reference to qualities of the quadruped 1500.

1. Come on then, horse and Chariots let vs haue *Tit. A.* II. ii. 18. b. Phr. *To take the h.*: (of the mare) to conceive. 3. Fifteene hundred Foot, fiue hundred Horse Are march'd vp 2 *Hen. IV*, II. i. 186. Phr. *H. and foot*: both divisions of an army; hence, whole forces; †*advb.* with all one's might. 4. If I tell thee a Lye, spit in my face, call me H. SHAKS.

II. Things resembling the quadruped. **1.** A contrivance on which a man rides, sits astride, or is carried, as on horseback 1597. **2.** A frame or structure on which something is mounted or supported 1703. **3.** An instrument, appliance, or device for some service suggesting that of a horse ME. **4.** *Naut.* See quots. 1626. †**5.** A lottery-ticket hired out by the day –1731. **6.** A mass of rock or earthy matter enclosed within a lode or vein; a fault or obstruction in the course of a vein; hence *to take h.* 1778. **7.** A 'crib' for students in preparing their work. *U.S.* **8.** *slang.* Among workmen, work charged for before it is executed. See *dead h.* LUCKOMBE 1770.

1. I saw the iron horses of the steam Toss to the morning air their plumes of smoke LONGF. A kind of rack called the h. 1895. 2. Horses, or Trussels 1703. Drying horses for their clothes 1826. 3. The engine to batter wals (called sometime the h., and now is named the ram) HOLLAND. 4. Horses for the Yards; a Conveniency for the Men to tread on, in going out to furl the Sails 1711. *Horse*, a thick iron rod..for the main sheet to travel on 1794. Horses are also called jackstays, on which sails are hauled out, as gaff-sails SMYTH.

Phrases. **To horse. a.** To horseback; used absol. as an order to mount. **b.** Of a mare: To the stallion. *To take h.*, to mount, start, or proceed on horseback; see also I. 1 b. and II. 6. *To talk h.*, to talk big or boastfully. **Dead h.** Taken as typical of that which has ceased to be of use, and which it is vain to attempt to revive. *To work*, etc. *for a dead h.*: to do work which has been paid for in advance, and so brings in nothing. *To flog a dead h.*: to engage in fruitless effort. **Flying h.** Pegasus; hence *Astron.* the constellation Pegasus. **Gift h.** (Earlier *given h.*) A horse bestowed as a gift. *To look a gift horse in the mouth*: to criticize a gift. **Great h.** (now *Hist.*) The horse used in battle or tournament. **High h. a.** *lit.* The war-horse or charger. **b.** *To mount* or *ride the high h.* (colloq.): to give oneself airs; to behave pretentiously or arrogantly. **White H. a.** The figure of a white h., reputed as the ensign of the Saxons when they invaded Britain, and the heraldic ensign of Brunswick, Hanover, and Kent; also, the figure of a h. cut on the face of chalk downs near Uffington in Berkshire, and elsewhere. **b.** A high white-crested racing wave. †**Wooden h.** The scaffold, the gallows; an instrument of torture. FULLER. *A h. that was foaled of an acorn*, the scaffold, the gibbet.

attrib. and *Comb.* **1.** General: as *h.-foal*, etc.; *h.-beef*, *-craft*, *-factor*, etc.; *h.-ball*, *-feed*, *-ferry*, *-path*, *-transport*, *-yard*, etc.; *h.-barge*, *-drill*, *-harrow*, *-rake*, *-tram*, etc.; *h.-artillery*, *-soldier*, *-troop*, *-trooper*, etc.; *h.-exercise*; *h.-breeder*, *-dealer*, etc.; *h.-towing*; *h. face*, *joke*, *mouth*, *vein*, etc.

2. Special: **a. h. aloes,** caballine, or fetid aloes; **-boot,** a leather covering for the hoof and pastern of a h., to protect them from interfering; **-bridge; -butcher; -doctor; -drench,** a draught of medicine administered to a h.; also, a horn, etc. by which it is administered; **-furniture,** the trappings of horses; **-iron** (see HORSE *v.* 9); **-knacker,** one who buys up old or worn-out horses, and slaughters them for their commercial products; **-monger; -pick, -picker,** a hooked instrument for removing a stone from a horse's foot; **-piece,** a large piece of whale's blubber; **h. pistol,** a large pistol carried at the pommel of the saddle when on horseback; †**-plea,** a special plea for delaying the cause and carrying it over the term; **-rough,** a calk fitted to a horse's shoe to prevent slipping in frosty weather; **-run,** a contrivance for drawing up loaded wheelbarrows from the deep cuttings by the help of a h., which goes backwards and forwards; **-towel,** a coarse towel, hung on a roller, for general use; **-tree,** the beam on which timber is placed previous to sawing; **-walk,** the path of a h. in working a gin, whim, etc.

b. In names of animals (sometimes denoting a large or coarse kind, sometimes with the sense 'infesting horses'): **h.-ant,** a large species of ant; **-bot,** the larva of the **horse-bee** or bot-fly (*Œstrus equi*); **-conch,** a large shell-fish (*Strombus gigas*); **-crab** = HORSESHOE-*crab*; **-emmet** = *horse-ant*; **-finch,** the chaffinch (*local*); **-lark,** the corn bunting (Cornwall); **-masher, -musher** = next (*a*); **-match, -matcher,** (*a*) the Stonechat or Wheatear (*Saxicola œnanthe*); (*b*) the Red-backed Shrike (*Lanius collurio*); **-mussel,** a large coarse kind of mussel of the genus *Modiola*; also a freshwater mussel, *Unio* or *Anodonta*; **-sponge,** the commercial bath-sponge (*Spongia equina*); **-stinger,** the Dragon-fly; **-tick** = HORSE-FLY; †**-whale,** the walrus; **-worm,** a maggot infesting horses, as the larva of the common bot-fly.

c. In names of plants, fruits, etc. (often denoting a large, strong, or coarse kind): **h.-balm,** a strong-scented labiate plant of the N. Amer. genus *Collinsonia*, with yellowish flowers; **-bane,** name for species of *Œnanthe*, supposed to cause palsy in horses; **-bean,** a coarse variety of the common bean, used for feeding horses; **-beech,** the Hornbeam (see BEECH 2); **-brier,** 'the common greenbrier or catbrier of N. America, *Smilax rotundifolia*' (*Cent. Dict.*); **-cane,** the Great Ragweed of N. America; **-cassia,** a leguminous tree (*Cassia marginata*), bearing long pods containing a purgative pulp used in the E. Indies as a medicine for horses; **-daisy,** the Ox-eye Daisy (see DAISY 2); †**-elder,** elecampane; **-eye, -eye bean,** the seed of the Cowage (*Mucuna pruriens*), a W. Indian leguminous plant; also that of *Dolichos Lablab*; **-fennel** (see FENNEL); **-gentian, -ginseng,** a N. American caprifoliaceous plant of the genus *Triosteum*, having a bitter root; **-parsley,** a large-leaved umbelliferous plant, *Smyrnium Olusatrum*; **-purslane,** a W. Indian plant, *Trianthema monogyna*; **-sorrel,** *Rumex Hydrolapathum*; **-sugar,** a shrub (*Symplocos tinctoria*), found in the southern U.S., also called *sweetleaf*, the leaves of which are used as fodder; **-thistle,** †(*a*) Wild Lettuce; (*b*) a thistle of the genus *Cirsium*; **-tongue,** (*a*) = DOUBLE-TONGUE 2; (*b*) the Hart's-tongue Fern; **-vetch** = HORSESHOE-*vetch*; **-weed,** name for two N. Amer. plants, *Erigeron canadensis*, also called *butter-weed* (now frequent in England), and *Collinsonia canadensis*, also called *horse-mint*; **-wood,** name for various W. Indian shrubs of the genus *Calliandra*.

Horse, *v.* OE. [f. prec. sb.] **1.** *trans.* To provide with a horse or horses; to set on horseback. Also *transf.* **2.** *intr.* To mount or go on horseback ME. **3.** *trans.* To raise or hoist up. Now *technical.* **4.** To elevate on a man's back, e.g. for flogging 1563. †**5.** *Naut.* Of a current, etc.: To carry with force –1726. **6.** Of a stallion: To cover (a mare) ME. **7.** To bestride. SHAKS. **8.** *Horse away*: to spend in a lottery. See HORSE *sb.* II. 5. FIELDING. **9.** *Horse up*: to drive (oakum) between the planks of a ship 1850.

1. Maron of Turin, who horsed oure Company from Lyons to Turin CORYAT. Guns horsed for service 1888. 4. The biggest boy..horsed me—and I was flogged THACKERAY. 9. *Horse iron*, an iron..used..by caulkers, to *horse-up* or harden in the oakum 1850.

Horse-back, horseback, *sb.* (*adv.*) ME. †**1.** (hǭ·ɹsˌbæ·k). The back of a horse –1704. **2.** (hǭ·ɹsbæk). See quots. ME. **3.** *Geol.* (hǭ·ɹsbæk) A low and somewhat sharp ridge of gravel or sand; a hog-back. *U.S.* 1857. **4.** *Coal-mining.* 'A portion of the roof or floor which bulges or intrudes into the coal' 1855. **5.** *adv.* Short for *on horseback* 1727.

2. Phr. *On h.* (†*a h.*): sitting or riding on a horse; (mounting) upon a horse. A couple of robbers a-horseback suddenly appeared SMOLLETT. Set a beggar on horse-back, and he'll ride to the devil COBBETT.

Ho·rse-block. 1753. **1.** A small platform, ascended by 3 or 4 steps, used in mounting a horse. **2.** 'A square frame of strong boards, used by excavators to elevate the ends of their wheeling-planks' (Gwilt) 1825.

Ho·rse-boat. 1591. **1.** A ferry-boat for conveying horses or carriages. **2.** (*U.S.*) A boat drawn by horses 1828.

Ho·rse-box. 1846. **1.** A closed carriage for transporting horses by railway. **2.** Applied joc. to large pews with high sides, formerly common 1884.

Ho·rse-boy. 1537. A stable-boy. (Often contemptuous.)

Ho·rse-bread. 1467. Bread made of beans, bran, etc. for food for horses.

Ho·rse-breaker. 1550. One who breaks in horses for use.

Ho·rse-car. *U.S.* 1864. **1.** A car drawn by a horse or horses. Also *attrib.* **2.** A railway car for the transport of horses. (*Cent. Dict.*)

Ho·rse-che·stnut. 1597. [tr. obs. Bot. L. *Castanea equina*.] **1.** The hard smooth shining brown seed or nut of the tree described in 2. 1611. **2.** A large ornamental tree, *Æsculus*

Hippocastanum (N.O. *Sapindaceæ*), introduced into England *c* 1550. Also, the allied genus *Pavia*, usu. called *buck-eye*.

Ho·rse-coper (-kōu:pəɹ), **-couper** (-kau:pəɹ). 1681. [f. HORSE + COPER¹, *couper* (see COUP *v.*¹).] A horse-dealer.

†**Ho·rse-corser, -courser.** 1552. [See CORSER, SCORSER.] A jobbing dealer in horses -1818. So †**Ho·rse-corsing, -coursing,** horse-jobbing.

Ho·rse-course. 1715. **1.** A horse-race. **2.** A race-course 1766.

Ho·rse-fai·r. ME. A fair or annual market for the sale of horses.

Ho·rse-fish. 1582. Any fish with a head more or less like that of a horse. **a.** The fish *Vomer setipinnis*, and the allied *Selene vomer*. **b.** The *Hippocampus* or sea-horse.

Ho·rse-flesh, horseflesh. ME. **1.** The flesh of a horse, esp. as food 1532. **2.** Living horses collectively ME. †**3.** = HORSE *sb.* II. 8. 1683. **4.** *attrib.* usu. in reference to the colour, a peculiar reddish bronze. **Horse-flesh ore,** an ore of copper, bornite.

2. Profoundly learned in Horse-flesh STEELE.

Ho·rse-fly. ME. [f. FLY *sb.*¹ 2.] One of various dipterous insects troublesome to horses, as the horse-tick (family *Hippoboscidæ*), the breeze or gadfly (*Tabanidæ*), the bot-fly (*Œstridæ*).

attrib. **Horse-fly-weed,** *Baptisia tinctoria*, also called *wild indigo*.

Horse-foot. ME. †**1.** A horse's foot -1597. †**2.** The plant Coltsfoot -1633. **3.** A crustacean of the genus *Limulus*, called *horseshoe-crab* 1672.

Ho·rsegate. 1619. [f. GATE *sb.*², going.] A right of pasturage for a horse, e.g. in a common field.

Ho·rse-go·dmother. *dial.* and *vulgar*. 1569. A large coarse-looking woman.

Horse guard (hǭ·ɹs gā:ɹd). 1645. **1.** One of a body of picked cavalry for special service as a guard; formerly also *collective* 1647. **b.** *pl.* The cavalry brigade of the English Household troops; *spec.* the third regiment of this body, the *Royal Horse Guards* 1661. **2.** *pl.* The barracks, head-quarters or guard-house of such cavalry; *spec.* a building in London, opposite Whitehall, bearing this name 1666. **3.** *pl.* The personnel of the office of the Commander-in-Chief and the military authorities at the head of the army 1826.

2. News that White Hall was on fire; and presently more particulars, that the Horse-guard was on fire PEPYS. 3. I can't say that I owe my successes to any favour or confidence from the Horse Guards WELLINGTON.

Horsehair (hǭ·ɹshēəɹ). ME. **a.** A hair from the mane or tail of a horse. **b.** A mass of such hair ME. **c.** *attrib.* and *Comb.*, as *h. chair*; **h.-lichen** = horsetail-lichen; **h.-worm,** a hairworm or Gordius.

Ho·rse-head. ME. **1.** The head of a horse, or a head like that of a horse. **2.** The stony inner cast of the fossil Trigonia 1708. **3.** *Zool.* = HORSE-FISH. †**4.** *Mining.* A kind of ventilator -1802.

Ho·rse-hoe, *sb.* 1731. [f. HORSE *sb.* + HOE *sb.*] A frame mounted on wheels and furnished with ranges of shares, each of which acts like a hoe. Hence **Horse-hoe** *v.* to work with a horse-hoe.

Ho·rse-hoof. ME. [f. HORSE *sb.* + HOOF.] **1.** The hoof of a horse 1539. **2.** The plant Coltsfoot ME. **3.** = HORSE-FOOT 3. 1699.

Ho·rse-jo·ckey. 1782. One hired to ride a horse in a race. (Now simply *jockey*.)

Horse latitudes, *sb. pl.* 1777. [?] The belt of calms and light airs which borders the northern edge of the N.E. trade-winds.

Horse-laugh (hǭ·ɹs,lɑf). 1713. A loud coarse laugh.

Horse-leech (hǭ·ɹs,lītʃ), *sb.* ME. [f. HORSE + LEECH :—OE. *lǽce*, *lēce*, physician.] †**1.** A farrier, a veterinary surgeon -1653. **2.** A large aquatic sucking worm (*Hæmopsis sanguisorba*) ME. **3.** *fig.* A rapacious insatiable person 1546. Hence †**Ho·rse-lee:chery, -leechcraft,** veterinary medicine.

Ho·rse-li·tter. ME. **1.** A litter hung on poles, carried between two horses, one in front and the other behind. **2.** A bed of straw or hay for horses. **b.** The manure consisting of such straw mixed with the excrements of horses. 1624.

Ho·rse-load. ME. A load for a horse; sometimes, a determinate weight; cf. LOAD. Also *fig.* a large quantity.

†**Ho·rsely,** *a.* Also **horsly(e.** [-LY¹.] Of the nature of a good horse. CHAUCER.

Ho·rse-ma·ckerel. 1705. A name for several fishes allied to the mackerel; *esp.* the Cavally or Scad (*Caranx vulgaris*).

Horseman (hǭ·ɹs,mǎn). *Pl.* **-men.** ME. **1.** One who rides on horseback; one skilled in riding and managing a horse. *spec.* a mounted soldier. **2.** A man who attends to horses 1882. **3.** An inferior variety of the carrier pigeon 1693. **4.** *Ichthyol.* A sciænoid fish of the genus *Eques* found on the coasts of Central America. Hence **Ho·rsemanship,** the art of riding on horseback, and (formerly) of breeding, rearing, and managing horses; the duties of the *manège*.

Horse-marine (hǭ·ɹs,mǎrī·n). 1824. [f. HORSE *sb.* + MARINE *sb.*] **1.** A marine mounted on horseback, or a cavalryman doing a marine's work 1878. **2.** *joc.* (*pl.*) An imaginary corps of mounted marine soldiers, as a type of men out of their element 1824.

Ho·rse-master. 1523. One who owns or manages horses; also, a horse-breaker.

Ho·rse-mill. 1467. A mill driven by a horse; usually, by one walking in a circle; *fig.* a monotonous round.

Ho·rse-mint. ME. **1.** A name of the wild mints, esp. *Mentha sylvestris* and *M. aquatica*. **2.** Applied in N. America to species of *Monarda*, etc.

Ho·rse-nail. ME. **1.** A horseshoe-nail. **2.** A tadpole (*local*) 1608.

Ho·rse-play. 1589. †**1.** Play in which a horse takes part; theatrical horsemanship. Also *transf.* -1668. **2.** Rough, coarse, or boisterous play 1589.

2. He [Collier] is too much given to horse-play in his raillery DRYDEN.

Ho·rse-plum. 1530. **1.** A small red variety of plum. **2.** (*U.S.*) The common wild plum of N. America (*Prunus americana*).

Ho·rse-pond. 1701. A pond for watering and washing horses; also, for ducking obnoxious persons.

Ho·rse-power. 1806. **1.** The power or rate of work of a horse in drawing; hence in *Mech.*, a unit for measuring the work of a prime motor, taken as = 550 foot-pounds per second (about 1½ times the actual power of a horse). Abbrev. H.P. **2.** *transf.* Power or rate of work as estimated by this unit. Also *fig.* 1860. **3.** A machine worked by a horse, by which the pull or weight of a horse is converted into power for driving other machinery 1853.

1. Nominal horse-power..has no fixed relation to indicated horse-power 1881. The term 'horse-power' has probably seen its best days PREECE. One 25 horse-power engine 1872. 2. What is the horse-power of the Niagara? MAURY. 3. An ordinary horse-power, such as is used for thrashing-machines [etc.] KNIGHT.

Ho·rse-pox. 1656. [See POX.] †**1.** A severe or virulent pox. (Used in coarse execrations.) -1694. **2.** A pustular disease of horses 1884.

Ho·rse-race. 1581. [RACE *sb.*¹] A race between mounted horses. Hence **Horse-racer, -racing.**

Ho·rse-radish. 1561. [See HORSE *sb. attrib.* 2 c.] **1.** A cruciferous plant (*Cochlearia Armoracia*), a native of middle Europe and western Asia; the thick rootstock of this plant, which has a pungent flavour, and is scraped or grated as a condiment 1625. **2.** *attrib.* and *Comb.*, as **horse-radish tree,** a tree (*Moringa pterygosperma*), a native of India, cultivated for its pod-like capsules, and for its winged seeds (*ben-nuts*), from which oil of ben is obtained; the root resembles horse-radish in flavour.

Horse-scorser, -scourser: see HORSE-CORSER.

Ho·rse-se·nse. *U.S. colloq.* 1870. Strong common sense, often found in ignorant and rude persons.

Horseshoe, horse-shoe (hǭ·ɹs,ʃū), *sb.* ME. **1.** A shoe for a horse, now usually formed of a narrow iron plate bent to the outline of the horse's hoof and nailed to the foot. **2.** Anything shaped like a horseshoe, or a circular arc larger than a semicircle 1489. **3.** *Bot.* = *horseshoe-vetch* 1578. **4.** *Zool.* A horseshoe-crab 1775. **5.** *attrib.*, as *h. arch, bend, table*, etc. 1796.

1. A Tradition, that 'tis a lucky thing to find a Horse-shoe BOYLE. 2. The river making a kind of a double horse-shoe DE FOE.

Comb.: **h.-bat,** any species of bat having a nose-leaf more or less horseshoe-shaped; **-crab,** a crab-like animal of the genus *Limulus*, so called from the shape of its shell; a king-crab; **h. head,** a disease in infants, in which the sutures of the skull are too open; **h. magnet,** one bent so that the two ends almost meet; **h.-nail,** a nail of soft iron for fastening on horseshoes; **-vetch,** a leguminous plant (*Hippocrepis comosa*) bearing umbels of yellow flowers, and jointed pods each division of which resembles a h. Hence **Ho·rseshoe** *v.* to provide with horseshoes; *Arch.* to make (an arch) horseshoe-shaped. **Ho·rse-sho:er. Ho·rse-shoeing,** the art or craft of shoeing horses.

Horse-tail, ho·rsetail. ME. **1.** A horse's tail. **b.** Used in Turkey as the symbol of war, and as an ensign denoting the rank of a pasha; see TAIL 1613. **2.** Name of the genus *Equisetum*, a cryptogamous plant with leafless jointed branches 1538. **b. Tree horsetail** = *horsetail-tree* 1884. **3.** A hippurite. **4.** *Anat.* The leash of nerves in which the spinal cord ends (in mod.L. *cauda equina*). **5.** *attrib.* and *Comb.*, as **horsetail-tree,** a tree of the genus *Casuarina*, esp. the Australian *C. equisetifolia*.

1. b. While all Christendom trembled at the sight of the horse-tails, Soliman died 1840.

Horsewhip (hǭ·ɹs,hwip), *sb.* 1694. A whip for driving or controlling a horse. Hence **Ho·rsewhip** *v.* to chastise with a h.

Horsewoman (hǭ·ɹs,wu:mǎn). 1564. A woman who rides on horseback.

Ho·rsing, *vbl. sb.* ME. [f. HORSE *v.* + -ING¹.] **1.** Provision of horses. **2.** The covering of a mare 1523. **3.** A mounting as on a horse; a flogging inflicted while on another's back 1688. *Comb.*: **h.-block, -stone** = HORSE-BLOCK.

Horst (hǭɹst). 1902. [G.] *Geol.* A term introduced by E. Suess for tracts of the earth's surface which have become immobile and formed buttresses against which surrounding tracts have been pressed.

Horsy (hǭ·ɹsi), *a.* 1591. [f. HORSE *sb.* + -Y.] **1.** Of, pertaining to, or of the nature of a horse or horses. **2.** Having to do with horses; devoted to horses or horse-racing; affecting the dress and language of a groom or jockey 1852. Hence **Ho·rsiness** (esp. in sense 2).

Hortation (hǭɹtē·ʃən). 1536. [ad. L. *hortationem*, *hortari*.] The action of exhorting or inciting; exhortation.

Hortative (hǭ·ɹtǎtiv). 1607. [ad. L. *hortativus*; see -IVE.]

A. *adj.* Characterized by exhortation; serving to exhort 1623.

B. *sb.* A hortatory speech.

Hortatory (hǭ·ɹtǎtəri), *a.* 1576. [ad. late L. *hortatorius*, f. *hortari*; see -ORY.] Of, pertaining to, or characterized by exhortation or encouragement; hortative.

Horte·nsial, *a.* ? *Obs.* 1655. [f. L. *hortensis*, *-ius* (f. *hortus*) + -AL.] Of or belonging to a garden. So **Horte·nsian** *a.* ? *Obs.*

†**Ho·rticultor.** *rare.* 1760. [f. L. *hortus* + *cultor*.] = HORTICULTURIST.

Horticulture (hǭ·ɹtikɒltiŭɹ, -tʃəɹ). 1678. [f. as prec. + *cultura*; after *agriculture*.] The cultivation of a garden; the art or science of cultivating or managing gardens, including the growing of flowers, fruit, and vegetables. So **Horticu·ltural** *a.* of or pertaining to h. **Horticu·lturist,** one who practises h.; esp. one who practises it scientifically as a profession.

Hortulan (hǭ·ɹtiŭlǎn), *a.* 1664. [ad. L. *hortulanus*, f. *hortulus*, dim. of *hortus*. In earlier form ORTOLAN, from It. *ortolano*.] Of or belonging to a garden or gardening.

‖ **Hortus siccus** (hǭ·ɹtŏs si·kŏs). 1687. [L., = dry garden.] An arranged collection of dried plants; a herbarium.
fig. The *hortus siccus* of dissent BURKE.

†**Ho·rtyard.** 1555. [Altered f. *orchard* (OE. *ortgeard*), infl. by L. *hortus.*] An ORCHARD; occas. a garden generally –1699.

Hory, horry, *a.* *Obs.* exc. *dial.* Also **howry.** [OE. *horig,* f. *horh* filth + -Y.] Foul, dirty, filthy; slanderous. TENNYSON.

Hosanna (hozæ·nă). OE. [ad. late L. *osanna, hosanna* (Vulg.), ad. Gr. ὡσαννά, ὡσαννά, repr. Hebr.]
A. *interj.* An exclam., meaning 'Save now!' or 'Save, pray!', occurring in Ps. cxviii. 25. Used by the Jews as an appeal for deliverance, and an ascription of praise to God, and in the Christian Church as an ascription of praise.
And the multitudes..cried, saying, H. to the sonne of Dauid *Matt.* xxi. 9. H. to the living Lord HEBER.
B. *sb.* A cry of 'hosanna'; a shout of praise 1641.

Hose (hōuz), *sb.* Pl. **hosen** (*arch.* or *dial.*), †**hoses;** *collect. pl.* **hose.** [OE. *hosa;* Com. Teut. (wanting in Goth.)] **1.** An article of clothing for the leg, sometimes also covering the foot. *collect. pl.* **hose.** In mod. use = Stockings reaching to the knee. *Half-hose,* short stockings or socks. ME. †**2.** Occas. = breeches, drawers; esp. in DOUBLET *and h.,* as the typical male apparel 1460. **3.** A flexible tube or pipe for conveying water or other liquid where it is wanted 1495. **4.** A sheath; *spec.* the sheath enclosing the ear or straw of corn; the sheath or spathe of an Arum 1450. **5.** A socket; in a printing press, a case connected by hooks with the platen to keep it in place. 1611.
1. Hir hosen weren of fyn scarlet reed CHAUCER. Hee beeing in loue, could not see to garter his h. *Two Gent.* II. i. 83. **2.** 1 *Hen. IV,* II. iv. 239. †*Shipman's hose,* wide trousers worn by sailors.
Comb.: **h.-bridge, -jumper, -protector, -shield,** devices for the protection of firemen's h. lying across a street or road; **-hook,** a hook for raising the h. of a fire-engine.

Hose (hōuz), *v.* ME. [f. HOSE *sb.*] **1.** *trans.* To provide with hose. **2.** To drench with a hose 1889.

Hosed (hōuzd), *a.* ME. [f. HOSE *v.* or *sb.* + -ED.] **1.** Wearing hose. **2.** Of a horse: Having the lower part of the legs covered with white hair 1720.

Hose-in-hose, *a.* and *sb.* 1629. [See HOSE *sb.* 4.] Said of flowers which appear to have one corolla within another, esp. a variety of *Primula* or Polyanthus.

Ho·se-net. Chiefly *Sc.* 1552. A small net resembling a stocking, affixed to a pole (Jam.); *fig.* a position from which escape is difficult.

Hosier (hōu·ʒiəɹ, hōu·ziəɹ). ME. [f. HOSE *sb.* + -IER.] One who makes or deals in hose (stockings and socks) and underclothing generally.

Hosiery (hōu·ʒiəri, hōu·ziəri). 1790. [f. prec.; see -ERY.] **1.** Hose collectively; extended to the whole class of goods in which a hosier deals. **2.** The business of a hosier 1789. **3.** A factory where hose is woven.

Hospice (hǫ·spis). 1818. [a. F., ad. L. *hospitium,* f. *hospitem;* see HOST *sb.*[2]] **1.** A house of rest and entertainment for pilgrims, travellers, or strangers, esp. that belonging to the monks of St. Bernard on the Alps; also, a home for the destitute. **2.** A hostel for students. RASHDALL.

Hospitable (hǫ·spităb'l), *a.* 1570. [a. obs. F. *hospitable,* f. *hospitare;* see HOSPITATE and -BLE.] **1.** Offering or affording welcome and entertainment to strangers; extending a generous hospitality to guests and visitors. **2.** *transf.* Disposed to receive or welcome kindly; open and generous in disposition 1655.
1. The savages in America are extremely h. KEATINGE. His h. gate DRAYTON. **2.** The religion of the Greeks..was h. to novelties 1887. Hence **Ho·spitableness. Ho·spitably** *adv.*

Hospitage (hǫ·spitédʒ). *Obs.* or *arch.* 1590. [ad. med.L. *hospitagium,* f. *hospitem;* see -AGE.] †**1.** Guestship. SPENSER. †**2.** Lodging. SPEED. **3.** A hospice 1855.

Hospital (hǫ·spităl), *sb.* ME. [a. OF. *hospital* (mod. *hôpital*), ad. med.L. *hospitale* adj. neut. sing. used subst. Cf. HOSTEL, HOTEL, SPITAL.] **1.** A place of rest and entertainment; a hospice. Hence, one of the establishments of the Knights Hospitallers. **2.** A charitable institution for the housing and maintenance of the needy, infirm, or aged. *Obs.* exc. in Eng. legal use and in proper names. ME. **b.** A university hall or hostel 1536. **c.** A charitable institution for the education and maintenance of the young 1552. **3.** *spec.* An institution for the care of the sick and wounded, or of those who require medical treatment. (The current use.) ME. †**4.** A place of lodging –1590.
3. *fig.* For the world, I count it not an Inne, but an Hospitall, and a place, not to live, but to die in SIR T. BROWNE.
Comb.: **h.-boy,** a charity-boy; **h. fever,** a kind of typhus fever arising in crowded hospitals from the poisonous atmosphere; **h. gangrene,** a spreading, sloughing, gangrenous inflammation starting from a wound and arising in crowded hospitals; **H. Saturday,** a particular Saturday in the year on which collections of money for the local hospitals are organized in the streets and elsewhere; **h.-ship,** a vessel fitted up as a floating h. for seamen; **H. Sunday,** a particular Sunday in the year on which collections of money are made in places of worship for the local hospitals; **h. ulcer** = *hospital gangrene.*

†**Ho·spital,** *a.* ME. [ad. L. *hospitalis,* f. *hospes, hospitem;* see -AL.] **1.** = HOSPITABLE –1697. **2.** Used as tr. L. *hospitalis* or Gr. ξένιος 'protector of the rights of hospitality', as in *h. Jove,* etc. –1807.

Hospitalism (hǫ·spitălizʼm). 1869. [-ISM.] The hospital system; used esp. with reference to its hygienic evils.

Hospitality (hǫspitæ·lĭti). ME. [a. OF. *hospitalité,* ad. L. *hospitalitas;* see HOSPITAL *a.*] **1.** The act or practice of being hospitable; the reception and entertainment of guests or strangers with liberality and goodwill. **b.** with *pl.* †**2.** Hospitableness –1711. †**3.** A HOSPITAL (sense 2) –1761.
1. 'Old English hospitality' SMOLLETT. **b.** In convivial and domestic hospitalities EMERSON. **3.** The h. of St. Leonard's near York HUME.

Hospitaller, -aler (hǫ·spităləɹ). ME. [a. OF. *hospitalier,* ad. med.L. *hospitalarius* hospitaller (senses 1 and 2), f. *hospitale* (see HOSPITAL *sb.*). HOSTELER, OSTLER are doublets.] **1.** = HOSTELER 1. 1483. **2.** *spec.* A member of a religious order formed for the care of the sick and infirm in hospitals. Such were orig. the *Knights Hospitallers* (see 3) ME. **3.** More fully, *Knights Hospitallers,* an order of military monks, which took its origin from a hospital founded at Jerusalem, *c* 1048, by merchants of Amalfi, for the benefit of poor pilgrims, but subsequently received a military organization, and became a bulwark of Christendom in the East. They were known as *Knights of the Hospital of St. John of Jerusalem,* etc., and, after the removal of the chief seat of the order to Malta, as *Knights of Malta.* ME. **4.** In St. Bartholomew's Hospital and St. Thomas's Hospital (orig. religious foundations): The title of the chaplain 1552.

†**Hospitate** (hǫ·spitēᵗt), *v. rare.* 1623. [f. L. *hospitat-, hospitari* to be a guest, med.L. *hospitare* to receive as a guest, f. *hospitem.*] †**1.** *trans.* To lodge or entertain. (Dicts.) †**2.** To lodge, take up one's abode. GREW. So **Ho·spitator.**

†**Hospi·tious,** *a.* 1588. [f. L. *hospitium* (see HOSPICE) + -OUS.] Hospitable –1784.

‖ **Hospitium** (hǫspi·ʃiŏm). 1650. [L.; see HOSPICE.] **1.** = HOSPICE 1. **2.** A hall or hostel for students in a university 1895.

‖ **Hospodar** (hǫ·spǫdāɹ). 1684. [a. Roumanian *hospodár,* of Slavonic origin.] A word meaning 'lord', a title formerly borne by the governors of the provinces of Wallachia and Moldavia.

Hoss (hǫs), dial. and U.S. var. HORSE.

Host (hōᵘst), *sb.*[1] ME. [a. OF. *ost, host, oost, hoost* army :—L. *hostem* (*hostis*) stranger, enemy.] **1.** An armed multitude of men; an army. Now *arch.* and *poet.* Also *fig.* and *transf.* **2.** *transf.* A great company; a multitude 1613. **3.** In Biblical uses (see below.) ME.
1. The sight of the armed h. which surrounded her 1840. *fig.* He was a h. of debaters in himself BURKE. **2.** A h. of thoughts M. PATTISON, of books JOWETT. **3.** *H.* or *hosts o heaven,* (*a*) the multitude of angels that attend on God; (*b*) the sun, moon, and stars. *Lord* (*God*) *of Hosts* (*Jehovah Ts'bāōth*): an O.T. title of Jehovah; app. referring sometimes to the heavenly hosts, sometimes to the armies of Israel, and hence in mod. use with the sense 'God of armies' or 'of battles'. Lord God of Hosts, be with us yet KIPLING. Hence **Ho·sted** *a.* in hosts.

Host (hōᵘst), *sb.*[2] ME. [a. OF. *oste, hoste* (mod. *hôte*) :—L. *hospitem* host, guest, etc.] **1.** A man who lodges and entertains another in his house; the correl. of *guest.* **2.** *spec.* A man who lodges and entertains for payment; the landlord of an inn ME. **3.** *Biol.* An animal or plant having a parasite or commensal habitually living in or upon it 1857. †**4.** A guest –1559.
1. Conduct me to mine H., we loue him highly *Macb.* I. vi. 29. **2.** Mine H. of the Garter SHAKS. Phr. *To reckon without one's h.;* to calculate one's score without consulting one's h.; to come to conclusions without complete data.

†**Host,** *sb.*[3] ME. [? ad. OF. *hosté, osté,* var. of *hostel, ostel* HOSTEL.] A hostel, inn –1590.
Phr. *To be* (or *lie*) *at h.*: to be put up at an inn; *fig.* to be at home *with.*

Host (hōᵘst), *sb.*[4] ME. [a. OF. *oiste, hoiste* :—L. *hostia.* See also HOSTIE.] †**1.** A victim for sacrifice; a sacrifice (*lit.* and *fig.*); often said of Christ –1653. **2.** *Eccl.* The bread consecrated in the Eucharist, regarded as the body of Christ sacrificially offered; a wafer used in celebrating Mass ME.

†**Host,** *v.* ME. [f. HOST *sb.*[2]] **1.** *trans.* To receive and entertain as a guest –1613. **2.** *intr.* To be a guest; to put up –1656.

Hostage (hǫ·stédʒ), *sb.*[1] ME. [a. OF. *ostage, hostage* (mod. *otage*) :—pop.L. **obsidaticum,* f. L. *obsidatus* hostageship, f. *obses, obsidem* hostage; infl. by *hospit-, hospes* HOST *sb.*[2]] †**1.** Pledge or security given to enemies or allies for the fulfilment of any undertaking by the handing over of one or more persons into their power; the state or condition of the persons thus handed over. (No pl.) –1731. **2.** with *pl.*) A (person thus given and held in pledge ME. **3.** *gen.* A pledge or security ME. †**4.** A treaty (*rare*). MALORY.
1. To give the young King..in H. to the Queen TINDAL. **2.** To solicit the exchange of hostages GIBBON. **3.** He that hath wife and children, hath given hostages to fortune BACON. Hence **Ho·stageship** = sense 1.

†**Ho·stage,** *sb.*[2] ME. [a. OF. (*h*)*ostage* :—late L. type **hospitaticum,* f. *hospes, hospitem* HOST *sb.*[2]] **1.** Entertainment; lodging, residence. **2.** A hostel, hostelry, inn. Also *attrib.* –1852.

Hostel (hǫ·stĕl), *sb.* ME. [a. OF. *ostel, -eil, hostel* (mod. *hôtel*) :—med.L. *hospitale* (see HOSPITAL).] †**1.** A place of sojourn; a lodging. Also *transf.* and *fig.* –1610. **2.** *spec.* An inn, a hotel. (Revived in 19th c. by Scott.) ME. **3.** A house of residence for students; esp. (in recent times) for students connected with a non-resident college; = HALL *sb.* 4 a. 1536. †**4.** A town mansion; = HOTEL 1. –1670. **5.** *attrib.* 1610.
2. The h., or inn SCOTT. **4.** His H. at Paris..was then the best House next to the Queen Mothers COTTON.

Hosteler (hǫ·stĕləɹ). Now *arch.* or *Hist.* ME. [a. OF. *ostelier, hostelier* (mod. *hôtelier*), f. *hostel;* see -ER. See also HOSTLER, OSTLER.] **1.** One who receives, lodges, or entertains guests or strangers; *spec.* in a monastery, one whose office was to attend to guests or strangers. *Obs.* exc. *Hist.* **2.** An innkeeper (*arch.*) ME. †**3.** A student who lives in a hostel (sense 3) –1655.

Hostelry (hǫ·stĕlri). Now *arch.* ME. [a. OF. (*h*)*ostelerie* (mod. *hôtellerie*); see prec. and -ERY 3, -RY.] **1.** An inn, a hostel. **2.** Hostel business (*nonce-use*) 1855.
1. A bashful child, homely brought up, In a rude hostelrie B. JONS.

Hostess (hōᵘ·stĕs). ME. [a. OF. *ostesse* (mod. *hôtesse*) f. (*h*)*oste* HOST *sb.*[2]; see -ESS.] **1.** A woman that lodges and entertains guests. **2.** *spec.* The mistress of an inn ME. Hence **Ho·stessship,** the office of h.

Hostie (hǫ·sti). *Obs.* or *arch.* 1483. [a. F., ad. L. *hostia.*] **1.** = HOST *sb.*[4] 1. **2.** = HOST *sb.*[4] 2. 1641.

Hostile (hǫ·stəil), *a.* (*sb.*) 1487. [ad. L. *hostilis*, f. *hostis* (see -ILE).] **1.** Of, pertaining to, or characteristic of an enemy; pertaining to or engaged in hostilities. **b.** Unfriendly 1782. **2.** Contrary, adverse, antagonistic 1791. **3.** *sb.* A hostile person; *spec.* (*U.S.*) a N. American Indian unfriendly to the Whites 1860.

1. The operations of h. armies WELLINGTON. Men of different and h. races FREEMAN. 2. Princes h. to the established faith MACAULAY. Hence **Ho·stilely** *adv.*, **Ho·stileness.**

Hostility (hǫsti·lĭti). 1473. [ad. late L. *hostilitas*, f. *hostilis*.] **1.** The state or fact of being hostile; hostile action; *esp.* such as involves war; *pl.* acts of warfare, war 1613. **2.** Opposition or antagonism 1632.

1. Open acts of sedition and h. 1706. A suspension of hostilities was agreed on PRESCOTT.

Hosting (hōu·stiŋ), *vbl. sb.* *Obs.* exc. *arch.* or *Hist.* ME. [f. HOST *v.*] The raising of a host or armed multitude; hostile encounter or array; †a military expedition. Also *attrib.*

That Angel should with Angel warr, And in fierce h. meet MILT. *P. L.* VI. 93.

Ho·stler. ME. [A syncopated form of *hosteler*. The form OSTLER is now more prevalent.] A man who attends to horses at an inn; a stableman, a groom. **b.** *U.S.* The keeper of the round-house for sheltering locomotives 1890.

Ho·stless, *a.* *rare.* 1590. [f. HOST *sb.*[2] + -LESS.] Without a host; †inhospitable.

Hostry (hōu·stri). *Obs.* or *arch.* ME. [a. OF. *hosterie*, *hostrie*, f. *hoste* (mod. *hôte*) HOST *sb.*[2]; see -ERY, -RY.] = HOSTELRY.

Hot, hott (hǫt), *sb.*[1] *Obs.* exc. *dial.* ME. [a. OF. *hotte* a panier or creel; perh. of Ger. origin.] **1.** A kind of basket or pannier for carrying earth, sand, lime, manure, etc. *n. dial.* **†2.** (Also **hut(t.**) A padded sheath for the spur of a fighting cock –1806.

Hot (hǫt), *a.* (*sb.*[2]) [Com. Teut.: OE. *hát* :—OTeut. **haito-z*, f. ablaut-stem *hit-*, *hît-*, *hait-*, whence also OE. *hǽtu* HEAT.] **1.** Having or communicating much heat; of or at a high temperature; the opposite of *cold*. (Differing from *warm* in degree.) **2.** Having or producing the sensation of heat (in a high degree). Usu. in predicate. ME. **†3.** In the physiology of the Middle Ages, expressing one of the fundamental qualities of humours, elements, planets, and bodies in general; see COLD *a.* –1670. **4.** Pungent, acrid, biting; corrosive; ardent 1548. **5.** *transf.* Excited; fervent OE.; angry, wrathful ME.; lustful; 'in heat' 1500. **6.** Intense, violent; raging, keen. (Chiefly of conflict or the like.) OE. **b.** *transf.* Uncomfortable 1611. **7.** *Hunting.* Of the scent: Strong, intense 1648. **b.** Of colour: Disagreeably intense 1896. **c.** Of a Treasury bill: Newly issued (*colloq.*) 1928. **d.** Of dance music: Highly elaborated 1928. **8.** That has not had time to cool down; said *esp.* of acts, and of a person fresh from an act ME. **†9.** *absol.* or as *sb.* Hot condition, heat –1667.

1. The wether was hoat HALL. Three h. dishes WOOD. 2. I am h. with haste SHAKS. Violent H. Pains 1702. 4. The Mustard is too h. a little *Tam. Shr.* IV. iii. 25. 5. Hotter wex his loue CHAUCER. She is so h. because the meate is colde *Com. Err.* I. ii. 47. 6. In the hottest of the fight 1845. 8. A h. corner 1896.

Phrases. *To blow h. and cold*: see BLOW *v.*[1] *Hot and hot*: said of dishes served in succession as soon as cooked; also *absol.* as *sb.* food thus served. Also *fig.* *To give it* (a person) *h.*: to administer a severe chastisement. So *to get* or *catch it h.* (colloq.). *To make it h. for*: to make the position uncomfortable for. *Too h. for* or *too h. to hold* (a person): said of a place, etc. which is made too disagreeable for him.

Comb.: **h. air,** vapourous or pretentious talk; also *attrib.*; **-drawn** *a.*, extracted with the application of heat (opp. to *cold-drawn*); **-plate,** a heated flat surface on a stove, etc., for cooking or the like; **h. spot** *spec.*, (*a*) a spot in the intake manifold of an internal-combustion engine specially heated from the exhaust; (*b*) a spot in the combustion chamber which becomes overheated and causes preignition; **h. with** (*colloq.*), h. spirits and water with sugar 1837.

Hot, *adv.* [OE. *háte*; afterwards levelled with the adj.] **1.** At a high temperature; pungently. **2.** *fig.* Ardently, violently, angrily, etc.; see the adj. ME.

Hot (hǫt), *v.* [OE. *hátian*, f. *hát* HOT *a.*] **†1.** *intr.* To be or become hot. (Only in OE.) **2.** *trans.* To heat. (Now *colloq.*) late ME.

Hot, obs. pa. t. and pple. of HIGHT.

Ho·tbed, ho·t-bed. 1626. **1.** A bed of earth heated by fermenting manure, for raising or forcing plants. **2.** *fig.* A place that favours the rapid growth or development of any condition, e.g. of corruption 1768. **3.** 'A platform in a rolling-mill on which rolled bars lie to cool' (Raymond) 1881. **4.** *attrib.* 1810.

2. Hotbeds of fever and ague KINGSLEY.

Hot blast. 1836. A blast of heated air forced into a furnace. Also *attrib.*, and short for *hot-blast process*, etc.

Hot-bloo·ded, *a.* 1598. Having hot blood; ardent or excitable; passionate.

Ho·t-brain. 1605. = HOT-HEAD. So **Ho·t-brained** *a.*, having an excitable brain.

Hotchkiss (hǫ·tʃkis). 1880. [Inventor's name.] A kind of machine gun and of rifle.

Hotchpot, hotch-pot (hǫ·tʃ,pǫt). ME. [a. F. *hochepot*, f. *hocher* to shake together + *pot* POT.] **1.** = HOTCHPOTCH 1. **2.** *Eng. Law.* The blending or gathering together of properties for the purpose of securing equality of division, *esp.* in the distribution of the property of an intestate parent; cf. COLLATION *sb.* 1. 1552. Also *fig.* **3.** *transf.* = HOTCHPOTCH 2. ME.

2. Bring the amount of their advancement into h. J. WILLIAMS. 3. A h. of true religion and poperye UDALL.

Hotchpotch, hotch-potch (hǫ·tʃ,pǫtʃ). ME. [A corruption of prec.] **1.** *Cookery.* A dish containing a mixture of many ingredients 1583. **2.** *fig.* A confused assemblage, a medley, jumble, farrago ME. **3.** *Eng. Law.* = HOTCHPOT 2. 1602. **4.** *adj.* Like a hotchpot, confused 1599.

2. A hotch-potch of errors 1728. 4. This h. Religion PURCHAS.

Hot cockles. *Obs.* exc. *Hist.* 1580. [f. HOT *a.* + ?COCKLE *sb.*[2]] A rustic game in which one player covers his eyes and being struck by the others in turn guesses who struck him. Also *attrib.*

Hot dog. *U.S. colloq.* 1908. A hot sausage enclosed as a sandwich in a roll of bread.

Hote: see HIGHT *v.*[1]

Hotel (hote·l, ote·l). 1644. [a. F. *hôtel*, later form of *hostel*.] **1.** (In Fr. use.) **a.** A town mansion. ‖**b.** A public official residence, *Hôtel de ville*, a town hall. ‖**c.** *Hôtel-Dieu*, a hospital. **†2.** A HOSTEL in a university 1748. **3.** An inn; esp. one of a superior kind 1765.

1. A few great men still retained their hereditary hotels between the Strand and the river MACAULAY.

Ho·t-foot. *adv.* ME. [f. HOT *a.* + FOOT *sb.*] With eager pace; in hot haste; hastily. Also as *adj.* 1582, as *sb.* 1869, and as *vb.* 1896.

Ho·t(-)head. 1660. A hot-headed person.

Hot-headed (hǫ·t,he:dėd,-he·dėd), *a.* 1641. **1.** Having a hot head (in *lit.* sense) 1693. **2.** *fig.* Excitable; impetuous, headstrong, rash 1641.

2. Too hot-headed and violent for a diplomatist 1887. Hence **Hot-hea·ded·ly** *adv.*, **-ness.**

Hot-house, hothouse (hǫ·thaus). 1451. **†1.** = BAGNIO 1. –1759. **†2.** A brothel –1699. **3.** A structure kept artificially heated for the growth of plants of warmer climates, or of flowers and fruits out of season. Also *attrib.* Also *fig.* 1749. **4.** A heated room or building for drying something 1555.

3. The technical system is a h. of mendacity BENTHAM.

‖**Hoti** (hǫ·ti). *Pl.* **hoties** (hǫ·tiz). 1638. [Gr. ὅτι conj., that.] A statement introduced by 'that'; an assertion, or fact asserted (opp. to DIOTI).

Poor sciolists who scarce know the Hoties of things HOWELL.

Hotly (hǫ·tli), *adv.* 1525. [-LY [2].] **1.** With great heat; so as to be hot or pungent 1592. **2.** *fig.* With fervour; ardently, passionately, keenly; excitedly.

2. The King h. retorted [etc.] GREEN. So **Ho·tness,** heat.

Ho·t-pot, hot pot. 1700. **1.** A hot drink of ale, etc. *local.* **2.** A dish composed of mutton or beef with potatoes, or potatoes and onions, cooked in an oven in an earthenware pot with a tight-fitting cover 1854. Also *attrib.*

Ho·t-press, *sb.* 1631. A contrivance for pressing paper or cloth between glazed boards and hot metal plates, to make the surface smooth and glossy. Also *attrib.* = *hot-pressed.* So **Hot-press** *v.* to subject to pressure in a hot-press; to make smooth and glossy by so doing. Usu. in pa. pple., or vbl. sb. **Hot-presser,** one whose occupation is hot-pressing paper or cloth.

Ho·t-short, *a.* 1798. [f. HOT *a.* + *short*, after RED-SHORT, etc.] Of iron: Brittle in its hot state; opp. to *cold-short.*

Hotspur (hǫ·tspʌɹ). 1460. **1.** One whose spur is hot with impetuous riding; hence, a heady or rash person. **2.** *attrib.* or *adj.* Fiery-spirited, hasty, rash 1596. **3.** An early pea 1700.

1. Herry Percy the yonger, whom the Scottis clepid Herry Hatspore CAPGRAVE. Hence **Ho·t-spurred** *a.* = 2.

Hottentot (hǫ·t'ntǫt). 1677. [a. Du. *Hottentot*, said by Dapper to mean 'stutterer' or 'stammerer'.] **1.** A member of a native S. African race of low stature and dark yellowish-brown complexion, who formerly occupied the region near the Cape of Good Hope. **b.** *transf.* A person of inferior intellect or culture 1726. **2.** *attrib.* Of or belonging to this race 1718.

1. b. The utmost I can do for him, is to consider him a respectable H. CHESTERF. *Comb.*: **Hottentot('s) bread,** *Testudinaria elephantipes*; **H. cherry,** *Cassine maurocenia.* Hence **Ho·ttentotism,** a practice characteristic of Hottentots, a species of stammering.

Hot water. ME. **1.** Water at a high temperature. Also *attrib.* **2.** *fig.* A state of ferment, trouble, or great discomfort; a scrape (*colloq.*) 1537.

2. Always getting into hot water R. H. DANA.

Hot well, hot-well. ME. **1.** A spring of naturally hot water. **2.** A reservoir in a condensing steam-engine, into which the hot water passes from the condenser 1766.

Houdah: see HOWDAH.

Hough (hǫk), *sb.* [Early ME. *hoȝ*, *houȝ*. See also HOCK *sb.*[2]] **1.** = HOCK *sb.*[2] 1. **2.** The hollow part behind the knee-joint in man; the adjacent back part of the thigh. Chiefly *Sc.* 1508. **3.** A joint of beef, venison, etc., consisting of the part extending from the hough (sense 1) some distance up the leg; the 'leg' of beef ME. Hence **Hough** *v.* to disable by cutting the sinew or tendons of the h.; to hamstring. **Hou·gher,** one who houghs or hamstrings; in Ireland, one of the Whiteboys.

Hough, var. spelling of HOE *sb.*[2] and *v.*

Hough-sinew, *sb.* (OE.) and *v.* (1472). = HOUGH *sb.*, *v.*

Houlet, obs. f. HOWLET.

Hoult, var. of HOLT.

Hound (haund), *sb.*[1] [Com. Teut.: OE. *hund* :—OTeut. **hundo-z*, taken to be a deriv. of base **hun-*, pre-Teut. **kun-*, in Gr. κύων, κυν-; cf. also L. *canis*.] **1.** A dog, generally. (Now only *arch.* or *poet.*) **2.** *spec.* A dog kept or used for the chase, usu. one hunting by scent. Now esp. applied to a foxhound; also to a harrier; (*the*) *hounds*, a pack of foxhounds. ME. Also *fig.* and *transf.* **3. a.** Applied opprobriously or contemptuously to a man; cf. DOG *sb.* OE. **b.** *transf.* A player who follows the 'scent' in *hare and hounds* 1857. **4.** Short for HOUND-FISH 1603. **5.** *attrib.* 1483.

2. Phr. *To ride to hounds*, *To follow the hounds*. *To hold with the hare and run with the hounds*: see HARE. *transf.* or *fig.* *The h. of hell*, Cerberus; *Orion's h.*, the dog-star. 3. Boy, false H. *Cor.* V. vi. 113. *Comb.* **h.-shark,** a small species of shark, *Galeus canis*, common on the Atlantic coast of N. America.

Hound (haund), *sb.*[2] 1495. [app. a corruption of an earlier **houn*, early ME. *hūn*, a. ON. *húnn* 'knob', esp. 'the knob at the top of the mast-head'. The *-d* is excrescent.] **1.** *Naut.* A projection or cheek, of which one or more are fayed to the sides of the masthead to serve as supports for the trestle-trees. **2.** One of the wooden bars connecting the fore-carriage of a springless wagon, etc., with the splinter-bar or shaft. *U.S.* and *local Eng.* 1860.

Hound (haund), *v.* 1528. [f. HOUND *sb.*[1]] **1.** *trans.* To hunt, chase, or pursue with hounds, or as a dog does. Also *absol.* Also *fig.* and *transf.* **2.** To set (a hound, etc.) *at* a quarry; to incite or urge *on* to attack or chase anything

1652. 3. *transf.* To incite or set (a person) *at* or *on* another; also *Sc.* with *out* 1570.

1. *transf.* To h. the fugitives from place to place 1897. 3. To h. the rabble upon them as tyrants MOTLEY.

Hou·nd-fish, hou·ndfish. ME. †1. = DOG-FISH. 2. Applied to: a. species of garfish of genus *Tylosurus*; b. *Blue hound-fish*, a former name in Massachusetts of *Pomatomus saltatrix*, now called the Bluefish; c. *Speckled hound-fish*, a former name of the Spanish Mackerel 1672.

Hou·nding, *sb.* 1860. [f. HOUND *sb.*[2]] *Naut.* The lower part of the mast, below the hounds.

Hounding (hau·ndiŋ), *vbl. sb.* 1854. [f. HOUND *v.*] The action of HOUND *v.*; *spec.* the tracking and driving of a deer, etc., by a hound or hounds, until it is brought under the hunter's gun. Also *fig.*

†Hou·nds-berry. ME. 1. The Black Bryony, *Tamus communis.* 2. The Black Nightshade, *Solanum nigrum* -1597. 3. The Wild Cornel or Dogwood. LYTE.

†Hou·ndsfoot. 1710. [ad. Du. *hondsvot*, Ger. *hundsfott*, scoundrel, lit. *cunnus canis.*] A scoundrel, a rascal. Also *attrib.* -1814.

Hound's-tongue. OE. [tr. Gr. *κυνόγλωσσον.*] Any plant of the genus *Cynoglossum* of boraginaceous plants, esp. *C. officinale.*

Hour (auᵊɹ). ME. [a. OF. *ure, ore,* later *hure, hore, h)eure,* mod.F. *heure* :—L. *hora* hour, a. Gr. *ὥρα* season, time of day.] 1. The twenty-fourth part of a civil day; sixty minutes. 2. A short or limited space of time, more or less than an hour ME.; *pl.* stated time of occupation or duty 1857. 3. Each of those points of time at which the twelve successive divisions after noon or midnight, as shown by a dial, are completed; hence, any definite 'time of day' ME. b. *pl.* Habitual time of getting up and (esp.) going to bed 1556. 4. A definite time in general; an appointed time; an occasion ME. 5. *Eccl. pl.* In full *canonical hours* (see also CANONICAL): The seven offices of mattins (with lauds), prime, terce, sext, none, vespers, and compline; a book containing these; *sing.* any of these. (The earliest recorded use.) ME. 6. *Mythol.* (*pl.*, with capital H, = L. *Horæ*, Gr. *Ὧραι.*) Female divinities supposed to preside over the changes of the seasons 1634. 7. *Astr.* and *Geog.* An angular measure of right ascension or longitude, being the 24th part of a great circle of the sphere, or 15 degrees 1777.

1. *Sidereal, solar hour*, 24th part of a sidereal, solar day. Thus this battaile continued .III. long houres HALL. 2. Sad houres seeme long *Rom. & Jul.* I. i. 167. A reduction of hours without any diminution of wages MILL. 3. Watchmen..called the hours of the night SERJT. BALLANTINE. *The eleventh h.*: see ELEVENTH. *Small hours*: the hours after midnight numbered one, two, etc. b. I keep early hours 1891. 4. Myne houre is not yett come TINDALE *John* ii. 4. Phr. *Of the h.*: of the present hour; as in 'the question of the h.' *In a good* (*happy*, etc.) *h.*: at a fortunate time; happily; so *in an evil* (*ill*, etc.) *h.* 6. The rosy-bosomed Hours MILT. *Comus* 986.

Comb.: **h.-angle,** *Astr.* the angular distance between the meridian and the declination-circle passing through a heavenly body, which is the measure of the sidereal time elapsed since its culmination; **-bell,** a bell rung every h., or that sounds the hours; **-book,** *Eccl.* a book of hours (sense 5 b); **-hand,** the short hand of a clock or watch which indicates the hours; **-plate,** the dial-plate of a clock or watch, inscribed with figures denoting the hours.

Hou·r-circle. 1674. 1. Any great circle of the celestial sphere passing through the poles; a meridian or declination-circle. Twenty-four of these are commonly marked on the globe, each distant from the next by one hour of right ascension. 1690. 2. A small brass circle at the north pole of an artificial globe, graduated into hours and divisions of an hour 1674. 3. A graduated circle upon an equatorial telescope, parallel to the plane of the equator, by means of which the hour-angle of a star is observed 1837.

Hou·r-glass. 1515. A contrivance for measuring time, consisting of a glass vessel with obconical ends connected by a constricted neck, through which a quantity of sand (or sometimes mercury) runs in exactly an hour. Often *fig.* Also *attrib.* referring to the shape of an hour-glass.

The figure of Time with an Hour-glass in one hand, and a Scythe in the other ADDISON.

‖**Houri** (hūᵊri, hauᵊ·ri). 1737. [a. F. *houri*, a. Pers. *ḥūrī*, f. (ult.) Arab. *ḥawira* to be black-eyed like a gazelle.] A nymph of the Mohammedan Paradise. Hence, a voluptuously beautiful woman.

Hourly (auᵊ·ɹli), *a.* 1513. [-LY[1].] 1. Of or belonging to an hour; of an hour's age or duration. 2. Occurring every hour; done, etc. hour by hour; frequent, continual 1530.

2. This is an accident of hourely proofe SHAKS.

Hourly (auᵊ·ɹli), *adv.* 1470. [-LY[2].] 1. Every hour; continually, very frequently. †2. For a short time -1549.

1. Two spoonfuls h. BYRON.

Housage (hau·zėdʒ). 1617. [f. HOUSE *v.*[1] + -AGE.] 1. A fee paid for housing goods. 2. The condition of being housed. COLERIDGE.

House (haus), *sb.*[1] Pl. **houses** (hau·zėz). [Com. Teut.: OE. *hūs*; referred by some to the verb root *hud-, hūd-* of *hȳdan* to HIDE, Indo-European stem *keudh-.*] 1. A building for human habitation; *esp.* a dwelling-place. b. The portion of a building occupied by one tenant or family. *Sc.* 2. A place of worship; a temple; a church. (Usu. *h. of God, of prayer*, etc.) OE. b. An inn, tavern 1550. 3. A building for the keeping of cattle, birds, plants, goods, etc. 1503. 4. a. A religious house, a convent; *transf.* the religious fraternity abiding there ME. b. A college in a university (i.e. either the building, or the fellows and students collectively) 1536. c. A boarding-house attached to a public school; the boys lodged there 1857. d. The building in which a legislative or deliberative assembly meets; *transf.* the assembly itself; a quorum of such an assembly 1541. e. Applied also to other deliberative assemblies; formerly also to a municipal corporation 1562. f. A place of business; *transf.* a mercantile firm. *The H.* (colloq.): the Stock Exchange. g. A theatre, PLAYHOUSE; *transf.* the audience or attendance 1662. 5. The persons living in one dwelling; a household, family OE. 6. A family including ancestors and descendants; a lineage, a race OE. 7. a. *fig.* Dwelling-place; place of abode, rest, deposit, etc. OE. b. *transf.* The habitation of any animal OE. 8. *Astrol.* a. A twelfth part of the heavens as divided by great circles through the north and south points of the horizon; the whole sky, excluding those parts that never rise and that never set, being thus divided into twelve houses, numbered eastwards, beginning with the *house of the ascendant* (see ASCENDANT B. 1), each having its special signification. b. A sign of the zodiac considered as the seat of the greatest influence of a particular planet; each of the seven planets, except the sun and moon, having two such houses, a *day house* and a *night house.* ME. †9. Each square of a chess-board 1562-1829.

1. His h. is his castle MULCASTER. *The H.*, a euphemism for the workhouse. 2. When my master goeth into the h. of Rimmon to worship there 2 *Kings* v. 18. On to God's h. the people prest TENNYSON. b. To drink freely..for the good of the h. GOLDSM. A tied house..is one..owned by a brewer for the sale of his goods 1891. 3. Doues with noysome stench Are from their..Houses driven away 1 *Hen. VI*, I. v. 24. 4. b. Heads of Houses 1856. *The H.*, Christ Church, Oxford. *Peterhouse*, St. Peter's College, Cambridge. d. Phr. *To make a h., keep a h.* (i.e. a quorum). f. The Rule of the House is sometimes a great bugbear to compositors 1892. g. Acted..to constantly crowded houses CIBBER. 5. The whole h. was down with influenza (*mod.*). 6. A plague a both your houses! *Rom. & Jul.* III. i. 111. 7. a. Yet if some voice that man could trust Should murmur from the narrow h. TENNYSON. b. The swallow..to build his hanging h. Intent THOMSON.

Phrases. *H. of call*: a. a h. where journeymen of a particular trade assemble, where carriers call for commissions, or where various persons may be heard of; b. a h. where one is wont to call. *H. of ill* (*evil*) *fame* (*repute*): a disreputable h.; *esp.* a brothel. *H. and home*: an alliterative strengthening of 'home'. *H. of office*: domestic apartment; †pantry; privy 1419. †*H. of religion* (also *h. of piety*): a religious house, a convent. *Keep h.* a. To maintain and preside over a household; also *fig.* b. To manage the affairs of a household. (See also HOUSEKEEPER, -KEEPING.) c. (Usu. *to keep the h.*) To stay indoors; to be confined to the h.; also *fig.* *Like a h. on fire* (*afire*): as fast as a h. would burn. *As safe as houses*: perfectly safe.

attrib. and *Comb.* 1. General: as *h.-drain, -rent, -room, -wall, -window*, etc.; *h.-broom, -clock, -flannel*, etc.; *h. affairs, h. work*; *h.-chaplain, -folk*, etc.; *h.-hunter, -hunting, -owner*, etc.; *h.-proud* adj., etc.

2. Special: as **h.-agent,** an agent employed in the sale and letting of houses, the collection of rents, etc.; **-barge** = HOUSE-BOAT; **-book,** a book for household accounts; **-boy**; **-car** (*U.S.*), 'a box-car; a closed railroad-car for carrying freight'; **-chambermaid,** a servant who is both chambermaid and housemaid; **-cricket,** the common species of cricket (*Acheta domestica*) frequenting houses (as dist. from the *field-cricket*); **-dinner, -supper,** (held at a club, school, boarding-house, etc., for members and their guests); **-duty,** a tax imposed on inhabited houses in England; **-engine** (*Mech.*), a steam-engine structurally dependent on the building in which it is contained; **-factor** = *house-agent*; **-flag,** the distinguishing flag of a shipping house; **-fly,** the common fly (*Musca domestica*); **-line** *Naut.*, a small line of three strands, used for seizings, etc. (also called *housing*); **-martin,** the common martin (*Chelidon urbica*); **-parlour-maid** (cf. *house-chambermaid*); **-party,** the guests staying in a h.; **-physician,** a resident physician in a hospital; **-shrew,** the common shrew-mouse (*Crocidura* (*Sorex*) *aranea*); **-snake,** *Ophibolus getulus*, found in N. America, also called *chain-snake*; **-sparrow,** the common sparrow (*Passer domesticus*); **-spider,** any species of spider infesting houses; **-surgeon,** a resident surgeon in a hospital; **-swallow,** the common swallow (*Hirundo rustica*); **-tablemaid** (cf. *house-chambermaid*); **-tax** = *house-duty*; **-waiting-maid** (cf. *house-chambermaid*); †**-wood,** wood for housebote.

House (haus), *sb.*[2] ME. [a. OF. *huche, houce*, mod.F. *housse*, perh. f. Arab.] A covering of textile material; usu. one attached to a saddle, so as to cover the back and flanks of a horse; a housing.

House (hauz), *v.*[1] [OE. *hūsian* (in sense 1), f. *hūs* HOUSE *sb.*[1]]

I. *trans.* 1. To receive or put into a house; to provide with a house to dwell in; to keep or store in a house or building. †b. To drive or pursue into a house -1715. 2. To receive, as a house does; to give shelter to 1610. 3. *transf.* and *fig.* To cover as with a roof; to harbour, lodge 1577. 4. a. *Naut.* To place in a secure or unexposed position; to lower and fasten 1769; to cover or protect with a roof 1821. b. *Carpentry.* To fix in a socket, mortice, or the like 1833. c. *pass.* Of hops: To become massed with bines at the top of the poles.

1. To h. plants BACON, an oat-rick G. WHITE, children 1832. b. *Com. Err.* v. i. 188. 2. Caves That h. the cold-crowned snake TENNYSON. 4. a. A large ship, with her top-gallant-masts housed R. H. DANA.

II. *intr.* †1. To erect a house; to build -1496. 2. To dwell in (or as in) a house; to harbour 1591. †3. *House in* (also in *pass.*): said of a ship of which the upper works are built narrower than the lower -1711.

2. Graze where you will, you shall not h. with me SHAKS. Where Saturn houses DRYDEN.

House (hauz), *v.*[2] 1500. [f. HOUSE *sb.*[2]; cf. F. *housser.*] *trans.* To cover (a horse) with a house or housing.

Hou·se-boat. 1790. A boat roofed over and fitted up as a house, for living in.

Hou·sebote. [OE. *hūsbōt*, f. *hūs* HOUSE + *bōt* BOOT *sb.*[1]] *Law.* The repair of a house; wood for this purpose; the right of a tenant to take this from the landlord's estate.

Housebreaker (hau·sˌbrēkəɹ). ME. 1. One who breaks open and enters a house with intent to commit a felony. 2. One whose business it is to demolish houses 1875. Hence **Hou·se-break** *v.* to break into a house with felonious intent. So **Hou·sebreaking,** the crime of breaking open and entering a house with felonious intent. Also *attrib.*

Hou·se-builder. 1769. One whose business is the building of houses; a builder.

House-builder Moth: a W. Indian insect (*Oiketicus Sandersii*).

Housecarl (hau·sˌkāɹl). [Late OE. a. ON. *húskarl* (HOUSE, CARL).] *Hist.* A member of the bodyguard or household troops of a (Danish or late Old English) king or noble.

Hou·se-dog. 1711. A watch-dog; a domestic dog.

Hou·se-dove. 1530. 1. A tame dove or pigeon. 2. *fig.* A stay-at-home 1579.

Hou·se-father. 1552. [tr. Ger. *hausvater.*] The father of a household or family; the male head of a collection of persons living together as a family.

Household (hau·s,hōuld). ME. [f. HOUSE *sb.*[1] + HOLD *sb.*[1]] I. †1. The maintaining of a house or family; housekeeping –1576. †2. The contents of a house collectively; household goods –1709. 3. The inmates of a house collectively; a domestic establishment ME. 4. Ellipt. for *h. bread, coal*, etc. 1638.

3. The master of the h. should be up early and before all his servants JOWETT. The housholde of fayth TINDALE *Gal.* vi. 10. *The Household* = the royal or imperial h.

II. *attrib.* (and *adj.*) a. Of or belonging to a household, domestic ME. b. Of or belonging to the royal household, as **h. troops,** troops specially appointed to guard the person of the sovereign 1711. c. *fig.* Familiar, intimate, homely (*arch.*) 1450.

c. Good plain houshold judgment STERNE.

Comb.: **h. bread,** bread for ordinary household use; now, white bread made of inferior flour; **h. franchise, suffrage,** the right of voting in parliamentary or other elections, consequent on being a householder (see HOUSEHOLDER); **h. gods** (*Rom. Antiq.*), the *Lares* and *Penates*, divinities supposed to preside over the h., whose images were kept in the *atrium* or central room of the house; *fig.* the essentials of home life; **h. loaf,** a loaf of h. bread; **h. servant; h. word,** a saying in familiar use; a name known to everybody.

Householder (hau·s,hōuldəɹ). ME. [f. HOUSE *sb.*[1] + HOLDER[1] 2.] The person who holds or occupies a house as his own dwelling and that of his household; esp., one qualified to exercise the franchise by the occupancy of a house or tenement. Hence, The head of a household or family.

With your head full of ten-pound householders MACAULAY. So **Hou·seholding** *sb.* †housekeeping; occupation of a house; also *attrib.*

Household-stuff. *arch.* 1511. The goods, utensils, vessels, etc. belonging to a household.

Housekeeper (hau·s,kīpəɹ). 1440. [f. HOUSE *sb.*[1] + KEEPER, i. e. keeper of a house.] 1. = HOUSEHOLDER. Now *rare* or *Obs.* †2. One who keeps a (good, bountiful, etc.) house; a hospitable person –1707. 3. a. A person in charge of a house, office, place of business, etc. 1632. †b. A watch-dog –1688. 4. A woman engaged in housekeeping; *esp.* the woman in control of the female servants of a household 1607. 5. One who 'keeps the house', or stays at home 1710.

2. John Barnston..a bountiful house keeper FULLER. 3. b. *Macb.* III. i. 97. 4. *Cor.* I. iii. 55.

Housekeeping (hau·s,kīpiŋ), *sb.* 1538. [f. HOUSE *sb.*[1] + KEEPING *vbl. sb.*] 1. The maintenance of a household; the management of household affairs 1550. †2. The keeping of a good (or other) table; hospitality –1849. b. *concr.* Provisions for household use (*pseudo-arch.*) 1826.

2. b. 'Tell me..what is in the pantry?' 'Small h. enough,' said Phoebe SCOTT.

Housel (hau·z'l), *sb. Obs.* exc. *Hist.* [OE. *húsl.*] The consecrated elements at the Eucharist; the administration or reception of the Holy Communion.

Housel (hau·z'l), *v. Obs.* exc. *Hist.* [OE. *húslian*, f. *húsl* HOUSEL *sb.*] *trans.* To administer, *pass.* (and *refl.*) to receive, the Holy Communion.

Houseleek (hau·s,līk). 1440. [OE. type **húsléac*, f. *hús* HOUSE *sb.*[1] + *léac* LEEK.] The plant *Sempervivum tectorum*, a succulent herb with pink flowers, thick stem, and leaves forming a dense rosette close to the root, which grows commonly on walls and roofs. Hence, any species of the genus *Sempervivum*, N.O. *Crassulaceæ*.

Houseless (hau·slės), *a.* ME. [-LESS.] 1. Not having a house; having no shelter; homeless. 2. Destitute of houses to shelter 1586.

1. Your House-lesse heads SHAKS. 2. The h. woods WORDSW. Hence **Hou·selessness,** h. condition.

Houseling (hau·sliŋ), *sb. Obs.* or *dial.* 1598. [-LING.] A stay-at-home; also, an animal bred up by hand (*dial.*).

Houseling, -lling (hau·z'liŋ), *vbl. sb. Obs.* exc. *Hist.* OE. [f. HOUSEL *v.* + -ING[1].] 1. Administration of the Eucharist; communion. 2. *attrib.* Sacramental 1474.

2. Phr. **Houseling people**: communicants.

Housemaid (hau·s,mēid). 1694. A female domestic servant, having charge esp. of the reception-rooms and bed-rooms. Also *attrib.*

Housemaid's knee: an inflammation of the bursa over the knee-cap, induced by kneeling on hard floors.

Housemaster (hau·s,ma:stəɹ). 1878. 1. The master of a house or household (*rare*). 2. (*Hou·se-ma·ster.*) The master of a boarding-house at a public school 1884.

Housemate (hau·s,mēit). 1809. One who lives in the same house with another. Also *fig.*

Hou·se-mother. 1837. [tr. Ger. *hausmutter.*] The mother of a household or family; the female head of a community living together as a family.

Hou·se-place, houseplace. 1812. The common living-room in a farm-house or cottage (*local*).

Hou·se-room. 1586. Room in a house for a person or thing; lodging. Also *fig.*

Hou·se-top. 1526. The top or roof of a house. b. *fig.* A public place (cf. Luke xii. 3).

Hou·se-warming. 1577. The action of celebrating the entrance into the occupation of a new house or home with an entertainment; also, the entertainment.

I dined at Chiffinch's house-warming EVELYN. Hence **House-warm** *v.* to give, or take part in, a h.

Housewife (hau·s,wəif, hʊ·zwif, hʊ·zif), *sb.* Pl. **housewives** (hau·s,wəivz, hʊ·z(w)ivz). [ME. (12th c.) *hus(e)wif*, f. *hūs* HOUSE *sb.*[1] + *wīf* woman, WIFE. Elision of *w* (cf. *Chiswick*, etc.) gave the forms *huzzif, hussive.*] 1. The mistress of a family; the wife of a householder. Often, A woman who manages her household with skill and thrift, a domestic economist. †2. A light, worthless, or pert woman or girl. Usu. *huswife*; now HUSSY, q.v. –1705. 3. (Usu. hʊ·zif). A pocket-case for needles, pins, thread, scissors, etc. (Still often spelt *huswife, hussive.*) 1749.

1. There is..but An Hour in one whole Day between A H. and a Slut 1710.

Hou·sewife (see prec.), *v.* Now *rare.* Also -wive. 1566. [f. prec. sb.] 1. *intr.* To act the housewife; to manage a household with skill and thrift; to practise economy. 2. *trans.* To manage with skill and thrift; to economize, make the most of. (Cf. *to husband.*) 1632.

2. The vndrest Hearth, and the ill house-wif'd roome 1649. I must h. the money DE FOE.

Housewifely (hau·s,wəifli, hʊ·z(w)ifli), *a.* 1526. [f. as prec. + -LY[1].] 1. Of the character of a housewife; skilful and thrifty in the management of a house. 2. Belonging to or befitting a housewife 1560.

2. A most h. bunch of keys C. BRONTË.

Housewifery (hau·s,wəifri, hʊ·z(w)ifri). 1440. [f. as prec. + -RY.] 1. The function or province of a housewife; domestic economy; housekeeping. 2. *concr.* Articles of household use. ? *Obs.* 1552.

Housewright (hau·s,rəit). Now *rare.* 1549. [f. HOUSE *sb.*[1] + WRIGHT.] A builder of houses; a house-carpenter.

Housing (hau·ziŋ), *sb.*[1] ME. [f. HOUSE *v.*[1] or *sb.*[1] + -ING[1].] 1. The action of HOUSE *v.*[1] 2. a. Shelter of or as of a house; lodging ME. b. Houses collectively; house-property; *spec.* outhouses or outbuildings ME. †c. A house ME. d. Provision of houses 1899. †3. *Arch.* A canopied niche for a statue, etc.; also *collect.* tabernacle-work –1521. (*Hist.*) 4. *Naut.* a. A covering or roofing for a ship when laid up, or under stress of weather. b. The part of a lower mast between the heel and the upper deck, or of the bowsprit between the stem and the knight-heads. c. = *house-line* (see HOUSE *sb.*[1]). 1821. 5. *Carpentry.* A space excavated out of one body for the insertion of the extremity of another 1823. 6. *Mech.* a. 'One of the plates or guards on the railway-carriage or truck, which form a lateral support for the axle-boxes'. b. 'The framing holding a journal-box.' c. 'The uprights supporting the cross-slide of a planer.' (KNIGHT.) 1875. *Comb.* **h.-box** = JOURNAL-BOX.

Housing (hau·ziŋ), *sb.*[2] ME. [f. HOUSE *sb.*[2] and *v.*[2] + -ING[1].] 1. A covering. (Often in *pl.*) Rare in gen. sense. 2. *spec.* A cloth covering put on a horse, etc., for defence or ornament; caparison, trappings 1645. b. 'The leather fastened at a horse's collar to turn over the back when it rains' (Halliwell). 3. *attrib.*, as in **h.-cloth,** a cloth used for a housing 1607.

Housling: = HOUSELING.

Houss, var. of HOUSE *sb.*[2]

‖**Houstonia** (hustōu·niă). 1838. [mod.L., f. Dr. W. *Houston*, a botanist (died 1733).] *Bot.* A N. American genus of plants (N.O. *Rubiaceæ*), with delicate four-parted flowers of various colours; the best known is *H. cærulea*, the Bluet.

Hout, var. of HOOT.

Houting (hau·tiŋ). 1880. A species of whitefish, *Coregonus oxyrhynchus*, found in some freshwater lakes.

Houve, hoove. *Obs.* or *Sc.* [OE. *hūfe* :— OTeut. **hūƀōn* wk. fem. Cf. HIVE.] A covering for the head; a turban, a coif; a cap, a skull-cap; in Sc. (*how, hoo*) a night-cap.

Houyhnhnm (hwi·hn'm, hwi·n'm). 1727. [A combination of letters to suggest the neigh of a horse.] Swift's name in *Gulliver's Travels* for one of a race of beings described as horses endowed with reason and bearing rule over a degraded brutish race of men, called the Yahoos. Hence *transf.*

†**Hove,** *v.*[1] ME. [Deriv. unkn. In 16th c. largely replaced by HOVER.] 1. *intr.* To HOVER –1590. 2. To wait, linger, stay, remain –1595. 3. To come or go floating or soaring; to be borne, move, or pass away –1650.

Hove, *v.*[2] *Obs.* or *dial.* ME. [app. f. HEAVE *v.* (pa. t. *hove*, pa. pple. *hoven*).] †1. *trans.* To lift –1570. 2. *trans.* To swell, inflate, puff up or out. Chiefly in pa. pple. Hoved = HOVEN. 1601. 3. *intr.* (for *refl.*) To rise; to swell up 1590.

Hove, *v.*[3] Abbrev. for BEHOVE.

Hove, pa. t. and pple. of HEAVE (see also HOVEN).

Hovel (hǫ·v'l, hʊ·v'l), *sb.* ME. [?] 1. An open shed; an outhouse used as a shelter for cattle, a receptacle for grain or tools. 2. A rude or miserable dwelling-place; a wretched cabin 1625. 3. The conical building enclosing a porcelain oven or kiln 1825. 4. A stack of corn, etc. 1591.

Hovel, *v.*[1] 1583. [f. HOVEL *sb.*[1]] a. *trans.* To shelter as in a hovel or shed. b. (*Archit.*) To form like an open hovel or shed; as 'to hovel a chimney' 1823.

a. To houell thee with Swine and Rogues forlorne *Lear* IV. vii. 39.

Hovel, *v.*[2] 1880. [? f. HOVELLER, q.v.] a. *intr.* To pursue the occupation of a hoveller. b. *trans.* To bring (a vessel) into harbour, moor and unload it, etc. Hence **Hovelling** *vbl. sb.* the business of a hoveller, piloting.

Hoveller (hǫ·v'ləɹ, hʊ·v'ləɹ). Also -eler. 1769. [Of unkn. origin.] 1. An unlicensed pilot or boatman, esp. on the Kentish coast; often applied to a boatman who goes out to wrecks, occas. with a view to plunder. 2. The craft used by these boatmen 1880.

Hoven (hōu·v'n), *ppl. a.* Now *dial.* Also hove. 1555. [pa. pple. of HEAVE *v.*] Swollen, bloated, puffed out; as cattle with over-feeding. Also *fig.* Cf. HOOVE.

Hover (hǫ·vəɹ, hʊ·vəɹ), *sb.* 1513. [f. HOVER *v.*] 1. An act of hovering 1893. 2. The action or condition of remaining in suspense 1513. 3. Any overhanging stone or bank under which a fish, otter, etc., can hide. Chiefly *s. dial.* 1602.

Comb. **H.-fly,** a dipterous insect of the order *Bombyliidæ*, which hovers over flowers without settling.

Hover (hǫ·vəɹ, hʊ·vəɹ), *v.* ME. [In 16th c. repl., and perh. an iterative deriv. of, HOVE *v.*] 1. *intr.* To hang or remain suspended in the air *over* or *about* a particular spot. 2. *transf* and *fig.* To keep hanging or lingering *about* (a person or place), to wait near at hand, move to and fro near or around 1581. 3. †To hesitate before taking action; to waver in indecision; hence, to hang *on the verge of* 1440. †4. *trans.* Of a bird: To flap or flutter (the wings) -1687. 5. To brood over; to cover (the young) with wings and body 1776.

1. This hauke hovereth to longe above PALSGR. Cloudes alwaies hovering about the tops thereof 1600. 2. Pestilence was hovering in the track of famine GEO. ELIOT. 3. A mind hovering on the verge of madness (*mod.*). 5. Capons..h. chickens like hens G. WHITE. Hence **Ho·verer**, an animal or thing that hovers. **Ho·veringly** *adv.*

How (hau), *sb.*[1] *north.* ME. [a. ON. *haug-r* mound, cairn, app. related to OTeut. *hauh-* high.] 1. A hill, hillock; as in Great H., Silver H., etc. 2. An artificial mound, tumulus, or barrow 1669.

How (hau), *adv.* (*sb.*[2]) [OE. *hú* :—**hwō* :—OTeut. **hwô*, advb. f. interrog. pron. stem *hwa-* who?] An adverb primarily interrog., used also in exclams., and in conjunctive and relative constructions.

I. In direct questions. 1. In what way or manner? By what means? 2. In what condition or state? ME. 3. To what effect? With what meaning? Also, By what name? *arch.* (Repl. by 'What?') ME. 4. *ellipt.* for 'How is it?' or 'How say you?' and used interjectionally. (Now 'What?' or 'What!') *arch.* (exc. in *how about ...?*) OE. 5. To what extent? In what degree? OE. 6. At what rate or price? 1597.

1. How schulen deede men ryse a3en? WYCLIF 1 *Cor.* xv. 35. How saidst thou, She is my sister? *Gen.* xxvi. 9. *As how* (ellipt.): see As *adv.* *How if..?* = 'How will (would) it be if..?' 2. Phr. *How are you? How do you do?* (formerly *How do you?*). How's little Miss Sharp? THACKERAY. *How's that?* in *Cricket*, an appeal to the umpire to say whether a batsman is 'out' or not. 3. How art thou call'd? SHAKS. 4. How! signior..have you not authority? DE FOE. Don't say 'How?' for 'What?' O. W. HOLMES. 5. How old..are you? 1573. 6. How do you sell the plums? (*mod.*).

II. In direct exclams. In what a way! to what an extent or degree! OE.

How are the mightie fallen! 2 *Sam.* i. 19.

III. In dependent questions and exclams. 1. In what way, manner, condition, etc.; by what means OE. 2. Followed by an infinitive: In what way; by what means ME. 3. After verbs of saying, perceiving, and the like: = That OE. 4. To what extent; in what degree OE.

1. Shakespeare has taught us how great men should speak and act JOWETT. Be wary how you engage THACKERAY. 2. There is no better lesson how not to do it 1897. 3. Shee had heard..how that the Lord had visited his people *Ruth* i. 6.

IV. Introducing a relative clause. 1. In what way, manner, condition, etc.; by what means; in the way that; however; as ME. †2. To what extent, in what degree (that); HOWEVER -1602. †b. Correlative to *so*: To what extent; in what degree; as... as -1879. †3. With sb. as antecedent: In which (way); by which (name) -1690.

1. Be that how it will 1695. 2. b. Phr. *By how much..by so much* = L. *quantum..tantum.* (A Latinism.)

V. With indef. adj. or adv.: In (some, any) way or manner (*rare*) OE.

He found means, some how or other, to go DE FOE. Phrase. **How so.** ME. a. *interrog.*: How is it so? How is that? †b. *relative*: Howsoever. †c. However much; although.

B. *sb.*[2] (often in collocation with *why.*) 1. A question or query as to the way or manner 1533. 2. The way or manner (in which) 1551.

1. Bother your hows and whys! (*mod.*). 2. Must we in all things look for the how, and the why, and the wherefore? LONGF.

How, howe, *int.* (*sb.*[3]) *Obs.* or *dial.* ME. [A natural utterance.] 1. = Ho *int.*[1] Also *sb.* as name for this. 2. A cry of sailors in heaving the anchor up, etc.: usu. with *hale, heave.* Also *sb.* as name for this. 1450.

Howbeit (hau,bī·it). ME. [Orig. three wds. *how be it*, with pa. t. *how were it* (= however it were).]

A. *adv.* However it may be; be that as it may; nevertheless; however (*arch.*) 1470.

†**B.** *conj.* or *conj. adv.* (orig. with *that*). Though, although -1634.

‖**Howdah** (hau·dă). *E. Indies.* Also **houda(h.** 1774. [Pers. and Urdū *haudah*, f. Arab. *haudaj*, a litter carried by a camel or an elephant.] A seat to contain two or more persons, usually fitted with a railing and a canopy, erected on the back of an elephant.

How-do-ye, how-d'ye, howdy, *phr.* and *sb.* Now *Obs.* or *dial.* 1563. 1. The phr. *how do ye? how do you?* = how are you? 2. *sb.* = next 2. 1575. 3. *attrib.* or *adj.* 1600.

How-do-you-do, how-d'ye-do, *phr.* and *sb.* 1632. 1. A phrase inquiring after the health of the person addressed; see Do *v.* 1697. 2. *sb.* Used as a name for the inquiry 1632. 3. A 'business'; an awkward state of things 1835. Hence **How-d'ye-do** *v.* to say 'How d'ye do?' to.

Howdy, -ie (hau·di). *Sc.* and *n. dial.*, *vulgar.* 1725. [?] A midwife.

Howel (hau·ĕl), *sb.* 1846. [prob. f. LG.; cf. MHG. *hovel, hobel*, Ger. *hobel*, etc.] A plane with a convex sole, used by coopers for smoothing the insides of casks, etc. Hence **How·el** *v.* to plane or smooth with a h.

However (hau,e·vəɹ); contr. **howe'er** (hauē·ᵊɹ), *adv.* ME. [f. How *adv.* + EVER *adv.*] 1. In whatever manner; by whatever means: to whatever extent. b. However much; although. *Obs.* or *arch.* 1591. †2. In any case, at all events, at any rate. (Now merged in 3.) -1790. 3. For all that, nevertheless, notwithstanding; yet; = *but* at the beginning of the sentence 1613. 4. Interrog. (and conjunctive): How, in any circumstances or way whatever? (See EVER *adv.*) *colloq.* 1871.

1. I coniure you..(How ere you come to know it) answer me *Macb.* IV. i. 51. His innocence, h. manifest, could not save him M. PATTISON. 3. I, h., Must not omit [etc.] MILTON. 4. H. did you manage it? (*mod.*).

†**Howish** (hau·iʃ), *a. colloq.* 1694. [f. How *adv.* + -ISH.] Having a vague sense of indisposition; 'all-overish' -1802.

†**Howitz, haubitz.** 1687. [a. Ger. *haubitze*, earlier *haufnitz*, ad. Boh. *houfnice* sling, catapult.] = next. (Usu. unchanged in pl.) -1781.

Howitzer (hau·itsəɹ). 1695. [A deriv. of prec.] A short, comparatively light gun, which fires a heavy projectile at a high angle of elevation and low velocity. *Comb.*, as *h.-boat.*

Howker, var. of HOOKER[2].

Howl (haul), *sb.* 1599. [f. HOWL *v.*] 1. The prolonged and mournful cry of a dog, wolf, etc., which dwells upon the vowel *u*; the similar sound of the wind, etc. 1605; or in a wireless receiver during tuning-in 1921. 2. A loud wail of pain or anguish; a savage yell of rage or disappointment. (Often *contempt.*)

1. The Wolfe, Whose howle's his Watch *Macb.* II. i. 54.

Howl (haul), *v.* [ME. *houlen* = MDu. *hûlen*, etc.; echoic. Cf. Gr. ὑλᾶν, L. *ululare*, etc.] 1. *intr.* To utter a prolonged, loud, and doleful cry, in which the sound of *u* (*ū*) prevails. Said of dogs, wolves, etc.; formerly also of the owl. 2. Of a human being: To utter a similar sound; to wail, lament, esp. with pain. Now often used contemptuously. ME. 3. *trans.* To utter with howling. Also *h. out.* 1530. 4. *intr.* To make a prolonged wailing noise. Of an organ: To cipher. 1687. b. Of a wireless receiver (see prec.) 1920.

1. They heard Dogges howle on the shore PURCHAS. 2. Goo to nowe ye Ryche men. Wepe and howle TINDALE *Jas.* v. 1. He still howls about the expense of printing SCOTT. 3. Howling certaine Psalmes PURCHAS. 4. The wind was howling 1875.

Howler (hau·ləɹ). 1840. [f. HOWL *v.* + -ER[1].] 1. An animal that howls; *spec.* a S. American Monkey of the genus *Mycetes*. 2. A person hired to howl at a funeral 1844. 3. *slang.* Something 'crying'; *spec.* a glaring blunder 1872.

Howlet (hau·lĕt, *Sc.* hu·lĕt). *dial.* See also OWLET. 1450. [app. a. F. *hulotte*; cf. Ger. *eule*, MLG. *ûle.*] An owl, owlet.

How·ling, *ppl. a.* 1605. [f. HOWL *v.* + -ING[2].] 1. That howls. 2. Filled with howling; dreary. In the Biblical phr. *h. wilderness*, etc., merely intensive. 1611. 3. *fig.* (chiefly *slang.*) Glaring, 'screaming' 1865.

3. A h. swell SALA. Hence **How·lingly** *adv.*

Howsoever (hausou,e·vəɹ). *arch.* ME. [f. *how so* (see How *adv.*) + EVER *adv.*] 1. = HOWEVER 1. (Sometimes with ellipsis.) 2. With adj. or adv.: To what extent or in what degree soever 1557. †3. = HOWEVER 2. -1663. †4. = HOWEVER 3. -1709.

2. How low soeuer the matter SHAKS. H. well instructed he might be BOLINGBROKE.

Howsomever (hau·sǒme·vəɹ), *adv.* Now *dial.* or *vulgar.* ME. [A parallel formation with *howsoever*, with the conj. *sum, som* (= Da., Sw. *som* as, that) instead of *so.*] †1. = HOWEVER 1, 1 b. -1601. 2. = HOWEVER 3. 1562.

†**Hox,** *v. Obs.* or *dial.* ME. [Shortened from *hoxen* vb.] *trans.* To hough, to hamstring -1756.

Hoy (hoi), *sb.*[1] 1495. [app. ad. MDu. *hoei*, pl. *hoeyen*, mod.Du. †*heude, heu.* Ult. origin unkn.] 'A small vessel, usually rigged as a sloop, and employed in carrying passengers and goods, particularly in short distances on the sea-coast' (Smyth).

Hoy (hoi), *interj.* (*sb.*[2]) ME. [A natural exclam.] 1. A cry used to call attention; also to incite or drive hogs, etc. In naut. language used in hailing or calling aloft. 2. *sb.* A call of 'hoy!' 1641. Hence **Hoy** *v.* to urge on with cries of 'hoy!'; to drive with shouts; *intr.* to call 'hoy!'

‖**Hoya** (hoi·ă). 1851. [mod.Bot.L., f. Thomas *Hoy*, an English gardener (died 1821).] *Bot.* A large genus of climbing herbaceous plants (N.O. *Asclepiadaceæ*), bearing dense umbels of showy flowers; commonly known as *honey-plants, wax-plants*, or *wax-flowers*. They are cultivated in greenhouses for their beauty.

Hoyden (hoi·dĕn), *sb.* (*a.*) 1593. [? Connected with HOIT *v.*] †1. A clown, boor -1708. 2. A rude, or ill-bred girl (or woman); a romp 1676. 3. *attrib.* or *adj.* Belonging to, or of the character of a hoyden; inelegant in deportment, roystering 1728. Hence **Hoy·denhood**, the condition of a h. **Hoy·denish** *a.* having the character or manners of a h.; characteristic of a h. **Hoy·denishness.**

Hoy·den, *v.* 1709. [f. prec. sb.] *intr.* To play the hoyden.

†**Hoyle.** 1614. *Archery.* A mark when shooting at ROVERS -1845.

Hoyman (hoi·măn). 1666. [f. HOY *sb.*[1] + MAN.] A man in charge of a hoy.

Hr-, a frequent combination in OE. [:—OTeut. *hr-* :—Aryan *kr-*]. In initial *hr-*, the *h* was lost in the transition to ME.: e.g. OE. *hræfn, hróf*, etc., now RAVEN, ROOF, etc.

Huanaco, var. of GUANACO.

Hub (hɒb). 1511. [? same wd. as HOB *sb.*[2]] †1. The HOB of a fire-place -1825. 2. The central solid part of a wheel; the nave 1649. 3. *transf.* and *fig.* A central point of revolution, activity, life, interest, etc. 1858. 4. Techn., etc. uses:

a. *Die-sinking.* A cylindrical piece of steel on which the design for a coin is engraved in relief 1851. b. An abruptly raised piece of ground, a stumbling-block 1669. c. A thick sod 1828. d. A block for stopping the wheel of a vehicle 1856.

2. Phr. *Up to the h.* (U.S.): as far as possible; deeply or inextricably involved, as a wheel in mud. 3. Boston State-House is the hub of the solar system O. W. HOLMES. *Comb.* **h.-band**, a metal band to reinforce a wooden h. of a wheel.

Hub a dub. [Echoic.] The noise of beating a drum. MME D'ARBLAY.

Hubble-bubble (hɒ·b'l,bɒ·b'l). 1634. [Reduplication of BUBBLE, as suggestive of the sound.] 1. A rudimentary form of hookah in which the smoke bubbles through a coco-nut shell, or the like, half-filled with water. 2. A representation of a bubbling sound; also of confused talk 1740. 3. *attrib.* Of confused ideas, speech, etc. 1754.

2. There was a considerable roll and hubble-bubble of the tides as we rounded the point LADY BRASSEY.

Hubbub (hɒ·bɒb). 1555. [In 16th c. *hooboube, -boobe*, often referred to as an Irish cry.] 1. A confused noise of a multitude shouting or yelling. b. The din of a crowd, or of a multitude of speakers heard at once 1779. 2. Noisy turmoil; confusion, disturbance; a riot, row 1619.

1. b. The h...of Parliamentary discussion SEELEY. So Hu·bbuboo·, -aboo·, a confused yelling; esp. as a savage war-cry; hence, a tumult, turmoil.

Hubby, *a. U.S.* 1860. [f. HUB 4 b + -Y[1].] 'Full of hubs or projecting protuberances; as, a road that has been frozen while muddy is hubby' (Webster).

Hübnerite (hü·bnərəit). 1867. [f. *Hübner*, who analysed it.] *Min.* Tungstate of manganese, found in reddish-brown bladed crystals.

Hubristic (hiubri·stik), *a.* 1831. [irreg. (for *hybristic*) ad. Gr. ὑβριστικός, f. ὕβρις.] Insolent, contemptuous.

Huck (hɒk), *sb.*[1] *Obs.* exc. *dial.* 1788. (In comb. ME.) [perh. f. Teut. root *huk-*, *hūk-*, *hukk-* to be bent.] The hip, the haunch. *Comb.*: **H.-bone** = HUCKLE-BONE 1. **H.-backed, h.-shouldered** *adjs.* hump-backed, crump-shouldered.

Huck, *sb.*[2] 1851. Short for HUCKABACK, q. v.

Huck (hɒk), *v. Obs.* exc. *dial.* ME. [The base of HUCKSTER, q.v.] *intr.* To higgle in trading; to chaffer, bargain. Also *fig.*

Huckaback (hɒ·kăbæk). 1690. [?] A stout linen fabric, with the weft threads thrown alternately up so as to form a rough surface, used for towelling, etc. Also *attrib.* or as *adj.*

Huckle (hɒ·k'l), *sb.* 1529. [In form, a dim. of HUCK *sb.*[1]] 1. The hip or haunch. †2. ? The hock of a quadruped TOPSELL. *Comb.*: **H.-back**, a hump-back; **h.-backed** *a.*

†**Huckle**, *v.* 1620. [f. HUCK *v.* + -LE iterative.] *intr.* To haggle in bargaining -1655.

Huckleberry (hɒ·k'lˌberi). *U.S.* 1670. [? corrupt f. HURTLEBERRY, WHORTLEBERRY.] The fruit and plant of species of *Gaylussacia* (N.O. *Vacciniaceæ*), low berry-bearing shrubs, common in N. America. Also applied to N. American species of the closely allied *Vaccinium*, more properly called *blueberry*. Also *attrib.*

Huckle-bone (hɒ·k'lˌbōun). 1529. [See HUCKLE *sb.*] 1. The hip- or haunch-bone; the ischium or whole *os innominatum*. 2. The astragalus in the hock-joint of a quadruped; the knuckle-bone 1542.

Huckster (hɒ·kstəɹ), *sb.* ME. [See HUCK *v.* The history is obscure.] 1. A retailer of small goods, in a petty shop or booth, or at a stall; a pedlar, a hawker. b. As term of reproach: A regrater of corn, etc.; a broker, a middleman 1573. 2. *transf.* and *fig.* A person ready to make his profit of anything in a mean and petty way 1553.

Phr. †*In huckster's hands (handling)*: where it is likely to be roughly used or lost; unlikely to be recovered. Hence †**Hu·cksterage**, huckstering, haggling. **Hu·cksteress, -tress**, a female h. **Hu·ckstery**, the business, or place of business, of a h.; *pl.* the goods dealt in by a h.

Hu·ckster, *v.* 1592. [f. HUCKSTER *sb.*] 1. *intr.* To bargain, haggle (*lit.* and *fig.*). 2. *trans.* To traffic in, in a petty way; to retail; to bargain over (*lit.* and *fig.*) 1642. Hence **Hu·cksterer.**

Hud (hɒd). *Obs.* exc. *dial.* ME. [? f. Teut. root *hud-*, *hūd-*, to cover, whence *hide* vb., etc.] The husk of a seed, the hull or shell of a fruit; a pod or seed-vessel.

†**Hudder-mudder**, *sb.* 1461. [A reduplicated compound; app. related to ME. *hoder* vb. to huddle.] Concealment -1583.

Huddle (hɒ·d'l), *sb.* 1579. [app. f. HUDDLE *v.*] 1. A mass of things crowded together in hurried confusion 1586; a confused crowd of persons or animals 1642. 2. a. Confusion, disorder; confused utterance. b. Disorderly haste, hurry, bustle. 1606. †3. A miserly old hunks -1604.

1. The women..were all got in a h. together, out of their wits 1742.

Huddle (hɒ·d'l), *v.* 1579. [? f. as HUD + -LE.]

I. *trans.* †1. To put or keep out of sight; to hush *up* -1795. 2. To jumble; to pile or heap up confusedly 1579. b. To draw (oneself) together 'all of a heap' 1755. 3. To push or thrust in a disorderly mass or heap *into*, *out of* (etc.) 1655. b. with *on*: To put on (clothes) 'all of a heap' 1697. 4. To drive or push hurriedly; to hurry (a person or thing). ? *Obs.* 1649. Also with *over*, *through*, *up*.

1. The matter was hudled up, and little spoken of 1653. 2. Hudling iest vpon iest *Much Ado* II. i. 252. Huddled together in a flock GOLDSM. 3. They huddled the king's body into a postchaise THACKERAY. b. His clothes seem to be huddled on anyhow HELPS. 4. Let him forecast his Work with timely care, Which else is huddled DRYDEN. To h. up a compromise MACAULAY.

II. *intr.* 1. To gather or flock in a congested mass; to crowd together unceremoniously; to nestle closely in a heap. Also with *together*, *up.* 1596. †2. To hurry in disorder or confusion -1766.

1. The cattle huddled on the lea TENNYSON. 2. Fools h. on, and always are in haste ROWE.

†**Hu·ddle**, *a.* and *adv.* 1564. [f. HUDDLE *sb.* or *v.*]

A. *adj.* Huddled, confused, congested -1713.

B. *adv.* Confusedly; in a crowding mass; in disorderly haste -1606.

Hudibrastic (hiūdibræ·stik), *a.* (*sb.*) 1712. [f. *Hudibras*, after *fantastic*, etc.] In the metre or after the manner of *Hudibras*, by Samuel Butler, 1663-78; burlesque-heroic. *sb.* Hudibrastic verse or language 1739. Hence **Hudibra·stically** *adv.*

Hu·dsonite. 1842. [Named from the *Hudson* River, near which it is found.] *Min.* A variety of pyroxene, containing much iron.

Hue (hiū), *sb.*[1] [OE. *hīew*, *hīw* :—(ult.) OTeut. **hiwjom*.] †1. Form; appearance; species -1653. 2. External appearance of the face and skin; complexion. Also *transf.* ME. 3. Colour OE. b. *Chromatics.* Variety of any colour; tint or quality of a particular colour 1857.

2. She was not broun ne dun of hewe CHAUCER. 3. The ashen h. of age SCOTT. b. The first [crimson] is a red with a violet h. 1861.

Hue, *sb.*[2] ME. [a. OF. *hu*, *hui*, etc., f. *huer* to hoot, cry, shout, HUE *v.*[2]] Outcry, shouting, clamour, esp. that raised by a multitude in war or the chase. *Obs.* exc. in HUE AND CRY, q. v.

Hue (hiū), *v.*[1] [OE. *hīwian*, f. *hīw*, HUE *sb.*[1]] *trans.* To form, fashion, figure; esp. (in later use) to colour. Chiefly in pa. pple. Also *fig.*

Hue, *v.*[2] Now *local.* ME. [app. a. F. *huer*; prob. echoic in origin.] 1. *intr.* To shout, make an outcry; *spec.* in hunting, and now in the Cornish sea fisheries. 2. *trans.* To assail, drive, or guide with shouts 1590.

Hue and cry, *sb.* (Often hyphened.) 1502. [Anglo-Norman *hu e cri.*] 1. *Law.* Outcry calling for the pursuit of a felon, raised by the party aggrieved, by a constable, etc. b. A proclamation for the capture of a criminal or the finding of stolen goods 1601. 2. The pursuit of a felon with such outcry 1648. 3. *gen.* A cry of alarm or opposition; outcry 1584. Hence **Hue-and-cry** *v.* to raise the hue and cry; to pursue with hue and cry.

Hued (hiūd), *ppl. a.* OE. [f. HUE *v.*[1] or *sb.*[1] + -ED.] Having a hue, coloured.

Hueless (hiū·lės), *a.* [f. HUE *sb.*[1] + -LESS.] †1. (In OE. and ME.) Formless. 2. Colourless, pallid OE.

Huer (hiū·əɹ). Now *local.* 1530. [f. HUE *v.*[2] + -ER[1].] †1. One employed to drive deer with noise and shouting -1674. 2. *Fishing.* One who directs seine-fishing from high ground by the sea, as in the Cornish pilchard fishery. Cf. BALKER[2]. 1602.

Huff (hɒf), *sb.* 1599. [See HUFF *v.*] †1. A puff of wind; a slight blast -1725. 2. A gust *of* anger or annoyance 1599; a fit of petulance or offended dignity caused by an affront 1757. †3. Inflated opinion of oneself; arrogance, bluster, bounce -1697. †4. One who swaggers; a hector, a bully -1713. 5. *Draughts.* An act of huffing 1860.

2. She went out of the room quite in a h. MISS BURNEY. 4. Every Silly Huff [is call'd] a Captain T. BROWN.

Huff (hɒf), *v.* 1583. [Imitative of the sound of a blast of air through an orifice.] 1. *intr.* To blow, puff. *Obs.* exc. *dial.* †2. *trans.* To blow; esp. to blow or puff *up.* Also *fig.* -1719. 3. *intr.* To swell, swell up. *Obs.* exc. *dial.* 1656. †4. *intr.* To puff or swell with pride or arrogance; to storm, bluster, talk big; to bluff -1734. 5. *intr.* To swell with anger or irritation; to take offence 1598. 6. *trans.* To hector, bully; to chide, storm at. (Cf. 'to blow up'.) 1674. b. To treat with arrogance or contempt 1676. 7. To offend the dignity of; to put in a huff. Chiefly in *passive.* 1814. 8. *Draughts.* To remove (an opponent's man) from the board as a forfeit for failing to take a piece that is *en prise*. The removal was marked by blowing on the piece. 1688.

5. The..woman has huffed, and won't trust me MARRYAT. Hence †**Hu·ffer**, a swaggering, hectoring person. **Hu·ffingly** *adv.*

Huff-cap (hɒ·fˌkæp). *Obs.* or *arch.* 1577. [f. HUFF *v.* + CAP *sb.*, i.e. 'that huffs or raises the cap'.] A. *adj.* 1. Of liquor: Heady. *Obs.* exc. *Hist.* 1599. 2. Blustering, swaggering (*arch.*) 1597. B. *sb.* 1. Strong and heady ale 1577. †2. A swashbuckler -1706.

Hu·ffish, *a.* 1755. [f. HUFF *sb.* + -ISH.] Arrogant; petulant. **Hu·ffish-ly** *adv.*, **-ness.**

Huffle (hɒ·f'l), *v. Obs.* exc. *dial.* 1583. [dim. and freq. of HUFF *v.*: see -LE.] *trans.* To blow, inflate (*lit.* and *fig.*); also *intr.* to bluster; of the wind: to make a sound as of blowing in gusts (hence as *sb.*).

†**Huff-snuff**, *sb.* 1583. [f. HUFF *v.* + SNUFF, in the sense 'offence, resentment'.] A conceited fellow who is quick to take offence; a hector, bully -1653. Also *attrib.*

Huffy (hɒ·fi), *a.* 1677. [f. HUFF *sb.* + -Y[1].] 1. Windy, effervescent, puffy. *Obs.* or *dial.* †2. *fig.* Airy, unsubstantial -1681. †3. Puffed up; haughty; blustering -1691. 4. †a. Arrogant. b. Ready to take offence 1680.

1. Champaign, and other h. liquors 1765. 4. She is very apt to be h. Hence **Hu·ffily** *adv.* **Hu·ffiness.**

Hug (hɒg), *sb.* 1617. [f. HUG *v.*] 1. A strong clasp with the arms; an embrace of affection; the squeeze of a bear 1659. 2. A squeezing grip in wrestling; esp. *Cornish h.*; hence *fig.* 1617.

Hug (hɒg), *v.* 1567. [?] 1. *trans.* To clasp or squeeze tightly in the arms; usu. = embrace; but also said of a bear squeezing a man, etc., between its forelegs. Also *transf.* and *fig.* b. *fig.* To caress or court, *esp.* in order to get favour or patronage 1622. c. To cherish (an opinion, belief, etc.) with fervour 1649. 2. *refl.* †To make oneself snug -1757; *fig.* to felicitate oneself 1622. 3. *intr.* To lie close, cuddle 1595. 4. *trans.* (orig. *Naut.*) To cling to (the shore, etc.) 1824.

1. He bewept my Fortune, And hugg'd me in his Armes SHAKS. *To h. one's chains* (fig.): to delight in bondage. b. The sordid practice of hugging or caressing attorneys AUSTIN. 4. Hugging the Spanish coast MARRYAT. Hence **Hu·ggingly** *adv.*

Huge (hiūdʒ), *a.* [ME. *huge*, *hoge*, app. aphet. f. OF. *ahuge*, *ahoge*, in same sense. Origin unkn.] Very great, large, or big; immense, enormous, vast; *transf.* of very great power, rank, capabilities, etc.

He..made an hughe fire GOWER. A matter of..h. moment 1680. Hugest Heiress now going CARLYLE. Hence **Hu·ge·ly** *adv.*, **-ness.** var. **Hu·geous, -ly, -ness.**

Hugger (hɒ·gəɹ), *sb.*[1] 1682. [f. HUG *v.* + -ER[1].] One who hugs.

†**Hu·gger**, *sb.*[2] 1576. [Cf. HUGGER *v.*] Concealment.

Hugger (hɒ·gəɹ), *v. Obs.* exc. *dial.* 1520. [? short for HUGGER-MUGGER *v.*] †1. *intr.* To lie concealed. 2. *trans.* To conceal 1600. †3. *intr.* To get into confusion. SKELTON.

Hugger-mugger (hɒ·gəɹˌmɒ·gəɹ). 1526. [Earlier *hucker mucker.* Origin unkn.]

A. *sb.* 1. Concealment, secrecy; esp. in phr. *in h.* Now *arch.* or *vulgar.* 1529. 2. Disorder; a muddle 1674.

1. To clap up the marriage in hugger-mugger FORD.

B. *adj.* 1. Secret, clandestine 1692. 2. Disorderly, confused, makeshift 1840.

C. *adv.* 1. Secretly, clandestinely 1526. 2. In a muddle 1880.

Hugger-mugger, *v.* late ME. [f. prec.] 1. *trans.* To keep secret; to hush *up.* 2. *intr.* To proceed in a clandestine manner; to go *on* in a muddled way 1805.

Huggery (hɒ·gəri). 1804. [f. HUG *v.*, HUGGER *sb.*[1]; see -ERY.] The action or practice of hugging (see HUG *v.* 1 b).

Huggle (hʊ·g'l), *v.* Now *dial.* 1583. [? iterative of HUG *v.*] To hug.

†Hugmatee. 1699. [?] Cant name of a kind of ale –1704.

Huguenot (hiū·gĕnǫt), *sb.* (*a.*) 1562. [a. F. *Huguenot*, a popular alteration of Ger. *eidgenoss*, confederate, infl. by the name *Hugues* (Hatz.-Darm.).] **1.** A French Protestant in the 16th and 17th c. In French, orig. a nickname, said to have been imported from Geneva. **2.** *adj.* Of or belonging to the Huguenots 1682. Hence **Hu·guenotism**, the religious system of the Huguenots; Calvinism.

†Hu·gy, *a.* ME. [f. HUGE *a.* + -Y.] = HUGE –1728.

Huh (hʊ), *interj.* 1608. An exclam. of suppressed feeling.

Huia (hū·iă). Also **hui** (hū·i). 1845. [Native Maori; from the bird's whistle.] A New Zealand bird, *Heteralocha acutirostris*, the tail feathers of which are prized by the Maoris as ornaments.

†Huisher, husher, now as Fr. **‖huissier** (wisye), *sb.* ME. [a. OF. *huisier, huscier* (mod. *huissier*), f. (*h*)*uis* door :—pop.L. **ūstium* for *ostium* door.] = USHER. Hence **†Huisher** *v. trans.* to usher, precede.

‖Huitain (witē·n). 1589. [a. F., f. *huit* eight.] A set of eight lines of verse.

Huke (hiūk), *sb. Obs.* exc. *Hist.* ME. [a. OF. *huque, heuque*; in med.L. *huca*. Ult. origin unkn.] A kind of cape or cloak with a hood worn by women and afterwards by men. Applied also to the Arab *haïk*; see HAIK.

†Hulch, *sb.* (*a.*) 1611. [?] **1.** A hump. COTGR. **2.** *adj.* Hunched. Also in comb. **h.-backed** *a.* hunch-backed; also *transf.* of round-backed tools. –1708. Hence **Hu·lchy** *a.* humpy, hump-backed. (*Obs.* or *dial.*)

‖Huldee, huldi (hʊ·ldī). *E. Ind.* 1832. [Hindī, etc.] Vernacular name of the plant *Curcuma longa*, the tubers of which yield turmeric; also of the powdered turmeric.

Hulk (hʊlk), *sb.* [OE. *hulc*, ME. *hulke*, conjecturally referred to Gr. ὁλκάς a ship that is towed, etc.] **1.** A ship. Usually, in ME. and later, A large ship of burden or transport, often associated with the carrack. Now *arch.* = 'big, unwieldy vessel'. **†2.** The HULL of a ship –1829. **3.** The body of a dismantled ship (worn out and unfit for sea service), retained in use as a store-vessel, etc. (See also SHEER-HULK.) 1671. **b.** A vessel of this kind formerly used as a prison. Usu. *pl.* 1797. **4.** *transf.* and *fig.* A big, unwieldy person, or mass 1597.

1. The sooty h. Steered sluggish on THOMSON. **3.** Like Drake's old H. at Deptford COTTON. **b.** The sentence of death..would be commuted for—the hulks MEDWIN.

Hulk (hʊlk), *v.*[1] 1575. [var. of HOLK *v.* to hollow out.] **1.** *trans.* To disembowel. *dial.* **2.** *Mining.* To remove the 'gouge' or softer part of a lode before blasting 1881.

Hulk (hʊlk), *v.*[2] 1793. [f. HULK *sb.*] **1.** *trans.* **†a.** To condemn to the hulks (see HULK *sb.* 3 b). **b.** To lodge (sailors, etc.) temporarily in a hulk. 1827. **2.** *intr.* To act, hang about, or go in a hulking manner (*dial.*) 1793. **3.** (With *up.*) To rise bulkily 1880.

Hulking (hʊ·lkiŋ), *a. colloq.* 1698. [f. HULK *sb.* 4 + -ING[2].] Bulky, unwieldy; ungainly on account of bulk.

A great h. son JOWETT. So **Hu·lky** *a. colloq.*

Hull (hʊl), *sb.*[1] [OE. *hulu* husk, from *hul-*, *helan* to cover.] **1.** The shell, pod, or husk of pease and beans; the outer covering of any fruit or seed. **2.** *transf.* and *fig.* A covering, envelope; the case of a chrysalis; *pl.* clothes, garments 1718.

2. Blankets, and bibs, and other nameless hulls CARLYLE.

Hull (hʊl), *sb.*[2] 1556. [? same wd. as prec.] The body or frame of a ship, apart from the masts, sails, and rigging. Also of a flying boat or rigid airship. **†b.** = HULK *sb.* 3. –1666.

We discovered by her H. she was a Christian Frigot 1676. Phr. *To lie at h.* = HULL *v.*[2] 1 (see AHULL). *H. down*: so far away that the h. is below the horizon and invisible. So *H. out*: with the h. above the horizon.

Hull (hʊl), *v.*[1] ME. [f. HULL *sb.*[1]] *trans.* To remove the hull, shell, or husk of. Also *transf.* Hence **Hu·ller**, *spec.* a hulling-machine.

Hull (hʊl), *v.*[2] 1545. [f. HULL *sb.*[2]] **†1.** *intr. Naut.* Of a ship: To float or be driven on the hull alone; to lie a-hull –1708. Also *transf.* and *fig.* **2.** *trans.* To strike (a ship) in the hull with cannon shot 1726.

2. The Phœnix was thrice hulled by our shot 1776.

Hullabaloo (hʊ:lăbălū·), *sb.* (*int.*) 1762. [app. a riming duplication of *halloo*, thus, *halloo-baloo!*] **a.** Tumultuous noise; uproar; clamorous confusion. Also *fig.* **b.** as *int.* 1845.

Hulled (hʊld), *a.* 1577. [f. HULL *sb.*[1] and [2] + -ED[2].] Having a hull (of a particular kind).

Hulled (hʊld), *ppl. a.* ME. [f. HULL *v.*[1]] Stripped of the hull or husk.

Hullo, hulloa (hŏlōu·), *interj.* 1857. A call used to hail a person or to excite his attention.

Huloist, Hulotheism: see HYLOIST, -THEISM.

Hulver (hʊ·lvəɹ). *Obs.* exc. *dial.* [In late ME. *hulfere*, = ON. *hulfr*, explained as 'dogwood'.] Holly. *Knee h.*, Butcher's Broom. *Sea h.*, Sea Holly, Eryngo. Also *attrib.*

Hum (hʊm), *sb.*[1] 1469. [Cogn. w. HUM *v.*[1]] **1.** A low continuous sound made by a bee, etc., also by a spinning top, machinery in motion, etc. (Dist. from a *buzz* by not being sibilant.) 1601. **b.** A murmur of many distant voices or noises 1599. **2. a.** An inarticulate vocal murmur uttered with closed lips in a pause of speaking, from hesitation, embarrassment, affectation 1469. **b.** A like sound uttered in approbation, mild surprise, dissent, etc. 1653. **†3.** Strong or double ale –1719.

1. The h. of the mill EMERSON. **b.** The h. of expectation FROUDE. **2. a.** These Shrugs, these Hum's, and Ha's *Wint. T.* II. i. 74. **3.** Would I had some h. FLETCHER.

Hum, *sb.*[2] 1751. [Short for HUMBUG *sb.*] An imposition, a hoax (*slang* or *colloq.*).

Hum (hʊm), *v.*[1] [ME. *humme*; echoic.] **1.** *intr.* To make a low continuous murmuring sound or note, as a bee, etc.; also said of a spinning top, etc.; to sing with closed lips (cf. 4). **2.** *intr.* To make a low inarticulate vocal sound; *esp.* in expression of dissatisfaction, or †of approbation or applause ME. **b.** To make an inarticulate murmur in a pause of speaking, from hesitation, embarrassment, etc. Usu. in phr. *to h. and ha* (*haw*) ME. **3.** To give forth an indistinct sound by the blending of many voices, etc.; hence (*colloq.*) to be all astir 1726. **4.** *trans.* To sing with closed lips and without articulation 1602. **†5.** To greet with a hum (of applause) –1733.

1. Bees cluster and h. BOWEN. **2.** Upon which the Rabble hummed 1687. **b.** H. and stroke thy Beard *Tr. & Cr.* I. iii. 165. **3.** The whole country was humming with dacoits KIPLING. Phr. (colloq.) *To make things hum*: to keep in activity. **4.** Low humming..Some ancient Border gathering song SCOTT.

Hum, *v.*[2] *arch.* 1751. [Short for HUMBUG *v.*] To hoax, take in, humbug (*slang* or *colloq.*).

Hum, *v.*[3] *colloq.* or *slang.* 1927. [?] *intr.* To smell disagreeably. Hence as *sb.*

Hum (həm), *interj.* 1596. An inarticulate exclam. uttered with the lips closed, either in a pause of hesitation, etc., or as expressing slight dissatisfaction, dissent, etc.

Human (hiū·măn), *a.* (*sb.*) [ME. *humayn*(*e*, *humain*(*e*, a. F. *humain* :—L. *humanus*, f. same root as *homo, hominem*. Orig. stressed and spelt *huma·ne*. Differentiated early in the 18th c.] **1.** Of, belonging to, or characteristic of man. **2.** Of the nature of man; that is a man; consisting of men 1484. **b.** *Astrol.* Applied to signs of the zodiac, or constellations, figured in the form of men or women 1658. **3.** Mundane, secular. (Often opp. to *divine.*) 1533. **4.** Having the qualities or attributes proper to man 1727. **5.** *sb.* A human being, a man. (Now chiefly *joc.* or *affected.*) 1533. With *the*: The human race 1841.

1. The Structure of the h. Body Jos. BUTLER. **2.** Humane Sacrifices were offered to Diana PURCHAS. **3.** To err is humane, to forgive divine POPE. In all h. probability 1712. **4.** He was very h., and sent the poor Seamen Presents 1727.

†Hu·manate, *a.* [ad. med.L. *humanatus*, *humanare.*] Made human; converted into human flesh. CRANMER. So **†Humana·tion**, incarnation.

Humane (hiumē·n), *a.* 1500. [Earlier spelling of HUMAN, restricted after 1700 to particular senses, and assoc. w. L. *humanus.*] **1.** Characterized by such behaviour or disposition towards others as befits a man: †civil, courteous, obliging –1784; kind, benevolent 1603. **b.** Applied to certain implements, etc. which inflict less pain than others of their kind 1904. **2.** Applied to those branches of literature (*literæ humaniores*) which tend to humanize or refine, as the ancient classics, rhetoric, and poetry; hence, elegant, polite. (See HUMANITY.) 1691.

1. H. civility MARVELL. To be h. is human TRENCH. *H. Society*: a society for the rescue of drowning persons 1776. **2.** The more h. and polite Part of Letters 1712. Hence **Huma·ne·ly** *adv.*, **-ness**.

Humaniform (hiumæ·nifǫɹm), *a.* 1889. [f. L. *humanus*; see -FORM.] Of human form; anthropomorphous. So **†Humanifo·rmian**, an anthropomorphite 1550–1624.

Humanify (hiumæ·nifəi), *v.* 1629. [f. HUMAN *a.* + -FY.] To make human. Hence **Huma:nifica·tion.**

Humanism (hiū·măniz'm). 1812. [f. HUMAN *a.* + -ISM, after *humanist.*] **†1.** Belief in the mere humanity of Christ. COLERIDGE. **2.** The quality of being human; devotion to human interests 1836. **3.** Any system of thought or action which is concerned with merely human interests, or with those of the human race in general; the 'Religion of Humanity' 1860. **4.** Devotion to those studies which promote human culture; literary culture; *esp.* the system of the Humanists 1832.

3. Comtism or Positivism, or, as it might be called, H. 1876. **4.** The h. of Erasmus and More 1885.

Humanist (hiū·mănist). 1589. [ad. F. *humaniste*, ad. It. *umanista*; see HUMAN and -IST.] **1.** A student of human affairs, or of human nature 1617. **2.** One versed in the 'humanities'; a classical scholar; *esp.* a Latinist (*arch.*) 1589. **3.** *Literary Hist.* One of the scholars who, at the Renascence, devoted themselves to the study of Roman, and afterwards of Greek, antiquity; hence, applied to later disciples of the same culture 1670. Also *attrib.*

2. I might repute him as a good h., but I should ever doubt him for a good devine HARINGTON. **3.** Milton was born a h., but the Puritan temper mastered him M. ARNOLD.

Humani·stic, -al, *a.* 1716. [f. prec. + -IC, + -ICAL.] Pertaining to the humanists; pertaining to classical studies; classical.

Humanitarian (hiumænitēᵊ·riăn). 1819. [f. HUMANITY, after *unitarian*, etc.]

A. *sb.* **1.** *Theol.* One who affirms the mere humanity of Christ. **2.** One who professes the 'Religion of Humanity', holding that man's duty is chiefly or wholly comprised in the advancement of the welfare of the human race 1831. **3.** A philanthropist; *esp.* one who goes to excess in his humane principles 1844.

3. A man cannot be too really humane, but the typical h. is only sentimental 1891.

B. *adj.* **1.** Holding the views or doctrines of humanitarians; held or practised by humanitarians 1846. **2.** Having regard to the interests of humanity or mankind at large. Often *contemptuous* or *hostile.* 1855.

2. The nonsense of h. sentimentalists 1897. Hence **Humanita·rianism**, the system, principles, or practice of humanitarians.

†Humanitian (-i·ʃăn). 1577. [irreg. f. HUMANITY + -AN, after *logician.*] One versed in the humanities; a classical scholar –1691.

Humanity (hiumæ·nĭti). ME. [a. F. *humanité*, ad. L. *humanitatem.*]

I. Conn. w. *human.* **1.** The quality or condition of being human, manhood; human nature; man in the abstract. **b.** *pl.* Human attributes; traits or touches of human nature or feeling; points that appeal to man 1800. **2.** The human race; mankind 1579.

1. I would change my H. with a Baboone *Oth.* I. iii. 317. **b.** The fair humanities of old religion COLERIDGE. **2.** Their services to h. are very great BANCROFT.

II. Conn. w. *humane.* 1. The character or quality of being humane: †civility, courtesy; obligingness –1794; kindness, benevolence ME. b. *pl.* Instances or acts of humanity 1577. 2. Learning or literature concerned with human culture, as grammar, rhetoric, poetry, and esp. the ancient Latin and Greek classics. a. *sing.* (Still used in the Scottish Universities = 'the study of the Latin language and literature'.) 1483. b. *pl.* (Usu. with *the*; = Fr. *les humanités.*) 1702. Also *attrib.* c. One of the classes in a Jesuit school.

1. Great tenderness of heart, and h. of disposition BURKE. b. The courtesies and humanities of generous warfare SOUTHEY. 2. b. An Eton captain..critically learned in all the humanities EMERSON.

Humanize (hiū·mănəiz), *v.* 1603. [ad. F. *humaniser*, f. L. *humanus*; see -IZE.] 1. *trans.* To make or render human; to give a human character or form to; to conform to human nature or use; *spec.* to modify (lymph, milk) by communicating to it human characteristics. 2. To make humane; to civilize, soften, refine 1647. 3. *intr.* for *pass.* To grow humane 1790.

1. The Fijians humanized their gods 1895. 2. To h. the way in which war is carried on FREEMAN. 3. Humanizing by degrees, it [the law of nations] admitted slavery instead of death [as a punishment] FRANKLIN. Hence **Humaniza·tion; Hu·manizer,** one who or that which humanizes.

Humankind (hiū·măn,kəi·nd). 1645. [Prop. two wds.; written as one, after *mankind.*] The human race; mankind.

Humanly (hiū·mănli), *adv.* 1485. [f. HUMAN *a.* + -LY².] 1. After the manner of man, in accordance with human nature; by human means 1613. 2. From the standpoint of man 1581. 3. With the feelings distinctive of man; with human kindness 1485.

2. [The deed] was thought humanely impossible 1707. 3. Modestly bold, and h. severe POPE.

Hu·manness. 1727. [-NESS.] Human quality.

Humate (hiū·mēt), *sb.* 1844. [f. HUM-IC + -ATE⁴.] *Chem.* A salt of humic acid.

†Huma·tion. 1635. [ad. L. *humationem*, f. *humare.*] Burial; inhumation –1661.

†Hum-bird. 1634. [f. HUM *sb.*¹ or *vb.-stem* + BIRD.] = HUMMING-BIRD –1819.

Humble (hʊ·mb'l), *a.*¹ [ME. *umble, humble*, a. OF. *umble, humble*:—L. *humilem* low, f. *humus* ground. The pron. without initial aspirate is still heard.] 1. Having a low estimate of oneself; not self-asserting or assuming; lowly; the opposite of *proud.* 2. Of lowly condition, rank, or estate; modest, unpretentious ME.; †low-lying –1729; low-growing 1658.

1. Christ was h., they are proud 1640. Your faithful h. servant, Wm. Pinkey 1808. 2. I am from h., he from honored name SHAKS. The h. Plains below 1729. *H. plant*: the common Sensitive plant.

Humble, *a.*²: see HUMMEL *a.*

Humble, *v.*¹ ME. [f. HUMBLE *a.*¹] 1. *trans.* To render humble or meek; to cause to think more lowly of oneself 1591. 2. To lower in dignity, position, condition, or degree; to bring low, abase 1484. 3. *refl.* To render oneself humble; to do obeisance, bow (*arch.*) ME.

1. Loue's a mighty Lord, And hath so humbled me *Two Gent.* II. iv. 137. 2. The prowde shall be allway humbled CAXTON. 3. The army..humbled them selfes mekely before the crosse HALL. Hence **Hu·mblingly** *adv.*

†Humble, *v.*² ME. [Cf. Du. *hommelen*, MHG. *hummeln.*] *intr.* To rumble; to mumble; to hum or buzz as a bee –1617.

Humble, *v.*³: see HUMMEL.

Humble-bee (hʊ·mb'lbī). 1450. [Perh. repr. an OE. **humbol-béo.*] A large wild bee, of the genus *Bombus*, which makes a loud humming sound; a bumble-bee.

Humbleness (hʊ·mb'lnės). ME. [-NESS.] The quality of being humble; meekness, lowliness; unpretentiousness.

With bated breath, and whispring humblenesse SHAKS.

Humble pie. 1648. [For sense 1 see HUMBLES.]

†1. = UMBLE PIE, a pie made of the umbles of a deer. 2. *To eat humble pie*: to be very submissive; to submit to humiliation 1830.

Humbler (hʊ·mblər). 1611. [f. HUMBLE *v.*¹ + -ER¹.] One who or that which humbles.

†Humbles, *sb. pl.* 1460. Occas. sp. of UMBLES, the inwards of a deer, etc. –1709.

†Humblesse. ME. [a. OF. (*h*)*umblesse*; see HUMBLE *a.*¹ and -ESS².] Humbleness, humility –1736.

Humbly (hʊ·mbli), *adv.* ME. [f. HUMBLE *a.*¹ + -LY².] 1. In a humble manner; with humility. 2. Modestly; unpretentiously 1746.

Humbug (hʊ·mbʊg), *sb.* (*a.*) *colloq.* 1751. [?] †1. A hoax; an imposition –1799. 2. An imposture, fraud, sham 1751. 3. Deception, pretence; used interjectionally = 'stuff and nonsense!' 1825. 4. An impostor, a 'fraud' 1804. 5. A kind of sweetmeat (*dial.*) 1825. 6. *attrib.* Humbugging 1812.

Humbug (hʊ·mbʊg), *v.* 1751. [f. HUMBUG *sb.* In 18th c. stressed *humbu·g.*] 1. *trans.* To practise humbug upon; to impose upon, hoax, delude. b. To change or transfer by trickery 1821. 2. *intr.* To practise humbug; to be a humbug; 'to fool *about*' 1753. Hence **Humbugger,** a humbug, impostor. **Humbu·ggery,** humbug, imposture.

Humdrum (hʊ·m,drʊ·m, hʊ·mdrʊm). 1553. [app. reduplicated f. HUM *v.*¹]

A. *adj.* 1. Lacking variety; commonplace; monotonous, dull. †2. (*adj.* or *adv.*) Without distinction; undecided –1710.

1. A plain h. Sermon J. H. NEWMAN.

B. *sb.* 1. A dull, monotonous, commonplace fellow 1598. 2. Dullness, commonplaceness, monotony. Also with *a* and *pl.* 1727. Hence **Hu·mdru·m** *v.* to proceed in a h. fashion.

Humdudgeon (hʊ·mdʊ·dʒən). 1785. [Cf. HUM *sb.*² and DUDGEON *sb.*²] An imaginary illness.

Humect (hiume·kt), *v.* Now *rare.* 1531. [ad. L. *humectare*, f. *humectus*, f. *humere*; see HUMID, HUMOUR.] 1. *trans.* To moisten, wet. 2. *intr.* To become moist 1686.

Humectant (hiume·ktănt). ? *Obs.* 1659. [ad. L. *humectantem*; see prec.] a. *adj.* Moistening, wetting. b. *sb. Med.* A diluent 1822.

Humectate (hiume·kteit), *v.* Now *rare.* 1640. [f. L. *humectat-* ppl. stem.] = HUMECT 1. So **Humecta·tion,** the action of moistening; the condition of being moistened; †liquefaction 1425. **†Hume·ctative** *a.* tending to moisten.

Hume·ctive. *rare.* 1633. [irreg. f. HUMECT *v.* + -IVE. Cf. *adaptive.*] a. *adj.* Humectative. b. *sb.* = HUMECTANT *sb.* 1828.

Humeral (hiū·mĕrăl). 1615. [ad. late L. **humeralis*, used as sb. neut. (*h*)*umerale*, f. *humerus.*]

A. *adj.* 1. *Anat.* Of or pertaining to the HUMERUS. 2. Of or pertaining to the shoulder or shoulders 1853.

2. *H. veil* (Eccl.): an oblong vestment of silk worn round the shoulders in various rites and enveloping the hands when holding sacred vessels.

B. *sb.* 1. *Eccl.* †a. A part of the Jewish sacerdotal vestment, worn on the shoulder. TRAPP. b. = *Humeral veil* (A. 2).

Humero- (hiū·mĕro), comb. f. L. *humerus* shoulder, in the sense of 'pertaining to the humerus and ...', as *humero-cubital*, etc.

‖**Humerus** (hiū·mĕrʊs). Pl. **-i.** 1666. [L., = shoulder, (rarely) upper arm.] *Anat.* The bone of the upper arm, extending from the shoulder-joint to the elbow-joint; the homogenetic bone in other vertebrates.

†Humet, *sb.* 1500. [? a. OF. **heaumet* dim. of *heaume* the bar of the helm or rudder.] *Her.* A fess or bar so couped that its extremities do not touch the sides of the shield –1592. Hence **Hume·tty** *a.* said of an ordinary of which the extremities are couped so as not to reach the sides of the escutcheon.

Humic (hiū·mik), *a.* 1844. [f. L. *humus* + -IC.] *Chem.* Of or pertaining to humus or mould. *H. acid*, an acid found in humus or derived from it by boiling with an alkali.

Humicubation (hiūmi,kiubē·ʃən). 1656. [f. L. *humi* on the ground + *cubatio*, f. *cubare.*] Lying down on the ground, esp. by way of penitence or humiliation.

Humid (hiū·mid), *a.* 1549. [a. F. *humide.*] Slightly wet as with steam, vapour, or mist; moist, damp. b. Of diseases: Marked by a moist discharge 1813.

The h. Flours, that breathd Thir morning Incense MILT. Mouldering walls and h. floor GOLDSM. Hence **Humi·dify** *v.* to render h. **Hu·mid-ly** *adv.*, **-ness.**

Humidity (hiumi·dĭti). ME. [a. F. *humidité*, ad. L. *humiditatem*, f. *humidus* HUMID.] 1. The quality of being humid; moistness, dampness 1450. 2. *concr.* Moisture; damp; *pl.* the humours and juices of animals and plants ME.

1. *Relative H.* (of the atmosphere) in *Meteorol.*, the amount of moisture which it contains as compared with that of complete saturation at the given temperature.

Humifuse (hiū·mifiūs), *a.* 1854. [ad. mod.L. *humifusus*, f. *humi* on the ground + *fusus, fundere.*] *Bot.* Applied to the stalk of vegetables when it stretches over the surface of the ground, but without sending out roots.

Humify (hiū·mifəi), *v. rare.* Also **humefy.** 1651. [ad. late L. (*h*)*umificare.*] *trans.* To render humid; to moisten.

Humiliant (hiumi·liănt), *a. rare.* 1844. [ad. L. *humiliantem.*] Humiliating. MRS. BROWNING.

Humiliate (hiumi·lieit), *v.* 1533. [f. late L. *humiliat-, humiliare.*] †1. *trans.* To make low or humble in position, condition, or feeling; to humble. Also *refl.* 2. To subject to humiliation; to mortify 1757.

2. The country was humiliated by defeat GREEN. Hence **Humi·liatingly** *adv.* **Humi·liator.**

Humiliation (hiūmili,ē·ʃən). ME. [a. F., ad. late L. *humiliationem.*] The action of humiliating or condition of being humiliated; humbling, abasement. Formerly often = humility. Also with *a* and *pl.*

Where will the h. of this country end? *Junius Lett.* Incensed by multiplied wrongs and humiliations MACAULAY.

Humility (hiumi·lĭti). ME. [a. F. *humilité*, ad. L. *humilitatem.*] 1. The quality of being humble or having a lowly opinion of oneself; meekness, lowliness, humbleness; the opposite of *pride* or *haughtiness.* b. With *pl.* An act of self-abasement 1612. 2. Humble or low condition, rank, or estate; unpretentiousness 1623. 3. A local name of several N. American birds of the family *Scolopacidæ* 1634.

1. b. With these humilities..they satisfied the young king 1612. 2. The h. of the fare LAMB.

Humin (hiū·min). 1844. [f. HUMUS + -IN.] *Chem.* A neutral substance said to exist in black humus.

Humite (hiū·məit). 1814. [f. Sir Abraham *Hume*, of London.] *Min.* A fluo-silicate of magnesium, long considered a variety of chondrodite, but now made a distinct species.

Hummel (hʊ·m'l), **humble** (hʊ·mb'l), *a. Sc.* 1474. [Corresp. to LG. *hummel, hommel* hornless beast; ? conn. w. HAMBLE to mutilate.] 1. Of cattle: Hornless 1536. 2. Of corn or grain: Awnless 1474. †3. Chapped. HOLLAND.

Hummel, humble, *v. Sc.* and *n. dial.* 1800. [f. prec. adj.] 1. *trans.* To deprive of the horns. 2. To remove the awns from (barley) 1800. Hence **Hu·mmelled, -eled, hu·mbled** *a.* **Hu·mmeller, -eler,** one who, or a machine which, hummels.

Hummer (hʊ·mər). 1605. [f. HUM *v.*¹ + -ER¹.] A thing or person that hums. 1. An insect that hums; also a humming-bird. 2. A person or thing marked by extreme energy, activity, etc. (*colloq.* or *slang*) 1681.

Humming (hʊ·miŋ), *vbl. sb.* 1440. [f. HUM *v.*¹ + -ING¹.] The action of HUM *v.*¹

Humming, *ppl. a.* 1578. [f. as prec. + -ING².] 1. That hums; †that hums approbation. Sometimes hyphened to its noun, as *h.-bee, -top*, etc. 2. Of extraordinary activity, intensity, or magnitude; brisk, 'booming'; 'thumping', 'stunning' (*slang* or *colloq.*) 1654. b. Of liquor: Strong; ? frothing (*colloq.*) 1675.

2. b. A Tub of h. stuff would make a Cat speak 1675.

Humming-bird. 1637. Any bird of the large family *Trochilidæ*, the species of which make a humming sound by the rapid vibration of their wings.

They are all of very small size, and are usually brilliantly coloured. They are peculiar to America, and most frequent within the tropics.
attrib. **Humming-bird hawk-moth (sphinx)**, a species of hawk-moth (*Macroglossa stellatarum*), whose flight resembles that of a humming-bird.

Hummock (hɒ·mək). 1555. [Orig. naut.; source obscure. Not from *hump*, which is much later.] **1.** A boss-like protuberance, rising above the general level of a surface; a low hillock or knoll. **b.** A sand hill on the sea-shore 1793. **c.** *Geol.* An elevated or detached boss of rock 1808. **d.** A protuberance on an ice field or floe 1818. **2.** In southern U.S., an elevation rising above a plain or swamp and often densely covered with hardwood trees; a clump of such trees on a knoll. (The local form in Florida, etc. is *hammock.*) 1636. Hence **Hu·mmocked** *ppl. a.* thrown into hummocks; hummocky. **Hu·mmocking**, the forming of hummocks on an ice field.

Hummocky (hɒ·məki), *a.* 1766. [f. prec. + -Y.] **1.** Abounding in or characterized by hummocks. **2.** Of the form or nature of a hummock 1791.

‖**Hummum** (hɒ·mɒm). 1634. [Corruption of Arab. *ḥammām* hot bath (HAMMAM).] An Oriental bathing establishment; a Turkish bath; a HAMMAM.

Humoral (hiū·mŏrăl), *a.* 1543. [a. F., f. L. *humor*; see -AL.] **1.** *Med.* Of or belonging to, consisting of, or containing any of the humours or fluids of the body; caused by a disordered state of the humours 1547. **b.** Relating to the bodily humours; applied esp. to the ancient doctrine that all diseases were due to disorder in the humours; as, *humoral pathology* 1793. †**2.** *gen.* Humid, fluid. TIMME. Hence **Hu·moralism**, h. pathology. **Hu·moralist**, a believer in h. pathology. **Humorali·stic** *a.* of or belonging to the humoralists.

Humoresque (hiūmŏre·sk), *sb.* 1889. [ad. Ger. *humoreske*, f. L. *humor*; see -ESQUE.] *Mus.* A humorous or capricious composition.

Humorism (hiū·mŏriz'm). 1831. [f. as prec., after *humorist.*] **1.** *Med.* The doctrine of the four bodily humours (see HUMOUR *sb.*), and their relation to temperaments and to diseases 1832. **2.** The characteristics of a humorist (see HUMORIST 2). COLERIDGE.

Humorist, humourist (hiū·mŏrist). 1596. [a. F. *humoriste*, ad. med.L. *humorista*, f. L. *humor*; see -IST.] †**1.** A fantastical or whimsical person; a faddist –1830. **2.** A facetious or comical person, a wag; now *esp.* one skilled in the literary or artistic expression of humour. Also *fig.* 1599. **3.** = HUMORALIST 1846.

1. A humourist is one that is greatly pleased, or greatly displeased with little things WATTS. 2. Men ..prefer the Conversation of Humourists before that of the Serious 1707. Hence **Humori·stic** *a.* belonging to, characteristic of, or of the nature of a humorist; (*occas.*) humorous.

Humorize (hiū·mŏrəiz), *v.* 1598. [f. L. *humor* + -IZE.] †**1.** *intr.* To comply with the humour of a person or thing. MARSTON. **2.** To speak or think humorously 1609.

Humorous (hiū·mŏrəs), *a.* 1578. [With sense 1 cf. late L. (*h*)*umorosus* moist, wet. In other senses f. HUMOUR *sb.*] †**1.** Moist, humid, damp –1612. †**2.** = HUMORAL 1. –1831. †**3.** Full of, or subject to, humours; capricious, whimsical; odd, fantastic –1823; moody, peevish –1842. **4.** Full of, characterized by, or showing humour or drollery; facetious, comical 1705.

1. The hum'rous Fogges, night DRAYTON. 3. Pall'd Appetite is h., and must be gratify'd with Sauces rather than Food STEELE. He is h. to his Wife, he beats his Children PENN. 4. The Western American is always h. BESANT & RICE. Hence **Hu·morous-ly** *adv.*, **-ness.**

Humour, humor (hiū·məɹ, yū·məɹ), *sb.* ME. [a. AF. (*h*)*umour*, OF. (*h*)*umor*, *-ur*, mod.F. *humeur* :—L. *humorem*, *umorem* fluid, moisture. The form *humour* is now usual in Great Britain, *humor* in U.S. The pronunciation of the initial *h* is only recent. Cf. HONOUR.]

I. Physical senses. †**1.** Moisture; damp exhalation –1697. **2.** Any fluid or juice of an animal or plant, either natural or morbid. Now *rare* or *arch.* ME. **b.** *spec.* One of the four chief fluids (*cardinal humours*) of the body (blood, phlegm, choler, and melancholy or black choler), by the relative proportions of which a person's physical and mental qualities and disposition were formerly held to be determined (see TEMPERAMENT). *Obs.* exc. *Hist.* ME. **3.** One of the transparent fluid or semi-fluid parts of the eye, viz. the *aqueous humour* in front of the iris, and the *vitreous humour*, which fills most of the space between the iris and the retina; formerly including also the denser *crystalline lens* ME.

1. To..sucke vp the humours Of the danke Morning *Jul. C.* II. i. 262. 2. b. He answered me that choler was the cause of my sicknes 1581. †*Black h.*, black choler or melancholy.

II. 1. Mental disposition (orig. as determined by the proportion of the bodily humours; see I. 2 b); temperament 1475. †**b.** *transf.* Character, style; sentiment, spirit (of a writing, musical composition, etc.) –1717. **2.** Temporary state of mind; mood, temper 1525; †habitual frame of mind –1676. **3.** A state of mind having no apparent ground or reason; mere fancy, whim, caprice, freak, vagary 1565. **4. a.** That quality of action, speech, or writing, which excites amusement; oddity, comicality. **b.** The faculty of perceiving what is ludicrous or amusing, or of expressing it; jocose imagination or treatment of a subject. (Less purely intellectual than *wit*, and often allied to pathos.) 1682.

1. Thus Ile curbe her mad and headstrong humor *Tam. Shr.* IV. i. 212. 2. Was euer woman in this humour woo'd? SHAKS. Every Man in his Humour B. JONS. (*title*). 3. These are complements, these are humours *L.L.L.* III. i. 23. I haue an humor to knocke you indifferently well..and that's the humor of it *Hen. V*, II. i. 63. The humors of Election Day HAWTHORNE. 4. The happy compound of pathos and playfulness, which we style..h. 1854. Phrase. *Out of h.*: displeased; out of conceit *with.*

Humour, humor, *v.* 1588. [f. HUMOUR *sb.*] **1.** *trans.* To comply with the humour of; to indulge. **2.** *fig.* To comply with the peculiar nature or exigencies of; to adapt oneself to; to act in compliance with; to fit, suit (*with* something) 1588. †**3.** *trans.* To give a particular style to. WALTON.

1. To h. the ignorant *L.L.L.* IV. ii. 52. 2. The man That with smooth air couldst humour best our tongue MILT. (In wood-carving) to h. the wood. 3. This Song was well humor'd by the maker 1653.

Humoured, humored (hiū·məɹd, yū·məɹd), *a.* 1598. [f. HUMOUR *sb.* and *v.* + -ED.] **1.** Having a (specified) disposition, as GOOD-HUMOURED, etc. †**2.** Imaginary. PURCHAS. **3.** Indulged 1649.

Hu·mourless, -orless, *a.* 1847. [-LESS.] Devoid of humour.

Humoursome, humorsome (hiū·məɹsɒm), *a.* 1656. [f. HUMOUR *sb.* + -SOME.] **1.** = HUMOROUS 3. **2.** Indulgent 1876.

1. The Divine Will..not a meer arbitrary, H... thing CUDWORTH. Hence **Hu·moursome-ly** *adv.*, **-ness.**

Hump (hɒmp), *sb.* 1708. [First exemplified, 1681, in the comb. *hump-backed* = the earlier *crump-backed*. Of uncertain origin.] **1.** A protuberance; esp. a protuberance on the back occurring as a normal feature in the camel, bison, etc., or as a deformity in man. **2.** *transf.* A hummock 1838. **3.** A fit of ill humour; sulks (*slang*) 1727. **4.** *attrib.* 1807.

Hump, *v.* 1673. [f. prec.] †**1.** *intr.* To have a fit of ill humour, sulk. **2.** *trans.* To give (one) 'the hump'. THACKERAY. **3.** *trans.* To make hump-shaped; to hunch. Also *absol.* 1840. **4.** To hoist or carry (a bundle) upon the back (*Austral. slang*) 1853. **5.** *refl.* To exert oneself, make an effort (*U.S. slang*) 1835.

Humpback, hump-back, *sb.* (*a.*) 1697. [See HUMP *sb.*] **1.** (*hu·mp-ba·ck.*) A back having a hump. **2.** (*hu·mpback.*) A person with a humped back 1712. **3.** = *h. whale* 1725. **4.** *adj.* Having a hump on the back 1725.

4. **Humpback whale**, a whale of the genus *Megaptera*, so called because the low dorsal fin forms a characteristic hump on the back.

Hump-backed, *a.* 1681. [See HUMP *sb.* The stress varies.] Having a humped or crooked back; hunched. Also *transf.*

Humped (hɒmpt), *a.* 1713. [f. HUMP *sb.* + -ED [2].] Having a hump (or humps); having the back rounded.

Humph (hɒmf), *interj.* (and *sb.*) 1681. The syllable 'h'mf!' used as an expression of doubt or dissatisfaction. Also *sb.*, as a name for this utterance. Hence **Humph** *v.* to utter the syllable 'h'mf!'.

Hu·mpless, *a.* 1868. Having no hump.

†**Hump-shoulder.** 1704. [See HUMP *sb.*] A shoulder raised into a hump. Hence †**Hump-shouldered** *a.* having a hump-shoulder.

Humpty (hɒ·mᵖti), *a.* 1825. [? from next wd.] Humped, hump-backed. Also as *sb.*, a low padded cushion seat 1924.

Humpty-dumpty (hɒ·mᵖti dɒ·mᵖti). 1698. [In sense 1, ? f. HUM *sb.*[1] 3; in sense 2, from *hump* and *dump*, with intrusive *t.*]

A. *sb.* **1.** A drink, 'ale boiled with brandy'. **2.** A short, dumpy, hump-shouldered person; in the nursery rime explained as an egg (in reference to its shape); also allusively 1785.

B. *adj.* Short and fat 1785.

Humpy (hɒ·mpi), *sb.* 1873. [Native *oompi*, infl. by *hump.*] A native Australian hut.

Humpy (hɒ·mpi), *a.* 1708. [f. HUMP *sb.* + -Y[1].] Having humps; marked by protuberances; humped; hump-like.

Humstrum (hɒ·mstrɒm). 1739. [f. HUM *v.*[1] + STRUM *v.*] **1.** A musical instrument of rude construction or out of tune. **2.** Indifferently played music 1882.

‖**Humus** (hiū·mɒs). 1796. [L.] Vegetable mould; the dark-brown or black substance resulting from the slow decomposition of organic matter. It is a valuable constituent of soils Also *attrib.*

Hun (hɒn). 1607. [ad. med.L. *Hunni* app. ult. from *Hun-yü*, name of a Turkic tribe. (In OE. *Hūne, Hūnas.*)] **1.** One of an Asiatic race of warlike nomads, who invaded Europe *c* A.D. 375, and later, under their king Attila (styled *Flagellum Dei*, the scourge of God), overran and ravaged a great part of it. **2.** *transf.* A reckless destroyer of the beauties of nature or art; cf. 'Goth', 'Vandal' 1806. **b.** During the war of 1914–18, applied generally to the Germans, in allusion to their methods of warfare.

2. Where furious Frank, and fiery H., Shout in their sulphurous canopy CAMPBELL.

Hunch (hɒnʃ), *sb.* 1630. [In sense 1 from next; in sense 2 deduced from *hunch-backed.*] **1.** The act of hunching; a push, thrust, shove. *Obs.* exc. *dial.* **2.** A hump 1804. **3.** A lump, a hunk 1790. **4.** *U.S.* A presentiment 1904.

Hunch (hɒnʃ), *v.* 1581. [First traced in the comb. *hunch-backed*, substituted for *bunch-backed* in the second Quarto of *Rich. III.* IV. iv. 81.] **1.** *intr.* To push, thrust, shove. Also *fig. dial.* **2.** *trans.* To push, shove, thrust. *dial.* 1659. **3.** *trans.* To compress, bend, or arch convexly 1678.

2. Hunching and Justling one another 1668. 3. He sat..hunched up, with his knees and his chin together 1892.

Hunchback, hunch-back. 1712. [f. HUNCH *sb.* + BACK *sb.*] **1.** (hɒ·nʃ˛bæ·k) A hunched back 1718. **2.** (hɒ·nʃ˛bæk) = HUMPBACK *sb.* 2. 1712. **3.** *attrib.* Hump-backed 1850. So **Hu·nchbacked** *a.* having a protuberant or crooked back.

Hundred (hɒ·ndrĕd), *sb.* and *a.* [OE. *hundred*, pl. *-red, -redu*, *hundrað* neut., corresp. to a Gothic type **hunda-raþ*, lit. the tale or number of 100.] **1.** The cardinal number equal to ten times ten, or five score. Symbols 100 or C. **a.** As sb. or quasi-sb. In sing., usually *a* (arch. *an*) *h.*, emphatically *one h.*; in expressing rate, *the h.* In pl., *hundreds.* After a numeral adj., *hundred* is generally used as a collective pl. (Cf. *dozen.*) OE. **b.** As adj. or quasi-adj., followed immediately by a pl. (or collective) noun OE. **c.** The cardinal form *hundred* is also used as an ordinal when followed by other numbers, the last of which alone takes the ordinal form; e.g. 'the hundred-and-first', etc. **2.** Often used indef. for a large number ME.; also, for a definite number more than five score 1469. **3.** In England, etc.: A subdivision of a county or shire, having its own court; also formerly the court. *Chiltern Hundreds*: see CHILTERN. OE. **b.** A division of a county in Delaware 1621. **4.** = HUNDREDWEIGHT 1542.

1. Add one round h. POPE. Tickets fabricated by

the h. 1885. Some hundreds of men were present (*mod.*). Eight h. of the brave COWPER. **b.** The h. and one odd chances (*mod.*). Phr. *The Hundred Days*, the period of the restoration of Napoleon Bonaparte, after his escape from Elba, ending June 22, 1815. **2.** Phr. *Great* or *long h.*: usu. = 120. **3.** It is certain that in some instances the h. was deemed to contain exactly 100 hides of land F. W. MAITLAND. *Comb.* **Hundred-court,** in *Eng. Hist.* the court having civil and criminal jurisdiction within a territorial hundred.

Hundredal (hʊ·ndrĕdăl), *a.* 1862. [f. HUNDRED 3 + -AL.] Of or pertaining to a territorial hundred.

Hu·ndredary. 1700. [ad. med.L. *hundredarius*; see next and -ARY.] = HUNDREDER 1.

Hundreder, -or (hʊ·ndrĕdəɹ, -ǫ̆ɹ). 1455. [f. HUNDRED 3 + -ER²; in med.L. *hundredarius*.] **1.** The bailiff or chief officer of a hundred. **2.** An inhabitant of a hundred, esp. one liable to serve on a jury 1501.

Hundredfold (hʊ·ndrĕdfōuld). ME. [f. HUNDRED + -FOLD.] **1.** *adj.* A hundred times as much or as many. **2.** *adv.* A hundred times (in amount). Now always *a* (*an*) *h.* ME. **3.** *sb.* A hundred times the amount or number ME.

2. Armies which outnumbered them a h. MACAULAY. **3.** Some [brought forth] an h. *Matt.* xiii. 8.

Hundredth (hʊ·ndrĕdþ), *a.* (*sb.*) ME. [f. HUNDRED + -TH.] **1.** Coming last in order of a hundred successive individuals. **2.** *sb.* A hundredth part 1774.

1. *Hundredth part*: one of a hundred equal parts into which a whole is, or may be, divided.

Hundredweight (hʊ·ndrĕdwēⁱt). 1474. [f. HUNDRED + WEIGHT. The pl. is unchanged after a numeral or an adj. expressing plurality, as *many*.] An avoirdupois weight equal to 112 pounds; prob. orig. to 100 pounds, whence the name. Abbrev. cwt. (formerly C.).

Locally it has varied from 100 to 120 lb.; in U.S. it is now usu. 100 lb.

Hung (hʊŋ), *ppl. a.* 1641. [pa. pple. of HANG *v.*] **1.** Suspended; (of meat) suspended in the air to be cured by drying, or to become high 1655. **2.** Furnished *with* hanging things 1648; †having pendent organs -1785. **3.** *U.S.* Of a jury: see HANG *v.* I. 6 b.

Hung, pa. t. and pple. of HANG *v.*

†Hu·ngar. 1565. [a. Ger. *Ungar.*] **1.** A Hungarian -1606. **2.** A gold coin of Hungary, worth about 5*s.* -1756.

Hungarian (hʊŋgēᵊ·riăn). 1553. [f. med.L. *Hungaria.*] **A.** *adj.* **1.** Of, belonging to, or native of Hungary 1600. **†2.** Thievish; needy, beggarly (with play on *hungry*) -1608.

1. H. horse, H. leather. **2.** *Merry W.* I. iii. 23.

B. *sb.* **1.** A native or inhabitant of Hungary; a Hungarian horse; the language of Hungary 1553. **†2.** (With play on *hunger.*) A hungry person, a great eater -1632.

†Hunga·ric, *a.* 1661. [ad. med.L. *Hungaricus.*] = HUNGARIAN *a.* 1. -1694.

H. fever: an old name for typhus fever.

Hungary (hʊ·ŋgări). 1450. [ad. med.L. *Hungaria*, f. *Hungari, Ungari, Ungri, Ugri*, med.Gr. Οὔγγροι, Ger. *Ungarn*, names applied to the Magyars.] **1.** A country of central Europe, formerly a part of the Austro-Hungarian monarchy. **†2.** A Hungarian 1502.

H. water: a distilled water, made of rosemary flowers infused in rectified spirit of wine 1698.

Hunger (hʊ·ŋgəɹ), *sb.* [OE. *hungor, -ur* :—OTeut. **hungru-*.] **1.** The uneasy or painful sensation caused by want of food; craving appetite. Also, the exhausted condition caused by want of food. Often personified. **2.** Dearth; famine. *Obs.* or *arch.* OE. **3.** *transf.* and *fig.* Strong desire or craving 1548.

1. For strong hounguer he criede loude ME. The parent of all industries is H. DRUMMOND.

Comb. **h.-march,** a march undertaken esp. by unemployed to call attention to their condition; **h.-rot,** a disease in corn or †cattle due to deficient nourishment; **h.-strike** *sb.*, refusal by a prisoner to take food, in order to obtain release; also *vb.*

Hunger (hʊ·ŋgəɹ), *v.* [OE. *hyngran* (later *hingrian*), f. *hungr-*, HUNGER *sb.*] **†1.** *impers.* as in *it hungers me*: 'there is hunger to me', I am hungry -ME. **2.** *intr.* To feel or suffer hunger, be hungry OE. **3.** *transf.* and *fig.* To long *for*, to hanker *after* 1440. **†4.** *trans.* To have a hunger or craving for; to desire with longing -1563. **5.** To subject to hunger; to starve, famish 1575.

2. I hungerd and yhe me fedde HAMPOLE. **3.** Blessed are they which doe h. and thirst after righteousnesse *Matt.* v. 6.

Hu·nger-bit, *a.* ME. = next.

Hu·nger-bitten, *a.* [OE. *hungerbiten.*] Pinched with hunger; famished, starved.

Hungered (hʊ·ŋgəɹd), *a. arch.* ME. [Partly aphet. f. A-HUNGERED, partly pa. pple. of HUNGER *v.* 5.] Hungry; famished, starved.

Hu·ngerer. ME. [f. HUNGER *v.* + -ER¹.] One who suffers hunger; one who longs.

Hu·ngerly, *a. Obs.* or *arch.* ME. [f. HUNGER *sb.* + -LY¹.] Hungry-looking; having a famished look. So **Hu·ngerly** *adv.* hungrily, greedily. *Obs.* or *arch.* 1557.

†Hu·nger-starve, *v.* ME. [f. HUNGER *sb.* + STARVE *v.*] *trans.* To starve with hunger; to starve -1879.

Hungry (hʊ·ŋgri), *a.* [OE. *hungrig, -reg* :—WGer. type **hungrag-*, f. HUNGER *sb.*; see -Y¹.] **1.** Having the sensation of hunger; feeling pain or uneasiness from want of food; having a keen appetite. Also *transf.* **2. a.** Famine-stricken. ? *Obs.* ME. **b.** Of food: Eaten with keen appetite. Now *rare* or *Obs.* 1552. **3. a.** Of food, etc.: That leaves one hungry. Hence *fig.* Unsatisfying. Now *rare.* 1561. **b.** Inducing hunger (*rare*) 1611. **4.** *transf.* and *fig.* Eager, greedy, avaricious ME. **5.** 'More disposed to draw from other substances than to impart to them' (J.); esp. of land, etc.: Not rich or fertile, poor; of rivers: Not supplying food for fish. †Applied formerly also to hard waters, acrid wines, etc. 1420.

1. Hee hath filled the h. with good things *Luke* i. 53. *transf.* Yond Cassius has a leane and h. looke *Jul. C.* I. ii. 194. **2. a.** In the sowre h. tyme CHAUCER. **3. b.** A h. sermon THACKERAY. **4.** The h. flame devours the silent dead POPE. **5.** Flat tracts of h. pasture ground KEATINGE. Hence **Hu·ngrily** *adv.* **Hu·ngriness.**

Hunk (hʊŋk), *sb.* 1813. [Identical with West Flem. *hunke* (*een hunke brood* a hunk of bread).] A large piece cut off; a thick or clumsy piece, a lump; a hunch.

Hunker (hʊ·ŋkəɹ), *sb. U.S.* ? *Obs.* 1849. [app. f. HUNKS *sb.* + -ER.] In U.S. politics: A conservative, one opposed to innovation or change; a nickname first used in the State of New York about 1845. Hence **Hu·nkerism.**

Hunkers (hʊ·ŋkəɹz), *sb. pl. Sc.* 1785. [?] In the phr. *on one's hunkers*, in a squatting position, with the haunches, knees, and ankles acutely bent.

Hunks (hʊŋks), *sb.* Also **hunx.** 1602. [Origin unkn.] A surly, crusty old person; now usu., a close-fisted, stingy man; a miser.

They all think me a close old h. EARL ORRERY.

Hunnish (hʊ·niʃ), *a.* [f. HUN + -ISH¹.] Of, pertaining to, or like the Huns BYRON.

†Hunt, *sb.*¹ [OE. *hunta* hunter :—OTeut. type **hunton-*.] A hunter; a huntsman -1807.

Hunt (hʊnt), *sb.*² ME. [f. HUNT *v.*] **1.** The act of hunting; the act of chasing wild animals for sport or for food; the chase. **b.** *fig.* and *gen.* Pursuit, as of a wild animal; a search, esp. a diligent search 1605. **2. a.** A body of persons engaged in, or associated for the purpose of, hunting with a pack of hounds 1579. **†b.** Game killed in hunting. *Cymb.* III. vi. 90. **c.** The district hunted 1857. **3.** *Change-ringing.* (Cf. HUNT *v.* 7.) 1684.

1. The h. is vp, the morne is bright and gray *Tit. A.* II. ii. 1. **b.** On a h. for lodgings 1852. **2. c.** Within the Heythrop h. (*mod.*).

Hunt (hʊnt), *v.* [OE. *huntian* :—OTeut. type **huntōjan.*] **1.** *intr.* To go in pursuit of wild animals or game; to engage in the chase. Also of animals: to pursue their prey. **2.** *trans.* To pursue (wild animals or game) for the purpose of catching or killing; to chase for food or sport; often *spec.* to pursue with hounds. Also said of animals. OE. **3.** (*fig.* and *gen.*) *intr.* To search (*after* or *for* anything), esp. with eagerness ME.; *trans.* to search for (esp. with desire or diligence); to endeavour to capture, obtain, or find ME.; to track 1579. **4.** *trans.* To pursue with force, violence, or hostility; to chase or drive *away* or *out* ME. Also *fig.* **5.** To scour (a district) in pursuit of game; *spec.* to make (a district) the field of fox-hunting; *fig.* to examine every corner of 1440. **6.** To use in hunting 1607. **7.** *Change-ringing.* To alter the position of a bell in successive changes so as to shift it by degrees from the first place to the last (*hunting up*), or from the last to the first (*h. down*) 1684.

1. The dog kinds..love to h. in company GOLDSM. **2.** The King he is hunting the Deare *L.L.L.* IV. iii. 1. **3.** Sathanas..dayly hunteth to take thy soule 1526. He neuer huntit benefice 1573. I hunted the seams still farther up the glacier TYNDALL. **4.** He might lay his account with being hunted out of society SCOTT. **5.** He hunted the Cottesmore country 1875. **6.** To rear, feed, hunt, and discipline the pack SOMERVILLE.

Phrase. *To h. counter*: see COUNTER *adv.* 1; **h. the slipper,** a parlour game in which a ring of players passes a slipper covertly while a player in the middle tries to get hold of it 1766.

Hunter (hʊ·ntəɹ). ME. [f. HUNT *v.* + -ER¹.] **1.** A man who hunts; one engaged in the chase of wild animals; a huntsman. **b.** *fig.* and *gen.* One who searches eagerly for something. (Usu. in comb., as *fortune-h.*, etc.) ME. **2.** A horse used, or adapted for use, in hunting 1655. **b.** A dog used in or adapted for hunting 1591. **3.** An animal that hunts its prey; *spec.* = *hunting-spider* 1658. **4.** = *Hunting-watch* 1851. **5.** *attrib.* 1483.

Comb. **hunter's mass,** a shortened mass for hunters eager for the chase 1595; **hunter's moon,** a name for the full moon next after the HARVEST MOON.

Hunterian (hʊntīᵊ·riăn), *a.* 1807. [f. *Hunter* + -IAN.] Of or belonging to John Hunter (1728–1793), or his brother William Hunter (1718–1783), famous Scottish surgeons.

Hu·nting, *vbl. sb.* OE. [-ING¹.] The action of HUNT *v.* Also *Comb.* So **Hu·nting** *ppl. a.*

Comb.: **h.-box,** a small country-house for h.; **-case,** a watch-case with a hinged cover to protect the glass; **-crop,** a straight whipstock with a leather loop for insertion of a thong or lash; **-dog,** a dog used for hunting; also, the Hyena-dog of S. Africa, which hunts in packs; **-field,** the ground on which a hunt is going on; also, the body of mounted huntsmen following the hounds; **-flask**; **-horn,** a horn on which signals are blown in hunting; on a side-saddle, the second pommel on the near side; **h. leopard,** the Cheetah (*Felis jubata*); **-piece,** a picture representing a hunting scene; **-seat,** a country-house occupied only during the hunting season; **-shirt** *U.S.*, a trapper's shirt, orig. made of deerskin and ornamented; **-song,** a song sung during a hunt, or relating to hunting; **-watch,** a watch having a *hunting-case* to protect the glass.

Hu·nting-ground. 1777. [f. HUNTING *vbl. sb.*] A district or tract of country adapted for hunting, or in which hunting is practised. Also *fig.*

Happy hunting-ground(s): those expected by the American Indians in the world to come; hence, the future state. Also *fig.* a favourable place for hunting, collecting, etc.

Huntress (hʊ·ntrĕs). ME. [f. HUNTER + -ESS.] **1.** A woman (or goddess) who follows the chase. Also *transf.* and *fig.* **2.** A mare used for hunting 1858.

Huntsman (hʊ·ntsmăn). 1567. [f. *hunt's* genitive of HUNT *sb.* + MAN.] **1.** A man who hunts, a hunter. **2.** *spec.* The manager of a hunt, who takes charge of the hounds and directs the pursuit of game 1596.

Comb. **h.'s cup,** *Sarracenia purpurea*, a N. Amer. plant so called from its pitcher-shaped leaves.

Hu·ntsmanship. 1631. [-SHIP.] The position, office, or business of a huntsman; the art of hunting.

Hunt's-up. 1537. Orig. *the hunt is up*, an old song or tune sung or played to awaken huntsmen in the morning, and also used as a dance. Hence: **a.** An early morning song; **†b.** a disturbance, uproar. *Obs.* or *dial.*

a. Hunting thee hence, with Hunts-vp to the day SHAKS.

Hup, hupp (hʊp), *interj.* 1733. A call to a horse to quicken his pace. Hence **Hup** *v.* *intr.* to shout *hup*, to urge on a horse.

Hu·rcheon. *Sc.* and *north.* ME. [OF. *herichon.*] A hedgehog.

Hurden: see HARDEN.

Hu·rdies, *sb. pl. Sc.* 1535. [?] The buttocks, the hips. Also *fig.*

Hurdle (hɔ̄·ɹd'l), *sb.* [OE. *hyrdel*:—OTeut. type **hurdilo-z*, f. OTeut. **hurdi-s*, pre-Teut.

krtis*; cf. L. *cratis* hurdle, Gr. *κυρτία* wicker-work, Skr. *krt* to spin, *crt* to fasten together.] **1. A portable rectangular frame, orig. having horizontal bars interwoven or wattled with withes of hazel, willow, etc.; = wattle; but now often an open frame, like a field gate; used chiefly to form temporary fences, sheep-pens, etc. **b.** A kind of frame or sledge on which traitors used to be drawn through the streets to execution ME. **c.** *Fortif.*, etc. A wattled hurdle, used to lay upon marshy ground or across a ditch to provide a firm passage, or for other purposes ME. **2.** Anything formed, like a hurdle, of crossing bars or grating ME.

Comb. **h.-race,** a race in which the contestants have to jump over hurdles; also *the hurdles*. **Hu·rdler,** one who makes hurdles or runs in hurdle-races.

Hu·rdle, *v.* 1598. [f. prec. sb.] †**1.** *trans.* To construct like a hurdle; to wattle. **2.** To enclose or mark *off* with hurdles 1632. †**3.** To bush-harrow 1733. **4.** *intr.* To compete in a hurdle-race 1896.

Hurds: see HARDS.

Hurdy-gurdy (hɒ̄·ɹdi,gɒ̄·ɹdi). 1749. [App. echoic.] **1.** A lute-like instrument, having strings (two or more of which are tuned as drones); the strings are sounded by the revolution of a rosined wheel turned by the left hand, the notes being obtained by the action of keys which stop the strings. Now applied pop. to the barrel-organ. **2.** (More fully *hurdy-gurdy wheel*.) An impact wheel driven by a tangential jet of water which strikes a series of buckets on the periphery. *U.S.* 1872.

Hure. ME. [a. OF. *hure* hair of the head, head.] †**1.** A cap –1482. **2.** The head of a boar, wolf, or bear 1844.

Hurkaru, var. of HIRCARRA.

Hurl (hɒ̄ɹl), *sb.* ME. [f. HURL *v.*] **1.** The action or an act of hurling 1530. **2.** The stick or club used in the game of hurling 1791. **3.** Swirl (*rare*) ME. †**4.** Strife, contention; tumult –1653.

Hurl (hɒ̄ɹl), *v.* ME. [In early ME. confused with *hurtle*, also with *harl* to drag; assoc. later w. *whirl*.] **1.** *intr.* To move with violence or impetuosity; to rush; to dash. *Obs.* or *arch.* **2.** *trans.* To drive or impel with impetuous force or violence ME. **3.** *trans.* To precipitate, throw down, overthrow (*lit.* and *fig.*) ME. **4.** To throw or cast; to fling; †to 'throw' in wrestling ME. **b.** *spec.* To play the game of hurling 1766. **5.** *transf.* and *fig.* To throw out or forth (words, threats, rays, etc.) with force 1590. †**6.** *intr.* To roar or bluster as the wind; to howl –1598.

2. Amr hurled his troops..in vain against the solid walls of Babylon 1884. **3.** Raised to power and hurled from it MACAULAY. **4.** Hector and Ajax h. their lances at each other 1874. **5.** Hurling defiance toward the vault of Heav'n MILT. *P. L.* I. 669.

Hu·rlbat. 1440. [app. f. HURL *v.* + BAT *sb.*[2]] †**1.** ? Some form of club; rendering L. *aclys* a small javelin –1656. †**2.** Used to render L. *cæstus* CESTUS[2] –1791. **3.** = HURL *sb.* 2. 1820.

Hurl-bone, late var. of WHIRL-BONE.

†**Hurled,** *a.* 1460. [Cf. mod.Du. *horrel* (*-voet*).] Deformed or distorted, as a club-foot –1647.

†**Hurlement.** 1585. [f. HURL *v.* + -MENT.] Rush, violence; confusion –1618.

Hurler (hɒ̄·ɹləɹ). 1440. [f. HURL *v.* + -ER[1].] **1.** One who throws with violence 1532. **2.** *spec.* One who plays either game of HURLING 1602. **3.** One who contends or strives 1440.

Hurley (hɒ̄·ɹli). Also **hurly.** 1825. [f. HURL *v.*] **1.** The Irish game of hurling 1841. **2.** The stick or club used in this game; a club or cudgel of the same shape 1825. **3.** The ball used in hurling 1856.

†**Hurley-hacket.** *Sc.* 1529. [Cf. HURL *v.*] **1.** A sport consisting in sliding down a steep place in a trough or sledge, as in tobogganing –1810. **2.** An ill-hung carriage. SCOTT.

Hurling (hɒ̄·ɹliŋ), *vbl. sb.* ME. [f. HURL *v.* + -ING[1].] **1.** Throwing; esp. with violence. **2. a.** A game, closely akin to hand-ball, once popular in Cornwall 1600. **b.** In Ireland, a game resembling hockey 1366. †**3.** Strife; commotion –1576. †**4.** The violent rushing of wind; the sound of this; rolling of thunder –1668.

2. a. H. taketh his denomination from throwing of the ball CAREW.

†**Hurlpit, -pool,** var. ff. WHIRLPIT *Obs.*, WHIRLPOOL.

†**Hurlwind.** 1509. [f. HURL *v.* for WHIRL *v.*] = WHIRLWIND –1640.

Hurly (hɒ̄·ɹli). 1596. [f. HURL *v.*] Commotion; strife.

Hurly-burly (hɒ̄·ɹli,bɒ̄·ɹli), *sb.*, *a.*, and *adv.* 1539. [Formed on the phr. *hurling and burling*. The simple HURLY is later.] **1.** *sb.* Commotion, strife, uproar, confusion. (Formerly a dignified word.) **2.** *adj.* Attended with commotion or disturbance; tumultuous 1596. †**3.** *adv.* Tumultuously; confusedly –1704.

1. When the Hurley-burley's done, When the Battaile's lost, and wonne *Macb.* I. i. 3. Hence **Hurly-burly** *v.* to throw into, or make, a hurly-burly. *Obs.* or *arch.*

Huronian (hiurōu·niăn), *a.* 1862. [f. *Huron* + -IAN.] *Geol.* Of or belonging to Lake Huron; a term at one time applied to a division of the archæan series of rocks as found in Canada.

Hurr (hɒ̄ɹ, hʋrr), *v.* *Obs.* exc. *dial.* ME. [Echoic.] *intr.* To make a dull sound of vibration or trilling.

R is the Dogs Letter, and hurreth in the sound B. JONS.

Hurrah (hurā·, hʋ̆rā·), **hurray** (hurē̆i·, hʋ̆rē̆i·), *int.* and *sb.* 1686. [A later substitute for HUZZA. The form *hurrah* is literary and dignified; the popular form is *hooray*.]

A. *int.* A shout expressive of approbation, encouragement, or exultation; used esp. as a 'cheer' at public meetings, etc. 1716.

Hurrah for brown Autumn! hurrah! hurrah! 1845.

B. *sb.* **1.** A name for this shout 1686. ‖**2.** Repr. F. *houra*, Russian *urá*: The shout of attack of the Cossacks; hence, an attack 1841.

Hurrah's nest: a disorderly mass; a state of confusion or disorder. *U.S.*

Hurrah·, hurray·, *v.* 1798. [f. prec.] **1.** *intr.* To shout 'hurrah!' **2.** *trans.* To encourage with shouts of 'hurrah!'; to 'cheer' 1832.

†**Hurrer.** ME. [f. HURE *sb.* cap + -ER[1].] A maker of, or dealer in, hats and caps –1766.

Hurricane (hʋ·rikĕⁱn, -kĕn), *sb.* 1555. Also †**furicane.** [a. Sp. *huracan*, **furacan*, from Carib.] **1.** Primarily, one of the violent wind-storms or cyclones of the W. Indies; hence, any storm in which the wind blows with terrific violence. Also *transf.* and *fig.* †**2.** A crowded fashionable assembly at a private house –1805.

1. The winds are..stark mad in an herricano FULLER. *fig.* A h. of cheers 1882.

Comb.: **h.-bird,** the frigate-bird; **-deck,** a light upper deck or platform in some steamers; so **-decked** *a.*, having a h.-deck; **-house,** a shelter at the mast-head for the look-out man; also, a kind of round-house on deck; **-lamp,** a lamp so constructed as not to be extinguished by violent wind.

Hence **Hurricane** *v. intr.* to make a commotion; *trans.* to blow upon as a h.

†**Hurrica·no,** *sb.* 1605. Also †**furicano.** **1.** An early form of HURRICANE. **2.** Applied to a waterspout –1627.

2. The dreadfull spout, Which Shipmen doe the H. call *Tr. & Cr.* V. ii. 172. Hence **Hurrica·no** *v.* (*rare*), to whirl or drive as a hurricane.

Hurried (hʋ·rid), *ppl. a.* 1667. [f. HURRY *v.* + -ED[1].] Driven along, done or performed, with a rapidity due to pressure or want of time; characterized by hurry; full of haste; hasty.

1. Haste Of midnight march, and h. meeting here MILT. *P. L.* V. 778. A h. moment 1829, embrace 1855. Hence **Hu·rried-ly** *adv.*, **-ness.**

Hurrier (hʋ·riəɹ). 1611. [f. HURRY *v.* + -ER[1].] One who hurries (see the vb.).

Hurry (hʋ·ri), *sb.* 1600. [Orig. the sb. is identical in sense with HURLY. Senses 2 and 3, together with the earliest uses of the vb., based on the element *hurr*, have a more immediately onomatopœic origin.] †**1.** Commotion, agitation; tumult –1843; excitement, perturbation –1789. **2.** Excited, hasty, or impetuous motion; rush. Now *rare* or *Obs.* 1659. **3.** Action accelerated by pressure or want of time; undue haste; the condition of being obliged to act quickly; eagerness to get something done quickly 1692. **b.** Qualified by *no* or *any* (with neg. implication): Need for hurry 1849. **4.** *advb.* 1796.

1. Too much h. of spirits MME D'ARBLAY. **2.** A h. of hoofs in a village street LONGF. **3.** There is no h. in the designs of God 1879. **b.** Is there any h.? (*mod.*). **5.** as *adj.* (U.S.), hurried.

Hurry (hʋ·ri), *v.* 1590. [See HURRY *sb.*] **1.** *trans.* To carry, convey, or cause to go with excessive haste 1592; to carry or drive with impetuosity or without deliberation to some action, conduct, or condition of mind 1595; †to drive with impetuous motion –1696. **2.** *intr.* To move or act with excited haste, or effort at speed. *Hurry up!* make haste (*colloq.*) 1590. †**3.** *trans.* To agitate; to harass, worry. *Obs.* exc. *dial.* –1848. **4.** To urge to greater speed; to hasten unduly 1713.

1. A second fear..Which madly hurries her she knows not whither SHAKS. To h. you into an act of unjust aggression THIRLWALL. **2.** Nature never hurries, never takes leaps 1871. **3.** Her form wasted, her spirits were hurried HT. MARTINEAU. **4.** H. up the tea (*mod.*). Hence **Hu·rryingly** *adv.*

Hurrygraph (hʋ·rigraf). *U.S.* 1861. [f. HURRY + GRAPH.] A hurried sketch or impression.

Hurry-scurry (hʋ·ri,skʋ·ri), *adv.*, *adj.*, and *sb.* *colloq.* 1732. [Reduplicative f. HURRY *v.*: cf. SCURRY *v.*] **1.** *adv.* In disorderly haste, pell-mell 1750. **2.** *adj.* Characterized by hurry and commotion 1732. **3.** *sb.* The hurrying and disorderly rushing of a number; a rush 1754. Hence **Hu·rry-scu·rry** *v. intr.* to run or rush in confused and undignified haste.

Hurst (hɒ̄ɹst). Also **hirst,** etc. [OE. *hyrst* :—OTeut. type **hursti-z*. A freq. element in place-names, as in *Chislehurst*, *Amherst*, etc.]

I. 1. An eminence, hillock, knoll, or bank, esp. one of a sandy nature; a ford made by a bed of sand or shingle. **2.** A grove of trees; a copse; a wood; a wooded eminence OE.

1. We are bound to drive the bullocks All by hollows, hirsts, and hillocks SCOTT. **2.** Hursts that house the boar 1871.

II. Techn. senses. (Connexion with prec. is doubtful.) **1.** The frame of a pair of millstones 1710. **2.** The ring of the helve of a trip- or tilt-hammer, which bears the trunnions 1825.

Comb.: **h.beech,** the Hornbeam; **-frame** = sense II. 2.

Hurt (hɒ̄ɹt), *sb.*[1] ME. [app. a. OF. *hurte* (mod. *heurte*), f. *hurter*, *heurter*; see HURT *v.* The sense 'injury' is purely Eng.] †**1.** A knock, blow, or stroke causing a wound or damage –1844. **2.** Bodily injury so caused; a wound; a lesion; damage ME. **3.** *gen.* Harm, wrong, damage, detriment ME.

1. Of the great disordering of horses with the hurts of our English arrowes 1590. **2.** Herbes..To heele with youre hurtes hastily CHAUCER. A mortall h. SHAKS. **3.** What h. can it do you? DICKENS.

Hurt (hɒ̄ɹt), *sb.*[2] 1562. [a. F. *heurte*.] *Her.* A roundel azure; usu. held to represent a hurtleberry.

Hurt (hɒ̄ɹt), *sb.*[3] Now *dial.* 1542. [Of uncertain origin.] = HURTLEBERRY.

Hurt (hɒ̄ɹt), *v.* Pa. t. and pple. **hurt.** ME. [app. a. F. *hurter* (now *heurter*) to bring into collision, knock against, etc. Of obscure origin.]

I. Trans. uses. †**1.** To knock, strike, dash (a thing against another, or two things together) –1634. †**2.** To knock, strike, give a blow to (so as to wound or injure) –1662. **3.** To cause bodily or physical injury or pain to ME. **4.** *gen.* To injure, do harm to; to wrong ME. **5.** To give mental pain to; to distress, vex, offend 1526.

2. Whan þurgh þe body hurte was Diomede CHAUCER. **3.** I haue foughten with a knyght..I am sore hurte and he bothe MALORY. **4.** Tressilian..had much hurt his interest with her SCOTT. **5.** I own I was hurt to hear it SHERIDAN.

II. Intr. and absol. uses. †**1.** *intr.* To strike, dash (*on* or *against* something); to come into collision –1622. **2.** *absol.* To cause injury, do harm; to cause or inflict pain ME. **3.** *intr.* for *pass.* To suffer injury or pain. (Now only *colloq.*) ME.

2. They shall not h. nor destroy in all my holy mountaine *Isa.* xi. 9. **3.** Does your hand still h.? 1898.

Hurter[1] (hv̄·ɹtəɹ). 1472. [-ER [1].] One who or that which hurts or injures.
I shall not be a h. if no helper BEAUM. & FL.

Hurter[2] (hv̄·ɹtəɹ). ME. [ad. F. *hurtoir*, f. *hurter* HURT *v.*] 1. The shoulder of an axle, against which the nave of the wheel strikes; also, a strengthening piece on the shoulder of an axle. 2. a. A beam fixed on a gun-platform, to stop the wheels of the gun-carriage from injuring the parapet. b. A wooden or iron piece fastened to the top-rails of the lower gun-carriage or chassis, to check the motion of the gun. 1828.

Hurtful (hv̄·ɹtfŭl), *a.* 1526. [f. HURT *sb.*[1] + -FUL.] Causing hurt or injury; harmful, noxious, noisome. Hence **Hu·rtful-ly** *adv.*, -ness.

Hurtle (hv̄·ɹt'l), *sb. poet.* and *rhet.* 1773. [f. next.] The action or an act of hurtling; dashing together, collision, conflict; clashing sound.

Hurtle (hv̄·ɹt'l), *v.* Now only *lit.* or *arch.* ME. [app. a dim. and iterative of HURT *v.* to 'strike with a shock'.]
I. *trans.* 1. = HURT *v.* I. 1. 2. To strike or dash against; to come into collision with. Also *fig.* ME. 3. To drive violently or swiftly; to dash, dart, shoot, fling, cast. Often confounded with *hurl*. By Spenser, *erron.*, To brandish. 1590.
2. The ragged cindery masses hurtling one another in the atmosphere 1881. 3. An arrow, hurtel'd ere so high MARVELL.
II. *intr.* 1. To strike *together* or *against* something, esp. with violence or noise; to dash, clash, impinge; to meet in shock and encounter. Also *fig.* ME. 2. To emit a sound of collision; to clatter; hence, to move with clattering; to come with a crash 1509. 3. To dash, rush, hurry; esp. with noise 1509.
1. Together hurtled both their steedes FAIRFAX. 2. The noise of Battel hurtled in the Ayre *Jul. C.* II. ii. 22. 3. Pell mell the men came hurtling out 1873.

Hurtleberry (hv̄·ɹt'lberi). 1460. [app. a deriv. of HURT *sb.*[3]] The fruit of *Vaccinium Myrtillus*, or the shrub itself; the whortleberry or bilberry; also applied to other species of *Vaccinium*, and to the HUCKLEBERRY.

Hurtless (hv̄·ɹtlės), *a.* ME. [f. HURT *sb.*[1] + -LESS.] 1. Free from hurt; unhurt. 2. Causing no hurt; harmless 1549.
1. On lionet shalt hurtlesse soe, And on the dragon tread 1586. 2. H. blows DRYDEN. Hence **Hu·rtless-ly** *adv.*, -ness.

Husband (hv·zbănd), *sb.* [Late OE. *hūsbonda*, *-bunda*, f. *hūs* house + late OE. ? *bōnda*, *bunda*, a. ON. *bóndi*, peasant owning his own house and land, freeholder, franklin, yeoman; orig. pres. pple. of *búa*, *bóa* to dwell, have a household.]
I. †1. The master of a house, the male head of a household –ME. 2. A man joined to a woman by marriage. Correl. of *wife*. ME. Also *transf.* of animals and †plants 1553.
2. Thou hast no h. yet, nor I no wife: Giue me thy hand *Com. Err.* III. ii. 68. By marriage, the h. and wife are one person in law BLACKSTONE.
II. †1. One who tills and cultivates the soil; a cultivator, farmer, husbandman. In early north. use, a manorial tenant. –1697. 2. The manager of a household or establishment; a housekeeper; a steward. *Obs.* exc. in spec. applications. 1450. 3. With qualifying epithet. A saving, frugal, or provident man; an economist. (Cf. HOUSEWIFE.) Now *rare* or *arch.* 1510.
1. He was accounted..the greatest H., and most excellent Manager of Bees in Cornwall 1723. 2. *Ship's husband*: an agent appointed by the owners to attend to the business of a ship while in port; esp. to see that the ship is in all respects well found. Now little used. 3. I had been so good a h. of my rum, that I had a great deal left DE FOE.

Husband (hv·zbănd), *v.* ME. [f. prec. sb.]
I. 1. *trans.* To till (the ground), to dress or tend (trees); to cultivate. Also *fig.* 2. To administer as a good householder or steward; to manage with thrift and prudence; to economize; also, to save 1440.
1. Husbanding the Vallies which lie nearest to them HEYLIN. 2. We were obliged to h. our ammunition 1748.
II. 1. *trans.* To provide or match with a husband; to mate 1565. 2. To act the part of a husband to; to become the husband of, to marry 1601. b. *fig.* To espouse (an opinion) 1883.
1. I am husbanded with such a Clowne 1602. 2. Husbanding his means, with the hope of ultimately husbanding a wife 1843. Hence **Hu·sbandable** *a.* (*rare*), capable of being economically used; fit for cultivation.

Hu·sbandage. 1809. [f. HUSBAND *sb.* + -AGE.] The commission or allowance paid to a ship's husband.

Hu·sbandland. ME. [f. HUSBAND *sb.* + LAND.] An old northern term for the holding of a husband or manorial tenant, = yardland, virgate; the land occupied and tilled by the tenants of a manor, in contradistinction to the demesne lands.

Hu·sbandless, *a.* 1546. [-LESS.] Unwedded; widowed.

Hu·sbandlike, *a.* and *adv.* 1542. [LIKE *a.* and *adv.*] After the manner of a husband.

Husbandly (hv·zbăndli), *a.* 1573. [-LY [1].] 1. Belonging to or befitting a husband; marital 1581. 2. Pertaining to a husbandman or to husbandry. ? *Obs.* 1573. †3. Thrifty, saving, economical –1734. So **Hu·sbandly** *adv.* thriftily, frugally, economically.

Husbandman (hv·zbăndmæn). *Pl.* **-men.** ME. [f. HUSBAND *sb.* + MAN. In early use often two wds.] 1. A man who tills and cultivates the soil; a farmer. Also *fig.* †2. = HUSBAND *sb.* I. 1. ME. only. †3. = HUSBAND *sb.* II. 3. STEELE.

Husbandry (hv·zbăndri). ME. [-RY.] †1. Domestic economy. †b. *transf.* and *fig.* Management (as of a household) –1658. 2. The business of a husbandman; agriculture, farming ME.; †industrial occupation generally –1639. †3. *concr.* Household goods; agricultural produce; land under cultivation; the body of husbandmen on an estate –1628. 4. (Good or bad) economy; *absol.* economy, thrift, profit ME.
1. The h. and mannage of my house *Merch. V.* III. iv. 25. 2. The chief branch of h. is the rearing of sheep 1806. 3. Spoones and stooles, and al swich housbondrye CHAUCER. Ye are goddis husbandrye TINDALE 1 *Cor.* iii. 9. 4. Good h. and frugality are quite out of fashion 1745.

Hush (hvʃ), *sb.* 1601. [f. HUSH *v.*[1] Rare bef. 19th c.] Suppression of sound; silence; stillness, quiet.
It is the h. of night BYRON.

Hush (hvʃ), *a. arch.* 1602. [Modified f. HUSHT *a.*] Silent, still, hushed. *Haml.* II. ii. 508.

Hush (hvʃ), *v.*[1] 1546. [app. f. HUSHT *a.*] 1. *trans.* To make silent, still, or quiet; to silence. 2. *transf.* and *fig.* To suppress; to allay, lull, pacify. Also with *up.* 1632. 3. *intr.* To become or be silent, quiet, or still. Also *colloq.* with *up.* 1561.
2. Phr. *H. up*: to suppress mention of; to keep from getting known.

Hush *v.*[2] *dial.* 1613. To shoo.

Hush, *v.*[3] *n. dial.* 1750. [Echoic.] *trans.* To send or let forth (water) with a rush; *spec.* in *Lead Mining*, to send a rush of water over a sloping surface, in order to uncover ore, and separate it from earth and stones.

Hush (hvʃ), *int.* 1604. [Later form of HUSHT *int.*, or imper. of HUSH *v.*[1]] A command to be quiet; silence!

Hu·sh-boat, -ship. [HUSH *int.*, *v.*[1]] An armed ship disguised as a peaceful vessel to lure German submarines in the war of 1914–18.

Hushed (hvʃt), *ppl. a.* 1602. [Historically for HUSHT, but treated later as pa. pple. of HUSH *v.*[1]] Silenced, stilled, quieted.
No more; but hush'd as Midnight Silence go DRYDEN.

Husher = *usher*: see HUISHER.

Hush-hush. 1919. Reduplic. of HUSH *int.*, used attrib. to denote anything to be kept specially secret.

Hush-money. 1709. [See HUSH *v.*[1]] Money paid to prevent disclosure or exposure, or to hush up a crime, etc.

Husht, *int.* Now *dial.* ME. = HUSH *int.*

Husht (hvʃt), *a. arch.* ME. [Varies with HUST, and WHIST, from the interj. forms. It was at length felt as a pa. pple., as if *hush-t*, whence a new vb. HUSH. Now treated as a variant spelling of *hush'd*, HUSHED.] Silent, still, quiet; later, Rendered silent.
Euen as the wind is h. before it raineth SHAKS.

Husk (hvsk), *sb.*[1] [Late ME. *huske*; possibly f. OE. *hūs* house.] 1. The dry outer integument of certain fruits and seeds; a glume or rind; *spec.* in *U.S.*, the outer covering of an ear of maize or Indian corn. 2. †a. The coriaceous wing-case of an insect; an elytron. b. The shell or case of a chrysalis; a cocoon (? *arch.*). 1552. 3. *techn.* 'The supporting frame of a run of millstones' (Knight) 1875. 4. *transf.* and *fig.* The (usually worthless) outside or exterior of anything 1547.
1. The huskes that the swine did eate *Luke* xv. 16. 2. The dragon-fly..An inner impulse rent the veil Of his old h. TENNYSON. 4. A few huskes of reason 1644.

Husk (hvsk), *sb.*[2] 1722. [In sense 1 ? f. prec.; in sense 2 app. f. HUSKY *a.*] 1. A disease affecting cattle; a short dry cough. 2. Huskiness 1816.

Husk (hvsk), *v.*[1] 1562. [f. HUSK *sb.*[1]] *trans.* To remove the husk from.

Husk (hvsk), *v.*[2] *local.* 1577. [Goes with HUSK *sb.*[2]] *intr.* Of cattle: To cough as when suffering from the husk.

Husked (hvskt), *a.* 1583. [f. HUSK *sb.*[1] and *v.*[1]] †1. Furnished or covered with a husk –1686. 2. Stripped of the husk 1607.

Husking (hv·skiŋ), *vbl. sb.* 1721. [f. HUSK *v.*[1] + -ING [1].] The action of HUSK *v.*[1] *spec.* in *U.S.* The removal of the husk from Indian corn; hence, a gathering of neighbours and friends to assist a farmer in husking his corn; called also *h.-bee.*
Fair day; h. at Colo's 1712.

Husky (hv·ski), *sb.* 1864. [Corruption of Eskimo.] An Eskimo; the Eskimo language; an Eskimo dog.

Husky (hv·ski), *a.* 1552. [f. HUSK *sb.*[1] + -Y [1].] 1. Full of, containing, or consisting of husks; of the nature of a husk. 2. Dry as a husk; arid (*lit.* and *fig.*) 1599. 3. Of persons and their voice: Dry in the throat, so that the sound of the voice becomes more or less a hoarse whisper 1722. 4. *U.S.* and *Canadian colloq.* Tough, strong, hefty; also as *sb.* 1884.
3. His voice was h. with anger LONGF. Hence **Hu·skily** *adv.* **Hu·skiness** (in sense 3).

‖**Hu·so.** Also **huse.** 1706. [med. L., a. OHG. *hûso*; cf. HAUSEN.] The great sturgeon, *Acipenser huso*, of the Black and Caspian Seas.

Huss, *sb. dial.* Also **hurse.** 1440. [?] The dog-fish. Also *attrib.*

Hussar (huzā·ɹ). 1532. [a. Hungarian *huszar*, orig. 'freebooter, free-lance', later 'light horseman', (ult.) ad. It. *corsaro*, *corsare* CORSAIR. Not from Magyar *husz* twenty.] 1. One of a body of light horsemen organized in Hungary in the 15th c.; hence, the name of light cavalry regiments formed elsewhere in Europe in imitation of these. 2. *transf.* and *fig.* A skirmisher; a free-lance in literature or debate 1768.
1. *Black* or *Death H.*, one of the 'Black Brunswickers' (hussars with black uniform) who, in the war with France, 1809–13, neither gave nor received quarter; hence *fig.* I belong to the Black Hussars of Literature, who neither give nor receive criticism SCOTT.

Hussite (hv·səit, hu·səit). 1532. [ad. mod.L. *Hussita* (usu. pl.), f. John *Huss*, or *Hus*, orig. of *Husinec*, in Bohemia.] A follower of John Huss, the Bohemian religious reformer of the 15th c. Also *attrib.* or *adj.*

Hussy, huzzy (hv·zi), *sb.* 1530. [Phonetic reduction of HOUSEWIFE, q.v.] †1. = HOUSEWIFE 1. –1800. 2. A rustic, rude, opprobrious, or playfully rude mode of addressing a woman 1650. 3. In some rural districts = Woman, lass; hence, A light or worthless woman; an ill-behaved or mischievous girl; a jade, minx. Also joc. and in raillery. 1647. †4. = HOUSEWIFE 3. –1824.

†**Hust,** *interj.* [A natural utterance, enjoining silence.] A sharp whispered sound enjoining silence: = HIST! ST! HUSH! (Chaucer.) So †**Hust** *a.* silent, quiet, hushed.

Husting (hv·stiŋ). Usu. in pl. **hustings.** [OE. *hūsting*, a. ON. *hūs-þing*, house-assembly, a council held by a king, earl, etc., as dist. from the general assembly of the people (the

OE. *folc-ȝemót*).] 1. (In form *husting*.) An assembly for deliberative purposes, esp. one summoned by a king or other leader; a council. *Obs.* exc. *Hist.* 2. (In form *husting*, pl. *hustings*.) A court held in the Guildhall of London by the Lord Mayor, Recorder, and Sheriffs (or Aldermen), long the supreme court of the city OE. †3. (In form *hustings*, constr. as *sing.*) The upper end of the Guildhall, where this court was held; the platform on which the Lord Mayor and Aldermen took their seats –1761. 4. The temporary platform on which candidates for Parliament formerly stood for nomination, and while addressing the electors. Hence, the proceedings at a parliamentary election. 1719. Now *U.S.*, any place where political campaign speeches are made.

4. When the rotten hustings shake TENNYSON.

Hustle (hʊ·s'l), *v.* 1684. [ad. Du. *husselen*, *hutselen* to shake, to toss, freq. of Du. *hutsen*.] †1. *trans.* To shake to and fro, toss (money in a hat, etc.). Also *absol.* –1801. 2. To push or knock about unceremoniously; to jostle in a rough or violent fashion. Also *fig.* Also with *into*, *out of*, *through*. 1751. b. To urge forward in a rough unfastidious fashion 1887. 3. *intr.* To push roughly *against*. Also *absol.* 1823. b. *intr.* To push or elbow one's way 1855. 4. *intr.* To hurry, to bustle; to make a push 1821.

2. Dearling..was hustled by a gang of pickpockets 1798. b. He hustles the cob into a canter 1887. 4. The King..had hustled along the floor SCOTT. Hence **Hu·stle** *sb.* the act of hustling (*pitch and h.*, pitch-and-toss 1688); in *U.S.*, 'push'.

Hustle-cap (hʊ·s'lˌkæːp). ? *Obs.* 1709. [f. HUSTLE *v.* (sense 1) + CAP *sb.*] A form of pitch-and-toss, in which the coins were shaken in a cap before being tossed.

Hustlement (hʊ·s'lmĕnt). *Obs.* exc. *dial.* ME. [a. OF. *(h)ostillement*, later *out-*, f. *(h)ostiller*, mod. *outiller* to furnish, fit out with tools, f. OF. *(h)ostil*, mod. *outil* tool.] Household furniture; chiefly *pl.* household goods.

Hustler (hʊ·slər). 1825. [f. HUSTLE *v.* + -ER [1].] 1. One who hustles; one of a gang of pickpockets who work on this plan. 2. orig. *U.S.* One who works with impatient energy. 1886.

Huswife, etc.: see HOUSEWIFE, etc.

Hut (hʊt), *sb.* 1545. [a. F. *hutte*, a. MHG., Ger. *hütte*, perh. :—OTeut. **hudjā*, f. root *hud-*, *hūd-* of OE. *hȳdan* to hide.] 1. a. *Mil.* A wooden structure for the temporary housing of troops. Also *transf.* b. A small dwelling of rude and mean construction, often of branches, turf, or mud. In Australia, a stockman's cottage 1658. 2. The back end or body of the breech-pin of a musket 1853.

1. Dining off black bread..in a Swiss peasant's h. 1893.

Hut (hʊt), *v.* 1652. [a. F. *hutter* refl., f. *hutte*; see prec. sb.] 1. *trans.* To place in a hut or huts; to furnish with a hut or huts. 2. *intr.* To lodge or take shelter in a hut or huts; to go into winter quarters, as troops 1807.

1. Some of the men are hutted, but the officers are still in tents 1879.

Hutch (hʊtʃ), *sb.* [ME. *huche*, *hucche*, a. F. *huche* :—med.L. *hutica*; ult. etym. obscure.] 1. A chest or coffer, in which things are stored. 2. A box or box-like pen or house in which an animal is confined, as a *rabbit-hutch* 1607. b. Applied contemptuously to a hut or cabin, or joc. to a small house 1607. 3. Techn. a. Short for bolting-hutch 1619. b. A box for washing ore 1881. c. A box-like carriage, wagon, truck, etc. for use in agriculture, mining, etc. 1744. d. As a measure = about 2 cwt. 1802.

2. b. I cannot express what a satisfaction it was to me to come into my old h. DE FOE.

†**Hutch**, *a.* 1624. [app. a var. of HULCH *a.*; but cf. HUCK-.] Hunched, humped, gibbous; chiefly in *h. back* –1668.

Hutch, *v.* 1574. [f. prec. sb.] 1. *trans.* To put or lay up in a hutch or chest. Also *fig.* 2. To wash (ore) in a hutch. (Recent Dicts.)

†**Hutchet**. 1572. [ad. F., f. *hucher* to call.] *Her.* A bugle –1661.

Hutchinsonian (hʊtʃinsōᵘ·niăn). 1753. [See -IAN.] A. *adj.* Of or pertaining to John Hutchinson (died 1737), a writer on natural philosophy, who interpreted the Bible mystically, and opposed the Newtonian philosophy 1765. B. *sb.* An adherent of the above.

‖**Hutia** (hutī·ă). [Sp.] Any rodent of the West Indian genus *Capromys*.

Hutment (hʊ·tmĕnt). 1889. Accommodation in huts; an encampment of huts.

Huttonian (hʊtōᵘ·niăn), *a.* 1802. [See -IAN.] A. *adj.* Of or relating to James Hutton the geologist (1726–1796), who maintained against Werner the igneous or plutonic origin of basalt, granite, etc. B. *sb.* An adherent of Hutton's geological principles 1802.

Huxter, etc., obs. ff. HUCKSTER, etc.

Huyghenian (həigī·niăn), *a.* 1704. [f. *Huyghens* + -IAN.] Of or pertaining to Christian Huyghens, a Dutch mathematician and astronomer (1629–95).

H. eyepiece, a negative eyepiece invented by Huyghens, consisting of two plano-convex lenses, with their plane sides towards the eye.

Huzz (hʊz), *v.* 1555. [Echoic; cf. *whizz*.] *intr.* (rarely *trans.*) To buzz.

Wi' 'is kittle o' steam Huzzin' an' maäzin' the blessed feälds TENNYSON.

Huzza (hʊzā·, huzā·), *int.* and *sb.* 1573. [app. a mere exclam.] 1. *int.* A shout of exultation, encouragement, or applause; a hurrah 1682. 2. *sb.* The shout of huzza 1573.

2. They made a great h. or shout at our approch EVELYN.

Huzza (hʊzā·, huzā·), *v.* Also **-ah**, **-ay** (hʊzē̆ⁱ·), *v.* 1683. [f. prec.] 1. *intr.* To shout huzza. 2. *trans.* To acclaim with huzzas 1688.

2. The way of the world, which huzzays all prosperity THACKERAY.

Hw-, a freq. OE. initial element (:—OTeut. *χw-*, pre-Teut. *q-ʷ*), later WH-, q.v.

Hy, obs. f. HIGH.

Hyacine, corrupt f. HYACINTH (sense 1).

Hyacinth (həi·ăsinþ). See also JACINTH. 1553. [Ult. ad. Gr. ὑάκινθος hyacinth (flower and gem) of unkn. origin, explained in Greek myth as the name of a youth beloved by Apollo; see sense 2.] 1. A precious stone. a. Repr. Gr. ὑάκινθος, L. *hyacinthus*, a stone of a blue colour, prob. the sapphire. b. In mod. use, a reddish-orange variety of zircon; also applied to varieties of garnet and topaz of similar colour. c. *Her.* The name for the colour *tenné* or tawny 1704. 2. A plant. a. Repr. Gr. ὑάκινθος, L. *hyacinthus*, a name for some flower; according to Ovid a deep red or purple lily. It was said to have sprung up from the blood of the slain youth Hyacinthus, and to have the letters AI, or AIAI, on its petals. Now only *Hist.* or *poet.* 1578. b. Eng. name of the genus *Hyacinthus* (N.O. *Liliaceæ*), bulbous plants with spikes of bell-shaped six-parted flowers, of various colours; esp. *H. Orientalis*, a native of the Levant. Also applied to allied plants of similar habit. 3. A bird; a kind of water-hen with purple plumage, as the genera *Ionornis* and *Porphyrio*. 4. *attrib.*, esp. in reference to the reddish-orange colour of the gem, or the blue and purple colour of the flower 1694.

2. O hyacinths! for ay your AI keep still, Nay, with more marks of woe your leaves now fill DRUMM. OF HAWTH. b. **Wild** or **Wood H.** (of Britain), *Scilla nutans* (= BLUEBELL 2); (of N. America), *Scilla* or *Camassia Fraseri*. 4. The h.-hued hills OUIDA. Hence **Hyaci·nthian** *a.* of or pertaining to the h.: hyacinthine.

Hyacinthine (həiˌăsi·nþin, -əin), *a.* 1656. [ad. L. *hyacinthus*; see -INE.] 1. Of the colour of a hyacinth (gem or flower). (Chiefly as a poetic epithet of hair, after Hom. *Od.* VI. 231.) 2. Of, made of, or adorned with hyacinths 1675. 3. Like the boy Hyacinthus 1847.

1. Hyacinthin locks Round from his parted forelock manly hung Clustring MILT. *P. L.* IV. 301. 3. The h. boy, for whom Morn well might break and April bloom EMERSON.

‖**Hyades** (həi·ădīz), *sb. pl.* Rarely **Hyads**. ME. [a. Gr. Ὑάδες fem. pl., pop. conn. w. ὕειν to rain, but perh. f. ὗς, ὑός swine, the L. name being *suculæ* little pigs.] *Astron.* A group of stars near the Pleiades, the chief of which is the bright red star Aldebaran.

Thro' scudding drifts the rainy Hyades Vext the dim sea TENNYSON.

Hyæna, var. of HYENA.

Hyalescent (həiˌăle·sĕnt), *a.* [f. Gr. ὕαλος + -ESCENT.] Becoming hyaline or glassy. So **Hyale·scence**, the process of becoming or condition of being hyaline. 1864.

Hyaline (həi·ălin, -əin), *a.* and *sb.* 1661. [ad. L. *hyalinus*, a. Gr. ὑάλινος, f. ὕαλος, glass.]

A. *adj.* Resembling glass, transparent as glass, crystalline, vitreous. (Chiefly *techn.*)

B. *sb.* 1. 'A sea of glass like unto crystal' (Rev. iv. 6); hence poet. for the smooth sea, the clear sky, or anything transparent 1667. 2. *Anat.* and *Biol.* a. The HYALOID membrane of the eye. b. Hyaline cartilage, i.e. ordinary cartilage, as dist. from fibro-cartilage, etc. c. = *Hyaloplasm* (see HYALO-) 1864.

1. On the cleer H., the Glassie Sea MILT. *P. L.* VII. 619.

Hyalite (həi·ăləit). 1794. [f. Gr. ὕαλος glass + -ITE.] *Min.* A colourless variety of opal, occurring in globular concretions.

‖**Hyalitis** (həiˌăləi·tis). 1847. [f. as prec. + -ITIS.] *Path.* Inflammation of the vitreous humour of the eye.

Hyalo- (həiˌălo), comb. f. Gr. ὕαλος glass. **Hy·alograph** [Gr. -γραφος that writes], 'an instrument for etching on a transparent surface'; so **Hyalo·graphy**, 'the art of writing or engraving on glass' (Webster). **Hy·alophane** [Gr. -φανης], *Min.* a barium feldspar, found in transparent crystals. **Hy·aloplasm** [Gr. πλάσμα], *Biol.* transparent homogeneous protoplasm; hence **Hyalopla·smic** *a.* †**Hy·alotype**, a positive picture, copied on glass from a negative on glass.

Hyaloid (həi·ăloid). 1835. [a.F. *hyaloïde*, or ad.L., a. Gr. ὑαλοειδής, f. ὕαλος; see HYALINE.]

A. *adj.* (Chiefly *Anat.*) a. Glassy, hyaline. b. Connected with the hyaloid membrane.

a. *H. coat* or *membrane*, a thin transparent membrane enveloping the vitreous humour of the eye. b. *H. artery*, *canal*, *vein* (*Syd. Soc. Lex.*).

B. *sb.* 1. *Anat.* The hyaloid membrane; see A. a. 1838. 2. = HYALINE B. 1. 1844.

‖**Hyalonema** (həiˌălonī·mă). 1855. [mod.L., f. Gr. ὕαλος + νῆμα thread.] The glass-rope sponge, which roots itself to the sea-bed by a long stem twisted of fine siliceous threads.

Hybern-, erron. sp. of HIBERN-.

Hyblæan (həiblī·ăn), *a.* Also **Hyblean**. 1614. [f. L. *Hyblæus* (f. *Hybla*, Gr. Ὕβλη) + -AN.] Of or pertaining to the town of Hybla in Sicily celebrated for its bees; hence *poet.* honied, sweet, mellifluous.

Busy as H. swarms 1682. So **Hy·blan** *a.*

Hybodont (hi·bodǫnt). 1836. [f. Gr. ὕβος hump + ὀδούς, ὀδοντ- tooth.]

A. *sb.* A shark of the extinct genus *Hybodon* or family *Hybodontidæ*, with conical compressed teeth.

B. *adj.* Belonging to the *Hybodontidæ* 1872.

Hybrid (həi·brid). 1601. [f. L. *hybrida*, more correctly *hibrida* (*ibrida*), offspring of a tame sow and wild boar; hence, half-breed.]

A. *sb.* 1. The offspring of two animals or plants of different species, or (less strictly) varieties; a half-breed, cross-breed, mongrel. 2. *transf.* and *fig.* Anything derived from heterogeneous sources; in *Philol.* a composite word formed of elements belonging to different languages 1850.

1. Grotesque hybrids, half-bird, half-beast 1851. At the best we [English] are but hybrids 1861. The common Oxlip..is certainly a h. between the primrose and the cowslip DARWIN.

B. *adj.* 1. Produced by the interbreeding of two different species or varieties; mongrel, cross-bred, half-bred 1775. 2. *transf.* and *fig.* Derived from heterogeneous sources; composed of incongruous elements; mongrel 1716.

2. *H. bill*, a bill in Parliament combining the characteristics of a public and private bill, which is referred to a *h. committee*, i.e. a committee nominated partly (as in a public bill) by the House of Commons, and partly (as in a private bill) by the Committee of Selection.

Hence **Hybri·dity**, h. condition.

Hybridism (həi·bridiz'm, hi·b-). 1845. [f. prec. + -ISM.] 1. The fact or condition of being hybrid; also, the production of hybrids;

cross-breeding. **2.** *Philol.* The formation of a word from elements belonging to two different languages 1862. So **Hy·bridist**, a hybridizer.

Hybridize (həi·bridəiz, hi·b-), *v.* 1845. [f. HYBRID + -IZE.] **1.** *trans.* To cause to interbreed and thus to produce hybrids. **2.** *intr.* **a.** To produce a hybrid or hybrids between two distinct species or varieties 1853. **b.** To cross or interbreed 1862. Hence **Hy·bridi·zable** *a.* capable of hybridization. **Hy:bridiza·tion**, the formation of hybrids; cross-breeding. **Hy·bridizer**, one who produces hybrids by cross-breeding.

Hy·bridous, *a.* Now *rare* or *Obs.* 1691. [f. L. *hybrida* + -OUS. (The only word of the group in Johnson.)] = HYBRID *a.*

Hydage, obs. f. HIDAGE.

Hydatic (həidæ·tik), *a.* 1710. [ad. Gr. ὑδατικός watery. Cf. F. *hydatique.*] Pertaining to or of the nature of a hydatid; watery. So †**Hyda·tical** *a.*

Hydatid (həi·dătid, hi·d-), *sb.* (*a.*) Chiefly in *pl.*; formerly in L. form **hydatides** (hidæ·tidīz). 1683. [ad. Gr. ὑδατίς, ὑδατιδ- a drop of water, etc. Cf. F. *hydatide.*] *Path.* **1.** A cyst containing a clear watery fluid, occurring as a morbid formation in the tissues of animal bodies; *esp.* one formed by and containing the larva of a tapeworm (esp. of *Tænia echinococcus*) in its encysted state. **2.** *attrib.* or *adj.* Of or belonging to hydatids; of the nature of a hydatid; containing or affected with hydatids 1807.

Hence **Hydati·diform** (also contr. **Hy·datiform**) *a.* having the form or character of a h.

Hydr-, the usual form of HYDRO- bef. a vowel.

Hydra (həi·dră). ME. (first as **ydre, idre**, from Fr.). [a. L., a. Gr. ὕδρα.]

I. 1. *Gr. Myth.* The fabulous many-headed snake of the marshes of Lerna, whose heads grew again as fast as they were cut off; at length killed by Hercules. **2.** *transf.* and *fig.* An evil resembling the Lernæan hydra, *esp.* in the difficulty of its extirpation 1494. **3.** *rhet.* Any terrific serpent or reptile 1546. **4.** A water-snake 1608. **5.** *Astron.* An ancient southern constellation, represented as a water-snake or sea-serpent. Its chief star is Alphard or Cor Hydræ 1559.

1. Worse Then Fables yet have feign'd, or fear conceiv'd, Gorgons and Hydra's, and Chimera's dire MILT. *P. L.* II. 628. 2. The h. of revolt lay stunned and prostrate MERIVALE.

II. *Zool.* (pl. usu. **hydræ.**) A genus of Hydrozoa, consisting of freshwater polyps of very simple structure, the body forming a cylindrical tube, with a mouth surrounded by a ring of tentacles with stinging thread-cells. (So named by Linnæus (1756), because cutting it in pieces only multiplies its numbers.) **b.** The sexual bud or medusa of any hydroid hydrozoan; so called from its resemblance to an individual of the genus Hydra 1865. **c.** *Hydra tuba*: a larval or non-sexual form of hydroid in certain Hydrozoa, of a trumpet-like form 1847.

Hydracid (həidæ·sid). 1826. [f. HYDR(O- d + ACID. Cf. F. *hydracide.*] *Chem.* An acid containing hydrogen, as dist. from an *oxyacid*, or *oxacid*, containing oxygen; now applied esp. to the halogen acids, or simple compounds of hydrogen with chlorine, bromine, iodine, etc.

‖**Hydræmia** (həidrī·miă). Also **hydremia.** 1845. [f. HYDR(O- b + Gr. -αιμία, f. αἷμα blood.] *Path.* A watery condition of the blood. Hence **Hydræ·mic, -emic** *a.* of the nature of or affected with h.

Hydragogue (həi·drăgǫg). 1638. [a. F. *hydragogue*, or ad. L., a. Gr. ὑδραγωγός conveying water, f. ὑδρ- + ἄγειν.]

A. *adj.* Of medicines: Having the property of removing water or serum, or of causing watery evacuations.

B. *sb.* [sc. *medicine* or *drug.*] 1658.

Hydramide (həi·drămәid). 1865. [f. HYDR(O- d + AMIDE.] *Chem.* A tertiary diamide formed by the action of ammonia on certain aldehydes.

Hydramine (həi·drămәin). 1877. [f. HYDR(O- d + AMINE.] *Chem.* An oxethene base; an amine containing hydroxyl substitution compounds of ethyl.

‖**Hydrangea** (həidræ·ndʒiă). 1753. [mod.L. *Hydrangēa* (Linn.), f. Gr. ὑδρ- (HYDRO-) + ἄγγος vessel (in allusion to the cup-like form of the seed-capsule). Cf. F. *hydrangée.*] A genus of shrubs (N.O. *Saxifragaceæ*), with white, blue, or pink flowers in large globular clusters; esp. the Chinese species *H. hortensis*, commonly cultivated in Great Britain.

Hydrant (həi·drănt). 1828. [Irreg. f. Gr. ὑδρ- (HYDRO-) + -ANT[1]. Of U.S. origin.] An apparatus for drawing water directly from a main, consisting of a pipe with one or more nozzles, or with a spout or the like.

Hydranth (həi·drænþ). 1874. [f. HYDRA II + Gr. ἄνθος flower.] *Zool.* One of the non-sexual zooids occurring in colonial Hydrozoa. Sometimes extended to any hydroid (free or colonial).

‖**Hydrargyrum** (həidrā·ɹdʒirǒm). 1563. [mod.L. *hydrargyrum*, altered from L. *hydrargyrus*, a. Gr. ὑδράργυρος artificial quicksilver, f. ὑδρ- (HYDRO-) + ἄργυρος silver.] Quicksilver, mercury. Symbol Hg. Hence **Hydra·rgyral, -ate, -ic, -ous** *adjs.* mercurial. **Hydra·rgyrism,** ‖**Hydrargyro·sis,** mercurial poisoning.

‖**Hydrarthrosis** (həidrāɹþrōᵘ·sis). 1861. [f. HYDR(O- b + ARTHROSIS.] *Path.* Dropsy of the joints.

Hydrastine (həidræ·stәin). 1876. [f. mod. L. *Hydrastis* + -INE.] **a.** An alkaloid obtained from the root of *Hydrastis Canadensis*, a N. American ranunculaceous plant. **b.** A medicine consisting of this alkaloid mixed with berberine and resin.

Hydrate (həi·drĕ't), *sb.* 1802. [f. Gr. ὑδρ- (HYDRO-) + -ATE[1] 1 c.] *Chem.* A compound of water with another compound or an element, e.g. hydrate of chlorine. Formerly, and still by some, applied also to a HYDROXIDE, e.g. KOH, potassium hydrate; NH_4OH, ammonium hydrate. Hence **Hy·drate** *v. trans.* to combine chemically with water; to convert into a h. **Hy·drated** *a.* chemically combined with water or its elements; formed into a h. **Hydra·tion**, the action of hydrating or condition of being hydrated; as *water of h.*, as contrasted with *water of constitution.*

Hydraulic (həidrǭ·lik). 1626. [ad. L. *hydraulicus*, a. Gr. ὑδραυλικός, f. ὕδωρ, ὑδρ- water + αὐλός pipe. Cf. F. *hydraulique.*]

A. *adj.* **1.** Pertaining to water (or other liquid) as conveyed through pipes or channels, esp. by mechanical means; belonging to hydraulics 1661. **2.** Applied to various mechanical contrivances operated by water-power, or in which water is conveyed through pipes; e.g. a *h. crane, engine, machine, motor* 1656. **3.** Applied to substances which harden under water and so become impervious to it; as *h. cement, lime, mortar* 1851.

1. *H. mining*: a method of mining in which the force of a powerful jet of water is used to wear down a bed of auriferous gravel or earth, and to carry the debris to the sluices where the particles of gold are separated. 2. *H. belt*, an endless woollen band passing over rollers for raising water by absorption and compression. *H. block* (*Shipbuilding*), a hydraulic lifting-press made to occupy the place of a building-block beneath the keel of a vessel in a repairing-dock, so as to raise the vessel when needed. *H. elevator, lift*, a lift or hoist worked by h. power. *H. main*, in gas-works, a large pipe containing water, and receiving the pipes from the several retorts, which dip below the surface of the water so that the raw gas is partly purified on its way to the condenser. *H. press* = HYDROSTATIC *press*. *H. ram*, an automatic pump in which the kinetic energy of a descending column of water in a pipe is used to raise some of the water to a height above that of its original source; also applied to the lifting piston of a hydrostatic press. *H. valve*, a valve formed by an inverted cup with its edge under water over the upturned open end of a pipe, so as to close the pipe against the passage of air.

B. *sb.* **a.** Short for *h. engine, press*, etc. **b.** Applied hydraulic force. 1729.

Hence †**Hydrau·lical** *a.* = prec. A. **Hydrau·lically** *adv.* by means of h. power or appliances. **Hydrau·licking** *vbl. sb.* h. mining.

Hydraulico-, comb. f. Gr. ὑδραυλικός HYDRAULIC.

‖**Hydrau·licon.** *Pl.* **-a.** 1570. [a. Gr. ὑδραυλικόν (ὄργανον): see HYDRAULIC.] An ancient musical instrument in which water was used, prob. to regulate the pressure of the air; a water-organ.

Hydraulics (həidrǭ·liks). 1671. [Pl. of HYDRAULIC; see -ICS.] The department of science which deals with the conveyance of water or other liquids through pipes, etc., and with the mechanical applications of the force exerted by moving liquids. Often used more widely, as = *hydrokinetics* or *hydrodynamics.*

Hydrazine (həi·drăzәin). 1887. [mod. f. HYDR(OGEN + AZO- (for *azote*) + -INE.] *Chem.* A colourless stable gas, with strong alkaline reaction, N_2H_4. Also extended to a class of compounds in which one or more of the hydrogen atoms in this are replaced by a univalent radical, as *Ethyl h.* $N_2H_3.C_2H_5$.

Hydremia, -ic: see HYDRÆMIA, -IC.

‖**Hydria** (həi·driă, hi·driă). *Pl.* **-æ.** 1850. [L., a. Gr. ὑδρία a water-pot.] A water-pot; in *Archæol.* a large Greek jar or pitcher for carrying water, with two or three handles.

Hydriad (həi·driæd). 1864. [a. Gr. ὑδριάς (νύμφη).] A water-nymph.

Hydric (həi·drik), *a.* 1854. [f. HYDR(OGEN) + -IC.] *Chem.* Of hydrogen, containing hydrogen in chemical combination; as in *h. chloride* = *hydrogen chloride* or *hydrochloric acid.*

Hydride (həi·drәid). 1849. [f. HYDR(O- d + -IDE.] *Chem.* †**a.** = HYDRATE in the earlier sense. **b.** Now, a substance formed by the union of hydrogen with an element or a radical.

Hydriform (həi·drifǭɹm), *a.* 1822. [See HYDRA and -FORM.] Hydra-shaped; having the form of the hydra polyp.

†**Hydriodate** (həidrəi·odĕ't). 1823. [f. as next + -ATE[1] 1 c.] *Chem.* A hydriodide –1851.

Hydriodic (həidrəi,ǫ·dik), *a.* 1819. [f. HYDR(OGEN) + IOD(INE) + -IC.] *Chem.* Containing hydrogen and iodine in chemical combination. **H. acid,** the simple combination of hydrogen and iodine, also called *hydrogen iodide* (HI), a colourless very soluble gas, of strongly acid properties and suffocating odour. So **Hydriodide** (həidrəi·odәid), a compound of h. acid with an organic radical (or, formerly, with an element).

Hydro- (həidro), bef. a vowel also **hydr-**, = Gr. ὑδρ(o-, comb. f. ὕδωρ water. Hence:

a. Miscellaneous terms, in which *hydro-* has the sense of 'water', as in *hydrography*, etc.; or is loosely combined, as in *hydrogeology*, etc.

b. In medical and pathological terminology, *hydro-* is prefixed (*a*) to names of parts of the body, to denote that such part is dropsical or affected with an accumulation of serous fluid, as *hydrocardia*, etc.; also, in the combination *hydropneumo-*, to express the presence of water and air, as in *hydropneumopericardium*, etc.; (*b*) to names of diseases or diseased formations, denoting the accompaniment of dropsy or of an accumulation of serous fluid, as *hydrocachexia, -y, -diarrhœa*, etc.

c. Prefixed to names of minerals, *hydro-* denotes a hydrous compound.

d. In mod. chemical terms, the prefix *hydro-* originally meant combination with water. Hence, as this often implies combination with the hydrogen of the water, *hydr(o-* has become the regular combining form of *hydrogen*, like *oxy-* for *oxygen*, etc. Prefixed to the name of a compound substance *hydro-* usually means the addition or substitution of hydrogen in its constitution, e.g. *benzoin* $C_{14}H_{12}O_2$, *hydrobenzoin* $C_{14}H_{14}O_2$, etc.

e. In mod. zoological terminology, *hydro-* is used in the nomenclature relating to members of the class HYDROZOA and their organs or parts.

f. Derivs. of Gr. ἱδρώς 'sweat' have been erron. written *hydro-* instead of *hidro-*, e.g. *hydroadenitis* inflammation of the sweat glands.

Hydrobaro·meter, an instrument for determining the depth of the ocean from the pressure of the superincumbent water. **Hy·drobranch** [Gr. βράγχια gills], *Zool.* a member of the *Hydrobranchiata*, a division of gastropods containing species which breathe water only; so **Hydrobra·nchiate** *a.*, pertaining to the *Hydrobranchiata*. **Hydrocau·line** [Gr. καυλός stem] *a.*, *Zool.* pertaining to or characteristic of the ‖**Hydrocau·lus** or main stem of the cœnosarc of a hydrozoan. ‖**Hydroce·phalis** [Gr. κεφαλή, the oral and stomachal regions of a hydroid. **Hydroco·ralline** [CORALLINE] *a.*, *Zool.* pertaining to the *Hydrocorallinæ*, an order or sub-order of *Hydroidea*, the coral-making hydroid hydrozoa; *sb.* one of this order. **Hy·drocycle** [CYCLE *sb.*], a velocipede adapted for propulsion on the surface of water. **Hy·drocyst** [Gr. κύστις CYST], *Zool.* one of the tentacles or feelers, resembling immature polypites, attached to the cœnosarc in certain Hydrozoa, as in the family *Physophoridæ*; hence **Hydrocy·stic** *a.* **Hydrœ·cial** *a.*, pertaining to the ‖**Hydrœ·cium** [Gr. οἰκίον, f. οἶκος], a sac into which the cœnosarc can be retracted in certain Hydrozoa, as the *Calycophoridæ*. **Hydro-extractor**, a centrifugal machine for drying clothes, etc. **Hydroferricya·nic, -ferridcyanic** *a.*, *Chem.* in *h. acid* = hydrogen ferricyanide, $H_6Fe_2Cy_{12}$; hence **Hydroferri(d)cy·anate**, a salt of this acid. **Hydroferrocya·nic** *a.*, *Chem.* in *h. acid* = hydrogen ferrocyanide, H_4FeCy_6; hence **Hydroferrocy·anate**, a salt of this acid. **Hydrogalva·nic** [GALVANIC] *a.*, pertaining to the production of galvanic electricity by means of liquids. †**Hydro·gnosy** [Gr. -γνωσια], a history and description of the waters of the earth. **Hydroˌio·dic** = HYDRIODIC. **Hydroma·gnesite**, *Min.* hydrous carbonate of magnesium, found in white silky crystals or earthy crusts. **Hydromedu·san** [MEDUSA] *a.*, belonging or related to the *Hydromedusæ*, now a subclass of Hydrozoa (called also *Craspedota*), formerly a synonym of Hydrozoa; *sb.* a member of this subclass. **Hydrome·tallurgy** [METALLURGY], 'the act or process of assaying or reducing ores in the wet way, or by means of liquid re-agents' (Webster). **Hydrome·teor**, an atmospheric phenomenon which depends on the vapour of water, as rain, hail, and snow; hence **Hy:drometeorolo·gical** *a.*, pertaining to **Hy:drometeoro·logy**, that part of meteorology which deals with atmospheric phenomena depending on the vapour of water. **Hydromi·ca**, *Min.* a variety of potash mica containing more water than ordinary muscovite; hence **Hydromica·ceous** *a.* **Hydroperitonæ·um**, *Path.* same as ASCITES. **Hy·drophid** [Gr. ὄφις serpent], *Zool.* a venomous sea-snake of the genus *Hydrophis* or family *Hydrophidæ*, found in the Indian Ocean. **Hy·drophyll**, *Bot.* Lindley's name for plants of N.O. *Hydrophyllaceæ*, of which the typical genus is *Hydrophyllum*, the Waterleaf of N. America. **Hydrophyllia·ceous** *a.*, having the characters of the ‖**Hydrophy·llium** [Gr. φύλλιον] = BRACT 2. **Hy·dropult** [*-pult* in CATAPULT], a force-pump worked by hand; a garden-pump. ‖**Hydro·rachis, -o·rrhachis**, *Path.* extensive serous accumulation within the spinal canal. ‖**Hydrorhi·za** [Gr. ῥίζα root], the root-stock or rooting fibres by which a colony of Hydrozoa is attached to some foreign object; hence **Hydrorhi·zal** *a.* **Hy·drospire** [Gr. σπεῖρα coil, SPIRE], one of the system of lamellar tubes lying between and below the ambulacra in blastoids, supposed to have been respiratory in function. **Hydrota·lcite** [TALC], *Min.* a hydrous oxide of aluminium and magnesium, a fibrous white mineral of pearly lustre and greasy feel. **Hydrotellu·ric** *a.*, *Chem.* formed by hydrogen and tellurium in chemical combination; *h. acid*, telluretted hydrogen, H_2Te, an offensive gas; its salts are **Hydrote·llurates**. ‖**Hydrothe·ca** [L. *theca*, Gr. θήκη receptacle], *Zool.* one of the perisarcal cups or calycles in which the polypites in certain Hydrozoa (as the *Sertularidæ*) are lodged; hence **Hydrothe·cal** *a.*

Hy:dro-ae·roplane. 1914. [See HYDRO-.] An aeroplane adapted for rising from and landing on water.

†**Hydrobro·mate.** 1836. [f. as next + -ATE[1] I c.] *Chem.* A bromide, viewed as a salt of hydrobromic acid; also, a hydrobromide –1876.

Hydrobromic (həidroˌbrōᵘ·mik), *a.* 1836. [f. HYDRO- d + BROMIC.] *Chem.* Containing hydrogen and bromine in combination.

H. acid, also called *hydrogen bromide* (HBr), a colourless gas with a pungent odour and strongly acid taste, fuming in the atmosphere and very soluble in water. So **Hydrobro·mide**, a compound of h. acid with an organic radical.

Hydrocarbon (həidroˌkā·ɹbǫn). 1826. [f. as prec. + CARBON.] *Chem.* A chemical compound of hydrogen and carbon. (These compounds, the *paraffins, olefines, acetylenes, benzenes*, etc., are very numerous, and constitute the subject-matter of organic chemistry.) **b.** *attrib.*, as *h. radical, series*, etc. **H. gas**: any gaseous h. Hence **Hy:drocarbona·ceous** *a.* pertaining to, of the nature of, or containing a h. **Hydrocarbo·nic, Hydroca·rbonous** *adjs.* of the nature of a h.

Hydrocarbonate (-kā·ɹbŏnėt). 1800. [f. HYDRO(GEN + CARBONATE.] *Chem.* A hydrocarbon; †formerly, carburetted hydrogen (CH_4).

†**Hydroca·rburet.** 1815. [f. HYDRO- d + CARBURET.] *Chem.* A hydrocarbon; *spec.* carburetted hydrogen gas –1850.

Hydrocele (hai·drosīl). 1597. [a. L., a. Gr. ὑδροκήλη, f. ὑδρο-water + κήλη tumour.] *Path.* A tumour with a collection of serous fluid; *spec.* a tumour of this kind in the cavity of the *tunica vaginalis* of the testis; dropsy of the testicle or of the scrotum. Hence **-ce·lous** *a.*

‖**Hydrocephalus** (həidrose·fălŏs). 1670. [Medical L., ad. Gr. ὑδροκέφαλον, f. ὑδρο- + κεφαλή.] *Path.* An accumulation of serous fluid in the cavity of the cranium, resulting in gradual expansion of the skull, and finally inducing general weakness, with mental failure; water on the brain. The acute form is often called *tubercular meningitis*.

Children are more liable to hydrocephali than adults CHAMBERS. Hence **Hydrocepha·lic** *a.* pertaining to, or characteristic of, h.; affected with h. **Hydroce·phaloid** *a.*, resembling h., as in *hydrocephaloid disease*, a condition of coma incident to young children and resulting apparently from cerebral anæmia. **Hydroce·phalous** *a.* affected with h. var. **Hydroce·phaly.**

†**Hydrochlo·rate.** 1819. [f. as next + -ATE[1] I c.] *Chem.* An old name for a chloride; also for a hydrochloride –1880.

Hydrochloric (həidroˌklōᵊ·rik), *a.* 1817. [f. HYDRO- d + CHLORIC.] *Chem.* Containing hydrogen and chlorine in chemical combination.

H. acid, called also *hydrogen chloride* (HCl), a colourless gas of strongly acid taste and pungent odour, extremely soluble in water. (Earlier names were *muriatic acid, spirit of salt, chlorhydric acid.*)

Hydrochloride (həidroˌklōᵊ·rəid). 1826. [f. HYDRO- d + CHLORIDE.] *Chem.* A compound of hydrochloric acid with an organic radical (formerly, also, with an element).

†**Hydrocyanate** (həidroˌsəi·ănėt). 1818. [f. as next + -ATE[1] I c.] *Chem.* An old name for a cyanide, considered as a salt of hydrocyanic acid –1854.

Hydrocyanic (həidroˌsəiˌæ·nik), *a.* 1818. [f. HYDRO- d + CYANIC.] *Chem.* Containing hydrogen and cyanogen in chemical combination.

H. acid, or *hydrogen cyanide* (HCN or HCy), the combination of hydrogen with cyanogen (CN or Cy), an extremely poisonous volatile liquid with an odour like that of bitter almonds, the solution in water being known as *prussic acid*.

Hydrodynamic, -al (həi:droˌdəi-, -dinæ·mik, -ăl), *a.* 1828. [ad. mod.L. *hydrodynamicus*; see next and DYNAMIC.] Pertaining to the forces acted upon or exerted by water or other liquids; belonging to HYDRODYNAMICS.

Hydrodynamics (həi:droˌdəi-, -dinæ·miks). 1779. [ad. mod.L. *hydrodynamica*; see HYDRO- a and DYNAMICS. The Latin word was first used by Daniel Bernoulli.] The branch of Physics which treats of the forces acting upon or exerted by liquids. Orig. = HYDROKINETICS; now usually including Hydrokinetics and Hydrostatics.

Hydrodynamometer (-dəinămǫ·mītəɹ). 1890. [f. HYDRO- a + DYNAMOMETER.] An instrument for measuring the force exerted by a liquid in motion.

Hydro-ele·ctric, *a.* 1832. [f. HYDRO- a + ELECTRIC.] †**1.** Of or pertaining to hydro-electricity; galvanic –1855. **2.** Effecting the development of electricity by the friction of water or steam 1863. **3.** Producing electricity by utilizing the motive power of water 1905. So **Hy:dro-electri·city.**

†**Hydroflu·ate.** 1841. [f. HYDRO- d + FLUATE.] *Chem.* An old name for a fluoride viewed as a salt of hydrofluoric acid; also for a hydrofluoride.

Hydrofluoric (həidroflūˌǫ·rik), *a.* 1822. [f. HYDRO- d + FLUORIC.] *Chem.* Containing hydrogen and fluorine in chemical combination.

H. acid, or *hydrogen fluoride* (HF), a colourless gas, fuming in moist air and rapidly absorbed by water.

Hydrofluosilicic (həi:droˌflūˌosili·sik), *a.* 1842. [f. HYDRO- d + FLUO- + SILICIC.] *Chem.* Containing hydrogen, fluorine, and silicon in chemical combination.

H. acid (H_2SiF_6), or *hydrogen silicofluoride*, a fuming liquid which gradually attacks glass, esp. on heating. So **Hydrofluosi·licate**, a salt of h. acid; a silico-fluoride.

Hydrogen (həi·drǒdʒĕn). Also †**hydrogene.** 1791. [a. F. *hydrogène*, f. Gr. ὕδωρ, ὑδρ- water; see -GEN I.] *Chem.* **1.** One of the elements; a colourless, invisible, odourless gas; it burns with a pale-blue flame, whence its former name of *inflammable air*. It is the lightest substance known, having a specific gravity of about one-fourteenth of that of air. Symbol H; atomic weight 1.

It occurs free in nature in small quantities in certain volcanic gases, and is an essential constituent of all animal and vegetable matter. It forms two-thirds in volume and one-ninth in weight of water (H_2O), which is the sole product of the combustion of h. in ordinary air. It is a constituent of all acids, in which it can be replaced by bases to form salts.

2. *attrib.* **a.** *h. lamp*, etc.; **h. acid** = HYDRACID; †**h. air, gas**, old names for h. **b.** In systematic names of chemical compounds of h. with an element or radical = 'of hydrogen'; as *h. bromide* HBr; *h. dioxide* H_2O_2 (oxygenated water); *h. sulphide* H_2S (also sulphuretted h.); etc. On the analogy of h. chloride, etc., acids are often named as salts of h., e.g. *h. chlorate* $HClO_3$ (= chloric acid), etc.

Hydrogenate (həi·drǫdʒĕnēˑt, həidrǫ·dʒĕnēˑt), *v.* 1809. [f. prec. + -ATE[3].] *Chem.* To charge, or cause to combine, with hydrogen; to hydrogenize. Hence **Hydrogena·tion.**

Hydrogenium (həidroˌdʒī·niǒm). 1868. [f. as prec. + -IUM.] *Chem.* Hydrogen regarded as a metal.

Hydrogenize (həi·drǫdʒĕnəi:z), *v.* 1802. [f. as prec. + -IZE.] *Chem.* To charge, or combine with hydrogen.

Hydrogenous (həidrǫ·dʒĕnəs), *a.* 1791. [f. HYDROGEN + -OUS.] *Chem.* Of, pertaining to, or consisting of hydrogen.

Hydrogeology (həi:droˌdʒīˌǫ·lŏdʒi). 1824. [f. HYDRO- a + GEOLOGY.] That part of geology which treats of the relations of water on or below the earth's surface. Hence **Hydrogeolo·gical** *a.* relating to this.

Hydrographer (həidrǫ·grăfəɹ). 1559. [f. Gr. ὕδωρ, ὑδρ- water, after *geographer*.] One skilled in hydrography; *spec.* one who makes hydrographic surveys and constructs charts of the sea, its currents, etc. So **Hydrogra·phic, -al** *a.* pertaining or relating to hydrography. **Hydrogra·phically** *adv. rare.*

Hydrography (həidrǫ·grăfi). 1559. [See prec.] **1.** The science which has for its object the description of the waters of the earth's surface, comprising the study and mapping of their forms and physical features, of the contour of the sea-bottom, shallows, etc., and of winds, tides, currents, and the like. (In earlier use, including the principles of Navigation.) Also, a treatise on this science. **2.** The subject-matter of this science 1852. †**3.** [Gr. γραφή, -γραφία.] Writing with water. Also *fig.* –1659.

3. *fig.* In Grief's Hydrography CLEVELAND.

†**Hydro·guret.** 1819. [f. HYDROGEN + -URET (after *sulphuret*).] *Chem.* A hydruret or hydride. Hence †**Hydro·guretted** *a.* chemically combined with hydrogen.

Hydroid (həi·droid). 1864. [f. HYDRA II + -OID.]

A. *adj. Zool.* Resembling or allied to the genus *Hydra* of Hydrozoa; belonging to the order or subclass *Hydroidea*, of which *Hydra* is the typical genus.

B. *sb. Zool.* **a.** One of the *Hydroidea*. **b.** One of the two forms of zooids occurring in Hydrozoa, resembling *Hydra* in structure, but typically asexual; opp. to *Medusa*. 1865. So **Hydroi·dean** = prec. B. **a.**

Hydrokinetic, -al (-kəine·tik, -ăl), *a.* 1873. [f. HYDRO- a + KINETIC + -AL.] Relating to the motion of liquids. So **Hydrokine·tics**, the kinetics of liquids; that branch of hydrodynamics which deals with the motion of liquids.

Hydrology (həidrǫ·lŏdʒi). 1762. [ad. mod.L. *hydrologia*, f. Gr. ὑδρο- water; see -LOGY.] The science which treats of water, its properties and laws, its distribution over the earth's surface, etc. Hence **Hydrolo·gic, -al** *a.* pertaining or relating to h. **Hydro·logist**, one skilled in h.

Hydrolysis (həidrǫ·lisis). 1880. [f. Gr. ὕδωρ, ὑδρο- + λύσις, f. λύειν to dissolve.] A decomposition of water in which the two constituents (H and OH) are separated and fixed in distinct compounds. So **Hydroly·tic** *a.* of or pertaining to h.

Hydromancy (hai·dromænsi). ME. [ad. late L. *hydromantia*, f. Gr. ὑδρο- + μαντεία; see -MANCY.] Divination by means of water, or the pretended appearance of spirits therein.

Hydromania (haidromē^i·niă). 1793. [f. HYDRO- + MANIA.] A mania for water; *Path.* an excessive craving for liquids.

Hydromantic (haidromæ·ntik). 1590. [ad. med.L. *hydromanticus*, f. Gr. ὑδρο- + μαντικός; see -MANTIC.]

A. *adj.* Of or pertaining to hydromancy 1651.

†**B.** *sb.* **1.** = HYDROMANCY 1590. **2.** One skilled in hydromancy 1638.

Hydromechanics (hai:dromikæ·niks). 1851. [f. HYDRO- a + MECHANICS.] The mechanics of liquids; hydrodynamics (in its wider sense); esp. in relation to its application to mechanical contrivances.

Hydromel (hai·dromel). ME. [a. L., ad. Gr. ὑδρόμελι, f. ὑδρο- + μέλι.] A liquor consisting of honey and water, which when fermented is called *vinous h.* or *mead.*

Hydrometer (haidrǫ·mɪtəɪ). 1675. [f. Gr. ὑδρο- + -METER. F. *hydromètre* has commonly the sense 'rain-gauge'.] **1.** An instrument for determining the specific gravity of liquids, or, in some forms, of either liquids or solids.

The common type consists of a graduated stem having a hollow bulb and a weight at its lower end, so as to float with the stem upright in a liquid, the specific gravity of which is indicated by the depth to which the stem is immersed.

2. An instrument used to determine the velocity or force of a current; a current-gauge 1727.

Hydrometry (haidrǫ·mètri). 1727. [ad. mod.L. *hydrometria*, f. Gr. ὑδρο- + -μετρία.] The determination of specific gravity by means of the hydrometer; hence, that part of hydrostatics which deals with this. (In early use app. coextensive with 'hydrodynamics' in the mod. sense.) So **Hydrome·tric, -al** *a.* of or pertaining to h.; relating to the measurement of the velocity and force of currents.

‖**Hydronephrosis** (hai:dronɪfrō^u·sis). 1847. [mod.L., f. Gr. ὑδρο- + νεφρός kidney + -OSIS.] *Path.* A distended condition of the ureter, the pelvis, and the renal calices, caused by an obstruction of the outflow of urine; dropsy of the kidney. So **Hydronephro·tic** *a.* relating to, characteristic of, or affected with h.

Hy·dropath. 1842. [f. HYDROPATHY.] = HYDROPATHIST.

Hydropathy (haidrǫ·păþi). 1843. [mod., f. HYDRO-, after *allopathy*, etc., the second element being apprehended as = 'treatment' or 'cure' of disease.] A kind of medical treatment, consisting in the external and internal application of water; the water-cure. Hence **Hydropa·thic, -al** *a.* of, pertaining to, or of the nature of h.; practising h. **Hydro·pathist,** one who practises or advocates h. **Hydro·pathize** *v.* to practise h.

Hydrophane (hai·drŏfē^in). 1784. [f. Gr. ὑδρο- + -φανής apparent, φανός bright, f. φαίνειν.] *Min.* A variety of opaque or partly translucent opal which absorbs water upon immersion and becomes transparent. Hence **Hydro·phanous** *a.* having the property of becoming transparent by immersion in water.

Hydrophobe (hai·drŏfo^ub). [a. F., ad.L. *hydrophobus*, a. Gr., f. ὑδρο- water + φόβος dread.] One affected with hydrophobia.

Hydrophobia (haidrŏfō^u·biă). Also 7–8 hydrophoby (haidrǫ·fŏbi). 1547. [a.L., a. Gr. ὑδροφοβία; see prec.] **1.** *Path.* A symptom of rabies or canine madness when transmitted to man, consisting in an aversion to liquids, and difficulty in swallowing them; hence, rabies, esp. in human beings. **2.** In etym. sense: Horror of water; *fig.* Madness 1759.

2. I am mortally sick at sea, and regard with..a kind of h. the great gulf that lies between us HUME. Hence **Hydropho·bial, Hydropho·bic, Hydro·phobous** *adjs.* of or pertaining to h.; affected with h. **Hydro·phobist,** one who treats cases of h.

Hydrophoran (haidrǫ·fŏrăn). [f. mod.L. *Hydrophora* (f. HYDRA + Gr. -φόρος bearing) + -AN.] **a.** *adj.* Belonging to the *Hydrophora*, one of the three subclasses of Hydrozoa, comprising *Hydra* and compound forms bearing zooids similar to *Hydra*. **b.** *sb.* One of the *Hydrophora*. So **Hydro·phorous** *a.*

Hydrophore (hai·drofō^əɪ). 1842. [ad. Gr. ὑδροφόρος water-carrying.] An instrument for procuring specimens of water from any desired depth, in a river, lake, or ocean.

Hydrophyte (hai·drŏfəit). 1832. [f. Gr. ὑδρο- + φυτόν plant.] *Bot.* An aquatic plant; applied esp. to the *Algæ*. Hence **Hydrophyto·graphy,** the description of aquatic plants. **Hydrophyto·logy,** the branch of botany which deals with aquatic plants.

‖**Hydrophyton** (haidrǫ·fitǫn). 1885. [f. as prec.] *Zool.* The branched plant-like structure supporting the zooids in certain colonial Hydrozoa. Hence **Hydro·phytous** *a.* having the character of a h.

Hydropic (haidrǫ·pik). ME. [a. OF. *ydropique, -ike*, ad. L. *hydropicus*, a. Gr. ὑδρωπικός, f. ὕδρωψ HYDROPS. Subseq. refash. after L.]

A. *adj.* **1.** = DROPSICAL 1, 2. 1483. †**2.** Having an insatiable thirst, like a dropsical person; hence *fig.* 13..–1763. **3.** Charged with water; swollen 1651. †**4.** Curing dropsy –1710.

3. It..swels like an hydropick cloud JER. TAYLOR.

B. *sb.* **1.** A dropsical person. Now *rare.* 1549. **2.** A medicine for the dropsy 1694.

So **Hydro·pical** *a.* (now *rare*) = prec. A. 1–3; of thirst, unquenchable. **Hydro·pically** *adv.* with or as with dropsy.

Hydroplane (hai·droplē^in). [f. HYDRO- + PLANE *sb.*[3]] **1.** A plane for lifting a boat above the surface of the water; a boat designed to skim upon the surface 1907. **2.** The bow-rudder of a submarine. 1911. **3.** = HYDRO-AEROPLANE. 1914.

Hydro-pneumatic (hai:dro,niumæ·tik), *a.* (*sb.*) 1794. [f. HYDRO- a + PNEUMATIC.] Pertaining to water and air or gas; applied to apparatus involving the combined action of water and air.

‖**Hydrops** (hai·drǫps). Now only *Path.* ME. (ydrope). [L. *hydrops, hydropem*, a. Gr. ὕδρωψ dropsy, f. ὕδωρ, ὑδρ-.] Dropsy.

Hydropsy (hai·drǫpsi). [ME. *id-, ydropisie*, a. OF. = med.L. (*h*)*ydropisĭa* for L. *hydropisis* (Pliny), a. Gr. *ὑδρώπισις, f. ὕδρωψ HYDROPS. Formerly *hydro·pesie, hydro·psy*, whence the aphetic *dropesie* DROPSY.] Dropsy. Hence †**Hydro·psic, -ical** *adjs.* hydropic.

Hydroptic (haidrǫ·ptik), *a.* *Obs.* exc. *arch.* 1631. [Erron. f. HYDROPSY, after *epilepsy, epileptic.*] = HYDROPIC. So †**Hydro·ptical** *a.*

Hydroquinone (haidro,kwəi·no^un). Also -chinon(e, -kinone. 1865. [f. HYDRO(GEN + QUINONE.] *Chem.* A diatomic phenol, $C_6H_4(OH)_2$, prepared from quinone, $C_6H_4O_2$, by reduction with sulphurous acid, crystallizing from water in colourless rhombic prisms. Now used as a developer in photography.

Hydroscope (hai·dro,sko^up). 1678. [ad. Gr. ὑδροσκόπος water-seeker, and ὑδροσκόπιον water-clock.] †**1.** A hygroscope. **2.** A kind of water-clock; a cylindrical graduated tube, filled with water, which measured time by trickling through an aperture in the bottom. *Hist.* 1727. **3.** A telescope for use under water 1909.

Hydrosome (hai·drosō^um). 1861. [ad. mod.L. *hydrosoma* (also used), f. HYDRA + Gr. σῶμα.] *Zool.* The entire body of any hydrozoan, esp. that of a colonial hydrozoan consisting of a number of zooids connected by a cœnosarc. Hence **Hydroso·mal, Hydroso·matous** *adjs.* of or belonging to a h.

Hydrosphere (hai·drosfiəɪ). 1887. [f. HYDRO- a + SPHERE, after *atmosphere.*] The waters of the earth's surface collectively.

Hydrostat (hai·drostæt). 1858. [f. HYDRO- a + *-stat*, as in AEROSTAT.] **1.** An apparatus for preventing the explosion of steam-boilers. **2.** An electrical device for detecting the presence of water 1871.

Hydrostatic (haidro,stæ·tik), *a.* 1671. [Ult. f. Gr. ὑδρο- water + στατικός (see STATIC); but cf. Gr. ὑδροστάτης a hydrostatic balance, which prob. originated mod.L. *hydrostaticus.*] **1.** Relating to the equilibrium of liquids, and the pressure exerted by liquids at rest; belonging to hydrostatics. **2.** Used to denominate various instruments and appliances involving the pressure of water or other liquid as a source of power or otherwise 1681. **3.** Used in reference to certain aquatic animals having air-bladders which enable them to float upon the surface of the water 1840.

1. *H. paradox*: the principle (depending on the law of uniform pressure of liquids) that any quantity of a perfect liquid, however small, may be made to balance any quantity (or any weight), however great. **2.** *H. balance*: a balance for ascertaining the specific gravity of substances by weighing them in water. *H. bed*: a water-bed. *H. bellows*: a contrivance for illustrating the law of uniform distribution of pressure in liquids; it consists of a bellows-like chamber, into which water, being introduced by a narrow vertical tube, supports a weight placed on the upper board of the bellows. *H. press*: a machine in which the pressure of a body of water is transmitted from a cylinder of small sectional area to one of greater, and thus multiplied in accordance with the law of h. pressure. Also called *hydraulic press* or *Bramah's press.*

So **Hydrosta·tical** *a.* dealing with or referring to hydrostatics; also = prec. **Hydrosta·tically** *adv.* in accordance with, or by means of hydrostatics. **Hy:drostati·cian,** one versed in hydrostatics.

Hydrostatics (haidro,stæ·tiks). 1660. [In form pl. of HYDROSTATIC. Cf. STATICS.] That department of Physics which treats of the pressure and equilibrium of liquids at rest; the statics of liquids; a branch of *Hydrodynamics* in the wide sense.

†**Hydrosulphate** (haidrosɒ·lfēt). 1828. [f. HYDRO(GEN + SULPHATE.] *Chem.* Now called a *hydrosulphide* or *sulphydrate* –1872.

Hydrosulphide (haidrosɒ·lfəid). 1849. [f. HYDRO(GEN + SULPHIDE.] *Chem.* A compound obtained by the union of hydrogen sulphide (sulphuretted hydrogen) with a metal or radical; a sulphydrate.

†**Hydrosulphuret** (-sɒ·lfiuret). 1800. [f. HYDRO(GEN + SULPHURET.] *Chem.* An old name for a hydrosulphide –1826. So **Hydrosu·lphuretted** *a.* charged or combined with sulphuretted hydrogen.

†**Hydrosulphuric** (-sɒlfiū^ə·rik), *a.* 1823. [f. HYDRO(GEN + SULPHURIC.] *Chem.* Containing or consisting of hydrogen and sulphur only; as *h. acid*, an old name for hydrogen sulphide (H_2S), also called sulphydric acid –1872.

†**Hydrosulphurous** (-sɒ·lfiurəs), *a.* 1855. [f. as prec. + SULPHUROUS.] In *h. acid*, a name given first to dithionic acid; afterwards to hydrogen hyposulphite, $H_2S_2O_4$.

Hydrotherapeutic (hai:dro,þerăpiū·tik), *a.* 1885. [f. HYDRO- b + THERAPEUTIC.] Hydropathic. So **Hy:drotherapeu·tics** *pl.* [see -ICS], that part of medicine which treats of the therapeutical application of water; water-cure.

Hydrotherapy (haidro,þe·răpi). 1876. [f. Gr. ὑδρο- + θεραπεία.] Hydrotherapeutics.

Hydrothermal (haidroþə·ɪmăl), *a.* 1849. [f. Gr. ὑδρο- + θερμός; see THERMAL.] *Geol.* Of or relating to heated water; *spec.* applied to its action in bringing about changes in the earth's crust.

‖**Hydrothorax** (haidroþō^ə·ræks). 1793. [Medical L., f. Gr. ὑδρο-HYDRO- b + θώραξ.] *Path.* A disease characterized by an effusion of serous fluid into one or both of the pleural cavities; dropsy of the chest.

Hydrotic (haidrǫ·tik). 1671. [Erron. for HIDROTIC, through confusion with derivs. of ὑδρο- HYDRO-.] **a.** *adj.* Sudorific; also sometimes, Causing a discharge of water. **b.** *sb.* A sudorific medicine, or in wider sense, a hydragogue. So **Hydro·tical** *a.* 1616, **-ly** *adv.*

Hydrotropic (haidro,trǫ·pik), *a.* [f. Gr. ὑδρο- + -τροπος turning + -IC. Cf. HELIOTROPIC.] *Bot.* Turning towards or under the influence of water. So **Hydro·tropism,** the property, exhibited esp. by roots, of bending or turning under the influence of moisture.

Hydrous (hai·drəs), *a.* 1826. [f. Gr. ὕδωρ, ὑδρο- + -OUS.] *Chem.* and *Min.* Containing water, as an additional chemical or mineral constituent.

Hydroxide (haidrǫ·ksəid). 1851. [f. HYDRO- d + OXIDE.] *Chem.* A compound of an element or radical with oxygen and hydrogen, not with water; by some restricted to compounds whose reactions indicate the presence of the group hydroxyl (OH). (Formerly used interchangeably with HYDRATE.)

Hydro·xy-. *Chem.* Bef. a vowel **hydrox-.** 1872. [f. HYDRO(GEN + OXY(GEN.] An element signifying the addition or substitution of oxygen and hydrogen or the radical hydroxyl.

Hydroxyl (hǝidrǫ·ksil). 1866. [f. HYDR(OGEN + OXY(GEN) + -YL, repr. Gr. ὕλη matter.] *Chem.* The monad radical HO or OH, consisting of an atom of hydrogen in combination with an atom of oxygen, which is a constituent of many chemical compounds. Also *attrib.* **b.** in *Comb.* indicating the addition or substitution of the group OH in the compound, as *h.-benzol*, etc. 1872.

Hydroxylamine (hǝidrǫ·ksilămǝin). 1869. [f. prec. + AMINE.] *Chem.* A basic substance, NH_2OH, allied to ammonia, which combines with acids to form a well-defined series of salts.

‖**Hydrozoa** (hǝidrǒzōu·ă), *sb. pl.* 1843. [mod.L., f. HYDRO- e, as comb. f. HYDRA II + Gr. ζῷον.] *Zool.* A class of Cœlenterate animals, chiefly marine. Familiar examples are the freshwater Hydra, and the various organisms called Acalephs, Medusæ, or Jelly-fishes. Also in sing. **Hydrozo·on**, one of these. Hence **Hydrozo·al, -an, -ic** *adjs.* of or belonging to this class. **Hydrozo·an** *sb.* an animal of this class.

†**Hydruret** (hǝi·druret). 1812. [f. HYDR(OGEN + -URET (taken from *sulphuret*).] *Chem.* A compound of hydrogen with a metal or organic radical; a hydride. Hence **Hy·druretted** *a.* combined with hydrogen.

‖**Hydrus** (hǝi·drǒs). 1667. [L., ad. Gr. ὕδρος water-snake; cf. HYDRA.] **1.** A fabulous sea-serpent. **b.** A former name for the genus *Hydrophis* of venomous sea-snakes 1838. **2.** *Astron.* One of the southern constellations 1796.

1. Cerastes hornd, H., and Ellops drear MILT. *P.L.* x. 525.

Hye, obs. f. HIE.

Hyemal, etc., var. of HIEMAL, etc.

Hyena, hyæna (hǝi,ī·nă). ME. [a. L. *hyæna*, a. Gr. ὕαινα, app. a fem. f. ὗς, ὑ- pig. Cf. F. *hyène*.] **1.** A carnivorous quadruped of a family *Hyænidæ* allied to the Dog-tribe, though in the skull approaching the *Felidæ* or Cat-kind; having powerful jaws, neck, and shoulders, but poor hind quarters.

There are three extant species, the Striped H. (*Hyæna striata*), inhabiting northern Africa and much of Asia; the Brown H. (*H. brunnea*), and Spotted H. or Tiger-wolf (*H. crocuta*), natives of southern Africa. The extinct Cave H. (*H. spelæa*) inhabited many parts of the Old World. The name *Laughing H.*, orig. applied to the Striped H., is considered by some to be more appropriate to the Spotted H.

2. *transf.* Applied to a cruel, treacherous, and rapacious person 1671. **3.** A name of the Thylacine or Tasmanian Tiger 1832. †**4.** A fabulous stone said to be taken from the eye of the hyena; also called *hyæneum* -1855. **5.** *attrib.*, as *h. foeman, laughter* 1818.

2. Out, out, Hyæna MILT. *Sams.* 748.

Hye·na-dog. 1837. **1.** A S. African quadruped (*Lycaon pictus*), superficially resembling the hyenas. †**2.** The AARD-WOLF of S. Africa 1838.

Hyetal (hǝi·ĕtăl), *a. rare.* 1864. [f. Gr. ὑετός rain + -AL.] Of or belonging to rain.

Hyeto- (hǝi,ĕto), comb. f. Gr. ὑετός rain, as in:

Hy·etograph, a chart showing the rainfall (*Syd. Soc. Lex.*); hence **Hyetogra·phic, -al** *a.*; **Hyetogra·phically** *adv.*; **Hyeto·graphy**, the branch of meteorology that deals with the distribution and mapping of the rainfall. **Hyetolo·gical** *a.*, of or pertaining to **Hyeto·logy**, the branch of meteorology that treats of rain. **Hyeto·meter**, a rain-gauge 1730. **Hyetome·trograph**, an automatic instrument for registering the amount of rainfall during successive periods.

‖**Hygeia** (hǝidʒī·ă). 1737. [a. Gr. ὑγεία, late form of ὑγίεια health, Ὑγίεια the goddess of health, f. ὑγιής. A rare variant *Hygiea* represents Gr. ὑγίεια.] **1.** In *Gr. Myth.* the goddess of health, daughter of Æsculapius; health personified; *transf.* a system of sanitation or medical practice. **2.** *Astron.* The 10th asteroid. Hence **Hygei·an** *a.* pertaining to Hygeia, or to health; healthy; sanitary. **Hy·geist**, one versed in hygiene.

Hygiene (hǝi·dʒi,īn, hǝi·dʒīn). 1796. [a. F. *hygiène*, in mod.L. *hygieina*, ad. Gr. ὑγιεινή (τέχνη). Formerly used in L. or Gr. form.] Knowledge or practice as relating to the maintenance of health; a system of principles or rules for preserving or promoting health; sanitary science. Hence **Hygie·nic** *a.* belonging or relating to h.; sanitary. **Hygie·nically** *adv.* **Hygie·nics** *pl.* [see -ICS] = HYGIENE. **Hy·gienist**, one versed in h.

Hygiology (hǝidʒi,ǫ·lŏdʒi). 1855. [f. Gr. ὑγεία (see HYGEIA) + -(O)LOGY.] The science of health; hygiene.

Hygrine (hǝi·grǝin). 1865. [f. Gr. ὑγρός moist + -INE.] *Chem.* An alkaloid obtained from coca-leaves in the form of a thick pale yellow oil of a burning taste.

Hygro- (hǝi·gro), bef. a vowel **hygr-**, repr. Gr. ὑγρο-, ὑγρ-, comb. f. ὑγρός wet, moist, fluid.

Hy·grodeik [Gr. δεικνύναι], a form of hygrometer consisting of a wet-bulb and a dry-bulb thermometer together with a scale on which the degree of humidity is shown by an index whose position depends on the height of the mercurial column in each. **Hy·grograph** [Gr. γραφος], an instrument for registering automatically the variations in the humidity of the air. **Hygro·phanous** [Gr. ὑγροφανής] *a.*, *Bot.* of moist appearance; also, appearing translucent when moist and opaque when dry (*Syd. Soc. Lex.*). **Hygro·philous** [Gr. φίλος] *a.*, *Bot.* affecting moist places. **Hy·groplasm** [Gr. πλάσμα a thing moulded], a term for the fluid part of protoplasm. †**Hygrosta·tics**, 'the art of finding the specific weights of moist bodies' (Bailey).

Hygrology (hǝigrǫ·lŏdʒi). 1790. [f. HYGRO- + -LOGY.] That department of physics which relates to the humidity of the atmosphere or other bodies. ¶Erron. explained in mod. Dicts.

Hygrometer (hǝigrǫ·mĭtǝɹ). 1670. [f. Gr. ὑγρο- + -METER.] An instrument for measuring the humidity of the air or a gas, or the ratio of the amount of moisture actually present in it to that required for saturation. (Formerly often applied to a contrivance to which the name HYGROSCOPE is more properly given.)

Hygrometric (hǝigrome·trik), *a.* 1794. [f. mod.L. *hygrometricus*; see -IC.] **1.** Belonging to hygrometry; measuring, or relating to, the degree of humidity of the atmosphere or other bodies 1819. **2.** = HYGROSCOPIC 2. 1794. **3.** Said of water, etc. so diffused as to be apparent only by the humidity it imparts 1835. So **Hygrome·trical** *a.*, **-ly** *adv.*

Hygrometry (hǝigrǫ·mètri). 1783. [f. Gr. ὑγρο- HYGRO- + μετρία.] That branch of physics which relates to the measurement of the humidity of the air.

Hygroscope (hǝi·grŏskoup). 1665. [f. as prec. + -σκοπος observing.] An instrument which indicates (without accurately measuring) the degree of humidity of the air.

Hygroscopic (hǝigro,skǫ·pik), *a.* 1775. [f. as prec. + -IC.] **1.** Pertaining to the hygroscope or hygroscopy; hygrometric. **2.** *spec.* Said of bodies which are sensitive to moisture, and thus indicate roughly the presence or absence of humidity 1790. **3.** = HYGROMETRIC 3. 1862. So **Hygrosco·pical** *a.*, **-ly** *adv.* **Hygroscopi·city**, h. quality.

Hygroscopy (hǝigrǫ·skŏpi). 1855. [f. Gr. ὑγρο- HYGRO- + -σκοπία.] The observation of the humidity of the air or other substance.

Hyke (hǝik), *int.* ? *Obs.* 1764. [Cf. HEY and HI, used in same sense.] A call to incite dogs to the chase SCOTT. Hence **Hyke** *v.*

‖**Hyla** (hǝi·lă). 1842. [mod.L., ad. Gr. ὕλη wood, forest.] A tree-frog or tree-toad, as *Hyla pickeringi* of the U.S.

Hyla, var. of HYLE.

Hylactic (hilæ·ktik), *a. rare.* 1861. [ad. Gr. ὑλακτικός.] Of the nature of barking. So **Hyla·ctism**, barking.

‖**Hylæosaurus** (hǝilīosǭ·rǒs). Also **hylæ·osaur.** 1833. [mod.L., f. Gr. ὑλαῖος belonging to forests + σαῦρος lizard.] *Palæont.* A gigantic fossil saurian, found in the Wealden formation of Tilgate forest, chiefly characterized by a dermal ridge of large bony spines.

†**Hyla·rchic**, †**-al**, *a.* 1676. [ad. Gr. *ὑλαρχικός = ὑλάρχιος, f. ὕλη + ἄρχειν]. Ruling over matter -1713.

†‖**Hyla·smus.** [mod.L., f. (ult.) Gr. ὕλη.] Materialization. H. MORE. So †**Hyla·stic** *a.*, **-ally** *adv.* 1639.

†‖**Hyle** (hǝi·lī). ME. [med.L. *hyle*, a. Gr. ὕλη.] Matter, substance; the first matter of the universe -1774. So **Hy·lic**, †**-al** *a.* material. (In Gnostic theology opp. to *psychic* and *pneumatic.*) **Hy·licism**, materialism. **Hy·licist**, a materialist.

Hyleg (hǝi·leg). 1625. [Origin obscure. In Pers. (and Turkish) *hailāj*, 'a nativity', said to be a Greek wd.] *Astrol.* Ruling planet of a nativity; apheta. Hence †**Hylegi·acal** *a.* of or pertaining to the h.; *sb.* = hylegiacal place.

Hylo- (hǝilo) = Gr. ὑλο- (ῡ), comb. f. ὕλη wood, material, matter (see HYLE).

Hy·lobate [ad. mod.L. *Hylobates*, a. Gr. ὑλοβάτης wood-walker], a long-armed ape or gibbon. **Hylo·ide·al** *a.*, pertaining to **Hy·lo·ide·alism**, the doctrine that reality belongs to the immediate object of belief as such; material or somatic idealism; hence **Hy·lo·ide·alist.** **Hylomo·rphic, -al** *a.*, pertaining to **Hylomo·rphism** [Gr. μορφή], (*a*) the doctrine that primordial matter is the First Cause of the universe; (*b*) the scholastic theory of matter and form; so **Hylomo·rphist.** †**Hylopa·thian** *a.*, pertaining to, or holding the view that all things are affections of matter; *sb.* one who holds this view. †**Hylopa·thic** *a.*, capable of affecting or being affected by matter. **Hylo·pathism**, the doctrine that matter is sentient; hence **Hylo·pathist.** †**Hylo·pathy** [Gr. πάθος, -παθεια affection], a spirit's power of affecting matter. **Hylo·phagous** [Gr. -φαγος] *a.*, wood-eating (said of certain beetles). †**Hylosta·tic, -al** [Gr. στατικός STATIC] *a.*, that places or arranges matter. **Hylo·theism** [THEISM], the doctrine that God and matter are identical; material pantheism; hence **Hylo·theist**; **Hy·lothei·stic** *a.*

‖**Hylodes** (hǝilōu·dīz). 1858. [mod.L., a. Gr. ὑλώδης woody.] *Zool.* A genus of American toads; one of these.

Hyloist (hǝi·lo,ist). 1818. [erron. for *hylist*, f. Gr. ὕλη.] One who affirms that matter is God.

Hylozoic (hǝilozōu·ik), *a.* 1678. [f. HYLO- + Gr. ζωή life + -IC.] Of or pertaining to hylozoism; materialistic.

Hylozoism (hǝilozōu·iz'm). 1678. [f. as prec. + -ISM.] The theory that matter has life, or that life is merely a property of matter. Hence **Hylozo·ist**, a believer in h. **Hylozo·istic** *a.*

Hymen[1] (hǝi·mĕn). 1590. [a. L. *Hymen*, a. Gr. Ὑμήν.] **1.** In *Gr.* and *Rom. Myth.*: The god of marriage, represented as a young man carrying a torch and veil. **2.** Marriage; wedlock; nuptials. Now *rare.* 1608. **3.** A hymeneal song (*rare*) 1613.

1. Would..That..at the marriage-day The cup of H. had been full of poison MARLOWE. *Hymen's fane, temple*, etc., the church at which a marriage is solemnized.

Hymen[2] (hǝi·mĕn). 1615. [a. Gr. ὑμήν, ὑμένος membrane.] **1.** *Anat.* The virginal membrane, stretched across and partially closing the external orifice of the vagina. **2.** *Conch.* The ligament between the opposite valves of a bivalve shell.

Hymenaic (hǝimĕnē·ik), *a. rare.* [ad. L. *hymenaicum*, f. Gr. ὑμέναιος; see HYMEN[1].] *lit* Of or pertaining to Hymen; used to invoke Hymen.

H. dimeter, a dactylic dimeter acatalectic (-⏑⏑-⏑⏑).

Hymeneal (hǝimĕnī·ăl). 1602. [f. L. *hymenæus*, a. Gr. ὑμέναιος + -AL.]

A. *adj.* Pertaining to marriage.

Views of h. connexions MME. D'ARBLAY.

B. *sb.* **1.** A wedding-hymn 1717. **2.** *pl.* Nuptials 1655.

2. I will not talk any more politically but turn to hymeneals H. WALPOLE. Hence **Hymene·ally** *adv.* So **Hymene·an** *a.* and †*sb.* (in sense B. 1).

Hymenial (hǝimī·niăl), *a.* 1874. [f. HYMENIUM + -AL.] *Bot.* Pertaining to the hymenium.

‖**Hymenium** (həimī·niǒm). Pl. **-ia.** 1830. [mod.L., ad. Gr. ὑμένιον, dim. of ὑμήν HYMEN².] *Bot.* The spore-bearing surface in fungi. In the common mushroom it covers the gills. Also *attrib.*

Hymeno- (həi:mĕnǫ), repr. Gr. ὑμενο-, comb. f. ὑμήν, ὑμένος membrane, HYMEN², as in HYMENOPTEROUS.

Hymeno·geny [-GENY], the production of membranes by the simple contact of two liquids. **Hy·menomyce·te** [ad. mod.L. *hymenomycetes* pl., f. Gr. μύκητες mushrooms], one of the *Hymenomycetes*, an order of fungi in which the hymenium is on the exposed surface of the sporophore; hence **Hy:meno-myce·tal, -tous** *adjs.*, belonging to or having the nature of a hymenomycete; **Hy:menomyce·toid** *a.*, resembling a hymenomycete. **Hy·menophore,** ‖**Hymeno·phorum** [Gr. -φόρος carrying], the part of a fungus which supports the hymenium. **Hymeno·tomy** [Gr. -τομία, τομή], incision of the hymen.

Hymenopter (həimĕnǫ·ptəɹ). 1828. [ad. F. *hymenoptère*; see next.] A hymenopterous insect.

‖**Hymenoptera** (həimĕnǫ·ptĕră), *sb. pl.* 1773. [mod.L. (Linn.), a. Gr. ὑμενόπτερα adj. neut. pl.; see HYMENOPTEROUS.] *Zool.* An extensive order of insects (including the ants, wasps, bees, etc.), having four membranous wings (sometimes caducous or absent); the females have an ovipositor, which may also serve as a sting. Hence **Hymeno·pteral** *a.* hymenopterous. **Hymeno·pteran,** one of this order. **Hymeno·pterist,** an entomologist whose special study is H.

Hymenopterology (həi:mĕnǫptĕrǫ·lŏdʒi). 1855. [f. prec. + -(O)LOGY.] The branch of Entomology which deals with Hymenoptera. Hence **Hymenoptero·logist. Hymenoptero-lo·gical** *a.*

Hymenopterous (həimĕnǫ·ptĕrəs), *a.* 1813. [f. mod.L. *hymenopterus*, a. Gr. ὑμενόπτερος (f. ὑμενο- membrane + πτερόν wing) + -OUS.] Having membranous wings; belonging to the Hymenoptera.

Hymn (him), *sb.* OE. [f. L. *hymnus*, a. Gr. ὕμνος a song in praise of gods or heroes. Late eccl. L. *ymnus* was adopted in OE. as *ymen*; but ME. forms repr. OF. *ymne*, finally modified under classical influence to *hymn*.] **1.** A song of praise to God; *spec.* a metrical composition adapted to be sung in a religious service; sometimes dist. from *psalm* or *anthem*, as not being part of the text of the Bible. **2.** An ode or song of praise in honour of a deity, a country, etc. 1513. **3.** *attrib.*, as in **h.-book.**

1. The earliest h. of Christian devotion..Hosanna to the Son of David STANLEY. 2. Every noone-tide they sing Hymnes to the Sunne PURCHAS.

Hymn (him), *v.* 1667. [f. prec. sb.] **1.** *trans.* To worship or praise in song; to sing hymns to. **2.** To sing as a hymn; to express in a song of praise 1727. **3.** *absol.* To sing hymns 1715.

1. Hymning th' Eternal Father MILT. *P.L.* VI. 96. 2. They h. their praises JOWETT. 3. The lark that hymned on high 1827. Hence **Hymner** (hi·məɹ, hi·mnəɹ), a singer of hymns 1816.

Hymnal (hi·mnăl), *a.* (*sb.*). ME. [f. L. *hymnus* + -AL. The sb. use repr. a med.L. *hymnale*.] **1.** Of or pertaining to a hymn or hymns 1644. **2.** *sb.* A collection of hymns; a hymn-book. So **Hy·mnary** 1888.

Hymnic (hi·mnik), *a.* (*sb.*) 1589. [f. HYMN *sb.* + -IC.] **1.** Of, pertaining to, of the nature of, a hymn or hymns. **2.** *sb.* A composition of the nature of a hymn. LAMB.

Hymnist (hi·mnist). 1621. [f. L. *hymnus* HYMN *sb.* + -IST.] A composer of hymns.

Hymnody (hi·mnŏdi). 1711. [ad. med. L. *hymnodia*, a. Gr. ὑμνῳδία singing of hymns, f. ὕμνος + ἀείδειν. Cf. PSALMODY.] **1.** The singing, or composition, of hymns. **2.** Hymns collectively; the body of hymns belonging to any age, country, church, etc. 1864.

1. The Moravians being great in h. 1876. 2. The jewels of German h. SCHAFF.

Hymno·grapher. 1619. [f. Gr. ὑμνογράφος + -ER¹.] A composer of hymns. So **Hymno·graphy,** the history and bibliography of hymns 1864.

Hymnology (himnǫ·lŏdʒi). 1638. [Orig. ad. Gr. ὑμνολογία the singing of hymns; but now app. f. HYMN *sb.* + -(O)LOGY.] †**1.** The singing of hymns -1855. **2.** The composition of hymns 1839. **3.** The study of hymns, their history, use, etc.; also, hymns collectively 1818.

3. A handbook of h. 1880. Hence **Hymnolo·gic, -al** *a.* of or pertaining to h.; **-ly** *adv.* in relation to h. **Hymno·logist,** a composer or student of hymns.

Hynd, hyne, obs. ff. HIND.

Hynder, obs. f. HINDER *a.*, *v.*

Hyne (həin), *adv. dial.* ME. (Sc.) [Contr. form of *hethen*; cf. SYNE.] Hence.

Hyo- (həi,ǫ). 1811. [f. Gr. ὑο- in ὑοειδής; see HYOID.] A formative element referring to the hyoid bone in connexion with adjoining parts of the body.

Hyobra·nchial *a.*, pertaining to the hyoid bone and the branchiæ. **Hy:o-epiglo·ttic, Hy:o-epi-glotti·dean** *adjs.*, connecting the hyoid bone with the epiglottis. **Hyoga·noid, Hy:oganoi·dean** [GANOID] *adjs.*, belonging to, or characteristic of, the *Hyoganoidei*, a subclass of ganoid fishes, having the hyoid apparatus like those of the teleosts. **Hyo-glo·ssal, Hyoglo·ssian** [Gr. γλῶσσα] *adjs.*, connected with the hyoid bone and the tongue. ‖**Hyo-glo·ssus,** a muscle of the hyoid bone and tongue. **Hyome·ntal** [L. *mentum*] *a.*, pertaining to the hyoid bone and the chin. ‖**Hyopla·stron** [PLASTRON] = HYOSTERNAL *sb.*; hence **Hyopla·stral** *a.* **Hyo-sca·pular** *a.*, pertaining to the hyoid bone and the scapula. **Hyothy·roid** *a.*, pertaining to the hyoid bone and the thyroid cartilage: as *sb.* = hyothyroid muscle.

Hyoid (həi·oid). 1811. [ad. F. *hyoïde*, ad. mod.L. *hyoïdes*, Gr. ὑοειδής, shaped like the letter υ. Cf. HYO-] *Anat.*

A. *adj.* **1.** *H. bone*: the tongue-bone or *os linguæ*, situated between the chin and the thyroid cartilage. In man it is a horseshoe- or U-shaped bone (whence the name) embedded horizontally in the root of the tongue, with its convexity pointing forwards. **2.** Pertaining to the hyoid bone 1842.

2. *H. arch, h. apparatus*, the second visceral arch in Vertebrates, lying between the hyomandibular and hyobranchial clefts.

B. *sb.* **1.** The hyoid bone; see A. 1. 1872. **2.** The hyoid artery 1883.

Hence **Hyoi·dal, Hyoi·dan** *adjs.* = next.

Hyoidean (həi,oi·dĭ,ăn), *a.* 1835. [f. mod. L. *hyoideus* (f. *hyoides* HYOID B.) + -AN.] *Anat.* Of or belonging to the hyoid (bone).

Hyomandibular (həi:ǫ,mændi·biŭlăɹ). 1872. [f. HYO- + MANDIBULAR.] *Anat.*

A. *adj.* Pertaining to the hyoid bone and the mandible or lower jaw 1875.

H. bone, in fishes, the bone of the suspensorium which articulates with the cranium. *H. cleft*, the cleft between the mandibular and hyoid arches in the embryo of Vertebrates.

B. *sb.* The hyomandibular bone.

Hyoscine (həi·ǫsəin). 1872. [Arbitrarily f. HYOS(CYAMUS + -INE.] *Chem.* An amorphous alkaloid isomerous with hyoscyamine.

Hyoscyamine (həi,ǫsəi·ăməin). 1836. [f. next + -INE.] *Chem.* An extremely poisonous alkaloid ($C_{17}H_{23}NO_3$), obtained from the seeds of *Hyoscyamus niger* and some other *Solanaceæ*, isomerous with atropine; used in medicine as a sedative. So ‖**Hy:oscya·mia.**

‖**Hyoscyamus** (həi,ǫsəi·ămɒ̆s). 1799. [ad. Gr. ὑοσκύαμος (f. ὑός, gen. of ὗς pig + κύαμος bean).] A genus of plants belonging to the N.O. *Solanaceæ*; the British species is *Hyoscyamus niger*, HENBANE. Also, the tincture of henbane.

Hyosternal (həi,ǫstɔ̄·ɹnăl), *a.* (*sb.*) 1835. [f. HYO- + STERNAL.] **1.** Pertaining to the hyoid apparatus and the sternum or breastbone 1870. **2.** *sb.* Each of the second pair of plates in the plastron of a turtle, also called the hypoplastron.

‖**Hyosternum** (həi,ǫstɔ̄·ɹnɒ̆m). [f. HYO- + STERNUM.] = prec. 2.

Hyostylic (həi,ǫstəi·lik), *a.* 1880. [f. HYO- + Gr. στῦλος pillar + -IC.] *Anat.* Having the lower jaw suspended from the cranium by a hyomandibular bone (opp. to *autostylic* and *amphistylic*). Also said of the lower jaw itself.

Hyp (hip). Also *pl.* **hyps.** *colloq.* ? *Obs.* 1705. [Abbrev. of HYPOCHONDRIA. Cf. HIP *sb.*³, *v.*³] Usu. *the h., the hyps*: hypochondria.

Heav'n send thou hast not got the hyps! SWIFT.

Hyp-, the form of HYPO- used bef. a vowel.

Hypæthral, -ethral (həip-, hipī·þrăl), *a.* 1794. [f. L. *hypæthrus, hypæthros* adj. and sb., ad. Gr. ὕπαιθρος under the sky + -AL.] **1.** Open to the sky; having no roof. **2.** Open-air 1879.

1. The internal colonnade to the hypaethral temple is a peristyle 1794.

‖**Hypallage** (həipæ·lădʒi, hip-). 1577. [L., a. Gr. ὑπαλλαγή interchange, f. ὑπό + ἀλλάσσειν (stem ἀλλαγ-).] A figure of speech in which there is an interchange of two elements of a proposition, their natural relations being reversed. (In Quintilian VIII. vi. 23 = METONYMY.)

The phrase 'you also are become dead to the law', ..is a h. for 'the law has become dead to you' 1874.

‖**Hypanthium** (h(ə)ipæ·nþiɒ̆m). 1855. [mod. L., f. HYPO- 2 + Gr. ἄνθος flower.] *Bot.* An enlargement or other development of the torus under the calyx. GRAY. Hence **Hypa·nthial** *a.*

Hypapophysis (həipăpǫ·fisis, hip-). *Pl.* **-ses.** 1854. [f. HYPO- 2 (*b*) + APOPHYSIS.] *Anat.* An APOPHYSIS or spinous process on the lower or ventral side of a vertebral centrum. Hence **Hypapophy·sial** *a.*

Hyparterial (-aɹtīᵊ·riăl), *a.* [f. HYP(O- 2 + ARTERIAL.] *Anat.* Situated beneath the artery or trachea. (Mod. Dicts.)

Hypaspist (həipæ·spist, hip-). 1827. [ad. Gr. ὑπασπιστής shield-bearer; see HYPO- 1.] A shield-bearer; one of a picked body of troops in the Macedonian army.

‖**Hypate** (hi·pătī). 1603. [L., a. Gr. ὑπάτη (sc. χορδή CHORD) uppermost string.] The name of the lowest tone in the lowest two tetrachords of ancient Greek music.

Hypaxial (həipæ·ksiăl, hip-), *a.* 1872. [f. HYPO- 2 + AXIS + -AL.] *Compar. Anat.* Lying beneath, or on the ventral side of, the vertebral axis.

Hyper (həi·pəɹ), joc. or colloq. abbrev. (*a*) of *hypercritic*, (*b*) of *hyper-Calvinist.*

Hyper- (həipəɹ), *prefix*, repr. Gr. ὑπερ- (ὑπέρ prep. and adv., 'over, beyond, over much, above measure').

I. Formations with prepositional force of 'over, beyond, or above' (what is denoted by the second element). **1.** General formations: **a.** adjs., as *hyper-angelical*, etc. **b.** Rarely in sbs. and vbs.; e.g. *hypergoddess, hyperdeify.* **2.** *Mus.* In *hyperæolian*, etc., denoting either (*a*) the acute modes in ancient Greek music, which began at a definite interval above the ordinary *Æolian*, etc., or (*b*) the 'authentic' modes in mediaeval music (the same as *Æolian, Dorian*, etc.) as contrasted with the 'plagal' modes *hypoæolian*, etc. **3.** In *Math.*, as in *hyperconic, hyper-elliptic*, etc. See also HYPERDETERMINANT.

II. Formations with adverbial sense of 'over much, to excess, exceedingly'. **1.** General formations: as *hyperacid*, etc.; *hyperacidity*, etc.; *hypervitalize*. **2.** Spec. and techn. terms, as *hyperalbuminosis*, etc.

III. **1.** Formations in which *hyper-* qualifies the second element adverbially or attributively; as in HYPERAPOPHYSIS, etc. **2.** In *Chem.*, *hyper-* denotes the highest in a series of oxygen compounds (cf. HYPO- 5); e.g. *hyperoxide*; now usually expressed by PER-.

Some words belonging to the above groups follow here: for the more important see in their alphabetical places.

‖**Hyperalbumino·sis,** *Path.* excess of albumen in the blood. **Hyperbra:chycepha·lic** *a.*, *Craniol.* extremely brachycephalic; applied to a skull of which the cranial index is over 85; so **Hyperbrachy-ce·phaly,** h. condition. **Hyperbra·nchial** *a.*, *Zool.* situated above the gills or branchiæ. ‖**Hyper-ca·rdia** [Gr. καρδία], *Path.* hypertrophy of the heart. **Hyperchro·matism,** abnormally intense coloration. **Hyperco·nic** *a.*, *Geom.* relating to the intersection of two conicoids or surfaces of the second order. ‖**Hyperge·nesis,** excessive production or growth. **Hyperhidro·sis, -idro·sis** (erron. *-hydrosis*), *Path.* excessive sweating. **Hyperidea·tion,** excessive mental activity or restlessness. **Hypermne·sia** [Gr. μνῆσις], unusual power of memory. **Hyper-nutri·tion** = HYPERTROPHY. **Hyperorga·nic** *a.*, beyond or independent of the organism. **Hyper-orthogna·thic** *a.*, *Craniol.* excessively orthognathic; applied to a skull in which the cranial index is over 91; so **Hyperortho·gnathy,** h. condition. **Hy-perpyre·tic** [Gr. πυρετός] *a.*, *Path.* pertaining to or affected with ‖**Hyperpyre·xia,** a high or excessive degree of fever; whence **Hyperpyre·xial, Hyper-pyre·xic** *adjs.* = *hyperpyretic.* ‖**Hypersarco·ma, Hypersarco·sis,** *Path.* proud or fungous flesh. **Hy·perspace,** *Geom.* space of more than three dimensions. ‖**Hypertricho·sis** [Gr. τρίχωσις, f. τριχ-, θρίξ], excessive growth of hair.

‖**Hyperæmia** (həipərī·miă). Also **-hæmia, -emia.** 1836. [mod.L., f. HYPER- II. 2 + Gr. -αιμία (cf. *anæmia*), f. αἷμα blood.] *Path.* An excessive accumulation of blood in a particular part; congestion.

Active or *arterial h.*, congestion arising from increased flow through the arteries. *Passive* or *venous h.*, congestion due to obstruction in a vein. Hence **Hyperæ·mic, -e·mic** *a.* of, pertaining to, or affected with h.

‖**Hyperæsthesia** (-es-, -īsþī·siă). 1849. [mod.L., f. HYPER- II. 2 + Gr. -αισθησία, αἴσθησις.] *Path.* Excessive and morbid sensitiveness of the nerves or nerve-centres. Also *transf.* So **Hyperæsthe·tic** *a.* affected with h.

Hyperapophysis (-ăpǫ·fisis). 1872. [HYPER- III. 1.] *Anat.* A process of bone extending backward from the neural spine of one vertebra to that of another, or developed from the postzygapophysis. Hence **Hyperapophy·sial** *a.*

†**Hyperaspist** (-æ·spist). 1638. [ad. Gr. ὑπερασπιστής, f. ὑπερασπίζειν to hold a shield over, f. ἀσπίς.] A defender, champion –1747.

‖**Hyperbaton** (həipɔ̄·ɹbătǫn). 1579. [L., a. Gr. ὑπέρβατον, lit. 'overstepping', f. ὑπερβαίνειν.] *Gram.* and *Rhet.* A figure of speech in which the natural order of words or phrases is inverted, esp. for the sake of emphasis. Also, an instance of this.

The sence..ys 'the fende makethe this' for whiche Chaucer vsethe..(accordinge to the rethoricall figure Hiperbatone), 'This makethe the fende' THYNNE. Hence **Hyperba·tic** *a.* pertaining to or of the nature of h.; inverted. **Hyperba·tically** *adv.*

Hyperbola (həipɔ̄·ɹbŏlă). 1668. [a. mod. L. *hyperbola*, ad. Gr. ὑπερβολή, lit. 'excess', f. ὑπερβάλλειν (ὑπέρ over + βάλλειν to throw). So named because the inclination of its plane to the base of the cone exceeds that of the side of the cone (see ELLIPSE).] *Geom.* One of the conic sections; a plane curve consisting of two separate, equal and similar, infinite branches, formed by the intersection of a plane with both branches of a double cone (i.e. two similar cones on opposite sides of the same vertex). It may also be defined as a curve in which the focal distance of any point bears to its distance from the directrix a constant ratio greater than unity. It has two foci, one for each branch, and two asymptotes, which intersect in the centre of the curve, midway between the vertices of its two branches. (Often applied to one branch of the curve.) **b.** Extended (after Newton) to algebraic curves of higher degrees denoted by equations analogous to that of the common hyperbola 1727. Hence †**Hyperboliform** *a.* of the form of, or resembling, a h. (Dicts.)

Hyperbole (həipɔ̄·ɹbŏlī). 1529. [a. Gr. ὑπερβολή excess, exaggeration; cf. prec.] **1.** *Rhet.* A figure of speech consisting in exaggerated statement, used to express strong feeling or produce a strong impression, and not intended to be taken literally. Also, an instance of this. **b.** *gen.* Excess, extravagance (*rare*) 1652. †**2.** *Geom.* = HYPERBOLA –1716.

1. Scriptural Examples of H...Deut. 9. 1, Cities fenced up to heaven..Joh. 21. 25, The whole world could not contain the books J. SMITH. var. †**Hype·rboly** (in sense 1) 1598.

Hyperbolic (həipəɹbǫ·lik), *a.* 1646. [ad. Gr. ὑπερβολικός, f. ὑπερβολή.] **1.** *Rhet.* = HYPERBOLICAL 1. **2.** *Geom.* Of, belonging to, or of the form or nature of a hyperbola; having some relation to the hyperbola 1676.

2. *H. curvature*, the same as ANTICLASTIC curvature. *H. function*: a function having a relation to a rectangular hyperbola similar to that of the ordinary trigonometrical functions to a circle; as the *h. sine, cosine, tangent*, etc. (abbrev. *sinh, cosh, tanh*, etc.). *H. logarithm*: a logarithm to the base *e* (2·71828..), a natural or Napierian logarithm; so called because proportional to a segment of the area between a hyperbola and its asymptote. *H. spiral*: a spiral in which the radius vector varies inversely as the angle turned through by it.

Hyperbolical (həipəɹbǫ·likăl), *a.* ME. [f. as prec. + -AL.] **1.** *Rhet.* Of the nature of, involving, or using hyperbole; exaggerated, extravagant. †**b.** *gen.* Excessive, enormous –1859. **2.** *Geom.* = HYPERBOLIC 2. 1571. Hence **Hyperbo·lically** *adv.*

Hyperbolism (həipɔ̄·ɹbŏliz'm). 1653. **1.** *Rhet.* [f. HYPERBOLE + -ISM.] Use of or addiction to hyperbole; exaggerated style, or an instance of this. **2.** *Geom.* [ad. mod.L. *hyperbolismus* (Newton).] A curve whose equation is derived from that of another curve by substituting *xy* for *y*, as that of the hyperbola is from that of the straight line 1861. So **Hype·rbolist**, one given to the use of hyperbole 1661. **Hype·rbolize** *v.* to exaggerate (*trans.* and *intr.*) 1594.

Hyperboloid (həipɔ̄·ɹbŏloid). 1684. [f. HYPERBOLA + -OID.] †**1.** = HYPERBOLA b. –1796. **2.** A solid or surface of the second degree, some of whose plane sections are hyperbolas, the others being ellipses or circles. Formerly restricted to those of circular section, generated by the revolution of a hyperbola about one of its axes; now called *hyperboloids of revolution* 1743.

There are two kinds of h.: *the h. of one sheet* and *of two sheets*, e.g. those generated by revolution about the conjugate and transverse axes respectively.

Hyperborean (həipəɹbō·rĭăn). 1591. [ad. late L. *hyperboreanus* = cl. L. *hyperboreus*, ad. Gr. ὑπερβόρεος, -βόρειος, f. ὑπερ- HYPER- I + βόρειος northern, βορέας BOREAS.]

A. *adj.* Of, pertaining to, or characterizing the extreme north of the earth, or (*colloq.* or *joc.*) of a particular country; in ethnological use, cf. B. **b.** Of or pertaining to the fabled Hyperboreans 1613.

Even to the h. or frozen sea 1633.

B. *sb.* An inhabitant of the extreme north of the earth; in *pl.* members of an ethnological group of Arctic races. *loosely* and *fig.* One who lives in a northerly clime. 1601.

In Greek legend the Hyperboreans were a happy people who lived in sunshine and plenty beyond the north wind.

Hypercatalectic (-kætăle·ktik), *a.* 1704. [ad. late L. *hypercatalecticus*; see HYPER- I. and CATALECTIC.] *Pros.* Of a verse or colon: Having an extra syllable after the last complete dipody. Also applied to the syllable. †Formerly also = HYPERMETRIC.

Hypercritic (həipəɹkri·tik), *sb.* (*a.*) 1618. [HYPER- II. 1. Cf. F. *hypercritique* (Boileau).] **1.** †A master critic; a severe critic; an over-critical person 1633. †**2.** Hypercriticism; also, a critique –1757. **3.** *adj.* = next. KEATS.

Hypercri·tical, *a.* 1605. [HYPER- II. 1.] Unduly critical; addicted to hypercriticism; as *h. carpers.* Hence **Hypercri·tically** *adv.*

Hypercriticism (-kri·tisiz'm). 1678. [HYPER- II. 1.] Excessive, unduly severe, or minute criticism. So **Hypercri·ticize** *v.*

Hyperdete·rminant. 1845. [HYPER- I. 3.] *Math.* **a.** *sb.* A determinant of operative symbols; a symbolic expression for an invariant or covariant; invented by Cayley. **b.** *adj.* Of the nature of a hyperdeterminant.

‖**Hyperdulia** (həipəɹduləi·ă). 1530. [HYPER- II. 1.] The superior DULIA or veneration paid by Roman Catholics to the Virgin Mary. Hence **Hyperdu·lic, -al** *a.* of the nature of h.

Hypergamy (həipɔ̄·ɹgămi). 1881. [f. HYPER- III. 1 + Gr. γάμος marriage.] Marriage with one of equal or superior caste: in reference to Hindu customs.

‖**Hypericum** (həipe·rikŏm, *etym.* hipərəi·kŏm). 1471. [L. *hypericum, hypericon*, a. Gr. ὑπέρεικον, f. ὑπέρ over + ἐρείκη heath.] **1.** *Bot.* A large genus of plants (herbs or shrubs), the type of the N.O. *Hypericaceæ*, having pentamerous yellow flowers, and leaves usually marked with pellucid dots; commonly known as St. John's-worts. †**2.** *Pharm.* (in form *hypericon*). A drug prepared from a plant of this genus –1691.

‖**Hyperinosis** (həi:pərinōu·sis). 1845. [f. HYPER- II. 2 + Gr. ἴς, ἰνός fibre + -OSIS.] *Path.* A diseased state of the blood in which it contains an excessive amount of fibrin. Hence **Hyperino·sed, -o·tic** *adjs.* having excess of fibrin.

Hypermetamorphosis (həi:pəɹ,metămǭ·ɹfŏsis). 1875. [HYPER- II. 2.] *Entom.* An extreme form of metamorphosis occurring in certain insects, in which the animal passes through two or more different larval stages. So **Hypermetamo·rphism**, the character of undergoing h. **Hypermetamo·rphic, -morpho·tic** *adjs.* characterized by h.

Hypermeter (həipɔ̄·ɹmītəɹ). 1656. [ad. Gr. ὑπέρμετρος, f. μέτρον.] **1.** *Pros.* A hypermetric verse. **2.** *joc.* A person taller than ordinary. ADDISON. Hence **Hyperme·tric, -ical** *a.*

Hypermetrope (həipəɹme·trōup). 1864. [f. Gr. ὑπέρμετρος + ὤψ, ὦπα eye.] *Path.* A person affected with hypermetropia.

‖**Hypermetropia** (həi:pəɹmītrōu·piă). Also **-metropy** (-me·trŏpi). 1868. [mod.L., f. as prec. + *-ia* -IA[1].] *Path.* An affection of the eye, usually due to a flattened form of the eyeball, in which the focus of parallel rays lies behind instead of on the retina; long-sightedness. Hence **Hypermetro·pic** *a.*

‖**Hyperoödon** (həipərōu·ŏdǫn). 1843. [mod. L., f. Gr. ὑπερῷος superior, or ὑπερῴη palate + ὀδούς, ὀδον(τ- tooth.] *Zool.* A genus of Cetacea, containing the bottle-nosed whales.

‖**Hyperopia** (-ōu·piă). 1884. [f. HYPER- II. 2 + Gr. ὤψ, ὦπα eye + *-ia* -IA[1].] *Path.* = HYPERMETROPIA. So **Hypero·pic** *a.*

‖**Hyperostosis** (həi:pərǫstōu·sis). *Pl.* **-oses.** 1835. [f. as prec. + Gr. ὀστέον, ὀστο- bone; see -OSIS.] *Path.*, etc. An overgrowth of bony tissue; hypertrophy of bone; exostosis.

Hyperoxida·tion. 1876. [HYPER- II. 1.] Excessive oxidation. HARLEY.

Hyperoxide (-ǫ·ksəid). 1855. [HYPER- III. 2.] *Chem.* = PEROXIDE.

Hyperoxygenate (-ǫ·ksidʒĕne't), *v.* 1793. [HYPER- II. 1.] *trans.* To supersaturate with oxygen. (Chiefly in pa. pple.) **b.** *joc.* To impart excess of sourness to 1811.

b. An old huckstering grocer..whose natural sourness..is hyperoxygenated by Methodism SOUTHEY. So **Hyperoxygena·tion**, the action of hyperoxygenating; hyperoxygenated condition. **Hypero·xygenize** *v.* = HYPEROXYGENATE (chiefly in pa. pple.).

†**Hyperoxymuriate** (həi:pərǫksimiūə·riĕt). 1794. [HYPER- III. 2.] *Chem.* A salt of 'hyperoxymuriatic' (now called chloric) acid; a chlorate –1854.

†**Hyperoxymuria·tic,** *a.* 1794. [HYPER- III. 2.] *Chem.* In *H. acid*, the old name of chloric acid $HClO_3$ –1807.

Hyperper (həipɔ̄·ɹpəɹ). 1598. [ad. med. L. *hyperperum, -pyrum*, ad. Gr. ὑπέρπυρον, f. ὑπέρ + πῦρ; applied to gold highly refined by fire.] *Numism.* A Byzantine coin; the gold solidus.

Hyperphysical (həipəɹfi·zikăl), *a.* 1600. [HYPER- I. 1.] Above or beyond what is physical; supernatural. Hence **Hyperphy·sically** *adv.* So **Hyperphy·sics**, the science or subject of the supernatural.

‖**Hyperplasia** (həipəɹplē·ziă). 1861. [mod. L., f. HYPER- II. 2 + Gr. πλάσις formation.] *Path.* A form of hypertrophy consisting in abnormal multiplication of the cellular elements of a part or organ; excessive cell-formation. So **Hy·perplasm** = prec. **Hyperpla·sic, -pla·stic** *adjs.* of, pertaining to, or exhibiting h.

Hypersthene (həi·pəɹsþīn). 1808. [ad. F. *hypersthène*, f. HYPER- II. 1 + Gr. σθένος; from its superior hardness as compared with hornblende.] *Min.* A silicate of iron and magnesium, of the pyroxene group, a greenish-black or greenish-grey mineral, closely allied to hornblende, often exhibiting a peculiar metalloidal lustre. Also *attrib.* Hence **Hypersthe·nic** *a.*[1] related to or containing h. **Hypersthe·nite**, a dark granite-like aggregate of h. and labradorite.

‖**Hypersthenia** (həipəɹsþī·niă). 1855. [mod. L., f. HYPER- II. 2 + Gr. σθένος.] *Path.* Extreme or morbid excitement of the vital powers; the opposite of *asthenia.* Hence **Hypersthe·nic** *a.*[2] relating to, characterized by, or producing h.

Hyperthesis (həipɔ̄·ɹþĭsis). 1882. [a. Gr. ὑπέρθεσις, f. ὑπέρ HYPER- + θέσις placing.] Transposition, metathesis. So **Hyperthe·tic** *a.* pertaining to or exhibiting h. †**Hyperthe·tical** *a.* superlative. CHAPMAN.

Hypertrophy (həipɔ̄·ɹtrŏfi), *sb.* 1834. [ad. mod.L. *hypertrophia*, f. Gr. ὑπέρ (see HYPER- II. 2) + -τροφία, τροφή; cf. ATROPHY.] *Physiol.*

and *Path.* Excessive growth or development of a part or organ, produced by excessive nutrition. The opposite of ATROPHY. *fig.* Overgrowth. Hence **Hypertro·phic, -al** *a.* of the nature of, affected with, or producing h. **Hype·rtrophous** *a.* characterized by h. **Hype·rtrophy** *v.* to affect with or undergo h.

‖**Hypha** (həi·fă). *Pl.* **-phæ** (-fī). 1866. [mod.L., ad. Gr. ὑφή web.] *Bot.* The structural element of the thallome of Fungi, consisting of long slender branched filaments, usually having transverse septa, and together constituting the *mycelium.* Hence **Hy·phal** *a.*

Hyphæresis, -eresis (hi-, həifiə·rīsis). 1890. [a. Gr. ὑφαίρεσις; cf. *aphæresis.*] *Gram.* The omission of a letter or syllable in the body of a word.

Hyphen (həi·fĕn), *sb.* 1620. [a. late L., a. late Gr. ἡ ὑφέν, subst. use of ὑφέν together, in one, f. ὑφ', ὑπό under + ἕν one.] **1.** A short dash or line (-) used to connect two words together as a compound; also, to join the separated syllables of a word, as at the end of a line; or to divide a word into parts. **b.** Applied to the 'plus' sign (+). DAUBENY. **2.** *transf.* A short pause between two syllables in speaking 1868; a connecting link 1868. Hence **Hy·phen** *v.* to join by a h.; to write (a compound) with a h. So **Hy·phenate** *v.*

Hy·phenated *ppl.a.* (orig. *U.S.*), applied to persons whose nationality is designated by a hyphened form; hence, to a person whose patriotic allegiance is assumed to be divided 1893. So **Hy·phenate** *sb.*

Hyphomycetous (hi:f-, həi:fo,məisī·təs), *a.* 1887. [f. mod.L. *Hyphomycetes* (f. Gr. ὑφή web + μύκητες fungi) + -OUS.] *Bot.* Of or belonging to the *Hyphomycetes*, a group of fungi consisting simply of hyphæ.

Hypinosis (hipinōu·sis). 1845. [f. HYPO- 4 + Gr. ἴς, ἰνός tissue + -OSIS.] *Path.* A diseased state of the blood in which the quantity of fibrin is below the normal. Hence **Hypino·tic** *a.*

Hypnagogic (hipnăgǫ·dʒik), *a.* 1886. [ad. F. *hypnagogique*, f. Gr. ὕπνος + ἀγωγός leading, f. ἄγειν.] *Properly*, Inducing sleep; in use = that accompanies falling asleep.

Hypno- (hi·pno), bef. a vowel **hypn-**, comb. f. Gr. ὕπνος sleep. Used chiefly in new pathological terms.

Hy·pnobate [Gr. -βατης walker], a sleep-walker. **Hy·pnocyst,** *Biol.* an encysted protozoan which remains quiescent and does not develop spores. **Hypnoge·nesis, Hypno·geny,** induction of the hypnotic state; so **Hypnogene·tic, -ge·nic, Hypno·genous** *adjs.*, producing the hypnotic state; *rarely*, producing sleep. **Hypnogene·tically** *adv.*, by hypnogenesis. **Hypno·logy,** the science of the phenomena of sleep; hence **Hypnolo·gic, -al** *a.* **Hypno·logist,** one versed in hypnology. **Hy·pnosperm, -spore,** *Bot.* an oospore or zygospore (in the *Algæ*) which, after fertilization, passes through a period of rest before germinating; a resting cell or spore; so **Hy·pnospora·nge, Hy:pnospora·ngium,** *Bot.* a sporangium containing hypnospores; **Hypnospo·ric** *a.*, of the nature of a hypnospore.

Hypnoid, *a.*[1]: see under HYPNUM.

Hypnoid (hi·pnoid), *a.*[2], **hypnoidal** (hipnoidăl), *a.* *U.S.* 1904. [f. Gr. ὕπνος sleep + -OID.] Resembling hypnosis; hypnotic.

Hypnosis (hipnōu·sis). 1876. [f. Gr. ὑπνοῦν to put to sleep.] *Phys.* **1.** The inducement or the gradual approach of sleep. **2.** Artificially produced sleep; esp. the hypnotic state 1882.

Hypnotic (hipnǫ·tik). 1625. [ad. F. *hypnotique*, ad. late L. *hypnoticus*, a. Gr. ὑπνωτικός, f. ὑπνοῦν to put to sleep. In 2, short for *neuro-hypnotic.*]

A. *adj.* **1.** Inducing sleep; soporific. **2.** Pertaining to or of the nature of hypnotism or 'nervous sleep'; accompanied by or producing hypnotism 1843. **3.** Susceptible to hypnotism 1881.

1. H. Draughts 1758. 2. The h. or so-called mesmeric state MAUDSLEY. 3. The trained h. subject 1892.

B. *sb.* **1.** An agent that produces sleep; a sedative or soporific drug 1681. **2.** A person under the influence of hypnotism 1888.

†**Hypno·tical** *a.* = A. 1. **Hypno·tically** *adv.*

Hypnotism (hi·pnǒtiz'm). 1842. [f. HYPNOTIC + -ISM. First used as a shortened form of *neuro-hypnotism* by Dr. James Braid of Manchester, who introduced the term.] **1.** The process of hypnotizing, or artificially producing a state in which the subject appears to be in a deep sleep, without any power of changing his mental or physical condition, except under the influence of some external suggestion or direction. On recovering from this condition, the person has usually no remembrance of what he has said or done during the hypnotic state. Also, the branch of science which deals with the production of this state. See BRAIDISM, MESMERISM.

The usual way of inducing the state consists in causing a person to look fixedly, for several minutes, with complete concentration, at a bright object placed above and in front of the eyes at so short a distance that the convergence of the optic axes can only be accomplished with effort.

2. The hypnotized or hypnotic condition 1843. **3.** Sleepiness or sleep artificially induced by any means; also *fig.* 1860.

So **Hy·pnotist,** a hypnotizer. **Hy·pnotize** *v.* to put into a hypnotic state; to mesmerize; also *absol.* **Hypnotiza·tion,** the action of hypnotizing; hypnotized condition. **Hy·pnotizer,** one who hypnotizes.

‖**Hypnum** (hi·pnǒm). *Pl.* **-nums, -na.** 1753. [mod.L., ad. Gr. ὕπνον 'moss growing on trees'.] *Bot.* A large genus of pleurocarpous mosses; feather-moss. Hence **Hy·pnoid** *a.*[1] belonging or akin to the genus *H.* **Hypno·philous** *a.* growing among the mosses.

Hypo[1] (hi·po). ? *Obs.* 1711. [Abbrev. of HYPOCHONDRIA; cf. HYP.] Morbid depression of spirits.

Hypo[2] (həi·po). 1861. [Abbrev. of HYPOSULPHITE.] *Photogr.* The salt formerly called hyposulphite, now thiosulphate, of soda, used for fixing photographic pictures. Also *attrib.*

Hypo- (həipo, hipo), bef. vowels also **hyp-**, *prefix*, repr. Gr. ὑπο-, ὑπ- (f. ὑπό prep. and adv. 'under' = L. *sub*). The first vowel in Gr. ὑπο-, L. *hypo-*, is short, but *y* is now usually treated in all positions except before two consonants as (əi), against both etymology and history.

1. In words from Greek; as *hypochondria*, *hypocrisy*, *hypotenuse*, etc.

2. In modern formations, with sense 'under, beneath, below'; as (*a*) *hypobasal*, HYPODERMIC, etc.; (*b*) HYPOBLAST, *hypozoa* (animals low in the scale).

3. *Mus.* In *hypoæolian*, *-dorian*, etc., used to denote either (*a*) the grave modes in ancient Greek music, beginning at a definite interval below the ordinary *Æolian*, *Dorian*, etc., or (*b*) the 'plagal' modes in mediæval music, each of which has a compass a fourth below that of the corresponding 'authentic' mode.

4. 'To some extent', 'slightly', 'somewhat' in adjs.; 'slight' or 'deficient' in sbs.; the opposite of HYPER- II.

5. In Chemistry, *hypo-* (in contrast with HYPER- III. 2) is used to name an oxygen compound lower in the series than that having the simple name without *hypo-*; thus *sulphurous acid* = H_2SO_3, *hyposulphurous acid* = H_2SO_2.

Some words belonging to the above groups follow here: for the more important see in their alphabetical places.

‖**Hypoa·ria** *pl.* [Gr. ᾠάριον little egg], *Ichthyol.* a pair of protuberant oval ganglia developed beneath the optic lobes of osseous fishes; hence **Hypoa·rian** *a.* **Hypoba·sal** *a.*, *Bot.* applied to the lower of the two cells or portions of the oospore of vascular cryptogams (cf. EPIBASAL). ‖**Hypo·bole** [Gr. ὑποβολή suggestion], *Rhet.* the mentioning and refuting of objections which might be brought against the speaker's case by an opponent. ‖**Hypocatha·rsis,** *Med.* a slight purging; so **Hypocatha·rtic** *a.* ‖**Hypocli·dium** [Gr. κλείς, κλειδ- key], *Ornith.* the interclavicular element of the clavicles of a bird, seen in the merry-thought of a fowl; hence **Hypocli·dian** *a.* **Hy·pocone,** *Zool.* the sixth cusp of the upper molar tooth of mammals of the group *Bunodonta.* **Hypocry·stalline** *a.*, *Min.* consisting of crystals contained in a non-crystalline or massive mineral substance. ‖**Hypoda·ctylum** [Gr. δάκτυλος], *Ornith.* the lower surface of a bird's toe. **Hy:poderma·tomy** [Gr. δέρμα skin + τομή cutting], *Med.* incision of a subcutaneous part. **Hypodermo·clysis** [Gr. κλύσις a drenching], *Med.* the injection of nutrient fluids under the skin in the collapse from cholera, etc. ‖**Hypodia·stole** [Gr. ὑποδιαστολή], *Gr. Gram.* = DIASTOLE 3. **Hypodi·crotous** *a.*, *Phys.* having a slight secondary wave in each pulse-beat. **Hypo-elli·psoid,** *Geom.* a curve traced by a point in the circumference of a circle or ellipse rolling along the inside of an ellipse. **Hypogæ·ate,** *Chem.* a salt of hypogæic acid. **Hypogæ·ic** [f. mod.L. (*Arachis*) *hypogæa* the earth-nut] *a.*, in *h. acid*, $C_{16}H_{30}O_2$, discovered in oil of earth-nut. **Hypo·genous** [Gr. -γενής produced] *a. Bot.*, (*a*) growing upon the under surface of leaves; (*b*) growing beneath the surface. **Hypo·gnathism,** hypognathous conformation. **Hypo·gnathous** [Gr. γνάθος jaw] *a.*, *Ornith.* having the under mandible longer than the upper. **Hypohy·al** [see HYO-, HYOID] *a.*, *Anat.* forming the base of the hyoid arch; *sb.*, that part of the hyoid arch which lies between the stylohyal and basibranchial. **Hypo·menous** [Gr. μένειν] *a.*, *Bot.* arising from below an organ, without adhering to it. **Hy·pomere** [Gr. μέρος], *Biol.* the lower half of certain sponges; hence **Hypo·meral** *a.*, pertaining to a h. **Hypopho·nic** [Gr. φωνή] *a.*, serving as an accompaniment or response; so **Hypo·phonous** *a.* ‖**Hypophy·llium** [Gr. φύλλιον little leaf], *Bot.* a small abortive leaf, like a scale, placed below a cluster of leaf-like branches or leaves. **Hypophy·llous** [Gr. φύλλον] *a.*, *Bot.* growing under, or on the under side of, a leaf. **Hypophy·sics,** matters that lie beneath physics. ‖**Hypopla·stron,** *Zool.* the third lateral piece of the plastron of Chelonia: = *hyposternal*; hence **Hypopla·stral** *a.* ‖**Hypo·ptilum** [Gr. πτίλον feather], *Ornith.* the subsidiary shaft or plume of a feather, which springs from the main stem at the junction of quill and rachis; the after-shaft, the hyporachis; hence **Hypo·ptilar** *a.* ‖**Hy·popus** [Gr. ὑπόπους having feet beneath], *Zool.* a heteromorphous nymphal form of certain acaroids; hence **Hypo·pial** *a.* ‖**Hypopy·gium** [Gr. ὑποπύγιον rump, tail, πυγή buttocks], *Entom.*, (*a*) the last ventral segment of the abdomen; (*b*) the clasping organ at the end of the abdomen of many male dipterous insects. ‖**Hypo·rachis (-rrhachis)** [Gr. ῥάχις spine], *Ornith.* the accessory rachis or shaft of a bird's feather, the hypoptilum; hence **Hyporachi·dian (hyporrh-)** *a.* ‖**Hypora·dius,** *Ornith.* one of the barbs of the hyporachis of a feather; hence **Hypora·dial** *a.* **Hyporrhy·thmic** *a.*, deficient in rhythm; said of a heroic hexameter when the cæsura is not observed. **Hyposke·letal** *a.*, *Anat.* = HYPAXIAL (cf. EPISKELETAL). **Hyposte·rnal** [Gr. ὑπόστερνος: see STERNUM] *a.*, *Anat.*, in *h. bone*, also *hyposternal* as *sb.*, the hypoplastron of a chelonian; also called ‖**Hyposte·rnum.** **Hyposti·gma** [Gr. ὑποστιγμή a comma], *Palæogr.* the comma, which anciently had the form of a modern full stop. **Hyposto·matous, hypo·stomous** [Gr. στόμα, στοματ-] *a.*, *Zool.* having the mouth inferior, as certain fishes and infusoria (*Hypostomata*). ‖**Hypo·strophe** [Gr. ὑποστροφή turning back], (*a*) *Path.* a turning or tossing as of the sick in bed; a relapse; a falling back, as of the womb; (*b*) *Rhet.* reversion to a subject after a parenthesis. **Hy·postyle** [Gr. ὑπόστυλος: see STYLE] *a.*, *Arch.* having the roof supported on pillars. **Hyposyllogi·stic** *a.*, having the value, but not the strict form, of a syllogism. **Hypota·ctic** [Gr. ὑποτακτικός] *a.*, *Gram.* dependent, subordinate in construction. ‖**Hypota·rsus,** *Ornith.* a process of the hinder part of the tarso-metatarsus of most birds; the talus or so-called calcaneum; hence **Hypota·rsal** *a.* **Hypota·xis** [Gr. ὑπόταξις], *Gram.* subordination, subordinate construction. ‖**Hypothe·cium** [Gr. θηκίον, dim. of θήκη case], *Bot.* the mass of fibres lying beneath the sub-hymenial layer; hence **Hypothe·cial** *a.* **Hypo·thenar** [Gr. ὑποθέναρ, f. θέναρ palm of the hand] *a.*, *Anat.* of or pertaining to the eminence on the inner side of the palm, over the metacarpal bone of the little finger. **Hypo·trichous** [Gr. θρίξ, τριχ-] *a.*, *Zool.* of or pertaining to the *Hypotricha*, an order of the class *Ciliata* of *Protozoa*, having the locomotive cilia confined to the ventral surface. **Hypotympa·nic** *a.*, *Anat.* situated beneath the tympanum; applied esp. to the lower bone of the jaw-pier in osseous fishes; *sb.* the quadrate. ‖**Hypozeu·gma,** *Gram.* the combination of several subjects with a single verb or predicate. ‖**Hypozeu·xis,** *Gram.* the use of several parallel clauses, each having its own subject and verb. ‖**Hypozo·a** [Gr. ζῷον], *Zool.* = PROTOZOA; hence **Hypozo·an** *a.* **Hypozo·ic** *a.*, *Geol.* lying beneath the strata which contain remains of living organisms; *Zool.* of or pertaining to the *Hypozoa.*

Hypoblast (həi·po-, hi·poblæst). 1875. [HYPO- 2.] **1.** *Bot.* The flat dorsal cotyledon of a grass. ? *Obs.* 1882. **2.** *Biol.* The inner layer of cells in the BLASTODERM 1875. Hence **Hypobla·stic** *a.*

Hypobranchial (həipo-, hipobræ·ŋkiăl), *a.* 1848. [HYPO- 2.] *Anat.* **a.** *adj.* Situated under the branchiæ or gills. **b.** *sb. pl.* The lower portion of the branchial arch.

Hypobromite (həipo-, hipobrōu·məit). 1877. [HYPO- 5.] *Chem.* A salt of hypobromous acid.

Hypobromous (həipo-, hipobrōu·məs), *a.* 1865. [f. HYPO- 5 + BROM(INE + -OUS.] *Chem.* In *h. acid*, an acid (HBrO) derived from bromine, having strong oxidizing and bleaching properties.

Hypocaust (həi·pǒkǭst, hi·po-). 1678. [ad. late L. *hypocaustum*, *-causton*, a. Gr. ὑπόκαυστον, *lit.* room or place 'heated from below', f. ὑπό HYPO- 1 + καυ-, καίειν to burn.] *Rom. Antiq.* A hollow space extending under the floor of the *caldarium*, in which the heat from the furnace (*hypocausis*) was accumulated for the heating of the house or of a bath. b. *transf.* A stove. SCOTT.

Hypochlorite (həipo-, hipoklōᵊrəit). 1835. [HYPO- 5.] *Chem.* A salt of hypochlorous acid.

Hypochlorous (həipo-, hipoklōᵊrəs), *a.* 1841. [HYPO- 5.] *Chem. H. acid*, an oxy-acid of chlorine (HClO), which possesses strong oxidizing and bleaching qualities.

Hypochonder, -chondre (hipokǫ·ndəɹ). ? *Obs.* 1547. [a. F. *hypocondre*; see next.] = HYPOCHONDRIUM. Also *pl.* = HYPOCHONDRIA 1.

Hypochondria (həipokǫ·ndriă, hipo-). 1563. [ad. late L. *hypochondria* pl., a. Gr. τὰ ὑποχόνδρια, neut. pl. of ὑποχόνδριος, f. ὑπό HYPO- 1 + χόνδρος cartilage, esp. that of the breast-bone.] ‖ 1. as pl. of HYPOCHONDRIUM. Those parts of the human abdomen which lie immediately under the ribs and on each side of the epigastric region. †b. The viscera situated in the hypochondria; the liver, gall-bladder, spleen, etc., formerly supposed to be the seat of melancholy and 'vapours' -1652. †c. Erron. as *sing.* -1727. 2. as *sing.* General depression, melancholy, or low spirits, for which there is no real cause 1668.

2. Will Hazard was cured of his h. by three glasses 1710. Hence **Hypocho·ndrial** *a.*

Hypochondriac (həipokǫ·ndriæk, hipo-). 1615. [a. F. *hypocondriaque*, ad. med.L. *hypochondriacus*; see prec.]

A. *adj.* 1. Of states: Proceeding from the hypochondria, regarded as the seat of melancholy; hence, consisting in a settled depression of spirits. ? *Obs.* b. Of persons, their dispositions, etc.: Affected by hypochondria 1641. 2. *Anat.* Situated in the hypochondria 1727. *H. region*, the part of the abdomen occupied by the hypochondria. 1727.

1. b. Complaints founded only in an h. imagination 1782.

B. *sb.* 1. A person affected with or subject to hypochondria 1639. †2. = HYPOCHONDRIA 2. -1796.

2. Abbreviations exquisitely refined: as..Hypps, or Hippo, for Hypochondriacks SWIFT.

So **Hypochondri·acal** *a.* = prec. A. **Hypochondri·acally**, *adv.* **Hypochondri·acism** = HYPOCHONDRIA 2.

Hypochondriasis (həi:po,kǫndrəi·ăsis, hi:po-). 1766. [f. HYPOCHONDRIA + -ASIS. But the suffix *-asis* is almost entirely limited to names of cutaneous diseases.] *Path.* A disorder of the nervous system, generally accompanied by indigestion, but chiefly characterized by the patient's unfounded belief that he is suffering from some serious bodily disease. So **Hypocho·ndriasm** (in same sense). **Hypocho·ndriast** = HYPOCHONDRIAC *sb.* 1.

Hypocho·ndric, *a. rare.* 1681. [f. as prec. + -IC.] = HYPOCHONDRIAC *a.*

‖ **Hypochondrium** (həipokǫ·ndriŏm, hi·po-). 1696. [mod.L., ad. Gr. ὑποχόνδριον; see HYPOCHONDRIA.] Each of the two hypochondriac regions which are distinguished as 'right' and 'left'.

†**Hypocho·ndry.** 1621. [ad. L. *hypochondrium, -ia.*] 1. = HYPOCHONDRIUM. Chiefly *pl.* -1685. 2. = HYPOCHONDRIA 2. -1874.

†**Hy·pocist.** 1751. [Cf. F. *hypociste.*] = next.

†**Hypocistis.** 1425. [a. L., a. Gr. ὑποκιστίς, f. ὑπό + κίστος the plant Cistus. (The early forms *h)ypoquistid(os* represented the Gr. genitive.)] *Med.* The solidified juice of *Cytinus hypocistis*, a parasitic plant of the South of Europe, growing on the roots of Cistus; it contains gallic acid, and was formerly used as a tonic and astringent -1751.

Hypocorism (həip-, hipǫ·kŏriz'm). *rare.* 1850. [ad. Gr. ὑποκόρισμα, -κορισμός, f. ὑποκορίζεσθαι to play the child, f. ὑπό + κόρη.] A pet-name.

Hypocoristic (həi:po-, hi:pokŏri·stik), *a.* 1796. [ad. Gr. ὑποκοριστικός; see prec.] Of the nature of a pet-name; pertaining to the habit of using endearing or euphemistic terms.

Harry..is the free or h. name for Henry PEGGE. So †**Hypocori·stical** *a.* 1609, -ly *adv.* 1652.

Hypocotyl (həipo-, hipo,kǫ·til). 1880. *Bot.* Name for the hypocotyledonous stem. Hence **Hypoco·tylous** *a.*

Hypocotyledonary (həi:po-, hi:po,kǫtilī·dŏnări), *a.* 1875. [HYPO- 2.] Placed under, or supporting, the cotyledons. So **Hypocotyle·donous** *a.*

Hypocrateriform (həi:po-, hi:po,krătīᵊri·fǭım), *a.* 1760. [f. Gr. ὑποκρατήριον (f. ὑπό HYPO- 1 + κρατήρ CRATER 1) + -FORM.] *Bot.* Having the form of a salver raised on a support: said of a corolla in which the tube is long and cylindrical, with a flat spreading limb at right angles to it, as the periwinkle and phlox. So **Hypocrate·rimorphous** *a.*

‖ **Hypo·crisis.** ME. [L.; see next.] Hypocrisy.

Hypocrisy (hipǫ·krĭsi). ME. [a. OF. *ypocrisie* (mod. *hypocrisie*), f. eccl. L. *hypocrisis*, a. Gr. ὑπόκρισις, f. ὑποκρίνεσθαι to answer, play a part, pretend, f. ὑπό HYPO- + κρίνειν to decide, judge.] The assuming of a false appearance of virtue or goodness, with dissimulation of real character or inclinations, esp. in respect of religious life or belief; hence, dissimulation, pretence, sham. Also, an instance of this.

It is the law of goodness to produce h. MOZLEY.

Hypocrite (hi·pǫkrit). ME. [a. OF. *ypo-*, *ipocrite* (mod. *hypocrite*), ad. eccl. L. *hypocrita*, ad. Gr. ὑποκριτής an actor, pretender, f. ὑποκρίνεσθαι; see prec.] One who falsely professes to be virtuously or religiously inclined; one who pretends to be other and better than he is; hence, a dissembler, pretender. Also *attrib.* or *adj.*

Woe vnto you, Scribes and Pharisees, hypocrites *Matt.* xxiii. 13. Her cousins, seeing her with red eyes, set her down as a h. JANE AUSTEN. *attrib.* H. fanatics SWIFT. Hence **Hypo·crital** *a.* (now *rare*), hypocritical. †**Hy·pocritely** *a.* and *adv.*

Hypocritic (hipǫkri·tik). 1540. [ad. Gr. ὑποκριτικός; see HYPOCRISY.]

A. *adj.* = HYPOCRITICAL.

His silken smiles, his h. air CHURCHILL.

B. *sb. rare.* 1. = HYPOCRITE 1818. †2. The art of declamation with appropriate gesture. BURNEY.

Hypocritical (hipǫkri·tikăl), *a.* 1538. [f. as prec. + -AL.] Of the nature of, characterized by, hypocrisy; (of persons) addicted to hypocrisy.

They are exceedingly subtill, hypocriticall and double-dealing PURCHAS. Formal or h. professions FREEMAN. Hence **Hypocri·tically** *adv.* 1548.

Hypocycloid (həipo-, hiposəi·kloid). 1843. [HYPO- 2.] *Geom.* A curve traced by a point in the circumference of a circle which rolls round the interior circumference of another circle (cf. EPICYCLOID). Hence **Hypocycloi·dal** *a.*

Hypoderm (həi·po-, hi·podə̄ɹm). 1855. [ad. next.] = HYPODERMA 1.

‖ **Hypoderma** (həipo-, hipodə̄·ɹmă). *Pl.* **-dermata.** 1826. [mod.L., f. Gr. ὑπό + δέρμα skin; cf. HYPODERMIS.] 1. *Zool.* A tissue or layer lying beneath the skin or outer integument in Arthropoda and other invertebrates; 'the subcutaneous areolar tissue of the skin of mammals' (*Syd. Soc. Lex.*). 2. *Bot.* A layer of cells lying immediately under the epidermis of a leaf or stem 1877. Hence **Hypode·rmal** *a.*

Hypodermatic (həi:po-, hi:po,dəɹmæ·tik), *a.* 1855. [HYPO- 2.] = HYPODERMIC. Also as *sb.* = hypodermic injection. Hence **Hypoderma·tically** *adv.*

Hypodermic (həipo-, hipodə̄·ɹmik), *a.* 1865. [f. HYPODERMA + -IC.] 1. *Med.* Pertaining to the use of medical remedies introduced beneath the skin of the patient; esp. in *h. injection*, the introduction of drugs into the system in this manner. b. as *sb.*: A hypodermic remedy 1875. 2. *Anat.* Lying under the skin; pertaining to the hypoderm 1877. Hence **Hypode·rmically** *adv.* subcutaneously.

‖ **Hypodermis** (həipo-, hipodə̄·ɹmis). 1866. f. HYPO- 2 + Gr. -δερμις, *-dermis* as in EPIDERMIS.] 1. *Bot.* The inner layer of the spore-case of an urn-moss. 2. *Zool.* = HYPODERMA 1. 1874.

Hypogæic, etc.: see HYPO-.

Hypogastric (həipo-, hipogæ·strik). 1656. [ad. F. *hypogastrique*, f. *hypogastre*; see next.]

A. *adj.* Pertaining to, or situated in, the hypogastrium.

H. region = HYPOGASTRIUM. So †**Hypoga·strical** *a.* 1615.

†B. *sb. pl.* The hypogastric arteries (*rare*) 1722-1797.

‖ **Hypogastrium** (həipo-, hipogæ·striŏm). 1681. [mod.L., ad. Gr. ὑπογάστριον, f. ὑπό + γαστήρ, γαστρ- belly.] The lowest region of the abdomen; *spec.* the central part of this, lying between the iliac regions. So **Hypoga·strocele** (*Path.*), a hernia in the hypogastric region.

Hypoge·al, *a.* 1686. [f. as next + -AL.] = next.

Hypogean (həipo-, hipodʒī·ăn), *a.* 1852. [f. L. *hypogeus*, ad. Gr. ὑπόγειος (f. γῆ earth) + -AN.] Existing or growing underground; subterranean.

Hypogene (həi·po-, hi·podʒīn), *a.* 1833. [f. HYPO- 2 + Gr. γεν-, γίγνεσθαι. Cf. F. *hypogène.*] *Geol.* Formed under the surface; applied to rocks otherwise called primary and metamorphic; also, subterranean, hypogean. Hence **Hypoge·nic** *a.*

Hypogeous (həipo-, hipodʒī·əs), *a.* Also -gæous. 1847. [f. as HYPOGEAN + -OUS.] = HYPOGEAN.

‖ **Hypogeum** (həipodʒī·ŏm, hipo-). Also -gæum. *Pl.* -gea (-ʒī·ă). 1706. [L. *hypogeum*, *hypogæum*, ad. Gr. ὑπόγειον, ὑπόγαιον adj. neut. sing. used subst.; see HYPOGEAN.] An underground chamber or vault. var. **Hy·pogee** (*rare*) 1656.

Hypoglossal (həipo-, hipoglǫ·săl), *a.* 1831. [f. mod.L. HYPOGLOSSUS + -AL.] *H. nerve*, the motor nerve of the tongue proceeding from the medulla oblongata and forming the twelfth or last pair of cranial nerves. Also *absol.* = HYPOGLOSSUS.

‖ **Hypoglossus** (həi·po-, hipoglǫ·sŏs). 1811. [mod.L., f. Gr. ὑπό + γλῶσσα tongue.] *Anat.* The hypoglossal nerve.

Hypogyn (həi·po-, hi·podʒin). 1847. [ad. F. *hypogyne.*] *Bot.* A hypogynous plant. So **Hypogy·nic** *a.* = next.

Hypogynous (həip-, hipǫ·dʒinəs), *a.* 1821. [f. mod.L. *hypogynus* (1789), f. Gr. ὑπό + γυνή taken as = 'pistil' + -OUS.] *Bot.* Situated below the pistils or ovary; said of stamens when these grow on the receptacle and are not united to any other organ; also of plants having the stamens so placed. So **Hypo·gyny**, h. state.

Hyponasty (həi·po-, hi·ponæsti). 1875. [f. HYPO- 2 + Gr. ναστός pressed + -Y. Cf. EPINASTY.] *Bot.* A tendency in plant-organs to grow more rapidly on the under or dorsal side than on the upper or ventral. Hence **Hypona·stic** *a.* pertaining to or characterized by h.

†**Hyponitric** (həipo-, hiponəi·trik), *a.* 1854. [HYPO- 5.] *Chem.* In *h. acid*, an old name for tetroxide (or peroxide) of nitrogen, pernitric acid, NO_2 or N_2O_4 -1876.

Hyponitrite (həipo-, hiponəi·trəit). 1836. [HYPO- 5.] *Chem.* A salt of hyponitrous acid.

Hyponitrous (həipo-, hiponəi·trəs), *a.* 1826. [HYPO- 5.] *Chem.* In *h. acid*, an unstable acid $(HNO)_2$, obtained in combination as a potassium salt.

Hypopharynx (həipo-, hipofæ·riŋks). 1826. [a. F., f. HYPO- 2 + PHARYNX.] *Entom.* A median projection from the internal surface of the lower lip in insects. Hence **Hy:popharyngeal** *a.* situated beneath, or in the lower part of, the pharynx; belonging to the h.

Hypophosphate (həipo-, hipofǫ·sfēt). 1864. [HYPO- 5.] *Chem.* A salt of hypophosphoric acid.

Hypophosphite (həipo-, hipofǫ·sfəit). 1818. [HYPO- 5.] *Chem.* A salt of hypophosphorous acid.

Hypophosphoric (hǝipo-, hipofǫsfǫ·rik), *a.* 1854. [HYPO- 5.] In *h. acid*, $P_2O_2(OH)_4$, a tetrabasic acid, obtained as an odourless liquid.

Hypophosphorous (hǝipo-, hipofǫ·sfŏrǝs), *a.* 1818. [HYPO- 5.] In *h. acid*, a monobasic acid of phosphorus, PH_3O_2.

‖**Hypophysis** (hǝip-, hipǫ·fisis). 1706. [a. Gr. ὑπόφυσις offshoot, outgrowth.] †1. *Path.* Cataract in the eye. 2. *Bot.* A part of the embryo in angiosperms, from which the root and root-cap are developed 1875. 3. *Anat.* (In full *H. cerebri*) The pituitary body of the brain 1864. Hence **Hypophy·sial** *a.* of or pertaining to the h. of the brain.

‖**Hyposcenium** (hǝiposī·niŏm, hipo-). 1753. [f. Gr. *ὑποσκήνιον = τὰ ὑποσκήνια the parts beneath the stage.] *Gr. Antiq.* The low wall supporting the front of the stage in a Greek theatre.

‖**Hypospadias** (hǝipospē·diǣs, hipo-). 1855. [a. Gr., f. ὑπό + σπᾶειν to draw.] *Path.* A congenital malformation consisting in a fissure of the lower wall of the male urethra, the result of arrested development. Hence **Hypospa·diac, -dial, Hypospa·dic** *adjs.* of the nature of, pertaining to, or affected with h.

Hypostasis (hǝip-, hipǫ·stăsis). *Pl.* **-ses** (-sīz). 1529. [a. late L., a. Gr. ὑπόστασις, lit. that which stands under; see HYPO- 1.] 1. *Med.* a. Sediment, deposit; *spec.* that of urine 1590. b. Hyperæmia in dependent organs of the body, caused by subsidence of the blood into these parts 1855. †2. Base, foundation, support -1621. 3. *Metaph.* That which subsists, or underlies anything; substance: (*a*) as opp. to attributes or 'accidents'; (*b*) as dist. from what is unsubstantial 1605. 4. Essence, principle, essential principle 1678. 5. *Theol.* Personality, personal existence, person: (*a*) dist. from *nature*, as in the one h. of Christ as dist. from his two *natures* (human and divine), (*b*) dist. from *substance*, as in the three 'hypostases' of the Godhead, which are said to be the same in 'substance' 1529. 6. *Bot.* The suspensor of an embryo 1866.

3. Either as a property or attribute or as an h. or self-subsistence COLERIDGE. 5. That two natures could be concentred into one h. (or person) JER. TAYLOR. So †**Hypo·stasy** = HYPOSTASIS 1, 5.

Hypostasize (hǝip-, hipǫ·stăsǝiz), *v.* 1809. [f. prec. + -IZE.] *trans.* = HYPOSTATIZE *v.* Hence **Hypostasiza·tion.**

Hypostatic (hǝip-, hipostæ·tik), *a.* 1678. [ad. Gr. ὑποστατικός (f. ὑποστατός set under, supporting); used as adj. to ὑπόστασις.] 1. *Theol.* Of or pertaining to substance, essence, or personality (see HYPOSTASIS). 2. *Path.* Of the nature of hypostasis or excess of blood in the dependent parts of the body 1866.

1. *H. union*: (*a*) the union of the divine and human natures in the 'hypostasis' of Christ; (*b*) the consubstantial union of the three 'hypostases' in the Godhead. So **Hyposta·tical** *a.* = prec. sense 1 1561; †of or pertaining to the essential principles or elements of bodies; hence **-a·lity** 1545. **Hyposta·tically** *adv.* 1593.

Hypostatize (hǝip-, hi·pǫ·stătǝiz), *v.* 1829. [f. Gr. ὑποστατός (see prec.) + -IZE.] *trans.* To make into or treat as a substance. Hence **Hypostatiza·tion.**

Hypostome (hǝi·postoum, hi·po-). 1862. [ad. F. *hypostome*, mod.L. *hypostoma* (also used), f. HYPO- 2 + Gr. στόμα mouth.] A part of the mouth in some invertebrates; e.g. the clypeus of dipterous insects, the labium or under lip of trilobites, the proboscis of Hydrozoa.

†**Hyposu·lphate.** 1819. [HYPO-5.] *Chem.* A salt of hyposulphuric acid. (Now called a DITHIONATE.)

Hyposulphite (hǝipo-, hiposʋ·lfǝit). 1826. [ad. F. *hyposulfite*; see HYPO-5 and SULPHITE.] *Chem.* A salt of hyposulphurous acid. a. Orig. (and still commercially) applied to the salts now called by chemists *thiosulphates*. b. Now, a salt of the acid $H_2S_2O_4$, formerly called a *hydrosulphite* 1872.

†**Hyposulphu·ric,** *a.* 1819. [ad. F. *hyposulphurique*; see HYPO- 5.] *Chem.* In *h. acid*, an old name of DITHIONIC acid.

Hyposulphurous (hǝipo-, hiposʋ·lfiŭrǝs), *a.* 1817. [HYPO- 5.] In *h. acid*: †a. The orig. name for *thiosulphuric acid*. b. Now, the acid $H_2S_2O_4$; formerly called *hydrosulphurous acid* 1872.

Hypotenusal (hǝip-, hipǫtĕniū·săl). Also hypothenusal. 1571. [ad. late L. *hypotenusalis*, f. *hypotenusa*.]

A. *adj.* Pertaining to, of the nature of, or forming a hypotenuse. Now *rare*.

†B. *sb.* (sc. *line*) = HYPOTENUSE -1661.

Hypotenuse (hǝip-, hipǫ·tĕniūs). Also hypothenuse. 1571. [ad. late L. *hypotenusa*, a. Gr. ὑποτείνουσα pr. pple. (fem.), (the full expression being ἡ τὴν ὀρθὴν γωνίαν ὑποτείνουσα (sc. γραμμή or πλευρά), the line or side subtending the right angle), f. ὑπό + τείνειν to stretch. The erron. sp. with *th* was formerly the more usual.] The side of a right-angled triangle which subtends, or is opposite to, the right angle.

‖**Hypothallus** (hǝipo-, hipoþæ·lŏs). 1855. [mod.L.; see HYPO- 2.] *Bot.* The fibrous or filamentary substratum on which the thallus of lichens is developed. Hence **Hypotha·lline** *a.*

Hypothec (hǝip-, hipǫ·þĕk). Also **hypotheca** (h(ǝ)ipoþī·kă). 1592. [a. F. *hypothèque* or ad. late L. *hypotheca*, ad. Gr. ὑποθήκη, f. ὑποτιθέναι to deposit as a pledge.] 'A security established by law in favour of a creditor over a subject belonging to his debtor, while the subject continues in the debtor's possession' (*Bell's Dict. Law Scot.*). a. *Rom. Law.* 'An agreement without delivery' (Poste). b. *Scots Law.* The lien or prior claim of a landlord for his rent over the crop and stock of a tenant farmer (but see now *Act* 43 *Vict.* c. 12 § 1), and over the furniture and other effects of a tenant in urban property 1730. So **Hypo·thecal** (? *Obs.*), **Hypo·thecary** *adjs.*, of, pertaining to, of the nature of, an h. or mortgage.

Hypothecate (hǝip-, hipǫ·þĭkeᶦt), *v.* 1681. [f. *hypothecat-*, ppl. stem of med.L. *hypothecare*, f. *hypotheca* HYPOTHEC; see -ATE[3].] *trans.* To give or pledge as security; to pawn, mortgage.

He had no power to h. any part of the public revenue MACAULAY. Hence **Hypo·thecator,** one who hypothecates or pledges something as security.

Hypothecation (hǝip-, hipǫþĭkē·ʃǝn). 1681. [f. prec.; see -ATION.] The act of pledging as security; pledging or pawning. In some legal systems applied only to a lien upon immovable property; in others to a lien on any kind of property.

Hypothenusal, hypothenuse, erron. ff. HYPOTENUSAL, HYPOTENUSE.

Hypothesis (hǝip-, hipǫ·þĭsis). Pl. **-ses** (-sīz). 1596. [a. Gr. ὑπόθεσις foundation, f. ὑπό + θέσις placing.] †1. A subordinate thesis; a particular case of a general proposition -1721. 2. A proposition or principle put forth or stated merely as a basis for reasoning or argument, or as a premiss from which to draw a conclusion. In *Logic*, The antecedent or protasis of a conjunctive or conditional proposition. 1656. b. A case or alternative considered or dealt with as a basis for action 1794. 3. A supposition or conjecture put forth to account for known facts; *esp.* in the sciences, a provisional supposition which accounts for known facts, and serves as a starting-point for further investigation by which it may be proved or disproved 1646. 4. A supposition in general; something assumed to be true without proof; an assumption 1654. b. Hence *spec.* A mere assumption or guess 1625.

1. If the thesis be true, the h. will follow FILMER. 2. Collusion being, by h., out of the question BABBAGE. b. In each of these last hypotheses, you will observe the necessity that we should be within reach of each other WELLINGTON. 3. The celebrated nebular hypotheses of Herschel and of Laplace 1803. 4. b. Your reasoning..seems plausible; but still it is only h. SCOTT. Hence **Hypo·thesize** *v. intr.* to frame a h.; *trans.* to assume 1738.

Hypothetic (hǝip-, hipoþe·tik), *a.* (*sb.*) 1680. [ad. Gr. ὑποθετικός pertaining to ὑπόθεσις; see prec.] = next.

Hypothetical (hǝipoþe·tikăl, hipo-), *a.* (*sb.*) 1588. [f. as prec. + -AL.] 1. Involving hypothesis; conjectural 1617. b. *Logic.* Of a proposition: Conditional; opp. to CATEGORICAL. Of a syllogism: Having a hypothetical proposition for one of its premisses. 1588. 2. Depending on hypothesis; supposed, assumed 1665. 3. *sb.* A hypothetical proposition or syllogism 1654.

2. It would be..impossible..to declare..what would be our conduct upon any h. case WELLINGTON. Phr. †*H. necessity*: that kind of necessity which exists only on the supposition that something is or is to be; repr. Aristotle's ἀναγκαῖον ἐξ ὑποθέσεως. Hence **Hypothe·tically** *adv.*

Hypothetico-disjunctive, *a.* 1837. *Logic.* Combining the 'hypothetical' (conjunctive) and disjunctive forms of statement; applied to a conditional proposition of which the consequent is disjunctive (e.g. If A is B, C is either D or E); also to the DILEMMA. b. as *sb.* A proposition or syllogism of this kind.

Hypo·thetize, *v. rare.* 1852. [f. Gr. ὑπόθετος + -IZE.] = HYPOTHESIZE.

‖**Hypotrachelium** (h(ǝ)ipotrăkī·liŏm). 1563. [L., ad. Gr. ὑποτραχήλιον, f. ὑπό HYPO- 1 + τράχηλος neck.] *Arch.* The lower part or neck of the capital of a column; in the Doric order, the groove between the neck of the capital and the shaft.

Hypotrochoid (h(ǝ)ipotrōu·koid, h(ǝ)ipǫ·trokoid). 1843. [HYPO- 2.] *Geom.* The curve described by a point rigidly connected with the centre of a circle which rolls on the inside of another circle. Hence **Hypotrochoi·dal** *a.* of the form of, or pertaining to, a h.

‖**Hypotyposis** (h(ǝ)ipǫt(ǝ)ipōu·sis). 1583. a. Gr. ὑποτύπωσις sketch, outline, f. ὑποτυπόειν, f. τύπος TYPE.] *Rhet.* Vivid description of a scene, event, or situation.

Hypoxanthine (hǝip-, hipǫksæ·nþǝin). 1850. [HYPO- 5.] *Chem.* A nitrogenous substance, $C_5H_4N_4O$, found in the muscle, spleen, heart, etc. of vertebrates, and forming a white crystalline powder; also called *sarcine*. Hence **Hypoxa·nthic** *a.* derived from, or of the nature of, h.

Hypped (hipt), *ppl. a.* 1710. Now HIPPED *a.*[2], q.v. So **Hy·ppish** *a.*

Hypsi- (hi·psi), repr. Gr. ὕψι *adv.* on high, aloft, in comb. also = high, lofty. See also HYPSO-.

Hypsiloid (hipsǝi·loid, hi·psiloid), *a.* 1886. [ad. Gr. ὑψιλοειδής, f. ῦ ψιλόν UPSILON; see -OID.] V-shaped or U-shaped.

Hypsistarian (hipsistēᵊ·riăn). 1705. [f. Gr. Ὑψιστάριος (f. ὕψιστος highest) + -AN.] *Eccl. Hist.* a. *adj.* Belonging to an eclectic sect (4th c.), so called from worshipping God under the name of the Most High (ὕψιστος). b. *sb.* A member of this sect.

Hypso- (hi·pso), repr. rare Gr. ὑψο-, used with same force as ὑψι- HYPSI-; in mod. use, occas. as comb. f. ὕψος 'height'.

Hypsometer (hipsǫ·mĭtǝɹ). 1840. [f. prec. + -METER.] An instrument for measuring altitudes, esp. one consisting essentially of a delicate thermometer, by which the boiling-point of water is observed at particular elevations. Hence **Hypsome·tric, -al** *a.* pertaining to hypsometry or the h. **Hypsome·trically** *adv.* **Hypso·metry,** the measuring of altitudes; the science which treats of this; also, the condition of a part of the earth's surface in reference to height above (or depth below) the level of the sea.

Hypt, variant of HYPPED.

Hypural (hǝip-, hipiūᵊ·răl), *a.* (*sb.*) 1871. [f. Gr. ὑπ(ό HYPO- 2 + οὐρά tail + -AL.] Situated beneath the tail; *spec.* in *Ichthyol.* applied to the bones beneath the axis of the tail, which support fin-rays. Also *absol.* as *sb.*

Hyraci-, hyraco- (bef. a vowel **hyrac-**), L. and Gr. comb. forms respectively of HYRAX.

Hyracoid (hǝiᵊ·răkoid), *a.* [f. L. *hyrac-*, stem of HYRAX + -OID.] Resembling a hyrax; pertaining to or characteristic of the order or sub-order *Hyracoidea*, containing the Hyrax and its congeners.

‖**Hyrax** (hǝiᵊ·ræks). 1832. [mod.L., a. Gr. ὕραξ, ὕρακ- shrew-mouse.] *Zool.* A genus of small rabbit-like quadrupeds, containing the

DAMAN, cony, or rock-rabbit of Syria, an Abyssinian species or sub-species, and the Cape Hyrax or rock-badger (*klipdas*) of S. Africa. It is now made the type of an order or sub-order *Hyracoidea*. So **Hyra·cid** *a.* belonging to the family *Hyracidæ*, or its sole genus *Hyrax*.

Hyrse, obs. f. HIRSE.

Hyrst: see HURST.

Hyson (həi·sən). 1740. [ad. Chinese *hsi-ch'un*, in Cantonese *hei-ch'un*, 'bright spring', the name of coarse green tea. *Young Hyson* is *yü-ch'ien* = 'before the rains' (when picked).] A species of green tea from China. *Young H.*, a fine green tea (see above).

Hy-spy (həi spəi). Also **I spy**. 1777. A boy's game played by hiders and seekers, in which a seeker cries 'hy spy!', on discovering one of the hiders.

Hyssop (hi·sǫp). OE. [ad. L. *hyssopus*, *hyssopum*, ad. Gr. ὕσσωπος, ὕσσωπον, app. an eastern word.] **1.** A small bushy aromatic herb of the genus *Hyssopus* (N. O. *Labiatæ*); esp. *H. officinalis*. **2.** In Biblical use: A plant, prob. the Thorny Caper (*Capparis spinosa*), the twigs of which were used for sprinkling in Jewish rites; hence, a bunch of this used in ceremonial purification, and allusively OE. **b.** As the type of a lowly plant (1 Kings iv. 33); whence *fig.* ME. **3.** Applied in the western U.S. to species of *Artemisia* 1807.

2. Purge me with hyssope, and I shalbe cleane *Ps.* li. 7. **b.** And hee spake of trees, from the Cedar tree that is in Lebanon, euen vnto the Hyssope that springeth out of the wall 1 *Kings* iv. 33.

Hyst-: see HIST-.

Hysteranthous (histĕræ·nþəs), *a.* 1835. [f. Gr. ὕστερος later + ἄνθος + -OUS.] *Bot.* Of plants: Having the flowers appearing before the leaves. (The word should mean the reverse of this.)

Hysterectomy (histĕre·ktŏmi). 1881. [f. HYSTERO- + Gr. ἐκτομή.] Excision of the uterus.

‖**Hysteresis** (histĕrī·sis). 1881. [a. Gr. ὑστέρησις a coming late, f. ὕστερος.] *Electr.* The lagging of magnetic effects behind their causes. So **Hystere·sial** *a.*

‖**Hysteria** (histi°·riă). 1801. [medical L.; f. HYSTERIC.] **1.** *Path.* A functional disturbance of the nervous system, characterized by anæsthesia, hyperæsthesia, convulsions, etc., and usually attended with emotional disturbances or perversion of the moral and intellectual faculties. (Colloq. called *hysterics.*) Women being more liable than men to this disorder, it was originally thought to be due to a disturbance of the uterus. **2.** *transf.* and *fig.* Unhealthy emotion or excitement 1839.

2. A wave of humanitarian h. 1897.

Hysteric (histe·rik). 1657. [ad. L. *hystericus*, ad. Gr. ὑστερικός (f. ὑστέρα womb).]

A. *adj.* **1.** = HYSTERICAL A. 1. **2.** = HYSTERICAL A. 2. 1751. †**3.** Of medicines: Good for diseases of the uterus –1732.

2. The united pangs..produced a sort of h. laugh SMOLLETT.

B. *sb.* †**1.** A remedy for uterine disorders –1757. **2.** One subject to hysteria 1751. **3.** *pl.* **Hysterics** (also *sing.*). An equivalent of HYSTERIA, but chiefly = hysterical fits or convulsions; hence in sing.: A convulsive fit of laughter or weeping 1727.

3. Sobs, And indications of hysterics BYRON. Hence **Hyste·ricism**, h. state; hysteria.

Hysterical (histe·rikăl). 1615. [f. as prec. + -AL.]

A. *adj.* **1.** Of, pertaining to, or characteristic of hysteria; affected with hysteria. **2.** *transf.* and *fig.* Morbidly emotional or excited 1704.

B. *sb.* †**1.** = HYSTERIC B. 1. –1671. **2.** *pl.* = HYSTERIC B. 3 (*rare*) 1834.

Hence **Hyste·rically** *adv.*

Hystero-[1] (hi·stĕro), bef. a vowel **hyster-**, comb. f. Gr. ὑστέρα womb. Used in recent formations with the senses: **a.** Of the womb, uterine, as in *h.-paralysis*, etc. **b.** Accompanied or associated with hysteria, hysterical, as *h.-catalepsy*, etc.

Hy·sterocele [Gr. κήλη tumour], *Path.* a hernia containing the uterus or part of it. ‖**Hystero-dy·nia** [Gr. ὀδύνη pain], *Path.* pain of the womb. **Hy·stero-e·pilepsy**, a form of hysteria characterized by the occurrence of epileptiform convulsions; occurring chiefly among females; hence **Hy·stero-epile·ptic** *a.* and *sb.* **Hy·sterophore** [Gr. -φόρος], *Surg.* a pessary for supporting the uterus.

Hy·stero-[2], comb. f. Gr. ὕστερος later.

Hysteroge·nic, *a.* 1886. [HYSTERO-[1].] *Path.* Producing hysteria; relating to the production of hysteria. So **Hystero·genous** *a.* **Hystero·geny**, the production of hysteria.

Hysteroid, -al (hi·stĕroid, -ăl), *a.* 1855. [Irreg. f. HYSTERIA + -OID + -AL.] Resembling or having the form of hysteria.

†**Hystero·logy**[1]. 1623. [ad. late L. *hysterologia*, a. Gr., f. ὑστερο- HYSTERO-[2] + λόγος.] *Gram.*, etc. = HYSTERON PROTERON –1842.

Hystero·logy[2]. 1855. [f. HYSTERO-[1] + -LOGY.] *Med.* A treatise on the uterus.

‖**Hysteron proteron** (hi·stĕrǫn prǫ·tĕrǫn), *sb.* (*a.* and *adv.*) 1565. [late L., a. Gr. ὕστερον πρότερον, the latter (put as) the former.] **1.** *Gram.* and *Rhet.* A figure of speech in which what should come last is put first. **2.** *gen.* The position or arrangement of things in the reverse of their natural or rational order 1589. **3.** as *adj.* 1646. †**4.** as *adv.* By or with an inversion of the natural order of things –1617.

In these woordes..'Take ye: Eate ye: This is my Bodie', They have founde a Figure called Hysteron Proteron JEWEL. **3.** This *hysteron proteron* Stuff NORTH.

Hysterophyte (hi·stĕrŏfəit). 1855. [ad. mod.L. *hysterophytum*, f. Gr. ὑστέρα womb + φυτόν plant.] *Bot.* A plant of the class *Hysterophyta* or *Fungi*; any fungus growing upon, and deriving its nourishment from, organic matter. Hence **Hy·stero·phytal** *a.* fungal.

‖**Hysterosis** (histĕrōᵘ·sis). 1620. [med. or mod.L., f. Gr. ὕστερος, after *anadiplosis*, etc.] = HYSTERON PROTERON.

Hysterotomy (histĕrǫ·tŏmi). 1801. [ad. mod.L. *hysterotomia*, f. HYSTERO-[1] + Gr. -τομία.] *Surg.* The operation of cutting into the uterus; the Cæsarean section; also = HYSTERECTOMY. So **Hy·sterotome**, a knife for performing h.

Hystricid (hi·strisid). [ad. mod.L. *Hystricidæ*, f. *hystrix*, *hystricem*, a. Gr. ὕστριξ, ὑστριχ- porcupine; see -ID.] *Zool.* A rodent of the family *Hystricidæ*; a porcupine. So **Hy·stricine** *a.* pertaining to the sub-family *Hystricinæ* 1883.

Hystricomorph (hi·strikomǭɹf). 1882. [f. Gr. ὕστριξ, ὑστριχ-, L. *hystric-* (see prec.) + Gr. -μορφος.] *Zool.* A member of the *Hystricomorpha*, a primary division of Rodents including the porcupine and its congeners. So **Hy·stricomo·rphic, -phine** *adjs.* of, belonging to, or having the characters of the *Hystricomorpha*.

I

I (əi), the ninth letter and third vowel of the Roman alphabet, going back through the Greek *Iota* to the Semitic *Yod*. The Semitic letter represents a consonant (= English *y* in *yellow*, *yoke*, etc.); by the Greeks, who had no *y* consonant, it was adopted as the symbol of the *i* vowel. In the Latin alphabet, on the other hand, it was used with both values, viz. that of *i* vowel (long and short), and *y* consonant, as in *ibīdem*, *ībis*; *iacui*, *Iouis*. When the consonant sound (y) passed in Romanic into the 'soft g' sound (dʒ), it continued to be symbolized by I until the early part of the 17th century, when it came to be denoted by J j, a differentiated form of I i, which was then confined to the vowel-sounds.

The original value of the Græco-Roman I vowel when long was that of the 'high-front-narrow' vowel of Bell's scale, as in French *machine*, etc. In Teutonic, the short *i* has prob. always been the corresponding 'wide' vowel (i), as in Eng. *finny*, *missing*. Long *i*, on the other hand, has changed into a diphthong with *i* as its second element. The English diphthong is here symbolized by (əi), the first element being taken as the 'mid-mixed-wide' vowel of Bell's scale, the general 'obscure vowel' of English; but it varies locally. Cf. OE., OHG., OLG. *mīn* with Eng. *mine*, Ger. *mein*, Du. *mijn*.

For other values of the letter *i* see the key to the pronunciation.

The dot surmounting the minuscule or 'small letter' i is derived from a diacritic mark, like an acute accent, used in Latin MSS. to indicate the *i* in positions in which it might have been mistaken for part of another letter. The same cause led finally to the growth in English of a kind of scribal canon that *i* must not be used as a final letter, but must in this position be changed to *y*; though in inflected forms, where the *i* was not final, it was retained; hence *city*, *cities*; *holy*, *holier*, *holiest*, etc.

I. The letter and its name. (Pl. *Is*, *I's*, *is*, *i's*.) *I per se*, or *I per se I*, the letter *I* forming a syllable by itself, esp. the pronoun *I*. Also *fig.* esp. in *To dot the i's*, etc.; see DOT *v.*[1]

II. **1.** Used to denote serial order; marking, e.g., the ninth sheet of a book, etc. **2.** In *Logic*, a particular affirmative. **3.** The Roman numeral symbol for ONE. (This was not originally the letter, but a single line denoting unity.) **4.** *Math.* In Higher Algebra, *i* or ι often stands for $\sqrt{-1}$. In Quaternions, *i*, *j*, *k*, are symbols of vectors.

III. *Abbreviations*. I (*Chem.*) = Iodine. I (*Zool.*) = incisor. I.D.B. = illicit diamond buyer. *i.h.p.* (*Mech.*) = indicated horse-power. I.L.P. = Independent Labour Party. See also IHS, and IOU.

I (əi), *pers. pron.*, *1st sing. nom.* [OE. *ic* :—OTeut. **ek*, *ik*; cf. L. *ego*, Gr. ἐγώ(ν, Skr. *ahám* :—primitive type **egóm*, **egō*. The oblique cases of the singular are supplied from a stem *me-* common to the whole Aryan family. The plural nom. *we* has a Germanic form **wi-z* from a primitive stem *wei-*, Skr. *vay-ám*; its oblique cases are from a stem *uns-* (:— **n̥s*), co-radicate with L. *nos*, Skr. *nas*. The paradigm of the pronoun in modern English is:

	SINGULAR.	PLURAL.
Nom.	I	we
Dat. Acc.	me	us
Poss. *Pron.* { *absol.*	mine	ours.
{ *adj.*	my	our.]

I. As pronoun. **1.** The pronoun by which a speaker or writer denotes himself, in the nominative case. **2.** Sometimes used for the objective after a verb or preposition. (This is now considered ungrammatical.) 1596.

1. I care not, I, to fish in seas 1653. Poor I to be a nun DRYDEN. **2.** My father hath no childe but I SHAKS.

II. As substantive. **1.** The pronoun as a word 1599. **2.** *Metaph.* The subject or object of self-consciousness; the *ego* 1710.

1. Phr. *Another I* = a second self. **2.** A manifestation of power from something which is *not I* CARLYLE. Phrase. I AM, the Lord Jehovah, the Self-existent (*Exod.* iii. 14).

I, obs. f. AYE, yes, and of EYE; var. of †HI, they.

I', i, weakened f. IN *prep.* bef. a cons., as in *i'faith*; now *dial.* or *arch.*

†**I-**[1], *prefix*, also written Y-, OE *ge-*, forming collective sbs., deriv. adjs., advbs., and vbs.; esp. used with the pa. pple. of verbs.

I-[2], reduced f. IN-[3] (q. v.), occurring in words of L. origin bef. *gn-* (later *n*), as *ignoble*, *ignominy*, etc.

-i, *suffix*: a learned or technical pl. ending, as in *cirri*, *foci*, *radii*, *banditti*, *dilettanti*, *literati*. It is also freq. (without a sing.) in mod.L. names of groups in Nat. Hist., as *Acanthopterygii*, etc.

-i-, connective or quasi-connective L. *-i-*, being the stem-vowel, as in *omni-vorus*, or a weakened representative thereof, as in *herbi-vorus* (*herba-*), or merely connective, as in *gramin-i-vorus* (*gramin-*). So in many English words.

Ia-: obs. sp. of JA-.

-ia, *suffix*[1], a termination of L. and Gr. sbs. [= *-i-*, *ι-*, stem or connective vowel + -A *suffix* 2]. Examples in Eng. use are *hydrophobia*, *mania*, *militia*, etc.; hence frequent in mod.L. terms of Pathology, of Botany, in names of countries, and in names of alkaloids (after *ammonia*), as *aconitia*, *atropia*, etc., in which the ending *-ine* is now preferred.

-ia, *suffix*[2] [f. *-i-* stem or connective vowel + -A *suffix* 4], forming plurals of L. and Gr. sbs. in *-ium*, *-e* (*-i*), *-ιον*, some of which are in Eng. use, as *paraphernalia*, *regalia*, etc.; hence freq. in mod.L. names of classes, etc. in Zoology, as *Mammalia*, etc.

-ial, *suffix*, repr. L. *-ialis*, *-iale*, as in *curialis*, etc.; freq. in Eng. to form deriv. adjs. from L. adjs. in *-is*, *-ius*, as *cælestis*, *celestial*, *dictatorius*, *dictatorial*. See -AL *suffix* 1.

Iamb (əiˑæmb). 1842. [a. F. *ïambe*.] *Pros.* = IAMBUS.

Iambic (əi,æˑmbik). 1575. [ad.L. *iambicus*, a.Gr., f. ἴαμβος IAMBUS.]

A. *adj.* Of a verse, rhythm, etc.: Consisting of, characterized by, or based on iambuses. Of a foot: Consisting of, or of the nature of, an iambus. 1586. 2. Of a poet: Employing iambic metres 1581.

1. The feet of our verses are either iambick, as 'aloft, create'; or trochaick, as 'holy, lofty' JOHNSON. 2. Th' Iambick Muse P. FLETCHER. So **Iaˑmbical** *a.*, -ly *adv.*

B. *sb.* (Usu. *pl.*) An iambic foot or verse. Also *transf.* a piece of invective or satire in verse (cf. IAMBUS) 1575.

Ĭāmbics mārch frŏm shōrt tŏ lōng COLERIDGE.

Iambist (əi,æˑmbist). 1839. [ad. Gr. ἰαμβιστής, f. ἰαμβίζειν.] A writer of iambics. So **Iaˑmbize** *v.* (*rare*), to attack in iambic verse; to satirize.

Iambographer (əi,æmbǫˑgrăfəɹ). 1625. [f. Gr. ἰαμβογράφος + -ER [1].] A writer of iambics.

‖**Iambus** (əi,æˑmbɒ̆s). 1586. [L., a. Gr. ἴαμβος, f. ἰάπτειν to assail (in words); the iambic trimeter being first used by Greek satiric writers.] A metrical foot consisting of a short followed by a long syllable; in accentual verse, of an unaccented followed by an accented syllable.

-ian, *suffix*, repr. L. *-ianus*, i.e. an original or connective vowel *-i-*, with suffix *-anus*; see -AN 1, 'of or belonging to'. In mod. formations, esp. from proper names, the number of which is without limit, as *Addisonian*, *Bodleian*, *Gladstonian*, *Wordsworthian*; *Aberdonian*, *Oxonian*, etc. In sbs. like *theologian*, *-ian* is a refashioning of F. *-ien*.

Ianthine (əi,æˑnþin), *a.* 1609. [ad.L. *ianthinus*, ad. Gr. ἰάνθινος.] Violet-coloured.

Iatraliptic (əi,ætrăliˑptik). *rare.* 1656. [ad. (ult.) Gr. ἰατραλειπτικός, f. ἰατραλείπτης, f. ἰατρός + ἀλείπτης.] a. *adj.* Relating to the cure of diseases by the use of unguents. b. *sb.* A physician who follows this method.

Iatric (əi,æˑtrik), *a. rare.* 1851. [ad. Gr. ἰατρικός, f. ἰᾶσθαι.] Medical; medicinal. So **Iaˑtrical** *a.* medical 1688; **Iaˑtrico-scriˑptural** *a.* 1716.

I..am..still under Iatrical advice BYRON.

Iatro- (əi,ēˑtro, əi,æˑtro), repr. Gr. ἰατρο-, ἰατρός physician.

Iatro-cheˑmical *a.* = CHEMIATRIC; so **Iatro-cheˑmist**, one belonging to the iatro-chemical school; also *gen.* one who applies chemistry to medical practice. **Iaˑtromathemaˑtical** *a.*, †practising medicine in conjunction with astrology; relating to or holding a mathematical theory of medicine; hence **Iaˑtromathemaˑtically** *adv.* 1603; so **Iaˑtromathemaˑtician**, one belonging to the iatromathematical school.

Iberian (əibīᵊriăn). 1601. [f. L. *Iberia*, the country of the *Iberi* or *Iberes*, a. Gr. Ἴβηρες the Spaniards; also an Asiatic people near the Caucasus. See -AN, -IAN.]

A. *adj.* 1. Of or pertaining to ancient Iberia in Europe, or its inhabitants; hence a. Basque; b. Of Spain and Portugal unitedly. 1618. 2. Of or pertaining to ancient Iberia in Asia, corresp. to modern Georgia 1671.

2. The Hyrcanian cliffs Of Caucasus, and dark I. dales MILT. *P. R.* III. 318.

B. *sb.* 1. a. A Basque; a Spaniard 1623. b. The Basque language. 2. An inhabitant of ancient Iberia in Asia 1601.

Ibex (əiˑbeks). Pl. **ibexes**, rarely **ibices** (əiˑbisīz). 1607. [L. *ibex* (*ibicem*).] A species of wild goat (*Capra ibex* or *Ibex ibex*) inhabiting the Alps and Apennines, the male of which has very large strongly ridged recurved horns, and brownish or reddish grey hair; the female, shorter horns and grey hair; also called *bouquetin* and *steinbock*.

‖**Ibidem** (ibəiˑdem). 1663. [L., f. *ibi* there + *-dem*, as in *idem*, *tandem*, etc.] In the same place. Abbrev. *ibid.* or *ib.*

Ibis (əiˑbis). *Pl.* **ibises**; also (now rarely) **ibides** (əiˑbidīz), **ibes** (əiˑbīz). ME. [a. L. *ibis* (gen. *ibis*, *ibidis*, pl. *ibes*), a. Gr. ἶβις the ibis, an Egyptian bird.] A genus of large grallatorial birds of the family *Ibididæ*, allied to the stork and heron, comprising many species with long legs and slender decurved bill; a bird of this genus, esp. (and originally) the Sacred Ibis of Egypt (*Ibis religiosa*), with white and black plumage, venerated by the ancient Egyptians.

Other species are the Glossy, Scarlet, and White I.

-ible, the form of the suffix -BLE, repr. L. *-ĭbilis*, and *-ībilis*; as *legible*, *visible*, *audible*, etc. Often displaced by *-able* in words that have come through Fr., or are formed on an Eng. verb, as *referable*, *tenable*, *dividable*, etc.

Ibsenism (iˑbsəniz'm). 1891. [f. the name of Henrik *Ibsen* (1828–1906), Norwegian dramatist and poet + -ISM.] The dramatic principles and aims characteristic of the writings of Ibsen and the Ibsenites, which expose conventional hypocrisies. Hence **Ibseˑnian** *a.* and *sb.* **Iˑbsenite**, an admirer or imitator of Ibsen.

Ic, obs. f. I *pron.*

-ic (formerly **-ick**, **-ik(e**, **-ique**) *suffix*, primarily forming adjs., many of which are used as sbs. having also the form **-ics**; see 2.

1. In adjs., immediately repr. F. *-ique*, ad.L. *-ic-us*, occurring in words of L. formation, as *civicus*, *classicus*, or in L. words adopted from Gr., as *comicus* κωμικός. This suffix in Gr., formed adjs. with the sense 'after the manner of', 'of the nature of', 'pertaining to', 'of'. In L. it was used chiefly in the compound suffix *-aticus* (-ATIC, -AGE), and in wds. formed from Gr., or on Gr. types. b. In *Chem.*, the suffix is used to form the names of oxygen acids and other compounds having a higher degree of oxidation than those whose names end in *-ous*; e.g. *chloric acid* HO_3Cl, *chlorous acid* HO_2Cl.

2. Already in Gr., adjs. in -ικός were used absol. as sbs., e.g. in sing. masc., as Στωικός (man) of the porch, Stoic, hence in L. *Stoicus*; also, in sing. fem., in names of arts (sc. τέχνη), or systems of thought, knowledge, or action (sc. θεωρία, φιλοσοφία), e.g. ἡ μουσική music, ἡ ἠθική ethics, etc.; and in neut. pl., as τὰ οἰκονομικά things pertaining to domestic economy, a treatise on this, economics.

In English, words of this class in use bef. 1500 had the singular form, as *arsmetike*, *magike*, *logike* (*-ique*), etc.; this form is retained in *arithmetic*, *logic*, *magic*, *music*, *rhetoric*. Subseq., forms in **-ics** (*-iques*) occur as names of treatises, e.g. *etiques* = τὰ ἠθικά; and towards 1600 this form is applied to the subject-matter of such treatises, in *mathematics*, *economics*, etc. From 1600 onward this has been the accepted form with names of sciences, as *acoustics*, etc., or matters of practice, as *æsthetics*, *politics*, *tactics*, etc. The names of sciences, even though ending in *-ics*, are construed as singular; while names of practical matters, as *gymnastics*, *politics*, *tactics*, remain plural, in construction as well as in form.

3. Besides the preceding, there are many other sbs. formed directly from adjs. in *-ic* taken absol., as *emetic*, *cosmetic* (pl. *emetics*, etc.); *epic*, *lyric*, *Anacreontics*, *iambics*; *domestic*, *rustic*, *classic*, *mechanic*, *lunatic*.

-ical, a compound suffix, f. -IC + -AL, forming an adj. from a sb. in *-ic*, as *music*, *musical*, or a secondary adj., as *comic*, *comical*. Many adjs. have a form both in *-ic* and *-ical*, that in *-ical* being usually the earlier and the more commonly used. Often also the form in *-ic* is restricted to the sense 'of' or 'of the nature of' the subject in question, while that in *-ical* has wider or more transferred senses.

-ically, advb. ending, f. -ICAL + -LY[2], forming advs. from adjs. in *-ical*, which are used also as the advs. from the corresponding adjs. in -IC. Thus *poetic*, *poetical*, adv. *poetically*.

Icarian (əikēᵊriăn), *a.* 1595. [f. L. *Icarius* = Gr. Ἰκάριος, f. *Icarus*, Ἴκαρος the son of Daedalus, in Gr. Myth.] Of, pertaining to, or characteristic of Icarus, who, in escaping from Crete, flew so high that the sun melted the wax with which his wings were fastened on, so that he fell into the sea; hence, applied to ambitious acts which end in ruin.

G. DANIEL *Poems* 1639.

†**Icasm.** [ad. Gr. εἴκασμα.] A figurative expression. H. MORE.

Ice (əis), *sb.* [Com.Teut.: OE. *īs* :—OTeut. **īso-*.] 1. Frozen water; water rendered solid by cold. b. With *pl.*: A mass or piece of ice OE. 2. *The ice*: the layer of ice on a river, lake, sea, etc. ME. 3. *fig.* ME. 4. A congelation resembling ice. BACON. 5. a. A frozen confection. Now with *an* and *pl.* An ice-cream or water-ice 1773. b. = ICING 1727. 6. *attrib.*, as *ice-beach*, *-chart*, *-cutter*, etc. 1591.

2. Phr. *To break the ice*: to make a passage for boats, etc. by breaking the frozen surface of a river, lake, etc.; *fig.* to make a beginning; in mod. usage, to break through cold reserve. *To cut no ice*: to effect nothing. 3. Tut, tut, thou art all Ice SHAKS.

Comb.: **i.-action**, the action of ice upon the surface of the earth, esp. during the ice-age; **-age**, the glacial period (see GLACIAL); **-anchor**, a grapnel for holding a ship to an ice-floe; **-apron**, a pointed structure for protecting a bridge-pier from ice carried down by the stream; **-axe**, an axe used by Alpine climbers, for cutting steps; **-bag**, an india-rubber bag filled with ice for application to some part of the body; **-beam**, a beam placed at the stern or bow of a ship to resist the pressure of ice; **-bearer**, a CRYOPHORUS; **-bed**, a stratified glacial deposit; **-belt** = ICE-FOOT; **-boulder**, a boulder conveyed by glacial action; **-box**, a box for holding ice, an ice-chest; **-calk** = CALK *sb.* 2; **-canoe**, a canoe with iron runners for use on frozen lakes or rivers; **-chair**, a sledge-chair; **-chamber**, a compartment containing, or cooled by, ice; a refrigerating chamber; **-chest**, a refrigerator; **-claw**, an iron claw for grappling and lifting blocks of ice; **-closet**, an ice-chamber or ice-chest; **-creeper** = *ice-calk*; **-drift**, drifted ice in the mass; **-escape**, an apparatus for rescuing persons who have fallen through the ice; **-fender**, a fender or guard to protect a vessel from injury by ice; **-ferns**, the fern-like formations produced on glass by the action of frost; **-fish**, the capelin; **-flow**, an ice-stream; **-fox**, the Arctic fox; **-glass** = *crackle-glass* (CRACKLE *sb.*); **-gull**, U.S. name for the glaucous gull and the ivory gull; **-ladder** = *ice-escape*; **-ledge** = ICE-FOOT; **-machine**, a machine for making ice artificially; **-mark**, a mark, scratch, or groove produced by ice-action, esp. during the ice-age; **-mill**, a glacier-mill; **-pack**, a body of separate pieces of drift-ice closely packed so as to form one great ice-field; **-pail**, a pail for holding ice, in which bottles of wine, etc. are cooled; **-paper**, transparent gelatine in thin sheets used in copying drawings; **-period**, the ice-age; **-pit**, a pit in which ice is stored for preservation; **-pitcher**, a pitcher with double sides, or the like, for holding broken ice or iced water; **-plane**, an instrument for smoothing ice; an instrument for shaving off fragments of ice for cooling drinks; **-poultice**, a bag or bladder filled with pounded ice for application to parts of the body; **-pudding**, a frozen confection in the form of a pudding; **-pulse**, the throbbing movement which precedes an ice-quake; **-quake**, a convulsion which accompanies the break-up of an ice-field or ice-floe; **-raft**, a floating sheet of ice; **-river** = ICE-STREAM; **-saw**, a large saw employed by Arctic voyagers and in ice harvesting for cutting ice; **-ship**, one specially built to resist ice-pressure; **-shoe**, a spiked shoe for walking on ice; **-striæ**, thin lines of scoring made in rocks by ice passing over them; **-system**, a connected system or group of glaciers; **-whale**, the great polar whale; **-yacht** = ICE-BOAT 1; hence **-yachting**, **-yachtsman**.

Ice (əis), *v.* ME. [f. the sb.] 1. *trans.* To cover with ice; to convert into ice. Also *fig.* 2. To cover or garnish (cakes, etc.) with a concretion of sugar (cf. ICING). Also *fig.* 1602. 3. To refrigerate with ice; to cool (esp. wine) by placing it among ice 1825. 4. To make cold; to freeze, chill. Chiefly *fig.* 1804. 5. *intr.* To turn to ice; to freeze. Also *fig.* 1839.

-ice, *suffix*, in ME. also **-is(e**, **-ys(e**, etc.

1. a. OF. *-ice* (*-ise*), of non-popular origin, ad. L. *-itia*, or *-itius*, or *-itium*. Thus *avarice*, etc. (ad. L. *avaritia*, etc.), the later *police* (ad. L. *politia*), *novice*, *precipice*, *service* (= L. *novitius*, *precipitium*, *servitium*). Cf. -ISE [2].

2. The ending *-ice* has various other origins, partly through assimilation to the preceding; as in (*ac*)*complice*, (*ap*)*prentice*, *bodice*, *poultice*.

Iceberg (əiˑsbəɹg). 1774. [prob. from Du. *ijsberg*.] †1. An Arctic glacier, which comes close to the coast, and is seen from the sea as a hill or 'hummock' –1821. 2. A detached portion of a glacier carried out to sea; a huge floating mass of ice, often rising to a great height above the water 1820. Also *fig.*

2. Ice-berg. [*Note*] This term..I restrict..to detached ice, in contradistinction to the glacier or ice *in situ* KANE. *fig.* Captain Thelwal is a perfect i. 1840.

Iˑce-bird. 1620. *Ornith.* 1. The little auk or sea-dove. 2. The Indian night-jar 1862.

Iceblink (əi·sbliŋk). 1817. [= Du. *ijsblink*; f. ICE *sb.* + BLINK *sb.*[2]] 1. A luminous appearance on the horizon, caused by the reflection of light from ice. See BLINK *sb.*[2] 4. 2. The name of a range of ice-cliffs in Greenland. Also generally: An ice-cliff. ? *Obs.* 1819.

I·ce-boat. 1819. 1. A boat mounted on runners for propulsion on the ice. 2. A boat or barge for breaking the ice in a river or canal 1838.

I·ce-bolt. 1789. [f. BOLT *sb.*[1]] **a.** A sudden deadly chill. **b.** An avalanche.

Ice-bound (əi·s,baund), *ppl. a.* 1659. [f. ICE *sb.*] Held fast by ice; frozen in; hemmed in by ice.

I·ce-brea:ker. 1838. [f. ICE *sb.* + BREAKER [1].] 1. Anything that breaks up moving ice; *spec.* an ice-apron. 2. A vessel for breaking a channel through ice 1875. 3. A whaler's name for the Greenland whale.

I·ce-cap. 1854. 1. A permanent cap or covering of ice over a tract of country, as e.g. at either pole 1875. 2. *Med.* A bladder or bag containing pounded ice, for application to the head in congestion of the brain, etc. 1854.

I:ce-crea·m. 1769. [Earlier *iced cream*, 1688.] Cream or custard flavoured, sweetened, and congealed. Also *attrib.*

Iced (əist), *ppl. a.* 1688. [f. ICE *sb.* or *v.* + -ED.] Covered with ice; cooled by means of ice. Of a cake, etc.: Covered with icing.

I·ce-fall. 1817. [After *waterfall.*] 1. A cataract of ice; a part of a glacier resembling a frozen waterfall. 2. The fall of a mass of ice 1861.

I·ce-field. 1694. A wide flat expanse of ice.

Ice-floe (əi·s,flōu). 1819. [See FLOE.] A large sheet of floating ice, smaller than an ice-field.

I·ce-foot. 1856. [ad. Da. *isfod*, in same sense.] **a.** A belt or ledge of ice extending along the coast in Arctic regions. **b.** Also, the margin of an ice-floe 1897.

I·ce-hill. 1694. A hill or mound of ice; an elevated glacier; a slope covered with ice, for tobogganing, etc. †Also, a floating iceberg.

I·ce-hook. 1694. †**a.** A kind of boat-hook, used to push large flakes of ice away from a ship. †**b.** An ice-anchor. **c.** A hook used in hoisting ice for storage.

I·ce-house. 1687. A structure, often underground, and with non-conducting walls, in which ice is stored for use during the year.

Ice-island. 1777. = ICEBERG 2. So **I·ce-isle** 1808.

Iceland [1] (əi·s,lænd). 1842. A country covered with ice; the region of perpetual ice.

Iceland [2] (əislănd). [ME. *Island, Yslond*, etc., ad. ON. *Ísland*, f. *íss* ICE + *land* LAND.] The name of a large island lying on the border of the Arctic Ocean, between Norway and Greenland; used *attrib.* in names of articles imported from or peculiar to that country, as **I. cur, I. dog** (also short **I.**), a shaggy sharp-eared white dog, formerly in favour as a lap-dog in England; **I. lichen, I. moss,** a species of edible lichen, *Cetraria islandica*, having medicinal properties; **I. poppy,** a variety of *Papaver nudicaule*, the yellow Arctic poppy; **I. spar,** a transparent variety of calcite, used in demonstrating the polarization of light.

Icelander (əi·slăndəɹ). 1613. [f. prec. + -ER [1].] An inhabitant or native of Iceland.

Icelandic (əislæ·ndik). 1674. [See -IC.]

A. *adj.* Pertaining to Iceland, or to Icelandic (see B.).

B. *sb.* The language of Iceland, which in all essential points retains the form of Old Norse 1833.

Iceman, ice-man (əi·smæn). 1855. 1. A man skilled in traversing ice. 2. A man appointed to look after the ice on a skating-pond and assist in cases of accident 1860. 3. One engaged in the ice trade, or in harvesting ice (*U.S.*) 1864. Hence **I·cemanship,** ice-craft.

I·ce-ma:ster. 1853. A pilot skilled in navigating vessels among ice-floes.

I·ce-mou:nt(ain. 1694. = ICEBERG.

I·ce-plant. 1753. A plant (*Mesembryanthemum crystallinum*), having leaves covered with pellucid watery vesicles looking like ice; a native of the Canary Islands, S. Africa, etc.

I·ce-plough. 1858. An instrument used in America for cutting grooves in ice, for the purpose of removing large blocks which are stored for summer use.

I·ce-sheet. 1873. A sheet or layer of ice covering an extensive tract of land; as e.g. during the ice-age.

I·cespar. 1816. [ad. Ger. *eisspath*; from its appearance.] *Min.* Glassy orthoclase, first found in the lava of Vesuvius.

I·ce-stream. 1853. 1. A stream of ice-floes carried in a particular course; esp. that which sweeps round Cape Farewell in Greenland 1878. 2. A valley glacier.

I·ce-work. 1729. 1. Frosted work. 2. *Geol.* Work done by glaciers or icebergs 1843.

Ich, obs. f. I *pron.*, EACH.

Ichneumon (iknịū·mǫn). 1572. [a. L., a. Gr. ἰχνεύμων, lit. 'tracker', f. ἰχνεύειν, f. ἴχνος track, footstep.] 1. A small brownish-coloured slender-bodied carnivorous quadruped, *Herpestes* (formerly *Viverra*) *ichneumon*, closely allied to the mongoose, and resembling the weasel tribe in form and habits. It is found in Egypt, and is noted for destroying the eggs of the crocodile, on which account it was venerated by the ancient Egyptians. (Called also *Pharaoh's Rat*, and formerly *Indian Mouse.*) Cf. COCKATRICE. 2. A small parasitic hymenopterous insect (family *Ichneumonidæ*), which deposits its eggs in or on the larva of another insect, upon which its larvæ feed when hatched; an ichneumon-fly 1658.

1. I., a beaste of Egypte..who creepeth into the body of a Crocodyle, when in sleape he gapeth and eating his bowels, sleaeth him BOSSEWELL.

Comb.: **I.-fly** = 2; †**i. maggot,** the larva of the i.-fly.

Ichneumon-, comb. stem of prec. (in sense 2), as in **Ichneumo·nidan** *a.*, pertaining to the family *Ichneumonidæ* of hymenopterous insects; *sb.*, an insect of this family 1815. **Ichneumo·niform** *a.*, having the form or characters of an ichneumon-fly.

Ichnite (i·knəit). 1854. [f. Gr. ἴχνος track + -ITE.] *Geol.* A fossil footprint.

Ichnography (iknǫ·grăfi). 1598. [a. F. *ichnographie*, or ad. late L. *ichnographia*, a. Gr., f. ἴχνος + -γραφία.] A ground-plan; a horizontal section of a building or of part of it; also, the plan or map of a place. Also *transf.* and *fig.* Hence **Ichnogra·phic, -al** *a.* pertaining or relating to i. **Ichnogra·phically** *adv.*

Ichnolite (i·knǒləit). 1846. [f. Gr. ἴχνος + λίθος, -LITE.] = ICHNITE.

Ichnolithology (i:knǫ,liþǫ·lŏdʒi). 1882. [f. as prec. + -LOGY.] = ICHNOLOGY. Hence **I:chnolitholo·gical** *a.*

Ichnology (iknǫ·lŏdʒi). 1851. [f. Gr. ἴχνος + -LOGY.] **a.** That part of palæontology which treats of fossil footprints. **b.** The ichnological features of a district collectively. Hence **Ichnolo·gical** *a.*

‖**Ichoglan** (i·tʃǫglæn). 1677. [obs. Turk., f. *īch* interior + *oγlān* young man.] A page in waiting in the palace of the Sultan.

Ichor (əi·kǭɹ). 1638. [a. Gr. ἰχώρ.] 1. *Gr. Myth.* The ethereal fluid, not blood, supposed to flow in the veins of the gods 1676. 2. *transf.* and *fig.* Blood; a fluid likened to the blood of animals 1638. 3. *Path.* A watery acrid discharge from certain wounds and sores 1651.

2. The azure i. of this élite of the earth FORD *Handbk. Spain.* Hence **Ichorous** (əi·kŏrəs), *a.* of the nature of i.; containing or discharging i.

‖**Ichorrhæmia** (əikǫ̆rī·miă). Also **-emia.** 1854. [f. Gr. ἰχώρ + -αιμία, f. αἷμα.] *Path.* Poisoning of the blood from the absorption of sanious matter.

Ichthyic (i·kþi,ik), *a.* 1844. [ad. Gr. ἰχθυϊκός fishy, f. ἰχθύς.] Of, pertaining to, or characteristic of fishes; piscine. So **I·chthyal, I·chthyan** *adjs.*

Ichthyo- (i·kþi,o), bef. a vowel **ichthy-,** comb. f. Gr. ἰχθύς, ἰχθύος fish.

I·chthydin, I·chthyin (-thin), **I·chthylin** (-ulin), *Chem.* names of albuminoid substances got from the egg-yolk of various fishes. **Ichthyoco·prolite** [COPROLITE], *Palæont.* the fossilized excrement of a fish; also *ichthyocoprus.* **I·chthyodo·nt** [Gr. ὀδοντ-], *Palæont.* a fossil tooth of a fish. **Ichthyo·latry** [-LATRY], the worship of fishes, or of a fish-god, as Dagon. **I·chthyoma·ncy** [-MANCY], divination by means of the head or entrails of fishes; so **Ichthyoma·ntic** *a.* **Ichthyophthi·ran** [Gr. φθείρ louse] *a.*, *Zool.* belonging to the crustacean order *Ichthyophthira*, parasites upon fishes; *sb.* a fish-louse. **Ichthyo·tomist** [Gr. -τομος cutting], an anatomist of fishes; so **Ichthyo·tomy. I·chthy·ta·xidermy,** the taxidermy or stuffing of the skins of fishes as zoological specimens.

‖**Ichthyocolla** (ikþi,okǫ·lă). 1601. [L., a. Gr., f. ἰχθυο- fish + κόλλα glue.] Fish-glue, isinglass. Also *attrib.*

Ichthyodorylite,-dorulite (i:kþi,odǫ·riləit, -dǫ·rịūləit). 1837. [f. ICHTHYO- + Gr. δόρυ spear + -LITE.] *Palæont.* A fossil spine of a fish or fish-like vertebrate.

Ichthyo·grapher. 1677. [f. as prec. + Gr. -γραφος + -ER [1].] A writer on fishes. So **Ichthyo·graphy. Ichthyogra·phic** *a.*

Ichthyoid (i·kþi,oid). 1855. [f. as prec. + -OID.]

A. *adj.* Fish-like. So **Ichthyoi·dal** *a.*

B. *sb.* A vertebrate of the fish type; *spec.* = ICHTHYOPSID 1863.

Ichthyol (i·kþi,ǫl). 1885. [f. ICHTHY(O- + L. *oleum.*] *Med.* A brownish-yellow syrupy liquid obtained by the dry distillation of bituminous rocks containing remains of fossil fishes; used as a remedy in skin diseases. (Proprietary term.) Hence **Ichthyo·lic** *a.*

Ichthyolite (i·kþi,ŏləit). 1828. [f. as prec. + -LITE.] *Palæont.* A fossil fish; any fossil of ichthyic origin. Hence **Ichthyoli·tic** *a.*

Ichthyology (ikþi,ǫ·lŏdʒi). 1646. [f. Gr. ἰχθύς, ἰχθυο- + -LOGY.] The natural history of fishes as a branch of zoology. **b.** The ichthyological features (*of* a district), the fishes (*of* a region) as subjects of scientific study. Hence **Ichthyolo·gic, -al** *a.* of or pertaining to i. **Ichthyolo·gically** *adv.* **Ichthyo·logist,** an expert, or student, in i.

Ichthyomorphic (i:kþi,omǭ·ɹfik), *a.* 1879. [f. ICHTHYO- + Gr. μορφή + -IC.] **a.** Having the form of a fish, as the fish-god Dagon. **b.** Possessing the zoological characters of fishes; ichthyoid.

‖**Ichthyophagi** (ikþi,ǫ·fădʒəi), *sb. pl.* 1555. [L., pl. of *ichthyophagus*, a. Gr., f. ἰχθυο- fish- + -φάγος eating.] Fish-eaters. (Rarely in *sing.*) So †**Ichthyo·phagan** (*rare*), **Ichthyo·phagist, -gite,** a fish-eater. **Ichthyo·phagous** *a.* fish-eating. **Ichthyo·phagy,** the practice of eating fish.

Ichthyophthalmite(ikþi,ǫfþæ·lməit). 1805. [f. Gr. ἰχθύς + ὀφθαλμός + -ITE.] *Min.* = APOPHYLLITE.

‖**Ichthyopsida** (ikþi,ǫ·psidă), *sb. pl.* 1871. [mod.L., f. ICHTHYO- + Gr. ὄψις appearance; see -ID.] *Zool.* The lowest of the three primary groups of *Vertebrata* in Huxley's classification, comprising the amphibians, the fishes, and fish-like vertebrates. Hence **Ichthyo·psid, -o·psidan, -opsi·dian** *adjs.* of or belonging to the *I.*; *sbs.* a vertebrate of this group.

Ichthyopterygian (i:kþi,ǫptěri·dʒiăn). [f. Gr. ἰχθυο- + πτέρυξ, πτερυγ- wing, πτερύγιον wing, fin + -AN.] *Palæont.* **a.** *adj.* Belonging to the *Ichthyopterygia*, an order of extinct marine reptiles, so named from the paddle- or fin-like character of the digits of the fore and hind limbs, the type of which is the ichthyosaurus. **b.** *sb.* An ichthyosaurian.

Ichthyornis (ikþi,ǭ·ɹnis). 1872. [mod.L., f. Gr. ἰχθύς fish + ὄρνις, ὄρνιθος bird.] *Palæont.* An extinct order of toothed birds (*Odontornithes*) belonging to the sub-class *Odontotormæ*, having socketed teeth and biconcave vertebræ, the remains of which occur in the cretaceous rocks of N. America. Hence **Ichthyorni·thic** *a.* **Ichthyorni·thid,** a bird of the family *Ichthyornithidæ*.

Ichthyosaur (i·kþi,osǭɹ). 1830. [See next.] = next, **b.**

Ichthyosaurus (i:kþi,osǭ·rǫ̆s). *Pl.* **-i.** 1832. [mod.L., f. Gr. ἰχθύς, ἰχθυο- + σαῦρος

(= σαύρα) lizard.] *Palæont.* A genus of extinct marine animals, combining the characters of saurian reptiles and of fishes with some features of whales, and having an enormous head, a tapering body, four paddles, and a long tail. (Found chiefly in the Lias.) **b.** An animal of this genus. Hence **Ichthyosau·rian** *a.* of or pertaining to the i.; belonging to the order *Ichthyosauria*; *sb.* an animal of this order. **Ichthyosau·rid,** an animal of the I. family, *Ichthyosauridæ.* **Ichthyosau·roid** *a.* having the form or characters of an i.

‖**Ichthyosis** (ikþi͵ōu·sis). 1815. [mod.L., f. Gr. ἰχθύς + -OSIS.] *Path.* A congenital disease of the skin in which the epidermis assumes a dry and horny appearance. (Also called *fish-skin disease* and *porcupine disease.*) Hence **Ichthyo·tic** *a.* subject to or affected with i.

-ician (i·ʃăn), a compound suffix, in F. *-icien*, consisting of -IAN (ME. and F. *-ien*) added to names of arts or sciences in L. *-ica*, F. *-ique*, Eng. -IC, -ICS, to denote a person skilled in the art or science; e.g. *arithmetician, politician, statistician*; occas. formed by analogy on names not ending in -IC, as *academician*, etc.; cf. also *patrician*, f. L. *patricius.*

‖**Icica** (i·sikă). 1865. [Native name in Guiana.] *Bot.* Name of a genus of S. American trees (N.O. *Burseraceæ*), of which *I. altissima* is the Cedar-wood and *I. heptaphylla* the Incense-wood of Guiana. **I. resin,** a fragrant resin obtained from the Incense-wood; hence **I·cican, I·cacin,** a crystalline resin, obtained from this.

Icicle (əi·sik'l). [OE. *ises gicel*, f. gen. of *is* ICE + *gicel* ICKLE.] **1.** A pendent rod-like ice-formation, produced by the freezing of falling or dripping water. Also *transf.* **2.** *Her.* (See quot.) 1830.

1. Eaves of snow, from which long icicles depended TYNDALL. *transf.* Saltpeter in long icicles 1644. 2. *Icicles*, depicted in shape as guttées, but reversed ROBSON. Hence **I·cicled** *a.* overhung with icicles; also, †frozen.

Icily (əi·sili), *adv.* 1848. [f. ICY *a.* + -LY [2].] Freezingly. Also *fig.* So **I·ciness,** the quality of being icy. Chiefly *fig.*

Icing (əi·siŋ), *vbl. sb.* 1769. [f. ICE *v.* + -ING [1].] **1.** The process of encrusting or adorning with crystallizations of sugar; *concr.* an incrustation of sugar. **2.** The process of cooling or preserving by means of ice 1837.

-icity (i·sĭti), a compound suffix, a. F. *-icité*, ad. L. *-icitatem* (nom. *-icitas*), formed by the addition of *-tāt-* (see -TY) to adj. stems in *-ic(i)-*, as *rusticitas*, f. *rusticus.* On the analogy of these, abstract sbs. in *-icité* in Fr. and *-icity* in Eng. are formed upon adjs. of any origin in *-ic*; e.g. *atomicity, electricity, publicity*, etc.

Icker (i·kəɹ). 1513. Sc. form of EAR *sb.*[2]

Ickle (i·k'l). *Obs.* exc. *dial.* [OE. *giecel (*gicel, gycel*), f. (ult.) OTeut. *jekon-, in ON. *jaki* piece of ice.] = ICICLE. Also *transf.*

†**Icod** (ikǫ·d), *int.* 1697. Var. of ECOD, q.v. -1790.

I-come(n, ME. pa. pple. of COME *v.*

Icon (əi·kǫn). Also **ikon, eikon.** 1572. [a. late L. *icōn* (Pliny), ad. Gr. εἰκών, εἰκον- likeness, image, picture.] †**1.** An image, figure, or representation; a portrait; an illustration in a book -1727. **b.** An image in the solid; a statue 1577. **2.** *Eastern Ch.* A representation of some sacred personage, itself regarded as sacred, and honoured with a relative worship 1833. †**3.** *Rhet.* A simile -1676.

1. b. The I. of an Elephant SIR T. HERBERT. 2. Behind them were carried..six censers, and six sacred ikons PINKERTON.

Iconic (əikǫ·nik), *a.* Also **eiconic.** 1656. [ad. late L. *iconicus*, ad. Gr., f. εἰκών.] Of or pertaining to an icon; of the nature of a portrait; *spec.* in *Art*, applied to the ancient portrait statues of victorious athletes, and hence to memorial statues and busts of a fixed type. So **Ico·nical** *a. rare* 1652.

†**I·conism.** 1656. [ad. late L. *iconismus*, a. Gr., f. εἰκονίζειν.] A representation of some image or figure; imagery; metaphor -1680.

†**I·conize,** *v.* [ad. Gr. εἰκονίζειν.] *trans.* To form into an image; to figure, to represent. CUDWORTH.

Icono-, Gr. εἰκονο-, comb. f. εἰκών ICON.

Iconodu·ly [see DULIA], the veneration of images; so **I·conodu·lic** (*-doulic*) *a.*; **I·conodule, Iconodu·list,** a venerator of images. **I·conoma·nia,** an infatuated devotion to images; a mania for collecting icons or portraits. **I·conophile, Icono·philist** [Gr. φίλος], a connoisseur of pictures, engravings, book illustrations, and the like; hence **Icono·philism, -phily,** the taste for these.

Iconoclasm (əikǫ·nǒklæz'm). 1756. [f. Gr. εἰκών + κλάσμα, f. κλᾶν to break; after next.] The breaking or destroying of images; *esp.* of images and pictures set up as objects of veneration; hence *transf.* and *fig.*

Iconoclast (əikǫ·nǒklæst), *sb.* (*a.*) 1641. [ad. late L. *iconoclastes*, a. late Gr., f. εἰκών + -κλάστης breaker.] **1.** A breaker or destroyer of images; *spec.* one who took part in the movement in the 8th and 9th centuries to put down the use of these in religious worship in the Christian churches of the East; hence, applied analogously to Protestants in the 16th and 17th centuries. **2.** *transf.* and *fig.* One who assails cherished beliefs or venerated institutions on the ground that they are erroneous or pernicious 1842. **3.** *attrib.* or *adj.* Iconoclastic 1685.

1. The Puritans .. seem mere savage Iconoclasts CARLYLE. 2. Kant was the great i. J. MARTINEAU. 3. An i. riot 1845. Hence **Iconocla·stic** *a.* of or pertaining to iconoclasts or iconoclasm. **Iconocla·stically** *adv.* **Iconocla·sticism,** the principles or practice of iconoclasts.

Ico·nograph. 1884. [f. Gr. εἰκών + -γραφος written, γραφή writing.] A drawing, engraving, or illustration for a book; = ICON 1.

Iconography (əikǫnǫ·grăfi). 1628. [ad. med.L. *iconographia*, ad. Gr., f. εἰκών + -γραφία -GRAPHY.] †**1.** *concr.* A pictorial representation; a drawing or plan -1678. **2.** The description of any subject by means of drawings or figures; any book in which this is done; also, the branch of knowledge which deals with representative art in general 1678.

2. The i. of the altar-canopy 1874. Hence **Icono·grapher,** one who makes figures or drawings of objects. **Iconogra·phic, -al** *a.* of or pertaining to i.

Iconolater (əikǫnǫ·lătəɹ). 1654. [f. Gr. εἰκών, after *idolater.*] A worshipper of images. So **Icono·latry,** image-worship.

Iconology (əikǫnǫ·lŏdʒi). 1730. [f. Gr. εἰκών, εἰκονο-; see -LOGY.] **1.** That branch of knowledge which deals with the subject of icons; also icons collectively, or as objects of investigation, etc. **2.** Symbolical representation; symbolism 1849. Hence **Iconolo·gical** *a.*, **-lo·gically** *adv.* 1730. **Icono·logist.**

Iconomachy (əikǫnǫ·măki). 1581. [ad. eccl. L. *iconomachia*, a. eccl. Gr. εἰκονομαχία, f. εἰκών + -μαχία.] A war against images; hostility to images in connexion with worship. So †**Icono·machal** (*erron.* **-mical**) *a.* hostile to images.

‖**Iconostas** (əikǫ·nostæs). 1833. [Russ., f. Gr. εἰκονόστασις; see next.] = next.

‖**Iconostasis** (əikǫnǫ·stăsis). 1833. [eccl. L., a. eccl. Gr. εἰκονόστασις, f. εἰκών ICON + στάσις station.] *Eastern Ch.* The screen separating the sanctuary or 'bema' from the main body of the church, and on which the icons are placed.

Icos-, icosa-, icosi-, repr. Gr. comb. forms of εἴκοσι twenty.

Icosaco·lic [Gr. κῶλον member, COLON] *a.*, *Anc. Pros.* consisting of twenty cola or members. **Icosase·mic** [Gr. σῆμα mark, σημεῖον mark, mora] *a.*, *Anc. Pros.* consisting of or containing twenty moræ or units of time, i.e. the equivalent of twenty short syllables. **Ico·sian** *a.*, of or pertaining to twenty.

Icosahedron (əi:kosăhī·drǫn, -he·drǫn). 1570. [a. Gr. εἰκοσάεδρον adj. neut., used subst., f. εἴκοσι + ἕδρα.] *Geom.* A solid contained by twenty plane faces; *spec.* the *regular icosahedron*, contained by twenty equilateral triangles. Hence **Icosahe·dral** *a.* having twenty faces.

‖**Icosandria** (əikosæ·ndriă). 1753. [mod.L. (Linn.), f. Gr. εἴκοσι + ἀνήρ, ἀνδρ- taken as = 'stamen'.] *Bot.* A Linnæan class, containing plants with twenty or more stamens inserted on the calyx. Hence **Icosa·nder,** a plant of this class. **Icosa·ndrian, Icosa·ndrous** *adjs.* belonging to this class.

I:cosite:trahe·dron. 1831. [f. Gr. εἴκοσι + τετρα- four + ἕδρα base.] *Geom.* and *Cryst.* A solid figure contained by twenty-four plane faces; *esp.* a *deltohedron* or *trapezohedron.*

I-cried, ME. pa. pple. of CRY *v.*

-ics *suffix*: see -IC 2.

Icteric (ikte·rik). 1600. [ad. L. *ictericus*, a. Gr., f. ἴκτερος (see ICTERUS).]

A. *adj.* Belonging to, of the nature of, or affected with jaundice. So **Icte·rical** *a.* **b.** Used for the cure of jaundice 1710.

I. Oriole: a N. American bird (*Icterus vulgaris*), having black and yellow plumage; also called *troopial.*

B. *sb.* **1.** A person affected with jaundice 1634. **2.** A remedy for jaundice 1727.

Icterine (i·ktĕrəin), *a.* 1855. [f. ICTERUS + -INE.] *Zool.* **a.** Yellowish. **b.** Belonging to the family *Icteridæ* or sub-family *Icterinæ* of American passerine birds (typical genus *Icterus*) 1884.

Icteritious (-i·ʃəs), *a.* 1609. [f. med.L. *icteritia* jaundice + -OUS.] Jaundiced; also *fig.*

Icteroid (i·ktĕroid), *a.* 1855. [f. Gr. ἴκτερος jaundice + -OID.] Resembling or characteristic of jaundice.

‖**Icterus** (i·ktĕrǒs). 1706. [L., a. Gr. ἴκτερος jaundice; also, a certain yellowish-green bird.] **1.** *Path.* Jaundice. **b.** *Bot.* A disease of plants in which the leaves turn yellow 1866. **2.** *Zool.* A genus of American passerine birds, now restricted to the American orioles 1713.

Ictic (i·ktik), *a. rare.* 1847. [irreg. f. L. *ictus* (*u*-stem); see -IC.] **1.** Of the nature of a blow or stroke; abrupt and sudden. **2.** *Pros.* Pertaining or due to the ictus 1898.

‖**Ictus** (i·ktǒs). 1707. [L., = blow, stroke, thrust, f. *icere.*] **1.** *Pros.* Stress on a particular syllable of a foot or verse 1752. **2.** *Med.* **a.** The beat of the pulse. **b.** *Ictus solis* (L.): sunstroke 1811.

Icy (əi·si), *a.* OE. [f. ICE *sb.* + -Y [1]. Formed anew in 15th c.] **1.** Abounding in ice; covered or overlaid with ice. **2.** Consisting of ice 1600. **3.** Resembling ice; extremely cold, frosty; slippery 1590. Also *fig.*

1. The flowers of the I. Zones 1796. Greenland's i. mountains HEBER. 3. An i. current 1886. *fig.* If he be leaden, ycie, cold, vnwilling, Be thou so too SHAKS. *Comb.*, as *icy-pearled* (having pearls or sparkling drops of ice), *-wheeled*, etc.

Id (id). 1893. [A German formation.] *Biol.* In Weissmann's theory of heredity: A unit of germ-plasm or idioplasm.

-id, *suffix* [1], repr. F. *-ide*, L. *-idus*, used to form adjs., chiefly from verbs with *e*-stems, as *acidus* from *acere*, etc.; occas. from verbs with *i*- or consonant stems, and from sbs., as *fluidus*, f. *fluere*, *morbidus*, f. *morbus*, etc. Not a living formative in Eng.

-id, *suffix* [2], corresp. to Fr. *-ide*, in sbs. derived from L. sbs. in *-is*, *-idem*, adopted from Gr. sbs. in -ις, -ιδα; as *chrysalid*, *pyramid*, etc. In botanical terms, as *orchid*, etc., this formative denotes a member of the order *Orchidaceæ*, etc.

-id, *suffix* [3]. (*a*) In zoological appellatives, sb. and adj.: (i) formed from L. names of Families in *-idæ*, pl. of *-ides*, repr. Gr. -ιδης = 'son of'; as *Araneid*, a member of the Family *Araneidæ.* (ii) formed from L. names of Classes, etc., in *-ida*, taken as neut. pl. of *-ides* = Gr. -ιδης; as *Arachnid*, a member of the Class *Arachnida.* See -IDAN. (*b*) *Astron.* Applied to groups or showers of meteors radiating from a constellation, after which they are named, as *Leonid*, *Quadrantid.*

-id, *suffix* [4], early spelling of the chemical suffix -IDE, still used by some, esp. in U.S.

-idan, in zoological appellatives, sb. and adj., formed on -ID [3] with suffix -AN, meaning 'of or pertaining to', or 'a member of' the group designated by the suffix *-ida* or *-idæ*; as *arachnidan* (f. *Arachnida*) = *arachnid*, etc.

Idant (əi·dănt). 1893. [Arbitrarily f. ID.] *Biol.* One of the chromatin bodies in the nucleus of a reproductive or other cell, regarded as consisting of 'ids' (see ID).

Ide[1] (əid). 1839. [ad. mod.L. *idus*, ad. Sw. *id*.] A freshwater cyprinoid fish (*Leuciscus idus* or *I. melanotus*), of northern Europe.

Ide[2]: see IDES.

-ide, *Chem.*, a suffix used to form names of simple compounds of an element with another element or a radical. It is added to the stem or an abbreviated form of the word, and was first used in *ox-ide* from *oxygen*. It sometimes displaced other derivs. in *-et*, *-uret*.

Idea (əidī·ă), *sb.* Also *erron.* †**idæa.** Pl. **ideas;** formerly sometimes **ideæ.** 1531. [a. late L. *idea* (in Platonic sense), a. Gr. ἰδέα, f. root ἰδ-, ἰδεῖν to see. Cf. the earlier IDEE.]

I. Archetype, pattern, plan, standard. 1. In Platonic philosophy: An eternally existing pattern of any class of things, of which the individual things are imperfect copies, and from which they derive their existence 1563. 2. A standard of perfection; an ideal. *Obs.* or *arch.* 1586. 3. The conception of a standard or principle to be realized or aimed at; the plan or design according to which something is created or constructed 1581. 4. In weaker sense: A notion of something to be done; an intention, plan of action 1617. †5. A pattern, type; a preliminary sketch or draft; an outline; something in an undeveloped state –1702. 6. *Mus.* A musical theme, phrase, or figure as sketched 1880.

1. How widely we are fallen from the pure Exemplar and I. of our Nature SIR T. BROWNE. 3. This new created World..how good, how faire, Answering his great I. MILT. *P.L.* VII. 557. 4. The i. of short parliaments is..plausible enough BURKE.

†II. A figure, representation, image, symbol (*of* something) 1531–1714; form, figure (as a quality or attribute); shape; aspect; nature or character –1737.

III. 1. †a. The mental image of something previously seen or known, and recalled by the memory –1764. b. More generally: A conception 1612. c. Something merely imagined 1588. 2. More widely: Any product of mental apprehension or activity, existing in the mind as an object of knowledge or thought; a thought, conception, notion; an item of knowledge or belief; a way of thinking 1645. b. A vague belief, opinion, or estimate; a supposition, impression, fancy 1712.

1. Th' I. of her life shal sweetly creepe Into his study of imagination SHAKS. b. Then gay Ideas crowd the vacant brain POPE. c. Which make.. Predestination a meere Idæa PRYNNE. Phr. *In idea* (= F. *en idée*), in mind, in thought; opp. to *in reality*. 2. To teach the young i. how to shoot THOMSON. b. I had no i. you would be flooded 1866.

IV. Mod. Philosophy. 1. [from III.] With Descartes and Locke: The immediate object of thought or mental perception 1666. 2. [from I. 1.] a. In the Kantian and transcendental schools: One of the *noumena* or ultimate principles apprehended by reason. b. In Hegelianism: The absolute truth of which all phenomenal existence is the expression; *the Idea*, the Absolute. 1838.

1. The leading doctrine of Locke, as is well known, is the derivation of all our ideas from sensation and from reflection HALLAM.

Idea'd, ideaed (əidī·ăd), *a.* 1753. [f. IDEA *sb.* + -ED[2].] Having an idea or ideas, *esp.* of a specified kind.

Ideal (əidī·ăl). 1611. [a. F. *idéal*, ad. late L. *idealis*, f. *idea*.]

A. *adj.* 1. Existing as an idea or archetype; relating to or consisting of ideas (see IDEA *sb.* I. 1) 1647. 2. Conceived as perfect in its kind. Cf. IDEA *sb.* I. 2, 3. 1613. 3. Of, pertaining to, or of the nature of an idea or conception 1611; representing an idea 1846. 4. Existing only in idea; opp. to *real* or *actual*. Hence sometimes, Not real or practical; visionary 1611. 5. *Philos.* Idealistic 1764. 6. *Math.* Applied to a number or quantity which has no actual existence, but is assumed in a system of complex numbers 1860.

1. The Natural existence of things is founded upon their I. existence 1691. 2. I. perfection BOLINGBROKE, beauty RUSKIN, enjoyment 1861. 3. The crucifix..is an i., not a realistic representation 1874. 4. They despised the i. terrors of a foreign superstition GIBBON.

B. *sb.* 1. A conception of something, or a thing conceived, as perfect in its kind; a perfect type; a standard of excellence 1798. 2. An imaginary thing 1884.

1. The Chinese i. of making all people alike MILL. [Confucius] as the i. of a sage MAX MÜLLER.

¶See also BEAU-IDEAL.

Idealess (əidī·ă,lės), *a.* 1818. [-LESS.] Destitute of ideas; conveying no idea.

Idealism (əidī·ăliz'm). 1796. [ad. F. *idéalisme*, or Ger. *idealismus*, f. IDEAL.] 1. *Philos.* Any system in which the object of external perception is held to consist, either in itself, or as perceived, of ideas (see IDEA *sb.*).

Subjective Idealism is the opinion that the object of external perception consists, whether in itself or as known to us, in ideas of the perceiving mind; *Critical* or *Transcendental I.*, the opinion (of Kant) that it consists, as known to us, but not necessarily in itself, of such ideas; *Objective I.*, the opinion (of Schelling) that while, as known to us, it consists of such ideas, it consists also, as it is in itself, of ideas identical with these; *Absolute I.*, (*a*) the opinion (of Hegel) that it consists, not only as known to us, but in itself, of ideas, not however ours, but those of the universal mind; (*b*) also applied more generally to other forms of idealism which do not suppose an independent reality underlying our ideas of external objects.

2. The practice of idealizing; imaginative treatment in art or literature; ideal style or character; opp. to *realism*. Also, aspiration after an ideal. 1829. b. (with *pl.*) An act or product of idealizing 1822.

2. The perfected i. which reigns in his [Titian's] greatest works 1841.

Idealist (əidī·ălist). 1701. [f. IDEAL + -IST.] 1. *Philos.* One who holds a doctrine of idealism; see prec. 1. 2. One who idealizes; an artist or writer who treats a subject imaginatively. Opp. to *realist*. 1805. 3. One who conceives, or follows after ideals. Sometimes *depreciatively*, A visionary. 1829. 4. *attrib.* or *adj.* = next 1875.

Idealistic (əidi,ăli·stik), *a.* 1829. [f. prec. + -IC.] Pertaining to or characteristic of an idealist; belonging to or having the character of idealism. Hence **Ideali·stical** *a.*, **-ly** *adv.*

Ideality (əidi,æ·lĭti). 1701. [f. IDEAL + -ITY.] †1. The faculty of forming ideas (see IDEA *sb.* I. 1). NORRIS. 2. The imaginative faculty. (Orig. a term of *Phrenology*.) 1828. 3. The quality of being ideal 1817. 4. with *pl.*: Something ideal or imaginary 1844.

4. Amiable idealities about 'love in a cottage' 1844.

Idealize (əidī·ăləiz), *v.* 1786. [f. IDEAL + -IZE.] *trans.* To make ideal; to represent in an ideal form or character; to exalt to an ideal perfection 1795. b. *absol.* or *intr.* To conceive an ideal or ideals 1786.

b. [Men's] natural propensity to i. 1786. Hence **Idealiza·tion. Ide·alizer.**

Ideally (əidī·ăli), *adv.* 1598. [f. IDEAL *a.* + -LY[2].] †1. In 'idea' or archetype –1701. 2. Imaginarily 1598. 3. In conformity with the ideal 1840. 4. *Biol.* In relation to a general plan or archetype (of a class) 1859.

Idealogical, etc. erron. ff. IDEOLOGICAL, etc.

Ideate (əidī·eɪt), *v.* 1610. [f. IDEA *sb.*; see -ATE[3].] 1. *trans.* To form the idea of; to imagine, conceive. 2. *absol.* or *intr.* a. To form ideas, to think. b. To devise something imaginary. 1862.

1. A State which Plato Ideated DONNE. Hence **Idea·tion,** the formation of ideas of things not present to the senses. **Idea·tional, Ide·ative** (*rare*) *adjs.* of or pertaining to ideation.

Ide·ate, *a.* and *sb.* 1677. [ad. mod.L. *ideatus*; cf. prec.]

A. *sb.* Produced by or deriving its existence from a (Platonic) idea; see IDEA *sb.* I. 1.

B. *sb.* The external object of which an idea is formed 1677.

Idee (əidī·). *Obs.* exc. in vulgar use. ME. (LYDGATE). [a. F. *idée*; see IDEA *sb.*] = IDEA.

‖**Idée fixe** (*ide fiks*). 1836. [Fr.] A fixed idea.

‖**Idem** (əi·dem, i·dem). ME. [L. *īdem* masc., *ĭdem* neut. 'the same'.] The same word, name, title, author, etc.. Abbrev. *id.*

I·dent, -ant, *a.* *Sc.* 1567. [Later form of ITHAND *a.*: cf. EIDENT.] Diligent, persistent. Hence **I·dently** *adv.* 1438.

Identic (əide·ntik), *a.* 1649. [ad. scholastic L. *identicus* (cf. IDENTITY).] 1. = IDENTICAL 1, 2. 2. In diplomacy, applied to action or language in which two or more governments agree to use precisely the same form, in their relations with some other power; esp. in *identic note* 1863.

Identical (əide·ntikăl), *a.* 1620. [f. med.L. *identicus* (see prec.) + -AL.] 1. The same; the very same. (Often emphasized by *same*, *very*.) 1633. 2. Agreeing entirely in material, constitution, properties, qualities, or meaning 1677. 3. *Logic.* Said of a proposition, the terms of which denote the same thing; as *man is a human being* 1620. 4. *Alg.* Expressing or effecting identity, as *i. equation*, *i. operation* 1875.

1. In the same identicall path 1633. 2. Crystals.. are cases of..cohesion of i. particles 1896. Hence **Ide·ntical·ly** *adv.*, **-ness.**

†**Identi·fic,** *a.* 1678. [see IDENTIFY.] Doing the same; concurring in action. GALE. So †**Identi·fically** *adv.*, identically 1475; †**Identifica·lity** 1716.

Identification (əide:ntifikē·ʃən). 1644. [f. IDENTIFY; see -FICATION.] The action of identifying or fact of being identified.

The i. of Serbâl with Sinai STANLEY, of habitual offenders 1887.

Identify (əide·ntifəi), *v.* 1644. [ad. late L. *identificare*; see IDENTITY and -FY.] 1. *trans.* To make identical (*with*, †*to* something); to regard or treat as the same. b. To make one *with*; to associate inseparably. Chiefly *refl.* and *pass.* 1780. †c. *intr.* To be made, become, or prove to be the same –1834. 2. To determine the identity of; in *Nat. Hist.* to refer a specimen to its proper species 1769.

1. Osiris, whom he identifies with Serapis GIBBON. b. Let us i...ourselves with the people BURKE. c. Your taste and mine do not always i. LAMB. 2. To i. stolen goods (*mod.*). Hence **Ide·ntifiable** *a.* able to be identified.

Identism (əide·ntiz'm). 1857. [f. *ident(i)-*, comb. f. L. *idem*, + -ISM.] The system or doctrine of (absolute) identity (see IDENTITY 1).

Identity (əide·ntĭti). 1570. [ad. F. *identité*, ad. late L. *identitas*, peculiarly formed from *ident(i)-*, f. L. *idem* + *-tas*, *-tatem*; see -TY.] 1. The quality or condition of being the same; absolute or essential sameness; oneness. Also with *an* and *pl.* 2. Individuality, personality 1638; individual existence (? *Obs.*) 1683. 3. *Alg.* An identical equation, i.e. one which is true for all values of the literal quantities 1859. 4. The condition of being identified in feeling, interest, etc. (*rare*) 1868. 5. *attrib.* = 'that serves to identify the holder', as *identity card*, *disk*, etc. 1900.

1. *Absolute identity*, that asserted in the doctrine of Schelling that mind and matter are phenomenal modifications of the same substance. I. of conviction FROUDE. 2. *Personal i.*: continuity of the personality. 4. He is..in visible i. with the age GLADSTONE. Phr. *Law* or *Principle of I.*: the so-called principle that 'Every A is A'.

Ideo- (əi·di,o), combining f. Gr. ἰδέα IDEA, as in **Ideo-motor** [MOTOR] *a.*, applied by W. B. Carpenter to automatic muscular movements arising from complete occupation of the mind by an idea, and to the cerebral centres controlling such movements; so **Ideomo·tion,** ideo-motor movement. **I·deophone** [Gr. φωνή], a sound or group of sounds denoting an idea, i.e. a spoken word (A. J. Ellis). **Ideopra·xist** [Gr. πρᾶξις; see -IST], one whose practice is actuated by an idea.

Ideogram (əi·dio,græm). 1838. [f. Gr. ἰδέα IDEA + -GRAM.] = next.

Ideograph (əi·dio,graf). Also *erron.* **idea-.** 1835. [f. as prec. + -GRAPH.] A character or figure symbolizing the idea of a thing, without expressing the name of it, as the Chinese characters, etc.

Thus in English, the i. + may be pronounced 'plus', 'added to', or 'more' according to the pleasure of the reader SAYCE. Hence **I:deogra·phic** *a.* of the nature of an i.; relating to or composed of ideographs; *sb.* an ideographic character; *pl.* a method of writing in ideographic characters. **Ideogra·phical** *a.*, **-ly** *adv.*

Ideography (əidi,ǫ·grăfi). Also *erron.* **idea-.** 1836. [f. as prec. + -GRAPHY.] The representation of ideas by graphic signs; writing consisting of ideographs.

Ideolo·gic, -ical, *a.* 1797. [f. IDEOLOG-Y + -IC + -AL.] Belonging or relating to ideology.

Ideologist (əidi,ǫ·lŏdʒist). Also *erron.* idea-. 1798. [ad. F. *idéologiste*; see next and -IST.] 1. One versed in ideology (sense 1). 2. A person occupied with an idea or ideas; esp. a visionary, a mere theorist 1818. So **Ide·o·logue** 1815.

Ideology (əidi,ǫ·lŏdʒi). 1796. [ad. F. *idéologie*: see IDEO-, -LOGY.] 1. The science of ideas; the study of the origin and nature of ideas. b. *spec.* The system of Condillac, which derived all ideas from sensations. 2. Ideal or abstract speculation; visionary theorizing 1813. 3. A system of ideas concerning phenomena, esp. those of social life; the manner of thinking characteristic of a class or an individual.

Ides (əidz), *sb. pl.* Rarely in sing. **ide.** ME. [a. F., ad. L. *Idus* sb. pl.] In the ancient Roman calendar, the eighth day after the nones, i.e. the 15th of March, May, July, October, and the 13th of the other months.

The days after the nones were reckoned forward to the ides; hence 'the sixth of the ides' (or 'the sixth ide') 'of June', loosely rendering L. *ante diem sextum Idus Junias* = June 8. Cæsar..Beware the Ides of March *Jul. C.* I. ii. 17.

‖**Id est.** 1598. [L., = 'that is'.] Two Latin words, used in Eng. in the sense 'that is to say'. Abbrev. *i. e.* (formerly often *i.*).

Idiasm (i·di,æz'm). 1868. [ad. Gr. ἰδιασμός.] A peculiarity, mannerism.

Idic (i·dik), *a.* 1893. [f. ID + -IC.] Pertaining to an id or ids.

Idio- (i·diǝ), repr. Gr. ἰδιο-, comb. f. ἴδιος own, personal, private, peculiar, separate, distinct.

I·dioblast [-BLAST], *Bot.* an individual plant-cell of different nature or content from the surrounding tissue. **Idiocyclo·phanous** [CYCLO-] *a.*, = *idiophanous.* **Idiodi·nic** [Gr. ὠδίς, ὠδιν- birth-pains] *a.*, *Zool.* having a special opening for the extrusion of genital products. †**Idio-ele·ctric** *a.*, capable of being electrified by friction. **Idiogo·naduct**, the gonaduct of an idiodinic animal. **I·diograph**, one's private mark or signature; hence **Idiogra·phic** *a.* **Idio·meter** [-METER], an instrument for measuring the personal equation of an observer, by observation of the transit of an artificial star whose actual motion is exactly known. **Idiomu·scular** *a.*, *Path.* a term for the local contraction, under physical stimulus, of a muscle which is fatigued or dying. **Idio·phanism**, idiophanous nature or property. **Idio·phanous** [Gr. -φανής] *a.*, exhibiting axial interference figures without the use of polarizing apparatus. **I·dioplasm**, *Biol.* a term for the special portion of protoplasm in a germ or cell which is supposed to determine the character of the resulting organism; hence **Idioplasma·tic** *a.* **Idiopsycho·logy**, the psychology of one's own mind; hence **Idiopsycholo·gical** *a.* **Idiorepu·lsive** *a.*, self-repelling. **Idiosta·tic** [STATIC] *a.*, not employing any auxiliary electrification in the measurement of electricity (opp. to HETEROSTATIC).

Idio·crasy. 1654. Now *rare.* [ad. Gr. ἰδιοκρασία, f. ἰδιο- IDIO- + -κρασία, κρᾶσις mixing.] = IDIOSYNCRASY -1755. Hence **Idiocra·tic, -al** *a.* idiosyncratic.

Idiocy (i·diǒsi). 1487. [perh. f. IDIOT, as *prophecy* from *prophet*, etc.] The state or condition of being an idiot; extreme mental imbecility.

I. is a defect of mind which is either congenital, or due to causes operating during the first few years of life MAUDSLEY.

Idiom (i·diəm). 1588. [ad. L. *idioma*, Gr. ἰδίωμα, f. (ult.) ἴδιος own, private, peculiar.] 1. The form of speech peculiar to a people or country. b. A dialect 1598. 2. = IDIOTISM I. 2. 1598. 3. A form of expression, construction, phrase, etc. peculiar to a language; a peculiarity of phraseology approved by usage, and often having a meaning other than its grammatical or logical one 1628. 4. Specific form or property; peculiar nature; peculiarity. *Obs.* exc. as *fig.* of 1 or 2. 1644.

1. Our Vernacular I. ADDISON. The classics of the Tuscan i. GIBBON. 2. The I. of it, as to the main, appears to be Teutonick 1683. 3. Every speech hath certaine Idiomes, and customary Phrases of its own HOWELL. 4. The idioms of national opinion and feeling MACAULAY.

Idiomatic (idiǒmæ·tik), *a.* 1712. [ad. Gr. ἰδιωματικός, f. ἰδίωμα (ἰδιώματ-) IDIOM.] 1. Peculiar to or characteristic of a particular language; vernacular; colloquial. 2. Given to or marked by the use of idioms 1839.

2. Like most i...writers, he [Dryden] knew very little about the language historically or critically LOWELL. So **Idioma·tical** *a.* Hence **Idioma·tical-ly** *adv.*, -ness.

Idiomorphic (idiǝmǭ·ɹfik), *a.* 1887. [f. IDIO- + Gr. μορφή + -IC.] *Min.* Having its own characteristic form; *spec.* having its characteristic crystallographic faces: said of one of the constituent minerals of a rock. Hence **Idiomo·rphically** *adv.*

Idiopathic, -al (idiǝpæ·þik, -ăl), *a.* 1669. [f. IDIOPATHY + -IC + -AL.] 1. *Path.* Of a disease: Of the nature of a primary morbid state; not consequent upon another disease. 2. Of the nature of a particular affection or susceptibility 1846. Hence **Idiopa·thically** *adv.* So **I·diopathe·tic, -al** *a. rare.*

Idiopathy (idi,ǫ·păþi). 1640. [ad. mod.L. *idiopathia*, a. Gr. ἰδιοπάθεια (Galen); see IDIO- and -PATHY.] †1. A feeling or sensation peculiar to an individual or class -1688. 2. *Path.* A disease not preceded or occasioned by any other; a primary disease 1640.

2. This moral i...this itch for seeing memorable places..is peculiarly English 1833.

Idiosyncrasy (idiǒsi·ŋkrăsi). 1604. [ad. Gr. ἰδιοσυγκρασία, also -σύνκρασις; see IDIO- and CRASIS.] A peculiarity of constitution or temperament. 1. The physical constitution of an individual or †class. Now only *Med.* 2. The mental constitution peculiar to a person or class; individual bent of mind or inclination 1665. 3. A mode of expression peculiar to an author 1837.

1. Something in the i. of the patient that puzzles the physician BERKELEY. 2. The pertinacious i. of the Gallic genius STUBBS. 3. The style of Bacon has an i. 1837. Hence **Idiosyncra·tic, -al** *a.* pertaining to, or of the nature of, i. **Idiosyncra·tically** *adv.* by peculiarity of constitution.

Idiot (i·diət), *sb.* ME. [a. F. *idiot*, ad. L. *idiota*, ad. Gr. ἰδιώτης private person, 'layman', f. ἴδιος.] †1. An ignorant, uneducated man; a simple man; a clown -1722. †b. *spec.* A layman -1660. †c. One not professionally learned; also, a private man -1663. 2. A person so deficient mentally as to be incapable of ordinary reasoning or rational conduct. Applied to one permanently so afflicted. ME. b. A term of reprobation: A blockhead, an utter fool ME. †c. A man of weak intellect maintained as a professional fool or jester -1711. 3. *attrib.* or quasi-*adj.*, as *i. boy, laugh*, etc. ME.

1. The bisshop repreuyd hym sore as unconnyng and an ydeote CAXTON. b. For he would not Take orders but remaine an Idiote 1611. 2. Idiots make very few or no Propositions, and reason scarce at all LOCKE. b. You i., do you know what peril you stand in? DICKENS. Hence **Idiot** *v. trans.* to call (any one) i. TENNYSON. **I·diotcy** = IDIOCY. **Idio·tic** *a.* devoid of intellect; utterly stupid, senseless, foolish. †**Idiotish** *a.* idiotic.

Idio·tical, *a.* 1646. [f. late L. *idioticus* + -AL.] †1. Uneducated, plain, ignorant -1725. †2. Private, personal (*rare*) -1660. 3. = IDIOTIC 1656. Hence **Idio·tical-ly** *adv.*, -ness.

‖**Idioticon** (idi,ǭ·tikǒn). 1842. [a. Gr. ἰδιωτικόν.] A dictionary confined to a particular dialect, or containing words and phrases peculiar to one part of a country.

Idiotism (i·diǒtiz'm). 1588. [In branch I. = F. *idiotisme*, ad. late L. *idiotismus* common or vulgar manner of speaking, a. Gr. ἰδιωτισμός. In II., f. IDIOT + -ISM.]

I. †1. = IDIOM 1. -1716. †2. The peculiar character or genius of a language -1731. 3. = IDIOM 3. 1615. †b. *transf.* A peculiarity of action, manner, or habit -1639.

II. 1. Ignorance; lack of knowledge or culture 1635. 2. = IDIOCY (now *rare*) 1611. b. Extreme folly, senselessness, or stupidity 1592.

2. Direct Lunacie and Ideotism 1632. b. What i. it would be in me to trust myself to a ministry capable of such baseness WILKES.

Idiotize (i·diǒtəiz), *v.* 1716. [f. IDIOT + -IZE.] †1. *intr.* To act in a way peculiar to themselves. 2. *intr.* To become idiotic or stupid 1800. 3. *trans.* To make idiotic; to befool 1831.

I·diotry. 1494. [f. IDIOT + -RY.] a. *Sc. Law.* = IDIOCY. b. Idiotic conduct, madness 1757.

Idle (əid'l), *a.* (*sb.*) [OE. *idel*; cf. Ger. *eitel* bare, etc. The orig. sense was app. 'empty'.] †1. Empty; void (*of*) -ME. 2. Void of any real worth, usefulness, or significance; hence, ineffective, vain, frivolous, trifling OE. †b. Void of meaning or sense; also (of persons) light-headed -1658. c. Groundless 1590. 3. Of things: Useless OE. 4. Doing nothing, unemployed OE. b. Of things, esp. time: Unoccupied ME. 5. Of things: Inactive, not moving or in operation 1522. 6. Lazy, indolent ME. †7. quasi-*adv.* = IDLY -1633.

1. I am idel erþe & voide, til þou illumyne me 1450. 2. He is no i. talker 1576. I. conjectures 1802. c. I. or malicious reports MACAULAY, hopes BROWNING. 3. Vsurping Iuie, Brier, or i. Mosse SHAKS. 4. Vacaboundes and ydell persones 1530. b. *I. bread* = bread of idleness (IDLENESS). Dozing out all his i. noons COWPER. Phr. *I. worms*, worms said joc. to breed in the fingers of the i. (*Rom. & Jul.* I. iv. 65, Qo. 1597). 5. We don't keep the pits i. for the fun of the thing 1898. **I. wheel, i.-wheel**, an intermediate wheel used for connecting two geared wheels when they cannot be brought sufficiently near to gear directly, or when it is necessary that the follower should revolve in the same direction as the leader, which it would not do if they geared directly. *I. pulley*, the loose pulley of the 'fast-and-loose-pulley' arrangement. 6. †*I. bellies*, indolent sluggards or gluttons (cf. *Titus* i. 12).

Comb. **i.-tongs** = LAZY-TONGS.

B. *sb.* (the *adj.* used *absol.*). †1. *In* (earlier *on, an*) *i.*: in vain -1500. †2. Idleness -1606. †3. An idler -1709.

1. Euery man that taketh goddes name in ydel CHAUCER.

Idle (əid'l), *v.* 1592. [f. prec. adj.] 1. *intr.* To move idly. 2. To be idle 1668. b. quasi-*trans. To i.* (time) *away*, to pass in idleness 1652. 3. *trans.* To cause to be idle 1826.

†**I·dle-hea·ded**, *a.* 1598. [f. *idle head.*] 1. Of little understanding; silly; crazy -1631. 2. Off one's head; distracted, delirious -1694.

1. The superstitious idle-headed-Eld SHAKS.

I·dleman. *rare.* ME. 1. One who has no occupation; †formerly, in Ireland, a gentleman. 2. One employed to do odd jobs 1845.

Idleness (əi·d'lnės). [OE. *idelnes*; see -NESS.] †1. Vanity -ME. 2. Groundlessness, worthlessness; triviality; ineptitude, futility 1645. †3. Light-headedness; delirium; also folly (*rare*) -1645. 4. The condition of being idle; want of occupation; habitual indolence; an instance of this. (Now the ordinary sense.) OE.

2. The i. of the proceedings 1885. 4. *Bread of i.*, bread not earned by labour; [She] eateth not the bread of i. *Prov.* xxxi. 27.

Idler (əi·dləɹ). 1534. [f. IDLE *v.* + -ER [1].] 1. One who idles or is idle; one who spends his time in idleness; an indolent person. 2. *Naut.* One of those who, being liable to constant day duty on board a ship-of-war, are not subjected to keep the night-watch 1794. 3. *Machinery.* An idle wheel (see IDLE *a.* 5) 1875.

Idlesse (əi·dlės). *arch.* Also **idless.** 1596. [Pseudo-antique f. IDLE *a.*; see -ESS [2].] Idleness; *dolce far niente.*

Idly (əi·dli), *adv.* OE. [f. IDLE *a.* + -LY [2]. (Formerly *idlely.*)] 1. Vainly, in vain; uselessly; carelessly, frivolously, ineffectively. †b. Incoherently, deliriously -1632. 2. In an idle or lazy way; indolently, inactively ME.

Ido (ī·dǝ). 1907. [In this language, = offspring.] An artificial language, based on Esperanto. Hence **I·doist.**

Idocrase (əi·dǒkrēˈs). 1804. [a. F., f. Gr. εἶδος form + κρᾶσις mixture.] *Min.* = VESUVIANITE.

Idol (əi·dəl, əi·d'l), *sb.* ME. [a. OF. *idole*, ad. late L. *idolum*, a. Gr. εἴδωλον, f. εἶδος form, shape.]

I. From Jewish and Christian use. 1. An image or similitude of a deity or divinity, used as an object of worship; applied to those used by pagans, whence, in scriptural language, = 'false god' (1 Cor. viii. 4). b. Applied polemically to any material object of adoration in a Christian Church 1545. 2. *fig.* Any thing or person that is the object of excessive or supreme devotion 1562.

1. Their dumb idols, whom they called by the name of the holy gods DE FOE. b. This mischievous i. the mass 1554. 2. Money, the I. of other People, was the least of his Care 1737. A hero who was the i. of his army THIRLWALL.

II. From classical Greek (and Latin) use. †1. An image, effigy, or figure of a person or thing; esp. a statue -1605. †b. A counterpart, likeness -1667. 2. An incorporeal phantom 1563. 3. A mental fiction; a phantasy 1577. b. *Logic.* = IDOLUM 2. 1678. †4. A fictitious personation; a sham; a pretender -1660. 5. *attrib.* 1585.

1. b. Th' Apostat in his Sun-bright Chariot sate I. of Majestie Divine MILT. *P. L.* VI. 101. 3. Vain idols and phantoms of blessedness 1899. b. This is but another i. of the Atheists den CUDWORTH. 5. I. shapes KEBLE.

Phr. *Idol shepherd* (Zech. xi. 17): used in 17th c. polemics, sometimes with allusion to idolatry, sometimes with *idol* taken as = 'counterfeit' or 'sham', sometimes associated with *idle*, 'neglectful of duty'. *Comb.* **i.-shell,** a tropical mollusc of the family *Ampullariidæ*.

Hence **†I·dol** *v.* (*rare*), to make an i. of; to idolize.

†Idola·ster. ME. [a. OF. *idolastre* (mod. *idolâtre*), var. of *idol-, ydolatre*; see IDOLATER.] = IDOLATER 1. -1616.

Idolater (əidǫ·lătəɹ). ME. [ad. OF. *idolatre*, mod. *idolâtre*, shortened f. eccl. L. *idololatra*, earlier *-latres*, ad. Gr. εἰδωλολάτρης (N. T.) IDOLOLATER, q.v.] 1. A worshipper of idols; one who pays divine honours to an image or representation of a god, or to any natural object as a deity. 2. An adorer, devoted admirer (*of*) 1566.

2. Old covetous men, ydolaters of their treasures 1566. var. **†Ido·latrer.** Hence **Ido·latress,** a female i. Also *fig.*

Idolatric, †-al (əidǫlæ·trik, -ăl), *a.* 1550 [ad. mod.L. *idolatricus*; see -IC and -AL.] Idolatrous.

Idolatrize (əidǫ·lătrəiz), *v.* 1592. [f. IDOLATRY + -IZE.] †1. *intr.* To worship idols; to commit idolatry -1706. 2. *trans.* To make an idol of; to worship idolatrously. Chiefly in *fig.* use. 1615. †3. To render idolatrous. CUDWORTH. Hence **Ido·latrizer.**

Idolatrous (əidǫ·lătrəs), *a.* 1550. [f. IDOLATER, F. *idolâtre* + -OUS.] 1. Of, pertaining to, or of the nature of idolatry. 2. Used in idol-worship. ? *Obs.* 1613. 3. Given to the worship of idols or false gods 1600.

1. I. veneration of the state 1863. 2. He saw an i. altar at Damascus FULLER. 3. The Philistines I., uncircumcised, unclean MILT. *Samson* 1364. Hence **Ido·latrous-ly** *adv.*, **-ness.**

Idolatry (əidǫ·lătri). ME. [a. OF. *idol-, ydolatrie*, mod. *-âtrie*, shortened f. eccl. L. *idololatria* IDOLOLATRY; see IDOL and LATRIA.] 1. The worship of idols or images 'made with hands', or of any created object. †b. *pl.* Idolatrous objects. MILT. 2. Immoderate attachment to or veneration for any person or thing; admiration savouring of adoration ME.

1. b. To worship Calves, the Deities Of Egypt..And all the Idolatries of Heathen round MILT. *P. R.* III. 418.

†I·dolish, *a.* 1530. [f. IDOL *sb.* + -ISH[1].] Heathenish; idolatrous -1641.

Idolism (əi·dǒliz'm). 1608. [f. IDOL *sb.* + -ISM.] 1. The practice of idolatry. 2. The action of idolizing; an idolization 1825. 3. A false mental image or notion; cf. EIDOLON 1671.

Idolist (əi·dǒlist). 1614. [f. as prec. + -IST.] A worshipper of idols. Also *attrib.*

Idolize (əi·dǒləiz), *v.* 1598. [f. IDOL *sb.* + -IZE.] 1. *trans.* To make an idol of, to render idolatrous worship to; hence, to adore, or love to excess. b. To make into an idol. ? *Obs.* 1669. 2. *intr.* To practise idolatry 1631.

1. They [my soldiers] do not i. me, but look upon the Cause they fight for CROMWELL. 2. To i. after the manner of Egypt 1864. Hence **I·doliza·tion. I·dolizer.**

Idolo-, comb. f. Gr. εἴδωλον IDOL, as in ‖**Idolodouli·a** [Gr. δουλεία DULIA], veneration of an inferior kind given to idols or images. **Idologra·phical** *a.* descriptive of idols. **Idolo·mancy** [Gr. μαντεία], divination by idols. **Idoloma·nia, †Idolo·many,** zealous idolatry.

Idoloclast (əidǫ·lǒklæst). 1843. [f. IDOLO- + Gr. -κλάστης, after *iconoclast.*] A breaker of idols; an iconoclast. Hence **Idolocla·stic** *a.*

†Idolo·later. 1608. [ad. eccl. L. *idololatres*, later *-latra.*] = IDOLATER. Hence **†Idolola·tric, †-al** *a.* idolatrous. So **†Idolo·latry** [eccl. L. *idololatria*, Gr. εἰδωλολατρεία] = IDOLATRY 1550.

Idolothyte (əidǫ·lǒþəit). ? *Obs.* 1562. [ad. eccl. L. *idolothytus*, a. Gr., f. εἴδωλον IDOL + θυτός sacrificed.] A. *adj.* Offered to an idol. B. *sb.* A thing offered to an idol. Chiefly *pl.* 1579.

Hence **Idolothy·tic** *a.* of or characterized by the eating of meats offered to idols. HUXLEY.

†Idolous, *a.* 1546. [f. IDOL *sb.* + -OUS.] a. Of the nature of an idol. b. Idolatrous. -1617.

‖**Idolum, -on** (əidōᵘ·lǒm, -ǫn). *Pl.* **idola** (†-aes, †-ums). 1619. [L., a. Gr. εἴδωλον IDOL.] 1. An image or unsubstantial appearance; a phantom; a mental image or idea. 2. A false mental image; a fallacy 1640.

2. What Bacon expressively termed Idola, empty assumptions and misconceptions SAYCE.

Idoneous (əidōᵘ·nɪ̆əs), *a.* Now *rare.* 1615. [f. L. *idoneus* + -OUS.] Apt, fit, suitable.

An Ecclesiastical Benefice..ought to be conferr'd on an I. Person AYLIFFE. So **Idone·ity,** fitness, suitableness, aptitude. **Ido·neousness.**

Idorgan (i·dǭɹgăn). 1883. [Arbitrarily f. ID-EAL + ORGAN.] *Biol.* An ideal or potential organism.

Idrialin (i·driălin). 1838. [a. F. *idrialin* (Dumas, 1832), f. as next + -IN.] 1. *Min.* Original name of IDRIALITE 1844. 2. *Chem.* The essential constituent of idrialite, $C_{42}H_{28}O$, forming colourless scales which melt at a very high temperature.

Idrialite (i·driăləit). 1849. [f. *Idria* in Austria, where found in the quicksilver mines; see -LITE.] *Min.* A mineral hydrocarbon, called also inflammable cinnabar.

Idyll, idyl (əi·dil). 1601. [ad. L. *idyllium*, a. Gr. εἰδύλλιον, dim. of εἶδος form, picture.] 1. A short poem, descriptive of some picturesque scene or incident, chiefly in rustic life. 2. *transf.* An episode or a series of events or circumstances suitable for an idyll 1841. 3. *Mus.* A pastoral or sentimental composition.

1. Phr. *Prose idyll*, an idyllic composition in prose. Those amatorious eidyls and eclogues of Theocritus HOLLAND. Auld Licht Idylls (*title*) BARRIE. [in prose.] 2. The pairing of the birds is an i. EMERSON. Hence **Idy·llian** (*rare*), **Idy·llic, -al** *adjs.* of, belonging to, or of the nature of an i.; forming a suitable theme for an i. **Idy·llically** *adv.* **I·dyllist. I·dyllize** *v.* to make into an i.; to render idyllic.

‖**Idy·llium, -on.** *Pl.* **idyllia** (-ums, -ons). 1579. [a. L., a. Gr.; see IDYLL.] = IDYLL.

Ie-, former sp. of JE-, as in *Iesus*, etc.; see I, the letter.

-ie, earlier form of -Y [6] suffix; in mod. use chiefly known as the Sc. spelling, now also often adopted in Eng., as in *birdie, doggie*, etc.

-ier, a suffix forming nouns designating position, employment, or profession, derived from sbs., rarely agent-nouns from vbs., (1) in words of ME. age, in which the suffix is unstressed, and varies with *-yer*, as *collier, bowyer*, (2) in words of later date, in which the suffix is stressed, and varies with -EER, as *bombardier, cashier*, etc.

1. In words of ME. age, the suffix is of obscure and app. of diverse origin. Cf. *cottier* (*cotier* = med.L. *cotarius*), *tilier, bowyer*, etc. In other words, as *carrier, courtier, currier, soldier*, the suffix is really *-er* (or earlier *-our*), the *i* belonging to the vb. stem.

2. In words of later introduction, the suffix is the F. *-ier* (:—L. *-arius*: see -ARY[1]). Many of these also occur with *-eer*, expressing the Eng. pronunciation; in some of these -EER has been established, and from them has become a living Eng. suffix, as in *auctioneer, charioteer*, etc.

‖**Ier-oe** (ĭ̄ěrōᵘ·). *Sc.* 1701. [Gael.] A great-grandchild.

If (if), *conj.* (*sb.*) [OE. *gif.* By many considered to represent one or more cases of the sb. represented by ON. *if, ifi* 'doubt, hesitation'; OHG. *iba*, 'condition, stipulation, doubt', the conj. thus meaning originally 'on condition', 'on the stipulation (that)'.]

I. Introducing a clause of condition or supposition (the protasis of a conditional sentence).

On condition that; given or granted that; in (the) case that; supposing that; on the supposition that.

1. *With the protasis in the indicative.* The indicative after *if* implies that the speaker expresses no adverse opinion as to the truth of the statement in the clause; he may accept it. 2. *With the protasis in the subjunctive, and the apodosis in the indicative or imperative.* The subjunctive after *if* implies that the speaker guards himself against endorsing the truth of the statement; he may doubt it OE. 3. *With both protasis and apodosis in the subjunctive.* Expressing a mere hypothesis. OE. 4. The conditional clause is often elliptical; thus *if not* (= if a thing is, be, or were not), formerly sometimes = 'unless, except' ME. 5. The conditional clause alone is sometimes used as an exclam. to express (*a*) a wish or determination, e.g. *If I had only known!* (sc. I would have done so-and-so); (*b*) surprise or indignation, e.g. *If ever I heard the like of that!* OE.

1. She 's six and fifty if she 's a day SHERIDAN. Declare if thou knowest it all *Job* xxxviii. 18. 2. If thou be the sonne of God, command that these stones bee made bread *Matt.* iv. 3. If euer I were Traitor, My name be blotted from the booke of Life *Rich. II*, I. iii. 201. 3. If I were you, I would not do it (*mod.*). 4. He weighed eighteen stone, if a pound 1884.

Phrases. **An if, and if** (see AN *conj.* 2) = If. *arch.* **As if,** followed by a clause containing a past subj. (sometimes ellipt.), or an infinitive expressing purpose or destination: As the case would be if; as though. **If so be (that),** if it happen that, supposing that. *arch.* and *dial.*

II. Introducing a noun-clause depending on the verb *see, ask, learn, doubt, know*, or the like: Whether OE.

Hee sent foorth a doue from him, to see if the waters were abated *Gen.* viii. 8.

B. *sb.* The conditional conjunction used as a name for itself; hence, a condition, a supposition 1513.

Thou seruest me, I wene, with iffes and with andes SIR T. MORE.

I'faith. 1420. = in faith: see FAITH *sb.* III. 2.

Ife·cks, I'fe·gs, *int. Obs.* exc. *dial.* 1610. [Perversion of prec.] Used as a trivial oath: In faith, by my faith.

I-fere: see YFERE *sb.* and *adv.*

-iferous, -ific, -ification, -ify, comb. ff. -FEROUS, -FIC, -FICATION, -FY, q. v.

†Igad, i'gad (igæ·d), *int.* 1671. Var. of EGAD -1728.

Igasuric (igăsiūᵊ·rik), *a.* 1830. [ad. F. *igasurique*, f. *igasur*, Malay name for St. Ignatius' Bean: see -IC.] *Chem.* In *i. acid*, an acid contained in small quantities in St. Ignatius' bean, *nux vomica*, and the root of *Strychnos colubrina*. So **Igasu·rate,** a salt of i. acid. **Igasu·rine,** a poisonous alkaloid found in *nux vomica*.

Igdrasil: see YGGDRASIL.

‖**Igloo** (i·glu). 1856. [Eskimo, = house.] 1. An Eskimo dome-shaped hut, esp. one built of snow. 2. The cavity in the snow above a seal's breathing-hole 1882.

†Igna·ro. 1620. [a. It.] An ignoramus -1686.

Ignatian (ignē̆ⁱ·ʃiăn), *a.* (*sb.*) 1605. [f. *Ignatius* (see def.) + -AN.] 1. Pertaining to Ignatius Loyola (1491-1556), or to the Order of Jesus founded by him. 2. Of or belonging to St. Ignatius, bishop of Antioch, martyred at Rome in the 2nd century; esp. in *I. Epistles*, letters doubtfully attributed to him 1832. 3. *sb.* A follower of Ignatius Loyola; a JESUIT 1613.

Ignatius' Bean. 1751. = Bean of St. Ignatius, the poisonous seed of *Strychnos Ignatii*.

Igneous (i·gnɪ̆əs), *a.* 1664. [f. L. *igneus* + -OUS.] 1. Of, pertaining to, or of the nature of fire; fiery. 2. Resulting from, or produced by, the action of fire; *esp.* in *Geol.* Produced by volcanic agency (opp. to AQUEOUS) 1665.

1. I. exhalations LYELL. 2. The i. origin of basalts 1796.

Ignescent (igne·sĕnt). 1828. [ad. L. *ignescentem, ignescere* to take fire.] A. *adj.* Kindling, bursting into flame; firing up. B. *sb.* An ignescent body or substance 1828.

Ignicolist (igni·kǒlist). 1816. [f. L. *ignis* + *-cola* (f. *colere* to worship) + -IST.] A fire-worshipper.

Igniferous (igni·fĕrəs), *a.* 1618. [f. L. *ignifer*, f. *ignis*; see -FEROUS.] Producing fire. Also *fig.*

†**Igni·fluous,** *a. rare.* 1623. [f. late L. *ignifluus* + -OUS.] Flowing with fire -1659.

Igniform (i·gnifǭɹm), *a. rare.* 1744. [f. L. *ignis* + -FORM.] Of the form of fire.

Ignify (i·gnifəi), *v. rare.* 1586. [f. as prec.; see -FY.] *trans.* To cause to burn.

Ignigenous (igni·dʒĕnəs), *a. rare.* 1727. [f. L. *ignigena* fire-born, f. *ignis* + *-genus*, from *gen-* (*gignere*) + -OUS.] Produced by the action of fire.

Ignipotent (igni·pǒtĕnt), *a.* 1656. [f. L. *ignipotentem* (epithet of Vulcan), f. *potens.*] Ruling or having power over fire.

Th' pow'r i. her word obeys POPE.

Ignipuncture (ignipʊ·ŋktiŭɹ). 1886. [f. L. *igni-* + PUNCTURE.] *Surg.* Puncture with a white-hot styliform cautery.

‖**Ignis fatuus** (i·gnis fæ·tiu,ʊ̆s). 1563. [med. or mod.L., = foolish fire.] A phosphorescent light seen hovering or flitting over marshy ground, supposed to be due to the spontaneous combustion of an inflammable gas (phosphuretted hydrogen) derived from decaying organic matter; pop. called *Will-o'-the-wisp*, *Jack-a-lantern*, etc. **b.** *fig.* Any delusive guiding principle, hope, aim, etc. 1599.

An *Ignis Fatuus* that bewitches And leads Men into Pools and Ditches BUTLER *Hud.* I. i. 509.

†**Ignite,** *a.* 1560. [ad. L. *ignitus*, pa. pple. of *ignire* to set on fire.] In a white or red heat; glowing with heat, fiery -1704.

Ignite (ignəi·t), *v.* 1666. [f. prec.] **1.** *trans.* To subject to the action of fire, to make intensely hot; in chemical use, to heat to the point of combustion or chemical change. **2.** To set fire to, to kindle; also *fig.* 1823. **3.** *intr.* To take fire; to begin to burn 1818.

1. A piece of the substance was ignited to whiteness 1795. 2. To i. a lamp TYNDALL. 3. The gas ignited 1885. Hence **Igni·table, -ible,** *a.* capable of being ignited. **Igni·ter,** one who or that which ignites.

Ignition (igni·ʃən). 1612. [f. med. or mod.L. *ignitionem.*] **1.** The action of igniting; *esp.* Heating to the point of combustion, or of chemical change; the condition of being so heated or on fire. **2.** The action of setting fire to anything; the process of taking fire; also, *loosely*, burning 1816. **b.** A means of igniting. GREENER. **c.** The process or the means of igniting the mixture in the cylinder of an internal combustion engine 1894.

Ignivomous (igni·vǒməs), *a.* 1603. [f. late L. *ignivomus*, f. *ignis* + *vomere*; see -OUS.] Vomiting fire; also *fig.*

Ignobility (ignəbi·lĭti). 1483. [ad. L. *ignobilitas*, f. *ignobilis*, after *nobility*; see -ITY.] The quality of being ignoble.

Ignoble (ignōu·b'l), *a.* 1494. [a. F., ad. L. *ignobilis*, f. I-[2] = *in-* not + *gnobilis*, *nobilis* NOBLE.] **1.** Of persons: Not noble in respect of birth, position, or reputation; of low birth or humble station. Also of animals, things, places, etc. **2.** Not noble in disposition, nature, or quality; dishonourable 1592.

1. I was not i. of Descent SHAKS. Any i. occupation JOWETT. The old division of noble and i. hawks R. MUDIE. (*Note.* The term 'ignoble' was applied to the short-winged hawks, e.g. the goshawk and the sparrow-hawk, which rake after the quarry, as dist. from the long-winged falcons, which stoop to the quarry at a single swoop.) This Clermont is a meane and i. place CORYAT. 2. Thus Belial..Counsel'd i. ease MILT. *P.L.* II. 227. Hence **Igno·bleness. Igno·bly** *adv.*

Ignoble (ignōu·b'l), *v. rare.* 1590. [f. prec., as the opposite to ENNOBLE.] *trans.* To make ignoble or infamous. Also *fig.*

Ignominious (ignǒmi·niəs), *a.* 1450. [a. F. *ignominieux*, or ad. L. *ignominiosus.*] **1.** Full of ignominy; involving shame, disgrace, or obloquy; discreditable. Also sometimes: Lowering to one's dignity or self-respect. **2.** Of persons: Covered with, or deserving, ignominy; infamous 1577.

1. The i. terms of peace were rejected with disdain GIBBON. 2. Then first with fear surpris'd and sense of paine, Fled i. MILT. *P.L.* VI. 395. Hence **Igno·mi·nious·ly** *adv.*, **-ness.** So †**Igno·mious** *a.* 1574.

Ignominy (i·gnǒmini). 1540. [a. F. *ignominie*, ad. L. *ignominia*, f. I-[2] = *in-* not + **gnomen*, *nomen.*] **1.** Dishonour, disgrace, infamy; the condition of being in disgrace, etc. **2.** Ignominious or base quality or conduct; that which entails disgrace 1564.

1. Even his successes had been purchased with i. THIRLWALL. 2. [Death is] the very disgrace and i. of our natures SIR T. BROWNE. So †**I·gnomy** 1534.

Igno·rable, *a.* [ad. L. *ignorabilis.*] Capable of being ignored; of which one may be ignorant. FERRIER.

Ignoramus (ignǒrē·mʊ̆s). *Pl.* **-uses** (-ʊ̆sėz), also †**-us.** 1577. [L., = 'we do not know', (in legal use) 'we take no notice of (it)'.] †**1.** The endorsement formerly made by a Grand Jury upon a bill or indictment, when they considered the evidence insufficient to warrant the case going to a petty jury. Hence quasi-*sb.*, or *ellipt.* Also *transf.* an answer which admits ignorance of the point in question; *fig.* a state of ignorance. (The endorsement now used is 'not a true bill', or 'not found', or 'no bill'.) **b.** *attrib.* as in *i. jury*, *crew*, *Whig* (alluding to the Grand Jury which rejected the bill against the Earl of Shaftesbury, 1681). **2.** An ignorant person. [f. *Ignoramus*, used as a name for a lawyer. See N.E.D.] 1616.

1. As for Medusa's brother I return i. 1658. 2. I. and Dulman his Clearke 1634. Hence †**Ignora·mus'd** *ppl. a.* freed from prosecution by the *ignoramus* of the Grand Jury 1734.

Ignorance (i·gnǒrăns). ME. [a. F., ad. L. *ignorantia*, f. *ignorantem.*] **1.** The fact or condition of being ignorant; want of knowledge (general or special). Also with *an* and *pl.* (*rare*) 1749. †**2.** With *an* and *pl.* An act due to want of knowledge; an offence or sin caused by ignorance -1611.

1. Marvell is the daughter of Ignorance 1573. National i. of decent art RUSKIN. 2. Our ignorances haue reached vp vnto heauen 1 *Esdras* viii. 75. So †**I·gnorancy** (in sense 1) 1526.

Ignorant (i·gnǒrănt), *a.* (*sb.*) ME. [a. F., ad. L. *ignorans*, *ignorantem*; see IGNORE.] **1.** Destitute of knowledge; unknowing, unlearned. Also *fig.* or *transf.* of things. **2.** with *of*: Having no knowledge of; hence †unconscious of, innocent of, having no share in 1483. **3.** *transf.* Resulting from ignorance 1509. †**b.** That keeps one in ignorance. SHAKS. †**4.** Of things: Unknown -1634. **5.** *sb.* An ignorant person (now *rare*) 1480.

1. There were..none so i. as not to know his deeds MOTLEY. *fig. Cymb.* III. i. 27. 2. Of cards and dice they are happily i. 1615. 3. Alas, what i. sin haue I committed *Oth.* IV. ii. 70. b. *Wint. T.* I. ii. 397. 4. Whence he is, tis i. to vs CHAPMAN. 5. Church authorities..too often entrust their buildings to ignorants 1874.

Ignorantine (ignǒræ·ntin), *a.* and *sb.* 1861. [ad. F. *ignorantin*, f. *ignorant* IGNORANT, after *capucin*, etc.; see -INE.] *I. friars*, *Ignorantines*: a name taken by the Brethren of Saint-Jean-de-Dieu, an order founded in 1495 to minister to the sick poor; they subsequently devoted themselves to the instruction of the poor. Hence, the name is given in France to the 'Brethren of the Christian Schools' or 'Christian Brothers', a community founded *c* 1680, for the education of the poor.

I·gnorantism. *rare.* 1856. [f. IGNORANT + -ISM.] = OBSCURANTISM. So **I·gnorantist.**

Ignorantly (i·gnǒrăntli), *adv.* 1495. [f. as prec. + -LY[2].] In an ignorant manner; without knowledge.

Whom ye then i. worship, hym shewe I vnto you TINDALE *Acts* xvii. 23.

Ignoratio elenchi: see next, 3.

Ignoration (ignorē·ʃən). 1588. [ad. L. *ignorationem.*] †**1.** The fact or condition of being ignorant 1612. **2.** The action of ignoring; the being ignored 1865. **3.** *Ignoration of the Elench*, repr. scholastic L. **Ignoratio elenchi** (ignorē·ʃio ile·ŋkəi), a logical fallacy consisting in disproving some statement different from that advanced by an opponent; also extended to any argument irrelevant to the object in view 1588.

Ignore (ignōə·ɹ), *v.* 1611. [ad. F. *ignorer*, or L. *ignorare* not to know, to disregard, f. I-[2], *in-* not + **gnorare*, f. stem *gno-* to know (cf. *gnarus*).] **1.** *trans.* To be ignorant of. *Obs.* or *rare.* **2.** Said of a Grand Jury: To return (a bill) with the endorsement 'not found' (see IGNORAMUS 1); to refuse acceptance of 1830. **3.** To refuse to take notice of; to leave out of consideration, shut one's eyes to 1801.

1. The little that I know, and they i. BOYLE. 3. To i. an invitation 1832, an important feature of necessary evidence FROUDE.

†**Ignote.** 1623. [ad. L. *ignotus.*] **a.** *adj.* Unknown. **b.** *sb.* A person unknown.

a. Th' i. are better than ill known COWLEY.

Iguana (igwā·nă). 1555. [a. Sp. *iguana*, repr. Carib name *iwana.*] A large arboreal lizard of the W. Indies and S. America, *I. tuberculata*, which attains to a length of five feet or more; also, in Zool., the name of the genus, which includes the *horned i.* of San Domingo, and other species; loosely applied to lizards of allied genera. Hence **Igua·nian** *a.* resembling an i., belonging to the i. family *Iguanidæ*; *sb.* one of this family; also **Igua·nid. Igua·noid** *a.* and *sb.* = *iguanian.*

Iguanodon (igwæ·nǒdǫn). 1830. [f. prec. + Gr. ὀδούς, ὀδοντ-, after *mastodon*, etc.] *Palæont.* A large herbivorous lizard found fossil in the Wealden formation; it was from 25 to 30 feet long, and its teeth and bones resembled those of the iguana; whence the name. So **Iguano·dont** *a.* having teeth like those of the iguana; *sb.* a saurian so characterized; one of the family *Iguanodontidæ* of extinct dinosaurs, typified by the i.

‖**Ihram** (irā·m, iχrā·m). Also †**hir(r)awem.** 1704. [Arab. *iḥrām*, f. *ḥarama* to forbid.] **1.** The dress worn by Mohammedan pilgrims, consisting of two pieces of white cotton. **2.** The state in which a pilgrim is held to be while he wears this garb, during which many acts are unlawful 1704.

IHS, in ME., med.L., etc., repr. a Greek MS. abbrev. of the word IH(ΣΟΥ)Σ, Jesus; also used as a symbol or monogram of the sacred name.

Often looked upon as a Latin contraction, and explained variously as standing for *Iesus Hominum Salvator*, Jesus Saviour of men, *In Hoc Signo* (*vinces*), in this sign (thou shalt conquer), or *In Hac Salus*, in this (cross) is salvation.

Ik, ME. form of I *pron.*

Il-[1], assim. form of the prefix IN-[2] before initial *l*, as in *il-lation*, etc. See IN-[2].

Il-[2], assim. form of the neg. prefix IN-[3] before initial *l*, as in *il-legal*, etc.; also ILLOGICAL.

-il, -ile, *suffixes*, repr. L. *-ilis* and *-ĭlis*, forming adjs., and occas. sbs., as in *fossilis* fossil, *agilis* agile. These suffixes are in origin the same, viz. *-lis* with connective *-i-*, which with *-i-* stems as *civi-s*, etc. gave *-īlis*. The mod. tendency is to pronounce (-əil), with some exceptions, in all cases.

†**Ile**[1]. 1601. [ad. L. *ile* or *ileum.*] = ILEUM -1656.

Ile[2], var. of AIL *sb.*[2], awn of barley, etc.

Ile, obs. f. ILL, ISLE, AISLE.

I·leac, *a.* 1822. A refash. of ILIAC *a.* after L. *ileus*, or ILEUM.

Ileitis (ili,əi·tis). 1855. [f. ILEUM + -ITIS.] *Path.* Inflammation of the ileum.

Ileo-, comb. f. ILEUM; as,

Ileo-cæ·cal *a.*, relating to or connected with the ileum and the cæcum; as in *ileo-cæcal valve*, a valve consisting of two semilunar folds at the opening of the ileum into the cæcum; the name is occas. restricted to the lower of these. **Ileo-co·lic** *a.*, relating to or connected with the ileum and the colon; *ileo-colic valve* = *ileo-cæcal valve* (sometimes restricted to the upper fold of this). **Ileo-coli·tis,** inflammation of the ileum and colon.

†**I·leon.** 1495. [med.L. (in Gr. form).] = ILEUM -1767.

‖**Ileum** (i·li,ʊ̆m, əi·-). 1682. [Late or med. L. Cl. L. had only *ilia* (pl. of *ile* or *ilium*). The form *ileum* (*ileon*, *-os*) is app. due to a confusion of this with *ileus* (see next).] *Anat.* The third portion of the small intestine, succeeding the jejunum and opening into the cæcum.

‖**Ileus** (i·li,ʊ̆s, əi·-). 1706. [L. *ileus*, *ileos*, a. Gr. ἰλεός or εἰλεός colic, app. f. εἴλειν to roll.] **1.** *Path.* A painful affection due to intestinal obstruction, esp. in the ileum; also called *iliac passion.* **2.** *Anat.* = ILEUM 1706.

Ilex (əi·leks). ME. [a. L.] **1.** The holm-oak or evergreen oak (*Quercus Ilex*). Also *attrib.* ‖**2.** In mod. Botany, a genus of *Aquifoliaceæ*, including the common holly (*I. Aquifolium*), and numerous other trees 1565.

Iliac (i·liǣk), *a.* (*sb.*) 1519. [a. F. *iliaque*, or ad. late L. *iliacus*; the L. is in form a deriv. of *ilia*, but the suffix is Gr. (-ακός), and the sense goes with L. *ileus*, Gr. εἰλεός, ἰλεός colic.] **1.** Properly, Of the nature of the disease called ILEUS; but taken as = Pertaining to or affecting the ILEUM. **2.** Pertaining to the flank, or to the ilium or flank-bone 1541. **3.** *sb.* Short for *i. passion* (*Obs.*); also for *i. artery*, etc. 1782.

1. *Iliac passion* [late L. *passio iliaca*] = ILEUS 1. 2. *I. artery*, each of the two arteries, right and left, into which the abdominal aorta divides. *I. bone*, the ilium. So †**Ili·acal** *a.* = ILIAC *a.*

Iliad (i·liǣd). 1579. [ad. L. *Ilias, Iliad-*, a. Gr. Ἰλιάς, sc. ποίησις, the Iliad; f. Ἴλιος, Ἴλιον Ilium, Ilion, Troy.] **1.** A great epic poem of ancient Greece traditionally attributed to Homer, describing the ten years' siege of Ilium or Troy by the Greeks. **2.** *transf.* and *fig.* **a.** An epic poem like that of Homer 1619. **b.** A long series of disasters or the like (Gr. Ἰλιὰς κακῶν, Demosthenes); a long story 1609.

2. b. It opens another I. of woes to Europe BURKE. Hence **I·liadist**, a rhapsodist; a writer of Iliads.

Ilicic (əili·sik), *a.* 1861. [f. L. *ilex, ilicem* (see ILEX 2) + -IC.] *Chem.* Of or pertaining to the holly; in *i. acid*, an acid contained in the leaves of the holly. So **I·licate**, a salt of i. acid. **I·licin**, the non-nitrogenous bitter principle of the holly.

Ilio- (i·lio), comb. f. ILIUM 3; as,

Ilio-do·rsal *a.*, relating to the dorsum of the ilium. ‖**Iliopso·as**, the iliac and psoas muscles regarded as one muscle. Esp. in comb. with adjs. relating to other parts of the body with sense 'relating to or connecting the ilium and..', as **ilio-fe·moral, -lu·mbar, -perone·al** [Gr. περόνη fibula] (applied to muscles connecting the ilium and the fibula; also as *sb.*), etc.

Ilion, obs. var. of ILIUM.

-ility, compound suffix (F. *-ilité*, L. *-ilitas*), consisting of -ITY added to adjs. in *-il* (*civility*), *-ile* (*servility*), or *-le* (*ability*).

Ilium (i·liŏm). *Pl.* **ilia.** Also formerly **ilion**, *pl.* **ilia.** ME. [L. *ilium*; in cl. L. only in pl. *ilia* flanks, sides, also entrails. See also ILEUM.] *Anat.* †**1.** The ILEUM –1827. †**2.** *pl.* The flanks (L. *ilia*) –1706. **3.** The anterior or superior bone of the pelvis, the hip-bone; usually (as in man) articulating with the sacrum, and anchylosing with the ischium and pubis, forming together with these latter the *os innominatum* 1706.

Ilixanthin (əiliksæ·nþin). 1865. [f. ILEX holly + ξανθός yellow + -IN.] *Chem.* A yellow colouring matter obtained from the holly.

Ilk (ilk), *a.*[1] (*pron.*) Now *Sc.* [OE. *ilca* m., *ilce* f. and n., app. f. the pronominal stem *i-, ī-* (cf. L. *i-s, i-dem*) + *-līc* = Goth. *-leiks* (see LIKE).] †**1.** Same, identical –1556. †**2.** *absol. The, that ilk*: the same (person or persons, or thing) –1650.

Phr. *Of that ilk*, of the same place, territorial designation, or name; as *Wemyss of that i.* = Wemyss of Wemyss. *Sc.* Hence *ilk* is erron. used for 'family, class, set'; any member of that ilk 1845.

Ilk, *a.*[2] (*pron.*) Now *Sc.* OE. [North. and midl. form of *ilch, iche* = south. *ælch, æche*, EACH.] = EACH 1 a; every.

Ill (il), *a.* and *sb.* [Early ME. (*a* 1200) *ill*, a. ON. *illr* ill, bad, etc. Ult. etym. unkn.; not conn., though synonymous, w. OE. *yfel* EVIL. Now used less as an adj. than as an adverb; and several senses of the adj. survive only in arch. use or in particular collocations.]

A. *adj.* **1.** Morally evil; wicked, vicious, blameworthy. **b.** Imputing or implying evil 1483. **2.** Malevolent, unfriendly, unkind, harsh, cruel ME. **3.** Doing or tending to do harm; hurtful; dangerous ME. **4.** Causing pain, discomfort, or inconvenience; offensive, objectionable ME. **5.** Of conditions, fortune, etc.: Wretched, unlucky; unfavourable, disastrous ME. **6.** Difficult, troublesome. (Usu. with *dative inf.*, as 'ill to please'.) ME. **7.** In privative sense: Not good ME. **8.** Of health, etc.: Unsound, disordered. Hence, of persons, etc.: Out of health, not well; almost always used predicatively. (The prevailing mod. sense.) 1460.

1. I. company 1680, actions BUTLER, habits LANDOR. b. He that hath an yll name, is halfe hangd 1546. 2. I. tongues SHELLEY, offices MACAULAY. 3. There's some i. Planet raignes SHAKS. *I. weeds grow apace* Provb. 4. Great raine and yll wether HALL. 5. Woe vnto the wicked, it shall be i. with him *Isa.* iii. 11. *It's an i. wind that blows nobody good* Provb. 7. I am i. at these Numbers SHAKS. I. Manners occasion Good laws FULLER. 8. My eye was very red and i., in the morning PEPYS. Children are well and i. in a day 1849.

Phrases (often unnecessarily hyphened): **i. desert**, demerit, blameworthiness (so *i. deserving*); **i. ease**, discomfort; **i. fame** (see 1 b.); esp. in *house of i. fame*; **i. grace** (see GRACE *sb.*); **i. part** (see PART *sb.*); **i. success**, imperfect success (sense 6); often = failure (cf. 5); **i. temper** (see TEMPER *sb.*). See also Main Words.

B. *sb.* [the adj. used absol.] **1.** = EVIL *sb.* 1 a; the opposite of good ME. **2.** Moral evil; wickedness, sin, wrong-doing (*arch.*) ME. †**b.** A wicked act –1741. **3.** Something blameful, unfavourable, unfriendly, or injurious. (Perh. orig. the adv.) ME. **4.** Evil as caused; harm, injury, mischief ME. **5.** Evil as suffered; misfortune, disaster, trouble, distress; (with *pl.*) a calamity, etc. ME. **6.** Bodily disorder. (Chiefly *Sc.*) ME.

1. Great good must have great i. as opposite 1605. 2. Forgive..The i. that I this day have done KEN. 3. I can think no i. of him (*mod.*). 4. Loue worketh no i. to his neighbour *Rom.* xiii. 10. 5. To know if good or i. shall befall them 1660. No sense have they of ills to come GRAY. 6. An i. no doctor could unravel SHELLEY.

Ill (il), *adv.* [Early ME. *ille*, f. ILL *a.*] In an ill manner; badly.

Phr. *To speak, think*, etc. *i.* (*of*); *to like i., to take i. I. at ease* (see EASE *sb.*). *I.-to-do*: in poor circumstances. *I.-off*: badly off (the opposite of *well-off*: see OFF). My youth i.-spent 1601. I. fares the land..Where wealth accumulates, and men decay GOLDSM. He.. behaved extremely i. 1793. We can i. spare him 1832.

Ill (il), *v.* Now *dial.* ME. [f. ILL *a.*] † **1.** *trans.* To harm, wrong –1614. **2.** To speak ill of 1530.

I'll, formerly †**Ile**, abbrev. of *I will.* 1591.

Ill-, in comb.

A. General uses. **I.** From ILL *a.* See ILL BLOOD, ILL BREEDING, etc.

II. From ILL *sb.* See ILL-WILLER, -WILLING, -WISH, -WISHER, etc.; also *ill-deceived* (deceived by evil).

III. From ILL *adv.* 1. With verbs, as ILL-TREAT, ILL-USE. 2. With adjs. derived from verbs, as *ill-manageable*, etc. 3. With pres. pples., or adjs. of ppl. form, forming adjs., as *ill-according*; ILL-FARING, -JUDGING, -LOOKING, etc. 4. With pa. pples., or adjs. of the same form, forming adjs., as ILL-AFFECTED, -DISPOSED, -GOT, -GOTTEN, etc.; ILL-ADVISED, -BRED, -SORTED, etc.

IV. Parasynthetic combs., in which *ill-* is sometimes of adverbial, sometimes of adjectival origin. See ILL-CONDITIONED, -FAVOURED, -HUMOURED, -MANNERED, -NATURED, -STARRED, -TEMPERED, -TONGUED, etc.

B. Special Combs.: **ill-accu·stomed** *a.*, (*a*) little habituated to something; (*b*) little frequented by customers; **ill-born** *a.*, of evil birth or origin; **ill-content, -contented** *adjs.*, discontented, †displeased; **ill-fashioned** *a.*, of an i. fashion, or badly fashioned; **ill-friended** *a.*, ill provided with friends; **ill-lived** (-ləivd) *a.*, leading a bad or immoral life; etc.

†**Illa·bile**, *a. rare.* 1740. [f. IL-[2] + LABILE.] Not liable to slip, fall, or err; infallible. CHEYNE.

†**Illa·borate**, *a. rare.* 1631. [ad. late L. *illaboratus.*] Unlaboured; unfinished –1751.

†**Illa·chrymable**, *a. rare.* 1623. [ad. L. *illacrimabilis.*] Unmoved by tears; incapable of weeping. (Dicts.)

Ill-advi·sed, *a.* 1592. [ILL- III. 4.] Done without wise consideration, injudicious; *occas.*, ill-counselled, following bad advice. Hence **Ill-advi·sedly** *adv.*

Ill-affe·cted, *a.* 1596. [ILL- III. 4.] †**1.** Affected with illness; diseased –1727. **2.** Unfriendly, disaffected 1596. Hence **Ill-affe·ctedness.**

†**Illa·psable**, *a.* [f. IL-[2] + LAPSABLE.] Not liable to fall. GLANVILL.

Illapse (ilæ·ps, ill-), *sb.* Now *rare.* 1614. [ad. L. *illapsus*, f. *illabi* to slip, etc. in; see IL-[1] and LAPSE.] **1.** The act of gliding, slipping, or falling in, of gently sinking into or permeating something. **2.** A gentle gliding movement (*rare*) 1835.

1. Praying for the i. of the Holy Ghost 1881.

Illapse (ilæ·ps, ill-), *v.* Now *rare.* 1666. [f. L. *illapsus*, pa. pple. of *illabi.*] *intr.* To fall, glide, or slip in.

The illapsing of Souls into prepared Matter HALE.

†**Illa·queable**, *a.* [See ILLAQUEATE and -BLE.] Capable of being ensnared. CUDWORTH.

Illaqueate (ilæ·kwi,e¹t), *v.* ? *Obs.* 1548. [f. L. *illaqueat-, illaqueare*, f. *il-* (IL-[1]) + *laqueare*, f. *laqueus* noose, snare.] *trans.* To catch as in a noose; to ensnare, entangle.

Let not..his scholastic retiary versatility of logic i. your good sense COLERIDGE. So †**Illa·queate** *ppl. a.* ensnared. **Illaquea·tion**, the action of catching or entangling in a noose; the being ensnared; also, 'a snare' (J.).

Illation (ilē¹·ʃən). 1533. [ad. late L. *illationem*, f. *inferre, illatum*, to bring in, INFER.] **1.** The action of drawing a conclusion from premisses; hence, an inference, deduction, or conclusion. **2.** *Eccl.* The Eucharistic Preface to the *Ter-sanctus.* 1863.

1. In the process of syllogising there is not really an i. or inference AUSTIN.

Illative (ilē¹·tiv). 1591. [ad. late L. *illativus*, f. *illat-* (see prec.).]

A. *adj.* **1.** Of words: Introducing or stating an inference; esp. in *illative particle* 1611. **2.** Of the nature of an illation; inferential 1637. **3.** Of, pertaining to, or characterized by illation 1870.

3. The Ratiocinative or I. Sense J. H. NEWMAN.

†**B.** *sb.* An illative particle –1659; an illative clause –1651. Hence **Illa·tively** *adv.*

Illaudable (ilǭ·dăb'l), *a.* 1589. [ad. late L. *illaudabilis.*] Not laudable; unworthy of praise or commendation. Hence **Illau·dably** *adv. rare.*

I·ll-being. 1840. [f. ILL *adv.* + BEING *vbl. sb.*] The antithesis of *well-being.* CARLYLE.

Ill blood, i·ll-bloo·d. 1624. [See ILL *a.* 2, and BLOOD *sb.* II. 2.] Unfriendly feeling, animosity; strife.

I·ll-bo·ding, *a.* [ILL- II.] That bodes evil; of evil omen. *1 Hen. VI*, IV. v. 6.

Ill-bred, *a.* 1622. [f. ILL *adv.* + BRED *ppl. a.*] **1.** Badly brought up; unmannerly, rude. †**2.** Of a bad breed. *rare.* 1796. So **Ill breeding, i·ll-bree·ding**, bad bringing up; hence, bad manners, rudeness.

Ill-condi·tioned, *a.* 1614. [f. *ill condition* + -ED[2].] Having bad qualities; in a bad condition or state; now usually, of an evil disposition, malignant. In Geometry, applied to a triangle which has very unequal angles.

I·ll-dee·dy, *a.* Now *Sc.* 1460. [f. *ill deed* + -Y[1].] Given to evil deeds; mischievous.

Ill-dispo·sed, *a.* ME. [f. ILL *adv.* + DISPOSED.] **1.** Having a bad disposition; wicked; malignant, malevolent; unpropitious. †**2.** Unwell, indisposed –1645. **3.** Badly arranged 1726. **4.** Disinclined (*to do* something). GOLDSM.

†**Illecebra·tion.** *rare.* 1624. [f. late L. *illecebrare*, f. *illecebra* charm, lure.] The action of alluring; enticement –1704. So †**Ille·cebrous** *a.* alluring, enticing 1531.

†**Ille·ct**, *v. rare.* 1529. [f. L. *illect-, illicere* to allure.] *trans.* To allure, entice –1534.

Illegal (ilī·găl), *a.* 1626. [a. F. *illégal*, or ad. med.L. *illegalis*; see IL-[2].] Not legal; contrary to, or forbidden by, law.

They have set aside a return as i. *Junius Lett.* I. commerce 1817. Hence **Ille·gal·ly** *adv.*, **-ness.**

Illegality (iligæ·lĭti). 1639. [See prec. and -ITY.] **1.** The quality or condition of being illegal; also, an instance of this. †**2.** = ILLEGITIMACY. Fielding.

1. The I. of Ship-money CLARENDON.

Illegible (ile·dʒib'l), *a.* 1640. [f. IL-[2] + LEGIBLE.] Not legible; undecipherable. †**b.** Unreadable, because of language or matter –1828.

I. writing RUSKIN. b. Sir Michael Scott, again—being all magic, witchcraft, and mystery—is absolutely i. 1828. Hence **Illegibi·lity. Ille·gibly** *adv.*

Illegitimacy (ilĭdʒi·timăsi). 1680. [f. next; see -ACY.] The quality or state of not being legitimate; *spec.* bastardy.

Illegitimate (ilĭdʒi·timĕt), *a.* (*sb.*) 1536. [f. L. *illegitimus*, after LEGITIMATE *a.*] 1. Not legitimate, not in accordance with law; unauthorized; spurious; irregular, improper 1645. 2. *spec.* a. Not born in lawful wedlock; spurious, bastard. (The earliest sense in Eng.) 1536. b. Not correctly deduced or inferred; illogical 1599. c. Naturally or physiologically abnormal 1615. 3. *sb.* A bastard 1583.

1. I. government BURKE, curiosity 1876. 2. a. I am a Bastard..in euery thing i. SHAKS. b. O i. construction SHAKS. c. These i. plants, as they may be called, are not fully fertile DARWIN. Hence **Ille·gi·timately** *adv.* 1633. **Illegitima·tion**, the action, or an act, of declaring i.; † = ILLEGITIMACY 1553.

Illegitimate (ilĭdʒi·timeit), *v.* 1611. [f. prec.] *trans.* To declare or pronounce illegitimate; to bastardize. So **Illegi·timatize** *v.*, **Illegi·timize** *v.*

Illeism (i·lĭ,iz'm). 1809. [f. L. *ille* he; after *egoism*.] Excessive use of the pronoun *he*. COLERIDGE. So **I·lleist.**

†**Ille·viable**, *a. rare.* 1642. [f. IL-² + LEVIABLE.] That cannot be levied –1706.

Illfare (i·l,fēəɹ). ME. [f. ILL *a.* + FARE *sb.*¹] The condition of getting on badly; the opposite of *welfare*.

Ill-faring, *a.* 1400. [f. ILL *adv.* + FARING *ppl. a.*] Faring badly.

Ill-fa·ted, *a.* 1710. 1. Having or destined to an evil fate. 2. Fraught with bad fortune 1715.

Ill-fa·voured, -ored, *a.* 1530. *Sc.* ill-fa(u)rd, etc. [f. ILL *a.* + FAVOUR *sb.* + -ED².] Having an unpleasing appearance; ill-looking, uncomely; *transf.* offensive; objectionable.

The seuen thin and ill fauoured kine *Gen.* xli. 27. Democracy is an ill-favoured word to English ears 1865. Hence **Ill fa·voured-ly** *adv.*, **-ness.**

Ill-got, *a.* 1593. [f. ILL *adv.* + *got*, pa. pple. of GET *v.*] = next.

Things ill got had ever bad success SHAKS.

Ill-go·tten, *a.* 1552. [f. ILL *adv.* + *gotten*, pa. pple. of GET *v.*] Gained by evil means; *esp.* in *i. goods.*

Ill humour, i·ll-hu·mour. 1568. [Prop. two wds.: ILL *a.* + HUMOUR *sb.*] †1. A disordered bodily humour (see HUMOUR *sb.* 2) –1665. 2. A disagreeable mood; crossness, sullenness, bad temper. (Often hyphened.) 1748. Hence **I·ll-hu·moured** *a.*, **-ly** *adv.*

Illiberal (ili·bĕrăl, ill-), *a.* (*sb.*) 1535. [a. F., ad. L. *illiberalis*, f. *il-* (IL-²) + *liberalis*.] 1. Not befitting a free man; not pertaining to or acquainted with the liberal arts (see LIBERAL), unscholarly; ill-bred, ungentlemanly; base, mean, vulgar, rude. 2. Not generous in respect to the opinions, rights, or liberty of others; narrow-minded, bigoted; opposed to liberal principles 1649. 3. Not free in giving; stingy 1623. 4. *sb.* One who is not liberal; one opposed to Liberalism in politics 1818.

1. I. Latin CHESTERF., occupation JOWETT. 2. Popery..of the most..i. kind ROBERTSON. 3. An over-sparing or i. Hand 1695. 4. I am a violent I.; but it does not follow that I must be a Conservative RUSKIN. Hence **Illi·beralism, Illi·beralness**, illiberality, i. principles. **Illibera·lity**, the quality of being i. **Illi·beralize** *v.* to render i. **Illi·berally** *adv.*

Illicit (ili·sit, ill-), *a.* 1652. [a. F. *illicite*, ad. L. *illicitus*, f. *il-* (IL-²) + *licitus, licere* to be allowed.] Not authorized or allowed; improper, irregular; *esp.* not sanctioned by law, rule, or custom; unlawful, forbidden.

I. commerce 1748, love 1806, distillation MCCULLOCH. *Illicit process* (Logic): the fallacy in which a term not distributed in the premisses of a syllogism is distributed in the conclusion 1827. Hence **Illi·cit-ly** *adv.*, **-ness.** So †**Illi·citous** *a.* 1611.

†**Illiga·tion.** [ad. L. *illigationem*, f. (ult.) *il-* (IL-¹) + *ligare* to bind.] Entanglement. FELTHAM.

†**Illi·ghten**, *v.* 1555. [app. altered f. *alighten* (see ALIGHT *v.*³), after *illuminate*, etc.] *trans.* To illuminate, enlighten (*lit.* and *fig.*) –1693.

Illimitable (ili·mităb'l, ill-), *a.* (*sb.*) 1596. [f. IL-² + LIMITABLE.] 1. That cannot be limited; having no determinable limits; boundless. 2. *sb.* That which is illimitable 1884.

1. The heauens i. hight SPENSER. Hence **Illi·mitabi·lity, Illi·mitableness**, boundlessness. **Illi·mitably** *adv.*

†**Illi·mitate**, *a.* 1602. [ad. late L. *illimitatus*, f. *il-* (IL-²) + *limitare*.] Unlimited, unbounded –1640.

Illimitation (ilimitē¹·ʃən). *rare.* 1610. [f. IL-² + LIMITATION.] The condition or fact of being free from limitation.

Illimited (ili·mitĕd, ill-), *a.* 1602. [f. IL-² + LIMITED.] Not limited; unrestrained.

Some plead for an i. toleration of all Religions 1645. Hence **Illi·mited·ly** *adv.*, **-ness.**

Illinition (ilini·ʃən). Also *erron.* **-ation.** 1678. [f. L. *illinire*, late var. of *illinere* to smear.] 1. A smearing or rubbing in or on, of ointment, liniment, etc.; *concr.* that which is smeared or rubbed in 1684. 2. *transf.* †a. A calcining process, in which metals were anointed with certain solutions –1683. b. *concr.* A thin crust or coating of extraneous matter on the surface of metals, etc. 1796.

2. b. A thin crust or i. of black manganese KIRWAN.

†**Illiqua·tion.** 1612. [f. *il-* (IL-¹) + *liquatio* melting.] *Chem.* The melting or infusing of one substance into another –1678.

Illiquid (ili·kwid, ill-), *a.* 1694. [f. IL-² + LIQUID.] *Law.* Of a right, debt, or claim: Not clear or manifest; not ascertained or legally constituted. Of an asset, etc.: Not easily realizable. Hence **Illiqui·dity.**

I·llish, *a. rare.* 1637. [-ISH¹.] Somewhat unwell.

Illision (ili·ʒən, ill-). Now *rare.* 1603. [ad. L. *illisionem*, f. *illidere*.] The action of striking against something.

Illiteracy (ili·tĕrăsi). 1660. [f. ILLITERATE; see -ACY.] The quality or condition of being illiterate; ignorance of letters; absence of education; *esp.* inability to read and write. b. An error due to want of learning. POPE.

To reform the i. of the clergy WARTON. Comparative i., as tested by marks instead of names 1888.

Illiteral (ili·tĕrăl, ill-), *a.* 1765. [f. IL-² + LITERAL.] Not literal.

Illiterate (ili·tĕrĕt), *a.* (*sb.*) 1556. [ad. L. *illitteratus* (*illit-*), f. *il-* (IL-²) + *litteratus* (*lit-*) learned, liberally educated (see LITERATE).] 1. a. Of persons: Ignorant of letters or literature; without education; *spec.* (in reference to census returns, voting by ballot, etc.) Unable to read, i.e. totally illiterate. b. Of things: Characterized by ignorance of letters, or absence of learning or education 1597. 2. In L. sense: Not written upon; not expressed in words (*rare*) 1645. 3. *sb.* An illiterate, unlearned, or uneducated person; *spec.* one unable to read 1628.

1. a. The I. fishermen of Galilee E. IRVING. b. Bookless or i. religions MAX MÜLLER. 3. In Ireland the illiterates were 21 per cent. of the electors 1893. So †**Illi·terated** *a.* = prec. 1. Hence **Illi·terate-ly** *adv.*, **-ness. Illi·terature**, illiteracy; want of learning 1592.

Ill-judged, *a.* 1717. [f. ILL *adv.* + *judged*.] Done without judgement, injudicious.

An ill-judged economy 1828 So **I·ll-ju·dging** *a.* judging malevolently; judging mistakenly; uncritical; injudicious.

†**Ill-looked**, *a.* 1636. [f. ILL *a.* + LOOK *sb.* + -ED².] Having evil looks; ill-looking, ugly –1821. So **I·ll-loo·king** *a.* of evil or repulsive appearance, ugly 1633.

Ill luck, i·ll-lu·ck. 1548. [f. ILL *a.* 5 + LUCK *sb.*] Unfavourable luck; bad fortune, misfortune. Also *attrib.* MILT.

Ill-ma·nnered, *a.* ME. [f. ILL *a.* + MANNER *sb.* + -ED².] Unmannerly, rude. Hence **I·ll-ma·nneredly** *adv.* Also **I·ll-ma·nnerly** *a.*

Ill nature, i·ll-na·ture. 1691. [f. ILL *a.* + NATURE.] Malevolent disposition or character; unkindly feeling.

Ill-na·tured, *a.* 1635. [f. prec. + -ED².] †1. Of evil or bad nature or character; malignant –1788. 2. Of evil disposition; unkindly, churlish, spiteful 1635.

1. Must the earth..be sad, because some ill-natured star is sullen? FULLER. 2. People say such ill-natured things 1869. Hence **I·ll-na·tured-ly** *adv.*, **-ness** (*rare*).

Illness (i·lnĕs). 1500. [f. ILL *a.* + -NESS.] †1. Bad moral quality; badness –1718. †2. Unpleasantness; troublesomeness; noxiousness; badness –1718. 3. Bad or unhealthy condition of the body (or, formerly, of a part); the condition of being ill (ILL *a.* 8); disease, ailment, sickness. Also with *an* and *pl.* (The only current mod. sense.) 1689.

1. Ambition..without The illnesse that should attend it *Macb.* I. v. 21. 2. The i. of the Weather LOCKE. 3. In the family circle Sir Walter Scott seldom spoke of his i. LOCKHART.

Illocal (ilō̆u·kăl, ill-), *a.* 1601. [ad. late L. *illocalis*; see IL-² and LOCAL.] 1. Not local, having no location in space. †2. Out of place, *nonce-use.* 1804. Hence **Illoca·lity**, the condition of being i. 1678. **Illo·cally** *adv.* 1678.

Illogic (ilǫ·dʒik, ill-). 1856. [f. IL-² + LOGIC, after next.] The opposite of logic; illogicalness.

Illogical (ilǫ·dʒikăl, ill-), *a.* 1588. [f. IL-² + LOGICAL.] Not logical; devoid of or contrary to logic; ignorant or negligent of the principles of sound reasoning.

A foolish and i. antipathy 1850. Hence **Illogica·lity**, i. quality or character; unreasonableness; an instance of this. **Illo·gically** *adv.* **Illo·gicalness**, illogicality.

Ill-o·mened, *a.* 1685. [f. *ill omen* + -ED².] Having bad omens; ill-starred; inauspicious.

Illoricated (ilǫ·rikeitĕd, ill-), *a.* 1861. [f. IL-² + LORICATED.] *Zool.* Without a lorica or hard shell-like covering. So **Illo·ricate** *a.*

Ill-placed, *a.* 1655. Badly placed; also, misplaced, inopportune.

Ill-so·rted, *a.* 1691. [f. ILL *adv.* + *sorted*.] Badly assorted; ill-matched.

He and his wife were an ill-sorted pair BYRON.

Ill-starred, *a.* 1604. [f. ILL *a.* + STAR *sb.* + -ED².] Born under an evil star (according to astrology); unfortunate, unlucky, ill-fated. *transf.* Disastrous 1704.

How dost thou looke now? Oh ill-Starr'd wench *Oth.* v. ii. 272.

Ill-te·mpered, *a.* 1601. [partly f. ILL *adv.* + *tempered*; partly f. *ill temper* + -ED².] †1. Having the 'humours' badly tempered or mixed; unhealthy, distempered –1685. 2. Having a bad temper; morose, cross, peevish 1601.

1. *Jul. C.* IV. iii. 115. 2. You cross-grained, ill-tempered, good for nothing whelp 1825.

Illth (ilþ). 1860. [f. ILL *a.* + -TH.] The reverse of *wealth* or 'well-being'. Coined by RUSKIN.

Ill-timed, *a.* 1692. [f. ILL *adv.* + *timed*.] Badly timed; unseasonable.

Ill-tongued, *a.* 1300. [f. ILL *a.* + TONGUE *sb.* + -ED².] Having an evil tongue.

Ill-treat (i·l,trī·t), *v.* 1794. [f. ILL *adv.* + TREAT *v.*] *trans.* To treat badly; to ill-use, maltreat. So **Ill-trea·tment** 1825.

†**Ill-turned**, *a.* 1637. [f. ILL *adv.* + *turned*.] Badly turned, shaped, or expressed; also, ill-disposed –1774.

Illucidate (il¹ū·sideit), *v. rare.* 1545. [After L. *elucidare*, with prefix IL-¹.] *trans.* To shed light upon; to clear up, elucidate. Hence **Illu·cidative** *a.*

Illude (il¹ū·d), *v.* Now *rare.* 1420. [ad. L. *illudere*, f. *il-* (IL-¹) + *ludere* to play.] †1. *trans.* To mock, deride –1704. 2. To trick, deceive with false hopes 1447. †3. To evade, elude –1820.

Illume (il¹ū·m), *v.* 1602. [Short for ILLUMINE.] = ILLUMINE; almost exclusively *poetic.*

A second sun array'd in flame, To burn, to kindle, to i. SHELLEY. Thou camest Thy Disciples to i. NEALE.

Illuminable (il¹ū·minăb'l), *a.* 1730. [ad. L. *illuminabilis*, f. *illuminare* to ILLUMINATE.] Capable of being illuminated.

Illuminant (il¹ū·minănt). 1644. [ad. L. *illuminantem*.] a. *adj.* Lighting up, enlightening 1677. b. *sb.* That which illumines or illuminates; an illuminating agent; a source of illumination.

Illuminate (il¹ū·minĕt), *ppl. a.* and *sb.* ME. [ad. L. *illuminatus, illuminare*; see next.]

A. *pa. pple.* and *adj.* 1. Lighted up; made bright by light (*arch.*) 2. Enlightened †spiritually or intellectually 1563.

2. Speaking to the i. or Baptized 1672. I. by learning BACON.

B. *sb.* A spiritually or intellectually enlightened person, or one claiming to be so or to have the inner light (*arch.*) 1600.

Illuminate (il¹ū·mineit), *v.* 1535. [f. L. *illuminat-, illuminare*; f. IL-¹ + *lumen* light.] 1. *trans.* To light up, give light to. (*lit.* and *fig.*) 2. To throw light upon (a subject); to elucidate. Also *absol.* 1586. 3. To make resplendent; to shed a lustre upon 1601. 4. To decorate profusely with lights, as a sign of festivity or rejoicing 1702. 5. To set alight (*rare*) 1658. Also *intr.* (for *refl.*) 6. To decorate (an initial letter, word, or text) with gold, silver, and colours, or with tracery and miniature designs, executed in colours; to adorn (a manuscript, inscription, text, etc.) with such decorative letters and miniatures. (Repl. ENLUMINE.) 1706.

1. Two great lights..To i. the Earth MILT. *P. L.* VII. 350. *fig* I. mine eies..O good Lord T. BENTLEY. Disciplines i. the intellect 1635. 3. *Jul. C.* I. iii. 110. 4. The whole City being..illuminated 1702. Hence **Illu·minated** *ppl. a.* in senses of the vb.; *spec.* of or belonging to the ILLUMINATI (see next). **Illu·minatingly** *adv.*

‖**Illuminati** (ilʿūminēⁱ·təi, ilūminā·tī), *sb. pl.* Also *sing.* -ato (-ā·to); †pl. -oes. 1599. [Pl. of L. *illuminatus*, It. *-ato* 'enlightened', in fig. sense.] Persons claiming special enlightenment in religious, or (later) intellectual matters. a. A sect of Spanish heretics which existed in the 16th c. under the name of *Alumbrados* or 'enlightened'; also, a similar but obscure sect of French Familists in Louis XIII's reign. b. As tr. Ger. *Illuminaten*, the name of a secret society, founded at Ingolstadt in Bavaria, in 1776, by Prof. Adam Weishaupt, holding deistic and republican principles; hence applied to other thinkers regarded as atheistic or free-thinking, e.g. the French Encyclopædists 1797. c. *gen.* Persons affecting to possess special enlightenment on any subject; often used satirically 1816.

Illumination (ilʿūminēⁱ·ʃən). ME. [a. F., ad. L. *illuminationem.*] 1. The action of illuminating; the being illuminated; a lighting up, a supplying of light 1563. Also *fig.* b. *Optics.* Degree of lighting up 1863. 2. Spiritual enlightenment; divine inspiration; †*spec.* baptism. (The earliest sense in Eng.) ME. 3. Intellectual enlightenment; information, learning; †occas. in *pl.*, intellectual gifts. Also, the doctrines of the *Illuminati.* 1634. 4. The lighting up of a building, town, etc., in token of festivity or rejoicing. Also with *an* and *pl.* An instance of this; also *pl.* the lights themselves. 1691. †5. Elucidation (*rare*) –1658. 6. The embellishment of a letter or writing with colours, etc.: see ILLUMINATE *v.* 6. b. with *pl.* The designs, etc., employed in such embellishment. †c. The colouring of maps or prints. 1678.

2. A praier for illuminacion of mynde 1450. 4. When London had a grand i. BYRON. 6. I. admits no shadows, but only gradations of pure colour RUSKIN.

Illuminatism (ilʿū·minĕtiz'm). 1798. [f. ILLUMINATI + -ISM.] = ILLUMINISM. So **Illu·minatist** = ILLUMINIST.

Illuminative (ilʿū·minēⁱtiv, -ĕtiv), *a.* 1644. [f. L. *illuminat-*, *illuminare*; see -ATIVE.] 1. Having the property of illuminating or affording light. Also *fig.* 2. Pertaining to the illumination of writing 1870.

1. Ordinary i. gas 1870. *fig.* The purgative, i., and unitive stages of devotion SOUTHEY. 2. I. art 1870. Hence **Illu·minatively** *adv.* NASHE.

Illuminator (ilʿū·minēⁱtəɹ). 1485. [ad. L. *illuminator.*] 1. He who or that which illuminates, an illuminant 1598; *techn.* an instrument or device for concentrating or reflecting the light 1837. 2. One who illuminates spiritually. (The earliest sense in Eng.) 1485. 3. One who illuminates intellectually; applied contemptuously to the 18th c. Illuminati 1777. 4. One who embellishes letters or manuscripts with gold and colours: see ILLUMINATE *v.* 6. 1699.

Illu·minatory, *a. rare.* 1762. [f. L. *illuminat-* ppl. stem + -ORY.] Illuminative; explanatory.

Illumine (ilʿū·min), *v.* ME. [a. F. *illuminer*, ad. L. *illuminare.*] = ILLUMINATE *v.*

The long-illumined cities TENNYSON. What in me is dark I. MILT. *P. L.* I. 23. Sonnets..illumined with letters of gold POPE.

Illuminee·. 1800. [ad. F. *illuminé*; see -EE.] One of the Illuminati.

Illuminer (ilʿū·minəɹ). Also -or. 1450. [f. ILLUMINE *v.* + -ER [1].] 1. An illuminator; an enlightener (*lit.* and *fig.*). †2. A source of light; a luminary –1686. †3. One who illuminates manuscripts, etc. –1824.

Illuminism (ilʿū·miniz'm). 1798. [ad. F. *illuminisme*, f. *illuminer*; see -ISM.] The doctrines or principles of the ILLUMINATI, or of any sect so called; also *gen.*

In Spain, I. associated itself with freemasonry 1840. So **Illu·minist**, one who holds the doctrine of i. Also *attrib.* **Illumini·stic** *a.*, pertaining to i., or the illuminists.

Illuminize (ilʿū·minəiz), *v.* 1800. [f. ILLUMINE *v.* + -IZE.] 1. *intr.* To be an illuminist. COLERIDGE. 2. *trans.* 'To initiate into the doctrine or principles of the Illuminati' (Webster).

†**Illu·minous,** *a.*[1] 1485. [f. IL- [1] + LUMINOUS.] Bright –1745.

Illuminous (ilʿū·minəs, ill-), *a.*[2] *rare.* 1656. [f. IL- [2] + LUMINOUS.] Non-luminous, dark.

‖**Illupi** (i·lupi). *East-Ind.* 1832. [Tamil *iluppai* or *iruppai.*] An evergreen tree, *Bassia longifolia* (N.O. *Sapotaceæ*), a native of Southern India. *I. oil*, a fixed solid oil obtained from i. seeds.

†**Illu·re, Illu·rement.** Alterations of ALLURE, ALLUREMENT, after words having prefix *il-*. –1661.

Ill usage, i·ll-u·sage. 1621. [Prop. two wds., but commonly hyphened after *ill-used.*] The action of using ill; bad or unkind treatment.

Ill-use (i·l,yū·z), *v.* 1841. [Prop. two wds.; see prec.] *trans.* To use badly; to treat cruelly, unkindly, or inconsiderately.

Ill-used (i·l,yū·zd), *pa. pple.* and *ppl. a.* 1594. [Orig. two wds., hyphened when used attrib.; now taken as pa. pple. of prec. vb.] Badly used; ill-treated.

Illusion (ilʿū·ʒən). ME. [a. F., ad. L. *illusionem*, f. *illudere* to ILLUDE.] †1. The action of deriding or mocking; derision, mockery –1567. 2. †a. The action, or an act, of deceiving the bodily or the mental eye by what is unreal or false; deception, delusion, befooling –1695. b. The fact or condition of being deceived by false appearances; a false conception or idea; a deception, delusion, fancy 1571. 3. A deceptive or illusive appearance, statement, belief, etc.; in early use often *spec.* An apparition, phantom ME. 4. Sensuous perception of an external object, involving a false belief or conception; often including *hallucination.* Also (with *pl.*) an instance of this. 1774. 5. Name of a thin transparent kind of tulle 1887.

2. a. *Hen. VIII*, I. ii. 178. b. A sense of universal i...follows the reading of metaphysics H. SPENCER. 3. Stay I.: If thou hast any sound, or vse of Voyce, Speake to me *Haml.* I. i. 127. 4. As distinguished from hallucinations, illusions 'must always have a starting-point in some actual impression, whereas a hallucination has no such basis' J. SULLY. Hence **Illu·sionable** *a.* (*rare*) liable to illusions. **Illu·sionary** *a.* illusory.

Illusionism (ilʿū·ʒəniz'm). 1843. [f. ILLUSION + -ISM.] The theory that the material world is an illusion.

Illusionist (ilʿū·ʒənist). 1843. [f. as prec. + -IST.] 1. One who holds the theory of illusionism. 2. A sleight-of-hand performer 1864. 3. One given to illusion. WEBSTER.

Illusive (ilʿū·siv), *a.* 1679. [f. L. *illus-*, *illudere* + -IVE.] That tends to illude; productive of illusion or false impression; deceptive, illusory.

A vain i. show, That melts whene'er the sunbeams glow SCOTT. Hence **Illu·sive·ly** *adv.*, **-ness.**

Illusor (ilʿū·səɹ). *rare.* ME. [ad. late L. *illusor, -orem.*] A deceiver, deluder.

Illusory (ilʿū·səri), *a.* 1599. [ad. late L. *illusorius*; see prec. and -ORY.] Tending to deceive by unreal prospects; of the nature of an illusion; illusive. In first quot. as *sb.* = an illusion.

To trust him uppon pledges is a meare illusorye Q. ELIZ. The price given..is i. ROGERS. Hence **Illu·sorily** *adv.* **Illu·soriness.**

†**Illu·strable,** *a.* 1658. [f. L. *illustrare*; see -BLE.] = next –1668.

Illustratable (i·lŏstrēⁱtăb'l, -lʊ·strĕtăb'l), *a.* 1850. [f. ILLUSTRATE *v.* + -ABLE.] Capable of being illustrated.

Illustrate (i·lŏstrēⁱt, ilʊ·strēⁱt), *v.* 1526. [f. L. *illustrat-*, *illustrare* to light up, set off, etc.] †1. *trans.* To light up, illumine –1717. b. *fig.* (*Obs.* or *arch.*) 1526. †2. To make lustrous, luminous, or bright; *gen.* to beautify, adorn –1748. 3. To set in a good light. Now *rare.* 4. To shed lustre upon; to make illustrious; to confer honour or distinction upon. Now *rare* or *Obs.* 1530. 5. To elucidate, clear up, explain 1538. 6. To make clear by means of examples; to exemplify 1612. 7. To elucidate by means of pictures; to ornament (a book, etc.) with elucidatory designs. Said also of the pictures. 1638.

3. Pitt..apt enough to take any step to i. his own measures H. WALPOLE. 4. Mr. Wedderburne..who now illustrates the title of Lord Loughborough GIBBON. 5. You have..illustrated it by quotations and metaphors 1874. 6. To i. the advantages of vigilance and foresight 1786. 7. To i. the results of an expedition with photographs 1873. So †**Illu·strate** *ppl. a.* illustrated, illuminated, enlightened, etc.; *adj.* illuminated, resplendent, clear; lustrous, illustrious. **I·llustrated** *ppl. a.* †made bright; having pictorial illustrations; *sb.* an illustrated newspaper or magazine.

Illustration (ilŏstrēⁱ·ʃən). ME. [a. F., ad. L. *illustrationem.*] †1. Illumination (spiritual, intellectual, or physical) –1764. 2. The action of making or fact of being made illustrious; distinction. Also, an example, means or cause of distinction. 1616. 3. The action or fact of making clear or evident; elucidation; exemplification 1581. Also with *an* and *pl.* 4. The pictorial elucidation of any subject 1813; an illustrative picture, drawing, cut, or the like 1817.

Illustrative (ilʊ·strĕtiv, i·lŏstrēⁱtiv), *a.* 1643. [f. L. *illustrat-*, *illustrare* + -IVE.] Serving or tending to illustrate; explanatory; exemplificatory. Const. *of.* Hence **Illu·stratively** *adv.*

Illustrator (i·lŏstrēⁱtəɹ). 1598. [f. ILLUSTRATE *v.*] One who or that which illustrates (see the vb.). So **I·llustratress.**

Illu·stratory, *a.* 1734. [f. L. *illustrat-* ppl. stem + -ORY.] Illustrative.

†**Illustre,** *a.* 1500. [a. F.] Illustrious –1653.

†**Illustre,** *v.* 1490. [a. F. *illustrer*, ad. L. *illustrare.*] 1. *trans.* To illumine –1606. 2. To render illustrious –1657.

2. As ye valew your places, i. them 1657.

Illustrious (ilʊ·striəs), *a.* 1566. [f. L. *illustris* + -OUS.] †1. Lighted up, having lustre; luminous, shining, bright –1886. †2. Clearly manifest –1792. 3. Possessing lustre; distinguished; renowned, famous 1566. †¶. Not lustrous (IL- [2]). *Cymb.* I. vi. 109. (Some read *illustrous.*)

2. The final cause of uniformity is i. KAMES. 3. This high i. Prince *Lear* V. iii. 135. One leaf of the i. folio LAMB. Hence **Illu·strious·ly** *adv.*, **-ness.**

‖**Illustrissimo** (ilŏstri·simo, It. illustri·ssimo), *a.* and *sb.* 1623. Also anglicized -issim(e 1609. [It.] a. *adj.* Most illustrious; used as a title of courtesy in speaking to or of Italian nobles (and others). b. *sb.* A man of noble rank.

Illustrous: see under ILLUSTRIOUS.

Ill will, i·ll-wi·ll, *sb.* ME. [In early use northern, corresp. to ON. *illvili.*] Evil feeling or intention towards another; malevolence, enmity, dislike. Hence †**Ill-will** *v. trans.* to wish evil to. **I·ll-wi·lled** *a.* (*Obs.* exc. *dial.*) malevolent; †reluctant. **I·ll-wi·ller,** an ill-wisher. **Ill-wi·lling** *a.* wishing ill.

Ill-wisher (i·l wi·ʃəɹ). 1607. [f. ILL *adv.* (or *sb.*) + WISHER.] One who wishes evil to another. So **I·ll-wi·sh** *v.* to wish evil to 1865.

Illy (i·l,li), *adv.* Now chiefly *U.S.* 1549. [f. ILL *a.* + -LY [2].] Badly; ill.

Ilmenite (i·lmĕnəit). 1827. [f. the *Ilmen* Mountains (in southern Urals), where found.] *Min.* Oxide of iron and titanium found in brilliant black crystals.

Ilvaite (i·lvă,əit). 1816. [f. *Ilva*, Elba, where found.] *Min.* A black crystalline silicate of iron and calcium, called also lievrite.

Im- [1], assim. form of the suffix IN- [2], before *b, m, p.* Many words taken into ME. from Fr. have both *em-* and *im-*, and in some, as *empanel, impanel*, the variation still continues; see EM- and IN- [2]. In words more recently derived from Latin (or from Italian) *im-* is the regular form.

Im- [2], assim. form in L. of the neg. prefix IN- [3] before *b, m, p,* which retains the same form in English, as *immemorial, impossible.*

I'm (əim), colloq. contr. of *I am.*

Image (i·mėdʒ), *sb.* ME. [a. F. *image,* earlier *ima·gene,* ad. L. *imago, imaginem*; app. f. same root as *imitari* to IMITATE.] **1.** An artificial imitation or representation of the external form of any object, esp. of a person. **a.** A statue, effigy, sculptured figure. (Often applied to figures as objects of worship.) **b.** (Less usually) A likeness, portrait, picture, carving, or the like. (Now *rare* or *Obs.* exc. in allusions to Matt. xxii. 20.) ME. †**c.** Applied to the constellations, as figures, etc. -1674. **d.** *fig.* 1548. **2.** An optical appearance or counterpart of an object, such as is produced by rays of light either reflected as from a mirror, refracted as through a lens, or falling on a surface after passing through a small aperture ME. **b.** *transf.* (*a*) A collection of heat-rays concentrated at a particular point or portion of space, analogous to an image formed by light-rays. (*b*) *Electr.* (See quot.) 1873. **3.** *abstractly.* Appearance, form; semblance, likeness. (Now only with reference to biblical language, esp. Gen. i. 26, 27.) ME. Also *concr.* (*Obs.* or *arch.*) 1530. **4.** A counterpart, copy ME.; a symbol, emblem, representation 1566; a type, typical example, embodiment 1548. **5.** A mental representation of something (esp. a visible object); a mental picture or impression; an idea, conception ME. **6.** A vivid or graphic description 1522. **7.** *Rhet.* A simile, metaphor, or figure of speech 1676.

1. a. An ymage þat haþ .iiij. hedes MAUNDEV. The ymage of godde Hamone 1450. **b.** Whos is this ymage, and the wrytyng aboue? WYCLIF *Matt.* xxii. 20. **2.** *Negative* or *accidental i.*: that seen after looking intently at a bright-coloured object, and having a colour complementary to that of the object. (See also AFTER-IMAGE.) *Real i.* in *Optics,* an image produced by reflection or refraction, when the rays from each point of the object actually meet at a point; when they diverge as if from a point beyond the reflecting or refracting body, it is called a *virtual i.* **b.** (*b*) An imaginary electrified point, which has no physical existence..but which may be called an electrical i., because the action of the surface on external points is the same as that which would be produced by the imaginary electrified point if the spherical surface were removed MAXWELL. **3.** God created man in his owne I. *Gen.* i. 27. *concr.* Diverse ymages lyke terrible develles HALL. **4.** Sleepe is the i. of death 1620. This Play is the I. of a murder done in Vienna *Haml.* III. ii. 248. An awful i. of calm power SHELLEY. **5.** She endeavoured to dismiss his i. from her mind 1797. **6.** Theocritus..has only given a plain i. of the way of life amongst the peasants 1717. *Comb.,* as *i.-graver, -monger,* etc.

Image (i·mėdʒ), *v.* 1440. [f. IMAGE *sb.*; earlier, a. F. *imager.*] **1.** *trans.* To make an image of; to represent by an image; to figure, portray, delineate. Also *fig.* 1790. **2.** To reflect, mirror 1792. **3.** To copy (*rare*) 1611; to resemble (*rare*) 1701. **4.** †**a.** To devise, plan -1460. **b.** To imagine, represent *to oneself* 1708. **5.** To describe (esp. vividly or graphically) 1628. **6.** To symbolize, typify 1816.

1. Shrines of imag'd saints WARTON. **2.** Structures imaged in the wave ROGERS. **4. b.** We i. to ourselves the Tarpeian Rock as a tremendous precipice 1781. **6.** O stream!..Thou imagest my life SHELLEY. Hence **I·mageable** *a.* capable of being imaged, esp. in the mind.

I·mage-brea·ker. 1596. One who destroys images; an iconoclast. So **I·mage-brea·king** *sb.* and *a.*

Imaged (i·mėdʒd), *a.* 1718. [f. IMAGE + -ED.] **1.** [f. the vb.] Represented by an image (physical or mental). **2.** [f. the sb.] Of porcelain: Decorated with human figures 1797.

I·mageless, *a.* 1821. [-LESS.] Without an image or images.

I·mage-ma·ker. 1500. A maker of images (usu. in sense 1 a).

Imager (i·mėdʒəɹ). [ME. *ym-, imageour,* a. OF. *ym-, imageur,* f. *image.*] †A sculptor, carver -1603; †a painter (*rare*) 1591.

Imagery (i·mėdʒəri, i·mėdʒri). ME. [a. OF. *imagerie,* f. *imagier* IMAGER; see -ERY.] **1.** Images collectively; image-work. Rarely including pictures. Also in *pl.* †**b.** Figured work on a textile fabric; embroidery -1777. **c.** *transf.* Scenery; nature's image-work 1647. †**2.** Idolatry -1624. †**3.** The art of statuary or carving; *rarely,* of painting -1611. †**4.** Workmanship, make, figure, form, fashion -1667. †**5.** = IMAGE *sb.* 4. -1649. **6.** †**a.** Imagination, fancy, groundless belief. **b.** The result of this; mental images collectively or generally. 1611. **7.** The use of rhetorical images, or such images collectively; figurative illustration, esp. of an ornate character 1589.

1. His cup embost with I. SPENSER. **b.** A counterpoynt of arras silk with ymagery 1480. **c.** The visible scene With all its solemn i., its rocks, Its woods WORDSW. **4.** Dress your people unto the i. of Christ JER. TAYLOR. **6. b.** Like a dream's dim i. SHELLEY. **7.** The glowing i. of prophets 1858.

I·mage-wo·rship. 1628. The worship of images; idolatry. So **I·mage-wo·rshipper. I·mage-wo·rshipping** *sb.* and *a.*

†**Imagilet.** [? for *imagelet*; see -LET.] A statuette. FULLER.

Imaginable (imæ·dʒinăb'l), *a.* ME. [ad. late L. *imaginabilis,* f. *imaginare*; see -BLE.] Capable of being imagined; conceivable.

Such a dreadfull noyse, as is scarce i. SIR T. HERBERT. Guilty of the greatest crimes i. 1692. So **Imaginabi·lity** (*rare*), **Ima·ginableness,** quality of being i. **Ima·ginably** *adv.*

†**Ima·ginal,** *a.*[1] *rare.* 1647. [app. f. IMAGINE *v.* + -AL.] Of or pertaining to the imagination; imaginable -1658.

Imaginal (imæ·dʒinăl), *a.*[2] 1877. [f. L. *imagin-,* stem of IMAGO + -AL.] *Entom.* Of or pertaining to an insect imago.

Imaginal disks: certain regularly arranged discoidal masses of indifferent tissue, which the apodal maggot carries in the interior of its body when it leaves the egg. These undergo little or no change until the larva encloses itself in its hardened last-shed cuticle, and becomes a pupa.

†**Ima·ginant.** 1605. [ad. L. *imaginantem.*] **A.** *ppl. a.* That imagines. BACON. **B.** *sb.* One who imagines -1663.

Imaginary (imæ·dʒĭnări), *a.* (*sb.*) ME. [ad. L. *imaginarius,* f. *imago, imagin-* IMAGE; see -ARY.] **1.** Existing only in imagination or fancy; not really existing. (Opp. to *real, actual.*) **b.** Said of lines, etc., assumed to be drawn through or between certain points 1601. **c.** *Math.* Applied to quantities or loci having no real existence, but assumed to exist; e.g. the square root of a negative quantity, or any expression involving this, or any point, curve, etc. denoted algebraically by such an expression. Also *transf.* Relating to imaginary quantities or loci, as *i. geometry, projection,* etc. (Opp. to *real.*) 1706. †**2.** Imaginative -1677. †**3.** Of the nature of an image -1669. †**4.** Putative. DONNE. †**5.** Imaginable -1687. †**6.** *sb.* An imagination; a fancy -1748. **7.** *sb.* (*Math.*) An imaginary quantity or expression; see 1 c above 1864.

1. After giving me i. wit and beauty, you give me i. passions, and you tell me I'm in love LADY M. W. MONTAGU. **2.** SHAKS. *Sonn.* xxvii. **3.** SHAKS. *Lucr.* 1422. Hence **Ima·ginarily** *adv.* 1593.

†**Ima·ginate,** *ppl. a.* Chiefly *Sc.* 1533. [ad. L. *imaginatus.*] Imagined; imaginary -1601.

Imagination (imædʒinēɪ·ʃən). ME. [a. F., ad. L. *imaginationem.*] **1.** The action of imagining, or forming a mental concept of what is not actually present to the senses (cf. sense 3); the result of this, a mental image or idea (freq. characterized as *vain, false,* etc.). †**2.** The mental consideration of actions or events not yet in existence. **a.** Scheming or devising; a device, scheme, plot; a fanciful project. *Obs.* exc. as a biblical archaism. ME. **b.** Expectation, anticipation -1654. **3.** That faculty of the mind by which we conceive the absent as if it were present (freq. including memory); the 'reproductive imagination' ME. **4.** The power which the mind has of forming concepts beyond those derived from external objects; the 'productive imagination'. **a.** Fancy ME. **b.** The creative faculty; poetic genius 1509. **5.** The operation of the mind; thinking; thought, opinion. Now *rare* or *Obs.* ME.

1. They..accounted his undoubted divinations, madde immaginations 1576. Could such an i. ever have been entertained by him? HUME. **2. a.** I., or Compassing..was punishable by our Law 1660. **b.** To tell you truly mine own i., I thought [etc.] MARVELL. **3.** The beauty of her countenance haunting his i. 1797. **4. a.** Looke how i. blowes him SHAKS. **b.** And as i. bodies forth The forms of things vnknowne; the Poet's pen Turnes them to shapes, and giues to aire nothing, A locall habitation, and a name SHAKS. Hence **Imagina·tional** *a.*

Imaginative (imæ·dʒinēɪtiv, -ĕtiv), *a.* (*sb.*) ME. [a. OF. *imaginatif,* ad. late L. *imaginativus*; see IMAGINE *v.* and -ATIVE.] **1.** Of persons: Given to imagining. †**a.** Full of thoughts, plans, or devices. **b.** Full of idle fancies. **c.** Having inventive genius. **2.** Of, pertaining to, or concerned in the exercise of imagination as a mental faculty ME. †**3.** Existing only in imagination; imaginary -1646. **4.** Characterized by, or resulting from, the productive imagination; bearing evidence of high creative fancy 1829. †**5.** *sb.* Imagination -1641.

1. The Witches themselues are I., and beleeue ofttimes, they doe that, which they doe not BACON. **2.** Milton had a highly i., Cowley a very fanciful mind COLERIDGE. **4.** The i. tale of Sintram and his Companions SCOTT. Hence **Ima·ginative-ly** *adv.* 1430, **-ness** 1664.

Imagine (imæ·dʒin), *v.* ME. [a. F. *imaginer,* ad. L. *imaginare, -ari,* f. *imaginem.*] **I.** *trans.* **1.** To form a mental image of, to represent to oneself in imagination, to picture to oneself. **2.** To create as a mental conception, to conceive; to assume, suppose (a mathematical line, etc.) ME. **3.** To devise, plot, plan, compass. Now a biblical or legal archaism. ME. †**4.** To ponder, meditate -1582. **5.** To conjecture, suspect, suppose ME. **6.** To form an idea or notion with regard to something not known with certainty, to suppose, 'take into one's head' (*that*) 1548.

1. A thing..that it is not possible for man to ymagine the like without seeing 1566. **2.** I. your self in the same case MORE. **3.** Why do..the people i. a vaine thing? *Ps.* ii. 1. To i. the Death of the Prince..is made High Treason 1707.

II. *intr.* †**1.** To meditate; to form designs -1589. **2.** To exercise the imagination 1631. **3.** *Imagine of*: = sense I. 1. 1586.

2. Women may be trained to reason and i. as well as men 1809. Hence **Ima·giner,** one who imagines.

Imagist (i·mėdʒist). 1919. [f. IMAGE *sb.* + -IST.] One of a group of modern poets who, in revolt against romanticism, seek clarity of expression through the use of precise images. Also *attrib.* Hence **I·magism,** the practices and work of the imagists.

Imago (imēɪ·go). *Pl.* **imagines** (-ēɪ·dʒiniz) and **imagos.** 1797. [An application of L. *imago* IMAGE (Linn.).] *Entom.* The final and perfect stage or form of an insect after its metamorphoses; the 'perfect insect'.

‖**Imam, imaum** (imā·m). 1613. [a. Arab. *imām,* f. *amma* to go before, precede.] **1.** The officiating priest of a Mohammedan mosque. **2.** A title given to various Mohammedan leaders and chiefs; as, the Caliph, or other independent princes, etc. 1662.

‖**Imaret** (imā·ret, i·măret). 1613. [a. Turk., a. Arab. *'imārat* 'rendering habitable', hence 'hospice'.] A hospice for pilgrims and travellers in Turkey.

Imb-: see EMB-.

Imba·n, *v.* [See IM-[1] and BAN *v.*] To put under a ban. J. BARLOW.

Imba·nd, *v.* [f. IM-[1] + BAND *sb.*[3]] To form into a band. J. BARLOW.

†**Imba·rge,** *v.* 1596. [f. IM-[1] + BARGE *sb.*] *trans.* To embark -1627.

Imbarge, -bargo: see EMBARGE, etc.

Imbark (imbā·ɹk), *v.* 1647. [f. IM-[1] + BARK *sb.*[1]] *trans.* To enclose in or clothe with bark. Also *fig.*

Imbark, -ation, etc.: see EMBARK, etc.

†**Imba·rn,** *v.* 1610. [f. IM-[1] + BARN *sb.*] *trans.* To gather into a barn or barns; to garner. Also *fig.* -1796.

Imbase: see EMBASE.

†**Imba·stardize,** *v.* [f. IM-[1] + BASTARDIZE.] *trans.* To render bastard or degenerate. MILTON.

Imbathe, -battle, -bay: see EMB-.

Imbecile (i·mbisil, i·mbisīl), *a.* (*sb.*) 1549. [Earlier *imbecill(e,* a. F. *imbécille,* now *imbécile,* ad. L. *imbecillus, -is* (of unkn. composition). The single *l* is due to an erron. impression that the L. word was *imbecilis.*] **1.** Weak, feeble; esp. of body. **2.** Mentally weak; of weak character or will through want of mental power; hence, Fatuous, idiotic. (The chief current sense.) 1804. **b.** Of actions: Stupid, absurd, idiotic 1861. **3.** *sb.* A person of weak intellect 1802.

2. But he had the misfortune to be 'imbecile'..in fact, he was partially an idiot DE QUINCEY. Hence **I·mbecilely** *adv.* stupidly, idiotically.

†Imbe·cile, *v.* 1539. [Confused with EMBEZZLE *v.*, q.v.] **1.** *trans.* To make imbecile, weak, or impotent –1651. **2.** In senses of EMBEZZLE *v.*, q.v. 1546.

1. To i. and hinder health NEWTON. **2.** The dede of the foundacion was lost or imbecilled away 1546.

Imbecilitate (imbĕsi·liteᵻt), *v.* 1653. [f. IMBECILITY; see -ATE³. In 17th c. *imbecill-.*] *trans.* = IMBECILE *v.* **1.**

Imbecility (imbĕsi·lĭti). 1533. [Earlier *imbecillitie*, a. F. *imbécillité*, ad. L. *imbecillitatem*, f. *imbecillus*. For the single *l*, see IMBECILE *a.*] **1.** Weakness, feebleness, impotence. Also with *an* and *pl.* **b.** Incompetency or incapacity (*to do* something) 1767. **2.** Weakness of mind, esp. as characterizing action; hence, silliness, absurdity, folly; an example of this. (Pathologically, *imbecility* is a defect of mental power of less degree than idiocy, and not congenital.) 1624.

1. The i. of the Irish administration MACAULAY. **2.** I. is..weakness of mind owing to defective mental development MAUDSLEY.

Imbed, Imbellish: see EMBED, etc.

†Imbellic, *a.* [f. IM-² + L. *bellicus*.] Unwarlike. FELTHAM.

Imber, obs. and var. f. EMBER.

Imbesel(l, etc., obs. ff. EMBEZZLE.

Imbibe (imbəi·b), *v.* ME. [Partly a. F. *imbiber*; partly ad. L. *imbibere*, f. *im-* (IM-¹) + *bibere*.]

†I. *trans.* To soak, imbue, or saturate with moisture; to steep. Also *fig.* –1804. **†b.** With inverted construction: To instil *into* –1812.

II. 1. *trans.* To take into one's mind or moral system 1555. **2.** To drink in (liquid), absorb (moisture) 1621. **3.** To take up, absorb, or assimilate (a gas, etc.); to take (solids) into solution or suspension 1626. **†4.** *transf.* To absorb, swallow up –1712.

1. They may also herewith i. trewe religion EDEN. **2.** So barren sands i. the shower COWPER. To i. brandy-and-water 1859, fresh air HELPS. **3.** Such salts are readily imbibed by water BERKELEY. The heat of the sun's rays, which the earth imbibes 1834. Hence **Imbi·ber,** one who or that which imbibes or drinks.

Imbibition (imbibi·ʃən). 1471. [a. F., ad. L. **imbibitionem*.] The action of imbibing (see the vb.).

Phr. †*To lie in i.*: to lie a-soak or a-steep. When wood distends on i. 1875. The i. of truth HOLLAND.

Imbitter, Imblaze: see EMBITTER, etc.

Imbody, -bog, -boil, -bolden: see EMBODY, etc.

†Imbo·nity. [ad. late L. *imbonitas* (Tertullian), f. *im-* (IM-²) + *bonitas*.] The reverse of goodness; unkindness. BURTON.

Imborder, var. of EMBORDER.

†Imbo·rdure, *v.* 1486. [f. IM-¹ + BORDURE.] *trans.* To encompass with a border; *spec.* in *Her.* to furnish with a bordure of the same tincture –1658.

†‖Imboscata (imbǫskā·ta). Also **em-.** 1595. = AMBUSH, q.v. –1820.

†Imbosk, *v.* 1562. [ad. It. *imboscare*, f. *im-* (IM-¹) + *bosco* wood. Cf. EMBOSS *v.*²] *refl.* To hide or conceal oneself –1657. Also *intr.* for *refl.* 1641.

Imbosom, -boss(e, -bosture, -bound, -bow, -bowel, -bower, -box, -brace, -braid, etc.: see EMBOSOM, etc.

†Imbra·nch, *v.* Also **en-, in-.** 1577. [f. IM-¹ + BRANCH *sb.*] To graft on the stock –1598.

Imbrangle, Imbrase: see EMB-.

Imbreathe (imbrī·ð), *v.* 1574. [f. IM-¹ + BREATHE *v.*; cf. EMBREATHE, INBREATHE.] **1.** *trans.* To breathe in, inhale. Also *fig.* **2.** To inspire, instil; to inspire *with* 1601.

Imbred, -breed: see INBRED, INBREED.

Imbreviate (imbrī·viˌeᵻt), *v.* 1609. [f. med.L. *imbreviat-*, *imbreviare*.] *trans.* To put into the form of a brief; to enrol, register.

‖Imbrex (i·mbreks). *Pl.* **imbrices** (i·mbrisīz). 1857. [L., f. *imber* a rain-shower.] **1.** *Archæol.* A curved roof-tile. **2.** One of the scales of an imbrication 1890.

Imbricate (i·mbrikĕt), *a.* (*sb.*) 1656. [ad. L. *imbricatus*, *imbricare* to form like a gutter-tile, f. *imbrex, imbricem*.] **†1.** Formed like a gutter-tile or pantile –1661. **2.** Covered with or composed of scales or scale-like parts overlapping like roof-tiles; e.g. said of the scaly covering of reptiles and fishes, of leaf-buds, the involucre of *Compositæ*, etc. 1656. **b.** Of leaves, scales, etc.: Overlapping like tiles 1796. **3.** = IMBRICATED 3. 1890. **4.** *sb.* A reptile, fish, etc. covered with imbricated scales 1862. Hence **I·mbricately** *adv.* in an imbricated manner or order.

Imbricate (i·mbrikeᵻt), *v.* 1784. [f. L. *imbricat-* ppl. stem; see prec.] **1.** *trans.* To place so as to overlap like roof-tiles. **2.** *trans.* and *absol.* To overlap like tiles 1820. Hence **I·mbricative** *a.* = IMBRICATE *a.* 2.

Imbricated (i·mbrikeᵻtėd), *ppl. a.* 1704. [f. prec.] **†1.** Of leaves: Hollowed in like a gutter-tile –1741. **2.** = IMBRICATE *a.* 2, 2 b. 1753. **3.** Resembling in pattern a surface of overlapping tiles 1875.

2. I. like the cone of the Scotch fir GEIKIE. **3.** [Majolica] ornamented..with..i. patterns 1875.

Imbrication (imbrikā·ʃən). 1650. [See IMBRICATE *v.* and *a.*] **†1.** ? The dropping of water from roof-tiles. BULWER. **†2.** 'A covering with tile' –1658. **3.** An overlapping as of tiles; a decorative pattern imitative of this 1713.

Imbrica·to-. Comb. f. L. *imbricatus*, = imbricately-, imbricated and —; as *i.-granulous*.

†Imbri·er, *v.* 1605. [f. IM-¹ + BRIER *sb.*] To entangle as among briers –1690.

†Imbroca·do¹. 1600. [Altered f. It. *imbroccata*: see -ADO.] = IMBROCCATA –1657.

†Imbroca·do². 1656. [Altered f. It. *imbroccato*.] = BROCADE. (Dicts.)

†Imbrocca·ta. 1595. [a. It., f. *imbroccare* 'to giue a thrust at fence ouer the dagger', f. *brocco*, †*brocca* stud, nail (cf. BROACH *sb.*).] A pass or thrust in fencing.

Imbroglio (imbrōᵘ·lyo). Also **em-.** 1750. [a. It., f. *broglio* confusion; see BROIL *sb.*¹ and *v.*²] **1.** A confused heap. **2.** A state of confused entanglement; a complicated or difficult situation; a serious misunderstanding, embroilment 1818. **3.** *Mus.* 'A passage in which the vocal or instrumental parts are made to sing, or play, against each other, in such a manner as to produce the effect of.. confusion' (Grove) 1880.

1. Papers and books, a huge i. GRAY. **2.** A financial i. 1833.

Imbrown, obs. f. EMBROWN.

Imbrue (imbrū·), *v.* ME. [Late ME. *enbrowe, -brewe*, prob. a. OF. *embroer, -ouer, -uer* to cover with mud, sully, bedabble.] **†1.** *trans.* To stain, dirty, defile –1593. **2.** To stain, dye (*in* or *with*) 1529. **b.** Said of blood, etc. Now *rare.* 1597. **†3.** In pregnant sense (*with blood* understood) –1749. **†4.** To soak *in*, saturate *with*. Also *absol.* –1634. **†5.** *fig.* To steep *in*; to imbue *with*; to infect –1674. **¶6.** To pour, to emit moisture. SPENSER *F. Q.* II. v. 33.

2. Wretches, who have imbrued their hands in so much innocent blood CROMWELL. **3.** *absol.* What? shall wee haue Incision? Shall wee embrew? SHAKS. **5.** Imbrewed with Heresies 1565. Hence **Imbrue·d** *ppl. a.*; *spec.* in *Her.* stained with blood. **Imbrue·ment** (*rare*).

Imbrute (imbrū·t), *v.* Also **em-.** 1634. [f. IM-¹ + BRUTE *sb.*¹] **1.** *trans.* To degrade to the level of a brute; to make bestial 1640. **2.** *intr.* To sink to the level of a brute 1634.

1. MILT. *P. L.* IX. 166. **2.** The soul grows clotted by contagion, Embodies, and embrutes MILT. *Comus* 468. Hence **Imbru·tement,** brutalization.

Imbue (imbiū·), *v.* 1555. [ad. L. *imbuere* to wet, stain, etc. In earlier examples only in the pa. pple. *imbued* answering to the L. pa. pple. *imbutus*.] **1.** *trans.* To saturate; to dye, tinge, impregnate (*with*) 1594. **b.** To imbrue (with blood) 1850. **2.** To impregnate, permeate, pervade, or inspire (*with* opinions, etc.) 1555.

1. Cere-cloth, imbued with unguents and spices 1878. **2.** Thy words with Grace Divine Imbu'd MILT. *P. L.* VIII. 216. Hence **Imbue·ment,** imbuing; the fact of being imbued.

Imburse (imbɔ̄·ɹs), *v.* Now *rare.* 1530. [ad. late and med.L. *imbursare*, f. *im-* (IM-¹) + *bursa* purse.] **1.** *trans.* To put into one's (or a) purse; to store up. **2.** **†a.** To enrich 1646. **b.** To pay, refund 1721. Hence **Imbu·rsement** (*rare*), supplying with money; payment 1665.

†Imbu·te, *v.* 1657. [f. L. *imbut-*, *imbuere*.] *trans.* To steep, soak. TOMLINSON. Hence **†Imbu·tion,** steeping, soaking.

Imide (i·məid, iməi·d). 1850. [Purposely altered from AMIDE.] *Chem.* A name for derivatives of ammonia (NH_3), in which two atoms of hydrogen are exchanged for a metal or organic radical; these being viewed as compounds of the metal, etc., with a hypothetical radical **Imidogen** (iməi·doˌdʒen), NH. Often in comb., as in *succinimide* NH.CO. Hence **Imi·do-,** comb. form of prec.

Imitable (i·mităb'l), *a.* 1550. [a. F., ad. L. *imitabilis*, f. *imitari*; see -ABLE.] **1.** Capable of being imitated 1598. **†2.** Deserving of imitation –1781.

1. Pindar is i. by none COWLEY. **2.** The worst of times afford i. examples of virtue SIR T. BROWNE. Hence **I·mitabi·lity, I·mitableness,** i. quality. **†I·mitably** *adv.*

I·mitancy. *nonce-wd.* [f. L. *imitantem*; see -ANCY.] The quality or property of imitating; imitativeness. CARLYLE.

Imitate (i·miteᵻt), *v.* 1534. [f. L. *imitat-*, *imitari*.] **1.** *trans.* To do or try to do after the manner of; to follow the example of; to copy in action. **b.** *occas.*, To mimic, counterfeit 1613. **2.** To copy, reproduce 1590. **3.** To be, become, or make oneself like; to assume the aspect of; to simulate 1588. **†4.** To make in imitation of.

1. The Children imitating their Parents DAMPIER. **b.** Of Apes and Monkies there are..that will i. all they see 1660. **2.** To i. the workes of others 1638, an ode GAY. **3.** In habite they i. the Italians 1615. **4.** The counterfet Is poorely imitated after you SHAKS. *Sonn.* liii.

Imitation (imitā·ʃən). 1502. [ad. L. *imitationem*; perh. through F.] **1.** The action or practice of imitating. **2.** The product of imitating; a copy, an artificial likeness; a counterfeit 1601. **3.** *Literature.* 'A method of translating looser than paraphrase, in which modern examples and illustrations are used for ancient, or domestick for foreign' (J.); an example of this 1656. **4.** *Mus.* The repetition of a phrase or melody, usually at a different pitch, either with the same intervals, rhythm, motion, etc. (*exact i.*), or with these more or less modified (*free i.*) 1727. **5.** *attrib.* Made (of cheaper material) in imitation of a real or genuine article or substance 1858.

1. I. is the sincerest of flattery COLTON. Phr. *In i. of.* **2.** Modern imitations of ancient coins 1876. **3.** In i. of Horace his second Ode, B. 4. COWLEY. **5.** I. tortoise-shell 1895. Hence **Imita·tional** *a.* of, pertaining to, or characterized by i. **Imita·tionist,** one who practises i., or gives imitations.

Imitative (i·miteᵻtiv), *a.* (*sb.*) 1584. [ad. late L. *imitativus* (see -ATIVE).] **1.** Characterized by or consisting in imitation. **2.** Given to imitation; prone to copy or mimic 1752. **3.** Simulative; fictitious; counterfeit 1838. **†4.** *sb.* A verb expressing any kind of imitation. PHILLIPS.

1. *Imitative arts*, the arts of painting and sculpture. *I. word*, a word which reproduces a natural sound. Walking..in a manner feebly i. of the human gait 1867. **2.** Human beings are very i. SYD. SMITH. Hence **I·mitative·ly** *adv.*, **-ness.**

Imitator (i·mitēᵻtəɹ). 1523. [ad. F. *imitateur*, ad. L. *imitatorem*.] One who imitates another; one who produces an imitation of anything. Also *transf.* of things. Hence **I·mita·torship,** the office of an i. So **I·mitatress, Imita·trix,** a female i.

Immaculacy (imæ·kiŭlăsi). 1799. [see -ACY.] Immaculate condition or quality.

Immaculate (imæ·kiŭlĕt), *a.* ME. [ad. L. *immaculatus*, f. *im-* (IM-²) + *maculatus* spotted.] **1.** Free from spot or stain; pure, unblemished, undefiled. **2.** Free from fault or flaw. (Chiefly in neg. or ironical use.) 1832. **3. a.** Spotlessly clean or neat 1735. **b.** *Nat. Hist.* Without coloured spots or marks 1797.

1. *Immaculate Conception*, the conception of the Virgin Mary, as held to have been free from the taint of original sin. *I. lamb*, applied to Christ, after L. *agnus immaculatus* (Gr. ἀμνὸς ἄμωμος) 1 *Pet.* i. 19. 2. The Sceptical philosophy is by no means so i. 1856. 3. a. A white-glov'd Chaplain..in immac'late trim POPE. Hence **Imma·culate-ly** *adv.*, **-ness.**

†Immai·led, *a.* [f. IM-[1] + MAIL *sb.* + -ED.] Clad in mail. W. BROWNE.

Imma·lleable, *a. rare.* 1675. [IM-[2].] Not malleable.

Imma·nacle, *v. rare.* 1634. [IM-[1].] *trans.* To put manacles on; to handcuff; to fetter. MILT. *Comus* 665.

Immana·tion. [IM-[1], after EMANATION.] A flowing in. LAMB.

Immane (imē¹·n), *a. arch.* 1602. [ad. L. *immanis*, f. *im-* (IM-[2]) + *manus* hand.] **1.** Monstrous in size or strength; huge, tremendous 1615. **2.** Inhumanly cruel or savage.

1. A man in shape i., and monsterous CHAPMAN. Hence **Imma·ne·ly** *adv.*, **-ness.**

Immanence (i·mănĕns). 1816. [f. IMMANENT *a.*; see -ENCE.] The fact or condition of being immanent; indwelling. So **I·mmanency,** indwellingness 1659.

Immanent (i·mănĕnt), *a.* 1535. [ad. late L. *immanentem*, *immanere*, f. *im-* (IM-[1]) + *manere.*] **1.** Indwelling, inherent; actually present or abiding *in*; remaining within. (Opp. to *transcendent.*) **2.** *I. act* (*action*): an act which is performed entirely within the mind of the subject, and produces no external effect; opp. to a *transient* or *transitive act.* Now *rare.* 1613.

1. They have not cared to recognize it [the external world] as the shrine of i. Deity J. MARTINEAU. 2. A cognition is an i. act of mind SIR W. HAMILTON. Hence **I·mmanently** *adv.* Also **Immanental** (imăne·ntăl), *a.* pertaining to the doctrine of immanence 1885; **I·mmanentism,** the doctrine of immanence 1907; **I·mmanentist** *a.* 1917.

Imma·nifest, *a. rare.* 1646. [IM-[2].] Not manifest or evident.

†Imma·nity. 1557. [ad. L. *immanitas*, f. *immanis.*] The quality of being immane; enormity –1667; monstrous cruelty –1669.

Immantle (imæ·nt'l, imm-), *v.* 1601. [f. IM-[1] + MANTLE.] **1.** *trans.* To cover or enwrap with, or as with, a mantle. **†2.** To place round as a fortification. HOLLAND.

Imma·rble, *v. rare.* 1642. [IM-[1].] *trans.* To convert into marble; to make cold, hard, etc., as marble.

Immarcescible (imaɹse·sib'l), *a.* Now *rare.* 1432. [ad. late L. *immarcescibilis*, f. *im-* (IM-[2]) + *marcescere*, *marcere.*] Unfading; imperishable; esp. in *i. crown* (*of glory*). Hence **Immarce·scibly** *adv.*

Immarginate (imā·ɹdʒinĕt, imm-), *a.* 1826. [f. IM-[2] + MARGINATE.] *Entom.* Having no distinct or separate margin.

Imma·rtial, *a. rare.* [IM-[2].] Unwarlike. CHAPMAN.

†Imma·sk, *v.* [f. IM-[1] + MASK *sb.* or *v.*] *trans.* To cover as with a mask; to disguise. SHAKS.

†Imma·tchable, *a.* 1596. [IM-[2].] Unmatchable –1630.

Immaterial (imătīᵊ·riăl), *a.* (*sb.*) ME. [ad. med.L. *immaterialis*, f. *im-* (IM-[2]) + *materialis.*] **1.** Not consisting of matter; incorporeal; spiritual. **b.** *pl.* as *sb.* Non-material things 1661. **2.** Having little substance. *Tr. & Cr.* v. i. 35. **†3.** Not pertinent to the matter –1632. **4.** Of little or no importance 1698.

1. That strange i. Power of the Loadstone 1641. 4. The question of notice becomes i. after my finding that there was no agreement CHITTY. Hence **Immateriality,** the quality or character of being i.; an i. thing, existence, or essence. **Immate·rial·ly** *adv.*, **-ness.**

Immaterialism (imătīᵊ·riăliz'm). 1713. [f. prec. + -ISM, after *materialism.*] **1.** The doctrine that matter does not exist in itself as a substance or cause, but that all things have existence only as the ideas or perceptions of a mind. **2.** = *Immateriality.* BYRON. So **Immate·rialist,** one who holds the doctrine of i.

Immaterialize (imătīᵊ·riălaiz), *v.* 1661. [f. as prec. + -IZE.] *trans.* To render immaterial or incorporeal.

†Immate·riate, *a.* 1626. [IM-[2].] = IMMATERIAL –1653.

Immature (imătiūᵊ·ɹ), *a.* 1548. [ad. L. *immaturus*, f. *im-* (IM-[2]) + *maturus.*] **1.** Untimely, premature. (Mostly of death.) *Obs.* or *arch.* **2.** Not mature; not perfect or complete; unripe 1599.

2. I. fruit BRADLEY, polypi DARWIN, student 1823. Hence **Immatu·re·ly** *adv.*, **-ness. Immatu·rity,** the quality or condition of being i.

Immeability (imī¦ăbi·lĭti). 1731. [f. IM-[2] + L. *meabilis* passable; see -BILITY.] Inability to pass or flow through a channel.

Immeasurable (ime·ʒiŭrăb'l, imm-), *a.* 1440. [IM-[2].] That cannot be measured; immense.

The vast i. Abyss MILT. *P.L.* VII. 211. Hence **Immea·surabi·lity, Immea·surableness,** incapability of being measured. **Immea·surably** *adv.*

Immeasured (ime·ʒiŭd, imm-), *a.* 1456. [IM-[2].] Not measured; immense, vast.

†Immecha·nical, *a.* 1715. [IM-[2].] Not mechanical –1796. Hence **Immecha·nically** *adv.* So **†Imme·chanism,** non-mechanical property; inertia.

Immediacy (imī·diăsi). 1605. [f. next; see -ACY.] **1.** Freedom from intermediate agency; direct relation or connexion; directness. **b.** *Logic*, etc. (See IMMEDIATE 2, quots.) 1834. **2.** The condition of being the immediate lord or vassal (see IMMEDIATE 1 b.) 1762. **3.** The condition of being immediate in time 1856.

1. *Lear* v. iii. 65. 2. Varel lost its i. or independency, and stands at present under the superiority of Oldenburg 1762. 3. I. of enjoyment 1856.

Immediate (imī·diĕt), *a.* (*adv.*) 1533. [ad. med.L. *immediatus*, f. *im-* (IM-[2]) + *mediatus* MEDIATE.] **1.** That has no intermediary or intervening member, medium, or agent; that is in actual contact or direct relation 1548. **b.** *spec.* In *Feudal* language, said of the relation between two persons, one of whom holds of the other directly, as in *i. lord, tenant, tenure*; also ellipt. = Holding directly of the sovereign or lord paramount, *spec.* in Germany, of the Emperor 1543. **2.** Acting or existing without any intervening medium or agency; involving actual contact or direct relation; opp. to *mediate* and *remote* 1533. **3.** Having no person, thing, or space intervening, in place, order, or succession; proximate, nearest, next; close, near; often used *loosely*, of a distance which is of no account 1602. **4.** Of time: Present or next adjacent; of things: Pertaining to the time current or instant 1605. **b.** Taking effect without delay; instant 1568. **5.** Having a direct bearing 1725. **†6.** *adv.* [partly L. *immediātē.*] Immediately 1508–1626.

1. His [the Emperor's] more i. servants GIBBON. The i. object of all art is either pleasure or utility BUCKLE. 2. By Our owne ymmediate commaunde 1625. Phr. *Immediate inference* (Logic): an inference drawn from a single premiss, without the intervention of a middle term. *I. knowledge* (Philos.): knowledge of self-evident truth; intuitive knowledge. *I. auscultation* (Med.): auscultation performed without the stethoscope. 3. You are the most i. to our throne *Haml.* I. ii. 109. In the i. neighbourhood (*mod.*) 4. The i. future FROUDE. An i. reply will oblige (*mod.*). 5. Destitute of obvious or i. utility 1896. Hence **Imme·diateness.**

Immediately (imī·diĕtli), *adv.* (*conj.*) ME. [f. L. *immediatus* + -LY [2], orig. to render L. *immediate* adv. (cf. prec. 6).] **1.** In an immediate way; by direct agency; directly. **2.** With no person, thing, or distance intervening in time, space, order, or succession; closely; proximately; directly 1466. **3.** Without any delay; instantly ME. **b.** as *conj.* (ellipt. for *immediately that*). The moment that 1839.

1. Canow..was immediatly vnder the dominion of the Tartars HAKLUYT. I. holden of the Crown 1647. 3. He bade me goe immeadiatlye 1500.

Immediatism (imī·diĕtiz'm). 1825. [f. IMMEDIATE *a.* + -ISM.] **1.** Immediateness. *rare.* **2.** The principle of immediate action; in *U.S. Hist.* the policy of the immediate abolition of slavery 1835; hence **Imme·diatist** 1835.

Immedicable (ime·dikăb'l), *a.* 1533. [See IM-[2] and MEDICABLE.] Incapable of being healed, incurable. Also *transf.* and *fig.*

I. wounds 1596, disaffection MILT. **Imme·dicably** *adv.*

Immelodious (imĭlōᵘ·diəs, imm-), *a.* 1601. [IM-[2].] Unmelodious.

Immemorable (ime·mŏrăb'l), *a.* 1552. [See IM-[2] and MEMORABLE.] **1.** Not memorable; not worth remembering. **†2.** = IMMEMORIAL –1796.

Immemorial (imĭmōᵊ·riăl), *a.* 1602. [See IM-[2] and MEMORIAL.] That is beyond memory or out of mind; ancient beyond memory or record; extremely old.

The moan of doves in i. elms TENNYSON. *I. usage* (Law): a practice which has existed time out of mind; custom; prescription. Hence **Immemo·rially** *adv.*

Immense (ime·ns), *a.* (*sb.*) 1490. [a. F., ad. L. *immensus*, f. *im-* (IM-[2]) + *mensus*, pa. pple. of *metiri* to measure.] **1.** Unmeasured; hence, immeasurably large; boundless; infinite. ? *Obs.* 1599. **2.** Extremely great or large; vast, huge 1490. **3.** *slang.* Splendid 1762. **4.** *sb.* Immensity 1791.

1. That i. and boundless ocean Of nature's riches DANIEL. 2. I. Armies 1660. At i. length 1895. An i. eater (*mod.*). Hence **Imme·nse·ly** *adv.*, **-ness.**

†Imme·nsible, *a.* 1579. [a. F. or ad. L. **immensibilis*, f. *im-* (IM-[2]) + *mens-*, *metiri* to measure; see -IBLE.] Immeasurable; immense –1630.

Immensity (ime·nsĭti). 1450. [a. F. *immensité*, or ad. L. *immensitas.*] **1.** The quality or condition of being immense; boundlessness, infinity. **2.** Vast magnitude; hugeness 1652; an immense deal 1778. **3.** That which is immense 1631.

1. The i. of God STILLINGFL. Thou, whose exterior semblance doth belie Thy Soul's i. WORDSW. 2. The i. of the disaster 1883. 3. Thou..shutt'st in little room I. DONNE. Yon blue i. BYRON.

†Imme·nsive, *a.* 1604. [ad. obs. f. *immensif*; see -IVE.] Immeasurable, immense –1648.

Immensurable (ime·nsiŭrăb'l, -ſŭr-), *a.* 1535. [a. F.; see IM-[2] and MENSURABLE.] Immeasurable.

What an i. space is the Firmament DERHAM. Hence **Immensurabi·lity, Imme·nsurableness.**

†Imme·nsurate, *a.* 1654. [ad. late L. *immensuratus*, f. *im-* (IM-[2]) + *mensuratus.*] Unmeasured, immense –1766.

Immerd (imə̄·ɹd), *v. rare.* 1635. [f. (ult.) *im-* (IM-[1]) + *merda* dung.] *trans.* To bury in or cover with ordure.

Immerge (imə̄·ɹdʒ, imm-), *v.* Now *rare.* 1611. [ad. L. *immergere*, f. *im-* (IM-[1]) + *mergere* to MERGE.] **1.** *trans.* To dip, plunge, put under the surface of a liquid; to immerse 1624. Also *transf.* and *fig.* **2.** *intr.* (for *refl.*) To plunge or dip oneself in a liquid; to sink. Also *transf.* and *fig.* 1706. **†b.** *spec.* of a celestial body: To enter the shadow of another in an eclipse, or to disappear behind another in an occultation; to sink below the horizon –1787.

1. To i. birds in spirits 1770. *fig.* We..I. ourselves in luxury JOHNSON. 2. I. up to the Breast in a warm Bath WESLEY. Hence **Imme·rgence,** the action of immerging.

†Immergent, *a.* Erron. sp. of EMERGENT, in sense 'urgent' –1792.

†Imme·rit, *sb.* 1628. [f. IM-[2] + MERIT.] Demerit –1750.

†Imme·rited, *ppl. a.* 1600. [IM-[2].] Unmerited. Hence **†Imme·rit** *v.* not to deserve or merit (only in *pres. pple.* and *ppl. a.*).

†Imme·ritous, *a.* [f. L. *immeritus* + -OUS.] Undeserving, without merit. MILTON.

Immerse (imə̄·ɹs), *v.* 1605. [f. L. *immers-*, *immergere* (see IMMERGE).] **1.** *trans.* To dip or plunge into a liquid; to put overhead in water, etc.; *spec.* to baptize by immersion. Also *transf.* and *†fig.* **2.** *transf.* and *fig.* To plunge or sink into a (particular) state of body or mind; to steep, absorb in some action or activity. Chiefly *pass.* or *refl.* 1664. **3.** *intr.* for *refl.* To plunge oneself, sink, become absorbed (*lit.* and *fig.*). Now *rare* or *Obs.* 1667.

1. To i. meat in a solution of salt 1879. *transf.* More than a mile immers'd within the wood DRYDEN. *fig.* Other formes..are more immersed into matter BACON. 2. A youth immersed in Mathematics COWPER.

†**Imme·rse**, *ppl. a.* 1626. [ad. L. *immersus.*] Immersed –1647.
After long Inquiry of Things, I. in Matter BACON.

Immersed (imɔ̄·ɹst), *ppl. a.* 1667. [f. IMMERSE *v.* + -ED[1].] Dipped, plunged, or sunk in, or as in, a liquid 1678. **b.** Growing wholly under water. GRAY. **c.** *Biol.* Sunken or embedded in a surface 1826. †**d.** *Astron.* Plunged in darkness, eclipsed –1854.

†**Immersible** (imɔ̄·ɹsĭb'l), *a.*[1] *rare.* 1693. [f. (ult.) *im-* (IM-[2]) + *mergere, mers-*; see -IBLE.] That cannot sink in water. Hence **Immersibi·lity.**

Imme·rsible, *a.*[2] *rare.* 1846. [f. IMMERSE *v.* + -IBLE.] Capable of being immersed.

Immersion (imɔ̄·ɹʃən). 1450. [ad. late L. *immersionem.*] The action of immerging or immersing. **1.** Dipping or plunging into water or other liquid, and *transf.* into other things 1658. **b.** The administration of Christian baptism by dipping the whole person in water; dist. from *affusion* or *aspersion* 1629. **c.** *Alch.* Reduction of a metal in some solvent 1683. **2.** *transf.* and *fig.* Absorption in some condition, action, interest, etc. 1647. **3.** *Astron.* The disappearance of a celestial body behind another or in its shadow, as in an occultation or eclipse; opp. to *emersion* 1690. **4.** *Microscopy.* The introduction of a liquid between the object-glass and the object 1875. **5.** *attrib.*, as (sense 1) *i. bath*, (4) *i. fluid, lens, objective*, etc. 1875.
1. Two or Three total Emersions in the Cold Bath ADDISON. **2.** His i. in the Peninsular War ALISON. **5.** *I. lens*, an achromatic objective for the microscope, which is used with a drop of water between the front lens and the slide, to prevent the extreme refraction of the luminous pencils if air is present. Hence **Imme·rsionism**, the doctrine or practice of i. in baptism. **Imme·rsionist**, one who adheres to immersionism.

Immesh, var. of ENMESH *v.*

Immethodic, -al (imeþǫ·dik, -ăl, imm-), *a.* 1605. [IM-[2].] Having no method; unmethodical. Hence **Immetho·dical·ly** *adv.*, **-ness.**

Immethodize (ime·þǫdəiz), *v.* 1811. [f. IM-[2] + METHOD + -IZE.] *trans.* To emancipate from method; to render unmethodical. LAMB.

Immetrical (ime·trikăl, imm-), *a.* 1598. [IM-[2].] Not metrical; unmetrical. Hence **Imme·trical·ly** *adv.*, **-ness.**

Immigrant (i·migrănt). 1787. [ad. L. *immigrantem*, after *emigrant.*] **A.** *adj.* Immigrating 1805. **B.** *sb.* One who or that which immigrates; a person who migrates into a country as a settler. (orig. in N. Amer. use.)

Immigrate (i·migre[i]t), *v.* 1623. [f. L. *immigrat-, immigrare*, f. *im-* (IM-[1]) + *migrare* to MIGRATE.] **1.** *intr.* To come to settle in a country (which is not one's own); to pass into a new habitat (*lit.* and *fig.*). **2.** *trans.* To bring in as settlers 1896.
2. The expense of immigrating coolie labour from the East Indies 1898. Hence **Immigra·tion**, entrance into a country for the purpose of settling there. **I·mmigrator**, an immigrant. **I·mmigratory** *a.* of or pertaining to immigration.

†**Immi·nd, inmi·nd**, *v.* 1647. [IM-[1].] *trans.* To remind –1660.

Imminence (i·minĕns). 1606. [ad. late L. *imminentia*, f. *imminent-*; see -ENCE.] **1.** The fact or condition of being imminent or impending 1655. **2.** That which is imminent; impending evil or peril 1606.
1. The i. of any danger or distress FULLER. **2.** I.. dare all i. that gods and men Addresse their dangers in SHAKS. So **I·mminency**, imminent quality or character.

Imminent (i·minĕnt), *a.* 1528. [ad. L. *imminens, -entem, imminere* to overhang, impend, be near, f. *im-* (IM-[1]) + *-minere* as in *eminere*; cf. EMINENT.] **1.** Of an event, etc. (usu. of evil or danger): Impending threateningly, hanging over one's head; ready to overtake one; coming on shortly. †**2.** Remaining intent (*upon* something) 1641. **3.** In lit. sense: Overhanging 1727. †**4.** Confused with IMMANENT –1856.
1. Haire-breadth scapes i' th' i. deadly breach SHAKS. Invasion was i. STUBBS. **2.** Their eyes ever i. upon worldly matters MILT. Hence **I·mminently** *adv.*

Immingle (imi·ŋg'l, imm-), *v.* 1606. [IM-[1].] *trans.* To mix or blend intimately; to mingle. Also *intr.* for *refl.*
intr. Where..with the chestnut the oak-trees i. CLOUGH.

†**I·mminute**, *a.* 1681. [ad. L. *imminutus, imminuere*, f. *im-* (IM-[1]) + *minuere* to lessen.] Lessened. So †**Imminu·tion**, lessening, decrease.

Immiscible (imi·sĭb'l), *a.* 1671. [f. IM-[2] + MISCIBLE.] That cannot be mixed; incapable of mixture.
Like water and oil, they are i. 1833. Hence **Immiscibi·lity**, i. quality. **Immi·scibly** *adv.*

Immission (imi·ʃən, imm-). Now *rare.* 1526. [ad. L. *immissionem*, f. *immittere* to IMMIT.] The action of immitting; insertion, injection, admission, introduction. The opposite of *emission.* **b.** That which is immitted 1526.

Immit (imi·t), *v.* Now *rare* or *Obs.* 1578. [ad. L. *immittere*, f. *im-* (IM-[1]) + *mittere* to send.] *trans.* To put in, inject, infuse; to introduce; the opposite of *emit.*

Immitigable (imi·tigăb'l), *a.* 1576. [ad. L. *immitigabilis*; see IM-[2] and MITIGABLE.] That cannot be mitigated, softened, or appeased. Hence **Immi·tigably** *adv.*

Immix (imi·ks), *v.* Now *rare.* ME. [f. *immixt* pa. pple., analysed as implying a present *immix.* See MIX *v.*] *trans.* To mix in (*with* something else); to mix intimately, mix up, commingle. Also *refl.* and *intr.*
Samson with these immixt, inevitably Pulled down the same destruction on himself MILT. *Sams.* 1657.

†**Immi·xable**, *a.* 1641. [IM-[2].] Immiscible.

†**Immixt, immixed** (imi·kst), *a.* 1622. [orig. ad. L. *immixtus*, f. *im-* (IM-[2]) + *mixtus.*] Not mixed, pure, simple –1659.
They [the Chinese] are the most ancient and i. people in the Universe SIR T. HERBERT. Hence **Immi·xtness, -edness.** So †**Immi·xt** *v.* (*rare*) = IMMIX.

†**Immi·xture**[1]. *rare.* 1648. [IM-[2].] The condition of being unmixed; purity; simplicity.

Immixture[2] (imi·kstiŭɹ). 1859. [f. L. *immixt-, immiscere* to IMMIX + -URE; cf. *admixture*, etc.] The action of immixing or mixing up; commingling; the fact of being mixed up (*in* something).
To avoid an i. in political strife BRYCE.

Immobile (imō̆u·bil), *a.* ME. [a. F., ad. L. *immobilis*; see IM-[2] and MOBILE.] Incapable of moving or being moved; immovable (*lit.* and *fig.*); fixed, stable. Also loosely: That does not move; motionless, stationary. var. †**Immoble.**

Immobility (imobi·lĭti). 1483. [a. F. *immobilité*, or ad. L. *immobilitas, -tatem*, f. *immobilis.*] The quality or condition of being immobile; fixedness, stability; motionlessness (*lit.* and *fig.*). **b.** *concr.* = IMMOVABLE B. Browning.

Immobilize (imō̆u·biləiz), *v.* 1871. [ad. F. *immobiliser*, f. *immobile*; cf. *mobilize.*] *trans.* To render immobile; to keep (a joint or limb) without motion for surgical purposes; to render (troops) incapable of being mobilized; to withdraw (specie) from circulation, holding it against bank-notes.
To oblige the enemy to i. around us considerable forces 1871. Hence **Immobiliza·tion**, the action or process of immobilizing; *concr.* specie withdrawn from circulation.

†**Immo·deracy.** *rare.* 1682. [f. IMMODERATE; see -ACY.] Want of moderation; excess –1686. So †**Immoderancy.** SIR T. BROWNE.

Immoderate (imǫ·dĕrĕt), *a.* ME. [ad. L. *immoderatus*; see IM-[2] and MODERATE.] **1.** Not moderate; exceeding usual or proper limits; excessive, extravagant; unreasonable; extreme. †**2.** Unrestrained; intemperate –1696. †**3.** Boundless; very great (*rare*) –1656.
1. I. slepe ELYOT, expenses 1601. Pindarus was i. in the ornaments of his poesie 1638. Hence **Immo·derate·ly** *adv.*, **-ness.**

Immoderation (imǫdĕrē[i]·ʃən). 1541. [a. F., or ad. L. *immoderationem*; see IM-[2] and MODERATION.] The opposite of moderation; immoderateness, excess. †**b.** *pl.* Excesses –1679.

Immodest (imǫ·dĕst), *a.* 1570. [ad. L. *immodestus*; see IM-[2] and MODEST.] Not modest, void of modesty. **1.** Arrogant, forward, impudent. **2.** Improper, indelicate, indecent, lewd, unchaste 1590.
1. With this i. clamorous outrage SHAKS. **2.** To speak lewd words and sing i. songs DE FOE. **Immo·destly** *adv.*

Immodesty (imǫ·dĕsti). 1597. [ad. L. *immodestia*; see IM-[2] and MODESTY.] Want of modesty; arrogance; impudence 1605; impropriety, indelicacy; unchastity 1597.
She shames to think that ought within her face Should breed th' opinion of i. DANIEL.

†**Immo·dish**, *a.* 1649. [IM-[2].] Unfashionable –1690.

Immo·dulated, *ppl. a. rare.* 1765. [f. IM-[2] + *modulated.*] Not modulated; without vocal modulation.

†**Immolate**, *ppl. a. Obs.* or *arch.* 1534. [ad. L. *immolatus*; see next.] Sacrificed, immolated –1830.

Immolate (i·mole[i]t), *v.* 1548. [f. L. *immolat-, immolare*, orig. to sprinkle with sacrificial meal, f. *im-* (IM-[1]) + *mola* meal.] **1.** *trans.* To sacrifice, offer in sacrifice; to kill as a victim. (Now only of sacrifices in which life is taken.) †Also *absol.* or *intr.* **2.** *transf.* and *fig.* To give up to destruction or severe loss for the sake of something else; to sacrifice 1634.
1. Human victims were immolated to the Thunderer 1851. **2.** To i. their own inclinations..to their Vanity BOYLE.

Immolation (imolē[i]·ʃən). 1533. [ad. L. *immolationem.*] **1.** The action of immolating; sacrificial slaughter of a victim; sacrifice. **b.** Applied to the sacrifice of the mass 1548. **c.** *concr.* That which is immolated; a sacrifice, an oblation 1589. **2.** *fig.* Sacrifice 1690.
1. The I. of Isaac SIR T. BROWNE. **2.** This i. of genius and fame at the shrine of conscience EMERSON.

I·mmolator. 1652. [ad. L., f. *immolare.*] One who immolates or offers in sacrifice.

†**Immo·ment**, *a.* [Arbitrary f. IM-[2] + MOMENT *sb.*] Of no moment; trifling. *Ant. & Cl.* V. ii. 166. So **Immome·ntous** *a.* (*rare*), unimportant 1726.

Immoral (imǫ·răl), *a.* (*sb.*) 1660. [f. IM-[2] + MORAL. Cf. F. *immoral.*] The opposite of *moral.* **1.** Not consistent with, or not conforming to, moral law; opposed to or violating morality; now often, morally evil or impure; vicious, dissolute. †**2.** Non-moral. SHERLOCK.
1. The same dissolute i. temper of mind BUTLER. **B.** *sb.* An immoral lesson; *pl.* bad morals; also, an immoral person 1863.
Hence **Immo·rally** *adv.* in an i. manner. Also **Immo·ralism**, i. practice 1918; **Immo·ralist**, one who practises immorality 1691.

Immorality (imoræ·lĭti). 1566. [f. prec. + -ITY, after *morality.*] **1.** Immoral quality, character, or conduct; wickedness, viciousness. (Now often used spec. of sexual impurity.) **2.** An immoral act or practice; a vice 1631.
1. The educated Greeks..had no horror of i. as such FROUDE. **2.** Deceit and falsehood are not regarded as immoralities in the eyes of Asiatics 1859.

Immo·ralize, *v. rare.* 1754. [f. IMMORAL + -IZE.] *trans.* To render immoral.

†**Immorigerous**, *a.* 1623. [f. IM-[2] + MORIGEROUS.] Unyielding; rebellious; uncivil –1732. Hence †**Immori·gerousness**, uncomplying obstinacy 1649.

Immortal (imǭ·ɹtăl). ME. [ad. L. *immortalis* (in pl. = the gods), f. *im-* (IM-[2]) + *mortalis.* Cf. F. *immortel.*]
A. *adj.* **1.** Not mortal; not subject to death; undying; living for ever. **b.** *transf.* Pertaining to immortal beings or immortality; heavenly, divine 1535. **2.** In wider sense: Everlasting, unfading, incorruptible 1630. **b.** *spec.* Of fame, etc.: Lasting through all time 1514. **3.** In hyperbolical use: Lasting, perpetual, constant 1538; †*colloq.* excessive –1627.
1. Lyke a þyng inmortal semede sche CHAUCER. Now vnto yͤ king eternal, i., inuisible..be honour and glory for euer & euer TINDALE 1 *Tim.* i. 17. **b.** I haue Immortall longings in me *Ant. & Cl.* v. ii. 283. **2.** The race, where that immortall garland is to be run for MILT. **b.** Aires, Married to i. verse MILT. †*I. herb* = IMMORTELLE. **3.** I have made myself an i. enemy by it PEPYS.
B. *sb.* **1.** An immortal being; one not subject to death. In *pl.*, a title for the gods of mythology. 16.. **2.** *fig.* **a.** In *pl.* a title for the

royal bodyguard of ancient Persia; also, for other troops 1803. **b.** A person, esp. an author, of enduring fame. Usu. in *pl.* 1882. **3.** That which is immortal; immortality 1841.

1. Under yon great city fight no few Sprung from Immortals COWPER.

Hence **Immo·rtalism**, a doctrine of or belief in immortality. **Immo·rtalist**, one who believes in immortality. **Immo·rtally** *adv.* eternally; perpetually; *colloq.* infinitely.

Immortality (imǫɹtæ·līti). ME. [a. F. *immortalité*, ad. L. *immortalitatem.*] **1.** The quality or condition of being immortal; exemption from death or annihilation; endless existence; eternity; perpetuity. **2.** Enduring fame or remembrance 1535.

1. Phr. *Conditional i.*: the theological doctrine that human i. is conditional upon faith in Christ. This mortall must put on immortalite TINDALE 1 *Cor.* xv. 53. The Sadducees denied..the i. of the Soul BAXTER. 2. Shakspeare's i. is secure 1866.

Immortalization (imǭ·ɹtăləizēⁱ·ʃən). 1603. [f. next + -ATION.] The action of immortalizing, or fact of being immortalized.

Immortalize (imǭ·ɹtăləiz), *v.* 1566. [f. IMMORTAL + -IZE.] **1.** *trans.* To render immortal; to exempt from death 1633; to perpetuate 1566; to confer enduring fame upon (the prevailing sense); also *absol.* 1589. **2.** *intr.* To become immortal (*rare*) 1737.

1. A genius..who has immortalized Edinburgh,—Walter Scott LD. COCKBURN. Hence **Immo·rtalizer.**

‖**Immortelle** (imǫɹte·l, ‖Fr. *i*mmortel). 1832. [Fr. (short for *fleur immortelle*).] A name for various composite flowers of papery texture (esp species of *Helichrysum*, *Xeranthemum*, etc.) which retain their colour after being dried; = EVERLASTING.

Immortification (imǭ·ɹtifikēⁱ·ʃən). 1626. [ad. eccl.L. *immortificatio*; see IM-² and MORTIFICATION.] Want of mortification; a condition of the soul in which the passions are not mortified.

†**Immo·te**, *a.* 1601. [ad. L. *immotus.*] Unmoved –1685.

Immotile (imōᵘ·til, -əil), *a.* 1872. [f. IM-² + MOTILE.] Not motile; incapable of movement. So **Immo·tive** *a.* 1627.

Immovable (imū·văb'l), *a.* (and *sb.*) ME. [f. IM-² + MOVABLE.]

A. *adj.* **1.** *lit.* That cannot be moved physically; firmly fixed; incapable of movement. Often loosely: Motionless, stationary, fixed. **2.** *fig.* Not subject to change; unalterable, fixed ME.; steadfast, unyielding 1534; emotionless, impassive 1639. **3.** *Law.* Not liable to be removed; permanent; opp. to *movable* 1449.

1. I. as Statues 1662. 2. *Immovable feast*: see FEAST *sb.* Resting immooveable in his counsels 1600. His features were i. DICKENS. 3. All commodities, Moveable and Immoveable HOBBES.

B. *sb.* (*Law.*) A piece or article of property that is immovable (see A. 3); usu. in *pl.* Immovable property, as land and things adherent thereto, as trees, buildings, servitudes 1588.

Hence **Immovabi·lity, Immo·vableness**, i. quality or condition. **Immo·vably** *adv.* in an i. manner (*lit.* and *fig.*).

Immund (imɒ·nd), *a. rare.* 1621. [ad. L. *immundus.* Cf. F. *immonde.*] Unclean, foul.

†**Immundi·city.** 1530. [ad. obs. F. *immondicité*, irreg. f. *immondice* impurity, ad. L. *immunditia.*] Uncleanness, impurity; filthiness; in *pl.* impurities –1660.

Immune (imiū·n), *a.* ME. [ad. L. *immunis* exempt, f. *im-* (IM-²) + *munis* ready to serve, *munus* service, duty.] **1.** Free (*from* some liability); exempt. *Obs.* exc. *fig.* from 2. **2.** *spec.* Having immunity *from* poison, contagion, etc., esp. through inoculation, etc. 1881; serving to develop immunity 1902.

Immunity (imiū·nīti). ME. [ad. L. *immunitas*, f. *immunis* IMMUNE; see -ITY, and cf. F. *immunité.*] **1.** *Law.* Exemption from a service, obligation, or duty; freedom from liability to taxation, jurisdiction, etc.; privilege granted to an individual or a corporation conferring particular exemptions. Also less strictly: Non-liability, privilege. Also with *pl.* **2.** *spec.* (*Eccl.*) Exemption of eccl. persons and things from secular or civil liabilities, burdens, or duties. Chiefly with *an* and *pl.* 1513. †**3.** Undue freedom, licence –1680. **4.** Exemption *from* any usual liability, or from anything injurious 1592. **5.** The condition of being immune; immunization; see IMMUNE *a.* 2. 1879.

1. I. from taxation without consent of parliament HALLAM. 2. The immunite..of that sacred Sanctuarie MORE. 4. I. from Trouble HALE, from snakes 1894. 5. The i. of vipers from their own poison 1887.

Immunize (i·miŭnəiz), *v.* 1892. [f. IMMUNE + -IZE.] *trans.* To render immune from poison or infection. Hence **Immuniza·tion**, immunizing or being immunized.

Immure (imiūə·ɹ), *v.* 1583. [ad. med.L. *immurare*, f. *im-* (IM-¹) + *murus* wall. Cf. F. *emmurer.*] †**1.** *trans.* To wall in, to surround with walls; to fortify –1746. **2.** To enclose within walls; to imprison; to confine as in a prison 1588. Also *transf.* and *fig.* (now *rare*). **3.** To build into a wall; to entomb in a wall. Also *transf.* 1675.

1. An Altar..immured by a Square Wall 1698. 2. Immur'd (in the Fleet) HOWELL, in the walls of a cloister 1791. *fig.* Loue..Liues not alone emured in the braine SHAKS. *refl.* To i. himself..in a German University 1826. Hence †**Immu·re** *sb.* something that immures; a wall SHAKS. **Immu·rement**, imprisonment, confinement.

Immu·sical, *a.* Now *rare.* 1626. [IM-².] Not musical or harmonious.

Immutable (imiū·tăb'l), *a.* ME. [ad. L. *immutabilis*; see IM-².] Not mutable; not subject to or susceptible of change; unalterable. **b.** *techn.* Invariable; used e.g. of the markings of a species 1621.

We speak of eternal and i. justice JOWETT. Hence **Immutabi·lity, Immu·tableness. Immu·tably** *adv.*

Immutate (i·miutĕt), *a. rare.* 1788. [ad. L. *immutatus*, f. *im-* (IM-²) + *mutatus.*] Unchanged. So †**Immu·te** *a.* 1639.

†**Immuta·tion.** 1540. [ad. L. *immutationem*; see next.] Mutation, change, alteration, transformation –1704.

†**Immu·te**, *v.* 1613. [ad. L. *immutare*, f. *im-* (IM-¹) + *mutare.*] *trans.* To produce a change in; to alter, transform –1661.

Imp (imp), *sb.* [OE. *impa* (or ? *impe*), pl. *impan*, related to *impian* to IMP; see next.] †**1.** A young shoot; a sapling; a sucker, slip, scion –1672. †**2.** A graft –1706. **3.** Scion (esp. of a noble house); offspring, child (usu. male). *Obs.* since 17th c., exc. as a literary archaism, or as in 5. ME. **b.** = 'Child' (*fig.* and *transf.*). *Obs.* or *arch.* ME. **4.** *spec.* A child of the devil or of hell 1526; hence, a little devil or demon, an evil spirit 1584. **5.** A mischievous child; a young urchin; often used playfully 1642. †**6.** A youth; fellow, lad, boy –1889. **7.** A piece added on, to eke out, lengthen out, or enlarge something; e.g. †an additional tag to a bell-rope; an addition to a beehive to increase its height (*dial.*); a length of twisted hair in a fishing-line (*dial*) 1595.

3. Prince Edward, that goodly ympe HALL. b. Art thou..that Impe of Glory? QUARLES. 4. The Devil's Impe the Pope 1648. A scoffing man..shows more of the i. than of the angel CARLYLE. Small i. of blackness, off at once LOCKER *To Printer's Devil.* 5. I was..an incorrigibly idle i. SCOTT.

Imp (imp), *v.* [OE. *impian* (rare) = OHG. *impfōn* (G. *impfen*), ? ult. from Gr. ἐμφύειν.] †**1.** *trans.* To graft, engraft –1681. **2.** *transf.* and *fig.* To engraft, implant; to inlay, set or fix in (*arch.*) ME. **3.** *Falconry.* To engraft feathers in a damaged wing, so as to restore or improve the powers of flight; hence, allusively 1477. **4.** To extend, lengthen, enlarge, add to; to eke *out*; to repair; to add on a piece to 1592.

2. They were imped in the wicked family of Ahab TRAPP. 3. Ymping a fether to make me flye LYLY. Phr. *To i. the wings of*: to strengthen the flight of; Their Buzzard-wings, imp'd with our Eagles Plumes DRAYTON. If I imp my wing on thine, Affliction shall advance the flight in me GEO. HERBERT. Imp'd with Wings, The Grubs proceed to Bees with pointed Stings DRYDEN. 4. To i. out unavoidable defects with [etc.] CLARENDON.

Imp. Abbrev. of *imperator*, *imperial*, *imprimatur*, etc.

†**Impa·cable**, *a.* 1571. [f. IM-² + L. *pacare* + -ABLE.] That cannot be appeased; implacable –1602. Hence †**Impacabi·lity.**

Impack (impæ·k), *v. rare.* 1590. [f. IM-¹ + PACK *v.*] *trans.* To pack in; to press closely together into a mass. Hence **Impa·ckment**, impacking or being impacked.

Impact (i·mpækt), *sb.* 1781. [ad. L. type **impactus*, f. ppl. stem of *impingere.*] The act of impinging; the striking of one body against another; collision. Chiefly in *Dynamics*, in reference to momentum. Also *fig.*

The i. of the vibrations of the luminous ether on the retina HUXLEY. *fig.* The i. of barbarian conquest STUBBS.

†**Impa·ct**, *ppl. a.* 1563. [ad. L. *impactus*, *impingere.*] = IMPACTED. Const. as *pple.* or *adj.* –1652.

Impact (impæ·kt), *v.* 1601. [orig. and usu. in pa. pple. *impacted*, f. L. *impactus* + -ED¹; the vb. is from this.] **1.** *trans.* To press closely into or in something; to fix firmly in; to pack in. **2.** To stamp or impress (*on* something). GALE. **3.** To make impact *with* 1916.

Impa·cted, *ppl. a.* 1683. [See prec.] Pressed closely in, firmly fixed.

Impaction (impæ·kʃən). 1739. [ad. L. *impactionem.*] The action of becoming, or condition of being, impacted or firmly fixed in. So **Impa·ctment.**

Impaint (impēⁱ·nt), *v.* 1596. [f. IM-¹ + PAINT *v.*] *trans.* To paint upon something, depict. 1 *Hen. IV*, v. i. 80.

Impair (impēᵊ·ɹ), *sb.*¹ *Obs.* or *arch.* 1568. [f. IMPAIR *v.*] An act of impairing; the being impaired; impairment.

I·mpair, *a.* (and *sb.*²). 1606. [Cf. F. *impair* unequal.] †**1.** (?) 'Unsuitable' (T.), unfit; inferior. (But the reading is disputed.) *Tr. & Cr.* IV. v. 103. **2.** Not paired, odd 1839. **b.** *sb.* An unpaired or odd one 1880.

Impair (impēᵊ·ɹ), *v.* [ME. *empaire empeire*, a. OF. *empeirer* to make worse :—L. type **impeiorare*, f. *im-* (IM-¹) + *peior.* Refash. after L. in 15th c.] **1.** *trans.* To make worse, less valuable, or weaker; to lessen injuriously; to damage, injure. **2.** *intr.* (for *refl.*) To grow or become worse; to suffer injury or loss; to deteriorate ME.

1. It never wastes nor empairs an Estate FULLER. Truth No years i. YOUNG. 2. Flesh may empaire.. but reason can repaire SPENSER. Hence **Impai·rable** *a.* (*rare*) that can be impaired. **Impai·rer. Impai·rment**, the action of impairing; the being impaired; deterioration ME.

Impalace (impæ·lĕs), *v.* 1611. [IM-¹.] *trans.* To place or install in a palace.

†**Impa·latable**, *a. rare.* 1787. [IM-².] Not palatable –1814.

Impale (impēⁱ·l), *v.* 1530. Also †**em-**. [a. F. *empaler*, ad. med.L. *impalare*, f. *im-* (IM-¹) + *palus* stake.] **1.** *trans.* To enclose with pales or stakes; to surround with a palisade; to fence in. Also *transf.* and *fig.* Now *rare.* †**b.** *Mil.* To enclose or surround (troops) for defence, as with other troops, or with wagons, etc. (Improp., To set in array.) –1670. **2.** To surround for adornment; to encircle, as with a crown or garland; to border, edge. *Obs.* or *arch.* 1553. **3.** *Her.* To marshal (two coats of arms) side by side on one shield, divided palewise 1605. †**b.** *fig.* To place side by side –1659. **4.** To thrust a pointed stake through the body of; to fix upon a stake thrust up through the body 1613. Also *transf.*

1. Their country goeth under the tearme of *The English Pale*, because the first Englishmen..did empale for themselves certaine limits in the East part of the Iland *Camden's Brit.* II. 73 (Ireland). **b.** The Legionaries stood..impal'd with light armed MILTON. 3. **b.** The Admission of St. Patrick..to be match'd and impaled with the Blessed Virgin in the Honour thereof FULLER. 4. Let them..be..empal'd and left To writhe at leisure round the bloody stake ADDISON. *transf.* The falcon often impales himself on the long and sharp beak [of the heron] 1807.

Impalement (impēⁱ·lmĕnt). 1598. Also †**em-**. [a. F. *empalement*, f. *empaler*; see -MENT.] **1.** The action of enclosing with pales; *concr.* an enclosing fence or palisade 1611. Also *transf.* and *fig.* †**2.** *Bot.* Applied to the calyx, and, in composite flowers, to the involucre –1799. **3.** *Her.* The marshalling of two coats of arms side by side on one shield divided palewise; the arms so marshalled 1774. **4.** The torture or punishment of impaling (see IMPALE *v.* 4) 1630. **5.** The act or fact of being impaled upon the spikes of a gate, etc. 1887.

†**Impa·ler.** 1671. [f. IMPALE *v.* + -ER [1].] Applied by Grew to each of the calyx-leaves or sepals of a single flower, and the bracts of a composite.

†**Impa·llid,** *v. rare.* [f. IM-[1] + PALLID.] *trans.* To render pallid or pale. FELTHAM.

Impalm (impā·m), *v. rare.* 1611. [f. IM-[1] + PALM *sb.*] *trans.* To take or grasp in the palm of the hand; also *fig.*

†**Impa·lmed,** *a.* [f. IM-[1] + *palmed*, repr. L. *palmatus.*] Embroidered with palm-branches: said of the tunica worn by Roman generals in their triumphal processions. FELTHAM.

Impalpable (impæ·lpăb'l), *a.* 1509. [a. F.; see IM-[2] and PALPABLE.] 1. Incapable of being felt; imperceptible to the touch; intangible. Said of things immaterial; also, of very fine powder, in which no grit is felt. 2. *fig.* Not (readily) apprehensible by the mind; producing no definite impression; 'intangible' 1774.

1. A thing i., A shadow COWPER. An i. transparent gas 1873. 2. The almost i. beauties of style and expression 1838. Hence **Impalpabi·lity,** i. quality. **Impa·lpably** *adv.*

Impalsy (impǭ·lzi), *v.* 1750. [f. IM-[1] + PALSY *sb.*] To affect with or as with palsy, to paralyse.

Impaludism (impæ·liudiz'm). 1881. [f. IM-[1] + L. *palus, paludem* marsh + -ISM.] The general morbid state occurring in inhabitants of marshy districts.

Impanate (impē·nĕt, i·mpănĕt), *ppl. a.* 1550. [ad. med.L. *impanatus*; see IMPANE.] Contained or embodied in bread; see IMPANATION. So **Impanate** *v.* (*rare*), to embody in bread.

Impanation (impănē·ʃən). 1548. [ad. med.L. *impanationem*, f. *impanare*; see IMPANE.] In Eucharistic theory: A local presence or inclusion of the body of Christ in the bread after consecration: one of the modifications of the doctrine of the real presence.

Impanator (i·mpănētəɹ). 1855. [ad. med. L. *impanatorem*, f. *impanare* (see next).] One who holds the doctrine of impanation.

†**Impa·ne,** *v.* 1547. [ad. med.L. *impanare*, f. *im-* (IM-[1]) + *panis* bread.] *trans.* To embody in bread; see IMPANATION –1548.

Impa·nel, impa·nnel, *v.* 1514. Var. of EMPANEL *v.*

Imparadise, em- (impæ·rădəis, em-), *v.* 1586. [See IM-[1] and PARADISE.] 1. *trans.* To place in, or as in, Paradise; to transport, ravish 1592. 2. To make a paradise of (a place or state).

1. Imparadis't in one anothers arms MILT.

†**Imparalleled** (impæ·răleld), *a.* 1604. [f. IM-[2] + *paralleled.*] Without parallel, matchless –1680.

†**Impa·rdonable,** *a.* 1523. [IM-[2].] Not to be pardoned, unpardonable –1797. Hence †**Impa·rdonably** *adv.*

Imparidigitate (impæ:ridi·dʒitĕt), *a.* 1864. [f. L. *impar* + DIGITATE.] *Zool.* Having an odd number of fingers or toes on each limb; perissodactyl.

Imparipinnate (-pi·nĕt), *a.* Also **-pennate.** 1847. [ad. mod.L. *imparipinnatus* (Linn.); cf. prec. and PINNATE.] *Bot.* Pinnate (as a leaf) with an odd terminal leaflet.

Imparisyllabic (impæ:risilæ·bik), *a.* 1730. [f. L. *impar* + SYLLABIC.] *Gram.* Applied to Greek and Latin nouns which have not the same number of syllables in all the cases: e g. nom. *lapis*, gen. *lapidis*; etc. Also †**-ical** 1671.

Imparity (impæ·rĭti). Now *rare* or *Obs.* 1563. [ad. late L. *imparitas*; see IM-[2] and PARITY.] 1. = DISPARITY 1. †2. = DISPARITY 2. –1687. †3. Of numbers: The quality of not being divisible into two equal (integral) parts; unevenness; an uneven or odd number –1659.

1. That there might be no imparitie nor inequality at all among his citizens HOLLAND. 3. By two and three, the first parity and i. SIR T. BROWNE.

Impark (impā·ɹk), *v.* Also †**em-.** ME. [a. AF. *enparker*, OF. *emparquer*, f. *em-* (IM-[1]) + *parc* PARK.] 1. *trans.* To enclose in a park, as beasts of the chase; hence *gen.* to confine, shut up. 2. To enclose (land) for a park 1535.

1. Their Deer are no where imparked 1665. Hence **Imparka·tion,** enclosure of land for a park (also *gen.*).

Imparl (impā·ɹl), *v.* Also **em-.** *Obs.* exc. *Hist.* 1461. [a. obs. F. *emparler* to speak, plead.] †1. *intr.* To speak *together*, or *with* another, upon a matter; to parley –1600. 2. *Law.* 'To have license to settle a litigation amicably; to obtain delay by adjustment' (Wharton). *Obs.* in practice; see next, 2. 1461. †3. *trans.* To talk over (*rare*) –1805.

Imparlance (impā·ɹlăns). *Obs.* exc. *Hist.* 1579. [a. AF. **emparlaunce*; see prec. and -ANCE.] †1. Conference, discussion, parleying –1828. 2. *Law.* An extension of time to put in a response in pleading a case, on the (real or fictitious) ground of a desire to negotiate for an amicable settlement; a continuance of the case to another day; a petition for, or leave granted for, such delay. (Abolished in 1853.) Also *fig.*

2. But with rejoinders and replies..Demur, i., and essoign, The parties ne'er could issue join SWIFT.

Imparsonee (impāɹsŏnī·), *a.* 1607. [f. med.L. *impersonata*, f. *im-* (IM-[1]) + *persona* PARSON; see -EE [1].] *Eccl. Law.* In phr. *Parson imparsonee*, a clergyman duly presented, instituted, and inducted into a parsonage or rectory.

Impart (impā·ɹt), *v.* 1471. [a. OF. *empartir*, ad. L. *impartire* (usu. *impert-*) to share, f. *im-* (IM-[1]) + *partire* to PART.] 1. *trans.* To give a part or share of; to make another a partaker of; to bestow, communicate. (Usu. (now only) with immaterial object.) Also *absol.* 1477. 2. To communicate as knowledge or information; to make known, tell, relate (*arch.*) 1547. †b. *refl.* To make known one's mind –1653. †3. To give a share of to each of several persons; to distribute –1601. †4. To have or get a share of; to partake –1655. †b. *intr.* To partake *in* –1615.

1. Thee stars imparted no light 1583. *absol.* He that hath two coats, let him i. to him that hath none *Luke* iii. 11. 2. When I did first i. my loue to you SHAKS. b. Imparting himself equally to all Men CLARENDON. Hence **Impa·rtance** (*rare*; not on L. analogies), **Imparta·tion,** the action of imparting; communication. **Impa·rter,** one who or that which imparts.

Impartial (impā·ɹʃăl), *a.* 1593. [IM-[2].] 1. Not partial; not favouring one more than another; unprejudiced, unbiased, fair, just, equitable. †2. Not fragmentary; entire, complete (*rare*) 1716. ¶3. Misused for *partial. Rom. & Jul.* Qo. 1, I. 1856.

1. An i. Conscience SOUTH, Sovereign *Junius Lett.*, tribunal 1838. 2. An i. and universal Obedience BLACKALL. Hence **Impa·rtialist** (*rare*), one who professes impartiality. **Impa·rtial-ly** *adv.*, **-ness** (*rare*).

Impartiality (impāɹʃiæ·lĭti). 1611. [f. prec. + -ITY.] 1. The quality of being impartial; freedom from prejudice or bias; fairness. †2. Completeness. BLACKALL.

1. I. to children FIELDING. A tone of historic i. 1836.

Impartible (impā·ɹtib'l), *a.*[1] (*sb.*) 1398. [ad. late L. *impartibilis*; see IM-[2] and PARTIBLE.] 1. Incapable of being parted or divided; not subject to partition; indivisible. Now chiefly legal. 2. *sb.* Something that is indivisible 1788.

1. The question..whether the estate..was partible or i. 1890. Hence **Impartibi·lity** [1], i. quality 1656. **Impa·rtibly** *adv.* 1631.

†**Impartible,** *a.*[2] *rare.* 1631. [f. L. *impartiri*; see -IBLE.] Capable of being imparted. Hence **Impartibility** [2], communicability.

Imparticipable (impāɹti·sipăb'l), *a.* (*sb.*) 1789. [IM-[2].] 1. Incapable of being participated or shared. 2. *sb.* An imparticipable thing 1789.

Impartment (impā·ɹtmĕnt). 1602. [f. IMPART *v.* + -MENT.] The fact of imparting, or that which is imparted; communication; a communication.

It beckons you to go away with it, As if it some i. did desire To you alone *Haml.* I. iv. 59.

Impassable (impɑ·săb'l), *a.* 1568. [IM-[2].] 1. That cannot be passed along, through, or across. †2. That cannot pass (away or through) –1832. 3. That cannot be made to pass (*rare*) 1865.

1. I. Woods DAMPIER, bounds 1844. 3. To make half-sovereigns practically i. 1887. Hence **Impassabi·lity, Impa·ssableness,** i. quality or condition. **Impa·ssably** *adv.*

‖**Impasse** (ǣnpā·s, impɑ·s). 1851. [F., f. *im-* (IM-[2]) + stem of *passer.*] A road or way having no outlet; a blind alley, 'cul-de-sac'. Also *fig.*

Impassible (impæ·sib'l), *a.* ME. [a. F.; see IM-[2] and PASSIBLE.] 1. Incapable of suffering; not subject to pain. 2. Incapable of suffering injury or detriment 1491. 3. Incapable of feeling or emotion; impassive, insensible, unimpressible 1592. †4. Insufferable (*rare*) –1665.

1. That i. state, where all tears shall be wiped from our eyes 1667. 2. I. as air BAILEY. 3. He was i. before victory, before danger, before defeat THACKERAY. Hence **Impassibi·lity, Impa·ssibleness,** the quality of being i. **Impa·ssibly** *adv.*

Impassion (impæ·ʃən), *v.* Also †**em-.** 1591. [ad. It. *impassionare*, f. *im-* (IM-[1]) + *passione* PASSION.] *trans.* To fill or inflame with passion; to excite deeply or strongly. Also *absol.* Hence **Impa·ssionable** *a.* easily roused to passion. (Dicts.)

Impassionate (impæ·ʃənĕt), *a.*[1] Now *rare.* 1590. [ad. It. *impassionato*; see prec.] = IMPASSIONED. Hence **Impa·ssionately** *adv.*

Impassionate, *a.*[2] Now *rare.* 1621. [f. IM-[2] + PASSIONATE.] Free from passion; dispassionate.

Impassionate (impæ·ʃəneit), *v.* 1639. [f. IMPASSIONATE *a.*[1]; see -ATE [3].] 1. *trans.* = IMPASSION 1641. †2. *intr.* To be or become impassioned –1646.

Impassioned (impæ·ʃənd), *ppl. a.* Also †**em-.** 1603. [f. IMPASSION *v.* + -ED [1].] Filled or inflamed with passion; deeply moved; passionate, ardent.

The Tempter all impassiond thus began MILT. *P. L.* IX. 678. Hence **Impa·ssioned-ly** *adv.*, **-ness.**

Impassive (impæ·siv), *a.* 1667. [IM-[2].] 1. = IMPASSIBLE 1. 2. Naturally without sensation; not susceptible of physical impression or injury, invulnerable 1687; insensible, unconscious 1848. 3. Deficient in, or void of, mental feeling or emotion; unimpressionable, apathetic; also, in good sense, imperturbable, serene 1699. 4. Intolerable (*rare*) 1828.

1. MILT. *P. L.* VI. 455. 2. On the i. Ice the light'nings play POPE. 3. An attitude of i. reserve FROUDE. Hence **Impa·ssively** *adv.* 1828, **-ness** 1648. **Impassi·vity** 1794.

Impastation (impæstē·ʃən). 1727. [f. next.] The formation of a paste; also *concr.* a sort of mason's work, made of stucco, or stone ground small, and wrought up again in manner of a paste.

Impaste (impē·st), *v.* 1548. [ad. It. *impastare*, f. *im-* (IM-[1]) + *pasta* PASTE. Cf. F. *empâter.*] 1. *trans.* To enclose in or encrust with or as with a paste. 2. To make into a paste or crust 1576. 3. *Painting.* To paint by laying on colour thickly 1727.

2. *Haml.* II. ii. 481. 3. Heavily impasted pictures 1865.

‖**Impasto** (impɑ·sto). 1784. [It., f. *impastare* (see prec.).] *Painting.* The laying on of colour thickly; impasting, as a characteristic of style; see prec. 3. Also *attrib.*

attrib. It is impossible to clean i. work 1880.

†**Impa·sture,** *v.* 1612. [f. IM-[1] + PASTURE *sb.*] 1. *trans.* To place in a pasture; to turn out to graze –1614. 2. To enclose for pasture. BLITHE.

†**Impa·tible,** *a.* 1541. [ad. L. *impatibilis*, f. *im-* (IM-[2]) + *patibilis*, f. *pati* to suffer.] 1. = IMPASSIBLE 1, 2. 2. Intolerable –1659.

1. The Devil..is a Spirit, and so i. of materiall Fire FULLER.

Impatience (impē·ʃĕns). ME. [a. OF. *impacience, -patience*, ad. L. *impatientia*, f. *im-* (IM-[2]) + *patientia*; see -ENCE.] The fact or quality of being impatient. 1. Want of endurance; failure to bear suffering, annoyance, etc. with equanimity; irascibility. Often with *of*, or *inf.* 2. *esp.* Intolerance of delay; restlessness of desire or expectation; restless eagerness 1581.

1. [Thou] makest fortune wroth and Aspere by thine in-pacience CHAUCER. I. of cold and wet TOPSELL, of contradiction D'ISRAELI. 2. I wait with i.

for..your return 1712. So †Impa·tiency (esp. as a quality or disposition).

Impatient (impē·ʃĕnt), *a.* (*sb.*) ME. [a. OF. *impacient, impatient*, ad. L. *impatientem*, f. *im-* (IM-²) and *pati.*] 1. Not patient; not bearing or enduring (pain, etc.) with composure; easily provoked. Also *transf.* of action or speech: Indicating impatience. Often with *of, inf.*, or *dependent clause*. 2. That does not willingly endure delay; restless in desire or expectation. Const. *for*, or *inf.* 1588. b. *transf.* and *fig.* Characterized by, or attended with, impatience of delay 1703. †3. 'Not to be borne' (J.) -1646. 4. *sb.* An impatient person 1502.

1. An i. Spirit is never without Woe STEELE. I. of advice STEELE, of heat 1893. 2. I. for the day POPE. *transf.* This one i. Minute 1703. 3. SPENSER *F. Q.* II. i. 44. Hence **Impa·tiently** *adv.*, †**-ness** (*rare*).

†**Impa·tronize,** *v.* 1577. [a. F. *impatroniser* to make master of, f. *patron*, L. *patronus*; see IM-¹.] 1. *trans.* To put in possession *of*; usu. *refl.* -1681. b. *transf.* To take possession of -1799. 2. To patronize 1629.

1. To i. themselves of many Cities and Strong-holds 1681. Hence †**Impa:troniza·tion,** absolute seigniory or possession; the act of impatronizing.

Impave (impē·v), *v. rare.* 1833. [IM-¹.] To pave in; to set in a pavement.

Impaved with rude fidelity Of art Mosaic WORDSW.

Impavid (impæ·vid), *a. rare.* 1857. [ad. L. *impavidus.*] Fearless, undaunted. Hence **Impa·vidly** *adv.*

Impawn (impǭ·n), *v.* 1596. [f. IM-¹ + PAWN *v.* or *sb.*] 1. *trans.* To put in pawn; to pledge. Also *fig.* 2. *fig.* To risk the safety of 1613.

‖**Impayable** (impē·ăb'l, Fr. ɛ̃pɛyabl'), *a.* ME. [a. F., f. *im-* (IM-²) + *payer.* Now often treated as Fr.] †1. Unappeasable. HAMPOLE. 2. That cannot be paid or discharged 1797. ‖3. Beyond price. b. *colloq.* 'Beyond anything'. 1818.

3. The cheese, the fruits, the salad..were *impayables* SCOTT.

Impeach (impī·tʃ), *v.* [ME. *em-, enpechen*, later *empesche*, a. OF. *empechier, empescher*, mod.F. *empêcher*:—late L. *impedicare*, f. *im-* (IM-¹) + *pedica* fetter, f. *pes, pedem* foot. In senses 4 and 5 repr. L. *impetere*. Cf. IMPEACHMENT.] †1. *trans.* To impede, hinder, prevent -1690. †2. To hinder the action, progress, or well-being of; to affect prejudicially; to hurt, endamage, impair -1691. 3. To challenge, call in question, attack; to discredit, disparage 1590. 4. *gen.* To bring a charge against; to accuse *of*, charge *with* ME.; to 'peach' upon 1617; to find fault with, to censure 1813. 5. *spec.* To accuse of treason or other high crime or misdemeanour (usu. against the state) before a competent tribunal 1568. Also applied transf. to analogous judicial processes 1734.

1. A Ditch..to i. the Assaults of an Enemy 1690. 3. To i. one's credit 1600, a general rule FIELDING, a contract BLACKSTONE. 4. Nothing..that might i. me either with error or vntrueth 1590. 5. Latimer was impeached and accused by the voice of the Commons 1863. Hence **Impea·ch** *sb.* †hindrance, impediment 1551; †detriment 1575; challenge, impeachment 1590. **Impea·chable** *a.* capable of being impeached; liable to impeachment; chargeable 1503. **Impea·cher,** one who impeaches 1552.

Impeachment (impī·tʃmĕnt). ME. [a. OF. *empechement, empeschement*, mod. *empêchement*; see prec. and -MENT.] The action of impeaching. †1. Hindrance, obstruction; impediment -1674. †2. Detriment -1648. 3. A calling in question or discrediting; disparagement 1478. 4. Accusation, charge. *Obs.* exc. in *the soft i.* ME. 5. The accusation and prosecution of a person for treason or other high crime or misdemeanour before a competent tribunal; in Great Britain, 'the judicial process by which any man, from the rank of a peer downwards, may be tried before the House of Lords at the instance of the House of Commons'; in U.S., a similar process in which the accusers are the House of Representatives and the court is the Senate 1640.

1. Boris..without i. now ascended the throne MILT. 3. Without an i. to their honour 1658. 4. A considerable i. of heresy 1865. Phr. *Without impeachment of waste* (= law L. *absque impetitione vasti*): 'a reservation frequently made to a tenant for life, that no man shall proceed against him for waste committed' (Wharton). 5. The articles of Strafford's i. HALLAM.

Impearl (impɔ̄·ɹl), *v.* 1586. [ad. F. *emperler*; see IM-¹ and PEARL.] 1. *trans.* To deck with or as with pearls 1591. 2. To make pearly or pearl-like 1639. 3. To form into pearl-like drops 1586.

1. The flowry Meads, Impearl'd with tears SYLVESTER. 3. Dew-drops, which the Sun Impearls on every leaf and every flouer MILT. *P. L.* v. 747.

Impeccable (impe·kăb'l), *a.* (*sb.*) 1531. [ad. late L. *impeccabilis*, f. *im-* (IM-²) + *peccare*; see -BLE.] 1. Of persons: Not liable to sin; exempt from the possibility of doing wrong. 2. Of things: Faultless, unerring 1620. 3. *sb.* One who is impeccable 1748.

1. The Pope is not only infallible, but also i. 1670. Hence **Impeccabi·lity,** the quality or character of being i. **Impe·ccably** *adv.* without liability to sin.

Impeccancy (impe·kănsi). 1614. [ad. eccl. L. *impeccantia*; see -ANCY.] Sinlessness; inerrancy.

Impeccant (impe·kănt), *a.* 1763. [f. IM-² + L. *peccans, peccantem.*] Not sinning; unerring.

Impectinate (impe·ktinĕt), *a.* [IM-².] *Entom.* Not pectinate; not comb-toothed: said of antennæ, etc. (Recent Dicts.)

Impecunious (impĭkiū·niəs), *a.* 1596. [f. IM-² + PECUNIOUS.] Having no money, penniless; in want of money.

A poore i. creature NASHE. var. **Impecu·niary.** Hence **Impecunio·sity,** lack of money; pennilessness.

Impedance (impī·dăns). 1886. [f. IMPEDE *v.* + -ANCE.] *Electr. lit.* Hindrance; virtual resistance due to self-induction in an electrified body.

Impede (impī·d), *v.* 1605. [ad. L. *impedire*, f. *im-* (IM-¹) + *pes, ped-* foot.] *trans.* To obstruct in progress or action; to hinder; to stand in the way of.

My load, light as it was, impeded me TYNDALL. Hence †**Impe·dible** *a.* that can be impeded or hindered.

Impedient (impī·diĕnt), *a.* (*sb.*) 1596. [ad. L. *impedientem*; see prec.] 1. Obstructive, hindering. 2. *sb.* [sc. *agent*] 1661.

Impediment (impe·dimĕnt), *sb.* ME. [ad. L. *impedimentum* hindrance, pl. *-menta* baggage, f. *impedire* to IMPEDE.] 1. The fact of impeding or condition of being impeded; *concr.* something that impedes; a hindrance, an obstruction. 2. †A (physical) defect -1657; *esp.* a stammer or stutter 1494. 3. (Chiefly *pl.*) Baggage, esp. of an army; IMPEDIMENTA 1540. 4. The impedited condition of a planet; see IMPEDITE *v.* 2. 1819.

1. Thus farre..Haue we marcht on without i. SHAKS. Hence †**Impe·diment** *v.* to obstruct. **Impedime·ntal** *a.* obstructive; impeditive.

‖**Impedimenta** (impedime·ntă), *sb.pl.* 1600. [L.; see prec.] Things which encumber progress; baggage; travelling equipment (of an army, etc.).

†**I·mpedite,** *ppl. a.* 1544. [ad. L. *impeditus.*] Impeded, obstructed, hindered; having an impediment. *Astrol.*: see IMPEDITE *v.* 2. -1671.

Impedite (i·mpĭdəit), *v.* Now *rare* or *Obs.* 1535. [f. L. *impedit-*, ppl. stem of *impedire.*] 1. = IMPEDE 1. 2. *Astrol.* Said of a planet when its influence is hindered by the position of another 1647. So †**Impedi·tion,** hindering; being hindered. **Impe·ditive** *a.* of the nature of an impediment; obstructive.

Impel (impe·l), *v.* 1490. [ad. L. *impellere*, f. *im-* (IM-¹) + *pellere* to drive.] 1. *trans.* To drive, force, or constrain (a person) *to* some action, or *to do* something; to urge on, incite. 2. *lit.* To drive or cause to move onward; to impart motion to; to propel 1611.

1. Human nature will i. him to seek pleasure instead of virtue JOWETT. 2. The heart..impels the blood through the arteries BEDDOES. Hence **Impe·ller,** one who, or that which, impels.

Impellent (impe·lĕnt). 1620. [ad. L. *impellentem*; see prec.] a. *adj.* That impels; impelling. b. *sb.* A thing which impels 1644.

†**Impe·n,** *v.* 1627. [f. IM-¹ + PEN *sb.*¹ or *v.*¹] *trans.* To shut up in a pen or fold -1661. Hence †**Impe·nt** *pa. pple.* 1633.

†**Impe·nd,** *v.*¹ 1486. [ad. L. *impendĕre*, f. *im-* (IM-¹) + *pendĕre* to weigh, pay out.] *trans.* To pay; to expend; to apply (money); to bestow -1690.

Impend (impe·nd), *v.*² 1599. [ad. L. *impendēre*, f. *im-* (IM-¹) + *pendēre* to hang.] 1. *intr.* To hang or be suspended (*over*) 1780. 2. *transf.* and *fig.* Of evil or danger: To hang threateningly (*over*) as about to fall 1599. 3. Hence *gen.* To be about to happen; to be imminent 1674. 4. *trans.* To overhang, hover over (*rare*). 1652.

2. Barbarism is ever impending over the civilized world J. H. NEWMAN. 3. A war which was..impending THIRLWALL.

Impendent (impe·ndĕnt), *a.* Now *rare.* 1592. [ad. L. *impendentem*; see prec.] 1. Overhanging 1611. 2. Imminent; near at hand.

2. If..I. horrors, threatning hideous fall One day upon our heads MILT. *P. L.* II. 177. So **Impe·nding** *ppl. a.* Hence **Impe·ndence,** imminence. **Impe·ndency,** imminent or threatening character; an impending circumstance.

Impenetrability (impe:nĭtrăbi·lĭti). 1665. [f. next; see -ITY.] 1. The quality or condition of being impenetrable; inscrutability; unfathomableness; 'unsusceptibility of intellectual impression' (J.) 1706. 2. *Nat. Philos.* That property of matter in virtue of which two bodies cannot occupy the same place at the same time 1665.

Impenetrable (impe·nĭtrăb'l), *a.* 1460. [a. F., ad. L. *impenetrabilis*; see IM-² and PENETRABLE.] 1. That cannot be penetrated or pierced; impossible to get into or through. Const. *to, by.* 2. *transf.* and *fig.* Inscrutable; unfathomable 1531. 3. Impervious to intellectual or moral influences, impressions, or ideas 1596. 4. *Nat. Philos.* Possessing impenetrability (see prec. 2) 1666.

1. Woods i. To Starr or Sun-light MILT. *P. L.* IX. 1086. I. mist WORDSW. 2. An i. secret LINGARD, countenance 1800. 3. It is the most i. curre That euer kept with men SHAKS. Hence **Impe·netrableness,** impenetrability. **Impe·netrably** *adv.*

Impe·netrate, *v.* 1859. [IM-¹.] *trans.* To penetrate intimately.

Impenitence (impe·nitĕns). 1624. [ad. late L. *impœnitentia*; see -ENCE.] The fact or condition of being impenitent; want of repentance; hardness of heart; obduracy.

Denouncing wrauth to come On thir i. MILT. *P. L.* XI. 816. So **Impe·nitency,** the quality or state of being impenitent.

Impenitent (impe·nitĕnt). 1532. [ad. L. *impœnitentem*, f. *im-* (IM-²) + *pœnitens* PENITENT.] A. *adj.* Not penitent; having no contrition or sorrow for sin; unrepentant, obdurate.

After thy hardnesse, and i. heart N.T. (Rhem.) *Rom.* ii. 5. I. Criminals and Malefactors STEELE. Hence **Impe·nitently** *adv.*

B. *sb.* An impenitent person 1532.

†**Impe·nitible,** *a.* 1614. [f. IM-² + stem of L. *pœnitere* + -IBLE.] Incapable of repentance -1637.

Impennate (impe·nĕt), *a.* and *sb.* 1842. [f. IM-² + PENNATE.] a. *adj.* Featherless, wingless; *spec.* applied to the *Impennes*, certain swimming birds which have small wings covered with scale-like feathers, as the penguins. b. *sb.* A bird of this kind.

†**Impe·nnous,** *a.* [f. IM-² + L. *penna* + -OUS.] Wingless. SIR T. BROWNE.

Impeople (impī·p'l) *v.*, var. of EMPEOPLE.

†**I·mperance.** [f. L. *imperant-*, *imperare*; see -ANCE.] Commandingness. CHAPMAN. So †**I·mperant** *a.* commanding, ruling 1617.

†**I·mperate,** *ppl. a.* 1470. [ad. L. *imperatus, imperare.*] a. as *pa. pple.* commanded, ruled -1677. b. as *adj.* 'Commanded' *sc.* by the will; opp. to ELICIT *a.*, q.v. -1710.

b. All the actions elicite or i., which a sinner must performe..that God may be pacified 1624.

†**I·mperate,** *v.* 1599. [f. L. *imperat-*, *imperare.*] *trans.* To command, rule, govern -1660. **Impera·tion,** the action of commanding (*rare*). BENTHAM.

Imperative (impe·rătiv). 1530. [ad. late L. *imperativus*, f. *imperare, imperat-*; see -IVE.] A. *adj.* 1. *Gram.* Expressing command: applied to the verbal mood or forms which express a command, request, or exhortation. 2. Having the quality or property of commanding;

commanding, peremptory 1598. 3. Demanding obedience; that must be done or performed; urgent; of the nature of a duty; obligatory 1823.

2. The suits of kings are i. Bp. Hall. 3. The condition of our sick men made it i. that I should return at once Kane.

B. *sb.* 1. *Gram.* The imperative mood, or a verbal form belonging to it 1530. 2. An imperative action, speech, condition, etc.; a command 1606.

2. The unconditional i. of the moral law Sir W. Hamilton. Hence **Imperati·val** *a.*, **Impe·ratively** *adv.*, **-ness.**

‖**Imperator** (impĕrē·tǫɹ). 1579. [L.] a. In Roman History, a word orig. meaning 'commander', under the Republic, conferred by salutation of the soldiers on a victorious general; afterwards, under the Empire, confined to the head of the state, in whose name all victories were won, and thus = Emperor, q.v. b. *gen.* Absolute ruler, emperor; commander, ruler 1588.

a. Pompeyes souldiers saluted him by the name of I. North. Hence **Impera·torship**, the office of i.

Imperatorial (imperătōə·riăl), *a.* 1660. [f. L. *imperatorius* + -al.] 1. Of or pertaining to an imperator, emperor, or commander; imperial. †2. Imperative 1690.

1. A speech of i. grandeur De Quincey. Hence **Imperato·rially** *adv.* vars. †**Imperato·rian** 1640, †**Imperato·rious** 1625, †**Impe·ratory** 1616.

Imperatorin (imperătōə·rin). Also **imperatrin.** 1838. [f. Bot. L. *Imperatoria* + -in.] *Chem.* A neutral substance discovered in the root of masterwort, *Imperatoria Ostruthium*; the same as peucedanin.

†**Impe·ratrice.** 1460. [a. F., ad. L. *imperatrix, -tricem.*] Empress –1542. So ‖**Impera·trix.**

Imperceivable (impəɹsī·văb'l), *a.* Now *rare.* 1617. [Im-[2].] Imperceptible. Hence **Impercei·vableness. Impercei·vably** *adv.*

†**Imperceived,** *a. rare.* 1624. [Im-[2].] Not perceived –1691.

†**Impercei·verant,** *a.* [Im-[2].] Not perceiving, undiscerning. *Cymb.* IV. i. 15.

Imperceptible (impəɹse·ptĭb'l), *a.* (*sb.*) 1526. [a. F., ad. med.L. *imperceptibilis*; see Im-[2].] Not perceptible. a. Naturally incapable of affecting the perceptive faculties. b. So slight, gradual, subtle, or indistinct as not to be perceptible 1635.

a. As for the soule, it is..i. to all the naturall senses Holland. b. I. gradations 1853.

B. *sb.* An imperceptible thing or creature; with *the*: that which is imperceptible 1709.

Hence **I·mperceptibi·lity**, incapability of being perceived. **Imperce·ptibleness. Imperce·ptibly** *adv.*

Imperception (impəɹse·pʃən). 1662. [Im-[2].] Absence or want of perception.

Imperceptive (impəɹse·ptiv), *a.* 1661. [Im-[2].] 1. Not perceptive; impercipient. 2. In pass. sense: Imperceptible (*rare*). Mozley. Hence **Imperce·ptiveness. Impercepti·vity.**

Impercipient (impəɹsi·piĕnt), *a.* (*sb.*) 1813. [Im-[2].] Not perceiving; lacking perception. b. *sb.* One who lacks perception 1898. So **Imperci·pience**, lack of perception.

†**Impe·rdible,** *a. rare.* [f. Im-[2] + L. *perdere* + -ible.] That cannot be lost or destroyed. Feltham. Hence †**Imperdibi·lity**, i. quality.

Imperence (i·mpĕrĕns). 1766. A vulgar corruption of Impudence. So **I·mperent** *a.*

Imperfect (impɔ̄·ɹfĕkt), *a.* (*sb.*) [ME. *imparfit(e, imperfit(e,* a. F. *imparfait* :—L. *imperfectus*, f. *im-* (Im-[2]) + *perfectus*. Subseq. refash. after L.]

I. 1. Wanting some part; not fully formed, made, or done; unfinished, incomplete; deficient. 2. Not coming up to the standard; defective, faulty ME. †3. Vicious, evil –1630. 4. Not fully instructed or accomplished *in* 1570.

1. Inperfit cercles Chaucer. 2. Your other Senses grow i. By your eyes anguish *Lear* IV. vi. 5. 4. I. in the Doctrine of Meteors Sir T. Browne.

II. Techn. senses. 1. *Gram.* Applied to a tense which denotes action going on but not completed; usually to the past tense of incomplete or progressive action ('past imperfect'), as *I was writing* 1530. †2. *Arith.* a. Applied to a number which is not equal to the sum of its aliquot parts; opp. to *perfect*. b. Applied to a power (square, cube, etc.) whose root is an incommensurable quantity; opp. to a *perfect square, cube*, etc. –1706. 3. *Mus.* †a. In mediæval music, applied to a note when reckoned as twice (not three times) the length of a note of the next lower denomination; and hence to 'modes', etc. characterized by such relative value of the notes. b. Applied to Plain Chant melodies which do not extend through the entire compass of the mode in which they are written (Grove). c. Sometimes applied to a diminished fourth, fifth, or triad; see Diminished 1597. 4. *Bot.* Applied to flowers in which any normal part is wanting 1704. 5. *Law.* (See quots.) 1832.

3. *Imperfect cadence*: one ending not on the direct chord of the tonic, but usually on that of the dominant, and having the effect of a partial close or stop; a *half-close*. *I. concords* or *consonances*: a name for the thirds and sixths, major and minor. 5. An i. law ..is a law which wants a sanction and which therefore is not binding Austin. *I. obligations*, moral duties, which cannot be enforced by law. *I. trusts*: executory trusts (Executory *a.* 3).

B. as *sb.* 1. *Gram.* The imperfect (i.e. past imperfect) tense 1871. †2. *Mus.* An imperfect concord 1667.

Hence **Impe·rfect·ly** *adv.*, **-ness.**

†**Impe·rfect,** *v.* 1555. [f. prec. adj.] *trans.* To render imperfect; to destroy the perfection of –1682.

Imperfe·ctible, *a.* 1869. [Im-[2].] Incapable of being made perfect. Hence **Imperfectibi·lity**, incapability of being made perfect 1836.

Imperfection (impəɹfe·kʃən). ME. [a. F., or ad.L. *imperfectionem.*] 1. The condition or quality of being imperfect; incompleteness; defectiveness, faultiness. 2. (with *pl.*) A defect, fault, blemish ME. †3. *Mus.* The making of a note imperfect, or the condition of its being imperfect –1880.

1. The necessary i. of language Jowett. 2. Sent to my account With all my imperfections on my head Shaks.

Imperfective (impəɹfe·ktiv), *a.* 1677. [f. Imperfect *a.* + -ive.] †1. Characterized by imperfection –1684. 2. *Slavonic Grammar.* Applied to a form or 'aspect' of the verb expressing action not completed (either continuous, or repeated); opp. to *perfective* 1844.

Imperforable (impɔ̄·ɹfŏrăb'l), *a.* 1658. [Im-[2].] That cannot be perforated.

Imperforate (impɔ̄·ɹfŏrĕt), *a.* 1673. [Im-[2].] Not perforated; having no perforation, foramen, or opening. Chiefly in scientific and technical use. So **Impe·rforated** *a.* 1650.

Imperforation (impɔ̄ɹfŏrē·ʃən). 1656. [Im-[2].] The condition of being imperforate; a case of this.

Imperial (impī·riăl). ME. [a. OF. *em-, imperial*, ad. L. *imperialis*, f. Imperium; see -al.]

A. *adj.* Pertaining to an empire or emperor.

I. 1. Of or pertaining to the (or an) empire. 2. Of or pertaining to a sovereign state, which in its independence and importance ranks with an empire 1532. 3. Of or pertaining to the (or an) emperor ME.; *spec.* belonging to the party of the (Romano-German) Emperor 1470. 4. *fig.* and *transf.* Of the nature or rank of an emperor; commanding, supreme in authority ME. 5. Majestic, august, exalted ME.; domineering, imperious 1581. 6. Befitting an emperor; of special excellence; magnificent 1731.

1. *Imperial chamber*, is a sovereign court, established for the affairs of the immediate states of the empire Chambers *Cycl.* The I. double eagle 1861. 2. The imperiall lawes of the Realme of Englande 1556. The United Kingdom is an 'Imperial' State—a State exercising 'imperium', or dominion over the colonies and other dependencies 1888. 3. The I. titles and I. pretensions of the English Kings in the tenth and eleventh centuries Freeman. A series of i. coins from Augustus to Diocletian D. Wilson. 4. And the imperiall Votresse passed on, In maiden meditation, fancy free Shaks. 5. The Lily's height bespoke command, A fair i. flower Cowper. 6. These are I. Works, and worthy Kings Pope.

II. *spec.* 1. Applied to those weights and measures appointed by statute to be used throughout the United Kingdom 1838. 2. In names of products and commodities of special size and quality, as *I. tea* 1664. b. Name of a size of paper: of printing-paper usually 22 by 32 inches, of writing-paper 22 by 30. 1668.

Phrases. *I. blue*: an aniline blue dye, also called *spirit-blue*. *I. city*: (*a*) a city that is the seat of empire, or that is itself a sovereign state; (*b*) any city of the old German Empire which owned allegiance to the Emperor alone. †*I. crown*: = Crown Imperial (*Fritillaria imperialis*). *I. drink* (formerly †*i. water*): a drink made of cream of tartar flavoured with lemons and sweetened. *I. yellow*: name of a kind of porcelain made in China, having a uniform yellow glaze, reserved for the use of the i. court; hence transf.

B. *sb.* 1. = Imperialist 1. 1524. b. An imperial personage 1588. 2. A Russian gold coin, formerly worth 10 silver roubles, now 15. 1839. 3. A case or trunk for luggage, adapted for the roof of a coach or carriage. Also the roof itself (F. *impériale*). 1794. 4. A trade name for articles of special size or quality; as, a large decanter 1858; a size of paper (see A. II. 2 b) 1712; etc. †5. Short for *cloth imperial*, a textile fabric in use in the Middle Ages, with figures woven in gold; app. so called as being made at Constantinople –1876. 6. A small tuft of hair left growing beneath the lower lip; so called because the Emperor Napoleon III wore such a tuft 1839.

Imperialism (impī·riăliz'm). 1858. [f. Imperial *a.* + -ism.] 1. The rule of an emperor, esp. when despotic. 2. The principle or spirit of empire; advocacy of imperial interests 1881.

1. I., or, indeed, any worse form of despotism 1869. 2. I mean the greater pride in Empire which is called I... a larger patriotism Ld. Rosebery.

Imperialist (impī·riălist). 1603. [f. as prec. + -ist; cf. F. *impérialiste.*] 1. An adherent of the (or an) emperor (usu., 1600–1800, of the German Emperor); one of the emperor's party. 2. An advocate of imperialism 1800. 3. *attrib.* or *adj.* Adhering or pertaining to imperialism 1868. Hence **Imperiali·stic** *a.* = prec. 3. **Imperiali·stically** *adv.*

Imperiality (impīəriˌæ·lĭti). 1534. [f. as prec. + -ity.] †1. Imperial rank, power, or authority –1629. 2. A joc. title for an imperial personage; also *collect.* = imperial personages (cf. *royalty*) 1870. ¶*Erron.* An imperial right or privilege (Dicts.). (Based on a misprinted quot. from Tooke; see Imperialty 2.)

Imperialize (impī·riălaiz), *v.* 1634. [f. as prec. + -ize.] †1. *intr.* To act imperially. Sir T. Herbert. †2. *trans.* To attach to the party of the Emperor (e.g. against the Papacy). Fuller. 3. To render imperial 1805.

Imperially (impī·riăli), *adv.* 1550. [f. Imperial *a.* + -ly[2].] 1. In an imperial manner. 2. *Her. I. crowned*: said of charges represented with an imperial crown 1823.

Imperialty (impī·riălti). *rare.* 1600. [f. Imperial, after *royalty*.] †1. Imperial state or government –1616. 2. An imperial right or privilege; a tax levied by an emperor or empress. (Cf. *royalty*.) 1799.

2. The late empress having..relinquished her imperialties on the private mines W. Tooke.

Imperil (impe·ril), *v.* Also **em-**. 1596. [f. Em-, Im-[1] + Peril *sb.*] *trans.* To bring into or put in peril; to endanger. Hence **Impe·rilled, -iled** *ppl. a.*; also **Impe·rilment**, imperilling, or being imperilled.

Imperious (impī·riəs), *a.* 1541. [ad. L. *imperiosus*, f. *imperium*; see -ous.] †1. Imperial –1703. 2. Ruling, sovereign, dominant; commanding; majestic, stately. *Obs.* (or merged in 3 or 4.) –1819. 3. Overbearing, dictatorial, domineering. (The prevailing mod. sense.) 1555. 4. Urgent, overmastering, imperative 1541.

1. King, be thy thoughts I. like thy name Shaks. 2. It is Emperious, both o'r Love and Hate Drayton. The i. Mountaine Taurus Sir T. Herbert. 3. A proud, i. aristocrat, contemptuous..of popular rights Froude. 4. The i. necessity which urges us on 1877. Hence **Impe·rious·ly** *adv.*, **-ness.**

†**Impe·rish,** *v.*, var. of Emperish, q.v.

Imperishable (impe·riʃăb'l), *a.* 1648. [Im-[2].] That cannot perish; not subject to decay; indestructible, immortal, enduring.

Good deeds Do no i. record find Save in the rolls of heaven Wordsw. Hence **Impe·rishabi·lity, Impe·rishableness,** the quality of being i. **Impe·rishably** *adv.* indestructibly.

‖**Imperium** (impīᵊ·riŏm). 1651. [L.] Command; absolute power; supreme or imperial power; EMPIRE.

L. phr. *Imperium in imperio*, an empire within an empire, an independent authority exercised or claimed within the jurisdiction of another authority.

Impermanent (impə̄·ɹmănĕnt), *a.* 1653. [IM-².] Not permanent or lasting. Hence **Impe·rmanence**, the fact or condition of being i. **Impe·rmanency**, the quality or state of being i.

Impermeable (impə̄·ɹmĭăb'l), *a.* 1697. [a. F., or ad. L. *impermeabilis*; see IM-² and PERMEABLE.] Not permeable; that cannot be passed through or traversed; *spec.* in *Physics*, that does not permit the passage of water or any fluid, liquid or gaseous.

A bed of hard and i. clay 1827. Hence **Impermeabi·lity, Impe·rmeableness**, i. quality. **Impe·rmeably** *adv.*

Impermi·ssible, *a.* 1858. [IM-².] Not permissible.

†**Impermi·xt,** *a.* Also **in-**. 1500. [ad. L. *impermixtus*.] Unmixed, unmingled -1677.

Imperscri·ptible *a.* 1832. [f. IM-² + L. **perscriptibilis*, f. *perscribere* to write down.] For which no written authority can be adduced; unrecorded; as, an *imperscriptible right*.

†**Imperscru·table,** *a.* 1526. [ad. L. *imperscrutabilis*, f. *im-* (IM-²) + *perscrutare*; see -BLE.] Not to be searched out; inscrutable -1681.

†**Imperse·verant,** *a.* [IM-².] Not persevering. BP. ANDREWES.

Impersonal (impə̄·ɹsənăl). 1520. [ad. late L. *impersonalis*; see IM-² and PERSONAL.]

A. *adj.* **1.** *Gram.* A term applied to verbs when used only in the third person singular, as *it rains, methinks*, etc. (Many ordinary verbs have impersonal constructions.) **2.** Having no personal reference or connexion; said of things 1630. **3.** Not possessing personality 1842.

3. Slaves being regarded as i. men POSTE.

B. *sb.* **1.** *Gram.* An impersonal verb 1509. **2.** An impersonal thing or creature (*rare*) 1796.

Hence **Impersona·lity**, i. quality; an impersonal being or creation. **Impe·rsonalize** *v.* to render i. **Impe:rsonaliza·tion**, the action of rendering i.; an impersonalized condition or form. **Impe·rsonally** *adv.* in an i. manner.

Impersonate (impə̄·ɹsəneᶦt), *v.* 1624. [f. L. *im-* (IM-¹) + *persona*.] †**1.** *trans.* To embody in a person. **2.** To invest with a supposed personality; to personify 1624; to embody in one's own person; to typify 1855. **3.** To act (a character); to personate 1715.

2. His position was dignified and important, as impersonating the unity of the race STUBBS. 3. To i. his [Shakspere's] characters 1863. Hence **Impe·rsonator**, one who plays a part.

Impersonate (impə̄·ɹsənĕt), *ppl. a.* 1820. [Short for *impersonated*; see -ATE².] Embodied in a person; impersonated.

Impersonation (impə̄ɹsənēᶦ·ʃən). 1800. [f. prec. vb.] **1.** The action of impersonating or fact of being impersonated; personification; *concr.* an instance of this. **2.** The dramatic representation of a character 1825.

1. The very i. of good-humour DICKENS.

Impersonify (impəɹsǫ·nifəi), *v.* 1804. [IM-¹.] *trans.* To represent in personal form; to personify. Hence **Imperso:nifica·tion** 1799.

†**Impe·rspicable** *a.* 1665. [ad. late L. *imperspicabilis*.] Not to be discerned; invisible.

Imperspicu·ity. 1659. [IM-².] The reverse of perspicuity; obscurity. So **Imperspi·cuous** *a.* (*rare*), obscure.

Imperspi·rable, *a.* Now *rare.* 1684. [IM-².] Incapable of perspiration. Hence **Imperspirabi·lity.**

Impersua·dable, *a.* 1704. [IM-².] Not persuadable. Hence **Impersua·dableness.**

†**Impersua·sible,** *a.* 1576. [ad. med.L. *impersuasibilis*.] = prec. Hence †**Impersuasibi·lity** 1549. †**Impersua·sibly** *adv.* 1659.

†**Impe·rtinacy,** erron. f. IMPERTINENCY.

Impertinence (impə̄·ɹtinĕns), *sb.* 1603. [a. F., f. *impertinent* IMPERTINENT; see -ENCE.] **1.** The fact or character of not pertaining to the matter in hand; want of pertinence; irrelevance 1626; (with *pl.*) an irrelevance 1612. **2.** Inappropriateness, incongruity; triviality, trifling, folly, absurdity 1629; (with *pl.*) something which is inappropriate, etc. 1603. **3.** Interference with what lies beyond one's province; presumptuous or forward behaviour or speech, esp. to a superior; insolence. (The chief current sense in colloq. use.) 1712. **b.** (with *pl.*) An instance of this; a piece of impertinence 1822.

2. Unacquainted with the vain i. of forms *Junius Lett.* 3. Masters and mistresses sometimes provoke i. from their servants MRS. CHAPONE. **b.** We resent wholesome counsel as an i. HAZLITT. Hence **Impe·rtinence** *v.* to treat with i. (H. WALPOLE). So **Impe·rtinency** (in all senses) 1589.

Impertinent (impə̄·ɹtinĕnt), *a.* (*sb.*) ME. [a. F., or ad. L. *impertinens, -entem*; see IM-² and PERTINENT.] †**1.** Not appertaining (*to*); unconnected; inconsonant. ? *Obs.* **2.** Not pertaining to the matter in hand; not pertinent; not to the point; irrelevant. Now *rare* exc. in *Law.* ME. **3.** Not suitable to the circumstances; not consonant with reason; absurd, trivial, silly 1590. **4.** Const. *to* (*unto*): in senses 2 and 3. 1532. **5.** Of persons, etc.: Meddling beyond one's province; intrusive, presumptuous; insolent or saucy in speech or behaviour. (The chief current sense in colloq. use.) 1681. **6.** *sb.* An impertinent †matter, or person 1628.

1. I. to each other and to any common purpose COLERIDGE. 2. *Temp.* I. ii. 138. 3. In comparison of this, all other Knowledge is vain, light and i. HALE. 4. I thynke it not impartinent vnto this matter 1564. 5. I have been i. in interrupting you 1681. 6. An inquisitive i...medling where he has nothing to do 1710. Hence **Impe·rtinently** *adv.*

†**Impertra·nsible,** *a.* 1677. [f. IM-² + med. L. *pertransibilis*, f. *pertransire*.] That cannot be passed through or crossed. Hence †**Impertransibi·lity.**

Imperturbable (impəɹtə̄·ɹbăb'l), *a.* 1450. [ad. late L. *imperturbabilis*; see IM-² and PERTURBABLE.] Not liable to be mentally perturbed, agitated, or excited; serene, calm.

Great was the embarrassment..even of the i. Burleigh MOTLEY. Hence **Imperturbabi·lity, Impertu·rbableness**, i. quality or condition. **Impertu·rbably** *adv.* in an i. manner; calmly.

Imperturba·tion. 1648. [ad. L. *imperturbationem* (Jerome).] Freedom from perturbation; calmness.

Impertu·rbed, *a.* 1721. [f. IM-² + *perturbed*.] Not perturbed; undisturbed, unmoved.

Imperviable (impə̄·ɹviăb'l), *a.* 1816. [f. L. *impervius*; ? by confusion with *impermeable*.] Impervious; impermeable. Hence **Imperviabi·lity. Impe·rviableness.**

Impervious (impə̄·ɹviəs), *a.* 1650. [f. as prec.; see IM-².] Through which there is no way; not affording passage (*to*); impermeable. Also *fig.*

1. The western channel into it is i., by reason of rocks PENNANT. *fig.* To deal with men i. to argument BUCKLE. Hence **Impe·rvious-ly** *adv.*, **-ness.**

†**I·mpery.** ME. Var. of EMPERY -1657.

Impest (impe·st), *v.* Also †**em-**. 1618. [ad. F. *empester*, f. *em-* = IM-¹ + *peste* PEST, plague.] *trans.* To infect with a plague or pestilence. Hence **Impesta·tion**, the action of impesting.

†**Impe·ster,** *v.* Also †**em-**. 1601. [a. OF. *empestrer* (now *empêtrer*), f. late L. **impastoriare*, f. *im-* (IM-¹) + late L. *pastorium, -a*, a hopple for a horse.] *trans.* To hobble (a horse); to entangle, embarrass, encumber -1807.

Impeticos, *v.* A burlesque word; cf. *impocket* and *petticoat*. *Twel. N.* II. iii. 27.

‖**Impetigo** (impĭtəi·go). Pl. **-igines** (-i·dʒiniz). ME. [L., f. *impetere* to assail; cf. *vertigo*.] A name for various pustular diseases of the skin, and in *pl.* for such diseases in general.

The leprosy of the Romans before the time of Cicero was the i. 1803. Hence **Impeti·ginous** *a.* pertaining to or of the nature of i.; 'scurfy; covered with small scabs' (J.).

†**I·mpetrable,** *a.* 1599. [ad. L. *impetrabilis*; see -BLE.] **1.** That may be obtained by request. HOBBES. **2.** Capable of effecting something, successful NASHE.

†**I·mpetrate,** *ppl. a.* 1528. [ad. L. *impetratus*; see next.] Obtained by request; impetrated -1722.

Impetrate (i·mpĕtrēᶦt), *v.* 1533. [f. L. *impetrat-, impetrare*, f. *im-* (IM-¹) + *patrare* to effect.] **1.** *trans.* To obtain by request or entreaty; to procure. Now chiefly *Theol.* (also in *Rom. Law*). **2.** To request, beseech, ask for. Now *rare*. 1565. Hence **I·mpetrative** (*rare*), **I·mpetratory** *adjs.* having the quality of obtaining by or as by request. var. †**Impetre** ME.

Impetration (impĕtrēᶦ·ʃən). 1484. [ad. L. *impetrationem*; see prec.] **1.** The action of procuring by request or entreaty. (Chiefly *Theol.*) 1518. **b.** *Law.* The obtaining (of a writ) 1648. **c.** 'The pre-obtaining of church benefices in England from the court of Rome, which belonged to the gift and disposition of the king, and other lay-patrons of this realm' (Tomlins) 1484. **2.** Petition, supplication, request 1618.

1. **c.** That..penalties..should be attached to all i. of benefices from Rome by purchase or otherwise FROUDE.

Impetuosity (impe:tiuǫ·sĭti). 1585. [a. F. *impétuosité*; see next and -ITY.] The quality or character of being impetuous; sudden or violent energy of movement, action, etc.; vehemence; (with *pl.*) an impetuous movement, action, or feeling.

You know the i. of my brother's temper FIELDING. Flames..issued forth with great i. 1811.

Impetuous (impe·tiuᵢəs), *a.* ME. [a. F. *impétueux, -euse*, ad. L. *impetuosus*, f. *impetus*; see -OUS.] **1.** Of physical things or actions: Having much impetus; moving with great force or violence; very rapid, forcibly rushing, violent 1489. **2.** Of feelings, etc., and hence of persons: Acting with or marked by great, sudden, or rash energy; vehement, violent, passionate ME.

1. Impietouse wyndes 1547; impittious haste SHAKS. That great and i. River RAY. 2. The i. vivacity of youth JOHNSON. The i., ready to go at that which others are afraid to approach JOWETT. Hence **Impe·tuous-ly** *adv.*, **-ness.**

Impetus (i·mpĭtŏs). 1641. [a. L., f. *impetere*, f. *im-* (IM-¹) + *petere* to seek.] **1.** The force with which a body moves and overcomes resistance; energy of motion; impulse, impulsion 1656. **b.** *Gunnery.* The altitude due to the initial velocity of a projectile, i.e. the space through which it must fall to attain an equal velocity; the force of projection as measured by this 1807. **2.** In ref. to feelings, actions, etc.: Moving force, impulse, stimulus 1641.

2. Fugitive Huguenots gave a fresh i. to weaving YEATS.

Impeyan (i·mpiăn), *a.* (*sb.*) Also **Impeian.** 1870. [Named in 1787, after Sir Elijah and Lady *Impey*, who tried to naturalize the bird in England.] *Impeyan pheasant*: a kind of E. Indian pheasant (*Lophophorus impeyanus*), with crested head; the male has plumage of metallic hues. Also other species of *Lophophorus*. **b.** Of or belonging to this pheasant. **c.** *sb.* = I. pheasant.

‖**Imphee** (i·mfi). 1857. [*imfe*, native name in Natal.] A species of sugar-cane, *Holcus saccharatus* (Linn.), also called African or Chinese Sugar-cane, Broom Corn, Sorgho, and Planter's Friend.

‖**I·mpi.** 1879. [Zulu, = body or company, esp. of armed men.] A body of Caffre warriors; a force, detachment, army.

Impicture (impi·ktiŭɹ), *v.* 1520. Also †**en-**, **em-**. [f. IM-¹ + PICTURE.] **1.** *trans.* To portray. †**2.** To impress as with a picture. SPENSER.

Impie·rce, var. of EMPIERCE *v.*

†**Impie·rceable,** *a.* ME. [IM-².] Not pierceable; that cannot be pierced -1691.

Impiety (impəi·ĕti). ME. [a. F. *impiété*; see IMPIOUS and -ITY.] **1.** Want of reverence for God or religion; ungodliness; unrighteousness, wickedness. Also with *an* and *pl.* **2.** Absence of natural piety, as of child to parent; want of dutifulness; hence, want of reverence generally 1588.

1. The impietie of Arrius and other heretikes 1600. When I .. had seene impieties without number 2 *Esdras* iii. 29. 2. An instance of filial i. (*mod.*).

†**Impi·gnorate,** *pa. pple.* 1548. [ad. med.L. *impignoratus, impignorare*, f. *im-* (IM-¹) +

pignus, pignor- pledge, etc.] Pledged, pawned, mortgaged -1684. So **Impi·gnorate** *v.* (chiefly *Sc.*) to place in pawn; to pledge, mortgage. **Impi·gnora·tion**, pledging, pawning, mortgage.

Imping (i·mpiŋ), *vbl. sb.* ME. [f. IMP *v.* + -ING¹.] The action of IMP *v.*; grafting, engrafting; the repairing of a hawk's wing with adscititious feathers. Also *attrib.*

Impinge (impi·ndʒ), *v.* 1535. [ad. L. *impingere*, f. *im-* (IM-¹) + *pangere* to fix, drive in.] **1.** *trans.* To fasten or fix on forcibly (*rare*). **2.** To strike, dash, hurl a thing *upon* something else; *refl.* = 4. 1660. **3.** To strike; to collide with. Now *rare*. 1777. **4.** *intr.* To strike or dash; to come into (violent) contact; to collide 1605. Also *fig.* **5.** To encroach or infringe *on* or *upon* 1758.

4. A ship that is void of a Pilot, must needs i. upon the next rock or sands BURTON. Rays of light impinging on the retina give rise to sensory impulses FOSTER. Hence **Impi·ngement**, impact, collision (*lit.* and *fig.*); encroachment. So **Impi·ngent** *a.* (*rare*), impinging.

†**Impi·nguate**, *v.* 1620. [f. ppl. stem of late L. *impinguare*, f. *im-* (IM-¹) + *pinguis*.] *trans.* To make fat; to fatten -1693. Hence †**Impingua·tion.**

Impious (i·mpiəs), *a.* 1575. [f. L. *impius* (f. *im-* (IM-²) + *pius*) + -OUS.] **1.** Not pious; without piety or reverence for God and his ordinances; presumptuously irreligious, wicked, or profane. **2.** Wanting in natural reverence and dutifulness, esp. to parents (*rare*) 1613.

1. Canst thou with i. obloquie condemne The just Decree of God? MILT. *P. L.* v. 813. E'er i. plow to wound the earth began T. BROWN. Hence **I·mpious·ly** *adv.*, **-ness.**

Impish (i·mpiʃ), *a.* 1652. [f. IMP *sb.* + -ISH¹.] Having the characteristics of an imp. Hence **I·mpish·ly** *adv.*, **-ness.**

Impiteous (impi·tiəs), *a.* 1877. [IM-².] Pitiless.

Implacable (implæ·kăb'l, -plē·kăb'l), *a.* 1450. [a. F., ad. L. *implacabilis*; see IM-² and PLACABLE. By Spenser and Longfellow stressed on first (or third) syllable.] **1.** That cannot be appeased; irreconcilable; inexorable. †**2.** That cannot be assuaged or mitigated -1862.

1. The i. enemy of Bourbon 1769. Sectaries..i. to those who differed from them 1785. **2.** O how I burne with i. fire SPENSER *F. Q.* II. vi. 44. Hence **Implacabi·lity**, the condition of being i. **Impla·cableness. Impla·cably** *adv.*

Impla·cement, var. of EMPLACEMENT.

Implacental (implăse·ntăl). 1839. [IM-²; cf. mod.L. *Implacentalia* neut. pl., name of the group.] *Zool.* **a.** *adj.* Having no placenta, a term applied to the group of mammals consisting of the marsupials and monotremes (*Implacentalia*). **b.** *sb.* A mammal having no placenta 1864. So **Implace·ntate** *a.* (Dicts.)

Implant (impla·nt), *v.* 1541. Also †**em-.** [a. F. *implanter*; see IM-¹ and PLANT.] **1.** *trans.* To plant in, insert, infix. Chiefly *pass.* 1545. **2.** To fix or instil (a principle, etc.) *in* one. Chiefly *pass.* (The ordinary use.) 1541. †**b.** To engraft (a bud). Also *fig. rare.* -1675. **3.** To plant. Also *fig.* 1610.

2. They are both inclinations of nature, implanted of God 1541. **3.** Those [herbs] which the gardiner implanteth 1753. *fig.* Minds well implanted with solid and elaborate breeding MILT. Hence **Impla·nter.**

Implantation (implantē·ʃən). 1578. [a. F., f. *implanter* to IMPLANT.] The action or process of implanting; the fact or manner of being implanted. Also *attrib.*

Implate (implē·t), *v. rare.* [f. IM-¹ + PLATE *sb.*] *trans.* To cover with plates; to sheathe (Dicts.).

Implausible (implǭ·zib'l), *a.* 1602. [IM-².] †**1.** Not worthy of applause; unacceptable. WARNER. **2.** Not having the appearance of truth, probability, or acceptability; not plausible 1677.

2. The art of making plausible or i. harangues SWIFT. Hence **Implausibi·lity, Implau·sibleness**, want of plausibility. **Implau·sibly** *adv.*

Impleach (implī·tʃ), *v. poet.* 1597. Also †**em-.** [f. IM-¹ + PLEACH.] To entwine, interweave.

Implead (implī·d), *v.* [ME. *en-, emplede*, ad. AF. *en-, empleder*, f. *em-* (EM-, IM-¹) + OF. *plaidier* (mod. *plaider*) to PLEAD.] **1.** *trans.* To sue (a person, etc.) in a court of justice, raise an action against. Now only *arch.* or *Hist.* †**2.** To arraign, accuse, impeach. Const. *of.* -1846. **3.** *nonce-use.* To plead *with* 1839.

1. To sue or be sued, i. or be impleaded BLACKSTONE. Hence †**Implea·dable** *a.*¹ that may be sued (as a person) or prosecuted (as a suit) 1570; capable of being pleaded 1648. †**Implea·der**, a prosecutor, accuser, or impeacher 1577.

†**Implea·dable**, *a.*² 1607. [f. IM-² + PLEADABLE.] Not to be pleaded against, or met by any plea -1614.

†**Implea·sing**, *a. rare.* 1602. [IM-².] Unpleasing -1613.

Impledge (imple·dʒ), *v.* 1548. Also †**em-.** [f. IM-¹ + PLEDGE.] *trans.* To pledge, pawn; to give as security; to engage.

Implement (i·mplĭmĕnt), *sb.* 1454. [app. ad. L. *implementum* a filling up, taken as = 'that which serves to fill up or stock (a house, etc.)'. Sometimes referred to EMPLOY *v.*, and taken as = 'thing employed or used'.]

I. 1. *pl.* Things that serve as equipment or outfit, as household furniture, ecclesiastical vestments, etc. In *sing.* An article of furniture, dress, etc. †**b.** *gen.* Requisites -1752. **2.** *pl.* The apparatus, instruments, etc. employed in any trade or in executing any piece of work; as *agricultural implements, flint implements*, etc. In *sing.* A tool, instrument. 1538. Also *fig.*

2. *fig.* Those Sciential rules, which are the implements of instruction MILTON.

II. †**1.** Something necessary to make a thing complete (*rare*) -1650. **2.** *Sc. Law.* Full performance 1678.

Hence **Impleme·ntal** *a.* of the nature of an i. or implements 1676.

Implement (i·mplĭmĕnt), *v.* Chiefly *Sc.* 1806. [f. prec. sb.] **1.** *trans.* To complete, perform; to fulfil. **2.** To complete, supplement 1843. **3.** To provide with implements 1886.

1. To i. an obligation 1806, an order of court 1833. The chief mechanical requisites of the barometer are implemented in such an instrument as the following NICHOL. **2.** To i. wages by pauper relief BURTON.

Implete (implī·t), *v. U.S.* 1862. [f. L. *implet-, implere*; see IM-¹.] *trans.* To fill.

Impletion (implī·ʃən). 1583. [ad. late L. *impletionem*; see prec.] **1.** The action of filling; the being filled; fullness. †**2.** Fulfilment (of prophecy) -1716.

†**Imple·tive**, *a. rare.* 1647. [f. L. *implet-*, ppl. stem + -IVE.] Having the quality of filling -1677.

†**I·mplex**, *a. rare.* 1710. [ad. L. *implexus, implectere*; see IM-¹.] Involved; having a complicated plot. ADDISON *Spect.* No. 297, ¶ 2. So †**Implexed** *ppl. a.* 1619. **Imple·xion**, complication, intertwining 1678.

Impliable (impləi·ăb'l), *a.*¹ *rare.* 1734. [IM-².] Not pliable; inflexible.

Impli·able, *a.*² 1865. [f. IMPLY *v.* + -ABLE.] Capable of being implied.

Implicate (i·mplikĕt), *a.* and *sb.* 1450. [ad. L. *implicatus*; see IMPLICATE *v.*]

A. *adj.* **1.** Intertwined, twisted together; also, wrapped up *with*, entangled *in*. †**2.** Intricate -1637. Hence †**I·mplicateness.**

B. *sb.* †**1.** Entanglement, confusion. SANDERSON. **2.** That which is implied 1881.

Implicate (i·mplikeᵉt), *v.* 1600. [f. L. *implicat-, implicare*, f. *im-* (IM-¹) + *plicare* to fold, twist.] **1.** *trans.* To intertwine; to entwine, entangle 1610. **2.** To involve; to bring into connexion *with* 1600.

1. [They] i., and intangle themselves together so, as to make, as it were, little knots BOYLE. **2.** It implicates a contradiction 1600. In no conspiracy against the government had a Quaker been implicated MACAULAY. The brain is pathologically implicated in insanity 1887. Hence **I·mplicative** *a.* having the quality of implying 1602; †*sb.* a statement or writing implying more than it expressly states 1589. **I·mplicatively** *adv.* ? *Obs.* 1579.

Implication (implikē·ʃən). ME. [ad. L. *implicationem*; see prec.] **1.** The action of implicating; the condition of being implicated. Also *fig.* **2.** The action of implying; the fact of being implied or involved, without being plainly expressed; that which is involved or implied in something else 1581. **3.** The process of involving or fact of being involved in some condition, etc. 1873.

1. The implications of the sinewes of the arme 1578. The mystic i. of his nature with ours J. MARTINEAU. **2.** Phr. *By i.*: by what is implied, by natural inference. Either expressly or by i. 1793.

Implicit (impli·sit), *a.* 1599. [a. F. *implicite* or ad. L. *implicitus*, later form of *implicatus*.] †**1.** Entangled, entwined; involved -1803; involved in each other; overlapping, as, *i. years* -1704. **2.** Implied though not plainly expressed; naturally or necessarily involved in something else 1599. **3.** Resting on the authority of another without doubt or inquiry; unquestioning, absolute; as, *i. faith, belief, confidence, obedience, submission*, etc. 1610. †**b.** Hence, *erron.*: Absolute, unmitigated -1651. **c.** *transf.* Of persons: Characterized by implicit faith, credulity, or obedience. ? *Obs.* 1694.

1. The..bush with frizl'd hair i. MILT. *P. L.* VII. 323. **2.** I. threats 1665, Atheists EARL MANCH., desires GEO. ELIOT. The undeveloped conceptions that lay i. in it SAYCE. **3. b.** When the Peace is grounded, but vpon an implicite ignorance BACON. Hence **Impli·cit·ly** *adv.*, **-ness.** So †**Impli·city**, entanglement, complication, involution.

Implied (impləi·d), *ppl. a.* 1529. [f. IMPLY *v.* + -ED¹.] Contained or stated by implication; involved in what is expressed; necessarily intended though not expressed; see IMPLY *v.*

Phr. *I. contract, trust, warranty*, etc.: see these wds. So **Impli·edly** *adv.* by implication, implicitly 1400.

Implode (implōᵘ·d), *v.* 1881. [f. IM-¹ + L. *plodere, plaudere* to clap, after EXPLODE.] **1.** *intr.* and *trans.* To burst inwards. **2.** *trans.* To utter or pronounce by implosion. Hence **Implo·dent**, an implosive sound.

Imploration (implorē·ʃən). 1577. [ad. L. *implorationem*.] The action of imploring; earnest supplication.

†**Implora·tor.** [f. L. *implorare*.] 1602. One who implores.

Meere implorators of vnholy Sutes *Haml.* I. iii. 129. So **Implo·ratory** *a.* (*rare*), of imploring or beseeching nature 1832.

Implore (implōᵊ·ɹ), *v.* 1500. [ad. L. *implorare*, f. *im-* (IM-¹) + *plorare*.] **1.** *trans.* **a.** To beg or pray for (aid, pardon, etc.) with touching entreaties; to ask for in supplication; to beseech. †Formerly sometimes with two objects. 1540. **b.** To beseech (a person) with deep emotion (to do something) 1603. **2.** *intr.* To utter touching supplications 1500.

1. **a.** Hee might plainely discerne her dolorous gesture in the act of imploring his succour 1632. Hence †**Implo·re** *sb.* imploration, entreaty. **Implo·rer** (*rare*). **Implo·ring·ly** *adv.*, **-ness.**

Implosion (implōᵘ·ʒən). 1877. [f. IMPLODE; cf. EXPLOSION.] **1.** The bursting inward of a vessel from external pressure 1880. **2.** *Phonetics.* (See quot.) 1877.

2. The i. consists in closing the glottis simultaneously with the stop position, and then compressing the air between the glottis stoppage and the mouth one SWEET. So **Implo·sive** *a.* and *sb.* (a sound) formed by implosion.

Implume (implⁱū·m), *v. rare.* 1612. = EMPLUME *v.*

Implu·med, *a. rare.* 1604. [IM-².] Unfeathered, unfledged; deprived of feathers.

Implunge (implʊ·ndʒ), *v.* 1590. [f. IM-¹ + PLUNGE *v.*] *trans.* To plunge *in* or *into*. Now *rare.*

‖**Impluvium** (implⁱū·viŏm). 1811. [L., f. *impluere* to rain into.] In ancient Roman houses, the square basin situated in the middle of the atrium or hall, which received the rainwater from the COMPLUVIUM or open space in the roof. (But occas. = *compluvium*.)

Imply (impləi·), *v.* ME. [a. OF. *emplier* :—L. *implicare* to enfold, f. *im-* (IM-¹) + *plicare.* See also EMPLOY.] †**1.** *trans.* To enfold, enwrap, entangle, involve; in *lit.* and *fig.* senses -1823. **2.** To involve or comprise logically; to involve the truth or existence of (something not expressly asserted or maintained) 1529. **b.** Of a word or name: To involve by signification; to import, mean 1630. **3.** To express indirectly; to insinuate 1581. †**4.** = EMPLOY *v.* -1659. ¶ **5.** To refer, ascribe; = APPLY *v.* I. 9. *Obs.* 1655.

1. Phœbus..His blushing face in foggy cloud implyes SPENSER. 2. In Job..mention is made of fish-hooks, which must i. Anglers in those times WALTON. There are situations in which despair does not i. inactivity BURKE. 5. Whence might this distaste arise?..Is it..your perverse and peevish will, To which I most i. it? WEBSTER & ROWLEY.

Impo·cket, *v.* Also **em-**. 1728. [IM [1].] *trans.* To put into one's pocket; to pocket.

Impoison, obs. f. EMPOISON.

†**Impo·larily**, *adv.* 1646. [f. IM- [2] + POLARY + -LY [2].] Not according to polarity.

Impolder (impōu·ldəɹ), *v.* 1899. [ad. Du. *inpolderen*: see IM-[1] and POLDER.] *trans.* To make a polder of; to reclaim from the sea.

Impolicy (impǫ·lisi). 1747. [f. IM-[2] + POLICY, after *impolitic.*] The quality of being impolitic; bad policy; inexpediency.

An act of such flagrant i. and injustice 1798.

Impolite (impŏləi·t), *a.* 1612. [ad. L. *impolitus*, f. *im-* (IM-[2]) + *politus* polished, POLITE.] Not polished; wanting polish; rude, rough; discourteous. **Impoli·te·ly** *adv.*, **-ness.**

Impolitic (impǫ·litik), *a.* 1600. [IM-[2].] Not politic; not according to good policy; unsuitable for the end desired; inexpedient.

The most unjust and i. of all things, unequal taxation BURKE. So †**Impoli·tical** *a.* Hence **Impoli·tically**, **Impo·liticly** *advs.* in an i. manner. **Impo·liticness**, impolicy.

Imponderable (impǫ·ndĕrăb'l). 1794. [IM-[2].] **A.** *adj.* Not ponderable; *spec.* in *Physics*, having no weight, as the luminiferous ether. **b.** Having no appreciable weight 1846. **B.** *sb.* An imponderable substance, etc. 1842.

Hence **Imponderabi·lity**, i. quality. **Impo·nderableness.** **Impo·nderably** *adv.* without any weight.

Imponderous (impǫ·ndĕrəs), *a. rare.* 1646. [IM-[2].] Without weight; imponderable; *loosely*, extremely light. Hence **Impo·nderousness.**

†**Impo·ne**, *v.* 1529. [ad. L. *imponere*, f. *im-* (IM-[1]) + *ponere.*] *trans.* To place upon something; to impose –1729. **b.** To 'lay', stake, wager. (Doubtful. Cf. IMPAWN.) *Haml.* V. ii. 155 (1623).

Imponent (impōu·nĕnt). 1842. [ad. L. *imponentem*; see prec.] **A.** *adj.* That imposes. T. H. GREEN. **B.** *sb.* One who imposes 1842.

†**Impoo·r**, *v.* 1613. [IM-[1].] To impoverish.

†**Impo·pular**, *a.* 1721. [IM-[2].] Unpopular. Hence †**Impo·pularly** *adv.*

Imporous (impō̆ə·rəs), *a.* ? *Obs.* 1646. [IM-[2].] Not porous; having no pores. var. †**Imporo·se.** Hence †**Imporo·sity** (*rare*) 1626.

Import (i·mpoɹt, *formerly* impō̆ə·ɹt), *sb.* 1588. [f. IMPORT *v.*]

I. 1. The fact of importing or signifying something; that which a thing imports; purport, meaning 1601. **2.** Consequence, importance 1588.

1. Words of dubious i. BYRON. 2. Most serious designes, and of great i. indeed too *L. L. L.* V. i. 106.

II. 1. That which is imported or brought in from abroad. (Usu. in *pl.*) Opp. to *export.* Also *attrib.* 1690. **2.** The action of importing; importation 1797.

1. The Imports exceed the Exports CHILD. 2. It is an error..to look on the balance of trade as a mere question of i. and export GOSCHEN.

Import (impō̆ə·ɹt), *v.* ME. [ad. L. *importare*, f. *im-* (IM-[1]) + *portare.* Also, in part, ad. F. *emporter* to carry away.]

I. From cl. L. *importare.* **1.** *trans.* To bring in; to introduce from abroad, or from one use or connexion to another 1508. **2.** *spec.* To bring in (goods or merchandise) from a foreign country, in international commerce. Opp. to *export.* 1548. **3.** To convey to another, communicate (information). Merged in I. 1 and 5. 1565. †**4.** To bring about; to carry with it as a consequence or result –1705. **5.** To involve; to imply 1529; to convey in its meaning; to signify, denote 1533; to bear as its purport; to express, state, make known ME.; to portend 1591.

1. They imported with them into England the old Runic language and letters WARTON. 2. We i. things of great value, and, in return, export little or nothing BURKE. 5. Release..by deed under seal..imports valuable consideration and creates an estoppel 1884. The levee was exactly what the word imports MACAULAY. They..passed a resolution importing [etc.] MACAULAY. Comets importing change of Times and States SHAKS.

II. From med.L., It. *importare*, F. *importer.* **1.** *intr.* To involve a considerable result (actual or possible); to be important, signify, matter. (Only in 3rd person.) *arch.* 1588. **2.** *trans.* To concern. (Only in 3rd person.) 1561.

1. Neither imported it where we lodged MORYSON. 2. A question that imports us nearly 1865. Let me say..what it imports thee to know SCOTT.

III. From Fr. *emporter.* †**1. a.** To lead (a person *to do* something). EVELYN. †**b.** To influence in feeling, carry away. EVELYN. †**2.** To gain, win (victory). **b.** *intr.* To gain the victory, prevail. **c.** *trans.* To overcome. –1624.

2. b. But Scipio imported and prevailed in the end HOLLAND.

†**Importable**, *a.*[1] ME. [a. F., ad. L. *importabilis*; see IM-[2] and PORTABLE.] That cannot be carried or borne; usu. *fig.* unendurable –1651. Hence †**Impo·rtableness.** †**Impo·rtably** *adv.*

Importable (impō̆ə·ɹtăb'l), *a.*[2] 1533. [f. IMPORT *v.* + -ABLE.] Capable of being imported or introduced. Hence **Importabi·lity**, capability of being imported or introduced.

Importance (impǭ·ɹtăns, -pō̆ə·ɹ-). 1505. [a. F.; see IMPORTANT and -ANCE.]

I. 1. The fact or quality of being important; moment, significance, gravity, consequence 1508. **b.** Personal consequence 1678. †**2.** An affair of consequence –1670. †**3.** Urgency; importunity –1781.

1. Emploienge treasour..on thynges..of small importaunce ELYOT. b. A family..of some i. (*mod.*). 2. *Cymb.* I. iv. 45. 3. *John* II. i. 7.

†**II. 1.** Income, revenue. *Sc. Obs.* 1505–33. **2.** = IMPORT *sb.* I. –1709. **b.** Bearing 1691.

2. The wisest beholder..could not say if th' i. were Ioy, or Sorrow SHAKS. So †**Impo·rtancy**, = prec. I.

Important (impǭ·ɹtănt, -pō̆ə·ɹ-), *a.* 1586. [a. F., ad. med.L. *importans, -tantem*, f. *importare* 'to be of consequence, weight, or force'; see IMPORT *v.* II.] **1.** Having much import or significance; weighty, grave, significant. **2.** Having an air of importance; consequential 1713. †**3.** Urgent, pressing, importunate –1630.

1. How..i. is it to every man to be frequented with learning 1586. 2. Discoursing, with i. face, On ribbons, fans, and gloves and lace SWIFT. 3. *Much Ado* II. i. 74. Hence **Impo·rtantly** *adv.* weightily; consequentially.

Importation (impoɹtē̆·ʃən). 1601. [f. IMPORT *v.* (Hence in F.)] **1. a.** *Commerce.* The action of importing goods, etc. from abroad; opp. to *exportation.* **b.** *gen.* Bringing in, introduction 1666. **2.** *concr.* †Imports collectively; an imported article 1664.

2. Solomon's i., Gold and apes POPE.

Importer (impō̆ə·ɹtəɹ). 1700. [f. IMPORT *v.* + -ER [1].] One who or that which imports or introduces; *esp.* a merchant who imports goods from abroad.

Impo·rting, *ppl. a.* 1579. [f. as prec. + -ING [2].] †**1.** That imports or signifies; important –1654. **2.** That imports merchandise 1812.

†**Impo·rtless**, *a.* [f. IMPORT *sb.* + -LESS.] Without import; trivial. *Tr. & Cr.* I. iii. 71.

†**Impo·rtunable**, *a.* 1482. [f. IMPORTUNE *a.* (or ? *v.*) + -ABLE.] **1.** Burdensome, heavy –1611. **2.** Troublesome. DRANT.

Importunacy (impǭ·ɹtiunăsi). 1548. [f. IMPORTUNATE *a.*; see -ACY.] = IMPORTUNITY 3.

Importunate (impǭ·ɹtiunět), *a.* 1477. [f. L. *importunus* + -ATE [2]; perh. after *obstinate*, *fortunate*, etc.] †**1.** Inopportune, untimely –1659. †**2.** Burdensome; grave –1824; troublesome –1691. **3.** Pressing, urgent; busy. *Obs.* or *arch.* 1542. **4.** Persistent in solicitation; pertinacious 1477.

3. I. busines 1542. 4. I. creditors 1863. Hence **Impo·rtunate·ly** *adv.*, **-ness.**

Importunate (impǭ·ɹtiuneit), *v.* 1598. [f. F. *importuner*; see IMPORTUNE *v.* and -ATE [3].] = IMPORTUNE *v.* 3. Hence **Impo·rtunator**, one who importunes.

Importune (impǫɹtiū·n, impǭ·ɹtiun), *a.* (*sb.*) ME. [a. F. *importun, -une*, ad. L. *importunus* unfit, troublesome, grievous, f. *im-* (IM-[2]) + the same stem as in *opportunus* OPPORTUNE.] †**1.** Inopportune, untimely; unfit –1704. †**2.** Troublesome, burdensome; vexatious; heavy, exacting –1864. †**3.** = IMPORTUNATE *a.* 3. –1647. **4.** Persistent in solicitation; pertinacious; irksome through importunity 1447. †**5.** *sb.* One who is importune. [= F. *importun.*] –1734.

1. A Wild Ass, with Brayings I. SWIFT. 4. Yet seynge this weddowe is so i. vpon me I will delyuer her COVERDALE *Luke* xviii. 5. Hence **Importu·nely** *adv.* (now *rare*).

Importune (impǫɹtiū·n, impǭ·ɹtiun), *v.* 1530. [a. F. *importuner*, f. *importunus*; see prec.] †**1.** *trans.* To burden; to trouble, worry, pester, annoy –1788. †**2.** To press, urge. Also *absol.* –1615. **3.** To solicit pressingly or persistently; to beset with petitions 1530. **4.** To ask for (a thing) urgently and persistently 1588. **5.** *intr.* To be importunate 1548. ¶**6.** To import, portend. (A Spenserian misuse.) 1590.

2. *Meas. for M.* I. i. 57. 3. Ye were importun'd the passing it MILT. 5. Too poor for a bribe, and too proud to i.; He had not the method of making a fortune GRAY. Hence **Importuner.**

Importunity (impǫɹtiū·nĭti). 1450. [a. F. *importunité*, ad. L. *importunitas*; see IMPORTUNE *a.* and -ITY.] †**1.** The condition of being inopportune; unseasonableness; an unsuitable time –1589. †**2.** Burdensomeness, trouble –1739. **3.** Troublesome pertinacity in solicitation 1460.

3. Because of hys importunite he woll ryse and geve hym as many as he nedeth TINDALE *Luke* xi. 8.

Imposable (impōu·zăb'l), *a. rare.* 1660. [f. IMPOSE *v.* + -ABLE.] **1.** That may be imposed or laid on. **2.** That may be imposed upon; gullible 1734. Hence **Impo·sableness.**

Impose (impōu·z), *v.* 1484. Also †**-em-**. [a. F. *imposer*, f. *im-* (IM-[1]) + *poser*, repr. L. *imponere*; see COMPOSE, POSE.]

I. *trans.* **1.** To lay on or set on; to put, place, or deposit (*arch.*) 1597. **b.** *Eccl.* To lay on hands in blessing, or in ordination, confirmation, etc. 1582. **c.** *Printing.* To lay pages of type or stereotype plates in proper order on the imposing-stone or the bed of a press, and secure them in a chase 1652. **2.** *fig.* **a.** *gen.* To put, place; to place authoritatively 1681. **b.** To bestow (a name or title) *upon, on,* †*to* 1500. †**c.** To put authoritatively (an end, conclusion, etc.) to –1611. †**3.** To lay (a crime) to the account of; to impute. (The earliest use.) –1663. **4.** To lay on; to inflict (something) *on* or *upon* 1581. **5.** To 'put' (a thing) *upon* (a person) by false representations; to palm off 1650.

1. She impos'd a stone Close to the cauernes mouth CHAPMAN. 2. b. The name was imposed antecedent to his birth 1774. 4. What Fates i., that men must needs abide SHAKS. Minos..imposed upon the Athenians a cruel tribute JOWETT. To i. duties on foreign merchandise 1863. 5. To i. such a Cheat upon the World 1681.

II. *intr.* **1.** To put oneself *upon* (in various senses) 1625. **2.** To put a tax, to levy an impost (*upon*). ? *Obs.* 1618. **3.** To practise imposture; also with *on, upon* 1662.

1. When it [Truth] is found, it imposeth vpon mens Thoughts BACON. To i. upon a generous person 1694, on the good nature of others 1883. 2. To restraine the Crowne from imposing upon the people without their consent 1642. 3. To be imposed upon by fine Things and false Addresses STEELE.

Hence †**Impo·se** *sb.* (*rare*), the imposition of a charge, duty, or task 1591–1605. **Impo·sement** (*rare*), imposition 1664. **Impo·ser** 1597.

Imposing (impōu·ziŋ), *vbl. sb.* 1610. [f. IMPOSE *v.* + -ING [1].] The action of imposing; imposition. **b.** *Printing.* The arrangement of pages of type in a forme 1727.

attrib. **I.-stone, -table**, a slab of stone or metal on which pages of type or stereotype plates are imposed.

Imposing (impōu·ziŋ), *ppl. a.* 1651. [f. as prec. + -ING [2].] **1.** That peremptorily enjoins; exacting. **2.** That impresses by appearance or manner 1786. **3.** Using deception; practising imposture 1754.

2. Mountains..of i. magnitude TYNDALL. Hence **Impo·sing·ly** *adv.*, **-ness.**

Imposition (impŏzi·ʃən). ME. [ad. L. *impositionem*, f. *imponere* to IMPOSE.] **1.** The action of putting, placing, or laying on 1597.

b. *spec.* The laying on of hands in blessing, ordination, confirmation, etc. ME. **c.** *Printing.* The imposing or arranging of pages of type in the forme 1824. **2.** The action of attaching, affixing, or ascribing; bestowal (of a name, etc.) ME. †**3.** Accusation. *Wint. T.* I. ii. 74. **4.** The action of imposing; the action of inflicting, levying, or enjoining 1593; †taxation -1628. **5.** Anything imposed, levied, or enjoined; an impost; tax, duty 1460; †an injunction -1664; an exercise or task imposed as a punishment at school or college 1746; †in 17th cent. Puritanical use, a dogma or ceremony imposed without scriptural warrant. **6.** The action of deceiving by palming off what is false or unreal; an instance of this, an imposture 1632.

1. The i. of my hand on his forehead, instantly put a stop to his spasms MEDWIN. b. Thus..the grace of God is given by the i. of hands JER. TAYLOR. 4. The superstitious impositions of fasts BURTON. 6. The predictions..were mere impositions on the people SWIFT.

Impossibilist (impǫ·sibilist). 1900. [f. L. *impossibilis* IMPOSSIBLE + -IST.] One who advocates a policy which is impossible of realization. So **Impo·ssibilism.**

Impossibi·litate, *v. rare.* 1633. [f. next + -ATE [3].] *trans.* To render impossible.

Impossibility (impǫsibi·lĭti). ME. [a. F. *impossibilité*; see IMPOSSIBLE and -ITY.] **1.** The quality of being impossible; (with *an* and *pl.*) an impossible thing. †**2.** Impotence, inability -1796.

1. The i. that his Intelligence could be true CLARENDON. Is not every genius an i. till he appear? CARLYLE.

Impossible (impǫ·sĭb'l). ME. [a. F., or ad. L. *impossibilis*; see IM- [2] and POSSIBLE.]

A. *adj.* **1.** Not possible; that cannot be done, exist, or come into being; that cannot be, in existing or specified circumstances. Const. *to* or *for.* **2.** *Math.* Having no possible or real value, imaginary 1673. **3.** In recent use, with ellipsis of some qualification implied by the context; as, impossible to deal with or recognize, etc.; 'out of the question' 1858.

1. They..laughed therat as at an i. lye MORE. Craggie cliff..i. to climbe MILT. *P. L.* IV. 548. 3. Oxford..home of..i. loyalties! M. ARNOLD. The.. ghosts..made the place absolutely i. 1884.

B. *sb.* = IMPOSSIBILITY (*rare* in *sing.*) ME. With *the*: That which is or seems impossible 1845. Hence **Impo·ssibleness** (*rare*). **Impo·ssibly** *adv.*

Impost [1] (i·mpoust). 1568. [a. OF. *impost*, now *impôt*, ad. med.L. *impostus* or *impostum*, from L. *impostus, impositus, imponere* to IMPOSE.] **1.** A tax, duty, imposition, tribute; *spec.* a customs-duty levied on merchandise. Now chiefly *Hist.* (Dicts., following Cowell, make *impost* a duty on *imported* goods; but this limitation wants evidence.) **2.** *Racing slang.* The weight which a horse has to carry in a handicap race 1883.

1. A bench of Judges..declared the new i. [ship-money] to be legal GREEN.

Impost [2] (i·mpoust). 1664. [a. F. *imposte*, ad. It. *imposta*, f. as prec.] *Arch.* **1.** The upper course of a pillar or abutment, frequently projecting in the form of an ornamental moulding or capital, on which the foot of an arch rests. (Where there is no projection, the impost is called *continuous.*) **2.** A horizontal block supported by upright stones, as at Stonehenge. Also *attrib.* 1768.

†**Impo·sterous,** *a.* 1562. [f. *imposter* IMPOSTOR, or ? f. IMPOSTURE + -OUS.] **1.** Of the nature of an imposture; false -1665. **2.** Having the character of an impostor -1652.

Imposthume: see IMPOSTUME.

Impostor (impǫ·stəɹ). 1586. [a. F. *imposteur*, ad. late L. *impostor*, f. *imponere* (*imposit-, impost-*). At first confused with IMPOSTURE.] One who imposes on others; a deceiver, swindler, cheat; now chiefly, one who passes himself off as some one other than he is. Also *attrib.*

Being found a meere I., he dyed most miserably 1624. So †**Imposto·rious** 1623, **Impo·storous** 1548 *adjs.* having the character of an i. or imposture. Hence **Impo·storship,** the office or character of an i. 1620. †**Impo·story** (*rare*), = IMPOSTURE 1653. **Impo·stress** 1614, †**Impo·strix** 1655 (both *rare*), a female i.

Impostrous (impǫ·strəs), *a.* 1612. [Abbrev. of IMPOSTEROUS; cf. *monster, -trous.*] **1.** Having the character of an impostor. **2.** Of the nature of an imposture 1635.

1. An i. pretender to knowledge GROTE. 2. I. lies 1635.

†**Impo·stumate, -thumate,** *ppl. a.* 1601. [Altered f. *apostumate*, APOSTEMATE *ppl. a.*, after IMPOSTUME.] Affected with impostumes; of the nature of an impostume. Also *fig.* -1764.

†**Impo·stumate, -thumate** *v.* 1592. [Altered f. *apostumate*, APOSTEMATE *v.*, after IMPOSTUME; cf. prec.] **1.** *trans.* To affect with an impostume. -1758. **2.** *intr.* To swell into an impostume; to fester, gather. -1762. So **Impostuma·tion, -thuma·tion** (now *rare*), suppuration; = IMPOSTUME *sb.* 1524.

Impostume, -thume (impǫ·stiŭm), *sb.* Now *rare.* ME. [a. OF. *empostume*, altered f. *apostume, aposteme*; see APOSTEM, and N.E.D.] **1.** A purulent swelling or cyst in any part of the body; an abscess. **2.** *fig.* **a.** A moral or political festering sore; the swelling of pride, etc. 1565. †**b.** Applied to a gathering cloud. DRAYTON.

1. An Error in the judgment, is like an impostem in the Head SOUTH. 2. The imposthume I prick to relieve thee of,—Vanity BROWNING. Hence †**Impo·stume, -thume** *v.* = IMPOSTUMATE *v.* ME.

†**Impo·sturage.** *rare.* 1654. [f. next + -AGE.] Imposture -1656.

Imposture (impǫ·stiŭɹ). 1537. [a. F., ad. late L. *impostura*, f. *impost-, imponere.*] **1.** The action or practice of imposing on others; wilful and fraudulent deception. †**b.** Illusion -1794. **2.** A cheat, a fraud 1548; a thing (or person) which is pretended to be what it is not 1699.

1. There's a sure market for i. BYRON. 2. Many of the Bones which were carried about by Monks, were none of their Bones but Impostures BURNET.

Imposturous (impǫ·stiŭrəs), *a.* 1608. [f. IMPOSTURE + -OUS.] **1.** Of the nature of imposture (now *rare*). †**2.** Given to imposture; having the character of an impostor -1697.

2. The shamefull vntruth of those i. liers SPEED.

†**Impo·stury.** [f. as prec. + -Y.] Imposture. G. SANDYS.

Imposure (impōu·ʒ'ŭɹ). *rare.* 1682. [f. IMPOSE *v.* + -URE.] An imposing, a laying on.

Impot (i·mpǫt). Schoolboys' abbreviation of IMPOSITION (sense 5).

Impo·table, *a.* 1608. [IM- [2].] Undrinkable.

Impotence (i·mpǒtěns). ME. [a. F., ad. L. *impotentia*, f. *impotens* IMPOTENT.] **1.** Want of strength or power; utter inability or weakness; helplessness. **2.** Want of physical power; feebleness of body, as through illness, etc. ME. **b.** *Path.* Want of sexual power; usu. said of the male 1655. †**3.** Lack of self-restraint, violent passion -1720.

1. O i. of mind, in body strong! MILT. *Sams.* 52. 2. A condition of i. and dotage 1836. 3. MILT. *P. L.* II. 156. So **I·mpotency** ME.

Impotent (i·mpǒtěnt), *a.* (*sb.*) ME. [a. F., ad. L. *impotentem*; see IM- [2] and POTENT.] **1.** Having no power or ability to do anything; helpless; ineffective 1444. **2.** Physically weak; without bodily strength; helpless, decrepit ME. **b.** Wanting in sexual power; incapable of reproduction 1615. †**3.** Not master of oneself; unrestrained, headlong, passionate. Also with *of.* 1596. **4.** *sb.* An impotent person 1425.

1. The works of man are i. against the assaults of nature GIBBON. 2. He was feble and Oold, And impotent LYDG. 3. But Juno, i. of passion, broke Her sullen silence POPE. 4. Impotents of all sorts PETTY. Hence **I·mpotently** *adv.*

†**Impo·tionate,** *v.* [f. med.L. *impotionat-, impotionare*, f. *im-* (IM- [1]) + *potionem* (poisoned) draught.] *trans.* To poison. FOXE.

Impound (impau·nd), *v.* 1554. Also †**em-.** [f. IM- [1] + POUND *sb.* [2]] **1.** *trans.* To shut up in or as in a pound. **2.** To seize or secure by legal right; to take possession of (a document or the like) to be held in custody of the law 1651.

1. Some cattle..had been impounded for tithe-payment HT. MARTINEAU. How to i. the Rebels, that none of them might escape BACON. Hence †**Impou·ndage, Impou·ndment,** the act of impounding. **Impou·nder,** one who impounds.

Impoverish (impǫ·věriʃ), *v.* 1440. [ad. OF. *empoveriss-, empov(e)rir, -pauvrir*, f. *em-* :—L. *im-* (IM- [1]) + *povre, pauvre* POOR.] **1.** *trans.* To make poor; to reduce to poverty. †**b.** To make bare *of* (some form of wealth) -1726. **2.** To make weak or poor in quality; to exhaust the strength or native quality of 1631.

1. Corruption .. impoverishes and enslaves the country *Junius Lett.* 2. To i. the blood ALLBUTT. Hence **Impo·verisher. Impo·verishment,** the fact or process of impoverishing; impoverished condition; loss of wealth or means.

Impower, obs. var. of EMPOWER.

Impracticability (impræ:ktikăbi·lĭti). 1747. [f. IMPRACTICABLE; see -ITY.] **1.** The quality or condition of being impracticable; practical impossibility. **b.** Intractability, stubbornness 1764. **2.** with *an* and *pl.* Something impracticable 1797.

Impracticable (impræ·ktikăb'l), *a.* (*sb.*) 1653. [IM- [2].] **1.** Not practicable; that cannot be carried out or done; practically impossible 1677. **2.** That cannot be put to use or practically dealt with; unmanageable, intractable, unserviceable 1653. **3.** *sb.* An impracticable person 1829.

1. An i. design 1696. 2. Idle and i. wastes W. IRVING. An i. way CROMWELL, pass GROTE. A poor i. creature! GOLDSM. 3. An utter i. 1829. Hence **Impra·cticableness. Impra·cticably** *adv.*

Impra·ctical, *a. rare.* [IM- [2].] **1.** Impracticable (now *U.S.*) 1774. **2.** Unpractical 1865.

Imprecate (i·mprĭkeɪt), *v.* 1613. [f. L. *imprecat-, imprecari*; in senses 1 and 2, f. *im-* (IM- [1]) + *precari.*] **1.** *trans.* To pray for, invoke. **b.** To beg for (*rare*) 1636. **2.** To pray (a deity), supplicate. Now *rare* or *Obs.* 1643. †**3.** *absol.* or *intr.* To pray; to invoke evil -1673. **4.** *trans.* To invoke evil upon; to curse. Now *rare.* 1616.

1. She..imprecated a thousand curses upon his head SMOLLETT. b. He..would only i. patience till [etc.] LOWELL. 4. His co-religionists were imprecating him as the man who had brought this persecution upon them 1879. Hence **I·mprecatingly** *adv.* in the way of a curse 1652.

Imprecation (imprĭkē·ʃən). 1585. [ad. L. *imprecationem*; see prec.] **1.** The action of imprecating, or invoking evil upon any one, in an oath or adjuration; cursing 1589; (with *pl.*) a curse 1603. †**2.** A prayer, invocation, entreaty -1631.

1. At each fierce i. he quenched a light, and dashed down a candle FROUDE.

Imprecatory (i·mprĭkeɪtəri, -kētəːri, imprĭkē·təri), *a.* 1587. [f. L. *imprecat-*, ppl. stem + -ORY.] Expressing or involving imprecation; invoking evil; cursing.

The i. Psalms 1881. **I·mprecatorily** *adv.*

Imprecise (imprĭsəi·s), *a. rare.* 1805. [IM- [2].] Not precise. So **Impreci·sion** (*rare*), want of precision; inexactness 1803.

Impredicable (impre·dikăb'l), *a. rare.* 1623. [IM- [2].] That cannot be predicated.

Impregn (imprī·n), *v.* Now only *poet.* 1425. [ad. late L. *impraegnare*, f. *im-* (IM- [1]) + *praegnare* to be PREGNANT.] = IMPREGNATE *v.* (in all senses).

Impregnable (impre·gnăb'l), *a.* ME. [Corrupted from *imprenable*, a. F. *imprenable*, f. *im-* (IM- [2]) + *pren-*, stem of *prendre* to take. The *g* is inserted.] Of a fortress, etc.: That cannot be taken by arms; incapable of being reduced by force; able to hold out against all attacks. Also *fig.*

1. The Seas, Which he hath giu'n for fence i. 3 *Hen. VI*, IV. i. 44. *fig.* A man politely i. to the intrusion of human curiosity CARLYLE. Hence **Impregnabi·lity,** i. condition or quality. **Impre·gnableness** (*rare*). **Impre·gnably** *adv.*

Impregnant (impre·gnănt), *a.*[1] (*sb.*) 1641. [In sense 1, f. IM- [1] + PREGNANT; in sense 2, ad. L. *impraegnantem.*] †**1.** Impregnated, pregnant. Also *fig.* **2.** Impregnating. Also as *sb.* That which impregnates. 1661.

†**Impregnant,** *a.*[2] *rare.* [IM- [2].] Sterile. OSBORN.

Impregnate (impre·gnĕt), *ppl. a.* 1545. [ad. late or med.L. *impraegnatus*; see IMPREGN.] **1.** Impregnated (*lit.* and *fig.*). ¶**2.** Erron. for IMPREGNABLE 1632.

Impregnate (impre·gneɪt), *v.* 1605. [f. prec.; see -ATE [3].] **1.** *trans.* To make preg-

ǫ̈ (Ger. Kǫ̈ln). ǿ (Fr. peu). ü (Ger. Müller). ü (Fr. dune). ɒ (curl). ē (ēə) (there). ē (eɪ) (rein). ɛ (Fr. faire). ə (fir, fern, earth).

nant; to cause to conceive; to fertilize; in *Biol.*, also, to fecundate the female reproductive cell or ovum 1646. Also *fig.* **b.** *intr.* for *pass.* To become pregnant. ADDISON. **2.** To fill *with* some active principle, element, or ingredient, diffused through it or mixed intimately with it; to imbue, saturate. Earlier = to fill. (Usu. in *pass.*) 1605. Also *fig.* **3.** Said of the active principle or influence: To be diffused through (something); to permeate, interpenetrate, fill, saturate 1664.

2. Water impregnated with some penetrating Salt ARBUTHNOT. *fig.* To i. his colleagues with the same loftiness of principle LYTTON. 3. Light impregnates air, air impregnates vapour BERKELEY. Hence **Impre·gnatory** *a.* having the function of impregnating.

Impregnation (impregnēⁱ·ʃən). 1605. [f. prec. vb.] **1.** The action or process of making pregnant; fecundation, fertilization. **2.** The action of imbuing or fact of being imbued with something; diffusion of an active element through a substance; saturation. Also *fig.* 1641. **3.** *concr.* That with which something is impregnated 1713; in *Geol.*, a mineral deposit consisting of a rock impregnated with ore, not forming a true vein 1881.

2. The I. of the Blood with Air RAY.

†Impreju·dicate, *ppl. a.* 1640. [f. IM-² + PREJUDICATE *ppl. a.*] Unprejudiced –1677.

Impren(i)able, etc., obs. ff. IMPREGNABLE.

Imprepara·tion. 1597. [IM-².] Unpreparedness.

†Impre·sa. 1589. [a. It. *impresa* (imprē·za) undertaking, device, etc. :—late L. **imprensa*; see EMPRISE, etc.] **1.** An emblem or device, usu. with a motto –1653. **2.** The sentence accompanying an emblem; hence, a motto, maxim, proverb –1641.

1. In an i., the figures express and illustrate the one part of the author's intention, and the word the other DRUMM. OF HAWTH. var. **†Impre·so.**

‖**Impresario** (imprezā·rio). Also erron. **impress-.** 1746. [It. *impresario* undertaker, f. *impresa*; see prec.] One who organizes public entertainments; *esp.* the manager of an operatic or concert company.

Imprescriptible (imprĭskri·ptib'l), *a.* 1563. [a. F.; see IM-² and PRESCRIPTIBLE.] Not subject to prescription; that cannot in any circumstances be taken away or abandoned; esp. in *i. right(s.*

The author of an ideal creation..has an i. property in the fame of his work W. J. COURTHOPE. Hence **Imprescriptibi·lity** (*rare*), the quality of being i. **Imprescri·ptibly** *adv.*

†Impre·se, i·mprese. 1588. [a. obs. F. *imprese*, ad. It. *impresa* IMPRESA.] = IMPRESA. –1811.

Emblazon'd Shields, Impreses quaint MILT.

Impress (i·mpres), *sb.*¹ 1590. [f. IMPRESS *v.*¹ Formerly also stressed *impre·ss.*] **1.** The act of impressing or stamping; the 'stamp' (*of* anything); *concr.* a mark or indentation made by pressure, e.g. of a seal or stamp 1592. **†b.** A cast, mould (*rare*) 1695. **c.** = IMPRINT; impression 1877. **2.** *fig.* **a.** Characteristic or distinctive mark; stamp 1590. **b.** An impression upon the mind or senses. Now *rare.* 1591. **3.** *Comb.*, as *i. copy*, a press-copy 1885.

1. The..I. of thy Feet WATTS. b. Having taken the Impresses of the Insides of these Shells WOODWARD. 2. Lucerne bears most strongly the i. of the middle ages 1832. b. *Two Gent.* III. ii. 6.

Impress (i·mpres), *sb.*² Now *rare.* 1602. [f. IMPRESS *v.*² Formerly stressed *impre·ss.*] Impressment; enforced service in the army or navy. Also *attrib.*, as **i.-gang** = PRESS-GANG.

We are all much alarmed..with a military i. 1803.

Impress (i·mpres), *sb.*³ *Obs.* exc. *Hist.* 1611. [var. of IMPRESE. In 16th–17th c. also *impre·ss.*] = IMPRESA.

Their shields broken, their impresses defaced BURKE.

†Impress, *sb.*⁴ 1569. [var. of IMPREST *sb.*¹] **1.** = IMPREST *sb.*¹ –1633. Also *attrib.* **2.** A charge made upon the pay of a naval officer who has not satisfactorily accounted for public money advanced to him 1803.

Impress (impre·s), *v.*¹ ME. [f. L. *impress-*, *imprimere*, f. *im-* (IM-¹) + *premere* to press. Partly answering to OF. *empresser.*]

I. *trans.* **1.** To apply with pressure; to produce by pressure (a mark *on*, †*in*); to imprint, stamp. **2. a.** *fig.* To stamp (a character or quality) *upon* anything ME. **b.** *transf.* To produce or communicate (motion), exert (force) by pressure. Const. *on, upon.* 1717. **3.** *fig.* To imprint (an idea, etc.) *on* (†*in, to*) the mind; to enforce, urge (a rule of conduct, etc.) *on* another ME. **†4.** To print –1781.

1. He did i. On the green moss his tremulous step SHELLEY. 2. The image of virtue, which Nature had impressed upon his heart 1791. b. The force impressed upon a ship by the wind 1765. 3. A few such examples impressed a salutary consternation GIBBON.

II. *trans.* **1.** To exert pressure upon; to press; to mark by means of pressure, esp. with a stamp, seal, etc. Const. *with.* 1588. Also *fig.* **2.** To affect or influence strongly. Usu. said of the instrument. 1736.

1. His hart like an Agot with your print impressed *L. L. L.* II. i. 236. *fig.* Real property..impressed.. with an implied trust for sale 1884. 2. The letter.. does not i. me favourably DICKENS. He tried to i. me with his importance (*mod.*).

†III. *intr.* To press in; to throng about –1480.

Impress (impre·s), *v.*² 1596. [f. IM-¹ + PRESS *v.*²] *trans.* To levy or furnish (a force) for military or naval service, to enlist; *spec.* to compel (men) to serve in the army or navy (in recent use, only the latter); to force authoritatively into service. **b.** To take by authority for royal or public service 1749. **c.** *fig.* or *transf.* 1657.

Yesterday sailed the Diamond..to i. men 1803. b. I impressed his wagons WASHINGTON. c. Hypotheses into the service of which Philology was impressed 1869.

†Impre·ss, *v.*³ *rare.* 1665. [Erron. for IMPREST *v.*¹] **1.** *trans.* = IMPREST *v.*¹ 1 –1819. **2.** To charge with a deduction (the pay of an officer) in respect to public moneys or stores not accounted for by him 1803.

†Impre·ssa¹. 1586. Erron. form of IMPRESA –1656.

†Impre·ssa². Erron. form of IMPRESS *sb.*¹ (2 a) –1647.

Impre·ssed, *ppl. a.* ME. [f. IMPRESS *v.*¹ + -ED¹.] In the senses of IMPRESS *v.*¹ I; in *Zool.* and *Bot.*, having an appearance of being stamped in; sunk in, depressed.

Impressible (impre·sib'l), *a.* 1626. [f. as prec. + -IBLE.] Capable of being impressed (on something); susceptible, impressionable. Hence **Impressibi·lity,** also **-ability,** the quality of being i. **Impre·ssibleness. Impre·ssibly** *adv.*

Impression (impre·ʃən), *sb.* ME. [a. F., ad. L. *impressionem*, f. *imprimere* (ppl. stem *impress-*); see IMPRESS *v.*¹] **1.** The action or process of impressing: *esp.* **a.** The action involved in the pressure of one thing upon or into the surface of another; also, the effect of this 1444. **†b.** A charge, onset –1799. **c.** The impact of any atmospheric or physical force. ? *Obs.* 1694. **†d.** A stress, emphasis –1824. **2.** A mark produced upon any surface by pressure. Hence, a depression, indentation; also, a mould, cast, copy. Also *fig.* ME. **†b.** A mark, trace, indication –1658. **3.** The process of printing. Now *rare.* 1509. **b.** The result of printing; a print; a printed copy 1559. **c.** The printing of one issue (of a book, etc.); hence, the aggregate of copies thus printed; see EDITION 3 b. 1570. **4.** The effective action of one thing upon another; influence; the effect of such action ME. **†5.** *spec.* An atmospheric influence, condition, or phenomenon –1684. **6.** The effect produced by external force or influence on the senses or the mind; a sensation 1632; an effect produced on the intellect, conscience, or feelings ME. **7.** A notion, remembrance, or belief, impressed upon the mind; *esp.*, in mod. use, a vague or indistinct survival from more distinct knowledge 1613. **8.** *Painting.* **a.** 'The ground-colour'. **b.** A stratum of a single colour laid upon a wall or surface for ornament, or for protection from humidity. 1864.

1. a. The i. of order on..chaos 1875. 2. As..a seal [is said] to make an i. upon wax BERKELEY. *fig.* The stamp and clear i. of good sense COWPER. 3. The i. of the fourth volume had consumed three months GIBBON. b. Very early impressions of Dürer's engravings 1869. c. Of this translation there were six impressions before the year 1601 WARTON. 4. One of the hardest of the metals; a file can scarcely make any i. on it IMISON. 5. *Fiery impression*, a comet, meteor, or the like. 6. Those perceptions, which enter with most force and violence, we may name *impressions* HUME. An i. of sound..is carried to the brain BAIN. His Sermons made no I. on his English Auditory FULLER. 7. I have an i. that I have met him before (*mod.*). Phr. *Under the impression.* Hence **Impre·ssion** *v.* (*rare*), to stamp; to affect with an impression; (in *pass.*) to be affected 1612.

Impressionable (impre·ʃənăb'l), *a.* 1836. [a. F.; see -ABLE.] **1.** Easily susceptible of impressions; sensitive. **2.** Capable of being impressed 1878.

1. She had a pretty face and an i. disposition T. HOOK. 2. Tinfoil thin enough to be i. by the metal style 1878. Hence **Impressionabi·lity,** susceptibility to impressions 1835. So **Impre·ssional** *a.* = IMPRESSIONABLE.

Impre·ssionary, *a.* 1889. [-ARY.] = IMPRESSIONISTIC.

Impressionism (impre·ʃəniz'm). 1839. [f. IMPRESSION *sb.* + -ISM.] **†1.** Applied to the philosophy of Hume. *nonce-use.* J. ROGERS. **2.** [after F. *impressionnisme*, 1876] The theory or practice of the impressionist school of painting (see next) 1882. **3.** The literary presentation of salient features, done in a few strokes 1883.

Impressionist (impre·ʃənist). 1881. [ad. Fr. *impressionniste* 1876; see IMPRESSION and -IST.] A painter who endeavours to express the general impression produced by a scene or object, to the exclusion of minute details or elaborate finish; also, a writer who practises a similar method. Hence **Impressioni·stic** *a.* of or pertaining to impressionism; in the style of the impressionists. **Impressioni·stically** *adv.*

Impre·ssionless, *a. rare.* 1864. [-LESS.] Without impression; unimpressible.

Impressive (impre·siv), *a.* 1593. [f. IMPRESS *v.*¹ + -IVE.] **†1.** Capable of being easily impressed; impressible –1665. **2.** Characterized by making a deep impression on the mind or senses; able to excite deep feeling. Rarely said of persons. 1775.

1. Men..of..i. tempers, and weak intellectuals 1665. 2. An i. actress LAMB, scene TYNDALL. Hence **Impre·ssive·ly** *adv.*, **-ness.**

Impre·ssment¹. *rare.* 1854. [f. IMPRESS *v.*¹ + -MENT. In sense 2 for F. *empressement.*] **1.** Exertion of pressure. BUSHNELL. **2.** Earnestness, ardour 1854.

Impressment² (impre·sment). 1796. [f. IMPRESS *v.*² + -MENT.] The act or practice of impressing or forcibly taking for the public service. Also *fig.*

†Impre·ssor. *rare.* 1631. [f. L. *imprimere* to IMPRESS (cf. L. *pressor*, etc.).] One who, or that which, makes impressions –1663.

Impressure (impre·ʃiŭi). Now *rare.* 1600. [f. IMPRESS *v.*¹ + -URE, after *pressure.*] **1.** The action of exerting pressure upon 1649. **2.** An impression; an indentation 1600. **3.** A mental or sensuous impression 1607.

Imprest (i·mprest), *a.* and *sb.*¹ 1568. [For the earlier PREST *a.* and *sb.* The *im-* may be partly due to the phr. *in prest (money)*; see PREST *a.*]

†A. *adj.* Of money: Lent, or advanced, esp. to soldiers, sailors, and public officials –1755.

B. *sb.* An advance (of money) made to one who is charged with some business by the state. †Formerly, also, advance-pay of soldiers or sailors. 1568. **†b.** *gen.* An advance, a loan –1704.

Vpon euery Contract we make, we giue the Victualers an i. before hand MORYSON. *Bill of I.*, an order authorizing a person to draw money in advance; so *i.-bill.*

†Imprest, *sb.*² 1610. [f. IMPREST *v.*²] = IMPRESSMENT². –1651.

†Impre·st, *v.*¹ 1565. [ad. It. (and med.L.) *imprestare* to lend.] **1.** *trans.* To advance, lend (money) –1810. **b.** To furnish (a person) with an advance of money 1612. **2.** To draw (a bill or money by a bill) –1661.

†Impre·st, *v.*² 1589. [f. *imprest, impressed*, pa. pple. of IMPRESS *v.*²] *trans.* To impress for the army or navy –1708.

†Impre·valency. [IM-².] Want of prevailing power. BP. HALL. So **†Impre·valence.**

Impreve·ntable, *a. rare.* 1864. [IM-².] That cannot be prevented. Hence **Impreventabi·lity,** i. state or quality.

Imprimatur (imprimēⁱ·tə̆ɹ). 1640. [L.; = 'let it be printed'.] 1. The formula, signed by an official licenser of the press, authorizing the printing of a book; hence as *sb.* an official licence to print. 2. *fig.* Sanction 1672.

†**Imprime**, *v.* 1575. Also **em-**. [f. IM-[1] + PRIME *a.* or *sb.*, or L. *primus*.] 1. *trans. Hunting.* (See quot.) –1775. 2. To begin. WOTTON.

1. When he is hunted and doth first leave the herde we say that he is syngled or emprymed TURBERVILE. Hence †**Impri·me** *sb.* the act of impriming a deer. †**Impri·ming** *vbl. sb.* beginning, commencement.

†**I·mpriment.** [ad. L. *imprimentem*.] Something that impresses or imprints. STERNE.

†**Impri·mery.** Also **-ie.** 1663. [a. F. *imprimerie*, f. *imprimer*; see -ERY.] 1. A printing-office or printing-house –1696. 2. Printing. WOOD. 3. A print or impression. BLOUNT.

‖**Imprimis** (imprəi·mis), *adv.* or *adv. phr.* 1465. [L., assim. form of *in primis*.] In the first place, first. Now unusual.

Imprint (i·mprint), *sb.* 1480. [ME. type *empreynte, -printe*, a. F. *empreinte*, ppl. sb. from *empreindre*; subseq. refash. after L.; see next.] 1. A figure impressed or imprinted on something; a mark produced by pressure; an impression, stamp 1483. Also *fig.* 2. †a. The condition of being printed (in phr. *in enprinte*) –1485. b. The printing of a book, etc. (*mod.*). c. An impression *of* a writing 1882. 3. The name of the publisher, place of publication, and date, printed in a book, usually at the foot of the title-page (*publisher's i.*); also, the name of printer and place of printing, printed at the end of a book, or on the back of the title-page (*printer's i.*) 1790. †4. An onset. CAXTON.

3. The i...' At the Clarendon Press' 1790.

Imprint (impri·nt), *v.* [ME. *empreynten, -prent-, -print-*, a. OF. *empreinter* :—(ult.) late pop. L. *impremere*, for cl. L. *imprimere*; refash. after L.] 1. *trans.* To mark by pressure; to impress, stamp. †2. To impress (letters or characters) on paper or the like by means of type; to PRINT –1822. 3. *fig.* a. To impress *on* or *in* the mind, memory, etc. ME. b. To impress (a quality, etc.) *on* or *in* a person or thing; to communicate. In *pass.* of a quality: To exist strongly marked *in* or *on* a person, etc. 1526. 4. *transf.* To stamp or impress (something) *with* a figure, etc. ME. b. *fig.* To impress *with* some feeling, quality, etc. 1765.

1. The Volto Santo or print of our Saviour's face, which he imprinted in the handkerchief of St. Veronica 1670. 2. Imprinted at London by Robert Barker BIBLE (1611) *title-p.* 3. a. I. this in thy memorie 1576. b. That wisedome which the Divine hand hath imprinted in his workes G. SANDYS. Hence **Impri·nter**, one who or that which imprints; †a printer 1548.

Imprison (impri·z'n), *v.* ME. [a. OF. *en-, emprisoner*, mod. *emprisonner*, f. *en-, in-* (IN-[2]) + *prison* PRISON.] 1. *trans.* To put in prison; to detain in custody; to confine. 2. *transf.* and *fig.* To confine, shut up; in various connexions 1533.

1. Lord, they know that I imprisoned..them that beleeued on thee *Acts* xxii. 19. Since imprison'd in my mother Thou me freed'st C'TESS PEMBROKE. 2. Try to i. the resistless wind DRYDEN. Hence **Impri·sonable** *a.* capable of or liable to imprisonment. **Impri·soner**, one who imprisons.

Imprisonment (impri·z'nmĕnt). [ME. *en-, emprisonement*, a. AF. *enprisounement*, OF. *emprisonement*, f. *emprisoner* + -MENT.] The action of imprisoning, or fact or condition of being imprisoned; confinement; incarceration. Also *transf.* and *fig.*

Imprisonment, is when a man is by publique Authority deprived of liberty HOBBES. *fig.* Into the slavishe i. of vices most detestable FLEMING.

Improbability (imprǫbăbi·lĭti). 1598. [f. IMPROBABLE; see -ITY.] The quality of being improbable; unlikelihood; (with *an* and *pl.*) something unlikely.

Improbable (imprǫ·băb'l), *a.* 1598. [ad. L. *improbabilis*; see IM-[2] and PROBABLE.] 1. Not probable; not likely to be true; not easy to believe; unlikely. 2. In pregnant sense: Unlikely to 'do', suit, etc. 1659.

1. If this were plaid vpon a stage now, I could condemne it as an i. fiction SHAKS. I. of success LD. ORRERY. 2. In the most i. soile HAMMOND. Hence **Impro·bableness. Impro·bably** *adv.*

†**Improbate**, *v.* [f. L. *improbat-, improbare*, f. *im-* (IM-[2]) + *probare* to make good, approve.] *trans.* To disapprove, disallow. BLOUNT.

Improbation (imprŏbēⁱ·ʃən). 1551. [ad. L. *improbationem*; see prec.] †1. Disapprobation, disapproval –1789. †2. Disproof, confutation (*rare*) –1657. 3. *Sc. Law.* Disproof of a writ; an action brought to prove a document to be false or forged 1575.

Improbative (imprǫ·bătiv), *a.* 1677. [f. L. *improbat-, improbare* + -IVE.] 1. Liable to improbation or disproof. 2. = IMPROBATORY 1876.

Improbatory (imprǫ·bătəri), *a.* 1828. [f. as prec. + -ORY.] Having the function of disproving; in *Sc. Law*, made in improbation of a writ.

Improbity (imprǭ·bĭti, imprǫ·bĭti). ME. [ad. L. *improbitas*, f. *improbus*.] 1. Persistency, perseverance. *Obs.* or *nonce-use.* 2. Wickedness, want of principle or integrity 1594.

2. The exuberant I. of ill Men 1695.

†**Improdu·ction.** *rare.* 1662. [IM-[2].] The condition of not having been produced from anything else –1678.

†**Improfi·cience.** *rare.* 1605. [IM-[2].] Lack of proficiency. So **Improfi·ciency** (now *rare*).

†**Impro·fitable**, *a.* ME. [IM-[2].] Unprofitable –1725.

Improgressive (imprǫgre·siv), *a.* 1809. [IM-[2].] Not progressive; unprogressive. **Improgre·ssive·ly** *adv.*, **-ness.**

†**Improli·fic, †-al**, *a.* 1646. [IM-[2].] Not prolific –1686.

†**Improli·ficate**, *v.* [IM-[1].] To render prolific, to fertilize. SIR T. BROWNE.

†**Impro·mpt**, *a.* [ad. L. *impromptus*; see IM-[2] and PROMPT.] Not ready; unready. STERNE.

Impromptu (imprǫ·mᵖtiū). 1669. [ad. L. *in promptu* in readiness, written as one word.] A. *adv.* Without preparation; off-hand.

This was made almost *impromptu* BOSWELL.

B. *sb.* Something composed or uttered without preparation; an extemporaneous composition or performance; an improvisation. Also, a musical composition having the character of an improvisation. 1683.

C. *adj.* 1. Composed or uttered without premeditation; improvised 1789. 2. Made or done on the spur of the moment; extemporized, makeshift 1764.

1. I. poems 1789, replies D'ISRAELI. 2. An i. visit 1856. Hence **Impro·mptuary** *a.* = C. 1 (BENTHAM).

Improper (imprǫ·pəɹ), *a.* 1531. [IM-[2].] Not proper; the opposite of proper. 1. Not strictly belonging to the thing under consideration; not in accordance with truth, fact, reason, or rule; abnormal; incorrect, wrong. b. Not properly so called 1575. 2. Not in accordance with the circumstances or the end in view; unsuitable, ill-adapted 1570. 3. Unbecoming; indecorous, indecent. Also *transf.* of a person. 1739. †4. ? Not peculiar to an individual; general, common (*rare*) 1610.

1. To eate Christs flesh—to pluck out our right eye ..We cannot read any of these literally and properly ..therefore we must seek for a spiritual and i. sense 1649. b. *Improper fraction*: a fraction whose numerator is greater than (or equal to) its denominator. *I. diphthong*: see DIPHTHONG. They are not to be adorned with any art but such improper ones as nature is said to bestow, as singing and poetry FLETCHER. [This quot. is taken in sense 4 in recent Dicts.] 2. As i. to be approached as a rocky lee shore 1774. 3. I am too old to be i. H. WALPOLE. Hence †**Impro·perty**, impropriety 1555–1663.

†**Improper**, *v.* [ME. *en-, empropre*, app. repr. an AFr. var. of OF. *aproprier*, ad. L. *appropriare* to APPROPRIATE.] = IMPROPRIATE *v.* 1, 2. –1642.

If he would..i., and inclose the Sun beames, to comfort the rich JEWEL.

†**Impropera·tion**[1]. 1502. [f. late L. *improperare* to taunt, upbraid.] The action of upbraiding or reviling; a reproach, taunt.

†**Impropera·tion**[2]. 1536. Erron. f. IMPROPRIATION –1624.

Improperly (imprǫ·pəɹli), *adv.* ME. [f. IMPROPER *a.* + -LY[2]. Occurs once only in ME.; then not till 1531.] In an improper manner; wrongly, incorrectly, unsuitably, unbecomingly.

†**Impropi·tious**, *a.* [IM-[2].] Not propitious; unfavourable. WOTTON.

†**Impropo·rtion.** 1450. [IM-[2].] Want of proportion, disproportion –1675. Hence †**Impropo·rtionable**, †**Impropo·rtionate** *adjs.* disproportionate.

Impropriate (imprōᵘ·pri,eⁱt), *v.* 1538. [f. ppl. stem of med. or mod.L. *impropriare*; cf. APPROPRIATE.] †1. *trans.* To make one's (or some one's) own; to appropriate –1703. 2. *spec.* To annex (an ecclesiastical benefice) to a corporation or person, as their corporate or private property 1538; esp. b. (in later use) to place tithes or ecclesiastical property in lay hands 1613.

1. To i. the Preaching of the Gospell to one certain Order of men HOBBES. Hence **Impro·priator**, one to whom a benefice is impropriated; esp. = *lay impropriator*; †also *gen.* **Impro·pria·trix**, a female i.

Impropriate (imprōᵘ·pri,ēt), *ppl. a.* 1538. [ad. med. or mod.L. *impropriatus*; see prec.] 1. Appropriated to some person or persons. ? *Obs.* 1600. 2. Of a benefice or tithes: Impropriated.

Impropriation (imprōᵘpri,ēⁱ·ʃən). 1535. [f. IMPROPRIATE *v.*; see -ATION.] 1. The action of impropriating (see IMPROPRIATE *v.* 2). b. The proprietorship thus conveyed 1631. c. An impropriated benefice 1578. †2. *gen.* The action of making proper to some person or thing; appropriation –1728. †b. Something appropriated; a property –1651.

1. c. An i. which the Lord Gray of Wilton..restored to the Church FULLER.

Impropriety (imprǫ,prəi·ĕti). 1611. [ad. F. *impropriété*, or L. *improprietas*, f. *improprius* IMPROPER *a.*] 1. The quality of being improper; incorrectness; inappropriateness 1697; unseemliness; morally improper conduct 1751. 2. With *an* and *pl.* An instance of improper language, conduct, etc.; a breach of propriety 1674.

1. We may..say, without i., that [etc.] MILL. The i. of holding a public discussion with such men JOWETT. The i. of my conduct JOHNSON. 2. Every language has likewise its improprieties and absurdities JOHNSON.

†**Impro·pry, -rie**, *v.* 1526. [f. as *impropre*, IMPROPER *v.*] *trans.* To appropriate, impropriate –1571.

†**Improspe·rity.** 1528. [f. L. *improsper* + -ITY.] Want of, or the opposite of, prosperity; unprosperousness –1722.

†**Impro·sperous**, *a.* 1598. [f. as prec. + -OUS.] 1. Not prosperous; unsuccessful –1829. 2. Of fortune, etc.: Unpropitious –1656. Hence †**Impro·sperous·ly** *adv.* 1594, †**-ness** 1647.

Improvable (imprū·văb'l), *a.* Also improveable. 1646. [f. IMPROVE *v.*[2] + -ABLE.] 1. Capable of being turned to profit; that may be taken advantage of; serviceable. Now *rare.* 2. Of land: Capable of being profitably cultivated; capable of being made more productive 1659. 3. Capable of being made better 1677.

1. Finding this project of a penny-post..apparently i. NORTH. 2. A fine spread of improveable lands ADDISON. 3. With Moral principles .. i. by the exercise of his Faculties HALE. Hence **Improvabi·lity, Impro·vableness**, the quality of being i. **Impro·vably** *adv.*

†**Improve**, *v.*[1] 1449. [a. OF. *improver*, F. *improuver*, ad.L. *improbare* to condemn, f. *improbus*.] 1. *trans.* To disprove, refute, confute –1678. 2. To disapprove as bad; to disallow; to reprove; to censure, condemn –1642.

1. We..will in due place i. their error therein 1606. 2. When they had improued and disallowed my savinges 1551.

Improve (imprū·v), *v.*[2] 1509. [Orig. *en-, emprow(e*, a. AFr. *en-, emprower*, a parallel form of *aprower*; f. OF. *en* into + *pro, prou, preu*, oblique case of *pros* profit; see APPROVE *v.*[2]] †1. *refl. To i. oneself (of)*: to make one's profit (of) –1655. 2. *trans.* To make good use of, turn to profit or good account; *spec.* to enlarge upon for spiritual edification 1539. †b. To invest (money); in N. America, to enclose and cultivate (land). c. To employ to advantage, as a means or instrument 1529; later American: *spec.* to occupy (a place). †3. To enhance in monetary value –1750. †4. To make greater in amount or degree; to advance. (Now merged in 5.) –1771. †b. To augment (what is evil), to make worse –1800. 5. To advance or raise to a better quality or condition; to make better; to ameliorate. (The prevailing mod. sense.) 1617. 6. *absol.* To make improvements 1699. 7. *intr.* To increase, augment, advance, develop. *Obs.* (exc. as merged in 8). 1650. 8. *intr.* To increase in value or excellence; to become better 1727.

1. The Townsmen..unconscionably improving themselves on the Scholars necessities FULLER. 2. How doth the little busy bee I. each shining hour! WATTS. To i. an opportunity LINGARD, the occasion FREEMAN. b. To i. Lands for the proffit thereof 1653. To i., and put it [his Talent] out BUTLER. c. Places..improved for Trading and Fishing 1677. Every Corner is improved for Cupboards and necessarys CELIA FIENNES. 3. They i. their commodities to a treble price MORYSON. 4. b. As wholesome Medicines the Disease i., There where they work not well COWLEY. 5. The habit of attention may be improved by exercise SIR B. BRODIE. 6. Phr. *To i. on* or *upon*: to make something better than. We cannot i. upon nature 1867. 8. Trade has improved (*mod.*).

†Improve, *v.*[3] 1612. [var. of *aprove*, APPROVE *v.*[1]] 1. *trans.* To prove, establish, show to be true or real –1670; *intr.* to prove or turn out to be (*rare*) 1612. 2. *trans.* To approve, countenance. C. MATHER.

Improvement (imprū·vmĕnt). 1453. [a. AF. *emprowement*, f. *emprower* IMPROVE *v.*[2] + -MENT.] 1. The turning of a thing to profit or good account; making the most of a thing; realization of the profits of anything; *concr.* profit. *Obs.* in *lit.* sense. 2. *spec.* †The turning of land to better account; cultivation and occupation of land; merged at length in sense 5. 1549. b. *concr.* A piece of land improved by inclosure, building, etc. *Obs.* exc. in *U.S. dial.* 1473. c. *fig.* Bodily or mental cultivation or culture; an accomplishment. *Obs.* exc. as merged in 5, 6. 1711. 3. The turning to account of any person or thing (now *Obs.* or *U.S. dial.*), or of any event or season 1611. b. *spec.* The profitable spiritual application of a text or incident 1655. †4. The action or process of enhancing, or an instance of this 1548–1788. †b. quasi-*concr.* An advanced stage, development (*of* something) –1716. †c. *concr.* Increase, produce –1719. 5. The action or process of making or becoming better; betterment, amelioration 1647. 6. With *an* and *pl.*: a. An act of making or becoming better; that by which anything is made better 1697. b. With *on* or *upon*: An advance upon (something previous); hence, a thing that is an advance upon (the former thing) 1712.

2. b. My aunt's bell rings for our afternoon's walk round the improvements GOLDSM. c. I look upon your city as the best place of i. SOUTH. 3. Prompt i. of the opportunity (*mod.*). 4. This was nothing but ..an improuement of his griefe 1617. 5. The i. of Trade 1662, of body and mind JOWETT. 6. It is a great i. to add the juice of two Seville oranges MRS. GLASSE. b. The sons are no great i. upon the sires SPURGEON.

Improver (imprū·vəɹ). 1647. [f. IMPROVE *v.*[2] + -ER[1].] 1. One who or that which improves; †a cultivator, occupier. 2. Short for *dress-improver* 1884. 3. A person who works at a trade, and accepts the opportunity of improvement wholly or in part instead of wages 1858; in the Civil Service, applied to a grade of clerks intermediate between boy clerks and assistant clerks.

2. Her 'improver' was found to be so arranged as to hold 6 lb. of smuggled tobacco 1884.

†Improvi·ded, *a.* 1548. [IM-[2].] 1. Unprovided; unprepared –1622. 2. Unforeseen. SPENSER.

Improvidence (imprǫ·vidĕns). 1425. [ad. L. *improvidentia*; see IM-[2] and PROVIDENCE.] The fact or quality of being improvident; want of foresight; thriftlessness.

Shee'le lift thee to i., And breake thy neck from steepe securitie MARSTON.

Improvident (imprǫ·vidĕnt), *a.* 1514. [f. IM-[2] + PROVIDENT; cf. L. *improvidus*.] 1. Unforeseeing; that does not forecast the future. 2. Not circumspect; heedless; unwary 1591. 3. Thriftless 1624.

1. The i...conduct of the German powers 1795. 2. Improuident Souldiors, had your Watch been good, This sudden Mischiefe neuer could haue falne SHAKS.

†Improvide·ntially, *adv.* 1797. [IM-[2].] = next –1819.

Impro·vidently, *adv.* 1607. [f. IMPROVIDENT *a.* + -LY[2].] 1. In an improvident manner; without providing for the future. 2. In an unforeseen manner (*rare*) 1885.

1. Agricultural labourers marry early and i. 1868.

Improving (imprū·viŋ), *vbl. sb.* 1602. [f. IMPROVE *v.*[2] + -ING[1].] The action of IMPROVE *v.*[2]; improvement.

Improving lease (Sc. Law): a lease granted to a tenant for a longer period than the usual one, with the object of encouraging him to make permanent improvements on the holding.

Improvisate (imprǫ·vizeɪt), *v.* 1832. [f. F. *improviser*; see IMPROVISE and -ATE[3].] = IMPROVISE (*trans.* and *intr.*). So **Impro·visate** *ppl. a.* (*rare*), improvised; impromptu.

Improvisation (i:mprǒvəizēɪ·ʃən, imprǫvizēɪ·ʃən). 1786. [f. IMPROVISE, IMPROVISATE.] 1. The action of improvising; also *concr.* verse, music, etc. so improvised. 2. The production or execution of anything off-hand; anything so produced or executed 1874.

1. The thrush-like i...that charm[s] us in our Elizabethan drama LOWELL.

Impro·visatize, *v. rare.* 1847. [irreg. f. IMPROVISATE + -IZE.] = IMPROVISATE.

Improvisator (imprǫ·vizēɪtəɹ). 1795. [f. IMPROVISATE, after It. and F.] One who composes extempore; an improviser.

‖**Improvisatore, -provvisatore** (*improv-* (*v*)*izatō·re*). Pl. -ori (-ō·ri), also -ores. 1765. [It., f. *improv*(*v*)*isare* to IMPROVISE.] An improvisator (Italian or of the Italian type).

Improvisatorial (imprǫvizătō°·riăl), *a.* 1822. [f. IMPROVISATOR; see -ORY and -AL.] Of, pertaining to, or having the nature of an improvisator; relating to or having the power of improvisation. Hence **Improvisato·rially** *adv.* So **Improvi·satory** *a.* 1806.

‖**Improvisatrice, -provvisa-** (*improv*(*v*)*izatrī·tʃe*). Pl. -trici (-trī·tʃi). 1804. [It., fem. of *improv*(*v*)*isatore*; see -TRICE.] A woman who improvises.

Improvise (i·mprǒvəiz, improvəi·z), *v.* 1826. [a. F. *improviser*, ad. It. *improv*(*v*)*isare*, f. *improv*(*v*)*iso* IMPROVISO.] 1. *trans.* To compose, utter, or perform extempore. 2. To get up on the spur of the moment; to provide for the occasion 1854. 3. *intr.* To compose, utter, or perform verse or music impromptu; to speak extemporaneously; to do anything on the spur of the moment 1830.

1. The singular faculty of being able to i. quotations DISRAELI. 2. To i. a dance 1854, a tent DICKENS. Hence **Improvi·se** *sb.* an improvisation 1820. **Impro·vi·sedly** *adv.* **Improvi·ser.**

†Improvi·sion. 1646. [IM-[2].] Want of provision or forethought –1649.

†Improviso (improvəi·zo), *a.* 1786. [It., = L. *improvisus*, f. *im-* (IM-[2]) + *provisus*, *providere* to foresee.] Improvised, extempore –1789.

Improvvisatore, -trice: see IMPROVIS-.

Imprudence (imprū·dĕns). 1445. [ad. L. *imprudentia*, f. *imprudens* IMPRUDENT; see -ENCE. Cf. F. *imprudence* (14th c.).] The quality or fact of being imprudent; want of prudence; rashness; (with *an* and *pl.*) an imprudent act.

Not taking those precautions against the weather.. I soon suffered for my i. 1831. Love at first sight sounds like an i. LUBBOCK. So **†Impru·dency** 1576.

Imprudent (imprū·dĕnt), *a.* (*sb.*) ME. [ad. L. *imprudens*, *imprudentem*, f. *im-* (IM-[2]) + *prudens*, contracted from *providens*, *providere* to see before one; see PRUDENT.] 1. Not prudent, wanting in prudence or discretion; rash, heedless, indiscreet, incautious. †2. *sb.* An imprudent person –1767.

1. I. men are call'd Fools 1710. Loss for the folly of i. actions R. COKE. Hence **Impru·dently** *adv.*

†Imprude·ntial, *a.* [IM-[2].] Not prudential. MILT.

Impuberal (impiū·bĕrăl), *a. rare.* 1836. [f. L. *impubes*, *impuberem* + -AL.] Not come to puberty or maturity; immature. So **Impu·berate**, **Impu·bic** *adjs.* (*rare*).

Impuberty (impiū·bəɹti). 1785. [f. as prec. + -TY, after *puberty*.] The condition of not having reached the state or age of puberty.

Impudence (i·mpiŭdĕns). ME. [ad. L. *impudentia*, f. *impudens* IMPUDENT; see -ENCE.] The quality or fact of being impudent. †1. Shamelessness; immodesty –1712. 2. Shameless effrontery; insolence; unabashed presumption 1611. b. Applied to an impudent person. DRYDEN. 3. In a neutral sense: Freedom from shamefastness 1619.

1. *All's Well*, II. i. 173. 2. Some with I. invade the Court DRYDEN. 'Confound his impudence!' muttered Squeers DICKENS. 3. I had not enterprise nor i. enough to venture from my concealment W. IRVING. So **I·mpudency** (now *rare*), in all senses 1529.

Impudent (i·mpiŭdĕnt), *a.* (*sb.*) ME. [ad. L. *impudens*, *impudentem*, f. *im-* (IM-[2]) + *pudens* ashamed, modest, orig. pres. pple. of *pudere* to make or feel ashamed.] †1. Wanting in modesty; shameless, unblushing; indelicate –1732. 2. Possessed of unblushing effrontery; shamelessly forward, insolently disrespectful 1563. 3. *sb.* A person of unblushing effrontery or insolence 1586.

1. Inpudent is he that..hath no shame of hise synnes CHAUCER. 2. A wicked, i., bold-faced hussy DICKENS. An i. reply 1873. Hence **I·mpudently** *adv.*

Impudicity (impiudi·sĭti). 1528. [a. F. *impudicité*, f. L. type **impudicitas*, for cl. L. *impudicitia*, f. *impudicus* shameless.] Shamelessness, immodesty.

Impugn (impiū·n), *v.* ME. [a. F. *impugner*, ad. L. *impugnare* to attack, f. *im-* (IM-[1]) + *pugnare*.] †1. *trans.* To fight against; to attack, assail, assault (a person, city, etc.) –1651. †b. To withstand, resist, oppose –1660. 2. To assail by word or argument; to call in question; to oppose as false or erroneous ME. b. To find fault with, accuse (now *rare*) ME.

2. The saint was scarcely canonised, before his claims to beatitude were impugned DISRAELI. Hence **Impu·gnable** *a.*[1] (*rare*), **Impu·gnant** *a.*, opposed *to*, **Impugna·tion** ME., **Impu·gner**, **Impu·gnment.**

Impugnable (impʋ·gnăb'l), *a.*[2] ? *Obs.* 1570. [f. IM-[2] + L. *pugnare* + -ABLE.] That cannot be assailed or overcome.

Impuissance (impiū·isăns). 1483. [a. F.; see IM-[2] and PUISSANCE. (Also *impu*,*i·ssance*.)] Impotence, powerlessness, weakness.

An i. to conserve himself 1602.

Impuissant (impiū·isănt), *a.* 1629. [a. F.; see IM-[2] and PUISSANT.] Impotent, powerless, weak.

Impulse (i·mpʋls), *sb.* 1647. [ad. L. *impulsus*, f. ppl. stem of *impellere* to IMPEL.] 1. An act of impelling; an application of sudden force causing motion; a thrust, a push 1650. Also *fig.* 2. *Dynamics.* a. An indefinitely large force enduring for an inappreciably short time but producing a finite momentum; such as the blow of a hammer, etc. 1796. b. The product of the average value *of* any force multiplied by the time during which it acts (CLERK MAXWELL) 1875. 3. a. Force or influence exerted upon the mind by some external stimulus; suggestion, incitement 1660. b. Incitement arising from some state of mind or feeling 1647. c. Sudden inclination to act without premeditation 1763. 4. The effect produced by impulsion; momentum, impetus 1715. Also *fig.* b. *Path.* 'The wave of change which travels through nerve and muscle in passing from rest into action' (*Syd. Soc. Lex.*) 1886. 5. *attrib.* 1825.

1. We cannot conceive how any thing but i. of body can move body LOCKE. *fig.* The blind impulses of Fatality and Fortune BENTLEY. 3. a. A..Divine I. and Impression 1674. b. Under an i. of curiosity 1833. c. Guided by i. rather than by judgement FREEMAN. 4. *fig.* Orseolo gave a new i. to navigation YEATS.

Impu·lse, *v.* Now *rare.* 1611. [f. the sb.] *trans.* To give an impulse to; to impel; to instigate.

Impulsion (impʋ·lʃən). ME. [a. F., ad. L. *impulsionem*, f. *impuls-*, *impellere*; cf. IMPULSE *sb.*] 1. The action of impelling or forcing onward; also of striking upon, pushing, or pressing against without producing motion; the condition of being impelled. Also *transf.* and *fig.* †b. An impelling cause or occasion. BACON. 2. a. Instigation, incitement 1533. b. Determination to action from natural tendency or temporary excitement; impulse 1530. 3. Impetus 1795.

1. The centrifugal force, or force of I., is still un-

known 1794. **2. a.** Atreus and Thyestes..at the i. of their mother slew this Chrysippus HOBBES. **b.** The like i. from which a drowning man catches at a twig 1793. **3.** The i. which Kant had given to philosophy SIR W. HAMILTON.

Impulsive (impʋ·lsiv), *a.* (*sb.*) ME. [a. OF. *impulsif*, or ad. med.L. *impulsivus*, f. L. *impuls-*, *impellere*; see -IVE.] **1.** Having the property of impelling; characterized by impulsion or impetus 1604. **2.** Impelling or determining to action 1555. **3.** Of persons, etc.: Actuated or characterized by impulse; apt to be moved by sudden impulse or swayed by emotion 1847. †**4.** *sb.* An impelling agent or cause -1659.

1. The force Of the i. chariot CHAPMAN. When a force produces it's effect instantaneously, it is said to be i. 1803. **2.** The love of God was the i. (= originating) cause HORNECK. Hence **Impu·lsive-ly** *adv.*, **-ness.** **Impu·lsivist**, one who acts on impulse. **Impulsi·vity**, impulsiveness.

†**Impu·lsor.** 1653. [a. L.] One who, or that which, impels -1700. So **Impu·lsory** *a.* (*rare*), that tends to impel 1659.

Impu·nctate, *ppl. a.* 1819. [IM-2.] Not punctate; not marked with points or dots.

Impu·nctual, *a.* 1864. [IM-2.] Not punctual; behind time. So **Impunctua·lity**, want of punctuality 1790.

†**Impune** (impiū·n), *a.* [ad. L. *impunis*, f. *im-* (IM-2) + *pœna*, *punire* to punish.] Unpunished; enjoying impunity. T. ADAMS.

Impunible (impiū·nĭb'l), *a.* *rare.* 1660. [f. IM-2 + L. *punire* + -IBLE.] Not punishable; unpunishable. Hence **Impu·nibly** *adv.*

Impunity (impiū·nĭti). 1532. [ad. L. *impunitas*; see IMPUNE and -TY.] Exemption from punishment or penalty; exemption from injury or loss.

Delay of punishment is no sort nor degree of presumption of final i. BUTLER. The venom of the most deadly snakes may be swallowed with i. PRINGLE.

†**Impura·tion.** [f. L. *impurus* + -ATION.] Pollution (*lit.* and *fig.*). BP. HALL.

Impure (impiū̆ə·ɹ), *a.* 1536. [ad. L. *impurus*, f. *im-* (IM-2) + *purus*. Cf. F. *impur(e.*]

I. 1. Containing some defiling or offensive matter; dirty, unclean 1597; not pure ceremonially; unhallowed 1612. **2.** Not pure morally; defiled by sin; unchaste; filthy 1536.

1. An i. atmosphere 1807. The invader, who had touched the hallowed soil with i. feet THIRLWALL. **2.** Defaming as i. what God declares Pure MILT.

II. Mixed with some extraneous matter; contaminated, adulterated 1626. **b.** Of a language, style, etc.: Containing foreign idioms or grammatical blemishes 1613. **c.** Of a colour: Containing an admixture of some other colour or colours; also said of a spectrum when the colours overlap 1860.

I. mercury 1816, thought 1704. **c.** The rainbow is an imperfect or i. spectrum TYNDALL. Hence †**Impu·re** *v.* to make, or become, i. 1597. **Impu·re-ly** *adv.*, **-ness.**

Impu·ritan. 1617. [f. IMPURE *a.*, after PURITAN.] One who practises impurity; also, a dyslogistic term for one opposed to Puritanism.

Impurity (impiū̆ə·rĭti). 1450. [a. OF. *impurité* = mod.F. *impureté*, ad. L. *impuritas*; see IMPURE *a.* and -TY.] **1.** The quality or condition of being impure, in any sense; foulness; defilement 1548. **2.** That which is or makes impure; dirt; corruption; foreign matter 1450.

1. The i. of the ayr 1660, of thought 1704. I. or beastlinesse is not hard to be defined HEALEY. **2.** Novels..full of impurities, impieties 1639. Ashes or other impurities 1799.

Impurple, obs. f. EMPURPLE *v.*

Imputable (impiū·tăb'l), *a.* 1626. [ad. med.L. *imputabilis*; see IMPUTE and -BLE.] **1.** That may be imputed *to* or assigned to the account of; chargeable, attributable. †**2.** Liable to imputation; open to accusation or censure; culpable -1784.

1. The errour is i. onely to the Transcriber 1626. **2.** Some justly blameable and i. Act SHAFTESB. Hence **Imputabi·lity, Impu·tableness**, the quality of being i. **Impu·tably** *adv.*

Imputation (impiutēˑʃən). 1545. [ad. late L. *imputationem.*] **1.** The action of imputing or charging; the fact of being charged with a crime, fault, etc.; (with *pl.*) accusation, charge 1581. **2.** *Theol.* The attributing to believers of the righteousness of Christ, and to Christ of human sin, by vicarious substitution; also, the imputing of the guilt of Adam's sin to all his descendants 1545. †**3.** The making a merit of a thing. EARLE.

1. I would humour his men, with the i. of beeing neere their Mayster SHAKS. The i. of a new violation of faith BURKE. **2.** I. is the attributing of a character to a person which he does not really possess HOOK.

Imputative (impiū·tătiv), *a.* 1579. [ad. late L. *imputativus*; see IMPUTE and -IVE.] Characterized by being imputed; existing or arising by imputation.

A man would think we need no i. wickedness 1691. Hence **Impu·tative-ly** *adv.*, **-ness.**

Impute (impiū·t), *v.* ME. [a. F. *imputer*, ad. L. *imputare*, f. *im-* (IM-1) + *putare* to reckon.] **1.** *trans.* To bring (a fault, etc.) into the reckoning against; to lay to the charge of; to attribute or assign *to*. **b.** Occas. in a good sense: To set to the credit of; to ascribe or reckon *to* 1574. **2.** *Theol.* To attribute or ascribe (righteousness, guilt, etc.) *to* a person by vicarious substitution 1583. **3.** To arraign or tax *with* fault; to accuse. ? *Obs.* 1596. †**4.** To reckon or take into account; to consider -1794. †**5.** To impart -1675.

1. We usually ascribe good, but i. evil JOHNSON. **b.** It was imputed to him for righteousnesse *Rom.* iv. 22. **2.** Thy merit Imputed shall absolve them who renounce Thir own both righteous and unrighteous deeds MILT. *P.L.* III. 291. **4.** [K. Henry VI] for his holy life was imputed a Saint SPEED. Hence **Impu·tedly** *adv.* by imputation.

Imputrescence (impiutre·sĕns). 1658. [IM-2.] Absence of decomposition.

Imputre·scible, *a.* 1656. [IM-2.] Not subject to decomposition. **Imputrescibi·lity.**

†**Imputrid** (impiū·trid), *a.* 1684. [IM-2.] Not putrid; applied to a fever -1824.

In, *sb.* 1764. [f. IN *adv.*] **1.** *pl.* **a.** The party that is in office, usu. in phr. (*the*) *ins and outs*. **b.** In games: The side whose turn it is to play 1862. **2. Ins and outs.** Windings or turnings in and out in a road, a course of action, etc.; sinuous ramifications 1670. **b.** Those who are constantly entering and leaving the workhouse 1884.

1. a. Everything the Ins do the Outs denounce SPURGEON. **2.** The ins and outs of legal method R. H. HUTTON.

In, *a.* 1599. [IN *adv.* used *attrib.*, or as positive of INNER, INMOST.] That is in; that lies, remains, lives, is situated, or is used in or within; internal. (Usu. hyphened to the sb.)

In (in), *v.* OE. [Conn. w. *inn* IN *adv.* and INN *sb.* Cf. OHG. *innôn*, from the adv. *inn.*] **1.** *trans.* †To give or put in; to take in, include, enclose; *esp.* to take in or reclaim (waste land). Now *dial.* **2.** To gather into the barn, stackyard, etc.; to harvest or house ME. **3.** To get in, gather in, collect 1615. †**4.** To take in mentally. FLORIO. †**5.** *intr.* To go in, to enter; in 17th c. to begin -1639.

2. He taryed tyll they had inned all their corne 1525. **5.** We inne diversely, but end alike 1639.

In (in), *prep.* [Com. Teut., cogn. w. L. *in*, Gr. ἐν. The apocopated *i* became common in early ME. in certain dialects.] *General sense*:— The preposition expressing the relation of inclusion, situation, position, existence, or action within limits of space, time, condition, circumstances, etc. In ancient times, expressing also (like L. *in*) motion or direction from a point outside to one within limits (now ordinarily *in-to*, INTO).

I. Of position or location. **1.** Within the limits or bounds of, within (any place or thing). †**2.** = ON (of position) -1730. †**b.** = AT -1671. **3.** *In* is now regular with collectives thought of as singular (*in an army*, *a crowd*) OE. **4.** With numerals, nouns of quantity, etc., expressing ratio or rate 1436. **5.** Defining the particular part of anything in which it is affected ME. **6.** Expressing relation to that which covers, clothes, or envelopes, its material, its colour, etc., = clothed in, wearing, bound in, etc. OE. **7.** With non-physical realms, regions of thought, departments or faculties of the mind, spheres of action, etc., treated as having extension or content OE.

1. Summe in þe Eir, and summe in þe Eorþe, and summe in helle deope LANGL. In the green woods SHELLEY; in the East DICKENS. *With the article omitted: *In bed, in chancery, in church, in school, in town*; in Capernaum 1526 in Europe 1686. **2. b.** Ere in the head of nations he appear MILT. *P.R.* I. 98. **4.** A debtor..offered 6*s.* 8*d.* in the pound 1892. **5.** A masked battery took them in flank 1795. **6.** Martirs clothed alle in purpul ME. A lady in a Gainsborough hat (*mod.*). **7.** I discover an arrant laziness in my soul FULLER. Opposed in politics MACAULAY.

II. 1. Of situation, i.e. kind or nature of position OE. **b.** Situation within the range of sensuous observation or the sphere of action of another ME. **2.** Of condition or state, physical, mental, or moral OE. **3.** Of occupation or engagement ME. **b.** In the process or act of, in case of ME. **4.** Of manner (way, mode, style, fashion) ME. **b.** Of form, shape, conformation, arrangement, order OE. **c.** Of manner of speech or writing OE. **d.** *colloq.* Within the sphere of (a particular class or order of things) 1866. **5.** Of means or instrumentality (now usually *with*) OE. **6.** Of material, constituents, and the like ME. **7.** Of degree, extent, measure ME. **8.** Expressing object, aim, or purpose ME. **9.** In reference to; in the case, matter, or province of ME.

1. *In the dust, in hot water*, etc.; *in chains, in a leash*, etc.; *in the sunshine, in all weathers*, etc. **b.** In sight of God's high Throne MILT. **2.** *In a blaze, in debt, doubt, sickness*, etc.; *in cash, in liquor, in tears*. **3.** In search of plunder DICKENS. **b.** Drowned in crossing the river (*mod.*). **4.** *In confidence, in piteous terms*, etc. **b.** Did he..begin in rogue, and end in enthusiast? SOUTHEY. **d.** The newest..thing in pinnacles RUSKIN. **5.** A French Ship..ballasted in mahogany 1804. Progne, with her Bosom stain'd in Blood DRYDEN. I drinke to you in a Cup of Sack SHAKS. **6.** Half-length portraits, in crayons DICKENS. **7.** Differing but in degree MILT. **8.** *In affirmation, memory, recompense, scorn, witness*, etc.

III. Of time. **1.** Within the limits of a period or space of time OE. **2.** In the course of ME. **3.** Before or at the expiration of; within the space of ME. **4.** Formerly (and still occas.) used, where *at, on, during, for* are now in use, or where the prep. is omitted OE.

1. Between.. Twelve and Four in the Morning STEELE. The prince in his childhood THIRLWALL. The..houses you see in a railway excursion 1859. **2.** In a moment and in the twincklynge of an eye TINDALE 1 *Cor.* xv. 52. **3.** I rallied in a day or two 1843. **4.** The Duke in Counsell? In (= *at*) this time of the night? SHAKS. Looke you..that our Armies ioyn not in (= *on*) a hot day SHAKS. To Westminster Hall, where I have not been..in (= *for*) some months PEPYS. This engine..set out in (*in* now omitted) four hours after my landing SWIFT.

IV. Pregnant uses; sometimes due to ellipsis. **1.** With reflexive pronouns: *In himself, in itself*, etc.: in his or its own person, essence, or nature; absolutely ME. **2.** In spiritual or mystical union with ME. **3.** In the person or case of ME. **4.** Belonging to, as a quality, attribute, faculty, or capacity; hence, within the ability, capacity, thought, etc. of ME. **5.** In the hands of; legally vested in 1460. **6.** Partaking, sharing, associated, or actually engaged in 1728. **7.** Of representative character or capacity, as *in* NAME *of, in* RIGHT *of*; see the sbs. **8.** Ellipt. for 'in the character of' 1831.

1. Of things absolutely or in themselves MILL. **2.** Blessed are the dead which die in the Lord *Rev.* xiv. 13. **3.** Good against fits in women 1707. **4.** To prefer evil to good is not in human nature JOWETT. **5.** The minerals, therefore, are in the trustees 1884. **6.** Phr. *To be in it*, to be an actual competitor, partner, etc.; to be in the running, to count for something. **8.** I am to come out in Bianca FR. A. KEMBLE.

V. Of motion or direction. See also II. 8. **1.** = INTO OE. †**2.** Hence formerly used where *upon, on, towards, unto, to* are now in use -1557.

1. And broghte hire hoom with hym in his contree CHAUCER. He..in the Billows plung'd his hoary Head DRYDEN.

Phrases. **In so far**: in such measure or degree (as); to such extent (that). **In that**: in the fact that; in its being the case that; seeing that; as, because. See also INASMUCH, INSOMUCH, etc.

In (in), *adv.* (*a.*) [Com. Teut.; OE. *in(n.* See also INNE.]

I. Of motion or direction. [OE. *inn, in.*] **1.** Expressing motion from a point without to a place within certain limits (see also under COME, GO, PASS, PUT, etc.). **b.** Used after *may, must, shall*, etc., or absol. with imperative force, with omission of 'go', 'enter', etc. (cf. IN *v.* 5). Now chiefly *poet.* or *rhet.* OE. **2.** Expressing motion in the direction of some central point; hence, in proximity to some point specified or implied; into or in close quarters 1702. **3.** Into the bargain; in addition (to the legal amount); over and above, besides; as in to *get, give, throw in* 1634.

1. In comes my nephew DE FOE. b. The door is open! I'll in, and take my leave of her 1668. Phr. *Day in, day out*: continually. 2. About five yards in, it [the path] took a turn 1888. 3. And so you have the fight in gratis DICKENS.

II. Of position. **1.** Within a certain space; esp. inside a house ME. **b.** On the inside, within ME. **2.** In various special senses (see quots.) 1588.

1. Dame, art thow in? 1475. b. A sheepskin coat with the woolly side in 1873. 2. †a. = Engaged, involved; All my plots Turn back upon myself: but I am in, And must go on MASSINGER. b. = In office, in power; Who's in, who's out *Lear* v. iii. 15. c. = In possession of the field, etc.; having the turn or right to play; He scored 33..while he was in 1884. d. In legal possession of (an estate); In by descent CRUISE. e. Of fire or light: Burning, lighted; The law..which orders the Fire to be always kept in ADDISON. f. Of a train, coach, mail, etc.: Come in, arrived. g. = In the market, in season; Savoys are in 1891.

Phrases. **In for.** a. Engaged or involved *in* some business, etc. *for* a specified time; finally committed or destined to do or suffer something. b. *esp.* in phr. *in for it*: Committed to a course of action; also, certain to meet with punishment, etc. c. In the competition for something. d. *In for a penny, in for a pound*; see PENNY. **In with.** a. In agreement with; on friendly terms with. b. *Naut.* Close in to, near (the land). c. †*To come in with*, to overtake; also = *to fall in with* (see FALL *v.*).

Combs. 1. Pples. and vbl. sbs., nouns of action, and agent-nouns, from vbs. qualified by *in*, are formed by prefixing *in-*, when used as adjs. or sbs. Their number is practically unlimited. See IN- *pref.*[1]

2. With sbs. Usu. opp. to *out-*. (Cf. IN *a.*) Thus **i·n-brother**, a resident brother of a fraternity or guild; **i·n-burgess**, one resident in the burgh; **i·n-case**, a case of an in-patient; **i·n-patient**, one who remains in a hospital while under treatment; **i·n-pensioner**, one resident in a charitable institution.

3. With verbs: see IN- *pref.*[1]

4. With advs. and prepositions; as IN-BETWEEN.

‖**In** (in). The Latin prep. *in* (with the ablative case) 'in', (with accusative) 'into', occurs in many phrases, of which the chief are given below.

1. **in ca·pite**, in chief (see CHIEF *sb.*), holding directly from the crown 1558. 2. **in exte·nso**, at full length 1826. 3. **in extre·mis**, in the last agonies 1530. 4. **in fo·rma pau·peris**, in the form of a poor person (exempted from liability to pay the costs of an action; see PAUPER *sb.*); hence, in a humble or abject manner 1592. 5. **in infini·tum**, to infinity, without end 1564. 6. **in li·mine**, on the threshold, at the very outset 1804. 7. **in lo·co**, in the place of; esp. **in loco pare·ntis**, in the place or position of a parent 1710. 8. **in me·dias re·s**, into the midst of affairs, into the middle of a narrative 1786. 9. **in memo·riam**, to the memory of. Hence as *sb.* = A memorial poem or writing. 1850. 10. **in nu·bibus**, in the clouds; not yet settled; also, incapable of being carried out 1583. 11. **in pa·rtibus (infide·lium)**, in parts inhabited by unbelievers. In *R.C.Ch.* describing a titular bishop in an uncivilized or a heretical country 1687. 12. **in perpe·tuum**, to all time 1642. 13. **in pontifica·libus**, in pontificals, in the proper vestments of a pope, cardinal, etc. 1494. 14. **in pro·pria perso·na**, in his (her, etc.) own person 1654. 15. **in si·tu**, in its (original) place; in position 1817. 16. **in sta·tu quo· (ante, prius, or nunc)**, in the same state (as formerly or now) 1602. 17. **in terro·rem**, as a warning, in order to terrify others 1612. 18. **in to·to**, as a whole, absolutely, completely 1798. 19. **in tra·nsitu**, in passing, on the way. 20. **in va·cuo**, in a vacuum or empty space 1660.

In-, *pref.*[1], the prep. and adv. IN, in comb. with vbs., vbl. derivs., and other words. In OE. the adv. *inn, in*, was freely used in collocation with vbs. of motion or change of state. In the infinitive the adv. generally stood before the vb., and in derived vbl. sbs. and adjs. always so. In this position the adv. came at length to be written in comb. with the vb.; hence, many regular compounds with stress on *in-*, thus *incoming, income, incomer, indweller, inlet, insight*, etc. Other formations, in which the prefix usually has the sense 'in, within, internal', are *inborn, inside, inward*, etc.

In- *pref.*[2], repr. L. *in-* adv. and prep., used in comb. with vbs. or their derivatives, less commonly with other parts of speech, with the senses 'into, in, within; on, upon; towards, against', sometimes expressing onward motion or continuance, sometimes intensive, sometimes transitive, and in other cases with no appreciable force. For *Form-history*, see EN-, IL-[1], IM-[1], IR-[1].

In-, *pref.*[3], the L. *in-*, cogn. w. Gr. *α-, αν-*, Com. Teut. *un-*, prefixed to adjs. and their derivatives, rarely to other wds., to express negation or privation. In Eng. the modern tendency is to restrict *in-* to words obviously answering to Latin types, and to prefer the OE. negative *un-* in other cases, as *unavailing, uncertain, undevout*.

In-, *pref.*[4], of Teut. origin, prefixed to OE. and ME. adjs., with the sense 'inly', 'intimately', 'thoroughly', and hence 'exceedingly', 'very'.

-in, *suffix*[1]. *Chem.* A modification of the chemical suffix -INE[5], used for the names of neutral substances, such as glycerides, glucosides, bitter principles, colouring matters, which are thus distinguished from names of alkaloids and basic substances in -INE. Some of these were formerly spelt with *-ine*, esp. *dextrine, gelatine, margarine*, and are still so spelt in non-scientific use.

-in, *suffix*[2], obs. var. of -INE[1] in adjs., as *feminin, genuin*, etc.; also occas. var. of -INE[4]:—L. *-ina*, as in *ruin*.

-ina, *suffix*[1], L. fem. suffix found in *regina* queen, extended in It. or Sp., and thence in Eng. use, to form feminine titles, as *czarina*, and female Christian names, as *Alexandrina*, etc. It occurs also in *concertina, seraphina*, etc., names of musical instruments.

-ina, *suffix*[2], in wds. which are the neut. pl. of L. adjs. in *-inus*, and in mod.L. wds. formed after them, used (in agreement with *animalia*, understood) to form names of groups of animals related to some typical genus, as *Bombycina* (genus *Bombyx*), etc.

Inability (inăbi·lĭti). ME. [a. OF. *inhabilite* or ad. med.L. *inhabilitas*: see IN-[3] and ABILITY.] The condition of being unable; want of ability, physical, mental, or moral; lack of power, capacity, or means. †b. *spec.* Bodily infirmity –1834.

My distressing i. to sleep at night DICKENS.

Inable, -ment, obs. ff. ENABLE, -MENT.

Ina·bstinence. 1667. [IN-[3].] Want of abstinence; failure to abstain. MILT. *P. L.* XI. 476.

†**Inabstra·cted**, *ppl. a. rare.* 16.. [IN-[3].] Not abstracted.

†**Inabu·sively**, *adv.* 1677. [IN-[3].] Not abusively, properly. LD. NORTH.

Inaccessible (inækse·sĭb'l), *a.* †Also *erron.* -able. 1555. [a. F., ad. late L. *inaccessibilis*; see IN-[3].] 1. That cannot be reached, entered, or got to; that cannot be scaled or penetrated. 2. *fig.* Unapproachable 1583. †3. (tr. Gr. ἄαπτος.) 'Not to be touched, resistless, invincible'. CHAPMAN.

1. Its i. acropolis defied them GROTE. 2. This savage hero was not i. to pity GIBBON. Hence **I:naccessibi·lity**, quality or condition of being i.; unapproachableness. **Inacce·ssibleness. Inacce·ssibly** *adv.*

Inacco·rdant, *a.* 1822. [IN-[3].] Not accordant; inharmonious. So **Inacco·rdance, -ancy**, i. quality. **Inacco·rdantly** *adv.*

Inaccuracy (inæ·kiŭrăsi). 1757. [f. next; see -ACY, and cf. *accuracy*.] The quality or condition of being inaccurate; want of accuracy; also with *an* and *pl.*

An appearance of i. in the use of terms 1772. Historical inaccuracies 1883.

Inaccurate (inæ·kiŭrĕt), *a.* 1738. [IN-[3].] Not accurate; inexact, incorrect, erroneous.

I. modes of expression JOWETT. **Ina·ccurate-ly** *adv.* 1669, **-ness.**

Inacquai·ntance. 1607. [IN-[3].] The being unacquainted; want of acquaintance.

Inacquie·scent, *a.* [IN-[3].] Not acquiescent. SCOTT. So †**Inacquie·scency** 1647.

†**Inact** (inæ·kt), *v.*[1] 1647. [f. IN-[2] + ACT *v.*] *trans.* To actuate –1662.

Inact, *v.*[2], obs. f. ENACT.

Inaction (inæ·kʃən). 1707. [f. IN-[3] + ACTION *sb.*] Absence of action or activity; inertness, supineness.

Inactive (inæ·ktiv), *a.* 1725. [IN-[3].] Not active; not disposed to act; inert, indolent, sluggish; passive, quiescent.

The seeming Charms of an idle and i. life POPE. A converter of i. or free, into active or combined oxygen ODLING. An i. market 1883. Hence **Ina·ctively** *adv.* So **Ina·ctiveness** 1678.

Inactivity (inækti·vĭti). 1646. [IN-[3].] The quality or state of being inactive; want of activity; inertness, sluggishness; passiveness, quiescence.

Poor Fenton..died..of Indolence and I. POPE. The Government should be taught that the highest wisdom of a state is a wise and *masterly i.* CALHOUN.

†**Inactuate** (inæ·ktiu,eɪt), *v.* 1651. [IN-[2].] *trans.* To make active, put in action –1662. Hence **Inactua·tion.**

Inadaptabi·lity. 1840. [IN-[3].] Want of adaptability.

So **Inada·ptable** *a.*, **Inadapta·tion, Inada·ptive** *a.*

Inadequate (inæ·dĭkwĕt), *a.* 1675. [IN-[3].] Not adequate; not equal to requirement; insufficient.

I. conceptions BOYLE, terms 1792, remuneration 1880. Resources..i. to meet the expenses of war GREEN. Hence **Ina·dequacy**, insufficiency. **Ina·dequate-ly** *adv.*, **-ness. Inadequa·tion** *arch.* 1630.

Inadhe·rent, *a.* 1855. [IN-[3].] Not adherent; free. So **Inadhe·sion**, non-adhesion 1796. **Inadhe·sive** *a.* not adhesive 1811.

Inadmissible (inădmi·sĭb'l), *a.* 1776. [IN-[3].] Not admissible; not to be admitted, entertained, or allowed.

Tea, coffee, and alcohol are I. ALLBUTT. Hence **Inadmissibi·lity**, the fact or quality of being i.

†**Inadu·lterate**, *a.* [IN-[3].] Unadulterated. HERRICK.

Inadventurous (inădve·ntiŭrəs), *a.* 1853. [IN-[3].] Not adventurous; unenterprising.

Inadvertence (inădvə̄·ɹtĕns). 1568. [ad. Schol. L. *inadvertentia*; see next and -ENCE.] The fact or habit of being inadvertent; failure to observe or pay attention; inattention; also = next. b. with *an* and *pl.* An act or fault of inattention; an oversight 1725.

The said letter..was, through i., laid before the board BURKE. Marriage is one of those inadvertences which can hardly go for nothing even in the easiest life 1876.

Inadvertency (inădvə̄·ɹtĕnsi). 1592. [ad. Schol. L. *inadvertentia*; see IN-[3] and ADVERTENCY.] The quality or character of being inadvertent; also = prec.

Inadvertent (inădvə̄·ɹtĕnt), *a.* 1653. [IN-[3].] 1. Not properly attentive; inobservant, negligent; heedless. 2. Of actions, etc.: Characterized by want of attention; hence, unintentional 1724.

2. An i. step may crush the snail, That crawls at evening in the public path COWPER. Hence **Inadve·rtently** *adv.*

†**Inadve·rtisement.** [f. IN-[3] + ADVERTISEMENT 1.] Want of attention; inadvertence. SIR T. BROWNE.

Inadvisable (inădvəi·zăb'l), *a. rare.* 1870. [IN-[3].] Unadvisable. Hence **Inadvisabi·lity**, unadvisableness 1864.

Inadvisedly (inădvəi·zĕdli), *adv. rare.* 1894. [IN-[3].] Unadvisedly. So **Inadvi·sedness** 1652.

-inæ, *suffix*, in wds. which are the fem. pl. of L. adjs. in *-inus*, used (in agreement with *bestiæ*, understood) to form names of subfamilies of animals, as *Caninæ* (L. *caninus* canine), *Felinæ* (L. *felinus* feline).

Inæsthetic (inĭsþe·tik), *a.* 1846. [IN-[3].] Not æsthetic; void of taste.

†**Ina·ffable**, *a.* 1656. [IN-[3].] Not affable. So †**Inaffabi·lity** 1611.

†**Inaffe·cted**, *ppl. a. rare.* 1617. [IN-[3].] = UNAFFECTED. Hence †**Inaffe·cted-ly** *adv.*, †**-ness.**

†**Inai·dible**, *a.* [IN-[3].] That cannot be assisted; helpless. *All's Well* II. i. 122.

Inalienable (inē·liĕnăb'l), *a.* 1645. [IN-[3].] Not alienable; that cannot be transferred from its present ownership or relation.

The i. character of alimony 1884. Hence **Ina:lienabi·lity**, i. quality. **Ina·lienably** *adv.*

Inalime·ntal, *a. rare.* 1626. [IN-[3].] Not affording aliment or nourishment.

Inalterable (inǭ·ltərăb'l), *a.* 1533. [IN-³.] Not alterable; unchangeable, immutable; unalterable. Hence **Inalterabi·lity**, unchangeableness. **Ina·lterably** *adv.*

Inamissible (inămi·sĭb'l), *a.* Now *rare.* 1649. [IN-³.] Not liable to be lost. Hence **Inamissibi·lity. Inami·ssibleness.**

Inamorata (inæmorā·tă). Also **en-**. 1651. [a. It. *in(n)amorata*, fem. pa. pple. of *in(n)amorare*; see INAMORATO.] A female lover, mistress, sweetheart.

The faire I. who from farre Had spy'd the Ship which her hearts treasure bare SHERBURNE.

Ina·morate, *a.* and *sb.* 1602. [ad. It. *in(n)amorato*; see below.] **a.** *adj.* Enamoured, in love. †**b.** *sb.* One in love, a lover -1612. Hence †**Ina·morately** *adv.* lovingly 1599.

Inamorato (inæmorā·to). Also **en-**. 1592. [a. It. *in(n)amorato* lover, masc. pa. pple. of *in(n)amorare* 'to enamour, to fall in loue' (Florio), f. *in-* (IN-²) + *amore*.] A lover.

Inamour, -ed, obs. ff. ENAMOUR, -ED.

Inamo·vable, *a. rare.* 1851. [IN-³.] Not removable. Hence **Inamovabi·lity,** the quality of being i. 1849.

In and in, in-and-in. 1630. [IN *adv.*]

A. *adv.* Further and further in; continually inwards. Also *attrib.* (in quasi-*adj.* use).

Phr. *To breed in and in*, to breed always within a limited stock 1765. So *to marry in and in*.

B. *sb.* †**1.** The name given to a throw made with four dice, when these fell all alike or as two doublets -1668. †**b.** A gambling game played with four dice; the player who threw *in and in* (see above) took all the stake -1674. **2.** A space which opens up and ever discloses something further in 1890.

In and out, in-and-out, *adv.* ME. [Cf. also *ins and outs*, IN *sb.* 2.] **1.** Alternately in and out; now in, now out. †**2.** Inside out -1591. **3.** Both in and out 1895. **4.** *attrib.* (quasi-*adj.*) in various senses 1640.

1. Her feet beneath her petticoat Like little mice stole in and out SUCKLING. He was much in and out 1855. **3.** To know a man in and out 1895. **4.** *In-and-out cottage*, a cottage of irregular plan. *In-and-out running*, alternate winning and losing of races.

Inane (inē¹·n). 1662. [ad. L. *inanis*.]

A. *adj.* **1.** Empty, void. **2.** Of persons, etc.: Destitute of sense; silly; empty-headed.

1. Vast i. infinities KINGSLEY. **2.** Some i. and vacant smile SHELLEY.

B. *sb.* **1.** That which is inane; void or empty space; vacuity; the 'formless void' 1677. **2.** An empty-headed person. POPE.

1. Atoms..dispers'd and dancing in the great I. 1700. Hence **Ina·nely** *adv.* emptily, senselessly.

†**Ina·ngular,** *a.* 1646. [IN-³.] Not angular.

Inanimate (inæ·nimĕt), *a.* (*sb.*) 1563. [ad. late L. *inanimatus* lifeless; see IN-³ and ANIMATE.] **1.** Not animated; lifeless; *spec.* not endowed with animal life, as in *inanimate nature*, i.e. all outside the animal world. **2.** Without the activity of life (*lit.* and *fig.*); spiritless, dull 1704. **3.** *sb.* An inanimate thing 1652.

1. And Ardennes waves above them her green leaves, Dewy with nature's tear-drops, as they pass, Grieving, if aught i. e'er grieves, Over the unreturning brave BYRON. **2.** The stock markets were quite i. 1893. So †**Ina·nimated** *a.* 1646-1826. Hence **Ina·nimate·ly** *adv.*, **-ness.**

†**Ina·nimate,** *v.* 1600. [f. ppl. stem of late L. *inanimare*; see IN-² and ANIMATE *v.*] *trans.* To put life into (*lit.* and *fig.*) -1689. Hence †**Inanima·tion¹**, infusion of life, spirit, or vitality 1614-1647.

Inanima·tion². 1784. [IN-³.] Inanimate condition; absence of life or liveliness.

Inanition (inăni·ʃən). ME. [ad. L. *inanitionem*, f. *inanire* to make empty, f. *inanis* empty.] The action or process of emptying; the condition of being empty, or (*spec.*) exhausted from want of nourishment. Also *fig.*

Hunger and thirst are inanitions of the body JOWETT. *fig.* Anarchy..usually..perishes of i. FROUDE.

Inanity (inæ·nĭti). 1501. [ad. L. *inanitas*, f. *inanis* INANE.] **1.** The quality or condition of being empty or void; emptiness 1607. **2.** *fig.* **a.** Want of substance or solidity; unsatisfactoriness; vanity; hollowness 1603. **b.** Lack of ideas or sense; frivolity, senselessness, silliness 1753. **c.** Vacuity of existence; idleness, inaction 1782. **3.** with *an* and *pl.* An inane remark or practice 1661.

1. What shall fill..the I. and Vacuity of the heart of man? 1631. **2. b.** To treat a topic with i. 1803. **3.** The vanities and inanities of fashion HOLLAND.

Ina·pathy. *rare.* 1846. [IN-³.] The opposite of apathy.

†**Inapo·state,** *a.* [IN-³.] Not apostate; loyal. HERRICK.

†**Inappa·rent,** *a.* 1626. [IN-³.] Not apparent; invisible; latent -1753.

†**Inappea·lable,** *a.* 1651. [IN-³.] = INAPPELLABLE.

Inappea·sable, *a.* 1840. [IN-³.] Not to be appeased.

Inappellable (inăpe·lăb'l), *a.* 1825. [f. IN-³ + L. *appellare* + -BLE.] From which there is no appeal. Hence **Inappellabi·lity.**

Inappetent (inæ·pĭtĕnt), *a.* 1796. [IN-³.] Not appetent; without desire or longing. So **Ina·ppetence** 1691, **-ency** 1611, lack of appetence.

Inapplicable (inæ·plikăb'l), *a.* 1656. [IN-³.] Not applicable; incapable of being applied (*to* some case); unsuitable (*to* the purpose).

Döppler's method was practically i. LUBBOCK. Hence **Ina·pplicabi·lity,** the quality of being i. **Ina·pplicably** *adv.*

Inapplication (inæplikē¹·ʃən). 1721. [IN-³.] **1.** Want of application, e.g. to one's duties. **2.** Inapplicability 1784.

Inapposite (inæ·pŏzit), *a.* 1661. [IN-³.] Not apposite, not to the point, out of place; impertinent. Hence **Ina·ppositely** *adv.*

Inappreciable (inăprī·ʃiăb'l), *a.* Also **-tiable.** 1787. [IN-³.] Not appreciable; †priceless -1868; too inconsiderable to be estimated; imperceptible 1802.

A barrier of i. value SCOTT. An inappretiable quantity 1802. Hence **Inappre·ciably** *adv.*

Inappreciation (inăprīʃi,ē¹·ʃən). 1864. [IN-³.] Want of appreciation; failure to estimate duly.

Inappreciative (inăprī·ʃiĕtiv), *a.* 1868. [IN-³.] Wanting in appreciation. Hence **Inappre·ciative·ly** *adv.*, **-ness.**

Inapprehensible (inæprĭhe·nsib'l), *a.* 1641. [IN-³.] Not apprehensible; that cannot be grasped by the senses or intellect.

Inapprehension (inæprĭhe·nʃən). 1744. [IN-³.] Want of apprehension.

Inapprehe·nsive, *a.* 1651. [IN-³.] Not apprehensive; without apprehension; unconcerned. Hence **Inapprehe·nsiveness.**

Inapproachable (inăprōᵘ·tʃăb'l), *a.* 1828. [IN-³.] That cannot be approached; inaccessible, unapproachable. Hence **Inapproa·chably** *adv.*

Inappropriate (inăprōᵘ·priĕt), *a.* 1804. [IN-³.] Not appropriate; not suitable to the case; unfitting, improper. Hence **Inappro·priate·ly** *adv.*, **-ness.**

Inapt (inæ·pt), *a.* 1744. [IN-³. Cf. INEPT.] **1.** Unsuitable, inappropriate, inapposite. **2.** Not apt; unskilful, awkward 1860. Hence **Ina·pt·ly** *adv.*, **-ness.**

Inaptitude (inæ·ptitiūd). 1620. [IN-³.] Want of aptitude.

†**Ina·quate,** *ppl. a.* 1550. [ad. L. *inaquatus*, *inaquare* to turn into water; see IN-².] Converted into water. Hence †**Inaqua·tion,** conversion into water.

Inarable (inæ·răb'l), *a.* 1656. [IN-³.] Not arable.

Inarch (inā·ɹtʃ), *v.*¹ 1629. [f. IN-² + ARCH *v.*] *trans.* To graft by connecting a growing branch without separating it from its parent stock; to graft by approach; see APPROACH *sb.* 7. Hence **Ina·rching** *vbl. sb.* grafting by approach; *transf.* = ANAPLASTY (*rare*).

Ina·rch, *v.*² *rare.* 1882. [f. IN-¹ + ARCH *v.*] To arch in, encompass like an arch.

†**Ina·rk,** *v. rare.* 1595. [f. IN-¹ or ² + ARK *sb.*] *trans.* To put or enclose in an ark -1646.

Inarm (inā·ɹm), *v.* Also **en-**. 1612. [f. as prec. + ARM *sb.*¹; cf. F. *embrasser.*] *trans.* To clasp within or as with the arms; to embrace; to throw the arms round.

Inarticulate (inaɹti·kiŭlĕt), *a.* 1603. [ad. L. *inarticulatus*; see IN-³ and ARTICULATE.] Not articulate; the opposite of ARTICULATE. **1.** Not jointed or hinged; esp. in *Zool.* and *Bot.* Not composed of segments united by joints 1607. **b.** Of or belonging to the division *Inarticulata* of Brachiopods, now called *Ecardines* (*mod.*). **2.** Of sound or voice: Not of the nature of articulate speech; not uttered with intelligible modulations. Also, indistinctly pronounced. 1603. **b.** Not able to use articulate speech; dumb 1754. **c.** *transf.* Having no distinct meaning 1855.

2. Solemn Musick, which is I. Poesie DRYDEN. **b.** The poor Earl, who is i. with the palsy H. WALPOLE. **c.** I. gibberish 1855. So **Inarti·culated** *ppl. a.* Hence **Inarti·culate·ly** *adv.*, **-ness.**

†**Inarticula·tion¹.** 1578. [IN-².] = ENARTHROSIS -1634.

Inarticula·tion². *rare.* 1765. [IN-³.] Absence of distinct articulation; inarticulate utterance.

Inartificial (inaɹtifi·ʃăl), *a.* 1588. [ad. L. *inartificialis* (Quintilian); see IN-³ and ARTIFICIAL (as tr. Gr. ἄτεχνος).] Not artificial. **1.** Not produced by art or constructive skill; natural. Now *rare.* 1656. **2.** Rude, clumsy; inartistic 1613. †**3.** Of an argument: Not according to the art of Logic, but derived from testimony or authority -1725. **4.** Artless, unaffected, natural 1664. **5.** Plain, simple, straightforward 1823.

2. Unskilfull and i. buildings 1671. An i. classification HERSCHEL. **3.** An i. Argument is the Testimony of another WATTS. Hence **Inartificia·lity. Inartifi·cially** *adv.*, **-ness.**

Inartistic, -al (inaɹti·stik, -ăl), *a.* 1849. [IN-³.] Not in accordance with the principles of art; also, having no appreciation for art. **Inarti·stically** *adv.*

Inasmuch (inĕzmʌ·tʃ), *adv.* ME. [orig. *in as much*, occas. later *in asmuch*, now written as one wd.]

I. In phr. *Inasmuch as.* **1.** In so far as, to such a degree as, according as. **2.** In that; seeing that; considering that; since, because.

1. In as much as ye haue done it vnto one of the least of these my brethren, ye haue done it vnto me *Matt.* xxv. 40. **2.** I. as 'he was delivered for our sins' WESLEY.

†**II.** Without *as*: In an equal degree, likewise. SWIFT.

Inattention (inăte·nʃən). 1710. [IN-³.] Want of attention; failure to attend; want of observant care or notice; heedlessness, negligence. **b.** Want of courteous personal attention 1792.

The universal Indolence and I. among us 1710.

Inattentive (inăte·ntiv), *a.* 1741. [IN-³.] Not attentive; not applying the mind steadily; not observant; negligent.

An unsteady and i. habit of mind WATTS. Hence **Inatte·ntive·ly** *adv.*, **-ness.**

Inaudible (inǭ·dib'l), *a.* 1601. [ad. L. *inaudibilis*; see IN-³ and AUDIBLE.] Not audible; not capable of being heard.

Th' i., and noiseless foot of time SHAKS. Hence **Inaudibi·lity,** the quality or condition of being i. **Inau·dibly** *adv.*

Inaugur (inǭ·gɘɹ), *v.* Now *rare.* 1555. Also **-ure.** [a. F. *inaugurer*, or ad. L. *inaugurare* to INAUGURATE.] †**1.** *trans.* = INAUGURATE *v.* 1. -1706. **2.** = INAUGURATE *v.* 5. 1890.

Inaugural (inǭ·giŭrăl), *a.* (*sb.*) 1689. [a. F., f. *inaugurer*, after L. *auguralis*.] **1.** Of or pertaining to inauguration; forming part of the formal commencement of any course or career. **2.** *sb.* An inaugural speech or address. *U.S.* 1860.

1. Mr. Thwaites Greek Professor made his I. Speech 1708.

†**Inau·gurate,** *a.* 1600. [ad. L. *inauguratus*; see next.] Inaugurated, formally installed into office -1681.

Inaugurate (inǭ·giŭrē¹t), *v.* 1606. [f. L. *inaugurat-*, *inaugurare* to take auguries from the flight of birds, to install after taking auguries, f. *in-* (IN-²) + *augurare* to take auguries; see AUGUR *sb.* and *v.*] **1.** *trans.* To admit or induct to an office or dignity by a formal ceremony; to consecrate, install, invest. †**2.** To invest with a sacred character, etc. F. JUNIUS. **3.** To make auspicious; to sanctify, consecrate (*rare*) 1639. 4. 'To begin with good omens' (J.); to begin with some formal ceremony or notable act; to enter upon; to usher in; to initiate. (Sometimes merely grandiose for 'begin'.) 1755. 5. To introduce into public use by a formal opening ceremony 1852.

1. To i. a King DRAYTON, a bishop 1637, a Caliph 1708. 4. To i. the revolution 1851, a new era 1865, the daily work of a school GRANT. 5. To i. a statue 1852. Hence **Inau·gurator**, one who inaugurates; an initiator. **Inau·guratory** *a.* = INAUGURAL.

Inauguration (inǫgiŭrēⁱ·ʃən). 1569. [ad. L. *inaugurationem*; see prec.] The action of inaugurating. 1. Formal induction, institution, or ushering in with auspicious ceremonies. 2. The formal commencement or introduction of a course of action, an important era or period of time, etc. 1856. 3. *attrib.* = INAUGURAL 1686.

1. The King's Anniversary I. 1627. 2. The i. of privateering YEATS. 3. An i.-speech 1772.

Inaunter, var. of ENAUNTER, in case (that).

Inaurate (inǭ·rĕt), *a. rare.* 1826. [ad. L. *inauratus.*] a. Gilded, covered with gold. b. *Entom.* Applied to parts having a metallic lustre.

†**Inau·rate**, *v. rare.* 1623. [f. ppl. stem of L. *inaurare.*] *trans.* To gild. Hence †**Inaura·tion**, gilding.

†**Inau·spicate**, *a.* 1632. [ad. L. *inauspicatus*; see IN-³ and AUSPICATE.] Ill-omened, inauspicious -1668.

Inauspicious (inǭspi·ʃəs), *a.* 1592. [IN-³.] Not auspicious; ill-omened, unlucky, unfortunate.

The yoke of i. starres SHAKS. A tardy and i. season KANE. Hence **Inauspi·cious-ly** *adv.*, **-ness.**

Inauthe·ntic, *a. rare.* 1860. [IN-³.] Not authentic. Hence **Inauthenti·city.**

Inautho·ritative, *a.* 1659. [IN-³.] Not authoritative; having no authority.

In banco: see BANCO *sb.*

Inbardge, var. of EMBARGE *v.*

I·n-bea·ming, *vbl. sb.* 1662. [f. IN *adv.* + BEAMING *vbl. sb.*] A beaming or shining in.

In-being, inbeing (i·nbī·iŋ). 1587. [f. IN *adv.* + BEING *vbl. sb.*] 1. Inherence, immanence 1617. 2. Inward or essential nature 1661. †3. An indwelling being: applied to the 'persons' of the Trinity -1643.

3. In the same most single essence are three Persons or In-beings GOLDING.

I·nbe·nt, *ppl. a.* 1586. [f. IN *adv.* + BENT *ppl. a.*] Bent or curved inwards; turned or directed inwards.

In-betwee·n. 1815. [Phr. *in between*, used subst. or attrib.] a. quasi-*sb.* An interval; also, a person who intervenes. b. quasi-*adj.* Placed between.

†**Inblow·**, *v.* [OE. *inblāwan*, f. IN-¹ + BLOW *v.*, tr. L. *inflare, inspirare.*] *trans.* To blow or breathe into; to inflate; to inspire -1678. Hence †**Inblown** *ppl. a.*

Inboard (i·nbōᵊɹd). 1850. [Prop. a phr., IN *prep.* + BOARD *sb.* V.]

Naut. A. *adv.* Within the sides of a ship or vessel 1853.

Luckily, those who were upset managed to fall i. 1863.

B. *prep.* Inside, within (a vessel) 1864.

C. *adj.* Situated within or towards the centre of the vessel 1850.

Inbond (i·nbǫnd), *a.* 1842. [f. IN-¹ + BOND *sb.*¹] *Building.* Said of a brick or stone laid with its length across a wall (also called a *header*); also of a wall built of these. Opp. to *outbond*.

Inborn (i·nbǭ·ɹn, i·nbǫɹn), *ppl. a.* OE. [f. IN *adv.* + BORN *ppl. a.*] †1. Born in a place; aboriginal -1875. 2. Of a quality, etc.: Born in a person; innate 1513. b. *transf.* Of a person: That was born such (*rare*) 1818.

2. Some i. sense Of courtesy PALGRAVE. b. The Arab is..an i. gentleman BOSW. SMITH.

†**Inbow·**, *v.* ME. [f. IN-¹ + BOW *v.*¹] 1. *trans.* To bend into a curved or arched form; to incurve, arch -1625. 2. To bow or bend (towards); to incline. WYCLIF.

†**I·nbowed, in-bowed**, *a.* 1586. [f. IN *adv.* + *bowed.*] Bowed or bent inwards or concavely; as, an *inbowed bone* -1658.

Inbreak (i·nbrēⁱk). *rare.* 1837. [f. IN *adv.* + BREAK *sb.*¹, after *outbreak.*] A breaking in, invasion, forcible incursion. So **I·nbrea·king** *vbl. sb.* 1652.

Inbreathe (inbrī·ð), *v.* ME. [f. IN-¹ + BREATHE *v.*, after L. *inspirare.*] 1. *trans.* To breathe (something) in (*lit.* and *fig.*). 2. To inspire (a person) 1851. Hence **Inbrea·ther.**

Inbred (i·nbre·d, i·nbred), *ppl. a.* Also †**im-.** 1592. [f. IN *adv.* + BRED.] 1. Bred within; innate. †2. Bred in a place, native 1638. 3. (Prop. *in-bred.*) Bred in-and-in. STEVENSON.

1. Your i. Curiosity, and love of Experimental Learning BOYLE.

Inbreed (inbrī·d), *v.* Also **im-.** 1599. [f. IN-¹ + BREED *v.*] 1. *trans.* To engender or produce within. †2. To breed or bring up *in* a course of action. HOLLAND.

1. To i. and cherish in a great people the seeds of vertu MILT.

In-breeding (i·nbrī:diŋ), *vbl. sb.* 1842. [f. IN *adv.* + BREEDING *vbl. sb.*] Breeding in-and-in.

In-breeding..generally results mischievously 1881.

Inbri·ng, i·n-bri·ng, *v.* Now *rare* or *Obs.* Chiefly *Sc.* [OE., f. IN-¹ + BRING *v.*] *trans.* To bring in; to introduce; *esp.* in *Sc. Law*, to bring in by legal authority. So **I·nbri·nging** *vbl. sb.*

Inburning (i·nbɒ̄:miŋ), *ppl. a.* [f. IN *adv.* + BURNING *ppl. a.*] Burning internally. SPENSER.

Inburst (i·nbɒɹst), *sb. rare.* 1837. [f. IN *adv.* + BURST *sb.*; cf. *outburst.*] A bursting in, irruption. So **Inbu·rst** *v.* (*rare*), to burst in 1540.

‖**Inca** (i·ŋkă). 1594. [Peruvian, 'lord, king, emperor', also, 'man of the blood royal'.] The title of the emperor or king of Peru before its conquest by the Spaniards; also, one of the royal race of Peru.

attrib. **I. Cockatoo**, an adaptation of Ger. *Inka Kakadu*, name of the Pink or Leadbetter's Cockatoo of Australia. **I. tern**, a species of tern (*Nænia inca*), the Bearded Tern.

Inca·ge, etc., obs. var. of ENCAGE, etc.

Incalculable (inkæ·lkiŭlăb'l), *a.* 1795. [IN-³.] 1. That cannot be calculated, computed, or forecast. 2. Of a person, etc.: That cannot be reckoned upon 1876.

1. I. mischiefs BURKE. An i. course BURKE. 2. An i. temper 1879. Hence **Inca:lculabi·lity**, i. quality. **Inca·lculableness. Inca·lculably** *adv.*

†**Inca·lendared**, *pa. pple.* 1622. [f. IN-² + CALENDAR *v.* or *sb.* + -ED¹.] Canonized.

Incalescent (inkăle·sĕnt), *a.* Now *rare.* 1680. [ad. L. *incalescentem*, *incalescere*, f. *in-* (IN-²) + *calescere* to grow warm.] Becoming hot or warm; increasing in warmth (*lit.* and *fig.*). Hence **Incale·scence** 1646, †**Incale·scency** 1658, the action or process of becoming i.; rise of temperature; heating.

In-calf (in,kā·f), *a.* 1556. [phr. *in calf* used *attrib.*] Of a cow: That is in calf. So **Inca·lver**, a cow in calf.

†**Incameration** (inkæmĕrēⁱ·ʃən). 1670. [a. F., f. *in-* (IN-²) + It. *camera* chamber, the papal treasury; see CAMERA.] Annexation to the papal domain -1741.

Incamp, -ment: see ENCAMP, -MENT.

Incan (i·ŋkăn), *a.* 1885. [f. INCA + -AN.] Pertaining to the Incas of Peru.

Incandesce (inkænde·s), *v.* 1874. [ad. L. *incandescere*, f. *in-* (IN-²) + *candescere* to become white.] 1. *intr.* To be or become incandescent; to glow with heat. Chiefly in pres. pple. 2. *trans.* To render incandescent 1883.

Incandescent (inkænde·sĕnt), *a.* 1794. [ad. L. *incandescentem*; see prec.] 1. Luminous or glowing with heat. b. *gen.* Glowing, brilliantly luminous 1867. c. *techn.* Applied to that form of electric light produced by the incandescence of a filament or strip of carbon; the *glow-lamp* as dist. from the *arc light*. Hence *transf.* of gas and other lamps. 1881. 2. *fig.* Ardent, fiery; 'flaming up' 1859.

1. The hypothesis of an originally i. globe PAGE. b. The i. snow 1872. 2. The 'incandescent passions' of the Anti-Semites 1894. Hence **Incande·scence**, the state of being i. (*lit.* and *fig.*). **Incande·scency**, the quality or state of being i.

Incanescent (inkăne·sĕnt), *a. rare.* 1866. [f. L. *incanescentem*, *incanescere* to become white.] = CANESCENT.

Incanous (inkēⁱ·nəs), *a.* 1864. [f. L. *incanus* hoary + -OUS.] *Bot.* Hoary with white pubescence.

†**Inca·nt**, *v.* 1546. [ad. L. *incantare.*] a. *intr.* To use incantation or enchantment. b. *trans.* To enchant, charm. -1665.

Incantation (inkæntēⁱ·ʃən). ME. [a. F., ad. L. *incantationem*, f. *incantare*; see prec.] The use of a formula of words spoken or chanted to produce a magical effect; the utterance of a spell or charm; more widely, The use of magical ceremonies or arts; sorcery, enchantment. b. with *pl.* An instance of this; *concr.* a spell, charm ME.

Like the demons of old summoned by i. BURTON. So **I·ncanta·tor** (*rare*), one who uses i. **Inca·ntatory** *a.* (*rare*), using, or of the nature of, i.

Incanton (inkæ·ntǫn), *v.* 1705. [f. IN-² + CANTON *sb.*¹] *trans.* To make into or admit as a canton.

Incapable (inkēⁱ·păb'l), *a.* (*sb.*) 1591. [ad. med.L. *incapabilis*; see IN-³ and CAPABLE.]

I. Not capable; the opposite of capable. †1. Unable to take in, contain, hold, or keep -1841. †b. Unable to put up with; impatient *of* -1712. 2. Not open to or susceptible of; insensible to. Const. *of.* *Obs.* or *arch.* 1601. 3. Of such a nature, or in such a condition, as not to allow or admit of; not susceptible of. Const. *of*, or (formerly) with *inf.* 1712. 4. Not having the capacity, power, or fitness for; unable. Const. *of*, or (formerly) with *inf.* 1610. b. In a good sense: Not having the depravity, moral weakness, etc. for 1755. 5. *absol.* Incompetent; without ordinary capacity 1594. 6. Not (legally) qualified or entitled; disqualified. Const. *of*, or (formerly) with *inf.* 1651.

1. I. of more SHAKS. *Sonn.* cxiii. 2. As one i. of her owne distresse *Haml.* IV. vii. 179. 3. Not i. to be beloved 1712. 4. Growne incapeable Of reasonable affayres SHAKS. I. of much exertion 1842. b. My foes..have laid things to my charge whereof I am i., even in thought SCOTT. 5. Phr. *Drunk and i.*, i.e. so drunk as to be incapable of taking care of himself. 6. I. of holding any public employment MACAULAY.

†II. In passive sense: That cannot be received or apprehended (*rare*). Const. *to.* -1625.

B. *sb.* A thoroughly incompetent person 1809.

Hence **Incapabi·lity**, the quality or condition of being i. **Inca·pableness. Inca·pably** *adv.*

Incapacious (inkăpēⁱ·ʃəs), *a.* 1617. [f. L. *incapax*, *incapaci-* + -OUS.] 1. Not of sufficient size to take in something. b. Not able to contain much; narrow, limited. (*lit.* and *fig.*) 1635. 2. Not having mental capacity for something. Const. *of*, or (formerly) with *inf.* Also *absol.* 1617.

2. Buzzing them into popular eares and capacities, i. of them BP. MOUNTAGU.

Incapacitate (inkăpæ·siteⁱt), *v.* 1657. [f. INCAPACITY + -ATE³.] 1. *trans.* To deprive of capacity; to disqualify, unfit 1661. 2. To disqualify in law.

1. My lameness does not i. me..for the work of the day school 1882. 2. You have incapacitated public Preachers from sitting in Parliament CROMWELL. Hence **Incapacita·tion**, the action of incapacitating or fact of being incapacitated; disqualification.

Incapacity (inkăpæ·sĭti). 1611. [ad. med. L. *incapacitas*, F. *incapacité*; see IN-³ and CAPACITY.] 1. Want of capacity; inability, powerlessness; incompetence; (with *an* and *pl.*) an instance of this. b. Inability to take, receive, or deal with in some way. Const. *of*, *for.* 1655. 2. Legal disqualification, disability; an instance of this 1648.

1. His i. and ignorance were equal to his presumption GIBBON. 2. Persons..lying..under an I. *c* 1680.

Incapsulate (inkæ·psiŭleⁱt), *v.* Also **en-.** 1874. [f. IN-² + L. *capsula* + -ATE³.] *trans.* To enclose in a capsule. Hence **Inca·psulating** *ppl. a.*; applied *fig.* to certain languages in which modifying elements are inserted in the body of a word 1868. Hence **Incapsula·tion**, the action or process of incapsulating 1860.

Incarcerate (inkā·ɹsĕrĕt), *ppl. a. arch. a* 1500. [ad. med.L. *incarceratus*, *incarcerare*, f. *in-* (IN-²) + *carcer* prison.] Incarcerated; confined, shut in.

Incarcerate (inkā·ɹsĕreⁱt), *v.* 1560. [f. L. *incarcerat-*, *incarcerare*; see prec. and -ATE ³.] *trans.* To shut up in, or as in, prison; to confine.

What is it..to i. the Liberty of the Subject under the Iron and weighty Chains of an Arbitrary Government? 1640. Hence **Inca·rcerated** *ppl. a.*; *spec.* in *Path.*, variously used of a strangulated, obstructed, or otherwise irreducible hernia and of a retained placenta. **Incarcera·tion**, imprisonment 1536. **Inca·rcerator**, one who incarcerates or imprisons.

†**Inca·rdinate**, *a.* Used joc. for *incarnate*. Hee's the verie diuell i. *Twel. N.* v. i. 185.

Incardinate (inkā·ɹdineⁱt), *v.* 1609. [f. ppl. stem of med.L. *incardinare* to institute into an ecclesiastical benefice, f. *in-* (IN-²) + *cardo, cardinem* hinge, *cardinalis* a chief presbyter, a CARDINAL.] *trans.* **a.** To institute as principal priest, deacon, etc. at a particular church or place. **b.** To institute to a cardinalship. So **Incardina·tion.**

Incardinated..that is Mortized or riueted to a Church, as a hinge to a dore 1609.

Incarn (inkā·ɹn), *v.* Also †**en-**. ME. [a. F. *incarner*, ad. L. *incarnare* to make flesh, f. *in-* (IN-²) + *caro, carn-*.] **1.** *trans.* To cover with flesh, heal over (a wound, etc.); *absol.* to cause flesh to grow 1541. **b.** *intr.* To become covered with flesh, to heal 1689. **2.** To incarnate (*rare*) 1563.

Incarnadine (inkā·ɹnădin, -əin). 1591. [a. F. *incarnadin, -ine*, ad. It. *incarnadino*, var. of *incarnatino* flesh-colour, deriv. of *incarnato* INCARNATE.]

A. *adj.* Prop., Flesh-coloured, carnation, pale red or pink; also, crimson or blood-red (cf. CARNATION ²); in mod. use occas. = Blood-stained (from Shaks.; see INCARNADINE *v.*)

You'll..calmly wash those hands i. BYRON.

B. *sb.* Flesh-colour, blush colour; also, a crimson or blood-red colour 1622.

Inca·rnadine, *v. arch.* 1605. [f. prec.] *trans.* To dye or tinge with incarnadine; to redden. (From Shaks. onward associated with the colour of blood.)

This my Hand will rather The multitudinous Seas incarnardine, Making the Greene, one Red *Macb.* II. ii. 62.

Incarnate (inkā·ɹnĕt), *a.* ME. [ad. L. *incarnatus* made flesh; see INCARN. In sense 2 = Fr. *incarnat, -ate.*] **1.** Clothed or invested with flesh; embodied in flesh; in a human (or animal) bodily form. **b.** Of a quality, etc.: Impersonated 1532. **2.** Flesh-coloured; light pink or crimson. *Obs.* exc. in *Bot.* 1533.

1. And slay th' i. Deity WESLEY. Phr. *Devil incarnate*: applied hyperbolically to a person, but the adj. often becomes nearly = 'out-and-out', 'arrant'. **b.** The quack is a Falsehood I. 1839. **2.** The common red and i. clovers DARWIN.

Incarnate (inkā·ɹneⁱt), *v.* 1533. [f. prec.] **1.** *trans.* To render incarnate; to embody in flesh. **2.** *transf.* and *fig.* **a.** To actualize, embody (an abstraction) 1591. **b.** To impersonate (a quality, etc.) 1806. †**3.** = INCARN **1.** –1725. †**b.** *intr.* for *refl.* = INCARN 1 b. –1759. †**4.** To make carnal; to despiritualize –1683. **5.** To convert (vegetable matter) into flesh. PLAYFAIR.

1. I must not ask why God took this way to i. his Son DONNE. **2. b.** This friar incarnated the Venetian spirit SYMONDS. **3. b.** My uncle Toby's wound was near well..'twas just beginning to i. STERNE. **5.** To 'i.' Indian corn [i. e. by feeding cattle with it] 1882.

Incarnation (inkaɹnēⁱ·ʃən). ME. [a. F., ad. late L. *incarnationem*; see INCARN.] **1.** The action of incarnating or fact of being incarnated or 'made flesh'; assumption of, or existence in, a bodily (esp. human) form. **a.** *spec.* of Christ, or of God in Christ. Often absol. *The Incarnation.* (The earliest sense. In early use often in reference to the date of the incarnation or birth of Christ.) **b.** *fig.* Embodiment. ? *Obs.* 1615. **2.** *concr.* **a.** An incarnate or embodied form (*of*) 1742. **b.** A living type or embodiment (*of* a quality, etc.) 1833. **c.** Loosely: A thing which is an embodiment (*of*) 1821. **3.** The formation of new flesh upon or in a wound or sore; healing up; granulation; *concr.* a growth of new flesh 1544. **4.** Flesh-colour, carnation; a pigment or dye of this colour. *Obs.* or *arch.* 1485. **b.** *attrib.* or as *adj.* = INCARNATE *a.* 2. 1562.

1. He was borne after the Incarnacion of oure lord ij. c. yeres 1477. **2. a.** His [Vishn'u's] first i. was that of a fish 1843. **b.** William Rufus..a foul i. of selfishness STUBBS.

†**Incarnative** (inkā·ɹnătiv). ME. [a. obs. F. *incarnatif, -ive*: see INCARNATE *v.* and -IVE.]

A. *adj.* **1.** Promoting the growth of flesh in a wound or sore –1694. **2.** Used joc. for *incarnate* (= 'arrant'). GREENE & LODGE.

B. *sb.* [sc. *medicine, application*] 1568–1720.

†**Inca·rve**, *v. rare.* Also **en-**. 1596. [IN-² = EN-¹ B. 3.] *trans.* To carve or engrave in or upon something –1615.

Incase, -ment, vars. of ENCASE, -MENT.

†**Inca·sk**, *v.* 1611. [f. IN-¹ or ² + CASK *sb.*] *trans.* **a.** To put into a cask. **b.** To cover with, or as with, a casque or helmet. SHELTON.

†**Inca·stellate, en-**, *v.* 1538. [f. ppl. stem of med.L. *incastellare*; see IN-² and -ATE ³.] *trans.* To make into a castle; to fortify; to enclose with masonry –1601. So †**Inca·stle** *v.*

†**Inca·stellated**, *ppl. a.* 1611. [ad. It. *incastellato* 'hoof-bound' (Florio).] Hoof-bound (as a horse). (Dicts.) So †**Inca·stled, inca·stelled** *ppl. a.* in same sense.

Incatenation (inkætĭnēⁱ·ʃən). 1762. [f. med.L. *incatenare* to enchain.] Putting in or fastening with chains; harnessing; a linking or being linked together. So **Inca·tenate** *v.* 1839.

†**Incau·telous**, *a.* 1610. [IN-³.] Incautious –1734.

Incaution (inkǭ·ʃən). 1715. [IN-³.] Want of caution.

Incautious (inkǭ·ʃəs), *a.* 1703. [IN-³; after L. *incautus.*] Not cautious; wanting in caution; heedless, unwary, rash.

An i. moment 1800, employment of language LEWIS. Hence **Incau·tious-ly** *adv.*, **-ness.**

Incavate (i·nkăveⁱt), *a. rare.* [ad. L. *incavatus.*] Hollowed, bent inwards. (Dicts.)

Incavation (inkăvēⁱ·ʃən). 1799. [f. L. *incavare.*] The action of making hollow; also, a hollow on a surface; a hollowed place.

†**Inca·ve**, *v.*¹ [ad. L. *incavare*, f. *in-* (IN-²) + *cavare.*] To make hollow; to bend inwards. SIDNEY.

Incave, encave (inkēⁱ·v, en-), *v.*² 1604. [f. IN-², EN-¹ + CAVE *sb.* Cf. F. *encaver.*] *trans.* To enclose or shut up in, or as in, a cave. So **Inca·vern, encavern** *v.* 1611.

Incede (insī·d), *v. rare.* 1669. [ad. L. *incedere* to go on; see IN-²] *intr.* To move on, advance; to move with measured or stately pace. Hence **Ince·dingly** *adv.* (often with allusion to Virgil, *Æn.* I. 46).

Incele·brity. 1803. [IN-³.] Want of celebrity.

Incend (inse·nd), *v. Obs.* (exc. as *nonce-wd.*) 1502. [ad. L. *incendere* to set on fire.] **1.** *trans.* To set alight 1597. †**2.** To engender (bodily heat); to heat, inflame –1621. †**3.** To inflame, excite (the mind, passions, etc.); to incite to action –1684.

Incendiarism (inse·ndiăriz'm). 1674. [f. INCENDIARY + -ISM.] The practice or commission of arson. *fig.* Inflammatory agitation.

Incendiary (inse·ndiări). 1606. [ad. L. *incendiarius*, f. *incendium* conflagration; see -ARY.]

A. *adj.* **1.** Consisting in, or pertaining to, the malicious setting on fire of buildings or other property 1611. **b.** *Mil.* Adapted for setting on fire an enemy's buildings, ships, etc. 1871. **2.** *fig.* Tending to stir up strife, violence, or sedition; inflammatory 1614.

1. An i. outrage at Norwich SPEED. **b.** A shower of i. shells 1871. **2.** I. publications 1853.

B. *sb.* **1.** One who wilfully or criminally causes a conflagration; one who commits arson 1606. **2.** *fig.* One who stirs up civil strife or violence; an inflammatory agitator; a firebrand 1631. †**b.** An incentive to evil –1726.

2. The Jesuits had been the incendiaries of the late insurrection H. WALPOLE.

†**Ince·ndious**, *a.* 1823. [ad. L. *incendiosus*; see -OUS.] = INCENDIARY *a.* Hence †**Ince·ndiously** *adv.*

Incensation (insensēⁱ·ʃən). 1853. [f. med. L. *incensare* to INCENSE.] The action of censing.

Incense (i·nsens), *sb.* [ME. *ansens, encenz*, a. OF. *encens, ancens*, ad. eccl. L. *incensum* incense, lit. 'that which is set on fire', f. *incendere.* Altered after L.] **1.** An aromatic gum, etc., or a mixture of fragrant gums or spices, used for producing a sweet smell when burned. **2.** The smoke or perfume of incense, esp. when burned as an oblation or in religious ceremonial ME. **3.** *transf.* and *fig.* ME.

1. And moore encens in to the fyr he caste CHAUCER. **2.** A thicke cloud of i. went vp *Ezek.* viii. 11. **3.** *transf.* The humid Flours, that breathd Thir morning I. MILT. *P. L.* IX. 194. *fig.* Offer pure i. to so pure a shrine SHAKS. *Lucr.* 194.

Comb.: **i.-boat**, a boat-shaped vessel used to hold i. for transfer to a censer; †**-brass**, tr. Gr. χαλκολίβανον in Rev. i. 15 (1611 'fine brass', but also explained as 'yellow frankincense'); **-breathing** *a.*, exhaling fragrance; **-cedar**, the genus *Libocedrus*, esp. the White Cedar (*L. decurrens*); **-tree**, a name for various trees yielding i., esp. of the genera *Boswellia* and *Icica*; also applied to a species of *Pittosporum*, from its fragrant flowers; **-wood**, the wood of *Icica heptaphylla.*

Incense (i·nsens), *v.*¹ ME. [a. F. *encenser*, f. *encens* INCENSE *sb.*] **1.** *trans.* To fumigate or perfume with incense, esp. in connexion with a religious ceremony; to burn or offer incense before, or to; to cense. Also *transf.* and *fig.* **2.** To burn or offer as incense (*lit.* and *fig.*) 1605. **3.** *intr.* To burn or offer incense ME.

1. To i. Idols 1709. *transf.* Wild roses incensed the fresh air 1861. **3.** To i. unto Idols 1638.

Incense (inse·ns), *v.*² ME. [a. OF. *incenser* (? *encenser*), f. L. *incens-*, *incendere*; see INCEND.] †**1.** *trans.* To set on fire, kindle; to consume with fire, burn –1700. †**2.** To inflame (passion, etc.) –1809. **3.** †To fire (a person *with* passion, etc.) –1664. **b.** *spec.* To inflame with wrath, excite to anger, enrage, exasperate. (The current sense.) 1494. Also *fig.* †**4.** To incite to some action; to stir up, set on –1639.

1. Like pretious Odours, most fragrant, when they are incensed, or crushed BACON. **2.** Will God i. his ire For such a petty Trespass? MILT. *P. L.* IX. 692. **3. b.** This so incensed her father, that [etc.] FIELDING. *fig.* Winds wrastling with great fires, i. the flames DEKKER. Hence **Incensed** (inse·nst, *poet.* inse·nsĕd) *ppl. a.* kindled (*lit.* and *fig.*); inflamed with wrath; in *Her.* said of an animal depicted with fire issuing from mouth and ears. **Ince·nsement** (now *rare*), anger, exasperation.

Incenser ¹ (i·nsensəɹ). 1555. [a. F. *encenseur*; see INCENSE *v.*¹ and -ER ¹ 2.] One who burns or offers incense; also *fig.*

Incenser ²: see INCENSOR.

†**Ince·nsion.** ME. [ad. L. *incensionem*, *incendere* to INCEND.] **1.** Burning; setting on fire; conflagration –1656. **2.** Bodily inflammation –1745. **3.** Incensement. BAXTER.

†**Ince·nsive**, *a.* (*sb.*) *rare.* 1563. [a. obs. F. *incensif, -ive*; see INCEND and -IVE.] **1.** Of inflamed disposition, full of rage. FOXE. **2.** Inflammatory –1677. **3.** *sb.* = INCENTIVE *sb.* RALEIGH.

†**Ince·nsor, -er.** 1555. [a. L. *incensor*; see INCEND *v.*] One who kindles, inflames, or incites; an instigator –1627.

Incensory (i·nsensŏri). 1611. [ad. med.L. *incensorium*, f. *incensum* INCENSE *sb.*: see -ORY.] †**1.** ? A burnt offering. CHAPMAN. **2.** A censer 1645.

Incensurable (inse·nsiŭrăb'l, -ʃŭr-), *a. rare.* 1846. [IN-³.] Not censurable. Hence **Ince·nsurably** *adv. rare.*

Incentive (inse·ntiv). ME. [ad. L. *incentivus* setting the tune, inciting, f. *incinere* to sing to. In sense 2, app. confounded with INCENSIVE.]

A. *adj.* **1.** Having the quality of inciting; provocative 1603. †**2.** Having the property of kindling –1708.

1. An i. speech in the House of Lords NORTH. **2.** Part i. reed Provide, pernicious with one touch to fire MILT. *P.L.* VI. 519. Hence **Ince·ntively** *adv.*

B. *sb.* [L. *incentivum.*] Something that arouses feeling, or incites to action; an exciting cause or motive; an incitement, provocation, spur ME.

An I. to the Love of our Country STEELE.

Incentor (inse·ntəɹ). Now *rare.* 1563. [a. L., f. *incinere* to sing to.] **1.** One who excites (strife, etc.); one who incites *to* action. †**2.** 'He that singeth the descant'. BLOUNT.

Incentre, en- (in-, ensɛ·ntəɹ), *v. rare.* 1611. [f. IN-², EN-¹ + CENTRE.] *trans.* To centre *in* something; to fix in the centre.

Incept (insɛ·pt), *v.* 1569. [f. L. *incept-*, *incipere* to begin.] 1. *trans.* To undertake; to begin, enter upon. 2. *intr.* = COMMENCE *v.* 4. (Retained in the University of Cambridge until 1926.) Hence *gen.* to enter upon one's career or office 1852. 3. *trans.* (*Biol.*) To take in, as an organism or cell 1863.
2. The 'Licentiate' was not regarded as a full 'Master' or 'Doctor' till he had 'incepted' RASHDALL.

Inception (insɛ·pʃən). 1483. [ad. L. *inceptionem*, f. *incipere* to begin.] 1. Origination, beginning, commencement. 2. In Univ. use: The action of incepting (cf. COMMENCEMENT 2) 1680. 3. The action of taking in, as an organism 1849.
1. Between the i. and the execution of the project LECKY.

Inceptive (insɛ·ptiv). 1612. [a. obs. F. *inceptif, -ive*, f. *incept-*, *incipere* to begin; see -IVE.]
A. *adj.* 1. Beginning, incipient; initial 1662. 2. *Gram.* and *Logic.* Expressing the beginning of action, as *i. verb, proposition*, etc. 1656. Hence Ince·ptively *adv.* in an i. way.
2. Verbs I., the same as Inchoatives 1706.
B. *sb.* 1. An inceptive verb or proposition 1612. †2. (*pl.*) Initial circumstances; beginnings -1734.

Inceptor (insɛ·ptəɹ, -ǭɹ). 1479. [a. L., f. *incipere* to begin.] 1. One who incepts at a University. 2. *gen.* A beginner (*rare*) 1706.

†I·ncerate, *v. rare.* 1623. [f. ppl. stem of L. *incerare.*] To cover with wax -1727. Hence †Incera·tion, the action of covering with wax, or of making a substance like moist wax.

†Ince·rtain. 1491. [a. F., f. *in-* (IN-³) + *certain*, after L. *incertus.*] A. *adj.* = UNCERTAIN -1741. B. *sb.* 1. Uncertainty 1502. 2. An obs. game at cards. SHADWELL. So †Ince·rtainly *adv.*

†Ince·rtainty. 1484. [a. OF. *incertaineté.*] = UNCERTAINTY -1792.

Incertitude (insɔ̄·ɹtitiūd). 1601. [a. F., f. L. *in-* (IN-³) + *certitudo.*] 1. Subjective uncertainty. 2. Objective uncertainty; insecurity 1603.
1. Thus we were brought back to our old i. BURKE. 2. The i. and instabilitie of this life HOLLAND.

Incessable (insɛ·săb'l), *a.* Now *rare.* 1545. [ad. L. *incessabilis*, f. *in-* (IN-³) + *cessare* to CEASE. Formerly assim. to *cease.*] Ceaseless, incessant. Hence Ince·ssably *adv.* ME.

Incessancy (insɛ·sănsi). 1615. [f. next + -ANCY.] The quality of being incessant or unceasing; unbroken continuance.

Incessant (insɛ·sănt), *a.* 1532. [prob. a. F. *incessant*, f. L. *in-* (IN-³) + *cessantem*, *cessare* to cease.] 1. That does not cease; unceasing, ceaseless, continual, either in duration or repetition. †2. Unending, endless, everlasting -1564. 3. quasi-*adv.* Without intermission or pause 1557.
1. The i. weepings of my wife SHAKS. The rude flint Yields to the i. drop SMOLLETT. 3. Do they not ..call I. on his tardy Vengeance? ROWE. Hence Ince·ssantly *adv.* unceasingly; instantly ME. Ince·ssantness.

†Ince·ssion. *rare.* 1651. [ad. L. *incessionem*, f. *incedere* to go on, walk.] Onward motion; progression -1845.
The i. or locall motion of animals SIR T. BROWNE.

Incest (i·nsest). ME. [ad. L. *incestus* (*u* stem) or *incestum* adj. neut., f. *in-* (IN-³) + *castus* chaste.] The crime of sexual intercourse or cohabitation between persons related within the degrees within which marriage is prohibited by law.
Spiritual i. (in *R.C.Ch.*): (*a*) Marriage or sexual connexion between persons related by spiritual affinity, or with a person under a vow of chastity, etc. (*b*) The holding by the same person of two benefices, one of which depends on the collation of the other.

Incestuous (insɛ·stiuəs), *a.* 1532. [ad. L. *incestuosus*; see -OUS.] 1. Guilty of incest 1552. †b. Loosely: Adulterous -1681. 2. Of the nature of or involving incest 1532. †3. Begotten of incest -1621.
1. Caius Caligula, that wicked and i. emperor 1592. 2. He had ever trampled on the laws of Persia by an i. union with his sisters THIRLWALL. Hence Ince·stuous-ly *adv.*, -ness.

Inch (inʃ), *sb.*¹ [OE. *ynce*:—**unkia*, a. L. *uncia* twelfth part, inch (cf. OUNCE). Not in other Teut. langs.] 1. A measure of length, the twelfth part of a foot. Hence, a measure of surface and of solidity (explicitly *square* or *superficial, cubic* or *solid inch*). Used also as the unit of measurement of rainfall, of atmospheric pressure, and of the flow of water. 2. *transf.* and *fig.* The least amount or part (of space, time, material or immaterial things); a very little; a bit ME. 3. *attrib.* See quots. 1646.
1. The gill contains 8·665 cubic inches (*mod.*). *Inch of rain*: that quantity which would cover a surface to the depth of an i.; = 3,630 cubic feet on an acre. *I. of pressure*: that amount which balances the weight of a column of mercury, an inch high, in the mercurial barometer. *Miner's i. of water*: that amount that will pass in 24 hours through an opening of 1 square inch under a constant pressure of 6 inches. 2. I'll flog you within an i. of your life DICKENS. 3. (*a*) Of the length, thickness, etc. of an inch; as *i.-board* (board an inch thick); of the focal length of an inch, as *i. object-glass.* (*b*) With prefixed numeral (*two-i.*, etc.); Of the length, diameter, etc. of (so many) inches.
Phrases. *By inches, i. by i.*: by small degrees, very gradually. *Inches* = stature; I would I had thy inches SHAKS. *Give him an i. and he'll take an ell*: undue advantage will be taken of slight concessions.
Comb.: i.-measure, etc., one divided into inches; -pound (*Dynamics*), the work done in raising a pound weight vertically through an i. (cf. *foot-pound* s.v. FOOT *sb.*); -worm, a geometer caterpillar.

Inch (inʃ), *sb.*² ME. [a. Gael. *innis* (iniʃ), gen. *innse* (ī·nʃe) island.] A small island; also, locally, a meadow by a river (as the Inches of Perth).

Inch (inʃ), *v.* 1599. [f. INCH *sb.*¹] 1. *intr.* To move, advance, or retreat by inches or small degrees. 2. *trans.* To drive by inches or small degrees 1667. 3. To measure or compute the number of inches in 1673.
1. With slow paces measures back the field, And inches to the walls DRYDEN. 2. And so i. him and shove him out of the world DRYDEN.
Phr. *I. out*: to eke out by small amounts †to deal out sparingly.

Incha·mber, *v. rare.* 1611. [IN-².] *trans.* To lodge in or as in a chamber.

†Incha·ngeable, *a. rare.* 1583. [IN-³.] Unchangeable -1654. So †Inchangeabi·lity, unchangeableness.

Inchant, etc.: see ENCHANT, etc.

†Incha·ritable, *a.* 1496. [IN-³.] Not charitable; uncharitable -1670.

†Incha·rity. 1589. [IN-³.] Want of charity -1679.

Inchase: see ENCHASE *v.*²

†Incha·stity. 1586. [IN-³.] Unchastity -1671.

Inched (inʃt), *a.* 1605. [f. INCH *sb.*¹ or *v.* + -ED.] Containing (so many) inches in length or other dimension.

Inchest, var. of ENCHEST *v.*

Inchmeal (i·nʃ,mīl), *adv.* (*sb.*) 1530. [f. INCH *sb.*¹ + -MEAL.] By inches; little by little. Also with *by.*
To die, as it were, by inch-meal FLAVEL.

Inchoate (i·nko,ĕt), *a.* 1534. [ad. L. *inchoatus* (*incohatus*), pa. pple. of *inchoare* (*incohare*) to begin.] Just begun, incipient; in an initial or early stage; hence elementary, imperfect, undeveloped, immature.
It was a Church i., beginning, not perfect 1581. Hence I·nchoate-ly *adv.*, -ness.

Inchoate (i·nko,eit), *v.* 1612. [f. L. *inchoatus*; see prec.] 1. *trans.* To begin; also, to cause to begin, bring about. 2. *intr.* To make a beginning 1654.

Inchoation (inko,ē¹·ʃən). 1530. [ad. late L. *inchoationem* (prop. *incohationem*).] Beginning, commencement; origination; early stage. †b. *pl.* Beginnings -1660. †c. A prefix 1661.
But the i. of those graces, the consummation whereof dependeth on mysteries ensuing HOOKER.

Inchoative (inkōu·ătiv, i·nko,eⁱtiv). 1530. [See INCHOATE *v.* and -IVE.]
A. *adj.* 1. That is in an incipient stage; rudimentary, inchoate; initial 1631. 2. *Gram.* Of verbs: Inceptive 1530. Hence Incho·atively *adv.* in an i. manner.
1. The solution..is still in its i. stages CARLYLE.
B. *sb.* (*Gram.*) An inchoative verb 1530.

†I·nchpin. 1571. [app. f. INCH *sb.*¹ + PIN *sb.*; or (in sense 1) a corruption of some other word.] 1. The sweetbread of a deer; also explained as 'the lower gut', etc. -1688. 2. ? A pin an inch long. GOLDING.

Inchu·rch, obs. var. of ENCHURCH *v.*

†Inci·curable, *a. rare.* 1657. [ad. mod.L. *incicurabilis*, f. *in-* (IN-³) + *cicurare* to tame; see -ABLE.] That cannot be tamed; hence, of plants, that cannot be naturalized -1776.

Incide (insəi·d), *v.*¹ ? *Obs.* 1597. [ad. L. *incidere* to cut into, f. *in-* (IN-²) + *cædere*; cf. INCISE *v.*] 1. *Surg.* To cut into, make incision (*trans.* or *intr.*). †2. *Med.* To sever, loosen, disperse, resolve (a viscid humour, phlegm, etc.); = CUT *v.* II. 4. -1797.

Incide (insəi·d), *v.*² *rare.* 1774. [ad. L. *incidere*, f. *in-* (IN-²) + *cadere* to fall; cf. INCIDENT *a.*] *intr.* To fall *upon*; to have incidence.

Incidence (i·nsidĕns). ME. [a. F., f. *incident*; see -ENCE.] †1. = INCIDENT *sb.* 1. -1651. 2. The act or fact of falling upon, or coming in contact with 1656. 3. *Physics.* The falling of a line, or anything moving in a line (as a ray of light, etc.), upon a surface; the manner of such falling 1626. 4. *Astron.* = IMMERSION 3. 1727. 5. The range or scope of a thing, the extent of its influence or effects 1825.
1. Many operations have been invented sometimes by a casual i. and occurrence BACON. 2. The i. of a heavy gale KANE. 3. *Angle of Incidence*, the angle which the incident line, ray, etc. makes with the perpendicular to the surface at the point of i. *Axis of i.*, the perpendicular to the surface at the point of i. 5. The i. and effect of taxes and regulations MᶜCULLOCH.

†I·ncidency. 1611. [See prec. and -ENCY.] 1. An incident -1701. 2. The quality of being liable to fall *to*; (with *pl.*) a thing incident *to* -1683. 3. *Physics.* = INCIDENCE 3. -1704. 4. The meeting of lines. MORSE.

Incident (i·nsidĕnt), *sb.* ME. [a. F. *incident* adj. used subst.] 1. Something that occurs casually in connexion with something else; an event of accessory or subordinate character. 2. An occurrence viewed as a separate circumstance 1462. †b. A matter, an affair (*rare*) -1761. 3. A distinct piece of action in a play or poem 1695; a single feature in a picture 1705. 4. †An accessory circumstance -1755; in *Law*, a privilege, burden, custom, etc. commonly or invariably attaching to an office, estate, or the like 1628. †b. An incidental expense -1776.
3. No person, no i. in the play, but must be of use to carry on the main design DRYDEN. A sweet piece of rock i. RUSKIN. 4. The 'incidents' of tenure by knight-service DIGBY.

Incident (i·nsidĕnt), *a.* 1488. [a. F., or ad. L. *incidentem*, *incidere*, f. *in-* (IN-²) + *cadere* to fall.] 1. Liable to befall or occur *to*; likely to happen; hence, naturally attaching. 2. *Law.* Attaching itself, as a privilege, burden, or custom, *to* an office, position, etc. 1491. †3. Relating or pertinent *to* -1614. †4. Apt to fall into; liable *to*; subject *to* -1767. 5. = INCIDENTAL 1. Now *rare* or *Obs.* 1523. 6. Subordinate, subsidiary, accessory 1725. 7. Falling or striking upon or against, as light upon a surface. Const. *upon.* 1667.
1. The fallacies i. to categorical syllogisms REID. 2. Fealtie is incydent to everye manner of Service 1574. 5. By occasion i. there was talke of a text of Scripture 1581. With all the Charges i. BUTLER. 6. Phr. †*Incident proposition*, a proposition inserted in a principal one, and introduced by a relative pronoun; a subordinate relative clause.

Incidental (insidɛ·ntăl), *a.* (*sb.*) 1616. [f. INCIDENT *sb.* + -AL.] 1. Occurring or liable to occur in fortuitous or subordinate conjunction with something else; casual 1644. b. Of a charge or expense: Such as is incurred apart from the primary disbursements 1739. 2. Casually met with (*rare*) 1856. 3. *sb.* An incidental circumstance, event, charge, etc. 1707.
1. Those i. discourses which we have wandered into MILT. b. The house rent, and the i. charges of a family 1804. Phr. *Incidental images, colours*: such as are perceived by the eye as a consequence of visual impressions no longer present. *Incidental music*, marches, dances, songs, etc. introduced during the action of a play. Hence Incide·ntal-ly *adv.*, -ness.

†**I·ncidently,** *adv.* 1529. [f. INCIDENT *a.* + -LY [2].] Incidentally -1824.

Incinerable (insi·nĕrăb'l), *a. rare.* [f. med.L. *incinerare* + -ABLE.] Capable of being burnt to ashes. SIR T. BROWNE.

†**Inci·nerate,** *ppl. a.* 1471. [ad. med.L. *incineratus*; see next.] Incinerated -1626.

Incinerate (insi·nĕreⁱt), *v.* 1555. [f. ppl. stem of med.L. *incinerare*, f. *in-* (IN- [2]) + *cinis, cinerem* ashes; see -ATE [3].] **1.** *trans.* To reduce to ashes, consume by fire. **2.** *intr.* To become reduced to ashes 1800.

1. It is the Fire only that Incinerates Bodies BOYLE. Hence **Incinera·tion,** reduction to ashes 1529; *spec.* (esp. in U.S.) the cremation of the dead.

Incipience (insi·piĕns). 1864. [f. INCIPIENT; see -ENCE.] Beginning, commencement; the fact or condition of being incipient; with *pl.* A beginning. So **Inci·piency,** the quality or state of being incipient 1817.

Incipient (insi·piĕnt). 1589. [ad. L. *incipientem, incipere* to begin.]

A. *adj.* Beginning; coming into, or in an early stage of, existence; in an initial stage 1669. Hence **Inci·piently** *adv.*

I. madness JOHNSON, fermentation SIR H. DAVY.

B. *sb.* †**1.** = INCEPTOR -1598. **2.** *Heb. Gram.* The verbal 'tense' or form with prefixed servile letters, variously called Future, Present, and Imperfect 1866.

‖**Incipit** (i·nsipit). [L., = begins: used, as in old MSS., to introduce the title of a literary work.] The opening words of a poem or other piece. Cf. EXPLICIT.

Incircle, obs. f. ENCIRCLE *v.*

†**Inci·rclet.** [f. IN- [1] or [2] + CIRCLET.] A little circular curl or spiral. SIDNEY.

†**Incircumscri·ptible,** *a.* 1550. [ad. med.L. *incircumscriptibilis*; see IN- [3].] Incapable of being circumscribed or limited -1652.

Incircumscri·ption. *rare.* 1651. The condition of being uncircumscribed; boundlessness.

†**Incircumspe·ct,** *a.* 1531. [IN- [3].] Not circumspect; incautious, heedless -1651.

†**Incircumspe·ction.** 1646. [IN- [3].] Want of circumspection; heedlessness, unwariness -1683.

Incise (insəi·z), *v.* 1541. [a. F. *inciser*, for OF. *enciser*, f. L. *incis-, incidere*; see INCIDE *v.* [1]] **1.** *trans.* To cut into, make an incision in; to cut marks upon, engrave *with* figures. Also *absol.* **2.** To form by cutting; to carve, engrave 1631.

2. I on thy Tombe this Epitaph i. CAREW.

Incised (insəi·zd), *ppl. a.* 1597. [f. INCISE *v.* + -ED [1].] **1.** Cut into; marked by cutting. **b.** *Bot.* and *Zool.* Having marginal notches; as a leaf or an insect's wing 1826. **2.** Produced by incision; engraved 1807.

Incision (insi·ʒən). ME. [a. F., ad. L. *incisionem*, f. *incidere* INCIDE *v.* [1]] **1.** The action of cutting into something 1474. **2.** The effect of cutting into something; a division produced by cutting; a cut, a gash ME. **b.** *Bot.* and *Zool.* A deep indentation or notch 1578. †**3.** *Med.* The loosening and removal of viscid humours; cf. INCIDE *v.* [1] 2. BACON. **4.** *fig.* Incisiveness 1862. ¶**5.** Used erron. for INSITION, engrafting 1601.

Incisive (insəi·siv), *a.* (*sb.*) 1528. [ad. med.L. *incisivus*; see INCISE *v.* and -IVE.] **1.** Having the quality of cutting into something; cutting, penetrating with a sharp edge 1597. **2.** *Anat.* Applied to the incisor teeth; and hence to the *incisive bones* = the premaxillary bones 1804. †**3.** Cutting, piercing; 'cutting' viscid humours (see INCIDE *v.* [1] 2) -1694. **4.** *fig.* Sharp or keen in mental qualities; penetrating, acute, trenchant 1850. **5.** *sb.* An incisor tooth 1804.

4. Her i. smile MRS. BROWNING. An i. and pungent style 1880. Hence **Inci·sive-ly** *adv.*, **-ness.**

Inciso- (insəi·so), comb. advb. f. L. *incisus*, used in the sense 'incisedly—', 'incised and —', as *i.-dentate*, etc.

Incisor (insəi·səɪ, -ǭɪ). 1672. [a. med. and mod.L. *incisor* lit. 'cutter', f. *incidere* INCIDE *v.* [1]] *Anat.* and *Zool.* A tooth adapted for cutting; any one of the front teeth in either jaw, situated between the canine teeth on each side. **b.** *attrib.* Adapted for cutting, as *i. forceps, tooth*; connected with the incisor teeth, as *i. artery*, etc. 1837.

Incisory (insəi·sŏri), *a.* 1594. [f. as INCISOR; see -ORY.] Having the property of cutting, incisive; applied to the incisor teeth.

Incisure (insi·ʒ'ŭɪ). 1597. [ad. L. *incisura*, f. *incis-, incidere* INCIDE *v.* [1]; see -URE.] A cut, notch, slit, cleft.

Incitable (insəi·tăb'l), *a. rare.* 1800. [f. INCITE *v.* + -ABLE.] Capable of being incited or urged to action. Hence **Incitabi·lity.**

Incitant (i·nsitănt, insəi·tănt). 1802. [ad. L. *incitantem*, f. *incitare* to INCITE.] **A.** *adj.* That incites, stimulating 1886. **B.** *sb.* That which incites.

†**I·ncitate,** *v.* 1597. [f. L. *incitat-, incitare.*] *trans.* To incite -1623. So †**I·ncitate** *ppl. a.* 1568.

Incitation (insəitēⁱ·ʃən, insitēⁱ·ʃən). 1477. [a. F., ad. L. *incitationem.*] **1.** The action of inciting; incitement, stimulation. †**2.** That which incites; a stimulus, incitement -1709. †**3.** Power of inciting -1684.

2. This passion..the..noblest I. to honest Attempts STEELE.

†**Inci·tative,** *a.* and *sb. rare.* 1490. [a. obs. F. *incitatif, -ive.*] = INCITANT *a.* and *sb.* -1620.

Incite (insəi·t), *v.* 1483. [a. F. *inciter*, ad. L. *incitare*, f. *in-* (IN- [2]) + *citare*, freq. of *ciere, citum* to put in motion; see CITE.] *trans.* To urge or spur on; to stir up, instigate, stimulate. Const. *to, unto*; *to do* something.

The Pope incited the King of Spain to make war against the Republick BRAMHALL. Manufactures were incited 1812. Hence **Inci·ter.** **Inci·tingly** *adv.*

Incitement (insəi·tmĕnt). 1594. [f. INCITE *v.* + -MENT.] **1.** The action of inciting. †Also, the condition of being incited. **2.** That which incites or rouses to action; an exciting cause; a stimulus, incentive, spur 1600.

1. Chiefly by the i. of the Cardinal 1647. 2. Pleasure, the greatest i. of evil JOWETT.

Incito-motor (insəi·tomōᵘ·təɪ, -ǒɪ), *a. rare.* 1886. [f. INCITE *v.* + MOTOR, after EXCITO-MOTOR, q.v.] Inciting to motion or muscular action; applied to the action of the nervous centres which determine the contraction of the muscles through the intermediation of the motor nerves. Also erron. identified with *excito-motor*. So **Inci·to-mo·tory** *a.* 1884.

†**Inci·vil,** *a.* 1586. [a. F., ad. late L. *incivilis*; see IN- [3] and CIVIL.] **1.** Not according to civil law. DANIEL. **2.** Savage, barbarous. MARLOWE. **3.** Rude, clownish -1707.

Incivility (insivi·lĭti). 1584. [ad. F. *incivilité*, ad. late L. *incivilitatem*; see prec. and -ITY.] The quality or condition of being incivil or uncivil. †**1.** Want of civilization; savageness, barbarism -1811. †**2.** Want of good manners or good breeding -1673. **3.** Want of civility or politeness; discourtesy, rudeness. Also with *an* and *pl.* 1612.

1. That barbarous relic of feudal i., duelling 1811. 3. [Guildford] was treated by Jeffreys with marked i. MACAULAY. No person offered me the least i. LUDLOW.

Incivilization (insi·vilizēⁱ·ʃən, -əiz-). 1823. [IN- [3].] Uncivilized condition; want of civilization. So †**Inci·vilize** *v.* 1603.

Incivism (i·nsiviz'm). 1794. [ad. F. *incivisme*; see IN- [3] and CIVISM.] The opposite of CIVISM; want of good citizenship; *orig.*, want of loyalty to the principles of the French Revolution: regarded as a crime against the Republic.

Socrates is to be..exculpated from the charge of i. GROTE.

†**Inclama·tion.** *rare.* 1612. [ad. late L. *inclamationem*; see IN- [2].] A calling upon, invocation. Also, a cry, a loud call. -1613.

Inclasp, obs. f. ENCLASP *v.*

Inclau·dent, *a.* [IN- [3].] *Bot.* Not closing. PAXTON.

†**Incla·vate,** *v. rare.* 1666. [f. med.L. *inclavat-, inclavare*; see -ATE [3].] *trans.* To nail or bolt in, fix firmly.

Inclave, obs. f. ENCLAVE *a. Her.*

Incle, var. of INKLE *sb.* and *v.*

I·n-clea·ring. 1872. [IN *adv.*] The cheques, bills of exchange, etc., collectively, payable by a bank, and received through the Clearing-house for settlement; also *attrib.*

Inclemency (inkle·mĕnsi). 1559. [ad. L. *inclementia*; see next and -ENCY.] The quality or condition of being inclement. **1.** Severity of weather; (with *pl.*) an instance of this 1699. †**2.** Want of kindliness of disposition; pitilessness, unmercifulness -1658.

1. The I. of the weather 1725. The inclemencies of a cold climate 1748. 2. The inclemencie of the late Pope laboring to forestall him in his just throne BP. HALL.

Inclement (inkle·mĕnt), *a.* 1621. [ad. L. *inclementem*; see IN- [3] and CLEMENT.] Not clement. **1.** Of climate, etc.: Not temperate; extreme; severe 1667. †**2.** Not kindly; pitiless, harsh, severe, cruel -1725.

1. To shun Th' i. Seasons, Rain, Ice, Hail and Snow MILT. *P.L.* x. 1063. 2. Pope Clement the fift, was i. and cruell 1621. Hence **Incle·ment-ly** *adv.*, **-ness.**

Inclinable (inkləi·năb'l), *a.* 1449. [a. OF. *enclinable*, f. *encliner*, later *incliner*, ad. L. *inclinare*; see INCLINE *v.* and -ABLE.] **1.** Having a (mental) leaning in some direction; inclined, disposed 1494. **2.** Favourably disposed; favourable; amenable 1449. **3.** Having a tendency to some physical quality, character, condition, or action 1607. **4.** Capable of being inclined 1766.

1. Of a Noble Nature, and i. to mercy FELTHAM. Too i. for factions 1654. 2. An argument that the nabob is i. to the French W. HASTINGS. 3. His Hair i. to Red 1683. Hence †**Incli·nableness.** †**Incli·nably** *adv.*

Inclination (inklinēⁱ·ʃən). 1483. [ad. F., ad. L. *inclinationem*, f. *inclinare* to INCLINE.] **I. 1.** The action or an act of inclining. †**b.** Decantation, or tilting a vessel for pouring -1758. **2.** The fact or condition of being inclined; deviation from the normal vertical or horizontal position or direction; leaning or slanting position; slope, slant 1530. **b.** The amount of slope or deviation from the horizontal position 1799. **c.** *Dialling.* The amount by which the plane of an inclining dial deviates from the vertical 1593. **d.** The dip of the magnetic needle. Hence *attrib.* in *i.-chart*, etc. 1678. **3.** *gen.* (chiefly in *Geom.*) The direction of a line, surface, or body, with respect to another line, surface, or body which has a different direction; the difference of direction of two lines, etc. regarded as tending towards each other; usually, the amount of such difference measured by the *angle of inclination*. In *Astron.* occas. *spec.* the position of the plane of a planet's orbit in relation to that of the ecliptic, measured by the angle between them 1570.

1. A courteous i. of the head 1850. 2. b. The drain has an i. of one foot in 100 yards 1799.

II. 1. The action of inclining, bending, or directing the mind to something. ? *Obs.* 1509. **2.** Disposition, propensity ME.; liking, affection 1647; †natural disposition; nature, character -1713. **3.** Formerly, the general character or nature (of a thing); now only as *fig.* from prec. 1593. **4.** *transf.* An action or practice to which one is inclined 1526; †a person for whom one has a liking -1712.

2. Each his several way Pursues, as i. or sad choice Leads him perplext MILT. *P.L.* II. 524. 3. The whole i. of the War depending on him 1653. 4. Thieving is a very prevalent i. among them MORSE. Jack had, of late, been her i. ARBUTHNOT.

III. *Gr.* and *L. Gram.* The throwing of the accent of an enclitic upon the last syllable of the word to which it is attached 1842.

Inclina·tional, *a. rare.* 1821. [f. prec. + -AL.] **a.** Relating to inclination to the horizon 1879. **b.** Of or pertaining to mental disposition.

Inclinatory (inkləi·nătəri), *a.* ? *Obs.* 1613. [f. L. *inclinat-, inclinare* to INCLINE + -ORY.] Relating to or characterized by inclination or dip. *I. needle* = DIPPING-NEEDLE. Hence **Incli·natorily** *adv.*

Incline (inkləi·n, i·nˌkləin), *sb.* 1600. [f. the vb.] †**1.** = INCLINATION II. 2. **2.** An inclined plane or surface; a slope, declivity; an inclined roadway along which mineral is conveyed 1846.

Incline (inklәi·n), *v.* [ME. *encline*, a. OF. *encliner*, f. (ult.) L. *inclinare* to bend inwards or towards; see IN-[2].]

I. *trans.* 1. To bend or bow (the head, the body, etc.) towards a person or thing, and hence forward or downward. †Also *fig.* 2. To give a tendency to (a person, the mind, will, etc.); to dispose ME. 3. To cause to lean; to slope, tilt 1590; †to direct (something immaterial) towards a particular object –1626. 4. *Gr.* and *L. Gram.* To cause (a dependent word) to lean its accent upon the preceding word (see ENCLITIC *a.*) 1751.

1. Thou oughtest to enclyne and bowe thy kne CAXTON. Enclyne thine eares to me COVERDALE *Ps.* xvi[i]. 6. 2. Such advice as God shall i. him.. to propound MILT. 3. Just as the Twig is bent, the Tree's inclin'd POPE. Oure God..hath enclyned mercy vnto vs COVERDALE *Ezra* ix. 9.

II. *intr.* 1. To bend the head or body forward or downward; to bow. ?*Obs.* ME. 2. *fig.* To bow, submit, yield *to*; to condescend; to accede (*to*) 1440. 3. To turn in mind, etc. in a given direction; to apply oneself (*to*). (Now mostly with mixture of next.) ME. 4. To have a mental leaning towards something; to be disposed or inclined ME. 5. To slope, slant, bend downwards. Const. *to, towards*. 1568. b. *Dialling.* Said of a dial the plane of which leans forwards; opp. to *recline* 1593. 6. *gen.* To have an oblique position or direction, so as to make angles with something else 1553. b. *Mil.* To move in a direction at angles with the front, so as to gain ground to the flank while advancing 1796. 7. *fig.* To have a tendency, tend (*to*) 1509; to have some quality in an incipient degree 1589.

2. To enclyne to theyr desyre MORE. 3. To..i. to virtue 1580. 4. Their hearts inclined to follow Abimelech: for they said, He is our brother *Judg.* ix. 3. 6. A course directly East, or inclining to the side of the South PURCHAS. 7. Victory inclined to the side of the allies GIBBON. He was stout and well-built, inclining to corpulence MARRYAT.

Inclined (inklәi·nd), *ppl. a.* ME. [f. INCLINE *v.* + -ED[1].] 1. Leaning or falling away from the vertical or horizontal; sloping, slanting 1541; making an angle with something else (const. *to*) 1813. 2. Disposed; in the mood or mind for something ME. †3. Having a particular disposition, character, or nature –1616.

1. Phr. *Inclined plane*, a material plane surface inclined at an acute angle to the horizon, constituting one of the mechanical powers. 2. Every Ryver to the see Enclyned ys to goo by kynde CHAUCER. *Dishonestly i., well-inclined.*

Incliner (inklәi·nәɹ). 1609. [f. as prec. + -ER[1].] One who or that which inclines; an inclining dial.

Inclining (inklәi·niŋ), *vbl. sb.* ME. [f. as prec. + -ING[1].] 1. A bending forward or downward; a bowing of the head or body; a slope, declivity. †Also *fig.* 2. Tendency, bent ME.; party, following (*Obs.* or *arch.*) 1604.

2. Hold your hands Both you of my i. and the rest SHAKS.

Inclinometer (inklinǫ·mǐtәɹ). 1842. [irreg. f. L. *inclinare* + -METER; cf. DECLINOMETER.] An instrument for measuring the vertical intensity of the earth's magnetic force, as shown by the inclination or dip of the magnetic needle.

Inclip (inkli·p), *v. arch.* 1608. [f. IN-[1] + CLIP *v.*[1]] *trans.* To clasp, enclose.

What ere the Ocean pales, or skie inclippes SHAKS.

Incloister, var. of ENCLOISTER *v.*

Inclose (inklōu·z), *v.* ME. Var. form of ENCLOSE, being the legal and statutory form, in reference to the inclosing of common and waste lands; still occas. in other senses; see ENCLOSE.

Inclosure (inklōu·ʒʼŭɹ, -ʒәɹ). 1517. Var. form of ENCLOSURE, being the statutory form in reference to the inclosing of waste lands, commons, etc. Formerly also in other senses.

Your letter..with the i., was duly received 1776. The I. Commissioners for England and Wales 1845.

Incloude, -owd, obs. ff. ENCLOUD.

Include (inklū·d), *v.* ME. [ad. L. *includere*, f. *in-* (IN-[2]) + *claudere*.] 1. *trans.* To shut or close in; †to shut up, confine. Now only in *pass.* Also *fig.* b. To enclose (in an area) 1662. 2. To contain, comprise, embrace: a. as a member of an aggregate, or a constituent part of a whole ME.; b. as a subordinate element, corollary, or secondary feature 1526. 3. To place in a class or category; to embrace in a general survey; to reckon in a calculation, etc. 1560. †4. To bring to a close. SHAKS.

1. He [Ashmole] shew'd me a toade included in amber EVELYN. b. It was after included in its circuit STILLINGFL. 2. a. Dispersed are the glories it included SHAKS. It includes..the Pie, Jay, Nutcracker, etc. BEWICK. b. The losse of such a Lord, includes all harmes SHAKS. 3. Men of feeble parts..are not to be included in this number 1794. 4. *Two Gent.* v. iv. 160. Hence **Inclu·dible, -able** *a.* capable of being included.

Included (inklū·dėd), *ppl. a.* 1552. [f. prec. + -ED[1].] Shut in, enclosed, contained, comprised. b. *Bot.* Said of parts (esp. the style or stamens) which do not protrude beyond the corolla 1847.

Including (inklū·diŋ), *ppl. a.* 1670. [-ING[2].] 1. That includes (see the vb.). 2. Often = Inclusive of. (Syntactically, it agrees sometimes with the word for the group previously (or afterwards) mentioned, but oftener with an indef. pron. *one, we, you* understood.) 1853.

2. These premises..were..in the occupation of several other warehousemen, i. Mr. T. Tapling 1864. Hence **Inclu·dingly** *adv.* 1449.

Inclu·se. *Obs.* exc. *Hist.* ME. [ad. L. *inclusus, includere.*] A. *adj.* Enclosed. B. *sb.* An anchorite. So †**Inclu·se** *v. trans.* to enclose, shut up.

Inclusion (inklū·ʒәn). 1600. [ad. L. *inclusionem*, f. *includere* to INCLUDE.] 1. The action of including; the fact or condition of being included; an instance of this. 2. *concr.* That which is included; *spec.* in *Min.*, A gaseous or liquid substance, or a small body, contained in a crystal or a mineral mass 1839.

1. In this Kingdome the name of Frenchman hath by i. comprehended all kind of Aliens SELDEN.

Inclusive (inklū·siv), *a.* (*sb.*) 1515. [ad. med.L. *inclusivus*, f. *inclus-, includere* to INCLUDE: see -IVE. Cf. F. *inclusif, -ive.*] 1. Including, enclosing, comprehending 1594; comprehensive 1601; characterized by including or taking in, as opp. to excluding or leaving out 1651. †2. Characterized by being included in something else –1735. 3. quasi-*adv.* = INCLUSIVELY 2. 1515. 4. *sb.* An inclusive proposition or particle 1533.

1. The inclusiue Verge Of Golden Mettall, that must round my Brow SHAKS. Phr. *I. terms, payment*, etc.: such as include all accessory payments. *I. of*, including or embracing. 3. From Monday till Saturday i. 1873. Hence **Inclu·siveness.**

Inclusively (inklū·sivli), *adv.* 1578. [f. prec. + -LY[2].] 1. In a way that includes; so as to include or be included. 2. With inclusion of the term or limit mentioned; one or both extremes being included 1597.

†**Incoa·ched**, *ppl. a.* Also **en-**. 1599. [f. IN-[2] + COACH + -ED[1].] Conveyed in a coach or carriage –1618.

†**Inco,a·cted**, *a. rare.* [f. L. *incoactus* + -ED[1].] Uncompelled, unconstrained. HALE.

Incoagulable (inko,æ·giŭlăb'l), *a.* 1667. [IN-[3].] Not coagulable; incapable of coagulation.

Inco,ale·scence. *rare.* 1846. [IN-[3].] Non-coalescence.

†**Inco·cted**, *a.* 1645. [f. L. *incoctus* + -ED[1] 2.] Uncooked, raw; hence, indigestible –1657. So †**Inco·ctible** *a.* 1684.

Incoercible (inko,ɔ̄·ɹsĭb'l), *a.* 1710. [IN-[3].] 1. That cannot be coerced, restrained, or overpowered by force 1756. 2. That cannot be confined; volatile 1710. †b. Incapable of being liquefied by pressure; formerly said of some gases 1861.

Incoexistence (in,kōu,ėgzi·stěns). [IN-[3].] Absence of coexistence; the fact of not existing together. LOCKE.

Incoffin (inkǫ·fin), *v.* 1570. [IN-[2].] *trans.* To enclose in, as in, or like, a coffin.

Incog (inkǫ·g). 1700. [Colloq. abbrev. of INCOGNITO, INCOGNITA.] A. *adj.* = INCOGNITO, INCOGNITA *adjs.* 1705. B. *adv.* = INCOGNITO *adv.* C. *sb.* = INCOGNITO *sb.*, INCOGNITA *sb.*[1]

Incogitable (inkǫ·dʒităb'l), *a.* 1522. [ad. late L. *incogitabilis*; see IN-[3] and COGITABLE.] Unthinkable, inconceivable. Hence **Incogitabi·lity** (*rare*), the quality of being i.

†**Inco·gitance.** *rare.* 1637. [f. as next; see -ANCE.] = next –1659.

†**Inco·gitancy.** 1612. [ad. L. *incogitantia*, f. *incogitantem*; see next.] 1. Want of thought or reflection; thoughtlessness; inadvertence –1759. 2. Want of the faculty of thought –1673.

1. Infirmities..are, vsually, sins of incogitancie 1612.

Incogitant (inkǫ·dʒitănt), *a.* 1628. [ad. L. *incogitantem*, f. *in-* (IN-[3]) + *cogitans, cogitare* to think.] That does not think; thoughtless; without the faculty of thought.

A light i. young man 1679. Hence **Inco·gitantly** *adv.*

Incogitative (inkǫ·dʒitĕ[i]tiv), *a. rare.* 1690. [IN-[3].] Unthinking; without the faculty of thought.

A mere, bare, pure, i. Matter CLARKE. Hence **Inco·gitati·vity** (*rare*), the quality of being i.

‖**Incognita** (inkǫ·gnită), *a.* and *sb.*[1] 1668. [It., fem. of *incognito* unknown.]

A. *adj.* Of a female: Unknown or disguised; having one's identity unavowed.

She would go to Naples *incognita* 1884.

B. *sb.* 1. An unknown or disguised woman; one whose identity is not made known 1718. 2. Unknown or unavowed character (of a woman) 1882.

2. The Queen will not assume her i. until [etc.] 1882.

‖**Inco·gnita**, *sb.*[2] *pl.* 1846. [L., adj. neut. pl.] Unknown things or places.

†**Inco·gnite**, *a.* 1609. [ad. L. *incognitus.*] Unknown –1678.

Inco·gnitive, *a.* [IN-[3].] Destitute of the faculty of cognition. F. HALL.

‖**Incognito** (inkǫ·gnito), *a., adv., sb.* Pl. -**ti** (-tī). 1638. [It. *incognito* adj., adv., ad. L. *incognitus.*]

A. *adj.* Unknown; whose identity is concealed or unavowed; concealed under a disguised or assumed character 1649.

A Fool is very troublesome, when he Presumes he is I. 1676.

B. *adv.* With one's real name, title, or character undisclosed or disguised; used esp. in reference to royal or dignified personages who wish not to be openly recognized 1649.

'Twas long ago Since Gods came down *Incognito* PRIOR.

C. *sb.* 1. An unknown man; one who conceals his identity 1638. 2. The condition of being unknown, anonymity; fictitious character; disguise.

2. Few writers would have preserved their i. so long 1874.

Incognizable, -isable (inkǫ·gni-, -kǫ·nizăb'l), *a.* 1767. [IN-[3].] Not cognizable; incapable of being known, perceived, or apprehended; incapable of recognition.

On life's incognisable sea M. ARNOLD.

Incognizance (inkǫ·gni-, -kǫ·nizăns). 1856. [IN-[3].] Want of knowledge or recognition.

Incognizant (inkǫ·gni-, -kǫ·nizănt), *a.* 1837. [IN-[3].] Not cognizant; without knowledge or apprehension *of*; unaware, unconscious *of*.

A man..is never altogether incognisant..of himself FERRIER.

Incognoscible (inkǫgnǫ·sĭb'l), *a.* 1691. [IN-[3].] Unknowable, beyond cognizance. Hence **Incognoscibi·lity**, the quality or condition of being i.

Incoherence (inkohīә·rěns). 1611. [IN-[3].] 1. *lit.* Want of cohesion 1672. 2. Want of connexion; incompatibility, incongruity of subjects or matters 1665. 3. Want of coherence in thought or language; incongruity, inconsistency. Also with *an* and *pl.* 1611.

1. The..shale..from its i. has been denuded for the most part MURCHISON. 3. A Petition fraught with Nonsense and I., Confusion and Impertinence SOUTH. This mythic theory is a mass of incoherences 1859. So **Incohe·rency** (in senses 2, 3).

Incoherent (inkohīә·rěnt), *a.* 1626. [IN-[3].] 1. Without physical coherence or cohesion; unconnected, disjoined, loose 1695. Also *transf.* and *fig.* 2. Of abstract things, actions, thought, language, etc.: Consisting of incongruous parts; not logically connected or unified; inconsistent, uncoordinated; disjointed 1626.

3. Incapable of cohering or coalescing; naturally different; incongruous 1643.

2. An i. fortuitous system, governed by chance BERKELEY. She muttered an i. sentence 1791. **3.** His armour was patched up of a thousand i. pieces SWIFT. Hence **Incohe·rent-ly** *adv.*, **-ness** (*rare*).

Incohesive (inkohī·siv), *a.* 1846. [IN-[3].] Not cohesive.

Incoincident (inko,i·nsidĕnt), *a.* 1636. [IN-[3].] Not coinciding; not necessarily existing together; not identical. Hence **Inco,i·ncidence**, want of coincidence or agreement.

†**Incolu·mity.** 1533. [a. OF. *incolumité*, ad. L. *incolumitas*, f. *incolumis* safe, sound; see -TY.] Safety, soundness, freedom from danger -1672.

Incomber, obs. var. of ENCUMBER.

†**Incombi·ning**, *a.* [IN-[3].] Not combining; incompatible. MILT.

Incombustible (inkǫmbʊ·stĭb'l), *a.* (*sb.*) 1460. [See IN-[3] and COMBUSTIBLE.] **1.** Incapable of being burnt or consumed by fire. **2.** *sb.* That which is incombustible 1807.

1. An infusible and i. substance, as chalk or magnesia 1874. Hence **Incombustibi·lity, Incombu·stibleness.**

Income (i·nkǫm), *sb.*[1] ME. [f. IN *adv.* + COME *v.*; cf. INCOME *v.*] **1.** Coming in, entrance, arrival, advent; beginning. Now *rare.* **b.** *spec.* Spiritual influx or communication. (Now *Obs.* or *rare.*) 1647. †**2.** A fee paid on coming in; entrance-money -1712. †**3.** A new-comer, immigrant -1804. †**4.** Something added or incidental -1602. **5.** *spec.* That which comes in as the periodical produce of one's work, business, lands, or investments (commonly expressed in terms of money); annual or periodical receipts accruing to a person or corporation; revenue. Formerly also in *pl.* = Receipts, profits 1601. *National income*, the income of a nation as a whole.

1. Pain pays the i. of each precious thing SHAKS. **b.** The pure Incomes of his holy Life..flow in upon them R. BARCLAY. **5.** No Fields afford So large an I. to the Village Lord DRYDEN. The incomes of the poor clergy GEO. ELIOT. *attrib.* **Income bonds,** bonds of a corporation or company, the interest of which is not cumulative, secured by a lien upon the net income of each year, after payment of prior charges.

Income (i·nkʊm), *sb.*[2] *Sc.* and *n. dial.* 1808. [f. IN *adv.* + COME. Cf. ANCOME.] A morbid affection of any part of the body, a swelling, impostume, or the like.

†**Inco·me**, *v.* [OE. *incuman*; a collocation of IN *adv.* + COME *v.* Now repl. by *come in.*] *intr.* To come in, enter -1565.

Incomer (i·nkʊ:məɹ). 1514. [f. IN *adv.* + COMER.] One who comes in; opp. to *outgoer*; also *spec.* **a.** a visitor, immigrant, or foreign resident; **b.** an intruder; an invader; **c.** a successor; **d.** *Sport.* a bird that flies towards the sportsman.

I·ncome-tax. 1799. [INCOME *sb.*[1] 5.] A tax levied in some countries on incomes.

In Great Britain first introduced as a war-tax in 1799; re-introduced in 1842, and maintained since. Assessed at a rate annually fixed by Parliament. The existing income-tax..certainly is a tax that should not be retained a moment after it can be dispensed with McCULLOCH.

Incoming (i·nkʊ:miŋ), *vbl. sb.* ME. [f. IN *adv.* + COMING *vbl. sb.*] **1.** The action or fact of coming in; entrance; arrival. (Opp. to *outgoing.*) **2.** = INCOME *sb.*[1] 5. (Usu. in *pl.*) 1596.

1. The i. of spring 1825. **2.** The nominal incomings are 900 *l.* (*mod.*).

I·ncoming, *ppl. a.* 1753. [f. IN *adv.* + COMING *ppl. a.*] That comes in or enters; also *spec.* **a.** succeeding; **b.** immigrant; **c.** coming in as profit; **d.** (of a period of time) about to begin.

†**Incomme·nd,** *v.* 1574. [IN-[2].] = COMMEND *v.* 1 -1621.

In commendam: see COMMENDAM.

Incommensurable (inkǫme·nsiŭrăb'l, -ʃŭr-), *a.* (*sb.*) 1557. [ad. med.L. *incommensurabilis*; see IN-[3] and COMMENSURABLE.] **1.** *Math.* Not commensurable; having no common measure (integral or fractional). Said of two or more quantities or magnitudes, or of one in relation to another; also sometimes *absol.* = incommensurable with ordinary or rational quantities, as the natural numbers 1570. **b.** (in *Arith.*) Having no (integral) common measure except unity 1557. **2.** *gen.* Having no common standard of measurement 1660. **b.** *spec.* Not worthy to be measured *with*; utterly disproportioned to 1799. **3.** *sb.* An incommensurable quantity, etc.; usu. in *pl.* 1741.

1. That the Diameter of every Square is I. with the Sides CUDWORTH. **2. b.** Solutions, which I still dismissed as i. with the facts 1892. Hence **Incomme·nsurabi·lity, Incomme·nsurableness** (*rare*) i. quality. **Incomme·nsurably** *adv.*

Incommensurate (inkǫme·nsiŭrĕt, -ʃŭr-), *a.* 1650. [IN-[3].] **1.** Not commensurate; not of corresponding measure or degree; out of proportion, inadequate. Const. *with, to.* 1684. †**b.** Disproportioned. BULWER. **2.** = INCOMMENSURABLE 1687.

1. Power, unfortunately, i. with good will 1856. **2.** Difficulty and doubt are i. J. H. NEWMAN. Hence **Incomme·nsurate-ly** *adv.*, **-ness.**

Incommiscible (inkǫmi·sib'l), *a.* *rare.* 1620. [IN-[3].] Incapable of being mixed together. Hence **Incommiscibi·lity.**

†**Incommi·xed, -mi·xt,** *a.* 1513. [IN-[3].] Not mixed together, or with something -1660. So †**Incommi·xture,** unmixed condition.

†**Inco·mmodate,** *v.* 1555. [f. L. *incommodat-*, *incommodare*; see INCOMMODE *a.*] = INCOMMODE *v.* -1693. So †**Inco·mmodate** *ppl. a.* incommoded. **Incommoda·tion** (now *rare*), inconvenience.

†**Incommo·de,** *a.* (*sb.*) 1518. [a. F., ad. L. *incommodus*; see IN-[3] and COMMODE *a.*] **1.** = INCOMMODIOUS 1, 4. -1771. **2.** *sb.* An inconvenience. WOLSEY.

Incommode (inkǫmōᵘ·d), *v.* 1598. [a. F. *incommoder*, ad. L. *incommodare.*] **1.** *trans.* To subject to inconvenience or discomfort; to trouble, annoy, molest, embarrass. **2.** To hinder, impede, obstruct (an action, etc.) 1702.

1. At first, the confinement of a chamber incommoded us W. IRVING. So †**Incommo·dement,** condition of being incommoded.

Incommodious (inkǫmōᵘ·diəs), *a.* 1551. [IN-[3].] **1.** Causing inconvenience or discomfort; troublesome, disagreeable. †**2.** Hurtful, injurious -1655. †**3.** Unprofitable, unfit, unsuitable; unbefitting -1714. **4.** Of places, etc.: Not convenient for shelter, travelling, etc.; inconveniently small, narrow, etc.; uncomfortable 1615.

1. Their life is nothing hard or i. 1551. **4.** An i. port POPE, prison HOWARD. Hence **Incommo·dious-ly** *adv.*, **-ness.**

Incommodity (inkǫmǫ·dĭti). ME. [a. F. *incommodité*, ad. L. *incommoditas*; see INCOMMODE *a.* and -ITY.] **1.** Incommodious quality, condition, or state of things; inconvenience, disadvantage, discomfort. **2.** With *pl.* An incommodious thing or circumstance ME.

1. Moche teene and incommodité Foloweth age 1500. **2.** The Incommodities and Commodities of Vsury BACON.

Incommunicable (inkǫmiū·nikăb'l), *a.* 1568. [IN-[3].] **1.** Not communicable; incapable of being imparted or shared 1577. **2.** Incapable of being told or uttered; ineffable, unspeakable 1664. **3.** Not communicative 1568. **4.** Not in communication (with others or with each other); without intercourse 1646.

1. The i. power of the crown 1760. **3.** Terrible judges, seuere, intractable, collerick, i. NORTH. **4.** The two worlds..were not i. GROTE. Hence **Incommu·nicabi·lity, Incommu·nicableness,** the quality of being i. **Incommu·nicably** *adv.*

†**Incommu·nicated,** *ppl. a.* 1646. [IN-[3].] Not communicated; that is without communication -1664. So **Incommu·nicating** *a.* not communicating, without communication. †**Incommunica·tion,** absence of communication or imparting 1611.

Incommunicative (inkǫmiū·nikĕtiv), *a.* 1670. [IN-[3].] Not communicative; not disposed for intercourse or conversation; uncommunicative.

A silent and i. sort of character HAWTHORNE. Hence **Incommu·nicative-ly** *adv.*, **-ness.**

Incommutable (inkǫmiū·tăb'l), *a.* 1450. [ad. L. *incommutabilis.* In sense 2 f. IN-[3] + COMMUTABLE.] **1.** Not changeable; not liable to alteration; immutable. **2.** Not commutable; unexchangeable 1775.

1. The giver of a perfect and i. law CHALMERS. Hence **Incommutabi·lity, Incommu·tableness. Incommu·tably** *adv.*

Incompact (inkǫmpæ·kt), *a.* 1616. [IN-[3].] Not compact; loosely put together; of loose consistency. Also *transf.* and *fig.*

transf. The empire of the Czars being already i. and vast LANDOR. Hence **Incompa·ct-ly** *adv.*, **-ness.**

Incompa·cted, *a.* 1680. [IN-[3].] Incompact.

Incomparable (inkǫ·mpărăb'l), *a.* (*adv.*, *sb.*) ME. [a. F.; see IN-[3] and COMPARABLE.] **1.** With which there is no comparison; matchless, peerless, transcendent. **2.** Not to be compared (*with* or *to*) 1614.

1. She was afterwards his i. wife FULLER.

†**B.** *adv.* Incomparably -1664.

C. *sb.* An incomparable person or thing 1704.

Such a succession of incomparables PENN. Hence **Inco·mparabi·lity, Inco·mparableness,** the quality of being i. **Inco·mparably** *adv.* ME.

†**Incompa·red,** *a.* [IN-[3].] Unmatched. SPENSER.

†**Incompa·ssion.** 1625. [IN-[3].] Absence of compassion or pity -1675.

†**Incompa·ssionate,** *a.* 1611. [IN-[3].] Not compassionate; void of compassion or pity -1679. Hence †**Incompa·ssionate-ly** *adv.*, †**-ness.**

Incompatible (inkǫmpæ·tĭb'l), *a.* (*sb.*) 1563. [ad. med.L. *incompatibilis* (said of benefices); see IN-[3] and COMPATIBLE.] Not compatible. **1.** Of benefices, etc.: Incapable of being held together. **2.** Mutually intolerant; incapable of existing together in the same subject; discordant, incongruous, inconsistent 1592. †**3.** Unable to 'get on' together; at variance -1722. †**4.** Irreconcilable -1635. **5.** *sb.* An incompatible person or thing 1711.

2. The use of the shield is i. with that of the bow GIBBON. He felt that to be a politician and a preacher of righteousness was to combine two vocations practically i. 1871. Hence **Incompatibi·lity, Incompa·tibleness. Incompa·tibly** *adv.*

Incompetence (inkǫ·mpĭtĕns). 1663. [a. F. *incompétence*; after INCOMPETENT.] †**1.** Inadequacy. **2.** The fact or condition of being incompetent; want of the requisite ability, power, or qualification; incapacity 1716. **3.** Of a logical conclusion: Want of legitimacy; faultiness 1837.

2. I. of the aortic and mitral valves 1876. **3.** The competence or i. of any Conclusion SIR W. HAMILTON.

Incompetency (inkǫ·mpĭtĕnsi). 1611. [f. prec. or next; see -ENCY.] **1.** The quality of being incompetent; = INCOMPETENCE 2. Also, with *pl.*, an instance of this. **2.** Legal incapacity or disqualification 1650. **3.** Logical illegitimacy 1837.

1. [The] utter i. of the bishops PRIESTLEY. **2.** The testator's alleged i. to enter into the agreement 1833.

Incompetent (inkǫ·mpĭtĕnt), *a.* (*sb.*) 1597. [a. F. *incompétent*, ad. late L. *incompetentem*; see IN-[3] and COMPETENT.] †**1.** Inadequate -1823. **2.** Of inadequate ability or fitness; not having the requisite capacity or qualification; incapable. Rarely of things. 1635. **3.** Not legally competent or qualified 1597. **4.** Logically illegitimate 1835. **5.** *sb.* An incompetent person 1866.

1. A purse i. to this demand LAMB. **2.** The Nabob, who was totally i. to his own defence JAS. MILL. **3.** Subjects..judges i. To judge their king DANIEL. **5.** A dauber, an i., not fit to be a sign-painter STEVENSON. Hence **Inco·mpetent-ly** *adv.*, **-ness.**

†**Incompe·tible,** *a.* 1513. [f. IN-[3] + COMPETIBLE.] **1.** Incompetent. **2.** Not competible; not within one's competence or capacity; not properly applicable *to*; inappropriate. 1533. Occas. confused with *incompatible.* -1684.

Puffed vp with incomparable and i. Titles of Learning BP. MOUNTAGU. Hence †**Incompetibi·lity,** incompetency, incapacity.

Incomplete (inkǫmplī·t), *a.* ME. [ad. L. *incompletus*; see IN-[3] and COMPLETE.] Not complete; not fully formed, made, or done; not whole or thorough; wanting some part; unfinished, defective.

It pleaseth him in mercy to account himself i. and maimed without us HOOKER. *Incomplete flower*, a flower wanting one or more of the normal parts (calyx, corolla, stamens, or pistils). *I. metamorphosis* (in insects, etc.), imperfect metamorphosis. Hence **Incomple·te-ly** *adv.*, **-ness.**

Incomple·tion. 1804. [IN-³.] Incomplete condition.

Incomplex (inkǫ·mpleks, *formerly* inkǫ̆mple·ks), *a.* 1658. [ad. late L. *incomplexus*; see IN-³ and COMPLEX.] Not complex; not involved; simple. Hence †**Incomple·xly** *adv.*

†**Incompli·able,** *a.* 1625. [IN-³.] Not able or ready to comply or act in concord; unconformable -1664.

Incompliance (inkǫ̆mpləi·ǎns). Now *rare.* 1655. [IN-³.] †1. Want of conformity. †2. Unaccommodating disposition; want of complaisance -1805. 3. Failure to comply; non-compliance 1708.

2. A martial man..is apt to have a tincture of sowerness and incomplyance in his behaviour COLLIER.

Incompliant (inkǫ̆mpləi·ǎnt), *a.* Now *rare.* 1647. [IN-³.] Not compliant. 1. Not yielding to the desires or requests of others; unaccommodating 1707. 2. Of things: a. Incompatible. b. Unpliant, unyielding. 1647. Hence **Incompli·ancy** (*rare*), i. character. **Incompli·antly** *adv.*

†**Incompo·rtable,** *a.* [IN-³.] Not to be borne. NORTH.

†**Incomposed** (inkǫ̆mpōu·zd), *a.* 1608. [IN-³; cf. L. *incompositus.*] 1. Not composite; simple, uncompounded -1683. 2. Wanting in composure or orderly arrangement; disordered; agitated, discomposed 1608. 3. Indisposed (*to*) 1660.

2. The Anarch old With faultring speech and visage incompos'd MILT. *P. L.* II. 989. †**Incompo·sed·ly** *adv.* 1612, †**-ness.**

Incomposite (inkǫ·mpǒzit), *a.* (*sb.*) 1677. [ad. L. *incompositus*; see IN-³ and COMPOSITE.] 1. Not composite; simple, uncompounded. As *sb.* Something uncompounded. 2. Not properly composed or put together 1879.

1. *Incomposite number* (Arith.): a prime number. ? *Obs.*

Incompossible (inkǫ̆mpǫ·sĭb'l), *a.* Now *rare.* 1605. [ad. schol.L. *incompossibilis*; see IN-³ and COMPOSSIBLE.] Not possible together; that cannot exist or be true together; wholly incompatible or inconsistent.

To adopt the Hamiltonian word, the two Judgments are i. BOWEN. Hence **Incompossibi·lity,** i. quality; also, with *pl.*, an instance of this.

†**Incompo·sure.** 1644. [IN-³.] Discomposure, disorder -1706.

†**Incomprehe·nse,** *a.* [ad. L. *incomprehensus.*] Not comprehended within limits; boundless. MARSTON.

Incomprehensible (i:nkǫmprĭhe·nsĭb'l), *a.* (*sb.*) ME. [ad. L. *incomprehensibilis*; see IN-³ and COMPREHENSIBLE.] 1. That cannot be contained within limits. (Chiefly *Theol.*) *arch.* 2. That cannot be grasped by the understanding; beyond the reach of intellect. *Obs.* or *arch.* exc. as in b. ME. b. That cannot be understood; inconceivable, unintelligible 1604. †3. That cannot be grasped (physically); impalpable (*rare*) -1745. 4. *sb.* An incomprehensible being or thing (in sense 1 or 2) 1548.

1. The father i., the sonne i.: and the holy ghost i. *Athan. Creed.* The Firmament..And all her numberd Starrs, that seem to rowle Spaces i. MILT. *P. L.* VIII. 20. 2. b. She was perfectly i. to me DICKENS. 4. That notion..is nothing but a bundle of incomprehensibles CUDWORTH. Hence **Incomprehensibi·lity, Incomprehe·nsibleness. Incomprehe·nsibly** *adv.*

Incomprehension (i:nkǫmprĭhe·nʃən). 1605. [IN-³.] The fact of not grasping with the mind; want of comprehension; failure to understand.

Our ignorance and i. of the least things in Nature GALE.

Incomprehensive (i:nkǫmprĭhe·nsiv), *a.* 1652. [IN-³.] 1. Not comprehensive; not understanding. 2. Not inclusive 1774. †3. Incomprehensible -1791. Hence **Incomprehe·nsive·ly** *adv.*, **-ness.**

Incompressible (inkǫ̆mpre·sĭb'l), *a.* 1730. [IN-³.] That cannot be compressed or squeezed into smaller compass; incapable of compression. Also *fig.*

Liquids in general are treated in hydrostatics as i. bodies LARDNER. Hence **Incompressibi·lity,** the quality of being i.

†**Inco·mpt,** *a.* 1631. [ad. L. *incom(p)tus* unadorned, rough.] Void of neatness; inelegant -1669. Hence †**Inco·mptness.**

Incomputable (inkǫ̆mpiū·tăb'l, inkǫ·mpiutăb'l), *a.* 1606. [IN-³.] That cannot be computed.

†**Inconcea·lable,** *a.* [IN-³.] That cannot be concealed. SIR T. BROWNE.

Inconceivable (inkǫ̆nsī·văb'l), *a.* (*sb.*) 1631. [IN-³.] 1. That cannot be conceived or realized in the imagination; unthinkable. Often merely = 'hardly credible', 'extraordinary'. 2. *spec.* As a philosophical term.

(*a*) Opposed to the fundamental laws of thought, self-contradictory. (*b*) Repugnant to recognized axioms or laws of nature. (*c*) Involving a combination of facts which appears incredible. (*d*) Incapable of being represented by a mental image 1655.

1. With an i. dexterity 1646. 2. What is i. or contradictious, is nothing at all to us H. MORE. Power without substance is inconceiveable REID. The i. qualities of space 1875. Hence **Inconceivabi·lity,** the quality of being i.; something that is i. **Inconcei·vableness. Inconcei·vably** *adv.*

B. *sb.* A thing or quality that cannot be conceived 1706.

†**Inconce·ptible,** *a.* [IN-³.] Inconceivable. HALE.

†**Inconce·rning,** *a.* *rare.* 1642. [IN-³.] That does not matter; unimportant -1650.

†**Inconci·liable,** *a.* *rare.* Also **-cilable, -cileable.** 1643. [f. IN-³ + CONCILIABLE.] Incapable of being conciliated; irreconcilable -1694.

†**Inconci·nn, -e,** *a.* *rare.* 1660. [f. IN-³ + CONCINNE.] Not adjusted or adapted; incongruous -1678. So †**Inconci·nnate** *a.* awkward; not adapted; unsuitable 1533. †**Inconci·nnately** *adv.* inelegantly.

Inconci·nnity. *Obs.* or *arch.* 1616. [ad. L. *inconcinnitas*; see INCONCINN and -ITY.] Want of concinnity; inelegance; impropriety, unsuitableness.

†**Inconci·nnous,** *a.* 1662. [f. L. *inconcinnus* + -OUS.] 1. Incongruous. 2. *Mus.* Inharmonious -1811.

†**Inconclu·dent,** *a.* 1671. [f. IN-³ + CONCLUDENT.] = next. So †**Inconclu·dency** 1654.

†**Inconclu·ding,** *a.* 1644. [IN-³.] Inconclusive -1677.

Inconclu·sion. 1847. [IN-³.] The condition of reaching no conclusion; an inconclusive result.

Inconclusive (inkǫ̆nklū·siv), *a.* 1690. [IN-³.] 1. Not conclusive in argument or evidence; that does not bring to an end (a doubt, dispute, etc.); not decisive. b. Given to inconclusion. SIR H. TAYLOR. 2. Not conclusive in action 1841.

1. Long and i. debates..on the legality of a Papal abdication MILMAN. 2. The i. nature of his Indian operations 1841. Hence **Inconclu·sive·ly** *adv.*, **-ness.**

†**Inconco·ct,** *a.* 1596. [IN-³.] = next -1626.

†**Inconco·cted,** *a.* 1605. [IN-³.] Not concocted; not fully digested or matured; not softened by ripening; raw -1677.

†**Inconco·ction.** 1626. [IN-³.] The fact or condition of being unconcocted or undigested.

Inconcre·te. *a.* Now *rare.* 1626. [ad. late L. *inconcretus*; see IN-³ and CONCRETE.] Not concrete; abstract; immaterial.

†**Inconcu·rrent,** *a.* 1651. [IN-³.] Not concurrent. So †**Inconcu·rring** *a.* 1646.

†**Inconcu·ssible,** *a.* Also **-able.** 1589. [a. obs. F. *inconcussible*, f. *in-* (IN-³) + L. *concuss-*, *concutere*; see -IBLE.] That cannot be shaken; firmly fixed, stable -1715.

Incondensable (inkǫ̆nde·nsăb'l), *a.* Also *erron.* **-ible.** 1736. [f. IN-³ + CONDENSABLE.] That cannot be condensed; incapable of being made more dense or compact; *spec.* incapable of being reduced to the liquid or solid condition. Hence **Incondensabi·lity** (*erron.* **-ibility**), i. quality.

Incondite (inkǫ·ndit), *a.* 1539. [ad. L. *inconditus*, f. *in-* (IN-³) + *conditus*, *condere* to put together.] 1. Ill constructed, ill composed: said esp. of literary and artistic compositions 1634. 2. Unformed; rude, unpolished, unrefined 1539.

1. An i. collection..of..rules AUSTIN. 2. The Negresses..forgot themselves..and were altogether i. KINGSLEY. Hence **Inco·nditely** *adv.*

†**Incondi·tional,** *a.* [IN-³.] Unconditional. SIR T. BROWNE.

Inconditionate (inkǫ̆ndi·ʃənět), *a.* (*sb.*) 1654. [IN-³; cf. F. *inconditionné.*] 1. Not limited by conditions; unconditioned. 2. *sb.* (*Philos.*) An entity which is unconditioned; a form under which the Unconditioned is conceived 1829.

1. The power of Government..is..not i. 1654. 2. The Unconditioned and the species, or Inconditionates which it contains—viz., Absolute and Infinite VEITCH.

†**Inconfi·rmed,** *a.* [IN-³.] Not become firm or strong. SIR T. BROWNE.

†**Inconfo·rm,** *a.* 1659. [IN-³.] Not conformed *to* -1663. So **Inconfo·rmable** *a.* not conformable; unconformable 1612. †**Inconfo·rmist** = NONCONFORMIST.

Inconformity (inkǫ̆nfǭ·ɹmĭti). 1594. [IN-³.] Want of conformity. b. *spec.* = NONCONFORMITY 1633.

Inconfused (inkǫ̆nfiū·zd), *a.* 1626. [IN-³; cf. L. *inconfusus.*] Not confused; free from mixture of the elements.

†**Inconfu·sion.** [IN-³.] Unconfused condition. BACON.

†**Inconfu·table,** *a.* [IN-³.] Not confutable. PENN. Hence †**Inconfu·tably** *adv.* 1664.

Incongealable (inkǫ̆ndʒī·lăb'l), *a.* ? *Obs.* 1623. [IN-³.] Incapable of being congealed.

†**Incongе·nerous,** *a.* [IN-³.] Not of the same kind; the opposite of CONGENEROUS. SIR T. BROWNE.

Incongenial (inkǫ̆ndʒī·niăl), *a.* 1797. [IN-³.] Not congenial; uncongenial. Hence **Incongenia·lity.**

Incongruent (inkǫ·ŋgru,ěnt), *a.* 1531. [ad. L. *incongruentem*; see IN-³ and CONGRUENT.] Not congruent; disagreeing, unsuitable, incongruous. Hence **Inco·ngruence, Inco·ngruency** (? *Obs.*), want of congruence; incongruity. **Inco·ngruently** *adv.*

Incongruity (inkǫ̆n,grū·iti). 1532. [ad. med.L. *incongruitas*; see IN-³ and CONGRUITY.] 1. The quality, condition, or fact of being incongruous; want of accordance or harmony; inconsistency. Also with *an* and *pl.* 1610. 2. Want of accordance with what is reasonable or fitting; unsuitableness, inappropriateness, absurdity. Also with *an* and *pl.* 1597. 3. Want of harmony of parts or elements; incoherence. Also with *an* and *pl.* 1532. †4. *Gram.* Grammatical incorrectness; solecism -1612.

1. Such I. and Nonconformity in their furniture MARVELL. 2. Without i...we cannot speak of geometrical beauty JOHNSON. 3. The i. of the clerk's apparel SCOTT.

Incongruous (inkǫ·ŋgru,əs), *a.* 1611. [f. L. *incongruus* (see IN-³ and CONGRUOUS) + -OUS.] Not congruous. 1. Disagreeing in character or qualities; not in keeping; discordant, inconsistent, inharmonious, unsuited. Const. *with, to.* (Often with a mixture of sense 2.) 2. Unbecoming, unsuitable, inappropriate, absurd, out of place 1623. 3. Not self-consistent; incoherent 1658. †4. *Gram.* Grammatically incorrect -1678. 5. *Theory of Numbers.* Of two numbers: Not congruent; giving different remainders when divided by the modulus (see CONGRUENCE 3) 1864.

1. The cart way of the village divides..two very i. soils G. WHITE. 2. How i. and irrational the common Temper of Mankind is DE FOE. 3. Of all human characters a fanatic philosopher is the most i. H. WALPOLE. Hence **Inco·ngruous·ly** *adv.*, **-ness.**

†**Inconjunct** (inkǫ̆ndʒʌ·ŋkt), *a.* 1603. [IN-³.] Not in conjunction; *spec.* in *Astrol.*, said of two planets or their positions when neither affects the operation of the other -1819.

Inconne·cted, *a.* *rare.* 1732. [IN-³.] Not connected; disconnected. Hence **Inconne·ctedness.**

Inconnexion, -ection (inkǫ̆ne·kʃən). ? *Obs.* 1620. [IN-³.] Want of connexion; unconnectedness; an instance of this.

Insconscient (inkǫ·nʃiěnt), *a.* *rare.* 1885. [IN-³.] Unconscious.

Whether you believe that Creation was the work of design or of i. law LD. SALISBURY.

†**Inco·nscionable,** *a* 1596. [IN-³.] Not having, or not regarding, conscience; uncon-

scionable -1800. Hence †Inco·nscionableness. †Inco·nscionably *adv.*

Inconscious (inkǫ·nʃəs), *a.* Now *rare.* 1670. [f. late L. *inconscius* + -OUS.] †1. Not privy to some deed. MILT. 2. Not conscious; unconscious 1678. Hence **Inco·nsciously** *adv.*

Inconsecutive (inkǫnse·kiŭtiv), *a.* 1836. [IN-[3].] Not consecutive; inconsequent. Hence **Inconse·cutive·ly** *adv.*, **-ness.**

Inconsequence (inkǫ·nsĭkwĕns). 1588. [ad. L. *inconsequentia*, f. *inconsequentem.*] 1. Want of logical sequence; inconclusiveness, illogicalness; an instance of this. 2. Want of natural connexion of ideas, actions, or events; an irrelevant action or circumstance 1842. 3. The practice or habit of drawing inconsequent inferences, or of speaking or acting disconnectedly 1817. †4. The being of no consequence -1812.

1. Mr. S. himself could not but see the i. of his own argument GATAKER. 3. That mingling of i. which belongs to us all, and not unhappily GEO. ELIOT. So †**Inco·nsequency.**

Inconsequent (inkǫ·nsĭkwĕnt), *a.* (*sb.*) 1579. [ad. L. *inconsequentem*; see IN-[3] and CONSEQUENT.] 1. Not following as a logical conclusion; falsely inferred 1627. b. Not following in the natural order of events; irrelevant 1881. 2. Wanting in logical reasoning; involving erroneous inference 1579; disconnected, inconsecutive; irrelevant 1869. 3. *transf.* Of a person: Characterized by inconsequence 1794. 4. Of no consequence (*rare*). STERNE. †5. *sb.* An illogical inference; a *non sequitur.* PRYNNE.

1. His illation from thence deduced [is] i. HAKEWILL. 2. Confused thought and i. reasoning 1877. 5. A meer i. 1643. Hence **Inco·nsequent·ly** *adv.*, **-ness** (*rare*).

Inconsequential (inkǫnsĭkwe·nʃăl), *a.* 1621. [IN-[3].] = INCONSEQUENT. Hence **Inconsequentia·lity**, i. quality or character. **Inconseque·ntially** *adv.*

Inconsiderable (inkǫnsi·dərăb'l), *a.* 1598. [a. F. *inconsidérable.*] Not considerable. †1. Incalculable (*rare*) -1631. 2. Not to be considered; beneath notice; insignificant 1637. b. Hence, of very small value, amount, or size 1648. †3. Inconsiderate, thoughtless (*rare*) -1726.

2. I never heard of the fellow. He is i. 1658. b. I. sums 1654. An i. stream MORSE. I. in numbers 1812. Hence **Inconsi·derableness**, i. quality. **Inconsi·derably** *adv.*

†**Inconsi·deracy.** *rare.* 1748. [f. INCONSIDERATE; see -ACY.] Inconsiderateness -1847. So †**Inconsi·derance** (*rare*) 1549.

Inconsiderate (inkǫnsi·dərĕt), *a.* (*sb.*) 1450. [ad. L. *inconsideratus*; see IN-[3] and CONSIDERATE.] 1. Not properly considered; thoughtless, unadvised, precipitate, rash. 2. Of persons, etc.: Acting without deliberation; thoughtless, imprudent, indiscreet 1595. 3. Without consideration for others 1842. †4. Of no importance -1703. 5. *sb.* An inconsiderate or thoughtless person 1588.

1. Sauls i. and rash oath 1612. 2. The i. multitude MILT. They are younger and more i. JOWETT. 3. Of an i. temper 1842. So **Inconsi·derate·ly** *adv.* 1460, **-ness. Inconsi·dered** *a.* (in sense 1).

Inconsideration (inkǫnsidərē¹·ʃən). 1526. [a. F., or ad. late L. *inconsiderationem.*] 1. Want of consideration; indiscretion. 2. Absence of consideration for others 1872.

1. Faults of i. and thoughtlessness JANE AUSTEN. 2. [Nature's] merciless i. for the individual where the interests of the Race are in question W. R. GREG.

Inconsistence (inkǫnsi·stĕns). Now *rare* or *Obs.* 1643. [f. INCONSISTENT (after *consistence*); see -ENCE.] = INCONSISTENCY.

Inconsistency (inkǫnsi·stĕnsi). 1647. [f. as prec. (after *consistency*); see -ENCY.] 1. Want of consistency; lack of accordance or harmony (*with* something, or *between* things); incompatibility, contrariety, opposition 1699. 2. Want of agreement between two things or parts of a thing; a discrepancy, an incongruity 1647. 3. Of persons: Want of consistency in thought or action; an inconsistent act 1665.

1. The i. of our Religion with Magic ADDISON. 2. Nor is there any i. in wise and good fathers having foolish..sons JOWETT. 3. I.—the only thing in which men are consistent HOR. SMITH. The inconsistencies of which Pitt had been guilty MACAULAY.

Inconsistent (inkǫnsi·stĕnt), *a.* (*sb.*) 1646. [IN-[3].] Not consistent. 1. Of a substance: Without consistence; of incoherent nature (*rare*) 1677. 2. Not consisting; not agreeing in substance, spirit, or form; not in keeping; at variance, discordant, incompatible, incongruous 1646. 3. Wanting in harmony; self-contradictory; involving inconsistency 1651. 4. Of a person: Not consistent in thought or action. Const. *with*, †*to*, or *absol.* 1709. 5. *sb.* (*pl.*) Things, statements, etc. which are inconsistent with each other or with something else 1652.

1. The parts..of dust [are] i. RUSKIN. 2. Resentment is not i. with good-will BUTLER. 4. You..are i. with your own principles *Junius Lett.* *absol.* Thoughtless, thankless, i. man! YOUNG. Hence **Inconsi·stent·ly** *adv.*, **-ness** (*rare*).

Inconsolable (inkǫnsōu·lăb'l), *a.* 1596. [ad. L. *inconsolabilis*; see IN-[3] and CONSOLABLE.] Not admitting of consolation; that cannot be consoled, alleviated, or assuaged.

I. woe 1862. Still i. for his loss C. BRONTË. Hence **Inconso·labi·lity, Inconso·lableness**, i. condition. **Inconso·lably** *adv.*

Inconsolate (inkǫ·nsŏlĕt), *a.* *rare.* 1656. [IN-[3].] Unconsoled, disconsolate. Hence **Inco·nsolately** *adv.*

Inconsonant (inkǫ·nsŏnănt), *a.* 1658. [IN-[3].] Not consonant or agreeable *to*, †*unto*; not agreeing *with*.

A Fiction utterly i. to the whole Method of Nature HALE. Hence **Inco·nsonance,** †**Inco·nsonancy** (*rare*) 1650, want of consonance or agreement. **Inco·nsonantly** *adv.*

Inconspicuous (inkǫnspi·kiu,əs), *a.* 1624. [f. late L. *inconspicuus* + -OUS; see IN-[3] and CONSPICUOUS.] †1. That cannot be seen or discerned -1793. 2. Not readily seen; not prominent or striking 1828.

2. Small and i. flowers 1845. **Inconspi·cuous·ly** *adv.*, **-ness.**

†**Inco·nstance.** ME. [a. F., ad. L. *inconstantia*, f. *inconstantem* INCONSTANT: see -ANCE.] = INCONSTANCY -1712.

Inconstancy (inkǫ·nstănsi). 1526. [ad. L. *inconstantia*; see prec. and -ANCY.] Want of constancy. 1. Fickleness; changeableness; an instance of this. 2. Mutability; irregularity; absence of uniformity 1613. †3. Inconsistency (in statements, etc.); an instance of this -1605.

1. Lightnesse and inconstancie in love SPENSER. 2. The silent Moone..constant image of the worlds inconstancie PURCHAS.

Inconstant (inkǫ·nstănt), *a.* (*sb.*) ME. [a. F., ad. L. *inconstantem*: see IN-[3] and CONSTANT.] Not constant. 1. Not steadfast; fickle, changeable. 2. Of things: Frequently changing; variable, irregular 1526. 3. *sb.* An inconstant person or thing 1647.

1. The fickle, i., volatile temper of the people 1844. 2. Th' i. Moone, That monethly changes SHAKS. 3. Let us eliminate the inconstants RUSKIN. Hence **Inco·nstant-ly** *adv.*, †**-ness.**

Inconsumable (inkǫnsiū·măb'l), *a.* 1646. [IN-[3].] 1. Not consumable by fire, etc. 2. *Pol. Econ.* Not consumable in use 1785.

2. The i. things, like machinery, leather, coin 1884. Hence **Inconsu·mably** *adv.*

†**Inconsu·mmate,** *a.* *rare.* 1641. [ad. late L. *inconsummatus.*] Not consummated or completed; unfinished -1695.

†**Inconsu·mptible,** *a.* 1579. [ad. late L. *inconsumptibilis.*] Incapable of being consumed -1708. So †**Inconsu·mptive** 1513.

Inconta·minate, *a.* 1508. [ad. L. *incontaminatus.*] Uncontaminated, undefiled.

Incontestable (inkǫnte·stăb'l), *a.* Also *erron.* **-ible.** 1673. [a. F., f. *in-* (IN-[3]) + *contestable.*] That cannot be contested or disputed; unquestionable, incontrovertible.

I. proof 1748, beauty SCOTT, evidence 1885. Hence **Inconte·stabi·lity**, i. quality. **Inconte·stableness. Inconte·stably** *adv.*

†**Inconte·sted,** *a.* 1712. [IN-[3].] Undisputed -1794.

†**Inconti·guous,** *a.* *rare.* 1660. [f. late L. *incontiguus* + -OUS.] Not in contact; unconnected -1685. Hence †**Inconti·guously** *adv.*

Incontinence (inkǫ·ntinĕns). ME. [a. F., or ad. L. *incontinentia*; see IN-[3] and CONTINENT *a.*] 1. Want of continence or self-restraint; inability to contain or restrain: a. Unchastity. b. *gen.* (Const. *of.*) 1836. 2. *Path.* Inability to retain a natural evacuation 1754.

1. b. [They] do not waste themselves by i. of tongue CARLYLE. So †**Inco·ntinency** 1485.

Incontinent (inkǫ·ntinĕnt), *a.* (*sb.*) ME. [a. F., or ad. L. *incontinentem*; see IN-[3] and CONTINENT.] 1. Not continent; wanting in self-restraint, esp. with reference to sexual appetite. 2. Unable to contain or retain. Usu. with *of.* 1641. 3. Unable to retain natural evacuations. WEBSTER. 4. *sb.* An unchaste person. B. JONS. Hence **Inco·ntinently** *adv.*[1] in an i. manner.

Incontinent (inkǫ·ntinĕnt), *adv.* *arch.* ME. [a. F., ad. late L. *in continenti* (sc. *tempore*) in continuous time, without any interval.] Straightway, at once, immediately.

The Lords will be here i. SCOTT. So **Inco·ntinently** *adv.*[2] 1484.

Inconti·nuous, *a.* *rare.* 1862. [IN-[3].] Not continuous. So **Incontinu·ity.**

Incontrollable (inkǫntrōu·lăb'l), *a.* 1599. [IN-[3].] 1. That cannot be controlled; uncontrollable. †2. That cannot be interfered with; fixed, unchangeable -1646. †3. Incontrovertible -1646. Hence **Incontro·llably** *adv.*

Incontrovertible (inkǫntrǫvə̄·ɹtib'l), *a.* 1646. [IN-[3].] That cannot be controverted; indisputable. Hence **Incontrovertibi·lity, Incontrove·rtibleness. Incontrove·rtibly** *adv.*

Inconvenience (inkǫnvī·niĕns), *sb.* ME. [a. OF. *inconvenience* (mod. *inconvenance*), ad. late L. *inconvenientia* inconsistency, f. *inconvenientem* INCONVENIENT: see -ENCE.] The fact or quality of being inconvenient. †1. Want of agreement; inconsistency with reason or rule, absurdity; an instance of this -1706. †b. Unsuitableness -1684. †2. Moral unsuitableness; unseemly behaviour; impropriety; also with *an* and *pl.* -1560. †3. Harm, injury, mischief; misfortune, trouble. †Also with *an* and *pl.* -1796. 4. Want of adaptation to personal ease; discomfort; incommodity. Also with *an* and *pl.* 1578.

2. They fall..sometime from hot words to further i. *Homilies.* 3. Rapine, ruine, and a thousand inconveniences, follow ARMIN. 4. She could have spared him without the smallest i. DICKENS. Hence **Inconve·nience** *v.* to cause i. to; to put to i.; to incommode. So **Inconve·niency** = INCONVENIENCE.

Inconvenient (inkǫnvī·niĕnt). ME. [a. F. *inconvénient*; see IN-[3] and CONVENIENT.]

A. *adj.* †1. Not agreeing or consonant; incongruous; absurd -1674. †2. Unsuitable, inappropriate, out of place -1840. †3. Morally unsuitable; unseemly, improper -1694. 4. Unfavourable to comfort; incommodious, embarrassing, disadvantageous, awkward 1651.

2. If it appeare not inconuenient to you *A. Y. L.* v. ii. 73. 4. A good choice of i. lodgings DICKENS.

†B. *sb.* That which is inconvenient -1658.

Hence **Inconve·nient·ly** *adv.*, †**-ness** (*rare*).

Inconversable (inkǫnvə̄·ɹsăb'l), *a.* ? *Obs.* Also *erron.* **-ible.** 1577. [f. IN-[3] + CONVERSE *v.* + -ABLE.] Not conversable; †unsociable; uncommunicative.

Inconversant (inkǫ·nvəɹsănt), *a.* *rare.* 1679. [IN-[3].] Not conversant; not versed *in* or familiar *with*.

†**Inconve·rted,** *a.* [IN-[3].] Not turned or changed; unconverted. SIR T. BROWNE.

Inconvertible (inkǫnvə̄·ɹtib'l), *a.* 1646. [IN-[3].] 1. Incapable of being changed into anything else; †*spec.* indigestible. 2. Not interchangeable. Usu. of terms: Not equivalent. 1706. b. *Logic.* Of a proposition: That cannot be converted 1864. 3. Not exchangeable for something else. *spec.* of paper money, That cannot be converted into specie. 1833.

3. I. bank paper would have been everywhere refused 1833. Hence **Inconvertibi·lity, Inconve·rtibleness. Inconve·rtibly** *adv.*

Inconvincible (inkǫnvi·nsĭb'l), *a.* 1674. [IN-[3].] Incapable of being convinced; not open to conviction.

None are so i. as your half-witted people 1674. Hence **Inconvincibi·lity. Inconvi·ncibly** *adv.* 1646.

†**Inco·ny,** *a.* 1588. [A cant word that rimed with *money*. Origin unkn.] ? Rare, fine, delicate, pretty, nice. *L. L. L.* III. i. 136. -1633.

Incoordinate (inkoₗǭ·ɹdinĕt), *a.* 1889. [IN-[3].] Not co-ordinate. So **Incoo·rdinated**; **Incoordina·tion**, want of co-ordination; esp in *Phys.* in reference to muscular action (see CO-ORDINATION) 1876.

†**Inco·rd,** *v. rare.* 1611. [ad. It. *incordare.*] *Incordare,* ..to incord or burst as a horse FLORIO. So †**Inco·rded** *ppl. a.* (of a horse) ruptured; suffering from hernia 1607. †**Inco·rding** *vbl. sb.* rupture or hernia in a horse 1598.

†**Inco·rnished,** *ppl. a. rare.* [f. IN-² + *cornish* CORNICE + -ED; after It. *incorniciare.*] Furnished with a cornice or cornices. EVELYN.

Incoronate (inkǫ·rǒnĕt), *a.* 1867. [ad. It. *incoronato*; cf. CORONATE.] Wearing or having a crown; crowned. So **Incorona·tion,** coronation, crowning 1470.

Inco·rporable, *a.* 1607. [f. L. *incorporare* + -ABLE.] Capable of being incorporated.

†**Inco·rporal,** *a.* (*sb.*) 1551. [ad. L. *incorporalis*; see IN-³ and CORPORAL.] **1.** = INCORPOREAL; immaterial –1646. **2.** *sb.* An incorporeal thing or place. CUDWORTH. Hence †**Inco·rporality,** the quality of being incorporeal. †**Inco·rporally** *adv.* immaterially.

Inco·rporate, *a. rare.* 1540. [ad. rare L. *incorporatus* not embodied; see IN-³ and CORPORATE.] Without body or material substance; unembodied.

Incorporate (inkǭ·ɹpŏrĕt), *ppl. a.* ME. [ad. late L. *incorporatus*; see the vb.] **1.** United in one body (*lit.* and *fig.*). Now *rare.* **2.** Of a company, etc.: Formally constituted as a corporation. Also of persons; United in a corporation. 1480. †**b.** Associated with others, as members of the same corporation –1684. **3.** Having a bodily form ME.

1. It is Caska, one i. To our Attempts SHAKS. 2. b. The Welshmen our neighbours, or rather our i. countrimen CAMDEN. 3. Ideals never yet i. GEO. ELIOT.

Incorporate (inkǭ·ɹpŏreit), *v.* ME. [f. late L. *incorporat-, incorporare*; see IN-² and CORPORATE *v.*]

I. *trans.* **1.** To combine or unite into one body or substance; to mix or blend thoroughly together (a number of things or one thing *with* another). Also *fig.* 1544. **2.** To put into or include in the body or substance of something else; to embody, include ME. **b.** To include as a part or parts of itself (*esp.* of literary material) 1824. **3.** To combine into a society or organization; *esp.* to constitute as a legal corporation 1460. **b.** To admit (a person) as member of a company or association 1530. **4.** To furnish with a body; to embody (*rare*) 1623.

1. A melted Cement, made of Pitch, Rosin, and Wood-ashes, well incorporated BOYLE. *transf.* You shall not stay alone, Till holy Church i. two in one SHAKS. 2. b. The best edition, incorporating all the works of the author DIBDIN. 3. b. Yesterday was incorporated A. M. Mr. Stevens HEARNE.

II. *intr.* **1.** Of one thing: To unite or combine with something else so as to form one body. Const. *with,* occas. *into.* 1594. **2.** Of two or more things: To unite so as to form one body; to grow into each other; to form an intimate union (*lit.* and *fig.*). ? *Obs.* 1625.

1. Grace can no more i. with sin, than oyle with water FLAVEL. 2. Truth and Falshood..may Cleaue, but they will not I. BACON. Hence **Inco·rporated** *ppl. a.* in senses of the vb.; †embodied 1644; constituted as a legal or formal corporation 1677. **Inco·rporating** *ppl. a.*; as *I. union* (said orig. of the Union between England and Scotland in 1707).

Incorporation (inkǭɹpŏrē·ʃən). ME. [ad. late L. *incorporationem.*] **1.** The action of incorporating; the being incorporated. **b.** *Philol.* The combination of two or more parts of speech in one word. SAYCE. **2.** The action of forming into a community or (legal) corporation 1460. †**b.** The document creating or legalizing a corporation; a charter –1605. **3.** An incorporated society or company 1530. **4.** Embodiment (*rare*) 1645.

1. The i. of two independent legislatures 1812. 2. The Patent for the I. of the Parish Clerks 1640. 3. An eminent member of the Goldsmiths' I. SCOTT.

Incorporative (inkǭ·ɹpŏrĕtiv), *a.* 1592. [f. INCORPORATE *v.* + -IVE.] Characterized by or tending to incorporation.

Incorporator (inkǭ·ɹpŏreitəɹ). 1670. [f. as prec.] **1.** One who incorporates, or combines into one body or substance 1829. **2.** One who takes part in the formation of an incorporated company; one of the original members of an incorporated company 1670. **3.** A member of one University who is incorporated in another 1887.

Incorporeal (inkǫɹpōᵊ·rĭăl), *a.* (*sb.*) 1532. [f. L. *incorporeus* (Macrobius) + -AL.] Not corporeal. **1.** Having no material structure; not composed of matter; immaterial. **2.** Of, pertaining to, or characteristic of immaterial beings 1667. **3.** *Law.* Having no material existence in itself, but attaching as a right or profit to some actual thing; esp. *i. hereditament* 1628. **4.** *sb.* (*pl.*) Things incorporeal 1628.

1. Two active i. principles, heat and cold HALLAM. 2. MILT. *P.L.* VIII. 37. 3. Property called i., such as an annuity BENTHAM. Hence †**Incorpo·realism,** the doctrine that i. spirit or substance exists. †**Incorpo·realist,** one who holds this view. **Incorporea·lity. Incorpo·really** *adv.*

Incorporeity (inkǭɹpŏrī·iti). 1601. [ad. med.L. *incorporeitas,* f. L. *incorporeus*; see -ITY.] The quality of being incorporeal; immateriality; with *pl.,* an incorporeal quality.

Incorpsed (inkǭ·ɹpst), *a. rare.* 1602. [f. IN-² + CORPSE + -ED².] Made into one body (with something).

Incorrect (inkǫre·kt), *a.* 1432. [ad. L. *incorrectus*; see IN-³ and CORRECT.] †**1.** Uncorrected; unchastened –1602. **2.** Of a book: Containing many scribal or typographical errors 1484. **3.** Not in conformity with a recognized standard; faulty 1672. **4.** Not in accordance with fact; erroneous, inaccurate 1828.

1. *Haml.* I. ii. 95. 3. The Wit of the last Age was yet more i. than their Language DRYDEN. A practice that was considered i. 1883. 4. An i. statement, narration or calculation 1828. Hence **Incorre·ct-ly** *adv.,* **-ness.**

†**Incorre·ction.** *rare.* 1598. [IN-³; cf. F. *incorrection.*] **1.** The action of making incorrect. **2.** The condition of being uncorrected 1649. **3.** Incorrectness, faultiness. H. WALPOLE.

Incorrespo·ndence. *rare.* 1667. [IN-³.] Want of correspondence or harmony. So **Incorrespo·ndency** (*rare*).

†**Incorrespo·ndent,** *a. rare.* 1599. [IN-³.] Not in agreement or harmony –1667. So **Incorrespo·nding** *a.*

Incorrigible (inkǫ·ridʒĭb'l), *a.* (*sb.*) ME. [a. F.; see IN-³ and CORRIGIBLE.] **1.** Bad beyond correction or reform. †**2.** Of something faulty: That cannot be set right. Of disease: Incurable. –1804. **3.** *sb.* One who is incorrigible 1746.

1. An habituated, infatuated, i., cauterized Drunkard 1655. 2. An i. ulcer ABERNETHY. Hence **Inco·rrigibi·lity, Inco·rrigibleness. Inco·rrigibly** *adv.*

Incorro·dible, *a.* 1855. [IN-³.] Incapable of being corroded.

Incorro·sive, *a. rare.* 1871. [IN-³.] Having no tendency to corrosion.

Incorrupt (inkǒrɒ·pt), *a.* Now *rare.* ME. [ad. L. *incorruptus*; see IN-³ and CORRUPT *a.*] Not corrupt; free from corruption. **1.** Of organic matter: Free from decomposition or putrefaction; not decayed; not infected with decay. **2.** Not debased or perverted; pure, sound 1550. **b.** Of a text, etc.: Not affected by error or corruption. 1624. **3.** Morally uncorrupted; pure in life; *esp.* not to be bribed into wrong-doing 1545.

2. The first churche of the Apostles..was moste pure and incorrupte CRANMER. 3. The most juste and i. juge 1545. So †**Incorru·pted** *a.* (in all senses). Hence **Incorru·pt-ly** *adv.,* **-ness.**

Incorruptible (inkǒrɒ·ptĭb'l), *a.* (*sb.*) ME. [a. F.; see IN-³ and CORRUPTIBLE.] **1.** Not corruptible; that cannot decay or perish; everlasting, eternal. **2.** That cannot be perverted or bribed 1667. **3.** *sb.* (*pl.*) An ancient Christian sect, the Aphthartodocetæ, who maintained the incorruptibility of the body of Christ 1727.

1. The deed shall ryse i. TINDALE 1 *Cor.* XV. 52. 2. Suppos'd Not i. of Faith, not prooff Against temptation MILT. *P. L.* IX. 298. Hence **Incorruptibi·lity, Incorru·ptibleness. Incorru·ptibly** *adv.*

Incorruption (inkǒrɒ·pʃən). *arch.* 1526. [a. F.; see IN-³ and CORRUPTION.] **1.** Freedom from physical corruption. Now *arch.* and only in reference to 1 Cor. XV. 42, etc. †**2.** Freedom from corrupt conduct –1677. †**3.** Of texts: Freedom from erroneous alterations –1662.

1. Hit is sowen in corrupcion and ryseth in incorrupcion TINDALE 1 *Cor.* XV. 42.

†**Incorru·ptive,** *a.* [IN-³.] Not liable to decay. AKENSIDE.

†**Incourse.** *rare.* 1440. [ad. L. *incursus,* after *concourse,* etc.] Running in; inrush; assault, attack –1668.

Incrassate (inkræ·sĕt), *a.* 1608. [ad. L. *incrassatus*; see next.] †**1.** Thickened (in consistence); condensed –1685. †**2.** *fig.* Of the mind: Dulled –1660. **3.** *Zool.* and *Bot.* Of a thickened or swollen form 1760.

3. Peduncle..I., thickened towards the Flower 1760.

Incrassate (inkræ·seit), *v.* 1601. [f. L. *incrassat-, incrassare,* f. *in-* (IN-²) + *crassare,* f. *crassus* CRASS.] **1.** *trans.* To thicken in consistence; to condense, inspissate. Now *rare.* Also *absol.* and †*intr.* †**2.** *fig.* To make gross (the mind, etc.); to dull –1666. **3.** To thicken in †sound or form 1668.

1. Liquors, which time hath incrassated into gellies SIR T. BROWNE. *intr.* These naturally subtile Parts ..i. and grow clumsy CHEYNE.

Incrassated (inkræ·seitĕd), *ppl. a.* 1657. [f. prec. + -ED¹.] Thickened. †**b.** Used as = aspirated –1691.

Incrassation (inkræsē·ʃən). 1633. [f. L. *incrassare.*] **1.** The action of incrassating, or condition of being incrassated; thickening; *concr.* a thickened formation 1822. †**2.** Phonetic thickening; aspiration. WILKINS.

Incrassative (inkræ·sătiv). ? *Obs.* 1666. [f. L. *incrassat-, incrassare* + -IVE.] **A.** *adj.* Having the quality of incrassating the 'humours'. **B.** *sb.* [sc. *medicine,* etc.]

Increasable (inkrī·săb'l), *a.* 1534. [f. INCREASE *v.* + -ABLE.] Capable of being increased.

A low quit-rent, i. at definite periods 1806. Hence **Increa·sableness. Increa·sably** *adv.*

Increase (i·nkrīs, *formerly* inkrī·s), *sb.* ME. [f. INCREASE *v.*]

I. The action of increasing. **1.** The action, process, or fact of becoming or making greater; augmentation, growth, enlargement, extension. †**b.** *spec.* The advance of daylight from sunrise to noon; the waxing of the moon –1665. **2.** The becoming numerous or more frequent; multiplication ME. **b.** *spec.* The multiplication of a family or race; the production of offspring; reproduction, procreation, propagation, breeding ME. †**3.** *spec.* Advancement, progress –1719.

1. As if encrease of Appetite had growne By what it fed on SHAKS. With i. of business came i. of expense 1870. b. Seeds will grow soonest..if they be Set..in the I. of the Moone BACON. 2. b. Drie vp in her the Organs of i. SHAKS. Phr. *On the increase*: becoming greater or more frequent.

II. †**1.** The result of increasing; an increased amount, addition, increment ME. **2.** Offspring, progeny, brood. Properly collective. 1552. **3.** Vegetable produce, crops (*arch.*). Also *transf.* and *fig.* 1535.

1. Thou wilt but adde encrease vnto my Wrath SHAKS. 2. And all the i. of thine house shall die in the floure of their age 1 *Sam.* ii. 33. 3. The teeming autumn, big with rich i. SHAKS. *transf.* Behold.. the Seas with her merveilous increse 1559. *fig.* Thou shalt not..lend him thy victuals for i. *Lev.* XXV. 37.

Increase (inkrī·s), *v.* [ME. *encres(se,* a. AF. *encres-, encress-* = OF. *encreis(s)-, encreistre,* later *encroistre* :—L. *increscere,* f. *in-* (IN-²) + *crescere* to grow. The *ea* represents ME. open *ē.*]

I. *intr.* **1.** To become greater in size, amount, duration, or degree; to wax, grow. Also with *in.* **2.** To grow in numbers, to multiply; *esp.* by propagation ME. **3.** To advance in wealth, fortune, power, influence, etc.; to thrive; to prosper. *Obs.* or *arch.* ME. **4.** *Lat. Gram.* Of a noun, etc.: To have one syllable more in the genitive 1612.

1. The Poo..That Estward ay encresseth in his cours CHAUCER. He..encreased in stature and in wisdom 1814. 2. And bad euery creature in his kynde encrees LANGL. 3. He must increase: and I muste decreace TINDALE *John* iii. 30.

II. *trans.* **1.** To cause to wax or grow; to make greater in amount or degree. Also with *in.* ME. **2.** To make more numerous, multiply ME. †b. To cause to yield increase. DRYDEN. 3. To make more wealthy, prosperous, or powerful; to cause to thrive; to promote. *Obs.* or *arch.* ME.

1. Thou shalt encrease the price thereof *Lev.* xxv. 16. 2. Take ye wiues..that ye may bee increased there *Jer.* xxix. 6. 3. Cicero..increased the latine tounge after another sorte ASCHAM. Hence **Increa·sedly** *adv.* (*rare*), in an increased degree. **Increa·singly** *adv.* more and more.

†Increa·seful, *a. rare.* 1593. [f. INCREASE *sb.* + -FUL.] Full of increase; productive, fruitful -1599.

Increasement (inkrī·sment). Now *rare.* ME. [f. INCREASE *v.* + -MENT.] 1. = INCREASE *sb.* I. 1, 2. 1509. 2. = INCREASE *sb.* II. 1-3.

Increaser (inkrī·səɹ). 1528. [f. INCREASE *v.* + -ER¹.] One who or that which increases (see the vb.).

Increate (inkrīˌeˈt), *a.* ME. [ad. med.L. *increatus.*] Not created, uncreated; said of divine beings or attributes.

Bright effluence of bright essence i. MILT. *P. L.* III. 6. So †**Increated** *ppl. a.* in same sense.

Incredible (inkre·dĭb'l), *a.* ME. [ad. L. *incredibilis*; see IN-³ and CREDIBLE.] 1. Not credible; that cannot be believed. b. In weakened sense: Inconceivable 1482. c. Of a person (*rare*). BENTHAM. †2. Unbelieving (*rare*) -1761.

1. Why should it be thought a thing i. with you, that God should raise the dead? *Acts* xxvi. 8. b. These stories do i. mischief BURKE. Hence **Incredibi·lity,** the quality or fact of being i.; that which is i. **Incre·dibleness. Incre·dibly** *adv.* in an i. manner or degree.

†Incre·ditable, *a.* 1695. [IN-³.] Discreditable. -1732.

†Incre·dited, *a.* 1633. [IN-³.] Disbelieved.

Incredulity (inkrĭdiū·lĭti). [Late ME., a. F. *incrédulité*, ad. L. *incredulitatem.*] 1. A disbelieving frame of mind; unwillingness to believe; disbelief. †2. Want of religious faith; unbelief -1619.

1. The i. of St. Thomas H. WALPOLE. 2. Either in the faith of Christ or..in i. 1560.

Incredulous (inkre·diŭləs), *a.* 1579. [f. L. *incredulus* + -OUS.] 1. Unbelieving; not ready to believe; sceptical. Not now used of religious unbelief. b. Of action, etc.: Indicating or prompted by incredulity 1613. †2. = INCREDIBLE -1750.

They call it philosophical to be i. on holy things LANDOR. b. I. smiles PURCHAS. 2. Miracles.. will be thought i. in this age 1631. Hence **Incre·dulous-ly** *adv.*, **-ness.**

†I·ncremable, *a. rare.* [f. IN-³ + L. *cremare* + -ABLE.] That cannot be consumed by fire; incombustible. SIR T. BROWNE.

Incremation (inkrĭmēˈ·ʃən). Now *rare* or *Obs.* 1826. [f. IN-² + CREMATION.] = CREMATION (now the usual word).

Increment (i·nkrĭment). ME. [ad. L. *incrementum*, f. stem of *increscere*; see INCREASE and -MENT.] 1. The action or process of becoming greater, or (with *pl.*) a case of this; increase, augmentation, growth. b. Advancement. *Obs.* or *arch.* 1609. c. The waxing of the moon; *spec.* in *Heraldry* 1610. d. *Rhet.* 'An ascending towards a climax' (= L. *incrementum* in Quintilian) 1753. 2. Amount of increase; an addition; an amount gained, profit 1631. b. *Math.* and *Phys.* A small (or sometimes infinitesimal) amount by which a variable quantity increases (*e.g.* in a given small time); *spec.* the increase of a function due to a small increase in the variable, as in the *Method of Increments*, now called the Calculus of Finite Differences (see DIFFERENCE *sb.*) 1721. 3. A quantity obtained from another by increase or addition. Const. *of.* (*rare.*) 1864.

1. We add daily increments to our knowledge and science KIRBY. d. *Increment*..4. (*Rhet.*) An amplification without strict climax, as in the following passage: 'Finally, brethren, whatsoever things are true..' Phil. iv. 8. WEBSTER. 2. *Unearned increment*: see UNEARNED. Hence **Increme·ntal** *a.* of or relating to an i. or increments.

†I·ncrepate, *v.* 1570. [f. L. *increpat-*, *increpare*, f. *in-* (IN-²) + *crepare* to make a noise, etc.] *trans.* To chide, rebuke, reprove -1657. So **Increpa·tion** (*Obs.* or *arch.*), chiding, reproof, rebuke; with *pl.* a reproof 1502.

Increscent (inkre·sĕnt). 1572. [ad. L. *increscentem*, *increscere*; see -ENT.]

A. *adj.* Increasing, becoming greater. Chiefly of the moon: Waxing, in her increment 1658.

B. *sb.* (Chiefly *Her.*) The moon in her increment, represented as a crescent with the horns towards the dexter side. (Opp. to *decrescent.*) So †**Incre·scence,** increase 1533.

†Incre·st, *v. rare.* Also **en-.** 1611. [f. IN-² + CREST *sb.*] *trans.* To adorn with or as with a crest -1616.

Incriminate (inkri·mineˈt), *v.* 1730. [See IN-² and CRIMINATE; cf. F. *incriminer.*] *trans.* To charge with a crime; to involve in an accusation or charge. So **Incrimina·tion** (*rare*), the action of incriminating; the fact or condition of being so incriminated 1651. **Incri·minator,** an accuser. LANDOR. **Incri·minatory** *a.* tending to i.

Incro·tchet, *v. rare.* Also **en-.** 1806. [f. IN-², EN-¹ + CROTCHET *sb.*] *trans.* To enclose within crotchets or brackets.

‖**Incroyable** (ęŋkrwayab'l). 1797. [F. *incroyable* incredible.] Name for the French fop or dandy of the period of the Directory.

†I·ncruent, *a. rare.* 1624. [ad. L. *incruentus.*] Bloodless; not attended with shedding of blood -1660. So †**Incrue·ntal,** †**Incrue·ntous** *adjs.*

Incrust, etc., var. of ENCRUST, **etc.**

Incrustate (inkrʊ·stĕt), *ppl. a.* 1626. [ad. L. *incrustatus*, f. *in-* (IN-²) + *crustare*, f. *crusta* CRUST.] †1. Formed or hardened into a crust -1731. 2. Enveloped with a crust. *Obs.* exc. *Bot.* 1671. 3. *Zool.* and *Bot.* Having the form of a crust, as a polyzoan or lichen; *spec.* of or pertaining to the *Incrustata*, a division of cyclostomatous Polyzoa.

Incrustate (i·nkrʊsteˈt), *v.* Now *rare.* Also **en-.** 1570. [f. L. *incrustat-*, *incrustare*; see prec.] 1. = ENCRUST 2. †2. In the arts: a. = ENCRUST 1. b. To attach as or like an incrustation. -1764.

Incrustation (inkrʊstēˈ·ʃən). Also **en-.** 1607. [ad. late L. *incrustationem.*] 1. The action of encrusting; the formation of a crust, the fact or condition of being encrusted 1656. 2. A facing of marble, mosaic, etc. on a building. †Also *fig.* 1607. 3. A crust or hard coating formed naturally on an object; *esp.* a calcareous or crystalline concretion or deposit 1671. Also *fig.* 4. A scab or eschar on the surface of a body 1656.

2. *fig.* The old popishe ceremonies..are, as it were, an I. both vnlawful and vnseemly 1607. 3. *fig.* Hidden under the incrustations of sense and evil habit J. MARTINEAU.

†Incry·stal, *v.* 1611. [f. IN-² + CRYSTAL *sb.*] 1. *trans.* (and *intr.*) To CRYSTALLIZE. 2. To enclose in crystal 1648.

2. The humour was..But lovers tears inchristalled HERRICK.

Incry·stallizable, *a. rare.* 1807. [IN-³.] Incapable of being crystallized; uncrystallizable.

Incubate (i·nkiubeˈt), *v.* 1641. [f. L. *incubat-*, *incubare*, f. *in-* (IN-²) + *cubare* to lie; see -ATE³.] 1. *trans.* To sit upon (eggs) in order to hatch them; to hatch (eggs) thus or by some equivalent process 1721. Also *fig.* 2. *intr.* To sit upon eggs, to brood 1755. Also *fig.* 3. a. *intr. Path.* Of a disease: To pass through the process of INCUBATION. b. *trans. Biol.* To place in an incubator (for developing bacteria). 1896.

Incubation (inkiubēˈ·ʃən). 1614. [ad. L. *incubationem*; see prec.] 1. The action of sitting on eggs in order to hatch them; the hatching of eggs by sitting on them 1646. Also *transf.* and *fig.* 2. *Path.* The process or phase through which the germs of disease pass between contagion or inoculation and the development of the first symptoms 1835. 3. *Gr. Antiq.* The practice of sleeping in a temple or sacred place for oracular purposes 1871. 4. *attrib.*, as *i.-period*, etc. 1858.

1. *fig.* He who, by his i. upon the waters of the creation, hatched that rude mass into the beautiful form we now see GURNALL. 2. Phr. *Period of i.*, the space of time occupied by this process, which varies greatly for different diseases. Hence **Incuba·tional** *a.*

Incubative (i·nkiubeˈtiv), *a.* 1835. [See INCUBATE and -IVE.] Of or pertaining to incubation, esp. the incubation of disease; characterized by incubation.

Incubator (i·nkiubeˈtəɹ). 1854. [a. L., f. *incubare.*] 1. A bird which incubates. Also *fig.* 1858. 2. An apparatus for hatching birds by artificial heat 1854. b. An apparatus for rearing children born prematurely. 3. An apparatus for the artificial development of bacteria 1896. 4. *fig.* and *transf.* A breeder, author, source 1864.

Incubatory (i·nkiubētəri), *a.* 1877. [See INCUBATE and -ORY.] Incubative.

†Incu·be, *v.* [f. IN-² + CUBE *sb.*] To infix like a cube. MILT.

†I·ncubee. A distortion of INCUBUS. B. JONS.

†Incu·biture. 1653. [f. L. *incubit-*, *incubare* + -URE.] = INCUBATION 1. -1743.

Incubous (i·nkiubəs), *a.* 1857. [f. L. *incubare* + -OUS.] *Bot.* Having the leaves so disposed that the tip of one leaf or other part lies flat over the base of the next above it.

‖**Incubus** (i·nkiubʊs). Pl. **-bi** (-bəi); also **-buses,** etc. ME. [late L. (Augustine) = cl.L. *incubo* nightmare.] 1. A feigned evil spirit or demon, supposed to descend upon persons in their sleep, and especially to seek carnal intercourse with women. In the Middle Ages, their existence was recognized by law. 2. The nightmare 1561. 3. A person or thing that weighs upon and oppresses like a nightmare 1648. 4. *Entom.* Name of a parasitic genus of hymenopterous insects.

1. Belial the dissolutest Spirit that fell The sensuallest, and after Asmodai The fleshliest I. MILT. *P. R.* II. 152. 3. The many years preaching of such an Incumbent, I may say, such an I. oft-times MILT. The i. of evil habits MCLAREN.

†Incu·lcate, *ppl. a.* 1608. [ad. L. *inculcatus*; see next.] Inculcated, taught -1653.

Inculcate (i·nkʊ̆lkeˈt, inkʊ·lkeˈt), *v.* 1550. [f. L. *inculcat-*, *inculcare* to stamp in, tread in, f. *in-* (IN-²) + *calcare*, f. *calc-*, *calx* heel.] *trans.* To endeavour to force (a thing) into or impress (it) on the mind of another by emphatic admonition, or by persistent repetition; to urge on the mind; to teach forcibly.

That commandement which Christ did so often i. vnto Peter HOOKER. An opinion..difficult to i. upon the minds of others 1802. Hence †**Inculcatedly** *adv.* by impressive repetition. **Inculca·tion,** the action of impressing on the mind by forcible admonition or frequent repetition. †**Incu·lcative** *a.* (*rare*), tending to i.; impressive. **Inculcator** (see the vb.), one who inculcates. **Incu·lcatory** *a.* (*rare*), fitted or tending to i.

†Incu·lk, *v.* 1528. [ad. L. *inculcare.*] = INCULCATE *v.* -1576.

†Incu·lp, *v.* [ad. L. *inculpare.*] = INCULPATE *v.* SHELTON.

Inculpable (inkʊ·lpăb'l), *a.* Now *rare.* 1491. [See IN-³ and CULPABLE.] Not culpable; free from blame.

Suche personages..whose lyues be i. ELYOT. Hence **Inculpabi·lity, Incu·lpableness,** blamelessness. **Incu·lpably** *adv.*

†Incu·lpate, *a. rare.* 1612. [ad. L. *inculpatus*, f. *in-* (IN-³) + *culpatus*, *culpare* to blame.] Unblamed, inculpable -1647.

Inculpate (i·nkʊlpeˈt, inkʊ·lpeˈt), *v.* 1799. [f. med.L. *inculpat-*, *inculpare*, f. *in-* (IN-²) + *culpare*; cf. *exculpate.*] 1. *trans.* To bring a charge against; to accuse; to blame. 2. To involve in a charge; to incriminate 1839.

1. We should be slow to i. motives 1833. 2. Attempting to exculpate himself and i. Dr. Nassau for [etc.] 1897. Hence **Inculpa·tion,** blame, censure, incrimination. **Incu·lpative, Incu·lpatory** *adjs.* tending to incriminate; attributing fault or blame.

Incult (inkʊ·lt), *a.* Now *rare.* 1599. [ad. L. *incultus.* Cf. F. *inculte.*] 1. Uncultivated, untilled 1621. 2. Unpolished, untrimmed, inartistic, rude. 3. Of persons, etc.: Wanting in culture; inelegant, rough, coarse 1621.

1. Germany then, saith Tacitus, was i. and horrid, now full of magnificent Cities BURTON. 2. His style is diffuse and i. 1851. 3. He is i., but clever 1862.

†Incu·ltivated, *a.* 1665. [IN-³.] Uncultivated; unpolished, rude -1716. So **Incultiva·tion** 1784.

†Incu·lture. *rare.* 1627. [IN-³.] Want of culture or cultivation -1867.

†**Incu·mbence.** 1677. [f. INCUMBENT; see -ENCE.] **a.** The fact of being incumbent. **b.** A matter that is incumbent; a duty or obligation. -1768.

Incumbency (inkʊ·mbĕnsi). 1608. [f. INCUMBENT; see -ENCY.] **1.** The condition of lying or pressing upon something; brooding; a spiritual overshadowing. Now *rare* or *Obs.* 1651. **b.** With *an* and *pl.*: An incumbent weight or mass 1679. **2.** The quality of being incumbent as a duty; an incumbent duty or obligation. Now *rare.* 1608. **3.** The position or office of an incumbent; now only *Eccl.* (or *transf.* from this). Also, the sphere, or period of tenure, of an incumbent. 1656.

2. All the incumbencies of a family DONNE. 3. He has retired from his i. and given up his benefice 1886.

Incumbent (inkʊ·mbĕnt), *sb.* ME. [ad. L. *incumbentem*; see next. App. from a med.L. sense of L. *incumbere* = 'obtinere, possidere'.] The holder of an ecclesiastical benefice; hence *gen.*, of any office (now *rare*) 1672.

The I. lent me the Church WHITEFIELD. The i. of the coronership 1884.

Incumbent (inkʊ·mbĕnt), *a.* 1548. [ad. L. *incumbentem*, *incumbere*, f. *in-* (IN-²) + *cumbere* to lie.] **1.** That lies, leans, rests, or presses with its weight upon something else 1624. **2.** *spec.* **a.** *Physics.* Of air, fluid, or other weight, as exerting downward pressure 1660. **b.** *Geol.* Superincumbent, as a stratum 1789. **c.** *Bot.* Said of an *anther* when it lies flat against the inner side of the filament; of *cotyledons* when the back of one is applied to the radicle 1760. **d.** *Zool.* Of hairs, spines, etc.: Lying along the surface on which they grow. **e.** *Ornith.* Of the hind toe of a bird: Resting on the ground with its whole length, its insertion being on a level with the anterior toes. **3.** Resting or falling upon a person as a duty or obligation. Const. *on, upon.* 1567. †**4.** Impending, imminent, threatening -1793. †**5.** Bending one's energies to some work -1814. †**6.** In occupation of a benefice. Const. *on.* -1661.

1. He stears his flight Aloft, i. on the dusky Air MILT. *P. L.* I. 226. 3. That there was a duty i. upon us CROMWELL. 5. Habits of firm and i. application SCOTT. Hence **Incu·mbently** *adv.*

‖**Incumber, Incumbrance,** etc., var. ENCUMBER, ENCUMBRANCE, etc.

†**Incumbi·tion.** [irreg. f. L. *incumbere.*] The action of lying or pressing upon; also *fig.* STERNE.

‖**Incunabula** (inkiunæ·biŭlă), *sb. pl.* 1824. [L. (neut. pl.), f. *cunæ* cradle.] **1.** The earliest stages in the development of anything. **2.** (With sing. *incunabulum*): Books produced in the infancy of printing; *spec.* those printed before 1501. var. **Incu·nable.** 1861. **3.** *Ornith.* The breeding-places of a species of bird. Hence **Incuna·bular** *a.* of or pertaining to early printed books. **Incuna·bulist,** one who collects or is interested in incunabula.

Incur (inkʊ̄·ɹ), *v.* ME. [ad. L. *incurrere*, f. *in-* (IN-²) + *currere* to run.]

I. *intr.* †**1.** To run, flow, fall, or come *to* or *into* -1677. †**b.** To come in so as to meet the eye, etc. -1692. †**2.** To run *into* (danger, etc.); to render oneself liable *to* (damage) -1620.

1. b. They are Inuisible, and incurre not to the Eie BACON.

II. *trans.* †**1.** To run into; to come upon, meet with -1680. **2.** To run or fall into (some consequence, usu. undesirable); to bring upon oneself ME. †**3.** To cause to be incurred; to entail -1784.

2. I should haue..incurred the suspicion of fraud LYLY. 3. This sickness has necessarily incurred expences 1784.

Incurable (inkiū̊ə·răb'l), *a.* (*sb.*) ME. [a. OF.; see IN-³ and CURABLE.] **1.** That cannot be cured; incapable of being healed by medicine or medical skill. **2.** *transf.* and *fig.* Not admitting of remedy or correction ME. **3.** *sb.* A person suffering from an incurable disease. Usu. in *pl.* 1652.

1. God..him..smoot With invisible wounde, ay i. CHAUCER. 2. Ignorance is not so i. as error BERKELEY. Hence **Incurabi·lity, Incu·rableness. Incu·rably** *adv.* in an i. manner; to an i. degree.

Incurious (inkiū̊ə·riəs), *a.* 1570. [ad. L. *incuriosus*; see IN-³ and CURIOUS.]

I. Subjectively. **1.** Without care or concern; negligent, heedless; untroubled (*arch.*). **2.** Devoid of curiosity 1613. **3.** Inattentive, careless 1691. †**4.** Not precise; uncritical; undiscriminating -1749.

1. In his Cloaths and Habit..he was not now only i., but too negligent CLARENDON. 2. I. and indifferent about truth 1774. 3. The more careless and i. Observer RAY.

II. Objectively. †**1.** Not carefully prepared, made, composed, or done -1824. **2.** Unworthy of careful notice; not curious. (Esp. in neg. forms of expression.) 1747.

2. The inscriptions..are not i. TWISS. Hence **Incurio·sity, Incu·riousness,** want of care; want of curiosity or interest in things. **Incu·riously** *adv.*

Incurrent (inkʊ·rĕnt), *a.* 1563. [ad. L. *incurrentem*; see INCUR and -ENT.] Running in; penetrating into the interior; †falling within (a period).

The most principal matters in his time i. FOXE. Hence **Incu·rrence,** the action or fact of incurring, e.g. liabilities; the entrance of sensations or impressions.

Incursion (inkʊ̄·ɹʃən). ME. [ad. L. *incursionem.*] **1.** The action of running in or of running against 1615. **2.** A hostile inroad or invasion; esp. a sudden attack ME. Also *transf.* and *fig.* †**3.** The action of incurring (blame, etc.) HEALEY.

1. The inevitable i. of new images JOHNSON. 2. Against the Scythian, whose incursions wild Have wasted Sogdiana MILT. *P. R.* III. 301. Phr. †*Sins of daily incursion*: the small sins which make daily inroads upon a holy life.

Incursive (inkʊ̄·ɹsiv), *a.* 1592. [f. L. *incurs-*, *incurrere* + -IVE.] Given to making incursions; aggressive, invasive.

Incurtain, obs. var. of ENCURTAIN *v.*

Incurvate (inkʊ̄·ɹvĕt), *ppl. a.* 1647. [ad. L. *incurvatus.*] = INCURVED.

Incurvate (inkʊ̄·ɹveʼt, i·n-), *v.* 1578. [f. L. *incurvat-*, *incurvare.*] **1.** *trans.* To bring into a curved shape; to bend; to crook; now, *spec.*, to bend or curve inwards. †**2.** *intr.* To take or have a curved shape -1697.

Incurvation (inkʊɹvēʼ·ʃən). 1607. [ad. L. *incurvationem.*] **1.** The action or process of bending or curving; an instance of this 1608. †**b.** *spec.* Bowing in reverence or worship -1702. **2.** The condition of being bent; curvature; a curve or bend. Also *fig.* 1647. **3.** A curving inwards, or the condition of being curved inwards 1822.

1. b. Must i. towards the East be still continued? 1607. 2. *fig.* The incurvations of practice..when compared with the rectitude of the rule BLACKSTONE. 3. It [whitlow] is also occasioned by an i. of the nails 1822. So **Incu·rvature** (*rare*), in sense 3.

Incurve (inkʊ̄·ɹv), *v.* 1610. [ad. L. *incurvare*; see IN-² and CURVE *v.*] **1.** *trans.* = INCURVATE *v.* 1; in mod. use, To curve or bend (something) inwards. **2.** *intr.* To curve or bend inwards 1704.

2. Those fair open fields that i. to thy beautiful hollow CLOUGH.

Incurved (inkʊ̄·ɹvd), *ppl. a.* 1623. [f. prec. + -ED¹.] Bent into or having a curved form; in mod. use, Having an inward curvature. (Now chiefly in *Zool.* and *Bot.*)

†**Incu·rvity.** [f. L. *incurvus* + -ITY; cf. L. *curvitas.*] The quality of being incurved; inward curvature. SIR T. BROWNE.

‖**Incus** (i·ŋkʊ̆s). 1669. [L., f. *incudere*; see INCUSE *v.*] *Anat.* and *Zool.* **1.** The middle one of the three small bones of the ear (*malleus, incus,* and *stapes*). **2.** A part of the mouth-apparatus in *Rotifera*, upon which the two mallei work 1877.

Incuse (inkiū̆·z). 1818. [ad. L. *incusus*, *incudere* (see next).] *adj.* Hammered or stamped in; said of a figure or impression upon a coin or the like. *sb.* A figure stamped in; an impression in intaglio upon a coin, etc. 1818.

sb. The head of Proserpine in an i. surrounded by dolphins 1879.

Incuse (inkiū̆·z), *v.* 1864. [f. L. *incus-*, *incudere* to work on the anvil (*incus*).] *trans.* To impress by stamping; to mark with an impressed figure. Chiefly in pa. pple.

†**Incuss,** *v.* 1527. [f. L. *incuss-*, *incutere*, f. *in-* (IN-²) + *quatere* to shake, etc. Cf. CONCUSS.] *trans.* To strike in, impress; to strike (terror, etc.) into the mind; to inspire a person with (some feeling) -1613.

Incut (i·nkʊt), *ppl. a.* 1888. [f. IN *adv.* + CUT *ppl. a.*] Set in by or as by cutting; *spec.* in *Printing*, inserted in a space left in the outside of the text, instead of in the margin; also called *cut-in.*

†**Incu·te,** *v.* 1542. [ad. L. *incutere*; see INCUSS *v.*] = INCUSS.

Incysted, obs. f. ENCYSTED.

Ind (ind). ME. [a. F. *Inde*:—L. *India.*] **1.** = INDIA. Now *arch.* or *poet.* †**2.** *pl.* Indians -1526.

1. From the east to westerne Inde *A. Y. L.* III. ii. 93.

Ind-, *Chem.*: see INDI-, INDO-.

‖**Indaba** (indā·bă). 1894. [Zulu *in-daba* subject, topic, matter, business.] A communication or transaction of affairs, a conference between or with South African natives.

Indagate (i·ndăgeʼt), *v.* ? *Obs.* 1623. [f. L. *indagat-*, *indagare.*] *trans.* To search into, investigate. So **Indaga·tion** (? *Obs.*), the action of tracking out; investigation 1589. †**Indaga·tive** *a.* inclined to seek (JER. TAYLOR). **I·ndagator** (now *rare*), a searcher, investigator.

Indam(m)age, obs. var. ENDAMAGE.

Indart (indā·ɹt), *v.* 1598. [IN-¹.] *trans.* To dart in.

†**Inde.** ME. [a. F. *inde*, AF. *ynde*, ad. L. **indium* = *indicum*, lit. Indian, as sb. indigo.] A blue dye obtained from India, now called INDIGO; the colour of this, or a fabric dyed with it -1658. **b.** *attrib.* or as *adj.* Blue. ME. only.

Indear, obs. var. of ENDEAR.

Inde·bt, *v.* Now *rare.* 1565. [Inferred from INDEBTED, perh. after F. *endetter.*] **1.** *trans.* To involve in debt. **2.** To bring under an obligation 1603.

2. Thy Fortune hath indebted thee to none DANIEL.

Indebted (inde·tĕd), *ppl. a.* [ME. *endetted*, after OF. *endetté*; see EN- and DEBT *sb.*] **1.** Owing money; in debt. **2.** Under obligation to another on account of some liability incurred or claim unsatisfied; bound. *Obs.* or *arch.* ME. **3.** Owing gratitude; beholden 1561.

1. He being..gretly endetted ME. 2. When I have promised, I am i.; and debts may be claimed, must be paid BP. HALL. 3. For this observation I am i. to an ingenious and worthy friend PRIESTLEY. Hence **Inde·btedness,** the condition of being indebted; the sum owed; debts collectively. **Inde·btment** (*rare*), indebtedness.

†**Inde·cence.** *rare.* 1714. [? a. F. *indécence.*] = INDECENCY 1. -1797.

Indecency (indī·sĕnsi). 1589. [ad. L. *indecentia*, f. *indecentem*; see next and -ENCY.] **1.** Unseemliness; unbecoming or outrageous conduct; an instance of this. †**2.** Uncomeliness of form -1648. **3.** Immodesty; a quality savouring of obscenity; an indecent act 1692.

1. These Bishops..were fain to descend to many indecencies and indignities to support themselves FULLER. 3. The hatred of i...is a modern virtue DARWIN.

Indecent (indī·sĕnt), *a.* 1563. [a. F. *indécent*; see IN-³ and DECENT.] **1.** Unbecoming; in extremely bad taste; unseemly. †**2.** Uncomely -1743. **3.** Offending against propriety or delicacy; immodest; suggesting or tending to obscenity 1613.

1. With i. haste 1839. 3. Their Dances were lascivious, their Gestures i., and their Songs immodest 1676. Hence **Inde·cent·ly** *adv.*, **-ness.**

Indeciduate (ind si·diuʼĕt), *a.* 1879. [IN-³.] Not deciduate, as a placenta; not having a decidua; belonging to the *Indeciduata* (a division of mammals comprising the Ruminantia, Edentata, and Cetacea).

Indeciduous (indĭsi·diuʼəs), *a.* 1646. [IN-³.] †**1.** Not liable to fall off or be shed -1656. **2.** *Bot.* Of a leaf: Not deciduous. Of a tree or plant: Not losing the leaves annually; evergreen. 1755.

1. The indiciduous and unshaven locks of Apollo 1646.

†**Inde·cimable,** *a.* [f. IN-³ + L. *decimare* to tithe + -ABLE.] Not decimable; not liable to pay tithe. COKE.

Indecipherable (indĭsəi·fərăb'l), *a.* 1802. [IN-³.] Incapable of being deciphered or made out. Hence **Indeci·pherabi·lity, Indeci·pherableness.**

Indecision (indĭsi·ʒən). 1763. [a. F. *indécision*; see IN-³ and DECISION.] Want of decision; inability to make up one's mind; hesitation.

The term i...implies an idea very nicely different from that of irresolution; yet it has a tendency to produce it SHENSTONE.

Indecisive (indĭsəi·siv), *a.* 1726. [IN-³.] 1. Not decisive; not such as to settle (a question, contest, etc.); inconclusive. 2. Characterized by indecision; undecided; hesitating; irresolute 1787. 3. Uncertain; not definite, indistinct 1816.

1. An i. predatory war MACAULAY. 2. Perplexed and i. whether to go forwards or backwards MOZLEY. Hence **Indeci·sive-ly** *adv.*, **-ness.**

Indeclinable (indĭkləi·năb'l), *a.* (*sb.*) ME. [a. F. *indéclinable*; see IN-³ and DECLINABLE.] †1. Incapable of declining, or being caused to decline; undeviating, fixed, constant –1637. †2. That cannot be turned aside from; inevitable –1660. 3. *Gram.* Incapable of being declined grammatically; having no inflexions 1530. 4. *sb.* An indeclinable word 1530.

3. Adjectives are i., having no variation either of Gender, Case, or Number 1748. Hence **Indecli·nably** *adv.*

Indecomposable (indĭkǫmpōu·zăb'l), *a.* 1812. [IN-³.] Incapable of being decomposed or resolved into constituent elements.

Indecorous (indĭkōᵊ·rəs, -de·kŏrəs), *a.* 1680. [f. L. *indecorus* (see IN-³ and DECOROUS) + -OUS.] †1. Unbecoming –1692. 2. Contrary to, or wanting, decorum or propriety of behaviour; in bad taste 1682; indecent (*rare*) 1829.

2. Among savages especially haste is i. KANE. I. statues MACAULAY. **Indecorous-ly** *adv.*, **-ness.**

Indecorum (indĭkōᵊ·rŏm). 1575. [a. L. *indecorum* adj. neut. sing. used subst.] 1. An indecorous or unbecoming action or proceeding; an impropriety. 2. The quality of being indecorous; impropriety, now esp. of behaviour 1664.

2. The charge is not..for i., or indiscretion, but for falsehood BURKE.

Indeed (indī·d), *adv. phrase.* ME. [f. IN *prep.* + DEED *sb.*; written as two wds. till 1600.] 1. In actual fact, in reality, in truth. b. Freq. placed after a word in order to emphasize it 1575. 2. In reality, in real nature or essence ME. 3. With confirming and amplifying force: In point of fact, as a matter of fact 1535. 4. With concessive force = It is true, it must be admitted 1563. 5. In dialogue, used to emphasize the reply to a question or remark 1583; also in echoing the question asked by another speaker 1766. 6. Interrogatively = 'Is it so?' 'Really?' 1598. 7. As an exclam., expressing irony, contempt, amazement, incredulity, or the like 1710 SWIFT.

1. The lorde is risen in dede TINDALE *Luke* xxiv. 34. b. This is Musick i. WALTON. Marvellous i. 1742. 3. I am..a cautious man, i. a timid one 1885. 4. Latin, not classical i., but good of its kind 1894. 5. Can you tell me? I. I cannot JOWETT. 'Who is this Mr. Grey?' 'Who, i.!' DISRAELI. 6. 'That's Jarsper's.' 'I.?' said Mr. Datchery DICKENS. 7. 'O, i.', I said, 'what a wonderful thing!' JOWETT. Phr. *Indeed and indeed*, really and truly (*colloq.*).

Indefatigable (indĭfæ·tigăb'l), *a.* 1586. [a. obs. F. *indéfatigable*, ad. L. *indefatigabilis*, f. *in-* (IN-³) + *defatigare* to wear out; see -BLE.] Incapable of being wearied; that cannot be tired out; unremitting in labour or effort.

Upborn with i. wings Over the vast abrupt MILT. *P. L.* II. 408. A man of..industry i. SIR T. BROWNE. Hence **Indefa·tigabi·lity, Indefa·tigableness,** the quality of being i. **Indefa·tigably** *adv.*

Indefeasible (indĭfī·zĭb'l), *a.* 1548. [IN-³.] Not defeasible; not liable to be made void, or done away with; that cannot be forfeited.

A good and indefeisible estate BLOUNT. The great writers..have mostly asserted freedom of conscience as an i. right MILL. Hence **Indefeasibi·lity, Indefea·sibleness. Indefea·sibly** *adv.*

Indefectible (indĭfe·ktĭb'l), *a.* 1659. [IN-³.] Not defectible. 1. Not liable to failure, defect, or decay; unfailing. 2. Faultless 1833.

1. The burning, and not consuming bush, signifies the i. splendor of the church 1736. 2. An i. wisdom 1852. Hence **Indefectibi·lity,** quality of being i. 1624. **Indefe·ctibly** *adv.*

Indefective (indĭfe·ktiv), *a.* ? *Obs.* 1641. [IN-³.] Not defective; free from defect; faultless, flawless.

Upon Condition of absolute i. obedience SOUTH.

Indefensible (indĭfe·nsĭb'l), *a.* 1529. [IN-³.] Not defensible; admitting of no defence.

I. small townes and villages 1569. An i. hypothesis 1799, quarrel FROUDE. Hence **Indefensibi·lity, Indefe·nsibleness. Indefe·nsibly** *adv.*

†**Indefe·nsive,** *a.* 1586. [IN-³.] Defenceless –1634.

The sword awes the i. villager SIR T. HERBERT.

†**Indeficient** (indĭfi·ʃent), *a.* 1508. [a. OF. *indéficient*; see IN-³ and DEFICIENT.] Unfailing, exhaustless –1851.

The Lamb His people feeds from i. streams TRENCH. Hence **Indefi·ciency.** †**Indefi·ciently** *adv.*

Indefinable (indĭfəi·năb'l), *a.* 1810. [IN-³.] That cannot be defined or exactly described. Hence **Indefi·nableness. Indefi·nably** *adv.*

Indefinite (inde·finit), *a.* (*sb.*) 1530. [ad. L. *indefinitus*; see IN-³ and DEFINITE.] Undefined, unlimited.

I. *gen.* 1. Without distinct limitation of being or character; indeterminate, vague, undefined 1561. 2. Of indetermined extent, amount, or number 1594. †b. Formerly *occas.*, Boundless, infinite –1745.

1. Some generall i. promises 1651. A fine, though i., emotion 1885. 2. Commodities that admitted of i. multiplication 1884. b. I. and omnipresent God, Inhabiting eternity! 1745.

II. *spec.* 1. *Gram.* Applied to various adjs., pronominal words, and advs.; as *any, other, some, such, anyhow*, etc.; esp. in *indefinite article*, the individualizing adj. *a, an* (A *adj.*²), or its equivalents in other langs. 1530. 2. *Logic.* Applied to propositions in which the subject has no mark of quantity 1697. 3. *Bot.* a. Said of inflorescence; also called CENTRIPETAL (q.v.), or *indeterminate* 1876. b. Said of the stamens or other parts of the flower when numerous and not clearly multiples of the number of the petals, etc. 1845.

B. *sb.* (the adj. used ellipt.) An indefinite thing, word, statement, etc.; something which cannot be definitely specified, described, or classed 1591.

So **Inde·finite-ly** *adv.* 1471, **-ness** 1589.

Indefinitive (indĭfi·nĭtiv), *a. rare.* 1580. [IN-³.] Not definitive; not characterized by definition; indefinite.

A school of opinion..fixed in its principles, i. and progressive in their range J. H. NEWMAN. Hence **Indefi·nitive·ly** *adv.*, **-ness.**

Indefinitude (indĭfi·nitiud). 1677. [IN-³.] †1. The condition of having no known limit; undefined or undefinable number or amount. HALE. 2. Indefiniteness, undefined state 1827. So **Indefi·nity** (*rare*), in both senses 1623.

Indehiscent (indĭhi·sĕnt), *a.* 1832. [IN-³.] *Bot.* Not dehiscent; said of fruits which do not split open when mature, but liberate the seed by decay. Hence **Indehi·scence.**

Indele·ctable, *a. rare.* 1585. [IN-³.] Unpleasant.

Indeliberate (indĭli·bĕrĕt), *a.* 1617. [IN-³.] †1. Of persons, etc.: Wanting in deliberation; hasty or rash –1677. 2. Done without deliberation; unpremeditated. Now *rare*. 1655. So †**Indeli·berated** *a.* (in sense 2). Hence **Indeli·berate·ly** *adv.* (*rare*), **-ness** (*rare*). **Indelibera·tion,** want of deliberation or forethought 1614.

Indelible (inde·lĭb'l), *a.* 1529. [In 16–17th c. *indeleble*, ad. L. *indelebilis*, f. *in-* (IN-³) + *delebilis* DELIBLE.] That cannot be deleted, blotted out, or effaced; ineffaceable, permanent.

Phr. *Indelible ink*, ink which makes i. marks. An indeleble note of infamy SANDERSON. Man still bears in his bodily frame the i. stamp of his lowly origin DARWIN. An i. impression DISRAELI. The i. (= indefeasible) rights of mankind BLACKSTONE. Hence **Inde·libleness. Inde·libly** *adv.*

Indelicacy (inde·likăsi). 1712. [IN-³; see next and -ACY.] Want of delicacy; want of a nice sense of propriety, refinement, or good taste; coarseness of character, manners, etc.

Your Papers would be chargeable with something worse than I., they would be Immoral STEELE. The i. of the Hindus 1818.

Indelicate (inde·likĕt), *a.* 1742. [IN-³.] 1. Wanting in, or offensive to, delicacy or propriety; coarse, unrefined. 2. Wanting in fine tact 1800. †3. Of food: Coarse –1777.

1. The..most i. sarcasms 1804. 2. She felt that..it would be i. to attempt more 1800. Hence **Inde·licately** *adv.*

Indemnification (inde:mnifikēⁱ·ʃən). 1732. [f. INDEMNIFY; see -FICATION.] 1. The action of compensating for actual loss or damage sustained; also the fact of being compensated; *concr.* the payment made with this object. b. The action of compensating for trouble, annoyance, etc.; *concr.* the recompense so rendered 1774. †2. Indemnity.

1. Giving him a full i. and equivalent for the injury thereby sustained BLACKSTONE.

Indemnify (inde·mnifəi), *v.*¹ 1611. [f. L. *indemnis* unhurt + -FY.] 1. *trans.* To keep free *from*, secure *against* (any hurt, harm, or loss); to give an indemnity to. 2. To compensate *for* loss suffered, expenses incurred, etc. 1693. b. To compensate *for* disadvantages, annoyances, hardships, etc. 1707.

1. The fact indemnified the peace officers..if they killed any of the mob in endeavouring to suppress ..riot BLACKSTONE. 2. b. The high price of provisions indemnifies the cultivator for the hard life 1836.

†**Inde·mnify,** *v.*² *rare.* 1583. [f. IN-² + DAMNIFY.] *trans.* To hurt, harm –1593.

Indemnity¹ (inde·mnĭti). 1467. [a. F. *indemnité*, ad. late L. *indemnitas*, f. *indemnis.*] 1. Security or protection against contingent hurt, damage, or loss; safety. 2. A legal exemption from the penalties or liabilities incurred by any course of action 1670. 3. Compensation for loss, etc.; indemnification 1793; a sum paid by way of compensation 1872. 4. *attrib.*, as *i. bill*, etc. 1818.

1. Thei would prouide sufficiently for thindemnity of the wytnes in that behalfe MORE. Insurance ought to be a contract of i. LUBBOCK. 2. Receiving beforehand an i. for every excess BUCKLE. *Act* (or *Bill*) *of Indemnity*, an act of Parliament or other authority granting exemption from the penalties attaching to any unconstitutional or illegal proceeding. Also *fig.* 3. Within four years, France had to pay to Germany a war i. of £240,000,000 FAWCETT.

†**Inde·mnity**². *rare.* 1556. [ad. OF. *indampnité*, f. *in-* (IN-²) + L. *damnum* loss.] Damage, hurt –1629.

Indemonstrable (indĭmǫ·nstrăb'l), *a.* 1570. [IN-³.] Incapable of being demonstrated or proved. (Said *esp.* of axiomatic truths, principles, etc.) Hence **Indemo:nstrabi·lity, Indemo·nstrableness. Indemo·nstrably** *adv.*

Indenize, etc.: see ENDENIZE, etc.

Indent (inde·nt, i·ndent), *sb.*¹ 1589. [f. INDENT *v.*¹] 1. An incision in the edge of a thing; a deep recess; an indentation 1596. 2. *Printing.* = INDENTION 2. 1884. 3. = INDENTURE *sb.* 2. 1551. b. A certificate of a money claim; *spec.* an indented certificate issued by the U.S. Government, at the end of the War of Independence, for the principal or interest due on the public debt. *Obs.* exc. *Hist.* 1788. 4. An official requisition for stores. (Orig. by a covenanted servant of the E. I. Company.) 1772. 5. *Comm.* An order for goods, esp. one sent to England from abroad 1800.

Indent (i·ndent), *sb.*² 1690. [f. INDENT *v.*²] A dint or depression in the surface of anything; an indentation.

Indent (inde·nt), *v.*¹ [ME. *endent*, ad. F. *endenter*, f. *in-* (IN-²) + L. type **dentare* to furnish with teeth, f. *dens, dentem.*] 1. To make a tooth-like incision or incisions in the edge or border of; to notch or jag; now, chiefly, to give a strongly serrate outline to. b. To penetrate deeply (a coast-line, etc.). Also *transf.* 1555. c. *intr.* To form a recess 1784. 2. *trans.* To sever the two halves of a document, drawn up in duplicate, by a toothed, zigzag, or wavy line, so that the two parts exactly tally with each other; hence, to draw up (a document) in two or more exactly corresponding copies. See INDENTURE *sb.* 2. ME. †3. *intr.* To enter into an engagement by indenture; hence, to covenant; to engage. Also *fig.* –1759. †4. *trans.* a. To covenant, stipulate, agree about, promise –1631. †b. To engage (a person) as a servant, etc. by or as by indentures –1804. 5. *intr.* To make out a written order with a duplicate or counterfoil; hence, to make a requisition *on* or *upon*. (Orig. Anglo-Indian.) Also, later, to draw *upon*. 1829. 6. *trans.* To make an incision in (a board, etc.) for the purpose of dovetailing, etc.; to join or joint together by this method 1741. 7. *Printing.* To set back (from the margin) the beginning of (one or more lines); to insert (notes) in the text 1676. †8. *intr.* To move in a zigzag or indented line; to double -1643. †b. *trans. To i. the way*: in same sense -1622.

1. b. Lochleven, an arm of the sea which deeply indents the western coast of Scotland MACAULAY. 3. He indented not what reward he should have ABP. SANDYS. 5. I have indented largely, (to use our Indian official term,) for the requisite books MACAULAY. 7. You must i. your Line four Spaces at least MOXON.

Indent (inde·nt), *v.*[2] ME. [f. IN-[2] + DENT *v.* In actual use not regarded as distinct from prec.] †1. *trans.* To inlay, set, emboss -1730. 2. *trans.* To form as a dint, dent, or depression; to impress ME. 3. To make a dint or dints in (a thing) with or as with a blow; to dint or dent 1586. 4. *intr.* To become indented or furrowed 1653.

2. Deep Scars were seen indented on his Breast DRYDEN. 3. Shields indented deep in glorious wars POPE.

Indentation (indentē·ʃən). 1728. [f. INDENT *v.*[1] and [2]; see -ATION.]

I. f. INDENT *v.*[1] 1. The action of indenting; the condition of being indented; denticulation; toothing 1836. 2. A cut, notch, or angular incision in anything; a deep recess in a coastline, or the like 1728. 3. *Printing.* = INDENTION I. 2. 1864.

2. The Greek coast is full of indentations BUCKLE.

II. f. INDENT *v.*[2] The action of impressing so as to form a dent or dint; the dent, hollow, or depression thus formed; any depression in a surface 1847.

Indented (inde·ntėd), *ppl. a.*[1] ME. [f. INDENT *v.*[1] + -ED [1].] 1. Having the edge deeply cut with angular incisions; serrated 1440. b. Having a serrated or zigzag figure, direction, or course; constructed with salient and re-entrant angles, as a battery, parapet, etc. 1600. 2. *Her.* Of an ordinary, etc.: Having a series of similar indentations or notches ME. 3. Of a legal document: Cut zigzag or wavy at the top or edge; having counterparts severed by a zigzag line ME. 4. Bound by an indenture 1758. 5. *Printing.* Set in, so as to break the line of the margin 1840.

1. *Indented Line* (in *Fortif.*), a serrated line, forming several angles, so that one side defends another. 3. Deeds are divided into two sorts; deeds poll, or cut in a straight line; and deeds indented CRUISE.

Indented (inde·ntėd), *ppl. a.*[2] 1635. [f. INDENT *v.*[2] + -ED [1].] Impressed, struck, or dinted in, so as to make a depression in a surface. b. Marked with sharp depressions on the surface, as if caused by blows. Hence **Inde·ntedly** *adv.*

Indentee (indentī·), *a.* 1727. [ad. F. *endenté*, ad. med.L. *indentatus*; see INDENT *v.*[1]] *Her.* Having indents not joined to each other, but set apart.

Indenting (inde·ntiŋ), *vbl. sb.*[1] ME. [f. INDENT *v.*[1] + -ING [1].] The action of INDENT *v.*[1], or its result. a. = INDENTATION I. 1, 2. b. The making of an INDENTURE (I. 2) or INDENT (*sb.*[1] 3-5) 1472.

Indenting (inde·ntiŋ), *vbl. sb.*[2] 1580. [f. INDENT *v.*[2] + -ING [1].] = INDENTATION II.

Indention (inde·nʃən). 1733. [Irreg. f. INDENT *v.*[1] and [2].]

I. f. INDENT *v.*[1] 1. = INDENTATION I. 1, 2. 2. *Printing.* The indenting of a line in printing or writing; the leaving of a blank space at the beginning of a line at the commencement of a new paragraph, etc.; the blank space so left 1824.

2. *Hanging* or *reverse i.*, the projection of the first line of a paragraph, etc., beyond the vertical line of those that follow.

II. f. INDENT *v.*[2] = INDENTATION II. 1839.

†**Inde·ntment.** 1597. [f. INDENT *v.*[1] + -MENT.] 1. Indentation -1713. 2. An indenture, covenant -1611.

Indenture (inde·ntiŭɹ), *sb.* [ME. *endenture*, a. OF. *endenteure* (later *-ure*), ad. L. type **indentatura*; see INDENT *v.*[1] In sense repr. also INDENT *v.*[2]]

I. f. INDENT *v.*[1] 1. The action of indenting; an indentation 1671. 2. A deed between two or more parties with mutual covenants, executed in two or more copies, all having their tops or edges correspondingly indented for identification and security. Hence, any deed or sealed agreement between two or more parties. ME. b. *spec.* The contract by which an apprentice is bound to a master 1463. c. An official list, inventory, certificate, etc., prepared (orig. in duplicate) for purposes of control, as a voucher, etc. ME. d. *fig.* Contract, mutual engagement 1540. †3. A zigzag line or course; a doubling -1781.

2. And our Indentures Tripartite are drawne SHAKS. b. *To take up one's indentures*, to receive the i. back from the master in evidence of the completion of apprenticeship or service. d. My heart hath past Indentures with mine eye, Not to behold a Maid QUARLES.

II. f. INDENT *v.*[2] †1. An inlaying or embossing 1664. 2. = INDENTATION II. 1793.

Inde·nture, *v.* 1631. [f. INDENTURE *sb.*] †1. *intr.* To enter into an indenture. R. FRANCK. 2. *trans.* To bind by indentures 1676. †3. *intr.* To move in a zigzag line -1635. 4. *trans.* To indent, furrow 1770.

4. Age may creep on, and i. the brow WOTY.

I·ndentwise, *adv.* 1758. [f. INDENT *sb.*[1] + -WISE.] After the form of an indenture, with a counterpart.

Independence (indǐpe·ndĕns). Also †-ance. 1640. [f. INDEPENDENT; see -ENCE. Cf. F. *indépendance*.] 1. The condition or quality of being independent; the fact of not depending on another (see the adj.); exemption from external control or support; individual liberty of thought or action. Rarely in bad sense: Insubordination. 2. *concr.* A competency; = INDEPENDENCY 3 c. 1815. 3. *attrib.* 1860.

1. The charms of i. let us sing SHENSTONE. The dignified clergy..pretended to a total i. on the State HUME. 3. *Independence Day*, July 4, the day on which, in 1776, the Declaration of I. was made; celebrated annually in U.S. as a national holiday.

Independency (indǐpe·ndĕnsi). Also †-ancy. 1611. [f. as prec. + -ENCY.] 1. = prec. 1. Now *rare*. 2. = CONGREGATIONALISM 1. 1642. 3. *concr. pl.* Independent things 1659. b. An autonomous state 1818. c. A competency; a fortune on which the possessor can live without earning his bread 1748.

3. c. The deceased had something in the nature of an i., however modest 1886.

Independent (indǐpe·ndĕnt). Also †**-ant.** 1611. [f. IN-[3] + DEPENDENT; cf. F. *indépendant*.] Not dependent.

A. *adj.* 1. Not depending upon the authority of another; not in position of subordination; not subject to external control or rule; self-governing, free. 2. (with capital *I.*) = CONGREGATIONAL 2. 1642. 3. Not contingent on or conditioned by anything else 1614; not depending on the existence or action of others, or of each other 1790. 4. Not dependent on another for support or supplies 1670. b. *simply.* (*a*) Not dependent on any one else for one's living; (*b*) not needing to earn one's living. 1732. c. *transf.* Constituting a competency 1790. 5. Not influenced or biased by the opinions of others; thinking or acting for oneself 1735. b. (cf. 4), Refusing to be under obligation to others (*mod.*). 6. *Math.* Not depending on another for its value. *I. variable*: a quantity whose variation does not depend on that of another. 1852.

1. An i. workman, such as a weaver or shoemaker A. SMITH. It has been said..that the church is i. on the state 1785. 3. Beauty and Merit are Things real, and i. on Taste and Opinion STEELE. An i. inquiry has been instituted by the Local Board of Health (*mod.*). Phr. *Independent of* (†*on*, †*from*): = Independently of, without regard to, irrespective of. 4. b. *transf.* A dry but i. crust COWPER. c. A person of i. means 1885. 5. A person capable of taking an i. stand HAWTHORNE. *I. Labour Party* (see LABOUR). b. The widow..is very i., and refuses all pecuniary aid (*mod.*).

B. *sb.* 1. An adherent of Independency; a member of an Independent church; a Congregationalist 1644. 2. A person who acts independently of any organized party; also, a member of any organized party called *Independent* 1808.

Hence **Indepe·ndentism**: †a. = INDEPENDENCY 2; b. the principles of any party called *Independent*. **Indepe·ndently** *adv.*

†**Indepe·nding**, *a.* 1604. [f. IN-[3] + *depending* ppl. adj.] = INDEPENDENT *a.* -1675.

Indepo·sable, *a. rare.* [IN-[3].] That cannot be deposed. STILLINGFL.

†**Inde·pravate**, *a.* 1609. [ad. L. *indepravatus*.] Uncorrupted.

†**Indeprehe·nsible**, *a.* 1633. [ad. L. *indeprehensibilis* (Quintil.).] Incapable of being mentally apprehended; undiscoverable -1652.

Indeprivable (indǐprəi·văb'l), *a.* Now *rare.* 1585. [IN-[3].] 1. Incapable of being taken away. 2. That cannot be deprived of something. WEBSTER.

Indescribable (indǐskrəi·băb'l), *a.* (*sb.*) 1794. [IN-[3].] A. *adj.* That cannot be described; indefinite, vague; transcending description. B. *sb.* (*pl.*) Things which cannot be described; (*slang*) trousers 1794. Hence **Indescribabi·lity**, incapacity of being described; something that cannot be described. **Indescri·bably** *adv.*

Indescri·ptive, *a. rare.* 1828. [IN-[3].] Not descriptive.

Indesert (indǐzə·ɹt). Now *rare.* 1612. [f. IN-[3] + DESERT *sb.*[1]] Absence of desert 1646. *pl.* Demerits, faults.

Indesignate (inde·zignět), *a.* 1844. [f. IN-[3] + DESIGNATE *ppl. a.*] *Logic.* Not quantified, indefinite. Also as *sb.*

The I. is..often not thought in any relation of quantity at all MILL.

†**Inde·sinent**, *a.* 1601. [See IN-[3] and DESINENT.] Unceasing, perpetual -1799. Hence †**Inde·sinency.** †**Inde·sinently** *adv.*

†**Indesi·rable**, *a.* 1846. [IN-[3].] Undesirable.

Indestructible (indǐstrɒ·ktĭb'l), *a.* 1674. [IN-[3].] That cannot be destroyed; incapable of destruction. Hence **Indestructibi·lity, Indestru·ctibleness. Indestru·ctibly** *adv.*

Indeterminable (indǐtō·ɹmināb'l), *a.* (*sb.*) 1486. [ad. L. *indeterminabilis* (Tertullian).] †1. Not capable of being limited in respect of range, number, etc. (*rare*) -1690. 2. Of disputes, etc.: Incapable of being settled 1611. 3. Incapable of being definitely fixed; *spec.* in *Nat. Hist.* 1646. 4. *sb.* An indeterminable point or problem. SIR T. BROWNE. Hence **Indete·rminableness. Indete·rminably** *adv.*

Indeterminate (indǐtō·ɹmině̆t), *a.* (*sb.*) ME. [ad. L. *indeterminatus* (Tertullian).] Not determined; undetermined. †1. Not definitely set down. CHAUCER. 2. Not fixed in extent, number, character, or nature; indefinite, indistinct, uncertain 1603. b. Of statements, words, etc.: Wanting in precision, vague 1774. c. *Math.* Of a quantity: Not limited to a fixed value or number of values. (Also as *sb.*) Of a problem: Having an unlimited number of solutions. 1706. d. *Bot.* (*a*) = INDEFINITE II. 3 a, 1731; (*b*) of æstivation; Having parts which do not come into contact in the bud 1842. 3. Not established; uncertain 1626. 4. Not decided; left doubtful 1656. 5. Not determined by motives (regarded as external forces); acting freely 1836.

2. Empires of great extent but i. limits 1782. b. Some is an i. adjective JEVONS. c. *I. analysis*, the branch of analysis which deals with the solution of i. problems. *Method of i. coefficients* (more prop. of *undetermined coefficients*), a method of analysis invented by Descartes. *I. equation*, an equation in which the unknown quantities are i. *I. form*, a form consisting of two i. quantities. *I. series*, a series whose terms proceed by the powers of an i. quantity. 3. An i. future GEO. ELIOT. 5. In positive morality, the mandate is conceived as emanating from an i. superior GROTE. Hence **Indete·rminacy** (*rare*). **Indete·rminate-ly** *adv.*, **-ness.**

Indetermination (indǐtōɹminē·ʃən). 1619. [f. prec.; see -ATION.] Absence of determination; the fact or condition of being undetermined or indeterminate 1649. †b. An indeterminate number or quantity. FOTHERBY.

Indetermined (indǐtō·ɹmind), *a.* Now *rare.* 1611. [f. IN-[3] + DETERMINED *ppl. a.*] Not determined, UNDETERMINED. †b. *Math.* = INDETERMINATE 2 c. -1743.

Indeterminism (indĭtə̄·rminiz'm). 1874. [f. IN-³ + DETERMINISM.] The theory that human action is not necessarily determined by motives, but is in some sense free. So **Indete·rminist**, one who holds the doctrine of i.

†**Indevi·rginate**, *a. rare.* 1616. [IN-³.] Undeflowered. Also *fig.* Unsullied. -1822.

†**Indevo·te**, *a. rare.* [ad. late L. *indevotus.*] = INDEVOUT. Bentley.

†**Indevo·ted**, *a.* 1647. [IN-³.] Not devoted; disaffected or disloyal -1759.

Indevotion (indĭvōu·ʃən). 1526. [IN-³.] Want of devotion; indevout feeling or action. The sloth and i. of the clergy 1866.

Indevout (indĭvau·t), *a.* 1450. [IN-³.] Not devout, irreverent, irreligious. Hence **Indevou·t·ly** *adv.*, **-ness.**

Indew, obs. f. ENDUE.

Index (i·ndeks), *sb.* Pl. **indexes** and **indices** (i·ndisīz). ME. [a. L., f. *in-* (IN-²) + **dic-* to point out; see INDICATE. The pl. *indexes* is usual in sense 5 only.] **1.** The forefinger; so called because used in pointing. Now chiefly *Anat.* **2.** A piece of wood, metal, etc., which serves as a pointer; *esp.* in scientific instruments, a pointer on a graduated scale, which indicates movements or measurements 1594. **b.** An alidade 1571. **3.** The hand of a clock or watch; also, the gnomon of a sundial. Now *rare.* 1594. **4.** That which serves to direct *to* a particular fact or conclusion; a guiding principle 1598. **b.** A sign, token, or indication *of* something 1607. **5.** †**a.** A table of contents prefixed to a book, an argument; also, a preface, prologue. **b.** An alphabetical list (usually) at the end of a book, of the names, subjects, etc. occurring in it, with indication of the places where they occur 1580. Also *fig.* **6.** *spec.* (short for *Index librorum prohibitorum*). The list, published by authority, of books which Roman Catholics are forbidden to read, or may read only in expurgated editions 1613. **b.** ‖*Index expurgatorius* (L.), *Expurgatory I.*, an authoritative specification of the passages to be expunged or altered in works otherwise permitted. Also *transf.* and *fig.* 1611. †**7. a.** *Mus.* = DIRECT *sb.* 2. -1869. **b.** *Printing.* = HAND *sb.* IV. 1. ? *Obs.* 1727. **8.** *Math.* **a.** *Alg.* = EXPONENT *sb.* 2. 1674. †**b.** The integral part, or characteristic, of a logarithm -1828. **9.** In various sciences, a number or formula expressing some property, form, ratio, etc. of the thing in question. See quots. 1829.

4. Lest when my lisping guiltie Tongue should hault, My Lookes might prove the I. to my Fault DRAYTON. **b.** That olde saying is vntrue 'the face Is i. of the heart' 1616. **9.** *I. of refraction* or *refractive i.* (of a medium), in *Optics*, the ratio between the sines of the angles of incidence and refraction of a ray of light passing from some medium (usually air) into the given medium. In *Craniometry*, a formula expressing the ratio of one diameter, etc. of the skull to another, as *alveolar* or *basilar*, *cephalic*, etc., *i.* In *Cryst.*, each of the three (or four) whole numbers which define the position of a face of a crystal. *I. of friction*, in *Dynamics*, the coefficient of friction; see COEFFICIENT.

Comb.: **i.-arm** = sense 2 b; **-correction**, a correction for i.-error; **-digit** = sense 1; **-error**, the constant error in the reading of a mathematical instrument, due to the zero of the i. not being exactly adjusted to that of the limb; **-finger**, (*a*) = sense 1, (*b*) = sense 2; **-gauge**, a measuring instrument in which the distance between the measuring-points is shown by an i.; **-glass**, a mirror at the fixed point of the i.-arm in an astronomical or surveying instrument, from which the light is reflected to the horizon-glass; **-hand** = senses 2 and 3; **i. machine**, a machine for fancy weaving, being a modification of the Jacquard loom.

Index (i·ndeks), *v.* 1720. [f. prec. sb.] **1.** *trans.* To furnish with an index. **2.** To enter (a word, name, etc.) in an index 1761. **3.** To place on the INDEX (*sb.* 6) 1791. **4.** To indicate 1788. Hence **I·ndexer**, one who compiles an index.

Indexical (inde·ksikăl), *a.* 1828. [irreg. f. INDEX *sb.* + -ICAL.] **a.** Arranged like an index. **b.** Relating or pertaining to, or of the nature of, an index. So **Inde·xically** *adv.* in the manner of an index, alphabetically 1728.

Indexte·rity. *rare.* 1611. [IN-³.] Want of dexterity; awkwardness.

Indi-. *Chem.* [f. L. *Indus*, as root of *indicum, indigo.*] A comb. element used in naming substances derived from or related to indigo, as *indifulvin*, etc.

India (i·ndiă). OE. [a. L. *India*, a. Gr. Ἰνδία, f. Ἰνδός the (river) Indus, a. Pers. *hind*, OPers. *hiñd'u*, Skr. *sindhu* 'river', *spec.* the river Indus; hence, all the country east of the Indus.] **1.** A country of Southern Asia, lying east of the river Indus and south of the Himalaya mountains (also called *Hindustan*); also extended to include *Farther* or *Further India*, between this and China. See also EAST INDIA. †**2.** Formerly applied to America, or some parts of it; cf. INDIES, WEST INDIES -1772. †**3.** *pl.* = INDIES -1604. **4.** Short for *India silk, paper*, etc. 1712. **5.** *attrib.*, as *India cloth, muslin, silk*, etc.; also *India bonds, stock*, etc. 1658.

Comb.: **I. Docks**, docks in East London, formerly appropriated to vessels trading with the East and West Indies; †**I. House**, the office of the E. I. Company in London; **I. ink** (see INDIAN INK); **I. Office**, that department of the British Government which deals with Indian affairs; **I. proof** = *I. paper proof*: see INDIA PAPER 1; **I. red** = *Indian red* (see INDIAN A.); †**I. wood**, logwood.

Indiademed (indəi·ădemd), *ppl. a.* [f. IN-¹ or ².] Set in a diadem. SOUTHEY.

Indiaman (i·ndiămæ̆n). Pl. **-men.** 1709. [f. INDIA + MAN, as in *man of war*, etc.] A large ship engaged in the trade with India.

Indian (i·ndiăn). 1390. [f. INDIA: cf. -AN.]

A. *adj.* **1.** Belonging or relating to India, or the East Indies, or to the British Indian Empire; native to India 1566. **b.** Of Indian manufacture, material, or pattern 1673. **2.** Belonging or relating to the original inhabitants of America and the West Indies 1618. **3.** Made of Indian corn or maize, as *I. bread, I. meal, I. dumpling* 1635.

1. Ganges or Hydaspes, I. streams MILT. *P.L.* III. 436. **2.** *I. house*, a wigwam.

Special collocations. **a.** of India or the East Indies (sense 1), or so originally supposed: **I. almond**, a large tree (*Terminalia Catappa*), the seeds of which resemble almonds; **I. berry** = COCCULUS INDICUS, or the plant which yields this; **I. blue**, indigo; **I. cane**, the Bamboo; **I. club**, a club of varying weight, for use in gymnastic exercises; †**I. cock**, the turkey (but the bird is a native of N. America); **I. crocus**, a name for the dwarf orchids of the subgenus *Pleione* (genus *Cœlogyne*); **I. eye**, a species of pink (*Dianthus plumarius*), so called from the eye-shaped marking on the corolla; **I. fire**, a composition of sulphur, realgar, and nitre, burning with a brilliant white flame, used as a signal-light; **I. geranium**, a grass of the genus *Andropogon*, which yields a fragrant oil used in perfumery; †**I. grass**, an old name of silk-worm gut used by anglers (see also in b below); **I. heart**, a plant of the genus *Cardiospermum*; **I. hemp**: see HEMP 5 (see also in b below); **I. hog**, the Babiroussa; **I. leaf**, the aromatic leaf of a species of *Cinnamomum*; **I. light** = BENGAL *light*; **I. oak**, the teak-tree; **I. Ocean**; **I. red**, a red pigment orig. obtained from the East Indies in the form of an earth containing oxide of iron; now prepared artificially by roasting iron sulphate; **I. reed** = next (see also in b below); **I. shot**, the plant *Canna indica* (N.O. *Marantaceæ*), so called from its round hard black seeds; **I. yellow**, a bright yellow pigment obtained from India, consisting mainly of euxanthate of magnesium.

b. of North America or the West Indies: **I. balm**, the purple Trillium or Birth-root (*Trillium erectum* or *T. pendulum*); **I. bean**, *Catalpa bignonioides*; **I. bread**, †(*a*) the Cassava; (*b*) bread made from I. corn; **I. cress, cresses**, the Nasturtium, so called from the flavour of the leaves; †**I. drug**, tobacco; **I. file**, the same as *single file*, so called because the N. Amer. Indians usually march in this order; **I. gift**, a gift for which an equivalent return is expected; **I. grass**, *Sorghum nutans* and *Molinia cœrulea*; **I. hemp**, *Apocynum cannabinum*, a plant having a fibrous integument used by the N. Amer. Indians for the same purposes as hemp; †**I. herb**, tobacco; **I. path**, a footpath through the woods, such as is made by N. Amer. Indians; **I. physic**, *Gillenia trifoliata*, a N. Amer. rosaceous plant with a medicinal root; **I. pipe**, *Monotropa uniflora*, a leafless plant with a solitary drooping flower, of a uniform pinkish-white throughout, parasitic on the roots of trees; **I. plantain**, the genus *Cacalia* of composite plants; **I. poke**, the White Hellebore of N. America, *Veratrum viride*; **I. pudding**, a pudding made with I. meal, molasses, and suet; also, the same as *hasty-pudding*; **I. reed**, a blow-pipe such as the N. Amer. Indians use for shooting arrows; **I. rice** = CANADA *rice*; **I. shoe**, (*a*) a moccasin; (*b*) an American name for the plant *Cypripedium* or Lady's Slipper; **I. tobacco**, *Lobelia inflata*; **I. turnip**, (*a*) the tuberous root of *Arisæma triphyllum* (N.O. *Araceæ*), or the plant itself; (*b*) the edible tuberous root of *Psoralea esculenta*; **I. weed**, tobacco; †**I. wheat**, an old name for Indian corn.

B. *sb.* **1.** A native of India or the East Indies; an East Indian. Now *rare*; usu. repl. by *Hindoo.* **b.** An Anglo-Indian 1751. **2.** A member of any of the aboriginal races of America or the West Indies; an American Indian 1553. **3.** Name of a constellation (*Indus*) lying between Sagittarius and the south pole 1674.

2. *Red Indian*: one of the aboriginal race of N. America; so called from the coppery colour of their skin.

Indian corn. 1621. [INDIAN *a.* 2.] The common name of *Zea Mays*, or of the grain produced by it; cultivated by the Americans at the time of the discovery of America. Also called MAIZE, and in U.S. simply CORN.

Indian fig. 1594. **1.** The Prickly Pear 1712. **2.** *Indian fig-tree.* **a.** The BANIAN tree 1594. †**b.** The BANANA 1613.

Indian ink. Also **India ink.** 1665. A black pigment made in China and Japan, sold in sticks; it consists of lampblack made into a paste with a solution of gum and dried. Called also *China ink* (CHINA ¹ I).

Indianist (i·ndiănist). 1851. [-IST.] One versed in the languages, history, etc. of India.

Indian summer. 1794. [INDIAN *a.* 2.] A period of calm, dry, mild weather, with hazy atmosphere, occurring in the late autumn in the Northern U.S. Also *fig.*

India paper. 1768. (*Indian p.* 1750.) **1.** A soft absorbent paper of creamy-yellow or pale buff colour, imported from China, and used for the proofs of engravings. Also used loosely of similar papers. Hence *India paper proofs* (also *India proofs*). **2.** (*Oxford India paper.*) A very thin tough opaque printing-paper made by the Oxford University Press in imitation of paper from the East 1875.

I·ndia-ru·bber, India rubber. 1799. **1.** = CAOUTCHOUC, q.v. In later use shortened to *rubber.* **2.** *attrib.*, as *india-rubber ball, band*, etc.; *india-rubber plant, tree, vine*; *india-rubber works* 1833.

†**I·ndiary**, *a.* [f. INDIA + -ARY.] Relating to India. SIR T. BROWNE.

†**I·ndical**, *a.* 1661. [f. L. *indicem* INDEX + -AL.] Pertaining to an index or indexes.

Indican (i·ndikæ̆n). 1859. [f. L. *indicum* INDIGO + -AN I. 2; cf. ALLOXAN.] *Chem.* The natural glucoside ($C_{26}H_{31}NO_{17}$) formed in plants which yield indigo, by the decomposition of which indigo-blue is produced; it forms a light-brown syrup, of bitter taste, and slightly acid reaction. **b.** *Indican of urine*: an incorrect name for the potassium salt of indoxyl sulphuric acid, a normal constituent of the urine of animals.

Indicant (i·ndikănt). 1607. [ad. L. *indicantem.*] **A.** *adj.* That indicates; indicative. **B.** *sb.* (*Med.*) That which indicates the remedy or treatment suitable 1623.

Indicate (i·ndikeᵉit), *v.* 1651. [ad. L. *indicat-, indicare*; f. *in-* (IN-²) + *dicare* to make known; cf. INDEX.] **1.** *trans.* To point out, point to, make known, show (more or less distinctly). In *Med.* to point out as a remedy or treatment. **2.** To be a sign or symptom of; to betoken 1706. **3.** *trans.* Of persons: To point out, direct attention to. *Occas.*, To point to with the hand or by gesture. 1808. **4.** To state or express; *esp.* to express briefly, lightly, or without development; to give an indication of 1751.

1. Above the steeple shines a plate, That turns and turns, to i. From what point blows the weather COWPER. **2.** Large noses..were considered as indicating prudence 1798. **4.** The waves are indicated on the plinth ELLIS.

Indication (indikēᵉ·ʃən). 1541. [a. F., ad. L. *indicationem.*] **1.** The action of indicating; that in which this is embodied; a hint, suggestion, etc. 1626. **b.** *spec.* in *Med.* A suggestion or direction as to the treatment of a disease, derived from the symptoms 1541. **2.** A sign, token, or symptom; an expression by sign or token 1660.

1. The indications of the senses are always imperfect,

and often misleading TAIT. 2. Modesty is the certain I. of a great Spirit STEELE.

Indicative (indi·kătiv, i·ndikeᶦtiv), *a.* (*sb.*) 1490. [ad. F. *indicatif, -ive*, ad. L. *indicativus*; see INDICATE and -IVE. The first pronunciation is that used in senses 1 and 3.] 1. *Gram.* That points out, states, or declares: applied to that mood of a verb which states a relation of objective fact between the subject and predicate 1530. 2. That indicates, points out, or directs; that hints or suggests; also with *of* 1490. 3. *sb. Gram.* The indicative mood; a verb in the indicative mood 1530.

1. The I. Mood sheweth or declareth, as *laudo* I praise MILT. 2. I. Signs of any changes in States and times 1663. Hence **Indicatively** *adv.*

Indicator (i·ndikeᶦtəɹ). 1666. [a. late L.; cf. F. *indicateur.*] 1. One who or that which points out, or directs attention to, something 1831. b. *Anat.* The muscle which extends the index or forefinger; the *extensor indicis* 1696. c. In a microscope, A pointer which indicates the position of an object 1837. 2. That which serves as an indication *of* something 1666. b. Anything used in a scientific experiment to indicate the presence of a substance or quality, change in a body, etc.; *esp.* a chemical reagent 1842. 3. *techn.*:

a. An instrument which indicates the pressure of steam on the piston of a steam-engine at each portion of its stroke. b. In a blast-furnace, a gauge which indicates the proper height of a charge. c. The dial and mechanism by which messages are indicated in a dial-telegraph. d. An instrument which indicates at any moment the position of the cage in the shaft of a mine. e. A contrivance in a lending library for showing what books are out or in. 1839.

4. *Ornith.* A honey-guide, a bird of the genus *Indicator*, or family *Indicatoridæ* 1835.

1. Birds..were celestial indicators of the gods' commands FROUDE.

Comb.: **i.-card**, the card on which an i.-diagram is traced; **-cylinder**, the cylinder of a steam-engine i.; **-diagram**, a figure traced by the i. of a steam-engine, showing the pressure at different points of the stroke; **-muscle** = sense 1 b; **-pointer**, the pointer in a telegraph i.; **-telegraph**, a form of telegraph in which the letters of a message are indicated by a pointer on a dial-plate.

Indicatory (i·ndikătəri, i·ndikeᶦtəri), *a.* 1590. [f. L. *indicat-*, ppl. stem; see INDICATE and -ORY.] †1. *Med.* Symptomatic; cf. INDICANT *a.* -1624. 2. Serving to indicate or point out something. Also with *of.* 1734.

Indicatrix (indikēᶦ·triks). 1841. [mod.L., fem. of INDICATOR; see -TRIX. Cf. DIRECTRIX.] 1. *Geom.* The curve in which a given surface is cut by a plane indefinitely near and parallel to the tangent-plane at any point; so called because it indicates the nature of the curvature of the surface at that point. 2. *Optical indicatrix*: L. Fletcher's name for a surface (sphere, spheroid, or ellipsoid) devised to indicate by its geometrical characters the optical characters of rays of light refracted through a crystal of any kind 1892.

‖**Indicavit** (indikēᶦ·vit), *sb.* 1607. [L.; = 'he has pointed out'; 3rd sing. perf. ind. used subst.] *Law.* A writ of prohibition, by which, in certain cases, a suit might be removed from the eccl. court to the king's court at the instance of the patron of the defendant.

†**I·ndice.** *rare.* 1595. [a. F.] An indication, sign -1645.

Indices, Indicia, pl. of INDEX, INDICIUM.

†**Indi·cible**, *a.* 1480. [ad. med.L. *indicibilis*; see IN-³.] Unspeakable, inexpressible -1685.

O vnparalell'd loss! O griefe i. EVELYN.

‖**Indicium** (indi·ʃiə̆m). Pl. **indicia.** 1625. [L.] An indication, sign, token. Chiefly in *pl.*

Indicolite (indi·kŏləit). 1808. [f. Gr. ἰνδικόν INDIGO + -LITE.] *Min.* An indigo-coloured variety of tourmaline.

Indict (indəi·t), *v.*¹ [ME. *enditen*, a. AF. *enditer*, corresp. in form to OF. *enditer*, answering to a late L. type **indictare*, f. *in-* (IN-²) + *dictare* to declare, DICTATE. Refash. after L., and (since 1600) written *indict*, though pronounced *indite.*] 1. *trans.* To bring a charge against; to accuse (a person) *for* (†*of*) a crime, *as* (†*for*) a culprit. 2. To make (it) matter of indictment (*rare*) 1670.

1. They indicted our friends as rioters ELLWOOD.

Hence **Indi·ctable** *a.* liable to be indicted; on account of which an indictment may be raised. **Indictee·**, a person indicted. **Indi·cter**, one who indicts.

†**Indi·ct**, *v.*² 1538. [f. L. *indict-*, *indicere*, f. *in-* (IN-²) + *dicere* to say, tell, declare.] To declare authoritatively, announce, proclaim -1720.

To i. a new Parliament 1648, a day for prayer with fasting C. MATHER, war EVELYN.

Indict, obs. erron. f. INDITE.

Indiction (indi·kʃən). ME. [ad. L. *indictionem*; see INDICT *v.*²] 1. The action of announcing authoritatively and publicly; an appointment, declaration, proclamation 1563. 2. The decree of the Roman Emperors fixing the valuation on which the property-tax was assessed at the beginning of each period of fifteen years; hence, the amount paid on this basis. Also *transf.* 1586. 3. The fiscal period of fifteen years, instituted by the Emperor Constantine in A.D. 313, and reckoned from the 1st of Sept. 312, which became a usual means of dating ordinary events, etc. Also called *Cycle* or *Era of i.* or *indictions.* ME. Also *transf.* 4. A specified year in the cycle of fifteen years, counting from A.D. 312-13, indicated by its numerical position in the cycle; the number thus indicating a year ME. †5. An eccl. observance authoritatively enjoined, or the period of it; *esp.* a public fast -1685.

1. The cruell indictions of warres FERNE. 5. The frequency of our Theatrical pastimes during that I. [Lent] EVELYN. Hence **Indi·ctional** *a.* of or pertaining to an i. or cycle of years.

†**Indictive** (indi·ktiv), *a. rare.* 1656. [ad. L. *indictivus*; see INDICT *v.*² and -IVE.] Proclaimed or appointed by authority -1741.

Indictment (indəi·tmĕnt). ME. [a. AF. *enditement, endictement*, f. *enditer* INDICT *v.*¹] 1. The action of indicting or accusing; spec. in *Eng. Law*, the legal process in which a formal accusation is preferred to and presented by a Grand Jury. b. The legal document containing the charge 1506. 2. *Sc. Law.* A form of process by which a criminal is brought to trial at the instance of the Lord Advocate; the formal written charge 1773.

Phr. *Bill of i.*, the written accusation as preferred to the Grand Jury, before it has been by them either found a true bill or ignored.

Indies (i·ndiz), *sb. pl.* 1555. [Pl. of *Indie* or INDY, adaptation of L. *India.*] 1. A name given to the lands and regions now distinguished as EAST and WEST INDIES, q. v. †2. Used allusively for a region or place yielding great wealth -1742.

2. They shall be my East and West Indies SHAKS.

Indifference (indi·fĕrĕns). late ME. [f. as next; see -ENCE.] †1. = INDIFFERENCY 1. -1754. 2. Absence of feeling for or against; hence *esp.* Absence of care for or about a person or thing; unconcern, apathy. Const. *to, towards.* 1659. 3. Indetermination of the will, or of a body to rest or motion; neutrality 1728. 4. †The quality of being neither good nor bad (TILLOTSON); mediocrity 1864. 5. = INDIFFERENCY II. 1. 1656. 6. The fact of making no difference; unimportance; a thing or matter of no importance 1644. 7. *Magnetism. I. point, point of i.*: the middle zone of a magnet where the attractive powers of the two ends neutralize each other 1886.

2. The human mind is often..in a state neither of pain nor pleasure, which I call a state of i. BURKE. 6. The Necessity or I. of observing the Mosaic Rites 1708.

Indifferency (indi·fĕrĕnsi). late ME. [ad. L. *indifferentia*; see INDIFFERENT and -ENCY.] I. 1. Absence of bias, prejudice, or favour; impartiality, equity. Now *rare.* 2. = INDIFFERENCE 2. Now *rare.* 1625. †3. Indetermination of the will; freedom of choice -1699. 4. Of a word: Capability of being applied to different things; neutral or equivocal sense. Now *rare* or *Obs.* 1596. †5. Of a place: Neutrality in point of advantage -1645. †6. The condition of being neither good nor bad -1692.

2. How long will you halt in this I.? BP. HALL. 3. This I. to do or not to do, cannot be the true Notion of Liberty BURNET.

II. 1. Want of difference in nature or character; substantial equivalence. Now *rare.* 1568. 2. Absence of difference in respect of consequence, effect, meaning, or importance; the fact of its being of no consequence either way 1564. †b. A matter of indifference -1668.

1. You have arrived at a fine Pyrrhonism, at an equivalence and i. of all actions EMERSON. 2. It is a matter of meere i. FULKE.

Indifferent (indi·fĕrĕnt), *a.* (*sb.* and *adv.*) ME. [a. F., or ad. L. *indifferentem*, f. *in-* (IN-³) + *differentem* DIFFERENT.]

I. 1. Without difference of inclination; unbiased, impartial, disinterested; fair, just, even-handed. *arch.* 2. Having no inclination or feeling for or against a thing; hence, Unconcerned, apathetic, insensible. Const. *to.* 1519. †3. Of neutral disposition; equally disposed or indisposed *to* -1690. †4. Having a neutral relation *to* (two or more things); impartially pertinent or applicable -1678. †5. Not more advantageous to one person or party than to another -1655. 6. †Of medium quality or character -1699; fairly large; tolerable (*Obs.* or *arch.*) 1546. 7. Of neutral quality; neither good nor bad 1532. b. Hence, by euphemism: Not particularly good. (Often preceded by *but* or *very.*) 1638. c. In poor health. *Obs.* or *dial.* 1753. 8. In scientific use: a. Neutral in chemical, electrical, or magnetic quality, as *i. point.* b. Undifferentiated, as *i. cell, tissue*, etc. 1855.

1. I leave to all worthy and i. men to judge RALEIGH. Phr. *I. justice*, impartial or even-handed justice. 2. These mighty cliffs..I. to the sun or snow SCOTT. 6. I. wealth to maintaine his family..nothing superfluous LYLY. 7. Bards and bardlings, good, bad, and i. 1821. b. After an ill supper, he was shewed an i. bed CLARENDON.

II. †1. Not different; equal, even; identical, the same -1721. 2. Regarded as not mattering either way. Cf. I. 2. 1513. b. Of no consequence either way; immaterial 1611. c. *spec.* Of an observance, etc.: That may be equally well observed or neglected; non-essential 1563.

2. I am arm'd, And dangers are to me i. *Jul. C.* I. iii. 115. b. Many haue sinned for a smal matter [*marg.* thing i.] *Ecclus.* xxvii. 1.

Hence **Indi·fferent-ly** *adv.* ME., **-ness.**

B. *sb.* †1. One who is disinterested -1602. 2. One who is neutral or unconcerned, esp. in religion or politics 1556. 3. *pl.* Things indifferent; non-essentials (*rare*) 1626.

†C. *adv.* To some extent; moderately, tolerably, fairly -1826.

You have seen me act my part i. well SCOTT.

Indiffere·ntiated, *a. rare.* 1878. [IN-³.] Not differentiated; not specialized.

Indifferentism (indi·fĕrĕntiz'm). 1827. [f. INDIFFERENT *a.* + -ISM.] 1. A spirit of indifference professed and practised 1831. b. *esp.* Adiaphorism; absence of zeal or interest in religious matters 1827. 2. *Philos.* A theory in which the characteristic differences of mind and matter are supposed to disappear 1866. Also, = ADIAPHORISM, IDENTISM.

1. b. His anxiety to promote Christian charity converted into i. PUSEY. So **Indi·fferentist**, one who professes or practises indifference, neutrality, or unconcern.

Indifulvin (indifʊ·lvin). 1865. [f. INDI- + L. *fulvus* yellow + -IN.] *Chem.* A brittle, friable, reddish-yellow resin ($C_{22}H_{20}N_2O_3$), obtained from indican.

Indifuscin (-fʊ·sin). 1859. [f. INDI- + L. *fuscus* dark + -IN.] *Chem.* A brown powder ($C_{24}H_{20}N_2O_9$) obtained from indican.

Indigen, var. of INDIGENE.

‖**Indi·gena.** Pl. **-næ.** 1591. [L., f. *indu-*in, within + *-gena* from *gen-*, stem of *gignere* to beget.] = INDIGENE *sb.* Hence **Indi·genal** *a.* = INDIGENOUS; *sb.* = INDIGENE *sb.*

Indigence (i·ndidʒĕns). ME. [a. F., ad. L. *indigentia*; see INDIGENT and -ENCE.] †1. The fact or condition of wanting or needing (a thing); lack, deficiency; requirement -1775. 2. *spec.* Want of the means of subsistence; poverty, penury, destitution ME. †3. A want, a need -1694.

2. As they had before been reduced from affluence to i. BURKE. So **I·ndigency** (in all senses).

Indigene (i·ndidʒīn). 1598. [a. F. *indigène*, ad. L. *indigena*, f. *indi-* (*indu-*), ancient deriv. form of *in* prep. + *gon-*, *gignere*, in passive 'to be born'.] †**A.** *adj.* = INDIGENOUS -1697. **B.** *sb.* Anative 1664.

Indigenous (indi·dʒĭnəs), *a.* 1646. [f. late L. *indigenus* (f. *indigena*: see prec.) + -OUS.] **1.** Born or produced naturally in a land or region; native *to* (the soil, region, etc.). **b.** *transf.* and *fig.* Inborn, innate 1864. **2.** Native, vernacular 1844.

1. Yet were they [Negroes] all transported from Africa..and are not i. or proper natives of America SIR T. BROWNE. b. Joy and hope are emotions i. to the human mind 1864. 2. I. schools H. H. WILSON. Hence **Indi·genous-ly** *adv.*, **-ness.**

Indigent (i·ndidʒĕnt), *a.* (*sb.*) ME. [a. F., ad. L. *indigentem*, *indigere* to lack, f. *indu-* (IN-[2]) + *egere* to want.] **1.** Lacking in what is requisite; wanting, deficient (*arch.*). Also with *of*. **2.** *spec.* Lacking the necessaries of life; needy, poor ME. **3.** *sb.* An indigent person 1563.

1. How low, how little are the Proud, How i. the Great GRAY. 2. I. faint Soules, past corporall toyle SHAKS. Hence **I·ndigent-ly** *adv.*, **-ness.**

†**Indige·st**, *a.* (*sb.*) ME. [ad. L. *indigestus* unarranged, f. *in-* (IN-[3]) + *digestus*, *digerere*.] **1.** Undigested; crude; shapeless, confused; unarranged -1806. **2.** *sb.* A shapeless mass 1595.

1. A chaos rude and i. W. BROWNE. 2. *John* v. vii. 26.

Indigested (indidʒe·stĕd), *a.* 1587. [f. IN-[3] + DIGESTED *ppl. a.*] **1.** Not arranged; without form; shapeless, chaotic 1593. **b.** Not ordered in the mind; ill-considered 1587. **2.** Not digested in the stomach 1620. †**3.** Not purified or rectified by heat; crude, raw. WOTTON. †**4.** 'Not brought to suppuration' (J.) 1676.

1. A rude and i. Chaos, or confusion of matters PURCHAS. b. The wild and i. Notion of raising my Fortune DE FOE.

Indigestible (indidʒe·stĭb'l), *a.* 1528. (Earlier †*-able*.) [ad. L. *indigestibilis*; see IN-[3] and DIGESTIBLE.] Incapable of being digested, or difficult to digest; not easily assimilated as food. Also *fig.* and *transf.*

fig. Indigestable malice PURCHAS. Hence **Indigestibi·lity, Indige·stibleness.**

Indigestion (indidʒe·styən). 1450. [a. F., ad. late L. *indigestionem*; see IN-[3] and DIGESTION.] **1.** Want of digestion; incapacity of or difficulty in digesting food. Also *fig.* **b.** with *pl.* A case or attack of indigestion 1702. **2.** Undigested condition; disorder, imperfection. Also, an instance of this. 1656.

1. I. is learnedly spoken of as dyspepsia BEALE.

Indigestive (indidʒe·stiv), *a.* 1632. [IN-[3].] **1.** Suffering from indigestion; tending to indigestion; dyspeptic. †**2.** Not ready to digest offences. COTTON.

Indigitate (indi·dʒiteit), *v.* 1617. [f. L. *indigitat-*, *indigitare* to call upon, invoke (a deity), etc.; of obscure origin, erron. associated w. *digitus* finger.] †**1.** *trans.* **a.** To call, to indicate by a name. **b.** To proclaim, declare. -1680. †**2.** To point out with or as with the finger; to indicate -1716. **3.** *intr.* To interlock like the fingers of two hands. 1835.

1. b. The Scriptures did i. he would rise again the third day HACKET. 2. Their lines did seeme to i. and point at our times SIR T. BROWNE. Hence **Indigita·tion**, †the action of indigitating; in *Anat.*, interlocking of the fingers of two hands; hence, the mode of junction of muscle and tendon.

Indiglucin (indiglū·sin). 1865. [f. INDI- + Gr. γλυκύς + -IN.] *Chem.* A light yellow 'sugar', $C_6H_{10}O_6$, one of the constituents of indican.

Indign (indəi·n), *a.* Now only *poet.* 1450. [a. F. *indigne*, ad L. *indignus*, f. *in-* (IN-[3]) + *dignus* worthy.] **1.** Unworthy; undeserving (*arch.*). **2.** Unbecoming; fraught with shame or dishonour; disgraceful 1545.

1. A cursyd foole and Indygne hounde CAXTON. 2. All indigne, and base aduersities, make head against my Estimation SHAKS. Hence †**Indi·gnly** *adv.*

Indi·gnance. *rare.* 1590. [f. INDIGNANT; see -ANCE.] Indignation; the being indignant. So **Indi·gnancy** (*rare*).

Indignant (indi·gnănt), *a.* 1590. [ad. L. *indignantem*, *indignari* to regard as unworthy, f. *indignus*; see INDIGN.] Affected with indignation; provoked to wrath by something unworthy, unjust, or ungrateful; 'inflamed at once with anger and disdain' (J.). Also *fig.* of things.

Full of fiers fury and i. hate To him he turned SPENSER. *fig.* His seat..I. spurns the cottage from the green GOLDSM. Hence **Indi·gnantly** *adv.*

Indignation (indignē·ʃən). ME. [ad. L. *indignationem*, or immed. a. F.] †**1.** The action of counting or treating as unworthy of regard; disdain, contempt -1530. **2.** Anger at what is unworthy or wrongful; wrath excited by a sense of wrong, or by meanness, injustice, wickedness, or misconduct; righteous or dignified anger ME. †**3.** The turning of the stomach against unwelcome food, etc. -1668.

2. Go, my puple..be hid a litil while, to the tyme that passe myn indignacioun WYCLIF *Isa.* xxvi. 20. So great was the i. against Wolsey FROUDE. *fig.* Ready mounted are they to spit forth Their Iron i. 'gainst your walles SHAKS.

†**Indi·gnify**, *v.* 1595. [f. L. *indignus* + -FY.] To treat with indignity; to dishonour; to represent as unworthy -1743.

Indignity (indi·gnĭti). 1584. [ad. L. *indignitatem*, f. *indignus*.] †**1.** The being unworthy; unworthiness. In *pl.*, Unworthy qualities. -1677. †**2.** The quality of being unbecoming, dishonourable, or disgraceful; want of dignity or honour. **b.** Disgraceful conduct; a disgraceful act. -1766. **3.** Unworthy treatment; contemptuous or insolent usage. With *an* and *pl.*: A slight; an insult or affront. 1584. †**4.** = INDIGNATION 2. -1784.

1. Accept my Zeale, and pardon mine Indignitie SYLVESTER. 2. Oh, i.! oh, blot To honour and religion! MILT. *Sams.* 411. 3. Their contempts and indignities offered to our Countrey and Prince HAKLUYT. 4. God..took this their affront in high i. FULLER.

Indigo (i·ndigo), *sb.* (*a.*) 1555. [Occurs from 16th c. in two forms *indico*, *indigo*; f. L. *indicum* (Pliny), a. Gr. ἰνδικόν the blue Indian dye, lit. 'the Indian (substance)', adj. neut. used subst.] **1.** A substance obtained in the form of a blue powder from plants of the genus *Indigofera*, N. O. *Leguminosæ*, and largely used as a dye.

It is produced by the decomposition of the glucoside INDICAN, which exists also in woad and various other plants. Its essential constituent is indigo-blue; besides which, however, *commercial* or *crude indigo* contains indigo-red, indigo-brown, and some earthy matters (indigo-gluten).

b. *pl.* Sorts or samples of indigo 1609. **2.** A plant from which indigo is obtained, INDIGO-PLANT, including several species of *Indigofera*; esp. *I. tinctoria*, *I. Anil*, and *I. floribunda* 1600. **3.** The colour yielded by indigo, reckoned by Newton as one of the seven prismatic or primary colours 1622.

B. *adj.* (attrib. use of 3.) Of a deep violet-blue colour 1856.

A sky of..a streaky i. hue H. S. WILSON.

Comb.: **i.-berry**, the fruit of *Randia latifolia* and *R. aculeata*, from which a blue dye is obtained; **-brown**, a brown resinous substance, a mixture of indihumin and indiretin, existing in all kinds of commercial i.; **-carmine**, indigo-disulphonate of sodium or potassium, used for dyeing silk and as a water-colour; **-copper**, the mineral COVELLINE; **-finch** = INDIGO-BIRD; **-gelatine, -gluten**, the glutinous matter found in commercial i.; **-green**, a green substance obtained from i. by adding potash to an alcoholic solution of an alkaline hyposulphindigotate; **-purple**, purple obtained from i. by the action of fused sodium sulphate; **-purpurin, -red**, synonyms of INDIRUBIN; **-snake** (*U.S.*), the gopher-snake; **-yellow**, 'a substance produced by heating hyposulphindigotate of calcium with lime-water in contact with air; it is a transparent yellow mass (Watts).

I·ndigo-bi·rd. 1864. A N. American bird, a species of finch, *Cyanospiza cyanea*, family *Fringillidæ*, the male of which has the head and upper parts of rich indigo-blue.

Indigo-blue. 1712. **A.** *sb.* **1.** The blue-violet colour of indigo. **2.** The blue colouring matter of indigo, also called *indigotin*, crystallizing in fine right rhombic prisms of blue colour and metallic lustre; pure indigo 1838. **B.** *adj.* Of the blue colour of indigo 1836.

Indigogen (i·ndigoˌdʒən). 1838. [f. INDIGO + -GEN 'producing'.] *Chem.* An obs. name for INDIGO-WHITE.

Indigometer (indigǫ·mĭtəɹ). 1828. [f. as prec. + -METER.] An instrument for ascertaining the strength of indigo. So **Indigo·metry**, the art or method of determining the colouring power of indigo.

Indigo-plant. 1757. A plant yielding indigo; *spec.* a plant of the genus *Indigofera*.

I·ndigotate. 1838. [f. as next + -ATE.[1]] *Chem.* A salt of indigotic acid; a nitrosalicylate.

Indigotic (indigǫ·tik), *a.* 1838. [f. as INDIGOTIN + -IC.] Of, pertaining to, or produced from indigo.

I. acid, = ANILIC *acid*.

Indigotin (i·ndigotin). 1838. [f. INDIGO + *t* euphonic + -IN.] *Chem.* = INDIGO-BLUE. Also *attrib.* and *Comb.*

Indigo-white. 1874. *Chem.* Reduced or deoxidized indigo, also called *leucindigo*, a white crystalline powder obtained by reduction from commercial indigo; it is re-converted by oxidation to indigo-blue.

Indihumin (indiˌhiū·min). 1865. [f. INDI- + L. *humus* soil + -IN.] *Chem.* A product of the decomposition of indican, which occurs with indiretin in indigo-brown.

†**Indi·latory**, *a.* *rare.* 1654. [IN-[3].] Not dilatory.

†**Indi·ligence.** 1496. [ad. L. *indiligentia*; see IN-[3] and DILIGENCE.] **1.** Want of diligence -1658. **2.** Want of attention -1651. So †**Indi·ligent** *a.* idle, slothful; inattentive. †**Indi·ligently** *adv.*

Indime·nsional, *a.* [IN-[3].] Having no dimensions. TAIT.

†**Indimi·nishable**, *a.* *rare.* 1641. [IN-[3].] That cannot be diminished or lessened -1799.

Indin (i·ndin). 1845. [f. IND- indigo- + -IN.] *Chem.* A crystalline substance of a beautiful rose-colour, isomeric with indigo-blue.

Indirect (indire·kt), *a.* ME. [a. F., or ad. L. *indirectus*; see IN-[3] and DIRECT.] Not direct. **1.** Of a way, etc.: Not straight; crooked; devious; of a movement: Oblique. (Chiefly *fig.*) 1474. **b.** Of actions, etc.: Not straightforward; not fair and open; crooked, deceitful, corrupt 1570. **2.** Not taking the straight or nearest course to the end aimed at; roundabout 1584. **b.** *Logic.* 1727. **c.** *Pol. Econ.* Of taxation: Not levied directly upon the person on whom it ultimately falls 1801. **3.** *Gram.* Of speech or narration: Put in a reported form, not in the speaker's own words; oblique; opp. to *direct* 1866. **4.** Not directly aimed at or attained; not immediately resulting from an action or cause 1823.

1. Heauen knowes..By what by-pathes, and i. crook'd-ways I met this Crowne SHAKS. b. Livings ..may not by corrupt and i. Dealings be transferred to other Uses 1570. 2. Implicite or i. proofs WATERLAND. b. *I. Modes*, of syllogisms..are the five last modes of the first figure..It is the conversion of the conclusion which renders the modes i. 1727. Showing that something impossible or absurd follows from contradicting our conclusion is called i. demonstration ABP. THOMSON. c. They [i. taxes] consist in the levy of imposts on articles of consumption [etc.] ROGERS. 4. Happiness is not the direct aim, but the i. consequence of the good government JOWETT. Hence **Indire·ct-ly** *adv.*, **-ness.**

Indire·cted, *a.* *rare.* 1601. [IN-[3].] Not directed or guided -1819.

Indirection (indire·kʃən). 1595. [f. INDIRECT, after DIRECTION.] **1.** Indirect movement or action; roundabout means or method 1602. **2.** Want of straightforwardness in action; deceit; malpractice.

1. And thus doe we..By indirections finde directions out *Haml.* II. i. 65. 2. *Jul. C.* IV. iii. 75.

Indiretin (indirī·tin). 1865. [f. INDI- + Gr. ῥητίνη resin + -IN.] *Chem.* A dark-brown shining resin, one of the components of indigo-brown, obtained from indican.

Indirubin (indirū·bin). 1859. [f. INDI- + L. *ruber* red + -IN.] *Chem.* A substance, isomeric with indigo-blue, obtained by decomposition of indican. Also called *indigo-purpurin* and *indigo-red*.

Indiscernible (indizə·mĭb'l). Also †*-able*. 1635. [f. IN-[3] + DISCERNIBLE; cf. F. *indiscernable*.] **A.** *adj.* **1.** Incapable of being discerned; imperceptible, undiscoverable. **2.** Indistinguishable. *Obs.* or *arch.* 1646.

1. A rapid look, i. by male eye READE.

B. *sb.* **1.** An animal, etc. that cannot be

discerned by the senses. KIRBY. **2.** *Metaph.* A thing that cannot be distinguished from some other thing or things 1717.

2. Where there is no difference, there is no activity, and hence no substance or individuality. This is the meaning of the celebrated 'identity of indiscernibles' E. CAIRD. Hence **Indisce·rnibleness. Indisce·rnibly** *adv.*

†Indisce·rpible, *a.* 1659. [IN-[3].] = INDISCERPTIBLE -1839. Hence **†Indiscerpibi·lity, †Indisce·rpibleness. †Indisce·rpibly** *adv.*

Indiscerptible (indisə·ɹptĭb'l), *a.* 1736. [IN-[3].] Incapable of being divided into parts; not destructible by dissolution of parts.

The soul has no parts to be separated; in Butler's phrase, it is i. 1848. Hence **Indiscerptibi·lity, Indisce·rptibleness. Indisce·rptibly** *adv.*

Indisciplinable (indi·siplinăb'l), *a.* 1600. [IN-[3].] Incapable of being disciplined; intractable.

Indiscipline (indi·siplin). 1783. [IN-[3].] Absence or lack of discipline; want of the order and method acquired by training.

Indiscoverable (indiskʊ·vərăb'l), *a.* 1640. [IN-[3].] Not discoverable; undiscoverable.

†Indiscovered, *a.* [IN-[3].] Not discovered. COWLEY.

†Indisco·very. 1629. [IN-[3].] Non-discovery -1646.

Indiscreet (indiskrī·t), *a.* ME. [prob. a. F. *indiscret, -crète,* or ad. L. *indiscretus,* in a med.L. sense; see DISCREET *a.* Cf. INDISCRETE.] **†1.** Without sound judgement -1675. **2.** Imprudent in speech or action; inconsiderate; unadvised 1588.

1. I. chroniclers 1617. 2. It would ill become me to be vaine, i., or a foole *L. L. L.* IV. ii. 31. Hence **Indiscree·t-ly** *adv.*, **-ness.**

Indiscrete (indiskrī·t), *a.* 1608. [ad. L. *indiscretus* unseparated; see IN-[3] and DISCRETE, and cf. prec.] **†1.** Not distinctly distinguishable from contiguous objects or parts -1661. **2.** Not divided into distinct parts 1782.

2. Next all was water, all a chaos i. 1883. Hence **Indiscre·tely** *adv.* without separation or division.

Indiscretion (indiskre·ʃən). ME. [a. F., ad. late L. *indiscretionem*; see IN-[3] and DISCRETION.] **1.** Want of discretion; in early use, chiefly, want of discernment or discrimination; in later, want of judgement; imprudence. **2.** An indiscreet act or step. (Sometimes *euphem.*, for an immoral act or practice.) 1601.

2. A youth, gu'lty only of an i. MACAULAY.

Indiscriminate (indiskri·minĕt), *a.* 1597. [IN-[3].] **1.** Of things: Not marked by discrimination or discernment; done without making distinctions; confused, promiscuous 1649. **2.** Of persons: Undiscriminating; making no distinctions 1792. **3.** quasi-*adv.* Indiscriminately 1597.

1. I. vengeance 1777, slaughter THIRLWALL, censure and applause STANLEY. 2. An i. admirer 1840. Hence **Indiscri·minate·ly** *adv.*, **-ness.**

Indiscriminating (indiskri·mineˑtiŋ), *a.* 1754. [IN-[3].] Not discriminating. Hence **Indiscri·minatingly** *adv.*

Indiscrimination (indiskriminē·ʃən). 1649. [IN-[3].] The fact of not discriminating; the condition of not being discriminated; absence of distinction; want of discernment.

Indiscriminative (indiskri·minĕtiv), *a.* 1854. [IN-[3].] Not characterized by, or inclined to, discrimination. So **†Indiscri·minatively** *adv.* 1684.

†Indiscu·ssed, *a. rare.* 1534. [IN-[3].] Undiscussed -1631.

†I·ndish, *a.* 1548. [f. IND + -ISH[1].] = INDIAN *a.* -1601.

Indispensable (indispe·nsăb'l), *a.* (*sb.*) Also **†-ible.** 1533. [ad. med.L. *indispensabilis*; see IN-[3] and DISPENSABLE.] Not to be dispensed with. **†1.** Not subject to eccl. dispensation; not to be permitted, allowed, or condoned -1654. **2.** Of a law, duty, etc.: That cannot be remitted, set aside, or neglected 1649. **3.** That cannot be done without; absolutely necessary or requisite. Const. *to, for.* 1696. **4.** *sb.* An indispensable thing or person 1681; *pl.* (*colloq. euphemism*) Trousers 1841.

1. [He] absolutely condemnes this marriage as incestuous and i. BP. HALL. 2. Our obligations to obey all God's commands..are absolute and i. BUTLER. 3. The knowledge of anatomy is i. to him 1793. Hence **Indispensabi·lity, Indispe·nsableness. Indispe·nsably** *adv.*

†Indispe·rsed, *a. rare.* 1647. [IN-[3].] Undispersed -1686.

Indispose (indispōu·z), *v.* 1657. [f. IN-[3] + DISPOSE *v.*] **1.** To put out of the proper disposition for some action or result; to render unfit or incapable; to disqualify. **2.** To put out of health, disorder. (See INDISPOSED.) 1694. **3.** To affect with mental indisposition, disincline, render averse or unwilling 1692. **4.** To cause to be unfavourably disposed; to set at variance. (Now unusual.) 1748. **5.** To render not liable or subject (*to* something) 1822.

1. Not to get one's Sleep..indisposes one..for the Day 1863. 3. Indisposing landlords to let long leases of farms MALTHUS. 4. Polemical conversations.. certainly do i., for a time, the contending parties towards each other CHESTERF. 5. Inoculation indisposes the constitution to infection 1830.

Indisposed (indispōu·zd), *ppl. a.* late ME. [f. IN-[3] + DISPOSED.] **†1.** Not put in order, out of order -1691. **†2.** Unfitted, unqualified -1646. **†3.** Evilly disposed, ill-conditioned 1464-1597. **4.** Out of health, unwell; not very well. (Mostly predicative.) SHAKS. **5.** Not disposed or inclined mentally or physically; unwilling, unfriendly (now *rare*) 1646. **†6.** Not disposed *of* 1669.

Hence **Indispo·sedness** (now *rare* or *Obs.*), the condition of being indisposed; indisposition.

Indisposition (i:ndispŏzi·ʃən). 1440. [IN-[3].] The fact or condition of being indisposed. **†1.** Want of adaptation; unfitness; incapacity -1750. **†2.** Want of apt arrangement; displacement or misplacement; disorder -1677. **†3.** Evil disposition 1553. **4.** Disordered bodily condition; ailment; esp. of a slight character 1598. **5.** Disinclination, unwillingness 1594. **6.** The state of being unfavourably disposed *to* or *towards* 1647. **7.** The condition of not being liable or subject (*mod.*).

4. A long i. of Health hath much hindred..me HALE. 5. A great i. to prayer 1628. 6. An i. to the interests of Ireland BURKE. 7. The two substances showed an i. to combine (*mod.*).

Indisputable (indi·spiutăb'l, indispiū·tăb'l), *a.* 1551. [ad. late L. *indisputabilis*; see IN-[3] and DISPUTABLE.] **1.** That cannot be disputed; unquestionable. **†2.** Undisputing. RICHARDSON. Hence **Indisputabi·lity, Indisputableness. Indisputably** *adv.*

†Indispu·ted, *a.* 1643. [IN-[3].] Not disputed -1804.

Indissociable (indisōu·ʃiăb'l), *a.* 1855. [IN-[3].] Incapable of being dissociated.

Indissoluble (indi·sǫliŭb'l, indisǫ·liŭb'l), *a.* 1542. [ad. L. *indissolubilis*; see IN-[3] and DISSOLUBLE.] Not dissoluble. **1.** That cannot be dissolved or decomposed; that cannot be destroyed, put an end to, or abolished; indestructible 1568. **†2.** That cannot be dissolved in a liquid. (Repl. by INSOLUBLE.) -1794. **b.** That cannot be melted or liquefied. ? *Obs.* 1751. **3.** That cannot be dissolved, undone, or broken; firm, stable, lasting. (The prevailing sense.) 1542.

1. Well fenced with an i. wall HOLLAND. 2. b. Some bodies, i. by heat, can set the furnace and crucible at defiance JOHNSON. 3. An i. tye SHAKS., chain of circumstances PRIESTLEY. Hence **Indissolubility** (indi·sǫl-, indisǫ·liubi·lĭti), **Indissolubleness,** the quality of being i. **Indissolubly** *adv.*

†Indisso·lvable, *a.* Also **†-ible.** 1531. [IN-[3].] = INDISSOLUBLE (in all senses) -1788. Hence **†Indissolvabi·lity, †Indisso·lvableness. †Indisso·lvably** *adv.*

†Indi·stance. 1624. [ad. med.L. *indistantia*; cf. IN-[3] and DISTANCE.] The quality or character of being 'indistant'. So **†Indi·stancy.** -1659.

†Indi·stant, *a.* 1644. [ad. late or med.L. *indistans, -stantem,* tr. Gr. ἀδιάστατος; see IN-[3] and DISTANT.] **1.** Not distant, not separated by an interval; continuous. **2.** Without material extension. CUDWORTH. Hence **†Indi·stantly** *adv.*

Indistinct (indisti·ŋkt), *a.* late ME. [ad. L. *indistinctus*; see IN-[3] and DISTINCT.] **1.** Not seen or heard clearly; confused, blurred; hence, faint, dim, obscure. Also *transf.* Also of the act of perception, or a perceiving faculty. **2.** Not distinct; not kept separate or apart in the mind or perception; not clearly defined or marked off 1604. **3.** Of judgement or action: Not distinguishing between different things; undiscriminating, indiscriminate. Now *rare* or *Obs.* 1650.

1. The public haunt..Hums i. THOMSON. An i. recollection JOWETT. 2. Three sacred persons in Trinitie, distinguished really, and yet i. essentially 1604. 3. Some in an i. voracity eating almost any SIR T. BROWNE. So **Indisti·nctly** *adv.* 1420.

†Indisti·nctible, *a.* [f. IN-[3] + *distinctible,* f. L. *distinct-, distinguere* + -IBLE.] Undistinguishable. WARTON.

Indistinction (indisti·ŋkʃən). Now *rare.* 1624. [IN-[3].] **1.** The fact of not distinguishing. **2.** The condition or fact of not being distinct or different; undistinguishableness 1644. **†3.** Indistinctness, obscurity, dimness -1795.

1. That scandalous i. between the worthy and the worthless 1768. 2. In a body there cannot be i. of parts, but each must possesse his own portion of parts JER. TAYLOR.

Indistinctive (indisti·ŋktiv), *a.* 1699. [IN-[3].] **1.** Not distinguishing; undiscriminating. **2.** Without distinctive character or features 1846. Hence **Indisti·nctive-ly** *adv.*, **-ness.**

Indisti·nctness. 1727. [f. INDISTINCT *a.* + -NESS.] The quality or condition of being indistinct; obscurity, dimness.

The ambiguity or i. of terms WHATELY. I. of outline 1880.

Indistinguishable (indisti·ŋgwiʃăb'l), *a.* 1606. [IN-[3].] **1.** Incapable of being discriminated or recognized as different *from* something else, or from each other 1658. **b.** *transf.* Of which the parts are not distinguishable 1606. **2.** That cannot be clearly perceived; not discernible; imperceptible 1642.

1. The true seeds of Cypresse and Rampions are i. by old eyes SIR T. BROWNE. b. You whorson i. Curre SHAKS. 2. The..i. lapse of time COLERIDGE. Hence **Indistinguishabi·lity, Indisti·nguishableness. Indisti·nguishably** *adv.*

Indisti·nguished, *a.* Now *rare.* 1605. [IN-[3].] Not distinguished; undistinguished.

†Indisti·nguishing, *a.* 1828. [IN-[3].] Undiscriminating; as, *i. liberalities.* (WEBSTER.)

Indistributable (indistri·biutăb'l), *a.* 1847. [IN-[3].] That cannot be distributed.

Indisturbable (indistɜ̄·ɹbăb'l), *a.* 1660. [IN-[3].] Incapable of being disturbed.

Indisturbance (indistɜ̄·ɹbăns). Now *rare.* 1659. [IN-[3].] Absence of disturbance; quietness, tranquillity.

†Indi·tch, *v.* 1597. [f. IN-[1] or [2] + DITCH *sb.*] **1.** *trans.* To cast into or bury in (or as in) a ditch -1630. **2.** To surround with a ditch; to entrench -1610.

Indite (indəi·t), *v.* [ME. *endite,* a. OF. *enditer*:—L. type **indictare*; see INDICT *v.*[1]] **†1.** *trans.* = DICTATE *v.* 1. Also *absol.* -1815. **†2.** = DICTATE *v.* 2. -1709. **3.** To put into words, compose (a poem, etc.); to express or describe in a literary composition ME. Also *absol.* or *intr.* **4.** *trans.* To put into written words, to pen; to set down in writing. In later use, passing into 3. ME. ¶**5.** *Catachr.* for *invite. Rom. & Jul.* II. iv. 135.

3. He hadde deuised his artycles so wysely, and endicted the[m] so well MORE. My heart is inditing a good matter *Ps.* xlv. 1. 4. To endite Tickets for the Bear-garden MARVELL. Hence **Indi·tement,** composition in prose or verse. **Indi·ter,** one who indites, composes, or dictates; an author, writer, etc.

Indium (i·ndiŏm). 1864. [f. radical of *ind-icum* INDIGO + *-ium,* after *sodium,* etc.; in reference to the two indigo lines which form the characteristic spectrum of the metal.] *Chem.* A soft silver-white metal of extreme rarity, occurring in association with zinc and other metals; discovered by means of spectrum analysis in the zinc-blende of Freiberg. Symbol In. Also *attrib.*

Indivertible (indivɜ̄·ɹtĭb'l), *a.* 1821. [f. IN-[3] + *divertible.*] Incapable of being diverted or turned aside.

†**Indivi·dable,** *a.* 1602. [IN-³.] Indivisible -1637.

†**Indivi·ded,** *a.* 1563. [IN-³.] Undivided -1695.

Individual (indivi·diu̦ăl). ME. [f. med.L. *individualis*, f. *individuus* indivisible, inseparable (see INDIVIDUUM) + -AL; cf. F. *individuel.*]

A. *adj.* †**1.** One in substance or essence; indivisible -1678. †**2.** Inseparable -1667. **3.** Existing as a separate indivisible entity; numerically one, single; particular, special 1613. †**b.** Identical, selfsame, very same -1804. **4.** Distinguished from others by attributes of its own 1646. **5.** Characteristic of an individual 1605.

1. The holy and indiuiduall Trinitie 1623. 2. To have thee by my side Henceforth an i. solace dear MILT. *P. L.* IV. 486. 3. Every man in his physical nature is one i. single agent BUTLER. A determination in each i. man to go his own way FROUDE. b. Which I do believe to be this i. Book 1701. 4. He is so quaint and so i. in his views 1894. 5. As touching the Manners of learned men, it is a thing personall and individuall BACON.

B. *sb.* †**1.** *pl.* Inseparable things; see A. 2. -1661. **2.** A single object or thing, or a group of things regarded as a unit; a single member of a class, group, or number 1605. **b.** *Logic* and *Metaph.* An object which is determined by properties peculiar to itself and cannot be subdivided into others of the same kind; *spec.* in *Logic*, An object included in a species, as a species is in a genus 1628. **c.** *Zool.* and *Bot.* A single member of a species; a single specimen of an animal or plant 1859. **d.** *Biol.* An organism regarded as having a separate existence 1776. **3.** A single human being, as opp. to Society, the Family, etc. 1626. **b.** A human being, a person. (Now chiefly vulgar or disparaging.) 1742. †**4.** Short for *i. person*; person, personality, self -1800.

2. That individuals die, his will ordains DRYDEN. 3. b. The i. whom I desired to meet KANE.

Individualism (indivi·diu̦ăliz'm). 1835. [a. F. *individualisme*, or f. INDIVIDUAL + -ISM.] **1.** Self-centred feeling or conduct as a principle; free and independent individual action or thought; egoism. **2.** The social theory which advocates the free and independent action of the individual. Opp. to COLLECTIVISM and SOCIALISM. 1884. **3.** = INDIVIDUALITY 2, 3. 1854. **4.** *Philos.* **a.** The doctrine that reality is constituted of individual entities. **b.** The doctrine that the self is the only knowable existence; egoism 1877.

Indivi·dualist. 1840. [f. INDIVIDUAL + -IST.] An adherent of individualism. Also *attrib.* or as *adj.* Hence **Indivi:duali·stic** *a.* of or pertaining to individualism or individualists.

Individuality (individiu̦æ·lĭti). 1614. [f. as prec. + -ITY.] **1.** The state or quality of being indivisible or inseparable; an indivisible or inseparable entity 1645. **2.** The fact or condition of existing as an individual; separate and continuous existence 1658. **3.** The aggregate of properties peculiar to an individual; the sum of the attributes which distinguish an object from others of the same kind; individual character. **b.** Idiosyncrasy. 1614. **c.** *pl.* Individual characteristics 1647. **4.** An individual personality 1775.

1. There ought to be an i. in Mariage MILT. 3. The Puritan i. is nowhere so overpowering as in Milton 1874. 4. Here sit poor I, with nothing but my own solitary i. JOHNSON.

Individualize (indivi·diu̦ălaiz), *v.* 1637. [f. as prec. + -IZE.] **1.** *trans.* To render individual; to characterize by distinctive marks or qualities; to mark out from other persons or things. Also *absol.* **2.** To specify, particularize. Also *absol.* 1656.

1. The peculiarities which i. and distinguish the humour of Addison 1805. Hence **I:ndividualiza·tion.**

Individually (indivi·diu̦ăli), *adv.* 1597. [-LY ².] †**1.** Indivisibly; inseparably, undividedly -1627. **2.** In individual identity. ? *Obs.* 1624. **3.** Personally; in an individual capacity 1660. **4.** In an individual or distinctive manner; as single persons or things; each by each, one by one; opp. to *collectively* 1641.

1. An attribute.. i. proper to the Godhead HAKEWILL. 2. Phr. *I. the same*, identically the same. *I. different*, different as individuals (though possibly of the same species). 4. The sacrifice which they collectively made was i. repaid to them JOWETT.

Indivi·duate, *ppl. a.* 1606. [ad. med.L. *individuatus*; see next.] †**1.** Undivided, indivisible, inseparable -1751. **2.** Rendered individual; individualized (*arch.*) 1606.

Individuate (indivi·diu̦eⁱt), *v.* 1614. [f. med.L. *individuare* to render individual, f. L. *individuus*; see -ATE ³.] **1.** *trans.* To form into an individual entity 1646. **2.** To give an individual character to; to distinguish from others of the same species; to individualize; to single out 1614. †**3.** To appropriate to an individual. TRAPP.

1. There was a seminality and contracted Adam in the rib, which..was individuated into Eve SIR T. BROWNE. 2. Circumstances i. actions 1641. Hence **Indivi·duator,** one who or that which individuates.

Individuation (i:ndividiu̦ēⁱ·ʃən). 1628. [ad. med.L. *individuationem*; see prec.] **1.** The action or process of individuating. *spec.* in Scholastic Philosophy, The process leading to individual existence, as distinct from that of the species. **2.** The condition of being an individual; individuality, personal identity 1642. **3. a.** *Biol.* The sum of the processes on which the life of the individual depends 1867. **b.** The unification of parts or forces necessary to constitute an individual or organic unity. MIVART.

†**Individu·ity.** 1605. [ad. med.L. *individuitatem*, f. L. *individuus.*] **1.** The quality of being indivisible -1695. **2.** The quality that constitutes an individual -1656.

†**Indivi·duous,** *a.* 1642. [f. L. *individuus* undivided, indivisible + -OUS.] Of undivided nature; indivisible. MORE.

‖**Individuum** (indivi·diu̦ŏm). Pl. **-a, -ums.** 1555. [L., adj. neut. sing. used subst.; see IN-³ and DIVIDUOUS.] **1.** The indivisible; an indivisible entity 1599; †an atom -1706. **2.** *Logic.* A member of a species 1555. **3.** An individual person or thing 1591.

2. Phr. *I. vagum*: something indicated as an individual, without specific identification; From particular propositions nothing can be concluded, because the *Individua vaga* are..barren POPE.

†**Indivi·nity.** [IN-³.] Absence of divine character. SIR T. BROWNE.

Indivisible (indivi·zĭb'l). ME. [ad. late L. *indivisibilis*; see IN-³ and DIVISIBLE.]

A. *adj.* Not divisible; incapable of being divided, distributed, or †separated.

Dominion (that is) supreme power is i., insomuch as no man can serve two Masters HOBBES.

B. *sb.* That which is indivisible; an infinitely small particle or quantity 1644.

One instant or i. of time DIGBY. *Method of indivisibles*: a method of calculating areas, volumes, etc., based on the conception of indivisibles, published by Bonaventura in 1635. Hence **Indivisibi·lity, Indivi·sibleness. Indivi·sibly** *adv.*

Indivision (indivi·ʒən). 1624. [ad. late L. *indivisionem.*] Absence of division; undivided condition.

Indo-¹ (i·ndo), comb. f. Gr. Ἰνδός, L. *Indus*, employed in modern compounds, in which it qualifies another word, sb. or adj., or denotes the combination of Indian with some other characteristic (chiefly ethnological); as *I.-British, -Briton, -English*, etc.; **I.-Chinese,** belonging to Further India, or the region between India and China; etc.

Indo-². Bef. a vowel **ind-.** [f. Gr. Ἰνδός, L. *Indus*, as root of *indicum*, INDIGO.] *Chem.* A formative of names of compound bodies relating to indigo, or belonging to the INDOLE group; see INDOGEN, etc.

†**Indo·cible,** *a.* 1555. [IN-³.] Incapable of being taught or instructed; unteachable -1774. Hence †**Indocibi·lity,** †**Indo·cibleness.**

Indocile (indōu·səil, -dǫ·sil), *a.* 1603. [a. F., or ad. L. *indocilis.*] Unwilling or unapt to be taught; not readily submitting to instruction or guidance; intractable. Hence **Indocility** (indosi·lĭti) 1648.

Indoctrinate (indǫ·ktrineⁱt), *v.* Also †**en-.** 1578. [f. L. type **indoctrinare, -inat-*: see IN-² and DOCTRINE.] **1.** *trans.* To imbue with learning, to teach. **b.** To instruct *in* a subject, principle, etc. 1656. **c.** To imbue *with* a doctrine, idea, or opinion 1832. **d.** To bring *into* a knowledge of something 1841. **2.** To teach, inculcate (a subject, etc.) (*rare*) 1800.

1. They are altogether unlearned, even the Priests meanly indoctrinated HEYLIN. c. Fully indoctrinated with a sense of the magnitude of their office M. ARNOLD. Hence **Indo:ctrina·tion,** instruction; formal teaching. var. †**Indo·ctrine** *v.* 1450.

I:ndo-Europe·an. 1813. [f. INDO-¹ + EUROPEAN.]

A. *adj.* Common to India and Europe; applied to the great family or class of cognate languages (also called INDO-GERMANIC and ARYAN, q. v.) spoken over the greater part of Europe and extending into Asia as far as northern India, and to the race or its divisions using one or other of these languages. **b.** Pertaining or belonging to the Indo-European family of languages or peoples, as *Indo-European root, philology, culture*, etc.

B. *sb.* A member of the Indo-European race; an Aryan 1871.

Indogen (i·ndŏdʒĕn). 1886. [f. INDO-² + -GEN 1.] *Chem.* A name for the group $C_6H_4\langle{}^{CO}_{NH}\rangle C$, the double molecule of which (di-indogen) constitutes indigo-blue. **Indo·genide,** any compound of i. with another radical.

I:ndo-Ge·rman, *a. rare.* 1826. = next.

I:ndo-Germa·nic, *a.* 1835. [f. INDO-¹ + GERMANIC, ad. Ger. *indogermanisch.*] = INDO-EUROPEAN *a.*, ARYAN *a.* (The term is faulty as not including Celtic.) Hence **I:ndo-Ge·rmanist,** a student of Indo-Germanic philology.

Indoin (i·ndo̦in). 1884. [f. INDO-² + -IN.] *Chem.* A blue dye-stuff, related to indigo.

Indole (i·ndōul). Also (*improp.*) **indol.** 1869. [f. IND(O-² + -OLE, from L. *oleum.*] *Chem.* A crystallizable substance, also called *ketole*, formed in large shining colourless laminæ, having a peculiar odour; it is obtained artificially by reduction of indigo-blue; *pl.* alkylated derivatives of indole.

I. group, the group including indole, isatin, indigo, and related compounds and derivatives.

Indolence (i·ndŏlĕns). 1603. [a. F., or ad. L. *indolentia* freedom from pain.] †**1.** Insensibility to pain; want of feeling -1723. †**2.** Freedom from pain; a neutral state, in which neither pain nor pleasure is felt -1751. **3.** The disposition to avoid trouble; love of ease; laziness; sluggishness 1710.

2. I. is like the state of a sleeping Man STANLEY. 3. Some men fail as preachers through intellectual i. 1878. So †**I·ndolency,** in all senses.

Indolent (i·ndŏlĕnt), *a.* (*sb.*) 1663. [ad. late L. *indolentem*, f. *in-* (IN-³) + *dolens* grieving.] **1.** *Path.* Causing no pain, painless; esp. in *i. tumour, ulcer.* **2.** Averse to toil or exertion; slothful, lazy, idle 1710. †**3.** *sb.* An indolent person -1810.

2. A good-natured i. Man STEELE. Hence **I·ndolent-ly** *adv.*, **-ness.**

‖**Indoles** (i·ndolīz). *rare.* 1673. [L., f. *indu-* in, within + **ol-* to grow (cf. ADULT, etc.).] Innate quality or character.

Indoline (i·ndŏləin). 1884. [f. INDOLE + -INE.] *Chem.* A polymer of indole, formed by heating leucindigo with barium hydrate, zinc-dust, and water, crystallizing in long bright yellow needles.

†**Indo·mable,** *a. rare.* 1450. [ad. L. *indomabilis*, f. *in-* (IN-³) + *domare* to tame.] Untameable -1728.

Indomitable (indǫ·mităb'l), *a.* 1634. [ad. late L. *indomitabilis*, f. *in-* (IN-³) + *domitare* to tame.] **1.** Untameable. ? *Obs.* **2.** That cannot be overcome or subdued by labour, difficulties, or opposition; unyielding. Usually approbative. (The ordinary use.) 1830.

1. I. pride SCOTT. 2. I. strength 1830, energy 1865. Hence **Indomitabi·lity, Indo·mitableness,** the quality of being i. **Indo·mitably** *adv.*

Indonesian (indonī·ʃiăn). 1881. [f. INDO-¹ + Gr. νῆσος island + -IAN.] **a.** *adj.* Of or belonging to the East Indian islands. **b.** *sb.* An inhabitant of these islands.

Indoor, in-door (i·ndōəɹ), *a.* (*adv.*) 1711. [For earlier *within-door* (Bacon).] **1** Pertaining to the interior of a house, etc.; situated or done within doors or under cover. **b.** Within the workhouse or poorhouse 1864. **2.** *adv.* = next. TENNYSON.

1. b. I. and outdoor poor 1864. I. relief FAWCETT.

Indoors, in-doors (i·ndōᵊ·ɹz), *adv.* 1799. [repr. earlier *within doors.*] Within or into a house, etc.; under cover. †b. *attrib.* = INDOOR *adj.* WASHINGTON.

Indophenol (-fī·nǫl). 1892. [f. INDO-[2] + PHENOL.] *Chem.* A coal-tar colour used in dyeing, produced by the simultaneous oxidation of a phenol and a paradiamine; one of its commercial forms is *naphthol blue.*

Indorsation (indǭɹsē·ʃən). 1540. [f. *indorse,* ENDORSE *v.*; chiefly *Sc.*] Indorsement.

Indo·rse, etc., variant of ENDORSE, etc.

Indorse is the form found in legal and statutory use; it is also approved in all American Dicts.; but *Endorse* is now almost universal in Eng. commercial use.

Indow, -ment, obs. ff. ENDOW, -MENT.

Indoxyl (indǫ·ksil). 1886. [f. INDO-[2] + OXYL.] *Chem.* A brownish oil, isomeric with oxindole, formed when indoxylic acid is heated above its melting-point. Hence **Indoxy·lic** *a.*, in *I. acid,* a white crystalline precipitate, slightly soluble in water; its salts are **Indo·xylates.**

†**Indrape,** *v.* 1622. [f. IN-[2] + DRAPE *v.*] *trans.* To make into cloth; to weave -1843.

Indraught, indraft (i·nˌdraft). 1570. [f. IN *adv.* + DRAUGHT; cf. *indrawn,* etc.] **1.** The act of drawing in; inward attraction 1682. **2.** An inward flow, stream, or current, as of water or air; *esp.* a current setting towards the land or up an estuary, etc. Also *transf.* and *fig.* 1594. †**3.** A place where the water flows into the land; an inlet; inward passage. Also *fig.* -1706.

2. To avoid the I. of the Bay or Gulf of Mexico DE FOE.

Indraw·al. 1869. [f. IN *adv.* + DRAW *v.*, after *withdrawal.*] = prec.

I·ndraw:ing, *ppl. a.* 1598. [IN *adv.*] That draws in or inward.

Like some old wreck on some i. sea TENNYSON.

Indrawn, *ppl. a.* 1751. [IN *adv.*] Drawn in. **a.** as *adj.*, or bef. sb. (i·nˌdrǭn). **b.** as *pple.*, or after sb. (inˌdrǭ·n) 1865.

†**Indre·nch,** *v.* Also †**en-.** 1593. [f. IN-[2], EN-[1] + DRENCH *v.*] *trans.* To drench or drown in something; to immerse -1609.

‖**Indri** (i·ndri). Also **indris.** 1839. [A Malagasy exclam. *indry!* 'lo! behold!', mistaken by Sonnerat for the name of the animal; the only Malagasy name is *babakoto,* lit. 'father-child'.] A name given to the BABACOOTE, a lemurine animal of Madagascar (*Indris* or *Lichanotus brevicaudatus*), living in trees, with soft woolly hair, very long hind legs, and very short tail.

Indubious (indiū·biəs), *a.* 1624. [IN-[3].] **1.** Not admitting of doubt; indubitable. †**2.** Feeling no doubt; free from doubt 1665.

1. Am I not free to attend for the ripe and i. instinct? CLOUGH.

Indubitable (indiū·bităb'l), *a.* (*sb.*) 1625. [a. F., or ad. L. *indubitabilis*; see IN-[3] and DUBITABLE.] That cannot be doubted; perfectly certain or evident. As *sb.* An indubitable thing or fact. WATTS. Hence **Indu·bitableness. Indu·bitably** *adv.* unquestionably.

†**Indu·bitate,** *a.* 1475. [ad. L. *indubitatus,* f. *in-* (IN-[3]) + *dubitare* to DOUBT.] Undoubted -1678. So †**Indu·bitated** 1641.

†**Indu·bitate,** *v. rare.* 1646. [f. IN-[2] + L. *dubitatus* doubted.] *trans.* To render doubtful or uncertain; to call in question -1660.

To i. a thing of so constant credit 1660.

Induce (indiū·s), *v.* ME. [ad. L. *inducere,* f. *in-* (IN-[2]) + *ducere* to lead.] **1.** *trans.* To lead (a person) by persuasion or some influence *to* (†*into,* †*unto*) some action, condition, belief, etc.; to move, influence, prevail upon (any one) *to do* something. **2.** To bring in, introduce. *Obs.* or blended with 3. ME. **3.** To bring about, bring on, produce, cause, give rise to ME. **b.** *spec.* To produce (an electric current or magnetic state) by induction 1812. †**4.** To lead to (something) as a conclusion or inference; to suggest, imply -1646. **5.** To infer; *esp.* in recent use, to derive as an induction 1563. †**6.** To draw (something) on or over -1784.

1. If he coulde not by fayre and gentle speche i. them vnto his opinion 1551. These considerations i. me to believe [etc.] 1796. 2. To i. peace HALL, doubt into a question PALEY. A thinge written by me to i. children to the latin tongue WITHALS. 3. Gentle walking without inducing fatigue 1780. 5. From a sufficient number of results a proposition or law is induced 1888. Hence **Indu·cer.**

Induced (indiū·st), *ppl. a.* 1585. [f. prec. + -ED[1].] In the senses of the vb. (see esp. INDUCE *v.* 3 b).

Induced current, an electric current excited by INDUCTION. *I. magnet,* a magnet affected by induction.

Inducement (indiū·smĕnt). 1594. [f. as prec. + -MENT.] †**1.** The action of inducing -1648. **2.** That which induces; something attractive by which a person is led on or persuaded to action 1594; †an incentive -1691. †**3.** A preamble or introduction to a book or subject -1617. **b.** *Law.* (See below.) †**4.** A leading to some conclusion or inference; that which leads to a conclusion. SIR T. BROWNE.

2. Inducements to foreign artisans to come over and settle in this country SMILES. 3. b. *Matters of i.* (Law): introductory averments stating the circumstances, etc., leading up to the matter in dispute, but not stating such matter.

Indu·cible, *a. rare.* 1643. [f. INDUCE *v.* + -IBLE.] **1.** Capable of being brought on, brought about, or caused 1677. †**2.** Capable of being inferred. SIR T. BROWNE.

Induct (indɒ·kt), *v.* ME. [f. L. *induct-*, *inducere.*] **1.** *trans. Eccl.* To introduce formally into possession of a benefice or living. **b.** To introduce into office 1548. **c.** To install in a seat, room, etc. 1706. **2.** To lead, conduct *into* (*lit.* and *fig.*) (*rare*) 1600. **3.** To introduce (*to*); to initiate (*into*) 1603. **4.** *absol.* To form an induction WHEWELL. **5.** *Electr.* = INDUCE *v.* 3 b. 1839.

1. c. Inducting himself into the pulpit SCOTT.

Inductance (indɒ·ktăns). 1888. [f. prec. + -ANCE.] *Electr.* Capacity for magnetic induction; also, self-induction, or the coefficient of self-induction. *ellipt.* = i. coil.

attrib. **i. coil,** a coil of large inductance; *spec.* a wireless tuning coil.

Inductile (indɒ·ktil, -təil), *a.* 1736. [IN-[3].] Not ductile; not pliable; unyielding to influences. Hence **Inducti·lity.**

Induction (indɒ·kʃən). ME. [a. F., or ad. L. *inductionem.*] †**1.** The action of inducing by persuasion; inducement -1588. **2.** The action of initiating in the knowledge of something; the process of being initiated; introduction, initiation. Now *rare.* 1526. **3.** An introduction; a preface, preamble (*arch.*) 1533. †**b.** An initial step in any undertaking. SHAKS. **4.** *Eccl.* The action of formally introducing a clergyman into a benefice, together with all rights, profits, etc. pertaining to it ME. **b.** *gen.* The formal introduction to an office, position, or possession; installation 1460. **5.** The action of introducing (a person, custom, etc.). *rare.* 1604. **6.** The adducing *of* a number of separate facts, particulars, etc., esp. for the purpose of proving a general statement 1551. **7.** *Logic.* The process of inferring a general law or principle from the observation of particular instances (opp. to DEDUCTION, q. v.) 1553; a conclusion derived from induction; formerly used in the wider sense of 'inference' 1440. **8.** *Math.* The process of proving that a theorem is true, because it *is* true in a certain case, and therefore in the next case, and hence in the next but one, and so on 1838. **9.** *Electr.* and *Magnetism.* The action of inducing or bringing about an electric or magnetic state in a body by the proximity (without contact) of an electrified or magnetized body 1812.

2. I have never yet seen any service, and must have my i. some time or other DE FOE. 3. That which hee takes for the second Argument..is no argument, but an i. to those that follow MILT. b. These promises are faire, the parties sure, And our i. full of prosperous hope SHAKS. 7. You must take up with I., and bid adieu to Demonstration BERKELEY. The contrast between his wide inductions and the apparently flimsy foundation on which they are made to rest 1868. 9. Phr. *Electrodynamic* or *voltaic i.*, the production of an electric current (*induced current*) by the influence of another independent current. *Electromagnetic i.*, the production of a state of magnetic polarity in a body over or round which an electric or galvanic current passes, or the generation of an electric current by the action of a magnet (the latter called more properly *magneto-electric i.*). *Electrostatic i.*, the production of an electrical charge upon a body by the influence of a neighbouring body charged with statical electricity, as exemplified in Volta's electrophorus. *Magnetic i.*, the production of magnetic properties in iron or other substances when placed in a magnetic field. *Mutual i.*, the reaction of two electric circuits upon each other; *self-i.*, the reaction of different parts of the same circuit upon each other.

Comb.: (sense 9) **i.-balance,** an electrical apparatus so contrived that the currents induced in the secondary wires of two induction-coils balance each other; **-coil,** an apparatus for producing electric currents by induction, consisting of two separate coils of wire generally surrounding a soft-iron core, the primary coil being connected with an external source of electricity, and having an arrangement for causing the electric current to vary in intensity, the effect of which is to produce a current of different character in the secondary coil; (sense 3) **-pipe,** the pipe through which the live steam is introduced into the cylinder of a steam-engine; **-port,** the opening by which steam passes from the steam-chest into the cylinder; **-valve,** the valve which controls the passage of steam into the cylinder. Hence **Indu·ctional** *a.* of, pertaining to, or of the nature of i.

Inductive (indɒ·ktiv), *a.* 1607. [ad. L. *inductivus,* f. *induct-*, *inducere*; see -IVE.] **1.** Leading on (*to* some action, etc.); inducing. †**2.** Productive *of* -1772. **3.** *Logic.* Of the nature of, based upon, or using induction 1764. **4.** Of the nature of, pertaining to, or due to electric or magnetic induction 1849. **5.** Introductory 1868.

1. Ungovern'd appetite..a brutish vice, I. mainly to the sin of Eve MILT. *P. L.* XI. 519. 3. The i. mind of a Davy or a Faraday 1842. 4. I. retardation in long ocean cables 1879. Hence **Indu·ctive-ly** *adv.* by i. reasoning; by electric induction; **-ness. Inducti·vity,** inductive quality 1888.

Inducto- (indɒ·kto), comb. form of INDUCTION; as in:

Inducto·meter, an instrument for ascertaining the force of electrical induction 1839.

Inductor (indɒ·ktəɹ). 1652. [a. L.; see INDUCT *v.*] **1.** One who introduces or initiates (*rare*). **2.** One who inducts a clergyman to a benefice 1726. **3.** Any part of an electric apparatus which acts inductively on another 1849.

Inductorium (indɒktōᵊ·riɒm). 1875. [mod. L., neut. of late L. *inductorius* INDUCTORY; see -ORIUM.] A name for the induction-coil as adapted for the display of the electric spark.

Indu·ctory, *a.* 1632. [ad. late L. *inductorius,* f. *inducere* to INDUCE: see -ORY.] Introductory.

†**Indu·ctric,** *a.* 1849. [irreg. f. INDUCTION, after *electric.*] *Electr.* Operating by induction. So **Indu·ctrical** *a.*

Indue, etc., var. of ENDUE, etc.

Indulge (indɒ·ldʒ), *v.* 1638. [ad. L. *indulgere.* (*Indulgence, Indulgent* are earlier.)] **I.** *trans.* **1.** To treat (a person) with complaisance; to gratify by compliance, or by absence of restraint or strictness; to humour. Const. *in.* 1660. Also *fig.* **b.** *refl.* To give free course to one's inclination; to take one's pleasure. Const. *in.* 1659. **c.** To gratify (a person) *with* something given or granted 1790. **2.** To grant an indulgence to; see INDULGENCE *sb.* II. 1662. **3.** To gratify (a desire or inclination); to give oneself up to, yield to. Occas. merely: To entertain, cherish. 1656. **4.** To bestow or grant (something) as a favour, or as a matter of free grace; to concede as an indulgence. Now *rare.* 1638. **5.** *Comm.* To grant an indulgence on (a bill). Cf. INDULGENCE *sb.* II. 3. 1766.

1. b. Pleasing anticipations in which he indulged himself MAR. EDGEWORTH. 3. To i. my own fancy, I began to compile this work BLOUNT. 4. Scarce indulging himself necessary Relaxations 1648.

II. *intr.* (with prep.) †**1.** *Indulge to*: to grant indulgence *to,* to give way to, gratify (a propensity = I. 3; rarely a person = I. 1) -1790. **2.** *Indulge in* (ellipt. for *indulge oneself in,* I. 1 b): To give free course to one's inclination for; to take one's pleasure freely in 1706.

2. Any little amusement in which he could i. DICKENS. Hence †**Indu·lgement,** indulgence. **Indu·lger. Indu·lgingly** *adv.*

Indulgence (indɒ·ldʒĕns), *sb.* ME. [a. F., or ad. L. *indulgentia,* f. *indulgentem*; see -ENCE.]

I. *gen.* 1. The action of indulging (a person), or the fact of being indulgent; favouring forbearance or relaxation of restraint. Sometimes dyslogistic: Over-lenient treatment. **b.** With *an* and *pl.* An instance of this 1591. **2.** The action of indulging (desire, inclination, etc.); the yielding to some propensity (const. *of, in,* †*to*); the action of indulging *in* some practice, luxury, etc. 1638. Also *absol.*

1. Left to her self..Shee first his weak i. will accuse MILT. *P. L.* IX. 1186. **b.** He..supplied [them] with every i. MACAULAY. **2.** The i. of private malice 1769. I. in sin 1843. *absol.* To grow Rich, that he may live in figure and i. LAW.

II. *spec.* (from I. 1 b). **1.** *R. C. Ch.* A remission of the punishment which is still due to sin after sacramental absolution, this remission being valid in the court of conscience and before God, and being made by an application of the treasure of the Church on the part of a lawful superior ME. **2.** *Eng. Hist.* Applied to the grant or offer to Nonconformists, in the reigns of Charles II and James II, of certain religious liberties as special favours, but not as legal rights 1672. **3.** *Comm.* An extension, made as a favour, of the time within which a bill of exchange or a debt is to be paid 1827.

1. Among others he had recourse to a sale of Indulgences ROBERTSON. **2.** *Declaration of Indulgence,* a royal proclamation, e.g. that of Charles II in 1672, offering certain religious liberties.

Indu·lgence, *v.* 1599. [f. prec. sb.] †**1.** *trans.* = INDULGE *v.* I. 4. **2.** *R. C. Ch.* To attach an indulgence to (a particular act or object); see next 1866.

Indulgenced (indʊ·ldʒĕnst), *ppl. a.* 1841. [f. prec. sb. or vb. + -ED.] *R. C. Ch.* Having an indulgence attached to it; applied to prayers, material objects, etc., the use of which is declared to convey an indulgence.

Indulgency (indʊ·ldʒĕnsi). Now *rare.* 1547. [ad. L. *indulgentia*; see -ENCY.] = INDULGENCE *sb.* I. 1, 2, II. 1.

Indulgent (indʊ·ldʒĕnt), *a.* 1509. [ad. L. *indulgentem.*] **1.** That indulges or tends to indulge; disposed to comply with desire or humour or to overlook faults or failings; not strict or severe; not exercising restraint. Often dyslogistically, Not exercising due restraint, weakly lenient. Also *fig.* of things. †**2.** SELF-INDULGENT -1705.

1. Such in thy behalf shall be Th' i. censure of posterity WALLER. The most i. of landlords 1839. *fig.* I. summer 1860. **2.** The feeble old, i. of their ease DRYDEN. Hence **Indu·lgent-ly** *adv.*, **-ness.**

†**Indulge·ntial,** *a.* [f. L. *indulgentia* + -AL.] Of or pertaining to indulgences; see INDULGENCE *sb.* II. 1. BREVINT.

†**Indu·lgiate,** *v. rare.* 1615. [irreg. f. INDULGE *v.* + -ATE[3].] *trans.* = INDULGE *v.* -1628.

Induline (i·ndiŭləin). 1882. [f. IND(O-[2] + *-ul-* dim. + -INE.] *Chem.* A general name for a series of compounds related to aniline, yielding blue-black, blue, and greyish dyes, known in commerce as nigrosine, violaniline, Elberfeld blue, aniline grey, etc.

Indult (indʊ·lt). 1535. [a. F., or ad. L. *indultum*, pa. pple. neut. of *indulgere* used subst.] †**1.** A special privilege granted by authority -1625. **2.** *R. C. Ch.* 'A licence or permission granted by the Pope..authorising something to be done which the common law of the Church does not sanction' (*Cath. Dict.*) 1536. **3.** *Hist.* A duty paid to the king of Spain or Portugal on imported goods. (Dicts.) So ‖**Indulto** [Sp. and Pg.], in all senses 1645.

†**Indument.** 1494. [In I, ad. L. *indumentum* garment; in II = ENDUEMENT, ENDOWMENT.]

I. **1.** Clothing, investiture; a garment, robe, vesture. Also *fig.* -1684. **2.** *Nat. Hist.* A covering, as of hair, feathers, etc.; an integument; an investing membrane. (Also in L. form *indumentum.*) -1864.

II. **1.** = ENDUEMENT -1659. **2.** = ENDOWMENT 1602.

‖**Induna** (indū·nă). 1875. [Zulu.] An officer under the king or chief of the Zulus, Matabele, and other S. African tribes.

Induplicate (indiū·plikĕt), *a.* 1830. [IN-[2].] *Bot.* Folded or rolled in at the edges, without overlapping; said of leaves and petals in vernation or æstivation. So **Induplica·tion,** folding or doubling in; an example of this. **Indupli·ca·tive** *a.* = INDUPLICATE.

Indurance, obs. f. ENDURANCE.

Indurate (i·ndiurĕt), *ppl. a.* Now *rare.* ME. [ad. L. *induratus, indurare,* f. *in-* (IN-[2]) + *durus* hard. Formerly stressed *indu·rate.*] **1.** Made hard, hardened 1530. **2.** Of persons, etc.: Morally hardened, rendered callous; also, stubborn, obstinate.

2. They are as indurat as Pharaoh 1667.

Indurate (i·ndiureit), *v.* 1538. [f. L. *indurat-* ppl. stem; see prec. Formerly stressed *indu·rate.*] **1.** *trans.* To make hard or hardy; to harden. **2.** To harden (the heart, etc.); to render callous or unfeeling; to make stubborn 1538. **3.** *intr.* To become or grow hard; (of a custom) to become fixed 1626.

1. They [slaves] had been indurated to want, exposure and toil TOURGEE. **2.** More like to i. than to mollify LATIMER. **3.** The prescription will soon grow, and begin to i. 1881. Hence **I·ndurative** *a.* of hardening tendency or quality 1592.

Induration (indiurēⁱ·ʃən). ME. [a. F., or ad. med.L. *indurationem*; see prec.] **1.** The action of hardening; the process of being hardened or becoming hard; also, hardened condition. Now chiefly in *Geol.* or *Path.* **2.** A hardening of character or feeling; stubbornness; callousness 1493.

2. To what a degree of i. and searedness must you have brought yourself 1873.

Indusial (indiū·ziăl), *a.* 1833. [f. INDUSIUM + -AL.] *Geol.* Containing, or composed of, indusia or larva-cases.

I. limestone, a form of freshwater limestone in Auvergne, so called from the cases of the larvæ of Phryganea, great heaps of which have been encrusted, as they lay, and formed into a rock. LYELL.

Indusiate (indiū·ziĕt), *ppl. a.* 1830. [ad. L. *indusiatus*; see INDUSIUM and -ATE[2].] *Bot.* Furnished with an indusium. So **Indu·siated.**

Indusiform (indiū·zifǭrm), *a.* 1857. [f. INDUSIUM + -FORM.] *Bot.* Having the shape of an indusium.

‖**Indusium** (indiū·ziŏm). Pl. **-ia.** 1706. [L., app. f. *induere* to put on; see ENDUE.] **1.** *Anat.* The amnion of the fœtus. **2.** *Bot.* **a.** The membranous scale covering the sorus of a fern 1807. **b.** A collection of hairs united into a sort of cup, and enclosing the stigma in the *Goodeniaceæ.* LINDLEY. **3.** *Entom.* The case of a larva 1832.

Industrial (indʊ·striăl). [Occurs 1590; then app. not till late in 18th c. Orig. f. L. *industria* + -AL. In 19th c., ad. mod.F. *industriel.*]

A. *adj.* Pertaining to, or of the nature of, industry or productive labour; resulting from industry. Of persons: Engaged in or connected with an industry or industries. **b.** Of a quality suitable only for industrial use 1904.

Industrial school: a school for teaching one or more branches of industry; *spec.* a school established for the compulsory attendance of neglected children, where they are instructed in some industry or trade.

B. *sb.* **1.** One engaged in industrial pursuits 1865. **2.** *pl.* Shares in a joint-stock industrial enterprise 1894.

Hence **Indu·strialize** *v.*, **Indu·strially** *adv.*

Indu·strialism. 1831. [f. prec. + -ISM.] A system of things arising from or involving the existence of great industries; the organization of industrial occupations. So **Indu·strialist,** a worker or manufacturer 1864.

Industrious (indʊ·striəs), *a.* 1523. [ad. post-cl.L. *industriosus* (see -OUS), or F. *industrieux.*] Characterized by industry. †**1.** Skilful, able, clever, ingenious -1687. **2.** Characterized by application; painstaking, zealous, attentive, careful 1552. †**3.** Intentional, designed, purposed, voluntary -1817. **4.** Characterized by or showing assiduous and steady work. (The prevailing sense.) 1591.

2. I. to seeke out the trueth of these thinges SPENSER. I. after wisdom MILT., of the common good DRYDEN. **4.** Solomon seeing the young man that he was i. 1 *Kings* xi. 28. I. habits GOLDSM., toil COWPER. Hence **Indu·strious-ly** *adv.*, **-ness.**

Industry (i·ndŏstri). 1477. [a. F. *industrie,* or ad. L. *industria* diligence.] †**1.** Intelligent or clever working; skill, ingenuity, dexterity -1613. †**2.** A device, contrivance; a crafty expedient -1621. **3.** Diligence or assiduity in any task or effort; close and steady application to the business in hand 1531. **4.** Systematic work or labour; habitual employment, now esp. in the productive arts or manufactures 1611. **5.** A particular branch of productive labour; a trade or manufacture 1566.

3. By industrie and diligence any perfection may be attained 1576. **4.** The Leaders of I...are virtually the Captains of the World CARLYLE. *House of i.*, a workhouse. *School of i.*, an industrial school. **5.** The rights and properties of our national industries DISRAELI.

Phr. †*Of industry*, on purpose (after L. *de* or *ex industria*) 1613.

Indutive (indiū·tiv), *a.* 1866. [f. L. *indut-*, *induere* to put on + -IVE.] *Bot.* Of seeds: Having the usual integument or covering.

‖**Induviæ** (indiū·vi,ī), *sb. pl.* 1835. [L. *induviæ* clothing, f. *induere* to put on.] *Bot.* Leaves which not being articulated with the stem cannot fall off but decay upon it. LINDLEY. Hence **Indu·viate** *a.* clothed with i.

Indwell (i·n,dwe·l), *v.* Pa. t. and pple. indwelt. ME. [f. IN-[1] + DWELL.] **1.** *trans.* To dwell in, inhabit, occupy as a dwelling. Also *fig.* **2.** *intr.* To dwell, abide, have one's abode (*in*). Also *fig.*

1. *fig.* The Holy Ghost became a Dove, not as a symbol, but as a constantly indwelt form MILMAN. Hence **Indweller, in-dweller** (i·n,dwe·ləɹ), one who dwells in a place; an inhabitant; a sojourner.

Indwelling (i·ndwe:liŋ), *vbl. sb.* ME. [f. IN *adv.* + DWELLING *vbl. sb.*; cf. prec.] The action of dwelling in a place. Usu. *fig.* The abiding of God or the Divine Spirit in the heart or soul.

By the i. of God all objects are infused, and contained within TRAHERNE.

†**Indy, Indie.** 1509. [ad. L. *India*; cf. *Italy*, etc.] = INDIA -1647.

-ine, *suffix* [1], forming adjs., repr. L. *-īnus, -ina, -inum*, with the sense 'of' or 'pertaining to', 'of the nature of'. Examples are L. *adulterinus* adulterine, *divinus* divine, *femininus* feminine, etc.; also, *Alpinus* Alpine, etc. The termination is now greatly used in *Nat. Hist.*, in forming adjs. on the names of genera, as *acarine, accipitrine,* etc. In these Nat. Hist. adjs. the pronunciation is (-əin), usually unstressed; but in other words it is very various; cf. *divine* (-əi·n), *marine* (-ī·n), *feminine* (-in), *leonine* (-əin). Also *riverine.*

-ine, *suffix* [2], forming adjs., repr. L. *-inus*, a. Gr. *-ινος*, as *adamantinus* adamantine, *pristinus* pristine, etc. The etym. and historical pronunciation is (-in), e.g. (pri·stin), (ædăma·ntin); but cf. *crystalline* (-əin), etc.

-ine, *suffix* [3], repr. F. *-ine*, L. *-ina*, Gr. *-ίνη*, forming fem. titles, as in Gr. *ἡρωΐνη*, L. *heroina*, F. *héroïne* heroine. See also *landgravine, margravine.*

-ine, *suffix* [4], forming sbs., repr. F. *-ine* (-in), L. *-ina* (*-inus*), in origin identical with -INE [1]. The adjs. in *-inus, -ina* were also used subst., as in *concubinus, -ina* concubine, *Antoninus* Antonine, etc. The Eng. form of those in *-ina* is *-ine*, occas. *-in*; those in *-inus* give F. and Eng. *-in*, but in Eng. often *-ine.*

In Romanic, and hence in Eng. in the F. form *-ine* (-ī·n), this suffix is greatly used in forming names of derived substances, similative appellations, diminutives, etc.; e.g. *dentine, grenadine,* etc.

-ine, *suffix* [5], *Chem.*, in origin an offshoot of -INE [4], as occurring in the names of some derived substances; see GELATIN, -INE. At first the ending *-ine* was by some reduced to *-in*; but recently, in systematic nomenclature, *-ine* is now used (1) in forming names of alkaloids and basic substances, as *aconitine,* etc., which are thus distinguished from names of neutral substances, proteids, etc., in *-in* (see -IN [1]); and (2) in Hofmann's systematic names of hydrocarbons of the form C_nH_{2n-2}, as *ethine* or acetylene, C_2H_2, etc. In the names of the elements, etc., *-ine* is retained. In pop. and commercial use, *-ine* is still current in some cases where systematic nomenclature requires *-in*; see -IN [1].

-ine, as used to form the names of minerals, has in later use been changed, in the names of

species, to *-ite*; thus *chalcosine, erythrine* are in Dana *chalcocite, erythrite*.

Inearth (inǝ·ɹþ), *v.* 1801. [IN-[1].] To inter. Chiefly *poet.*

Inebriant (inī·briǎnt). 1819. [ad. L. *inebriantem*; see INEBRIATE *v.*] **a.** *adj.* Intoxicating. **b.** *sb.* An intoxicant.

Inebriate (inī·briět), *ppl. a.* and *sb.* 1497. [ad. L. *inebriatus*; see next.] **1.** *ppl. a.* Inebriated; intoxicated (*lit.* and *fig.*). **2.** *sb.* An intoxicated person; now only, a habitual drunkard 1794.

1. Thus spake Peter as a man i. and made drounken with the swetenesse of this vision UDALL. 2. An Asylum for Inebriates 1864.

Inebriate (inī·brieɪt), *v.* 1497. [f. ppl. stem of L. *inebriare*, f. *in-* (IN-[2]) + *ebriare* to intoxicate, f. *ebrius* drunk.] **1.** *trans.* To make drunk; to intoxicate. Also *absol.* 1555. **2.** *transf.* and *fig.* **a.** To excite or stupefy, as with liquor 1497. †**b.** To refresh as with drink; to drench -1649. †**3.** *intr.* To become intoxicated. BACON.

1. The cups That cheer but not i. COWPER. 2. a. A sophistical rhetorician, inebriated with the exuberance of his own verbosity DISRAELI.

Inebriation (inībri‚ēɪ·ʃǝn). 1526. [ad. L. *inebriationem* (Augustine); see prec.] The action of inebriating, or condition of being inebriated; intoxication 1646. **b.** *fig.* Intoxication of the mind or feelings; excitement or emotion such as to cause loss of mental or moral balance.

b. They did not preserve him from the i. of prosperity 1828.

†**Ine·briative**, *a.* 1615. [f. INEBRIATE *v.* + -IVE.] Intoxicating; of or pertaining to inebriation -1628.

Inebriety (inibrəi·ėti). 1775. [f. IN-[2] + EBRIETY.] The state or habit of being inebriated; drunkenness; esp. habitual drunkenness, regarded as a disease. Also *fig.*

Inebrious (inī·briǝs), *a. rare.* 1450. [f. L. type **inebriosus*, after L. *ebriosus* (see EBRIOUS).] †**1.** Inebriating, intoxicating -1704. **2.** Drunken; addicted to drunkenness 1837.

Inedible (ine·dib'l), *a.* 1822. [IN-[3].] Not edible; unfit to be eaten. Hence **Inedibi·lity.**

Inedited (ine·ditėd), *a.* 1760. [IN-[3].] Not edited; unpublished; not described in any published work.

Her letters, still extant although i. 1855.

Ineffable (ine·făb'l), *a.* (*sb.*) 1450. [a. F., ad. L. *ineffabilis* unutterable, f. *in-* (IN-[3]) + *effabilis*.] **1.** That cannot be expressed in words; unspeakable, unutterable, inexpressible. **2.** That must not be uttered 1597. †**3.** *Math.* Irrational, surd -1729. **4.** *sb. pl.* (*colloq.*) Trousers 1823.

1. Thankes be vnto God for his i. gyfte TINDALE 2 *Cor.* ix. 15. 2. To thee, the i. Name BROWNING. Hence **Ineffabi·lity, Ine·ffableness, Ine·ffably** *adv.* in an i. manner, or to an i. extent or degree.

Ineffaceable (inėfē¹·săb'l), *a.* 1804. [IN-[3].] That cannot be effaced or obliterated; indelible (*lit.* and *fig.*). Hence **Ineffaceabi·lity**, i. quality. **Ineffa·ceably** *adv.*

Ineffectible (inėfe·ktĭb'l), *a. rare.* Also -able. 1649. [IN-[3].] †**1.** Ineffectual, ineffective. BP. HALL. †**2.** Not to be effected by ordinary means; supernatural. BP. HALL. **3.** Impracticable 1806.

Ineffective (inėfe·ktiv), *a.* (*sb.*) 1651. [IN-[3].] **1.** Insufficient to produce any, or the intended, effect; hence, ineffectual; inoperative. **2.** Of a person: Inefficient 1653. **3.** *sb.* A person unfit for work or service 1856.

1. I. remedies 1651. I. architecture 1858. An i. appeal 1898. 2. I. age SOUTHEY. Hence **Ineffe·ctive-ly** *adv.*, **-ness.**

Ineffectual (inėfe·ktiu̯ăl), *a.* ME. [IN-[3].] Not effectual; without any, or the intended, effect; unavailing. **b.** Of things: Not producing the usual effect; weak or tame in effect 1784. **c.** Of a person: That is a failure 1865.

All his efforts were i. 1704. b. A white face,—shivering, i. lips MRS. BROWNING. c. Pope Stephen III,..a weak and i. man 1897. Hence **Ineffectua·lity, Ineffe·ctualness. Ineffe·ctually** *adv.*

Ineffervescence (inefǝɹve·sěns). *rare.* 1794. [IN-[3].] The fact of not effervescing; absence of effervescence. So **Ineffervescent** *a.* (*rare*), having the quality of not effervescing. **Ineffervescibi·lity**, incapability of effervescing.

Inefficacious (inefikē¹·ʃǝs), *a.* 1658. [IN-[3].] Of a remedy, treatment, etc.: Not efficacious; without efficacy.

The precaution..is quite i. DICKENS. Hence **Ineffica·cious-ly** *adv.*, **-ness** 1646.

Ineffica·city. 1721. [ad. F. *-ité*.] = next.

Inefficacy (ine·fikăsi). 1612. [ad. late L. *inefficacia*, f. *inefficax, -cac-*.] Want of efficacy; incapacity to produce the desired effect.

The i. of advice is usually the fault of the counsellor 1751.

Inefficiency (inėfi·ʃěnsi). 1749. [f. as next + -ENCY.] Want of efficiency; inability to effect something; ineffectiveness, inefficient character.

The scandalous i. of the Government LECKY.

Inefficient (inėfi·ʃěnt), *a.* (*sb.*) 1750. [IN-[3].] **1.** Not efficient; failing to produce, or incapable of producing, the desired effect; ineffective. Of a person: Not effecting something; not having the ability or industry required for what one has to do; not fully capable. **2.** *sb.* An inefficient person 1898.

1. Ploughs of an i. structure 1804. He..rarely promoted an i. person KEIGHTLEY. 2. 'Inefficients' by birth 1898. Hence **Ineffi·ciently** *adv.*

Inelaborate (inĭlæ·bŏrět), *a.* 1650. [IN-[3].] Not elaborate; not having much labour expended on it; simple or slight in workmanship. Hence **Inela·borately** *adv.*

Inelaborated (inĭlæ·bŏreɪtėd), *a.* 1623. [IN-[3].] Not laboriously worked out; not thoroughly formed by natural or chemical process.

Inelastic (inĭlæ·stik), *a.* 1748. [IN-[3].] Not elastic; void of elasticity or springiness.

I. fluids, a name for liquids, as being void of 'elasticity' in the older sense (see ELASTIC A. 2). So **Inelasti·city**, absence of elasticity; rigidity.

Inelegant (ine·lĭgănt), *a.* 1509. [a. F. *inélégant*, ad. L. *inelegantem*; see IN-[3] and ELEGANT.] **1.** Wanting in grace of form or manner; unrefined; clumsy, coarse, unpolished. Used *esp.* of language and literary style. **2.** Wanting in æsthetic refinement or delicacy 1667. **3.** (*nonce-use* from late L.) Not in harmony with the main body of the Law. AUSTIN.

1. When the forms..are i., that is, when they are composed of unvaried lines HOGARTH. His imitation of Horace on Lucilius is not i. JOHNSON. 2. Order, so contriv'd as not to mix Tastes, not well joynd, i. MILT. *P. L.* v. 335. Hence **Ine·legance, Ine·legancy. Ine·legantly** *adv.*

Ineligible (ine·lidʒĭb'l), *a.* 1770. [IN-[3].] **1.** Incapable of being elected; disqualified for election to an office or position. **b.** Hence, Unfit to be chosen 1828. †**2.** Of actions: Such as one would not choose to do; inexpedient; undesirable -1797. **3.** *absol.* with *pl.* as *sb.* One not eligible as a suitor or husband 1896.

1. b. As a son-in-law he was quite i. TROLLOPE. Hence **Ine·ligibi·lity, Ine·ligibleness**, the quality or fact of being i. **Ine·ligibly** *adv.* in an i. manner.

Ineloquent (ine·lŏkwěnt), *a.* 1530. [IN-[3].] Not eloquent; void of eloquence.

The i. Brindley, behold he has chained seas together CARLYLE. Hence **Ine·loquence. Ine·loquently** *adv.*

Ineluctable (inĭlʌ·ktăb'l), *a.* 1623. [ad. L. *ineluctabilis*, f. *in-* (IN-[3]) + *eluctari* to struggle out.] From which one cannot escape by struggling; inescapable.

Struggling in the grip of some force outside themselves, inexorable, i. MRS. H. WARD. Hence **Inelu·ctably** *adv.*

Ineludible (inĭl'ū·dĭb'l), *a.* Also -able. 1662. [IN-[3].] That cannot be eluded or escaped. Hence **Inelu·dibly** *adv.*

Inembryonate (ine·mbri‚ŏnět), *a.* 1846. [IN-[3].] *Biol.* Not embryonate; having no embryo.

†**Ine·narrable**, *a.* 1450. [a. F. *inénarrable*, ad. L. *inenarrabilis*, f. *in-* (IN-[3]) + *enarrare* to narrate.] That cannot be narrated, told, or described; unspeakable -1716.

Earth's i. continent CHAPMAN.

Inept (ine·pt), *a.* 1561. [ad. L. *ineptus*; see IN-[3] and APT.] **1.** Not adapted or adaptable; without aptitude; unsuitable, unfit (*arch.*) 1603. **b.** Inappropriate 1675. **2.** Absurd; silly, foolish 1604. **3.** *Law.* Void, of no effect 1561.

1. The differences between *apt* and *inept* Counsellours HOBBES. b. I. words, which do not affect the ..absolute gift 1883. 2. She look'd on you as an I. Animal 1710. So **Ine·pt-ly** *adv.* 1523. **Ine·ptness.**

Ineptitude (ine·ptitiud). 1615. [ad. L. *ineptitudo*, f. *ineptus*; see -TUDE.] **1.** Want of aptitude; inaptness, unfitness; incapacity. **2.** Want of mental capacity; silliness; a silly act or remark 1656.

1. That I. for Society, which is frequently the Fault of us Scholars STEELE. 2. The i. of statesmen 1885.

Inequable (inī·k-, -e·kwăb'l), *a. rare.* 1717. [ad. L. *inæquabilis*; see IN-[3] and EQUABLE.] Uneven; not uniform. So †**Inequabi·lity** (*rare*) 1581.

Inequal (inī·kwăl), *a.* ME. [ad. L. *inæqualis*; see IN-[3] and EQUAL.] = UNEQUAL. **b.** Of a surface: Uneven 1661. Hence **Ine·qual-ly** *adv.*, **-ness.**

Inequality (inĭkwǫ·lĭti). 1484. [a. OF. *inequalité*, ad. med.L. *inæqualitas*, f. *inæqualis* INEQUAL.] The condition of being unequal; want of equality. **1.** Want of equality between persons or things; disparity; as in physical qualities; in dignity, rank, or circumstances, etc. **b.** A condition of superiority or inferiority in relation to something, *esp.* the being unequal *to* a task, insufficiency 1553. **2.** †**a.** Of persons: Unequal treatment of others; partiality. **b.** Of things: Want of due proportion, uneven distribution. 1538. **3.** Want of uniformity: **a.** in surface or outline 1607; **b.** in motion, action, or condition; in duration or recurrence; in rate or proportion; in manner, quality, degree, etc. 1626. **4.** *Astron.* A deviation from uniformity in the motion of a heavenly body 1690. **5.** *Math.* **a.** The relation between quantities that are unequal in value or magnitude. *Sign of i.*, either > ('is greater than') or < ('is less than'). **b.** An expression of this relation; dist. from *equation*. 1875.

1. Inequalities in the wages of labour and profits of stock ADAM SMITH. The i. between the rich and the poor 1802. b. Conscious of the I. of a Female Pen to so Masculine an Attempt MRS. CENTLIVRE. 2. Inequalities in the pressure of the income-tax 1858. 3. a. Fine inequalities of hill and dale 1801. b. The i. of the Pulse SALMON, of our climate HANWAY. In Wordsworth there are no inequalities COLERIDGE.

Inequation (inĭkwē¹·ʃǝn). 1855. [f. L. *inæquatus*, after EQUATION.] A formula expressing inequality; = INEQUALITY 5 b.

Ine·qui-, combining element, in sense 'unequal', 'unequally', not of L. formation, but f. IN-[3] + EQUI-: e.g.

ine·quia·xed, ine·quia·xial *a.* having unequal axes; **ine·quidi·stant** *a.* not equidistant; **ine·quilo·bate, ine·quilobed** *a.* having unequal lobes.

Inequilateral (inīkwilæ·těrăl), *a.* 1662. [IN-[3].] Having unequal sides.

I. shell: one in which a transverse line drawn through the apex of the umbo divides the valve into two unequal and unsymmetrical parts.

In equilibrio: see EQUILIBRIUM.

Inequitable (ine·kwităb'l), *a.* 1667. [f. IN-[3] + EQUITABLE.] Not equitable; unfair, unjust. Hence **Ine·quitably** *adv.*

†**Ine·quitate**, *v.* [f. L. *inequitat-*, *inequitare* to ride on or over.] *trans.* To ride over or through; hence, to pervade, permeate. H. MORE.

Inequity (ine·kwĭti). 1556. [IN-[3].] Want of equity or justice; the fact or quality of being unfair; unfairness, partiality. **b.** with *pl.* An unfair or unjust matter or action 1857.

Many of her statesmen confess its i. and inexpediency BANCROFT.

Inequivalve (inī·kwivalv), *a.* 1776. [f. INEQUI- + VALVE.] *Conch.* Having valves of unequal size. So **Ine·quivalved, Ine·quiva·lvular** *a.*

Ineradicable (inĭræ·dikăb'l), *a.* 1818. [IN-[3].] Incapable of being eradicated or rooted out. Also *fig.*

This i. taint of sin BYRON. Hence **Inera·dicably** *adv.*

Inerasable (inĭrē¹·săb'l), *a.* Also -ible. 1811. [IN-[3].] That cannot be erased. Hence **Inera·sably, -ibly** *adv.*

†**Inerge·tic**, †**-al**, *a.* 1691. [f. IN-[3] + (EN)ERGETIC(AL).] Without energy; inactive, sluggish -1852.

Inerm (inə·ɹm), *a.* 1760. [ad. L. *inermis*, f. *in-* (IN-[3]) + *arma*.] *Bot.* Destitute of prickles or thorns; unarmed. So **Ine·rmous** *a.* (Dicts.)

Inerrable (ine·răb'l), *a.* 1613. [ad. post-cl.L. *inerrabilis*, f. *in-* (IN-[3]) + *errare*.] Incapable of erring; infallible.

Catholic Christianity rested on an i. Church as the teacher of truth 1879. Hence **Inerrabi·lity, Ine·rrableness**, infallibility. **Ine·rrably** *adv.*

Inerrant (ine·rănt), *a.* 1652. [f. L. *inerrantem*, f. *in-* (IN-[3]) + *errare*.] †1. *Astron.* Of a star: Fixed; not planetary. GAULE. 2. That does not err; unerring 1837. So **Ine·rrancy**, the quality of being i.

Inerratic (inerӕ·tik), *a.* 1655. [IN-[3].] Not erratic or wandering; fixed (as a star); following a fixed course.

†**Ine·rring**, *a.* [IN-[3].] = UNERRING. Howell. So †**Ine·rringly** *adv.* unerringly.

Inert (inə·ɹt), *a.* 1647. [ad. L. *inertem* unskilled, inactive, f. *in-* (IN-[3]) + *artem* ART.] 1. Having no inherent power of action, motion, or resistance; having the property of INERTIA. b. Without active chemical, physiological, or other properties; neutral 1800. 2. Of persons, animals, and (*transf.*) moving things: Inactive, sluggish, not inclined for or capable of action. Also of mental faculties. 1774.

1. Matter is said to be passive and i. BERKELEY. *fig.* The i. mass of accumulated prejudices HAZLITT. b. Carbon..is totally i. at ordinary heats H. SPENCER. *I. gas* (Chem.), a gaseous element such as helium, argon, neon, krypton, and xenon which are chemically inactive; also *ellipt.* as *sb.* 2. Timid as a Minister and i. as a statesman BRIGHT. An i. little town DICKENS. Hence **Ine·rtion**, i. condition; inactivity; sloth. **Ine·rt-ly** *adv.*, **-ness.**

Inertia (inə·ɹʃiă). 1713. [L., f. *iners, inertem*. The L. term was introduced into physics by Kepler.] 1. *Physics.* That property of matter by virtue of which it continues in its existing state, whether of rest or of uniform motion in a straight line, unless that state is altered by external force. Also called *vis inertiæ*. Also *fig.* 2. *transf.* Inactivity; disinclination to act; inertness, apathy 1822.

Ine·rtial *a.* of, pertaining to, or of the nature of i.

Inerudite (ine·rudəit), *a.* 1801. [ad. L. *ineruditus*; see IN-[3] and ERUDITE.] Not erudite; unlearned, uninstructed. So †**Inerudi·tion**, want of erudition 1685.

Inescapable (inĕskē·păb'l), *a.* 1792. [IN-[3].] That cannot be escaped or avoided; inevitable.

†**Ine·scate**, *v.* 1602. [f. L. *inescat-, inescare* to allure with bait, f. *in-* (IN-[2]) + *esca* food, bait.] *trans.* To allure with or as with a bait; to entice.

They i. and circumvent poore silly Soules 1602. So †**Inesca·tion**, alluring; an allurement.

Ine·sculent, *a.* 1831. [IN-[3].] Inedible.

Inescutcheon (inĕskʊ·tʃən). 1610. [f. IN *adv.* + ESCUTCHEON.] *Her.* An escutcheon of pretence, or other small escutcheon, charged on a larger escutcheon.

In esse: see ESSE 1.

Inessential (inĕse·nʃăl), *a.* (*sb.*) 1677. [IN-[3].] 1. Devoid of essence; unsubstantial, immaterial. 2. Not of the essence of a thing; not necessary to the constitution or existence of any thing 1836. 3. *sb.* That which is inessential 1778.

1. His i. figure cast no shade Upon the golden floor SHELLEY. Hence **Inesse·ntia·lity**, i. quality.

Inestimable (ine·stimăb'l), *a.* ME. [a. F., ad. L. *inæstimabilis*; see IN-[3] and ESTIMABLE.] 1. Incapable of being estimated; too great, profound, or intense to be computed. b. Priceless; invaluable 1579. †2. quasi-*adv.* Inestimably –1581.

1. The wealth consumed was i. DE FOE b. This charter, the i. monument of English freedom BURKE. †**Ine·stimabi·lity, -ableness, Ine·stimably** *adv.*

Ineunt (i·niˌɒnt). 1836. [ad. L. *ineuntem* entering, beginning, f. *inire*.] A. *adj.* Entering. B. *sb.* A point of a curve. Also *i.-point*. 1859.

Ineva·sible, *a.* 1846. [IN-[3].] Not evasible; that cannot be evaded.

Inevidence (ine·vidĕns). Now *rare.* 1654. [IN-[3].] Lack of evidence; obscurity (*rare*) 1671; †uncertainty –1677.

Inevident (ine·vidĕnt), *a.* Now *rare.* 1614. [ad. late L. *inevidentem* (Boeth.); see IN-[3] and EVIDENT.] Not evident; not clear or obvious; obscure.

Inevitable (ine·vităb'l), *a.* ME. [ad. L. *inevitabilis*; see IN-[3] and EVITABLE.] That cannot be avoided; not admitting of escape or evasion; that cannot fail to occur, etc.

All..Await alike th' i. hour GRAY. *The i.* (absol.), what cannot be avoided or escaped; There is no good in arguing with the i. LOWELL. Hence **Ine·vitabi·lity, Ine·vitableness. Ine·vitably** *adv.*

Inexact (inegzӕ·kt), *a.* 1828. [IN-[3].] Not exact; not strictly correct or precise. b. Of a person: Characterized by inexactness 1849. Hence **Inexa·ct-ly** *adv.*, **-ness.**

Inexactitude (inegzӕ·ktitiud). 1786. [IN-[3].] The quality or character of being inexact; want of exactitude, accuracy, or precision; inexactness. Also, an instance of this.

The author's i. of thought and expression 1869.

Inexcitable (ineksəi·tăb'l), *a.* *rare.* 1616. [In sense 1 (stressed *ine·xcitable*), ad. L. *inexcitabilis*; in 2, f. IN-[3] + EXCITABLE.] †1. From which one cannot be roused –1651. 2. Not excitable; not liable to excitement 1828.

1. In this i. sleepe CHAPMAN. Hence **Inexci·tabi·lity** (*rare*), the quality of being i.

Inexcommu·nicable, *a.* *rare.* 1610. [IN-[3].] That cannot be excommunicated.

A multitude is i. 1617.

Inexcusable (inekskiū·zăb'l), *a.* late ME. [ad. L. *inexcusabilis*; see IN-[3] and EXCUSABLE.] Not excusable; incapable of being justified.

Therfore arte thou i. o man TINDALE *Rom.* ii. 1. An i. affront LYTTON. Hence **Inexcu·sabi·lity, Inexcu·sableness. Inexcu·sably** *adv.*

†**Ine·xecrable**, *a.* ? An intensive of EXECRABLE, or a misprint.

O be thou damn'd, i. dogge *Merch. V.* IV. i. 128.

Inexecutable (inekse·kiutăb'l), *a.* 1833. [IN-[3].] That cannot be executed.

The arbitrary..provisions of this edict made it i. M. ARNOLD.

Inexecution (ineksĭkiū·ʃən). 1681. [IN-[3].] Lack or neglect of execution; non-performance.

His i. of orders baffled that effort JEFFERSON.

Inexertion (inegzə·ɹʃən). 1794. [IN-[3].] Want of exertion; failure to exert (oneself) or exercise (a faculty); inactivity.

Inexha·lable, *a.* [IN-[3].] Not exhalable; that cannot be evaporated. SIR T. BROWNE.

†**Inexhau·st**, *a.* 1612. [ad. L. *inexhaustus*; see IN-[3] and EXHAUST *ppl. a.*] = next –1665.

Inexhausted (inegzǭ·stĕd), *a.* 1626. [IN-[3].] Unexhausted.

I. Sources of Perfection ADDISON. Hence **Inexhau·stedly** *adv.* without exhaustion.

Inexhaustible (inegzǭ·stĭb'l), *a.* Also **-able.** 1601. [IN-[3].] Not exhaustible. 1. Incapable of being consumed or spent; exhaustless 1631. 2. Incapable of being emptied of contents 1601. 3. Incapable of being worn out in strength or vigour 1762.

1. Our inexhaustable strata of coal PENNANT. 2. An i. purse 1646. 3. Almost i. by toil 1848. Hence **Inexhau·stibi·lity, Inexhau·stibleness. Inexhaus·tibly** *adv.*

Inexhaustive (inegzǭ·stiv), *a.* 1728. [IN-[3].] Not exhaustive; exhaustless. Hence **Inexhau·stively** *adv.*

Inexhau·stless, *a.* 1739. [Confusion of *inexhaustible* and *exhaustless*.] Exhaustless.

Inexist (i:negzi·st), *v.* 1678. [f. IN *adv.* + EXIST *v.*] *intr.* To exist or have its being *in* something else.

The roundness inexists in the clay, and the thought of it inexists in my understanding TUCKER.

Inexistence[1] (inegzi·stĕns). 1635. [IN-[2].] The fact or condition of existing in something; inherence.

Inexi·stence[2]. Now *rare.* 1623. [IN-[3].] The fact or condition of not existing; non-existence.

†**Inexi·stency**[1]. 1674. [IN-[2].] = INEXISTENCE[1]; also (with *pl.*) something inexistent or inherent –1774.

†**Inexistency**[2]. 1659. [IN-[3]]. = INEXISTENCE[2].

Inexistent (i:negzi·stĕnt), *a.*[1] Also †**-ant.** 1553. [ad. late L. *inexistentem* (Boeth.), f. *in-* (IN-[2]) + *ex(s)istentem*.] Existing or having its being in something else; inherent.

Inexi·stent, *a.*[2] ? *Obs.* 1646. [IN-[3].] Not existing; not having existence.

Inexorable (ine·ksŏrăb'l), *a.* 1553. [ad. L. *inexorabilis*; see IN-[3] and EXORABLE.] Incapable of being persuaded by entreaty; not to be moved from one's purpose or determination; relentless, rigidly severe.

More i. farre, Then emptie Tygers, or the roaring Sea SHAKS. Lawes..are things deafe and i. HOLLAND. How entirely i. is the nature of facts 1858. Hence **Ine·xorabi·lity, Ine·xorableness**, the quality of being i. **Ine·xorably** *adv.* relentlessly.

Inexpansible (inekspӕ·nsĭb'l), *a.* 1878. [IN-[3].] Not expansible; incapable of being expanded.

Inexpectable (inekspe·ktăb'l), *a.* [IN-[3].] Not to be expected. BP. HALL.

Inexpe·ctant, *a.* 1853. [IN-[3].] Devoid of expectation. So **Inexpe·ctancy**, absence of expectancy 1643. **Inexpecta·tion**, absence of expectation 1627.

†**Inexpe·cted**, *a.* 1586. [IN-[3].] Not expected; unlooked-for –1651. Hence †**Inexpe·cted-ly** *adv.*, †**-ness.**

Inexpedience (inekspī·diĕns). Now *rare.* 1608. [See next and -ENCE.] = next.

Inexpediency (inekspī·diĕnsi). 1641. [f. INEXPEDIENT; see -ENCY.] The quality of being inexpedient; disadvantageousness, impolicy.

The i. of attempting to raise any considerable revenue by means of income-taxes McCULLOCH.

Inexpedient (inekspī·diĕnt), *a.* 1608. [IN-[3].] Not expedient; disadvantageous in the circumstances; unadvisable, impolitic.

Nothing could be more correctly lawful; but..few things would be more manifestly i. BENTHAM. Hence **Inexpe·diently** *adv.*

Inexpensive (inekspe·nsiv), *a.* 1837. [IN-[3].] 1. Not expensive or costly; cheap. 2. Not given to expenditure 1859. Hence **Inexpe·nsive-ly** *adv.*, **-ness.**

Inexperience (inekspīə·riĕns). 1598. [a. F., ad late L. *inexperientia*; see IN-[3] and EXPERIENCE.] Want of experience; hence, want of adequate knowledge or skill.

Those Failings which are incident to Youth and I. DRYDEN.

Inexperienced (inekspīə·riĕnst), *a.* 1626. [IN-[3].] Not experienced; having no (or little) experience; lacking the knowledge or skill derived from experience. Const. *in*.

We were not i. in sledging over the ice KANE.

Inexpert (inekspə·ɹt), *a.* 1450. [a. OF. *inexpert, -e*, ad. L. *inexpertus*; see IN-[3] and EXPERT *a.*] †1. Not experienced; having no (or little) experience. Const. *in, of*. –1697. 2. Wanting the aptitude or dexterity derived from experience; unskilled 1597. Hence **Inexpe·rt-ly** *adv.*, **-ness.**

Inexpiable (ine·kspiăb'l), *a.* 1570. [ad. L. *inexpiabilis*; see IN-[3] and EXPIABLE.] 1. Of an offence: That cannot be expiated or atoned for. 2. Of a feeling, etc.: That cannot be appeased by expiation; irreconcilable. (Also *transf.* of an action.) 1598.

1. His mirth is an i. sin 1728. 2. To raise in me i. hate MILT. *Sams.* 839. I. war BURKE. Hence **Ine·xpiableness, Ine·xpiably** *adv.*

Inexpiate (ine·kspiĕt), *a.* 1611. [ad. late L. *inexpiatus* (Augustine).] 1. Not expiated or atoned for 1819. †2. Unappeased.

2. To rest i. were much too rude a part 1611.

Inexplainable (ineksplē·năb'l), *a.* *rare.* 1623. [IN-[3].] That cannot be explained; inexplicable.

†**Ine·xpleble**, *a.* Also erron. **inexpleable.** 1569. [ad. L. *inexplebilis*, f. *in-* (IN-[3]) + *explere*; see EXPLETE *v.*] That cannot be filled; insatiable –1788. Hence †**Ine·xplebly** *adv.* (erron. **inexpleably**), insatiably.

Inexplicable (ine·ksplikăb'l), *a.* (*adv.*) late ME. [a. F., ad. L. *inexplicabilis*; see IN-[3] and EXPLICABLE.] †1. That cannot be unfolded, untwisted, or disentangled; inextricable; very complex –1656. †b. as *adv.* Inexplicably. CAXTON. †2. That cannot be unfolded in words; inexpressible –1691. 3. That cannot be explained; unintelligible; (in recent use) unaccountable 1546.

1. Mazes..of knottes i. EDEN. 2. The i. benefite of knowledge 1551. 3. I. dumbe shewes SHAKS., mysteries MAURY. Hence **Ine·xplicabi·lity, Ine·xplicableness. Ine·xplicably** *adv.*

Inexplicit (inekspli·sit), *a.* 1802. [IN-3.] Not explicit; indefinite; not clear in terms or statement. So **Inexpli·cit-ly** *adv.* 1757, **-ness.**

Inexplo·rable, *a.* 1646. [IN-3.] That cannot be explored; inscrutable.

Inexplo·sive, *a.* 1867. [IN-3.] Not liable to or capable of explosion.

Inexpressible (inekspre·sĭb'l). 1625. [IN-3.]

A. *adj.* That cannot be expressed in words; unutterable, unspeakable, indescribable. (Often as an emotional intensive.)

Ere mid-day arriv'd In Eden, distance i. By Numbers that have name MILT. *P.L.* VIII. 113. Its seclusion gives it an i. charm TYNDALL.

B. *sb.* 1. Something inexpressible 1652. 2. *pl.* (*colloq.*) Breeches or trousers 1790.

Hence **Inexpressibi·lity, Inexpre·ssibleness. Inexpre·ssibly** *adv.* (as an emotional intensive).

Inexpressive (inekspre·siv), *a.* 1652. [IN-3.] 1. = INEXPRESSIBLE *a.* (*arch.*). 2. Not expressive; wanting in expression 1744.

2. His i. eye 1860. Hence **Inexpre·ssive-ly** *adv.*, **-ness.**

Inexpugnable (inekspʊ·gnăb'l), *a.* 1490. [a. F., ad. L. *inexpugnabilis*; see IN-3 and EXPUGNABLE.] That cannot be taken by assault or storm; incapable of being overthrown by force; impregnable, invincible. *lit.* and *fig.*

How the i. walles of Jerico were ouerthrowen MORE. *fig.* An i. desire of sleeping 1590. Hence **Inexpu·gnably** *adv.*

†Inexsu·perable, *a.* 1623. [ad. L. *inexsuperabilis*; see IN-3 and EXSUPERABLE.] That cannot be overcome.

Inexte·nded, *a. rare.* 1739. [IN-3.] Without extension.

Inextensible (inekste·nsĭb'l), *a.* 1840. [IN-3.] Not capable of extension; that cannot be stretched or drawn out in length.

The assumption..that the ether is i. and incompressible 1881. Hence **Inextensibi·lity**, the quality of being i.

Inexte·nsion. 1827. [IN-3.] Want of extension; unextended state.

In extenso: see IN *Lat. prep.*

Inexte·rminable, *a. rare.* 1586. [ad. post-cl.L. *inexterminabilis*; see IN-3 and EXTERMINABLE.] †1. Having no possible end; interminable –1668. 2. That cannot be exterminated 1828.

Inexti·nct, *a. rare.* 1623. [ad. L. *inexstinctus*; cf. IN-3 and EXTINCT.] Unextinguished.

†Inexti·nguible, *a.* ME. [a. F. or ad. L. *inextinguibilis*; see IN-3.] = next –1677.

Inextinguishable (inekstiŋgwiʃăb'l), *a.* 1509. [IN-3.] That cannot be extinguished (see the vb.); unquenchable, indestructible, etc.

I. rage MILT., laughter COWPER, hope SOUTHEY. Hence **Inexti·nguishably** *adv.*

Inexti·nguished, *a.* 1746. [IN-3.] Not extinguished; still burning; unextinguished.

Inextirpable (inekstə·ɹpăb'l), *a.* 1623. [ad. L. *inexstirpabilis* (Pliny), f. *in-* (IN-3) + *exstirpare* to EXTIRPATE.] That cannot be extirpated or rooted out.

In extremis: see IN *Lat. prep.*

Inextricable (ine·kstrikăb'l), *a.* late ME. [ad. L. *inextricabilis*, f. *in-* (IN-3) + *extricare* to EXTRICATE.] 1. From which one cannot extricate oneself (*lit.* and *fig.*). 2. Of a knot, etc.: That cannot be disentangled or untied. Also *transf.* 1610. †3. Of a problem: That cannot be solved –1664. 4. Intricately involved, confused, or perplexed; incapable of being put straight 1655. 5. Intricate, elaborate, exquisitely wrought (*rare*) 1691.

1. We..lose our selves in i. Mazes 1720. Struggling with an i. trouble HAWTHORNE. 4. The ecclesiastical polity of the realm was in i. confusion MACAULAY. 5. The i. richness of the fully developed Gothic jamb and arch RUSKIN. Hence **Ine·xtricabi·lity, Ine·xtricableness. Ine·xtricably** *adv.*

†Ineye (in,əi·), *v.* ME. [f. IN-2 + EYE, after L. *inoculare*.] *trans.* To put an eye or bud into (the bark of a tree); to inoculate –1708.

Infall (i·nfǭl). 1645. [f. IN *adv.* + FALL *sb.*; = Ger. *einfall.*] An inroad, attack, incursion, or descent (*upon* or *into*). Now *rare.*

Infallibilism (infæ·libiliz'm). 1870. [f. as next + -ISM.] The principle of the infallibility of some person or thing, esp. of the Pope.

Infallibilist (infæ·libilist). Also **-blist.** 1870. [f. L. *infallibilis* + -IST.] One who upholds the infallibility of some person or thing, esp. of the Pope. Also *attrib.*

Infallibility (infælĭbi·lĭti). 1611. [f. as INFALLIBLE + -ITY.] 1. The quality or fact of being infallible or exempt from liability to err. 2. The quality of being unfailing; unfailing certainty 1631.

1. The Pope sitting in his Chaire,..may yet erre for all his i. GATAKER. *His I.*, a title given to the Pope; also, a mock title. 2. The i. of a gun KANE.

Infallible (infæ·lĭb'l), *a.* (*sb.*) late ME. [ad. med.L. *infallibilis* (in Bæda), f. *in-* (IN-3) + *fallibilis* FALLIBLE.] Not fallible. 1. Not liable to be deceived or mistaken; incapable of erring. 2. Not liable to fail; unfailing; sure; certain 1526. 3. *sb.* One who or that which is infallible 1816.

1. Parliaments are not i. *Junius Lett.* 2. An i. Maxime 1654, ointment and plaister ARBUTHNOT, fruit of Unwisdom 1843. Hence **Infa·llibleness**, infallibility. **Infa·llibly** *adv.* indubitably; unerringly.

†Infa·llid, *a.* 1635. [f. IN-3 + (app.) an assumed *fallid, or L. *fallidus, from *fallere* to deceive.] = INFALLIBLE 2.

†Infama·tion. 1533. [a. F., ad. L. *infamationem*; see INFAME *v.*] The action of holding up to infamy; defamation –1651.

Infa·matory, *a. rare.* 1612. [ad. med.L. *infamatorius*; see -ORY.] †a. = DEFAMATORY. b. Bringing infamy.

†Infa·me, *sb.* ME. [a. OF. *infame* :—late L. *infamium* = L. *infamia.*] = INFAMY –1616. So **†Infa·me** *a.* = INFAMOUS 1572.

Infame (infēi·m), *v. arch.* ME. [a. F. *infamer*, ad. L. *infamare*, f. *infamis.*] 1. *trans.* To render infamous; to reprobate. †2. To defame –1604. †3. To accuse of something infamous –1797.

1. This inhuman Practice will i. your Government PENN.

Infamize (i·nfămǝiz), *v.* 1596. [f. L. *infamis* + -IZE.] = INFAME *v.* 1, 2. Hence (by perversion) **†Infa·monize** *v.* (*L. L. L.* v. ii. 684).

Infamous (i·nfăməs), *a.* ME. [Corresponds to rare OF. *infameux*, med.L. *infamosus* = L. *infamis.* Formerly stressed *infa·mous.*] 1. Of ill fame or repute; notorious *for* badness of any kind; held in infamy or public disgrace. 2. Deserving of infamy; of shameful badness, vileness, or abominableness; of a character or quality deserving utter reprobation. (A strong adj. of detestation.) 1489. 3. *Law.* Of a person: Deprived of civil rights, in consequence of conviction of certain crimes 1548. b. Of a crime or punishment: Involving or entailing infamy 1555.

1. Those that be neere..shall mocke thee which art i. *Ezek.* xxii. 5. The high-way betwixt Jericho and Jerusalem is i. for theeving FULLER. 2. False erraunt knight, i., and forswore SPENSER. Detest the very ground on which was acted such an i. Treachery 1703. 3. They are condemned to lose the Franchise or Freedom of the Law, that is, become I., and of no Credit 1707. b. And so had two wives at once, which is by the civil law a thing i. 1555. Phr. *I. crime*, a term now chiefly applied to sodomy and kindred offences. Hence **I·nfamous-ly** *adv.*, **-ness.**

Infamy (i·nfămi). 1473. [a. F. *infamie*, ad. L. *infamia.*] 1. Evil fame or reputation; public reproach, shame, or disgrace. Also with *an* and *pl.* 2. The quality or character of being infamous or of shameful vileness; (with *pl.*) an infamous act. 1513 3. *Law.* The loss of all or certain of the rights of a citizen, consequent on conviction of certain crimes; see INFAMOUS 3. 1609.

1. Ye are taken vp in the lips of talkers, and are an i. (= an object of public reproach) of the people *Ezek.* xxxvi. 3. 2. The i. of the peace was more deeply.. felt GIBBON.

Infancy (i·nfănsi). 1494. [ad. L. *infantia* inability to speak, f. *infantem* INFANT *sb.*1; see -ANCY.] 1. The condition of being an infant; early childhood, babyhood. 2. *Law.* The condition of being a minor; the period of life during which a person remains under guardianship (extending, in common law, to the end of the twenty-first year); minority, nonage 1658. 3. *fig.* The earliest period in the history of anything; the rudimentary stage in any process of growth 1555. 4. *concr.* (chiefly *rhet.*) Infants collectively 1598. †5. In etym. sense: Speechlessness; silence. MILT.

1. Heaven lies about us in our i. WORDSW. 2. The defendant pleaded i., the goods having been supplied before he was of age (*mod.*). 3. Thrice happy was the worlds first infancie P. FLETCHER. 4. Old age and i. Promiscuous perished SHELLEY.

Infa·nd, *a. Obs.* exc. as *nonce-wd.* 1608. [ad. L. *infandus.*] = next.

†Infa·ndous, *a.* 1644. [f. as prec. + -OUS.] Unspeakable, not to be spoken of; nefarious –1708.

I·nfangthief. [OE. *infangenþēof*, f. IN *adv.* + *fangen*, pa. pple. of *fōn* to seize (see FANG *v*1.) + *þēof* thief; lit. 'thief seized within'.] *O.E. Law.* The right of the lord of a manor to try and to amerce a thief caught within its limits.

Infant (i·nfănt), *sb.*1 ME. [a. OF. *enfant*, *-aunt* (F. *enfant*) child :—L. *infans, infantem*, sb. use of *infans* unable to speak, f. *in-* (IN-3) + *fans, fari* to speak.] 1. A child during the earliest period of life (or still unborn); esp. a child in arms; often, any child under seven years of age. Also *fig.* and *transf.* 2. A person under (legal) age; a minor. In common law, a person under the age of twenty-one years; in the case of a ruler, one under the age at which he becomes constitutionally capable of exercising sovereignty 1513. †3. A youth of noble or gentle birth –1600. 4. Applied joc. to various productions of exceptional size, strength, etc. 1832. 5. *attrib.* (or *adj.*) a. That is an infant or like an infant, as *i. heir, martyr*, etc. 1595. b. In its earliest stage, undeveloped, nascent, incipient, as *i. blossom, civilization, navy*, etc. 1593. c. Of or belonging to an infant or infants, proper to or intended for infants; infantile; as *i. class, years*, etc. 1586.

1. An i. crying in the night: An i. crying for the light: And with no language but a cry TENNYSON. *transf.* The Canker Galls, the Infants of the Spring SHAKS. 3. The noble I. [Rinaldo] stood a space Confused, speechless FAIRFAX. 4. The heaviest gun..the Woolwich I...weighs 35 tons 1874. *Comb.* **i.-baptism**, the baptism of infants, pædobaptism.

Infant (i·nfănt), *sb.*2 1555. [ad. Sp., Pg. *infante*; see INFANTE.] A prince or princess of Spain or Portugal; = INFANTE, INFANTA.

†I·nfant, *v.* 1483. [a. F. *enfanter*, f. *enfant.*] *trans.* To bring forth (a child). Also *fig.* –1642.

This worthy Motto, No Bishop, no King is of the same batch, and infanted out of the same feares MILT.

‖**Infanta** (infa·ntă). 1601. [Sp., Pg., fem. of INFANTE.] A daughter of the king and queen of Spain or Portugal; *spec.* the eldest daughter who is not heir to the throne. †Also *transf.* and *fig.* of other young ladies.

transf. Lady Catherine grew frightened, lest her i. [her daughter] should vex herself sick H. WALPOLE.

‖**Infante** (infa·nte). 1555. [Sp., Pg. *infante* :—L. *infantem* INFANT *sb.*1] A son of the king and queen of Spain or Portugal other than the heir to the throne (who is called *principe*); *spec.* the second son.

I·nfanthood. 1862. = INFANCY.

Infa·nticidal, *a.* 1835. [f. INFANTICIDE2 + -AL.] Of or practising infanticide.

Infanticide1 (infæ·ntisəid). 1680. [a. F., ad. late L. *infanticida*, f. *infantem* + *cædere, -cidere*; see -CIDE 1.] One who kills an infant.

Infanticide2 (infæ·ntisəid). 1656. [a. F., ad. late L. *infanticidium*; see prec. and -CIDE 2.] The killing of infants, *esp.* the killing of new-born infants, as a custom among savages, and in the ancient world. b. *spec.* The crime of murdering an infant after its birth, perpetrated by or with the consent of its parents, esp. the mother 1789.

Infantile (i·nfăntəil, -til), *a.* 1696. [ad. late L. *infantilis*, f. *infantem.*] Of or pertaining to an infant, infants, or infancy: belonging to a person when an infant; existing in its infancy. b. Infant-like 1772.

I. diseases 1800, literature 1864.

Infantilism (infæ·ntiliz'm). 1895. [f. prec. + -ISM.] *Path.* The state of being mentally or physically undeveloped.

Infantine (i·nfăntəin), *a.* 1603. [a. F. *infantin, -ine*, var. of *enfantin, -ine*; see INFANT *sb.*[1] and -INE[1].] = INFANTILE.

A degree of credulity next to i. BURKE.

†**I·nfantly,** *a.* 1618. [-LY[1].] Infant-like.

Infantry (i·nfăntri). 1579. [a. F. *infanterie*, ad. It. *infanteria* foot-soldiery, f. *infante* a youth, foot-soldier :—L. *infantem.*] **1.** The body of foot-soldiers; foot-soldiers collectively; that part of an army which consists of men who march and manœuvre on foot and carry small arms, now a rifle. **2.** Infants collectively. Now *joc.* 1613. **3.** *attrib.*, as *i. brigade*, etc. 1813.

1. *Mounted I.*, soldiers mounted for the sake of transit, but who fight on foot.

I·nfantryman. 1883. A soldier of an infantry regiment.

I·nfant-schoo·l. 1833. A school for young children (usually under seven years of age).

Infarce, -se, var. of ENFARCE *v. Obs.*

Infarct (infā·ɹkt), *sb.* 1873. [ad. med. or mod.L. *infarctus*, f. ppl. stem of *infarcire*, f. *in-* (IN-[2]) + *farcire* to stuff.] *Path.* A portion of tissue that has become stuffed with extravasated blood, serum, or other matter; the substance of an infarction. So **Infa·rct** *v. trans.* to affect with infarction 1822.

Infarction (infā·ɹkʃən). 1689. [f. L. *infarcire.*] *Path.* The action of stuffing up or condition of being stuffed up, obstruction; *concr.* = INFARCT *sb.* Now usually restricted to morbid conditions of the tissues resulting from obstruction of the circulation, as by an embolus.

Infare (i·nfeᵊɹ). [OE. *innfær*, f. *inn*, IN *adv.* + *fær* going, FARE *sb.*[1], f. *faran* to go.] †**1.** (OE. and early ME.) The act of going in; an entrance, way in. **2.** *Sc.*, *n. dial.*, and *U.S.* A feast or entertainment given on entering a new house; *esp.* at the reception of a bride in her new home ME.

†**Infa·shionable,** *a. rare.* 1635. [IN-[3].] Unfashionable –1787.

†**Infa·tigable,** *a.* 1510. [a. F., ad. L. *infatigabilis*; see IN-[3] and FATIGABLE.] = INDEFATIGABLE –1713.

Infatuate (infæ·tiu,ĕt), *ppl. a.* 1471. [ad. L. *infatuatus*, *infatuare*; see next.] Infatuated.

Infatuate (infæ·tiu,eᶦt), *v.* 1533. [f. L. *infatuat-*, *infatuare*, f. *in-* (IN-[2]) + *fatuus* foolish.] †**1.** *trans.* To turn (counsels, etc.) into folly, to exhibit the foolishness of; to confound, frustrate, bring to nought –1724. **2.** To make (a person) utterly foolish or fatuous; to inspire with an extravagant passion 1567.

1. God hath infatuated your high subtle wisdom TINDALE. 2. The short-lived joy that infatuated the public BOSWELL. Hence **Infa·tuatedly** *adv.*

Infatuation (infætiu,ēᶦ·ʃən). 1649. [f. L. *infatuare.*] The action of infatuating or condition of being infatuated; an extravagantly foolish or unreasoning passion.

The I. of the Enthusiast, sets him above the Fear of Death 1718. Your i. about that girl blinds you 1815.

Infaust (infǭ·st), *a. rare.* 1658. [ad. L. *infaustus.*] Unlucky, unfortunate, ill-omened. So †**Infau·sting,** a rendering i., a boding of ill-luck 1622.

Infeasible (infī·zĭb'l), *a.* Now *rare.* 1533. [IN-[3].] Not capable of being accomplished or carried out; impracticable. So **Infeasibi·lity, Infea·sibleness,** the quality of being i.

†**Infect,** *ppl. a.* ME. [a. F., or ad. L. *infectus*, *inficere*; see next.] Infected. Often construed as pa. pple. of next. –1617.

Infect (infe·kt), *v.* ME. [ad. L. *infect-*, ppl. stem of *inficere* to dip in, stain, spoil, etc., f. *in-* (IN-[2]) + *facere* to make, do, put.] **1.** *trans.* To affect, influence, or imbue with some quality or property by immersion or infusion. *Obs.* or *rare.* 1495. †**2.** To spoil or corrupt by noxious influence, admixture, or alloy; to adulterate –1693. **3.** To fill (the air, etc.) with noxious corruption or the germs of disease ME. **4.** To affect with disease; to act upon by infection or contagion. Also *absol.* ME. Also *transf.* and *fig.* **5.** To taint with moral corruption; to deprave ME. **6.** To taint with crime; to involve in crime or its penalties 1580. **b.** *Internat. Law.* To taint with illegality 1758. **7.** To imbue with an opinion or belief, esp. heresy or seditious views. Also said of the opinion. 1483. **8.** To affect (a person) with some feeling. Also of feelings: To take hold of. 1595. **9.** To affect or influence with some quality or by introducing something extraneous 1605. **b.** *spec.* Of a sound: To affect and alter the sound in a neighbouring syllable 1872. †**10.** To infest –1712.

3. If her breath were as terrible as [her] terminations, ..she would i. to the north starre SHAKS. 4. Persons infected with plague DE FOE. *fig.* With a Son's death t'i. a Father's sight DRYDEN. 7. Whan the heresye of the arryans had enfected al Italye CAXTON. 8. 'Twas a feare Which oft infects the wisest SHAKS. 10. Much infected with serpents, moskittos [etc.] 1712. Hence **Infe·cter** (? *Obs.*), -or, one who infects. **Infe·ctible** *a.* (*rare*), capable of being infected.

Infection (infe·kʃən). ME. [a. F. *infection*, ad. late L. *infectionem*, f. *inficere*; see prec.] †**1.** The action or process of affecting injuriously, or the fact of being so affected; corrupt condition –1621. †**2.** Contamination of air or water, etc. –1801. **3.** The agency, substance, germ, or principle by which an infectious disease is communicated or transmitted ME. **b.** *pl.* Morbific influences, principles, or germs 1533. **4.** The communication of disease, esp. by the agency of the atmosphere or water (hence, strictly, dist. from *contagion*); the action or process of infecting; the fact of being infected 1548. **5.** Disease caused by infection; a plague, epidemic, pestilence; †*occas.*, A disease, a seizure with disease 1563. **6.** Moral contamination; an instance of this 1529. **7.** Communication of harmful opinions or beliefs 1529. **8.** *Internat. Law.* Contamination by illegality: see INFECTIOUS 6. 1879. **9.** The contagious or 'catching' influence or operation of example, sympathy, etc. 1616. †**10.** The process of moistening, colouring, etc. by immersion or infusion (*rare*) –1686. **11.** *Celt. Gram.* Alteration of a sound under the influence of a neighbouring sound 1872. ¶ **12.** Misused *joc.* for *affection*, liking. SHAKS.

3. The i. may be in the very air DE FOE. b. All the infections that the Sunne suckes vp From Bogs, Fens, Flats, on Prosper fall *Temp.* II. ii. 1. 4. As a man suspected of i. is refused admission into cities JOHNSON. 5. He found himself shunned in public places as an i. THIRLWALL. 7. A heart that..throws off the i. of these times YOUNG. 9. The i. of his..enthusiasm 1873. Hence **Infe·ctionist** (*rare*), one who lays stress upon i. as a cause of disease.

Infectious (infe·kʃəs), *a.* 1542. [f. INFECT-ION + -IOUS.] **1.** Having the quality or power of communicating disease by infection; infecting with disease; pestilential, unhealthy. **2.** Of diseases: Apt to be communicated by infection (dist. from CONTAGIOUS) 1592. **b.** *transf.* Of or for infectious diseases 1887. †**3.** Infected with disease –1727. **4.** Tending to contaminate character, morals, etc. Now *rare.* 1547. **5.** Of actions, emotions, etc.: 'Catching', contagious 1611. **6.** *Internat. Law.* Tainting with illegality (said of contraband or hostile goods in their effect on the rest of a cargo, or on the ship) 1878.

1. There is something i. in the atmosphere LYTTON. 2. The fever was highly i. 1790. b. The i. hospital 1887. 3. *Oth.* IV. i. 21 [*Qos.* infected]. 5. An i. good humour and urbanity 1899. Hence **Infe·ctious-ly** *adv.*, **-ness.** var. †**Infe·ctuous** 1495.

Infective (infe·ktiv), *a.* ME. [ad. L. *infectivus*; see INFECT *v.* and -IVE. Recently revived in medical use.] **1.** Infectious. **2.** Producing moral infection 1576. †**3.** Producing an emotion, feeling, etc. by infection –1703.

1. The i. matter shown to exist in the blood serum 1883. Hence **Infe·ctiveness, Infecti·vity.**

Infecund (infe·kʊnd), *a.* ME. [ad. L. *infecundus*, f. *in-* (IN-[3]) + *fecundus* FECUND. Formerly *infecu·nd.*] Not fecund; barren, unproductive. So †**Infecu·ndous** *a. rare.*

Infecundity (infĭkʊ·ndĭti). 1605. [ad. L. *infecunditas*; see prec. and -ITY.] Unfruitfulness, barrenness (*lit.* and *fig.*).

Infeeble, obs. f. ENFEEBLE *v.*

Infeft (infe·ft), *v. Sc. Law.* 1462. Variant of ENFEOFF. So **Infe·ftment** 1456 = ENFEOFFMENT.

Infelicific (infīlisi·fik), *a.* 1874. [f. L. *infelix*, *infelici-*, after FELICIFIC.] *Ethics.* Productive of unhappiness.

Infelicitous (infĭli·sĭtəs), *a.* 1835. [IN-[3].] Unhappy, unfortunate; *esp.* not apt or appropriate; the opposite of FELICITOUS.

An i. idea 1857, illustration 1884. **Infeli·citously** *adv.*

Infelicity (infĭli·sĭti). ME. [ad. L. *infelicitas*, f. *infelix.*] **1.** The state of being unhappy or unfortunate; an unhappy condition; unhappiness; bad fortune, ill luck, misfortune. **b.** An instance of bad fortune; a misfortune; a cause or source of unhappiness 1577. **2.** Unlucky inaptness or inappropriateness; with *pl.* an inapt expression or detail of style 1617.

1. That pure i. which accompanies some people in their walk through life LAMB. 2. With how great i. or incongruity soever it be HALES.

Infelo·nious, *a.* [IN-[3].] Not of the nature of felony. GEO. ELIOT.

Infelt, *ppl. a.* 1586. [f. IN *adv.* + *felt* ppl. adj.] Inwardly felt or experienced

Infeodation: see INFEUDATION.

Infeof(f, -ment, obs. ff. ENFEOFF, -MENT.

Infer (infə̄·ɹ), *v.* Inflected **inferred,** etc. 1526. [ad. L. *inferre*, f. *in-* (IN-[2]) + *ferre* to bear. Cf. F. *inférer* (16th c.).] †**1.** *trans.* To bring on, bring about, induce, occasion, cause, procure –1754. †**b.** To confer –1614. †**c.** To cause to be. MILT. *P.L.* VII. 116. †**2.** To bring in, introduce; to mention, report; to adduce, allege –1710. **3.** To bring in or draw as a conclusion; in *Logic*, To derive by deduction or induction from something known or assumed; to accept from evidence or premisses; to conclude 1529. Also *absol.* **4.** To lead to as a conclusion; to involve as a consequence; to imply. (Said of a fact or statement.) 1530.

1. Inferre faire Englands peace by this Alliance SHAKS. 2. Full well hath Clifford plaid the Orator, Inferring arguments of mighty force SHAKS. 3. What I never meant Don't you i. PRIOR. *absol.* To *infer* is to be regarded as the proper office of the Philosopher;—to *prove*, of the Advocate WHATELY. 4. Consider first, that Great or Bright inferrs not Excellence MILT. *P.L.* VIII. 91. Hence **Inferable, -ible** (infə̄·răb'l, i·nfĕrĭb'l) *a.* that may be inferred; deducible.

Inference (i·nfĕrĕns). 1594. [ad. med.L. *inferentia* (Abelard), f. *inferentem*, *inferre*; used instead of cl. L. *illatio.*] **1.** The action or process of inferring; *esp.* in *Logic*, the forming of a conclusion from premisses, either by induction or deduction; = ILLATION 1. Also (with *pl.*), an act of inferring; the logical form in which this is expressed. **2.** That which is inferred, a conclusion drawn from data or premisses 1612.

1. Religion is..a matter of deduction and i. BUTLER. In any i., we argue either to something already implied in the premisses or not; if the latter, the i. is inductive, if the former, deductive. If the deductive i. contain only a single premiss, it is immediate; if it contain two premisses, and the conclusion be drawn from these jointly, it is mediate, and is called a syllogism FOWLER. 2. To draw inferences has been said to be the great business of life MILL.

Inferential (infĕre·nʃăl), *a.* 1657. [f. med. L. *inferentia* + -AL.] Of, pertaining to, or depending on, or of the nature of inference.

The belief was, probably, i. 1854. Hence **Infere·ntially** *adv.* in an i. manner; in the way of inference: *occas.* (qualifying the whole statement) = as may be inferred.

Inferior (infīᵊ·riəɹ). ME. [a.L., comp. of *inferus.*] Lower; opp. to *superior.*

A. *adj.* **1.** Lower in position; nether, subjacent. (Now chiefly techn.) **2.** Lower in degree, rank, importance, quality, amount, etc.; of less value or consideration; lesser; subordinate 1531. **3.** Of low degree, rank, etc.; in mod. use esp.: Of no great value or excellence; comparatively bad, poor, mean 1531. **4.** *Astron.* **a.** Applied to Venus and Mercury, whose orbits lie within that of the earth (orig., according to Ptolemaic astronomy, as having their spheres below that of the sun). **b.** *I. conjunction*: that of an inferior planet with the sun when between the earth and the sun. **c.** *I. meridian*: that part of the celestial meridian which lies below the pole; so *i. passage* (of the meridian), etc. 1658. **5.** *Bot.* Growing below some other part or organ; said of the calyx when growing below or free from the ovary, and of the ovary when adherent to the sides of the calyx so as to be below the lobes of it 1785. 6. *Anat.* and *Zool.* Applied to parts or organs situated below others of the same kind, or below the usual or normal position 1826. 7. *Printing.* Applied to small letters or figures cast or made to range at the bottom of the ordinary letters in a line of type, as in H_2, C_nH_{2n-2}. JACOBI.

1. The old Glacial drift..being observed in several places as an i. deposit DANA. 2. The labours of inferiour tenants 1607. The body, or, as some love to call it, our inferiour nature BURKE. I feel myself inferiour to the task BOSWELL. 3. The country with which he shows so i. an acquaintance 1878.

B. *sb.* 1. A person inferior to another (in rank, etc.); one of less consideration, attainments, etc.; a subordinate 1502. 2. A thing inferior to another; †also formerly (in *pl.*), things of this lower world, sublunary affairs or events 1589. 3. *Printing.* An inferior letter; see A. 7. 1884.

1. Love towards Inferiors is Courtesy and Condescension SHERLOCK.

Hence **Inferio·rity. Infe·riorly** *adv.*

Infernal (infɔ̄·ɹnăl). ME. [a. F., ad. L. *infernalis*, f. *infernus* adj.]

A. *adj.* 1. Of or relating to the world or regions below, i.e. to the realm of the dead in ancient mythology, or the abode of evil spirits in Jewish and Christian belief; of, pertaining or relating to, hell. 2. Like that of hell; hellish 1562. 3. Of the nature of the inhabitants of hell; diabolical, fiendish 1603. 4. *colloq.* 'Confounded'; execrable, detestable 1764.

1. The courte of i. Pluto EDEN. The flocking shadows pale, Troop to th' infernall jail MILT. 2. The i. hiss and crackle of the flame KINGSLEY. 3. Voltaire, With an i. sneer upon his lips 1827. Phr. †*I. stone*: an old name for lunar caustic 1706. *I. machine*: an apparatus (often harmless in appearance) contrived to produce an explosion and criminally destroy life or property; formerly, an explosive machine used in war 1810. 4. An i. ass 1897.

B. *sb.* 1. An inhabitant of the infernal regions or of hell. (Usu. in *pl.*) 1582. †2. *pl.* The infernal regions -1673.

Hence **Infe·rnally** *adv.* (Usu. *colloq.*)

‖**Inferno** (infɔ̄·ɹno). 1834. [It., :—late L. *infernus* hell.] Hell; a place compared to hell, or to Dante's *Inferno.*

Infero- (i·nfĕro), mod. comb. form of L. *inferus* low, used in *Zool.*, etc. to designate parts situated low down or on the under side; as:

infero·ante·rior *a.*, situated below and in front; **-fro·ntal** *a.*, in the lower part of the forehead; **-la·teral** *a.*, below and on one side; **-me·dian** *a.*, in the middle of the under side; **-poste·rior** *a.* below and behind.

Inferobranch (i·nfĕro‚bræŋk). 1836. [f. INFERO- + L. *branchiæ* gills.] *Zool.* One of the order or sub-order *Inferobranchiata* of gastropod molluscs, originally comprising those in which the gills are situated under the projecting border of the mantle, now including also allied forms without gills. So **I:nfero·bra·nchian, -bra·nchiate** *adjs.* belonging to the *Inferobranchiata*; *sbs.* = INFEROBRANCH.

Inferrible, -able (infɔ̄·rĭb'l, -ăb'l), *a.* 1646. [f. INFER *v.* + -ABLE; the sp. *inferrible* is of mongrel character between L. **inferibilis* and Eng. *infe·rrable*; see -BLE.] That may be inferred; deducible. Hence **Infe·rribly** *adv.*

Infertile (infɔ̄·ɹtəil, -til), *a.* 1597. [a. F., ad. late L. *infertilis*; see IN-³ and FERTILE.] Not fertile; unproductive, barren, sterile.

To sowe the same in an infertile grownde 1597. Hence **Infe·rtilely** *adv.* **Inferti·lity.**

†**Infe·st,** *a.* 1513. [ad. L. *infestus.*] Hostile -1641.

Infest (infe·st), *v.* 1477. [a. F. *infester*, or ad. L. *infestare*, f. *infestus.*] 1. *trans.* To attack, annoy, or trouble in a persistent manner; to molest; to harass. 2. To trouble (a country or place) with hostile attacks; to visit persistently or in large numbers (or even singly) with evil intent; to swarm in or about, so as to be troublesome 1602.

1. He sought all manner of ways to i. the Emperor FOXE. That complication of political diseases which infests the nation FIELDING. 2. The Turkish Pyrats, which..infested al those Seas PURCHAS. Wasps i. the Camp with loud Alarms DRYDEN. Hence **Infe·ster** *sb.* (*rare*), one who, or that which, infests.

Infestation (infestēⁱ·ʃən). 1492. [ad. late L. *infestationem* (Tertullian), f. *infestare.* Cf. F. *infestation.*] The action of infesting; now used esp. of insects which attack plants, grain, etc., usu. in large swarms. Also, an attack or assault of this kind.

The i. did much harm in young Fir woods MISS ORMEROD.

†**Infe·ster,** *v. rare.* 1563. [f. IN-² + FESTER *v.*] *trans.* To render (a sore) festered, to cause to rankle. Also *fig.* -1611.

†**Infe·stious,** *a.* 1593. Also **-uous.** [irreg. f. L. *infestus* or INFEST *v.*, after adjs. in *-ious, -uous.*] Hostile -1709. So †**Infe·stive** *a.*¹

†**Infe·stive,** *a.*² 1623. [ad. L. *infestivus*; see IN-³ and FESTIVE.] 'Without mirth or pleasantness'. (Dicts.) So **Infesti·vity** (*rare*), absence of festivity; dullness 1727.

Infeudation (infiudēⁱ·ʃən). 1473. [ad. med.L. *infeudationem*; see FEUD², FEE *sb.*² Cf. F. *inféodation*, formerly *infeudation.*] 1. a. The granting of an estate to be held in fee; enfeoffment. b. *I. of tithes*, the granting of tithes to laymen. 2. A deed of enfeoffment 1647.

Infibulate (infi·biuleⁱt), *v. rare.* 1623. [f. L. *infibulat-*, *infibulare*, f. *in-* (IN-²) + *fibula* a clasp, etc.] *trans.* To fasten with a clasp or buckle. Hence **Infi:bula·tion,** the action of infibulating; *spec.* the fastening of the sexual organs with a fibula or clasp.

Infidel (i·nfidĕl). 1460. [a. OF. *infidèle*, ad. L. *infidelis*, f. *in-* (IN-³) + *fidelis* faithful.]

A. *sb.* †1. An unbeliever 1526. 2. *spec.* a. An adherent of a religion opposed to Christianity; esp. a Mohammedan, a Saracen (the earliest sense in Eng.); also, *occas.*, a Jew or a pagan. Now chiefly *Hist.* 1470. b. From a non-Christian point of view: = Gentile, Giaour, etc. 1534. 3. A disbeliever in religion generally; esp. one in a Christian land who denies the divine origin and authority of Christianity; a professed unbeliever. Usu. a term of opprobrium. 1526. 4. *gen.* One who does not believe in something specified. (Freq. *fig.* from 3.) 1606.

2. a. Two honderd sarasyns or Infydeles MALORY. b. I sought to wed The daughter of an I. MILT. *Sams.* 221. 4. Spiritual communications, as regards which Mrs. Browning is a believer, and her husband an i. 1858.

B. *adj.* 1. Unbelieving; pagan, heathen, etc. 1460; †incredulous, sceptical (*rare*) -1704. 2. Of, pertaining to, or characteristic of, infidels or infidelity 1742.

Infidelity (infide·lĭti). ME. [ad. L. *infidelitas*, f. *infidelis.* Cf. F. *infidélité.*] 1. Want of faith; unbelief, esp. disbelief in the truth or evidences of Christianity; the attitude of an infidel. †b. Mohammedanism; Heathenism (*rare*) -1613. 2. *gen.* Disbelief, incredulity 1579. 3. Unfaithfulness or disloyalty to a person; esp., in mod. use, to a husband or wife 1529; an act or instance of this 1714. †4. Untrustworthiness; an instance of this -1785.

1. I. is the proper opposite of faith MANNING. 3. Mischiefs arising from conjugal i. and impunity 1700. 4. The i. of that conveyance [the post] BURKE.

Infield, in-field (i·n‚fīld), *sb.* 1551. [f. IN *adv.* + FIELD *sb.*] 1. The land of a farm which lies around or near the homestead; hence, arable land as opp. to pasture; land regularly manured and cropped 1733; orig. *attrib.*, in *i. land* 1551. 2. *Base-ball.* The diamond. b. The four fielders placed on the boundaries of the in-field. 3. *Cricket.* The part of the ground near the wicket, or the fieldsmen stationed there (hence **In-fieldsman**) 1910.

1. *Infield and outfield*, a system of husbandry which confines manuring and tillage to the infield land.

Infie·ld, *v.* 1856. [f. IN-² + FIELD *sb.*] To enclose, as a field.

I·n-fi:ghting, *vbl. sb.* 1812. [IN *adv.*] *Pugilism.* Fighting or boxing at close quarters; the practice of getting close up to an opponent.

Infi·gured, *ppl. a.* Also **en-.** 1611. [IN-², EN-¹.] Marked or adorned with figures.

Infile, obs. var. of ENFILE *v.*

Infilm, *v.* 1864. [f. IN-² + FILM *v.*] To cover with a film; to coat thinly.

Infilter (infi·ltəɹ), *v.* 1846. [f. IN *adv.* + FILTER *v.*, or ad. F. *infiltrer.*] = next, 1.

Infiltrate (infi·ltreⁱt), *v.* 1758. [f. IN-² + FILTRATE *v.*] 1. *trans.* To introduce by filtration; to cause (a fluid) to permeate through pores or interstices. Also *fig.* 2. To pass into or permeate by filtration 1758. 3. *intr.* To pass through or into a substance by filtration; to percolate through pores or interstices 1828. Also *fig.*

2. Carbonized remains, often infiltrated with mineral matter HUXLEY. 3. Education infiltrates from the upper and governing classes to the lower 1861.

Infiltration (infiltrēⁱ·ʃən). 1796. [f. INFILTRATE *v.*] 1. The action or process of infiltrating; percolation. Also *fig.* b. The penetration by settlement, etc. of one people into another 1904. 2. The action of infiltrating a substance with something; the process, fact, or condition of being infiltrated or permeated 1830. 3. An infiltrated deposit 1812.

1. The i. of sea-water through lavas KIRWAN. *fig.* The i. of tribal ideas MAINE. 2. Fatty I.—which is often described as 'fatty degeneration'—consists in the i. of the tissues with fat, which is deposited in them from the blood 1873. 3. Calcareous infiltrations filling the cavities of other stones KIRWAN.

In fine, *adv. phr.*: see FINE *sb.*¹ I. 1.

Infinitary (infi·nitări), *a.* [= Ger. *infinitär*, as in *infinitärkalkul* (Du Bois Raymond); see -ARY¹.] *Math.* Relating to infinity, or to an infinite value of a quantity.

Infinitate (infi·niteⁱt), *v.* 1864. [f. ppl. stem of Schol.L. *infinitare* (Abelard), f. *infinitus*; see -ATE³.] *trans.* To render infinite; in *Logic*, to make (a term, or predicate) 'infinite' or indefinite in extent, by prefixing a negative. Hence **Infinita·tion,** the action of infinitating; the condition of being infinitated; hence, applied to *permutation* or *obversion* 1652.

Infinite (i·nfinit), *a.* (*adv.*) and *sb.* ME. [ad. L. *infinitus* unbounded, f. *in-* (IN-³) + *finitus* FINITE. In hymns occas. rimed with (-əit).]

A. *adj.* 1. Having no limit or end; boundless; immeasurably great in extent, duration, etc. Chiefly of God or His attributes; also of space, time, etc. b. Loosely: Exceedingly great; immense, vast ME. †c. Immensely long, 'endless' -1638. 2. with *sb. pl.* Unlimited in number; very many, 'no end of'. Now *arch.* or *rare.* ME. †3. Indeterminate in nature, meaning, etc. -1663. 4. *Math.* †a. Of indefinite length or magnitude. BARROW. b. Having no limit; opp. to *finite*, also to *closed* 1692. 5. *Mus.* Of a canon: Made continually to recur to the beginning, so as never to come to a regular close; circular 1811. 6. *Gram.* Applied to those parts of the verb which are not limited by person and number. Opp. to *finite.* 1871. 7. *Logic.* Infinitated 1860.

1. Greate is oure Lorde,..yee his wyszdome is i. COVERDALE *Ps.* cxlvi[i]. 5. No man can have in his mind an image of i. magnitude HOBBES. b Gratiano speakes an i. deale of nothing SHAKS. 2. I. other Instances of like nature may be given HALE. 4. *I. series* (Math.): a series of quantities or expressions which may be indefinitely continued without ever coming to an end 1706. So **i. decimal** 1796.

†B. *adv.* Infinitely; in hyperbolical sense = very greatly -1673.

C. *absol.* or as *sb.* 1. That which is infinite; an infinite being, thing, quantity, extent, etc. Now usu. in *sing.* with *the*, esp. as a designation of God 1587. 2. In hyperbolical use: A very great amount or number; very much or many; 'no end' 1563. 3. *Math.* An infinite quantity: see A. 4 b. 1656.

1. The Presence-chamber of the I. J. MARTINEAU. 2. There was i. of new cakes placed PEPYS. That Calais tower has an i. of symbolism in it RUSKIN.

Infinitely (i·nfinitli), *adv.* ME. [-LY².] 1. In an infinite degree, or to an infinite extent. b. *Loosely*, Exceedingly, immensely, vastly 1584. †2. To an indefinite distance or extent -1695. †3. In an indefinite manner or sense; generally -1591. 4. *Math.* Without limit 1692.

1. Every particle of matter is i. divisible PRIESTLEY. b. Dear Prue—I have yours of the 14th, and am i. obliged to you for the length of it STEELE.

I·nfiniteness. Now *rare.* 1534. [f. INFINITE *a.* + -NESS.] The quality or condition of being infinite; infinity; immensity, vastness.

The Schools talk of the I. of Space 1700. The i. of her sensuality FORD.

Infinitesimal (infinite·simăl). 1655. [f. mod.L. *infinitesimus*, f. L. *infinitus* (cf. *cente-*

simus, etc.). Orig. an *ordinal*, viz. the 'infiniteth' in order; but, like other ordinals, also used to name fractions, thus *i. part* or *i.* came to mean unity divided by infinity ($\frac{1}{\infty}$), and thus an infinitely small part or quantity.

A. *sb.* (or *absol.*) †**1.** As ordinal: The 'infiniteth' member of a series. H. MORE. **2.** (Chiefly *Math.*) As a fraction. The inverse or reciprocal of an infinite quantity; †an infinitely small fraction *of* anything. Hence **b.** (*Math.*) An infinitely small quantity, a quantity less than any assignable quantity. **3.** *Loosely.* An extremely small quantity or amount 1840.

B. *adj.* **1.** (Chiefly *Math.*) **a.** Infinitely or indefinitely small. (Correl. to *infinite*, and, with it, opp. to *finite.*) **b.** *transf.* Relating to infinitesimal quantities; esp. in *i. calculus*, a name for the differential and integral calculuses considered as one. 1710. **2.** *Loosely*, Too small to be measured or reckoned; extremely minute or insignificant 1733.

2. The i. Vessels of the Nervous System HARTLEY. Hence **Infinite·simally** *adv.* in an i. degree; usu. qualifying *small.*

Infiniteth, *a. nonce-wd.* 1708. [f. INFINITE + -TH, termination of ordinal numerals.] *Math.* The ordinal numeral corresponding to *infinite.* E. HALLEY. (**Infinitieth,** from *infinity*, is now in oral use.)

Infinitival (infi:nitəi·văl), *a.* 1869. [f. L. *infinitivus* + -AL.] *Gram.* Of or belonging to the infinitive.

Infinitive (infi·nitiv). 1470. [ad. L. *infinitivus*, f. *in-* (IN-[3]) + *finitivus* defining, definite.]

A. *adj.* **1.** *Gram.* The name of that form of a verb which expresses simply the notion of the verb without predicating it of any subject. Usu. classed as a *mood*, though strictly a substantive with certain verbal functions, esp. those of governing an object, and being qualified by an adv. 1520.

(Called by Quintilian and Priscian *infinitus modus*, by Diomedes *infinitivus* 'because it has not definite persons and numbers'.)

In mod. Eng., the infinitive has the simple uninflected form of the vb. In OE., the infinitive had (in the nom.-acc. case) the suffix *-an*, ME. *-en*, *-e*; it had also a dative form in *-anne*, ME. *-enne*, *-ene*, *-en*, *-e*. The latter is sometimes called by mod. grammarians the *gerundial* or *gerundive infinitive.* (It answers more to the L. supine.) The OE. nom.-acc. infinitive is the source of the simple infinitive, as in 'we saw him *come*', etc. The dative infinitive is formally the source of the infinitive with *to*; but *to* is now prefixed also to the nom.-acc. infinitive, where OE. had the simple form in *-an*, as in '*to see* is to believe', etc.

†**2.** Infinite, endless. Also as *adv.* HARDING.

B. *sb.* **1.** *Gram.* The infinitive 'mood' or form of a verb 1530. †**2.** An infinite amount; an infinity. MARKHAM.

1. *Split* (or *cleft*) *i.*, an i. with an adv. between *to* and the verbal part. The following is an example:—
To sit on rocks, to muse o'er flood and fell,
To slowly trace the forest's shady scene.
BYRON, *Ch. Harold* II. xxv.

Hence **Infi·nitively** *adv.* in the i. mood; †infinitely (*rare*).

Infinito- (infinəi·to), comb. f. L. *infinitus* INFINITE, with the sense 'infinitely, to an infinite degree', as in *i.-infinitesimal* (used by Hartley to describe an infinitesimal of the second degree). Also loosely with sense 'infinite and', as in *i.-absolute.*

Infinitude (infi·nitiūd). 1641. [f. L. type **infinitudo* (after *multitudo*, etc.). Cf. FINITUDE.] **1.** The quality or attribute of being infinite; boundlessness. Also, *loosely*, Immensity, vastness. **2.** (with *pl.*) Something that is infinite (or, *loosely*, indefinitely great); a boundless (or vast) extent, space, amount, number, etc.; infinity 1667.

1. The universe fatigues with its **i.** GARNETT. **2.** I am who fill I. MILT. *P. L.* VII. 168. An i. of complex relations DARWIN.

‖**Infinitum** (infinəi·tŏm). 1682. [L.; = INFINITE; also as sb.] = INFINITY; see AD INFINITUM, etc.

Infinituple (infi·nitiup'l), *a.* 1722. [f. L. *infinitus*, after *centuple*, etc.] Infinitely as much or as many; an infinite number of times (something else). WOLLASTON.

Infinity (infi·nĭti). ME. [a. F. *infinité*, ad. L. *infinitas*, f. *infinitus*; see -ITY.] **1.** The quality of being infinite or having no limit; boundlessness (esp. as an attribute of Deity). **2.** Something that is infinite; infinite extent, amount, duration, etc.; a boundless space; an endless or unlimited time ME. **3.** Loosely (from 1 and 2): Immensity, vastness; a very great amount or number, 'no end' (*of*) ME. **4.** *Math.* **a.** Infinite quantity (see INFINITE A. 4 b): denoted by the symbol ∞. Also, an infinite number (*of* something) 1692. **b.** *Geom.* Infinite distance, or that region of space which is infinitely distant; usu. in phr. *at i.* 1873.

1. One whose..i. passeth all nombre, that is almightye God himselfe MORE. **2.** There cannot be more infinities than one; for one of them would limit the other RALEIGH. Man's point of life 'between two infinities' (of that expression Marcus Aurelius is the real owner) M. ARNOLD. **3.** An i. of pains JOWETT. Phr. *To i.* (= L. *ad* or *in infinitum*): endlessly, without limit.

Infirm (infə̄·ɹm), *a.* ME. [ad. L. *infirmus*, f. *in-* (IN-[3]) + *firmus* FIRM.] **1.** Of things: Not firm or strong; weak, unsound; frail, shaky, feeble. Also *transf.* of arguments, titles, etc. Now *rare.* **2.** Of persons, etc.: Not strong and healthy; physically weak or feeble, esp. through age. Also *transf.* of age. 1605. **3.** Not firm or strong in character or purpose; weak, irresolute 1526.

1. Those that build on sandie or infirme ground 1624. The i. title of the House of Lancaster LD. BROUGHAM. **2.** A poore, infirme, weake, and despis'd old man *Lear* III. ii. 20. What is infirme, from your sound parts shall flie SHAKS. **3.** Infirme of purpose: Giue me the Daggers SHAKS. Hence **Infi·rm-ly** *adv.*, **-ness** (now *rare*).

Infirm (infə̄·ɹm), *v.* Now *rare.* 1449. [ad. L. *infirmare* to weaken, etc., f. *infirmus* INFIRM *a.*] To make infirm; to weaken; to invalidate (a law, custom, etc.).

The bad faith of the Habsburgs could not i. Magyar rights 1890.

Infirmarer (infə̄·ɹmărəɹ). ME. [a. OF. *enfermerier*; app. f. *enfermerie* INFIRMARY.] *Hist.* In mediæval monasteries, the person who had charge of the infirmary. So **Infi·rmaress** [-ESS[1]]. **Infirma·rian,** in same sense.

Infirmary (infə̄·ɹmări). 1451. [ad. med.L. *infirmaria*, f. *infirmus*; see -ARY[1] B. 3. See also FERMERY.] **1.** A building or part of a building for the treatment of the sick or wounded; a hospital. Also *fig.* †**2.** A conservatory. SLOANE.

Infirmation (infəɹmē·ʃən). [ad. L. *infirmationem.*] The action of weakening or invalidating (evidence).

Infirmative (infə̄·ɹmătiv), *a.* (*sb.*) *rare.* 1611. [a. F. *infirmatif*, *-ive.*] Tending to weaken or invalidate. As *sb.* That which tends to weaken.

†**Infi·rmatory.** *rare.* 1598. [ad. med.L. *infirmatorium.*] = INFIRMARY –1678. var. †**Infi·rmitory** 1538–1645.

Infirmity (infə̄·ɹmĭti). ME. [ad. L. *infirmitatem*, f. *infirmus* INFIRM *a.* (see -ITY). Cf. F. *infirmité.*] The condition of being infirm. **1.** Weakness or want of strength; inability; an instance or case of this. **b.** Of an argument or title: Want of validity 1614. **2.** Physical weakness, debility, frailty, feebleness of body, resulting from some defect, disease, or (now mostly) old age ME. **3.** A special form or variety of weakness; †an illness, disease; now esp. a failing in some faculty or sense ME. **4.** Weakness of character; moral weakness or frailty; also with *an* and *pl.* ME.

1. When I could no longer hurt them, the revolutionists have trampled on my i. BURKE. **2.** I. that decaies the wise *Twel. N.* I. v. 82. **3.** He is a little deaf and has a similar i. in sight JOWETT. **4.** The head of the house..was a byword for i. of purpose BURTON. Fame..(That last i. of Noble mind) MILT. *Lycidas* 71.

Infix (i·nfiks), *sb.* 1881. [f. L. *infix-*; see next.] *Gram.* A modifying element inserted in the body of a word.

Infix (infi·ks), *v.* Also **en-.** 1502. [Partly f. L. *infix-*, *infigere* to fix in; partly f. IN-[1] or [2] + FIX *v.*] **1.** *trans.* To fix or fasten *in*; to implant or insert firmly. Also *fig.* **b.** To fix or fasten on something 1601. **2.** To fix (a fact, etc.) *in* the mind or memory; to impress 1542. **3.** *Gram.* To insert (a formative element) in the body of a word (cf. prec.) 1868.

1. Infixing their Nailes in the Fronts of them, they claw off the skin 1650. *fig.* The vices which they introduced, and the habits they infixed LAMB. **2.** First soundly i. in thy mind what thou desirest to remember FULLER. Hence **Infi·xion** (*rare*), the action of infixing; the condition of being infixed.

Inflamable, obs. var. of INFLAMMABLE.

Inflame (inflē̆·m), *v.* Also **en-.** [ME. *enflamme*, a. OF. *enflammer*:—L. *inflammare*, f. *in-* (IN-[2]) + *flamma* FLAME.]

I. *trans.* **1.** To cause to blaze; to set on fire; to kindle. **b.** *transf.* To light up or redden as if with flame 1477. **2.** *fig.* To fire with passion, strong feeling, or desire; to kindle (passion, etc.) ME. **3.** To heat, make hot; *esp.* to raise (the body or blood) to a feverish heat; to excite inflammation in 1530. **4.** To add heat or fuel to, to aggravate 1607; †to augment (a price, etc.) –1773.

1. Gardiner had inflamed many Martyrs, and hath now his body inflamed 1631. **b.** The red, reflected sky Inflames the river 1892. **2.** Having their minds enflamed with passion 1726. **3.** My father's face.. Inflamed with wrath TENNYSON. **4.** To i. an animosity 1879, a reckoning GOLDSM.

II. *intr.* **1.** To burst into flame; to catch fire 1638. **2.** To become hot with passion; to glow with feeling 1559. **3.** To be affected with inflammation 1607.

Hence **Infla·med** *ppl. a.* set on fire, etc.; *Her.* depicted as in flames. **Infla·mer,** one who or that which inflames; an instigator.

Inflammable (inflæ·măb'l), *a.* (*sb.*) Also †inflameable. 1570. [See INFLAME and -BLE. Cf. F. *inflammable.*] **1.** Capable of being inflamed; susceptible of combustion; easily set on fire. **2.** Excitable, hasty-tempered, passionate 1800. **3.** *sb.* An inflammable substance 1770.

1. Alcohol is very i. ROSCOE. *I. air*, old name for hydrogen gas. **2.** A sanguine and i. disposition 1845. Hence **Inflammabi·lity, Infla·mmableness,** i. quality. **Infla·mmably** *adv.*

Inflammation (inflămē̆·ʃən). 1533. [ad. L. *inflammationem.*] **1.** The action of inflaming; setting on fire or catching fire; the condition of being in flames 1563. †**b.** *concr.* Something in flames –1772. **2.** The action of inflaming mentally; the condition of being so inflamed; excitement, fervour. Also, an instance of this. 1597. **3.** *Path.* A morbid process affecting some part of the body, characterized by excessive heat, swelling, pain, and redness; also, an instance of this 1533. †**4.** Augmentation of charge 1821.

1. The i. of the Cities of the Plain 1650. **2.** The means of calming a people in a state of extreme i. BURKE. **4.** The i. of his weekly bills BYRON.

Inflammative (inflæ·mătiv), *a.* and *sb.* *rare.* 1685. [f. ppl. stem of L. *inflammare*: see -IVE.] = INFLAMMATORY *a.* and *sb.*

Inflammatory (inflæ·mătəri), *a.* and *sb.* 1681. [f. as prec. + -ORY.] †**1.** Of, pertaining to, characterized by, or causing a blazing condition –1796. **2.** Tending to excite desire, passion, anger, or animosity. (Now usu. in a bad sense.) 1711. **3.** That tends to inflame the blood; exciting the brain or senses; stimulating 1733. **4.** *Path.* Of the nature of, pertaining to, indicative of, or characterized by inflammation 1732. **5.** *sb.* That which inflames, excites, or rouses feeling or passion 1681.

2. I. libels 1767, powers of art GIBBON, speeches 1834. **4.** I. Distempers ARBUTHNOT. Hence **Infla·mmatorily** *adv.*

†**Inflate,** *ppl. a.* late ME. [ad. L. *inflatus*; see next and -ATE *suffix*[2].] = INFLATED.

Inflate (inflē̆·t), *v.* 1502. [f. L. *inflat-*, *inflare*, f. *in-* (IN-[2]) + *flare* to blow.] **1.** *trans.* To blow out or distend with wind or air; to fill with air or gas; also *absol.* to cause flatulence 1533. **2.** To puff up (a person) *with* high spirits, pride, etc.; to elate. Also *absol.* 1502. **3.** To dilate, distend, or swell; to enlarge 1705. **4.** To swell or expand artificially or unduly 1843.

1. To i. the lungs 1834, a balloon ROSCOE, (*fig.*) vanity 1870. **2.** Character that prosperity could not i. 1803. **3.** When Passion's tumults in the bosom rise, I. the features, and enrage the eyes J. SCOTT. **4.** We i. our paper currency EMERSON. Hence **Infla·table** *a.* that can be inflated. **Infla·tingly** *adv.* **Infla·ter, -or,** one who or that which inflates.

Inflated (inflē̆·tėd), *ppl. a.* 1652. [f. prec. + -ED[1].] **1.** Puffed out or swollen by air or gas 1681. **2.** Of language: Turgid, bombastic

1652. 3. Expanded, as if by inflation 1726. 4. Elated with vanity or false notions 1784. 5. Raised in price artificially 1881.

1. Bridges on..i. skins 1853. 2. The account..is long and i. GOLDSM. 4. I. and astrut with self-conceit, He gulps the windy diet COWPER. 5. An i. state of prices that could not possibly be maintained GLADSTONE.

Inflation (inflē·ʃən). ME. [ad. L. *inflationem*. Cf. obs. F. *inflation*.] 1. The action of inflating with air or gas 1601. 2. The condition of being inflated with air or gas, or of being distended as if with air ME. 3. The condition of being puffed up with vanity, pride, or false notions 1526. 4. Turgidity, bombast 1603. 5. Increase beyond proper limits; esp. of prices, the issue of inconvertible paper money, etc. 1864. Hence **Infla·tionary** *a.*, marked by inflation of prices; **Infla·tionist**, one who advocates an increase of the paper currency; also *attrib.*; so **Infla·tionism**.

‖**Inflatus** (inflē·tŭs). [L.; cf. prec.] A blowing or breathing into; inflation; inspiration. MRS. BROWNING.

Inflect (infle·kt), *v.* ME. [ad. L. *inflectere*, f. *in-* (IN-²) + *flectere* to bend.] 1. *trans.* To bend inwards; to bend into a curve or angle; hence, to bend, to curve. Also *fig.* †2. *Optics.* = DIFFRACT *v.* -1811. 3. *Gram.* To vary the termination of (a word) in order to express different grammatical relations 1668. 4. To modulate (the voice); spec. in *Music*, to flatten or sharpen (a note) by a chromatic semitone 1828.

2. Are they [rays of light] not reflected, refracted, and inflected by one and the same principle? NEWTON.

Inflected (infle·ktėd), *ppl. a.* 1646. [f. prec. + -ED¹.] 1. Bent or curved; bent inwards. 2. *Gram.* Having inflexions; characterized by grammatical inflexion 1775.

Inflection: see INFLEXION.

Inflective (infle·ktiv), *a.* 1666. [f. INFLECT *v.* + -IVE.] 1. Inflecting; tending to inflect. 2. Pertaining to or characterized by grammatical inflexion 1799.

2. The glories of a completely i. language WHITNEY.

Inflesh, obs. f. ENFLESH *v.*

†**Infle·x**, *a.* 1753. [ad. L. *inflexus*.] *Bot.* = INFLEXED -1794.

Inflexed (infle·kst), *ppl. a.* 1661. [f. as prec. + -ED¹.] Bent inwards; incurved.

Inflexibility¹ (infleksĭbi·lĭti). 1611. [f. INFLEXIBLE¹ + -ITY.] The quality or condition of being inflexible; incapability of being bent; unyielding stiffness, rigidity; firmness of purpose, obstinacy.

Features arranged into the utmost i. of expression SCOTT. Bone..cannot swell, in consequence of its i. 1876. Hence **Infle·xibleness** (*rare*). **Infle·xibly** *adv.* 1534.

Inflexibility²: see INFLEXIBLE².

Inflexible (infle·ksĭb'l), *a.*¹ ME. [ad. L. *inflexibilis*; see IN-³ and FLEXIBLE.] Not flexible. 1. Incapable of being bent; not pliant; rigid, stiff. 2. Unbending in temper or purpose; immovable, inexorable ME. 3. Unalterable, rigidly fixed 1693.

2. He is i., stedfast, and faileþ not TREVISA. 3. Nature's laws are more i. than iron 1871.

†**Infle·xible**, *a.*² *rare.* ME. [f. L. *inflex-* (see INFLEX *a.*) + -IBLE.] Capable of being inflected; in *Optics*, diffrangible -1857. Hence †**Inflexibi·lity**².

Inflexion, inflection (infle·kʃən). 1531. [ad. L. *inflexionem*. As to the spelling cf. CONNEXION, etc.] 1. The action of inflecting; the condition of being inflected; *concr.* a bending, bend, curvature, or angle. Also *fig.* †2. *Optics.* = DIFFRACTION -1831. 3. *Geom.* Change of curvature from convex to concave at a particular point on a curve; *point of i.*, the point at which this takes place 1721. 4. *Gram.* The modification of the form of a word to express different grammatical relations; including the declension of sbs., adjs., and pronouns, the conjugation of vbs., and the comparison of adjs. and advs. 1668. b. *concr.* An inflected form; also, the inflexional suffix 1668. 5. Modulation of the voice; in speaking or singing, a change in the pitch or tone of the voice 1600.

Hence **Infle·xional, infle·ctional** *a.* pertaining to or characterized by grammatical inflexion.

Inflexive (infle·ksiv), *a.*¹ [f. L. *inflex-*, *inflectere* + -IVE.] = INFLECTIVE. (Dicts.).

†**Inflexive**, *a.*² [IN-³.] Inflexible. CHAPMAN.

†**Infle·xure.** 1578. [f. L. *inflex-*, *inflectere*, after FLEXURE.] A bend, curve, or turn inwards -1658.

Inflict (infli·kt), *v.* 1566. [f. L. *inflict-*, *infligere*.] 1. *trans.* To lay on as a stroke, blow, or wound; to impose; to cause to be borne 1593. 2. With inverted construction: To afflict (a person) *with* something painful or disagreeable. (Now *rare.*) 1566.

1. To i. paine, lasting shame SHAKS., a penalty HOBBES. 2. We should be inflicted with less . twaddle 1883. Hence **Infli·ctable** *a.* that can or may be inflicted. **Infli·cter, -or**, one who inflicts. **Infli·ctive** *a.* tending to i.; pertaining to infliction.

Infliction (infli·kʃən). 1534. [ad. late L. *inflictionem*.] The action of inflicting (pain, punishment, annoyance, etc.); the fact of being inflicted (*Meas. for M.* I. iii. 28). b. Something inflicted, as pain, punishment, etc.; an annoyance, a 'visitation' 1586.

b. Such Persecutions, as seem to be Divine Inflictions 1665.

Inflood (inflʊ·d), *v.* 1855. [f. IN-¹ or ² + FLOOD *v.*] *intr.* To flow in, to enter as a flood.

The silent inflooding of the day STEVENSON.

Inflorescence (inflore·sėns). 1760. [ad. mod.L. *inflorescentia* (Linn.), f. L. *inflorescere* to come into flower.] *Bot.* 1. The mode in which the flowers of a plant are arranged in relation to the axis and to each other; the flowering system. b. The collective flower or blossom of a plant 1851. 2. The process of coming into flower; blossoming. Also *fig.* 1800.

1. I. affords the truest, and in most Genera the most elegant Distinction 1760.

Inflow (i·nflōu), *sb.* 1839. [f. IN *adv.* + FLOW *sb.*¹] = INFLUX.

Inflow (inflōu·), *v.* 1651. [f. IN-¹ + FLOW *v.*] †1. *intr.* *Astrol.* = INFLUE *v.* -1670. 2. To flow in 1882. †3. *trans.* To cause to flow in. HOBBES.

†**Influe**, *v. rare.* 1426. [a. F. *influer*, ad. L. *influere* to flow in.] *intr.* To shed (heavenly) influence -1618.

Influence (i·nfluĕns), *sb.* ME. [a. F. *influence* emanation from the stars (also inflow of water; affluence), f. L. *influentem*, *influere*. The astrological sense was common in med.L.] †1. The action or fact of flowing in; inflow, influx -1702. 2. *spec.* in *Astrol.* The supposed flowing from the stars of an ethereal fluid acting upon the character and destiny of men, and affecting sublunary things generally. In later times taken as an exercise of occult power. ME. b. *transf.* The exercise of analogous power by human beings. Now only *poet.* ME. †c. Disposition, or temperament, as held to be due to astral influence -1663. †3. The inflowing or infusion (*into* a person or thing) of any kind of divine, moral, or other secret power or principle; that which thus flows in or is infused -1677. 4. The exertion of action of which the operation is unseen, except in its effects, by one person or thing upon another; the action thus exercised. Orig. const. *into*; now *on*, *upon*, *in*. 1588. 5. The capacity of producing effects by insensible or invisible means; ascendancy of a person or social group; control not formally or overtly expressed 1652. 6. A thing or person that exercises influence 1736. 7. *Electr.* = INDUCTION 9. 1870.

2. Canst thou bind the sweete influences of the Pleiades? *Job* xxxviii. 31. What euill starre On you hath frownd, and pourd his i. bad? SPENSER *F. Q.* I. viii. 42. b. Ladies, whose bright eyes Rain i. MILT. c. Germans and Bohemians, nations by i. heavie, slowe 1601. 3. MILT. *P. L.* v. 695. 4. Before they had much i. on my thoughts JOHNSON. Phr. *Undue i.*: see UNDUE. 5. To owe a position to i., not to merit (*mod.*).

Influence (i·nfluĕns), *v.* 1658. [f. prec.] 1. *trans.* To exert influence upon, to affect by influence. Sometimes esp. to move by undue influence; †formerly *spec.* of astral influence. 2. *intr.* To exert influence 1670. †3. *trans.* To cause to flow in; to infuse, instil -1705.

1. The Sovereign can i. the conduct of public affairs LD. BROUGHAM. Expenditures to 'influence' city council 1891. Hence **I·nfluencer**, one who or that which influences. **I·nfluencive** *a.* (*rare*), having the quality of influencing.

Influent (i·nfluĕnt), *a.* (*sb.*) ME. [ad. L. *influentem*.] 1. Flowing in. Also *transf.* and *fig.* 1445. †2. Exercising astral influence or occult power -1856. †3. Influential -1657. 4. *sb.* A tributary, an affluent 1859.

1. Thames, with i. tide COWPER. 2. Multitudinous mountains..panting..Beneath the i. heavens MRS. BROWNING. [Humility] is more..i. upon others, then any other vertue 1654.

Influential (influe·nʃăl), *a.* 1570. [f. med. L. *influentia* INFLUENCE + -AL.] †1. *Astrol.* Possessing or exercising astral influence; of, pertaining to, or of the nature of such influence -1664. †b. *transf.* Working by hidden processes -1745. 2. Having or exerting influence, power, or effect 1655. 3. Having great influence; powerful 1734.

2. Hurtful errours, i. on practice BARROW. 3. Very i. among the Citisens NORTH. I precepts H. SPENCER. Hence **Influe·ntially** *adv.* with influence; in an i. manner; *Electr.* by induction.

Influenza (influ,enză). 1743. [a. It. *influenza*, lit. 'influence':—med.L. *influentia*.

It. *influenza* has the sense (developed, app., from the notion of 'astral' or 'occult influence') of 'visitation' of any epidemic disease; hence, absol., that of 'an epidemic'; applied spec. to the epidemic of 1743 (called also *la grippe*), for which it became the English specific name.]

A specific febrile zymotic disorder, highly contagious, and occurring usually in widespread epidemics. Its symptoms and sequelæ include rapid prostration and severe catarrh. Applied loosely to any severe catarrh of the respiratory mucous membrane, *esp.* to an *influenza-cold*. *attrib.* and *Comb.*, as *i. bacillus*, etc.; **i.-cold**, a severe cold with symptoms resembling those of i.

Influx (i·nflʊks). 1626. [a. F., or ad. late L. *influxus*, f. *influere* to flow in.] 1. The act or fact of flowing in; an inflow. b. The mouth of a river 1652. 2. *transf.* The continuous ingression of persons or things into some place or sphere 1652. †3. = INFLUENCE 2. -1650. †4. = INFLUENCE 3-5. -1703.

1. A strong i. of light 1823. b. The Kennet, near its I. into the Thames 1675. 2. An i. of unruly people 1652, of new opinions 1775, of Greek EARLE, of settlers from the Slave States BRYCE.

Influxion (inflʊ·kʃən). Now *rare.* 1605. [ad. late L. *influxionem*.] 1. Inflow, influx. †2. = INFLUENCE 2. -1642.

†**Influ·xious**, *a.* [f. prec.; see -OUS.] Shedding (astral) influence. HOWELL.

†**Influ·xive**, *a.* 1624. [f. L. *influx-*, *influere* + -IVE.] Infusing or communicating influence; influential -1657. Hence †**Influ·xively** *adv.* by influxion.

Info·ld, obs. var. of ENFOLD.

†**Info·liate**, *v. rare.* 1640. [f. IN-² + L. *folium* leaf, after It. *infogliare*. See -ATE³.] *intr.* To put on leaves, to become leafy -1656.

Inform (infǭ·ɹm), *a.* 1555. [a. F. *informe*, ad. L. *informis* shapeless, f. *in-* (IN-³) + *forma*.] 1. Having no regular form; unshapen, misshapen (*arch.*). 2. Without form; formless; of the nature of matter unendowed with 'form' 1654.

Inform (infǭ·ɹm), *v.* [ME. *enforme*, a. OF. *enformer* (mod. *informer*), ad. L. *informare* to give form to, f. *in-* (IN-²) + *forma* FORM.]

I. †1. *trans.* To put into form or shape; to shape -1643; to arrange; to compose -1666. †2. *intr.* To take shape; to form -1652.

2. It is the bloody Businesse, which informes Thus to mine Eyes *Macb.* II. i. 48.

II. *trans.* To give 'form' or formative principle to; hence, to stamp, impress, or imbue *with* some specific quality or attribute; to inspire, animate ME.

The God of Souldiers..informe Thy thoughts with Noblenesse *Cor.* v. iii. 71. Long as Breath informs this fleeting Frame PRIOR.

III. 1. *trans.* To form (the mind, character, etc.), esp. by imparting learning or instruction; hence, To instruct, teach; †to advise. Now *rare.* ME. †b. To direct, guide -1846. 2. To impart knowledge of some particular fact or occurrence to; to tell (one) of something; to apprise. The prevailing mod. sense. ME. Also *refl.* 3. *absol.* or *intr.* †a. To give information; to report -1683. **b.** To lay or exhibit an information, bring a charge or complaint (*against*, rarely *on*) 1586.

1. Nor are we informed by nature, in future contingencies and accidents BUTLER. **b.** MILT. *Comus* 180. **2.** Some have enformed me that my realme was never so riche HALL. **3. a.** *Macb.* I. v. 34. **b.** You must not i. against him GOLDSM.

IV. †**1.** *trans.* To impart the knowledge of; to instruct in, to teach -1621. †**2.** To make known, report, relate, tell -1810.

1. To i. religion BACON. **2.** It is informed us that your young and ryotous people will ryse HALL. *All's Well* IV. i. 91.

Informal (infǭ·ɹmăl), *a.* 1584. [IN-³.] Not formal. **1.** Not done or made according to a regular or prescribed form; not observing forms; not according to order; irregular; unofficial, disorderly. **b.** Unceremonious 1828. †**2.** ? Disordered in mind 1603.

1. An i. overture W. IRVING. **b.** An i. visit (*mod.*). **2.** These poore informall women SHAKS. Hence **Informa·lity**, the quality or fact of being i.; absence of formality; an instance of this. **Info·rmally** *adv.*

Informant (infǭ·ɹmănt). 1661. [f. L. *informantem*, *informare* to INFORM.]

A. *adj. Metaph.* Informing; giving form; actuating; see INFORM *v.* II.

B. *sb.* †**1.** That which informs, animates, or actuates GLANVILL. **2.** One who gives information of some fact or occurrence 1693. **b.** *Law.* One who lays an information against a person; an informer 1783.

2. b. It was the last evidence of the kind. The i. was hanged BURKE.

In forma pauperis: see IN *Lat. prep.*

Information (infǭɹmēⁱ·ʃən). [ME. *enformacion*, a. OF. *enformacion* (mod. *information*), ad. L. *informationem*, f. *informare* to INFORM.]

I. 1. The action of informing (in sense III. 1 of the vb.); training, instruction; communication of instructive knowledge. Now *rare* or *Obs.* †Also with *an* and *pl.* An instruction -1760. **2.** The action of telling or fact of being told of something ME. **3.** That of which one is apprised or told; intelligence, news 1450. †Also with *an* and *pl.* 1527. **4.** The action of informing against, charging, or accusing (a person). Now *Obs.*, exc. as transf. from 5. 1480. **5.** *Law.* **a.** A complaint or charge against a person lodged with or presented to a court or magistrate, in order to the institution of criminal proceedings without formal indictment. (The original object of this procedure was to dispense with the previous finding of a grand jury.) 1467. **b.** A complaint of the Crown in respect of some civil claim, in the form of a statement of the facts by the attorney-general or other proper officer, either *ex officio*, or on the relation of a private individual 1624.

1. For the i. of our judgment and the conduct of our lives BUTLER. **2.** This I have by credible informacion learned MORE. **3.** Some informations from an eminent person SWIFT. **4.** *Hen. VIII*, v. iii. 110.

†**II.** The action of informing with some active or essential quality (see INFORM *v.* II); inspiration, animation (e.g. of the body by the soul) -1870.

That..no i. of pride may enter into us CLARENDON. Hence **Informa·tional** *a.* of, pertaining to, or conveying i.

Informative (infǭ·ɹmătiv), *a.* 1626. [f. L. *informat-*, *informare* + -IVE.] Having the quality of informing; animative 1647; instructive 1655; of the nature of legal information. Hence **Info·rmatively** *adv.*

Informatory (infǭ·ɹmătŏri), *a.* 1881. [f. as prec. + -ORY.] Having the quality of instructing or communicating information.

†**Info·rmed**, *a.* 1526. [f. IN-³ + FORMED, after L. *informis*.] **1.** Of faith: Not vitalized or animated by charity. (An awkward use.) -1630. **2.** Unformed; imperfectly formed -1686.

Info·rmed, *ppl. a.* 1549. [f. INFORM *v.* + -ED¹.] Instructed; enlightened; now usu. *well-*, *ill-informed*.

Informer (infǭ·ɹməɹ). ME. [f. INFORM *v.* + -ER¹.] †**1.** An instructor, teacher -1662. **2.** One who communicates information ME. **3.** One who informs against another, or lays an information; *spec.* one who makes it his business to detect offenders against penal laws and to lay informations against them; a *common informer* 1503. **4.** An inspirer, animator, vitalizer (see INFORM *v.* II) 1727.

4. Nature! i. of the Poet's art POPE.

Informidable (infǭ·ɹmidăb'l), *a. rare.* 1667. [IN-³.] Not formidable; not to be dreaded.

Of limb Heroic built..Foe not i. MILT. *P. L.* IX. 486.

Informity (infǭ·ɹmĭti). Now *rare* or *Obs.* 1583. [ad. late L. *informitatem*, f. *informis*; see -ITY.] Unformed condition, shapelessness; deformity. Also *fig.*

†**Info·rmous**, *a.* 1610. [app. f. L. *informis* + -OUS.] Having no definite form, shapeless; unshapely -1701.

†**Info·rtunate**, *a.* ME. [ad. L. *infortunatus* (see IN-³, FORTUNATE).] Unfortunate -1682.

The day i. that I was bore 1440. An i. dream PURCHAS, planet 1671. Hence †**Info·rtunate·ly** *adv.*, †**-ness.**

Infortune (infǭ·ɹtiŭn). ME. [a. F.; see IN-³ and FORTUNE.] †**1.** Want of good fortune; ill fortune, ill luck. †Also with *an* and *pl.* -1653. **2.** *Astrol.* A malevolent planet or aspect 1632. So †**Infortuned** *ppl. a.* unfortunate. CHAUCER.

†**Infortu·nity.** 1477. [a. OF. *infortunité*, ad. late L. *infortunitas*.] Unfortunate condition; misfortune; a misfortune -1720.

†**Infou·nd**, *v.* ME. [ad. obs. F. *infondre*, *-fundre*, or ad. L. *infundere*.] *trans.* To pour in; to infuse. (Usu. in *fig.* sense.) -1589.

Infra- (i·nfră), *prefix*, repr. L. *infra* adv. and prep. 'below, underneath, beneath'. Regularly opposed to *supra-* (or *super-*).

A. In prepositional relation to the sb. represented in second element. **1.** Denoting 'below', 'beneath' (i.e. 'lower down than') in respect of local situation or position. **2.** Denoting 'below' or 'beneath' in respect of status or condition, as *infrabestial*, etc. **3.** Denoting 'within' (as in med.L.), as *infraterritorial*, etc.

B. In attrib. or advb. relation to the second element: 'lower', 'inferior', 'under-', as *infraposition*, etc.

The use of the hyphen is practically optional, though it is usually omitted in recognized terms, except when the second element begins with a vowel. **infraaxi·llary** *a.*, *Anat.* lying below the armpit; *Bot.* situated below the axil of a leaf or branch; **infrabra·nchial** *a.*, *Zool.* situated below the branchiæ or gills; **infraclavi·cular** *a.*, *Anat.* situated below the clavicle or collar-bone, as in *i. bone*; also as *sb.* = *infraclavicular bone*; **infrahu·man** *a.*; **infrahy·oid** *a.*, *Anat.* lying below the hyoid bone; **infrala·bial** *a.*, *Anat.* situated below the lips; **infrali·ttoral** *a.*, pertaining to the zone of the sea below the littoral region; **inframa·rginal** *a.*, situated beneath the margin or border, as in *i. convolution*, the superior temporal convolution; **inframaxi·llary** *a.*, situated below the jaw, as in *i. nerve*; *sb.* the lower jaw-bone; **inframe·dian** *a.*, applied to the zone of the ocean below the median zone; **infrana·tural** *a.*, below what is natural; hence **infrana·turalism**; **infra-o·rbital** *a.*, *Anat.* situated below the orbit of the eye; **infrapo·sed** *a.*, placed below something else (cf. *superposed*); so **infraposi·tion**; **infrasca·pular** *a.*, *Anat.* situated below the shoulder-blade; **infraspi·nal** *a.*, *Anat.* situated beneath the spine of the scapula; so **infraspi·nate**, **-spi·nous** *adjs.*; **infrastape·dial** *a.*, situated below the axis of the stapes of the middle ear in birds; **infraste·rnal** *a.*, *Anat.* situated below the sternum or breast-bone; **infrate·mporal** *a.*, *Anat.* situated below the temples; **infraterrito·rial** *a.*, lying within a territory; **infratro·chlear** *a.*, *Anat.* situated beneath the trochlea of the trochlearis muscle in the eye.

†**Infract**, *a.* 1566. [ad. L. *infractus*, f. *in-* (IN-³) + *fractus*, *frangere*.] Unbroken; unweakened; whole -1613.

Infract (infræ·kt), *v.* 1798. [f. L. *infract-*, *infringere*.] *trans.* To break; to violate, infringe. Chiefly *U.S.* So **Infra·ctible** *a.* capable of being infracted or broken.

Infraction (infræ·kʃən). 1623. [ad. L. *infractionem*.] **1.** The action of fracturing; *concr.* a fracture. **2.** The action of infringing (a bond or obligation); breach, violation 1673. †**3.** *Optics.* = REFRACTION 1635.

Infractor (infræ·ktəɹ). 1524. [a. med.L. *infractor*, f. *infringere*; cf. F. *infracteur*.] One who breaks or infringes; a violator, infringer.

‖**Infra dig.** (i·nfră di·g), *adj. phr.* 1824. [Colloq. abbrev. of L. *infra dignitatem*.] Beneath one's dignity; unbecoming one's position; undignified.

Infragrant (infrēⁱ·grănt), *a.* 1813. [IN-³.] Malodorous.

Infralapsarian (i:nfrălæpsēᵊ·riăn). 1731. [f. L. *infra* under + *lapsus* fall + *-arian*, as in *Trinitarian*, etc.] *Theol.* **A.** *sb.* A term applied in the 17th c. to Calvinists holding the view that God's election of some to everlasting life was consequent to his prescience of the Fall of man, or that it contemplated man as already fallen, and was thus a remedial measure; opp. to SUPRALAPSARIAN. **B.** *adj.* Of or pertaining to the Infralapsarians or their doctrine. Hence **Infralapsa·rianism**, the doctrine of Infralapsarians.

SUBLAPSARIAN is, in English writers, more usual than *Infralapsarian*. But some distinguish the two, associating *Sublapsarian* with the view that the Fall was foreseen, and *Infralapsarian* with the view that it was permitted, by God.

Infranchise, etc. obs. ff. ENFRANCHISE, etc.

Infrangible (infræ·ndʒĭb'l), *a.* 1597. [IN-³.] **1.** That cannot be broken; unbreakable. Also *fig.* **2.** That cannot be infringed; inviolable 1834.

1. I. Atomes 1603. And link'd their fetlocks with a golden band, I., immortal POPE. Hence **Infrangibi·lity**, **Infra·ngibleness.** **Infra·ngibly** *adv.*

Infrequence (infrī·kwĕns). *rare.* 1644. [f. as next; see -ENCE.] = next.

Infrequency (infrī·kwĕnsi). 1600. [ad. L. *infrequentia*, f. *infrequentem*; see -ENCY.] †**1.** The fact or state of being unfrequented; also, Small attendance; paucity, fewness -1658. **2.** The fact or state of rarely occurring; uncommonness, rarity 1677.

1. The solitude and i. of the place HOLLAND. **2.** The i. of marriage GIBBON.

Infrequent (infrī·kwĕnt), *a.* 1531. [ad. L. *infrequentem*, f. *in-* (IN-³) + *frequentem*. Cf. F. *infréquent*.] Not frequent; †little used (ELYOT); not occurring often 1612; (qualifying an agent-noun) that does something rarely 1722; not plentiful 1682.

Words of i. occurrence JOHNSON. A sparing and i. worshiper of the Deity WOLLASTON. Hence **Infre·quently** *adv.*

Infrigidate (infri·dʒideⁱt), *v.* Now *rare.* 1545. [f. late L. *infrigidat-*, *infrigidare*, f. *in-* (IN-²) + *frigidus* cold.] *trans.* To make cold; to chill, cool. Hence **Infrigida·tion**, the action of cooling or condition of being cooled; refrigeration.

Infringe (infri·ndʒ), *v.* 1533. [ad. L. *infringere*, f. *in-* (IN-²) + *frangere*.] †**1.** *trans.* To break, shatter (*rare* in physical sense); to crush; to defeat, frustrate; to invalidate -1671. **2.** To violate or break (an oath, pledge, treaty, etc.); to contravene 1533. †**3.** To refute; to contradict -1660. †**4.** To weaken, impair; to mitigate -1694. **5.** *intr.* To break in or encroach *on* or *upon* 1760.

2. Ioue for your Loue would i. an oath SHAKS. **5.** They did not i. upon this boundary for some time COOK. Hence **Infri·ngement**, the act or fact of infringing; breach, violation; encroachment; †contradiction. **Infri·nger**, one who infringes.

†**Infri·ngible**, *a.* Also **-eable.** 1548. [var. of INFRANGIBLE, after L. *infringere*.] That cannot be infringed or broken; unbreakable -1642; irrefragable -1629.

Infructuose (infrʊ·ktiu͵ōus), *a.* 1727. [ad. L. *infructuosus*; see IN-³.] = next.

Infructuous (infrʊ·ktiu͵əs), *a.* 1615. [f. as prec.; see IN-³ and FRUCTUOUS.] Not producing fruit, unfruitful, unprofitable (*lit.* and *fig.*). Hence **Infru·ctuously** *adv.*

‖**Infula** (i·nfiulă). 1610. [L. (in sense 1).] **1.** *Rom. Antiq.* A sort of fillet of red and white wool, worn on the forehead by priests, worshippers, and suppliants, or similarly placed on victims for sacrifice, etc. 1727. **2.** *Eccl.* Each of the two lappets of a bishop's mitre. Also in *Her.* var. †**I·nfule** (in sense 1).

Infumate, *v. rare.* 1721. [f. L. *infumat-*, *infumare* (Pliny), f. *in-* (IN-²) + *fumare*, f. *fumus*.] *trans.* To smoke, to dry by smoking. Hence **Infumated** *ppl. a.* **Infuma·tion.** (Dicts.)

†**Infu·me**, *v.* 1601. [ad. L. *infumare*; see prec.] = prec. -1623.

‖**Infundibulum** (infʊndi·biŭlŏm). 1706. [L., = funnel, f. *infundere* + *-bulum*, suffix forming names of instruments.] †1. A funnel (*rare*). 2. *Anat.* Applied to various funnel-shaped cavities or structures of the body; as, *i. of the brain* (*i. cerebri*), a funnel-shaped prolongation downwards and forwards of the third ventricle of the brain, at the extremity of which is the pituitary body; *i. of the lungs*, the funnel-shaped sacs in which the air-passages terminate 1799. b. *Zool.* (*a*) A tubular organ in the Cephalopoda through which the water is driven from the gills. (*b*) The gastric cavity of Ctenophora with which the œsophageal tube communicates. (*c*) The dilated upper extremity of the oviduct of a bird. 1877. Hence **Infundi·bular** *a.* funnel-shaped. **Infundi·bulate** *a.* having an i.; funnel-shaped. **Infundi·buliform** *a.* funnel-shaped.

†Infu·neral, *v.* [f. In-[2] + Funeral *sb.* or *v.*] *trans.* To entomb. G. Fletcher.

Infuriate (infiūə·riĕt), *a.* 1667. [ad. med.L. *infuriatus, infuriare*, f. *in-* (In-[2]) + *furiare*, f. *furia.*] Excited to fury; maddened; raging, frantic, furious. Also *fig.* of things.

Th' i. hil that shoots the pillar'd flame Thomson.

Infuriate (infiūə·rieɪt), *v.* 1667. [f. med.L. *infuriat-, infuriare*; see prec.] *trans.* To fill with fury; to render mad with anger; to enrage.

This insulting allusion to his dark skin infuriates Neville Dickens. Hence **Infu·riatingly** *adv.*

†Infu·scate, *v.* 1650. [f. L. *infuscat-, infuscare*, f. (ult.) *in-* (In-[2]) + *fuscus.*] *trans.* To make dark-coloured or dusky; to darken –1727. Hence **Infusca·tion,** the action of darkening; darkened condition.

†Infu·se, *sb.* 1568. [ad. L. *infusus* a pouring in.] = Infusion –1596.

Infuse (infiū·z), *v.* ME. [f. L. *infus-, infundere* to pour in.] 1. *trans.* To pour in; †to pour *into*; to introduce (a liquid ingredient). 2. *transf.* and *fig.* To introduce as by pouring; to instil, insinuate 1526. †3. To pour *on* or *upon*; to shed, diffuse –1672. 4. To steep or drench in a liquid, so as to extract the soluble properties; to macerate 1533. b. *intr.* To undergo infusion or maceration 1615. 5. With inverted construction: To affect (a liquid) by steeping some soluble substance in it; hence, to imbue or inspire (a person) *with* some infused quality. In wider use, to impregnate (*with* some quality, opinion, etc.). 1560.

1. 'Tis of great consequence, what is infus'd Into a Vessell when it first is vs'd Heywood. 2. These words, these lookes, I. new life in me Shaks. He infused his own intrepid spirit into the troops Gibbon. 4. While I am infusing my tea Barrie. 5. Thou didst smile, Infused with a fortitude from heauen *Temp.* I. ii. 154. Hence **Infu·ser,** one who, or that which, infuses; †*spec.* a retort.

Infusible (infiū·zĭb'l), *a.*[1] 1555. [f. In-[3] + Fusible.] Not fusible; incapable of being fused or melted.

Pure lime, except placed in clay, is i. Kirwan. Hence **Infusibi·lity**[1], **Infu·sibleness,** i. quality.

Infu·sible, *a.*[2] *rare.* 1660. [f. L. *infus-*; see Infuse *v.*] Capable of being fused.

The doctrines being i. into all Hammond. Hence **Infusibi·lity**[2]. (Dicts.)

Infu·sile, *a.* 1825. [In-[3].] Not fusile.

Infusion (infiū·ʒən). 1425. [a. F., or ad. L. *infusionem.*] 1. The action of pouring in, or fact of being poured in; that which is poured in. Now chiefly *fig.* 1532. b. *spec.* in *Surg.* Injection 1601. 2. The process of pouring water over a substance, or steeping the substance in water, in order to impregnate the liquid with its properties or virtues 1573. b. A dilute liquid extract obtained from a substance by soaking it with, or steeping it in, water; also any water containing dissolved organic (esp. vegetable) matter 1550. 3. An infused element, admixture, tincture 1626. 4. = Affusion 1751.

1. *fig.* I.—the doctrine which regarded our *a priori* Ideas as infused into the Intellect by an act of God 1857. The continual i. into it of new blood to perform its functions J. H. Newman. 2. Oil of Ivy-berries, made by expression or i. Walton. b. Spunges wetted in I. of Tobacco Boyle. 3. He..was a gentleman with a slight i. of the footman Lamb. 4. Baptism by i. Jortin. Hence **Infu·sionism,** the doctrine that the soul is a divine emanation, infused into the body at conception or birth. **Infu·sionist,** an adherent of this doctrine.

Infusive (infiū·siv), *a.* 1630. [f. L. *infus-, infundere* + -ive.] 1. Having the quality or power of infusing 1728. †2. Naturally or divinely infused; innate. Brathwait.

1. Th' i. force of Spring on Man Thomson.

‖Infusoria (infiusōə·riă), *sb. pl.* 1787. [Neut. pl. (sc. *animalcula*) of mod.L. *infusorius* Infusory.] A class of Protozoa, comprising ciliated, tentaculate, and flagellate animalcula, essentially unicellular, free-swimming, or sedentary; so called because found in infusions of decaying animal or vegetable matter.

Orig. the *Infusoria* comprehended an assemblage of minute, usually microscopic, organisms, of many diverse kinds, including some now classed as vegetables, as the *Diatomaceæ* and the *Desmidiaceæ*. As now constituted, the *Infusoria* are Protozoa characterized by a half-liquid endosarc, a firm cortical ectosarc, an outer membraneous cuticle, a mouth and anus, and a contractile vesicle which injects fluid.

Hence **Infuso·rial** *a.* of or pertaining to the I.; consisting of or formed by I. **Infuso·rian** *a.* of or pertaining to the I.; *sb.* a member of the I.

‖Infuso·rium. 1876. [mod.L., sing. of prec.] An individual animalcule of the Infusoria.

Infusory (infiū·səri). 1684. [f. L. *infus-, infundere*; see -ory.]

A. *adj.* †1 Of or pertaining to (surgical) injection. 2. = Infusorial. 1826.

B. *sb.* A member of the Infusoria 1835.

Ing (iŋ). *local.* ME. [a. ON. *eng* f., *enge, engi* neut., meadow, meadow-land, MDu. *enc, enge.* (Not in OE.)] A meadow; esp. one by the side of a river, and low-lying. Also *attrib.*

-ing[1], suffix forming verbal derivs., orig. abstract nouns of action: OE. *-ung, -ing*:— OTeut. type **-ungā* (and ?**-iŋgā*) str. fem.; not identified exc. in Teut. In ME. *-ing* (*-inge*) became the regular form.

1. The original function of the suffix was to form nouns of action; as *ácsung* Asking, *féding* Feeding. Originally abstract, these sbs., even in OE., came to express a completed action, a process, habit, or art, as *leornung* Learning, *tídung* Tidings, etc., and sometimes became concrete, as in *bedding*, etc. By extension, similar formations have been made from sbs., as *ballooning*, etc., and, by ellipsis, from advs., as *outing*, etc.

2. The vbl. sb. in *-ing* came also to be used as a gerund, i.e. a sb. with certain verbal functions; e.g. the habit of *speaking loosely* (= loose speaking); he practises *writing* (= the writing of) *leading articles*; etc. This use is peculiar to English; it was unknown to OE. and early ME.

3. In Wyclif, etc., the form in **-inge, -ynge** also appears for the Dative Infinitive, OE. *-enne*, ME. *-ene, -en.* This is a case of phonetic confusion. See N.E.D.

-ing[2], suffix of the pr. participle, and of adjs. thence derived, or so formed; an alteration of OE. *-ende* = L. *-ent-*, Gr. *-οντ-*, Skr. *-ant-*.

-ing[3], a suffix forming derivative masc. sbs., with the sense of 'one belonging to', or 'of the kind of', hence 'one possessed of the quality of', and also as a patronymic = 'one descended from, a son of', and as a diminutive. See also -ling (= *-l* + *-ing*).

Ingan (i·ŋən). 1725. Dial. f. Onion.

†Inganna·tion. 1646. [ad. It. *ingannazione*, f. *ingannare*, f. *inganno* fraud, deceit; see -ation.] Deceiving; deception –1658.

Ingate (i·ngeɪt), *sb.*[1] *n. dial.* 1496. [f. In *adv.* + Gate *sb.*[2]] 1. The action or faculty of entering; ingress. 2. An entrance 1591. †3. *concr.* That which enters. Usu. in *pl.*: Ingoings, incomings, imports; also import duties or dues –1714.

I·ngate, *sb.*[2] 1858. [f. In *adv.* + Gate *sb.*[3]] *Founding.* An aperture in a mould for pouring in metal.

Ingather (i·ngæ·ðəɹ), *v.* 1575. [f. In *adv.* + Gather *v.*] *trans.* To gather in. *lit.* and *fig.*

Ingathering (i·ngæ:ðəriŋ), *vbl. sb.* 1535. [f. In *adv.* + Gathering *vbl. sb.*] The action of gathering in or collecting (esp. the harvest); a gathering in.

Feast of I. = Feast of Tabernacles.

Ingem (indʒe·m), *v.* 1611. [f. In-[2] + Gem *sb.*, chiefly after It. *ingemmare.*] To set or adorn with gems.

†Inge·minate, *ppl. a. rare.* 1637. [f. L. *ingeminatus, ingeminare*, f. *in-* (In-[2]) + *geminare.*] Doubled, redoubled; repeated –1676.

Ingeminate (indʒe·mineɪt), *v.* 1594. [f. L. *ingeminat-*; see prec.] 1. *trans.* To repeat, reiterate; to emphasize by repetition. †2. To double (a thing); to repeat (an action) (*rare*) –1686.

1. [Falkland] often..would with a shrill and sad accent, i. the word, Peace, Peace Clarendon. Hence **Ingemina·tion,** the action of ingeminating; a repetition (*arch.*); duplication (*rare*) 1576.

Ingender, obs. f. Engender.

†Inge:nerabi·lity. 1598. [f. Ingenerable; see -ity.] The quality of being ingenerable –1691.

Ingenerable (indʒe·nĕrăb'l), *a.* Now *rare.* ME. [ad. med.L. *ingenerabilis*; see In-[3] and Generable.] Incapable of being generated. (Chiefly in 17th c. phr. *i. and incorruptible.*) Hence **Inge·nerably** *adv.*

Ingenerate (indʒe·nĕrĕt), *a.* 1656. [ad. late L. *ingeneratus*; see In-[3] and Generate *ppl. a.*] Not generated; self-existent.

The Soul is Incorruptible, I., and Immortal 1656. Hence †**Inge·nerateness.** Cudworth.

Ingenerate (indʒe·nĕrĕt), *ppl. a.* 1531. [ad. L. *ingeneratus*; see next.] 1. Inborn, innate; (of diseases) congenital (*rare*). †2. Engendered, begotten (*lit.* and *fig.*) (*rare*) –1611.

1. That gravitie and sternesse, whiche is in you as it were by nature i. Elyot.

Ingenerate (indʒe·nĕreɪt), *v.* Now *rare.* 1528. [f. L. *ingenerat-, ingenerare*, f. *in-* (In-[2]) + *generare.*] *trans.* To generate within, engender, produce.

To shew..how these opynyons were ingenerated Fox. Hence **Ingenera·tion** (*rare*), the action of ingenerating.

†Inge·niary, *a.* [ad. med.L. *ingeniarius*, f. L. *ingenium.*] Inventive. Evelyn.

†Inge·niate, *v. rare.* [f. med.L. *ingeniat, ingeniare*, f. L. *ingenium*; cf. F. *ingénier.*] *trans.* To devise, contrive, plan, design. Daniel.

Ingenie, var. of Ingeny *Obs.*

†Ingenio (indʒī·nio). 1600. [a. Sp.:—L. *ingenium* Engine.] A sugar-mill or -works in the West Indies. –1722.

Ingeniosity (indʒīniǫ·sĭti). Now *Obs.* or *rare.* 1607. [a. F. *ingéniosité*, f. L. *ingeniosus*; see next and -ity.] The quality of being ingenious; ingenuity.

Ingenious (indʒī·niəs), *a.* late ME. [a. F. *ingénieux, -euse*, or ad. L. *ingeniosus*, f. *ingenium*; see -ous.]

I. †1. Having high intellectual capacity; able, talented, possessed of genius. *Obs.* in gen. sense. –1807. †b. Of a composition, etc.: Showing these qualities –1809. †2. Intelligent; sagacious –1824. 3. Having an aptitude for invention or construction; skilful (now usually in a light sense) 1576; of things, actions, etc.: Showing cleverness of invention or construction. (The current sense.) 1548.

1. Wine gives all things, it makes the dull i. T. Brown. b. A good i. Sermon Hearne. 3. I. in tormenting ourselves 1885. An i. contrivance Maury.

II. Used by confusion for Ingenuous –1776. *Tam. Shr.* I. i. 9.

Inge·niously *adv.* in an i. manner; with skilful contrivance; †Ingenuously. **Inge·niousness.**

†Inge·nit, -ite, *a.*[1] 1604. [ad. L. *ingenitus* inborn.] Inborn, innate; native –1728.

An ingenite ardor of Navigation Gale.

†Ingenit, -ite, *a.*[2] 1677. [ad. late L. *ingenitus* unborn, f. *in-* (In-[3]) + *genitus, gignere.*] Not born or begotten; not made or produced; uncreated –1678.

As the Monad is Ingenit or Unmade Cudworth.

‖Ingénue (æ̃nʒenü). 1848. [Fr., fem. of *ingénu* Ingenuous.] An artless innocent girl, esp. of the type represented on the stage. Hence **Ingénueism.**

Ingenuity (indʒĭniū·ĭti). 1592. [ad. L. *ingenuitas*, f. *ingenuus* Ingenuous; cf. F. *ingénuité.* The use of the word as the abstract sb. from *ingenious* is Eng. only.]

I. †1. The condition of being free-born or well-born –1658. †b. Liberal quality (of education); hence, Liberal education –1662. †2. Nobility of character or disposition; high-mindedness, generosity –1716. 3. Freedom from dissimulation; honourable dealing; openness, candour, frankness. (Now usu. *ingenuousness.*) 1614.

1. b. A seminary of religion and i. FULLER. 3. Melchior Canus..for a Papist a man of singular i. JACKSON.
II. Senses conn. w. INGENIOUS. †1. High intellectual capacity; genius, talent, wit. *Obs.* in gen. sense. –1795. †2. Intellectual capacity; intelligence; (one's) senses or wits –1675. †b. *transf.* Wisdom –1660. 3. Capacity for invention or construction. Also an attribute of the thing, action, etc.: Skilfulness of contrivance or design. (The current sense.) 1649. Also with *an* and *pl.* 1650.

3. The i. of his knavery 1664, of our weavers PENNANT. [A] kind-hearted schemer..rich in petty ingenuities 1829.

Ingenuous (indʒe·niuəs), *a.* 1598. [f. L. *ingenuus* (f. *in-* (IN-²) + *gen-*, stem of *gignere* to beget) + -OUS.] 1. Of free or honourable birth. (Chiefly in references to Roman History.) 1638. 2. Noble in nature, character, or disposition; generous, high-minded. *Obs.* or *arch.* 1599. †b. Also of animals or things –1664. †3. Befitting a free-born or high-born person; liberal –1757. 4. Honourably straightforward; open, candid, frank. (The current sense.) 1598. b. Guileless, innocent; artless. (= F. *ingénu, -ue.*) 1673. ¶5. In 17th c. freq. misused for *ingenious*. *Obs.* –1795.

2. They scoffe him; an iniury hardly indured by any i. man 1631. b. An i. soil 1664. 3. That great opener of the mind, i. science BURKE. 4. An i. confession 1621. Language..well weighed and well guarded, but clear and i. MACAULAY. 5. *Cymb.* IV. ii. 186. Hence **Inge·nuously** *adv.* in an i. manner; †liberally. **Inge·nuousness**, the condition or quality of being i.; †(by confusion) *ingeniousness*.

†I·ngeny. 1474. [ad. L. *ingenium*, f. *in-* (IN-²) + *gen-*, stem of *gignere* to beget.] 1. Mind; mental tendency, disposition –1708. 2. Mental ability, genius –1697.

Ingerminate, *v.* 1860. [IN-².] To cause to germinate. (Dicts.)

Ingest (indʒe·st), *v.* 1617. [f. L. *ingest-*, *ingerere*, f. *in-* (IN-²) + *gerere* to carry, bear; cf. *digest*.] †1. *trans.* To put in, thrust in. COLLINS. 2. *spec.* To introduce (aliment) into the stomach (or mouth); to take in (food) 1620. Hence **Inge·stive** *a.* having the function of taking in aliment.

‖**Ingesta** (indʒe·stă), *sb. pl.* 1727. [L., neut. pl. of *ingestus*; see prec.] *Phys.* Substances introduced into the body as nourishment.

Ingestion (indʒe·styən). 1597. [ad. late L. *ingestionem*, f. *ingerere*. Cf. F. *ingestion*.] †1. Introduction. 2. The action of ingesting or taking in aliment 1620.

Inghamite (i·ŋəməit). 1743. A member of the religious body founded in 1742 by Benjamin *Ingham*, on principles resembling those of Moravians and Methodists.

Ingine, Sc. f. ENGINE.

Ingirt, var. of ENGIRT *v.*

Ingle (i·ŋg'l), *sb.*¹ Orig. *Sc.* 1508. [?] 1. Fire; a fire burning upon the hearth; a house-fire. ¶2. *erron.* An open fireplace 1841. 3. *attrib.* 1853.

1. His wee bit i., blinkin bonilie BURNS. *Comb.*: **i.-bench**, a bench beside the fire; **-cheek** (*Sc.*), the jamb of a fireplace; **-nook** (orig. *Sc.*), the chimney-corner; **-side**, a fireside.

†Ingle, *sb.*² 1592. [?] A catamite. ¶Misused for 'familiar friend'. SCOTT.

†Ingle, *v.* 1595. [f. prec.] 1. *trans.* To fondle, caress –1631. 2. To wheedle, coax –1602. 3. *intr.* To fondle *with* 1611.

Inglobate (inglōᵘ·bᵉt), *a. rare.* 1852. [IN-².] Formed into a globe or globular mass.

Inglobe, obs. f. ENGLOBE.

Inglorious (inglōᵊ·riəs), *a.* 1573. [ad. L. *ingloriosus* (Pliny); see IN-³ and GLORIOUS.] 1. Not glorious; not known to fame; humble, obscure. Now *rare.* 1591. †Also with *of*. GIBBON. 2. Bringing no glory (to a person); hence, shameful, disgraceful, ignominious 1573.

1. I. may they liue, i. die, That suffer learning liue in misery 1602. Some mute i. Milton here may rest GRAY. 2. The victory over the senate was easy and i. GIBBON. Hence **Inglo·rious-ly** *adv.*, **-ness.**

Inglut, -glutte, obs. ff. ENGLUT *v.*

‖**Ingluvies** (inglū·vi,īz). 1727. [L., prob. f. *glū- to swallow.] *Anat.* The crop of a bird, the first stomach of a ruminating animal, an insect, etc. Hence **In,glu·vial** *a.* (*rare*), of or pertaining to the i. or crop.

†In,glu·vious, *a.* 1569. [ad. L. *ingluviosus*; see prec. and -OUS.] Greedy, gluttonous –1659. Hence **†Inglu·viously** *adv.*

I·n,go:ing, *vbl. sb.* Now *rare.* ME. [f. the phr. *go in* (see IN-¹) + -ING¹.] A going in; entrance; way in. b. The sum paid by a tenant or purchaser for fixtures, etc. on taking over business or other premises 1905.

I·n-go:ing, *ppl. a.* 1825. [f. as prec. + -ING².] That goes in or inwards; that enters; as, an *i. tenant*. b. Penetrating, thorough 1928.

Ingorge, Ingrace, etc., var. ENGORGE, etc.

Ingot (i·ŋgǫt). ME. [Of uncertain origin. F. *lingot* is app. adopted from Eng., with coalescence of the article, for *l'ingot*. Cf. LINGOT.] †1. A mould in which metal is cast; an ingot-mould –1799. 2. A mass (usu. oblong or brick-shaped) of cast metal, esp. of gold, silver, or (now) of steel 1547. 3. *attrib.* 1558.

1. And fro the fir he took vp his mateere And in thyngot putte it CHAUCER. 2. Not, like a Miser, to gaze only on his Ingots STEELE.

†Ingra·cious, *a.* 1600. [IN-³.] Ungracious –1676.

I·ngrain, *a.* (*sb.*) 1766. [f. the phr. *in grain*; see GRAIN *sb.*¹ III. 1. Now usu. *i·ngrain* bef. a sb., *ingrai·n* after it or in the predicate.] 1. Dyed in grain; dyed with fast colours before manufacture; dyed in the fibre; thoroughly dyed. b. (*U.S.*) *Ingrain carpet*, a two-ply carpet, in which the pattern goes through and through and appears on both sides 1836. Also *ellipt.* as *sb.* 2. Of qualities, habits, etc.: Inborn, firmly fixed, inveterate, ingrained 1852; thorough 1865.

Ingrain, obs. or arch. var. of ENGRAIN *v.*

Ingrained (ingrē̆ⁱ·nd), *ppl. a.* 1548. [app. orig. a var. of *engrained* ppl. a.; but now taken as if from *in* adv. + *grained*. Stressed *i·ngrained* bef. a sb., otherwise *ingrai·ned*.] †1. Dyed in grain. 2. *fig.* Wrought in the inmost texture; deeply rooted, inveterate 1599. b. Of persons: Out-and-out 1630.

2. I. wickedness 1855. b. He is an i. sceptic LOWELL.

†In,gra·pple, *v.* 1597. [f. IN-² + GRAPPLE *v.*] To join in grappling; to grapple together (*intr.* and *trans.*) –1661.

Then shall young Hotspur..I. with thy sonne 1597.

Ingrate (ingrē̆ⁱ·t), *a.* (*sb.*) ME. [ad. L. *ingratus*, f. *in-* (IN-³) + *gratus*. Cf. F. *ingrat*.] 1. Not grateful; †unpleasant –1702; †unfriendly –1563; unthankful (*arch.*) 1528. 2. *sb.* An ungrateful person 1570. Hence **†In,gra·tely** *adv.*

†In,gra·teful, *a.* 1547. [IN-³.] 1. Displeasing, disagreeable –1754. 2. Not feeling or showing gratitude –1759.

1. The Oil is of an i. Odor 1694. 2. Desirous of pleasures, and ingratefull for benefits 1547. Hence **†In,gra·teful-ly** *adv.*, **†-ness.**

Ingratiate (ingrē̆ⁱ·ʃi,eⁱt), *v.* 1622. [app. f. 16th c. It. *ingratiare*, f. phrase *in gratia* (now *grazia*), L. *in gratiam* into favour.] †1. *trans.* To bring into favour *with*; to render agreeable *to* –1755. 2. *refl.* To get oneself into favour *with*; to render oneself agreeable *to* 1622. †Also *intr.* for *refl.* †3. *trans.* To make (a thing) pleasant, agreeable, or acceptable (*to* or *with*) –1748.

1. All this would not i. this Usurper with them FULLER. 2. If he did not do somewhat to i. himself to the People CLARENDON. 3. Things, when wanted, are ingratiated to us, as warmth after cold 1656. Hence **Ingra·tia·tingly** *adv.* in an ingratiating manner. **Ingratia·tion**, the action or process of ingratiating oneself. **Ingra·tiatory** *a.* that tends to i.

Ingratitude (ingræ·titiūd). ME. [a. F., ad. late L. *ingratitudo*, f. L. *ingratus*; cf. GRATITUDE.] 1. Want of gratitude; indisposition to acknowledge or reciprocate benefits received; ungratefulness. †2. Unfriendliness, unkindness –1566.

1. I. is monstrous *Cor.* II. iii. 10. I. to benefactors is the first of revolutionary virtues BURKE.

†In,gra·ve, *v.* Also **†en-.** 1535. [f. IN-¹ or ² + GRAVE *sb.*¹ or *v.*¹] *trans.* To put in a grave; to bury –1683.

Ingrave, etc. obs. f. ENGRAVE *v.*, etc.

Ingravescent (ingrăve·sĕnt), *a.* 1822. [f. L. *ingravescentem*, *ingravescere* to grow worse.] Increasing in gravity or severity. Hence **Ingrave·scence.**

Ingravidate (ingræ·videⁱt), *v.* 1642. [f. late L. *ingravidat-*, *ingravidare*, f. *in-* (IN-²) + *gravidus* heavy, GRAVID.] 1. *trans.* To load or weigh; to render gravid, to impregnate. 2. *intr.* To become heavy. TOMLINSON. Hence **Ingravida·tion**, the action of ingravidating or state of being ingravidated; pregnancy 1615.

†Ingrea·t, *v.* Also **†en-.** 1619. [f. IN-² + GREAT *a.*] *trans.* To make great, to magnify –1627.

†Ingre·dience. 1526. [f. as INGREDIENT; see -ENCE. In sense 1, orig. a misspelling of *ingredients*, and subseq. confused with the sing. *ingredient*.] 1. That which enters into a mixture. a. The ingredients, separately or collectively –1694. b. (with *pl.*) A single ingredient –1661. 2. The fact or process of entering in –1677.

1. a. This euen-handed Iustice Commends th' I. of our poyson'd Challice To our owne lips SHAKS. b. Ale requireth two ingrediences COGAN. So **†Ingre·diency.**

Ingredient (ingrī·diĕnt). 1460. [ad. L. *ingredientem*, *ingredi* to enter, f. *in-* (IN-²) + *gradi* to step; cf. F. *ingrédient* sb.]

A. *adj.* That enters in; entering into a thing or place (*Obs.* or *arch.*) 1611.

The generosity that is i. in the temper of the soul 1713.

B. *sb.* †1. One who, or that which, enters in –1624. 2. Something that enters into the formation of a compound or element; a component part, constituent, element. Primarily used of medical, etc. mixtures. 1460. †b. Chief ingredient. *Oth.* II. iii. 311.

1. [The air] being a perpetual ambient and i. WOTTON. 2. Stupidity, I told you, is no i. in piety GAUDEN.

Ingress (i·ngres), *sb.* ME. [ad. L. *ingressus* entering, f. *ingredi*; see prec.] 1. The action or fact of entering. Also, Capacity or right of entrance, esp. in legal phr. *i., egress, and regress* 1543. b. A place or means of entrance ME. 2. The action of entering upon a thing; a beginning, an attempt; also, The beginning of an action, period, etc. (*arch.*) ME. 3. a. *Astrol.* The arrival of a planet at that part of the heaven occupied by another planet, or at the ascendant, or the mid-heaven 1603. b. *Astron.* The entrance of the sun into a sign of the zodiac. ? *Obs.* 1652. c. The first contact of an inferior planet with the sun, or of a satellite with its planet, at a transit 1751.

†Ingre·ss, *v.* ME. [f. L. *ingress-*, *ingredi*; see prec.] To enter (*trans.* and *intr.*) –1817.

Ingression (ingre·ʃən). 1470. [ad. L. *ingressionem*; see INGRESS *sb.*] The action of going in; entrance; invasion.

Ingreve, -grieve, -groove, -gross(e, varr. ENGRIEVE, etc.

Ingrowing (i·ngrōᵘ:iŋ), *ppl. a.* 1869. [IN *adv.*] Growing inwards or within something; *spec.* of a nail: Growing into the flesh.

Ingrown (i·ngrōᵘn), *ppl. a.* 1670. [IN *adv.*] That has or is grown within something; native, innate. b. Of a nail: That has grown into the flesh 1878.

Ingrowth (i·ngrōᵘþ). 1852. [IN *adv.*] a. The action of growing inwards. b. That which grows inwards. (Opp. to *outgrowth*.) 1877.

‖**Inguen** (i·ŋgwen). 1706. [L.] The groin.

Inguilty, erron. f. UNGUILTY.

Inguinal (i·ŋgwinăl), *a.* 1681. [ad. L. *inguinalis* (Pliny), f. *inguen*, *inguin-*.] *Anat.*, etc. Of, belonging to, or situated in the groin.

Inguino- (i·ŋgwino), comb. f. L. *inguen*, *inguin-*; as in **i.-scro·tal** *a.*, belonging to the groin and the scrotum; etc.

Ingulf, etc., var. of ENGULF, etc.

Ingurgitate (ingɒ̄·ɹdʒiteⁱt), *v.* 1570. [f. L. *ingurgitat-*, *ingurgitare* to pour in (like a flood), f. *in-* (IN-²) + *gurges, gurgitem* a gulf.] 1. *trans.* To swallow greedily or immoderately. Also *fig.* Also *absol.* b. To gorge, to cram with food or drink 1583. 2. *trans.* To swallow up as a gulf or whirlpool; to engulf (*lit.* and *fig.*) 1619.

2. Bankers who..do not absorb and i. your principal 1849.

Ingurgitation (ingɒ̄ɹdʒitēⁱ·ʃən). 1530. [ad. late L. *ingurgitationem*; see prec.] 1. The action of ingurgitating; guzzling or swilling.

b. Engulfment 1826. ¶**2.** *erron.* A gurgling noise. HAWTHORNE.

1. A large draught and i. of wine BACON.

†**Ingu·stable,** *a.* Also *erron.* **-ible.** 1623. [ad. L. *ingustabilis*; see IN-[3] and GUSTABLE.] Tasteless; not perceptible by the sense of taste –1656.

†**Inhabile,** *a.* 1678. [a. F., or ad. L. *inhabilis*; see IN-[3] and ABLE, HABILE.] Unfit, unable; unqualified –1830. So †**Inhabi·lity** (doublet of *inability*), incapacity, disability; INABILITY 1488.

Inhabit (inhæ·bit), *v.* *Pa. pple.* **inhabited,** †**inhabit.** [ME. *enhabit(e,* a. OF. *enhabiter,* ad. L. *inhabitare,* f. *in-* (IN-[2]) + *habitare* to dwell; see HABIT *v.*] **1.** *trans.* To dwell in, occupy as an abode. Said of men and animals. Also *transf.* and *fig.* **2.** *intr.* To dwell, live; to have one's abode; to abide, lodge (*arch.*) ME. Also *transf.* and *fig.* †**3.** *trans.* To occupy or people (a place) –1651. †**4.** To settle (a person) in a place; to locate, house; *refl.* to take up one's abode; *pass.* to be domiciled or resident –1600.

1. They shall builde houses, and i. them *Isa.* lxv. 21. The..fishes..which i. the mid ocean 1881. *fig.* The High and loftie One that inhabiteth eternitie *Isa.* lvii. 15. **2.** To learn What creatures there i. MILT. *P. L.* II. 355. *fig.* See, on the Shoar inhabits purple Spring DRYDEN. **4.** O knowledge ill inhabited, worse then Ioue in a thatch'd house SHAKS.

Inha·bitable, *a.*[1] 1601. [f. prec. + -ABLE.] Capable of being inhabited.

Hence **Inha·bitabi·lity**[1], **Inha·bitableness.**

†**Inha·bitable,** *a.*[2] ME. [a. F., ad. L. *inhabitabilis*; see IN-[3] and HABITABLE.] Not habitable, uninhabitable –1742. **b.** Uninhabited 1529.

The frozen ridges of the Alpes, Or any other ground i. SHAKS. Hence **Inha·bitabi·lity**[2].

†**Inha·bitance.** 1482. [f. as INHABITANT + -ANCE.] **1.** An inhabiting; inhabitation; residence –1630. **2.** An abode, dwelling –1611.

1. The ruines yet resting in the wilde Moores, which testifie a former i. CAREW.

Inhabitancy (inhæ·bitănsi). 1681. [f. INHABITANT; see -ANCY.] **1.** The fact of inhabiting or of being an inhabitant; occupation by an inhabitant or inhabitants; residence as an inhabitant, *esp.* during a specified period, so as to gain the rights and privileges of an inhabitant. **2.** A place of habitation. GROTE.

Inhabitant (inhæ·bitănt). 1462. [a. AF. and OF. *inhabitant,* ad. L. *inhabitantem.*]

A. *adj.* Inhabiting, dwelling, resident (*arch.* or *Obs.*) 1526.

Specially if he be there i. 1625.

B. *sb.* One who inhabits; a human being or animal dwelling in a place; a permanent resident. (In early use only in *pl.*)

Leopards, Bores, Iaccalls, and such like sauage inhabitants 1615. Without the good will of a single English-born i. of England FREEMAN.

†**Inha·bitate,** *v.* 1600. [f. L. *inhabitat-* ppl. stem.] To inhabit –1720.

Inhabitation (inhæ:bitēⁱ·ʃən). ME. [ad. late L. *inhabitationem.*] **1.** The action of inhabiting; the being or becoming inhabited. **b.** *fig.* Spiritual indwelling 1615. †**2.** A place of dwelling; an inhabited region or building; an abode –1639. †**3.** A collection of inhabitants; population; settlement (*rare*) –1818.

1. The first i. of this Realme GRAFTON. **b.** The i. of the Holy Spirit GALE. **3.** Or universal groan As if the whole i. perish'd MILT. *Sams.* 1512.

Inhabita·tiveness. 1838. [f. as INHABITATE + -IVE + -NESS.] *Phrenology.* = INHABITIVENESS.

†**Inha·bited,** *a.* 1614. [IN-[3].] Uninhabited –1621.

Inha·bited, *ppl. a.* 1570. [f. INHABIT *v.* + -ED[1].] Dwelt in; having inhabitants.

Inhabiter (inhæ·bitəɹ). *arch.* ME. [f. as prec. + -ER[1].] One who inhabits, an inhabitant; †a colonist.

Inhabitiveness (inhæ·bitivnės). 1815. [f. INHABIT *v.* + -IVE + -NESS.] *Phrenology.* The disposition to remain always in the same abode; attachment to country and home.

You know my (what the phrenologists call) i. LOWELL.

Inhalant (inhēⁱ·lănt), *a.* (*sb.*) 1822. [ad. L. *inhalantem, inhalare* to INHALE.] **1.** Inhaling; serving for inhalation 1825. **2.** *sb.* An inhalant opening or pore 1822; an apparatus for inhaling; a medicinal preparation for inhalation (*mod.*).

Inhalation (inhălēⁱ·ʃən). 1623. [f. L. *inhalare.*] **1.** The action, or an act, of inhaling; *spec.* inhaling of medicines or anæsthetics in the form of gas or vapour. **2.** *Med.* A preparation to be inhaled 1882.

Inhale (inhēⁱ·l), *v.* 1725. [ad. L. *inhalare* to breathe upon, f. *in-* (IN-[2]) + *halare* to breathe out. Taken in Fr. and Eng. as the opposite of *exhale*; hence the current sense.] **1.** *trans.* To breathe in; to take into the lungs. Also *fig.* **2.** *loosely.* To absorb (fluid) 1841.

1. We are continually inhaling and exhaling atmospheric air TYNDALL.

Inhaler (inhēⁱ·ləɹ). 1778. [f. prec. + -ER[1].] **1.** One who inhales 1835. **2.** A contrivance for inhaling. **a.** An apparatus for administering a medicinal or anæsthetic gas or vapour by inhalation 1778. **b.** An appliance for enabling a person to breathe with safety in a deleterious atmosphere or under water 1864.

Inhance, inhanse, obs. ff. ENHANCE *v.*

Inharmonic, -al (inhaɹmǫ·nik, -ăl), *a.* 1674. [IN-[3].] Not harmonic; dissonant, inharmonious; not according to the principle of harmony.

Inharmonious (inhaɹmōᵘ·niəs), *a.* 1711. [IN-[3]. Cf. F. *inharmonieux.*] **1.** Of sound: Not in harmony; sounding disagreeably; discordant, untuneful. **2.** Not harmonious in relation, action, or sentiment; disagreeing; conflicting 1748.

1. Sounds i. in themselves and harsh COWPER. Hence **Inharmo·nious-ly** *adv.*, **-ness.**

Inharmony (inhā·ɹmŏni). *rare.* 1799. [IN-[3].] Want of harmony; discord.

Inhaul (i·nhǫl). 1860. [f. IN *adv.* + HAUL *sb.*] *Naut.* = next.

Inhauler (i·nhǫ:ləɹ). 1793. [f. IN *adv.* + HAULER.] An appliance for hauling in; *spec.* (*Naut.*) 'the rope used for hauling in the clue of a boomsail, or jib-traveller' (Smyth).

Inhaust (inhǭ·st), *v. rare.* 1547. [f. IN-[2] + L. *haust-, haurire* to draw; cf. *exhaust.*] *trans.* To draw or suck in; to inhale; to imbibe. So **Inhau·stion,** inhalation.

Inhearse, obs. f. ENHEARSE.

Inhell (inhe·l), *v.* 1607. [f. IN-[1] + HELL *sb.*] *trans.* To put into or confine in hell.

†**Inherce,** obs. f. ENHEARSE *v.* 1 *Hen. VI,* IV. vii. 45.

Inhere (inhīᵊ·ɹ), *v.* Also †**inhære.** 1586. [ad. L. *inhærere,* f. *in-* (IN-[2]) + *hærere* to stick; cf. *adhere,* etc.] **1.** *intr.* To stick *in*; to be or remain fixed or lodged *in* something (*rare* or *Obs.*). Also *fig.* 1608. **2.** To exist, abide, or have its being, as an attribute, quality, etc., *in* a subject or thing. (The current sense.) 1586. **b.** To be vested or inherent *in,* as a right, power, etc. 1840.

1. *fig.* So strongly does it i. in our constitution, that very few are able to conquer it BURKE. **2.** Knowledge and perception i. in mind alone BAIN.

Inherence (inhīᵊ·rĕns). Also †**inhærence.** 1577. [f. med.L. *inhærentia,* f. *inhærentem*; see -ENCE.] The fact or condition of inhering; the state or quality of being inherent; permanent existence (as of an attribute) *in* a subject; indwelling. So **Inhe·rency** (in mod. use chiefly as a quality).

Inherent (inhīᵊ·rĕnt), *a.* Also †**inhærent.** 1578. [f. L. *inhærentem.*] **1.** Sticking in; fixed, situated, or contained in something (in physical sense). Also *fig.* (Now *rare* or *Obs.*) **2.** Existing in something as a permanent attribute or quality; forming an element, esp. an essential element, of something; intrinsic, essential 1588. **3.** Vested *in* or attached to a person, office, etc., as a right or privilege 1628.

1. *fig.* Least I..teach my Minde A most i. Basenesse SHAKS. **2.** The melancholy i. in his constitution JOHNSON. **3.** The legislative authority was i. in the general assembly GIBBON. Hence **Inhe·rent-ly** *adv.*

Inherit (inhe·rit), *v.* [ME. *enherite,* a. OF. *enheriter* to put (one) in possession as heir, f. *en-* (EN-[1], IN-[2]) + *heriter*:—late L. *hereditare*; see HERIT *v.* Cf. F. *hériter* for the change of sense.] †**1.** *trans.* To make heir, put in possession. (Cf. *disinherit.*) –1593. **2.** *trans.* To take or receive (property, *esp.* realty or a right, title, etc.) as heir of the former possessor (usu. an ancestor) at his decease; to get by legal descent or succession ME. **b.** To derive (a quality, etc., physical or mental) from one's progenitors by natural descent; to possess by transmission from parents or ancestry 1597. **c.** To receive from a predecessor in office. Chiefly *fig.* 1847. **3.** *transf.* To receive, obtain, have, or hold as one's portion ME. **4.** To succeed as heir 1533. **5.** *absol.* or *intr.* To succeed as an heir; to come into or take possession of an inheritance. Also *fig.* 1533.

1. *Rich. II,* I. i. 85. **2.** Lat him as ayre, quen I am erþed, enherit my landis ME. **b.** The cold blood hee did..inherite of his Father SHAKS. **3.** Good master, what shall I doe to i. eternall life? *Luke* xviii. 18. **4.** Our sons i. us TENNYSON. **5.** His Issue [were] barred from Inheriting TYRRELL. Hence **Inhe·ritage** (*rare*), a heritage, inheritance. **Inhe·ritor,** one who inherits, in various senses; an heir. **Inhe·ritress,** †**-trice,** †**-trix,** an heiress.

Inheritable (inhe·rităb'l), *a.* Also †**en-.** 1470. [a. AF. *en-, inheritable,* able to be made heir, f. *enheriter*; see INHERIT and -ABLE.] **1.** Capable of inheriting (see the vb.). **2.** Capable of being inherited. **a.** *lit.* = HERITABLE 1. 1483. **b.** *fig.* = HERITABLE 2. 1828.

1. In England..upon deficiency of I. Blood, Lands escheat to the Crown 1774. **2. a.** The British Crown was in those early days i. by females SYD. SMITH. **b.** I. deviations of structure DARWIN. Hence **Inhe·ritabi·lity, Inhe·ritableness,** i. quality. **Inhe·ritably** *adv.* so as to be i., by inheritance.

Inheritance (inhe·rităns). ME. [a. AF. *enheritance* being admitted as heir, etc.; see INHERIT *v.* and -ANCE.]

I. The action or fact of inheriting. **1.** *lit.* Hereditary succession to property, a title, etc.; 'a perpetual or continuing right to an estate, vested in a person and his heirs' (Wharton). **2.** *transf.* and *fig.* **a.** Possession, ownership, of something as one's birthright; right of possession 1535. **b.** Natural derivation of qualities or characters from parents or ancestry 1859.

1. The realme of Fraunce to him..by lyneall enheritaunce aperteyning HALL. **2. a.** But you hath the Lorde taken..that ye shulde be the people of his enheritaunce COVERDALE *Deut.* iv. 20. **b.** These characters may be attributed to i. from a common progenitor DARWIN.

II. That which is inherited. **1.** *lit.* Property, or an estate, which passes by law to the heir on the decease of the possessor 1473. Also *fig.* **2.** *transf.* and *fig.* Something that one comes into possession of by right or divine grant; birthright. In biblical use applied to persons, etc., as God's possession (κλῆρος), and to possessions or blessings as received or enjoyed by such persons. (Cf. HERITAGE *sb.*) 1535.

1. He [the minister] is the tenant of the day, and has no interest in the i. *Junius Lett.* *fig.* His name, The sole i. he left BYRON. **2.** O helpe thy people, geue thy blessynge vnto thy enheritaunce COVERDALE *Ps.* xxvii[i]. 9.

Inhesion (inhī·ʒən). Also †**inhæsion.** 1631. [ad. late L. *inhæsionem*; see INHERE.] The action or fact of inhering, esp. as a quality or attribute; inherence.

Phr. *Subject of i.,* that in which a quality or attribute inheres.

†**Inhe·sive,** *a. rare.* 1639. [f. L. *inhæs-*; see INHERE and -IVE.] Having the quality of inhering; inherent. Hence †**Inhe·sively** *adv.* inherently 1600.

Inhiate (i·nhi,eⁱt), *v.* 1543. [f. L. *inhiat-, inhiare*; see IN-[2] and HIATE.] *intr.* To gape, open the mouth wide. Hence †**Inhia·tion,** the act of gaping *after.*

Inhibit (inhi·bit), *v.* Pa. pple. **inhibited;** also †**inhibit(e.** 1460. [f. L. *inhibit-, inhibere,* f. *in-* (IN-[2]) + *habere* to hold.] **1.** *trans.* To forbid, prohibit, interdict (a person); **b.** without const.: *esp.* to forbid (an ecclesiastic) to exercise clerical functions 1531. **2.** To forbid, prohibit (a thing, action, etc.). Now *rare.* 1494. **3.** To restrain, check, hinder, prevent, stop 1535.

1. The said Peckam inhibited all from selling victuals to him or his family FULLER. **b.** He did never i. me in my life LATIMER. **2.** Burial may not be inhibited or deny'd to any one AYLIFFE. Hence **Inhi·biter, -or,** one who inhibits.

Inhibition (inhibi·ʃən). ME. [a. OF. *inhibicion,* later *inhib-,* ad. rare L. *inhibitionem.*] **1.**

The action of inhibiting or forbidding; a prohibition. **2.** *spec.* †**a.** In *Eng. Law*, formerly = PROHIBITION. **b.** In *Eccl. Law*, The order of an eccl. court, stopping proceedings in inferior courts; also, now *esp.*, the command of a bishop or eccl. judge, that a clergyman shall cease from exercising ministerial functions. 1532. **3.** The action of preventing, hindering, or checking. Now esp. in *Physiol.* 1621.

3. By i. we mean the arrest of the functions of a structure or organ, by the action upon it of another, while its power to execute those functions is still retained L. BRUNTON.

Inhibitory (inhi·bitəri), *a.* 1490. [ad. med. L. *inhibitorius* (see INHIBIT *v.* and -ORY).] **1.** Of the nature of an inhibition; prohibitory. **2.** *Physiol.* That restrains, checks, or hinders action 1855.

1. This Original Right of the Archbishop, I. of our Liberty..is the very Point in Question 1701. 2. *I. nerve*, a nerve of which the stimulation represses or diminishes action; The hypothesis that alcohol narcotises the i. nerve of the heart 1882.

†**Inhi·ve**, *v. rare.* 1611. [IN-1 or 2.] *trans.* To put into a hive; to HIVE –1622.

†**Inho·ld**, *v.* 1614. [f. IN-1 + HOLD *v.*] **1.** *trans.* To hold within; to contain, enclose –1628. **2.** *intr.* To contain oneself, keep *from.* FULLER.

†**Inho·lder.** 1599. [f. prec., or as prec.] **1.** A tenant. SPENSER. **2.** That which holds or contains –1674.

†**Inhoo·p**, *v.* [f. IN-1 or 2 + HOOP *sb.* or *v.*] *trans.* In *Cockfighting*: To place or enclose in a hoop, to surround with a hoop. *Ant. & Cl.* II. iii. 38.

Inhospitable (inhǫ·spităb'l), *a.* 1570. [a. OF., ad. med. or mod.L. *inhospitabilis* (= L. *inhospitalis*); see IN-3 and HOSPITABLE.] Not hospitable. **1.** Not disposed to welcome and entertain strangers; withholding hospitality from guests or visitors. **2.** *transf.* Of a region or coast: Not offering shelter or entertainment 1616.

1. Jael, who with i. guile Smote Sisera sleeping through the Temples nail'd MILT. 2. The Coast is i. as well as the People 1727. Hence **Inhospitabi·lity, Inho·spitableness, Inho·spitably** *adv.* var. †**Inho·spital** *a.*

Inhospitality (inhǫspitæ·līti). 1570. [ad. L. *inhospitalitas*, f. *inhospitalis*; see -ITY.] The quality or practice of being inhospitable; want of hospitality.

Inhuman (inhiū·măn), *a.* 1481. [ad. L. *inhumanus*, f. *in-* (IN-3) + *humanus.* The spelling was *inhumane* till after 1700. The stress was orig. on the final syllable.] **1.** Of persons: Not having the qualities proper or natural to a human being; *esp.* destitute of natural kindness or pity; brutal, unfeeling. Also *fig.* of things. **b.** Of actions, etc.: Brutal, barbarous, cruel 1489. **2.** Not of the ordinary human type 1568.

1. E'er sounding Hammers forg'd th' inhumane Sword DRYDEN. b. Inhumane Cruelties CLARENDON. 2. The human and i. wonders painted thrice the size of life D. JERROLD. Hence **Inhu·man-ly** *adv.*, **-ness.**

Inhumane (inhiumē·n), *a.* 1598. [ad. L. *inhumanus*; see prec. In later use f. IN-3 + HUMANE.] †**1.** = INHUMAN 1. –1777. †**2.** Uncivilized, uncultured, impolite. BUTLER. **3.** Not humane; destitute of compassion for suffering 1822. Hence **Inhuma·nely** *adv.*

Inhumanity (inhiumæ·nīti) 1477. [a. F. *inhumanité*, or ad. L. *inhumanitatem*, f. *inhumanus.*] **1.** The quality of being inhuman or inhumane; want of human feeling; brutality, barbarous cruelty. **b.** With *an* and *pl.* An inhuman or cruel deed 1647. †**2.** Want of politeness or courtesy –1648.

1. Man's i. to Man Makes countless thousands mourn BURNS.

Inhumate (inhiū·meᵗt, i·nhiumeᵗt), *v. rare.* 1612. [f. L. *inhumat-*, *inhumare* to INHUME.] *trans.* To inhume, bury.

Inhumation (inhiumē·ʃən). 1612. [f. L. *inhumare* (see prec. and -ATION).] **1.** The action or practice of burying in the ground; the fact or condition of being buried; interment 1636. **2.** The burying of a thing under ground. Also *fig.* 1658. †**3.** An obsolete chemical process, in which vessels were buried in earth, within a circular fire, for purposes of distillation –1650.

Inhume (inhiū·m), *v.* Also †en-. 1610. [ad. L. *inhumare* (Pliny), f. *in-* (IN-2) + *humus* ground.] **1.** *trans.* To inter, bury (the dead); to lay in the grave. Also *fig.* **b.** *transf.* Of the earth or tomb: To cover (the dead). ? *Obs.* 1621. **2.** To bury in the ground; to cover with soil. Now *rare.* 1621.

1. Here 's a storm Able to wake all of our name inhumed MIDDLETON. 2. By which the Cities were inhumed LYELL.

Inial (i·niăl), *a.* 1803. [f. INI-ON + -AL.] *Anat.* Of or belonging to the inion. So **I·niad** *adv.*, towards the inial aspect.

†**Inima·ginable**, *a.* 1533. [ad. mod.L. *inimaginabilis* (Erasmus); see IN-3 and IMAGINABLE.] Unimaginable –1759.

Inimical (ini·mikăl), *a.* 1513. [ad. late L. *inimicalis*, f. *in-* (IN-3) + *amicus* friend; see -AL.] **1.** Having the disposition or temper of an enemy; unfriendly, hostile. Const. *to.* **2.** Adverse or injurious in tendency or influence; harmful, hurtful. Const. *to.* 1643.

1. A prince i. to civil and religious liberty 1765. 2. Practices i. to health JOWETT. Hence **Inimica·lity, Ini·micalness. Ini·mically** *adv.*

†**Inimici·tious**, *a.* Also †en-. 1641. [f. L. *inimicitia* + -OUS.] = INIMICAL –1761. So †**Ini·micous** *a.* 1597; †**Inimicity**, hostility 1561.

Inimitable (ini·mităb'l), *a.* 1531. [ad. L. *inimitabilis*; see IN-3 and IMITABLE.] **1.** Incapable of being imitated; surpassing or defying imitation; peerless. **2.** Not to be imitated. WASHINGTON.

1. I. eloquence ELYOT, stile HOLLAND. The i. chemistry of nature 1756. Hence **Ini·mitabi·lity, Ini·mitableness. Ini·mitably** *adv.*

Ini·mitative, *a.* 1836. [IN-3.] = prec.

In infinitum: see IN *Lat. prep.*

Inion (i·niǫn). 1803. [a. Gr. ἰνίον nape of the neck.] *Anat.* A ridge of the occiput; *spec.* the external occipital protuberance.

†**Inique**, *a.* 1521. [ad. L. *iniquus*, f. *in-* (IN-3) + *æquus* equal, just, fair.] Unjust; iniquitous. –1730.

†**Ini·quitable**, *a.* 1734. [f. IN-3 + EQUITABLE, after *iniquitous*, etc.] Unjust; iniquitous.

Iniquitous (ini·kwitəs), *a.* 1726. [f. INIQUITY + -OUS; cf. *felicitous.*] Characterized by iniquity; grossly unjust; wicked.

I. opinions SWIFT, prosecutions 1770. I. in price RUSKIN. Hence **Ini·quitous-ly** *adv.*, **-ness.**

Iniquity (ini·kwiti). ME. [a. OF. *iniquité*, ad. L. *iniquitas*, f. *iniquus*, INIQUE.] **1.** The quality of being unrighteous, or (more often) unrighteous action or conduct; wickedness, sin; *occas.*, esp. in early use, Injurious or wrongful action towards another; now generally connoting gross injustice or public wrong. **b.** *pl.* Sins; wrongful acts, injuries 1477. †**2.** Want of equity; injustice, unfairness. *Obs.* exc. as implied in 1. 1587. **3.** The name of a comic character in the old morality plays, also called the VICE, representing some particular vice, or vice in general. 1594. †**4.** Unfavourableness, adverse operation. (A Latinism.) –1619.

1. Departe from me all ye workers off iniquytie TINDALE *Luke* xiii. 27. b. The oppressions and iniquities of the Oude government 1804. 3. Thus, like the formall Vice, Iniquitie, I morallize two meanings in one word SHAKS. 4. They all were destroyed by the iniquitie of Fortune 1619.

†**Ini·quous**, *a.* 1654. [f. L. *iniquus* (see prec.) + -OUS.] Unjust, unfair; wicked, iniquitous –1724.

Inirritable (ini·rităb'l), *a.* 1794. [IN-3.] Not irritable or susceptible of excitement. Hence **Ini·rritabi·lity.**

Ini·rritative, *a.* ? *Obs.* 1796. [IN-3.] Characterized by absence of irritation, as *i. debility.*

Inisle, var. of ENISLE *v.*

Initial (ini·ʃăl). 1526. [ad. L. *initialis*, f. *initium* beginning; see -AL.]

A. *adj.* **1.** Of or pertaining to a beginning; existing at, or constituting, the beginning; primary; occas. = elementary, rudimentary. **2.** Standing at the beginning of a word, etc., or of the alphabet; as *i. letter* SIR T. MORE.

1. The square of the i. velocity PLAYFAIR. The i. stage of mental disease 1880. The cells from which these..masses of nascent tissues arise are known as *i. cells* GOODALE.

B. *sb.* †**1.** A beginning *of* something –1839. **2.** An initial letter; *esp.* (in *pl.*) the initial letters of a person's name and surname 1627. **3.** *Mus.* Each of the prescribed notes (usu. called *absolute initials*) on which a Plain-song melody may begin in any given mode. W. S. ROCKSTRO.

Initial (ini·ʃăl), *v.* 1864. [f. prec. B. 2.] *trans.* To mark or sign with initials; to put one's initials to or upon. Hence **Ini·tialed** (-alled) *ppl. a.* **Ini·tialing** (-alling) *vbl. sb.* and *ppl. a.*

Initially (ini·ʃăli), *adv.* 1628. [f. INITIAL *a.* + -LY 2.] In relation to, or in the way of, a beginning; at the outset, at first.

Initiate (ini·ʃi,eᵗt), *v.* 1603. [f. L. *initiat-*, *initiare* to begin.] **1.** *trans.* To begin, commence, enter upon; to introduce, set going, originate 1604. **b.** *intr.* To commence. ? *Obs.* 1618. **2.** *trans.* To admit with proper introductory rites or forms into some society or office, or to knowledge of or participation in some principles or observances, esp. of an occult character; hence, To instruct in the elements of any subject or practice. Const. *into*, *in* (†*to*). 1603. **3.** *intr.* **a.** To perform the first rite. POPE. **b.** To undergo initiation 1896.

1. They feared (for the present) to i. their attempt SPEED. 2. Our author in his old age..initiated himself in the sacred rites of Delphos DRYDEN. To i. young people in the elements of Physical Science HUXLEY. Hence **Ini·tiated** *ppl. a.* (often *absol.* in *pl.* sense; rarely as sb. sing.).

Initiate (ini·ʃi,ĕt), *ppl. a.* and *sb.* 1605. [ad. L. *initiatus*, *initiare*; ? also as short for *initiated.*]

A. *ppl. a.* Initiated. **1.** Admitted into some society, office, or position; instructed in some secret knowledge 1610. †**b.** *transf.* Pertaining to a novice. *Macb.* III. iv. 143. **2.** Begun, commenced, introduced 1767.

1. We..that are i. Divines BURTON. 2. As soon..as any child was born, the father began to have a permanent interest in the lands..and was called *tenant by the courtesy initiate* BLACKSTONE.

B. *sb.* A person who has been initiated; hence, a beginner 1811.

Initiation (iniʃi,ē·ʃən). 1583. [ad. L. *initiationem*; cf. F. *initiation.*] **1.** The action of initiating, or fact of being initiated; beginning, origination 1641. **2.** Formal introduction by preliminary instruction or initial ceremony into some office, society, etc., or to participation in some principles or observances; hence, Instruction in the elements of any subject or practice 1583.

1. The Church of Germanie had its i. or beginning in Martin Luther 1641. The i. of Parliamentary measures 1863. 2. A large school is a most valuable i. into actual life 1876.

Initiative (ini·ʃiĕtiv), *sb.* 1793. [a. F., f. as INITIATIVE *a.*] **1.** That which initiates, begins, or originates; the first step; hence, the act, or action, of taking the first step or lead; beginning, origination. **2.** The power, right, or function of initiating something. Hence *to possess* or *have the i.* 1793. **b.** *spec. Pol. Sci.* The right of a citizen or defined number of citizens, outside the Legislature, to initiate legislation, as in some of the Swiss cantons, and in Switzerland as a Federal Republic 1889.

1. Phr. *On one's own i.*, by one's own origination. *To take the i.* (F. *prendre l'initiative*): to make the first step, originate some action. 2. b. Both Referendum and I. are institutions which have grown up gradually in the Cantons, spreading from one to another 1889.

Initiative (ini·ʃiĕtiv), *a.* 1642. [f. L. *initiat-*, *initiare* + -IVE.] Characterized by initiating; having the function, power, or faculty of beginning or originating something; initiatory.

Initiator (ini·ʃi,eᵗtəɹ). 1676. [a. late L.] One who or that which initiates. So **Ini·tiatress, -atrix**, a female i.

Initiatory (ini·ʃiĕtəri), *a.* (*sb.*) 1612. [f. L *initiat-*, *initiare* + -ORY.] **1.** Such as pertains to the beginning or first steps; initial, introductory. **2.** Pertaining or tending to initiation; serving to initiate (see INITIATE *v.* 2) 1632. **3.** *sb.* An initiatory rite 1675.

1. The i. stage of legal proceedings STUBBS. 2. The i. Rite of water-baptism WARBURTON.

Inition (ini·ʃən). *rare.* 1463. [a. OF., ad. L. type **initionem*, f. *inire* to enter.] Entrance, beginning, initiation.

Inject (indʒe·kt), *v.* 1599. [f. L. *inject-*, *injicere*, f. *in-* (IN-²) + *jacĕre* to throw.] **1.** *trans.* To throw in. *Obs.* in general sense. –1646. **b.** *spec.* To drive or force (a fluid, etc.) into a passage or cavity; cf. INJECTION 1 b. 1601. **2.** *fig.* To throw in, as a thought or feeling into the mind, etc.; to suggest; to interject. Now *rare.* 1639. **3.** *transf.* To fill or charge (a cavity, etc., or an animal body) by injection. Const. *with.* 1731. †**4.** To throw *on* something –1725.

1. b. I..injected Barley Water up the Nose 1758. 2. Our Adversary injects..bad motions into our hearts FULLER. 3. To i. the bladder with warm water 1844. 4. Iniect the same on hot coales, and sitt therover 1599. Hence **Inje·cted** *ppl. a.*; *spec.* in *Path.* having the capillaries or small vessels distended with blood, bloodshot.

Injection (indʒe·kʃən). 1541. [ad. L. *injectionem*; cf. F. *injection.*] **1.** The action of injecting. *Obs.* in general sense. –1686. **b.** *spec.* The action of forcing a fluid, etc. into a passage or cavity, as by means of a syringe, pump, etc.; *esp.* the introduction in this way of a liquid or other substance into the vessels or cavities of the body, either for medicinal, or (in a dead body) preservative purposes 1541. **2.** *Path.* The fact of being charged with injected matter; injected or bloodshot condition 1806. **3.** *concr.* That which is injected; *spec.* a liquid or solution injected into an animal body, for medicinal or other purposes, as an enema, etc. 1607. **4.** *fig.* The throwing in of something from without, as of an idea into the mind, etc.; a suggestion, a hint. Now *rare.* 1622. **5.** *attrib.*, as *i. powder, syringe, theory*; *i.-cock, -condenser, -engine, -pipe, -valve, -water*, etc. (in relation to condensing steam-engines in which the steam is condensed by the injection of a jet of cold water) 1752.

4. Satans Injections are like Weeds that fall Into thy Garden, darted or'e the Wall QUARLES.

Injector (indʒe·ktəɹ). 1744. [f. L. *injicere.*] **1.** A contrivance for injecting; an apparatus for injecting water into the boiler of a steam-engine. **2.** A person who injects 1897.

Injelly (indʒe·li), *v. rare.* 1842. [IN-¹ or ².] To set or enclose in jelly.

Injoin: see ENJOIN.

†**Injoint**, *v.*¹ [IN-².] *intr.* To unite, join. *Oth.* I. iii. 35.

†**Injoi·nt**, *v.*² [IN-³.] *trans.* To unjoint, disjoint. HOLLAND.

Injucu·ndity. *rare.* 1623. [ad. L. *injucunditas*, f. *injucundus*; see IN-³ and -ITY.] Unpleasantness, disagreeableness.

Injudi·cial, *a. rare.* 1607. [IN-³.] Not judicial; †injudicious; not according to the forms of law; not becoming a judge. Hence **Injudi·cially** *adv.*

Injudicious (indʒudi·ʃəs), *a.* 1649. [IN-³.] Not judicious. †**1.** Wanting sound judgement; deficient in the power of judging aright –1694. **2.** Not manifesting practical judgement or discretion; showing want of judgement; unwise, ill-advised, ill-judged 1710.

1. The hearts of the in-judicious multitude 1654. 2. To vindicate a man..against an i. biographer 1792. Hence **Injudi·ciously** *adv.*, **-ness.**

Injunction (indʒʊ·ŋkʃən). 1480. [ad. late L. *injunctionem*; cf. F. *injonction.*] **1.** The action of enjoining or authoritatively directing; an authoritative or emphatic admonition or order. **2.** *Law.* A judicial process by which one who is threatening to invade or has invaded the legal or equitable rights of another is restrained from commencing or continuing such wrongful act, or is commanded to restore matters to the position in which they stood previously to his action 1533. †**3.** Conjunction, union. MILT.

1. The high I. not to taste that Fruit MILT. *P. L.* x. 13. Forgetful of his Mother's parting injunctions 1898. 2. He may with an I., out of the Chancery stop their proceedings FULLER.

Injure (i·ndʒŭɹ), *v.* 1583. [f. INJURY *sb.*; repl. INJURY *v.*] **1.** *trans.* To do injustice to; to wrong 1592. †**2.** To do outrage to in speech; to insult, revile, calumniate –1659. **3.** To do hurt or harm to; to damage; to impair 1586. Also *intr.* for *refl.* 1848.

1. When haue I iniur'd thee? when done thee wrong? SHAKS. 3. He had..injured himself in crossing the Gemmi TYNDALL. Hence **I·njurer.**

Injurious (indʒūə·riəs), *a.* 1480. [a. F. *injurieux*, ad. L. *injuriosus*, f. *injuria.*] **1.** Wrongful; hurtful to the rights of another; wilfully inflicting injury or wrong 1494. **2.** Wilfully hurtful or offensive in language; insulting; calumnious. (Now only of words or speech.) 1480. **3.** Tending to hurt or damage; harmful, detrimental, deleterious 1559.

1. A wronged servant shall have right..from his i. master 1634. 2. Call me their Traitor, thou iniurious Tribune SHAKS. 3. It would be i. to the public trade of England 1817. Hence **Inju·riously** *adv.*, **-ness.**

Injury (i·ndʒŭri), *sb.* ME. [ad. L. *injuria*, sb. use of fem. of *injurius* unjust, wrongful, f. *in-* (IN-³) + *jus, jur-* right.] **1.** Wrongful action or treatment; violation or infringement of another's rights; suffering or mischief wilfully or unjustly inflicted. Also, A wrongful act; a wrong inflicted or suffered. †**2.** Intentionally hurtful or offensive speech or words; insult, calumny; a taunt, an affront –1710. **3.** Hurt or loss caused to or sustained by a person or thing; harm, detriment, damage; an instance of this ME.

1. By [wholesome laws]..we are bridled..from doing of iniuries 1611. I., as distinct from harm, may raise sudden anger BUTLER. 2. He began to raile upon them with a thousand injuries FLORIO. 3. Having sustained a heavy blow without i. SCOTT.

†**I·njury**, *v.* 1484. [a. F. *injurier*, ad. late L. *injuriare*, f. *injuria.* Repl. *c* 1600 by INJURE.] = INJURE –1651.

†**Inju·st**, *a.* ME. [a. F. *injuste.*] = UNJUST –1711. Hence †**Inju·stly** *adv.*

Injustice (indʒʊ·stis). ME. [a. F., ad. L. *injustitia*, f. *injustus* UNJUST.] The opposite of justice; unjust action; wrong; unfairness. Also, An unjust act.

The many iniustices of yoʳ last edict 1601. All briberie and iniustice shall be blotted out *Ecclus.* xl. 12.

†**Inju·stifiable**, *a. rare.* 1646. [IN-³.] Unjustifiable –1714.

Ink (iŋk), *sb.*¹ [ME. *enke*, a. OF. *enque* (mod. *encre*) :—late L. *encaustum*, a. Gr. ἔγκαυστον the purple ink used by the Greek and Roman emperors for their signatures, f. ἐγκαίειν to burn in (see ENCAUSTIC).] The coloured (usually black) fluid ordinarily employed in writing with a pen on paper, parchment, etc. (*writing ink*), or the viscous paste used in printing (*printing* or *printer's ink*). Also *fig.* and *transf.*

The word *ink* without qualification commonly means black writing ink. Inks are distinguished by their colour, as *black, red, blue, gold ink*, etc.; by the purpose which they serve, as *copying, lithographic, marking, printing* (or *printer's*), *writing ink*; by some special quality, as *indelible, invisible, sympathetic ink*; by the place of manufacture, as *China, Indian ink*, q.v.

Deformed monsters, fowle, and blacke as inke SPENSER. Battles..fought only by i. CARLYLE.

b. The black inky liquid secreted by the cuttle-fish and allied cephalopods, and stored in a sac or bladder 1586.

Comb. 1. General: as *i.-drop, -maker, -stained*, etc.; *i.-bottle, -case, -reservoir*, etc.

2. Special: **i.-bag**, the bladder-shaped sac in the cuttle-fish, etc. containing the 'ink'; **-ball**, (*a*) = BALL *sb.*¹ 12; (*b*) a kind of oak-gall used in making i.; **-eraser**; **-fish**, a cuttle-fish or squid; **-gland** = *ink-bag*; **-nut** = MYROBALAN; **-pad**; **-pencil**; **-plant**, the European shrub *Coriaria myrtifolia*, or N. Zealand species *C. thymifolia*; **-powder**, the powdered ingredients of i.; **-sac** = *ink-bag*; **-spot**, (*a*) a stain of i.; (*b*) a dark spot on the skin; **-well**, an ink-cup adapted to occupy a hole in a desk; **-writer**, a telegraph instrument which records messages in i.

Ink, *sb.*² 1572. [?] †**1.** *orig.* A mill-rind. Used as a charge in *Her.* **2.** Now, 'The socket which holds the toe of a vertical shaft or spindle' (Knight) 1875.

Ink (iŋk), *v.* 1562. [f. INK *sb.*¹] *trans.* To mark, stain, or smear with or as with ink. **b.** To cover types with ink 1727.

I·nk-be:rry. 1716. A name given, from their colour or juice, to various shrubs, and their berries; *esp.* **a.** A small shrub of the holly family (*Prinos glaber* or *Ilex glabra*), a native of the Atlantic coast of N. America. **b.** The W. Indian indigo-berry (*Randia aculeata*).

Inker (i·ŋkəɹ). 1882. [f. INK *v.* + -ER¹.] One who or that which inks. **1.** A telegraph-instrument which records the message in ink. **2.** *Printing.* An inking-roller 1884.

I·nk-horn. ME. [f. INK *sb.*¹ + HORN *sb.*] **1.** A small portable vessel (orig. made of a horn) for holding writing-ink; now seldom used. **2.** *attrib.* **a.** †**ink-horn mate, varlet**, a mere scribbler. SHAKS. **b. ink-horn term**, a learned or bookish word (*arch.*) 1543.

1. The man that..hadde an enk-horn in his rigge WYCLIF *Ezek.* ix. 11. 2. b. Soche are your Ynkehorne termes BALE. Hence †**I·nkhornism** (*rare*), an ink-horn term.

Inking (i·ŋkiŋ), *vbl. sb.* 1818. [-ING¹.] The action of INK *v.*; *spec.* the covering of type with ink. **b.** *attrib.*, chiefly in terms relating to printing or to inking the type, as *i.-roller*, etc. 1790.

Inkle (i·ŋk'l), *sb.* Now *rare.* 1532. [? Not conn. w. *lingle.*] A kind of linen tape, or the thread or yarn from which it is made.

Inkle (i·ŋk'l), *v. rare.* ME. [Cf. INKLING.] **1.** *trans.* To utter in an undertone, to hint. (In later use a back-formation from INKLING 2.) **2.** *dial.* To get an inkling of 1866.

2. She inkled what it was BLACKMORE.

Inkling (i·ŋkliŋ), *vbl. sb.* ME. [f. INKLE *v.* + -ING¹.] **1.** Mentioning in an undertone; a faint or slight report or rumour. *Obs.* exc. *dial.* **2.** A hint, a slight intimation 1531. **3.** A hint received; hence, a vague notion; a suspicion 1546. **4.** *dial.* An inclination 1787.

1. There was an ynkling, that it wold not be long er you came 1576. 2. Geuyng an incklyng of his secound cummyng UDALL. 3. If he gets but an i.,..our project is marr'd FOOTE.

In-kneed (in,nī·d, i·n,nīd), *a.* 1724. [f. IN *adv.* + KNEE *sb.* + -ED².] Having the legs bent inwards at the knees.

†**In,knit**, *v.* [f. IN-¹ + KNIT *v.*] *trans.* To knit up, draw close together. CHAUCER.

Inknot (in,nǫ·t), *v. rare.* 1611. [f. IN-¹ + KNOT *v.*] To include in or with a knot; to tie in; also, = INNODATE *v.*

Inkpot (i·ŋk,pǫt). 1553. [INK *sb.*¹] **1.** A small pot for holding writing-ink. **2.** *attrib.* **inkpot term** = ink-horn term (see INK-HORN 2 b) 1553.

Inkshed (i·ŋk,ʃed). *joc.* 1672. [f. INK *sb.*¹ + *-shed*, after BLOODSHED.] The shedding or spilling of ink; consumption or waste of ink in writing.

With no bloodshed..but with immense beershed and i. CARLYLE.

Inkstand (i·ŋk,stænd). 1675. A stand for holding one or more ink-bottles or ink-glasses (often with a tray, etc.); occas. applied to an inkpot. So †**I·nk-sta:ndish.**

I·nkster. [f. INK *v.* or *sb.*¹ + -STER.] A scribbler. READE.

Inky (i·ŋki), *a.* 1581. [f. INK *sb.*¹ + -Y.] **1.** Of or pertaining to, written with, using ink; literary. **2.** As black as ink; very black or dark 1593. **3.** Stained with ink, inked 1683.

1. England..is now bound in with shame, With I. blottes, and rotten Parchment bonds SHAKS. 2. A little i. tarn HAUGHTON. 3. I. fingers 1894.

Inlace, var. of ENLACE.

†**Inla·gary.** 1607. [ad. med.L. *inlagaria*, f. ME. *inlaȝe* INLAW; see -ARY¹.] The restitution of an outlaw to the benefit and protection of the law. So †**Inlaga·tion**, in same sense.

Inlaid (i·nlēɪd, inlēɪ·d), pa. pple. of INLAY *v.*

Inland (i·nlănd, i·nlænd). OE. [f. IN *adv.* + LAND *sb.*]

A. *sb.* **1.** The inner part of an estate, feudal manor, or farm; in OE. and feudal tenure, the land around the house occupied or cultivated by the owner, not held by any tenant (cf. DEMESNE II. 1.). **2.** *sing.* and *pl.* The inland country, the interior. †Formerly, also, the inlying districts near the capital and centres of population. 1573.

B. *adj.* (attrib. use of sb.) **1.** Of or pertaining to the interior part of a country or region; remote from the sea or border 1456. **2.** Carried on or operating within the limits of a country. Opp. to *foreign.* 1546.

1. *I. sea*, a large body of salt water, entirely or nearly severed from the ocean; applied also to large

lakes. The improvement of our i. navigation 1792. 2. The i. trade of England 1745. Phr. *I. bill of exchange. I. duty*, a duty on i. trade, etc., as the excise and stamp duties. *I. revenue*, the part of the national revenue consisting of taxes and i. duties.

C. *adv.* In or towards the interior or heart of a country, as opp. to the coast or border, or to wild outlying districts 1600.

Yet am I in-land bred, And know some nourture SHAKS.

Inlander (i·nlăndəɹ). 1610. [f. as prec. + -ER[1].] One who dwells in the interior of a country.

Inlandish (inlæ·ndiʃ), *a.* 1657. [f. as prec. + -ISH.[1]] †1. Home, domestic, native; opp. to *outlandish*. REEVE. 2. Of an inland nature or character 1849.

†Inla·pidate, *v.* [f. IN-[2] + L. *lapidem* + -ATE[3].] *trans.* To convert into stone, to petrify. BACON.

Inlard, var. of ENLARD *v.*

Inlaw (i·nlǭ), *sb.* [ME. *inlaȝe*, f. IN-[1] + *laȝe* LAW, after *utlaȝe* outlaw.] One who is within the domain and protection of the law; opp. to *outlaw*. Now *Hist.*

Inlaw (inlǭ·), *v.* [OE. *inlagian*, f. IN-[1] + *lagu* LAW; cf. *útlagian* to outlaw.] *trans.* To bring within the authority and protection of the law, to reverse the outlawry of (a person).

-in-law. [f. IN *prep.* + LAW *sb*] A phrase appended to names of relationship, as *father, mother, son*, etc., to indicate that the relationship is not by nature, but in the eye of the Canon Law, with reference to the degrees of affinity within which marriage is prohibited. These forms can be traced back to the 14th c. Formerly *-in-law* was also used in the sense of *step-*. Hence **In-law**, a relation by marriage 1894.

I·nlawry. [f. INLAW *v.* + -RY; cf. INLAGARY.] = INLAGARY. Lytton.

Inlay (i·nlēⁱ, inlēⁱ·), *sb.* 1656. [f. next.] 1. The process or art of inlaying (*rare*). 2. Material inlaid or prepared for inlaying; inlaid work 1697. Also *fig.* †3. The layering of plants. SIR T. BROWNE.

2. With rich i. the various floor was graced POPE. *fig.* The Violet, Crocus, and Hyacinth with rich i. Broiderd the ground MILT. *P. L.* IV. 701.

Inlay (inlēⁱ·), *v.* 1596. [f. IN-[1] + LAY *v.*] †1. *trans.* To lay in, or as in, a place of concealment or preservation. DONNE. 2. To lay or embed (a thing) in the substance of something else so that its surface becomes continuous with that of the matrix 1598. b. To insert a page of a book, a plate, or a cut, in a space cut in a larger and stouter page, for its preservation, or to enlarge the margin, and thus the whole size 1810. 3. To furnish or fit *with* a substance of a different kind embedded in its surface; to diversify or ornament (a thing) by such insertion of another material disposed decoratively 1596. Also *fig.* b. *transf.* Said of the material embedded 1784.

2. The moorstone courses, inlaid into the frame of the building SMEATON. 3. Looke how the floore of heauen Is thicke inlayed with pattens of bright gold SHAKS. *fig.* But these things are..thence borrow'd by the Monks to i. thir story MILT. b. The stream, That, as with molten glass, inlays the vale COWPER.

Inlayer (i·nlēⁱ:əɹ). 1660. [f. INLAY *v.* + -ER[1].] One who inlays (see the vb.).

Inleague, obs. var. of ENLEAGUE *v.*

†Inlea·guer, *v.* [f. IN-[1] + LEAGUER *sb.*[1], camp.] *intr.* To encamp with a besieging or beleaguering force. HOLLAND.

Inlet (i·nlet), *sb.* ME. [f. IN *adv.* + LET *v.*[1]] 1. Letting in, admission. Now *rare.* 2. A way of admission; an entrance 1624. 3. A narrow opening by which the water penetrates into the land; a small arm of the sea; an indentation in the sea-coast or the bank of a lake or river; a creek 1570. 4. A piece let in or inserted 1798. 5. *attrib.*, as *i. area, valve*, etc. 1882.

2. These In-lets of Men and of Light [i. e. doors and windows] WOTTON. *fig.* An increase of our possessions is but an i. to new disquietudes GOLDSM.

Inlet (in,le·t), *v.* ME. [f. IN-[1] + LET *v.*[1] Orig. two wds. = *let in.*] To let in. †1. *trans.* To allow to enter -1661. 2. To let in or insert (one thing) in another 1860. So **†I·nle:tter** (*rare*), one who gives admittance.

Inlighten, -list, etc.: see ENLIGHTEN, etc.

In loco: see IN *Lat. prep.*

Inlook (i·nluk). 1869. [f. IN *adv.* + LOOK *sb.*, after OUTLOOK.] Looking within, introspection.

†I·nly, *a.* [OE. *in(n)lic*, f. *inn*, IN *adv.* + *lic*, -LY[1]. App. re-coined from next in 15th c.] Inward, interior; inwardly felt -1612.

Didst thou but know the i. touch of Loue SHAKS.

Inly (i·nli), *adv.* [OE. *in(n)lice*, f. *in(n)lic*; see prec. and -LY[2].] a. Inwardly; in the heart, spirit, or inner nature; in regard to the inner life. b. In a way that goes to the heart; heartily; thoroughly, extremely.

Friends year by year more i. known EMERSON.

I·nlying, *vbl. sb.* 1734. = LYING-IN. So **I·nlying** *ppl. a.*, lying inside 1844; lying in 1864.

Inmate (i·nmēⁱt), *sb.* (*a.*) 1589. [f. IN *adv.* (or perh. orig. INN *sb.* 1) + MATE *sb.*] 1. One who dwells with others in the same house (now *rare*). In early use, A lodger or subtenant. b. Sometimes, A foreigner, stranger. Often *fig.* 1600. 2. In relation to the house: An occupant along with others; hence, *occas.*, = Indweller, inhabitant, occupier. Const. *of.* (*lit.* and *fig.*) 1597. 3. *attrib.* or *adj.* That is an inmate (*lit.* and *fig.*); dwelling in the same house with, or in the house of, another; indwelling. ? *Obs.* 1630.

1. Taking an i. in to his hous 1601. b. He is but a new fellow, An in-mate here in Rome B. JONS. 2. So spake the Enemie of Mankind, enclos'd In Serpent, I. bad MILT. *P. L.* IX. 495. An i. of a lunatic asylum MEDWIN. 3. I. guests MILT. Hence **I·nmatecy** [irreg.: see -CY], the position of an i. 1806.

Inmeat (i·nmīt); usu. in pl. **inmeats.** Now *rare* exc. *dial.* 1616. [f. IN *adv.* + MEAT *sb.*] Those internal viscera of an animal which are used for food; hence *gen.* Entrails, inwards.

In medias res, In memoriam: see IN *Lat. prep.*

Inme·sh, var. of ENMESH *v.*

†Inmew·, *v.* [? f. IN-[1] + MEW *v.*] *trans.* ? To mew or coop up. BEAUM. & FL.

†In mid, *prep.* ME. only. [Analytical var. of ME. *on midde, amidde*, AMID.] Amid, in the middle or centre of.

Inmost (i·nmoust, -mǒst), *a.* (*sb.*, *adv.*) [OE. *innemest* (f. *innem-a, -e + -est), double superl. of *inne* IN *adv.*; see -MOST.] 1. *lit.* Situated farthest within, most inward, most remote from the outside. Also *fig.* 2. *absol.* or *sb.* That which is inmost; the inmost part (*lit.* and *fig.*). Rarely in *pl.* OE. 3. *adv.* Most inwardly (*rare*) OE.

1. Into thir i. bower Handed they went MILT. *P. L.* IV. 738. *fig.* In the inmoste affeccion of their hertes UDALL. 2. Lodge it in the i. of thy bosom FORD. 3. Thro' all their i.-winding caves POPE. So **†I·nmore** *a.* inner. HOLLAND.

Inn (in), *sb.* [OE. *inn* neut. :—OTeut. **innom*; agreeing, exc. in stem suffix, with ON. *inne, inni* (:—OTeut. **innjom*), f. *inn, inne* IN *adv.*] †1. A dwelling-place, habitation, lodging; a house (in relation to its inhabitant). †2. 'Dwelling-place', 'abode', 'place of sojourn', in fig. uses -1615. 3. A public house for the lodging and entertainment of travellers, wayfarers, etc.; a hostelry or hotel; occas., *erron.*, a tavern which does not provide lodging ME. b. *fig. esp.* A temporary lodging as opp. to a permanent abode 1529. 4. A lodging-house or house of residence for students (cf. HOSTEL *sb.*); now *Obs.*, exc. as in b and c. †a. At the Universities. 1346. (Preserved till 19th c. in *New Inn Hall*, Oxford.) b. *Inns of Chancery*: certain sets of buildings in London, orig. places of residence and study for students and apprentices of law; also the societies by which they were occupied 1458. c. *Inns of Court*: the four sets of buildings in London (the Inner Temple, the Middle Temple, Lincoln's Inn, and Gray's Inn) belonging to the four legal societies which have the exclusive right of admitting persons to practise at the bar; hence, these four societies themselves. (Formerly also colloq. *inns a court.*) 1396. d. *Serjeants' Inn*: a collegiate building of the now extinct order of Serjeants-at-Law, esp. that in Chancery Lane, sold in 1877. 1646. 5. *attrib.* as **†i.-house** = sense 3; etc. 1694.

1. To let the world wag, and take mine ease in mine in HEYWOOD. Phr. **†***To take (up) one's i.* (or *inns*): to take up one's residence, quarters -1647; With me ye may take up your In For this same night SPENSER. 2. My people shal dwel in the ynnes of peace COVERDALE *Isa.* xxxii. 18. 3. He still has found The warmest welcome at an i. SHENSTONE. b. To that dark i., the grave SCOTT.

Inn (in), *v.* Now *rare.* [f. INN *sb.* (In OE. and ME. inseparable in form from IN *v.*, q.v.)] 1. *trans.* To lodge, house. Often *refl.* 2. *intr.* (? for *refl.*) To lodge, sojourn; now, to put up (at an inn or hostel) ME. b. Of a coach: To stop or put up (at an inn) 1748. c. *fig.* and *transf.* 1591.

1. Whan he had broght hem in to his Citee And Inned hem euerich in his degree CHAUCER. 2. b. You had better send for them where the machine inns H. WALPOLE.

Inn, obs. f. IN *prep.*, *adv.*, and *v.*

Innascibility (inæsibi·lĭti, inn-). 1602. [ad. late L. *innascibilitas.*] The attribute of being independent of birth: said of God the Father.

Innate (i·nnēⁱt, innēⁱ·t, inēⁱ·t), *a.* ME. [ad. late L. *innatus* (Tertullian), f. *in-* (IN-[2]) + *natus*, *nasci* to be born.] 1. Existing in a person (or organism) from birth; belonging to the original or essential constitution (of body or mind); inborn, native, natural. a. Of qualities, principles, etc. (esp. mental); opp. to *acquired*, esp. in *innate ideas*. b. Of a vegetable formation: Originating within the matrix or substance of the plant. Of a mineral: Originating within the matrix; native. 1887. 2. *transf.* Inherent. ? *Obs.* 1600. 3. *Bot.* Said of a part or organ borne on the apex of another; as, an *i. anther* 1830.

1. a. It is an establish'd Opinion amongst some Men, That there are in the Understanding certain I. Principles..which the Soul receives in its very first Being, and brings into the World with it LOCKE. It has been disputed whether there be any i. ideas, or whether all ideas be derived from sensation and reflexion HUME. var. **†Inna·ted** *a.* Hence **Inna·te·ly** *adv.*, **-ness.** **Inna·tive** *a.* (now *rare* or *Obs.*), innate, native 1513.

†Innate, *v. rare.* 1602. [f. prec.] *trans.* a. To make innate; to produce within something. b. (In Fuller) To imbue or endow by nature (*with* something); usu. in *pass.*

Innato-, comb. f. L. *innatus* INNATE *a.*, forming adjs. in which it adverbially qualifies the second element, as **inna:to-se·ssile**, innately sessile; etc.

Innavigable (inæ·vigăb'l, inn-), *a.* 1527. [ad. L. *innavigabilis*; see IN-[3] and NAVIGABLE.] Not navigable; that cannot be navigated.

There is no..Sea innauigable 1527. When a Ship ..is rendered i. [etc.] MAGENS. Hence **Inna·vigabi·lity, Inna·vigableness. Inna·vigably** *adv.*

†I·nne, *adv.* and *prep.* OE. [f. OE. *in* IN.] A. *adv.* 1. Of position: In, within, inside, indoors -1470. 2. Of motion: In (to a place). Not in OE. -1486.

B. *prep.* 1. Of position: In, within. Not in OE. -1450. 2. Of motion: Into. ME. only.

Inner (i·nəɹ), *a.* (*sb.*) [OE. *inne(r)r-a*, *in(n)r-a, -e* adj. (compar. of *inne, inn*, IN *adv.*). Only used attrib., and not followed by *than.*] 1. Situated more within; more or further inward; interior. Often with a positive force, antithetical, not to *in*, but to *outer*: Situated within; inward; internal. Also *fig.* and *transf.* b. *Mus.* Applied to parts or voices intermediate between the highest and lowest of the harmony (also called *middle*). 2. Mental or spiritual OE. 3. *sb.* That division of a target next outside the bull's-eye, or, in some targets, the division immediately outside the centre; also, *ellipt.* a shot which strikes this 1887.

1. Into an I. chamber ME. An inner tube of india-rubber..separate from the outer cover 1902. 2. The sense By which thy i. nature was apprised Of outward shows SHELLEY. Phr. *The i. man*, the i. part of man; the soul or mind; *joc.* the stomach or inside, esp. in reference to food. *I. Temple*: see TEMPLE *sb.*[1]

I·nnerly, *adv. Obs.* or *rare.* ME. [f. INNER *a.* + -LY[2].] †More within; inwardly, internally.

Innermost (i·nəɹmǒust, -mǒst). ME. [f. INNER *a.* + -MOST.] A. *adj.* Inmost. B. *sb.* The inmost part 1674. Hence **I·nnermostly** *adv.* MRS. BROWNING.

Innerness (i·nəɹnės). 1880. [f. INNER *a.* + -NESS.] Inwardness.

Innervate (inə̄·ɹveit, inn-), *v.* 1870. [f. IN-² + L. *nervus* + -ATE³; cf. *enervate.*] *Physiol.* To supply (some organ or part) with nerve-force, or with nerves.

The ganglionic mass, whence the jaws and foot-jaws are innervated ROLLESTON.

Innervation (inəɹvēⁱ·ʃən). 1832. [f. as prec. + -ATION.] The action or process of innervating; the fact of being innervated; supply of nerve-force from a nerve-centre to some organ or part by means of nerves; stimulation of some organ by its nerves.

Innerve (inə̄·ɹv, inn-), *v.* 1828. [f. IN-² + NERVE *sb.* or *v.*] = INNERVATE; also *fig.* to animate.

Inness (i·n,nės). *rare.* 1866. [f. IN *adv.* or *a.* + -NESS.] **a.** The quality of being *in* (something). **b.** Inner quality or state.

Innholder (i·nhōᵘ:ldəɹ). Now *rare.* 1464. [f. INN *sb.* + HOLDER¹]. = INNKEEPER.

Inning (i·niŋ), *vbl. sb.* [OE. *innung*; f. IN *v.*, or INN *v.* + -ING¹.]

I. From IN *v.* †1. A putting or getting in; what is put or got in; contents; income. OE. only. 2. The action of taking in, inclosing, etc.; *esp.* the reclaiming of marsh or flooded land 1530. **b.** *pl.* Lands taken in or reclaimed 1706. 3. The action of getting in; ingathering, harvesting 1522. 4. In *Cricket, Base-ball*, etc. (in Great Britain always in *pl.* form **innings**, whether in sing. or pl. sense): That portion of the game played by either side while 'in' or at the bat. In *Cricket* also used of the play of, or score of runs made by, any one batsman during his turn 1746. **b.** *transf.* (in Great Britain always in *pl.*) The time during which a person, party, principle, etc. is in power; a turn 1855.

4. **b.** The new ideas of 'peace, retrenchment and reform' got their innings W. R. GREG.

II. The action of INN *v.*; lodging, housing; *concr.* a lodging, house OE.

Innkeeper (i·n,kīːpəɹ). 1548. [f. INN *sb.* 3 + KEEPER.] One who keeps an inn or public house; an innholder, taverner. Hence **I·nnkee·ping** *sb.* the keeping of an inn (also *attrib.*); *adj.* that keeps an inn.

Innocence (i·nŏsĕns). ME. [a. F., ad. L. *innocentia*; see next and -ENCE.] 1. Freedom from sin, guilt, or moral wrong in general; moral purity. 2. The fact of not being guilty of that with which one is charged; guiltlessness 1559. 3. Freedom from cunning or artifice; guilelessness, simplicity; hence, ignorance, silliness ME. 4. Of things: Innocuousness 1828. 5. *concr.* An innocent person or thing ME. 6. *U.S.* A popular name of *Houstonia cærulea*, which has small blue flowers 1845.

1. How came our first Parents to sin, and to lose their Primitive I.? SOUTH. 2. Where the guilt is doubtful, a presumption of it should in general be admitted *Junius Lett.* 3. The servants, who had traded on my i. 1883. 5. Well said, I.! SHERIDAN.

Innocency (i·nŏsĕnsi). Now *rare* or *arch.* ME. [ad. L. *innocentia*, f. *innocentem*; see next and -ENCY.] = prec.

Innocent (i·nŏsĕnt). ME. [a. F. *innocent*, OF. pl. *-enz, -ens*, ad. L. *innocentem*, f. *in-* (IN-³) + *nocentem, nocere* to hurt.]

A. *adj.* 1. Doing no evil; free from moral wrong, sin, or guilt; pure, unpolluted. Now always implying 'unacquainted with evil'; but formerly sometimes (*e.g.* of God or Christ), Sinless, holy. Also *transf.* and *fig.* 2. Free from specific wrong or guilt; not deserving of the suffering inflicted; not guilty, guiltless, unoffending ME. **b.** *colloq.* with *of*: Free from; devoid of 1706. 3. Simple, guileless, unsuspecting; hence, naïve, ingenuous ME. **b.** Silly, half-witted. Now *dial.* 1548. 4. Of actions, etc.: Free from guilt or moral evil (Often blending with 5.) 1514. 5. Of things: Doing no harm; not injurious; harmless, innocuous. (In *Path.* opp. to *malignant.*) 1662. **b.** Lawful 1828.

1. When we say that God made man i., What do we mean? MAURICE. *fig.* She woos the gentle air To hide her guilty front with i. snow MILT. 2. *I. blood*, the blood (or life) of the i.; I haue sinned, in that I haue betraied the i. blood *Matt.* xxvii. 4. The Peasant, i. of all these Ills DRYDEN. **b.** The Sermon..was quite i. of meaning WESLEY. 3. For all she looks so i. as it were, take my Word for it she is no Fool STEELE. 4. I think no pleasure i., that is to man hurtful FRANKLIN. 5. His Powder upon Examination being found very i. BUDGELL.

B. *sb.* 1. **a.** An innocent person; one not disposed to do harm, or unacquainted with evil ME. †**b.** A guiltless person –1748. 2. *esp.* A young child; *spec.* in *pl.* (with capital), the young children slain by Herod after the birth of Jesus (Matt. ii. 16), reckoned from early times as Christian martyrs (also called *the Holy Innocents*) ME. 3. A guileless, simple, or unsuspecting person; hence **b.** A simpleton; a half-wit, an idiot ME.

1. Thou hast kill'd the sweetest i., That ere did lift vp eye *Oth.* v. ii. 199. 2. (*Holy*) *Innocents' Day*, the 28th of December, observed as a church festival in commemoration of the slaughter of the Innocents. (Formerly called CHILDERMAS.) 3. In Scotland..a natural fool [was called] an i. SCOTT.

Hence **I·nnocently** *adv.* in an i. manner ME.

Innocuity (inokiū·iti). 1855. [f. L. *innocuus* + -ITY; cf. F. *innocuité.*] The quality of being innocuous.

Innocuous (inǫ·kiu,əs), *a.* 1598. [f. L. *innocuus* (f. *in-* (IN-³) + *nocuus* (rare), f. root of *nocere* to hurt) + -OUS.] Not hurtful or injurious; harmless. In *Zool.* applied *spec.* to the non-venomous snakes (constituting the order *Innocua*).

But over Diomedes' left shoulder passed The point i. COWPER. Hence **Inno·cuous-ly** *adv.*, **-ness.**

†**I·nnodate**, *v.* 1635. [f. L. *innodat-*, *innodare*, f. *in-* (IN-²) + *nodare* to knot, f. *nodus* NODE.] *trans.* To fasten in or with a knot; *spec.* to include or involve in an anathema or interdict –1655. Hence †**Innoda·tion.**

Inno·minable, *a. arch.* ME. [ad. L. *innominabilis*; see IN-³ and NOMINABLE.] Incapable of being or unfit to be named.

Innominate (in(n)ǫ·minĕt), *a.* 1638. [ad. late L. *innominatus* (Boeth.), f. *in-* (IN-³) + *nominatus.*] 1. Not named, unnamed, anonymous. 2. *Rom. Law.* Of a contract: Unclassified 1774. 3. Anat. *I. bone* (*os innominatum*), the hip-bone, a union of three original bones, ilium, ischium, and pubis. *I. artery* (*arteria innominata*), a large artery given off from the arch of the aorta, just before the left carotid artery. *I. vein* (*vena innominata*), each of the two veins formed by the junction of the subclavian and the internal jugular veins behind the inner ends of the clavicle. 1866. **b.** *absol.* as *sb.* (also in L. form *innominatum*, *-ata*): = *i. bone, artery*, or *vein.* 1879.

Innovate (i·nŏveit), *v.* 1548. [f. L. *innovat-*, *innovare*, f. *in-* (IN-²) + *novare* to make new, f. *novus.*] †1. *trans.* To change into something new; to alter; to renew –1818. †2. To bring in (something new); to introduce as new –1738. 3. *intr.* To bring in or introduce novelties; to make changes *in* something established; to introduce innovations. Occas. const. *on* or *upon.* 1597.

1. Attempts to i. the constitutional or habitual character JOHNSON. 2. Some words which I have innovated..upon his Latin DRYDEN. 3. To i. is not to reform BURKE. So †**Innovate** *a.* newly introduced 1600. Hence **I·nnovative** *a.* having the character of innovating; †revolutionary. **I·nnovator**, one who innovates; †a revolutionist 1598; **I·nnovatory** *a.* 1853.

Innovation (inŏvēⁱ·ʃən). 1548. [ad. L. *innovationem*; see prec.] 1. The action of innovating; the introduction of novelties; the alteration of what is established. †Formerly const. *of.* 1553. †**b.** Revolution (= L. *novæ res*) –1633. 2. A change made by innovating; something newly introduced; a novel practice, method, etc. 1548. †**b.** A rebellion or insurrection –1726. 3. *Bot.* The formation of a new shoot at the apex of a stem or branch; *esp.* that which takes place at the apex of the thallus of mosses; also (with *pl.*) a new shoot thus formed 1835.

1. The innouation of new honors SELDEN. 2. The tribute you demand from the Hindûs..is an i. and an infringement of the laws of Hindustân 1800. Hence **Innova·tional** *a.* of, pertaining to, or characterized by i. 1817. **Innova·tionist**, one who favours innovations.

Innoxious (in(n)ǫ·kʃəs), *a.* 1623. [ad. L. *innoxius*; see IN-³, NOXIOUS, and -OUS.] 1. Not noxious; harmless, innocuous 1638. †2. Innocent, blameless.

1. Even lions, when surfeited, are i. 1831. 2. The good man walk'd i. thro' his age POPE. Hence **Inno·xious-ly** *adv.*, **-ness.**

†**Innu·bilous**, *a. rare.* 1656. [f. L. *innubilus* + -OUS.] Cloudless –1708.

Innuendo (iniu,e·ndo). Also *erron.* **inuendo.** *Pl.* -does (†-do's, †-dos). 1564. [L., = 'by nodding at, pointing to, intimating'.] 1. The med.L. formula used to introduce a parenthetical explanation; = meaning, to wit, that is to say. 2. Hence, as sb. The parenthetical explanation itself; *esp.* the injurious meaning alleged to be conveyed by words not *per se* injurious or actionable, which, in an action for libel or slander, is usually introduced into the record and issue by the words 'meaning thereby', after the expressions alleged to have been used 1701. **b.** The words or expressions thus explained or needing explanation; a blank to be filled up with the name of the person to whom it is alleged to refer 1755. 3. An oblique hint or suggestion; an insinuation, esp. one of a depreciatory kind 1678.

2. No *I.* can make such Words actionable SCROGGS. **b.** An indictment for a libel, with all the *inuendos* filled up 1802. 3. [He] sought by nods and winks and inuendoes to intimate his authorship W. IRVING.

Innue·ndo, *v.* 1705. [f. prec. sb.] 1. *intr.* To utter or make innuendoes. 2. *Law.* To interpret or construe by attaching an innuendo 1851.

Innumerable (in(n)iū·mĕrăb'l), *a.* ME. [ad. L. *innumerabilis*; see IN-³ and NUMERABLE.] Incapable of being numbered or reckoned; not to be counted for multitude, numberless. Often with exaggerative force. **a.** With sing. sb.; now only with *host, multitude*, etc. **b.** Now usu. with pl. sb. 1450.

a. An i. company of Angels *Heb.* xii. 22. An i. flight Of harmefull fowles SPENSER. **b.** Cedars, with i. boughs MILT. Murmuring of i. bees TENNYSON. Hence **Innu·merabi·lity, Innu·merableness**, the quality of being i. **Innu·merably** *adv.*

Innumerous (in(n)iū·mĕrəs), *a. arch.* 1536. [ad. late L. *innumerosus*; see IN-³ and NUMEROUS.] 1. Without number; innumerable, countless. Now only *poet.* or *rhet.* 2. Void of metrical or rhythmical number (*rare*) 1886.

Innutrient (in(n)iū·triĕnt), *a.* 1822. [IN-³.] Not nourishing.

Innutrition (in(n)iutri·ʃən). 1796. [IN-³.] Lack of nutrition, failure of nourishment. *I. of the bones* = RICKETS.

Innutritious (in(n)iutri·ʃəs), *a.* 1796. [IN-³.] Not nutritious.

Ino- (əi·no), comb. f. Gr. ἴς, ἰνός muscle, fibre, nerve, strength, as in INOGEN, q. v.

†**Inobe·dience.** ME. [a. OF., or ad. late L. *inobedientia* (Augustine); see IN-³ and OBEDIENCE.] = DISOBEDIENCE –1684.

†**Inobe·dient**, *a.* ME. [a. OF., or ad. late L. *inobedientem* (Augustine); see IN-³ and OBEDIENT.] = DISOBEDIENT –1805. Hence **Inobe·diently** *adv.*

Inobno·xious, *a. rare.* 1659. [IN-³.] Not obnoxious; not exposed *to*; inoffensive.

Inobservable (inǫbzə̄·ɹvăb'l), *a.* Now *rare.* 1600. [ad. L. *inobservabilis*; see IN-³ and OBSERVABLE.] Incapable of being observed; not noticeable.

Inobservance (inǫbzə̄·ɹvăns). 1611. [a. F., ad. L. *inobservantia*; see next and -ANCE.] 1. Failure to observe or notice; inattention. 2. The not keeping of a law, custom, bond, promise, etc. 1626. So **Inobse·rvancy** (*rare*).

Inobservant (inǫbzə̄·ɹvănt), *a.* 1663. [ad. L. *inobservantem*; see IN-³ and OBSERVANT.] That does not observe or notice. Hence **Inobse·rvantness**, inobservance 1659.

Inobservation (inǫbzəɹvēⁱ·ʃən). *rare.* 1579. [IN-³.] †1. The non-observance *of* a law, promise, etc. –1653. 2. Want of observation or attention; inobservance 1727.

Inobtrusive (inǫbtrū·siv), *a. rare.* 1796. [IN-³.] Not obtrusive; modest, retiring. Hence **Inobtru·sive·ly** *adv.*, **-ness.**

Inoca·rpin. 1865. [f. mod. Bot.L. *Inocarpus* (f. INO- fibrous + Gr. καρπός fruit) + -IN.] *Chem.* A red colouring matter contained in the juice of *Inocarpus edulis*, a tree of Asia and the E. India islands.

Inoccupa·tion. 1786. [IN-³.] Want of occupation; unoccupied condition.

Inoculable (inǫ·kiŭlăb'l), *a.* 1847. [f. L. *inoculare* to INOCULATE; see -ABLE.] Of a person: Capable of being infected with a disease by inoculation. Of a disease: Capable of being communicated by inoculation. Of matter or virus: That may inoculate a person or transmit a disease. Hence **Ino·culabi·lity.**

Inocular (inǫ·kiŭlăɹ), *a.* 1826. [IN-².] *Entom.* Of an antenna: Inserted in a sinus in the inner margin of the compound eye, which thus partly surrounds its base.

Inoculate (inǫ·kiŭleᶦt), *v.* ME. [f. L. *inoculat-*, *inoculare* to engraft, implant, f. *in-* (IN-²) + *oculus* eye, bud.] **1.** *trans.* (*Hort.*) To set or insert (an eye, bud, or scion) in a plant for propagation; to subject (a plant) to the operation of budding; to propagate by inoculation; to bud (one plant) *into*, *on*, or *upon* (another). Also *absol.* Also *fig.* †**2.** *transf.* To join or unite by insertion –1668. **b.** *intr.* To become joined or united with continuity of substance –1720. **3.** *trans.* (*Path.*) To engraft or implant (a disease, or the germ or virus) upon a person by INOCULATION, q.v. 1722. **b.** To impregnate (a person or animal) with the virus or germs of a disease; *spec.* for the purpose of inducing a milder form of the disease and rendering the subject immune 1722. **c.** *absol.* or *intr.* To perform inoculation 1765. **d.** *fig.* (*trans.*) To imbue (a person) *with* 1824.

1. *fig.* The Pelhams..always inoculated private quarrels on affairs of state H. WALPOLE. **3. d.** My parents had tried in vain to i. me with wisdom W. IRVING. Hence **Ino·culative** *a.* characterized by or pertaining to inoculation. **Ino·culator.**

Inoculation (inǫkiŭlēᶦ·ʃən). late ME. [ad. L. *inoculationem*; see prec.] **1.** *Hort.* Grafting by budding; an instance of this. Also *transf.* **2.** *Path.* The introduction into the body, by puncture of the skin, or through a wound, of the virus or germs of an infectious disease. (Orig. applied, after 1700, to the intentional introduction of the virus of small-pox, but now also to the introduction (accidentally or otherwise) of the virus or germs of any bacterial disease into the body through a wound.) 1714. **b.** *fig.* The imbuing of a person *with* feelings, opinions, etc. 1824.

2. b. The popular pursuit of natural beauty, the i. of the crowd with it MOZLEY.

†**Ino·diate,** *v.* 1657. [f. L. type **inodiare* (f. *in-* (IN-²) + *odium*) + -ATE³.] *trans.* To render odious or hateful –1721.

†**Ino·dorate,** *a.* [IN-³.] Unscented. BACON.

Inodorous (inōᵘ·dŏrəs), *a.* 1666. [f. L. *inodorus* + -OUS.] Destitute of odour; without smell or scent. Hence **Ino·dorous·ly** *adv.*, **-ness.**

Inoffensive (inǫfe·nsiv), *a.* 1598. [IN-³.] **1.** Doing or causing no harm; harmless, unoffending. **2.** Not objectionable; not offending the senses; not a cause of offence 1622.

1. An i. man for life and conversation..nothing of viciousness could be charged upon him FULLER. Useful and i. animals 1790. **2.** An i. medicine 1744. Hence **Inoffe·nsive·ly** *adv.*, **-ness.**

Inofficial (inǫfi·ʃăl), *a. rare.* 1632. [IN-³.] Not official; unofficial.

Inofficious (inǫfi·ʃəs), *a.* 1603. [ad. L. *inofficiosus*, f. *in-* (IN-³) + *officiosus* obliging, officious; see -OUS.] †**1.** Not ready to do one's duty or office; not inclined to do good offices; disobliging –1706. **b.** *Law.* Not in accordance with moral duty 1663. **2.** Without office, function, or operation 1884.

1. Thow drown'st thy selfe in i. sleep 1603. **b.** *I. testament*, a will not in accordance with the testator's natural affection and moral duties WHARTON. **2.** Where the operative part and the recital are at variance, the recital must be treated as i. 1885. Hence **Inoffi·cious·ly** *adv.*, **-ness.**

Inogen (əi·nodʒen). 1889. [f. INO- + -GEN 1.] *Physiol.* Hermann's term for a hypothetical complex substance supposed to exist in muscular fibre and to be the energy-yielding substance of muscle. Hence **Inoge·nic** *a.* of or pertaining to i.

†**Inopera·tion.** 1620. [ad. late L. *inoperationem* (Hilary), f. *inoperare.*] A working within; inworking –1645.

Inoperative (inǫ·pĕrĕtiv), *a.* 1631. [IN-³.] Not operative; not working; in *Law*, without practical force, invalid.

The resolutions..not having been so ratified, were i. 1885. Hence **Ino·perativeness.**

Inope·rcular, *a. rare.* 1864. [IN-³.] *Conch.* = next.

Inoperculate (inopɔ̄·ɹkiŭlĕt), *a.* 1835. [IN-³.] Not having an operculum or lid; *spec.* in *Conch.*, of or belonging to the *Inoperculata*, a division of *Pulmonifera* containing those univalves, such as snails, whose shell has no operculum. So **Inope·rculated** *a.*

†**Ino·pinable,** *a.* ME. [ad. L. *inopinabilis*, f. *in-* (IN-³) + *opinabilis* opinable.] Not opinable; unthinkable, inconceivable; not to be thought of –1581.

This..is inopynable, incredible and a very paradox 1555.

Ino·pinate, *a.* 1598. [ad. L. *inopinatus*, f. *in-* (IN-³) + *opinatus*, *opinari* to think.] Not thought of; unlooked for; unexpected –1807.

Inopportune (inǫ·pǫ̈ɹtiū·n), *a.* 1533. [ad. late L. *inopportunus* unfitting; see IN-³ and OPPORTUNE. Rare till 19th c.] Not opportune; inappropriate or inconvenient, esp. with regard to time; unsuited to the occasion; unseasonable.

No visit could have been more i. T. HOOK. Turbulent and i. in their demands LECKY. Hence **Ino·pportu·ne·ly** *adv.*, **-ness.**

Inopportunist (inǫ·pǫ̈ɹtiū·nist), *sb.* (*a.*) 1880. [f. INOPPORTUNE + -IST, after *opportunist.*] **1.** One who believes a policy or course of action to be inopportune; *esp.* one who, on that ground, opposed the doctrine of Papal Infallibility at the Vatican Council, 1870; one opposed to the OPPORTUNISTS. **2.** *adj.* Of or belonging to the inopportunists 1888.

Inopportunity (i·nǫpǫ̈ɹtiū·nĭti). 1500. [ad. late L. *inopportunitas.*] The quality or fact of being inopportune; unseasonableness.

Inoppressive (inǒpre·siv), *a. rare.* 1627. [IN-³.] Not oppressive; unoppressive.

†**Ino·pulent,** *a.* [IN-³.] Not opulent; poor. SHERLEY.

Inorb (inǭ·ɹb), *v.* 1847. [IN-².] *trans.* To place in an orb or sphere; to surround with or as with an orb; to encircle.

Inordinacy (inǭ·ɹdinăsi). Now *rare.* 1617. [f. INORDINATE; see -ACY.] The quality or condition of being inordinate; inordinateness; also, an inordinate act.

That wantonness of power, and i. of ambition 1785.

†**Ino·rdinance.** 1638. [IN-³.] An inordinate action or practice; an excess –1799.

Inordinate (inǭ·ɹdinĕt), *a.* ME. [ad. L. *inordinatus* disordered, irregular, f. *in-* (IN-³) + *ordinatus*, *ordinare.*] **1.** Not ordered; irregular, disorderly; not controlled or restrained. **2.** Not kept within orderly limits, immoderate, excessive ME. **3.** Of persons: Not conforming or subject to law or order, disorderly; immoderate, intemperate 1450.

1. To keep i. hours 1625. A rude and i. heap RAY. **2.** I. drinking 1665, vanity BURKE, prices 1872. **3.** I. admirers of antiquity BUCKLE. Hence **Ino·rdi·nate·ly** *adv.*, **-ness.**

†**Inordina·tion.** 1612. [ad. late L. *inordinationem*; see IN-³ and ORDINATION.] The condition of being inordinate (in conduct, etc.); an instance of this –1788.

That intrinsick I., and Deviation from right Reason inherent in it [a Lye] SOUTH.

Inorganic (inǫɹgæ·nik), *a.* 1794. [f. IN-³ + ORGANIC.] **1.** Not characterized by having organs; not formed with the organs of life; destitute of organized physical structure; said of inanimate matter and bodies formed of it without vital action. **b.** *Chem.* Of elements, compounds, etc.: Not entering into the composition of organized bodies; not formed under the action of the vital forces 1831. **2.** = INORGANICAL 1. 1821. **3.** Not belonging to the organism or structure; that does not arise by natural growth; spec. in *Philol.* of sounds or forms not arising from regular phonetic development 1843; *Path.* of abnormal heart-sounds not due to disease of the heart substance. **4.** Without systematic arrangement. CARLYLE.

1. *I. world, nature*, the material world outside the animal and vegetable kingdoms; the world of matter, with its forces. **b.** *I. Chemistry*, that branch which investigates i. compounds; the chemistry of mineral substances. **3.** The yoke of an i. and alien despotism MERIVALE. These languages will hardly ever agree in what is anomalous or i. MAX MÜLLER.

†**Inorga·nical,** *a.* 1621. [IN-³.] **1.** Without organs or instruments; not having, or not acting by, organs. Said of the soul or mind. –1688. **2.** = INORGANIC 1. –1690. Hence **Inorga·nically** *adv.* without organs or organization.

†**Inorga·nity.** *rare.* 1643. [f. IN-³ + L. *organum*, Gr. ὄργανον + -ITY.] The condition of being without organs –1727.

The i. of the Soul SIR T. BROWNE.

Ino:rganiza·tion. 1839. [IN-³.] Absence of organization; unorganized condition.

Ino·rganized, *a.* 1649. [IN-³.] Not organized; not having organization.

Inornate (inǭ·ɹnĕᶦt), *a.* 1510. [ad. L. *inornatus.*] Not ornate; unadorned, plain.

†**Inortho·graphy.** 1779. [IN-³.] Incorrect spelling.

Inosculate (inǫ·skiŭleᶦt), *v.* 1671. [f. IN-² + L. *osculare* to furnish with a mouth or outlet, f. *osculum*, dim. of *os* mouth.] **1.** *intr.* Of blood-vessels, etc.: To open into each other; to have connexion terminally; to anastomose 1683. **2.** Of solid parts: To unite by interpenetrating or fitting closely into each other 1713. **3.** *trans.* To cause (blood-vessels, or the like) to open into each other; to connect by anastomosis 1734. **4.** To cause (fibres, or the like) to pass into each other 1671. **5.** *transf.* and *fig.* **a.** *intr.* To join or unite so as to become continuous; to blend 1836. **b.** *trans.* To cause to grow together or unite so as to become continuous 1829.

Inosculation (inǫskiŭlēᶦ·ʃən). 1672. [f. prec.] The action of inosculating; the opening of two vessels of an animal body, or of a vegetable, into each other; anastomosis; junction by insertion; hence, applied generally to the passing of one thing into another.

The i. of veins 1672.

Inosite (əi·nosəit). 1857. [f. a potential **inose* (f. INO- muscle + -OSE) + -ITE.] *Chem.* A non-fermentable saccharine substance ($C_6H_{12}O_6 + 2H_2O$), isomeric with glucose, discovered by Scherer (1850) in the fluid contained in the cardiac muscular tissue of the ox, and since found in other parts of the body and in plants.

Inoxidizable (inǫksidəi·zăb'l), *a.* 1864. [IN-³.] Not oxidizable; incapable of rusting.

Ino·xidize, *v.* 1881. [IN-³.] *trans.* To render not liable to oxidize.

Inp-: see IMP-, as in *inpale*, etc.

In partibus, etc.: see IN *Lat. prep.*

I·n-pa:tient. 1760: see IN *adv.* Combs. 2.

I·n-phase. 1916. [attrib. use of phr. *in phase.*] *Electr.* Of the same phase.

Input (i·nput), *sb.* 1753. [IN *adv.* Combs. 1.] **1.** A sum put in (*Sc.*). **2.** That which is put or taken in; esp. of electrical apparatus 1893.

†**Input,** *v.* late ME. [IN-¹.] **1.** *trans.* To put on, impose. **2.** *Sc.* To put in, set (in some position) 1557–1839.

Inquarta·tion. *rare.* 1881. [?a. F. *inquartation* (Littré).] A process of separating gold and silver; see QUARTATION.

Inquest (i·nkwest). [ME. *enqueste*, a. OF. *enqueste* = Rom. and med.L. *inquesta*, sb. from fem. pa. pple. of Com. Rom. **inquērĕre* to INQUIRE. Pronounced *inque·st* (whence aphetic *'quest*) till end of 17th c.] **1.** A legal or judicial inquiry to ascertain or decide a matter of fact, esp. one made by a jury in a civil or criminal case. Formerly, a general term for all formal or official inquiries. Now mostly = 'coroner's inquest' (see CORONER). Also *fig.* **2.** The body of men appointed to hold a legal inquiry; a jury; now *esp.* a coroner's jury ME. **3.** *gen.*

†An inquiry or question; a questioning –1853; †a pursuit, a research; †a quest –1667; inquiry or investigation (now *rare*) 1625.

1. *Great I.*, an occasional name for the Domesday inquiry and valuation. *I. of Office*, an inquiry made by the king's officer, or by commissioners appointed for the purpose, concerning any matter that entitles the king to the possession of lands or tenements, goods or chattels. *fig. Great, last, general i.*, the last Judgement. 2. *Grand* or *great i.* = Grand JURY. *Grand* (or *great*) *i. of the nation*, applied to the House of Commons. 3. This is the laborious and vexatious i. that the soul must make after science SOUTH.

Inquiet (inkwəi·ĕt), *a.* ME. [ad. L. *inquietus*, f. *in-* (IN-³) + *quietus*.] Not quiet; †restless, troublesome –1552; uneasy, anxious (*rare*) 1502. Hence †**Inqui·etness.**

Inquiet (inkwəi·ĕt), *v.* Now *rare.* ME. [a. F. *inquiéter*, ad. L. *inquietare*, f. *inquietus*.] *trans.* To destroy the quiet of; †to disquiet, disturb (in mind) –1828.

Inquietation (inkwəi,ĕtē¹·ʃən). *arch.* 1461. [a. OF., ad. med.L. *inquietationem*.] The action of disturbing or molesting; the condition of being disturbed or disquieted.

Inquietude (inkwəi·ĕtiūd). 1440. [a. F. *inquiétude*, or ad. late L. *inquietudo*.] †1. Disturbed condition; disturbance –1797. 2. *Med.* Restlessness (of the body), caused by pain, uneasiness, or debility 1597. 3. Disturbance of mind; disquietude 1658. b. *pl.* Anxieties 1652.

Inquiline (i·nkwiləin), *sb.* (*a.*) *rare.* 1641. [ad. L. *inquilinus* an indweller in a place not his own, f. *in-* (IN-²) + *colere* to dwell.] †1. A sojourner, a lodger, an indweller. BP. MOUNTAGU. 2. *Zool.* An animal which lives in the nest or abode of another; a commensal or guest 1879. 3. *attrib.* or as *adj.* 1716.

2. There are several genera of gall-flies which..are known as guest gall-flies or inquilines 1884.

†**I·nquinate,** *v.* 1542. [f. L. *inquinat-*, *inquinare* to pollute, etc.] *trans.* To pollute, defile, corrupt –1682. So **Inquina·tion** [ad. late L. *inquination-em*] (now *rare*), pollution; polluted condition; a defilement; a defiling agent (*lit.* and *fig.*) 1447.

Inquirable, enquirable (in-, ĕnkwəi³·rǎ-b'l), *a.* Now *rare.* 1485. [f. INQUIRE *v.* + -ABLE.] That calls for inquiry; open to inquiry. (Chiefly in legal use.) Also with *into.*

†**Inquirance, enquirance.** [ME. *enquerance* (prob. OF. or AF.), f. *enquerant, enquerre* to INQUIRE; see -ANCE.] Inquiry –1567.

Inquire, enquire (in-, ĕnkwəi³·ɹ), *v.* [ME. *enquere(n*, a. OF. *enquerre*, mod.F. *enquérir* :—Common Romanic **inquērĕre* for *inquærere* (analytical for cl.L. *inquirere*), f. *in-* (IN-²) + *quærere* to ask. Refash. after cl.L. in 15th c., but the half-latinized *enquire* still subsists beside *inquire.*] †1. *trans.* To search into, seek knowledge concerning, investigate, examine –1787. 2. To seek knowledge of (a thing) by putting a question; to ask about; to ask (something) *of*, Sc. *at* (a person) ME. b. with interrog. clause as object: To ask ME. †3. To address a question to, question, interrogate; to ask (some one) –1682. 4. *intr.* To make investigation; to search, seek; to make inquisition. Const. *into*, †*of*, †*after.* ME. 5. *intr.* To seek information by questioning; to put a question or questions; to ask. Const. *of*, also (now Sc.) *at, about, after.* ME. b. To make request *for* a thing; to ask to see a person. Const. *for.* 1500. †6. *trans.* To seek, search for, try to find. With *out* (rarely *forth*): To seek till one finds; to seek out, find out by seeking (often including the notion of *asking*). –1790. †7. *trans.* (or *absol.*) To ask for, demand (*rare*) –1656. ¶8. *erron.* To name. SPENSER *F. Q.* II. x. 12.

1. A Probe..to enquire the depth of a wound WOODALL. 2. You must enquire your way *Cor.* III. i. 54. b. I will i...if he has gone out GALT. 3. Thou no more..Shalt be enquir'd at Delphos MILT. *P.R.* I. 458. 4. Of faery lond yet if he more inquyre..He may it fynd SPENSER. 5. Goe and i. diligently of the childe N.T. (Rhem.) *Matt.* ii. 8. Dauid enquired of the Lord 1 *Sam.* xxiii. 2. b. Hath any body enquir'd for mee here to day? SHAKS. 6. Enquire the Iewes house out SHAKS. Hence **Inqui·rer, en-**, one who inquires; a seeker, investigator; a questioner. **Inqui·ringly, en-,** *adv.* in an inquiring manner.

‖**Inquirendo** (inkwəire·ndo). 1607. [L., = 'by inquiring'.] *Law.* 'An authority given to some official person to institute an enquiry concerning the Crown's interests' (Wharton). b. An investigation 1846.

Inquiry, enquiry (in-, ĕnkwəi³·ri). 1440. [Earlier *enquery*, f. *enquere*, INQUIRE *v.* + -Y⁴; subseq. refash. after the vb.] The action, or an act or course, of inquiring. 1. The action of seeking, esp. (now always) for truth, knowledge, or information concerning something; search, research, investigation, examination. b. (with *pl.*) A course of inquiry, an investigation 1512. 2. The action of asking or questioning; interrogation. (*Comm.* = DEMAND *sb.* 4.) 1565. b. A question; a query 1548.

1. To reject the christian religion without i. 1743. b. Enquiries into Antiquity STEELE. 2. We coulde learne nothinge therof by enquiry 1565. b. Our reply to this reasonable enquiry is simple SCRIVENER.

Phr. *Court of I.*, a court legally constituted to inquire into and investigate any charge against an officer or soldier of the army, or any transaction which may possibly be found to call for proceedings before a court-martial. *Writ of I.*, a writ directing an i. or inquest.

†**Inqui·sible,** *a.* [irreg. f. *inquisite, inquisition* + -IBLE.] Capable of being inquired into; subject to inquisition. HALE.

†**Inquisite,** *v.* 1639. [f. L. *inquisit-, inquirere*; perh. f. next.] 1. *trans.* To inquire into, investigate, examine. Also *absol.* –1734. 2. To proceed against (a person) by inquisition or by the method of the Inquisition –1736.

1. *absol.* He inquisited with justice and decorum NORTH.

Inquisition (inkwizi·ʃən), *sb.* ME. [a. OF., ad. L. *inquisitionem.*] 1. The action or process of inquiring or searching into matters; search, investigation, examination; †scrutiny, inspection. Also with *an* and *pl.* 2. A judicial or official investigation or inquiry, an inquest; also the document recording such inquiry and its result ME. 3. *R. C. Ch.* (with capital *I.*) An ecclesiastical tribunal (officially styled the Holy Office) for the suppression of heresy and punishment of heretics, organized in the 13th c. under Innocent III, under a central governing body at Rome called the Congregation of the Holy Office 1502. 4. *attrib.* 1612.

1. To make i. of the truth 1570. The i. of the curious F. HALL. I heartily abhor an i. in faith BERKELEY. 2. R. became a lunatic, and was so found by i. 1896. 3. By Order of the Tribunal of the I. at Toledo..Eight Jews were burnt alive 1691. 4. If I left them..To these I. dogs and the devildoms of Spain TENNYSON. Hence **Inquisi·tional** *a.* of or pertaining to the I. or to inquiry; inquisitorial 1644. So **Inquisi·tionary** *a.* (*rare*).

Inquisi·tion, *v.* 1644. [f. prec. sb.] *intr.* To make inquisition or investigation; *trans.* to proceed against by the Inquisition.

Inquisitive (inkwi·zitiv), *a.* (*sb.*) ME. [a. OF. *inquisitif, -ive*, ad. late L. *inquisitivus* (Boeth.), f. L. *inquisit-, inquirere* to INQUIRE; see -IVE.] 1. Given to inquiry, questioning, or research; desirous of, or eager for, knowledge; curious ME. b. Now usu. in bad sense: Unduly or impertinently curious; prying 1529. 2. *sb.* An inquisitive person 1589.

1. So many learned, wise and i. men BERKELEY. b. I. Persons..who have a Mind to pry into the Thoughts and Actions of their Neighbour SOUTH. Hence **Inqui·sitive-ly** *adv.*, **-ness.**

Inquisitor (inkwi·zitəɹ). 1504. [a. OF. *inquisiteur*, in AF. *-itour*, ad. L. *inquisitorem*, f. *inquirere.*] 1. One who makes inquisition or inquiry; an investigator; an inquisitive person. Const. *of, into.* 2. One whose official duty it is to inquire, examine, or investigate, in matters of crime, taxation, etc. 1513. †b. A detective, informer, or spy –1797. c. *transf.* and *fig.* 1734. 3. An officer of the Inquisition; see INQUISITION 3. 1545.

1. Curious Inquisitors of the causes of all naturall things 1586. 2. c. What 's that to you, brother? Who made you the i. of my actions? FIELDING.

Inquisitorial (inkwizitōº·riăl), *a.* 1761. [f. med.L. *inquisitorius* + -AL.] 1. Of or pertaining to an (official) inquisitor or inquisitors; having or exercising the function of an inquisitor. 2. Of the character of an inquisitor; prying 1796.

1. An i. tribunal..was erected in the kingdom HUME. The Cruel and Dangerous I. System of the Church of Rome in Ireland 1821. 2. The i. or secret system [of criminal procedure] 1900. Hence **Inquisito·rial-ly** *adv.*, **-ness.** So †**Inquisito·rious** *a.* (in sense 2). MILTON.

Inqui·sitory *a.* 1639. = INQUISITORIAL.

†**Inquisitu·rient,** *a.* [f. L. type **inquisiturientem*, f. (ult.) *inquirere* to INQUIRE.] Eager to play the inquisitor. MILTON.

Inra·cinate, *v. rare.* 1882. [f. F. *enraciner* + -ATE³, after DERACINATE.] *trans.* To enroot, to implant.

†**Inrai·l,** *v.* 1594. [f. IN-¹ + RAIL *v.*] *trans.* To rail in, inclose with a railing –1724.

‖**In re.** [See IN *Lat. prep.* and RE *sb.*²]. a. In fact, in reality 1602. b. In the matter or case of 1877.

Inregister, obs. f. ENREGISTER *v.*

Inroad (i·nrōud), *sb.* 1548. [f. IN *adv.* + ROAD *sb.*, in sense 'riding'.] 1. A hostile incursion into a country; a raid or foray. 2. *transf.* or *fig.* A powerful or sudden incursion; a forcible encroachment 1637. †3. An opening or passage in –1697.

1. Aggressive war, as distinguished from mere plundering inroads FREEMAN. 2. Papal inroads on the liberties of the Church GREEN.

Inroad, *v.* Now *rare.* 1625. [f. prec. sb.] †*trans.* To invade; to make an inroad into –1656. Also *intr.*

The Saracens..inroded Aquitain FULLER.

Inrol(l, obs. ff. ENROLL.

I·nro·lling, *ppl. a.* 1851. [IN *adv.*] That rolls in (like a wave).

I·nru·nning, *vbl. sb.* ME. [IN *adv.*] †a. Incursion, attack (tr. L. *incursus*). WYCLIF. b. Inflowing, the place of inflowing. TENNYSON.

Inruption (inrʊ·pʃən). 1809. [Refash. of IRRUPTION, emphasizing *in-*.] A breaking or bursting in.

Inrush (i·nrʊʃ), *sb.* 1817. [IN *adv.*] A rushing or pouring in; inflow, influx (*lit.* and *fig.*).

The..i. of tourists 1883. So †**Inru·sh** *v.* to rush in 1610–1773.

†**Insa·bbatist.** *rare.* 1634. [f. F. *insabbaté*, or med.L. *insabbatus, -sab(b)atatus*; see -IST. But now referred to the peculiar shoe (*sabate* = F. *sabot, savate*) worn by the sect.] A member of the sect of the Waldenses.

They were supposed falsely to neglect the Sabbath, and called Insabbathists RANKEN.

†**Insa·fety.** 1635. [IN-³.] Unsafeness; risk.

Insalivate (insæ·liveɪt), *v.* 1855. [IN-².] *trans.* To mix or impregnate (food) with saliva in the act of mastication. So **Insaliva·tion** 1833.

Insalubrious (insăliū·briəs), *a.* 1638. [f. L. *insalubris* + -OUS.] Not salubrious; detrimental to health. (Now chiefly of climate or surroundings.)

Insalubrity (insăliū·briti). 1663. [a. F. *insalubrité*; see prec. and -ITY.] Unhealthy character (of locality, climate, etc.); †unwholesomeness (of food).

Insalutary (insæ·liutări), *a.* 1694. [ad. late L. *insalutaris*, f. *in-* (IN-³) + *salutaris.*] Not salutary. †1. Injurious to health; insalubrious –1773. 2. Not having a healthy mental or social influence or effect. LYTTON.

Insa·nable, *a. rare.* 1547. [ad. L. *insanabilis*, f. *in-* (IN-³) + *sanare* to heal.] That cannot be healed, cured, or remedied; incurable. Hence †**Insanabi·lity,** †**Insa·nableness,** i. quality. †**Insa·nably** *adv.*

Insane (insē¹·n), *a.* (*sb.*) 1560. [ad. L. *insanus*, f. *in-* (IN-³) + *sanus* SANE.] 1. Of persons: Not of sound mind, mad, mentally deranged. Also of the mind: Unsound. b. *absol.* An insane person. Hence (*attrib.* use of the *pl.*), Set apart for the insane, as *i. asylum, ward*, etc. 1786. 2. Of actions (also colloq. of things): Mad, idiotic, irrational 1842. †3. Causing insanity. SHAKS.

2. The i. and excessive passion for athletics 1869. 3. Haue we eaten on the i. Root, That takes the Reason Prisoner? SHAKS. Hence **Insa·ne-ly** *adv.*, **-ness.**

†**Insa·niate,** *v.* [irreg. f. L. *insania* + -ATE³.] *trans.* To make unsound or insane. FELTHAM.

†**Insa·nie.** *rare.* 1572. [a. obs. F. *insanie*, ad. L. *insania*, f. *insanus.*] Madness.

Insanitary (insæ·nitări), *a.* 1874. [IN-³.] Not sanitary or healthful; injurious to health. Hence **Insa·nitariness.**

Insanitation (insænitē·ʃən). 1884. [IN-³.] Want of sanitation; insanitary condition; absence of sanitary requirements.

Insanity (insæ·nĭti). 1590. [ad. L. *insanitatem*, f. *insanus*; see -ITY.] **1.** The condition of being insane; unsoundness of mind as a consequence of brain-disease; madness, lunacy. Orig. called *i. of mind.* **2.** Extreme folly; an instance of this 1844.

1. D. Skae's..definition of i. as 'a disease of the brain affecting the mind' is not disputable 1897. 2. The insanities of idealism H. SPENCER.

†**Insa·pory**, *a. rare.* [irreg. f. IN-³ + L. *sapor* taste + -Y.] Unsavoury. SIR T. HERBERT.

Insatiable (insēⁱ·ʃiăb'l), *a.* ME. [a. OF. *insaciable* (mod. *insatiable*), or ad. L. *insatiabilis*; see -ABLE.] Not satiable; that cannot be satiated, satisfied, or appeased; that always craves for more. Const. *of*, rarely *with*. Also *fig.* of things.

I. of antiquity MILT., with war COWPER. *fig.* Insaciable whyrlepoles MORE. Hence **Insatiabi·lity, Insa·tiableness. Insa·tiably** *adv.*

Insatiate (insēⁱ·ʃiĕt), *a.* 1509. [ad. L. *insatiatus* (Statius), f. *in-* (IN-³) + *satiatus, satiare.*] That is not satiated or satisfied; never satisfied; insatiable. Const. *of*, †*for*.

Satan..i. to pursue Vain Warr with Heav'n MILT. *P. L.* II. 8. I. of battle 1848. *fig.* I. hell, still crying, More MARSTON. So **Insa·tiated** *a.* (*rare*). Hence **Insa·tiate·ly** *adv.*, **-ness.**

Insati·ety. *rare.* 1578. [a. obs. F. *insatieté* (Godef.), ad. L. *insatietas*; see IN-³ and SATIETY.] The condition of being insatiate; unsatisfied desire or demand.

†**Insatisfa·ction.** 1568. [IN-³.] Absence of satisfaction; dissatisfaction -1682.

†**Insa·turable**, *a.* ME. [ad. L. *insaturabilis* insatiable, f. *in-* (IN-³) + *saturare* to SATURATE.] Insatiable -1755.

Inscience (i·nʃiĕns). Now *rare.* 1578. [ad. L. *inscientia*, f. *inscientem*, after *scientia.*] The condition of not knowing; want of knowledge; ignorance.

Inscient (i·nʃiĕnt), *a.*¹ Now *rare.* 1578. [ad. L. *inscientem*, f. *in-* (IN-³) + *sciens, scient-, scire.*] Not knowing; lacking knowledge; nescient, ignorant. So †**I·nscious** *a.* 1633.

I·nscient, *a.*² [f. IN-² + L. *scientem.*] Having inward knowledge. MRS. BROWNING.

Insconce, obs. f. ENSCONCE.

Inscribable (inskrəi·băb'l), *a.* 1846. [f. next + -ABLE.] Capable of being inscribed.

No rectangular parallelogram is i. in a circle (*mod.*).

Inscribe (inskrəi·b), *v.* 1552. [ad. L. *inscribere*, f. *in-* (IN-²) + *scribere.*] **1.** *trans.* To write, mark, or delineate in or on something, e.g. on a monument, tablet, etc. Also *fig.* **b.** To enroll on an official document or list 1605. **c.** *Comm.* To issue a state (or other) loan in the form of shares with registered holders (see INSCRIBED) 1884. **2.** To mark (a surface, column, etc.) with writing or other characters 1637. **b.** To dedicate *to* a person by a short inscription less formal than an ordinary dedication 1645. **3.** *Geom.* To delineate or trace (a figure or line) within a figure, so that some particular points of it lie in the boundary or periphery of that figure 1570.

An angular figure (polygon or polyhedron) is said to be inscribed in another figure when the angular points of the former lie in the bounding line or lines, or surface or surfaces, of the latter. A curved figure (plane or solid) is said to be inscribed in an angular figure when the former touches each of the bounding lines or surfaces of the latter. More rarely, a line is said to be inscribed in a figure when its extremities lie in the boundary of that figure.

1. We raise the marble and i. the flattering epitaph 1864. 2. Like to that sanguine flower inscrib'd with woe MILT. b. An author may with great propriety i. his work to him by whose encouragement it was undertaken JOHNSON. Hence **Inscri·ber**, one who inscribes; the writer of an inscription. So **I·nscript**, something inscribed; an inscription. **Inscri·ptible** *a.* (*rare*) = INSCRIBABLE.

Inscribed (inskrəi·bd), *ppl. a.* 1571. [f. prec.] In the senses of INSCRIBE *v.* **b.** Of a state (or other) loan: Issued not in the form of bonds passing from hand to hand, but as shares of which the names of the holders are registered or entered in a list kept at the head office of the issuing state or company 1882.

Inscription (inskri·pʃən). ME. [ad. L. *inscriptionem.*] **1.** The action of inscribing. Also *fig. rare.* 1652. **2.** *concr.* That which is inscribed; a piece of writing or lettering upon something; *esp.* a legend, description, or record traced upon some hard substance for the sake of durability, as on a monument, building, stone, tablet, medal, coin, vase, etc. 1538. Also *fig.* **3.** *spec.* **a.** A title, heading, superscription. (Now *rare* or *Obs.* as dist. from 2.) ME. **b.** A brief dedication of a book or work of art to a person; the superscription of a letter 1742. **4.** *Anat.* A marking upon some organ or part produced by another in contact with it; *esp.* on the fleshy part of a muscle where a tendon crosses it 1578. **5.** *Comm.* The action of inscribing stock; in *pl.* inscribed stocks (see INSCRIBED) 1797. Hence **Inscri·ptional** *a.* †bearing an inscription; characteristic of, or of the nature of, an i. or inscriptions.

Inscriptive (inskri·ptiv), *a.* 1740. [f. L. *inscript-, inscribere* + -IVE.] **1.** Of the nature of an inscription; belonging to or used in inscriptions. †**2.** Bearing an inscription. DYER.

Inscroll (inskrōᵘ·l), *v.* 1596. [f. IN-¹ or ² + SCROLL.] *trans.* To inscribe or enter upon a scroll. *Merch. V.* II. vii. 72.

Inscrutable (inskrū·tăb'l), *a.* (*sb.*) 1450. [ad. late L. *inscrutabilis*, f. *in-* (IN-³) + *scrutari*; see -ABLE.] **1.** That cannot be searched into or found out by searching; impenetrable, unfathomable; entirely mysterious. Rarely of things physical, as an abyss. **2.** *sb. pl.* Inscrutable things 1663.

1. The herte of man is i., and onely god knoweth it 1526. As i. a mystery as the origin of Life 1894. Hence **Inscrutabi·lity, Inscru·tableness. Inscru·tably** *adv.*

Insculp (inskʊ·lp), *v.* Now *rare* or *Obs.* Pa. pple. **insculped, insculpt.** ME. [ad. L. *insculpere*, f. *in-* (IN-²) + *sculpere* to carve, or F. *insculper*. Used first in pa. pple. *insculpt*, ad. L. *insculptus*; whence perh. the finite vb.] **1.** *trans.* To carve, engrave, or sculpture (upon something). Also *fig.* **2. a.** To shape artistically by cutting. **b.** To sculpture (stone, etc.); to CARVE. Also *fig.* 1578.

1. Which he insculped in two likely stones DRAYTON. 2. b. The sacred Tables..insculpt of God's own hand 1830. So †**Inscu·lpt** *v.* 1487. †**Inscu·lption**, the action of carving or sculpturing upon something; a carved figure or inscription. Also *fig.*

Inscu·lpture, *sb.* ? *Obs.* 1607. [a. obs. F. *insculpture*, f. L. *insculpere*; see -URE.] A figure or inscription carved or sculptured upon something.

On his Grauestone, this I. *Timon* v. iv. 67.

Inscu·lpture, *v.* Also **en-.** 1787. [f. IN-² = EN- + SCULPTURE.] *trans.* To carve or sculpture upon something.

Shapes..That yet survive ensculptured on the walls WORDSW.

†**Inscutcheon.** 1562. = INESCUTCHEON.

Inseam, obs. f. ENSEAM *v.*¹

Insearch(**e, -er**, var. of ENSEARCH, -ER.

†**Insecable**, *a. rare.* 1623. [ad. L. *insecabilis.*] Incapable of being cut -17..

Insect (i·nsekt), *sb.* 1601. [ad. L. *insectum*, ellipt. for *animal insectum* animal notched or cut into (Pliny), f. *insectus, insecare*; tr. Gr. ἔντομον; cf. ENTOMO-.] **1.** A small invertebrate animal, usually having a body divided into segments, and several pairs of legs, and often winged; in pop. use comprising, besides the animals scientifically so called (see 2), many other arthropods, as spiders, mites, centipedes, wood-lice, etc., and other invertebrates, as the 'coral-insect'; still applied by the uneducated to earthworms, snails, etc., and even some small vertebrates, as frogs and tortoises. **2.** *Zool.* An animal belonging to the class *Insecta* of *Arthropoda*; see INSECTA 2. 1601. **3.** *fig.* Applied to any insignificant or despicable person 1684.

3. He, the little I., was recommended to King William HEARNE.

attrib. and *Comb.* **1.** General: as *i. pest, vermin*, etc.; *i. quire, race*, etc.; *i. understanding*; *i. egg, larva*, etc.; *i.-box, -cabinet, -trap*.

2. Special: as **i.-beds**, the calcareous bands of the British Lias, in which the relics of i.-life are very abundant; **-feeder**, a creature that feeds on insects; **-powder**, a powder (usually prepared from the dried flowers of species of *Pyrethrum*) used to kill or drive away insects.

†**Insect**, *a.* 1589. [ad. L. *insectus*, pa. pple.; see prec.] Having the body divided into segments; chiefly in *i. animals* = L. *animalia insecta*; see INSECTA.

‖**Insecta** (inse·ktă), *sb. pl.* 1609. [L., pl. of *insectum* INSECT; formerly also *insecta animalia* 'cut-waisted animals'.] †**1.** Former pl. of INSECT, as used pop. -1651. †**b.** Also erron. *insectæ, insecta's.* Also *fig.* -1658. **2.** *Zool.* A class of invertebrate animals; formerly comprising the whole of the ARTHROPODA, or all these except the *Crustacea* and *Arachnida*; now restricted to the *Hexapoda*, having the body divided into three regions (head, thorax, and abdomen), with six legs (all borne upon the thorax), and usually two or four wings (but in some cases none); constituting the largest class of *Arthropoda* 1727.

Insectarium (insektēᵊ·riɒm). Also **Insektary** (i·nsektări). 1881. [f. INSECTA + -ARIUM.] A place for keeping and breeding insects; an entomological vivarium.

†**Insecta·tion.** *rare.* 1535. [ad. L. *insectationem* pursuit, f. *insectari* to pursue, rail at.] Railing, calumniation -1658.

Insected (inse·ktĕd), *ppl. a. rare.* 1645. [f. L. *insectus* (see INSECT *a.*) + -ED¹.] Cut into; divided, as it were, into segments, as an insect.

Insecticide¹ (inse·ktisəid). 1865. [f. L. *insectum* INSECT + *-cida*, -CIDE¹, killer.] One who or that which kills insects; *spec.* a preparation used for destroying insects. **b.** *attrib.* or as *adj.* Having the property of destroying insects. So **Insectici·dal** *a.* 1857.

Inse·cticide². 1865. [f. as prec. + -CIDE².] The killing of insects.

Insectile (inse·ktil, -təil), *a.*¹ and *sb.* 1615. [f. L. *insectum*; cf. L. *sectilis*, f. *sectus.*]

A. *adj.* Of, pertaining to, or of the nature of an insect; consisting of insects; also *fig.* infesting like insects. Now *rare.* 1626.

†**B.** *sb.* = INSECT *sb.* -1666.

†**Inse·ctile**, *a.*² *rare.* [IN-³.] Incapable of being cut or divided -1683.

Insection (inse·kʃən). 1653. [f. L. *insect-, insecare*; cf. *dissection.*] The action of cutting into, incision; division into sections; *concr.* an incision, division, indentation.

‖**Insectivora** (insekti·vŏră), *sb. pl.* 1836. [mod.L., neut. pl. of *insectivorus* insect-eating (sc. *animalia*).] *Zool.* **1.** An order of *Mammalia*, comprising numerous small quadrupeds, as the mole, shrew, and hedgehog, most of which feed on insects. **b.** A group of *Cheiroptera*; the insectivorous Bats. **2.** *Entom.* A group of *Hymenoptera* which feed on other insects (Westwood).

Insectivore (inse·ktivoᵊɹ). Also **-vor.** 1863. [a. mod.F. *insectivore* (Cuvier), ad. L. *insectivorus.*] An insectivorous animal or plant; *spec.* one of the *Insectivora.*

Insectivorous (insekti·vŏrəs), *a.* 1661. [f. mod.L. *insectivorus* + -OUS.] Feeding on insects; applied to the *Insectivora* among mammals, and various birds, such as swallows; also to those plants which capture and absorb insects, as the sundew, Venus's fly-trap, etc.

Insectology (insektǫ·lŏdʒi). 1766. [a. F. *insectologie*, f. L. *insectum* + -(O)LOGY.] A term formerly used as = ENTOMOLOGY; but now usually applied to the study of insects in their economic relations to man, as producers of silk, cochineal, etc., and as agricultural pests or benefactors. Hence **Insecto·loger, Insecto·logist**, a student of i.

Insecure (insǐkiūᵊ·ɹ), *a.* 1649. [ad. med.L. *insecurus*; see IN-³ and SECURE.] Not secure. †**1.** Wanting assurance, confidence, or certainty; uncertain; without certainty *of* -1807. **2.** Unsafe; exposed to danger; liable to give way, fail, or be overcome 1654.

1. Troubled with sorrow and i. apprehensions JER. TAYLOR. 2. So in-secure did overmuch security make them 1654. Hence †**Insecu·re** *v.* (*rare*), to render i. **Insecu·re·ly** *adv.*, **-ness.**

Insecurity (insǐkiūᵊ·rĭti). 1646. [ad. med. L. *insecuritas*, f. *in-* (IN-³) + *securus.*] †**1.** The condition of not being sure; want of confidence; (subjective) uncertainty. SIR T. BROWNE. 2. The state or quality of being unsafe; liability to give way, fail, or suffer loss or damage; want of firmness; a condition of danger. With *pl.* An instance of this. 1649.

2. The i. of all human acquisitions JOHNSON, of titles 1822, of great prosperity J. H. NEWMAN.

†Insecu·tion. [ad. late L. *insecutionem*, f. *insequi*, f. *in-* (IN-[2]) + *sequi* to follow.] The action of following closely upon; close pursuit. CHAPMAN.

Inseminate (inse·mineɪt), *v.* 1623. [f. L. *inseminat-*, *inseminare*, f. *in-* (IN-[2]) + *seminare* to sow.] *trans.* To sow in; to cast in as seed. Also *fig.* Hence **Insemina·tion.**

Insensate (inse·nsĕt), *a.* (*sb.*) 1500. [ad. late L. *insensatus* (Tertull.), f. *in-* (IN-[3]) + *sensatus* gifted with sense, f. *sensus*; see -ATE [2] 2.] 1. Without sensation, senseless, inanimate. 2. Wanting in mental or moral feeling; devoid of sensibility 1553. †b. With *of*, *to*: Not feeling; unconscious of; unaffected by –1813. 3. Lacking sense or understanding; unintelligent, senseless, foolish 1529. 4. *sb.* An insensate person. [= F. *insensé.*] 1877.

1. The silence and the calm, Of mute i. things WORDSW. 2. b. The Suitors souls, i. of their doom POPE. 3. Projects the most i. [were] formed ALISON. Hence **Inse·nsate·ly** *adv.*, **-ness.**

Insense (inse·ns), *v.* *Obs.* exc. *n. dial.* [ME. *ensens(e*, a. OF. *ensenser* to enlighten, f. *en-* in, into + *sens*; subseq. assim. to L. type **insensare*.] *trans.* To cause (a person) to understand or know; to inform.

Insensibility (insensibi·liti). 1510. [ad. late L. *insensibilitas*, f. *insensibilis*; see -ITY.] The quality or condition of being insensible.

I. In passive sense. The quality of being imperceptible, or not appreciable by the senses (*rare*) 1635.

II. In active sense. 1. Incapability, or deprivation, of (physical) feeling or sensation; unconsciousness; a swoon 1510. b. Physical insensitiveness (*to* something) 1808. 2. Incapacity of mental feeling or emotion; want of moral susceptibility; apathy, indifference 1691.

1. I fell from my horse in a state of i. 1841. b. I. to the changes of the seasons W. IRVING. 2. I. to the goodness of the Creator PALEY.

Insensible (inse·nsĭb'l), *a.* (*sb.*) ME. [ad. L. *insensibilis*, f. *in-* (IN-[3]) + *sensibilis*, f. *sentire*, *sens-* to feel.]

I. Passively. 1. a. Imperceptible by the senses; non-material (now *rare*) ME. b. So small, slight, etc. as to be inappreciable by the senses or by the mind. (The prevailing sense.) 1584. †2. Unintelligible; without sense or meaning. (Chiefly in legal use.) –1884.

1. a. The names which stand for i. actions and notions, are derived from sensible objects MANSEL. b. There is an i. transition H. SPENCER. 2. The words are i. and uncertain words 1657.

II. Actively. 1. a. Not having the faculty of sensation. Now *rare.* ME. b. Deprived of sensation; unconscious ME. c. Incapable of physically feeling or knowing (something specified). Const. *of*, *to*. 1526. 2. a. Incapable of mentally feeling, perceiving, or being affected by (something specified); unconscious; unsusceptible, indifferent. Const. *of*, *to*, etc. 1612. b. Incapable of feeling or emotion; callous, apathetic 1617. †3. Destitute of sense or intelligence; irrational –1794.

1. a. The i. spot on the retina BREWSTER. b. He fell down in a fit, and remained long i. MACAULAY. c. I. to wounds GEO. ELIOT. 2. a. I. of your kindness 1802. Hence **†Inse·nsibleness**, the quality or condition of being i. **Inse·nsibly** *adv.* 1425.

Insensitive (inse·nsitiv), *a.* 1610. [IN-[3].] Not sensitive; destitute of feeling or sensation; not susceptible of impressions. Also *transf.*

One spot on the retina, not very far from the most sensitive portion, is entirely i. to light HARLAN. Hence **Inse·nsitiveness.**

Insensuous (inse·nsiuəs), *a.* *rare.* 1861. [IN-[3].] Not sensuous; that is not an object of sense. MRS. BROWNING.

Insentient (inse·nʃiĕnt), *a.* 1764. [IN-[3].] Not sentient; destitute of sensation or consciousness; indifferent (*rare*).

An i. inert substance REID. Shall I return it [a stone] thanks, the i. thing? BROWNING. Hence **Inse·ntience.**

Inseparable (inse·părăb'l), *a.* (*sb.*) ME. [ad. L. *inseparabilis*, f. *in-* (IN-[3]) + *separabilis*.] 1. Not separable; incapable of being separated or disjoined. 2. *sb.* Usu. *pl.* Things or persons that cannot be separated; inseparable companions 1520.

1. An i. union 1662. My i. companion during eleven years MRS. CARLYLE. *I. accident, attribute, quality*, etc. (*Logic*), an accident, etc., that cannot be separated from its subject. *I. prefix* or *preposition* (*Gram.*), a prefix found only in combination, and incapable of being used as a separate word; e.g. *mis-*, *un-*. Hence **Inseparabi·lity, Inse·parableness. Inse·parably** *adv.*

Inseparate (inse·părĕt), *a.* 1550. [ad. L. *inseparatus* (Tertull.); see IN-[3] and SEPARATE.] Not separate *from*; undivided; hence often = INSEPARABLE.

We live linked, i.—heart in heart SWINBURNE. Hence **Inse·parately** *adv.*

Insert (i·nsɜɹt), *sb.* 1890. [f. next.] An insertion; a rider on a proof; *U.S.* a circular or the like placed between the leaves of a magazine or the folds of a newspaper.

Insert (insɜ̄·ɹt), *v.* 1529. [f. L. *insert-*, *inserere*, f. *in-* (IN-[2]) + *serere* to join together, put into.] 1. *trans.* To set, put, or place in; to push or thrust in; to fit or fix in; to introduce; to engraft. Said primarily of putting any solid object into a space which it fits, or fills up. b. To put in or introduce; to include 1533. 2. *Anat.*, *Zool.*, *Bot.* To attach; to join at a specified point of attachment. Only in *pa. pple.* 1828.

1. It inserts its long tongue into the holes through which the ants issue BEWICK. To i. vaccine matter in the arm 1799, a key in a lock DICKENS. b. Something he had inserted into the Magazine J. H. NEWMAN. To i. an advertisement in a newspaper (*mod.*). Hence **Inse·rter.**

Inse·rted, *ppl. a.* 1598. [f. INSERT *v.* + -ED[1].] Set or put in; fitted in, engrafted. b. *Entom.* Set deeply; not free 1826.

Insertion (insɜ̄·ɹʃən). 1578. [ad. L. *insertionem*, f. *inserere*.] 1. The action of inserting; see INSERT *v.* 1598. 2. That which is inserted; an inserted addition, piece, or part 1624. b. *Needlework.* Embroidery or ornamental needlework, made to be sewed into plain material, for decorative purposes; a piece of such work 1858. 3. *Anat.*, etc. The attachment of a muscle, external organ, etc., as to place and manner 1578.

1. The i. of artificial teeth 1878, of trade notices, advertisements, etc. in a newspaper (*mod.*). 2. b. A white straw hat, trimmed with buff i. 1881. 3. Anthers erect, i. basal HOOKER.

†Inse·rve, *v.* *rare.* 1683. [ad. L. *inservire*, f. *in-* (IN-[2]) + *servire*.] *intr.* To be of service or use *to*; to conduce *to*.

†Inse·rvient, *a.* 1646. [ad. L. *inservientem*; see prec.] 1. Serving, servile. SIR T. BROWNE. 2. Subservient *to* some end; serviceable, conducive, assisting –1802. Hence **†Inse·rvience** 1657.

1. The i. and brutall faculties 1646.

†Inse·ssion. 1559. [ad. late L. *insessionem*, f. *insidere*, f. *in-* (IN-[2]) + *sedere* to sit.] The action of sitting in a bath –1684. b. A hip- or sitz-bath 1559–1657.

b. *Insessions* be bathing tubs..wherein the patient may sit vp to the middle or aboue HOLLAND.

Insessor (inse·səɹ). *rare.* 1835. [a. L., f. *insidere*; see prec.] One who sits in or on.

The I. of the chariot of the cherubim 1835.

‖**Insessores** (insesŏ^ə·rīz), *sb. pl.* 1823. [mod.L., pl. of prec.] *Ornith.* The Perchers or Perching birds, having feet with three toes in front and one behind, adapted for perching on trees. (The composite character of the group has caused the use of the name to be given up.) Hence **Insesso·rial** *a.* of or pertaining to the *Insessores*, or Perchers.

Inset (i·nset), *sb.* 1559. [f. IN *adv.* + SET *sb.*] 1. A setting in, inflow, influx (of water); hence, †a channel. Also *attrib.* 2. That which is set in or inserted. a. A folded section of paper placed within another, completing the sequence of pagination; an extra page or set of pages inserted in a sheet or book; an advertisement on a separate leaf inserted in a magazine, etc. 1875. b. A smaller map, picture, etc. inserted within the border of a larger one 1881. c. A piece of cloth let into a dress 1894.

1. There are tidal influences combined with the general insets from the Atlantic LYELL.

Inse·t, *v.* Pa. pple. **inset**; also **insetted.** ME. [f. IN-[1] or IN *adv.* + SET *v.*] †1. To insert, engraft. Const. *to*. ME. only. 2. To set in, insert; *spec.* to insert as an inset (INSET *sb.* 2 a) 1890. Hence **Insetter,** one employed to inset sheets.

Inseverable (inse·vərăb'l), *a.* 1661. [IN-[3].] Incapable of being severed or broken; inseparable. Hence **Inse·verably** *adv.* 1640.

†Insha·de, *v.* [f. IN-[2] + SHADE *v.*] *trans.* To shade; to tint or vary one colour with another. W. BROWNE.

Inshave (i·nʃēiv). 1875. [f. IN *adv.* + SHAVE.] A tool used by coopers for shaving or planing the inner face of staves.

Insheath, obs. f. ENSHEATH.

Inshell, enshell (inʃe·l, en-), *v.* *rare.* 1607. [f. IN-[1], EN-[1] + SHELL *sb.*] *trans.* To withdraw within the shell. Also *fig.*

†Inship, *v.* 1591. [f. IN-[1] + SHIP *sb.*] *trans.* To put into a ship; to embark –1615.

In shore, i·n-sho·re, *adv. phr.* (*adj.*) 1701. [f. IN *adv.* + SHORE.] 1. *adv.* From seaward in towards the shore; close to the shore 1748. 2. *attrib.* or *adj.* Lying, situated, or carried on near or close to the shore 1701. b. Moving in towards the shore 1882.

1. She was..driven inshore by some boats 1812. The Havilah passing in-shore of the Bombay 1859. 2. The i. fishing 1855, waters 1885. b. An i. wind 1882.

Inshrine: see ENSHRINE.

Inside (i·nsəi·d, insəi·d, i·nsəid), *sb.*, *adj.*, *adv.*, and *prep.* 1504. [f. IN *adj.* (*adv.* used *attrib.*) + SIDE. The opposite of *outside.*]

A. *sb.* 1. The inner side or surface; that side which is within, or nearer to the centre, or farther from the outer edge or surface. 2. The interior 1550. b. *spec.* (i·nsəi·d) The interior of the body; the internal organs, esp. the stomach and bowels; the entrails. (Also in *pl.* in same sense.) *colloq.* and *dial.* 1741. c. Inward nature, mind, thought, or meaning 1599. d. The middle or main portion of a period of time, exclusive of the beginning and end 1890. 3. (adj. or adv. used ellipt.) An inside passenger or place in a coach or other vehicle (*colloq.*) 1798. 4. In advb. phr. *inside ou·t*: so that the inner side becomes the outer.

1. Look'd he o' th' i. of the Paper? SHAKS. The i. of the pavement 1894. 2. Shew the in-side of your Purse to the out-side of his hand, and no more adoe SHAKS. b. My i. cries cupboard KINGSLEY. c. Here's none but friends here, we may speak Our insides freely MASSINGER. d. Home for the i. of a fortnight T. HARDY. 3. The four insides of a Dover coach are taken for to-morrow morning SOUTHEY.

B. *adj.* (i·nsəid). Situated on or in the inside; of, belonging to, or used for the inside (*lit.* and *fig.*); interior, internal 1611. b. *U.S.* Of a person: Working indoors 1892. c. *fig.* Coming from 'the inside'; not generally available 1888.

Is whispering nothing?..Kissing with in-side Lip? SHAKS. *I. cylinder*, *framing*, *gear*, used techn. in reference to locomotive engines having the driving-gear within the main frame. *I. callipers*, etc., i.e. used for the interior of cylindrical or hollow work. (*To cut, do*) *the i. edge* (*Skating*): a particular form of fancy skating on the inner edge of the skate-iron. *I. track*: in *Racing*, the inner, and therefore shorter, side of a curved track; hence *fig.* a position of advantage. c. Inside information 1888.

C. *adv.* (insəi·d). On or in the inside. 1. On the inner side 1803. 2. In or into the inner part; internally 1851.

2. Full, i., sir 1851. Now then, ladies and gentlemen, walk i.! 1866.

Phr. *I. of* (in reference to time): Within the space of; before the end of. *U.S.* and *Colonial colloq.*

D. *prep.* Inside of; on the inner side, or in the inner part, of; within 1791.

To run i. the Bermudas R. H. DANA.

I·nsi·der. 1875. [f. INSIDE + -ER[1].] One who is inside; a person who is within the limits of some place, society, etc.; hence, one who is in possession of special information.

†Insi·diate, *v.* 1624. [f. ppl. stem. of L. *insidiari* to lie in ambush, f. *insidiæ* ambush.] 1. *trans.* To lie in wait for; to plot against –1656. 2. *intr.* To lie in wait; to plot –1639. So **†Insidia·tion** 1612. **†Insi·diator** 1539.

Insidious (insi·diəs), *a.* 1545. [ad. L. *insidiosus*, f. *insidiæ*; see -OUS.] Full of wiles or plots; lying in wait or seeking to entrap or ensnare; sly, treacherous, deceitful, underhand, artful, cunning. (Of persons and things.)

A false, i. Tongue, may whisper a Lye so close, and low SOUTH. A more powerful and i. enemy J. H. NEWMAN. A victim to an i. disease (*mod.*). Hence **Insi·dious-ly** *adv.*, **-ness.**

Insight[1] (i·nsəit). ME. [f. IN *adv.* + SIGHT *sb.* Orig. = 'internal sight', i.e. with the eyes of the mind; but subseq. analysed as sight or seeing *into* a thing or subject.] †1. Internal sight, mental vision or perception, discernment; in early use occas., Understanding, wisdom -1647. 2. A glimpse or view beneath the surface; the faculty or power of thus seeing 1580. †3. A mental looking *to* or *upon* something; consideration; respect, regard -1491. †4. Sight (of the bodily eyes); looking; looking in, inspection; a look -1663.

1. Much better is..the i. of the mind than the light, or eyesight, of the body 1578. 2. This thorough I. into the Man..makes me disesteem him 1718. Hence **†I·nsighted** *a.* having i. 1602.

†Insight[2]. *north.* and *Sc. Obs.* 1522. [?] Goods, *esp.* household furniture.

‖**Insignia** (insi·gniă), *sb. pl.* Less freq. in sing. **insigne** (insi·gni). 1648. [L., pl. of *insigne* mark, sign, badge of office. See ENSIGN *sb.*] 1. Badges or distinguishing marks of office or honour; emblems of a nation, person, etc. b. Erron. used as sing., with pl. *-as* 1774. 2. (usu. *fig.*) Marks or tokens indicative of anything 1796.

1. The *insignia* of the Order of the Bath WELLINGTON. b. A slender white wand, the dreaded insignia of his office W. IRVING. 2. The i. of immortality BREWSTER.

Insignificance (insigni·fikăns). 1699. [f. INSIGNIFICANT; see -ANCE.] The fact or quality of being insignificant. 1. Want of signification or meaning 1754. 2. Want of significance; unimportance; contemptibility.

2. A sufficient apology for a whole life of i. SCOTT. So **Insigni·ficancy** 1651.

Insignificant (insigni·fikănt), *a.* (*sb.*) 1627. [IN-[3].] 1. Devoid of signification; meaningless 1651. 2. Devoid of significance, weight, or force; †ineffective; immaterial·trivial; contemptible 1627. 3. Small in size; petty 1748. 4. *sb.* a. A word or thing without signification. b. An unimportant or contemptible person. 1710.

1. The frequency of i. speech HOBBES. 2. An i. blockhead 1751. The Roman loss was i. in this battle FROUDE. 3. Thebes had sunk to an i. village THIRLWALL. Hence **Insigni·ficantly** *adv.*

†Insigni·ficative, *a.* 1660. [ad. late L. *insignificativus*, f. *in-* (IN-[3]) + *significare.*] Not significative, not denoting by external signs -1751.

Insignment, obs. f. ENSIGNMENT.

†Insi·mulate, *v.* 1532. [f. L. *insimulat-*, *insimulare* to bring a plausible charge against, accuse, f. *in-* (IN-[2]) + *simulare* to SIMULATE.] *trans.* To charge, accuse -1663. So **†Insimula·tion,** accusation 1586-1604.

Insincere (insinsīə·ɹ), *a.* 1634. [ad. L. *insincerus* not genuine, f. *in-* (IN-[3]) + *sincerus.*] Not sincere or genuine; assuming a false guise in speech or conduct; dissembling, disingenuous.

Things stand..but ticklish and i. betwixt us and Holland MARVELL. Hence **Insince·rely** *adv.* 1625.

Insincerity (insinse·riti). 1548. [f. L. *insincerus* + -ITY.] †1. Want of purity, corruption. UDALL. 2. The opposite of sincerity; the quality of being insincere; dissimulation; an instance of this 1699.

2. Manfredi, a statesman of the Italian school, who takes i. for wisdom GOUV. MORRIS. The fashionable insincerities of his day A. DOBSON.

†Insi·new, *v.* Also **en-.** 1597. [f. IN-[2] + SINEW.] *trans.* To furnish with sinews; to innerve; to inspire with vigour or strength -1611.

All members of our Cause..That are insinewed to his Action 2 *Hen. IV*, IV. i. 172.

Insinuant (insi·niuˌănt), *a. rare.* 1639. [ad. L. *insinuantem*, *insinuare* to INSINUATE.] 1. Insinuating; wheedling, ingratiating. 2. That steals its way in 1877.

Insinuate (insi·niuˌeɪt), *v.* 1529. [f. L. *insinuat-*, *insinuare*, f. *in-* (IN-[2]) + *sinuare* to curve.] 1. *trans.* To introduce tortuously, sinuously, indirectly, or by devious methods; to introduce by imperceptible degrees or subtle means 1647. Also *refl.* and †*intr.* (for *refl.*). 2. *trans.* To introduce (a person) by sinuous, stealthy, or artful ways into some position or relation; esp. *refl.* to worm oneself into the favour, etc. of another 1579. †Also *intr.* (for *refl.*). 3. *refl.* Of an immaterial thing: To instil itself subtly; to win its way *into* men's minds, favour, or notice 1594. †4. *trans.* To draw, win, or attract (a person, etc.) subtly or covertly *to* or *unto* something -1677. 5. To introduce to the mind indirectly, covertly, or privily; to infuse or instil subtly or imperceptibly 1529. 6. To convey indirectly; to hint obliquely; now generally with implication of cunning or underhand action 1561. Also *absol.* 7. To signify indirectly; to suggest, imply. *Obs.* or *arch.* 1533. 8. *Law.* To register (a deed or document); to lodge for registration 1529.

1. Trees, which i. their roots into the fissures KENDALL. 2. *refl.* They insinuated themselves into families to betray them 1832. 3. A pure and humble religion gently insinuated itself into the minds of men GIBBON. 5. In which wisdom was to be insinuated not enforced MAURICE. 6. Hints and allusions, expressing little, insinuating much BERKELEY. 7. He did i. with his eyes, unto me, I should depart and leave them 1641.

Insi·nuating, *ppl. a.* 1591. [f. prec. vb. + -ING[2].] 1. That penetrates sinuously between the particles of a body; subtly penetrating 1615. 2. That artfully works his way into company, position, favour, etc.; wily, wheedling, ingratiating.

1. Black smoak..of the most subtile and i. nature 1799. 2. [An] i. Hypocrite H. MORE. Englishmen of honourable name..and i. address MACAULAY. Hence **Insi·nuatingly** *adv.*

Insinuation (insiniuˌēɪ·ʃən). 1526. [ad. L. *insinuationem*; cf. F. *insinuation.*] The action of insinuating. 1. A winding or twisting 1661. 2. Introduction or entrance by winding, indirect, or stealthy motion; stealing in 1614. 3. The action of stealing into the favour of any one by winning, persuasive, or subtle means; a winning or ingratiating action or speech 1553. 4. The subtle or insensible instilling of anything into the mind 1526. 5. The suggestion or hinting of anything indirectly or covertly; (with *pl.*) an indirect or covert suggestion 1532. †6. *Law.* The production or delivery of a will for official registration, as a step towards procuring probate -1726.

2. The resistance of adamant is insufficient to defeat the i. of a fibre 1806. 3. I never advanced a Step by way of I., to curry Favour or Affection, as they say, on any Side 1728. 4. The i. of divine truth CUDWORTH. 5. A modest title should only informe the buyer what the book containes without furder i. MILT.

Insinuative (insi·niuˌeɪtiv, -ĕtiv), *a.* 1592. [f. L. *insinuat-*, *insinuare* + -IVE.] 1. Having the property of stealing into favour or confidence; subtly ingratiating. 2. Tending to insinuate into the mind 1786. 3. Characterized by or involving insinuation or suggestion; given to insinuations; suggestive, hinting 1648.

1. His Discourse [was] plausible and i. 1683. Hence **Insi·nuative-ly** *adv.*, **-ness.**

Insinuator (insi·niuˌeɪtəɹ). 1598. [a. L.] a. One who artfully creeps into favour; b. One who hints subtly.

Insi·nuatory, *a.* 1871. [f. L. *insinuat-*, ppl. stem + -ORY.] Insinuative.

Insipid (insi·pid), *a.* (*sb.*) 1620. [ad. late L. *insipidus*, f. *in-* (IN-[3]) + *sapidus* SAPID; cf. F. *insipide.*] 1. Without taste; having only a very slight taste; without perceptible flavour. 2. *fig.* Wanting the qualities which excite interest or emotion; lifeless, dull, flat 16.. †3. Devoid of taste, intelligence, or judgement; stupid, foolish, dull -1784. †4. *sb.* An insipid person or thing -1834.

1. No water can be pure that is not quite i. 1756. *I. diabetes* (*diabetes insipidus*), a form of diabetes dist. from *saccharine diabetes* (*diabetes mellitus*): see DIABETES. 2. I. compliments DISRAELI. 3. To church, where a most i. young coxcomb preached PEPYS. Hence **Insipi·dity,** the quality of being i.; an i. person, remark, etc. **Insi·pid-ly** *adv.*, **-ness.**

Insipient (insi·piĕnt). 1494. [ad. L. *insipientem*; see IN-[3] and SAPIENT.] A. *adj.* Void of wisdom; foolish. (Now mostly disused to avoid confusion with *incipient.*) 1528. †B. *sb.* An unwise or foolish person. -1633. So **Insi·pience,** the quality of being i. 1422.

Insist (insi·st), *v.* 1586. [ad. L. *insistere*, f. *in-* (IN-[2]) + *sistere* to stand; cf. F. *insister.*] 1. *intr.* To stand or rest *on* or *upon.* ? *Obs.* 1598. 2. To continue steadfastly *in* a course of action, to follow steadfastly *in* (*on*) a person's steps, etc.; to continue with urgency; to persevere (*arch.*) 1586. 3. To dwell at length or with emphasis *on* or *upon* (†*of*, †*in*) a matter; hence, *to i. on* = to assert or maintain persistently 1596. 4. To make a demand with persistent urgency; to take a persistent or peremptory stand (*on*, *upon*, †*for*, †*against*, etc.) 1623.

1. Angles likewise which i. on the Diameter, are all Right Angles 1709. 2. To caste our eyes upon Nature, and to i. in her steps 1638. 3. I cannot now i. Upon particulars B. JONS. Protarchus..insists that..all pleasures are good JOWETT. 4. To i. on the..appointment being made 1896. Hence **Insi·ster,** one who insists. **Insi·stingly** *adv.*

Insistence (insi·stĕns). Also †**-ance.** 1611. [f. prec. + -ENCE. The sp. in *-ance* follows *assistance*, etc.] The action of insisting; the fact, or quality, of being insistent.

Insistency (insi·stĕnsi). Also †**-ancy.** 1859. [f. as prec.; see -ENCY.] The quality of being insistent; urgency, pertinacity; an instance of this.

Insistent (insi·stĕnt), *a.* (*sb.*) Also †**-ant.** 1624. [ad. L. *insistentem*, *insistere.*] 1. Standing or resting on something (*rare*). 2. Dwelling firmly on something asserted, demanded, etc.; persistent, urgent. Hence, Enforcing attention. 1868. 3. *Ornith.* [F. *insistant.*] Applied to the hind toe of birds when it is inserted so high that it touches the ground only with its tip; opp. to *incumbent* 1886. 4. *sb.* An insistent person 1868.

2. The i. facts of sin, suffering, and misery 1888. Hence **Insi·stently** *adv.* in an i. manner.

†Insi·sture. [f. INSIST *v.* + -URE.] Continuance, persistence. *Tr. & Cr.* I. iii. 87.

†Insi·tiency. 1701. [f. IN-[3] + L. *sitientem*, *sitire* to thirst; see -ENCY.] Freedom from thirst.

†Insi·tion[1]. 1589. [ad. L. *insitionem*, *inserere.*] The action of engrafting, engraftment; *concr.* a graft. Also *transf.* and *fig.* -1855.

†Insition[2], obs. erron. f. INCISION.

Insititious (insiti·ʃəs), *a.* 1639. [f. L. *insiticius* (erron. *-itius*) engrafted; see INSITION[1] and -ITIOUS.] Of engrafted or inserted nature; introduced from without.

In situ (1803): see IN *Lat. prep.*

Insnare, Insnarl, obs. ff. ENSNARE, etc.

Insobriety (insobrəi·ĕti). 1611. [IN-[3].] Want of sobriety; intemperance (either generally, or *spec.* in drinking).

Insociable (insōu·ʃiăb'l), *a.* Now *rare.* 1581. [ad. L. *insociabilis*; see IN-[3] and SOCIABLE.] †1. That cannot be associated or combined; incompatible -1678. 2. Unsociable 1588.

1. Lime and wood are i. WOTTON. 2. This austere i. life SHAKS. Hence **Insociabi·lity, Inso·ciableness,** i. disposition or state. **Inso·ciably** *adv.*

†Inso·ciate, *a.* [f. IN-[3] + L. *sociatus.*] Not associated; solitary. B. JONS.

Insolate (i·nsoleɪt), *v.* 1623. [f. L. *insolat-*, *insolare* to place in the sun, f. *in-* (IN-[2]) + *sol.*] *trans.* To place in, or expose to the rays of, the sun.

Insolation (insolē·ʃən). 1612. [ad. L. *insolationem*; see prec.] The action of placing in the sun; exposure to the sun's rays; *occas.*, the effect of this. 1. *gen.* 1654. 2. *spec.* a. Exposure of some substance to the sun's rays, as for the purpose of drying, bleaching, or maturing 1612. b. Exposure of the body to the sun's rays for medical treatment 1626. c. Injurious exposure to the sun's rays or to excessive heat; sunstroke 1758.

Insole (i·nsōul). 1851. [f. IN *a.* + SOLE *sb.*] a. The inner sole of a boot or shoe. b. A flat piece of warm or waterproof material laid inside the shoe.

Insolence (i·nsŏlĕns). ME. [ad. L. *insolentia*, f. *insolentem* INSOLENT; see -ENCE.]

1. The quality of being insolent, esp. as manifested in action. †a. Pride; arrogance, contempt for inferiors. b. Offensive contemptuousness of action or speech due to presumption; sauciness 1668. c. An insolent act; a piece of insolence (now *rare*) 1491. †2. Exultation. SPENSER. †3. Inexperience -1500. †4. The quality or character of being unusual; unaccustomedness 1631.

1. a. I do wonder, his i. can brooke to be commanded vnder Cominius SHAKS. *Cor.* I. i. 266. The rich Man's I. ROWE. b. When their I. was such, as to make Kings the Instruments of their Ambition 1683. c. The Assaults and Insolences of Night Robbers 1680.

I·nsolency. Now *rare.* 1494. [ad. L. *insolentia*; see prec. and -ENCY.] = prec.

Insolent (i·nsǒlěnt), *a.* (*sb.*) ME. [ad. L. *insolentem* unaccustomed, f. *in-* (IN-³) + *solere* to be accustomed.]

A. *adj.* I. †1. Proud, disdainful, arrogant, overbearing; offensively contemptuous of the rights of others. 2. Contemptuous of rightful authority; presumptuously contemptuous; impertinently insulting 1678. †3. Immoderate, going beyond the bounds of propriety -1712.

1. How i. is upstart pride! GAY. 2. God will not gratifie their i. demand BAXTER. An idle, drunken, i. fellow 1884. 3. All the Extremities of Houshold Expence, Furniture, and i. Equipage STEELE.

II. †1. Unaccustomed, unusual -1665. †2. Unused to a thing; inexperienced -1598.

B. *sb.* An insolent person 1595.

Out i. *John* II. i. 122.

Hence I·nsolent·ly *adv.*, †-ness.

Insolidity (insoli·dĭti). ? *Obs.* 1578. [IN-³.] Absence of solidity; want of firmness or stability; frailty, flimsiness, weakness.

Insolubility (insǫliubi·lĭti). 1620. [f. L. *insolubilis*, see -ITY.] The quality of being insoluble. †1. Indissolubility. BRENT. 2. Incapability of being solved; also, an insoluble problem 1837. 3. Incapability of being dissolved in a liquid 1791.

1. The i. of Marriage 1620. 2. The i. of this problem 1837.

Insoluble (insǫ·liub'l), *a.* (*sb.*) ME. [ad. L. *insolubilis*; see IN-³ and SOLUBLE.] 1. That cannot be dissolved, undone, or loosed; indissoluble. Now *rare.* †b. Of arguments: Irrefragable (*rare*) -1676. 2. That cannot be solved or explained, as a difficulty, problem, etc.; unsolvable ME. 3. Incapable of being dissolved in a liquid 1713. 4. *sb.* Something insoluble; a difficulty or problem that cannot be solved or explained ME.

1. Like a strong and i. wall HOLLAND. 2. An i. question concerning the origin of evil WARBURTON. 3. The i. salts 1857. Hence Inso·lubleness. Inso·lubly *adv.*

Insolvable (insǫ·lvăb'l), *a.* 1652. [IN-³.] 1. = INSOLUBLE *a.* †2. Of a debt: 'That cannot be paid' (J.) 1755. Hence Insolvabi·lity, Inso·lvableness. Inso·lvably *adv.*

Insolvency (insǫ·lvěnsi). 1660. [f. INSOLVENT *a.*; see -ENCY.] The condition of being insolvent; the fact of being unable to pay one's debts or discharge one's liabilities; an instance of this. Also *transf.* and *fig.*

Prisoners..who intend to take the Benefit of the Act of I. 1725.

Insolvent (insǫ·lvěnt), *a.* (*sb.*) 1591. [IN-³.] Not solvent. 1. Unable to pay one's debts or discharge one's liabilities; bankrupt. †2. Not able to be cashed or realized -1728. 3. Pertaining or relating to insolvents or insolvency 1837. 4. *sb.* An insolvent debtor 1725.

1. The cruel treatment of the i. debtors of the state GIBBON. 3. He had been through the I. Court THACKERAY. 4. An i. as distinguished from a bankrupt, was an i. who was not a trader; for originally only a trader could be made bankrupt WHARTON.

‖**Insomnia** (insǫ·mniă). 1758. [L., f. *insomnis* sleepless, f. *in-* (IN-³) + *somnus*.] Inability to sleep; sleeplessness. Also †Insomnie 1623, †Insomnium 1694-1856.

Insomnious (insǫ·mniəs), *a.* *rare.* 1658. [ad. L. *insomniosus*, f. prec.; see -OUS.] Affected with insomnia; sleepless.

Insomnolence (insǫ·mnǒlěns). 1822. [IN-³.] Insomnia. So Inso·mnolency 1843, Inso·mnolent *a.* 1840. (All *rare.*)

Insomuch (insǒmʊ·tʃ), *adv.* ME. [The three words *in so much*, now usu. written as one.] 1. *absol.* So much, so far. 2. *Insomuch as.* a. Inasmuch as, seeing that, since 1485. †b. = sense 3. -1658. c. To such an extent as, so as 1651. 3. *Insomuch that*: To such an extent that, so that. (The most usual construction.) †4. With ellipsis of *as*: = 2 a. -1605.

2. a. In so much as I am not French by birth, but born..in the city of Marseilles CAXTON. c. In so much and in so far as they are susceptible of becoming [etc.] BENTHAM. 3. The rain fell in torrents, i. that ..the soldiers were often ankle-deep in water ALISON. 4. *A. Y. L.* v. ii. 60.

Insonorous (insǒnōə·rəs), *a.* *rare.* 1795. [IN-³.] Not sonorous; giving a dull or muffled sound.

Insooth, *adv.*, for *in sooth*; see SOOTH *sb.*

Insorb (insǭ·ɹb), *v.* *rare.* 1878. [f. IN-¹ + L. *sorbere*.] *trans.* To absorb *into.* So Inso·rbent *a.* absorbent 1756.

‖**Insouciance** (ɛ̃nsusyā·ns, *occas.* insū·siăns). 1799. [F., f. next; see -ANCE.] Carelessness, indifference, unconcern.

‖**Insouciant** (insū·siănt, Fr. ɛ̃nsusyaṅ). 1829. [F., f. *in-* (IN-³) + *souciant*, *soucier* to care:— L. *sollicitare* to disturb, agitate.] Careless, indifferent, unconcerned.

Insoul, var. of ENSOUL *v.*

Inspan (inspæ·n), *v.* *S. Afr.* 1850. [a. Du. *inspannen*, f. *in* adv. + *spannen* to stretch, tighten.] *trans.* To yoke (horses, oxen, etc.) in a team to a vehicle; to harness (a wagon).

†**I·nspect**, *sb.* 1489. [app. ad. L. *inspectus*. (Stress orig. *inspe·ct*, in 18th c. *i·nspect*.)] The act of looking into a matter; inspection, examination -1746.

Inspect (inspe·kt), *v.* 1623. [f. L. *inspect-*, ppl. stem of *inspicere*, and its freq. *inspectare*.] 1. *trans.* To look carefully into; to view closely and critically; to examine; now *spec.* to investigate or oversee officially. †2. *intr.* To look closely or carefully; to examine *into* or *among* -1799.

1. He inspected nature with the close eye of a naturalist D'ISRAELI. 2. That..you would please to i. among your father's papers SWIFT.

Inspection (inspe·kʃən). ME. [a. F. *inspection*, *-cion*, ad. L. *inspectionem*, f. *inspicere* to INSPECT.] 1. The action of inspecting or looking narrowly into; careful scrutiny or survey; close examination; *spec.* official investigation or oversight. †2. Insight, perception -1709. †3. A plan of a piece of ground, etc. which has been inspected; a design, survey, view -1795.

1. The I. of the Intrails of Beasts, to learn the will of Heaven BOYLE. *Trial by I.*, a mode of trial in which some point or issue, being evidently the object of sense, was decided by the judges of the Court upon the evidence of their own senses. Hence Inspe·ctional *a.* of, pertaining or relating to i.; *spec.* that can be read or understood at sight.

Inspective (inspe·ktiv), *a.* 1609. [ad. late L. *inspectivus*, f. *inspect-*, *inspicere*; see -IVE.] 1. Given to inspection; watchful, attentive 1684. †2. Concerned with investigation; theoretical -1660.

Inspector (inspe·ktəɹ). 1602. [a. L., from *inspicere*.] 1. One who inspects or looks carefully at or into; an overseer, a superintendent; *spec.* an officer appointed to examine into, and supervise or report upon, the working of some department or institution, or the due observance of certain laws and regulations, as *I. of schools*, *of weights and measures*, *of mines*, etc. b. One who looks *into* something for information, from curiosity, etc. 1667. c. An officer of police ranking next below a superintendent and above a sergeant 1840. 2. *Gr. Antiq.* = EPOPT 1818. 3. Inspector-General: An officer at the head of a system of inspection, having under him a body of inspectors 1702. Hence Inspe·ctoral *a.*

Inspectorate (inspe·ktǒrět). 1762. [f. prec.; see -ATE¹.] 1. a. The office or function of an inspector; supervision by inspectors. b. A body or staff of inspectors. Also *attrib.* 2. A district under official inspection 1853.

Inspectorial (inspektōə·riăl), *a.* 1753. [f. INSPECTOR + -IAL; after words from L. *-orius* + -AL.] Of, pertaining or belonging to inspectors; having the rank or position of an inspector.

Inspectorship (inspe·ktəɹʃip). 1753. [f. as prec. + -SHIP.] The office or position of an inspector; inspectorate.

Inspectress (inspe·ktrės). 1785. [f. INSPECTOR + -ESS.] A female inspector.

†**Inspe·rge**, *v.* 1599. [ad. L. *inspergere*, f. *in-* (IN-²) + *spargere* to scatter.] *trans.* To sprinkle on; to scatter on or in -1683.

†**Inspe·rse**, *v.* *rare.* 1577. [f. L. *inspers-*, *inspergere*.] = prec. -1721. So †Inspe·rsion, the action of sprinkling on; that which is sprinkled on 1568.

‖**Inspeximus** (inspe·ksimŏs). 1628. [L., = 'we have inspected'; the first word in recital of the inspection of charters, etc.] *Law.* A charter in which the grantor avouches to have inspected an earlier charter which he recites and confirms. Also *attrib.*

Insphere, -spheare, var. of ENSPHERE *v.*

Inspinne, var. of INCHPIN (sense 1).

Inspirable (inspəiə·răb'l), *a.* 1656. [f. INSPIRE *v.* + -ABLE.] Capable of being inspired (see the vb.).

†**Inspirate** (i·nspireit), *v.* 1615. [f. L. *inspirat-*, *inspirare*.] = INSPIRE *v.* -1810.

Inspiration (inspirē·ʃən). ME. [a. OF., ad. L. *inspirationem*.]

I. Lit. senses. †1. The action of blowing on or into (*rare*) -1710. 2. The action, or an act, of inhaling; the drawing in of the breath into the lungs in respiration. (Opp. to EXPIRATION.) 1564. Also *transf.*

2. In I. the lungs are passive TODD.

II. Fig. senses. 1. The action of inspiring; the fact or condition of being inspired; a breathing or infusion into the mind or soul. a. *spec.* (*Theol.*, etc.) A special immediate action or influence of the Spirit of God (or of some divine or supernatural being) upon the human mind or soul; said *esp.* of that divine influence under which the books of the Bible are held to have been written ME. b. *gen.* A breathing in of some idea, purpose, etc. into the mind; the suggestion of some feeling or impulse, esp. of an exalted kind SHAKS. c. The prompting (from some influential quarter) of the utterance or publication of particular views or information on some public matter 1880. 2. *transf.* Something inspired; an inspired utterance or product 1819; an inspiring principle 1865.

1. a. *Verbal i.* of the Bible, the view according to which every word written was dictated by the Spirit of God. *Plenary i.*, the view that the inspiration of the writers extends to all subjects treated of, so that all their statements are to be received as infallibly true. The Prophets, who teach us by diuine i. BIBLE *Transl. Pref.* 3. b. There is i. in numbers, in men acting at once and together MOZLEY. 2. Whatever motive your own souls supply As i. BROWNING. Hence Inspira·tional *a.* of or pertaining to i.; inspired, inspiring.

Inspira·tionist. 1846. [f. prec. + -IST.] A believer in a theory of inspiration; as *plenary i.*, a believer in plenary inspiration.

Inspirator (i·nspireitəɹ). 1624. [a. L.] †1. One who or that which inspires -1848. 2. a. A kind of injector in a steam-engine 1890. b. A kind of respirator 1898.

Inspiratory (inspəiə·rătəri, i·nspireitəri), *a.* 1773. [f. L. *inspirat-*, *inspirare* + -IVE.] Belonging to inspiration or inhalation; serving to draw in the air in respiration.

Inspire (inspəiə·ɹ), *v.* ME. [a. OF. *enspirer*, *inspirer*, ad. L. *inspirare*, f. *in-* (IN-²) + *spirare* to breathe.]

I. Lit. senses. 1. *trans.* To breathe or blow upon or into. *Obs.* or *arch.* †Also *intr.* †2. *trans.* To blow or breathe (air, etc.) upon or into -1697. b. To breathe (life, a soul) *in* or *into*. In later use, *fig.* ME. 3. *trans.* To take into the lungs by breathing, inhale. (Opp. to EXPIRE.) 1528. b. *intr.* or *absol.* To draw in the breath 1661.

1. Descend, ye Nine!..The breathing instruments i. POPE. 2. MILT. *P. L.* IV. 804. 3. The Air we walk in and i. 1761.

II. Fig. senses. 1. *trans.* To infuse some thought or feeling into (a person, etc.), as if by breathing; to animate by some mental or spiritual influence. a. *spec.* (*Theol.*, etc.) To influence or actuate by special divine or supernatural agency; used esp. in reference to the prophets, apostles, and Scripture writers ME. **b.** *gen.* To influence, animate, or actuate (a person) *with* a feeling, idea, impulse, etc. Also said of the feeling, influence, etc. ME. **2.** To breathe in or infuse (a feeling, thought, principle, etc.) into the mind or soul ME. Also *absol.* **3.** *transf. trans.* To suggest or prompt the utterance of particular views or information on some public matter, or to prompt a speaker or writer to such utterance 1883.

1. **a.** As god inspired hir forth sho went 1450. **b.** Poverty inspires necessity with daring JOWETT. What zeale, what furie, hath inspir'd thee now? SHAKS. **2.** Al scripture of God ynspyrid is profitable to teche WYCLIF. He inspired terror to the enemy and a just confidence to the troops GIBBON. Hence **Inspi·rer,** one who or that which inspires. **Inspi·ringly** *adv.*

Inspired (inspəi·ɹd), *ppl. a.* 1450. [f. prec. + -ED¹.] **1.** Blown on or into; inflated. *Obs.* or *arch.* 1649. **2.** Breathed in; inhaled. (Opp. to *expired.*) 1649. **3.** Actuated or animated by divine or supernatural influence 1667. **4.** Infused or communicated by divine or supernatural power; having the character of inspiration 1450. **5.** *transf.* Prompted by, or emanating from, an influential (but unavowed) source 1887.

3. Th' inspir'd Castalian Spring MILT. *P. L.* IV. 273. 4. These abilities, wheresoever they be found, are the i. gift of God MILT. 5. An i. paragraph, journal (*mod.*). Hence **Inspi·redly** *adv.* by or as by inspiration.

Inspirit (inspi·rit), *v.* 1610. [f. IN-² + SPIRIT *sb.*] **1.** *trans.* To put spirit, life, or energy into; to animate; to encourage; to incite (*to,* or *to do* something). **2.** To fill with, or cause to be possessed by, a spirit or supernatural being 1675.

1. To i. the doubtful courage of his soldiers SCOTT.

†**Inspi·ssate,** *ppl. a.* 1603. [ad. late L. *inspissatus, inspissare*; see next.] Inspissated, thickened –1720.

Inspissate (inspi·seⁱt, i·nspiseⁱt), *v.* 1626. [f. late L. *inspissare* (Boeth.), f. *in-* (IN-²) + *spissare, spissus* thick.] **1.** *trans.* To thicken, condense. Also *fig.* **2.** *intr.* To become thick or dense 1755.

1. Pitch is tar inspissated BERKELEY.

Inspissation (inspisēⁱ·ʃən). 1603. [ad. med.L. *inspissationem.*] The action of making, or process of becoming, thick or dense; thickening, condensation; an instance of this. So **Inspissative** *a.*, producing inspissation 1425.

Instability (instăbi·lĭti). ME. [a. F. *instabilité,* ad. L. *instabilitatem,* f. *instabilis.*] The quality of being unstable; lack of stability in regard to position, condition, or moral qualities; want of steadiness, fixity, or firmness of purpose or character. With *an* and *pl.*, an instance of this.

Some lamentyng the instabilitee of the Englishe people, iudged thim to be spotted with perpetuall infamie HALL.

Instable (instēⁱ·b'l), *a.* Now *rare.* 1483. [ad. L. *instabilis,* f. *in-* (IN-³) + *stabilis* STABLE.] Not stable; lacking in stability; unstable. Hence †**Insta·bleness,** instability 1460.

Install (instǭ·l), *v.* Also **instal.** 1483. [ad. med.L. *installare,* f. *in-* (IN-²) + *stallum*; see STALL. Cf. F. *installer.*] **1.** *trans.* To invest with an office or dignity by seating in a stall or official seat. Hence, To instate in an office, rank, etc. with the customary ceremonies or formalities. **b.** To place in any office or position, esp. one of dignity; to establish in any place or condition 1647. **2.** To place (an apparatus, a system of lighting, heating, or the like) in position for service or use 1867.

1. The Bishop of Ostia..consecrates and instals the Pope HOWELL. **b.** What station charms thee? I'll i. thee there YOUNG. Hence **Insta·llant, -er.**

Installation (instǫlēⁱ·ʃən). 1606. [ad. med.L. *installationem,* f. *installare*; see prec.] **1.** The action of installing or fact of being installed; the ceremony of formally inducting (a person) into an ecclesiastical dignity, an order of knighthood, or an official position; hence, formal establishment in any office or position. **2.** The action of setting up or fixing in position for service or use (machinery, apparatus, etc.); a mechanical apparatus set up or put in position for use; *spec.* used to include all the necessary plant, materials, and work required to equip rooms or buildings with electric light 1882.

1. The ceremony of his [the Nizam's] i. MACAULAY.

Instalment¹, installment (instǭ·lmĕnt). 1589. [f. INSTALL *v.* + -MENT.] **1.** The action of installing or fact of being installed; installation. **b.** Establishment in any position, seat, or place 1646. †**2.** A place or seat wherein some one is installed (*rare*) –1610.

1. The instalement of this noble Duke, In the seate royall of this famous Ile SHAKS. **2.** Each faire I., Coate, and seu'rall Crest, With loyall Blazon, euermore be blest SHAKS.

Instalment² (instǭ·lmĕnt). Also **install-.** 1732. [f. IN-² + STALMENT.] †**1.** The arrangement of the payment of a sum of money by fixed portions at fixed times –1775. **2.** 'The payment, or the time appointed for payment, of different portions of a sum of money, which, by agreement . . is to be paid in parts, at certain stated times' (Tomlins) 1776. **3.** Each of several parts into which a sum payable is divided, in order to be paid at different fixed times; a part of a sum due paid in advance of the remainder 1776. Also *attrib.* (freq. in recent use).

3. *fig.* His conclusion may be accepted as a large i. of the truth H. SPENCER.

Instamp, obs. f. ENSTAMP.

Instance (i·nstăns), *sb.* ME. [a. F., ad. L. *instantia* presence, urgency, etc., in med. Schol.L. transl. Gr. ἔνστασις; f. *instantem* INSTANT *a.*]

I. 1. Urgency in speech or action; urgent entreaty; earnestness; persistence. (*arch.* exc. in phr. *at the i. of.*) †**b.** Chiefly *pl.* An urgent entreaty, repeated solicitation –1862. †**2.** Impelling motive; cause –1665.

2. Tell him his Feares are shallow, without i. SHAKS.

II. Instant time. †**1.** A being present, presence; the present time –1597. †**2.** An instant, a moment –1674.

1. *2 Hen. IV,* IV. i. 83. **2.** Those continued instances of time which flow into thousand yeares SIR T. BROWNE.

III. In Scholastic Logic, etc. †**1.** A case adduced in objection to or disproof of a universal assertion (= med.L. *instantia,* Gr. ἔνστασις) –1696. **2.** A fact or example brought forward in support of a general assertion or an argument, or in illustration of a general truth. Hence, a case, an illustrative example. Also, in broader sense, a case occurring, a recurring occasion. 1586. †**b.** A detail, circumstance –1745. †**3.** Something which proves or indicates; a proof, evidence; a sign, token, mark –1791.

1. To conclude upon an enumeration of particulars, without i. contradictory, is no conclusion, but a conjecture BACON. **2.** Noy..is an i. that mere knowledge is not true wisdom D'ISRAELI. Phr. †*To make* or *give i.* (*in*): = INSTANCE *v.* 2. 1614. *For i.*: for example 1657. **3.** SHAKS. *Lucr.* 1511.

IV. In legal use, etc. [From L. *instantia* in Ulpian.] **1.** A process or proceeding in a court of justice, a suit 1661. **2.** Hence, *In the first i.*: as the first step in proceeding; in the first place 1676.

1. *Court of first i.*, court of primary jurisdiction; The loser is seldom satisfied with the decision of a Court of first i. 1865. *I. court,* a branch of the former Admiralty Court, having jurisdiction in cases of private injuries to private rights occurring at sea or closely connected with maritime subjects and in contracts of a maritime nature 1802. **2.** The penalty is in the first i., corrective not penal 1850.

Instance (i·nstăns), *v.* late ME. [f. prec. sb.] †**1.** *trans.* To urge, entreat urgently, importune –1736. **2.** *intr.* To cite an instance, to adduce an example in illustration or proof. Const. *in* (the example adduced). Now *rare.* 1601. †**b.** Of a thing: To be exemplified 1667. **3.** *trans.* To illustrate, prove, or show, by means of an instance; to exemplify. Now *rare.* 1608. **4.** To cite as an instance or example. In imper. = 'Take as an instance'; cf. WITNESS. 1622.

2. It would be needless to i. in sheep which constantly flock together G. WHITE. **b.** This story doth not only i. in kingdoms, but in families too JER. TAYLOR. **4.** I may i. olive oil, which is mischievous to all plants JOWETT.

Instancy (i·nstănsi). 1515. [ad. L. *instantia*; see -ANCY.] **1.** The quality of being instant; urgency, earnestness, solicitation; pressure, pressing nature. **2.** Imminence (*rare*) 1658. **3.** Instantaneity (*rare*) 1851. †**4.** = INSTANCE III. 2. JACKSON.

1. Those heauenly precepts, which our Lord and Sauiour with so great instancie gaue as concerning peace and vnitie HOOKER.

Instant (i·nstănt), *sb.* ME. [ellipt. use of INSTANT *a.*] **1.** The time now present, or regarded as present; hence, point of time, moment 1500. **2.** An infinitely short space of time; a moment ME. †**3.** = INSTANCE *sb.* III. 2. JEWELL. †**4.** = INSTANCE *sb.* I. 1. HOLLAND.

1. Of all the extent of time, onely the i. is that which we can call ours FULLER. **2.** He was not an i. too soon 1891. Phr. *In an i.*, *on* (†*upon,* †*in*) *the i.*, etc. *The i.*, ellipt. = 'the very moment that', 'as soon as ever'.

Instant (i·nstănt), *a.* (*adv.*) 1477. [a. F. *instant,* ad. L. *instantem, instare,* f. *in-* (IN-²) + *stare* to stand.] **1.** Pressing, urgent; importunate. *Obs.* or *arch.* **2.** Now (or then) present, existing, or happening (*arch.*) 1527. **b.** Said of the current calendar month; now ellipt. as in *the 10th instant.* Abbrev. *inst.* 1547. **3.** Close at hand, imminent 1520. **4.** Following immediately 1596. **5.** *adv.* (*poet.*) Instantly, at once 1602.

1. They were i. with loud voyces, and required that he might be crucified BIBLE (Genev.) *Luke* xxiii. 23. He has i. need of you 1856. **2. b.** The 20 or 21 of that i. 1583. The 3d of this i. March 1796. **3.** The abrupt Fate's footstep i. now BROWNING. **4.** The shame it selfe doth speake For i. remedy *Lear* I. iv. 268. **5.** You my sinnewes, grow not i. Old *Haml.* I. v. 94.

Instantaneous (instăntēⁱ·niəs), *a.* 1651. [f. L. *instantem,* after *momentaneus*; see -EOUS.] **1.** Occurring or operating in an instant; done without any perceptible lapse of time. **2.** Existing at or pertaining to some particular instant. Chiefly in *Dynamics,* as *i. axis, i. centre of rotation* 1837.

1. Justification is a continued Act, and not any I. Act BAXTER. The motion of electricity..appears to be i. IMISON. Hence **Instantane·ity, Instanta·neousness. Instanta·neously** *adv.* 1644.

‖**Instanter** (instæ·ntəɹ), *adv.* 1688. [L. adv.] Immediately, forthwith, at once. (Orig. a law term, but now chiefly emphatic for *instantly.*)

He was at your service *instanter* 1883.

Insta·ntial, *a. rare.* 1647. [f. L. *instantia* INSTANCE *sb.* + -AL.] Of, pertaining to, or furnishing an instance or instances.

Instantly (i·nstăntli), *adv.* 1477. [f. INSTANT *a.* + -LY².] **1.** Urgently, with importunity (*arch.*). †**2.** At this or that very moment; now, just now, just –1632. **3.** In a moment; forthwith, at once 1552. **b.** *conjunctively.* The moment that, as soon as 1793. **4.** Immediately (in position). RUSKIN.

1. They..besought him i. TINDALE *Luke* vii. 4. **3. b.** He ran across the grass i. he perceived his mother THACKERAY.

Instar (instā·ɹ), *v.* 1592. [IN-¹.] **1.** *trans.* To set as a star; to make a star of. **2.** To set or adorn with or as with stars 1652.

1. Our heart is high instarr'd in brighter spheres FORD.

Instate (instēⁱ·t), *v.* Also †**en-.** 1603. [f. IN-² + STATE *sb.* Cf. *reinstate.*] **1.** *trans.* To put (a person) into a certain state or condition; to install, establish. Const. *in* (*into, to*). 1613. †**2.** To endow or invest (a person) *with* –1659.

1. It will not be my fault if she is not at once instated in her rights 1864. **2.** *Meas. for M.* V. i. 429. Hence **Insta·tement** (now *rare*), instating; establishment.

†**Instau·rate,** *v.* 1583. [f. L. *instaurat-, instaurare*; see INSTORE.] *trans.* = INSTORE *v.* –1666.

Instauration (instǫrēⁱ·ʃən). 1603. [ad. L. *instaurationem*; see INSTORE *v.*] **1.** The action of restoring or repairing; renovation, renewal. †**2.** Institution, founding, establishment –1778.

1. His [Bacon's] grand i. of the sciences 1761. **2.** The i. and advancement of states BP. LOWTH.

Instaurator (i·nstǫrēⁱtəɹ). 1660. [a. late L., f. *instaurare.*] **a.** One who restores or renews. **b.** A founder.

The great i. of all knowledge, Bacon M. PATTISON.

Instead (inste·d), *phrasal comb.* ME. [The two words *in stead* = 'in place'; before 1620 usu. written separately, but after *c* 1640 conjunctly. See STEAD *sb.*] **1.** Phr. *Instead of*, †*in stead of*: In place of, in lieu of, in room of; for, in substitution for. Also used ellipt. bef. a prep., adv., adj., or phrase. **2.** Without *of*: In its stead, in place of the thing mentioned; as a substitute 1667.

1. Catholicon the drugge, that it is in stead of all purges BIBLE *Transl. Pref.* 3. I. of money he gave promises GOLDSM. *ellipt.* I found the patient worse i. of better (*mod.*). 2. To rase Quite out thir Native Language, and i. To sow a jangling noise of words unknown MILT.

Insteep (instīˑp), *v.* Now *rare.* 1599. [f. IN-[1] + STEEP *v.*, after L. *immergere.*] *trans.* To immerse; to steep or soak *in*; to imbrue.

Where in gore he lay insteeped *Hen. V*, IV. vi. 12.

Instep (iˑnstep). 1530. [app. f. IN-[1] + STEP.] **1.** The upper surface of the human foot between the toes and the ankle. **2.** That part of the hind-leg of a horse which extends from the hock to the pastern-joint. Also the corresponding parts in birds, etc. 1720. **3.** That part of a shoe, stocking, etc. fitting or covering the instep 1599. **4.** A part of a hill, a tree trunk, etc., resembling the human instep in shape or position 1681.

Instigate (iˑnstigeˈt), *v.* Pa. pple. **-ated**; also †-at. 1542. [f. L. *instigat-*, *instigare*, f. *in-* (IN-[2]) + **stigare*; cf. Gr. στίζειν (root στιγ-) to prick.] **1.** *trans.* To spur, urge on; to stir up, stimulate, incite (now mostly to something evil). **2.** To stir up, foment, provoke 1852.

1. To i. Princes to warre upon one another HOBBES. 2. What he and they called levying war was, in truth, no better than instigating murder THACKERAY. Hence **Iˑnstigatingly** *adv.* **Iˑnstigative** *a.* tending to i.; stimulative 1642. **Iˑnstigator** 1598, **Instigaˑtrix** 1611.

Instigation (instigēˑʃən). ME. [ad. L. *instigationem.*] The action of instigating or goading; incitement, stimulation; an incentive, stimulus, spur.

That this foul deed was done by the i...of his stepmother FREEMAN.

Instil, instill (instiˑl), *v.* 1533. [ad. L. *instillare*, f. *in-* (IN-[2]) + *stillare* to drop; cf. F. *instiller.*] **1.** *trans.* To put in by drops; to introduce in small quantities 1547. **2.** To introduce little by little into the mind, soul, heart, etc.; to cause to enter by degrees; to infuse gradually; to insinuate 1533. †**b.** To teach or urge stealthily -1807. †**3.** To imbue *with*. MILT.

1. Michael..from the Well of Life three drops instill'd MILT. *P. L.* XI. 416. 2. How hast thou instill'd Thy malice into thousands MILT. *P. L.* VI. 269. Hence **Iˑnstillator, Instiˑller**, one who instils or infuses. **Instiˑlment**, the action of instilling.

Instillation (instilēˑʃən). 1540. [ad. L. *instillationem.*] The action of instilling; that which is instilled.

†**Instiˑmulate**, *v.* 1570. [f. L. *instimulat-*, *instimulare.*] *trans.* To incite, instigate, stimulate -1670. Hence †**Instimulaˑtion**.

Instinct (iˑnstiŋkt), *sb.* ME. [ad. L. *instinctus*, f. *instinguere*, f. *in-* (IN-[2]) + *stinguere* orig. to prick, stick; root *stig-* as in *instigate*. Formerly stressed *instiˑnct.*] †**1.** Instigation; impulse; prompting -1730. **2.** Innate impulse; natural or spontaneous tendency or inclination. In mod. use assoc. w. sense 3. 1568. **3.** *spec.* An innate propensity in organized beings (esp. in the lower animals), varying with the species, and manifesting itself in acts which appear to be rational, but are performed without conscious adaptation of means to ends. Also, the faculty supposed to be involved in this operation. 1596. **b.** Any faculty acting like animal instinct; intuition; unconscious dexterity or skill 1597.

2. There is a natural i. in all heavy bodies to lean and press upon the lowest parts 1726. Our love of the Alps is..a Teutonic i. SYMONDS. Edward was by i. a lawgiver STUBBS. 3. The operation of i. is more sure and simple than that of reason GIBBON. The very essence of an i. is that it is followed independently of reason DARWIN. b. The true i. of genius HAMERTON.

Instinct (instiˑŋkt), *ppl. a.* Usu. const. as *pa. pple.* 1538. [ad. L. *instinctus*, pa. pple. of *instinguere* (see prec.) Revived about 1800 in sense 3, which is app. due to a misunderstanding of sense 2.] †**1.** Implanted naturally; innate -1628. †**2.** Impelled, moved, excited, inflamed, animated -1720. **3.** In recent use: Imbued or charged *with* something, as a moving or animating force or principle 1797.

2. Forth rush'd..The Chariot..undrawn, It self i. with Spirit MILT. *P. L.* VI. 752. 3. I. with life to its finger-ends CARLYLE.

†**Instiˑnct**, *v.* 1538. [f. L. *instinct-*, *instinguere* to instigate; see INSTINCT *sb.*] **1.** *trans.* To instigate, prompt, impel internally -1694. **2.** To implant naturally or as an instinct; to infuse as an animating principle -1732.

†**Instiˑnction.** 1440. [f. (ult.) L. *instinguere* to instigate; see INSTINCT *sb.*] **1.** Instigation; prompting; inspiration -1670. **2.** Innate impulse; instinct -1753.

Instinctive (instiˑŋktiv), *a.* (*adv.*) 1649. [f. L. *instinct-*, *instinguere* + -IVE; see INSTINCT *sb.*, and cf. F. *instinctif.*] Of the nature of instinct; operating by or resulting from innate prompting. **b.** *poet.* as *adv.* 1715.

I. intimations of the death of some absent friends BP. HALL. The i. fondness natural to parents 1718. The alternation of the lower limbs is i. in man BAIN. Hence **Instiˑnctively** *adv.* in an i. manner; by instinct 1610.

Instinctiˑvity. [f. prec. + -ITY.] The quality of being instinctive; proneness to instinctive action. COLERIDGE.

Instipulate (instiˑpiŭlět), *a.* 1847. [IN-[3].] *Bot.* Not stipulate, having no stipules, exstipulate.

Institor (iˑnstitǫɹ). 1657. [a. L., f. *insistere*; see INSIST.] A factor or agent; a broker; a retailer, huckster, vendor. (Chiefly in *Rom.* and *Sc. Law.*) So **Institoˑrial** *a.* of or pertaining to an i.

Institute (iˑnstitiŭt), *sb.*[1] 1520. [ad. L. *institutum* purpose, design, plan, etc., sb. use of neut. of *institutus*, *instituere* to INSTITUTE. In sense 3, corresp. to F. *institute*, *-s*, ad. late L. *instituta* pl., in sense of cl. L. *institutiones.*] †**1.** Purpose, design -1670. **2.** Something instituted; an established law, custom, usage, or organization; an institution 1546. †**b.** The act of instituting -1657. **3.** A principle or element of instruction; usu. in *pl.*, a digest of the elements of a subject, esp. of jurisprudence. (So in F.) 1579. **4.** A society or organization instituted to promote literature, science, art, education, or the like; also, the building in which such work is carried on. Often specialized as *Literary, Philosophical, Mechanics' I.* 1829.

2. The institutes and customs of civil life MILT. b. Water, sanctify'd by Christ's i. MILT. 3. *Institutes of Justinian* (*Institutiones Justiniani*), an elementary treatise on Roman Law, compiled by order of the Emperor Justinian in A.D. 533. *Institutes of medicine*, the statement of the principles on which medicine is based. 4. The title of Member of the I. is the highest distinction to which a Frenchman of culture can aspire 1889.

Iˑnstitute, *sb.*[2] 1681. [ad. L. *institutus* (person) instituted (as heir).] *Rom.* and *Sc. Law.* The person to whom an estate is first given in a testament or destination.

†**Iˑnstitute**, *ppl. a.* ME. [a. AF. *institut* (Britton), ad. L. *institutus*, *instituere.*] Instituted -1671.

Institute (iˑnstitiŭt), *v.* ME. [f. L. *institut-*, *instituere*, f. *in-* (IN-[2]) + *statuere* to set up; see STATUTE.] **1.** *trans.* **a.** To set up, establish, found, ordain; to introduce, bring into use or practice 1483. †**b.** To order, arrange, put into form, frame -1745. **c.** To set on foot, initiate, start (an inquiry, etc.) 1797. **2.** To establish in an office, charge, or position; to appoint; now only, to place in a spiritual charge. Const. *to*, *into* (*in*), or *absol.* ME. **b.** *Rom. Law.* To appoint as heir or executor 1590. †**3.** To ground or establish in principles; to train, educate, instruct -1831.

1. The artists have instituted a yearly exhibition of pictures and statues JOHNSON. c. Mythological comparisons instituted by scholars MAX MÜLLER. 2. Cosin of Yorke, we i. your Grace To be our Regent in these parts of France SHAKS. Young..was instituted to the united vicarages of St. Peter and St. Mary MASSON. 3. Instituted..in all the learning of Greece and Rome MIDDLETON. Hence **Iˑnstituter** = INSTITUTOR.

Institution (institiŭˑʃən). late ME. [a. OF. *institution*, ad. L. *institutionem*; see prec.] **1.** The action of instituting or establishing; foundation; ordainment; the fact of being instituted 1450. **b.** *spec.* The establishment or ordination of a sacrament of the Christian Church, esp. of the Eucharist, by Christ. Hence, that part of the office of Baptism, and of the prayer of consecration in the Eucharist, which consists in reciting the words used in institution (more fully *words, commemoration*, or *recital of i.*) 1538. †**2.** The giving of form or order to a thing; orderly arrangement; regulation. **b.** System; constitution. -1821. **3.** Establishment in a charge or position. **a.** *Eccl.* In Episcopal churches, the establishment of a clergyman in the office of the cure of souls, by the bishop or his commissary. In the Church of England, the investment of the presentee to a living with the spiritual part of his benefice. ME. **b.** *Rom. Law.* The appointment of an heir 1880. †**4.** Training, instruction, education, teaching -1790. †**5.** Usu. in *pl.* **a.** Elements of instruction; first principles. **b.** An elementary treatise; = INSTITUTE *sb.*[1] 3. -1800. **6.** An established law, custom, usage, practice, organization, or other element in the political or social life of a people 1551. **b.** *colloq.* A well-established or familiar practice or object 1839. **7.** An establishment, organization, or association, instituted for the promotion of some object, esp. one of public utility, religious, charitable, educational, etc. The name is often popularly applied to the building appropriated to the work of a benevolent or educational institution. 1707. **b.** Often = INSTITUTE *sb.*[1] 4. 1800.

1. The i. of coined money ADAM SMITH. 3. a. The i. by the bishop enables the clerk..to enter into his parsonage-house and take his tithes or ecclesiastical dues; but previous to induction he cannot lease them 1845. 6. The i. of property 1871. b. The pillory was a flourishing i. in those days THACKERAY. 7. The testator leaves £10,000 in charitable legacies to various institutions (*mod.*). b. The Royal I. of Great Britain (incorporated 1800); the Smithsonian I. at Washington, U.S. (1830), etc.

Institutional (institiŭˑʃənăl), *a.* 1617. [f. prec. + -AL.] **1.** Of, pertaining to, or originated by institution; having the character of an institution; furnished with institutions. **b.** Of religion: Expressed by means of or taking shape in definite institutions, as a church, a hierarchy, sacramental ordinances. **2.** Dealing with or pertaining to legal institutes or the elements of a subject 1765. **3.** Of or pertaining to an organized society, or the building in which its work is carried on 1882.

3. The dull monotony of i. life 1896. Hence **Institu·tionalism**, the system of institutions; *spec.* the principles of institutional religion; the system of housing people in institutions. **Institu·tionalist**, one who writes on legal institutes, or on the elements of a science or art. **Institu·tionalize** *v.*, to render institutional; to bring up in an institution.

Institutionary (institiŭˑʃənări), *a.* 1646. [f. as prec. + -ARY[1].] †**1.** Of or pertaining to instruction or elements of instruction; educational -1734. **2.** Of or pertaining to legal institutes 1734. **3.** Relating to ecclesiastical institution 1814. **4.** Of or pertaining to institutions 1882.

Institutive (iˑnstitiŭtiv), *a.* (*sb.*). 1627. [f. as INSTITUTE *v.* + -IVE.] **1.** Having the quality of instituting; pertaining to the institution of something. †**2.** Characterized by being instituted -1651. †**3.** *sb.* A person or thing that institutes 1644.

2. An i. decencie MILT. Hence **Iˑnstitutively** *adv.*

Institutor (iˑnstitiŭtəɹ). 1546. [a. L.; cf. F. *instituteur.*] **1.** One who institutes or establishes; a founder; an organizer. †**2.** An instructor -1822. **3.** *U.S.* In the American Episcopal Church: A bishop, or a presbyter acting for him, who institutes a minister into a parish or church 1804. So **Iˑnstitutress** 1786, **Instituˑtrix** 1706, a female i.

†**Instoˑp**, *v.* [f. IN-[1] + STOP *v.*] *trans.* To stop, close up. DRYDEN.

†**Instoˑre**, *v.* Also **instaur(e.** ME. [ad. L. *instaurare*; OF. *instaurer.*] **1.** *trans.* To restore, repair, renew -1563. **2.** To erect, establish, institute, commence -1450. **3.** To furnish, provide, supply; to store *with* (*of*) -1633.

Instra·tified, *ppl. a.* 1828. [IN *adv.*] 'Stratified within something else' (Webster).

†**Instru·ct**, *ppl. a.* 1440. [ad. L. *instructus*, pa. pple. of *instruere.*] **1.** Educated, taught, informed –1671. **2.** Furnished or equipped *with* something –1615.

2. Neither ship i. with oars, Nor men CHAPMAN.

Instruct (instrʊ·kt), *v.* 1477. [f. L. *instruct-*, *instruere*, f. *in-* (IN-[2]) + *struere* to pile up, build, etc.; see STRUCTURE and cf. F. *instruire.*]

I. 1. *trans.* To furnish with knowledge or information; to teach, educate 1526. †**b.** To teach (a thing) –1670. **2.** To apprise, inform concerning a particular fact or circumstance 1500; also †*absol.* **b.** *Eng. Law.* To give information as a client to a solicitor, or as a solicitor to a counsel; to authorize one to appear as advocate 1836. **3.** To furnish with authoritative directions as to action 1557. **b.** *U.S.* To direct (a representative) how to vote, etc. 1841.

1. If we be ignorant, they [the Scriptures] will i. vs BIBLE *Transl. Pref.* 3. A teacher to i. me in latin BORROW. **2.** Being instructed in the precise time of his Nativity, calculates his fortunes SIR T. HERBERT. **3.** And she, being before instructed of her mother, said, Giue me heere Iohn Baptists head in a charger *Matt.* xiv. 8. I instructed him to take two grains only of the Digitalis daily 1800.

II. †**1.** (Chiefly *poet.*) To put in order; to form; to 'inform'; to make ready, prepare, equip, furnish –1774. **2.** *Sc. Law.* To furnish (a statement) with evidence or proof; to vouch, verify; to prove clearly 1681.

Hence **Instru·cter**, one who instructs (now usu. INSTRUCTOR). **Instru·ctible** *a.* (*rare*), open to instruction.

Instruction (instrʊ·kʃən). ME. [a. OF., ad. L. *instructionem*, f. *instruere.*] **1.** The action of instructing or teaching; the imparting of knowledge or skill; education; †information 1506. **2.** The knowledge or teaching imparted. With *an* and *pl.* An item of knowledge imparted; a precept, a lesson. ME. †**3.** Information. With *an* and *pl.* An item of information imparted or acquired, an account, a narrative. –1655. **4.** A making known to a person what he is required to do; a direction, an order, a mandate. Now usu. *pl.* ME. **b.** Direction given to a solicitor or counsel 1734.

2. To profit by the instructions of the pulpit 1873. **4.** Some of the company had..secret i...to take hym MORE. Hence **Instru·ctional** *a.* of or pertaining to i. or teaching; conveying information.

Instructive (instrʊ·ktiv), *a.* 1611. [f. L. *instruct-*, ppl. stem (see INSTRUCT *v.*) + -IVE.] Having the character or quality of instructing; conveying instruction.

Essays and Characters Ironicall and I. J. STEPHENS (*title*). Hence **Instru·ctive-ly** *adv.*, **-ness.**

Instructor (instrʊ·ktəɪ). 1460. [a. L., f. *instruere.*] One who instructs; a teacher. **b.** *spec.* in Amer. colleges: A college teacher inferior in rank to a professor. So **Instru·ctress**, †**-trice**, a female i.; also *fig.*

Instrument (i·nstrŭmĕnt), *sb.* ME. [a. F., or ad. L. *instrumentum*, f. *instruere* to instruct.] **1.** A thing with or through which something is done or effected; a means. **b.** A person made use of by another person or being, for the accomplishment of a purpose (cf. *tool*) ME. **2.** A tool, implement, weapon. (Now usu. dist. from a *tool*, as being used for more delicate work or for artistic or scientific purposes.) ME. †**b.** *collect.* Apparatus. (A Latinism.) MILT. **3.** *spec.* A contrivance for producing musical sounds ME. (in early 19th cent. *spec.* the pianoforte). †**4.** A part of the body having a special function; an organ –1718. **5.** *Law.* A formal legal document whereby a right is created or confirmed, or a fact recorded; a formal writing of any kind, as an agreement, deed, charter, or record, drawn up and executed in technical form 1483.

1. The Gods are iust, and of our pleasant vices Make instruments to plague vs SHAKS. Among the Tartars..cattle are the instruments of commerce ADAM SMITH. **b.** God used him as an i. to reform his Church BRAMHALL. **2.** Threshing instruments 1611. Instruments of torture 1843. Mathematical instruments (*mod.*). **b.** Much i. of war MILT. *P. R.* III. 388. **3.** I am a mynstrell as thou seest here by myne instrumentes LD. BERNERS.

Instrument (i·nstrŭmĕnt), *v.* 1719. [f. prec. sb.] **1.** *Law.* **a.** To draw up an instrument (see prec. 5). **b.** *trans.* To petition by means of an instrument. **2.** *Mus.* To arrange or score (a piece of music) for instruments, esp. for an orchestra 1822.

Instrumental (instrŭme·ntăl). ME. [a. F., ad. med.L. *instrumentalis*; see INSTRUMENT *sb.* and -AL.]

A. *adj.* **1.** Of the nature of or serving as an instrument or means. **b.** Serving well for the purpose; useful; effective, efficient. Now *rare* or *Obs.* 1602. **2.** Of, pertaining to, performed with, or arising from a material instrument; due to the instrument (as *i. error*) 1644. **3.** Of music: Performed on, or composed for, an instrument or instruments. (Opp. to *vocal.*) 1509. **b.** Of the nature of, or belonging to, a musical instrument (*rare*) 1683. †**4.** *Old Physiol.* Serving for some special vital function; organic –1607. **5.** *Gram.* The name of a case in Sanskrit, Slavonic, etc., denoting that *with* or *by* which something is done 1806.

1. I. in bringing about revolutions BUTLER. **b.** The Head is not more Natiue to the Heart, The Hand more Instrumentall to the Mouth SHAKS. **2.** To have recourse to i. aids HERSCHEL. **3.** Rare music, vocal and i. EVELYN. **b.** The nightingale..breathes such sweet loud music out of her little i. throat WALTON.

B. *sb.* †**1.** That which is instrumental; an instrument, means –1643. †**2.** A bodily organ –1564. **3.** *Gram.* The instrumental case, the 'ablative of the instrument' 1806.

Hence **Instrume·ntalist**, a performer of i. music (opp. to *vocalist*) 1823. **Instrumenta·lity**, the quality or condition of being i.; agency; (with *pl.*) a means, an agency. **Instrumentaliza·tion**, (mere) execution of music on an instrument 1872. †**Instrume·ntalize** *v.* to make i. to some end 1594; to make an instrument of; to measure by means of instruments. **Instrume·ntally** *adv.* in an i. manner; as an instrument or means 1581; by an instrument or means; with or upon a musical instrument 1716; in the instrumental case 1846. †**Instrume·ntalness**, instrumentality.

†**Instrumentary** (instrŭme·ntări), *a.* 1564. [f. INSTRUMENT + -ARY.] **1.** = INSTRUMENTAL *a.* 1. –1657. **2.** = INSTRUMENTAL *a.* 4. –1638.

Instrumentation (i:nstrŭmentē¹·ʃən). 1845. [a. F.; see INSTRUMENT *v.* and -ATION.] **1.** *Mus.* The composition or arrangement of music for instruments, esp. for an orchestra; orchestration. ¶**b.** Erron. used for: Playing on instruments (with reference to style) 1856. **2.** The use of a scientific, surgical, or other instrument 1874. **3.** Operation, or provision, of instruments or means; instrumental agency, instrumentality 1858.

1. The cantatas..possess..an i. far more brilliant and spirited 1845. **2.** The first principle of i. in the urethra is to avoid the use of force VAN BUREN. **3.** If I am caught, whether by your i. or not [etc.] 1883.

Instrume·ntist. *rare.* [f. INSTRUMENT + -IST.] Instrumentalist. DOULAND.

†**Insty·le**, *v.* 1596. [f. IN-[2] + STYLE *sb.* or *v.*] *trans.* To style, denominate –1759.

Insuavity (inswæ·vĭti). *rare.* 1621. [ad. L. *insuavitas*; see IN-[3] and SUAVITY.] Lack of suavity or sweetness; unpleasantness.

Insubjection (insŏbdʒe·kʃən). *rare.* 1818. [IN-[3].] Want of subjection; the state of not being subject to authority or control.

Insubmergible (insŏbmɔ̄·ɪdʒĭb'l), *a.* 1808. [IN-[3].] That cannot be submerged or sunk under water. So **Insubme·rsible** *a.*

Insubmi·ssion. *rare.* 1828. [IN-[3].] Want of submission; insubordination. WEBSTER.

Insubmi·ssive, *a.* 1841. [IN-[3].] Not submissive; unyielding to power or authority; unsubmissive.

Insubordinate (insŏbǭ·ɪdinĕ̄t), *a.* (*sb.*) 1849. [IN-[3].] **1.** Not subordinate; not obedient to the orders of superiors. **2.** *sb.* One who is insubordinate 1886. Hence **Insubo·rdinately** *adv.*

Insubordination (insŏbǭɪdinē¹·ʃən). 1790. [IN-[3].] The fact or condition of being insubordinate; resistance to or defiance of authority; disobedience.

Insubstantial (insŏbstæ·nʃăl), *a.* 1607. [ad. late and med.L. *insubstantialis*, f. *in-* (IN-[3]) + *substantialis.*] **1.** Not existing in substance; not real; non-substantial 1610. **2.** Void of substance; not of stout or solid substance. Also *fig.*

1. This insubstantiall Pageant *Temp.* IV. i. 155. Hence **Insubstantia·lity**, unsubstantiality.

†**Insu·ccate**, *v. rare.* 1623. [f. L. *insuccare*, prop. *insucare*, f. *in-* (IN-[2]) + *succus*, *sucus* juice; see -ATE[3].] *trans.* To soak, steep. (Dicts.) So †**Insucca·tion**, the action of soaking or steeping.

Insuccess (insŏkse·s). 1646. [IN-[3].] Want of success. So †**Insucce·ssful** *a.*

Insucken (i·nsʊk'n), *a. Sc. Law.* 1546. [f. IN *prep.* + SUCKEN.] Situated within a certain sucken or jurisdiction having its own mill; astricted to a certain mill.

Insue, obs. f. ENSUE.

Insuetude (i·nswĭtiūd). *rare.* [ad. L. *insuetudo* (post-cl.), f. *insuetus* unaccustomed.] The quality of not being in use. LANDOR.

Insufferable (insʊ·fəɪăb'l), *a.* 1533. [IN-[3].] Not sufferable; intolerable, unbearable.

A vain Person is the most i. Creature living in a well-bred Assembly STEELE. Hence **Insu·fferably** *adv.*

Insufficience (insŏfi·ʃĕns). Now *rare.* ME. [a. OF. *insufficience*, ad. late L. *insufficientia*; see next and -ENCE.] = INSUFFICIENCY.

Insufficiency (insŏfi·ʃĕnsi). 1488. [ad. late L. *insufficientia*, f. *insufficientem*; see next and -ENCY.] **1.** Of a person: Inability to fulfil requirements; incapacity, incompetence. *Obs.* or *arch.* Also with *an* and *pl.* **2.** Of a thing: Deficiency, inadequacy 1488. **3.** Physical incapacity or impotence; inability of a bodily organ to do its work 1714.

1. A due sense of his own faults and insufficiencies 1773. **2.** An i. of data CHALMERS. **3.** The marriage afterwards being declared Null, by Reason of his I. STEELE.

Insufficient (insŏfi·ʃĕnt), *a.* ME. [a. OF., or ad. L. *insufficientem*; see IN-[3] and SUFFICIENT.] Not sufficient. †**1.** Of a person: Of inadequate ability; unfit; incompetent –1657. **2.** Of a thing: Deficient in force, quality, or amount; inadequate 1494.

1. Some of those that were ministers were much i. BACON. Hee is i. in lands 1620. **2.** But a single hand is i. for such a harvest DRYDEN. Hence **Insuffi·cient-ly** *adv.*, †**-ness.**

Insufflate (i·nsʊflē¹t), *v.* 1657. [f. L. *insufflat-*, *insufflare* (post-cl.), f. *in-* (IN-[2]) + *sufflare* to blow upon.] **1.** *trans.* To blow or breathe in. EVELYN. **b.** *spec.* To breathe upon catechumens, or on the water of baptism. **2.** *Med.* To blow (air, gas, etc.) into some opening of the body; to treat by insufflation 1670. Hence **Insuffla·tor**, a contrivance for insufflating.

Insufflation (insʊflē¹·ʃən). 1580. [ad. L. *insufflationem* (post-cl.); see prec.] **1.** The action of blowing or breathing on or into 1621. **b.** *spec.* Blowing or breathing upon a person or thing to symbolize the influence of the Holy Spirit and the expulsion of evil spirits; a rite of exorcism used in some churches 1580. **2.** The blowing or breathing (*of* something) in; in *Med.* of air, etc. into the lungs, or of gas, vapour, or powder into or on some part of the body 1823. **3.** The condition of being inflated 1866.

†**Insui·table**, *a. rare.* 1612. [IN-[3].] Unsuitable –1692. Hence †**Insuitabi·lity.**

‖**Insula** (i·nsiŭlă). Pl. **-æ.** 1832. [L., an island, etc.] **1.** *Rom. Antiq.* A block of buildings; a square or space mapped out or divided off. **2.** *Anat.* **a.** The central lobe of the cerebrum; the lobule of the corpus striatum or Sylvian fissure, the Island of Reil. **b.** A term applied to a clot of blood floating in serum. 1886.

Insular (i·nsiŭlăɪ), *a.* (*sb.*) 1611. [ad. L. *insularis*, f. *insula*; see -AR[1].] **1.** Of or pertaining to an island; inhabiting or situated on an island. **2.** Of the nature of an island; composing or forming an island 1662. Also *transf.* **3.** Having the characteristic traits of islanders; *esp.* isolated; self-contained; narrow or prejudiced in feelings, ideas, or manners 1775. **4.** *sb.* An inhabitant of an island 1744.

1. Our i. feuds BURKE. The west coasts of continents enjoy i...climates R. H. SCOTT. **3.** The penury of i.

conversation JOHNSON. Without ceasing to be English, he has escaped from being i. LOWELL. Hence **I·nsularism**, the quality of being i.; esp. narrowness of ideas, feelings, or outlook. **I·nsularly** *adv.* var. **I·nsulary** *a.* and *sb.* (now *rare* or *Obs.*) 1585.

Insularity (insiulæ·rĭti). 1755. [f. prec. + -ITY.] **1.** The state or condition of being an island, or of being surrounded by water 1790. **2.** The condition of living on an island; hence, narrowness of mind or feeling, contractedness of view 1755.

1. The i. of Britain was first shown by Agricola, who sent his fleet round it PINKERTON. 2. The proverbial i. of the average Briton EARL DUNMORE.

Insulate (i·nsiulět), *a.* Now *rare.* 1712. [ad. L. *insulatus*, f. *insula*; see -ATE[2] 2.] Detached, isolated, insulated.

Insulate (i·nsiuleit), *v.* 1538. [f. L. *insula* + -ATE[3], or *insulatus* adj.] **1.** *trans.* To make into an island by surrounding with water; to convert into an island. **2.** *transf.* and *fig.* To cause (a thing, person, etc.) to stand detached from its surroundings; to separate from the rest; to place apart; to isolate 1785. **3.** *Electr.* and *Heat.* To cut off or isolate from conducting bodies by the interposition of non-conductors, so as to prevent the passage of electricity or heat 1755. †**4.** *Chem.* and *Phys.* To free from combination with other elements; to isolate –1834.

1. Trent..turneth aside his streame Northward.. and so almost insulateth or encompasseth Burton HOLLAND. Phr. *Insulating stool*, one with glass legs, or other non-conducting supports, to i. a body placed on it.

Insulated (i·nsiuleitĕd), *ppl. a.* 1727. [f. prec. + -ED[1].] **1.** Made into an island; surrounded by water 1776. **2.** *transf.* and *fig.* Placed or standing apart; separated from intercourse with others; solitary, isolated 1727. **3.** Electrically cut off from (the earth or other conducting bodies) by being surrounded with non-conductors 1791.

2. I. pyramidal hills PENNANT. An i. life COWPER.

Insulation (insiulēi·ʃən). 1798. [f. INSULATE *v.*; see -ATION.] **1.** The action of insulating; the fact or condition of being insulated; *concr.* an insulated object. **2.** The action of insulating electrically or physically; the condition of being isolated by non-conductors so as to prevent the passage of electricity or heat 1822. **b.** *concr.* Insulating material 1870.

Insulator (i·nsiuleitəɹ). 1801. [f. INSULATE *v.*; see -OR.] One who or that which insulates; *spec.* a contrivance, usu. of glass or porcelain, for supporting or carrying telegraph-wires without carrying off the current.

Insulin (i·nsiulin). 1922. [f. L. *insula* islet + -IN[1].] *Pharm.* A drug extracted from the islets of Langerhans in the pancreas, used in the treatment of diabetes.

Insu·lse, *a.* Now *rare.* 1609. [ad. L. *insulsus*, f. *in-* (IN-[3]) + *salsus* witty, lit. salted, f. (ult.) *sal* salt.] **1.** Lacking wit or sense; dull, stupid; absurd. **2.** *lit.* Tasteless, insipid 1675.

Insu·lsity. Now *rare.* 1623. [ad. L. *insulsitas*; see prec.] The quality of being insulse; stupidity, senselessness. MILTON.

Insult (i·nsɒlt), *sb.* 1603. [a. F. *insult*, now *insulte*, or ad. late L. *insultus*, f. *in-* (IN-[2]) + *saltus* leap; cf. next.] **1.** An act, or the action, of attacking or assailing; attack, assault, onset (*lit.* and *fig.*). *arch.* †**b.** *Mil.* An open and sudden attack, without preparations. **2.** An act, or the action, of insulting (in sense 1 or 2 of vb.); injuriously contemptuous speech or action; an affront 1671. †**3.** The act of leaping upon; 'covering'. DRYDEN.

2. The ruthless sneer that i. adds to grief SAVAGE. *Phr.* To add insult to injury.

Insult (insɒ·lt), *v.* 1570. [ad. L. *insultare* to leap at or on, etc. Cf. F. *insulter.*] †**1.** *intr.* To manifest arrogant or scornful delight by speech or behaviour; to exult proudly or contemptuously; to vaunt, glory, triumph –1857. **2.** *trans.* To assail with scornful abuse or offensive disrespect; to offer indignity to; to affront, outrage 1620. †**3.** *intr.* To make an attack or assault (*lit.* and *fig.*) –1670. **4.** *trans.* To attack, assault, assail (now only *fig.* in general sense). †**b.** *spec.* (*Mil.*) To attack openly and suddenly without preparations. 1697. †**5.** *intr.* To leap wantonly. GAULE.

1. They know how, The Lyon being dead euen Hares i. DANIEL. The Dutch do mightily i. of their victory PEPYS. Whilst the infidel..insults over their credulous fears PALEY. 2. Whatever the canting Roundhead had regarded with reverence was insulted MACAULAY. 4. Having no Fleet at Sea, the Portugueze insulted his Sea-coasts 1727. Hence **Insu·ltable** *a.* (*rare*), capable of being insulted. **Insu·lter. Insu·ltingly** *adv.*

Insultation (insɒltē̆·ʃən). *Obs.* or *arch.* 1513. [a. F., or ad. L. *insultationem.* Common in 17th c.] **1.** The action, or an act, of insulting (in sense 1 or 2 of vb.); injuriously contemptuous speech or behaviour; insult. †**2.** Attack, assault –1657.

†**Insultment.** [f. INSULT *v.* + -MENT.] The action of insulting; contemptuous triumph; insult. *Cymb.* III. v. 145.

†**Insu·me**, *v.* 1675. [f. IN-[2] + L. *sumere*; cf. *assume*, etc.] *trans.* To take in, absorb –1733. So †**Insu·mption**, absorption.

†‖**Insuper, in super** (insiū·pəɹ), *adv.* 1624. [L., f. *in* in + *super* above.] Over; *to stand in super*, to stand over as a balance or unsettled claim.

Insuperable (insiū·pərăb'l), *a.* (*sb.*) ME. [ad. L. *insuperabilis*, f. *in-* (IN-[3]) + *superare* to overcome. Cf. obs. F. *insuperable.*] **1.** That cannot be overcome; unconquerable, invincible. *Obs.* or merged in 3. **2.** That cannot be surmounted or passed over 1660. **3.** *fig.* Of difficulties, etc.: That cannot be got over or overcome; invincible; insurmountable 1657. **4.** Unsurpassable. RUSKIN.

1. Invincible soldiers, and appointed with armes i. HOLLAND. 2. I. highth of loftiest shade, Cedar, and Pine, and Firr MILT. *P. L.* IV. 138. 3. His i. disinclination to entering into holy orders 1744. Hence **Insu·perabi·lity, Insu·perableness**, the quality of being i. **Insu·perably** *adv.*

Insupportable (insŏpōə·ɹtăb'l), *a.* 1530. [a. F., or ad. eccl. L. *insupportabilis*, f. *in-* (IN-[3]) + *supportare*; see SUPPORTABLE.] **1.** That cannot be supported; unendurable; unbearable. **b.** Unjustifiable, indefensible 1649. †**2.** That cannot be sustained; irresistible –1697.

1. I. Insolence COWLEY, distress 1791. 2. He gan advaunce With huge force and i. mayne SPENSER. Hence **Insuppo·rtableness. Insuppo·rtably** *adv.*

Insupposable (insŏpōu·zăb'l), *a.* 1668. [IN-[3].] That cannot be supposed.

Insuppressible (insŏpre·sĭb'l), *a.* 1610. [IN-[3].] That cannot be suppressed; irrepressible. Hence **Insuppre·ssibly** *adv.*

Insuppressive (insŏpre·siv), *a. rare.* 1601. [IN-[3].] Insuppressible. *Jul. C.* II. i. 134.

Insurable (inʃūə·răb'l), *a.* 1810. [f. INSURE *v.* + -ABLE.] Capable of being, or proper to be, insured; sufficient to form a ground for insurance. **Insurabi·lity.**

Insurance (inʃūə·răns). 1553. [Var. of *ensurance* (a. OF. *enseurance*), with IN-[2] for EN-[1].] †**1.** The action or a means of insuring or making certain –1788. †**2.** = ASSURANCE 3. 1706. †**3.** Betrothal, engagement to marry. UDALL. **4.** *Comm.* The act or system of insuring property, life, etc.; a contract by which the one party undertakes, in consideration of a payment (called a *premium*), to secure the other against pecuniary loss, by payment of a sum of money in the event of destruction of or damage to property (as by disaster at sea, fire, etc.), or of the death or disablement of a person; the department of business which deals with such contracts. Also called ASSURANCE (and in 17th c. occas. *ensurance*). 1651.

Assurance, the earlier term, is now rarely used of marine, fire, or accident insurance, and is retained in Great Britain in the nomenclature and use of most life insurance companies. But in general popular use, *insurance* is the prevalent term.

b. The sum paid for insuring; the premium 1666. **c.** The amount for which property or life is insured 1838. **d.** The act or system of insuring employed persons against sickness or unemployment, esp. in accordance with the Acts of 1911 and 1920. **5.** *attrib.*, as *i. company, policy*, etc. 1651.

4. Money was taken up upon bottomary and i., and the ship left by the master and seamen upon rocks where..she must perish PEPYS. Hence †**Insu·rancer**, one who gives i. or assurance; one who insures or makes sure.

Insu·rant. 1858. [f. INSURE *v.* + -ANT[1].] One who effects or obtains an insurance.

Insure (inʃūə·ɹ), *v.* 1440. [Var. of ENSURE (with IN-[2] for EN-[1]).] †**1.** *trans.* To make (a person) sure (*of* a thing) –1686. †**2.** = ENSURE 2, 3. –1560. **3.** *Comm.* To secure the payment of a sum of money in the event of loss of or damage to property (esp. by casualty at sea, by fire, etc.), or of the death or disablement of a person, in consideration of the payment of a premium and observance of certain conditions; to effect an insurance upon. Said either of the person who pays the premium, or of the office or underwriters who undertake the risk. For the latter many offices and writers prefer *assure* (esp. in reference to life insurance). 1635. **b.** *absol.* or *intr.* To undertake insurance risks; to effect an insurance 1651. **4.** *trans.* To make certain, to secure, to guarantee (some thing, event, etc.) 1681. **5.** To make safe, to secure (*against, from*) 1724.

3. As much more insured upon his ship and goods as they were worth PEPYS. To i. his House ADDISON, a life 1883. **c.** (Cf. INSURANCE 4 d). 4. An ardour which could hardly fail to i. success BUCKLE. 5. The evidence of trials past does not i. them against trials that may come 1864.

Insurer (inʃūə·rəɹ). 1638. [f. INSURE + -ER[1].] One who or that which insures; *esp. Comm.* One who contracts, for a premium, to indemnify a person against losses; an underwriter. Also called *Assurer* (*Assuror*).

Insurge (insɒ̄·ɹdʒ), *v.* Now *rare.* 1523. [ad. L. *insurgere*, f. *in-* (IN-[2]) + *surgere* to rise.] †**1.** *intr.* To arise, spring up –1576. †**2.** To rise in opposition *against*; to make insurrection, revolt –1610. **3.** *trans.* To stir up; to raise in insurrection. *Obs.* exc. as *nonce-wd.* 1796.

Insurgent (insɒ̄·ɹdʒĕnt). 1765. [ad. L. *insurgentem, insurgere*; see prec. and -ENT.]

A. *adj.* **1.** Rising in active revolt. Also *fig.* 1814. **2.** Of the sea or a flood Surging up or rushing in 1849.

1. The i. barons 1845. 2. The broad volume of the i. Nile M. ARNOLD.

B. *sb.* One who rises in revolt against constituted authority; a rebel who is not recognized as a belligerent 1765.

The colonial insurgents 1812. Hence **Insu·rgence**, a rising, revolt. **Insu·rgency**, the quality or state of being i.

Insurmountable (insŏɹmau·ntăb'l), *a.* 1696. [IN-[3].] That cannot be surmounted, overcome, or passed over.

This difficulty is i. LOCKE. Hence **Insurmountabi·lity, Insurmou·ntableness. Insurmou·ntably** *adv.*

Insurrection (insŏre·kʃən). 1459. [a. F., ad. rare L. *insurrectionem*, f. *insurgere*; see INSURGE.] **1.** The action of rising in arms or open resistance against established authority or governmental restraint; with *pl.*, an armed rising, a revolt; an incipient or limited rebellion. Also *fig.* **2.** Upheaval. RUSKIN.

1. He [Jack Cade]..wrote letters to many Citees.. to have made a comon i. 1459. Insurrections are generally wrong; revolutions are always right BUCKLE. *fig.* It is not the insurrections of ignorance that are dangerous, but the revolts of intelligence LOWELL. Hence **Insurre·ctional** *a.* of, pertaining to, or of the nature of i. **Insurre·ctionary** *a.* insurrectional; addicted to i. **Insurre·ctionist**, one who takes part in an i., or who advocates revolt against authority.

Insusceptible (insŏse·ptĭb'l), *a.* 1603. [IN-[3].] Not susceptible; not able or apt to receive impressions; not liable to be affected by something or in some way.

I. of mutation HOLLAND, to the infection of the small-pox 1808. I. or, as I may call them, not poisonable people MACCORMAC. Hence **Insusceptibi·lity.** So **Insusce·ptive** *a.*

†**Insuspe·ct(ed**, *a.* 1606. [IN-[3].] Unsuspected –1646.

Insusurra·tion. *rare.* 1614. [ad. L. *insusurrationem*, f. *insusurrare*, f. *in-* (IN-[2]) + *susurrare* to whisper.] A whispering in the ear; an insinuation –1653.

Inswathe, var. of ENSWATHE *v.*

In't, arch. abbrev. of *in it.* **I'n't, i'nt**, obs. abbrev. of *isn't, is not.*

Intablature, obs. f. ENTABLATURE.

Intact (intæ·kt), *a.* 1450. [ad. L. *intactus*, f. *in-* (IN-[3]) + *tactus, tangere.*] Untouched; kept or left entire; unblemished; unimpaired.

†**Inta·ctible**, *a.* [IN-[3].] = next. (Dicts.)

Inta·ctile, *a. rare.* 1659. [ad. L. *intactilis*; see IN-³ and TACTILE.] Not tactile; intangible.

Intagliated (intæ·lyeɪtėd), *ppl. a.* 1782. [f. It. *intagliato*, *intagliare* to engrave (f. *in-* (IN-²) + *tagliare* to cut) + -ED¹.] Carved on the surface; engraved in or as in intaglio.

‖**Intaglio** (intæ·lyo), *sb.* Pl. **intaglios**, rarely **intagli** (inta·lyi). Also *erron.* †**intaglia**; pl. -as. 1644. [It., = engraving, engraved work, a carving (pl. *intagli*), f. *intagliare*; see prec.] 1. A figure or design incised or engraved; a cutting or engraving in stone or other hard material. Also *fig.* and *transf.* b. The process or art of carving or engraving in a hard material; incised carving; the condition or fact of being incised. Chiefly in phr. *in intaglio*, as opp. to *in relievo* or *in relief*. Also *fig.* 1762. 2. Anything ornamented with incised work; esp. an incised gem. Opp. to *cameo.* 1654. b. A countersunk die 1825. Hence **Inta·glio** *v. trans.* to engrave with a sunk pattern or design; to execute in i.

Intail, obs. f. ENTAIL *sb.* and *v.*

Intake (i·nteɪk). Chiefly *Sc.* and *n. dial.* 1523. [IN *adv.*; cf. *take in*, TAKE *v.*] 1. The act of taking in from outside; the quantity taken in 1808. 2. (Chiefly *n. dial.*) An inclosure 1523. 3. The place where water is taken into a channel or pipe 1559. 4. *Mining.* The airway of a mine. Also *attrib.* 1851. 5. A narrowing or abrupt contraction made in the width of a tube, a stocking, etc.; the point at which this is made 1808.

2. When horses in the sunburnt i. stood WORDSW.

†**Inta·minated**, *a.* [f. med.L. *intaminatus*, *intaminare* + -ED¹.] Uncontaminated, uncorrupted, pure. WOOD.

Intangible (intæ·ndʒĭb'l), *a.* 1640. [ad. med.L. *intangibilis*, f. *in-* (IN-³) + L. *tangibilis* TANGIBLE.] Not tangible; incapable of being touched; not cognizable by the sense of touch; impalpable. Also *fig.*

This wonderful i. aether TYNDALL. Hence **Inta·ngibi·lity**, **-ta·ngibleness**. **Inta·ngibly** *adv.*

†**Inta·ngle**, etc., obs. ff. ENTANGLE, etc.

†**Inta·stable**, *a.* [IN-³.] Incapable of being tasted. GREW.

Integer (i·ntĭdʒəɪ). 1509. [a. L., f. *in-* (IN-³) + *tag-*, *teg-*, root of *tangere* to touch. Cf. ENTIRE.]

A. *adj.* (Now *rare* or *Obs.*) †1. Whole, entire. WOLSEY. †2. Marked by moral integrity; upright. VICARS. 3. *Math.* = INTEGRAL A. 4 a. 1660.

3. A whole or i. number HUTTON.

B. *sb.* 1. *Math.* A number or quantity denoting one or more whole things or units; a whole number or undivided quantity. Opp. to *fraction.* 1571. 2. A particular quantity of any kind (as money, weight, etc.) taken as the unit of measurement. Now *rare* or *Obs.* 1822. 3. *gen.* A whole or entire thing or entity 1848.

2. The Carat serves as the I. 1868.

Integrable (i·ntĭgrăb'l), *a.* 1727. [f. L. *integrare* to make whole + -ABLE.] Capable of being integrated (see INTEGRATE *v.* 2, 3). Hence **I:ntegrabi·lity.**

Integral (i·ntĭgrăl). 1551. [ad. late L. *integralis*, f. *integr-*; see INTEGER and -AL.]

A. *adj.* 1. Of or pertaining to a whole. Said of a part or parts: Belonging to or making up an integral whole; constituent, component; *spec.* necessary to the completeness of the whole. 2. Made up of component parts which together constitute a unity; in *Logic*, said of a whole consisting of or divisible into parts actually (not merely mentally) separable. Now *rare* or *Obs.* exc. in techn. use. 1588. 3. Having no part or element lacking; unbroken, whole, entire, complete. Now somewhat *rare.* 1611. 4. *Math.* a. Consisting of a whole number or undivided quantity; not fractional, or not involving a fraction 1658. b. Relating to, or involving integrals; obtained by, belonging to, or proceeding by integration 1727.

1. The arms, legs, etc. are *integral* parts; body and soul *essential* parts of a man CHAMBERS. 3. Excerpta of Writers whose i. works are lost for ever MATHIAS. Repent with an i...repentance JER. TAYLOR. 4. b. *Integral calculus*: the calculus of integrals; that branch of the infinitesimal calculus which deals with the finding and properties of integrals of functions, also used to include the solution of differential equations, and parts of the theory of functions, etc.

B. *sb.* 1. Something entire or undivided; a whole. *Obs.* exc. as *transf.* from 3 = total sum. 1620. †2. An integral part or element; a constituent, component -1685. 3. *Math.*

a. (of a function): That quantity of which the given function is the differential or differential coefficient; so called because it may be regarded as the whole sum of a series of consecutive values assumed by an infinitesimal function (differential) of the variable while the latter changes continuously from any one value to any other. When such limits of variation are fixed or determinate, it is called a *definite i.* An i. is denoted by the sign ∫ (orig. a long *s*, for L. *summa* sum); in a definite i. the inferior and superior limits are indicated at the bottom and top of the sign, thus $\int_a^b$. b. (of a differential equation, or a system of such equations): An equation or system of equations from which the given equation or system can be derived by differentiation. 1727.

Integrality (intĭgræ·lĭti). 1611. [f. late L. *integralis* INTEGRAL; see -ITY. Cf. F. *intégralité.*] The condition of being integral; wholeness, entirety, completeness.

Integrally (i·ntĭgrăli), *adv.* 1471. [f. as prec. + -LY².] In an integral manner; as a whole; entirely.

Integrant (i·ntĭgrănt), *a.* (*sb.*) 1637. [ad. L. *integrantem*, *integrare*; see INTEGRATE *v.*] 1. Of parts: = INTEGRAL A. 1. 2. *sb.* That which integrates; a component 1824.

1. The Church consisteth of two i. parts, *viz.* Pastors and Sheepe GILLESPIE.

Integrate (i·ntĭgrėt), *a.* 1485. [ad. L. *integratus*; see next.] = INTEGRAL A. 2, 3.

Integrate (i·ntĭgreɪt), *v.* 1638. [f. L. *integrat-*, *integrare* to make whole.] 1. *trans.* To render entire or complete; to make up (a whole); said of the parts or elements. ? *Obs.* b. To complete (what is imperfect) by the addition of the necessary parts 1675. 2. To combine (parts or elements) into a whole 1802. 3. *Math.* To find or calculate the integral of; see INTEGRAL B. 3. Also *absol.* to perform the operation of integration. 1727. b. *transf.* and *fig.*; *spec.* to indicate or register the mean value, or the total sum of all the portions or elements, of some physical quantity 1864.

1. The particular doctrines which i. Christianity CHILLINGW. b. The fragmentary contribution of one being integrated by the fragmentary contributions of others DE QUINCEY. 3. b. *Integrating spectroscope*, a spectroscope in which the slit receives light from all parts of a luminous object and blends it all together to form a single united spectrum; opp. to *analysing spectroscope.* Hence **I·ntegrative** *a.* integrating; tending to i.

Integration (intĭgrēɪ·ʃən). 1620. [ad. L. *integrationem* (in L. only in sense 'renewal, restoration to wholeness').] The action or process of integrating. 1. The making up of a whole by adding together or combining the separate parts or elements; a making whole or entire. (Often opp. to *differentiation.*) 2. *Math.* The operation of finding the integral of a given function or equation; the inverse of differentiation 1727.

2. *I. by parts*: i. by means of the formula $\int udv = uv - \int vdu$, where u and v are any functions of the same variable. *Constant of i.*: an arbitrary constant which must be added to get the complete expression for an integral. *Sign of i.*: the sign ∫ denoting an integral (see INTEGRAL B. 3 a).

Integrator (i·ntĭgreɪtəɪ). 1879. [a. L., f. *integrare.*] One who or that which integrates; *spec.* an instrument for indicating or registering the total amount or mean value of some physical quantity, as area, temperature, etc.; see INTEGRATE *v.* 3 b.

Integripallial (intĭgripæ·liăl), *a.* Also **integro-**. 1862. [f. L. *integri-*, comb. f. *integer* + *pallium* cloak + -AL. The form *integro-* is not analogical.] *Zool.* Having the pallial line not broken or indented; applied to a division of lamellibranchiate molluscs, in which the siphons are small or absent. Also **Integripa·lliate** *a.* (Opp. to *sinupallial*, *-ate.*)

Integrity (inte·grĭti). 1450. [ad. L. *integritas*, f. *integer*, *integr-* whole, INTEGER.] 1. The condition of having no part or element wanting; unbroken state; material wholeness, completeness, entirety. 2. Unimpaired or uncorrupted state; original perfect condition; soundness 1450. 3. †a. Innocence, sinlessness -1678. b. Soundness of moral principle; the character of uncorrupted virtue; uprightness, honesty, sincerity 1548.

1. The walls were standing..though not in their i. 1870. 2. He did but restore the law to her integritie 1561. 3. b. Better is the poore that walketh in his i., then he that is peruerse in his lippes, and is a foole *Prov.* xix. 1.

†**Integuma·tion.** *rare.* 1803. [Short for *integumentation.*] The formation of integuments -1828.

Integument (inte·giŭmĕnt). 1611. [ad. L. *integumentum* covering, f. *integere.*] That with which anything is covered, enclosed, or clothed; *spec.* the natural covering or investment of the body, or of some part or organ, of an animal or plant; a skin, shell, husk, rind, etc. Hence **Integume·ntal** *a.* of or belonging to the i.; **Integume·ntary** *a.* integumental, of the nature of an i.; cutaneous. **Integumenta·tion** (*rare*), the action of covering or condition of being covered with an i.

Intellect (i·ntėlekt). ME. [ad. L. *intellectus* (*u* stem), f. ppl. stem of *intellegere*; see INTELLIGENT.] 1. That faculty, or sum of faculties, of the mind or soul by which one knows and reasons (excluding sensation, and sometimes imagination; dist. from *feeling* and *will*); power of thought; understanding. Rarely in reference to the lower animals. 2. *transf.* †a. An intellect embodied; an 'intelligence', a spirit. b. Intellect embodied; also, intellectual persons collectively. 1602. 3. *pl.* Intellectual powers; 'wits', 'senses'. Now *arch.* or *vulgar.* 1698. 4. That which one is to understand by something; the sense, purport (of a word or passage) -1588.

1. Hath Bullingbrooke Depos'd thine I.? SHAKS. 2. It walked the town awhile, Numbering good intellects MILT. 3. A man of sound intellects SMOLLETT. 4. I will looke againe on the i. of the Letter *L. L. L.* IV. ii. 137.

I·ntellected, *a. rare.* 1791. [f. prec. + -ED².] Endowed with intellect.

Intelle·ctible, *a.* 1557. [ad. med.L. *intellectibilis.*] †a. = INTELLECTIVE 1. b. = INTELLIGIBLE 3.

Intellection (intėle·kʃən). 1449. [ad. late and med.L. *intellectionem*, f. *intellegere*; see INTELLIGENT.] 1. The action or process of understanding; *spec.* simple apprehension 1614. b. (with *pl.*) A particular act of understanding; *occas.*, the permanent result of such an act; a conception, notion, idea 1579. †c. The faculty of understanding; intellect -1797. †d. Understanding, information -1509. †2. *Gram.* and *Rhet.* The figure SYNECDOCHE -1553.

Intellective (intėle·ktiv), *a.* 1477. [ad. late L. *intellectivus*, f. *intellect-*, *intellegere* + -IVE. Cf. F. *intellectif.*] 1. Having the faculty of understanding; possessed of intellect. Applied, after Aristotle, to one of the parts of the soul (ψυχή). 1480. †2. = INTELLECTUAL A. 3 b -1632. 3. = INTELLECTUAL A. 1. 1477. †4 = INTELLECTIBLE b -1656.

1. The Greek philosophers acknowledged several kinds of ψυχή, the nutritive, the sensitive, and the i. MILL. Hence **Intelle·ctively** *adv.*

Intellectual (intėle·ktiuăl). ME. [ad. L. *intellectualis*, f. *intellectus* INTELLECT.]

A. *adj.* 1. Of, or belonging to, the intellect or understanding. b. That appeals to or engages the intellect 1834. †2. Apprehensible or apprehended only by the intellect; non-material, spiritual; ideal -1711. †3. Characterized by or possessing intellection or understanding; intelligent -1797. b. Possessing a high degree of understanding; given to pursuits that exercise the intellect 1819.

1. Easy Credulity, which is the third cause of Intellectuall slavery 1654. b. The more i. branches of warfare FREEMAN. 3. Who would loose, Though full of pain, this i. being? MILT. *P. L.* II. 147. b. But—oh! ye lords of ladies i., Inform us truly, have they not hen-peck'd you all? BYRON. Hence **Intelle·ctual·ly** *adv.*, **-ness**.

B. *sb.* †1. The intellectual faculty; the intellect, mind -1667. 2. *pl.* = INTELLECT *sb.* 3. (*arch.*) 1615. 3. *pl.* Things pertaining to the intellect 1650. 4. An intellectual being; a person having superior powers of intellect 1652.

1. The Woman, opportune to all attempts, Her

Husband..not nigh, Whose higher i. more I shun MILT. *P. L.* IX. 483. **2.** Your fear for Hartley's intellectuals is just and rational LAMB. **4.** A dinner of intellectuals 1884.

Intellectualism (intèle·ktiuăliz'm). 1829. [f. prec. + -ISM.] **1.** *Philos.* The doctrine that knowledge is wholly or mainly derived from the action of the intellect, i.e. from pure reason. **2.** Devotion to merely intellectual culture or pursuits 1838.

Intelle·ctualist. 1605. [f. as prec. + -IST.] A devotee of the intellect or understanding; in *Philos.*, one who holds the doctrine of intellectualism.

Intellectuality (intèlektiu,æ·lĭti). 1611. [ad. late L. *intellectualitas* (Tertullian).] The quality or state of being intellectual; intellectual power or ability.

Intellectualize (intèle·ktiu,ălaiz), *v.* 1819. [f. INTELLECTUAL *a.* + -IZE.] **1.** *trans.* To render intellectual; to give an intellectual character or quality to. Also *absol.* **2.** *intr.* [after *moralize.*] To exercise the intellect; to talk or write intellectually; to philosophize 1827.

1. It..refines and intellectualizes life 1821. Hence **Intelle·ctualiza·tion** 1821.

Intelligence (inte·lidzĕns), *sb.* ME. [a. F., ad. L. *intelleg-*, *intelligentia*; see INTELLIGENT and -ENCE.] **1.** The faculty of understanding; intellect. **2.** Understanding as a quality admitting of degree; *spec.* superior understanding; quickness of mental apprehension, sagacity ME. **3.** The action or fact of mentally apprehending something; understanding, knowledge, comprehension (*of* something). Now *rare* or *Obs.* 1450. **4.** An impersonation of intelligence; an intelligent or rational being; esp. a spirit 1589. **5.** Mutual conveyance of information; communication, intercourse. Now *rare* or *Obs.* 1531. **†6.** A relation of intercourse between persons or parties. Also *fig.* –1827. **7.** Information, news, tidings 1450. **†b.** *pl.* A piece of information or news –1750. **c.** The obtaining of information; the agency for obtaining secret information; the secret service. 1697. (Revived in modern wars.)

1. He is led to the conception of a Power and an I. superior to his own HERSCHEL. 2. Some learned Englisheman of good i. GRAFTON. 3. I write, as he that none i. Of metres hath, ne floures of sentence 1530. 4. How fully hast thou satisfi'd mee, pure I. of Heav'n, Angel serene MILT. *P. L.* VIII. 181. 5. They took it into their heads..that he was of i. with the enemy 1717. 6. He sent an embassy..to renew the good i. between them 1734. 7. I. poured in from all quarters, that one place after another was assailed JAS. MILL. c. Comb., as *i. department, man, officer.*

†Inte·lligence, *v.* 1593. [f. prec.] **1.** *trans.* To bring intelligence of (an event, etc.); to inform (a person) –1642. **2.** *intr.* To convey intelligence; to tell tales 1616.

Intelligenced (-ĕnst, *poet.* -ĕnsĕd), *a.* 1602. [f. prec. sb. + -ED [2].] **a.** Having understanding. **b.** Informed.

Intelligencer (inte·lidzĕnsəɹ). 1581. [f. INTELLIGENCE *sb.* + -ER; cf. obs. F. *intelligencier.*] One who conveys intelligence or information; an informer, a spy, a secret agent 1581; a bringer of news 1632. **b.** *fig.* Applied to things 1586; †as the title of a newspaper, etc. 1641–1801.

An I., which in real truth is no better than a Spie 1658.

†Inte·lligencing, *ppl. a.* 1608. [f. INTELLIGENCE *v.* or *sb.* + -ING [2].] Conveying intelligence or information; playing the spy –1711. *Wint. T.* II. iii. 68.

Intelligency (inte·lidzĕnsi). Now *rare.* 1598. [ad. L. *intelligentia*; see -ENCY.] **1.** = INTELLIGENCE *sb.* **1.** BROWNING. **2.** = INTELLIGENCE *sb.* 4. 1652. **†3.** = INTELLIGENCE *sb.* 5. –1711. **†4.** = INTELLIGENCE *sb.* 7 b. –1748.

Intelligent (inte·lidzĕnt). 1509. [ad. L. *intelleg-*, *intelligentem*, pr. pple. of *intellegere* (later *intelligere*), f. *inter* between, within + *legere* to bring together, choose, read, etc. Cf. F. *intelligent.*]

A. *adj.* **1.** Having the faculty of understanding; possessing intelligence or intellect 1598. **2.** Having or showing a high degree of intelligence; knowing, sensible, sagacious 1509. **3.** That understands (a particular thing, etc.); cognizant *of*; acquainted *with*; versed *in* 1546. **†4.** 'Bearing intelligence, giving information, communicative' (Schmidt *Shaks. Lex.*).

1. The work of an i. mind BUTLER. 2. It is..in order of nature for him to govern that is the more i. BACON. 3. I. of seasons MILT. 4. Our Postes shall be swift, and i. betwixt vs SHAKS.

B. *sb.* **1.** An intelligent or rational being. **b.** A person of intelligence. Now *rare.* 1601. **†2.** An intelligencer, a spy –1751.

1. God..must of necessitie..be the first i. GALE.

Intelligential (intelidze·nʃăl), *a.* 1611. [f. L. *intelligentia* + -AL.] **1.** = INTELLECTUAL A. **1.** **2.** Possessing, or of the nature of, intelligence 1646.

1. The Devil enterd, and his brutal sense..soon inspir'd With act i. MILT. *P. L.* IX. 190. 2. An i. creature 1646.

†Intellige·ntiary. 1577. [f. as prec. + -ARY.] **1.** *adj.* Relating to or conveying intelligence or news. WOTTON. **2.** *sb.* = INTELLIGENCER.

Intelligently (inte·lidzĕntli), *adv.* 1671. [f. INTELLIGENT *a.* + -LY [2].] In an intelligent manner; sagaciously, sensibly.

‖**Intelligentsia, -tzia** (intelidze·ntsiă). 1920. [Russian, f. L. *intelligentia* INTELLIGENCE.] The class consisting of the educated portion of the population and regarded as capable of forming public opinion.

Intelligible (inte·lidzĭb'l), *a.* (*sb.*) ME. [f. L. *intellegi-*, *intelligibilis*, f. *intellegere* + -IBLE.] **†1.** Capable of understanding; intelligent –1777. **2.** Capable of being understood; comprehensible 1509. **b.** Of a person in reference to his words 1655. **3.** *Philos.* Capable of being apprehended only by the understanding (not by the senses); objective to intellect. (Opp. to *sensible*) ME. **4.** *sb.* That which is intelligible; an object of intellect or understanding; *spec.* in *Philos.* (see sense 3) 1601.

1. A meere Scholer is an i. Asse OVERBURY. 2. What you say now is very i. BERKELEY. b. He spoke so fast as to be hardly i. (*mod.*). 3. The I. world..is ..a world of a nature purely spiritual and intellectual 1701. Hence **Inte·lligibi·lity, Inte·lligibleness,** the quality of being i.; *transf.* an i. thing.

Inte·lligibly, *adv.* 1607. [f. prec. + -LY [2].] **1.** In an intelligible manner; comprehensibly. **†2.** In relation to the understanding; as an object of intellect. (Opp. to *sensibly.*) –1701.

Intemerate (inte·mĕrĕt), *a.* 1491. [ad. L. *intemeratus*, f. *in-* (IN- [3]) + *temeratus*, *temerare* to violate.] Inviolate, undefiled, unblemished. So **†Inte·merated** *a.* Hence **Inte·merate·ly** *adv.*, **-ness. †Intemera·tion,** inviolate condition.

Intemperament (inte·mpĕrămĕnt). *rare.* 1698. [f. IN- [3] + TEMPERAMENT.] An untempered or distempered condition (esp. of the body, blood, etc.).

Intemperance (inte·mpĕrăns). ME. [a. F., ad. L. *intemperantia*, f. *in-* (IN- [3]) + *temperantia.*] Want of temperateness. **†1.** Intemperateness, inclemency, severity of the air, weather, or climate –1707. **2.** Lack of moderation or restraint; excess in any kind of action; *spec.* excessive indulgence of any passion or appetite 1547. **b.** with *pl.* An instance of this 1613. **3.** *spec.* Immoderate indulgence in intoxicating drink; addiction to drinking 1617.

2. Some..by violent stroke shall die,..by I. more In Meats and Drinks MILT. *P. L.* XI. 472. 3. [Indifference] to the crying evils of *intemperance* 1841. So **†Inte·mperancy** (in all senses) 1532.

†Inte·mperant, *a. rare.* 1542. [ad. L. *intemperantem*, f. *in-* (IN- [3]) + *temperantem*, *temperare* to qualify, etc.; see -ANT.] Wanting moderation or self-restraint; incontinent, intemperate –1598.

Intemperate (inte·mpĕrĕt), *a.* ME. [ad. L. *intemperatus*, f. *in-* (IN- [3]) + *temperatus*, *temperare.*] **1.** Not temperate, excessive, extreme; esp., of climate or weather, inclement, severe. Now *rare.* 1526. **2.** Of persons, etc.: Without temperance or moderation; immoderate, unbridled; violent 1508. **3.** Characterized by excessive indulgence in a passion or appetite ME. **b.** *spec.* Given to an excessive use of intoxicating drink 1677.

1. *I. zone*, the Torrid or Frigid zone, as opp. to the Temperate zone. 2. Many i. Speeches and passages happend 1688. The i. zeal of the reformers 1777. 3. His concupiscible i. lust SHAKS. Hence **Inte·mperately** *adv.*

Inte·mperateness. Now *rare.* 1555. [f. prec. + -NESS.] The quality of being intemperate. **1.** = INTEMPERANCE **1.** **2.** = INTEMPERANCE **2.** 1571.

1. The intemperatenes of the ayer and region of Dariena EDEN. 2. I. of language 1653.

†Inte·mperature. 1559. [a. obs. F. *intempérature*, f. *in-* (IN- [3]) + *température.*] **1.** = INTEMPERANCE **1.** –1820. **2.** Abnormal or distempered condition of the body; intemperament –1799.

‖**Intemperies** (intempe·ri,īz). 1676. [L., f. *in-* (IN- [3]) + *temperies* temperature, temper.] Disordered condition of the body, dyscrasy; rarely, of the weather.

Intempestive (intempe·stiv), *a.* 1548. [ad. L. *intempestivus*, f. *in-* (IN- [3]) + *tempestivus* seasonable.] Untimely, unseasonable, inopportune.

Loud and i. laughter 1891. Hence **Intempe·stively** *adv.* So **†Intempesti·vity,** unseasonableness, untimeliness.

†Inte·nable, *a.* 1650. [IN- [3].] That cannot be held or maintained; untenable –1752.

Intend (inte·nd), *v.* [ME. *entend(e*, a. F. *entendre*:—L. *intendere* to stretch forth or out, etc., f. *in-* (IN- [2]) + *tendere* to stretch, TEND.]

I. †1. *trans.* To stretch forth, extend; to point forwards –1633. **†2.** To stretch, strain, make tense; to expand, dilate (*lit.* and *fig.*) –1837. **†3.** To intensify (*trans.* and *intr.*) –1705.

2. As when a bow is successively intended and remitted CUDWORTH. 3. The Church hath power to i. our Faith but not to extend it JER. TAYLOR.

II. 1. *trans.* To direct (the eyes, mind, etc.) *to, into, towards* something. Now a conscious Latinism. ME. **2.** *intr.* and *trans.* To direct one's course; to proceed on (a journey, etc.). (L. *intendere, intendere iter.*) *Obs.* or *arch.* ME. **†b.** *intr.* To start on a journey, to set out; *occas.*, ellipt. for 'intend to go or start' –1817. **†3.** *trans.* To refer, attribute, ascribe (a thing) *to* some one 1615.

1. I. thine eye Into the dim and undiscovered sky PATMORE. 2. *Per.* I. ii. 116. b. I i. for England this spring, where I have some affairs to adjust BYRON.

III. [Ult. f. L. *intendere* = *intendere animum.*] **†1.** *intr.* To direct the mind or attention; to pay heed; to apply oneself assiduously. Const. *to, unto*, rarely *about, on, at.* –1613. **†b.** *refl.* To devote oneself –1627. **†c.** *absol.* –1603. **†2.** To apply oneself *to do* something; to endeavour, strive –1674. **†3.** *intr.* To give ear, hearken –1568. **†b.** *trans.* To hearken to. LATIMER. **†4.** *intr.* To be in attendance or waiting; to attend –1644. **†b.** *trans.* To attend on or to –1633. **†5.** *trans.* To turn one's thoughts to; to occupy oneself with; to look after –1784.

1. Eche to his owene nede gan entende CHAUCER. c. But loe the eyes of God entend And watch to ayde the iust STERNHOLD & H. 4. I wish that one of your number..may i. and appear at that Committee CROMWELL. 5. I. at home..what best may ease The present misery MILT.

IV. †1. *trans.* To have understanding of (something); to apprehend *that* something is –1620. **†2.** *intr.* To have or come to an understanding; to agree; to be in accord. [F. *s'entendre.*] –1509. **†3.** To apprehend, conceive; to think; to judge –1638. **†4.** *trans.* To construe, interpret, or hold legally –1798.

4. The law will i. it to be so BLACKSTONE.

V. 1. *intr.* To have a purpose or design; to be minded. *Obs.*, exc. as absol. use of 2. ME. **2.** *trans.* To have in the mind as a fixed purpose; to purpose, design. (The chief current sense.) ME. **3.** To design (a thing) for some purpose; to destine (a thing or person) to a fate or use; to purpose to bestow; to mean (a thing) *to be* or *to do* something 1590. **4.** To design to express; to mean 1572. **†b.** To designate as something; to call (*rare*) –1605.

2. I know not Gentlemen what you i. SHAKS. He intended his son should have it in remainder for his life only CRUISE. 3. A Play, Intended for great Theseus nuptiall day SHAKS. The second son is intended for the army (*mod.*). 4. By Profit I i. not here any Accession of Wealth HOBBES.

VI. Senses of uncertain position or origin. **†1.** *trans.* To expect. [OF. *entendre* = F. *attendre.*] –1485. **†2.** To assert, maintain; to pretend; to claim –1634. **†3.** *intr.* To tend or incline –1640. **4.** *trans.* To superintend, direct. Cf. INTENDANT. 1791.

4. Nine arbiters, appointed to i. The whole arrangements of the public games COWPER.

Hence **Inte·nder,** one who intends or purposes; †a pretender.

†Inte·ndance 1. ME. [a. OF. *entendance.*] Application of the mind; attention -1611.

Intendance 2 (inte·ndāns). 1739. [a. F., f. *intendant* INTENDANT *sb.*; see -ANCE.] The function of an intendant; superintendence, direction; intendancy; *spec.* a department of the French public service, or the officials conducting it, as the war commissariat, etc. **b.** The official quarters or office of an intendant 1895.

Intendancy (inte·ndānsi). Also 7-9 **-ency.** 1598. [f. INTENDANT *sb.*; see -ANCY.] **1.** The office, position, or function of an intendant; a body of intendants. **b.** *fig.* Superintendence. WARBURTON. **2.** A district in Spanish America under an intendant (*intendente*) 1810.

Intendant (inte·ndānt), *sb.* Also 7-9 **-ent.** 1652. [a. F., ad. L. *intendentem, intendere*; see INTEND *v.*] One who has the charge, direction, or superintendence of a department of public business, the affairs of a town or province, the household of a prince or nobleman, etc.; a superintendent, a manager. Used orig. and chiefly as the title of certain public officers in France and elsewhere.

The Marquess..appointed him..I. of his household DISRAELI.

†Inte·ndant, *a.* Also 4-5 **en-.** ME. [a. F. *entendant*, pr. pple. of *entendre* to INTEND.] Attentive -1581.

Intended (inte·ndėd), *ppl. a.* (*sb.*) 1576. [f. INTEND *v.* + -ED 1.] **1.** Purposed; designed, meant; intentional 1586. **†2.** Stretched out or forth; extended; increased in force or intensity, strained -1667. **†3.** Minded, resolved -1657. **4.** *sb. colloq.* An intended husband or wife 1767.

1. Your entended iourney 1594. 2. With sharpe i. sting SPENSER. Hence **Inte·ndedly** *adv.* designedly.

Intendence (inte·ndėns). *arch.* 1687. [f. INTEND *v.*; see -ENCE.] The paying of attention, attendance.

Writ of i. and respondence, a writ under the Great Seal in favour of one who received an appointment from the king, ordering all persons to attend and respond to his requests.

Intendency, etc.: see INTENDANCY, etc.

†Inte·ndiment. 1528. [ad. med.L. *intendimentum.*] **1.** = INTENDMENT 1. -1590. **2.** Intention, purpose -1628. **3.** Attention. SPENSER.

Intending (inte·ndiŋ), *ppl. a.* 1660. [-ING 2.] That intends. **b.** Qualifying an agent-noun: Purposing to be, that is (such) in intention 1788.

b. I. subscribers should communicate [etc.] 1884.

Intendment (inte·ndmėnt). ME. [a. F. *entendement* understanding, f. *entendre*; see INTEND *v.*] **†1.** The faculty or action of understanding -1601. **†2.** Way of understanding (something); interpretation; view -1630. **3.** Signification; import. Now *rare* or *Obs.* ME. **4.** *Law.* The construction put upon anything by the common law; true meaning as fixed by law 1574. **†5.** The act or fact of intending; intent; that which is intended; a design, project -1804. **†b.** The purpose or object of anything -1732. **†6.** Tendency, inclination -1620. **†7.** An office of supervision. FORD.

1. Maister Chaucer..Mirour of fructuous entendement HOCCLEVE. 3. A phrase of sinister and odious i. 1879. 4. *Common i.*, customary or reasonable interpretation, as determined by the law. The Ordinary (which is the Bishop by common i.) 1577.

Intenerate (inte·nĕrēit), *v.* Now *rare.* 1595. [f. L. *in-* (IN- 2) + *tener* tender; see -ATE 3.] *trans.* To make tender, soften, mollify (*lit.* and *fig.*).

Feare intenerates the heart, making it fit for all gracious impressions BP. HALL. So **Inte·nerate** *ppl. a.* intenerated. Hence **Intenera·tion,** the action of intenerating, or fact of being intenerated.

†Inte·nible, *a.* [f. IN- 3 + L. type **tenibilis*, f. *tenere* to hold.] Incapable of holding or containing. *All's Well* I. iii. 208.

Intensate (inte·nsēit), *v. rare.* 1831. [f. L. type **intensare* (f. *intensus*) + -ATE 3.] *trans.* To make intense; to intensify. Hence **Intensa·tion** 1826.

Intensative (inte·nsătiv). *rare.* 1853. [f. L. **intensat-*, **intensare* + -IVE.] **a.** *adj.* = INTENSIVE 4. 1870. **b.** *sb.* = INTENSIVE 7.

Intense (inte·ns), *a.* ME. [a. F. *intense*, ad. L. *intensus, intendere*; see INTEND *v.* Cf. INTENT *a.*] *Etymologically*, Stretched, strained, high-strung. Hence: **1.** Of a quality or condition: Raised to or existing in a very high degree; violent, extreme, excessive; of colour, very deep; of a feeling, ardent. Also *transf.* of a thing. 1653. **2.** Of personal, esp. mental, action, etc.: Strenuously directed to some end; intent, eager, earnest, ardent 1645. **3.** Of a person: **†a.** Intent *upon* (*about*) something -1724. **b.** Feeling, or susceptible to, intense emotion 1830; often in trivial sense, highly sensitive or impressionable 1878. Also *transf.* of language, aspect, etc. 1684.

1. I. cold EVELYN. *transf.* The yellow stars grew more i. overhead BLACK. 2. Somtime slackning the cords of i. thought and labour MILT. 3. b. 'The intense school' may be defined as always using the strongest possible word on every possible occasion MACKINTOSH. *transf.* The expression..i. and stern 1838. Hence **Inte·nsely** *adv.*, **Inte·nseness.**

Intensification (inte:nsifikē¹·ʃən). 1847. [f. INTENSIFY; see -FICATION.] The action of intensifying; intensified condition; *spec.* in *Photogr.*, the thickening or increasing of the opacity of the film of a negative.

Inte·nsifier (-fəi,əɹ). 1835. [f. next + -ER 1.] Something that intensifies; *spec.* in *Photogr.* (see next, 1 b).

Intensify (inte·nsifəi), *v.* 1817. [f. L. *intensus* + -FY.] **1.** *trans.* To render intense; to augment, strengthen, heighten, etc. **b.** *Photogr.* To make the chemically affected parts of (a negative) more dense or opaque, so as to produce a stronger contrast of light and shade 1861. **2.** *intr.* To grow in intensity 1853.

1. Her uneasiness will be greatly intensified DICKENS. 2. There is no relief: the action intensifies 1896.

Intension (inte·nʃən). 1603. [ad. L. *intensionem*; see INTEND, INTENSE, and cf. INTENTION, a doublet of this.] **1.** The action of stretching, tension; straining. ? *Obs.* **2.** Intentness; resolution, determination 1619. **3.** Intensification. (Opp. to *remission.*) 1610. **4.** Degree, esp. notable degree, of some quality, etc.; intensity, depth, strength, force. (Often contrasted with *extension.*) 1604. **5.** *Logic.* The COMPREHENSION of a notion or concept; the CONNOTATION of a term. (Opp. to EXTENSION.) 1836.

2. I found myself..listening with an agony of i. 1860. 3. Brightness is the I. of Light 1658. 4. The essence of farming on virgin soils is extension; on old land it is i. 1888.

Intensitive (inte·nsĭtiv), *a.* (*sb.*) *rare.* 1817. [irreg. f. INTENSITY + -IVE.] = INTENSATIVE, INTENSIVE.

Intensity (inte·nsĭti). 1665. [f. INTENSE + -ITY.] **1.** The quality of being intense; extreme force, strength, depth, brightness, etc. **2.** The degree or amount of some quality, condition, etc.; force, strength, energy, etc.; degree of some characteristic quality; *esp.* in *Physics*, as a measurable quantity 1794. **b.** *Photogr.* = DENSITY 4. 1855.

1. Such an i. of cold BOYLE. He..looked at the stranger for several seconds with a stern i. DICKENS. 2. Denoting the degrees of i. of some particular qualities by figures 1796.

Intensive (inte·nsiv), *a.* (*sb.*) 1450. [a. F. *intensif, -ive* = med. or mod.L. *intensivus*, f. *intens-, intendere* to stretch, strain; see INTEND, INTENSE.] **†1.** = INTENSE *a.* 1. -1687. **†2.** = INTENSE *a.* 2. -1669. **3.** Of, relating, or pertaining to intensity, as dist. from external spatial extent or amount; of or pertaining to logical intension 1604. **b.** Having the quality of intensity 1836. **4.** Having the property of making intense; intensifying; esp. in *Gram.*, expressing intensity; giving force or emphasis 1608. **5.** *Econ.* Applied to methods of cultivation, fishery, etc., which increase the productiveness of a given area; opp. to *extensive* 1832. **6.** Characterized by being intensified 1888. **7.** *sb.* Something that intensifies; *spec.* in *Gram.* an intensive word or prefix 1813.

2. I. thinking is tedious, and tires 1669. 3. The record of an i. as well as extensive development TRENCH. Hence **Inte·nsively** *adv.* intensely (now *rare*); †intently; in relation to intensity or to logical intension. **Inte·nsiveness.**

Intent (inte·nt), *sb.* [ME. had two forms: (1) *entent, intent*:—L. *intentus* a stretching out; (2) *entente, intente*, a. OF. *entente*:—pop. L. **intenta* sb., from fem. of *intentus* pa. pple. The form with *in-* is rare bef. 1400, with *en-* after 1550.] **1.** The act or fact of intending or purposing; intention, purpose (formed in the mind); design. Formerly also, Will, inclination; that which is willed, pleasure, desire. Now chiefly in legal use. **†2.** Attention, heed -1704. **†3.** Intent effort, endeavour -1483. **†4.** Mind, or an act of the mind; understanding; frame of mind, spirit; perception; notion, opinion, or thought of any kind -1623. **†5.** Meaning; purport -1676. **†b.** *Law.* = INTENDMENT 4. -1767. **6.** An end purposed; aim, purpose. *rare* or *Obs.* exc. in phr. *To* (*for*) *all intents and purposes.* ME. **†7.** Intended subject or theme -1670.

1. The bare i. to commit treason is many times actual treason BLACKSTONE. 4. She taketh in good entente The wyl of Crist CHAUCER. 6. I highly recommend the end and i. of Pythagoras's injunction CHATHAM.

Intent (inte·nt), *a.* 1606. [ad. L. *intentus, intendere.* A doublet of *intense*, but differentiated in sense.] **1.** Having the mind strenuously bent upon something; eager, assiduous; bent, resolved 1610. **2.** Of the faculties, looks, etc.: Directed with strained attention; eager, keen; intense 1606. **†3.** Intensely active. SIR T. BROWNE.

1. I. our prayers to heare 1610, on high designs GOLDSM. 2. The i. Application with which he pursues Trifles STEELE. Hence **Inte·ntly** *adv.* in an i. manner. **Inte·ntness.**

†Intenta·tion. *rare.* 1612. [ad. L. *intentationem.*] An accusation; a threatening -1656.

Intention (inte·nʃən). ME. [a. OF. *en-, intention*, ad. L. *intentionem.*]

I. General senses. **†1.** The action of straining or directing the mind or attention to something -1749. **†2.** The action or faculty of understanding; way of understanding (something); notion. Also, the mind generally. -1526. **†3.** Meaning, import -1668. **4.** The action of intending; volition; purpose ME. **5.** That which is intended; a purpose, design ME. **b.** *pl.* (*colloq.*) Purposes in respect of a proposal of marriage 1796. **6.** Ultimate purpose; aim of an action ME. **†7.** = INTENSION 1. -1654. **b.** Forcible application or direction (*of* the mind, eye, thoughts, etc.). (With more of the notion of *tension* than in sense 1.) 1638. **†8.** = INTENSION 3. -1758.

4. You never open your mouth but with i. to give pain JOHNSON. 5. Sir, Hell is paved with good intentions JOHNSON. b. Colonel Fitzwilliam had made it clear that he had no intentions at all, and..she did not mean to be unhappy about him JANE AUSTEN. 6. To..loke wel to what entention the yeft is gyuen CAXTON. 7. b. The toil and labour, and racking i. of the brain SOUTH.

II. Spec. uses. **1.** *Surg.* and *Med.* An aim or purpose in a healing process; hence, a plan or method of treatment (*arch.*) ME. **2.** *Logic.* The direction of the mind to an object; a conception formed by directing the mind to some object; a general concept 1532. **3.** *Theol.* One of the three things necessary, according to the Schoolmen, to the effectual administration and validity of a Sacrament, the others being *Matter* and *Form* 1690. **4.** (*Special*) *i.*, a special direction of prayer at mass, etc., to a certain object 1594.

1. *Healing by first intention*, the healing of a lesion or fracture by the immediate reunion of the severed parts, without granulation; *by second i.*, the healing of a wound by granulation after suppuration. 2. *First intentions* (Logic), primary conceptions of things, formed by the direct application of the mind to the things themselves; e.g. the concepts of *a tree, an oak.* *Second intentions*, secondary conceptions formed by the application of thought to first intentions in their relations to each other; e.g. the concepts of *genus, species, difference*, etc. Logic was said [by Avicenna] to treat of *second intentions applied to first* MANSEL.

Intentional (inte·nʃənăl), *a.* 1530. [ad. med.L. *intentionalis*, f. *intentionem.*] **1.** Of or pertaining to intention or purpose; existing (only) in intention. **2.** Done on purpose; intended 16.. **3.** *Schol. Philos.* Pertaining to the operations of the mind; mental; existing in or for the mind 1624.

2. An i. insult SCOTT. 3. I. species H. MORE. Hence **Inte·ntionally** *adv.* in an i. manner or relation.

Intentionality (inteːnʃənæ·liti). 1611. [ad. Schol.L. *intentionalitas*; see prec. and -ITY.] The quality or fact of being intentional.

Intentioned (inte·nʃənd), *a.* 1647. [f. INTENTION + -ED[2].] Having intentions (of a specified kind); as, *equitably i.*

Intentive (inte·ntiv), *a. Obs.* or *arch.* ME. [a. OF. *en-, intentif, -ive*, ad. late L. *intentivus*, f. *intent-, intendere*; see -IVE.] 1. Of persons: Attentive, heedful, intent. 2. Of the faculties, etc.: Intently bent or directed ME.

2. His too i. trust to flatterers 1592. **Inte·ntive·ly** *adv.*, **-ness.**

Inter (intǝ̄·ɹ), *v.* ME. [a. OF. *enterrer*, ad. prob. late pop. L. *interrare*, f. *in-* (IN-[2]) + *terra*, for cl.L. *inhumare.*] 1. *trans.* To deposit (a corpse) in the earth; to inhume, bury. Also *transf.* and *fig.* †2. Said of a tomb: To enclose the corpse of 1631. †3. = BURY *v.* 3. –1741.

1. Dead and enterr'd DONNE. 2. This rich marble doth i. The honoured wife of Winchester MILT.

‖**Inter** (i·ntəɹ), the L. prep. = 'between', 'among', occurs in L. phrases occasional in Eng., e.g. *inter alia*, amongst other things (less usu. *inter alios*, amongst other persons); *inter nos*, between ourselves; *inter se*, between or among themselves.

Inter-, *prefix.* The Latin prep. and adv., *inter* 'between, among, amid, in between, in the midst', used as an Eng. formative element.

I. In adverbial or adjectival relation to the second element.

1. Prefixed to vbs., pples., vbl. sbs., and ppl. adjs., to form verbs, etc.; as in: a. *interbreathe, -cloud, -dash, -distinguish, -lie, -mention, -receive, -set*, etc.; b. *interaccuse, -arch, -balance, -chase, -grapple, -jangle, -oscillate, -talk, -vary, -wed, -wish*, etc. 2. Prefixed in adjectival relation to sbs., or in adverbial relation to adjs.; as in: a. *inter-absorption, -colonization, -combat, -combination, -comparison, -mobility, -mutation; inter-comparable, -repellent, -visible*, adjs., etc.; b. *intercalm* (an interval of calm), *-canal* (a canal connecting two others), etc.

II. In prepositional relation to the sb. expressed or implied in the second element.

1. Prefixed to *sbs.*, forming sbs.; as in: a. *interjoist, inter-modillion, interspiral*, etc.; also *interworld*; b. *interpapacy, inter-parliament*, INTERREGNUM. 2. Prefixed to *adjs.*, in prepositional relation to the sb. implied (as *interacinous*, 'that is *inter acinos*, between the acini'); as in: a. INTERALVEOLAR, -ARTICULAR, -CELLULAR, *-epimeral, -mandibular, -peduncular, -sternal*, etc.; b. *inter-equinoctial, -sessional*, etc.; c. *interclerical* (between clergymen), *-collegiate, -departmental*, etc.; d. *intercranial* (prop. *intracranial*), *-imperial, -trinitarian*, etc. 3. Prefixed to sbs., forming adjs.; as in *inter-club* (between different clubs), *-county, -empire, -school, -town, -university* (-'*varsity*), etc.

The main stress is on the radical word, exc. in I. 2 b; but, when this is a monosyllable, it tends to shift to *inter-*.

The following adjs., mostly belonging to II. 2, are given as being of subordinate importance, but not quite self-explanatory. **Intera·cinous**, situated or occurring between or among the acini of a gland. **Interauri·cular**, 'situated between the auricles of the heart' (*Syd. Soc. Lex.*). **Intercaro·tic, Intercaro·tid**, situated between the two carotid arteries. **Interca·rpal**, situated or occurring between the bones of the carpus. **Interco·smic, -al**, situated or existing between worlds. **Intercra·nial**, situated within the skull (prop. *intracranial*). **Interimpe·rial**, carried on between or connecting the various countries of the (British) Empire. **Interme·mbral**, subsisting (as a relation) between members or limbs, as *i. homology*. **Intermercu·rial** (prop. *intra-*), *Astron.* situated within the orbit of Mercury. **Intermetaca·rpal**, situated between the bones of the metacarpus; so also **Intermetata·rsal. Intermo·ntane**, situated between mountains. **Intero·cular**, situated or occurring between the eyes. **Interpe·talary**, *Bot.* situated between petals. **Interphala·ngeal**, situated between two successive phalanges of a finger or toe. **Interta·rsal**, *Anat.* situated between the bones of the tarsus. **Interti·dal**, inhabiting the sea-shore between the limits of high and low tide. **Intertrochante·ric**, situated between two trochanters; spec. applied to a line or ridge between the greater and lesser trochanter of the femur. **Intertu·bular**, situated between tubes or tubuli. **Interu·ngular, Interu·nguiate**, situated between the hoofs (e.g. in sheep).

Interact (i·ntərˌæːkt), *sb.* 1750. [f. INTER- II. 1 + ACT *sb.*, after F. *entr'acte.*] The interval between two acts of a play; an interlude; hence, an intermediate employment.

Interact (intərˌæ·kt), *v.* 1839. [INTER- I. 1 b.] *intr.* To act reciprocally, to act on each other. Hence **Intera·ction**, reciprocal action; action or influence of persons or things on each other 1832. **Intera·ctive** *a.* reciprocally active.

Interadditive (intərˌæ·ditiv). 1819. [f. INTER- I. 2 a + ADDITIVE.] Something added or inserted between or among other things.

Inter-agent (intərˌē·dʒěnt). 1728. [f. as prec. + AGENT.] An intermediate agent; a go-between. So **Inter-a·gency.**

Interall, obs. f. ENTRAIL.

Interalveolar (intərˌælvī·ǒlǎr), *a.* 1834. [INTER- II. 2 a.] *Anat.* 1. Situated between the alveoli or air-cells of the lungs. 2. Situated between the alveoli or sockets of the teeth of a sea-urchin 1877.

‖**Interambulacrum** (-ē·krǒm). *Pl.* **-acra.** 1870. [INTER- II. 1.] *Zool.* One of the imperforate plates occupying the intervals of the ambulacra or perforate plates in the shells of echinoderms. Hence **Interambula·cral** *a.* of or pertaining to interambulacra; situated between ambulacra.

Interamnian (intərˌæ·mniǎn), *a.* 1774. [f. L. *interamnus* lying between two rivers (f. *inter* INTER- II. 2 a + *amnis*) + -IAN.] Lying between rivers, like Mesopotamia; enclosed by rivers.

Intera·nimate, *v. rare.* [INTER- I. 1 b.] *trans.* To animate mutually. DONNE.

†**Interarbora·tion.** [f. INTER- I. 2 a + L. *arbor* + -ATION.] Intermixture of the branches of trees on opposite sides. SIR T. BROWNE.

Interarticular (i:ntərˌaɹti·kiulǎɹ), *a.* 1808. [f. INTER- II. 2 a + L. *articulus* joint.] Lying or prevailing between the contiguous surfaces in a joint.

Interatomic (i:ntərˌătǫ·mik), *a.* 1863. [INTER- II. 2 a.] Existing or acting between atoms.

Interaulic (intərˌǭ·lik), *a. nonce-wd.* 1864. [f. INTER- II. 2 a + L. *aula* court; see AULIC.] 'Existing between royal courts' (Webster).

Interauri·cular, etc.: see INTER- *pref.*

Interaxis (intərˌæ·ksis). *Pl.* **-axes** (-æ·ksīz). 1842. [INTER- II. 1.] *Arch.* The space between the axes. So **Intera·xal** *a.* pertaining to the i., situated between the axes.

†**Interba·state**, *v. rare.* 1657. [f. F. *interbaster* to quilt; see -ATE[3].] *trans.* To sew between (cotton, etc.) so as to keep in place; to quilt. Hence †**Interbasta·tion**, quilting. So †**Interba·ste** *v.* (*rare*) 1611.

Interbed (intəɹbe·d), *v.* 1858. [INTER- I. 1 a.] *trans.* To embed amongst or between, to interstratify.

Interbrachial (-brē·kiǎl), *a.* (*sb.*) 1877. [f. INTER- II. 2 a + L. *brachium* arm.] 1. *Zool.* = INTERAMBULACRAL, INTERRADIAL. 2. *sb.* An interbrachial part or member.

I·nter-brain. 1887. [INTER- I. 2 b.] *Anat.* = DIENCEPHALON.

Interbranchial (-bræ·ŋkiǎl), *a.* 1880. [INTER- II. 2 a.] *Zool.* Situated between the branchiæ or gills.

Interbreed (intəɹbrī·d), *v.* 1859. [INTER- I. 1 b.] 1. *intr.* Of animals of different race or species: To breed with each other 1864. 2. *intr.* or *absol.* To cause animals to interbreed 1859. 3 *trans.* To cross-breed. Also *fig.* 1865.

†**Inte·rcalar**, *a.* 1533. [ad. L. *intercalaris.*] = INTERCALARY 1. –1699.

Intercalary (intǝ̄·ɹkǎlǎri), *a.* 1614. [ad. L. *intercalarius* or *intercalaris*, f. *intercalare* to INTERCALATE.] 1. Of a day, days, or month: Inserted at intervals in the calendar in order to bring an inexact reckoning of the year into harmony with the solar year. b. Of a year: Having intercalated days or an additional month 1648. †2. Of a line or stanza: Inserted at intervals in a composition; of the nature of a refrain –1803. 3. Of the nature of an insertion; interpolated, intervening 1798.

1. Since the reform of the calendar by Julius Cæsar (B.C. 46), an i. day (now Feb. 29) is required only once in four years; see BISSEXTILE and LEAP-YEAR. 2. Having a double burthen or i. verse oft recurring HAMMOND. 3. I. spines OWEN. Last of the I. Kaisers CARLYLE.

Intercalate (intǝ̄·ɹkălēˈt), *v.* 1614. [f. L. *intercalat-, intercalare* to proclaim the insertion of (a day, etc.) in the calendar, f. *inter* + *calare* to proclaim solemnly; cf. CALENDS.] 1. *trans.* To insert (an additional day, days, or month) in the calendar. Also *absol.* 2. *transf.* To insert or interpose something additional, extraneous, etc. among other things; to interpolate. Chiefly in *pass.* 1824. b. *Geol.* in *pass. pple.* Interstratified, interbedded with the original series 1833.

2. b. Harder beds of rock, intercalated with the softer ones H. MILLER. var. †**Intercale** *v.* 1613.

Intercalation (intəɹkălē·ʃən). 1577. [ad. L. *intercalationem*; see prec.] 1. The insertion of an additional day, days, or month into the ordinary year; an intercalated day or space of time. 2. *transf.* The insertion of any addition between the members of an existing or recognized series; the occurrence of a layer or bed of a different kind between the regular strata of a series; (with *an* and *pl.*) the thing or matter thus interjected 1648.

2. Successive intercalations indicative of more than one period of glaciation A. R. WALLACE.

Intercartilaginous (-kāɹtilæ·dʒinəs), *a.* 1872. [INTER- II. 2 a.] *Anat.* Situated between cartilages.

Intercede (intəɹsī·d), *v.* 1578. [ad. L. *intercedere*, f. *inter* between + *cedere* to go. Cf. F. *intercéder.*] 1. *intr. Rom. Hist.* Of the tribunes: To interpose a veto 1581. †2. To come *between* in time, space, or action; to intervene –1799. †3. *trans.* To come, pass, or lie between; to intervene between –1799. †4. *intr.* To come in the way –1673. 5. *intr.* To interpose on behalf of another or others 1606.

4. Subjects are bound..to obey the Magistrate Actively in all things where their Duty to God intercedes not MARVELL. 5. I heare not one man open his mouth to i. for the offender BP. HALL. Hence **Interce·der.**

†**Interce·dent**, *a.* 1578. [ad. L. *intercedentem*; see prec.] Coming between; intervening –1683. Hence †**Interce·dence** (*rare*), intervention 1640.

Intercellular (intəɹse·liǔlǎɹ), *a.* 1835. [INTER- II. 2 a.] Situated between or among cells.

Only two cells form an i. passage, not three or four LINDLEY. So **I·nterce:ll, Interce·llulary** *adjs.*

Intercensal (intəɹse·nsǎl), *a.* 1887. [Improp. f. INTER- II. 2 b + L. *census* + -AL; see CENSUAL.] Of or belonging to the interval between two censuses, occurring between two censuses.

Intercentral (intəɹse·ntrǎl), *a.* 1870. [INTER- II. 2 a.] *Phys.* a. Situated between the centra of the vertebræ; see CENTRUM. b. Connecting, or relating to the connexion of, nerve-centres.

‖**Interce·ntrum.** 1878. [f. INTER- II. 1 + CENTRUM.] *Comp. Anat.* A wedge- or chevron-shaped process, generally situated between the centra, occurring on the ventral aspect of the vertebral column in many Vertebrates, and esp. in Reptiles; = HYPAPOPHYSIS.

Intercept (i·ntəɹsept), *sb.* 1821. [ad. L. *interceptum, intercipere*; see next.] 1. An interception. 2. *Math.* The part of a line lying between two points at which it is intersected by lines or planes 1864.

Intercept (intəɹse·pt), *v.* 1545. [f. L. *intercept-, intercipere*, f. *inter* + *capere* to take, seize.] 1. *trans.* To seize, catch, or carry off on the way from one place to another; to cut off from the destination aimed at 1548. b. To stop the natural course of (light, heat, etc.); to cut off (light) *from* anything 1545. †c. To interrupt –1759. d. To check, cut off (passage or motion) from one place to another 1596. †e. *absol.* or *intr.* –1682. 2. To prevent, check, stop, hinder 1576. 3. To mark off or include (a certain space) between two points or lines; hence, to contain, enclose. *spec.* in *Math.* (see INTERCEPT *sb.* 2). 1571. 4. To cut off (one thing) *from* another, or (*ellipt.*) from sight, access, etc. 1662.

1. I..Marcht toward S. Albons, to i. the Queene SHAKS. To i. Ships STEELE, supplies 1847. b. God

will shortely i. your brethe..if ye repent not JOYE. **d.** Vessels, sent out..to i. his passage 1683. **2.** Causes less excusable also i. its influence J. MARTINEAU. **4.** The glass which now intercepts from the eye of the mind the realities of the future world CHALMERS. Hence †**Interce·pter** (*rare*), **-or**, one who or that which intercepts. **Interce·ption**, the action of intercepting; †*spec.* in *Med.* the interruption of the motion or passage of bodily humours. **Interce·ptive** *a.* having the quality of intercepting.

Intercession (intəɹse·ʃən). 1500. [ad. L. *intercessionem*.] **1.** The action of interceding or pleading on behalf of (*rarely* against); entreaty, solicitation, or prayer for another; mediation 1534; †a petition or pleading on one's own behalf –1742. **2.** *Rom. Hist.* The action of interposing a veto 1573. †**3.** Interposition, intervention –1638. ¶**4.** Intermission –1683.

1. I will send to the kyng, and make humble i. for your pardon HALL. Hee euer liueth to make i. for them *Heb.* vii. 25. Hence **Interce·ssional** *a.* of or pertaining to i.

†**Interce·ssionate**, *v.* 1593. [f. as prec. + -ATE [3].] **1.** *intr.* = INTERCEDE *v.* –1598. **2.** *trans.* To entreat. NASHE.

Intercessor (intəɹse·səɹ). 1482. [a. L., f. *intercedere*.] **1.** One who intercedes on behalf of another; a mediator. **b.** In religious use: A Mediator 1526. †**2.** An intermediary; a go-between –1598. **3.** *Eccl.* A bishop, who, during a vacancy, administered the see, until a successor had been elected 1727.

Intercessorial (intəɹsesōᵊ·riăl), *a.* 1776. [f. as next + -AL.] Of or pertaining to an intercessor.

Intercessory (intəɹse·səri), *a.* 1576. [f. L. *intercessor*; see -ORY.] Having the function or purpose of intercession; that intercedes for others; as, an *i. prayer*.

†**Interchain**, *v. rare.* 1590. [INTER- I. 1 b.] *trans.* To chain or link one to another –1649. *Mids. N.* II. ii. 49.

Interchange (i·ntəɹtʃēⁱndʒ), *sb.* 1548. [a. OF. *entrechange*, f. *entrechangier*; see next.] **1.** Giving and receiving with reciprocity; reciprocal exchange between two persons or parties. **2.** The change of each of two (or more) things, conditions, etc. for the other, or of one thing, etc. for another; the taking by each of the place or nature of the other 1581. **3.** Alternate or varied succession in time, order, or space; alternation, vicissitude 1559. **4.** *attrib.*, as in *i. service, station*, etc. (for the passage of traffic from one railway line to another) 1887.

1. Enter-change of Gifts, Letters, louing Embassies SHAKS. An i. of commodities betwixt two countries 1804. **2.** Enterchange of war for peace DRUMM. OF HAWTH. **3.** Sweet i. Of hill and Vallie, Rivers, Wood and Plaines, Now Land, now Sea MILT.

Interchange (intəɹtʃēⁱ·ndʒ), *v.* Also †**enter-**. ME. [a. OF. *entrechangier* to change, disguise, f. *entre-* (INTER- I. 2) + *changier*, *changer* to CHANGE.] **1.** *trans.* To exchange mutually; to give and receive in reciprocity. **b.** Of one person or party: To exchange (something) *with* another person 1566. **2.** To put each of (two things) in the place of the other; †also, to exchange (one thing) *for* another; †to change (clothes) ME. **3.** To cause (things) to follow each other alternately or in succession 1561; *intr.* to alternate *with*; to become by turns 1483.

1. To i. presents 1624, opinions MACAULAY. **b.** I interchanged signals with His Majesty's Ship, L'Aimable 1805. **2.** Once more I shall enterchange My wained state, for Henries Regall Crowne SHAKS. **3.** *intr.* Those [Insecta] that Enterchange from Wormes to Flyes BACON.

Interchangeable (intəɹtʃēⁱ·ndʒăb'l), *a.* (*adv.*) 1450. [a. OF. *entrechangeable*; see prec. and -ABLE.] †**1.** Mutual, reciprocal –1665. †**b.** as *adv.* Mutually –1644. †**2. a.** Of two or more things: Coming or following in place of each other –1783. †**b.** Of one thing: Changeable –1749. **3.** Admitting an exchange of place or function 1569.

2. a. Darknesse and light hold i. dominions SIR T. BROWNE. **b.** I. Weather 1749. **3.** Not one..recognizes it [*for the nonce*] as i. with 'for the occasion' F. HALL. Hence **Interchangeabi·lity**, **Intercha·ngeableness**. **Intercha·ngeably** *adv.* 1375.

†**Intercha·ngement**. 1601. [f. prec. vb. + -MENT.] = INTERCHANGE *sb.* 1. –1796.

†**Inte·rcident**, *a.* 1603. [ad. L. *intercidentem* falling between.] **1.** *Med.* Of days in an illness: Falling between the critical and judicial days –1685. **2.** *Path.* Of the pulse: characterized by irregular rhythm. HARVEY. Hence †**Inte·rcidence**, the fact of being i. HOLLAND.

†**Interci·pient**. 1656. [ad. L. *intercipientem* intercepting.] **A.** *adj.* That intercepts or stops the flow of humours 1684. **B.** *sb.* An application which does this –1684.

†**Interci·sion**. 1578. [ad. L. *intercisionem*, f. *intercidere* to cut through.] **1.** The action of cutting through; section, intersection. Also with *an*: A cross-section. –1726. **2.** The action of stopping or interrupting, esp. temporarily; the fact of being interrupted or ceasing for a time –1660. Also with *an* and *pl.* –1813. **3.** Falling away, failing –1651.

Interclavicle (intəɹ͵klæ·vik'l). 1870. [f. INTER- II. 1 + CLAVICLE.] *Anat.* A bone occurring between the clavicles in certain vertebrates. So **I:nterclavi·cular** *a.* lying between the clavicles; esp. in *i. bone, ligament, notch* 1831.

†**Interclo·se**, *v. rare.* 1457. [f. INTER- I. 1 a + CLOSE *v.*] *trans.* To shut up; to enclose within –1680.

†**Interclu·de**, *v.* 1524. [ad. L. *intercludere*, f. *inter* + *claudere* to close.] **1.** *trans.* To close, shut up, block (a passage); to prevent the passage of –1683. **2** To shut up, confine within bounds –1806. **3.** To shut off, cut off *from* –1621.

1. Like as the voice is sometimes intercluded by a hoarseness 1669. So †**Interclu·sion**, shutting up.

Intercolline (intəɹkǫ·ləin), *a.* 1858. [f. INTER- II. 2 a + L. *collis* a hill, *collinus* relating to a hill.] *Geol.* Lying between hills; applied by Sir Charles Lyell to the hollows lying between hills formed by accumulation of erupted volcanic matter.

Intercolonial (i:ntəɹkǒlōᵘ·niăl), *a.* 1855. [f. INTER- II. 2 c + COLONIAL.] Existing, carried on, etc. between different colonies. Hence **Intercolo·nially** *adv.*

I:nterco·lumn. ? *Obs.* 1665. [ad. L. *intercolumnium* (f. *inter* + *columna*).] *Arch.* The space between two columns.

Intercolumnar (i:ntəɹkǒlʊ·mnăɹ), *a.* 1842. [f. INTER- II. 2 a + L. *columna*; cf. F. *intercolumnaire*.] **1.** *Arch.* Lying or placed between two columns 1862. **2.** *Anat.* Extending between the columns of the external abdominal rings. So **Intercolu·mniary** *a.* in sense 1. 1663.

†**Intercolumna·tion.** 1664. = next –1757.

Intercolumniation (i:ntəɹkǒlʊmniēⁱ·ʃən). 1624. [f. L. *intercolumnium* + -ATION.] **1.** = INTERCOLUMN. **2.** The placing of columns, with reference to the space between them 1847.

Interco·mmon, *v.* [ME. *entrecomon*, ad. AF. *entrecomuner*, f. *entre-* (INTER- I. 1 b) + *comuner* to COMMON, COMMUNE.] †**1.** *intr.* To have intercourse *with* others; to associate *with* or together –1675. **2.** *intr.* To share in the use of the same common 1598. †**3.** *intr.* To share or participate *with* others, or mutually –1661. †**4.** *trans. Sc. Law.* To denounce by 'letters of intercommuning'; hence, to outlaw –1717.

3. He and hogs did in some sort entercommon both in their diet and lodging FULLER. **4.** The numbers and desperate tempers of those who were intercommoned BURNET. Hence **Interco·mmonage**, the practice of sharing with others, esp. of using common pasture. **Interco·mmoner**, one who participates with others, esp. in the use of common pasture. Chiefly in *pl.*

Intercommune, *v.* Now *rare* or *Obs.* ME. [a. AF. *entrecomuner*; see prec., and cf. COMMUNE *v.* Stressed at first *co·mmune*, later prob. *commu·ne*.] **1.** *intr.* To have mutual communion; to hold conversation with each other or with another. †**2.** To have intercourse, relations, or connexion, esp. in *Sc. Law*, with rebels or denounced persons –1828. †**3.** To participate in the use of the same pasture or the like. HOLLAND. †**4.** *trans. Sc.* To denounce by letters or writ of intercommuning; to prohibit 'intercommuning with' –1730.

Interco·mmuner. 1620. [f. prec. (sense 4) + -ER [1].] *Sc. Law.* One who holds intercourse or correspondence with a person denounced by law. Now *Hist.*

Intercommu·nicable, *a.* 1822. [f. INTERCOMMUNICATE *v.*, after COMMUNICABLE.] Capable of or suitable for intercommunication.

Intercommunicate (i:ntəɹkǒmiū·nikeⁱt), *v.* 1586. [f. Anglo-Lat. *intercommunicat-*, *-communicare*; see INTER- I. 1 b and COMMUNICATE.] **1.** *intr.* To communicate mutually; to have mutual intercourse; to have free passage into each other. **2.** *trans.* To communicate, impart, or transmit to and from each other 1603.

1. The branchial chambers i. both above and below.

Intercommunication (-kǒmiūnikēⁱ·ʃən). 1586. [ad. Anglo-Lat. *intercommunicatio*.] **1.** Intercourse. **2.** Interchange of speech; mutual conference 1603. **3.** Passage to and fro by channels or lines of communication 1866.

Intercommunion (-kǒmiū·niən, -yen). 1761. [INTER- I. 2 a.] **1.** Communion with one another; intimate intercourse. **2.** The mutual action or relation between things in regard to functions 1817.

2. When all these studies reach the point of i. and connection with one another JOWETT.

Intercommunity (-kǒmiū·nĭti). 1587. [INTER- I. 2 a.] The quality of being common to various parties; the condition of having things in common.

Intercomparison, etc.: see INTER- *pref.*

Intercondylar (-kǫ·ndilăɹ), *a.* 1884. [f. INTER- II. 2 a + L. *condylus*, a. Gr. κόνδυλος knuckle.] Situated between condyles or rounded bone-ends. So **Interco·ndyloid** 1836.

Interconnect (-kǒne·kt), *v.* 1865. [INTER- I. 1 b.] *trans.* To connect each with the other. Chiefly in *pa. pple.*

Interconnexion, -connection (-kǒne·kʃən). 1822. [INTER- I. 2 a.] Mutual connexion.

Intercontine·ntal, *a.* 1855. [INTER- II. 2 c.] Situated or subsisting between, or connecting, different continents; including persons of different continents; as *i. railways*.

Interconvertible (-kǒnvə̄·ɹtĭb'l), *a.* 1802. [INTER- I. 2 a.] Mutually convertible; interchangeable; as, *i. expressions*. Hence **Interconvertibi·lity**. **Interconve·rtibly** *adv.*

Intercostal (-kǫ·stăl). 1597. [ad. mod.L. *intercostalis*, f. INTER- II. 2 a + L. *costa* rib; see COSTAL.] **A.** *adj.* Situated between the ribs of the body; also *transf.*

transf. A keelson with i. plates SIR E. REED.

B. *sb. pl.* Intercostal parts 1681.

Two sets of muscles, called intercostals HUXLEY.

Intercourse (i·ntəɹkoᵊɹs). Also †**enter-**. 1467. [a. OF. *entrecours* exchange, commerce, f. *entrecorre* :—L. *intercurrere*.] **1.** Communication to and fro between countries, etc.; mutual dealings between the inhabitants of different localities. In early use only with reference to trade. **2.** Social communication between individuals; dealings; discourse 1547. **b.** With *of* (= in respect of) 1613. **c.** Sexual connexion 1798. **3.** Communion between man and that which is spiritual or unseen 1561. †**4.** Intercommunication between things or parts –1787. †**5.** Passage in; entrance –1658. **6.** Continuous interchange *of* (letters, etc.). Now *rare*. 1576. †**7.** Alternation –1655. †**8.** Intervention; an intervening course or space; an interval –1646.

1. They had free entercourse of trade one with another BINGHAM. **2.** Those with whom time and i. have made us familiar JOHNSON. **3.** A devout i. with God PUSEY. **6.** This sweet i. Of looks and smiles MILT.

Intercross (i·ntəɹkrǫs), *sb.* 1859. [INTER- I. 2 a.] An instance of cross-breeding or cross-fertilization.

Intercross (intəɹkrǫ·s), *v.* 1711. [INTER- I. 1 b.] **1.** *trans.* **a.** To cross each other (also *intr.* for *refl.*). **b.** To lay or place across each other. **2.** *intr.* Of plants or animals of different stocks or species: To breed or propagate with each other. Also *trans.* in *pass.* 1859.

2. The almost universal sterility of species when intercrossed DARWIN.

Intercrural (intəɹkrūᵊ·răl), *a.* 1693. [INTER- II. 2 a.] *Anat.* Situated between the crura, legs, or limbs, of the body, or of some part of it; see CRUS 2.

†**Intercu·r**, *v.* 1527. [ad. L. *intercurrere.*] 1. *intr.* To run, come, or pass *between* persons or things –1625. 2. To intervene, come in the way –1677.

Intercurrence (intəɹkʋ·rĕns). 1603. [f. next; see -ENCE.] Intervention; an intervening occurrence.

Intercurrent (intəɹkʋ·rĕnt), *a.* (*sb.*) 1611. [ad. L. *intercurrentem.*] That runs or comes between. 1. †Lying or situated between –1685; intervening 1611. 2. *spec.* in *Med.* a. Of a disease: Occurring during the progress of another disease. Also, Recurring at intervals. Formerly (of a fever), Happening at any period of the year. 1684. b. Of the pulse: Having an extra beat 1707. †3. *sb.* An incident. HOLLAND. Hence **Intercu·rrently** *adv.*

†**Intercuta·neous**, *a.* 1651. [f. late L. *intercutaneus* + -OUS. Cf. F. *intercutané.*] Subcutaneous. Also, lying between the bark and stem of a tree –1664.

†**I·nterdeal**, *sb.* 1591. [f. INTER- I. 2 a + DEAL *sb.*[2]] Mutual dealing, negotiation; intercourse; ado –1612.

Interdea·l, *v.* 1601. [f. INTER- I. 1 b + DEAL *v.*] *intr.* To deal or negotiate mutually.

I:nterdenomina·tional, *a.* 1877. [INTER- II. 2 c.] Common to several religious denominations.

Interdental (intəɹde·ntăl), *a.* 1874. [INTER- II. 2 a.] 1. Situated or placed between the teeth (of a person or animal, or of a toothed wheel). 2. *Phonology.* Pronounced by placing the tip of the tongue between the teeth 1877.

2. French (t) and (d) are dental, often also i. SWEET.

Interdepend (i:ntəɹdǐpe·nd), *v.* 1848. [INTER- I. 1 b.] *intr.* To depend upon each other mutually.

Interdependence (i:ntəɹdǐpe·ndĕns). Also -ance. 1822. [INTER- I. 2 a.] Mutual dependence. So **Interdepe·ndency** 1838.

Interdependent (i:ntəɹdǐpe·ndĕnt), *a.* 1817. [INTER- I. 2 a.] Dependent each upon the other. Hence **Interdepe·ndently** *adv.* in mutual dependence.

Interdict (i·ntəɹdikt), *sb.* [ME. *entredit*, a. OF. *entredit*, mod. *interdit*, ad. L. *interdictum*, pa. pple. neut. of *interdicere* to INTERDICT.] 1. *gen.* An authoritative prohibition; an act of forbidding peremptorily 1626. 2. *Law.* a. *Rom. Law.* A provisional decree of the prætor, in a dispute of private persons relating to possession, commanding or (more usually) forbidding something to be done 1611. b. *Sc. Law.* An order of the Court of Session, or of an inferior court, corresponding to an INJUNCTION in English Law 1810. 3. *R.C.Ch.* An authoritative sentence debarring a particular place or person (esp. the former) from ecclesiastical functions and privileges ME.

1. These are not Fruits forbidden, no i. Defends the touching of these viands pure MILT. *P. R.* II. 369.

Interdict (intəɹdi·kt), *v.* [ME. *entredite-n*, f. *entredit* INTERDICT *sb.*; subseq. refash. after L. *interdict-* ppl. stem.] 1. *trans.* To declare authoritatively against the doing of (an action) or the use of (a thing); to forbid, prohibit; to debar by or as by a command 1502. 2. To restrain (a person) by authority from the doing or use of something; to forbid to do something 1575. 3. *Eccl.* To lay under an interdict (see INTERDICT *sb.* 3) ME.

1. Firm wisdom interdicts the soft'ning tear POPE. 2. Who..will..i. thee his tabernacle ABP. SANDYS.

Interdiction (intəɹdi·kʃən). 1494. [ad. L. *interdictionem.*] The action of interdicting, or fact of being interdicted. 1. Authoritative or peremptory prohibition 1579. 2. *Eccl.* The issuing of an interdict; the action of laying, or condition of being laid, under an interdict 1494. 3. a. *Sc. Law.* A restraint imposed upon a person incapable of managing his own affairs on account of unsoundness of mind, etc. b. *Law.* = INTERDICT *sb.* 2 a, b. 1575.

1. This I. of sepulchral Rites WARBURTON.

Interdi·ctive, *a. rare.* 1609. [f. L. *interdict-* ppl. stem + -IVE.] = INTERDICTORY.

Interdictor (intəɹdi·ktəɹ, -ǫı). 1681. [a. late L. *interdictor*, f. *interdicere* to interdict.] One who interdicts; esp. in *Sc. Law* (see INTERDICTION 3 a).

Interdictory (intəɹdi·ktəri), *a.* 1755. [ad. late L. *interdictorius*; see -ORY.] Having the quality or effect of interdicting; prohibitory.

Interdiffuse (intəɹdifiū·z), *v.* 1882. [INTER- I. 1 a.] *trans.* To diffuse between or among other things. So **Interdiffu·sion**, mutual diffusion 1864. **Interdiffu·sive** *a.* tending to mutual diffusion 1859.

Interdigital (intəɹdi·dʒităl), *a.* 1836. [ad. L. *interdigitalis.*] Situated between, or connecting, digits (fingers or toes).

Interdigitate (intəɹdi·dʒiteit), *v.* 1847. [f. INTER- I. 1 b + L. *digitus* + -ATE[3].] 1. *intr.* To interlock like the fingers of the two hands when clasped; to inosculate by reciprocal serrations. 2. *trans.* To cause to interlock or inosculate in this way (*rare*) 1864. Hence **I:nterdigita·tion**, the action or condition of interdigitating; *concr.* an interdigitating structure or process.

†**Intere·mption.** *rare.* 1656. [ad. late L. *interemptionem*, f. *interimere* to destroy.] Destruction, slaughter –1664.

†**Interess**, *sb.* [ME. and AF. *interesse*, a. med.L. *interesse* compensation for loss, sb. use of L. *interesse* to be between, etc. Cf. Pr., It., Ger. *interesse.*] = INTEREST *sb.* –1716.

†**Intere·ss**, *v.* *Pa. pple.* **interessed, -est.** 1570. [f. prec. sb.; cf. F. *intéresser* to invest with a share, etc.] 1. *trans.* = INTEREST *v.* 1. Chiefly in *pass.*, *to be interessed*, to have a right or share. –1674. 2. = INTEREST *v.* 2. Chiefly in *pass.* –1663. 3. To affect injuriously; to endamage –1641. 4. = INTEREST *v.* 4. –1711. 5. To affect with a feeling of concern; *refl.* To concern oneself. –1697. Hence **Interessee·** (*rare*), an interested party.

‖**Intere·sse termini.** 1658. [med.L., = interest of term or end.] *Law.* A right of entry on a leasehold estate, acquired through a demise.

†**Intere·ssor.** [a. med.L., f. *interesse* to be among.] A partner. PETTY.

Interest (i·ntĕrĕst), *sb.* 1450. [An alteration of INTERESS, app. after OF. *interest*, mod. *intérêt*, app. a sb. use of L. *interest* it makes a difference, etc.]

I. 1. The relation of being objectively concerned in something, by having a right or title to, a claim upon, or a share in. a. Legal concern *in* a thing; esp. right or title to property, etc. Also *fig.* b. Right or title to spiritual privileges 1607. c. Share, part 1586. d. *esp.* A pecuniary share or stake in, or claim upon anything 1674. 2. The relation of being concerned or affected in respect of advantage or detriment; esp. an advantageous relation of this kind 1533. b. Good, benefit, profit, advantage 1579. 3. A thing in which one has an interest or concern 1618. 4. A business, cause, or principle, in which a number of persons are interested; the party interested; a party having a common interest 1674. 5. = SELF-INTEREST 1622. 6. Influence due to personal connexion; personal influence *with* (†*in*) a person or body of persons 1600. 7. The feeling of one who is concerned or has a personal concern in any thing; hence, the state of feeling proper to such a relation; a feeling of concern for or curiosity about a person or thing 1771. b. *transf.* Power of exciting this feeling, interesting character or quality 1821. 8. The fact or quality of mattering; concernment, importance 1809.

1. a. All your I. in those Territories Is vtterly bereft you SHAKS. c. Ah so much i. haue [I] in thy sorrow, As I had Title in thy Noble Husband SHAKS. d. Those fractional and volatile interests in trading adventures which go by the name of 'shares' KINGLAKE. 2. To have an i. in the welfare of a country BURKE. b. One who has our i. at heart BURKE. *In the interest(s) of*: on the side of what is beneficial or advantageous to. SHAKS. *Lear* V. iii. 85. *Mod.* He represented Ipswich in the Liberal i. 4. The notion of creating a new, that is, a moneyed i., in opposition to the landed i. BOLINGBROKE. 6. To raise the people in the counties..where his i. lay HUME. 7. A man with wide interests 1898. b. Questions of great i. JOWETT. 8. Matters of subordinate i. 1845.

II. Senses related to med.L. *interesse*, as used in the phrase *damna et interesse*, Fr. *dommages et intérêts*, the indemnity due to any one for the damage done to him. Cf. OF. *interest* in sense 'damage', also 'damages'. †1. Injury, detriment. b. Compensation for injury, damages (*rare*). –1607. 2. Money paid for the use of money lent (the *principal*), or for forbearance of a debt, according to a fixed ratio (*rate per cent.*) 1545. b. *fig.* esp. in phr. *with interest*, with increase or augmentation 1589.

2. *Simple i.*, the i. paid on the principal as lent. *Compound* (†*compounded*) *i.* (*i. upon i.*), the i. eventually paid on a principal periodically increased by the addition of interest remaining unpaid. b. The latter..returned the blows with i. W. IRVING.

Interest (i·ntĕrĕst), *v.* 1608. [Altered f. INTERESS *v.*, after INTEREST *sb.*] 1. *trans.* To invest with a share in or title to something, esp. a spiritual privilege. Const. *in.* 1610. 2. To cause to have an objective interest or concern in the progress or fate of a matter; to involve; chiefly in *pass.* 1608. 3. Of a thing: To concern; to affect; to relate to. *rare* or *Obsol.* 1638. 4. To cause to take a personal interest, share, or part in; to engage *in*. *refl.* To take active part *in*. 1630. 5. To affect with a feeling of concern; to excite the curiosity or attention of 1780.

1. By faith we become interested in the propitiation 1864. 3. Their private opinions..doe not i. our beliefs 1638. 4. They seek to i. in their design the City of London 1647. I am not called upon to i. myself in his behalf (*mod.*). 5. Your account of the first night interested me immensely DICKENS.

Interested (i·ntĕrĕstĕd), *ppl. a.* 1665. [f. prec. + -ED[1].] 1. Concerned, affected; having an interest or share in something 1828. 2. Self-seeking, self-interested. (The opposite of *disinterested.*) 1705. 3. Characterized by a feeling of concern, sympathy, or curiosity 1665.

1. An i. witness 1828. 2. The wretched consequences of i. marriages THACKERAY. 3. An i. auditor (*mod.*). Hence **I·nterested-ly** *adv.*, -**ness.**

Interesting (i·ntĕrĕstiŋ), *ppl. a.* 1711. [f. INTEREST *v.* + -ING[2]. Formerly (and still dial.) *intere·sting.*] †1. That concerns, touches, or affects; important –1813. 2. Adapted to excite interest; of interest 1768.

1. In defence of what they thought most dear and i. to themselves 1769. 2. An i. conversation 1843. All knowledge is i. to a wise man M. ARNOLD. *In an i. condition* (*situation*): pregnant 1748. Hence **I·nteresting-ly** *adv.*, -**ness.**

Interfacial (intəɹfēi·ʃăl), *a.* 1837. [f. INTER- II. 2 a + L. *facies*; cf. FACIAL.] Included between two faces of a crystal or other solid; as in *i. angle.*

Interfascicular (-făsi·kiŭlăı), *a.* 1836. [INTER- II. 2 a.] *Anat.* and *Bot.* Situated between fascicles or bundles of tissue.

Interfemoral (-fe·mŏrăl), *a.* 1828. [INTER- II. 2 a.] *Anat.* Extending between the femora or thighs; as, *the i. web of a bat.*

Interfenestration (i:ntəɹfenĕstrēi·ʃən). 1823. [INTER- I. 2 a.] *Archit.* The spacing of the windows of a building.

†**Interfe·re**, *v.*[1] late ME. [a. obs. F. **entre-*, *interferer* to introduce, app. f. L. *inter* + *ferre* to carry.] *trans.* To interpose, intersperse; *intr.* to be intermingled *with.*

Interfere (intəɹfiə·ɹ), *v.*[2] 1530. [a. OF. *s'entreférir* to strike each other, f. *entre-* INTER- I. 1 b + *férir* :—L. *ferire.*] 1. *intr.* Of a horse: To strike the inside of the fetlock with the shoe or hoof of the opposite foot; to knock one leg against another. Said also of the feet. (Rarely of persons.) 2. *intr.* Hence, of things generally: To strike against each other; to come into collision; to clash; to get in each other's way. Now chiefly in *Physics*, of waves of light, heat, sound, etc.: To exercise reciprocal action, so as to increase, diminish, or nullify the natural effect of each. †Also *fig.* 1613. †3. *intr.* To run into each other; to intercross, intersect –1725. 4. a. Of things, actions, etc.: To come into collision or opposition, so as to affect the course of 1662. b. Of persons: To meddle *with*; to interpose in something, esp. without having the right to do so 1632. 5. To interpose, so as to affect some action; to intervene. Const. *in.* 1743.

1. She [a mare] enterfears a little behind 1684. 2. *fig.* When public duty and private feeling i...then justice calls for punishment 1836. 4. a. No scruples of conscience to i. with his morality *Junius Lett.*

6. *U.S. Football.* To interpose between the player with the ball and a would-be tackler so as to help the

former 1920. Hence **Interfe·rer. Interfe·ringly** *adv.*

Interference (intəɹfīə·rĕns). 1783. [irreg. f. prec. + -ENCE, after derivs. of L. *ferre*, e.g. *difference*.] **1.** The action or fact of interfering or intermeddling. **2.** *Physics.* The mutual action of two waves or systems of waves, in reinforcing or neutralizing each other, when their paths meet or cross 1830.

Orig. introduced to designate phenomena observed in the mutual action of two rays of light, before the establishment of the undulatory theory; subseq. extended to sound-waves, the undulations on the surface of water, etc. **b.** *Wireless.* The intrusion of electrical disturbances which interfere with reception 1902.

3. The action of interfering (of a horse). (Dicts.) **4.** *U.S.* The conflict of claims arising when two applications are made for a similar patent 1888. **5.** *U.S. Football*: see prec. 6.

1. Active i. in the struggles of the Continent 1874.

Comb.: **i. figure,** the figure produced when a section of crystal, appropriately cut, is viewed in converging polarized light; **i. fringe,** one of a series of alternate light and dark bands produced by a diffraction-grating. Hence **Interfere·ntial** *a.* of, pertaining to, or operating by, wave-interference.

Interferometer (i:ntəɹfīərǫ·mǐtəɹ). 1899. [f. INTERFERE + -(O)METER.] An instrument for measuring lengths by means of the interference phenomena of two rays of light.

Interflow (intəɹflōu·), *v.* 1610. [f. INTER- I. 1 + FLOW *v.*] **1.** *intr.* To flow between (*rare*). **2.** *intr.* To flow into each other; to intermingle 1844. So **I·nterflow** *sb.* 1610.

Interfluent (intɔ̄·ɹfluˌĕnt), *a.* 1651. [ad. L. *interfluentem*, *interfluere*.] **1.** Flowing between. Now *rare*. **2.** Intermingling; in which there is an interflow 1872. So **Inte·rfluence** 1817. **Inte·rfluous** *a.* 1656.

Interfold (intəɹfōu·ld), *v.* 1579. [f. INTER- I. 1 b + FOLD *v.*] *trans.* (and *refl.*) To fold together or within each other; to involve in common folds.

Interfoliaceous (-fōuliēi·ʃəs), *a.* 1760. [INTER- II. 2 a.] *Bot.* Situated alternately between a pair of opposite leaves.

Interfo·liate, *v.* 1696. [f. INTER- I. 1 a + L. *folium* + -ATE[3].] *trans.* To interleave.

Interfre·tted, *ppl. a.* 1828. [INTER- I. 1 b.] *Her.* Interlaced.

Interfulgent (-fɒ·ldʒĕnt), *a. rare.* 1721. [ad. L. *interfulgentem* (Livy).] Shining among or between.

Interfuse (intəɹfiū·z), *v.* 1593. [f. L. *interfus-*, *interfundere*, f. *inter* + *fundere* to pour.] **1.** *trans.* To permeate or intersperse. **2.** To pour in, infuse 1667. **3.** To fuse or blend (*trans.* and *intr.*) 1851. **4.** *trans.* Of one thing: To penetrate or permeate and blend with 1876.

1. Abundantly interfused with Greek and Latin quotations HAWTHORNE. **2.** The ambient Aire wide interfus'd Imbracing round this florid Earth MILT. *P. L.* VII. 89. **4.** The genius which interfused the plays 1876.

Interfusion (-fiū·ʒən). 1817. [f. prec.] The action of interfusing or fact of being interfused.

Interganglio·nic, *a.* 1835. [INTER- II. 2 a.] *Anat.* Situated between or connecting ganglia, as the nerves of the sympathetic system.

†Inte·rgatory. Syncopated f. INTERROGATORY. *Merch. V.* V. i. 298.

Interglacial (-glēi·ʃiăl), *a.* 1867. [INTER- II. 2 b.] *Geol.* Lying between glacial periods; formed or occurring between two such periods.

Intergla·ndular, *a.* 1873. [INTER- II. 2 a.] *Anat.* Lying between glands.

Interglobular (-glǫ·biŭlăɹ), *a.* 1859. [INTER- II. 2 a.] *Anat.* Lying between globules (of dentine).

I·ntergrowth. 1844. [INTER- I. 2 a.] The growing (of things) into each other.

Interhæ·mal. 1846. [INTER- II. 2 a.] *Anat.* **A.** *adj.* Situated between hæmal spines. **B.** *sb.* An interhæmal bone or spine 1880.

Interhyal (-həi·ăl). 1884. [f. INTER- II. 2 a + HY(OID) + -AL.] *Anat.* **A.** *adj.* Situated between two parts of the hyoid arch of a fish. **B.** *sb.* An intermediate bone or cartilage in the hyoid arch 1888.

Interim (i·ntərim). 1548. [L. *interim* adv., f. *inter* + advb. ending *-im*.]

‖**A.** *adv.* In the meantime, meanwhile 1580.

I., take courage, and make your calculations anew 1804.

B. *sb.* **1.** An intervening time; the meantime; now usu. in phr. *in the i.* = A. 1563. **†2.** Something done in the interim; an interlude –1633. **3.** A provisional arrangement, adopted in the meanwhile 1558. **b.** *Ch. Hist.* (with capital *I.*) Each of three provisional arrangements for the adjustment of religious differences between the German Protestants and the Roman Catholic Church, promulgated, one in 1541 and two in 1548, pending a settlement by a General Council 1548.

1. Betweene the acting of a dreadfull thing, And the first motion, all the I. is Like a Phantasma, or a hideous Dreame *Jul. C.* II. i. 64. **2.** *L. L. L.* I. i. 172.

C. *adj.* Done, made, occurring, etc. in or for the meantime; provisional. Formerly also of time: Intervening. 1604.

I. orders for payment of alimony 1858. **I. dividend** 1882.

Hence **I·nterimist,** one who accepted or advocated one of the Interims (B. 3 b) 1560. **I:nterimi·stic** (†-ical 1643) *a.* = INTERIM C.; also, belonging to the Interimists; pertaining to or in accordance with the Interim 1859.

Interior (intīə·riəɹ). 1490. [a. L. *interior*, compar. adj. from *inter* (superl. *intimus*).]

A. *adj.* **1.** Situated more within, or (simply) within something; internal. **b.** Inland; belonging to the interior 1777. **2.** Existing within limits figured as spatial: **a.** Internal, domestic; as opp. to *foreign* 1768; **b.** Inner, as distinct from what appears on the surface or is publicly declared 1775. **3.** Mental or spiritual; 'inward' 1513. **b.** Devoted to spiritual things; pious, devout 1756.

1. *I. angle* (Geom.): any one of the angles included between the sides of a rectilineal figure within the figure; also, an angle included between a straight line falling upon two other straight lines and either of the latter on the side towards the other. *I. planets*: Mercury and Venus, whose orbits are within that of the earth (more usu. called INFERIOR). *I. screw*, one cut on an i. or hollow surface, as of a nut, burr, or tap-hole. **b.** In the interiour parts of the empire SIR W. JONES. **2. a.** The i. trade, or that from place to place within the country JAS. MILL. **b.** There was to be no i. cabinet MACAULAY. **3. b.** Difference.. between the i. and the worldly man W. G. WARD.

B. *sb.* **1.** The interior part of anything; the inside 1828. **b.** The inland parts of a country, island, or continent; an inland region 1796. **c.** The inside of a building or room; also, a picture of this. (Usu. with *an* or in *pl.*) 1864. **2.** Inner nature or being; inward mind; soul, character 1596. **3.** The internal or home affairs of a country or state; the department concerned with these; in the titles *Secretary*, *Department of the I.* (U.S. and Canada), and *Minister of the I.*, used in reference to France, Germany, Italy, etc. 1838.

1. In the i. of the earth HUXLEY. **c.** A photographer noted for his interiors (*mod.*). **2.** *Merch. V.* II. ix. 28. Hence **Inte·riorly** *adv.* internally; inwardly.

Interiority (intīəriˌǫ·rĭti). *rare.* 1701. [ad. med.L. *interioritas*; see -ITY.] The quality or state of being interior; inner character or nature; an inner element.

Interja·cence. *rare.* 1864. [f. INTERJACENT; see -ENCE.] The fact of lying between.

Interjacency (intəɹdʒēi·sĕnsi). 1646. [f. as prec. + -ENCY.] The quality or state of lying between; also, something lying between.

The I. of two Provinces between your Seat of Government and the Places to which you would now extend your Jurisdiction 1773.

Interjacent (intəɹdʒēi·sĕnt), *a.* 1594. [ad. L. *interjacentem*, *interjacere*.] Lying or existing between; intervening; as, *i. nations*.

Interja·culate, *v.* [f. INTER- I. 1 a + *jaculat-*, *jaculari* to throw.] To interject (an ejaculation). THACKERAY. Hence **Interja·culatory** *a.* expressed in parenthetical ejaculations 1827.

Interject (intəɹdʒe·kt), *v.* 1578. [f. L. *interject-*, *interjicere* (*-jacere*), f. *inter* + *jacere* to throw.] **1.** *trans.* To throw in between; to introduce abruptly; to insert, interpose. **b.** To remark parenthetically or as an interruption 1791. **†2.** *intr.* for *refl.* **a.** To cross one another, as two lines. **b.** To come between; to intervene, interpose –1676.

Interjection (intəɹdʒe·kʃən). ME. [a. F., ad. L. *interjectionem*; see prec.] **1.** The utterance of ejaculations expressive of emotion; an exclamation. **2.** *Gram.* A natural ejaculation expressing emotion, viewed as a Part of Speech 1530. **3.** The action of interjecting or interposing anything; also, that which is interjected 1598. **†4.** *Rhet.* = PARENTHESIS 1678.

1. The I. of Laughing BACON. **2.** How now! interiections? why then, some be of laughing, as ha, ha, he SHAKS. The i. may be defined as a form of speech which is articulate and symbolic but not grammatical EARLE. Hence **Interje·ctionary, Interje·ctory** *adjs.* characterized by i.

Interjectional (intəɹdʒe·kʃənăl), *a.* 1761. [f. prec. + -AL.] **1.** Of the nature of something thrown in between or among other remarks 1788. **2.** Of, belonging to, or of the nature of an interjection in language.

2. A number of i. sounds uttered with a strange variety of intonation SCOTT. Hence **Interje·ctionally** *adv.*

Interje·ctionalize, *v.* [-IZE.] *trans.* To make into an interjection. EARLE.

Interje·ctural, *a.* [f. L. *interjectura* an insertion + -AL.] Of the nature of what is interjected; interjectional.

†Interjoi·n, *v.* [INTER- I. 1 b.] *trans.* To join reciprocally. *Cor.* IV. iv. 22.

Interju·nction. *rare.* 1836. [f. L. *interjungere*.] A mutual joining.

Interknit (intəɹni·t), *v.* 1805. [INTER- I. 1 b.] **1.** *trans.* To knit each into the other; to intertwine. **2.** *intr.* To intertwine. KEATS.

†Interknow·, *v.* Also **en-.** 1603. [INTER- I. 1 b.] To know mutually –1652. Hence **†Interknow·ledge,** mutual or reciprocal knowledge.

Interlace (intəɹlēi·s), *v.* [ME. *entrelace*, a. F. *entrelacer*, f. *entre-* (ENTER-, INTER- I. 1) + *lacer* to LACE.] **1.** *trans.* To unite two (or more) things by intercrossing laces, strings, etc.; hence, to connect intricately; to entangle, involve. (*rare* in physical sense.) **2.** To intercross two series of threads, etc. with constant alternation 1523. **b.** *fig.* To alternate, to interweave 1576. **†3.** To interweave; to introduce as by interweaving; to insert, interpolate. Chiefly *fig.* or *transf.* –1677. **4.** To intersperse, vary, mingle, or mix *with*. Chiefly *transf.* and *fig.* 1531. **5.** *intr.* for *refl.* To cross each other intricately, as if woven together; to lie like the fingers of two interlaced hands 1596.

1. Ice..is built up of crystalline particles interlaced together HUXLEY. **2.** Trees..Now i. your trembling tops above DRUMM. OF HAWTH. *fig.* Interlacing of talke and communication 1576. **3.** SHAKS. *Lucr.* 1390. **5.** Through boughs that i. 1855. Hence **Interla·ced** *ppl. a.*; *spec.* in *Her.* applied to annulets, rings, etc. that are linked together as are the links of a chain.

Interlacement (intəɹlēi·smĕnt). 1603. [f. prec. + -MENT.] **1.** The action of interlacing or condition of being interlaced; *concr.* an interlaced arrangement or structure. **2.** Intricate intermingling 1872.

Interlamellar (intəɹlæ·mĕlăɹ), *a.* 1846. [INTER- II. 2 a.] *Zool.* Situated between or among lamellæ (*e.g.* of the gills).

Interlaminar (intəɹlæ·minăɹ), *a.* 1831. [INTER- II. 2 a.] *Anat.* Situated between laminæ or plates.

Interlaminate (intəɹlæ·minēit), *v.* 1816. [INTER- I. 1 a.] *trans.* To insert in or between alternate laminæ or plates. Hence **Interlamina·tion,** the action of interlaminating; an interlaminated formation 1833.

I·nterlapse. 1658. [INTER- I. 2 a.] The lapse of time between any two events.

Interlard (intəɹlā·ɹd), *v.* 1533. [a. F. *entrelarder*, f. *entre-* (INTER- I. 1 a) + *larder* to LARD.] **†1.** *trans.* To mix with alternate layers of fat; in *Cookery*, to insert strips of fat, bacon, etc. into (lean meat) before cooking; to lard –1741. †Also *transf.* **2.** *fig.* To mix, mingle, or intersperse *with* 1563. **†3.** To interpose, interpolate –1755.

1. *transf.* Grey Marble, interlarded with white Alabaster 1632. **2.** To i. talk with oaths 1694, English composition with foreign words 1872. **3.** Speeches in which he often interlarded the words O tempora, O mores 1755.

Interlay (intəɹlēⁱ·), *v.* Pa. t. and pple. -laid. 1609. [f. INTER- I. 1 a + LAY *v.*] *trans.* To lay or place between or among. Also *fig.*

Interleaf (i·ntəɹlīf). Pl. **-leaves.** 1741. [INTER- I. 2 b.] A leaf inserted between the ordinary leaves of a book, usu. blank; also *transf.*

Interleague (intəɹlī·g), *v.* Now *rare.* 1590. [f. INTER- I. 1 b + LEAGUE *v.*; or ? f. phr. *to enter league.*] *intr.* and *refl.* To enter into a league *with* another, or with each other.

Interleave (intəɹlī·v), *v.* 1668. [f. INTER- I. 1 a + LEAF *sb.* (pl. *leaves*).] *trans.* To insert leaves, usu. blank, between the ordinary leaves of (a book). Also *transf.* and *fig.*

fig. To i. days of hardship with days of ease DE QUINCEY.

†**Interli·bel,** *v. rare.* 1626. [f. INTER- I. 1 b + LIBEL *v.*] *trans.* To libel (one another).

Interline (intəɹləi·n), *v.*[1] [ME. ad. med.L. *interlineare*, f. *inter* + *linea* LINE *sb.*[2] Cf. F. *interligner* vb.] **1.** *trans.* To insert additional words between the lines of (a document). Chiefly *pass.*, const. *with.* Also *fig.* **2.** To insert (a word or words) between the lines in a written document 1589. **3.** *absol.* or *intr.* **a.** To make interlinear insertions 1576. †**b.** *fig.* To come between the lines –1655. †**4.** *trans.* To write or print in alternate lines. LOCKE. †**5.** To mark with lines, esp. of various colours –1661. †**6.** To place or insert something in lines between or among something else. Const. *with.* –1736.

1. The coopie..was interlined and sumwhear blotted 1563. **2.** Words accidentally omitted were also placed in the margin, or interlined 1882. **3. b.** As in night's gloomy page One silent star may i. H. VAUGHAN. **6.** I saw the foot..interlined among the horse DE FOE.

Interline (intəɹləi·n), *v.*[2] 1480. [f. INTER- I. 1 a + LINE *v.*[1]] *trans.* To insert a second or inner lining between the stuff and ordinary lining (of a garment).

Interlineal (-li·nĭăl), *a.* 1526. [INTER- II. 2 a.] †**1.** = INTERLINEAR **1.** –1826. **2.** Disposed in alternate lines. RUSKIN.

Interlinear (-li·nĭăɹ), *a.* 1440. [ad. med. L. *interlinearis*, f. *inter* + *linea* LINE. Cf. F. *interlinéaire.*] **1.** Written or printed between the lines. **2.** Of a book: Having the same text in different languages printed in alternate lines. ? *Obs.* 1624.

1. *I. Gloss*, Anselm's gloss on the Vulgate, placed in MSS. between the lines of the Latin text. *I. system*: see HAMILTONIAN *a.* **2.** The I. Bible BEDELL. Hence **Interli·nearly** *adv.*

Interlineary (intəɹli·nĭări). 1605. [See prec. and -ARY[2]. Cf. late ME. *entirlynarie.*]

A. *adj.* = INTERLINEAR.

B. *sb.* **1.** An interlinear version. Also *fig.* 1644. **2.** *ellipt.* for (a.) the Latin Interlinear version of the Bible by Arias Montanus (1568–72); (b.) the Interlinear Gloss on the Vulgate. 1659.

Hence **Interli·nearily** *adv.* between, or as between, the lines.

Interlineate (-li·nĭ,eⁱt), *v. rare.* 1693. [f. ppl. stem of med.L. *interlineare.* In mod. use, perh. f. next.] *trans.* and *absol.* = INTERLINE *v.*[1] Also *fig.*

Interlineation (-linĭ,ēⁱ·ʃən). 1602. [f. prec.; see -ATION.] The insertion of a word or words between the lines of a writing; that which is so inserted.

Interli·ning, *vbl. sb.* 1467. [f. INTERLINE *v.*[1] + -ING[1].] = INTERLINEATION.

Interlink (i·ntəɹliŋk), *sb.* 1634. [INTER- I. 2 b.] An intermediate or connecting link.

Interlink (intəɹli·ŋk), *v.* 1587. [INTER- I. 1 b.] *trans.* To link (two or more things) to one another, or (one thing) *with* something else. Often *fig.*

These are two Chains which are interlink'd DRYDEN.

Interlobate (-lōu·bēⁱt), *a.* 1881. [INTER- II. 2 a.] Situated between loops or lobes, esp. in *Geol.* between the terminal lobes of a glacier-moraine.

Interlobular (-lǫ·biŭlăɹ), *a.* 1834. [INTER- II. 2 a. Cf. F. *interlobulaire* (Littré).] *Anat.* and *Path.* Situated or occurring between the lobes of any organ.

Interlocation (-ləkēⁱ·ʃən). *rare.* 1611. [INTER- I. 2 a.] A placing between, interposition; also, something placed between.

Interlock (intəɹlǫ·k), *v.* 1632. [INTER- I. 1 b.] **1.** *intr.* To engage with each other by partial overlapping or interpenetration of alternate projections and recesses. Also *fig.*, of immaterial things. **2.** *trans.* To lock or clasp within each other. Chiefly *pass.* 1807.

1. I felt my fingers work and my hands i. C. BRONTË. **2.** Fibres..inextricably interlocked 1879.

Interlocution (-ləkiū·ʃən). 1534. [ad. L. *interlocutionem*, f. *interloqui*, f. *inter* + *loqui.*] **1.** The action (on the part of two or more persons) of talking or replying to each other. **a.** Talk, discourse, dialogue. †**b.** An alternate reading or speaking, as in making responses, etc. –1643. †**2.** The action of replying; a reply, response –1782. †**3.** The action of interrupting speech; an interruption; a parenthetical utterance –1683. †**4.** *Law.* An intermediate decree before final decision –1726.

Interlocutor[1] (-lǫ·kiŭtəɹ). 1514. [f. L. *interloqui*; see INTERLOCUTION, and cf. F. *interlocuteur.*] One who takes part in a dialogue, conversation, or discussion. In *pl.* the persons who carry on a dialogue. **b.** With *poss. pron.* One who takes part in conversation with another 1848.

b. Your true rustic turns his back on his i. GEO. ELIOT.

Interlocutor[2] (-lǫ·kiŭtəɹ). 1533. [a. F. *interlocutoire*, ad. L. *interlocutorium.* Occas. spelt *interloquitur.*] *Sc. Law.* A judgement or order of a court or of the Lords Ordinary, signed by the pronouncing or presiding judge.

Interlocutory (-lǫ·kiŭtəri). 1590. [See INTERLOCUTION and -ORY.]

A. *adj.* **1.** Of the nature of, pertaining to, or occurring in, dialogue or conversation 1597. **2.** Spoken intermediately 1821. **3.** *Law.* Pronounced during the course of an action; not finally decisive; esp. in *i. decree, injunction, judgement, order* 1590.

1. He knowes that interloquutory swearing is a sinne 1626. **2.** I. observations 1864.

B. *sb.* **1.** *Law.* An interlocutory decree. †**2.** A discussion. MOTTEUX.

Interlocutress (-lǫ·kiutrės). 1858. [f. INTERLOCUTOR[1] + -ESS.] A female interlocutor. So **Interlo·cutrice, -trix** 1848.

Interlope (intəɹlōu·p), *v.* 1603. [f. INTER- I. 1 + *lope*, dial. form of LEAP *v.*, as in *land-loper.*] **1.** *intr.* 'To run between parties and intercept the advantage that one should gain from the other; to traffic without a proper licence; to forestall; to anticipate irregularly' (J.); to intrude. †**2.** *trans.* To foist in; to intercalate –1659. †**3.** To intrude upon (*rare*) 1701.

2. Grotius interlopes the following passage HEYLIN.

Interloper (i·ntəɹlōupəɹ, intəɹlōu·pəɹ). 1590. [See prec. Fr. *interlope* is from English.] **1.** **a.** *orig.* An unauthorized trader; one who trespasses on the rights of a trade monopoly; †a ship engaged in unauthorized trading. **b.** *transf.* One who thrusts himself into any position or affair, which others consider as pertaining solely to themselves 1632. †**2.** An intercepter (*of* something). MILT.

1. b. He was a mere i., and we were entitled to use force to keep him out of our premises 1884.

†**Interlu·cate,** *v. rare.* 1623. [f. L. *interlucat-, interlucare*, f. *inter* + *lux, lucem* light.] To lop or thin a tree. (Dicts.) So **Interluca·tion,** the action of thinning a tree or wood 1656.

Interlucent (-l[i]ū·sėnt), *a. rare.* 1727. [ad. L. *interlucentem.*] Shining between.

Interlude (i·ntəɹl[i]ūd), *sb.* ME. [ad. med. (Anglo-) Lat. *interludium* (Du Cange), f. *inter-* (INTER- I. 2) + *ludus.*] **1.** A dramatic or mimic representation, usually light or humorous, such as was commonly introduced between the acts of the long mystery-plays or moralities, etc.; hence, a stage-play, a comedy, a farce. Now (after Collier) applied as a specific name to the earliest form of the modern drama, as represented by the plays of J. Heywood. †Also *transf.* or *fig.* **2.** An interval in the performance of a play; the pause between the acts, or the means employed to fill this up. Also *fig.* 1660. **b.** *Mus.* An instrumental piece played between the verses of a psalm or hymn, or in the intervals of a church-service, etc. 1838. **3.** *transf.* An interval in the course of some action or event; an intervening time or space of a different character 1751.

1. John Heywood's dramatic productions..are neither Miracle-plays nor Moral-plays, but what may be properly and strictly called Interludes: J. P. COLLIER. **2.** Dreams are but interludes which fancy makes; When monarch reason sleeps, this mimic wakes DRYDEN. **3.** We were confined to the inn, except for the i. of the custom-house MME. D'ARBLAY.

Interlude (i·ntəɹl[i]ūd), *v.* 1608. [f. prec.] †**a.** *intr.* To perform a play. **b.** *intr.* To come between, as an interlude. **c.** *trans.* To interrupt, as with an interlude. Hence †**Interluder,** a player in an interlude.

†**Interlu·ency.** [f. L. *interluentem, interluere* to flow between; see -ENCY.] A flowing between. HALE.

Interlunar (intəɹl[i]ū·năɹ), *a.* 1598. [INTER- II. 2 b; cf. F. *interlunaire.*] Pertaining to the period between the old and new moon.

The moon..Hid in her vacant i. cave MILT. So †**Interlu·nary** *a.* 1594.

Interlunation (-l[i]unēⁱ·ʃən). 1813. [See prec. and LUNATION.] The period between the old and the new moon; *fig.* a blank or dark interval. So **Interlune** (*rare*) 1561.

Intermarriage (intəɹmæ·rėdʒ). Also †**en-.** 1579. [INTER- I. 2 a.] **1.** The action or fact of intermarrying; union in or connexion by marriage. **a.** Of two persons, or of one person *with* another. Now only in legal phraseology. **b.** Marriage between members of different families, castes, tribes, nations, or societies 1602. **2.** *loosely.* Marriage between persons (or interbreeding between animals) nearly related 1882.

Intermarry (intəɹmæ·ri), *v.* Also †**en-.** 1574. [INTER- I. 1 b.] **1.** *intr.* To contract matrimony, to marry. **a.** Said of couple; hence of one person (*with* another). Now only in legal phraseology. **b.** Of members of different families, castes, tribes, nations, or societies 1611. **2.** *trans.* To join in marriage; also *fig.* (*rare*) 1863.

1. b. The Hollanders obtaining a garrison there, intermarried with the Native Women 1665.

‖**Intermaxilla** (i:ntəɹmæksi·lă). *Pl.* **-æ.** 1882. [mod.L., f. INTER- II. 1 + MAXILLA.] *Anat.* Each of two bones situated between the maxillary bones of the upper jaw, in man small and soon fusing with these, but in most mammals large, distinct, and situated in front of them (thus usu. called *premaxillæ*).

Intermaxillary (i:ntəɹmæ·ksilări, -mæksi·lări), *a.* (*sb.*) 1826. [INTER- II. 2 a.] *Anat.* and *Zool.* **1. a.** Situated between the maxillæ; as in *i. bone* (= prec.), *i. apodeme.* **b.** Belonging or attached to the intermaxilla; as *i. teeth.* **2.** *sb.* Short for *i. bone*, etc. 1834.

†**Intermea·n.** *rare.* 1599. [f. INTER- I. 2 b + MEAN *sb.*] An intermediate part, act, etc.; an interlude –1834.

Intermeddle (intəɹme·d'l), *v.* [ME. *entremedle*, a. AF. *entremedler* = OF. *entremesler*, F. *entremêler*, f. *entre-*, L. *inter-* + AF. *medler*, OF. *mesler* to MEDDLE.] †**1.** *trans.* To meddle or mix together; to intermix. Const. *with.* –1733. †**2.** *refl.* = next –1594. **3.** *intr.* To concern oneself *with* or *in*; to have to do *with*; to meddle, interfere (esp. in what is none of one's business) 1477.

3. The see of Rome was alway ready to entermedle 1561. To i. in a business BURKE, with a department 1834.

Intermeddler (intəɹme·dləɹ). 1576. [f. prec. + -ER[1].] †**a.** One who concerns himself or has to do with something –1577. **b.** *spec.* One who meddles with what is none of his business; in early use = INTERLOPER 1601.

Intermediacy (intəɹmī·diăsi). *rare.* 1713. [f. INTERMEDIATE *a.*; see -ACY.] The state of being intermediate; intervention.

†**Interme·dial.** 1599. [f. L. *intermedius* + -AL.] **A.** *adj.* **1.** = INTERMEDIATE *a.* –1852. **2.** = INTERMEDIARY *a.* **1.** –1846. **B.** *sb.* = INTERMEDIATE *sb.* –1654.

Intermediary (intəɹmī·diări). 1788. [f. L *intermedium*; cf. F. *intermédiaire.*]

A. *adj.* **1.** Acting or of the nature of action between two parties; mediatory 1818. **2.**

Situated or occurring between two things; intermediate 1788.

1. I. agents 1869. 2. This i. stage of her life 1882.

B. *sb.* 1. One who acts between others; a go-between, mediator 1791. 2. Something acting between persons or things, a medium, means; also *abstr.* Agency (*of* something) 1859. 3. An intermediate form or stage 1865.

Intermediate (intəɹmī·diĕt), *a.* and *sb.* 1567. [ad. med.L. *intermediatus*, f. L. *intermedius.*]

A. *adj.* Coming or occurring between two things, places, times, numbers, members of a series, etc.; 'holding the middle place or degree between two extremes' (J.); interposed, intervening.

I. points 1665, events HARTLEY, steps PALEY, stature 1823, agents MACAULAY. Phr. *I. state* (Theol.): the condition of souls between death and the resurrection or the last judgement 1777.

B. *sb.* Something intermediate or intervening; a middle term; a nexus between two things 1650. 2. A person who intervenes between others 1879.

Intermediate (intəɹmī·diēᵉt), *v.* 1610. [f. INTER- I. 1 + MEDIATE *v.*] †1. *intr.* To intervene. FRENCH. †2. To interfere, interpose -1716. 3. To act between others; to mediate 1624. 4. *trans.* To join by intermediate parts 1880.

Intermediately (intəɹmī·diĕtli), *adv.* 1730. [f. INTERMEDIATE *a.* + -LY [2].] 1. In an intermediate position or relation. 2. By intermediate agency; indirectly; opp. to *immediately* 1755.

Intermediation (intəɹmīdiē·ʃən). 1602. [f. prec. vb., or f. INTER- I. 2 a + MEDIATION.] The action of intermediating; interposition, intervention.

Intermediator (intəɹmī·diēⁱtəɹ). 1522. [f. INTERMEDIATE *v.*, after *mediator.*] One who or that which intermediates; a mediator.

†**Interme·dious**, *a. rare.* 1657. [f. L. *intermedius* + -OUS.] = INTERMEDIATE *a.* -1678.

Intermedium (intəɹmī·diŏm). *Pl.* -ia, -iums. 1589. [a. L. *intermedium* adj. neut., f. *inter* + *medius*; cf. MEDIUM.] 1. Something intermediate in position; an interval of space. ? *Obs.* 1611. 2. Something intermediate in time; †an interlude; an interval of time (? *Obs.*) 1589. 3. An intermediate agent, intermediary, medium; also *abstr.* intermediate agency, mediation (*of*) 1660. 4. *Comp. Anat.* [sc. *os.*] A bone of the carpus, situated between the ulnare and the radiale, or the corresponding bone of the tarsus between the tibiale and fibulare 1878.

†**Interme·ll**, *v. Obs.* (or rare archaism). ME. [a. OF. *entremeller*, var. of *entremesler*, mod.F. *entremêler* to INTERMEDDLE.] = INTERMEDDLE.

Intermembral, etc.: see INTER- *pref.*

Interment (intə̄·ɹmĕnt). ME. [f. INTER *v.* + -MENT.] The action of interring or burying in the earth.

‖**Intermezzo** (intəɹme·dzo). Pl. -i (-ī), -os (oz). 1834. [It. *intermezzo*, pop. form of *intermedio*, ad. L. *intermedium.*] 1. a. A short dramatic, musical, or other performance, of a light and pleasing character, introduced between the acts of a drama or opera. b. A short movement connecting the main divisions of a large musical work, instrumental or vocal. 2. *transf.* An interval; an episode 1851.

2. The purgatorial i. of the Catholic church 1875.

†**Intermi·ddle**, *a.* 1613. [f. INTER- I. 2 c + MIDDLE *a.*] = INTERMEDIATE.

Intermigration (-məigrē·ʃən). 1677. [INTER- I. 2 a.] Interchange of abode or habitat; reciprocal migration.

Interminable (intə̄·ɹminăb'l), *a.* ME. [a. F., or ad. late L. *interminabilis* (Tertull.), f. *in-* (IN- [3]) + *terminare*; see -ABLE.] That cannot be bounded or ended; boundless; endless. (In mod. use freq. implying impatience at the length of something.)

Possession..of lyf Intermynable CHAUCER. An i. controversy D'ISRAELI. Hence **Inte·rminabi·lity**, **Inte·rminableness**. **Inte·rminably** *adv.*

Interminate (intə̄·ɹminĕt), *a.* Now *rare.* 1533. [ad. L. *interminatus*, f. *in-* (IN- [3]) + *terminatus* ended.] 1. That is without end or limit; infinite. †2. quasi-*adv.* Without end, always. ABP. PARKER. So †**Inte·rminated** *a.*

†**Interminate**, *v.* 1631. [f. L. *interminat-*, *interminari*, f. *inter* + *minari* to threaten.] *trans.* To threaten, menace (a thing) -1656.

†**I:ntermina·tion.** 1526. [ad. L. *interminationem*; see INTERMINATE *v.*] Commination; a threat or menace -1684.

Intermi·ne, *v. rare.* 1622. [f. INTER- I. 1 + MINE *v.* or *sb.*] *trans.* To intersect with mines or veins.

Intermingle (intəɹmi·ŋg'l), *v.* 1470. [f. INTER- I. 1 + MINGLE *v.*] 1. *trans.* To mingle (two or more things) together; also, to introduce and mix (an element) *with* or *among* other things. 2. To intersperse *with*; †to variegate 1553. 3. *intr.* To mingle together or *with* something 1626.

1. Fuller has intermingled a great deal of gossip and rubbish with his facts 1842. 3. Shadow and sunshine intermingling quick COWPER.

‖**Interministerium** (-ministī°·riŏm). *rare.* [f. INTER- II. 1 + L. *ministerium*; formed by Walpole, after INTERREGNUM.] The period intervening between two ministries.

The I. still exists; no place is filled up H. WALPOLE.

†**Intermi·se.** 1612. [var. of ENTERMISE.] Intervention, mediation, agency -1715.

Intermission [1] (intəɹmi·ʃən). 1426. [ad. L. *intermissionem*, f. *intermittere.*] 1. The fact of intermitting, giving over, or ceasing for a time; a temporary pause, cessation, etc. *spec.* in *Path.* of a fever or the pulse. b. Temporary cessation, respite, relief, rest, pause. Const. *from.* Now *rare.* 1576. 2. The lapse of a space of time between events or periods of action; the time during which action temporarily ceases; interval; †vacation, recess 1563. 3. An interruption or break of continuity in a wall, line of cliffs, or the like 1624.

1. I did laugh, sans i., An houre by his diall SHAKS. Phr. *Without i.* b. Rest or i. none I find MILT. *P. L.* II. 802. 2. Chusing their Time in those Intermissions while the Preacher is at Ebb SWIFT.

†**Intermi·ssion** [2]. *rare.* 1628. [f. INTERMIT *v.* [2], after prec.] 1. = INTERMISE -1670. 2. Interposition, intervention (of a thing) -1667.

2. The third day that the Lords have, without i. of any other businesse, continued upon the question MARVELL.

Intermissive (intəɹmi·siv), *a.* 1586. [f. L. *intermiss-*, *intermittere* to INTERMIT *v.* [1] + -IVE.] Of the nature of, pertaining to, intermission; intermittent; coming at intervals.

Make Pleasure thy..i. Relaxation SIR T. BROWNE.

Intermit (intəɹmi·t), *v.* [1] 1542. [ad. L. *intermittere*, f. *inter* + *mittere* to send, let go, put.] 1. *trans.* To discontinue for a time; to suspend 1576. †b. To interrupt, cause intermission to -1704. †c. To omit, pass over -1692. 2. *intr.* To cease or stop for a time; to be intermittent 1571. b. *spec.* in *Path.* of a fever (pain, etc.) or of the pulse 1626.

1. To i. it..for a year or two,..and then to return to the use of it BOYLE. 2. Let me know the exact time when your Courts i. JOHNSON.

†**Intermit**, *v.* [2] ME. [Refash. of ENTERMETE, after L. *intermittere.*] 1. *refl.* = ENTERMETE 1. -1548. b. *intr.* = INTROMIT 3. -1548. 2. *trans.* = INTROMIT 1. -1676.

Intermittence (intəɹmi·tĕns). Also -ance. 1796. [a. F.; see INTERMITTENT and -ENCE.] 1. The fact of intermitting; discontinuance for a time. 2. Intermittent sequence. TYNDALL. So **Intermi·ttency**, intermission 1662.

Intermittent (intəɹmi·tĕnt), *a.* (*sb.*) 1603. [ad. L. *intermittentem.*] 1. That intermits or ceases for a time; coming or operating at intervals. *spec.* in *Path.* of the pulse, a fever, etc. 2. *sb. Path.* An intermittent fever. Also *fig.* 1693.

1. This disorder was not in its nature i. BURKE. Hence **Intermi·ttently** *adv.* in an i. manner.

Intermittingly (-mi·tiŋli), *adv.* 1654. [-LY [2].] In an intermitting manner; intermittently.

Intermix (intəɹmi·ks), *v.* 1562. [f. INTERMIXT, taken as pa. pple. of an Eng. vb.; see COMMIX, MIX.] 1. *trans.* To mix together, intermingle. 2. *intr.* To be or become mixed together; to blend or associate intimately 1722.

1. Hee, she knew would i. Grateful digressions, and solve high dispute With conjugal Caresses MILT.

Intermixed, intermixt (intəɹmi·kst), *ppl. a.* 1555. [orig. *intermixt*, ad. L. *intermixtus*, *intermiscere*, f. *inter* + *miscere* to mix. The form *intermixed* followed the formation of the vb. *intermix.*] Mixed together, intimately mixed. Hence **Intermi·xedly**, **intermi·xtly** *adv.* with intermixture, promiscuously. So †**Intermi·xtion** = next 1520.

Intermixture (intəɹmi·kstiŭɹ). 1586. [f. L. *intermixt-* ppl. stem + -URE.] 1. The action of intermixing or fact of being intermixed; intimate mixture 1592. 2. *concr.* or quasi-*concr.* Something, or a quantity or portion *of* something, intermixed with or added to something else.

1. From the i. of its houses with trees, it [Norwich] is called a city in an orchard 1778.

Intermobility, etc.: see INTER- *pref.*

Intermolecular (intəɹmole·kiŭlăɹ), *a.* 1843. [INTER- II. 2 a.] Existing, or occurring between the molecules of a body or substance.

Intermundane (intəɹmɒ·ndēⁱn), *a.* 1691. [f. INTER- II. 2 a + L. *mundus, mundanus.*] 1. Situated, or present, between different worlds. 2. Existing between worlds reciprocally 1858.

1. The vast distance, between these great bodies, are call'd i. spaces LOCKE. So †**Intermu·ndial**, †**Intermu·ndian.**

‖**Intermu·ndium.** 1817. [A mod. sing. of L. *intermundia* (pl.) the spaces between the worlds.] A space between two worlds.

†**Intermu·re**, *v.* 1606. [f. INTER- I. 1 a + L. *murus* wall.] *trans.* To inclose between walls, to wall in -1628.

Intermuscular (intəɹmɒ·skiŭlăɹ), *a.* 1822. [INTER- II. 2 a.] *Anat.* Situated between muscles, or between muscular fibres.

Intermutation: see INTER- *pref.* I. 2 a.

Intermutual (intəɹmiū·tiu͵ăl), *a.* 1595. [INTER- I. 2 a; pleonastic for *mutual.*] Mutual, reciprocal. Hence **Intermu·tually** *adv.*

Intern (intə̄·ɹn). Also †**interne.** 1578. [a. F. *interne* = It. *interno*, ad. L. *internus*, f. *in* adv. + *-ternus* suffix, as in *sempiternus*, etc.]

A. *adj.* (Now *poet.* or *arch.*) = INTERNAL *a.*

B. *sb.* (Also *interne* after Fr.) An assistant resident physician or surgeon in a hospital 1891. *U.S.*

Intern (intə̄·ɹn), *v.* Also †**interne.** 1606. [f. (ult.) It. *interno*, F. *interne*; see prec.] †1. *intr.* To enter or pass in; to become incorporated or united with another being. 2. *trans.* To confine within the limits of a country, district, or place; to oblige to reside within prescribed limits. Also *fig.* 1866. 3. To send (goods, etc.) into the interior of a country. *U.S.*

2. To disarm troops crossing the neutral frontier and to i. them till the conclusion of peace W. E. HALL.

Internal (intə̄·ɹnăl). 1509. [ad. late med.L. *internalis* (f. *internus*); see -AL. Opp. in all senses to *external.*]

A. *adj.* 1. Situated or existing within something; of or pertaining to the inside; inward 1590. b. *Anat.* Situated away from the surface of the body, or nearer the median line 1719. 2. Pertaining to the inner nature or relations of anything; belonging to the thing or subject in itself; intrinsic 1607. b. Of or pertaining to the domestic (as dist. from the foreign) affairs of a country 1795. 3. Of or belonging to the inner nature or life of man; mental or spiritual; inward; subjective 1509.

1. I. navigation 1804. *I. angle* (Geom.) = *interior angle* (see INTERIOR A. 1). *I. combustion*, (*a*) see COMBUSTION 2 b; (*b*) applied to gas and oil engines, in which the energy necessary to produce motion is developed in the engine cylinder and not in a separate chamber 1888. 2. The i. evidence for some statements renders them highly probable FREEMAN. b. The maintenance of i. peace STUBBS. 3. Sensations and ideas are both i. 1869.

B. *sb.* 1. *pl.* The inward parts or organs; inwards, entrails 1764. †2. *Med.* (usu. in *pl.*) A medecine or remedy to be taken internally -1704. 3. Something belonging to the thing in itself. (Now always in *pl.*) 1652. †4. (Usu. in *pl.*) The inner nature, soul, spirit -17..

3. To Guard the Internals of Religion SACHEVERELL.

Hence **Interna·lity**, the quality or fact of being **i.**; also with *an* and *pl.*

Internally (intɔ̄·ɹnăli), *adv.* 1597. [f. prec. + -LY [2].] **1.** In, on, or with respect to, the inside or interior. **2.** With respect to the inner nature or relations of anything, esp. the internal affairs of a country, etc. 1791. **3.** Mentally, spiritually 1646.

Interna·sal, *a.* 1866. [f. INTER- II. 2 a + L. *nasus.*] = *intranasal* (see INTRA-).

International (intəɹnæ·ʃənăl). 1780. [INTER- II. 2.] **A.** *adj.* Existing, constituted, or carried on between different nations; pertaining to the relations between nations. **b.** (with capital *I.*) Belonging to the International Working Men's Association, a society of working-men founded in London in 1864 (and dissolved in 1874), the objects of which were identified with those of the socialism of Marx.

The great science of i. law, the determining authority in questions of right between independent states HALLAM. An I. Exhibition 1861, yacht race 1888.

B. *sb.* **a.** A person belonging to two different nations (*e.g.* native of one and resident in another) 1870; one who takes part in an international contest 1895. **b.** (with capital *I*, and sometimes in Fr. form *-ale*) = International Working Men's Association (see A. b); also, a member or adherent of this.

b. *First I.*, that of 1864–74; *Second I.*, formed in 1889 at Paris and having later its seat in Brussels; *Third I.*, formed in 1919 by the Russian communists (Bolsheviks) on a revolutionary basis.

‖**Internationale** (-næʃiŏnā·l, ‖ ænṫęrnasyonal). [Fr. (sc. *chanson* song).] A revolutionary hymn composed by Eugène Pottier in 1871 and adopted by French socialists and later by others. (See also prec. B. b.)

Interna·tionalism. 1877. [f. INTERNATIONAL + -ISM.] International character or spirit; the principle of community of interests or action between different nations; *spec.* (with capital *I.*) the doctrine or principles of the International Working Men's Association.

Interna·tionalist. 1864. [f. as prec. + -IST.] **a.** An advocate of or believer in internationalism; *spec.* a member of or sympathizer with the International Working Men's Association. **b.** One versed in international law. **c.** One who takes part in an international contest.

Internationa·lity. 1864. [See -ITY.] International quality, condition, or character.

Interna·tionalize, *v.* 1864. [See -IZE.] *trans.* To render international in character or use; *spec.* to bring (a country, territory, etc.) under the combined government or protection of two or more different nations. Hence **Interna·tionaliza·tion.**

Interna·tionally, *adv.* 1864. [See -LY [2].] In an international manner; between or among different nations.

Interne: see INTERN.

Internecine (intəɹnī·səin), *a.* 1663. [ad. L. *internecinus*, f. *internecium* slaughter, destruction, f. *internecare*; see next. The etym. pronunc. would be *inte·rnecine.*] **1.** *orig.* Deadly, destructive, characterized by great slaughter. **2.** *esp.* (In mod. use.) Mutually destructive, aiming at the slaughter or destruction of each other 1755.

1. *I. war*, war for the sake of slaughter, war to the death. **2.** Eight thousand Zealots, who stabbed each other in i. massacre FARRAR.

Internecion (intəɹnī·ʃən). *rare.* 1610. [ad. L. *internecionem* massacre, etc., f. *internecare* to kill, destroy, f. *inter* (as in *interficere*) + *necare* to kill.] Destruction, massacre.

Internecive (intəɹnī·siv), *a. rare.* 1819. [ad. L. *internecivus*, (scribal) var. of *internecinus.*] = INTERNECINE 2.

†**Interne·ct**, *v.* 1694. [ad. L. *internectere* to bind to each other, f. *inter* + *nectere.*] *trans.* To interconnect. So †**Interne·xion, -ne·ction**, mutual connexion 1654.

Internee·. 1920. [f. INTERN *v.* 2 + -EE [1].] An interned person.

Sinn Fein internees. *Newspaper.*

Interneural (intəɹniūə·răl), *a.* (*sb.*) 1846. [f. INTER- II. 2 a + Gr. νεῦρον nerve; see NEURAL.] *Anat.* and *Zool.* Situated between nerves, or between neural spines or arches; applied *spec.* to the dermal spines or bones supporting the dorsal fin-rays in fishes (cf. INTERSPINAL). **b.** as *sb.* (*pl.*) = Interneural spines 1880.

†**Inte·rnity.** *rare.* 1760. [f. L. *internus* + -ITY.] The quality of being internal, inwardness; something internal. H. BROOKE.

Internment (intɔ̄·ɹnmĕnt). 1870. [f. INTERN *v.* 2 + -MENT.] The action of interning; confining within prescribed limits.

Interno-, comb. advb. form of L. *internus* INTERNAL; as in **inte·rno-me·dial, -me·dian** *adjs.*, *Entom.* situated within the median line or nervure, or between the internal and median nervures, of the wing 1826.

Internodal (intəɹnōu·dăl), *a.* 1835. [f. INTER- II. 2 a + L. *nodus*; cf. *nodal.*] *Bot.* and *Zool.* Situated between nodes; belonging to or constituting an internode.

Internode (i·ntəɹnōud). 1667. [ad. L. *internodium* (see below).] **1.** *Bot.* That part of a stem or branch intervening between two of the nodes or knots from which the leaves arise. **2.** *Zool.* and *Anat.* A slender part intervening between two nodes or joints; each bone of a finger or toe 1722.

†**Interno·dial**, *a.* [f. next + -AL.] = INTERNODAL. SIR T. BROWNE.

‖**Internodium** (intəɹnōu·diŏm). Pl. **-ia.** Now *rare.* 1644. [L., f. *inter* + *nodus*; see INTER- II. 1.] = INTERNODE. (*erron.* A joint.)

†**I·nternunce.** Also **-nonce.** 1647. [a. F. *internonce*, ad. L. *internuntius* (*-nuncius*); see INTERNUNCIUS.] = INTERNUNCIO. –1847.

Internuncial (intəɹnɒ·nʃiăl), *a.* 1845. [f. L. *internuntius* (see below) + -AL.] Having the function of conveying messages between two parties, etc.; used *fig.* of the nerves.

†**Internu·nciess.** *rare.* [irreg. f. INTERNUNCIO + -ESS.] A female internuncio or messenger. CHAPMAN.

Internuncio (intəɹnɒ·nʃio). Also †**-tio.** 1641. [ad. It. *internunzio*, ad. L. *internuntius* (*-nuncius*); see next.] **1.** A messenger between two parties. **2.** A representative or ambassador of the Pope at a foreign court while there is no nuncio, or at a minor court to which no nuncio is sent 1670. **3.** A minister representing a government, esp. that of Austria, at the Ottoman Porte 1700. Hence **Internu·ncioship**, the office or function of an i. or go-between.

‖**Internu·ncius.** 1675. [L. in med. spelling, for cl. L. *internuntius*, f. *inter* between + *nuntius* a messenger.] = prec. 1.

Internuptial (intəɹnɒ·pʃăl), *a.* 1850. [f. INTER- I. 2 or II. 2 + L. *nuptiæ*; cf. *nuptial.*] **1.** Pertaining to intermarriage. **2.** Intervening between two marriages or married states 1885.

Interoceanic (i:ntər,ōuʃi,æ·nik), *a.* 1855. [INTER- II. 2 b.] Situated between oceans; connecting two oceans, as a strait or canal.

Interocular, etc.: see INTER- *pref.*

Interopercular (i:ntər,opɔ̄·ɹkiŭlăɹ), *a.* 1854. [f. next + -AR; cf. *opercular.*] *Ichthyol.* Belonging to, or of the nature of, an interoperculum; chiefly in *i. bone* = next.

‖**Interoperculum** (i:ntər,opɔ̄·ɹkiŭlŏm). 1834. [INTER- I. 2 b.] *Ichthyol.* One of the bones forming the gill-cover; usually situated below the præoperculum, and partly between this and the operculum and suboperculum.

Interorbital (intər,ǭ·ɹbităl), *a.* 1852. [INTER- II. 2 a.] *Anat.* Situated between the eye-sockets.

Interosculant (intər,ǫ·skiŭlănt), *a.* 1855. [INTER- I. 2 a; cf. next.] Interosculating; forming a connecting link.

An 'i.' group,—a party of genera and species which connect families scientifically far apart KINGSLEY.

Interosculate (intər,ǫ·skiŭlēit), *v.* 1882. [f. INTER- I. 1 b + OSCULATE.] *intr.* **a.** To interpenetrate or inosculate with each other. **b.** To form a connecting link between two groups. Hence **I:nterosculа·tion.**

Intero·sseal, *a.* 1805. [f. as next + -AL.] = next.

Interosseous (intər,ǫ·siəs), *a.* 1745. [f. INTER- II. 2 a + L. *os, oss-* bone, *osseus* bony + -OUS.] *Anat.* Situated between bones; said of various ligaments, muscles, nerves, and vessels.

†**Interpa·le**, *v.* 1553. [f. INTER- I. 1 + PALE *v.*] **1.** *trans.* To divide by pales, as in Heraldry; to alternate in vertical divisions. BRENDE. **2.** = IMPALE *v.* 2. LOVELACE.

Interparietal (-părəi·ĕtăl), *a.* (*sb.*) 1835. [INTER- II. 2 a.] *Anat.* **1.** Situated between the parietal bones of the skull. **2.** *sb.* The interparietal bone.

†**Interpau·se**, *v.* 1534. [f. INTER- I. 1 + PAUSE *v.*] *intr.* To pause in the midst of something. MORE. So †**I·nterpause** *sb.* a pause between or in the course of something 1599.

Interpel (intəɹpe·l), *v.* Now only in *Sc. Law.* ME. [ad. L. *interpellare*, f. *inter* + *pellare*, secondary form of *pellere* to drive. Cf. F. *interpeller.*] †**1.** *trans.* To appeal to; to petition –1591. †**2.** To interrupt (a person) in speaking; to break in on or disturb –1647. **3.** *Sc. Law.* To intercept, cut off, prevent 1722.

2. No more now, for I am interpell'd by many businesses HOWELL.

Interpellant (intəɹpe·lănt). 1869. [a. F. *interpellant*, pr. pple. of *interpeller*, ad. L. *interpellare*; see prec.] One who addresses an interpellation (e.g. in the French Chamber).

Interpellate (intəɹpe·lēit), *v.* 1599. [f. ppl. stem of L. *interpellare.*] †**1.** *trans.* To interrupt or break in upon. **2.** To address an interpellation to (a minister in the French or other Chamber) 1874.

Interpellation (i:ntəɹpelēi·ʃən). 1526. [ad. L. *interpellationem*. Re-introduced from Fr. in sense 5 in 19th c.] †**1.** The action of appealing to or entreating; intercession –1670. †**2.** A summons, citation –1726. †**3.** The action of breaking in upon; interruption –1834. **4.** *Sc. Law.* Prevention, hindrance 1814. **5.** The action of interrupting the order of the day (in a foreign legislative Chamber) by asking from a minister an explanation of some matter belonging to his department 1837.

1. By the importunity of her i. BECON. **3.** Sophistic reasonings, and sarcastic interpellations LANDOR. **5.** An incessant fire of questions, interpellations, objurgations CARLYLE.

Interpenetrate (intəɹpe·nĭtrēit), *v.* 1809. [INTER- I. 1.] **1.** *trans.* To penetrate between the parts or particles of (anything); to pass through and through, permeate, pervade 1818. Also *intr.* **2.** *intr.* To penetrate each other; to unite or mingle by mutual penetration 1809. **b.** *trans.* To penetrate reciprocally 1843. **3.** *Arch.* (*trans.* and *intr.*) To appear as if penetrating or passing through a moulding, etc. 1840.

1. The water is everywhere interpenetrated by air, which the fishes breathe MEDWIN. **2.** Law and religion thus interpenetrating neutralized each other COLERIDGE. **3.** Their shafts interpenetrating the mouldings of the panels and tracery BOUTELL.

Interpenetration (i:ntəɹpenĭtrēi·ʃən). 1809. [INTER- I. 2 a.] **1.** The action of penetrating between or among; thorough penetration 1822. **2.** Mutual penetration 1809. **3.** *Arch.* The intersection of two forms; *spec.* an independent continuation of mouldings or other members past their intersection, so that the identity of a member is preserved after it has partly coincided with another or has been swallowed up in it 1840.

Interpe·netrative, *a.* 1860. [INTER- I. 2 a.] Intimately or reciprocally penetrative. Hence **Interpe·netratively** *adv.* 1834.

Interpetiolar (intəɹpe·tiŏlăɹ), *a.* 1830. [INTER- II. 2 a; see PETIOLAR.] *Bot.* Situated between petioles, or between a petiole and the axis. Also **Interpe·tiolary** *a.*

Interphalangeal: see INTER- *pref.*

Interpilaster (i:ntəɹpilæ·stəɹ). 1823. [INTER- II. 1.] *Arch.* The space between two pilasters.

†**Interpla·ce**, *v.* 1548. [INTER- I. 1 a, b.] *trans.* **a.** To place between or in the midst of. **b.** To place between each other or alternately. (Only in *pass.*) –1678.

Interplait (intəɹplæ·t), *v.* Also **-plat.** 1822. [INTER- I. 1 b.] *trans.* To plait together; to intertwine, interweave.

Interplanetary (-plæ·nĕtări), *a.* 1691. [INTER- II. 2 a.] Situated between the planets.

Interplay (i·ntəɹplēⁱ). 1862. [INTER- I. 2 a.] Reciprocal play, free interaction.

Interplead (intəɹplī·d), *v.* Also †**enter-ple(a)de.** 1473. [ad. AF. *enterpleder*: see INTER- I. 1 a, b and PLEAD *v.*] 1. *intr.* In *Law*: To litigate with each other in order to determine some point in dispute in which a third party is concerned. †2. *trans.* To raise as a plea –1716.

Interpleader (intəɹplī·dəɹ). Also †**enter-.** 1567. [a. AF. *enterpleder* (see prec.) inf. as subst.] *Law.* A suit pleaded between two parties to determine a matter of claim or right, on which the action of a third party depends, esp. to determine to which of them livery or payment ought to be made.

Interpleural (-plūə·răl), *a.* 1879. [f. INTER- II. 2 + Gr. πλευρά ribs.] Situated between the pleuræ of the right and left lungs.

Interpoint (intəɹpoi·nt), *v.* 1595. [INTER- I. 1 a.] a. *trans.* To put a point or points between (words); to punctuate. b. *intr.* or *absol.* To insert a point or points.

Her sighes should i. her words DANIEL.

Interpolable (intɜ·ɹpŏlăb'l), *a.* [f. L. *interpolare* to INTERPOLATE + -ABLE.] That may be interpolated; suitable for interpolation. DE MORGAN.

Interpolar (-pōu·lăɹ), *a.* (*sb.*) 1870. [INTER- II. 2 a.] Situated between the poles (of a galvanic battery, etc.). b. as *sb.* An interpolar wire 1882.

†**Inte·rpolate,** *ppl. a.* late ME. [ad. L. *interpolatus*, pa. pple. of *interpolare.*] Intermittent (esp. of fever); interpolated –1669.

Interpolate (intɜ·ɹpŏleⁱt), *v.* 1612. [f. ppl. stem of L. *interpolare* to furbish up, to alter, f. *inter* (INTER- I. 1 a) + *-polare*, related to *polire* to POLISH.] †1. *trans.* To polish up; to put a fresh gloss on (*rare*) –1706. 2. To alter or enlarge (a book or writing) by insertion of new matter; *esp.* to tamper with by inserting new or foreign matter 1612. Also *transf.* 3. To introduce (words or passages) into a pre-existing writing; *esp.* to insert (spurious matter) in a genuine work without note or warning 1640. b. *transf.* To intercalate 1802. 4. *intr.* or *absol.* To make insertions or interpolations 1720. †5. *trans.* To interrupt by an interval. (Only in *pass.*) HALE. 6. *Math.* To insert an intermediate term or terms in a series 1796.

2. A Manuscript of Sir Ralph Hoptons..interpolated with his own hand FULLER. 3. Words which no Vedelius can carp at as interpolated BP. HALL. b. By interpolating a month of 30 days WHEWELL.

Interpolation (intɜ:ɹpŏlēⁱ·ʃən). 1612. [a. F., or ad. L. *interpolationem*; see prec. and -ATION.] †1. The action of furbishing or polishing up –1678. 2. The action of interpolating a writing, or a word, etc. therein (cf. senses 2 and 3 of the vb.); the condition or fact of being interpolated 1612. b. With *pl.* An interpolated word or passage 1675. 3. The action of introducing or inserting among other things or between the members of any series. Also with *an* and *pl.* An insertion. 1849. b. *Math.* The process of inserting in a series an intermediate number or quantity ascertained by calculation from those already known 1763. †4. Interposition of time; interval. CROOKE.

1. A Refinement and I. of Paganism CUDWORTH. 2. This end was carried out by interpolations and falsification of ecclesiastical documents HUSSEY. 3. The i. of fossiliferous..rocks MURCHISON.

Inte·rpolator. 1659. [a. L.] One who interpolates.

Interpo·lish, *v. rare.* 1609. [INTER- I. 1 a.] To polish here and there or at intervals.

Interpone (intəɹpōu·n), *v.* 1523. [ad. L. *interponere*, f. *inter* + *ponere.*] *trans.* and *refl.* = INTERPOSE *v.* So †**Interpo·nent** (*rare*), one who or that which interposes 1592.

Interposal (intəɹpōu·zăl). 1607. [f. next + -AL.] = INTERPOSITION 1, 2.

Interpose (intəɹpōu·z), *v.* 1582. [a. F. *interposer*, f. L. *inter* + F. *poser* (see POSE); substituted for L. *interponere* (see INTERPONE), by form-assoc. with *interposition*, etc. Cf. *compose, dispose*, etc.] 1. *trans.* To place between, in space or time. Often with implication of obstruction or delay. 1599. 2. †*refl.* To place oneself between; to stand in the way –1745. Also *intr.* (for *refl.*). 3. *trans.* To put forth or introduce in the way of interference or intervention 1606. 4. *intr.* (and †*refl.*) To put oneself forward or interfere in a matter; to intervene 1603. 5. *trans.* To introduce, esp. in the midst of other matters as an interruption or digression 1582. b. *absol.* or *intr.* To interrupt, make a digression 1667. †6. *trans.* To come or be in the way of; to obstruct –1671.

1. Only a small part of the convexity of the globe is interposed between us and the sun MORSE. 2. What watchfull Cares doe i. themselves Betwixt your Eyes, and Night? SHAKS. 3. To i. arbitration 1798. 4. I shall not i. in their Quarrel ADDISON. 5. To i. a jocular, and perhaps ridiculous digression PETTY. Hence †**Interpose** *sb.* interposition. **Interpo·ser.**

Interposition (i:ntəɹpŏzi·ʃən). ME. [a. F., ad. L. *interpositionem*, f. *interponere.* Not derivationally related to INTERPOSE.] 1. The action of placing something or oneself between; the fact of being placed or situated between; intervention. b. An instance of this; *occas.*, that which is interposed 1650. 2. Interference, mediation; also, an instance of this 1461. †3. A parenthesis; a digression 1553.

2. By the immediate i. of Providence *Junius Lett.*

†**Interpo·sure.** 1627. [f. INTERPOSE *v.* + -URE; cf. *composure*, etc.] Interposition –1733.

Interpret (intɜ·ɹprėt), *v.* ME. [a. F. *interpréter*, or ad. L. *interpretari*, f. *interpres, -pretem*, f. *inter* + root corresp. to Skr. *prath-* to spread abroad.] 1. *trans.* To expound the meaning of; to render clear or explicit; to elucidate; to explain. †Formerly also, To translate. b. To explain to oneself 1795. c. In recent use: To give one's own interpretation of (a musical composition, a landscape, etc.); to render 1880. 2. To expound or take in a specified manner ME. 3. *absol.* or *intr.* To make an explanation; to give an exposition; *spec.* to act as an interpreter or dragoman. †Formerly also, To translate. ME. †4. *intr.* To signify, to mean. SELDEN.

1. And they shall call his name Emmanuel, which being interpreted is, God with vs *Matt.* i. 23. The law interprets..his wishes with regard to the disposal of his property FAWCETT. 2. As thou wouldst be well interpreted by others i. others well DONNE. This transaction was interpreted into a bribe SMOLLETT. 3. Unskilful with what words to pray, let mee I. for him MILT. *P.L.* XI. 33.

Interpretable (intɜ·ɹprėtăb'l), *a.* 1611. [ad. late L. *interpretabilis* (Tertull.), f. *interpretari* to INTERPRET; see -BLE.] Susceptible of interpretation, explicable.

†**Inte·rpretament.** *rare.* Also *erron.* **interprement.** 1645. [ad. L. *interpretamentum*, f. *interpretari*; see -MENT.] Interpretation –1802.

Inte·rpretate, *v.* Now *rare* or *Obs.* 1522. [f. L. *interpretat-*, *interpretari.*] = INTERPRET *v.*

Interpretation (intɜ:ɹprĭtēⁱ·ʃən). ME. [a. F. *interprétation*, or ad. L. *interpretationem.*] 1. The action of interpreting; explanation, exposition. †b. The faculty or power of interpreting –1552. 2. An explanation given; a way of explaining; †a comment ME. b. The representation of a part in a drama, or the rendering of a musical composition, according to one's conception of the author's idea 1880. 3. The way in which a thing ought to be interpreted; proper explanation; hence, Signification, meaning ME. †4. The action of translating; a translation –1646.

1. *I. of Nature*, Bacon's phrase to denote the discovery of natural laws by means of induction. The just i. of geological phenomena HUXLEY. b. To another [is geven] the interpretacion off tonges TINDALE 1 *Cor.* xii. 10. 2. The ambiguity of oracles, and their ambodextrous interpretations LILLY. They give mean Interpretations..to the worthiest Actions ADDISON. 4. Cephas: which is by interpretacion, a stone TINDALE *John* i. 42.

Interpretative (intɜ·ɹprĭtētiv), *a.* 1569. [f. L. *interpretat-*, *interpretari* + -IVE. Cf. F. *interprétatif.*] 1. Having the character, quality, or function of interpreting; explanatory, expository. 2. Deduced or deducible by interpretation; inferential, constructive (*arch.* or *Obs.*) 1610.

1. I. lexicography JOHNSON. 2. Constructive, or i. treasons 1798. Hence **Inte·rpretatively** *adv.* by way of interpretation (*rare*); †by inference, constructively.

Interpreter (intɜ·ɹprėtəɹ). [ME. *interpretour*, AF. form of OF. *interpreteeur, -teur*, ad. late L. *interpretatorem.* In 16th c. refash. after agent-nouns in *-er*; see -ER [1].] 1. One who interprets or explains ME. 2. One who translates languages ME. †3. One who makes known the will of another; a title of Mercury as messenger of the gods. (L. *interpres divum* Virgil.) –1678. †4. *Rhet.* = SYNONYMY 1589.

1. Then said Christian to the I., Expound this matter more fully to me BUNYAN. 2. Hee [Joseph] spake vnto them by an i. *Gen.* xlii. 23. 3. MILT. *P.L.* III. 657. Hence **Inte·rpretership.**

Interpretress (intɜ·ɹprėtrės). 1775. [f. INTERPRETER + -ESS.] A female interpreter. var. †**Inte·rpretess** 1717.

Interprovi·ncial, *a.* 1839. [INTER- II. 2 b.] Lying, extending, or carried on, between different provinces; pertaining to the mutual relations of provinces.

Interpubic (intəɹpiū·bik), *a.* 1836. [INTER- II. 2 a.] Situated between the pubic bones.

Interpunction (intəɹpɒ·ŋkʃən). 1617. [ad. L. *interpunctionem*, f. *interpungere*, f. *inter* + *pungere* to prick, etc.] The insertion of points between words, clauses, or sentences; punctuation. *concr.* A point inserted.

Interpunctuate (intəɹpɒ·ŋktiuˌeⁱt), *v.* 1850. [INTER- I. 1 a.] To insert the points between words and clauses; to punctuate. Also *fig.* So **Interpunctua·tion** = prec. sb. 1717.

Interradial (intəɹˌrēⁱ·diăl). 1870. [INTER- II. 2 a.] *Zool. adj.* Situated between radii or rays, as in an echinoderm. *sb.* An interradial part.

Interramal (intəɹˌrēⁱ·măl), *a.* 1874. [INTER- II. 2 a.] *Ornith.* Situated between the rami or branches of the lower jaw.

†**Interˌre·gency.** *rare.* 1600. [f. next; see -ENCY.] The tenure of an interrex or interregent –1674.

†**Interˌre·gent.** *rare.* 1600. [INTER- I. 2 b; after *interrex.*] = INTERREX.

‖**Interregnum** (intəɹˌre·gnɒm). *Pl.* **-regna, -regnums.** 1579. [L., f. *inter* (INTER- II. 1) + *regnum*; cf. next.] †1. Temporary authority or rule exercised during a vacancy of the throne or a suspension of the usual government –1770. 2. The interval between the close of a king's reign and the accession of his successor 1590. 3. A cessation or suspension of the usual ruling power. Also *fig.* 1648. 4. A breach of continuity; an interval, pause, vacant space 1659. Hence **Interˌre·gnal** *a.*

Interreign (i·ntəɹˌrēⁱn). Now *rare.* 1533. [f. INTER- II. 1 + REIGN, after prec.; cf. F. *interrègne.*] †1. = INTERREGNUM 1. –1611. 2. = INTERREGNUM 2. 1586.

Interrelated (i:ntəɹˌrĭlēⁱ·tėd), *ppl. a.* 1827. [INTER- I. 1 b.] Mutually related or connected.

Interrelation (i:ntəɹˌrĭlēⁱ·ʃən). 1848. [INTER- I. 2 a.] Mutual or reciprocal relation. So **I:nterˌrela·tionship.**

Interrenal (intəɹˌrī·năl). 1893. [f. INTER- II. 2 a + L. *renes* kidneys; see RENAL.] *Anat.* a. *adj.* Situated between the kidneys. b. *sb* An interrenal body.

Inte·rrer. 1611. [f. INTER *v.* + -ER [1].] One who inters.

‖**Interrex** (i·ntəɹˌreks). *Pl.* **-reges** (-rī·dʒīz). 1579. [L., f. *inter* (INTER- I. 2 b) + *rex.*] One who holds the supreme authority in a state during an interregnum.

The regents at that time called *Interreges* NORTH.

†**Inte·rrogate,** *sb. rare.* Also **-rogat.** 1633. [ad. L. *interrogatum*, or a. F. *interrogat.*] A question; an interrogation –1661.

Interrogate (inte·rŏgeⁱt), *v.* 1483. [f. L. *interrogat-*, *interrogare*, f. *inter* between, at intervals + *rogare* to ask.] 1. *trans.* To ask questions of, to question, esp. formally; to examine by questions. Also *fig.* †2. To ask about (something) (*rare*) –1698. 3. *absol.* or *intr.* To ask questions; *spec.* in *Law* (see INTERROGATORY B. 1) 1622.

1. *fig.* To i. Truth 1701, nature 1794, one's memory HELPS. 2. Interrogating the State of Europe FRYER. 3. The leave of the court to i. must be obtained 1883. Hence **Inte·rrogatee·**, one who is interrogated. **Inte·rrogatingly** *adv.*

Interrogation (inteːrǫgēⁱ·ʃən). ME. [a. F., or ad. L. *interrogationem*; see prec.] 1. The action of interrogating; a questioning; †request 1551. b. With *an* and *pl.* A question ME. 2. *Gram.* and *Rhet.* Questioning, or a question, as a form of speech 1532. b. *Point* (*mark*, *note*) *of interrogation*, also *i.-point* (and, formerly, *i.*): the symbol used in writing or printing to indicate a question, usually placed at the end of the sentence and having the form ? or ?.

A point of interrogation is also sometimes placed before a word or phrase, to query its correctness, existence, etc.

In Spanish, it is placed both before and after the question, in the former case inverted as in *¿Quien sabe?* who knows?

2. b. It is a mistake to be inquisitive. A walking i.-point is never a pleasant companion 1895. Hence **Interroga·tional** *a.* interrogative.

Interrogative (intərǫ·gătiv). 1520. [ad. late L. *interrogativus*; see INTERROGATE *v.* and -IVE.]

A. *adj.* 1. Of, pertaining to, or of the nature of questioning; having the form or force of a question 1597. 2. *Rhet.* and *Gram.* Of a word or form: Employed in asking a question 1520. 3. Given to asking questions; inquisitive (*rare*) 1709.

1. The i. method of Socrates JOWETT. 2. *I. pronouns*, the pronouns *who? which? what? whether? I. adverbs*, such as *where? when? why? wherefore?* Hence **Interro·gatively** *adv.* in an i. manner.

B. *sb.* 1. An interrogation 1581. 2. *Gram.* A word or form employed in asking a question; esp. an interrogative pronoun 1530.

Interrogator (inteˑrǫgeⁱtəɹ). 1751. [a. late L.; cf. F. *interrogateur.*] One who interrogates; a questioner.

Interrogatory (intərǫ·gători). 1533. [ad. late L. *interrogatorius*; see INTERROGATE *v.* and -ORY.] A. *adj.* = INTERROGATIVE *a.* 1576.

B. *sb.* 1 An interrogation, a question; *spec.* in *Law*: A question formally put, or drawn up in writing to be put, to an accused person or a witness 1533. 2. Examination (of an accused person) (*rare*). [= F. *interrogatoire.*] 1827.

1. A paper of interrogatories was laid before him by order of the Privy Council MACAULAY. Hence **Interro·gatorily** *adv.* interrogatively.

In terrorem: see IN *Lat. prep.*

†**Interru·pt**, *ppl. a.* ME. [a. OF. *interrupt*, ad. L. *interruptus*; see next.] Interrupted (see the vb.). In quot., Forming an interval or breach between two parts of something.

Our adversarie, whom no bounds Prescrib'd, no barrs of Hell..nor yet the main Abyss Wide i. can hold MILT.

Interrupt (intərʊ·pt), *v.* ME. [f. L. *interrupt-*, *interrumpere* to break asunder, break off, f. *inter* between + *rumpere* to break; cf. CORRUPT.] 1. *trans.* To break in upon (*esp.* speech or discourse); to break the continuity of; to break off, hinder the course of, cause to cease or stop (usu. temporarily). 2. To break in upon (a person) while doing something, *esp.* speaking; to hinder or cause to stop (usu. temporarily) in what one is doing ME. 3. *absol.* or *intr.*; also quasi-*trans.* = to say in interruption ME. †4. *trans.* To hinder, stop, prevent, thwart -1632. †5. To infringe, suspend (a law) -1587.

1. Not one of us but had his sleepe interrupted by fearfull dreames 1615. There being neither Tree nor Bush to i. his Charge CLARENDON. 2. It were a grosse incivility to i. them in their conversation 1639. 3. Please not to i., my good friend JOWETT.

Interrupted (intərʊ·ptėd), *ppl. a.* 1552. [f. prec. + -ED [1].] Broken in upon; broken off; having its course hindered or continuity broken; made discontinuous. b. *Bot.* (and *Zool.*) Having smaller, or otherwise differing, members (*e.g.* leaflets in a compound leaf) in the intervals between others in a series; also, discontinuous (as a linear marking) 1828.

Interru·ptedly, *adv.* 1663. [f. prec. + -LY [2].] With interruptions or void intervals; discontinuously. b. *Bot.* (and *Zool.*) With smaller or otherwise different members in the intervals between the others (see prec. b) 1753.

b. *Spiræa ulmaria*..leaves i. pinnate HOOKER.

Interrupter, -or (intərʊ·ptəɹ). 1511. [partly a. L., partly f. INTERRUPT *v.* + -ER [1].] One who interrupts (see the vb.). b. A device for interrupting an electric current 1868.

Interruption (intərʊ·pʃən). ME. [ad. L. *interruptionem*; cf. F. *interruption.*] The action of interrupting, or fact of being interrupted (see the vb.). 1. Hindrance of course or continuance; temporary stoppage or cessation 1489. 2. A breach of continuity in space or serial order; a break; the formation or existence of a gap ME. †b. Irruption. HALE. †3. The action, or an act, of hindering or thwarting -1595. 4. *Sc. Law.* The step legally requisite to stop the currency of a period of prescription 1615.

1. I still go on with the work I have in hand, but with terrible interruptions BURKE. 2. The Interruptions of the Strata WOODWARD. b. Places severed from the Continent by the i. of the Sea HALE. 3. SHAKS. *John* III. iv. 9.

Interruptive (intərʊ·ptiv), *a.* 1643. [f. as INTERRUPT *v.* + -IVE.] 1. Having the quality of interrupting 1651. †2. Characterized by interruption; interrupted. HERLE.

Interscapular (intəɹskæ·piŭlăɹ), *a.* (*sb.*) 1721. [INTER- II. 2 a.] 1. *Anat.* and *Zool.* Situated between the scapulæ or shoulder-blades. 2. *sb.* (in *pl.*) The interscapular feathers.

Interscendent (intəɹse·ndĕnt), *a. rare.* 1796. [ad. mod.L. *interscendens*, *-ent-em* (Leibnitz), f. *inter*; after *transcendens* TRANSCENDENT.] *Math.* Applied to expressions or equations involving incommensurable quantities in the exponents; regarded as being intermediate between *algebraic* and *transcendental*. Also **Interscende·ntal** *a.*

†**Interscri·be**, *v. rare.* 1656. [ad. L. *interscribere.*] To write between, to interline.

Interseam (intəɹsī·m), *v. Obs.* or *arch.* 1589. [ad. F. *entresemer* to sow among, f. *entre-* between + *semer* :—L. *seminare.* But app. often assoc. w. SEAM *v.*] *trans.* To sprinkle or scatter between or amongst other things; to intersperse. Chiefly in *pa. pple.*

†**Intersecant**, *a.* (*sb.*) *rare.* 1658. [ad. L. *intersecantem*, pr. pple. of *intersecare*; see next.] Intersecting. As *sb.* (in *pl.*) Intersecting lines.

Intersect (intəɹse·kt), *v.* 1615. [f. L. *intersect-*, *intersecare*, f. *inter* + *secare* to cut.] 1. *trans.* To divide (something) in two by passing through or lying across it; to cross. Freq. in *pass.* (const. *with* or *by*). b. *Geom.* Of a line or surface: To cut (see CUT *v.* IV. 1) 1646. c. To divide (two things) by passing between them 1784. 2. *intr.* (for *refl.*) To cross or cut each another; chiefly *Geom.* 1847.

1. Crevasses also i. the ice TYNDALL. b. Where these two Arches I., or cut each other, there is the Center MOXON. c. Lands intersected by a narrow frith Abhor each other COWPER. 2. Straight streets intersecting at right angles GROTE.

Intersection (intəɹse·kʃən). 1559. [ad. L. *intersectionem.* Cf. F. *intersection.*] 1. The action or fact of intersecting. 2. The place where two things intersect; chiefly *Geom.*, the point (or line) common to two lines or surfaces which intersect 1559. Hence **Interse·ctional** *a.*, of, pertaining to, or characterized by i.

Interseptal (intəɹse·ptăl), *a.* 1847. [f. L. *intersæptum* diaphragm, etc. (f. *inter* + *sæptum* fence) + -AL.] Situated between septa or partitions. (Chiefly *Anat.* and *Zool.*)

†**Interse·rt**, *v.* 1583. [f. L. *intersert-*, *interserere*, f. *inter* + *serere* to set, place, etc.] *trans.* To insert between other things; to interpolate -1691. So †**Interse·rtion**, the action of intersertìng; that which is interserted.

Interset; see INTER- *pref.* I. 1 a.

Intershock (intəɹʃǫ·k), *v. rare.* 1603. [f. INTER- I. 1 b + SHOCK *v.* With sense 1 cf. F. *s'entrechoquer.*] †1. *trans.* To shock or attack mutually -1605. 2. *intr.* To strike together, collide 1650.

Intershoot (intəɹʃū·t), *v.* 1845. [INTER- I. 1 a.] *intr.* To shoot or glance at intervals. *trans.* To variegate at intervals (chiefly in pa. pple. *intershot*, const. *with*).

Hues..intershooting, and to sight Lost and recovered WORDSW.

Intersidereal (iˑntəɹsəidīᵊ·rĭăl), *a.* 1656. [See INTER- II. 2 c and SIDEREAL.] = INTERSTELLAR.

Intersocial (intəɹsōᵘ·ʃăl), *a.* 1852. [See INTER- II. 2 c and SOCIAL.] Existing between associates; social.

Intersomnial (intəɹsǫ·mniăl), *a.* 1849. [f. INTER- II. 2 d + L. *somnium* dream + -AL; prop. *intrasomnial.*] Occurring in the midst of a dream. So **Interso·mnious** *a.* 'between sleeping and waking' (Worcester).

Interspace (i·ntəɹspēⁱs), *sb.* ME. [INTER- I. 2 b.] 1. A space between two things; interval. 2. An interval of time 1629. So **Interspa·tial** *a.* of or belonging to an i.

Interspace (intəɹspēⁱ·s), *v.* 1847. [INTER- I. 1.] *trans.* To put a space or interval between; to occupy or fill the space or interval between.

†**I·nterspeech.** 1579. [INTER- I. 2 a.] Speech between or among a number of persons; colloquy -1656.

Intersperse (intəɹspɔ̄·ɹs), *v.* 1566 (*entersparse*). [f. L. *interspers-*, **interspergere*, f. *inter* + *spargere.*] 1. *trans.* To scatter or sprinkle between or among other things; to mingle dispersedly or at intervals 1645. 2. To furnish, adorn, or diversify *with* things scattered about or mingled at intervals.

1. The way in which you have interspersed local traditions and stories KINGSLEY. 2. The face of the country was interspersed with groves GIBBON.

Interspersion (intəɹspɔ̄·ɹʃən). 1658. [f. prec.] The action of interspersing or condition of being interspersed.

Interspinal (intəɹspəi·năl), *a.* 1831. [INTER- II. 2 a.] = next.

Interspinous (intəɹspəi·nəs), *a.* 1839. [INTER- II. 2 a.] *Anat.* Situated between the spines or spinous processes of vertebræ.

†**Interspira·tion.** 1623. [ad. L. *interspirationem*; see next.] A taking breath between; a breathing space -1656.

†**Interspi·re**, *v.* 1647. [ad. L. *interspirare*, f. *inter* + *spirare* to breathe.] To take breath between; to pause, take rest. H. MORE.

Interstate, inter-state (i·ntəɹˌstēⁱt), *a.* *U.S.* 1845. [INTER- II. 3.] Lying, extending, or carried on between states; pertaining to the mutual relations of the States of the American Union.

Trusts are purely State, and not i. affairs 1899.

Interstellar (intəɹste·lăɹ), *a.* 1626. [INTER- II. 2 a.] Situated between the stars; occupying or passing through the spaces between the stars.

A comet arriving from remote i. space PROCTOR. So **Interste·llary** *a.* (Dicts.)

Intersternal: see INTER- II. 2 a.

Interstice (intɔ̄·ɹstis, i·ntəɹstis). 1603. [ad. L. *interstitium* space between, f. **interstit-*, *intersistere*, f. *inter* + *sistere* to stand; cf. F. *interstice.*] 1. An intervening space (usu. empty); *esp.* a relatively small or narrow space between things or the parts of a body; a narrow opening, chink, or crevice. 2. An intervening space of time; an interval between actions. Now *rare.* 1639. b. *spec.* in *Canon Law* (*pl.*) The intervals required between the reception of the various degrees of holy orders 1745.

1. The interstices of water are always found full of air 1756. 2. Long inter-regnums or interstices in government 1639. Hence **Intersticed** *a.* having interstices; also, fitted at intervals *with* something.

†**Intersti·nctive**, *a.* 1696. [f. L. *interstinctus*, *interstinguere* + -IVE.] Serving to divide or mark off. WALLIS.

Interstitial (intəɹsti·ʃăl), *a.* 1646. [f. L. *interstitium* (see INTERSTICE) + -AL.] 1. Of the nature of an interstice; forming interstices. 2. Of a thing: Pertaining to, existing in, or occupying interstices 1665. 3. Of a physical or morbid process: Taking place in the interstices of a body, and so affecting its internal structure 1807.

2. *I. tissue* (Anat.), the fine connective tissue lying between the cells of other tissue. *I. organs*, smaller organs of the body situated between larger ones. Hence **Intersti·tially** *adv.*

†**Intersti·tion.** ME. [ad. L. *interstitionem*; see INTERSTICE.] = INTERSTITIUM.

†‖**Interstitium** (intəɹsti·ʃiʊ̆m). *Pl.* **-stitia**, (†-a's), **-stitiums.** 1597. [L.; see INTERSTICE.] = INTERSTICE -1706.

Interstratification (-stræ·tifikē¹·ʃən). 1855. [INTER- I. 2 a.] The condition or fact of being interstratified; an interposed formation or deposit.

Interstratify (-stræ·tifəi), *v.* 1822. [INTER- I. 1 b.] 1. *trans.* in *pass.* Of geological strata: To be alternated or interspersed *with* other strata. 2. *intr.* To lie as strata between other strata 1880. Hence **Interstra·tified** *ppl. a.* placed as a stratum between other strata 1839.

Intertangle (intəɹtæ·ŋg'l), *v.* 1589. [INTER- I. 1 b.] *trans.* To tangle together; to intertwine confusedly. Hence **Interta·nglement**, intertangled state or condition.

Intertarsal: see INTER- *pref.*

†**Interte·x**, *v.* 1578. [ad. L. *intertexere*, f. *inter* + *texere* to weave.] *trans.* To weave together, intertwine –1666.

Intertexture (intəɹte·kstiŭɹ). 1649. [f. L. *intertext-*, ppl. stem of *intertexere* (see prec.) + -URE.] 1. The action of interweaving; the fact or condition of being interwoven. 2. quasi-*concr.* An intertwined or interwoven structure 1651.

2. I. firm Of thorny boughs COWPER.

Intertie (i·ntəɹtəi). 1703. [INTER- I. 2 b; but orig. a var. of *interdice*.] A horizontal piece of timber connecting two vertical pieces.

Intertissued (intəɹti·ʃiud), *ppl. a.* 1599. [f. OF. *entretissu* interwoven + -ED¹.] Interwoven.

†**Intertra·ffic.** 1603. [INTER- I. 2 a.] Traffic between two or more persons or places; reciprocal commerce –1640.

Intertranspi·cuous, *a.* [INTER- I. 2 a.] Transpicuous between or through each other. SHELLEY.

Intertransve·rse, *a.* 1831. [INTER- II. 2 a.] *Anat.* Situated between the transverse processes of the vertebræ.

Intertribal (intəɹtrəi·băl), *a.* 1862. [INTER- II. 2 c.] Existing or carried on between different tribes.

‖**Intertrigo** (intəɹtrəi·gō). 1706. [L. (for *interterigo*), f. **interterere* to rub against each other.] *Path.* Inflammation caused by the rubbing of one part of the surface of the skin against another.

Intertrochanteric: see INTER-.

Intertrochlear (-trǫ·kliăɹ), *a.* 1870. [INTER- II. 2 a.] Situated in the middle of the trochlear surface of a joint.

Intertropical (intəɹtrǫ·pikăl), *a.* 1794. [INTER- II. 2 a.] Of or pertaining to regions between the tropics; tropical.

Intertubular: see INTER-.

Intertwine (intəɹtwəi·n), *v.* 1641. [INTER- I. 1 b.] 1. *trans.* To twine (things) together; to interlace, intertwist, interweave. Also *intr.* for *refl.* 2. *trans.* To twine round and involve (*rare*) 1717. Hence **I·ntertwine** *sb.*, **Intertwi·nement**, the fact of intertwining; intertwined state; an intertwined formation. **Intertwi·ningly** *adv.* so as to i.

Intertwist (intəɹtwi·st), *v.* 1659. [INTER- I. 1 b.] *trans.* To twist one within another; to intertwine, intertangle. Hence **Intertwi·stingly** *adv.*

Interungular, -ungulate: see INTER-.

Interurban (intər,ɒ̄·ɹbăn), *a.* 1883. [f. INTER- II. 2 b + L. *urb-s* city + -AN.] Carried on between, or connecting, cities.

Interval (i·ntəɹvăl), *sb.* [ME. *enterval*, *intervall(e*, ult. (partly through Fr.) ad. L. *intervallum*, orig. 'space between ramparts', f. *inter* + *vallum* rampart.] 1. The period of time between two events, actions, etc., or between two parts of an action, etc.; a period of cessation; a pause, break. b. *spec.* The space of time intervening between two febrile paroxysms, or between any fits or periods of disease 1634. 2. The space of time intervening between two points of time; any intervening time 1616. 3. An open space lying between two things or two parts of one thing; a gap, opening 1489. 4. In N. America: = INTERVALE 3. 1684. 5. *Mus.* The difference of pitch between two musical sounds or notes 1609. 6. *fig.* Distance between persons in respect of position, beliefs, etc., or between things in respect of their qualities 1849.

1. The intervals of the play PEPYS. b. The interuals or good dayes of a Tertian Ague 1634. Phr. *Lucid i.*: see LUCID. 2. An i. of more than sixty years GROTE. Phr. *At* (†*by*) *intervals*, now and again, not continuously. 3. 'Twixt Host and Host but narrow space was left, A dreadful i. MILT. *P. L.* VI. 105. Short intervals of still water 1791. Phr. *At intervals*, here and there. Hence **Interva·llic** *a.* 1847.

Interval (i·ntəɹvăl), *v. rare.* 1630. [f. prec. sb.] †1. *intr.* To come between or in an interval; to form an interval –1632. 2. *trans.* (in *pass.*) To break or interrupt at intervals 1883.

2. A march of infinite light..intervaled indeed with eddies of shadow RUSKIN.

Intervale (i·ntəɹvēl). Now *Amer.* ME. [In former Eng. use, a var. of INTERVAL. Later, esp. in New England, assoc. w. *vale* (see sense 3).] †1. Of time: = INTERVAL *sb.* 1. –1682. †2. Of space: = INTERVAL *sb.* 3. –1684. 3. In N. America: A low level tract of land, esp. along a river; = INTERVAL *sb.* 4. Also *attrib.* 1653.

3. By intervales we mean those low lands which are adjacent to the rivers S. WILLIAMS.

†‖**Interva·llum.** *Pl.* **-valla, -vallums.** 1574. [L.; see INTERVAL *sb.*] = INTERVAL *sb.* 1, 2. –1647.

He shall laugh without Interuallums SHAKS.

Inter-'varsity, -vary: see INTER- *pref.*

Intervein (intəɹvē¹·n), *v.* 1615. [f. INTER- I. 1 a + VEIN *sb.* or *v.*] 1. *trans.* To intersect with or as with veins. 2. (In *pass.*) To place in alternate veins 1811.

1. White the rest With vermeil intervein'd CARY.

Intervene (intəɹvī·n), *v.* 1588. [ad. L. *intervenire*, f. *inter* + *venire*. Cf. F. *intervenir.*] 1. *intr.* To come in as something extraneous 1605. 2. To happen or take place between other events, or between points in time 1610. 3. To come in or between; to interpose (*spec.* in *Law*, cf. next) 1646. 4. To come, extend, or lie *between* 1621. †5. *trans.* To come between; to intercept; to prevent, hinder –1839.

1. What wonder if so near Looks i. and smiles MILT. *P. L.* IX. 222. 2. Some argument had intervened between them LAMB. 3. In all the Negotiations where he has intervened TEMPLE. 4. No clouds, no vapours i. DYER. 5. Woodlands of birch..and hazel ..intervening the different estates with natural sylvan marches DE QUINCEY.

Intervener¹ (intəɹvī·nəɹ). Rarely **-or.** 1621. [f. prec. vb. + -ER¹.] One who intervenes; *spec.* in *Law*, one who intervenes in a suit to which he was not originally a party.

Interve·ner². 1847. [f. INTERVENE *v.*, after *interpleader*, etc.] *Law.* The interposition of a person in a suit in an ecclesiastical court in defence of his own interest.

Intervenient (intəɹvī·niĕnt), *a.* (*sb.*) 1605. [ad. L. *intervenientem*, *intervenire*.] 1. That intervenes; that comes in as something extraneous. 2. Intervening in space, time, or action 1618. 3. *sb.* One who intervenes 1620.

2. On the horizon's verge, O'er i. waste WORDSW. Hence †**Interve·nience**, †**-ency**, intervention.

†**Interve·nt**, *v. rare.* 1593. [f. L. *intervent-*, *intervenire*.] *trans.* To come between, obstruct, thwart –1647.

Intervention (intəɹve·nʃən). ME. [ad. late L. *interventionem*. Cf. F. *intervention.*] 1. The action of intervening, 'stepping in', or interfering in any affair, so as to affect its course or issue. 2. Intermediate agency; the fact of coming in as an intermediary 1659. 3. The fact of coming or being situated between in space, time, or order 1645.

1. The i. of the allied powers between Greece and Turkey in 1827 BRANDE & COX. 2. Adam was framed immediately by God, without the i. of man or woman PEARSON. 3. Trade Winds..are frequently impeded by the i. of Islands 1671. Hence **Interve·ntionist**, one who favours i., esp. in international affairs 1839.

Interventor (intəɹve·ntəɹ). 1727. [a. L.] 1. *Eccl.* = INTERCESSOR 3. 2. *U.S.* A mine-inspector.

Interventricular (i:ntəɹventri·kiŭlăɹ), *a.* 1836. [INTER- II. 2 a.] *Anat.* Situated between the ventricles (of the heart or brain).

†**Intervenue.** [a. obs. F. *inter-*, *entrevenue*, f. *inter-*, *entrevenir* to INTERVENE; cf. *avenue*, *revenue*.] Intervention. SIR H. BLOUNT.

†**Interve·rt**, *v.* 1600. [ad L. *intervertere*, f. *inter* + *vertere* to turn.] 1. To divert another way; to alienate, misapply, misuse –1648; *esp.* to appropriate, embezzle –1850. 2. To give a different turn to –1825.

1. Interverting, embezeling their masters estates TRAPP. Hence †**Interve·rsion**, embezzlement 1676.

Intervertebral (intəɹvə̄·ɹtĭbrăl), *a.* 1782. [INTER- II. 2 a.] *Anat.* Situated between vertebræ. Hence **Interve·rtebrally** *adv.* between vertebræ.

Interview (i·ntəɹviū), *sb.* 1514. [a. F. *entrevue*, vbl. sb. from *entrevoir* to have a glimpse of, *s'entrevoir* to see each other, f. *entre-* (ENTER-) + *voir* :—L. *videre*.] 1. A meeting of persons face to face, esp. for the purpose of formal conference on some point. b. *spec.* A meeting between a representative of the press and some one from whom he seeks to obtain statements for publication 1869. †2. Mutual view (*of* each other) (*rare*) –1667. †3. Inspection –1586; a view, glance, glimpse (*of* a thing) –1719.

1. Of Ceremonies in the enterview of Kings FLORIO. b. It is claimed for him [Joseph M'Cullagh, of St. Louis] that he was the inventor of the modern newspaper i. 1897. 2. At i. both stood A while MILT. *P. L.* VI. 555.

†**Interview**, *v.*¹ 1548. [ad. F. *entrevoir*, *s'entrevoir*, pa. pple. *entrevu*, after VIEW *v.*] 1. a. *trans.* To have a personal meeting with (each other). b. *intr.* To meet together in person. HALL. 2. *trans.* To get a view of; to glance at –1624.

Interview (i·ntəɹviū), *v.*² 1869. [f. INTERVIEW *sb.*] *trans.* To have an interview with (a person); *spec.* To talk with so as to elicit statements for publication.

A northwest newspaper, in which I have been 'interviewed', and private conversation reported to the public LONGF. Hence **I·nterviewing** *vbl. sb.* **Interviewee·**, one who is interviewed.

Interviewer (i·ntəɹviū,əɹ). 1869. [f. prec. + -ER¹.] One who interviews; *spec.* a journalist who interviews a person with the object of obtaining matter for publication.

Intervisible: see INTER- *pref.* I. 2 a.

Intervisit (intəɹvi·zit), *v.* 1609. [ad. F. *entrevisiter*, f. *entre-* (INTER- I. 1 b) + *visiter*.] *intr.* To exchange visits.

Intervital (intəɹvəi·tăl), *a. rare.* 1850. [INTER- II. 2.] Existing between two lives or stages of existence.

[There] comes no faintest whisper from the i. gloom FARRAR.

Intervocal (intəɹvōᵘ·kăl), *a. rare.* 1891. [f. INTER- II. 2 a + L. *vocalis* vocal, a vowel.] Occurring between vowels. So **Intervoca·lic** *a.* (more usual) 1887.

Intervolution (intəɹvǫl¹ū·ʃən). 1850. [f. next.] Intervolved condition; a winding.

Intervolve (intəɹvǫ·lv), *v.* 1667. [f. L. *inter* (INTER- I. 1) + *volvere* to roll, wind; cf. *involve*.] *trans.* To wind or roll up (things) within each other; to wind or involve (something) within the coils of something else. Also *intr.*

Mazes intricate, Eccentric, intervolv'd MILT.

Interweave (intəɹwī·v), *v.* Pa. t. **-wove**, pa. pple. **-woven** (†**-wove**); also †**-weaved.** 1578. [f. INTER- I. 1 b + WEAVE *v.*] 1. *trans.* To weave together, as the warp and woof of a fabric; to interlace; to intertwine. 2. *transf.* and *fig.* To intermingle as if by weaving; to intertwine intricately; to blend intimately 1589.

1. Two Olives..With roots intwin'd, and branches interwove POPE. A..method of interweaving gold with wool or linen 1870. 2. The moral law is..interwoven into our very nature BUTLER.

Interwind (intəɹwəi·nd), *v.* Pa. t. and pple. **-wound** (waund). 1693. [INTER- I. 1 b.] *trans.* To wind (things) into or through each other; to wind together; to intertwine, intertwist. Also *fig.* Also *intr.* (for *refl.*)

Interwish, etc.: see INTER- *pref.*

Interwork (intəɹwɒ̄·ɹk), *v.* Pa. t. and pple. **-wrought** (-rǭ·t), **-worked** (-wɒ̄·ɹkt). 1603. [INTER- I. 1 b.] *trans.* To work one thing into and through another; to combine by interpenetration. b. *intr.* To interact 1855.

Interwoven (intəɪwōᵘ·v'n), *ppl. a.* 1647. [pa. pple. of INTERWEAVE *v.*] Woven together; interlaced; intricately entangled.

Interwreathe (-rī·ð), *v.* 1658. [INTER- I. 1 b.] *trans.* To wreathe together; to intertwine into, or as in, a wreath.

†**Inte·stable,** *a.* 1590. [ad. late L. *intestabilis*, f. *in-* (IN-³) + *testabilis*, f. *testari*; see INTESTATE.] 1. Legally incapable of making or of benefiting by a will -1767. 2. Disqualified from being a witness or giving evidence -1656. Hence †Intestabi·lity.

Intestacy (inte·stăsi). 1767. [f. INTESTATE *a.*; see -ACY.] *Law.* The condition or fact of dying intestate or without having made a will.

Intestate (inte·stĕt). ME. [ad. OF. *intestat*, L. *intestatus*, f. *in-* (IN-³) + *testatus*, *testari* to bear witness, to make a will.] A. *adj.* 1. Of a person: Not having made a will. 2. Of things: Not disposed of by will 1538.

1. He..died i. JOHNSON. *fig. Rich. III*, IV. iv. 128. 2. The admynystratyon of i. godys 1538.

B. *sb.* One who dies intestate 1658.

Intestinal (inte·stinăl, intestəi·năl), *a.* 1599. [ad. med. or mod.L. *intestinalis*. Cf. F. *intestinal*.] 1. Of or pertaining to the intestines; found in or affecting the intestines. b. Having an intestine or enteron; opp. to ANENTEROUS. 2. = INTESTINE *a.* 1. MRS. BROWNING.

1. I. worms 1797. The i. tube 1851.

Intestine (inte·stin), *sb.* 1533. [ad. L. *intestinum* (also used), adj. neut. used subst.; see next.] 1. The lower part of the alimentary canal, from the pyloric end of the stomach to the anus, called pop. the bowels or guts. In ordinary use, commonly pl.; the singular is applied to each of the two distinct parts, the *small intestine* (comprising the duodenum, jejunum, and ileum), and the *large intestine* (comprising the cæcum, colon, and rectum), and also, in scientific use, to the canal as a whole; in biology, it often includes the whole alimentary canal from the mouth downward 1597. †2. *fig.* The inmost part or member. LD. BERNERS.

Intestine (inte·stin), *a.* 1535. [ad. L. *intestinus*, f. *intus* within. Cf. F. *intestin*.] 1. Internal with regard to a country or people; domestic, civil. Also *fig.* †2. Internal with regard to human nature or the nature of things; inward, innate (*rare*) -1678. †3. Seated in the bowels; intestinal -1727. 4. Internal with reference to any thing or place. (*Obs.* exc. as *fig.* from 1 or 3.) 1664.

1. The i. shocke, And furious cloze of ciuill Butchery SHAKS. I. feuds PRIOR, foes 1764, division 1869. 4. All i. Works as Wainscot, floors [etc.] EVELYN. Phr. *I. motion*: motion entirely within, or among the molecules of, a body.

†**I·ntext.** [? ad. L. *intextus* an interweaving, or ? f. IN *adv.* + TEXT *sb.*] The text or matter of a book. HERRICK.

Intextine (inte·kstin). Also **intexine.** 1835. [f. L. *intus* + EXTINE.] *Bot.* An inner coating of the pollen grain within the extine.

Inte·xture, *v. rare.* 1856. [f. L. *intext-*, ppl. stem of *intexere* to weave in + -URE.] *trans.* To weave or work in. Hence Inte·xtured *ppl. a.*

Inthral(l, etc.: see ENTHRAL(L, etc.

†**Inthro·ng,** *v.* 1600 [f. IN-¹ + THRONG *v.*] *intr.* To throng, press, or crowd in. FAIRFAX.

†**Inthro·nizate,** *ppl. a.* Also **-tron-.** 1470. [ad. late L. *int(h)ronizatus*, *int(h)ronizare*.] *trans.* To enthrone -1577. Hence †Inthronization, obs. var. of ENTHRONIZATION.

Intice, etc., obs. var. ENTICE, etc.

Intil(l (ME.), Sc. and n. dial. ff. INTO.

Intimacy (i·ntimăsi). 1641. [f. INTIMATE *a.*; see -ACY.] 1. The quality or condition of being intimate; close familiarity; *euphem.* for illicit sexual intercourse 1676. b. Closeness of observation, knowledge, or the like 1714. 2. Intimate connexion or union (*rare*) 1720.

1. Sir Thomas, drawing back from intimacies in general JANE AUSTEN. 2. The Union and I. between Father and Son WATERLAND.

†**Intimado** (intimā·do). 1682. [Altered f. INTIMATE *sb.*; see -ADO.] = INTIMATE *sb.* -1823.

His *intimados*..were in the world's eye a ragged regiment LAMB.

Intimate (i·ntimĕt). 1632. [ad. L. *intimatus*, *intimare*, f. *intimus* inmost, as *sb.* a close friend, f. *intus* within; see INTIMATE *v.*]

A. *adj.* 1. Inmost, most inward, deep-seated; hence, Essential, intrinsic. Now chiefly in scientific use. 2. Pertaining to the inmost thoughts or feelings 1671. 3. Close in acquaintance or association; characterized by familiarity; very familiar. Also *transf.* of things: Pertaining to or dealing with such close personal relations. 1635. b. *euphem.* of illicit sexual intercourse 1889. 4. Of knowledge or acquaintance: Close 1680. 5. Of a relation between things: Very close 1692.

1. The i. structure of matter and ether 1878. 2. I knew From i. impulse MILT. *Sams.* 223. 3. A Knight who was an i. friend of his 1635. 4. An i. knowledge of his character *Junius Lett.* 5. Pride..is of such I...Connexion with Ingratitude SOUTH. Hence I·ntimate-ly *adv.* 1637, -ness (*rare*) 1642.

B. *sb.* A person with whom one is intimate; a very close friend or associate 1659.

Intimate (i·ntimeɪt), *v.* Pa. pple. **intimated**; also †**intimate.** 1538. [f. late L. *intimat-*, *intimare* to put or bring into, drive or press into, to make known, announce, notify, f. *intimus*.] 1. *trans.* To make known formally, to notify, state; †formerly, to proclaim, to declare (war). 2. To make known indirectly; hence, to signify, indicate; to imply, to hint at 1590. b. To mention indirectly 1634. †3. To make intimate, familiarize -1654.

1. He incontinente did proclaime and i. open warre HALL. This resolution she intimated to the leaders of both factions ROBERTSON. 2. The Apostle expresses one duty and intimates another JER. TAYLOR.

Intimation (intimēᵎ·ʃən). 1442. [a. F., ad. late L. *intimationem*; see prec.] 1. The action of intimating; formal notification; †formerly, declaration (of war). b. *Law.* Notification of a requirement made by law, and of the penalty in case of default. ? *Obs.* 1632. 2. An expression by sign or token; an indication; a suggestion, a hint 1531.

1. They made an edict, with an i., that whosoever killed a storke should be banished HOLLAND. 2. I have often had intimations in dreams JOWETT.

†**I·ntime,** *a.* 1618. [a. F. *intime*, or ad. L. *intimus*.] = INTIMATE *a.* -1678.

Intimidate (inti·mideɪt), *v.* 1646. [f. med. L. *intimidat-*, *intimidare*, f. *in-* (IN-²) + *timidus*; see -ATE³, and cf. F. *intimider*.] *trans.* To render timid, inspire with fear; to overawe, cow; now, *esp.* to force to or deter from some action by threats or violence.

Unless you can find means to corrupt or i. the jury *Junius Lett.* Hence Inti·midator. Inti·midatory *a.* of intimidating nature or tendency.

Intimidation (intimidēᵎ·ʃən). 1658. [n. of action from prec.] The action of intimidating or making afraid; the fact or condition of being intimidated; now, *esp.* the use of threats or violence to force to or restrain from some action.

What was denied to reason and policy is surrendered to i. J. W. CROKER.

Intimity (inti·mĭti). 1617. [f. L. *intimus* + -ITY; cf. F. *intimité*.] †1. = INTIMACY 1. COLLINS. 2. Intimate quality or nature; inwardness; privacy 1889.

†**I·ntimous,** *a.* 1619. [f. L. *intimus* + -OUS.] = INTIMATE *a.* -1665.

Intinction (inti·ŋkʃən). 1559. [ad. late L. *intinctionem*, *inting(u)ere*.] †1. The action of dipping in; a dyeing; that in which something has been dipped, an infusion -1658. 2. *Eccl.* The action of dipping the bread in the wine at the Eucharist, so that the two kinds may be administered conjointly 1872.

†**Intincti·vity.** 1794. [f. IN-³ + L. *tinct-*, *tingere* to dye + -IVE + -ITY; prob. after *inactivity*.] The quality of not communicating colour.

Intine (i·ntin). 1835. [f. L. *int-us* + -INE.] *Bot.* The inner membrane of the pollen grain.

Intire, Intitle, obs. ff. ENTIRE, ENTITLE.

Intitulation (intitiŭlēᵎ·ʃən). Also †**en-.** 1456. [? a. obs. F., or ad. med.L. or L. type *intitulationem.] 1. The action of entitling; a superscription, title. 2. The action of bestowing a title; a designation 1586.

Intitule (inti·tiŭl), *v.* Also †**en-.** 1483. [a. OF. *en-*, *intituler*, ad. late L. *intitulare*, f. *in-* (IN-²) + *titulus* TITLE.] 1. = ENTITLE *v.*, in various senses. †2. To prefix *to* a book the name of a person to whom it is dedicated -1691. †3. To dedicate *to* by name or title -1707.

2. I intituled Your Majesty to a Work EVELYN. 3. The Society [of the Garter] is entituled to St. George 1707.

Into (i·ntŭ), *prep.* OE. [Orig. the two words, *in* adv., *to* prep., in which the adv. expresses general direction, and the prep. has reference to a particular point or place.] *General sense*:—The prep. expressing the motion which results in the position expressed by IN, or which is directed towards that position.

I. Of motion or direction; ordinary uses. 1. Expressing motion to a position within a space or thing. Regularly after verbs of going, coming, bringing, putting, and the like. 2. In reference to non-physical things, treated as having extension or content OE. 3. a. Introducing the substance or form into which anything turns or grows, or is changed, moulded, fashioned, or made ME. b. Introducing the condition or result brought about by some action 1540. 4. Introducing the parts produced by division, breaking, folding, and the like ME. 5. Used techn. with the vb. MULTIPLY. 6. As an addition or accession to; as *into the bargain*. [Perh. = in, to the bargain; cf. IN *adv.* I. 3.] 1646. 7. Expressing direction without actual motion, after *turn*, *look*, *search*, etc. 1605. 8. Introducing a period of time to the midst of which anything advances or continues 1594.

1. Come into the garden, Maud TENNYSON. A.. limitation which can easily be read into deed or will 1895. *ellipt.* At dawn he is into Bonair KIPLING. 2. These things..beaing beaten into the Dukes minde MORE. To fall into errour 1551. What Measures the Allies must enter into STEELE. 3. a. The twilight thickened into night W. IRVING. b. Persecuted into insurrection 1849. 7. If you can looke into the Seedes of Time SHAKS. 8. We had now got into the month of March DICKENS.

II. Obs. senses. †1. Unto, even to; to the very..-1548. †2. Towards -1652. †3. Until, on to, up to (a time or date) -1534. †4. Unto, to (a thing or person) -1611. †5. Defining the part of anything in which it is penetrated, pierced, etc. -1788.

4. That he enchants Societies into him *Cymb.* I. vi. 167. 5. I..fired again, and shot him into the head DE FOE.

III. Of position: = IN. (After 1400, *Sc.*)

To laugh wi' tears into its een RAMSAY.

In-toed (stress variable), *a.* 1824. [IN *adv.*] Having the toes turned inwards.

Intolerable (intǫ·lĕrăb'l), *a.* (*adv.*) ME. [ad. L. *intolerabilis*; see IN-³ and TOLERABLE.] 1. That cannot be tolerated, borne, or put up with; unendurable, insupportable, insufferable. †b. Loosely, as a strong intensive: Excessive, extreme, very great. (Cf. *awful*.) -1725. 2. That cannot be withstood ME. 3. *adv.* Intolerably; also, Exceedingly, extremely -1716.

1. A cloudless, i. sun 1861. I. conduct FROUDE. b. But one halfe penny-worth of Bread to this intollerable deale of Sacke? SHAKS. 3. Her onely fault ..Is, that she is intollerable curst *Tam. Shr.* I. ii. 89. Hence Into·lerabi·lity, Into·lerableness. Into·lerably *adv.*

Intolerance (intǫ·lĕrăns). 1765. [ad. L *intolerantia*, f. *intolerantem*.] 1. The fact or habit of not tolerating (something); inability, or unwillingness, to tolerate or endure some particular thing. Const. *of*. 2. *spec.* Absence of tolerance for difference of opinion or practice, esp. in religious matters; denial of the right to differ 1790.

1. I. of official peculation 1844. 2. The great antagonist of i. is not humanity, but Knowledge BUCKLE. So †Into·lerancy 1623.

Intolerant (intǫ·lĕrănt), *a.* (*sb.*) 1735. [ad. L. *intolerantem*, f. *in-* (IN-³) + *tolerantem*, *tolerare* to TOLERATE.] 1. Not having the habit or capacity of tolerating (something); unable, or unwilling, to endure (something specified). Const. *of*. b. *Forestry.* Incapable of enduring shade. *U.S.* 1898. 2. *spec.* That does not tolerate opinions or practices different from one's own, esp. in religious matters; that denies the right to differ; disposed to persecute those who differ 1765. 3. *sb.* An intolerant person 1765.

1. The powers of human bodies being limited and i.

of excesses ARBUTHNOT (J.). Some patients are very *i.* of arsenic 1880. **2.** The national temper of the Jews was i. PALEY. Hence **Into·lerantly** *adv.* So †**Into·lerating** *a.* 1710.

Intoleration (intǫlĕrē¹·ʃən). *rare.* 1611. [IN-³.] Want of toleration; intolerance.

Intomb(e, obs. f. ENTOMB.

‖**Intonaco, -ico** (intǭ·năko, -iko). 1806. [It. *intonico,* †*intonaco* plaster, f. *intonicare,* L. type **intunicare,* f. *tunica* coat, TUNIC.] The final coating of plaster spread upon a wall or other surface, esp. for fresco painting.

†**I·ntonate,** *v.*¹ *rare.* 1626. [f. L. *intonat-, intonare,* f. *in-* (IN-²) + *tonare* to thunder.] *trans.* To thunder forth –1739.

Intonate (i·ntoneit), *v.*² 1795. [f. ppl. stem of med.L. *intonare,* f. *in-* (IN-²) + *tonus* TONE.] **1.** *trans.* To INTONE. **2.** To utter or pronounce with a particular tone 1823. **3.** *Phonetics.* To emit or pronounce with sonant vibration; to voice. WHITNEY.

1. Savonarola .. intonating .. the psalm *Exurgat Deus* ROSCOE.

Intonation (intonē¹·ʃən). 1620. [f. med.L. *intonare* to INTONE.] **1.** In *Church Music.* The opening phrase of a plain-song melody, preceding the reciting-note, and usually sung either by the priest alone, or by one or a few of the choristers; the recitation of this. **2.** The action of intoning, or reciting in a singing voice 1788. **3.** The utterance or production of musical tones; in reference to manner or style, esp. to exactitude of pitch 1776. **4.** Manner of utterance of the tones of the voice in speaking; accent 1791.

4. That unfortunate i. of Aberdeenshire 1791.

Intonator (i·ntonē¹tə1). 1875. [f. as INTONATION.] A monochord or single string stretched across a flat sound-board, for the study of musical intervals.

Intone (intōu·n), *v.* Also **en-.** 1485. [ad. med.L. *intonare;* in form *entone,* prob. a. OF. *entoner.*] **1.** *trans.* To utter in musical tones; to chant; *spec.* To recite in a singing voice; usu. to recite in monotone. Also *absol.* or *intr.* **2.** To sing the opening phrase of a plain-song melody at the beginning of a chant, canticle, etc. 1880. **3.** = INTONATE *v.*² 2. 1860. **4.** *intr.* 'To make a slow protracted noise' (J.) 1728.

1. The Clergy began to i. their Litany MILMAN. **4.** So swells each wind-pipe; Ass intones to Ass POPE. Hence **Into·nement, en-** (*rare*), intonation.

Intorsion (intǭ·ɹʃən). 1760. [a. F., ad. L. *intorsionem,* f. *intorquere;* see next.] The action of twisting; *spec.* in *Bot.* the twisting of the stem of a plant.

Intort (intǭ·ɹt), *v.* Now *rare.* 1615. [f. L. *intort-, intorquere,* f. *in-* (IN-²) + *torquere* to twist.] *trans.* To twist or curl inwards. Perh. only in the pa. pple. **Into·rted.**

In toto: see IN *Lat. prep.*

I·ntou:rist. 1930. [IN *adv.*] The name of the State Travel Bureau of the U.S.S.R.

Into·xicant. 1863. [ad. med.L. *intoxicantem;* see -ANT.] **a.** *adj.* Intoxicating 1882. **b.** *sb.* An intoxicating substance or liquor.

Intoxicate (intǫ·ksikĕt), *ppl. a.* (*sb.*) ME. [ad. med.L. *intoxicatus;* see next. In later use taken as short for *intoxicated.*] †**1.** Rendered poisonous; empoisoned –1637, killed by poison –1607. **2.** Intoxicated, inebriated (*lit.* and *fig.*) 1500. **3.** *sb.* One who is intoxicated. H. WALPOLE.

2. The mind i. With present objects WORDSW.

Intoxicate (intǫ·ksikeit), *v.* 1529. [f. med.L. *intoxicat-, intoxicare,* f. *in-* (IN-²) + *toxicare* to poison, f. *toxicum* = Gr. τοξικόν poison.] †**1.** *trans.* To poison –1684. **2.** To stupefy or render unconscious or delirious, madden with a drug or alcoholic liquor; to inebriate, make drunk 1598. Also *absol.* **3.** *fig.* †**a.** To 'poison'; to corrupt morally or spiritually –1860. **b.** To stupefy or excite as with a drug or alcoholic liquor 1591.

2. It..goeth downe very pleasantly, intoxicating weake braines HAKLUYT. *absol.* Cordials, which heat and i. BERKELEY. **3. b.** So new a Power will undoubtedly i. Persons who were not born to it CHAS. I. Hence **Into·xicated** (with alcoholic liquor 1576, *fig.* 1692). **Into·xicating** *ppl. a.,* **-ly** *adv.*

Intoxication (intǫksikē¹·ʃən). LYDGATE. [f. INTOXICATE *v.*] **1.** The action of poisoning; the state of being poisoned; an instance of this. *Obs.* exc. *Med.* **2.** The action of stupefying with a drug or alcoholic liquor; the making drunk or inebriated; the condition of being so stupefied or made drunk 1646. **3.** *fig.* †**a.** The poisoning of the moral or mental faculties; a cause of this –1728. **b.** The action or power of highly exciting the mind; elation beyond the bounds of sobriety 1712.

3. b. The i. of wealth and power THIRLWALL.

Intra- (intră), *prefix,* repr. L. *intra* 'on the inside, within'. Sometimes confused with INTER-. Chiefly in adjs., in which it stands in prepositional relation to the sb. implied in the second element.

Intra-a·cinous, occurring within an acinus or racemose gland. **Intraca·rpellary,** *Bot.* situated within a carpel; also (*erron.*) between or among carpels (prop. *intercarpellary*). **Intrace·llular,** *Biol.* situated or occurring within the substance of a cell (as digestion in Protozoa); hence **Intrace·llularly** *adv.* **Intra-ecclesia·stical,** existing or occurring within a church. **Intralo·cular,** situated within the loculi or chambers of some structure. **Intrama·rginal,** situated on the inner side of the margin, *e.g.* of a leaf. **Intramercu·rial, -ian,** *Astron.* situated within the orbit of Mercury. **Intrana·sal,** situated or occurring within the nose. **Intranu·clear,** situated within the nucleus of a cell. **Intraparo·chial,** existing or occurring within a parish. **Intrastro·mal,** situated within the stroma or connective tissue of an organ or structure. **Intraterrito·rial,** situated or contained within a territory. **Intrathora·cic,** situated or occurring within the thorax. **Intra-u·rban,** carried on within a city. **Intrava·lvular,** situated within or between valves (prop. *intervalvular*). **Intra-vite·lline** [L. *vitellus* yoke], occurring within the yolk of an egg.

Intracranial (-krē¹·niăl), *a.* 1847. [f. INTRA- + L. *cranium;* cf. *cranial.*] Situated or occurring within the cranium or skull.

Intractable (intræ·ktăb'l), *a.* (*sb.*) 1545. [ad. L. *intractabilis;* see IN-³ and TRACTABLE.] **1.** Of persons, etc.: Not to be guided; uncontrollable, refractory, stubborn. **2.** Of things: Not easily treated or dealt with; resisting treatment or effort 1607. **3.** *sb.* An unmanageable person 1883.

1. An i. people 1548, animal 1837, will 1878. **2.** Lands..of a boggy i. character 1861. Hence **Intractabi·lity, Intra·ctableness,** the quality of being i. **Intra·ctably** *adv.*

Intractile (intræ·ktil, -əil), *a. rare.* 1626. [IN-³.] †**1.** Not tractile; incapable of being drawn out in length; not ductile. BACON. **2.** = INTRACTABLE *a.* 2. 1880.

†**Intra·do.** 1640. [ad. Sp. *entrada* entry = late L. *intrata;* see ENTRADA and -ADO 2.] **1.** A formal entry –1716. **2.** Income; revenue –1672. **3.** An entering upon. H. L'ESTRANGE.

2. Their *Intrado* would never support their ordinary charges 1672.

Intrados (intrē¹·dǫs). 1772. [a. F., f. L. *intra* + F. *dos* the back.] *Arch.* The lower or interior curve of an arch; *spec.* the lower curve of the voussoirs or stones which immediately form the arch. Cf. EXTRADOS.

Intrafoliaceous (-fōu₁li₁ē¹·ʃəs), *a.* 1760. [f. INTRA- + L. *folium;* see FOLIACEOUS.] *Bot.* Situated on the inner side of a leaf.

Intralobular (intrălǫ·biŭlăɹ), *a.* 1839. [f. INTRA- + LOBULE; cf. *lobular.*] *Anat.* Situated or occurring within the lobes of an organ or structure; as, the *i. bile-vessels,* the biliary capillaries.

Intramolecular (-mole·kiŭlăɹ), *a.* 1884. [INTRA- *pref.*] Situated, existing, or occurring within a molecule or the molecules of a body or substance.

Intramundane (-mʊ·ndē¹n), *a.* 1845. [f. INTRA- + L. *mundus;* cf. *mundane.*] Situated or existing within the world (i. e. this world, or the material or created world).

Intramural (intrămiū°·răl), *a.* 1846. [f. INTRA- + L. *murus;* cf. *mural.*] **1.** Situated, existing, or performed within the walls of a city or building. **2.** *Anat., Path.,* and *Biol.* Situated within the substance of the wall of a hollow organ, or of a cell 1879.

Intranscalent (intrɑnskē¹·lĕnt), *a.* 1846. [f. IN-³ + TRANSCALENT, after *transparent.*] Impervious to heat. Hence **Intransca·lency.**

Intransferable (intrɑ·nsfĕrăb'l, intrɑnsfǝ̄·răb'l), *a.* 1853. [IN-³.] Incapable of being transferred.

Intransgressible (intrɑnsgre·sĭb'l), *a.* 1603. [IN-³.] That cannot or may not be transgressed.

†**Intra·nsient,** *a.* 1650. [IN-³.] Not passing over; not passing to another by succession –1717.

Intransigent (intrɑ·nsidʒĕnt). Also **-eant.** 1879. [a. F. *intransigeant* (ęntrănzizaṅ), from Sp. *los intransigentes,* the party of the Extreme Left in the Spanish Cortes, and in 1873–4 the extreme Republicans in Spain; f. L. *in-* (IN-³) + *transigentem, transigere* to come to an understanding, f. *trans* across + *agere* to act.]

A. *adj.* That refuses to come to terms; uncompromising, irreconcilable 1881.

The advancing tide of *intransigeant* radicalism 1883.

B. *sb.* An irreconcilable (in politics); an uncompromising Republican 1879.

Certain of the Intransigents..are averse to a reconciliation between Italy and the Papal See 1899. So **Intra·nsigence, -e·ance** 1882.

Intransitive (intrɑ·nsitiv), *a.* (*sb.*) 1612. [ad. L. *intransitivus* not passing over (Priscian), f. *in-* (IN-³) + *transire.*] **1.** *Gram.* Of verbs and their construction: Expressing action which does not pass over to an object; not taking a direct object. (See TRANSITIVE, NEUTER.) **b.** as *sb.* An intransitive verb 1824. **2.** That does not pass on to another person, or beyond certain limits (*rare*) 1641. **3.** *Math.* In the theory of groups, opp. to TRANSITIVE, q.v. 1902.

2. And then it is for the image sake, and so far is i.; but whatever is paid more to the image is transitive, and passes further JER. TAYLOR. Hence **Intra·nsitively** *adv.* in an i. manner.

In transitu: see IN *Lat. prep.*

Intransla·table, *a.* 1690. [IN-³.] Untranslatable.

Intransmi·ssible, *a.* 1656. [IN-³.] Not transmissible.

Intransmu·table, *a.* 1691. [IN-³.] Not transmutable or changeable into something else. Hence **Intransmutabi·lity.**

Intrant (i·ntrănt). 1560. [ad. L. *intrantem, intrare* to enter.] **A.** *sb.* **1.** One who enters; an incomer (*rare*). **b.** One who enters into holy orders 1637. **c.** One who makes legal entry 1592. †**2.** Formerly, in the University of St. Andrews, a student chosen by each nation for the election of the Rector –1819.

1. The school in which the i. had been previously educated is specified MASSON.

B. *adj.* Entering; that enters 1803.

Intra-ocular (intră₁ǫ·kiŭlăɹ), *a.* 1826. [f. INTRA- + L. *oculus;* cf. *ocular.*] Situated or occurring within the eyeball. (Also erron. for *interocular.*)

Intrap, obs. f. ENTRAP *v.*

Intrapetiolar (intrăpe·tiǒlăɹ), *a.* 1864. [f. INTRA- + PETIOLE; cf. *petiolar.*] *Bot.* Situated within, or on the inner side of, the petiole or leaf-stalk; applied **a.** to an axillary bud formed immediately under the base of the petiole and surrounded by it so as not to appear until the leaf has fallen; **b.** to a stipule, or pair of confluent stipules, between the petiole and the axis.

Intratropical (-trǫ·pikăl), *a.* 1811. [INTRA- *pref.*] Situated or occurring within the tropics.

Intra-uterine (intră₁yū·tĕrin, -əin), *a.* 1835. [f. INTRA- + L. *uterus;* cf. *uterine.*] Situated, occurring, or passed within the uterus or womb; relating to this stage of an animal's life.

Intravenous (intrăvī·nəs), *a.* 1847. [f. INTRA- + L. *vena* vein; cf. *venous.*] Existing or taking place within a vein or the veins.

Intraventricular (-ventri·kiŭlăɹ), *a.* 1882. [f. INTRA- + L. *ventriculus, -um* VENTRICLE; cf. *ventricular.*] *Anat.* Situated or contained within a ventricle of the brain or heart.

Intreasure, etc.: see ENTREASURE, etc.

†**Intreatable,** *a.* 1509. [ad. F. *intraitable,* f. *traiter* to treat, after L. *intractabilis;* see INTRACTABLE.] That cannot be treated with; inexorable –1598.

Intrench (intre·nʃ), *v.* 1754. [f. IN-[1] + TRENCH.] **1.** *trans.* To make a trench in; to furrow. **2.** Var. of ENTRENCH *v.*

†**Intre·nchant,** *a. rare.* [f. IN-[3] + TRENCHANT *a.*] Used passively: Incapable of being cut. *Macb.* V. viii. 9.

Intrenchment: see ENTRENCHMENT.

Intrepid (intre·pid), *a.* 1627. [ad. L. *intrepidus,* f. *in-* (IN-[3]) + *trepidus* alarmed.] Fearless; undaunted; daring; brave.

Is there to be no pride in i. patriotism? 1833. Hence **Intre·pidly** *adv.*, **-ness.**

Intrepidity (intrĭpi·dĭti). 1704. [f. as prec. + -ITY.] The quality of being intrepid; fearlessness; firmness of mind in the presence of danger; courage.

I. in the discharge of professional duty MACKINTOSH.

†**I·ntricable,** *a.* 1540. [f. L. *intricare* to entangle; see INTRICATE *a.* and -ABLE.] Entangling, perplexing; entangled –1621.

Intricacy (i·ntrikăsi). 1602. [f. next; see -ACY.] **1.** The quality of being intricate; complexity; complicated condition. **2.** quasi-*concr.* A complication; a perplexing difficulty 1611.

1. A buisines of much intricasie 1619. The beauty of a composed i. of form HOGARTH. **2.** A long i. of passages SCOTT.

Intricate (i·ntrikĕt), *a.* 1470. [ad. L. *intricatus, intricare,* f. *in-* (IN-[2]) + *tricæ* trifles, tricks, perplexities, *tricari* to raise difficulties, etc.] **1.** Perplexingly entangled or involved; complicated 1579. **2.** Of thoughts, statements, etc.: Perplexingly complicated in meaning; involved; obscure 1470. †**3.** Ensnared, entangled –1528.

1. Wrestling amongst i. paths of Rockes 1632. A Face I. as the Law COWLEY. I. and narrow lanes SCOTT. **2.** He..could..make the intricat'st anigmas plain 1683. The i. and subtle rule which was then in force 1849. Hence **I·ntricate-ly** *adv.*, **-ness.**

Intricate (i·ntrikeit), *v.* Now *rare.* 1548. [f. L. *intricat-, intricare*; see prec.] **1.** *trans.* To render intricate; to make involved; to complicate 1564. **2.** To entangle or ensnare; to involve in toils; to perplex.

1. How ever the matter may be intricated by passing through many perhaps unknowing hands BP. HALL.

†**Intrica·tion.** ME. [ad. med.L. *intricationem* (see INTRICATE *a.*).] The action of intricating; intricated condition; complication, entanglement –1773.

†‖**Intri·go.** 1648. [It.] = INTRIGUE *sb.* –1676. **b.** *spec.* The plot of a play –1672.

Intriguant, -gant (i·ntrigănt, F. ęntrigaṅ). 1781. [a. F. *intriguant, intriguer* to INTRIGUE; also *intrigant,* ad. It. *intrigante.*] An intriguer. So ‖**Intriguante, -gante** (intriga·nt, F. ęntrigā·nt), a female intriguer.

Intrigue (intrī·g), *sb.* 1647. [a. F., ad. It. *intrigo, -ico,* f. *intrigare, -care* :—L. *intricare*; see INTRICATE *a.*] †**1.** Intricacy, complexity; something complicated; a maze, a labyrinth –1686. †Also *fig.* **2.** The exertion of tortuous or underhand influence to accomplish some purpose; underhand scheming 1664. **b.** (with *pl.*) A plot to accomplish a purpose by such influence 1647. †**3.** The plot of a play, poem, or romance –1725. **4.** Clandestine illicit intimacy between a man and a woman 1668. **b.** *transf.* The combination of queen and knave in certain games of cards 1830.

2. A complicated scene..of plotting and i. JAS. MILL. **b.** He was made Cardinal by Intrigues, Factions, and Tumults DRYDEN. **4.** I., Philotis!..I have laid that word by; amour sounds better DRYDEN. Hence **Intri·guish** *a.* somewhat of the nature of i. NORTH.

Intrigue (intrī·g), *v.* 1612. [a. F. *intriguer,* ad. It. *intrigare* :—L. *intricare*; see INTRICATE *a.*] **1.** *trans.* To trick, deceive, cheat; to perplex. Now *rare.* **b.** As a recent gallicism: To excite the curiosity or interest of. **2.** To entangle, involve; to implicate. Now *rare.* 1677. **3.** *intr.* To carry on a secret amour or illicit intimacy; to have a liaison 1660. **4.** *intr.* To carry on underhand plotting or scheming; to employ secret influence for the accomplishment of designs 1714. **b.** To bring or get by intrigue 1673. **5.** To excite the interest or curiosity of; to interest so as to puzzle or fascinate 1894. (A gallicism.)

2. It doth not seem worth the while..with more subtilty to i. the Point BARROW. **b.** The story itself does not greatly i. us 1905. **3.** He had intrigued with a Vestal virgin FROUDE. **4.** **c.** Rigby..had already intrigued himself into a subordinate office DISRAELI. Hence **Intri·guer. Intri·guery,** the practice of intriguing. †**Intri·guess,** a female intriguer. **Intri·guingly** *adv.* with secret machinations.

†**Intri·nce,** *a.* Also **intrinse.** [? short for INTRINSICATE.] Intricate, involved. *Lear* II. ii. 81.

Intrinsic (intri·nsik), *a.* (*sb.*) 1490. [a. F. *intrinsèque,* ad. med. Schol.L. *intrinsecus* adj., f. L. *intrinsecus* adv. inwardly, inwards. Opp. to EXTRINSIC.] †**1.** Situated within; interior, inner –1665. **b.** *Anat.* Applied to a muscle of a member or organ which has its origin and insertion within that organ; so in *Path.* to a morbid growth arising in the part or tissue in which it is found 1839. †**2.** Inward, internal (in *fig.* sense); secret –1689. †**b.** Intimate –1651. **3.** Belonging to the thing in itself; inherent, essential, proper 1642. Const. *to.* †**4.** *sb.* (*ellipt.* for 'inmost part', 'intrinsic value', 'intrinsic quality') –1751.

3. The intrinsick Value of Silver consider'd as Money LOCKE. Confirmed..by i. probability THIRLWALL. The flower has no beauty..that is not i. and native to it 1873. *I. equation of a curve* (Math.): an equation expressing the relation between its length and curvature (and so involving no reference to external points, lines, etc., as in equations referred to co-ordinates). So **Intri·nsical,** †**-ecal** *a.* (*sb.*) Now *rare.* Hence **Intrinsica·lity, Intri·nsicalness** (*rare*). **Intri·nsically** *adv.*

†**Intri·nsicate,** *a.* Also **-secate.** 1560. [app. f. It. *intrinsecato, -sicato* familiar, confused in sense with *intricato.*] = INTRICATE, involved, entangled. *Ant. & Cl.* V. ii. 307.

Intro- (intro), *prefix.* L. *intro* adv. 'to the inside', used with vbs. and their derivatives, as *introducere* to lead in. Hence in English words derived from L. or formed of L. elements.

Intro·a·ctive *a.* internally active; also, *loosely,* mutually active. **Introce·ssion** (*rare*), a depression or sinking of any parts inwards. **Introfle·xed** *ppl. a.*, bent or curved inwards; so **Introfle·xion. Introgre·ssion,** a going or coming in, entrance, incoming. **Intromole·cular** *a.*, subsisting within a molecule, or between its constituent atoms (dist. from *intermolecular*). †**Intropre·ssion,** pressure inwards. **Intropu·lsive** *a.* [L. *puls-* ppl. stem], having the quality of driving inwards. **Introrece·ption,** the action of receiving within.

Introduce (intrŏdiū·s), *v.* 1475. [ad. L. *introducere* to lead or bring in, f. *intro* + *ducere.* Cf. F. *introduire.*] **1.** *trans.* To lead or bring into a place, or into the inside or midst of something; to bring in, conduct inwards 1639. **b.** To put in from without; to insert 1695. **c.** To usher or bring (a person) into a society or body 1766. **2.** To bring (a thing) into some sphere of action or thought; to bring in in the course of some action or in a composition; to add or insert as a (new) feature or element 1559. **3.** To bring into use or practice, vogue, or fashion; to institute (a law, custom, etc.) 1603. †**4.** To bring on, bring about, give rise to, occasion, induce –1692. **5.** To usher in (a time, action, matter, etc.); to start, open, begin 1667. †**6.** To bring (a person) into the knowledge of something; to teach, instruct –1500. **7.** To bring into personal acquaintance; to make known to a person or to a circle 1659. **b.** To present formally, as at court, etc. 1685. **c.** To bring out into society 1708. **8.** To bring to the notice or cognizance of a person, etc.; to bring a bill or measure before parliament, etc. 1766.

1. Byron gave orders to Tita to i. the monkey and bulldog MEDWIN. **b.** To i. metals into a flame TYNDALL. **c.** On the same day..Bute was..introduced into the Cabinet MACAULAY. **2.** To i. amendments into a bill 1849. **3.** The Julian calendar was introduced in the year 44 B.C. LOCKYER. **4.** Whatsoever introduces habits in children deserves the care and attention of their governors LOCKE. **5.** This discussion served to i. the young soldier's experiences SCOTT. **7.** He introduced himself to my acquaintance STERNE. **b.** The Chevalier..begged to i. us at court 1718. **8.** To i. to the company a ballad GOLDSM. Hence †**Introdu·cement, Introdu·cer, Introdu·cible, -eable** *a.*

†**Introdu·ct,** *v.* 1481. [f. L. *introduct-, introducere*; see prec.] **1.** *trans.* To teach, instruct –1500. **2.** To introduce; to bring in –1670.

Introduction (intrŏdʊ·kʃən). ME. [a. F., ad. L. *introductionem.*] **1.** The action of introducing or bringing in, etc. 1651. **b.** Something introduced; a practice or thing newly brought in, etc. 1603. †**2.** The action or process of leading to something; a preliminary step or stage –1660. †**3.** Initiation in the knowledge of a subject; elementary instruction –1702. **4.** That which leads to the knowledge or understanding of something 1529. **5.** The action of introducing or making known personally; *esp.* formal presentation of one person to another, or of persons to each other, with communication of names, etc. 1711.

1. The i. of a digression JOWETT, of metal LUBBOCK. **b.** This fish was a late i. ROGERS. **4.** His introductions or first lesson SIR T. BROWNE. The I. to the Work FIELDING. An I. to the Study of Electricity PRIESTLEY (*title*). The study of Etruscan art is a necessary i. to that of Roman J. FERGUSSON. **5.** To you..I owe my i. to a large circle of friends J. H. NEWMAN. Phr. *Letter of i.*

Introductive (intrŏdʊ·ktiv), *a.* 1631. [f. L. *introduct-, introducere*; see -IVE.] = INTRODUCTORY. Hence **Introdu·ctively** *adv.*

Introdu·ctor. *arch.* 1638. [a. late L.; cf. F. *introducteur.*] One who or that which introduces; an introducer; esp. *an i. of ambassadors.* Hence **Introdu·ctress** 1657.

Introductory (intrŏdʊ·ktəri). ME. [ad. late L. *introductorius,* f. *introduct-, introducere*; see -ORY.] **A.** *adj.* **1.** Serving to introduce; introductive *of* 1605. **2.** Leading up to or on to something; preliminary 1660. Hence **Introdu·ctorily** *adv.*

1. I. letters 1787. Testimony..i. of fraud 1800. **2.** I place Schools before Colledges, because they are i. thereunto 1661.

B. *sb.* †**1.** An introductory treatise 1391–1552. **2.** A preliminary step 1646.

Introit (i·ntrǫuit, i·ntroit). 1481. [a. F. *introït,* †*-ite,* ad. L. *introitus,* f. *introire.*] †**1.** A going in; entrance –1716. **2.** *Eccl.* A psalm, etc. sung by the choir as the priest approaches the altar to celebrate the Eucharist; a variable part of the Mass consisting of an antiphon with verses of a psalm and Gloria Patri, said by the priest before the Kyrie eleison 1483.

Intromission (intrŏmi·ʃən). 1545. [f. L. *intromittere,* or ? immed. a. F.] The action of intromitting. **1.** The action of sending, letting, or putting in; insertion; admission, admittance 1601. **2.** Intermeddling, interference; esp. in or from *Sc. Law,* intermeddling with the effects of another, either with or without legal authority; in the latter case called *vicious i.* 1545.

Intromit (intrŏmi·t), *v.* ME. [ad. L. *intromittere,* f. *intro* + *mittere* to send.] **1.** *trans.* To cause or allow to enter; to put in, insert, introduce; to send or let in, admit. Now *rare.* 1582. †**2.** *refl.* To interfere (*with* or *in*) –1657. **3.** *intr.* for *refl.* To interfere, intermeddle, have to do *with.* (Now only *Sc.*) ME. **b.** *Sc. Law.* To deal *with*; *esp.* to deal with property or effects; either *legally,* or *viciously* without legal right 1522.

1. Whether our reasons eye be clear enough To I. true light H. MORE (1647).

Intromittent (intrŏmi·tĕnt), *a.* 1836. [ad. L. *intromittentem*; see prec.] That intromits or introduces; having the function of intromission.

Chiefly in *Zool.* and *Physiol. i. apparatus, organ,* the male copulatory organ.

Intromitter (intrŏmi·təɹ). 1507. [f. INTROMIT + -ER[1].] One who intromits; *spec.* in *Sc. Law,* one who interferes or deals with the property of another.

Introrsal (intrǭ·ɹsăl), *a.* 1831. [f. as next + -AL.] = next.

Introrse (intrǭ·ɹs), *a.* 1842. [ad. L. *introrsus,* from *introversus* (turned) inwards.] *Bot.* Turned or directed inwards; of an anther which opens towards the centre of the flower. Hence **Intro·rsely** *adv.*

Introspect (introspe·kt), *v.* 1683. [f. L. *introspect-, introspicere,* or f. L. *introspectare.*] *trans.* To look into, esp. with the mind; to examine narrowly or thoroughly. Now *rare.*

Introspection (introspe·kʃən). 1677. [f. L. *introspicere* (see prec.).] **1.** The action of looking into, or under the surface of, things, esp. with the mind. ? *Obs.* exc. as in 2. **2.** *spec.* (with no object expressed): The action of looking within, or into one's own mind; examination or observation of one's own thoughts, feelings, etc. 1807.

2. In Homer's time..i. had not begun its work 1850. Hence **Introspe·ctionist**, one who practises i.; one who adopts the psychological method of i.

Introspective (introspe·ktiv), *a.* 1820. [f. L. *introspect-*, *introspicere* + -IVE.] Having the quality of looking within; examining into one's own thoughts, feelings, etc., or expressing such examination; of, pertaining to, characterized by, or given to introspection.

Whom I..remember as a mild, melancholy, i. man SOUTHEY. Hence **Introspe·ctive-ly** *adv.*, **-ness**. **Introspe·ctor.**

†Introsu·me, *v.* 1657. [f. INTRO- + L. *sumere* to take.] *trans.* To take in; to take (medicine) internally; to absorb (nutriment) –1664. So **†Introsu·mption**, **†Introsu·mptive** *a.*

Introsusception (i:ntrosʊse·pʃən). 1794. [f. INTRO- + L. *susceptionem*, f. *suscipere.*] The action of taking up or receiving within; = INTUSSUSCEPTION. **Introsusce·pted** *ppl. a.*

†Introve·nient, *a.* [ad. L. *introvenientem.*] Coming in. SIR T. BROWNE.

Introversible (introvə·ɪsĭb'l), *a.* 1883. [See INTROVERT *v.* and -IBLE.] Capable of being introverted, as the finger of a glove.

Introversion (introvə̄·ɹʃən). 1654. [ad. mod.L. *introversionem*; see below.] **1.** The action of turning the thoughts inwards. **2.** The action of (physically) turning inwards, esp. of withdrawing an outer part into the interior; the condition of being so turned inwards 1794. So **Introve·rsive** *a.* 1866.

I·ntrovert, *sb.* 1883. [f. next.] **1.** *Zool.* A part that is or can be introverted. **2.** *Psychol.* A person characterized by introversion 1916.

Introvert (introvə̄·ɹt), *v.* 1669. [f. L. type **introvertere*, f. INTRO- + *vertere* to turn; cf. L. *introversus* adv.] **1.** *trans.* To turn (the mind, thought, etc.) inwards upon itself. **2.** To turn or bend inwards (physically); in *Zool.* to turn (a part or organ) inwards upon itself; to withdraw within its own tube or base 1784.

2. His awkward gait, his introverted toes COWPER. Hence **Introve·rtive** *a.* 1855.

Introvolution (i:ntro,vol'ǖ·ʃən). *rare.* 1829. [f. INTRO- + *-volution* in *evolution*, etc.] The process of involving one thing within another.

Intrude (intrǖ·d), *v.* 1534. [ad. L. *intrudere*, f. *in-* (IN-²) + *trudere* to thrust.] **1.** *trans.* To thrust, force, or drive (any thing) in 1563. **2.** *trans.* To thrust or bring in without leave; to force *on* or *upon* a person 1586. **†3.** *refl.* and *intr.* To thrust oneself into any benefice, possession, office, or dignity to which one has no title or claim; to usurp *on* or *upon* –1682. **4.** To thrust oneself in without warrant, leave, or welcome. Also *transf.* and *fig.* of things, etc. 1573. **†5.** *trans.* To enter forcibly. SHAKS. *Lucr.* 848.

1. Their parts are wedged and intruded one into another GREW. 2. The tendency which intruded earthly Madonnas and saints between the worshipper and the spiritual Deity BRYCE. 4. Thy wit wants edge And manners, to intru'd where I am grac'd SHAKS. To what end shouldst thou i. thy self unwarrantably into their companies? 1659. Hence **Intru·ded** *ppl. a.*; *spec.* in *Geol.* = INTRUSIVE 2 b.

Intruder (intrǖ·dəɹ). 1534. [f. prec. + -ER¹.] **1.** One who intrudes into an estate or benefice or usurps on the rights or privileges of another. Now only in legal use. **2.** One who thrusts himself in without right or welcome 1588.

2. Vnmannerly I. as thou art *Tit. A.* II. iii. 65.

Intru·dress. [f. prec. + -ESS.] A female intruder. FULLER.

†Intru·nk, *v.* [f. IN-² + TRUNK *sb.*] *trans.* To enclose in or as in a trunk. FORD.

Intruse (intrǖ·s), *a.* 1870. [ad. L. *intrusus*, *intrudere.*] *Bot.* Having a form as if pushed or thrust inwards.

Intrusion (intrǖ·ʒən). ME. [a. OF. *intrusion*, med. L. *intrusio*, f. *intrudere* to INTRUDE.] **1.** The action of thrusting or forcing in, or fact of being thrust in; also *concr.* something thrust in 1639. **b.** *spec.* in *Geol.* The influx of rock in a state of fusion into fissures or between strata; a portion of intruded rock 1849. **2.** The action of thrusting oneself into a vacant estate or benefice to which one has no title or claim; *spec.* the entry of a stranger after the determination of a particular estate of freehold before the remainder-man or reversioner; also, a trespass on the lands of the crown. Hence, invasion; usurpation. (Now only in legal use.) ME. **b.** The settlement of a minister of the Church of Scotland without the consent of the congregation 1849. **3.** The action of thrusting oneself in without right or welcome; encroachment on something possessed or enjoyed by another 1592.

3. [George Fox's] i. of himself into assemblies where he was not wanted 1896. Hence **Intru·sional** *a.*

Intru·sionist. 1849. [f. prec. + -IST.] One who practises or supports intrusion (see INTRUSION 2 b). So **Intru·sionism** 1841.

Intrusive (intrǖ·siv), *a.* 1401. [f. L. *intrus-*, *intrudere* + -IVE.] **1.** Of intruding character; coming or entering without invitation or welcome. **2.** That has been intruded or thrust in 1847. **b.** *Geol.* Of an igneous rock: Forced, while in a state of fusion, into cavities or fissures of other rocks 1844.

1. Truth's i. voice severe SCOTT. Hence **Intru·sive-ly** *adv.*, **-ness.**

Intrust, var. f. ENTRUST.

Intubate (i·ntiubeɪt), *v.* 1612. [f. IN-² + L. *tuba* TUBE + -ATE³.] **†1.** *trans.* To form into tubes. STURTEVANT. **2.** *Med.* To treat by inserting a tube into an aperture, esp. into the larynx (see next). Also *absol.* 1889.

Intubation (intiubēɪ·ʃən). 1887. [f. prec.; see -ATION.] The insertion of a tube; esp. *i. of the larynx*, the insertion of a tube into the glottis to keep it open, in diphtheria, etc.

Intuent (i·ntiu,ĕnt), *a.* 1865. [ad. L. *intuentem*, *intueri.*] That knows by intuition.

Intuit (i·ntiu,it), *v.* Also **-ite.** 1776. [f. L. *intuit-*, *intueri*; see INTUITION.] **†1.** *trans.* To instruct. **2. a.** *intr.* To receive knowledge by direct perception 1840. **b.** *trans.* To know by intuition 1858. Hence **Intu·itable** *a.*

2. b. He is a being..who by the eternal necessity even of his nature, intuits everything BUSHNELL.

Intuition (intiu,i·ʃən). 1497. [a. F., ad. late or med.L. *intuitionem*, f. *intueri*, f. *in-* (IN-²) + *tueri* to look. Cf. L. *intuitus.*] **†1.** A looking upon or into; inspection; a sight or view. (= L. *intuitus.*) –1664. **†2.** The action of mentally looking at; contemplation; perception, recognition; mental view –1755. **†3.** Ulterior view; regard, respect, reference –1718. **4.** *Schol. Philos.* The immediate knowledge ascribed to angelic and spiritual beings, with whom vision and knowledge are identical 1652. **5.** *Mod. Philos.* The immediate apprehension of an object by the mind without the intervention of any reasoning process; a particular act of such apprehension 1600. **b.** Immediate apprehension by the intellect alone; an act of such apprehension 1659. **c.** Immediate apprehension by sense; an act of such apprehension 1819. **6.** Direct or immediate insight; an instance of this 1762.

3. Phr. *With i. to (of)*, with reference to. *In i. to*, in respect to, in view of. 4. Our Superiors are guided by I., and our Inferiors by Instinct ADDISON. 5. What we *feel*, and what we *do*, we may be said to know by i. PRIESTLEY. b. The truths known by i. are the original premises from which all others are inferred MILL. c. All our i. however takes place by means of the senses only RICHARDSON tr. *Kant's Proleg. to Metaph.* 6. The intuitions of genius unconscious of any process 1866.

Intuitional (intiu,i·ʃənăl), *a.* 1860. [f. prec. + -AL.] **1.** Of, pertaining to, or derived from intuition; of the nature of intuition. **2.** Pertaining to that theory, or philosophical school, which bases certain elements of knowledge on intuition (see prec. 5 b) 1865.

Intui·tionalism. 1850. [f. prec. + -ISM.] The theory of the intuitional school; the doctrine that the perception of truth, or of certain truths, is by intuition. So **Intui·tionalist** = INTUITIONIST (in both senses).

Intuitionism (intiu,i·ʃəniz'm). 1847. [f. INTUITION + -ISM.] **1.** The doctrine of Reid and others, that in perception, external objects are known immediately, without the intervention of a vicarious phenomenon. **2.** = INTUITIONALISM 1874. So **Intui·tionist**, one who holds the theory of i. (in either sense).

Intuitive (intiǖ·itiv), *a.* 1594. [ad. med.L. *intuitivus*, f. *intuitus.*] **†1.** Beholding. BULWER. **†b.** Of sight or vision: That consists in immediate looking upon an object, and sees it as it is –1656. **2.** Of knowledge or mental perception: That consists in immediate apprehension, without the intervention of any reasoning process 1645. **b.** Of a truth: Apprehended by intuition 1872. **3.** Of the mind or reason, or a mental act, etc.: That acts by intuition or immediate apprehension; opp. to *discursive* 1667. **4.** Of persons: Possessing intuition 1652. **5.** Of or pertaining to the school of moral philosophy that holds the first principles of ethics to be apprehended by intuition 1861.

2. The i. vision comes like an inspiration 1849. 3. Whence the soule Reason receives, and reason is her being, Discursive, or I. MILT. *P. L.* v. 488. 5. The i. moralist..believes that the utilitarian theory is profoundly immoral LECKY. Hence **Intu·itive-ly** *adv.*, **-ness.**

Intuitivism (intiǖ·itiviz'm). 1874. [f. prec. + -ISM.] The doctrine that the fundamental principles of ethics are matters of intuition. So **Intu·itivist**, one who holds this doctrine; *attrib.* holding, or pertaining to, this doctrine.

Intumesce (intiume·s), *v.* 1796. [ad. L. *intumescere*, f. *in-* (IN-²) + *tumescere*, inceptive of *tumere* to be tumid, to swell.] *intr.* To swell up, become tumid; to bubble up.

Intumescence (intiume·sĕns). 1656. [a. F., f. L. *intumescere*; see prec. and -ENCE.] **1.** The process of swelling up. Also *fig.* in reference to language. **2.** *Physiol.* A swelling of the tissue of any organ or part of the body, or of a plant. Also *concr.* 1822. **3.** The bubbling up of a fluid, etc. 1661. Also *fig.*

1. The i. of the tide JOHNSON. 3. The mixture melted without i. 1796. *fig.* The i. of nations would have found its vent JOHNSON. So **†Intume·scency**, intumescent quality or condition 1650.

Intumescent (intiume·sĕnt), *a.* 1870. [ad. L. *intumescentem.*] Swelling up; becoming tumid.

†Intu·mulate, *v.* Pa. pple. **-at(e** and **-ated.** 1535. [f. (ult.) L. *in-* (IN-²) + *tumulus.*] *trans.* To place in a tomb; to bury –1606.

Intune, var. of ENTUNE *v.*

†Intu·rbidate, *v. rare.* 1684. [f. IN-² + late L. *turbidat-*, *turbidare* to confuse, f. *turbidus.*] *trans.* To render turbid; to disturb, confuse –1834.

The confusion of ideas and conceptions under the same term painfully inturbidates his theology COLERIDGE.

Inturgescence (intəɹdʒe·sĕns). 1755. [f. late L. *inturgescere* to swell up + -ENCE.] The action of swelling up; a swollen condition. (Dicts.) So **†Inturge·scency** 1650.

Inturn (i·ntəɹn). 1599. [IN *adv.*] **†1.** An inward turn, bend, or curve 1690. **2.** The turning in of the toes; also, a step in dancing 1599. **†3.** In wrestling: The act of putting a leg between the thighs of an opponent and lifting him up. Also *fig.* 1602.

†I·ntuse. [f. L. *intusum*, *intundere.*] A bruise. SPENSER.

Intussuscept (i:ntəs,səse·pt), *v.* 1835. [f. L. *intus* + *suscept-*, *suscipere* to take up; after next.] *trans.* To take up within itself or some other part; to introvert, to invaginate; said spec. of part of a bowel. So **I:ntussusce·ptive** *a.* characterized by intussusception.

Intussusception (i:ntəs,səse·pʃən). 1707. [f. L. *intus* + *susceptionem* a taking up.] **1.** A taking within; absorption into itself. Also *transf.* and *fig.* **2.** *Phys.* and *Biol.* The taking in of foreign matter by a living organism and its conversion into organic tissue. In *Veg. Phys.* opp. to *apposition*. 1764. **3.** *Path.* The inversion of one portion of intestine and its reception within an adjacent portion; invagination; introversion; an instance of this 1811.

1. A particle of dry gelatine may be swelled up by the i. of water HUXLEY. 2. Some will have them [shells] increase by i., and others by juxtaposition 1771.

Intwine, etc., var. ENTWINE, etc.

‖Inula (i·niŭlă). 1822. [L., see ELECAMPANE.] A plant so called by Roman writers; identified by mediæval herbalists with Elecampane (*Inula Helenium* Linn.); hence, in *Bot.*, the name of the genus of *Compositæ* to which Elecampane belongs.

Hence **I·nulin** [-IN [1]] *Chem.*, a white starchy substance ($C_6H_{10}O_5$), obtained from the roots of Elecampane and other *Compositæ*. **I·nuloid**, a soluble modification of inulin, occurring in the roots of Jerusalem artichoke, dahlia, etc.

†Inu·mbrate, *v.* 1623. [f. L. *inumbrat-*, *inumbrare*, f. *in-* (IN-[2]) + *umbrare* to shade, f. *umbra*.] *trans.* To cast a shadow upon; to shade; to put in the shade –1822.

Inunct (inɒ·ŋkt), *v. rare.* 1513. [f. L. *inunct-*, *inunguere*, f. *in-* (IN-[2]) + *unguere* to anoint.] *trans.* To anoint; to smear.

Inunction (inɒ·ŋkʃən). 1483. [ad. L. *inunctionem*; see prec.] **1.** The action of anointing; smearing with, or rubbing in of, oil or ointment 1621. **b.** The anointing with oil in religious rites. Cf. UNCTION. 1483. **2.** *concr.* An ointment, liniment, or unguent 1601.

†Inu·nctuous, *a.* 1634. [IN-[3].] Not unctuous; without oil or grease. So **†Inunctuo·sity** 1794.

Inundant (inɒ·ndănt), *a.* 1629. [ad. L. *inundantem*; see next and -ANT.] Overflowing, inundating.

Inundate (i·nɒndeɪt, inɒ·ndeɪt), *v.* 1623. [f. L. *inundat-*, *inundare*, f. *in-* (IN-[2]) + *undare* to flow; see -ATE[3]. The stress is now mostly on the first syllable.] **1.** *trans.* To overspread *with* a flood of water; to overflow, flood 1791. **2.** *transf.* and *fig.* To fill with an overflowing abundance or superfluity 1623.

1. The period when the Nile inundates Ægypt 1791. 2. I was inundated with letters WASHINGTON.

Inundation (inɒndē·ʃən). ME. [ad. L. *inundationem*; see prec. and -ATION.] **1.** The action of inundating; the fact of being inundated with water; an overflow of water; a flood. **2.** *transf.* and *fig.* An overspreading or overwhelming in superfluous abundance; overflowing, superabundance 1589.

1. This place hath a great pond caused by the i. of Nilus HAKLUYT. 2. An I. of impertinent Visitors 1767.

†Inundersta·nding, *a.* [IN-[3].] Not understanding; without apprehension. PEARSON.

Inurbane (inɒɹbē·n), *a.* 1623. [ad. L. *inurbanus*; see IN-[3] and URBANE.] Not urbane; unpolished; esp. impolite. Hence **Inurba·ne·ly** *adv.* 1610, **-ness** 1727.

Inurbanity (inɒɹbæ·nĭti). 1598. [IN-[3].] Lack of urbanity; unpolished manner or deportment; esp. incivility.

The proverbial i. of these official Cerberi 1825.

Inure, enure (iniūə·ɹ, ėniūə·ɹ), *v.*[1] 1489. [f. IN-[2], EN-[1] + URE, work, operation, etc., a. F. *œuvre*.] **1.** *trans.* To bring by use, habit, or continual exercise to a certain condition or state of mind; to accustom, habituate. **†2.** To put into exercise or operation; to exercise, to practise, to commit (a crime). (Chiefly in form *enure*.) 1549. **3.** *intr.* Chiefly *Law* and *U.S.* To come into operation; to operate; to take or have effect 1589.

1. We see to what easie satisfactions..he had inur'd his conscience MILT. The poor, inured to drudgery and distress COWPER. 2. MILT. *P. L.* VIII. 239. 3. This shall enure by force and way of grant COKE. A burial dress that shall i. for salvation in the realms of death KINGLAKE.

†Inu·re, *v.*[2] 1619. [ad. L. *inurere*, f. *in-* (IN-[2]) + *urere* to burn.] **1.** *trans.* To burn in, brand –1679. **2.** To burn in a flame 1709.

Inurement (iniūə·ɹmĕnt). Also **†en-**. 1586. [f. INURE *v.*[1] + -MENT.] The action of inuring or state of being inured; habituation.

Inurn (inɒ̄·ɹn), *v.* Also **†en-**. 1602. [IN-[2].] *trans.* To put (the ashes of a cremated body) in an urn; hence *transf.* to entomb, inter. Also *fig.*

The body was sometimes burnt and inurned, but sometimes buried 1861.

Inusitate (iniū·ziteɪt), *a.* Now *rare.* 1546. [ad. L. *inusitatus*, f. *in-* (IN-[3]) + *usitatus*, *usitari* to use often.] Unwonted, unusual, out of use. So **Inusita·tion** (*rare*), disuse.

†Inu·st, *a. rare.* 1634. [ad. L. *inustus*, *inurere* (see INURE *v.*[2]).] Burnt in, branded –1647.

†Inu·stion. 1618. [f. L. *inurere*, *inust-*; see prec. and -TION.] **1.** Burning. T. ADAMS. **2.** The action of burning in or branding with fire. H. MORE (1647). **3.** Cauterization –1834.

Inutile (iniū·til), *a.* 1484. [a. F., ad. L. *inutilis*, f. *in-* (IN-[3]) + *utilis* useful. Recently re-adopted from Fr.] Useless, of no service, unprofitable.

Inutility (iniuti·lĭti). 1598. [a. F. *inutilité*, ad. L. *inutilitas*; see prec. and -ITY.] The quality or state of being useless; want of utility; unprofitableness. **b.** A thing or person that is useless 1802.

To find nothing in knowledge but its i. LYTTON.

Inu·tterable, *a.* Now *rare.* 1603. [IN-[3].] That cannot be uttered; unutterable.

In vacuo: see IN *Lat. prep.*

Invade (invē·d), *v.* 1491. [ad. L. *invadere*, f. *in-* (IN-[2]) + *vadere* to go, walk.] **1.** *trans.* To enter in a hostile manner, or with armed force 1494. **2.** *transf.* and *fig.* To enter or penetrate after the manner of an invader 1548. **3.** *intr.* or *absol.* To make an invasion or attack 1491. **4.** *trans.* To intrude upon, infringe, encroach on, violate 1514. **†b.** To usurp, seize upon –1712. **†5.** To make an attack upon (a person). *lit.* and *fig.* –1753. **†6.** (Latinisms): **a.** To enter (*lit.* and *fig.*). SPENSER. **b.** To go; traverse. GRENEWEY.

1. Asserhadon invades Babylon NEWTON. 2. The deer i. the crops TENNANT. A sense of loss, of loneliness invades her M. ARNOLD. 4. You did their Natural Rights i. COWLEY. Hence **Inva·der**, one who invades, intrudes, or seizes.

Inva·ginate, *a. rare.* 1887. [ad. mod.L. type **invaginatus*; see next.] Invaginated.

Invaginate (invæ·dʒineɪt), *v.* 1656. [f. mod.L. type **invaginare*, f. L. *in-* (IN-[2]) + *vagina* sheath; see -ATE[3].] **1.** *trans.* **a.** To put in a sheath. **b.** To turn (a tubular sheath) back within itself; to introvert. **2.** *intr.* To become invaginated 1887.

Invaginated (invæ·dʒineɪted), *ppl. a.* 1835. [f. prec. + -ED[1].] Sheathed; turned into a sheath; introverted.

Invagination (invædʒinē·ʃən). 1658. [f. as prec.] The action of sheathing or introverting; the condition of being sheathed or introverted; intussusception.

The Gastrula..was originated by an inversion or i. of the Blastula tr. *Haeckel's Evol. Man.*

Invalescence[1] (invăle·sĕns). *rare.* 1730. [f. IN-[3] + *-valescence* in *convalescence*.] Ill health.

Invalescence[2] (invăle·sĕns). *rare.* 1755. [f. L. *invalescere* to grow strong; see -ENCE.] Strength; health; force (Dicts.).

†Invaletu·dinary, *a. rare.* 1661. [ad. med.L. *invaletudinarius*, f. *invaletudinem*, f. *in-* (IN-[3]) + *valetudo* health.] Wanting health or strength; infirm, invalid –1661.

Invalid (invæ·lid), *a.*[1] 1635. [ad. L. *invalidus*, f. *in-* (IN-[3]) + *validus* strong.] Not valid. **†1.** Without power or strength; weak, feeble –1834. **2.** Of no force; *esp.* without legal force, void 1635.

2. That which was i. from the beginning, cannot become valid by prescription or tract of time BRAMHALL.

Invalid (i·nvălīd, -lid, invălī·d), *a.*[2] and *sb.* Also **-ide.** 1642. [f. as prec., with pronunciation after F. *invalide*. Orig. only a special sense of prec.]

A. *adj.* Infirm from sickness or disease; enfeebled or disabled by illness or injury. Now only an attrib. use of the sb.

His invalide and suffering sister 1869.

B. *sb.* **1.** An infirm or sickly person 1709. **2.** A soldier or sailor disabled for active service 1704. **3.** *attrib.* **a.** (See A.) **b.** Of or for invalids. 1845.

2. *Invalides*, the *Hôtel des Invalides*, a hospital or home for old and disabled soldiers in Paris.

Hence **I·nvalidish** 1855, **I·nvalidy** 1894 *adjs. colloq.*, somewhat of an invalid.

Invalid (invæ·lid), *v.*[1] Now *rare.* 1626. [f. INVALID *a.*[1]; cf. INVALIDATE *v.*] *trans.* To render invalid; to invalidate.

Invalid (i·nvălīd, invălī·d), *v.*[2] Also **-ide.** 1787. [f. INVALID *a.*[2]] **1.** *trans.* To make an invalid; to lay up or disable by illness or injury. (Chiefly in *pass.*) 1803. **2.** To enter on the sick-list; to report as unfit for active service 1787. **3.** *intr.* To become an invalid; of a soldier or sailor: To go on the sick-list; to leave the service on account of illness or injury 1829.

1. The Queen..was invalided at Windsor 1837. 2. He was invalided home, sorely against his will 1882. 3. The conscripts die first, they i. at an inexplicable rate 1885.

Invalidate (invæ·lideɪt), *v.* 1649. [f. L. type **invalidare*, perh. after F. *invalider*; see -ATE[3].] *trans.* To render invalid; to render of no force or effect; *esp.* to deprive of legal efficacy.

To i. an Obligation 1651, an argument 1674, evidence 1801. Hence **†Inva·lidable** *a.* ineffective 1634.

Invalidation (invælidē·ʃən). 1771. [f. prec.] The action of invalidating or rendering invalid.

It is no i. of this high claim 1863.

Invalidism (i·nvălīdiz'm, invălī·diz'm). 1794. [f. INVALID *sb.* + -ISM.] The state of being an invalid; chronic infirmity or ill health that prevents activity.

Invalidity (invăli·dĭti). 1550. [f. L. type **invaliditas*, f. *invalidus*; cf. *validity*.] **1.** [Related to INVALID *a.*[1]] The quality of being invalid; *esp.* want of legal validity. **†2.** Want of strength or efficacy; weakness, incapacity –1698. **3.** [Related to INVALID *a.*[2]] Want of bodily strength or health; condition of being an invalid; bodily infirmity 1698.

1. The I. of their Passports 1711, of the evidence 1841. 3. Allowances for both i. and old age 1891. So **Inva·lidness.**

Invalorous (invæ·lŏrəs), *a. rare.* 1846. [IN-[3].] Not valorous, cowardly.

Invaluable (invæ·liuăb'l), *a.* 1576. [IN-[3].] **1.** That cannot be valued; above and beyond valuation; inestimable. **2.** Without value, valueless 1640.

1. A free government..is an i. blessing BUTLER. Hence **Inva·luableness.** **Inva·luably** *adv.*

†Inva·lued, *a. poet. rare.* 1603. [IN-[3].] Invaluable –1806.

Invar (i·nvaɹ). 1902. [abbrev. of INVARIABLE.] An alloy of nickel and steel in which the coefficient of expansion is negligible.

Invariable (invē^ə·riăb'l), *a.* (*sb.*) 1457. [f. IN-[3] + VARIABLE, or a. F.] **A.** *adj.* Not subject to variation or alteration; unchangeable; constant; unvarying. **b.** *Math.* Of a quantity: Constant. Of a point, line, etc.: Fixed. 1704. **B.** *sb. Math.* An invariable quantity, a constant 1864. Hence **Invariabi·lity, Inva·riableness**, unchangeableness. **Inva·riably** *adv.*

A. The value of gold and silver is certainly not i. MᶜCULLOCH.

Invariance (invē^əriăns). 1878. [f. next; see -ANCE.] *Math.* The character of remaining unaltered after a linear transformation; the essential property of an invariant. So **Inva·riancy.**

Invariant (invē^ə·riănt). 1851. [IN-[3].]

A. *adj.* Unvarying 1874.

B. *sb. Math.* A function of the coefficients of a quantic, such that, if the quantic be linearly transformed, the same function of the new coefficients is equal to the first function multiplied by some power of the modulus of transformation. Hence **Inva·riantive** *a.* belonging to an i. **Inva·riantively** *adv.*

Invaried (invē^ə·rid), *a. rare.* 1677. [IN-[3].] Unvaried.

Invasion (invē·ʒən). 1508. [a. F., ad. late L. *invasionem*, f. *invadere*.] **1.** The action of invading; an entrance or incursion with armed force; a hostile inroad. Also *fig.* **2.** Infringement by intrusion; encroachment upon the property, rights, privacy, etc. of any one 1650. **†3.** Assault, attack (upon a person, etc.) –1757.

1. *fig.* An i. of Disease BOYLE, of doubt 1847.

Invasive (invē·siv), *a.* 1456. [a. F. *invasif, -ive*, in med.L. *invasivus*, f. *invas-*, *invadere*; see -IVE.] **1.** Of, pertaining to, or of the nature of, invasion; †(of weapons) offensive. **2.** Characterized by invasion 1598. Also *transf.* and *fig.* **3.** Intrusive, encroaching 1670.

1. An i. war 1788. 2. Th' i. foe's designs SHENSTONE.

Invecked (inve·kt), *ppl. a.* 1496. [f. *inveck* for *invect*, L. *invectus*, *invehere* (see IN-

VEIGH) + -ED.] Bordered by or consisting (as an edge) of a series of small convex lobes. Chiefly in *Her.*

†**Inve·ct**, *v.* 1548. [f. L. *invect-*, *invehere* (see INVEIGH).] **1.** *trans.* To bring in, import, introduce. UDALL. **2.** *intr.* To inveigh –1625.

Invected (inve·ktėd), *ppl. a.* 1641. [f. L. *invectus*, *invehere* + -ED [1].] Brought in, introduced; *spec.* in *Her.* = INVECKED.

†**Inve·ction.** 1450. [ad. L. *invectionem*, f. *invehere.*] **1.** The action of inveighing; an invective –1651. **2.** Importation –1658.

Invective (inve·ktiv). ME. [a. F. *invectif*, *-ive* adj., *invective* sb., ad. late L. *invectivus* 'reproachful, abusive'; see INVECT and -IVE.]

A. *adj.* **1.** Using or characterized by denunciatory or railing language; inclined to inveigh; vituperative, abusive. Now *rare.* †**2.** Carried or borne in (against something). FLORIO.

1. Divers i. speeches..had passed in the same 1576.

B. *sb.* **1.** A violent attack in words; a denunciatory or railing speech, writing, or expression 1523. **2.** (Without *pl.*) Vehement denunciation; vituperation 1602.

1. This it is that fills..Pamphlets with spightfull invectives BP. HALL. 2. A torrent of i. 1839.

Hence **Inve·ctively** *adv.* (now *rare*).

Inveigh (invē·ⁱ), *v.* 1486. [ad. L. *invehere* to carry or bear to or into, *invehi* to be borne, carry oneself, or go into, to attack, f. *in-* (IN- [2]) + *vehere.* For the spelling cf. *weigh.*]

I. †**1.** *trans.* To introduce (*rare*) –1550. †**2.** To entice, inveigle –1680. †**3.** To carry away (*to* a place) 1878.

II. 1. *intr.* To utter vehement denunciation, reproach, or censure; to rail loudly. Const. *against* (†*at*, *of*, *on*, *upon*). (The current sense.) 1529. †**2.** *trans.* To attack or assail with words 1670.

1. Williams inveighed against Laud as a Papist D'ISRAELI. Popular orators, who rose to power by inveighing against property FROUDE. Hence **Inveigher.**

Inveigle (invī·g'l), *v.* 1494. [In 15–16th c. *envegle* (occas. *enveugle*), app. a corruption of an earlier **avegle*, *aveugle*, a. F. *aveugler* to blind, f. *aveugle*:—late pop. L. *aboculum*, f. *ab-* without + *oculus* eye. Cf. *embraid* = *abraid*, etc.] †**1.** *trans.* To blind in mind or judgement; to beguile, deceive –1709. **2.** To gain over by deceitful allurement; to entice, seduce 1540. †**b.** To entrap, ensnare, entangle –1707.

1. The subtiltie of Satan inueagling vs, as it did Eue HOOKER. 2. Yet have they many baits, and guilefull spells To i. and invite th' unwary sense MILT. *Comus* 538. b. To enveigle and entangle his necessitous neighbour..till he have got a hank over his estate SANDERSON. Hence **Invei·glement,** cajolery, allurement, enticement. **Invei·gler.**

†**Invei·l**, *v.* 1592. [f. IN- [1] or [2] + VEIL *v.*] To cover with or as with a veil –1763.

Invendible (inve·ndĭb'l), *a. rare.* 1706. [IN- [3].] Not vendible; unsaleable. Hence **Inve:ndibi·lity,** unsaleableness.

Inveneme, etc., obs. ff. ENVENOM, etc.

Invent (inve·nt), *v.* 1475. [f. L. *invent-*, *invenire*, f. *in-* (IN- [2]) + *venire* to come. Cf. F. *inventer.*] **1.** *trans.* To come upon, find; to discover. (*Obs.* exc. in reference to the *Invention of the Cross*: see INVENTION I. 1.) **2.** To find out or produce by mental activity; †to devise –1821; to fabricate, feign, 'make up' 1535. **3.** To find out in the way of original contrivance; to devise first, originate (a new method, instrument, etc.). The chief current sense. 1538. †**4.** To bring into use formally or by authority; to found, establish, institute, appoint –1692. †**5.** With *inf.*: To devise, contrive, find out how (*to do* something) –1729.

1. It was in a bed of this tender herb [sweet basil] that Our Lord's Cross was invented 1887. 2. For laboured impiety, what apology can be invented? JOHNSON. The calumnies which..he had invented to blacken the fame of Anne Hyde MACAULAY. 3. They invented the arte of printing 1601. Galileo invented the telescope 1783. I only said I invented the word 'agnostic' HUXLEY. 5. They will i. to engage your attention BUTLER.

†**I·nventary, -arie.** 1459. [var. f. INVENTORY *sb.*, after L. *inventarium.*] = INVENTORY *sb.* –1763.

Inventer: see INVENTOR.

Inve·ntful, *a. rare.* 1797. [f. INVENT *v.* + -FUL.] Full of invention.

Inve·ntible, -able, *a. rare.* 1641. [f. INVENT *v.* + -IBLE (on L. analogy), -ABLE.] Capable of being invented. Hence **Inve·ntibleness.**

Invention (inve·nʃən). [ME. a. OF. *invencion*, *envention*, ad. L. *inventionem*; see INVENT *v.*]

I. 1. The action of coming upon or finding; discovery. *Obs.* or *arch.* **b.** *Rhet.* Selection of topics or arguments 1509. **2.** The action of devising, contriving, or making up; fabrication 1526. **3.** Contrivance or production of a new method, of an art, kind of instrument, etc. previously unknown; origination, introduction 1531. **b.** In art and literary composition: The devising of a subject, idea, or method of treatment, by exercise of the intellect or imagination 1638. **4.** The faculty of inventing or devising; inventiveness 1480. †**5.** Invented style, fashion, design –1715.

1. The i. and use of the four metals in Greece NEWTON. *Invention of the Cross*: the reputed finding of the Cross by Helena, mother of the Emperor Constantine, in A.D. 326; hence, the church festival observed on the 3rd of May in commemoration of this. 2. This proceeding is not of my own i. SWIFT. 3. The first inuention of Tobacco taking JAS. I. 4. He was not a man of much i. SMEATON. 5. Guns of several Sizes and Inventions ADDISON.

II. 1. Something devised; a device, contrivance, design, plan, scheme 1513. †**2.** A literary composition –1601. **3.** A fabrication, fiction, figment 1500. **4.** An original contrivance or device 1546. **5.** *Mus.* A short piece of music in which a single idea is worked out in a simple manner. GROVE.

1. God hath made man vpright: but they haue sought out many inuentions *Eccl.* vii. 29. 2. *Twel. N.* v. i. 341. 3. The Story..was all meer I. 1748. 4. Tyle and slate to couer houses were the inuencion of Sinyra 1546.

†**III.** Coming in, arrival. DRAYTON.

Hence **Inve·ntional** *a.* (*rare*), of, pertaining to, or of the nature of i. (Dicts.) †**Inve·ntious** *a.* = INVENTIVE 1, 2. 1591–1656.

Inventive (inve·ntiv), *a.* 1450. [a. OF. *inventif*, *-ive* = It. *inventivo*; ad. L. type **inventivus*; see INVENT and -IVE.] **1.** Having the faculty of invention; original in contriving or devising. **2.** Produced by or showing original contrivance 1601. †**3.** Invented, fictitious –1673.

1. Those that haue ye inuentiuest heades ASCHAM. 2. I. mockery and insult SCOTT. Hence **Inve·ntively** *adv.*, **-ness.**

Inventor (inve·ntəɹ). Also †**-er.** 1490. [a. L., f. *invenire* to come upon.] One who invents. †**1.** A discoverer. 1509–1744. **2.** One who devises something fictitious or false 1513. **3.** One who devises or produces something new (as an instrument, art, etc.) by original contrivance; 'the first finder-out'. (The prevailing sense.) 1490.

Inventorial (inventōᵊ·riăl), *a. rare.* [f. L. type **inventorius* (f. *inventor*) + -AL.] Pertaining to, or having the character of, an inventory; detailed. Hence **Invento·rially** *adv.* in detail 1604.

Inventory (i·nvĕntəri), *sb.* 1450. [ad. med. L. *inventorium*, for cl. L. *inventarium* (see INVENTARY).] **1.** A detailed list of articles, such as goods and chattels, or parcels of land, found to have been in the possession of a person at his decease or conviction, sometimes with a statement of the nature and value of each; hence any such detailed statement of property, goods or furniture, or the like. **2.** *gen.* or *fig.* A list, catalogue; a detailed account 1589. **3.** *transf.* The lot of goods, etc., which are or may be made the subject of an inventory 1691. **4.** *U.S.* = STOCK-TAKING.

1. There take an Inuentory of all I haue SHAKS. 2. What sects? What are their opinions? give us the I. MILTON.

Inventory (i·nvĕntəri), *v.* 1526. [f. prec. sb.] *trans.* To make an inventory or descriptive list of; to catalogue (goods, etc.). Also *gen.* or *fig.*

fig. It [my beauty] shal be inuentoried and euery particle and vtensile labell'd to my will SHAKS.

Inve·ntress. 1586. [-ESS.] A female inventor. So †**Inventri·ce** 1509–1546, **Inve·ntrix** 1604 (? *Obs.*).

Inveracious (invĕrē·ʃəs), *a.* 1885. [IN- 3.] Untruthful. So **Invera·city** 1864.

Inverisimilitude (inve:risimi·litiūd). 1818. [IN- [3].] Lack of verisimilitude; unlikelihood; improbability.

Inverminate (invɔ̄·ɹmineⁱt), *v.* 1830. [f. IN- [2] + L. *verminare* to have worms.] *trans.* To infest like worms; to swarm or burrow in. COLERIDGE. So **Inve:rmina·tion,** the condition of being infested with (intestinal) worms 1808.

Inverness (invəɹne·s). 1865. [a. Gael. *Inbhir-nis* mouth of the (river) Ness.] A town in the Highlands of Scotland. Hence *I. cloak*, *overcoat*, name of an overcoat with a removable cape (*I. cape*).

Inverse (invɔ̄·ɹs, i·nvəɹs). 1658. [ad. L. *inversus*, *invertere*, f. *in-* (IN- [2]) + *vertere*; orig. sense app., To turn outside in.]

A. *adj.* **1.** Turned upside down; inverted. **2.** Inverted in position, order, or relations 1831. **3.** *Math.* **a.** *Arith.* and *Alg.* Of such a nature in respect to another operation, relation, etc. that the starting-point of the one is the conclusion of the other, and *vice versa*; opposite in nature or effect. Opp. to *direct.* 1660. **b.** *Geom. Inverse point, line, curve*, etc., one related to another point, line, curve, etc., in the way of geometrical inversion (see INVERSION I. 3 b) 1873. **4.** *Cryst.* Opp. to *direct* 1878.

1. Make from these Piers i. Arches MOXON. 2. Go on..Seeking, an i. Saul, a kingdom to find only asses CLOUGH. 3. a. *Inverse ratio*: (*a*) a ratio in which the terms are reversed; (*b*) the ratio of two quantities which vary inversely, i. e. one of which increases in the proportion in which the other decreases, and *vice versa*; so *i. proportion.* *I. square*: often used for the relation of two quantities one of which varies inversely as the square of the other. *Rule of Three i.*: that case of the Rule of Three in which the antecedent of each of the ratios corresponds to the consequent of the other.

B. *sb.* **1.** An inverted state or condition; thus *CBA* is the inverse of *ABC* 1681. **2.** The result of inversion: **a.** *Math.* A ratio, proportion, or process in which the antecedents and consequents are interchanged. Also, short for *inverse function.* 1695. **b.** *Geom.* Short for *inverse curve, point*, etc. 1873. **c.** *Logic.* The proposition obtained by inversion 1896.

Inverse (invɔ̄·ɹs), *v.* Now *rare.* 1611. [f. prec.] *trans.* To turn upside down; to invert; to reverse in order or direction.

Inversely (invɔ̄·ɹsli), *adv.* 1660. [f. INVERSE *a.* + -LY [2].] In an inverse manner or order; as the inverse; by inversion. **b.** Invertedly; upside down 1776.

Inversion (invɔ̄·ɹʃən). 1551. [ad. L. *inversionem*; cf. F. *inversion.*]

I. 1. A turning upside down 1598. **b.** *Geol.* The folding back of stratified rocks upon each other, so that older strata overlie the newer 1849. **2.** A reversal of position, order, sequence, or relation 1599. †**b.** *Rhet.* = ANTISTROPHE 3 b. –1657. **c.** *Gram.* = ANASTROPHE 1586. **d.** *Mus.* The action of inverting an interval, chord, phrase, or subject (see INVERT *v.* I. 2 e); also, the interval, chord, etc. so produced 1806. **e.** *Logic.* An immediate inference in which the new subject is the negative of the original one 1896. **3.** *Math.* **a.** *Arith.* and *Alg.* The reversal of a ratio by interchanging the positions of the antecedent and consequent 1660. **b.** *Geom.* A transformation in which for each point of a given figure is substituted another point in the same straight line from a fixed point (called the *origin* or *centre of inversion*), and so situated that the product of the distances of the two points from the centre of inversion is constant (*cyclical* or *spherical inversion*). Also extended to similar transformations involving a more complex relation of corresponding points or lines, as *quadric inversion*, *tangential inversion.* 1873. **4.** *Mil.* An evolution by which ranks are converted into files 1635. **5.** *Chem.* A decomposition of certain carbohydrates into two different substances, as of cane-sugar into dextrose and lævulose, whereby the direction of the optical rotatory power is reversed 1864. †**6.** = METAPHOR –1589.

2. When we dress by a mirror we perform a series

of inversions, very difficult at first BAIN. **b.** You maye confute the same by inuersion, that is to saie, tournyng his taile cleane contrary 1551.

II. 1. *Her.* See INVERTED II. 1. 1638. **2.** A turning outside in, introversion; a turning inside out. *spec.* in *Path.* 1598.

†**III.** Diversion to an improper purpose; perversion –1755.

Invert (i·nvəɹt), *sb.* 1838. [f. INVERT *v.*] **1.** An inverted arch. **2.** *Psychol.* One whose sex instincts are inverted 1897.

Invert (invə̄·ɹt), *v.* 1533. [f. L. *invertere*, f. *in-* (IN-[2]) + *vertere*; *lit.* to turn in, to turn outside in, hence to turn the opposite way.]

I. 1. *trans.* To turn upside down 1613. †**b.** *fig.* To overthrow, upset; to subvert –1706. **2.** To reverse in position, order, or sequence; to turn in an opposite direction 1533. **b.** *fig.* 1552. †**c.** *Rhet.* To retort an argument upon an opponent –1796. †**d.** To use (words) in a non-literal sense. PUTTENHAM. **e.** *Mus.* To change the relative position of the notes of (an interval or chord) by placing the lowest note higher, usually an octave higher; also, to modify (a phrase or subject) by inverting the intervals between the successive notes, i.e. by reversing the direction of its motion 1838. **f.** *Logic.* To obtain the inverse of (a proposition) 1896. **g.** *Math.* To transform by inversion, obtain the inverse of. **3.** *Mil.* Cf. INVERSION I. 4. 1832. **4.** *Chem.* To break up (cane-sugar) into dextrose and lævulose 1864. †**5.** *intr.* To change to the opposite –1813.

1. Again the lab'ring hind inverts the soil SHENSTONE. 2. The way is the same, but the order is inverted HOBBES. b. Thus is all inverted, many Kings, and few subjects PURCHAS. c. They inverted, and retaliated the impiety BURKE.

†**II.** *trans.* To divert from its proper purpose; to pervert to another use –1678.

III. †**1.** *trans.* To turn in or inward –1646. **2.** To turn outside in, or inside out; *spec.* in *Path.* 1615.

I·nvert, *a.* 1880. [Short for INVERTED.] In **I. sugar:** Sugar formed by the breaking up of cane-sugar into dextrose and lævulose.

Invertant (invə̄·ɹtănt), *a.* 1828. [f. INVERT *v.* + -ANT[1].] *Her.* = INVERTED II. 1.

Invertebral (invə̄·ɹtĭbrăl), *a.* *rare.* 1816. [IN-[3].] = INVERTEBRATE *a.*

‖**Invertebrata** (invə̄ɹtĭbrē̆·tă), *sb. pl.* 1828. [mod.L., = *animalia invertebrata*; see INVERTEBRATE.] A name for all animals except the *Vertebrata* or back-boned animals; now only a convenient negative term for all groups below the Vertebrata.

Invertebrate (invə̄·ɹtĭbrĕt). 1826. [ad. mod.L. *invertebratus*, in neut. pl. INVERTEBRATA, f. L. *in-* (IN-[3]) + *vertebra* joint, esp. of the spine; see VERTEBRATE.]

A. *adj.* Not having a backbone or spinal column. **b.** *fig.* Without 'backbone' 1879. **B.** *sb.* One of the Invertebrata 1826. Also *fig.*

Inverted (invə̄·ɹtėd), *ppl. a.* 1598. [f. INVERT *v.* + -ED[1].]

I. 1. Turned upside down. **b.** *Mus.* Of chords or intervals: Having the lowest note transposed an octave higher 1811. **2.** Reversed in position or order; turned in the opposite direction 1602. **3.** Reversed in relations 1702. **b.** Reversed in meaning 1646. **4.** *Mil.* Cf. INVERSION I. 4, INVERT *v.* I. 3. 1832. **5.** *Math.* = INVERSE *a.* I. 3. 1885. **6.** *Chem.* Of cane-sugar: Exhibiting lævorotatory power 1857.

1. They had no covering but an i. boat 1806. 2. I live in an i. order. They who ought to have succeeded me are gone before me BURKE. 3. This i. Idolatry, wherein the Image did Homage to the Man STEELE.

II. 1. *Her.* Turned inwards or towards the middle of the field: said of animals or their members 1610. **2.** *Path.* Introverted; turned inside out 1787.

Hence **Inve·rtedly** *adv.* in an i. manner.

†**Invertible** (invə̄·ɹtib'l), *a.*[1] 1534. [ad. late L. *invertibilis*, f. *in-* (IN-[3]) + *vertere*; see -BLE.] That cannot be turned or reversed –1633.

An indurate and i. conscience CRANMER.

Inve·rtible, *a.*[2] 1881. [f. INVERT *v.* + -IBLE.] **a.** That can be inverted. **b.** That tends to invert the usual order.

Invertin (invə̄·ɹtin, i·nvəɹtin). 1879. [f. INVERT *v.* + -IN[1].] *Chem.* A chemical ferment, obtained as a white powder from yeast desiccated in air; it is the constituent which produces the inversion of sugar.

Invertor (invə̄·ɹtəɹ). [f. INVERT *v.* + -OR (here irreg.).] An instrument for reversing an electric current; a commutator. (Mod. Dicts.)

Invest (inve·st), *v.* 1489. [ad. L. *investire*, f. *in-* (IN-[2]) + *vestire* to dress, clothe.]

I. 1. *trans.* To clothe; to dress or adorn 1583; to put on as clothes or ornaments 1596. **2.** *transf.* To cover or surround as with a garment. Const. *with.* 1548. **b.** To cover as a garment does 1632. **3.** *fig.* 1604. **4.** To clothe *with* or *in* the insignia of an office; hence, *with* the dignity itself; to install *in* an office or rank with proper rites 1489. **5.** To establish in the possession of any office, position, property, etc.; to endow with power, authority, or privilege. Const. *in, with.* 1564. **6.** To settle, secure, or vest (a right or power) in (a person) 1590. **7.** *Mil.* To enclose or hem in; to besiege, beleaguer; †to attack 1600.

1. Ile show you, how the Bride, faire Isis, they i. DRAYTON. So faire a crew..Cannot find one this girdle to inuest SPENSER. 2. b. Thread-like down which invests the plant 1861. 4. The lord Thomas Stanley he inuested with the swoorde of the countie of Darby HALL. 5. To i. a person with lands 1861. 6. The powers invested in Congress 1794. 7. Astorga is invested WELLINGTON.

II. [after It. *investire* (13th cent.).] To employ (money) in the purchase of anything from which interest or profit is expected 1613. **b.** *absol.* or *intr.* To make an investment; *colloq.* to lay out money 1864.

b. *colloq.* To i. in a penny time-table (*mod.*).

†**Inve·stient,** *a.* 1695. [ad. L. *investientem*, *investire*; see -ENT.] Investing, coating, enveloping –1762.

Investigable (inve·stigăb'l), *a.*[1] 1594. [ad. late L. *investigabilis*; see INVESTIGATE and -ABLE.] Capable of being investigated, traced out, or searched into; open to investigation.

†**Inve·stigable,** *a.*[2] 1510. [ad. late L. *investigabilis* (Vulg.), f. *in-* (IN-[3]) + *vestigare* to track, trace.] Incapable of being traced; unsearchable –1701.

Investigate (inve·stigeˡt), *v.* 1510. [f. L. *investigat-*, *investigare*, f. *in-* (IN-[2]) + *vestigare*.] **1.** *trans.* To search or inquire into; to examine systematically or in detail. **2.** *intr.* To make search; to reconnoitre, to scout; to inquire systematically, to make investigation 1510.

1. To i. a question of law *Junius Lett.* 2. To i. into the nature of Society MANDEVILLE. Hence **Inve·stigatingly** *adv.* **Inve·stigative** *a.* **Inve·stigator.**

Investigation (investigē̆ˡ·ʃən). late ME. [a. F., ad. L. *investigationem*; see prec.] **1.** The action of investigating; search, inquiry; systematic examination; minute and careful research. Also with *an* and *pl.* **2.** The tracking of (a beast). T. TAYLOR.

1. I. of the truth 1602. Characters which require a long i. to unfold BURKE.

†**Inve·stion.** *rare.* 1586. [ad. med.L. *investionem*, for **investitionem*.] The action of investing; investment –1632.

Investitive (inve·stitiv), *a.* 1780. [f. ppl. stem of L. *investire* + -IVE.] Having the property or function of investing.

Investiture (inve·stitiŭɹ). ME. [ad. med.L. *investitura*, f. *investire*; Fr. *investiture*.] **1.** The action of clothing or robing; *concr.* that which clothes or covers. Chiefly *fig.* 1651. **2.** The action or ceremony of clothing in the insignia of an office; the formal investing of a person with an office or rank; the formal putting (a person) in possession of a fief or benefice. Often, spec., the livery and seizin of the temporalities of an eccl. dignity. ME. **3.** Clothing in attributes or qualities; establishment in any state of privilege or honour 1626. **4.** = INVESTMENT 4. Now *rare.* 1649. †**5.** = INVESTMENT 5. –1845.

1. The darkness of clouds is the accustomed i. of the Divine presence 1871. 2. The king..gave the bishop the i., or livery and seizin of his temporalities, by the delivery of a ring and staff BURKE. 3. One incapable of i. with any grandeur LAMB.

Investment (inve·stmĕnt). 1597. [f. INVEST *v.* + -MENT.] **1.** The act of putting clothes or vestments on; *concr.* clothing; vestments. Also *fig.* **2.** *transf.* An envelope; a coating 1646. **3.** = INVESTITURE 2, 3. 1649. **4.** *Mil.* The surrounding or hemming in *of* a town or fort by a hostile force; beleaguerment; blockade. Also *attrib.* 1811. **5.** *Comm.* The investing of money or capital; an amount of money invested in some species of property. Also *attrib.* 1615. **b.** A form of property viewed as a vehicle in which money may be invested 1837.

1. You, Lord Arch-bishop..Whose white Inuestments figure Innocence SHAKS. 3. The i. of the powers of nature with personal life and consciousness CLODD. 4. To draw the i. closer KINGLAKE. 5. Before the i. could be made, a change of the market might render it ineligible A. HAMILTON. b. 'I do not put myself in the way of hearing about profitable investments' 1837.

Investor (inve·stəɹ). Also †**-er.** 1586. [f. INVEST *v.* + -OR.] One who invests.

Investure (inve·stiŭɹ), *sb.* 1577. [f. INVEST + -URE. Not on L. analogies.] = INVESTITURE, INVESTMENT.

†**Inve·sture,** *v.* *rare.* 1552. [Partly f. prec.; partly f. IN-[1] or [2] + VESTURE.] **1.** *trans.* To invest *in* an estate or dignity. ASCHAM. **2.** To clothe, to vest –1661.

2. Our monks investured in their copes FULLER.

Inveteracy (inve·tĕrăsi). 1691. [f. next; see -ACY.] **1.** The quality of being inveterate; the state of being strong or deep-seated from long persistence 1719. **2.** Deep-rooted prejudice, hostility, or hatred; enmity of old standing 1691.

1. The i. of the people's prejudices ADDISON. 2. The I. of the Jews against the Christians 1703.

Inveterate (inve·tĕrĕt), *a.* late ME. [ad. L. *inveteratus* become old, pa. pple. of *inveterare*, f. *in-* (IN-[2]) + *veterare* to make old.] **1.** Of old standing; aged. **2.** Firmly established by long continuance; long-established; deep-rooted; obstinate. (Now mostly of things evil.) 1563. **3.** Full of obstinate prejudice or hatred; embittered, malignant; virulent. (Now *vulgar.*) 1528. **4.** Settled or confirmed in habit, condition, or practice; hardened, obstinate 1734.

1. An I. willow-tree EVELYN. 2. An Extirpation of i., sinfull Habits SOUTH. I. diseases COWLEY. His old and i. enemies ALISON. 3. I felt i. against him DICKENS. 4. An i. smoker 1859. Hence **Inve·terate·ly** *adv.*, **-ness.**

Inveterate (inve·tĕreˡt), *v.* *Obs.* or *arch.* 1574. [f. L. *inveterat-*, *inveterare*; or f. prec.] **1.** To make old; to establish or confirm by age or long continuance; †also, to harden (the bowels). **2.** To render inveterate in enmity. J. HARRINGTON.

†**Inve·teration.** *rare.* 1631. [ad. L. *inveterationem*; see INVETERATE and -ATION.] The action of rendering, or process of becoming, inveterate –1721.

†**Invi·ct,** *a.* 1494. [ad. L. *invictus*, f. *in-* (IN-[3]) + *victus*, *vincere*.] Unconquered –1678. So †**Invi·cted** *a.* 1600.

Invidious (invi·diəs), *a.* 1606. [ad. L. *invidiosus* (see -OUS), f. *invidia* ill will, ENVY.] **1.** Tending or fitted to excite ill will or envy. **2.** Of an action, duty, topic, etc.: Entailing odium or ill will upon the person performing, discharging, discussing, etc.; giving offence to others 1701; of a distinction, etc.: Offensively discriminating 1709. **3.** That looks with an evil eye; envious, grudging, jealous. Now *rare.* 1668. †**4.** Odious *to* a person (*rare*) –1720.

1. An i. Pamphlet 1755. His revenue..was ample without being i. BURKE. 2. The laws against the combinations of labourers..were seen to be unjust and i. ROGERS. 4. Joseph..became i. to his elder Brethren STEELE. Hence **Invi·dious·ly** *adv.*, **-ness.**

Invigilancy (invi·dʒilănsi). *rare.* 1611. [f. L. *in-* (IN-[3]) + *vigilantia*; see -ANCY.] Absence of vigilance or watchfulness. So **Invi·gilance** (*rare*) 1828.

Invigilate (invi·dʒileˡt), *v.* 1553. [f. L. *invigilat-*, *invigilare*, f. *in-* (IN-[2]) + *vigilare* to watch.] **1.** *intr.* To keep watch. Now *spec.* To watch over students at examination. †**2.** *trans.* To arouse; to make watchful (*rare*) –16.. Hence **Invi·gilator.** **Invigila·tion.**

Invigorate (invi·gŏre̋ⁱt), *v.* 1646. [f. L. type **invigorare* = OF. *envigorer*; see -ATE [3].] **1.** *trans.* To impart vigour to; to fill with life and energy; to strengthen, animate. **2.** *intr.* To become vigorous 1759.

1. Their minds and bodies were invigorated by exercise GIBBON. Hence **Invigora·tion. Invi·gorative** *a.* invigorating.

Invigour (invi·gəɹ), *v. rare.* Also †**en-.** 1611. [In form *envigour*, a. OF. *envigorer, -ourer,* f. *en-* (IN-[2]) + *vigueur*; subseq. refash. after L.] *trans.* To invigorate.

†**Invi·le,** *v. rare.* [f. IN-[2] + VILE *a.*] To render vile. DANIEL.

†**Invi·llage,** *v.* 1613. [f. IN-[2] + VILLAGE.] *trans.* To make or reduce into a village.

Invincible (invi·nsĭb'l), *a.* (*sb.*) ME. [a. F., ad. L. *invincibilis*, f. *in-* (IN-[3]) + *vincibilis*, f. *vincere* to conquer.]

A. *adj.* **1.** That cannot be vanquished, overcome, or subdued; unconquerable. **b.** *transf.* and *fig.* 1482. †**2.** Unsurpassable –1617. **3.** Of or pertaining to the Invincibles (see B. b) 1885.

1. *I. Armada*: see ARMADA. The name 'Invincible', so commonly given to this fleet, was not official J. K. LAUGHTON. **b.** An i. reason and an argument infallible HALL.

B. *sb.* One who is invincible 1640. **b.** A member of an Irish assassination society so called, developed from the Fenians about 1881–2.

Hence **Invincibi·lity** 1601, **Invi·ncibleness. Invi·ncibly** *adv.*

Inviolable (invəi·ŏlăb'l), *a.* 1530. [ad. L. *inviolabilis*, or a. F.] **1.** Not to be violated; not liable or allowed to suffer violence; to be kept sacredly free from profanation, infraction, or assault 1532. †**2.** That cannot be violated, broken, forced, or injured –1719.

1. Styx is the i. oath COWPER. Jove's i. altar POPE. A humble i. English home 1863. **2.** Th' i. Saints In Cubic Phalanx firm advanc't entire MILT. *P. L.* VI. 398. The strict and i. Harmony of the three Persons WATERLAND. Hence **Invi·olabi·lity, Invi·olableness** (now *rare*). **Invi·olably** *adv.*

Inviolacy (invəi·ŏlăsi). 1846. [f. next; see -ACY.] The condition of being inviolate; inviolateness.

Inviolate (invəi·ŏle̋t), *a.* ME. [ad. L. *inviolatus*, f. *in-* (IN-[3]) + *violatus, violare.*] Not violated; free from violation; unhurt, uninjured, unbroken; unprofaned, unmarred; intact.

With..fayth inuyolate LYDG. Clement VIII ordered that the relics should remain untouched, i. 1848. So **Invi·olated** *a.* 1548. Hence **Invi·olate·ly** *adv.*, **-ness.**

†**I·nvious,** *a.* 1622. [f. L. *invius* (f. *in-*, IN-[3] + *via*) + -OUS.] Having no roads or ways; pathless, trackless –1681.

Invi·rile, *a.* [IN-[3].] Unmanly, effeminate. LOWELL. So †**Inviri·lity**, effeminacy 1628.

Inviscate (invi·ske̋ⁱt), *v.* ME. [f. L. *inviscat-, inviscare* to smear with, or snare in, bird-lime, f. *in-* (IN-[2]) + *viscum*; see VISCID.] **1.** *trans.* To render viscid or sticky; to mix or cover with a sticky substance. **2.** To catch in some sticky substance (*rare*) 1646.

2. A..clammy substance like tar, in which..insects are inviscated WITHERING. Hence **Invisca·tion.**

†**Invi·scerate,** *v.* 1626. [f. ppl. stem of L. *inviscerare*, f. *in-* (IN-[2]) + *viscera* entrails.] *trans.* To put into the 'bowels' or heart –1648. Hence †**Inviscera·tion.**

Invisible (invi·zĭb'l). ME. [a. F., ad. L. *invisibilis*; see IN-[3] and VISIBLE.]

A. *adj.* **1.** That cannot be seen; that by its nature is not an object of sight. **2.** Not in sight; not to be seen 1555. **3.** Too small to be discerned; imperceptible 1665. **b.** *I. green*: a very dark shade of green, not easily distinguishable from black 1844.

1. *I. ink* (called also *sympathetic ink*), an ink which requires heat, vapour, or the like to make visible what is written in it. **2.** Langham called every day..but I was i. 1840.

B. *sb.* **1.** An invisible thing, person, or being 1646. **2.** One who denies the visible character of the Church; *spec.* in *pl.* certain German Protestants of the 16th c. 1818.

1. Swedenborg..with his invisibles LAMB. *The i.*, the unseen world; the Deity; The I. in things scarce seen reveal'd COWPER. Hence **Invisibi·lity, Invi·sibleness. Invi·sibly** *adv.*

†**Invi·sion.** [IN-[3].] Want of vision; blindness of young animals. SIR T. BROWNE.

Invitation (invite̋ⁱ·ʃən). 1598. [ad. L. *invitationem.*] **1.** The action of inviting to come, attend, or take part in something 1611. **b.** The spoken or written form in which a person is invited 1615. **c.** In the English Communion Service, the exhortation beginning 'Ye that do truly' 1883. **2.** *fig.* The presenting of attractions or inducements to come or advance; an instance of this; attraction; inducement 1598. **3.** *attrib.*, as *i.-performance*, one attended only by people invited 1808.

1. b. The invitations are out 1864. **2.** I spie entertainment in her;..she giues the leere of inuitation *Merry W.* I. iii. 50.

Invitatory (invəi·tătəri). ME. [ad. L. *invitatorius* inviting.] **A.** *adj.* That invites or tends to invite; containing or conveying an invitation. **B.** *sb.* **1.** [= med.L. *invitatorium.*] An invitation 1666. **2.** *Eccl.* A form of invitation used in religious worship; *spec.* in the breviary, the antiphon to *Venite exultemus* at matins; in the Prayer Book, the invitatory psalm or *Venite* 1450.

I. psalm (*Eccl.*): the *Venite*, Psalm xcv.

Invite (i·nvəit), *sb. colloq.* or *vulgar.* 1593. [f. next; cf. *request*, etc.] The act of inviting; an invitation.

Invite (invəi·t), *v.* 1533. [a. F. *inviter*, ad. L. *invitare.*] **1.** *trans.* Of a person: To ask (a person) graciously, kindly, or courteously, **a.** to come *to* (*into*, etc.) a place or proceeding 1553. **b.** *to do something* assumed to be agreeable 1583. **c.** To request 1854. †**d.** To try to attract or induce –1617. **e.** *fig.* Unintentionally to encourage (something) to come 1650. **2.** Of a thing: To present inducements to (a person) *to do* something or proceed *to* a place or action 1533. **b.** To tend to bring on 1599. †**c.** To attract physically –1800.

1. If thou be inuited of a mighty man, withdraw thy selfe, and so much the more will he inuite thee *Ecclus.* xiii. 9. **b.** She did not i. him to enter 1797. **c.** I never i. confidences BLACK. **e.** You threaten Peace, and you i. a War DRYDEN. **2.** The exemples of owre fathers..doo inuite vs hereunto EDEN. **b.** It seemed to i. discussion BURKE.

Invitee (invəitī·). 1837. [f. INVITE *v.* + -EE.] One who is invited.

Invitement (invəi·tmĕnt). Now *rare.* 1599. [ad. L. *invitamentum.*] †**1.** Inviting; an invitation –1639. **2.** Inducement; allurement 1627.

Inviter (invəi·təɹ). Also †**-or.** 1586. [f. INVITE *v.* + -ER [1].] One who invites. Hence **Invi·tress,** a female i. 1617.

Invitiate (invi·ʃie̋t), *a. rare.* 1590. [IN-[3].] Without blemish.

Invi·ting, *ppl. a.* 1600. [f. INVITE *v.* + -ING [2].] **1.** That invites. **2.** Attractive; alluring; tempting 1604.

2. This Fruit Divine, Fair to the Eye, i. to the Taste MILT. *P. L.* IX. 777. Hence **Invi·ting·ly** *adv.*, **-ness.**

Invitrifiable (invi·trifəiˌăb'l), *a.* 1796. [IN-[3].] That cannot be vitrified or converted into glass.

Invocate (i·nvŏke̋ⁱt), *v.* Now *rare.* 1526. [f. L. *invocat-, invocare.*] **1.** *trans.* = INVOKE. †**2.** *intr.* To make invocation –1802.

1. Those old nine [Muses] which rimers inuocate SHAKS.

Invocation (invŏke̋ⁱ·ʃən). ME. [a. OF., ad. L. *invocationem.*] **1.** The action or an act of invoking or calling upon (God, a deity, etc.) in prayer or attestation; supplication for aid or protection. **b.** *Eccl.* A form of invocatory prayer. Also, The name or appellation used in invoking a divinity, etc. 1827. **2.** The action or an act of conjuring or summoning a devil or spirit by incantation; a charm, spell ME. **3.** *Admiralty Prize Procedure.* The calling in of papers or evidence from another case 1806.

1. I woll make i...Unto the god of sleepe anone CHAUCER. **2.** 'Tis a Greeke inuocation, to call fools into a circle SHAKS.

Invocatory (invǫ·kătəri, i·nvŏke̋ⁱtəri), *a.* 1691. [f. L. *invocare, invocat-* + -ORY.] Of the nature of, characterized by, or used in, invocation.

Invoice (i·nvois), *sb.* 1560. [app. orig. = *invoyes*, pl. of INVOY = 16th c. F. *envoy* (now *envoi*), f. *envoyer* to send.] A list of the particular items of goods shipped or sent to a factor, consignee, or purchaser, with their value or prices, and charges. Also, *loosely*, A consignment of invoiced goods. Also *attrib.*

Invoice (i·nvois), *v.* 1619. [f. prec. sb.] *trans.* To make an invoice of, to enter in an invoice.

They should be invoiced at a reasonable and just price 1800.

Invoke (invōᵘ·k), *v.* 1490. [a. F. *invoquer*, ad. L. *invocare*, f. *in-* (IN-[2]) + *vocare* to call.] **1.** *trans.* To call on (God, a deity, etc.) in prayer or as a witness; to appeal to for aid or protection; to summon or invite in prayer. **2.** To summon (a spirit) by charms or incantation; to conjure; also *fig.* 1602. **b.** To utter (a sacred *name*) in invocation 1698. **3.** To make supplication for, to implore 1617. **4.** *Admiralty Prize Procedure.* To call in evidence from a parallel case, or from the papers of a sister ship of the same owners, etc. 1802.

1. In witness of this our league, we i. the holy name of the living God 1777. **2.** Thou shalt stand by my side while I i. the phantom LYTTON. **3.** The spirits.. who..i. the vengeance of Heaven on their destroyer 1832. Hence **Invo·ker,** one who invokes.

Involucel (invǫ·liusel). 1804. [ad. mod.L. *involucellum* (also used), dim. of INVOLUCRUM.] *Bot.* A whorl of bracts surrounding one of the divisions in an inflorescence; a partial or secondary involucre. So **Involuce·llate** *a.* furnished with involucels.

Involucre (i·nvŏl[i]ūkəɹ). 1578. [a. F., ad. L. *involucrum.*] **1.** That which envelops or enwraps; a case, covering, envelope; *spec.* in *Anat.*, a membranous envelope, as the pericardium. Also *fig.* **2.** *Bot.* A whorl or rosette of bracts surrounding an inflorescence, or at the base of an umbel. Also **b.** In ferns, sometimes applied to the indusium. **c.** In fungi, the velum. 1787. **3.** *Zool.* = INVOLUCRUM 3. So **Involu·cral** *a.* of or pertaining to an i. 1845. **Involu·crate(d** 1830, **I·nvolucred** 1806 *adjs.* furnished with an i. **Involu·criform** *a.* having the form of an i. 1851.

‖**Involucrum** (invŏl[i]ū·krǒm). Pl. **-a.** 1677. [L., f. *involvere* to INVOLVE.] **1.** = INVOLUCRE 1. **2.** *Bot.* = INVOLUCRE 2. 1753. **3.** *Zool.* A kind of sheath about the base of the thread-cells of acalephs. HUXLEY.

Involuntary (invǫ·lǒntări), *a.* 1531. [ad. L. *involuntarius*; see IN-[3] and VOLUNTARY.] **1.** Not voluntary; done or happening without exercise or without co-operation of the will; not done willingly or by choice; unintentional. **b.** *Physiol.* Concerned in bodily actions or processes which are independent of the will 1840. **2.** Unwilling 1597.

1. The i. closing of the eyelids when the surface of the eye is touched DARWIN. **2.** A vast i. throng POPE. Hence **Invo·luntarily** *adv.* **Invo·luntariness.**

Involute (i·nvŏl[i]ut). 1661. [ad. L. *involutus, -um*, pa. pple. of *involvere* to INVOLVE.]

A. *adj.* **1.** Involved; intricate; †obscure 1669. **2.** Rolled or curled up spirally; spiral; *spec.* in *Conch.* Having the whorls wound closely round the axis, and nearly or wholly concealing it 1661. **3.** *Bot.* Rolled inwards at the edges 1760. **4.** *Geom.* †*I. figure* or *curve* = B. 2. –1796.

1. This most i. of Lies is finally winded off CARLYLE.

B. *sb.* **1.** Something involved or entangled (*rare*) 1845. **2.** *Geom.* A curve traced out by the end of a flexible inextensible string if unwound from a given curve in the plane of that curve; the locus of a point in a straight line which rolls without sliding on a given curve. Correl. to EVOLUTE. 1796.

Involuted (i·nvŏl[i]utĕd), *a.* 1797. [f. prec. + -ED [1].] **1.** = INVOLUTE *a.* 2, 3. **2.** *Phys.* That has passed through the process of involution (see INVOLUTION 4) 1898.

Involution (invŏl[i]ū·ʃən). 1611. [ad. L. *involutionem*, f. *involvere*; cf. F. *involution.*] **1.** The action of involving or fact of being involved; implication; also, quasi-*concr.*, that which is involved. **b.** *concr.* Something that involves or enwraps; a covering, etc. SIR T. BROWNE. **2.** An involved or entangled condition; complication; also *concr.*, something complicated; an intricate movement, etc. 1611. 3. *Anat.* A rolling, curling, or turning inwards; *concr.* a part formed by this action 1851. 4. *Phys.* The retrograde change which occurs in the body or in some organ in old age. Also *attrib.* 1860. 5. *Math.* a. *Arith.* and *Alg.* The multiplication of a quantity into itself any number of times, so as to raise it to any assigned power 1706. b. *Geom.* A system of pairs of points on a straight line, so situated that the product of the distances of each pair from a fixed point on the line (the *centre of i.*) is constant 1847.

1. The i. or comprehension of Presbyter within Episcopus JER. TAYLOR. 2. The style of the first act has..more i., than the general style of Fletcher HAZLITT. The involutions of an intricate dance 1858.

Involve (invǫ·lv), *v.* Also †en-. ME. [ad. L. *involvere*, f. *in-* (IN-[2]) + *volvere* to roll.] 1. *trans.* To roll or enwrap in anything; to enfold, envelop. Const. *in*, †*with*. ME. 2. To wind in a spiral form; to wreathe, coil, entwine 1555. 3. *fig.* To envelop within the folds of some condition or circumstance ME.; to entangle, to render intricate 1533. 4. To entangle (a person) in trouble, difficulties, perplexity, etc.; to embarrass. Const. *in*, †*with*, †*into*. ME. 5. To implicate in a charge or crime 1655. 6. To include; to contain, imply; *esp.* to contain implicitly 1605. 7. To roll up within itself; to overwhelm and swallow up 1605. 8. *Math.* To multiply (a quantity) into itself any desired number of times; to raise to a power. Now *rare* or *Obs.* 1673.

1. I saw Fog only,.. I. the passive city MRS. BROWNING. 2. Some of Serpent kinde,..involv'd Thir Snakie foulds MILT. *fig.* He knows His end with mine involvd MILT. 3. This passage is involved in great obscurity PALEY. 4. Involved in financial difficulties 1898. 5. Let not my Crime i. the Innocent 1695. 6. Mighty mysteries involved in numbers BERKELEY. Every argument involves some assumptions WESTCOTT. When the safety of the nation was involved U. S. GRANT. 7. The gathering number, as it moves along, Involves a vast involuntary throng POPE. 8. Let $a+x$ be involved to the 5th power HUTTON.

Involved (invǫ·lvd), *ppl. a.* 1607. [f. prec. + -ED[1].] 1. In senses of prec. †2. Of persons, their actions, etc.; Not straightforward and open; underhand, reserved –1713.

Hence **Invo·lved·ly** *adv.*, **-ness.**

Involvement (invǫ·lvmĕnt). 1630. [f. as prec. + -MENT.] 1. The action or process of involving; the fact of being involved 1706; that which is involved 1821. †2. A covering 1630.

†**I·nvoy.** [Var. of ENVOY *sb.*[1]] An INVOICE. MORYSON.

†**Invu·lgar,** *a.* 1604. [IN-[3].] Not vulgar; refined; unusual –1627.

†**Invu·lgar,** *v.* 1599. [IN-[2].] *trans.* To divulge to the common people; to vulgarize.

Invu·lnerable, *a.* 1595. [ad. L. *invulnerabilis*; see IN-[3].] Incapable of being wounded, hurt, or damaged (*lit.* and *fig.*).

Hence **Invu·lnerabi·lity, Invu·lnerableness. Invu·lnerably** *adv.*

†**Invu·lnerate,** *a.* 1680. [ad. L. *invulneratus*.] Unwounded. So †**Invu·lnered** *a.* 1613–35.

Invultuation (invɒltiu|ēⁱ·ʃən). 1856. Also **invultation.** [n. of action f. med. L. *invultuare*, *invultare* to make a likeness, f. *in-* (IN-[2]) + *vultus* countenance.] The making of a likeness, esp. the waxen effigy of a person for purposes of witchcraft.

Inwall (i·nwǫl), *sb.* 1611. [IN *adv.*] An inner or inside wall.

Inwall, *v.*, var. of ENWALL.

Inward (i·nwǭɹd). Comp. †**inwarder,** superl. **inwardest** (now *rare*). [OE. *innanweard*, *inneweard*, *inweard*, f. *innan*, *inne*, *inn* adv. and prep. + *-weard* (see -WARD).]

A. *adj.* I. 1. Situated within; that is the inner or inmost part; that is in or on the inside. b. Of the voice or a sound: Uttered without due opening of the mouth; muffled, indistinct. Also *transf.* of the utterer. 1774. 2. Applied to the mind, thoughts, and mental faculties as located within the body; hence = mental or spiritual ME. †b. Deeply felt; hence, earnest, fervent –1627. c. Spiritually minded (? *Obs.*) 1450. †3. Intimate, familiar, confidential –1675. †b. Of a bird or beast: Domesticated, tame –1643. †4. Secret; private –1611. 5. Domestic, intestine. *Obs.* or *arch.* 1513. †6. Intrinsic –1620.

1. b. The marten..when it sings, is so i. as scarce to be heard G. WHITE. 2. Behold, thou desirest trueth in the i. parts *Ps.* li. 6. *Inward man* = *inner man* (see INNER *a.* 2). 3. Friendly to all men, i. but with few QUARLES. 4. All i. grudges and open discordes HALL. 5. I. war amongst our selues MORE.

II. [From the adv.] Directed or proceeding towards the inside, as *i. postages* 1849.

B. *sb.* [absol. use of the adj.] 1. The inward part, the inside; usu. *spec.* the internal parts or organs of the body, the entrails. (Now *rare* in *sing.*) OE. 2. The inner nature or essence of a thing or person; that which is within; the interior character, qualities, thoughts, etc. (*rare* in *sing.*, *Obs.* in *pl.*) OE. †3. = INTIMATE *sb.* –1607. 4. *pl.* Articles imported, or dues on such articles. Also *attrib.* 1761.

1. The intrailes or i. of beastes COGAN. The fat of the inwardes TINDALE. 3. Sir, I was an i. of his SHAKS.

Inward (i·nwǭɹd), *adv.* [OE. *innan-*, *inne-*, *inweard*; see prec.] 1. Towards the inside or interior. a. Of motion OE. b. Of position ME. 2. *fig.* Towards that which is within; into the mind or soul; into one's own thoughts ME. b. = INWARDLY *adv.* 3. OE.

1. a. Pathes..leading i. farr SPENSER. 2. Satiated with external pleasures, she turns i. 1766. b. We i. bled DRYDEN.

Inwardly (i·nwǭɹdli), *a. rare.* [OE. *inweardlic*, f. *inweard* + *-lic*, -LY[1].] †a. = INWARD *a.* –1504. b. Relating to what is inward or spiritual. COLERIDGE.

Inwardly (i·nwǭɹdli), *adv.* [OE. *inweardlīce*; see prec. and -LY[2].]

I. 1. In, on, or in reference to the inside or inner part; within 1483. b. With a voice that does not pass the lips; not aloud 1530. 2. Intimately, thoroughly; closely ME. 3. In heart; in mind or thought; in spirit ME. †b. In or from the inmost heart; fervently, earnestly –1632.

1. Therefore let Benedicke like couered fire..waste i. *Much Ado* III. i. 78. b. Half i., half audibly she spoke TENNYSON. 3. They blesse with their mouth, but they curse i. *Ps.* lxii. 4.

II. Towards the inside or inner part; *fig.* towards that which is within; into the mind or soul (now *rare*) 1667.

Inwardness (i·nwǭɹdnĕs). ME. [f. INWARD *a.* + -NESS.] †1. The inner part or region; *pl.* Inward parts, entrails. Usu. *fig.* –1530. 2. The inner nature, essence, or meaning 1605. 3. The quality of being inward to something else (*lit.* or *fig.*) 1611. †4. Intimacy, familiarity –1715. 5. Depth or intensity of feeling or thought 1836; spirituality 1859.

2. Sense cannot arrive to th' inwardnesse Of things H. MORE (1647). 4. In the..i. of conjugal conference STEELE. 5. This i. of the words of Christ JOWETT.

Inwards (i·nwǭɹdz), *adv.* [ME. *inwardes*, f. *inward* adv., with advb. gen. *-es*, *-s*, as in *besides*, etc.] = INWARD *adv.*

Inweave (inwī·v), **enweave,** *v.* Pa. t. **-wove.** Pa. pple. **-woven** (also †**-weav d, -wove**). 1578. [f. IN-[1] (or [2]), EN-[1] + WEAVE *v.* Chiefly in pa. pple.] 1. *trans.* To weave in; to weave (things) together; to interweave. Also *fig.* 2. To insert (one thing) in or into another by weaving in or entwining. Const. *in*, *into* (*among*, *through*). 1596. Also *fig.* 3. To combine *with* something inserted or entwined 1591. 4. To form by weaving or plaiting 1667.

1. A living link in that Tissue of History, which inweaves all Being CARLYLE. 4. Down they cast Thir Crowns inwove with Amarant and Gold MILT.

Inwheel, var. of ENWHEEL *v. Obs.*

†**Inwit.** ME. [f. IN *adv.* + WIT *sb.* Not related to OE. *inwit*, *inwid* deceit.] 1. Conscience; inward sense. Also *clean i.* = 'a clean heart'. ME. only. 2. Reason, understanding; wisdom –1587. 3. (tr. L. *animus.*) Heart, soul, mind; cheer, courage. WYCLIF.

Inwith (i·nwiþ). *Obs.* exc. *Sc.* ME. [f. IN *adv.* + WITH *prep.*] A. *prep.* Within, inside of. †1. Of place –1513. †2. Of time. ME. only.

1. This purs hath she i. her bosom hyd CHAUCER.

B. *adv.* †1. Denoting position: Within, inwardly –1565. 2. Denoting direction: Inwards. *Sc.* 1768. b. Hence as *adj. Sc.* 1768.

Inwork (i·nwɒ̄·ɹk), *v. rare.* 1681. [IN-[1] or IN *adv.* See also INWROUGHT.] To work in or within (*trans.* and *intr.*).

Inworn, *ppl. a.* 1641. [IN *adv.*] a. as *pa. pple.* of *wear in*: Worn or pressed in. b. as *adj.* inveterate.

Inwrap, -wreathe, etc.: see ENWRAP, etc.

Inwrought, *ppl. a.* Also **en-.** 1637. [f. IN *adv.* + *wrought*, pa. pple. of *work* vb.]

I. as *pa. pple.* (inrǭ·t). 1. Of a fabric: Having something worked in by way of decoration (*lit.* and *fig.*). 2. Of a pattern, etc.: Worked into a fabric. Also *transf.* 1740. 3. Worked together *with* something 1824; worked into anything as a constituent 1734.

1. His Mantle hairy, and his Bonnet sedge, I. with figures dim MILT. 2. Flowers enwrought On silken tissue WORDSW.

II. as *adj.* (i·nrǭt). (In senses as above.) 1830.

‖**Inyala** (inyā·lă). 1848. [Native name.] An antelope of S. Africa, *Tragelaphus angasi*, ranging from Nyasaland to Zululand.

Inyo·ke, *v. rare.* 1595. [IN-[1].] *trans.* a. To yoke or unite *to* something. b. To yoke in a wagon, etc.

Io (əi·o). 1592. [a. L. *io*, Gr. ἰώ.] (Also *Io pæan.*) An exclam. of joy or triumph; occas. as *sb.*, an utterance of '*Io!*', an exultant shout or song.

Io-, earlier spelling of **Jo-**; see **I, J,** the letters.

Iod- (əi,ǫd), comb. f. mod.L. *iodum* IODINE, used (chiefly before a vowel) in forming names of iodine compounds; as **iodhy·drin,** an iodine ether of glycerine; etc. Before a cons. usu. IODO-, q. v.

Iodal (əi·ǫ̆dăl). 1838. [f. IOD- + AL(COHOL), after CHLORAL.] *Chem.* A compound of iodine, an oily liquid, analogous to chloral.

Iodate (əi·ǫ̆dēⁱt), *sb.* 1826. [f. IODIC + -ATE[4].] *Chem.* A salt of iodic acid. So **I·odate** *v.* to impregnate or treat with iodine.

†**Iode.** 1826. [a. F. *iode* IODINE.] 1. = IODINE 1830. 2. = IODIDE.

Iodic (əi,ǫ·dik), *a.* 1826. [f. IOD- + -IC.] Of or pertaining to iodine. 1. *Chem.* Containing iodine in union with oxygen; as in *i. acid* (*hydrogen iodate*), an oxygen-acid of iodine. Also *Min.* in *i. silver* = IODYRITE. 2. *Path.* Caused by administration of iodine 1887.

Iodide (əi·ǫ̆dəid). 1822. [f. IOD- + -IDE.] *Chem.* A binary compound of iodine with a more positive element, or an organic radical.

Iodine (əi·ǫ̆din, -əin). 1814. [f. F. *iode* (ad. Gr. ἰώδης violet-coloured) from the colour of its vapour + -INE[3], as in *chlorine.*] *Chem.* One of the non-metallic elements belonging to the halogen group; at ordinary temperatures a greyish-black soft brittle solid with a metallic lustre, volatilizing into a dense vapour of a deep violet colour; in chemical properties resembling chlorine and bromine, but less energetic. Symbol I; atomic weight 127. Also *attrib.*, as in *i. fluid*, *i. injection*, *i. poisoning.*

Iodine exists in sea-water and mineral springs, and in sea-weed and many marine animals, and is extensively obtained from the mother-liquor of Chilian sodium nitrate.

Iodism (əi·ǫ̆diz'm). 1832. [f. IOD- + -ISM.] *ath.* A morbid state induced by excessive or long-continued medicinal use of iodine (or its compounds).

Iodize (əi·ǫ̆dəiz), *v.* 1841. [f. IOD- + -IZE.] *trans.* To treat or impregnate with iodine or an iodide. (Chiefly in *Photogr.* and *Med.*) Hence **I·odizer,** one who or that which iodizes.

Iodo- (əiǫ̆do), used as combining form of mod.L. *iodum* IODINE (chiefly bef. a cons.).

Iodoform (əi,ōᵘ·dofǭɹm, əi·ǫ̆dofǭɹm), *sb.* 1835. [f. IODO- + FORM(YL); cf. *chloroform.*] A compound of iodine (CHI_3), analogous to chloroform, obtained in light yellow scaly crystals, having an odour of saffron and a sweet taste; used medicinally, and as an antiseptic, esp. in surgical dressings. Hence **Io·doform, Iodofo·rmize** *vbs.* to treat or impregnate with i. **Iodofo·rmism,** poisoning by the medical use of iodoform.

I·odous, *a.* 1826. [f. IOD- + -OUS.] 1. *Chem.* Applied to compounds containing iodine in greater proportion to oxygen than those called *iodic*; e.g. a hypothetical *iodous acid*, HIO_2. 2. Having the quality of, or resembling, iodine.

Iodyrite (əi,ǫ·dirəit). 1854. [f. IODINE, after *argyrite*.] *Min.* Native iodide of silver, a sectile mineral, usu. of a yellow colour.

Iolite (əi·ǒləit). 1810. [= Ger. *iolith*, f. Gr. ἴον violet + λίθος; see -LITE.] *Min.* A silicate of aluminium, iron, and magnesium, occurring in short orthorhombic crystals, or granular, of various shades of blue or violet-blue. Also called CORDIERITE or DICHROITE.

Ion (əi·ǫ̆n). 1834. [a. Gr. ἰόν, neut. pr. pple. of ἰέναι to go.] Either of the products (see ANION, CATION) which appear at the respective poles when a substance is subjected to electrolysis; hence, any of the electrically charged particles which are released by dissociation in an electrolyte; a molecule or atom considered electrically; a gaseous particle electrically charged by the action of Röntgen or other rays, etc.

-ion, *suffix*, repr. F. *-ion*, L. *-io*, *-ionem*, a suffix forming sbs. of condition or action from adjs. or sbs., occas. from the vb.-stem, but chiefly from the ppl. or supine stem in *t-*, *s-*, *x-*, e.g. *damnationem* condemning, *missionem* sending, *co(n)nexionem* close union. Examples of all these occur in English, but chiefly those in *-tion* (*-sion*, *-xion*); the form in -ATION (q.v) is the most frequent, and has become a living formative.

Ionian (əi,ōᵘ·niăn). 1563. [f. L. *Ionius*, a. Gr. Ἰώνιος + -AN.] A. *adj.* Of or pertaining to Ionia or to the Ionians; Ionic 1594.

Ionian mode (*Mus.*) a. A mode in ancient Greek music, characterized as soft and effeminate. b. The last of the 'authentic' ecclesiastical modes, having C for its final, and G for its dominant, corresp. to the modern major diatonic scale.

B. *sb.* A member of that division of the Hellenic race which occupied Attica and the northern coast of the Peloponnesus, and established colonies, esp. in Asia Minor, where a large district was named from them Ionia.

Ionic (əi,ǫ·nik), *a.*[1] and *sb.* 1579. [ad. L. *Ionicus*, a. Gr. Ἰωνικός.] A. *adj.* 1. = IONIAN *a.* 2. *Arch.* Name of one of the three orders of Grecian architecture (Doric, Ionic, Corinthian), characterized by the two lateral volutes of the capital 1585. 3. *Mus.* (See *Ionian mode*, a, above.) ? *Obs.* 1579. 4. *Gr.* and *Lat. Pros.* Name of a foot consisting of two long syllables followed by two short ('ionic *a majore*'), or two short followed by two long ('ionic *a minore*'). *I. metre*, a metre consisting of Ionic feet. So †**Io·nical** *a.* 1624.

1. *I. dialect*, the most important of the three main branches of ancient Greek, of which also the Attic was a development. *I. School* or *Sect of philosophy*, that founded by Thales of Miletus in Asiatic Ionia.

B. *sb.* †1. = IONIAN *sb.*; a member of the Ionic School of philosophy -1613. 2. The Ionic dialect of ancient Greek 1668. 3. *Gr.* and *Lat. Pros.* An Ionic foot or verse; Ionic metre; see A. 4. 1612.

Hence **Io·nicize** *v. intr.* to use Ionic; *trans.* to render Ionic (in style or dialect).

Io·nic, *a.*[2] 1890. [f. ION + -IC.] *Physics.* Of or pertaining to ions.

I·onize, *v.* 1898. [f. ION + -IZE.] 1. *intr.* Of an electrolyte: To split into ions 1899. 2. *trans.* Of X rays, cathode rays, etc.: To produce ions in a gas and so make it a conductor. So **Ioniza·tion.**

-ior, *suffix*, repr. L. *-ior* of comparatives, as *inferior*, etc.; formerly *-iour* = F. *-ieur*.

Iota (əi,ōᵘ·tă). 1592. [a. Gr. ἰῶτα.] 1. The name of the Greek letter I, ι, corresp. to the Roman I, i, the smallest letter in the Greek alphabet 1607. 2. *fig.* (after Matt. v. 18; see JOT): The least, or a very small, particle or quantity; an atom. (Usu. with negative.)

1. *Iota subscript*, a small iota written beneath a long vowel, forming the second element of a diphthong, as in ᾳ, ῃ, ῳ. 2. Not an i. should be yielded of the principle of the bill BURKE.

Iotacism (əi,ōᵘ·tăsiz'm). 1656. [ad. L. *iotacismus*, a. Gr. ἰωτακισμός, a laying too much stress upon the ι, f. ἰῶτα.] Excessive use or repetition of the letter *iota* or I; *spec.* the pronunciation of other Greek vowels like *iota* (i.e. as Latin ī or mod. Eng. *ee*), as in mod. Greek. So **Io·tacist.**

I O U (əi·ōᵘ·yū̆). 1795. [= 'I owe you'. The abbreviation occurs 1618.] A document bearing these three letters followed by a specified sum, and signed, constituting a formal acknowledgement of a debt.

An I. O. U. is admissible evidence of a debt without a stamp ESPINASSE.

-iour, a compound suffix, viz. -OUR (OF. *-ur*, *-or*, F. *-eur*), preceded by an *i* representing *i*, *ei*, *e*, of another element; as in *saviour*, ME. and AF. *sauveour*, OF. *sauve-ur*, *-e-or*, early F. *salvedur*:—L. *salvatorem*; see also HAVIOUR and -OUR. Sometimes now written *-ior* (as *warrior*), *-ier* (as *soldier*).

-ious, a compound suffix, viz. *-ous*, added to an *i* which is part of another suffix, repr. L. *-iosus*, F. *-ieux*, with sense 'characterized by, full of'. See -ITIOUS and -OUS.

Ipecac, shortened form of next. 1788.

Ipecacuanha (ipⁱkækiu,æ·nă). 1682. [a. Pg. *ipecacuanha* (ipekakwa·nʸă), ad. Tupi-Guarani *ipe-kaa-guéne*, said to mean 'low or creeping plant causing vomit'.] 1. The root of *Cephaëlis Ipecacuanha*, N.O. *Cinchonaceæ*, a S. Amer. small shrubby plant, which possesses emetic, diaphoretic, and purgative properties; also applied to the forms in which the drug is employed. 2. The plant itself 1788. 3. Transferred to other plants whose roots have emetic properties, e. g.

Bastard or **Wild I.** (*Asclepias curassavica*); **Peruvian**, **Striated**, or **Black I.** (*Psychotria emetica*); **White I.** (*Richardsonia scabra*).

4. *fig.* Something that produces nausea 1763. 5. *attrib.*, as **i. wine**, the filtered infusion of the root in wine 1761.

4. An author, talking of his own works..is to me a dose of i. H. WALPOLE.

Ipocras, obs. f. HIPPOCRAS.

‖**Ipomœa** (əipomī·ă). Also **ipomæa**, ipomea. 1794. [mod.L. (Linn.), f. Gr. ἰπ-, stem of ἴψ a worm + ὅμοιος like.] *Bot.* A genus of twining or creeping plants, mostly tropical, N.O. *Convolvulaceæ*, with trumpet- or salver-shaped corolla; many of the species are cultivated as flowering plants, and one, *I. Batatas*, furnishes the sweet potato. Hence **Ipomœ·ic** *a.* of Ipomœa, in *i. acid*, named from *Ipomœa Jalapa*, jalap.

‖**Ipse dixit** (i·psĭ di·ksit). *Pl.* **ipse dixits.** 1572. [L., = Gr. αὐτὸς ἔφα 'he himself (the master) said it'.] An unproved assertion resting on the bare authority of some speaker; a dogmatic statement; a dictum.

The capricious *ipse dixit* of authority J. H. NEWMAN.

Ipseity (ipsī·,iti). 1659. [f. L. *ipse* self + -ITY.] Personal identity and individuality; selfhood.

‖**Ipso facto** (i·psoᵘ fæ·ktoᵘ), *advb. phr.* 1548. [L.] By that very fact; by the fact itself.

Ir-[1], assimilated form in L. of IN-[2] bef. initial *r*, used in the same way in Eng., as in *ir-radiate*, etc.

Ir-[2], assimilated form in L. of IN-[3] bef. initial *r*, used in the same way in Eng., as in *ir-rational*, etc.

Iracund (əiᵊ·răkʊnd), *a.* 1821. [ad. L. *iracundus*, f. *ira* + *-cundus* 'inclining to'.] Inclined to wrath; choleric, passionate. So †**Iracu·ndious** *a.* 1491–1662. **Iracu·ndity** 1840.

‖**Irade** (irā·de). 1883. [Turk., a. Arab. *irādah* will, desire.] A written decree issued by the Sultan of Turkey.

Iranian (əirēⁱ·niăn). 1789. [f. Pers. *īrān* Persia + -IAN.] A. *adj.* 1. Of or pertaining to Iran or Persia; in *Compar. Philol.* applied to one of the two Asiatic families of the Indo-European languages, comprising Zend and Old Persian and their cognates. †2. a. Aryan. b. Indo-Iranian. -1850. So **Ira·nic** *a.*

B. *sb.* A member of the Iranian race; a speaker of an Iranian language 1789.

Irascible (əiræ·sĭb'l, iræ·s-), *a.* ME. [a. F., ad. L. *irascibilis*, f. *irasci*.] Easily provoked to anger or resentment; prone to anger; irritable, choleric, passionate. b. Characterized by or arising from anger 1659.

A solitary and i. old gentleman 1873. b. I., and objurgatory speech 1659. Hence **Irascibi·lity**, **Ira·scibleness**. **Ira·scibly** *adv.*

Irate (əirēⁱ·t), *a.* 1838. [ad. L. *iratus*, pa. pple. of **irari*, inceptive *irasci* to be or become angry.] Excited to ire; incensed, enraged, angry.

He was at once hauled up before the i. Commandant LIVINGSTONE. Hence **Ira·tely** *adv.* in an i. manner.

Ire (əiᵊɹ). ME. [a. OF. *ire*, *yre*, ad. L. *ira*.] Anger; wrath. Now chiefly *poet.* and *rhet.*

Ireful (əiᵊ·ɹfŭl), *a.* ME. [f. IRE + -FUL.] 1. Full of ire; angry, wrathful. 2. Choleric, passionate ME. Hence **I·reful·ly** *adv.*, **-ness.**

Irenarch (əiᵊ·rīnāɹk). 1702. [ad. late L. *irenarcha*, a. Gr. εἰρηνάρχης; see EIRENARCH.] An Eastern provincial governor or keeper of the peace, under the Roman and Byzantine empires. Now *Hist.*

Irenic (əire·nik, əirī·nik). 1864. [ad. Gr. εἰρηνικός, f. εἰρήνη peace.] *adj.* Pacific, non-polemic. *sb. pl.* **Irenics:** irenical theology 1882.

Irenical (əire·nikăl, əirī·nikăl), *a.* 1660. [f. as prec. + -AL.] Peaceful, pacific; tending to promote peace, esp. in relation to theological or eccl. differences.

‖**Irenicon** (əirī·nikǫ̆n, əire·nikǫ̆n). 1618. [a. Gr. εἰρηνικόν adj. neut.; see IRENIC. Also spelt EIRENICON, q. v.] A proposal designed to promote peace; esp. in a church or between churches. So ‖**Ire·nicum.**

Irian (əiᵊ·riăn), *a.* 1857. [f. IRIS + -AN.] *Anat.* Belonging to the iris of the eye.

Iricism (əiᵊ·risiz'm). 1743. [irreg. f. IRISH, after *Scotticism*.] An Irishism.

Irid (əiᵊ·rid). *rare.* 1822. [f. L. *irid-*, Gr. ἰριδ-, stem of *iris*, ἶρις IRIS.] 1. The iris of the eye. 2. *Bot.* A plant of N.O. *Iridaceæ* 1866.

Iridaceous (əiᵊridēⁱ·ʃəs, iri-), *a.* 1851. [f. L. *irid-* (see prec.) + -ACEOUS.] *Bot.* Related to plants of the genus *Iris*; belonging to the N.O. *Iridaceæ*.

Iridal (əiᵊ·ridăl), *a. rare.* 1837. [f. as prec. + -AL.] Of or belonging to the rainbow.

Iridectomy (əiᵊride·ktŏmi, iri-). 1855. [f. as prec. + Gr. ἐκτομή + -Y.] *Surg.* Excision of a portion of the iris. Also *attrib.*

Iridescence (iride·sĕns). 1803. [f. IRIDESCENT; see -ENCE.] The quality of being iridescent; the interchange of colours as in the rainbow, mother-of-pearl, etc.; a play of glittering and changing colours. Also *fig.*

A rich metallic i. COUES. *fig.* Frequent iridescences of fancy 1803. So **Iride·scency** (? *Obs.*) 1799.

Iridescent (iride·sĕnt), *a.* 1796. [f. L. *irid-* IRIS + -ESCENT.] Displaying colours like those of the rainbow, etc.; glittering or flashing with interchanging colours. Also *fig.*

The i. colours produced by heat on polished steel and copper MRS. SOMERVILLE. **Iride·scently** *adv.*

Iridian (əiri·diăn), *a.* 1864. [f. L. *irid-* IRIS + -IAN.] 1. Pertaining to the iris of the eye. 2. Rainbow-like 1884.

Iridic (əiri·dik), *a.* 1845. [f. IRIDIUM + -IC.] *Chem.* Containing iridium; applied to compounds in which iridium is quadrivalent.

Iridious (əiri·diəs), *a.* 1865. [f. IRIDIUM + -OUS.] *Chem.* Containing iridium; applied to compounds in which iridium is trivalent.

Iridium (əiri·diə̆m). 1804. [f. L. *irid-* IRIS 2 + -IUM.] A white metal of the platinum group, resembling polished steel, and fusible with great difficulty, found (usu. with osmium) in native platinum, and in the native alloy IRIDOSMIUM. Chemical symbol Ir; atomic weight 193.

I should incline to call this metal *Iridium*, from the striking variety of colours which it gives, while dissolving in marine acid TENNANT.

Iridize (i·r-, əiᵊ·ridəiz), *v.* 1864. [f. L. *irid-* IRIS, or IRID-IUM + -IZE.] 1. *trans.* To make iridescent 1874. 2. To cover or tip with iridium. Hence **I·ridiza·tion**, irisation; in *Path.*, the coloured halo seen round a light by persons affected with glaucoma.

Irido- (əiᵊ·rido, i·rido), a. Gr. *ἰριδο-, comb. form of ἶρις IRIS, used in forming pathological and surgical terms, chiefly denoting diseases of the iris and operations upon it; as I:ridodia·lysis, the artificial separation of the iris from the ciliary ring; I:ridodone·sis [Gr. δονέειν to shake], tremulousness of the iris; etc.

Iridodesis (əiəridǫ·dĭsis). 1858. [f. Gr. ἶρις, ἰριδ- (IRIDO-) + δέσις binding.] *Surg.* An operation in which the iris is secured in a certain position by a ligature.

Iridoline (əiri·dǫləin). 1863. [f. L. *irid-* IRIS + *oleum* oil + -INE.] *Chem.* A base ($C_{10}H_9N$) occurring in coal-tar oil.

Iridosmine (əiəridǫ·sməin, iri-). 1827. [f. IRID-IUM + OSM-IUM + -INE[5].] A native alloy of the metals iridium and osmium, usually occurring in flattened grains with platinum. Also **Irido·smium,** and *osmiridium.*

Iridotomy (əiəridǫ·tŏmi, iri-). 1855. [f. IRIDO- + Gr. -τομία; cf. *lithotomy.*] Section of the iris.

Iris (əiə·ris), *sb.* Pl. **irides** (əiə·ridīz), **irises.** ME. [a. Gr. ἶρις, stem ἰριδ-. The pl. *irides* is chiefly used in sense 4.] **1.** *Gr. Myth.* The goddess who acted as the messenger of the gods, and displayed as her sign the rainbow; hence, allusively, a messenger 1593. **2.** A rainbow; a many-coloured refraction of light from drops of water 1490. **b.** *transf.* A rainbow-like appearance; a circle or halo of prismatic colours 1601. **c.** *fig.* 1821. **3. a.** A hexagonal prismatic crystal (Pliny *Nat. Hist.* XXXVII. ix. 52). **b.** A variety of rock crystal, having the property of reflecting the prismatic colours by means of natural flaws in its interior ME. **4.** *Anat.* A flat, circular, coloured membrane suspended vertically in the aqueous humour of the eye, and separating the anterior from the posterior chamber; in its centre is a circular opening called the pupil 1525. **b.** (*transf.*) *Entom.* The inner ring of an ocellated spot on an insect's wing 1826. **5.** *Bot.* A genus of plants, the type of the natural order *Iridaceæ*; most of the species have tuberous (less commonly bulbous or fibrous) roots, sword-shaped equitant leaves, and showy flowers; formerly often called Fleur-de-lis or Flower-de-luce. Also, a plant of this genus. 1578.

1. 2 *Hen. VI*, III. ii. 407. 2. His Crest, that prouder then blew I. bends SHAKS. b. In the Spring a livelier i. changes on the burnish'd dove TENNYSON. c. Is Virtue but a shade? And Freedom but the I. of a storm? DISRAELI.

Comb.: **i.-diaphragm,** a contractile diaphragm for lenses, contrived so as to imitate the action of the i.; **-disease,** a form of herpes, generally affecting the back of the hands; **-root,** the root of *Iris florentina*, orris-root.

Iris (əiə·ris), *v.* 1816. [f. prec.] *trans.* To make iridescent; to form into, or place as, a rainbow. Only in *pa. pple.*

Irisate (əiə·riseit), *v.* 1828. [irreg. f. IRIS *sb.* + -ATE[3].] *trans.* To render iridescent. Hence **I·risated** *ppl. a.*, **Irisa·tion.**

Iriscope (əiə·riskǒup). 1841. [irreg. f. IRIS *sb.* 2 + -SCOPE.] A device for exhibiting the primary colours by the action of the breath on a specially prepared plate of highly polished black glass.

Irised (əiə·rist), *a.* 1816. [f. IRIS *sb.* or *v.*] **1.** Having the colours of the rainbow. **2.** Having an iris or irises; as *large-irised* 1879.

Irish (əiə·riʃ). [Orig. *Ī'risc*, f. *Ī'r-*, stem of OE. *Ī'ras* the inhabitants of Ireland + *-isc*, -ISH. The stem *Ī'r-* is obscurely from OIr. *Ériu* Erin (see HIBERNIAN).]

A. *adj.* **1.** Of persons: Of, belonging to, or native to Ireland; orig. and esp. used of the Celtic inhabitants ME. †**b.** Belonging to the Scottish Highlands or the Gaelic inhabitants of them –1652. **2.** Of things: Of or pertaining to Ireland or its inhabitants (freq. denoting a species, variety, or quality peculiar to Ireland) ME. **3.** Epithet of the language of the Celtic inhabitants of Ireland. Hence applied to words, idioms, etc. belonging to that language, and to anything composed or written in it 1547. **4.** Having what are considered Irish characteristics 1589.

1. Irish Free State: see FREE STATE 3. 2. *I. car, frieze, whisky*, etc.; also *I. elk, greyhound, wolf, wolf-hound*, etc. **I. daisy,** the dandelion. **I. moss,** the edible seaweed *Chondrus crispus*, also called carrageen. **I. blackguard, bull, stew** (see the sbs.). **I. diamond,** rock crystal. 4. They laugh'd at such an i. blunder, To take the noise of brass for thunder SWIFT.

B. *sb.* (The adj. used ellipt.) **1. a.** as *pl.* The inhabitants of Ireland, or their descendants, esp. those of Celtic race ME. **b.** In *sing.* (with pl. *Irishes*). An Irishman. (Chiefly *Sc.*) 1613. **2.** The Irish language ME. †**b.** Scottish Gaelic; ERSE –1723. †**3.** An old game resembling backgammon –1664. **4.** *ellipt.*, e.g. for Irish linen, snuff, whisky, etc. 1799.

†*To weep I.*, to shed crocodile tears.

Irishism (əiə·riʃiz'm). 1734. [f. IRISH + -ISM.] An Irish peculiarity, esp. of expression; a Hibernicism; an Irish bull.

Irishman (əiə·riʃmæ̆n). *Pl.* **-men.** ME. [f. IRISH *a.* + MAN.] A native of Ireland; a man of Irish race. So **I·rishwoman** ME.

Irishry (əiə·riʃri). *Hist.* or *arch.* ME. [f. IRISH *a.* + -RY.] **1.** *collect.* The native Irish. **2.** Irish character or nationality; an Irish trait 1834.

1. They that refuse to be under lawes..are tearmed the I., and commonly the Wilde Irish HOLLAND.

Iritis (əirəi·tis). 1818. [f. IRIS + -ITIS.] *Path.* Inflammation of the iris. Hence **Iri·tic** *a.* pertaining to or affected with i.; affecting the iris.

Irk (ɔ̄ɹk), *v. arch.* [ME. *irken, yrken*, orig. n. and n. midl.; of uncertain origin.] †**1.** *intr.* To grow weary or tired; to feel disgusted; to be loath –1797. †**2.** *trans.* To be weary of or disgusted with; to loathe –1628. **3.** Of a thing: To affect with weariness, dislike, or disgust; to bore (*arch.*) 1513. **b.** impers. *It irks* (*me*), it wearies, annoys, troubles me; = L. *piget* 1483. *arch.*

3. Irks care the crop-full bird? BROWNING. b. It irk'd him to be here, he could not rest M. ARNOLD.

†So **Irk** *a.*, weary, disgusted. ME.

Irksome (ɔ̄·ɹksǒm), *a.* ME. [f. IRK *v.* + -SOME.] †**1.** Tired; disgusted; bored. Const. *of.* –1590. **2.** Wearisome, tedious; burdensome, annoying. Formerly also, Distressing; in early use, Loathsome 1513.

2. Not to irksom toile, but to delight He made us MILT. *P. L.* IX. 242. **I·rksome-ly** *adv.*, **-ness.**

Iron (əi·əɹn), *sb.*[1] [OE. *īren*, used beside *īsen*:—OTeut. type **īsarnom*; cogn. w. OCelt. **īsarnom* (whence OIr. *iarn*, etc.); ult. etym. unkn. The Eng. type *īren* became the standard form in ME. The form *iron* became universal about 1630.] **1.** A metal, the most abundant and useful of those used in the metallic state; very variously employed for tools, implements, machinery, constructions, and in many other applications.

Pure iron is soft and of a silver-white colour, but is scarcely known; the metal as commonly used has usually an admixture of carbon, and varies in colour from tin-white to dark grey. It is of three kinds, differing in the amount of carbon present: *malleable iron*, or WROUGHT IRON, which is comparatively soft, very tenacious, fusible only at a very high temperature, and capable at a red heat of being hammered or rolled into any required shape; CAST IRON, which is hard and brittle, and fusible at a lower temperature; and STEEL, which partakes of the properties of both. Iron is very rarely found native, but is obtained from its ores, which are chiefly oxides or salts of the metal. Chemically, iron is a metallic element; symbol Fe (*ferrum*); atomic weight, 56. In alchemy it was represented by the sign for the planet Mars (♂).

b. With *an* and *pl.* A variety or sort of iron 1858. **c.** *Med.* A preparation of iron, used in medicine as a tonic 1803. **2.** With defining attribute; see also BAR (*sb.*[1]), BOG (*sb.*[1]), CAST-, PIG-, WHITE, WROUGHT-IRON, etc. 1632. **3.** In fig. uses, as a type of extreme hardness or strength 1612. **4.** An instrument, utensil, or part of one, made of iron. (CURLING-*iron*, etc.) OE. **b.** *esp.* A brand-iron ME. †**c.** *pl.* Dies used in striking coins –1848. **d.** *Golf.* A golf-club having an iron head with an angle of loft between that of a mashie and that of a cleek 1857. **e.** *slang.* A portable fire-arm; a pistol 1836. **f.** *pl.* Iron supports for the legs, etc. **5.** *esp.* An implement of iron used when heated to smooth out linen, etc.; usu. defined, as BOX-*iron*, FLAT-IRON, etc. ME. **6.** †**a.** An iron weapon; a sword. **b.** Used (without *an* and *pl.*) with reference to warfare or slaughter. OE. **7.** An iron shackle or fetter; usu. in *pl.* OE. **8.** *attrib.* Of or pertaining to iron 1530.

3. Beare witnesse, all that haue not hearts of I. SHAKS. 4. b. Hauing their conscience seared with a hote i. 1 *Tim.* iv. 2. 6. Meddle you must that 's certain, or forsweare to weare i. about you SHAKS. Bismarck..is known throughout the world as 'the man of blood and iron' 1898. 7. *In irons*, said of a person having the feet or hands fettered. Also *fig.* (*Naut.*) A square-rigged vessel is said to be *in irons* when, the yards being so braced that some sails are laid aback in coming up into the wind, she will not 'cast' or turn either way. Phr. *The i. entered into his soul*, Ps. c[i]v. 18, a mistranslation of the Heb. (lit. 'his person entered into the iron', i.e. fetters, chains), now used fig. to express the impression made by captivity, affliction, or hard usage, upon the inmost being of the sufferer.

Phrases. *To strike while the i. is hot*: to act at the appropriate time. *To have* (or *put*) *many* (*too many*, etc.) *irons in the fire*: (*a*) to have or be engaged in (too) many occupations or undertakings; (*b*) to have or use several expedients to attain a purpose.

Combs. 1. General: as in *i.-filings, -furnace*, etc.; *i.-using* adj.; *i.-smelting* sb.; *i.-branded* adj.; *i.-black*; *i.-brown, -red* adjs.

2. Special: **i.-cement,** a kind of very hard cement; **-clay** *a.*, of mixed iron and clay; **-cloth,** chain-mail; **i. cross,** a Prussian order, conferred for bravery in war; **-fall,** a fall of meteoric i.; **-free** *a.*, free from i.; †proof against the force of i.; **i. period** (*Archæol.*) = IRON AGE 2; **-sponge,** i. in a loose state with little cohesion (see SPONGE); **-stain,** a stain produced by iron-rust or tincture of i., or on a plant by a fungus; **-yellow,** Mars yellow.

b. Esp. in names of chemical compounds and minerals; as **i.-clay,** same as *clay ironstone* (see CLAY *sb.*); **-flint,** ferruginous quartz; **-glance,** specular iron-ore (see GLANCE *sb.*[2]); **i. pyrites,** native bisulphuret of i. (see PYRITES).

†**Iron,** *sb.*[2] 1623. [app. a var. of *eren*, ERNE, eagle.] In 17th c. dicts., A male eagle –1688.

Iron (əi·əɹn), *a.* [OE. *īsern, īsen, īren*, f. **īsern-en*, etc. In most mod. uses indistinguishable from the sb. used attrib.] **1.** Of iron; consisting or formed of iron. (L. *ferreus.*) **2.** Having the appearance of iron; of the colour of iron (or iron-rust) 1613. **3.** *fig.* Resembling iron in some quality, esp. hardness. **a.** Extremely hard or strong ME. **b.** Extremely hardy or robust; enduring 1617. **c.** Firm, inflexible; unyielding 1602. †**d.** Unimpressionable –1651. **e.** Harsh, cruel, merciless; severe 1591. **f.** Of or pertaining to the IRON AGE (q.v.); debased; wicked. (Sometimes mixed with prec. sense.) 1592. **g.** In phr. *i. sleep* or *slumber*, tr. L. *ferreus somnus* (Virg. *Æn.* X. 745). Chiefly *poet.* 1624.

1. Luke's i. crown, and Damien's bed of steel GOLDSM. 2. A Knight of..i. hue 1632. 3. a. Thy necke is an yron Sinew *Isa.* xlviii. 4. b. The i. frame wasted by inward trouble 1864. c. Their ever-loyal i. leader TENNYSON. e. Her i. yoke BURKE. f. The bigots of the i. time SCOTT.

Phrases with specialized sense: **I. Crown,** the ancient crown of the kings of Lombardy, so called from having a circlet of i. inserted (reputed to have been made from one of the nails of the Cross); **i. horse,** a locomotive steam-engine; **i. walls,** the ironclad ships of the British navy, regarded as a defence to the country (cf. *wooden walls*).

Iron (əi·əɹn), *v.* ME. [f. IRON *sb.*[1]] **1.** *trans.* To fit, furnish, cover, or arm with iron. (Chiefly in pa. pple.) **2.** To shackle with irons; to put in irons 1653. **3.** To smooth or press with a heated flat-iron, as cloth, etc. 1680. **b.** *fig.* esp. with *out* 1863.

2. The miserable victimes were imprisoned, ironed, scourged BURKE. 3. The servants are all ironing 1789. b. The differences [are] amicably ironed out 1905.

Iron age. 1592. [See IRON *a.* 3 f.] **1.** *Gr. and Roman Mythol.* The last and worst age of the world, succeeding the Golden, Silver, and Brazen Ages. Hence *allusively*, An age or period of wickedness, debasement, etc. **2.** *Archæol.* That period, subsequent to the *stone age* and *bronze age*, in which iron weapons and implements were or are used by mankind. Hence *transf.*, a period characterized by the general use of iron. 1879.

I·ron-bark. 1802. [Austral-Eng., f. IRON *a.* or *sb.*[1] + BARK.] Any species of *Eucalyptus* having solid bark, as *E. resinifera, paniculata, Leucoxylon*, etc., trees valued for their timber. Also, the wood of any of these. Also *attrib.*

Iron-bound, *a.* ME. [f. IRON *sb.*[1] + pa. pple. of BIND *v.* (With shifting stress.)] **1.** Bound with iron; also, fettered. **2.** *transf.* Of a coast: Rock-bound 1769. **3.** *fig.* Rigorously confined or restricted; unimpressionable; hard and fast 1807.

1. Yren-bounde coffres ME. 2. An iron-bound coast 1852. 3. The old iron-bound, feudal France EMERSON.

I·ron-cased (-kēⁱst), *a.* 1859. [f. IRON *sb.*¹ + *cased*, pa. pple. of CASE *v.*] Cased in iron; applied to ships of war, now called IRONCLAD.

I·ronclad, iron-clad. 1852. [See CLAD *ppl. a.*]

A. *adj.* 1. Clad in iron; protected or covered with iron; *esp.* of a ship of war: Cased wholly or partly with thick plates of iron or steel, as a defence against shot, etc. 1859. 2. *fig.* (Chiefly *U.S.*) Of an extremely strict or rigorous character, as a regulation, agreement, etc. 1884.

1. Two powerful iron-clad rams 1878. 2. *I. oath*: an oath characterized by the severity of its requirements and penalties. Bills..full of the most arbitrary and 'iron-clad' provisions 1887.

B. *sb.* An ironclad ship: see A. 1. 1862.

Ironer (əi·ənəɹ). 1857. [f. IRON *v.* + -ER¹.] One who irons; *spec.* one whose occupation it is to iron clothes, etc.

I·ron-fou:nder. 1817. [f. IRON *sb.*¹ + FOUNDER *sb.*²] One who founds or casts iron. So I·ron-fou:nding; I·ron-fou:ndry 1784.

Iron-grey, -gray. [OE. *īsengrǣg.*]

A. *adj.* Of the grey colour of freshly broken iron, or of dark hair when turning grey. B. *sb.* 1. An iron-grey colour 1552. 2. An iron-grey horse or dog 1523.

Iron-handed, *a.* 1768. [f. *iron hand* + -ED².] Having a 'hand of iron'; inflexible; severe, rigorous, despotic.

The iron-handed goddess, Necessity TUCKER.

I·ronheads (-hedz). 1863. A local name of the Knapweed (*Centaurea nigra*), from its hard involucre.

I·ron-hea:rted, *a.* 1618. Extremely hard-hearted; unfeeling; cruel.

Ironic (əirǫ·nik), *a.* 1614. [ad. late L. *ironicus*, a. Gr. εἰρωνικός, f. εἰρωνεία dissimulation, IRONY.] Pertaining to irony; uttering or given to irony; of the nature of or containing irony.

An i. man..more especially an i. young man..may be viewed as a pest to society CARLYLE.

Ironical (əirǫ·nikăl), *a.* 1576. [f. as prec. + -AL.] 1. Of the nature of irony; meaning the opposite of what is expressed. 2. That uses or is given to irony 1589. †3. Dissembling; feigned, pretended (*rare*) -1727.

1. A bitterly i. compliment to Bentley's courtesy 1853. 2. Socrates..got the name of..the i. philosopher 1793. Hence Iro·nical-ly *adv.*, -ness.

Ironing (əi·əmiŋ), *vbl. sb.* 1710. [f. IRON *v.* + -ING¹.] 1. The pressing and smoothing of clothes, etc., with a heated iron. Also *attrib.* 2. The putting (*of* persons) in irons (*rare*) 1820.

I·ronish, *a.* Now *rare.* 1450. [f. IRON *sb.*¹ + -ISH.] †1. Of iron. 2. Partaking of the qualities of iron; irony; ferruginous 1641.

Ironist (əi°·rŏnist). 1727. [f. Gr. εἴρων dissembler, user of irony + -IST.] One who uses irony.

I·ronma:ster. 1674. The master of an iron-foundry or ironworks; a manufacturer of iron, esp. on a large scale.

I·ron-mine. 1601. 1. A mine from which iron-ore is obtained. 2. Iron-ore. Now *dial.* 1645.

Ironmonger (əi·ənmɒ:ŋgəɹ). ME. [f. IRON *sb.*¹ + MONGER.] A dealer in ironware; a hardware merchant.

Ironmongery (əi·ənmɒ:ŋgəri). 1711. [f. prec.; see -ERY.] 1. Hardware; a general name for all articles made of iron. b. An ironmonger's shop 1841. 2. Smith's work 1871. 3. *attrib.* 1769.

Iron-mould, -mold (əi·ənmōuld), *sb.* 1601. [f. IRON *sb.*¹ + MOULD, earlier *mole*, OE. *māl* mole, spot, mark.] A spot or discoloration on cloth, etc., caused by iron-rust or an ink-stain. Also *fig.* Hence I·ron-mou:ld, -mold *v.* to stain or become stained with iron-mould.

I·ron-o·re, iron ore. 1601. The ore of iron; any crude form in which iron is found in the earth. Also *attrib.*

I·ron-sa:nd. 1876. *Geol.* Sand containing particles of iron-ore, usually either magnetite or titaniferous oxide.

I·ron-si:ck, *a.* 1626. Said of a wooden ship when her bolts and nails are so corroded with rust that she has become leaky. Now *rare* or *Obs.*

Ironside (əi·ənsəid). Also (*sing.*) Ironsides. ME. 1. *sing.* A man of great hardihood or bravery. 2. *pl.* (*Ironsides.*) Applied to Cromwell's troopers in the Civil War; hence allusively. The sing. is sometimes used of one of these; a Puritan warrior. 1648. 3. An ironclad 1861.

1. Is eldoste sone, Edmond yrene syde R. GLOUC. Lieutenant General Cromwell *alias* Ironside 1644. Hence he [Cromwell] acquired that terrible Name of Ironsides 1663.

I·ron-sided, *a.* 1825. [f. *iron side* + -ED².] Having sides made of or resembling iron; ironclad.

I·ronsmith. Now *rare* or *Obs.* ME. [f. IRON *sb.*¹ + SMITH.] 1. An artificer in iron; a blacksmith. 2. As a rendering of the native name of a bird, a species of barbet (*Megalæma faber*) 1885.

Ironstone, iron-stone (əi·ənstōun, -stǒn). 1522. The name given to various hard iron-ores containing admixtures of silica, clay, etc. *attrib.* **Ironstone china, i. ware,** a hard kind of white pottery.

I·ron-tree. 1719. A name (more or less local) for various trees and shrubs with very hard wood, as *Ixora ferrea* of the W. Indies (also called *hardwood*), etc.

Ironware (əi·ənwēᵊɹ). 1447. A general name for all light articles made of iron; hardware.

I·ronweed. 1827. [f. IRON *sb.*¹ + WEED *sb.*; so called from the hard stem.] The Knapweed (*Centaurea nigra*), and the N. Amer. species of *Vernonia.*

Ironwood, iron-wood (əi·ənwud). 1657. A name (more or less local) for the extremely hard wood of various trees; also for the trees themselves.

Among these are the genus *Sideroxylon* (chiefly tropical); several species of *Diospyros* or Ebony; *Ostrya virginica*, *Bumelia lycioides*, *Carpinus americana*, etc. of N. America; *Erythroxylon areolatum*, etc. of the W. Indies; *Xylia dolabriformis*, *Mesua ferrea*, *Metrosideros vera*, etc. of the E. Indies; *Olea capensis* and *O. undulata* of S. Africa; *Notelæa ligustrina* of Tasmania and N. S. Wales; etc.

I·ronwork, iron-work (-wɔ̄ɹk). 1451. 1. Work in iron; usu. *concr.* parts of things made of iron, or articles made of iron collectively. 2. An establishment where iron is smelted, or where heavy iron goods are made. Now always in *pl.* form ironworks (sometimes construed as a *sing.*) 1581.

I·ronwort (-wɔ̄ɹt). 1562. [f. IRON *sb.*¹ + WORT, tr. L. *sideritis* (Pliny), a. Gr. σιδηρῖτις, a herb that heals sword-wounds, f. σίδηρος iron.] Name for plants of the labiate genus *Sideritis*; also for species of *Galeopsis.*

Irony (əi°·rŏni), *sb.* 1502. [ad. L. *ironia* (also used), a. Gr. εἰρωνεία 'dissimulation, ignorance purposely affected'. Cf. F. *ironie.*] 1. A figure of speech in which the intended meaning is the opposite of that expressed by the words used; usually taking the form of sarcasm or ridicule in which laudatory expressions are used to imply condemnation or contempt. Also with *an* and *pl.* 2. *fig.* A contradictory outcome of events as if in mockery of the promise and fitness of things. (In F. *ironie du sort.*) 1649. 3. In etym. sense: Dissimulation, pretence; esp. in reference to the ignorance feigned by Socrates as a means of confuting an adversary (*Socratic i.*) 1502.

1. A drayman, in a passion, calls out, 'You are a pretty fellow', without suspecting that he is uttering i. MACAULAY. *Dramatic* or *tragic i.*, use of language having an inner meaning for a privileged audience, an outer for those immediately concerned. 2. The i. of time 1884.

Irony (əi·əmi), *a.* ME. [f. IRON *sb.*¹ + -Y.] Of iron; of the nature of iron; resembling, abounding in, or containing iron.

I. quartz 1843. Crystals of a clear i. brown 1875.

†I·rous, *a.* ME. [a. AF. *irous*, OF. *iros*, *irus*, later *ireux* :—pop. L. type **irosus*, f. *ira.*] 1. Given to anger, irascible -1574. 2. Angry, enraged -1500. Hence †I·rously *adv.*

†Irpe, *sb.* 1599. [?] Some kind of gesture: ? a toss of the head, the act of perking.

From Spanish shrugs, French faces, smirks, irpes, and all affected humours, Good Mercury defend us B. JONS. So †Irpe ? *a.*, ? perk, smart B. JONS.

Irradiance (irēⁱ·diăns). 1667. [f. IRRADIANT; see -ANCE.] The fact of irradiating; emitted radiance. Also *fig.* So Irra·diancy, the fact or quality of being irradiant 1646.

Irradiant (irēⁱ·diănt), *a.* 1526. [ad. L. *irradiantem*, *irradiare.*] Emitting rays of light; shining brightly. Also *fig.*

As Fire extinguish'd by th' I. Sun 1710.

Irradiate (irēⁱ·diĕt), *ppl. a.* 1526. [ad. L. *irradiatus*, *irradiare* (see next).] Illumined; made bright or brilliant. Const. as pple. or adj.

The sky Erewhile i. only with his beam CARY.

Irradiate (irēⁱ·diēⁱt), *v.* 1603. [f. L. *irradiat-*, *irradiare*, f. *ir-* (IR-¹) + *radiare* to shine, f. *radius* ray.] 1. *trans.* To direct rays of light upon; to shine upon; to illumine 1623. †b. To influence with or as with rays of heat or anything radiant -1677. 2. *fig.* and *transf.* To illumine with spiritual or intellectual light 1627; to brighten as with light 1651. 3. To radiate; to send forth in or as in rays 1617. †4. *intr.* To radiate; to diverge in the form of rays -1794. 5. *intr.* To emit rays, to shine (*on* or *upon*) 1642. 6. *intr.* To become radiant 1800.

1. The midnight lightnings..That with their awful blaze, i. heaven SOUTHEY. 2. The priest's jovial good humour irradiated his happy countenance LEVER. 6. Lamb every now and then irradiates COLERIDGE. Hence Irra·diative *a.* of which the tendency or property is to i. Irra·diator.

Irradiation (irēⁱdiēⁱ·ʃən). 1589. [a. F., ad. L. **irradiationem*; see prec.]

I. 1. The action of irradiating; shining 1599. b. A ray of light, a beam 1643. 2. *fig.* a. A beaming forth of spiritual light 1633. b. Intellectual illumination 1589. 3. *Optics.* The apparent enlargement of the edges of an object strongly illuminated, when seen against a dark ground 1834.

3. People look larger in light clothes than in dark, which may also be explained as the effect of i. BERNSTEIN.

II. 1. The emission of heat-rays 1794. †2. In older Physiology: The emission or emanation of any fluid, influence, principle, or virtue, from an active centre -1706. †b. The (fancied) emission of an immaterial fluid or influence from the eye -1696. 3. *Physiol.* The transmission of excitation from a nerve-centre outwards 1847.

Irradicate (iræ·dikeⁱt), *v. rare.* [f. IR-¹ + *radicare*, *-ari* to take root.] *trans.* To fix by the root, to enroot. SIR W. HAMILTON.

Irrationable (iræ·ʃənăb'l), *a. Obs.* or *arch.* 1583. [ad. late L. *irrationabilis*, f. *ir-* (IR-²) + *rationabilis.*] = IRRATIONAL *a.* 1, 2. -1832. So †Irrationabi·lity.

Irrational (iræ·ʃənăl). 1470. [ad. L. *irrationalis*, f. *ir-* (IR-²) + *rationalis.*]

A. *adj.* 1. Not endowed with reason. 2. Not in accordance with reason; illogical, absurd 1641. 3. *Math.* Not rational; not commensurable with ordinary quantities such as the natural numbers; not expressible by an ordinary (finite) fraction, proper or improper. Usually applied to roots; the same as *surd.* 1551. 4. *Gr. Pros.* Said of a syllable having a metrical value not corresponding to its actual time-value, or of a metrical foot containing such a syllable 1844.

1. The more i. kinds of animals SCOTT. 2. Inconsiderate courage has given way to i. fear BURKE.

B. *sb.* 1. A being not endowed with reason; one not guided by reason 1646. 2. *Math.* An irrational number or quantity; a surd 1571.

Hence Irra·tionalism, a system of belief or action that disregards or contradicts rational principles. So Irra·tionalist, Irrationali·stic *a.* Irra·tionally *adv.*

Irrationality (iræʃənæ·lĭti). 1570. [f. prec. + -ITY.] 1. The quality of being irrational (see IRRATIONAL *a.*) 2. *Optics.* The inequality of the ratios of the dispersion of the various colours in spectra produced by refraction through different substances 1797.

1. Proof of the i. of mankind 1717.

Irrealizable (irīˑăləizăb'l), *a.* 1853. [IR-².] That cannot be realized; unrealizable.

Irrebuttable (irĭbʊˑtăb'l), *a.* 1834. [IR-².] That cannot be rebutted.

Irreceptive (irĭseˑptiv), *a.* 1846. [IR-².] Not receptive; incapable of receiving.

Irreciprocal (irĭsiˑprǒkăl), *a.* 1886. [IR-².] Not reciprocal; as, *i. conduction* (Electr.), unipolar conduction. So **Irreciproˑcity**.

Irreclaimable (irĭklēˑmăb'l), *a.* 1609. [IR-².] †1. Uncontrollable. HOLLAND. 2. That cannot be reclaimed 1662; of land 1814. 3. Irrevocable 1834. Hence **Irreclaiˑmably** *adv.*

Irrecognition (irekǫgniˑʃən). 1820. [IR-².] Absence of recognition; non-recognition.

Irrecognizable (ireˑkǫgnəiːzăb'l), *a.* 1837. [IR-².] Incapable of being recognized; unrecognizable. Hence **Irrecognizabiˑlity**, **-reˑcognizably** *adv.*

Irreconcilable (ireˑkǫnsəilăb'l, ireːkǫnsəiˑlăb'l), *a.* (*sb.*) Also **-cileable**. 1599. [IR-².] 1. That cannot be reconciled; implacably hostile. Const. *to*. 2. Incompatible. Const. *to, with*. 1646. 3. *sb.* A person who refuses to be reconciled; *esp.* One of a political party who refuses to come to any agreement or make any compromise 1748. b. *pl.* Principles, ideas, etc. which cannot be harmonized with each other 1895.

1. I. enemies GREEN. 2. Creeds..i. with salvation 1866. 3. From Oxford graduates down to Irish irreconcilables 1884. Hence **Irreˑconcilabiˑlity**, **Irreconcilableness**, the quality of being i. **Irreconcilably** *adv.* 1598. var. **Irreconciˑliable** *a. rare.*

†Irreˑconcile, *v.* 1647. [IR-².] *trans.* To render unreconciled; to make antagonistic; to estrange -1670. Hence **Irreˑconciˑlement**.

†Irreˑconciled, *a.* 1599. [IR-².] Not reconciled; *spec.* in a state of variance with God -1750.

†Irreconciliaˑtion. 1650. [IR-².] The fact or condition of being unreconciled -1678.

Irrecoverable (irĭkʊˑvərăb'l), *a.* 1533. [f. IR-² + RECOVER *v.* + -ABLE.] That cannot be †revoked, got back, restored to health or life; *fig.* not capable of being remedied or rectified. †b. That cannot be recovered from -1674.

An i. sentence of death TUCKER. I. debts 1782, ill health 1809. *fig.* A final and i. fall 1679. Hence **Irrecoˑverableness**. **Irrecoˑverably** *adv.*

†Irrecuperable (irĭkiūˑpərăb'l), *a.* ME. [a. OF., ad. late L. *irrecuperabilis*, f. *ir-* (IR-²) + *recuperare*; see -ABLE.] 1. That cannot be recovered or regained -1644. 2. That cannot be recovered from; incurable -1626.

1. Teares be lost upon a thing i. HACKET.

†Irrecuˑrable, *a. rare.* 1548. [f. IR-² + RECURE *v.* + -ABLE.] Incurable; irremediable -1579. So **†Irrecuˑred** *a.* (*rare*), incurable 1598.

Irrecusable (irĭkiūˑzăb'l), *a.* 1776. [a. F. *irrécusable*, or ad. late L. *irrecusabilis*; see RECUSANT and -ABLE.] Incapable of being refused acceptance.

I will give him an i. proof H. WALPOLE. **Irreˑcuˑsably** *adv.*

Irredeemable (irĭdīˑmăb'l), *a.* 1609. [IR-²; prob. after OF. (legal) *irredimible*.] 1. Incapable of being redeemed or bought back. b. Of paper currency: Not convertible into cash 1850. 2. *fig.* That admits of no release or change of state; absolute, hopeless 1839. 3. Beyond redemption; utterly depraved 1834.

1. The debt..for which annuities have been granted for a limited period is called the I. debt 1820. 2. He ..Wrought for his house an i. woe TENNYSON. Hence **Irredeemabiˑlity**, **Irredeeˑmableness**, the quality of being not redeemable. **Irredeeˑmably** *adv.*

Irredentism (irĭdeˑntiz'm). 1883. [See next and -ISM.] The policy or programme of the Irredentists.

Irredentist (irĭdeˑntist). 1882. [ad. It. *irredentista*, f. (*Italia*) *irredenta* unredeemed, unrecovered (Italy).] In Italian politics (since 1878), an adherent of the party which advocates the recovery and union to Italy of all Italian-speaking districts now subject to other countries. Also *attrib.* as *adj.*

Irreducible (irĭdiūˑsĭb'l), *a.* 1633. [IR-².] 1. That cannot be reduced to a desired form, state, condition, etc. b. *spec.* That cannot be reduced to a simpler or more intelligible form 1753. 2. *Path.* That cannot be reduced by treatment to a desired form or condition 1836. 3. Incapable of being reduced to a smaller number or amount 1860. 4. Invincible, insuperable 1858.

1. Fashions..i. to rule HALLAM. b. *I. case* (Alg.): that case of cubic equations where the root..appears under an impossible or imaginary form, and yet is real CHAMBERS. 2. An i. tumour in the right groin 1859. Hence **Irreducibiˑlity**, **Irreduˑcibleness**. **Irreduˑcibly** *adv.* var. **Irreduˑctible** *a.* (*rare*).

Irreflection, -flexion (irĭfleˑkʃən). 1861. [IR-².] Want of reflection; unreflecting action or conduct.

Irreflective (irĭfleˑktiv), *a.* 1833. [IR-².] Unreflecting. Hence **Irrefleˑctiveˑly** *adv.*, **-ness**.

Irreformable (irĭfǭˑɹmăb'l), *a.* 1609. [IR-².] 1. Incapable of being reformed. 2. Incapable of alteration 1812.

1. She was unteachable, i. 1892.

Irrefragable (ireˑfrăgăb'l), *a.* 1533. [ad. late L. *irrefragabilis*, f. *ir-* (IR-²) + *refragari*; see -ABLE.] 1. That cannot be refuted or disproved; incontrovertible, indisputable, undeniable. 2. That cannot or must not be broken; indestructible; inviolable; irresistible. Now *rare*. 1562. †3. Of persons: Obstinate, inflexible -1621.

1. Alexander of Hales, the i. Doctor CAMDEN. An i. answer to the popular theories STUBBS. 3. He is i. in his humour BURTON. Hence **Irreˑfragabiˑlity**, **Irreˑfragableness**. **Irreˑfragably** *adv.*

Irrefrangible (irĭfræˑndʒĭb'l), *a.* 1719. [f. IR-² + REFRANGIBLE (irreg. for *refringible*, after *refraction*).] 1. That cannot or must not be broken; inviolable. 2. *Optics.* Not refrangible; incapable of being refracted (*mod.*).

Irrefutable (irĭfiūˑtăb'l, ireˑfiutăb'l), *a.* 1620. [ad. L. *irrefutabilis*, f. *ir-* (IR-²) + *refutabilis*, f. *refutare* to REFUTE.] That cannot be refuted or disproved; incontrovertible, irrefragable. Hence **Irrefutabiˑlity**, the quality of being i. **Irrefutably** *adv.*

Irregenerate (irĭdʒeˑnĕrĕt), *a. rare.* 1657. [IR-².] Not regenerate; unregenerate. Hence **†Irregeˑneracy**, **†-generaˑtion**, unregenerate state.

Irregular (ireˑgiŭlăɹ). [ME. *irreguler(e*, a. OF. *irreguler*, ad. med.L. *irregularis*, f. *ir-* (IR-²) + L. *regularis*; see REGULAR.]

A. *adj.* Not regular. I. 1. Of things: Not in conformity with rule or principle; contrary to rule; disorderly in action or conduct; anomalous, abnormal 1483. b. Unregulated; morally disorderly. ? *Obs.* 1608. 2. Of persons: Not conforming to rule, law, or moral principle; lawless, disorderly ME. 3. Not of regular or symmetrical form; unevenly placed 1584. 4. In reference to time or motion: Unequal or uneven in continuance, occurrence, or succession. Hence of an agent: Doing something at irregular intervals or times. 1608.

1. The efforts of their i. valour GIBBON. An I. order 1894. b. I. appetite 1726, conduct 1804. 2. The i. and wilde Glendower SHAKS. 3. Two i. rows of tall meagre houses DICKENS. 4. I. breathing 1794. An i. attendant (*mod.*).

II. Techn. senses. 1. *Eccl.* Disqualified for ordination, or for exercise of clerical functions ME. 2. *Gram.* Inflected not according to the normal method. Said also of the inflexion. 1611. 3. *Math.* Having unequal sides 1700. 4. *Bot.* and *Zool.* a. Abnormal in form. b. Not symmetrical or uniform in shape or arrangement; *spec.* of a flower, Having the members of the same cycle (esp. the petals) unlike in form or size. 1794. 5. *Mil.* Of troops: Not belonging to the established army organization; not forming an organized military body 1856.

5. The Danes..put the i. English levies to flight FREEMAN.

B. *sb.* 1. *Gram.* An irregular noun, verb, etc. (*rare*) 1611. 2. One not belonging to the regular body; one not of the regular clergy; an irregular practitioner, attendant, etc. 1534. b. *Mil.* A soldier not of the regular army; usu. in *pl.* = irregular troops 1747.

2. b. With this small company of irregulars..we set out 1756. Hence **Irreˑgular-ly** *adv.*, **†-ness**.

Irregularity (iregiŭlæˑrĭti). ME. [a. F. *irrégularité*, ad. med. L. *irregularitas*, f. *irregularis*; see -ITY.] The quality or state of being irregular; something that is irregular; *spec.* in *Eccl.* Infraction of the rules as to entrance into or exercise of holy orders; an impediment or disqualification by which a person is debarred from ordination, exercise of clerical functions, or ecclesiastical advancement.

†Irreˑgulate, *a.* 1579. [ad. med.L. *irregulatus*; see IR-².] Unregulated; irregular, disorderly -1650. So **Irreˑgulated** *a. rare.* 1660.

Irreˑgulate, *v.* 1600. [f. prec.] *trans.* To render irregular; to disorder.

†Irreˑgulous, *a.* [f. IR-² + L. *regula* + -OUS.] Unruly, lawless. *Cymb.* IV. ii. 315.

†Irrejeˑctable, *a.* [IR-².] That cannot be rejected. BOYLE.

†Irrelaˑpsable, *a.* 1660. [IR-².] Not liable to relapse. H. MORE.

Irrelate (irĭlēˑt), *a. rare.* 1845. [f. IR-² + L. *relatus*, *referre*.] Not related, unrelated.

Irrelation (irĭlēˑʃən). 1848. [IR-².] Absence of relation, want of connexion.

Irrelative (ireˑlătiv), *a.* 1640. [f. IR-² + RELATIVE.] Not relative; unrelated, unconnected; hence, in *Metaph.*, without relations, absolute. b. Irrelevant 1649. c. *Mus.* (See quot.) 1811.

It seems evident, that they [colours, odours, etc.] have an absolute Being i. to Us BOYLE. c. *Irrelative*, a term applied to any two chords which do not contain some sound common to both BUSBY. Hence **Irreˑlativeˑly** *adv.*, **-ness**.

Irrelevance (ireˑlĭvăns). 1561. [IR-²; cf. RELEVANCE, -ANCY.] The fact or quality of being irrelevant; want of pertinence. Also with *an* and *pl.*

A second i. foisted in upon the back of the first 1872. So **Irreˑlevancy** 1592.

Irrelevant (ireˑlĭvănt), *a.* 1558 (orig. Sc.). [IR-².] Not relevant or pertinent to the case; that does not apply; said orig. of evidence or arguments.

No accumulation of facts can establish an i. conclusion 1877. Hence **Irreˑlevantly** *adv.*

Irrelievable (irĭlīˑvăb'l), *a.* 1670. [IR-².] Not relievable, that cannot be relieved.

Irreligion (irĭliˑdʒən). 1592. [ad. L. *irreligionem*, f. *ir-* (IR-²) + *religionem*.] 1. Want of religion; hostility to or disregard of religious principles; irreligious conduct 1598. †2. A false or perverted religion -1655. Hence **Irreliˑgionist**, one who supports or practises i.; a professed opponent of religion.

Irreligious (irĭliˑdʒəs), *a.* 1561. [ad. L. *irreligiosus*, f. *ir-* (IR-²) + *religiosus* RELIGIOUS.] 1. Not religious; hostile to or without regard for religion; ungodly. Also *transf.* of things. †2. Believing in, practising, or pertaining to a false religion -1634.

1. I. men, whose short prospects are filled with earth, and sense, and mortal life BERKELEY. 2. The issue of an I. Moore SHAKS. Hence **Irreliˑgiousˑly** *adv.*, **-ness**.

Irremeable (ireˑmĭăb'l, irīˑmĭăb'l), *a.* 1569. [ad. L. *irremeabilis*, f. *ir-* (IR-²) + *remeare* to go back, f. *re-* + *meare*; see -ABLE. Cf. *permeable*.] Admitting of no return.

The dark i. way POPE. Hence **Irreˑmeably** *adv.*

Irremediable (irĭmīˑdiăb'l), *a.* 1533. [ad. L. *irremediabilis*; see IR-² and REMEDIABLE.] Not remediable; that does not admit of remedy, cure, or correction; irreparable.

A person of a desperate fortune, i. and irrecoverable JER. TAYLOR. Hence **Irremeˑdiableness**. **Irremeˑdiably** *adv.* 1601.

Irremissible (irĭmiˑsĭb'l), *a.* Also *erron.* †-able. ME. [a. F. *irrémissible*, ad. L. *irremissibilis*; see IR-² and REMISSIBLE.] Not remissible; for or of which there can be no remission.

An irremissable sin HALES, annual Tribute 1728. Hence **Irremissibiˑlity**, **Irremiˑssibleness**, the quality or condition of being i. **Irremiˑssibly** *adv.*

†Irremiˑssion. 1631. [IR-².] Non-remission.

Irremiˑssive, *a.* 1817. [IR-².] Unremitting.

†Irremiˑttable, *a. rare.* 1587. [IR-².] = IRREMISSIBLE -1635.

Irremovable (irĭmū·văb'l), *a.* (*sb.*) 1597. [IR-².] 1. Not removable; not subject to removal; permanent 1598. †2. Immovable, inflexible (*lit.* and *fig.*) -1822. 3. *sb.* One whose position is permanent 1848. Hence **Irremovabi·lity, -mo·vableness, -mo·vably** *adv.*

Irremu·nerable, *a. rare.* 1623. [IR-².] That cannot be remunerated or paid.

†**Irrenow·ned**, *a.* [IR-².] Unrenowned. SPENSER.

Irrepair (irĭpēᵊ·ɹ). *rare.* 1822. [IR-².] = DISREPAIR.

Irreparable (ire·părăb'l), *a.* ME. [a. F. *irréparable*, ad. L. *irreparabilis*; see IR-² and REPARABLE.] Not reparable; that cannot be rectified, remedied, or made good.

I. is the losse, and patience Saies, it is past her cure SHAKS. **Irre·parabi·lity, Irre·parableness. Irre·parably** *adv.* var. **Irrepai·rable** (now *rare*).

Irrepealable (irĭpī·lăb'l), *a.* 1633. [IR-².] Incapable of being repealed or annulled; irrevocable.

Let..this inhibitory Statute..stand..i. 1642. **Irrepealabi·lity, Irrepea·lableness. Irrepea·lably** *adv.*

Irrepe·ntant, *a. rare.* 1573. [IR-³.] Not repentant; impenitent. So **Irrepe·ntance** (*rare*), non-repentance. **Irrepe·ntantly** *adv.*

Irreplaceable (irĭplēᵢ·săb'l), *a.* 1807. [IR-².] Not replaceable; that cannot be replaced.

Irrepleviable (irĭple·viăb'l), *a.* 1543. [ad. med.L. *irrepleviabilis*; see IR-² and REPLEVIABLE.] *Law.* = next.

Irreplevisable (irĭple·vizăb'l), *a.* 1621. [f. IR-² + REPLEVISABLE.] *Law.* Not replevisable; that cannot be replevied or delivered on sureties.

Irreprehensible (ireprĭhe·nsĭb'l), *a.* Now *rare.* ME. [ad. late L. *irreprehensibilis*; see IR-² and REPREHENSIBLE.] Not reprehensible or blameworthy; irreproachable. Hence **Irreprehe·nsibleness. Irreprehe·nsibly** *adv.*

Irrepresentable (ireprĭze·ntăb'l), *a.* 1673. [IR-².] Incapable of representation.

Progressive actions, as such, are i. by painting DE QUINCEY. Hence **Irreprese·ntableness.**

Irrepressible (irĭpre·sĭb'l), *a.* (*sb.*) 1818. [f. IR-² + REPRESS + -IBLE.] 1. Not repressible; that cannot be repressed, restrained, or put down. (Of persons, often *joc.*) 2. *sb.* An irrepressible person 1890.

1. The..uproar of the i. undergraduates 1879. **Irrepressibi·lity, -pre·ssibleness. Irrepre·ssibly** *adv.*

Irrepre·ssive, *a.* 1856. [IR-².] = prec.

Irreproachable (irĭprōᵘ·tʃăb'l), *a.* 1634. [a. F. *irréprochable*; see IR-² and REPROACHABLE.] Not reproachable; free from blame, faultless.

An exact and i. Piece of Architecture EVELYN. Hence **Irreproachabi·lity, Irreproa·chableness**, the quality of being i. **Irreproa·chably** *adv.*

Irreprovable (irĭprū·văb'l), *a.* 1504. [IR-².] 1. Not reprovable; blameless, irreproachable. Now *rare.* †2. That cannot be disproved; irrefutable -1646. Hence **Irrepro·vableness. Irrepro·vably** *adv.*

Irreption (ire·pʃən). 1598. [ad. late L. *irreptionem.*] Creeping or stealing in.

Irreptitious (irepti·ʃəs), *a.* 1673. [f. L. *irrept-*, *irrepere* to creep in or on + -OUS.] Characterized by creeping in or having crept in, esp. into a text.

†**Irre·putable**, *a.* 1709. [IR-².] Not reputable -1749.

Irresilient (irĭz-, irĭsi·liĕnt), *a.* [IR-².] Non-resilient; that does not spring back or rebound. H. SPENCER.

Irresistance (irĭzi·stăns). 1643. [IR-².] Absence of resistance; non-resistance.

Irresistible (irĭzi·stĭb'l), *a.* (*sb.*) Also †-able. 1597. [ad. late L. *irresistibilis*, f. *ir-* (IR-²) + *resistere*; see -IBLE.] 1. Not resistible; too strong, weighty, or fascinating to be resisted. †2. Not to be resisted lawfully. PRYNNE. 3. *sb.* An irresistible person 1774.

1. That Heroic, that Renown'd, Irresistible Samson MILT. The power of opinion is i. GIBBON. **Irresistibi·lity, Irresi·stibleness. Irresi·stibly** *adv.*

†**Irresi·stless**, *a.* 1669. [Erron. blending of *irresistible* and *resistless.*] Resistless, irresistible -1796.

Irresoluble (ire·zŏl'ŭb'l), *a.* 1646. [ad. L. *irresolubilis*; see IR-² and RESOLUBLE.] 1. Incapable of being resolved into elements; indissoluble; insoluble 1666. 2. Incapable of being loosened and dispelled or relieved 1646. 3. Incapable of being solved 1868.

2. With many moe almost i. scruples GAULE. Hence **Irre·solubleness**, the quality of being i.

Irresolute (ire·zŏl'ŭt), *a.* 1573. [ad. L. *irresolutus*; see IR-² and RESOLUTE.] †1. Not resolved; left ambiguous or obscure -1603. 2. Unresolved as to a course of action. Also *fig.* 1579. 3. Wanting in resolution; infirm of purpose; vacillating 1600.

2. I. what part to take FRANKLIN. 3. Cicero..was i., timid, and inconsistent J. H. NEWMAN. Hence **Irre·solute·ly** *adv.*, **-ness.**

Irresolution (irezŏl'ū·ʃən). 1592. [prob. a. F. *irrésolution*, f. *ir-* (IR-²) + *résolution.*] Want of resolution. †1. The condition of not having arrived at a settled opinion on some subject; uncertainty, doubt. With *pl.* An instance of this. -1813. 2. The condition of being irresolute; indecision of character; vacillation. With *an* and *pl.* An instance of this. 1601.

2. His i. of mind..induced him to listen to the suggestions of the French ambassadors 1823.

Irresolvable (irĭzǫ·lvăb'l), *a.* 1660. [IR-².] Not resolvable. 1. Incapable of being solved. 2. That cannot be resolved into elements or parts 1785. 3. That cannot be disentangled 1886.

2. *I. nebulæ*, nebulæ that cannot be resolved into stars by telescopic examination. Hence **Irresolvabi·lity, Irreso·lvableness.**

†**Irreso·lved**, *a.* 1621. [IR-².] Not resolved; not settled in opinion; undecided; irresolute -1864. Hence **Irreso·lvedly** *adv.*

Irrespective (irĭspe·ktiv), *a.* and *adv.* [IR-².] Not respective. †1. Disrespectful -1654. 2. Characterized by disregard of particular persons or circumstances. Now *rare.* 1650. 3. Existing or considered without respect or regard to something else; independent *of* 1694. b. Now chiefly advb.; = IRRESPECTIVELY. Const. *of.* 1839.

2. He..oversteps, in his i. zeal, every decency and every right opposed to his course COLERIDGE. 3. A speculative interest, which is i. of all practical considerations BUCKLE.

Irrespectively (irĭspe·ktivli), *adv.* 1624. [f. prec. + -LY².] †1. Disrespectfully. FEATLY. †2. In a manner showing disregard of particular persons or circumstances -1716. 3. Without regard to other things; independently 1648.

3. Prosperity, considered absolutely and i., is better and more desirable than adversity SOUTH.

Irrespirable (irĭspəiᵊ·răb'l, ire·spirăb'l), *a.* 1822. [f. IR-² + RESPIRABLE, or a. F.] Not respirable; unfit for respiration.

Irresponsible (irĭspǫ·nsĭb'l), *a.* Also †-able. 1648. [f. IR-² + RESPONSIBLE. Cf. F. *irresponsable.*] 1. Not responsible; not answerable for conduct or actions; not liable to be called to account; incapable of legal responsibility. Also, Acting or done without a sense of responsibility. 2. Insolvent 1890.

They left the crown..perfectly i. BURKE. The prisoner was idiotic and i. 1890. **Irresponsibi·lity, Irrespo·nsibleness. Irrespo·nsibly** *adv.*

Irresponsive (irĭspǫ·nsiv), *a.* 1846. [IR-².] Not responsive; not responding to a force or stimulus; giving no answer to a question or inquiry. Hence **Irrespo·nsiveness.**

Irrestrainable (irĭstrēᵢ·năb'l), *a.* 1643. [IR-².] Not restrainable; that cannot be held in check. Hence **Irrestrai·nably** *adv.*

Irresu·scitable, *a.* [IR-².] Not resuscitable; that cannot be restored to life. CARLYLE.

Irretention (irĭte·nʃən). [IR-².] Lack of retention; irretentiveness. DE QUINCEY.

Irretentive (irĭte·ntiv), *a.* 1749. [IR-².] Not retentive; lacking the power of retention. Hence **Irrete·ntiveness.**

Irretraceable (irĭtrēᵢ·săb'l), *a.* 1847. [IR-².] That cannot be retraced.

Irretractile (irĭtræ·ktil, -təil), *a.* [IR-².] Not retractile; incapable of being drawn back. H. SPENCER.

Irretrievable (irĭtrī·văb'l), *a.* 1695. [IR-².] That cannot be retrieved; irrecoverable; irreparable.

The i. decline of his brother's health GIBBON. **Irretrievabi·lity, Irretrie·vableness, Irretrie·vably** *adv.*

†**Irretu·rnable**, *a.* 1563. [f. IR-² + RETURN *v.* + -ABLE.] That cannot be turned back; admitting of no return -1600.

Irrevea·lable, *a.* [IR-².] That cannot be revealed. So **Irrevea·lably** *adv.* (Dicts.)

Irreverence (ire·vĕrĕns). ME. [ad. L. *irreverentia*, f. *irreverentem*; see -ENCE.] 1. The fact or quality of being irreverent; disrespect to a person or thing held sacred or worthy of honour. b. with *an* and *pl.* An instance of this 1744. 2. The condition of not being reverenced. CLARENDON.

Irreverend (ire·vĕrĕnd), *a.* 1576. [IR-².] 1. Not reverend; unworthy of veneration 1748. ¶2. Formerly confused with IRREVERENT.

2. I. Gesture or Behaviour GRINDAL. **Irre·verendly** *adv.*

Irreverent (ire·vĕrĕnt), *a.* Also †inr-. 1494. [ad. L. *in-*, *irreverentem*, f. *in-*, *ir-* (IR-²) + *reverentem*, *revereri* to REVERE. Cf. F. *irrévérent.* In OF. *reverent* represented L. *reverendus*; whence sense 1.] †1. = IRREVEREND. Fabyan. 2. Not reverent; wanting in reverence; showing disrespect to a sacred or venerable person or thing 1550.

2. Th' i. Son Of him who built the Ark MILT. *P. L.* XII. 101. The i. irony of Mephistopheles B. TAYLOR. **Irre·verently** *adv.*

Irreversible (irĭvɔ̄·ɹsĭb'l), *a.* Also †-able. 1625. [IR-².] That cannot be reversed. 1. That cannot be undone, repealed, or annulled; irrevocable. 2. That cannot be turned backwards, upside down, or in the opposite direction 1821.

1. The irreversable Decree of Fate 1728. **Irreversibi·lity, Irreve·rsibleness. Irreve·rsibly** *adv.*

Irrevocable (ire·vŏkăb'l), *a.* Also †irrevo·kable. ME. [ad. L. *irrevocabilis*, f. *ir-* (IR-²) + *revocabilis*, f. *revocare. Irrevokable* follows Eng. *revoke.*] That cannot be recalled. 1. That cannot be called, brought, fetched, or taken back; that is beyond recovery. 2. That cannot be revoked, repealed, annulled, or undone; unalterable, irreversible. (The prevailing sense.) 1490.

1. The i. yesterday KINGSLEY. 2. Bi the sentence irreuocable of theym [the gods] CAXTON. **Irre·vocabi·lity, Irre·vocableness. Irre·vocably** *adv.*

Irrevoluble (ire·vŏliub'l), *a. rare.* 1641. [f. IR-² + REVOLUBLE, ad. L. *revolubilis.*] That has no finite period of revolution; of infinite circuit.

The dateless and i. Circle of Eternity MILT.

Irrigable (i·rigăb'l), *a.* 1844. [f. L. *irrigare*; see -BLE.] Capable of being irrigated.

Irrigate (i·rigeᵢt), *v.* 1615. [f. L. *irrigat-*, *irrigare*, f. *ir-* (IR-¹) + *rigare* to water.] 1. *trans.* To supply with moisture; to moisten, wet. 2. *spec.* To supply (land) with water by means of channels or streams passing through it; to water. (The prevailing sense.) 1623. b. *Med.* To supply (a part, a wound, etc.) with a constant flow or sprinkling of some liquid, for cooling, cleansing, or disinfecting 1876. 3. *fig.* To refresh or make fruitful as with moisture 1686.

2. Country..artificially irrigated by a network of canals YEATS.

Irrigation (irigēᵢ·ʃən). 1612. [ad. L. *irrigationem*; see prec.] The action of supplying or fact of being supplied with moisture; *spec.* the action of supplying land with water by means of channels or streams. Also *attrib.*

The Sixth Helpe of Ground is by..I. BACON.

Irrigator (i·rigeᵢtəɹ). 1829. [a. late L.] 1. One who or that which irrigates. 2. *Med.* A contrivance for irrigating (sense 2 b) 1887.

Irriguous (iri·giu,əs), *a.* Now *rare.* 1651. [f. L. *irriguus*, f. *ir-* (IR-¹) + *riguus* watered, f. stem of *rigare.*] 1. Irrigated; moistened, wet; *esp.* of a region or tract of land: well-watered, moist, watery. 2. Having the quality of irrigating; watering, bedewing 1684.

1. The flourie lap Of som i. Valley MILT. *P. L.* IV. 255. 2. A lordly river..Through the meadows sinuous, wandered i. CLOUGH. Hence **Irri·guousness.**

†**Irrisible** (iri·zib'l), *a.* [ad. late L. *irrisibilis*, f. *irridere.*] Ridiculous. A. CAMPBELL.

Irrision (iri·ʒən). Now *rare* or *arch.* 1526. [ad. L. *irrisionem*, f. *irridere.*] The action of laughing at a person or thing in derision or contempt; mockery.

Appellatives of scorne, or i. JER. TAYLOR.

Irrisor (irəi·sǫ̈ɹ). *rare.* 1739. [a. L.; see prec.] 1. One who laughs at another; a mocker. 2. *Zool.* A bird of the genus *Irrisor* or family *Irrisoridæ*, so called from their cry; a wood-hoopoe. Hence **Irri·sory** *a.*

Irritability (i:ritäbi·lĭti). 1755. [ad. L. *irritabilitas*, f. *irritabilis*; see next and -ITY.] The quality or state of being irritable. 1. The quality or state of being easily annoyed or excited to anger; proneness to vexation or annoyance; petulance 1791. 2. *Path.* Of a bodily organ or part: The condition of being excessively or morbidly excitable or sensitive to the contact or action of anything 1785. 3. *Physiol.* and *Biol.* The capacity of being excited to vital action (e.g. motion, contraction, nervous impulse, etc.) by the application of an external stimulus; a property of living matter or protoplasm in general, and esp. of certain organs or tissues of animals and plants, particularly muscles and nerves 1755.

1. The gloomy i. of his [Johnson's] existence BOSWELL.

Irritable (i·rităb'l), *a.* 1662. [ad. L. *irritabilis*, f. *irritare*; see -BLE.] Capable of being irritated; susceptible of irritation. 1. Readily excited to anger or impatience; easily ruffled or annoyed. 2. Readily excited to action; highly responsive to stimulus; (of a bodily organ or part). Excessively or morbidly excitable or sensitive (see IRRITATE *v.*[1] 3) 1791. 3. *Physiol.* and *Biol.* Capable of being excited to vital action by the application of some physical stimulus; said *esp.* of muscles and nerves, as subject respectively to contraction and to motor or sensory impulse under the influence of the proper external forces 1793.

1. His ill health made him more suspicious and i. than ever ELPHINSTONE. Hence **I·rritably** *adv.*

I·rritament. Now *rare* or *Obs.* 1634. [ad. L. *irritamentum* a provocative; see IRRITATE *v.*[1] and -MENT.] Something that excites or provokes an action, feeling, or state; a provocative, an incentive; an irritant.

Irritancy[1] (i·ritănsi). 1831. [f. IRRITANT *a.*[1]; see -ANCY.] Irritating quality or character; irritation.

I·rritancy[2]. 1681. [f. IRRITANT *a.*[2]; see -ANCY.] *Rom., Civil,* and *Sc. Law.* The fact of rendering, or condition of being rendered, null and void.

Irritant (i·ritănt), *a.*[1] and *sb.* 1636. [ad. L. *irritantem*, *irritare* IRRITATE *v.*[1]]

A. *adj.* †1. That irritates or stirs up; exciting, provocative. 2. Causing irritation, physical or (*rarely*) mental; irritating 1828.

2. I. poisons 1834. I. or factious opposition 1885.

B. *sb.* An irritant substance, body, or agency; in *Path.* a poison, etc. which produces irritation; in *Physiol.* and *Biol.* anything that stimulates an organ to its proper vital action. Also *fig.* 1802.

fig. A persecution which pinches, but does not suppress, is merely an i., and not an absorbent HELPS.

I·rritant, *a.*[2] 1592. [ad. L. *irritantem*, *irritare* IRRITATE *v.*[2]] *Rom., Civil,* and *Sc. Law.* Rendering null and void.

The States elected Henry Duke of Anjowe for their king, with this clause i.; That if hee did violate any point of his oath, the people should owe him no allegeance HAYWARD.

Irritate (i·riteit), *v.*[1] 1531. [f. L. *irritat-*, *irritare* to incite, excite, provoke.] †1. *trans.* To stir up, excite, provoke (a person, etc.) to some action. Const. *to, into,* or *inf.* –1841. †b. To stir up, give rise to (an action, feeling, etc.); to heighten, aggravate –1824. 2. To exasperate, provoke; to vex, fret, annoy 1598. 3. *Path.* To excite (a bodily organ or part) to morbid action, or to abnormal condition; to produce irritation in 1674. 4. *Physiol.* and *Biol.* To stimulate (an organ of an animal or plant) to some characteristic action or condition, as motion, contraction, or nervous impulse 1803.

1. Cold maketh the Spirits vigorous, and irritateth them BACON. b. With us drink irritates quarrels SIR T. HERBERT. 2. Dismiss the man, nor i. the god POPE. 4. Irritating the soles, by tickling or otherwise CARPENTER. So †**I·rritate** *ppl. a.* irritated. **I·rritatedly, I·rritatingly** *advs.*

I·rritate, *v.*[2] 1605. [f. L. *irritat-*, *irritare* to make void, f. *irritus* invalid; see IRRITE *a.*] *Rom., Civil,* and *Sc. Law. trans.* To render void, nullify; = DEFEAT *v.* 5.

Irritation (iritē·ʃən). 1589. [ad. L. *irritationem.*] The action of irritating, or condition of being irritated. †1. The action of stirring up or provoking to activity; incitement –1859. 2. Exasperation, provocation, vexation, annoyance 1703. 3. *Path.* (and *Med.*) Excitement of a bodily part or organ to excessive sensitiveness or morbid action; the resulting condition 1685. 4. *Physiol.* and *Biol.* The inducement of some vital action or condition (as motion, contraction, or nervous impulse) in an organ, tissue, etc. of an animal or plant by application of a stimulus 1794.

1. The whole body of the arts and sciences composes one vast machinery for the i. and development of the human intellect DE QUINCEY. 2. Jacobinism which arises from penury and i. BURKE.

Irritative (i·riteitiv), *a.* 1686. [f. as IRRITATE *v.*[1] + -IVE.] 1. Having the quality of stirring up or exciting to action; now in *Physiol.* or *Biol.* Having the property of stimulating to vital action. 2. Tending to irritate; annoying 1878. 3. *Path.* Characterized by or accompanied with irritation of the system or of some organ 1807.

3. I. fever 1807, conditions of the bone 1873.

Irritatory (i·riteitəri, -ătəri), *a.* [f. as prec. + -ORY.] Irritative. HALES.

†**Irrite,** *a.* Also **irrit.** 1482. [ad. L. *irritus* invalid, f. *ir-* (IR-[2]) + *ratus* established, valid.] Void, of no effect –1741.

†**Irrite,** *v.* 1450. [a. F. *irriter.*] = IRRITATE *v.*[1] –1661.

Irrorate (i·rŏrĕt), *a.* 1826. [ad. L. *irroratus* bedewed.] Irrorated (see next 2).

Irrorate (i·rŏreit), *v.* 1623. [f. L. *irrorat-*, *irrorare*, f. *ir-* (IR-[1]) + *rorare* to drop dew, f. *ros, rorem.*] †1. *trans.* To wet or sprinkle as with dew; to bedew, besprinkle; to moisten –1676. 2. *Zool.*, esp. *Entom.* In *pa. pple.* = sprinkled minutely (*with* dots) 1843.

Irroration (irorē·ʃən). 1623. [f. IRRORATE *v.*] †1. A sprinkling or wetting as with dew; a moistening –1784. 2. *Zool.* A sprinkling of minute dots or spots of colour 1843.

Irrotational (irotē·ʃənăl), *a.* 1875. [IR-[2].] *Dynamics.* Not rotational; characterized by absence of rotation; said of fluid motion.

Irrubrical (irū·brikăl), *a.* 1846. [IR-[2].] Not rubrical; contrary to the rubric.

†**I·rrugate,** *v.* 1566. [f. L. *irrugat-*, *irrugare*, f. *ir-* (IR-[1]) + *rugare*, f. *ruga* a wrinkle.] *trans.* To wrinkle. So †**I·rrugation.**

Irrupt (irɒ·pt), *v. rare.* 1855. [f. L. *irrupt-*, *irrumpere*, f. *ir-* (IR-[1]) + *rumpere.*] 1. *trans.* To break into. 2. *intr.* To burst in, break in, make an irruption 1886.

Irruption (irɒ·pʃən). 1533. [ad. L. *irruptionem*; see prec.] 1. The action of bursting or breaking in; a violent entry, inroad, incursion, or invasion, esp. of a hostile force or tribe. ¶2. Confused with ERUPTION.

1. As if Nature made recompence for the irruptions of the seas HOLLAND. 2. Vesuvius had lately made a terrible i. LUTTRELL. Feverish Irruptions ARBUTHNOT.

Irruptive (irɒ·ptiv), *a.* 1593. [f. as IRRUPT + -IVE.] Making or tending to irruption.

Irvingite (ɔ̄·rviŋəit). 1836. [f. surname *Irving* + -ITE.] A member of a religious body founded about 1835 on the basis of principles promulgated by Edward Irving (1792–1834), a minister of the Church of Scotland, settled in London, and excommunicated in 1833. (The body itself assumes the title of *Catholic Apostolic Church.*) Also *attrib.* or *adj.* So **I·rvingism.**

Is (iz), *v.* 3 sing. pres. indic. of vb. BE, q.v.

Is-: see ISO-.

-is (-ys), ME. and esp. Sc. var. of the grammatical inflexion *-es*, *-s*, of the gen. sing., and the pl. of sbs., and of the 3rd pers. sing. of verbs. In MSS. sometimes treated as a separate word or element.

My Lord of Caunterbury is avis and agreement 1456.

Isabel (i·zăbel). 1828. [a. F. *isabelle* = ISABELLA.] 1. = ISABELLA 1. 2. A small variety of the Pouter pigeon; so called from its colour 1867. 3. A N. Amer. grape. LONGF.

Isabella (izăbe·lă), *a.* (*sb.*) 1600. [From the name *Isabella*, Fr. *Isabelle.*] 1. Greyish yellow; light buff. Also used as *sb.* (Not assoc. w. the Archduchess Isabella and the siege of Ostend, 1601–1604.) 2. Applied to varieties of fruits: a. A kind of peach. b. A species of N. Amer. grape (*Vitis Labrusca*) with large fruit, sometimes purple, often green and red. 1664.

Isabelline (izăbe·lin, -əin), *a.* 1859. [f. prec. + -INE.] Of an Isabella colour, greyish yellow.

Isagoge (əisăgōu·dʒi, -gōu·gi). 1652. [a. L., a. Gr. εἰσαγωγή introduction, f. εἰς + ἀγωγή leading.] An introduction.

Isagogic (əisăgǫ·dʒik), *a.* (*sb.*) 1828. [ad. L. *isagogicus*, a. Gr.; see prec.]

A. *adj.* Of or pertaining to isagoge; introductory to any branch of study.

The formal, introductory or i., studies 1887.

B. *sb.* (usu. in pl. *isagogics*). Introductory studies; *esp.* that part of theology which is introductory to exegesis 1864.

So †**Isago·gical** *a.* introductory 1529.

Isagon, -ic, erron. forms of ISOGON, -IC.

Isapostolic (əisæpǫstǫ·lik), *a.* 1860. [f. eccl. Gr. ἰσαπόστολος equal to an apostle + -IC.] Equal to, or contemporary with, the apostles; a name given in the Greek Church to bishops consecrated by the apostles, and to other persons eminent in the primitive church.

Isat-, an element derived from L. *isatis* (Gr. ἰσάτις) woad, used in *Chem.* to form the name of ISATIN, etc.

Isatic (əisæ·tik) *acid*, $C_8H_7NO_3$ (= isatin + H_2O); the salts of which are **Isatates** (əi·săteits). **I·satyde** (†isathyd), a substance bearing the same relation to isatin that indigo-white bears to indigo-blue, being formed from it by the addition of one atom of hydrogen.

Isatin (əi·sătin). Also **-ine.** 1845. [f. L. *isatis*, a. Gr. ἰσάτις the plant woad, whence a blue dye is obtained + -IN[1].] *Chem.* A crystalline, reddish-orange substance ($C_8H_5NO_2$), of brilliant lustre, obtained from indigo by oxidation.

-isation, freq. var. of -IZATION.

Isatis (əi·sătis). 1774. [from some northern native name.] The white or Arctic fox, *Canis lagopus.*

Iscariot (iskæ·riǫt). 1581. [ad. L. *Iscariota*, a. Gr. Ἰσκαριώτης, ? ad. Heb. *ish-q'riyōth* man of Kerioth (a place in Palestine).] The surname of Judas, the disciple who betrayed Jesus Christ. Hence, = an accursed traitor. Also *attrib.* Hence **Iscario·tic, -ical** *a.* of or relating to Judas Iscariot.

Ischiadic (iskiˌæ·dik), *a.* 1727. [ad. L. *ischiadicus*, a. Gr. ἰσχιαδικός, f. ἰσχιάς, ἰσχιαδ- pain in the hip, f. ἰσχίον hip-joint.] Of or pertaining to the ischium; ischiatic. So **I·schial** *a.*

Ischiatic (iskiˌæ·tik), *a.* 1656. [ad. med.L. *ischiaticus*, altered from *ischiadicus* (see prec.).] 1. Of or pertaining to the ischium or hip; sciatic 1741. 2. Affected with sciatica.

Ischio- (i·skio), ad. Gr. ἰσχιο-, comb. f. ἰσχίον ISCHIUM, with sense 'pertaining to or connecting the ischium and . . .', as **ischiore·ctal,** etc.

Hence also **Ischio-ca·psular** *a.*, relating to or connected with the ischium and the capsular ligament of the hip-joint. **Ischio·cerite** [Gr. κέρας horn], *Zool.* the third joint of a fully developed antenna of a crustacean. **Ischio·podite** *sb.* [Gr. πούς, ποδ- foot], *Zool.* the third joint of a fully developed limb of a crustacean.

‖**Ischium** (i·skiɒm). Pl. **ischia** (erron. †-ias). 1646. [L., a. Gr. ἰσχίον hip-joint; later as now used.] The lowest of the three parts of the *os innominatum*, the bone on which the body rests when sitting.

Ischuretic (iskiure·tik). 1706. [f. Gr. ἰσχουρέειν to suffer from retention of urine; cf. next and *diuretic.*] A. *adj.* Having the property of curing ischuria. B. *sb.* A medicine that cures ischuria.

‖**Ischuria** (iskiū̆ə·riă). Also **ischury** (i·skiŭri). 1675. [L. *ischuria*, a. Gr. ἰσχουρία retention of urine, f. ἴσχειν to hold + οὖρον.] Difficulty in passing urine, due either to suppression or retention. Hence **Ischu·ric** *a.*

Ise, I'se, dial. or arch. abbrev. of *I shall* or *I is* (= I am).

-ise [1], freq. spelling of -IZE, q. v.

-ise [2], suffix of sbs., repr. OF. *-ise*, properly :—L. *-itia*, but also, in words of learned formation, put for L. *-icia, -itia, -icium, -itium.* Hence it became a living suffix, forming abstract sbs. of quality, state, or function, as in *couard-ise, gaillard-ise*, etc. In the words from L., *-ise* was subseq. changed in F. to *-ice*, as in *justice, service*, in which form the suffix mostly appears in Eng.

Isentropic: see Iso-.

Isethionic (əisīþiˌǫ·nik), *a.* 1838. [f. Iso- + ETHIONIC.] *Chem.* In *isethionic acid*, a monobasic acid, $C_2H_6SO_4$, formed by boiling ethionic acid with water. Hence **Ise·thionate.**

Ish (iʃ). *Sc.* 1375. [f. *ish* vb. (ME. and later Sc., a. OF. *issir* :—L. *exire* to go out).] **a.** Exit, as in *ish and entry.* **b.** Expiry of a legal term.

-ish [1], a suffix forming adjs., of Com.Teut. origin; cogn. w. Gr. -ισκ-ος dim. suffix of sbs. Sometimes syncopated to *-sh* (spelt also *-ch*); in Sc. *-ish* becomes *-is* and *-s.* Old formations have vowel-mutation, as *English* (cf. *Angle*), *French* (cf. *Frank*), *Welsh* (cf. *Wales*).

1. In OE. and the cognate langs., chiefly forming gentile adjs. from national names; e.g. *British* (OE. *Brittisc*), *English* (OE. *Englisc*, Sc. †*Inglis*), *Scottish, Scotch* (OE. *Scyttisc*; Sc. †*Scottis*, later *Scots*), etc. 2. Added to other sbs., with the sense 'Of or belonging to a person or thing, of the nature or character of'. These were not numerous in OE., but in later times the ending is common, chiefly in a derogatory sense, 'Having the (objectionable) qualities of'; as in *apish, currish, womanish*, etc. Also from names of things, with sense 'Of the nature of, tending to', as *bookish, freakish*, etc.; or from other parts of speech, as *stand-offish*, etc. 3. Added to adjs. with the sense 'Of the nature of, approaching the quality of, somewhat'; e.g. *bluish* (*a* 1400), *blackish* (*a* 1500), etc. Now, in colloq. use, possible with nearly all monosyllabic adjs., and some others, e.g. *brightish, loudish, narrowish*, etc. 4. Added to names of hours of the day or numbers of years to denote: Round about, somewhere near.

Hence advs. in **-ishly** and sbs. in **-ishness.**

-ish [2], a suffix of vbs., repr. F. *-iss-*, extended stem of vbs. in *-ir*, e.g. *périr, perissant.* The F. *-iss-* originated in the L. *-isc-* of inceptive vbs. Examples are *abolish, blemish, nourish, vanish*, etc. See also ADMONISH, etc.

Ishmael (i·ʃmeˌĕl, i·ʃmẹ-). [Heb. proper name; = 'God will hear'.] Proper name of the son of Abraham by Hagar; hence, An outcast; one 'whose hand is against every man, and every man's hand against him' (Gen. xvi. 12), one at war with society 1899.

Hence **I·shmaelite** (a descendant of I., as the Arabs claim to be): *fig.* = ISHMAEL; **Ishmaelitic** (-i·tik), **I·shmaelitish** (-əi:tiʃ), *adjs.*

Isiac (əi·siæ̆k, i·siæ̆k). 1694. [ad. L. *isiacus*, a. Gr. ἰσιακός, f. *Isis.*] **A.** *adj.* Of or relating to Isis, the principal goddess of ancient Egyptian mythology 1740. **B.** *sb.* A priest or worshipper of Isis.

I. table, a copper tablet, now in Turin, containing figures of Egyptian deities with Isis in the middle. Hence **Isiacal** (əisəi·ăkăl) *a.* 1613.

Isicle, isi(c)kle, obs. ff. ICICLE.

Isidorian (isidō³·riăn), *a.* 1882. [f. *Isidorus* proper name; see -IAN.] Of or pertaining to Isidorus or Isidore; spec. to St. Isidore, archbishop of Seville 600–636, author of several historical and eccl. works, and of twenty books of *Origines* or Etymologies.

In the Middle Ages his name was attached to various other works, particularly to a collection of canons and decretals.

Isinglass (əi·ziŋglɑs). 1528. [Said to be a corruption of an obs. Du. *huisenblas*, Ger. *hausenblase* isinglass, lit. 'sturgeon's bladder'; see HAUSEN and HUSO.] 1. A whitish, semi-transparent, and very pure form of gelatin, obtained from the sounds or air-bladders of some freshwater fishes, esp. the sturgeon; used for making jellies, for clarifying liquors, etc. Also extended to similar substances made from hides, hoofs, etc. 2. A name given to mica, from its resembling in appearance some kinds of isinglass 1747. 3. *attrib.* and *Comb.*, as *i. glue, size*; **i.-stone,** mica 1688.

Islam (i·slăm, i·z-, islā·m). 1613. [a. Arab. *islām* lit. 'resignation, surrendering (to God)', inf. noun of *aslama.*] The religious system of Mohammed, Mohammedanism; the body of Mohammedans or Mussulmans, the Mohammedan world 1818. †**b.** An orthodox Mohammedan –1814.

Poor faint smile Of dying I. SHELLEY. Hence **Islamic** (islæ·mik, islā·mik), **Islami·tic** *adjs.* Mohammedan, Moslem. **I·slamism,** Mohammedanism. **I·slamite,** a Mohammedan; also *attrib.* **I·slamize** *v.* to convert or conform to Mohammedanism; also *intr.*

Island (əi·lænd), *sb.* [OE. *īgland* (*īegland*), *īland*, a compound of OE. *īeg, īg* 'isle' + LAND. The simple form *īeg* corresponded to Gothic type **ahwiô, aujô*, a substantivized fem. of an adj. derived from *ahwa* 'water' (OE. *ēa*), with sense of 'watery', 'watered', and hence 'watered place, meadow, island'. The ordinary ME. and early mod.Eng. form was *iland, yland.* In 15th c. the first part of the word began to be assoc. w. *ile, yle* (of Fr. origin); and when *ile* was spelt *isle, iland* erron. followed it as *isle-land, island.*] 1. A piece of land completely surrounded by water. (Formerly including a peninsula, a place insulated at high water or during floods, or begirt by marshes.) **b.** = ISLE *sb.* 1 b. 1535. †**c.** In full, *island of ice*: an iceberg, or the like –1769. 2. *transf.* Something resembling an island in position; an elevated piece of land surrounded by marsh land; a piece of woodland surrounded by prairie; a block of buildings [= L. *insula*] 1620. **b.** *Anat.* A detached or insulated portion of tissue or group of cells, entirely surrounded by parts of a different structure; *I. of Reil*, the central lobe of the cerebrum 1879. **c.** = REFUGE *sb.* 2 b. 1876. 3. *attrib.* 1613.

1. The Iland was called Melita *Acts* xxviii. 1. The i. [Britain] has produced two or three of the greatest men that ever existed EMERSON. 2. A small hill, or iland, in the meddow on the west side of Charles Riuer 1650. 3. The i.-fishing DRUMM. OF HAWTH. Our rough i.-story TENNYSON. The i.-home they won for us GEO. ELIOT. I.-belted shores 1884.

Comb.: **i.-continent,** an i. approaching the size of the continents, or containing several states, as Australia or Greenland; **-platform,** a platform at a railway station, with lines on each side of it.

Island (əi·lænd), *v.* 1661. [f. prec. sb.] 1. *trans.* To make into or as into an island; to place as an island; to place or set on, or as on, an island; to insulate. 2. To set or dot with or as with islands 1805.

1. Billowy mist..islanding The peak whereon we stand SHELLEY. 2. The waveless plain of Lombardy ..Islanded by cities fair SHELLEY.

Island, obs. f. ICELAND [2]. *Island crystal*, Iceland spar.

Islander (əi·lændəɹ). 1550. [f. ISLAND *sb.* + -ER [1].] A native or inhabitant of an island.

I·slandman. Now *rare* or *local.* 1577. = ISLANDER.

At Belfast applied to the ship-builders on Queen's Island, more fully *Queen's Islandmen.*

Isle (əil), *sb.* [ME. *ile* (*ilde*), a. OF. *ile* (AF. *ilde*), earlier *isle*, mod.F. *île* :—L. *insula* island. In 15th c. Fr. again often spelt *isle* (after L.), whence in Eng.] 1. An island; now more usually one of smaller size. Also *fig.* **b.** In O.T., after the equivalent Heb., applied to the lands beyond the sea; esp. in phr. *isles of the Gentiles* ME. 2. A building, or block of buildings, surrounded by streets. [L. *insula.*] 1670.

1. Great Ladie of the greatest I. SPENSER. **b.** The yles shall waite for his lawe *Isa.* xlii. 4.

Isle (əil), *v.* 1570. [f. prec. sb.] 1. *trans.* = ISLAND *v.* 1. 2. *intr.* To remain or lodge on an isle. TENNYSON.

1. Thank Him who isled us here TENNYSON.

I·sleman. *rare.* 1814. [In AF. context *yleman* (14th c.).] = ISLESMAN, ISLANDER.

Islesman (əi·lzˌmæ̆n). 1578. [Earlier Sc. *yllis(ch)man.*] An inhabitant or native of any group of isles, esp. the Hebrides, Orkneys, or Shetland Isles.

Islet (əi·lĕt). 1538. [a. F. *islette*, mod. *îlette*, dim. of ISLE *sb.*; see -ET.] 1. A little island, an eyot or ait. 2. *transf.* = ISLAND *sb.* 2. 1645. **b.** An isolated piece of animal or vegetable tissue 1851. 3. *attrib.* 1810.

1. Where there is an i. in the stream GOLDSM. 2. Islet..a spot of a different colour, included in a plaga or macula KIRBY & SP. 3. That i. angle of the west R. ELLIS. Hence **I·sleted** *ppl. a.* placed like an i.; studded with islets.

Islot, ilot (əi·lǫ̈t). 1772. [a. F. *islot*, now *îlot*, dim. of *isle, île*, ISLE *sb.*] An islet.

-ism, *suffix*, repr. F. *-isme*, L. *-ismus*, a. Gr. -ισμός, forming nouns of action from vbs. in -ίζειν, e.g. βαπτίζειν, βαπτισμός the action of dipping, baptism. An allied suffix was -ισμα(τ-), expressing the thing done, and which in some cases is the source of modern *-ism.* The following are the chief uses of the suffix:

1. Forming a simple noun of action, naming the process, or the completed action, or its result (rarely concrete); as in *agonism, aphorism, baptism, organism, syllogism*, etc. **b.** Expressing the action or conduct of a class of persons, as *heroism, patriotism, priggism, scoundrelism*, etc.; also the condition of a person or thing, as *barbarism, orphanism, parallelism*, etc.; also *Daltonism.*

2. Forming the name of a system of theory or practice, as *Arianism, Brahmanism, Chartism, Conservatism, Puseyism, Quietism*, etc. **b.** More of the nature of class-names or descriptive terms for doctrines or principles, are *agnosticism, altruism, bimetallism, jingoism, sansculottism, stoicism*, etc.

3. Forming a term denoting a peculiarity or characteristic, esp. of language, e.g. *Americanism, Græcism, Orientalism*, etc. To these add such as *archaism, colloquialism, modernism, solecism.*

Ism (i·z'm), *quasi-sb.* 1680. [The prec. suffix used generically.] A form of doctrine, theory, or practice having a distinctive character or relation; chiefly disparaging.

He is nothing,—no 'ist', professes no '-ism' but superbism and irrationalism SHELLEY.

Ismaelian, Ismaïlian (ismeˌī·liăn, -i·liăn), *sb.* and *a.* 1839. [f. proper name *Ismael* or *Ismaïl.*] A member of a sect of the Shiite branch of Islam which held that, at the death of Djafar Madeck, the Imamship ought to have descended to the posterity of his deceased elder son Ismail, and not to the surviving younger son Mousa, to whom he left it. **b.** as *adj.*

I·smaelite, *sb.* (*a.*) Also (in sense c) **I·smailite.** 1571. **a.** Another form of ISHMAELITE. **b.** A name formerly sometimes given (esp. by Jews) to the Arabs as descendants of Ishmael, and so to Mohammedans generally. **c.** *spec.* = ISMAELIAN.

Isn't, colloq. f. *is not.*

Iso- (əiso), bef. a vowel occas. **is-,** comb. f. Gr. ἴσος equal, used in numerous terms, nearly all scientific, the second element being properly and usually of Gr. origin, rarely of Latin (the proper prefix in the latter case being EQUI-). Some of the less important of these are:

Isentro·pic *a.* and *sb. Physics*, of equal entropy; (a line on a diagram) indicating successive states of a body in which the entropy remains constant. **I·sobath** (-bæþ) [Gr. βάθος depth], an inkstand with a float so contrived as to keep the ink in the dipping-well at a constant level. **Isobathytherm** (-bæ·piþəɹm) [Gr. βαθύς deep + θέρμη heat], a line connecting points having the same temperature in a vertical section of any part of the sea; so **Isobathythe·rmal, -the·rmic** *adjs.* **Isocephaly** (-se·făli), **-kephaly** (-ke·făli) [Gr. κεφαλή head], the principle observed in some ancient Greek reliefs, esp. in friezes, of representing the heads of all the figures at nearly the same level. **I·sochasm** (-kæz'm) [Gr. χάσμα gap], a line on a map, etc. connecting places having equal frequency of auroral displays; so **Isocha·smic** *a.* (lines or curves) bounding zones of equal auroral frequency. **Isochroous** (əisǫ·kroˌəs) [Gr. χρόα colour] *a.*, of the same colour throughout. **Isodimorphism** (əi:sodəimǭ·ɹfiz'm) [see DIMORPHISM], *Cryst.* 'isomorphism between the forms severally of two dimorphous substances' (Webster); so **I:sodimo·rphous** *a.*, exhibiting isodimorphism. **Isohyetal** (-həi·ĭtăl), **-hy·etose** [Gr. ὑετός rain] *adjs.* (*sbs.*), (a line on a map, etc.) connecting places having equal annual or seasonal rainfall. **Isoneph** (əi·sonef) [Gr. νέφος cloud], a line on a map, etc. connecting places at which the amount of cloud for a given period (e.g. a year) is the same; so **Isonephelic** (-nĭfe·lik) [Gr. νεφέλη] *a.*, indicating equality in respect of cloudiness. **Isopiestic** (-pəiˌe·stik) [Gr. πιέζειν] *a.*, denoting equal pressure. **Isoseismal** (-səi·smăl) [Gr. σεισμός earthquake] *a.* and *sb.*, (a line on a map, etc.) connecting points at which the intensity of an earthquake-shock is the same; so **Isosei·smic** *a.* **Isosporous** (əisǫ·spŏrəs) [Gr. σπόρος seed] *a.*, *Bot.* producing spores all of the same size or kind (opp. to *heterosporous*); so **Isospore** (əi·sospoəɹ), one of such spores. **Isostemonous** (-stī·mŏnəs) [Gr. στήμων in sense 'stamen'] *a.*, *Bot.*

having the stamens equal in number to the parts of the perianth; also said of the stamens; so **Isostemony** (-stī·mŏni), the condition of being isostemonous. **Isotrimorphism** (əisotraimǭ·ɹfiz'm), *Cryst.* 'isomorphism between the forms, severally, of two trimorphous substances' (Webster); so **I·sotrimo·rphous** *a.*, exhibiting isotrimorphism.

b. In *Chem.* sometimes prefixed to the name of a compound substance to denote another substance isomeric with it. The number of such names is unlimited.

Isobar (əi·sobāɹ). Also **isobare.** 1864. [f. Gr. ἰσοβαρής of equal weight, f. ἰσο-, Iso- + βαρε-, βάρος weight, βαρύς heavy.] *Phys. Geog.* and *Meteorol.* A line (drawn on a map, etc., or imaginary) connecting places on the earth's surface at which the barometric pressure is the same (at a given time, or on the average for a given period); an isobaric line.

Isobaric (əisobæ·rik), *a.* 1878. [f. prec. + -IC. (Not on Gr. analogies.)] Indicating equal barometric pressure; containing or relating to isobars.

Isobarism (əisǫ·băriz'm). 1882. [f. as prec. + -ISM.] Equality of weight. (Dicts.)

Isobarometric (əisobærome·trik), *a. rare.* 1864. [f. Iso- + BAROMETRIC.] = ISOBARIC.

Isocheim (əi·sokəim). Also **-chime.** 1864. [f. Gr. ἰσο-, Iso- + χεῖμα winter-weather.] *Phys. Geog.* An isochimenal line.

Isocheimal (əisokəi·măl), *a.* and *sb.* Also **-chimal.** 1839. [f. prec. + -AL.] = ISOCHIMENAL.

Isochimenal (-kəi·mĭnăl). Also **-cheimenal.** 1846. [f. F. *isochimène* (Humboldt), f. Gr. ἰσο-, Iso- + χειμαίνειν to be wintry, f. χεῖμα winter-weather, storm.] **A.** *adj.* Indicating equal mean winter temperatures; said of lines on a map, etc. **B.** *sb.* An isochimenal line, an isocheim.

Isochromatic (əi:soˌkromæ·tik), *a.* 1829. [f. Iso- + CHROMATIC.] **1.** *Optics.* Of the same colour or tint, as two lines or curves in an interference figure of a biaxial crystal. **2.** *Photogr.* = *orthochromatic*.

Isochronal (əisǫ·krŏnăl), *a.* †Also *erron.* **-cronal.** 1680. [f. mod.L. *isochronus* (Leibnitz), a. Gr. ἰσόχρονος (f. ἰσο-, Iso- + χρόνος time) + -AL.] = ISOCHRONOUS.

So **Isochro·nic, -al** *a.*

Isochronism (əisǫ·krŏniz'm). 1770. [f. as prec. + -ISM.] The character or property of being isochronous, or of oscillating or taking place in equal spaces of time.

Isochronous (əisǫ·krŏnəs), *a.* 1706. [f. as ISOCHRONAL + -OUS.] Taking place in or occupying equal times; equal in metrical length; equal in duration, or in intervals of occurrence; characterized by or relating to vibrations or motions of equal duration; vibrating uniformly, as a pendulum. **b.** Equal in duration (vibration-period, etc.) *to* or *with* something 1776. Hence **Iso·chronously** *adv.*

Isoclinal (əisoklǝi·năl), *a.* (*sb.*) 1839. [f. Iso- + Gr. κλίνειν to bend, slope.] **1.** *Phys. Geog.* Indicating equal magnetic inclination; applied to lines connecting points on the earth's surface at which the magnetic inclination or dip is the same; relating to or containing such lines. **2.** *Geol.* Of strata: Dipping all in the same direction 1882. **3.** *sb.* An isoclinal line: see sense 1. 1889. So **Isocli·nic** *a.* and *sb.*

Isocracy (əisǫ·krăsi). 1652. [ad. Gr. ἰσοκρατία equality of power or political rights, f. ἰσο-, Iso- + κράτος, κρατε- strength, power; see -CRACY.] Equality of power or rule; a system of government in which all the people possess equal political power.

A debasing i., which already views with suspicion the cultivation of the highest literature 1895.

Isocrymal (əisokrəi·măl). 1852. [f. Iso- + Gr. κρυμός cold + -AL.] *Phys. Geog.* **A.** *adj.* Applied to lines on a map, etc. connecting places at which the temperature is the same during a specified coldest part (*e.g.* the coldest 30 consecutive days) of the year. **B.** *sb.* An isocrymal line; also **I·socryme.**

Isodiabatic (əi:sodəiˌăbæ·tik), *a.* 1859. [f. Iso- + Gr. διαβατικός able to pass through; cf. ADIABATIC.] *Physics.* Relating to or indicating the transmission of equal amounts of heat to and from a body or substance.

Isodiametric, -al (əisodəiˌăme·trik, -ăl), *a.* 1884. [f. Iso- + DIAMETRIC.] Having equal diameters; *spec.* applied in *Bot.* to cells of rounded or polyhedral form; in *Cryst.* to crystals having equal lateral axes.

Isodynamic (əi:sodinæ·mik), *a.* (*sb.*) 1832. [f. Gr. ἰσοδύναμος + -IC; after *dynamic.*] Of or pertaining to equal force. **1.** *Phys. Geog.*, etc. Indicating equal (magnetic) force; applied to lines connecting points at which the intensity of the magnetic force is the same; or to a chart, etc. exhibiting these. Also as *sb.* An isodynamic line. **2.** Of equal force, value, or efficacy 1842. So **Isodyna·mical** *a.*, in sense 1.

Isodynamous (əisodi·năməs), *a.* 1835. [f. as prec. + -OUS.] *Bot.* Growing with equal vigour on both sides.

Isogeotherm (əisoˌdʒī·oþəɹm). 1864. [f. Iso- + Gr. γεω- earth + θέρμη, θερμός.] *Phys. Geog.* A line or surface (usu. imaginary) connecting points in the interior of the earth having the same temperature. Hence **Isogeothe·rmal, -the·rmic** *adjs.* of the nature of an i.

Isogonal (əisǫ·gŏnăl), *a.* (*sb.*) 1857. [f. Gr. ἰσογώνιος equiangular + -AL.] **1.** = ISOGONIC *a.*[1] and *sb.* **2.** Equiangular 1878.

Isogonic (əisogǫ·nik), *a.*[1] (*sb.*) 1851. [f. as prec. + -IC.] *Phys. Geog.* Indicating equal angles (of magnetic variation); applied to lines on a map, etc. connecting points of the earth's surface where the magnetic declination, or variation from the true north, is the same; or to a map, etc. exhibiting these. Also as *sb.* An isogonic line.

Isogo·nic, *a.*[2] [f. as next + -IC.] *Biol.* Characterized by isogonism. (Mod. Dicts.)

Isogonism (əisǫ·gŏniz'm). 1884. [f. Iso- + Gr. γόνος, γονή offspring + -ISM.] *Biol.* The production of sexual individuals of the same structure from different stocks, occurring in some *Hydrozoa*.

Isographic (əisogræ·fik), *a.* 1872. [f. Iso- + -GRAPHIC.] = HOMALOGRAPHIC. **Isogra·phically** *adv.* in the way of i. projection.

Isolable (əi·sŏlăb'l), *a.* 1855. [f. ISOLATE + -ABLE.] Capable of being isolated.

Isolate (əi·sŏlēˈt), *v.* 1807. [f. ISOLATED, or f. F. *isoler*, ad. It. *isolare* (:—L. *insulare*) + -ATE[3].] **1.** *trans.* To place apart or alone; to cause to stand alone, separate, detached, or unconnected with other things or persons; to insulate. **2.** *Chem.* To obtain as a separate substance 1836. **3.** *Electr.* = INSULATE *v.* 3. 1855. **4.** To cut off (an infected person or place) from all contact with others 1890.

1. Whatever isolates people from people is a mischievous partition wall 1845. High culture always isolates 1873.

Isolated (əi·sŏlēˈtĕd), *ppl. a.* 1763. [f. F. *isolé*, ad. It. *isolato* :—L. *insulatus* insulated, f. *insula*. Now ranking as pa. pple. of prec. vb.] Placed or standing apart or alone; detached or separate from other things or persons; unconnected with anything else; solitary.

Collective action is more efficacious than i. individual effort M. ARNOLD. Hence **I·solatedly** *adv.*

I·solating, *ppl. a.* 1861. [f. ISOLATE *v.* + -ING[2].] *Philol.* Applied to languages of which each element is an isolated or independent word, none being compounded or inflected.

Isolation (əisŏlēˈ·ʃən). 1833. [a. F., f. *isoler.*] The action of isolating; the fact or condition of being isolated; separation from other things or persons; solitariness. **b.** *attrib.* in *i. hospital, camp*, etc., one by which isolation is effected 1891.

I·solative, *a.* 1888. [f. ISOLATE *v.* + -IVE.] In *Phonetics*, said of sound-changes which take place without reference to neighbouring sounds.

I·solator. 1855. [f. ISOLATE *v.*; see -OR.] One who or that which isolates; an insulator.

Isologous (əisǫ·lŏgəs), *a.* 1857. [f. Iso- + Gr. λόγος + -OUS.] *Chem.* Having equality or parallelism of relations; applied to two or more hydrocarbon series, of each of which the members are related to each other in the same way.

The allylic, the benzoic, and the cinnamic series, are *i.* with that of alcohol W. A. MILLER.

Isomer (əi·soməɹ). 1866. [f. Gr. ἰσομερής sharing equally, f. ἰσο- Iso- + μέρος part, share; in F. *isomère.*] *Chem.* A substance isomeric with another; any one of a number of isomeric compounds.

Isomeric (əisome·rik), *a.* 1838. [f. as ISOMER + -IC; after Ger. *isomerisch* (Berzelius).] *Chem.* Composed of the same elements in the same proportions, and (ordinarily) having the same molecular weight, but forming different substances, with different properties (owing to the different grouping of the constituent atoms).

Isomeride (əisǫ·mĕrəid). 1857. [f. as ISOMER + -IDE.] *Chem.* = ISOMER.

Isomerism (əisǫ·mĕriz'm). 1838. [f. ISOMER + -ISM.] *Chem.* The fact or condition of being isomeric; identity of percentage composition in compounds differing in properties.

Bodies may conduct themselves chemically in exactly the same way, and yet differ in some of their physical properties, as in their action towards polarized light. To distinguish this kind of i...it is called *physical i.* 1896.

Isomeromorphism (əiso:mĕroˌmǭ·ɹfiz'm). 1864. [f. *isomero-*, comb. f. next + Gr. μορφή form + -ISM.] *Cryst.* Isomorphism between isomeric substances.

Isomerous (əisǫ·mĕrəs), *a.* 1857. [f. as ISOMER + -OUS.] **1.** *Bot.* Of a flower: Having the same number of parts in each whorl. (Said also of the whorls.) Opp. to HETEROMEROUS 2. **2.** *Chem.* = ISOMERIC 1864.

Isometric (əisome·trik), *a.* 1840. [f. Gr. ἰσομετρία (f. ἴσος + μέτρος) + -IC.] **1.** Of equal measure or dimensions 1855. **2.** Applied to a method of projection or perspective, in which the plane of projection is equally inclined to the three principal axes of the object, so that all dimensions parallel to these axes are represented in their actual proportions; used in drawing figures of machines, etc. 1840. **3.** *Cryst.* Applied to that system of crystalline forms characterized by three equal axes mutually at right angles (also called *cubic, tesseral*, etc.); belonging to this system 1868. So **Isome·trical** *a.* 1838. **Isome·trically** *adv.*

Isomorph (əi·somǭɹf). 1864. [f. Gr. ἰσο-, Iso- + μορφή form.] *Chem.* and *Min.* A substance or organism isomorphous with another.

Isomorphic (əisomǭ·ɹfik), *a.* 1862. [f. as prec. + -IC.] **1.** *Chem.* and *Min.* Exhibiting isomorphism, isomorphous; pertaining to or involving isomorphism. **2.** *Math.* Said of groups corresponding to each other in form, and in the nature and product of their operations 1897.

Isomorphism (əisomǭ·ɹfiz'm). 1828. [f. as prec. + -ISM.] The character of being isomorphous. **1.** *Chem.* and *Min.* The property of crystallizing in the same or closely related forms, esp. as exhibited by substances of analogous composition. **2.** *Math.* Identity of form and of operations between two or more groups.

1. The discovery by Professor Mitscherlich, of what is called the *isomorphism* of crystals, diminishes in some degree the value of crystalline form as a distinctive character TRIMMER.

Isomorphous (əisomǭ·ɹfəs), *a.* 1828. [f. as ISOMORPH + -OUS.] **1.** *Chem.* and *Min.* Having the property of crystallizing in the same or closely related geometric forms; said esp. of two compounds or groups of compounds of different elements, but of analogous composition. **2.** *Math.* = ISOMORPHIC 2.

-ison, suffix of sbs., repr. OF. *-aison, -eison, -eson, -ison* :—L. *-ationem* (adopted later in the learned form *-ation*, which is thus a doublet of *-ison*), *-etionem, -itionem.* Examples *comparison, garrison, jettison, venison*, etc.

Isonomic (əisonǫ·mik), *a.* 1864. [ad. Gr. ἰσονομικός 'devoted to equality', f. ἰσονομία: see ISONOMY.] **1.** Having equal laws or rights (*rare*). **2.** *Chem.* Having the same or a similar arrangement of elements; involving analogy of composition, as *isomorphism* in the stricter sense 1864. **3.** Of the same or like polarity; applied to contact of parts of the body in experiments on animal magnetism; opp. to HETERONOMIC, q. v.

Isonomy (əisǫ·nŏmi). 1600. [ad. It. *isonomia*, a. Gr. ἰσονομία, f. (ult.) ἰσο-, Iso- + νόμος law.] Equality of laws, or of people before the law.

Isopathy (əisǫ·păþi). *rare.* 1855. [f. Iso- + -PATHY.] *Med.* **a.** The theory that disease may be cured by a product of the disease, as small-pox by variolous matter. **b.** The popular notion that disease in a particular organ may be cured by eating the same organ of a healthy animal.

Isoperimeter (əi:sopĕri·mĭtəɹ). 1674. [ad. Gr. ἰσοπερίμετρος: see Iso- and PERIMETER.] *Geom.* A figure having a perimeter equal to that of another; usu. *pl.* Figures of equal perimeter.

Isoperimetrical (əi:soperime·trikăl), *a.* 1706. [f. Gr. ἰσοπερίμετρος (see prec.) + -ICAL.] *Geom.* **1.** Of figures: Having equal perimeters. **2.** Relating to or connected with isoperimetry 1743. So †**Isoperi·metral** *a.* 1625.

Isoperimetry (əisopĕri·mĕtri). 1811. [f. as ISOPERIMETER + -Y[3].] *Geom.* That branch of geometry which deals with isoperimetrical figures and problems.

Isopleural (əisoplūə·răl), *a.* [f. as next + -AL.] Having equal sides, equilateral; *spec.* in *Zool.* belonging to the sub-class *Isopleura* of gastropods, which have the body bilaterally symmetrical, as in the chitons. **Isopleu·rous** *a.*

†**I·sopleure.** Also **isopleuron.** 1592. [ad. Gr. ἰσόπλευρος equilateral, f. ἰσο-, Iso- + πλευρά rib, side.] An equilateral figure –1674.

Isopod (əi·sŏpǫd), *sb.* (*a.*) Also **isopode.** Pl. **isopods;** also freq. in L. form **iso·poda.** 1835. [a. mod.F. *isopode*, f. mod.L. *Isopoda* neut. pl., f. Iso- + Gr. πούς, ποδ-.] *Zool.* An animal of the order *Isopoda* of sessile-eyed Crustaceans, characterized by seven pairs of equal and similarly placed thoracic legs; comprising marine, freshwater, and terrestrial species, some being parasitic. Also as *adj.*

So **Iso·podan** *a.* and *sb.* = prec. **Isopo·diform** *a.* having the form of an i., as certain insect larvæ 1826. **Iso·podous** *a.* belonging to, or having the characters of, the *Isopoda*.

Isopolity (əisopǫ·lĭti). 1836. [ad. Gr. ἰσοπολιτεία.] Chiefly *Anc. Hist.* Equality of rights of citizenship between different communities or states; reciprocity of civic rights.

Between America and England..one would be glad if there could exist some i. CLOUGH.

Isosceles (əisǫ·sĭlīz), *a.* (*sb.*) 1551. [a. late L., a. Gr. ἰσοσκελής equal-legged, f. ἰσο- + σκέλος, σκελε- leg.] *Geom.* Of a triangle: Having two of its sides equal.

Also *Isoscele* (əi·sosīl) *sb.* BROWNING.

Isospondylous (əisospǫ·ndiləs), *a.* [f. mod.L. *Isospondylus* (in pl. *-yli*) (f. Iso- + Gr. σπόνδυλος, σφόν- vertebra, joint) + -OUS.] *Ichthyol.* Belonging to, or having the characters of, the *Isospondyli*, an order of physostomous fishes.

Isostasy (əisǫ·stăsi). [f. Iso- + Gr. στάσις station + -Y[3].] The equilibrium of the earth's crust; hydrostatic equilibrium. Hence **Isosta·tic** *a.* 1901.

‖**Isoteles** (əisǫ·tĭlīz). 1849. [a. Gr. ἰσοτελής, f. ἴσος equal + τέλος tax.] *Anc. Gr. Hist.* One of a class of *metœci* or resident aliens at Athens who enjoyed all civic (except political) rights. So **Iso·tely**, the condition of an i.

Isotheral (əisǫ·þĕrăl, əi·soþīərăl). 1839. [f. next + -AL.] **A.** *adj.* Applied to lines on a map, etc. connecting places having the same mean summer temperature. **B.** *sb.* An isotheral line.

Isothere (əi·soþiəɹ). 1852. [a. F. *isothère* sb. (= *ligne isothère*), a. Gr. ἰσο- Iso- + θέρος, θερε- summer.] *Phys. Geog.* An imaginary line passing through points on the earth's surface that have the same mean summer temperature.

Isotherm (əi·soþəɹm). 1860. [f. F. *isotherme*, f. Gr. ἰσο- Iso- + θέρμη heat, θερμός hot.] *Phys. Geog.* An imaginary line passing through points on the earth's surface that have the same mean temperature; an isothermal line.

Isothermal (əisoþə·ɹmăl). 1826. [f. F. *isotherme* (see prec.) + -AL.]

A. *adj.* Of, pertaining to, indicating, or corresponding to equal temperatures; **a.** *esp.* in *Phys. Geog.* applied to a line connecting places on the earth's surface at which the temperature for a particular period (e.g. a year) is the same; also to a map or chart exhibiting such lines. **b.** Applied to (imaginary) lines or surfaces of equal heat in a crystal or other body when heated 1854. **B.** *sb.* An isothermal line or surface; an isotherm 1852.

Hence **Isothe·rmobath** [Gr. βάθος depth], a line connecting points of equal temperature at various depths in a vertical section of the sea. **Isothe·rmous** *a.* = ISOTHERMAL *a.*

Isotope (əi·sotoup). 1913. [f. Iso- + Gr. τόπος place.] *Chem.* A chemical element possessing the same chemical character as another element occupying the same place in the periodic table, but distinguished from it in other ways, as by its radio-activity or the differing mass of its atoms. SODDY. Hence **Isoto·pic** *a.*, **I·sotopism, Iso·topy.**

Isotopic was used by Cohen and Miller in a different sense in 1904.

Isotropic (əisotrǫ·pik), *a.* 1864. [f. Iso- + Gr. τρόπος turn, etc. + -IC.] *Physics.* Exhibiting equal physical properties or actions in all directions; opp. to *æolotropic* or *anisotropic*. So **I·sotrope, Iso·tropous** *adjs.* in same sense. **Iso·tropy**, the condition or quality of being i.

Israel (i·zreɪĕl, i·zrė-). OE. [a. L. *Israel*, Gr. Ἰσραήλ, a. Heb. *yisrāēl*, lit. 'he that striveth with God', symbolic proper name conferred on Jacob, Gen. xxxii. 28.] **1.** The people descended from Israel or Jacob, the 'children of Israel' collectively; the Jewish or Hebrew nation or people. **2.** In *fig.*, uses; *esp.* the chosen people of God, the elect; the Christian Church, or true Christians collectively ME.

2. The greatest Troublers of our *Israel* 1692.

Israelite (i·zreɪĕləit, i·zrė-). ME. [ad. L. *Israelita*, ad. Gr. Ἰσραηλίτης; in Heb. *yisrĕēlī*; see prec. and -ITE.] **A.** *sb.* **1.** One of the people of Israel; a Hebrew; a Jew. **2.** *fig.* One of God's chosen people ME.

1. Behold an I. indeed in whom is no guile *John* i. 47.

B. *adj.* Pertaining to Israel; Jewish, Israelitish 1851.

So **I·sraeli·tic, †-al, I·sraeli·tish** *adjs.* belonging to the Israelites; Jewish.

Issuable (i·ʃiuăb'l, i·siu-), *a.* 1570. [f. ISSUE *sb.* and *v.* + -ABLE.] **1.** *Law.* In regard to which or during which issue may be joined. Also *transf.* **2.** That may be issued, as a writ or summons; authorized to be issued 1642. **3.** Liable to issue as the proceeds of any property, investment, or source of revenue 1674.

1. His Lordship held that there was no issueable matter in the paragraphs complained of 1890. Hence **I·ssuably** *adv.* so as to raise an issue.

Issuance (i·ʃiuăns, i·siu-). *U.S.* 1865. [f. next; see -ANCE.] The action of issuing; = ISSUE *sb.*

Issuant (i·ʃiuănt, i·siu-), *a.* 1610. [f. ISSUE *v.* + -ANT[1], after F. pr. pples. in *-ant*. Superseding earlier *issant.*] **1.** Issuing or proceeding from a place or source. Now *rare.* 1634. **2.** *Her.* Emerging from the bottom of a chief, or (less usually) rising from another bearing or from the bottom of an escutcheon. Said esp. of a beast of which the upper half alone is visible.

Issue (i·ʃiu, i·siu), *sb.* ME. [a. OF. *issue*, *eissue*, etc. (mod.F. *issue*) :—pop.L. **exuta* sb., from fem. of **exutus* pa. pple., for cl. L. *exitus*, f. L. *exire* to go out.]

I. 1. The action of going, passing, or flowing out; power of egress or exit; outgoing, outflow. Also *fig.* †**b.** A sortie –1685. **2.** Outgoing, termination, end, close 1483. **3.** *Med.* A discharge of blood or other matter from the body, either due to disease or produced surgically by counter-irritation 1526. **b.** An incision or artificial ulcer made for the purpose of causing such a discharge 1607.

1. The Lord kepe thin entre and thi issu WYCLIF *Ps.* cxx[i]. 8. To make i. HOLLAND. Place of i. TYNDALL. *fig.* Vnto God the Lord belong the issues from death *Ps.* lxviii. 20. **3. b.** He had a blister, or i., upon his neck PEPYS.

II. A place or means of egress; outlet ME.

This Sea [the Caspian] is..without any i. to other Seas PURCHAS.

III. 1. Offspring; a child or children; a descendant or descendants. Now chiefly in legal use. †Formerly occas. with pl. *issues*. ME. Also *fig.* †**b.** A race, stock; also *fig.* –1680. **2.** Produce, proceeds; profits arising from lands, tenements, amerciaments, or fines. Now only in legal use. ME. †**b.** A fine, an amerciament; an order for levying such –1752. **3.** Outcome, product 1601. †**b.** An action, a deed (in relation to the doer). SHAKS.

1. No i. from this marriage survived 1850. **2.** Profytes and issues of the maners ME. **3. b.** *Jul. C.* III. i. 294.

IV. Event, result, consequence. Also in pl. *In the i.*, in the event ME. †**b.** Luck in an undertaking –1639. †**c.** Decision, conclusion –1719. **d.** The upshot of an argument, evidence, etc. 1604.

The i. of a combat GOUGE. **b.** *Ant. & Cl.* I. ii. 97. **d.** *Oth.* III. iii. 219.

V. *Law.* The point in question, at the conclusion of the pleadings in an action, when one side affirms and the other denies 1511. **b.** *transf.* A point on the decision of which something depends or is made to rest; a point or matter in contention; the point at which a matter becomes ripe for decision 1566. **c.** A matter or point which remains to be decided 1836.

Issue of law, an issue raised by a demurrer or analogous proceedings, conceding the fact alleged, but denying the application of the law as claimed. *General i.*, an issue raised by simply traversing the allegations in the declaration, as in the plea 'not guilty'. **b.** Phr. *To put to* (†*on, upon, an, the*) *i.*: to bring to a point admitting of decision. **c.** There is a mighty i. at stake..the good or evil of the human soul JOWETT.

Phrases. **At i. a.** In *Law*: The term used, when, in the course of pleading, the parties come to a point which one affirms and the other denies. Hence *gen.* of persons or parties: In controversy; at variance. **b.** Of a matter: In dispute; in question. **To join i. a.** *Law.* To submit an issue jointly for decision; also, of one party, To accept the issue tendered by the opposite party. **b.** *transf.* To accept or adopt a disputed point as the basis of argument in a controversy. **c.** To take up the opposite side of a case, or a contrary view *on* a question.

VI. From ISSUE *v.* The action of sending or giving out officially or publicly; an emission of bills of exchange, notes, bonds, shares, postage-stamps, etc. **b.** The set number or amount (of coins, notes, copies of a newspaper, etc.) issued at one time, or distinguished in pattern, etc., from those issued at another time 1835. **c.** An item or amount given out 1861 (orig. *U.S.*).

Bank of issue: see BANK *sb.*[3] The first small i. of the French assignats JEVONS.

Comb. **i. pea**, a pea or other small globular body placed in a surgical issue (I. 3 b), to keep up irritation.

Issue (i·ʃiu, i·siu), *v.* ME. [f. prec. sb.]

I. *intr.* **1.** To go or come out; to flow out; to come forth, sally out. **b.** To start forth, to branch out; †to stick out 1533. **c.** *transf.* and *fig.* To emerge 1481. **2.** To be born, or descended. Now only in legal use. 1450. **3.** To come as proceeds or revenue; to accrue 1443. **4.** To take origin, be derived, spring 1481. **b.** To result 1576. **5.** To turn out (in a specified way); to end or result *in* 1665. **6.** To be published or emitted 1640.

1. Let's..i. forth, and bid them Battaile straight SHAKS. **b.** From his head i. foure great hornes SIR T. HERBERT. **3.** A fee farme rent issuing out of white acre of ten shillings BACON. **4.** It issues from the rancour of a Villaine SHAKS. **5.** A philosophy which issues in such conclusions FROUDE. **6.** Before money can legally i. from the Treasury [etc.] 1795.

II. *trans.* **1.** To give exit to; to send forth, or allow to pass out; to let out; to emit; to discharge 1442. †**2.** To give birth to; to bear (offspring), have issue –1672. **3.** To give or send out authoritatively or officially; to send forth or deal out formally or publicly; to emit, put into circulation 1601. †**4.** To bring to an issue; to settle, terminate. Chiefly Amer. –1706. **b.** To cause to end *in* something (now *rare*) 1676. **5.** To supply (an army, etc.) *with* 1925.

1. A gaping wound Issuing life blood SHAKS. **2.** *Temp.* I. ii. 59. **3.** To i. process BLACKSTONE, writs BURKE, tickets DICKENS, parts of a Dictionary 1897.

Issueless (i·ʃiulĕs, i·siulĕs), *a.* 1447. [-LESS.] Without issue; without offspring. **b.** Without result 1611.

Both their daughters i. 1791.

Issuer (i·ʃiuɪəɹ, i·siuɪəɹ). 1757. [f. ISSUE *v.* + -ER[1].] One who issues; see the vb.

I·ssuing, *vbl. sb.* 1481. [f. as prec. + -ING[1].] **1.** The action of ISSUE *v.* †**2.** *concr.* A place or point of issue; an outlet –1712.

-ist, *suffix*, corresp. to F. *-iste*, L. *-ista*, Gr. -ιστής, forming agent-nouns from verbs in -ίζειν (see -IZE), consisting of the agential -της added to the vb.-stem, as in βαπτίζειν, βαπτιστής, L. *baptista*, F. *baptiste* baptist. Cognate to the suffix -ισμός, -ISM.

In Eng. the suffix is used also in a multitude of terms having no corresponding words in *-ize* or *-ism*, which denominate the professed followers of some leader or school, the professional devotees of some principle, or the practisers of some art. In some cases the form in *-ist* is distinguished from the agent-noun in *-er* only by the more professional or systematic sense which it implies: cf. *copier*, *copyist*; *cycler*, *cyclist*; *philologer*, *philologist*.

Ist, quasi-*sb.* 1811. [The suffix *-ist* used generically.] A professor of some *ism*; a holder of some special doctrine, or adherent of some system; a votary of, or expert in, some science, art, or pursuit. Often disparaging or joc.

Is't (ist), arch., poet., colloq., or dial. abbrev. of *is it*.

-ister, †-istre, suffix repr. OF. *-istre*, a by-form of *-iste*, -IST, said to have arisen through false analogy with words like *ministre*. Hence *evangelistre*, beside *evangeliste*; so *choristre*, etc. From OF., these forms passed into English, where they were spelt first *-istre*, as in *queristre*, etc.; afterwards *-ister*, as in *chorister*.

†Isthm(e. 1609. [a. F. *isthme*, ad. L. *isthmus*.] = ISTHMUS -1646.

I·sthmian (see ISTHMUS), *a.* (*sb.*) 1601. [f. L. *isthmius*, a. Gr. ἴσθμιος + -AN.] **1.** Belonging to, situated upon, or forming, an isthmus or neck of land 1654. **2.** *spec.* Belonging to the Isthmus of Corinth; esp. in *Isthmian games*, one of the national festivals of ancient Greece, celebrated in the Isthmian sanctuary in the first and third years of each Olympiad 1603. **3.** *sb.* An inhabitant of an isthmus, e.g. of the Isthmus of Corinth 1601.

Isthmus (i·sþmŏs, i·stmŏs, i·smŏs). Pl. **isthmuses** (-ŏsēz), rarely **isthmi** (-əi). 1555. [a. L. *isthmus*, a. Gr. ἰσθμός neck, narrow passage, etc.] **1.** *Geog.* A narrow portion of land, enclosed on each side by water, and connecting two larger bodies of land; a neck of land. Also *fig.* **2.** *Anat.*, *Zool.*, and *Bot.* A narrow part or organ connecting two larger parts; *esp.* the narrow passage connecting the cavity of the mouth with that of the pharynx (more fully *i. of the fauces* or *throat*) 1706.

-istic, double suffix of adjs. and sbs., corresp. to F. *-istique*, L. *-isticus*, Gr. -ιστικός, viz. the suffix -ικός, -IC, added to sbs. in -ιστής, -IST. In Eng., supplying a derivative adj. to sbs. in *-ist*; e.g. *altruistic*, *atheistic*, *realistic*, etc.

Words in *-istic* are essentially adjs., but like other adjs. in -IC, they are sometimes used as sbs. Sometimes also, like other adjs. in -IC, they have a secondary form in **-istical**.

Istle (i·stli, improp. i·st'l). Also **ixtle, ixtli.** 1883. [Corruption of Mexican *ixtli*.] A valuable fibre obtained from *Bromelia sylvestris* and species of *Agave*, as *A. Ixtli*, and used for cordage, nets, carpets, etc. *attrib.* **i.-grass**, a name for *Bromelia sylvestris*.

It (it), *pron.* [OE. *hit*, the neuter nom. and acc. of the stem *hi-*, the nom. masc. of which is HE, q.v. The dative and genitive were *him*, *his*, as in the masc. During the ME. period, *hit* lost its initial *h*, first when unemphatic, and at length in all positions, in standard English. In the 16th c. the tendency arose to restrict the genitive *his* to the male sex. For the neuter was substituted at first *thereof* or *of it*, etc., and finally a new factitious genitive (possessive) *it's*, ITS.]

I. As nominative. **1.** The proper neuter pronoun of the third person sing. Used orig. of any neuter sb.; now only of things without life, and of animals when sex is not particularized; hence usually of all the lower animals, and sometimes of infants. **b.** *It* may refer to a matter expressed or implied in a statement, or occupying the mind of the speaker OE. Hence *mod. colloq.* predicatively, the supremely important or conventionally proper thing. **2.** As nom. of the vb. *to be*, *it* refers to the subject of thought, attention, or inquiry, whether impersonal or personal, in a sentence asking or stating what or who this is; as *What is it? It is I.* Often with a relative clause implied, as *Who is it* (that knocks)? So Fr. *ce*, Ger. *es*. **†b.** Used where *there* is now substituted. (Cf. Ger. *es ist, es sind*.) -1617. **c.** In archaic ballad style, the introductory *it* is sometimes = *there* 1603. **†d.** Used for *he*, *she*, or *that*. Cf. F. *c'est*, Ger. *es ist*. -1684. **3.** As the subject of an impersonal verb or impersonal statement, expressing action or a condition of things simply, without reference to any agent OE. **4.** When the logical subject of a verb is an infinitive phrase, a clause, or sentence, this usually follows the verb, and its place is taken by *it* as 'provisional' or 'anticipatory subject' OE. **b.** So also sometimes when the logical subject is a sb. OE. **c.** Also in a periphrastic construction; as *it was on a Monday that I met him* ME. **5.** The pronoun is also used pleonastically after the noun subject; now esp. in ballad poetry, or, in an interrog. sentence, in rhetorical prose, for the sake of emphasis ME.

1. And he was casting out a deuil, and it was dumbe *Luke* xi. 14. It is a hearty child BAIN. **b.** Sir, you and I must part, but that's not it SHAKS. **c.** *slang.* The *ne plus ultra* 1900. **d.** Sex appeal 1927. **2. c.** It is an ancient mariner, And he stoppeth one of three COLERIDGE. **d.** 'Tis a Good Boy, said his Master BUNYAN. **3.** Phr. *It rains, it is very late, it is Christmas day.* It is a far cry to Lochow SCOTT. O heart, how fares it with thee now? TENNYSON. In a cronique it telleth thus GOWER. It tells in the Bible how David slew Goliath (*mod.*). **4.** It was necessary to make a choice MACAULAY. It appears that you were present (*mod.*). **b.** What may it be, the heavy sound? SCOTT. **c.** It was by him that money was coined MACAULAY. **5.** The deck it was their field of fame CAMPBELL.

II. As objective case (accus. and dat.). **1.** The neuter accusative or direct object after a verb; having the same range of reference as the nominative OE. **b.** Also used as an anticipatory object. Cf. I. 4. 1596. **2.** After a prep. (In OE. *hit* or *him*, according to the regimen of the prep.) ME. **3.** As simple dative = 'to it'. (In OE. *him*.) ME. **4.** Often used as an indef. object of a verb; so in imprecations. And in this way verbs are formed for the nonce upon nouns; e.g. *to king it, queen it, cab it*, etc. The use is now colloq. 1548.

1. Let it be neither mine nor thine, but diuide it 1 *Kings* iii. 26. **b.** Publish it that she is dead *Much Ado* IV. i. 206. **2.** I to my office, and there hard at it till almost noon PEPYS. **3.** It grandame will Giue yt a plum SHAKS. **4.** Ile Queene it no inch farther SHAKS.

III. As possessive; = ITS. Now *dial.* ME.

It's had it head bit off by it young SHAKS. That which with it owne glory can make them happy BP. HALL.

IV. As reflexive pron. **1.** In accus. and dative = ITSELF 1595. **2.** As possessive = ITS (L. *suus*) 1548.

1. My heart hath one poore string to stay it by SHAKS.

V. 1. As antecedent pron. followed by relative expressed or understood. (Rare; usu. *that which, the one that, what*.) **2.** When the antecedent is the subject of a clause which precedes the relative, it may be used of persons as well as things 1596.

1. An if it please me which thou speak'st SHAKS. 2. It is a good Diuine that followes his owne instructions SHAKS.

Itacism (ī·tăsiz'm). 1854. [f. Gr. ἦτα, the name of the letter η; cf. IOTACISM.] The giving to the Greek vowel η the sound-value ī, like Eng. *ee* (opp. to ETACISM, in which it has the original value ē); also, reduction in pronunciation of different Greek vowels and diphthongs to the sound ī (represented in ancient Greek by the letter ι, iota); hence the substitution in MSS. of ι for any of these vowels or diphthongs. So **I·tacist**, one who favours i. 1837.

Itacolumite (ităkǫ·liumait). 1862. [f. *Itacolumi*, a mountain in Brazil + -ITE.] *Min.* A granular, quartzose, talcomicaceous slate.

Itaconic (ităkǫ·nik), *a.* 1865. [f. ACONITIC, by transposition of letters.] *Chem.* Of, pertaining to, or derived from aconitin.

I. acid, $C_5H_6O_4$, an acid isomeric with citraconic and mesaconic acids, obtained in the dry distillation of citric acid. Its salts are **Ita·conates.**

Italian (itæ·liăn). ME. [ad. L. *Italianus*, f. *Italia*.] **A.** *adj.* **1.** Of or pertaining to Italy or its people; native to or produced in Italy 1547. **†b.** Printing = ROMAN (type). STRYPE. **†c.** = ITALIC *a.* 3. -1723. **2.** As the designation of the modern language of Italy 1530. **3.** Applied to the form of handwriting developed in Italy, and now used in Great Britain, America, etc., which approaches in form to italic printing; opp. to the Gothic hand 1571.

1. Adde thus much more, that no I. Priest Shall tythe or toll in our dominions SHAKS. Phr. **I. cloth**, a kind of linen jean with satin face, largely used for linings. **I. roof**, a hip-roof. **I. sixth** (*Mus.*), a chord consisting of a note with its major third and augmented sixth. **I. warehouse**, a shop where I. groceries, fruits, olive oil, etc. are sold.

B. *sb.* **1.** A native of Italy ME. **2.** The Italian language 1485. **†3.** An Italian scholar. FLORIO.

1. The great merchants of Europe were the Italians 1818.

Italianate (itæ·liănēt), *a.* 1572. [ad. It. *Italianato*; see -ATE [2].] **1.** Rendered Italian; see ITALIANATE *v.* **2.** Of Italian character, form, or aspect 1592.

1. An Englishman Italionat is a Devill Incarnat HOWELL.

Italianate (itæ·liăneɪt), *v.* 1567. [Found first in pa. pple. *Italianated*, f. It. *Italianato*, whence the vb.] *trans.* To render Italian; to give an Italian character to. (Usu. depreciatory.) **Ita·lianated** *ppl. a.* = ITALIANATE *a.* 1553.

Ita·lian i·ron, *sb.* 1833. A hollow cylindrical iron and heater, used for fluting and crimping lace, frills, etc. Hence as *vb.*

Italianism (itæ·liăniz'm). 1594. [f. ITALIAN + -ISM.] **1.** An Italian practice, feature, or trait; *esp.* an Italian expression or idiom. **2.** Italian quality, spirit, or taste; attachment to Italian ideas; sympathy with Italy 1824.

Italianize (itæ·liănəiz), *v.* 1611. [a. F. *italianiser*; cf. ITALIAN and -IZE.] **1.** *intr.* To practise Italian fashions or habits; to become Italian (in character, etc.). **2.** *trans.* To make Italian in character or style 1673.

2. Nol's Latin clerks were somewhat Italianiz'd 1673. Hence **Ita·lianizer.**

Italic (itæ·lik). 1563. [ad. L. *Italicus*, a. Gr. Ἰταλικός, f. Ἰταλία, L. *Italia* Italy.]

A. *adj.* **1.** Of or pertaining to ancient Italy or its tribes; *spec.* in *Rom. Hist.* and *Law*, pertaining to parts of Italy other than Rome 1685. **b.** Pertaining to the Greek colonies in southern Italy; said of the school of philosophy founded in Magna Græcia by Pythagoras. (Occas. used to include the Eleatic school.) 1662. **c.** *Arch.* A name for the fifth of the classical orders, the COMPOSITE 1563. **†2.** = ITALIAN *a.* 1. -1734. **3.** (with small *i*) Applied to the species of printing type introduced by Aldus Manutius of Venice, in which the letters slope to the right. In early use also *Italica* (sc. *littera*). 1612.

2. The I. caution of the ambassador NORTH. 3. Documents .. profusely underlined .. in which the *machinations of villains* are laid bare with i. fervour THACKERAY.

B. *sb.* **1.** A member of the Italic school (see A. 1 b) 1594. **2.** (with small *i*) *pl.* (rarely *sing.*) Italic letters: now usually employed for emphasis or distinction. See A. 3. 1676.

2. We quote the passage; the italics are ours (*mod.*). Hence **†Italic** *v.*, to italicize 1683.

Italicism (itæ·lisiz'm). *rare.* 1773. [f. ITALIC *a.* + -ISM.] An Italian expression or idiom; an Italianism.

Italicize (itæ·lisəiz), *v.* 1795. [f. ITALIC + -IZE.] *trans.* To print in italics.

The lines we have italicized are lines of very great beauty 1865.

Italiot, -ote (itæ·liǫt, -out). 1660. [ad. Gr. Ἰταλιώτης, f. Ἰταλία Italy.] **A.** *sb.* A person of Greek descent dwelling in ancient Italy; an inhabitant of Magna Græcia. **B.** *adj.* Of or pertaining to the Greek colonies in southern Italy.

Italo-, used as comb. f. *Italian*, as in **I·talo-Byza·ntine** *a.*, pertaining to Byzantine art as developed in Italy; **I·taloma·nia**, mania for things Italian.

Ita-palm (i·tă,pām). 1866. [f. *ita*, native Brazilian name + PALM [2].] A palm-tree (*Mauritia flexuosa*) of tropical S. America.

Itch (itʃ), *sb.* [OE. *ȝicce*, sb. from stem of *ȝiccan*; see ITCH *v.* [1]] **1.** An uneasy sensation of irritation in the skin; *spec.* a contagious disease, in which the skin is covered with vesicles and pustules, accompanied by extreme irritation, now known to be produced by the itch-mite; scabies. **b.** Applied, with qualification, to forms of eczema and other skin diseases, as *bakers', bricklayers', grocers' i.* **2.** *fig.* An uneasy or restless hankering after something; usu. spoken contemptuously. Const. *of, for, after* (†*at*), or *inf.* 1532.

2. The i. of originality infects his thought and style LOWELL. *Comb.*: **i.-acarus, -insect, -mite, -tick,** a small parasitic arachnid (*Sarcoptes scabiei*) of the family *Acaridæ*, which burrows in the human skin, and gives rise to the disease called i. or scabies.

Itch (itʃ), *v.*[1] [OE. *giccan* :—WGermanic **jukkjan*, from stem *juk-*. In 14th–15th c. the form *ȝicch-, ȝitch-*, lost its initial *ȝ* before *i*, as happened in *Ipswich*.] **1.** *intr.* To have or feel irritation of the skin, such as causes an inclination to scratch the part affected; said of the part; also of the person affected. **2.** *fig.* To have an irritating desire or uneasy craving provoking to action. Const. with *inf.*; also *for.* ME.

1. Socrates dilates on the pleasures of itching and scratching JOWETT. **2.** His tongue itch'd to be let loose 1622. Hence **I·tchingly** *adv.*

†Itch, *v.*[2] 1579. [app. identical with HITCH *v.* and early ME. *icche*.] = HITCH *v.* 2. –1621.

†I·tchless, *a.* 1635. [-LESS.] Free from itching or the itch; incorruptible –1648.

Itchy (i·tʃi), *a.* Now *colloq.* 1530. [-Y[1].] Affected with itching or the itch; of the nature of the itch. Hence **I·tchiness** 1822.

-ite, *suffix*[1], corresp. to F. *-ite*, L. *-ita* (*-ites*), ad. Gr. *-ίτης*, forming adjs. and sbs. (of adj. origin) with the sense '(one) connected with or belonging to', 'a member of', as in *ὁπλίτης adj.* heavy-armed, *sb.* a heavy-armed soldier. In English:

1. Used to form names of persons (also adjectively), as in *Sybarite*; *Israelite, Sodomite*, etc.; *eremite, Monophysite*, etc.; also *Claphamite*, etc.; *Wycliffite, Puseyite*; *Shelleyite*; *Jacobite, Luddite, Peelite*, etc. **2. a.** *Palæont.* Used to form the names of fossil organisms; as *ammonite, dendrite, lignite*, etc. **b.** *Min.* The systematic ending of the names of mineral species, as *anthracite*, etc.; *chlorite, hepatite*, etc.; *azurite, graphite, syenite, wernerite*, etc. **3.** *Anat.* and *Zool.* Used to form terms denoting one of the constituent parts, segments, or joints of a body or organ; as in *somite* a segment of the body; so *pleurite, podite*, etc. **4.** *Chem.* Used to form the names of some saccharine substances, glucoses, and other organic compounds, as *dulcite*, etc.; also of explosives, as *cordite, dynamite*, etc.; and of commercial products, as *vulcanite*, etc. **b.** In Inorganic Chemistry, *-ite* is the systematic termination of the salts of acids denominated by adjs. in *-ous*; e.g. *nitrite* a salt of *nitrous acid.*

A few of the words in *-ite* have derivative adjs. in **-itic**, as *Semitic*, etc.; many of those in group 1 have adjs. in **-itish**, as *Israelitish*, etc.

-ite, *suffix*[2], an ending of adjs. adapted from L. pa. pples. in *-itus*, of vbs. in *-īre, -ĕre, -ēre*, as in *eruditus* erudite, *compositus* composite, etc.; of sbs. derived from the same or from the cognate L. sbs. in *-us*, as *appetitus* appetite; of verbs formed from the same ppl. stems, as *expedite, unite.*

Item (əi·tĕm), *adv.* and *sb.* ME. [a. L. *item* adv., just so, in like manner, moreover, f. *i-s, i-d* he, it + advb. ending *-tem*.]

‖**A.** *adv.* Likewise, also.

It shalbe Inuentoried..As, I. two lippes indifferent redde, I. two grey eyes, with lids to them SHAKS.

B. *sb.* **1.** A statement, maxim, or admonition such as was commonly introduced by the word *item.* Hence, generally, an intimation, a hint. Now *U.S. local.* 1561. **2.** An article or unit of any kind; an entry in an account, a clause of a document, etc. 1578. **b.** A detail of information or news 1819.

1. Getting i. thereof, he departed to the sea HEARNE. **2.** Tauern items DEKKER. **b.** The items in a newspaper 1865.

Item (əi·tĕm), *v.* 1601. [f. prec.] *trans.* To set down by items; to enter as an item.

I have Item'd it in my memory ADDISON.

Itemize (əi·tĕməiz), *v.* Chiefly *U.S.* 1860. [f. ITEM *sb.* + -IZE.] *trans.* To set down by items or enter as an item; to specify the items of (an account, etc.).

Iter (i·təɪ, əi·təɪ). Pl. **iters,** ‖**iti·nera.** 1598. [a. L.; in sense 1, med.L.] **1.** *Hist.* = EYRE 1. Also *transf.* 1647. **b.** The record of proceedings during a circuit 1598. **2.** A Roman road or line of travel 1751. **3.** *Anat.* A way or passage; *spec.* the tubular cavity leading from the third to the fourth ventricle of the brain 1897.

†Iterable (i·tĕrăb'l), *a. rare.* [ad. late L. *iterabilis* (Tert.), f. *iterare*; see -ABLE.] Capable of being iterated or repeated –1682.

Iterance (i·tĕrăns). 1604. [f. ITERANT; see -ANCE.] Iteration. So **I·terancy** 1889.

Iterant (i·tĕrănt), *a.* 1626. [ad. L. *iterantem*, *iterare*.] That iterates; repeating, echoing.

A Reflexion I., which we call Eccho BACON.

†I·terate, *ppl. a.* 1471. [ad. L. *iteratus*.] Iterated –1657. **†I·terately** *adv.* repeatedly.

Iterate (i·tĕreᵗt), *v.* 1533. [f. L. *iterat-*, *iterare* to do again, f. *iterum* again.] **1.** *trans.* To do over again; to perform a second time; to repeat; to renew. Now *rare.* **2.** To say or assert again or repeatedly; to repeat 1533.

1. To i. an experiment 1682. **2.** We i. the Psalms oftener then any other part of Scripture HOOKER.

Iteration (itĕrēⁱ·ʃən). 1450. [ad. L. *iterationem.* Cf. F. *itération.*] **1.** Repetition of an action or process (now usu. implying frequency or long continuance); an instance of this. **2.** The repetition of something said 1530.

2. Tedius I. therof I let passe 1556.

Iterative (i·tĕrĕⁱtiv), *a.* 1490. [a. F. *itératif, -ive*, ad. late L. *iterativus*, f. ppl. stem of *iterare*; see -IVE.] **1.** Characterized by repeating or being repeated. **2.** *Gram.* Frequentative 1827. Hence **I·terative·ly** *adv.*, **-ness.**

†Ithand, *a. Sc.* and *north. dial.* ME. [ad. ON. *iðinn* assiduous, diligent. Cf. EIDENT and IDENT.] **1.** Assiduous, diligent –1570. **2.** Constant, continual –1536. Hence **†Ithandly** *adv.*

Ithyphallic (iþifæ·lik). 1614. [ad. L. *ithyphallicus*, ad. Gr. *ἰθυφαλλικός*, f. *ἰθύς* erect + *φαλλός* PHALLUS; in neut. as sb., *ithyphallicum* sc. *carmen.*]

A. *adj.* Pertaining to the phallus carried in procession at the Bacchic festivals; *spec.* composed in the metre of the Bacchic hymns (the trochaic dimeter brachycatalectic) 1795. **b.** Grossly indecent 1864. **B.** *sb.* A poem in ithyphallic metre; also, an indecent poem.

Itineracy (əiti·nĕrăsi, it-). 1827. [f. late L. *itinerat-*; see -ACY 3.] = ITINERANCY.]

Itinerancy (əiti·nĕrănsi, it-). 1789. [f. next; see -ANCY.] **1.** The state or condition of being itinerant; the action of itinerating, esp. for a specific purpose, as preaching or public speaking; a journey from place to place 1802. **b.** A body of itinerants 1836. **2.** Itinerant preaching; *spec.* the system in practice in various Methodist churches, according to which the regular ministers are appointed not to a congregation, but to a circuit, which is changed triennially 1789. **b.** Itinerant ministry 1809.

Itinerant (əiti·nĕrănt, it-). 1570. [ad. late and med.L. *itinerantem*, pr. pple. of late L. *itinerari*, med.L. *itinerare* to travel.]

A. *adj.* Journeying; travelling from place to place; not fixed or stationary; travelling on circuit. **b.** Journeying or travelling in connexion with some employment or vocation; preaching in a circuit; of or pertaining to the regular Wesleyan ministry 1661. **c.** *fig.* and *transf.* 1634.

1. Such i. judges as go Oxford Circuit FULLER. **b.** To appoint to a Circuit as an I. Preacher 1829.

B. *sb.* One who travels from place to place, esp. in the pursuit of a trade or calling; a travelling preacher, etc. 1641.

Glad to turn i., To stroll and teach from town to town BUTLER. Hence **Iti·nerantly** *adv.*

‖**Itinerarium** (itinĕrēᵊ·riŏm). 1747. [late L., sb. use of neut. of *itinerarius* adj.; see ITINERARY *a.*] = ITINERARY *sb.* 2, 3.

Itinerary (əiti·nĕrări, it-), *sb.* 1450. [ad. L. *itinerarium*, sb. use of neuter of *itinerarius*; see next.] **1.** A line or course of travel; a route. **2.** A journal of travel; an account of a journey 1483. **3.** A road-book, a guide-book 1538. **b.** *transf.* A sketch of a proposed route 1856. **4.** An itinerant (*rare*) 1709.

2. Many may rede the itineraryes of them that hath ben at Ierusalem 1526.

Itinerary (əiti·nĕrări, it-), *a.* 1552. [ad. late L. *itinerarius*, f. *iter, itiner-*; cf. F. *itinéraire* adj.] **1.** Of or pertaining to a journey, travelling, or a route. **b.** Pertaining to roads (esp. Roman roads) or the description of roads 1552. **2.** = ITINERANT *a.* 1617.

1. b. The i. system of the Romans was..an effective instrument of centralization MERIVALE.

Itinerate (əiti·nĕreᵗt, it-), *v.* 1600. [f. late L. *itinerat-*, *itinerari* to travel.] **1.** *intr.* To travel or journey from place to place. **b.** To travel from place to place preaching; *spec.* of a Methodist minister (cf. ITINERANCY 2) 1775. **2.** *trans.* To journey through, traverse 1830. Hence **Itinera·tion,** the action of itinerating; a preaching or lecturing tour 1623.

-ition, *suffix*, repr. F. *-ition*, L. *-itionem*, forming nouns of action from vbs. with ppl. stem in *-it-*, as in *position* from *positus*, *audition* from *auditus.* It is really a case of the suffix -ION, q.v.

-itious[1], compound suffix of adjs., f. L. *-ici-us* + -OUS. These L. endings, from the confusion of *c* and *t* in late and med.L. MSS., were formerly written *-itius*, whence the current Eng. spelling. Examples are *ascriptitious, factitious*, etc.

-itious[2], a combination of the suffix -OUS, repr. L. *-osus*, with derivs. containing *iti-*, chiefly sbs. in *-itionem*; e.g. *ambition, ambitious*, L. *ambitiosus*, etc.; see -IOUS, -OUS.

-itis, *suffix*, a. Gr. *-ῖτις*, properly forming the fem. of adjs. in *-ίτης*; already in Gr. used to qualify *νόσος* disease, expressed or understood, e.g. *ἀρθρῖτις* (disease) of the joints, gout, *arthritis.* On the analogy of these, *-itis* has become in mod. medical L., and in Eng., the regular name for affections of particular parts, and *spec.* (though not etymologically) for inflammatory disease or inflammation of a part. Examples are *appendicitis, bronchitis, tonsilitis.*

Often jocularly used to denote something that is conceived as a disease; e.g. *suffragitis* = exaggerated advocacy of (woman's) suffrage.

-itous, compound suffix, containing the *-it-* of sbs. in -ITY, and the adj. ending -OUS; corresp. to Fr. *-iteux*, L. *-itosus*, contr. for *-itatosus*, as in *calamitosus* for *calamitatosus*; so *felicitous*, etc.

Its (its) *poss. pron.* [Formed *c* 1600 from IT + *-s* of the possessive or genitive case, and at first commonly written *it's*. See IT III.]

A. As *adj. poss. pron.* Of or belonging to it, or that thing (L. *ejus*); also *refl.*, Of or belonging to itself, its own (L. *suus*) 1598.

From translation all Science had it's of-spring FLORIO. The Gospel has its mysteries J. H. NEWMAN.

B. As *absolute possessive.* Its own. *rare.*

It's, its, contraction of *it is.*

Itself (itse·lf), *pron.* OE. [orig. two words, IT *pron.* and SELF. In 17–18th c. often treated as ITS + SELF; as still in *its own self*, and the like.]

I. Emphatic or limiting use. Usu. in apposition with a sb. in nom. or obj.: Very, the very, that very; alone (L. *ipsum*). Rarely alone as subject. **b.** Used alone in predicate, emphatically 1600.

The earth and tyme it selfe 1560. Or joy itself Without the touch of sorrow SHELLEY. **b.** An eye all pale Striving to be itself KEATS.

II. Reflexive use. = L. *sibi, se*; Ger. *sich* OE.

Th' offence pardons it selfe SHAKS. His heart gathereth iniquitie to it selfe *Ps.* xli. 6. The child will do itself a mischief (*mod.*).

Ittria, Ittrium, *Chem.*: See YTTRIA, etc.

-ity [ME. *-ite*, a. F. *-ité*, L. *-itatem*], the usual form in which the suffix (L. *-tas, -tatem*, expressing state or condition) appears, the *-i-* being orig. either the stem vowel of the radical (e.g. L. *suavi-tas* suavity), or its weakened repr. (e.g. L. *puro-, puri-tas* purity), rarely a mere connective (e.g. L. *auctor-i-tas* authority). Hence many playful or pedantic nonce-wds., as *between-ity, woman-ity.*

‖**Itzebu, -boo** (itsibū·). 1616. [Japanese: two words, *itse, itche* one, *bū* division, quarter.] A Japanese phrase meaning 'one quarter', commonly applied to a silver coin in use before 1871; it was worth about 1*s.* 4*d.* sterling.

Iu-, earlier spelling of IV-, and of JU-.

Iulidan (əiyū·lidăn). 1885. [f. mod.L. *Iulida*, *-idæ*, f. *Iulus* (see next).] *Zool.* A myriapod of the family *Iulidæ* (see next 2).

‖**Iulus** (əiyū·lɒs). 1658. [f. *iulus*, a. Gr. ἴουλος down, a catkin, etc.] †1. A catkin –1757. 2. A genus of animals of the class Myriapoda, order *Chilognatha* (*Diplopoda*); a millepede.

-ium, *suffix. Chem.*, used to form the names of metallic elements, as *cadmium*, *iridium*.

I've, colloq. contr. of *I have*.

-ive, *suffix*, forming adjs. (and sbs.) Formerly also *-if*, *-ife*; a. Fr. *-if*, fem. *-ive* :—L. *-ivus*. Largely used in Eng. to adapt L. words in *-ivus*, or form words on L. analogies, with the sense 'having a tendency to, having the nature, character, or quality of, given to (some action)'. Already in L. many of these adjs. were used subst.; hence in Eng.; e.g. *adjective*, *captive*, *derivative*, etc. Hence advs. in **-ively**, and abst. sbs. in **-iveness**, **-ivity**.

In the 17th cent. *-ive* is sometimes synonymous with *-ible*, as *extensive* = extensible, *inexpressive* = inexpressible.

Ivied, ivyed (əi·vid), *a.* 1771. [f. Ivy + -ED [2].] Overgrown or clothed with ivy.

Ivorine (əi·vŏrīn). 1897. [f. Ivory + -INE [4].] Trade-name for a substance imitating ivory.

Ivory (əi·vŏri). ME. [a. OF. *yvoire* (mod. *ivoire*) :—L. *eboreus* adj., from *ebur*, *ebor-* ivory; cf. Skr. *ibhas* elephant.] 1. The hard, white, elastic, and fine-grained substance (being dentine of exceptional hardness) composing the main part of the tusks of the elephant, mammoth (*fossil i.*), hippopotamus, walrus, and narwhal; it is employed as a material for many articles of use or ornament. 2. A substance resembling ivory, or made in imitation of it 1842. 3. *Black i.*: African negro slaves as an object of commerce. *slang.* 1873. 4. The colour of ivory; ivory-white; *esp.* whiteness of the human skin 1590. 5. An article made of ivory, esp. a carving in that material. b. *slang* (usu. *pl.*) Dice; also billiard balls 1830; piano keys 1855. 6. A tusk of an elephant, etc. 1894. 7. *slang.* (*sing.* and *pl.*) The teeth 1782. 8. *attrib.* a. Made or consisting of ivory ME. b. White or smooth as ivory 1586.

2. The tooth of an olyfaunt is yuorye CAXTON. 2. *Vegetable i.*, the i.-like albumen of the seed of the S. Amer. palm *Phytelephas macrocarpa*. 5. b. Suppose we adiourn to Fish Lane, and rattle the ivories LYTTON. 8. a. *I. gate*; see GATE *sb.*[1] 4. *I. tower*, (fig.) a position of lofty seclusion (after F. *tour d'ivoire*, used by Sainte-Beuve of Vigny's seclusion in a turret room).

Comb.: **i.-bill**, a species of woodpecker, *Picus* or *Campephilus principalis*; **-gull**, a small white Arctic gull, *Pagophila eburnea*; **-nut**, the corozo-nut; hence **-(nut-)palm**, **-plant**; **-paper**, a thick paper or thin cardboard with a finely prepared polished surface, used by artists; **-shell**, a univalve of the genus *Eburna*, of an i. colour.

Ivory-black. 1634. A fine soft black pigment, obtained by calcining ivory in a closed vessel.

Ivory-type. 1875. *Photogr.* A picture produced by placing a photograph, light in colour, made translucent by varnish, tinted on the back, over a stronger picture, so as to give the effect of a photograph in natural colours.

Ivy (əi·vi). *Pl.* **ivies** (əi·viz). [OE. *ifig*, obscurely related to OHG. *ebahewi*, *ebawi*, *ebah*.] 1. A climbing evergreen shrub (*Hedera Helix*), indigenous to Europe and Asia, having dark-green shining leaves, usu. five-angled, and bearing umbels of greenish-yellow flowers, succeeded by dark berries; it is an ornamental covering of walls, ruins, etc. The plant was anciently sacred to Bacchus. 2. Applied, with distinctive addition, to plants of other genera 1588. 3. *attrib.* OE.

1. *Black*, *English i.*, the common i., also termed *H. nigra*, from its black berries. Here are cool mosses deep, And thro' the moss the ivies creep TENNYSON. 2. **American** or **Five-leaved i.**, Virginia creeper, *Ampelopsis hederacea* or *quinquefolia*. **German i.**, *Senecio mikanoides*, a variety of Groundsel. **Japanese i.**, *Ampelopsis tricuspidata*. **West Indian i.**, *Marcgravia umbellata*. 3. I.-crowned Bacchus MILT.

Comb.: **i.-garland**, a garland of i., formerly the sign of a house where wine was sold; **-leaf**, a leaf of i., †a thing of little value; †*To pipe in* (*with*) *an ivy-leaf* (fig.), to console oneself with some frivolous employment; **-tod** (*arch.*) = IVY-BUSH.

Ivy-bush. 1576. A bushy branch of ivy; *fig.* a place of concealment or retirement. †b. *spec.* A bush of ivy, or a picture of it, placed outside a tavern as a sign that wine was sold there; hence, the tavern itself. †Hence *fig.* A sign or display (of anything).

Iwis, ywis (iwi·s), *adj.*, *adv.*, and *sb. arch.* [OE. *gewis* adj. (= MHG. *gewis*, Ger. *gewiss* certain), of which the neut. was used adverbially in ME.] A. *adj.* (*gewis*) Certain (subjectively and objectively). Only in OE. B. *adv.* (*gewis*, *iwis*, and *iwisse*) Certainly, assuredly, indeed. (The writing with capital I, and separation of the two elements, have led later authors to use it erron. as = *I wot*, *I know*, as if a present of *I wist*.) ME. †C. *sb.* [the adj. used absol.] Certainty –ME.

Ixia (i·ksiă). 1794. [L., a. Gr. ἰξία.] *Bot.* A genus of S. African iridaceous plants, with large showy flowers.

Ixtle, ixtli: see ISTLE.

‖**Izar** (i·zăr). 1836. [Arab. *izar*.] The outer garment of Moslem women, a long cotton mantle covering the whole figure.

Izard (i·zărd, ‖*izār*). Also **isard, izzard.** 1791. [ad. F. *isard*, Gascon *isart*.] A capriform antelope allied to the chamois, found in the Pyrenees.

-ization (also **-isation**), suffix forming nouns of action from vbs. in -IZE: see next.

-ize (also written **-ise**), suffix forming vbs. = F. *-iser*, It. *-izzare*, Sp. *-izar*, ad. late L. *-izare*, f. Gr. -ίζειν, extensive formative of verbs. The suffix, whatever the element to which it is added, is in its origin the Gr. -ίζειν, L. *-izare*; and, as the pronunciation is also with *z*, there is no reason why in English the special French spelling in *-iser* should ever be followed. Hence here the termination is uniformly written *-ize*. In current English the following are the chief groups:

1. Words from Greek, or formed on Greek elements; a. with the trans. sense of 'make or conform to, or treat in the way of, the thing expressed by the basic word', as *baptize*, *anathematize*, *monopolize*, etc.; b. with the intrans. sense 'to act some person or character, do or follow some practice', as *apologize*, *philosophize*, etc.

2. Words formed on Latin adjs. or sbs., mostly with the trans. sense 'to make (that which is expressed by the derivation)', as *actualize*, *colonize*, *satirize*, etc.; trans. or intrans., as *cicatrize*, *moralize*, etc.; occas. only intrans., as *temporize*.

3. Words from later sources, as *bastardize*, *jeopardize* trans., *gormandize* intr.

4. Words formed on ethnic adjs., and the like, chiefly trans., as *Americanize*, *Anglicize*, etc.

5. Words formed on names of persons, sometimes with the intrans. Gr. sense of 'to act like, or in accordance with', as in *Calvinize*, but usu. in the trans. sense of 'to treat like, or after the method of, or according to the (chemical or other) process of'; as in *Boucherize*, *Bowdlerize*, *galvanize*, etc.; with other terms, and nonce-words such as *Gladstonize*, etc., without limit.

6. From names of substances, chemical and other; in the trans. sense of 'to charge, impregnate, treat, or affect with'; as *alcoholize*, *oxidize*, etc.; so in nonce-words, as *Londonize* to make like London, etc.

-izer, suffix of agent-n. from vbs. in -IZE.

Izzard (i·zăɹd). *arch.* or *dial.* Also **izzet, izzart, uzzard.** 1738. [app. in origin the same wd. as *zed*.] The letter Z. Cf. EZOD.

Izzard, var. of IZARD.

J

J (dʒē̆), the tenth letter of the English alphabet, is, in its origin, a comparatively late modification of the letter I. From the 11th to the 17th c., the letter I i represented both the vowel sound of *i*, and a consonant sound (dʒ). To keep the inconspicuous small ı distinct, esp. in cursive writing, various scribal expedients were employed (see I). Among these, an initial ı was often prolonged above or below the line, or both; a final ı was generally prolonged below the line, and in both cases the 'tail' in cursive writing at length became a curve. The 'dot' was also used with the tailed form, and thus arose the modern j, *j*. But this was at first merely a final form of i, used in Latin in such forms as 'filij', and in numerals, as j, ij, xij. It was in the 17th c. that the differentiation of the two forms of the letter took place, i, *i* remaining for the vowel, and j, *j* being used for the consonant, and the capital forms of the latter, J, *J*, being introduced.

The sound regularly denoted by the letter J in English is the consonant (dʒ). In *hallelujah* it has the sound of the Roman i-consonant (y). So in proper names or alien terms from German and other languages in which the Roman value of *j* is retained, as *Jena* (yē·nă), *Jaeger*, etc. In a few French words, distinctly recognized as alien, *j* has the French sound (ʒ), as *déjeuner*, etc. In the transliteration of Oriental names, as *Jāt*, *Jenghiz*, etc., *j* is used with its English value.

I. 1. The letter. (pl. *J's*, J's, *js*, j's.) 2. Short for **J-pen**, a broad-pointed pen, stamped with the letter J.
II. 1. Rarely used to express serial order. In the alphabetical designations of the batteries of the Royal Artillery, A, B, C, etc., J is used for the tenth. 2. As a Roman numeral j was formerly used as a final form of i in j, ij, vj, etc.; this is retained in medical prescriptions. 3. In *Math.* and *Physics*, *J* is used to denote the Jacobian; also Joule's mechanical equivalent of heat.
III. Abbrevs. J. stands for various proper names, as *John*, *Jane*, etc. J., Judge. J.P., Justice of Peace. Jr., jr., Junior. J.C.R., junior COMMON-ROOM.

‖**Jaal-goat** (dʒē̆·ăl-, yā·ălˌgōᵘt). 1838. [ad. Heb.] The wild goat of Mount Sinai, Upper Egypt, Abyssinia, etc. (*Capra jaala*).

Jab (dʒæb), *v. colloq.* and *dial.* 1825. [var., orig. Sc., of JOB *v.*[1]] *trans.* To thrust; to poke roughly; to stab. Also *absol.* or *intr.* Hence **Jab** *sb.* (*colloq.* or *dial.*), an act of jabbing with something pointed, or with the fist.

Jabber (dʒæ·bəɹ), *sb.* 1727. [f. next.] The act of jabbering; gabble, chatter; gibberish.

Jabber (dʒæ·bəɹ), *v.* 1499. [app. onomatopœic, with frequentative form; cf. *gab*, *gabber*, *gabble*.] 1. *intr.* To talk rapidly and indistinctly or unintelligibly; to speak volubly and with little sense. 2. *trans.* To speak or utter rapidly and indistinctly; to express by jabbering. Often *contemptuously*. 1532.

2. To j. French ADDISON. Hence **Ja·bberer**, one who jabbers 1678. **Ja·bberingly** *adv.* in a jabbering manner. **Ja·bberment**, jabbering MILTON.

Jabbernowl, var. of JOBBERNOWL.

‖**Jabiru** (dʒæ·birū). Also **jaburu.** 1774. [Tupi-Guarani *jabirú*.] A large wading bird of tropical and subtropical America (*Mycteria americana*), of the stork family. Also applied to the allied *Xenorhynchus australis* and *indicus*, and *Ephippiorhynchus senegalensis*, of the Old World.

‖**Jaborandi** (dʒæbŏræ·ndi, *prop.* dʒabŏrandī·). 1875. [Tupi-Guarani *jaburandi*, also *jaburandiba* (*iba* plant, tree).] The dried leaflets of a Brazilian plant *Pilocarpus pinnatifolius*, N.O. *Rutaceæ*, having diuretic and sudorific properties.

Jaborine (dʒæ·bŏrəin). 1887. [f. prec. + -INE [5].] *Chem.* An alkaloid contained, together with pilocarpine, in the leaves of jaborandi.

‖**Jabot** (ʒabo). 1823. [F.; origin unkn.] 1. A frill formerly worn by men on the front of a shirt, edging the opening. 2. An ornamental frill on a woman's bodice 1881.

‖**Jacamar** (dʒæ·kămaɹ). 1825. [a. F., ad. Tupi-Guarani *Jacama-ciri*.] Any bird of the family *Galbulidæ*, natives of South America, somewhat resembling the bee-eaters in appearance, and the kingfishers in habits.

‖**Jacana** (dʒæ·kănă). 1753. [ad. Pg. *jacana*, ad. Tupi-Guarani *jasanā*.] Any bird of the genus *Parra* (*Jacana*) or family *Parridæ* (*Jacanidæ*), consisting of grallatorial aquatic birds inhabiting the warmer regions of the world, having enormous straight claws, which enable them to walk on the floating leaves of aquatic plants.

‖**Jacaranda** (dʒækăræ·ndă, *prop.* dʒakărandā·). 1753. [Tupi-Guarani.] Name given to various trees of tropical America yielding fragrant and ornamental wood; esp. to those of the genus *Jacaranda* (N.O. *Bignoniaceæ*). b. The wood of any of these. c. A drug obtained from a tree of this genus.

‖**Jacare** (dʒæ·kăre). 1753. [Tupi-Guarani.] A South American alligator.

Jacent (dʒē·sĕnt), *a.* ? *Obs.* 1602. [ad. L. *jacentem*, *jacēre* to lie.] Lying; recumbent; *fig.* sluggish.

Jacinth (dʒæ·sinþ, dʒē·sinþ). [ME. *iacynt*, *iacinct*, a. OF. *iacinte* or late L. *iacint(h)us*, *-inctus*, an alteration of *hiacint(h)us*, L. *hyacinthus*, a. Gr. ὑάκινθος HYACINTH; the *h* being lost and the initial *i* made consonantal.] **1. a.** Among the ancients, a gem of a blue colour, prob. sapphire. **b.** In mod. use, a reddish-orange gem, a variety of zircon. = HYACINTH 1. **c.** The colour of the gem (see b) 1572. †**2.** = HYACINTH 2. –1760. **3.** *attrib.* 1526.

Jack (dʒæk), *sb.*[1] [A pet-name or by-name, familiar for *John*; in ME. *Jakke*, *Jacce*, *Jacke*, a disyllable.]

I. Applied to a man, or the figure of one. **1.** (As proper noun.) A familiar by-form of *John*; hence, a generic proper name for a man of the common people. **b.** *Cousin Jack*: a familiar name for a Cornishman. †**2.** (As a common noun.) A man of the common people; a lad, fellow, chap; *esp.* an ill-mannered fellow, a 'knave' –1746. **3.** (As proper or common noun.) A familiar appellation for a sailor. Also JACK-TAR, q. v. 1659. **4.** Variously applied to a serving-man, a labourer, one who does odd jobs, etc. See also CHEAP *Jack*, STEEPLE *Jack*, etc. 1836. **5.** *Cards.* The knave of trumps in all-fours; hence *gen.* any one of the knaves 1674. **6.** A figure of a man which strikes the bell on the outside of a clock 1498.

1. And hee's now but Iacke Foord, that once were John HEYWOOD. A good J. makes a good Gill RAY. 2. A mad-cap ruffian and a swearing Iacke SHAKS. Phr. †*To play the j.*: to play the knave. *Every man j.*: every individual man (*colloq.*). 6. *Rich. III*, IV. ii. 117.

II. Applied to things which take the place of a lad or man, or save human labour; also more vaguely. **To separate contrivances, machines, utensils*, etc. **1.** A machine for turning the spit in roasting meat; a *bottle-jack* or a *smoke-jack* 1587. **2.** A name for various contrivances consisting (solely or mainly) of a roller or winch 1572. **3.** A wooden frame for sawing wood upon 1573. **4.** A machine, usually portable, for lifting heavy weights by force acting from below; in the commonest form, having a rack and a pinion wheel or screw and a handle turned by hand 1703. **5.** A contrivance for pulling off boots; a boot-jack. *rare* or *Obs.* (exc. in the compound). 1679. **6.** *Mining.* **a.** 'A kind of water-engine, turned by hand. *Staff.*' (Halliwell.) **b.** 'A wooden wedge or gad used in mining to assist in cleaving strata. 1858. ***To parts of instruments or machines.* **7.** In the virginal, spinet, and harpsichord: An upright piece of wood fixed to the back of the key-lever, and fitted with a quill which plucked the string as the jack rose on the key being pressed down. (By Shaks. and others erron. applied to the key.) 1598. **8.** In various machines.

a. An oscillating lever, e.g. in a stocking-frame or knitting-machine 1764. **b.** *Weaving* = Heck-box (see HECK) 1844. **c.** *Spinning.* A coarse bobbin and fly-frame operating on the sliver from the carding-machine 1875. **d.** *Telegr.*, etc. A terminal in a telegraph or telephone, consisting of a spring-clip by means of which instruments can be expeditiously introduced into the circuit.

9. In carriages: A small engine fixed to the bottom of the spring, and used to heighten or lower the body 1794. ****To things of smaller than the normal size.* **10.** The least bit; a whit. *Obs. colloq.* 1530. **11.** *Bowls.* A smaller bowl placed as a mark for the players to aim at 1611. **12.** *slang.* **a.** A farthing. **b.** A counter made to resemble a sovereign; so *half-j.* 1700. **13.** A quarter of a pint (*local*) 1736. **14.** *Naut.* Short for *jack cross-tree* (see IV. 1 b) 1840. *****To other things.* **15.** A post-chaise (*slang* or *colloq.*) 1812. **16.** A portable cresset or fire-basket used in hunting or fishing at night. *U.S.* 1895.

III. In names of animals. **1.** Applied to the male of various animals, chiefly in comb.; also simply: **a.** A male hawk, *esp.* merlin (= *jack-merlin*) 1623. **b.** (Short for JACKASS 1.) A male ass, *esp.* one kept for breeding mules. *U.S.* 1799. **2.** Name for various birds. **a.** Short for JACKDAW, *Jack-curlew*, *Cornish jack*, the Cornish chough, JACK SNIPE. **b.** In CURLEW-*jack*, JUMPING-*jack*, WHISKY JACK: see these wds. **3.** Name of various fishes, etc. **a.** A young or small pike 1587. **b.** Also applied to several American fishes; as the pike-perch, *Stizostedium vitreum*; a scorpænoid fish, *Sebastodes paucispinis*; several carangoid fishes, esp. *Caranx pisquetos* and *Seriola carolinensis*; and the pampano, *Trachynotus carolinus*. **c.** *Poor Jack* (also *dry* or *dried Jack*), dried hake; also called *Poor John* 1667.

IV. *Combs.*, etc. **1.** Combs. denoting things, etc.: **j.-back** [BACK *sb.*[2]], (*a*) in *Brewing*, a vessel with a perforated bottom for straining the wort from the hops (also called *hop-back*): (*b*) 'a tank which receives the cooled wort in a vinegar-factory' (Knight); **-engine** (*Coal-mining*), a donkey-engine; **-fishing**, (*a*) fishing for jack; (*b*) *U.S.*, fishing at night by means of a j. or cresset; **-hunting** *U.S.*, hunting by means of a jack-light (see II. 16); **-ladder** *Naut.*, 'one with wooden steps and side ropes' (Knight), = JACOB'S LADDER 2; **-lamp**, (*a*) a Davy-lamp with a glass cylinder outside the gauze; (*b*) *U.S.* = sense II. 16; **-pin** *Naut.*, a belaying-pin; **-pot**, in draw-poker, a pot or pool that has to accumulate until one of the players can open the betting with a pair of jacks or better; hence *fig.*; **-roll**, a winch or windlass turned directly by handles; **-sinker**, each of a series of thin metal plates suspended from the front end of the jacks in a stocking frame or knitting-machine, and serving, in conjunction with the *lead-sinkers*, to form loops upon the thread; **-towel**, a long towel with the ends sewed together, suspended from a roller.

b. In some uses *jack* has a diminutive force or meaning; as **j.-arch**, an arch whose thickness is only of one brick; **-block** *Naut.*, a small block seized to the topgallant-mast-head, for sending the topgallant-yards up and down; **-cross-tree** *Naut.*, an iron cross-tree at the head of a long topgallant mast, to support a royal or skysail mast; **-rafter**, **-rib**, **-timber**, one shorter than the full length.

2. Prefixed to another noun denoting a person, a thing personified, a trade, or a quality, so as to form a *quasi*-proper name or nickname; as *Jack Blunt* (a blunt fellow); *Jack boot(s* (the 'Boots' at an inn), *Jack Presbyter*, *Jack Priest*; **Jack Frost**, frost or frosty weather personified; †**Jack-sauce**, a saucy or impudent fellow; **Jack sprat**, a little fellow, a dwarf.

3. Substantive phrases with specific senses. *Jack at a pinch*, one who is ready for any emergency; 'a poor Hackney Parson'; *Jack in office*, a pretentious petty official; also *attrib.*; *Jack of (at) all trades*, a man who can turn his hand to any kind of business; *Jack of (on, o') both sides*, a person who sides first with one party and then with the other, a trimmer; †*Jack of the clock*, or *clock-house* = sense I. 6; also *transf.* of a person (*Rich. II*, v. v. 60); †*Jack out of office*, a person who has been dismissed from office; one whose 'occupation is gone'.

4. In names of animals (sometimes signifying *male*, sometimes *small*, *half-sized*). **a.** Denoting *male*, as *jack-hare*; esp. of falcons, as *jack-hobby*, *-kestrel*, *-merlin*. **b. Jack crow**, *Picathartes gymnocephalus*, a W. African corvine bird; **Jack curlew**, name for two small species of curlew: (*a*) the whimbrel, *Numenius phæopus*; (*b*) the *N. hudsonicus* of N. America; **Jack-fish**, the pike; also a name for other carangoid fishes; **Jack-salmon**, a pike-perch; **Jack-spaniard**, a large W. Indian species of wasp.

5. In popular names of plants. Sometimes denoting 'dwarf, undersized', as **Jack-by-the-hedge**, the hedge-garlic, *Sisymbrium Alliaria*; **Jack-in-the-bush**, local name for hedge-garlic; **Jack-in-the-pulpit** (*U.S.*), a N. American araceous plant, *Arisæma triphyllum*, so called from the appearance of the upright spadix partly surmounted by the enclosing spathe; **Jack oak**, a N. Amer. species of oak (*Quercus nigra*); also called *black jack*.

Jack, *sb.*[2] Now *arch.* ME. [a. F. *jaque*, in OF. also *jaques*. Ult. origin uncertain.] †**1. a.** A short and close-fitting jacket. ME. only. **b.** A coat of fence, usually of leather quilted, and in later times often plated with iron; *occas.*, a coat of mail (*arch.*) ME. **2.** A vessel for liquor; orig. of waxed leather coated outside with tar or pitch (= BLACK JACK 1); a (leathern) jug or tankard (*arch.*) 1573.

1. b. Like..the yron plates of a iacke, one lying on an other 1578. Phr. †*To be on* (a person's) *j.*: to lay blows on him; to be down upon him.

Jack (dʒæk), *sb.*[3] 1633. [Prob. a use of JACK *sb.*[1], as if short for 'jack-flag', i.e. small flag (as dist. from the ensign).] A ship's flag of smaller size than the ensign, used at sea as a signal, or as a mark of distinction; *spec.* the small flag, indicating nationality, which is flown from the jack-staff at the bow of a vessel, as in *British jack*, *Dutch jack*, etc.

In British use the jack has been since the 17th c. (except under the Commonwealth) a small-sized 'Union Flag' of the period (UNION JACK), which has also been, since 1707, inserted in the upper canton of the ensign; hence, the name 'union jack' is often improperly applied to the union flag itself, when this is not carried or used as a jack.

In the United States naval service the j. is a blue flag with a white five-pointed star for each State in the Union.

Jack, *sb.*[4] 1613. [ad. Pg. *jaca*, ad. Malayālam *chakka*.] The fruit of an East Indian tree (*Artocarpus integrifolia*), a large and coarse kind of bread-fruit. Also the tree itself.

†**Jack**, *sb.*[5] 1695. Colloq. abbrev. of JACOBITE –1732.

Jack (dʒæk), *v.* 1873. [f. senses of JACK *sb.*[1]; in sense 3 of obscure origin.] **1.** *trans.* *To jack up*: To hoist with a jack (see JACK *sb.*[1] II. 4) 1885. **2.** *intr.* To hunt or fish at night with a jack (see JACK *sb.*[1] II. 16). *U.S.* 1881. **3.** *dial.* or *colloq.* *To jack up*: **a.** *trans.* (*a*) To do for, ruin 1873. (*b*) To throw up, give up, abandon 1880. **b.** *absol.* or *intr.* To give up suddenly or promptly 1873.

Jack-a-dandy (dʒæ:kădæ·ndi). 1632. [See JACK *sb.*[1] IV and cf. DANDY *sb.*[1]] A little pert or conceited fellow; a beau, fop, dandy.

Jackal (dʒæ·kǫl). 1603. [Corruption of Turkish *chakāl*, ad. Pers. *shagāl*, cogn. w. Skr. *s'rgāla*, *ç'rgāla* jackal. Formerly stressed on the second syllable.] **1.** An animal of the dog kind, about the size of a fox; one of various species of *Canis*, as *C. aureus* or *C. anthus*, inhabiting Asia and Africa, hunting in packs by night with wailing cries, and feeding on dead carcases and small animals; formerly supposed to hunt up prey for the lion, hence termed 'the lion's provider'. **2.** *fig.* A person who acts like a jackal, *esp.* one who does mean work for another, or ministers to his requirements 1688.

1. I am a brother to jackals R.V. *Job* xxx. 29. Hence **Ja·ckal** *v. intr.*, to act as jackal (*for*).

Ja·ck-a-Le·nt. *arch.* Also **-o'-Lent, of Lent.** 1598. [See A *prep.*] **1.** A figure of a man, set up in Lent to be pelted. Hence *fig.* a butt for every one to throw at. **2.** *transf.* A puppet; an insignificant person 1598.

Jackanapes (dʒæ·kănēips). *Pl.* **-apes, -apeses**, (†-aps's). 1450. [Orig. *Jack Napes*, perh. a playful name for a tame ape, with *n-* as in *Ned*, *Nell*, etc., and *-s* as in *Hobbes*, etc.] **1.** Name for a tame ape or monkey 1526. **2.** A ridiculous upstart; a pert, impertinent fellow; a coxcomb. (The current use.) 1555.

2. That Iacke an-apes with scarfes SHAKS. *attrib.* A scurvy Iack a-nape Priest SHAKS.

Jackaroo (dʒæ·kărū). *Austral.* 1880. [f. JACK *sb.*[1] + *kang)aroo*.] An inexperienced colonist.

Jackass (dʒæ·kˌæs). 1727. [f. JACK *sb.*[1] + ASS.] **1.** A male ass, a he-ass. **2.** = ASS 2. 1823. **3. Laughing Jackass**: the Giant Kingfisher of Australia (*Dacelo gigas*), so called from its cry 1798. **4.** *Naut.* a kind of heavy rough boat used in Newfoundland.

Comb.: **j.-copal**, the raw copal of Zanzibar; **-deer**, an African antelope, the sing-sing; **-fish**, an Australian fish (*Chilodactylus macropterus*), esteemed as food; **j. penguin**, a common species of penguin (*Spheniscus demersus*), so called from its cry; **j. rabbit** = JACK-RABBIT.

Jack-boot, ja·ckboot. 1686. [?] A large strong boot, the top of which came above the knee, orig. worn by cavalry soldiers; later, by fishermen and others.

†**Ja·ck-boy.** 1573. [f. JACK *sb.*[1] + BOY.] A boy employed in menial work; *spec.* a stable-boy, groom, or postillion –1849.

Jack-chain. 1639. [f. JACK *sb.*[1] II. 1; because used in roasting-jacks.] A chain each link of which consists of a double loop of wire, resembling a figure of 8.

Jackdaw (dʒæ·kdǫ). 1543. [f. JACK *sb.*[1] + DAW.] **1.** The common name of the DAW (*Corvus monedula*), which frequents church towers, old buildings, etc.; noted for its loquacity and thievish propensities. **2.** *fig.* Applied *contempt.* a loquacious person 1605.

1. Iack dawes; the veriest theeves..especially for silver and gold HOLLAND.

Jackeen (dʒækī·n). *Anglo-Irish.* 1840. [Irish dim. of JACK *sb.*[1]] A self-assertive worthless fellow.

Jacket (dʒæ·kėt), *sb.* 1462. [a. OF. *jaquet, jacquet*, dim. of *jaque*, JACK *sb.*[2]] 1. An outer garment for the upper part of the body: the same as the jack; now, an outer garment with sleeves, reaching no lower than the waist; also a short coat without tails (as a *dinner jacket*). b. That worn by a jockey in horse-racing; now a loose-fitting blouse of silk or satin, of the owner's distinctive racing colours 1856. c. Applied to something worn round the body for other purposes than clothing; as a *strait-jacket*, etc. 2. An outer covering for anything, esp. one placed round a pipe, steam-cylinder, or boiler, to protect it, prevent escape or access of heat, etc. 1815. b. A paper wrapper in which a bound book is issued. 1894. 3. a. The natural covering or coat of various animals; the fleece (of a sheep), hair (of a dog), fur (of a cat), etc.; also the skin (of a seal, fish, etc.) 1613. b. The skin of a potato (when cooked with the skin on) 1856.

1. Phr. *To dust, swinge, thrash, trim*, etc. (a person's) *j.*, to give him a beating. b. *To send in* (a jockey's) *j., take away his j.*, etc.

Ja·cket, *v.* 1861. [f. prec. sb.] 1. *trans.* To cover with or enclose in a jacket. 2. *dial.* or *colloq.* To beat, thrash 1875.

Jacketed (dʒæ·kėtėd), *a.* 1552. [f. prec. sb. or v. + -ED.] Clothed, covered, or surrounded with a jacket.

Ja·cketing. 1851. [f. as prec. + -ING[1].] 1. = JACKET *sb.* 2. 1881. 2. Material for making jackets 1882. 3. *colloq.* A beating. 1851.

Jack-frame. 1703. [f. JACK *sb.*[1] II. 2 + FRAME.] 1. The frame in which a jack or winch is fixed. 2. *Cotton Manuf.* A contrivance consisting of a rotating can containing a bobbin, formerly much used for giving a twist to the roving as delivered by the drawing rollers, and simultaneously winding it upon the bobbin. Also called *jack-in-a-box*. 1875.

Jack-fruit. 1830. = JACK *sb.*[4]

Jack-in-the-box, Jack-in-a-box. 1546. †1. A sharper or cheat –1725. †2. Applied contemptuously to the consecrated host 1546. 3. A toy consisting of a box containing a figure with a spring, which leaps up when the lid is raised. Also *fig.* 1702. 4. Techn.:

†a. A self-acting valve for relieving water-mains from accumulations of air. b. A screw-jack or lifting-jack, esp. one used in stowing cargo. c. A kind of screw-press. d. An instrument with a small but powerful screw, used by burglars to break open safes or doors. e. = JACK-FRAME 2.

Jack-in-the-green. 1801. 1. A man or boy enclosed in a wooden or wicker pyramidal framework covered with leaves, in the May-day sports of chimney-sweepers, etc. 2. A variety of primrose in which the calyx is transformed into leaves 1876.

Jack Johnson. 1914. Name of a negro boxer (known as 'the Big Smoke'), applied in the war of 1914–18 to a German gun and shell.

Jack Ketch. 1705. [From the name of John or '*Jack' Ketch*, the common executioner 1663 (?) –1686. He became notorious on account of his barbarity at the executions of William Lord Russell and others.] An appellation for the common executioner or hangman.

He is then a kind of jack-catch, an executioner-general WESLEY.

Jack-knife (dʒæ·kˌnəif), *sb.* 1776. [app. of U.S. origin; perh. assoc. with some sense of JACK *sb.*[1]] 1. A large clasp-knife for the pocket; also, one with a lanyard, worn by seamen. 2. In a telephone station = JACK *sb.*[1] II. 8 d. **Jack-knife** *v.* to cut with a j.-k. 1855.

Jack-line. 1615. [f. JACK *sb.*[1]; cf. JACK-CHAIN.] A kind of thin rope or line used for various purposes.

Jackman (dʒæ·kmæ̆n). *Sc.* 1567. [app. f. JACK *sb.*[1] I. 4 + MAN. Referred by Scott to JACK *sb.*[2]] An attendant or retainer kept by a nobleman or landowner. Now *Hist.*

Jack-o'-la·ntern, jack-a-lantern. 1663. †1. A man with a lantern; a night watchman –1704. 2. An ignis fatuus or will-o'-the-wisp; *fig.* something misleading or elusive 1673. 3. A lantern made of the rind of a large turnip or a pumpkin, with holes to represent eyes, nose, and mouth. *North. Eng., Sc.*, and *U.S.*

2. I have followed Cupid's Jack-a-lantern, and find myself in a quagmire SHERIDAN.

Ja·ck-pla:ne. 1763. [JACK *sb.*[1]] A long heavy plane used for coarse work.

Ja·ck-pu·dding. *arch.* 1648. [JACK *sb.*[1] IV. 2.] A buffoon, clown, or merry-andrew, *esp.* one attending on a mountebank.

Ja·ck-ra·bbit. *U.S.* 1882. [Short for *jackass-rabbit*; so called from its long ears.] One of several species of large prairie-hares with remarkably long ears and legs.

Ja·ck-screw:. 1769. A lifting-jack with a screw.

Jack snipe, ja·ck-sni:pe. 1663. [See JACK *sb.*[1] III. 2.] A small species of snipe, *Scolopax* (*Gallinago*) *gallinula*; also called *half-snipe*. Also applied to the common American snipe, *Gallinago Wilsoni*, the Dunlin, *Tringa alpina* (Shetland), and the pectoral sandpiper of N. America, *Tringa maculata*.

Ja·ck-staff. 1692. [f. JACK *sb.*[3] + STAFF.] *Naut.* A short staff, usually set upon the bowsprit or at the bow of a ship, on which the jack (JACK *sb.*[3]) is hoisted.

Jackstay (dʒæ·kˌstēi). 1840. [JACK *sb.*[1] IV. 1.] *Naut.* a. A rope, rod, or batten placed along a yard or gaff to bend the sail to. b. A rod or rope running up and down on a mast, on which the square-sail yard travels.

Ja·ck-stone, ja·ckstone. 1814. [var. of CHECK-STONE; perh. assoc. w. JACK *v.*] A small round pebble or stone; esp., in *pl.*, a set of pebbles tossed up and caught in the game of dibs.

Ja·ck-straw·, ja·ckstraw. 1565. [See JACK *sb.*[1], in various senses. *Jack Straw* was a leader in the Rising of the Commons in 1381.] 1. A 'man of straw'; a man of no substance or consideration. 2. One of a set of straws, or strips of ivory, bone, wood, or the like, used in a game in which they are thrown on the table in a heap, and have to be picked up singly without disturbing the heap. Also, in *pl.*, the game thus played. 1801.

Jack-ta·r. 1781. [See JACK *sb.*[1] I. 3.] A familiar term for a common sailor.

Jacob (dʒē̆ı·kəb). 1662. [a. Heb., in Gr. Ἰάκωβος, L. *Jacobus*, whence also Eng. JAMES.] A personal name and surname; used also in deriv. and transf. senses, partly referring to JACOB'S LADDER. †1. = JACOBUS. Pepys. †2. *slang.* a. A housebreaker carrying a ladder –1753. b. A ladder –1803. c. A simpleton –1812.

Phr. **Jacob's coat, membrane** (*Anat.*), the layer of rods and cones of the retina of the eye (named after Arthur Jacob, an Irish ophthalmic surgeon, died 1874); **Jacob's shell**, the scallop-shell *Pecten Jacobæus*, the emblem of St. James the Greater; **Jacob's stone**, a name for the coronation stone of the Scottish kings at Scone, now in Westminster Abbey, fabled to be the stone of Jacob's pillow (*Gen.* xxviii. 11); **Jacob's ulcer**, a term for *Lupus* or rodent ulcer of the eye (from Arthur Jacob).

Jacobean (dʒækŏbī·ăn), *a.* (*sb.*) Also -æan. 1770. [f. late and mod.L. *Jacobæus* (f. *Jacobus*; see prec.).] 1. Of or pertaining to the reign or times of James I of England; *spec.* in *Arch.*, a term for the 17th-c. style in England, consisting of very late Gothic with a large Palladian admixture; also *transf.* in other arts 1844. 2. Of or pertaining to St. James the Less, or the Epistle written by him 1883. b. *Jacobean lily*, a bulbous plant (*Sprekelia formosissima*), named after St. James 1770. 3. *sb.* A statesman or writer of the time of James I 1885.

Jacobian (dʒăkōu·biăn). 1852. [f. *Jacobi* (see below) + -AN.] *Math.* A. *adj.* Pertaining to or named after K. G. J. Jacobi (1804–51), professor at Königsberg in Prussia; discovered, introduced, or investigated by Jacobi; as *J. function*, etc. B. *sb.* Short for *J. determinant*, an important functional determinant.

Jacobin (dʒæ·kŏbin), *sb.*[1] and *a.*[1] ME. [a. F. *Jacobin* (orig. an adj., *frère jacobin*), ad. med.L. *Jacobinus*, f. *Jacobus*; see JACOB.]

A. *sb.* 1. A Dominican friar. (Orig. applied to the French members of the order, from the church of *Saint-Jacques* (St. Jacobus) which was given to them, and near which they built their first convent.) Also *attrib.* or as *adj.* 2. A member of a French political club established in 1789, at Paris, in the old convent of the Jacobins (sense 1), to maintain and propagate the principles of extreme democracy and absolute equality 1790. b. *transf.* An extreme radical in politics, etc. 1793. About 1800, a nickname for any political reformer.

2. b. With the Jacobins I shall keep no terms BURKE.

B. *adj.* a. Of or belonging to the Jacobins or Dominican friars. b. Pertaining to the Jacobins (sense 2 above); hence, ultra-democratic. 1795. Hence **Jacobi·nic, -al** *a.* of, pertaining to, or characteristic of the French Jacobins; ultra-democratic.

†**Ja·cobin**, *sb.*[2] and *a.*[2] 1517. [= OF. *Jacobin*, ad. med.L. *Jacobinus*, f. *Jacobus*; see JACOBITE[1].] a. *sb.* = JACOBITE *sb.*[1] b. *adj.* Of or pertaining to this sect. –1768.

Jacobin (dʒæ·kŏbin), *sb.*[3] Also †**Jacobine.** 1668. [a. F. *Jacobine*, fem. of *Jacobin* (JACOBIN *sb.*[1] 1); so called from their cowl or hood.] An artificial breed of the domestic pigeon, with reversed feathers on the back of the neck, suggesting a cowl or hood.

Jacobinism (dʒæ·kŏbiniz'm). 1793. [f. JACOBIN *sb.*[1] + -ISM.] The doctrine or practice of the French Jacobins; ultra-democratic principles. b. A Jacobinical trait or notion 1888.

Jacobinize (dʒæ·kŏbinəiz), *v.* 1793. [f. as prec. + -IZE.] *trans.* To render Jacobin, to imbue with revolutionary ideas. Hence **Ja:cobiniza·tion** 1798.

Jacobite (dʒæ·kŏbəit), *sb.*[1] and *a.*[1] ME. [ad. med.L. *Jacobita*, f. *Jacobus*; see JACOB and -ITE.] A member of a Monophysite sect taking its name from Jacobus Baradæus, of Edessa, who revived the Eutychian heresy in the 6th c. Also *attrib.* or as *adj.*

†**Ja·cobite**, *sb.*[2] 1550. [ad. med.L. *Jacobita*, f. *Jacobus*; see -ITE.] = JACOBIN *sb.*[1] 1. –1818.

†**Ja·cobite**, *sb.*[3] 1658. [f. JACOB + -ITE.] A descendant of Jacob, an Israelite; also applied to the 17th-c. Puritan refugees.

Jacobite (dʒæ·kŏbəit), *sb.*[4] and *a.*[2] 1611. [f. L. *Jacobus* James (see JACOB) + -ITE.]

A. *sb.* An adherent of James II of England after his abdication, or of his son the Pretender; a partisan of the Stuarts after the Revolution of 1688. 1689.

A private form of prayers..used amongst the Jacobites, for King James in his afflictions LUTTRELL.

B. *adj.* †1. In *Jacobite piece* = JACOBUS 1611. 2. Of or pertaining to the adherents of James II and his family (see A.) 1692.

2. Atterbury was nothing more or less than a J. priest 1788. Hence **Jacobi·tic, -al** *a.* pertaining to the adherents of the Stuarts; holding Jacobite principles. **Jacobi·tically** *adv.* **Ja·cobitish** *a.* Jacobitical; -ly *adv.*

Jacobitism (dʒæ·kŏbəitiz'm). 1700. [See -ISM.] 1. The principles of the Jacobites or adherents of James II and his family; adherence to the Stuart cause. 2. The doctrines of the Jacobite sect of Christians 1882.

Ja·cob's la·dder. 1733. [In reference to Gen. xxviii. 12.] 1. A common garden plant, *Polemonium cæruleum*, having corymbs of blue (or white) flowers; so called from the ladder-like appearance of its leaves. 2. *Naut.* A rope ladder with wooden steps for ascending the rigging from the deck 1840. 3. *fig.* 1831.

Jacob's membrane, etc.: see JACOB.

Jacob's staff. 1548. [In sense 1, from St. James (*Jacobus*), whose symbols are a pilgrim's staff and a scallop shell. In other senses, app. fanciful.] †1. A pilgrim's staff –1656. 2. a. An instrument formerly used for taking the altitude of the sun; a cross-staff 1559. b. An instrument for measuring distances and heights, consisting of a square rod about three feet in length with a cursor which slips on the staff 1777. c. A straight rod shod with pointed iron, and having a socket-joint at the summit for supporting a surveyor's circumferentor instead of a tripod. †3. A staff containing a concealed sword or dagger –1656. 4. A plant, the Great Mullein or Aaron's Rod 1879.

Jacobus (dʒăkōu·bŏs). *Pl.* -uses. 1612. [a. L. *Jacobus* James; see JACOB.] The (unofficial) name of an English gold coin, struck in the reign of James I; it passed orig. for 20*s.*, later for 22*s.* or 24*s.*

Jaconet (dʒæ·kǒnėt). 1769. [Corruption of Urdū *Jagannāthī*, from *Jagannāth* (Juggernaut) or *Jagannāthpūrī* in Cuttack, where first made.] A cotton fabric orig. imported, but now manufactured in England; now, A plain cotton cloth of medium thickness or weight, lighter than a shirting, and heavier than a mull.

†**Jacou·nce, jagou·nce.** ME. [a. OF. *jacunce, jagonce* :—pop.L. type **iacuntius* for **hiacyntius*, in cl.L. *hyacinthius* (sc. *lapis*), adj. from *hyacinthus*.] The jacinth or hyacinth (precious stone) –1529.

Jacquard (dʒăkā·ɹd, dʒæ·kăɹd). 1835. Surname of Joseph Marie Jacquard of Lyons (died 1834), who invented an apparatus to facilitate the weaving of figured fabrics in the loom. Hence *J. apparatus, attachment, engine, machine, mechanism*; also **Jacquard loom,** a loom fitted with this apparatus, for the weaving of figured fabrics; *J. fabric, muslin, stripes,* etc. **b.** Also *ellipt.* as *sb.* = Jacquard apparatus, etc.

‖**Jacquerie** (ʒakəri·). 1523. [F., in OF. *jaquerie*, peasants or villeins collectively, spec. as in Eng.; f. *Jacques*; cf. JACK *sb.*[1]] *Hist.* The rising of the villeins or peasants of northern France against the nobles in 1357–8; hence, Any rising of the peasantry.

Jactance (dʒæ·ktăns). *rare.* 1491. [a. F., ad. L. *jactantia*, f. *jactantem, jactare*; see JACTATION and -ANCE.] Boasting; vainglorious speaking. So **Ja·ctancy,** boastfulness, vainglory; boasting.

Jactation (dʒæktē·ʃən). 1576. [ad. L. *jactationem*, f. *jactare*, freq. of *jacĕre* to throw; cf. F. *jactation*.] **1.** = JACTITATION 2. 1680. **2.** Boasting, bragging, ostentatious display 1576.

Jactitation (dʒæktitē·ʃən). 1632. [ad. med.L. *jactitationem* (in Canon Law) a false declaration tending to some one's detriment, f. L. *jactitare*, in sense 'to throw out publicly', freq. of *jactare*; see prec.] **1.** Public or open declaration, esp. boasting, bragging. **2.** *Path.* A restless tossing of the body: a symptom of distress in severe diseases. **b.** A twitching or convulsive movement of a limb or muscle. 1665. †**3.** Bandying to and fro. STERNE.

1. *J. of marriage* (Law): a giving out or boasting falsely by a person that he or she is married to another whereby a reputation of their marriage may ensue.

Jaculate (dʒæ·kiŭlėt), *v. rare.* 1623. [f. L. *jaculat-, jaculari* to dart, f. *jaculum*, f. *jacĕre* to throw.] *trans.* To dart, hurl; *intr.* (for *refl.*) to dart forward.

Jaculation (dʒækiŭlē·ʃən). *rare.* 1608. [ad. L. *jaculationem*; see prec.] The action of darting, hurling, or throwing; a hurl, a throw.

Hills Hurl'd to and fro with j. dire MILTON.

Jaculator (dʒæ·kiŭlētəɹ). 1763. [a. L., f. *jaculari* to JACULATE.] **1.** One who throws or hurls (*rare*) 1796. **2.** A fish (*Toxotes jaculator*); = ARCHER 5. Also *j. fish.*

Jaculatory (dʒæ·kiŭlătəri), *a. rare.* 1616. [ad. late L. *jaculatorius*, f. *jaculat-, jaculari*.] Pertaining to throwing or darting; that is thrown or darted; (of prayer) ejaculatory.

Jad (dʒæd). *local.* 1871. [?] In the Bath-stone quarries: 'A long deep holing or cutting made for the purpose of detaching large blocks of stone from their natural beds' (Gresley). Hence **Ja·dding** *vbl. sb.*, also *attrib.*

Jade (dʒēɪd), *sb.*[1] ME. [?] **1.** A contemptuous name for a horse; a horse of inferior breed; a sorry worn-out horse; a vicious, worthless horse. **b.** *occas.* used without depreciatory sense: = Horse 1553. **c.** *fig.* 1577. **2.** A term of reprobation applied to a woman. Also used playfully, like *hussy.* 1560. **b.** Applied to Fortune, Nature, etc. personified 1594. **c.** Rarely to a man 1596.

1. Be blithe though thou ryde vp-on a Iade CHAUCER. **c.** You alwaies end with a Iades tricke SHAKS. **2.** An expensive J. of a Wife ADDISON. **b.** When Fortune, fickle jade's unkind 1812. **c.** A iolly Prater, but a I. to doe SYLVESTER. Hence **Ja·dery,** behaviour of a j. 1612.

Jade (dʒēɪd), *sb.*[2] 1727. [= F. *le jade*, for †*l'ejade* = It. *giada*, ad. Sp. *ijada* in *piedra de ijada*, lit. 'colic stone', f. *ijada* flank, †colic, f. L. *ilia* flank; cf. NEPHRITE.] **1.** A name given to **a.** NEPHRITE, a silicate of lime and magnesia, a hard translucent stone, in colour light green, bluish, or whitish; **b.** JADEITE, a silicate of sodium and aluminium, closely resembling nephrite in appearance. Sometimes also applied to SAUSSURITE. **2.** *attrib.* 1865.

Jade (dʒēɪd), *v.* 1601. [f. JADE *sb.*[1]] **1.** *trans.* To make a jade of (a horse); to exhaust or wear out by driving or working hard; to fatigue, weary 1606. **2.** *intr.* To become tired or worn out; to grow dull or languid; to flag 1620. †**3.** *trans.* To befool; to jape –1679.

1. Our horses were jaded—perfectly 'done up' 1837. **2.** When I feel my Muse beginning to j., I retire to the solitary fireside of my study BURNS. **3.** I do not now foole my selfe, to let imagination iade mee SHAKS. Hence **Ja·ded** *ppl. a.* 1593; **Ja·ded-ly** *adv.*, **-ness.**

Jadeite (dʒē̆ɪ·dəit). 1865. [f. JADE *sb.*[2] + -ITE.] *Min.* See JADE *sb.*[2] The hardest and most highly prized variety of jade.

Jade-stone. 1775. [f. JADE *sb.*[2] + STONE.] = JADE *sb.*[2]

Jadish (dʒēɪ·diʃ), *a.* 1573. [f. JADE *sb.*[1] + -ISH[1].] Of the nature of, or having the characteristics of, a jade; of or pertaining to a jade. **a.** Of a horse 1576. **b.** Of a person, *esp.* a woman 1573. **Ja·dish-ly** *adv.*, **-ness.**

Jag (dʒæg), *sb.*[1] Also **jagg.** [*Jag* sb. and vb. are found from *c* 1400. App. onomatopœic. There are no cognates in Teut. or Rom.] **1.** A dag or pendant made by cutting the edge of a garment; also, a slash or cut in the surface of a garment to show a different colour underneath. †**b.** An attached pendant or fringe –1606. **2.** A shred of cloth; in *pl.* Rags, tatters. Also *transf.* and *fig.* A scrap, fragment. *Obs.* exc. *dial.* 1555. **3.** A hairy, bristly, or thread-like projection 1519. **4.** A sharp projection; a denticulation; a sharp or rugged point of rock, etc. 1578. **5.** A barb or dovetail which resists retraction 1875. **6.** *Sc.* A prick with anything sharp 1818.

Comb. **j.-bolt,** a bolt having a beard raised upon its angles with a chisel (hence **j.-bolt** *v.* to fasten with a jag-bolt).

Jag. *sb.*[2] *dial.* and *U.S.* 1597. [?] **1.** A load (usually a small cart-load) of hay, wood, etc. **b.** A pedlar's wallet. SCOTT. **c.** *slang.* A 'load' of drink; also, a drinking bout 1678. **2.** A portion or quantity; a 'lot'. *U.S.* 1834.

Jag (dʒæg), *v.*[1] ME. [See JAG *sb.*[1]] **1.** *trans.* To pierce with something sharp; †to stab; to prick (*Sc., north. Eng.,* and *U.S. dial.*) **2.** *trans.* To slash or pink (a garment, etc.) by way of ornament ME. **3.** To make indentations in the edge or surface of; to make ragged or uneven, rugged or bristling 1568. **4.** *Naut.* To lay in long bights, as a rope, and tie with stops. *U.S.*

Jag, *v.*[2] *dial.* 1747. [f. JAG *sb.*[2]] *trans.* To carry in a cart, or on a pack-horse.

Jagannāth, the better sp. of JUGGERNAUT.

‖**Jäger, jaeger** (yē̆·gəɹ). Also †**jager,** and YAGER, q.v. 1776. [Ger. *jäger* hunter, f. *jagen* to chase. Cf. CHASSEUR.] **1.** A (German or Swiss) huntsman or hunter 1823. **2.** A rifleman or sharpshooter in the German and Austrian armies 1776. **3.** An attendant upon a person of rank or wealth, dressed in a huntsman's costume. Cf. CHASSEUR 3. 1831. **4.** A predatory sea-bird of the family *Laridæ*; a skua-gull 1838.

Jagg; see JAG.

Jagged (dʒæ·gėd, dʒægd), *a.* 1440. [f. JAG *sb.*[1] and *v.*[1] + -ED. Now usu. disyllabic as adj., monosyllabic as pple.] **1.** Of a garment: Cut into jags; pinked, slashed. **2.** Having the edge irregularly cut, gashed, or torn 1577. **3.** Having deep irregular indentations and projecting points; laciniated; esp. of leaves, petals, etc. 1523. **b.** In names of plants: Having jagged leaves or flowers 1548. **4.** Irregularly and sharply pointed 1651.

2. A notched and j. knife DICKENS. **4.** Frowning cliffs and j. pinnacles MERIVALE. **Ja·gged-ly** *adv.*, **-ness.**

Jagger[1] (dʒæ·gəɹ). 1598. [f. JAG *v.*[1] + -ER[1].] One who or that which jags; *spec.* **a** jagging-iron, also a toothed chisel.

Ja·gger[2]. *dial.* 1514. [f. JAG *sb.*[2] or *v.*[2] + -ER[1].] **1.** A carrier; a hawker. **2.** *Mining.* A man who carries ore on pack-horses from a mine to the smelting-place 1747.

Jaggery (dʒæ·gəri). 1598. [a. Indo-Port. *jágara*, ad. Canarese *sharkare*; cf. SUGAR, Skr. *çarkarā*.] A coarse dark brown sugar made in India by evaporation from palm sap. Also applied to any kind of crude sugar.

J. palm, a palm-tree that yields j., esp. *Caryota urens.*

Jaggy (dʒæ·gi), *a.* 1717. [f. JAG *sb.*[1] + -Y[1].] Having jags; jagged; in *Sc.*, prickly.

‖**Jaghire** (dʒagīə·ɹ). *E. Indies.* Also **jaghir, jagir,** etc. 1622. [a. Urdū (Pers.) *jāgīr*, f. *jā* place + *gīr* holding, holder.] An assignment of the king's or government's share of the produce of a district to an individual or a body, as an annuity, either for private use or for the maintenance of a public (esp. military) establishment; also, the district, or the income, so assigned. Hence ‖**Jaghirdar** (dʒagīə·ɹdāɹ) [Pers. *-dār* possessor], the holder of a j.

Jaguar (dʒæ·gwaɹ, dʒæ·giu,āɹ). 1604. [a. Tupi-Guarani *yaguara, jaguara* (ya-, ʒawāra), orig. a class-name for all carnivorous beasts.] A large carnivorous feline quadruped, *Panthera onca*, yellowish-brown in colour and marked with ocellated spots, inhabiting wooded parts of America from Texas to Paraguay.

Of the large Spotted Cats, the largest is the J. 1875.

‖**Jaguarete.** 1753. [a. Tupi-Guarani *jaguareté*, f. as prec. + *-eté* 'true'; the specific name of the jaguar.] The Guarani name for the jaguar; long mistaken for a distinct species or variety, e. g. the Black Jaguar.

‖**Jaguarondi** (dʒægwărǫ·ndi, yægwa-). 1885. [Native name in Tupi-Guarani; cf. JAGUAR.] A large wild cat (*Felis yaguarundi*, Desmarest), dark brown or brownish grey in colour, with a long body and tail, inhabiting America from Texas to Paraguay.

‖**Jah** (dʒā). 1539. The form of the Heb. *Yah*, short for *Yahwe(h* (Jahveh) JEHOVAH, in the English Bible. See JEHOVAH.

Jahvism (yā·viz'm). Also **Jahveism, -ehism, Yahwism** (yā·ve,iz'm, yā·wiz'm). 1867. [f. *Jahveh, Jahve, Yahwe(h*, different transliterations of the Heb. (previously represented by JEHOVAH) + -ISM.] The religion of Jahveh; the system of doctrines and precepts connected with the worship of Jahveh. **b.** The use of *Jahve(h)* as a name for God.

So **Jahvist** (yā·vist), **a.** a worshipper of Jahveh; **b.** = JEHOVIST 2. **Jahvi·stic** *a.* of or pertaining to Jahvism or the Jahvist.

Jail, gaol (dʒēɪl), *sb.* [Two types: 1) ME. *gay(h)ole, -ol, gaill(e, gaile,* etc., a. ONF. *gaiole, gayolle, gaole*; 2) ME. *jaiole, jayle, jaile,* etc., a. OF. *jaiole, geole,* etc., F. *geôle* prison :—Rom. and pop.Lat. **gaviola*, for **caveola*, dim. of *cavea* cavity, cage, coop; see CAGE. The Norman Fr. and ME. *gaiole, gaole* survives in the spelling *gaol* (chiefly due to statutory and official tradition); the current pronunciation corresponds to the form *jail*, which in U.S. is the official spelling.] **1.** A place or building for the confinement of persons accused or convicted of a crime or offence; a prison. Now, a public building for the confinement of persons committed by process of law. **b.** Without the article: = imprisonment 1447. **c.** *transf.* and *fig.* Place of confinement ME.

At that period the gaols were..depositories of pestilence MCCULLOCH. **b.** Having been sent to gaol by him twice KINGSLEY. **c.** [Love] is..A plesaunt gayl and esy prisoun ME.

Comb.: †**j. damp,** the noxious exhalation formerly common in jails; **j. distemper** = JAIL-FEVER; **j.-house** (*U.S.*), a jail; **j. money,** money paid for the maintenance of a jail.

Jail, gaol (dʒēɪl), *v.* 1604. [f. prec.] *trans.* To confine in or as in a jail; to imprison.

One, whose bolts, That jail you from free life, bar you from death TENNYSON.

Jail-bird, gaol-bird (dʒēɪ·lbɔ̄ɹd). 1603. [With allusion to a caged bird; see JAIL *sb.*] A prisoner in jail; esp. a habitual criminal; as a term of reproach, an incorrigible rogue.

Jai·l-deli·very, gaol-delivery. 1461. [See DELIVERY.] 1. The clearing a jail of prisoners by bringing them to trial, esp. at the assizes; hence the judicial process by which every prisoner awaiting trial in a jail is either condemned or acquitted at the assizes. 2. Deliverance from jail or imprisonment, whether by force or otherwise 1592.

1. [He] came before the Iustices of Gaole deliuery at Newegate HALL. 2. The legislature has been obliged to make a general arbitrary jail-delivery BURKE.

Jailer, jailor, gaoler (dʒē¹·ləɹ). ME. [Two types corresp. to *gaol, jail*; see JAIL *sb.* and -ER [2] 2.] One who has charge of a jail or of the prisoners in it; a jail-keeper.

fig. His Iniury The Gaoler to his pitty SHAKS. Hence **Jai·leress, Jai·lership.**

Jail-fever, gaol-fever. 1753. [f. JAIL, GAOL *sb.* + FEVER *sb.*] A virulent type of typhus-fever, formerly endemic in crowded jails, and frequent in ships and other confined places.

Jain, ‖Jaina (dʒē¹n, dʒē¹·nă). 1805. [Hindī *jaina* :—Skr. *jaina* of or pertaining to a Buddha or saint, f. *jina* a Buddha, a (Jain) saint, lit. 'overcomer', f. root *ji* conquer.] **A.** *sb.* A member of a non-Brahminical East Indian sect, holding doctrines closely resembling those of Buddhism. **B.** *adj.* Of or pertaining to the Jains or their religion. **Jai·nism,** the religious system of the Jains. **Jai·nist** *sb.* and *a.* = JAIN.

Jakes (dʒē¹ks). Now *rare.* c 1530. [? conn. w. proper name *Jaques, Jakes*; or from *Jakke* 'Jack', quasi *Jakkes*, 'Jack's'.] A privy. Also *transf.* and *fig.*

Jalap (dʒæ·ləp, dʒǫ·ləp), *sb.* 1574. [= F. *jalap*, ad. Sp. *jalapa*, in full *purga de Jalapa*, from *Jalapa* formerly *Xalapa*, a city of Mexico, in Aztec *Xalapan* (ʃalā·pan), lit. 'sand by the water', f. *xalli* sand + *atl* water + *pan* upon.] A purgative drug obtained from the tuberous roots of a Mexican climbing plant, *Exogonium* (*Ipomœa*) *Purga* and some other convolvulaceous plants; the active principle is the resin contained in the tubers (*resin of j.*). Also applied to the plants themselves 1698.

False or Garden J., *Mirabilis Jalapa.* Hence **Ja·lap** *v.* to dose or purge with j.

Jalapin (dʒæ·lăpin). 1832. [f. mod.L. *jalāpa* (see prec.) + -IN.] *Chem.* A glucoside resin; the resin of jalap-stalks. It is a strong purgative. So **Jala·pic** *a.* in *jalapic acid*, $C_{68}H_{59}O_{35}$, an acid produced by dissolving j. in aqueous solutions of the alkalis or alkaline earths; hence **Ja·lapate,** a salt of this acid.

Jalouse (dʒălū·z), *v. Sc.* 1816. [a. F. *jalouser* to regard with jealousy, f. *jaloux, -ouse* JEALOUS.] 1. *trans.* To be suspicious about. 2. To suspect (that a thing is so); to surmise, guess 1816. ¶3. (*Misused by southern writers.*) To regard with jealousy; to begrudge jealously 1879.

‖Jalousie (ʒa·luzi). 1824. [F., = jealousy; also as here.] A blind or shutter made with slats which slope upwards from without, so as to exclude sun and rain, and admit air and some light. Hence **Ja·lousied** *a.* provided with a j. 1847.

Jam (dʒæm), *sb.*[1] Also **jamb.** 1806. [f. JAM *v.*] The action of jamming; a crush, a squeeze; a mass of things or persons tightly crowded or packed together; a block in a confined passage. **b.** The tight squeezing of one or more movable parts of a machine into or against another part so that they cannot move; the blocking of a machine from this cause 1890. Also *attrib.*

Comb.: **j.-nut,** an auxiliary nut screwed down upon the main nut to hold it; **-weld** (*Forging*), a weld in which the heated ends or edges of the parts are square butted against each other and welded.

Jam (dʒæm), *sb.*[2] 1730. [? f. JAM *v.* in sense 'to bruise or crush by pressure'.] A conserve of fruit prepared by boiling it with sugar to a pulp. Also *transf.* and *fig.*

Without Real J.—cash and kisses—this world is a bitterish pill 1885.

‖Jam (dʒām), *sb.*[3] ? *Obs.* 1793. [f. JAMA.] A kind of dress or frock for children.

‖Jam (dʒām), *sb.*[4] Also **jám, jām.** 1843. [?] A title given to certain native chiefs in Kutch, Kattywar, and the lower Indus.

Jam (dʒæm), *v.* Also **jamb.** 1706. [app. onomatopœic.] 1. *trans.* To press or squeeze (an object) tightly between two converging bodies or surfaces; to wedge or fix immovably in an opening 1719. **b.** To make fast by tightening 1726. **c.** To block (a passage, etc.) by crowding or crushing into it 1866. **d.** To bruise or crush by pressure 1832. 2. *intr.* To become fixed, wedged, or held immovably; to stick fast 1706. 3. *trans.* To cause the fixing or wedging of (some movable part of a machine) so that it cannot work; to render (a machine, gun, etc.) unworkable thus 1851; *intr.* to become unworkable thus 1885. **b.** Wireless. *trans.* To cause interference in (radio signals). Also *intr.* To be affected by such interference. 1914. 4. *trans.* To press, squeeze, or crowd together in a compact mass; to force together 1768. 5. To thrust or ram *into* a confined space 1793. Also with *against, down, in* 1836.

1. The Ship..stuck fast, jaum'd in between two Rocks DE FOE. **d.** He jamm'd his finger in the door 1840. 2. The Ice jam'd 1706. 5. Hats are jammed tightly on the head 1887. Hence **Jammed** *ppl. a.*

Jam, obs. f. JAMB.

‖Jama, jamah (dʒā·mă). *E. Ind.* 1776. [Urdū (Pers.) *jāmah* garment. Cf. *pyjamas.*] The long cotton gown worn by Hindoos.

Jamadar, var. of JEMADAR.

Jamaica (dʒămē¹·kă). 1756. The name of a large West Indian island. Used *attrib.* of things native to or imported from that island, as *Jamaica bark, ebony*, etc. Also **J. pepper** = ALLSPICE; **J. rum,** often called simply Jamaica; **J. wood** = BRAZILETTO. Hence **Jamai·can** *a.* and *sb.* 1681.

Jamb (dʒæm). ME. [a. F. *jambe* :—late L. *gamba* 'hoof', in later pop.L. 'leg'; ? f. (ult.) Celtic *camb-* crooked, bent (Diez).] 1. (also *jambe.*) *Her.* The leg of an animal represented on coat of arms 1725. **b.** *Armour.* A leg-piece made of metal or cuir-bouilli 1834. 2. *Arch.* Each of the side posts of a doorway, window, or chimney-piece, upon which rests the lintel; a cheek; esp. in pop. use, (*pl.*) the stone cheeks of a fire-place ME. 3. A projecting columnar part of a wall; a columnar mass or pillar in a quarry or mine 1687. 4. *Mining.* A bed of clay or stone running across a mineral vein or seam 1721.

Jamb: see JAM *sb.*[1] and *v.*

Jambeau (dʒæ·mbo). *Hist.* Pl. **-eaux.** ME. [In form repr. AF. **jambeau* deriv. of *jambe* leg.] A piece of armour for the leg; *pl.* leggings; a pair of jambes.

†Jambee. 1704. [f. *Jambi* a district, town, and large river of Sumatra.] A species of *Calamus* or *Dæmonorops* from the district of Jambi; a cane made of this, fashionable in Queen Anne's time –1709.

‖Jambo, jambu (dʒæ·mbo, -bū). *E. Ind.* 1598. [Vernacular forms repr. Skr. *jambu, jambū* 'rose-apple', and its derivs.] **a.** *Eugenia Jambos* (*Jambosa vulgaris*), the Rose Apple. **b.** *Eugenia Jambolana*, the Java Plum, also called *Jambolan* 1835. **c.** *Eugenia malaccensis*, the Malay Apple, and kindred species, native to the Malay archipelago 1727. So **Jambolan** = JAMBO b.

Jamboree·. [Of uncertain origin.] 1872. 1. A noisy revel; a carousal or spree. *U.S. slang.* 2. *Cards.* In railroad euchre, a hand containing the five highest trumps, which entitles the holder to score sixteen points. 3. A rally of Boy Scouts; orig. applied to the international rally held at Olympia in Aug. 1920.

‖Jamdani (dʒāmdā·nī). *E. Ind.* Also **-danee.** 1858. [Pers.] A species of fine cotton cloth with spots or flowers woven in the loom.

James (dʒē¹mz). ME. [a. OF. *James* :—late L. **Ja·comus*, f. L. *Ja·cobus* (learned form *Iaco·bus*), a. Gr. Ἰάκωβος, ad. Heb. = Jacob, a frequent Jewish name.]

I. A Christian name; hence *transf.* 1. A sovereign (*slang*). (Cf. JACOBUS.) 1858. 2. A burglar's crow-bar; = JEMMY *sb.* 4. 1812. 3. A sheep's head 1827.

II. St. James, either apostle of the name; esp. St. James the Greater, whose shrine at Compostella was a centre of pilgrimage. *St. James's day, tide*, the 25th of July, dedicated to St. James the Greater ME. *St. James's shell*, a scallop-shell worn by pilgrims to the shrine at Compostella; also the scallop *Pecten jacobæus*. 1500. **b.** *St. James's wort*, Ragwort, *Senecio Jacobæa* 1578.

III. Also, a surname; hence, **James's Powder,** a febrifuge, formerly very popular, prepared by Dr. Robert James (1703–1776).

Jamesonite (dʒē¹·msənəit). 1825. [f. Professor *Jameson*, of Edinburgh (1773–1854).] *Min.* Sulph-antimonide of lead, usually occurring in fibrous masses; feather-ore.

Jamestown-weed. *U.S.* Also **Jim(p)sonweed.** 1687. [f. *Jamestown*, in Virginia.] The Thorn-apple, *Datura Stramonium.*

Jammy (dʒæ·mi), *a.* [f. JAM *sb.*[2] + -Y [1].] Sticky with jam.

Jane (dʒē¹n). ME. [f. OF. *Janne(s*, F. *Gênes.*] †1. A small silver coin of Genoa –1671. 2. = JEAN, the fabric, q.v.

†Jane-of-apes. *joc. nonce-wd.* [f. after *Jack-of-apes.*] A female Jackanapes. MASSINGER.

‖Jangada (dʒæŋgā·dă). 1598. [Pg., ad. Malayālam *changādam* raft, etc., ad. Skr. *saṃghāṭa* 'joinery'.] A float or raft of logs joined together, and furnished with a lateen sail; used in parts of Brazil and Peru. **b.** *orig.* A raft used in the E. Indies.

Jangle (dʒæ·ŋg'l), *sb.* [In ME. a. AF. or OF. *jangle* sb. from *jangler*; later, from next.] †1. Idle talk, chatter; an idle word. ME. only. 2. Contention, altercation 1641. 3. Discordant sound, ring, or clang 1795. 4. Confused and noisy talk. (A blending of 1 and 3.) 1839.

1. Do manye goode werkes, and spek fewe Iangles CHAUCER. 3. The mad j. of Matilda's lyre GIFFORD.

Jangle (dʒæ·ŋg'l), *v.* ME. [a. OF. *jangler* (12th c.); ult. history unkn. Cf. JINGLE *v.*]

I. *intr.* †1. To chatter, babble, prate; said also of birds –1774. 2. To speak or sound harshly or discordantly ME.

1. Thy mynde is lorn, thou ianglest as a Iay CHAUCER. 2. Thus they go on, wrangling and jangling 1797.

II. *trans.* 1. To speak or utter in a noisy, babbling, discordant, or contentious manner ME. 2. To cause (a bell, etc.) to give forth a harsh discordant sound 1604.

2. Like sweet bells iangled out of time, and harsh SHAKS. Hence **Ja·ngler,** †a chatterer, a noisy disputant. **†Ja·ngleress.**

†Ja·nglery. ME. [a. OF. *janglerie*; see -ERY 1 b.] Idle talk; wrangling –1583.

Janitor (dʒæ·nitǫɹ). 1584. [a. L., f. *janua* door, with agent-suffix *-tor.*] 1. A doorkeeper, porter, ostiary 1630. †2. An usher in a school –1876. 3. *Sc.* and *U.S.* A caretaker of a building who has charge of the cleaning and heating of it 1878. Hence **Ja·nitoress, Ja·nitress, Ja·nitrix,** a female j.

Janizary, janissary (dʒæ·nizări, yæ·ni-). 1529. [Ult. ad. Turkish *yeñi-tsheri*, f. *yeñi* new, modern + *tsheri* soldiery, militia.] 1. One of a former body of Turkish infantry, constituting the Sultan's guard and the main part of the standing army. The body was composed mainly of tributary children of Christians, and was abolished in 1826. 2. Hence, any Turkish soldier; *esp.* one of an escort for travellers in the East 1615. 3. *fig.*, etc. 1565. 4. *attrib.* 1642. Hence **Janiza·rian** *a.*

3. The Romish Janizaries are the tribute Children of all Europe 1679.

Janker (dʒæ·ŋkəɹ). *Sc.* 1823. [?] A long pole on wheels, used for carrying logs and other heavy weights.

Jansenism (dʒæ·nsĕniz'm). 1656. [f. as next + -ISM.] The doctrinal system of the Jansenists.

Jansenist (dʒæ·nsĕnist), *sb.* (*a.*) 1664. [f. the surname *Jansen* + -IST.] A follower in the Roman Catholic Church of Cornelius Jansen, bishop of Ypres in Flanders (died 1638), who maintained after St. Augustine the perverseness and inability for good of the natural human will. Also *attrib.* or *adj.* Hence **Janseni·stic, -ical** *a.* 1711; **†Janse·nian** (*rare*).

Jant, etc.: see JAUNT, etc.

January (dʒæ·niŭări). [ME. *Ieniuer*, etc., a. ONF. *Jenever* = mod.F. *Janvier* :—L. *Januarium*, nom. *Januarius* (*mensis*), i.e. the month of JANUS, as presiding over the entrance into the year.] The first month of the year according to modern reckoning. Abbrev. Jan.

Janus (dʒē¹·nɒ̆s). 1508. An ancient Italian deity, regarded as having doors and entrances under his protection; represented with a face on the front and another on the back of his head; the doors of his temple in the Roman Forum were always open in time of war, and shut in time of peace. Often used *attrib.*, and allusively, referring to the two-faced figure.

Four faces each Had, like a double J. MILT. *P.L.* XI. 129. *attrib.* A friend is Janus-faced: he looks to the past and the future EMERSON.

Jap. 1880. Colloq. abbrev. of JAPANESE.

Japan (dʒăpæ·n), *sb.* (*a.*) 1577. [ad. Chinese *Jih-pŭn* (= Japanese *Ni-pon*), 'sunrise', 'orient', f. *jih* (Jap. *ni*) sun + *pŭn* (Jap. *pon, hon*) origin.] 1. A country of eastern Asia consisting of a long cluster of islands extending between Kamchatka in the north and the Philippines in the south. †b. *transf.* A Japanese 1588. 2. A hard varnish of the kind used in work orig. imitating lacquer of Japan 1688. 3. Japanese work, esp. with painted and varnished design 1742. 4. a. Japanese porcelain. †b. Japanese silk 1729. 5. *attrib.* Of, belonging to, native to, or produced in Japan; as **J. clover**, a leguminous annual introduced into southern U.S. in 1840 from China and Japan; **J. earth** = CATECHU; **J. ink**, a superior black writing ink, generally glossy when dry; **J. moth**, a moth of the genus *Adela* 1673. 6. *attrib.*, in sense 2, as *j. cabinet, frame*, etc. 1681; *J. varnish* (*tree*) = AILANTO 1789.

Japan (dʒăpæ·n), *v.* 1688. [f. prec., sense 2.] 1. *trans.* To lacquer with japan; to varnish with any material that gives a hard black gloss. 2. *transf.* To make black and glossy as in japanning 1714. 3. *slang.* To ordain. (With reference to the black coat.) 1756.

2. His gaiters, too, were fresh japann'd W. COMBE.

Japanese (dʒæpănī·z). 1604. [f. JAPAN + -ESE.] A. *adj.* Of or pertaining to Japan 1719. What more picturesque than the J. umbrellas? 1884. B. *absol.* or as *sb.* 1. A native of Japan. (Now only as adj. used absol. and unchanged for pl.) 1604. 2. The Japanese language 1828.

Japanesery (dʒæpănī·zəri). 1885. Also in Fr. form **japonaiserie**. [f. prec. + -ERY, after Fr. (cf. CHINOISERIE).] Japanese conduct, art, decoration, etc.; an instance of this.

Japanned (dʒăpæ·nd), *ppl. a.* 1693. [f. JAPAN *v.*] 1. Varnished, lacquered, etc., with japan 1693. b. Polished with blacking 1750. 2. Made or become Japanese 1889. So **Japa·nning** *vbl. sb.*, also *concr.* = JAPAN 2.

Japanner (dʒăpæ·nəɹ). 1614. [f. JAPAN *sb.* and *v.* + -ER¹.] †1. A Japanese; a Japanese ship –1764. 2. One who japans, one who follows the trade of varnishing with japan 1695: †*joc.* a shoe-black –1734.

Jape (dʒē¹p), *sb.* ME. [See JAPE *v.*] †1. A trick, a device to deceive or cheat. *Obs.* since *c* 1515, but used by Scott. 2. A device to amuse; a merry or idle tale; a jest, gibe. Revived in 19th c. ME. †3. A trifle, toy –1570. Hence **Ja·pish** *a.* 1745.

1. The japes and mockeries of evil spirits SCOTT.

Jape (dʒē¹p), *v.* ME. [Etym. unkn. Revived in 19th c. in sense 4.] †1. *trans.* To trick, beguile, befool, deceive –1463. †2. To seduce; to know carnally. †Also *intr.* –1589. 3. *trans.* To mock, deride, insult. Occas. used in 18–19th c. 1440. 4. *intr.* To say or do something in jest or mockery ME. Hence **Ja·per**, one who japes; *esp.* a professional jester. †**Ja·pery**, ribaldry; a jest.

Japhetic (dʒăfe·tik), *a.* Also **Japetic**. 1828. [f. *Japheth* (or L. *Japetus*) + -IC.] Of or belonging to Japheth, one of the sons of Noah; descended from Japheth: sometimes applied to the Indo-European family. So **Japhetite** (dʒē¹·fetəit), also **Japhethite**, a descendant of Japheth.

Japonic (dʒăpǭ·nik), *a.* 1673. [f. *Japon*, JAPAN.] Of or pertaining to Japan; Japanese. So †**Japo·nian** *a.* and *sb.* 1591.

J. earth: catechu, terra japonica.

Japonica (dʒăpǭ·nikă). 1819. [mod. L., fem. of *Japonicus* pertaining to Japan.] The name given to various ornamental plants orig. native to Japan, as the common camellia (*Camellia japonica*), the Japan quince (*Pyrus japonica*).

Jar (dʒāɹ), *sb.*¹ 1546. [Goes with JAR *v.*] I. 1. A harsh inharmonious sound; †*spec.* in *Mus.*, A discord 1553. †2. A vibration or tick of the clock. SHAKS. 3. A quivering or grating sound 1669. 4. A tremulous vibration resulting from concussion or physical shock 1815.

1. A little iarre in musick is not easily espied 1586. 2. *Wint. T.* I. ii. 43.

II. 1. Discord, want of harmony; a divergence or conflict of opinions, etc.; †a discrepancy of statement 1548. 2. Dissension, quarrelling 1546. b. A dissension; a petty (esp. domestic) broil 1583.

2. b. *Proverb.* Women's jars breed men's wars. Phr. *At* (*a*) *j.*: at discord (now *rare*).

III. A method of connecting the bit and the rods or cable in an apparatus for drilling rocks by impact, by means of which at each up-stroke a jar of the bit is produced which jerks it upwards 1864.

IV. A representation of the harsh vibratory sound made by certain birds and insects, whence their popular names, as JAR-BIRD, JAR-OWL; hence transf., as in NIGHTJAR.

Jar (dʒāɹ), *sb.*² 1592. [a. F. *jarre*, a. Arab. *jarrah*, earthen water-vessel.] 1. A vessel of earthenware, stoneware, or glass, without spout or handle (or two-handled), usu. more or less cylindrical in form. Orig. used only in its eastern sense of a large earthen vessel for holding water, oil, wine, etc. 2. Such a vessel and its contents; hence, a jarful. Formerly a measure of capacity 1598.

1. *Leyden jar*: see LEYDEN. 2. Sir, Spain has sent a thousand jars of oil POPE.

Jar, *sb.*³ *arch.* or *colloq.* 1674. [Later form of *char*, CHARE *sb.*¹, turn, turning; see AJAR *adv.*¹] In *on* or *upon the* (or *a*) *j.*, on the turn, partly open, AJAR *adv.*¹

Jar (dʒāɹ), *v.* Also †**gerre**, †**charre**. 1526. [This vb. and its sb., JAR ¹, are in origin prob. echoic.]

I. 1. *intr.* To emit or make a harsh grating sound; to sound in discord with other sounds. Also *fig.* †2. *intr.* Of a clock (or, of minutes): To tick. Also in Shaks. *trans.* To cause to tick. 1593. 3. *intr.* To strike against something with a grating sound, or so as to cause vibration; to clash 1665. 4. *intr.* To sound harshly *in* (*obs.*), or fall with harsh effect *on*, the ear. Hence, To strike with discordant or painful effect *upon* the nerves, feelings, mind, conscience, etc. 1538. 5. *intr.* To vibrate audibly; hence, to vibrate, shiver, or shake from an impact or shock 1735. 6. *trans.* To cause to sound discordantly 1633. 7. To cause to vibrate; to shake into vibration 1568. 8. To injure by concussion or impact 1875.

1. Iarringe, and snarringe at me like dogs 1576. 2. *Rich. II*, V. v. 51. 3. As broadsword upon target jarred SCOTT. 4. His laugh jars on one's ear THACKERAY. 7. The fine paved road..jars the nerves terribly MRS. PIOZZI.

II. 1. *intr.* To be out of harmony or at discord in character or effect; to disagree; to conflict 1541. b. To clash 1621. 2. *intr.* To be at strife; to quarrel; to dispute, wrangle 1550. †3. *trans.* To bring to discord –1628.

1. Orders and Degrees Jarr not with liberty, but well consist MILT. *P.L.* V. 793.

‖**Jararaca** (dʒărără·kă). 1613. [Native name.] A venomous serpent of Brazil (*Bothrops Jararaca*) of the family *Crotalidæ*.

Ja·r-bird. [JAR *sb.*¹ IV.] Local name of the Nut-hatch. G. WHITE.

‖**Jarde.** 1727. [F.] = JARDON.

‖**Jardinière** (ʒardinyę̄r). 1841. [Fr.] 1. An ornamental stand or receptacle for plants, flowers, etc. 2. *Cookery.* A preparation of mixed vegetables stewed in a sauce; *j. soup*, vegetable soup 1846.

‖**Jardon.** 1720. [F. *jardon*, ad. It. *giardone*, augm. of *giarda* JARDE.] *Farriery.* A callous tumour on the leg of a horse, on the outside of the hock –1797.

Jarful (dʒā·ɹful). 1866. [f. JAR *sb.*² + -FUL.] As much as a jar will hold.

†**Ja·rgle**, *v.* 1549. [a. OF. *jargoillier*, *-ouillier* (also *gar-*), prob. from an onomatopœic base *jarg-*, *garg-*; see JARGON *sb.*¹] *intr.* To utter a harsh or shrill sound; to chatter, jar –1600.

†**Jargogle**, *v.* *trans.* To confuse, jumble. LOCKE.

Jargon (dʒā·ɹgən), *sb.*¹ ME. [a. OF. *jargon*, *-oun*, *gargon*, etc., warbling of birds, chatter, talk; perh. containing the same radical *garg-*, *jarg-* as *jargoillier*: see JARGLE.] 1. Twittering, chattering. (Recently revived.) 2. Unintelligible or meaningless talk or writing; nonsense, gibberish ME. †3. A cipher, or other system of characters or signs having an arbitrary meaning –1708. 4. A barbarous, rude, or debased language or variety of speech; a 'lingo'; used esp. of a hybrid speech 1643. 5. Applied contemptuously to the language of scholars, the terminology of a science or art, or the cant of a class, sect, trade, or profession 1651. 6. A 'babel' of sounds 1711.

2. Alchymy..is found to be mere J. and Imposture 1722. 4. Others had the Levant J., which they call Lingua Frank DE FOE. 5. The j. of the trade 1704, of the Law 1717. Metaphysical j. KAMES. Hence **Jargonee·r**, a jargon-monger. **Jargo·nic.**¹

Jargon, jargoon (dʒā·ɹgən, dʒaɹgū·n), *sb.*² 1769. [a. F. *jargon*, ad. It. *giargone*; usually identified (ult.) with ZIRCON, Pg. *zarcão*, Arab. *zarqūn*.] A translucent, colourless, or smoky variety of the mineral zircon, found in Ceylon. Hence **Jargo·nic** *a.*² 1796.

Jargon (dʒā·ɹgən), *v.* ME. [a. OF. *jarg-*, *gargonner*, *-ouner*, F. *jargonner*, f. JARGON *sb.*¹] 1. *intr.* To warble, twitter, chatter. *Obs.* from 15th to 19th c. 2. *intr.* To utter jargon; to talk unintelligibly 1570.

2. Disappear, I say; away, and j. no more in that manner CARLYLE. Hence **Ja·rgoner.**

Jargonelle (dʒāɹgŏne·l). Also **-el.** 1693. [a. F. *jargonelle* 'a very gritty variety of pear', dim. of *jargon* JARGON *sb.*²] An early-ripening variety of pear.

Ja·rgonist. *rare.* 1782. [f. JARGON *sb.*¹ + -IST.] One who affects or uses a jargon.

Jargonize (dʒā·ɹgŏnəiz), *v.* 1803. [f. as prec. + -IZE.] a. *intr.* To talk jargon or a jargon. b. *trans.* To bring (*into* a condition) by means of jargon; to translate into jargon.

†**Jark.** *Old Cant.* 1561. A seal –1818.

‖**Jarl** (yāɹl). Also **yarl.** 1820. [ON. (= OE. *eorl* EARL), orig. 'a man of noble birth'.] An old Norse or Danish chieftain or under-king. *Hist.*

Jarosite (dʒæ·rosəit). 1854. [f. Barranco *Jaroso* in Spain; see -ITE.] *Min.* A hydrous sulphate of iron and potassium, occurring usually in yellowish rhombohedral crystals.

Jar-owl, jarr-owl. 1832. [f. JAR *sb.*¹ IV.] The goatsucker or nightjar (*local*).

Jarrah (dʒæ·ră). 1866. [Anglicized ad. *Jerryhl*, native name.] The mahogany gum-tree (*Eucalyptus marginata*) of West Australia; the durable timber of this tree. Also *attrib.*

Jarring (dʒā·riŋ), *vbl. sb.* 1555. [f. JAR *v.* + -ING¹.] The action of JAR *v.* 1. Harsh dissonance; discordant sound. 2. Vibration caused by concussion 1775. 3. Discordant action 1581. 4. Disputing, wrangling 1574.

1. The j. of a distant door BYRON. 3. A harsh j. of incongruent principles SIR J. REYNOLDS.

Ja·rring, *ppl. a.* 1552. [f. JAR *v.* + -ING².] That jars (see the vb.).

A violent j. Motion 1665. J. int'rests 1762, sectaries 1780. Hence **Ja·rring-ly** *adv.*, **-ness.**

Jarvey (dʒā·ɹvi). *colloq.* Also **jarvy**, jarvie. 1819. [By-form of *Jarvis* or *Jervis*, personal name.] 1. A hackney-coachman 1820. †2. A hackney-coach –1868.

1. The old j. with his many-caped Benjamin SALA.

Jasey (dʒē¹·zi). 1780. [app. = *Jersey*.] Humorous or familiar for a wig, esp. one made of worsted.

Jasmine, -in (dʒæ·smin), **jessamine, -in** (dʒe·sămin). 1548. [Like all the European forms, f. Arab. *yās(a)min*, adopted from Pers.

yāsmīn.] **1. a.** *orig.* The plant *Jasminum officinale*, a climbing shrub with fragrant white flowers, grown in England since the 16th c.; hence, **b.** Any species or plant of the botanical genus *Jasminum*, with white or yellow salver-shaped flowers. Also the flower of any of these.

Next to the Common or White Jasmine, the ordinary 'jessamine' of English literature, the best known is the Yellow-flowered, *J. fruticans*; the total number of species is about ninety.

c. Applied to plants of other genera 1760. **2.** A perfume derived from the flowers of the jasmine or jessamine 1670. **3.** *attrib.*, as *j. flower*, etc. 1644.

1. Where jasmine trails on either side the door CRABBE. **c. Cape J.**, *Gardenia florida* and *G. radicans*; **French J.**, *Calotropis procera*, a shrub found in Southern Asia and Africa; **Wild J.**, of Jamaica, a species of *Pavetta*; of the W. Indies, *Faramea odoratissima* and the genus *Ixora*.

Jasp (dʒasp). Now *rare* or *Obs.* ME. [a. F. *jaspe*, ad. L. *iaspis* JASPIS.] = JASPER 1.

Ja·spachate (-keˈt), **ja·spagate.** 1681. [a. F. *jaspagate*, ad. L. *iaspachates* (Pliny), a. Gr., f. ἴασπις jasper + ἀχάτης AGATE.] *Min.* The same as *agate jasper*; see JASPER *sb.* 1.

Jasper (dʒa·spəɹ), *sb.* [ME. *iaspre*, a. OF. *jaspre*, var. of *jaspe*, ad. L. *iaspis, iaspidem*, a. Gr. ἴασπις, ἰασπιδ- jasper, a word of oriental origin.] **1.** A kind of precious stone. **a.** As tr. Gr. ἴασπις or L. *iaspis*, any bright-coloured chalcedony except carnelian, the most esteemed being green. **b.** Now, an opaque cryptocrystalline variety of quartz, of various colours, usually red, yellow, or brown, due mostly to the presence of iron oxide.

Agate j., 'an agate consisting of j. with veinings and cloudings of chalcedony' (Dana). *Banded, striped*, or *ribbon j.*, a variety having the colours in broad stripes.

2. Short for *jasper-ware* 1825.

Comb.: **j.-opal**, an impure opal containing iron oxide and having the colour of yellow jasper; **j.-pottery, -ware**, a fine kind of porcelain invented by Wedgwood, and used by him for his cameos, etc.

†Ja·sper, *v.* 1620. [f. JASPER *sb.*] **1.** *intr.* To have a clouding or speckling of various colours, like some kinds of jasper; to be variegated. **2.** *trans.* To marble, to speckle 1799. So **Ja·spered** *a.*, marbled, speckled 1620.

Ja·sperated, *ppl. a.* [f. JASPER *sb.* + -ATE + -ED.] 'Mixed with jasper' (Webster).

Jasperize (dʒa·spərəiz), *v.* 1833. [f. as prec. + -IZE.] *trans.* To convert by petrifaction into jasper, or into a form of silica resembling jasper.

Jaspery (dʒa·spəri), *a.* 1797. [f. as prec. + -Y [1].] Of the nature of, resembling, or containing jasper.

†Jaspi·dean, *a.* 1796. [f. as next + -AN.] = next -1807.

Jaspideous (dʒæspi·dǐəs), *a.* 1804. [f. L. *iaspideus* + -OUS.] Of the nature of jasper.

‖**Jaspis** (dʒæ·spis). ME. [L. *iaspis* jasper, a. Gr.] = JASPER *sb.* 1 a; rarely 1 b.

Ja·spoid, *a.* 1855. [f. Gr. ἴασπις JASP + -OID.] Resembling jasper.

†Jaspo·nyx. 1616. [a. L. *iasponyx*, a. Gr., f. ἴασπις jasper + ὄνυξ ONYX.] An onyx partaking of the characters of jasper -1748.

‖**Jataka** (dʒæ·tăkă). 1861. [Skr., = nativity.] A narration of one of the incarnations of Buddha preceding Gautama.

Jauk (dʒǭk), *v. Sc.* 1568. [?] *intr.* To trifle, dawdle.

Jaunce, *v. Obs.* or *arch.* 1593. [prob. f. OF.] **a.** *trans.* ? To make (a horse) prance up and down. **b.** *intr.* ? To prance as a horse.

Spur-gall'd, and tyrd by iauncing Bullingbrooke SHAKS. So **†Jaunce** *sb.* = JAUNT *sb.* 1.

Jaundice (dʒǭ·ndis, dʒā·ndis), *sb.* ME. [a. F. *jaunice, jaunisse*, in 12th c. *jalnice*, lit. 'yellowness', f. *jalne, jaune*; see -ICE. The *d* is an accretion. Often treated as a pl. in *-yes, -ies, -ers*, like *measles, glanders*, etc.] **1.** A morbid condition caused by obstruction of the bile, and marked by yellowness of the conjunctiva, skin, fluids, and tissues, and by constipation, loss of appetite, and weakness. (Called *yellow, black, green j.*, according to the colour of the skin.) **b.** *White j.* = CHLOROSIS; *blue j.* = CYANOSIS 1727. **†2.** A disease of trees in which there is discoloration of the leaves -1669. **3.** *transf.* and *fig.* 1629.

3. The Love of Gold, (That J. of the Soul, Which makes it look so Guilded and so Foul) COWLEY.

Jaundice (dʒǭ·ndis, dʒā·n-), *v.* 1791. [app. f. JAUNDICED.] *trans.* To affect with jaundice; usually *fig.* To affect with envy or jealousy; to tinge the views of.

Her perceptions were jaundiced by passion 1791.

Jaundiced (dʒǭ·ndist, dʒā·n-), *a.* 1640. [f. JAUNDICE *sb.* + -ED [2].] **1.** Affected with jaundice. **2.** Yellow-coloured 1640. **3.** *fig.* 1699.

1. All looks yellow to the jaundic'd eye POPE. **3.** Here jealousy with jaundic'd look appears GARTH.

Jaunt (dʒǭnt, dʒānt), *sb.* 1592. [Goes w. JAUNT *v.*, which appears a little earlier.] **1.** A fatiguing or troublesome journey. (Now only as an ironical use of 2.) **2.** An excursion, trip, journey, *esp.* one taken for pleasure 1678.

1. I arrived here, after a very troublesome j. 1752. **2.** I have been a j. to Oxford H. WALPOLE.

Jaunt (dʒǭnt, dʒānt), *v.* 1570. [?] **†1.** *trans.* (?) To make (a horse) prance up and down; to tire a horse by riding him up and down -1611. **†2.** To carry up and down on a prancing horse; to cart about (*rare*) -1818. **3.** *intr.* Of a person: To trot or trudge about. *Obs.* or *arch.* 1575. **4.** *intr.* To take a jaunt, now, esp., for pleasure 1647. **5.** *intr.* To move jauntily. R. BRIDGES.

Jau·nting-ca:r. 1801. [f. *jaunting* vbl. sb. + CAR.] A light, two-wheeled vehicle, popular in Ireland, now carrying four persons seated two on each side, either back to back (*outside jaunting-car*) or facing each other (*inside jaunting-car*), with a seat in front for the driver.

Jaunty (dʒā·nti, dʒǭ·nti), *a.* 1662. [Formerly *jantee* and *janty*, repr. F. *gentil* (pronounced ʒañti·), noble, gentle, genteel.] **†1.** Well-bred; gentlemanly; genteel -1830. **b.** Of things: Elegant, stylish (? *Obs.*) 1662. **2.** Easy and sprightly in manner; affecting airy self-satisfaction or unconcern 1672. **b.** Lively, brisk 1719.

2. This sort of Woman is usually a janty Slattern STEELE. Hence **Jau·ntily** *adv.* **Jau·ntiness.**

Java (dʒā·vă). 1842. Name of an island in the Malay archipelago. Used *attrib.* in names of things connected with it in origin, as **J. almond**, *Canarium commune*; **J. plum**, *Eugenia Jambolana*; **J. sparrow**, a kind of weaver-bird (*Amadina oryzivora*). Also ellipt., **Java**, a variety of domestic fowl.

Javan (dʒā·văn). 1606. [f. JAVA + -AN.] *adj.* and *sb.* (A native) of Java. So **Javane·se.**

Javel [1] (dʒæ·v'l). ? *Obs.* ME. [?] A low fellow; a rascal.

†Ja·vel [2]. 1601. [a. F. *javelle* = ONF. *gavelle* GAVEL *sb.*[2]] = GAVEL *sb.*[2] -1611.

Javelin (dʒæ·v'lin), *sb.* 1513. [a. F. *javeline*; from radical *javel-*; cf. JAVELOT.] **1.** A light spear thrown with the hand; a dart. Also *fig.* **†2.** A pike or half-pike; a lance -1839. **b.** = JAVELIN-MAN 1. 1849. **†3.** A fish; app. the pilchard or anchovy 1655. **4.** *attrib.* 1513.

1. *fig.* Where the grey rocks strike Their javelins up the azure MRS. BROWNING. Hence **Ja·velin** *v. trans.* to strike or pierce with or as with a j. **Javelinee·r**, a soldier armed with a j.; a javelin-man.

Javelin-man. 1705. [f. JAVELIN *sb.* + MAN.] **1.** One of a body of men in the retinue of a sheriff who carried spears or pikes (JAVELIN *sb.* 2), and escorted the judges at assizes. **2.** A soldier armed with a javelin 1846.

†Ja·velot. 1489. [a. OF. *javelot*, perh. of Celtic origin.] A small spear or javelin thrown with the hand or from a catapult -1708. Hence **†Javelotie·r**, a soldier armed with a j.

Jaw (dʒǭ), *sb.* ME. [Occurs first as *jow(e*, later as *jaw(e*, and for a time as CHAW(E. App. not the F. *joue* cheek. For a hypothetical etymology see N.E.D.] **1.** One of the bones (or sets of bones) forming the framework of the mouth; in *sing.* more often the *lower* or *under jaw*, the inferior maxillary, than the *upper jaw* or superior maxillary. **2.** In *pl.* The bones and associated structures of the mouth including the teeth; hence, the cavity formed by these parts; the mouth, fauces, throat ME. **3.** *transf.* chiefly in *pl.* The two sides of a narrow pass, fissure, gorge, or channel; the narrow entrance into a valley, gulf, or sea; etc. ME. **4.** *pl.* Applied to the seizing or holding members of a machine, etc., arranged in pairs, and usually capable of an opening and closing movement; *spec. Naut.* the semicircular, concave, or forked end of a boom or gaff which clasps the mast with its projecting ends 1789. **5.** *fig.* (in *pl.*) The seizing action or capacity of any devouring agency, as death, time, etc. 1563. **6.** Vulgar loquacity; *esp.* cheeky or impudent talk; also, in vulgar language, A talk, a speech, a lecture, an address 1748.

1. The j. fell, and the eyes were fixed 1866. **2.** From his wide Jaws His Tongue unmoisten'd hangs SOMERVILLE. **5.** To winne renowne Euen in the iawes of danger, and of death SHAKS. **6.** Phr. *To hold* or *stop one's j.* (possibly at first literal).

Comb.: **j.-bit** (*U.S.*), a short bar placed beneath a journal box to unite the two pedestals in a car-truck; **-breaker**, a word hard to pronounce (colloq.); also, a machine with powerful jaws for crushing ore, etc.; **-rope** (*Naut.*), the rope which fastens the two horns or prongs of the boom or gaff round the mast; **-tooth**, a molar tooth; **-wedge** (*U.S.*), a wedge to tighten the axle-box in an axle-guard.

Jaw (dʒǭ), *v.* 1612. [f. prec.] **†1.** *trans.* To use the jaws upon. **2.** *slang.* **a.** *intr.* To use the vocal organs. (A vulgar or contemptuous equivalent for *speak.*) 1748. **b.** *trans.* To scold, lecture 1810. **3.** *To j. away*: to cut to the shape of jaws, or in a concave curve 1802.

Jawbation: see JOBATION.

Jaw-bone, jawbone (dʒǭ·bōun). 1489. [f. JAW *sb.* + BONE.] Any bone of the jaws; *spec.* each of the two forming the lower jaw.

Jawed (dʒǭd), *a.* 1529. [f. JAW *sb.* + -ED [2].] Having or furnished with jaws.

Jaw·-fall. 1660. **1.** Falling of the jaw; *fig.* dejection (*rare*). **†2.** Dislocation or subluxation of the lower jaw so that it cannot be shut. RUSH.

Jaw·-fa:llen, *a.* 1603. [f. JAW *sb.* + *fallen* pa. pple.] Chop-fallen; dejected.

†Jawn, obs. var. of CHAWN *sb.* and *v.*

Jawy (dʒǭ·i), *a. rare.* 1654. [f. JAW *sb.* + -Y [1].] Of or pertaining to the jaw; forceful in language.

Jay (dʒeⁱ). ME. [a. OF. *jay*, mod.F. *geai* = med.L. *gaius, gaia* (Papias). Not identical with F. *gai.*] **1.** A common European bird, *Garrulus glandarius*, in structure, etc. resembling the magpie, but in habits arboreal, and having a plumage in which vivid tints of blue are heightened by bars of jet-black and patches of white. **b.** Applied to birds of the sub-family *Garrulinæ* or family *Garrulidæ*, among which are the *Blue Jay* (*Cyanurus cristatus*) of N. America, the *Canada Jay* (*Perisoreus canadensis*), the *Grey Jay, Green Jay*, etc. 1688. **2.** Applied to: **a.** The Jackdaw; **b.** The Cornish chough, also called *Cornish jay*; **c.** The Missel thrush (*local*) 1484. **3.** *transf.* **a.** An impertinent chatterer. **b.** A showy, flashy, or light woman. **c.** A person absurdly dressed. **d.** A simpleton. 1523.

3. Some Iay of Italy..hath betraid him SHAKS. **d. j.-walker** (orig. *U.S.*), one who crosses a street without regard to traffic regulations.

Jay·-bird. 1851. A jay: in parts of England, the Common Jay; in U.S., the Blue Jay.

Jay·-haw:ker. *U.S.* 1865. A name given to the irregular soldiers who fought in and around eastern Kansas, in the free soil conflict, and the early part of the American civil war; hence, a raiding guerrilla.

Jazerant, jesserant (dʒæ·zĕrănt, dʒe·s-). Now only *Hist.* ME. [a. OF. *jaseran, -ant, jaz-, jac-, jesseran*, etc., orig. an adj.; of Saracen origin. According to Diez, prob. identical with Sp. *jazarino* Algerian, f. Arab. (*al-*)*jazirah* 'the island', in pl. *Al-jazā'-ir* Algiers.] 'A light coat of armour composed of splints or small plates of metal rivetted to each other or to a lining of some stout material' (Fairholt).

Jazz (dʒæz), *sb.* 1918. [American Negro.] A kind of music in syncopated time, as played by negro bands in U.S. Hence, any syncopated dance music; also, a dance to this music; attrib. as *j.-band, -dance, -music, -step.* Also applied to fantastic designs or vivid patterns. Hence **Jazz** *v. intr.* to dance jazz; *trans.* to arrange as jazz; **Ja·zzy** *a.*, resembling jazz.

Jealous (dʒe·ləs), *a.* [ME. *gelos*, etc., a. OF. *gelos* (mod. *jaloux, -ouse*):—med.L. *zelosus*, f. late L. *zelus*, a. Gr. ζῆλος zeal, jealousy; see -OUS.] †1. Vehement in wrath, desire, or devotion -1661. †2. Ardently amorous; fond, lustful -1555. 3. Vigilant in guarding; suspiciously careful or watchful. Const. *of* (*for, over*). ME. 4. Troubled by the belief, suspicion, or fear that the good which one desires to gain or keep for oneself has been or may be diverted to another; resentful towards another on account of known or suspected rivalry: **a.** in love or affection, esp. in sexual love ME.; **b.** in respect of success or advantage ME. **c.** In biblical language, said of God: Having a love which will tolerate no unfaithfulness in the beloved object ME. 5. Suspicious; apprehensive of evil, fearful. Now *dial.* 1532. †**b.** Doubtful, mistrustful -1682. 6. Suspiciously vigilant to prevent something (expressed or understood); vigilant in scrutinizing 1601. Also *transf.*

1. I haue beene very iealous for the Lord God of hostes 1 *Kings* xix. 10. 3. The people, j. of their hardly-won liberties BRYCE. 4. a. So young a husband's j. fears BYRON. b. Leading persons in the state were j. of his glory THIRLWALL. c. For I the Lorde thy God am a gelouse God COVERDALE *Exod.* xx. 5. 5. My master is very j. of the pestilence 1607. b. *Jul. C.* I. ii. 162. 6. Measures [of weight, etc.] were subject to j. supervision ROGERS. Phr. †*Jealous glass*, an old name for glass which is translucent but not transparent. Hence **Jea·lous·ly** *adv.*, **-ness.**

†**Jealous-hood.** So printed in 4th Fol. Shaks. (1685), *Rom. & Jul.* IV. iv. 13, and taken by some as a single word = 'jealousy'.

Jealousy (dʒe·ləsi). ME. [a. OF. *gelosie, jalousie*, f. *gelos* JEALOUS; see -Y [3].] The quality of being jealous. †1. Anger, wrath, indignation -1649. †2. Devotion, eagerness, anxiety to serve -1565. 3. Solicitude or anxiety for the preservation or well-being of something ME. 4. The state of mind arising from the suspicion, apprehension, or knowledge of rivalry: **a.** in love ME.; **b.** in respect of success or advantage ME.; **c.** see JEALOUS 4 c. ME. 5. Suspicion; apprehension of evil; mistrust. Now *dial.* ME.

1. How long, Lord, wilt thou be angry, for euer? shall thy ielousie burne like fire? *Ps.* lxxix. 5. 4. a. Gelousy [is mightie] as the hell COVERDALE *Song Sol.* viii. 6. b. Local jealousies FREEMAN. c. They prouoked him to iealousie with strange gods *Deut.* xxxii. 16.

Jeames. 1600. †**a.** Obs. f. JAMES. **b.** (After Thackeray), A ludicrous name for a liveried footman (pron. dʒīmz).

Jean (dʒēⁱn). 1488. [app. same as ME. *Gene, Jene*, etc. in OF. *Janne(s*, mod.F. *Gênes*, med.L. *Janua*, Genoa, a city of Italy.] †1. Genoa; *attrib.* = GENOESE -1607. 2. A twilled cotton cloth; a kind of fustian. Orig. *jene fustian*, shortened to *jean*. In U.S. *jeans*. 1567. **b.** *attrib.*, as *j. cap*, etc. 1801.

Jear(e, Jeat(e, obs. ff. JEER *sb.*[1], JET.

Jebusite (dʒe·biŭzəit). 1535. Name of a tribe of Canaanites, dispossessed of Jerusalem by David. In 17th c., a nickname for a Jesuit. Hence **Jebusite** *v.*, **Jebusi·tic, -i·tical, -itish** *a.*

Jedburgh, Jeddart staff: see STAFF *sb.* Whence **Jedwood-** (Scott) or **Jeddart-axe**, which is due to a misapprehension.

Jee (dʒī), *v. Sc.* 1722. [? Cf. GEE *v.*] 1. *intr.* To move, to stir; to move to one side; to move to and fro 1727. 2. *trans.* To cause to move; to move aside, shift, or displace slightly. Hence **Jee** *sb.* a move, motion 1829.

Jee, *adv.* and *int.* 1785. **a.** The verb-stem used advb. or as an exclam. **b.** = GEE *int.*, a word of command to a horse.

Jeer (dʒīᵊɹ), *sb.*[1] 1495. [?] *Naut.* Tackle for hoisting and lowering the lower yards. (Usu. in *pl.*) **b.** *Comb.*, as *j.-capstan*, etc.

Jeer (dʒīᵊɹ), *sb.*[2] 1579. [f. next.] 1. An act of jeering; a scoff, flout, gibe, taunt 1625. †**b.** The action of jeering; mockery, scoffing -1753. †2. Phr. *In a jeer*, (?) in a huff. NORTH.

1. A blow is much sooner forgotten than a j. SPURGEON.

Jeer (dʒīᵊɹ), *v.* 1553. [?] 1. *intr.* To speak in derision or mockery; to scoff derisively (*at*). 2. *trans.* To address or treat with scornful derision; to deride, flout 1590.

1. Here Grub-street Geese presume to joke and j. GRAY. 2. Yea, dost thou ieere & flowt me in the teeth? SHAKS. Hence **Jee·rer. Jee·ringly** *adv.*

Jeff (dʒef), *sb. Circus slang.* A rope. DICKENS.

Jeffersonian (dʒefəɹsōᵘ·niăn). *U.S.* 1856. [f. Thomas *Jefferson*, President of the U.S. 1801–1809.] *adj.* Pertaining to President Jefferson, or holding his political doctrines (now called DEMOCRATIC). *sb.* A supporter or follower of Jefferson; a Democrat 1880.

Jeffersonite (dʒe·fəɹsənəit). 1822. [Named after President *Jefferson*; see prec. and -ITE.] *Min.* A greenish-black variety of pyroxene, containing some zinc and manganese.

Jeg (dʒeg). 1875. [Cf. *jedge*, a Sc. form of GAUGE.] A templet or guage for verifying shapes of parts in gun and gun-stock making.

Jehad: see JIHAD.

‖**Jehovah** (dʒĭhōᵘ·vă). 1530. [The Eng. and common European representation, since 16th c., of the Hebrew divine name (IHUH, JHVH). This word (the 'sacred tetragrammaton'), as being too sacred for utterance, was pointed in the O.T. by the Masoretes with the vowels ᵉ (= a), ō, ā, of *ădōnāi*, as a direction to the reader to substitute ADONAI for the 'ineffable name'. Students of Hebrew at the Revival of Letters took these vowels as those of the sacred name itself, whence, in L. spelling, IeHoVa(H), i.e. *Iehoua(h)*. It is now held that the original name was IaHUe(H), i.e. *Jahve(h* = *Yahwe(h*, 'he that is', 'the self-existent', or 'the one ever coming into manifestation', but this meaning is conjectural.] The principal and personal name of God in the Old Testament; in English versions, 'the LORD'. Hence in mod. Christian use = God, the Almighty.

I appeared vnto Abraham Isaac and Iacob an allmightie God: but in my name Iehouah [*Wyclif* Adonay] was I not knowne vnto them TINDALE *Exod.* vi. 3.

Jehovist (dʒĭhōᵘ·vist). 1753. [f. JEHOV(AH + -IST.] †1. One who holds that the vowel-points annexed to the word Jehovah in Heb. represent the actual vowels of the word; opp. to ADONIST. 2. A name applied to the author (or authors) of those non-Deuteronomic parts of the Hexateuch in which the divine name is rendered 'Jehovah'; opp. to ELOHIST. (Now usu. JAHVIST or *Yahwist*.) 1844.

Hence **Jehovi·stic** *a.* of or pertaining to the J. or Jehovists, characterized by the use of the name 'Jehovah'; also (rarely) pertaining to the religion of Jehovah. In both senses now usu. JAHVISTIC (or *Yahwistic*).

Jehu (dʒī·hiu). *joc.* 1682. [See 2 Kings ix. 20.] **a.** A fast or furious driver. **b.** A driver, a coachman. Hence as *vb.*, to drive furiously 1779.

Jejunal (dʒĭdʒū·năl), *a.* 1878. [f. JEJUNUM + -AL.] Of or pertaining to the jejunum.

Jejune (dʒĭdʒū·n), *a.* 1615. [ad. L. *jejunus* fasting.] †1. Without food, fasting; hungry -1754. 2. Deficient in nourishing or substantial qualities; thin, scanty; meagre, unsatisfying; (of land) poor, barren 1646. 3. Unsatisfying to the mind or soul; dull, insipid, dry; thin, poor; wanting in substance. (The prevailing sense.) 1615.

3. Empty and j. speculations 1671. A very j. and unsatisfactory reason BLACKSTONE. Hence **Jeju·ne·ly** *adv.*, **-ness.**

Jejunity (dʒĭdʒū·nĭti). 1623. [ad. L. *jejunitas*, f. *jejunus* fasting.] The quality of being jejune; jejuneness.

‖**Jejunum** (dʒĭdʒū·nŏm). 1541. [Mediæval application of L. *jejunum*, neut. of *jejunus* fasting (sc. *intestinum*). So in F.] *Anat.* The second part of the small intestine, between the duodenum and ileum.

‖**Jelick** (dʒe·lik, *prop.* ye·lĕk). 1816. [Turk. *yelek* waistcoat.] A vest or bodice worn by Turkish women.

Jell (dʒel), *v. U.S. colloq.* 1830. [f. JELLY *sb.*] To congeal or jelly.

Jellied (dʒe·lid), *a.* 1593. [f. JELLY *sb.* and *v.* + -ED.] 1. Turned into jelly; congealed, coagulated. †2. Flavoured with jelly, sweet. CLEVELAND.

Jelly (dʒe·li), *sb.* [ME. *gelĕ*, a. F. *gelée* frost, also jelly:—L. *gelata* frozen, pa. pple. of *gelare*; see -ADE.] 1. An article of food, consisting chiefly of gelatin, obtained from various animal tissues by boiling and subsequent cooling, having a soft homogeneous consistence and usually semitransparent. Also, later, a preparation of the juice of fruit, etc., thickened into a similar consistence. †**b.** The substance GELATIN -1855. 2. *gen.* Anything of the consistence of jelly 1600. **b.** *spec.* Applied to the alga *Nostoc*, which appears as a jelly-like mass on dry soil after rain, and was supposed to be the remains of a fallen star 1641. **c.** A mixture of gelatin and glycerin used for mounting microscopic objects 1856.

1. The J...of Red Cabbage ARBUTHNOT. Thick j. made from chickens 1850. 2. I could have beaten the Woman into a J. D'URFEY. b. Like that falling Meteor, there she lies, A J. cold on Earth SOMERVILLE.

Comb.: **j.-bag**, a bag for straining j. through; **-mould**; **-plant**, an Australian seaweed, *Eucheuma speciosum*, from which j., size, cement, etc. are made.

Jelly (dʒe·li), *v.* 1601. [f. JELLY *sb.*] 1. *intr.* To come to the consistence of jelly; to congeal, coagulate. 2. *trans.* To convert into jelly; to cause to 'set'; to reduce to the consistence of jelly 1601.

Je·lly-fish. 1707. †1. An oceanic fish of the genus *Plagyodus* or *Alepisaurus*, family *Scopelidæ*. 2. Pop. name of various acalephs, medusas, or sea-nettles, from their gelatinous structure 1841. Also *fig.* Also *attrib.*

‖**Jemadar** (dʒe·mădāɹ). *E. Ind.* Also jemi-, jamadar. 1763. [Urdū, f. Pers. (Arab.) *jamaᶜ* collection (of men) + Pers. *dār* holder.] A native officer in a Sepoy regiment, corresponding to a lieutenant; also, a name for the head of a body of police, etc., or of servants. Hence **Jemadary**, the office of a j. 1863.

Jemima (dʒĕməi·mă). 1899. [Female personal name.] 1. A made-up tie. 2. *pl.* Elastic-sided boots 1902.

Jemmy (dʒe·mi), *sb.* Also **jimmy.** 1753. [A pet-form of James; cf. JEMMY *a.*] †1. A dandy; a finical fellow -1764. †2. A kind of riding-boot; also *j. boot* -1771. 3. A great-coat. DICKENS. 4. A crow-bar used by burglars, generally made in sections 1811. 5. A sheep's head as a dish 1836.

1. Phr. *Jemmy Jessamy* (*Jessamine*) attrib., dandified, foppish, effeminate. See JESSAMY. 5. You're all jaw like a sheep's jimmy HENLEY & STEVENSON.

Jemmy (dʒe·mi), *a. Obs.* exc. *dial.* Also gemmy, jimmy, etc. 1750. [deriv. of *Jim*, GIM *a.*] Spruce, neat; dexterous.

A smart cock'd beaver and a j. cane LAMB. Hence **Je·mmily** *adv.* **Je·mminess.**

Jenequen, var. HENEQUEN [Sp. *jeniquen*].

‖**Je ne sais quoi** (ʒənsękwà). 1656. [Fr., = I know not what.] An inexpressible something.

Jennet (dʒe·nĕt). 1463. [a. F. *genet*, a. Sp. *jinete*, †*ginete* light horseman. In Fr. and Eng. transferred from the horseman to the horse.] 1. A small Spanish horse. 2. A (Spanish) light horseman. *Obs.* exc. *Hist.* 1676.

1. Isabella, royally attired, rode on a Spanish j. PRESCOTT.

Jenneting (dʒe·nĕtiŋ). 1601. [app. f. F. *Jean* or *Jeannet*, in *pomme de Saint-Jean*, after *sweeting*, etc.] A kind of early apple.

Jenny (dʒe·ni). 1600. [A familiar or pet form of *Janet* (or of *Jane*), serving as a feminine of *Jack*, and hence used in similar applications.]

I. 1. The female name; hence, sometimes applied derisively to a man. (*Mod. Sc.*) 2. Used as a prefix to denote a female animal, as *j.-ass, j.-hooper*, and occas. applied without reference to sex 1600. **b.** Short for *j. ass, j. wren* 1808. 3. *Creeping J.*, the plant Moneywort 1882.

II. 1. Short for SPINNING-JENNY 1796. 2. A locomotive crane which runs backwards and forwards, and moves heavy weights 1861. 3. *Billiards.* A stroke made by a losing hazard into the middle or top pocket, from a ball lying near to the cushion 1856.

Jenny wren (dʒe·ni re·n). 1648. [See JENNY I. 2.] A pop. name for the wren; sometimes regarded in nursery lore as the wife, bride, or sweetheart of Robin Redbreast.

Jeofail (dʒe·feil), *sb.* 1541. [Anglo-Fr. *jeo fail, jo faill.* I am at fault, I mistake.] *Law.* A mistake or oversight in pleading; also, an acknowledgement of such error. *Hist.* †b. *transf.* A mistake –1828. Hence †**Jeo·fail** *v. intr.* to fail to meet an obligation 1599.

Jeopard (dʒe·pǎɹd), *v.* ME. [Back-formation from JEOPARDY.] 1. *trans.* To put in jeopardy; to expose to loss, injury, or death; to hazard. †b. *intr.* (for *refl.*) To run the risk; to venture –1598. †2. *trans.* To stake, bet –1580.
1. As ready to j. his life and fortune..as ever his.. forefathers had been FREEMAN. Hence **Jeo·parder**, one who puts in jeopardy.

Jeopardize (dʒe·pǎɹdəiz), *v.* 1646. [f. prec. or JEOPARD-Y + -IZE.] *trans.* = prec. 1.
That he should j. his wilful head Only for spite at me SIR H. TAYLOR.

†**Jeo·pardous,** *a.* 1451. Also **-ious** (1502). [f. JEOPARD-Y + -OUS.] 1. Fraught with risk –1661. 2. Venturesome –1593.
1. Shippes sailyng into so jeoperdous and ferre parties HEN. VII. 2. A lustye and iuperdous Knyght 1494. Hence †**Jeo·pardous-ly** *adv.*, **-ness.**

Jeopardy (dʒe·pǎɹdi), *sb.* [ME. *iuparti,* etc., a. OF. *iu parti,* later *ieu* (*geu*) *parti,* lit. 'divided play or game, even game', hence 'uncertain chance', a term of chess, etc.] †1. *Chess,* etc. A problem –1500. †b. A device, trick, stratagem –1536. †2. A position in a game, undertaking, etc. in which the chances of winning and losing are even; uncertainty –1597. 3. Risk of loss, harm, or death ME.
3. Why stand we in ieopardy euery houre? 1 *Cor.* xv. 30. Hence **Jeo·pardy** *v.* = JEOPARD *v.* 1.

Jequirity (dʒėkwi·riti). 1882. [ad. Fr., ad. Tupi-Guarani.] A twining shrub, *Abrus precatorius,* the particoloured beans of which are used as ornaments, etc., and in medicine.

‖ **Jerboa** (dʒəɹbōu·ǎ, dʒə̄·ɹbo̜ǎ). 1662. [mod. L., a. Arab.] A small rodent quadruped, *Dipus sagitta,* found in the deserts of Africa; it is of the size of a rat, has very long hind legs and short fore legs, and a long tufted tail, and is a remarkable jumper. Hence, any Jumping-mouse of the genus *Dipus* or family *Dipodidæ.*
Comb. **J.-mouse,** a N. Amer. rodent of the genus *Dipodomys,* one of the pouched mice or kangaroo-rats of the South-western U.S. and Mexico.

Jere, in *good jere,* altered f. GOODYEAR, q. v. SCOTT.

Jereed: see JERID.

Jeremiad (dʒerǐ·məi·æ̆d). Also **-ade.** 1780. [a. F. *jérémiade,* f. *Jérémie,* L. *Jeremias* Jeremiah, in reference to his Lamentations in the O.T.] A lamentation; a writing or speech in a strain of grief or distress; a doleful complaint; a complaining tirade.
I could sit down, and mourn, and utter doleful Jeremiads without end HELPS.

Jerfalcon, etc., obs. f. GERFALCON, etc.

Jericho (dʒe·riko). 1635. [A town in Palestine; see 2 Sam. x. 5.] Used in slang or colloq. phrases for a place of retirement or concealment, or a place far out of the way.
Let them all goe to J., And ne're be seen againe 1648.

‖ **Jerid, jereed** (dʒěrī·d), *sb.* Also **jerreed, jerrid,** etc. 1662. [Arab.] A wooden javelin, about five feet long, used in games by Persian, Turkish, and Arabian horsemen. Also, a game in which this is used. Hence †**Jeri·d** *v. intr.*, to throw the jerid 1698.

Jerk (dʒə̄ɹk), *sb.*[1] 1555. [App. echoic; see also YERK.] †1. A stripe, a lash –1796; *fig.* a lash of sarcasm –1741. 2. A sharp sudden pull, throw, push, thrust, or twist 1575. b. (in pl. *the jerks*). Involuntary spasmodic movements of the limbs or features, esp. resulting from religious excitement 1805. 3. *fig.* A short sharp witty speech; a sally 1588. †4. A short abrupt series of notes (of a bird) –1794.
2. His Jade gave him a Jerk B. JONS. b. These Methodis' sets people crazy with the jerks 1874. 3. Sir, use your jerks and quillets at the bar BROME.

Jerk, *sb.*[2] 1799. [f. JERK *v.*[2]; see also JERKY *sb.*[2]] Jerked meat, charqui.

Jerk (dʒə̄ɹk), *v.*[1] 1550. [App. echoic; see JERK *sb.*[1]] †1. *trans.* To strike with or as with a whip, switch, or wand –1709; †*fig.* to lash with satire or ridicule –1710. 2. To move (anything) by a sharp suddenly arrested motion; to give a sudden thrust, push, pull, or twist to 1589. b. To throw or toss with a quick sharp motion 1786. 3. *fig.* To utter (words or sounds) abruptly, or sharply and shortly 1602. 4. *intr.* To give a jerk; to jerk a bow or nod; to move with a jerk 1606. b. To move the limbs or features spasmodically 1874. †5. *intr.* To sneer, carp, gird –1704. †6. *intr.* To utter a short sharp abrupt series of notes –1773.
2. He jerked the horse's mouth roughly 1875. 4. The door jerked open 1833. 5. You must be jerking at the times, forsooth 1643.

Jerk (dʒə̄ɹk), *v.*[2] 1707. Also †**jirk.** [Corrupted from American Sp. *charquear,* f. *charque, charqui,* ad. Quichua (Peruv.) *ccharqui* 'dried flesh, unsalted, in long strips'.] *trans.* To cure (meat, esp. beef) by cutting it into long thin slices and drying it in the sun.

Jerker (dʒə̄·ɹkəɹ). 1596. [f. JERK *v.*[1] + -ER[1].] 1. One who jerks, esp. from religious excitement. 2. *U.S.* A fish, the river-chub, *Hybopsis kentuckiensis,* also called *hornyhead* 1884.

Jerker, variant of JERQUER.

Jerkin[1] (dʒə̄·ɹkin). *arch.* or *Hist.* 1519. [?] A close-fitting jacket, jersey, or short coat, often made of leather. Still used *dial.* for a waistcoat, an under vest, or a loose jacket.

†**Je·rkin**[2]. 1539. [? dim. of *jer-* in *jerfalcon,* GERFALCON.] The male of the gerfalcon.

†**Je·rkin**[3], *sb.* or *a.* 1612. In *j. beef* = jerked beef (see JERK *v.*[2]) –1657.

Jerkin-head. 1842. [? for *jerking-,* from JERK *v.*[1]] *Arch.* (See quot.)
'A form of roofing which is half-gable, half-hip. The gable generally goes as high as the ties of the couples, above which the roof is hipped off' (*Chambers' Encycl.* V. 697).

Jerky (dʒə̄·ɹki), *a.* and *sb.*[1] 1858. [f. JERK *sb.*[1] + -Y.] **A.** *adj.* Characterized by jerks or sudden abrupt or twitching movements; often *fig.* spasmodic.
Talkers that have what may be called j. minds 1858. A j. style 1887. Hence **Je·rkily** *adv.*, **Je·rkiness.**
B. *sb.* A springless wagon. *U.S.* 1884.

Je·rky, *sb.*[2] *U.S.* 1890. [ad. American Sp. *charqui, charque*; see CHARQUI and JERK *v.*[2]] Jerked beef.

Jerm-, obs. sp. of GERM-, in various words.

Jeroboam (dʒerǒbōu·ǎm). 1816. [So called in allusion to *Jeroboam* 'a mighty man of valour' (1 Kings xi. 28), 'who made Israel to sin' (xiv. 16).] A large bowl or goblet; a very large wine-bottle.

Jero·nymite, var. of HIERONYMITE.

Jeropiga, -pigia, var. of GEROPIGA.

Jerque (dʒə̄ɹk), *v.* Also †**jirk.** 1819. [Referred to It. *cercare* to search, but historical evidence is wanting.] *trans.* To search (a vessel) for unentered goods; to examine or search a ship's papers in order to ascertain whether the captain's and the customs officer's lists of cargo agree, and to see that all the cargo has been duly entered and described.

Jerquer (dʒə̄·ɹkəɹ). 1681. [See prec. vb.] A custom-house officer, a searcher; in the London Custom House, A clerical officer who examines and checks a ship's papers, to see that all the cargo has been duly entered and described.

Jerry (dʒe·ri), *sb.* 1834. [Familiar var. of *Jeremy* or *Jeremiah.*] 1. A machine for shearing cloth 1883. 2. Short for **j.-shop**: A low beer-house 1834. 3. Short for **j. hat**: A round felt hat 1841. 4. Short for JERRY-BUILDER 1890.

Je·rry, *a.* 1882. [prob. short for JERRY-BUILT.] Constructed unsubstantially of bad materials.

Je·rry-bui·lder. 1881. [?] A speculating builder who 'runs up' unsubstantially built houses of inferior materials. So **Je·rry-bui·lding. Je·rry-bui·lt** *a.* built unsubstantially of bad materials; built to sell.

Jersey[1] (dʒə̄·ɹzi). 1583. The name of the largest of the Channel Islands; used *attrib.* and *ellipt.* 1. *attrib.* Of Jersey; of Jersey worsted. 2. *sb.* a. Jersey knitted work; Jersey worsted; worsted generally 1587. †b. Wool that has been combed and is ready for spinning –1790. 3. A woollen knitted close-fitting tunic, with short or long sleeves, worn either as an outer tunic, or as an under-shirt or under-vest 1836. 4. One of a breed of cattle of the Channel Islands; a cow of the island of Jersey 1881.

Je·rsey[2]. *U.S.* 1770. = New Jersey.

Jert, *sb., v.* Now *dial.* 1540. = JERK *sb.*[1], *v.*[1]

Jerusalem (dʒerū·sălěm). 1615. The city in Palestine so named; the Holy City. Hence *attrib.* or *ellipt.* **J. letters,** letters or symbols tattooed on the arm or body in memory of a visit or pilgrimage to J.; **J. pony,** a donkey (in reference to Christ's riding into J. on an ass). See also ARTICHOKE, CROSS, etc.

Jervine (dʒə̄·ɹvəin). 1838. [Formerly also *jervina*; f. Sp. *jerva* the poisonous root of *Veratrum.*] *Chem.* An alkaloid occurring, together with veratrine, in the roots of *Veratrum album* and *V. viride.* Also called *jervia.*

Jess (dʒes), *sb.*; in pl. **jesses** (dʒe·sėz). [ME. *ges,* a. OF. *ges* (*gez, getz*) nom., sing. and pl., of *get,* mod.F. *jet* cast, JET *sb.*[3]:—L. *jactus* throw, cast, f. *jacĕre* to throw.] A short strap of leather, silk, etc., fastened round each of the legs of a hawk used in falconry; usually bearing on its free end a small ring or *varvel* to which the swivel of the leash is attached. Also *fig.*
Their talk was all of training, terms of art, Diet and seeling, jesses, leash and lure TENNYSON. Hence **Jess** *v. trans.* to put the jesses on (a hawk) 1860.

Jessamine, var. of JASMINE, q. v.

†**Jessamy.** 1633. [Corruption of *jessamine.*] 1. = JASMINE 1. –1733. 2. A dandy, fop. See JEMMY *sb.* –1802.

Jessant (dʒe·sǎnt), *a.* 1572. [In sense 1, a. OF. *gesant* (later *gisant*) lying, pr. pple. of *gésir* :—L. *jacēre* to lie. In sense 2, ?.] *Her.* 1. Said of a charge represented as lying over another and partly covering it 1610. 2. Said when an animal is represented with a branch, flower, etc. in its mouth or as if issuing from it.
2. *Jessant* stands between the names of the two charges, e. g. *a hart j. a branch of dittany.*

Jesse (dʒe·si). 1456. [Name of the father of David (1 Sam. xvi. 12).] A genealogical tree representing the genealogy of Christ from 'the root of Jesse' (cf. Isa. xi. 1); used in churches as a decoration for a wall, window, vestment, etc., or in the form of a large branched candlestick; *attrib.* **J. window.**

Jessed (dʒest), *a.* 1610. [f. JESS *sb.* or *v.* + -ED.] Of a hawk: Furnished with or wearing jesses; in *Her.* having the jesses of a specified tincture.

Jest (dʒest), *sb.* ME. [a. OF. *geste, jeste,* ad. L. *gesta*; see GEST *sb.*[1], of which this is a var. sp.] †1. A notable deed or action –1604. †2. A narrative of exploits; orig. in verse. ME. only. †3. An idle tale –1620. 4. A mocking speech; a taunt, a jeer. Also, A piece of raillery or banter. 1548. 5. A saying (or *transf.* recital) intended to excite laughter; a witticism, joke 1551. 6. a. Trifling sport, fun 1551. b. Jesting, merriment; ridicule 1597. c. A jocular affair 1732. 7. A sportive action, prank, or frolic; a practical joke. Now *rare.* 1566. †8. A pageant, masque, masquerade –1601. 9. A laughing-stock 1598.
1. Settyng furthe the iestes, actes and deedes, of the nobilitie HALL. 4. Too bitter is thy iest SHAKS. 5. Let not thy laughter handsell thy owne J. QUARLES. 6. a. His eyes do drop no teares: his prayres are in iest SHAKS. b. Alas poore Yorick,..a fellow of infinite Iest SHAKS. c. Life is a j., and all things shew it GAY. 7. Hold the sweete iest vp SHAKS. 9. Why then make sport at me, then let me be your iest SHAKS.

Jest (dʒest), *v.* 1526. [f. prec. : = GEST *v.*[1], of which this is a var. sp.] 1. *intr.* To utter gibes or taunts; to scoff, jeer, mock. b. *trans.* To jeer at; to ridicule; to banter 1721. 2. *intr.* To trifle 1530. 3. *intr.* To make witty or humorous remarks; to joke 1553. †b. *intr.* To disport oneself –1632.
2. Verily I do not iest with you; there came newes from him last night SHAKS. 3. Because Mirth is agreeable, another thinks fit eternally to j. STEELE. b. As gentle, and as iocond, as to iest, Go I to fight SHAKS.

Jest-book (dʒe·stbuk). 1750. [f. JEST *sb.*] A book of jests or amusing stories.

Jester (dʒe·stəɹ). ME. [var. sp. of GESTER, or f. JEST *v.* + -ER[1].] 1. A professional reciter of romances (*arch.*). 2. A mimic, buffoon, or merry-andrew; esp. one maintained in a prince's court or nobleman's household 1510. 3. One who jests, or speaks or acts in jest; a joker 1510.

1. A small whole length of Archee, the King's j. H. WALPOLE. 3. Iesters do oft proue Prophets SHAKS.

Je·stful, *a.* 1831. [-FUL.] Full of jesting.

Jesting (dʒe·stiŋ), *vbl. sb.* 1526. [f. JEST *v.* + -ING [1].] The action of JEST *v.*; pleasantry; trifling; ridicule.

J., said Arcite, suits but ill with pain DRYDEN.

Je·sting, *ppl. a.* 1551. [f. as prec. + -ING [2].] That jests; jocose; trifling; †jeering.

What is Truth; said j. Pilate BACON. **Je·stingly** *adv.* 1568.

†**Je·suist.** *rare.* 1582. [-IST.] = next -1645.

Jesuit (dʒe·ziu,it), *sb.* Also †**-ite.** 1550. [ad. mod.L. *Jesuita*, f. *Jesus* + *-ita*; see -ITE [1].] 1. A member of the 'Society of Jesus', a Roman Catholic order founded by Ignatius Loyola in 1534.

The object of the Society was to support and defend the Roman Church against the 16th-c. Reformers, and to propagate the faith among the heathen. The stringent organization of the order soon made it very powerful. Its secret power, and the casuistical principles maintained by many of its representatives, and generally ascribed to the body as a whole, have rendered its name odious not only in English, but in French and other languages, and have given rise to sense 2, and to the opprobrious sense attached to *Jesuitical*, *Jesuitry*, and other derivatives.

2. *transf.* A dissembling person; a prevaricator 1640. 3. A dress worn by ladies in the 18th century, a kind of indoor morning gown 1767. 4. *attrib.* or *adj.* That is a Jesuit; of or belonging to the Society of Jesus; Jesuitical 1660.

1. The diuels agents .. by the name of Iesuites STUBBES. Teach Jesuits that have travell'd far, to Lye, Teach Fire to burn, and Winds to blow COWLEY. 2. To humble the pride of some Jesuits, who call themselves Quakers 1777.

Comb. (genitival): **Jesuits' bark**, the bark of species of *Cinchona*, Peruvian bark (introduced into Europe from the Jesuit Missions in S. America); **Jesuits' drops**, 'name given to a preparation of garlic, Peruvian balsam, and sarsaparilla' (Mayne); **Jesuits' nut**, the seed of *Trapa natans*; †**Jesuits' powder**, an old name for powdered Peruvian bark; **Jesuits' tea**, an infusion of the leaves of *Psoralea glandulosa*, a S. Amer. leguminous shrub.

†**Je·suit**, *v.* 1600. [f. prec. sb.] 1. *intr.* To act the Jesuit (*rare*). 2. *trans.* To make a Jesuit of -1645. 3. To dose with Jesuits' bark (*nonce-use*). HARVEY.

†**Je·suited**, *a.* 1600. [f. JESUIT *sb.* or *v.* + -ED.] Made or become a Jesuit; imbued with the principles or character of the Jesuits; Jesuitical -1834.

Jesuitess (dʒe·ziu,itės). 1600. [f. JESUIT *sb.* + -ESS.] A female Jesuit; one of an order of nuns established on the principles of the Jesuits, but suppressed by Pope Urban VIII.

Jesuitic, -al (dʒeziu,i·tik, -ăl), *a.* 1600. [f. as prec.; see -IC, -ICAL.] 1. Of or pertaining to the Jesuits; belonging to the Society of Jesus; Jesuit. 2. Dissembling; practising equivocation or mental reservation of truth 1613. Hence **Jesui·tically** *adv.* 1600.

Jesuitism (dʒe·ziu,iti:z'm). 1609. [f. as prec. + -ISM.] 1. The principles or practice of the Jesuits. 2. Principles or practice such as those ascribed to the Jesuits; Jesuitry 1613. 3. A Jesuitical quibble or equivocation (*rare*) 1749.

Jesuitize (dʒe·ziu,itəiz), *v.* 1644. [See -IZE.] 1. *intr.* To play the Jesuit; to propound Jesuitical doctrines. 2. *trans.* To imbue with Jesuit principles 1679.

Jesuitry (dʒe·ziu,itri). 1832. [f. JESUIT *sb.* + -RY.] Subtle casuistry or prevarication; the doctrine that the end justifies the means.

Jesus (dʒī·zɒs). ME. [a. L. *Iesus*, a. Gr. Ἰησοῦς, ad. late Heb. or Aramaic *Jeshua*, for earlier *Jehoshua* or *Joshua* (explained as 'Jah (or Jahveh) is salvation'), a frequent Jewish personal name.

During the ME. period regularly used in its OF. (objective) form *Iesu* (*Jesu*). The (L. nom.) form *Iesus* (*Jesus*) was rare in ME., but became the regular Eng. form in 16th c. In later use, *Jesu* occurs in hymns, rarely in nom. or obj., but frequently in the vocative.

1. The name of the Founder of Christianity. 2. A figure or representation of Jesus Christ, as a CRUCIFIX or ECCE HOMO, or an emblem or device such as the letters IHS, etc. 1487.

1. Euen soo: come lorde Iesu TINDALE *Rev.* xxii. 20 [so Cov., *Great B.*; *Geneva*, *Bps.*, etc. Iesus]. Jesu, lover of my soul C. WESLEY.

Jet (dʒet), *sb.*[1] and *a.* ME. [a. OF. *jaiet*, *jayet* (F. *jais*) :—L. *gagātēs*, a. Gr. γαγάτης; see GAGATE.]

A. *sb.* 1. A hard compact black form of lignite, taking a brilliant polish. It is used in making toys, buttons, etc., and attracts light bodies when electrified by rubbing. †b. A piece of jet -1607. †2. Black marble -1648. 3. The colour of jet; a deep glossy black 1450.

1. b. Your lustre too'll..Draw courtship to you, as a jet doth strawes B. JONS. 3. The pansy freaked with jet MILT.

B. *attrib.* or *adj.* 1. Made or consisting of jet 1444. 2. Of the colour of jet 1716. b. *spec.* in **j. ant**, a kind of ant (*Formica fuliginosa*); †**-wood**, ebony 1607.

1. *fig.* J. memories (onely attracting straws and chaff unto them) FULLER. *Comb.* **j.-coal**, cannel coal.

†**Jet**, *sb.*[2] ME. [app. *jet* = F. *jet* throw, cast, for CAST *sb.* in certain senses.] 1. A device, a contrivance. ME. only. 2. Fashion, style, mode, manner -1526.

2. Phr. *Of the new j.*, *of the best j.*, etc.

Jet (dʒet), *sb.*[3] See also JUT *sb.*[2] 1610. [Partly from JET *v.*[2] (and *v.*[1]); partly from senses of F. *jet*, f. *jeter* to throw, cast.] †1. = JETTY *sb.* 2. G. FLETCHER. †2. A dart, spring, 'sprint'. H. MORE (1647). †3. An affected jerk of the body; a swagger -1719. 4. A stream of water or other liquid shot forward or thrown upwards (either in a spurt or continuously), esp. from a small orifice; hence, any similar emission of steam, gas, or (rarely) of solid bodies 1696. Also *transf.* and *fig.* 5. A spout or nozzle for emitting water, gas, etc. 1825. 6. *Metal-casting.* a. A channel or tube for pouring melted metal into a mould. b. The projecting piece of metal left at the end of a type in casting, and subsequently broken off. 1875. 7. A large ladle 1620.

Comb.: **j.-break**, the mark left, as on a metal type, by a jet or sprue when removed after casting; **-pump**, a pump in which fluid is impelled by a jet of air, steam, etc.

Jet, *sb.*[4] 1748. [By-form of GIST, a. Law Fr. *gist* (mod. *gît*), in the phr. *action gist* or *gît* 'action lies', taken subst.] = GIST *sb.*[3]

†**Jet**, *v.*[1] [ME. *gette*, *iett*(*e*, app. a. Anglo-Fr. *gett-re*, in 15th c. Fr. *getter*, *jetter*, mod. *jeter* to throw, cast, etc.; but the senses are those of L. *jactare se*, *jactari* to boast, brag, vaunt oneself, etc.]

I. 1. *intr.* To walk or move about in an ostentatious manner; to strut, swagger. Often with *up and down*. -1669. b. To caper, to trip -1700. 2. *intr.* To stroll -1777. 3. *trans.* To traverse ostentatiously 1530-1581.

1. The Pharisee, he goeth jetting bolt upright UDALL. Mistris Minx..iets it as gingerly as if she were dancing the Canaries NASHE.

II. 1. *intr.* To vaunt, to brag -1664. 2. *intr.* To revel, roister, riot -1640.

Jet (dʒet), *v.*[2] 1588. [a. F. *jeter* :—late L. or Com. Rom. type **jettare* :—*jectare* unexplained alteration of cl. L. *jactare*, freq. of *jacĕre* to throw, cast.]

I. †1. *intr.* To project, protrude, jut. Const. *out*, *over*. -1762. †b. *intr.* (*transf.*) To encroach *on* or *upon* -1636. †2. *trans.* To build *out* (part of a house, etc.); to cause to project -1714.

1. b. Insulting tyranny beginnes to iet Upon the innocent and lawlesse throane SHAKS.

II. 1. To throw, cast, toss. *Obs.* exc. *dial.* 1659. †2. *intr.* To spring, hop, bound, dart -1827. †3. *intr.* To jolt or jog -1676. †4. Of a bird: To jerk the tail up and down -1783.

2. Like as the haggard.. Jets oft from perch to perch QUARLES.

III. 1. *intr.* To spout or spurt forth; to issue in a jet or jets 1692. 2. *trans.* To emit in a jet or jets 1708.

2. Conflicting tides that..high their mingled billows J. SCOTT.

Je·t-bla·ck, *a.* 1475. Black like jet; glossy black.

‖**Jet d'eau** (ʒe,dō). Pl. **jets d'eau** (ʒe,dō). 1706. [F., = 'jet of water'.] An ornamental jet of water ascending from a fountain or pipe; the fountain or pipe from which this issues.

Jetsam (dʒe·tsăm). 1491. [Orig. *jetson*, syncopated f. *jetteson*, JETTISON, but soon perverted to *jetsom*(*e*, *jetsam*.] Goods thrown overboard to lighten a ship in distress (and afterwards washed ashore).

The last clause is no part of the etymological meaning, which should be 'that which has been thrown overboard to save the ship', without reference to whether it sinks or floats. Recent Law-books take the word as 'that which is *thrown* or *cast ashore* by the sea'; Spelman and Blackstone, as 'merchandise thrown overboard and sunk in the sea'. Both explanations evidently arose in the attempt to distinguish *jetsam* from *flotsam*.

†**Jetteau** (dʒetō·). 1705. A form confusing It. *getto* (*d'acqua*) and F. *jet d'eau*: see JET D'EAU -1763.

†**Je·tter.** [ME. *gettour*, a. AF. **gettour* = (in form) OF. *geteor*, *-our*, *-eur*, etc. :—pop.L. *jettatorem* = cl. L. *jactatorem* boaster, braggart, from *jactare*; see JET *v.*[1]] One who boasts, vaunts, or makes an ostentatious display; a braggadocio, bully, 'blade', 'spark' -1611.

Jettison (dʒe·tisən), *sb.* ME. [a. AF. *getteson*, in OF. *getaison* :—L. *jactationem* action of throwing; see JET *v.*[2] and -ISON. See also JETSAM.] *Maritime Law.* The action of throwing goods overboard, esp. to lighten a ship in distress. b. *fig.* Throwing overboard 1887. Hence **Je·ttison** *v.* to throw overboard, esp. to lighten a ship in distress 1848.

Jetton (dʒe·tən). 1762. [a. F. *jeton*, f. *jeter* to cast, to cast up (accounts), etc.; see JET *v.*[2]] A counter of metal, ivory, etc., formerly used in casting up accounts and in card-playing. Also applied to medals and tokens.

Jetty (dʒe·ti), *sb.* Also †**jettee.** See also JUTTY. [ME. *get*(*t*)*ey*, etc., a. OF. *getee*, *jetee*, subst. use of pa. pple. fem. of *jeter* to throw; see JET *v.*[2] Occas. written as F., *jetée*.] 1. a. A mole, pier, or the like, constructed at the entrance of a harbour, or running out into the sea or a lake, so as to defend the harbour or coast; any similar structure. b. A projecting part of a wharf. Also *transf.* and *fig.* †2. A projecting part of a building; *esp.* an overhanging upper story -1677. †3. A bulwark or bastion -1867.

Comb. **j.-head**, that part of a wharf which projects beyond the rest; *esp.* the front of a wharf, whose side forms one of the cheeks of a wet or dry dock.

Jetty (dʒe·ti), *a.*[1] 1477. [f. JET *sb.*[1] + -Y[1].] 1. Of the colour of jet; jet-black; also *advb.* 2. Of the nature of jet 1875. Hence **Je·ttiness.**

†**Je·tty**, *a.*[2] [f. JET *sb.*[3] or *v.*[2] + -Y[1].] Swelling. CHAPMAN.

Jetty (dʒe·ti), *v.* 1449. [f. JETTY *sb.*] †1. *trans.* To cause to project, furnish with projections. †2. *intr.* To project, jut -1615. 3. To furnish with a jetty 1889.

‖**Jeu** (ʒö). Pl. **jeux** (ʒö). [F. :—L. *jocum* JOKE.] The French for 'play' or 'game'; occurring in **jeu d'esprit** (ʒö desprī), a play or playful action in which some cleverness is displayed; now usu., a witty or humorous trifle 1712; **jeu de mots** (ʒö də mo), a play on words, a pun 1823.

Jew (dʒiū), *sb.* [ME. *gyu*, *giu*, *iu*, *iuw*(*e*, etc., a. OF. *giu*, *gyu*, *giue*, earlier *juieu*, etc. :—L. *iudæum* (nom. *-us*) Jew; in later F. *juif*, fem. *juive*. L. *iudæus* was a. Gr. Ἰουδαῖος, f. Aramaic *yehūdāi*, corresp. to Heb. *yehūdī* Jew, f. *yehūdāh* Judah, name of a Hebrew patriarch and the tribe descended from him.] 1. A person of Hebrew race; an Israelite. (Orig. a Hebrew of the kingdom of Judah; later, any Israelite who adhered to the worship of Jehovah as conducted at Jerusalem.) 2. *transf.* Applied to a grasping or extortionate usurer, or a trader who drives hard bargains or deals craftily 1606. 3. *attrib.* or as *adj.* That is a Jew, Jewish, as *Jew boy*, etc.; of or relating to Jews, as *Jew bill*, etc. 1613.

1. What is the reason? I am a Iewe; Hath not a Iew eyes? SHAKS. You forget Lady Lilac's as rich as a J. BYRON. *Jew's eye*: something valued highly; Pictures..Each 'worth a Jew's eye' 1844. 2. Jacob is a regular J., and practises all sorts of tricks and wiles COLERIDGE.

Comb.: **J.-bail**, insufficient bail; **-baiting** *sb.* [= Ger. *Judenhetze*], systematic harrying of Jews; **-bush**, the Milk plant; **-lizard**, a large Australian lizard, *Amphibolurus barbatus*. b. Genitival Combs.: **Jews' frankincense**, a plant of the genus *Styrax*, or the resin obtained from it (storax or benzoin); **Jews' houses,** remains of ancient tin-smelting furnaces in Cornwall; **Jews' thorn** = *Christ's thorn.*

Jew, *v. colloq.* 1845. [f. JEW *sb.* (sense 2).] *trans.* To cheat or overreach.

Jewel (dʒ'ū·ĕl), *sb.* [ME. *iuel, iuwele, iuall,* etc., a. AF. *juel, jeual* = OF. *joel* (mod.F. *joyau*); :—L. **jocale,* f. *jocus* play.] **1.** An article of value used for adornment, usu. of the person; a costly ornament, *esp.* one made of gold, silver, or precious stones. *Obs.* in *gen.* sense. **b.** An ornament worn as the badge of an order, or as a mark of distinction or honour 1672. **2.** A precious stone, a gem; *esp.* one worn as an ornament. (The prevailing mod. sense.) 1590. **b.** *Watch-making.* A precious stone, usu. a ruby, used for a pivot-hole, on account of its resistance to wear 1825. **3.** *fig.* A precious thing or person; a 'treasure', a 'gem' ME. †**4.** *Naut.* A heavy ring, used to press together the two parts of a cable or rope which is laid round an article and then rove through the ring. Also *attrib.* -1755.

1. Heere, weare this Iewell for me, tis my picture SHAKS. 2. A iewell rich he found That was a Ruby of right perfect hew SPENSER. *Comb.*: **j.-hole** (*Watch-making*), a hole drilled in a j. for a pivot. 3. Oh, 'tis a j. of a husband DRYDEN.

Jew·el, *v.* 1601. [f. prec.] **1.** *trans.* To furnish or adorn with jewels. **b.** *Watch-making.* To fit with jewels for the pivot-holes. Usu. in *pa. pple.* 1804. **2.** *fig.* To bedeck as with jewels 1859.

1 b. A gold hunting watch.. j-d in four holes 1844.

Jew·el-block. 1769. *Naut.* The name given to each of two small blocks suspended at the extremities of the main and fore-topsail yards, through which the halyards of the studding-sails are passed.

Jew·el-house. 1473. A house, building, or chamber in which jewels are kept. Now *rare.* **b.** *spec.* The room in the Tower of London in which the crown jewels are kept.

Jeweller, -eler (dʒ'ū·ĕləɹ). ME. [a. AF. *jueler* = OF. *juelier,* f. *juel*; in mod.F. *joaillier.*] A maker of jewels; a dealer in jewels or jewellery.

Jewellery, jewelry (dʒ'ū·ĕlri, dʒ'ū·ĕləri). ME. [a. OF. *juelerye,* f. *joel, juel*; see JEWEL and -ERY. In mod.Eng. app. from JEWELLER, and from JEWEL; see -ERY and -RY.] Jewellers' work; gems or ornaments made or sold by jewellers; jewels collectively, or as a form of adornment. Also *fig.*

In commercial use commonly spelt *jewellery.* The pronunc. with three syllables is usual with both forms.

Jewess (dʒ'ū·ĕs). ME. [f. JEW *sb.* + -ESS.] A female Jew; a Jewish woman.

Jew-fish. 1697. [app. f. JEW *sb.* + FISH.] A name given to various fishes, chiefly of the family *Serranidæ.*

The Jew-fish..I judge so called by the English, because it hath Scales and Fins, therefore a clean Fish, according to the Levitical Law DAMPIER.

Jewis, -ise, var. JUISE *Obs.*, judgement.

Jewish (dʒ'ū·iʃ), *a.* 1546. [f. JEW *sb.* + -ISH [1].] Of, belonging to, or characteristic of, the Jews; Israelitish, Hebrew. Also *fig.*

fig. You ask a J. price for it, Mr. Graves THACKERAY. Hence **Jew·ish-ly** *adv.*, **-ness.**

†**Jew·ism.** 1579. [f. JEW *sb.* + -ISM.] The religious system of the Jews; Judaism -1800.

Jewry (dʒ'ūə·ri). ME. [a. AF. *juerie* = OF. *juierie* (mod. *juiverie*): see JEW and -ERY.] **1.** The land of the Jews, Judea; occas. = Palestine. *Obs.* or *arch.* **2.** The Jews' quarter in a town or city; the Ghetto. (Hence *Old Jewry* in London.) *Obs.* exc. *Hist.* ME. †**3.** The Jewish religion -1552. **4.** The Jewish people, race, nation, or community; the Jews collectively ME.

1. In Iewry is God knowne; his name is greate in Israel BIBLE (Great) *Ps.* lxxvi. 1.

Jew's-ear. 1544. [Erron. tr. of med.L. *auricula Judæ* Judas's ear; so called from its shape, and from its being often found on the elder, on which tree Judas is said to have hanged himself.] An edible cup-shaped fungus (*Hirneola* or *Exidia Auricula-Judæ*), formerly in repute as a medicine.

Jews' harp, Jew's-harp. (Also occas. w. small j.) 1584. [var. of JEWS' TRUMP, q. v.] **1.** A musical instrument, consisting of an elastic steel tongue fixed at one end to a small lyre-shaped frame of brass or iron, and bent at the other end at right angles; it is played by holding the frame between the teeth and striking the free end of the metal tongue with the finger, variations of tone being produced by altering the size and shape of the cavity of the mouth. Called also *Jews' trump.* **2.** *Naut.* 'The shackle for joining a chain-cable to the anchor-ring' (Smyth) 1750.

Jews' stone, Jewstone. 1617. [tr. med.L. *lapis Judaicus.*] **1.** The fossil spine of a large sea-urchin, found in Syria, formerly used in medicine. ? *Obs.* 1633. **2.** A crystallized form of iron pyrites (also called *marcasite*), formerly used as a gem. ? *Obs.* 1617. **3.** A local name for hard unmanageable rocks 1803.

Jews' trump, Jew's-trump. Now *rare.* 1545. [Earlier than *Jews' harp.* In Scotland and N. of England called simply TRUMP, agreeing with the Fr. name *trompe,* now displaced by *guimbarde.* The first element was certainly *Jews* from the first. The attribution to the Jews occurs only in English.] = JEWS' HARP 1. †**b.** Applied to a usurer. CHAPMAN.

‖**Jezail** (dʒĕzai·l, -ē·l). *E. Ind.* 1838. [Pers. *jazā'il.*] A long and heavy Afghan musket.

Jezebel (dʒe·zĕbĕl). 1558. Name of the infamous wife of Ahab, king of Israel (1 Kings xvi. 31, etc.); hence, a wicked abandoned woman, or a woman who paints her face.

Jib (dʒib), *sb.*[1] 1661. [? abbrev. of *gibbet,* as being hung from the mast-head.] **1.** *Naut.* A triangular stay-sail stretching from the outer end of the jib-boom to the fore-topmast head in large ships, and from the bowsprit to the mast-head in smaller craft. **2.** *dial.* The under lip (in phr. *to hang the j.*). Also, the mouth, face, or nose. 1825.

1. *Flying j.*, a second sail of similar shape set before the jib on the *flying jib-boom*; in some large vessels as many as six jibs are carried, the outermost being the *jib of jibs.* Phr. *The cut of one's j.* (colloq.): one's personal appearance, countenance, or look; If she disliked what the sailor calls the cut of their j. SCOTT. *Comb.*: **j.-guy,** a stout rope which supports the jib-boom; **-halyard,** the halyard for raising and lowering the j.; **-header,** a topsail shaped like a j.; **-stay,** the stay on which the j. is set; **-traveller,** a circular iron hoop, with a hook and shackle, used to haul out the tack of the j.

Jib (dʒib), *sb.*[2] 1764. [app. abbrev. of *gibbet.*] The projecting arm of a crane; also, the boom of a derrick. *Comb.* **j.-crane,** a crane fitted with a j.

Jib (dʒib), *sb.*[3] 1801. [f. JIB *v.*[2]] **1.** The action of jibbing; a state of standstill. **2.** A jibbing horse, a jibber 1843.

Jib (dʒib), *v.*[1] Also **gibb, jibb**; see also GYBE *v.* 1691. [Etym. obscure.] **1.** *trans.* To pull (a sail or yard) round from one side of a vessel to the other, as in tacking, etc. **2.** *intr.* Of a sail, etc.: GYBE *v.* 1. 1719. **b.** *transf.* Of other things: To swing round 1891.

Jib, *v.*[2] Also **jibb,** rarely **gib.** 1811. [?] **1.** *intr.* Of a horse, etc.: To stop and refuse to go on; to move restively backwards or sideways. **2.** *fig.* To stop short, draw back, back out 1812. **b.** To start aside; to shy *at* 1882.

1. A backward swain is like a jibbing horse 1862. Hence **Ji·bber** *sb.* a horse that jibs.

Ji·bbah, Egyptian form of JUBBAH.

Jibber (dʒi·bəɹ), *v.* 1824. [Alternative spelling of GIBBER.] *intr.* To speak rapidly and inarticulately.

Jib-boom. 1748. [f. JIB *sb.*[1] + BOOM *sb.*[2]] *Naut.* A spar run out from the end of the bowsprit, to which the tack of the jib is lashed, and beyond which is sometimes extended the *flying jib-boom.*

Jib-door. 1800. [?] A door flush with the wall in which it stands, and usually made indistinguishable from it.

Jibe (dʒəib), *v. U.S.* Also **gibe.** 1813. [?] *intr.* To chime *in* (*with*); to agree.

Jibe, var. of GIBE *sb.* and *v.*, GYBE *v.*

Jiffy (dʒi·fi). *colloq.* 1785. [?] A very short space of time; e.g. *in a jiffy.* Also **Jiff** 1797.

Jig (dʒig), *sb.* 1560. [Origin uncertain. App. not conn. w. OF. *gigue* a kind of stringed instrument.] **1.** A lively, rapid, springy kind of dance. **2.** The music for such a dance; a rapid lively dance-tune; *spec.* one in triple rhythm (usually 6-8 or 12-8) 1588. †**3.** A song or ballad of lively, jocular, or mocking (often scurrilous) character -1673. †**4.** A light performance of a lively or comical character, given at the end, or in the interval, of a play -1728. **5.** A piece of sport, a joke; a trifle; a trick 1592. **6.** A name for various mechanical contrivances and simple machines, often merely with the sense 'dodge', 'device', 'contrivance'. *spec.* **b.** A contrivance for jigging or dressing ore by shaking it up jerkily in a fluid medium (see JIG *v.* 5) 1877. **c.** *Coal-mining.* A steep tramway on which the loaded trucks as they descend draw up the empty trucks 1866. **7.** Applied joc. to a horse, a person, etc. 1706.

1. Wooing..is hot and hasty like a Scotch ijgge SHAKS. 2. They sing to jigs, and dance to church music H. WALPOLE. 4. He's for a Iigge, or a tale of Baudry SHAKS. 5. Phr. *The j. is up* = the game is up (now *dial.* or *slang*). Her jigs, and her junketings, and her tears THACKERAY.

Comb.: **j.-pin,** a pin used by miners to hold the turn-beams, and prevent them from turning.

Jig (dʒig), *v.* Also †**gig.** 1588. [Closely related to JIG *sb.* (q. v.).] **1. a.** *trans.* To sing or play as a jig, or in the style of a jig (see JIG *sb.* 2, 3). ? *Obs.* **b.** *trans.* To dance (a jig or other lively dance) 1719. **c.** *intr.* To dance a jig; to dance in a rapid jerky fashion 1672. **2.** *intr.* To move up and down or to and fro with a rapid jerky motion 1604. **b.** *trans.* To jerk to and fro or up and down 1710. **3.** *intr.* To move in unison *with*; to agree, 'jump', chime *with* (*rare*) 1838. †**4.** *trans.* To put *off* with a trick. FORD. **5.** To dress (ore) by shaking it under water in a sieve or box with perforated bottom, or the like 1778. **6.** To shape an earthen vessel with a jigger (see JIGGER *sb.*[1] 4 a) 1865. **7.** In *Well-boring,* To bore with the aid of a spring-pole, which jerks up the rods and drill after the stroke. (*U.S.*)

1. To Iigge off a tune at the tongues end SHAKS. b. While this brave Carmagnole-dance has hardly jigged itself out CARLYLE. 2. *Haml.* III. i. 150.

Jigger (dʒi·gəɹ), *sb.*[1] 1675. [Partly f. JIG *v.*; partly ?.] **1.** One who jigs or dances a jig. Also, A 'guy' (*dial.*). **2.** *Naut.* **a.** A small tackle consisting of a double and a single block and a fall; *esp.* one used to hold on the cable when it is heaved into the ship 1726. **b.** A small sail 1831. **c.** Short for *jigger-mast* 1880. **d.** A small vessel of the smack type furnished with a 'jigger' sail (see b) 1860. **3.** *Mining.* **a.** One who jigs ore (JIG *v.* 5). **b.** An apparatus for dressing ore, consisting of a sieve, or a box with holes, which is shaken up and down in water, or into which water is forced 1778. **4.** A name for various mechanical contrivances: e.g. **a.** *Pottery.* A horizontal lathe used in china-making 1825. **b.** A loose chain used as a warehouse crane. 1891. **c.** *Billiards.* A slang name for the rest 1847. **d.** A small roller or set of rollers fitted in a suspended oscillating frame, for graining leather 1883. **e.** *Printing.* A guide-mark used by compositors. **f.** *Wireless.* An oscillation transformer 1902. **g.** *Golf.* A short iron-headed club used for approaching 1893.

Comb.: **j.-mast** (*Naut.*), (*a*) a small mast at the stern, on which a j. (sense 2 b) is hoisted; (*b*) the aftermost mast of a four-masted merchant ship; **-tackle** (*Naut.*) = sense 2 a; **-yard** (*Naut.*), a yard on which the j. (sense 2 b) is extended.

Jigger (dʒi·gəɹ), *sb.*[2] 1781. [Corruption of CHIGOE.] **1.** = CHIGOE. **2.** Applied in U.S. to various harvest-ticks, e.g. *Leptus americanus* and *L. irritans.*

Jigger (dʒi·gəɹ), *v.*[1] *colloq.* 1867. [? freq. of JIG *v.*] *intr.* To make a succession of rapid jerks; said of a fish struggling to free itself.

Ji·gger, *v.*[2] *slang* or *colloq.* 1837. [?] A vague substitute for a profane oath, esp. in asseverations. (Only in *pass.*)

Ji·ggery-po·kery. *colloq.* 1896. Humbug.

Jigget (dʒi·gĕt), *v. colloq.* 1687. [dim. of JIG *v.*] *intr.* To jig; to hop or skip about; to shake up and down; to fidget.

Jigging (dʒi·giŋ), *vbl. sb.* 1641. [f. JIG *v.* + -ING [1].] The action of JIG *v.*; *spec.* in

Mining, the method of dressing ore by the motion of a wire sieve in a vat of water, where the smallest particles pass through the sieve. *Comb.*: j.-**machine**, a machine for jigging; = JIGGER *sb.*[1] 3 b; -**sieve**, a sieve for jigging ore.

Jiggish (dʒi·giʃ), *a.* 1624. [f. JIG *sb.* + -ISH[1].] **1.** Inclined to jigging; frivolous, frolicsome 1634. **2.** Of the nature of, or suitable for, a jig or light dance.

1. She is never sad, and yet not j. HABINGTON.

Jiggle (dʒi·g'l), *v.* 1836. [dim. or freq. of JIG *v.*] To move backwards and forwards, or up and down, with a light unsteady motion; to move in a rapid succession of slight jerks; to rock lightly (*trans.* and *intr.*). Hence **Ji·ggle** *sb.* a jiggling movement.

Jiggumbob (dʒi·gəmbɒb). *colloq.* ? *Obs.* 1613. [A humorous formation from JIG *sb.* or *v.*] = THINGUMBOB.

Ji·g-saw. 1873. [f. JIG *v.*] A vertically reciprocating saw used to cut irregular patterns. *J. puzzle*, a puzzle consisting of a picture mounted on board and cut into irregular pieces.

‖**Jihad, jehad** (dʒihā·d). 1869. [Arab. *jihad.*] A religious war of Mohammedans against unbelievers in Islam, inculcated as a duty by the Koran and traditions. **b.** *transf.* A war or crusade for or against some doctrine, opinion, etc.; a war to the death.

Jill, var. of GILL *sbs.*3, 4.

Jillet (dʒi·lėt). *Sc.* 1755. [dim. of name *Jill* or GILL (*sb.*[4]).] A giddy or flighty young woman; a jilt; a wench.

Jill-flirt, var. of GILL-FLIRT.

Jilt (dʒilt), *sb.* 1672. [In sense **1**, perh. contr. f. *gillot*, early f. JILLET. In sense 2, infl. by JILT *v.*] †**1.** A harlot or strumpet; a kept mistress –1815. **2.** One who deceives or capriciously casts off a lover after giving him encouragement. (The current sense.) 1674. **3.** *Sc.* A wench 1816.

Jilt (dʒilt), *v.* 1660. [Origin unkn.] **1.** *trans.* To deceive after holding out hopes in love; to cast off (a lover) capriciously; to play the jilt towards. Orig. said only of a woman. 1673. Also *absol.* or *intr.* 1696. **2.** *gen.* To deceive, delude (*Obs.*); to prove false to (any one); to throw over for another. (Now chiefly *fig.* from 1.) 1660.

Jimcrack, obs. f. GIMCRACK.

Jim-crow (dʒi·m,krōᵘ). *U.S.* 1863. [app. f. *Jim*, var. of *Jem* (cf. JEMMY *sb.* 4).] An implement for bending or straightening iron rails by the pressure of a screw. Also *attrib.*, as *jim-crow planing-machine*, a planing-machine with a reversing tool, to plane both ways, and named because it is able to 'wheel about and turn about'.

Jim-jam (dʒi·mdʒæm). 1550. [A whimsical reduplication.] †**1.** A gimcrack, a knick-knack (*colloq.*) –1592. **2.** *pl.* Delirium tremens (*slang*) 1885. **b.** *pl.* A fit of the creeps 1904.

Jimmy (dʒi·mi), variant of JEMMY (q.v.), in most senses.

Jimp (dʒimp), *a.* (*adv.*) *Sc.* and *n. dial.* 1508. [?] **1.** Slender, slim, delicate, graceful, neat. (A Sc. or northern word, introduced in 19th c. into English literature.) **2.** Scanty; bare (measure) 1768. **3.** *adv.* Barely 1814. Hence **Ji·mp-ly** *adv.*, -**ness.**

Jim(p)son-weed: see JAMESTOWN-WEED.

Jin: see GIN, JINN.

Jingall, var. of GINGALL.

Jingle (dʒi·ŋg'l), *sb.* Also †**gingle.** 1599. [f. JINGLE *v.*] **1.** A noise such as is made by small bells, or loose pieces of metal when struck, etc. **b.** Applied depreciatively to other sounds 1827. **2.** Something that jingles; a jingling bell, etc. 1615. **3.** Affected repetition of the same or similar sounds; a catching array of words, whether in prose or verse. Chiefly contemptuous. 1645. **4.** A covered two-wheeled car used in the south of Ireland and in Australia. Also *attrib.* 1806. **5.** U.S. name for the shell of the saddle-oyster, *Anomia.* Also *attrib.* 1887.

1. The continual j. of our sledge-bells SYMONDS. **b.** The scolding and the j. of the piano M. ARNOLD. **2.** The tambourine,..and the Turkish j., used in the army HONE. **3.** Little gingles, and tinkling of words 1663.

Jingle (dʒi·ŋg'l), *v.* ME. [Echoic.] **1.** *intr.* To give forth a mingling of ringing sounds, as by the striking together of coins, keys, etc. Also *transf.* and *fig.* **b.** To proceed or move with a jingling sound 1732. **2.** *trans.* To cause to emit a mingling of ringing sounds 1508. **3.** *intr.* **a.** Of prose or verse: To sound with alliteration, rimes, or the like 1670. **b.** To play with words for the sake of sound; (*depreciatively*) to rime 1642.

1. The harness jingles, as it passes by 1871. **2.** Jingling his keys in one pocket 1874. **3. a.** A gingling verse,..*Ad mala patrata, sunt atra theatra parata* HOWARD. Hence **Ji·ngler**, one who or that which jingles; a rimer. **Ji·nglingly** *adv.*

Jingo (dʒi·ŋgo), *int.*, *sb.*, and *a.* 1670. [Orig. a piece of conjurer's gibberish. In 1694 *by jingo* is used by Motteux to render Fr. *par Dieu*; cf. *by Golly, Gosh, Jabers*, etc. In Scotland, *by jing* or *jings* is in common use.]

A. *int.* and *sb.* **I.** †**1.** (Usually *Hey* or *High Jingo!*) A conjurer's call for the appearance of something; the opposite of *Hey presto!* Hence, an exclam. of surprise at the appearance of something. –1730. **2.** *By jingo!* a strong form of asseveration (*colloq.* or *vulgar*) 1694.

2. By j., quoth Panurge, the Man talks somewhat like MOTTEUX *Rabelais* IV. lvi. 219. We don't want to fight, yet by Jingo! if we do, We've got the ships, we've got the men, and got the money too 1878.

II. [f. the expression 'by Jingo!' in the refrain of the music-hall song, quoted in sense 2 above.] A nickname for those who supported the policy of Lord Beaconsfield in sending a British fleet into Turkish waters to resist the advance of Russia in 1878; hence, a blatant 'patriot', a Chauvinist 1878.

B. *adj.* †**1.** Exhibiting vulgar dash. MILLAIS. **2.** Of or pertaining to the political jingo; characterized by jingoism 1879.

Jingoism (dʒi·ŋgo,iz'm). 1878. [f. prec. + -ISM.] The policy or practices of the jingoes. So **Ji·ngoist** = JINGO A. II. 1884.

Jink (dʒiŋk), *sb.* orig. *Sc.* 1700. [cf. JINK *v.*] **1.** The act of eluding; a quick turn so as to give the slip to a pursuer or a guard 1786. **2.** *Cards.* The winning of a game of spoil-five, twenty-five, or forty-five, by taking all the tricks in one hand 1887. **3. High Jinks**: app. orig. high pranks. †**a.** A name for various frolics at drinking parties (*Sc.*) 1700. **b.** Lively or boisterous sport. (Also simply *jinks.*) 1842.

1. Our billie's gien us a' the j. An' owre the sea BURNS. **3. a.** The evening ended in the full jollity of *High Jinks* LOCKHART. **b.** A scene for romps and jinks 1851.

Jink (dʒiŋk), *v.* Chiefly *Sc.* 1715. [app. onomatopœic, expressing nimble motion.] **1.** *intr.* To move with quick sudden action; to move jerkily to and fro 1785. **2.** *intr.* To make a quick elusive turn, so as to dodge a pursuer, etc. 1785. **3.** *trans.* To elude by dodging; to dodge 1774. **4.** To diddle 1785. **5.** *intr.* (*Cards.*) To win a game of spoil-five, twenty-five, or forty-five by taking all the tricks in one hand 1887. Hence **Ji·nker**, one who or that which jinks.

‖**Jinn** (dʒin). Also **djin, ginn, jin.** 1684. [a. Arab. *jinn*, collect. pl., demons, spirits; sing. *jinnī* (see next).] In Mohammedan demonology, an order of spirits lower than the angels, said to have the power of assuming human and animal forms, and to exercise supernatural influence over men. Oftener used as a *sing.* to denote one of these.

‖**Jinnee** (dʒinī·). Also GENIE. Also fem. **jinnee·yeh.** 1841. [a. Arab. *jinnī*, fem. *jinnīyeh* demon or spirit.] The sing. of prec.

Jinny (dʒi·ni). 1797. Pet-form of JANE, used locally in transf. uses. *Mining.* A stationary engine used to let down or draw up trucks on an inclined plane; also = **jinny-road**, a self-acting inclined plane.

‖**Jinricksha, jinrikisha** (dʒinri·kʃă, -ri·kiʃă). 1874. [a. Japanese *jin-riki-sha* (*j* = ʒ), f. *jin* man + *riki* power + *sha* vehicle.] A light two-wheeled hooded vehicle, drawn by one or more men. Shortened colloq. to *rickshaw.*

Jitney (dʒi·tni). *U.S.* 1915. [?] **a.** Five cents. **b.** An automobile that plies for a small fare.

Jiu-jitsu: see JU-JITSU.

Jo (dʒō). *Sc.* Also **joe.** 1529. [Sc. form of JOY, F. *joie.*] †**1.** Joy, pleasure –1570. **2.** A sweetheart, darling, beloved one 1529.

2. John Anderson, my jo BURNS.

Joan (dʒōᵘn). 1588. [orig. *Joanna* or *Johanna*, fem. of *Jo(h)annes* John; hence transf.] **1.** Generic name for a female rustic. **2.** A close-fitting cap worn by women about 1750.

1. Some men must loue my Lady, and some Ione SHAKS.

Job (dʒɒb), *sb.*[1] 1557. [?] **1.** A piece of work; *esp.* a small definite piece of work in one's own calling. **2.** A piece of work, or transaction, done for hire, or with a special view to profit 1660. **3.** A public service or trust turned to private gain or party advantage 1667. †**b.** Personal profit; private interest –1785. **4.** Anything one has to do 1694. **5.** An affair, business, occurrence, state of things: esp. in *good j.*, *bad j.* 1700. **6.** Short for *job-carriage*, *job-horse* –1863. **7.** *attrib.* Hired or used by the job or particular piece of work, or for a definite time, as *job-carriage*, *-gardener*, *-horse*, etc. 1701.

1. He..never lack'd a j. for Giles to do BLOOMFIELD. Phr. *By the j.* I do not design to hire one [gardener] ..but only employ him by the j. BERKELEY. **2.** Their Faith's a Dream, their Preaching but a J. 1778. **3.** Who makes a Trust or Charity a J., And gets an Act of Parliament to rob POPE. **4.** 'Tis an ugly j.: but soldiers obey commands BROWNING. Phr. *To do the j. for*, or *to do* (a person's) *j.*: (*a*) to do what is required by him; (*b*) *slang*, to 'do for', ruin, destroy. *To make a job of*: to manage successfully. *Bad j.*: a failure (see also sense 5).

Comb.: **j. lot**, a parcel of goods, of sundry kinds or qualities, bought as a speculation with a view to profit; hence (*depreciatively*) any miscellaneous lot of things, persons, etc.; -**price**, (*a*) a price paid for things hired or work done by the job; (*b*) a price paid for things bought as a job lot; -**work**, piece-work.

Job (dʒɒb), *sb.*[2] 1560. [f. JOB *v.*[1]] An act of 'jobbing'; an abrupt stabbing with the sharp end of anything; a peck, dab, thrust; a jerk or wrench of the bit in a horse's mouth.

Job (dʒōᵘb), *sb.*[3] 1553. Name of an ancient patriarch, whose story forms a book of the Old Testament; a type (*a*) of destitution, (*b*) of patience.

Phrases. **Job's comforter**, one who, under the guise of comforting, aggravates distress (cf. *Job* xvi. 2). **Job's news**, news of disaster; so **Job's post**, a messenger who brings such news; see *Job* i. 13–19. **Job's tears** (also †*Job's drops*), a species of grass (*Coix Lacryma*), having round shining grains resembling tears.

Job (dʒɒb), *v.*[1] 1490. [app. echoic.] **1.** *trans.* To peck, dab, stab, prod, etc., as with the point of something; to hurt a horse's mouth with the bit; in pugilistic language, to strike with a sharp or cutting stroke. **2.** To thrust (something pointed) abruptly into something else 1573. **3.** *intr.* To peck (*at*) as a bird; to thrust (*at*) so as to stab or pierce; to penetrate *into* 1566.

1. He measured his distance accurately, and jobbed his adversary about the head 1818.

Job (dʒɒb), *v.*[2] 1670. [f. JOB *sb.*[1]] **1.** *intr.* To do jobs; to work by the piece 1694. **2.** *trans.* To let out (a large piece of work) in separate portions to different contractors or workmen 1882. **3.** To hire (*occas.*, to let out on hire) for a particular job, or for a definite time (a horse, carriage, etc.). Also *absol.* 1786. **4.** To let or deal with for profit 1726. **5.** To buy and sell (stock or goods) as a broker; to deal with as a middleman 1670. **b.** *intr.* To buy and sell stock 1721. **6.** *intr.* To turn a public office or service, or a position of trust, improperly to private or party advantage; to practise jobbery 1732. **7.** *trans.* To make a job of (JOB *sb.*[1] 3, 4); to deal with in some way; *esp.* corruptly for private gain or advantage. Also with *away*, *into.* 1720. **8.** To put *off* by artifice 1876.

1. He had worked..and still jobbed about HONE. **3.** She went to the livery-man from whom she jobbed her carriage THACKERAY. **5.** The Essays are..jobb'd here by Scribners, New York WALT WHITMAN. **6.** I daresay he jobs, as all other people of consequence do, in elections and so forth SCOTT.

Jobation (dʒobē·ʃən). *colloq.* 1687. [f. JOBE *v.* + -ATION. Dialectally, usu. *jawbation*, as if from *jaw.*] The action of JOBE *v.*; a rebuke, reproof, *esp.* a long and tedious one; a 'lecture'.

Jobber 1 (dʒǫ·bəɹ). *dial.* 1580. [f. JOB *v.*1 + -ER 1.] One who or that which jobs, pecks, pokes, thrusts, etc.

Jobber 2 (dʒǫ·bəɹ). 1670. [f. JOB *v.*2 + -ER 1.] 1. One who does jobs or is employed by the job; a hack; a piece-worker 1706. 2. A jobmaster 1848. 3. A broker, a middleman; a small trader or salesman 1670. 4. A member of the Stock Exchange, who deals in stocks or shares on his own account; a STOCK-JOBBER; called, in the Stock Exchange itself, a *dealer* 1719. 5. One who improperly uses a public office, trust, or service for private gain or party advantage 1739.

1. Our translators have usually been the jobbers of booksellers D'ISRAELI. 5. He is an atrocious j. G. ROSE.

Jobbernowl (dʒǫ·bəɹnōul). *colloq.* 1592. [? f. *jobbard* a stupid fellow + NOLL, OE. *hnol*, head.] 1. A blockish or stupid head 1599. 2. A blockhead. Also *attrib.*

Jobbery (dʒǫ·bəri). 1832. [Cf. JOBBER 2 and -ERY.] 1. Jobs collectively; job-work. Also *attrib.* 2. The perpetration of corrupt jobs (see JOB *sb.*1 3) 1837.

Jo·bbing, *vbl. sb.* 1735. [f. JOB *v.*2 + -ING 1.] The action of JOB *v.*2 1. The doing of odd jobs 1800. 2. The practice of a middleman or stock-jobber. (See also STOCK-JOBBING.) 1735. 3. = JOBBERY 2. 1784. 4. *attrib.* 1775.

2. The jobbing of the public funds BURKE. 3. The system of Parliamentary jobbing MAY.

Jobbish (dʒǫ·biʃ), *a.* 1792. [f. JOB *sb.*1 + -ISH 1.] Of the nature of a job (see JOB *sb.*1 3).

†**Jobe** (dʒōub), *v. colloq.* Also **job.** 1670. [f. JOB *sb.*3, in allusion to the lengthy reproofs of Job's friends.] *trans.* To rebuke in a long and tedious harangue; to 'lecture' –1794.

A former president of St. John's college..would frequently Job his students for going constantly three or four times a day to chapel AMHERST.

Jobmaster, job-master (dʒǫ·b,mɑːstəɹ). 1802. [f. JOB *sb.*1 + MASTER *sb.*] A man who keeps a livery stable and lets out horses and carriages by the job.

†**Jo·cant**, *a.* 1440. [app. ad. L. *jocantem*, *jocari* (rarely *jocare*).] Mirthful, merry, jocund –1687. So †**Jo·cantry**, mirth, merriment.

Jockey (dʒǫ·ki), *sb.* 1529. [dim. or pet-form of *Jock*, by-form of John; orig. Sc. and n. Eng.] 1. A diminutive of the name *Jock* or John, usu. = 'little Jock, Jacky, Johnny'; hence, applied to any man of the common people (chiefly *Sc.*); also, a lad; an under-strapper. (Cf. JACK *sb.*1 2.) 2. A strolling minstrel or beggar; a vagabond. *Sc. Obs.* exc. *Hist.* 1683. 3. One who manages or has to do with horses; a horse-dealer. *Obs.* or *dial.* 1638. b. Hence, A crafty or fraudulent bargainer; a cheat 1683. †4. One who rides or drives a horse; a postillion; a charioteer –1850. 5. *spec.* A professional rider in horse-races. (The chief current sense.) 1641. 6. *attrib.* 1670.

3. I, and W. Hewer, and a friend of his, a j., did go about to see several pairs of horses, for my coach PEPYS. 5. The jockies whipp'd, the horses ran COMBE.

Comb.: **j.-cap**, a peaked cap of the style worn by jockeys; **-club**, a club for the promotion and regulation of horse-racing; *spec.* the Jockey Club established at Newmarket, which is the supreme authority in England on these matters 1758; **-coat**, a kind of great-coat (? formerly worn by horse-dealers); **-sleeve**, a sleeve like that of a jockey-coat.

So **Jo·ckeydom**, jockeys collectively. **Jo·ckeyism**, the style, phraseology, or practice of jockeys.

Jockey (dʒǫ·ki), *v.* 1659. [f. prec. sb.] 1. *trans.* To play the jockey with (see prec. 3 b); to trick, take in, 'do'. b. To play tricks with; to manipulate in a tricky way 1890. c. *intr.* To play the jockey, act fraudulently; to aim at an advantage by adroit management 1835. 2. *trans.* To ride (a horse) in a race, as a jockey 1825.

1. The way in which she jockied Jos, and which she described with infinite fun THACKERAY.

Jockeying (dʒǫ·ki,iŋ), *vbl. sb.* 1770. [f. JOCKEY *v.* + -ING 1.] The action of JOCKEY *v.* 1. Horse-dealing; the riding and management of horses. Also *attrib.* 2. Adroit management for the purpose of gaining an (unfair) advantage; trickery, cheating 1807.

Jockeyship (dʒǫ·kiʃip). 1763. [See -SHIP.] 1. a. The art of a jockey; skill in horse-racing. b. The practice of jockeying (see prec. 2). 2. A mock title for a jockey. COWPER.

1. b. To vie in j. or cunning at a bett SHENSTONE. 2. Where can at last his j. retire? 1781.

Jocko (dʒǫ·ko). Also **jacko.** 1847. [a. F. *jocko*, erroneously made by Buffon out of *engeco*, prop. *ncheko*, native name in the Gaboon country, W. Africa.] The chimpanzee; *occas.*, any ape.

Jockteleg (dʒǫ·ktĕleg). *Sc.* and *n. dial.* Also **jacklag, jackleg,** etc. 1672. [?] A (large) clasp knife.

Jocose (dʒokōu·s), *a.* 1673. [ad. L. *jocosus*, f. *jocus* jest; see -OSE.] 1. Full of jokes; given to joking; playful, sportive, waggish. 2. Of the nature of a joke, or characterized by jokes; playful in style or character 1699.

1. When they vouchsafe to..be j. and pleasant with an Adversary SHAFTESBURY. 2. J. talk GEO. ELIOT. Hence **Joco·se·ly** *adv.*, **-ness.**

Jocoserious (dʒōuko,sīə·riəs), *a.* 1661. [f. *joco-*, comb. f. L. *jocus* jest + SERIOUS.] Half jocular, half serious; blending jokes and serious matters.

Jocosity (dʒokǫ·sĭti). 1646. [f. L. *jocosus* JOCOSE; see -ITY.] Jocose quality or disposition; mirthfulness. b. A jocose saying or act 1859.

Jocular (dʒǫ·kiŭlăɹ), *a.* 1626. [ad. L. *jocularis*, f. *joculus*, dim. of *jocus* jest.] 1. Disposed to joking or jesting; mirthful, merry. 2. Of the nature of, or containing, a joke; said or done in joke; comic, humorous 1674.

1. Pardon me for being j. ADDISON. 2. Sheridan made some j. reply 1826. Hence **Jocula·rity**, the quality of being j. **Jo·cularly** *adv.*

‖ **Joculator** (dʒǫ·kiŭlēⁱtəɹ). *Obs.* exc. *Hist.* 1500. [a. L., f. *joculari* to jest; see JONGLEUR, JUGGLER.] A professional jester, minstrel, or jongleur. Hence †**Jo·culatory** *a.* characteristic of, or having the character of, a jester.

Jocund (dʒǫ·kŏnd, dʒōu·kŏnd), *a.* ME. Now only literary. [a. OF. *jocond*, *jocund* (also *ju-*), ad. late L. *jocundus*, modification (after L. *jocus* jest) of L. *jucundus* pleasant, f. *juvare* to help, delight.] Feeling, expressing, or communicating mirth or cheerfulness; merry, blithe, sprightly, light-hearted; pleasant, cheering. †b. Joyful, glad, well-pleased –1578.

Iocond day Stands tipto on the mistie Mountaines tops SHAKS. Hence **Jo·cund·ly** *adv.*, **-ness.** †**Jo·cundry**, j. action or disposition.

Jocundity (dʒokʊ·ndĭti). ME. [ad. late L. *jocunditas*, f. *jocundus* JOCUND.] 1. Jocund quality or condition; mirthfulness; mirth, merriment, glee. b. A pleasantry. NORTH. †2. Pleasure, joy, happiness (of a spiritual kind) –1628.

Jodel: see YODEL.

Joe (dʒōu), *sb.*1 1772. Abbrev. of *Joannes* or JOHANNES, a Pg. gold coin.

Joe (dʒōu), *sb.*2 *colloq.* or *slang.* [Familiar abbrev. of *Joseph.*] 1. Short for *Joe Miller* 1834. 2. A fourpenny piece = JOEY 1 1882. 3. **Joe Manton**, a name given to fowling-pieces made by Joseph Manton, a London gunsmith 1816. 4. **Joe Miller.** [From the name of Joseph Miller, a comedian (1684–1738), attached to a jest-book published after his death.] a. A jest-book 1789. b. A joke; *esp.* a stale joke, a 'chestnut' 1816. Hence **Joe-Millerism** MEREDITH 1879.

4. b. A fool and his money are soon parted, nephew: there is a Joe Miller for your Joe Manton SCOTT.

†**Joey** 1 (dʒōu·i). *slang* or *colloq.* 1865. [Dim. from prec.; see -Y 6. Named from Joseph Hume.] A fourpenny piece.

Joey 2 (dʒōu·i). 1839. [Native Austral. *joè.*] A young kangaroo; also *gen.* a young animal or child.

Jog (dʒǫg), *sb.*1 1611. [f. JOG *v.*] 1. An act of jogging; a shake; a slight push; a nudge 1635. 2. a. The act of moving mechanically up and down. b. The act of jogging along; also *transf.*, e.g. of the rhythm of verse. 1611.

1. A little breeze of wind..which..gave them a kind of a J. on their way towards the shore DE FOE. 2. The familiar j. of a hack carriage 1889.

Jog, *sb.*2 1715. [Cf. JAG *sb.*1 and JOGGLE *sb.*2] 1. = JAG *sb.*1 4; also, a protuberance, swelling (*rare*). ? *Obs.* 2. A right-angled notch, recess, or step, in a surface; any space cut out by such a notch (*U.S.*) 1881.

2. Her [Spain's] maritime advantages were indeed diminished by the j. which Portugal takes out of her territory MAHAN.

Jog (dʒǫg), *v.* 1548. [app. onomatopœic, and akin to SHOG. Not of Celtic origin.] 1. *trans.* To shake or move (a heavy body) with a push or jerk; also with *up*. Also *fig.* 2. To give a slight push to; to nudge; esp. so as to arouse attention 1589. Also *fig.* 3. *intr.* To move up and down or to and fro with a heavy unsteady motion; to move about as if shaken 1586. 4. *intr.* To walk or ride with a jolting pace; to trudge; hence, to move on, go on, be off 1565. Also *fig.*

1. The Seamans needle which is jogged and troubled BP. REYNOLDS. 2. Sudden I jogg'd Ulysses, who was laid Fast by my side POPE. *fig.* I jogged his memory by reverting to our water-party 1840. 3. His sisters-elect, jigging and jogging in a mad polka 1852. 4. The load jogg'd homeward down the lane CLARE. Iog-on, Iog-on the footpath way SHAKS. *fig.* My worldly matters j. on very well SCOTT. Hence **Jo·gger**, one who or that which jogs 1605.

Joggle (dʒǫ·g'l), *sb.*1 1727. [f. JOGGLE *v.*1] An act, or the action, of joggling.

Jo·ggle, *sb.*2 1703. [? from *jog* = JAG, a projection.] *Masonry* and *Carpentry.* A joint at the meeting of two adjacent pieces of stone or timber, to prevent them from sliding on one another; a notch in one piece, or a corresponding projection in the other, or a small piece let in between both, for this purpose. b. *Comb.*, as *j.-joint*, *-piece*, etc. 1703.

Joggle (dʒǫ·g'l), *v.*1 1513. [app. dim. or freq. of JOG *v.* Cf. SHOGGLE.] To jog continuously or repeatedly. 1. *trans.* To shake to and fro, as by repeated jerks; to cause to move from side to side. 2. *intr.* To move to and fro with repeated jerks; to shake or rock about, as something loose or unsteady; *dial.* to jog *along* 1683.

1. Something chanced to j. the magnets..and they instantly rushed together BREWSTER.

Joggle, *v.*2 1801. [f. JOGGLE *sb.*2] *Masonry* and *Carpentry.* *trans.* To join or fit together by means of a joggle; to fasten with a joggle.

Jo·g-jo·g, *adv.* and *adj.* 1780. [f. JOG *v.*] 1. *adv.* With a jogging motion or pace. 2. *adj.* = JOG-TROT B. 1837.

Jog-trot, *sb.*, *adj.*, *adv.* 1653. [f. JOG *v.* or *sb.*1 + TROT.] A. *sb.* (jǫ·g-trǫ·t). 1. *lit.* A jog-ging trot; a slow regular jerky pace (usu. of a horse) 1796. 2. *fig.* A slow, monotonous, or easy-going progression in any action 1756.

2. The monstrous jog-trot of daily life LEVER.

B. *adj.* (jǫ·g-trǫt). 1. *lit.* Of the nature of a jog-trot, jogging; adapted for jogging along 1797. 2. *fig.* Uniform and unhurried; according to routine; humdrum 1653. b. Acting in a jog-trot way 1766.

1. Pleasant jog-trot roads HUGHES.

C. *adv.* (jǫ·g-trǫt). At a jog-trot pace 1845. Hence **Jo·g-tro·t** *v.* to go or move at a jog-trot (*lit.* and *fig.*). **Jo·g-trotter.** SCOTT.

Johannean (dʒohæ·nĭăn), *a.* 1881. [f. L. *Johannes* + -AN.] = JOHANNINE.

Johannes, Joannes (dʒo(h)æ·nīz). 1756. [a. L. *Joannes* (see JOHN), in the legend of the coin.] The name in the British colonies for the Pg. *dobra de quatro escudos* or *peça* of Joannes or João V (1703–1750), a gold coin valued at 6,400 reis, or about 36*s.* sterling. (Also familiarly *jo*, or JOE.)

Johannine (dʒohæ·nəin), *a.* 1861. [f. as prec. + -INE 1.] Of, belonging to, or having the character of, the apostle John.

Johannisberger (dʒohæ·nisbǒɹgəɹ). 1822. [Ger.] A fine white wine produced at Johannisberg in the Rheingau.

John (dʒǫn). ME. [= OF. *Jehan*, F. *Jean* :—L. *Joannes* (later *Johannes*), a. Gr. Ἰωάννης, ad. Heb. *yōχānān*, in full *yehōχānān* Johanan, or Jehohanan, explained as 'Jah (or Jahveh) is gracious'.] 1. A masculine Christian name. b. Also used as a representative proper name for a footman, butler, waiter, messenger, or the like, and in other ways; cf. JACK, JOHNNY. †2. A plant; a variety of pink; usu. Sweet

John -1597. †3. *Sir John*: familiar or contemptuous designation for a priest; from *Sir* as rendering L. *dominus* at the Universities. Cf. also MESS JOHN. -1653.

3. Com neer thou preest, com hyder thou sir Iohn CHAUCER.

Phr., etc. **J.-a-dreams**, a dreamy fellow; **J. Company**, joc. appellation of the East India Company, taken over from the name *Jan Kompanie*, by which the Dutch E. I. C., and now the Dutch government, are known to natives in the East; **J. Doe** (*Eng. Law*), the name given to the fictitious lessee of the plaintiff in the (now obsolete) action of ejectment; **J.-go-to-bed-at-noon**, pop. name for the Goat's-beard, *Tragopogon pratensis*, or other flowers which close about midday, as the Pimpernel and the Star-of-Bethlehem; †**J. Trot**, a bumpkin.

b. St. John's, in comp. **St. John's bread**, the fruit of the carob-tree; also, the tree 1568. **St. John's-wort**, name for plants of the genus *Hypericum* ME.

†**Jo·hn-a-no·kes.** 1531. [orig. *John atten Oke*, i.e. *John* (who dwells) *at the oak*.] A fictitious name for one of the parties in a legal action; hence, indefinitely, any one -1815.

Jo·hn-apple. 1609. = APPLE-JOHN.

†**Jo·hn-a-sti·les.** 1531. [orig. *John atte Stile*, i. e. *John* (who dwells) *at the stile*.] A fictitious name for a party in a legal action (usu. coupled with JOHN-A-NOKES) -1714.

John Bull. 1772. [Name of a character representing the English nation in Arbuthnot's satire (1712).] 1. A personification of the English nation; Englishmen collectively, or the typical Englishman 1778. b. (with *a* and *pl.*) A typical Englishman 1772. 2. A kind of game of chance. STRUTT.

1. b. Both, like true John Bulls, fought with better will than justice for Old England MME. D'ARBLAY. Hence **John-Bu·llism**, the typical English character; a typically English act, utterance, or characteristic.

John Dory (dʒǫn dōᵊ·ri). 1609. [In sense 2, from *John* added to *Dorée* or DORY, the name of the fish. No doubt a joc. formation.] 1. As a proper name. 2. A popular name of a fish, *Zeus faber*, formerly called simply the *dorée* or *dory* 1754.

Johnian (dʒǭᵘ·niăn), *sb.* (*a.*) 1655. [f. JOHN + -IAN.] A member or student of St. John's College, Cambridge.

Johnny, Johnnie (dʒǫ·ni). 1673. [Familiar dim. of *John*; see -IE, -Y[6].] 1. A fellow, chap; *spec.* a nickname given to Englishmen in the Mediterranean, to the Confederate soldiers in the American civil war, etc.; now, chiefly, a fashionable young man of idle habits. 2. Applied to a tiger 1815, a kind of penguin 1898, etc. 3. *Johnny Raw*: nickname for a raw recruit, a novice 1813.

Jo·hnny-cake. Also **journey-cake.** 1775. [Of uncertain origin; perhaps = *Shawnee cake*.] a. *U.S.* A cake made of maize-meal, toasted before a fire, or baked in a pan. b. *Australia.* A cake made of wheat-meal, baked on the ashes or fried in a pan.

Johnsonese (dʒǫnsənī·z), *sb.* (*a.*) 1843. [f. Samuel *Johnson* + -ESE.] The language or style of Dr. Johnson, or an imitation of it.

B. *adj.* In the style of Dr. Johnson 1882.

Johnsonian (dʒǫnsǭᵘ·niăn). 1791. [f. as prec. + -IAN.] A. *adj.* Of, belonging to, or characteristic of Dr. Samuel Johnson (1709-1784); applied esp. to a style of English abounding in words of Latin origin. B. *sb.* A student or admirer of Dr. Johnson 1887. Hence **Johnso·nianism**, J. style or J. phrase. So **Jo·hnsonize** *v. trans.* to clothe in or imbue with the style or language of Dr. Johnson.

Join, *sb.* 1825. [f. JOIN *v.*] An act of joining, or the fact of being joined; *concr.* a line of junction, a joining.

Join (dʒoin), *v.* ME. [a. OF. *joign-*, stem of *joindre* :—L. *jungere* to join; root *jug-* = Gr. ζυγ-, Skr. *yuj-*, Indo-Eur. *yug-*, whence OTeut. *juk-*, Eng. *yoke*.]

I. *trans.* 1. To put (things) together, so that they become physically united or continuous; to fasten, attach, connect, unite. †b. To harness (horses, etc. together, or to a vehicle); to yoke -1728. †c. To combine in a mixture -1626. d. *Geom.* To connect (two points) by a straight line 1660. 2. To put or bring into close contact ME. 3. To put together, combine, unite (immaterial things) ME. †4. To add, annex; to add in contribution -1709. 5. To unite, combine (troops, etc.) into one body or company 1560. †b. *refl.* -1611. 6. To link or unite in marriage, friendship, or any kind of association; to associate, ally ME.

1. Seas but j. the regions they divide POPE. b. He bade the light-foot Houres without delay To joyn his Steeds 1621. 3. To j. Humanity and Policy together BACON. 4. While expletives their feeble aid do j. POPE. 5. *To j. forces* (fig.), to combine efforts. b. Then the Spirit saide vnto Philip, Goe neere, and ioyne thy selfe to this charet *Acts* viii. 29. 6. What therefore God hath joyned together, let not man put asunder *Matt.* xix. 6.

II. *intr.* 1. To come or be brought into material contact or connexion; to combine, unite physically ME. 2. To be in contact; to adjoin ME. 3. †a. To come close together in time. b. To come together or exist together, in operation ME. 4. Of two or more: To come together, come into company ME. †5. *Astrol.* To come into conjunction -1697. 6. To come together, meet, or engage in conflict. ? *Obs.* ME. 7. To enter into association or alliance ME.

1. The ryver of Tames begynneth where Tame and Yse ioyne togyther PALSGR. 2. Iustus..whose house ioyned harde to the sinagoge TINDALE *Acts* xviii. 7. 3. b. Tho' truths in manhood darkly j. TENNYSON. 6. Looke you pray..that our Armies ioyn not in a hot day SHAKS. 7. He makes it his business to j. in Conversation with Envious men STEELE.

III. *trans.* To form (a whole) by putting parts together, e.g. as a JOINER. *Obs.* exc. in phrases. ME.

IV. *trans.* To come into contact, contiguity, company, or union with; to associate oneself with; to become a member of; *ellipt.* for *join oneself to*, †*join to*. 1702.

The two hands that joyn one another are Emblems of Fidelity ADDISON. A young Fellow joyns us from t'other End of the Room STEELE. *absol.* When do you j.?—where is your regiment? LEVER. Phr. *To j. the* (*great* or *silent*) *majority*, to die. *To join up* (colloq.), to enlist.

Phrases. *To j. battle*: to come together and begin a battle; to enter upon a battle, or (*fig.*) a contest of any kind 1455. Also †*intr.* said of the battle 1650. *To j. hands* (from I. 2): a. *lit.* (*a*) To clasp one's hands together; (*b*) of two persons, To grasp each the hand of the other, in token of amity, or *spec.* of marriage; (*c*) of a third person (e.g. the priest at marriage), To cause two persons to grasp each other's hand. b. *fig.* (*j. hands*, *j. hand in hand*): To combine in some action or enterprise.

Join-, the vb.-stem used in comb., as in †**join-hand** *sb.* = JOINING-HAND.

Joinant (dʒoi·nănt), *a.* ME. [a. F. *joignant*, *joindre* to join; see -ANT[1].] †1. Adjoining, adjacent. ME. only. 2. *Her.* = CONJOINED 1828.

Joinder (dʒoi·ndəɹ). 1601. [a. F. *joindre* to join, pres. inf. taken subst.] The act of joining; conjunction, union; *spec.* in *Law* in various connexions.

Joiner (dʒoi·nəɹ), *sb.* [ME. *ioynour*, a. AF. *joignour*, OF. *joigneor*, f. *joigner* to JOIN, assim. to agent-nouns in *-er*; see -OR, -ER[1].] 1. One who joins (see JOIN *v.*[1]) 1483. 2. A craftsman who constructs things by joining pieces of wood; a worker in wood who does lighter and more ornamental work than that of a *carpenter* ME. 3. *transf.* A machine for doing various kinds of work in wood 1875. 4. *colloq.*, *U.S.* One who joins many organizations. **Joi·ner** *v. intr.* to do the work of a j.; also *trans.* **Joi·nering** *vbl. sb.*

Joinery (dʒoi·nəri). 1672. [f. JOINER + -Y[3]; see -ERY.] 1. The art or occupation of a joiner; also *concr.* things made by a joiner. 2. *transf.* and *fig.* Work analogous to that of a joiner 1774.

2. That hideous piece of female j., a patch-work counterpane MISS MITFORD.

†**Joining-hand.** 1583. [f. *joining* + HAND *sb.*] Handwriting in which the successive letters of each word are joined; cursive hand -1812.

Joint (dʒoint), *sb.* ME. [a. OF. *joint* and *jointe*, sb. use of *joint*, *-te* (:—L. *junctum*, *-ta*), pa. pple. of *joindre* to join.]

I. A junction. 1. A joining of two bones (or corresponding parts of an invertebrate animal), either rigidly, or (*esp.*) so as to move upon one another; an articulation. 2. A part of the stem of a plant from which a leaf or branch grows (esp. thickened, as in grasses); a node 1523. 3. That wherein or whereby two members or elements of an artificial structure or mechanism are joined or fitted together, either so as to be rigidly fixed (as *e.g.* bricks, stones, lengths of pipe, etc.), or as in a hinge, pivot, swivel ME. 4. *Geol.* A crack or fissure intersecting a mass of rock; usually occurring in sets of parallel planes, dividing the mass into blocks 1601.

1. Phr. *Out of j.* (ME.): *lit.* said of a dislocated bone; also of the part or member affected; *fig.* perverted, disordered, disorganized. The time is out of ioynt: Oh cursed spight, That euer I was borne to set it right *Haml.* I. v. 188. 3. *Universal j.*: see UNIVERSAL A. *adj.* 7. *To break j.*: see BREAK *v.* V. 2. 4. The partings which divide columnar basalt into prisms are joints LYELL.

II. 1. A part of an animal or plant body connected with another part by a joint or articulation ME. 2. *spec.* One of the portions into which a carcass is divided by the butcher, consisting of one or more bones with the meat thereon 1576.

III. *slang* or *colloq.* (chiefly *U.S.*) A meeting-place, esp. for an illicit purpose; *spec.* an illicit opium-den or drinking-saloon 1883.

Comb.: **j.-bedded** *a.* (*Masonry*), of a stone: placed so that its natural bed (or horizontal surface) forms a vertical j. of the work; **-chair** (*Railways*), a chair (see CHAIR *sb.*) supporting the rails at a j.; **-coupling**, a form of universal joint for coupling sections of shafting; **-hinge**, the same as a strap-hinge; **-oil**, †**-water**, synovia; also in names of cattle diseases, as *joint-ill*, *-murrain*.

Joint (dʒoint), *a.* ME. [a. F. *joint* (:—L. *junctum*), pa. pple. of *joindre* :—L. *jungere* to join. Occas. hyphened to the following sb., *esp.* in sense 2.] 1. Put together, joined, combined, united. *spec.* Of two or more lives: Contemporaneous, concurrent 1606. 2. Of a person or persons: Having or doing (what is expressed by the noun) together or in common ME. 3. Of a thing, action, etc. (in *sing.*): Held, done, made, etc. by two or more persons, parties, or things, in conjunction; common to two or more ME. †4. Made up of parts joined or combined -1711.

1. By their joynt endeavours 1641. During the j. lives of the trustees 1883. 2. Ioynt heires with Christ *Rom.* viii. 17. J.-owners of the Stockport and Woodley Junction 1878. 3. A ioynt burthen, laid vpon vs all SHAKS. J.-estates BLACKSTONE. A j. committee of the two Houses MACAULAY.

Joint (dʒoint), *v.* 1530. [f. JOINT *sb.*] I. *trans.* To connect by a joint or joints; to fasten, fit together, unite. Also *fig.* 1547. b. To fill up the joints of stone, brickwork, etc. with mortar or the like; to point 1703. c. *Carpentry.* To prepare (a board, stave, etc.) for being joined to another 1864. 2. *intr.* for *refl.* To fit exactly into each other as in the joints of masonry, etc. 1695. 3. *trans.* To divide at a joint or into joints; to disjoint, to dismember 1530.

1. The fingers are..jointed together for motion RAY. b. They j. the paving with mortar SMEATON. 3. He joints the Neck: And with a stroke so strong The Helm flies off DRYDEN. To j. a piece of Meat 1709.

Jointed (dʒoi·ntėd), *a.* ME. [f. JOINT *sb.* + -ED[2].] Furnished with, constructed with, or having joints (see the sb.). b. In *comb.*: Having joints of a specified kind 1591.

In j. Armour MILT. b. Iron-j. TENNYSON. **Joi·ntedly** *adv.*

†**Jointer**[1]. 1566. [? f. JOINT *a.* + -ER[1].] A joint possessor; one who holds a jointure -1590.

Jointer[2] (dʒoi·ntəɹ). 1678. [f. JOINT *v.* + -ER[1].] 1. Name of various tools. a. *Carpentry*, etc. A long kind of plane used in dressing the edges of boards, staves, etc. for jointing; also a machine used in jointing staves. b. *Masonry.* A tool used for pointing the joints of brick or stone work 1703. c. A bent piece of iron inserted into a wall to strengthen a joint 1864. 2. A workman employed in jointing; *esp.* one who makes the junctions between parts of an electric wire, etc. 1876.

Comb. **j.-plane** = sense 1 a.

Jointing (dʒoi·ntiŋ), *vbl. sb.* 1591. [f. JOINT *v.* + -ING[1].] The action of JOINT *v.* Also *concr.* The structure of a joint or junction 1668.

Comb.: **j.-plane**, (*a*) a plane of fissure, as in a rock;

(*b*) = JOINTER² 1 a; **-rule**, a long flat ruler used for guiding the jointer (JOINTER² 1 b) in marking the joints of brickwork.

Jointless (dʒoi·ntlės), *a.* 1559. [f. JOINT *sb.* + -LESS.] Without joints or the use of joints; stiff, rigid.

Jointly (dʒoi·ntli), *adv.* ME. [f. JOINT *a.* + -LY².] In a joint manner; so as to be joined; †together –1710; †continuously in space or time –1548; unitedly, conjunctly (the only current sense) ME.

A devise to two persons, to hold j. and severally 1767.

Jointress (dʒoi·ntrės). 1602. [f. JOINTER¹ + -ESS.] A widow who holds a jointure; a dowager.

Th' Imperiall Ioyntresse of this Warlike State SHAKS.

†Joint-ring. 1604. A finger-ring made of two separable halves; = GEMEL 3. –1703.

Joint stock, joint-stock. 1615. [f. JOINT *a.* + STOCK.] 1. Stock or capital held by a number of persons jointly; capital divided into shares; a common fund. 2. *attrib.* (joi·nt-stock). Holding a joint stock; formed or conducted on the basis of a joint stock; as *joint-stock bank, company, firm* 1797.

Joint-stool (dʒoi·nt,stūl). ME. [In sense 1, orig. *joined stool*; in 2, f. JOINT *sb.* I. 3.] 1. A stool made of parts joined or fitted together; a stool made by a joiner. *Obs.* exc. *Hist.* 2. *Mech.* A block holding up the ends of parts which belong in apposition, as railway rails, ways of vessels, etc. 1875.

Joint-tenant. 1531. [Law-Fr. *jointenant*: see JOINT *a.* and TENANT.] One who holds an undivided estate in the same right jointly with another or others, with right of survivorship, till the whole remains in a single hand. Also *fig.* So **Joint-te·nancy**, the holding of an estate by joint-tenants.

Jointure (dʒoi·ntiŭɹ), *sb.* ME. [a. F. :—L. *junctura*, f. *junct-*, *jungere* to join; see -URE.] †1. Joining, union –1606. 2. *concr.* A joining, a joint (now *rare*) ME. †3. The holding of an estate by two or more persons in joint-tenancy –1767. 4. *spec.* a. *orig.* The holding of property to the joint use of husband and wife for life or in tail, as a provision for the latter during widowhood. Hence, b. A sole estate limited to the wife, to take effect upon the death of her husband for her own life at least. 1451. †c. = *dowry*: see DOWRY 2. –1615.

4. He had married a widdow of 700 li. per annum joynter WOOD. Hence **Joi·nture** *v.* to settle a jointure upon; **Joi·ntureless** *a.*

Jointuress (dʒoi·ntiŭrės). 1693. [Altered f. JOINTRESS, after prec.] = JOINTRESS.

Jointweed (dʒoi·nt,wīd). 1866. Pop. name of various weeds with jointed stems. a. In U.S., *Polygonum articulatum.* b. Locally in Eng., various species of Horsetail (*Equisetum*); also the common Mare's-tail (*Hippuris vulgaris*).

Joi·nt-worm. 1706. 1. A tape-worm; as consisting of a series of joints. 2. *U.S.* The larva of various species of hymenopterous insects belonging to the genus *Isosoma*, which do great damage to grain.

Jointy (dʒoi·nti), *a.* 1578. [f. JOINT *sb.* + -Y¹.] Having numerous joints.

Joist (dʒoist), *sb.* [ME. *giste, gyste*, a. OF. *giste*, in mod.F. *gîte*, one of the small beams supporting a platform for artillery, a bed of mineral, etc., f. OF. *gesir* (mod. *gésir*) :—L. *jacere* to lie.] 1. One of the timbers, laid horizontally or nearly so, on which the boards of a floor or the laths of a ceiling are nailed; also, A timber which similarly supports the floor of a platform, a bridge, or other structure. †2. A mass of mineral in its natural bed. 1829.

Joist (dʒoist), *v.*¹ 1615. [f. prec.] *trans.* To furnish with, or fix on, joists.

Joist, *v.*² 1601. Obs. and dial. f. GIST *v.*

Joke (dʒōᵘk), *sb.* 1670. [app. ad. L. *jocus* jest, joke, sport; orig. slang.] 1. Something said or done to excite laughter or amusement; a witticism, a jest; jesting, raillery; also, a ridiculous circumstance. 2. *transf.* A laughing-stock 1791. 3. Something not serious or earnest; a jesting matter 1726.

1. Phr. *Practical j.*, a trick played upon some person usually in order to have a laugh at his expense. *To crack a j.*; *to turn a matter into a j.* The simple j. that takes the shepherd's heart THOMSON. 2. I shall be the standing j. of the mess-table 1823. Hence **Jo·ky** *a.*, jocular.

Joke (dʒōᵘk), *v.* 1670. [f. prec., or ad. L. *jocari* to jest, to joke.] 1. *intr.* To make a joke, to jest. 2. *trans.* To make the object of a joke or jokes; to chaff, banter, rally 1746.

1. Your Honour is pleas'd to j. with me STEELE. 2. Sir Joseph Banks joked her about Otoroo MRS. PIOZZI. Hence **Jo·kingly** *adv.* 1700.

Joker (dʒōᵘ·kəɹ). 1729. [f. JOKE *v.* + -ER¹.] 1. A jester; a merry fellow. 2. *slang.* Man, 'fellow', 'chap' 1811. 3. a. Something used in playing a trick 1858. b. An odd card in a pack, either left blank or ornamented, used in some games, counting usu. as a trump and sometimes as the highest trump 1885. 4. *U.S.* A clause unobtrusively inserted in a legislative enactment and affecting its operation in a way not immediately apparent 1904.

Jokesmith (dʒōᵘ·ksmiþ). 1813. [f. JOKE *sb.* + SMITH.] A manufacturer of jokes.

My j. Sidney, and all his kidney SOUTHEY.

‖**Jokul**, *prop.* **jökull** (yō·kul). Also **yokul.** 1780. [Icel. *jökull* icicle, hence ice, glacier; cf. ICICLE.] In reference to Iceland: A mountain permanently covered with ice and snow; a snow-mountain.

Jole, var. of JOWL. **Jolie, -if, -ife**, etc., obs. ff. JOLLY. **Joll(e**, obs. f. JOWL.

Jollification (dʒǫ:lifikēⁱ·ʃən). *colloq.* 1798. [f. JOLLY *a.* + -FICATION.] The action of jollifying; merrymaking, jollity.

We had a great j. here last week SCOTT.

Jollify (dʒǫ·lifəi), *v.* *colloq.* 1824. [f. as prec. + -FY.] To make merry; to make or become slightly intoxicated.

Jollily (dʒǫ·lili), *adv.* ME. [f. JOLLY *a.* + -LY².] In a jolly manner (see JOLLY *a.*) So †**Jo·lliment, Jo·lliness**, jollity, mirth.

Jollity (dʒǫ·lĭti). [ME. *jolivete, jolite*, etc., a. OF., f. *jolif, joli*; see JOLLY *a.* and -TY.] 1. The quality or condition of being jolly; exuberant mirth; †levity, giddiness. 2. Merrymaking, revelry; *pl.*, Festivities ME. †3. Pleasure; esp. sexual pleasure, lust –1615. †4. Insolent presumption or self-confidence –1614. †5. Splendour, magnificence; finery –1698. †6. Pleasantry; joke, jest –1608.

1. Omnia fert ætas, both health and iollitie BARCLAY. 2. It comes, like an arrest of Treason in a J. FELTHAM. 4. In this iollitie of conceit, he determined to fight RALEIGH. 5. Needie Nothing trimd in iollitie SHAKS.

Jolloped (dʒǫ·ləpt), *a.* 1610. [f. *jollop* sb., wattle (app. f. JOWL *sb.*² + LAP *sb.*¹ 2) + -ED².] *Her.* = WATTLED.

Jolly (dʒǫ·li), *sb.*¹ *slang.* 1829. [JOLLY *a.* used as *sb.*] A royal marine.

I'm a J.—'Er Majesty's J.—Soldier and Sailor too KIPLING. *Tame j.*, a militiaman.

Jo·lly, *sb.*² 1829. Short for JOLLY-BOAT.

Jo·lly, *sb.*³ *colloq.* Short for JOLLIFICATION.

Jolly (dʒǫ·li), *a.* and *adv.* [ME. *jolif, joly*, etc., a. OF. *jolif, joli* gay, festive, etc., of uncertain origin. For the loss of the final *f* cf. *hasty, tardy*.]

I. 1. Of gay disposition or character; lively; joyous; mirthful. Now *arch.* and chiefly of time. †2. Having the lively spirits of youth or health; fresh, sprightly –1586. 3. In high spirits; exhilarated ME.; *euphem.* slightly intoxicated 1652. 4. Indulging in, or fond of, conviviality; festive; jovial ME.

1. While the j. Hours lead on propitious May MILT. 3. Young Churchill and a dozen more grew j., stayed till seven in the morning and drank thirty two bottles H. WALPOLE. 4. *The j. god*, Bacchus. He became a viveur and j. dog about town THACKERAY.

II. †1. Of cheerful courage; high-hearted; brave –1642. †2. Overweeningly self-confident; arrogant, overbearing –1666.

†III. Amorous; wanton, lustful –1645.

In the Song of Songs, which is generally believed, even in the jolliest expressions, to figure the spousals of the church with Christ MILT.

IV. †1. Brilliant, showy, splendid –1688. †2. Finely dressed; = *Sc.* 'braw' –1593. 3. Good-looking; fair, pretty. Now only *dial.* ME. 4. Healthy and well developed; well-conditioned; plump (*dial.* and *colloq.*) 1661.

4. A dainty dame in her youth, and a j. woman in her age 1661.

V. 1. Splendid, fine, excellent; also *ironical* 1534. 2. Exceedingly pleasant, agreeable, or 'nice'. Now *colloq.* 1549. 3. As an admiring intensive: Admirably great, large, big, etc.; *ironically*, 'fine', 'nice'. Now *colloq.*

1. For he's a j. good fe-el-low FARRAR. 2. This Life is most iolly SHAKS. 3. The king had four-and-twenty daughters, a j. number FULLER.

B. *adv.* 1. In a jolly manner; merrily, pleasantly 1615. 2. Qualifying an adj. or adv.; orig. appreciatively, later also ironically, with intensive force: Extremely, very. Now *colloq.* 1549.

2. 'Tis like you'll proue a iolly surly groome SHAKS.

Jolly (dʒǫ·li), *v.* 1610. [f. JOLLY *a.*] 1. *intr.* To make merry, enjoy oneself (*rare*). 2. *slang.* To treat (a person) in an agreeable manner, in order to keep him in good humour, or the like. Const. *up, along*. orig. *U.S.* 1893. b. = CHAFF *v.*²

Jolly-boat (dʒǫ·libōᵘt). 1727. [?] A clinker-built ship's boat, smaller than a cutter, used chiefly as a hack-boat for small work.

†**Jo·llyhead.** [-HEAD.] Jollity. SPENSER.

Jolt (dʒōᵘlt), *sb.* 1599. [See next.] †1. A knock (of the head, etc.) against something –1618. 2. An abrupt shock or jerk which throws a person (or thing) up, to fall again by his (or its) own weight 1632; *fig.* a surprise 1905.

2. My daughter Evelyn going in the coach..a j. (the doore being not fast shut) flung her quite out EVELYN.

Jolt (dʒōᵘlt), *v.* 1599. [? an alteration of JOT *v.*¹, infl. by JOWL *sb.*³ or ⁴.] †1. *trans.* To butt or push; to give a knock to; to nudge –1778. 2. To shake up from one's seat or place with a jerk or jerks; to carry or transport with jolts. (Chiefly in *pass.*) 1599. 3. *intr.* To ride or move along with constant jolts 1703. 4. *intr.* To move up and down or to and fro in a jerky manner 1788.

2. A Coach? I cannot abide to be iolted 1607. 3. He whipped his horses, the coach jolted again JOHNSON. 4. The shoulders..jolting up and down in the convulsions of a hoarse laugh MME. D'ARBLAY. Hence **Jo·ltingly** *adv.*

Jolter (dʒōᵘ·ltəɹ), *sb.* 1611. [f. JOLT *v.* + -ER¹.] One who or that which jolts. So **Jo·lter** *v.* (*rare*) [-ER⁵], to jolt continuously (*trans.* and *intr.*).

Jolter-head, jolterhead. 1620. [An extension of JOLT HEAD.] 1. (dʒōᵘ·ltəɹhe·d) = JOLT HEAD 1. 1700. 2. (dʒōᵘ·ltəɹhed) = JOLT-HEAD 2. 1620. Hence **Jo·lter-hea:ded** *a.* So **Jolter-pate** (in sense 1). SCOTT.

Jolt head, jolt-head. ? *Obs.* 1533. [?] †1. *prop.* jolt head (dʒōᵘ·lt,he·d): A large, clumsy, or heavy head; a stupid head –1701. 2. (dʒōᵘ·lt,hed) A heavy-headed or thick-headed person; a blockhead. Also *attrib.* 1573. Hence **Jo·lt-hea:ded** *a.* (now only *fig.*). ? *Obs.*

Jolty (dʒōᵘ·lti), *a.* 1834. [f. JOLT *sb.* + -Y¹.] Having or causing jolts, as *a j. coach.*

Jonah (dʒōᵘ·nă), *sb.* Also **Jonas.** 1612. 1. A Hebrew prophet, the subject of the Book of Jonah; used allusively. 2. **Jonah-crab**, a large crab (*Cancer borealis*) of the eastern coast of N. America 1893. Hence **Jonah** *v.* *trans.* to bring ill luck to.

Jonathan (dʒǫ·năþăn). 1816. [A personal name; orig. that of the son of Saul, king of Israel.] (esp. in phr. *Brother J.*) A generic name for the people of the United States, and also for a representative United States citizen.

The expression *Brother Jonathan* (cf. 2 *Sam.* i. 26) is said to have been applied to Jonathan Trumbull, Governor of Connecticut, by Washington; hence, to a New Englander, and at length as above.

‖**Jongleur** (ʒoṅglör). 1779. [F. *jongleur*, altered f. *jougleur*, in OF. *jogleor* :—L. *joculatorem* jester.] = JUGGLER 1.

The Jongleurs (the reciters of the merry and licentious fabliaux) MILMAN.

Jonquil (dʒʊ·ŋkwil, dʒǫ·n,kwil). Also †**iunquilia.** 1629. [ad. mod.L. *jonquilla* = F. *jonquille* or Sp. *junquillo*, dim. of *junco*, L. *juncus* rush; so called from the rush-like leaves.] 1. A species of Narcissus (*N. Jonquilla*), having long linear leaves and spikes of fragrant white or yellow flowers; the rush-leaved Daffodil. 2. A pale yellow colour like that of the jonquil. [F. *jonquille.*] 1791. 3. A canary-bird of jonquil colour. Abbrev. *jonque.* 1865.

Joram: see JORUM.

Jordan (dʒǭ·ɹdăn). ME. [?] †**1.** A kind of pot or vessel formerly used by physicians and alchemists. ME. only. **2.** A chamber-pot. Now *vulgar* or *dial.* ME.

Jordan almond. 1440. [In ME. *jardyne almaunde*, app. f. F. or Sp. *jardin* garden; later assoc. w. the river Jordan.] A fine variety of almond, now coming chiefly from Malaga. Also simply *jordan*.

Jorum (dʒōᵊ·rəm). 1730. [?] A large drinking-bowl or vessel; also, its contents; *esp.* a bowl of punch. **b.** *fig.* A large quantity 1872.

Joseph (dʒōu·zĕf). 1578. [repr. Heb. *yōsēph*, name of one of the twelve sons of Jacob, and esp. of the husband of Mary the mother of Jesus Christ; hence in derived uses.] **1.** In allusion to the patriarch Joseph 1849. **2.** A long cloak, worn chiefly by women in the eighteenth century when riding; it was buttoned down the front and had a small cape 1659. **3.** In names of flowers, as **Joseph's coat** (see Gen. xxxvii. 3), a cultivated variety of *Amarantus tricolor*; **Joseph's flower** (in ref. to the bearded figure of St. Joseph in art), Goat's-beard 1578.

Joskin (dʒǫ·skin). 1798. [Cf. *bumpkin*, and *joss* dial. to bump.] A country bumpkin.
I hate the Joskins LAMB.

Joss (dʒǫs). 1711. [app. derived from Pg. *deos* god. 'Pidgin'-English, not Chinese.] A Chinese figure of a deity, an idol. Also *transf.*
Comb.: **j.-house**, a Chinese temple or building for idol-worship; **-stick**, a thin cylinder or stick of fragrant tinder mixed with clay, used by the Chinese as incense, etc.

Josser (dʒǫ·səɹ). *slang.* 1886. [f. JOSS + -ER[1].] **1.** *Austral.* A padre. **2.** A simpleton; a fellow, chap.

Jostle, justle (dʒǫ·s'l, dʒɒ·s'l), *sb.* 1607. [f. next.] †**1.** A just or joust; a tussle –1609. **2.** A collision; a push or thrust that shakes; the action of a pushing crowd (*lit.* and *fig.*) 1611.
2. The jostle of South African nationalities 1881.

Jo·stle, ju·stle, *v.* ME. [f. JUST *v.* + -LE.] **I.** *intr.* †**1.** To just or tilt –1759. **2.** To knock or push *against*, to come into collision *with*; also *absol.* to push and shove 1546. Also *fig.* **b.** To contend for a place, etc. by pushing another away from it; hence, to vie *with* some one *for* some advantage 1614. **3.** To push one's way 1612.
2. They [the charets] shall iustle one against another in the broad wayes *Nahum* ii. 4. **b.** None j. with him for the wall LAMB. 3. It requires a strong man to j. through a crowd SCOTT.

II. *trans.* **1.** To shake or drive by pushing; to knock or push against; to elbow, hustle 1575. Also *fig.* **2.** *Racing.* To push against (a competitor) so as to retard him. Also *absol.* 1723. Also *fig.* **3.** To cause (one thing) to push against another (*lit.* and *fig.*) 1641.
1. Who standeth still i' the street Shall be hustled and justled about CLOUGH. One atom can jostle another out of its place TYNDALL.

Jo·stlement. 1859. [f. JOSTLE *v.* + -MENT.] Jostling.

Jot (dʒǫt), *sb.*[1] 1499. [ad. L. *iota* (read as *jota*), a. Gr. ἰῶτα name of the letter I, ι, the smallest in the alphabet; see IOTA.] The least letter of any writing; hence *gen.* the least or a very little part, point, or amount; a whit. (Usu. with neg. expressed or implied.)
One iott or one tytle of the lawe shall not scape TINDALE *Matt.* v. 18. He..never..abated one j. of his claim 1868.

†**Jot**, *sb.*[2] [f. JOT *v.*[1]] A jolt. H. MORE (1647).

Jot, *v.*[1] Now *dial.* 1530. [app. onomatopœic.] To jog, jolt, bump (*trans.* and *intr.*).

Jot, *v.*[2] 1721. [app. f. JOT *sb.*[1] App. orig. *Sc.*] *trans.* To write down in the briefest form, to make a short note of. Usu. *to j. down.* Hence **Jo·tter**, one who jots.

Jougs (dʒugz, dʒɒgz), *sb. pl.* 1595. [app. a. F. *joug* or L. *jugum* yoke. The pl. form refers to its two hinged halves.] An old Scottish instrument of punishment; it consisted of an iron collar, which was locked round the culprit's neck, and was attached by a chain to a wall or post.
He set an old woman in the j. (or Scottish pillory) SCOTT.

†**Jouisance, -issance.** 1483. [a. late OF. *jouissance*, f. *jouissant*, *jouir* to enjoy; see -ANCE.] = ENJOYMENT –1750.

†**Jouk**, *v.*[1] ME. [a. OF. *jok-ier*, *joqu-ier*, *jouq-ier* to be at roost, at rest, etc., mod.F. *jucher*. Ult. etym. unkn.] **1.** *intr.* Of birds: To perch, sit (upon branches); in *Falconry*, to roost, to sleep upon its perch –1672. **2.** *intr.* To lie asleep or at rest; to lie close; also, To abide, remain. ME. only.

Jouk, jook (dʒuk), *v.*[2] *Sc.* and *n. dial.* 1450. [Of uncertain origin; partly coincident with DUCK *v.*] **1.** *intr.* To dodge in order to avoid a missile or blow; to duck 1513. **2.** *intr.* To dart or spring out of the way or out of sight; to hide oneself by such action; to skulk 1510. **3.** *trans.* To dodge by ducking, bending, or springing aside 1812. **4.** *intr.* †**a.** To bend oneself supply as an acrobat 1450. **b.** To bow (jerkily) in salutation or obeisance 1567; *fig.* to cringe, fawn; to dissemble 1573.
1. But we must jouk and let the jaw gang by SCOTT. 4. **b.** But why should we to nobles jouk? BURNS.

Joul(e, obs. f. JOWL.

Joule (dʒaul). 1882. [f. Dr. J. P. *Joule*, English physicist.] *Physics.* An electrical unit, the amount of work done or heat generated by a current of one ampère acting for one second against a resistance of one ohm.
Phr. **Joule's equivalent** = mechanical equivalent of heat: see EQUIVALENT *sb.* 3 c.

Jounce (dʒauns), *v.* 1440. [?] **1.** *intr.* To move violently up and down; to bump, bounce, jolt. **2.** *trans.* To jolt, bump, or shake up and down, as by rough riding; to give (a person) a shaking 1581. Hence **Jounce** *sb.* a bump, a jolt; a jolting pace 1787.

Journal (dʒɒ̄·ɹnăl). ME. [a. OF. *jur-*, *jor-*, *journal*, *-el* daily (*livre*, *registre*, *papier journal* a day-book); as sb. a day, a day's work, etc. :—late L. *diurnalem* DIURNAL.]
A. *adj.* **1.** Daily, diurnal. Now *rare* or *Obs.* **2.** Ephemeral (*rare*) 1685.
B. *sb.* **I.** †**1.** *Eccl.* = DIURNAL *sb.* 1. –1549. †**2. a.** = ITINERARY –1613. †**b.** A record of travel –1792. **3.** A daily record of commercial transactions, entered as they occur, in order to the keeping of accounts 1500. **4. a.** A daily record of events or occurrences kept by any one for his own use. Now usually implying something more elaborate than a *diary.* 1610. **b.** A register of daily transactions kept by a public body or an association; *spec.* in pl. *Journals*, the record of the daily proceedings in one or other of the Houses of Parliament, kept by the Clerk of the House 1647. **c.** *Naut.* A daily register of the ship's course, the distance traversed, the winds and weather, etc. 1671. †**5.** A record of public events or transactions noted down as they occur, without historical discussion. Also in *pl.* –1687. **6.** A daily newspaper or other publication; hence, by extension, Any periodical publication containing news in any particular sphere 1728.
II. †**1.** A day's travel; a journey –1633. †**2.** Provision for a journey 1629. **3.** As much land as can be ploughed in a day. Prop. the Fr. word *journal* (ʒurnal). 1656. **4.** in *Machinery.* The part of a shaft or axle which rests on the bearings. (No explanation of the origin of this sense has been given.) 1814.
Comb.: **j.-bearing**, the support of a shaft or axle; **-box**, the box or structure enclosing the j. and its bearings; **-packing**, any mass of fibrous material saturated with oil or grease, and inserted in a journal-box to lubricate the j. Hence **Jou·rnal** *v.* to record in a j. 1803; in *Machinery*, to provide with or fix as a j. 1875.

Jou·rnal-book. 1603. [f. JOURNAL *a.* + BOOK *sb.*, after F. *livre journal*, but now taken as 'book consisting of a journal'.] A day-book of any kind; a diary of events; a book containing daily records.

Journalese (dʒɒ̄ɹnălī·z). *colloq.* 1882. [f. JOURNAL *sb.* + -ESE.] 'Newspaper' or 'penny-a-liner's' English.

Journalism (dʒɒ̄·ɹnăliz'm). 1833. [a. F. *journalisme*, f. *journal*; see -ISM.] **1.** The occupation or profession of a journalist; journalistic writing; the public journals collectively. **2.** The practice of keeping a journal 1848.

Journalist (dʒɒ̄·ɹnălist). 1665. [f. JOURNAL *sb.* + -IST.] **1.** One who earns his living by editing or writing for a public journal or journals. **2.** One who keeps a journal 1712.

Journalistic (dʒɒ̄ɹnăli·stik), *a.* 1829. [f. prec. + -IC.] **1.** Of or pertaining to journals or journalism; connected with journalism. **2.** Addicted to journalism (*rare*) 1833.

Journalize (dʒɒ̄·ɹnăləiz), *v.* 1766. [See -IZE.] **1.** *trans.* To enter in a journal or book for daily accounts; *spec.* in *Book-keeping* (see JOURNAL *sb.* I. 3). **2.** To enter, record, or describe in or as in a private journal 1775. **3.** *intr.* To make entries in or keep a journal 1774. **4.** To do the work of a journalist 1864.

Journey (dʒɒ̄·ɹni), *sb.* ME. [a. OF. *jornee*, *journee*, F. *journée* day, day's travel, work, etc. :—pop.L. **diurnata*, f. *diurnum* adj. neut. used sb., f. *dies* day. See -ADE.]
†**I.** A day –1656.
†*Journeys accounts* (*Law*), med.L. *dietæ computatæ* 'days counted', the number of days (usually fifteen) after the abatement of a writ within which a new writ might be obtained.
II. 1. A day's travel; the distance travelled in a day or a specified number of days ME. **2.** A spell of going or travelling, viewed as a distinct whole; an excursion or expedition to some distance; a round of travel. Usu. applied to land-travel, as dist. from a *voyage* by sea. Also *fig.* and *transf.* ME. †**3.** A military expedition, a campaign, etc. –1617.
1. Trent is..thre dayes Iorney on this syde Venise 1560. We travelled onward by short journeys JOHNSON. 2. Phr. *A j. by rail, on foot*; *j. to London, into the country*, etc. *To make* or *undertake a j.* And at parting..they wish him a happy iourney MORYSON. *fig.* This life..is a j., or rather one stage of our j. through matter TUCKER.
III. 1. A day's work; hence, a certain fixed amount of daily labour; a daily spell or turn of work. *Obs.* exc. *dial.* ME. †**2.** A day's doings; *gen.* business, affair –1672. †**3.** *esp.* A day's fighting; a battle, a fight –1617. **4.** A round or turn of work, such as is done at one time, in a day or a shorter space 1600; colloq. phr. *this journey*, on this occasion 1884.

Journey (dʒɒ̄·ɹni), *v.* ME. [a. AF. *journeyer*, OF. *jo(u)rnoyer*, *-ier*, *-eer*, f. *journee*, *jornee* JOURNEY *sb.*] **1.** *intr.* To make or proceed on a journey; to travel. Also *fig.* **2.** *trans.* To travel, traverse. ? *Obs.* 1531. †**3.** To ride or drive (a horse) –1607.
1. Satan had journied on, pensive and slow MILT. *P. L.* IV. 173. 2. I journeyed many a land SCOTT. Hence **Jou·rneyer**, a traveller 1566.

Journeyman (dʒɒ̄·ɹnimæ̆n). 1424. [f. JOURNEY *sb.* III. 1 + MAN.] **1.** One who, having served his apprenticeship to a handicraft or trade, is qualified to work at it for days' wages; a qualified mechanic or artisan who works for another. Dist. on one side from *apprentice*, on the other from *master.* Also *fig.* a drudge, hireling. **2.** *Astron.* More fully, *journeyman clock*: a secondary clock in an observatory, used to compare with standard clocks 1764. **3.** *attrib.*, as *j. tailor*, etc. 1467.
1. *fig.* I haue thought some of Natures Iourneymen had made men, and not made them well SHAKS.

Journey-work (dʒɒ̄·ɹniwɒ̄ɹk). 1601. [f. as prec.] **1.** Work done for daily wages or for hire; the work of a journeyman. **2.** *fig.* Inferior or inefficient work; hackwork 1614.

Joust, *sb.* and *v.*, **Jouster**, etc., common variant spellings of JUST, JUSTER, etc.

Jove (dʒōᵘv). ME. [ad. L. *Jovem* accus. of OL. *Jovis*, repl. in cl. L. by *Juppiter*, *Jūpiter* (orig. vocative **djeu pəter.*] **1.** = JUPITER 1. **2.** The planet Jupiter (*poet.*) ME. **b.** *Her.* = Azure 1562; **c.** *Alch.* Tin 1599.
1. Colloq. in the asseveration *By J.*; cf. L. *pro Juppiter*, *pro Jovem.*

Jovial (dʒōᵘ·viăl), *a.* 1590. [a. F. *jovial* (Rabelais), ad. It. *gioviale* 'borne vnder the planet Ioue' (Florio), ad. L. *jovialis*, f. *Jovi-s*; see JOVE and -AL.] †**1.** Of or pertaining to Jove; Jove-like –1611. **2.** Of or belonging to the planet Jupiter 1665. †**3.** *Her.* Azure in colour. HOLLAND. †**4.** *Alchemy.* Of tin. SALMON. **5.** *Astrol.* Under the influence of the planet Jupiter, which made those born under it joyful and happy. Also *absol.* as *sb.* –1863. **6.** Merry, jolly; convivial 1592.
1. This princely j. fowl [the eagle] DRAYTON. 2. Saturn..hath several..lesser Planets, like the J.

Satellites 1690. 5. According to that Star..the Aspect of one is Saturnine, of another Jovial, etc. STANLEY. 6. Be bright and Iouiall among your Guests to Night *Macb.* III. ii. 28. Hence **Jo·vial·ly** *adv.*, **-ness.**

†Jo·vialist. 1569. [f. prec. + -IST.] 1. A person born under the planet Jupiter –1653. 2. A person of a jovial disposition –1656.

Joviality (dʒōuviæ·lĭti). 1626. [ad. F. *jovialité*, f. *jovial*; see -ITY.] The quality of being jovial; good-fellowship; conviviality. var. **Jo·vialty** (now *rare*) 1621.

Jovialize (dʒōu·viăləiz), *v.* 1614. [f. JOVIAL *a.* + -IZE.] To make or †be jovial.

Jovian (dʒōu·viăn), *a.* (*sb.*) 1530. [f. L. *Jovis* JOVE + -AN.] 1. Of, belonging to, or of the nature of Jove. 2. Of or belonging to the planet Jupiter 1794. 3. *sb.* One who resembles or imitates Jove. MARSTON.

Jovice·ntric, *a.* 1864. *Astron.* Referred to Jupiter as a centre; viewed as from the centre of Jupiter.

Jovinianist (dʒovi·niănist). 1449. [f. med.L. *jovinianista*, f. *Jovinianus* Jovinian; see -IST.] A follower or adherent of Jovinian, a monk of the 4th c., who denied the virginity of Mary, opposed certain forms of celibacy and asceticism, and maintained the equality of all sins, rewards, and punishments. Also *attrib.* So **Jovi·nian** = prec. 1585.

†Jo·vy, *a.* ME. [ad. L. *Jovius*, f. *Jovis* JOVE.] Jovial –1667.

Jowl, jole (dʒōul, dʒaul), *sb.*[1] [OE. *ceafl*, ME. *chavel*, whence *chauel*, *chawl*. The *j* is unaccounted for.] 1. A jawbone, a 'chaft'; a jaw; esp. the under jaw; *pl.* Jaws. 2. Idle or malicious talk; = JAW *sb.* 6. –1589. 3. The cheek, a cheek 1668.

1. His mouth was too large and his jowl too heavy BESANT. 3. *Cheek by jowl*, in earlier use *cheek by cheek*; see CHEEK *sb.*

Jowl, jole (dʒōul, dʒaul), *sb.*[2] [ME. *cholle*, *choll*, *chol*; the *j* is unaccounted for.] The external throat or neck when fat or prominent; the dewlap of cattle; the crop or the wattle of a bird, etc.

Jowl, jole (dʒōul, dʒaul), *sb.*[3] [ME. *choll(e*, *iol*, etc., of unkn. origin. The *j* forms prob. originated in this word, and passed thence to JOWL *sb.*[1] and [2].] †1. The head of a man or beast –1825. 2. *spec.* The head of a fish; hence (as a cut or dish) the head and shoulders of salmon, sturgeon, or ling ME.

Jowl, joll (dʒōul), *sb.*[4] Now *dial.* 1520. [f. JOWL, JOLL *v.*] 1. A bump; a blow, esp. on the head; a knock, a stroke. 2. A single stroke of a bell. Chiefly *dial.* 1822.

Jowl, joll (dʒōul), *v.* Now *dial.* ME. [? f. JOWL *sb.*[3], the notion being to knock a head or ball.] 1. *trans.* To strike (a ball) with a stick. 2. To bump; to strike, knock, or push; esp. to dash (the head) against something 1470. 3. *trans.* To strike (the wall of a coal-pit), as a signal, etc. 1825. 4. *intr.* and *trans.* To toll, knell, or ring slowly, as a bell. Chiefly *dial.*

2. That Scull..how the knaue iowles it to th' grownd *Haml.* V. i. 84.

Jowled (dʒōuld), *a.* 1614. [f. JOWL *sb.*[1] + -ED[2].] Having jowls or jaws (of a specified kind). The crowd about the..doors—blue-jowled Portuguese KIPLING.

Jowler (dʒōu·lər, dʒdu·lər). *Obs.* exc. *dial.* [f. as prec. + -ER[1].] A heavy-jawed dog. Also, a quasi-proper name for a dog.

Jowter (dʒau·tər). *dial.* 1463. A fish-hawker. Also, A hawker of any kind.

Joy (dʒoi), *sb.* ME. [a. OF. *joie*, *joye* joy jewel, F. *joie* (= It. *gioja*) :—pop.L. **gaudia* fem. for L. *gaudia*, pl. of *gaudium* joy.] 1. Pleasurable emotion due to well-being or satisfaction; the feeling or state of being highly pleased; exultation of spirit; gladness, delight. Also with *a* and *pl.* b. The expression of glad feeling; mirth ME. c. Used interjectionally 1719. 2. A pleasurable state or condition; a state of felicity; hence, the place of bliss, paradise. *Obs.* or *arch.* ME. 3. A source or object of joy; a delight ME. b. As a term of endearment (esp. *dial.*) 1590. †4. = GLORY 4. –1483. †5. A jewel –1824.

1. They that sow in teares: shall reape in ioy *Ps.* cxxvi. 5. A j. in which I cannot rejoice TENNYSON. b. Breake foorth into ioy, sing together, yee waste places *Isa.* lii. 9. 2. So that at the last we may come to hys eternall ioye *Bk. Com. Prayer* 1552. 3. The hyll of Sion is a fayre place, & the ioye of the whole earth BIBLE (Great) *Ps.* xlviii. 2. b. His remembrance lay In Egypt with his ioy SHAKS.

Comb.: **j.-bells, -fire, -gun,** bells rung, a bonfire lighted [F. *feu de joie*], or a gun fired to celebrate a joyful event; **-ride** (orig. *U.S.*), a ride in a motor-car without the owner's leave; hence *gen.*; **-stick,** the lever controlling the wing and tail planes of an aeroplane 1917; **-weed,** a plant of the genus *Alternanthera.*

Joy (dʒoi), *v.* ME. [a. OF. *joir*, F. *jouir* :—pop.L. **gaudire* = L. *gaudere* to rejoice.] †1. *refl.* To experience joy; to enjoy oneself; to rejoice –1712. 2. *intr.* To feel or manifest joy; to be glad; to rejoice or delight ME. †b. *trans.* To rejoice at –1647. 3. *trans.* To fill with joy; to gladden, delight ME. 4. To derive enjoyment from; to enjoy. †Formerly, also, To have the use or benefit of. ME. †5. *trans.* To salute with expressions of joy, welcome, or honour; in early use, to glorify, extol –1725. †b. To wish joy *of*; to congratulate. Const. *of* (*in*). –1701.

1. He has never joyed himself since ADDISON. 2. I shall neuer ioy in my herte vnto the tyme I haue slayne the LD. BERNERS. I j. to see you 1741. 3. It joyes mee to heere thy soule prospereth CROMWELL. 4. Who might have liv'd and joy'd immortal bliss MILT. *P. L.* IX. 1166. 5. The faithful servant joy'd his unknown lord POPE. b. I come to j. you of a Crown ROWE.

Joyance (dʒoi·ăns). Chiefly *poet.* 1586. [f. JOY *v.* + ANCE. App. coined by Spenser.] 1. Rejoicing; delight; enjoyment 1590. 2. Festivity, merrymaking 1586. 3. Joyous character or quality; delight, charm 1847.

1. Chearfull, fresh and full of ioyance glad SPENSER. 2. His sports were faire, his ioyance innocent SPENSER. 3. An illimitable distance of sylvan j. DISRAELI. So **Joy·ancy,** joyousness 1849. **Joy·ant** *a.* joyous 1670.

Joyful (dʒoi·ful), *a.* ME. [f. JOY *sb.* + -FUL.] 1. Full of joy; having and showing joy; delighted. 2. Expressing or manifesting joy; indicative of gladness ME. 3. Fraught with, or causing joy; delightful ME.

1. A ioyfull mother of two goodly sonnes SHAKS. 2. Make a ioyfull noise vnto God *Ps.* lxvi. 1. 3. J. news 1592. Hence **Joy·ful·ly** *adv.*, **-ness.**

Joyless (dʒoi·lės), *a.* ME. [-LESS.] 1. Destitute of joy; sad, cheerless. 2. Causing no joy; dismal, dreary ME.

1. A j. smile SHAKS. 2. Doomed To eat his j. bread, lonely 1804. Hence **Joy·less·ly** *adv.*, **-ness.**

Joyous (dʒoi·əs), *a.* ME. [a. AF. *joyous* = OF. *joios*, *-eus*, F. *joyeux*, f. *joie* JOY *sb.*] 1. = JOYFUL 1, 2. 2. = JOYFUL 3. 1450.

1. A citie full of bruit, a ioyous citie BIBLE (Genev.) *Isa.* xxii. 2. A j. laugh HARE. 2. That j. season [harvest] 1796. Hence **Joy·ous·ly** *adv.*, **-ness.**

Joy·some, *a.* *rare.* 1613. [f. JOY *sb.* + -SOME.] Fraught with joy, gladsome.

Juba (dʒū·bă). *U.S.* 1834. [Negro.] A breakdown performed by plantation negroes of the Southern U.S., accompanied by repeated cries of *juba.*

Jubardy: see JEOPARDY.

Jubate (dʒū·bėt), *a.* 1826. [ad. L. *jubatus* maned.] *Zool.* Having a mane, or a fringe of hair like a mane.

‖**Jubbah** (dʒv·bă, dʒu·bbă). 1548. [ad. Arab. *jubbah*. Cf. JIBBAH.] An outer garment worn by Mohammedans and Parsees, consisting of a long cloth coat, open in front, with sleeves reaching nearly to the wrists.

‖**Jube** (dʒū·bi). 1725. [a. L. *jube*, imper. of *jubere*; said to be from the words *Jube, domne, benedicere*, 'Please, sir, bless' addressed to the celebrant by the deacon before the reading of the Gospel.] 1. A rood-loft or screen and gallery dividing the choir from the nave 1767. †2. A chair for the preacher, ordinarily placed within the enclosure of the choir 1725.

Jubilant (dʒū·bilănt), *a.* 1667. [ad. L. *jubilantem*, f. *jubilare* to JUBILATE.] Making a joyful noise; now generally, Making demonstrations of joy, exultingly glad. b. Expressing joy 1784.

Amid a mighty nation j. COLERIDGE. Hence **Ju·bilance, -ancy. Ju·bilantly** *adv.*

†Ju·bilar, *a.* 1613. [f. L. *jubilum* wild cry, but in sense assoc. w. *jubilæus* JUBILEE + -AR.] = JUBILARY. **Jubila·rian** [f. med.L. *jubilarius* JUBILARY], *R. C. Ch.* a priest, monk, or nun who has been such for fifty years 1782. **†Ju·bilary** *a.* [ad. med.L. *jubilarius*, f. *jubilum* wild cry, but in sense assoc. w. JUBILEE], of or pertaining to a jubilee, jubilar 1537.

‖**Jubilate** (dʒūbilā·ti, yūbilā·te), *sb.* ME. [L., 'shout ye', the first word of the psalm.] 1. The hundredth psalm (*Jubilate Deo*, O be joyful in the Lord), used as a canticle in the Anglican service; also, the music to which this is set. 2. *transf.* A call to rejoice; an outburst of triumph 1767. 3. *R. C. Ch.* The third Sunday after Easter, so called because Ps. 66, which begins with *Jubilate*, is used as the introit on that day.

Jubilate (dʒū·bileit), *v.* 1604. [f. L. *jubilat-*, *jubilare* to halloo, shout, huzza, to shout for joy.] †1. *trans.* To make glad. T. WRIGHT. 2. *intr.* To utter sounds of joy or exultation; to rejoice, exult 1641.

Jubilation (dʒūbilē·ʃən). ME. [ad. L. *jubilationem*, f. *jubilare* to JUBILATE.] The action of jubilating; exultation, gladness; public rejoicing. Also with *a* and *pl.*

Disconsolate amidst the publique Iubilations 1634.

†Jubile·al, *a.* *Obs.* 1588. [f. next + -AL.] Of jubilee. So **Jubile·an** *a.* 1624.

Jubilee (dʒū·bilī). Also **†jubile.** ME. [a. F. *jubilé*, ad. late L. *jubilæus* adj. (sc. *annus*), used as sb., after Gr. ἰωβηλαῖος adj., f. ἰώβηλος 'jubilee', ad. Heb. *yōbēl* 'jubilee', orig. 'ram', hence 'ram's horn used as a trumpet'. Assoc. w. native L. *jubilum* wild cry, shout, and *jubilare.*] 1. *Jewish Hist.* (more fully *year of Jubilee*). A year of emancipation and restoration, which was to be kept every fifty years, and to be proclaimed by the blast of trumpets throughout the land; during it the fields were to be left untilled, Hebrew slaves were to be set free, and lands and houses in the open country or unwalled towns that had been sold were to revert to their former owners or their heirs. b. *fig.* or *transf.* A time of restitution, remission, or release 1584. 2. *R. C. Ch.* A year of remission during which plenary indulgence may be obtained by a pilgrimage to Rome and certain pious works ME. 3. The fiftieth anniversary of an event ME. †b. A period of fifty years –1726. 4. A season or occasion of general rejoicing 1592. 5. Exultant joy, jubilation 1526. b. Shouting; sound of jubilation 1526. 6. *attrib.* ME.

1. And ye shall hallow the fiftieth yeere..: It shalbe a Iubile vnto you *Lev.* xxv. 10. b. The first day of our J. is Death SIR T. BROWNE. 3. *Silver J.* (after *Silver Wedding*), celebration of the twenty-fifth anniversary. *Diamond J.*, a name applied to the celebration of the sixtieth year of the reign of Queen Victoria. 5. b. All along the crowded way Was j. and loud huzza SCOTT.

Jubilize (dʒū·biləiz), *v.* 1649. [f. L. *jubilum* shout + -IZE.] *intr.* a. To jubilate. b. To celebrate a jubilee.

Jucundity (dʒukv·ndĭti). ? *Obs.* 1536. [ad. L. *jucunditas*, f. *jucundus* (see JOCUND).] 1. The quality of being pleasant; enjoyableness 1620. 2. = JOCUNDITY 1536.

Judæo- (dʒiudī,o), used as comb. f. L. *judæus* Jewish, as in *Judæologist* (1858), *Judæo-Christian.*

Judaic (dʒudē·ik), *a.* 1611. [ad. L. *Judaicus*, a. Gr. Ἰουδαϊκός, f. Ἰουδαῖος JEW.] Of or pertaining to the Jews, Jewish. So **Juda·ical** *a.* 1470, **Juda·ically** *adv.* 1582.

Judaism (dʒū·dĕ,iz'm). 1494. [ad. L. *judaismus*, a. Gr. ἰουδαϊσμός; see -ISM.] 1. The profession or practice of the Jewish religion; the religious system or polity of the Jews. 2. The act of Judaizing; a practice or style of thought like that of the Jews 1641. 3. *Hist.* As tr. med.L. *Judaismus* = JEWRY 2; also, the revenue derived by the Crown from the Jews; the treasury which received the money 1782. Hence **Ju·daist,** a Judaizer. **Judai·stic** *a.* of, pertaining to, or characteristic of, Judaists.

Judaize (dʒū·dĕ,əiz), *v.* 1582. [ad. late L. *judaizare*, a. Gr. ἰουδαΐζειν; see -IZE.] 1. *intr.* To play the Jew; to follow Jewish customs, religious rites, or practice. 2. *trans.* To make Jewish; to imbue with Jewish doctrines or principles 1653.

1. That Vsurers should haue Orange-tawney Bonnets, because they doe Iudaize BACON. 2. Error..in

many other Points of Religion had miserably judaiz'd the Church MILTON. Hence **Judaiza·tion,** a becoming or making Jewish in character. **Ju·daizer,** one who adheres to Jewish ritual or practice.

Judas (dʒū·dǣs). 1453. [a. L. *Judas*, a. Gr. Ἰούδας, ad. Heb. *yehūdāh* Judah, name of one of the sons of Jacob, whence, later, a common Jewish name.] 1. The name of the disciple who betrayed Jesus Christ; hence: One who betrays under the semblance of friendship; a traitor of the worst kind 1489. 2. A painted socket of wood in which the paschal candle was set. *Hist.* 1453 (1310 in Anglo-Latin). 3. A small lattice or aperture in a door, through which a person can look without being noticed from the other side 1865.

Comb.: **J.-blossom,** the blossom of the JUDAS-TREE; **-colour, -coloured** *a.* (of the hair or beard) red (from a mediæval belief that Judas Iscariot had red hair and beard); **-hole, -trap** = sense 3; **kiss; -like** *a.* and *adv.* Hence †**Judasly** *adv.*, treacherously 1508–1659.

Ju·das-tree. 1668. [From a popular belief that Judas hanged himself on a tree of this kind.] 1. The common name of *Cercis Siliquastrum*, a leguminous tree of Southern Europe and parts of Asia, with abundant purple flowers which appear in spring before the leaves. 2. A local name for the Elder (*Sambucus nigra*); see under JEW'S EAR.

Judcock (dʒɒ·dkɒk). 1621. [app. for *judge-cock* from its black crown compared to the judge's black cap.] The Jack Snipe.

Judge (dʒɒdʒ), *sb.* [ME. *juge*, a. OF. *juge*, usually referred to L. *judicum*, *-us* by-form of *judicem*, *judex* (f. *jus* right, law + *-dicus* speaking, speaker), but by some regarded as conformed to the vb. *juger* to JUDGE.] 1. A public officer appointed to administer the law; one who has authority to hear and try cases in a court of justice. 2. Used of God or Christ, as supreme arbiter, pronouncing sentence on men and moral beings ME. 3. *Heb. Hist.* An officer (usually a leader in war) invested with temporary authority in ancient Israel in the period between Joshua and the kings. b. *pl.* (in full, *the Book of Judges*): the seventh book of the Old Testament, containing the history of this period. ME. 4. A person appointed to decide in any contest, competition, or dispute; an arbiter, umpire ME. 5. One who or that which judges of anything in question. Often in phr. *to be judge.* 1470. 6. A person qualified to form or pronounce an opinion 1560. 7. *Mining.* A staff used for gauging the depth of the holing 1875.

1. Ivdges ought to remember, that their office is *Ius dicere*, and not *Ius dare*; to interprete law, and not to make law, or giue Law BACON. *Circuit-j.*, a j. of a circuit court. *J. ordinary*, spec. the j. of the Court of Probate and Divorce, previous to 1875. *J.-advocate, j. in eyre, puisne j.*, etc.: see ADVOCATE, etc. 2. Shall not the Iudge of all the earth doe right? *Gen.* xviii. 25. 4. He was one of the judges at a flower-show (*mod.*). 5. Well, thou shalt see: thy eyes shall be thy judge SHAKS. 6. I here disallow thee to be a competent j. WALTON. *Comb.* **j.-made** *a.* (of law), constituted by judicial decisions. Hence **Ju·dgeship,** the office of a j. 1677.

Judge (dʒɒdʒ), *v.* ME. [a. OF. *jugier*, AF. *juger* :—L. *judicare*, f. *judicem* JUDGE.]

I. *trans.* 1. To try, or pronounce sentence upon (a person) in a court of justice; to sit in judgement upon. (Also said of God or Christ: cf. prec. 2.) †2. *spec.* To sentence, condemn –1675. 3. To give sentence concerning (a matter); to try (a cause); to decide (a question) 1513. 4. To decree, order ME. 5. To assign or award by judgement. Now *rare* or *Obs.* ME. 6. To govern or rule as an Israelitish judge (cf. prec. 3). Also *absol.* To hold the office of a judge. ME. 7. To declare authoritatively (a person) to be (so-and-so). ? *Obs.* ME. 8. To form an opinion about; to estimate; to appraise ME. 9. To criticize; *esp.* to condemn, censure. Also *absol.* ME. 10. To apprehend, think, consider, suppose; to conclude, suppose to be ME.

1. Then all thy Saints assembl'd, thou shalt j. Bad men and Angels MILT. *P. L.* III. 330. 3. J. and defend my cause, O Lord TATE & BRADY. 5. Ladies whose bright eyes..j. the prize Of wit or arms MILT. 6. The example of Debora..when she iudged Israel KNOX. 7. Hee was iudged an vnprofitable seruant MORYSON. 8. Men judge by the complexion of the Skie The state and inclination of the day SHAKS. 9. Iudge not lest ye be iudged. For as ye iudge so shal ye be iudged TINDALE *Matt.* vii. 1, 2. 10. Small townes I j. they were 1615. It was..judged better to begin the attack at once FREEMAN.

II. *intr.* 1. To act as judge; to sit in judgement ME. 2. To give a decision or opinion on any matter; *esp.* to arbitrate ME. 3. To form an opinion; to arrive at a notion, esp. a sound or correct notion, about something; in *Logic*, To apprehend mentally the relation of two objects; to make a mental assertion or statement. Const. *of.* ME.

1. As for Civill matters they may j. without appeale 1639. 2. God must j. 'twixt man and me BROWNING. 3. When the mind assents to a proposition it judges MILL. From its form and colour he could..j. of its condition TYNDALL.

Judgement, judgment (dʒɒ·dʒmĕnt). ME. [a. F. *jugement*, f. *juger* to JUDGE + -MENT.] 1. The action of trying a cause in a court of justice; trial. (Now *rare* or merged in 3.). 2. The trial of moral beings by God (or Christ) as Judge; *spec.* the final trial at the end of the world. Often in *day of j.* ME. 3. The sentence of a court of justice; a judicial decision or order in court ME. b. *Law.* (*ellipt.*) An assignment of chattels, etc. made by judgement or decree of court; the certificate of such judgement as a security 1677. 4. Divine sentence or decision; *spec.* a misfortune or calamity regarded as a divine visitation or the like ME. 5. Any formal or authoritative decision, as of an arbiter. (Now *rare.*) ME. 6. Criticism; censure ME. 7. An opinion, estimate ME. †b. A form of religious opinion or belief; a 'persuasion' –1687. 8. The faculty of judging; that function of the mind whereby it arrives at a notion of anything; the critical faculty; discernment 1535. b. Discernment, discretion, understanding, good sense 1576. †c. *transf.* A person having good judgement; a 'judge' –1682. 9. *Logic.* The action of mentally apprehending the relation between two objects of thought; predication, as an act of the mind. With *pl.* A mental assertion or statement. 1704. 10. In biblical uses, chiefly as tr. Heb. *mishpāt.* a. Justice, righteousness, equity ME. b. A (divine) decree, ordinance, law, statute ME. c. (One's) right 1611. †11. The function of a judge or ruler (in ancient Israel). KNOX. 12. *attrib.* 1526.

1. A Daniel come to iudgement, yea a Daniel SHAKS. Phr. *To sit in j.*: (*a*) *lit.* to preside as judge at a trial; (*b*) *fig.* to pass j. *upon* (see 6), to judge, criticize (with assumed superiority). 3. He confessed the Inditement, and so had Iudgement to bee hanged HALL. b. Upon a marriage, a mother assigned an unregistered judgment to a trustee for her daughter for life LD. ST. LEONARDS. 4. Hence I tooke a thought, This was a Iudgement on me SHAKS. 5. *Haml.* V. ii. 291. 6. You have my designs, and I desire your judgment of them RAY. 7. This waye in my iudgement doeth excell all the rest 1559. *Private j.*: formation of individual opinion (esp. in religious matters), as opp. to acceptance of a statement or doctrine on authority. 8. b. A deed..owing more To want of judgment than to wrong design COWPER. 9. A Judgment, then, is an expression that two notions can or cannot be reconciled ABP. THOMSON. 10. a. *Isa.* lxi. 8. b. *Exod.* xxi. 1. c. *Deut.* x. 18.

Comb.: **j. creditor,** a creditor in whose favour a j. has been given ordering the payment of the debt due to him; **j. debt,** a debt for the payment of which a j. has been given; **j. debtor,** a debtor against whom such a j. has been given; **j. summons,** a summons issued in a County Court against a *judgement debtor*, to show cause why he should not be imprisoned for default in payment. Hence †**Ju·dgemented** *a.* 1548–1821, **Ju·dgementless** *a.* 1590.

Ju·dg(e)ment-day. 1591. [= *day of judgement*; see prec. 2.] The day of God's final judgement; the last day; doomsday.

Ju·dg(e)ment-hall. 1534. A hall in which trials at law are held; a court of justice; a tribunal. (Chiefly *Hist.*)

Ju·dg(e)ment-seat. 1526. The seat on which a judge sits when trying a cause or pronouncing judgement; a tribunal.

He was driven from the judgement-seat with scorn FREEMAN.

Judger (dʒɒ·dʒəɹ). 1449. [f. JUDGE *v.* + -ER[1].] One who or that which judges.

Judgmatic, -al (dʒɒdʒmæ·tik, -ăl), *a. colloq.* 1774. [irreg. f. JUDGE + *-matic*, after *dogmatic*.] Judicious, discerning.

Judicable (dʒū·dikăb'l), *a.* Now *rare.* 1647. [ad. late L. *judicabilis*, f. *judicare* to judge; see -ABLE.] Capable of being judged; liable to judgement.

Judica·tion. 1625. [ad. L. *judicationem*, f. *judicare* to judge.] The action of judging, judgement.

Judicative (dʒū·dikĕtiv), *a.* 1641. [f. L. *judicat-*, *judicare* to judge + -IVE; see -ATIVE.] Having the function of judging; judicial.

Appeals to their j. faculties 1678.

Judicatory (dʒū·dikătŏri, -di·kătŏri), *sb.* 1575. [ad. late L. *judicatorium* adj. neut.; see next.] 1. A court of judicature; a tribunal. Chiefly *Sc.* 1606. Also *transf.* and *fig.* 2. Judicature; a system of judicature.

2. The Lords, as the Supreme Court of J. CLARENDON.

Ju·dicatory, *a.* ? *Obs.* 1603. [ad. late L. *judicatorius*, f. *judicat-*, *judicare* to judge; see -ORY.] 1. Having the function of judging or passing sentence; of or pertaining to judgement 1647. 2. By which a judgement may be made; critical.

1. A great Share in the j. Power PENN.

Judicature (dʒū·dikătiŭɹ, -eⁱtiŭɹ). 1530. [f. med.L. *judicatura*, f. L. *judicat-*, *judicare* to judge; see -URE.] 1. The action of judging; administration of justice; judicial process. 2. The office, function, or authority of a judge 1530. b. Extent of jurisdiction of a judge or court. BOUVIER. 3. A body of judges; a legal tribunal, or such tribunals collectively 1593. †4. *fig.* Mental judgement; criticism –1758. †5. Judicial (as opp. to moral) quality. MILT. 6. *attrib.* 1873.

1. We have demonstratively shewed .. that J. is nothing else but an Interpretation of the Laws HOBBES. *Supreme Court of J. in England*, that constituted by Acts of Parliament in 1873 and 1875, in which were united the Courts of Chancery, King's Bench, Common Pleas, Exchequer, Admiralty, etc. 5. Our Saviour disputes not here the J.,..but the morality of Divorce, whether it be Adultery or no 1643. 6. **Judicature Acts,** a name given to the statutes establishing the Supreme Court of J., and regulating its practice.

Judicial (dʒudi·ʃăl). ME. [ad. L. *judicialis*, f. *judicium* judgement; see -AL.]

A. *adj.* 1. Of or belonging to judgement in a court of law, or to a judge in relation to this function; pertaining to the administration of justice; proper to a legal tribunal; resulting from or fixed by a judgement in court. Also *fig.* b. Enforced by secular judges and tribunals; in *j. law*, opp. to *moral* and *ceremonial* ME. c. *Theol.* Inflicted by God as a judgement; of the nature of a divine judgement 1613. 2. Having the function of judgement 1561. 3. Of a judge; proper to a judge 1800. 4. Giving judgement upon any matter; forming or expressing a judgement; critical 1589. b. *Astrol.* Relating to the judgement of the influence of stars upon human affairs CHAUCER. †5. Judicious –1624.

1. J. separation is a new term introduced for the old divorce *a mensâ et thoro* LD. ST. LEONARDS. *Judicial murder*, an unjust though legal death sentence. c. What is called a j. blindness BURKE. 2. Parliaments were originally j. as well as legislative assemblies H. COX. *J. combat* (*duel*), one engaged in for formal decision of a controversy. *J. Committee of the Privy Council*: one of the two Appellate Tribunals in Great Britain, established in 1832 for the disposal of appeals made to the King in Council. 3. Phr. *Purity of the j. ermine.* Hence **Judicia·lity** 1621. **Judi·cial·ly** *adv.*, **-ness.**

B. *sb.* [The adj. used ellipt.] †1. A judicial law or ordinance; see A. 1 b –1721. †2. Determination, decision, judgement –1631. †b. *Astrol.* A determination as to a future event from the positions of the heavenly bodies 1496–1652. †3. A legal judgement –1660.

Judiciary (dʒudi·ʃări). Now *rare.* 1587. [ad. L. *judiciarius*, f. *judicium* judgement; see -ARY[1].] A. *adj.* = JUDICIAL A. 1604. B. *sb.* 1. Judicial astrology; a judicial astrologer. 1587. 2. = JUDICATURE 3. 1802.

Judicious (dʒudi·ʃəs), *a.* 1591. [ad. F. *judicieux*, *-euse*, f. L. *judicium* judgement; see -OUS.] 1. Having or exercising sound judgement; discreet, wise, sensible; *esp.* in relation to practical matters. 2. Proceeding from or showing sound judgement; marked by discretion, wisdom, or good sense 1600. †3. = JUDICIAL A. 1. –1632.

1. Now this ouer-done..cannot but make the Iudi-

cious greene *Haml.* III. ii. 29. A j. pilot 1704. 2. J. purchases 1833. A j. remark 1861. 3. His last offences to vs Shall haue Iudicious hearing *Cor.* v. vi. 128. Hence **Judi·cious-ly** *adv.*, **-ness.**

Judy (dʒū·di). 1812. [Familiar form of *Judith.*] Name of the wife of Punch in 'Punch and Judy'; hence (*slang*) applied disparagingly, *esp.* to a woman of ridiculous appearance.

Jug (dʒvg), *sb.*[1] 1569. A pet-name or familiar substitute for Joan, or Joanna; applied as a common noun to a homely woman, maidservant, sweetheart, or mistress; or in disparagement. Now *rare.*

Whoop Iugge I loue thee *Lear* I. iv. 245.

Jug (dʒvg), *sb.*[2] 1538. [? transf. use of prec.] 1. A deep vessel for holding liquids, usually with a swelling body, or one that tapers upward, having a handle on one side, and often a spout. Often differentiated, as *brown-, claret-, cream-jug*, etc. b. A jug with its contents; the liquid in a jug; *esp.* beer. Also, locally, A measure of capacity for ale or beer, usu. about a pint. 1635. 2. *slang.* A prison, jail; more fully STONE-JUG 1834.

Comb. **j.-handled** *a. fig.* (*U.S.*), unilateral, one-sided, unbalanced.

Jug (dʒvg), *sb.*[3] 1523. Imitation of one of the notes of a nightingale, etc.

Jug, *v.*[1] 1681. [f. JUG *sb.*[2]] †1. *intr.* To use a jug; to drink. 2. *trans.* To stew or boil in a jug or jar (esp. a hare) 1747. 3. *slang.* To shut up in jail. Also *transf.* To confine. 1841. **Jugged** (dʒvgd) *ppl. a.*, esp. in *jugged hare.*

Jug, *v.*[2] 1598. [Echoic; cf. JUG *sb.*[3]] *intr.* To utter a sound like 'jug', as a nightingale.

Jug, *v.*[3] 1600. [app. an altered by-form of JOUK *v.*[1] with specialized application.] *intr.* Of partridges, etc.: To crowd or nestle together on the ground; to collect in a covey. b. *trans.* To collect close together 1653.

Jugal (dʒū·găl), *a.* (*sb.*) 1598. [ad. L. *jugalis*, f. *jugum* yoke.] †1. Of or relating to a yoke; *esp.* conjugal –1656. 2. *Anat.* Of or pertaining to the zygoma or bony arch of the cheek; malar, zygomatic 1578. 3. *sb.* The jugal or malar bone 1854.

Jugate (dʒū·gět), *a.* 1887. [ad. L. *jugatus*, *jugare* to join together; see -ATE[2].] 1. *Bot.* Of a pinnate leaf: Having leaflets in pairs; usu. in comb. (see BIJUGATE, etc.). Of the leaflets: Paired. 2. *Numism.* = ACCOLLED 3. 1887.

Ju·gate, *v. rare.* 1623. [f. L. *jugat-*, *jugare* to yoke together; see -ATE[3].] *trans.* To yoke or couple together. Hence **Ju·gated** *ppl. a.*; in *Bot.* = JUGATE *a.* 1; **Juga·tion,** (*a*) joining, linking 1701; (*b*) a system of land assessment based on the number of yokes of oxen employed 1883.

Juger (dʒū·dʒəɹ). 1853. [ad. L. *jugerum* (formerly used in Eng.).] An ancient Roman measure of land, containing 28,800 (Roman) square feet, or 240 by 120 (Roman) feet, i. e. about three-fifths of an acre.

Jugful (dʒv·gful). 1834. [f. JUG *sb.*[2] + -FUL.] As much as fills a jug.

Juggernaut, ‖**Jagannath** (dʒv·gənǫt). 1638. [a. Hindī *Jagannāth* :—Skr. *Jagannātha* 'lord of the world', f. *jagat* world + *nātha* lord, protector. (The short *a* in Hindī is = *v*, whence the Eng. spelling).] 1. *Hindu Myth.* A title of Krishna, the eighth avatar of Vishnu; *spec.* the uncouth idol of this deity at Pūrī in Orissa, annually dragged in procession on an enormous car, under the wheels of which devotees are said to have thrown themselves to be crushed. Also *attrib.* 2. *fig.* Anything to which persons blindly devote themselves, or are ruthlessly sacrificed.

2. That remorseless J.—'the needs of man' EDISON.

Juggins (dʒv·ginz). *slang.* 1882. [?] A simpleton.

Juggle (dʒv·g'l), *sb.*[1] 1657. [f. JUGGLE *v.*] A piece of juggling; a conjurer's trick; hence, an imposture, cheat, fraud.

Ju·ggle, *sb.*[2] 1875. [Cf. JOGGLE *sb.*[2]] A block of timber cut to a length, either in the round or split.

Juggle (dʒv·g'l), *v.* ME. [a. OF. *jogler*, *jugler* (later *jougler*) :—late L. *joculare* for L. *joculari* to jest.] †1. *intr.* To act as a JUGGLER (sense 1) –1608. 2. To practise magic or legerdemain; to play conjuring tricks; to conjure 1440. 3. *transf.* and *fig.* To play tricks so as to cheat or deceive 1528. 4. *trans.* To deceive by jugglery; to trick, cheat, beguile 1531.

2. The conjurer juggles with two oranges 1885. 3. To j. with Scripture MILT. She never juggles or plays tricks with her understanding LAMB. 4. To j. men out of their Estates SELDEN. Hence **Ju·ggling** *vbl. sb.* and *ppl. a.* **Ju·gglingly** *adv.* (1647).

Juggler (dʒv·gləɹ). late OE. [a. OF. nom. *jog-, jug-, jouglere*, acc. *jogleor*, later *jougleur* :—L. *joculator, -atorem*, f. *joculari* to jest. See also JONGLEUR.] 1. One who entertains people by stories, songs, buffoonery, tricks, etc.; a jester, buffoon. (Often contempt.) –1591. 2. †A magician, wizard, sorcerer; a performer of legerdemain; a conjurer OE. 3. *transf.* and *fig.* One who deceives by trickery ME.

2. After dinner comes in a jugleur, which showed us very pretty tricks PEPYS. 3. The Sophist..is proved to be a dissembler and j. with words JOWETT.

Jugglery (dʒv·gləri). ME. [a. OF. *jogle-, juglerie*; see prec. and -ERY.] 1. The art or practice of a juggler; conjuring, legerdemain. 2. *transf.* Trickery, deception 1699.

2. An example of political j. and falsehood 1838.

Jugoslav (yūgo,slaˑv). 1880. Also **Y-.** [Russ. *iugo-* south.] A southern Slav; a member of the state of Jugoslavia, including the Serbs, Croats, and Slovenes. Also adj.

Jugular (dʒū·-, dʒv·giŭlăɹ). 1597. [ad. med. or mod.L. *jugularis*, f. L. *jugulum* collar-bone, neck, throat; see -AR.]

A. *adj.* 1. *Anat.* Of, pertaining to, or situated in the neck or throat; *esp.* an epithet of the great veins of the neck, as the *external j. vein*, which conveys the blood from the superficial parts of the head, and the *internal j. vein*, which conveys it from the inside of the skull. 2. *Ichthyol.* Of a fish: Having the ventral fins situated in front of the pectoral, i. e. in the region of the throat; said also of a ventral fin so situated 1766.

B. *sb.* 1. *Anat.* Short for *jugular vein* 1615. 2. *Ichthyol.* A jugular fish (see A. 2) 1835. So †**Ju·gulary** *a.*

Jugulate (dʒū·giŭlět), *v.* 1623. [f. L. *jugulat-*, *jugulare*, f. *jugulum*; see JUGULAR and -ATE[3].] 1. *trans.* To kill by cutting the throat; to put to death. 2. *fig.* To 'strangle'; *spec.* to stop the course of (a disease) by a powerful remedy 1876.

2. Misplaced attempts to 'jugulate' the disease [pneumonia] ALLBUTT. So **Jugula·tion** (*rare*).

‖**Jugulum** (dʒū·giŭlŏm). 1706. [L., dim. formation from *jug-*, *jungere* to join.] *Anat.* and *Zool.* A name for the collar-bone; also for the throat or lower front part of the neck, esp. in birds, the analogous part in insects.

‖**Jugum** (dʒū·gŏm). *Pl.* **juga.** 1857. [L., = 'yoke'.] *Bot.* a. A pair of leaflets in a pinnate leaf. b. Each of the ridges on the carpels of *Umbelliferæ.*

Juice (dʒūs), *sb.* ME. [a. F. *jus* :—L. *jus* broth, sauce, juice.] 1. The watery or liquid part of vegetables or fruits, which can be expressed or extracted; *spec.* that of the grape. 2. The fluid part of an animal body or substance; now usu. in *pl.* the bodily 'humours'; also used in *sing.* in the names of digestive secretions (*gastric j.*, etc.) ME. 3. *gen.* The moisture naturally contained in or coming from anything ME. 4. *fig.* Essence, spirit. ME. 5. *slang.* a. Petrol 1909. b. Electricity 1903.

1. Wines we have of Grapes; and Drinkes of other Iuyce BACON. 2. Marrow and Fat and Blood, and other Nutritious Juices BENTLEY. 3. The mineral Juyces in the Earth WOODWARD. 4. A theory, pickled in the preserving juices of pulpit eloquence BURKE. Hence **Juice** *v.* (*rare*), to moisten or suffuse with j. **Juiced** *a.* having j. (of a specified quality). **Jui·celess** *a.* devoid of j.; dry (*lit.* and *fig.*).

Juicy (dʒū·si), *a.* ME. [f. prec. + -Y[1].] 1. Full of juice; succulent. b. Of weather: Wet, rainy, soaking (*colloq.*) 1837. 2. *fig.* Rich in wealth, etc.; the opposite of 'dry' (*colloq.*) 1621. b. *Artists' slang.* Characterized by rich liquid colouring 1820. Hence **Jui·cily** *adv.* (*slang*), excellently. **Jui·ciness** (*lit.* and *fig.*).

†**Ju,ise.** ME. [a. OF. *juise*, for *juice*, ad. L. *judicium.* (See -ISE.)] Judgement, doom; penalty. Also *transf.* the gibbet –1480.

Ju-jitsu (dʒū,dʒi·tsu, dʒū·dʒitsu), *sb.* 1891. Also **jui-, jiu-jitsu, -jutsu.** [Japanese, = soft art.] The Japanese system of self-defence without weapons, now widely used as a form of physical training. Hence as *vb.* to overcome by ju-jitsu.

‖**Ju-ju, juju** (dʒū·dʒū). 1863. [W. African; said to be a. F. *joujou* toy.] An object of any kind superstitiously venerated by W. African native tribes, and used as a charm or amulet; a fetish. Also, the supernatural power attributed to such objects, or the system of observances connected therewith; also, a ban or interdiction effected by means of such an object (cf. *taboo*). Also *attrib.* Hence **Ju·juism, -ist.**

Jujube (dʒū·dʒūb). 1550. [a. F. *jujube* or med.L. (and Sp.) *jujuba*, a much altered form of Gr. ζίζυφον. See N.E.D.] 1. An edible berry-like drupe, the fruit of various species of *Zizyphus* (N.O. *Rhamnaceæ*). b. Any species producing this fruit, as *Z. vulgaris* of the Mediterranean countries, *Z. Jujuba* of China, *Z. Lotus* of N. Africa 1562. 2. A lozenge of gelatin, etc. flavoured with or imitating this fruit 1835.

1. The Lotus-eaters—whose favourite fruit still grows, under the name of the j., on the same coast THIRLWALL.

Comb.: **j. paste,** a jelly made from jujubes, or a confection flavoured with, or in imitation of, them; **-plum** = sense 1; **-tree** = sense 1 b.

Juke, obs. f. JOUK.

Julaceous (dʒulēⁱ·ʃəs), *a. rare.* 1880. [f. L. *julus*, prop. *iulus*, IULUS + -ACEOUS.] *Bot.* Catkin-like, amentaceous. GRAY.

Julep (dʒū·lep). ME. [a. F. *julep*, ad. Arab. *julāb*, a. Pers. *gulāb* rose-water, f. *gul* rose + *ab* water.] 1. A sweet drink variously prepared; *esp.* a liquid sweetened with syrup or sugar, and used as a vehicle. b. *transf.* and *fig.* Something to cool or assuage the heat of passion, etc. 1624. 2. *U.S.* A mixture of brandy, whisky, or other spirit, with sugar, ice, and some flavouring, usu. mint 1804.

1. Vse them with a iuleb of vyolettes TRAHERON.

Julian (dʒū·liăn), *a.* 1592. [ad. L. *Julianus*, f. *Julius.*] Pertaining to Julius Cæsar; used in *Chronol.* in connexion with the calendar instituted by him in the year 46 B.C.

Julian account, = 'old style' (see STYLE); *J. calendar* (see CALENDAR *sb.*); *J. epoch, era*, the time from which the Julian calendar dates (46 B.C.); *J. period*, a period of 7,980 Julian years, proposed by Joseph Scaliger in 1582 as a universal standard of comparison of chronology, consisting of the product of the numbers of years in the solar and lunar cycles and the cycle of the indiction (28×19×15); *J. year*, a year of the Julian calendar, or the average year (= 365¼ days) of that calendar.

‖**Julienne** (ʒülyeˑn). 1810. [F., f. *Jules* or *Julien*, proper name.] A soup made of various vegetables, esp. carrots, chopped and cooked in meat broth. Also *attrib.*

Julius, †**Julio.** 1547. [a. L. *Julius*, It. *giulio.*] A silver coin worth about sixpence, struck by Pope Julius II (1503–13).

July (dʒuləi·). [In OE. in L. form *Julius.* In ME. *Jule, Juil*, a. OF. *Jule, Juil, Julle* :—L. *Julium* acc. of *Julius*; also *Julie*, a. AF. *Julie*, ad. L. *Julius.* The latter form was accented *Ju·ly* as late as Dr. Johnson's time; the present accentuation is unexplained.] The seventh month of the year, so named after Julius Cæsar.

Cæsar..was borne..vpon the fourth day before the Ides of Quintilis, which moneth, after his death, was ..called for that cause, Iulie HOLLAND.

Julyflower, perversion of GILLYFLOWER.

Jumart (dʒū·maɹt). Also †**gimar.** 1690. [a. F. *jumart*, formerly *jumare*; of unkn. origin.] An imaginary hybrid animal, said to be the offspring of a bull and a mare or she-ass, or of a horse or ass and a cow.

Jumbal, jumble (dʒv·mb'l). 1615. [cf. GIMBAL 1, GIMMAL 1.] A kind of fine sweet cake or biscuit, formerly often made up in the form of rings or rolls; now in U.S., a thin crisp cake, composed of flour, sugar, butter, and eggs, flavoured with lemon-peel or sweet almonds.

Jumble (dʒv·mb'l), *sb.* 1661. [f. next.] 1. A confused mixture, a medley; also, disorder, muddle. **2.** A shock, shaking, or jolting; *colloq.* a ride in a carriage 1674.

2. The j. of the sea made shooting uncertain 1851.
Comb. **j.-sale,** a sale of miscellaneous cheap or second-hand articles at a charitable bazaar or the like.

Jumble (dʒʋ·mb'l), *v.* 1529. [Prob. onomatopœic.] **1.** *intr.* To move about in mingled disorder; to flounder about confusedly. **2.** *trans.* To muddle, confuse; often with *together* or *up* 1542. **3.** To stir up (a liquid, etc.) so as to mix the ingredients; to shake up; hence *colloq.* to take for a drive. ? *Obs.* 1616. **b.** *intr.* To travel with shaking or jolting 1748. **4.** *trans.* To put into mental confusion; to muddle 1668. †**5.** *intr.* To make a confused or rumbling noise; to strum on an instrument –1805.

1. In that fearfull Cave They [Furies] j., tumble, rumble, rage and rave SYLVESTER. 2. To j. the innocent and guilty into one mass, by a general indemnity BURKE. 3. That I might go abroad with my wife, who was not well, only to j. her PEPYS. Hence **Ju·mblement,** confused mixture 1707. **Ju·mbler.**

Jumble, var. of JUMBAL.

Jumbo (dʒʋ·mbo). 1823. [? from Mumbo *Jumbo*, name for a W. African divinity or bogy.] A big clumsy person, animal, or thing; popularized, esp., as the name of an elephant, famous for its size, in the London Zoological Gardens; hence, anything big or great in its kind.

†**Ju·ment.** ME. [ad. L. *jumentum* (contr. of *jugimentum*) yoke-beast, f. *jug-*, stem of *jungere* to join, *jugum* yoke.] A beast of burden; also a beast in general –1820.

Fit to fasten their Juments..unto them SIR T. BROWNE.

Jump (dʒʋmp), *sb.*[1] 1552. [f. JUMP *v.*] **1.** An act of jumping; a spring; a leap, a bound. **b.** esp. in reference to the distance cleared (*long j.*), or height jumped (*high j.*), as an athletic feat; also, a place to be jumped across, an obstacle to be cleared by jumping 1858. **2.** A sudden involuntary movement caused by a shock; a start. In *pl.* nervous starts; an affection marked by these, *spec.* (*a*) chorea, (*b*) delirium tremens (*slang*). 1879. **3.** Of things: A movement in which a thing is suddenly and abruptly thrown up or forward 1611. *spec.* in *Gunnery*: The vertical movement of the muzzle of a gun at the moment of discharge; the angle which measures this 1879. **4.** *fig.* A sudden abrupt rise, e. g. in price or the like; an abrupt change of level either upward or downward; a fault in stratification 1657. **5.** *fig.* A sudden and abrupt transition; an interval, gap, chasm, involving such sudden transition, *e.g.* in argument 1678. †**6.** *fig.* Critical point, crisis –1641. †**b.** Venture, hazard –1606.

1. The hare..goeth by iumpes TOPSELL. 4. A j. up of 100 in the majority 1896. 5. Their nimble nonsense..gains remote conclusions at a j. COWPER. 6. b. Our fortune lyes Vpon this iumpe SHAKS. Phr. *From the j.*, from the start. *On the j.*, on the move (*colloq.*).

Jump, *sb.*[2] *Obs.* exc. *dial.* 1653. [? corruption of F. *juppe*, obs. var. *jupe*, assim. to JUMP *v.* and *sb.*[1]] **1.** A kind of short coat worn by men in the 17th and 18th centuries. **2.** A kind of under (or undress) bodice worn by women, esp. in the 18th c.; often used instead of stays. From *c* 1740 usu. as pl. *jumps* (*a pair of jumps*). 1666. **3.** *attrib.*, as *j.-coat* 1660.

†**Jump,** *a.*, *adv.* 1539. [Conn. w. JUMP *v.* I. 4.] **a.** *adj.* Coinciding; even; exact, precise –1637. **b.** *adv.* With exact coincidence; exactly, precisely –1656.

a. J. concord between our wit and will SIDNEY.

Jump (dʒʋmp), *v.* 1511. [App. onomatopœic; cf. *bump*, etc.]

I. *intr.* **1.** To make a spring from the ground, etc. by flexion and sudden muscular extension of the legs, or the like; to throw oneself upward, forward, backward, or downward, from the point of support; to leap, spring, bound 1530. **b.** To move with a sudden involuntary jerk from excitement or shock; to start 1715. **2.** *transf.* Of things: To be moved or thrown up with a sudden jerk like a jump 1511. **3.** *fig.* To pass abruptly from one thing or state to another; to rise suddenly in amount, price, etc. 1579. **b.** To come *to* or arrive *at* (a conclusion, etc.) precipitately 1704. **4.** To act or come exactly *together*; to agree completely. Const. *with.* 1567.

1. Not the worst of the three, but iumpes twelue foote and a halfe by th' squire SHAKS. **b.** Phr. *To j. for joy*, said *lit.* of children, etc., also *fig.* to be joyfully excited 1775. 2. The sea was beginning to j. HALL CAINE. 3. Wool jumped up suddenly to 46*s.* per tod 1886. **b.** So given to jumping to conclusions is society 1884. 4. Our humors j. together completely W. IRVING. Phr. *To j. at*: To spring as a beast at its prey; *fig.* to accept eagerly 1769. *To j. upon*: To pounce upon as a beast upon its victim; hence (*colloq.*) to come down crushingly upon 1868.

II. *trans.* **1.** To pass clear over with a leap; to clear 1600. †**2.** To effect or do as with a jump –1684. **3.** To cause to jump; to startle. Also *fig.* 1815. **4.** To pounce upon; to rob, to cheat; to 'steal a march' upon 1789. **5.** To skip over, pass by, evade 1749. †**6.** To hazard. SHAKS. †**7.** To make up hastily (a marriage, a match) –1615. **8. a.** *Iron-forging.* To flatten, 'upset', or shorten and thicken by endwise blows. Also *transf.* 1851. **b.** To join by welding the flattened ends 1864. **c.** To join (rails, etc.) end on end. 1884. **9.** *Quarrying.* To drill by means of a jumper 1851.

1. Jumping these crevices KANE. 3. People..whose nerves have been jumped by scorchers 1898. 4. To j. the Transvaal 1899. Phr. *To j. a claim, etc.*: To take summary possession of a piece of land called a 'claim', on the ground that the former occupant has abandoned it, or has failed to comply with the legal requirements. Chiefly *U.S.* and *Colonial.* Also *transf.* 5. Phr. *To j. one's bail*, to abscond, leaving one's sureties liable. *U.S. slang.* 6. But heere.. Wee'ld iumpe the life to come *Macb.* I. vii. 7.

Jump-, the vb.-stem used in *Comb.*: **j.-joint,** (*a*) a joint in which the parts are welded end to end together; (*b*) a flush-joint in which the edges of the plates or planking are laid close together and make a smooth surface; **-seat,** a movable carriage-seat; also *adj.* and *sb.* (ellipt.) (a carriage) provided with such a seat; **-weld,** a weld effected by hammering together the heated ends of two pieces of metal; hence **-weld** *v.*

Jumper (dʒʋ·mpəɹ), *sb.*[1] 1611. [f. JUMP *v.* + -ER[1].] **1.** One who or that which jumps. **2.** A name applied in the 18th c. to a body of Welsh Methodists who used to jump and dance as a part of religious worship; also to more recent sects 1774. **3.** One who jumps a claim 1855. **4.** Applied to tools, etc. having a jumping motion. **a.** *Quarrying.* A heavy drill, used in making blasting-holes in rock, etc. Also *attrib.* 1769. **b.** A spring or click controlling the star-wheel of a repeating clock 1850. **c.** *Telegraphy.* A wire used to cut out an instrument or part of a circuit, or to close temporarily a gap in a circuit. **5.** A rough kind of sledge, usu. consisting of two saplings with the ends turned up, fastened by cross-pieces. *U.S.* 1823. **6.** *Naut.* A preventer-rope made fast so as to prevent a yard, mast, etc. from jumping or springing up in rough weather. Also *attrib.* 1856.

Hence **Ju·mper** *v. trans.* to bore (a hole) with a j. (sense 4 a). **Ju·mperism,** the principles of the Jumpers (sense 2).

Ju·mper, *sb.*[2] 1853. [prob. f. JUMP *sb.*[2]] A loose outer jacket or shirt reaching to the hips, worn by sailors, truckmen, etc.; also, a hooded fur jacket worn by Eskimos, and the like. In recent use (also *jumper-blouse*), A loose-fitting blouse without fastenings, worn over the rest of the dress and not tucked in at the waist; also, an outer garment consisting of bodice and short legs, worn by young children as a protection to their clothing.

Jumping (dʒʋ·mpiŋ), *vbl. sb.* 1565. [f. JUMP *v.* + -ING[1].] The action of JUMP *v.* **b.** *attrib.*, as **j.-sheet,** a stout sheet into which persons may jump from a burning building.

Jumping (dʒʋ·mpiŋ), *ppl. a.* 1567. [f. as prec. + -ING[2].] That jumps. **b.** In names of animals characterized by jumping or springing: **j.-deer,** the black-tailed deer of N. America, *Cariacus macrotis*; **-hare,** a rodent quadruped of S. Africa, *Pedetes caffer* or *Helamys capensis*, resembling the jerboa; **-louse,** a flea-louse, a jumping plant-louse; **-mouse,** (*a*) the American deer-mouse, *Zapus hudsonius*; (*b*) = *jumping-rat*; **-mullet,** a gray mullet, *Mugil albula*; **-rat,** a rodent of the family *Dipodidæ*; **-shrew,** the elephant-shrew of Africa, an insectivorous quadruped of the family *Macroscelididæ*; **-spider,** one of the group of spiders which leap upon their prey. **c. j.-bean, -seed,** the seed of a Mexican euphorbiaceous plant, which jumps about by reason of the movements of the larva of a tortricid moth (*Carpocapsa saltitans*) enclosed within it; **-jack,** a child's toy made out of the merrythought of a fowl; a toy figure of a man, which is made to jump by being pulled with strings; also *transf.*, the crested penguin. Hence **Ju·mpingly** *adv.*

Jumpy (dʒʋ·mpi), *a.* 1869. [f. JUMP *sb.*[1] + -Y[1].] Characterized by jumps (see JUMP *sb.*[1] 2, 5). **b.** Producing nervous excitement 1883. Hence **Ju·mpiness.**

Juncaceous (dʒʋŋkēⁱ·ʃəs), *a.* 1855. [f. mod.L. *Juncaceæ* (f. *juncus* rush) + -OUS; see -ACEOUS.] *Bot.* Belonging to the N.O. *Juncaceæ* (the rush family).

Juncat, -cate, obs. ff. JUNKET.

Junco (dʒʋ·ŋko). 1706. [a. Sp. *junco*, ad. L. *juncus* rush.] †**a.** The Reed-sparrow or Reed-bunting (*Emberiza schœniclus*). **b.** A N. American genus of Finches, the Snow-birds; one of these.

Juncous (dʒʋ·ŋkəs), *a.* *rare.* 1755. [ad. L. *juncosus*, f. *juncus* rush; see -OUS.] Rushy.

Junction (dʒʋ·ŋkʃən). 1711. [ad. L. *junctionem*, f. *jungere* to join.] **1.** The action of joining or fact of being joined; union, combination; coalition. **2.** The point or place at which two things join or are joined; *spec.* the place or station on a railway where lines meet and unite 1841. **3.** (In full, *junction canal*, *j. line*, *j. railway.*) A canal or railway forming a connexion between two other lines or with a centre of commerce 1796. **4.** *attrib.* 1839.

1. The J. of the French and Bavarian Armies ADDISON. The j. of a talent for abstruse reasoning with much literary inexperience M. ARNOLD.
Comb. **j.-plate,** a break-joint plate riveted over the edges of boiler-plates, which make a butt-joint.

Juncture (dʒʋ·ŋktiŭɹ, -tʃəɹ). ME. [ad. L. *junctura*, f. *junct-*, *jungere* to join; see -URE.] **1.** The action of joining together; joined condition; joining, junction 1589. **2.** The place at which, or structure by which, two things are joined; a joint, jointing, junction ME. †**b.** = JOINT *sb.* 1 –1717. **3.** Something that connects two things; a means of union (*rare*) 1677. **4.** A convergence of events or circumstances; a crisis, conjuncture 1656.

1. The j. with what precedes and follows FOSTER. 2. It stands at the j. of that great river with another 1763. 4. In the present critical j. of things BRIGHT.

June (dʒūn). [In OE. in L. form *Junius*, also *Juni*; in ME. a. F. *juin*, †*juing*:—L. *Junius.*] The sixth month of the year, in which the summer solstice occurs in the northern hemisphere.

The month of Iune is begynnynge of Somer ME.
Comb.: *J.-apple* = JENNETING; **-berry,** the fruit (also called *service-berry*) of a small tree, the shadbush (*Amelanchier canadensis*); also the tree; **-bug,** a name for various beetles which appear in June: (*a*) of the European genus *Rhinotrogus*; (*b*) of the genus *Lachnosterna* of the northern U.S.; (*c*) *Allorhina nitida*, of the southern U.S.; **-grass** (*U.S.*), the Kentucky blue-grass, *Poa pratensis*.

Juneating, perverted f. JENNETING.

Jungle (dʒʋ·ŋg'l). 1776. [a. Hindī and Marāṭhī *jangal* desert, waste, forest, Skr. *jaṅgala* dry, dry ground, desert.] **1.** In India, orig., Waste ground (= 'forest' in the original sense); hence, in Anglo-Indian use, **a.** Land overgrown with underwood, long grass, or tangled vegetation; also, the often impenetrable growth of vegetation covering such a tract 1776. **b.** with *a* and *pl.* A particular tract so covered; esp. as the dwelling-place of wild beasts 1783. **c.** Hence, used of similar tracts elsewhere 1849. **2.** *transf.* and *fig.* A wild, tangled mass 1850. **b.** *The Jungle* (*Stock Exch. slang*): the West African share market (*mod.*). **3.** *attrib.* 1810.

1. a. Land Waste for Five Years.. is called J. HALHED. **c.** The Jordan..threading its tortuous way through its tropical j. STANLEY.
Comb.: **j.-bear,** the Sloth-bear of India, *Prochilus labiatus*; **-cat,** the Marsh-lynx, *Felis chaus*; **-cock,** the male jungle-fowl; **-fever**; **-fowl,** (*a*) an East Indian bird of the genus *Gallus*, esp. *G. ferrugineus*

(*G. bankiva*); (*b*) a mound-bird of Australia, as *Megapodius tumulus*; **-hen**, the female jungle-fowl (*b*); **-market** (*Stock Exch.*), the market in shares of W. African Companies; **-ox**, the gayal; **-rice**, the millet-rice, *Panicum colonum*; **-sheep**, an Indian ruminant, *Kemas hypocrinus*. Hence **Ju·ngled** *a.*, covered with jungle 1842.

Jungly (dʒɒ·ŋgli), *a.* 1800. [f. JUNGLE + -Y [1].] Of the nature of or abounding in jungle; jungle-like.

Junior (dʒū·niəɹ), *a.* (*sb.*) 1526. [a. L. (for *juvenior*), compar. of *juvenis*.] **1.** The younger: used to denote the younger of two bearing the same name in a family, esp. a son of the same name as his father; also the younger of two boys of the same surname in a school. Abbrev. *jun.*, *junr.*, or *jr.* 1623. **2.** Of less standing; of lower position, in a class, rank, profession, etc. 1766. †**3.** Belonging to youth or earlier life –1772. **4.** Of later date; more modern. Now rarely of persons. 1621. **5.** *sb.* [the adj. used *absol.*] A person who is younger than another, or of more recent entrance or lower standing in a class, profession, etc. 1526. **b.** With possessive 1548.

1. Tho. Crabb, Sen. and Tho. Crabb, Jun. of Malborrow..Wooll-men 1708. 2. J. Sophisters 1766, flagship 1810, clerk 1870, partner 1871. 5. In an American college the students are classed by years, those of the first year being called freshmen, of the second year sophomores, of the third year juniors BRYCE. b. His j. she by thirty years BYRON. Hence **Ju·niorate**, in the Society of Jesus, a two-years' course for junior members before entering the priesthood.

Juniority (dʒūni,ǫ·rĭti). 1554. [f. JUNIOR + -ITY.] The state or condition of being junior.

Juniper (dʒū·nipəɹ). ME. [ad. L. *juniperus*. Cf. GENEVA [1].] **1.** A genus of coniferous evergreen shrubs and trees; spec. and orig., the common European species *Juniperus communis*, a hardy spreading shrub or low tree, having awl-shaped prickly leaves and bluish-black or purple berries, with a pungent taste, yielding a volatile oil (*oil of juniper*) used in medicine as a stimulant and diuretic, also in the manufacture of gin. The wood is occas. used in joinery. **b.** Used loosely of coniferous trees of other genera, as the American Larch, and the White Cedar 1748. **c.** In translations of the Bible, used, after the Vulgate, to render Heb. *rethem* or *rōthem*, a white-flowered shrub, *Retama Rœtam* ME. †**2.** A name for the Fieldfare. FLORIO. **3.** *attrib.* 1382.

1. The coals of J. raked up will keep a glowing Fire for the space of a year SIR T. BROWNE.

Comb.: **j.-water**, a cordial drink made from or flavoured with j.; **-worm**, the larva of a N. Amer. geometrid moth (*Drepanodes varus*), which feeds on juniper-leaves.

Junk (dʒɒŋk), *sb.*[1] ME. [a. OF. *jonc*, *junc* :—L. *juncus* rush.] †**1.** A rush –1491. **2.** *Surg.* A form of splint, orig. stuffed with rushes or bents 1612.

Junk (dʒɒŋk), *sb.*[2] ME. [?] †**1.** *Naut.* An old or inferior cable or rope; usu. *old j.* –1769. **b.** Pieces of old cable used for making fenders, reef-points, gaskets, oakum, etc. 1666. **2.** *transf.* A piece or lump of anything; a CHUNK 1726. **3.** orig. *Naut.* The salt meat used as food on long voyages, compared to pieces of rope 1762. **4.** *Whale-fishery.* The mass of thick oily cellular tissue beneath the case and nostrils of a sperm-whale, containing spermaceti 1839. **5.** *attrib.* 1800.

1. c. Worthless stuff, rubbish (*colloq.*) 1913.

Comb.: **j.-dealer**, *U.S.*, a marine-store dealer; **-hook**, a hook used in handling the j. of a whale; **-ring**, (*a*) a metal ring confining the hemp packing of a piston; (*b*) a steam-tight metal packing round a piston; **-shop**, a marine store; **-vat**, in tanning, a large vat for holding weakened vat-liquor; **-wad**, a wad for a gun made of j. or oakum bound with spun-yarn.

Junk (dʒɒŋk), *sb.*[3] 1617. [ad. Sp., Pg. *junco*, It. *giunco*, F. *jonque*, ad. Malay, Javanese *djong*.] A name for the common type of native sailing vessel in the Chinese seas. It is flat-bottomed, has a square prow, prominent stem, full stern, the rudder suspended, and carries lug-sails.

Junk (dʒɒŋk), *v.* 1803. [f. JUNK *sb.*[2]] *trans.* To cut *off* in a lump; to cut into junks or chunks. **b.** To treat as junk; to 'scrap' 1916.

Junk-bottle. *U.S.* 1805. A thick strong bottle made of green or black glass, 'the ordinary black glass porter bottle' (Bartlett).

‖**Junker** (yu·ŋkəɹ). 1554. [Ger. Cf. YOUNKER.] A young German noble; as a term of reproach, a narrow-minded, overbearing (younger) member of the aristocracy of Prussia, etc.; *spec.* a member of the reactionary party of the aristocracy, whose aim it is to maintain their own class privileges. Also *attrib.*

Bismarck is by instinct a J. 1891.

Junket (dʒɒ·ŋkĕt), *sb.* ME. [app. a. ONF. *jonket, jonquet, or *jonquette*, rush-basket, f. *jonc* rush.] **1.** A basket (orig. made of rushes); *esp.* for carrying or catching fish. Now *dial.* **2.** A cream-cheese or the like (orig. made in a rush-basket or served on a rush-mat); now, a dish consisting of curds sweetened and flavoured, served with a layer of scalded cream on the top 1460. †**3.** Any dainty sweetmeat, cake, or confection; a kickshaw –1764. **4.** A feast or banquet; also (now only in U.S.), an outing at which eating and drinking are prominent; a picnic-party 1530.

2. Milke, crayme, and cruddes, and eke the Ioncate, Þey close a mannes stomak..Þerfore ete hard chese aftir 1460. 4. With these junkets and feasts they joyned the celebration of the Lords Supper VINES.

Junket (dʒɒ·ŋkĕt), *v.* 1555. [f. prec. sb.] **1.** *intr.* To hold a banquet or feast; to make merry with good cheer; also (chiefly *U.S.*) to go on a pleasure excursion. **2.** *trans.* To entertain, feast. H. WALPOLE.

1. The Chancellor had intended to go junketting on the Rhine GREVILLE. Hence **Ju·nketer**, one who junkets; one who takes part in a junketing. **Ju·nketing** *vbl. sb.* feasting, merrymaking; also, picnicking; with *a* and *pl.* A feast, picnic, etc. †**Ju·nketry**, a sweetmeat 1599.

Juno (dʒū·nǫ). 1606. [L. *Juno*, in L. mythology the wife of Jupiter; the goddess of marriage and childbirth.] **1.** A woman resembling the goddess Juno, e.g. in stately beauty, in jealousy, etc. **2.** *Astron.* Name of the third of the asteroids 1834.

1. His be yon J. of majestic size POPE. Hence **Juno,e·sque**, *a.* resembling J. in stately beauty. **Juno·nian** *a.* pertaining to J.

Junta (dʒɒ·ntă). 1623. [a. Sp. (and Pg.) *junta* :—L. *juncta*, fem. pass. pple. of *jungere* to join, in Rom. used as a sb.] **1.** With reference to Spain or Italy: A deliberative or administrative council or committee. **2.** *gen.* = JUNTO **1.** 1714.

Junto (dʒɒ·ntǫ). Also †**juncto.** 1641. [Erron. form of JUNTA, by assim. to Sp. sbs. in *o* (cf. -ADO 2).] **1.** A body of men who have combined for a common purpose, esp. a political purpose; a clique, faction, or cabal; a club or coterie. †**2.** = JUNTA **1.** –1747.

1. The Juncto [the Rump] at Westminster have..received more Money in one year than all the Kings of England 1680. As..lately settled in a j. of the sex ADDISON.

Jupard(y(e, jupart(ye: see JEOPARD, -Y.

Jupe (dʒūp, Fr. ʒüp). Now only *Sc.* and *n. dial.* or as Fr. ME. [a. F. *jupe*, a. Arab. *jubbah*, *jibbah* JUBBAH.] †**1.** A loose jacket, kirtle, or tunic worn by men –1837. **2.** *Sc.* A woman's jacket, kirtle, or bodice. Also *pl.* a kind of stays. 1810. ‖**3.** [from mod.Fr.] A woman's skirt 1825.

Jupiter (dʒū·pitəɹ). ME. [a. L. *Jupiter*, *Juppiter*: see JOVE.] **1.** The supreme deity of the ancient Romans, corresponding to the Greek Zeus; the ruler of gods and men, and the god of the heavens, whose weapon was the thunderbolt. Also in exclams., e.g. *by Jupiter.* **2.** *Astron.* The largest of the planets in the solar system, revolving in an orbit lying between those of Mars and Saturn ME. †**b.** *Alch.* The metal tin –1758. †**c.** *Her.* Name for the tincture AZURE in blazoning by the names of heavenly bodies –1766. **3.** In names of plants, as **Jupiter's staff**, Mullein, *Verbascum Thapsus*, from its tall upright stem 1664.

1. [Adam] Smil'd..as J. On Juno smiles MILT.

Jupiter's beard. 1567. [tr. L. *Barba Jovis*.] A name for various plants.

a. *Anthyllis Barba-Jovis*, the Silverbush, a S. European evergreen leguminous shrub, having leaves covered with silvery down. b. The common houseleek, *Sempervivum tectorum*. c. *Hydnum Barba-Jovis*, a hymenomycetous fungus with a white fibrous margin.

Jupon (dʒū·pǫ̃n, dʒupǫ·n, Fr. ʒüpoñ). ME. [a. F. *jupon*, OF. also *juppon*, deriv. of *jupe* JUPE.] **1.** A close-fitting tunic or doublet; esp. one worn by knights under the hauberk; later, a sleeveless surcoat worn outside the armour. *Obs.* exc. *Hist.* †**2.** A short kirtle worn by women –1595. ‖**3.** A woman's skirt 1851.

Jural (dʒūᵊ·răl), *a.* 1635. [f. L. *jur-*, *jus* law, right + -AL.] **1.** Of or relating to law or its administration. **2.** *Moral Philos.* Of or pertaining to rights and obligations 18..

2. By the adjective j. we shall denote that which has reference to the doctrine of rights and obligations WHEWELL. Hence **Ju·rally** *adv.*

Jurament (dʒūᵊ·rămĕnt). *Obs.* exc. *Hist.* 1575. [ad. L. (post-cl.) *juramentum*; see -MENT.] An oath.

Jurassic (dʒuræ·sik), *a.* 1833. [ad. F. *Jurassique*, f. *Jura*, after *Liassic*, *Triassic*.] *Geol.* Of or pertaining to the Jura mountains: applied to formations belonging to the period between the Triassic and the Cretaceous, characterized by the prevalence of oolitic limestone, of which the Jura mountains between France and Switzerland are chiefly formed.

Jurat[1] (dʒūᵊ·ræt, F. ʒüra). late ME. [ad. med.L. *juratus*, lit. 'sworn man', sb. use of pa. pple. of *jurare* to swear.] **1.** One who has taken an oath; *spec.* one sworn to give information about the crimes committed in his neighbourhood, and to assist the administration of justice. *Obs.* exc. *Hist.* 1450. **2.** A municipal officer (esp. of the Cinque Ports) holding a position similar to that of an alderman 1464. **3.** In the Channel Islands, one of a body of magistrates, chosen for life, who with the Bailiff form the Royal Court for administration of justice 1537. **4.** With reference to France, etc.: **a.** [= F. *jurat*] A municipal magistrate in certain towns 1432. **b.** A member of a company or corporation, sworn to see that nothing is done against its statutes 1714.

Jurat[2] (dʒūᵊ·ræt). 1796. [ad. L. *juratum* that which is sworn.] *Law.* A memorandum as to when, where, and before whom an affidavit is sworn.

Juratory (dʒūᵊ·rătəri), *a.* 1553. [ad. late L. *juratorius* confirmed by oath; see JURAT[1] and -ORY.] Of or pertaining to an oath or oaths; expressed or contained in an oath.

Freed from his j. obligation 1647.

Juridic, -al (dʒuri·dik, -ăl), *a.* 1502. [ad. L. *juridicus*, + -AL.] **1.** Of or pertaining to law or legal proceedings; occas. = legal. **2.** Assumed by law to exist; juristic 1892.

1. Judges or juridical writers SIR C. BOWEN. 2. A Bill..extending to juridical persons, that is, duly registered corporations or partnerships [etc.] 1900. Hence **Juri·dically** *adv.* in a juridical manner.

Jurisconsult (dʒūᵊ:ris,kǫ̆nsɒ·lt). 1605. [ad. L. *jurisconsultus*, f. *juris*, gen. of *jus* law + *consultus* skilled.] One learned in law, esp. in civil or international law; a jurist; a master of jurisprudence.

Jurisdiction (dʒūᵊrisdi·kʃən). ME. [orig. a. OF. *jure-*, *juri-*, *jurdiction*, *-dicion* (F. *juridiction*), ad. L. *jurisdictionem*, f. *juris* (*jus*) + *dictio* declaration.] **1.** Administration of justice; exercise of judicial authority, or of the functions of a judge or legal tribunal; legal authority or power. **2.** Power or authority in general; administration, rule, control ME. **3.** The range of judicial or administrative power; the territory over which such power extends. Also *fig.* ME. **4.** A judicial organization; a judicature; a court, or series of courts, of justice 1765.

1. To declare the Law, which is not Judgment, but J. HOBBES. 2. To live exempt From Heav'n's high j. MILT. *P.L.* II. 319. 3. Basil's care of the churches ..extended far beyond the limits of his own j. J. H. NEWMAN. 4. The abolition of hereditary jurisdictions LECKY. Hence **Jurisdi·ctional** *a.*

Jurisdictive (dʒūᵊrisdi·ktiv), *a. rare.* 1640 [f. *jurisdiction*, after *administrative*, etc., but irreg.] Of or pertaining to jurisdiction.

Jurisprudence (dʒūᵊris,prū·dĕns). 1628. [ad. L. *jurisprudentia* (also *prudentia juris*), perh. through Fr.] **1. a.** Knowledge of or skill in law. **b.** The science which treats of human laws (written or unwritten) in general; the philosophy of law 1756. **2.** A system or body of law 1656.

1. b. The domain of Comparative J., of which English Law forms a small province 1861. 2. The history of our medical j. MACAULAY.

Jurispru·dent, *sb.* and *a.* 1628. [a. obs. F. *jurisprudent*, from *jurisprudence*: cf. *prudence*, *prudent*.] **1.** *sb.* One versed in, or treating of, jurisprudence; a jurist. **2.** *adj.* Versed or skilled in jurisprudence 1737.

Jurisprudential (-de·nʃăl), *a.* 1651. [f. L. *jurisprudentia* + -AL.] Of or pertaining to jurisprudence; rarely of persons: JURISPRUDENT 2. Hence **Jurisprude·ntially** *adv.* in relation to jurisprudence.

Jurist (dʒūə·rist). 1456. [a. F. *juriste*, ad. med.L. *jurista*, f. *jus, jur-* law, right; see -IST.] **1.** One who practises in law; a lawyer (now *U.S.*). **2.** One versed in the science of law; a legal writer 1626. **3.** A student of law, or one who takes a degree in law 1691.

2. This is not to be measured by the principles of Jurists BACON. Hence **Juri·stic, -al** *a.* of or pertaining to a j., or to the subject or study of law; legal; created by law. **Juri·stically** *adv.* in relation to law.

Juror (dʒūə·rəɹ). ME. [a. AF. *jurour* = OF. *jureor* (later *jureur*) :—L. *juratorem*, f. *jurare* to swear.] **1.** A member of a jury; a juryman. **†2.** One who brings false witness or a false presentment; a slanderer; an oppressor; a covetous man -1550. **3.** One of a body of persons appointed to award prizes in a competition 1851. **4.** One who takes or has taken an oath; one who swears allegiance to some body or cause. (Cf. NON-JUROR.) 1592.

1. The false verdict of jurors, whether occasioned by embracery or not, was antiently considered as criminal BLACKSTONE. 2. Sclaunderers, lyers, and iurours of the syse BARCLAY.

Jury (dʒūə·ri). ME. [a. AF. *juree, jure* = OF. *jurée* oath, juridical inquiry, inquest; med. L. *jurata*, sb. from fem. pa. pple. of *jurare* to swear (see -ADE suffix).]

I. A company of men sworn to render a 'verdict' or true answer upon some question or questions officially submitted to them; now, usually upon evidence delivered to them touching the issue; but orig. usually upon facts or matters within their own knowledge.

In England, juries in all criminal trials, in civil trials in the superior courts, and in writs of inquiry, consist of 12 men, who must be unanimous in their verdict. In Scotland, the number of the jury in a criminal trial is 15, and the verdict of a majority is accepted; in a civil trial the number is 12, and their verdict must be unanimous.

Coroner's jury: see CORONER and INQUEST. *Grand j.*: a jury of inquiry, accusation, or presentment, consisting of from 12 to 23 'good and lawful men of a county', who are returned by the sheriff to every session of the peace, and of the assizes, to receive and inquire into indictments, before these are submitted to a trial jury, and to perform such other duties as may be committed to them. Grand juries were abolished by the Administration of Justice Act 1933 exc. for certain indictments in London and Middlesex. They have been done away with in many states of U.S.A. *Petty jury* or *trial jury*: a jury which tries the final issue of fact in civil or criminal proceedings. *Special jury*: a jury consisting of persons on the jurors' book who are of a certain station or occupy premises of a certain rateable value.

II. *transf.* **1.** Applied to the body of DICASTS (δικασταί) of ancient Athens, or the *judices* of ancient Rome 1856. **2.** A body of persons selected to award prizes in an exhibition or competition 1851. **†3.** A dozen -1650.

Jury-, Jury *a.* (*Naut.*): see JURY-MAST.

Juryman (dʒūə·rimăn). 1579. A man serving on a jury; a member of a jury.

Ju·ry-ma:st. 1616. [?] **1.** *Naut.* A temporary mast put up in place of one that has been broken or carried away. **b.** *transf.* An apparatus used in Pott's disease, to keep the spinal column straight, and prevent lateral curvature 1883. **2.** Hence *jury-* is used in comb. to designate other parts of a ship contrived for temporary use, as **j.-rig**, etc.; and joc. of other things, as **j.-leg**, a wooden leg 1666. **b.** Hence **Jury** *a.* = temporary, makeshift 1821.

2. b. I have..some j. chairs and tables BYRON.

Jussive (dʒɒ·siv), *a.* 1846. [f. L. *juss-*, *jubere* to command; see -IVE.] *Grammar.* Expressing a command or order; as forms of the verb.

Just, joust (dʒɒst, dʒūst, dʒaust), *sb.* ME. [a. OF. *juste, joste, jouste*, F. *joute*, f. *juster*, etc. JUST *v.*] A combat in which two knights or men-at-arms on horseback encountered each other with lances; *spec.* a combat of this kind for exercise or sport; a tilt. Usu. in pl. *justs, jousts* (formerly construed as *sing.*), a series of these; a tournament.

For knightly giusts and fierce encounters fitt SPENSER.

Just (dʒɒst), *a.* ME. [a. F. *juste*, or ad. L. *justus*, f. *jus* right, law, justice.] **1.** That does what is morally right, righteous. Now chiefly a Biblical archaism. **2.** Upright and impartial in one's dealings; equitable ME. **†b.** Faithful. Const. *of, to.* -1809. **3. a.** Consonant with the principles of moral right; equitable; fair. Of rewards, punishments, etc.: Merited. ME. **b.** Constituted by law or by equity, lawful, rightful; †legally valid ME. **4.** Well-founded ME. **5.** Conformable to the standard; right; proper; correct ME. **b.** *Mus.* in *just interval*, etc.: Harmonically pure; sounding perfectly in tune 1811. **6.** In accordance with reason, truth, or fact; right; true; correct 1490. **†b.** Of a copy, calculation, etc.: Exact, accurate -1798. **†7.** Appropriate, suitable -1684. **†8.** Exact, as opp. to approximate. Also with defining word: = '(the) exact . .'. -1759. **†b.** Exact or uniform in operation, regular, even -1769. **†9.** Equal; even, level -1725. **†10.** That is such properly, fully, or in all respects; complete in amount or character; full; proper, regular -1778.

1. *J. before (with) God* or, simply, *j.*: Righteous in the sight of God; justified. Only the actions of the j. Smell sweet and blossom in the dust SHIRLEY. 2. The Gods are iust SHAKS. b. He was my Friend, faithfull, and iust to me SHAKS. 3. a. J. vengeance 1632. Is this fair, or reasonable, or j. to yourself? DICKENS. b. His country's j. liberties 1849. 4. Alas! my fears were j. 1796. 5. If they ffynd [the weights] not Iust: they breake them 1588. 6. A j. picture of American public opinion BRYCE. b. Like a j. map SWIFT. 7. Things to be done in their j. Season EVELYN. 8. If thou tak'st more Or lesse then a iust pound SHAKS. 9. The destin'd victim to dis-part In sev'n j. portions POPE. 10. Before he come to j. yeares (*i.e.* full age) 1588.

Just, joust (dʒɒst, dʒūst, dʒaust), *v.* ME. [a. OF. *juster, joster, jouster* :—late pop. L. *juxtare* to approach, meet, f. *juxta* near together. The historical Eng. sp. is *just* (cf. *adjust*), but *joust* is now more frequent.] **†1.** *intr.* To join battle, encounter, engage; *esp.* to fight on horseback as a knight or man-at-arms -1667. **2.** *spec.* To engage in a just or tournament; to tilt ME. **3.** *fig.* ME.

2. To Iust and Turney for her loue SHAKS. 3. Auster and Boreas justing furiously Under hot Cancer SYLVESTER.

Just (dʒɒst), *adv.* ME. [f. JUST *a.*; cf. advb. use of F. *juste.*] **1.** Exactly, precisely; verily, actually; closely: of place, time, manner, degree, number, sameness, etc. **†2.** In an exact or accurate manner; with precision; punctually; correctly -1743. **†3.** In replies, etc.; = 'Exactly so', 'just so', 'right' -1698. **4.** *absol.* of time: Exactly at the moment spoken of; precisely now (or then) 1667. **5.** No more than; only, merely; barely. Often preceded by *but* or *only.* 1665. **6.** No less than; absolutely; actually, positively; really; quite; simply. Chiefly *Sc.*, *dial.*, and *U.S.* 1726. **b.** As an emphatic expletive 1855.

1. *J. at, in, over* (etc.) *the* = at, in, over (etc.) the very. *J. to the*, to the very. A parted eu'n iust betweene Twelue and One SHAKS. I will do j. as you advise 1891. Nor cut thou lesse nor more But iust a pound of flesh SHAKS. 'Tis iust the fashion SHAKS. 3. *A. Y. L.* III. ii. 281. 4. His only child was j. dead 1818. 5. He can j. be said to live CHESTERF. J. a line to say that all goes well MRS. CARLYLE. I will j. walk on DISRAELI. 6. Isn't it j. splendid? (*mod. colloq.*). Phr. *Just now.* **a.** At this exact moment. **b.** But now; only a moment ago. **c.** Directly, presently.

||**Justaucorps** (ʒü·stokōr). 1656. [F., f. *juste* close-fitting + *au corps* to the body.] A close-fitting garment: *spec.* **a.** A body-coat reaching to the knees, worn in the 17th and 18th centuries. **b.** An outer garment worn by women in the 17th c. **c.** *Sc.* A jacket or waistcoat with sleeves.

Juster, jouster (dʒɒ·stəɹ, dʒū·stəɹ). ME. [a. AF. *justour* = OF. *justeor, justeur*, f. *juster* JUST *v.*; see -ER² 3.] One who justs; a tilter; hence, †an antagonist.

Justice (dʒɒ·stis), *sb.* OE. [a. OF. *justise*, *-ice* (*jostise*), ad. L. *justitia*, f. *justus* just.] **I. 1.** The quality of being (morally) just or righteous; the principle of just dealing; just conduct; integrity, rectitude. (One of the four cardinal virtues.) ME. **†2.** *Theol.* Observance of the divine law; righteousness; the state of being 'just before God' -1622. **3.** = JUSTNESS 2, 3. 1588.

1. COMMUTATIVE, DISTRIBUTIVE *justice*: see these words. The path of j. was the path of wisdom MACAULAY. 3. The j. of these observations 1885.

II. 1. Exercise of authority or power in maintenance of right; vindication of right by assignment of reward or punishment; requital of desert OE. **2.** The administration of law, or the forms and processes attending it; earlier, †Legal proceedings of any kind ME. **†b.** The persons administering the law; a judicial assembly, court of justice -1654. **†3.** Infliction of punishment, legal vengeance on an offender; *esp.* capital punishment; execution -1788. **4.** Personified, esp. in sense II. 1. 1599.

1. Phr. *Poetical j.*: the ideal justice in distribution of rewards and punishments supposed to befit a poem or the like. This rough j. of the world 1873. 2. Assassins, and all flyers from the hand Of J. TENNYSON. Phr. *Jedwood* or *Jeddart* (= Jedburgh) *j.*, trial after execution. So †*Cupar j. Justices' j.*, the kind administered by petty magistrates, esp. when disproportionately severe. 3. Phr. *To do j. on* or *upon* (*of*), to punish, esp. by death. 4. You are right Iustice, and you weigh this well: Therefore still beare the Ballance, and the Sword *2 Hen. IV*, v. ii. 102.

III. 1. *gen.* A judicial officer; a judge; a magistrate ME. **2.** *spec.* In Great Britain and U.S.: A member of the judicature. **a.** A judge presiding over or belonging to one of the superior courts; since 1875, a member of the Supreme Court of Judicature ME. **b.** A justice of the peace, or other inferior magistrate; esp. in pl. *the Justices* 1586. **3. Justice of the Peace** (†*J. of peace*), an inferior magistrate appointed to preserve the peace in a county, town, or other district, and discharge other local magisterial functions ME.

2. a. *Chief J.* or *Lord Chief J.*, formerly, the title of the judges presiding over each of the courts of King's Bench and of Common Pleas; both offices are now merged under the title of *Lord Chief J. of England.* The judges of the Court of Appeal are called *Lords Justices*; a judge of the High Court of Justice is called *Mr. Justice.*

Phrase. *To do j. to* (a person or thing): **a.** to render (one) what is his due, or vindicate his just claims; hence, To treat (a subject or thing) in a manner showing due appreciation. *To do oneself j.*, to do something in a manner worthy of one's abilities. **†b.** To pledge in drinking (*Oth.* II. iii. 90).

Comb.: **j.-eyre** (-ɛ̄ɹ): see EYRE; **-seat**, seat of j., judgement-seat.

Justice (dʒɒ·stis), *v.* ME. [a. AF. *justicer* = OF. *justicier*, ad. med.L. *justitiare* to exercise justice over, f. *justitia.*] **†1.** *trans.* To administer justice to; to rule, govern -1481. **†2.** To try in a court of law; to bring to trial; to punish judicially -1732. **3.** *intr.* To administer justice (as a justice of the peace) 1606.

Justicer (dʒɒ·stisəɹ). ME. [prob. orig. AF. form of OF. *justicier* = med.L. *justitiarius*; but commonly used as agent-noun from JUSTICE *v.*] **1.** One who maintains or executes justice (*arch.*). **2.** An administrator of justice; †a ruler or governor; a judge, magistrate (*arch.*) 1481. **†b.** *transf.* A judge, critic -1615. **3.** *spec.* = JUSTICE III. 2. 1535.

2. b. If some severe Censor and precise Iusticer blame this act HOLLAND.

Justiceship (dʒɒ·stisʃip). 1542. [f. JUSTICE *sb.* + -SHIP.] The office or dignity of a justice.

Justiciable (dʒɒsti·ʃiăb'l), *a.* 1656. [a. AF. and OF. (F.) *justiciable*, f. *justicier* to JUSTICE.] Liable to be tried in a court of justice; subject to jurisdiction. Hence **Justiciabi·lity.**

Justiciar (dʒɒsti·ʃiăɹ). 1485. [ad. med.L *justitiarius*; cf. next.] **1.** = JUSTICIARY *sb.* 1. 1579. **2.** = JUSTICE III. 2 a. *Obs.* exc *Hist.* 1485. **3.** *gen.* = JUSTICER 1, 2. 1623.

Justiciary (dʒɒsti·ʃiări), *sb.*[1] 1532. [ad. med.L. *justitiarius, -ciarius* judge, f. *justitia*;

see -ARY[1] B. 1.] 1. *Eng. Hist.* The chief political and judicial officer under the Norman and early Plantagenet kings, acting as regent in the king's absence; more fully, *Chief J.* 1700. 2. = JUSTICE III. 2 a, JUSTICIAR 2. *Obs.* exc. *Hist.* 1761. 3. = JUSTICER 1, 2. 1548. 4. Used to designate various foreign officers of state: = F. *justicier*, Sp. *justiciero*, It. *sindaco*, etc. 1763. †5. *Theol.* One who holds that man can of himself attain to righteousness –1716.

4. The j. of Arragon, a name dreadful to royal ears GIBBON.

Justiciary (dʒɒsti·ʃiări), *sb.*[2] *Sc.* 1473. [ad. med.L. *justitiaria, -ciaria*, f. *justitia*; see -ARY[1] B. 3.] The jurisdiction of a justiciar.

High Court of J., the supreme criminal tribunal of Scotland.

Justiciary (dʒɒsti·ʃiări), *a.* 1581. [ad. med. or mod.L. *justitiarius*, F. *justiciaire*.] 1. Pertaining to or connected with the administration of justice or the office of a justice. †2. *Theol.* Self-righteous; see JUSTICIARY *sb.*[1] 5. –1665.

‖**Justicies** (dʒɒsti·ʃiˌīz). 1534. [med.L., 2nd pers. sing. pres. subj. of *justiciare* to JUSTICE.] *Law.* A writ, now abolished, directed to a sheriff, empowering him to hold plea of debt in his county court for sums exceeding forty shillings; so called from the opening words.

Justicing (dʒɒ·stisiŋ), *vbl. sb.* 1606. [f. JUSTICE *v.* + -ING[1].] The administration of justice. Chiefly *attrib.*, esp. in *j.-room*, e.g. in the house of a justice of the peace.

Justico, -coat, -core, ff. JUSTAUCORPS.

Justifiable (dʒɒ·stifəiˌăb'l), *a.* 1523. [a. F., f. *justifier* to JUSTIFY.] †1. = JUSTICIABLE –1643. 2. Capable of being justified, or shown to be just 1561. †b. Of an assertion, etc.: Capable of being made good –1651. †3. Fitted to justify a claim or the like 1755.

2 *Justifiable homicide*: see HOMICIDE *sb.*[2] Emigration from one's own land seems hardly j. 1859. Hence **Ju·stifiabi·lity, Ju·stifiableness**, the quality of being j. **Ju·stifiably** *adv.*

Justification (dʒɒ:stifikē[i]·ʃən). ME. [ad. late L. *justificationem*, perh. through Fr.] †1. Administration of the law; execution of sentence; capital punishment –1480. †2. An ordinance; an ordained form –1609. 3. The action of justifying or showing something to be just, right, or proper; vindication of oneself or another; exculpation; †verification. b. That which justifies; an apology, a defence. 1494. 4. *Theol.* The action whereby man is justified, or freed from the penalty of sin, and accounted or made righteous by God; the fact or condition of being so justified 1526. 5. *Law.* The showing in court that one had sufficient reason for doing that which he is called to answer; the ground for such a plea 1483. b. The justifying of bail: see JUSTIFY 7 b. 6. The action of adjusting or arranging exactly, esp. in *Type-founding* and *Printing* 1672.

3. Nothing can with reason be urged in j. of revenge BUTLER. 4. The plain Scriptural notion of j. is pardon, the forgiveness of sins WESLEY. 5. If you have any thing of J., plead Not guilty 1660.

Justificative (dʒɒ·stifikē[i]tiv), *a.* 1611. [f. late L. *justificat-*, *justificare* + -IVE.] Serving to justify; justificatory.

Justificatory (dʒɒ·stifikē[i]təri), *a.* 1579. [f. late L. *justificat-*, *justificare* + -ORY.] Tending to justify; serving or intended to support a statement.

Justifier (dʒɒ·stifəiˌəɹ). 1526. [f. JUSTIFY + -ER[1].] 1. One who or that which justifies (see JUSTIFY *v.*). 2. *Type-founding* and *Printing*. a. A workman who 'justifies'; a wedge, etc. used in 'justifying' 1771.

1. Faith is the sole j. J. H. NEWMAN.

Justify (dʒɒ·stifəi), *v.* ME. [a. F. *justifier*, ad. late (chiefly eccl.) L. *justificare*, f. *justus* JUST; see -FY.] †1. *trans.* To administer justice to; to try as a judge; to have jurisdiction over, rule, control; to treat justly. b. *absol.* To judge. –1620. †2. *trans.* To execute justice upon; to sentence; to punish, esp. (*Sc.*) to execute –1860. 3. To show to be just or in the right; to vindicate (†*from* a charge) ME. 4. To absolve, acquit, exculpate; *spec.* in *Theol.*, to declare free from the penalty of sin on the ground of Christ's righteousness, or to make inherently righteous by the infusion of grace. Also *absol.* ME. 5. To corroborate, prove, verify ME. †b. To affirm, aver –1781. 6. To show or maintain the justice or reasonableness of; to defend as right or proper 1560. b. To furnish adequate grounds for, warrant 1658. †c. To render lawful –1725. 7. *Law. intr.* and *trans.* a. To show adequate grounds for (that with which one is charged) 1529. b. *To j. (†oneself) as bail, to j. bail*: to show by oath, as a person furnishing bail, that after the payment of his debts he is of adequate pecuniary ability. †8. To approve of; to ratify –1729. 9. To make exact; to fit or arrange exactly. Now only techn.; esp. (*Type-founding*), To adjust a 'strike' or 'drive', so as to form a correct matrix; (*Printing*) To adjust types together, so that they will exactly fill up the forme; to space out the line of type in the composing-stick properly; also *intr.* of type 1551.

2. Justified in the Grassmarket SCOTT. 3. Iustifie not thy self before God COVERDALE *Ecclus.* vii. 5. 4. The innocent and righteous slay thou not: for I will not iustifie the wicked *Exod.* xxiii. 7. 5. The narratives of antiquity are justified by the experience of modern times GIBBON. 6. That.. I may assert th' eternal Providence, And justifie the wayes of God to men MILT. *P. L.* I. 26. b. This very necessity had.. iustified the Act 1658. c. Till.. public nuptials j. the bride POPE.

Justle, var. of JOSTLE *v.*

Justly (dʒɒ·stli), *adv.* ME. [f. JUST *a.* + -LY[2].] In a just manner; righteously (*arch.*); rightfully, rightly; deservedly ME.; properly ME.; exactly, accurately (now *dial.*) ME.

To do iustly, and to loue mercy *Micah* vi. 8. This I j. fear PENN. J. popular 1849.

Justness (dʒɒ·stnės). ME. [f. JUST *a.* + -NESS.] The quality of being just: = JUSTICE in its non-legal senses. †1. Righteousness; uprightness –1726. 2. Rightfulness; fairness; validity, soundness 1559. 3. Conformity to truth or to a standard; correctness; propriety; †exactness 1666.

2. The j. of a title KNOX, of a cause 1759. 3. J. of perception to deal with facts M. ARNOLD.

Jut (dʒɒt), *sb.*[1] *Obs.* or *dial.* 1553. [As JUT *v.*[1]] A push, thrust, or shove against a resisting body; the shock of collision.

Jut (dʒɒt), *sb.*[2] 1709. [var. of JET *sb.*[3]] 1. A jutting out; that which juts; a projection or protruding point 1786. †2. = JET *sb.*[3] 3. CONGREVE.

Jut (dʒɒt), *v.*[1] *Obs.* or *dial.* 1548. [app. onomatopœic.] †1. *intr.* To strike, knock, or push *against* something –1628. 2. *trans.* To push, thrust, shove, jolt; to knock against something 1565.

1. One that would faine run an euen path.. and iutt against no man EARLE.

Jut (dʒɒt), *v.*[2] 1565. [var. of JET *v.*[2]] *intr.* To project or protrude. Often with *out* or *forth*. †b. *transf.* To encroach upon 1623.

Jute[1] (dʒūt). 1746. [ad. Bengāli *jhōṭo*, *jhuṭo*:—Skr. *jūṭa*, var. of *jaṭā* braid of hair.] The fibre from the bark of the plants *Corchorus capsularis* and *C. olitorius* (N.O. *Tiliaceæ*), imported chiefly from Bengal, and used in the making of gunny, canvas, bagging, cordage, etc. b. The plant itself, or any plant of the same genus. Also *attrib.*

Jute[2] (dʒūt). [In pl. *Jutes*, a mod. rendering of Bæda's *Jutæ* and *Juti*, = Icel. *Iótar* people of Jutland.] In *pl.* One of the three Low German tribes which invaded and settled in Britain in the 5th and 6th centuries; they occupied parts of Kent and Hampshire.

†**Jutty**, *sb.* late ME. [var. of JETTY *sb.*, a. F. *jetée*. The *u* for *e* as in JUT *v.*[2]] 1. = JETTY *sb.* 1 –1804. 2. = JETTY *sb.* 2. –1703.

2. No Iutty frieze, Buttrice [etc.] *Macb.* I. vi. 6.

Jutty (dʒɒ·ti), *v.* *Obs.* or *arch.* ME. [Related to prec. sb.] 1. *intr.* To project, jut (*arch.*). †2. *trans.* To project beyond, overhang. SHAKS. †3. = JET *v.*[2] 2. 1611.

†**Ju·venal.** 1588. [ad. L. *juvenalis* (= *juvenilis*), f. *juvenis* a young person.] 1. *adj.* Juvenile –1821. 2. *sb.* A youth; a juvenile –1664.

Juvenescent (dʒūvĭne·sĕnt), *a.* 1821. [ad. L. *juvenescentem*, *juvenescere*.] Becoming young or youthful. So **Juvene·scence**, the state of becoming young or youthful 1800.

Juvenile (dʒū·vĭnəil). 1625. [ad. L. *juvenilis*, f. *juvenis* a young person.]

A. *adj.* 1. Young, youthful. 2. Belonging to or characteristic of youth 1661.

1. Half a dozen j. messengers 1852. 2. Dressed in a very j. manner DICKENS. Hence **Ju·venile·ly** *adv.*, **-ness**.

B. *sb.* A young person; a youth 1733; in booksellers' language, a children's book.

Some bashful j. LONGF.

‖**Juvenilia** (dʒūvĭni·liă). 1622. [L. neut. pl. of *juvenilis* (see prec.).] Achievements or works of a person's youth.

Juvenility (dʒūvĭni·lĭti). 1623. [ad. L. *juvenilitas*, f. *juvenilis* JUVENILE; see -ITY.] 1. Juvenile condition; youthfulness; youthful manner, quality, character, or vigour. 2. *concr.* Juveniles collectively 1823. 3. *pl.* Juvenile characteristics, acts, or ideas 1661.

1. The Sallies of J. FOOTE. 3. Juvenilities unbecoming the character of old age 1706.

Juwise, -ys(e, var. JUISE, judgement.

Juxta- (dʒɒkstă), *pref.*, repr. L. *juxta* adv. and prep. 'near, by the side of, according to'; as in **j.-ampu·llary** *a.*, situated by the side of an ampulla; **-spi·nal** *a.*, situated by the side of the (or a) spine; **-ta·bular** *a.* (*Rom. Law*), according to a testament or written document.

Juxtapose (dʒɒkstăpōᵘ·z), *v.* 1851. [a. mod.F. *juxtaposer*, f. L. *juxta* + F. *poser*; see COMPOSE *v.*] *trans.* To place in juxtaposition. So **Juxtapo·sit** *v.* (*rare*) 1681.

Juxtaposition (dʒɒ:kstăpŏzi·ʃən). 1665. [a. F., f. L. *juxta* + F. *position*.] The action of placing two or more things close together or side by side; the condition of being so placed.

Allah is great, no doubt, and J. his prophet CLOUGH.

Jymold, var. of GIMMALED.

Jynx (dʒiŋks). *Pl.* **jynges** (dʒi·ndʒīz). 1649. [a. mod.L. *jynx*, pl. *jynges* = L. *iynx*, a. Gr. ἴυγξ, pl. ἴυγγες the wryneck, a bird made use of in witchcraft.] 1. A bird, the wryneck (*Jynx* or *Iynx torquilla*); also called *yunx*. 2. *transf.* A charm or spell. URQUHART.

K

K (kē[i]), the eleventh letter of the alphabet in English, was an original letter of the Roman alphabet, taken from the Greek *Kappa* K, originally ⋊, from Phœnician and general Semitic *Kaph* ⋊. Its sound in Greek and Latin was, as in English, that of the back voiceless stop consonant, or guttural *tenuis*. But at an early period of Latin orthography, the letter C (orig. repr. Gr. *Gamma*) was employed for the k sound, and the letter K fell into disuse, except in a few archaic spellings.

In Old English, K is merely a supplemental symbol occasionally used instead of C for the guttural sound. But after the Conquest, in accordance with the Norman usage, C was retained for the guttural only before *a, o, u, l, r*, and K was substituted for the same sound before *e, i, y*, and (later) *n*. Hence, in native words, initial K now appears only before *e, i, y*, and before *n* (:—OE. *cn-*), where it is no longer pronounced in Standard English. Medially and finally, *k* is used after a consonant (*ask, twinkle*), or long vowel (*make, like, week*); after a short vowel, *ck* is used instead of *cc* or *kk*, but the unstressed suffix, formerly *-ick* (*musick*), is now *-ic*, though, when a suffix in *e* or *i* follows, *k* reappears (*traffic, trafficker, trafficking*).

The native K words, being thus confined to Ke-, Ki-, Kn-, are few. But many foreign words of recent adoption, instead of being spelt with C before *a, o, u, l, r, h*, now take K in these positions; and in words from Greek also, many prefer to retain K, instead of latinizing it to C. In a very few words (not of English formation), K represents Gr. χ, esp. in the words in *kilo-*, as *kilogramme*, etc.

I. The letter. Pl. *K*s, K's, *k*s, k's. (Now pronounced (kē¹); formerly (kī) was also current.)

II. In serial order K is the 11th or 10th member, according as J is or is not reckoned as a member.

III. In *Chem.* K is the symbol for Potassium (mod.L. *Kalium*). In *Meteorol.* K = cumulus. In *Assaying*, etc. K = carat. In *Astron.* *k* designates Gauss's Constant, the square of which is a measure of the mass of the sun.

IV. *Abbreviations.* **a.** K. = *Kate, Katherine, Kenneth*, etc. **b.** = *King*: formerly used alone; now usu. in comb., as K.B., King's Bench; K.C., King's Counsel, King's College. **c.** = *Knight* (standing alone Kt.); in K.B., Knight Bachelor; K.B.E., Knight (Commander of the Order of the) British Empire; K.C.B., Knight Commander of the Bath; K.C.S.I., Knight Commander of the Star of India; K.G., Knight of the Garter; K.C.M.G., Knight Commander of the Order of St. Michael and St. George; K.P., Knight of the Order of St. Patrick; K.T., Knight of the Order of the Thistle; etc. **d.** *Electro-physiol.* = *Kathode* (also ka.), *Kathodic.* **e.** kg. = kilogramme; km. = kilometre.

Ka-, frequent var. of CA-, in ME., and in mod. representation of alien words; e.g. *kaaba, kadi, kaffeine*, etc.

||**Kaama** (kā·mă). Also **caama, kama, khama** (kgama). 1824. [Hottentot name.] The hartebeest, a S. Afr. antelope.

||**Kabassou** (kăbæ·su). 1774. [F. (Buffon), a. Galibi *capaçou*.] An armadillo of the genus *Xenurus*.

The K. .with twelve bands GOLDSM.

Kabbala(h, -ism, -ize, var. CABBALA, etc.

Kabob, var. of CABOB.

Kad-: see also CAD-.

||**Kaddish** (kæ·diʃ). 1613. [Aram. *qaddīsh* holy, holy one.] A portion of the daily ritual of the synagogue, composed of thanksgiving and praise, concluding with a prayer for universal peace; specially recited also by orphan mourners.

||**Kadi, kadee,** vars. of CADI.

Kaffir (kæ·fəɹ); prop. **Kafir** (kā·fīr). Also **kaffer, kaffre**; and see CAFFRE. 1801. [a. Arab. *kāfir* infidel.] **1.** = CAFFRE 1, 'infidel', Giaour 1814. **2.** = CAFFRE 2. Also *attrib.*, and as the name of their language 1801. **b.** *pl. Stock Exch.* The term for S. African mine shares. Also *attrib.* 1889. **3.** A native of Kafiristan in Asia 1854.

Kaffle, kafle, vars. of COFFLE, caravan.

Kafila, var. of CAFILA, caravan.

||**Kaftan,** var. of CAFTAN.

||**Kagu** (kā·gu). 1862. [Native name.] A grallatorial bird (*Rhinochetus jubatus*), of unusual type, peculiar to New Caledonia.

||**Kahau** (kā·hau). 1840. [Malay, so called from its cry.] The proboscis-monkey of Borneo (*Nasalis larvatus*).

Kail, var. of KALE, colewort, broth.

||**Kaimakam** (kaimăkā·m). 1645. [Turkish *qāimaqām*, ad. Arab. *qā'im maqām* one standing in the place (of another).] In the Turkish Empire: A lieutenant, deputy; a lieutenant-colonel; a deputy-governor; *spec.* the deputy of the Grand Vizier, and governor of Constantinople.

Kaiman, Kain: see CAYMAN, CAIN.

Kainite (kai·nəit). 1868. [ad. Ger. *kainit*, f. Gr. καινός new + -ITE; named with reference to its recent formation.] *Min.* Hydrous chlorosulphate of magnesium and potassium, found in Prussia and Galicia, largely used as a fertilizer.

Kainozoic, var. CAINOZOIC (*Geol.*).

Kairine (kai·rəin). 1883. [app. f. Gr. καιρός proper time + -INE [5].] *Chem.* A chinoline compound, *oxy-methyl-quinoline tetrahydride*, a strong antipyretic.

Kaiser (kai·zəɹ). ME. [Ult. ad. L. *Cæsar* CÆSAR, whence (perh. through Gr. καῖσαρ) the Teut. forms. OE. *cāsere* normally gave early ME. *caser* KASER; the usual ME. forms *kaiser, keiser*, were adopted afresh from other Teut. langs. The mod. form *kaiser* is directly adopted from German.] **a.** The Emperor; esp. The German Emperor (since 1871); cf. EMPEROR 1 and 2. **b.** An emperor, as a ruler superior to kings ME.

||**Kajawah** (kădʒā·wă, ka·dʒăwă). 1634. [Urdū (Pers.) *kajāwah*; also Pers. *kajawah*.] A camel-litter for women; a kind of large pannier or wooden frame, a pair of which are carried by a camel.

||**Kaka** (kā·kă). 1774. [Maori.] A New Zealand parrot of the genus *Nestor*, esp. *N. meridionalis*; its general colour is olive-brown, varied with red or yellow.

||**Kakapo** (kā·kăpo). 1843. [Maori, f. *kaka* parrot + *po* night.] The ground-parrot or owl-parrot of New Zealand, *Strigops habroptilus*, with green plumage, marked with dark-brown and yellow.

||**Kakaralli** (kākăræ·li). Also **-ali.** 1858. [Native name.] The wood and bark of *Lecythis Ollaria*, a tree of British Guiana, the timber of which is very durable in salt water.

||**Kakemono** (kækĕmōu·no). 180[illegible]. [Japanese, f. *kake-* to hang + *mono* thing.] A Japanese wall-picture, painted on silk or paper, and mounted on rollers.

Kakistocracy (kækistǫ·krăsi). 1829. [f. Gr. κάκιστος worst + -κρατία rule, after *aristocracy*.] The government of a state by the worst citizens.

Kako-, var. sp. of CACO-, repr. Gr. κακο- bad, evil, favoured by many recent writers; e.g. *kakodaimon, kakogenesis*, etc., and esp. **kakodyl(e.** See the words under C.

||**Kalan** (kalā·n, kē¹·lăn). 1861. [Native name.] The sea-otter of the Northern Pacific (*Enhydris lutris*).

Kale, kail (kē¹l, *Sc.* kēl). ME. [Northern form of COLE [1], q. v.] **1.** A generic name for various edible plants of the genus *Brassica*; cole, colewort, cabbage; *spec.* the variety with wrinkled leaves not forming a compact head (*B. oleracea acephala*), borecole. **2.** Broth in which Scotch kale or cabbage forms a principal ingredient; hence *Sc.* Broth or soup made with various kinds of vegetables 1470.

2. I will be back here to my kail (= dinner) against one o'clock SCOTT.

||**Kaleege, kalij** (kălī·dʒ, kā·lidʒ). *E. Ind.* 1864. [a. Hindī *kālij* (Yule).] An Asiatic pheasant of the genus *Euplocamus* or *Gallophasis*, found in the Himalayan region. (Corruptly *college-pheasant*.)

Kaleidophone (kăləi·dǫfoun). 1827. [f. as next + Gr. φωνή sound.] An instrument (invented by Wheatstone) for exhibiting the phenomena of sound-waves by means of a vibrating rod or plate with a reflector at the end.

Kaleidoscope (kăləi·dǫskoup). 1817. [f. Gr. καλός beautiful + εἶδος form + -SCOPE. Named by its inventor, Sir David Brewster.] An optical instrument, consisting of from two to four reflecting surfaces placed in a tube, at one end of which is a small compartment containing pieces of coloured glass; on looking through the tube, numerous reflections of these are seen, producing brightly-coloured symmetrical figures, which may be constantly altered by rotation of the instrument. Also *fig.*

fig. This rainbow look'd like hope—Quite a celestial k. BYRON. Hence **Kaleidosco·pic, -al** *a.* of or belonging to the k.; exhibiting constantly changing, brightly coloured figures.

Kalend, -ar, etc.: see CAL-.

Ka·le-, kai·l-yard. *Sc.* 1574. [f. KALE + YARD.] **1.** A cabbage-garden, kitchen-garden, as commonly attached to a small cottage. **2.** Used with reference to a class of recent fiction, affecting to describe, with much use of the vernacular, common life in Scotland; hence *attrib.* as *Kailyard School, dialect*, etc. 1895 (W. H. Millar). Hence **Kai·lyarder, -ism.**

[The appellation is taken from the Scottish Jacobite song 'There grows a bonnie brier bush in our kail-yard', from which 'Ian Maclaren' took the title of his book 'Beside the Bonnie Brier Bush' (1894).]

Kali (kæ·li, kē¹·li, kē¹·ləi). 1578. [Arab. *qalī*; see ALKALI.] **1.** = ALKALI 2. Also applied to Barilla (*Salsola Soda*), etc. †**2.** = ALKALI 1; hence, vegetable alkali, potash. (Latinized *kalium*, whence the symbol K for potassium.) –1819.

Hence **Kaliform** (kæ·lifǫɹm), *a.* having the appearance of Kali or Glasswort 1868. **Kaligenous** (kăli·dʒĭnəs), *a. Chem.* producing an alkali; said of metals that form alkalis with oxygen 1854.

||**Kalmia** (kæ·lmiă). Also **calmia.** 1776. [mod.L., f. *Kalm*, pupil of Linnæus.] *Bot.* A genus of American evergreen shrubs, N.O. *Ericaceæ*, with showy flowers, including the American Laurel, *K. latifolia*.

||**Kalon** (kē¹·lǫn). 1749. [Gr. καλόν, adj. neut. The (morally) beautiful; the 'summum bonum'; often *to kalon* (τὸ καλόν the beautiful).

||**Kalpa** (kæ·lpă). 1794. [Skr.] In Hindu cosmology: A great age of the world, a period of 4,320,000,000 years; a day of Brahma; a thousand yugas.

Kam, var. of CAM *a.* and *adv.*

Kama, var. of KAAMA.

||**Kamala** (kæ·mălă). 1820. [Skr.] A fine orange-coloured powder consisting of the glandular hairs from the fruit-capsules of an East Indian tree (*Mallotus philippinensis*), used for dyeing silks yellow, and as a vermifuge.

Kame, kaim (kē¹m). 1862. *north.* and *Sc.* form of COMB *sb.* (q. v.), esp. in the sense of a steep and sharp hill ridge; hence in *Geol.* an esker or osar.

||**Kami** (kā·mi). 1727. [Japanese, = 'superior, lord'.] **1.** A title given to daimios and governors, = 'lord'. **2.** In the Shinto or native religion of Japan: A divinity, a god (used by missionaries, etc. as = God).

||**Kamichi** (ka·miʃi). 1834. [Brazilian, through F. *kamichi* (Buffon).] The horned screamer (*Palamedea cornuta*), a bird of Guiana and the Amazon.

Kampseen, Kamsin, vars. of KHAMSIN.

Kamptulicon (kæmptiū·likǫn). 1844. [f. Gr. καμπτός flexible + οὖλος thick + -ικόν neut. adj. suffix.] Floor-cloth composed of a mixture of india-rubber, gutta-percha, and cork, mounted on canvas.

Kan: see CAN, KHAN.

||**Kanaka** (kæ·năkă, in Australia *improp.* kănæ·kă). 1840. [Hawaiian *kanaka* = 'man'.] A native of the South Sea Islands. Also *attrib.*

||**Kanchil** (ka·ntʃil). 1820. [Malay.] The smallest known species of chevrotain (*Tragulus Kanchil*), found in Borneo, Java, and Malacca.

Kand, var. of CAND, fluor-spar.

Kangaroo (kæŋgărū·). 1770. [Said by some to have been native Australian.] **1.** A marsupial mammal of the family *Macropodidæ*, remarkable for its strong hind-quarters and leaping-power. The species are natives of Australia, Tasmania, Papua, and some neighbouring isles; the larger kinds being known as *kangaroos*, the smaller as *wallabies*. Also as *collect. sing.* **2.** With qualifying words, as **Brush K.** = WALLABY; **Giant, Great** (†**Sooty**) **K.**, *Macropus giganteus*; HARE-K.; RAT-K.; ROCK K.; **Tree K.**, an arboreal kangaroo (genus *Dendrolagus*). **3.** *fig.*, esp. *joc.* A native of Australia 1827. **b.** *pl.* In Stock Exchange slang: West Australian mining shares; also, dealers in these shares 1896. **c.** Applied to a form of Parliamentary closure by which some amendments are selected for discussion and others excluded 1913. **4.** *attrib.* 1828.

Combs.: **k.-apple,** the edible fruit of the Australian plants *Solanum laciniatum* and *S. vescum*; also, the plants; **-bear,** the koolah; **-grass,** a tall fodder-grass (*Anthistiria australis*), found in Australasia, Southern Asia, and Africa; **-mouse,** (*a*) the Australian pouched mouse; (*b*) a small American rodent of the genus *Perognathus*; etc.

Kangaroo-rat. 1788. A small Australian marsupial; a rat-kangaroo, potoroo, bettong.

||**Kanoon** (kănū·n). 1714. [a. Pers. or Arab. *qānūn*.] A species of dulcimer, harp, or sackbut, with fifty to sixty strings.

Kant, obs. f. CANT *a.*, and CANT *sb.*[1]; also an oblique arm of a pier.

Kantian (kæ·ntiăn). 1803. [f. Immanuel *Kant*, German philosopher (1724–1804).]

A. *adj.* Of, pertaining to, or connected with Kant or his philosophy 1817. **B.** *sb.* One who holds the philosophical system of Kant. Hence **Ka·ntianism**; so **Ka·ntism, Ka·ntist, Ka·ntite** (*rare*).

Kantry, obs. f. CANTREF.

Kaolin (kā·ǫlin, kē¹·ǫlin). 1727. [a. F., ad. Chinese *kao-, kau-ling* (f. *kao* high + *ling* hill), name of a mountain in North China whence first obtained.] A fine white clay produced by the decomposition of feldspar, used in the manufacture of porcelain; first employed by the Chinese, but subseq. found in many places.

Hence **Kaoli·nic** *a.* **Kaolinite** (kā·-, kǣ·ǒlinəit), *Min.* a general name for those porcelain clays of which kaolin is the typical variety 1867. **Kaolinize** (kā·-, kǣ·ǒlinəiz), *v. trans.* to convert into kaolin 1874. **Kaoliniza·tion.**

‖**Kapelle** (kape·lĕ). 1838. [Ger. ad. med.L. *capella* CHAPEL.] In Germany, a musical establishment consisting of a band or orchestra, with or without a choir, such as used to be maintained at most of the German courts. Hence ‖**Kapellmeister** (kape·lməi·stər), the leader or conductor of a kapelle or orchestra.

‖**Kapok** (kǣ·pǫk, kā·-). Also **capoc.** 1750. [Malay *kāpoq.*] A fine short-stapled cotton wool, known as silk cotton, surrounding the seeds of the tree *Eriodendron anfractuosum*; used for stuffing cushions, etc. Also *k.-tree.*

Kapp (kæp). 1891. [f. Gisbert *Kapp*, a designer of dynamos; cf. *Ampere*, etc.] A workshop unit of magnetic lines of force, = 6,000 times the centimetre-gramme-second unit.

Karacul: see CARACUL.

‖**Karagan** (kā·rāgan). 1800. [Turkī, f. *kara* black.] A species of fox, *Vulpes karagan*, inhabiting Tartary.

Karaite (kē·ə·rā,əit). 1727. [f. Heb. *q'rāīm* scripturalists + -ITE [1].] A member of a Jewish sect which rejects rabbinical tradition and bases its tenets on a literal interpretation of the Scriptures. So **Ka·raism, Ka·raitism,** the religious system of the Karaites.

‖**Karatas** (kărǣ·tăs). 1727. [? Carib.] A West Indian and South American plant (*Bromelia Karatas*), allied to the pine-apple, and yielding a valuable fibre; silk-grass.

‖**Karma** (kā·ɹmă). 1828. [Skr. *karma*, *karman-*, action, fate.] In Buddhism, the sum of a person's actions in one of his successive states of existence, regarded as determining his fate in the next; hence, necessary fate or destiny, following as effect from cause. Hence **Ka·rmic** *a.*

Karmathian, Car- (kaɹmǣ·þiăn), *sb.* (*adj.*). 1819. [After *Karmat*, founder of the sect.] One of a sect of Mohammedans, founded in the 9th cent. As *adj.* Belonging to this sect.

Karn, -e, Karob, -e: see CAIRN, CAROB.

‖**Karoo, karroo** (kărū·). 1789. [Hottentot; of uncertain etym.] The name given to barren tracts in South Africa, consisting of extensive elevated plateaus, with a clayey soil, which during the dry season are entirely waterless and arid.

Kaross (kărǫ·s). 1731. Also **kross(e, cross.** [S. African *karos*; ? corrupt Du.] A mantle (or sleeveless jacket) made of the skins of animals with the hair on, used by the Hottentots and other natives of South Africa.

‖**Karri** (kæ·ri). 1870. [Native name (West Australia).] An Australian tree (*Eucalyptus diversicolor*, one of the 'blue gums'); also, its hard red timber, used in street-paving.

Karstenite (kā·ɹstĕnəit). 1844. [ad. Ger. *karstenit*, named after D. L. G. *Karsten*; see -ITE [1].] *Min.* = ANHYDRITE.

‖**Kartel** (kā·ɹt'l). Also **cartle.** 1880. [S. African Dutch; app. ad. Pg. *catel*, Tamil *kattil* bedstead.] The wooden bed or hammock in a S. African ox-wagon.

Karval, -vel, obs. ff. CARVEL.

Karyo- (kæ·riǒ), occas. **caryo-**, comb. f. Gr. κάρυον nut, kernel, employed in biological terms referring to the nucleus of an animal or vegetable cell, esp. to changes which take place in its structure. The earliest of these were *karyolysis*, *-lytic* (Auerbach, 1874), *karyokinesis* (Schleicher).

†**Ka·ser.** [OE. *cāsere*, repr. Com. Teut. type **kaisar-*, ad. L. *Cæsar* or Gr. καῖσαρ.] = KAISER -1605.

‖**Kat.** 1858. [Arab. *qat.*] A shrub, *Catha edulis*, N.O. *Celastraceæ*, a native of Arabia, where its leaves are used as tea.

Kat-: see also CAT-.

Kata-, *pref.*, a direct adoption of Gr. κατα-, in recent use often preferred to CATA- (q. v.).

‖**Katabasis** (kătæ·băsis). 1837. [a. Gr. κατάβασις; cf. ANABASIS.] A going down; a military retreat.

Katabatic (kætăbæ·tik), *a.* 1918. [ad. Gr. καταβατικός, f. καταβαίνειν to go down.] *Meteorol.* Of a wind: Caused by the local gravitation of cold air down a steep slope.

Katabolism (kătæ·bǒliz'm). 1876. [f. Gr. καταβολή a throwing down + -ISM.] Destructive metabolism. So **Katabo·lic** *a.*

‖**Katabothron** (kætăbǫ·þrǫn). Also **cata-.** Pl. **-a** (**-ons**). 1820. [a. Gr. καταβόθρον, f. κατά down + βόθρος a hole.] A subterranean channel or deep chasm formed by water.

Katastate (kătæ·stēt). 1889. [f. Gr. κατά down + στατός placed.] *Biol.* One of the simpler products of katabolism.

Katheter, Kathetometer: see CATHET-.

Katydid (kǣ·tidid). *U.S.* 1784. [Echoic]. A large green orthopterous insect of the family *Locustidæ*, of arboreal habits, which produces by stridulation a noise to which its name is due; the common or broad-winged species (*Cyrtophyllum concavum*) abounds in the central and eastern states of America.

Kauri (kau·ri). Also **cowry, -ie, cowdi(e, kourie,** etc. 1823. [Maori *kauri*, also written *kaudi*, *r* and *d* interchanging in Maori.] A tall coniferous tree of New Zealand (*Agathis* or *Dammara australis*), which furnishes valuable timber and a resin called kauri-gum.

Comb. **k.-gum, -resin,** the fossil resin of kauri, used as a varnish (cf. DAMMAR).

‖**Kava** (kā·vă). Also **cava, kaava, kawa**; also AVA. 1777. [Polynesian.] An intoxicating beverage prepared from the chewed, grated, or pounded roots of the Polynesian shrub *Piper methysticum* or *Macropiper latifolium* (N.O. *Piperaceæ*). Also, this plant, or its root. Also *attrib.* Hence **Ka·vain, Ka·wain,** a crystalline resin occurring in the kava root.

‖**Kavass** (kăvɑ·s). Also **cavass, kawass,** etc. 1819. [Turk. (Arab.) *qawwās* bow-maker, f. *qaws* bow.] An armed constable, an armed servant or courier (in Turkey).

Kaw, obs. f. CAW.

Kaw-: see CAW-, CAU-.

‖**Kayak** (kai·ăk). 1757. [Eskimo.] The canoe of the Greenlanders and other Eskimo, made of a framework of light wood covered with sealskins sewn together; the top has an opening in the middle to admit the single kayaker, who laces the covering round him to prevent the entrance of water. Hence **Kay·aker**, one who manages a k.

Kayan, see CAYENNE.

Kayles (kēlz), *sb. pl.* Now *dial.* or *Hist.* ME. [Corresp. to MDu. *keghel*, *kegel* (also *keyl-* in comb.) = OHG. *chegil* tapering stick, ninepin, cone, etc.] *pl.* The set of pins used in a kind of ninepins or skittles; usu., the game played with these. **b.** *sing.* One of these pins (*rare*) 1652.

Kaynard, var. of CAYNARD *Obs.*, sluggard.

‖**Kazi** (kā·zī). 1625. [a. Arab. *qādī* CADI.] A civil judge; = CADI.

‖**Kea** (kǣ·ă). 1862. [Maori; from its cry.] The Green Alpine Parrot of New Zealand (*Nestor notabilis*), which destroys sheep in order to prey upon their kidney-fat.

Kearn(e, obs. ff. KERN.

Keb (keb), *sb.* ME. [?] A ewe that has lost her lamb. Hence **Keb**, *v. dial. intr.* Of a ewe: **a.** To cast a lamb prematurely, or dead 1816. **b.** *To keb at*, to refuse to suckle (a lamb).

Bewitching the sheep, causing the ewes to 'keb' SCOTT.

Kebbuck (ke·bək). *Sc.* 1470. [?] A cheese.

A huge kebbock—a cheese, that is, made with ewe-milk mixed with cow's milk SCOTT.

†**Ke·chel.** [OE. *cœcil*, prob. *cǣcil* = MHG. *chüechel* :—**kōkilo-*; f. (ult.) **kōk-*, ablaut var. of **kak-*, whence CAKE (q. v.).] A little cake.

A God's k.: a cake given as alms in the name, or for the sake, of God. CHAUCER.

Keck, *sb.* Now *dial.* 1624. [A sing. of *kex* taken as a pl.] = KEX.

Keck (kek), *v.* 1601. [Echoic.] **1.** *intr.* To make a sound as if about to vomit; to retch; hence *to k. at*, to reject (food, etc.) with loathing. Also *fig.* **2.** *intr.* Of a bird: To utter a sound like *keck* 1844. Hence †**Ke·ckish** *a.* inclined to k.; squeamish 1603.

Keckle (ke·k'l), *sb. Sc.* 1820. [f. KECKLE *v.*[1]] A short spasmodic laugh; a chuckle.

Keckle (ke·k'l), *v.*[1] 1513. [var. of CACKLE *v.*[1], CHECKLE *v.*] **1.** *intr.* To cackle. **2.** To chuckle, laugh, giggle; *trans.* to utter with or express by chuckling 1857.

2. 'Ah, you're a wag, Sir', keckled the old man KINGSLEY.

Keckle (ke·k'l), *v.*[2] 1627. [?] *Naut. trans.* To case a cable or hawser with rope in order to prevent chafing: cf. CACKLE *v.*[2] Hence **Ke·ckling** *vbl. sb.* old ropes which are wound about a cable.

Ke·ckle, *v.*[3] *dial.* 1619. [freq. of KECK.] = KECK *v.* 1. Hence †**Ke·cklish** *a.* (*rare*), = KECKISH 1601.

Kecksy (ke·ksi). Chiefly *dial.* 1599. [f. *kexes* pl. of KEX, taken as = *kexies.*] = KEX, a hollow plant-stem.

Hatefull Docks, rough Thistles, Keksyes, Burres SHAKS.

†**Ke·cky**, *a.* 1711. [f. KECK *sb.* + -Y.[1]] = KEXY.

Ked, kade (ked, kēd). 1570. [?] A sheep-tick or sheep-louse (*Melophagus ovinus*).

Kedge (kedʒ), *sb.* 1769. [? short for KEDGE-ANCHOR. Also *catch*: see CATCH *sb.*[3]] = KEDGE-ANCHOR.

Kedge (kedʒ), *v.* 1627. [? specialized var. of CADGE *v.*] *intr.* **a.** To warp a ship, or move it from one position to another by winding in a hawser attached to a small anchor dropped at some distance; also *trans.* to warp. **b.** Of a ship: To move by means of kedging.

Kedge-anchor. Now *rare.* 1704. [f. KEDGE *v.*] A small anchor with an iron stock used in mooring or warping.

†**Ke·dger.** 1497. [f. KEDGE *v.* + -ER [1].] = prec. -1751.

‖**Kedgeree** (ke·dʒərī). 1625. [Hindī *khichrī*, Skr. *k'rsara* 'dish of rice and sesamum'.] An Indian dish of rice boiled with split pulse, onions, eggs, butter, and condiments; also, in European cookery, a dish made of cold fish, boiled rice, eggs, and condiments, served hot.

Kedlock (ke·dlǫk). *Obs.* exc. *dial.* ME. [app. repr. OE. *cedelc* 'herb mercury'; of unkn. etym.] **1.** = CHARLOCK. **2.** Identified with KEX 1694.

Keech (kītʃ). *Obs.* exc. *dial.* 1613. [?] A lump of congealed fat; the fat of a slaughtered animal rolled up into a lump.

Keek (kīk), *v.* Now only *Sc.* and *n. dial.* [ME. *kike*, with LG. cognates.] *intr.* To peep. Also *fig.* of things. Hence **Keek** *sb.* a peep 1773.

Keel (kīl), *sb.*[1] ME. [prob. a. ON. *kjǫl-r* :—**kelu-z*; not conn. w. Du. and G. *kiel* (KEEL *sb.*[2]).] **1.** The lowest longitudinal timber of a ship or boat, on which the framework of the whole is built up; in boats and small vessels forming a prominent central ridge on the under surface; in iron vessels, a combination of iron plates taking the place of the keel of a wooden vessel. **2.** A ship, vessel. (*poet.*, after L. *carina.*) 1547. **3.** That part of anything which corresponds to a ship's keel; a keel-like lower part 1726; esp. in aircraft 1888. **4.** A central ridge along the back or convex surface of any organ or structure, as a leaf, a petal, a glume of grass, the lower mandible of a bird, etc. 1597. **5.** *spec.* in *Bot.* and *Zool.*

a. The two lowest petals of a papilionaceous corolla, more or less united and shaped like the prow of a boat; the carina 1776. **b.** A prominent ridge along the breastbone of birds of the class *Carinatæ* 1766. **6.** *Arch.* A ridge or edge on a rounded moulding 1835.

The crooked k. the parting surge divides POPE. **False k.**, (*a*) an additional keel attached to the bottom of the true keel to protect it and increase the stability of the vessel; (*b*) an external keel subsequently added to a vessel. Phr. *On* (or *with*) *even k.*, with the keel level (see EVEN *a.*).

Comb.: **k.-block**, one of the short pieces of timber on which the keel of a vessel rests in building or in a dry dock; **-raking** = KEELHAULING; †**-rope**, a coarse rope formerly used for clearing the limber holes by drawing it backwards and forwards (Smyth).

Keel (kīl), *sb.*[2] ME. [a. MDu. *kiel* ship, boat, repr. a Com. Teut. wd. (**keuloz*), which appears as OE. *céol*, ON. *kjóll*, etc. Since the 16th c. the Du. and G. *kiel* has lost its sense of 'ship' and taken that of KEEL *sb.*[1]] **1.** A flat-bottomed vessel, esp. a lighter as used on the Tyne and Wear for loading colliers. **b.** The quantity of coals carried in a keel, now = 8 Newcastle chaldrons or 21 tons 4 cwt. 1750. **2.** Used to render OE. *céol* in the passage of the Saxon Chronicle relating to the first coming of the Angles to Britain 1605.

Keel, *sb.*[3] Chiefly *Sc.* 1480. [?] Ruddle, or a mark made with this.

Keel (kīl), *v.*[1] *Obs.* exc. *dial.* [Com. Teut.: OE. *cēlan*, *célan*; see COOL *a.* and *v.*] **1.** *trans.* To cool; *spec.* to cool (a hot liquid) by stirring, skimming, or pouring in something cold, in order to prevent it from boiling over. **2.** *intr.* To become cool or cold ME.

1. While greasie Ione doth keele the pot SHAKS. *fig.* Likely to lessen and k. the affections of the Subject MILT.

Keel (kīl), *v.*[2] 1808. [f. KEEL *sb.*[1]] **1.** *trans.* To plough (the sea) with a keel (*nonce-use*). **2.** *intr.* Of a ship: To roll on her keel 1867. **3.** Orig. *U.S.* *trans.* To turn up the keel of, show the bottom of. *K. over*, to turn over; to upset, capsize. 1828. **b.** *intr.* To turn or be turned over; to be upset; to fall over or be felled as if by a shock. 1860.

Keelage (kī·lėdʒ). *rare.* 1500. [f. KEEL *sb.*[1] + -AGE. Cf. med.L. *kylagium*, and F. *quillage*.] A toll or due payable by a ship on entering or anchoring in a harbour.

Keel-boat (kī·lbōut). 1695. [f. KEEL *sb.*[1] and [2].] †**a.** ? A small keel –1746. **b.** A large flat boat used on American rivers 1822. **c.** A yacht with a keel instead of a centre-board 1893.

Keeled (kīld), *a.* 1787. [f. KEEL *sb.*[1] + -ED[2].] **a.** Having a keel 1847. **b.** Having a central dorsal ridge; carinate.

a. The boat was..k. and clinker-built MEDWIN. b. A k. leaf 1848, sternum 1865.

Keeler[1] (kī·ləɹ). *rare.* ME. [f. KEEL *sb.*[2] + -ER[1].] †**a.** A keelman. **b.** A man employed in managing coal-barges and colliers in the Newcastle district 1875.

Keeler[2]. *Obs.* exc. *dial.* ME. [f. KEEL *v.*[1] + -ER[1].] A vessel for cooling liquids; a shallow tub.

Keelhaul (kī·lhǭl), *v.* 1622. [ad. Du. *kielhalen*.] *trans.* To haul (a person) under the keel of a ship, either by lowering him on one side and hauling him across to the other side, or, in the case of smaller vessels, lowering him at the bows and drawing him along under the keel to the stern.

Keeling (kī·liŋ). *Sc.* and *n. dial.* ME. [?] A cod-fish.

Kee·livine, keelie vine. *Sc.* and *n. dial.* 1782. [?] A black-lead pencil, or more generally, any coloured pencil enclosed in wood (as a *red k.*); also, locally, black-lead, plumbago. Also *attrib.*, as *k. pen*, a pencil. Hence **Kee·livined** *a.* marked with a pencil.

Keelman (kī·lmæn). ME. [f. KEEL *sb.*[2]] One who works on a keel or barge.

Keels, var. of KAYLES.

Keelson (also **Keelsale**), var. of KELSON.

Keen (kīn), *sb.* 1830. [a. Ir. *caoine* (kī·nə); cf. KEEN *v.*[2]] An Irish funeral wail.

Keen (kīn), *a.* (*adv.*) [Com. Teut.: OE. *céne* :—OTeut. **kōnjo-*.] †**1.** Wise, learned, clever –ME. †**2. a.** Brave, bold, daring –1605. †**b.** Of kings, etc.: Mighty, powerful, strong –1510. †**c.** Fierce, savage; cruel; harsh (*to* a person) –1622. †**d.** Bold, proud, insolent, heinous –1594. **3.** Having a very sharp edge or point; extremely sharp. (Now somewhat rhet., exc. in *keen edge*.) ME. **4.** *transf.* **a.** Operating on the touch or taste like a sharp instrument; acrid, pungent, stinging (now *unusual*) ME. **b.** Of cold, etc.: Piercing, intense. Of wind, air, etc.: Biting, piercing ME. **c.** Of sound, light, scent: Sharp, penetrating; shrill; vivid; clear; strong ME. **5.** Causing acute pain or deep distress; intense, bitter; sharp, cutting ME. **6.** Eager, ardent, fervid; intense ME.; const. *on*, *upon* 1714. **7.** Of the eyes, etc.: Sharp, penetrating. Hence, of other senses: Highly sensitive. 1720. **b.** Intellectually acute, shrewd; suggestive of mental sharpness 1704. †**8.** *adv.* Keenly –1667.

3. Out he caught a knyfe as A rasour kene CHAUCER. Plucke the keene teeth from the fierce Tygers jawes SHAKS. *fig.* Words K. to wound as sharpened swords SHELLEY. 4. a. K. mustard 1658, hail SHELLEY. b. While the Winds Blow moist and k. MILT. c. One star..with k. beams SHELLEY. 5. The keenest mental terrors DICKENS. K. speeches MACAULAY. 6. A k. sportsman 1827. K. competition 1862, enjoyment 1865. K. about money KINGSLEY. 7. Her glance is as the razor k. GAY. Dogs k. of scent 1875. b. A k. attorney CRABBE. His face was k. WORDSW. Hence **Kee·n-ly** *adv.*, **-ness.**

†**Keen**, *v.*[1] ME. [f. KEEN *a.*] †**a.** *intr.* To become keen. **b.** *trans.* To render keen; to sharpen 1599–1746.

Keen (kīn), *v.*[2] 1811. [f. Ir. *caoin-* (kīn), stem of *caoinim* I wail.] **1.** *intr.* To utter the keen for the dead; to wail bitterly. **2.** *trans.* To bewail with Irish wailing 1830.

Hence **Keener**, a professional mourner at Irish wakes and funerals.

Keep (kīp), *sb.* ME. [f. KEEP *v.*] †**1.** Care, attention, heed, notice. Const. *of*, *infin.*, or *cl.* –1647. **2.** Charge; orig. only in phr. †*to take k.* ME. **3.** *Hist.* The innermost and strongest structure or central tower of a mediæval castle, serving as a last defence; a tower; a stronghold, donjon 1586. **4.** A contrivance which serves for containing or retaining something 1615; e.g. a stop in a door-frame 1833; a part of the axle-box in a locomotive engine, fitted beneath the axle and serving to hold an oiled pad against it 1881. **5.** The act of keeping or maintaining; the fact of being kept 1763. **b.** The food required to keep a person or animal; provender, pasture; maintenance 1825.

2. Take euer a besy kepe of thy selfe CAXTON. Often he vsed of hys keepe a sacrifice to bring SPENSER. 3. Like the proud K. of Windsor rising in majesty of proportion, and girt [etc.] BURKE. Yon huge k. that hinders half the heaven TENNYSON. 5. Phr. *Out at k.*, said of animals in hired pastures. *In good k.*, well kept. *For keeps*: to keep, for good; hence, altogether. *colloq.* *Comb.* **k.-tower** = sense 3.

Keep (kīp), *v.* Pa. t. and pa. pple. **kept.** [Late OE. *cēpan*; ult. etym. unkn.]

I. Early senses (with *genitive* in OE., afterwards with *simple object*). †**1.** To seize, lay hold of; to snatch, take –ME. †**2.** To try to catch or get –ME. †**3.** To take in, receive, contain, hold –ME. †**4.** To take in with the eyes, ears, or mind; to mark, observe; to watch –1697. †**5.** To watch for, await –1485. †**6.** To lie in wait for; to intercept on the way –ME. †**7.** To encounter –ME. †**8.** To meet in a friendly way; to greet, welcome –1460.

4. While the stars and course of heaven I k., My wearied eyes were seiz'd with fatal sleep DRYDEN.

II. *trans.* (in early use also *intr.*) †**1.** To have regard, to care, to reck –1589. †**2.** *intr.* To have care, take care; to give heed, look *to* –1450. **3.** *trans.* To pay attention or regard to; to observe, stand to OE. **4.** To celebrate, solemnize ME. **5.** To observe by attendance, etc., or in some prescribed or regular way 1450. **5.** To guard, defend, protect, preserve, save ME. **6.** To take care of; to look after, watch over, tend ME. **7.** To maintain in proper order ME. **8.** To maintain continuously in proper form and order (a diary, books, etc.) 1552. **9.** To provide for the sustenance of; to maintain, support. Also *refl.* ME. **10.** To maintain in one's service, or for one's use or enjoyment 1548. **b.** *To k. a woman* as a mistress 1530. **11.** To have habitually in stock 1706. †**12.** *refl.* To conduct oneself, behave –ME. **13.** To preserve in being or operation ME. **14.** With complement: To preserve, maintain, retain, or cause to continue, in some specified condition, state, place, position, action, or course ME. Also *refl.* **15.** To hold as a captive or prisoner; to hold in custody; to prevent from escaping ME. **16.** To cause or induce to remain; to detain. Also *fig.* 1653. **17.** To hold back; to restrain, control. Const. *from* (*off*, *out of*). ME. Also *refl.* **18.** To withhold from present use, to reserve; to lay up, store up. Also *refl.* ME. **19.** Actively to hold in possession; to continue to have, hold, or possess. Also *absol.* (The opposite of *to lose*; now a leading sense.) ME. Also *fig.* **20.** To withhold (*from*) 1461. **21.** To hide, conceal; not to divulge ME. **22.** To continue to follow (a way, path, course, etc.) so as not to lose it or get out of it ME. **23.** To stay or remain in, on, or at (a place); not to leave ME. **b.** To stay or retain one's place in or on, against opposition 1599. **24.** To carry on, conduct ME. **25.** To conduct as one's own 1513. **26.** To carry on, maintain (an action, war, disturbance, or the like) ME.

1. Ne how the grekes pleye The wake pleyes ne kepe I nat to seye CHAUCER. 3. To kepe couenaunt LD. BERNERS. To k. rules 1668, Faith STEELE, an oath FREEMAN, an appointment 1891. 4. Phr. *To k. chapels*, *roll-call* (at college or school), *to k. terms*, *residence*, etc. *To k. regular* or *proper* (and so *late*, *early*) *hours.* 5. His goode shelde kept hym CAXTON. The horsemen were left..to..kepe the passage 1560. To keepe him from stumbling *Tam. Shr.* III. ii. 59. 6. Nor shall my Nel k. Lodgers SHAKS. Shall I keepe your hogs, and eat huskes with them? SHAKS. *To k. wicket* (see WICKET). Also *absol.* To act as wicket-keeper. 7. This space is kept with the scythe 1827. 8. No record was kept of the losses of the English 1869. 9. The land would barely k. the cows 1858. He kept the younger ladies in gloves 1890. 10. Because thou dost not keepe a dogge SHAKS. To k. pigs 1833, a gig 1853, a valet 1860. 13. Phr. *To k. silence*, *company*, *step*, *tune* (*with*); *to k. a look out*, *ward*, *watch*, etc. 14. Phr. *To k. a prisoner*, *at arm's length*, *at it*, *in repair*, *out of mischief*, etc. 16. Don't let me k. you 1885. 17. Kepe thy tonge from euell BIBLE (Great) *Ps.* xxxiv. 13. 18. To k. oneself for great occasions FREEMAN. 19. To get and kepe not is but losse of payne 1559. 21. Phr. *To k.* COUNSEL, a SECRET. 22. We kept no path DE FOE. 23. Phr. *To k. one's bed*, *one's room* (as in sickness); *to k. the house. To k. the deck*, *the saddle*, *one's ground*, etc. 25. I k. a Coffee-house STEELE. 26. What a catterwalling doe you keepe heere! SHAKS.

III. *intr.* **1.** To reside, dwell, live, lodge (now only *colloq.*, esp. at Cambridge and in U.S.) ME. **2.** To remain or stay for the time 1560. **3.** To remain or continue in a specified condition, state, position, etc. late ME. **4.** To continue, persevere, go on 1548. **5.** To remain in good condition; to last without spoiling. Also *fig.* 1586.

1. Where does Mr. Hollis 'keep'? inquired he of his bedmaker 1859. 2. I kept..within doors DE FOE. The wind kept in the proper quarter 1891. 3. Keepe in that minde, Ile deserue it *Merry W.* III. iii. 89. To k. friends 1883. 4. Turn to the left and k. straight on 1889. She kept tumbling off her horse 1892. 5. I had no hops to make it k. DE FOE. Your story..can k. 1889.

With preps. in specialized senses. **Keep at —.** To work persistently at. Also *to k. at it* (see AT *prep.* II. 2). **Keep from —.** To abstain from; to remain away from; to restrain oneself *from*. **Keep to —. a.** To stick to, abide by (a promise, etc.). **b.** To confine or restrict oneself to. **Keep with —.** To remain with; to keep company with; to keep up with.

With adverbs. **Keep away. a.** *trans.* To cause to remain absent or afar. **b.** *intr.* To remain absent or at a distance. **c.** *Naut.* *trans.* To cause to sail 'off the wind' or to leeward. *intr.* To sail off the wind or to leeward. **Keep back. a.** *trans.* To restrain; to detain; to hold back forcibly. **b.** To withhold; to reserve designedly; to conceal. **c.** *intr.* To hold oneself back. **Keep down. a.** *trans.* To hold down; to hold in subjection or under control; to repress. **b.** To keep low in amount or number; to prevent from growing or increasing. **c.** *Painting.* To keep low in tone. **d.** *Printing.* To set in lower-case type; to use capitals sparingly. **e.** *intr.* To remain subdued. **Keep in. a.** *trans.* To confine within; to hold in check; not to utter or give vent to; *spec.* to confine in school after hours. **b.** To keep (a fire) burning: see IN *adv.* II. 2 e. Also *intr.* of a fire. **c.** *Printing.* To set type closely spaced. **d.** *To keep one's hand in*: see HAND *sb.* **e.** *intr.* To remain indoors, or within a retreat, place, position, etc. **f.** To remain in favour or on good terms *with* (now *colloq.*). **Keep off. a.** *trans.* To hinder from coming near; to ward off; to avert. **b.** *intr.* To stay at a distance; not to come on. **Keep on. a.** *trans.* To maintain or retain in an existing condition or relation. **b.** To keep (a fire, etc.) going continuously. **c.** *intr.* To continue in a course or action; to go on with something. Now freq. with *pres. pple.* **d.** To remain fixed; to stay on. **Keep to.** *Naut.* *trans.* To cause (a ship) to sail close to the wind. **Keep together. a.** *trans.* To cause to remain in association or union. **b.** *intr.* To remain associated or united. **Keep under.** *trans.* To hold under control; to keep down. **Keep up. a.** *trans.* To keep shut up. †**b.** To keep undivulged. **c.** To support, sustain. Also *intr.* To bear up, so as not to break down. **d.** To maintain in proper condition;

to support; to keep in repair; to keep burning. **e.** To maintain, retain, preserve (a quality, state of things, etc.). **f.** To maintain, go on with (an action). **g.** To cause to remain out of bed. **h.** *Printing.* To keep (type or matter) standing; also, to use capitals freely. **i.** *To k. up to*: to prevent from falling below (a level, standard, etc.); to keep informed of. Also *intr.* for *refl.* **j.** *intr.* To continue alongside; to proceed at an equal pace *with* (*lit.* and *fig.*). †**k.** To stay within doors; to put up *at*.

Keeper (kī·pəɹ). ME. [f. KEEP *v.* + -ER [1].] One who or that which keeps.

I. 1. One who has charge, care, or oversight of any person or thing. **b.** An officer who has charge of a forest, woods, or grounds; now *esp.* = GAMEKEEPER 1488. **2.** One who observes or keeps a law, promise, etc. ME. **3.** One who owns or carries on some establishment or business 1440. †**4.** One who keeps a mistress –1748. **5.** One who or that which keeps or retains 1548. **6.** Any mechanical device for keeping something in its place; a clasp, catch, etc. *spec.* (*a*) a loop securing the end of a buckled strap; (*b*) the mousing of a hook; (*c*) the box into which the bolt of a lock projects when shot; etc. 1575. **b.** A bar of soft iron placed across the poles of a horseshoe magnet to prevent loss of power; an armature; also, a shoe 1837. **c.** A ring that keeps another (esp. the wedding-ring) on the finger; a guard-ring 1851.

1. And hee [Cain] said, I know not: Am I my brothers keeper? *Gen.* iv. 9. *K. of the Exchange and Mint*: the Master of the Mint, an office held by the Chancellor of the Exchequer. *K. of the Great* (†*Broad*) *Seal*: an officer in England and Scotland who has the custody of the Great Seal; in England the office is now held by the Lord High Chancellor. *K. of the Privy Seal*: (*a*) in England an officer through whose hands pass charters, etc. before coming to the Great Seal, now called Lord Privy Seal; (*b*) a similar officer in Scotland and the Duchy of Cornwall. 3. Isaac Beckett..Alehouse-keeper 1713.

II. 1. One who continues or remains *at* or *away from* a place 1611. **2.** A fruit, or other product, that keeps (well or ill) 1843.

Keepership (kī·pəɹʃip). 1485. [f. prec. + -SHIP.] The office or position of a keeper.

Keeping (kī·piŋ), *vbl. sb.* ME. [f. KEEP *v.* + -ING [1].] The action of KEEP *v.* **1.** Observance of a rule, institution, practice, promise, etc. **2.** Custody, charge, guardianship ME. **b.** Guard, defence. *Obs.* exc. *dial.* ME. **3.** The taking care of a thing or person; the state or condition in which a thing is kept ME. **4.** = KEEP *sb.* 5 b. 1644. †**b.** The maintaining of a mistress or lover; the fact or condition of being so maintained –1768. †**5.** Confinement; prison –1513. **6.** Retention; *pl.* things kept or retained ME. **7.** Reservation for future use 1560. **8. a.** In *Painting. orig.* The maintenance of the proper relation between the representations of nearer and more distant objects in a picture; hence, the maintenance of harmony of composition 1715. **b.** *gen.* Agreement, congruity, harmony 1819. **9.** Staying or remaining in a place or in a certain condition; remaining sound 1742.

1. The k. of Easter 1678. 2. As upright as a new Chancellor, who has the k. of the King's Conscience 1735. 4. b. Pray Madam were you ever in k.? GAY. 6. Good prize and worth the k. SIR T. HERBERT. 7. Fruits which spoil with k. JOWETT. 8. b. Phr. *In* or *out of k.* (*with*): in or out of harmony or agreement (with); Indications in k. with our view (*mod.*).

Kee·ping-room. *local* and *U.S.* 1790. [KEEP *v.* III. 1.] The living room of a person or a family; a parlour.

Keepsake (kī·psēⁱk). 1790. [f. KEEP *v.* + SAKE; cf. *namesake*.] Anything kept or given to be kept for the sake of the giver. *spec.* The name for certain literary annuals; so called as being designed for gifts. Also *attrib.*

Keerie: see KERRIE.

Keeve, kive (kīv, kəiv). [OE. *cȳf*.] A tub or vat; *spec.* a vat for holding liquid in brewing and bleaching; in *Mining*, a vessel in which tin or copper ore is washed.

‖**Kef, keif, kief** (kef, kəif, kīf). 1808. [Arab. *kaif*, colloq. *kef*, well-being, good-humour, etc.] **1.** A state of drowsiness or dreamy intoxication, such as is produced by the use of bhang, etc. **b.** The enjoyment of idleness; 'dolce far niente'. **2.** (In Morocco and Algeria, in form *kief, keef*.) Indian hemp or other substance smoked to produce this state. Also *attrib.* 1878.

1. I fell into *kef*, being incapable of sustained thought W. CORY.

‖**Keffiyeh** (kefī·ye). Also **kefiyeh, kefia,** etc. 1817. [Arab. *kaffiyah* or *kuffīyeh*, by some held to be ad. late L. *cofea, cuphia*; see COIF.] A kerchief worn as a head-dress by the Bedouin Arabs.

Keg (keg), *sb.* 1632. [Later form of CAG *sb.*[1], q. v.] A small barrel or cask, usu. of less than ten gallons. Also *attrib.*

‖**Kehaya** (kehăyā·). 1599. [Turk. *kiḥayā*, corrupt f. Pers., Turk. *katkhudā* (cf. *kad* house + *khudā* master).] A Turkish viceroy, deputy, etc.; a local governor.

Keilhauite (kəi·lhɑu,əit). 1846. [f. Prof. B. M. *Keilhau.*] *Min.* A titano-silicate of calcium, yttrium, and other metals.

Keir, var. of KIER.

‖**Keitloa** (kē·tlo,ă). 1838. [Sechuana *kgetlwa, khetlwa.*] A species of S. African rhinoceros (*Rhinoceros keitloa*), having two horns of nearly equal length.

Keld (keld). *n. dial.* 1697. [a. ON. *kelda.*] A well, fountain, spring. **b.** A deep, still, smooth part of a river. (Frequent in place-names, e. g. *How Keld, Sal(t)keld*, etc.)

Kele, obs. f. KEEL.

Kell (kel). *Obs.* exc. *dial.* ME. [A northern form corresp. to ME. *calle*, CAUL *sb.*[1]] **1.** = CAUL *sb.*[1] 1. **2.** Gossamer threads forming a kind of film on grass 1523. **b.** The web or cocoon of a spinning caterpillar 1612. **3.** *Anat.* = CAUL 4. 1540. **4.** *spec.* = CAUL 5. 1530.

4. I'le have him cut to the k., then down the seames BEAUM. & FL. Hence **Kelled** (†**keld**) *a.* webbed DRAYTON.

Kell, obs. f. KALE, KILN.

Keloid (kī·loid). 1854. [a. F. *kéloïde.*] *Path.* = CHELOID, q.v. Hence **Keloi·dal** *a.*

Kelp (kelp). [ME. *culp* or *culpe* (*ü*), of unkn. origin.] **1.** A collective name for large seaweeds (chiefly *Fucaceæ* and *Laminariaceæ*) which are burnt for the sake of the substances found in the ashes. **b.** *spec.* The giant or great kelp (*Macrocystis pyrifera* or *Fucus giganteus*) of the Pacific coast of America, the largest of seaweeds 1834. **2.** The calcined ashes of seaweed used for the sake of the iodine, etc. they contain; formerly much used in the manufacture of soap and glass 1678. **3.** *attrib.* 1833.

Comb.: **k.-fish**, the name given to several fishes found on the Pacific coast of U.S.; **k.-pigeon**, the sheathbill, an Antarctic sea-bird; **k. raft**, a mass of kelp floating on the sea.

Kelpie, kelpy (ke·lpi). *Sc.* 1747. [?] The Lowland Scottish name of a fabled spirit or demon, usu. appearing in the shape of a horse, reputed to haunt lakes and rivers, and to take delight in, or bring about, the drowning of travellers and others. Also *water-kelpie.*

Kelpies' feet, impressions in the old red sandstone of Forfarshire.

Kelson, keelson (ke·lsən). ME. [a. LG. *kielswîn* (whence G. *kielschwein*, Da. *kjølsvin*, Sw. *kölsvin*, Du. *kolsem* for *kolzwijn*). The first element is app. KEEL *sb.*[1], and the second is prob. SWINE (in obs. LG. = kelson). The tendency to spell *keelson* is recent; but the pronunc. (ke·lsən) still prevails.] **1.** A line of timber placed inside a ship along the floor-timbers and parallel with the keel, to which it is bolted, so as to fasten the floor-timbers and the keel together; a similar bar or combination of iron plates in iron vessels. **2.** Used as = KEEL *sb.*[1] 1 (*rare*) 1831.

Comb. **cross-k.**, a beam placed across the kelson to support the boilers or engines of a steamer.

Kelt [1] (kelt). Now only *Sc.* ME. [?] A salmon, sea-trout, or herling after spawning. Hence **Ke·lted** *a.*, that has spawned 1847.

Kelt [2]. *Sc.* and *n. dial.* 1577. [?] A kind of homespun cloth or frieze, usu. of black and white wool mixed. Also *attrib.* Also *fig.*

†**Ke·lter** [1]. *north.* 1502. [?; cf. KELT [2].] A coarse cloth –1600.

Kelter [2], **kilter** (ke·ltəɹ, ki·ltəɹ). 1606. [?] Good condition, order. (Freq. in U.S., in form *kilter.*)

I must rest awhile. My brain is out of kilter LOWELL.

Keltic, Kelto-, var. CELTIC, CELTO-.

Kemb, *v. Obs.* exc. *dial.* Pa. t. and pa. pple. **kembed, kempt.** [Com. Teut.: OE. *cęmban* :—OTeut. **kambjan*, f. *kamb-* COMB *sb.*[1] Now displaced by COMB *v.*, exc. in *kempt* and *unkempt.*] **1.** *trans.* = COMB *v.* 1. Now *dial.* **b.** *fig.* To trim. CHAUCER. **c.** *joc.* To beat, thrash 1566. †**2.** = COMB *v.* 2. Also *absol.* –1715.

1. His longe heer was kembd bihynde his bak CHAUCER.

Kemelin(e, etc.: see KIMNEL.

Kemp, *sb.*[1] *Obs.* exc. *dial.* [OE. *cempa* wk. masc. :—WGer. **kampjōn-*.] **1.** A big, strong, and brave warrior or athlete; a champion. **2.** *Sc.* A seed-stalk of the ribwort (*Plantago lanceolata*), used in a children's game 1825.

Kemp (kemp), *sb.*[2] ME. [a. ON. *kamp-r* beard, moustache, etc.] †A coarse or stout hair, as those of the eyebrows; now, hair of this kind occurring among wool. Also in *comb.* **k.-hair; k.-haired** *a.* Hence **Ke·mpy** *a.* abounding in kemps.

Kemple. *Sc.* 1565. [a. ON. *kimbill.*] A measure of hay or straw.

Kempt (kemᵖt), *ppl. a. arch.* OE. [f. KEMB *v.*] Of hair or wool: Combed; esp. in comb., as *well-k.*, etc.

Ken (ken), *sb.*[1] 1545. [f. KEN *v.*] †**1.** = KENNING *vbl. sb.* 3 b –1625. **2.** Range of vision. Now *rare.* 1590. †**3.** Sight or view *of* a thing, place, etc.; possibility or capacity of seeing –1745. **4.** Power or exercise of vision; look, gaze 1666. **b.** Mental perception or recognition 1560.

1. *Cymb.* III. vi. 6. 2. Beyond all K. by the best Telescopes RAY. The eye Is bounded in its k. to a stone's cast COWPER. 3. To drown in k. of shore SHAKS.

Ken (ken), *sb.*[2] 1567. [Vagabonds' slang.] A house; esp. one where thieves, beggars, or disreputable characters meet or lodge.

Ken (ken), *v.* [Com. Teut.: OE. *cęnnan* = Goth. *kannjan*, factitive of the preterite-pres. **kann-*, I know; see CAN *v.*[1] Now *arch.* (in sense II. 1), or *Sc.*]

I. In causative senses. (All *Obs.*) †**1.** *trans.* To make known –1567. †**2.** To direct, teach, or instruct (a person) –1529. †**3.** To direct, guide, show the way *to* (*unto, till*) a place or person –1560. †**4.** To consign, commend, deliver, bestow –1440.

II. In non-causative senses. **1.** To descry, see; to look at, scan. *arch.* ME. Also *absol.* (*Obs.* or *arch.*) 1577. **2.** To recognize; to identify. Now *north.* or *Sc.* ME. †**3.** To acknowledge, admit to be (genuine, valid, etc.) –1450. †**4.** To get to know –1586. **5.** To know (a person). Now *Sc.* ME. **6.** To know (a thing). Now chiefly *Sc.* ME. **7.** *intr.* or *absol.* To have knowledge (*of* or *about* something). Now *Sc.* ME.

1. As farre as I could k. thy Chalky Cliffes SHAKS. 2. 'Tis he, I k. the manner of his gate, He rises on the toe SHAKS. 6. He did k. the ambassador-craft as well as any in his age FULLER. 7. It was his father then ye kent o' SCOTT.

Kendal (ke·ndăl). ME. [f. *Kendal* in Westmorland, place of manufacture.] †**1.** A species of green woollen cloth –1687. Also †*attrib.* **2. Kendal green. a.** = sense 1. Now only *arch.* or *Hist.* 1514. **b.** The green colour of Kendal cloth; also, the plant Dyer's Greenweed, with which it was dyed 1866.

2. a. Three mis-begotten Knaues, in Kendall Greene SHAKS.

Kennel (ke·nĕl), *sb.*[1] ME. [app. a. ONF. **kenil* = F. *chenil* :—pop.L. **canile*, f. *canis* (cf. *ovile*).] **1.** A house or cot for a house-dog; a house or range of buildings in which a pack of hounds are kept. **b.** The hole or lair of a fox 1735. Also *transf.* and *fig.* **2.** A pack of dogs or allied animals 1470. Also *transf.* and *fig.* **3.** *attrib.* ME.

1. First let the K. be the Huntsman's Care SOMERVILLE. *transf.* He got us a room—we were in a k. before DICKENS. 2. *transf.* The howling of a k. of wolves 1765. *fig.* Hear the whole k. of Atheists come in with a full crie FULLER. *Comb.* **k.-book**, a book recording events of a kennel where dogs are bred.

Kennel (ke·nĕl), *sb.*[2] 1582. [Later form of CANNEL *sb.*[1] (q. v.).] The surface drain of a street; the gutter.

Kennel, *sb.*³, obs. f. CANNEL *sb.*²

Kennel (ke·nĕl), *v.* 1552. [f. KENNEL *sb.*¹] 1. *intr.* To lie or dwell in a kennel; to retire into a kennel or lair. Of a person (*contemptuous*): To lodge or lurk. Also *fig.* 2. *trans.* To put into, or keep in, a kennel 1592. Also *transf.* and *fig.*

1. Glad here to kennel in a Pad of Straw DRAYTON. 2. Kennelling the Wolfe and the Lamb together 1641. Hence **Ke·nnelling** *vbl. sb.*, also *concr.* provision of kennels.

Kenning (ke·niŋ), *vbl. sb.* Now only *Sc.* and *n. dial.* (exc. sense 5). ME. [f. KEN *v.* + -ING¹.] †1. Teaching, instruction. ME. only. †2. = KEN *sb.*¹ 3. –1697. †3. Range of sight –1601. †b. The distance that bounds the range of ordinary vision, *esp.* at sea; hence, a marine measure of about 20 or 21 miles –1694. 4. Mental cognition; knowledge, cognizance; recognition ME. b. A recognizable amount; a little 1786. 5. One of the periphrastic expressions used instead of the simple name of a thing, esp. in Old Norse poetry 1883.

3. b. Scylley is a Kenning..from the very Westeste Point of Cornewaulle 1538. 4. b. Tho' they may gang a kennin wrang, To step aside is human BURNS.

Keno, kino (kī·no). *U.S.* 1879. [?] A game of chance based on the drawing of numbers and covering of corresponding numbers on cards, in a manner similar to lotto.

Kenogenesis (kīnodʒe·nėsis). 1879. [irreg. for *cæno-* or *kainogenesis*, f. Gr. καινός new + γένεσις genesis.] Haeckel's term for the form of ontogenesis in which the true hereditary development of a germ is modified by features derived from its environment (opp. to *palingenesis*). Hence **Kenogene·tic** *a.*

‖**Kenosis** (kǐnōᵘ·sis). 1873. [a. Gr. κένωσις an emptying, with reference to *Phil.* ii. 7 ἑαυτὸν ἐκένωσε 'emptied himself'.] *Theol.* The self-limitation of the divine power and attributes by the Son of God in the Incarnation. Hence **Keno·tic** *a.* of or pertaining to k.; involving or accepting the doctrine of k.

Kenspeck (ke·nspek), *a. dial.* 1590. [? confused with *conspicuous.*] = next.

Kenspeckle (ke·nspek'l), *a. Sc.* and *n. dial.* 1714. [See prec. and -LE 1.] Easily recognizable; conspicuous.

Kentish (ke·ntiʃ), *a.* [OE. *Cęntisc*, f. *Cęnt* (ad. L. *Cantia* Kent) + *-isc*, -ISH¹.] 1. Of or belonging to Kent. Chiefly of the inhabitants or speech. 2. *absol.* as *sb.* a. *pl.* The natives or inhabitants of Kent (*rare*). OE. b. The dialect of Kent. 1866.

Phr. **K. fire**, a prolonged and ordered salvo or volley of applause, or demonstration of impatience or dissent (said to have originated in reference to meetings held in Kent in 1828–9, in opposition to the Catholic Relief Bill); †**K. Knocker** [f. *K. Knock*, the sand-bank before the mouth of the Thames], a Kentish smuggler; **Kentish man**, a native of Kent born west of the Medway (opp. to *man of Kent*).

Kentle, obs. f. QUINTAL.

Kentledge (ke·ntlėdʒ). 1607. [ad. F. *quintelage*, f. *quintal* QUINTAL + -AGE.] *Naut.* Pig-iron used as permanent ballast, usually laid upon the kelson-plates. Also *attrib.*

Kephalin (ke·fălin). 1878. [f. Gr. κεφαλή head + -IN¹.] *Chem.* Thudichum's term for a substance obtained from brain-matter.

Kephalo- (ke·fălo), var. f. CEPHALO-, preferred by some.

‖**Kepi** (kē·pi, F. ke·pī). Also **képi.** 1861. [F. *képi*, a. Ger. Swiss *käppi*, dim. of *kappe* a cap.] A French military cap, slightly tapering, with a flat top which slopes towards the front, and a horizontal peak.

Kept (kept), *ppl. a.* 1678. [f. KEEP *v.*] In senses of KEEP *v.*; *spec.* a. Maintained or supported by a paramour 1678. b. Financially supported and privately controlled by interested persons; as, *kept party*, *kept Press* 1888.

Kera- (ke·ră), from Gr. κέρας horn, occas. used in place of KERATO-, as **Ke·ralite** [-LITE], hornstone. **Ke·ratome** = *keratotome* (see KERATO-).

Keramic, -ist, vars. of CERAMIC, -IST.

Ke·rasine, *a.* 1864. [Improp. f. Gr. κέρας horn + -INE¹.] Horny, corneous.

Keratin (ke·rătin). 1847. [f. Gr. κέρας, κερατ- horn + -IN¹.] An organic substance found in horn.

Keratitis (kerătəi·tis). 1858. [f. Gr. κερατ- horn + -ITIS.] *Path.* Inflammation of the cornea.

Kerato-, bef. a vowel **kerat-**, var. of CERATO-, comb. f. Gr. κέρας, κερατ- horn, used in terms relating to horny substances, or to the cornea of the eye; as **Kerate·ctomy** [Gr. ἐκτομή], *Surg.* excision of part of the cornea. **Keratony·xis** [Gr. νύξις pricking], *Surg.* a method of operating for cataract. †**Ke·ratophyte** [Gr. φυτόν plant], *Zool.* a coral polyp with a horny axis. **Ke·ratotome** [Gr. -τομος cutting], *Surg.* a knife with triangular blade used for making incisions in the cornea. **Kerato·tomy**, incision of the cornea.

Keratode (ke·rătoud). 1872. [ad. Gr. κερατώδης horn-like.] = KERATOSE *sb.*

Keratoid (ke·rătoid), *a.* 1873. [ad. Gr. κερατοειδής; see above and -OID.] 1. *Math.* Resembling a horn in shape. *Keratoid cusp*: a cusp at which the two branches of the curve lie on opposite sides of the common tangent; a cusp of the first species. 2. Resembling horn in substance 1885.

Keratose (ke·ratōᵘs). 1851. [f. Gr. κερατ- horn + -OSE.] A. *adj.* Of a horny substance; applied to the texture of certain sponges. B. *sb.* A substance resembling horn forming part of the skeleton of certain sponges 1865.

Kerb (kɜ̄ɹb), *sb.* 1664. [Var. of CURB *sb.*, used in special senses.] 1. See CURB III. 2. *spec.* An edging of stone or the like, bordering a raised path, side-walk, or pavement.

2. *On the k.*: said of stock-exchange business done on the street-pavement, esp. after exchange hours.

Kerb (kɜ̄ɹb), *v.* 1861. [f. KERB *sb.*] *trans.* To furnish with a kerb. Hence **Ke·rbing** *vbl. sb.*, also *concr.* the stones forming a kerb.

Ke·rb-stone. Also **kirb-.** 1706. [KERB *sb.*] a. An edging of stone about the top of a well. b. One of the stones forming the kerb of a path; also, the kerb itself 1815.

attrib. **Kerb-stone broker** (*U.S.*), a broker, not a member of the stock exchange, who transacts business in the streets.

†**Kerch.** late ME. = CURCH.

Ke·rcher. *Obs.* exc. *dial.* [ME. *curcher*, *kercher*, by syncope from **cover-*, *kevercher*, a. OF. *couvre-*, *cuevrechier*, erron. ff. *couvrechief*, etc.] = KERCHIEF. Hence **Ke·rchered** *a.* covered with a k.

Kerchief (kɜ̄·ɹtʃif), *sb.* [ME. *curchef* and *kerchef*, syncopated forms of *coverchef* and *keverchef*, respectively a. OF. *couvrechief* and *cuevrechief*, in AF. also *courchief*; see COVERCHIEF.] 1. A cloth used to cover the head, formerly a woman's head-dress. †b. An amice. †c. A woman who wears a kerchief. DRYDEN. 2. A breast-kerchief or neckerchief ME. 3. A handkerchief 1815.

1. Her goodly countenance..Set off with k. starchd and pinners clean GAY.

Ke·rchief, *v.* 1600. [f. prec.] To cover with a kerchief; in *pa. pple.* and *ppl. a.* **Kerchiefed.**

Morn..kercheft in a comely cloud MILT.

Kerf (kɜ̄ɹf). [OE. *cyrf*, app. :—**kurƀi-*, f. *kurƀ-*, ablaut-form of *kerƀ-*, stem of OE. *ceorfan* to CARVE.] 1. The act of cutting; a cut, stroke; †power of cutting. Now *rare.* 2. The incision made by cutting, esp. by a saw 1523. 3. The cut end or surface on a tree or branch ME. 4. A cutting (of anything) 1678.

Kerite (kīᵊ·rəit). 1875. [f. Gr. κηρός wax + -ITE¹.] A kind of artificial caoutchouc for coating telegraph wires, made with tar or asphaltum, oils, and sulphur.

Kerl(e, obs. ff. CARL *sb.*¹

Kermes (kɜ̄·ɹmīz, -mėz). 1598. [= F. *kermès*, etc., ad. Arab. and Pers. *qirmiz.*] 1. The pregnant female of the insect *Coccus ilicis*, formerly supposed to be a berry; gathered in large quantities from a species of evergreen oak in S. Europe and N. Africa, for use in dyeing, and formerly in medicine; the red dye-stuff consisting of the dried bodies of these insects; = ALKERMES 1. 1610. 2. The species of oak (*Quercus coccifera*) on which this insect lives. More fully **kermes oak.** 1598. 3. Amorphous trisulphide of antimony, of a brilliant red colour. More fully **kermes mineral.** 1753. 4. *attrib.* 1671.

Kermesite (kɜ̄·ɹmėzəit). 1843. [f. KERMES + -ITE¹.] *Min.* Native red antimony, a compound of the oxide and sulphide, occurring in cherry-red six-sided prismatic crystals.

‖**Kermis** (kɜ̄·ɹmis). Also **kermess(e, kirmess(e.** 1577. [a. Du. *kermis* (earlier *ker-*, *kirmisse* :—orig. *kerk-*, *kirkmisse*), f. *kirk* KIRK + *mis* MASS.] In the Low Countries, etc.: A periodical (prop. annual) fair or carnival, characterized by much noisy merrymaking. *U.S.* a similar fair, usu. for charitable purposes.

Kern, kerne (kɜ̄ɹn), *sb.*¹ ME. [ad. Ir. *ceithern* (*ceatharn*), pronounced (ke·hĕrn) or (ke·ərn) band of foot-soldiers. Cf. CATERAN.] 1. *Hist.* A light-armed Irish foot-soldier; one of the poorer class among the 'wild Irish'. (Sometimes applied to Scottish Highlanders.) b. In collective sense; †*orig.* a band of Irish foot-soldiers ME. 2. *transf.* A rustic, boor; †vagabond. Now *rare.* 1553.

1. Now for our Irish warres, We must supplant those rough rug-headed Kernes SHAKS.

Kern, *sb.*² *rare.* 1570. [Conn. w. KERN *v.*¹ and KERNEL *sb.*¹] †1. Kernel (of a nut). 2. A grain (of wheat, sand, etc.). Hence **Kern-stone**, ? coarse-grained sandstone, or perh. oolite. 1753.

Kern (kɜ̄ɹn), *sb.*³ 1683. [for **carn*, a. F. *carne* 'projecting angle, nib of a quill pen' :—L. *cardinem* hinge.] *Printing.* A part of a metal type projecting beyond the body or shank, as the curled head of f and tail of j, etc.

Kern (kɜ̄ɹn), *v.*¹ Now chiefly *dial.* [ME. *kerne*, *curne*, app. repr. OE. **cyrnan* :—OTeut. **kurnjan*, f. *kurno-*; see CORN *sb.*¹] 1. *intr.* Of corn: To form the hard grains in the ear; to seed. Also of fruit: To set. †2. *trans.* To cause to granulate; to make (salt) into grains –1726. b. To salt (meat). *Obs.* exc. *dial.* 1613. c. *intr.* To granulate. *Obs.* exc. *dial.* 1657.

2. Salt kerned on the rocks very white HAKLUYT.

Kern (kɜ̄ɹn), *v.*² 1683. [f. KERN *sb.*³] *Printing.* To furnish (a type) with a kern. Hence **Kerned** *ppl. a.*

Kernel (kɜ̄·ɹnĕl), *sb.*¹ [OE. *cyrnel*, dim. of *corn* seed, grain, CORN :—OTeut. **kurnilo-*.] 1. A seed; esp. the seed contained within any fruit; a pip; a grape-stone. *Obs.* exc. *dial.* 2. The softer (usu. edible) part within the hard shell of a nut or stone-fruit OE. 3. The body of a seed (e. g. of wheat, etc.) within its husk, etc. ME. 4. A morbid formation of rounded form in any part of the body; *esp.* an enlarged gland in the neck or groin. Usu. in *pl.* Now chiefly *dial.* OE. 5. A gland; a tonsil; a lymphatic gland or ganglion; a rounded fatty mass. Now *rare* or *dial.* ME. 6. A nucleus; a core; a centre of formation 1641. Also *fig.*

2. He..casts away the Kirnell, because hee hath lost the Shell QUARLES. 6. This settlement, the k. of the great Norman Duchy FREEMAN. *fig.* The k. of Christianity—to be spiritually minded 1806.

†**Kernel**, *sb.*² ME. = CRENEL –1652.

Kernel (kɜ̄·ɹnĕl), *v.* 1483. [f. KERNEL *sb.*¹] †1. *intr.* To form kernels or seed. Of land: To produce grain or corn. –1722. 2. *trans.* To enclose as a kernel in its shell 1652.

Kernelled, -eled (kɜ̄·ɹnĕld), *a.* ME. [f. KERNEL *sb.*¹ + -ED².] †a. Of flesh: Full of kernels or glands. b. Of fruit: Having a kernel 1719.

Kernelly, -ely (kɜ̄·ɹnĕli), *a.* ME. [f. KERNEL *sb.*¹ + -Y¹.] †1. Of flesh: Glandular –1683. 2. Of the nature of a kernel 1655.

†**Ke·rnish**, *a. rare.* 1581. [f. KERN *sb.*¹ + -ISH¹.] Of, or of the nature of, a kern –1641.

Kerolite, var. of CEROLITE.

Kerosene (ke·rŏsīn). 1854. [irreg. f. Gr. κηρός wax + -ENE.] A mixture of liquid hydrocarbons, obtained by the distillation of petroleum; also from coal and bituminous shale; extensively used as a lamp-oil. The usual name is *paraffin oil* or *paraffin.*

‖**Kerrie, keerie** (ke·ri, kīᵊ·ri). 1731. [Hottentot or Bushman.] A short club or knobbed stick used as a weapon by natives of S. Africa.

Kers, -se, -ss, obs. or dial. ff. CRESS.

Kersey (kǭ·ɹzi). Now *rare*. ME. [? from *Kersey* in Suffolk.] **1.** A kind of coarse narrow cloth, woven from long wool, and usually ribbed. **2.** With *a* and *pl.* †A piece of kersey of a definite size; also, a make of kersey (chiefly in *pl.*) 1465. **3.** *pl.* Trousers made of kersey 1831. **4.** *attrib.* or *adj.* Made of kersey 1577; †*fig.* plain, homely 1588.

4. *fig.* Russet yeas and honest kersie noes SHAKS.

Kerseymere (kǭ·ɹzimīᵊɹ). 1798. [A corruption of CASSIMERE, assoc. w. KERSEY.] **1.** A twilled fine woollen cloth of a peculiar texture. **b.** *pl.* (rarely *sing.*) Trousers made of kerseymere 1840. **2.** *attrib.* 1836.

Kerseynette, corrupt f. CASSINETTE.

Kerve, obs. and dial. f. CARVE *v.*

Kesar, obs. f. KAISER.

Keslep, -lip, -lop, northern ff. CHEESELIP.

Kesse, obs. f. KISS *v.* **Kest, -e,** obs. ff. CAST *sb.* and *v.*

Kestrel (ke·strĕl). [Early mod.E. *castrel, kistrell, kestril,* of doubtful origin.] **1.** A species of small hawk (*Falco tinnunculus,* or *Tinnunculus alaudarius*), also called *Stannel* or *Windhover*. **b.** *fig.*, applied to persons, usually in contempt 1589. **2.** *attrib.* 1590.

1. b. Thou art thyself a kite, and k. to boot SCOTT.

Ket. Now *dial.* ME. [a. ON. *kjǫt* (:— **ketwo*ᵐ), flesh.] Raw flesh; carrion; *fig.* trash.

Ketch (ketʃ), *sb.*[1] 1655. [Later form of *cache,* CATCH *sb.*[2]] A strongly-built two-masted vessel, usually from 100 to 250 tons burden, formerly much used as a bomb-vessel (see BOMB-KETCH); now a similarly rigged small coasting vessel. Also *attrib.*

Ketch, *sb.*[2] 1681. [See JACK KETCH.] The hangman. Hence **Ketch** *v. trans.* to hang.

Ketchup (ke·tʃɒ̆p). Also CATCHUP. 1711. [app. ad. Chinese *kôechiap* or *kê-tsiap* brine of pickled fish.] A sauce made from the juice of mushrooms, walnuts, tomatoes, etc. Often qualified, as *mushroom k.*, etc.

Ketine (kī·tǝin). 1892. [f. KET(ONE + -INE [5].] *Chem.* An oily liquid, $C_6H_8N_2$, or one of a series of homologous bases $C_nH_{2n-4}N_2$, formed by the reduction of nitrosoacetone and its homologues by sodium (or tin) and hydrochloric acid.

Ketone (kī·tōun). 1851. [a. Ger. *keton,* a modification of ACETONE.] *Chem.* Name of a class of chemical compounds formed by oxidation of the secondary alcohols or carbinols, to which they stand in some respects in the relation of aldehydes. The lowest of the series, *dimethyl ketone,* is common ACETONE.

Hence **Keto·nic** *a.* of or pertaining to ketones, as in *ketonic acid.* So **Ke·tol,** a ketonic alcohol. **Ke·tose,** a sugar which is a ketonic alcohol, e.g. lævulose.

Kettle (ke·t'l). ME. [a. ON. *ketill* = OE. *cetel,* G. *kessel*; CTeut. ad. L. *catillus,* dim. of *catinus* vessel for food.] **1.** A vessel, commonly of metal, for boiling water, etc.; now *esp.* a covered metal vessel with a spout, a TEA-KETTLE. **2.** *transf.* **a.** 'The brass or metal box of a compass' 1867. **b.** = POT-HOLE 1874. †**3.** Short for KETTLEDRUM. *Haml.* v. ii. 286.

Phr. *A k. of fish.* **a.** On the Tweed, etc. A picnic, at which a kettle of fish cooked *al fresco* is the chief thing eaten; also simply *kettle* 1791. **b.** *fig.* A disagreeable or awkward state of things 1742.

Kettledrum (ke·t'l₁drɒm). 1542. **1.** A musical instrument of percussion consisting of a hollow hemisphere of brass or copper, over the edge of which parchment is stretched and tuned to a definite note 1602. †**2.** = KETTLE-DRUMMER –1755. **3.** *colloq.* An afternoon tea-party on a large scale. Cf. DRUM *sb.*[1] 8. 1861.

2. Trumpets and Kettle-Drums in rich Liveries 1669. Hence **Ke·ttledru·mmer,** one who plays the k. 1683.

Ke·ttle-stitch. 1818. [ad. G. *kettelstich* chain-stitch.] In bookbinding: A knot made at the head and tail of a book in sewing it, by which the thread holding one sheet is fastened to the thread in the next.

‖**Keuper** (koi·pǝɹ). 1842. [A German miners' term.] *Geol.* The upper member of the Triassic system, consisting in Germany of marls, shales, sandstones, gypsum, and clays, in England chiefly of marls and sandstones.

Kevel (ke·v'l), *sb.*[1] Now *Sc.* and *n. dial.* ME. [a. ON. *kefli* a round stick, small roller, gag, related to *kafli* a piece.] **1.** †**a.** A gag. **b.** A bit or twitch for a horse's mouth. **2.** A rounded piece of wood; a staff, cudgel 1807.

Kevel (ke·v'l), *sb.*[2] ME. [a. ONF. *keville* = Central F. *cheville* pin, peg, CHEVILLE.] *Naut.* A peg or cleat, usually fixed in pairs, to which certain ropes are belayed.

Kevel (ke·v'l), *sb.*[3] *Sc.* and *n. dial.* ME. [?] A kind of hammer for rough-hewing or breaking stone; also *k.-hammer, -mell.* Hence **Ke·vel** *v.* to break (stones).

†**Kevel,** *sb.*[4] 1759. [Said to be the native name in Senegal.] A gazelle –1834.

Kever, common ME. f. COVER *v.*[1] and [2] in midl. and s. dial.; rare obs. f. COVER *sb.*[1]

Kex (keks). *Obs.* exc. *dial.* ME. [Origin unkn.; W. *cecys* pl. is no doubt from Eng.] **1.** The dry, usually hollow, stem of various herbaceous plants, *esp.* of large umbelliferous plants, such as Cow Parsnip, Wild Chervil, etc. †**b.** Without *a*: collectively, or as a material –1725. **2.** An umbelliferous plant with a hollow stalk 1578. †**3.** The husk, sheath, or hard case of a chrysalis –1688. †**4.** *fig.* A dried-up sapless person –1711.

1. I should be as dry as a k. wi' travelling so far T. HARDY. 2. Tho' the rough k. break The starr'd mosaic TENNYSON. 3. When the k., or husk, is broken, he proveth a fair flying butterfly HOLLAND. Hence **Ke·xy** *a.* (now *dial.*), like a k.; dry and brittle; withered, sapless.

Key (kī), *sb.*[1] [OE. *cǣg* str. f. (pl. *cǣga*) and *cǣge* wk. f. (pl. *cǣgan*) = OFris. *kei, kay*; not in other Teut. langs.; ult. etym. unkn. Pronounced (kē) and often spelt *kay* till 1700; the mod. pronunc. is app. of northern origin. Cf. the surname *Kaye* or *Key* (*Caius*) in *Caius* (i.e. *Key's*) *College,* Cambridge.]

I. 1. An instrument, usually of iron, for moving the bolt or bolts of a lock forwards or backwards, and so locking or unlocking what is fastened by it. **b.** The representation of a key, in painting, sculpture, etc. 1450. **2.** In pregnant sense, with reference to the powers implied by the possession of the keys of any place; hence as a symbol of office, and *fig.* the office itself. OE. *Gold k.*, the groom of the stole.

1. The k. turns, and the door upon its hinges groans KEATS. Phr. *To get* (*have*) *the k. of the street* (ironical), to be shut out for the night, or have no house to go to. **b.** *St. Peter's keys,* the cross keys borne in the Papal arms. *Greek key,* each of the key-like bends of which the Greek fret consists. 2. All the townes in Acquitayne (except Bayon) delivered their keys, and became vassals HALL.

II. *fig.* **1.** Something compared to a key, with its power of locking and unlocking; that which opens up, or closes, the way to something; that which gives opportunity for, or precludes, an action, state of things, etc. OE. **2.** *Theol.* (See *Matt.* xvi. 19.) Usu. *pl.*: The ecclesiastical authority held by Roman Catholics to be conferred by Christ on St. Peter and transmitted to the Popes as his successors. More widely: The disciplinary power of priests as successors of the Apostles. OE. **3.** A place which gives its possessor control over the passage into or from a certain district, territory, inland sea, etc. 1440. **4.** That which serves to open up, disclose, or explain what is unknown, mysterious, or obscure OE. *spec.* an explanatory scheme for the interpretation of a cipher, etc., a set of solutions of problems, a translation of a text, etc. in a foreign language for the use of learners, and the like. **5.** *Mus.* †**a.** [after Guido Aretino's use of *clavis.*] The lowest note or tone of a scale or sequence of notes; the key-note. Hence, **b.** A scheme or system of notes or tones definitely related to each other, according to (or *in*) which a piece of music is written; such scheme being based upon and named after some particular note (the *key-note*), as *the key of C.* Hence, **c.** The sum of melodic and harmonic relations existing between the tones of such a system; tonality. 1590. **6. a.** *transf.* (High or low) tone (of the voice); pitch 1599. **b.** *fig.* Intensity or force, 'pitch' (of feeling or action); tone or style (of thought or expression); sometimes, prevailing tone or idea, 'key-note' 1594. **c.** Tone or relative intensity (of colour) 1851.

1. Love, the k. of hearts, will open the closest coffers FULLER. *Golden* or *silver k.*, money, employed as a bribe to obtain the opening of a door or to gain a purpose. 3. A very Important place, which is the K. of Sclavonia 1684. 4. Poetry is the k. to the hieroglyphics of nature HARE. A K. to Henry's Exercises 1870. It was the k. to his success; he knew the value of time 1883. 5. Both warbling of one song; both in one k. SHAKS. 6. a. Men speak in a high or a low k. BERKELEY. b. Let peace and love exalt your K. of mirth QUARLES.

III. Applied to mechanical devices, in function or form suggesting the key of a lock. **1.** A pin, bolt, wedge, etc., fitting into a hole or space contrived for it so as to lock various parts together; a cotter 1440. **2.** That which completes or holds together the parts of any fabric; *esp.* the key-stone of an arch, which holds the structure together ME. Also, the last board in a floor. Also †*fig.* **b.** That portion of a first coat of wall-plaster which passes between the laths and secures the rest; the roughness of a wall-surface which enables plaster to adhere to it 1825. **3.** In the organ, pianoforte, etc.: Each of the levers, which are pressed down by the fingers in playing, and actuate the internal mechanism so as to produce the notes 1500. Also, each of the small metal levers, actuated by the fingers, in the flute, oboe, clarinet, concertina, etc. 1688. **4.** Hence **a.** In telegraphy, A mechanical device for breaking and closing an electric circuit. **b.** In a type-writer, etc., each of a set of levers pressed by the fingers in the same manner as the keys of a pianoforte or organ 1837. **5.** An instrument for grasping a square or polygonal-headed screw, peg, or nut, and turning it by lever action 1610.

IV. A dry fruit with a thin membranous wing, usually growing in bunches, as in the ash and sycamore 1523.

Comb.: **k.-action,** the mechanism by which sounds are produced in musical instruments that have a key-board; **-bed** *Mech.*, the part of a shaft on or in which a key rests; **-bolt** *Mech.*, a bolt which is secured in its place by a key or cotter; **-bone,** (*a*) the collar-bone, clavicle (*nonce-use*); (*b*) a bone forming the key of a structure; **-groove** *Mech.* = *key-seat*; **-money,** a payment required from the tenant of a house before he is allowed to have the key; **-seat** *Mech.*, a key-bed or key-way; **-way** *Mech.*, a groove cut in a shaft, or in the boss of a wheel, to receive a key.

b. (in sense II. 4), as *key-map, -move, -sentence, -word*; passing into *adj.* in sense 'dominant', 'controlling', as **k. industry,** one which is essential to the carrying on of others; **k. man; k. position.**

Key (kī), *sb.*[2] Now written QUAY. ME. [a. OF. *kay, kai, cay.* For the ultimate etym. see CAY. In Eng., till 18th c., usually written *key* (less freq. *kay*), which latterly was pronounced as KEY *sb.*[1] The spelling *quay* is after later F. *quai.*] A wharf, a quay. †**b.** *transf.* A harbour, haven. QUARLES.

Key (kī), *sb.*[3] 1697. [var. of CAY, ad. Sp. *cayo* shoal, reef infl. in spelling and pronunc. by prec.] A low island, sand-bank, or reef, as in the W. Indies, etc. Cf. *Key West.*

Key (kī), *v.* [ME. *keiȝe(n, keie(n,* etc., f. *keiȝe* KEY *sb.*[1]] **1.** *trans.* To lock with a key. Also *fig. rare.* **2. a.** To fasten by means of a pin, wedge, bolt, or cross-piece 1577. **b.** To cause (plaster) to adhere (to laths) 1881. **3.** To regulate the pitch of the strings of a musical instrument. Hence *fig.*: To give a certain tone or intensity to (feelings, thoughts); *to k. up,* to raise to a high pitch 1636. **4.** To insert the keystone in (an arch). Also with *in.* 1735.

Keyage (kī·ėdʒ). Now written QUAYAGE. 1440. [a. OF. *kaiage, caiage,* etc.; see KEY *sb.*[2] and -AGE.] Quay-dues; quayage.

Keyboard (kī·bōᵊɹd). 1819. [KEY *sb.*[1] III. 3.] The set or row of keys in an organ, piano, type-writing machine, etc.

Key·-bugle. 1836. A bugle fitted with keys to increase the number of its sounds.

Key·-cold, *a.* Now *rare.* 1529. As cold as a key; very cold; *esp.* cold in death. Also *fig.*

Poore key-cold Figure of a holy King SHAKS.

Keyed (kīd), *a.* 1781. [f. KEY *sb.*[1] or *v.* + -ED.] **1.** Of a musical instrument: Furnished with keys. **2.** In carpentry, etc.: Secured by means of a key 1823. 3. Of an arch: Constructed with a keystone 1841.

Keyhole (kī·hōul). 1592. 1. The hole by which the key is inserted into a lock. 2. A hole made to receive a peg or key used in carpentry, etc. 1703.

attrib. and *Comb.*: **k. escutcheon**, an escutcheon-shaped plate of metal surrounding a keyhole; **k. limpet**, a gastropod of the family *Fissurellidæ*, having a shell with an aperture at the apex; **k. saw**, a narrow saw for cutting keyholes, etc.

Keyless (kī·lės), *a.* 1823. [KEY *sb.*[1]] Without a key; of a watch, etc.: wound up otherwise than by means of a key.

Key-note (kī·nōut). 1752. *Mus.* The first, i. e. lowest, note of the scale of any key, which forms the basis of, and gives its name to, the key; the tonic. Also *transf.* and *fig.*

Keys (kīz). ME. [Pl. of KEY *sb.*[1] in specialized use.] The elective branch of the Legislature of the Isle of Man. More fully *House of Keys.* (The reason for title is not clear.)

Keystone (kī·stōun). 1637. 1. The stone at the summit of an arch, which locks the whole together. Also *fig.* 2. A bond-stone 1823. 3. In chromolithography, the stone on which a general outline of the subject is made, serving as a guide in getting the colours in place 1875. 4. A block of cast iron used to fill up spaces in a lead-smelting furnace 1839.

1. *fig.* The tenet of predestination was the k. of his religion MACAULAY. *Comb.* **K. State**, *U.S.*, popular appellation of Pennsylvania, as being the seventh or central one of the original thirteen states 1841.

Khaki (kā·ki). 1857. [Urdū (Pers.) *khākī* dusty, f. *khāk* dust.] **A.** *adj.* **a.** Dust-coloured; dull brownish yellow. **b.** (*attrib.* use of B.) Made of khaki cloth. 1863. **B.** *sb.* A fabric of this colour largely employed since 1899 for field-uniforms. Orig. of stout twilled cotton (*K. drill*), but now also of wool (*K. Bedford*, *K. serge*) 1857.

The Infantry were dressed in khakee 1859.

C. As *adj.*, *adv.*, or *sb.* in such constr. as *to vote k.*, *a k. election*, *the k. loan* (*khakis*), etc., used in reference to the S. African War of 1899–1902, and the war spirit of that time 1900.

‖**Khalifa** (kălī·fă), var. of CALIPH.

‖**Khalsa(h** (kā·lsă). *E. Ind.* 1776. [Urdū (Pers.) *khāliçah*, *khālça(h*, fem. of Arab. *khāliç* pure, real, proper, etc.] 1. The state exchequer in Indian states. Also *attrib.*, as *k.-grain.* 2. The Sikh community or sect 1790.

‖**Khamsin** (kæ·msin). 1685. [Arab. *khamsīn*, mod. colloq. f. *khamsūn* fifty.] An oppressive hot wind from the south or south-east, which in Egypt blows at intervals for about 50 days in March, April, and May.

‖**Khan**[1] (kæn, kān). ME. [a. Turkī *khān* lord, prince, regarded as a modified form of *khāqān*; see CHAGAN.] **a.** *Hist.* Specific title given to the successors of Chingīz Khan, who were supreme rulers over the Turkish, Tartar, and Mongol tribes, as well as emperors of China, during the Middle Ages. **b.** A title (now of slight import) commonly given to rulers, officials, or men of rank in Central Asia, Afghanistan, etc.

‖**Khan**[2] (kæn, kān). ME. [Arab. *khān* inn.] In the East: A caravanserai.

Khanate (kæ·n-, kā·nēˡt). Also **khanat.** 1799. [f. KHAN[1] + -ATE[1].] A district governed by a khan; the position of a khan.

‖**Khansamah, -saman** (kansā·ma(n). *E. Ind.* 1645. (Corruptly *consumah*, *consumer.*) [Urdū (Pers.) *khānsāmān*, f. *khān* KHAN[1] + *sāmān* household goods.] In India: A house-steward; the head of the kitchen and pantry department.

‖**Khedive** (kėdī·v). 1867. [a. F. *khédive*, a. Turk. *khedīv*, *khidēv* prince, sovereign.] The title of the viceroy of Egypt, accorded to Ismail Pasha by the Turkish government in 1867. Hence **Khedi·val, Khedi·vial** *a.* **Khedi·vate, Khedi·viate**, the office, authority, or government of the k.

‖**Khidmutgar** (ki·dmʋtgār). 1765. [Urdū (from Pers.) *khidmatgār*, = *khidmat* service + *-gar*, agent-suffix.] In India: A male servant who waits at table.

‖**Khoja** (kōᵘ·dʒă). 1625. [Turk. and Pers. *khōjah*, prop. *khwājah.*] A professor or teacher in a Mohammedan school or college; a schoolmaster; a scribe, clerk.

‖**Khud** (kʋd). *E. Ind.* 1837. [Hindī *khaḍ.*] A deep ravine or chasm; a precipitous cleft in a hill-side.

‖**Khus-khus** (kʋ·skʋs). *E. Ind.* 1810. [Urdū (Pers.) *khas-khas.*] The sweet-scented root of an Indian grass, largely used in the manufacture of mats or screens ('tatties').

‖**Khutbah** (ku·tbă). 1800. [Arab. *khuṭbah*, *khoṭbeh*, f. *khaṭaba* to preach.] A form of sermon or oration used at meridian prayer on Fridays in Mohammedan mosques.

Kiang, var. KYANG, Tibetan wild horse.

Kibble (ki·b'l), *sb.*[1] 1671. [prob. ad. Ger. *kübel* 'tub'.] *Mining.* A large wooden or (later) iron bucket, for conveying ore or rubbish to the surface.

Ki·bble, *sb.*[2] 1891. [? Altered f. COBBLE.] = COBBLE *sb.*[1]

Kibble (ki·b'l), *v.*[1] 1790. [?] *trans.* To bruise or grind coarsely; to crush into small pieces. Also *absol.* **Ki·bbler. Ki·bblerman.**

Kibble (ki·b'l), *v.*[2] 1891. [f. KIBBLE *sb.*[1]] To convey ore or rubbish in a kibble.

Kibe (kəib), *sb.* ME. [Cf. Welsh *cibi* (also *cibwst*) of the same meaning.] 1. A chapped or ulcerated chilblain, *esp.* one on the heel. Also *fig.* 2. *transf.* **a.** A sore on a horse's foot. ? *Obs.* 1639. **b.** A breaking out at the top of the hoof in sheep. (So Welsh *cibi.*) 1846. †**c.** A hump or swelling. MAPLET.

1. *fig.* *To gall* or *tread on* (*one's*) *kibes*, to press upon closely so as to annoy. *To tread* or *follow on the kibes of*, to come closely at the heels of. Hence **Kibe** *v. rare*, to affect with kibes or chilblains; *erron.* to kick or gall 1757. **Kibed** *a.* affected with chilblains on the heels 1500.

‖**Kibitka** (kibi·tkă). 1799. [Russ., 'tent, tilt-wagon', f. Tartar *kibits*, with Russ. suffix *-ka.*] 1. A circular tent covered with thick felt, used by the Tartars; *transf.* a Tartar household or family. 2. A Russian wagon or sledge with a rounded cover or hood; a sledge with a tilt or covering 1806.

‖**Kiblah** (ki·blă). 1704. [Arab. *qiblah*, that which is placed opposite.] The point (the temple at Mecca) to which Mohammedans turn at prayer. **b.** A niche in a Mohammedan building on the side towards Mecca 1775.

Kibosh (kəi·bǫʃ, kibǫ·ʃ). *slang.* 1836. [? Yiddish.] 1. In phr. *To put the k. on*: to finish off, do for. 2. Nonsense, 'rot' 1873.

Kiby (kəi·bi), *a.* Now *dial.* 1523. [f. KIBE *sb.* + -Y[1].] Affected with kibes.

†**Ki·chel.** *rare.* [OE. *cicel*, of obscure etym.] A small cake –ME.

Kick (kik), *sb.*[1] 1530. [f. KICK *v.*]

I. 1. An act of kicking. **b.** Ability or disposition to kick 1885. Also *fig.* 2. *transf.* **a.** The recoil of a gun when discharged 1826. **b.** A jerk, jolt; jerking motion 1835. 3. One who kicks. Usu. with adj. 1857.

1. *More kicks than halfpence*: more harshness than kindness 1824. **b.** He had not a k. in him F. T. BULLEN. 2. **c.** *Electr.* A momentary high-voltage discharge in an inductive electric current 1910. **d.** *fig.* (orig. *U.S.*) A sharp stimulant effect, e.g. that of strong liquor or pungent seasoning; also, a thrill of excitement, fear, etc. 1903.

II. Slang senses. 1. *The kick*: the fashion, the newest style 1700. 2. A sixpence 1700. 3. *pl.* Breeches. ? *Obs.* 1700. 4. A pocket 1851. 5. *The kick*: 'the sack' (SACK *sb.*[1] I. 3) 1844.

Kick (kik), *sb.*[2] 1861. [?] 1. An indentation in the bottom of a glass bottle, making it hold less. 2. The projection on the tang of a pocket-knife blade, which prevents the edge of the blade from striking the spring 1864. 3. The piece of wood fastened to the upper side of a 'stock-board' to make a depression in the lower face of a brick as moulded 1875.

Kick (kik), *v.* [ME. *kike*, *kyke*, of unkn. origin. W. *cicio* is from Eng.]

I. 1. *intr.* To strike out with the foot. **b.** *slang.* To die 1725. 2. *fig.* To show temper; to rebel, be recalcitrant ME. 3. *transf.* **a.** Of firearms: To recoil when fired 1832. **b.** *Cricket.* Of the ground: To cause a ball to rebound in a more nearly vertical direction than usual 1882. 4. *trans.* To strike (anything) with the foot 1590. **b.** *transf.* Of things: To strike (anything) with a violent impact. Of a gun: To strike in the recoil. 1667. 5. With advs. or phrases: To impel, expel, eject, etc., with violence 1678. 6. To accomplish, make, or do by kicking 1857.

1. They.., like galled camels, k. at every touch B. JONS. Phr. *To k. against the pricks* (*spur*, *goad*): to strike the foot against these; also *fig.* to be recalcitrant to one's own hurt ME. *To k. over the traces*: (of a horse) to get a leg over the traces so as to kick more freely; *fig.* to throw off the usual restraints 1861. 2. *To k. against* or *at*, to object strongly to, rebel against; to spurn. 4. I should kicke being kickt, and being at that passe, You would keepe from my heeles SHAKS. *To k. the bucket*, to die (*slang*): see BUCKET *sb.*[2] *To k. one's heels*: see HEEL *sb.*[1] **b.** *To k. the beam*: see BEAM *sb.* 6. 5. **b.** *intr.* (To be or lie) *kicking about*: i.e. in danger of being kicked or otherwise damaged 1867.

II. With advs. **Kick off.** **a.** *trans.* To throw off (shoes) by kicking or jerking the foot. **b.** *Football. intr.* To give the first kick. **Kick out.** **a.** *trans.* To turn out with a kick, or in an ignominious fashion. **b.** *Football. intr.* To re-start the game by kicking the ball towards the opposite goal from (or behind) the 25-yard line; also, to kick the ball over a side line. **c.** *intr.* To die (*slang*). **Kick up.** **a.** *trans.* To raise (dust, etc.) by or as by kicking; hence, to make (any disturbance or nuisance). **b.** *Cricket. intr.* Of a ball: To rebound more or less vertically. Hence **Ki·ckable** *a.* **Ki·cker.**

†**Kickie-wickie.** [app. a joc. formation. Mod. editors usually adopt *kicksy-wicksy*, after the later folios.] A jocular or ludicrous term for a wife. *All's Well* II. iii. 297.

Kick-off (ki·k,ǫf). 1857. The first kick to the ball in a football match. Also *fig.*

†**Kicksey-winsey.** 1599. [app. a whimsical formation; cf. *kickshaws.*] **A.** *sb.* A fantastic device; a whim –1635. **B.** *adj.* Fantastic, whimsical, erratic –1652. **C.** *adv.* ? Topsy-turvy. J. TAYLOR.

Kickshaw, -shaws (ki·kʃǫ, -ʃǫz). 1597. [ad. F. *quelque chose* something. The wd. was sometimes correctly taken as sing., with pl. *-choses*; more often as a pl., with a sing. *kickshaw* afterwards formed from it.] 1. A fancy dish in cookery. (Chiefly contemptuous: A 'something' French.) 2. Something dainty or elegant, but unsubstantial; a toy, trifle, gewgaw 1601. 3. A fantastical frivolous person. *Obs.* exc. *dial.* 1644. 4. *attrib.* Frivolous, trifling 1658.

1. A ioynt of Mutton, and any pretty little tinie Kick-shawes SHAKS. 2. Art thou good at these kicke-chawses [Maskes, etc.] Knight? SHAKS.

Kicksie-wicksie: see KICKIE-WICKIE.

Kick-up (ki·k,ʋp). 1793. [f. the phr. *kick up.*] 1. The act of lifting the legs in, or as in, kicking 1861. 2. A row; a great to-do 1793. 3. A name given in Jamaica to two species of thrush, *Siurus noveboracensis* (Bessy Kick-up), and *S. aurocapillus* (Land Kick-up) 1847. 4. = KICK *sb.*[2] 1. 1901.

Kid (kid), *sb.*[1] [ME. *kide*, *kede*, *kid*, commonly regarded as ad. ON. *kið* (Sw., Da. *kid*).] 1. The young of a goat. 2. The flesh of a young goat ME. 3. **a.** The skin of a kid. **b.** Leather made from kid-skins, or from substitutes; chiefly used for gloves and shoes; *pl.* gloves (or boots) made of this leather. 1677. 4. *sing.* or *pl.* (Rendering L. *hædus* or *hædi.*) A pair of small stars in the constellation *Auriga*, represented as kids in the hand of the charioteer 1609. 5. *slang.* A child, esp. a young child. (Orig. low slang.) 1690.

1. She koude skippe and make game As any kyde or calf folwynge his dame CHAUCER.

Kid (kid), *sb.*[2] Now *dial.* ME. [Of unkn. origin; W. *cedys* pl. is prob. from Eng.] A faggot or bundle of twigs, brushwood, gorse, etc., used either for burning, or for embedding in a bank, beach, etc.

Kid (kid), *sb.*[3] 1769. [? var. of KIT *sb.*[1]] A small wooden tub; esp. a sailor's mess-tub.

Kid (kid), *sb.*[4] *slang.* 1873. [f. KID *v.*[3]] Humbug, 'gammon'.

Kid (kid), *v.*[1] ME. [f. KID *sb.*[1]] **a.** *trans.* To give birth to (a kid). **b.** *intr.* To bring forth a kid or kids.

Kid (kid), *v.*[2] Now *dial.* 1504. [f. KID *sb.*[2]] *trans.* **a.** To bind up in kids or faggots;

also *absol.* to make faggots. **b.** To secure (loose soil, etc.) by means of kids. Hence **Ki·dding** *vbl. sb.*; *concr.* kids used to secure loose soil, etc.; work in which kids are used.

Kid (kid), *v.*[3] *slang.* 1811. [perh. f. KID *sb.*[1] in sense 'to make a kid of'.] *trans.* To hoax, humbug, try to make (one) believe what is not true.

Kid, obs. f. KITH.

Kid, kidd(e, pa. t. and pple. of KITHE *v.*

Kidderminster (ki·dəɹminstəɹ). 1670. [Name of a town in Worcestershire.] **1.** *attrib.* Of or pertaining to Kidderminster; *spec.* a kind of carpet, originally manufactured there, in which the pattern is formed by the intersection of two cloths of different colours; also called *two-ply* and *ingrain* carpet. **2.** *absol.* = Kidderminster carpet or carpeting.

Kiddier. *Obs.* exc. *dial.* Also **kidder.** 1551. [?] = BADGER *sb.*[1] (q.v.).

Kiddle (ki·d'l). ME. [a. AF. *kidel, kydel,* OF. *quidel,* later *quideau,* also *guidel,* mod.F. *guideau.*] **a.** A dam, weir, or barrier in a river, having an opening in it fitted with nets, etc. for catching fish. **b.** An arrangement of stake-nets on the sea-beach for the same purpose. Also *attrib.*

Kiddy (ki·di), *sb.* 1579. [f. KID *sb.*[1] + -Y[6].] **1.** A little kid (young goat). **2.** *slang* and *colloq.* A little child 1889. **3.** *Thieves' slang.* A professional thief of 'flashy' dress and manner; one who dresses in a similar style 1780. **4.** *attrib.* as *adj.*: Pertaining to, appropriate to, 'kiddies' 1805.

3. Poor Tom was once a k. upon town BYRON.

Kiddy (ki·di), *v. slang.* 1851. [Cf. prec. and KID *v.*[3]] *trans.* To hoax, humbug.

Kid glove. 1832. **1.** A glove made of kid-skin or similar leather. **2.** *attrib.* as *adj.* (*Kid-glove*) Characterized by wearing kid gloves; dainty or delicate in action or operation; avoiding real work; free from roughness or harshness 1856.

1. Phr. *With kid gloves,* in a gentle, delicate, or gingerly manner. Hence **Kid-gloved** *a.* wearing kid gloves; *fig.* refined, dainty, delicate, etc.

Kidling (ki·dliŋ). 1586. [+ -LING.] A little kid.

Kidnap (ki·dnæp), *v.* 1682. [f. KID *sb.*[1] + NAP *v.*, to snatch, seize (cf. NAB).] Orig., to steal or carry off (children or others) for service on the American plantations; hence, to steal (a child), to carry off (a person) by illegal force.

I will k. her and send her to Virginia DE FOE. So **Ki·dna·pper,** one who kidnaps children or others; also *fig.* 1678.

Kidney (ki·dni). ME. [?] **1.** One of two glandular organs in the abdominal cavity of mammals, birds, and reptiles, which excrete urine and so remove effete nitrogenous matter from the blood. The kidneys of cattle, sheep, and pigs are eaten as food. **2.** *fig.* Temperament, nature; hence, class, stamp 1555. **3.** More fully *k. potato*; an oval variety of potato 1796. **4.** *attrib.*, as *k. disease, k. pie, k.-shaped,* etc. 1597.

1. Waiter, bring me a k. and some stout 1871. *fig.* A Youth, who officiates as the K. of the Coffee-house STEELE. 2. Thinke of that, a man of my K.; ..that am as subiect to heate as butter *Merry W.* III. v. 116. This fellow is not quite of a right k. FIELDING.

Phrase. †*Kidneys of wheat,* repr. 'fat of kidneys of wheat' *Deut.* xxxii. 14; cf. *Ps.* cxlvii. 14 'the fat of wheat', the finest of the wheat, in allusion to the kidney-fat as the choicest part of an animal, which was offered in sacrifice.

Comb.: **k.-cotton,** a variety of *Gossypium barbadense,* a cotton plant of which the seeds are in kidney-shaped masses; **k. ore,** hæmatite occurring in kidney-shaped masses; **-piece,** a cam with a kidney-shaped outline; **-potato** = 3; **-vetch,** a leguminous herb (*Anthyllis vulneraria*), Lady's-fingers.

Kidney bean, kidney-bean. 1548. **1.** Name for the dwarf French bean (*Phaseolus vulgaris*), and for the Scarlet Runner (*P. multiflorus*). See BEAN. **2. Kidney-bean tree.** The American Wistaria (*Wistaria frutescens*), also the Chinese (*W. chinensis*), both grown as wall-climbers in Great Britain 1741.

Ki·dneywort. 1640. [See WORT.] *Herb.* The plant *Cotyledon Umbilicus,* also called Navelwort; also *Saxifraga stellaris.*

Ki·d-skin. 1645. The skin of a kid, esp. as used for gloves; also skins of lambs, etc.

Kie, var. of *kye,* pl. of COW.

Kief, var. of KEF.

Kier (kīᵊɹ). 1573. [Cf. ON. *ker* vessel = OHG. *char,* Goth. *kas.*] †**a.** A brewing-vat. **b.** A large vat in which cloth is boiled for bleaching, etc.

‖**Kieselguhr** (kī·z'lgūr). 1875. [Ger., f. *kiesel* gravel, CHESIL[1] + GUHR.] A diatomaceous earth, used as an absorbent of nitro-glycerine in the manufacture of dynamite.

Kieserite (kī·zərəit). 1862. [f. D. G. *Kieser,* of Jena.] Hydrous magnesium sulphate, used in making Epsom salts, etc.

Kike, obs. f. KEEK *v.*, KICK *v.*

Kilderkin (ki·ldəɹkin). ME. [A corruption of MDu. *kinderkin,* also *kindeken, kinneken* (or *-kijn*), the fourth part of a tun, etc.; see -KIN.] **1.** A cask for liquids, fish, etc., holding 16 to 18 gallons. **2.** A cask of this size filled with some commodity; the quantity it contains; hence, a measure of capacity ME.

fig. A tun of man in thy large bulk is writ, But sure thow'rt but a k. of wit DRYDEN.

Kilkenny (kilke·ni). *K. cats*: two cats fabled to have fought until only their tails remained; used allusively. 1852.

Kill (kil), *sb.*[1] ME. [f. KILL *v.*] †**1.** A stroke, blow. ME. only. **2.** The act of killing an animal hunted as game 1852. **3.** A killed animal 1878. **4.** *Lawn Tennis* and *Rackets.* (Cf. KILL *v.* Phrases) 1903.

Kill (kil), *sb.*[2] *U.S. local.* 1669. [a. Du. *kil,* MDu. *kille* river-bed, channel.] A stream, 'creek', or tributary river; used esp. in place-names, as *Schuylkill.*

Kill, *sb.*[3] Also **kiln.** 1630. [?] On the Thames: An eel-trap or weel.

Kill (kil), *v.* Pa. t. and pa. pple. **killed** (kild). ME. [Origin unkn.; not in cogn. langs. Exceptionally the pa. pple. appears as **kilt,** now regarded as an Irishism.] †**1.** *trans.* To strike; to knock. Also *absol.* or *intr.* Also *fig.* ME. only. **2.** To put to death; to deprive of life; to slay. Also *fig.* ME. **b.** *absol.* To perform the act of killing, commit murder, cause death 1535. **c.** *intr.* in passive sense: To suffer killing; to yield (so much meat) when killed 1857. **d.** *trans.* To procure (meat) by killing animals 1560. **e.** To represent as killed or dead 1867. **3.** *transf.* To destroy the vitality or the activity of (an organism, a disease, etc.); to destroy, break up, or ruin. 1530. **4.** *fig.* To destroy, put an end to (a feeling, project, etc.) ME. **b.** To destroy (an appearance or quality) by contrast 1859. **5.** To consume (time), so as to bring it to an end 1728. **6.** In hyperbolic use: **a.** To overwhelm (a person) by a strong impression on the mind; to exhaust the strength of 1634. **b.** To injure seriously. (An Irishism.) 1800.

2. Yche other for to kylle With blody speris CHAUCER. What art thou, that telst of Nephews kilt? SPENSER. He was killing himself by late hours THACKERAY. Phr. *To k. out, off,* etc., to get rid of by killing. *To k. dead,* etc. **b.** They killed..near Blankney 1810. **c.** She [the cow] killed 34 stones 1888. **d.** To k. beefe and pork for 65 men of war 1689. **e.** He kills the hero in the last chapter (*mod.*). 3. Potatoes have quite killed the land YOUNG. The lye will have lost its causticity, or, in technical language..it is killed 1875. 4. [He] detected his wife..endeavouring to k. a laugh 1851. 6. **c.** *intr.* (orig. *U.S.*) To make an irresistible impression; as *dressed to k.* 1848. 7. *Printing.* To mark (matter) as not to be used.

Phrases. *To k. a ball*: (*a*) in tennis, to strike it so that it cannot be returned; (*b*) in football, to stop it dead. *To k. a bill* (in parliament): to prevent it from passing. *To k. with kindness*: to harm fatally by mistaken kindness. *K. or cure,* with reference to remedies which either cure or prove fatal.

Kill, obs. f. KILN.

Kill-, *vb. stem,* prefixed to sbs., forming *sbs.* with sense 'one who or that which kills ...', and *adjs.* = 'that kills ..., -killing', as **kill-courtesy,** a boorish person; **kill-duck** *a.*, suitable for killing ducks; etc.

‖**Killadar** (ki·lădāɹ). *E. Ind.* 1778. [Urdū (Pers.), f. Arab.; = 'fort-holder'.] The governor of a fort or castle.

Killas (ki·lăs). 1674. [Cornish.] Clay-slate; geologically, the clay-slate of Cornwall, of Devonian age, which rests on the granite.

Ki·ll-cow. *Obs.* exc. *dial.* 1581. [f. KILL *v.* + COW *sb.*[1]] **A.** *sb.* A bully, braggadocio; a terrible or great person; a man of importance 1589. **2.** *dial.* A serious affair. (Usu. in neg. phr.) 1825. **B.** *adj.* Bragging, bullying; terrifying 1581. Hence **Ki·llcow** *v.* to cow.

Ki·llcrop. *rare.* 1652. [ad. LG. *kilkrop,* G. *kielkropf*; etym. unkn.] An insatiate brat, popularly supposed to be a fairy changeling.

Killdee, killdeer (ki·ldī, -dīᵊɹ). Also **kil-.** 1731. [Imitative of its note.] The largest species of Ring-plover (*Ægialitis vocifera*) of N. America.

Ki·ll-devil, *sb.* (*a.*) 1590. [f. KILL *v.* + DEVIL.] **1.** A recklessly daring fellow. MARLOWE. **2.** W. Indian name for rum. ? *Obs.* 1651. **3.** *Angling.* An artificial bait, made to spin in the water like a wounded fish 1833. **4.** *adj.* That would kill devils 1831.

Killer (ki·ləɹ). 1535. [f. KILL *v.* + -ER[1].] **1.** One who or that which kills. **b.** *Humane k.*: see HUMANE 1 b.. **2.** (*k. whale*) A name of the grampus, *Orca gladiator,* and allied ferocious cetaceans 1725. **3.** An effective angler's bait 1681.

Ki·lles(s)e, var. CULLIS *sb.*[2], a groove or gutter; *spec.* in a cross-bow, or in a roof.

Killick, killock (ki·lik, -ək). 1630. [?] *Naut.* A heavy stone used on small vessels for an anchor; also a small anchor.

Killickinnick, var. of KINNIKINIC.

Killifish (ki·lifiʃ). Also **killy-.** 1836. [? f. KILL *sb.*[2] + FISH; but cf. KILLING *ppl. a.* 1 b.] Any of the small fish of several genera of *Cyprinodontidæ,* found in sheltered places on the east coast of N. America, and used as bait; esp. *Fundulus heteroclitus,* the *green k.*

Killing (ki·liŋ), *vbl. sb.* ME. [-ING[1].] **1.** Putting to death, murder. **2.** A dressing of slacked lime to 'kill' the grease in leather-dressing 1844.

Killing (ki·liŋ), *ppl. a.* ME. [-ING[2].] **1.** That kills (*lit.* and *fig.*). **b.** Of bait: Sure to kill 1681. **2.** In hyperbolic use: Able to kill. **a.** Fatal 1615. **b.** Overpoweringly attractive 1634. **c.** Exhausting 1850. **d.** That makes one 'die' with laughing (*colloq.*). **3.** As *adv.* Killingly 1670.

1. A Frost; a k. Frost SHAKS. Hence **Ki·lling·ly** *adv.*, **-ness.**

Ki·ll-joy, *sb.* and *a.* 1776. **A.** *sb.* One who or that which throws a gloom over social enjoyment. **B.** *adj.* That kills or puts an end to joy 1822.

Killock: see KILLICK.

†**Killow.** 1666. [?] A name given (orig. in Cumberland) to black-lead, plumbago, or graphite -1763.

Ki·ll-time, *sb.* (*a.*) 1748. [See KILL *v.* 5.] An occupation intended to 'kill time'. **b.** *adj.* Adapted to kill time 1759.

Kiln (kil, kiln), *sb.* [OE. *cylene,* etc.:— **cu·lina,* a. L. *culīna* kitchen, burning-place, etc. In ME. the final *n* became silent (in most districts).] A furnace or oven for burning, baking, or drying; esp. (*a*) for calcining lime (LIME-KILN); (*b*) for baking bricks (BRICK-KILN), tiles, etc.; (*c*) for drying grain, hops, etc. or for making malt. Also *attrib.*

Phr. *To set the k. on fire, to fire the k.*, to cause a serious commotion; He has contrived to set the k. on fire as fast as I put it out SCOTT. *Comb.* **k.-hole,** the fire-hole of a k. Hence **Kiln** *v. trans.* to burn, bake, or dry in a k.; so **Ki·ln-dry** *v. trans.*

Kilo-. Arbitrary deriv. of Gr. χίλιοι a thousand, introduced in French in 1795, used in the Metric system to form names of weights and measures containing 1,000 times the unit. Also **Kilo** (ki·lo) *sb.*, abbrev. of KILOGRAMME.

Kilocycle (ki·ləsəik'l). 1921. [f. KILO- + CYCLE *sb.*] One thousand cycles (see CYCLE *sb.* 10 b), esp. per second, as a unit in measuring the frequency of electrical oscillations. (Abbrev. kc.)

Kilogramme, -gram (ki·ləgræm). 1810. [a. F. *kilogramme* (1795); see KILO- and GRAMME, GRAM.] A weight containing 1,000 grammes, or about 2·205 lb. avoirdupois.

Kilogrammetre, -meter (ki·lǒgræm,mītəɹ). 1866. [a. F. *kilogrammètre*; see prec. and METRE.] *Physics.* The quantity of energy required to raise a weight of one kilogramme to the height of one metre.

Kilolitre, -liter (ki·lǒlītəɹ). 1810. [a. F. *kilolitre* (1798); see KILO- and LITRE.] A measure of capacity containing 1,000 litres.

Kilometre, -meter (ki·lǒmītəɹ). 1810. [a. F. *kilomètre* (1795); see KILO- and METRE.] A measure of length containing 1,000 metres, or 3280·89 feet, or nearly five-eighths of a mile. Hence **Kilome·tric, -al** *a.* of or pertaining to a k.; marking a k. on a road.

Kilowatt (ki·lǒwǫt). 1892. [f. KILO- + WATT.] *Electr.* A thousand watts.

Kilt (kilt), *sb.* 1730. [f. KILT *v.*] A part of the modern Highland dress, consisting of a skirt, usually of tartan cloth, deeply plaited, reaching from the waist to the knee; hence, any similar article of dress.

Hence **Ki·ltie**, a kilted Highland soldier.

Kilt (kilt), *v.* ME. [app. of Scand. origin; cf. Da. *kilte* (also *kilte op*) to tuck up, etc.] 1. *trans.* To tuck up (the skirts) round the body. Also with *up.* 2. To fasten or tie up; to 'string up' 1697. 3. *intr.* To go as with the loins girded 1816. 4. *trans.* To gather in vertical pleats, as in a kilt 1887.

Kilt, obs. or dial. pa. pple. of KILL *v.*

Kilted (ki·ltėd), *a.* 1809. [f. KILT *sb.* + -ED [2].] Wearing a kilt.

Kilted (ki·ltėd), *ppl. a.* 1724. [f. KILT *v.* + -ED [1].] Tucked up or having the skirts tucked up; also, gathered in vertical pleats.

Kilter, var. of KELTER.

Kilting (ki·ltiŋ), *vbl. sb.* 1521. [f. KILT *v.* + -ING [1].] The action of KILT *v.*; the act of girding or tucking up, or of plaiting like a kilt; the result of this.

Kimberlite (ki·mbəɹləit). 1887. [f. *Kimberley* in Cape Colony + -ITE [1] 2 b.] *Min.* The eruptive rock, or 'blue ground', which is the matrix of the diamond at Kimberley and elsewhere.

†Ki·mbo, *a.* = AKIMBO. Dryden. So **†Ki·mbo** *v.* -1808.

Kim-kam, *a.* and *adv. dial.* 1582. Crooked(ly); perverse(ly).

Kimmeridge (ki·məridʒ). 1832. A village on the Dorsetshire coast, where extensive beds of the Upper Oolite are developed. Hence *K. clay,* a bed of clay in the Upper Oolite, containing bituminous shales. *K. coal,* shale of the K. clay, containing so much bitumen that it may be burnt as coal.

Ki·mnel. *Obs.* exc. *dial.* [ME. *kem(b)elin, kim(e)lin, kim(e)nel,* app. rel. to OE. *cumb* COOMB [1].] A tub for household purposes.

‖**Kimono** (kimōᵘ·no). 1874. Earlier **kirimon** (1615). [Jap.] A long Japanese robe with sleeves. b. (Also *kimona.*) A European dressing-gown or wrap modelled on this 1902.

Kin (kin). [Com. Teut.: OE. *cyn(n* neut. :—OTeut. **kunjom*, from the weak grade of the ablaut-series *kin-, kan-, kun-* = Aryan *gen-, gon-, gn-* 'to produce, engender, beget', whence also Gr. γένος, γίγνομαι, L. *genus, gignere.*] 1. A group of persons descended from a common ancestor, and so connected by blood-relationship; a family, stock, clan. Now *rare.* 2. Ancestral stock or race; family; esp. in phr. *(come) of good (noble,* etc.) *k.* *Obs.* exc. *dial.* OE. 3. One's kindred, kinsfolk, or relatives, collectively. (Now the chief sense.) OE. b. In predicative use, = Related 1597. 4. Kinship, relationship. Now *rare.* 1548.

3. One of thy kin has a most weake *Pia-mater* SHAKS. One onely Daughter haue I, no Kin else SHAKS. b. One touch of nature makes the whole world kin SHAKS. 4. Within Prohibited Degrees of Kin BUTLER.

Phrases. **Of kin** = AKIN: Related by blood-ties. Also, Related in character or qualities. *Near of k.*, closely related. *Next (†nearest) of k.*, most closely related; chiefly *absol.* the person (or persons) standing nearest in blood-relationship to another, and entitled to share in his personal estate in case of intestacy 1548.

-kin (kin), *suffix,* forming dims., corresp. to MDu. *-kijn, -ken* = Ger. *-chen,* as in MDu. *husekijn, huusken,* G. *häuschen* a little house. Used first in some familiar forms of personal (chiefly male) names adopted or adapted from names current in Flanders and Holland (e.g. MALKIN, *Perkin, Simkin*). Other words are either adopted from Du. (e.g. *kilderkin, manikin*) or are of obscure origin. The only English formations which have obtained permanent currency are *bootikin* (1727), *lambkin* (1579).

A variant *-kins* has in later times become current in certain endearing forms of address, as *babykins, boykins.*

Kinæsthesis (kəinėsþī·sis). Also **-thesia.** 1880. [f. Gr. κινεῖν to move + αἴσθησις sensation.] The sense of muscular effort that accompanies a voluntary motion of the body. So **Kinæsthe·tic** *a.* belonging to k.

Kinchin (ki·ntʃin). *Cant.* 1561. [prob. corrupt f. G. *kindchen* little child.] 1. †a. *attrib.* in *k.-co(ve, -mort,* terms used by 16th c. tramps for a boy and girl respectively of their community. b. *absol.* A child, a 'kid'. (Now convicts' slang.) 2. *attrib.* in **Kinchin-lay,** the practice of stealing money from children sent on errands. Also *fig.* 1838.

2. 'Ain't there any other line open?' 'Stop', said the Jew..'The kinchin lay' *O. Twist* xlii.

Kincob (ki·ŋkǫb). *E. Ind.* 1712. [ad. Urdū (Pers.) *kimkhāb.*] A rich Indian stuff, embroidered with gold or silver; a piece or variety of this. Also *attrib.*

Kind (kəind), *sb.* [OE. *gecynd,* f. *ge-* (see I-, Y-) + root *kun-* (see KIN) + *-di-,* Indo-European *-ti.* The prefix *ge-* disappeared in late OE.]

I. Abstract senses. †1. Birth, origin, descent -1649. †2. The station, place, or property belonging to one by birth -ME. 3. Natural disposition, nature (in later use *rare*) OE. 4. Nature in general, or in the abstract, regarded as the established order (*rerum natura*). Rarely with *the.* *Obs.* (exc. as *arch.*) OE. †5. Gender; sex -1590. 6. The manner natural to any one; hence, mode of action; manner, way, fashion. *arch.* OE. 7. Generic or specific nature; esp. in phr. *in kind* (L. *in genere* or *in specie*), freq. contrasted with *in degree* 1628.

3. Sweet Grapes degen'rate there, and Fruits..renounce their K. DRYDEN. †*To do one's kind*: to do what is natural; *spec.* to perform the sexual function. 5. All they which be of the male k. [etc.] 1551. 6. I have done Wonders in this K. STEELE. 7. There are such wide differences in degree as to constitute almost differences in k. 1868.

II. A class of things. 1. A race; a natural group of animals or plants having a common origin OE. †b. A class of the same sex; a sex (in collective sense) -1735. †2. = KIN 1, KINDRED 2 -1697. 3. = KIN 2. *arch.* ME. 4. A genus or species; also, A sort, variety, or description. (= L. *genus.*) Now the chief sense. OE.

1. As when the total k. Of birds..Came summond over Eden MILT. *P. L.* VI. 73. Poets were ever a careless k. 1739. 3. [If she] came of a gentle k. SHAKS. 4. Something of the k. had been done FREEMAN. They had haversacks of a kind with them, but very little in them 1895. *In (under, †with) one k., both kinds* (Eccl.), referring to each of the elements (bread and wine) used in the Eucharist.

Phrases. **Kind of,** in *all kinds of trees* = 'trees of all kinds', *this k. of thing* = 'a thing of this kind'. As the original genitive phrase (see N.E.D. s.v. KIN *sb.*[1] 6 b) was in attrib. relation to the following sb., the natural tendency is still to treat *all kind of, no kind of,* etc., and, hence also, *kind of,* as an attrib. or adj. phrase qualifying the sb. Hence the use of *all, many, other, those,* and the like, with a pl. verb and pronoun, when the sb. was pl., as in *these kind of men have their use.* *A kind of..*: A sort of..; a (person or thing) of a kind; what might be called a... *Kind of* (colloq.) is used adverbially: In a way, as it were, to some extent. *In kind* (tr. L. *in specie*: see SPECIE). a. In the very kind of thing in question; usually of payment: In goods or natural produce, as opp. to money. b. Of repayment: In something of the same kind as that received (chiefly *fig.*).

Kind (kəind), *a.* [OE. *gecynde,* f. *gecynd* nature, KIND *sb.*]

I. Natural, native. †1. Of things, qualities, etc.: Natural; implanted by nature -1522; proper -1694. †2. Belonging to one by birth; lawful, rightful -1570. †3. Of persons: Rightful (heir, etc.) -ME.; natural -1589; related by kinship -1509.

1. What hay is kindest for sheep 1663.

II. 1. †a. Well-born, well-bred, gentle. b. Of a good kind; hence, good of its kind. Now only *dial.* ME. 2. Of persons: Naturally well-disposed; sympathetic; considerate; †generous, liberal, courteous. Also of disposition. Also *fig.* (This (with b and c) is now the main sense.) ME. b. Exhibiting a friendly disposition by one's conduct *to* a person or animal. Also *fig.* ME. c. Of action, etc.: Arising from or displaying a kind disposition ME. 3. Affectionate, loving, fond; on intimate terms. Also *euphem.* Now *rare* exc. *dial.* ME. †4. = KINDLY *a.* II. 3. -1774. 5. Grateful, thankful. *Obs.* exc. *dial.* 1450. 6. *dial.* or *techn.* Soft, tender; easy to work 1747.

1. b. A k. barley is one that malts well 1890. 2. Who does a kindness, is not therefore k. POPE. *fig.* Your kinder Stars a Nobler Choice have giv'n DRYDEN. b. Be kinde and curteous to this Gentleman *Mids. N.* III. i. 167. c. Your k. letter gave me very sincere pleasure TENNYSON. 3. Stiles where we stay'd to be k., Meadows in which we met TENNYSON. 5. He should declare himself thankful and k., for all those benefits 1563. 6. The importance of k. hair and good flesh in a feeding beast 1848.

III. As *adv.* = KINDLY. Now *colloq.* or *vulgar.* 1607.

He took it mighty k. H. WALPOLE.

Kindergarten (ki·ndəɹgā:ɹt'n). 1852. [a. Ger. *Kindergarten,* lit. 'children's garden'.] A school for developing the intelligence of young children by object-lessons, toys, games, singing, etc., according to a method devised by Friedrich Fröbel (1782–1852). Hence **Ki·ndergä·rt(e)ner, -ing,** a teacher (teaching) in a k.

Kind-hearted, *a.* 1535. [KIND *a.*] Having naturally a kind disposition.

To thy selfe at least kind harted proue SHAKS. *Sonn.* x. Hence **Kindhea·rtedness.**

Kindle (ki·nd'l), *sb.* ME. [app. a deriv. of *cynd-,* stem of *gecynd,* KIND *sb.*] †1. a. The young (of any animal), a young one. b. *collect.* A brood or litter (of kittens). -1486. 2. *In k.* (of a hare): With young 1877.

Kindle (ki·nd'l), *v.*[1] ME. [app. f. ON. *kynda* to kindle (*trans.* and *intr.*) + -LE. In most of the senses also with *up.*] 1. *trans.* To set fire to, light (a flame, fire, or combustible substance). 2. *intr.* To begin to burn, catch fire, burst into flame ME. 3. *fig. trans.* a. To inflame, inspire (a passion or feeling) ME. b. To fire, stir up (a person, the mind, etc.); to make ardent ME. c. To give rise to (†trouble, war, strife, etc.) ME. 4. *intr.* a. Of passion, etc.: To rise, to be excited ME. b. To become inflamed or ardent; to glow; to become animated ME. 5. *trans.* To light up as with fire 1715; *intr.* to become glowing or bright like fire 1797.

1. To k. wet straw into a flame BERKELEY. 2. My eye..caught a light kindling in a window C. BRONTË. 3. a. We kyndle Gods wrathe ouer vs 1547. b. Nothing remaines, but that I k. the boy thither *A. Y. L.* I. i. 179. c. He took measures for kindling a war with England HUME. 4. a. As their fury kindled [etc.] 1845. b. The words began thus to k. in my spirit BUNYAN. 5. The fires expanding..k. half the skies POPE. *intr.* Hereward's..eyes kindled KINGSLEY.

Kindle (ki·nd'l), *v.*[2] Now *dial.* ME. [Cf. KINDLE *sb.*] *trans.* To bring forth, give birth to (young). Also *fig.* b. *absol.* (Of hares and rabbits.) ME.

As the Conie that you see dwell where shee is kindled SHAKS.

Kindler (ki·ndləɹ). 1450. [f. KINDLE *v.*[1] + -ER [1].] One who or that which kindles, sets on fire, incites, or stirs up.

Kindlers of riot, enemies of sleep GAY.

Kindless (kəi·ndlės), *a.* ME. [f. KIND *sb.* + -LESS.] †1. Without natural power, feeling, etc.; unnatural -1602. 2. [As if f. KIND *a.*] Devoid of kindness (*rare*) 1847.

1. *Haml.* II. ii. 609. 2. A sad, gloomy, k. November night 1881.

Kindlily (kəi·ndlili), *adv.* 1826. [f. KINDLY *a.* + -LY [2].] In a kindly manner.

Ki·ndliness. 1440. [f. as prec. + -NESS.] 1. The quality or habit of being kindly; an instance of this. 2. Mildness (of climate, etc.) favourable to vegetation 1654.

2. We ascribe..k. to dews 1794.

Kindling (ki·ndliŋ), *vbl. sb.*[1] ME. [f. KINDLE *v.*[1]] 1. The action of KINDLE *v.*[1]

2. Material for lighting a fire. In *U.S.* usu. *pl.* 1513. Also Kindling wood.

Ki·ndling, *vbl. sb.*[2] ME. [f. KINDLE *v.*[2]] 1. The bringing forth of young 1440. 2. a. *collect.* A brood or litter; issue. b. *sing.* One of a brood or litter; a young animal ME.

Kindly (kəi·ndli), *a.* [OE. *gecyndelic*, f. *gecynde*, KIND + *-lic*, -LY[1].] I. †1. Natural; = KIND *a.* 1. -1727. †2. = KIND *a.* 2. -1670. 3. Having a right to one's position in virtue of birth or descent; rightful, lawful. Of children: Legitimate. Of a tenant (*Sc.*): Holding a lease of land which his ancestors have similarly held before him, and therefore usually on favourable terms. OE. b. Native-born (*arch.*) 1820.

1. Neither by lot of destiny Nor yet by k. death she perished SURREY. 'Tis lacke of kindely warmth, they are not kinde *Timon* II. ii. 226. 3. Your service is not gratuitous—I trow ye hae land for it. Ye're k. tenants SCOTT. b. God keep the k. Scot from the cloth-yard shaft SCOTT.

II. 1. Of good natural qualities; of a good sort; in good condition; goodly (*arch.* or *dial.*) ME. 2. Of persons: Kind-hearted, good-natured. Hence also of character, actions, etc. 1570. b. *transf.* and *fig.* Of things: Genial, benign; favourable to growth or *for* a particular crop 1655; also = KIND *a.* II. 6. 3. Acceptable, agreeable, pleasant, genial. In later use blending with 2 b. ME.

1. A thick, k. grass COOK. 2. The k. Force Of weeping Parents DRYDEN. b. A kind of white land ..k. for hops 1789. The k. feel of skin 1766. 3. As a lustie winter, Frostie, but kindely SHAKS.

Kindly (kəi·ndli), *adv.* [OE. *gecyndelīce*, f. as prec. + *-līce*, -LY[2].] 1. †Naturally -1586; fittingly (now esp. of processes which successfully follow their natural course) ME.; in an easy, natural way (now *dial.* or *colloq.*) ME.; †properly; exactly -1592. 2. Affectionately; with sympathy, benevolence, or good nature ME. 3. Agreeably, pleasantly 1596.

1. The Suppuration proceeding k., the Wound becomes a simple Wound 1758. Thou hast most k. hit it SHAKS. 2. Tell him he is an ass,—but say so k. ABP. TAIT.

Phrases. *To take k.*, to accept pleasantly, or as a kindness. *To take k. to*, to be naturally attracted to. *To thank k.*, to thank heartily, as for kindness shown.

Kindness (kəi·ndnės). ME. [f. KIND *a.* + -NESS.] †1. Kinship; natural affection arising from this -1677. †2. *Sc.* Natural right or title derived from birth or descent; the status of a kindly tenant -1578. †3. Natural inclination or aptitude (*rare*) -1674. 4. The quality or habit of being kind; an instance of this ME. 5. Kind feeling; affection, love. Also, Good will, favour, friendship. Now *rare*. ME.

4. Yet doe I feare thy Nature, It is too full o' th' Milke of humane kindnesse, To catch the neerest way *Macb.* I. v. 18. 5. It is not in my power..to hide a k. where I have one LADY M. W. MONTAGU.

Kindred (ki·ndrėd). [Early ME. f. KIN + *-reden*, -RED, OE. *rǣden*. The *d* is excrescent between *n* and *r*, as in *thunder*, etc.]

A. *sb.* 1. The being of kin; relationship by blood (occas., but erron., by marriage); kinship. b. *fig.* Affinity in respect of qualities 1577. 2. = KIN 1. Now *rare*. ME. †3. = KIN 2. -1513. 4. = KIN 3. ME.

1. Wee plead not kinred Or neare propinquity HEYWOOD. b. Thy k. with the great of old TENNYSON. 4. Her kindred's wishes, and her sire's commands POPE.

B. *attrib.* or *adj.* 1. Of the same kin; related by birth or descent 1530. Also *fig.* b. Belonging to, existing between, or done by, relatives 1593. 2. Allied in nature, character, or properties; having similar qualities ME.

1. *fig.* Carrick's k. shore SCOTT. b. K. bloud SHAKS. 2. Some k. spirit GRAY. The formation of rain and k. phenomena HUXLEY.

Kine, arch. pl. of COW *sb.*[1]

Kinema: see CINEMA.

Kinematic (kəinĭmæ·tik, kin-). 1864. [f. Gr. κίνημα, κινηματ- (f. κινεῖν to move) + -IC.] A. *adj.* Relating to pure motion, i.e. to motion considered abstractly, without reference to force or mass. B. *sb.* = KINEMATICS 1873. So **Kinema·tical** *a.* of or pertaining to kinematics 1864.

Kinema·tics. 1840. [See prec. and -IC 2.] The science of pure motion, considered without reference to matter or force. (Cf. KINETICS.)

Kinematograph; see CINEMATOGRAPH.

Kinesi- (kəinī·si), bef. a vowel also **kines-,** comb. f. Gr. κίνησις motion, as in:

Kinesia·trics [-IC 2], treatment of diseases by means of gymnastics or muscular action. **Kinesio·logy** (Bentham), the science of motion. **Kinesi·pathy** 1855, **Kinesithe·rapy** [Gr. θεραπεία healing] = *Kinesiatrics*. **Kineso·dic** [Gr. ὁδός a path] *a. Physiol.* transmitting motor impulses, efferent.

Kinetic (kəine·tik), *a.* (*sb.*) 1855. [ad. Gr. κινητικός moving; see -IC.] 1. Producing or causing motion. MAYNE. 2. Of, pertaining or relating to, motion; due to or resulting from motion 1864. 3. *sb.* = KINETICS 1873.

2. *K. energy*, the power of doing work possessed by a moving body by virtue of its motion. *K. theory of heat, of gases*: the theory that heat, or the gaseous state, is due to motion of particles of matter.

Kine·tics. 1864. [See prec. and -IC 2.] The branch of dynamics which investigates the relations between the motions of bodies and the forces acting upon them; opp. to *Statics*, which treats of bodies in equilibrium.

Kineto- (kəinī·to), repr. Gr. κινητο-, comb. f. κινητός movable, as in:

Kinetoge·nesis, the (theoretical) origination of animal structures in animal movements 1884. **Kine·tograph**, an apparatus for photographing a scene of action in every stage of its progress 1891. **Kine·toscope**, (*a*) a sort of movable panorama; (*b*) an apparatus for reproducing the scenes recorded by the kinetograph; (*c*) an instrument for illustrating the combination of circular movements of different radii in the production of curves.

King (kiŋ), *sb.* [Com. Teut.: OE. *cyning* :—OTeut. **kuniŋgo-z*, a deriv. of **kunjom*, OE. *cynn*, KIN, race, etc. Explained either (*a*) as 'scion of the kin or tribe' or 'scion of a (or the) noble kin', or (*b*) as 'son or descendant of one of (noble) birth'.] 1. The usual title of the male sovereign ruler of an independent state, whose position may be either purely or partly hereditary, or elective. A King is held to rank below an Emperor. 2. Applied to a woman (*rare*) ME. 3. Applied to God or Christ. Freq. in phr. *K. of heaven, of glory, K. of kings*, etc. OE. 4. A title given to one who holds a real or pretended authority or rank, or to one who plays the king 1656. 5. One who has pre-eminence compared with that of a king, as a *railway-k.*, etc. ME. b. Applied to things personified, as *K. Caucus, K. Cotton, K. of terrors* (death), etc. 1592. 6. *fig.* Something which has supremacy in its class ME. 7. †a. The queen-bee. -1747. b. A fully developed male termite 1895. 8. In games. a. In chess: The piece which each player has to protect against the moves made by the other, so as to avoid being finally checkmated ME. b. *Cards.* One card in each suit, bearing the representation of a king, and usually ranking highest except the ace 1563. c. *Draughts.* A crowned piece 1611. 9. *ellipt.* a. A toast in which the king's health is drunk 1763. b. A king-post 1842.

1. *K. designate, possessive*: see the adjs. *Uncrowned k.*, one who has the power, but not the rank, of a king. *The Books of Kings*: certain books of the O.T. which contain the history of the kings of Israel and Judah. Also ellipt. *Kings*. *K. of Kings*, a king who has other kings under him, an emperor. *K. of men*, tr. Gr. ἄναξ ἀνδρῶν. *K. Charles*, short for *K. Charles's Spaniel* (see SPANIEL); *K. Harry*, the goldfinch. 2. She [Maria Theresa] lived and died a K. BURKE. 4. *K. of Heralds*, the King Herald or King-of-Arms. 5. The old sugar kings of Jamaica 1894. 6. *K. of beasts*, the lion. *K. of birds*, the eagle. *K. of the Mullets*, (*a*) a Mediterranean fish (*Mullus imberbis*); (*b*) the common bass. John Barleycorn, Thou K. o' grain BURNS.

Combs. 1. General: as, *k.-bishop, -cardinal*, etc.; *k.-worship*, etc.; *k.-born*, etc.

2. Special: as, **k.-bee**, the queen-bee (see 7 a); **-card**, the best card left in a suit, e.g. the queen, if king and ace are out; **-cobra** = HAMADRYAD 2 a; **-conch, -conk**, a collector's name for a variety of conch; **-herald** (see HERALD); **-mullet**, the goat-fish (*Upeneus maculatus*) of the W. Indies; **-rod**, an iron rod used in place of a king-post; **-salmon**, the Californian Salmon (*Oncorhynchus quinnat*); **-snake**, a large N. Amer. snake (esp. *Ophibolus getulus*) which attacks other snakes; **-truss**, a roofing-truss which has a king-post; **-wood**, a Brazilian wood, prob. from a species of *Dalbergia*.

b. in names of birds, as **k.-auk** [tr. Norw. *alkekonge*], the little auk or rotche; **-crow**, the leader of a flock of crows; also the name of several species of drongo, esp. *Dicrurus ater*; **-duck, -eider**, *Somateria spectabilis*, allied to the eider-duck; **-hunter**, several species of African and Australian birds related to the kingfisher, but which do not feed on fish; **-lory, -parrakeet, -parrot**, several species of small parrots of the genus *Aprosmictus*, kept as cage-birds; **-penguin**, *Aptenodytes longirostris*; **-rail**, *Rallus elegans*; **-vulture**, *Gypagus* (*Cathartes*) *papa*, of tropical America, having a gaudy-coloured head.

c. in names of plants, as **k.-cob** = KING-CUP; **-fern**, the royal fern (*Osmunda regalis*); **-pine**, †(*a*) the pine-apple; (*b*) a large and stately Himalayan fir, *Picea Webbiana*; etc.

3. Combs. with **king's**. a. With sense Of, belonging to, in the service of the king, as head of the State, royal; as *King's* COUNSEL, ENGLISH, EVIDENCE, HIGHWAY, PEACE, REMEMBRANCER, SHIP, THANE, etc., for which see these words; **King's Advocate**, the Scottish Attorney-General. b. **king's (bad) bargain**, a malingerer, a soldier or sailor who shirks his duty; **king's cushion**, a seat made by the crossed hands of two persons; **king's friends**, *Hist.*, a political party which supported George III and the power of the crown; **king's silver**, (*a*) silver blessed by the king, and intended for cramp-rings; (*b*) money paid into the Court of Common Pleas for licence to levy a fine; **king's yellow**, orpiment. c. in names of plants, as **king's bloom**, the peony; **king's spear**, a kind of asphodel; **king's taper**, the Great Mullein.

Phraseological comb.: **King Charles's Spaniel** (see SPANIEL).

King (kiŋ), *v.* ME. [f. prec.] 1. *intr.* (usu. with *it*). To act the king; to rule, govern. 2. *trans.* To make king 1593; †at *Draughts* 1679. 3. To govern, as a king (*rare*) 1599.

2. Those traiterous Captains of Israel, who kinged themselves by slaying their masters SOUTH.

Ki·ng-bird. 1779. 1. A species of bird of paradise, *Paradisea regia*. 2. ? The eagle. BROWNING. 3. An American tyrant fly-catcher, usually *Tyrannus carolinensis* (also called 'Bee-Martin'), remarkable for its intrepidity during the breeding season 1828. 4. A sailor's name for species of tern (Newton).

Ki·ng-bolt. 1825. A main or large bolt in a mechanical structure; *esp.* a vertical bolt passing through the axle of a carriage or railway car, and forming a pivot on which the axle swings in taking curves.

Ki·ng-crab. 1698. [f. KING *sb.* + CRAB *sb.*[1]] A large arthropodous animal of the genus *Limulus*, having a convex carapace somewhat horseshoe-shaped; the horseshoe or Molucca crab. Now classed among the *Arachnida*.

Ki·ng-craft. 1643. The art of ruling as a king; *esp.* the use of crafty diplomacy in dealing with subjects.

Ki·ng-cup. 1538. The common buttercup; also, the Marsh Marigold.

Kingdom (ki·ŋdəm). [OE. *cyningdōm*; see KING and -DOM.] †1. Kingly function, authority, or power; sovereignty; kingship -1679. 2. A monarchical state or government ME. 3. The territory or country subject to a king; a realm ME. b. A familiar name for the Scottish county of Fife, which was one of the seven Pictish kingdoms 1710. 4. *transf.* and *fig.* ME. 5. A realm or province of nature; *esp.* the *animal, vegetable*, and *mineral kingdoms* 1691.

1. Monarchy..which Government, if he limit it by Law, is called K.; if by his own will, Tyranny HOBBES. 2. *United K.*, Great Britain and Ireland, so called since the Act of Union in 1800. A kingdom of the Just then let it be POPE. 3. The utmost border of his K. MILT. 4. *The k. of God*: the spiritual sovereignty of God or Christ, or the sphere over which this extends; the spiritual state of which God is the head. The Kingdome of perpetuall Night SHAKS. His mind his k., and his will his law COWPER.

Phrase. *Kingdom-come* (from *thy k. come* in the Lord's Prayer). a. The next world. *slang*. 1785. b. The millennial kingdom of Christ. Also *attrib.* 1848.

Kingdomed (ki·ŋdəmd), *a.* 1606. [f. prec.] 1. Furnished with, or constituted as, a kingdom. 2. Consisting of (so many) kingdoms; as *ten-k.*, etc. 1854.

1. K. Achilles in commotion rages SHAKS.

Ki·ng-fish. 1750. A name given to fishes remarkable for their size, appearance, or value as food; esp. (*a*) the opah; (*b*) a scombroid fish of Florida (*Cybium regale*); (*c*) an American sciænoid fish (*Menticirrus nebulosus* or related species); (*d*) a sciænoid fish of S. Australia (*Sciæna antarctica*).

Kingfisher (ki·ŋfi:ʃəɹ). 1440. 1. A small European bird (*Alcedo ispida*) with a long cleft beak and brilliant plumage, feeding on fish, etc., which it captures by diving. Hence, extended to other birds of the family *Alcedinidæ* or *Halcyonidæ*. **2.** An artificial salmon-fly. ? *Obs.* 1787.

1. That a Kings fisher hanged by the bill sheweth where the winde is SIR T. BROWNE.

Kinghood (ki·ŋhud). ME. [f. KING *sb.* + -HOOD.] Kingship; the rank, authority, or office of king; kingly spirit or character.

Ki·ng-ki:ller. SHAKS. A regicide. So **Ki·ng-killing** *sb.* and *adj.*

Kingless (ki·ŋlės), *a.* ME. [f. KING *sb.* + -LESS.] Without a king; having no king.

Kinglet (ki·ŋlėt). 1603. [f. KING *sb.* + -LET.] **1.** A petty king; one ruling over a small territory. Usu. *contemptuous.* **2.** Pop. name of the Golden-crested Wren, *Regulus cristatus*; also of two allied N. Amer. species, *R. satrapa* and *R. calendula* 1839.

Kinglihood (ki·ŋlihud). [f. KINGLY *a.* + -HOOD.] Kingly state; royalty. TENNYSON.

Kinglike (ki·ŋləik). 1561. **A.** *adj.* Resembling a king; kingly; regal. **B.** *adv.* Like, or in a manner befitting, a king 1884.

Kingliness (ki·ŋlinės). 1548. [f. KINGLY *a.* + -NESS.] Kingly quality or character.

Kingling (ki·ŋliŋ). 1598. [f. KING *sb.* + -LING.] A little or petty king. (Less contemptuous than *kinglet.*)

Kingly (ki·ŋli), *a.* ME. [f. KING *sb.* + -LY[1].] **1.** Of the nature of a king or kings; royal; of royal rank. **2.** Of or belonging to a king; held, exercised, or issued by a king; suitable for a king; royal, regal ME. **b.** Of government: Monarchical 1658. **3.** Kinglike; dignified, majestic, noble 1593. Also *fig.*

1. Geue eare, o thou k. house COVERDALE *Hos.* v. 1. 2. I thrice presented him a K. Crowne SHAKS. Leave k. backs to cope with k. cares COWPER. b. The k. form of government THIRLWALL. 3. I am..More like a King, more K. in my thoughts SHAKS. *fig.* The kingliest Abbey in all Christian lands TENNYSON. So **Ki·ngly** *adv.* in a k. manner, royally, regally 1586.

Ki·ng-ma:ker. 1599. One who sets up kings; *spec.* an epithet of the Earl of Warwick, in the reigns of Henry VI and Edward IV.

King-of-Arms. Also (less correctly) **King-at-Arms.** 1449. [See ARM *sb.*[2] IV.] Title of the three chief heralds of the College of Arms, viz. Garter, the principal King of Arms, and Clarenceux and Norroy, provincial Kings of Arms, the former having jurisdiction south, and the other north, of the Trent. There are also the Lyon King of Arms of Scotland, and the Ulster King of Arms of Ireland; also Bath King of Arms.

King-piece. 1664. = KING-POST.

King-pin. 1895. = KING-BOLT. Also *transf.*

Ki·ng-post. 1776. *Carpentry.* An upright post in the centre of a roof-truss, extending from the ridge to the tie-beam.

King's Bench. ME. [See BENCH *sb.*] A former court of record and the supreme court of common law in the kingdom; now represented by the King's Bench division of the High Court of Justice.

King's evil. ME. [tr. med.L. *regius morbus* (in class. L. = jaundice).] Scrofula, which was formerly supposed to be curable by the king's (or queen's) touch. Also *fig.*

King's Highway: see HIGHWAY.

Kingship (ki·ŋʃip). ME. [f. KING *sb.* + -SHIP.] **1.** The office and dignity of a king; the fact of being king; reign. Also *fig.* **2.** Monarchical government 1648. **3.** With poss. pron.: (His) royal majesty. Also *fig.* 1648. **4.** The dominion of a king 1864.

King's man, ki·ngsman. 1639. **1.** A royalist. **2.** A custom-house officer 1814.

King's Peace: see PEACE.

Kingston (ki·ŋstən). 1666. The angel-fish or monk-fish (*Squatina angelus*).

Kinic, obs. f. QUINIC.

Kink (kiŋk), *sb.*[1] 1561. [prob. a. Du *kink* twist, curl, app. from a root *kink-, *kik-, to bend, twist.] †**1.** *pl.* Twist or wool prepared for weaving. **2.** A short twist or curl in a rope, thread, hair, etc., at which it is bent upon itself. (Orig. naut.) 1678. Also *transf.* of a crick in the neck, etc. 1851. **3.** *fig.* (orig. *U.S.*) A mental twist; a faddy notion or device 1803.

3. To bring up young people without kinks W. CORY.

Kink, *sb.*[2] *Sc.* and *n. dial.* 1788. [f. next.] A fit or paroxysm, as of laughter or coughing.

Kink (kiŋk), *v.*[1] *Sc.* and *n. dial.* [North. form of CHINK *v.*[1], OE. *cincian*, app. a nasalized var. of Teut. **kîkan*, whence MHG. *kîchen* to gasp, etc. Cf. CHINCOUGH, KINK-COUGH, etc.] *intr.* To gasp convulsively for breath, as in hooping-cough or with laughing.

Kink (kiŋk), *v.*[2] 1697. [prob. a. Du. *kinken*, f. *kink* KINK *sb.*[1]] **1.** *intr.* To form a kink; to twist or curl stiffly, esp. at one point. **2.** *trans.* To cause to kink; to form a kink upon; to twist stiffly. Also *fig.* (Usu. in *pass.*) 1800.

‖**Kinkajou** (ki·ŋkădʒū). Also **kincajou.** 1796. [a. F. *quincajou*, f. N. Amer. Indian. The same word orig. as CARCAJOU.] A carnivorous quadruped (*Cercoleptes caudivolvulus*) of Central and S. America, allied to the racoon; it is about the size of the common cat, has a prehensile tail, and is nocturnal in its habits. Also called *potto* or *honey-bear.*

Kinkcough (ki·ŋkkǭf). *n. dial.* 1568. [f. KINK *v.*[1] + COUGH *sb.*] The hooping-cough.

Kinkhost (ki·ŋkhǫst). *Obs.* exc. *Sc.* ME. [f. KINK *v.*[1] + HOAST.] = prec.

Kinkle (ki·ŋk'l), *sb.* 1862. [f. KINK *sb.*[1]] **1.** A little kink or twist. **2.** *fig.* A 'wrinkle', a hint. LYTTON. Hence **Ki·nkled** *a.* having kinkles; frizzed, crisped, as hair.

Kinky (ki·ŋki), *a.* 1860. [f. KINK *sb.*[1] + -Y.[1]] **1.** Full of kinks; closely curled or twisted, as hair 1865. **2.** *fig.* (*U.S. colloq.*) Queer, crotchety.

‖**Kinnikinic** (ki:nikini·k). Also **killickinnick, killikinik.** 1799. [Algonquin; lit. 'mixture'.] **1.** A mixture used by N. Amer. Indians as a substitute for tobacco, or for mixing with it; mostly dried sumach-leaves and the inner bark of dogwood or willow. **2.** Plants used for this, as the Silky Cornel, *Cornus sericea*, and esp. Bearberry, *Arctostaphylos Uva-ursi* (also *trailing k., k.-vine*) 1839.

Kino (kī·no). 1788. [app. of W. African origin; cf. Mandingo *cano* = Gambia kino.] **1.** A substance resembling catechu, usually of a dark reddish-brown colour, consisting of the inspissated gum or juice of various tropical trees and shrubs; used in medicine and tanning as an astringent, and (in India) for dyeing cotton. Occas. called *Gum Kino.*

African or **Gambia K.** (the kind first known in Europe, but now out of use) is the produce of *Pterocarpus erinaceus*; **Botany Bay K.** or **Australian K.**, of *Eucalyptus resinifera* and other species; **East India K., Malabar K.,** or **Amboyna K.** (the kind most used), of *Pterocarpus Marsupium.*

2. Any of the plants which yield this 1876.

Kinology (kəinǫ·lŏdʒi). 1890. [irreg. f. Gr. κινέειν to move + -(O)LOGY.] That branch of physics which treats of motion; kinematics.

Kinone, Kinoyl, Kinquina, etc.: see QUIN-.

-kins, *suffix*, variant of -KIN in certain mild oaths, as *bodikins, lakins, maskins, pittikins.* See also -KIN.

Kinsfolk(s (ki·nzfōuk(s). Now *rare.* 1450. [f. KIN + FOLK, after *kinsman.*] Persons of the same kin; relations by blood; relatives.

They sought him among their kinsefolke and acquaintance *Luke* ii. 44.

Kinship (ki·nʃip). 1833. [f. KIN + -SHIP.] Relationship by descent; consanguinity.

She was of k. with the queen 1880.

Kinsman (ki·nzmæ̆n). [Early ME. f. *cunnes, kinnes*, gen. of KIN + MAN.] A man of one's own kin; a relative by blood (or, loosely, by marriage). Now chiefly literary. Also *fig.* Hence **Ki·nsmanship,** kinship.

Ki·nswoman. ME. [f. as *kinsman* + WOMAN.] A woman of one's own kin; a female relative. Now only literary.

Kintlage, -ledge, -lidge, obs. ff. KENTLEDGE.

‖**Kiosk** (ki,ǫ·sk). 1625. [= F. *kiosque*, a. Turk. *kiūshk* pavilion, Pers. *kūshk* palace, portico.] **1.** A light open pavilion or summer-house, often supported by pillars; common in Turkey and Persia. **2.** A light structure resembling this, for the sale of newspapers, a band-stand, etc. 1865.

Kip (kip), *sb.*[1] 1525. [?] **1.** The hide of a young or small beast (as a calf, a lamb, etc.) as used for leather 1530. **2.** A set or bundle of such hides, containing a definite number.

Kip, *sb.*[2] *slang.* 1766. [Cf. Da. *kippe* mean hut; *horekippe* brothel.] †**1.** A brothel. GOLDSM. **2.** A common lodging-house; a lodging in such a house; hence, a bed 1879.

Hence **Kip** *v. intr.*, to go to bed, sleep.

Kipe (kəip). Now *dial.* [OE. *cȳpe* wk. f., app. = LG. *küpe* (*keupe*) basket carried in the hand or on the back.] A basket; †*spec.* an osier basket used for catching fish; a basket used as a measure (*dial.*).

Kippage (ki·pėdʒ). *Sc.* 1567. [Aphetic f. F. *équipage.*] †**1.** A ship's crew or company. **2.** Disorder, confusion; a state of excitement or irritation 1814.

Kipper (ki·pəɹ), *sb.*[1] [OE. *cypera*, of unkn. origin.] The male salmon (or sea trout) during the spawning season. Also *attrib.* or as *adj.* 1533. **b.** A (young) person, a child (*slang*) 1905.

Comb. †**k.-time,** the period of close-time for salmon.

Kipper (ki·pəɹ), *sb.*[2] 1769. [Obscure.] A kippered fish; now *esp.* a herring so cured (see KIPPER *v.*).

Ki·pper, *v.* 1773. [? f. prec. sb.] *trans.* To cure (fish) by cleaning, rubbing repeatedly with salt and pepper or other spice, and drying in the open air or in smoke.

Kipper-nut. 1597. [?] = EARTH-NUT.

Kirk (kəɹk, *Sc.* kėrk), *sb.* ME. [Northern f. CHURCH; cf. ON. *kirkja.*] The Northern Eng. and Sc. form of CHURCH, in all its senses. **b.** In official use, the name 'Kirk of Scotland' gave place to 'Church of Scotland' at the date of the Westminster Assembly. But (c) in subsequent Eng. usage, 'kirk' often = the Church of Scotland, as dist. from the Church of England, or from the Episcopal Church in Scotland. So *Free K.* for the Free Church of Scotland 1674.

Comb. **Kirk·garth** ME. = CHURCHYARD. **Kirk·man** ME. 1. An ecclesiastic. 2. A member of the 'kirk', i.e. the Church of Scotland 1650. **Kirk·session,** the lowest court in the Established Church of Scotland and other Presbyterian Churches, composed of the minister and elders 1717. **Kirkyard** ME., now *Sc.* = CHURCHYARD.

Kirk, *v.* Now *Sc.* ME. [f. KIRK *sb.*] *trans.* = CHURCH *v.*

Kirmess, -mish, var. of KERMIS.

Kirn [1]. *sb.* and *v.* ME. north. and Sc. f. CHURN.

Kirn [2]. *Sc.* and *n. dial.* 1777. [?] **1.** Harvest-home, harvest-supper. **2.** The cutting of the last handful of corn in the harvest-field 1808.

‖**Kirschwasser** (ki·rʃvasər). Also **kirschen-.** 1819. [Ger., f. *kirsche* cherry + *wasser* water.] An alcoholic spirit distilled from a fermented liquor obtained by crushing wild cherries. Also abbrev. **Kirsch** (also **kirsh**) 1869.

Kirtle (kə·ɹt'l). [OE. *cyrtel* = ON. *kyrtill* tunic :—**kurtil-*, app. a dim. of **kurt-* 'short', said to be ad. L. *curtus.* But 'short coat' does not suit the Eng. use.] **1.** A man's tunic or coat, orig. a garment reaching to the knees or lower. **2.** A woman's gown. **b.** A skirt or outer petticoat. OE. **3.** *fig.* A covering of any sort; a coating of paint ME.

2. Ladies and gentlewomen were forbidden..to go abroad with wide-hoop'd gowns or kirtles HOWELL.

Hence **Ki·rtled** *a.*, clothed in a kirtle 1634.

Amid'st the flowry-kirtl'd Naiades MILT.

Kish [1] (kiʃ). 1776. [a. Ir. *cis* (kiʃ), *ceis* (keʃ) basket, hamper.] A large wickerwork basket, used in Ireland for carrying turf, etc.

A k. of turf burns 2 barrels of lime A. YOUNG.

Kish [2] (kiʃ). 1812. [?] A form of impure graphite, which separates from certain kinds of iron in smelting. Also, A dross on the surface of melted lead.

‖**Kismet** (ki·smet). 1849. [Turk., a. Arab. *qisma(t* portion, lot, fate, f. *qasama* to divide.] Destiny, fate.

Kiss (kis), *sb.* [ME. *kiss* from the vb. (The original OE. *coss* (:—OTeut. **kuss-oz*) continued till the 16th century.)] **1.** A touch or pressure given with the lips, in token of affection, greeting, or reverence; a salute or caress so given. **2.** *fig.* A light touch 1588. **b.** *Billiards.* Impact between balls both of which are in motion 1836. **3.** A sugar-plum 1825. **4.** A name for a drop of sealing-wax accidentally dropped beside the seal 1829.

1. Speake cosin, or..stop his mouth with a kisse SHAKS. Can danger lurk within a k.? COLERIDGE. 2. *L. L. L.* IV. iii. 26. 4. 'It 's Peggy O'Dowd's fist', said George, laughing. 'I know it by the kisses on the seal' THACKERAY.

Kiss (kis), *v.* Pa. t. and pple. **kissed** (kist). [OE. *cyssan* (pa. t. *cyste*, pa. pple. *cyssed*) :—OTeut. **kussjan*, f. **kuss-*; see prec.] **1.** *trans.* To press or touch with the lips, in token of affection, greeting, or reverence; to salute or caress with the lips; to give a kiss to. **2.** *intr.* or *absol.* ME. **b.** *trans.* with cognate obj.; also, to express by kissing 1830. **3.** *fig.* To touch lightly, as if in affection or greeting ME. Also *intr.* **b.** *spec.* in *Bowls*, *Billiards*, etc. said of a ball touching another ball lightly when both are in motion 1579. **4.** *trans.* with *adv.*, *prep.*, or *compl.* To put, get, or bring by kissing 1606.

1. With vs the wemen giue their mouth to be kissed, in other places their cheek, in many places their hand PUTTENHAM. 2. K. and be friends, sirrah SWIFT. b. To k. good-night 1883. 3. When the sweet winde did gently kisse the trees SHAKS. *intr.* Like fire and powder; Which as they kisse consume SHAKS. 4. We haue kist away Kingdomes, and Prouinces *Ant. & Cl.* III. x. 7.

Phrases. *To k. the book*, i.e. the Bible, New Testament, or Gospels, in taking an oath. *To k. the dust*, to be overthrown, humiliated, ruined, or slain; so *to k. the ground*. *To k. the hand* (*hands*) of a sovereign or superior, as a ceremonial greeting or leave-taking, or on appointment to an office of state; formerly, merely = to pay one's respects, to salute or bid farewell. *To k. the rod*, to accept correction submissively.

Kisser (ki·səɹ). 1537. [f. KISS *v.* + -ER [1].] One who kisses. **b.** The mouth (*vulgar*) 1860.

Kissing (ki·siŋ), *vbl. sb.* ME. [f. KISS *v.* + -ING [1].] The action of KISS *v.*

attrib. and *Comb.*, as †**k.-comfit**, a perfumed comfit for sweetening the breath; **k. dance** = CUSHION-*dance*; **-gate**, a small gate swinging in a U- or V-shaped enclosure, which allows only one person to pass at a time.

Kissing, *ppl. a.* 1590. [-ING [2].] That kisses.

Comb. **k.-crust** (*colloq.*), the soft part of the crust of a loaf where it has touched another in baking; **-kind** *a.*, on affectionate terms. **Ki·ssingly** *adv.*

Kist (kist), *sb.* [1] *Sc.* and *n. dial.* ME. [Northern f. CHEST *sb.* [1]; cf. ON. *kista*, etc.] **1.** A chest, box, coffer. **2.** A chest in which money is kept; a treasury; also *transf.* the store of money itself 1619. **3.** A coffin ME. **b.** *Archæol.* = CIST 1, KISTVAEN 1853. Hence **Kist** *v.* to put into a k. or coffin.

‖**Kist**, *sb.* [2] *E. Ind.* 1764. [Urdū (Pers., Arab.) *qist* portion.] An instalment (of the yearly land revenue or other payment).

Kistvaen, cistvaen (ki·stvain). 1715. [Anglicized sp. of Welsh *cist faen*, i.e. *cist* chest, cist + *faen* (pron. *vaen*) aspirated form of *maen* stone.] *Archæol.* = CIST 1.

Kit (kit), *sb.* [1] ME. [app. a. MDu. *kitte* a wooden vessel made of hooped staves (Du. *kit* tankard).] **1.** A circular wooden vessel made of hooped staves; *esp.* a tub- or pail-shaped vessel, often with a lid, for carrying milk, butter, fish, etc.; hence, *occas.*, a square box for the same purpose. **b.** A basket of straw or rushes, for holding fish 1847. **2.** A collection of articles forming part of the equipment of a soldier, and carried in a valise or knapsack; also, the valise; occas. = outfit, 'turn-out', uniform 1785. **b.** A collection of personal effects, esp. as packed for travelling 1833. **c.** The outfit of tools required by a workman 1851. **3.** *colloq.* A set, lot, collection of things or persons 1785.

Comb. **k.-bag**, a stout bag in which to carry a soldier's or traveller's k.

Kit (kit), *sb.* [2] Now *rare.* 1519. [? repr. first part of Gr. κιθάρα CITHARA.] A small fiddle, formerly much used by dancing masters.

Pray let me see you dance: I play upon the K. STEELE.

Kit (kit), *sb.* [3] 1562. Short f. KITTEN.

Kit (kit), *sb.* [4] 1533. **1.** Pet form of Catherine or Kate (cf. KITTY [1]). †**2.** A light woman –1639.

2. Kits of Cressides kinde GASCOIGNE.

Kit, *sb.* [5] 1584. [Pet form of *Christopher*.] In phr. *Kit with the canstick* or *candlestick* = JACK-O'-LANTERN.

Kit, *sb.* [6] 1740. [a. G. *kitt*.] A composition of resin, pitch, and tallow applied to canvas.

Kit, *sb.* [7] 1885. [?] *Photogr.* A frame inserted in a plate-holder to adapt it to a smaller size of plate.

Kit (kit), *v.* 1725. [f. KIT *sb.* [1]] *trans.* To put into a kit or kits; esp. fish for market.

Kit, obs. inf., pa. t. and pa. pple., of CUT *v.*

Kit-cat [1] (ki·tkæt). Now *dial.* 1664. [Redupl. from CAT *sb.*] The game of tip-cat.

Kit-cat [2] (ki·tkæt). Also **kit-kat**. 1704. [f. *Kit* (= Christopher) *Cat* or *Catling*, keeper of the pie-house where the club originally met.] **1.** *attrib.* with *Club*: A club of Whig politicians and men of letters founded in James II's time 1705. Also *absol.* **b.** A member of this club 1704. **2.** *attrib.* with *size*, *portrait*, etc.: A size of portrait, less than half-length, but including the hands. So called because the dining-room of the club was hung with portraits of the members, and was too low for half-size portraits. Also *absol.* Also *fig.* 1754.

Kitchen (ki·tʃĕn), *sb.* [OE. *cycene* wk. fem. :—pop.L. *cucina*, *cocina*, var. of *coquina*, f. *coquere* to COOK.] **1.** That room or part of a house where food is cooked. Also *fig.* **b.** = CUISINE 1679. †**2.** A utensil in which food is prepared; e.g. a Dutch oven (*U.S.*) –1858. **3.** (Formerly also *k. meat*.) Food from the kitchen; hence, any kind of food eaten with bread, etc., as a relish. Chiefly *Sc.* and *north. Ir.* ME. **4.** *attrib.* ME

1. The first foundation of a good House must be the K. 1616. b. The German k. is..execrable, and the French delicious CHESTERF. 3. Hunger is the best k. *Mod. Sc. Prov.* 4. *K.-fee*, dripping (so called as being a perquisite of the cook). *K.-garden*, a garden in which fruit and vegetables for the table are grown; also *attrib.* *K.-maid*, a girl employed in the k., usu. under the cook. *K.-physic* (joc.), nourishment for an invalid 1592. *K.-stuff*, requisites for the k., as vegetables, etc.; refuse of the kitchen, dripping, etc.; also *attrib.* of persons or things.

Kitchen (ki·tʃĕn), *v.* 1590. [f. prec. sb.] †**1.** *trans.* To entertain in the kitchen. *Com. Err.* V. i. 415. **2.** *Sc.* To serve as 'kitchen' or relish; to season 1721.

Kitchener (ki·tʃĕnəɹ). late ME. [f. as prec. + -ER [1].] **1.** One employed in a kitchen; *esp.* in a monastery. **2.** A cooking-range with its appliances 1851.

Kitchenette (kitʃĕne·t). orig. *U.S.* 1922. [See -ETTE.] A small room, alcove, etc. in a house or flat, combining kitchen and pantry.

Kitchen-midden (ki·tʃĕnmiːd'n). 1863. [tr. Da. *kjökken-* or *kökkenmödding*, f. *kökken* KITCHEN; see MIDDEN.] A refuse-heap of prehistoric date, consisting chiefly of the shells of edible molluscs and bones of animals, etc.

†**Ki·tchenry.** *rare.* 1609. [See -RY.] **1.** The body of servants employed in a kitchen –1658. **2.** The art of cooking. HOLLAND.

Kite (kəit), *sb.* [OE. *cȳta* (:—**kūtjon-*); no cognates.] **1.** A bird of prey of the family *Falconidæ* and subfamily *Milvinæ*, with long wings, tail usually forked, and no tooth in the bill. **a.** *orig.* and *esp.* the European species *Milvus ictinus*, also called *Red K.* and *Glede*, formerly common in England. **b.** Also, other species of the genus, or of the subfamily; e.g. the **Brahminy K.**, *Haliastur indus* of Hindustan; **Indian** or **Pariah K.**, *Milvus govinda*; **Swallow-tailed K.**, *Elanoides forficatus* of N. America; etc. 1813. **2.** *fig.* One who preys upon others; a sharper; also vaguely, as a term of detestation 1553. **3.** [From its hovering in the air like the bird.] A toy consisting of a light frame, with paper or other thin material stretched upon it; mostly in the form of an isosceles triangle with a circular arc as base, or a quadrilateral; constructed to be *flown* in a strong wind by means of a string attached and a tail to balance it 1664. **4.** *Comm. slang.* A bill of exchange, etc., used for raising money on credit; an accommodation bill. A person thus raising money is said *to fly a k.* 1805. **5.** *Naut.* (*pl.*) The highest sails of a ship, which are set only in a light wind. Also *flying-kites*. 1856. **6.** *Geom.* A quadrilateral figure symmetrical about one diagonal 1893.

2. Ah you K. *Ant. & Cl.* III. xiii. 89. 3. Phr. *To fly* (or *send up*) *a k.* (fig.): to try 'how the wind blows', i.e. in what direction things are tending.

Comb. **k. balloon**, sausage-shaped captive balloon for military observations.

Kite, *v.* 1863. [f. prec. sb.] **1.** *intr.* To fly with a gliding motion like that of a kite; *trans.* to cause to fly high like a paper kite. **2.** *Comm. slang.* **a.** *intr.* To 'fly a kite'; see KITE *sb.* 4. **b.** *trans.* To convert into a kite or accommodation bill. 1864.

Kite, obs. f. KYTE, belly.

Kit-fox. 1812. [? f. KIT *sb.* [3]] A small fox (*Vulpes velox*), of North-western America.

Kith (kiþ), *sb.* [OE. *cȳðð*, *cȳð* :—OTeut. **kunþiþā*, abstr. sb. from **kunþ-* known, OE. *cūð*, COUTH.] †**1.** Knowledge; information –1450. †**2.** One's native land; country –1513. **3.** The persons who are known, taken collectively; one's friends, fellow-countrymen, or neighbours; later, occas. confused with *kin*. *Obs.* or *arch.*, exc. in *Kith and kin*. OE.

Phr. *Kith and kin*: *orig.* Country and kinsfolk (see 2); in later use, Acquaintance and kinsfolk; now often taken as pleonastic for Kinsfolk, relatives.

Kithe, kythe (kəið), *v.* Now *Sc.* and *north.* [Com. Teut.: OE. *cȳðan* (ME. *cüþen*, *kyþen*, *kiþen*, *keþen*) :—OTeut. **kunþjan*, f. *kunþ-* known, COUTH.] **1.** *trans.* To make known; to manifest; *refl.* to show oneself, appear ME. **2.** *intr.* for *refl.* To come forth to sight; to become known; to appear ME. †**3.** *trans.* To manifest practically (a feeling, quality, etc.); hence, to practise, do –1724. †**4.** To own; to recognize –1613. Hence **Ki·thing, kything** *vbl. sb.* a making known, telling, showing, manifestation, etc.

Kitish (kəi·tiʃ), *a.* 1566. [f. KITE *sb.* + -ISH [1].] Like or of the nature of a kite; greedy.

Kitling (ki·tliŋ). Now *dial.* ME. [Etym. uncertain.] †**1.** The young of any animal –1603. **2.** A young cat, a kitten (now *dial.*) 1530. †**3.** Applied to a person –1745. **4.** *attrib.* or *adj.* Resembling a kitten or that of a kitten; inexperienced; diminutive 1604.

2. Whether goe you, now?..to drowne kitlings? B. JONS.

Kitten (ki·t'n), *sb.* [ME. *kitoun*, app. a. AFr. **kitoun*, **ketun* = OF. *chitoun*, *cheton*, var. of F. *chaton* kitten.] The young of the cat; a young cat. Also *transf.* and *fig.* Hence **Ki·ttenhood**, the state of being a k. **Ki·ttenish** *a.* like a k. or that of a k.

Ki·tten, *v.* 1495. [f. prec. sb.] Of a cat: To bring forth kittens; also of some other animals: To litter. *intr.* and *trans.*

†**Kittisol** (ki·tisǫl). 1588. [a. Pg. and Sp. *quitasol*, f. *quitar* to take away + *sol* sun.] A sunshade; *spec.* a Chinese umbrella made of bamboo and oiled paper –1875.

Kittiwake (ki·tiwēⁱk). 1661. [Imitative of its cry.] Any sea-gull of the genus *Rissa*; esp. (and primarily) *R. tridactyla*, the common species of the North Atlantic and Arctic Oceans, a small gull having white plumage with black markings on the primaries, and the hind toe rudimentary. Also *k. gull*.

Kittle (ki·t'l), *a.* Orig. *Sc.* and *n. dial.* 1560. [f. KITTLE *v.* [1]] Ticklish; difficult to deal with; risky, precarious, nice, delicate.

K. points of law 1728. *Kittle cattle*: people difficult to manage.

Kittle (ki·t'l), *v.* [1] Now *dial.* and chiefly *Sc.* [ME. *kytylle*, *kityll*, with Teut. cognates; perh. onomatopœic.] **1.** *trans.* To tickle (in physical sense). **2.** *fig.* To stir with feeling or emotion, usually pleasurable; to 'tickle' ME. **3.** To puzzle with a question, etc. 1824.

1. *transf.* The best fiddler that ever kittled thairm with horse-hair SCOTT.

Ki·ttle, *v.* [2] Now *Sc.* and *n. dial.* 1530. [? from KITLING.] **1.** = KITTEN *v.* **2.** *fig.* (*intr.* and *pass.*) To come into being 1823.

Kitty [1] (ki·ti). 1500. [Pet form of Catherine.] †**1.** A young girl or woman; occas. a light woman (*Sc.*) –1572. **2.** Local name for the wren; also *kitty-wren* 1681.

Ki·tty[2]. 1719. [f. as KIT *sb.*[3] + -Y.[6]] Pet name for a kitten.

Ki·tty[3]. 1825. [?] 1. Prison, lock-up. *dial.* 2. The pool at card games 1892. b. Applied to other kinds of pool or joint fund 1904. 3. *Bowls.* The jack 1909.

Kitysol, Kive: see KITTISOL, KEEVE.

Kiver, obs. and dial. f. COVER *sb.* and *v.*

‖**Kiwi** (kī·wi). Also **kiwi-kiwi, kivi.** 1835. [Maori.] Native New Zealand name of the APTERYX, now used in English.

Kl-, occas. ME. spelling for *Cl-*, now only in words of foreign origin.

Klaxon (klæ·ksən). 1914. [Name of manufacturing company.] An (electric) motor-horn. Hence as *vb.*

‖**Kleenebok** (klē·nĕbǫk, klī·nbǫk). 1834. [S. Afr. Du., = little buck.] A small S. Afr. antelope (*Cephalophus monticola*), also called Blue Duiker.

Klepht (kleft). Also **kleft.** 1820. [ad. mod.Gr. κλέφτης, ancient Gr. κλέπτης thief. One of those Greeks who after the conquest of Greece by the Turks in the 15th c. held out in the mountains. Hence, later, A brigand, bandit. Hence **Kle·phtism.**

Kleptomania (kleptomē̆·niă). 1830. [f. Gr. κλεπτο-, comb. f. κλέπτης thief + MANIA.] An irresistible tendency to theft in persons who are well-to-do, a supposed form of insanity. Hence **Kleptoma·niac,** one affected with k. (also *attrib.* or as *adj.*).

Klick, -er, -et, obs. ff. CLICK, etc.

Klino- (kləino), var. of CLINO-, as in *klinometer*, etc.; also **Klinocephalic** (-sĭfæ·lik), **-cephalous** (-se·făləs), *adjs.*, having a saddle-shaped depression at the vertex of the skull; hence **Klinoce·phalism, -ce·phaly. Klinostat** (kləi·nostæt), a stand on which germinating seeds, etc. are placed, and which is made to revolve so as to counteract the influence of gravity on their growth.

‖**Klipdas** [S. Afr. Du.]: see HYRAX.

‖**Klipspringer** (kli·pspri:ŋəɹ). 1785. [S. Afr. Du., f. *klip* rock + *springer* SPRINGER.] A small S. Afr. antelope (*Oreotragus saltatrix*).

Kloof (klūf). 1731. [a. Du. *kloof* (klōf) cleft; see CLOVE *sb.*[4]] In S. Africa: A deep narrow valley; a ravine.

Kn-, an initial combination still retained by most Teut. langs. In English the *k* is now silent.

Knab (næb), *v. Obs.* exc. *dial.* 1630. [Imitative.] To bite lightly, to nibble.

Knab: see NAB *sb.* and *v.*

†**Kna·bble,** *v.* 1567. [dim. or freq. of KNAB *v.*; cf. NIBBLE *v.*] To bite, gnaw, nibble. Usu. *intr.* or *absol.* with *at, upon.* –1684.

Knack (næk), *sb.*[1] [ME. *knak.* Of echoic origin. Cf. Du. *knak*, Ger. *knack, knacke*, etc.] †1. A sharp sounding blow, stroke, or rap. ME. only. 2. A crack or snap such as is made by striking a stone with a hammer 1565.

Knack (næk), *sb.*[2] ME. [? same wd. as prec.] 1. A trick; a device, artifice; formerly often, a crafty device, an underhand trick; later, a clever expedient, a dodge. 2. The faculty of doing something cleverly, adroitly, and successfully. (Now the leading sense.) 1581. b. A trick of action, speech, etc. 1674. 3. *concr.* An ingenious contrivance; a toy, trinket, KNICK-KNACK. ? *Obs.* 1540. †b. A choice dish; a dainty –1642. †c. A quaint device or conceit in writing –1660.

1. She ne used no suche knakkes smale CHAUCER. He has some k., or trick of the trade CARLYLE. 2. Our Holland had the true k. of translating FULLER. b. The Lady..has..a K. of saying the commonest Things STEELE. 3. Why 'tis..A knacke, a toy, a tricke, a babies cap SHAKS. b. As some teachers give to Boyes Junkets and Knacks, that they may learne apace MILT.

Knack (næk), *v.* ME. [Of echoic origin; with senses 2 and 3 cf. Du. *knakken*, MHG. *knacken* (also *gnacken*), etc.] †1. *intr.* To deal (sharp sounding) blows 1575. 2. *trans.* To strike (things, etc.) together so as to produce a sharp abrupt noise; to gnash (the teeth); to snap (the fingers). Now *dial.* 1489. 3. *intr.* To make a sharp abrupt noise, as when stones are struck together. Now *dial.* 1603. †4. *trans.* To 'break' (notes); to sing with trills or runs; to trill forth. ME. only. b. *intr.* To talk mincingly (*dial.*) 1674.

Knacker[1] (næ·kəɹ). Now *dial.* 16.. [f. KNACK *v.* + -ER[1].] Something that makes a sharp cracking noise; *spec.* a castanet.

Knacker[2] (næ·kəɹ). 1573. [?] 1. A harness-maker, a saddler (*dial.*). 2. One who buys worn-out horses, and slaughters them for their hides and hoofs, and for making dog's-meat, etc. 1812. b. One who buys old houses, ships, etc., for what he can make of them 1890. 3. *transf.* An old worn-out horse (*dial.*) 1864. Hence **Kna·ckery,** a knacker's yard.

†**Kna·ckish,** *a. rare.* 1660. [f. KNACK *sb.*[2] + -ISH[1].] Artful, tricky; artificial –1694. Hence †**Kna·ckishness,** artificiality.

Knacky (næ·ki), *a.* 1710. [f. as prec. + -Y.[1]] Having a knack; artful, clever, adroit, ingenious.

Knag (næg). 1440. [ME. *knag* or *knagge* = G. (orig. LG.) *knagge* knot, peg, etc.] 1. A short or stiff projection from the trunk or branch of a tree; hence, a peg or hook for hanging anything on. †2. One of the knobs of a stag's horn; a tine –1657. 3. A knot in wood, the base of a branch 1555. 4. A pointed rock or crag 1552. Hence †**Kna·gged** *a.* furnished with protuberances, knobs, or knots; toothed, jagged 1400. **Kna·ggy** *a.* knotty, rough, rugged 1552. **Kna·gginess.**

Knap (næp), *sb.*[1] Chiefly *dial.* [OE. *cnæp(p* top, summit (of a hill); perh. cogn. w. ON. *knapp-r* knob, etc. (see KNOP *sb.*).] The summit of a hill; a hillock or knoll; a rising ground.

Knap, *sb.*[2] *Obs.* exc. *dial.* ME. [Echoic; goes with KNAP *v.*[1]] 1. An abrupt stroke or blow; a smart knock. 2. The clapper of a mill 1622. †3. A cheating trick with dice –1680.

Knap, var. of KNOP *sb.*

Knap (næp), *v.*[1] Now *dial.* 1470. [Echoic, going with KNAP *sb.*[2]; cf. Du. and G. (orig. LG.) *knappen* to crack, crackle, etc.] 1. *trans.* To strike with a hard short sound; to knack, knock, rap. Also *absol.* or *intr.* 2. *trans.* To snap or break by a smart blow. Now used *spec.* of the breaking of stones for the road. 1535. b. *intr.* To snap 1545. 3. To utter smartly; to talk, chatter (a language). Also *intr. Sc.* and *n. dial.* 1581.

2. He hath knapped the speare in sonder COVERDALE *Ps.* xlv[i]. 9. 'Tis but silke that bindeth thee, K. the thread and thou art free HERRICK. 3. He answered ..that he could k. English with any one SCOTT.

Knap (næp), *v.*[2] Now *dial.* 1575. [Cf. KNAB *v.*; also Du. and G. (orig. LG.) *knappen* to crack, snap, bite.] *intr.* and *trans.* To bite in a short or abrupt way; to snap; to nibble.

†**Kna·p-bottle.** *Herb.* The Bladder-campion, *Silene inflata*, so called from its inflated calyx, which snaps when suddenly compressed. PARKINSON.

Knapper (næ·pəɹ). *dial.* and *local.* 1787. [f. KNAP *v.*[1] + -ER[1].] One who or that which knaps; one who breaks stones, flints, or the like; *esp.* one who shapes flints with a hammer 1870. b. A knapping-hammer.

†**Kna·ppish,** *a. Obs.* exc. *dial.* 1513. [f. KNAP *v.*[2] + -ISH[1].] Rudely abrupt or froward, testy –1629.

†**Kna·pple,** *v.* 1611. [Freq. of KNAP *v.*[2]; see -LE.] To bite shortly and repeatedly; to nibble –1878.

Kna·ppy, *a.* Now *dial.* 1552. [f. KNAP *sb.* and *v.* + -Y.[1]] Full of knaps; lumpy; also, testy.

Knapsack (næ·psæk). 1603. [a. LG. *knapsack*; perh. f. LG. and Du. *knappen* = KNAP *v.*[2], G. *knapp* eating, food + SACK.] A bag or case of canvas or leather for strapping to the back and carrying a soldier's necessaries; any similar receptacle used by travellers.

He packed up his k., and started for the train LYTTON.

Knapweed (næ·pwīd). ME. [Orig. *knopweed*, f. KNOP *sb.* + WEED *sb.*; from the hard rounded involucre.] Common name of species of *Centaurea* (N.O. *Compositæ*), esp. *C. nigra*, with a hard tough stem, and light purple flowers set on a rough dark-coloured globular involucre.

Knar (nāɹ). [ME. *knarre* = LG. *knarre(n*, Du. *knar* stump, knot, knob. Cf. KNUR.] 1. A rugged rock or stone. Now *dial.* 2. A knot in wood; *spec.* a protuberance covered with bark on the trunk or root of a tree ME. †3. A knotted, thick-set fellow. CHAUCER. Hence **Knarred** *a.* knotted, gnarled. **Kna·rry** *a.* (*rare*), having knars; knotty ME.

†**Knarl** (nāɹl). *rare.* 1598. [Related to prec.] A tangle, knot. GRENEWEY.

Knarle, Knarled, obs. ff. GNARL, -ED.

‖**Kna·ster,** Ger. sp. of CANASTER 2, a kind of tobacco.

Knave (nēᵻv), *sb.* [OE. *cnafa* :—OTeut. **knaƀon-*.] †1. A male child, a boy –1460. 2. A boy or lad employed as a servant; hence, a menial; one of low condition. (Freq. opp. to *knight.*) *arch.* OE. 3. An unprincipled man; a base and crafty rogue. (Now the main sense.) ME. b. *joc.* Now *rare.* 1553. 4. *Cards.* The lowest court card of each suit, bearing the figure of a soldier or servant; the jack 1568.

2. Every Horseman hath two or thre horses, and to every horse a k. DYMMOK. 3. The veriest k. and bufflehead that ever he saw in his life PEPYS. b. How now, my pretty knaue, how dost thou? SHAKS. Hence **Knave** *v.* to call (any one) k.; to make a k. of; to steal like a k.; to force knavishly. (All nonce-uses.) 1545.

†**Kna·ve-child.** ME. only. A male child.

Knavery (nēᵻ·vəri). 1528. [f. KNAVE *sb.* + -ERY.] 1. Practices characteristic of a knave; dishonest and crafty dealing; trickery, roguery; an instance of this. †2. Roguishness, waggishness, playing of tricks –1646; tricks of dress (*Tam. Shr.* IV. iii. 58). †3. Pop. name for Bog Asphodel –1640.

1. The Sun sees much Knauery in a yere, and the Moone more in a quarter DEKKER. 2. Full of iests, and gypes, and knaueries, and mockes SHAKS.

Knaveship (nēᵻ·vʃip). 1550. [f. KNAVE *sb.* + -SHIP.] 1. The condition of being a knave: used as a mock title 1589. †2. *Sc.* A small due, in meal, payable to the miller's servant, on each lot of corn ground at a thirlage mill –1818.

Kna·vess. [-ESS.] A she-knave. CARLYLE.

Knavish (nēᵻ·viʃ), *a.* ME. [f. KNAVE *sb.* + -ISH[1].] Characteristic, or having the character, of a knave. †1. Low, vulgar; obscene –1529. †2. Roguish, rascally, impertinent –1603. 3. Unprincipled, fraudulent 1570.

2. Cupid is a knauish lad, Thus to make poor females mad SHAKS. 3. 'Tis a knauish peece of worke SHAKS. Hence **Kna·vish-ly** *adv.*, **-ness.**

Knaw(e, obs. ff. GNAW.

Knawel (nǭ·ĕl). 1578. [a. Ger. *knauel, kneuel* knot-grass.] A book-name of the German knot-grass, *Scleranthus.*

Knead (nīd), *v.* Pa. t. and pa. pple. kneaded. [Orig. a strong vb.: OE. *cnedan*, pa. t. *cnæd*, pl. *cnǣdon*, pa. pple. *cneden* :—OTeut. type **kned-, knad-, knǣdum, knedano-.*] 1. *trans.* To mix and work up into a homogeneous plastic mass, by drawing out, folding over, and pressing together; *esp.* to work up (moistened flour or clay) into dough or a paste; to make (bread, pottery, etc.) thus. 2. *fig.* a. To reduce to a common mass, as if by kneading. b. To shape, as by kneading. ME. 3. *transf.*, esp. in reference to massage 1606.

1. Take some flour and k. it with oil MRS. GLASSE. 2. K. and shape her to your thought B. TAYLOR. 3. I will knede him, Ile make him supple SHAKS. Hence **Knea·dable** *a.* capable of being kneaded. **Knea·der,** one who, or that which, kneads. **Knea·dingly** *adv.* in the manner of one who kneads.

Knea·ding-trough. ME. A wooden trough or tub in which to knead dough.

Knebelite (nēᵻ·bĕləit). 1818. [ad. G. *Knebelit*, named after Major von *Knebel*; see -ITE[1].] *Min.* Hydrous silicate of iron and manganese.

Knee (nī), *sb.* [Com. Teut.: OE. *cnéo(w)*, neut. :—OTeut. **knewom* = pre-Teut. **gneuo-*; cf. L. *genu*, Gr. γόνυ, Skr. *jānu* knee.] 1. The joint, or region about the joint, between the thigh and the lower leg. 2. A joint in an animal regarded as corresponding to the human knee; e.g. the carpal articulation of the foreleg of a horse, etc. 1450. 3. The part of a garment covering the knee 1662. 4. Anything resembling the knee in position or shape; e.g. a piece of timber or metal having a natural or artificial angular bend; *spec.* in *Shipbuilding* and *Mech.* ME. †5. *Bot.* A bent joint in some grasses -1878.

1. Stories learned at a mother's k. 1858. Phr. *To offer* or *give a k.*, to act as second in a pugilistic encounter, and give a principal the support of a knee between the rounds. *On the knees of the gods* (Gr. θεῶν ἐν γούνασι, Hom.), beyond human control 1879. 3. My riding-cloth suit with close knees PEPYS. 4. The sydes, knees, and feete of those hills 1640.

Comb.: **k.-bone**, the patella, knee-cap; **-boot**, a boot reaching to the k.; a leathern apron to draw over the knees in a carriage; **-breeches**, breeches reaching down to, or just below, the k.; **-brush**, (*a*) a tuft of long hair, immediately below the carpal joint, on the legs of some antelopes; (*b*) a hairy mass covering the legs of bees, on which they carry pollen; **-jerk**, a sudden extension of the leg occasioned by striking the tendon below the patella; **-piece**, a bent piece of timber used in shipbuilding; also = *knee-rafter*; **-rafter**, a rafter the lower end of which is bent downwards; **-reflex** = *knee-jerk*; **-roof** = CURB-ROOF; **-swell**, in the American organ, a lever operated by the k., for crescendo and diminuendo effects.

Knee (nī), *v.* [In sense 1, OE. *cnēowian*, f. *cnēo(w)* KNEE *sb.* Since 16th c., f. KNEE *sb.*] 1. *intr.* To go down on, or bend, the knee or knees. b. *trans.* with complement 1607. 2. *trans.* To supplicate, or do obeisance to, by kneeling or bending the knee (*arch.*) 1592. 3. To strike or touch with the knee 1892. 4. *Carpentry.* To fasten with a knee or knees 1711.

1. b. K. The way into his mercy *Cor.* v. i. 5.

Knee-cap (nī·kæp). 1660. [f. KNEE *sb.* + CAP.] 1. A cap or protective covering for the knee. 2. The convex bone in front of the knee-joint; the patella, knee-pan 1869.

Kneed (nīd), *a.* 1597. [f. KNEE *sb.* and *v.* + -ED.] 1. Furnished with knees; as *broken-*, *weak-*, KNOCK-KNEED 1652. b. *Bot.* Having joints like knees; bent like a knee; geniculate 1597. c. Having an angle like a knee; also *techn.*, Having a knee or knees 1775. 2. Of trousers: Bulged at the knee 1887.

1. b. *K. grass*, a name of *Setaria verticillata*.

Knee-deep, *a.* ME. 1. So deep as to reach to the knee 1535. 2. Sunk to the knee (*in* water, mud, etc.). Also *fig.*

1. Decks..almost constantly knee-deep in water 1748. 2. Oxen..standing knee-deep in the cool water 1895.

Knee·-hole. 1862. A hole or space between the pedestal drawers of a writing-table, to receive the knees. Also *attrib.* b. *ellipt.* A knee-hole table.

Knee·-joint. 1648. 1. The joint of the knee. 2. *Mech.* A joint formed of two pieces hinged together endwise so as to resemble a knee, a toggle-joint. Also *attrib.* So **Knee·-joi:nted** *a.* geniculate.

Kneel (nīl), *v.* Pa. t. and pple. **kneeled** (nīld), **knelt** (nelt). [Early ME. *cneol(i)en* :— OE. *cnēowlian*; deriv. of *cnēow*, KNEE *sb.*] *intr.* To fall on the knees or a knee; to remain thus, as in supplication or homage. Const. *to*; also, with indirect passive. b. With *down*: To go down on the knees ME.

On these stones St. Peter kneeled 1756. *fig.* Who in heart not ever kneels HERBERT. b. But as for Cæsar, Kneele downe, kneele downe, and wonder SHAKS.

Kneeler (nī·ləɹ). ME. [f. prec. + -ER [1].] 1. One who kneels; *spec.* in 16–17th c., one who received the Lord's Supper kneeling. 2. *Ch. Hist.* a. One belonging to the third class of penitents in the early Eastern church, so called because they knelt during the whole of divine service. b. In the Apostolic Constitutions, one of the second class of catechumens, who received the bishop's blessing on bended knee. 1719. 3. A board, stool, or hassock on which to kneel 1848.

Knee-pan (nī·pæn). ME. [f. KNEE *sb.* + PAN.] The bone in front of the knee-joint; the patella, knee-cap.

Knee·-ti:mber. 1607. Timber having a natural angular bend, suitable for making knees in shipbuilding or carpentry. Also *fig.* b. with *pl.* A bent piece of timber used in carpentry, etc. 1739.

Knell (nel), *sb.* [OE. *cnyll* masc. :— **cnulli-*, from stem of *cnyllan*, KNELL *v.*] The sound made by a bell when struck or rung, esp. when rung slowly and solemnly, as after a death or at a funeral. b. *fig.* A sound announcing a death or the passing away of something; an omen of death or extinction 1613. c. *transf.* A doleful cry, dirge, etc. 1647.

A K., That summons thee to Heauen, or to Hell SHAKS. The curfew tolls the k. of parting day GRAY. *fig.* Men whose names are a k. to all hope of progress EMERSON.

Knell (nel), *v.* Now chiefly *arch.* [OE. *cnyllan* :—**knulljan*.] †1. *trans.* To knock; also *absol.* -ME. †2. *trans.* To ring (a bell); later, *esp.* to ring slowly and solemnly, as for a death etc., to toll; also *absol.* -1651. 3. *intr.* a. Of a bell: To ring; now esp. for a death or at a funeral ME. b. *fig.* To sound ominously 1816. 4. *trans.* To summon or call by or as by a knell (*into*, etc.) 1800. b. To proclaim by or as by a knell 1840.

3. a. Not worth a blessing, nor a bell to k. for thee FLETCHER. b. The words of the warlock are knelling in my ears SCOTT. 4. Each matin bell, the Baron saith, Knells us back to a world of death COLERIDGE.

Knicker [1] (ni·kəɹ). 1694. [a. Du. *knikker.*] 1. A boy's marble of baked clay. 2. (Also *nicker.*) A large flat button or disk of metal, used as a pitcher, in the boys' game 'on the line' 1899.

Knicker [2] (ni·kəɹ). 1881. In pl. *knickers*: colloq. contr. of KNICKERBOCKERS. Also *attrib.*, as *k. suit.*

Knickerbocker (ni·kəɹbǫkəɹ). 1848. [Pretended author of W. Irving's *History of New York.*]

I. (*with capital initial*). 1. A descendant of the original Dutch settlers of the New Netherlands in America; hence, a New Yorker. 2. *attrib.* or as *adj.* Of or pertaining to the Knickerbockers of New York 1856.

2. The dreadful K. custom of calling on everybody LONGF.

II. (*with small initial*). *pl.* Loose-fitting breeches, gathered in at the knee; also extended to the whole costume worn with these. (Rarely in *sing.*) 1859.

The name is said to have been given to them from their resemblance to the knee-breeches of the Dutchmen in Cruikshank's illustrations to W. Irving's *History of New York.*

Knick-knack, nick-nack (ni·kˌnæk). 1618. [Redupl. of KNACK *sb.*[2]] †1. A petty artifice -1673. 2. Any curious or pleasing trifle of furniture, dress, or food; a trinket, gimcrack, kickshaw 1682. Hence **Knick-kna·ckatory, nick-n.**, a repository of knick-knacks. **Kni:ck-kna·ckery, nick-n.**, knick-knacks collectively; also = sense 2. **Kni·ck-kna:ckish** *a.* of the character of a knick-knack; trifling, flimsy. **Kni·ck-kna:cky** *a.* addicted to knick-knacks; affected, trifling.

Knife (nəif), *sb.* Pl. **knives** (nəivz). [Late OE. *cnīf* :—OTeut. **knīƀo-z*, of uncertain etym.] A cutting-instrument, consisting of a blade with a sharpened longitudinal edge fixed in a handle, either rigidly as in *table-* or *sheath-k.*, or with a joint as in *pocket-k.* b. A knife used as a weapon; applied to a short sword, cutlass, or hanger ME. c. A sharpened cutting-blade, as in a straw-cutter, turnip-cutter, etc. 1833.

Bought a large kitchen k., and half a dozen oyster knives PEPYS. b. Phr. *War to the k.*: war to the last extremity (*lit.* and *fig.*). *To get* or *have one's knife into* (a person): to exhibit a malicious or vindictive spirit towards; to persecute unrelentingly.

Comb.: **k.-boy**, a boy employed to clean table-knives; **-file**, a thin and tapering file, with a very sharp edge; **-grass**, a stout American sedge (*Scleria latifolia*) with sharp-edged leaves; **-rest**, a small metal or glass device on which to rest a carving-knife or -fork at table.

Knife (nəif), *v.* 1865. [f. KNIFE *sb.*] *trans.* To cut, strike, or stab with a knife. b. *U.S. slang.* To strike at secretly 1888.

Knife and fork. 1727. 1. *lit.* as used in eating. Hence in phrases, as *to play a good knife and fork*, to eat heartily. Also *attrib.* 2. A name of Herb Robert and the common club-moss 1879.

Knife-board. 1848. 1. A board on which knives are cleaned. 2. Pop. name for the original roof-seat on omnibuses, consisting of a double bench placed lengthways 1852.

Kni·fe-e:dge. 1818. 1. The edge of a knife; also *transf.* Also *attrib.* = knife-edged. 1876. 2. A wedge of hard steel, on which a pendulum, scale-beam, etc. is made to oscillate 1818. Also *transf.* and *fig.*

2. On a knife-edge of ice between two crevasses L. STEPHEN. Hence **Knife-edged** *a.*

Knife-grinder. 1611. 1. One whose trade it is to grind knives, etc. 2. A grindstone, emery-wheel, or the like for grinding tools 1875. 3. a. A species of cicada. b. The nightjar or goatsucker. 1859.

Knight (nəit), *sb.* [Com. WGer.: OE. *cniht*, *cneoht* = Ger. *knecht* lad, servant, soldier.] †1. A boy, youth, lad. OE. only. †2. A boy or lad as an attendant or servant; hence, any male servant or attendant -ME. 3. With genitive, or poss. pron.: A military servant or follower; later, one devoted to the service of a lady as her attendant, or her champion in war or the tournament; hence also *fig.* OE. 4. a. In the Middle Ages: A military servant of the king or other person of rank; a feudal tenant holding land from a superior on condition of serving in the field as a mounted and well-armed man. Later: One raised to honourable military rank by the king or other qualified person, usually only a person of noble birth who had served as page and squire. b. One upon whom corresponding rank is conferred by the sovereign in recognition of personal merit, or of services rendered to crown or country. OE.

The distinctive title of a knight is *Sir* prefixed to the name, as 'Sir John Falstaff'; *Knight* (*Knt.* or *Kt.*) may be added, but this is now unusual. The honour of knighthood is conferred by the accolade, by letters-patent, etc. Modern knights rank below baronets, and the dignity is not hereditary.

c. More fully *Knight of the Shire*: A gentleman representing a shire or county in parliament; orig. one of two of the rank of knight. Now only techn. or *Hist.* CHAUCER. †5. Applied to personages of ancient history or mythology -1606. 6. a. *Rom. Antiq.* (tr. L. *eques* horseman). One of the class of *equites*, who originally formed the cavalry of the Roman army, and later were a wealthy and important class ME. b. *Gr. Antiq.* (tr. Gr. ἱππεύς horseman). A citizen of the second class at Athens in the constitution of Solon 1820. 7. a. *Chess.* One of the pieces, now usually distinguished by the figure of a horse's head 1440. †b. The knave in cards 1585.

3. O find him, giue this Ring to my true K. SHAKS. In all your quarrels will I be your k. TENNYSON. 4. She leaned against..The statue of the armed k. COLERIDGE. 5. This Aiax..This blended k., halfe Troian, and halfe Greeke SHAKS.

Phrases. a. †*K. of the carpet* (see CARPET *sb.*). †*K. of the community* or *parliament* = Knight of the Shire (see 4 c). *K. of the Round Table*, one of King Arthur's knights (see ROUND TABLE).

b. *K. of the* BATH, GARTER, THISTLE, etc. (see these wds.). *K. of St. John, of Malta, of Rhodes* = HOSPITALLER 3. *K. of Windsor*, one of a small number of military officers who have pensions and apartments in Windsor Castle. A title of the higher classes of the Order of the British Empire: see G.B.E. (s.v. G), K.B.E. (s.v. K).

c. In jocular phr., e.g. *k. of the brush*, a painter, *k. of the pestle*, an apothecary, †*k. of industry* (F. *chevalier d'industrie*), a sharper, swindler.

d. *Knights of Labour*, an extensive association in the U.S., embracing many of the Trade Unions.

Knight (nəit), *v.* ME. [f. prec.] *trans.* To dub or create (one) a knight.

Knightage (nəi·tėdʒ). 1840. [f. KNIGHT *sb.* + -AGE.] The whole body of knights; a list and account of those who are knights.

Kni·ght-e·rrant. *Pl.* **knights-errant.** ME. [See ERRANT *a.* 1.] 1. A mediæval knight who wandered in search of adventures. 2. *transf.* A person of a chivalrous or adventurous spirit. Occas. in ridicule. 1751.

Knight-e·rrantry. 1654. [f. prec. + -RY.] 1. The practice of a knight-errant; the action of knights who wandered in search of adventures. 2. Readiness to engage in romantic adventure. Often depreciative: Quixotic behaviour. 1659. 3. The body of knights-errant (*rare*) 1860.

2. It is a noble Piece of Knight-Errantry to enter the Lists against so many armed Pedagogues STEELE.

Knight-head (nəi·tˌheːd). 1711. *Naut.* One of two large timbers in a vessel that rise obliquely from the keel behind the stem, one on each side, and support the bowsprit; called also bollard timbers.

Knighthood (nəi·tˌhud). [OE. *cnihthád*, f. *cniht* boy, lad + *-hád* -HOOD.] †1. Boyhood, youth. OE. only. 2. The rank or dignity of a knight ME. 3. The profession or vocation of a knight ME. †b. (tr. L. *militia*.) Military service –1552. 4. Chivalrousness ME. 5. The collective body of knights; a company of knights ME. †b. (tr. L. *militia*.) Military force, host. ME. only.

2. I would not take a K. for my Fortune SHAKS. 3. The old virtues of k.—its truth and honour, its chastity and courage 1856. 4. The noble knighthode that was in them reconforted them LD. BERNERS. 5. The k. now-a-days are nothing like the k. of old time CHAPMAN.

†**Kni·ghtless**, *a. rare.* 1590. [-LESS.] Unbecoming a knight; unknightly –17..

Knightlike (nəi·tləik). ME. [-LIKE.] 1. *adj.* Like or befitting a knight; knightly. 2. *adv.* = KNIGHTLY *adv.* ME.

2. If, knight-like, he despises fear SCOTT.

Knightly (nəi·tli), *a.* OE. [f. KNIGHT *sb.* + -LY [1].] †1. Boyish. OE. only. 2. Having the rank or qualities of a knight; noble, chivalrous. Now *rare.* ME. 3. Of, belonging to, suitable or appropriate to a knight ME. 4. Consisting of knights (*rare*) 1845.

2. He was..k. in his attributes BYRON. 3. As one for k. giusts and fierce encounters fitt SPENSER. K. deeds DRYDEN. The k. sword 1834. 4. The k. order S. AUSTIN. Hence **Kni·ghtlihood, Kni·ghtliness**, k. condition or qualities.

Knightly (nəi·tli), *adv.* ME. [f. KNIGHT *sb.* + -LY [2].] In a manner befitting a knight; gallantly, chivalrously.

Say..why thou com'st thus k. clad in Armes? SHAKS.

Knight Marshal: see MARSHAL.

Knight of the post. 1580. [i. e. (?) of the whipping-post or pillory.] A notorious perjurer; one who got his living by giving false evidence; a false bail.

A knight of the post, whome in times past I haue seen as highly promoted as the pillory CHETTLE.

Kni·ght-se·rvice. Also **knight's service.** ME. *Feudal System.* The military service which a knight was bound to render as a condition of holding his lands; hence, the tenure of land under condition of performing military service. Also *fig.*

Knight's fee. ME. *Feudal System.* The amount of land for which the services of an armed knight were due to the sovereign.

Knipperdolling (ni·pərdǫliŋ). 1594. *Ch. Hist.* An adherent of Bernhard Knipperdolling, a leader of the Münster Anabaptists in 1533–5; an Anabaptist; hence, a religious fanatic.

Knit (nit), *sb.* 1596. [f. KNIT *v.*] †1. The style or stitch in which anything is knitted; knitted work; texture –1603. b. The action or process of knitting 1924. 2. *Mining.* A small particle of ore. RAYMOND.

1. Let..their garters [be] of an indifferent k. SHAKS.

Knit (nit), *v.* [OE. *cnyttan*, wk. vb. :—OTeut. **knuttjan*, f. stem *knutt-*, of OE. *cnotta*, KNOT *sb.* The pa. pple. is *knitted*, contr. *knit*; but *knitten* has also been used.] 1. *trans.* To tie in or with a knot; to fasten by or as by knotting. *arch.* and *dial.* 2. *trans.* †a. To net –1687. b. To form (a close texture) by the interlooping of successive series of loops of yarn or thread. (Now the chief specific sense.) 1530. Also *absol.* or *intr.* 3. *trans.* To interlock; to twine, weave, or plait together. *arch.* or *Obs.* 1470. 4. To draw closely together; to contract in folds or wrinkles; †to clench (the fist) ME. b. *intr.* Said of the brows 1815. 5. *trans.* To make close, dense, or hard; to compact; to concentrate ME. b. *intr.* (for *refl.*) To become consolidated 1605. c. *intr.* Of fruit: To form, set. Also of the tree or blossom: To form fruit. ME. †d. Of a female animal: To conceive 1732. 6. *trans.* To conjoin or unite closely (contiguous members, broken parts) 1578. b. *intr.* To become closely united 1612. c. *intr.* Of bees: To cluster. Now *dial.* 1577. 7. *fig.* To connect firmly; to unite or combine intimately ME. Also *intr.* (for *refl.*). 8. *trans.* To constitute by joining (a covenant, etc.); to establish (a relation); to tie, cement ME. 9. *intr.* To effervesce. [? A different word.] 1743.

1. A greate shete knytt at the iiij. corners TINDALE *Acts* x. 11. I knit my hand-kercher about your browes SHAKS. 2. b. She can k. him a stocke SHAKS. 3. Com, knit hands MILT. *Comus* 143. 4. He knits his Brow, and shewes an angry Eye SHAKS. 5. Knitting all his force, [he] got one hand free SPENSER. 6. Nature cannot k. the bones while the parts are under a discharge WISEMAN. 7. They [merchants] k. Mankind together in a mutual Intercourse of good Offices ADDISON. 8. When peace was knit again HOLLAND.

Comb. **Knit up.** ME. a. *trans.* To tie up, to fasten up, to string up; to compose or repair by knitting (*lit.* and *fig.*). b. To close up; to conclude. †c. To sum up.

Hence **Knit** *ppl. a.*, made by knitting (as *knit stocking*).

Knitch (nitʃ). Now *dial.* [ME. *knücche, knycche* :—OE. *gecnycc*(*e* 'bond'; f. same root as LG. *knuck*(*e*, Ger. *knocke*, a bundle of heckled flax.] A bundle (of wood, hay, corn, etc.) tied together; a sheaf or faggot.

If I dared break a hedge for a k. o' wood, they'd put me in prison KINGSLEY. Hence **Kni·tchel**, †**Knitchet**, a small k.; a handful (of reeds, etc.).

†**Kni·tster.** 1648. [f. KNIT *v.* + -STER.] = KNITTER 2.

Knitter (ni·təɹ). 1440. [f. KNIT *v.* + -ER [1].] 1. One who or that which ties, knots, or closely joins together (*lit.* and *fig.*). 2. One who knits yarn or thread for hosiery, etc. 1515. b. A knitting-machine 1890.

Knitting (ni·tiŋ), *vbl. sb.* ME. [f. KNIT *v.* + -ING [1].] 1. The action of KNIT *v.* 2. *spec.* The formation of a fabric by looping. *concr.* Knitted work. 1711.

attrib. and *Comb.*, as *k.-cotton, -machine*, etc.; **k.-needle**, a long straight blunt 'needle' or slender rod, used, two or more at a time, in knitting 1598; so **k.-pin** 1870; **-sheath**, a cylindrical sheath for holding a knitting-needle steady in knitting; etc.

Knittle (ni·t'l). ME. [A deriv. of KNIT *v.*; see -LE, -EL [1].] †1. A string for tying or fastening. ME. only. 2. *spec.* a. *Naut.* A small line made of yarn, used on board ship. Also *attrib.* 1627. b. A string fastened to the neck of a bag to draw it together 1847.

Knive (nəiv), *v.* 1850. [f. KNIFE *sb.*, after *wife, wive*, etc.] = KNIFE *v.*

Knob (nǫb), *sb.* ME. [= MLG. and mod.G. *knobbe* knot, knob, bud, etc.] 1. A small rounded lump or mass, esp. at the end or on the surface of something; a rounded protuberance, boss, stud; a bump, hump, wart, pimple, etc. b. *Arch.* A boss of carved work 1730. 2. A knoll; a hill in general; esp. in U.S. 1650. 3. A small lump (of sugar, coal, etc.) 1676. 4. *slang.* The head. Usually NOB, q. v. 1725. 5. = KNOBSTICK 2. 1838.

1. The bolt is moved by..a fixed k. or handle, as in the common door catch 1833. *Hen. V*, III. vi. 108. The rocky k. called Whitemoss Howe JENKINSON. 3. A k. of sugar TUCKER. *Comb.* **k.-lock**, a lock which is opened with a k.

Knob (nǫb), *v.* 1566. [f. prec.] 1. *trans.* To form knobs upon 1879. 2. *intr.* To form a knob or knobs, to bunch 1566. 3. *trans.* To free from knobs, to rough-dress (stone in the quarry) 1890.

Knobbed (nǫbd, nǫ·bėd), *a.* 1440. [f. KNOB *sb.* or *v.* + -ED.] Having a knob or knobs; formed into or ending in a knob.

Knobber (nǫ·bəɹ). ? *Obs.* 1700. [f. KNOB *sb.* + -ER [1].] *Venery.* A male deer in its second year; a brocket.

Knobble (nǫ·b'l). 1485. [dim. of KNOB *sb.*] A small knob. Hence **Kno·bbly** *a.*

Knobbler (nǫ·bləɹ). 1686. [f. prec. + -ER [1].] 1. = KNOBBER. 2. *Metall.* A shingler; also *nobbler.*

Knobby (nǫ·bi), *a.* 1543. [f. KNOB *sb.* + -Y [1].] 1. Full of, bearing, or covered with knobs or protuberances; knotty. 2. Of the nature of a knob, knob-shaped 1764. Hence **Kno·bbiness** 1611.

Knobkerrie (nǫ·bkeːri). Also **-keerie, -kerry.** 1849. [f. KNOB *sb.* + KERRIE, after Cape Du. *knopkirie, -kieri.*] A short thick stick with a knobbed head, used as a weapon or missile by S. Afr. tribes. Also *transf.*

Knobstick (nǫ·bˌstik). 1824. 1. A knobbed stick; a knobkerrie. 2. = BLACK-LEG 3. Also *attrib.* 1826.

Knock, *sb.*[1] ME. [f. KNOCK *v.*] An act of knocking; a hard stroke or thump; *spec.* a rap at a door to gain admittance, etc.

Knock (nǫk), *sb.*[2] 1587. [In sense 1, a. Gael. *cnoc* knoll. With 2 cf. Da. dial. *knok* little hillock.] 1. A hill, a knoll 17.. 2. A Lincolnshire name for a sandbank. Cf. *Kentish K.*, a sandbank near the mouth of the Thames; also *K. Sand.*

Knock (nǫk), *v.* [Late OE. *cnocian*; prob. echoic.] 1. *intr.* To strike as with the fist or something hard; *esp.* to rap upon a door, etc., to gain admittance (const. *at*, †*on*, †*upon*). Also *fig.* b. *trans.* with indef. obj. *it*, To give knocks; also, with cognate obj. 1613. 2. *trans.* To give a hard blow or blows to; to hit, strike, beat, hammer OE. b. To make a strong impression on; to 'fetch' (*slang*) 1883. 3. *trans.* To drive or bring (a thing) violently against something else ME. 4. *intr.* To come into violent collision with something; to strike, bump, clash 1530. b. Of mechanism: To rattle on account of parts being loose and striking each other 1869. Of a steam or internal combustion engine: To make a peculiar thumping noise 1904. c. with *adv.* or *advb. phr.*: To stir or move energetically, clumsily, and noisily, or at random, about a place 1825. 5. *trans.* With extension: To drive by striking 1610. b. To rouse or summon by knocking at the door. *colloq.* 1706.

1. Knocke ȝe, and it shal be opnyd to ȝou WYCLIF *Matt.* vii. 7. *fig. Temp.* I. ii. 8. 2. I haue an humor to knocke you indifferently well SHAKS. b. Phr. *To k. on* (†*in*) *the head*: *esp.* to stun or kill by a blow on the head; often *loosely*, to kill in a summary way; *fig.* to put an end to. c. *U.S. colloq.* To speak ill or slightingly of, criticize captiously. Also *intr.* 1901. 3. Phr. *To k. one's head against*: (*fig.*) to hurt oneself by coming into collision with resisting facts or conditions. 4. c. A..Navy Captain..who has knocked about Africa half his life 1839. 5. He yeeld him thee asleepe, Where thou maist knocke a naile into his head SHAKS.

Phr. *To k. the bottom out of*: (*fig.*) to make of no effect (*colloq.*). *To k. into a* COCKED *hat, to k.* SPOTS *off* or *out of, to k. into the middle of next* WEEK, etc. (*slang*, or *colloq.*).

Comb. with advs. **Knock about.** a. *trans.* To treat roughly. b. *intr.* To move about in an irregular way; to lead an irregular life (*colloq.*). **Knock down.** a. *trans.* To fell to the ground with a blow or blows; also *fig.* b. To dispose of (an article) to a bidder at an auction sale by knock of hammer or mallet. c. To call upon (*for* a song, etc.) *colloq.* d. To lower effectively (prices, etc.). *colloq.* e. *U.S. slang.* To embezzle (passengers' fares) 1860. **Knock in.** a. *trans.* To drive in by or as by blows. b. *intr.* (*Univ. slang.*) To knock so as to get into college after the gate is closed. **Knock off.** a. *trans.* To strike off by or as by a blow; also *fig. To k. a person's head off*, to beat him easily. b. To cause to leave off work. c. *intr.* To leave off. d. *trans.* To stop, give up (work). e. To complete or do hastily. *colloq.* f. To strike off from an amount or sum. **Knock out.** a. *trans.* To resell by auction among themselves goods bought by confederates at a nominal price. b. *fig.* To vanquish, exhaust. *To k. out of time* (Pugilistic), to disable an opponent so that he is unable to respond to the call of 'Time'. c. To make roughly or hastily. *colloq.* d. *intr.* (*Univ. slang.*) To get out of college by knocking at the gate after it has been shut. **Knock together.** *trans.* To put together hastily or rudely. **Knock under.** *intr.* Short for *knock under board*, to succumb in a drinking-bout; to give in, knuckle under. **Knock up.** a. *trans.* To drive upwards by knocking. b. *intr.* To be driven up so as to strike something. *To k. up against*, to come into collision with; *fig.* to come across. c. To make up or arrange hastily. d. In *Cricket*, to make (so many runs) by striking the ball. *colloq.* e. To arouse by knocking at the door. f. To exhaust, tire out (esp. in *pass.*). g. *intr.* To become exhausted, to break down. h. *trans.* To put an end to.

Knock-, the vb.-stem or noun of action in Comb. K.-bark (*Mining*), ore that has been crushed. Also with advs., as **k.-under**, an act of knocking under; etc.

Kno·ck-about, knockabout, *a.* (*sb.*) 1876. [The phr. *knock about* used attrib. and as sb.] A. *adj.* 1. Characterized by knocking about, or dealing blows 1885. b. *Theatr. slang.* Of noisy and violent character 1892. 2. Characterized by wandering irregularly about 1886. b. Of clothes: Suitable for knocking about 1880.

c. *Australia.* Applied to a labourer on a station who will turn his hand to anything 1876.

1. This k. sport [football] 1885. **b.** A k. entertainment 1897. **2. b.** Any make,..from k. suits to dress-clothes 1895.

B. *sb.* **1.** A knockabout performer or performance (see A. 1 b) 1887. **2.** *Australia.* A knock-about man (see A. 2 c) 1889.

Knock-down. 1690. [The phr. *knock down* used attrib. and as sb.]

A. *adj.* **1.** Such as to knock down; *fig.* overwhelming. **2.** *Knock-down price*, the price below which an article will not be knocked down at an auction 1895.

B. *sb.* **1.** Something overpowering; *e.g.* strong liquor (*slang*) 1698. **2.** A blow that knocks down; also *fig.* Also, A stand-up or free fight 1809.

Knocker (nǫ·kəɹ). ME. [f. KNOCK *v.* + -ER [1].] **1.** One who or that which knocks. **b.** A goblin imagined to dwell in mines, and to indicate the presence of ore by knocking 1747. **2.** An appendage, usually of iron or brass, fastened to a door, and hinged so that it may be made to strike against a metal plate, to attract attention. (The most usual sense.) 1598.

2. One could hardly find a K. at a Door in a whole Street after a Midnight Expedition of these *Beaux Esprits* STEELE. Phr. *Up to the k.*, in first-rate condition, in fine style (*slang*). **3.** *U.S. colloq.* A captious critic 1911.

Knocking (nǫ·kiŋ), *vbl. sb.* ME. [-ING [1].] **1.** The action of KNOCK *v.* **2.** *pl.* **a.** *Mining.* Ore that has been broken with a hammer before being crushed. **b.** Small pieces broken off from stone by hammering or chiselling. 1747.

Knock-knee (nǫ·kˌnī). 1827. [f. KNOCK *v.* + KNEE *sb.*] *pl.* Knees that knock together in walking from inward curvature of the legs. *sing.* Knock-kneed condition. Hence **Knock-kneed** *a.* having the legs bent inwards so that the knees knock together in walking; *fig.* halting 1806.

Kno·ck-me-dow·n. *colloq.* 1756.

A. *adj.* Such as to knock one down (*lit.* or *fig.*); riotous; overbearing; prostrating 1760. He's so positive, so knock-me-down J. H. NEWMAN.

B. *sb.* = KNOCK-DOWN B. 1.

Kno·ck-out. 1818. **A.** *adj.* Characterized by knocking out; *spec.* **a.** of, or in connexion with, an auction sale; **b.** of a blow, etc.: Such as to knock out of the contest.

a. Combinations, by a set of men who attend real sales, and drive, by various means, respectable purchasers away, purchase at their own price, and afterwards privately sell the goods, under a form of public auction, termed 'Knock-out Sales' 1818.

B. *sb.* **1.** The practice of knocking out at auctions, etc.; a knock-out sale; also, one of the confederates who 'knock out' 1854. **2.** A knock-out blow 1894; hence, a defeat; also *slang*, something that excels or outdoes everything.

Knoll (nōul), *sb.*[1] [OE. *cnoll* hill-top, etc., f. same root as Du. *knol*, formerly *knolle* clod, ball, turnip, Ger. *knollen*, etc.] **1.** The rounded top of a mountain or hill. *Obs.* exc. *dial.* **2.** A small eminence of more or less rounded form; a hillock, a mound OE.

2. A Knole fitly placed..for a Cittadell 1628.

Knoll (nōul), *sb.*[2] ME. [f. same root as KNELL.] An act, or the action, of tolling a bell; the sound of a large bell (*arch.* and *dial.*).

Knoll (nōul), *v.* 1440. [Goes with prec.] **1.** *trans.* To ring, toll (a bell); = KNELL *v.* 2. Also *fig.* Now *arch.* and *dial.* **2.** *intr.* = KNELL *v.* 3. Now chiefly *dial.* 1582. **b.** *trans.* To ring a knell for 1597. **c.** To ring or toll out. TENNYSON. **3.** *trans.* To summon by the sound of a bell 1600.

1. And so his Knell is knoll'd SHAKS. **2.** Where bels haue knoll'd to Church SHAKS. **b.** As a sullen Bell Remembred, knolling a departing Friend SHAKS. Hence **Kno·ller.**

Knop (nǫp), *sb.* [ME. *knop*, with Teut. cognates. Ult. etym. obscure.] **1.** A small rounded protuberance, a knob; a boss, stud, button, tassel, or the like; in *Arch.* = KNOB *sb.* 1 b. *Obs.* or *arch.* exc. *spec.* **2.** The bud of a flower (*arch.*) ME.

1. Sex silver spones with knopis of oure Ladie 1527. *Comb.* **k.-sedge**, the bur-reed, *Sparganium*.

†**Knop**, *v.* ME. [f. prec.] *trans.* To furnish or adorn with knops -1539.

Knopped (nǫpt), *a.* ? *Obs.* ME. [f. KNOP *sb.* or *v.* + -ED.] Having knops; knobbed; bearing buds; knob-shaped.

Knopweed, Knor, see KNAPWEED, KNUR.

Knosp (nǫsp). *rare.* 1808. [ad. Ger. *knospe* bud, boss, etc.] An ornament in the form of a bud, bunch, or rounded protuberance; a knob, boss. SCOTT. Hence **Knosped** *a.* furnished with knosps.

Knot (nǫt), *sb.*[1] [OE. *cnotta* :—OTeut. **knutton-* (whence KNIT *v.*).]

I. 1. An intertwining of the parts of one or more ropes, cords, or the like, made for the purpose of fastening them together, or to something else, and drawn tight; a tie in a rope, necktie, etc.; also a tangle accidentally drawn tight. **2.** A tie worn as an ornament or adjunct to a dress; a bow of ribbon; a cockade or epaulette ME. **3.** *Naut.* A piece of knotted string fastened to the log-line, one of a series fixed at such intervals that the number of them that run out while the sand-glass is running indicates the ship's speed in nautical miles per hour; hence, each division so marked on the log-line, as a measure of the rate of motion. Also *attrib.* = 'running (so many) knots', 1633. **b.** Hence, *loosely*, = 'nautical mile' 1748. **4.** A definite quantity of thread, yarn, etc., being so many coils tied by a knot 1398. **5.** Also *Porter's knot*: A kind of double shoulder-pad, with a loop passing round the forehead, used by London market-porters for carrying burdens 1719. **6.** A design or figure formed of crossing lines ME. **7.** A flower-bed laid out in an intricate design; any laid-out garden plot; a *flower-k.* Now chiefly *dial.* 1494. **8.** A central thickened meeting-point of lines, nerves, mountain-chains, etc. 1861. **9.** *Geom.* A unicursal curve in three-dimensional space, which, on being distorted so as to bring it into a plane without passing one part through another, will always have nodes 1877.

1. Mounsieur Parrolles..that had the whole theoricke of warre in the k. of his scarfe SHAKS. *Bowline k.*, *diamond k.*, *granny's k.*, *loop-k.*, *reef-k.*, *running k.*, *slip-k.*, *surgeon's k.*, etc.; see the first element in these. **2.** The Officers to wear..a mourning K. on their left Arm 1708. **3.** A ten-knot breeze 1860. **b.** The ship went ten knots an hour 1748. **8.** The k. of Pasco, a great ganglion, as it were, of the system [of the Andes] HERSCHEL.

II. Fig. applications. **1.** A tangle or difficulty; a knotty point or problem OE. **b.** The main point in a problem; the complication in the plot of a story or drama, etc. ME. **2.** A bond of union; a tie, link ME. **b.** *spec.* The marriage tie ME. †**3.** A bond; a binding condition; a spell that binds -1813.

1. *Gordian k.*: see GORDIAN. The death of John cut the k. FREEMAN. **2. b.** Send for the Countie,.. Ile haue his k. knit vp to morrow morning *Rom. & Jul.* IV. ii. 24. **3.** This was the first K. upon their Liberty HOBBES.

III. *transf.* **1.** A hard lump in an animal body; a swelling or protuberance; a knob in a bone; a tumour, ganglion, wart, pimple, or the like ME. **2.** A thickened part in the tissue of a plant; an excrescence on a stem, branch, or root; a node on a stem; the hard mass formed in a trunk at the insertion of a branch, causing a rounded cross-grained piece in a board. Also, a bud. Also (*pl.*) a disease of plum and cherry trees. ME. **3.** A knob or embossed ornamentation in carved or hammered work; a stud; a boss ME. **4.** A hill of moderate height; esp. a rocky summit. Freq. in proper names in the north-west of England. ME. **5.** A mass formed by the aggregation and cohesion of particles; a lump, clot, concretion 1625. **6.** A small group, cluster, band, or company of persons or things ME.

1. Let grow thy Sinews till their knots be strong SHAKS. The Queen, who sat With lips severely placid, felt the k. Climb in her throat TENNYSON. **2.** Blunt wedges riue hard knots SHAKS. **6.** All do conclude Mr. Coventry, and Pett, and me, to be of a k. PEPYS.

Comb.: **k.-hole,** (*a*) a hole in a board, etc., caused by the falling out of a k.; (*b*) the hollow formed in the trunk of a tree by the decay of a branch; **-stitch,** a stitch by which ornamental knots are made; **-wood,** wood that is full of knots; *esp.* pine.

Knot (nǫt), *sb.*[2] 1452. [Obscure. Camden's conjecture (see quot.) has no basis.] A bird of the Snipe family (*Tringa Canutus*), also called Red-breasted Sandpiper; it breeds within the Arctic Circle, but is common on the British coasts in late summer and autumn.

Knotts, i. *Canuti aves* vt opinor, e Dania enim aduolare creduntur CAMDEN.

Knot (nǫt), *v.* 1509. [f. KNOT *sb.*[1]] **1.** *trans.* To tie in a knot; to make knots in; to do up or secure with a knot 1547; *intr.* to form a knot or knots 1611. **2.** *intr.* To make or knit knots for fringes 1701; *trans.* to make or form (fringes) thus 1750. **3.** *trans.* To form protuberances, bosses, or knobs on or in; to make knotty; to knit (the brows) 1509. †**b.** *intr.* Of plants: To form knots or nodes; to bud; to form a close head; to 'set' -1660. **4.** *trans.* To combine firmly or intricately; to entangle, complicate 1611. †**b.** *intr.* To unite or gather together in a knot; to congregate; to concrete; to become knotted. **5.** *techn.* **a.** To cover the knots in (wood) before painting 1823. **b.** To remove knots from (cloth, etc.) 1875.

1. I wore The rope..Twisted as tight as I could k. the noose TENNYSON. **3.** The Gout had knotted all his Joynts 1697. **4. b.** A Cesterne, for foule Toades To k. and gender in *Oth.* IV. ii. 62. Hence **Kno·tting** *vbl. sb.* in all senses.

Knotberry. Also **knoutberry.** 1633. [? f. KNOT *sb.*[1] + BERRY.] Local name of the Cloudberry, *Rubus Chamæmorus*.

Knot-grass. 1538. [f. KNOT *sb.*[1] + GRASS; from the knotted stem.] **1.** The plant *Polygonum aviculare*, a common weed in waste ground, with intricately-branched creeping stems, and small pink flowers; an infusion of it was formerly supposed to stunt the growth. Also *P. maritimum*, *P. virginianum*, etc. **2.** Applied to other plants with knotty stems, etc.; as Marsh Bent, Mare's-tail, etc. 1578.

1. You dwarfe You minimus, of hindring knot-grasse made SHAKS.

Knotless (nǫ·tlės), *a.* ME. [-LESS.] Without a knot, free from knots; unknotted.

Ye'll slip frae me like a k. thread BURNS.

Knotted (nǫ·tėd), *a.* OE. [f. KNOT *sb.*[1] and *v.* + -ED.] **1.** Having knots; tied in a knot; fastened with a knot. **b.** *fig.* Entangled, intricate 1648. **2.** Formed or decorated with knots or bosses. **b.** Of a garden, laid out in knots. 1588. **3.** Characterized by knobs, protuberances, excrescences, or concretions; gnarled, as a trunk; having swollen joints, as a stem; knitted (as the brows) 1440. **b.** Forming a close head of blossom (*dial.*) 1744.

1. K. scourges COWPER. **b.** They're catch'd in k. law like nets BUTLER *Hud.* II. iii. 18. **2.** The West corner of thy curious k. garden SHAKS. **3.** The knees of k. Oakes *Tr. & Cr.* I. iii. 50. K. joints 1701, branches 1776.

Knotty (nǫ·ti), *a.* ME. [f. KNOT *sb.*[1] + -Y.[1]] **1.** Having or full of knots. **2.** *fig.* Full of intellectual complications; hard to explain; puzzling ME. **3.** Hard and rough in character 1568.

1. She bare a skourge, with many a knottie string GASCOIGNE. Like knots in a k. board 1594. **2.** Auoid ..Subtill and knottie Inquisitions BACON. **3.** To soften and dispell rooted and k. sorrowes MILT. *Comb.* **k.-pated** *a.* blockheaded. Hence **Kno·ttily** *adv.* **Kno·ttiness.**

Knotweed (nǫ·twīd). 1578. [f. KNOT *sb.*[1] + WEED *sb.*] †**a.** Knawel. **b.** Name for species of *Centaurea* (Knapweed, etc.), from the knobby heads 1827. **c.** Name for species of *Polygonum* 1884.

Knotwork (nǫ·twɔɹk). 1851. **1.** Ornamental work consisting of, or representing, cords intertwined and knotted together. **2.** A kind of fancy needlework 1882.

Knotwort (nǫ·twɔɹt). 1845. [See WORT.] **a.** Knot-grass (*Polygonum aviculare*). **b.** *pl.* Lindley's name for the N.O. *Illecebraceæ*.

Knout (naut, nūt), *sb.* 1661 (**knūte**). [a. Fr. spelling of Russ. *knut.*] A kind of scourge, often fatal in its effects, formerly used in Russia for flogging criminals. Hence **Knout** *v.* to flog with the k.

Know (nōu), *sb.* 1592. [f. KNOW *v.*] The fact of knowing; knowledge. *In the k.* (colloq.), in possession of inside information.

Know (nōu), *v.* Pa. t. **knew** (niū). Pa. pple. **known** (nōun). [Com. Teut. and Com. Aryan vb., now retained in Eng. alone of the

Teut. langs.: OE. (*ge*)*cnáwan*; = L. **gno-*, whence (*g*)*noscere*; Gr. *γνω-, whence γι-γνώ-σκειν; Skr. *jñā-* know. Generally held to be from the same root (*gen-*, *gon-*, *gn-*) as CAN *v.* and KEN. In Sc. KEN has supplanted *knaw.*] I. 1. *trans.* To recognize; to identify; to distinguish. †2. *trans.* To acknowledge the claims or authority of –1560.

1. Whether that in the life everlasting, we shal k. one an other DAUS. We'll teach him to know Turtles from Iayes *Merry W.* III. iii. 44. 2. I..k. the for my lorde 1450.

II. 1. To be acquainted with (a thing, place, person); to be familiar with (= F. *connaître*, Ger. *kennen*) ME. b. To have personal experience of (something) as affecting oneself. Also *fig.* Usu. with negatives. ME. 2. To be personally acquainted or on familiar terms with (a person) ME. †b. *intr.* Of two persons: To be (mutually) acquainted (= F. *se connaître*) SHAKS. 3. *trans.* To have carnal acquaintance with. (A Hebraism.) *arch.* ME.

1. He knew the Tauernes wel in al the toun CHAUCER. *refl.* K. thy selfe ELYOT. b. He has never known trouble 1877. 2. They are neighbours of ours, but we do not k. them (*mod.*). b. *Ant. & Cl.* II. vi. 86.

III. 1. To be aware or apprised of (= F. *savoir*, Ger. *wissen*); †to become cognizant of, ascertain ME. 2. To be conversant with; *esp.* to be versed or skilled in; †to learn ME. 3. To apprehend or comprehend as fact or truth. Formerly, *occas.*, †To get to understand ME. b. *absol.* or *intr.* To have understanding or knowledge ME. 4. To be cognizant of (a fact); to apprehend (with the mind), to understand ME. b. *absol.* Often parenthetically, esp. in colloq. use, in *you k.*, *we k.*, *do you k.* ME.

1. Pray let me k. your mind in this POPE. I do not k. his age exactly 1776. 2. Of course you k. your ABC L. CARROLL. Phr. *To k. better* (*than to do something*). *To k. by heart.* 3. He did not k. his own mind MACAULAY. b. Large-brow'd Verulam, The first of those who k. TENNYSON. 4. The Hollander..knows it right well, that there are none like English for Courage at Sea STURMY. When he knew himself insolvent 1817. He who does not k. what is true will not k. what is good JOWETT. b. Do you k., I saw the prettiest hat you can imagine JANE AUSTEN. Phr. *Not if I know it*, i.e. I will take care not to do the thing referred to.

IV. 1. *To k. how* (formerly also *to k.*): to understand the way, or be able (*to do* something) 1548. b. *ellipt.* in colloq. phr. *All one knows*, all one can; also *advb.*, to the utmost of one's ability 1872. †2. To make known –1450. 3. In biblical language: To take notice of, care for; to look after, protect; to approve ME. 4. Used (chiefly in sense III. 1) in colloq. and slang phrases expressing sagacity, cunning, or 'knowledge of the world', as *to k. what's what*, *to k. a thing or two*, *to k. the time of day*, etc. 1520.

1. I k. how to curse SHAKS. b. It cost him all he knew to restrain his anger 1883. 3. Thou hast knowne my soule in aduersite COVERDALE *Ps.* xxxi. 7. 4. The foreigner who does not 'k. the ropes'—that is to say, who is crassly ignorant SALA.

Comb. (with prep.). **Know of —**, a. To be cognizant of (something as existing, an event as having occurred). b. *Colloq. phrase. Not that I k. of*, not so far as I k. †*Not that you k. of*, an expression of defiance 1742. Hence **Know·er**, one who knows.

Knowable (nōu·ăb'l), *a.* (*sb.*) 1449. 1. That may be known; capable of being apprehended, understood, ascertained, or recognized 2. *sb.* A knowable thing; usu. in *pl.* 1661.

1. The k. Relations of unknown things HARTLEY. The body..was too much..disfigured to be k. 1806. Hence **Knowabi·lity**, **Know·ableness.**

Know-all. 1895. [f. KNOW *v.*] One who knows or professes to know everything.

Know(e (nau), Sc. and north. forms of KNOLL *sb.*[1]

Know-how (nōu·hau). *slang* (orig. *U.S.*). Knowledge of how to do some particular thing.

Knowing (nōu·iŋ), *vbl. sb.* ME. [f. KNOW *v.* + -ING[1].] The action or fact denoted by KNOW *v.* †1. Recognition. ME. only. †2. Personal acquaintance. ME. only. 3. The action of getting to understand, or fact of understanding; knowledge ME. 4. The fact of being aware of something; cognizance; intimation ME. †b. An experience. *Macb.* II. iv. 4.

3. K. is the acquiring and retaining knowledge and not forgetting JOWETT. 4. There is no k. how young women will act 1794.

Knowing (nōu·iŋ), *ppl. a.* ME. [f. KNOW *v.* + -ING[2].] 1. That knows (see KNOW *v.*). 2. Shrewd, cunning, acute, wide-awake. (Often implying the air of possessing information which one does not impart.) 1503. 3. Showing knowledge of 'what is what' in fashion, dress, etc.; stylish, smart. *colloq. Obs.* or merged in 2. 1796.

1. Our ordinary k. faculties M. ARNOLD. A man who is k. about horses JOWETT. 2. 'I believe you', replied George, with a k. jerk of his head 1852. Hence **Know·ing·ly** *adv.*, **-ness.**

Knowledge (nǫ·ledʒ), *sb.* [ME. (n. dial.) *knaulage*, in Wyclif *knowleche*, f. stem of KNOW *v.* + *-leche* (unexplained; see N.E.D.). Pronounced (nōu·ledʒ) by some, after *know.*] I. †1. Acknowledgement, confession; recognition of the position or claims (of any one) –1548. †2. Recognition –1611. †3. Legal cognizance. Chiefly *Sc.* –1732. †4. *gen.* Cognizance, notice; in phr. *to take k. of* –1623.

4. Wherefore haue wee afflicted our soule, and thou takest no k.? *Isa.* lviii. 3.

II. 1. The fact of knowing a thing, state, etc., or person; acquaintance; familiarity ME. †2. Personal acquaintance, friendship, intimacy. b. One's acquaintances. –1600. 3. Sexual intimacy. Now only in *carnal k.* (*arch.* and *legal*) ME. 4. Acquaintance with a fact; state of being aware or informed; consciousness (of anything) ME. b. *absol.* Acquaintance with facts, range of information, ken 1542. 5. Intellectual acquaintance with, or perception of, fact or truth; the fact, state, or condition of understanding. †Formerly, also, intelligence, intellect. ME. b. with *pl.* A mental apprehension; a cognition (*rare*) 1563. 6. Theoretical or practical understanding *of* an art, science, language, etc. ME. 7. The fact or condition of being instructed; information acquired by study; learning 1477. †8. Information; intelligence; intimation –1722. 9. The sum of what is known 1534. 10. (with *pl.*) A branch of learning; a science; an art. (Rarely in sing.) 1581. †11. A sign, mark, or token –1555.

1. His k. of human nature 1771. Phr. †*To grow out of k.*: to cease to be known. 4. The k. that a person is poor (*mod.*). b. Phr. *To one's k.*, so far as one is aware; also, as one is aware (in latter sense, also, *of one's k.*). *To come to one's k.* 5. K...implies..firm belief,..of what is true..on sufficient grounds WHATELY. K. of nature JEVONS. 6. Practical K. of Navigation at Sea STURMY. 7. Hee that increaseth k. increaseth sorrow *Eccles.* i. 18. 9. Abundance of emptie and unprofitable k. 1628.

Comb. **k.-box**, joc. name for the head.

†**Know·ledge**, *v.* [Early ME. *cnawlechien*, in 14th c. *knowleche(n*, prob. f. *cnaw* sb., and ult. f. *cnáwan*, *knowen* to KNOW + *-lechien* (unexplained). The ending *leche* became later *-lege*, whence *-ledge*. (Cf. *Grinnidge* = *Greenwich*.)] 1. *trans.* = ACKNOWLEDGE *v.* 1. –1582. b. *absol.* or *intr.* To make acknowledgement –1526. †c. *intr.* with *to* (in biblical versions): To give thanks to, to praise –1535. 2. *trans.* = ACKNOWLEDGE *v.* 2. –1643. 3. = ACKNOWLEDGE *v.* 3. –1797. 4. *trans.* To recognize and identify (a disease), to diagnose –1618.

2. They k. thee to be the Father of an infinite majesty 1535. Hence **Know·ledgement**, †formal acknowledgement; knowledge, cognizance (*arch.*). †**Know·ledging** *vbl. sb.* the action of the vb.; also, = KNOWLEDGE *sb.*

Knowledgeable (nǫ·ledʒăb'l), *a.* 1607. [f. KNOWLEDGE *sb.* and *v.* + -ABLE.] †1. [f. the vb.] Capable of being perceived or recognized –1619. 2. [f. the sb.] Possessing or showing knowledge or mental capacity. *colloq.* (orig. *dial.*). 1831. Hence **Know·ledgeableness.** **Know·ledgeably** *adv.*

Known (nōun), *ppl. a.* ME. [pa. pple. of KNOW *v.*] 1. Become an object of knowledge; learned; familiar; often, familiar to all. †2. Possessed of knowledge; learned *in*; informed or aware *of* –1655.

1. Men of k. courage 1647. A k. Non-juror 1704.

Know-nothing (nōu·nɒ:þiŋ), *sb.* and *a.* 1825. [KNOW *v.*] *sb.* 1. a. An ignoramus. b. An agnostic. 2. A member of a political party in U.S.A., called also the American party (1853–6). *adj.* Ignorant, agnostic. Hence **Know·no·thingism**, the profession of agnosticism 1866.

Knub (nɒb). Now *dial.* or *techn.* 1570. [Early mod.E. = LG. *knubbe*, etc.; see KNOB.] 1. = KNOB *sb.* 1. 2. The innermost wrapping of the chrysalis in a silk cocoon; usu. NUB 1812.

Knuckle (nɒ·k'l), *sb.* [ME. *knokel*; app. dim. of a word for 'bone' which appears as MLG. *knoke*, MHG. *knoche* (G. *knochen*).] †1. The end of a bone at a joint –1658. 2. *spec.* The bone at a finger-joint; esp. applied to those at the roots of the fingers 1440. 3. The projection of the carpal or tarsal joint of a quadruped; hence, a 'joint' of meat, *esp.* veal or ham, consisting of the knuckle-joint with the parts above and below it 1625. 4. Something shaped or protruding like a knuckle of a bone. *spec.* †a. A thickened joint of a plant, a node. b. *Anat.* A projecting bend of the intestine. c. *Mech.* The projecting tubular part of a hinge through which the pintle runs. d. *Shipbuilding.* An acute angle in certain timbers. 1601. 5. = KNUCKLE-DUSTER 1861.

2. Phr. *Near the knuckle* (colloq.): all but indecent. *Comb.*: **k.-bow**, **-guard**, a guard on a sword-hilt to cover the knuckles; **-end**, the small end of a leg of mutton or pork.

Knuckle (nɒ·k'l), *v.* 1740. [f. prec.] 1. *intr.* To place one's knuckles on the ground in playing at marbles. Usu. *k. down.* 2. *intr.* (*fig.*) To give in. Usu. *k. down* or *k. under.* 1740. 3. *trans.* To tap, strike, press, or rub with the knuckles 1793.

2. He had to k. and comply in all points CARLYLE. Hence **Knuckle-down** as *sb.*: a. a game at marbles; b. submission; as *adv.* = submissively.

Knu·ckle-bo·ne. 1440. 1. Any bone forming a knuckle 1577. 2. In an animal: a. A limb-bone with a ball-like knob at the joint-end, or the rounded end of such a bone; also, = KNUCKLE *sb.* 3. 1440. b. One of the metacarpal or metatarsal bones of a sheep or the like; hence (usu. *pl.*) a game played with these; also called *huckle-bones* or *dibs* 1759.

Knuckled (nɒ·k'l'd), *a.* ME. [f. KNUCKLE *sb.* + -ED[2].] †1. Knobbed, rugged; thick-jointed, as the stem of a plant –1626. 2. Having (prominent) knuckles; protuberant like a knuckle 1842.

Knu·ckle-du·ster. 1858. [f. KNUCKLE *sb.* + DUSTER. (orig. criminals' slang, U.S.)] A metal instrument to protect the knuckles from injury in striking, and to add force to a blow.

Knu·ckle-joi·nt. 1863. 1. *lit.* Each joint of the knuckles (of the hands), or the joint of the leg of an animal called a knuckle. 2. *Mech.* A joint in which a projection in one part is inserted into a corresponding recess in the other (like knuckles clasped together); also extended to universal joints, etc. 1863.

Knuffe, Knulling, see GNOFF, NULLING.

Knur, knurr (nɒ̄ɹ). [ME. *knorre*, *knurre*; etym. unkn.] †1. A hard excrescence or concretion in the flesh –1621. 2. A knot or hardened excrescence on the trunk of a tree; a kernel in stone; any swollen formation 1545. 3. A wooden ball used in the north country game of *Knur and spell*, resembling trap-ball. Also, A similar ball used in hockey, etc. 1852.

Knurl, nurl (nɒ̄ɹl), *sb.* 1608. [? dim. of KNUR.] 1. A knot, knob, boss, nodule, etc.; a small bead or ridge on a metal surface. 2. A thick-set stumpy person (*dial.*) 1674. Hence **Knurl, nurl** *v.* to make knurls, beadings, or ridges (on an edge or surface); to mill, to crenate. **Knurled, nurled** *a.* having knurls so wrought; crenated, milled 1611. **Knu·rly** *a.* having knurls; knurl-like, dwarfish 1602.

†**Knu·rry**, *a.* 1513. [f. KNUR + -Y.[1]] 1. Full of knurs, knotty, gnarled –1664. 2. *fig.* Knotty, perplexing –1652.

Knut, joc. sp. and pron. of NUT (= dandy) 1911.

Koala (koua·lă), prevalent form of KOOLAH.

‖**Kob** (kǫb). 1774. [? native Senegalese.] An African water-antelope of the genus *Kobus*. So ‖**Ko·ba.**

‖**Kobold** (kōu·bǫld). 1830. [G. *kobold*, *kobolt*; etym. unkn.] In German folklore: a. A familiar spirit, haunting houses and occas. helping the inmates; a brownie. b. An underground spirit haunting mines, etc.; a gnome.

Kobold, obs. f. COBALT.

Kodak (kōu·dæk), *sb.* 1888. [A trade-mark name invented by Mr. G. Eastman.] A kind of portable photographic camera with a continuous roll of sensitized film upon which successive negatives are made; also erroneously applied to any hand camera. **b.** *transf.* A photograph taken with a kodak 1895. Hence **Ko·dak** *v. intr.* to photograph with a kodak; *fig.* to catch or describe quickly or vividly.

‖**Koel** (kōu·ĕl). 1826. [Hindī *kōil*, f. Skr. *kokila*.] A cuckoo of the genus *Eudynamis*, esp. *E. honorata* of India, and *E. flindersi* of New Guinea and Australia.

‖**Koff** (kǫf). *rare.* 1794. [Du. *kof*.] *Naut.* A clumsy two-masted sailing-vessel, used by the Dutch, Danes, etc.

‖**Koftgari** (kǫftgărī·). *E. Indian.* 1874. [Urdū (Pers.) *kuft-*, *koftgarī* 'beaten-work'.] A kind of Indian damascene-work, in which a pattern traced on steel is inlaid with gold. Also abbrev. **Koft**, *attrib.* in *k.-work* 1880.

‖**Koh-i-noor** (kōu·hi,nūᵊɹ). 1849. [Pers. *kōh-i nūr* mountain (*kōh*) of light (*nūr*).] A famous Indian diamond, which became one of the British Crown jewels on the annexation of the Punjaub in 1849; hence *fig.* anything superb of its kind.

‖**Kohl**[1] (kō·h'l, kōul). 1799. [Arab.; see ALCOHOL.] A powder (usu. of antimony) used in the East to darken the eyelids.

Kohl[2], abbrev. of next.

‖**Kohlrabi, kohl-rabi** (kōulrā·bi). Also erron. **khol-**. 1807. [Ger. *kohlrabi*, 16th c. ad. It. *cavoli* (or *cauli*) *rape*, pl. of *cavolo rapa* (F. *chou-rave*) 'cole-rape'; cf. COLE[1].] A cabbage with a turnip-shaped stem; the turnip-cabbage.

‖**Kokoon** (kǫkū·n), **kokong** (kǫkǫ·ŋ). 1806. [Sechuana *kgokoñ* or *khokong*.] A large antelope (*Antilope taurina*) of S. Africa.

Kon, kon(n)e, obs. ff. CAN *v.*, CON *v.*

Ko·nilite. 1821. [f. Gr. κόνις dust + -LITE.] *Min.* A powdered form of silica found in the cavities of trap.

Koodoo, kudu (kū·dū). 1777. [Xosa-Kaffir *iqudu*.] A large African antelope (*Strepsiceros Kudu*), having a brown coat marked with white stripes; the male has long spirally-twisted horns.

Koolah (kū·lă), **koala.** *Australia.* 1808. [Native name. (The form *koala* is perh. orig. a misreading.)] An arboreal marsupial mammal of Australia (*Phascolarctos cinereus*), of an ashen-grey colour, somewhat like a sloth in form. Also called the *Australian* or *Native Bear*.

Kopec(k, -peek, -pek, var. of COPECK.

‖**Kopje** (kǫ·pi). 1881. [Du. *kopje*, dim. of *kop* head, COP *sb.*[2]] In S. Africa: A small hill.

Koran[1] (korā·n, kōᵊræ·n). 1625. [a. Arab. *qurān*, *qorān* recitation; cf. ALCORAN.] The sacred book of the Mohammedans, consisting of oral revelations by Mohammed collected in writing after his death; it is in Arabic. Hence **Kora·nic** *a.*

Koran[2] (kŏrā·n). 1775. [ad. S. Afr. Du. *kor-* or *knorhaan*, f. *kor-*, *knor-*, the bird's cry + *haan* cock.] A S. Afr. bustard, of the genus *Eupodotes*, esp. *E. afra*.

‖**Kosher** (kǫ·ʃəɹ), *a.* (*sb.*) Also **cosher**, etc. 1851. [Heb. *kāshēr* fit, proper.] **1.** Applied to food prepared according to the Jewish law. Hence of shops, houses, etc., where this is sold or used. **2.** *sb.* (*ellipt.*) Kosher food; also, a kosher shop 1886.

‖**Kotal** (kōu·tæl). *E. Ind.* 1880. [Pushtō *kōtal* mountain pass.] The pass over a mountain; a col; the ridge or summit of a pass.

‖**Kotow** (kōtau·), *sb.* Also **kow-tow, -too**, etc. 1804. [Chinese *k'o-t'ou*, f. *k'o* knock + *t'ou* the head.] The Chinese custom of touching the ground with the forehead, as an expression of respect, submission, or worship. **b.** *fig.* An act of obsequious respect 1834. Hence **Kotow·**, *v. intr.* to perform the k.; *fig.* to act in an obsequious manner.

‖**Kotwal** (kǫ·twāl). *E. Ind.* 1582. [Hindī *kotwal* porter or keeper of a castle or fort, magistrate.] A chief officer of police for a city or town in India; a native town magistrate. Hence ‖**Kotwa·lee**, police station.

‖**Koulan, kulan** (kū·lăn). 1793. [Tartar.] A species of equine quadruped (*Equus onager*), closely allied to the Dziggetai (with which it is united by some); the wild ass of Mesopotamia, Persia, and the banks of the Indus.

‖**Koumiss** (kū·mis). 1607. Cf. COSMOS[2]. [= F. *koumis*, Ger. *kumiss*, a. Tartar *kumiz*.] A fermented liquor prepared from mare's milk, used as a beverage by the Tartars; also, a spirituous liquor distilled from this. Imitations are also prepared from ass's milk and cow's milk.

‖**Kourbash, koorbash** (ku·rbaʃ), *sb.* Also courbash, etc. 1814. [a. Arab. *qurbāsh*, ad. Turk. *qirbāch* whip.] A whip made of hippopotamus or other hide; an instrument of punishment in Turkey, Egypt, and the Soudan. Hence **Kou·rbash** *v. trans.* to flog with the k.

‖**Kousso** (ku·so). 1851. [Abyssinian.] The dried flowers of an Abyssinian plant, *Hagenia* (*Brayera*) *abyssinica*, used as an anthelmintic.

Kow-tow: see KOTOW.

Kraal (krāl), *sb.* 1731. [a. Colonial Du. *kraal*, a. Pg. *curral*, *corral*; see CORRAL.] **1.** A village of S. or Central African natives, consisting of a collection of huts surrounded by a fence or stockade. Also *transf.* the community of such a village. **b.** *loosely.* A hovel 1832. **2.** An enclosure for cattle or sheep; a stockade, pen, fold 1796. Hence **Kraal** *v. trans.* to enclose in a k.

‖**Krait** (krait). *E. Ind.* 1874. [Hindī *karait*.] A venomous snake of the genus *Bungarus*, esp. *B. cæruleus*, common in Bengal.

‖**Kraken** (krā·kĕn, krāᵊ·kĕn). 1755. [Norw.] A mythical sea-monster of enormous size, said to have been seen at times off the coast of Norway.

Far, far beneath in the abysmal sea,..The K. sleepeth TENNYSON.

‖**Krameria** (krămīᵊ·riă). 1855. [Mod.L.; f. J. G. H. *Kramer*, an Austrian botanist.] **a.** *Bot.* An anomalous genus of *Polygalaceae*, comprising branched spreading undershrubs, natives of America, having astringent properties. **b.** *Med.* The root of *K. triandra* (rhatany-root), or a drug made from this.

Krang, var. of KRENG.

‖**Krantz, kranz** (krænts). *S. Africa.* 1834. [a. S. Afr. Du., = Du. *krans* coronet, chaplet; cf. Ger. *kranz*.] A wall of rock encircling a mountain or summit; hence, any precipitous or overhanging wall of rocks.

Kreatic, Kreatine, etc., var. of CREATIC, CREATINE, etc.

Kreil, krele, obs. ff. CREEL.

Kremlin (kre·mlin). 1662. [a. F., f. Russ. *kreml* citadel, of Tartar origin.] The citadel or fortified enclosure within a Russian town or city; *esp.* that of Moscow, which contains the imperial palace.

Kreng (kreŋ). Also **krang**, CRANG. 1820. [a. Du. *kreng* carrion, carcass; etym. unkn.] The carcass of a whale from which the blubber has been removed. Hence **Kre·nging-hook**, an instrument for stripping the blubber from a dead whale; so **Kre·nger**.

Kreosote: see CREOSOTE.

‖**Kreutzer** (kroi·tsəɹ). Also **creutzer, kreuzer**, etc. 1547. [Ger. *kreuzer*, f. *kreuz* cross; from the cross orig. stamped upon it.] A small copper (orig. silver) coin formerly current in Germany and Austria.

‖**Kriegspiel** (krī·g,spīl, ‖krī·kʃpīl). 1878. [Ger., = war-game.] A game in which blocks representing troops, guns, etc., are moved about on maps.

Kris, var. of CREESE, Malay dagger.

Krishnaism (kri·ʃnă,iz'm). 1885. [f. *Krishna*, a great deity of later Hinduism, worshipped as an incarnation of Vishnu.] The worship of or belief in Krishna. So **Kri·shnaist, Kri·shnaite**, a worshipper of Krishna.

Kritarchy (kri·taɹki). [f. Gr. κριτής judge + -αρχία rule, after *monarchy*, etc.] The rule of the Judges in Israel. SOUTHEY

Kroci-, krokydolite, var. CROCIDOLITE.

‖**Krone** (krō·nĕ). 1875. [Ger. *krone* (pl. *kronen*), Da. *krone* (pl. *kroner*), Sw. *krona* (pl. *kronor*) crown; cf. CROWN *sb.*] **1.** A silver coin of Denmark, Norway, and Sweden, worth 1*s.* 1½*d.* **2.** The German 10 mark gold piece 1898. **3.** An Austrian silver coin, = 10*d.* 1898.

Kroo, Krou, Kru (krū). 1835. [W. Afr.] *attrib.* or as *adj.* Of or pertaining to a negro race so named on the coast of Liberia, skilful as seamen. Hence **Kru-man**, one of this race.

‖**Krummhorn** (kru·mhǫɹn). 1694. [Ger., f. *krumm* crooked + *horn* HORN.] *Mus.* **a.** An obsolete wind-instrument of a curved form. **b.** An organ reed-stop of 8 ft. pitch, resembling the clarinet in tone; called also corruptly CREMONA[2].

Kryo- (krəi,o), var. sp. of *cryo-*, comb. f. Gr. κρύος frost.

Krypton (kri·ptǫn). 1898. [ad. neut. of Gr. κρυπτός hidden.] *Chem.* A rare inert gaseous element discovered by Sir W. Ramsay. Symbol Kr; atomic number 36; atomic weight 83·7.

Ksar, obs. f. CZAR.

‖**Kshatriya, Kshatri** (kʃa·tri,ya, -trī). *E. Ind.* 1782. [Skr. *kshatriya*, f. *kshatra* rule.] A member of the military caste, the second of the four great castes or classes among the Hindus.

‖**Kudos** (kiū·dǫs). 1793 (COLERIDGE). [a. Gr. κῦδος.] Glory, fame, renown (*Univ. slang* and *colloq.*). Hence **Ku·dize** *v.*, **Ku·dos** *v.* (*nonce-wds.*), to praise, glorify.

Kufic, var. CUFIC.

‖**Kukang** (kū·kæŋ). 1861. [Malay.] The slow-paced lemur or loris.

Ku-Klux(-Klan) (kiū·klɒks,klæ·n). 1868. [Superseded *Klan*.] A secret society formed in the Southern U.S. after the civil war of 1861–5 to protect the whites and to oppose negro influence; its activities are associated with murder and outrage.

‖**Kukri** (ku·krī). 1811. [Hindī *kukrī*.] A curved knife, broadening towards the point, used by the Gorkhas of India.

Kulan, var. of KOULAN.

‖**Kultur** (kultū·r). [Ger., = culture.] Applied derisively to German civilization, esp. as exemplified by their method of warfare.

Kumis, -iss, -ys, var. of KOUMISS.

‖**Kümmel** (kü·mĕl). 1882. [Ger. Cf. CUMIN.] A liqueur, flavoured with cumin, made in North Germany.

‖**Kunkur** (kɒ·ŋkɒɹ). *E. Ind.* Also **concher, kankar**, etc. 1793. [Hindī *kankar*.] A coarse kind of limestone found in India, in large tabular strata, or interspersed throughout the surface soil, in nodules of various sizes; used for lime, and also in road-making.

‖**Kupfernickel** (ku·pfəɹ,ni:k'l). 1796. [Ger., f. *kupfer* copper + *nickel* NICKEL.] *Min.* = NICCOLITE.

‖**Kuphar** (ku·fāɹ). 1800. [ad. Arab. *quffah*.] A circular coracle of wicker-work covered with skins, used on the Euphrates.

‖**Kurgan** (kurga·n). 1889. [Russ., of Tartar origin.] A prehistoric sepulchral tumulus or barrow in Russia and Tartary.

‖**Kursaal** (kū·r,zāl). 1849. [Ger., f. *kur*, *cur*, CURE *sb.*[1] + *saal* hall, room.] A public building at a German health resort, provided for the use of visitors.

‖**Kusima·nse.** 1861. [Native name.] A small burrowing carnivorous animal, *Crossarchus obscurus*, of W. Africa.

Kuskus, var. of KHUS-KHUS (= CUSCUS[2]).

Kutch, Kutcha, var. of CUTCH[2], CUTCHA.

‖**Kuttar** (kɒtā·ɹ). *E. Ind.* 1696. [Hindī *kaṭṭār*:—Skr. *kaṭṭāra*.] A short Indian dagger, having a handle of two parallel bars, joined by a cross-piece.

‖**Kvass** (kvas). 1553. [Russ. *kvas*.] A fermented beverage in use in Russia; rye beer.

Ky, pl. of COW (now *Sc.* and *n. dial.*).

‖**Kyabuka, kiabooca** (kəiăbū·kă). 1831. [Malay *kayu-buku* knot-wood.] A Malaysian tree (*Pterospermum indicum*) furnishing an ornamental wood, also called *Amboyna wood*.

‖**Kyang** (kyæŋ *monosyll.*). Also **kiang.** 1882. [Tibetan.] A Tibetan species of wild horse or ass (*Equus kiang*).

Kyanite, var. CYANITE, now more usual.

Kyanize (kəi·ănəiz), *v.* 1837. [f. J. H. *Kyan*, inventor of the process + -IZE.] *trans.* To treat (wood) with a solution of corrosive sublimate, to prevent decay.

Kyano-, var. f. CYANO-; **Kyanophyll** (kəi,æ·nŏfil) [Gr. φύλλον leaf], Kraus's name for a blue-green substance, supposed to be a constituent of chlorophyll.

Kyanol (kəi·ănǫl). 1855. [f. Gr. κύανος CYANO- + -OL.] A synonym of ANILINE.

†**Kyd, kydde,** *v.* (*pseudo-arch.*) 1530. [Evolved from ME. *kyd, i-kyd*, pa. pple. of KITHE *v.*, misused by Spenser.] *trans.* To know. *Sheph. Cal.* Dec. 92, 93.

Kye, pl. of Cow (now *Sc.* and n. dial.).

Kyke, obs. f. KEEK.

Kyle (kəil). *Sc.* 1549. [a. Gael. *caol* (kōl), 'narrow strait or sound'.] A narrow channel between two islands, or an island and the mainland; a sound, a strait.

‖**Kylie** (kəi·li). *W. Austral.* 1839. [Native name.] A boomerang.

‖**Kylin** (kī·li·n). Also **kilin.** 1857. [ad. Chinese *ch'i-lin* (Wade), f. *ch'i* male + *lin* female.] A fabulous animal of composite form, figured on Chinese and Japanese pottery.

Kylix: see CYLIX.

Kyloe (kəi·lŏ). *Sc.* 1727. [? related to KYLE.] One of a small breed of cattle with long horns reared in the Highlands and Western Islands of Scotland.

Kymnel(l(e, etc.: see KIMNEL.

Kymograph (kəi·mǫgraf). 1867. [f. Gr. κυμο-, comb. f. κῦμα wave + -GRAPH.] An instrument for graphically recording variations of pressure of a fluid, esp. in the vessels of a living animal. Also called *kymogra·phion.* Hence **Kymogra·phic** *a.*

Kymric, Kyphosis: see CYMRIC, etc.

‖**Kyrie** (kəiᵊri, -i,ĭ, ki·rie). 1519. [Short for *Kyrie eleison*; see next.] **1.** = next. **b.** *esp.* A musical setting of the Kyrie eleison in the Ordinary of the Mass, or of the Responses to the Commandments in the Anglican Communion Service. †**2.** = next, 2. –1582.

‖**Kyrie eleison, eleëson** (ki·rie ėlē·isǫn). ME. [The Gr. words Κύριε ἐλέησον 'Lord, have mercy', occurring in the Gr. text of *Ps.* cxxii. 3, etc. Very variously pronounced in English.] **1.** *Eccl.* The words of a short petition used in Eastern and Roman Churches, esp. at the beginning of the Mass; represented in the Anglican service by the words, 'Lord, have mercy upon us'. **b.** A musical setting of these words. †**2.** *transf.* A complaint; a scolding –1630.

‖**Kyrielle** (kirie·l). 1887. [a. F.; shortened from *Kyrie eleison*; see prec.] A form of French poetry divided into little equal couplets, and ending with the same word which serves for the refrain.

Kyriologic, var. of CYRIOLOGIC.

Kyte (kəit). *Sc.* and *n. dial.* 1540. [?] The belly, stomach, paunch.

Kythe, var. sp. of KITHE *v.*

L

L (el), the twelfth letter of the modern and the eleventh of the ancient Roman alphabet, represents historically the Gr. *lambda* and ultimately the Semitic *lamed.*

The sound normally expressed by the letter is the 'point-side' consonant, i.e. a sound produced by the emission of breath at the sides, or one side, of the oral passage when it is partially closed by contact of the point of the tongue with the gums or palate.

I. **1.** An object shaped like the letter L. (Also written *ell.*) **a.** An extension of a building at right angles to the main block. **b.** An elbow-joint of a pipe. **2.** *attrib.* and *Comb.*, as *L-shaped* adj.

II. Symbolical uses. **1.** Used to denote serial order; applied e.g. to the twelfth, or more usually the eleventh (I or J being omitted) group or section, the eleventh sheet of a book, etc. **2.** The Roman numeral for 50.

III. Abbrevs. L. = †Lord, Lordship (pl. LL.); in *Bot.* Linnæus; Latin; in Stage directions, etc., left; Licentiate, as L. D. S. = Licentiate of Dental Surgery; (*Chem.*) Lithium. L or l [L. *libra*] = pound of money, now often repr. by £; e.g. 100*l.* or £100; see also L. S. D. l = in ship's log-book, lightning; in references, line, as bk. 4, l. 8; in solmization, la. l.b.w. (*Cricket*), leg before wicket; *l.c.* (*Printing*), lower case. L. C. M. (*Arith.*), least common multiple. L. M. (*Prosody*), long metre. See also LL., LXX.

La (lā), *sb.* ME. [Orig. first syllable of L. *labii*; see GAMUT.] The sixth note in Guido d'Arezzo's hexachords, retained in solmization as the sixth note of the octave.

La (lā, la), *int.* 1598. [Cf. LO (OE. *lá* and early ME. *la*).] An exclam. formerly used to introduce or accompany a conventional phrase, an address, or an emphatic statement; in recent use, an expression of surprise. Now only *dial.*, *vulgar*, and *arch.* †**b.** Repeated as an expression of derision (*Timon* III. i. 22).

‖**Laager** (lā·gəɹ), *sb.* Also **lager.** 1850. [S. Afr. Du., = Ger. *lager*, Du. *leger* (see LEAGUER *sb.*[1]).] A camp, encampment; esp. one in the open marked out by a circle of wagons. Hence ‖**Laa·ger** *v. trans.* to form (wagons) into a l.; to encamp (persons) in a l. Also *absol.* or *intr.*

Lab (læb), *v. Obs.* or *dial.* ME. Also **labb.** [? Onomatopœic.] *trans.* and *intr.* To blab –1475. So **Lab** *sb.*, a blab, tell-tale.

Lab. Abbrev. of LABORATORY (sense 1).

Labadist (læ·bădist). 1753. [ad. F.] *Eccl. Hist.* A follower of Jean de *Labadie* (1610–74), who seceded from the Roman Church and founded a sect holding Quietist views. So **La·badism.**

‖**Labarum** (læ·bărǒm). 1658. [L., = Gr. λάβαρον; etym. unkn.] The imperial standard of Constantine the Great (306–337 A. D.), being the Roman military standard of the late Empire with Christian symbols added; hence *gen.*, a symbolical banner.

‖**Labba** (læ·bă). 1825. [? native name.] A cavy, *Cœlogenys paca*, native to Guiana.

Labby (læ·bi). 1901. [?] At Monte Carlo, a system in which the stakes are so arranged that a win cancels two previous losses.

‖**Labdanum** (læ·bdănǒm). Also †**lap-.** 1502. [med.L., f. L. *ladanum.*] = LADANUM.

Heap cassia, sandal-buds, and stripes Of l. BROWNING.

Labefactation (læ:bĭfæktē·ʃən). [ad. L. *labefactationem.*] = next. JOHNSON.

Labefaction (læbĭfæ·kʃən). 1620. [n. of action corresp. to LABEFY; see -FACTION.] A shaking, weakening; overthrow, downfall.

†**La·befy,** *v.* 1620. [ad. L. *labefacere* (f. root of *labare* to fall, totter + *facere* to make); see -FY.] *trans.* To weaken, impair.

Label (lē·bĕl), *sb.* ME. [a. OF. *label* (also *lablel*) ribbon, fillet, file (in *Her.*); etym. unkn.] **1.** A narrow band of linen, cloth, etc.; the infula of a mitre. †**2.** A strip of paper or parchment attached to a document by way of supplement; hence, a supplementary note or clause, a codicil. Also *fig.* –1706. †**3.** *Astron.* and *Surveying.* In an astrolabe, etc., a narrow thin brass rule used chiefly in taking altitudes –1674. †**4.** *gen.* A slip or strip of anything; e.g. of land, of iron, etc. –1686. **5.** *Her.* A mark of cadency distinguishing the eldest son of a family and consisting in a band drawn across the upper part of the shield having (usu. three) dependent points (*label of three points*); cf. FILE *sb.*[2] I. 5. ME. **6.** A narrow strip of material attached to a document to carry the seal 1494. **7.** A slip of paper, cardboard, metal, etc. for attaching to an object and bearing its name, description, or destination. (The chief current sense.) Also *fig.* 1679. †**b.** An adhesive postage-stamp, etc. 1840–1900. **8.** *Arch.* (also *l.-mould, -ing*) A moulding over a door, window, etc.; a dripstone 1823.

1. A knit night-cap..With two long labels button'd to his chin BP. HALL. **2.** *Cymb.* v. v. 430. **7.** The hamper was directed by a l. on the cording DE FOE. **b.** Sheets of 1*d.* Labels containing 240 Stamps 1840.

Comb.: **l.-stop** *Arch.*, a boss or corbel supporting the end of a l.

Label (lē·bĕl), *v.* Also †**lable.** 1601. [f. prec.] *trans.* To attach a label to; *fig.* to designate as with a label, to set down in a category (*as* so-and-so).

fig. It would be most unjust to l. Byron..as a rhetorician only M. ARNOLD. Hence **La·beller.**

‖**Labellum** (lăbe·lǒm). 1826. [L., dim. of *labrum* lip.] **1.** *Bot.* The lower division or lip of an orchidaceous corolla 1830. **2.** *Entom.* One of a pair of tumid lobes terminating the proboscis of certain insects. Hence **Labe·lloid** *a. Bot.* lip-shaped.

Labial (lē·biăl). 1594. [ad. med.L. *labialis*, f. *labium* lip.]

A. *adj.* **1.** Of or pertaining to the lips 1650. **b.** *Anat.*, *Zool.*, etc. Pertaining to a lip, lip-like part, or LABIUM; like or serving as a lip 1656. **2.** *Phonetics.* Of a vocal sound: Formed by complete or partial closure of the lips, as p, b, m, f, v, w, and the 'rounded' vowels 1594.

1. The l. muscles that swelled with Vehement evolution of yesterday Marseillaises CLOUGH. *L. pipe*, an organ-pipe furnished with lips, a flue-pipe.

B. *sb.* **1.** A labial sound 1668. **2.** A labial part or organ, e. g. one of the labial palpi of insects, etc. 1885.

Hence **La·bialism,** tendency to labialize sounds. **La·bialize** *v.* to render (a sound) labial in character; to round (a vowel); hence **Labializa·tion.**

Labiate (lē·bi,ĕt). 1706. [ad. mod.L. *labiatus*, f. LABIUM; see -ATE [2].]

A. *adj.* **1.** *Bot.* **a.** Lipped; having the corolla or calyx divided into two parts which suggest lips; bilabiate. **b.** Belonging to the N.O. *Labiatæ*, consisting of plants usually having bilabiate flowers, opposite leaves, and square stalks, e. g. the mints, ground-ivy, etc. **2.** *Anat.* and *Zool.* Resembling a lip or labium (Dicts.). So **La·biated** *a.* 1707

B. *sb. Bot.* A labiate plant 1845.

Labiatiflorous (lē:bi,ēⁱtiflōᵊrəs), *a.* 1855. [f. mod.L. *labiatus* + *-florus* + -OUS.] *Bot.* Having labiate flowers.

Labidometer (læbidǫ·mĭtəɹ). 1853. [f. Gr. λαβιδο-, λαβίς forceps + μέτρον -METER.] *Surg.* A pair of obstetric forceps with a scale attached for measuring the fœtal head.

Labile (lē·bil, læ·bil), *a.* 1447. [ad. L. *labilis*, f. *labi*; see -ILE.] **1.** Liable or prone to lapse. †**2.** Slippery (*lit.* and *fig.*) –1654. **3.** Prone to undergo displacement or change; unstable. Now only in *Physics* and *Chemistry.* 1603. **4.** *Electr.* Said of the application of a current by moving an electrode over an affected region 1888.

3. A l. state of equilibrium LD. SALISBURY. Hence **Labi·lity,** proneness to lapse, instability.

Labio- (lē·bio), comb. f. L. *labium* lip, (*a*) *Phonetics*, 'formed with lips and —', as *labio-dental*, etc.; (*b*) *Path.*, 'having to do with lips and —', as *labio-alveolar*, etc.

‖**Labium** (lē·biǒm) 1597. [L., = 'lip'.] A lip or lip-like part. **1.** *Anat.* †**a.** One of the sides of the aperture of a vein. **b.** Chiefly in pl. **labia,** in full *labia pudendi*: The lips of the female pudendum 1722. **2.** In insects, crustaceans, etc., the floor of the mouth, which serves as an under lip 1828. **b.** *Conch.* The inner lip of a univalve shell 1839. **3.** *Bot.* The (lower) lip of a labiate corolla 1823.

Lablab (læ·blæb). 1823. [Arab.] The Egyptian or black bean, a native of India, but naturalized in most warm countries.

†**Laborant.** 1665. [ad. L. *laborantem.*] A laboratory workman; chemist's assistant –1694.

Laboratory (læ·bǒrătəri). 1605. [ad. med.L. *laboratorium*, f. L. *laborare*; see -ORY. Cf. ELABORATORY.] **1.** A building set apart for experiments in natural science, orig. and esp. in chemistry, and for the manufacture of chemicals, etc. Also *transf.* and *fig.* **2.** *Mil.* 'A department of an arsenal for the manufacture and examination of ammunition and combustible stores' (Voyle) 1716. **3.** *Metall.* 'The space between the fire and flue-bridges of a reverberatory furnace in which the work is performed; also called the *kitchen* and the *hearth*' (Raymond) 1839. **4.** *attrib.*, as *l.-work*, etc. 1769.

1. *fig.* A notion neatly turned out of the l. of the mind J. H. NEWMAN. Hence **La·borato·rial** *a.*

Laborious (lăbōᵊriəs), *a.* ME. [ad. F. *laborieux*, or ad. L. *laboriosus*, f. *labor*; see

-IOUS.] **1.** Given to labour; hard-working. **b.** = LABOURING *ppl. a.* **1.** 1777. **2.** Toilsome ME. **b.** Of concrete objects: Entailing labour in construction, execution, or working. **3.** *Midwifery.* Attended with severe labour 1637. †**4.** Pertaining to labour. QUARLES.

1. All..combine to drive The lazy Drones from the l. Hive DRYDEN. b. The l. classes BURKE. 2. Hate not l. worke, neither husbandrie *Ecclus.* vii. 15. b. L. orient ivory sphere in sphere TENNYSON. Hence **Labo·rious-ly** *adv.*, **-ness.** So †**La·borous** *a.* ME. -1782.

Labour, labor (lēⁱ·bəɹ), *sb.* ME. [a. OF. *labor, labour* (mod.F. *labeur*), ad. L. *laborem.* In the British Isles the sp. with *-our* is usual, in U.S. *-or* is preferred.] **1.** Bodily or mental toil, esp. when painful or compulsory. **2.** *spec.* in mod. use: Physical exertion directed to the supply of the material wants of the community 1776. **b.** The general body of labourers and operatives who take this part in production. Chiefly *attrib.* 1880. **3.** An instance of bodily or mental toil ME. **4.** The product or result of toil. Also *pl. Obs.* exc. *arch.* ME. †**5.** Trouble taken. (Occas. *pl.*) -1656. **6.** The pains of childbirth; travail 1545. Also *fig.* †**7.** Eclipse. DRYDEN.

1. Man goeth forth vnto his worke: and to his l., vntill the euening *Ps.* civ. 23. Pleasure is l. too, and tires as much COWPER. Phr. *Hard l.*: see HARD *a.* IV. 2. 2. L., therefore, is the real measure of the exchangeable value of all commodities ADAM SMITH. b. The parliamentary representation of l. (*mod.*). 3. *A l. of Hercules*, a task requiring enormous strength. *L. of love*: see LOVE *sb.* 4. The waxen L. of the Bees DRYDEN. 6. The Queens in Labor They say in great Extremity SHAKS. *fig.* As if nature were..in l. to produce excellency BACON.

attrib. and *Comb.*, as *l. member, question*, etc.; *l.-saving* adj.; *l.-dimmed* adj.; also **l. exchange,** a State office where workers and employers of labour may be accommodated; **-market,** the supply of unemployed l. with reference to the demand for it; **-party** (also *Independent Labour Party*), a political party claiming to further the interests of the labouring or wage-earning classes; **-yard,** a yard in a workhouse or prison, where enforced l. is done by the inmates.

Hence **La·bourless, la·borless** *a.* without l.; requiring or doing no l.

Labour, labor (lēⁱ·bəɹ), *v.* ME. [a. F. *labourer*, ad. L. *laborare*, f. *labor-, labor* (see prec.).]

I. *trans.* **1.** To spend labour upon (the ground, etc.); to cultivate (now *poet.* or *arch.*); to work (a mine). **2.** *gen.* To work upon; to produce or execute with labour. *Obs.* or *arch.* ME. †**3.** To use labour upon in rubbing, or the like; *hence*, to rub, pound, beat, etc. -1661. **4.** To belabour. *Obs.* exc. *dial.* 1594. **5.** To treat with great pains; to work out in detail, elaborate (a point, a question) 1449. **6.** To work with a view to (a result); to work hard for (a cause, etc.). *Obs.* or *arch.* ME. †**7.** To endeavour to influence or persuade -1633. †**8.** (with compl.) To bring into a specified condition or position by strenuous exertion -1697. †**9.** To work; to use in some work -1671; to cause to undergo fatigue. *arch.*

1. The English labourer..hazards much when he labours land for himself A. YOUNG. 2. They..l. Honey to sustain their Lives DRYDEN. 5. Though he labours this point, yet [etc.] BURKE. In a single figure, parts are often highly laboured 1846. 6. How earnestly I laboured that re-union BURKE. 8. Sisyphus that labours up the Hill The rowling Rock in vain DRYDEN.

II. *intr.* **1.** To exert oneself, toil; to work hard or against difficulties ME. **2.** To strive (*for* some end or *to* do something) ME. †**3.** To exert one's influence. Const. *to* (a person). -1587. **4.** To move, *esp.* with painful exertion (*lit.* and *fig.*) Now *rare.* ME. **5.** To be troubled or distressed, as by disease, want, etc.; to suffer from some impediment or defect. Const. *under* (†*of, with, on, in*). ME. †**6.** Of women: To travail. Also *fig.* -1711. **7.** Of a ship: To roll or pitch heavily 1627.

1. He that laboryth not, let him not eate BRINKLOW. 2. I laboured for peace COVERDALE *Ps.* cxx. 7. L. not to comfort me *Isa.* xxii. 4. 4. Make not all the people to l. thither *Josh.* vii. 3. 5. To l. under an entire misapprehension KINGSLEY. 6. All women labouryng of chylde *Bk. Com. Prayer.* Hence †**La·bourable** *a.* capable of being laboured. **La·boured, la·bored** *ppl. a.* highly elaborated; showing indications of excessive labour; heavy, wanting in spontaneity.

Labourer, laborer (lēⁱ·bərəɹ). ME. [f. LABOUR *v.* + -ER[1].] One who labours. **1.** One who performs physical labour as a service or for a livelihood; *spec.* one who does work requiring chiefly bodily strength (often differentiated as *agricultural, dock, mason's l.*, etc.). **2.** *gen.* One who does work of any kind ME. **3.** A working insect, 'worker' 1601.

1. *Statute of Labourers*, mod. designation of the statute *De Servientibus* (23 Edw. III), regulating the rate of wages. An intelligent villager—not a labourer, but a man of the working-class 1891. 2. The l. is worthy of his hire *Luke* x. 7.

Labouring, laboring (lēⁱ·bəriŋ), *vbl. sb.* ME. [f. as prec. + -ING[1].] The action of LABOUR *v.* Also *attrib.*

Labouring, laboring (lēⁱ·bəriŋ), *ppl. a.* ME. [f. as prec. + -ING[2].] **1.** That labours; *esp.* performing unskilled labour, as in *l. man, population.* †**2.** Of a woman: Suffering the pangs of childbirth. Also *transf.* -1704. **3.** Striving against pressure or some obstacle; that is in trouble or distress; (of the heart) struggling under emotion or suppressed feeling, also heaving, palpitating; (of a ship) rolling or pitching heavily. (Often with some reference to 2.) ME. †**b.** Of the moon: Eclipsed. (A Latinism.) -1665.

1. I..oar'd with lab'ring arms along the flood POPE. Phr. *Labouring oar* the oar which requires most labour to work it; hence *fig.* 2. The l. mountain must bring forth a mouse DRYDEN. Hence **La·bouringly** *adv.*

Labourism (lēⁱ·bəriz'm). 1903. [f. LABOUR *sb.* + -ISM.] The principles and practice of the Labour Party. Hence **La·bourist, -ite.**

Laboursome, laborsome (lēⁱ·bəɹsɒm), *a.* 1551. [f. LABOUR *sb.* + -SOME.] †**1.** = LABORIOUS **1.** -1620. **2.** = LABORIOUS **2.** Now *rare* or *dial.* 1577. **3.** Of a ship: Liable to pitch and roll in a heavy sea 1691. Hence **La·boursome-ly** *adv.*, **-ness.**

Labrador (læ:brădō·ɪ), name of a large peninsula in British N. Amer.: **L. blue,** the blue of labradorite; **L. dog,** a variety of the Newfoundland dog; **L. duck,** a sea-duck of N. Amer.; **L. feldspar, spar, stone** (also simply *labrador*) = LABRADORITE; **L. tea,** *Ledum latifolium* and *L. palustre* of N. Amer., which have leaves that have been used for tea.

Labradorite (læbrădō·rəit). 1814. [f. prec. + -ITE.] *Min.* A kind of feldspar from Labrador, which shows a brilliant variety of colour when turned in the light.

†**Labras.** Pistol's blunder for L. *labra*, pl. of *labrum* lip. *Merry W.* I. i. 166.

Labret (lēⁱ·brĕt). 1857. [f. next + -ET.] An ornament inserted in the lip.

‖**Labrum** (lēⁱ·brɒm). *Pl.* **labra.** 1816. [L., cogn. w. LABIUM.] A lip or lip-like part. **a.** In insects, etc.: The upper border or covering of the mouth. **b.** *Conch.* The outer lip of a univalve shell. Hence **La·bral** *a.*

Laburnum (lăbɒ̄·ɹnɒm). 1578. [L. (Pliny).] A small leguminous tree, *Cytisus Laburnum*, with profuse racemes of bright-yellow flowers. Applied also to similar plants.

Labyrinth (læ·birinþ), *sb.* 1548. [ad. L., a. Gr. λαβύρινθος, of unkn. origin.] **1.** An intricate structure of intercommunicating passages, through which it is difficult to find one's way without a clue; a maze 1549. **2.** *transf.* An intricate or tortuous arrangement (of physical features, buildings, etc.) 1615. **b.** (*a*) *Metall.* A series of channels used for distributing and separating the ores in the order of the coarseness of grain 1839. (*b*) A chamber of many turnings for the condensation of fumes arising from dry distillation, etc. 1875. **3.** *Anat.* A complex cavity hollowed out of the temporal bone, consisting of a bony capsule (*osseous l.*) and a delicate membranous apparatus (*membranous l.*) contained by it; the internal ear 1696. **b.** Applied to other organs of intricate structure 1774. **4.** *fig.* An entanglement, maze of things, events, ideas, etc. 1548.

1. Crete will boast the L. SPENSER. Labyrinths are only proper for large gardens, and the finest in the world is said to be that of Versailles 1753. 2. Leyden lies..in the midst of a l. of rivulets and canals 1777. 4. The l. of the statutes under which London is governed 1885. *Comb.* **l. fret** *Arch.*, a fret, with many turnings, in the form of a l. Hence **La·byrinth** *v. trans.* to enclose in or as in a l.; to arrange in the form of a l. **Labyri·nthian, Labyri·nthic, -al, Labyri·nthine** *adjs.* pertaining to, of the nature or form of, a l.; *fig.* intricate, inextricable. So **Labyri·nthiform** *a.*

Labyrinthodon (læbiri·nþŏdǫn). 1847. [mod.L., f. Gr. λαβύρινθος + ὀδοντ-, ὀδούς tooth.] *Palæont.* Any large fossil amphibian of the genus *Labyrinthodon*, characterized by teeth of labyrinthine structure having the enamel folded and sunk inward. So **Labyri·nthodont. A.** *sb.* = prec. 1841. **B.** *adj.* Having labyrinthine teeth; *spec.* pertaining to the genus *Labyrinthodon* of fossil amphibians 1867.

Lac[1] (læk). 1553. [ad. Hindustani *lākh* :—Skr. *lākshā*, also *rākshā*.] **1.** (Also *gum-lac.*) The dark-red resinous incrustation produced on certain trees by the puncture of an insect (*Coccus lacca*), and used in the East as a scarlet dye. When melted, strained, and formed into irregular thin plates, it is known as *shell-lac* or SHELLAC. †**2.** The colour of lac; crimson; a pigment prepared from lac -1763. †**3.** = LACQUER 2 a, b. -1727. **4.** Ware coated with lac 1662.

attrib. and *Comb.*: **l.-cochineal,** the insect that produces l. (*Coccus lacca*); **-dye,** a scarlet dye prepared in India from l.; **-lake,** the purple pigment obtained from l. Hence †**Lac** *v.* to lacquer 1698-1727.

Lac[2], **lakh** (læk). *Anglo-Ind.* 1613. [ad. Hindustani *lākh* :—Skr. *laksha* masc. and neut., *lakshā* fem.] One hundred thousand; *occas.*, an indefinite number; *spec.* of coins, esp. in *a l. of rupees.*

Laccic (læ·ksik), *a.* 1794. [f. mod.L. *lacca* LAC[1] + -IC.] *Chem.* Only in *l. acid*, the acid procured from lac.

Laccin (læ·ksin). 1838. [f. as prec. + -IN.] The colouring principle in lac.

Laccolite (læ·kŏləit). 1877. [f. Gr. λάκκος a reservoir + -LITE.] *Geol.* A mass of igneous rock thrust up through the sedimentary beds, and giving a dome-like form to the overlying strata. var. **La·ccolith.**

Lace (lēⁱs), *sb.* [ME. *las*, ad. OF. *laz, las* (mod.F. *lacs*), f. pop.L. **lacium* (L. *laqueum*) a noose.] †**1.** A net, noose, snare. Usu. *fig.* -1603. †**2.** A cord, line, string, thread, or tie. Also *transf.* and *fig.* -1650. **3.** *spec.* **a.** A string or cord serving to draw together opposite edges, e. g. of bodices, boots, etc., by being passed through eyelet-holes or over hooks, etc. and pulled tight ME. †**b.** A cord used to support a sword, etc.; a baldric, belt -1597. **4.** Braid for trimming men's coats, etc. Now only in *gold, silver l.* 1530. **5.** A delicate open-work fabric of linen, cotton, silk, woollen, or metal threads, usually with inwrought or applied patterns 1555. **6.** A dash of spirits mixed with some beverage, esp. coffee 1704.

3. She was indeed a Pedler's daughter, and sold many Laces SHAKS. 4. In a scarlet waistcoat, with rich gold l., and a gold-lace hat BOSWELL. 6. He drinks his coffee without l. (or perh. = 'sugar') PRIOR. *Comb.*: **l.-bark (tree),** (*a*) a W. Indian shrub (*Lagetta lintearia*), so called from the lace-like layers of its inner bark; (*b*) in New Zealand, *Plagianthus betulinus*, ribbon-wood; **-glass,** Venetian glass with lace-like designs; **-pillow,** the pillow or cushion which is laid on the lap of a woman making pillow-lace; **-woman,** one who works or deals in l.

Lace (lēⁱs), *v.* ME. [ad. OF. *lacier* (F. *lacer*):—pop.L. **laciare* to ensnare, f. **lacium*; see prec.] †**1.** *trans.* To catch in, or as in, a noose or snare -1485. **2.** To fasten or tighten with, or as with, a lace or string. In mod. use *spec.* to fasten or tighten (boots, stays, etc.) with laces. Also with *down, on, together.* Also *transf.* and *fig.* ME. **b.** *intr.* (quasi-*pass.*) To admit of being fastened or tightened with laces 1792. **3.** To compress the waist of (a person) by drawing the laces tight. Also *fig.* 1566. **b.** *refl.*, and *intr.* for *refl.* 1650. **4.** *trans.* To thread or interlace (a fabric) *with* a lace, string, etc.; to embroider. Chiefly in *pa. pple.* 1483. **b.** To pass (a cord, etc.) in and out *through* a fabric, *through* holes, etc. Also *fig.* 1638. **5.** To trim with lace 1599. **6.** To diversify *with* streaks of colour 1592. **7.** To lash, beat, thrash 1599. †**8.** *Cookery.* To make incisions in (the breast of a bird) -1796. **9.** To mingle or dash (*with* spirits or †sugar) 1677.

2. Hir shoes were laced on hir legges hye CHAUCER.

3. Rather straitly laced in her Presbyterian stays SCOTT. Phr. *To l. in*: to compress the waist by lacing. *intr.* I can..l. in to sixteen inches 1871. **4.** Oblong vellum binding laced with cat-gut 1880. **5.** Cloth a gold, and cuts, and lac'd with siluer SHAKS. **6.** Here lay Duncan, His Siluer skinne, lac'd with his Golden Blood SHAKS. **7.** If I meet thee, I will l. thee roundly 1615.

Comb., as *l.-boots* 1827; also *l.-up* adj. and sb. 1836.

Laced (lēⁱst), *ppl. a.*[1] 1533. [f. LACE *v.* + -ED[1].] In the senses of the vb.

Phr. †*L. mutton* (slang): a strumpet. *Two Gent.* I. i. 102.

†**Laced,** *ppl. a.*[2] 1486. [orig. *lassed*, for *lessed*, pa. pple. of LESS *v.*] *Her.* Lessened, diminished –1586.

Lacedæmonian (læ:sĭdĭmōᵘ·niăn). 1545. [f. L. *Lacedæmonius*, Gr. Λακεδαιμόνιος + -AN.] **A.** *adj.* **a.** Of or pertaining to Lacedæmon (Sparta) or its people. **b.** Of speech, etc. = LACONIC. **B.** *sb.* A Spartan.

La·ce-piece. 1874. [? f. LACE *sb.* + PIECE.] The part of the prow of a wooden vessel above the cut-water and behind the figure-head.

Lacerable (læ·sĕrăb'l), *a.* 1656. [ad. late L. *lacerabilis*, f. *lacerare*.] Susceptible of laceration. Hence **Lacerabi·lity.**

Lacerate (læ·sĕrĕt), *ppl. a.* 1542. [ad. L. *laceratus*, *lacerare*.] **1.** Mangled, torn, lacerated. Also *fig.* **2.** *Bot.* and *Zool.* Having the edge or point irregularly cut or cleft; jagged 1776. Hence **La·cerately** *adv.*

Lacerate (læ·sĕrēⁱt), *v.* 1592. [f. L. *lacerat-*, *lacerare*, f. *lacer* mangled.] **1.** *trans.* To tear, mangle; to tear to pieces. **2.** *esp.* To afflict, distress, harrow (the heart) 1645.

1. Feet..lacerated by the thorns FARRAR. Hence **Lacera·tion, La·cerative** *a. rare.*

†**Lacert**[1]. *rare.* ME. [ad. L. *lacerta* or *lacertus*.] A lizard –1696.

†**Lacert**[2]. ME. [a. OF. *lacerte*, ad. L. *lacertus* fleshy part of the arm (? similative use of *lacertus* lizard; cf. *musculus* muscle, lit. 'little mouse').] A muscle –1696. So †**Lacertose, lacertous** *adjs.* muscular.

Lacertian (lăsɔ̄·ɹtiăn, -ʃiăn). 1822. [f. L. *lacerta* lizard + -IAN.] **A.** *adj.* Of or pertaining to the lizards or *Lacertilia*; lizard-like, saurian 1843. **B.** *sb.* A lacertilian; a lizard. So **Lace·rtine** *a.*

Lacertilian (læ:sɔɹti·liăn). 1854. [f. mod.L. *Lacertilia*, pl. the lizard tribe + -AN.] **A.** *adj.* Belonging to the *Lacertilia*. **B.** *sb.* [sc. *animal*].

Lacery, *sb.* (lēⁱ·səri). 1893. [f. LACE *sb.* + -ERY.] Lace-like work.

Lacet (lēⁱse·t). 1862. [f. LACE *sb.* + -ET.] Applied to a kind of braid used with crochet work or lace stitches.

Laches (læ·tʃẽz), *sb.* [ME. *lacchesse, lachesse*, a. OF. *laschesse*, f. OF. *lasche*; see LASH *a.* and -ESS[2]. Cf. *riches*.] †**1.** Remissness, negligence; also, an act of neglect –1494. **2.** *Law.* Negligence in the performance of a legal duty; delay in asserting a right, claiming a privilege, or applying for redress 1574. **b.** *transf.* Culpable negligence in general 1844. Also †**Laches** *a.* remiss; whence †**Lachesness.**

2. b. The l. of this ministry DISRAELI.

‖**Lachesis** (læ·kĕsis). 1872. [mod.L., a. Gr. Λάχεσις, one of the Fates.] *Zool.* A genus of venomous American snakes of the rattlesnake family (*Crotalidæ*).

†**Lachrymable, lacrymable,** *a.* 1490. [ad. L. *lacrimabilis*.] **1.** Meet for tears; lamentable –1648. **2.** Expressive of mourning –1635.

‖**Lachryma Christi** (læ·krimă kri·stəi). Also †**lachrymæ Christi,** and *simply* **lacrima, -mæ.** 1670. [L., = Christ's tear(s.] A strong sweet red wine of southern Italy.

Lachrymal (læ·krimăl). 1541. [ad. med.L. *lacrimalis, lachrymalis*, f. L. *lacrima, lacruma*, OL. *dacruma*, cogn. w. Gr. δάκρυ a tear. The *ch* is the med.L. *ch* written for *c* before L. *r*, as in *anchor*, etc. The correct sp. of this and the allied words would be *lacrim-*.]

A. *adj.* **1.** *Anat.* and *Phys.* Designating the organs concerned in the secretion of tears, and connected structures, etc. 1597. **2.** Of or pertaining to tears; *occas.*, given to, or indicative of, weeping. *L. vase*, one to hold tears. 1803.

2. The l. and suspirious clergy SYD. SMITH.

B. *sb.* **1.** *pl.* The lachrymal organs 1541. **b.** *Anat.* A lachrymal bone. MIVART. **2.** *pl.* Fits of weeping 1753. **3.** = LACHRYMATORY *sb.* 1769.

Lachrymation (lækrimēⁱ·ʃən). 1572. [ad. L. *lacrimationem*, f. *lacrimare* to shed tears.] The shedding of tears; weeping.

Lachrymatory (læ·krimătəri). 1658. [ad. L. type **lacrimatorius*, f. as prec.]

A. *adj.* Of or pertaining to tears; causing a flow of tears. *L. vase* = B. 1849.

B. *sb.* A vase to hold tears 1658.

No .. Lachrymatories, or Tear-Bottles SIR T. BROWNE. So **La·chrymary** *a.* and *sb.* 1705.

La·chrymist. 1620. [f. L. *lacrima* tear + -IST.] A weeper.

Lachrymose (læ·krimōᵘs), *a.* 1661. [ad. L. *lacrimosus*.] †**1.** Having the nature of tears. LOVELL. **2.** Given to tears; tearful 1727; mournful 1822. Hence **La·chrymosely** *adv.* var. **La·chrymous** 1490.

Lacing (lēⁱ·siŋ), *vbl. sb.* ME. [f. LACE *v.* + -ING[1].] **1.** The action of LACE *v.* **2.** *concr.* or quasi-*concr.* **a.** A fastening, tie; a shoestring ME. **b.** Braiding for men's clothes 1593. **c.** The coloured border on the petal of a flower, etc. 1844. **d.** = LACE *sb.* 6. 1862. **3.** *techn.* **a.** *Bridge-building.* (See quot.) **b.** *Mining.* (*a*) Timbers placed across the tops of bars or caps to secure the roof between the gears. (*b*) Strips or light bars of wrought iron bent over at the ends and wedged in tight between the bars and the roof. 1883.

1. The sound l. which the young rascal should inevitably receive 1893. **3. a.** *Lacing*, a system of bars, not intersecting each other at the middle, used to connect the two channels of a strut in order to make them act as one member 1885.

‖**Lacinia** (lăsi·niă). Pl. **-iæ.** 1668. [L., = lappet.] **1.** *Bot.* A slash in a leaf, petal, etc.; the slender lobe thus produced. **2.** *Entom.* The apex of the maxilla, esp. when slender 1826.

Laciniate (lăsi·niĕt), *a.* Also *erron.* lacinate. 1760. [f. prec. + -ATE[2].] *Bot.* and *Zool.* Cut into deep and narrow irregular segments; jagged, slashed. So **Laci·niated** *ppl. a.* 1668. **Lacinia·tion,** a cutting into laciniæ or fringes 1846. **Laci·niolate** *a. Bot.* having minute laciniæ (Dicts.).

Lack (læk), *sb.*[1] [Early ME. *lac* = MLG. *lak*, MDu. *lac* deficiency, fault, blame.] †**1.** A defect; failing; a fault, offence, crime –1598. **2.** Deficiency, want, need (*of* something desirable or necessary); an instance of this ME. **3.** Indigence; also, famine, starvation 1555. †**4.** Absence –1605. **5.** quasi-*concr.* The thing wanting (*rare*) 1549.

1. The lacke is not in the law, but in vs LATIMER. **2.** L. of money 1753, of judgment RUSKIN. Phr. *No l.* (*of*): enough, plenty (of). *For* (*by, from, through*) *l. of*: for want (*rarely* loss) of. **5.** One great l. here and elsewhere is the green sod 1848.

†**Lack,** *sb.*[2] 1638. [See ALACK *int.* and GOOD *a.* II. 2.] Only in exclam. *Good l.!* –1807.

†**Lack,** *a.* 1479. [ad. ON. *lak-r* :—OTeut. **lako-*, cogn. w. LACK *sb.*[1]] **1.** Of a quantity: Short, wanting –1644. **2.** Missing 1591.

1. *Little l. of*: not far short of: Sicke, sicke, alas, and little l. of dead SPENSER.

Lack (læk), *v.* ME. [f. LACK *sb.*[1] or *a.* Cf. MDu. *laken* to be wanting, to blame.] **1.** *intr.* To be wanting or missing; to be deficient. Now only in *to be lacking*. **2.** *trans.* To be without; to be destitute of or deficient in ME. †**b.** with *cannot*: To do or go without –1592. †**c.** To perceive the absence of, miss. SHAKS. **3.** To stand in need of 1530. **4.** *intr.* To be short *of* something. Now *rare*. 1523.

1. In him lacked neither good will nor courage HALL. **2.** It withered away, because it lacked moisture *Luke* viii. 6. Learning we l., not books CRABBE. **c.** I shall be lou'd when I am lack'd SHAKS. **3.** What do you lacke? what is't you buy? B. JONS. **4.** He that giueth vnto the poore, shall not lacke *Prov.* xxviii. 27. *Comb.* **l.-all,** one who is in want of everything.

Lackadaisical (lækădēⁱ·zikăl), *a.* 1768. [f. next + -IC + -AL.] Like one who is given to crying 'Lackaday!'; full of vapid feeling or sentiment; affectedly languishing.

L. misses 1852, letters 1870. Hence **Lackadai·sical-ly** *adv.*, **-ness.**

Lackadaisy (læ·kădēⁱ:zi), *int.* (*sb.*, *a.*) 1792. [Extended f. LACKADAY.] = LACKADAY, hence as *sb.* the utterance of the interjection; as *adj.* = prec.

La·ckaday, *int. Obs.* or *arch.* 1695. [Aphet. f. ALACK-A-DAY.] = ALACK-A-DAY.

Lacker, var. of LACQUER *sb.* and *v.*

Lackey, lacquey (læ·ki), *sb.* 1529. [Earlier *alakay*, a. F. (*a*)*laquais* †kind of soldier, (later) servant, a. Cat. *al*(*a*)*cay*, Sp. *alacayo*, ad. Arab. *alkaid* ALCAYDE.] **1.** A (liveried) footman or valet. Also *fig.* †**2.** A camp follower 1556.

1. He was not her lackey, and..she might send some one else with her errands MOTLEY. **2.** The.. lackeys and dross of the camp LYTTON.

Comb.: **l.-caterpillar,** the caterpillar of the lackey-moth; **-moth,** a bombycid moth of the genus *Clisiocampa*, so called from the bright colours of the caterpillars, which are striped and decorated like footmen.

Lackey, lacquey (læ·ki), *v.* 1568. [f. prec.] †**1.** *intr.* To do service as a lackey, esp. as a running footman; to dance attendance, do menial service. Often *fig.* **2.** *trans.* To wait upon as a lackey; to dance attendance upon. Chiefly *transf.* and *fig.* 1596.

1. The Minutes (that lackey at the heeles of Time) run not faster away then do our joyes DEKKER. **2.** He had lacqueyed and flattered WALPOLE 1881.

Lackland (læ·klænd). 1594. [f. LACK *v.* + LAND *sb.*] **A.** *sb.* One who has no land. **B.** *adj.* Having no land.

John who inherited no territory.. was thence commonly denominated L. HUME.

Lack-Latin (stress variable). 1534. [f. LACK *v.* + LATIN *sb.*] †**A.** *sb.* One who knows little or no Latin; chiefly in *Sir John Lack-latin* = an ignorant priest. **B.** *adj.* Ignorant of Latin; unlearned.

Lack-lustre (stress variable). 1600. [f. LACK *v.* + LUSTRE.] **A.** *adj.* Wanting in brightness; orig. of the eye, after Shaks. **B.** *sb.* The absence of lustre (*rare*) 1788.

Lacmus (læ·kmɔ̆s). 1794. [ad. Du. *lakmoes*, f. *lak* LAC[1] + *moes* pulp.] = LITMUS.

Laconian (lăkōᵘ·niăn). 1602. [f. L. *Laconia* + -AN.] **A.** *adj.* Of or pertaining to Laconia or its inhabitants; Spartan. **B.** *sb.* An inhabitant of Laconia.

Laconic (lăkǫ·nik). 1583. [ad. Gr. Λακωνικός, f. Λάκων LACONIAN.] **A.** *adj.* **1.** = LACONIAN *a.* **2.** Laconian-like, esp. in speech and writing; brief, sententious 1589.

1. The severe L. Disciplin 1683. **2.** This l. fool makes brevity ridiculous DAVENANT.

B. *sb.* (The adj. used absol.) †**1.** A laconic speaker –1692. **2.** Laconic speech. *pl.* Brief or concise sentences. 1718.

2. Shall we never again talk together in l.? ADDISON. So †**Laco·nical** *a.* 1576–1698, **-ly** *adv.* **Laco·nicism** = LACONISM 2 and 2 b.

Laconism (læ·kǒniz'm). 1570. [ad. Gr. λακωνισμός, f. λακωνίζειν to LACONIZE.] **1.** Partiality for the Lacedæmonians (*rare*) 1655. **2.** The practice of imitating the Lacedæmonians, esp. in brevity of speech 1570. **b.** A laconic speech 1597.

2. His will was brief to l. 1858. **b.** The highway l. of 'your money or your life' D. JERROLD.

Laconize (læ·kǒnəiz), *v.* 1603. [ad. Gr. λακωνίζειν, f. Λάκων LACONIAN; see -IZE.] **1.** *intr.* To favour the Lacedæmonians, their customs, mode of speech, interests, etc. **2.** *trans.* To render Lacedæmonian 1873.

Lacquer, lacker (læ·kəɹ), *sb.* 1579. [ad. obs. F. *lacre* a kind of sealing-wax; conn. w. Pg. *lacca* LAC[1]. *Lacquer* is app. after F. *laque*.] †**1.** = LAC[1] 1. –1714. **2. a.** A gold-coloured varnish, chiefly pale shellac dissolved in alcohol, and tinged with saffron, anatta, etc.; used esp. as a coating for brass 1673. **b.** Any of various kinds of resinous varnish, esp. the 'Japanese lacquer', capable of taking a hard polish, and used for coating articles of wood, etc. 1697. **3.** Articles of wood coated with lacquer (sense 2 b); chiefly made in Japan, China, and India 1895.

2. b. Japanese l. is the product of a tree, the *Rhus vernicifera* 1889.

Comb.: l.-**ware** = sense 3; -**work**, the making of lacquer-ware; also = *lacquer-ware*.

Lacquer, lacker (læ·kəɹ), *v.* 1688. [f. prec. sb.] *trans.* To coat with lacquer; hence *gen.* to varnish. Also *transf.* and *fig.* Also with *over*.

fig. Lackered over with an outer coating of fair-seeming 1831. Hence **La·cquerer, la·ckerer.**

Lacquey, var. of LACKEY *sb.* and *v.*

Lacrim-, lacrym-: see LACHRYM-.

Lacrosse (lakrǫ·s). 1867. [F. *la* the + *crosse* a hooked stick.] A N. Amer. game resembling hockey, but the ball is driven and caught with a CROSSE.

Lactary (læ·ktări). *rare.* 1646. [ad. L. *lactarius*, f. *lact-, lac* milk.] A. *adj.* Of, pertaining to, or concerned with milk; milky. B. *sb.* A dairy 1669.

Lactate (læ·kteͥt). 1794. [f. LACT-IC + -ATE[4].] *Chem.* A salt of lactic acid.

Lactation (læktēͥ·ʃən). 1668. [f. L. *lactare* to suckle.] 1. The action of suckling. 2. The secretion of milk from the mammary glands 1857.

Lacteal (læ·ktiăl). 1633. [f. L. *lacteus* (f. *lact-, lac* milk) + -AL.]

A. *adj.* 1. Of, pertaining to, or consisting of milk 1658; like milk 1633. 2. *Anat.* Conveying a milky fluid, *sc.* chyle 1664.

2. They have l. vessels, or lymphatics 1843. Hence **La·cteally** *adv.* var. **La·ctean** *a.*

B. *sb. pl.* 1. *Anat.* The lymphatic vessels of the mesentery, conveying the chyle from the small intestine to the thoracic duct 1680. †2. *Bot.* The lactiferous ducts. GREW.

Lacteous (læ·ktiəs), *a.* 1646. [f. L. *lacteus* (see LACTEAL) + -OUS.] 1. Of the nature of milk. 2. Resembling milk, *esp.* in colour 1646. †3. = LACTEAL *a.* 2. BENTLEY.

2. †*L. circle*: the Milky Way. †*L. star*: one belonging to the Milky Way. **La·cteously** *adv.*

Lactescence (lækte·sĕns). 1684. [f. next; see -ENCE.] 1. A milky appearance. 2. *Bot.* Flow of sap from plants when wounded, usu. white, but occas. red 1760. So †**Lacte·scency** (in sense 1) 1756.

Lactescent (lækte·sĕnt), *a.* 1668. [ad. L. *lactescentem*, f. *lactescere*, inchoative vb. f. *lactēre* to be milky.] 1. Becoming milky in appearance. 2. Of plants: Yielding a milky juice 1673. ¶3. Used for: Producing or secreting milk 1796.

Lactic (læ·ktik), *a.* 1790. [f. L. *lact-, lac* milk + -IC.] *Chem.* Of or pertaining to milk.

L. acid ($C_3H_6O_3$), the acid formed in sour milk. *L. fermentation*, the souring of milk, by the decomposition of the milk sugar.

Lactiferous (lækti·fĕrəs), *a.* 1673. [f. L. *lactifer* (f. *lact(i)-, lac* milk + *-fer* bearing) + -OUS.] 1. Producing, secreting, or conveying milk 1691. 2. Conveying or yielding a milky fluid (in plants).

Lactifluous (lækti·fluəs), *a.* 1699. [f. L. *lact(i)-, lac* milk + *flu-, fluere* to flow + -OUS; cf. L. *mellifluus*.] Flowing with milk.

Lacto- (læ·kto), comb. f. L. *lact-, lac* milk; as in **lacto·meter, la·ctoscope,** instruments for gauging the purity of milk; **la·cto-pro·tein,** an albuminous constituent of milk.

Lactose (læ·ktōͧs). 1858. [f. L. *lact-, lac* + -OSE[2].] A saccharine substance in milk, commonly called sugar of milk.

Lacuna (lăkiū·nă). *Pl.* -æ (-ī), -as (-ăz). 1663. [a. L. *lacuna* a hole, f. *lacus* LAKE *sb.*[2]] 1. A hiatus, blank, missing part. 2. A gap, an empty space, spot, or cavity 1872. b. *Anat.* A mucous follicle; also, a space in the connective tissue giving origin to a lymphatic 1706. c. *Anat.* A small cavity in the bone substance 1845. d. *Bot.* An air-cell 1836. Hence **Lacu·nal** *a.* of, pertaining to, or like a l. **Lacu·nar** *a.* of or pertaining to a l. or lacunæ; characterized by lacunæ.

Lacunar (lăkiū·năr), *sb.* Pl. **-ars, -aria.** 1696. [a. L., f. *lacuna*.] a. A ceiling consisting of sunk or hollowed compartments. b. *pl.* The sunken panels in such a ceiling.

Lacunary (lăkiū·nări), *a.* 1716. [f. LACUNA + -ARY[2].] = LACUNAL *a.*, LACUNAR *a.*

Lacu·ne (1701), anglicized f. LACUNA.

Lacunose (lăkiū·nōͧs), *a.* 1777. [ad. L. *lacunosus*.] Full of lacunæ; *spec.* in *Nat. Hist.* Hence *lacunoso-*, comb. form.

Lacu·stral, *a. rare.* 1843. [f. as next + -AL.] = next.

Lacustrine (lăkʊ·strin), *a.* 1830. [f. L. *lacus* LAKE *sb.*[2], after analogy of *palustri-, paluster*, f. *palud-, palus* marsh + -INE.] Of or pertaining to a lake or lakes. Said *esp.* of plants or animals inhabiting lakes, and *Geol.* of strata, etc., which originated by deposition at the bottom of lakes; also with reference to 'lake dwellings'.

L. age, period, the period when lake-dwellings were common.

Lacy (lēͥ·si), *a.* Also **lacey.** 1804. [f. LACE *sb.* + -Y[1].] Consisting of, or resembling, lace.

Lad (læd). [ME. *ladde*, of unkn. etym.] †1. A serving-man; a man of low birth and position; a varlet -1721. 2. A boy, youth; a young man, young fellow. Applied familiarly (occ. ironically) to a man of any age. 1535.

Lad, obs. pa. t. and pple. of LEAD *v.*

‖**Ladanum** (læ·dănʊ̆m). 1551. [L., à. Gr. λάδανον, λήδανον, f. λῆδον mastic.] 1. A gum resin which exudes from plants of the genus *Cistus*, esp. *C. ladaniferus* and *C. creticus*. †2. = LAUDANUM 1627.

Ladder (læ·dəɹ), *sb.* [OE. *hlǣd(d)er* str. fem.:—OTeut. **hlaidrjā*, f. Teut. root *hlī-*: *hlai-* (whence LEAN *v.*[1]):—Aryan *klī-*; cf. Gr. κλῖμαξ ladder.] 1. An appliance made of wood, metal, or rope, usu. portable, consisting of a series of bars ('rungs') or steps fixed between two supports, for ascent and descent. †b. *esp.* The steps to a gallows -1655. c. *fig.* ME. 2. Applied to things resembling a ladder ME.; recently, a ladder-like hole in a stocking.

1. [He] oft a lather tooke To gather fruit 1621. c. Northumberland, thou L. wherewithall The mounting Bullingbrooke ascends my Throne SHAKS. Phr. *To kick down the l.*: to repudiate the friends or means that have helped one to rise in the world. 2. *Cart-l.*, a rack or framework at the front, back, or sides of a cart, to increase its carrying capacity ME. *Fish-l.* (see FISH *sb.*[1]).

Comb.: l.-**dredge,** a dredge with buckets carried round on a ladder-like chain; l. **shell,** a marine shell of the genus *Scalaria*, a wentletrap; l. **way,** a way by which one ascends or descends by means of a l., (*a*) in the deck of a ship, (*b*) in the shaft of a mine.

Hence **La·dder** *v.* to furnish with a l. or ladders; (of a stocking) to be worn into 'ladders'.

Laddie (læ·di). Chiefly *Sc.* 1546. [f. LAD + -IE.] A young lad, a lad. (A term of endearment.)

Lade (lēͥd), *sb.* 1706. [north. form of LODE (OE. *-lād, -gelād* in *wætergelād*, etc., ME. *waterlade*).] 1. A channel for leading water to a mill-wheel; a mill-race. Chiefly *Sc.* 1808. ¶2. Channel, water-course, mouth of a river (evolved from place-names in *-lade*, as Cricklade, etc.) 1706.

Lade (lēͥd), *v.* Pa. pple. **laden, laded.** [Com. Teut. str. vb.: OE. *hladan* (*hlōd, gehladen*).]

I. To load (pa. pple. *laden*). 1. *trans.* To put cargo on board (a ship). Also (now only in *pass.*) to load (a vehicle, an ass, etc.). b. To load *with*: To charge or fill abundantly. Now only in pa. pple. *laden*. 1481. c. To load oppressively. Now only (somewhat *arch.*) in pa. pple., burdened *with* sin, etc. 1538. 2. To put as a burden, freight, or cargo; now only, to ship (goods) as cargo OE. Also *absol.* or *intr.* †3. To load (a gun); also, to load (cartridges) in a gun -1690.

1. They laded their asses with the corne *Gen.* xlii. 26. He..help'd At lading and unlading the tall barks TENNYSON. b. A tree wel laden and charged of fruyte 1484. c. L. him with irons 1602. Laden with the sin which they had committed LANE. 2. It is impossible to l. or deliver Cargoes COLQUHOUN. *absol.* A pier..at which vessels..l. and unlade MORSE.

II. To draw water (pa. pple. *laded*). 1. *trans.* To draw (water); to take up or remove (water, etc.) from a river, a vessel, etc., with a ladle, scoop, or the like; to bale. (Now chiefly *techn.* and *dial.*) OE. Also *absol.* or *intr.* †2. To empty by 'lading' -1628.

1. To l. off the Whey clear from Curd TWAMLEY. 2. Like one that..chides the Sea..Saying hee'le l. it dry SHAKS.

Laden (lēͥ·d'n), *v.* 1514. [f. LADE *v.* + -EN.] = LADE *v.*

Lader (lēͥ·dəɹ). 1456. [f. as prec. + -ER[1].] One who lades; *esp.* one who freights a ship.

La-di-da (lādidā·). *slang.* 1883. [Imitative of 'swell' modes of utterance. The refrain of a comic song in 1880. Cf. LARDY-DARDY.] A derisive term for one who affects gentility; a 'swell'. Also *attrib.* or *adj.* and as *vb.*

Ladify; see LADYFY.

Lading (lēͥ·diŋ), *vbl. sb.* late ME. [f. LADE *v.* + -ING[1].] 1. The action of LADE *v.*; *esp.* the loading of a ship with its cargo. 2. *concr.* Freight, cargo 1526.

1. *Bill of l.* (see BILL *sb.*[3]).

Ladle (lēͥ·d'l), *sb.* [OE. *hlædel*, f. *hladan* LADE *v.*; see -EL.] 1. A large spoon with a cup-shaped bowl and long handle for lading liquids, etc. 2. *techn.* a. *Gunnery.* An instrument for charging with loose powder 1497. b. *Founding.* A pan with a handle, to hold molten metal for pouring. So in *Glass-making*, a similar instrument for conveying molten glass from the pot to the cuvette. 1483. 3. One of the float-boards of a water-wheel 1611.

1. Some stird the molten owre with ladles great SPENSER. *Comb.* l.-**board** = sense 3. Hence **La·dleful,** as much as fills a l.

Ladle (lēͥ·d'l), *v.* 1525. [f. prec.] *trans.* a. To fit up (a water-mill) with ladle-boards. b. To lift out with a ladle. Also with *out, up*; and *fig.* Hence **La·dler.**

b. He can l. you out Latin by the quart 1797.

Ladrone (lădrōͧ·n). 1745. [ad. Sp. *ladron* :—L. *latronem* robber.] Used *occas.* in books on Spain or Spanish America for: A highwayman. Also *attrib.*

La·d's love. *dial.* 1825. [Cf. BOY'S LOVE.] The Southernwood (*Artemisia Abrotanum*).

Lady (lēͥ·di), *sb.* [OE. *hlǣfdīge* wk. fem.; f. *hlāf* LOAF + root *dīg-* to knead; see DOUGH. The gen. sing. (OE. *hlǣfdīgan*) became in ME. coincident in form with the nom.; hence *lady-bird, Lady-day, Lady-chapel*, etc., where *lady* = (Our) Lady's.]

I. †1. The female head of a household -ME. 2. A woman who rules over subjects; the feminine corresp. to *lord*. Now *poet.* or *rhet.*, exc. in *lady of the manor*. OE. †b. *transf.* and *fig.* -1610. c. A woman who is the object of a man's devotion; a mistress, lady-love ME. 3. *spec.* The Virgin Mary. (Usu. *Our Lady* = L. *Domina Nostra*). OE. 4. A woman of superior social position; in mod. use, above a loosely-defined but not very high standard. Orig. the fem. analogue of *lord*; in mod. use, corresp. to *gentleman*. Often, merely a courteous synonym for 'woman', *esp.* in 'this lady'. See also YOUNG LADY. ME. b. *vocatively.* (*a*) In *sing.*, now only *poet.* or *rhet.* (*b*) In *pl.*, the usual term of address. ME. 5. A woman whose manners, habits, and sentiments are those characteristic of the higher ranks of society 1861. 6. As an honorific title (see below) ME. 7. Wife, consort. Now chiefly restricted to instances in which the formal title of 'Lady' is involved in the relationship; otherwise vulgar. ME. b. The female of an animal (cf. *Comb.* 1 a).

2. Great Ladie of the greatest Isle SPENSER. b. Rome, once the L. of the world 1601. c. Never a line from my l. yet! TENNYSON. 3. Phr. †*Our Lady's bands*: pregnancy. By Gods blessed Ladie (that was euer his othe) MORE. 4. What L. is that same? *L. L. L.* II. i. 192. This is giving the ladies reason, 'It is so because it is' TUCKER. Poor l. l.. But if she were a real l. she would never be an opera-singer 1886. b. Know you this paper, L.? SHELLEY. Phr. *L. of the lake*, the designation of a personage in the Arthurian legends, Nimue or Vivien. *L. of pleasure*, a courtesan. *L. of easy virtue*, a woman whose chastity is easily assailable. *L. of Babylon, of Rome*, abusive terms for the Roman Catholic Church, with reference to the 'scarlet woman' of the Apocalypse. *L. of the bedchamber, l.-in-waiting*, an attendant to a queen or princess. 6. (*a*) *Lady* is used as a less formal substitute for the designation of rank in speaking of a marchioness, countess, viscountess, or baroness; thus 'The Marchioness (of) A.' is spoken to, and of, as 'Lady A. (*b*) *Lady* (or more formally, *The Lady*) is prefixed to the Christian names of the daughters of dukes, marquises, and earls. (*c*) The wife of the holder of a courtesy title of *Lord* John B., etc., is known as '(The) Lady John B.' (*d*) The wife of a baronet or

other knight ('Sir John C.') is commonly spoken of as 'Lady C.' *L. Mayoress*: see MAYORESS. (*c*) *Lady* is prefixed to designations of relationship, by way of respectful address or reference; Answer for yourself, l. cousin FIELDING. 7. About the end of May, Duke Lauderdale came down with his L. in great pomp BURNET.

II. In transf. applications. **1.** A kind of butterfly; now *painted l.* 1611. **2.** The calcareous structure in the stomach of a lobster, fancifully supposed to resemble the outline of a seated female figure 1653. **3.** The smallest size of Welsh (and Cornish) roofing slates 1803.

Comb. **1.** General: **a.** with sense 'female', as in *l. actor, clerk, doctor, farmer, friend, president*, etc.; also with names of animals, as *l.-dog, -pack*, etc. **b.** with sense 'claiming to be regarded as a lady', as in *l.-cook, -housekeeper*, etc.

2. Special (in many cases orig. uses of *lady* genitive, in sense I. 3): **L.-altar,** an altar in a Lady chapel; so †*lady-mass*, †*-priest*; **l.-clock** = LADY-BIRD; **(Our) L. eve, even,** the day before a Lady day; **l.-help,** a woman engaged to perform domestic service and treated as a lady; **-killer** *joc.*, a man who is credited with power of fascination over women; **L.-tide,** the time of the year about Lady day. **b.** In names of plants: **l.-bracken,** the brake, *Pteris aquilina*; **-fern,** an elegant fern, *Athyrium Filix-femina*, etc.

3. With the genitive *lady's* (occas. *ladies'*): **ladies' gallery,** a gallery in the House of Commons reserved for ladies; **lady's maid,** a womanservant who attends to the toilet of a l.; **lady's** or **ladies' man,** a man who is devoted to female society; **ladies' school,** a school for the education of 'young ladies'. **b.** In names of plants, etc. (*Lady's* being here orig. a shortening of *Our Lady's*): **Lady's bedstraw** (see BEDSTRAW); **lady's bower,** clematis; **lady's comb,** the Shepherd's Needle, *Scandix Pecten*; **lady's delight,** the violet; **(Our) Lady's hair,** (*a*) the grass *Briza media*; (*b*) *Adiantum Capillus-veneris*, also called Venus' hair; **lady's thigh,** repr. F. *cuisse-madame*, a variety of pear; **lady's thimble,** (*a*) the Harebell; (*b*) the Foxglove; **lady's thumb** *U.S.*, *Polygonum Persicaria*.

Lady (lēⁱ·di), *v.* 1600. [f. LADY *sb.*] †**1.** *trans.* To make a lady of; to address as 'lady' –1614. **2.** *intr. To l. it*: to play the lady or mistress (*rare*).

Lady-bird (lēⁱ·di,bɔ̄ɹd). 1592. [In sense 1, f. LADY *sb.* I. 3 (genitive, as in LADY DAY).] **1.** Name for the coleopterous insects of the genus *Coccinella* 1704. **2.** A sweetheart, darling.

2. What Lamb: what Lady-bird *Rom. & Jul.* I. iii. 3.

Lady chapel. Orig. **Our lady** (or **Lady's**) **chapel.** 1439. A chapel dedicated to the Virgin, attached to large churches, often placed eastward of the high altar.

Lady-cow (lēⁱ·di,kau). 1606. [f. LADY *sb.* I. 3 (genitive).] = LADY-BIRD.

Lady day (lēⁱ·di,dēⁱ). Orig. **Our Lady day.** ME. [f. LADY *sb.* I. 3 (genitive).] Now only March 25th, the Feast of the Annunciation; formerly also Dec. 8th, the Conception of the Virgin, Sep. 8th, the Nativity, and Aug. 15th, the Assumption.

Lady-fish (lēⁱ·di,fiʃ). 1712. A name applied to many different species of fish, as *Albula vulpes, Harpe rufa, Scomberesox saurus, Sillago domina*.

Ladyfy, ladify (lēⁱ·difəi), *v.* 1602. [f. LADY *sb.* + -FY.] *trans.* To make a lady of; to call 'Lady'.

Ladyhood (lēⁱ·dihud). 1820. [f. LADY *sb.* + -HOOD.] **1.** The condition of being a lady; the qualities pertaining to a lady. **2.** Ladies collectively 1821.

Ladykin (lēⁱ·dikin). 1853. [f. LADY *sb.* + -KIN.] A little lady; *occas.* used as a term of endearment.

Ladylike (lēⁱ·diləik), *a.* 1586. [-LIKE.] **1.** Having the distinctive appearance or manner of a lady. Also *sarcastically* of men: Effeminate. 1601. **2.** Befitting a lady; sometimes depreciatory, effeminately delicate or graceful.

1. He is a very lady-like poet HAZLITT. **2.** You have not a very lady-like way of expressing yourself 1877. Hence **La·dylikeness.**

La·dy-love. Also pseudo-*arch.* **ladye-love.** 1733. [f. LADY *sb.*] **1.** A sweetheart. **2.** Love for ladies. BYRON.

Lady's cushion. Also †**Our Lady's cushion.** 1578. †**a.** The plant Thrift, *Armeria maritima*. **b.** The Mossy Saxifrage, *Saxifraga hypnoides*.

Lady's finger, lady-finger. *Pl. occas.* **ladies' fingers.** 1670. **1.** *sing.* and *pl.* The plant *Anthyllis vulneraria*, the Kidney Vetch. **2. a.** A kind of cake (cf. *finger-biscuit*). 1820. **b.** *Austral.* A kind of grape. Also, a banana. 1892. **3.** *U.S.* (*a*) A variety of the potato; (*b*) One of the branchiæ of the lobster; (*c*) A variety of apple.

Lady's glove. 1538. [Orig. LADY *sb.* I. 3.] The foxglove, *Digitalis purpurea*.

Ladyship (lēⁱ·diʃip). ME. [See LADY and -SHIP.] **1.** The condition of being a lady. **2.** The personality of a lady ME. †**3.** Kindness befitting a mistress. GOWER. **4.** A district governed by a lady. STEELE.

2. *Her, your l.*, a respectful substitute for *she, you*, referring to a lady; now only to one of the rank of 'Lady'. Also used *sarcastically*.

Lady's laces. 1597. The striped garden variety of *Phalaris arundinacea*.

Lady's mantle. 1548. [LADY *sb.* I. 3.] The rosaceous herb *Alchemilla vulgaris*. Also, with qualification, of other species.

Lady-smock. Also **lady's, ladies' smock.** 1588. The Cuckoo-flower, *Cardamine pratensis*. (Locally also, *Convolvulus sepium*.)

Ladie-smockes all siluer white SHAKS.

Lady's slipper. Also **ladies', lady slipper.** 1597. The orchidaceous plant *Cypripedium Calceolus*. Also applied to the cultivated Calceolaria, and the Bird's-foot Trefoil.

Lady's traces, tresses. 1548. Name for orchids of the genus *Spiranthes*; also, locally, for grasses of the genus *Briza*.

Læn (lēⁱn). [OE. *lǣn*; see LOAN *sb.*[1]] *OE. Law.* An estate held as a benefice. *Comb.*: **l.-land,** land held as 'læn'; **-right,** beneficiary right.

Læotropic (lī,otrǫ·pik), *a.* Also *erron.* leio-. 1883. [f. Gr. λαιός left + τροπικός turning.] Turned or turning to the left: said of the whorls of a shell; opp. to *dexiotropic*.

Læt (lēⁱt). [OE. *lǣt* (found once) :—OTeut. **lǣto-z*; cf. OE. *lǣtan* LET *v.*[1]] OE. term for a person of status intermediate between that of a freeman and a slave. *Hist.*

Lævigate, obs. erron. f. LEVIGATE.

Lævo-, levo- (lī·vo), comb. f. L. *lævus*, in sense '(turning or turned) to the left', chiefly having reference to the property of causing the plane of a ray of polarized light to turn to the left: as in **a. lævo-gy·rate, -gy·rous** *adjs.*, characterized by turning the plane of polarization to the left; **-rota·tion,** rotation to the left; **b. lævo-co·mpound,** a chemical compound which causes lævo-rotation; **-glu·cose** = LÆVULOSE; etc.

Lævulin, levulin (lī·viŭlin). 1888. [f. LÆVUL-OSE + -IN.] *Chem.* A substance resembling dextrin, obtained from the roots of certain composite plants. Hence **Lævuli·nic,** only in *l. acid*, $C_5H_8O_3$.

Lævulose, levulose (lī·viŭlōus). 1871. [f. L. *lævus* left + -ULE + -OSE.] *Chem.* The form of GLUCOSE which is lævo-rotatory to polarized light; fruit-sugar. Hence **Lævulosane** [+ -ANE], a substance into which l. is converted by heating to 338°.

Lafayette (lafeye·t). *U.S.* 1859. [f. General *Lafayette*.] **1.** A sciænoid fish of the Northern U.S. (*Liostomus xanthurus*). **2.** A stromateoid fish (*Stromateus triacanthus*) 1884.

Laft(e, obs. pa. t. and pa. pple. of LEAVE.

Lag (læg), *sb.*[1] and *a.* 1514. [Belongs to LAG *v.*[2] Perh. an arbitrary distortion of *last* (cf. *fog, seg, lag*, used in children's games for 'first, second, last'). Or ? an alteration of *lack*, after FLAG *v.*[1], FAG *sb.*[2]]

A. *sb.* **1.** The last or hindmost person (in a race, etc.). Now *rare* exc. in schoolboy use. †**2.** *pl.* Dregs, lees –1703. **3.** [f. the vb.] The condition of lagging 1837. **b.** *Physics.* Retardation in a current or movement of any kind; the amount of this 1855.

1. In threats the foremost, but the l. in fight DRYDEN. **3. b.** *L. of the tide*: the interval by which the tide-wave falls behind the mean time in the first and third quarters of the moon. The l. of the steam-valve of a steam-engine 1855.

B. *adj.* †Last, hindmost (*obs.*); belated, lagging, tardy (now *rare*) 1552.

Some tardie Cripple..That came too lagge to see him buried SHAKS. *Comb.* **l.-end,** the fag end (now *rare*); †**-tooth,** a wisdom tooth.

Lag (læg), *sb.*[2] 1672. [app. a. ON. *lǫgg*; cf. Sw. *lagg* 'rim of a barrel', also 'stave'.] **1.** A stave of a barrel. Now *dial.* **2.** One of the staves or laths forming the covering of a band-drum or a steam boiler or cylinder, or the upper casing of a carding machine 1847.

Comb. **l.-screw,** (*a*) a flat-headed screw used to secure lags to cylinders or drums; (*b*) U.S. = *coach-screw*.

Lag (læg), *sb.*[3] *Cant.* 1811. [f. LAG *v.*[3]] **1.** A convict under sentence of transportation or penal servitude. **2.** A term of transportation or penal servitude 1821.

Lag, *sb.*[4] *dial.* 1875. A long, narrow, marshy meadow. W. S. BLUNT.

†**Lag,** *v.*[1] 1440. [?] **1.** *trans.* To daggle, render wet or muddy. ME. only. **2.** *intr.* To become wet or muddy. BUNYAN.

Lag (læg), *v.*[2] 1530. [See LAG *sb.*[1] and *a.*] **1.** *intr.* To progress too slowly; to fail to keep pace with others; to hang back, fall behind, remain in the rear. Also *fig.* **2.** *trans.* To cause to lag. *Obs.* exc. *dial.* 1570.

1. I shall not l. behinde, nor erre The way, thou leading MILT. *P. L.* x. 266. Hence **La·gger** *sb.*[1] 1523; **Lag-last** 1855.

Lag, *v.*[3] 1573. [?] †**1.** *trans.* To steal. **2. a.** To transport or send to penal servitude 1812. **b.** To catch, apprehend 1823.

Hence **La·gger** *sb.*[2] a convict undergoing or having undergone penal servitude.

Lag (læg), *v.*[4] 1887. [Back-f. LAGGING *vbl. sb.*] *trans.* To cover (a boiler, etc.) with wooden lags, strips of felt, etc.

Lagan (læ·găn). Also †**ligan.** 1491. [a. OF. *lagan, laguen, lagand*; perh. Scand., from root of LIE, LAY *vbs.*] *Law.* Goods or wreckage lying on the bed of the sea.

†‖**Laga·rto.** 1577. [Sp.; see ALLIGATOR.] An alligator –1600.

Lagenian (lădʒī·niăn), *a.* 1890. [f. L. *lagena* a flagon + -IAN.] *Zool.* Like or pertaining to the genus *Lagena* of *Foraminifera*, having a straight chambered shell.

Lageniform (lădʒī·nifǫɹm), *a.* 1826. [f. as prec. + -(I)FORM.] *Zool.* and *Bot.* Shaped like a bottle or flask.

Lager beer (lā·gəɹ,bīᵊɹ). Also simply **lager.** 1853. [ad. Ger. *lager-bier* beer brewed for keeping, f. *lager* a store + *bier* beer.] A light beer, originally German.

Laggard (læ·găɹd). 1702. [f. LAG *v.*[1] + -ARD.] **A.** *adj.* Lagging, hanging back, slow. L. hounds SCOTT. A l. obedience MANNING. Hence **La·ggard-ly** *adv.*, **-ness.**

B. *sb.* One who lags behind; a lingerer, loiterer 1808.

A l. in love, and a dastard in war SCOTT.

Lagging (læ·giŋ), *vbl. sb.* 1837. [f. LAG *sb.*[2] and LAG *v.*[4] + -ING[1].] **1.** *pl.* and *coll. sing.* The strips of wood or felt with which a boiler, an arch, a wall, etc. are covered. Also the action of covering with these.

Lagging (læ·giŋ), *ppl. a.* 1593. [f. LAG *v.*[2] + -ING[2].] That lags; lingering, tardy.

Foure l. Winters, and foure wanton springs End in a word SHAKS. Hence **La·ggingly** *adv.*

†**La·gly,** *adv.* [f. LAG *a.* + -LY[2].] Lastly. FLORIO.

Lagomorph (læ·gŏmǫɹf). 1882. [f. Gr. λαγώς hare + μορφή form.] *Zool.* One of the *Lagomorpha*, a group of rodents of which the hares form one family. Hence **Lagomo·rphic** *a.*

Lagoon[1] (lăgū·n). 1612. [ad. It., Sp. *laguna*, or F. *lagune* :—L. *lacuna* pool.] **1.** An area of salt or brackish water separated from the sea by low sand-banks, *esp.* one of those near Venice. **2.** The lake-like stretch of water enclosed in an atoll 1769.

Comb. **l.-island,** an atoll.

Lagoon[2] (lăgū·n). *rare.* 1868. [Anglicized f. It. *lagone*, augm. of *lago* :—L. *lacus* LAKE *sb.*[2]] In Tuscany, the basin of a hot spring from which borax is obtained.

‖**Lagophthalmus** (læg*ǫ*fþæ·lmǫs). 1657. [mod.L., ad. Gr. λαγώφθαλμος adj. 'hare-eyed' (i.e. unable to close the eyes, as hares were supposed to be), f. λαγώς hare + ὀφθαλμός eye.] *Path.* A morbid condition in which the eye remains wide open. Also called ‖ **Lagophthalmia**, and †**Lagophthalmy**. Hence **Lagophthalmic** *a.*

Lagune, var. of LAGOON[1].

Laic (lē·ik). 1491. [ad. late L. *laicus*, Gr. λαικός, f. λαός the people.] A. *adj.* = LAY *a.* The prosecution [of Socrates] was truly laick 1736. B. *sb.* One of the laity; a layman 1596. No person, whether l. or priest BUSHNELL. So **La·ical** *a.* **Laica·lity**, the state or condition of a layman. **La·ically** *adv.* in a laical manner.

Laicize (lē·isəiz), *v.* Also **-ise.** 1870. [f. LAIC *a.* + -IZE.] *trans.* To make lay; to secularize; *esp.* to throw open (a head-mastership or other office) to laymen 1870. Hence **La·iciza·tion**, **La·icizer**.

Laid (lēd), *ppl. a.* 1547. [pa. pple. of LAY *v.*] In senses of LAY *v.* **Laid paper**, paper having a ribbed appearance, from parallel wires in the mould.

Laidly (lē·dli), *a.* *Sc.* and *arch.* ME. [North. var. of LOATHLY.] Hideous, repulsive. Her l. wooer, whose income was better than his looks 1878.

Laigh (lēχ), *a.*, *adv.*, and *sb.* *Sc.* ME. [See Low *a.*] 1. *adj.* = Low *a.* 2. *adv.* In a low position; to a low point; in a low tone 1583. 3. *sb.* A hollow; a low-lying ground.

Lain, pa. pple. of LIE *v.*[1]

Lainer (lē·nəɹ). *Obs.* in literary use. ME. [a. F. *lanière*; cf. LANYARD.] A lace, strap, thong, lash.

Lair (lēəɹ), *sb.* [OE. *leger* str. neut. :—OTeut. **legro-*, f. root *leg-*; see LIE *v.*[1]] †1. The action or fact of lying –1631. 2. The resting place of a corpse; a grave, tomb. Now only *Sc.*, a plot in a graveyard. OE. 3. That whereon one lies down to sleep; a bed, couch OE. 4. A place for animals to lie down in; *esp.* for beasts of chase or of prey ME. 5. *Agric.* Nature or kind of soil 1519. 4. Low of distant cattle..dropping down to l. CLARE.

Lair (lēəɹ), *v.* ME. [f. prec.] †1. *trans.* To prostrate. ME. only. 2. a. *intr.* To lie (*on* a bed). b. Of cattle: To go to their lair. c. *trans.* To place in a lair. d. To serve as a lair for. 1607.

Lairage (lēə·rėdʒ). 1866. [f. LAIR *sb.* or *v.* + -AGE.] The placing of cattle in a lair or lairs; space so occupied, or an establishment of such lairs.

Laird (lēəɹd). *Sc.* 1450. [Sc. form of LORD (repr. north. ME. *laverd*).] A landed proprietor; orig. only one who held immediately from the king. Hence **Lai·rdship**, the condition, dignity, or estate of a l.; also, lairds as a whole 1649.

Laiser, obs. f. LEISURE.

‖**Laissez-aller** (lē·se æ·le; Fr. lese ale). Also **laisser-aller**. 1818. [Fr.; as next + *aller* to go, i.e. let (persons or things) go.] Absence of restraint; unconstrained freedom.

‖**Laissez-faire** (lē·se fēəɹ; Fr. lese fer). Also **laisser-faire**. 1825. [Fr.; *laissez* let + *faire* to do, i.e. let (people) do (as they think best).] A phr. expressive of the principle of non-interference by government with the action of individuals, esp. in trade and in industrial affairs. Also *attrib.* The 'orthodox' *laissez-faire* political economy 1887. Hence **Laissez-faireism.**

Laity (lē·iti). 1541. [f. *lai* LAY *a.* + -(I)TY.] 1. The condition or state of a layman 1616. 2. The body of the people not in orders as opp. to the clergy; laymen collectively 1541. 3. Unprofessional people, as opp. to lawyers, doctors, artists, etc. 1832. 2. The clergy were now retrograding, while the l. were advancing HALLAM. 3. Artists are wont to think the criticisms of the l. rather weak and superfluous HELPS

†**Lake**, *sb.*[1] ME. [a. ON. *leik-r* play :—OTeut. **laiko-*, a vbl. sb. from **laikan* to play, LAKE *v.*] 1. Play, sport, fun. In *pl.* games, tricks. –1570. 2. A fight, contest –1515.

Lake (lēk), *sb.*[2] [Early ME. *lac*, a. OF. *lac*, ad. L. *lacus*.] 1. A large body of water surrounded by land; in recent use often applied to an ornamental piece of water in a park, etc. Also *transf.* and *fig.* †2. A pond, a pool –1609. †3. After L. *lacus* = a wine-vat –1657. 1. Never more Shall the l. glass her. flying over it M. ARNOLD. *The Great L.* (a phrase borrowed from the N. Amer. Indians): the Atlantic Ocean. *The Great Lakes*: the five lakes Superior, Huron, Michigan Erie, and Ontario, which form the boundary between Canada and the U.S. 2. Ne noon so grey goo. gooth in the l. CHAUCER.

attrib. and *Comb.* 1. General: as *l.-fishery*, *-fowl*, *-shore*, etc.; *l.-trout*, etc.; *l.-reflected* adj.; *l.-diver*. 2. Special: **l.-basin**, a depression which contains, or has contained, a l.; **-country** = LAKE-LAND; **-crater**, a crater which contains or has contained, a l.; **-fly**, a fly that frequents lakes; *U.S.*, an ephemerid (*Ephemera simulans*) which swarms in the Great Lakes in July; **-lawyer** *U.S.*, joc. name for the bow-fin and the burbot in allusion to their voracity; **-weed**, water-pepper (*Polygonum hydropiper*). b. **Lake poets, school**, terms applied to Coleridge, Southey, and Wordsworth, who lived among the English Lakes; **L. poetry**, their poetry. c. **lake-dweller**, one who n prehistoric times lived in a **l.-dwelling** or **l.-habitation**, i.e. one built upon piles driven into the bed of a l.; **l.-hamlet**, **-settlement**, **-village**, a collection of such dwellings; **-man** = *lake-dweller*.

†**Lake**, *sb.*[3] ME. [prob. a. Du. *laken*, corresp. to OE. *lachen* 'clamidem'.] Fine linen –1603.

Lake (lēk), *sb.*[4] 1616. [Orig. a var. of LAC[1].] 1. A pigment of a reddish hue, orig. obtained from lac (LAC[1]), and now from cochineal treated as in 2. b. *transf.* as the name of a colour 1660. 2. A pigment obtained by the combination of some colouring matter with metallic oxide or earth. Often qualified, as *crimson*, *madder*, *yellow*, etc. *l.* *Indian l.*, a crimson pigment prepared from stick-lac treated with alum and alkali. 1684.

Lake (lēk), *v.* Now chiefly *dial.* [a. ON. *leika* = OE. *lácan*; CTeut. verb.] †1. *intr.* To exert oneself, leap, spring; hence, to fight –ME. 2. To play, sport; *occas.* in amorous sense; *dial.* to take a holiday; to be out of work ME.

La·ke-land, la·keland. 1829. [f. LAKE *sb.*[2] + LAND.] The land of lakes; *spec.* the region of the English lakes, in Cumberland, Westmorland, and Lancashire.

Lakelet (lē·k,lėt). 1796. [f. LAKE *sb.*[2] + -LET.] A small lake. Also *transf.*

Laker (lē·kəɹ). 1798. [f. LAKE *sb.*[2] + -ER[1].] †1. A visitor to the English lakes. [A pun, with reference to LAKE *v.*] 2. One of the Lake poets 1819. 2. The Lakers all..first despised, and then patronised 'Walter Scott' E. FITZGERALD.

Lakh: see LAC[2].

†**Lakin.** 1496. [Contr. f. LADY + -KIN.] Only in *By* (*our*) *l.*, a trivial form of *By Our Lady* –1625.

Lakke, obs. f. LACK.

Laky (lē·ki), *a.*[1] 1611. [f. LAKE *sb.*[2] + -Y[1].] Of or pertaining to a lake; lake-like.

Laky (lē·ki), *a.*[2] 1849. [f. LAKE *sb.*[4] + -Y[1].] Of the colour of lake; *spec.* of the blood, when the red corpuscles are acted upon by some solvent.

La-la (lā·lā·), *a.* 1785. [adj. use of *la la* interj.; see LA *int.* b.] So-so, poor.

Lallation (lælē·ʃən). 1647. [f. L. *lallare* to sing lalla or lullaby.] †a. Childish utterance. b. An imperfect pronunciation of *r*, in which it sounds like *l*; lambdacism.

Lam (læm), *sb.* 1688. *local.* [Earlier *lame*, a. F. *lame*.] *Weaving. pl.* Pieces of wood in a loom connected with the treadles and healds.

Lam (læm), *v.* 1595. [Cf. ON. *lemja*, lit. 'to lame', but used chiefly with reference to thrashing.] 1. *trans.* To beat soundly; to thrash; to whack. Now *colloq.* or *vulgar.* 2. *intr.* Chiefly school-boy slang, as *to l.* (*it*) *into one*, *to l. out* 1875. Hence **La·mming** *vbl. sb.* a beating.

Lama (lā·mă). Also *erron.* **llama.** 1654. [Tibetan *blama*, the *b* being silent.] A Buddhist priest of Mongolia or Tibet. *Dalai* (*dalae* or *delli*)-*l.*, title of the chief L. of Tibet; *Tesho-* or *Teshu-l.*, that of the chief L. of Mongolia. The former ranks highest, and is known to Europeans as the 'Grand Lama'. He receives almost divine honours. Hence **La·maic** *a* of or pertaining to the lamas; believed or taught by the lamas. **La·maism** (also **la·mism**), the doctrine and observances inculcated by the lamas. **La·maist, La·maite**, one who professes lamaism; also *attrib.* **Lamai·stic, Lamai·tic** *adjs.*, of or pertaining to the lamaists.

Lama, erron. f. LLAMA.

Lamantin (lămæ·ntin). 1706. [a. F.] The manatee.

Lamarckian (lămā·ɹkiăn). 1846. [f. *Lamarck*, French botanist and zoologist (1744–1829) + -IAN.] A. *adj.* Of or pertaining to Lamarck or to his theory ascribing organic evolution to inheritable modifications produced in the individual by habit, appetency, and the environment. B. *sb.* One who holds these views. So **Lama·rckianism, Lama·rckism**, Lamarck's doctrine of the origin of species. **Lama·rckite** = LAMARCKIAN *sb.*

Lamasery (lamā·səri). 1867. [a. F. *lamaserie*, app. formed irreg. by Huc from *lama*; see LAMA.] A Tibetan or Mongolian monastery of lamas.

Lamb (læm), *sb.* [Com. Teut.: OE. *lamb*, *lambor*, *lemb* str. neut. :—OTeut. **lamboz-*, **lambiz-*.] 1. The young of the sheep. 2. *fig.* a. A young member of a 'flock', esp. of the church OE. b. One who is as meek, gentle, innocent, or weak as a lamb OE. c. A simpleton 1668. 3. *The Lamb*, †*God's Lamb*, *the Lamb of God*, a title of Christ. (After John i. 29, Rev. v. 6, etc.) OE. b. (*Her.*) *Holy Lamb* = AGNUS DEI b. 1823. 4. *pl.* a. The name given to the ferocious soldiers of Col. Kirke's regiment in 1684–6, in ironical allusion to the device of the Paschal Lamb on their flag 1744. b. The name given to bodies of ruffians hired to commit acts of violence at elections. 1844. 5. The flesh of the lamb as food 1620. b. Short for LAMBSKIN 1527. 1. Ewes and thir bleating Lambs MILT. *P. L.* XI. 645. As well be hanged for a sheep as a l. *Mod. Provb.* 3. Worthy the L...for He was slain for us WATTS.

Comb.: **l.-ale**, an annual feast at lamb-shearing; **l.-florin** *Hist.*, a florin stamped with the 'Agnus Dei'; **lamb's fry**, the product of lamb's castration. **lamb's lettuce** = CORN-SALAD (*Valerianella olitoria*); **lamb's tails**, the catkins of the hazel.

Lamb (læm), *v.* 1456. [f. LAMB *sb.*] 1. *trans.* (*pass.* only.) To bring forth; to drop (a lamb). 2. *intr.* To bring forth a lamb; to yean 1611. 3. Of a shepherd: To tend (ewes) at lambing-time. Also, *to l. down*. 1850.

Lamb, obs. f. LAM *v.*

†**Lamback**, *v.* 1589. [? f. LAM *v.* + BACK *sb.*] *trans.* To beat, thrash. Also *fig.* So **Lamba·ste** *v.* (*slang* and *dial.*) 1637.

Lambda (læ·mdă). ME. [Gr. λάμβδα (or λάβδα).] 1. The 11th letter of the Greek alphabet, Λ, λ. 2. *Anat.* The point of junction of the sagittal and lambdoidal sutures 1888. *L. moth*, a moth marked with a l. on its wings.

Lambdacism (læ·mdăsiz'm), **labdacism** (læ·bd-). 1658. [ad. L., a. Gr. λα(μ)βδακισμός, f. λά(μ)βδα LAMBDA.] 1. A too frequent repetition of the letter *l* in speaking or writing. 2. A confusion of *l* and *r* in pronunciation; lallation 1864.

Lambdoid (læ·mdoid), *a.* 1597. [a. F. *lambdoïde*, ad. mod.L. *lambdoides*, ad. Gr. λαμβδοειδής; see LAMBDA and -OID.] = next.

Lambdoidal (læmdoi·dăl), *a.* Also **lamdoidal.** 1653. [f. prec. + -AL.] Resembling the Gr. letter lambda (Λ) in form. *L. suture* (*Anat.*), the suture connecting the two parietal bones with the occipital. *L. ridge*, the edge of the occipital bone forming the lambdoid suture.

Lambency (læ·mbĕnsi). 1817. [f. next; see -ENCY.] The state or quality of being lambent. Also *fig.*: *spec.* Brilliance and delicate play of wit or fancy 1871. The soft l. of the streamlet RUSKIN.

Lambent (læ·mbĕnt), *a.* 1647. [ad. L. *lambentem*, *lambere* to lick.] 1. Of a flame (fire, light): Playing lightly upon a surface without burning it, like a tongue of fire; shining with a soft clear light and without fierce heat. b. Hence, of eyes, the sky, etc.: Softly radiant 1717. c. *fig.* Of wit, style, etc.: Playing lightly and brilliantly over its subjects 1871. 2. In etym. sense: Licking, that licks 1706. 1. L., diffuse flashes of lightning without thunder 1834. *fig.* L. dulness played around his face DRYDEN. b. Eyes..l. with interior light 1867. c. The style so picturesque and l. DISRAELI. **La·mbently** *adv.*

Lambes, obs. f. LAMMAS.

†**La·mbitive.** 1646. [ad. mod.L. *lambitivum*, f. *lambere*; see -IVE.] **A.** *adj.* Of medicines: Taken by licking up with the tongue. **B.** *sb.* A medicine so taken. –1710.

Lambkin (læ·mkin). 1579. [f. LAMB *sb.* + -KIN.] A little lamb. Also *transf.*, chiefly as a term of endearment.

Lamb-like, lamblike (læ·mləik), *a.* 1599. [-LIKE.] Like a lamb, or that of a lamb.

Lambling (læ·mliŋ). *rare.* 1591. [-LING.] A young or little lamb.

Lamboys (læ·mboiz). 1548. [In quot. (the source of the word) possibly a mistake for JAMBEAUX.] *Antiq.* An imitation in steel of the 'bases' or skirt, reaching from the waist to the knee; occas. found in Tudor armour.

The tasses, the l., the backpece HALL.

Lambrequin (læ·mbrĕkin). 1725. [a. F.] **1.** A scarf or piece of stuff worn over the helmet as a covering: in *Her.* represented with one end (which is cut or jagged) pendent or floating. **2.** *U.S.* A short curtain or piece of drapery (with the lower edge scalloped or straight) placed over a door or window or suspended for ornament from a mantel-shelf. 1883. **3.** *Ceramics.* Ornamentation consisting of solid colour with a lower edge of jagged or scalloped outline 1873.

Lambskin (læ·mˌskin), *sb.* Also **lamb's skin.** ME. **1. a.** The skin of a lamb with the wool on. **b.** The same dressed and used for clothing, for mats, etc. In *collect. sing.* fur so prepared. **2.** Leather made from the skin of lambs 1745. **3.** Woollen cloth made to resemble lambskin (Ogilvie). †**4.** *punningly.* A heavy blow. (Cf. LAM *v.*) –1622. **5.** *Mining.* Anthracite slack 1873.

1. He is wolf in lamskine hyd ME. Hence †**Lambskin** *v. trans.* to beat, to thrash.

Lamb's tongue. 1578. **1.** A name for species of plantain (tr. med.L. *arnoglossa*, Gr. ἀρνόγλωσσον), and other plants. **2.** A sort of plane with a deep narrow bit for making quirks; also, the moulding made by this 1858.

Lamb's-wool (læ·mzˌwul). 1429. **1.** The wool of lambs, used for hosiery, etc.; clothing-material made of this. Also *attrib.* **2.** A drink of hot ale mixed with the pulp of roasted apples, sugared and spiced 1592.

Lamda, -doidal: see LAMBDA, -DOIDAL.

Lame (lēⁱm), *sb. techn.* 1586. [a. F. *lame* :—L. *lam(m)ina, lamna* thin piece or plate.] A thin plate, esp. of metal; a lamina; *spec.* applied to the small overlapping steel plates used in old armour.

Lame (lēⁱm), *a.* [OE. *lama, lǫma* :—OTeut. **lamo-*.] **1.** Crippled; weak, infirm; paralysed; unable to move. *Obs.* exc. *arch.* **b.** Crippled through injury to, or defect in, a limb, esp. in the foot or leg; limping, unable to walk OE. Also *transf.* of inanimate objects. **c.** Said of the limb; also of footsteps, etc. ME. **2.** *fig.* Maimed, halting; imperfect or defective. Said esp. of an argument, excuse, account, etc. ME. **b.** Of metrical feet, or verses composed of them: Halting, metrically defective 1600.

1. b. Another l. of a hande SAVILE. I was an eye unto the blynde, and a fote to the l. COVERDALE *Job* xxix. 15. 2. Oh most l. and impotent conclusion SHAKS. A very l. story FREEMAN. b. The Prose is Fustian, and the Numbers l. DRYDEN.

Phr. *L. duck*: see DUCK *sb.*[1] 6. Hence **La·me·ly** *adv.*, **-ness.**

Lame (lēⁱm), *v.* ME. [f. LAME *a.*] *trans.* To make lame; to cripple.

Lamel (læ·mĕl). Now *rare.* 1676. [ad. L. *lamella.*] = next.

‖**Lamella** (lăme·lă). Pl. **lamellæ** (lăme·lī). 1678. [L., dim. of *lamina.*] A thin plate, scale, layer, or film, esp. of bone or tissue e.g. one of the thin plates or scales which compose some shells, one of the erect scales appended to the corollas of some flowers, etc. Hence **Lame·llar** *a.* (chiefly *scientific*), consisting of, characterized by, or arranged in lamellæ. **Lame·llarly** *adv.* in thin plates or scales.

Lamellate (læ·melĕt), *a.* 1826. [ad. mod.L. *lamellatus*; see LAMELLA and -ATE [2].] Furnished with or arranged in lamellæ; lamellar Hence **Lame·llately** *adv.* **La·mellated** *a.* 1713.

Lamellibranch (lăme·libræŋk), *sb.* (*a.*) 1855. [ad. mod.L. *lamellibranchia* pl., f. LAMELLA + Gr. βράγχια gills.] *Zool.* A lamellibranchiate mollusc. **b.** *attrib.* or *adj.* = next 1867.

Lamellibranchiate (lămelibræ·ŋkiˌĕt), *a.* (*sb.*) 1842. [ad. mod.L. *lamellibranchiatus*; see prec. and -ATE [2].] *Zool.* Belonging to the group *Lamellibranchiata* of molluscs (so called as having lamellate gills), including oysters, mussels, etc. 1855. **b.** *sb.* A lamellibranch.

Lamellicorn (lăme·likǭɹn). 1835. [ad. mod.L. *lamellicornis*, f. L. *lamella* thin plate + *cornu* horn.] *Entom.* **A.** *adj.* Belonging to the *Lamellicornes* or the group *Lamellicornia* of beetles, having antennæ characterized by a lamelliform club. **B.** *sb.* A lamellicorn beetle, as the dung-beetle, cockchafer, etc. So **Lamelli·co·rnate, -co·rnous** *adjs.* = A.

Lamelliferous (læmĕli·fĕrəs), *a.* 1832. [f. LAMELLA + -(I)FEROUS.] Bearing or having lamellæ; lamellate.

Lamelliform (lăme·lifǭɹm), *a.* 1819. [f. LAMELLA + -(I)FORM.] Having the form of a lamella or thin plate.

Lamellirostral (lămelirǫ·străl). 1835. [f. mod.L. *lamellirostris*, f. LAMELLA + L. *rostrum* beak + -AL.] *Ornith.* **A.** *adj.* Belonging to the family *Lamellirostres* of birds, so called as having lamellose bills. **B.** *sb.* A lamellirostral bird.

Lamellose (lăme·lōᵘs), *a.* 1752. [f. LAMELLA + -OSE.] = LAMELLATE.

Lament (lăme·nt), *sb.* 1591. [ad. L. *lamentum.*] **1.** An act of lamenting; a passionate expression of grief. Also *poet.* lamentation. **2.** A conventional form of mourning; an elegy; a dirge; also, the air to which a lamentation is sung or played 1698.

1. A voice of weeping heard, and loud l. MILTON.

Lament (lăme·nt), *v.* 1530. [ad. L. *lamentari*, f. *lamentum.*] **1.** *trans.* To express or feel sorrow for or concerning; to mourn for; to bewail 1535. **2.** *intr.* To express or feel profound grief; to mourn passionately 1530. †**3.** *causative.* To distress –1704.

1. Samuel died, and all the Israelites..lamented him 1 *Sam.* xxv. 1. This stone laments the death of Andrea Pisano 1756. 2. He loves not most that doth l. the most 1595. Hence **Lame·nter. Lame·ntingly** *adv.*

Lamentable (læ·mĕntăb'l), *a.* ME. [a. F., or ad. L. *lamentabilis*; see prec. and -ABLE.] **1.** Full of or expressing sorrow; mournful, doleful. Now *rare* or *arch.* **2.** That is to be lamented; pitiable, deplorable ME. **b.** In joc. or trivial use: 'Pitiful, despicable' (J.); wretchedly bad 1699.

2. A l. change from that simplicity of manners STEELE. b. The result was something l. 1876. Hence **La·mentably** *adv.*

Lamentation (læmĕntēⁱ·ʃən). ME. [a. F., or ad. L. *lamentationem.*] The action of lamenting; the passionate expression of grief; mourning; in weakened sense, regret. **b.** A lament ME.

They all made gret lamentasyon for his departyng LD. BERNERS. b. Take thou vp a l. for the princes of Israel *Ezek.* xix. 1. *The Lamentations of Jeremiah*, or, shortly, *Lamentations*: a book of the O.T., ascribed to Jeremiah, and having for its subject the destruction of Jerusalem by the Chaldeans.

Lamented (lăme·ntĕd), *ppl. a.* 1611. [f. LAMENT *v.* + -ED [1].] Mourned for; bewailed; regretted.

Your late l. father 1864.

Lameter, lamiter (lēⁱ·mitəɹ). *Sc.* and *n. dial.* 1804. [obscurely f. LAME *a.*] A lame person; a cripple.

‖**Lametta** (lăme·tă). 1858. [It., dim. of *lama* = LAME *sb.*] Brass, silver, or gold foil or wire.

‖**Lamia** (lēⁱ·miă). Pl. **-iæ, -ias.** ME. [L. *lamia*, a. Gr. Λαμία a fabulous monster, also, a fish of prey. Cf. F. *lamie.*] **1.** A fabulous monster with the body of a woman, who was said to prey upon human beings and suck children's blood. Also, a witch, she-demon. †**2.** *Ichth.* A genus of sharks –1776. **3.** *Entom.* A genus of longicorn beetles.

Lamin (læ·min). Also **lamen.** 1489. [Anglicized f. next.] A lamina; a plate of metal used as an astrological instrument or as a charm.

‖**Lamina** (læ·mină). *Pl.* **laminæ** (læ·minī). 1656. [L. *lam(m)ina.* Cf. LAME *sb.*] A thin plate, scale, layer, or flake (of metal, etc.). **b.** *Anat.*, etc. A thin layer of bone, membrane, etc. 1706. **c.** *Geol.* The thinnest separable layer in stratified rock deposits 1794. **d.** *Bot.* (*a*) A thin plate of tissue. (*b*) The expanded portion of a leaf. (*c*) The (usually expanded) upper part of a petal. (*d*) The expanded part of the thallus or frond in algæ, etc. 1760.

Hence **La·minal, La·minar, La·minary, La·minose, La·minous** *adjs.* consisting of, arranged in, or formed into laminæ.

Laminable (læ·minăb'l), *a.* 1796. [See LAMINATE *v.* and -ABLE.] Capable of being formed into thin plates or layers. Hence **Laminabi·lity**, l. quality.

Laminarian (læminēᵊ·riăn), *a.* 1851. [f. mod.L. *Laminaria*, name of a genus of seaweeds known as sea-tangle, f. L. *lamina.*] *L. zone*: the zone of the sea, extending from low-water mark to a depth of ninety feet, in which seaweeds of the genus *Laminaria* are found.

Laminarite (læ·minărəit). 1839. [f. as prec. + -ITE.] *Geol.* A fossil seaweed supposed to be allied to the genus *Laminaria.*

Laminate (læ·minĕt), *a.* 1668. [ad. mod.L. *laminatus*; see next and -ATE [2].] Having the form of or consisting of a lamina or thin plate; furnished with a lamina or laminæ.

Laminate (læ·mineⁱt), *v.* 1664. [f. L. **laminat-*, **laminare*, f. LAMINA; see -ATE [3].] **1.** *trans.* To beat or roll (metal) into thin plates. **2.** To separate or split into layers or leaves. Also *intr.* for *refl.* 1668. **3.** To overlay with plates (of metal) 1697. **4.** To make by placing layer upon layer of material 1858.

Laminated (læ·mineⁱtĕd), *ppl. a.* 1668. [f. LAMINATE *v.* + -ED [1].] Consisting of, arranged in, or furnished with laminæ; made of a succession of layers of material.

Lamination (læminēⁱ·ʃən). 1676. [f. as prec.; see -ATION.] The action of laminating or condition of being laminated; also *concr.* in *pl.* laminæ.

Lamini- (læ·mini), comb. f. LAMINA, as in **Lamini·ferous** *a.*, having a structure consisting of laminæ or layers; **Laminipla·ntar** *a. Ornith.* having laminate tarsi, as the *Laminiplantares* of Sundevall's classification.

‖**Laminitis** (læminəi·tis). 1843. [f. LAMINA + -ITIS.] Inflammation of the sensitive laminæ of a horse's hoof.

La·mish, *a.* 1592. [f. LAME *a.* + -ISH [1].] Somewhat lame.

Lamm, obs. f. LAM *v.*

Lammas (læ·măs). [OE. *hlāfmæsse*, f. *hlāf* LOAF + *mæsse* MASS *sb.*[1]; subseq. felt as if f. LAMB + MASS.] **1.** The 1st of August, in the early English church a harvest festival, at which loaves of bread were consecrated, made from the first ripe corn. (In Scotland, a usual quarter-day.) Also, the season of this festival. **2.** *Latter L.* (†*day*), (joc.) a day that will never come; *at latter L.*, never. 1567.

1. Six years old last l. ADDISON.

attrib. and *Comb.*: chiefly with the sense of 'ripening at Lammas', as *L.-apple*, etc.; **L.-day**, August 1; **L.-land**, land that was private property till L. day (Aug. 1), but thereafter subject to common rights of pasturage till the spring; **L.-wheat** = *winter-wheat.*

Lammergeyer (læ·məɹgəiəɹ). 1817. [a. G. *lämmergeier*, f. *lämmer*, pl. of *lamm* lamb + *geier* vulture, GEIR.] The Bearded Vulture, *Gypaetus barbatus*; it is the largest European bird of prey, and inhabits lofty mountains in Southern Europe, Asia, and Northern Africa.

Lamp (læmp), *sb.*[1] ME. [ad. F. *lampe*, ad. L. *lampas*, Gr. λαμπάς, f. λάμπειν to shine.] **1.** A vessel containing oil, which is burnt at a wick, for the purpose of illumination. Now also a vessel of glass or the like, enclosing a candle, oil, a gas-jet, or an incandescent wire. Often defined, as *arc, Argand, Davy, electric, gas*, etc. *l.* **b.** Used for *torch*; (occas. with allusion to the Grecian torch-race: see LAMPADEDROMY) ME. **c.** = *safety-lamp* 1839. **2.** *transf.* **a.** *sing.* The sun, moon, a star or meteor; also, a flash (of lightning). *pl.* The stars or heavenly bodies in general. ME. **b.** *pl.* The eyes (formerly *poet.*; now *slang*) 1590. **3.** *fig.* A source or centre of light, spiritual or intellectual. Also, *l. of beauty, joy, life*, etc. 1500.

1. Darke Night strangles the trauailing Lampe SHAKS. Phr. *To smell of* (or †*taste*) *the l.* (said of a literary composition): to be manifestly the product of nocturnal or laborious study. b. Still the race of Hero-spirits pass the l. from hand to hand KINGSLEY. **2. a.** When they see Sun, we see the Lamps of night SIR T. HERBERT. 3. Ages elapsed ere Homer's l. appeared COWPER. The Seven Lamps of Architecture (cf. *Exod.* xxv. 37, etc.) RUSKIN (*title*).

attrib. and *Comb.* **1.** General: as *l.-chimney, -shade, -wick*, etc.; *l.-bearer, -cleaner*, etc.; *l.-lighting* adj. and sb.; *l.-lighted, -lit, -warmed* adjs., etc. **2.** Special: **l.-fly**, ? a glow-worm; **-furnace**, a furnace in which a l. was used as the means of heating; **-jack** *U.S.*, a hood over a lamp chimney on the roof of a car; **-man**, (*a*) a maker of or dealer in lamps; (*b*) one who tends lamps; **-shell**, a brachiopod, esp. one of the genus *Terebratula* or family *Terebratulidæ*.

†**Lamp**, *sb.*[2] [? for *lampne, ad. L. *lamina* (cf. LAME *sb.*).] ? A plate. CHAUCER.

Lamp (læmp), *v.* 1600. [f. LAMP *sb.*[1]] **1.** *intr.* To shine. Also *fig.* 1609. **2.** *trans.* To supply with lamps 1600. **3.** *transf.* To light as with a lamp 1808.

2. To play with Luna or newe lampe the starres 1600.

Lampad (læ·mpæd). *poet. rare.* 1796. [ad. Gr. λαμπαδ-, λαμπάς LAMP *sb.*[1]] In *pl.*, the seven 'lamps of fire' burning before the throne of God (Rev. iv. 5).

Lampadedromy (læ:mpade·drŏmi). 1848. [ad. Gr. λαμπαδηδρομία, f. λαμπαδ-, λαμπάς torch + -δρομία running. Many Dicts. have the incorrect form *lampadrome*.] *Gr. Antiq.* A torch-race; a race (on foot or horseback) in which a lighted torch was passed from hand to hand. So ‖ **La:mpadepho·ria, -doph·oria.**

Lampadist (læ·mpădist). 1838. [ad. Gr. λαμπαδιστής, f. λαμπαδίζειν, f. λαμπάς torch.] *Gr. Antiq.* A competitor in a torch-race.

Lampas (læ·mpăs), *sb.*[1] Also **lampers**, etc. 1523. [a. F. *lampas* (in 16th c. also *lampast*). Origin unkn.] A disease of horses, consisting in a swelling of the fleshy lining of the roof of the mouth behind the front teeth.

His horse..troubled with the Lampasse SHAKS.

Lampas (læ·mpăs), *sb.*[2] ME. [With sense 1, cf. MDu. *lampers*. In sense 2, a. F. *lampas*. Etym. unkn.] †**1.** A kind of glossy crape –1559. **2.** A kind of flowered silk, orig. from China 1816.

†**La·mpate.** 1819. [f. LAMP-IC + -ATE[4].] *Chem.* A salt of lampic acid; an aldehydate –1839.

Lamp-black (læ·mpblæ:k, læ:mpblæ·k), *sb.* 1598. A pigment consisting of almost pure, finely divided carbon; made by collecting the soot produced by burning oil or (now usually) gas. Also *attrib.* Hence **Lamp-bla·ck** *v.* to paint, smear, or coat with l.

Lamper-eel. 1824. [? f. *lampre*, var. of LAMPREY + EEL.] **1.** = LAMPREY. **2.** *U.S.* The mutton-fish or eel-pout (*Zoarces anguillaris*) of N. America 1885.

Lampern (læ·mpəɹn). ME. [a. OF. *lamproyon, lamprion, lampreon*, dim. of *lampreie* LAMPREY.] The river lamprey (*Petromyzon fluviatilis*).

Lampers, var. of LAMPAS *sb.*[1]

†**La·mpic**, *a.* 1819. [f. LAMP *sb.*[1] + -IC.] *Chem.* In *l. acid*: an earlier name of aldehyde. (It was first prepared by burning ether in a lamp with a platinum wire twisted round the wick.) –1839.

Lamping (læ·mpiŋ), *ppl. a.* 1590. [f. LAMP *v.* + -ING[2].] Flashing, resplendent.

Emongst th' eternall spheres and l. sky SPENSER.

Lampion (læ·mpiən). 1848. [a. F., ad. It. *lampione*, augm. of *lampa* LAMP *sb.*[1]] A pot or cup, often of coloured glass, containing oil with a wick, used in illuminations.

Lampless (læ·mplės), *a.* 1625. [-LESS.] Destitute of lamps.

Your Ladies eyes are lamplesse to that vertue FLETCHER.

La·mplet. 1621. [-LET.] A small lamp.

Lamplight (læ·mp,ləit). 1579. [f. LAMP *sb.*[1] + LIGHT *sb.*] The light given by a lamp or lamps.

Lamplighter (læ·mp,ləitəɹ). 1750. [f. as prec. + LIGHTER *sb.*[2]] **1.** One who lights lamps; one whose business it is to light the street lamps. **2.** *local U.S.* The calico bass 1888.

1. *Like a l.*, i.e. as quickly as the l. ran up his ladder: Skim up the rigging like a l. MARRYAT.

Lamp oil. 1581. Oil for burning in a lamp; also *fig.* nocturnal labour.

Lampoon (læmpū·n), *sb.* 1645. [a. F. *lampon*, orig. a drinking-song; from the exclam. *lampons* = let us drink (Littré).] A virulent or scurrilous satire upon an individual.

The rancorous lampoons of Gregory Nazianzen against his sovereign DE QUINCEY. Hence **Lampoo·n** *v.* to make the subject of a l. **Lampoo·ner. Lampoo·nery**, the practice of writing lampoons; lampooning quality or spirit.

Lamp-post (læ·mp,pōust). 1790. [f. LAMP *sb.*[1] + POST.] A post, usu. of iron, used to support a street-lamp. In the French Revolution also for hanging a victim of popular fury.

†**Lamprel.** 1526. [? f. *lampre* LAMPREY + -EL[1].] Some fish like a lamprey –1688.

Lamprey (læ·mpri). ME. [a. OF. **lampreie* (OF. and mod.F. *lamproie*) :—med.L. *lampreda*, said to be a var. of *lampetra*, f. L. *lambere* to lick + *petra* stone; the lamprey attaches itself by a sucker to stones. But *lampetra* may be an etymologizing perversion.] A pseudo-fish of the genus *Petromyzon*, resembling an eel in shape and in having no scales. It has a sucker-mouth, pouch-like gills, seven spiracles on each side of the head, and a fistula or opening on the top of the head.

Comb. **l.-eel**, the Sea-lamprey (*Petromyzon marinus*).

Lampro- (læ·mpro), repr. Gr. λαμπρο-, comb. f. λαμπρός bright, shining, as in **Lamprotype** [Gr. τύπος type], *Photogr.* a paper print glazed with collodion and gelatine; etc.

Lampron, -roon, etc., obs. ff. LAMPERN.

Lampyrine (læ·mpĭrin, -əin). 1842. [f. L. *lampyris* glow-worm, a. Gr. λαμπυρίς, f. λάμπειν to shine.] **A.** *adj.* Of or pertaining to the *Lampyrinæ* or fire-flies. **B.** *sb.* One of the *Lampyrinæ*.

Lanarkite (læ·năɹkəit). 1835. [f. *Lanarkshire*, where first found.] *Min.* Sulphocarbonate of lead, found in greenish-white, grey, or yellowish crystals.

Lanate (lē·nėt), *a.* 1760. [ad. L. *lanatus*, f. *lana* wool; see -ATE[2].] *Bot.* and *Ent.* Having a woolly covering or surface. So **Lanated** *a.*

Lancashire (læ·ŋkăʃəɹ). 1834. [f. *Lancaster* name of the county town + SHIRE.] The name of an English county, used *attrib.* in *L. boiler*, a horizontal, cylindrical, internally fired boiler, having two flues; also (*ellipt.* as *sb.*) as the designation of a breed of cattle.

Lancaster (læ·ŋkæstəɹ). 1857. [f. C. W. *Lancaster*, the inventor (died 1878).] In full *L. gun, rifle*, the name of a cannon and rifle (respectively) having a slightly oval bore.

Lancasterian (læŋkæsti°·riăn), *a.* Also **Lancastrian.** 1807. [f. proper name *Lancaster* + -IAN.] Of or pertaining to Joseph Lancaster (1778–1838) and the monitorial system which he established in schools.

Lancastrian (læŋkæ·striăn). 1548. [f. *Lancaster* + -IAN. Cf. YORKIST.]

A. *adj.* Pertaining to the English royal family which descended from John of Gaunt, Duke of Lancaster (died 1399), or to the party (whose emblem was the Red Rose) that supported this family in the Wars of the Roses.

B. *sb.* An adherent of the house of Lancaster; one of the Lancastrian faction in the Wars of the Roses.

Lance (lɑns), *sb.*[1] ME. [a. F. *lance* :—L. *lancea*. All Teut. langs. have adopted the Fr. wd.] **1.** A weapon, consisting of a long wooden shaft and an iron or steel head, held by a horseman in charging at full speed. Also *transf.* and *fig.* **2.** A similar weapon, used for various purposes, e. g. for spearing fish 1727. **3.** = LANCET. Now *rare.* 1475. **4.** A horse-soldier armed with a lance; a lancer 1602. **b.** *Hist.* A man-at-arms with his attendant retinue. Cf. F. *lance fournie*. 1818. †**5.** A branch of a tree –1669. **6.** *techn.* **a.** *Carpentry.* A pointed blade, usually employed to sever the grain on each side of the intended path of a chipping-bit or router 1875. **b.** *Mil.* An instrument which conveys the charge of a piece of ordnance and forces it home into the bore 1802. **c.** *Pyrotechny.* A thin case containing compositions which burn with a white or coloured flame 1634.

1. The l. was the..peculiar weapon of the knight GIBBON. Phr. *To break a l.*: see BREAK *v.* I. 1. *L. in rest* (see REST). 2. *Bomb-, gun-, hand-l.*, in *Whale-fishing*, an instrument for killing the whale, after he has been harpooned and wearied out. 4. A l., in other words, a belted knight, commands this party SCOTT.

Comb.: **l.-corporal** [after LANCEPESADE], one who acts as corporal, receiving pay as a private; **-fish** = LAUNCE[2]; **-head** = *lance-snake*; **-sergeant**, a corporal acting as a sergeant; **-snake**, a venomous snake of the American genus *Bothrops* (or *Craspedocephalus*), esp. *B. lanceolatus*, of the W. Indies; = FER-DE-LANCE 2.

†**Lance**, *sb.*[2] 1669. [f. LANCE *v.*] A cut, incision, slit. WORLIDGE.

Lance (lɑns), *v.* ME. [a. OF. *lancier* (F. *lancer*) :—L. *lanceare*, f. *lancea* LANCE *sb.*[1] In branch II f. LANCE *sb.*[1]]

I. 1. *trans.* To fling, launch, throw (a dart, also fire, etc.); to shoot out (the tongue). Now *rare* (chiefly *poet.*). **2.** *intr.* for *refl.* To spring, move quickly, rush. *Obs.* exc. *dial.* ME. †**3.** *intr.* To launch forth, push *out* –1595.

1. The torpedo-boat lances one of her horrid needles of steel 1898.

II. 1. To pierce with or as with a lance or a lancet; to cut, gash, slit. Also, To slit open. *Obs.* exc. *poet.* ME. **b.** *trans.* To wound or kill with a lance (*mod.*). **2.** *Surg.* To make an incision in (the gums, a sore, etc.) with a lancet; to cut open. Occas. with person as object. Also, to fetch *out* or let out by lancing. 1474. Also *fig.* Also *absol.*

1. Then they Lanced his flesh with Knives BUNYAN. 2. To l. and dress the..Tumours DE FOE.

Lancegay (lɑ·nsgē¹). *Obs.* exc. *Hist.* ME. [a. OF. *lancegaye*, f. *lance* LANCE *sb.*[1] + *zagaye* (see ZAGAIE, ASSAGAI).] A kind of lance.

La·nce-knight. *Hist.* 1523. [ad. Ger. *lanzknecht* (*lanz* = LANCE *sb.*[1]), perversion of *landsknecht*, f. *lands*, genitive of *land* LAND *sb.* + *knecht* servant. Orig. the G. word denoted the mercenary foot-soldiers belonging to the imperial territory, as dist. from the Swiss.] A mercenary foot-soldier, esp. one armed with a lance or pike.

Lancelet (lɑ·nslėt). 1565. [f. LANCE *sb.*[1] + -LET.] †**1.** A lancet –1656. **2.** *Zool.* = AMPHIOXUS 1836.

†**La·ncely**, *a.* [f. LANCE *sb.*[1] + -LY[1].] Proper to a lance; lance-like. SIDNEY.

Lanceolar (lɑ·nsiŏlăɹ), *a.* 1810. [f. L. *lanceola* (see next) + -AR.] = next.

Lanceolate (lɑ·nsiŏlėt), *a.* 1760. [ad. L. *lanceolatus*, f. *lanceola* small lance, dim. of *lancea* LANCE *sb.*[1]] Like a spear-head in shape; narrow and tapering to each end. ¶**b.** Lancet-shaped 1883.

Toadflax has linear leaves inclining to l. MARTYN. b. L. windows 1883. Hence **La·nceolately** *adv.* So **La·nceola:ted** *a.* 1752.

Lancepesade, lanceprisado (lɑns,pėzā·d, lɑ:ns,prizā·do). *Hist.* 1578. [a. F. *lancepessade* (now *anspessade*), ad. It. *lancia spezzata*, lit. 'broken lance', ? = one who has seen much service. The Fr. and Eng. sense (= lance-corporal) can be accounted for only conjecturally. For the quasi-Sp. form, see -ADO; the forms with *r* are influenced by Sp. *presa* grip, clutch.] **a.** *pl.* Soldiers of a superior class not included in the ordinary companies. **b.** A non-commissioned officer of the lowest grade; a lance-corporal 1611. **c.** *transf.* 1605.

†**La·ncer**[1]. ME. [ad. OF. *lanceor, lanceur*, f. *lancer* to throw, or f. LANCE *v.* + -ER[1].] **1.** One who lances or throws (a dart). ME. only. **2.** = LANCET –1688.

La·ncer[2] (lɑ·nsəɹ). 1590. [a. or ad. F. *lancier*, f. *lance* LANCE *sb.*[1]] **1.** A (cavalry) soldier armed with a lance; now only, one belonging to one of the regiments officially called Lancers. **2.** *pl.* A species of quadrille. Also the music for this. 1862. **3.** *attrib.* 1844.

1. The l. has sword [now carbine] and pistol besides his lance 1879.

Lancet (la·nsėt). ME. [ad. OF., F. *lancette*, dim. of *lance* LANCE *sb.*[1]] †1. ? A small lance. ME. only. b. In whale-fishing = LANCE *sb.*[1] 2. 1752. 2. A surgical instrument usually with two edges and a point, used for bleeding, opening abscesses, etc. 1440. 3. Short for *lancet arch, light, window* 1848.

2. Veins that seemed to invite the L. SHERIDAN.

Comb.: **l.-fish**, the doctor-fish (*Acanthurus*). b. *Arch.*, as **l. arch**, one with a pointed head like that of a l.; **l. window**, a high and narrow window terminating in a lancet arch; so, *l. Gothic, light, style.*

Lancewood (la·ns,wud). 1697. [f. LANCE *sb.*[1] + WOOD *sb.*] a. A tough elastic wood imported chiefly from the W. Indies, used for carriage-shafts, fishing-rods, cabinet-work, etc. b. A tree yielding this wood; e.g. *Duguetia quitarensis* from Cuba; etc.; and *Oxandra virgata* from Jamaica.

Lanch, obs. f. LAUNCH *sb.* and *v.*

Lanciform (la·nsifǭım), *a.* 1855. [f. LANCE *sb.*[1] + -(I)FORM.] Lance-shaped.

Lancinate (la·nsinėᵗt), *v. rare.* 1603. [f. L. *lancinat-*, *lancinare* to rend, etc.] *trans.* To pierce, tear. Hence **La·ncinating** *ppl. a.*, (chiefly of pain) acute, shooting, piercing. **Lancina·tion**, cutting, lancing; *transf.* a cutting *into*; *fig.* acute agony.

Land (lænd), *sb.* [Com. Teut.: OE. *land*, *lǫnd* str. neut. :—OTeut. **lando*ᵐ, cogn. w. OCelt. **landa* fem., whence Fr. *lande* heath, moor.] 1. The solid portion of the earth's surface, as opp. to *sea, water.* Cf. *firm land* (see FIRM *a.*), DRY LAND. †b. A tract of land. Also *transf.* of ice. -1669. 2. Ground or soil, esp. as having a particular use or particular properties. Often defined as *arable l., corn-l., plough-l., stubble l.* OE. 3. A part of the earth's surface marked off by natural or political boundaries; a country, territory OE. b. *fig.* = Realm, domain OE. ¶c. *U.S.* Euphem. for *Lord*, in phrases *the land knows, good land!* 1849. 4. Ground or territory as public or private property; landed property OE. b. *pl.* Territorial possessions OE. c. *Law.* (See quots.) 1628. †5. The country, as opp. to *the town* -1800. 6. Expanse of country of undefined extent. *rare* exc. with qualifying word, as *down-l.*, HIGHLAND, etc. 1610. 7. One of the strips into which a corn-field or a ploughed pasture-field is divided by water-furrows. Often taken as a measure of land-area and of length. OE. 8. *Sc.* A building divided into flats or tenements for different households 1456. 9. *techn.* a. [*transf.* from 7.] The space between the grooves of a rifle bore; also, the space between the furrows of a mill-stone 1854. b. In a steam-engine, the unperforated portion of the face-plate of a slide-valve 1875. c. The lap of the strakes in a clincher-built boat. Also called *landing* 1875.

1. Ye seken lond and see for yowre wynnynges CHAUCER. Naut. Phr. *L. to!* l. within sight. *L. ho!*: a cry of sailors when first sighting l. †*To set (the) land* to take the bearings of l. *L. shut in*: a phrase used when another point of land hinders the sight of that which a ship came from *How the land lies*: primarily *Naut.*; now chiefly *fig.* = what is the state of affairs. 2. In England, the l. is rich, but coarse HUME. 3. Phr. *The l. of Egypt, the l. of the midnight sun, the l. of the chrysanthemum*, etc. Go, view the l., euen Iericho *Josh.* ii. 1. Ill fares the l., to hastening ills a prey, Where wealth accumulates, and men decay GOLDSM. *L. of promise, promised l.*: see PROMISE *sb.*, etc. *L. of cakes* (Sc.): applied to Scotland, or the Scottish Lowlands. Also HOLY LAND. b. *L. of the leal* (Sc.): the realm of the blessed departed, heaven. *L. of the living*: the present life. *In the l. of the living* (a Hebraism): alive. *L. of Nod*: see NOD. 4. *Common, copyhold, debatable, demesne*, etc.: see the defining words. †*Concealed l.*: land privily held from the king by a person having no title thereto. This fellow might be in 's time a great buyer of L. *Haml.* v. i. 113. b. Messuages, lands, and tenements JARMAN. c. L. in the legall signification comprehendeth any ground, soile or earth whatsoeuer, as meadowes, pastures, woods, moores, waters, marishes, furses and heath...It legally includeth also all castles, houses, and other buildings COKE *On Litt.* 4. L. hath also, in its legal signification, an indefinite extent, upwards as well as downwards BLACKSTONE. 6. And sweet is all the l. about TENNYSON. 7. Green balks and furrowed lands COWPER.

attrib. and *Comb.* 1. General: a. *l.-boom, -development, -revenue, -tenure*, etc.; *l.-buyer, -monopolist, -nationalization*, etc.; *l.-surrounded* adj., etc.; *l.-army, -battle, -trade, -travel, -war*, etc. b. Prefixed to names of animals to indicate that they are terrestrial in their habits, and esp. to distinguish them from aquatic animals of the same name; as *l.-animal, -bird, †-cormorant, -fowl, -spaniel*, etc.; **l.-beetle**, a terrestrial predatory beetle, one of the group *Geadephaga*; **l. chelonian**, a tortoise; **-leech**, a leech of the genus *Hæmodipsa*, abounding in Ceylon; **-pike** = HELLBENDER 1; **-snail**, a snail of the family *Helicidæ*. **-sole**, the common red slug, *Arion rufus*; **-tortoise, -turtle**, any tortoise or turtle of terrestrial habits; **†-urchin**, the hedgehog; **†-winkle**, a snail.

2. Special: **l.-agency**, the occupation of a land-agent; **-agent**, a steward or manager of landed property also, an agent for the sale of land; **-blink**, an atmospheric glow seen from a distance over snow-covered l. in the arctic regions; **-boc**, *Hist.* a charter of land; **-cast**, an orientation; **-chain**, a surveyor's chain; **-fish**, (*a*) ? a fresh-water fish; (*b*) a fish that lives on l.; hence, an unnatural creature; **†-frigate**, a strumpet; **-fyrd** *OE.* and *Hist.*, the land force; **-hunger**, keenness to acquire l.; hence **-hungry** *a.*; **-ice**, ice attached to the shore, as dist. from floe; **-lead**, a navigable opening in the ice along the shore; **-office** *U.S.* and *Colonial*, an office in which the sales of new l. are registered, warrants issued for the location of l., etc.; **-reeve**, a subordinate officer on an estate, who acts as assistant to the land-steward; **-score** *Hist.*, a division of l. [repr. OE. *landscoru*]; **†-scot**, a tax on l. formerly levied in some parishes for the maintenance of the church; **-scrip** *U.S.*, a negotiable certificate, entitling the holder to the possession of certain portions of public land; **-shark**, (*a*) one who lives by preying upon seamen when ashore; (*b*) *rarely*, a land-grabber; **-sick** *a.*, (*a*) sick for the sight of l.; (*b*) *Naut.*, (of a ship) impeded in its movements by being close to l.; **-steward**, one who manages a landed estate for the owner; **-stream**, a current in the sea due to river waters; **-swell**, the roll of the water near the shore; **-trash**, broken ice near the shore; **-valuer**, one whose profession it is to value l. or landed estates; **-war**, (*a*) a war waged on l., opp. to a *naval war*; (*b*) a contention about l. or landed property; **-warrant** *U.S.*, a title to a lot of public l.; **-wash**, the wash of the tide near the shore.

Land (lænd), *v.* ME. [f. LAND *sb.*]

I. *trans.* 1. To bring to land; to set on shore; to disembark. 2. To bring into a specified place, e.g. on a journey; to bring into a certain position; usu. with advb. phr. Also *fig.* 1649. b. To set down from a vehicle 1851. c. *Naut.* To lower on to the deck or elsewhere by a rope or tackle 1867. d. *slang.* To get (a blow) home 1888. e. *Sporting colloq.* To bring (a horse) 'home', i.e. to the winning post. Also *intr.* to get in first, win. 1853. f. In uses corresponding to II. 2 c. 1918. 3. *Angling.* To bring (a fish) to land. Also, *to l. the net.* 1613. b. *fig.* of a person, or a sum of money 1854. 4. To fill or block *up* with earth; to silt up 1605.

1. He Landed an Army in Apulia 1678. 2. A jerk that nearly landed me on his [the horse's] back BURNAND. e. A shower of flukes at the latter end landed him the winner 1890.

II. *intr.* 1. To come to land; to go ashore; to disembark ME. 2. *lit.* and *fig.* To arrive at a place, a stage in a journey, etc.; to end *in* something 1679. b. To alight upon the ground, *e.g.* from a vehicle, after a jump, etc. 1693. c. Of aircraft: To come to earth from the air. Of a seaplane: To return to the water. 1899.

1. We..sailed into Syria, and landed at Tyre *Acts* xxi. 3. 2. b. The spot where the horse took off to where he landed is above eighteen feet 1814.

‖**Landamman(n** (la·ndaman). 1796. [Swiss Ger.; f. *land* LAND *sb.* + *amman*(*n* = G. *amtmann*, f. *amt* office + *mann* man.] In Switzerland, the chief magistrate or officer in certain cantons or certain smaller districts.

Landau (læ·ndǫ). 1743. [f. *Landau* in Germany, where first made.] A four-wheeled carriage, with a top in two parts, so that it may be closed or thrown half or entirely open. Also *l. carriage.*

Landaulet (lændǫle·t) Also **-ette.** 1771. [See -LET.] a. A small landau; a coupé with a folding top like a landau. b. A motor-car having a body the top back part of which may be opened or closed 1902. Also *demi-landau.*

La·nd-bank. 1696. A banking institution which issues notes on the security of landed property.

La·nd-breeze. 1667. A breeze blowing from land seawards.

La·nd-crab. 1638. Any species of crab that lives mostly on land but resorts to the sea for breeding.

†**Land-damn**, *v. trans.* ? To make a hell on earth for (a person). *Wint. T.* II. i. 143.

‖**Landdrost** (læ·nd,drǭᵘst). Also *erron.* **landro(o)st.** 1731. [S. Afr. Du.; f. *land* LAND *sb.* + *drost* bailiff.] A kind of magistrate in S. Africa.

Landed (læ·ndėd), *a.* ME. [f. LAND *sb.* + -ED [2].] 1. Possessed of land; having an estate in land. 2. Consisting of land; consisting in the possession of land; (of revenue) derived from land 1711.

1. The old l. aristocracy ALISON. Phr. *L. interest*: interest in land as a possession; the class having such interest. 2. A l. estate in Yorkshire TROLLOPE.

Lander (læ·ndəɹ). 1847. [f. LAND *v.* + -ER [1].] 1. One who lands or goes ashore 1859. 2. *Mining.* The man who lands the kibble at the mouth of the shaft 1847.

Landfall (læ·ndfǭl). 1627. 1. *Naut.* An approach to or sighting of land, esp. for the first time on a sea-voyage. b. *concr.* The first land 'made' 1883. 2. 'A sudden translation of property in land by the death of a rich man' (J.).

1. *To make a good* (or *bad*) *l.*: to meet with land in accordance with (or contrary to) one's reckoning.

La·nd-flood. ME. Overflowing of land by water from inland sources. Also *fig.*

Land-gavel (læ·ndgæ:vĕl). *Hist.* (Also †**langabull**, †**longable.**) [OE. *landgafol*, f. *land* LAND *sb.* + *gafol* GAVEL *sb.*[1]] Land-tribute, land-tax; rent for land, ground-rent.

La·nd-gra:bber. 1872. One who grabs or seizes upon land, esp. in an unfair manner; *spec.* in Ireland, a man who takes a farm from which a tenant has been evicted.

Landgrave (læ·ndgrēᵗv). 1516. [a. MHG. *lantgrâve* (G. *landgraf*); see LAND *sb.* and GRAVE *sb.*[3]] In Germany, a count having jurisdiction over a territory, and having under him several inferior counts; later, the title of certain German princes. Hence **La·ndgraveship** = next.

Landgraviate (lændgrēᵗ·vi,ėt). Also **-gravate** (1761). 1656. [ad. med.L. *landgraviatus*, f. LANDGRAVE; see -ATE [1].] The office, jurisdiction, or province of a landgrave.

Landgravine (læ·ndgrăvīn). 1682. [ad. G. *landgräfin*, Du. *landgravin.*] The wife of a landgrave; a female ruler of a landgraviate.

La·ndho:lder. ME. A holder, proprietor, or occupier of land; now occas. (opp. to *land-owner*), a tenant holding land from a proprietor. So **La·ndho:lding** *a.*

Landing (læ·ndiŋ), *vbl. sb.* 1440. [f. LAND *v.* + -ING [1].]

I. The action of LAND *v.* 1. Disembarkation. b. Arrival at a stage or place of landing, e.g. on a staircase 1705. c. Coming to ground at the end of a jump 1881. 2. *Angling.* (See LAND *v.* I. 3) late ME.; esp. in *l.-hook* 1847, *-net* 1837. 3. *Mining.* Receiving the loaded skip at the mouth of a shaft 1860.

II. Concrete senses. 1. A landing-place 1609. 2. A platform at the top of a flight of stairs or between two flights of stairs 1789. b. Stone used for staircase landings 1837. c. *Mining.* A stopping-place for a cage in a shaft, etc., or for a train on an incline 1886.

2. The five bedrooms all opened on a square l. 1882.

Comb.: **l. charges, rates**, charges or fees paid on goods unloaded from a vessel; **l. floor** = sense II. 2; **l.-stage**, a platform, often a floating one, for the landing of passengers and goods from vessels; **-strake** *Boat-building*, 'the upper strake but one' (Weale); **-waiter**, a customs officer who superintends the landing of goods and examines them.

La·nding-place. 1512. 1. A place where passengers and goods are or can be landed. 2. = LANDING *vbl. sb.* II. 2 (now the usual word) 1611. 3. *transf.* and *fig.* A place at which one arrives; a stopping- or resting-place 1727.

Landlady (læ·ndlēᵗdi). 1536. [f. LAND *sb.* + LADY *sb.*] 1. 'A woman who has tenants holding from her' (J.); †*fig.* a mistress (*rare*). 2. The mistress of an inn, lodging- or boarding-house 1654. †b. A gentleman's housekeeper 1618.

Land-law. [In sense 1 repr. OE. *landlagu*, f. *land* LAND *sb.* + *lagu* LAW *sb.*[1]; otherwise modern.] 1. (Also †*land's law*.) The law of a land or country; the 'law of the land'. 2. Law, or a law, relating to land 1878.

Land league. 1880. An association of Irish tenant farmers and others, organized in 1879 under the name of 'The Irish National Land League' (and suppressed in 1881), having for its object primarily the reduction of rent, and ultimately the substitution of peasant proprietors for landlords. Hence **La·nd-leaguer, -leaguism.**

†La·nd-leaper. ME. [f. LAND *sb.* + LEAP *v.* (in sense 'to run') + -ER [1].] = LAND-LOPER -1706.

Landless (læ·ndlės), *a.* OE. [-LESS.] 1. Having no landed property. 2. Without land 1605.

1. A List of Landlesse Resolutes *Haml.* I. i. 98. 2. In an unknown l. sea MORRIS.

La·nd-line. 1875. 1. The outline of the land against sky and sea. 2. An overland telegraphic line, as opp. to a cable 1884.

Landlocked (læ·ndlǫkt), *pa. pple.* and *ppl. a.* 1622. [See LOCK *v.*] Shut in or enclosed by land; nearly surrounded by land. Also *transf.* of fish: Living in landlocked waters so as to be shut off from the sea.

The taking of..land-locked salmon 1868. Hence **La·nd-lock** *sb. rare*, †l. condition; l. country.

Land-loper, -louper (læ·ndlōᵘ:pəɹ, -lɑu:-pəɹ). Now chiefly *Sc.* 15.. [ad. Du. *landlooper*, f. *land* LAND *sb.* + *loopen* to run; see LEAP *v.*] 1. A vagabond; *fig.* †a renegade; an adventurer. †2. = LAND-LUBBER -1725.

1. This High-German land-louper, Dousterswivel SCOTT. Hence **La·nd-lo·ping, -lou·ping** *ppl. a.* Now *Sc.*

Landlord (læ·ndlǫɹd). ME. [OE. had *landhlāford*, but the mod. word is f. LAND *sb.* + LORD *sb.*] 1. Orig., a lord or owner of land; in recorded use only *spec.* the person who lets land to a tenant. Hence (as correl. to *tenant*): A person of whom another person holds any tenement, whether a piece of land, a building, or part of a building. 2. The keeper of a boarding house; an innkeeper 1674. 3. A host (in private). Chiefly *Sc.* 1725.

1. L. of England art thou, and not King SHAKS. 3. Persons still persist among us in calling the head of the family, or the host, the l. RAMSAY.

Landlordism (læ·ndlǫɹdiz'm). 1844. [f. prec. + -ISM.] The principles or practice of landlords; the system according to which land is owned by landlords to whom tenants pay a fixed rent (chiefly used with reference to Ireland); advocacy or practice of such a system.

†La·ndlordry. [-RY.] Landlords as a class. BP. HALL.

La·ndlordship. 1828. [-SHIP.] The position or condition of a landlord; the tenure of such a position.

Land-lubber (læ·ndlʊ:bəɹ). 1700. [See LUBBER *sb.*] A sailor's term of contempt for a landsman. Hence **La·ndlubberly** *a.*

Landman (læ·ndmæ̆n). [OE. *landmann*, f. *land* LAND *sb.* + *mann* MAN *sb.* Cf. LANDSMAN.] 1. = COUNTRYMAN 1 (*rare*) -1641. 2. A countryman, peasant (after G. *landmann*) ME. 3. = LANDSMAN 2. Now *rare* or *Obs.* 1480. †4. A man having landed property -1708.

Landmark (læ·ndmāɹk). [OE. *landmearc* fem.; see LAND *sb.* and MARK *sb.*] 1. The boundary of a country, estate, etc.; an object set up to mark a boundary line. Also *fig.* 2. Any conspicuous object in the landscape, which serves as a guide (*orig.* and *esp.* to sailors in navigation); hence, any prominent object in a district, etc. 1570. 3. (In mod. use.) An object which is associated with some event or stage in a process; *esp.* an event which marks a period or turning-point in history 1859.

1. Cursed be he that remooueth his neighbours land-marke *Deut.* xxvii. 17. 2. Ith' midst an Altar as the Land-mark stood MILT. *P. L.* XI. 432.

La·nd-measure. 1611. †a. Measurement of land. b. Any of the denominations of measurement used in stating the area of land (e.g. the acre, the rood, etc.); also, a name for the system in current use. So **La·nd-measuring, -measurement,** the art or process of determining by measurement the area of lands, fields, farms, etc.; prop. a branch, but often used as a synonym, of land-surveying.

†La·nd-meter. 1582. [f. LAND *sb.* + METER, f. METE *v.* to measure.] A surveyor -1693.

Landocracy (lændǫ·krăsi). *joc.* 1848. [f. LAND *sb.*; see -CRACY.] The class which owes its influence to its possession of land.

Landowner (læ·nd,ōᵘnəɹ). 1733. [f. LAND *sb.* + OWNER.] An owner or proprietor of land. Hence **La·ndownership.** So **La·nd-owning** *sb.* and *a.*

Landrail (læ·ndrēɪl). 1766. [See RAIL *sb.*[3]; cf. *water-rail*.] The corn-crake, *Crex pratensis.*

La·nd-rat. 1596. [Cf. G. *landratte* land-rat, land-lubber.] A rat that lives on land. †Also as a term of abuse (*Merch. V.* I. iii. 24).

Landscape (læ·ndskeɪp). Also **landskip.** 1598. [a. Du. *landschap*, f. *land* LAND *sb.* + *-schap* (see -SHIP). Orig. a painters' term. The corrupt form in *-skip* was the earliest form.] 1. A picture representing inland scenery, as dist. from a sea picture, a portrait, etc. †b. *spec.* A background of scenery in a portrait or figure-painting -1676. 2. A prospect of inland scenery, such as can be taken in at a glance from one point of view; a piece of country scenery 1632. 3. *gen.* Inland natural scenery, or its representation in painting 1602. †4. *transf.* and *fig.* a. A view *of* something -1711. b. A distant prospect; a vista -1698. c. A sketch, outline; *occas.* a shadowy representation -1709. d. A compendium -1679. e. A bird's-eye view; a map -1723. f. The depiction of something in words -1712.

1. The landscapes exhibited on this occasion by Constable 1899. 2. Streit mine eye hath caught new pleasures Whilst the Lantskip round it measures MILTON. 3. The feeling for l. is often described as a modern one PATER. 4. d. That Landskip of iniquity, that Sink of Sin, and that Compendium of baseness, ..our Protector 1656.

Comb.: **l.-gardening,** the art of laying out grounds so as to produce the effect of natural scenery; so **l.-architecture** (*U.S.*); **l. marble,** a variety of marble which shows dendritic markings. Hence **La·ndscapist** (-skeɪpist) a painter of l.

La·nd-se:rvice. 1586. Service performed on land; military, as opp. to naval, service.

La·nd-side. ME. †1. The shore -1533. 2. The side towards the land; the landward side 1840. 3. The flat side of a plough, which is turned towards the unploughed land 1765.

Landslide (læ·ndsləid). orig. *U.S.* 1856. = next. b. *fig.* A great majority of votes, an overwhelming victory, esp. in an election 1895.

Landslip (læ·ndslip). 1679. The sliding down of a mass of land on a mountain or cliff side; land which has so fallen. Also *fig.*

Landsman (læ·ndzmæ̆n). *Pl.* **landsmen.** OE. [f. genitive of LAND *sb.* + MAN *sb.*] †1. A native of a particular country -ME. b. One's fellow-countryman (*rare*) 1598. 2. One who lives or works on land. b. *Naut.* 'The rating formerly of those on board a ship who had never been to sea' (Smyth). 1666.

La·nd-spring. 1642. A spring which comes into action through the overfulness of patches of soil. Also *fig.*

‖**Landsturm** (la·ntʃturm). 1814. [Ger.; lit. 'land-storm'.] In Germany, etc., a general levy in time of war; the forces so called out; the militia force consisting of those men not serving in the army or navy or in the *landwehr.*

La·nd-survey·ing. 1771. The process or art of making surveys of land. **La·nd-survey·or.**

La·ndswoman. 1837. A woman who lives on land, or is skilled in land-work.

‖**Land-tag** (la·nt,tāχ). Also *anglicized* **land-day.** 1591. [Ger.] In Germany, the diet of a state; formerly, the Diet of Empire or of the German Confederation.

La·nd-tax. 1689. A tax on landed property.

La·nd-tie. 1715. A rod, beam, piece of masonry, etc. securing a face-wall, etc. to a bank.

La·nd-va·lue. 1880. The economic value of land, esp. as a basis of rating or taxation.

Landward (læ·ndwǫ̈ɹd), *adv.* and *a.* 1513. [f. LAND *sb.* + -WARD.] A. *adv.* Towards the land. 1610. B. *adj.* †1. Pertaining to the country (as opp. to town) 1513. 2. Situated towards the land (as opp. to the sea); *occas.* belonging to the land 1845. So **La·ndwards** *adv.*

La·nd-wa:ter. 1531. a. Water that flows through or over land, as opp. to sea-water. b. A land-flood. c. Water free from ice along a frozen shore.

Landwehr (la·ndvēr). 1815. [Ger.; = 'land-defence'.] In Germany and elsewhere, that part of the organized land forces of which continuous service is required only in time of war. Also *transf.* Also *attrib.*

La·nd-wind. 1598. A wind blowing from the land seawards.

Lane (lēɪn). [OE. *lane*, *lǫne* wk. fem.] I. A narrow way between hedges or banks; a narrow road or street between houses or walls; a bye-way.

It is a long l. that has no turning *Proverb.* Phr. *Blind l.*: a cul-de-sac.

II. Transf. senses. 1. A narrow passage or way, or something resembling this; *esp.* a channel of water in an ice-field (also called a *vein*); the course prescribed for ocean steamers ME. 2. *slang.* The throat; chiefly in *the l.*, *the narrow, red l.*, etc. 1542. b. Short for *Drury L.* (*Theatre*), *Petticoat L.*, etc. 1856.

1. The people..made a l. for hym to passe thorough 1525. A black l. of open water stopped our progress KANE.

Lane, Sc. f. LONE *a.*

Lang, Lang-; see LONG, LONG-.

Langate, obs. var. LANGUET.

Langobardic (læŋgōᵘbā·ɹdik), *a.* 1724. [ad. late L. *Langobardicus*, f. *Langobardi* the Lombards.] = LOMBARDIC.

Langrage (læ·ŋgrėdʒ). Also **langridge.** 1769. [?] Case-shot loaded with pieces of iron of irregular shape, formerly used to damage the rigging and sails of an enemy. Also *attrib.* So **†Langrel** *sb.*, in same sense 1595.

†La·ngret. 1550. A kind of false die -1600.

Langshan (læ·ŋʃæn). 1871. [Name of a locality near Shanghai; in Chinese = 'wolf hill'.] A breed of black fowl, from China.

Langsyne (læ·ŋsəi·n), *adv.* (*sb.*) *Sc.* 1500. [Prop. two wds.; see LONG *adv.* and SYNE *adv.*] Long since, long ago. Also *sb.* esp. in *auld lang syne.*

Langteraloo, var. of LANTERLOO.

Language (læ·ŋgwėdʒ), *sb.* ME. [a. F. *langage*:—pop.L. type **linguaticum*, f. *lingua* tongue, language (F. *langue*; see LANGUE). The *u* is after F. *langue.*] 1. The whole body of words and of methods of combining them used by a nation, people, or race; a 'tongue'. b. *transf.* Method of expression otherwise than by words 1606. 2. *gen.* Words and the methods of combining them for the expression of thought 1599. b. Faculty of speech; ability to speak a foreign tongue. Now *rare.* 1526. 3. Manner or style of expression ME. b. The phraseology or terms of a science, art, profession, etc., or of a class 1502. c. The style (of a composition); the wording (of a document, statute, etc.) 1712. d. *vulgar.* Short for *bad language* 1886. †4. The act of speaking; the use of speech -1514. †b. That which is said, words, talk, report -1636. 5. A community having the same form of speech, a nation. *arch.* [A literalism of translation.] ME.

1. They haue beene at a great feast of Languages, and stolne the scraps *L. L. L.* v. i. 40. *Dead l.*: a language no longer in vernacular use. b. Ther's a l. in her eye, her cheeke, her lip SHAKS. *Finger l.* = DACTYLOLOGY. *L. of flowers*: a method of expressing sentiments by means of flowers. Choughs l., gabble enough, and good enough SHAKS. 2. There is not chastitie enough in l., Without offence to vtter them SHAKS. b. Oh that those lips had l.! COWPER. 3. *Bad l.*: oaths or coarse expressions. *Strong l.*: expressions indicative of excited feeling. Heretick is the best l. he affords me SIR T. BROWNE. b. I can drinke with any Tinker in his owne L. SHAKS. d. That rude eloquence which is known in Ivy Lane as 'language' BESANT. 5. All people, nations, and languages trembled..before him *Dan.* v. 19.

Hence **La·nguage** *v. trans.* to express in l. **La·nguageless** *a.*

Languaged (læ·ŋgwėdʒd), *ppl. a.* ME. [f. prec. + -ED [2].] 1. Skilled *in* a language or languages. Also *well l.* b. Provided with or having a language. Chiefly with qualifying word prefixed, as *many-, new-l.*, etc. 1605. 2.

Having (good, etc.) speech, (well or fair)-spoken. ? *Obs.* 1470. 3. Worded 1646.

1. Well l. in the French and Italian 1593. 2. Well-languag'd Daniel W. BROWNE.

‖**Langue** (lāṅg). ME. [Fr.] †1. A tongue or language –1665. 2. A national division or branch of a religious and military Order, *e.g.* of the Hospitallers 1799.

Langued (læŋgd), *a.* 1572. [f. F. *langue* tongue + -ED²; cf. F. *langué.*] *Her.* Of a charge: Represented with a tongue of a specified tincture.

†**Langue de bœuf.** ME. [Fr.; lit. 'ox tongue'.] 1. Any of certain plants with rough leaves, now mostly called BUGLOSS, q. v. –1732. 2. A spike or halberd, with a tongue-shaped head –1488.

‖**Languedoc** (lāṅgdǫk). 1664. Wine produced in the old French province of Languedoc.

Languescent (læŋgwe·sěnt), *a. rare.* 1837. [ad. L. *languescentem, languescere,* f. *languere*; see LANGUISH *v.*] Growing faint or languid.

Languet (læ·ŋgwět). Also **languette.** ME. [a. F. *languette,* dim. of *langue* tongue.] †1. The tongue of a balance. ME. only. †2. A tongue-shaped ornament; *esp.* a 'drop' of amber, jet, etc. –1548. †3. The latchet of a shoe –1787. 4. Anything resembling a tongue in shape or use 1580; *spec.* in the flue-pipes of an organ, the flat plate fastened by its edge to the top of the foot, and opposite the mouth 1852. 5. *Zool.* One of the row of little tongue-like processes along the dorsal edge of the branchial sac of an ascidian 1849.

4. At the point of a long L., or tongue of Rock HEYLIN.

Languid (læ·ŋgwid), *sb.* Also **language.** 1852. [Corruption of prec.] *Organ-building.* = LANGUET 4. (Also *attrib.*)

Languid (læ·ŋgwid), *a.* 1597. [a. F. *languide* or ad. L. *languidus,* f. *languere* to LANGUISH.] 1. Faint; inert; wanting in vigour or vitality. b. Indisposed to physical exertion 1728. 2. Spiritless, apathetic. Of interest, impressions: Faint, weak. 1713. b. Of ideas, style, language, a writer: Wanting in force, vividness, or interest 1677. 3. Of business, etc.: Sluggish, dull 1832. 4. Of inanimate things, physical motion, etc.: Weak, wanting in force; slow of movement. Of colour: Faint. 1646.

1. This recent illness had still left him l. 1876. *transf.* All round the coast the l. air did swoon TENNYSON. 2. I'll hasten to my troops, And fire their l. souls with Cato's virtue ADDISON. In him dislike was a l. feeling MACAULAY. 3. The market for exports was exceedingly l. ROGERS. 4. The l. flames at length subside POPE. Hence **La·nguid-ly** *adv.*, **-ness.**

Languish (læ·ŋgwiʃ), *sb.* ME. [f. the vb.] 1. The action or state of languishing. 2. A tender look or glance 1715.

1. One desparate greefe cures with anothers l. SHAKS. 2. A most bewitching l. carried all before it W. IRVING.

Languish (læ·ŋgwiʃ), *v.* ME. [a. F. *languiss-, languir* :—pop.L. **languire,* for class. L. *languere*; perh. cogn. w. L. *laxus* (see LAX *a.*) and Teut. **slako-* SLACK *a.*] 1. *intr.* To grow weak, faint, or feeble; to lose health or vitality; to continue in a state of feebleness and suffering. †In early use: To be sick (*of*). b. To live under lowering or depressing conditions 1489. 2. To grow slack, lose vigour or intensity 1626. 3. To droop in spirits; to pine with love or grief. Also with *for.* ME. b. To put on a languid look, as an indication of sentimental tenderness. Also quasi-*trans.* 1714. 4. a. quasi-*trans.* (usu. with *out*): To pass (a period of time) in languishing 1611. †b. *causal.* To make to languish (*rare*) –1603.

1. What is it..the King languishes of? *Laf.* A Fistula, my Lord *All's Well* I. i. 37. He did not live, but languished through life MRS. JAMESON. b. To l. in poverty CARLYLE. 2. The appetite languishes 1871. 3. Languysshe no more, but plucke up thyne herte 1509. I l. for Relief WESLEY. b. When a visitor comes in, she smiles and languishes, you'd think that butter wouldn't melt in her mouth THACKERAY. Hence **La·nguisher.**

Languishment (læ·ŋgwiʃměnt). 1541. [f. prec. + -MENT.] 1. Sickness, illness; physical weakness, pining, or suffering; *pl.* sufferings. ? *Obs.* 1596. b. Languor; inertness 1620. c. *fig.* of things 1617. 2. Mental pain, distress, or pining; trouble, grief; depression of spirits, sadness 1591. 3. *esp.* Amorous grief or pain 1541. b. Expression of sentimental emotion 1709.

3. Yet do I sometimes feel a l. For skies Italian KEATS. b. A look full of l. SMOLLETT.

Languor (læ·ŋgəɹ, læ·ŋgwǫ̈ɹ), *sb.* ME. [a. OF. *languor, lango(u)r* (mod. *langueur*), ad. L. *languorem,* f. *languere*; see LANGUISH *v.*] †1. Disease, sickness, illness –1609. †2. Sad case –1590. †3. Mental distress, pining, sorrow –1614. 4. Faintness, lassitude 1656. b. Tenderness or softness (of mood, feeling, etc.); lassitude of spirit caused by sorrow, amorous longing, or the like 1751. 5. Of immaterial things: Depressed condition, want of activity or interest; slackness, dullness 1748. b. Of the air, sky, etc.: Heaviness, oppressive stillness 1728.

3. My harts deepe l., and my soules sad teares SHAKS. 4. Great Evacuations produce L. of Spirits 1707. b. Whene'er The languors of thy love-deep eyes Float on to me TENNYSON. 5. Extreme l. now characterizes the trade for field seeds 1895. b. The l. of Rome—its weary pavements, its little life HAWTHORNE. So †**La·nguor** *v.* = LANGUISH *v.* (in various senses).

Languorous (læ·ŋg(w)ŏrəs), *a.* 1490. [ad. OF. *lango(u)reux,* f. *langor* LANGUOR *sb.*] †1. Distressful, sorrowful, mournful –1834. 2. Full of, characterized by, or suggestive of languor 1821.

2. To wile the length from l. hours TENNYSON.

Laniard, var. of LANYARD.

Laniariform (læniĕ·ᵊrifǭɹm), *a.* 1847. [f. L. *laniarius* LANIARY *a.* + -FORM.] Shaped like laniary teeth.

Laniary (læ·niări). 1826. [ad. L. *laniarius* pertaining to a butcher, f. *lanius* butcher, f. *laniare* to tear.] A. *adj.* Of teeth: Adapted for tearing, canine. B. *sb.* A canine tooth.

Laniate (læ·niēᵊit), *v. rare.* 1721. [f. L. *laniat-, laniare.*] *trans.* To tear to pieces.

Lanier, obs. f. LANNER.

Laniferous (lēᵊni·fěrəs), *a.* 1656. [f. L. *lanifer* (f. *lana* wool + *-fer* bearing) + -OUS.] Wool-bearing.

Lanific (lēᵊni·fik), *a. rare.* 1693. [ad. L. *lanificus,* f. *lana* wool + *-ficus* making; see -FIC.] a. Wool-producing. b. Busied in spinning wool. So †**Lani·fical** *a.* 1656.

†**La·nifice.** *rare.* 1626. [a. obs. F. *lanifice,* ad. L. *lanificium,* f. *lanificus*; see prec.] A spinning or weaving of wool; *concr.* wool-work –1633.

Lanigerous (lēᵊni·dʒěrəs), *a.* 1608. [f. L. *laniger* (f. *lana* wool + *ger-* carrying) + -OUS.] Wool-bearing; woolly.

‖**Lanista** (lăni·stă). 1834. [L.] A trainer of gladiators.

Lank (læŋk), *a.* (*sb.*) [OE. *hlanc*; not in other Teut. langs.; cf. Ger. *lenken* to bend, turn aside. See also LINK *sb.*²] 1. Loose from emptiness; not plump; shrunken, spare; flabby, hollow. Of grass: Long and flaccid 1634. Also *fig.* 2. Of hair: Not wavy, straight and flat 1690. †3. *sb.* Leanness, scarcity, thinness –1727.

1. The bard was a l. bony figure, with short black hair BOSWELL. My Purse..is but l. D'URFEY. A poem l. and long COWPER. 2. The extreme Puritan was at once known..by..his l. hair MACAULAY. Hence †**Lank** *v.* to make or become l. †**La·nk-ly** *adv.*, **-ness.**

Lanky (læ·ŋki), *a.* 1637. [f. LANK *a.* + -Y¹.] Awkwardly lean and long. †Also (of hair) somewhat lank. **La·nkily** *adv.*, **La·nkiness.**

Lanner (læ·nəɹ). ME. [ad. F. *lanier,* app. OF. *lanier* cowardly, used subst.] A species of falcon, found in countries bordering on the Mediterranean, *Falco lanarius* or *F. feldeggi.* In *Falconry,* the female of this species. So **La·nneret** (†lan(n)ard), the male of the l.

Lanolin (læ·nŏlin). Also **lanoline.** 1882. [f. L. *lana* wool + *ol-eum* oil + -IN¹.] *Chem.* The cholesterin-fatty matter extracted from sheep's wool, used as a basis for ointments.

Lansquenet (lɑ·nskěnet). Also **lamb-skin-it** (in sense 2 only). 1607. [a. F. *lansquenet,* ad. G. *landsknecht,* f. *lands* (genitive) country + *knecht* servant. *Landsknecht* was written early *lanzknecht,* as if f. *lanz* lance: see LANCE-KNIGHT.] 1. *Hist.* One of a class of mercenary soldiers in the German and other armies in the 16th and 17th centuries. 2. A game at cards, of German origin 1687.

2. He..sits down to Macco and l. THACKERAY.

Lant (lænt), *sb.*¹ Now *rare.* [OE. *hland, hlond.* The form *lant* is app. n. w. dial.] Urine; chamber-lye. Hence †**Lant** *v.* to mingle with l. 1630.

Lant (lænt), *sb.*² 1620. A fish = LAUNCE².

Lant, *sb.*³ *dial.* 1706. Short for LANTERLOO.

Lantanium, var. of LANTHANUM.

†**La·nterloo.** 1668. [ad. F. *lantur(e)lu,* orig. the unmeaning refrain of a popular 17th c. song.] The older form of LOO *sb.*¹

Lantern (læ·ntəɹn), *sb.* Also **lanthorn.** ME. [ad. F. *lanterne,* ad. L. *lanterna,* ad. Gr. λαμπτήρ (f. λάμπειν, see LAMP *sb.*¹), with ending after L. *lucerna.* Lanterns were formerly made of horn, hence prob. the form *lanthorn.*] 1. A transparent case, e. g. of glass, horn, talc, enclosing and protecting a light. b. *spec.* = MAGIC LANTERN. Chiefly *attrib.* c. *transf.* and *fig.* ME. 2. †A lighthouse –1705; the chamber at the top of a lighthouse, in which the light is placed 1796. 3. *Arch.* An open erection, on the top of a dome or of a room, having the apertures glazed, to admit light; a similar structure for ventilation, etc. ME. 4. A name of certain fishes; *esp.* the whiff, *Arnoglossus megastomus* 1674. 5. a. The luminous appendage of the lantern-fly 1750. b. *Aristotle's Lantern*: a name for the masticating apparatus of *Echinus,* from its shape 1841. 6. *techn.* a. *Calico-printing,* etc. A steam chamber in which the colours of printed fabrics are fixed 1839. b. *Electricity.* The part of the case of the quadrant electrometer which surrounds the mirror and suspension-fibres 1872. c. *Founding.* A perforated barrel to form a core upon 1839. d. *Mech.* A form of cog-wheel; 'a cylinder, in which the top and bottom are formed by circular plates or boards, connected by staves inserted at equal distances along their circumferences, serving as teeth' 1659.

1. By..the l. dimly burning C. WOLFE. †*L. and candle-light*: the old cry of the London bellman at night. c. Camden l..lanterne unto late succeeding age SPENSER.

Comb.: l.-**carrier** (also *-bearer*) = *lantern-fly*; **-fish,** the smooth sole; **-fly,** one of several species of insects of the family *Fulgoridæ*; **-jaws,** long thin jaws, giving a hollow appearance to the cheek; hence **-jawed** *a.*; **-light,** (*a*) the light from a l.; (*b*) a light (i. e. a glazed frame or sash) in the side of a l. (sense 3); (*c*) an arrangement for giving light through the roof of an apartment; **-pinion** = *lantern-wheel*; **-shell,** the bivalve genus *Anatina,* with a translucent shell; **-wheel** = sense 6 d.

Lantern (læ·ntəɹn), *v.* Also **lanthorn.** 1789. [f. the sb.] 1. a. *trans.* To enclose as in a lantern. b. To furnish, or light, with a lantern. 2. To put to death by hanging on a lamp-post. (= F. *lanterner.*) 1855.

Lanthanite (læ·nþănəit). 1849. [f. next + -ITE.] *Min.* Hydrous carbonate of lanthanum, found in white tabular crystals.

Lanthanum (læ·nþănŏm). Also **lant(h)anium.** 1841. [f. Gr. λανθάνειν to lie hid.] *Chem.* A rare element belonging to the group of earth metals, found in certain rare minerals, e. g. cerite; so called because it had lain concealed in oxide of cerium, etc. Symbol Ln.

Lanthopine (læ·nþǒpīn). 1880. [f. Gr. λανθάνειν (see prec.) + OP-IUM + -INE⁵.] *Chem.* An alkaloid found in opium.

Lanthorn, var. of LANTERN.

Lanuginous (lăniū·dʒinəs), *a.* 1575. [ad. L. *lanuginosus,* f. *lanugin-* (*lanugo*) down, f. *lana* wool; see -OUS.] Covered with down or fine soft hair; of the nature of down; downy. So **Lanu·ginose** 1693.

‖**Lanugo** (lăniū·go). 1677. [L., f. *lana* wool.] Fine soft hair or down, or a surface resembling this; *spec.* that covering the human fœtus.

Lanyard (læ·nyăɹd). 1425. [A re-adoption of F. *lanière* (see LAINER).] 1. = LAINER. Now *dial.* 2. *Naut.* 'A short piece of rope or line made fast to anything to secure it, or as a handle' (Smyth). Used: **a.** to secure the shrouds and stays 1626; **b.** for firing a gun 1825; **c.** for various other purposes 1669. **d.** The material of lanyards 1862.

2. **c.** Four ladders (each of which to have a l. four fathoms long) NELSON.

Lanzknecht (Ger.): see LANSQUENET.

Laodicean (lēⁱōdisī·ăn). 1564. [f. L. *Laodicea* (a. Gr. Λαοδίκεια) a city of Asia Minor + -AN.]

A. *adj.* **a.** Of or pertaining to Laodicea. **b.** 'Lukewarm, neither cold nor hot' (*Rev.* iii. 16), *esp.* in religion, politics, etc. 1633.

b. This L. cant of tolerance MRS. H. WARD.

B. *sb.* **a.** An inhabitant of Laodicea 1611. **b.** One who is lukewarm in religion, politics, etc. 1625 (BACON). Hence **Laodice·anism,** indifference.

Lap (læp), *sb.*¹ [OE. *lappa, læppa* wk. masc.; cf. ON. *lepp-r* clout, rag, lock of hair. ? Conn. w. Gr. λοβός LOBE, with Skr. *ramb-, lamb-*, to hang loose, or with Lith. *lópas* patch.] †1. A part (of a garment or the like) hanging down or projecting; a flap, lappet. In later use chiefly, a piece that hangs down at the bottom of a garment, one of the skirts of a coat, a portion of the skirt of a robe. Hence *pl.* (*colloq.*) a tail-coat. **2. a.** Of the ear, liver, lungs: = LOBE. *Obs.* exc. in *ear-lap.* OE. †**b.** A fold of flesh or skin -1615. †**3.** A cloth, clout -14.. **4.** The 'lap' (sense 1) used as a receptacle. †**a.** The fold of a robe over the breast; hence, the bosom -1643. **b.** The front portion of a skirt when held up ME. **5.** The front part from waist to knees of a person seated, as, with its covering garments, the place *in* or *on* which a child is nursed or an object held ME. **b.** *transf.* A hollow among hills 1745.

1. When David had cut off the l. of Saul's Garment HALES. 4. **b.** Girls with laps full of flowers LYTTON. 5. A Saylors Wife had Chestnuts in her Lappe SHAKS. She lays me upon my Face in her L. STEELE. **b.** A little valley, or rather l. of land, among high hills W. IRVING. Phr. *In fortune's, pleasure's l.*; *in the l. of* (luxury, etc.); *in the l. of Providence, the future* (all *fig.*). †*To fall into the l.* or *laps of*: to come within the reach, or into the power, of. (*Lapse* is occas. written for *laps*, by confusion with LAPSE *sb.*) *Comb.* **l.-board,** a board to lay on the l., as a substitute for a table.

Lap (læp), *sb.*² ME. [f. LAP *v.*¹] **1.** Something that is lapped; *esp.* liquid food for dogs. Also, *slang* and *dial.*, any weak beverage. 1567. **b.** *slang.* Liquor in general 1618. **2.** The action or an act of lapping; also, so much as may be taken up thus. Also *fig.* ME. **3.** A sound resembling that of lapping; e. g. that of wavelets on the beach 1884.

Lap (læp), *sb.*³ 1673. [f. LAP *v.*²] †**1.** ? A bundle. **2.** The amount by which one thing overlaps another; hence *concr.* the overlapping part 1800. **b.** *Steam-engine.* The distance traversed by a slide-valve beyond what is needed to close the passage of steam to or from the cylinder 1869. **c.** *U.S.* Any portion of a railroad track used in common by the trains of more than one system 1895. **3.** *Euchre.* In a series of games: Counting upon the score of the ensuing game all the points made over and above the five of which the game consists 1886. **4.** A layer or sheet (usually wound upon a bobbin or roller) into which cotton, wool, or flax is formed in certain stages of its manufacture 1825. **5.** The act of encircling, or the length of rope required to encircle, a drum or wheel. Also, enough thread, etc., to go once round something. 1867. **b.** *Racing.* One circuit of the track 1861.

2. The hand-made cigarette.. having a smaller 'l.' 1897. *Half-l.*: an arrangement, consisting in cutting away half the thickness of the two ends of rails, shafts, etc., to be joined, and fitting them together 1816. 5. **b.** A running track, three laps to the mile 1884.

attrib. and Comb., as (sense 2) *l.-dovetail, -jointed; l.-weld* sb. and vb. Also **l.-joint** = *half-l.* (see above).

Lap (læp), *sb.*⁴ 1812. [? a use of prec.] A rotating disk of soft metal or wood, used to hold polishing powder in cutting or polishing gems or metal. **b.** *Gun-making.* An iron rod round which is secured a leaden plug of the exact size of the tube of the gun barrel to be polished 1881.

Lap (læp), *v.*¹ [OE. *lapian*:—OTeut. *lap- (cogn. w. L. *lambĕre*, Gr. λάπτειν to lick, lap). The form *lappe, lap* (superseding the normal *lape*) is perh. after F. *laper.*] **1.** *intr.* To take up liquid with the tongue. **2.** *trans.* Of animals, *rarely* of human beings: To take up (liquid, *rarely* food) with the tongue; to drink greedily up. Also with *up.* **3.** *intr.* Of water: To move with a sound like that made in lapping 1823. **4.** *trans.* To beat upon (the shore, etc.) with a lapping sound 1854.

1. Vncouer Dogges, and l. *Timon* III. vi. 95. 2. They'l take suggestion, as a Cat laps milke SHAKS. 3. I heard the water lapping on the crag TENNYSON.

Lap (læp), *v.*² [ME. *lappe*, in *bi-lappe*, etc. Prob. f. LAP *sb.*¹ in sense 'fold' or 'piece of cloth'. A form *wlappe* which occurs is prob. after WRAP *v.*] **1.** *trans.* To coil, fold, wrap (a garment, etc.). Also *intr.* for *refl.* (now *dial.*). **2.** To fold, fold *up, together*; to roll *up* in successive layers. Const. *into.* Now only *dial.* ME. **3.** To enfold in a wrap or wraps, to enwrap, swathe; hence, to clothe, to bind up, tie round ME. Also *transf.* †**b.** To fold (*in the arms*); to embrace -1513. **4.** †**a.** To involve; to imply, include; to implicate; to wrap *up* in a disguise -1677. **b.** Of conditions, etc.: To enfold, surround, *esp.* with soothing, stupefying, or seductive effect. Often with *round.* ME. **5.** To enfold caressingly; to nurse, fondle; to surround with care. Now chiefly *pass.*, to be nursed *in* luxury, etc. ME. **6.** *trans.* **a.** To lay (something) *on, over* (another thing) so as partly to cover it. **b.** Of a slide-valve: To pass over and close (a port). Also, to cause (a slide-valve) to overlap the port. **c.** ? *U.S.* Of a boat, in racing: To come partly alongside (another). 1607. **7.** *Racing. trans.* To get one or more laps ahead of (a competitor) 1890. **b.** To travel over (a distance) as a lap 1923. **8.** [Prop. f. LAP *sb.*³ sense 4.] *trans.* To reduce raw cotton to a lap 1851.

3. The good old Prelate lies lapp'd in lead SCOTT. Phr. *To l. on*: to fix on with a lapping of thread or the like. 4. **b.** And ever against eating Cares, L. me in soft Lydian Aires, Married to immortal verse MILTON. 5. Lapped in idle luxury HAZLITT.

Phr. *To l. into* (something): to project *into* (something). *To l. over* (with *over* adv.): to project beyond something else, forming a lap or flap; *fig.* to extend beyond some limit. *Comb.* **l.-work,** work in which one part is interchangeably lapped over another.

Lap (læp), *v.*³ 1881. [f. LAP *sb.*⁴] *trans.* To polish (steel, etc.) with a lap (see LAP *sb.*⁴).

Laparo- (læ·părо), rarely bef. a vowel lapar-, comb. f. Gr. λαπάρα flank, f. λαπαρός soft, in terms of *Anat., Surg.*, etc. **Lapare·ctomy** [Gr. ἐκτομ-, ἐκτέμνειν], an excision of a portion of the intestine at the side. **Laparo·tomy** [Gr. -τομία cutting], a cutting through the abdominal walls into the cavity of the abdomen.

La·p-dog. 1645. [f. LAP *sb.*¹ 5 + DOG.] A small dog, such as may lie in a lady's lap.

Lapel (lăpe·l). Also †**lapell(e, lappel.** 1789. [f. LAP *sb.*¹ + -EL.] That part of the front of a coat which is folded over towards either shoulder. Hence **Lape·lled** *a.* furnished with a l.; folded over so as to form a l. 1751.

Lapful (læ·pful). 1611. [f. LAP *sb.*¹ + -FUL.] So much as will fill a person's lap.

Lapicide (læ·pisəid). 1656. [ad. L. *lapicida* for *lapidicida*, f. *lapid-, lapis* stone; see -CIDE 1.] One who cuts stones, or inscriptions on stone.

Lapidarian (læpidēᵊ·riăn), *a. rare.* 1683. [f. L. *lapidarius* + -AN.] **a.** Versed in the knowledge of stones. **b.** Executed in, or inscribed on, stone.

Lapidary (læ·pidări). ME. [ad. L. *lapidarius* adj and sb. (Cf. F. *lapidaire.*) In A. 2 and 3 ad. L. *lapidarium* or **lapidaria.*]

A. *sb.* **1. a.** An artificer who cuts, polishes, or engraves precious stones ME. †**b.** One skilled in gems or precious stones; a connoisseur of lapidary work -1796. **2.** A treatise on (precious) stones. *Obs.* exc. *Hist.* ME. †**3.** *collect.* Precious stones, jewellery -1609.

Comb. **lapidary('s-mill, -wheel,** the grinding and polishing apparatus of the l.

B. *adj.* **1. a.** Engraved on stone. **b.** Of style, etc.: Characteristic of or suitable for monumental inscriptions. 1724. **2.** Concerned with stones. *rare* exc. in *l. bee.* 1831.

1. In l. inscriptions a man is not upon oath JOHNSON. 2. The l. red-tipped bees, that built..in old dry stone walls H. MILLER.

Lapidate (læ·pideⁱt), *v.* 1623. [f. L. *lapidat-, lapidare*, f. *lapid-, lapis.* Cf. F. *lapider.*] *trans.* To throw stones at; also, to stone to death. So **Lapida·tion,** stoning to death; pelting with stones 1611.

Lapideous (lăpi·dĭəs), *a.* Now *rare.* 1646. [f. L. *lapideus*, f. *lapid-, lapis.*] **1.** Of the nature of stone, stony. †**2.** Consisting of or inscribed on stone, as *l. records.* G. CHALMERS.

Lapidescent (læpide·sĕnt), *a.* (*sb.*) ? *Obs.* 1644. [ad. L. *lapidescentem, lapidescere* to become stony.] That is in process of becoming stone; having a tendency to solidify into stone. Said chiefly of petrifying waters and the salts dissolved or suspended in them. *sb.* [sc. *substance*]. Hence **Lapide·scence,** l. condition; petrifaction. **Lapide·scency.**

Lapidific, †-al (læpidi·fik, -ăl), *a.* 1646. [f. L. *lapid-, lapis* + -(I)FIC, + -AL.] Adapted to or concerned with the making of stones.

Lapidify (lăpi·difəi), *v.* 1657. [ad. F. *lapidifier*, ad. med.L. *lapidificare*; see -FY.] To †become or make into stone. Hence **Lapi:difica·tion** 1626.

†**La·pidist.** *rare.* 1647. [f. L. *lapid-, lapis* + -IST.] = LAPIDARY *sb.* 1 a or b -1691.

Lapidose (læ·pidōᵘs), *a.* ME. [ad. L. *lapidosus.*] **1.** Abounding in stones; of stony nature. **2.** Growing in stony ground 1866.

‖**Lapilli** (lăpi·ləi), *pl.* 1747. [L., pl. of *lapillus*, dim. of *lapis.* In the spec. sense orig. pl. of It. *lapillo.*] Small stones or pebbles; now only *spec.* of the fragments of stone ejected from volcanoes.

‖**Lapis** (læ·pis). 1641. The Latin word for 'stone'. **1.** Used in: **l. Armenus,** Armenian stone, a blue carbonate of copper; **l. calaminaris,** calamine; **l. causticus,** caustic potash; **l. infernalis,** lunar caustic; **l. judaicus** = JEWS' STONE 1; **l. ollaris,** potstone, or soapstone; etc. **2.** Short for: **a.** med.L. *lapis philosophicus*, philosophers' stone; **b.** LAPIS LAZULI. 1666.

‖**Lapis lazuli, lapis-lazuli** (læ·pis læ·ziŭləi). Also shortened LAZULI. ME. [L. *lapis* + med.L. *lazuli* gen. of *lazulum*: see AZURE.] *Min.* A complex silicate containing sulphur, of bright blue colour, used as a pigment (see ULTRAMARINE). Also, the colour of this.

Some lump, ah God, of *lapis lazuli*,..Blue as a vein o'er the Madonna's breast BROWNING.

Lapland (læ·plǽnd). 1590. [a. Sw. *Lappland*; see LAPP and LAND.] The most northerly portion of the Scandinavian peninsula; formerly, the fabled home of witches and magicians, who had power to send winds and tempests. Often *attrib.* †**b.** A native of this region; a Lapland witch -1635. Hence **La·plander,** an inhabitant of L.; a Lapp. So **Lapla·ndian, -ic, La·plandish** *adjs.* of or pertaining to L., its people, or their language.

†**La·pling.** 1627. [f. LAP *sb.*¹ + -LING.] One who loves to lie on a (lady's) lap -1658.

Lapp (læp). 1846. [a. Sw. *lapp*, ? orig. a term of contempt. In med.L. *Lap(p)o* (pl. *Lap(p)ones*), whence F. *Lapon.*]

A. *sb.* One of a Mongoloid race (called by themselves *Sabme*), of dwarfish stature, inhabiting the north of Scandinavia.

B. *adj.* Pertaining to this race, Lappish; also *absol.* the Lappish language.

Lappaceous (læpēⁱ·ʃəs), *a.* 1707. [f. L. *lappaceus* (f. *lappa* a bur) + -OUS.] *Bot.* Of, pertaining to, or resembling a bur.

Lapper¹ (læ·pəɹ). 1606. [f. LAP *v.*¹ + -ER¹.] One who laps, or takes up (liquid) with the tongue.

Lapper² (læ·pəɹ). 1732. [f. LAP *v.*² + -ER¹.] One who laps or folds up (linen).

Lapper³ (læ·pəɹ). 1877. [f. LAP *v.*³ + -ER¹.] One who uses a lap or lapidary wheel.

Lappet (læ·pĕt), *sb.* 1573. [f. LAP *sb.*¹ + -ET.] **1.** A loose or overlapping part of a garment; a flap, fold. **b.** *gen.* A part of anything that hangs loose 1677. **2. a.** A fold or pendent piece of flesh, skin, membrane, etc. 1605. **b.** A lobe of the ear, liver, lungs, etc. 1609. **3.** The flap or skirt (of a coat). Also, the lapel. 1726. **4.** One of the streamers attached to a lady's head-dress; or any appendage to head-gear. In clerical attire, = BAND *sb.*[2] 4 b. 1720. **5.** Short for *lappet-moth* 1857.

4. A sealskin cap with ear lappets 1869.

Comb.: **l.-end**, the free end of a l. of lace, etc., often highly ornamented; **-moth**, one of several species of bombycid moths; **-weaving**, a method of weaving by which figures are produced on the surface of cloth by means of needles placed in a sliding frame; so **l.-muslin.**

Hence **La·ppet** *v. trans.* to cover with, or as with a l. 1864. **La·ppeted** *ppl. a.* wearing lappets; (of a head-dress) provided with lappets 1797.

Lappic (læ·pik), *a.* (*sb.*) [f. LAPP + -IC.] Pertaining to the Lapps. Also *absol.* the L. language.

Lapping (læ·piŋ), *vbl. sb.* ME. [f. LAP *v.*[2] + -ING[1].] †**1.** The action of LAP *v.*[2] Also *concr.* A wrapping; wraps, trappings. **2.** The process of forming into laps; *attrib.* in *l. cylinder, machine* 1825.

Lappish (læ·piʃ). 1875. [f. LAPP + -ISH[1].] **A.** *adj.* Of or pertaining to the Lapps or their language. **B.** *sb.* Their language.

Lapponian (læpōᵘ·niăn). 1607. [ad. med.L. *Lap(p)onem* (see LAPP) + -IAN.] **A.** *adj.* = LAPPISH *a.* **B.** *sb.* A Lapp.

Lapsable, lapsible (læ·psăb'l, -ib'l), *a.* 1678. [f. L. *lapsare* (see LAPSE *v.*) or *laps-, labi* to fall, slip.] **1.** Liable to pass or change; liable to err or fall. Const. *into.* ? *Obs.* **2.** *Law.* Liable to lapse 1751. Hence **Lapsabi·lity, -ibi·lity** 1661.

Lapse (læps), *sb.* 1450. [ad. L. *lapsus*, f. *labi* to glide, slip, fall.] †**1.** Utterance (of words). **2.** A slip of memory, tongue, pen, or †understanding; a slight error 1526. **3.** A weak or incautious falling from rectitude; a moral slip 1582. †**b.** *Theol.* The 'Fall' (of Adam) -1774. **c.** A lapsing *from* the faith, or *into* heresy; a deviation *from* one's rule of action 1660. **4.** A decline to a lower state or degree 1533. **5. a.** *Law.* The termination of a right or privilege through neglect to exercise it within the limited time, or through failure of some contingency 1570. **b.** *gen.* A falling into disuse 1838. **c.** A falling into ruin (*rare*) 1605. **6.** A gliding, flow (of water); a gliding flood. Also *occas.* a gentle downward motion. 1667. **b.** The gliding away (of life, time, etc.); a period elapsed 1758. **c.** *L. rate*, the rate of fall of temperature with height 1928.

3. The severe training which he had undergone made him less charitable for the lapses of others PRESCOTT. **c.** It is from their lapses and deviations from their principle, that alone we have any thing to hope BURKE. **5. a.** By the l. of some annuities on lives not so prolonged as her own, she found herself straitened H. WALPOLE. **6.** Sunnie Plaines, And liquid L. of murmuring Streams MILT. *P. L.* VIII. 263. **b.** Thou hast not felt the l. of hours M. ARNOLD.

Lapse (læps), *v.* 1611. [ad. L. *lapsare* to slip, stumble, fall, f. *laps-, labi.* In some senses, prob. f. LAPSE *sb.*]

I. *intr.* **1.** To fall away by slow degrees; to sink gradually through want of effort or vigour. Also with *away, back.* Const. *from, into.* 1641. †**b.** *simply.* To fall into error, heresy, or sin -1667. †**2.** To fall into decay -1654. **3.** *Law.* Of a benefice, an estate, a right, etc.: To fall in, pass away, revert (*to* some one) by non-fulfilment of conditions or failure of persons entitled to possession. Of a devise or grant: To become void. 1726. **4.** To glide, pass with an effortless motion; to descend gradually, sink 1798. **b.** Of a stream: To glide, flow. Also with *along.* Occas. of a person, a vessel: To float, glide gently over the water. 1832. **c.** Of time: To glide past, pass *away* 1702.

1. Should the British constitution ultimately l. into a despotism MALTHUS. **b.** To l. in Fulnesse Is sorer, then to lye for Neede *Cymb.* III. vi. 12. **3.** The income..lapses and goes to the..next of kin 1884. **4. b.** I saw the river lapsing calmly onward HAWTHORNE.

II. *trans.* (causative). †**1.** To cause to slip or fall, to draw down. Const. *into.* -1681. †**2.** To let slip (time, a term); to let pass unused -1726. †**3.** To allow (a right) to lapse; to suffer the lapse of (a living); to forfeit, lose -1697. ¶**4.** ? Assoc. w. *lapse* = *laps* pl. (LAP *sb.*[1] Phr.): ? To pounce upon as an offender 1601.

4. For which if I be lapsed in this place I shall pay deere *Twel. N.* III. iii. 36.

Lapsed (læpst), *ppl. a.* 1617. [f. LAPSE *v.* + -ED[1].] **1.** That has glided away, dropped out of use, disappeared, or fallen into decay 1667. **2.** Of a person: Fallen into a lower grade or condition; esp. fallen into sin, or from the faith; applied *Hist.* to Christians who denied the faith during persecution. Also *absol.* 1638. **3.** Said of a fief, devise, etc., the right to which has passed from the original holder, devisee, etc. 1617.

1. Once more I will renew His l. powers, though forfeit MILT. *P. L.* III. 176.

Lapser (læ·psəɹ). 1695. [f. LAPSE *v.* + -ER[1].] One who lapses (†esp. *from* the Christian faith).

Lapsible, etc.: see LAPSABLE, etc.

Lapsided, var. of LOP-SIDED.

La·pstone. 1778. [f. LAP *sb.*[1] + STONE.] A stone that shoemakers lay in their laps to beat leather upon.

La·p-streak. 1771. [f. LAP *sb.*[3] + STREAK.] A boat in which each streak overlaps the one below; a clinker-built boat.

‖**Lapsus** (læ·psɒ̆s). 1667. [L.; see LAPSE *sb.*] A lapse, slip, or error. Chiefly in **l. linguæ**, a slip of the tongue, and **l. calami**, a slip of the pen.

Laputan (lăpiū·tăn). In Swift **Laputian.** 1726. [f. *Laputa*, the flying island in *Gulliver's Travels*, whose inhabitants were addicted to visionary projects; see -AN, -IAN.]

A. *adj.* Of or pertaining to Laputa; hence, chimerical, visionary, absurd.

B. *sb.* An inhabitant of Laputa.

Swift's idea of extracting sunbeams out of cucumbers, which he attributes to his L. philosophers HERSCHEL.

Lapwing (læ·pwiŋ). [OE. *hlēapewince*, str. fem., f. *hlēapan* to leap + **winc-* to totter, waver. Named from its manner of flight. The current form is connected in pop. etym. with LAP *v.*[2] and WING *sb.*] A bird of the plover family, *Vanellus vulgaris* or *cristatus*, common in the temperate parts of the Old World. Called also PEWIT, from its cry. Its eggs are the 'plovers' eggs' of the London markets. Also *attrib.* as *l. stratagem*, etc., in allusion to its habit of leading a stranger away from its nest.

This L. runs away with the shell on his head SHAKS. In the Spring the wanton l. gets himself another crest TENNYSON.

Laquais, -ay, obs. ff. LACKEY.

‖**Laquear** (læ·kwiaɹ). 1706. [f. L. *laqueus* noose, band; see LACE *sb.*] *Arch.* A ceiling consisting of compartments sunk or hollowed, with bands between the panels.

Laquearian (lækwiē°·riăn), *a.* [f. L. *laquearius* + -AN.] Of a gladiator: Armed with a noose to entangle his opponent. BYRON. So †**La·queary** *a.* SIR T. BROWNE.

‖**Lar** (lāɹ). *Pl.* ‖**lares** (lē°·rīz), **lars** (lāɹz). Also †**larre.** 1586. [L. *lar*, pl. *lares.*] **1.** *Rom. Myth.* **a.** *pl.* The tutelary deities of a house; hence, the home. Often coupled with *Penates.* **b.** *sing.* A household or ancestral deity; also *fig.* **2.** *Zool.* The white-handed gibbon of Burmah, *Hylobates lar* 1819.

1. On the holy Hearth, The Lars, and Lemures moan with midnight plaint MILTON. Build houses; joyne to ours anothers lares 1647. **b.** Thomas Pitt.. the great *lar* of not fewer than five families in the English peerage 1889.

Larboard (lā·ɹbōᵊɹd, -bəɹd), *sb.* (*a.*) [ME. *lad(d)eborde, latheborde*, altered later to *ler-, leere-, larbord*, after *ster-, steere-, starbord*; f. *ladde-, lathe-* + OE. *bord* ship's side (BOARD *sb.* V. 1). Some connect the first component with LADE *v.*, taking it to mean 'the side on which cargo was received'.] *Naut.* **1.** The side of a ship which is to the left hand of a person looking from the stern to the bows. Opp. to STARBOARD. (Now repl. by *port*, to avoid confusion with *starboard.*) †**b.** as *adv.* = To larboard -1667. **2.** *attrib.* or *adj.* Belonging to or situated on the left or port side of a vessel 1495. **b.** *joc.* for: Left 1781.

2. On the l. quarter FALCONER. **b.** My l. eye COWPER.

Larcener (lā·ɹsĕnəɹ). 1634. [f. LARCENY + -ER[1].] One who commits larceny. Also *fig.* So **La·rcenist** 1803.

Larcenous (lā·ɹsĕnəs), *a.* 1742. [f. LARCENY + -OUS.] Pertaining to or characterized by larceny; thievish.

The l. and burglarious world SYD. SMITH. Hence **La·rcenously** *adv.* thievishly.

Larceny (lā·ɹsĕni). 1460. [app. f. AF. *larcin* (see LARCIN and -Y[3,4]), perh. infl. by L. *latrocinium.*] *Law.* The felonious taking and carrying away of the personal goods of another with intent to convert them to the taker's use. Also *gen.* theft.

Distinction was formerly made between *grand* and *petty l.*, the former being larceny of property of more, the latter of less, than 12 pence in value. *Simple l.*, plain theft unaccompanied by any aggravating circumstance; *mixed* or *compound l.*, larceny including the aggravation of a taking from one's house or person.

Larch (lāɹtʃ). 1548. [Introduced by Turner, ad. G. *lärche* :—MHG. *lerche, larche* :—OHG. **lerihha*, **larihha*, early ad. L. *laricem, larix* (whence late Gr. λάριξ).] **1.** A well-known coniferous tree, *Abies Larix* or *L. europæa*, a native of the Alps, largely cultivated. Its timber is tough. It yields Venetian turpentine, and the bark is used in tanning. **b.** Any tree of the genus *Larix*, e. g. the American Larch, *L. Americana.* **2.** The wood of this tree 1867.

1. When rosy plumelets tuft the l. TENNYSON.

Comb. **l.-bark**, the bark of the larch-tree; the *laricis cortex* of the British Pharmacopœia. Hence **La·rchen** *a.* consisting of larches, larch-.

†**La·rcin.** ME. [a. AF. and F. *larcin*, OF. *larrecin* (also *larcine* fem.) :—L. *latrocinium*, f. *latro* robber.] **1.** = LARCENY -1679. **2.** A larcener 1596-1656.

Lard (lāɹd), *sb.* ME. [a. OF. (mod.F.) *lard* bacon :—L. *lardum, laridum*, ? cogn. w. Gr. λαρινός fat, λαρός pleasant to the taste.] †**1.** The fat of a swine; (fat) bacon or pork; *rarely*, other fat meat used for larding -1725. **2.** (Often *hog's lard.*) The fat of a swine, esp. the internal fat of the abdomen, rendered and clarified, much used in cooking and in pharmacy ME. Also *transf.* **3.** *attrib.* 1555.

2. Fritters of flour fried in bear's l. W. IRVING. *Neutral l.*, l. made from the best internal fat. *Compound l.*, l. made from vegetable oils.

Comb.: **l.-oil**, an oil made from l., now used chiefly for lubricating machinery.

Lard (lāɹd), *v.* ME. [ad. F. *larder*, f. *lard* (see prec.).] **1.** *Cookery.* (*trans.*) To insert small strips of bacon, etc., in (meat, poultry, etc.) before cooking. Also *absol.* †**2.** To enrich with or as with fat; to fatten -1687. Also †*intr.* for *refl.* or *pass.* **3.** *transf.* To stick all over *with*; to cover, line, or strew *with.* *Obs.* or *arch.* 1543. Also †*fig.* **4.** To garnish (speech or writing) with particular words, expressions, ideas, etc.; to interlard 1549. **5.** To smear, cover, or mix with lard or fat; to grease (*rare*) ME. †**6.** *intr.* To ooze with lard. HANMER.

1. Nearly all lean meat may be larded with advantage 1884. **2.** Falstaffe sweates to death, and Lards the leane earth as he walkes along SHAKS. **3.** Their sides were altogether larded with arrowes SPEED. **4.** Monkes began to l. the lives of their Saints with lies FULLER. **5.** His Buff Doublet, larded o'er with Fat Of slaughter'd Brutes SOMERVILLE.

Lardacein (laɹdē¹·si,in). 1873. [f. as next + -IN[1].] *Chem.* A nitrogenous substance found deposited under morbid conditions in certain minute arteries and tissues of the body.

Lardaceous (laɹdē¹·ʃəs), *a.* 1822. [f. LARD *sb.* + -ACEOUS.] *Med.* Of the nature of or resembling lard; containing lardacein; *spec.* applied to amyloid degeneration; also said of the patient.

Larder[1] (lā·ɹdəɹ). ME. [a. OF. *lardier*, AF. *larder* :—med.L. *lardarium*, f. *lardum* LARD *sb.*] **1.** A room or closet in which meat (? orig. bacon) and other provisions are stored. Also *transf.* and *fig.* †**2.** *fig.* Chiefly in phr. *to make l. of*: to turn into meat for the larder; hence, to slaughter; *to larder*, to the slaughter-house. Also *occas.* simply = slaughter. ME.

1. Dress drains our cellar dry, And keeps our larder lean COWPER. **2.** Than [in November] is the l. of the swine GOWER.

Comb.: **l.-beetle**, *Dermestes lardarius*, an insect which devours stored animal foods; **-house** = sense 1.

Larder [2]. [f. LARD *v.* + -ER [1].] One who lards. FLORIO.

Larderer (lā·ɹdĕrəɹ). 1483. [? after CELLARER.] One who has charge of a larder.

Larderie, -ery, var. of LARDRY.

Lardiner (lā·ɹdinəɹ). ME. [a. AF. *lardiner*, altered f. *larder*, OF. *lardier*; see LARD *sb.*] †1. = LARDER [1] 1. *n.* and *Sc.* –1710. 2. An official who has charge of a larder. *Obs.* exc. as the title of an honorary office. ME.

Lardon (lā·ɹdən), **lardoon** (laɹdū·n). 1450. [a. F. *lardon* (= It. *lardone*), f. *lard*; see LARD *sb.*] *Cookery.* One of the pieces of bacon or pork used in larding meat.

†**La·rdry.** 1538. [ad. OF. *larderie*; see LARD *sb.* and -ERY.] = LARDER [1] 1. –1661.

Lardy (lā·ɹdi), *a.* 1881. [f. LARD *sb.* + -Y [1].] Full of or containing lard; fat.

La·rdy-da·rdy, *a. slang.* 1861. [Cf. LA-DI-DA.] Affected and languidly foppish.

Lare: see LAIR, LAYER, LORE.

Lares: see LAR.

Large (lāɹdʒ), *a.*, *adv.*, and *sb.* ME. [a. F. *large*, now chiefly in the sense 'broad, wide':—L. *larga*, fem. of *largus*, abundant, profuse, etc.]

A. *adj.* †I. Liberal in giving; munificent; open-handed. Also, liberal in expenditure, prodigal, lavish –1688.

The poore King Reignier, whose l. style Agrees not with the leannesse of his purse SHAKS.

II. †1. Ample in quantity; copious, abundant –1667. †2. Ample in spatial extent; spacious, roomy, capacious –1697. b. *fig.* Of the heart: Capacious 1535. †3. = BROAD *a.* 1. Often in *long and l.* –1715. †4. With definite measures of space and time = GOOD *a.* V. 2. –1737. †b. Of the time of day: Full –1470. 5. Wide in range or capacity; comprehensive ME. b. With reference to artistic treatment: Broad 1782. 6. Of discourse, etc.: Copious, lengthy. Now *rare.* 1477. †b. Of persons: Diffuse, prolix –1788. 7. In mod. Eng., a general designation for considerable magnitude, without the emotional implication of *great*. The more colloq. synonym is *big*. ME. 8. Of speech or manner: Pompous, 'big' 1605.

1. And we have yet l. day, for scarce the Sun Hath finisht half his journey MILT. *P. L.* v. 558. 2. Two Golden Horns on his l. Front he wears DRYDEN. 3. Southward through Eden went a River l. MILT. *P. L.* IV. 223. 4. A l. League from Friburg 1678. b. It was l. mydnycht 1470. 5. A l. memory SWIFT. The court had a l. discretion as to the joinder of parties 1886. L. in his offers of friendship (*mod.*). 6. Mr. Wyatt spake a l. speech by hart WOOD. b. I could be very l. upon this point PENN. 7. A l. vpper roome 1611. Great Theron, l. of Limb DRYDEN. L. profits (*mod.*). A l. lunch KIPLING. *Comb.* l.-paper, a size of paper used for a special edition of a book, having extra large margins; also *attrib.* 8. Your l. speeches, may your deeds approue *Lear* I. i. 187.

III. [Developed from sense II. 2.] †1. Indulgent, lax; not strict or rigorous –1733. †2. Having few limitations or restrictions; allowing considerable freedom –1793. †3. Of language: Loose, inaccurate (*rare*). ME. only. 4. Of speech, etc.: Free, unrestrained; lax, licentious, gross –1599. 5. *Naut.* Said of a wind that crosses the line of the ship's course in a favourable direction, esp. on the beam or quarter 1591.

1. A l. conscience sticketh at nothing BIBLE (Douay) 1 *Sam.* xxiv. Comm. 4. I neuer tempted her with word too l. *Much Ado* IV. i. 53. 5. When the wind came larger we waied anchor and set saile 1591.

Comb.: l.-eyed *a.*, having a l. eye or l. eyes; characterized by wide open eyes; -lunged *a. Path.*, characterized by enlargement of the lungs; -minded *a.*, having a liberal mind; marked by breadth of ideas; taking a l. view of things; hence *large-mindedness*.

B. *adv.* †1. Amply; fully, quite, by a great deal; abundantly. Chiefly *n.* and *Sc.* –1667. †2. Generously –1667. †3. Of speech and writing: At length, fully –1676. †4. With ample gait –1695. 5. *Naut.* a. With a large wind; with the wind on the quarter or abaft the beam; 'with the wind free when studding sails will draw' (Smyth); off the wind; chiefly in *to sail, go l.* 1627. b. ? Wide of a particular course 1670.

1. Provisions laid in l. For Man and Beast MILTON. 2. Well we may..l. bestow From l. bestowd MILT. *P. L.* v. 317. 3. *New Presbyter* is but *Old Priest* writ L. MILT. 4. A black Gelding..Trotts l. 1695. 5. *By and l.*: to the wind (within six points) and off it. †Also *fig.* All ways. *To go* or *lead l.*: in a manœuvre, to break off at a particular point from the course marked out, and proceed straight ahead.

C. *sb.* †1. Liberality, bounty; ? also = LARGESS 2 –1537. 2. *Mus.* The longest note recognized in the early notation, equivalent to two or three 'longs', according to the rhythm employed; also, the character by which it was denoted, viz. ▜ or ⊏. 1547.

Phrases. **At large.** a. At liberty, free. †*At more l.*: at greater liberty. †*To set at l.* b. Unsettled; not limited or confined one way or another. ? *Obs.* c. Of speech, etc.: At length, fully. †d. In full size. *A. Y. L.* IV. iv. 175. e. As a whole; in general; (taken) altogether. f. In a general sense; without particularizing. Now *rare.* g. In the open sea (*rare*). †h. Over a large area; abroad. i. *Naut.* = 'going large' (see LARGE B. 5 a). j. *Law.* In *Common at l.*: 'such as is neither appendant nor appurtenant to land, but is annexed to a man's person' (Blackstone). k. *U. S.* Said of electors or elected who represent the whole of a State and not merely a district of it. l. Without definite aim or application. †**At one's l.**: at liberty. **In l.**: on a l. scale; opp. to *in little.* †**With the largest**: in the most liberal fashion. LD. BERNERS.

Hence **La·rgely** *adv.* in a l. manner. **La·rgeness.**

Large (lāɹdʒ), *v.* ME. [f. LARGE *a.* Cf. OF. *largir* and F. *larguer.*] †1. *trans.* To enlarge, increase, widen –1647. 2. *Naut.* Of the wind: To become 'large' 1622.

Large-handed, *a.* 1607. †1. *fig.* Rapacious. *Timon* IV. i. 11. 2. *fig.* Open-handed 1628. 3. *lit.* Having large hands 1896. Hence **Large-ha·ndedness.**

Large-hearted, *a.* 1640. Having a large heart (see LARGE *a.* II. 2 b); magnanimous, generous; having wide sympathies. Hence **Large-hea·rtedness.**

Largen (lā·ɹdʒ'n), *v. poet.* 1844. [f. LARGE *a.* + -EN [5].] To grow or make large or larger.

Eyes, large always, slowly l. PATMORE.

Largess, largesse (lā·ɹdʒes). *arch.* and *literary.* ME. [a. F. *largesse*:—late L. **largitia*, f. *largus* (see LARGE *a.*).] †1. Liberality, bountifulness, munificence. Also *personified.* –1623. 2. Liberal or bountiful bestowal of gifts; *occas.* †lavish expenditure; *concr.* money or gifts freely bestowed ME. b. A free gift or dole 1561. 3. *fig.* (from 2). A generous or plentiful bestowal; something freely bestowed 1533. †4. Freedom, liberty –1594.

2. Our Coffers, with too great a Court, And liberall Largesse, are growne somewhat light SHAKS. Your proposed largess to the Church BROWNING. *Largess!* or †*A largess!*: a call for a gift of money, addressed to a person of position on some special occasion. Only *Hist.*, except as surviving locally at 'harvest home'. b. A largess or bounty of five dollars a man DE FOE. 3. He 's like the sun, a largesse to the world CROWNE.

Larget (lā·ɹdʒĕt). 1875. [a. Fr.; f. *large* LARGE *a.*] A short piece of bar-iron for rolling into a sheet.

†**Largi·fical,** *a. rare.* 1656. [f. L. *largificus* + -AL.] Liberal, bountiful –1709.

Largish (lā·ɹdʒiʃ), *a.* 1754. [f. LARGE *a.* + -ISH [1].] Somewhat large.

Largition (laɹdʒi·ʃən). Now *rare.* 1533. [ad. L. *largitionem*, f. *largiri*, f. *largus* (see LARGE *a.*).] The bestowal of gifts or largess; bountiful giving.

‖**Largo** (lā·ɹgo). 1683. [It., = broad.] *Mus.* A direction: In slow time with a broad dignified treatment. Also as *sb.*

Lariat (læ·riăt), *sb.* 1835. [a. Sp. *la reata* (see RIATA).] A rope used for picketing horses or mules; a cord or rope with a noose used in catching wild cattle; the lasso of Mexico and S. America. Hence **La·riat** *v. trans.* to secure with a l.

Larid (læ·rid). [ad. mod.L. *Laridæ*, f. *larus* gull.] *Ornith.* A bird of the *Laridæ* or gull family. Hence **La·ridine** *a.* having the characters of the gull family 1877.

Larigot (læ·rigŏt). 1811. [ad. F. *larigot.*] An organ stop.

Larikin, var. of LARRIKIN.

Lark (lāɹk), *sb.*[1], **laverock** (læ·vərək, *Sc.* lē·vrək). [OE. *lǽwerce*, *láwerce*, older *láurice*, later *láferce* wk. fem.; ult. etym. unkn.] 1. A general name for any bird of the family *Alaudidæ*, but usu., when used without a prefix, the SKYLARK (*Alauda arvensis*). The lark has a sandy-brown plumage, and remarkably long hind-claws (cf. LARKSPUR). 2. Applied with defining prefix to birds not belonging to the *Alaudidæ*; e.g. to certain buntings and pipits. Also TITLARK. 1766.

1. On þe morwe wan it was day, & þe larke by-gan to synge ME. Rise with the Larke LYLY. With your Theame, I could O're-mount the Larke SHAKS. *Crested L., Horned L., Red L., Shore-l.*; also SKYLARK, WOODLARK (members of the genus or family). 2. The Mud-Lark, Rock-Lark, Titlark, and Tree-Lark are Pipits NEWTON.

Lark (lāɹk), *sb.*[2] *colloq.* (orig. *slang.*) 1811. [Goes with LARK *v.*[2]] A frolic, a spree. Also *to go on, have, take a l.*

Lark (lāɹk), *v.*[1] [f. LARK *sb.*[1]] *intr.* To catch larks (*mod.*). So **La·rker** [1], one whose occupation it is to catch larks 1634.

Lark (lāɹk), *v.*[2] *colloq.* (orig. *slang.*) 1813. [Goes with LARK *sb.*[2] ? A use of LARK *sb.*[1] (cf. *skylark*); or ? = northern LAKE *v.*] 1. *intr.* To play tricks, frolic; to ride across country. 2. *trans.* To tease sportively, 'gammon'; to ride (a horse) across country 1848.

1. Jumping the widest brooks, and larking over the newest gates in the country THACKERAY. Hence **La·rker** [2], one given to larking.

Lark-heel, lark's-heel. 1597. 1. a. = LARKSPUR. b. The garden nasturtium (*Tropæolum*). 2. The elongated heel common among negroes 1865. Hence **Lark-heeled** *a.*

Larkspur (lā·ɹkspɒɹ). 1578. [f. LARK *sb.*[1] + SPUR.] *Bot.* Any plant of the genus *Delphinium*; so called from the spur-shaped calyx. The common larkspur is *D. Consolida.*

Larky (lā·ɹki), *a. colloq.* 1851. [f. LARK *sb.*[1] + -Y [1].] Inclined or ready for a lark.

Larmier (larmi*e*). 1696. [a. F., f. *larme* a tear.] 1. *Arch.* = CORONA 4, DRIP *sb.* 4. 2. *Anat.* The 'tear-bag' in the lachrymal fossa 1848.

Larmoyant (laɹmoi·ănt), *a.* 1824. [ad. F. *larmoyant*, *larmoyer* to be tearful, f. *larme.*] Given to tears, lachrymose.

†**Laron.** Also **laroone,** etc. ME. [ad. OF. *laron* (F. *larron*) :—L. *latronem.* Cf. LADRONE.] A robber –1656.

Villanie, La-roone: Rugby, my Rapier SHAKS.

Larrikin (læ·rikin). Chiefly *Austral.* Also larikin. 1870. [Originated in Melbourne; ? f. *Larry* (a dim. pet. form of Lawrence, common in Ireland) + -KIN.] A (usu. juvenile) street rowdy; the Australian equivalent of the 'Hoodlum' or 'Hooligan'. Also *attrib.*

Larrup (læ·rɒ̆p), *v. dial.* and *colloq.* Also larrop. 1823. [?] *trans.* To beat, flog, thrash.

Is this a land of liberty, where a man can't l. his own nigger? FONBLANQUE.

Larry, var. of LORRY.

Larum (lēə·rɒ̆m, læ·rɒ̆m), *sb.* 1533. [Aphetic f. ALARUM.] = ALARM *sb.* II. Also *attrib.*

†**Larum** (læ·rɒ̆m), *v. Obs.* exc. *dial.* 1595. [f. prec.] 1. *trans.* a. To sound *forth* loudly. b. To alarm. –1758. 2. *intr.* To rush *down* with loud cries. POPE.

La·rum-bell. *Obs.* exc. *poet.* 1568. [f. LARUM *sb.* + BELL.] = ALARM-BELL.

Larva (lā·ɹvă). *Pl.* **larvæ.** 1651. [L. *larva* a ghost; also, a mask.] 1. A ghost, hobgoblin, spectre. *Obs.* exc. *Hist.* 2. a. An insect in the grub state, i.e. from the time of leaving the egg till its transformation into a pupa. b. Applied to the immature form of other animals characterized by metamorphosis. 1768. Also *attrib.*

2. *fig.* The larvæ of future controversies 1854.

Larval (lā·ɹvăl), *a.* 1656. [ad. L. *larvalis* pertaining to larvæ or ghosts.] †1. Belonging to a ghost or goblin; ghastly. BLOUNT. 2. Of or pertaining to a larva or grub 1848; in the condition of a larva 1864. 3. *Path.* Of a disease: Latent, undeveloped 1897.

Larvate (lā·ɹvēɪt), *a.* 1846. [ad. mod.L. *larvatus*, f. *larva*; see -ATE [2] 2.] Masked, covered as by a mask. So **La·rvated** *a.* 1623.

Larve (lāɹv). 1603. [a. F. *larve*, ad. L. *larva.*] 1. = LARVA 1. †2. A mask (*lit.* and *fig.*) –1677. 3. = LARVA 2. 1769.

Larvi- (lā·ɹvi), comb. f. L. *larva*, LARVA. **La·rviform** *a.*, having the form of a larva. **Larvi·parous** [L. *parere*; see -OUS] *a.*, producing young in the condition of larvæ; produced in the form of larvæ.

Laryngeal (lări·ndʒĭăl), *a.* Also †**laringeal.** 1795. [f. mod.L. *laryngeus* (f. *laryng-*, LARYNX) + -AL.] *Anat.* and *Surg.* Of or pertaining to, affecting or seated in, or used in dealing with, the larynx.

‖**Laryngismus** (lærindʒi·zmɒ̆s). 1822. [mod.L., f. *laryng-*, LARYNX.] *Path.* Spasm of the muscles closing the larynx; laryngeal suffocation.

‖**Laryngitis** (lærindʒəi·tis). 1822. [mod.L., f. as prec. + -ITIS.] *Path.* Inflammation of the lining membrane of the larynx. Hence **Laryngi·tic** *a.*

Laryngo- (lări·ŋgo), bef. a vowel **laryng-**, comb. f. LARYNX. **Laryngo·logy,** that branch of medical science which treats of the larynx and its diseases; whence **Lary:ngolo·gical** *a.*, **Laryngo·logist.** **Laryngo·pha·rynx,** the larynx and the pharynx together; whence **Lary:ngo-phary·ngeal** *a.* **Laryngo·phony** [Gr. -φωνία sounding], the sound of the voice as heard through the stethoscope applied over the larynx. **Lary:ngotra·cheal** *a.*, pertaining both to the larynx and to the trachea or windpipe. **Lary:ngotracheo·tomy,** the operation of opening the larynx, and part of the trachea also. **Lary:ngo-ty·phus,** a form of typhus in which there is secondary ulceration of the larynx and necrosis of its cartilages.

Laryngoscope (lări·ŋgǒskōup). 1860. [f. LARYNGO- + -SCOPE.] An apparatus which by a combination of mirrors enables an observer to inspect a patient's larynx. Hence **Lary:ngosco·pic, -al** *a.* of or pertaining to the l., or to inspection of the larynx. **Lary:ngosco·pically** *adv.* with respect to, or by the use of the l. **Laryngo·scopist,** one who uses, or is skilled in using, the l. **Laryngo·scopy,** inspection of the larynx; the use of the l.

Laryngotome (lări·ŋgotǒum). 1855. [f. LARYNGO- + Gr. -τόμος cutter.] *Surg.* An instrument for performing laryngotomy.

Laryngotomy (læriŋgǫ·tŏmi). 1661. [ad. Gr. λαρυγγοτομία, f. λαρυγγο- LARYNX + -τομία cutting.] *Surg.* The operation of cutting into the larynx from without, esp. in order to provide an aperture for respiration. Hence **Lary:ngoto·mic** *a.*

Larynx (læ·riŋks). *Pl.* **larynges** (lări·ndʒīz). 1578. [a. Gr. λάρυγξ, mod.L. *larynx.*] *Anat.* A cavity in the throat with cartilaginous walls, containing the vocal cords, by means of which sounds are produced. In man and most of the higher animals this cavity forms the upper part of the trachea or wind-pipe. In birds there are two larynges, one at each end of the trachea; the lower of these, called SYRINX, is the true organ of sound.

Las (lɑs), *int.* 1604. Aphetic f. ALAS.

Las, obs. form of LACE, LASS, LESS.

Lascar (læ·skăɪ, læskā·ɪ). 1625. [Either Urdu *lashkar* army, camp, used erron., or abbrev. of *lashkarī* (see LASCARINE).] **1.** An E. Indian sailor. Also *attrib.* **2.** *Anglo-Ind.* 'A tent-pitcher'; also, an inferior class of artilleryman (in full *gun-l.*) 1798.

†**Lascaree** (læskărī·). 1712. [a. Urdu (Pers.) *lashkarī*; see next.] = LASCAR 1. E. COOKE.

†**Lascari·ne.** *Indian.* 1598. [ad. Pg. *lasquarin, -im*, a. Urdu (Pers.) *lashkarī* (adj., military; hence as sb., a soldier), f. *lashkar* army; see LASHKAR.] An E. Indian soldier; also, one of the native police –1825.

†**Lasci·vient,** *a.* 1653. [ad. L. *lascivientem*, pr. pple. of *lascivire* to be wanton, f. *lascivus.*] Wantoning, lascivious –1703. Hence †**Lasci·viency.**

Lascivious (lăsi·viəs), *a.* ME. [ad. late L. *lasciviosus* (Isidore), f. L. *lascivia* (f. *lascivus*); see -OUS.] Inclined to lust, lewd, wanton. **b.** Inciting to lust or wantonness; †voluptuous 1589.

Hee on Eve Began to cast l. Eyes MILT. *P. L.* IX. 1014. **b.** L. pictures 1602, meats BURTON. Hence **Lasci·vious-ly** *adv.*, **-ness.**

Laser (lē̆·səɪ, lē̆·zəɪ). *Hist.* 1578. [a. L. *laser.*] A gum-resin mentioned by Roman writers, obtained from an umbelliferous plant called *laserpicium* or *silphium* (σίλφιον). *Comb.* **l.-wort,** any plant of the genus *Laserpitium*, esp. *L. latifolium.*

Lash (læʃ), *sb.*[1] ME. [? f. LASH *v.*[1]] **1.** †**a.** *gen.* A sudden or violent blow; a sweeping stroke. **b.** *spec.* A stroke with a thong or whip. Also *transf.* and *fig.* **2.** The flexible part of a whip; now occas., the piece of whipcord, etc. forming the extremity of this ME. **b.** *poet.* and *rhet.* = 'whip, scourge' (*lit.* and *fig.*) 1586. **c.** *The l.*: the punishment of flogging 1694. **3.** Short for EYE-LASH 1796.

1. *fig.* How smart a l. that speech doth giue my Conscience *Haml.* III. i. 50. **2. b.** With all this..she has not escaped the l. of scandal MME. D'ARBLAY. **c.** He expired under the l. GIBBON.

Lash (læʃ), *sb.*[2] 1440. [? LASH *sb.*[1] substituted for other wds. of similar sound; or ? var. of LATCH *sb.*] †**1.** A string, cord, thong. Cf. LACE *sb.* 2, LATCH *sb.* 1. †**2.** = LASSO *sb.* 1 (*rare*) 1748. **3.** *Weaving.* = LEASE *sb.*[4] or LEASH 1731.

Lash (læʃ), *a.* *Obs.* exc. *dial.* ME. [a. OF. *lasche* (F. *lâche*), f. (ult.) L. *laxus* loose. With sense 3, cf. LUSH *a.*] †**1.** Culpably remiss –1694. †**2.** Loose, lax, relaxed –1546. **3. a.** Of food, fruits, grass, etc.: Soft, watery. **b.** Of weather: Raw, wet. **c.** Of a hide: Tender. 1440.

Lash (læʃ), *v.*[1] ME. [In branch I, perh. onomatopœic. Cf. also F. *lâcher.* In branch II, f. LASH *sb.*[1]]

I. 1. To make a sudden movement; to dash, fly, rush, spring, start. Of light: To flash. Of tears, water: To pour, rush. Also with *about, away, back, down, out.* Const. *at, from, into, out of, to.* **2.** To let fly *at*, make a dash or rush *at*, aim a blow *at* ME. **3.** *trans.* To dash, throw, or move violently. Now only *techn.* ME. †**4.** To lavish, squander. Chiefly with *out.* –1657. †**b.** To pour *out* or forth impetuously (words, etc.) –1653. **5.** *intr.* with *out*: To rush, launch out, into excess 1560.

1. When it [sin] finds the least vent, it lashes out to the purpose SOUTH. **2.** To laugh at Follies, or to l. at Vice DRYDEN. Phr. *To l. out*: to strike out violently; (of a horse) to kick out. **5.** To l. out excessively in dress STRYPE.

II. Senses referring to LASH *sb.*[1] **1.** *trans.* To beat, strike with a lash, etc.; to flog, scourge ME. **b.** *transf.*, esp. of the action of waves upon the shore. Occas. *intr.* (*on* the shore). 1694. **c.** *fig.*; esp. 'To scourge with satire' (J.); to castigate in words, rebuke 1590. **2.** With *adv.* or phr.: To urge or drive by, or as by, lashes 1594.

1. Lashing the pony until they reached their journey's end DICKENS. **b.** The rain lashed the panes C. BRONTË. **c.** Why, headstrong liberty is lasht with woe SHAKS. **2.** A glassy lake..Lashed into foaming waves COWPER.

Lash (læʃ), *v.*[2] 1440. [? f. LASH *sb.*[2], or a. OF. *lachier*, dial. var. of *lacier*; see LACE *v.*] †**1.** *trans.* To lace (a garment) –1611. **2.** Chiefly *Naut.* To fasten or make fast with a cord, rope, etc.; †to truss (clothes); to fasten *to* (something) 1624.

2. We had not a gun on board lashed 1748.

Lasher (læ·ʃəɪ). 1602. [f. LASH *v.*[1], 2 + -ER[1].] One who or that which lashes. †**1.** One who beats or whips. Also *fig.* –1611. **2.** *Naut.* The cord, etc. used to fasten any object 1669. **3.** Chiefly *local* (on the Thames): The body of water that lashes or rushes over an opening in a barrier or weir; hence, the opening; a weir 1677. **b.** The pool into which this water falls 1851.

3. The huge rafts..shoot the lashers in safety 1884. **b.** Men who..To bathe in the abandon'd l. pass M. ARNOLD.

Lashing (læ·ʃiŋ), *vbl. sb.*[1] ME. [f. LASH *v.*[1] + -ING[1].] The action of LASH *v.*[1]; beating, flogging. **b.** *pl.* (*Anglo-Irish*). 'Floods', abundance 1829.

†*L. out*, squandering. **b.** 'Lashings' of whiskey-punch LEVER.

Lashing (læ·ʃiŋ), *vbl. sb.*[2] 1669. [f. LASH *v.*[2] + -ING[1].] The action of LASH *v.*[2]; the action of fastening any movable body with a cord. Hence *concr.* the cord.

‖**Lashkar** (læ·ʃkaɪ). *Indian.* 1616. [Urdu (Pers.) *lashkar* army, camp. See LASCAR.] †**a.** A camp of native Indian soldiers –1634. **b.** A body of Afridi soldiers 1897.

Lask (lɑsk), *sb.* 1542. [a. ONF. *lasque*, f. **lasquer*: see next.] **1.** Diarrhœa; = LAX *sb.*[2] 2. Now only in veterinary use. †**2.** A laxative 1550.

Lask (lɑsk), *v.* ME. [a. ONF. **lasquer* = Central OF. *laschier* (F. *lâcher*) :—pop.L. **lascare* = class. L. *laxare*, f. *laxus.*] †**1.** *trans.* To lower in quality, quantity, or strength, relax. ME. only. †**2.** *intr.* To become loose in the bowels –1634. **3.** *Naut.* To 'go large', to sail neither 'by the wind' nor 'before the wind' 1622. Hence **La·sking** *vbl. sb.* and *ppl. a.* *Naut.* '(going) large'.

Lasket (lɑ·skět). 1704. [Perh. altered f. F. *lacet* (see LATCHET).] One of the loops by which a bonnet is attached to the foot of a sail.

Laspring (læ·spriŋ). 1760. Young salmon.

Lass (læs). [ME. *lasce, las(se*; cf. MSw. *lösk kona* unmarried woman.] **1.** A girl. (Not much used in the south.) **b.** *spec.* A maid-servant. *Sc.* and *n. dial.* **2.** A sweetheart 1596.

2. It was a Louer, and his lasse SHAKS. *Comb.* †**l.-lorn** *a.* forsaken by one's sweetheart. Hence **La·ssie,** a young l. **La·ssock,** a little girl.

Lass, freq. obs. f. LESS.

Lassitude (læ·sitiūd). 1533. [a. F., ad. L. *lassitudo*, f. *lassus.*] The condition of being weary; a flagging of the bodily or mental powers; indifference to exertion; weariness.

Periods of renewed enthusiasm after intervals of l. RUSKIN.

Lasso (læ·so), *sb.* 1808. [Sp. *lazo* (in America pronounced la·so) = OF. *laz*; see LACE *sb.*] **1.** A long rope of untanned hide, having a noose at the end to catch cattle and wild horses; used chiefly in Spanish America. **2.** *Mil.* = *lasso-harness* 1847.

Comb.: **l.-cell,** one of the urticating cells of the *Cœlenterata*, which eject the contained thread in the manner of a l.; **-harness,** a kind of girth placed round a cavalry horse, with a l. or long rope attached, for use in helping to draw guns, etc.

Hence **La·sso** *v. trans.* to catch with a l.; *Mil.* to draw (guns, etc.) with lasso-harness.

Last (lɑst), *sb.*[1] [OE. *lást* masc., footstep, *lǽst* fem., boot, *lǽste* fem., shoemaker's last; referred to a Teut. root **lais-* (: *lĭs-*) to follow a track, cogn. with L. *lira* furrow.] †**1.** A footstep, track, trace. After OE. only in Sc. *Not a l.*: nothing, not at all. –1500. **2.** A wooden model of the foot, on which shoemakers shape boots and shoes OE. **b.** *transf.* and *fig.* 1592–1647.

2. Great evil may arise from the cobbler leaving his l. and turning into..a legislator JOWETT. **b.** Here's gallants of all sizes, of all lasts 1607.

Last (lɑst), *sb.*[2] [OE. *hlæst* neut.; now referred to a pre-Teut. type **klat-sto-* (*-sti-*), parallel with **klat-to-*, repr. by ON. *hlass* neut., load; f. **klat-* root of LADE *v.*] †**1.** A load, burden, weight carried –ME. **2.** A commercial denomination of weight, capacity, or quantity varying for different goods and localities. As a weight, it is estimated at 2 tons or 4,000 lb. In wool weight, it is 4,368 lb. (= 12 sacks). As a measure for grain and malt, it is now 10 quarters = 80 bushels. A last of cod and herrings is 12 barrels (but of red herrings and pilchards 10,000 to 13,200 fish). Cf. Ger. *last.* ME. †**b.** *transf.* A huge indefinite number –1712. †**3.** A unit in the measurement of a ship's burden = 2 tons (occas. 1 ton) –1796.

Last (lɑst), *sb.*[3] ME. [f. LAST *v.*[1]] **1.** Continuance, duration. Now *rare.* **2.** Staying power 1857.

1. Things memorable, of perpetuitie, fame, and l. 1587.

Last (lɑst), *sb.*[4] *Obs.* exc. *Hist.* OE. [ad. Anglo-Latin *lastum, lestum* (Domesday Book *lest*), used as = OE. *lǽþ* LATHE[1].] = LATHE[1]. Also, the name for an administrative assembly; more fully *l.-court.*

Last (lɑst), *a.*, *adv.*, and *sb.*[5] [OE. *latost*, Northumb. *lætest*, superl. of *læt* adj., *late* adv. Syncopation before *st* originated in inflected forms; for *last*:—*latst* cf. BEST. (Cf. LATEST.)]

A. *adj.* **1.** Following all the others in a series, order, or enumeration; subsequent to all others in occurrence, existence, etc. ME.

b. *ellipt.* The last day (of a month). Now *local.* **c.** Utmost ME. **2.** Belonging to the end, *esp.* of life or of the world ME. **3.** Next before a point of time expressed or implied; the present time or next before; most recent, latest ME. **b.** With ellipsis of *letter.* Now chiefly *commercial.* 1638. **c.** ellipt. (*colloq.*) (A person's) latest joke, freak, characteristic action or saying, etc. 1843. **4.** That comes after all others in rank or estimation; lowest. Chiefly *ellipt.* ME. **5.** The only remaining ME. **b.** Often = 'most unlikely', 'most unwilling', 'most unsuitable' 1450. **6.** Final, conclusive, definitive. ? Now only in *l. word.* 1654. **7.** Reaching its ultimate limit; utmost, extreme. Now chiefly in phr. *of the l. importance.* 1674.

1. Fairest of Starrs, l. in the train of Night MILT. *P. L.* v. 166. Phr. *The two* (*three*, etc.) *l.* (the more frequent form till 17th c.). *The l. two* (*three*, etc.): the form now preferred, exc. where *last* = 'last-mentioned'. *The second last*: the last but one. *The last sacraments*: those administered in preparation for death. In the l. two Columns STURMY. Though l., not least in loue SHAKS. **c.** The land's l. verge Holds him R. ELLIS. **2.** Phr. *The four l. things* (Theol. ; = L. *quatuor novissima*); Death, Judgement, Heaven, and Hell. Hosius..with his l. breath, abjured the heresy J. H. NEWMAN. *The l. day*: the Day of Judgement, the end of the world. *The l. days*: the closing period of the life or history *of* (a person, etc.); also the days including and immediately preceding the Day of Judgement. **3.** Having writ to you l. post saves me [etc.] MARVELL. †*The last age*: the last century or so. *L. Wednesday, l. Christmas* (formerly †*Wednesday last was*, etc.); *l. evening*, yesterday evening; †*the l. day*, yesterday. **b.** I informed you in my l. FIELDING. **4.** The l. of nations now, though once the first COWPER. **5.** To the l. peny SHAKS. That l. infirmity of Noble mind MILTON. **b.** She was the l. person to be approached with undue familiarity PRESCOTT. **7.** Even shame, the l. of evils MILTON.

Special collocations: **l. brood, l. spring,** terms denoting a young salmon at a certain stage of growth. *L.cast, extremity,gasp,legs,post,will*, etc., see the sbs.

II. *absol.* (quasi-*sb.*) **a.** With a demonstrative or relative adj.: The last-mentioned person or thing 1560. **b.** The conclusion (now *rare*) 1607. **c.** The last day or last moments; the end of life, death. Chiefly with a possessive. ME. **d.** *One's l.*: the last thing a person does or can do; *esp.* in *to breathe one's l.* (sc. *breath*), *to look one's last* (sc. *look*), etc. ME. †**e.** The extremity. T. STAFFORD. **f.** *mod. colloq.* The end of one's dealings with something 1854.

a. Which two l. were not agreed upon 1560. **b.** Heare the l. of our sea-sorrow *Temp.* I. ii. 107. **c.** As he drew nigh his l. 1860. **d.** Eyes looke your l. Armes take your l. embrace SHAKS. **e.** To endure the l. of misery 1633. **f.** I shall never hear the l. of it (*mod.*). **g.** *U.S.* The end (of a week or month).

Phrases (with preps.). **At last** [ME. *attě laste*, for *at the* (earlier *than*) *laste*]: at the end, in the end, finally, ultimately. So *At* (*the*) *long l.*: at the end of all. **To the l.**: †(*a*) to the utmost; (*b*) up to or until the end, *esp.* of life, to the point of death; also *till the l.*

B. *adv.* **1.** After all others; at the latest time; at the end. (*Occas.* coupled with *least.*) OE. **2.** On the occasion next before the present; in the last instance; most lately; latest ME. **3.** In the last place, lastly 1560. **4.** In the end, finally 1667.

1. Nor Man the least Though l. created MILT. *P. L.* III. 278. **2.** He came l. from Astracan DE FOE. †*L. past*: (with dates) said of the period next before the time of writing or speaking; also (of a period of time) extending to the present, (the) past (year, etc.). Sermons..preached in Lente l. past LATIMER. **3.** First, my Feare: then, my Curtsie: l., my Speech SHAKS. **4.** To fall In universal ruin l. MILTON.

Last (lɑst), *v.*[1] [OE. *lǽstan* wk. vb., f. OTeut. *laisti-*: see LAST *sb.*[1]] †**1.** *trans.* **a.** In OE. only: To follow (a leader; with *dat.*), to follow, pursue (a course, etc.; with *accus.*). **b.** To carry out (a command, a promise); to pay (tribute), to abide by, maintain (peace). -1480. **2.** *intr.* To continue, endure, go on OE. †Also with complement -1667. **3.** To hold out, continue fresh, unexhausted, etc. ME. **b.** With indirect obj.: To suffice for a specified time 1530. **c.** quasi-*trans.* (*a*) To continue in vigour as long as or longer than (something else). Now only with *out.* †(*b*) To hold out under or against. 1500. †**4.** To reach, stretch -1577.

2. While the civil war lasted MACAULAY. **3.** Dwelling-houses built to l. RUSKIN. **c.** Old Families l. not three Oakes SIR T. BROWNE.

Last (lɑst), *v.*[2] 1880. [f. LAST *sb.*[1]] *trans.* To put (a boot or shoe) on the last.

Lastage (lɑ·stėdʒ). ME. [a. AF. and F. *lestage*, f. *lest* = LAST *sb.*[2]] **1.** A toll payable by traders attending fairs and markets. *Obs.* exc. *Hist.* †**2.** The ballast of a ship -1736. **3.** A port duty for liberty to load a ship, levied at so much per last 1592. **4.** An impost levied on the catch of herrings at so much per last 1601. **5.** = TONNAGE 1858. †**6.** Garbage. BLOUNT.

Laster (lɑ·stəɹ). 1878. [f. LAST *sb.*[1] + -ER[1].] A workman who shapes a boot or shoe, by fixing the parts smoothly on a last.

Lasting (lɑ·stiŋ), *sb.* 1782. [Ellipt. use of ppl. a.] A durable kind of cloth; = EVERLASTING B. 3 b. Also *attrib.*

Lasting (lɑ·stiŋ), *vbl. sb.*[1] ME. [f. LAST *v.*[1] + -ING[1].] The action of LAST *v.*[1]; continuance, duration, permanence. **b.** Staying power 1860. Also *attrib.*

Lasting (lɑ·stiŋ), *vbl. sb.*[2] 1875. [f. LAST *v.*[2] + -ING[1].] The action of shaping a boot or shoe on the last; chiefly *attrib.*, as *l.-awl, -machine*, etc.

Lasting (lɑ·stiŋ), *ppl. a.* and *adj.* ME. [f. LAST *v.*[1] + -ING[2].] **1.** Continuing, enduring; permanent. **2.** Durable ME. **3.** *Sporting slang.* Having staying power 1811.

2. A l. colour STURMY, cloth BERKELEY. Hence **La·sting-ly** *adv.*, **-ness.**

Lastly (lɑ·stli), *adv.* ME. [f. LAST *a.* + -LY[2].] **1.** At the end; in the last instance; ultimately. *Obs.* or *arch.*, exc. as used in a discourse or the like. †**2.** Conclusively, finally -1637. †**3.** Very lately, recently -1641.

2. As he pronounces l. on each deed MILT. *Lycidas* 83.

Lat, obs. f. LET *v.*

Latakia (lætăkī·ă). 1833. [Short for *Latakia tobacco.*] A fine kind of Turkish tobacco produced near and shipped from Latakia (the ancient Laodicea), a sea-port of Syria.

Latch (lætʃ), *sb.* ME. [In sense 1, perh. a. OF. *lache* lace, f. *lachier* :—pop.L. **laciare*, f. **lacium* LACE *sb.*; or else f. LATCH *v.*[1] (cf. *catch* sb.).] **1.** A loop or noose; a gin, snare; a tangle; a latchet, thong. *Obs.* exc. *dial.* and *techn.* **2.** A fastening for a door or gate, usu. consisting of a small bar which falls or slides into a catch, and is lifted or drawn by means of a thumb-lever, string, etc. from the outside. Now also, a kind of spring-lock (*drop-l., night-l.*) for a front door, which is opened from the outside by a key. ME. **3.** *Naut.* = LASKET 1710. †**4.** *Mil. Antiq.* A cross-bow with a trigger working like a door latch -1786.

Latch (lætʃ), *v.*[1] [OE. *læcc(e)an* wk. vb.; not in other Teut. langs.; f. OTeut. **lakk-*, repr. either pre-Teut. **laqn-* cogn. w. L. *laqueus* (see LACE *sb.*), or **lagn-* cogn. w. Gr. λάζεσθαι to take.] †**1.** *trans.* To take hold of, grasp, seize (esp. with the hand or claws); to clasp, embrace. Also *intr.* or *absol.* with *at, on, till.* -ME. †**2.** To take with force; to capture, seize upon -1535. **3.** To catch (something falling); to catch *in* (a receptacle). *Obs.* exc. *dial.* 1530. **4.** To be the recipient of; to receive (a name, gift; a blow, injury); to catch (a disease). *Obs.* exc. *dial.* ME. **5.** *intr.* To alight, settle (*dial.*) 1825.

3. Some l. the firebrands as they flew HOLLAND. **4.** *Macb.* IV. iii. 192.

Latch (lætʃ), *v.*[2] 1530. [f. LATCH *sb.*] *trans.* To fasten or secure with a latch.

The street door was to be latched, but not bolted 1882.

Latch(e, var. of LEACH *v.*

Latchet (læ·tʃėt). ME. [ad. OF. *lachet*, dial. var. of *lacet*, dim. of *laz, las*, LACE *sb.*] †**1.** A loop; a narrow strip of anything, a thong -1709. †**b.** *Naut.* = LASKET -1627. **c.** A thong to fasten a shoe. Now only *dial.* exc. in Biblical allusions. 1440. **2.** A catch for a shutter-bar. [? f. LATCH *sb.* + -ET.] 1842.

Latching (læ·tʃiŋ), *vbl. sb.* ME. [f. LATCH *v.*[1] + -ING[1].] †**1.** The action of LATCH *v.*[1] ME. only. **2.** *Naut.* = LASKET 1794.

Latch-key (læ·tʃ,kī). 1839. A key used to draw back the latch of an outer door.

Comb. *Latch-key vote*, the lodger-franchise.

La·tch-string. 1861. A string passed through a hole in a door so that the latch may be raised from the outside. Hence *fig.* in *U.S.* in colloq. phrases.

'Our latch string is out' has become a classic expression of cordial hospitality 1893.

Late (lēⁱt), *a.* (*sb.*) [Com. Teut.: OE. *læt* :—OTeut. **lato-*; f. **lat-* (:—pre-Teut. **lad-*, cf. L. *lassus* weary = **lad-tus*), ablaut var. of **let-*; see LET *v.*[1]] **1.** Slow, tardy; *dial.* slow in progress, tedious. Const. *to* with *inf.*; also with gen. or *of.* Now *dial.* **2.** After the due or customary time; delayed in time. Const. *to* with *inf.*, and *for.* OE. **b.** Of plants, fruit, etc.: Backward in flowering, ripening, etc. 1440. **3.** Far on in the day or night OE. Also *fig.* **4.** Belonging to an advanced stage in a period, development, etc. ME. **5.** Of a person: Recently deceased 1490. **b.** That was recently (what is implied by the sb.) but is not now (cf. LATE *adv.* 4 b) 1548. **6.** Recent in date; belonging to a recent period. Now *Obs.* of persons, and chiefly in phr. *of l. years.* 1513. **7.** Having to do with persons or things that arrive late (*colloq.*) 1862.

2. Phr. (impers.) *It is* (*too*) *l. to* do something. Don't be l. for the train 1884. L. learners BACON. My l. spring MILTON. **b.** The l. Narcissus DRYDEN. **3.** Phr. *It is l.* = the time is advanced. *L. hours*: hours after the proper time for sleep. Hence *colloq.* of persons 'keeping l. hours, rising or going to bed l.' *fig.* A sage reflection, But somewhat l. i' the day BYRON. **4.** The l. Latin hymn metres SWEET. **5.** Her..l. amyable husbonde CAXTON. **b.** Our late dwelling GOLDSM. His l. master 1842. **6.** The l. war 1817. During the l. reign MACAULAY. **7.** *L. fee* (earlier *l.-letter fee*), an increased fee paid to secure the dispatch of a letter posted after the advertised time of collection. Hence **La·te-ly** *adv.*, **-ness.**

B. *absol.* or quasi-*sb.* †**1.** Lateness. ME. only. **2. Of late:** during a comparatively short time extending to the present; recently, lately 1470.

Late (lēⁱt), *adv.* [OE. *late*, f. *læt-, lat-* LATE *a.*] †**1.** Slowly. OE. only. **2.** After the proper or usual time; at an advanced period; after delay OE. Also *transf.* **3.** Of the time of day: At or till a late hour ME. **4.** Recently, of late, lately; but now; †not long (*ago, before*). Now only *poet.* ME. **b.** Not long since (but not now); recently (but no longer) 1474. **5.** Relatively near the end of a period, history, etc. 1849.

2. Better three houres too soone, than a mynute too l. SHAKS. A weight..which crushes soon or l. BYRON. **3.** After supper, her aunt sat l. 1794. **4.** Those climes where I have l. been straying BYRON. **b.** L. king, now captive SPENSER. **5.** So l. as the days of the Stuarts MACAULAY.

Comb. With a following ppl. adj., usu. hyphened, as (sense 2) *l.-born, -lamented*, etc.; (sense 4) *l.-lost, -transformed* adjs.

Lated (lēⁱ·tėd), *ppl. a. poet.* 1592. [as if f. **late* vb. (f. LATE *a.*) + -ED[1].] = BELATED.

Lateen (lætī·n), *a.* (*sb.*) 1727. [Phonetic sp. of F. *latine* (in *voile latine* 'Latin sail', so named as used in the Mediterranean), fem. of *latin* LATIN *a.*] *L. sail*: a triangular sail suspended by a long yard at an angle of about 45 degrees to the mast. Hence *attrib.*, belonging to or having such a rig, as *l. mizzen, vessel.*

Latency (lēⁱ·tĕnsi). 1638. [f. LATENT *a.*; see -ENCY.] The condition or quality of being latent; *spec.* in *Biol.* So **La·tence** (*rare*).

Latent (lēⁱ·tĕnt), *a.* 1616. [ad. L. *latentem, latere* to be hidden.] Hidden, concealed; present or existing, but not manifest, exhibited, or developed; esp. in *Path.* of a disease. ? *Obs.* of material things. **b.** Disguised (*rare*) 1662.

The meaning l. under this specious phrase MACAULAY. *L. ambiguity*: in *Law*, a doubt as to the meaning of a document, not patent from the document itself, but raised by the evidence of some collateral or extrinsic matter. *L. heat* (Physics): see HEAT *sb.* 2. *L. buds* (Bot.): buds lying dormant till excited by some particular stimulus. Hence **La·tent-ly** *adv.*, **-ness.**

Later (lēⁱ·təɹ). 1450. [f. LATE *a.* + -ER[3].] **A.** *adj.* More late 1559. **B.** *adv.* At a later time or period; subsequently. *L. on*: subsequently.

Later, obs. f. LATTER *a.*

-later: see -LATRY.

Laterad (læ·tĕræd), *adv.* 1803. [f. L. *later-, latus* side + -AD II (see DEXTRAD).] *Anat.* Towards the side.

Lateral (læ·tĕrăl). 1600. [ad. L. *lateralis*, f. *later-*, *latus* side. Cf. F. *latéral*.] **A.** *adj.* **1.** Of or pertaining to the side; at or from the side; side-. †**2.** Existing or moving side by side. Of winds: Coming from the same half (eastern or western) of the horizon –1667. **3.** *spec.* **a.** *Anat.* and *Zool.* Situated on one side or other of the mesial plane, as *l. eye*, *fin*, *lobe*, etc. 1722. **b.** *Bot.* Belonging to, situated or borne upon the side of an organ, as *l. bud*, *flower*, etc. 1764. **c.** *Path.* Of diseases: (*a*) Affecting the side or sides of the body; (*b*) confined to one side of the body; (*c*) (of curvature of the spine) directed sideways 1724. **d.** Surg. *L. operation*: a mode of cutting for the stone, in which the prostate gland and neck of the bladder are divided laterally. Also *l. lithotomy*. 1727. †**e.** *Math.* Of a quantity or equation: Of the first power or degree; linear –1706. **f.** *Cryst.* Applied to those axes of a crystal or crystalline form which are inclined to the vertical axis; also to edges, faces, or angles, connected with such axes 1805. **g.** *Physics* and *Mech.* Acting or placed at right angles to the line of motion or of strain 1803.

1. *L. branch* (of a family): a branch descended from a brother or sister of a person in the direct line of descent. *L. moraine*: see MORAINE. The river and its l. streams HUXLEY. **2.** Eurus and Zephir with thir l. noise, Sirocco, and Libecchio MILT. **3. g.** *L. pressure* or *stress*, a pressure or stress at right angles to the length, as of a beam or bridge. *L. strength*, strength which resists a tendency to fracture arising from l. pressure.

B. *sb.* A lateral or side part, member, or object (as a shoot, tooth, branch, etc.) 1635.

Hence **Latera·lity**, the quality of having (distinct) sides; (right- or left-) sidedness; excessive development on one side. **La·teralized** *ppl. a.* rendered l. in position. **La·terally** *adv.* 1561.

Lateran (læ·tĕrăn). ME. [ad. L. *Laterana*, *Lateranum*.] The name of a locality in Rome, orig. the site of the palace of the Plautii Laterani, afterwards of that of the popes of the same name, and the cathedral church known as St. John Lateran [L. *Sancti Joannis in Laterano*]. Also *attrib.* or as *adj.* (= Eccl. L. *Lateranensis*), esp. with reference to the five general councils of the Western Church held in the church of St. John Lateran.

Lateri- (læ·tĕri), comb. f. L. *later-*, *latus* side, in scientific terms; cf. LATERO-. **Laterifio·ral**, **-flo·rous** [L. *flor-*, *flos*] *adjs.*, *Bot.* having lateral flowers. **Laterifo·lious** [L. *folium*] *a.*, *Bot.* (of a flower) growing from the stem at the base of a leaf, axillary.

Laterite (læ·tĕrəit). 1807. [f. L. *later* brick + -ITE [1].] *Min.* A red, porous, ferruginous rock, forming the surface covering in parts of India, etc. Hence **Lateri·tic** *a.* of the nature of or resembling l.

Lateritious (lætĕri·ʃəs), *a.* 1656. [f. L. *lateritius*, f. *later* brick; see -ITIOUS.] Pertaining to or resembling brick; brick-red; said chiefly of urinary deposits.

Latero- (læ·tĕro), comb. f. L. *later-*, *latus* side; cf. LATERI-. Usu. hyphened, (*a*) in sense 'pertaining to the side (and another part)', 'pertaining to the side of (a specified structure)', e. g. *l.-anterior*, *-nuchal* adjs.; (*b*) 'on or towards the side', e. g. *l.-flexion*, etc.

Latescent (lĕⁱte·sĕnt), *a.* 1836. [ad. L. *latescentem*, *latescere*, inceptive of *latere* to be hid.] Becoming latent, hidden, or obscure. So **Late·scence**, l. condition or quality.

Latest (lēⁱ·tĕst), *a.* (*adv.*) 1588. [Mod. superl. f. LATE *a.* + -EST. Cf. LAST *a.*] **1.** = LAST. Now *arch.* and *poet.* **2.** Most late; most recent 1593. **b.** *The l.*, the most recent piece of news, fashion, etc. 1889. **3.** *adv.* 1667.

1. Now at the last gaspe of Loues l. Breath DRAYTON. **2.** The l. newes we heare SHAKS. Phr. *At (the) l.*: at the most advanced hour or date. **3.** My fairest, my espous'd, my l. found MILT.

Late-wake, corrupt f. LYKE-WAKE.

†**La·teward.** 1456. [f. LATE *a.* + -WARD.] **A.** *adj.* **1.** Late, slow, backward –1745. **2.** Pertaining to a late period 1577. **B.** *adv.* **1.** Of late, recently –1649. **2.** Late, after the due time or season –1659. †**La·tewardly** *adv.* of late, lately; at a late date.

‖**Latex** (lēⁱ·teks). 1662. [L., = liquid, fluid.] †**1.** *Old Phys.* The name for juice of any sort in the body; esp. the watery part of the blood, etc. –1766. **2.** *Bot.* A milky liquid found in many plants, which exudes when the plant is wounded, and coagulates on exposure to the air 1835; *spec.* that of rubber-trees 1909.

Lath (lɑþ), *sb.* [OE. *lætt* sb. fem., ME. *laþþe*. Usu. taken as cogn. w MHG. *lade* plank (mod.G. *laden* counter, shop).] **1.** A thin narrow strip of wood used to form a groundwork for slates or tiles or plaster, and in the construction of lattice or trellis work and Venetian blinds. **b.** *collect.* Laths as a material used in building to form a wall or partition. Freq. in *l. and plaster* (usu. hyphened when used *attrib.* or quasi-*adj.*). 1490. **2.** *gen* A thin, narrow, flat piece of wood. Also *transf.* 1592. **3.** The bending part of an arbalest or cross-bow 1545.

1. b. L.-and-plaster work ROGERS. **2.** A sword of l. SCOTT. *transf.* His ribs are laths QUARLES.

Comb.: **l.-brick**, a long narrow brick used for the floors of grain-kilns; **-nail**, a nail for fixing laths upon battens 1330.

Lath (lɑþ), *v.* 1532. [f. prec.] *trans.* To cover or furnish (a wall or ceiling) with laths for plastering. Also with *over*, and *absol.*

Lathe [1] (lēⁱð). [Late OE. *læð* str. neut., corresp. to ON. *lāð* (poet.) landed possessions, land :—OTeut. **laþom*; cf. OE. *un-læd(e* wretched.] One of the administrative districts (now five in number) into which Kent is divided, each containing several hundreds.

Comb.: †**l. reeve**, the official charged with the administration of a l.; †**l. silver**, the chief rent payable to the crown.

Lathe [2] (lēⁱð). Now only *dial.* ME. [a. ON. *hlaða*, conn. w. *hlaða* LADE *v.*] A barn.

Lathe [3] (lēⁱð). Also †**lath.** 1476. [prob. cogn. w. Da. *lad* 'stand, support', as found in compounds, e. g. *savelad* saw-bench, *væverlad* loom, etc. The Da. word is prob. a spec. use of *lad* pile, heap regularly built up :—ON. *hlað*, related to *hlaða* to LADE. Or ? a modification of LATH *sb.*] †**1.** ? *gen.* A supporting structure, stand, scaffold. **2.** *spec.* (In full *turning-l.*) A machine for turning wood, metal, ivory, etc., in which the article to be turned is held in a horizontal position by means of adjustable centres and rotated against cutting tools 1611. **b.** A machine for throwing and turning pottery-ware, the article being placed upon a revolving horizontal disk; a *potter's l.* 1727.

2. Could turn his Word and Oath and Faith As many ways as in a Lath BUTLER. *Engine-*, *foot-*, *hand-l.*, lathes driven by an engine, etc. *Centre-*, *chuck-*, *duplex-*, *mandrel-*, *pole-l.*, etc., special forms of lathes. *Chasing-*, *fluting-*, *oval-*, *screw-cutting-l.*, etc., lathes doing work of these kinds.

Lathe [4] (lēⁱð). 1633. [Cogn. w. G. *lade*, Sw. *lad*; cf. prec. and LAY *sb.*[5]] The movable swing-frame or batten of a loom.

‖**Lathee** (latī·). 1850. [Hindi.] A long heavy stick, usu. of bamboo.

Lathen (lɑ·þ'n), *a. rare.* 1843. [f. LATH *sb.* + -EN [4].] Made of lath.

Lather (læ·ðəɹ), *sb.* [OE. *lēaðor* str. neut. :—OTeut. type **lauþrom* :—pre-Teut. **loutrom* (= Gr. λουτρόν bath), f. root **lou-* to wash (= L. *lavare*) + *-tro-* instrumental suffix.] **1.** †**a.** Washing soda. OE. only. **b.** A froth or foam from soap and water. **c.** *transf.* Violent perspiration, esp. the frothy sweat of a horse 1660. **2.** The action of lathering 1626. Hence **La·thery** *a.* chiefly *fig.* frothy, unsubstantial.

Lather (læ·ðəɹ), *v.* [f. prec. OE. had **lēaðran*, *leðran* :—OTeut. **lauþrjan*, f. **lauþrom*.] **1.** *trans.* To cover with or as with a lather; to wash in or with a lather. **2.** *intr.* To become covered with foam; now chiefly of a horse ME. **3.** *intr.* To produce and form a lather or froth 1608. **4.** *trans.* To beat, thrash. Also *intr.* with *into.* Also *fig.* 1797.

1. Nello skipped round him, lathered him, seized him by the nose, and scraped him GEO. ELIOT.

Lathing (lɑ·þiŋ), *vbl. sb.* Also †**latting.** 1486 [f. LATH *v.* + -ING [1].] **1.** The action of LATH *v.* **2.** *concr.* Lath-work 1756.

Lathy (lɑ·þi), *a.* 1672. [f. LATH *sb.* + -Y [1].] **1.** Like a lath; thin, or long and thin. Said esp. of a very thin person. **2.** Made of lath (and plaster) 1804.

1. Duns Scotus his picture—a leane lathie man WOOD.

Lati- (lēⁱti, læti), comb. f. L. *latus* broad, as **Latico·state** *a.*, *Zool.* having broad ribs. **Latide·ntate** *a.*, *Zool.* having broad teeth. **Latifo·liate**, **-fo·lious** *adjs.*, *Bot.* having broad leaves. †**Latiro·strous** [L. *rostrum* beak + -OUS] *a.*, *Ornith.* having a broad beak; so **Latiro·stral**, **-ro·strate** *adjs.* **Latiste·rnal** *a.*, having a broad breast-bone.

Latian (lēⁱ·ʃiăn), *a.* 1598. [f. L. *Latium* (see LATIN) + -AN.] Of or belonging to Latium; Latin.

†**Latibule.** *rare.* 1623. [ad. L. *latibulum*, f. *latere* to be hidden.] A hiding-place.

Latibulize (lăti·biŭləiz), *v. rare.* 1802. [f. as prec. + -IZE.] *intr.* To retire into a hiding-place or retreat (for the winter).

Laticiferous (lætisi·fĕrəs), *a.* 1835. [f. L. *latic-*, LATEX + -(I)FEROUS. Cf. F. *laticifère*.] *Bot.* Bearing or containing latex.

L. tissue, tissue containing l. tubes or vessels.

Laticlave (læ·tiklēⁱv). 1658. [ad. late L. *laticlavium*, *laticlavus*, f. *latus* broad + *clavus* purple stripe. (In cl. L. *latus clavus*.)] *Rom. Antiq.* A badge consisting of two broad purple stripes on the edge of the tunic, worn by senators and other persons of high rank.

‖**Latifundia** (lēⁱtifɒ·ndiă), *sb. pl.* 1630. [L. pl. of *latifundium*, f. *latus* broad + *fundus* estate.] Large estates Hence **Latifu·ndian** *a.* possessing l. NORTH.

†**La·timer.** ME. [a. OF. *latim(m)ier*, corrupt f. *latinier*, f. *Latin*; see LATIN *sb.*] An interpreter –1480.

Latin (læ·tin). [ad. L. *Latinus* adj., f. *Latium*, the part of Italy which included Rome. As sb., adopted in OE. as *læden* (see LEDEN).] **A.** *adj.* **1.** Of or pertaining to Latium or the ancient Latins (or Romans) ME. **2.** Pertaining to, characteristic of, or composed in the language of the ancient Latins or Romans. Of a writer, etc.: Versed in the Latin language. OE. Also *transf.* (*joc.*) **3.** Distinctive epithet of that branch of the Catholic Church which acknowledges the primacy of the Bishop of Rome, and uses the Latin tongue in its rites, etc. Also applied to its rites, clergy, etc. 1560. **4. a.** Applied (in opposition to *Greek*) to what pertains to the peoples of Western Europe, viewed in their relations with the Eastern Empire and with the Saracens and Turks. **b.** Applied to the European peoples which speak languages derived from Latin (though not all of Roman descent). 1788.

1. Learned in the Latyne tongue *Bk. Com. Prayer* (1552). **2.** Remuneration, O, that's the Latine word for three-farthings *L. L. L.* III. i. 138. A L. Grammar 1668, translation 1777. *transf.* Hang-hog is latten for Bacon SHAKS. **4.** *L. union*: the monetary alliance formed in 1865 by France, Belgium, Italy, and Switzerland, and afterwards joined by Greece, for the adoption and maintenance of a uniform system of bimetallic coinage in each of these states, and the recognition by each state of the coins of the others as legal tender. Phr. *L. cross*: see CROSS *sb.* 13.

B. *absol.* and as *sb.* **1.** The language of the people of ancient Rome; the Latin language OE. **2.** An inhabitant or native of Latium; one who possessed the Latin right of citizenship ME. **3.** (Chiefly in *pl.*) **a.** *Hist.* = FRANK *sb.*[1] 2. **b.** A member or adherent of the Latin or Western Church; now *rare* or *obs.* exc. with reference to subjects of the Turkish Empire. ME. †**4.** A translation into Latin, as a school exercise. Chiefly *pl.* –1679.

1. And though thou hadst small Latine, and lesse Greeke B. JONS. *Dog-L.*: see DOG *sb.* 8. *False L.*: L. which is faulty in construction; hence *transf.*, a breach of manners. *Thieves' L.*, the secret language or cant of thieves. **3. b.** The Catholics (here [at Jerusalem] called 'Latins') LADY HERBERT.

Hence †**La·tin** *v. trans.* to render or turn into L. 1553–1678. **La·tiner** (*colloq.*), a L. scholar; one who speaks L. 1691. **Lati·nic** *a.* of or pertaining to the ancient Latins or to the modern L. nations 1875. **Lati·nically** *adv.* 1784. **La·tinless** *a.* ignorant of L. 1599. †**La·tinly** *adv.* 1388–1656.

Latinism (læ·tiniz'm). 1570. [f. LATIN + -ISM.] **1.** A Latin idiom, esp. one used by a writer in another language; conformity in style to Latin models. **2.** The influence or sphere of action of the Latin races, or the Latin Church 1920.

1. Milton's L. is so pronounced as to be un-English 1875.

Latinist (læ·tinist). 1538. [f. LATIN + -IST.] 1. One versed in the Latin language; a Latin scholar; †*occas.* a writer of Latin. 2. A theologian of the Latin Church. COVERDALE. Hence **Latini·stic** *a.* pertaining to or characterized by latinism; characteristic of a l. So **Latini·stical** *a.* 1723.

Latinity (lăti·nĭti). 1619. [ad. L. *latinitatem*, f. *Latinus*; see LATIN and -ITY.] 1. The manner of speaking or writing Latin; Latin (with reference to its construction or style). 2. *Rom. Law.* The status of a Latin citizen 1880.

1. His l. is pure GIBBON.

Latinize (læ·tinəiz), *v.* 1589. [ad. L. *latinizare*, f. *Latinus*; see -IZE.] 1. *trans.* To turn into Latin, to write in Latin, to give a Latin form to (a word, etc.). 2. To make Latin or Latin-like, to make conformable to the ideas, customs, etc. of the Latins, or to the rites, etc. of the Latin Church 1603. 3. *intr.* To use Latin forms, idioms, etc. 1642.

1. The tendency to l. our speech TRENCH. 2. The Roman Catholic Church has..made great efforts to L. its Oriental branches 1882. 3. One pretended crime..that I l. too much DRYDEN. Hence **Latiniza·tion, La·tinizer.**

†**Lation.** 1603. [ad. L. *lationem*, f. *lat-*, ppl. stem of *ferre* to bear, carry.] *Astrol.* The action of moving, or the motion of a body from one place to another; motion of translation –1690.

Latish (lē̆·tiʃ), *a.* Also **lateish.** 1611. [f. LATE *a.* + -ISH [1].] Somewhat late. Also as *adv.*

Latitancy (læ·tĭtănsi). 1646. [f. next; see -ANCY.] The state of lying concealed or hid. Of an animal: Hibernation.

Latitant (læ·tĭtănt), *a.* (*sb.*) 1646. [ad. L. *latitantem*, *latitare* to lie hid.] That lies concealed; lurking, latent; (of an animal) hibernating. As *sb.* One who is in hiding 1887.

Latitat (læ·titæt). *Obs.* exc. *Hist.* 1523. [a. L. *latitat*, = 'he lies concealed'.] *Law.* A writ which supposed the defendant to lie concealed and which summoned him to answer in the King's Bench. So **Latita·tion** 1623.

Latitude (læ·tĭtiūd). ME. [ad. L. *latitudo*, f. *latus* broad; see -TUDE.]

I. 1. Transverse dimension; breadth, width as opp. to length; also *occas.* spaciousness. Now only *joc.* †b. A wide compass or extent –1791. 2. Extent, range, scope. Also, great or full extent. Now *rare.* 1605. †b. The range within which anything may vary –1796. †c. Local range –1638. 3. Freedom from narrow restrictions; liberality of construction or interpretation; tolerated variety of action or opinion 1605. †b. Laxity –1702.

1. The l. and bredth of the Zodiack is .xij. degrees 1559. b. A chace with a vengeance all the l. of the land FULLER. 2. His great learning and l. of knowledge SIR T. BROWNE. 3. The l. which a court of equity allows itself in enforcing agreements against the letter LD. ST. LEONARDS.

II. In Geography and Astronomy. 1. *Geog.* a. Angular distance on a meridian; only in *degree, minute*, etc. *of l.* b. The angular distance on its meridian (of any place on the earth's surface) north or south from the equator. ME. c. A locality as defined by parallels of latitude; usu. in *pl.* = regions, climes, parts of the world. Also *fig.* 1632. 2. *Astron.* The angular distance of a heavenly body from the ecliptic; called spec. *celestial l.* ME.

1. *Circle, parallel of l.*, see those words. A degree of l. measured on any meridian is about 69 miles everywhere 1867. c. Those latitudes and altitudes where no crops will grow W. R. GREG.

Hence **Latitu·dinal** *a.* relating to breadth or width (*rare*); relating to, connected with, or depending on geographical l.; corresponding with lines of l. **Latitu·dinally** *adv.*

Latitudinarian (læ:tĭtiūdinē^ə·riăn), *a.* and *sb.* 1662. [f. L. *latitudin-*, *latitudo* LATITUDE, after *trinitarian*, etc.]

A. *adj.* Allowing, favouring, or characterized by latitude in opinion or action, esp. in religious matters; not insisting on strict adherence to any code, standard, formula, etc.; tolerating free thought on religious questions; characteristic of the latitudinarians 1672.

His opinions respecting ecclesiastical polity and modes of worship were l. MACAULAY.

B. *sb.* One who practises or favours latitude in thought, action, or conduct, esp. in religious matters; *spec.* one of the English divines of the 17th c., who, while attached to episcopal government and forms of worship, regarded them as things indifferent; hence, one who, though not a sceptic, is indifferent as to creeds and forms.

Dr. Wilkins, my friend, the Bishop of Chester..is a mighty rising man, as being a L. PEPYS. *Latitudinarian*, one who fancies all religions are saving WESLEY *Eng. Dict.*

Hence **La·titudina·rianism**, l. doctrine, opinions, principles, or practice 1676. So †**Latitu·dinism** 1667–1685. **Latitu·dinous** *a.* characterized by latitude of interpretation. *U.S.* 1838.

Laton: see LATTEN.

Latonian (lătōᵘ·niăn), *a.* (*sb.*) 1591. [f. L. *Latonius*, f. *Latona*, a. Gr. (Æolic) Λάτων, (Attic) Λητώ; see -AN.] A. *adj.* Pertaining to Latona (= Gr. Leto), the mother of Apollo and Diana. B. *sb.* *The Latonian*: Apollo.

A. L. Twins..why hide you so your shining Fronts? SYLVESTER.

Latoun, obs. or arch. f. LATTEN.

Latrant (lē̆·trănt), *a.* 1702. [ad. L. *latrantem*, *latrare* to bark.] Barking; also *fig.*

†**Latrate**, *v.* 1623. [f. as next.] To bark like a dog; also *fig.*

Latration (lătrē̆·ʃən). 1623. [f. L. *latrare.*] A barking; also *fig.*

†**Latrede**, *a.* *rare.* [OE. *lætrǣde*, f. *læt* LATE *a.* + *rǣd* counsel, REDE.] Slow, tardy.

Whan a man is so l. or tarying CHAUCER.

Latreutic, -al (lătrū·tik, -ăl), *a.* *rare.* 1627. [ad. Gr. λατρευτικός (f. λατρεύειν: see next), + -AL.] Of the nature of LATRIA.

‖**Latria** (lătrəi·ă). Also †**latreia.** 1526. [late L., a. Gr. λατρεία, f. λατρεύειν to serve, serve with prayer.] *Theol.* In R. C. language: The supreme worship which is due to God alone (dist. from DULIA and HYPERDULIA).

Latrine (lătrī·n). 1642. [a. F. (chiefly in pl. *latrines*), a. L. *latrina*, contr. f. *lavatrina*, f. *lavare* to wash.] A privy.

†**Latrociny.** ME. [ad. L. *latrocinium*, f. *latro* robber. Cf. LARCENY.] 1. Highway robbery, brigandage –1657. 2. A band of robbers. Also *transf.* –1732.

-latry, -olatry, repr. Gr. -λατρεία worship, as in εἰδωλολατρεία IDOLATRY, *Mariolatry*, etc. Hence, in joc. nonce-use, *babyolatry* (q. v. s. v. BABY), etc. So -(*o*)*later*, repr. Gr. -λάτρης worshipper, as in *idolater, bibliolater*, etc.

Latten (læ·tĕn). ME. [a. OF. *laton, leiton*, mod.F. *laiton*:—pop. L. type **lactonem*; or, if Sp. *laton* was the original, perh. a deriv. of Com. Rom. **latta* lath, tin-plate (see LATH).] 1. A mixed metal of yellow colour, either identical with or very like brass; often hammered into thin sheets. Now only *arch.* and *Hist.* 2. Iron tinned over, tin-plate; more explicitly *white l.* Also, any metal made in thin sheets. Now *dial.* 1611. 3. *attrib.* or *adj.* Consisting or made of latten 1492. ¶4. Used with a pun on *Latin* 1607.

1. A dome of yellow laton from Andalusia R. F. BURTON. *Black l.* = latten-brass. *Shaven l.*, a thinner kind than black l. *Roll l.*, latten polished on both sides ready for use. 3. **L.-brass**, milled brass in thin plates or sheets, used by braziers and for drawing into wire. 4. I faith Ben: I'le e'en give him a douzen good Lattin Spoones, and thou shalt translate them SIR N. L'ESTRANGE.

Latter (læ·təɹ), *a.* (*adv.*) [OE. *lætra* (fem. and neut. -*e*) adj., *lator* adv., compar. of *læt* LATE. The mod. LATER is a new formation on LATE *a.*]

A. *adj.* †1. Slower –ME. 2. Later; *occas.* = 'second' (cf. LATTERMATH). Now only *poet.* or *arch.* ME. 3. Pertaining to the end of life, of a period, the world, etc.; = LAST. *Obs.* exc. *arch.* in *l. days.* 1513. 4. That has been mentioned second of two; opp. to *former* 1555. Also *absol.* or *ellipt.* 1608.

2. The opinion and practice of the l. Cato SWIFT. *L. Lammas*: see LAMMAS. 3. *L. end*: the concluding part (of a period, etc.); the end of life, (one's) death. Also *joc.*, the posteriors. ME. Hence **La·tterly** *adv.*, at the l. end; lately. **La·ttermost** *a.* last.

†B. *adv.* a. More slowly. b. Later. –1590.

b. My wife, more carefull for the l. borne SHAKS.

La·tter-day, *adj. phr.* 1842. Belonging to 'the latter days'; modern.

Latter-day Saints, the name the Mormons give themselves.

Latterkin (læ·təɹkin). 1659. A glazier's tool used in making lead-lights.

Lattermath (læ·təɹmaþ). *dial.* 1530. [f. LATTER *a.* + MATH (OE. *mǣþ*) mowing.] The latter mowing; the aftermath. Also, the crops then reaped.

La·ttermint. [f. LATTER *a.* + MINT *sb.*] ? A late kind of mint. KEATS.

Lattice (læ·tis), *sb.* ME. [a. OF. and F. *lattis*, f. *latte* LATH.] 1. A structure made of laths, or of wood or metal crossed and fastened together, with open spaces left between; used as a screen, e.g. in window openings; a window, gate, screen, etc. so constructed. Also *fig.* †b. A window of lattice-work (usu. painted red), or a pattern on the shutter or wall resembling this (see CHEQUER *sb.*[1] I. 4), formerly a sign of an alehouse or inn –1735. c. Lattices collectively; = LATTICE-WORK. Also *fig.* 1577. 2. *transf.* 1657. †3. A part of the auditorium of a theatre 1818. 4. *attrib.* ME.

1. Ahaziah fel downe thorow a lattesse in his vpper chamber 2 *Kings* i. 2. Thro' a l. on the soul Looks thy fair face and makes it still TENNYSON. b. If he draw not A L. to your doore, and hang a bush out 1639.

Comb.: **l.-bar** *Bridge-building*, a bar belonging to a system of latticing; **l. beam** = *lattice girder*; **l.-bridge**, a bridge consisting of a top and bottom flange connected by a number of flat iron bars forming a l.; **l. frame, girder**, a girder consisting of two horizontal bars connected by diagonal bars crossed so as to resemble lattice-work; **l. leaf (plant)**, the *Ouvirandra fenestralis* or lace-leaf of Madagascar; also **l. plant.**

Hence **Lattice** *v.* *trans.* to furnish with a l. or lattice-work. Also with *up, over* 1428. **La·tticed** *a.*, *spec.* in *Nat. Hist.* having a conformation or marking resembling lattice-work; *Her.* of a pattern resembling fretty, but placed cross-ways.

Lattice-window. 1515. A window furnished with a lattice; also, now, one composed of small diamond-shaped panes set in lead-work.

Lattice-work. 1487. = LATTICE *sb.* 1. Also, something resembling this.

Latticing (læ·tisiŋ). 1885. [f. LATTICE *sb.* or *v.* + -ING [1].] The process of making a lattice or lattice-work; in *Bridge-building* (see quot.).

Latticing, a system of bars crossing each other at the middle of their lengths, used to connect the two channels of a strut, in order to make them act as one member WADDELL.

‖**Latus** (lē̆·tŏs). 1702. [L., = side.] *Math.* In *Conic sections*: **l. rectum**, a straight line drawn through the focus of a conic at right angles to the transverse diameter, the parameter.

Laud (lǭd), *sb.* ME. [a. OF. *laude*, ad. L. *laudem*, *laus* praise.] 1. Praise, high commendation. Now *rare*, exc. in hymns. 2. *pl.* The first of the day-hours of the Church, the Psalms of which always end with Pss. cxlviii–cl, sung as one psalm and technically called *laudes* ME. Also *transf.* 3. A hymn or ascription of praise 1530.

1. Pursevantes and herauldes That crien ryche folkes laudes CHAUCER. 2. Now midnight lauds were in Melrose sung SCOTT.

Laud (lǭd), *v.* ME. [ad. L. *laudare*, f. *laud-*, *laus.*] *trans.* To praise, to sing or speak the praises of; to celebrate. Often *to l. and bless* (*praise, magnify*). Orig. implying an act of worship.

So ye shal be happy, & your werkes lauded 1477. Hence **Lau·der** = LAUDATOR.

Laudable (lǭ·dăb'l), *a.* Also †**laudible.** ME. [ad. L. *laudabilis*, f. *laudare*; see prec. and -ABLE.] 1. Praiseworthy, commendable. †Also, in early use, laudatory. 2. Of satisfactory nature, quality, or operation; healthy, sound, wholesome. Now only *Path.* of secretions, *esp.* pus. 1514. †3. *sb.* in *pl.* Laudable qualities, good points 1715.

1. A l. ambition WALTON. L. curiosity RUSKIN. 2. To promote a l. growth of flesh 1720. Healthy or l. pus 1878. Hence **Laudabi·lity** (*rare*), **Lau·dableness. Lau·dably** *adv.*

Laudanine (lǭ·dănəin). Also **-in.** 1888. [f. LAUDANUM + -INE [5].] *Chem.* A colourless to pale red crystalline alkaloid contained in opium.

Laudanum (lǫ·d'nǒm). Also †**lodanum.** 1602. [a. mod.L. *laudanum*, used by Paracelsus for a costly medicament, in which opium was early suspected to be the active ingredient. The wd. thus used may be a var. of LADANUM, or ? suggested by *laudare* to praise, or quite arbitrary.] **1.** In early use, any of various preparations in which opium was the main ingredient. Now: The simple alcoholic tincture of opium. †**2.** = LADANUM 1. -1702.

Laudation (lǫdē·ʃən). 1470. [ad. L. *laudationem*.] The action or an act of praising. Also, the condition of being praised.

As we read the long l. on the pedestal STANLEY.

Laudative (lǭ·dătiv). *rare.* 1605. [ad. L. *laudativus*, f. *laudat-*, *laudare*. Cf. F. *laudatif*.] **A.** *adj.* Expressive of praise; laudatory. Const. *of.* 1609. †**B.** *sb.* A laudative expression or discourse; a eulogy, panegyric.

Laudator (lǫdē·təɹ). 1825. [a. L.] One who praises; a eulogist.

Laudatory (lǭ·dătəri). 1555. [ad. L. *laudatorius* adj., f. *laudare*.]

A. *adj.* Expressive of praise; eulogistic.

†**B.** *sb.* A laudatory discourse, a eulogy -1642.

B. A l. of itself obtruded in the very first word MILT.

Hence **Lau·datorily** *adv.*

Laudian (lǭ·diăn), *a.*, *sb.* Also †**Laudean.** 1691. [f. William *Laud*, archbishop of Canterbury 1633-45 + -IAN.] Of, pertaining to, or characteristic of Laud; favouring the tenets of Laud; instituted by Laud. As *sb.*, a follower of Laud. Hence **Lau·dianism,** the principles and practice of Laud and his followers; also **Lau·dism.**

Laugh (lɑf), *sb.* 1690. [f. next.] **1.** The action of laughing; laughing, or an inclination to laugh; laughter (*rare*). **2.** An act, or the manner, of laughing. Also *fig.* 1713. **3.** = LAUGHING-STOCK (*rare*) 1817.

1. Do you find jest, and I'll find l. GOLDSM. 2. The heart's light l. pursued the circling jest S. ROGERS. Phr. *To have* or *get the l. on one's side*; *to have the l. of*, *to raise the l. against*.

Laugh (lɑf), *v.* [Com. Teut. str. vb. OE. *hlęhhan*, *hliehhan*, Anglian *hlæhhan*; the Teut. root **hlah-* (: **hlōh-* : **hlag-*) represents a pre-Teut. **klak-*, prob. echoic; cf. **klok-* in Gr. κλώσσειν to cluck. The mod. Eng. form descends from the Anglian *hlæhhan*.] **1.** *intr.* To manifest the spasmodic utterance, facial distortion, shaking of the sides, etc., which form the instinctive expression of mirth, amusement, sense of the ludicrous, scorn, etc. Also *transf.* to have the emotion which is expressed by laughing. **b.** Attributed *poet.* and *rhet.* to inanimate objects, chiefly with reference to movement or play of light and colour ME. **2.** quasi-*trans.* with cognate obj. Also, to utter laughingly or with laughter. 1470. **3.** With *dat.* of person, and *to* with sb., as in *to l. to scorn* (now *arch.* and *literary*) ME. **4.** With obj. and compl., adv., or advb. phr.: To produce a specified effect upon by laughing ME.

1. Then the whole quire hold their hips, and loffe SHAKS. Phr. *To l. in one's sleeve*: to l. to oneself. *To l. on the other, wrong side* (*of one's face, mouth*): to change to sadness and vexation from laughter and exultation. b. The heavens l. with you in your jubilee WORDSW. The wood fire..laughs broadly through the room HAWTHORNE. †*L. and lay* (or *lie*) *down*: an obsolete game at cards. 2. The large Achilles..laughs out a loud applause SHAKS. 3. All they that see me, l. me to scorne *Ps.* xxii. 7. †*To l. on, upon* (rarely *up*, *to*): to smile on. *To l. at*: to make fun of; to deride, ridicule. 4. Will you l. me asleepe, for I am very heauy SHAKS. Whose whole life is to eat, and drink..and l. themselves fat TRAPP. *To l. away*: †(*a*) to let go with a laugh; (*b*) to get rid of with a laugh; (*c*) to while away (time) with laughter. *To l. down*: to subdue or silence with laughter. *To l. off*, *out* = *to laugh away* (*b*). *To l. over*: to recall or repeat with laughter or mirth.

Hence **Lau·ghable** *a.* that may be laughed at; to be laughed at. **Lau·ghably** *adv.* **Lau·ghableness.** **Laughee·**, the person laughed at (CARLYLE). **Lau·gher,** one who laughs; one addicted to laughing; also, a scoffer; also, a variety of pigeon (1735).

Laughing (lɑ·fiŋ), *vbl. sb.* ME. [f. LAUGH *v.* + -ING[1].] The action of LAUGH *v.*; laughter.

Comb. **l.-matter,** a subject for laughter; **-muscle,** the *risorius*, or the muscle that produces the contortions attendant on laughter; †**-post, -stake** = LAUGHING-STOCK.

Laughing (lɑ·fiŋ), *ppl. a.* ME. [f. as prec. + -ING[2].] That laughs.

In names of animals, so called from their cry or aspect: **l. hyena, jackass** (see the sbs.); **l.-bird** *dial.*, the green woodpecker; **-crow,** any of various Asiatic birds; **-goose,** the white-fronted goose (*Anser albifrons*); **-thrush,** any of various Asiatic birds. Hence **Lau·ghingly** *adv.* 1530.

Laughing gas. 1842. Nitrous oxide, N_2O; so called from its exhilarating effects when inhaled.

Laughing-stock. 1519. [f. LAUGHING *vbl. sb.* + STOCK.] An object of laughter; a butt for ridicule.

You'll be a laughing stock to the whole bench, and a byword with all the pig-tailed lawyers SHERIDAN.

Laughsome (lɑ·fsǒm), *a. rare.* 1620. [f. LAUGH *sb.* + -SOME.] Addicted to laughing; (of things) laughable.

Laughter[1] (lɑ·ftəɹ). [OE. *hleahtor* str. masc. :—OTeut. **hlahtro-z*, f. root **hlah-*; see LAUGH *v.*] The action of laughing; *occas.* a manner of laughing. **b.** A laugh (now *rare*) OE. **c.** Used for: A subject or matter for laughter 1596.

1. *Homeric l.* (see *Iliad* i. 599 ἄσβεστος γέλως), irrepressible laughter. Then shal oure mouth be fylled with l. COVERDALE *Ps.* cxxv. 3. *Personified*, L. holding both his sides MILT. *L'Alleg.* 32. b. Exchanging quick low laughters BROWNING. c. L. for a Moneth, and a good iest for euer SHAKS. Hence **Lau·ghterless** *a.*

Laughter[2] (lɑ·ftəɹ). *dial.* 1601. [a. ON. **lahtr*, *látr* :—OTeut. **lahtro*m, f. **lag-*, root of LAY *v.*] The whole number of eggs laid by a fowl before she is ready to sit.

Lau·ghworthy, *a. rare.* 1616. Deserving to be laughed at, ridiculous.

Laughy (lɑ·fi), *a. rare.* 1837. [f. LAUGH *sb.* or *v.* + -Y[1].] Inclined to laugh.

Laumontite (lǭ·mǫntəit). 1805. [f. Gillet de *Laumont*, its discoverer; see -ITE.] *Min.* Hydrous silicate of aluminium and calcium.

†**Launce**[1]. [ad. L. *lancem* (*lanx*), It. *lance*.] A scale, balance. SPENSER.

Launce[2] (lɑns). 1623. [? same as LANCE *sb.*[1]] A fish of the genus *Ammodytes*; the sand-eel; = LANT *sb.*[2] Also called *sand-la(u)nce*. *Sable l.*: the capelin.

Launch (lǭnʃ, lānʃ), *sb.*[1] 1558. [f. LAUNCH *v.*] †**1.** The action or an act of lancing; a prick -1596. **2. a.** The action or process of launching a vessel. Also *fig.* with *out*. **b.** The starting off of a bird in flight. 1814. **3.** *concr.* in *Ship-building*. The slip or descent whereon the ship is built, including the machinery used in launching 1711. **4.** *dial.* An eel-trap 1847. **5.** *attrib.*, as **l.-block, -ways** = *launching-ways, launching-planks* 1720.

Launch (lǭnʃ, lānʃ), *sb.*[2] 1697. [ad. Sp. *lancha* pinnace, perh. of Malay origin.] **1.** The largest boat of a man-of-war, for use in shallow water, usually sloop-rigged. **2.** A large boat propelled by electricity, steam, etc. (*electric l.*, *steam-l.*), used for transporting passengers, or as a pleasure-craft 1865.

Launch (lǭnʃ, lānʃ), *v.* ME. [ad. ONF. *lancher* = Central OF. *lancier*; see LANCE *v.*] †**1.** *trans.* = LANCE *v.* II. 1, 2. -1724. **2.** To hurl, shoot, discharge, send off (a missile, a blow, etc.). (Cf. LANCE *v.* I. 1.) ME. **b.** To dart forward (a weapon, a limb, etc.). Now only, to dart *out* (something long and flexible). ME. **3.** *intr.* for *refl.* To rush, plunge, start or shoot forth; †to leap, vault; *transf.* to skip in reading ME. **b.** *fig.* (Now usually with *out*.) To enter boldly or freely into a course of action; to rush *into* expense; to burst *out* into (violent) speech 1608. **4.** *trans.* To cause (a vessel) to move or slide from the land, or the stocks, into the water; to set afloat; to lower (a boat) into the water ME. **b.** To send off, start upon a course, send adrift 1627. **c.** *fig.* To start (a person) *in*, *into*, or *on* a business, career, etc.; to set on foot (a project); to commence (an action). Also with *out.* 1602. **5.** *intr.* Of the ship: To be launched (now *rare*). **6.** To push *forth*, *out* from land, put to sea, advance seawards (*lit.* and *fig.*) 1534. **7.** *trans. Naut.* †**a.** To set up, hoist (a yard). **b.** To move (casks, etc.) by pushing. 1627.

1. Nine Bulls were launch'd by his victorious arm DRYDEN. *fig.* Thy Prophets..Rubb'd where they should haue launcht QUARLES. 2. To l. a thunderbolt SCOTT, the censures of the church against offenders FREEMAN. 3. b. I want time to l. into an ample discourse BOYLE. 4. Was this the face that launch'd a thousand ships? MARLOWE. c. The Mississippi scheme launched by John Law YEATS. *To l. into eternity*: rhet. for 'to put to death'. 6. To l. out into an ocean of common-place HUME. *To l. into eternity*: rhet. for 'to die'.

Launching (lǭ·nʃiŋ, lā·nʃiŋ), *vbl. sb.* 1592. [-ING[1].] The action of LAUNCH *v.*

Comb. †**l.-knife,** a lancet; **l.-planks,** a set of planks mostly used to form the platform on each side of the ship, whereon the bilgeways slide for the purpose of launching; **l.-ways** = *launching-planks.*

Laund (lǭnd). *Obs.* exc. *arch.* See also LAWN *sb.*[2] ME. [a. OF. *launde*, F. *lande* wooded ground, a. OCelt. **landa*; see LAND *sb.*] An open space among woods, a glade (= L. *saltus*); untilled ground, pasture.

Through this L. anon the Deere will come SHAKS.

Launder (lǭ·ndəɹ, lā·ndəɹ), *sb.* ME. [Contr. f. LAVENDER *sb.*[1]] †**1.** A man or woman who washes linen -1603. **2. a.** A trough for water, either cut in the earth, or formed of wood; *esp.* in *Mining*, one for washing the ore clean from dirt. **b.** A rain-water gutter. 1667. Now *local.*

Launder (lǭ·ndəɹ, lā·ndəɹ), *v.* 1597. [f. prec. sb.] **1.** *trans.* To wash and get up (linen). Also *transf.* and *fig.* †**2.** To sweat (gold or plate). B. JONS. **3.** Of a fabric: To bear laundering (well, etc.) 1909.

1. His linen [was] soft and badly laundered 1883. So **Lau·nderer,** one who launders (linen) (*Obs.* exc. *local* and *U.S.*) 1440; †one who sweats gold or plate.

Laundress (lǭ·ndrės, lā·ndrės), *sb.* 1524. [f. LAUNDER *sb.* + -ESS[1].] **1.** A woman who washes and gets up linen, etc. **2.** A caretaker of chambers in the Inns of Court 1592.

2. It's a curious circumstance, Sam, that they call the old women in these inns, laundresses DICKENS. Hence †**Lau·ndress** *v trans.* to furnish with laundresses, act as l. to; *intr* to act as a l. 1612-36.

Laundry (lǭ·ndri, lā·ndri). 1530. [Altered f. ME. *lavendry* (ad. OF. *lavan-*, *lavenderie*) after LAUNDER.] †**1.** The action or process of washing -1626. **2.** An establishment for washing and getting up linen 1577. **b.** Articles washed and got up. *recent.* ¶**3.** Used for LAUNDRESS. *Merry W.* I. ii. 5. **4.** *attrib.*, as *l.-man*, etc. 1585.

‖**Laura** (lǭ·ră). 1727. [a. Gr. λαύρα lane, passage, alley.] *Christian Antiq.* An aggregation of detached cells, tenanted by recluse monks under a superior, in Egypt and elsewhere.

Lauraceous (lǭrē·ʃəs), *a.* [f. mod.L. *Lauraceæ* + -OUS.] *Bot.* Belonging to the N.O. *Lauraceæ* or laurel family. (Rec. Dicts.)

Laurate (lǭ·rēt). 1873. [f. L. *laurus* laurel + -ATE[4]. See LAURIC.] *Chem.* A salt of lauric acid.

†**Laure.** [OE. ad. L. *laurus*.] The laurel or bay-tree; also, its leaves woven into a chaplet -1567.

†**Laureal,** *a. Obs. rare.* late ME. [ad. L. **laurealis*, f. *laurea* laurel.] Laureate -1756.

Laureate (lǭ·ri,ĕt). ME. [ad. L. *laureatus*, f. *laurea* laurel-tree, laurel crown, fem. of *laureus* adj., f. *laurus*; see LAUREL.]

A. *adj.* **1.** Crowned with laurel (as a symbol of distinction) ME. **b.** Of a crown, wreath: Consisting of laurel, or imitating one composed of laurel. Hence (*poet.*) *l. shade.* ME. **2.** Worthy of special distinction or honour, preeminent in a sphere or faculty. **a.** *gen.* ? *Obs.* 1508. **b.** *spec.* Distinguished as a poet, worthy of the Muses' crown ME. **3.** *transf.* Of things: Worthy of the laurel-wreath. Also, Of or pertaining to poets, or to a poet laureate. late ME.

1. To strew the Laureat Herse where Lycid lies MILT. b. The l. wreath, that Cecil wore GRAY. †*L. letters* [tr. L. *litteræ laureatæ*], a letter or dispatch announcing a victory. 2. a. No, Faustus, Thou art conjuror laureat, That canst command great Mephistophilis MARLOWE. b. *Poet Laureate*: in early use, a title given generally to eminent poets, and sometimes conferred by universities; in mod. use, the title given to a poet who receives a stipend as an officer of the Royal Household, writes court-odes, etc. The first recorded appointment by authority to the office of Poet Laureate was a 'warrant for a grant' to Dryden, on 13 April, 1668; confirmed by

patent of 18 Aug., 1670. **3.** Langage l. LYDGATE. The laureat strain of Pindar GROTE.

B. *sb.* **1.** = *Poet laureate* 1529. **b.** A court panegyrist 1863. **2.** *U.S.* A degree title awarded in some institutions to women. BRYCE. **3.** *Numism.* = LAUREL *sb.* 4. 1727.

1. The courtly laureat pays His quit-rent ode, his pepper corn of praise COWPER. Hence **Lau·reateship.**

Laureate (lǭ·riˌeit), *v.* *Obs.* exc. *Hist.* ME. [f. L. *laureatus*; see prec. and -ATE [3].] **1.** *trans.* To crown with laurel as victor, poet, or the like; to confer honourable distinction upon. **2.** *spec.* **a.** To graduate or confer a University degree upon. **b.** To appoint (a poet) to the office of Laureate. 1637.

1. By his reygne is all Englonde lawreat 1509.

Laureation (lǭriˌēⁱ·ʃən). 1637. [f. LAUREATE *v.*; see -ATION.] The action of crowning with laurel or making laureate; in the Sc. Universities, a term for graduation or admission to a degree; also, the creation of a poet laureate.

Laurel (lǫ·rĕl), *sb.* ME. (**lorer, laurer,** later, **lorel,** etc.) [ad. F. *laurier* for *lorier*, f. OF. *lor*:—L. *laurus*; the *l*, as often, repl. the second *r* in the word.] **1.** The Bay-tree or Bay-laurel, *Laurus nobilis*; see BAY *sb.*[1] 2. Now *rare*, exc. as in 2. **b.** Any plant of the genus *Laurus* or the N.O. *Lauraceæ*. LINDLEY. **2.** The foliage of this tree as an emblem of victory or of distinction in poetry, etc. **a.** *collect. sing.* ME. **b.** *pl.* 1585. **c.** A branch or wreath of this tree (*lit.* and *fig.*) ME. †**d.** The dignity of Poet Laureate –1814. **3.** In mod. use, applied to *Cerasus laurocerasus* and other trees having leaves like those of the true laurel 1664. **4.** *Numism.* One of the English gold pieces (esp. those of 20*s.*), first coined in 1619, on which the monarch's head was figured with a wreath of laurel 1623. **5.** *attrib.* ME.

1. The victor palm, the laurer to deuyne CHAUCER. **2. a.** Gyff lawrelle to that lord of myght 1460. **b.** Phr. *To reap, win one's laurels, to repose, rest, retire on one's laurels. To look to one's laurels*: to beware of losing one's pre-eminence. **c.** Fame flies after with a l. PRIOR. **3.** **Alexandrian Laurel,** *Ruscus racemosus*; **American Dwarf** or **Mountain L.** = KALMIA; **Cherry L.,** *Cerasus laurocerasus*; **Great L.,** U.S. name for *Rhododendron maximum*; **Japan L.** = AUCUBA; **Portugal L.,** *Cerasus Lusitanica*; **Spurge L.,** *Daphne Laureola*. For *Ground-, Rose-, Sheep-l.*, see the first element.

Comb.: **l.-bay** = *Bay-laurel* (sense 1); **-thyme** = LAURUSTINUS; **-tree** = sense 1; **-water,** the water obtained by distillation from the leaves of the cherry laurel and containing a small proportion of prussic acid.

†**Lau·rel,** *a.* 1606. [f. LAUREL *sb.*] Crowned or wreathed with laurel; hence, renowned. Vpon your Sword Sit Laurell victory SHAKS.

Laurel (lǫ·rĕl), *v.* 1631. [f. as prec.] *trans.* To wreathe with laurel; to adorn with or as with laurel.

Laurelled (lǫ·rĕld), *ppl. a.* 1682. [f. LAUREL *sb.* or *v.* + -ED.] **a.** Crowned or wreathed with laurel. Hence *fig.* honoured, illustrious; cf. LAUREATE. **b.** Covered with a growth of laurel; also, made of laurel.

a. *L. letters*: cf. LAUREATE *a.* 1 (quot.). **b.** Here no sepulchre built In the laurell'd rock M. ARNOLD.

Laurentian (lǫre·nʃiăn), *a.* 1863. [f. L. *Laurentius* + -AN.] *Geol.* Epithet of certain sedimentary strata found in Canada near the river St. Lawrence. Also quasi-*sb.* in collective sense.

†**Laureole.** Also **lauriol(e.** ME. [a. F., ad. L. *laureola*.] Spurge Laurel –1596.

Laurestinus, erron. f. LAURUSTINUS.

Lauric (lǭ·rik), *a.* 1857. [f. L. *laurus* + -IC.] *L. acid*, a white crystalline compound ($C_{12}H_{24}O_2$) obtained from the berries of *Laurus nobilis*. Hence in *L. aldehyde, ether*, compounds derived from this acid.

Laurin (lǭ·rin). 1838. [f. L. *laurus* + -IN [1].] *Chem.* A crystalline substance ($C_{22}H_{30}O_3$) obtained from the berries of *Laurus nobilis*.

Laurite (lǭ·rəit). 1866. [f. Mrs. *Laura* Joy; see -ITE.] *Min.* Sulphide of ruthenium, found with platinum in small brilliant crystals.

Laurustine (lǫ·rɒstəin). Also *erron.* †**lauri-, laure-.** 1683. [Englished form of next.] = next.

Laurustinus (lǫ·rɒstəi·nɒs). 1664. [a. mod.L. (orig. two wds.) *laurus tinus* (L. *laurus* laurel, *tinus* a plant, perh. the laurustinus).] An evergreen winter-flowering shrub, *Viburnum Tinus*.

Laus(e, obs. ff. LOOSE *a.*

†**Lauti·tious,** *a.* [f. L. *lautitia* (f. *lautus* washed) + -OUS.] Sumptuous. HERRICK.

Lauwine (lǭ·win, Ger. lauvī·nə). Also law-. 1818. [ad. Ger. *la(u)wine*, of Swiss origin, f. *lau* mild, tepid (Kluge).] An avalanche.

Lava (lā·vă). 1750. [a. It. *lava* (f. *lavare* to wash; see LAVE *v.*[1]), orig. a stream or gutter suddenly caused by rain, applied to a lava-stream from Vesuvius.] †**1.** A stream of molten rock issuing from the crater of a volcano or from fissures in the earth. **2.** The fluid or semi-fluid matter flowing from a volcano 1760. Also *fig.* **3.** The substance that results from the cooling of the molten rock 1750. **b.** A kind of lava, a bed of lava 1796. **4.** *attrib.* 1811.

Comb.: **l.-millstone,** a hard and coarse basaltic millstone, obtained from quarries near Andernach on the Rhine; **-ware,** a kind of stoneware, manufactured and coloured to assume the semi-vitreous appearance of l.

‖**Lavabo** (lăvēⁱ·bo). 1740. [L., = 'I will wash'.] **1.** *Eccl.* **a.** The ritual washing of the celebrant's hands at the offertory, accompanied by the saying of Ps. xxv[i]. 6–12, beginning *Lavabo inter innocentes manus meas.* **b.** The small towel, also the basin, used in this rite. **2.** A washing-trough used in some mediæval monasteries 1883.

Lavage (læ·vėdʒ). 1895. [a. F., f. *laver*.] *Med.* A cleansing of the stomach by means of emetics administered in large quantities of water.

Lavant (læ·vănt). *Sussex* and *Hants.* 1774. [?] A land-spring.

Lavatic (lăvæ·tik), *a.* 1830. [f. LAVA + -ATIC.] Consisting of or resembling lava.

Lavation (lăvēⁱ·ʃən). 1627. [ad. L. *lavationem*, f. *lavare* to wash.] The action or an act of washing; *concr.* water for washing.

Lavatory (læ·vătŏri), *sb.* ME. [ad. L. *lavatorium* a place for washing; see LAVE *v.*[1]] **1.** A vessel for washing, a laver, a bath. Also †*fig.* **2.** *Eccl.* The ritual washing of the celebrant's hands: (*a*) at the offertory (cf. LAVABO 1 a); †(*b*) at the taking of the ablutions. 1512. †**3.** A lotion –1694. **4.** An apartment with apparatus for washing the hands and face; now often combined with water-closets, etc. 1656. **5.** A laundry 1661. **6.** A place for washing gold 1727.

Lavatory (læ·vătŏri), *a.* 1846. [f. L. *lavare*; see LAVE *v.*[1]] Of or pertaining to washing.

†**Lavature.** 1601. [ad. L. type **lavatura* (= cl. L. *lotura*), f. *lavare*.] A lotion, a wash.

Lave (lēⁱv), *sb.* *Obs.* exc. *Sc.* [OE. *láf*:—OTeut. **laibā* str. fem.; see LEAVE *v.*] What is left over; the remainder, the rest.

†**Lave,** *a.* ME. [See LAVE *v.*[2]] Of ears (esp. a horse's ears): Drooping, hanging –1675. Hence **Lave-eared** (corruptly **leaf-eared**) *a.*, having lave ears.

Lave (lēⁱv), *v.*[1] Now chiefly *poet.* [App. a fusion of two formations. (1) OE. *lafian* to wash by affusion, to pour (water), ? ad. L. *lavare* to wash. (2) In ME. the representative of the OE. vb. blended with the vb. a. F. *laver* :—L. *lavare* = Gr. λούειν, f. OAryan root **lou-* to wash (whence LATHER).] **1.** *trans.* To wash, bathe. Also *fig.* Also *intr.* for *refl.* **2.** *trans.* Of a body of water: To wash against, to flow along or past 1623. **3.** To pour out with or as with a ladle; to ladle. Also *absol.* OE. †**4.** *trans.* To draw (water) out or up with a bucket, ladle, or scoop; to bale. Also with *out, up*, and compl., and *absol.* –1708.

1. Basons, and ewers, to laue her dainty hands SHAKS. *intr.* In her chaste current oft the goddess laves POPE. **2.** Where Torridge laves its banks of green CAPERN. **3.** L. the water..in slight handfuls.. over the head and face 1862.

†**Lave,** *v.*[2] [Cf. ON. *lafa* to droop.] Of the ears: To droop, hang down. BP. HALL.

Laveer (lăvīᵊ·ɹ), *v.* *Obs.* exc. *literary.* 1598. [ad. Du. *laveeren*, MDu. *laeveren, loveren*, ad. F. (16th c.) *loveer*, now *louvoyer*, f. *lof* windward (of Du. or LG. origin; see LUFF).] *intr.* To beat to windward; to tack. Hence **Lavee·rer,** one who laveers.

Lavement (lēⁱ·vˌmĕnt). 1650. [a. F., f. *laver* to wash.] **1.** The action of washing or cleansing (*rare*). **2.** *Med.* An injection 1794.

†**La·vender,** *sb.*[1] ME. [a. OF. *lavandier* masc., *lavandiere* fem. (mod.F. *lavandière* fem.), ad. late L. *lavandarius, -aria*, f. *lavanda*, f. *lavare* to wash; see LAVE *v.*[1]] A washerwoman, laundress. †Formerly also (*rarely*), a man who washes clothes. –1567.

Enuye..is lauender In the grete court alway CHAUCER.

Lavender (læ·vĕndəɹ), *sb.*[2] and *a.* ME. [a. AF. *lavendre* for **lavendle*:—med.L. *lavendula*. Ult. etym. obscure. See N.E.D.]

A. *sb.* **1.** The plant *Lavandula vera* (N.O. *Labiatæ*), a small shrub with small pale bluish flowers, and narrow oblong or lanceolate leaves; cultivated extensively for its perfume. Also applied to *L. Spica* (distinguished as *French L.* and †*L. spike*), and *L. Stœchas* (formerly †*L. gentle*), and to certain other plants. **2.** The flowers and stalks of *Lavandula vera*, laid among linen or other clothes to preserve them from moths when stored. **3.** The colour of lavender-flowers, a very pale blue with a trace of red 1882.

1. Here 's flowers for you: Hot Lauender, Mints, Sauory, mariorum SHAKS. **Sea L.,** *Statice Limonium*; also called †*Marsh L., L. Thrift.* †**L. of Spain** = LAVENDER COTTON. **2.** Phr. *To lay (up) in l.*: (*a*) to lay aside carefully for future use; (*b*) *slang*, to pawn; (*c*) to put out of the way of doing harm.

B. *adj.* Of the colour of lavender-flowers (see A. 3) 1882.

Too much of a lavender-kid-glove gentleman 1897. Hence **La·vender** *v. trans.* to perfume with l.; to put l. among (linen).

La·vender co·tton. 1530. Ground cypress (*Santolina Chamæcyparissus*); formerly confused with *Artemisia Abrotanum* or *maritima*.

La·vender-wa·ter. 1563. A perfume compounded, with alcohol and ambergris, from the distilled flowers of lavender.

Laver (lēⁱ·vəɹ), *sb.*[1] OE. [a. L. *laver*.] †**1.** A water-plant; = Gr. σίον –1601. **2.** A name for various marine algæ, esp., now, the edible species 1611. Also *attrib.*

2. **Purple l.,** *Porphyra laciniata.* **Green l.,** *Ulva latissima* and *Ulva lactuca.*

Laver (lēⁱ·vəɹ), *sb.*[2] ME. [a. OF. *laveoir*, *lavur*:—L. *lavatorium*; see LAVATORY.] **1.** A vessel, basin, or cistern for washing, in early use, chiefly a (metal) water-jug; *occas.* a pan or bowl for water. Now only *poet.* or *rhet.* **b.** The large brazen vessel for the ablutions of the Jewish priests (= Heb. *kiyyōr*, Vulg. *labrum*) 1535. **c.** The basin of a fountain. *Obs.* exc. *arch.* 1604. **2.** *transf.* and *fig.* The baptismal font; the spiritual 'washing' of baptism; any spiritually cleansing agency. After Gr. λουτρὸν παλιγγενεσίας Tit. iii. 5. ME. †**3.** A process or mode of ablution –1684.

Laveroc(k, etc.: see LARK *sb.*[1]

Lavic (lā·vik), *a.* 1835. [f. LAVA + -IC.] Of or pertaining to lava.

†**Lavish,** *sb.* 1483. [a. OF. *lavasse, lavache* deluge of rain.] Profusion, excessive abundance; prodigality, lavishness. Phr. *To make l.* –1597.

Lavish (læ·viʃ), *a.* 1475. [f. LAVISH *sb.*] **1.** Effusive 1485; †unrestrained; loose, wild, licentious –1640. **2. a.** Expending or bestowing without stint; profuse; prodigal. Const. *of, in.* In early use often: Wasteful, extravagant. 1475. **b.** Expended, bestowed, or produced unstintedly; profuse, abundant 1576.

1. Phr. *L. of (one's) tongue.* When Meanes and lauish Manners meete together SHAKS. **2.** Your l. wasting servants..will be glad of a crust before they dye 1643. **b.** Let her haue needfull but not lauish meanes SHAKS. Hence **La·vish·ly** *adv.*, **-ness.**

Lavish (læ·viʃ), *v.* 1542. [f. LAVISH *a.*] **1.** *intr.* To be lavish, e.g. of words, etc. 1567. **2.** *trans.* To bestow, distribute, or spend profusely and recklessly; also with *away, out* 1542.

2. They lauish gold out of the bagge *Isa.* xlvi. 6. To l. pity on any one FULLER. Hence La·visher. **La·vishingly** *adv.* **La·vishment** (now *rare*), the action of lavishing.

Lavolta (lăvǫ·ltă), *sb.* *Obs.* exc. *arch.* *Englished* **lavolt.** 1580. [f. It. *la* the + *volta* turn.] 'A lively dance for two persons, consisting a good deal in high and active bounds' (Nares). Also *transf.* and *fig.*

Behold the sunne-beames.., Dancing Lauoltoes on the liquid floare 1600. Hence †**Lavo·lta** *v.* to dance a l.; to caper as in the l. †**Lavoltetee·r,** one who dances the l.

Lavrock, var. of LARK *sb.*[1]

Lavy (læ·vi). 1698. A St. Kilda name for the guillemot.

Law (lǭ), *sb.*[1] [Late OE. *lagu* str. fem. (pl. *laga*; in comb. *lah-*), a. prehistoric ON. **lagu* (whence OIcel. *lǫg*), pl. of *lag* neut.; in sing. the word meant in OIcel. 'something laid or fixed'; the pl. had the collective sense 'law', and in ONorw. its form became (as in OE.) a fem. sing. The ON. *lag* corresponds to OS. *-lag* neut. :—OTeut. **lagom*, f. root **lag-* :—Indo-Eur. **logh-* : see LAY, LIE *vbs.* The L. *leg-*, *lex* is not now generally believed to be cognate. The native word in OE. was *ǽ*; see Æ *sb.*[2]]

I. **Human law.* 1. The body of rules, whether formally enacted or customary, which a state or community recognizes as binding on its members or subjects. (In this sense usually *the law.*) †Also, in early use, a code or system of such rules. b. Often personified as an agent 1513. †c. What the law awards –1593. 2. One of these rules. In early use only *pl.*, often with a collective sense (after L. *iura, leges*). OE. 3. *gen.* a. Laws as obeyed or enforced; controlling influence of laws; the condition of society in which laws are observed ME. b. (*a*) Laws in general, as a human institution. (*b*) The science of which laws are the subject-matter; jurisprudence. ME. c. Rules or injunctions that must be obeyed ME. 4. Often defined according to the matter with which it is concerned, as *commercial, ecclesiastical*, etc. *l.*, *the l. of evidence*, etc.; or according to the source from which it is derived, as *statute l., customary l., case-l.* (see CASE *sb.*[1]), etc. (*The*) *Canon l.* : see CANON. Also CIVIL LAW, COMMON LAW, *Martial l.* (see MARTIAL). b. *Both laws* [after med.L. (*doctor*, etc.) *utriusque iuris*]: in mediæval use, the Civil and Canon Law; in modern Scotland, the Roman Civil Law and the municipal law of the country 1577. c. *International law, the l. of nations*, under which nations, as individual members of a common polity, are bound by a common rule of agreement or custom; opp. to *municipal l.*, the rules binding in local jurisdictions (see MUNICIPAL) 1548. 5. In English technical use, the Statute and Common Law, in contradistinction to EQUITY 1591. 6. Applied predicatively to legal decisions or opinions to denote that they are correct. Also *good* or *bad l.* 1593. 7. (Usu. *the law.*) The legal profession. Orig. in *man of l.* (now somewhat *arch.*), a lawyer. ME. b. Legal knowledge 1630. 8. The action of the courts of law, as a means of procuring redress of grievances, etc.; judicial remedy. *Occas.* = recourse to the courts, litigation. 1450.

1. The Venetian Law Cannot impugne you as you do proceed SHAKS. b. 'If the law supposes that,' said Mr. Bumble,..'the law is a ass—a idiot' DICKENS. Phr. *The l. of the Medes and Persians* (see Dan. vi. 12): often used as a type of something unalterable. *Wager of L.*: see WAGER *sb.* 2. A L. is the Command of him, or them that have the Soveraign Power HOBBES. 3. a. Phr. *L. and order. Necessity knows* (or *has*) *no law.* b. Phr. *Court of l.* = COURT *sb.*[1] IV. 2. He consults men learned in the l. J. H. NEWMAN. c. Phr. *To give* (*the*) *l.* (*to*): to exercise undisputed sway; to impose one's will †*upon* (another). His father's wishes were l. 1853. 4. c. The L. or Custom of Nations HOBBES. 7. Three of his brothers are in the l. (*mod.*). 8. Phr. *To go to* (†*the*) *l.*, *to have* or *take the l. of* or *on* (a person). *To take the l. into one's own hands* (transf.): to redress one's own grievance, or punish an offender, without judicial aid. *Halifax l., Lidford l.*: the summary procedure of certain local tribunals which acted on the maxim 'hang first, try afterwards'.

***Divine law.* 9. The body of commandments which express the will of God with regard to the conduct of His intelligent creatures. Also (with *a, the*, and *pl.*) a particular commandment. a. *gen.* OE. b. as revealed, esp. in the Bible. Hence *occas.* the Scriptures themselves. OE. c. as implanted in the mind by nature, or as demonstrable by reason ME. 10. The precepts contained in the Pentateuch; esp. the ceremonial precepts considered separately OE. b. The Mosaic dispensation (as opp. to *the Gospel*); also, the system of Divine commands and of penalties contained in the Scriptures, considered apart from the offer of salvation by faith in Christ ME. c. The Pentateuch by itself ME. †11. A dispensation –1542. †12. A religious system; the Christian, Jewish, Mohammedan, or Pagan religion –1685.

9. a. Phr. *God's* (*Christ's*) *l.*, *the l. of God.* b. His delight is in the L. of the Lord *Ps.* i. 2. c. Phr. †*L. of kind, natural l.* (now rarely *the l. of nature*), *l of reason*, etc. 10. Phr. *The l. of Moses, the Mosaic* or *Jewish l.*, etc. The Gentiles which haue not the L., doe by nature the things contained in the L. *Rom.* ii. 14. b. Vain were all the deeds of the L. J. H. NEWMAN. 11. *The old l.* the Mosaic dispensation, the 'Old Covenant'; also, the books of the O.T. *The new l.* the Gospel dispensation. 12. Phr. *By my l.*: by my faith; By my lawe sire sayd Mopsius I see no way CAXTON.

****Combined applications.* 13. Often used as the subject of propositions equally applying to human and divine law 1594.

My designe being not to shew what is L. here, and there, but what is L. HOBBES.

II. Without reference to an external commanding authority. †1. Custom, customary rule or usage; habit, practice, ways –15.. †b. *Old Cant.* A (specified) branch of the art of thieving –1591. †2. What is or is considered right or proper –ME. 3. A rule of action or procedure, e.g. in an art or department of action, a game, etc. †Also, manner of life. ME. b. The code or body of rules recognized in a specified department of action ME.

1. *L. of* (*the*) *land*: custom of the country. 3. These [the Gentiles] hauing not the L., are a L. vnto themselues *Rom.* ii. 14. Self-protection is the first l. of life FROUDE. b. Phr. *L. of arms*: the settled custom of professional soldiers. *L. of honour* (see HONOUR *sb.*).

III. Scientific and philosophical uses. 1. In the sciences of observation, a theoretical principle deduced from particular facts, expressible by the statement that a particular phenomenon always occurs if certain conditions be present. In the physical sciences, etc., called more explicitly *l. of nature* or *natural l.*, and in early use viewed as a command imposed by the Deity upon matter. 1665. 2. Laws (of Nature) in general; the order and regularity in Nature expressed by laws 1853.

1. The conformity of individual cases to the general rule is that which constitutes a L. of Nature WHATELY. *Laws of motion*: chiefly used *spec.* for Newton's three propositions concerning motion and force. In certain sciences, particular laws are known by the names of their discoverers, as *Bode's law* concerning the distances of the planets, and *Kepler's laws* of planetary motions; *Avogadro's law* concerning the number of molecules in equal volumes of different gases, *Boyle's law* concerning the volume and pressure of a gas, *Charles's law* concerning the volume and temperature of a gas, and *Dulong and Petit's law* of atomic heats; *Grimm's, Verner's, and Grassmann's laws* relating to certain sound changes in the Indo-European languages. 2. In the argument against miracles the first objection is that they are against l. MOZLEY.

IV. *Sport.* An allowance in time or distance made to an animal that is to be hunted, or to a competitor in a race; a start 1600. b. Hence, Indulgence, mercy 1649.

So Huntsmen fair unto the Hares give L. DENHAM. b. The 'on dit' is that he has ten days more l. 1849.

attrib. and *Comb.* 1. General: as in *l. dictionary, -faculty, -library, -system*, etc.; *l.-list*; *l.-charges, -costs, -reports*, etc.; *l.-binding, -calf, -sheep*, etc.

2. Special: **l.-bible,** Irish R.C. name for the Authorized Version; **-French,** the corrupt Norman French used in English law-books; **-Latin,** the barbarous Latin of early English statutes; **-lord,** one of the members of the House of Lords qualified to take part in its judicial business; **-neck-cloth,** joc. for a pillory; **-office** (*U.S.*) a lawyer's office; **-officer,** a public functionary employed in the administration of the l., or to advise the government in legal matters; *spec.* (in England) *law-officer* (*of the Crown*), either the Attorney or Solicitor General; †**-prudent** *a.* [after *iuris prudentia*], marked by legal learning; **-term,** (*a*) a word or expression used in l.; (*b*) one of the periods appointed for the sitting of the law-courts; **-writer,** †(*a*) a legislator; (*b*) one who writes books on l.; (*c*) one who copies or engrosses legal documents.

Law (lǭ), *sb.*[2] *Sc.* and *north.* ME. [Northern repr. OE. *hlāw* LOW *sb.*[1]] 1. A (more or less conical) hill, as *North Berwick L.*, etc. †2. A monumental tumulus of stones. CAMDEN.

Law (lǭ), *v.* [OE. *lagian*, f. *lagu* LAW *sb.*[1]] †1. *trans.* To ordain (laws); to render lawful –1651. b. *Sc.* To give the law to. BURNS. 2. *intr.* To go to law, litigate. Also *to l. it.* Also quasi-*trans.* 1485. b. *trans.* To go to law with 1647. 3. To mutilate (an animal) so as to make it incapable of doing mischief; usu. *spec.* to EXPEDITATE (a dog). *Obs.* exc. *Hist.* 1534.

Law (lǭ), *int.* Now *vulgar.* 1588. [Cf. LA, LO; in later use coalescing with *lor'* = LORD as an exclam.] An exclam. of astonishment; in early use chiefly asseverative.

Law·-abi·ding, *a.* 1867. [f. LAW *sb.*[1] + pr. pple. of ABIDE *v.*] Abiding by, i.e. maintaining or submitting to the law.

Law·-book. ME. [f. LAW *sb.*[1] + BOOK.] 1. A book containing a code of laws. 2. Chiefly *pl.* A book treating of law 1555.

Law·-breaker. ME. [Cf. OE. *lahbreca.*] One who violates the law.

Law·-day. *Obs.* exc. *Hist.* ME. [f. LAW *sb.*[1]] The day for the meeting of a court of law, esp. of a sheriff's court, or of the court leet; hence, the session of such a court, or the court itself.

Laweour, -er(e, -eyer(e, obs. ff. LAWYER.

Lawful (lǭ·fŭl), *a.* ME. [f. LAW *sb.*[1] + -FUL.] 1. According or not contrary to law; permitted by law. †b. Permissible; justifiable –1717. 2. Appointed, sanctioned, or recognized by law; legally qualified or entitled ME. b. Of offspring: Legitimate 1513. †3. Law-abiding, loyal –1642.

1. It is lawfull for all men, to saue themselues from violence 1560. 2. Phr. *L. heir, king money, succession, title*, etc.; also *l. captive, prey, prize*, (*to be*) *l. game.* Truly she must be giuen or the marriage is not lawfull SHAKS. Phr. *L. age, years*: the age at which a person attains his legal majority. *L. day*, one on which it is lawful to transact business, or some particular kind of business. *L. money*, in certain American colonies, the local currency at the coin value upon which that which circulated in the colony was based before Queen Anne's proclamation of 1704. Hence **Law·ful-ly** *adv.*, **-ness.**

Lawgiver (lǭ·givəɹ). ME. [f. LAW *sb.*[1] + GIVER.] One who gives, i.e. makes or promulgates, a law or code of laws; a legislator. So **Law·-giving** *ppl. a.* that gives or makes laws; also *occas.* that gives the law to.

Law·-hand. 1731. The style of handwriting used for legal documents. Also *occas.* matter written in this hand.

An immense desert of law-hand and parchment DICKENS.

Lawk, lawks (lǭk(s), *int.* 1768. [Vulgar f. LACK *sb.*[2] or perversion of LORD.] = Lord! Also *Lawk-a-mussy* = Lord have mercy! *Lawk-a-daisy* (*me*) = LACKADAISY.

Lawless (lǭ·lės), *a.* ME. [f. LAW *sb.*[1] + -LESS.] 1. Without law; ignorant of, or not regulated by law. Of a law: Not based on right. Now *rare.* b. Exempt from law, above or beyond the reach of law ME. 2. Regardless of, or disobedient to law. Of passions, etc.: Unbridled. ME.

1. A barbarous..people whose law is lawlesse HAKLUYT. 2. Lawlesse desires are seas scorning all bounds DEKKER. L. violence 1855. Hence **Law·less-ly** *adv.*, **-ness.**

Law·-ma·ker. ME. [f. LAW *sb.*[1] + MAKER.] One who makes laws; a legislator.

Law·-me·rchant. 1622. [f. LAW *sb.*[1] + MERCHANT *a.*, after med.L. *lex mercatoria.*] A special system of rules for the regulation of trade and commerce, differing in some respects from the Common Law.

Lawn (lǭn), *sb.*[1] ME. [f. *Laon* in France (Skeat).] 1. A kind of fine linen, resembling cambric; *pl.* pieces or sorts of this. Also *transf.* and *fig.* 2. *spec.* This fabric used for the sleeves of a bishop. Hence, the dignity or office of a bishop. 1732. †3. An article of dress, etc., made of lawn –1812.

2. A Saint in Crape is twice a Saint in L. POPE.

Comb. **l.-sieve**, a fine sieve, made of l. (or silk), used in cookery, porcelain-manufacture, etc.

Lawn (lǭn), *sb.*[2] 1548. [Later form of LAUND.] **1.** = LAUND. Now *arch.* and *dial.* **b.** A stretch of untilled or grass-covered ground 1674. **2.** A portion of a garden, etc., covered with grass, which is kept closely mown 1733. Also *attrib.*

1. The thistly l., the thick-entangled broom THOMSON. 2. This L., a carpet all alive With shadows flung from leaves WORDSW.

Comb.: **l.-meet**, the meeting of a hunt in front of a gentleman's house; **-mower**, a machine provided with revolving spiral knives for cutting the grass on a l.; **-sprinkler**, a machine with revolving tubular arms from which water is sprinkled like rain. Hence **Lawn** *v. trans.* to turn into l. or grass-land; to make lawn-like.

Lawn sleeves, lawn-sleeves. 1640. Sleeves of lawn, as part of the episcopal dress. Hence, the dignity or office of a bishop; also, a bishop or bishops. **Lawn-sleeved** *a.*

Law·n-te·nnis. 1874. [LAWN *sb.*[2]] A modification of the game of tennis, played in the open air on a lawn or other prepared ground.

Lawny (lǭ·ni), *a.*[1] 1598. [f. LAWN *sb.*[1] + -Y [1].] **1.** Made of lawn. **b.** Dressed in lawn; also, pertaining to a wearer of lawn, i. e. a bishop 1647. **2.** Lawn-like 1615.

Lawny (lǭ·ni), *a.*[2] 1613. [f. LAWN *sb.*[2] + -Y [1].] †**a.** Containing lawns or glades. **b.** Resembling a lawn; covered with smooth grass.

b. There was a little l. islet SHELLEY.

Law·-sta:tioner. 1836. [f. LAW *sb.*[1] + STATIONER.] A tradesman who keeps in stock stationery and other things required by lawyers, and takes in manuscripts, etc. to be engrossed.

Lawsuit (lǭ·siūt). 1624. [f. LAW *sb.*[1] + SUIT *sb.*] A suit in law; a prosecution of a claim in a court of law.

Law·-wo:rthy, *a.* ? *Hist.* [f. LAW *sb.*[1] + WORTHY; a mod. rendering of OE. *þæra laga weorðe* (*þe*, etc.), 'worthy of (i. e. entitled to) the laws (which, etc.)'.] **a.** Of persons: Having a standing in the law-courts. **b.** Of things: Within the purview of the law; able to be dealt with by a court of law.

Lawyer (lǭ·yəɪ). ME. [f. LAW *sb.*[1] + -YER; see also -IER.] **1.** One versed in the law; a member of the legal profession, one whose business it is to advise clients, or to conduct suits in the courts. Colloquially often limited to attorneys and solicitors. †**2.** A lawgiver. MORE. **3.** *dial.* A long bramble 1857. **4.** *Penang lawyer* (see below). **5.** *Zool.* Local name in U.S. for: **a.** the Black-necked Stilt (*Himantopus nigricollis*); **b.** the Burbot (*Lota maculosa*), and the Bowfin or Mudfish (*Amia calva*). 1850.

1. A l. thus educated to the bar BLACKSTONE. 4. *Penang l.*: a kind of walking-stick, made from the stem of a dwarf palm having prickly stalks, and much used in settling disputes at Penang.

Comb. **Lawyer-like** *a.* and *adv.* Hence **Law·yerly** *a.*

Lax (læks), *sb.*[1] *Obs.* (revived as an alien wd. from the Continent.) [OE. *leax* = OHG. *lahs* (G. *lachs*), ON. (Sw., Da. *lax*).] A salmon; in later use, some particular kind of salmon.

Lax, *sb.*[2] 1526. [?f. LAX *v.*] †**1.** A laxative medicine –1544. **2.** = LASK *sb.* **1.** *Obs.* exc. *dial.* 1540.

Lax (læks), *a.* ME. [ad. L. *laxus*; cogn. w. *languere* to languish.] **1.** Of the bowels: Acting easily, loose. **2.** Slack; not tense, rigid, or tight. Hence of body or mind: Wanting in tone or tension. Now somewhat *rare.* 1660. **b.** Loose, relaxed 1782. **3. a.** Of organic tissue, stone, soils, etc.: Loose in texture; porous 1615. **b.** *Bot.* and *Zool.* Loosely or openly arranged, as an inflorescence, etc. 1796. **4.** Of clothes: Loose-fitting, worn loosely. Of persons: Negligent in attire and deportment. 1621. **5.** Loose, slack; vague, not precise 1450. **6.** quasi-*adv.* So as to have ample room. [A Latinism.] MILT. *P. L.* VII. 162.

1. The bowels l. ABERNETHY. 2. Persons of weak l. fibre 1789. 4. L. in their gaiters, laxer in their gait H. & J. SMITH. 5. In a l. way of speaking Jos. BUTLER. L. metre 1847. L. in conduct 1874, in attendance 1884. Hence **La·x-ly** *adv.*, **-ness.**

†**Lax,** *v.* ME. [ad. L. *laxare*, f. *laxus* LAX *a.*] *trans.* To make lax; to loosen, relax; to purge. Also *absol.* –1685.

†**La·xate,** *v.* 1623. [f. L. *laxatus*, *laxare*.] *trans.* To loosen, relax. Also *absol.* –1661.

Laxation (læksē·ʃən). ME. [ad. L. *laxationem*; see LAX *v.* and -ATION.] The action of loosening or relaxing; loosened or relaxed state; *occas.* an instance or means of relaxing.

Laxative (læ·ksătiv). ME. [a. F. *laxatif, -ive*, ad. L. *laxativus*; see LAX *v.* and -ATIVE.]

A. *adj.* **1.** Having the property of relaxing. **2.** Of the bowels, or bodily constitution: Loose, subject to flux or free discharge of the fæces. Of a disease: Characterized by such discharge. Now *rare.* 1546. **b.** *transf.* Unable to contain one's speech or emotions. ? *Obs.* 1601.

2. b. Fellowes of practis'd and most laxatiue tongues B. JONS. Hence **La·xativeness.**

B. *sb.* **1.** A laxative medicine ME. †**2.** ? Relaxed condition of the bowels, flux –1527.

†**Laxator.** 1799. [mod.L., f. L. *laxare*.] *Anat.* A (supposed) muscle of the external ear.

Laxist (læ·ksist). 1865. [f. LAX *a.* + -IST.] One who favours lax views or interpretation; *spec.* the designation given to the school of casuists in the Roman church who held that it was justifiable to follow any probability, however slight, in favour of liberty. Also *attrib.*

Laxity (læ·ksĭti). 1528. [a. F. *laxité*, ad. L. *laxitatem*; see LAX *a.*] The quality of being lax: **a.** in physical senses; **b.** in moral and intellectual senses 1623.

b. Such tales..engender l. of morals among the young JOWETT.

†**Lay,** *sb.*[1] ME. [a. OF. *lei*, mod.F. *loi* :– L. *legem*, *lex* law.] Law; *esp.* religious law; hence, a religion, a faith –1599.

Lay (lē), *sb.*[2] ME. [a. OF. *lai* = Pr. *lais*, *lays*; prob. of Teut. origin. Cf. OHG., MHG. *leich*, play, melody, song.] **1.** A short lyric or narrative poem intended to be sung. Often *poet.* for 'song'. **b.** *poet.* Applied to the song of birds ME. †**2.** Strain, tune –1581.

1. The L. of the Last Minstrel SCOTT (*title*). These brief lays, of Sorrow born TENNYSON *In Mem.* b. The thrustelcok made eek his l. CHAUCER.

†**Lay,** *sb.*[3] ME. [? aphet. f. ALLAY *sb.*[1]] Alloy. Chiefly *attrib.* in *l. metal*, name of a kind of pewter. –1794.

Lay, *sb.*[4] 1558. [f. LAY *v.*] †**1.** A wager, stake –1769. **2.** A place of lying or lodging; lair, couch (of animals); an oyster-or mussel-bed 1590. †**3.** A layer; a course (of masonry) –1769. **4.** The act of imposing a tax; an impost, assessment, rate. Now *dial.* 1558. **5.** *slang.* A line or plan of business, occupation, adventure, etc.; a (particular) job, line, or tack 1707. **6.** The way, position, or direction in which anything is laid or lies (*esp.* said of country) 1819. **b.** *Naut.* Of a rope: The direction or amount of twist given to the strands. Also in *Spinning.* 1800. **c.** *Printing.* The relative position of the sheet of paper and the type or plate on the press 1871. **7.** A share in a venture; *esp.* in *Whaling*, the proportion of the proceeds of a voyage which is allotted to a man 1825. **8.** *In* (*full, good*) *l.*: laying eggs 1885.

1. It is an even laie, that an idiot shall conjecture right R. SCOT. 3. First they layed a l. of Brickes, then a Mat made of Canes, square as the Brickes HAKLUYT. 5. He 's not to be found on his old l. DICKENS. 6. I..steered by the l. of the land THOREAU.

Lay (lē), *sb.*[5] *dial.* 1789. [var. of LATHE [3] and [4].] **1.** *Weaving.* = LATHE [4]. **2.** Used for LATHE [3] 2. 1797.

Lay (lē), *a.* (and *sb.*) ME. [a. F. *lai* (now repl. by *laïque*) :—eccl. L. *laicus*, a. Gr. λαϊκός (cf. LAIC).] **1.** Of persons: Belonging to the 'people' as dist. from the clergy; non-clerical. (Often hyphened with official titles.) **2.** Characteristic of, connected with, occupied or performed by, laymen or the laity 1609. **3.** *transf.* †**a.** Unlearned (*rare*) –1535. **b.** Non-professional, *esp.* with reference to law and medicine 1810. †**c.** Unsanctified; secular, worldly, *esp.* in phr. *l. part.* –1668.

1. He expressed the most rooted prejudice against Lay-Preachers WESLEY. 2. The bishop strove to get up a little l. conversation TROLLOPE. 3. b. The prevention of disease..is too technical for l. interference 1897.

Special collocations. **L. abbot,** a layman in possession of abbey property. **L. baptism,** baptism administered by a layman. **L. brother,** a man who has taken the habit and vows of a religious order, but is employed mostly in manual labour. **L. clerk,** (*a*) a 'singing man' in a cathedral or collegiate church; (*b*) a parish clerk. **L. communion,** (*a*) the condition of being in communion with the Church as a layman; (*b*) the communicating of the laity in the Eucharist. **L. deacon,** a man in deacon's orders who follows a secular employment. **Lay-elder** (see ELDER *sb.*[2] 4). **L. lord,** a peer who is not a lawyer; opp. to *law lord.* †**L. presbyter,** ? = 'lay elder'. **L. reader,** a layman licensed to conduct religious services. **L. rector** (see RECTOR). **L. sister,** the analogue of 'lay brother'. **L. vicar** (see VICAR).

†**B.** *absol.* and *sb.* The lay people, laity; also, a layman –1680.

Lay (lēi), *v.* Pa. t. and pple. **laid** (lēid). [OE. *lęcgan*, f. **lag-* ablaut-var. of OTeut. **leg-*; see LIE *v.*[1]] General sense: To cause to lie.

I. To prostrate. **1.** *trans.* To bring or cast down from an erect position; †*fig.* to cast down, abase. Now only with compl. **b.** Of wind or rain: To beat down (crops). Chiefly in *pass.* (In 16–17th c. spelt *ledge.*) 1590. **2.** To 'bring to bed' *of* a child; to deliver (a mother). *Obs.* exc. *dial.* 1460. **3.** To cause to subside (the sea, wind, dust, anxiety, anger, appetite, etc.). Now *arch.* or *dial.* exc. in *to l. the dust.* ME. **b.** To prevent (a spirit) from walking 1592. **4.** †To reduce (a swelling); to make to lie evenly 1579. **5.** *Naut.* To sail out so far as to bring (an object) to or below the horizon. (Opp. to *raise.*) 1574. **6.** *Gardening.* = LAYER *v.* 1 b. ? *Obs.* 1565.

1. One third of the town was laid in ashes 1890. *To l. low*: see the adj. b. Like flaws in summer laying lusty corn TENNYSON. 2. The midwife that laid my mother of me BUNYAN. 3. See how I l. the dust with my teares SHAKS. b. He faced the spectres of the mind And laid them TENNYSON.

II. To deposit. **1.** To place in a position of rest *on* the ground or other surface; to deposit OE. **2. a.** To place in a recumbent posture in a specified place ME. **b.** To deposit *in* the grave; to bury. Only with adv. or phr. indicating the place. OE. **3.** To produce and deposit (an egg). Also *absol.* OE. †**4.** With advb. phr. as compl., e.g. *to wed, in pawn*: To deposit as a pledge or in pawn; hence, to mortgage (lands) –1698. **5.** To deposit as a wager; to stake. Also *to l. a wager.* ME. **b.** *absol.* or *intr.* ME.

1. b. = *To lay on* or *upon the table* (see TABLE *sb.* II. 1. Phr.). 2. a. The bent grass where I am laid M. ARNOLD. b. Part, in the Places where they fell, are laid DRYDEN. Phr. *To l. to sleep, asleep*: to put to rest; to bury; also *fig.* Also *to l. to rest.* 3. There shall the great owle make her nest, and l. and hatch *Isa.* xxxiv. 15. 5. Hee would l. ten to one, the king was dead 1632.

III. To place, set, apply. **1.** To place close *to*; to apply; sometimes const. *on, upon* OE. Also, †*To l. from, off* –1611. †**b.** To put *in* or commit *to* (prison) –1560. **c.** To put (dogs) *on* a scent. Also *to l. a trail on* (a quarry). 1781. **2.** To place (affection, hope, etc.) *on* or *in* a person or thing ME. **b.** *To l.. before*: to bring to the sight of; hence, to submit to the consideration of OE. **3.** To set (a snare, a trap, an ambush); †to set (watch) ME. **b.** intr. *To l. for*: to set an ambush or a trap for; to waylay 1494. †**c.** *trans.* To set watch or guard in (a place); to beset; to search (a place) *for* –1645. †**4.** To post or station (soldiers, etc.); to station (post-horses) along a route. Also, to beset (a place) with soldiers. –1862. **b.** To place or locate (a scene) 1570. **5.** With object denoting a member of the body (see quots.) OE. **6.** *To l. hold* (*up*)*on, of*: to grasp, seize on; to avail oneself of (a pretext) 1535. **7.** *refl.* and *intr.* To apply oneself *to* 1535. **8.** *Mil.* To set (a gun, etc.) in the correct position for hitting a mark. Also *absol.* 1480. **9.** To put into a condition (usually one of subjection, passivity, or exposure), which is expressed by a complementary phrase ME.

1. Phr. *To l. to heart*: see HEART *sb.* And now also the axe is laid vnto the root of the trees *Luke* iii. 9. He laid his robe from him *Jonah* iii. 6. 2. Phr. *To l. store upon*: to value (*arch.*). b. I shall this Day l. before my Reader a Letter ADDISON. 3.

Thou layd'st a Trap to take my Life SHAKS. b. Men in debt..layd for by their creditors MASSINGER. c. I ..durst not peepe out, for all the Country is laid for me SHAKS. Phr. *To l. siege to*: to besiege; also *fig.* to attack. 4. b. In faire Verona, where we l. our Scene SHAKS. 5. Her arms across her breast she laid TENNYSON. Phr. †*To l. eyes on*: to look at. *To l. hands on* or *upon* a person or thing: (*a*) to place one's hands on or apply them to, esp. for purposes of appropriation or violence; hence (*b*) to seize, get hold of, appropriate; (*c*) to do violence to; now *to l. violent hands on* (with *oneself* = to commit suicide); (*d*) to perform the rite of imposition of hands in confirmation or ordination. *To l. a finger* or *one's finger*(*s*) *upon*: see FINGER *sb.* 2. 6. I laid hold of all Opportunities to exert it ADDISON. 9. Phr. *To l. fallow, idle*; *to l.* (land) *dry, under water*; *l. under necessity, obligation, difficulty, a command*, etc. *To l. bare*: (*a*) to denude, remove the covering from; (*b*) to expose to view, reveal. *To l. under contribution*: see CONTRIBUTION 1. *To l. open, waste*: see the adjs. *To l. by the heels*: see HEEL *sb.*[1] *To l. alongside, by the lee*, etc. (*Naut.*). *To l. aback* (Naut.): to brace (a yard) in such a way that the wind will blow against the forward side of the sail. *To l...aboard* (Naut.): to run into or alongside (a ship), usually in order to board her. So *to l. close, to l. athwart the hawse.*

IV. To present, put forward. 1. To put forward, allege (a claim, etc.) ME. b. To present (an information, indictment) in legal form 1798. c. *Law.* To state or describe *as*; to fix (damages) *at* a certain amount 1770. 2. To bring forward as a charge, accusation, or imputation; to impute, attribute, ascribe. Const. *to, on.* ? *arch.* ME.

1. We muste not l. excuses LD. BERNERS. c. He laid his damages at 20,000*l.* 1891. 2. There was leyde to him hye tresone 1473. E. G. with child, layd on the tapster WOOD. Phr. *To l. to* (a person's) *charge, at* or *to* (his) *door*: to charge upon. Also *to l. to one's credit*, etc.

V. To impose as a burden. 1. To impose (a penalty, command, obligation, burden, tax, etc.). Const. *on, upon.* OE. 2. To cast (blame, etc.) *on* or *upon* ME. 3. *To l. stress, weight, emphasis on* or *upon*: to emphasize, attach importance to 1666. 4. To bring (a stick, etc.) down *upon*; to inflict (blows). Also *to l. it on* (lit. and fig.) ME. 5. *absol.* and *intr.* To deal blows; to make an attack. Chiefly in phrases with preps.; e.g. *to lay on* or *upon*; *to l. at* (now chiefly *dial.*); *to l. into* (slang or colloq.); *to l. about one*; occas. (trans.) *to l.* (a weapon) *about one*; whence *fig.* to act vigorously. †6. To strike, beat (a person) *on* the face, *over* the head, etc. (The personal obj. is prob. a dative.) –1712.

1. An additional duty..was laid on windows 1845. The burden of proof being laid on the accused person ROGERS. 3. The great teachers laid all the stress on dogma 1890. 4. I have laid it on Walpole..unsparingly MACAULAY. 5. The sword of him that layeth at him cannot hold *Job* xli. 26. They laid about them with their staves DISRAELI. 6. Phr. †*To l. on the lips*: to kiss.

VI. To dispose or arrange properly over a surface. 1. *trans.* To place in the proper horizontal position (a foundation (often *fig.*), a floor, stones or bricks) OE. b. To set out (a table), to spread (the cloth), place in order (plates, dishes, etc.); hence, in later use, to set out the table for (a meal). Also *absol.* †Also, to prepare (a bed). ME. c. To trace (a ground-plan) 1594. d. *To l. a fire*: to place the fuel ready for lighting 1876. e. *Printing.* (*a*) To place and arrange (pages) for a forme upon the imposing stone; (*b*) to put (new type) in the cases. Also *to lay the case.* 1683. 2. *Rope-making.* To twist yarn to form (a strand), or strands to form (a rope) 1486. 3. *trans.* To fix the outlines of, arrange (a plan, plot, scheme); †to establish (a law), settle (a principle) OE. †b. *gen.* To contrive, arrange –1712. c. *intr.* †To make plans *for*; to plan, contrive, or intend *to do* something (now *dial.* and *U.S.*) 1450. 4. *Naut. To l. one's* (or *a*) *course*: to be able to sail in the direction wished for, however barely the wind permits it (Smyth) 1669. †5. To set down *in* writing; to put into, express *in* (certain terms, or language) –1775. 6. *Art.* a. To put upon a surface in layers; to put or arrange (colours, †a picture) on canvas 1570. b. *To l. a ground*: to spread a coating over a surface, as a basis for colours. So in Photogr., *to l. the grain.* 1762. 7. To cover, spread, or coat (*with* something), esp. by way of ornament ME.

1. Thou Lord in the beginning hast layed the foundation of the earth *Heb.* i. 10. The first submarine cable was laid 1890. b. I found that the table was laid for three MARRYAT. 2. The manner of laying the yarns into ropes 1853. 3. His Design had been long laid W. WOTTON. 4. The steamer's course was laid for Michipicoten 1890. 6. Epithetes thick laid As varnish on a Harlot's cheek MILT. 7. Black steel, Laid with gold tendrils 1879.

VII. In intr. uses, coinciding with or resembling those of LIE *v.*[1] (Now only an illiterate substitute for *lie.*) ME. b. *Naut.* To put oneself in a position indicated by the accompanying phr. or adv., e.g. *to l. at anchor, to l. by the wind*, etc. *To l. on the oars*, to cease rowing.

Thou..dashest him again to earth:—there let him l. BYRON. Phr. *To l. in wait*: see WAIT *sb.*

Comb. (with advs.) **Lay about.** †a. *trans.* To surround, beset. †b. *intr.* To contrive (*to do* something); to look out *for*. †c. To strike out with vigour. **L. abroad.** *trans.* To spread out (*arch.*). **L. aside.** *trans.* a. To put away from one's person; to put on one side. b. To dismiss from one's consideration or action; to abandon or postpone, to discontinue. †c. To get rid of. d. *pass.* To be incapacitated by illness. **L. away.** *trans.* = *lay aside*, a, b. **L. by.** a. *trans.* = *lay aside* a, b. b. To store up; to save (money). Also *absol.* c. To put away for future disposal or for safety. d. *pass.* To be 'laid aside' by illness. e. *intr.* (*Naut.*) = *lay to.* **L. down.** *trans.* a. To put down upon the ground, etc. *To l. down* (*one's*) *arms*: to surrender. b. To relinquish (office, hopes, etc.). c. To place in a recumbent or prostrate position. Often *refl.* d. To put down (money) as a wager or payment. e. To sacrifice (one's life). f. To construct (roads, railways, ships). Also *to l. down a keel.* g. To formulate definitely (a principle, rule, course of action, etc.). *To l. down the law*: to declare what the law is; hence *colloq.* to dogmatize. h. To set down on paper. i. *Agric.* To plant or sow (a field) with a certain crop, e.g. grass, etc. j. To store (wine) in cellars. k. *Sporting slang. To l. himself* (or simply *lay*) *down to his work*: of a horse, etc. to put all his strength into a race. **L. in.** a. *trans. To l. in the oars*: to unship them. b. To provide oneself with a stock of. Also said of 'taking in' food; hence *absol.* to feed vigorously (now *vulgar*). †c. To put in (a claim). Also *absol.* d. *Gardening.* To place in position (the new wood of a trained tree). e. To paint (a picture, etc.) in its first unfinished stage. f. To deliver (a blow). g. To discontinue working (a colliery). **L. off.** a. *trans.* To take off (now *U.S.*). †b. *Naut.* To steer (a ship) away from the shore. c. To mark off (plots of ground, etc.); to plot out land. d. To set off (distances) upon a surface. e. *Shipbuilding.* To transfer (plans) from the paper in the full size on the floor of the mould-loft. f. *dial.* and *U.S.* To discontinue; to discontinue the working of; to dismiss (a workman), usu. temporarily. Also *intr.*, to take a rest. **L. on.** a. *trans.* To impose (an injunction, penalty, tax). b. *intr.* To deal blows with vigour; to assail. c. *trans.* To inflict (blows); to ply (the lash). Also *to l. it on.* d. *To l.* (*it*) *on*: †(*a*) to be lavish in expense; (*b*) to pile on the charge for goods, etc. e. To apply a coat of (paint, etc.) to a surface. f. *Agric.* Of cattle: To put on (flesh); also *absol.* g. To put (dogs) on the scent. Also *transf.* in joc. use. h. To provide for the supply of (water, gas, etc.) through pipes from a reservoir. **L. out.** a. *trans.* To extend at length; to take out and expose to view, to the air, etc.; to spread out in order; to lay so as to project outwards. b. To stretch out and prepare (a body) for burial; hence (*slang*) to lay low, to 'do for'; (*fig.*) to put 'hors de combat'. c. To spend, expend (money). Also *absol.* †d. To exercise (powers, effort). e. *refl.* †To exert oneself *in, upon*; to take measures with a view to something. Const. *for*, to with *inf.* f. *intr.* With *for*: †To look out for; to take measures to win or get. Also, to scheme, plan *to* effect something. g. To display; to set forth, expound, demonstrate. ? Now *rare.* h. To apportion (land) for a purpose; to plot or plan out (grounds, streets, etc.). i. To map out; to set as a task or duty. j. *intr.* (*Naut.*). To go out towards the yard arms for the purpose of manipulating the sails. (Cf. *lie out.*) **L. over.** a. *trans.* To overlay. b. *U.S. colloq.* To allow to pass by; to postpone. c. ? *U.S. colloq.* To excel, put in the shade. **L. to.** *intr.* (*Naut.*) = *lie to* (see LIE *v.*[1]). **L. together.** a. *trans.* To place in juxtaposition; to add together. b. *To l...heads together*: to confer. **L. up.** a. *trans.* To put up and extend (one's limbs) on a couch. b. *Agric.* (*a*) To throw up (land) in ridges for sowing; often with *dry, rough, in ridges.* (*b*) To reserve for hay. c. To deposit in a place for safety; to store up; to put by. Often *absol.* to save money. Also *To l. up in lavender*: see LAVENDER *sb.*[2] 2. d. To cause to keep indoors or in bed through illness; often in *pass.* to be (taken) ill, to keep one's bed. e. To put away (a ship) in dock, etc. Also *intr.* for *pass.* or *refl.* f. *Rope-making* = sense VI. 2.

Lay, pa. t. of LIE *v.*[1]; dial. var. LEA *sb.*[2], *a.*

Lay-by (lēⁱ·bəi). 1879. [f. LAY *v.* + BY *adv.*] 1. A slack part of a river in which barges are laid by out of use. b. A railway siding 1906. 2. Something laid by; savings 1894.

Lay-day (lēⁱ·dēⁱ). 1845. [app. f. LAY *v.*] *Comm.* One of a certain number of days allowed according to a charter-party for the loading and unloading of cargo.

Layer (lēⁱ·əɹ), *sb.* ME. [f. LAY *v.* + -ER [1].] 1. One who or that which lays (see LAY *v.*). 2. Something laid; a thickness of matter spread over a surface; *esp.* one of a series; a stratum, course, or bed ME. Also *fig.* 3. *Gardening* and *Agric.* a. A shoot or twig of a plant fastened down and partly covered with earth, so that it may strike root while still attached to the parent stock 1664. b. *pl.* Patches of laid corn 1634. c. A field of grass or clover 1793.

Layer (lēⁱ·əɹ), *v.* 1796. [f. LAYER *sb.* 3.] 1. *Gardening.* a. *intr.* To bend down layers to the ground and cover them partly with earth so that they may strike root and propagate the plant. b. *trans.* To propagate by layers. c. To make a layer of. 2. Of crops: To be laid flat through weakness of growth 1882.

‖**Layette** (leye·t). 1874. [Fr.] Outfit of garments, toilet articles, and bedding for a new-born child.

Lay-fee. *Obs.* exc. *Hist.* ME. [a. AF. *lai fe.*] 1. A fee or estate in land held by secular services, as dist. from an eccl. fee. †2. The laity. Orig. in phr. *of the lay fee.* –1641.

Lay figure (lēⁱ· fi·gəɹ). 1795. [f. **lay* (in LAY-MAN [2]) + FIGURE *sb.*] A jointed wooden figure of the human body, used by artists for the arrangement of draperies, posing, etc. b. *fig.* A person of no consequence, a nonentity; an unreal character in a novel 1835.

Laying (lēⁱ·iŋ), *vbl. sb.* ME. [f. LAY *v.* + -ING [1].] 1. The action of LAY *v. Laying-on* = IMPOSITION (of hands). 2. *concr.* a. What is laid. b. A layer, bed, stratum 1683. c. An oyster-bed 1846. d. *Building.* 'The first coat on lath of two-coat plaster, or set-work' 1823.

Lay-land: see LEA-LAND.

Layloc(k, obs. and dial. f. LILAC.

Layman [1] (lēⁱ·mæ̆n). ME. [Orig. two wds.; see LAY *a.*] 1. One of the laity. 2. *transf.* An 'outsider' or non-expert (esp. in relation to law or medicine) 1477.

2. To declare and expresse to the lay men that be not learned in the law *Littleton's Tenures.* So Lay·woman.

†**Lay-man** [2]. 1688. [a. Du. *leeman*, for *ledeman*, f. *led*, now *lid* limb, joint + *man* MAN *sb.*[1]] = LAY FIGURE –1796.

Layner, obs. f. LAINER.

Lay·-off. 1904. [cf. *lay off* f, LAY *v.*] A period during which a workman is temporarily discharged.

Lay·-out. 1869. Chiefly *U.S.* [See *lay out*, LAY *v.*] The act or process of laying out or planning in detail; that which is laid or spread out.

Lay-shaft. 1908. A secondary shaft of a machine, driven by gearing from the main shaft.

†**Lay·ship.** [f. LAY *a.* + -SHIP.] The condition of a layman. MILT.

Laystall (lēⁱ·stǭl). 1527. [f. LAY *v.* + STALL.] †1. A burial-place –1556. 2. A place where refuse and dung are laid 1553.

2. The common Lay-stall of a Citie DRAYTON. So †Laystow.

Lazar (lēⁱ·zăɹ), *sb.* (*a.*) *arch.* ME. [ad. med.L. *lazarus*, an application of the proper name *Lazarus*, Luke xvi. 20.] 1. A poor and diseased person, usu. one afflicted with a loathsome disease; *esp.* a leper. 2. *adj.* Leprous 1483. Hence †La·zarous *a.* leprous.

Lazaret (læzăre·t). 1611. [a. F. *lazaret*, ad. It. *lazzaretto*: see next.] = next.

Lazaretto (læzăre·to). 1549. [ad. It. *lazzareto* (Florio), now *lazzeretto*, f. †*lazzaro* LAZAR.] 1. A house for the reception of the diseased poor, esp. lepers. (Chiefly with reference to foreign countries.) 2. A building, occas. a ship, set apart for the performance of quarantine 1605. 3. *Naut.* A space between decks, in some merchant vessels, used as a storeroom 1711.

La·zar-house. 1440. = prec., 1.

Lazarist (læ·zărist). 1747. [ad. F. *lazariste*, f. *Lazare*, Lazarus.] One of the Congregation of the Priests of the Mission founded by St. Vincent of Paul in 1624, and established in the College of St. Lazare at Paris.

Lazarus (læ·zărŏs). *rare*. 1508. [Proper name used allusively.] A leper; a beggar.

Laze (lēⁱz), *sb. colloq.* 1862. [f. next.] The action of LAZE *v.*; an instance of this.

Laze (lēⁱz), *v.* 1592. [Back-formation from LAZY *a.*] **1.** *intr.* To lie, move, act, or enjoy oneself lazily. Also with advs. †Also *refl.* **2.** quasi-*trans.* To pass *away* in indolence 1627.

2. So the bloudless Tortoise..lazeth his life away FELTHAM.

La·zule. ? *Obs.* 1598. [ad. L. *lazulum* (see LAPIS LAZULI).] = LAPIS LAZULI. Chiefly attrib. *l.-stone*.

Lazuli (læ·ziŭləi). 1789. Short for LAPIS LAZULI. Also *attrib.*, as **l.-finch**, a brilliant fringilloid bird (*Passerina amœna*) of western U.S.

Lazuline (læ·ziŭləin), *a.* 1877. [f. LAZULI + -INE [1].] Of the colour of lapis lazuli. PATMORE. Also *sb.* 1850.

Lazulite (læ·ziŭləit). 1801. [f. med.L. *lazulum* (see LAPIS LAZULI) + -ITE.] *Min.* Hydrous phosphate of aluminium and magnesium, found in blue monoclinic crystals; also the colour of this. ¶Occas. used = LAPIS LAZULI.

Lazurite (læ·ziŭrəit). 1892. [f. med.L. *lazur* (see AZURE) + -ITE.] *Min.* The blue part of lapis lazuli.

Lazy (lēⁱ·zi). 1549. [Orig. *laysy*, perh. f. LAY *v.* + *-sy*, as in *tipsy, tricksy*.]

A. *adj.* **1.** Averse to labour, indolent; idle; inactive, slothful. Also *transf.* of things, places, or conditions, favourable or appropriate to laziness. **2.** Of things: Sluggish, dull, slow-moving; now only *transf.* from sense 1. †Formerly of literary style, also of heat or chemical agents: Languid, having little energy. 1568. †**3.** *dial.* Bad –1787.

1. All..combine to drive The l. Drones from the laborious Hive DRYDEN. 2. L. leaden-stepping Hours MILT.

Comb.: **l.-bed**, a bed for potato-growing, about six feet wide, with a trench on each side, from which earth is taken to cover the potatoes; also *attrib.*; **-boots, -bones** (*colloq.*), a l. person; **-pinion**, a pinion serving as a transmitter of motion between two other pinions or wheels; **scissors, -tongs**, a system of several pairs of levers crossing and pivoted at their centres in the manner of scissors, for picking up objects at a distance. Hence **La·zily** *adv.*, **La·ziness.**

†B. *sb.* A name for the SLOTH. SIR T. BROWNE.

‖**Lazzarone** (læzărōᵘ·ne, latsarō·ne). Chiefly *pl.* **lazzaroni** (-ī). 1792. [It., augm. of *lazzaro* (Florio) LAZAR.] One of the lowest class at Naples, who lounge about the streets, living by odd jobs, or by begging.

About 30,000 lazaroni, or black guards MORSE.

lb. ME. Abbrev. of L. *libra* 'pound', *pl.* lb., lbs., now only of weight, but formerly of sterling.

-le, *suffix*, pron. ('l), of various origin.

1. Mod. Eng. form of ME. *-el(e, -le*, repr. OE. *-el, -ela, -(e)le* in sbs. and *-ol, -ul, -el* in adjs. (The form -EL is retained after *ch, g* soft, *n, r, sh, th*, and *v*. After *m* the suffix becomes *-ble*.) The sbs. formed on noun-stems have occas. a dim. sense, as *bramble*, or that of 'appliance or tool', as in *thimble, handle*. In those formed on vb.-stems the suffix is agential as in *beadle*, instrumental as in *bridle, girdle*, or less definite as in *bundle*. Adjs. formed on vb.-stems have the sense 'apt or liable' (to do what the vb. expresses), as in *brittle, fickle, nimble*, etc.

2. Occas. representative of ME. *-el(l, -elle*, in sbs. adopted from Fr. This, in *castle, mantle*, is OF. *-el*:—L. *-ellum* dim. suffix (see -EL); in *cattle* it is OF. *-el*:—L. *-āle*, the neut. sing., and in *battle* it is OF. *-aille* the neut. pl., of the adjective suffix *-ālis* (see -AL); in *bottle* it is OF. *-eille*:—L. *-icula* dim. suffix.

3. A verbal formative, repr. ME. *-(e)len*, OE. *-lian* :—OTeut. type *-ilōjan*, with freq. or dim. sense, as in *crackle, dazzle, gabble, sparkle, wriggle*, etc.

Lea (lī), *sb.*[1] [OE. *lēa(h* masc., and *lēah* fem.; app. cogn. w. OHG. *lôh*, mod.Ger. dial. *loh*, Flem. *-loo* as in *Waterloo*, and with L. *lucus* grove; supposed by some to be from root **leuq-* to shine (whence L. *lucere*, Eng. LIGHT *sb.*, etc.; for the sense cf. *clearing*).] A tract of open ground, either meadow, pasture, or arable land. After OE. chiefly poet. or rhet., ordinarily applied to grass land.

The lowing herd winds slowly o'er the l. GRAY.

Lea, ley, lay (lī, lēⁱ), *sb.*[2] Now *dial.* ME. [Ellipt. use of LEA (*ley, lay*) adj.] Land that has remained untilled for some time; arable land under grass; land 'laid down' for pasture, grass-land. Also *attrib.*

The husbandman..had turned his acres into leyes, his syths and ploughs into swords DRUMM. OF HAWTH.

Lea (lī), *sb.*[3] ME. [? f. F. *lier* (:—L. *ligare*) to bind, tie. But cf. LEASE *sb.*[4]] A measure of yarn of varying quantity; in worsted 80 yards; in cotton and silk 120 yards.

Lea, ley, lay (lī, lēⁱ), *a.* Now *dial.* [? repr. OE. *lǣge* (implied in comb. *lǣghrycg* LEA-RIG), f. root of LAY, LIE *vbs.* Cf. LOW *a.*] Of land: Fallow, unploughed. Also *fig.*

Leach (līʧ), *sb.* 1673. [app. f. LEACH *v.* In senses 1–3 prob. short for attributive combs.] **1.** A perforated vessel or trough used for making lye from wood ashes by pouring water over them. *Obs.* exc. *dial.* **2.** *Tanning.* The pit in which the tan-liquors are mixed 1777. **3.** *Salt-making.* The brine which drains from the salt, or is left in the pan when the salt is drawn out 1886. **4.** The action of leaching. **5.** 'A quantity of wood-ashes, through which water passes, and thus imbibes the alkali' (Webster) 1828.

Leach (līʧ), *v.* Also **leech, latch, letch.** 1614. [Prob. repr. OE. *leccan* to water (tr. L. *rigare*) :—OTeut. **lak(k)jan*, f. **lak-* denoting moisture. The form *letch* is normal; *leach* is obscure.] †**1.** *intr.* To soften, melt. *rare.* **2. a.** *trans.* To cause (a liquid) to percolate through some material 1796. **b.** To subject (bark, ores, etc.) to the action of percolating water, etc., with the view of removing the soluble constituents; to lixiviate 1840. **c.** *intr.* To pass through by percolation 1864. Also *intr.* for *refl.* Of ashes: To be subject to the action of percolating water 1883. **3.** *trans.* To take *away, out* by percolation 1860.

Leach(e, obs. ff. LEECH.

Leachy (lī·ʧi), *a.* ? *U.S.* 1879. [f. LEACH *v.* + -Y [1].] Of soil: Of a nature to let water percolate through; not capable of holding water; porous.

Lead (led), *sb.*[1] [OE. *lēad* str. neut. = Du. *lood* lead, MHG. *lôt* (mod.G. *lot, loth*) plummet, also solder.] **1.** The heaviest of the base metals, of a dull pale bluish-grey colour, easily fusible, soft and malleable. Chemical symbol Pb. Rarely *pl.* = kinds of lead. †**b.** Sometimes called *black lead* (= L. *plumbum nigrum*) in contradistinction to *white lead* (*plumbum album*), a name for tin –1753. **2.** See RED LEAD, WHITE LEAD. **3.** Short for BLACK LEAD, graphite, or plumbago. Hence, a small stick of graphite for filling a pencil. 1840. **4.** The metal as fashioned into a leaden coffin, a bullet, etc.; the leaden part of anything ME. **5. a.** A large pot, cauldron, or kettle. (Orig., one made of lead.) Now only *dial.* OE. **b.** *dial.* A leaden milk-pan. **6.** A sounding-lead 1440. **7.** *pl.* **a.** The strips of lead used to cover a roof; often *collect.* for a lead flat, a lead roof, †occas. construed as sing. 1578. **b.** The lead frames of the panes in lattice or stained glass windows 1705. **8.** *Printing.* A thin strip of type-metal, used in type-composition to separate lines 1808.

1. Phr. †*To lie, be wrapt in l.*: to be buried in a l. coffin. So †*to lay, lap in l.* 4. Heauen keepe L. out of mee SHAKS. 6. Phr. *To cast, heave the l.* *To arm the l.*: to fill the hollow in it with tallow in order to discover the nature of the bottom by the substances adhering (Smyth). 7. **a.** A Goodly Leads upon the Top, railed with Statua's interposed BACON.

Combs.: **l.-arming**, the tallow used for arming a lead (see 6); **-ash, -ashes**, litharge; **-bath**, (*a*) the mass of melted l. in a lead-furnace; (*b*) the molten l. with which gold and silver ores are melted before cupellation; **l. glance** [= Du. *loodglans*], galena; **-light**, a window in which small panes are fixed in leaden cames, also *attrib.*; **-line**, (*a*) a sounding-lead or plumb-line; (*b*) a line loaded with leaden weights, running along the bottom of a net; (*c*) a bluish grey line along the gums at their junction with the teeth, indicating lead-poisoning; **-mill**, (*a*) an establishment for producing milled or sheet l.; (*b*) a circular plate of l. used by the lapidary for grinding or roughing; **-nail** (mostly *pl.*), a nail used to fasten a sheet of l. on a roof; **-ochre** = MASSICOT; **-paper**, a test-paper treated with a preparation of l.; **-pencil**, a pencil of graphite, often enclosed in cedar or other wood; **-plant** (*U.S.*), a shrub (*Amorpha canescens*) found in the west of the Mississippi valley, and believed to indicate the presence of l. ore; **-plaster** = DIACHYLON; **-poisoning**, poisoning by the introduction of l. into the system; **-spar** = ANGLESITE or CERUSSITE; **-tree**, (*a*) a W. Indian name for the tropical leguminous tree *Leucæna glauca*; (*b*) a crystalline deposit of metallic l. or zinc that has been placed in a solution of acetate of l.; **-vitriol** = ANGLESITE; **-water** (= Ger. *bleiwasser*), dilute solution of acetate of l.; **-work**, plumbers' work and material; work in l., *esp.* glaziers' work; **-works** *pl.*, an establishment for smelting lead-ore; **-wort**, a herbaceous plant of southern Europe (*Plumbago europæa*); also, any plant of the genus *Plumbago* or the order *Plumbaginaceæ*.

Lead (līd), *sb.*[2] ME. [f. LEAD *v.*[1]] †**1.** The action of LEAD *v.*[1]; leading –1510. **b.** Direction given by going in front; example; esp. in phr. *to follow the l. of* 1863. **c.** *spec.* in *Hunting*, etc., chiefly in phr. *to give a l.*, i.e. to go first in leaping a fence, etc. 1859. **d.** A guiding indication 1851. **2.** The front or leading place; the place in front *of* (something). Also, the position or function of leading (e.g. a party), leadership 1570. **3.** *concr.* Something that leads. **a.** An artificial watercourse: cf. MILL-LEAD. **b.** A channel in an ice-field 1835. **c.** A path; a garden path; an alley. *Blind l.* = *blind alley* (see BLIND *a.* 10). **d.** A leash or string for leading a dog 1893. **4.** *Card-playing.* The action or right of playing the first card in a round or trick; also, the card so played, or proper to be played, or the suit to which it belongs 1742. **5.** *Curling.* The first player or the stone first played. 1685. **6.** *Mining.* **a.** = LODE 5. 1812. **b.** *Gold-mining.* An alluvial deposit of gold along the bed of an ancient river 1855. **7.** *Theatr.* The principal part in a play; also, one who plays such a part 1874. **8.** *Friendly lead* (see FRIENDLY *a.* 2). Also simply *lead*. 1851. **9.** *techn.* **a.** *Electricity.* (*a*) The angle between the plane through the lines of contact of the brushes or collectors of a dynamo or electric motor with the commutator and the transverse plane bisecting the magnetic field. (*b*) A conductor conveying electricity from the source to the place where it is used. 1881. **b.** *Engineering*, etc. The distance to which ballast, coal, soil, etc. has to be conveyed (see LEAD *v.*[1] 1 b) to its destination 1841. **c.** *Horology.* The action of a tooth, as a tooth of a wheel, in impelling another tooth or pallet 1880. **d.** *Naut.* The direction in which running ropes lead fair, and come down to the deck (Smyth) 1860. **e.** *Steam-engine.* (See quots.) 1838.

2. Phr. *To take the* (or *a*) *l.*, to occupy the front place, to assume the function of leader. Each of our porters took the l. in turn TYNDALL. 4. Phr. *To return one's partner's l.*: to play from the same suit on getting the l. 9. **e.** *L. of the crank*, the setting of the crank of one engine a little in advance of the right angle to the other; namely at 100° or 110° in place of 90°. This assists in rendering the motion of the piston more uniform, by moderating its velocity at the end of the stroke. *L. of the valve*, the amount of opening which a valve has when the engine is on the centre 1881.

Comb.: **l.-off**, a commencement; also that which leads off, the first of a series; **-reins** *Coaching*, the leaders' reins; **-screw**, 'the main screw of a lathe, which gives the feed motion to the slide-rest' (Webster).

Lead (līd), *v.*[1] Pa. t. and pa. pple. **led.** [Com. Teut. wk. vb.: OE. *lǣdan* :—OTeut. **laidjan*, f. **laidā* road, journey (see LOAD, LODE *sbs.*), related to OE. *līðan* to go, travel.]

I. To conduct. **1.** *trans.* To cause to go along with oneself. †**a.** To bring or take (a person or animal) to a place. (Phrases like *to l. captive* are now understood in sense 2.) –1704. **b.** To carry or convey, usu. in a cart, etc. Now only *n. dial.*: To cart (coal, corn, etc.). *To l. in* (grain): to house. OE. **c.** To bring forward, adduce (testimony); to bring (an action). Now only in *Sc. Law.* ME. **2.** To conduct, guide, esp. by going on in advance OE. **b.** Of motives, circumstances, etc.: To guide, direct to a place ME. **c.** Of a clue, light, sound, etc.: To serve (a person) as an indication of the way; to mark the course for. Also absol. *to l. in* (Naut.): to mark the course for entering port. 1697. **d.** *absol.* 1580. **e.** Phr. *To l. the way*: †(*a*) to guide, show the way to; (*b*) in later use, to take the lead in an expedition, etc. ME. **3.** Of a commander: To march at the head of and direct the movement of. Also with *on.* OE. **4.** To conduct (a person) by holding the hand, etc., (an animal) by means of a halter, bridle, etc. Const. *by* (the hand, etc.). **b.** *fig.* (*a*) To guide by persuasion (in opposition to *drive*). (*b*) *To l. by the nose* (see quot.): to cause to obey submissively. ME. **5.** To guide with reference to action or opinion; to conduct by argument, etc., *to* a conclusion; to induce *to* do something ME. **6.** Of a way, road, etc.: To conduct (a person) *to* or *into* a place. Hence *absol.* or *intr.*: to have a specified direction. ME. **b.** *intr.* To form a channel *into*, a connecting link *to* (something) 1833. **c.** *intr. To l. to*: to have as a result 1770. **7.** *To l.* (a person) *a dance*: *transf.* and *fig.*, to put to the trouble of hurrying from place to place; hence, to compel to go through a course of irksome action. So *to l.* (a person) *a chase, a life.* 1529. **8. a.** To conduct (water, steam) through a channel or pipe ME. **b.** To guide the course or direction of (something flexible; e. g. a rope, etc. *over* a pulley, *through* a hole, etc.) OE. **c.** Naut. *intr.* Of a rope: To admit of being led 1860. †**9.** To conduct (affairs); to manage, govern –1579.

1. b. Faith, sir, ha's led the drumme before the English Tragedians SHAKS. c. No evidence has yet been led to show SIR W. HAMILTON. 2. Therefore shall not Moses..his people into Canaan l. MILT. *P.L.* XII. 309. b. Instinct early led him into the political arena 1892. c. L., Kindly Light, amid the encircling gloom, L. Thou me on J. H. NEWMAN. d. Pray you l. on *Oth.* I. i. 311. 3. The Prince..led them on with great gallantry 1736. 4. The captive soldier was led forth GOLDSM. Phr. *To l. apes* (*in hell*): see APE *sb.* *To l.* (*a bride*) *to the altar, to church*: to marry. b. The Moore..will as tenderly be lead by th' Nose As Asses are *Oth.* I. iii. 407. 5. Tintoret..may l. you wrong if you don't understand him RUSKIN. 6. Broad steps l. down into a garden 1861. c. Several seizures of English cargoes led to reprisals on our part; reprisals led to a naval war M. PATTISON. 7. She had led him the life of a dog 1892. 8. b. Ropes..led through blocks fixed to stakes 1892.

II. To carry on. †**1.** To engage or take part in, to perform (dances, songs), to utter sounds. Cf. L. *ducere carmen, choros.* –1493. **2.** To go through, pass (life, †a portion of time). Cf. L. *ducere vitam.* Rarely, †To support life *by* (bread). OE.

2. Do l. your own life and let ours alone! BROWNING.

III. To precede, be foremost. (Cf. sense I. 2.) **1.** To have the first place in; *lit.* and *fig.* esp. in *to l. the dance, the van* ME. **b.** *absol.* To go first. Also with *off.* 1798. **2.** *trans.* To direct by one's example; to set (a fashion); to take the directing or principal part in (a proceeding, performance, etc.); to be chief of (a party, a movement); to have the official initiative in the proceedings of (a deliberative body) 1642. **3.** Of a barrister: *trans.* To act as leading counsel in (a cause); to act as leader to (another barrister); to take precedence of. Also *absol.* or *intr.* 1806. **4.** *Card-playing.* **a.** *intr.* To play the first card. Also with *off.* Said also of the card. Also in *indirect passive.* **b.** *trans.* As first player, to play (a specified card); to play one of (a specified suit). Also with *out.* 1731.

1. b. The Admiral's frigate led 1900. 2. To l. an insurrection 1841, the singing 1859, the prayers 1866, the chorus 1883, the orchestra 1891. Disraeli still led the House of Commons 1891 4. a. *To l. to* or *l. up to*: to play a card in order to bring out (cards held by another player). b. I l. a heart SWIFT.

Combs. (with advs.). **Lead away. a.** *trans.* To induce to follow unthinkingly. Chiefly in *pass.* **b.** Naut. *To l. it away*: to take one's course. **Lead off.** *trans.* To open (a dance, a ball); hence *gen.* to begin. Also *intr.* or *absol.* **Lead on. a.** *trans.* To induce gradually to advance; to beguile into going to greater lengths. **b.** *intr.* To direct conversation *to* a subject. **Lead out.** *trans.* = *Lead off.* Also, to conduct (a partner) to the dance. **Lead up. a.** *trans.* = *Lead off.* ? *Obs.* **b.** intr. *To l. up to* to form a gradual preparation for.

Lead (led), *v.*² ME. [f. LEAD *sb.*¹] **1.** To cover with or enclose in lead. Also with *over.* **2.** To arm, load, or weight with lead 1481. **3.** To fix (glass of a window) with leaden cames 1530. †**4.** To line (pottery) with lead or lead-glaze; to glaze –1686. **5.** *Printing.* To separate lines of type with leads (see LEAD *sb.*¹ 8) 1841. **6.** *passive* and *intr.* Of a gun-barrel: To become foul with a coating of lead 1875.

1. She leaded and paved the Friday Market Cross in Stamford FULLER. Hence **Lea·ded** *ppl. a.* (of panes of glass) fitted into leaden cames (1855); *Printing*, having the lines separated by leads (1805).

Leadage (lī·dėdʒ). 1891. [f. LEAD *v.*¹ + -AGE.] Distance that coal has to be conveyed from the mine to a sea-board or railway.

Leaden (le·d'n), *a.* [OE. *lēaden*: see LEAD *sb.*¹ and -EN ⁴.] **1.** Consisting or made of lead. Also *fig.* **2.** *transf.* and *fig.* **a.** Of base quality; opp. to *golden* 1577. **b.** Heavy as if made of lead 1579. **c.** Inert, depressing 1592. **d.** Dull grey, like lead ME.

1. What says this l. casket? *Merch. V.* II. vii. 15. *L. key, sceptre*, poet. for the powers of sleep or dullness. *L. sword*, type of a useless weapon. 2. a. Base l. Earles, that glory in your birth MARLOWE. b. L. handes LYLY, feet 1585, slumbers 1725. c. Saturne, that l. planet 1647. d. Colour..wan and of leden hewe CHAUCER. **Lea·den-ly** *adv.*, **-ness.**

Leaden (le·d'n), *v.* 1552. [f. LEAD *sb.*¹ + -EN ⁵ or f. LEADEN *a.*] †**a.** *trans.* To fasten with molten lead. **b.** To make leaden or dull. **c.** *intr.* To press down like lead; only in Leadening *ppl. a.*

Leader (lī·dəɹ). OE. [f. LEAD *v.*¹ + -ER¹.]

I. One who leads. **1.** *gen.* in various senses of the vb.; †a carrier. *Follow my l.*: a game in which each player must do what the leader does, or pay forfeit; also *fig.* **2.** *esp.* **a.** *L. of the House of Commons*: the member of the government who has the official initiative in the proceedings of the House. **b.** A counsel who leads (see LEAD *v.*¹ III. 3) in a case; a King's Counsel, whose status entitles him to lead. Also, the senior counsel of a circuit. 1856. **3.** One who leads a choir or band of dancers, musicians, or singers 1530. **4.** Among Methodists, the presiding member of a class (see CLASS *sb.* 7). Usu. *class-l.* 1743. **5.** One of the front horses in a team, or the front horse in a tandem 1700.

1. Ample Plains, Where oft the Flocks without a L. stray DRYDEN. All this day..they will gather to their leader's standard SCOTT. 3. *Much Ado* II. i. 157.

II. A thing which leads. **1. a.** *gen.* ME. **b.** *colloq.* A remark or question intended to lead conversation (cf. FEELER 3) 1882. **2.** In a tree or shrub: The shoot which grows at the apex of the stem, or of a principal branch; also, a bine 1572. **3.** A tendon 1708. **4.** = LEADING ARTICLE 1. 1844. **5.** *Mining.* **a.** A drain or stream that by its colour indicates the presence of minerals 1809. **b.** A small and insignificant vein which leads to a larger and better 1670. **6.** *Fishing* (U.S.). The end portion of a reel-line, having the snells of the fly-hooks attached to it 1859. **7.** *Printing.* A line of dots or dashes to guide the eye 1824.

4. Give me a man who can write a l. DISRAELI. Hence **Lea·deress**, a female l. **Leaderette** (līdəre·t), a short editorial paragraph printed in the same type as the leaders in a newspaper 1880. **Lea·derless** *a.* without a l. **Lea·dership**, the dignity, office, or position of a l.; also, ability to lead.

Lea·dhillite. 1835. [f. *Leadhills* in Scotland, where found; see -ITE.] *Min.* A sulphato-carbonate of lead, found in whitish pearly crystals.

Lead-in. 1913. [LEAD *v.*¹] A conducting wire joining a wireless receiver with an external aerial.

Leading (lī·diŋ), *vbl. sb.*¹ ME. [f. LEAD *v.*¹ + -ING ¹.] **1.** The action of LEAD *v.*¹; †carriage. **b.** *Light or l.* (Milton) = illumination or guidance 1644; hence Burke's phr., *men of light and l.* 1790. **2.** *Lead-mining.* One of the fine slender threads connecting the branches of a vein 1653. **3.** A directing influence or guidance; a term used by the Quakers 1889.

Comb.: **l.-block**, a fixed pulley, which alters the direction of the power, but does not increase it; **-business** (*Theatr.*), the parts usually taken by the leading actor; **-rein**, a rein to lead a horse, etc.; also *fig.*; **-staff**, †(*a*) a staff borne by a commanding officer; (*b*) a staff to lead a bull by means of a ring through its nose; **-string** (chiefly *pl.*), strings with which children used to be guided and supported when learning to walk 1677; hence in fig. phr.; a cord for leading an animal.

Leading (le·diŋ), *vbl. sb.*² 1440. [f. LEAD *v.*² + -ING ¹.] The action of LEAD *v.*²; esp. *concr.* = CAME; leadwork in general.

Leading (lī·diŋ), *ppl. a.* 1597. [f. LEAD *v.*¹ + -ING ².] That leads (see LEAD *v.*¹).

Special collocations: **l.-buoy**, one placed as a guide in sailing; **l. case** *Law*, one that serves as a precedent to decide other cases; **l. lady, man**, the chief actress or actor in a theatrical company; **l.-mark** *Naut.*, one of 'those objects which, kept in line or in transit, guide the pilot while working into port, as trees, spires, buoys, etc.' (Smyth) · **l.-motive** *Mus.*, occas. tr. LEITMOTIV, q.v.; **l. note** *Mus.*, the seventh note of the scale, so called from its tendency to lead up to the tonic 1752; **l. question**, one that suggests the answer expected; **l. seventh** *Mus.*, the chord of the seventh on the leading note.

Hence **Lea·dingly** *adv.* in a l. manner.

Leading article. 1807. **1.** A large-type article in a newspaper, expressing at length editorial opinion on any subject. **2.** *Comm.* **a.** A principal article of trade 1818. **b.** An article which is sold at a low price in order to attract customers for other things.

Leadless (le·dlės), *a.* 1809. [f. LEAD *sb.*¹ + -LESS.] Without lead.

L. pistol BYRON. L. glaze 1898.

Leadsman (le·dzmăn). 1857. [f. gen. of LEAD *sb.*¹ + MAN.] The man who heaves the lead in taking soundings.

Leady (le·di), *a.* ME. [f. LEAD *sb.*¹ + -Y ¹.] Resembling lead, usu. in colour.

Leaf (līf), *sb.* Pl. **leaves.** [OE. *lēaf* str. neut. (pl. *lēaf*) :—OTeut. **laubo-*; cf. Du. *loof*, Ger. *laub* neut., etc.]

I. 1. An expanded organ of a plant, usually green, produced laterally from a stem or branch, or springing from its root. When complete, it consists of a blade, footstalk, and stipules; pop., the word *leaf* denotes the blade alone. Some mod. botanists use the term to include also 'modified leaves', such as stamens, carpels, parts of the floral envelope, bracts, etc. **2.** *pop.* A petal; esp. in *rose-l.* 1565. **3.** *collect.* Foliage; leafage, leaves. Chiefly in *fall of the l.* *In* (*full*) *l.*: covered with foliage. 1537. **b.** Of wine: 'season', 'year' 1432. **4.** *spec.* The leaves: **a.** of the tobacco-plant 1618; **b.** of the tea-plant 1883. **5.** A representation of a leaf; esp. in *Archit.* 1459.

1. *fig.* This is the state of Man; to day he puts forth The tender Leaues of hopes, to morrow Blossomes SHAKS. 3. *fig.* My way of life Is falne into the Seare, the yellow Leafe SHAKS. 4. a. Tobacco in the leafe 1641.

II. Similative uses. **1.** A single fold of a folded sheet of paper, parchment, etc.; *esp.* in a book or manuscript (= two pages); hence, what is printed or written thereon OE. **2.** The layer of fat round the kidneys of a pig; also the inside fat of other animals. Now *dial.* and *U.S.* ME. **3.** A very thin sheet of metal, esp. gold or silver ME.; a lamina (of horn, marble, wood, etc.) 1601. **4. a.** A hinged part of a door, gate, or shutter ME. **b.** A hinged flap of a table; also *gen.* any movable addition to the top of a table 1558. **c.** The hinged part of a draw-bridge or bascule-bridge 1442. **d.** A hinged sight on a rifle barrel 1875. **5.** One of the teeth of a pinion 1706. **6.** The brim of a hat. Chiefly *Anglo-Irish.* 1767. **7.** Weaving. *L. of heddles*: all the heddles connected by the same two shafts of wood. *Twill of three, four,* etc. *leaves*: twill woven upon three, four, etc. leaves of heddles; hence *attrib.*, as *eight-leaf twill* 1831.

1. Phr. *To take a l. out of* (a person's) *book*: see BOOK *sb.* *To turn over a new l.*: to begin to mend one's ways; earlier, †*to turn the leaf* (1548).

Combs. **1.** General: as *l.-axil, -blade*, etc.; *l.-eater*; *l.-bearing* adj.; *l.-latticed, -strewn* adjs.; *l.-bladed* adj., etc.

2. Special: **l.-bearing** *a.*, having a leaf-like appendage; applied *spec.* to worms of the family *Phyllodocidæ*, which have gills in the form of leaves; **-beetle**, a beetle of the family *Chrysomelidæ*, which feed upon leaves only; **-bridge**, a bridge constructed with a leaf or leaves (sense II. 4c); **-bud**, a bud rom which leaves are produced (opp. to *flower-bud*); **-bundle**, the bundle of fibres running from the stem into the l. of a plant; **-butterfly**, one of the genu *Kallima*; **-climber**, a climber in which support is gained by the action, not of the stem, but of the leaves it bears; so **-climbing** *a.*; **-crumpler**, a moth, *Phycis indiginella*, of N. America, the caterpillars of which draw together and crumple the leaves on which they feed; **-cutting**, a l. used as a cutting in the propagation of certain plants; **-fat**, the fat round a pig's kidneys; **-flea**, an insect of the family *Psyllidæ* which lives on plants; **-folder**, a moth whose larvæ fold leaves together to form a protective covering; **-footed** *a.*, having leaf-like feet; **-frog**, a frog of the genus *Phyllomedusa*; **-gap** *Bot.*, a division in the fibre of a plant, caused by the protrusion of a leaf-bud; **-green** *a.*, of the colour of green leaves; also quasi-*sb.*; *sb.* = CHLOROPHYLL; **-hopper**, a name for insects of the family *Tettigoniadæ* which live mostly on the leaves of plants; **-insect**, a name for insects of the family *Phasmidæ*, esp. the genus *Phyllium*, in which the wings and sometimes the legs resemble leaves in shape and colour; **-lard**, lard from the flaky fat of the hog; **-lichen**, a lichen of the genus *Parmelia* or N.O. *Parmeliaceæ*; **-louse**, one of the aphides which infest the leaves of plants; a plant-louse; **-metal**, metal in thin leaves; **-miner**, a small caterpillar of a tineid moth which eats its way between the cuticles of leaves; so *leaf-mining caterpillar*; **-mould**, mould having a large proportion of decayed leaves in it; **-nosed** *a.*, having a leaf-like appendage on the snout; *spec.* applied to the phyllostomoid and rhinolophoid bats; **-opposed** *a. Bot.*, having opposite leaves; **-plant**, a plant cultivated for its leaves; **-red** = ERYTHROPHYLL; **-roller**, the caterpillar of certain (tortricid) moths, which rolls up the leaves of plants which it infests; so *leaf-rolling* adj.; **-rosette** *Bot.*, a cluster of leaves resembling a rosette; **-rust**, a mould which attacks trees, producing rusty spots on the leaves; **-scale**, a scale on a plant-stem which develops into a l.; **-scar**, the cicatrix left on the bark by the separation of the leaf-stalk of a fallen l.; **-sheath**, a sheath at the base of a leaf, embracing the stem, as in grasses; **-sight** (see II. 4 d); **-spine**, a l. which has developed into a long, conical, pointed, woody body; **-table**, a table with a leaf or flap; **-tendril**, a tendril consisting of a modified leaf or part of a leaf; **-thorn** = *leaf-spine*; **-tobacco**, the raw material as imported with the stalk on it; **-trace** *Bot.*, a 'vein' or fibrovascular bundle running down from a leaf into the stem; **-valve**, a valve which moves on a hinge; **-wasp**, a saw-fly; **-work**, ornamental work consisting of leaf-forms.

Leaf (līf), *v.* See also LEAVE *v.*[2] 1611. [f. LEAF *sb.*] 1. *intr.* To put forth leaves. Also *to l. out* (U.S.). 2. a. To turn or turn *over* (the leaves of a book). Now *U.S.* b. To number (a leaf of a book). 1663.

Leaf, private soldier's form of LEAVE *sb.*

Leafage (lī·fėdʒ). 1599. [f. LEAF *sb.* + -AGE.] 1. Leaves; foliage. b. The representation of these, *esp.* as an ornamentation 1703. 2. Lamination (*rare*) 1833.

Lea·f-cutter. 1815. An insect that cuts or eats out portions of the leaves of trees; *spec.* in *leaf-cutter ant, bee.* So **leaf-cutting** *ppl. a.*, in *l.-cutting ant, bee* 1802.

Leaf-eared: see LAVE *a.*

Leafed (līft), *a.* See also LEAVED *a.* 1552. [f. LEAF *sb.* + -ED[2].] 1. Having leaves; as *broad-, thick-, two-l.* 2. (Broad-) brimmed 1841.

Leaf-gold. 1598. 1. = GOLD-LEAF. Also *fig.* 2. Native gold in the form of laminæ. RAYMOND.

†**Lea·fit.** 1787. [f. LEAF *sb.* + *-it*, ? = -ET.] = LEAFLET 1. –1830.

Leafless (lī·flės), *a.* Also †LEAVELESS. 1590. [f. LEAF *sb.* + -LESS.] Without a leaf; destitute of leaves. Also *fig.*

L., yet soft as spring, The tender purple spray on copse and briers! M. ARNOLD. Hence **Lea·flessness.**

Leaflet (lī·flėt). 1787. [f. LEAF *sb.* + -LET.] 1. †a. *Bot.* A sepal. b. *Bot.* One of the divisions of a compound leaf. c. *pop.* A young leaf; *rarely*, a petal. 2. *Anat.* and *Zool.* An organ or part of one resembling a small leaf 1826. 3. A small-sized leaf of paper or a sheet folded into leaves but not stitched, and containing printed matter, chiefly for gratuitous distribution 1867.

3. Leaflets (as Spurgeon and Co. have christened very young tracts) MISS BROUGHTON.

Leafy (lī·fi), *a.* (See also LEAVY.) 1552. [f. LEAF *sb.* + -Y[1].] 1. Having, or abounding in, leaves; clothed with, made or consisting of, leaves. b. *spec.* in *Bot.* Foliate 1776. 2. Of the nature of, or resembling, a leaf 1671; laminate 1754.

1. In the l. month of June COLERIDGE. Hence **Lea·finess.**

League (līg), *sb.*[1] [Late ME. *leuge, leuke, lege, leghe*, etc., ad. late L. *leuga, leuca* (= late Gr. λευγη, λεύγα), said to be a Gaulish word.] An itinerary measure of distance, varying in different countries, but usu. estimated at about 3 miles; in Eng. use, only poet. or rhet. *Marine l.*: a unit of distance = 3 nautical miles or 3,041 fathoms. *Comb.* **l.-long** *a.* that extends the length of a l. 1860.

League (līg), *sb.*[2] Also †**le(a)ge,** †**ligue.** 1452. [The form *ligue* is a. F. *ligue*, ad. It. *liga*, var. of *lega*, vbl. sb. f. *legare* to bind :—L. *ligare*. The form *le(a)ge* is perh. ad. It. *lega*.] 1. A covenant or compact made between parties for their mutual protection and assistance, the prosecution of joint interests, and the like; a body of states or persons associated in such a covenant, a confederacy. b. In recent use, often adopted in the names of associations or societies having a common object 1846. 2. *gen.* A covenant, compact, alliance. Now *rare*. 1509.

1. Y^e^ l. offensive and defensive wth ye States Gen^ll^ 1678. *The League*, a l. formed in 1576 under the direction of the Guises, to prevent the accession of Henry IV to the French throne. *Holy L.*, a name given to several leagues, e.g. that formed by Pope Julius II against the French in 1511 and the Nuremberg L. of 1538. *Solemn L. and Covenant*: see COVENANT *sb.* 8. b. *Anti-Corn-Law L.*: a political association formed in 1838 to procure the abolition of the existing Corn Laws. *L. of Nations*, an association of self-governing states, dominions, etc. created by a covenant incorporated in the peace treaty of 1919 after the war of 1914–18, having as its object the maintenance of the peace of the world. ('The League of Nations Society' was formed in 1916.) 2. Linkt in happie nuptial L. MILT. *P.L.* IV. 339.

League (līg), *v.* 1611. [f. LEAGUE *sb.*[2] Cf. F. *liguer*.] 1. *trans.* To form or join into a league. †2. To bind, connect, join –1660. 3. *intr.* To join in or form a league or alliance. Also *to l. against* in indirect pass. 1638.

1. Hotspur..leagued himself with the Scots GREEN. 3. Where kings first leagued against the rights of men SHELLEY.

Leaguer (lī·gəɹ), *sb.*[1] 1577. [a. Du. *leger* camp; cf. LAIR *sb.*] 1. A military camp, esp. one engaged in a siege; an investing force. 2. A siege 1598. ¶3. Occas. confused with *leager* LEDGER 1678.

1. I came into the imperial l. at the siege of Leipsic DE FOE. Phr. *In l.*: in camp; engaged in a siege. 2. The l. of Lucknow SMILES.

Leaguer (lī·gəɹ), *sb.*[2] 1590. [f. LEAGUE *sb.*[2] + -ER[1].] A member of a league; e.g. of the League formed against the Huguenots in the reign of Henry III, the Anti-Corn-Law League, the Irish Land League, etc.

Leaguer (lī·gəɹ), *sb.*[3] 1683. [?ad. Du. *ligger* a tun, f. *liggen* LIE *v.*[1]] a. A measure of arrack 1712. b. A cask of wine or oil, ? of a certain size 1772. c. *Naut.* The longest water-cask, of 159 English imperial gallons 1683.

Lea·guer, *v.* 1596. [f. LEAGUER *sb.*[1]] †1. *refl.* and *intr.* To set one's leaguer, to encamp; also, to lie, lodge –1676. 2. *trans.* To besiege, beleaguer 1715.

2. Two mighty hosts a leaguer'd town embrace POPE.

†**Lea·guerer.** 1635. [f. LEAGUER *sb.*[1] + -ER[1].] A (Dutch) trooper –1654.

Leak (līk), *sb.* 1487. [perh. a. ON. *leke* str. masc. The relation between sb., adj., and vb. is unkn.] 1. A hole or fissure in a vessel containing or immersed in a fluid, which lets the fluid pass into or out of the vessel; said orig. and esp. of ships; also in phr. *to spring a l.* Also *transf.* and *fig.* 2. The action of leaking; leakage 1828.

1. Many little leaks may sink a ship FULLER. *transf.* A l. in the waistcoat-pocket in which you carry all your money 1806.

†**Leak,** *a.* [In OE. *hlec*; but the (app.) cogn. words in other Teut. langs. show no trace of the *h*. In 16th c., perh. a LG., MDu. *lek* (inflected *lěke-*); cogn. w. ON. *lekr*, and w. LEAK *sb.* and *v.*] = LEAKY. –1678.

Leak (līk), *v.* 1440. [a. or cogn. w. ON. *leka* str. vb. (pa. t. *lak*) to drip, to leak; f. Teut. root **lek-*, ablaut var. of **lak-*; see LACK *a.* Perh. formed afresh later from LEAK *sb.* or *a.*] 1. *intr.* To pass (*out, away, forth*) by a leak or leakage. Also *fig.* to pass *away* by gradual waste. 2. To let fluid pass in or out through a leak 1513. †b. To 'make water' (*vulgar*) –1796. †3. *pass.* To have sprung a leak; to be emptied by leakage –1748. 4. *trans.* To let (water, etc.) in or out through a leak. ? Now *U.S.* only. †Also *fig.* 1655. 5. *Brewing.* To cause (liquor) to run *over, on, off,* in small quantities or gradually 1674.

1. A democracy that has allowed its chief political interests to l. away 1890. Phr. *To l. out* (fig.): to come to be known in spite of efforts at concealment 1840. 2. The starboard boiler began to l. SIR J. ROSS. 4. The pipe leaks gas; the roof leaks rain 1889.

Leakage (lī·kėdʒ). 1490. [f. LEAK *v.* + -AGE.] 1. The action of leaking; loss of fluid by this means. 2. *transf.* and *fig.* Diminution resulting from gradual waste or escape 1642. 3. *concr.* That which leaks out. Also *fig.* 1661. 4. Allowance for waste of fluid by leakage from the containing vessels 1591.

2. The Cabinet..was not famous for its power of preventing the l. of state matters KINGLAKE.

Leaky (lī·ki), *a.* 1606. [f. LEAK *sb.* + -Y[1].] Having a leak or leaks; full of leaks. b. Incontinent of urine 1727. c. *fig.* Not reticent, blabbing; not retentive 1692.

L. casks 1872. A l. gas pipe 1881. Hence **Lea·kiness.**

Leal (līl), *a.* Now *Sc.* and *n. dial.* ME. [a. OF. *leel*, mod.F. *loyal* (see LOYAL) :—L. *legalis* LEGAL.] 1. Loyal, faithful, honest, true. 2. True, genuine; real, actual; exact, accurate; very (truth). Of a blow or shot: Well-aimed. ME. †3. Lawful; also, just, fair –1727.

1. The leelest maid o them a' 1776. L. service 1884. *Land of the l.*: see LAND *sb.* Hence **Lea·lly** *adv.* **Le·alty** (now *arch.*) faithfulness, loyalty.

Lea-land, lay-land (lī·lænd, lē·lænd). ME. [f. LEA *a.* + LAND *sb.*] Fallow land; land 'laid down' to grass.

Leam (līm), *sb.*[1] Now *Sc.* and *n. dial.* [OE. *léoma* str. masc. :—OTeut. **leuhmon-*, f. **leuh-* (see LIGHT *sb.*).] Light, flame; a flash, ray, or gleam of light; brightness, gleam. Also *fig.*

Leam (līm), *sb.*[2] *dial.* 1601. A drain or watercourse in fen districts.

Leam (līm), *v.* Now *Sc.* and *n. dial.* ME. [f. LEAM *sb.*[1]] *intr.* To shine, gleam; to light *up.*

Leamer, var. of LIMER[1], a hound.

Lean (līn), *sb.*[1] 1610. [f. LEAN *v.*] 1. The act or condition of leaning; inclination. *On the l.*: inclining. 1776. †2. *concr.* Something to lean on; a support. HEALEY.

Lean (līn), *a.* and *sb.*[2] [OE. *hlǣne* :—OTeut. type **hlainjo-*; ult. etym. unkn.] 1 Wanting in flesh; not plump; thin. Also *transf.* b. *Shipbuilding.* 'Sharp', opp. to *bluff* 1769. 2. *fig.* Poor in quantity or quality, meagre; slight, mean. Somewhat *arch.* Of diet: Poor, innutritious. ME. 3. Of flesh or meat: Containing little or no fat ME. 4. Wanting in rich elements or qualities. Now somewhat *rare*. ME. 5. Scantily provided ME. b. Of seasons, etc.: Marked by scarcity 1670. 6. *Printing.* (See quots.) 1676.

1. Yond Cassius has a leane and hungry looke, He thinkes too much SHAKS. *transf.* The l. Statue of a starv'd Renown 1693. 2. My leane and low ability SHAKS. Their l. and flashy songs MILT. A l. diet 1890. 4. A thick l. Mortar 1726. A country rough, l., and solitary 1817. L. fields 1899. 5. Cash is very lene 1623. Dress..keeps our larder l. COWPER. b. L. times DRYDEN, years 1890. 6. *L. strokes* are the narrow strokes in a Letter, as the Left Hand stroke in the letter A MOXON. *L. work*, the opposite of fat work—that is, poor unprofitable work 1871. Hence **Lea·n-ly** *adv.*, **-ness.**

B. *sb.* 1. The lean part of anything; the muscular tissue of meat as dist. from the fat 1450. 2. *Printing.* †a. A thin part or stroke of a letter 1683. b. Ill-paid work 1882.

1. Some fat to my leane 16..

Lean (līn), *v.*[1] Pa. t. and pa. pple. **leaned** (līnd), leant (lent). [ME. *lēnen* :—OE. *hleonian, hlinian*, f. Teut. root *hlī-* (ablaut-var. of *hlai-*: see LADDER) :—Indo-Eur. *klī-* represented in Gr. κλῖμαξ ladder, L. *clivus* declivity, Skr. *çri* to lean.] 1. *intr.* To recline, lie down, rest. *Obs.* exc. *Sc.* in reflexive construction. **2.** To incline the body against an object for support; to support oneself *on, against* something. Also *transf.* of inanimate objects. ME. **b.** To press *upon*; to lay emphasis *upon* 1736. **3.** *fig.* To rely or depend *on* or *upon*. Also *refl.* ME. **4.** To bend or incline *from, over, towards, back, out,* †*up* OE. **b.** To move or be situated obliquely; to swerve (*aside*); *U.S.* to 'make tracks' ME. **5.** To incline *towards, to* some quality, etc. Also, to have a tendency favourable *to.* ME. **6.** To be somewhat partial or favourable; to be inclined or disposed *to* or *towards* 1530. †**b.** To defer *to* an opinion –1611. **7.** (causal) *trans.* **a.** To cause to lean or rest, to prop *against*, etc. ME. **b.** To cause to bend or incline ME.

1. Lenynge on myn elbowe and my syde CHAUCER. 2. I leaned with my backe against an oke to rest me 1530. *transf.* Where the broad ocean leans against the land GOLDSM. Phr. *To l. upon* (*Mil.*): to be close up to something serving as a protection. 3. Trust in the Lord..and leane not vnto thine owne vnderstanding *Prov.* iii. 5. 4. A cone of ice forty feet high leaned quite over our track TYNDALL. *fig.* Ev'n his failings lean'd to virtue's side GOLDSM. 5. The Government leans towards Democracy BROUGHAM. 6. Aristotle leanes to the contrary opinion 1604. Phr. *To l. against*: to be unfavourable to. Chiefly *legal.* **b.** *Cymb.* I. i. 78. 7. **a.** Leane thine aged Back against mine Arme SHAKS. **b.** I..l. mine ear to the sounds of the air BOWEN.

†**Lean,** *v.*[2] [OE. *hlǣnian*, f. *hlǣne* LEAN *a.*] To become or to make lean –1616.

Leaning (lī·niŋ), *vbl. sb.* OE. [f. LEAN *v.*[1] + -ING[1].] **1.** The action of LEAN *v.*[1]; inclination; reclining. **2.** *fig.* Inclination, bias; tendency, 'penchant' 1587.

2. A l. towards Rome 1849.

Comb.: **l.-note** *Mus.* = APPOGGIATURA; **-stock,** (*a*) a support (*lit.* and *fig.*); (*b*) in an organ, the ledge on which a pipe rests.

Lean-to (lī·ntu), *sb.* (*a.*) 1461. [f. LEAN *v.*[1] + TO *adv.*] **1.** A building with rafters resting against the side of another; a penthouse. **2.** *attrib.* (or *adj.*) Belonging to or of the nature of such a building. Also, placed so as to lean against something. 1649.

2. They had set fire to the lean-to outhouse 1882.

†**Lea·ny,** *a.* ME. [f. LEAN *a.* + -Y[1].] Lean –1602.

Leap (līp), *sb.*[1] [OE. *hlȳp*, Anglian **hlēp* str. masc. :—OTeut. type **hlaupi-z*; f. root of LEAP *v.*] **1.** An act of leaping; a bound, jump, spring. **b.** *transf.* and *fig.* An abrupt movement or change OE. **2.** A leaping-place; something to be leaped over or from. Also, the place or distance leaped. (Freq. in place-names, as *Deerleap, Hindlip*, etc.) ME. **3.** Of animals: The action of leaping (the female) 1607. Also *transf.* **4.** The sudden fall of a river to a lower level 1796. **5.** *Mining.* A fault 1747. **6.** *Mus.* A passing from one note to another by an interval greater than a degree of the scale 1674.

1. Our elders took leaps, now they are all jumps 1825. Phr. *A l. in the dark*: a hazardous action of which the consequences are unforeseen. *By leaps, by leaps and bounds*: with startling rapidity of advance or increase. 2. This Place was therefore called *The Lover's L.* ADDISON. *Salmon l.*, a precipitous fall in a river over which salmon leap in going up river to breed. 4. The quiet stream is a succession of leaps and pools RUSKIN.

Comb.: **l.-day,** an intercalary day in the calendar, esp. February 29th.

Leap (līp), *sb.*[2] [OE. *lēap* str. masc.] **1.** A basket. Now *dial.* **2.** A basket in which to catch or keep fish OE.

Leap (līp), *v.* Pa. t. and pa. pple. **leaped** (līpt), **leapt** (lept). [Com. Teut.; OE. *hlēapan* :—OTeut. **hlaupan.* (Cf. LOUP from ON.)] †**1.** *intr.* To run, rush, 'throw oneself' –1716. **2.** To rise with both (or all) feet suddenly from a standing-place and pass through the air to some other position; to jump, spring OE. **b.** To spring *upon* a horse, *into* the saddle OE. **c.** Of a fish: To spring from the water ME. **3.** To spring or jump (with joy, mirth, etc.) OE. **4.** To spring suddenly *to* or *upon* one's feet, *from* a sitting or recumbent position, or *up* ME. **5.** *transf.* of a thing: To move with a leap or bound ME. **b.** Of the heart (or pulse): To beat vigorously, throb 1526. **6.** *fig.* To pass abruptly (from one condition or position to another) ME. **b.** *Mus.* To pass from one note to another by an interval greater than a degree of the scale. **7.** *trans.* To pass from one side of (a thing) to the other by leaping. late ME. **8.** Of a male animal: To spring upon (the female) in copulation 1530.

1. Hameward with clever strides he lap RAMSAY. 2. His hors for fere gan to turne, And leepe aside CHAUCER. He leaped up the stone steps by two at a time GEO. ELIOT. *Prov.* Look before you leap. **c.** Whenever a salmon leaps you must keep a slack line 1867. 3. Reioice yee in that day, and leape for ioy *Luke* vi. 23. 4. Arethusa leaping from her Bed DRYDEN. 5. I thought ten thousand swords must have leaped from their scabbards BURKE. The echos.. leaped from cliff to cliff TYNDALL. **b.** His heart leapt high as he look'd PALGRAVE. 7. The Nimrod ..Leaps every fence but one COWPER.

Leaper (lī·pəɹ). [OE. *hlēapere*; see LEAP *v.* and -ER[1].] One who or that which leaps.

Lea·p-frog. 1599. [f. LEAP *v.* + FROG[1].] A boys' game in which one player places his hands upon the bent back or shoulders of another and leaps or vaults over him. Also, a jump or leap of this description. Hence **Leap-frog** *v.* to leap or vault as at leap-frog (*intr.* and *trans.*).

†**Lea·pful.** OE. [f. LEAP *sb.*[2] + -FUL.] A basketful –ME.

Leaping (lī·piŋ), *vbl. sb.* OE. [f. LEAP *v.* + -ING[1].] The action of LEAP *v.*

attrib. and *Comb.*: **l.-head** 1862, **l.-horn** 1859, the lower pommel on a side-saddle; †**l.-house,** a brothel; **l.-time,** the time of activity, youth.

Leaping (lī·piŋ), *ppl. a.* OE. [-ING[2].] That leaps, etc.; see the vb.

l. spider, a jumping spider, one of the *Saltigradæ*. Hence **Lea·pingly** *adv.* by leaps.

Lea·p year. late ME. [Cf. ON. *hlaupár.*] A year having one day (now Feb. 29) more than the common year; a bissextile year.

(Perhaps because in the bissextile year any fixed festival after Feb. falls on the next week-day but one to that on which it fell in the preceding year, not on the next week-day as usual.)

Lear[1] (līəɹ). Now *Sc.* and *n. dial.* ME. [f. LERE *v.*; in mod.Sc. a var. of *lair, lare*; see LORE.] Instruction, learning; in early use, †a lesson; †also, a doctrine, religion.

†**Lear**[2]. ME. [a. OF. *lieure, lyeure, liure* :—L. *ligaturam* (see LIGATURE).] **1.** Tape; binding –1736. **2.** *Cookery.* A thickening for sauces, soups, etc.; a thickened sauce –1837.

Lear[3] (līəɹ). 1601. [? use of *lear*, LAIR *sb.* 5.] Colour (of sheep or cattle), due to the nature of the soil.

Lear: see LAIR, LEER, LERE, LIAR.

Lea·-rig. *dial.* [OE. *lǣghrycg*, f. **lǣge* LEA *a.* + *hrycg* back, RIDGE.] A ridge left in grass at the end of a ploughed field.

Learn (lɜ̄ɹn), *v.* Pa. t. and pa. pple. **learned** (lɜ̄ɹnd), **learnt** (lɜ̄ɹnt). [OE. *leornian*, f. (ult.) **lis-*, weak grade of **lais-*, root of OTeut. **lairā* LORE.]

I. 1. *trans.* To get knowledge of (a subject) or skill in (an art, etc.) by study, experience, or teaching. Also, to commit to memory, esp. in phrases *to l. by heart, by rote,* for which see the sbs. **2.** *intr.* To acquire knowledge of a subject or matter; to receive instruction OE. **3.** *trans.* To become informed of; to hear of, ascertain ME. **b.** *intr.* To be informed, ascertain, hear (*of*) 1756.

1. To l. True patience MILT. Henceforth I learne, that to obey is best MILT. L. to labour and to wait LONGF. Phr. *I am* (*yet*) *to l.*: I do not yet know. 2. Sir, I am too old to learne *Lear* II. ii. 134. 3. This good newes I have learned by a letter of yours 1638. Phr. *To l. out*: to discover (now *dial.*).

II. To impart knowledge. Now *vulgar.* **1.** *trans.* To teach ME. †**2.** To inform (a person) of something –1697.

1. No doubt the chickens crowed as the cocks had learned them FULLER. L. to know the House; l. the House to know you DISRAELI. To l. him a lesson 1889. 2. Learne me the Proclamation *Tr. & Cr.* II. i. 22.

Hence **Lea·rnable** *a.* that may be learnt. **Lea·rner,** one who receives instruction; †a teacher.

Learned (lɜ̄·ɹnėd), *ppl. a.* ME. [f. LEARN *v.* + -ED[1].] **1.** Of a person: In early use, that has been taught; educated. Later, deeply-read, erudite. Const. *in,* †*of.* **b.** *absol.* Chiefly in pl. *the l.* 1586. **c.** Said of one 'learned in the law'; hence by courtesy of any lawyer 1485. **d.** *transf.* of a trained pig, etc. 1833. **2.** Of things: Pertaining to, manifesting, or characterized by, profound knowledge gained by study 1613. **b.** In art-criticism, with reference to draughtmanship, colouring, etc.: Exhibiting thorough knowledge of method 1748. **c.** Of a language, profession, or science: Pursued or studied chiefly by men of learning. Of words: Introduced or used by men of learning. 1581.

1. And Moyses was lernd in al the wysdom of Egipcians WYCLIF *Acts* vii. 22. That dreaded phenomenon, a l. lady SCOTT. 2. If Jonson's l. Sock be on MILT. A l. sermon FULLER, education 1763. **c.** The l. languages L. MURRAY, professions 1850, words 1869. Hence **Lea·rned·ly** *adv.*, **-ness.**

Learning (lɜ̄·ɹniŋ), *vbl. sb.* [OE. *leornung, -ing*, f. *leornian*; see LEARN *v.* and -ING[1].] **1.** The action of LEARN *v.* †**2.** What is learnt or taught: **a.** a lesson –1611; **b.** information –1606; **c.** a doctrine, *esp.* a maxim in law –1626; **d.** a science –1613; **e.** an acquirement SHAKS. **3.** Knowledge, esp. of language or literary or historical science, got by study; also, learnedness ME.

1. There's nothing so good for l., as teaching R. OWEN. 2. **e.** *Haml.* V. ii. 35. 3. Oxenford.. a norishe of l., and a famous universitie 1559. What we want is not l., but knowledge LOWELL. *The new l.*: the studies, esp. that of Greek, introduced into England in the 16th c.; also applied to the doctrines of the Reformation 1530.

Leary: see LEERY *a.*

Leasable (lī·săb'l), *a.* 1611. [f. LEASE *v.* + -ABLE.] That may be leased.

Lease, *sb.*[1], **leaze** (līz). Now *dial.* [OE. *lǣs* str. fem. :—OTeut. type **lǣswā*. Occas. confused with the pl. of LEA *sb.*[1] Orig. meaning prob. land 'let alone', not tilled.] Pasture; pasturage; meadow-land; common.

Lease *sb.*[2]: see LEASE *a.*

Lease (līs), *sb.*[3] 1450. [a. AF. *les* = OF. *lais, leis, lez*, etc., a letting, leaving, vbl. noun f. *laisser* to let, leave.] **1.** A contract between parties, by which the one conveys lands or tenements to the other for life, for a term of years, or at will, usually in consideration of rent or other periodical compensation. **b.** The instrument by which the conveyance is made. **c.** The period of time for which the contract is made. **2.** *fig.*; esp. in phr. *a* (*new*) *l. of life* 1586. **3.** *Austral.* 'A piece of land leased for mining purposes' (Morris) 1890.

1. He got possession, on easy leases, of the revenues of Bath, Worcester and Hereford HUME. **b.** The l. ..had been lent..to the plaintiff..for perusal 1893. 2. Our high plac'd Macbeth Shall liue the L. of Nature *Macb.* IV. i. 99.

Lease (līs), *sb.*[4] ME. [app. a var. of LEASH *sb.*] †**1.** A certain quantity of thread –1457. **2.** The crossing of the warp-threads in a loom; the place at which they cross 1839. **3.** = LEASH *sb.* 6 a. 1824.

†**Lease,** *a.* and *sb.*[2] [Com. Teut.: OE. *lēas* :—OTeut. **lauso-*, f. **laus-*, an extension of the Indo-Eur. root **leu-* (Gr. λύειν to loosen).] **A.** *adj.* Untrue, false, lying –1450.

An Autbour..That halt not dremes false ne lees CHAUCER.

B. *sb.* Untruth, falsehood, lying.

Thus seyt the bok withoutyn ony les CHAUCER.

Lease (līz), *v.*[1] Now *dial.* [Com. Teut. str. vb.: OE. *lesan* to gather, glean.] **1.** *trans.* and *intr.* To glean. (In OE. used in wider sense: To gather, collect.) **2.** To pick ME.

†**Lease,** *v.*[2] [OE. *lēasian*, f. *lēas* LEASE *a.*] *intr.* To tell lies –1594.

Lease (līs), *v.*[3] 1570. [ad. AF. *lesser*, spec. use of OF. *lesser, laissier* (mod.F. *laisser*) to let, let go :—L. *laxare*, f. *laxus* loose, LAX *a.*] **1.** *trans.* To grant the possession or use of (lands, etc.) by a lease; to let *out* on lease. Also *transf.* and *fig.* **2.** To take a lease of; to hold by a lease 1877.

1. This land..Is now Leas'd out SHAKS. 2. Angling ..is hardly to be obtained unless by leasing a rod 1898.

Leasehold (lī·shōuld). 1720. [f. LEASE *sb.*[3] after *freehold.*] A tenure by lease; real estate so held. **b.** *attrib.* or *adj.* Held by lease 1731. Hence **Lea·seholder,** one who possesses l. property.

†**Lease-parole.** 1592. [f. LEASE *sb.*[3] + PAROLE.] A lease by word of mouth, not in writing –1672.

Leaser[1] (lī·zəɹ). Now *dial.* ME. [f. LEASE *v.*[1] + -ER[1].] A gleaner.

†**Lea·ser**[2]. *rare.* [OE. *lēasere*; see LEASE *v.*[2] and -ER[1].] A liar –1641.

Leaser[3] (lī·səɹ). 1607. [f. LEASE *v.*[3] + -ER[1].] One who leases; a leaseholder.

Leash (līʃ), *sb.* ME. [a. OF. *lesse, laisse* (mod.F. *laisse*)? :—L. *laxa* fem. of *laxus* LAX *a.*] **1.** The thong in which hounds or coursing-dogs are held. **2.** A set of three hounds, hawks, hares, etc.; hence *gen.* (*a leash of* = three) ME. **3.** *Hawking.* The thong or string which is passed through the varvels of the jesses to secure the hawk 1497. **4.** *fig.*; esp. in phr. *To hold* or *have in l.*, to have control over, keep in bondage ME. †**5.** A snare, noose –1814. **6.** *Weaving.* **a.** One of the cords (having an eye in the middle to receive the warp-thread) which extend between the parallel laths of the heddle of a loom. Also *leish.* 1731. **b.** = LEASE *sb.*[4] 2. 1888.

1. The hounds, hunted on the l. 1888. Phr. *The l.*: †(*a*) the department concerned with the keeping of the king's hounds; (*b*) the art or practice of coursing. 2. I contrived to bag a l. of trout 1882. 3. Terms of art, Diet and seeling, jesses, l. and lure TENNYSON. 4. For God hathe them in lease. Yea..they are his slaues BECON.

Leash (līʃ), *v.* 1503. [f. prec.] **1.** *trans.* To attach or connect by a leash 1599. **b.** *fig.* To link *together*, esp. in threes 1854. **2.** †To lash with a leash; to whip (*dial.*) 1503.

1. And, at his heeles, (Leasht in, like Hounds), should Famine, Sword, and Fire, Crouch for employment *Hen. V*, Prol. 7.

Leasing (lī·ziŋ), *sb.* *Obs.* or *arch.* exc. *dial.* (*Sc.* and *n.*) [OE. *lēasung*, f. *lēasian*; see LEASE *v.*[2] and -ING[1].] Lying, falsehood; a lie.

Comb.: **l.-maker**, a liar; *spec.* in *Sc. Law* (now *Hist.*), one who utters untrue and slanderous statements such as may prejudice the relations between the king and his subjects; so **l.-making**, verbal sedition.

Leasow (lī·so, le·zə), *sb.* Now *dial.* (*Sc. lizzure*, etc.) OE. [See LEASE *sb.*[1]] Pasture; pasturage; meadow-land.

Lea·sow, *v.* *Obs.* or *dial.* [OE. *lǣswian* (also *lǣsian*), f. *lǣsw-*, *lǣs* LEASOW *sb.*, LEASE *sb.*[1]] *trans.* and *intr.* To pasture, graze.

Least (līst), *a.* (*sb.*) and *adv.* [OE. *lǣst, lǣsest* :—prehist. **laisisto-*, superl. f. **laisiz-* LESS.] Used as the superl. of LITTLE. **A.** *adj.* **I.** In concord with *sb.* expressed or understood. **1.** Smallest; slightest; †fewest. Often coupled with *last.* **2.** Lowest in power or position; meanest. *arch.* OE.

1. Nor l. in Number, nor in Name the last DRYDEN. Phr. *The l.*: often used, esp. after negs., for 'Any, however small'. *L. common multiple*: see MULTIPLE. 2. Thou..art not the l. among the Princes of Iuda *Matt.* ii. 6.

II. Absol. uses (quasi-*sb.*). **1.** That which is least; the least quantity, amount, or †part *of* something ME. †**2.** as *sb.* A most minute quantity or part; a minimum –1813.

1. The very l. I can do is to apologize for the mistake (*mod.*). Phr. *To say the l.* (*of it*). *At l.*, *at the l.*: qualifying an expression of amount or number := '(so much or many) at any rate, if not more'; hence, characterizing a statement as certainly valid, even if a wider one be not allowable; = 'at any rate', 'at all events'. *In the l.* †(*a*) At the lowest estimate. (*b*) In the smallest or slightest degree. 2. There being in Nature no l. which cannot be divided STANLEY.

B. *adv.* In the least degree ME.

Mammon, the least erected Spirit that fell From heav'n MILT. Phr. *The l.*: in the least degree.

Least, obs. form of LEST.

Leastways (lī·stˌweⁱz), *adv.* ME. [See WAY.] †**a.** Orig. two wds. in the phr. *at* (*the*) *least way*(*s* = 'at least'. **b.** As one word, in the same sense. *dial.* and *vulgar.*

Leastwise (lī·stˌwəiz), *adv.* 1534. [See WISE *sb.*, -WISE, and cf. prec.] †**a.** As two wds. in certain phrases: *at* (*the*) *least wise* = 'at least'; *in the least wise* = 'in the least'. **b.** As one word = 'at least'. Now *dial.* or *vulgar.*

Leat (līt). Chiefly *s.w. dial.* 1642. [OE. (*wæter-*)*gelǣt*(*e* water-conduit, f. *ge-* prefix (see Y-) + root of *lǣtan* LET *v.*[1]] An open water-course to conduct water for mills, mining works, etc.

Leather (le·ðəɹ), *sb.* [OE. *leðer* (only in compounds) :—OTeut. **leþrom* neut. :—pre-Teut. **letrom*, whence Irish *leathar*, Welsh *lledr*, Breton *ler* (earlier *lezr*).] **1.** Skin prepared for use by tanning, etc. ME. **b.** *pl.* Kinds of leather 1853. **2.** Something made of leather, e.g. a strap, a thong; a piece of leather for a plaster or to tighten a tap; the leathern portion of a bellows, or of a pump-sucker ME. **b.** *pl.* Articles for wear made of leather, e.g. shoes, slippers, leggings, breeches 1837. **c.** *Cricket* and *Football.* The ball 1868. **3.** Skin. Now only *slang.* ME. **4.** *attrib.* or *adj.* Consisting or made of leather, or of a material resembling it OE.

1. *American l.*, a kind of oil-cloth; *patent l.*, l. having a fine black varnished surface. *Morocco, russia, Spanish, Turkey l.*: see those wds. Phr. *L. and prunella*: indifferent stuff. (A misinterpretation of Pope, *Essay on Man* iv. 204.) *Prov. phr.* A Currier, being present, said..If you have a Mind to have the Town well fortified and secure, take my Word, there is Nothing like L. 1767. 2. *Upper l.*: see UPPER. 3. Phr. *To lose l.*: to suffer abrasion of the skin. 4. Where is thy L. Apron, and thy Rule? *Jul. C.* I. i. 7.

Comb.: **l.-back**, a large soft-shelled turtle, *Sphargis coriacea*; **-bark**, a tree of the genus *Thymelæa*; **-board**, a composition of leather scraps, paper, etc., glued together and rolled into sheets, used in shoe-making; **-carp**, a scaleless variety of the carp; **-coat**, a name for a russet apple, from the roughness of its skin; **-flower**, a N. American climbing plant (*Clematis Viorna*) with thick leathery purplish sepals; **-head**, (*a*) *slang*, a blockhead; (*b*) *Austral.*, the friar-bird; **-leaf**, a low evergreen shrub of the northern U.S. (*Cassandra calyculata*), with coriaceous leaves; **-mouthed**, hard-mouthed, as fishes, horses, etc.; **-neck**, a sailor's name for a soldier, from the l. stock he used to wear; **-plant**, a composite plant of the genus *Celmisia*, a native of New Zealand; **-turtle** = *leather-back*; **-wing**, a bat; **-wood**, (*a*) a N. American shrub of the genus *Dirca*, with a very tough bark; (*b*) a Tasmanian tree with wood of a pale reddish mahogany colour, *Eucryphia billardieri* (Morris).

Leather (le·ðəɹ), *v.* ME. [f. LEATHER *sb.*] **1.** *trans.* To cover or arm with leather. **2.** To beat with a leathern thong; hence *gen.* to beat, thrash 1625. **b.** *fig. intr.* To work hard; with *away*, *on* 1869.

2. I'd like to l. 'im black and blue TENNYSON.

Leatherette (leðəre·t). 1880. [f. LEATHER *sb.* + -ETTE.] A fabric made of paper and cloth, in imitation of leather.

Lea·ther-ja·cket. 1770. [f. LEATHER *sb.* + JACKET.] **1.** Any of various fishes having a thick skin; e.g. *Balistes capriscus*, *Oligoplites saurus*, and species of *Monacanthus.* **2.** *Austral.* A kind of pancake 1846. **3.** *Austral.* Any of various trees having a tough bark; e.g. *Eucalyptus punctata* 1874. **4.** The grub of the crane-fly 1881.

Leathern (le·ðəɹn), *a.* [OE. *leðeren*, f. *leðer* LEATHER *sb.* + -EN[4]; cf. Du. *lederen*, G. *ledern.*] **1.** Consisting or made of leather. **b.** Used of the skin of living animals ME. **2.** Leather-like. Said esp. of the bat's wings, hence of its flight, and of the bat itself. 1513.

1. *L. convenience, -ency*: a Quakers' term for a coach; hence used joc. At the duly appointed hour, creaked forth the l. convenience SCOTT. **b.** *A. Y. L.* II. i. 37. 2. The weak-eyed bat..flits by on l. wing COLLINS.

Leatheroid (le·ðəroid). 1882. [f. LEATHER *sb.* + -OID.] Cotton paper chemically treated so as to resemble raw-hide.

Leathery (le·ðəri), *a.* 1552. [f. LEATHER *sb.* + -Y[1].] Resembling leather in appearance or texture; in botanical use = CORIACEOUS.

L. leaves of Conifers BOWER & SCOTT.

Leave (līv), *sb.* [OE. *lēaf*, str. fem. :—OTeut. type **laubā*, whence **laubjan* LEVE *v.*[1] Orig. sense prob. 'pleasure, approval'; the root is that of LOVE, LIEF, BELIEVE.] **1.** Permission *to do* something. †**2.** Leave-taking; in phr. *audience of l.* –1734. **3.** [f. LEAVE *v.*[1]] *Billiards.* The position in which the balls are left for the following play 1901.

1. Phr. *To ask, beg, get, give, grant, have, obtain l.*; *by, with, without* (*the*) *l.* (*of*). *By your l.*: an apology for taking a liberty; often *ironical*, to introduce an unwelcome remark. †*To give l.* (*fig.* of conditions or circumstances): to allow, permit. *L. of absence*, or simply *l.*, permission to be absent from a post of duty. (See also *sick-leave.*) *On l.*: absent from duty by permission. Hence, the period of such absence. *To take* (*one's*) *l.*: orig. †to obtain permission to depart (*rare*); hence, to bid farewell. (See also FRENCH LEAVE.)

Leave (līv), *v.*[1] [OE. *lǣfan* trans. and intr. :—OTeut. **laibjan*, f. **laibā* remainder, relic (see LAVE *sb.*). The OTeut. **laibjan* is the causative of **līban* str. vb., represented by the compounds OE. *belīfan* (see BELIVE *v.*), OHG. *belīban* (mod.G. *bleiben*) to remain, etc.]

I. To have a remainder; to cause or allow to remain. **1.** *trans.* Of a deceased person: To have remaining after one (a widow, property, etc.). **b.** Of things or conditions: To have remaining as a trace, etc. after removal or cessation 1756. **2.** To transmit at one's death *to* heirs or successors. Hence, to bequeath or devise. OE. **b.** In passive: *To be* (*well*, etc.) *left*: to be well provided for by legacy, etc. 1606. **3.** To allow to remain in a certain place or condition; to abstain from taking or dealing with. *To be left*: to remain. OE. †**b.** *absol.*; also with *over* –1642. **c.** To have as a remainder (in subtraction); to yield as a remainder when deducted from some larger amount. ME. **4.** †**a.** To neglect or omit to perform (some action, etc.); also to omit *to do* something –1624. **b.** To allow (an action, etc.) to stand over 1559. **5.** To commit, refer to another person or agent instead of oneself. Const. *to* or *dat.*; also *with.* ME. **b.** To allow (a person or thing) *to do* something, *to be* done or dealt with, without interference. 1456. **c.** *To l.* (*something*, etc.) *to be desired*: to be (more or less) unsatisfactory. **6.** To deposit or give in charge (some object) or station (a person) to remain after one's departure; to give (instructions, orders, information, e.g. one's name or address) for use during one's absence. Phr. *To l. a card on* (a person). ME.

1. In case he should..l. no lawful heir CRUISE. 2. Poore cosin Brooks hath left me 10 *l.* 1676. 3. For, what place is left now for honestie? where lodgeth goodnes? FLEMING. Persons who..have..very little liver left BUDD. *To l. undone, unsaid*, etc. = to abstain from doing, saying, etc. To l. the argument without proofs, is to l. it without effect PALEY. **c.** Three from eleven leaves eight (*mod.*). 4. **b.** Hee leaues repentance for gray hayres EARLE. 5. I..leave such theories to those that study Meteors SIR T. HERBERT. **b.** He left him to shift for himself COBBETT. 6. He left word that he would soon be home DICKENS.

II. To depart from, quit, relinquish. **1.** To quit (a place, person, or thing); to deviate from (a line of road, etc.) ME. **b.** *colloq.* (orig. *U.S.*) *To get* (or *be*) *left*: to be left in the lurch 1891. **2.** To go away from permanently; to cease to reside at (a place), to belong to (a society, etc.); to quit the service of (a person) ME. **3.** To abandon, forsake (a habit, etc.); to lay aside (a dress). Now *rare* exc. in *l. off.* ME. **4.** To cease, desist from, stop. Now only *arch.* = *l. off.* ME. †**b.** *intr.* –1633. †**5.** To cease speaking of –1604. †**b.** *intr.* To stop, break off in a narrative –1614.

1. We..steered.., leaving those isles on the east DE FOE. Pray, sir, l. the room BYRON. They left him dead 1883. *absol.* (*colloq.*) We left about eleven 1867. 3. The confession of a faulte is a profession to leaue the same BP. WATSON.

†**III.** *intr.* To remain; to remain *behind*, *over*; to continue or stay in one place –1541.

Phrases. *To l...alone*: = 'to let alone' (see ALONE I and LET *v.*[1]). *To l. go* (*of*) 1810, *to l. hold* (*of*), *to l. loose* (*of*) colloq.: to cease holding, to let go.

Combined with *advs.* **Leave behind.** †(*a*) To leave undone. (*b*) To go away without. (*c*) To have remaining after departure or removal, as a trace or consequence. **Leave off.** (*a*) *trans.* To cease from (an action, a habit). Also, to cease to wear or use (something). †(*b*) To give up; to forsake the society of. (*c*) *absol.* and *intr.* To cease doing; to make an end or interruption; to stop. Of a narrative: To end. Also *Comm.* of shares, etc.: To end (*at* a certain price) on the closing of the market. **Leave out.** To omit, not to insert or include. **Leave over.** To let 'stand over' for future consideration. *To l. it at that*: to proceed no farther with a matter 1902.

Leave (līv), *v.*[2] [ME. *lēve*, f. *lēf* LEAF *sb.*] *intr.* = LEAF *v.* 1.

†**Leave**, *v.*[3] [ad. F. *lever*: see LEVY.] *trans.* To raise (an army). SPENSER *F. Q.* II. x. 31.

Leaved (līvd), *a.* ME. [f. LEAF *sb.* or LEAVE *v.*[2] + -ED.] **1.** Having leaves; 'in leaf'. *lit.* and *fig.* Also *Her.* **b.** Having leaves (of a specified number or kind) ME. **2.**

Resembling a (plant-) leaf 1841. †3. Laminate -1658. 4. Of a door: Having (two) leaves 1610. 5. Furnished with leaves (of paper) 1629.

1. A foursquare stem..leaued like vnto an Oke HOLLAND. b. Thick-leaved platans TENNYSON. 2. L. forms 1865.

†Lea·veless, *a.* 1581. [var. of LEAFLESS.] Without leaves -1638.

Leaven (le·v'n), *sb.* ME. [a. F. *levain* = Prov. *levam* :—L. *levamen* means of raising, f. *levare* to raise.] 1. A substance which is added to dough to produce fermentation; *spec.* fermenting dough reserved from a previous batch. b. In wider sense; = FERMENT *sb.* 1. 1658. 2. *fig.* a. An agency which transforms by progressive inward operation (cf. Matt. xiii. 33, etc.) ME. b. Used for: A tempering or modifying element 1576.

1. b. The l. of typhus 1822. 2. a. There is a very sour l. of malevolence in many English and in many American minds against each other J. ADAMS. b. Pleasure with pain for l. SWINBURNE.

Phrases. *Of the same l.*: of the same sort or character. *The old l.*: after 1 *Cor.* v. 6, 7, the traces of the unregenerate condition.

Leaven (le·v'n), *v.* ME. [f. LEAVEN *sb.*] 1. *trans.* To cause (dough) to ferment by means of leaven. 2. *fig.* To permeate with a transforming influence; to imbue *with* some modifying element; †*rarely*, to corrupt by admixture 1550.

1. Know ye not that a little leauen leaueneth the whole lumpe? 1 *Cor* v 6. 2. The indolent, evil thought would still insinuate itself until it leavened their entire character 1862.

Leavenous (le·v'nəs), *a.* 1649. [f. LEAVEN *sb.* + -OUS.] Having the properties of leaven.

Leaver (lī·vəɹ). 1548. [f. LEAVE *v.*[1] + -ER[1].] One who leaves (see LEAVE *v.*[1]). *Ant. & Cl.* IV. ix. 22.

Leave-taking (lī·vtēˈkiŋ), *vbl. sb.* ME. [f. LEAVE *sb.*] The taking leave of a person; saying farewell; †parting speech. So **Lea·ve-ta:ker** KIPLING.

Leaving (lī·viŋ), *vbl. sb.* ME. [f. LEAVE *v.*[1] + -ING[1].] 1. The action of LEAVE *v.*[1] Also in Comb., as *leaving-off*. 2. *concr.* †a. *sing.* What is left; remainder -1596. b. *pl.* in same sense. (Cf. L. *reliquiæ*.) ME. 3. *attrib.* 1865.

2. b. The poorer sort..carried the leavings or fragments home HORNECK. 3. *L. certificate, examination, exhibition*, in connexion with leaving school or college. **L.-book** (at Eton), a book presented by friends on the occasion of one's 'leaving'. **L.-shop** (*slang*), an unlicensed pawnshop.

Leavy (lī·vi), *a.* ME. [More normal f. LEAFY.] 1. Having leaves. *Obs.* exc. *poet.* b. Consisting of or made of leaves (natural or ornamental) 1610. †2. Of a gate: Having leaves. CHAPMAN. Hence †**Lea·viness.**

‖**Leban** (le·băn). Also **lebban, leben.** 1698. [Arab. *laban*, f. root meaning 'to be white'.] Coagulated sour milk, used as a drink among the Arabs.

Lecanomancy (le·kănomænsi). 1610. [ad. Gr. λεκανομαντεία, f. λεκάνη dish, pan, pot + μαντεία divination.] Divination by the inspection of water in a basin.

Lecanoric (lekănǫ·rik), *a.* 1852. [f. *Lecanora*, name of a genus of lichens.] *Chem.* In *l. acid*: a crystalline substance obtained by Schunck from certain lichens of the genus *Lecanora*. So **Lecanorate** (-ō·rĕt), a salt of l. acid; **Lecano·rin** = *lecanoric acid* 1844.

Lech (lek). 1768. [ad. W. *llech* (flat) stone. Cf. CROMLECH.] A Celtic monumental stone.

Leche (lī·tʃī). 1857. [Sechuana.] A S. African water-buck, *Kobus leche*.

Lecher (le·tʃəɹ), *sb. arch.* ME. [a. OF. *lecheor, -eur, -ur*, etc., f. *lechier* to live in debauchery or gluttony, mod.F. *lécher* to lick :—OTeut. **likkōjan* to LICK.] A lewd or grossly unchaste man, a debauchee. Hence †**Le·cher** *a.* lecherous; also, base, vile. †**Le·cher** *v. intr.* to play the l. †**Le·cherer,** a l. [AF. *lecheryer*].

Lecherous (le·tʃərəs), *a. arch.* ME. [a. OF. *lecheros*, etc., f. *lecheur* LECHER *sb.*; see -OUS.] 1. Addicted to lechery; consisting in, characterized by, or inciting to lechery. †2. = LICKEROUS -1535.

1. A leccherous thing win WYCLIF *Prov.* xx. 1. Hence **Le·cherous-ly** *adv.*, **-ness.**

Lechery (le·tʃəri). ME. [a. OF. *lecherie, licherie*, f. *lecheur* LECHER *sb.*] Habitual indulgence of lust; lewdness of living. Also *fig.* †b. *transf.* Inordinate pleasure. MASSINGER.

Lecithin (le·siþin). Also **-ine.** 1861. [f. Gr. λέκιθος yolk of egg + -IN.] *Chem.* A nitrogenous fatty substance found in the nerve tissues, the yolk of eggs, blood, and other fluids of the body.

Lectern (le·ktəɹn). Also †**lettern, lecturn,** etc. [ME. *lettrun*, etc., a. OF. *lettrun, leitrun*, semi-pop. f. late L. *lectrum*, f. *leg-*, root of *legere* to read; cf. *mulctrum* milking-pail, f. *mulgere* to milk.] A reading- or singing-desk in a church, esp. that from which the lessons are read; often in the form of an eagle with outspread wings supported on a column.

Lection (le·kʃən). ME. [a. OF. *lectiun*, ad. L. *lectionem*, f. *lect-*, *legere* to read, to choose.] †I. = ELECTION. ME. -1535.

II. †1. The act of reading (*rare*); a particular way of reading or interpreting a passage -1702. b. *concr.* A reading of a text found in a particular copy or edition 1649. 2. *Eccl.* A 'lesson' 1608.

Lectionary (le·kʃənări). 1491. [ad. eccl. L. *lectionarium* (also used), f. L. *lectionem*; see prec. and -ARY.] A book containing (the list of) 'lessons' or portions of Scripture appointed to be read at divine service.

‖**Lectisternium** (lektistō·miŏm). 1597. [L., f. *lecti-*, *lectus* couch, bed + *sternere* to spread.] *Rom. Antiq.* A sacrifice of the nature of a feast, in which images of the gods were placed on couches with food before them.

Lector (le·ktǫɹ). 1483. [a. L.] 1. *Eccl.* An ecclesiastic belonging to one of the minor orders, who read the lessons. 2. A reader; *spec.* a reader or lecturer in a college or university (now chiefly *Hist.* and with reference to foreign use) 1563.

†**Le·ctuary.** ME. [Aphet. f. ELECTUARY.] An electuary -1578.

Lecture (le·ktiŭɹ, -tʃəɹ), *sb.* ME. [ad. L. *lectura*; see -URE.] †1. The action of reading. Also *fig.* Also, that which is read. -1835. †2. The way in which a text reads; a lection -1680. 3. The action of reading aloud. Also, a lection or lesson. *arch.* 1526. 4. A discourse before an audience or class (e.g. in a university) upon a given subject, usu. for the purpose of instruction 1536. b. A discourse of the nature of a sermon, delivered on an occasion outside the regular order of services 1556. c. A lecture or course or series of lectures, given at stated periods; a foundation for a lecturer, a lectureship 1615. †5. A lesson given by a teacher to a pupil -1765. †Also *fig.* 6. An admonition, esp. by way of reproof. Phr. *To read* (a person) *a l.* 1600.

4. The Common Law School, where the Vinerian Professor reads his Lectures 1827. c. The L. founded by the late rev. and pious John Bampton M.A. 1780. 6. Our young bridegroom receiv'd a terrible l. 1732.

Le·cture, *v.* 1590. [f. LECTURE *sb.*] 1. *intr.* To deliver a lecture or lectures. 2. *trans.* To deliver lectures to or before (an audience) 1681. 3. To admonish, rebuke, reprimand 1706.

Le·cturer. 1570. [f. LECTURE *v.* + -ER[1].] †1. = LECTOR 1. -1797. 2. An assistant preacher in the Church of England, who delivers afternoon or evening lectures 1583. 3. One who gives a lecture or lectures; *spec.* one appointed to deliver a course of lectures in a university or college, esp. as subordinate to a professor 1615. Hence **Le·cturership 1891.**

Le·ctureship. 1634. [f. LECTURE *sb.* (sense 4 c) + -SHIP; commonly used in place of the more regular *lecturership*.] The office of a lecturer.

Lecturn: see LECTERN.

Lecyth (le·siþ). 1846. [ad. mod.L. *Lecythis* (see below).] *Bot.* A plant of the order *Lecythidaceæ* (typical genus *Lecythis*). So **Le·cythid** *a.* 1871.

‖**Lecythus** (le·siþŏs). *Pl.* **lecythi** (-þəi). 1857. [ad. Gr. λήκυθος.] *Gr. Antiq.* A vase or flask with a narrow neck. Hence **Le·cythoid** *a.*, resembling a l.

Led (led), *ppl. a.* 1553. [Pa. pple. of LEAD *v.*[1]] In various uses (see the vb.).

Phrases. *Led horse*, a spare horse, led by an attendant or groom; also a sumpter-horse. *L.-captain*, a hanger-on, dependant, parasite.

†**Lede.** *Obs.* [OE. *léod, léode, -a.* Cf. G. *leute.*] A people, nation; persons collectively; (one's own) people; a man -1650.

Le·den. *Obs.* exc. *dial.* [OE. *lǣden*, repr. a Celtic or early Rom. pronunc. of L. *Latinum* Latin, confused with *léden* language, f. *léode* people.] †1. Latin. Only OE. †2. The language of a nation, etc.; a 'tongue' -ME. †b. Form of speech; way of speaking -1596. †c. *poet.* Applied to the 'language' of birds -1612.

Ledge (ledʒ), *sb.* [? ME. formation from *legge* (ledʒə), LAY *v.*] 1. A transverse bar or strip of wood, etc. fixed upon a door, gate, piece of furniture or the like. Now *dial.* and *techn.* b. *Naut.* A name for the small pieces of timber placed athwartships, under the decks of a ship, in the intervals between the beams ME. c. *Arch.* A small moulding; a string-course 1828. †2. A raised edging running along the extremity of a board or the like -1802. 3. A narrow horizontal surface, formed by the top of some projection in the vertical face of a wall, etc. 1558. b. A shelf-like projection on the side of a rock or mountain 1732. c. *Fortif.* = BERM 1729. 4. A ridge of rocks, esp. such as are near the shore beneath the surface of the sea; †a range of hills; a ridge of earth 1555. 5. †A course or layer (WOTTON); *Mining*, a stratum of metal-bearing rock; a quartz-vein 1847. 6. *attrib.* **l.-door** = *ledged door* 1825.

3. b. We clung to the crannies and ledges of the rock L. STEPHEN. 4. Three of the ships on invisible ledges the South winds drave BOWEN. Hence **Ledged** *ppl. a.* having or furnished with a l. or ledges; as, *ledged door*, one in which vertical boards are held together by three horizontal ledges.

Ledge, *v.*[1] *Obs.* exc. *dial.* Also †**lage,** etc. Aphet. f. *alegge, aledge* ALLEGE *v.*[2]

Nay 'tis no matter sir, what he leges in Latine SHAKS.

Ledge, *v.*[2] *rare.* 1598. [f. LEDGE *sb.*] 1. *intr.* To form a ledge. 2. *trans.* To furnish with a ledge; to form as a ledge 1599.

Ledgement, ledgment (le·dʒmĕnt). *Arch.* ME. [App. f. LEDGE *sb.* + -MENT.] 1. A string-course or horizontal suit of mouldings, such as the base-mouldings, etc., of a building. 2. The development of a surface, or the surface of a body stretched out on a plane, so that the dimensions of the different sides may be easily ascertained 1842.

Ledger (le·dʒəɹ). Also †**lidger, lieger,** leiger, etc. 1401. [perh. formed on Eng. *liggen, leggen*, dial. forms of LIE *v.*[1], LAY *v.* + -ER[1], after Du. *ligger, legger.*]

A. *sb.* 1. A book that lies permanently in some place; e.g. †a bible 1538; †a large copy of the breviary -1691; a register (now *U.S.*). b. *Comm.* The principal book of the set of books employed for recording mercantile transactions, in which all debtor-and-creditor accounts are set down 1588. 2. A horizontal timber in a scaffolding, lying parallel to the face of the building and supporting the putlogs. (Cf. *ligger.*) 1571. 3. A flat stone covering a grave 1510. 4. The nether millstone. Now *dial.* 1530. 5. *Angling.* Short for *ledger-bait* (see below). 1653. 6. A resident ambassador; also, a papal nuncio. *Obs.* exc. *Hist.* in form *lieger.* 1548. 7. *transf.* and *fig.* a. A (permanent) representative; a commissioner; an agent. *Obs.* or *arch.* in form *lieger.* 1603. †b. A resident in a place -1661.

6. A Nuncio differed from a Legate, almost as a Lieger from an extraordinary Ambassadour FULLER. 7. b. Hee's a lieger at Horne's ordinarie yonder B. JONS.

Comb.: **l.-bait,** a fishing bait which is made to remain in one place (also *attrib.*) WALTON; so *l.-hook, -line, -tackle*; **-blade,** in a cloth-shearing machine, the stationary straight-edged blade acting with a spiral revolving blade, and used to trim the nap and make it uniform; **-millstone** = sense 4; **-stone** = sense 3; **-wall** = *foot-wall* (FOOT *sb.* Combs. 2).

B. *adj.* **I.** In *attrib.* use. †1. *L.-ambassador*

or *ambassador l.*: resident ambassador 1550. †2. Resident in a place; permanent; stationary. Also *fig. L. side*: the side on which something lies. -1662. 3. *Mus.* **Ledger line**, a short line added temporarily above or below the stave to extend its compass 1700.

2. *L.-jests*: standing, stock jests. Like a bruised Codling Apple a little corrupted on the Leiger side GAYTON.

II. In predicative use, esp. in *to be, lie l.* 1. Resident as ambassador, commissioner, or agent. *Obs.* exc. *arch.* 1560. †2. Lying or resting in a place; stationary; resident -1661.

1. One that lay lieger at London for their dispatches HACKET. 2. Shiloh, where the Ark was long leiger FULLER.

Le·dger, *v.* Also **leger**. 1688. [f. LEDGER *sb.* (sense 5).] *intr.* To use a ledger-bait.

Le·dger-book. Now *Hist.* 1553. A book containing records; a register; a cartulary; a book of accounts.

Ledget, -it (le·dʒėt). 1805. [f. LEDGE *sb.* + -ET.] A projecting piece.

Ledgy (le·dʒi), *a.* 1779. [f. LEDGE *sb.* + -Y[1].] Abounding in or consisting of ledges or ridges of rock.

Lee (lī), *sb.*[1] Also *dial.* **lew.** [OE. *hlēo* (gen. *hlēowes*) str. neut. or masc. :—OTeut. **hlewo-*, whence ON. *hlý* shelter, warmth, *hlýja* to protect.] 1. Protection, shelter, rarely *pl.* †Also, a resting-place. 2. Chiefly *Naut.* The sheltered side of any object; hence, the side away from the wind ME. †3. A sheltered position or condition; hence, calmness, peace, tranquillity ME. 4. *attrib.* a. Indicating that an object is on the lee-side of a vessel, or to leeward of some other object, e.g. *l.-bowline*, etc. 1513. b. Implying motion to leeward 1726.

1. Phr. *In, under (the) l. of.* Rob Roy's cave under the Lea of Ben Lomond 1847. 2. We run in as much under the l. of the point as we could DE FOE. Phr. †*At l.*: (*a*) windbound; (*b*) under shelter. †(*To bring, fall*) *by the l.*: to leeward; also *fig.* †(*To bring, lay, lie*) *upon the l.*: with sails aback. *On, under (the) l.*: to leeward = ALEE. 4. b. The.. leisurely weather-roll and l.-roll R. H. DANA.

Comb.: **l.-anchor**, the anchor on the leeward side; **-bow**, the bow of a vessel that is turned away from the wind; hence *lee-bow* vb., to run under the lee-bow of; **-gage** (see GAUGE *sb.* I. 5); **-latch**, 'dropping to leeward of the course' (Smyth); **-most** *a.*, farthest to leeward; **-port**, a sheltered port; **-wheel**, 'the assistant to the helmsman' (Smyth).

Lee (lī), *sb.*[2] *Obs.* exc. in *pl.* ME. [a. F. *lie*, Gaulish L. *lia*, pl. *liæ* (10th c.); ? of Celtic origin.] The sediment from wine and other liquids. †a. *sing.* Also *fig.* Also *upon the l., to drain to the l.* -1813. b. *pl.* ME. c. *fig.* Basest part, dregs, refuse 1593. d. *pl.* construed as *sing. Macb.* II. iii. 100.

c. In these Lees and Dregges of time 1621. Phr. *To drain, drink the lees, to the lees*, i.e. to the last drop; (*to settle*) *on* or *upon the lees.*

†**Lee**, *a.* Cf. LEW *a.* ME. [f. LEE *sb.*[1]] Sheltered from the wind -1674.

†**Lee·-board**[1]. ME. [a. ON. *hlé-borð*, f. *hlé* LEE *sb.*[1] + *borð* BOARD.] The lee side (of a vessel).

Lee-board[2] (lī·bōᵊɹd). 1691. [f. LEE *sb.*[1] + BOARD.] A strong frame of plank, fixed to the side of a flat-bottomed vessel, and let down into the water to diminish her drift to leeward.

Leech (lītʃ), *sb.*[1] [OE. *lǽce* str. masc. (once *lǽca* wk.) :—OTeut. **lǣkjo-z* :—pre-Teut. **lēgio-s*; cf. Ir. *liaigh.*] 1. A physician; one who practises healing. Now *arch.* (chiefly *poet.*) or *jocular*. Also *transf.* and *fig.* 2. *attrib.*, as **l.-fee**, a physician's fee.

1. A farrier and bullock-leach 1776. Grudging the l. his growing bill PRAED.

Leech (lītʃ), *sb.*[2] [OE. *lǽce*, Kentish *lýce* str. masc. = MDu. *lake, lieke, leke* fem.] One of the aquatic blood-sucking worms of the order *Hirudinea*; esp. one of the genus *Hirudo* or *Sanguisuga*, used medicinally for drawing blood. b. *Artificial l.*: an apparatus consisting of a scarifier and glass tube for drawing blood by suction 1858. c. *fig.* One who sticks to another to suck gain out of him 1784.

Phr. *To stick like a l.* c. The spendthrift, and the l. That sucks him COWPER.

Comb.: **l.-extract**, an extract prepared from leeches, used experimentally for intravenous or intraperitoneal injections; **-gaiter**, a kind of gaiter worn in Ceylon for protection against land-leeches; **-glass** *Surg.*, a glass tube to hold a l. which is to be applied to a particular spot.

Leech (lītʃ), *sb.*[3] 1336. [App. conn. w. ON. *lík*, Du. *lijk*, Ger. *liek*, leech-line.] *Naut.* The perpendicular or sloping side of a sail. Also qualified, as *mast-l.*, etc. b. *attrib.* in **l.-line**, a rope attached to the l., serving to truss the sail close up to the yard; **-rope**, a name for that part of the bolt-rope to which the border or skirt of a sail is sewed.

Leech (lītʃ), *v.*[1] *arch.*, now *rare.* [Early ME., f. LEECH *sb.*[1]] *trans.* To cure, heal.

Leech, *v.*[2] 1828. [f. LEECH *sb.*[2]] *trans.* To apply leeches to medicinally. Also *absol.*

Leechcraft (lī·tʃ,kraft). *arch.* [OE. *lǽce-cræft*: see LEECH *sb.*[1], CRAFT.] The art of healing; medical science. †Also *concr.* Remedy, medicine. So **Lee·chdom** *arch.* [OE. *lǽce-dōm*] remedy.

Lee·cher. *rare.* ME. [f. LEECH *v.*[1] + -ER[1].] One who leeches; a physician. So **Lee·chery** (*rare*), leechcraft.

Leef, obs. f. LIEF.

†**Lee·ful**, *a.* [ME. *leveful*, f. LEAVE *sb.* + -FUL.] Permissible, right, lawful; just -1814.

Leek (līk). [OE. *lēac* str. neut. :—OTeut. **lauko-*; only Teut.] 1. A culinary herb, *Allium Porrum*, allied to the onion, but having the bulbous part cylindrical and the leaves flat and broad. 2. Referring to the colour of the leek, to its being the national emblem of the Welsh, etc. ME. 3. *attrib.* ME.

1. The Leeke is hot and dry, and doth attenuate GERARDE. **Wild L.**, *Allium ursinum.* 2. Nowe cherrye redde, nowe pale and greene as leekes 1575. *To eat the* (or *one's*) *l.*: to pocket a deliberate affront. *Hen. V*, V. i. 10.

†**Leer**, *sb.*[1] [OE. *hlēor* neut., cheek = OS. *hleor, hlear, hlier*, ON. *hlýr* (only pl.).] 1. The cheek -1586. 2. The face, countenance; hence, look, hue, complexion -1806.

2. *Tit. A.* IV. ii. 119.

Leer (lîᵊɹ), *sb.*[2] 1598. [f. LEER *v.*] A side glance; a look or roll of the eye expressive of slyness, malignity, lasciviousness, etc.

Damn with faint praise, assent with civil l. POPE.

Leer, *sb.*[3] Also **lear, lier.** 1662. *Glass-making.* An annealing-furnace. Also *attrib.*, as **l.-pan** = FRACHE.

Leer (lîᵊɹ), *a.*[1] Also **lear.** [OE. **lǽre* (in *lǽrnes* emptiness) :—WGer. **lǣri*, of uncertain origin; cf. Ger. *leer*, Du. *laar.*] †1. Empty. Also, clear *of.* -1567. 2. Having no burden or load; (of a horse) without a rider. *Obs.* exc. *dial.* ME. 3. *dial.* Empty of food; hungry, faint for want of food 1848. Hence **Leerness**, emptiness.

2. Leir and sumpter horses 1688. A l. waggon 1787. 3. I'm rather lear at supper JEFFERIES.

†**Leer**, *a.*[2] 1629. [app. f. LEER *v.*] Looking askance; oblique; sly, underhand -1830.

Leer (lîᵊɹ), *v.* 1530. [Perh. f. LEER *sb.*[1], with sense 'to glance over one's cheek'.] 1. *intr.* To look obliquely or askance. Now only, to glance with a sly, immodest, or malign expression in one's eye. †2. To walk stealthily or with averted looks -1878. 3. *trans.* To give a leer with (the eye) 1835.

1. Here Fannia leering on her own good man POPE. 3. [A parrot] cocking his head, leering his eye, and working his black tongue D. JERROLD. Hence **Lee·ringly** *adv.*

Leery (lîᵊ·ri), *a.*[1] *Obs.* exc. *dial.* 1676. [f. LEER *a.*[1] + -Y[1].] = LEER *a.*[1] in various senses.

Leery (lîᵊ·ri), *a.*[2] *slang.* 1796. [? f. LEER *a.*[2] + -Y[1].] Wide-awake, knowing, 'fly'. Hence **Lee·rily** *adv.*

Lees, *pl.* (dregs): see LEE *sb.*[2]

†**Leese**, *v.* [Com. Teut. str. vb.: OE. *-lēosan*, only in compounds, f. root **leus-*: *laus-*: *los-*, whence also LEASING *sb.*, -LESS, LOOSE *a.* and *v.*, LOSE *v.*, LOSS.] 1. *trans.* = LOSE, in its various senses -1675. 2. *absol.* and *intr.* To lose, be a loser -1610. 3. *trans.* To destroy; to bring to ruin or perdition; to spoil. = L. *perdere* -1553. ¶4. Incorrectly used by Spenser in the str. pa. t. and pa. pple. (*lore, lorn*) with sense 'to forsake, desert, leave'.

1. Flowers Pressed or Beaten, do l. the Freshness and Sweetness of their Odour BACON. 4. SPENSER *F. Q.* I. iv. 2, III. i. 44. Hence †**Lee·ser**, a destroyer, a loser. †**Lee·sing** *vbl. sb.* losing, loss; *occas.* destruction, perdition.

Lee shore. 1579. [LEE *sb.*[1]] 1. A shore that the wind blows upon. †2. A shore that shelters from the wind -1711.

Lee side. Also *dial.* **lew side.** 1577. [LEE *sb.*[1]] That side which is turned away from the wind. Opp. to *weather side.*

Leet (līt), *sb.*[1] *Obs.* exc. *Hist.* [ME., ad. AF. *lete* or AL. *leta*, ? ad. OE. *lǽþ*; see LATHE[1].] 1. = COURT LEET. 2. The jurisdiction of a court leet; the district over which this jurisdiction extended 1477. 3. *attrib.* as *l.-jury*, etc. 1651.

Leet (līt), *sb.*[2] Now chiefly *Sc.* 1441. [app. aphet. f. ME. *elite* (a. OF. *eslite, eslete*), election.] 1. A list of persons designated as eligible for some office. 2. *pl.* The candidates forming a leet 1533. Hence **Leet** *v.* (*Sc.*), to place in a l.

1. Phr. *To be in l., to be on the leets, to put in l., to put on the l.*, etc.

†**Leet**, *sb.*[3] 1571. [repr. OE. (*wega*) *gelǽte* :—OTeut. type **galǣtjom*, f. **ga-* together, Y- + **lǣt-* (see LET *v.*[1]).] A meeting of ways; in *two-, three-, four-way l.* -1691.

Leet, obs. f. LET *v.*

Leetle (lī·t'l). 1687. A joc. hesitating or emphatic pronunciation of LITTLE.

Leeward (lī·wǫɹd, liū·ǝɹd), *a.* (*sb.*) and *adv.* 1549. A. *adj.* †1. Of a ship: That makes much leeway -1769. 2. *gen.* Situated, or having a direction, away from the wind. Opp. to *windward.* Const. *of.* Hence *occas.* Sheltered. 1666. 3. *absol.* or quasi-*sb.* = LEE *sb.*[1] 2. 1549.

2. *L. shore* = LEE SHORE. *L.-tide*: a tide running the way the wind is blowing. *L.-way* = *Lee-way.* 3. Phr. *On, upon, to (the) l. of.*

B. *adv.* Toward the lee (LEE *sb.*[1] 2) 1785.

Hence **Lee·wardly** *a.* (of a ship) apt to fall to l. Opp. to *weatherly.* **Lee·wardmost** *a.* situated furthest to l. †**Lee·wardness**, tendency to fall to l.

Lee·-way, lee·way. 1669. [f. LEE *sb.*[1] + WAY.] The lateral drift of a ship to leeward of her course; the amount of deviation thus produced. Also *fig.*

Phr. *To make, fetch up, make up l.* *Angle of l.*: the angle made by the direction of a ship's keel with that of its actual course. *fig.* We have a great deal of leeway to make up with the Australians 1884.

Left (left). [ME. *left, lift* :—OE. *left* (Kentish), *lyft*; primary sense 'weak, worthless', represented in E.Fris. *luf*, Du. dial. *loof.*] A. *adj.* 1. Distinctive epithet of the hand which is normally the weaker (see LEFT HAND), and of the other parts on the same side of the body (occas. of their clothing, as in *l. boot, glove*, etc.); hence also of what pertains to the corresponding side of anything else. Opp. to *right*. 2. That has the relative position of the left hand with respect to the right. In predicative use with const. *of*; in attrib. use now LEFT-HAND is usual. ME.

1. Who stooping op'nd my l. side, and took From thence a Rib MILT. *L. side*, †*half* (also LEFT HAND): The position or direction (relative to a person) to which the l. hand points. *Over the l. shoulder*, now *over the l.* simply, a slang phrase implying that the meaning is the reverse of what is said. 2. *L. wing* (of an army), *l. branch* (of a stream). *L. bank* (of a river): that to the l. of a person looking down the stream. That part of the shield which appears on the l. side is called the dexter CUSSANS. *L. side, l. wing* in politics, = LEFT *sb.* 1 c. *L. centre*: in the French Chamber, those deputies of the centre (CENTRE *sb.* II. 4) who incline to the opinions of the Left and occupy seats adjacent to them.

B. *adv.* On or towards the left side ME.

Squadrons—l. wheel! 1796.

C. *sb.* 1. a. = LEFT HAND ME. b. *Mil.* The left wing (of an army). Also in *pl.*, the men whose place is on the left. 1707. c. In continental legislatures, the section of the members sitting on the left side of the chamber (as viewed from the president's chair), by custom those holding relatively liberal or democratic opinions. Hence *transf.* the more advanced or innovating section of a philosophical school, a religious sect, a political party, etc. 1837. 2. A glove, etc., for the left hand, etc. 1864.

1. a. In her right a civic wreath, In her l. a human

head TENNYSON. Cannon to l. of them,..Volley'd and thunder'd TENNYSON. **b.** Their Centres and Lefts move up 1832.

Left (left), *ppl. a.* 1586. [pa. pple. of LEAVE *v.*¹] **1.** In senses of LEAVE *v.*¹ Now rare exc. in *l.-luggage* (*office*, etc.). **2.** With advs. or advb. phr. 1783.

2. He came to thank me for some left-off clothes COWPER.

Left hand. ME. See LEFT *a.* 1. Also *attrib.* (usu. *left-hand*).

Phrases. *On, to the left hand* (*of*): on the l. side (of), in the direction of the l. side; also *fig.* *To take the l. hand* (*of*): to place oneself on the l. side (of). *To marry with the l. hand*, to marry morganatically; hence *a wife of the l. hand*; (*a daughter*) *by the l. hand*, one born of such a marriage; *occas.* an illegitimate daughter.

Comb.: **left-hand blow**, one delivered with the l. hand; **left-hand man**, †(*a*) a left-handed man; (*b*) one placed at one's left; **left-hand marriage** = *marriage with the left hand* (see above); so *left-hand wife*, *queen*; **left-hand rope**, rope laid up and twisted 'against the sun'; †**left-hand tongue**, a language written from right to left, as Hebrew.

Left-handed, *a.* (Stress variable.) 1485. [-ED ².] **1.** Having the left hand more serviceable than the right; using the left hand by preference. **2.** *fig.* Awkward; clumsy, inapt 1613. **3.** Ambiguous, questionable. †In medical language: Spurious. 1612. **4.** Ill-omened, sinister. Of a deity: Unpropitious. (Cf. L. *lævus*.) ? *Obs.* 1609. **5.** Of a marriage: Morganatic (from the custom in Germany by which the bridegroom gave the bride his left hand in such marriages). Said also of the parties so married, and of their issue. Occas. applied also to fictitious or illegal marriages, or to unions without marriage, and to their offspring. 1642. **6.** Adapted to the left hand or arm, or for use by a left-handed person; (of a blow) delivered with the left hand 1629. **7.** Characterized by a direction or rotation to the left; producing such a rotation in the plane of a polarized ray. (Cf. LÆVO-.) 1812.

1. A left-handed bowler is nearly always a right-handed bat 1892. **2.** A good artist is left-handed to no profession FULLER. **3.** A very left-handed compliment 1881. **4.** The (Left-handed) stroaks of fortune 1650. **5.** The children of a left-handed alliance are not entitled to inherit H. WALPOLE. **6.** Hall met him with a left-handed facer 1814. **7.** Left-handed, or reversed varieties of spiral shells WOODWARD. Hence **Leftha·nded-ly** *adv.*, **-ness.**

Le·ft-ha·nder. 1861. [f. LEFT HAND + -ER ¹.] A left-handed person or blow.

Left-handiness. [f. *_left-handy_ adj. (= LEFT-HANDED 2) + -NESS.] Awkward manner. Cf. F. *gaucherie*. CHESTERF.

Le·ftmost, *a.* Also **leftermost.** 1863. [-MOST.] Situated furthest to the left.

Left-over. 1897. *adj.* and *sb.* (Something) left or remaining over; also, a survival (1911).

Leftward (le·ftwǒɹd), *adv.* and *a.* 1483. [f. LEFT *a.* + -WARD.] **1.** *adv.* On, or in the direction of, the left hand. **2.** *adj.* Situated on the left. Also *occas.*, Directed towards the left. 1813.

1. L. and behind us is the desert 1898. **2.** A l. bend 1886. So **Le·ftwards** *adv.* = LEFTWARD *adv.* 1844.

Leg (leg), *sb.* ME. [a. ON. *legg-r* leg, limb:—OTeut. type *_lagjo-z_. Some connect with root *_laq-_ of Gr. λακτίζειν to kick, L. *lacertus* arm.]

I. The limb. **1.** One of the organs of support and locomotion in an animal body; in narrower sense, the part of the limb between the knee and foot. Also *transf.* and *fig.* **2.** The leg cut from the carcass of an animal or bird for use as food 1533. **b. Leg-of-mutton** *adj. phr.*, resembling a leg of mutton, *esp.* in shape 1840. **3.** An obeisance made by drawing back one leg and bending the other; a bow, scrape. Now *arch.* or *joc.* 1589. **4.** Short for BLACK-LEG 2. 1815. **5.** *Cricket.* **a.** *L. before wicket*: the act of stopping with the leg a straight-pitched ball (a fault for which the batsman may be given 'out'). Also, simply, *l. before.* Abbrev. *l. b. w.* 1795. **b.** (Also *the l.*) (*a*) That part of the 'on' side of the field which lies behind, or about in a line with, the batsman. Chiefly in (a hit) *to* (*the*) *l.* 1843. (*b*) The side of the pitch on which the batsman stands 1843. **c.** Hence, the position of a fieldsman placed to stop balls hit 'to leg'; also, the fieldsman so placed 1816.

1. Vse your legs, take the start, run awaie SHAKS. *fig.* One l. by truth supported, one by lies, They sidle to the goal COWPER. Phrases. **a.** *All legs and wings*, said of an overgrown awkward young person; *Naut.* = overmasted. *On the l.*, (of a dog) long in the leg, leggy. *The boot is on the other l.* (see BOOT *sb.*³). *To pull* (or *draw* Sc.) *a person's l.*, to 'get at', befool him (colloq.). *To give a person a l. up*, to help him to climb up, mount (a horse, etc.), or get over an obstacle (*lit.* and *fig.*). *To have a bone in one's l.*: a feigned excuse to avoid the use of one's legs. *To lift* (or *heave up*) *the l.*: said of a dog voiding urine. **b.** *To change l.*, (of a horse) to change step. *To have the legs of*, to outrun. *To put* (or *set*) *one's best l. foremost*, to exert oneself to the utmost. *To shake a l.*, to dance. *To stretch one's legs*, to exercise them by walking. *To take to one's legs*, †*to take one's legs*, to run away. **c.** *On one's legs*: (*a*) standing, *esp.* to make a speech; so joc. *on one's hind legs*; (*b*) well enough to go about; (*c*) *fig.* in a prosperous condition, established, *esp.* in *to set* (a person) *upon his legs*; also *transf.* of things. *To fall on one's legs*: to get well out of a difficulty. *To get on one's hind legs*: *lit.* of a horse, hence *joc.* of a man, to go into a rage. *To stand upon one's own legs*: to be self-reliant. *Not a l. to stand on*: no support whatever. **d.** *On one's last legs*, near the end of one's life, or (*fig.*) resources; said also of things. **e.** *To dance* (*run*, *walk*, etc.) a person *off his legs*: to cause (him) to dance, etc. till he can do no more. **f.** Put for 'the power of using one's legs', as in *to feel*, *find one's legs*. *To keep one's legs*, to remain standing or walking. See also SEA LEGS. **2.** Then came up a l. of mutton DE FOE. **b. Leg-of-mutton sail,** a kind of triangular sail; so *leg-of-mutton rig*. **Leg-of-mutton sleeve,** one full and loose on the arm but close-fitting at the wrist. **3.** Phr. *To make a l.* **5. c.** *Long*, *short*, *square l.*, the fieldsman, or his position, far from or near to the wicket or about square with it.

II. Something more or less like a leg in shape or function. **1.** A representation of a leg; *esp.* in *Her.* 1500. **2.** An artificial leg ME. **3.** That part of a garment which covers the leg 1580. **4.** A bar, pole, etc. used as a support or prop; *esp.* in *Shipbuilding* and *Mining* 1430. **5.** One of the supports of a chair, table, stool, etc. 1680. **6.** One of the branches of a forked, jointed, or curved object 1683. **b.** One of the sides of a triangle, viewed as standing upon a base (so Gr. σκέλος); one of the two parts on each side of the vertex of a curve 1659. **7.** *Naut.* **a.** A name for various short ropes, which branch out into two or more parts 1627. **b.** A run made on a single tack. Chiefly in *long*, *short l.*, *a good l.* 1867.

5. Mr. Pickwick grated the legs of his chair against the ground DICKENS. **7. b.** Valkyrie..preferred a series of short legs off Wemyss Bay to weather the Skelmorlie 1895.

Comb.: **l.-bone**, the shin-bone, tibia; **-rest**, a contrivance for resting the l. of an invalid when seated; **-worm**, the GUINEA WORM (q.v.) which attacks the legs. **b.** in *Cricket*: **l. bail, stump**, that nearest the batsman; **l. ball, break**, a ball which pitches on or breaks from the l. side; **-bye** (see BYE 1 a); **l. hit, stroke**, a hit to l.; **-theory**, bowling to leg with fieldsmen massed on that side.

Leg (leg), *v.* 1601. [f. LEG *sb.*] **I.** *intr.* *To l. it*: To walk fast or run. †**2.** *To l. it*, to 'make a leg'. *To l. unto*, to bow to. *rare.* –1633. **3.** *trans.* To work (a boat) through a canal-tunnel by pressing with the feet against the top or sides of the tunnel; to navigate (a tunnel) thus; also *to l. through* 1836. **4.** To catch by, or hit on, the leg 1852. Hence **Le·gger** (in sense 3).

Legacy (le·găsi), *sb.* ME. [a. OF. *legacie* a legateship, ad. med.L. *legatia* (see -ACY) the district of a legate, f. *legatus* LEGATE *sb.*]

†**I. 1.** The function or office of a delegate or deputy –1583. **b.** *spec.* The function or office of a papal legate. *To send in l.*: to send as legate. –1726. **2.** The message or business committed to a delegate or deputy –1654. **3.** A body of persons sent on a mission, or as a deputation, to a sovereign, etc.; also, the act of sending such a body –1598.

II. †**1.** = BEQUEST 1. –1606. **2.** A sum of money, etc. bequeathed to another: = BEQUEST 2. †Formerly also in gen. sense, what one bequeaths. 1460. **b.** *transf.* and *fig.*; esp. = anything handed down by an ancestor or predecessor 1586. **3.** *attrib.*, as *l.-duty*, etc.

2. You have paid..his l., at the hazard of ruining the estate *Junius Lett.* **b.** Leaving great legacies of thought TENNYSON. **3. L.-hunter, -monger,** one who pays court to old and rich persons in hope of obtaining a l.; so *legacy-hunting*.

Hence †**Le·gacy** *v.* to give or leave as a l.; to bequeath a l. to.

Legal (lī·găl), *a.* 1500. [ad. L. *legalis* (? through F. *légal*), f. *leg-*, *lex* law. Cf. LEAL, LOYAL.] **1.** Of, pertaining to, or falling within the province of law 1529. **b.** Belonging to or characteristic of the profession of the law 1819. **c.** *nonce-uses.* Observant of law; devoted to law 1872. **2.** Such as is required or appointed by law 1610. **b.** Such as is recognized by 'law' as dist. from 'equity' 1818. **3.** Permitted, or not forbidden, by law; lawful 1647. **4.** *Theol.* **a.** Of, pertaining to, or based upon the Mosaic law. **b.** Of, pertaining to, or concerned with the law of works, i. e. salvation by works, not faith. 1500. **5.** quasi-*sb.* Something legal; a legal formality, etc.; *Sc. Law*, the legal period within which reversion is permitted 1526.

1. A l. artifice BOYLE. L. debt MILTON, advice 1898. Phr. *L. man* = Law Latin *legalis homo*, a man who has full l. rights. So *l. person*. **b.** A l. face BYRON, mind (*mod.*). **c.** Edward..lived in a l. age STUBBS. **2.** L. possession 1751, tribunals 1844. *L. tender*: coin or other money, which a creditor is bound by law to accept, when tendered in payment of a debt. (See *Act* 33 *Vict.* c. 10 § 4.) **3.** It is as l...for the king to pardon, as for the party to accuse CLARENDON. Hence **Le·gal-ly** *adv.*, **-ness** (*rare*).

Legalism (lī·găliz'm). 1838. [f. LEGAL + -ISM.] **1.** *Theol.* Adherence to the Law as opp. to the Gospel; the doctrine of justification by works, or teaching which savours of it. **2.** A disposition to exalt the importance of law or formulated rule 1878.

Legalist (lī·gălist). 1641. [f. LEGAL + -IST.] **1.** *Theol.* An adherent or advocate of legalism. **2.** A stickler for legality 1865. **3.** One who views things from a legal standpoint 1829. Hence **Legali·stic** *a.*

Legality (lĭgæ·lĭti). 1460. [ad. F. *légalité*, med.L. *legalitas*, f. L. *legalis* LEGAL.] **1.** Attachment to law or rule. **b.** *Theol.* Insistence on the letter of the law; reliance on works for salvation, rather than on free grace. Also personified. 1678. **c.** The spirit of the legal profession 1880. **2.** The quality of being legal; lawfulness. In early use, Legitimacy. 1533.

1. c. L. delights in the ingenious contrivance of delays W. CORY. **2.** To try the l. of the proceedings ..against him H. COX.

Legalize (lī·gălәiz), *v.* 1716. [f. LEGAL + -IZE.] *trans.* To make legal; to authorize, justify, sanction.

A period..when oppression was legalised HOOK. Hence **Legaliza·tion**, the action of legalizing.

Legantine (le·gæntin), *a.* 1533. [as if ad. L. *_legantinus_, f. *legant-*, pr. pple. of *legare*; see LEGATE and -INE.] Erron. synonym of LEGATINE.

Legatary (le·gătări). 1542. [ad. L. *legatarius*, f. *legatum* a bequest.] **A.** *adj.* Of or pertaining to, or of the nature of a bequest 1676. **B.** *sb.* One to whom a bequest is left; a legatee.

Legate (le·gĕt), *sb.* OE. [a. OF. *legat*, ad. L. *legatus*, pa. pple. of *legare* to send as a deputy, etc.] **1.** An ecclesiastic deputed to represent the Pope and armed with his authority. **b.** The ruler of a LEGATION (sense 5) 1653. **2.** *gen.* An ambassador, delegate, messenger ME. **3.** *Rom. Hist.* The deputy or lieutenant of a general, or of the governor of a province; under the empire, the governor himself. Also *transf.* 1474.

1. *L. a* (or †*de*) *latere* (†also, *of latere, of the side*): a l. of the highest class, one whose acts are virtually those of the Pope himself. **2.** There stands The l. of the skies COWPER. Hence **Le·gateship.**

Legate (lĭgē¹·t), *v.* 1546. [f. L. *legat-*, *legare*.] *trans.* To give by will, to bequeath. Hence **Legatee·**, one to whom a legacy has been bequeathed.

Legatine (le·gătin), *a.* 1450. [f. LEGATE *sb.* + -INE ¹.] Of, pertaining to, or having the authority of, a legate. (Earlier LEGANTINE and LEGATIVE.)

L. constitutions: ecclesiastical laws, enacted in national synods, held under legates from Pope Gregory IX and Pope Clement IV. *L. synod*: one held under the presidency of a (papal) legate.

Legation (lĭgē¹·ʃən). 1460. [ad. L. *legationem*; see LEGATE *sb.*] **1.** The action of sending a deputy, esp. a (papal) legate; the fact of his being sent. **2.** His mission or commission 1470. **3.** *concr.* The body of deputies sent on a mission; a diplomatic minister (*now*, not being an 'ambassador') and his suite. Also *attrib.* 1603. **b.** The official residence of a diplomatic minister 1863. **4.** The dignity and office of a legate 1603. **5.** Formerly, one of the provinces of the Papal States, governed by a legate 1841.

1. The Divine L. of Moses WARBURTON. 3. A secretary of l...supplying their place 1756. *attrib.* The L. buildings 1886. Hence **Lega·tionary** *a.* of or pertaining to a l.; qualified or ready to go on a l. CARLYLE.

Legative (le·gătiv), *a.* 1537. [ad. late L. *legativus*; see LEGATE *v.* and -ATIVE.] **a.** In *l. bull, commission*: Deputing; conferring the authority of a legate. **b.** Of or pertaining to a legate, or (*rarely*) to an ambassador.

‖**Legato** (legā·to), *a.* (*adv.* and *sb.*) 1811. [It.: lit. 'bound', pa. pple. of *legare* :—L. *ligare* to bind.] *Mus.* A direction: Smooth and connected, without breaks. (Opp. to *staccato*.)

Legator (ligē·tǫ̆ɪ). 1651. [a. L., f. *legare*.] One who gives something by will; a testator.

†**Le·gature.** [f. LEGATE *sb.* + -URE.] The dignity and office of a legate; legateship. CLARENDON.

Leg-bail. 1774. In *to give leg-bail*, to decamp. Hence *occas.* = 'French leave', etc.

Lege, obs. f. LEDGE *v.*[1]

Legend (le·dʒĕnd), *sb.* ME. [a. F. *légende*, ad. med.L. *legenda* 'what is read', f. *legere*.] **1.** The story of the life of a saint. **2.** A collection of saints' lives or of similar stories ME. †**3.** A story, history, account –1671. †**4.** A roll, list, record –1601. **5.** *Eccl.* A book of readings or lessons for use at divine service, containing passages from Scripture and the lives of saints. *Obs.* exc. *Hist.* 1440. **6.** An unauthentic story handed down by tradition and popularly regarded as historical 1613. **7.** An inscription or motto; chiefly *spec.*, the words or letters impressed on a coin or medal, the title affixed to a picture 1611. **b.** *gen.* Written character; writing (*rare*) 1822. ¶**8.** Misused for LEGION. *Merry W.* I. iii. 99.

2. A gloryous legende Of goode women CHAUCER. *The L.* (now usu. called *the Golden L.*), a 13th century collection of saints' lives written by Jacobus de Voragine, Archbishop of Genoa. I had rather beleeue all the fables in the L., and the Alcaron, then that this vniuersall frame is without a minde BACON. 6. The l. which would attribute to Alfred the foundation of the University of Oxford HOOK. 7. No l. or effigy marks the graves of these royal Ladies FREEMAN. Hence †**Le·gend** *v. trans.* to tell as a l.

Legendary (le·dʒĕndări). 1513. [ad. med.L. *legendarius* adj. and sb., f. *legenda*; see LEGEND *sb.* and -ARY.] **A.** *adj.* **1.** Pertaining to or of the nature of a legend; connected or concerned with legends; related in legend 1563. **b.** Of writers: Relating legends 1646. **2.** Containing the legend on a coin 1830.

1. *L. period, age*, one of which the accounts are mostly of the nature of legends. Relics of a mythical or l. past 1900.

B. *sb.* **1.** A collection of legends, esp. of lives of saints; *occas.* = The Golden Legend 1513. **2.** A writer of legends 1625.

Legendry (le·dʒĕndri). 1849. [f. LEGEND *sb.* + -RY.] Legends collectively.

†**Le·ger**, *a.* 1481. [a. F. *léger* :—pop.L. type **leviarius*, f. *levis* light.] Light, not heavy; slight, trifling. Also, nimble. –1598. Hence †**Le·gerly** *adv.*

Leger, obs. f. LEDGER.

Legerdemain (le:dʒəɹdĭmē·n). ME. [a. F. *léger de main*, lit. 'light of hand'; cf. LEGER *a.*] **1.** Sleight of hand; jugglery; conjuring tricks. **2.** *transf.* and *fig.* Trickery, hocus-pocus 1532; †a trick, a juggle –1663. †**3.** A conjurer. CIBBER. **4.** *attrib.* or *adj.* Pertaining to or of the nature of legerdemain; juggling, tricky 1576.

1. Will ye see any feates of activity, Some sleight of hand, leigerdemaine? BEAUM. & FL. 2. There is a certain Knack or L. in argument SHAFTESB. 4. L. Tricks 1707. Hence **Legerdemai·nist**, a conjurer.

†**Lege·rity.** 1561. [ad. F. *légèreté*; see LEGER *a.* and -ITY.] Lightness (*lit.* and *fig.*); nimbleness –1830.

†**Legge**, *v. rare.* ME. only. [Aphet. f. ALLEGE *v.*[1]] To alleviate.

Legge, obs. f. LEDGE *v.*[1]

Legged (legd), *a.* 1470. [f. LEG *sb.* + -ED[2].] Having legs (*esp.* such or so many); as in BAKER-*l.*, *bare-l.*, BOW-LEGGED, *two-l.*, etc. In *Her.*, having legs of a specified tincture.

Leg'd like a man *Temp.* II. ii. 35.

†**Leggiadrous**, *a. rare.* 1648. [f. It. *leggiadro* light, sprightly + -OUS.] Graceful, elegant. JOS. BEAUMONT.

Legging (le·giŋ), *sb.* Chiefly *pl.* 1763. [f. LEG *sb.* + -ING[1] (but cf. -ING[3]).] In *pl.* A pair of outer coverings (usu. of leather or cloth) to protect the legs in bad weather, reaching from the ankle to the knee, or sometimes higher.

Legging (le·gin), *vbl. sb.* 1872. [f. LEG *v.* + -ING[1].] Making a leg or obeisance.

Leggy (le·gi), *a.* 1787. [f. LEG *sb.* + -Y[1].] Conspicuous for legs; lanky-legged.

†**Leg-harness.** ME. Armour for the leg –1840.

Leghorn (legǭ·ɹn, le·ghǭɹn). 1753. [Place-name *Leghorn*, ad. It. *Legorno* (16–17th c.), now *Livorno*, repr. L. *Liburnus*.] **1.** Name of a straw plaiting for hats and bonnets, made from a particular kind of wheat, cut green and bleached, and imported from Leghorn in Tuscany; a hat or bonnet made of this or straw like this. Also *attrib.*, as *L. bonnet, chip, plait*, etc. **2.** Name of a breed of the domestic fowl 1854.

Legible (le·dʒĭb'l), *a.* (*sb.*) ME. [ad. late L. *legibilis*, f. *legere* to read; see -BLE.] **a.** Of writing: Plain; easily made out. **b.** Of compositions: Accessible to readers (*nonce-use*); also, easy to read, readable (*rare*) 1676. **c.** *transf.* and *fig.* 1595.

a. A fair, fast, l. hand 1620. c. The trouble l. in my countenance LAMB. Hence **Legibi·lity. Le·gibly** *adv.*

Legific (lĭdʒi·fik), *a.* [f. L. *legi-*, *lex* law + *-ficus*; see -FIC.] Pertaining to the making of laws. J. GROTE.

Legion (lī·dʒən). ME. [a. OF. *legiun*, *legion* (mod.F. *légion*), a. L. *legionem*, *legio*, f. *legere* to choose, levy (an army); cf. -ION.] **1.** *Rom. Antiq.* A body of infantry in the Roman army, ranging in number from 3,000 in early times to 6,000 under Marius, usually with a large complement of cavalry. **b.** Applied to certain bodies in modern armies 1598. **2.** Vaguely: A host of armed men ME. **3.** A vast host (of persons or things); *esp.* in the (inaccurate) phr. *their name is L.* = 'they are innumerable' (cf. Mark v. 9) ME. **4.** *L. of Honour* [= F. *Légion d'honneur*]: a French order of distinction, conferred for civil or military services, etc. 1827. **b.** *American L.*, a national association of ex-service men instituted in 1919. *British L.*, a similar association founded in 1921 and incorporated by Royal Charter in 1925. **5.** *Nat. Hist.* An occasional term repr. an assemblage of objects intermediate in extent between a class and an order 1859. **6.** *attrib.* or *adj.* Multitudinous 1678.

1. b. *Foreign l.* [= F. *légion étrangère*]: a body of foreign volunteers in the French army in the 19th c., employed in the colonies, etc. 3. He..call'd His Legions, Angel Forms, who lay intrans't MILT. *P. L.* I. 301. A legioun is name to me; for we ben manye WYCLIF *Mark* v. 9.

Legionary (lī·dʒənări). 1577. [ad. L. *legionarius*, f. *legionem* LEGION; see -ARY.]

A. *adj.* **1.** Of or belonging to a legion. **b.** Of an inscription, mark, etc.: Designating a particular Roman legion 1851. **2.** Constituting or consisting of a legion or legions 1646.

1. The whole multitude of l. soldiers ARNOLD. b. The l. mark of the title 1863.

B. *sb.* A soldier of a legion, ancient or modern. Also, a member of the Legion of Honour. 1598.

The cowering l., with whom to hear was to obey DE QUINCEY.

Legioned (lī·dʒənd), *a. poet.* 1818. [f. LEGION + -ED[1].] Arrayed in legions.

Legislate (le·dʒislēˈt), *v.* 1719. [Back-formation f. LEGISLATOR, LEGISLATION.] **1.** *trans.* To make laws for. D'URFEY. **2.** *intr.* To make or enact laws 1805. **3.** *quasi-trans.* To bring or drive by legislation *into* or *out of*. Also rarely *trans.* to bring about or control by legislation. 1845.

2. Solon, in legislating for the Athenians, had an idea of a more perfect Constitution than he gave them BP. WATSON. 3. The legislated depreciation of this one estate..had cost him..£120,000. 1898.

Legislation (ledʒislēˈ·ʃən). 1655. [a. late L. *legis-lationem*, prop. two wds. = 'bringing of a law' (*legis* + *lationem*).] **1.** The action of making or giving laws; the enactment of laws, lawgiving. **2.** The enactments of a legislator or legislature; enacted laws collectively 1838.

1. Pythagoras, who join'd L. to his Philosophy, and ..pretended to Miracles..to give a more venerable Sanction to the Laws he prescribed LD. LYTTELTON. Hence **Legisla·tional** *a.* pertaining to l.

Legislative (le·dʒislĕtiv). 1641. [After LEGISLATION, LEGISLATOR; see -ATIVE. Cf. F. *législatif* (14th c.).]

A. *adj.* **1.** That legislates; having the function of making laws 1651. **2.** Of or pertaining to the making of laws 1641; enacted or appointed by legislation 1855. Hence **Le·gislatively** *adv.* by legislation.

1. On the 30th of September [1791], this National Assembly..dissolved itself, and gave place to the succeeding L. National Assembly 1797. 2. L. remedies 1855, penalties 1872, emancipation of Scotch industry LECKY.

B. *sb.* The power of legislating; the body in which this is vested, the legislature. Opp. to *executive*. Now *rare*. 1642.

Legislator (le·dʒislēˈtəɹ). 1605. [a. L. *legis-lator*, prop. two wds., = 'proposer of a law' (*legis*, *lex* + *lator*, used as agent-n. to *ferre* to bring).] One who makes laws (for a people or nation); a lawgiver; a member of a legislative body.

Legislators have long since discovered the absurdity of attempting to fix prices by law JEVONS. *transf.* The alleged l. of science BREWSTER. Hence **Le·gislatorship**, the position of l.

Legislatorial (ledʒislătō·riăl), *a.* 1774. [f. mod.L. type **legislatorius* (f. *legislator*) + -AL.] **1.** Having the power to legislate, acting as a legislator or legislature 1819. **2.** Of or pertaining to a legislator or legislation.

Legislatress (le·dʒislēˈtrĕs). 1711. [f. LEGISLATOR + -ESS.] A female legislator.

Nature, a beneficent l. MAINE. So **Legisla·trix** 1677.

Legislature (le·dʒislēˈtiŭɹ). 1655. [After LEGISLATOR; cf. -URE.] **1.** 'The power that makes laws' (J.); a body of persons invested with the power of making the laws of a country or state; *spec.* (*U.S.*) the legislative body of a State or Territory, as dist. from Congress. †**2.** The exercise of the function of legislation –1765.

1. 'Twas April, as the bumpkins say, The l. called it May COWPER. 2. It was very inconvenient to have both the l. and the execution in the same hands BURNET.

Legist (lī·dʒist). 1456. [ad. F. *légiste*, ad. med.L. *legista*, f. *leg-*, *lex* LAW; see -IST.] One versed in the law. (Cf. JURIST.) So †**Le·gister** ME.–1555.

‖**Le·git.** [L., pres. or pa. t. 3rd pers. sing. of *legere* to read.] Claim to 'Benefit of Clergy' based upon the fact of being able to read a verse of the Bible. BAXTER.

Legitim: see LEGITIME.

Legitimacy (lĭdʒi·timăsi). 1691. [f. LEGITIMATE; see -ACY.] **1.** The fact of being a legitimate child. **2.** Of a government or the title of a sovereign: The condition of being in accordance with law or principle. Now often, with reference to a sovereign's title: The fact of being derived by regular descent; *occas.* the principle of lineal succession to the throne. 1817. **3.** *gen.* Conformity to rule or principle, or (*Logic*) to sound reasoning 1836.

2. The Doctrine of Divine Right, which has now come back to us, like a thief from transportation, under the *alias* of L. MACAULAY. 3. The l. of our assumption 1836.

Legitimate (lĭdʒi·timĕt), *a.* 1494. [ad. med.L. *legitimatus*, *legitimare* to declare to be lawful, f. L. *legitimus*, f. *leg-*, *lex* law. The strict ppl. sense, = *legitimated*, is not found in English.] **1.** Of a child: Having the status of one lawfully begotten; entitled to full filial rights. Said also of a parent, and of lineal descent. (The only sense in Johnson.) †b. *transf.* Genuine, real; opp. to 'spurious' –1818. **2.** Conformable to law or rule; lawful, proper 1638. **b.** Normal, regular; conformable to a standard type 1669. **c.** Of a sovereign's title: Resting on hereditary right. Hence, said of a sovereign, a kingdom, etc. 1821. **d.** Logically admissible 1797.

1. The common law had deemed all those bastards who were born before wedlock: By the canon law they were l. HUME. 2. They [Moors] are a nation.. without a l. country or a name W. IRVING. b. A l. English classic MACAULAY. *The l. drama*: the body of plays, Shaksperian or other, that have a recognized theatrical and literary merit; also ellipt. (*Theatr. slang*) *the l.* d. Both [methods] were l. logical processes MILL. Hence **Legi·timate-ly** *adv.*, **-ness.**

B. *sb.* **1.** A legitimate child 1583; a legitimate sovereign; also, one who supports the title of such sovereigns 1821. †**2.** Something to which one has a legitimate title. MILT.

Legitimate (lĭdʒi·timeᶦt), *v.* 1531. [f. med.L. *legitimat-*, *legitimare* (see prec.). Cf. F. *légitimer.*] **1.** *trans.* To render legitimate by authoritative declaration or decree. Also *fig.* 1597. **2.** To make legal by enactment. In early use, To give (a person) a legal claim *to* (something). 1531. **3.** To affirm or show to be legitimate; to justify 1611.

1. To l. the duke of Lancaster's ante-nuptial children HALLAM. 3. Necessity legitimates my advice; for it is the only way to save our lives DE FOE.

Legitimation (lĭdʒitimēⁱ·ʃən). 1460. [ad. med.L. *legitimationem.* Cf. F. *légitimation.*] **1.** The rendering or authoritatively declaring (a person) legitimate. †**2.** Legitimacy –1689. **b.** *transf.* Of a literary work: Authenticity, genuineness. Now *rare.* 1635. **3.** The action of making lawful; authorization 1660.

3. The l. of Money, and the giving it its denominated value 1799.

Legi·timatist. *rare.* 1860. [f. as next + -IST.] = LEGITIMIST.

Legitimatize (lĭdʒi·timătəiz), *v.* 1791. [f. LEGITIMATE *a.* + -IZE.] *trans.* To render legitimate or lawful, *esp.* to render (a child) legitimate.

Legitime (le·dʒĭtim). Also †**legitim.** ME. [a. F. *légitime* adj. and sb., ad. L. *legitimus*, f. *leg-*, *lex* LAW.] †**A.** *adj.* = LEGITIMATE *a.* –1795. **B.** *sb. Civil* and *Sc. Law.* The portion of his movable estate to which children are entitled on the death of their father. = L. *legitima* (*pars*) 1768.

Legitimism (lĭdʒi·timiz'm). 1877. [ad. F. *légitimisme*; see -ISM.] In Fr. or Sp. politics: Adherence to the claim of the so-called 'legitimate pretender to the throne'.

Legitimist (lĭdʒi·timist). 1841. [ad. F. *légitimiste.*] A supporter of legitimate authority, esp. of a monarchical title claimed on the ground of direct descent; *spec.* in France, a supporter of the elder Bourbon line. Also *attrib.* or *adj.*

Legi·timize, *v.* 1833. [f. L. *legitimus* + -IZE.] = LEGITIMATIZE. **Legi:timiza·tion.**

Legless (le·glės), *a.* ME. [-LESS.] Having no legs.

Leglet (le·glėt). 1821. [f. LEG *sb.* + -LET.] **1.** A little leg. **2.** An ornament for the leg. (After *armlet*, etc.) 1836.

Leg-pull (le·gpul). *slang.* 1920. The act of 'pulling a person's leg' (see LEG *sb.* I. 1 phr.). So **Le·g-pu:ller, -pu:lling** (1908).

Leguleian (legiulī·ăn). 1631. [f. L. *leguleïus* (f. *leg-*, *lex*) + -AN.]

A. *adj.* Pettifogging. **B.** *sb.* A pettifogger. So **Legulei·ous** *a.* 1660.

Legume (le·giʉm, lĭgiū·m). 1676. [a. F. *légume*, ad. L. *legumen*, f. *legere* to gather, so called because the fruit may be gathered by hand.] **1.** The fruit or edible part of a leguminous plant, e.g. beans, peas, pulse. Hence, A vegetable used for food; chiefly in *pl.* 1693. †**2.** A leguminous plant –1725. **3.** The pod of a leguminous plant 1785.

Legumen (lĭgiū·mėn). *Pl.* **legumens,** ‖**legumina.** ME. [a. L.; see prec.] = prec.

Legumin (lĭgiū·min). Also **-ine.** 1827. [f. LEGUME + -IN.] *Chem.* A proteid substance resembling casein, found in leguminous and other seeds.

Leguminous (lĭgiū·minəs), *a.* 1656. [f. L. *legumin-*, *legumen* + -OUS.] **1.** Of, pertaining to, or of the nature of, pulse. **2.** *Bot.* Of or pertaining to the N.O. *Leguminosæ*, which includes peas, beans, and other plants bearing legumes or pods 1677. **b.** Like what pertains to a leguminous plant 1688.

Leibnitzian (ləibni·tsiăn). Also **Leibnitian,** **-izian.** 1754. [f. the name of G. W. *Leibnitz* (1646–1716) + -IAN.] **A.** *adj.* Pertaining to Leibnitz or his philosophy or mathematical methods 1765. **B.** *sb.* A follower of Leibnitz.

Leicester (le·stəɹ). 1834. [Name of an English county town.] Used *attrib.* and hence *ellipt.* as sb., to designate a long-woolled variety of sheep and a long-horned variety of cattle originally bred in Leicestershire.

Leiger, leigier: see LEDGER.

Leio- (ləi·o), also **lio-**, comb. f. Gr. λεῖος smooth; as in: **Leiophy·llous** [Gr. φύλλον] *a.*, *Bot.* having smooth leaves; **Leio·trichous** [Gr. τριχ-, θρίξ hair] *a.*, smooth-haired, belonging to the group ‖**Leio·trichi,** one of the two so-called primary divisions of mankind.

Leip(o)-: see LIP(O)-.

Leister (lī·stəɹ). 1533. [a. ON. *ljóstr*, f. *ljósta* str. vb., to strike.] A pronged spear for striking and taking salmon, etc. Hence **Lei·ster** *v. trans.* to spear with a l.

Leisurable (le·ʒ'ŭrăb'l, lī·-), *a.* 1540. [f. LEISURE + -ABLE; cf. *pleasurable*, etc.] **1.** Leisurely, deliberate. **2.** Not requiring haste; leisure (time). *rare.* 1607. Hence **Lei·surably** *adv.* (now *rare*).

Leisure (le·ʒ'ŭɹ, *local* lī·ʒ'ŭɹ). [ME. *leiser*, a. OF. *leisir* (mod. *loisir*), subst. use of inf. *leisir*:—L. *licere* to be permitted.] †**1.** Freedom or opportunity to do something –1640. †**b.** An opportunity. ME. only. **2.** Opportunity afforded by unoccupied time ME. **b.** Time allowed before it is too late. Now *rare.* 1553. **3.** The state of having time at one's own disposal; free time ME. **b.** A spell of free time. Now *rare.* 1449. †**4.** Leisureliness, deliberation –1677. **5.** *attrib.* 1669.

2. If your l. seru'd, I would speake with you SHAKS. b. For whose sanction there was no l. to wait JAS. MILL. 3. The Desire of L. is much more Natural, than of Business and Care TEMPLE. Phr. *To tarry, attend*, or *stay* (*upon*) a person's *l.*: to wait his time. Also *fig. arch.* 5. Let us pass a l. hour in story telling JOWETT.

Phrases. *At l.*: with time at one's disposal; without haste, with deliberation. *At one's l.*: when one has time; at one's ease or convenience. †*By l.* (also *by good l.*): with deliberation: at one's l.; by degrees; slowly. Also (= Gr. σχολῇ), barely.

Leisured (le·ʒ'ŭɹd, lī·-), *a.* 1631. [f. LEISURE + -ED².] **1.** Characterized by leisure. **2.** Having ample leisure, esp. in *the l. class(es* 1794.

Leisurely (le·ʒ'ŭɹli, lī·-), *a.* 1604. [f. LEISURE + -LY¹.] **1.** Having leisure; proceeding without haste 1613. **2.** Of actions or agents: Performed or operating at leisure; deliberate.

1. The men of l. minds COLERIDGE. 2. A l. journey across the south of France 1875. Hence **Lei·sureliness.** So **Lei·surely** *adv.* 1486.

‖**Leitmotiv** (ləi·tmotīf). Also **-motif, -motive.** 1876. [Ger., f. *leit-* leading + *motiv* MOTIVE.] *Mus.* In the musical drama of Wagner and his imitators, a theme associated throughout the work with a particular person, situation, or sentiment.

Lek (lek), *v.* 1884. [? a. Sw. *leka* to play; see LAKE *v.*] *intr.* Said of grouse: To congregate. Also **Lek** *sb.* a gathering or congregating 1871.

Leman (le·măn, lī·măn). *arch.* [Early ME. *leofmon*, f. *leof* LIEF, dear + MAN.] **1.** A lover or sweetheart; †*occas.* a husband or wife. **2.** In bad sense (cf. *paramour*): An unlawful lover or (chiefly in later archaistic use) mistress ME.

2. Yea! none did love him—not his lemans dear BYRON.

Leme, obs. f. LEAM *sb.*¹ and *v.*

Lemma¹ (le·mă). *Pl.* **lemmas,** ‖**lemmata.** 1570. [(ult.) a. Gr. λῆμμα, pl. λήμματα (f. root of λαμβάνειν to take) something received or taken, something taken for granted. Cf. F. *lemme.*] **1.** *Math.*, etc. A proposition assumed or demonstrated, preliminary to the demonstration of some other. **2. a.** The argument or subject of a literary composition, prefixed as a heading or title; a motto appended to a picture, etc. **b.** The heading or theme of a scholium, annotation, or gloss. 1616.

2. b. He marks off the l. from the body of the note in cases in which a l. is given W. G. RUTHERFORD.

Lemma² (le·mă). Pl. **lemmata** (le·mătă). 1880. [ad. Gr. λέμμα, f. λέπειν to peel.] *Embryol.* The primary or outer layer of the germinal vesicle.

Lemming (le·miŋ). Also **leeming.** 1713. [a. Norw. *lemming.*] A small arctic rodent, *Myodes lemmus*, resembling a field-mouse, about 6 in. long, with a short tail, prolific, and remarkable for its annual migrations to the sea. Also *l.-mouse*, *-rat.*

Collared or **Snowy l.**, *Cuniculus torquatus.*

Lemnian (le·mniăn), *a.* 1611. [f. L. *Lemnius*, Gr. Λήμνιος (f. Λῆμνος the island Lemnos) + -AN.] Of or pertaining to Lemnos.

L. earth (L. *terra Lemnia*), sigillated earth, sphragide. *L. reddle*, an ochre of a deep-red colour and firm consistence, occurring in conjunction with the Lemnian earth, and used as a pigment. *L. smith*: Hephæstus or Vulcan.

Lemniscate (lemni·skēt). 1781. [ad. mod. L. *lemniscata*, fem. of L. *lemniscatus* adj., adorned with ribbons, f. *lemniscus*; see next.] **a.** *Geom.* The designation of certain closed curves, having a general resemblance to the figure 8. **b.** *Alg.* Used *attrib.* in *l. function*, one of a class of elliptic functions first investigated by Gauss, in connexion with formulæ relating to this class of curves.

‖**Lemniscus** (lemni·skŏs). *Pl.* **-ci** (-səi). Also †**lemnisc** (1706–18). 1849. [L. *lemniscus*, Gr. λημνίσκος ribbon.] **1.** The character ÷ used by ancient textual critics in annotations. **2.** One of the minute ribbon-like appendages of the generative pores of some entozoans 1855.

Lemon (le·mən), *sb.*¹ ME. (*c* 1400). [ad. F. *limon* = med.L. *limonem*, related to F. *lime*; see LIME *sb.*² Prob. of Oriental origin; cf. Arab. *laimūn*, Pers. *līmūn*, etc., fruits of the citron kind.] **1.** An ovate fruit with a pale yellow rind, and an acid juice. The juice yields citric acid; the rind yields *oil* or *essence of lemons*, used in cookery and perfumery. **b.** *slang* (orig. *U.S.*). Something worthless or distasteful 1863. **2.** The tree (*Citrus Limonum*) which bears this fruit 1615. **3.** The colour of the lemon; pale yellow. More fully *l.-colour.* 1796. **4.** *attrib.*, as *l.-bloom*, *l.-cake*, *l.-coloured*, etc. 1598. **5.** quasi-*adj.*, short for *lemon-coloured* 1875.

Comb.: **l.-balm,** *Melissa officinalis*; **-cheese,** a confection made from lemons, butter, and eggs; **-cutting,** the feat of cutting a suspended l. in two with a sword when riding at full speed; **-grass,** a fragrant E. Indian grass (*Andropogon schœnanthus*) yielding the grass oil used in perfumery; also *attrib.*; **-kali,** a mixture of tartaric acid and sodium bicarbonate, which when dissolved form an effervescing drink; **-plant** (*Aloysia citriodora*), the so-called lemon-scented verbena; **-squash,** a drink made from soda-water, lemon-juice, and sugar; **-squeezer,** an instrument for squeezing out the juice of lemons; **-thyme,** a lemon-scented variety of thyme; **-tree,** (*a*) = sense 2; (*b*) = *lemon-plant*; **-verbena** = *lemon-plant*; **-wood,** a New Zealand tree, the Tarata.

Hence **Le·mon** *v.* to flavour with l. **Le·mony** *a.*

Lemon (le·mən), *sb.*² 1835. [app. a. F. *limande.*] In **lemon-dab, lemon-sole,** names for certain species of plaice or flounder.

Lemonade (lemənēⁱ·d). Also †**limonade.** 1663. [ad. F. *limonade*, f. *limon* lemon.] A drink made from lemons, with (aerated) water and sugar. So †**Lemona·do** 1640–76.

Lemur (lī·mŏɹ). *Pl.* **lemurs,** ‖**lemures** (le·miŭrīz). 1580. [a. L. **lemur*, pl. *lemures.*] **1.** *Rom. Myth.* In *pl.* The spirits of the dead. **2.** *Zool.* A genus of nocturnal mammals of the family *Lemuridæ*, found chiefly in Madagascar, allied to the monkeys, but having a pointed muzzle like that of a fox; an animal of this genus 1795.

1. The Lars, and Lemures moan with midnight plaint MILT. Hence **Lemu·ridous** *a.* belonging to the family *Lemuridæ*. **Le·murine** *a.* and *sb.* = next.

Lemuroid (le·miŭroid). 1873. [f. LEMUR + -OID.] **A.** *adj.* Resembling the lemurs; pertaining to the sub-order *Lemuroidea*, of which the genus *Lemur* is the type. B. *sb.* A lemuroid animal 1873.

†**Lend,** *sb.*^{1} [OE. **lęnden* (only in pl. *lęndenu*).] Chiefly *pl.* The loins; also, the buttocks -1550.

Lend, *sb.*^{2} *Sc.* 1575. [f. LEND *v.*^{1}] A loan.

Lend (lend), *v.*^{1} Pa. t. and pple. **lent.** [OE. *lǽnan* (giving ME. *lene*, Sc. *len*), f. *lǽn* (see LOAN *sb.*). The substitution of *lend-* for *len-* in the present stem, due to the ambiguity of the pa. t. *lende*, is early ME.] 1. *trans.* To grant temporary possession of (a thing) on condition of the return of the same or its equivalent. b. *spec.* To let out (money, etc.) at interest OE. c. *absol.* or *intr.* To make a loan or loans OE. 2. To grant, bestow; to impart, afford (usu. something not in the possession of the subject, or something viewed as a temporary possession or attribute) OE. †b. To hold out (a hand) to be taken -1611. c. *To l. an ear* or *one's ears*: to listen ME. d. To afford the use or support of; esp. in *to l. a hand*, etc., to assist. e. To give or deal (a blow). Now *dial.* 1460. f. To devote (one's strength) *to. rare.* 1697. 3. *refl.* To accommodate oneself *to*. Of things: To admit of being applied *to* a purpose or subjected *to* a certain treatment 1854.

1. To lende one his house to solemnise a mariage 1573. To l. a volume of poems 1785, a lease for perusal 1893. b. Thou shalt not..l. him thy victuals for increase *Lev.* xxv. 37. c. Hee that hath pity vpon the poore, lendeth vnto the Lord *Prov.* xix. 17. Phr. *To l. out*: = 1, 1 b; now esp. used of lending libraries. 2. While Heaven lends us grace MILT. *Comus* 938. 'Tis distance lends enchantment to the view CAMPBELL. b. L. me thy hand, and I will giue thee mine SHAKS. c. The young king seemed to l. a willing ear GEO. ELIOT. d. Lend 's a Hand here MOTTEUX. 3. None lends itself better to architectural purposes 1874.

Hence **Le·ndable** *a.* that may be lent.

†**Lend,** *v.*^{2} *Obs.* [OE. *lęndan* :—OTeut. **landjan*, f. *lando*^{m} LAND *sb.*] *intr.* To arrive, light (*up*)*on*, remain, tarry -1535.

Lender (le·ndəɹ). Also †**lenner.** [orig. OE. *lǽnere*, f. *lǽnan* LEND *v.*^{1}; later f. the vb. + -ER^1.] One who lends, esp. at interest.

Lending (le·ndiŋ), *vbl. sb.* ME. [f. LEND *v.*^{1} + -ING^1.] 1. The action of LEND *v.*^{1}; *esp.* the letting out of money at interest. 2. *concr.* Something lent 1602; †*spec. pl.*, money advanced to soldiers when the regular pay cannot be given -1637.

2. Mowbray hath receiu'd eight thousand Nobles, In name of lendings for your Highnesse Soldiers SHAKS.

Le·nding, *ppl. a.* 1586. [f. as prec. + -ING^2.] That lends.

L. library, one from which books are lent.

†**Lene,** *a.* and *sb.* 1751. [ad. L. *lenis* smooth.] *Phonetics.* Applied to the smooth breathing (*spiritus lenis*) in Greek; also to a stopped (esp. voiceless) consonant, opp. to *aspirate* -18..

Lene: see LEND *v.*^{1}

†**Leng,** *adv.* [OE. *lęng* :—OTeut. **langiz*, advb. compar. of **lango-* LONG *a.*] Longer -ME.

†**Lenger,** *a.* and *adv.* [OE. *lęngra*, neut. and fem. *lęngre* :—OTeut. **langizon-*, compar. of LONG *a.*] A. *adj.* Longer -1561. B. *adv.* Longer -1590.

†**Lengest,** *a.* and *adv.* [OE. *lęngest* :—OTeut. **langisto-*, f. **lango-* LONG *a.*; cf. prec.] A. *adj.* Longest, very long -1530. B. *adv.* Longest -1485.

Length (leŋþ), *sb.* [OE. *lęngðu* fem. :—OTeut. **langiþâ*, f. as prec.]

I. Quality of being long. 1. Linear measurement of any thing from end to end; the greatest of the three dimensions of a body or figure. 2. Extent from beginning to end, e.g. of a period of time, a series, a word, etc. ME. 3. The quality or fact of being long; opp. to *shortness* ME.; prolixity (now *rare*) 1593. b. An instance of this; *esp.* a long period 1697. 4. A distance as long as something specified ME. b. *Sport.* The length of a boat, a horse, etc., taken as a unit in stating the amount by which a race is won 1664. 5. With a demonstrative or other defining word: Distance 1450. b. *fig.* in advb. phrases, as, *to go* (*to*) *the l. of*, *a* (*great*, etc.) *l.*, (*all*, etc.) *lengths* 1697. †6. Reach -1628. 7. *Pros.* Quantity (of a sound or syllable). Also, long quantity (opp. to *shortness*). 1575. 8. *Cricket.* The proper distance for pitching a ball in bowling. Also = *length ball.* 1776.

1. The full l. of the rope between us TYNDALL. Phr. *To find, get, know the l. of* (a person's) *foot*; see FOOT *sb.* *The l. of one's tether*; see TETHER. 2. The lenght of the siege LD. BERNERS. b. To see a friend after a l. of absence LANDOR. 3. Such Customes have their force, onely from L. of Time HOBBES. Excuse my l. BURKE. 4. *At arm's l.*: see ARM *sb.*^{1} *Cable('s) l.*: see CABLE *sb.* 2 b. *One's l.*; I fell all my l. 1870. b. The Oxford crew won by three and a half lengths 1894. 5. He [Essex] had marched to the l. of Exeter CLARENDON. b. The cunningest of men, able to lie all lengths CARLYLE. 6. If I can get him within my Pistol's l. SHAKS. 8. How to stop a ball dropped rather short of a l. 1833.

II. Concrete senses. 1. a. A long stretch or extent 1595. b. A piece of a certain or distinct length 1565. 2. *Theatr. slang.* A portion of an actor's part, consisting of forty-two lines 1736. 3. *Brewing.* The quantity of wort drawn off from a certain quantity of malt 1742.

1. Large lengths of seas and shores SHAKS. 2. Kean said that 'Iago was three lengths longer than Othello' LD. BROUGHTON.

Phr. **At length. a.** To the full extent; in full; without curtailment. Also *at full, great, some*, etc. *l.* b. After a long time; at or n the end. †c. (*a*) At a distance; (*b*) in an extended line; tandem-fashion; (*c*) of a portrait = FULL LENGTH 1. d. With the body fully extended. Now usu. *at* (*one's*) *full l.*

Comb. **l. ball** *Cricket*, a ball pitched a l. (see sense I. 8).

Hence †**Length** *v.* to make or become longer ME.

Lengthen (le·ŋþ'n). 1440. [f. LENGTH *sb.*; cf. prec. and -EN^5.] 1. *trans.* To make longer. Also with *out.* †b. Used for: To eke out, cause to last longer. Also with *out.* -1748. 2. *intr.* To become longer 1695.

1. Then will I l. thy dayes 1 *Kings* iii. 14. To l. a vowel 1755. b. We agreed for the Gallapagos to get Turtle to l. our Provisions 1712. 2. Phr. *To l. out* (Mil.): to stride out.

Lengthful (le·ŋþfŭl), *a. poet.* (Now *rare.*) 1611. [f. LENGTH *sb.* + -FUL.] Of great length, long.

Lengthways (le·ŋþwēⁱz), *adv.* 1599. [f. LENGTH *sb.* + WAY with advb. *-s.*] In the direction of the length (*of* something).

Lengthwise (le·ŋþwəiz). 1580. [-WISE.] A. *adv.* = prec. B. *adj.* Following the direction of the length 1871.

Lengthy (le·ŋþi), *a.* 1689. [f. LENGTH *sb.* + -Y^1. Orig. an Americanism.] Characterized by length; having great length; often (of speeches, etc.) prolix, tedious.

I grow too minute and l. J. ADAMS. L. correspondence 1844, pleadings FREEMAN. A l. and stupendous cliff line H. M. STANLEY. Hence **Le·ngthily** *adv.* **Le·ngthiness.**

Lenience (lī·niĕns). 1796. [f. LENIENT; see -ENCE.] Lenient action or behaviour; indulgence.

Leniency (lī·niĕnsi). 1780. [See -ENCY.] The quality of being lenient.

Lenient (lī·niĕnt). 1652. [ad. L. *lenientem*, pr. ppl. of *lenire* to soothe, f. *lenis* soft.]

A. *adj.* 1. Softening, soothing, relaxing; emollient. Somewhat *arch.* 2. Indisposed to severity; gentle, mild, tolerant 1787.

1. L. of grief and anxious thought MILT. The l. hand of time FOSTER. 2. L. laws 1787, measures 1828. Hence **Le·niently** *adv.*

†B. *sb.* An emollient -1794.

Lenify (lī·nifəi), *v.* 1568. [f. L. *lenis* soft + -FY.] †1. *trans.* To relax, make soft or supple (some part of the body); to render (cider) mellow. Also, to mitigate (a physical condition). 1574. 2. To assuage, mitigate, soften, soothe (pain, suffering, etc.). Also, to mitigate (a sentence). Now *rare.*

Lenitive (le·nĭtiv). late ME. [ad. med.L. *lenitivus*, f. L. *lenire* to soften, soothe. In sense 2, as if f. LENITY + -IVE.]

A. *adj.* 1. Tending to allay or soften; mitigating, soothing; gently laxative; esp. in *l. electuary.* †2. Of persons, etc.: Displaying leniency, gentle -1655.

1. Such Writers..use the most l. language in expressing distastfull matter FULLER. Hence **Le·nitive·ly** *adv.*, **-ness.**

B. *sb.* 1. A lenitive medicine or appliance. Also *fig.* 1563. 2. Anything that softens or soothes; a palliative 1614.

2. He hath under his greatest Misery the L. of Hope HALE.

Lenitude (le·nitiūd). *rare.* 1627. [ad. L. *lenitudo*, f. *lenis.*] †a. In a material sense: Smoothness. b. = LENITY.

Lenity (le·nĭti). 1548. [ad. OF. *lenité* or L. *lenitatem.*] Mildness, gentleness, mercifulness. Also, an instance of this.

Hee is the verie soule of lenitie 1592.

Leno (lī·no). 1804. [? corruption of F. *linon* (linoṅ).] A kind of cotton gauze, used for caps, veils, curtains, etc. Also *attrib.*

†**Leno·cinant,** *a.* 1664. [ad. L. *lenocinantem*, *lenocinari*, f. *leno* pander.] Inciting to evil. H. MORE.

Lens (lenz). *Pl.* **lenses**; also formerly **lens, lens's,** and in L. form **lentes.** 1693. [a. L. *lens* lentil, from the form.] 1. A piece of glass, or other transparent substance, with two curved surfaces, or one plane and one curved, serving to cause regular convergence or divergence of the rays of light passing through it. (Now sometimes applied to analogous contrivances, as *acoustic l.*, *electric l.*) b. *spec.* A lens or combination of lenses used in photography 1841. 2. *Anat.* a. = *crystalline lens* (see CRYSTALLINE *a.*) 1719. b. One of the facets of a compound eye 1868. 3. *attrib.*, as *l.-shutter*, etc.; also, **l.-eye** = 2 b; **-form** = LENTIFORM 1787. Hence **Lensed** *a.* provided with a l. or lenses; **Le·nsless** *a.* having no l.

Lent (lent), *sb.*^{1} ME. [Shortened from LENTEN.] 1. The season of spring. *Obs.* exc. in *Comb.* ME. 2. *Eccl.* The period including 40 weekdays extending from Ash-Wednesday to Easter-eve, kept as a time of fasting and penitence, in commemoration of Our Lord's fasting in the wilderness ME. b. *transf.* and *fig.* 1598. c. *pl.* At Cambridge: The Lent-term boat-races 1893. †3. Hence, **a.** A period of forty days, esp. in *l. of pardon*, an indulgence of forty days -1535. †b. A period of fasting prescribed by any religious system -1781.

2. What is a Ioynt of Mutton..in a whole L.? SHAKS.

attrib. and *Comb.*, as (sense 1) *l.-corn*, etc.; (sense 2) *L.-diet*, *-sermon*, etc.; **l.-lily**, the yellow daffodil, *Narcissus Pseudonarcissus*; **l.-rose** = *lent-lily*; also, in S. Devon, *N. biflorus*; **L.-term** (at the Universities), the term in which L. falls.

†**Lent,** *sb.*^{2} Also **lente.** ME. only. [ad. L. *lentem*, *lens.*] Lentils.

Lent (lent), *a.* Also **lente.** ME. [a. F. *lent*, ad. L. *lentus.*] †1. Slow, sluggish; said esp. of a fever, a fire -1732. 2. *Mus.* = LENTO. Now *rare.* 1724.

Lent (lent), *ppl. a.* ME. [pa. pple. of LEND *v.*^{1}] In senses of LEND *v.*^{1} (Formerly often = 'borrowed'.)

Lent, obs. pa. t. and pple. of LEAN *v.*

-lent, *suffix*, in adjs. from L. The L. ending *-lentus* nearly = Eng. -FUL. Normally it is preceded by *u*, as in *turbulentus* turbulent; exceptions are *pestilentus* pestilent, *violentus* violent, *sanguinolentus* bloody.

‖**Lentamente** (lentame·nte), *adv.* 1762. [It., f. *lento* slow.] *Mus.* Slowly, in slow time.

Lenten (le·nt'n), *sb.* and *a.* †Also *Sc.* and *north.* **lentern, lentrin, -on.** [OE. *lęncten* str. masc.; prob. a derivative, through a shorter form appearing as MLG., MDu., Du. *lente*, Ger. *lenz*, etc., of **lango-* LONG *a.*, with reference to the lengthening of the days in spring. The eccl. sense is peculiar to Eng.; in the other Teut. langs. the only sense is 'spring'. In attrib. use *lenten* is now apprehended as an adj., as if f. LENT + -EN^4.]

†A. As separate *sb. Obs.*; superseded by LENT *sb.*^{1} 1. Spring; = LENT *sb.*^{1} 1. -ME. 2. = LENT *sb.*^{1} 2. -1553.

B. *attrib.* or *adj.* 1. Of or pertaining to Lent, observed or taking place in Lent, as in *L. day, fast, sermon*, etc. OE. 2. Appropriate to Lent; hence of provisions, etc., such as may be used in Lent, meagre; of clothing, looks, etc., mournful-looking, dismal 1577.

1. The Divell whipt St. Jerom in a l. dream, for reading Cicero MILT. 2. L. fare WESLEY. Dabitur's l. face BROWNING.

Comb.: †**l.-chaps**, applied to a person having a lean visage; **L.-corn**, corn sown about Lent; **l. fig**, †(*a*) a dried fig; (*b*) a raisin; **L. lily** (*rare*) = *Lent-lily*; **l. pie**, a pie containing no meat.

Lenticel (le·ntisel). 1870. [ad. mod.L. *lenticella*, dim. f. *lentem*, *lens* lentil.] 1. *Bot.* A lenticular corky spot on young bark, corresponding to one of the epidermal stomata. 2. *Anat.* A lenticular gland 1888. So **Lentice·llate** *a.* producing lenticels; having corky spots on the bark 1855.

Lenticular (lenti·kiŭlăɹ). 1658. [ad. late L. *lenticularis*, f. *lenticula*, dim. of *lent-*, *lens* lentil; see LENS.]

A. *adj.* 1. Having the form of a lens or of a lentil; double convex. 2. a. Of or pertaining to a lens. BEDFORD. b. Of or pertaining to the (crystalline) lens of the eye 1822.

L. bed *Geol.*, 'a bed which thins away in all directions' (Green); **l. ore**, beds of red argillaceous ore, so called from the flattened grains which compose it.

†B. *sb.* a. A lenticular glass or lens. b. A lenticular knife, i.e. a scraper used in osteotomy. -1802.

Hence **Lenti·cularly** *adv.* in a l. manner; after the fashion of a lens.

Lentiform (le·ntifǭɹm), *a.* 1706. [f. L. *lent-*, *lens* + -(I)FORM.] Having the form of a lentil or of a lens.

Lentigerous (lenti·dʒĕrəs), *a.* 1889. [f. L. *lenti-*, *lens* + *-ger-* carry + -OUS.] Having a crystalline lens: said of the eyes of some molluscs.

‖**Lentigo** (lentəi·go). *Pl.* **lentigines** (lenti·dʒiniz). ME. [f. L. *lentem*, *lens.*] A freckle or pimple; now usu. *collect.* for a freckly affection of the skin. Hence **Lenti·ginous** *a.* full of freckles; affected with l. 1597.

Lentil (le·ntil). [ME. *lentille*, a. F. *lentille* :—pop.L. **lenticula*, for *-icula*, dim. of *lent-* LENS.] 1. Chiefly *pl.*, in early use occas. *collective sing.* The seed of a leguminous plant (*Ervum Lens*, *Lens esculenta*); also the plant itself, cultivated for food. †b. = DUCKWEED (*Lemna*). More fully *Water l.* [= F. *lentilles d'eau*]. -1597. †2. *pl.* Freckles on the skin. (Cf. LENTIGO.) -1694. 3. *attrib.*, as *l.-soup*, etc.; **l.-shell** (*Zool.*), the genus *Ervillia*. 1555.

‖**Lentiscus** (lenti·skǝs). *Pl.* **lentisci**, **lentiscus's**. 1587. [L.] = next.

Lentisk (le·ntisk). late ME. [ad. L. *lentiscus.*] The mastic tree (*Pistacia Lentiscus*).

Lentitude (le·ntitiūd). 1623. [ad. L. *lentitudo*, f. *lentus.*] Slowness, sluggishness.

Lento (le·nto). 1724. [It.] *Mus.* A direction: Slow; slowly.

Lentoid (le·ntoid), *a.* 1879. [f. L. *lent-* LENS + -OID.] Having the form of a lens or lentil.

Lentor (le·ntəɹ, le·ntǭɹ). 1615. [ad. F. *lenteur* or L. *lentor* (sense 1), f. *lentus* slow.] 1. Of the blood, etc.: Clamminess, tenacity, viscidity. Now *rare.* †b. *concr.* A viscid component of the blood -1722. 2. Slowness; want of vital activity 1763.

†**Le·ntous**, *a.* 1646. [f. L. *lentus* + -OUS.] Clammy, viscid. SIR T. BROWNE.

L'envoy, **lenvoy**. ME. See ENVOY *sb.*[1] 1.

Pag. Is not *lenuoy* a *salue*? *Ar.* No, Page, it is an epilogue SHAKS.

‖**Leo** (lī·o). OE. [L.; see LION.] The Lion, the zodiacal constellation lying between Cancer and Virgo. Also, the fifth sign of the zodiac (named from this constellation). *Leo Minor*, a minor constellation, lying between the Great Bear and Leo.

Leon, obs. f. LION.

Leonid (lī·ŏnid). Also *pl.* in L. form **Leonides** (lī,ǭ·nidīz). 1876. [f. L. *leon-* LION (LEO) + -ID.] *Astron.* One of the meteors which appear to radiate from Leo.

Leonine (lī·ŏnəin, -nin), *a.*[1] ME. [a. L. *leoninus*, f. *leon-* LION. Cf. F. *léonin.*] 1. Lion-like; resembling that of a lion. 2. Of or relating to a lion 1500. Hence **Le·oninely** *adv.*

1. A man of l. aspect 1887. *L. monkey*: the *Macacus leoninus.*

L. convention or *partnership* (Rom. Law): one made 'on the terms that one should take all the profits and another bear all the loss' (Poste); held by Cassius to be not binding.

Leonine (lī·ŏnəin, -nin), *a.*[2] and *sb.* 1658. [ad. L. *leoninus*, f. *Leon-*, *Leo* proper name; see -INE[1].] A. *adj.* 1. Pertaining to one of the popes named Leo 1870. 2. *L. verse*: Latin verse consisting of hexameters, or alternate hexameters and pentameters, in which the final word rimes with that preceding the cæsural pause. So *l. poet*, *rime.* (For conjectures as to the identity of the inventor see Du Cange.) 1658. B. *sb. pl.* Leonine verse 1846.

L. city [mod.L. *Civitas Leonina*], that part of Rome, including the Vatican, which was walled and fortified by Leo IV (*c* 850).

‖**Leontiasis** (līǭntəi·ăsis). 1753. [mod.L., a. Gr., f. λεοντ-, λέων LION; see -ASIS.] *Med.* 1. A form of leprosy in which the face looks somewhat lion-like. 2. Hypertrophy of the bones of the face and skull, inducing a lion-like expression.

‖**Leontodon** (līǭ·ntŏdǭn). 1807. [mod.L., f. as prec. + ὀδοντ-, ὀδούς tooth; tr. DANDELION.] A plant of the genus *Leontodon*, of which the Dandelion was the original type.

Leopard (le·pəɹd). [ME. *leopard*, also *lebard*, *lubard*, *leupard*, *libbard*, etc., a. OF. *leopard*, *lebard*, etc. (mod.F. *léopard*), ad. late L. *leopardus*, ad. late Gr. λεόπαρδος, also λεοντόπαρδος, f. λεοντ-, λέων- LION + πάρδος PARD. Cf. Plin. *N.H.* VIII. xvii.] 1. A large carnivorous quadruped, *Panthera pardus*, also called the Panther, a native of Africa and southern Asia. Its coat is yellowish fawn shading to white under the body, with dark brown or black rosette-like spots. (In pop. language, the smaller varieties only are leopards, the larger being called panthers.) 2. A figure of a leopard in painting, heraldry, etc. ME. b. *Anc. Her.* A lion passant guardant [F. *lion léopardé*], as in the Arms of England ME. c. A gold coin of Edward III having on the obverse a lion passant guardant. 3. **Sea leopard** = *leopard-seal*: see SEA. 4. *attrib.*, as *l. skin*, *whelp*, etc. ME.

1. **American L.**, the jaguar, *Felis onca.* **Hunting L.**, the cheetah; **Snow L.**, the ounce, *F. irbis.* Can the blacke More change his skin? or the l. his spottes BIBLE (Genev.) *Jer.* xiii. 23. 2. With Libbards head on knee *L.L.L.* v. ii. 551. 4. **L. cat**, (*a*) the African wild cat, *Felis serval*; (*b*) the wild cat of India and the Malay Archipelago, *F. bengalensis*; (*c*) the American ocelot, *F. pardalis.* **L. wood**, the wood of a S. Amer. tree, *Brosimum Aubletii.*

Hence **Leo·pardess**, a female l. 1567.

Leopard's bane. 1548. [See BANE *sb.*] A plant of the genus *Doronicum*, esp. *D. Pardalianches.* Also applied to *Arnica montana*, *Paris quadrifolia* (Herb Paris), etc.

Lep, obs. or Sc. f. LAP, LEAP.

Lepadoid (le·pădoid). 1843. [f. Gr. λεπαδ-, λέπας limpet + -OID.] a. *adj.* Resembling a barnacle. b. *sb.* A lepadoid animal.

Le·pal. 1835. [f. Gr. λεπίς scale, after *petal*, etc.] *Bot.* A barren stamen transformed into a scale.

†**Le·per**, *sb.*[1] [ME. *lepre*, a. OF. *lepre*, *liepre* (mod.F. *lèpre*), ad. L. *lepra*, a. Gr. λέπρα, prop. fem. of λεπρός adj., scaly, f. λέπος scale.] Leprosy -1588.

Leper (le·pəɹ), *sb.*[2] and *a.* ME. [? prec. used attrib.] A. *sb.* One affected with leprosy. Also *attrib.*, as **leper('s) window**, name given to a supposed hagioscope for lepers. B. *adj.* Leprous ME. Hence **Le·per** *v.* to affect with leprosy; *fig.* to taint (CLOUGH).

Lepid (le·pid), *a.* Now *rare.* 1619. [ad. L. *lepidus.*] Pleasant, jocose, facetious. Occas., Charming, elegant. Hence †**Lepi·dity**, facetiousness. **Le·pidly** *adv.*

Lepidine (le·pidəin). 1855. [f. Gr. λεπιδ-, λεπίς scale; see -INE[5].] *Chem.* A volatile oily base obtained by distilling quinine, cinchonine, and other alkaloids.

Lepido- (le·pido), repr. Gr. λεπιδο-, comb. f. λεπίς scale: **Le:pidode·ndroid** *a.*, pertaining to or resembling plants of the genus *Lepidodendron*; *sb.* a plant of this genus or of the group of which it is the type. ‖**Le:pidode·ndron** [Gr. δένδρον tree], a genus of fossil plants common in coal-measures, having leaf-scars on the trunk; a plant of this genus. **Le:pidoga·noid**, **-ganoi·dean** *adjs.* pertaining to the *Lepidoganoidei*, a group of ganoid fishes having regular scales instead of plates. **Le:pidomela·ne** [Gr. μέλας, μέλαν-ος black], *Min.* a highly ferruginous mica, usu. found in aggregations of small black scales. **Le:pidosau·rian** *a.*, pertaining to the sub-class *Lepidosauria* of Reptiles, characterized by a scaly integument; *sb.* one of the *Lepidosauria.* **Le:pidosi·ren**, a genus of dipnoan fishes; a fish of this genus.

Lepidoid (le·pidoid). 1836. [f. Gr. λεπιδ-, λεπίς scale + -OID.] *adj.* and *sb.* Pertaining to, One of, the *Lepidoidei*, a family of fossil fishes having large rhomboidal scales.

Lepidolite (le·pidŏləit). 1796. [f. as prec. + -LITE.] A variety of mica containing lithia.

‖**Lepidoptera** (lepidǭ·ptĕră), *sb. pl.* 1773. [mod.L., f. Gr. λεπιδο-, LEPIDO- + πτερόν wing.] *Entom.* A large order of insects having four membranous wings covered with scales; it comprises the butterflies and moths. Hence **Le·pidopter**, one of the Lepidoptera 1828. **Lepido·pteral**, **Lepido·pteran**, **Lepido·pterous** *adjs.*, of or pertaining to the L. **Lepido·pterist**, one who studies the Lepidoptera.

Lepidote (le·pidout), *a.* 1836. [ad. mod.L. *lepidotus*, a. Gr., f. λεπιδ-, λεπίς scale.] *Bot.* Covered with scurfy scales; leprose, leprous. So **Le·pidoted** *a.*

Leporicide. [f. L. *lepor(i)-*, *lepus* hare + -CIDE 1.] A killer of hares. BURKE.

Leporine (le·pŏrəin). 1656. [ad. L. *leporinus*, f. *lepor-*, *lepus*; see -INE[1].] A. *adj.* Pertaining to a hare or hares; of the nature or form of a hare; lagomorphic. B. *sb.* An alleged cross between a hare and a rabbit 1862.

‖**Lepra** (le·pră). ME. [Late L., a. Gr. λέπρα; see LEPER *sb.*[1]] *Path.* A skin disease characterized by desquamation: (*a*) formerly = psoriasis; (*b*) now applied to leprosy (*Lepra cutanea* or *Elephantiasis Græcorum*). b. *Bot.* 'A white mealy matter, which exudes or protrudes from the surface of some plants' (*Treas. Bot.*) 1866.

Lepre: see LEPER and LEPRY.

‖**Leprechaun** (leprĕχǭ·n). 1604. [Middle Irish *luchrupán*, altered f. OIrish *luchorpán*, f. *lu* small + *corp* body.] In Irish folk-lore, A pigmy sprite.

Leprose (le·prous), *a.* 1856. [ad. L. *leprosus*, f. LEPRA.] *Bot.* Having a scaly or scurfy appearance. Hence **Leproso-**, comb. f., meaning 'leprose and . . .'

Leprosery (le·prŏsəri). 1897. [ad. F. *léproserie*, f. late L. *leprōsus* LEPROUS: see -ERY.] A leper hospital or colony.

†**Lepro·sity.** 1555. [ad. med.L. *leprositatem*, f. *leprosus* LEPROUS.] Leprous quality or condition. In *Alch.*, metallic impurity. -1635.

Leprosy (le·prŏsi). 1535. [? ad. med. L. **leprosia*, f. *leprosus* LEPROUS.] 1. A loathsome disease (*Elephantiasis Græcorum*), which slowly eats away the body, and forms shining white scales on the skin; common in mediaeval Europe. (In the Eng. Bible, the Heb. and Gr. words rendered 'leprosy' were app. used as comprehensive terms for various skin diseases.) 2. A leper-house (*rare*) 1834.

1. *fig.* Idleness is a moral l., which soon eats its way into the heart 1836.

Leprous (le·prəs), *a.* Also †**leperous**, etc. ME. [a. OF. *lepros*, *leprous* (mod.F. *lépreux*), ad. late L. *leprosus*, f. *lepra.*] 1. Afflicted or tainted with leprosy. Also *fig.* †b. Inducing leprosy -1602. c. Pertaining to, resembling, or accompanying leprosy 1635. 2. *transf.* Covered with white scales. In *Bot.* = LEPROSE. 1620.

1. The hous of Symon l. where as our lord dyned CAXTON. Behold, his hand was l. as snowe *Exod.* iv. 6. 2. One old l. screen of faded Indian leather DICKENS. Hence **Le·prous-ly** *adv.*, **-ness.**

†**Lepry.** ME. [f. LEPER *sb.*[2] + -Y[3].] = LEPROSY. -1660.

Lepto-, comb. f. Gr. λεπτός fine, small, thin, delicate: used in various scientific terms, as *leptocepha·lic* narrow-skulled, *leptoda·ctyl* adj. and sb. (a bird) having slender toes.

Lepton (le·ptǭn). *Pl.* **lepta** (-ă), *erron.* eptas. 1727. [a. Gr. λεπτόν slight (sc. νόμισμα coin), adj. neut.] a. An ancient Gr. coin worth about one-fourth of a farthing; the 'mite' of the N.T. b. The smallest coin ('centime') of modern Greece, being the one-hundredth part of a drachma.

†**Lere**, *v.* [OE. *læran* :—OTeut. **laizjan*, f. **laizâ* Lore *sb.*[1]] 1. *trans.* To teach; = Learn *v.* II. 1. –1852. 2. To inform; = Learn *v.* II. 2. –1643. 3. To learn, acquire knowledge of (something); to study, read (a book); to learn *to* do something –1818. 4. *absol.* and *intr.* = Learn *v.* I. 2, 3 b. –1721. Hence Le·red *ppl. a.* (*dial.*) = Learned.

Les, obs. f. Leash.

Lesbian (le·zbiăn), *a.* 1601. [f. L. *Lesbius*, Gr. Λέσβιος + -an.] 1. Of or pertaining to the island of Lesbos, in the Grecian archipelago. 2. *Lesbian vice*, Sapphism.

L. rule: a mason's rule made of lead, which could be bent to fit the curves of a moulding (Aristotle *Eth. Nic.* v. x. 7); *fig.*, a pliant principle of judgement. 2. L. passion, as the Greeks called it 1908. Irais.. A very scarce L. novel 1949. Hence **Le·sbianism.**

†**Lesed**, *pa. pple.* and *ppl. a.* ME. [f. L *læsus*, pa. pple. of *lædere* to hurt + -ed[1].] Damaged, injured –1741.

Lese-majesty (lī·zˌmæ·dʒĕsti). Also **leze-**. 1536. [ad. F. lèse-majesté (also in Eng. use), ad. L. *læsa majestas* hurt majesty, i.e. of the sovereign people.] Any offence against the sovereign authority; treason. Also *transf.*

¶Both in Fr. and Eng., *lese-* has been treated as a vb.-stem, taking a sb. in an objective relation, as in *lese-humanity*, an outrage upon the dignity of humanity, etc.

Lesion (lī·ʒən). 1452. [ad. F. *lésion*, ad. L. *læsionem*, f. *lædere* to hurt.] 1. Damage, injury; a hurt or flaw. 2. Damage or detriment to one's property or rights. Now chiefly in *Civil* and *Scots Law*, as a ground for setting a contract aside. 1582. 3. *Path.* Any morbid change in the exercise of functions or the texture of organs. Also *fig.* 1747.

Less (les), *a.* (*sb.*), *adv.*, and *conj.* [OE. *læs* adv. = OFris. *lês*; OE. *læssa* adj. = OFris. *lêssa*; both (ult.) :—OTeut. type **laisiz*, f. **laiso-* small + *-iz* comparative suffix (cf. -er [3]).] A. *adj.* As comparative of Little.

I. In concord with sb. (expressed or implied). 1. Of not so great size, extent, or degree (as something); smaller. Opp. (in mod.Eng.) to *greater*. Repl. by *smaller* with reference to material dimensions. b. Not so much; opp. to *more* ME. c. Fewer. Now regarded as incorrect. OE. 2. Of lower station, condition, or rank; inferior. *Obs.* exc. as in *no less a person than*, etc. OE. 3. Used *spec.* to characterize the smaller, inferior, or (after L. use) younger, of two persons or things of the same name; = L. *minor*. *Obs.* exc. in *James the Less*, and imitations of this. OE. 4. Before (formerly also, after) a numeral, etc.; = Minus. Also *transf.*, used (like *minus*) for 'not including', 'except'. OE. ¶5. Used by Shaks. in neg. expressions, where the sense requires 'more'.

1. Of too Evelis þe lasse Evill is to be chosyn 1440. b. I owe him little Dutie, and lesse Loue Shaks. 2. Phr. †*L. of, in*: inferior in point of. 3. †*L. Britain*, †*Britain the l.*: Brittany. †*The l. world* = Microcosm. 4. The space of a xi. wekes, thre dayes lesse Ld. Berners. 5. *Wint. T.* iii. ii. 57, *Cymb.* i. iv. 23.

II. *absol.* (quasi-*sb.*) 1. *The l.*: That which is smaller (of two things compared). Also of persons. ME. 2. A less amount, quantity, or number (*than* one specified or implied) OE.

1. The haire that couers the wit, is more then the wit; for the greater hides the lesse Shaks. 2. Phr. *L. than no time*; joc. for a very short time. *Far, little, much, nothing, something l.* *No l.* = 'nothing less'. *Nothing l. than*: quite equal to, the same thing as; see also B.

B. *adv.* To a smaller extent; in a lower degree OE.

Much l., still l. (†formerly also simply *l.*); The world thou hast not seen, much l. her glory Milt. †*Nothing l.*: anything rather. *Nothing l. than*: anything rather than; = F. *rien moins que.* Now *rare.* 1548. *More or less*: see More.

†C. *conj.* Unless. In early use *l. than, l. that* 1422–1772.

And the mute Silence hist along, 'L. Philomel will daign a Song Milt. *Pens.* 56.

†**Less**, *v.* [ME. *lasse, lessi*, f. *lasse, lesse* Less *a.*] To make or become less –1633.

-less (lès), *suffix*, forming adjs. The OE. *léas* was used in the sense 'devoid (of)', 'free (from)', (*a*) in OE. only, as a separate adj., governing the genitive; (*b*) subseq., as a suffix, attached to sbs. to form adjs. with privative sense. On the supposed analogy of instances of (*b*) in which the sb. taking the suffix was of the same form with the stem of a related vb., as *countless, numberless*, the suffix has been appended to many verbs, as in *abashless, dauntless, resistless, tireless*, †*topless* (= not overtopped), etc.

Lessee (lesī·). 1495. [a. AF. *lessee*, OF. *lessé*, pa. pple. of *lesser, lessier*, mod.F. *laisser* to leave; see Lease *v.*[3] and -ee.] A person to whom a lease is granted; a tenant under a lease. Hence **Lessee·ship**.

Lessen (le·s'n), *v.* ME. [f. Less *a.* + -en [5] 1.] 1. *intr.* To become less; to decrease. 2. To decrease in apparent size by the effect of distance, as a bird flying 1611. 3. *trans.* To make less; to diminish ME. †b. *pass.* To suffer loss or curtailment *of*; to be reduced *in* –1793. 4. To make less in estimation; to extenuate (faults); to disparage. *Obs.* or *arch.* 1585. †5. To humble; to degrade, lower –1788.

1. The river..lessened every step we went De Foe. 2. The sky-lark..lessening from the dazzled sight Gray. 3. To l. the value of money 1793, the hours of work Jevons. 4. To l. a heroic figure 1877. 5. The making of new Lords lessens all the rest Selden.

Lesser (le·səɹ). 1459. [Double comparative, f. Less *a.* + -er [3].] A. *adj.* 1. = Less *a.* Now only used *attrib.* 2. In spec. or techn. use, opposed to *greater*. a. *Astron.*, as in *The Lesser Bear*. Also *Geog.* in *L. Asia* (now *arch.*), Asia Minor. 1551. b. *Mus.* = Minor (intervals) 1674. c. In names of plants and animals, as *l. spotted woodpecker, l. celandine* 1678. d. *Anat.* 1842.

1. Woman is the l. man Tennyson.

†B. *adv.* Less –1625.

†**Lesses**, *sb. pl.* ME. [a. obs. F. *laisses*, *quasi* 'leavings', f. *laisser* to leave.] The dung of a 'ravenous' animal, as a wild boar, wolf, or bear –1807.

Lessive (le·siv). *rare.* 1826. [ad. F. *lessive* :—L. *lixiva* adj. neut. pl. used as sb.] A lye of wood-ashes, soap-suds, etc., used in washing.

Lessness (le·snĕs). *rare.* 1635. [f. Less *a.* + -ness.] Inferiority.

Lesson (le·sən, les'n), *sb.* ME. [ad. OF. *lecon*, F. *leçon* :—L. *lectionem*. Cf. Lection.] †1. The action of reading. Wyclif. †b. A public reading; a lecture; a course of lectures –1724. 2. *Eccl.* A portion of Scripture or other sacred writing read at divine service; a lection. (Now chiefly, the portion of the O.T. ('first lesson') and that of the N.T. ('second lesson') read at Morning and Evening Prayer in the Church of England.) ME. 3. A portion of a book or the like, to be studied by the pupil for repetition to the teacher. Hence, something that is or is to be learnt. ME. 4. A continuous portion of teaching given to a pupil or class at one time; one of the portions into which a course of instruction is divided. Hence occas. in text-books, a section of suitable length for continuous study. ME. b. *transf.* An instructive occurrence or example; a rebuke or punishment calculated to prevent a repetition of an offence 1586. †5. *Mus.* a. An exercise; a composition serving an educational purpose. b. A piece to be performed. –1811.

3. To learne Any hard L. that may do thee good Shaks. 4. *To give, take lessons*: to give, receive systematic instruction *in* a specified subject. Mr. Blagrave..did give me a l. upon the flageolette Pepys. b. His self-denial..was a constant l. 1882. *attrib.*, *l. book*, (*a*) a book from which lessons are learnt; †(*b*) a lectionary.

Lesson (le·sən), *v.* 1555. [f. prec. sb.] 1. *trans.* To give a lesson or lessons to, to instruct; to admonish, rebuke. Also, To bring *into* or *to* (a state) by lessoning. 2. To teach (a thing) as a lesson 1821.

1. It ought to l. us into an abhorrence of the abuse of our own power in our own day Burke.

Lessor (lesǭ·ɹ). 1487. [a. AF. *lessor, lessour*, f. *lesser*; see Lease *v.*[3] and -or.] One who grants a lease; one who lets property on lease.

Lest (lest), *conj.* [OE. phrase *þý læs þe*, lit. 'whereby less' = L. *quominus*. In ME. *þý* was dropped, and *les þe* became *les te*, *þ* after *s* changing normally into *t*.] 1. = L. *nē*, Eng. *that.. not, for fear that.* †Also *l. that*, in the same sense. 2. Used after verbs of fearing, or the like, to introduce a clause expressing the event that is feared; often admitting of being replaced by *that* (without neg.) OE.

1. Take hede l. eny man deceave you Tindale *Mark* xiii. 5. Lord God of Hosts, be with us yet, L. we forget, l. we forget R. Kipling. 2. Fearing l. they should succumb 1881.

Lest, obs. f. Last, Least, List *sb.* and *v.*

Let (let), *sb.*[1] ME. [f. Let *v.*[2]] 1. Hindrance, obstruction; also, something that hinders, an impediment. Now *arch.*: most common in *without l. or hindrance.* 2. In *Bowls, Fives, Rackets*, etc. Obstruction of the ball in specified ways, requiring it to be served again 1608.

1. The enemy wrought his will without l. or hindrance 1867.

Let (let), *sb.*[2] 1838. [f. Let *v.*[1]] A letting for hire or rent.

Let (let), *v.*[1] Pa. t. and pple. **let.** [Com. Teut. reduplicating str. vb.: OE. *lǽtan*. The root, Teut. **lǣt-* :—pre-Teut. **lēd-*, is related by ablaut to Teut. **lat-* (whence Late *a.*) :—pre-Teut. **lad-* (whence L. *lassus* weary). Primary sense app. 'to let go through weariness, to neglect'. Cf. F. *laisser* to let :—L. *laxare*, f. *laxus* loose.]

I. To leave; to allow to pass. †1. *trans.* To allow to remain –1651. †2. To leave undone; to omit (in reading, etc.) –ME. †b. with *inf.* as *obj.*: To omit or forbear *to* do something –1653. †c. *absol.* or *intr.* To desist, forbear –1554. †3. To leave *to* some one else –1612. †4. To quit, abandon, forsake; to abandon *to* (the flames) –1599. †5. To lose (one's life, honour, virtue, etc.) –1587. 6. To allow (fluid) to escape; to shed (tears, blood); to emit (breath, etc.). Also, to discharge (a gun). *Obs.* or *dial.* OE. 7. To grant the temporary possession and use of, in consideration of rent or hire. †Formerly also, to lend (money) at interest. OE. b. *intr.* in passive sense = *to be let* 1855. †8. To set free, liberate –1670. 9. To allow to pass or go. ME.

1. *Wint. T.* i. ii. 41. 2. b. Shaks. *Lucr.* 10. 6. *To l. blood* (Surg.): see Blood *sb.* I. 1. I'll..L. blood from her weasand Shelley. *To l. at* (now Sc.): to discharge missiles at; to assail; to aim at. *To l. into* (slang): to attack. 7. To l. his labour where it would obtain a better reward 1833. b. The mortgaged houses would speedily l. 1885. 8. Phr. *To l. free, at large.* 9. They would not l. a single Englishman on board of her Ld. Lonsdale.

Comb. with preps. *To l. into*: (*a*) to admit to, allow to enter (*lit.* and *fig.*); †also *absol.*; (*b*) to insert in the surface or substance of; (*c*) to introduce to the knowledge of, make acquainted with, inform about; also, †*to l. into one's knowledge.* *To l.* (a person) *off* a penalty, etc. (Cf. *let off* below.)

II. Uses requiring an inf. (normally without *to*). 1. *trans.* To suffer, permit, allow OE. b. The use of *to* before the inf. occurs chiefly when *let* is used in the passive 1523. 2. To cause. Now *arch.* exc. in *to l.* (a person) *know* = to inform (of something). OE. 3. The imperative with sb. or pronoun as obj. often serves as an auxiliary ME. b. with ellipsis of *go.* (Freq. in Shaks.; now *arch.*) 1590.

1. I was not let see him J. H. Newman. b. If they be..let to run wild Keble. 2. Pray l. me know your mind in this, for I am utterly at a loss Pope. 3. Leat vs call to memorie, the princes of times past Ld. Berners. b. But com let's on Milt. *Comus* 599.

†III. To behave, appear, think. 1. *intr.* To comport oneself; to have (a particular) behaviour or appearance; to make *as though* –1787 (*dial.*). 2. To think (highly, etc.) *of* (occas. *by, to*). *To l. well of*: to be glad of. –1600. 3. *trans.* with *complement.* To regard as. Also with obj. and inf., or clause: To consider *to be, that* (a person or thing) *is.* –1450.

Phraseological combs. * *with adj. as complement.* **Let alone.** †a. To leave in solitude. b. To abstain from interfering with, attending to, or doing. *To l. well alone*: see Well. Also *absol.* c. *colloq.* in imper.: *Let me* (*him*, etc.) *alone to* (do so and so) =

I (he, etc.) may be trusted to do, etc. Also with *for* and †*ellipt.* **d.** The imper. *let alone* is used colloq. with the sense 'not to mention'. (The obj. in this use follows the adj.). **e.** as *sb.* (*let-alone*); now only *attrib.* in the sense of 'laisser-aller'. **L. loose.** †**a.** To liberate, set free. **b.** To loose (one's hold, etc.), slacken (a bridle). **c.** To give free course to, allow to have full swing. †**d.** *intr.* To give way *to*.

** *with a verb in the inf.* **L. be. a.** = *let alone*, **b.** *absol.* **c.** = *let alone*, **d.** Chiefly *Sc.* **L. fall. a.** To lower (a bridge, a veil, etc.); *Naut.* to drop an anchor; also, a sail loosed from its gaskets. **b.** To proceed no further with, drop (a business). ? *Obs.* **c.** To drop (a word, a hint), esp. inadvertently. **d.** To shed (tears). **e.** *Geom.* To draw (a perpendicular) to a line from a point outside it. **L. fly**: see FLY *v.*[1] **L. go. a.** *trans.* To set at liberty, release; to relax (one's hold); to drop (an anchor). **b.** *intr.* = to let go one's hold. Const. *of.* **c.** To dismiss from one's thoughts; to cease to attend to or control. †**d.** To fire off (ordnance), discharge (missiles). **e.** To cease to restrain. *To l. oneself go*: in recent use, to give free vent to one's enthusiasm. **f.** as *sb.* An act of letting go. **L. run.** *Naut.* 'To cast off at once' (Smyth). **L. slip. a.** To let go (*gen.*), e.g. to unloose (a knot), to let loose (a hound) from the leash. Also *fig.* **b.** To allow (an opportunity) to pass without profit.

*** *with advs.* †**L. abroad.** To permit or cause to get about. **L. down. a.** To lower (a drawbridge, steps of a carriage, etc.); in narrower sense, to cause or allow to descend by gradual motion or short stages. Also occas. *intr.* for *pass.* **b.** To lower in position, intensity, strength, †value; to abase, humble. Also, to disappoint. **c.** *techn.* (*a*) To lower the temper of (metal). (*b*) To reduce or dissolve (shellac, etc.) by means of spirit solvents. **d.** *To be let down*: (of the claws of a hound) to be in contact with the ground. Also, of the sinew of a horse, to give way. **e.** *To l.* (a person) *down gently* or *softly*: to deal with him so as to spare his self-respect. **f.** as *sb.* (*let-down*). An act or instance of letting down: (*a*) a drawback; (*b*) a come-down; (*c*) a disappointment. *slang.* **L. in. a.** To admit; *esp.* to open the door of a house or room to; hence *refl.* to enter a building or room, usu. by means of a key. **b.** To give admittance to (light, water, air, etc.). Also *transf.* and *fig.* **c.** To insert into the surface or substance of a thing. **d.** To give rise to. *Obs.* or *arch.* **e.** Of ice, etc.: To give way and allow (a person) to fall through into the water. Hence *fig.* (colloq.) To involve in loss or difficulty, by fraud, etc. *To l. in for*: to involve in the performance, payment, etc. of. **L. off.** †**a.** *intr.* To cease. **b.** To discharge with an explosion. Hence *fig.* To 'fire off' (a joke, speech, etc.). **c.** To allow to escape; to excuse from punishment, service, etc. **d.** To allow or cause (fumes, sediment, etc.) to pass away. **e.** To lease in portions. **f.** as *sb.* (*let-off*). (*a*) A festivity. (*b*) An outlet. (*c*) A failure to utilize a chance in a game; e.g. in *Cricket*, to get a batsman out by a catch. (*e*) *Weaving.* The 'paying off' of the yarn from the beam; *concr.* a contrivance for regulating this; also *attrib.* **L. on.** *intr.* To disclose or betray a fact by word or look. *dial.* and *U.S.* **L. out. a.** To give egress to; to cause or allow to escape by an opening, esp. through a doorway (also *absol.*); to liberate. *To l. the cat out of the bag*: see BAG *sb.* **b.** To give vent to. †**c.** To allow to go forth freely *to* (an object). **d.** To make (a garment) looser. **e.** *Naut.* To shake out (a reef). **f.** To lend (money) at interest (? *obs.*); to put out to hire; to distribute among several tenants or hirers. **g.** To divulge; freq. with clause as obj. **h.** To strike out with (the fist, the heels, etc.). Chiefly *absol.* or *intr.* To strike or lash out. Hence, to use strong language. **i.** To give (a horse) his head. Also *absol.*, to ride with increased speed. *colloq.* **Let up.** *U.S. colloq.* **a.** To become less severe; to diminish, cease, stop; *to let up on*, to cease to have to do with 1882. **b.** as *sb.* (*let-up*). Cessation, pause; relaxation 1856.

Let (let), *v.*[2] [OE. *lęttan*, f. OTeut. **lato-* LATE *a.*] **1.** *trans.* To hinder, stand in the way of (a person, thing, action, etc.). *arch.* †**b.** *absol.* To be a hindrance –1642. †**2.** *intr.* To withhold oneself, to desist, refrain; to omit *to do* (something) –1653. †**b.** To tarry, wait –ME.

1. Persons who wilfully l. or hinder any sheriff or constable 1799. 'Sir King, mine ancient wound is hardly whole, And lets me from the saddle' TENNYSON. **2. b.** And in that yle half a day he lette CHAUCER.

-let, *suffix*, appended to sbs. The oldest words in Eng. with this ending are adoptions of OF. words formed by adding the dim. suffix *-et, -ete* (see -ET) to sbs. in *-el* (repr. the L. dim. suffix *-ellum, -ellam*, or the L. ending *-ale* of neut. adjs.; see -AL). Examples are *bracelet, chaplet, crosslet, frontlet, hamlet*, etc. Of these only *crosslet* suggests by its form and sense a dim. of an Eng. word. Possibly Fr. dims. were directly imitated by some Eng. writers.

An early dim. in *-let* is *armlet* (sense 2, 'little arm of the sea', recorded 1538); others are *townlet* (*a* 1552), *ringlet* (Shaks.), *kinglet* (Florio, after F. *roitelet*). But the formation did not become common until the 18th c.

In a few words (*anklet, armlet, necklet*, etc.) the suffix is appended to sbs. denoting parts of the body, forming names for articles of ornament or attire. The oldest word of this type, *armlet*, was perh. suggested by a false analysis of *frontlet*; in the later words the analogy of *bracelet* has prob. been chiefly operative.

Let-alone, *sb.* and *attrib.*: see LET *v.*[1]

Letch (letʃ), *sb.*[1] *Sc.* and *n. dial.* [? f. OE. *lęccan* vb.; cf. LEACH *sb.*] A stream flowing through boggy land; a muddy ditch or hole; a bog.

Letch (letʃ), *sb.*[2] 1796. [? f. LATCH *v.*[1]] A craving, longing.

The l. for blood which characterizes the savage 1862.

Letch, var. of LEACH *sb.*

Lethal (lī·þăl), *a.* 1583. [ad. L. *let(h)alis*, f. *let(h)um* death.] **1.** That may or will cause death; deadly, mortal. Now *esp.* of a dose of poison: Sufficient to cause death. 1613. **2.** Causing or resulting in spiritual death; deadly 1583. **3.** Of or pertaining to death 1607.

1. *L. chamber*: a chamber containing gases for killing animals painlessly. **3.** On thy wan forehead starts the l. dew COLERIDGE. †**Le·thally** *adv.*

Lethality (līþæ·lĭti). *rare.* 1656. [f. LETHAL *a.* + -ITY.] Lethal condition or quality; deadliness.

Lethargic (līþā·ɹdʒik). ME. [ad. L. *lethargicus*, ad. Gr., f. ληθαργος; see LETHARGY.] **A.** *adj.* **1.** Affected with lethargy. **b.** *transf.* Dull, sleepy, sluggish, apathetic 1612. **2.** Of or belonging to lethargy 1595. **3.** Causing lethargy 1715.

3. Found to possess l. properties DICKENS.

B. *sb.* A lethargic person. ? *Obs.* 1470.

So **Letha·rgical** *a.*, **-ly** *adv.*, **-ness.** †**Letha·rgious** *a. rare*, lethargic.

Lethargize (le·þăɹdʒəiz), *v.* 1614. [f. LETHARGY *sb.* + -IZE.] *trans.* To affect with lethargy.

Lethargy (le·þăɹdʒi), *sb.* ME. [a. L. *lethargia*, a. Gr., f. λήθαργος forgetful, f. ληθ-, λανθάνειν, λανθάνεσθαι to forget.] **1.** *Path.* Morbid drowsiness or prolonged and unnatural sleep. **2.** A condition of torpor, inertness, or apathy ME. Also *transf.*

2. Falling..into a carelessness, and (as I may call it) a L. of thought DRYDEN. Hence †**Le·thargy** *v. rare*, to affect with l.

Lethargy, obs. f. LITHARGE.

‖**Lethe** (lī·þi). 1567. [L., a use of Gr. λήθη forgetfulness. No river is called Λήθη by the Greeks; the river is Λήθης ὕδωρ 'water of oblivion'.] **1.** *Gr. Myth.* A river in Hades, the water of which produced, in those who drank it, forgetfulness of the past. Hence, 'the waters of oblivion' or forgetfulness of the past. ¶**2.** [? Infl. by L. *let(h)um*.] Death. *Jul. C.* III. i. 206. **3.** *attrib.*, as *L.-flood*, etc. 1579.

3. The fat weede That rots it selfe in ease, on L. Wharfe *Haml.* I. v. 33. Hence **Lethe·an** *a.* pertaining to the river L.; hence, pertaining to or causing forgetfulness of the past.

†**Le·thied,** *a.* [app. for *Lethe'd* (as printed in mod. edd.), f. LETHE + -ED.] ? = LETHEAN. *Ant. & Cl.* II. i. 27.

Lethiferous (līþi·fĕrəs), *a.* Also **letiferous.** 1651. [f. L. *let(h)ifer*, f. *let(h)um* death; see -FEROUS.] That causes or results in death; deadly. So **Lethi·feral** *a. rare.*

†**Lethy,** *a.* 1613. [f. LETHE + -Y[1].] = LETHEAN. Marston.

Let-off, *sb.*: see LET *v.*[1]

Let-pass (letpɑ·s). 1635. [f. phr. *let pass.*] A permission to pass; a permit.

Lett (let). 1831. [a. G. *Lette*, ad. *Latvi*, native name.] **a.** One of a people who inhabit parts of the Baltic provinces of Russia. **b.** = LETTISH.

Lettable (le·tăb'l), *a.* Also **letable.** 1611. [f. LET *v.*[1] + -ABLE.] That may be let.

Letter (le·təɹ), *sb.*[1] ME. [a. or ad. OF. and F. *lettre*:—L. *littera*, also *lītera*, letter of the alphabet (pl. *litteræ* an epistle, records, etc.), of unkn. origin.]

I. 1. A character representing one of the elementary sounds used in speech; an alphabetic symbol. **b.** *sing. collective* for *pl.* Now only in *before the l.* (= the more usual *before letters*): a proof taken from a plate before the lettering is added ME. **2.** *Printing.* A type; usu. in *pl.* types; also, a style of printed characters; a fount of type; types collectively 1519.

1. Ouer whose hedde was written in letters of Romayn in gold, *faicte bonne chere quy voudra* HALL.

II. Something written. †**1. a.** *sing.* Anything written; an inscription, document, text; a written warrant –1534. **b.** *pl.* Writings, written records –1789. **2.** A missive in writing; an epistle ME. **b.** *pl.* with sing. meaning, after L. *litteræ* ME. **3.** The precise terms of a statement; the signification on the surface ME. **4.** *pl.* Literature; also, the study of literature, erudition, learning; occas. (later), the profession of literature ME.

1. a. Magicien was noon That koude expounde what this lettre mente CHAUCER. **2.** By penny-post to send a l. PRIOR. **b.** *Letters dimissory, patent, testimonial*, etc. (see the adjs.). *Letters of administration, horning*, etc. (see those words). **L. of advice** (Comm.), a letter notifying, e.g. the drawing of a bill on, or the consignment of goods to, the correspondent. **L. of attorney** = *power of attorney* (see ATTORNEY *sb.*[2]). **Letters of brotherhood** (or **fraternity**), letters granted by a convent or an order to its benefactors entitling those named in them to a share in the benefits of its prayers and good works. **3.** *The l.*: the literal tenor of a law or statement, opp. to *the spirit* (see 2 *Cor.* iii. 6). *To the l.*: to the fullest extent; I shall obey you to the l. BYRON. **4. b.** *Man of letters* [= F. *homme de lettres*]: a scholar; now usu., a literary man, an author. *Commonwealth, republic of letters*, the whole body of those engaged in literary pursuits. Letters kept pace with art PRESCOTT.

attrib. and *Comb.* **1.** General: as *l.-bag, -clip, -post*, etc.; *l.-sorter*, etc.; *l.-copying, -writing.*

2. Special: as **l.-balance**, a contrivance for weighing a l.; **-book**, a book in which letters are filed, or in which copies of letters are kept for reference; **-bound** *a.*, enslaved by the letter of a law; **-box**, one in which letters are posted or deposited on delivery; **-card** [F. *carte-lettre*, G. *Kartenbrief*], a folded card with gummed and perforated edges for writing a l. upon 1892; **-case**, a case to hold letters; **-cutter**, one who makes punches for type-founding; so *letter-cutting*; **-founder, -founding, -foundry** (see FOUNDER *sb.*[2], etc.); **-head**, a sheet of letter-paper with a printed or engraved heading giving address, date, etc.; **-high** *a.* (*Printing*), of the height of the ordinary printing-type; **-lock**, a lock which can be opened only by arranging letters on it so as to form the word to which the lock is set; **-paper**, quarto-size paper for writing letters, the smaller sizes being called *note-paper*; **-perfect** *a.* (*Theatr.*), knowing one's part to the l.; **-punch**, a steel punch used in making matrices for type; **-rack**, (*a*) a tray with divisions to hold types; (*b*) a small frame in which letters or papers are kept; **-stamp**, an official stamp for cancelling postage-stamps or for impressing notifications on letters or parcels; **-weight** = *paper-weight*; **-wood**, another name for *leopard-wood* (see LEOPARD); **-worship**, undue attention to the l. of a law, etc.; **-writer**, (*a*) one who writes letters (hence, a title for manuals of letter-writing 1759); (*b*) a machine for copying letters.

Le·tter, *sb.*[2] ME. [f. LET *v.*[1] + -ER[1].] One who lets (blood, property, loose, etc.).

†**Le·tter,** *sb.*[3] ME. [f. LET *v.*[2] + -ER[1].] One who lets or hinders –1616.

Letter (le·təɹ), *v.* 1460. [f. LETTER *sb.*[1]] †**1.** *trans.* To instruct in letters. **2.** To exhibit or distinguish by means of letters 1668. **3.** To affix a name or title in letters upon (a book, a shop, etc.); to inscribe (a name) in letters 1712.

2. Fraunhofer..lettered them and made accurate maps of them TYNDALL.

Lettered (le·təɹd), *ppl. a.* ME. [f. LETTER *sb.*[1] or *v.*] **1.** Acquainted with letters; literate. **2.** Of or pertaining to learning or learned men; characterized by literary culture 1709. **3.** Composed of (so many) letters. WILLET. **4.** Inscribed with letters; *spec.* of a book: Having the title on the back in gilt or coloured letters 1665.

1. Mounsier, are you not lettred? *L. L. L.* v. i. 48. In lettered ease and calm content BP. MANT. **2.** He was a man of l. tastes DISRAELI.

Lettering (le·təriŋ), *vbl. sb.* 1645. [f. LETTER *v.* or *sb.*[1] + -ING[1].] †**1.** Letter-writing –1813. **2.** Putting letters upon (anything) by inscribing, marking, painting, gilding, printing, stamping, etc. Also, the letters inscribed. 1811.

1. I hate l. BYRON.

Letterless (le·təɹlĕs), *a.* 1618. [-LESS.] Devoid of letters. **1.** Illiterate. Also *absol.*

2. Having no correspondence 1837. 3. Having no letters inscribed 1881.

Lettern, obs. f. LECTERN.

Le·tter-press. 1758. [f. LETTER *sb.*[1]] 1. (Now usu. *letterpress.*) Matter printed from letters or types, as dist. from plates. Also *attrib.*, as in *l. printing.* 2. A letter-weight 1848. 3. A copying-press 1901.

Letter(r)ure, var. of LETTRURE.

Lettic (le·tik), *a.* (*sb.*) 1872. [f. LETT + -IC.] = LETTISH. Also, in wider sense, applied to the Baltic group of langs., comprising Lettish, Lithuanian, and Old Prussian, and to the peoples speaking these. As *sb.*, the Lettic or Lettish language. Also Letto-.

‖**Lettiga** (lettī·ga). 1805. [It. :—L. *lectica* a litter.] A kind of sedan chair carried by mules and seating two persons vis-à-vis.

Lettish (le·tiʃ), *a.* (*sb.*) 1831. [f. LETT + -ISH[1].] *adj.* Pertaining to the Letts or their language. *sb.* The language of the Letts.

†**Lettrure.** †Also **letterure.** ME. [ad. OF. *letreüre*, *lettreüre* :—L. *litteratura.*] 1. A writing, a written book. *Holy lettrure* = Holy Scripture. –1450. 2. Knowledge of letters; learning –1483.

Lettuce (le·tis). [ME. *letuse* conn. w. OF. *laitue* (mod.F. *laitue*) :—L. *lactuca*, f. *lact-*, *lac* milk, with reference to the milky juice of the plant.] 1. Any plant of the genus *Lactuca*; esp. *L. sativa* or Garden Lettuce, the leaves of which are used as a salad; often *collect.* in *sing.* for the plants or their leaves. 2. *attrib.* 1540.

1. *Wild l.*: some plant of this genus growing wild; *spec.* in England, *L. Scariola* and *L. virosa*; in U.S., *L. Canadensis.* For *Cabbage*, *Cos*, *Hare*, *Lamb's L.*, etc., see the first member.

Comb.: **l.-opium**, the inspissated juice of various kinds of lettuce, used as a drug; **-water**, a decoction of l.

Letuare, -ie, -y(e, var. LECTUARY.

Let-up, *sb.*: see LET *v.*[1]

Leucæthiop (liusī·þiǫp). Also **leucoethiop**, leucœthiop. 1819. [f. Gr. λευκός white (see LEUCO-) + Αἰθιοπ-, Αἰθίοψ an Ethiopian.] An albino of a negro race. So **Leu:cæthio·pia**, the constitution of a l. **Leu:cæthio·pic** *a.* characterized by leucæthiopia.

‖**Leuchæmia** (liukī·miă). Less correctly leuc-, leukæmia. 1855. [mod.L., f. Gr. λευκός white + αἷμα blood.] *Path.* A disease in which there is an excess of white corpuscles in the blood; leucocythæmia. Hence **Leuchæ·mic** *a.*

Leucic (liū·sik), *a.* 1865. [f. LEUC(IN + -IC.] *Chem. L. acid*, a fatty acid obtained from leucin. *L. ether*, an oily liquid obtained by the action of zinc-ethyl on oxalic ether.

Leucin (liū·sin). Also **-ine.** 1826. [f. Gr. λευκός + -IN.] *Chem.* A white crystalline substance, produced by the decomposition of proteins; amido-caproic acid.

Leucite (liū·səit). Also †**leucit.** 1799. [a. G. *leucit*, f. Gr. λευκός white; see -ITE.] *Min.* A glassy silicate of aluminium and potassium, occurring in volcanic rocks. Hence **Leuci·tic** *a.* **Leu·citoid** (*Cryst.*), the trapezohedron or tetragonal trisoctahedron; so called as being the form of the mineral l.

Leuco- (liū·ko), bef. a vowel **leuc-**, a. Gr. λευκο-, comb. f. λευκός white, as in:

Leuca·niline, *Chem.* a white crystalline substance obtained from rosaniline, etc. **Leuco·pathy** = ALBINISM. **Leu·cophyll** [Gr. φύλλον leaf], *Bot.* a colourless substance found in etiolated plants, capable of being transformed into chlorophyll. **Leu·coplast** [Gr. πλαστός moulded], **-pla·stid**, *Biol.* one of the colourless corpuscles found in the protoplasm of vegetable cells around which starch accumulates. **Leu·coscope**, an instrument contrived by Helmholtz for comparing the relative whiteness of lights or colours.

Leucocyte (liū·kǒsəit). 1870. [f. LEUCO- + -CYTE.] *Phys.* A colourless or 'white' corpuscle of the blood, lymph, etc. Hence **Leu:cocyto·sis**, Virchow's name for a temporary increase in the number of white corpuscles in the blood.

‖**Leucocythæmia** (liū:kosiþī·miă). Also **-themia.** 1852. [f. LEUCO- + Gr. κύτος -CYTE + αἷμα blood.] *Path.* = LEUCHÆMIA.

Leucoethiop: see LEUCÆTHIOP.

Leucoline (liū·kŏləin). 1852. [f. LEUCO- + -OL + -INE[5].] A coal-tar base, identical with quinoline. Also **Leu·col** (-kol) 1844.

‖**Leucoma** (liukōu·mă). 1706. [mod.L., a. Gr., f. λευκοῦν to make white, f. λευκός.] *Path.* = ALBUGO.

Leucomaine (liukōu·meɪ,əin). 1887. [f. LEUCO- after *ptomaïne.*] *Physiol. Chem.* An alkaloid found in the living body as a decomposition product of a protein.

Leucophane (liū·kŏfēⁱn). 1844. [f. late Gr. λευκοφανής, f. λευκός white + φαν-, φαίνεσθαι to appear, from its showing whitish reflexions.] *Min.* Silicate of glucium, calcium, and sodium. Also **Leuco·phanite.**

†**Leucophle·gmacy.** 1664. [ad. Gr. λευκοφλεγματία, f. λευκός white + φλεγματ- PHLEGM.] *Path.* A dropsical tendency, denoted by a phlegmatic condition of body –1732. So **Leu:cophlegma·tic** *a.* 1668.

‖**Leucorrhœa** (liū·kŏrī·ă). 1797. [f. Gr. λευκός white + ῥοία flow.] *Path.* A mucous discharge from the female genital organs; the whites.

‖**Leucosis** (liukōu·sis). 1706. [a. Gr., f. λευκοῦν to make white.] **a.** Albinism. **b.** Abnormal whitening of some part of the body.

Leucous (liū·kəs), *a.* 1842. [f. Gr. λευκός + -OUS.] White-skinned; blonde; albino.

Leud (liūd). *Hist.* Also in L. pl. form leudes (liū·dīz). 1756. [repr. med.L. *leudes*, a. OHG. *liudi*, *liuti.*] In the Frankish kingdoms: A vassal or feudatory.

Levancy (le·vănsi). 1695. [f. LEVANT *a.*; see -ANCY.] *Law.* In phr. *L. and couchancy*: the fact of being levant and couchant.

Levant (lĭvæ·nt), *sb.*[1] 1497. [a. F. *levant*, pr. pple. of *lever*, used subst. for the point where the sun rises. (In Milt. stressed *le·vant.*)] 1. *Geog.* †**a.** The countries of the East. **b.** *spec.* The eastern part of the Mediterranean, with its islands and the countries adjoining. 2. An easterly wind blowing up the Mediterranean; a levanter. ? *Obs.* 1628. 3. = *levant morocco* 1880. 4. *attrib.* †**a.** = 'east-, eastern', as *l. sea*, *wind* 1601. **b.** (sense 1 b, 'coming from the Levant'), as *L. feathers*, *morocco*, etc. 1503.

1. a. *The High L.* = the far East. 4. a. Forth rush the L. and the Ponent Windes MILT. *P.L.* x. 704.

Levant (lĭvæ·nt), *sb.*[2] 1714. [transf. use of prec. 1. Cf. F. '*faire voile en Levant*, to bee stolne, filched, or purloyned away' (Cotgr.).] *To come the l.*, *run* or *throw a l.*: to make a bet with the intention of absconding if it is lost.

Levant (le·vănt), *a.* 1496. [a. F. *levant*, pr. pple. of *lever* to raise, *refl.* to rise.] *Law.* Only in phr. *Levant and couchant*: lit. 'rising up and lying down'; said of cattle.

Levant (lĭvæ·nt), *v.* 1760. [f. LEVANT *sb.*[2]] 1. *intr.* To steal away, 'bolt'. Now *esp.* of a betting man: To abscond. 1781. †2. *trans.* To cheat by absconding 1776. In *L. me!*, a mild imprecation. FOOTE. Hence **Leva·nter**[2].

Levanter[1] (lĭvæ·ntəɪ). 1668. [f. LEVANT *sb.*[1] + -ER[1].] 1. **a.** = LEVANTINE *sb.* 1 (*rare*). **b.** A ship trading to the Levant (*rare*). 2. A strong and raw easterly wind in the Mediterranean (Smyth) 1790. Also *fig.*

Levantine (lĭvæ·ntin, le·văntin). 1649. [f. LEVANT *sb.*[1] + -INE[1].] **A.** *adj.* Of or pertaining to the Levant; in early use, †eastern. Also, recalling or resembling the manners of the Levantines. Of a vessel: Trading to the Levant. **B.** *sb.* 1. An inhabitant or native of the Levant 1706. 2. [F. *levantine.*] A very rich stout twilled black silk material 1831.

†**Levation.** ME. [ad. L. *levationem*, f. *levare* to raise.] 1. *Eccl.* The elevation of the Host –1559. 2. *concr.* Something levied; a duty, tax. CHILD.

Levator (lĭvē·tǫɪ). 1615. [a. late L., f. as prec.] 1. *Anat.* = ELEVATOR 1. †2. *Surg.* = ELEVATOR 2. –1789. Also †**Levatory** (in sense 2).

†**Leve**, *sb.* [OE. *geleafa*, *léafa* str. masc.; related to Goth. *galaubjan*; see BELIEVE *v.*] Belief, faith; *occas.* trust –ME.

†**Leve**, *v.*[1] [OE. (Anglian) *léfan*, (WS.) *lýfan*, f. OTeut. **lauƀâ* LEAVE *sb.*] To allow, permit. Also (esp. of God or Christ), to grant. –1513.

And leue me nevere swich a cas be-falle CHAUCER.

†**Leve**, *v.*[2] [OE. (Anglian) *léfan*, (WS.) *líefan*, short f. *gelefan*, *geliefan*; see BELIEVE.] 1. *intr.* = BELIEVE I. 1. –1535. 2. *trans.* = BELIEVE II. 1–3. –1570.

Leve, obs. f. LEAF, LIEF, LIVE *v.*

Levee (lĭvī·, le·vi), *sb.*[1] *U.S.* Also **levy.** 1718. [a. F. *levée*, fem. of *levé*, pa. pple. of *lever* to raise.] 1. An embankment to prevent the overflow of a river. 2. A landing-place, pier, quay 1842.

Levee (le·vi), *sb.*[2] Also †**levy, levée.** 1672. [ad. F. *levé*, var. of *lever* rising (subst. use of *lever* inf.); cf. COUCHEE. The pronunc. (lĭvī·) or (levī·) is preferred in the U.S.] †1. The action of rising, *spec.* from one's bed –1827. 2. A reception of visitors on rising from bed; a morning assembly held by a prince, etc. 1672. **b.** In Great Britain and Ireland, an assembly held (in the early afternoon) by the sovereign or his representative, at which men only are received 1760. **c.** A miscellaneous assemblage of visitors, irrespective of the time of day; applied (*U.S.*) to the President's receptions 1766. †3. The company assembled at a levee –1771.

2. b. He goes to the Levée once a year THACKERAY. c. The evening l. of the Minister of the Home Department 1831.

Levee (lĭvī·), *v.*[1] *U.S.* 1858. [f. LEVEE *sb.*[1]] *trans.* To raise levees or embankments along (a river) or in (a district).

†**Le·vee**, *v.*[2] 1725. [f. LEVEE *sb.*[2]] *trans.* To attend the levees of; to pursue at levees –1770.

Leveful(le, var. of LEEFUL.

Level (le·vĕl), *sb.* ME. [a. OF. *livel*, later *nivel*, mod.F. *niveau* :—pop.L. **libellum* = class.L. *libella*, dim. of *libra* balance.]

I. 1. An instrument which indicates a line parallel to the plane of the horizon, used in testing the relation to the horizontal of a surface to which it is applied. Also *fig.* †2. Level condition or position; horizontality –1726. 3. Position as marked by a horizontal line; an imaginary line or plane at right angles to the plumb-line, considered as determining the position of one or more points or surfaces 1535. 4. Position, plane, standard, in social, moral, or intellectual matters 1609. 5. A level or flat surface 1634. 6. A level tract of land; applied *spec.* (as a proper name) to *Bedford L.* or *the Great L.* in the fen district of England; *The Levels* (formerly *The L.*), the tract including Hatfield Chase in Yorkshire; etc. 1623. 7. *Mining.* **a.** A nearly horizontal drift, passage, or gallery in a mine. 1606. **b.** A 'drift' for drainage purposes.

1. *fig.* We steal by lyne and leuell, and 't like your grace *Temp.* IV. i. 239. 2. Phr. *On*, *upon a l.*, in a horizontal line or plane. *The l.*, the horizontal; *in l.*, on the ground (cf. L. *in plano*). 3. Phr. *On a l. with*: in the same horizontal plane as. *To find one's* or *its l.*: said of persons or things arriving at their proper place with respect to those around or connected with them. †*To hold its l. with*: to be on an equality with (Shaks.). 4. The calamity..had reduced all to one l. 1832. 5. He..Came on the shining levels of the lake TENNYSON. *The l.*, the earth's surface (*rare*).

II. From the vb. †1. **a.** The action of aiming a gun, etc., aim –1718. †**b.** That which is aimed at; a mark –1600. †**c.** *fig.* Aim, purpose, design –1605. 2. (*Surveying*) †*To make a l. of*: to ascertain the differences of elevation in (a piece of land). Also, *to take a l.* = LEVEL *v.* I. 4 (absol.). 1693.

1. As if that name shot from the dead leuell of a Gun, Did murder her *Rom. & Jul.* III. iii 103.

Comb.: **l.-error**, 'the microscopic deviation of the axis of a transit instrument from the horizontal position' (Smyth); **-range** (in *Gunnery*), 'the same as Point-blank Shot, or the Distance that a piece of Ordinance carries a Ball in a direct Line' (Phillips); **-staff** = *levelling staff* (LEVELLING *vbl. sb.*).

Level (le·vĕl), *a.*, *adv.* 1538. [f. LEVEL *sb.*] **A.** *adj.* 1. Having an even surface; 'not having one part higher than another' (J.). **b.** *fig.* Of quantities: Expressed in whole numbers. Of a race: Even. 1826. 2. Horizontal; at right angles to the plumb-line 1559. 3. On a level *with* something else. Also *fig.*, on an equality *with*; readily accessible or intelligible *to.* 1559. **4.** Of two or more things: Situated in the same level or plane. Also *fig.* 1601. **5.** Lying, moving, or directed in a (more or less) horizontal plane; esp. *poet.*, e. g. of the rays of the sun when it is low 1667. **6.** Of even quality, tone, or style; of even tenor 1655. **7.** †**a.** 'Equipoised, steady' (Schmidt). See 2 *Hen. IV*, II. i. 123, *Twel. N.* II. iv. 32. **b.** Well balanced: said of the head, etc. Orig. *U.S.* 1870. **8.** Plain, point-blank. KEATS. **9.** *One's l. best*: one's very best; one's utmost (*colloq.* or *slang*; orig. *U.S.*) 1851.

1. Along the l. Seas they flew POPE. 2. Phr. *L. lines* (Shipbuilding), lines determining the shape of a ship's body horizontally, or square from the middle line of the ship. 3. We should..apply ourselves to that which is l. to our capacities BUTLER. *L. crossing*: a place at which a road and a railway, or two railways, cross each other at the same l. 5. The last l. rays were glittering on the stream 1832. 6. A leisured and l. life 1899. 7. b. To tell a woman her head is l. is apparently a compliment in America 1870. Hence **Le·vel·ly** *adv.*, **-ness.**

†**B.** *adv.* With direct aim; on a level *with* –1659.

As l. as the cannon to his blank *Haml.* IV. i. 42.

Level (le·vĕl), *v.* Inflected **levelled, levelling** (*U.S.* **leveled, leveling**). ME. [f. LEVEL *sb.*]

I. 1. *trans.* To make level or even; to remove inequalities in the surface of. †Also, to spread levelly. 1440. **b.** *Dyeing.* To make (colour) even 1874. **2.** To place on the same level or plane. Also *fig.* 1563. **3.** To bring to the level of the ground; to lay low, to raze 1614. **b.** To knock (a person) down 1760. **c.** *transf.* and *fig.* To reduce or remove (inequalities) 1642. **4.** *Surveying.* To ascertain the differences of level in (a piece of land); to 'run' a section of; hence, to lay out. Also *absol.* or *intr.*, to take levels. 1598.

1. Phr. *To l. out*: to extend on a level; †*fig.* to contrive, procure (an opportunity). The road that grandeur levels for his coach EMERSON. 2. Gunpowder leveled peasant and prince W. PHILLIPS. Phr. *To l.* (a person or thing) *with* (now rare), *to*, †*unto*: to put on a level, equality, or par with. Also occas. *intr.* for *pass.* to be on a par with; With such Accomodation and besort As leuels with her breeding SHAKS. *To l. up, down*: to bring up, down to the level of something; Sir, your levellers wish to l. *down* as far as themselves; but they cannot bear levelling *up* to themselves JOHNSON. 3. Phr. *To l. to* or *with the ground, in the dust.* c. The mercantile spirit levels all distinctions LAMB.

II. 1. To aim (a missile weapon); to lay (a gun) 1530. †**b.** To shoot (a missile) *out* (*of* a weapon) –1664. **c.** To direct (one's looks); to dart (rays) 1594. **d.** *fig.* To aim, direct, point 1576. **2.** *absol.* or *intr.* To aim with a weapon; †*occas.* said of the weapon. Also freq. *transf.* and *fig.* Somewhat *arch.* 1500. †**b.** To guess *at* –1596.

1. Phr. *To l. one's aim*; Each at the Head Level'd his deadly aime MILT. b. [He] leuelled a quarrel out of a cros bowe STOW. d. This fellow's writings ..are levelled at the clergy FIELDING. 2. To leuell at perfection 1626. b. *Merch. V.* I. ii. 41.

†**Level-coil.** 1594. [Corruptly ad. Fr. phr. (*faire*) *lever le cul* (*à quelqu'un*), to make a person rise from his seat (*lever* to raise, *cul* buttock). The Fr. name of the game is *lève-cul.*] A rough, noisy game, formerly played at Christmas, in which each player in turn is driven from his seat and supplanted by another. Hence = riotous sport, noisy riot; phr. *to keep level-coil.* Also *advb.* = turn and turn about. –1684.

Leveller (le·vĕlər). Also (now *U.S.*) **leveler.** 1598. [f. LEVEL *v.* + -ER [1].] **1.** One who or that which levels. **2.** One who would level all differences of position or rank among men 1607. **3.** *pl.* Name of a rebel secret society in Ireland in the 18th c. 1762.

1. Sleep is equally a l. with death JOHNSON.

Levelling (le·vĕliŋ), *vbl. sb.* Also (now *U.S.*) **leveling.** 1580. [f. LEVEL *v.* + -ING [1].] **1.** Aiming, aim. **2.** The action of bringing to a uniform horizontal surface, or of placing in a horizontal position by means of a level. Also *fig.* 1598. **3.** *Surveying.* 'The art of determining the relative heights of points on the surface of the ground as referred to a hypothetical surface which cuts the direction of gravity everywhere at right angles' (Gen. Walker) 1812.

Comb.: **l.-instrument,** an instrument consisting essentially of a telescope fitted with a spirit-level, used in surveying; **l. pole, rod, staff,** a graduated pole with a vane sliding upon it, used in levelling; **-stand** (*Photogr.*), an instrument used to support a glass plate in a horizontal position.

Le·velling, *ppl. a.* Also (now *U.S.*) **leveling.** 1635. [-ING [2].] That levels; also, of or pertaining to levellers and their principles.

Leven. ME. Clipped f. ELEVEN, ELEVENTH. LEVENTH, clipped f. ELEVENTH.

Leven, var. of LEVIN; obs. f. LEAVEN.

Lever (lī·vər), *sb.* [ME. *levere, levour*, a. AF. **levere*, OF. *leveour* (F. *leveur*), f. *lever* to raise. The usual F. word is *levier.*] **1.** A bar of iron or wood serving to prize up or dislodge some heavy or firmly fixed object; a crowbar, handspike, etc. Also *fig.* †**b.** *gen.* A bar, pole, or rod –1613. **2.** *Mech.* Name for a rigid structure of any shape (normally a straight bar) fixed at one point called the fulcrum, and acted on at two other points by two forces, tending to cause it to rotate about the fulcrum 1648. **3.** *spec.* **a.** *Steam-engine.* †(*a*) = BEAM *sb.* 10; (*b*) a starting-bar. 1758. **b.** The piece by which the barrel of a breech-loader is opened 1881. **c.** In *Dentistry* and *Surg.* = ELEVATOR 2. 1846. **d.** Short for *l.-watch.*

The force to be resisted by the use of the lever is called the *weight*, and the force applied for this purpose the *power*. Levers are said to be of the *first*, *second*, or *third kind* or *order* according as the fulcrum, the weight, or the power is midmost of the three.

1. *fig.* Jealousy is a potent l. for quickening love 1831.

attrib. and *Comb.* **1.** General: **a.** with sense 'belonging to a l.', as *l.-pin*, etc. **b.** with sense 'acting as a l., worked by a l.', as *l.-corkscrew, -press*, etc. **2.** Special: as **l.-beam** (see BEAM *sb.* 10); **l. escapement** (*Watch-making*), an escapement in which the connexion between the pallet and the balance is made by means of two levers; **l. watch,** a watch with a l. escapement; **-wood,** the Virginian hop-hornbeam or ironwood, *Ostrya virginica.*

Lever (lī·vər), *v.* 1856. [f. LEVER *sb.*] **1.** *intr.* To apply, or work with, a lever. **2.** *trans.* To lift, push, or otherwise move with or as with a lever 1876.

Lever, obs. f. *liever*, compar. of LIEF *a.*

Leverage (lī·vərĕdʒ). 1724. [f. LEVER *sb.* + -AGE.] **1.** The action of a lever; the arrangement by which lever-power is applied; *concr.* a system of levers. **2.** The power of a lever; the mechanical advantage gained by the use of a lever 1830. **b.** *fig.* Means of accomplishing a purpose; power of action 1858.

2. Phr. *L. of a force*: the distance of the direction of a force from the axis. 2. b. With regard to such men the moralist has no l. whatever 1883.

Leveret (le·vərĕt). late ME. [ad. OF. *levret*(*t*)*e*, dim. of *levre* (F. *lièvre*) hare.] **1.** A young hare, esp. one in its first year. †**2.** *transf.* and *fig.* **a.** A pet, a mistress. **b.** A spiritless person. –1640. **3.** *attrib.*: **l.-skin,** a Japanese glaze, supposed to resemble a leveret's fur. (Rec. Dicts.)

2. b. Arrogant Boasters,..leverets in dangers 1630.

†**Le·vesel.** ME. [? repr. OE. **léafsele*, f. *léaf* LEAF + *sęle* hall.] A bower of leaves; a canopy or lattice –1480.

†**Levet.** 1625. [? ad. It. *levata*, f. *levare* to raise.] A trumpet call or musical strain to rouse soldiers and others in the morning –1705.

Leviable (le·viăb'l), *a.* 1484. [f. LEVY *v.* + -ABLE.] **1.** Of a duty, tax, etc.: That may be levied. **2.** Of a person: That may be called upon for contribution 1897. **b.** *U.S.* Of a thing: That may be levied upon (*rec.*).

Leviathan (lĭvəi·ăþăn). ME. [a. L. (Vulg.), a. Heb. *livyāthān.* Ult. origin unkn.] **1.** A (real or imaginary) sea monster, frequently mentioned in Hebrew poetry. **b.** *transf.*; esp. = a ship of huge size 1816. **c.** *fig.* A man of vast power or wealth 1607. †**2.** (After *Isa.* xxvii. 1.) Satan –1595. **3.** Applied to the commonwealth as an organism 1651. **4.** *attrib.* or *adj.* Huge, monstrous 1624; applied recently to coarse kinds of material.

1. There is that Leuiathan, whom thou hast made, to take his pastyme therin COVERDALE *Ps.* ciii[i]. 26. 3. The multitude so united in one person, is called a Commonwealth..This is the generation of that great L. [etc.] HOBBES.

Levier (le·viər). 1494. [f. LEVY *v.* + -ER [1].] One who levies (see LEVY *v.*).

Levigable (le·vigăb'l), *a.* 1670. [ad. med. L. *levigabilis*; see LEVIGATE *v.*] That can be †(*a*) polished, (*b*) reduced to powder (*rare*).

†**Le·vigate,** *pple.* [ad. late L. *lĕvigatus*, pa. pple. of *lĕvigare*, f. *lĕvis* light.] Lightened. ELYOT.

Levigate (le·vigĕt), *ppl. a.* Also *erron.* **læv-.** 1826. [ad. L. *lēvigatus* (see next).] *Bot.* and *Ent.* Smooth as if polished.

Levigate (le·vigeɪt), *v.* Also *erron.* **læv-.** 1612. [f. L. *lēvigat-*, *lēvigare*, f. *lēvis* (erron. *lævis*) smooth.] †**1.** *trans.* To make smooth; to polish –1835. **2.** To reduce to a fine smooth powder; to rub down; to make a smooth paste of (*with* some liquid). Also *fig.* 1694.

2. Levigating it with the oil of sweet almonds 1782. So **Leviga·tion** [ad.L. *levigation-em*], the action of the vb. 1471.

Levin (le·vin). *arch.* Also **leven.** [ME. *leven*(*e*, of unkn. origin.] Lightning; a flash of lightning; any bright light or flame. **b.** *attrib.*, as *l.-brand* 1599.

Leviner, corrupt f. LIMER [1], kind of hound.

Levir (lī·vəɪ). 1865. [a. L. *lēvir* brother-in-law; an Indo-Eur. wd. = Skr. *dēvar*, Gr. δαήρ, OE. *tácor*, etc.] A brother-in-law, or one acting as such under the custom of the LEVIRATE.

Levirate (lī·virĕt). 1725. [f. L. *levir* (see prec.) + -ATE [1].] The custom among the Jews and some other nations, by which the brother or next of kin to a deceased man was bound under certain circumstances to marry the widow. Hence **Levira·tic, -al** *a.* **Levira·tion,** leviratical marriage.

Levitate (le·viteɪt), *v.* 1665. [f. L. *levis* light, after GRAVITATE *v.*] **1.** *intr.* To rise by virtue of lightness; opp. to GRAVITATE 2 b. Now only with reference to 'spiritualism'. **2.** *trans.* †**a.** To make of less weight. **b.** To cause to rise in the air in consequence of lightness. Chiefly with reference to 'spiritualism'. 1686.

2. b. Tables turn, furniture dances, men are 'levitated' 1884. Hence **Levita·tion,** the action of levitating, in any sense 1668. **Le·vitative** *a.* **Le·vitator.**

Levite (lī·vəit). (Now with capital L.) ME. [ad. L. *levita*, also *levites*, ad. Gr. λευίτης, f. Λευί Levi (Heb. *Lēvī*, which also means 'Levite').] **1.** *Israel. Hist.* **a.** One of the tribe of Levi. **b.** One of that portion of the tribe who acted as assistants to the priests in the temple-worship. †**2.** *transf.* A deacon –1604. †**3.** A clergyman (*disparaging*). Also, a domestic chaplain (cf. *Judges* xvii. 12). –1849. †**4.** A kind of loose dress. [After F. *lévite.*] H. WALPOLE.

3. A young L.—such was the phrase then in use—might be had for his board, a small garret, and ten pounds a year MACAULAY. Hence **Levi·tic** *a.* = next.

Levitical (lĭvi·tikăl), *a.* 1535. [f. late L. *leviticus* + -AL.] **1.** Pertaining to the Levites or the tribe of Levi. **2.** Of or pertaining to the ancient Jewish system of ritual administered by the Levites; also, pertaining to the book of Leviticus 1540. †**b.** Pertaining to ritual. MILT.

1. A L. city 1867. 2. *L. degrees*: the degrees of consanguinity within which marriage is forbidden in *Lev.* xviii. 6–18. Hence **Levi·tical-ly** *adv.*, †**-ness.**

Leviticus (lĭvi·tikŏs). ME. [a. late L. *Leviticus* adj. (sc. *liber* book).] Name of the third book of the Pentateuch, which contains the Levitical law and ritual.

Levity [1] (le·viti). 1564. [ad. OF. *levité*, ad. L. *lēvitatem*, f. *lēvis* light; see -ITY.] **1.** The quality or fact of having comparatively little weight; lightness. Also *fig.* 1597. **b.** In pre-scientific physics, regarded as a positive property inherent in bodies in different degrees, in virtue of which they tend to rise. *Obs.* exc. *Hist.* or *allusively.* 1601. †**2.** Agility –1610. **3.** Want of serious thought; frivolity; unseasonable jocularity (the prevalent sense) 1564; instability, fickleness, inconstancy 1613; 'light' behaviour (said esp. of women) 1601.

1. Phr. †*Specific l.*: cf. *specific gravity* (GRAVITY II. 1 c). Hydrogen..rises in the air on account of its l. 1869. b. Hee..gave to every nature his proper forme; the forme of levitie to that which ascended RALEIGH. 3. Our grauer businesse Frownes at this leuitie *Ant. & Cl.* II. vii. 128. The Sarmatians soon forgot, with the l. of Barbarians, the services which they had so lately received GIBBON. Her elder sister ..had been distinguished by beauty and l. MACAULAY.

†**Le·vity**[2]. 1613. [ad. L. *lēvitatem*, f. *lēvis* smooth.] Smoothness.

Levo-, Levulin, var. LÆVO-, LÆVULIN.

Levy (le·vi), *sb.* ME. [a. F. *levée*, f. *lever* :—L. *levare* to raise.] 1. The action of levying: a. an assessment, duty, tax, etc.; b. men for war or other purposes 1607. 2. The amount or number levied: a. †A duty, impost, tax. In a benefit society, etc.: A call of so much per head. 1640. b. A body of men enrolled; also *pl.* the individual men 1611.

1. b. *L. in mass* [F. *levée en masse*]: a levy of all the able-bodied men. As to the levies, the men enlist unwillingly FROUDE. 2. a. Great and heavy Leavies upon a poor people PETTY. b. The leuie was thirtie thousand men 1 *Kings* v. 13.

Comb. l.-money, †(*a*) bounty-money paid to recruits; (*b*) the proceeds of calls from the members of a trade or benefit society.

Levy (le·vi), *v.* ME. [f. LEVY *sb.*] 1. *trans.* To raise (contributions, taxes); to impose (a rate, toll, etc.). Const. †*of, on, upon.* †b. To raise (a sum) as a profit or rent; to collect (a debt); also, to take the revenues of (land) –1768. c. To raise (a sum) by legal execution or process. Const. *on* (*the goods of*). Also, *To l. execution for* (a sum named). Also *absol.* 1506. d. To impose (service) *upon*; to require (a person's) attendance 1862. 2. *Law. To l. a fine*: see FINE *sb.*[1] II. b. (See also sense 1.) b. To draw up (an objection, protest) in due form 1660. †3. a. To set up (a fence, weir, etc.); to erect (a house) –1741. b. To plan out (ground) 1500. c. To weigh (an anchor) 1648. 4. To enlist, enrol (armed men); to muster the forces of (a district). Also *to l. up.* Also *fig.* 1500. 5. To undertake, commence, make (war) 1471. †6. To raise (a siege); to break up (a camp) –1628. ¶7. Erron. used for LEVEL *v.* 1618.

1. The pension..is levied by the emperor's officers SWIFT. A fine should be levied on the delinquent BABBAGE. 4. An army of twelve thousand men was suddenly levied HUME. 5. The Syrian King.. Assassin-like had levied Warr, Warr unproclam'd MILT. 6. Albeit hee saw that the siege was levied.. yet [etc.] HOLLAND.

Levyne (le·vin). 1825. Also **le·vynite** (1868). [after Prof. A. *Levy*.] *Min.* A white or light-coloured silicate of aluminium and calcium.

Lew (liū, lū). Now *dial.* Also **loo(e.** [OE. **hlēow*, *gehlēow* = ON. *hlýr* warm, mild.] A. *adj.* 1. †Warm; sunny (in OE.); lukewarm, tepid. 2. Sheltered from the wind 1674. B. *sb.* 1. Warmth, heat. *Obs.* exc. *Sc.* 1591. 2. Shelter.

Lew, *v.* *Obs.* exc. *dial.* [OE. *hlēwan*, f. *hlēow* LEW *a.*] 1. To make or †become warm. 2. To shelter 1664.

Lewd (liūd), *a.* [OE. *lǣwede*, of obscure etym.] †1. Lay, not clerical. Also *absol.* –1819. †2. Unlearned, unlettered. Also *absol.* –1601. †3. Belonging to the lower orders; common, low, vulgar –1640. †4. Ignorant (implying a reproach); unskilful, bungling; ill-bred, ill-mannered –1710. †5. Of persons: Bad, wicked, base; unprincipled, ill-conditioned; good-for-nothing –1709. †6. Of things: Worthless, poor, sorry –1692. 7. [From 5.] Lascivious, unchaste. (The surviving sense.) ME.

7. He had been seen in the company of l. women 1712. Hence Lew·d-ly *adv.*, -ness.

Lew·dster. [See -STER.] A lewd person. *Merry W.* v. iii. 23.

-lewe, ME. *suffix*, OE. *-lǣwe*, with sense 'affected by, liable to, or characterized by' (something undesirable). Etym. obscure.

Lewis (lū·is), *sb.*[1] 1743. [? f. *Lewis* as a name.] An iron contrivance for raising heavy blocks of stone, consisting of three pieces dovetailed together. Also called *lewisson*. Also *attrib.*, as l.-hole, the hole into which a lewis is fitted. Lewis *v.* to fit with a lewis 1837.

Lewis (lū·is), *sb.*[2] 1835. [f. the inventor's name.] A kind of shears used in cropping woollen cloth.

Lewis gun. 1913. [f. the name of the inventor, Col. Isaac Newton *Lewis* of the U.S. army.] A kind of magazine-fed, gas-operated, and air-cooled machine-gun.

Lewth (liūþ). Now *dial.* [OE. *hlēowþ*; see LEW *a.* and -TH.] Warmth; shelter.

Lew-warm, *a.* Now *dial.* Also **loo-**. 1450. [f. LEW *a.* (used advb.) + WARM *a.*] Lukewarm.

Lexical (le·ksikăl), *a.* 1836. [f. Gr. λεξικός, λεξικόν + -AL.] 1. Pertaining or relating to the words of a language. Often opp. to *grammatical.* 2. Pertaining to, of the nature of, or connected with a lexicon 1873. Hence Le·xically *adv.* in respect of vocabulary; according to the lexicons; in the manner of a lexicon.

Lexicographer (leksikǫ·grăfəɹ). 1658. [f. late Gr. λεξικογράφος, f. λεξικόν LEXICON + -γράφος: see -ER[1].] A writer or compiler of a dictionary. So **Lexicogra·phic, -al** *a.* pertaining to lexicography; **-ally** *adv.* **Lexico·graphist** (*rare*), a l. **Lexico·graphy**, writing or compilation of a dictionary or dictionaries.

Lexicon (le·ksikǭn). 1603. [mod.L., a. Gr. λεξικόν (sc. βιβλίον), neut. sing. of λεξικός of or for words, f. λέξις word, f. λεγ- to speak.] A word-book or dictionary; chiefly a dictionary of Greek, Hebrew, Syriac, or Arabic. b. *fig.* (*a*) A special vocabulary. (*b*) A list of words or names. 1647.

Lexigraphy (leksi·grăfi). 1828. [f. Gr. λέξις word + -γραφία -GRAPHY.] A system of writing in which each character represents a word. Hence **Lexigra·phic, -al** *a.*

‖**Lexiphanes** (leksi·fănīz). 1767. [a. Gr. Λεξιφάνης phrase-monger (title of one of Lucian's dialogues), f. λέξις word, phrase + φαν-, φαίνειν to show.] One who uses bombastic phraseology. Hence **Lexipha·nic** *a.*

‖**Lex talionis** (leks tæli,ōu·nis). 1597. [L.] The law of retaliation, 'an eye for an eye, a tooth for a tooth'.

Ley, obs. f. LAY, LEE *sb.*, LYE.

Ley, dial. var. LEA *sb.*[2], *a.*; also, a laying down (see *lay down* i, LAY *v.*).

Leyden (lɔi·dən). 1755. Name of a city in Holland, used in the names of certain electrical apparatus invented there in 1745–6: *L. jar* (formerly *phial* or *bottle*), an electrical condenser consisting of a glass bottle coated inside and outside with tinfoil, and having a brass rod surmounted by a knob passing through the cork, and communicating with the internal armature. Also *L. battery*, a battery consisting of several L. jars.

‖**Lhiamba, liamba.** 1861. [Native Afr. name.] Hemp.

‖**Li**[1] (lī). 1588. [Chinese.] The Chinese itinerary measure; 27⅛ *li* = 10 miles.

‖**Li**[2] (lī). 1771. [Chinese.] A Chinese weight, one-thousandth part of a liang. (A li of silver = CASH *sb.*[2])

li. 1450. Obs. abbrev. of L. *libra* pound, *libræ* pounds –1634.

Liability (lɔiăbi·lĭti). 1794. [f. LIABLE + -ITY.] 1. *Law.* The condition of being liable or answerable by law or equity. 2. The condition of being subject *to* something, apt or likely *to do* something 1809. 3. That for which one is liable; *pl.* debts, pecuniary obligations 1842.

1. *Limited l.* (Comm.): the being legally responsible only to a limited extent for the debts of a trading company of which one is a member. Also *attrib.* in *limited l. company*. Also *transf.* 2. L. to error 1874, to military service FROUDE.

Liable (lɔi·ăb'l), *a.* 1475. [? a. AF. **liable* = med.L. **ligabilis* that can be bound, f. *ligare*.] 1. *Law.* Bound or obliged by law or equity; answerable (*for*, also †*to*); legally subject or amenable *to*. 2. a. Exposed or subject to or likely to suffer from (something prejudicial); in older use with wider sense, †subject to (any agency or change). Normally const. *to*. 1593. b. Const. *inf.* Subject to the possibility of (doing or undergoing something undesirable). 1682. ¶3. Erron. used for: Incident *to* 1631–1746. †4. Subject or subservient *to*; belonging *to* –1616. †5. Suitable, apt –1595. 6. *U.S.* Likely 1901.

1. L. to serve on juries 1825, to income-tax 1867. 2. a. Not l. to fear or flight or paine MILT. Reasons ..l. to dispute 1801. b. Difficulties may be l. to occur BENTHAM. Ground l. to be overflowed 1896. 5. Apt, l. to be employ'd in danger SHAKS. Hence Li·ableness (now *rare*), liability.

‖**Liaison** (li,ē·zǭn, Fr. lyęzoṅ). 1648. [Fr. :—L. *ligationem*, f. *ligare* to bind.] 1. *Cookery.* A thickening for sauces; †also, the process of thickening. 2. †a. *gen.* A close connexion 1809. b. *spec.* An illicit intimacy between a man and a woman 1821. 3. *Fr. Phonetics.* The joining of a final consonant (otherwise silent) to a following word beginning with a vowel or mute *h* 1884. 4. *Milit.* Combination and co-operation of allied forces or arms of the same force. Hence *liaison-officer*. 1915.

Liana, liane (li,ā·nă, li,ā·n). 1796. [The form *liane* is a. F. *liane*, ? f. *lier* to bind; *liana* is perh. a latinization of *liane*.] Name for the various climbing and twining plants in tropical forests.

‖**Liang** (lyæŋ). 1827. [Chinese.] A Chinese weight, about 1⅓ oz. avoirdupois; this weight in silver as a money of account. Also called *tael.*

Liar (lɔi·əɹ). [OE. *lēogere*, f. *lēogan* LIE *v.*[2] See -AR[3], -ER[1] 2.] One who lies; an untruthful person.

Lyers had nede to haue good memories *Provb.*

‖**Liard** (lyar). 1542. [Fr.; prob. subst. use of *liard* adj. grey (see LYARD, LYART *a.*).] A small French coin worth ¼ of a sou. Hence, typically, a coin of small value.

Liard, var. of LYARD, LYART, grey.

Lias (lɔi·ăs). ME. [Introduced into mod. geology from dialects: a. OF. *liois* (mod.F. *liais*) a kind of limestone.] 1. A blue limestone rock occurring in s.w. counties of England. 2. *Geol.* The lower division of the Jurassic series, consisting of thin layers of blue argillaceous limestone 1833. Hence **Lia·ssic** *a.*, also **liasic**, pertaining to the l. formation.

Lib (lib), *v.*[1] Now *dial.* ME. [? repr. an OE. **lybban* = MDu. *lubben* to maim, f. Teut. root **lub-*; see LEFT *a.*] *trans.* To castrate.

†**Lib**, *v.*[2] *Cant.* 1567. [?] *intr.* To sleep –1859.

†**lib.**, abbrev. of L. *libræ* pounds. ME.

Li·bament. *arch.* 1582. [ad. L. *libamentum*, f. *libare* (see below).] = LIBATION.

Libant (lɔi·bănt), *a.* [f. L. *libantem*, *libare.*] Tasting; touching lightly. LANDOR.

Libard, obs. form of LEOPARD.

Libate (lɔibē·t), *v.* 1866. [f. L. *libat-*, *libare* to taste, pour out as an offering, etc.] a. *trans.* To pour out (wine, etc.) in honour of a god. Also, to make a libation to. b. *intr.* To pour out libations.

Libation (lɔibē·ʃən). ME. [ad. L. *libationem*; see prec.] The pouring out of wine, etc., in honour of a god; the liquid poured out; a drink-offering. b. *transf.* (somewhat *joc.*) Liquid poured out to be drunk; hence, a potation 1751.

The solemne libations at sacrifices HOLLAND. b. Libations to his health, or, in plain english, bumpers 1751.

Libatory (lɔi·bătŏri). 1609. [ad. L. *libatorius*; see LIBATE *v.* and -ORY.] A. *adj.* Pertaining to or consisting of libations 1834. †B. *sb.* A libatory vessel. BIBLE (Douay) 1 *Macc.* i. 23.

Libbard, arch. var. of LEOPARD.

‖**Libeccio** (libe·tʃo, It. libe·tʃo). Also *erron.* -ecchio. 1667. [It., f. L. *Libs* (also *Lips*), a. Gr. Λίψ, Λιβ-.] The south-west wind.

Libel (lɔi·bĕl), *sb.* ME. [a. OF. *libel* masc., *libelle* fem. (mod.F. *libelle*), ad. L. *libellus*, dim. of *liber* book.] †1. A little book; a short writing –1715. †b. A written paper. *Occas.* = LABEL *sb.* –1689. 2. A formal document; a written declaration. *Obs.* exc. *Hist.* and *Law.* ME. 3. a. *Civil Law.* The writing of the plaintiff containing his allegations and instituting a suit. b. *Eccl. Law.* The first plea in a cause. **c.** *Sc. Law.* The form of complaint on which a prosecution takes place. ME. †**4.** A leaflet, bill, or pamphlet posted up or publicly circulated; *spec.* one defaming some person's character (orig. *famous l.* = Law L. *libellus famosus*) –1776. **5.** *Law.* Any published statement damaging to the reputation of a person. In wider sense, any treasonable, seditious, or immoral writing. Also, the act of publishing such a statement or writing. 1631. **b.** In pop. use: Any false and defamatory statement. Also *transf.* of an unsuccessful portrait, a thing or circumstance that brings undeserved discredit on a person, country, etc. 1618.

1. b. With his testament there were three litle libels or codicils 1603. 2. Moses permitted a libell of diuorce 1565. 4. Singeing a pig with a new purchased l. SWIFT. 5. b. A rich knave's a l. on our laws YOUNG.

Libel (lǝi·bĕl), *v.* 1561. [f. LIBEL *sb.*; cf. OF. *libeller*, med.L. *libellare*.] †**1.** *intr.* To make libellous accusations; to spread defamation 1570–1637. **2.** *trans.* To defame by circulating libellous statements; to accuse falsely and maliciously; *spec.* in *Law*, to publish a libel against 1601. **3. a.** *Eccl.* and *Sc. Law.* To institute a suit against (a person) by means of a libel 1561. **b.** To bring suit in admiralty against (a vessel, a cargo, or its owner) 1805.

1. What's this but Libelling against the Senate? *Tit. A.* IV. iv. 17. 2. Some wicked wits have libell'd all the fair POPE. Hence **Libellee·**, *Law*, one against whom a libel has been filed. **Li·beller. Li·bellist.**

Libellant (lǝi·bĕlănt). Also **libelant.** 1726. [f. LIBEL *v.* + -ANT; after *appellant*, etc.] *Law.* One who institutes a suit in an eccl. or admiralty court. Also as *adj.*

Libellous (lǝi·bĕlǝs), *a.* 1619. [f. LIBEL *sb.* + -OUS.] Containing or constituting a libel, of the nature of a libel; also, engaged upon libels.

The l. pen of Martin Mar-prelate HALLAM. Hence **Li·bellously** *adv.*

‖**Liber** (lǝi·bǝɹ). 1753. [L., = 'bark'.] *Bot.* The inner bark of exogens; bast.

Liberal (li·bĕrăl). ME. [a. OF. *liberal* (F. *libéral*), ad. L. *liberalis* pertaining to a free man, f. *liber* free.]

A. *adj.* **1.** Orig., epithet of those 'arts' or 'sciences' (see ART *sb.* II. 1) that were 'worthy of a free man'; opp. to *servile* or *mechanical*. Later, of conditions, pursuits, etc.: 'Becoming a gentleman' (J.). Now *rare*, exc. of education, etc.: Directed to general intellectual culture; not narrowly technical or professional. **2.** Free in giving; generous, open-hearted. Const. *of.* ME. **b.** Abundant, ample, large ME. †**3.** Free from restraint; free in speech or action. In 16–17th c. often: Licentious. –1709. **b.** Of construction, etc.: Not rigorous; free 1778. **4.** Free from narrow prejudice; open-minded 1781; *esp.* open to the reception of new ideas or proposals of reform 1846. **5.** Of political opinions: Favourable to changes and reforms tending in the direction of democracy. Hence, epithet of a party; opp. to *Conservative*. 1801. **6.** *Comb.*, as *liberal-minded* adj. JOHNSON.

1. L. habits HALLAM, curiosity MACAULAY. 2. I see sir you are liberall in offers SHAKS. b. A l. gift 1602, foundation 1672, offer SCOTT. Women of l. outline 1897. 3. Your liberall jests Upon his person 1613. 4. *L. Christian*: in U.S. chiefly applied to the Unitarians and Universalists; in England to those who consider large parts of the traditional system of belief unessential; so *l. Christianity*, *l. theology*. 5. The L. Government had outlived its popularity 1881. *L. Conservative*, a member of the Conservative party not prejudiced against reform. *L. Unionist*, a member of the party formed by those Liberals who refused to support the Irish Home Rule Bill in 1886.

B. *sb.* **1.** A member of the Liberal party (see A. 5): **a.** in continental politics 1820; **b.** in British politics 1822. **2.** One who holds liberal views in theology. Chiefly *U.S.* 1887.

1. a. Our travellers..continue to resort to Paris.. and occasionally take part with *Ultras* or with *Liberals* 1820.

Hence **Li·beralism**, the holding of l. opinions in politics or theology; the political tenets of a L. **Li·beralist**, an advocate of liberalism. **Liberali·stic** *a.* pertaining or tending to liberalism. **Li·berally** *adv.*, **-ness** (*rare*).

Liberality (libĕræ·liti). ME. [a. OF. *liberalité*, ad. L. *liberalitatem*, f. *liberalis*.] **1.** The quality of being liberal or free in giving; generosity, munificence. **b.** An instance of this (now *rare*) 1526. **2.** Freedom from bias or prejudice; liberal-mindedness 1808. ¶**3.** Liberalism; liberals collectively 1843.

1. His l. knew no bottom but an empty purse FULLER. 2. Where look for l., if men of science are illiberal to their brethren? LYTTON.

Liberalize (li·bĕrălǝiz), *v.* 1774. [f. LIBERAL + -IZE.] **1.** *trans.* To render liberal; to free from narrowness; to enlarge the intellectual range of. **b.** To make Liberal in politics 1853. **2.** *intr.* To be or become liberal 1791.

1. It [the law] is not apt..to open and to l. the mind BURKE. 2. Russia must l., or be convulsed 1848. Hence **Li·beraliza·tion. Li·beralizer.**

‖**Liberate** (libĕrē¹·ti), *sb.* *Obs.* exc. *Hist.* 1475. [L., 'deliver ye', the first word of the writ, used subst.] *Law.* **1. a.** A writ issued out of Chancery for the payment of a pension or other royal allowance. **b.** A writ to the sheriff of a county for the delivery of land and goods taken upon the forfeiture of a recognizance. **c.** A writ issued out of Chancery to a jailer for the delivery of a prisoner who has put in bail for his appearance. **2.** *attrib.*, as *l. roll*, the account formerly kept of pensions and other allowances under the great seal.

Liberate (li·bĕreit), *v.* 1623. [f. L. *liberat-*, *liberare*.] *trans.* To set free, set at liberty; to release *from* (something). *Chem.* To set free from combination 1805.

To l. the public revenue 1776, acid 1805, slaves 1867.

Liberation (libĕrē¹·ʃǝn). 1440. [ad. L. *liberationem*; see prec.] The action of liberating or condition of being liberated; setting free.

L. Society: short for the 'Society for the L. of Religion from State Patronage and Control', which advocates disestablishment and disendowment of all established churches. Hence **Libera·tionist**, one who belongs to this society; an advocate of disestablishment. **Libera·tionism**, the principles or practice of liberationists.

Liberator (li·bĕreitǝɹ). 1650. [f. LIBERATE *v.*] One who liberates; a deliverer. So **Li·beratress, -trice, -trix,** a female l.

Liberatory (li·bĕrătŏri), *a.* *rare.* 1592. [f. L. *liberat-*, *liberare* + -ORY.] That liberates or favours liberation.

Libertarian (libǝɹtē°·riăn), *sb.* (*a.*) 1789. [f. LIBERTY + *-arian*, after *unitarian*, etc.] **1.** One who holds the doctrine of the freedom of the will. Opp. to *necessitarian*. Also *attrib.* or *adj.* **2.** One who approves of or advocates liberty 1878. Hence **Liberta·rianism**, l. principles or doctrines.

Liberticide (libɔ̄·ɹtisǝid), *sb.*[1] and *a.* 1793. [a. F., f. *liberté* LIBERTY + *-cide*, -CIDE 1.]

A. *sb.* A killer or destroyer of liberty 1795.

B. *adj.* Destructive of liberty.

A. Cæsar..the great l. SOUTHEY. Hence **Liberti·cidal** *a.*

Liberticide (libɔ̄·ɹtisǝid), *sb.*[2] *rare.* 1819. [f. as prec.; see -CIDE 2.] Destruction of liberty.

Libertine (li·bǝɹtin). ME. [ad. L. *libertinus*, f. *libertus* made free, cogn. w. *liber* free.]

A. *sb.* **1.** *Rom. Antiq.* A freedman; one manumitted from slavery; also, the son of a freedman. **2. a.** *pl.* The name given to certain antinomian sects of the early 16th c. **b.** Later, One who holds loose opinions about religion; a free-thinker. 1563. **c.** *transf.* One who goes his own way 1599. **3.** A man (†rarely a woman) who is not restrained by moral law; one who leads a licentious life 1593.

2. c. The Ayre, a Charter'd L. SHAKS. 3. Like a puft, and recklesse l. Himselfe, the Primrose path of dalliance treads *Haml.* I. iii. 49.

B. *adj.* **1.** Manumitted from slavery (*rare*) 1600. **2.** Acknowledging no law in religion or morals; free-thinking; antinomian. Also *occas.* Pertaining to the sects called 'Libertines'. 1577. **3.** Free or unrestrained generally. Now *rare* or *Obs.* 1589. **4.** Loose in morals; licentious, dissolute; characteristic of or resembling a libertine 1605.

3. The l. ant will choose her own settlement 1768. The transitions are as sudden as those in Pindar, but not so l. H. WALPOLE. 4. That l. humanism which stamps the Renascence 1886. Hence **Li·bertinage** = LIBERTINISM 1, 2.

Libertinism (li·bǝɹtiniz'm). 1611. [f. prec. + -ISM.] **1.** Free-thinking in religious matters 1641. **2.** Habitual licentiousness, *esp.* with regard to the relation of the sexes; the conduct or practice of a libertine 1611. **3.** Unrestrained liberty (*rare*) 1647.

1. Heathen false freedom and l. TRENCH. 2. Thus are wickedness and l., called a knowledge of the world, a knowledge of human nature RICHARDSON. So †**Li·bertism** (in sense 1) 1644.

Liberty (li·bǝɹti), *sb.* ME. [a. F. *liberté*, ad. L. *libertatem*, f. *liber* free.] **1.** Exemption or release from captivity, bondage, or slavery. **b.** In religious use ME. **2.** Freedom from arbitrary, despotic, or autocratic rule or control 1484. **3.** Faculty or power to do as one likes ME. **b.** *Philos.* Freedom from the control of fate or necessity. (Now chiefly in expressed antithesis to *necessity*.) 1538. **4.** Free opportunity or scope *to* do something; hence, leave, permission ME. **b.** *Naut.* Leave of absence 1758. **5.** Unrestrained action, conduct, or expression; licence. (*Occas.* personified.) Now only in sense: An instance of freedom; a licence. 1558. **6.** *Law.* **a.** = FRANCHISE *sb.* I. 2 b ME. **b.** *pl.* Privileges, immunities, or rights enjoyed by prescription or by grant ME. **c.** †Hence *occas.* a person's domain or property. The district over which a person's or corporation's privilege extends. Also (in England bef. 1850), a district within the limits of a county, but exempt from the jurisdiction of the sheriff, and having a separate commission of the peace. 1455. **7.** *L. of the tongue*: space for the tongue of a horse, made by the bit's arching in the middle 1727.

1. To proclaime libertie to the captives *Isa.* lxi. 1. b. Where is the spirit of God, there is liberte WYCLIF 2 *Cor.* iii. 17. 2. Fredome and lyberte is better than ony gold or syluer CAXTON. *Cap of l.*: see CAP *sb.*[1] *Natural l.*: the state in which every one is subject only to the laws of nature. *Civil l.*: natural l. restricted by the nature and necessities of the community. *L. of conscience*: freedom to follow without interference the dictates of conscience in matters of creed or worship. *L. of the press*: the right to print and publish whatever one pleases without previous governmental permission. 3. I me reioysed of my libertee, That selde tyme is founde in mariage CHAUCER. 4. There is no l. for causes to operate in a loose and stragling way SIR T. BROWNE. 5. Libertie plucks Iustice by the nose SHAKS. Phr. *To take the l. to* do or *of* doing something: to go so far, be so presumptuous as to (etc.). *To take liberties*: to be unduly familiar (*with* a person; occas. *euphem.*); to deal freely *with* (rules, facts, etc.). The Mountain Nymph, sweet L. MILT. 6. b. *Cor.* II. iii. 223. c. *L.* or *liberties of a city*: the district, extending beyond the bounds of the city, subject to the municipal authority. *Liberties of a prison*: the limits outside a prison, within which prisoners were occas. permitted to reside.

Phr. *At l.*: not in captivity or confinement; esp. in phr. *to set at l.*, to liberate. Also, free to act, move, think, etc. Also, (of persons or things) unoccupied, disengaged.

Comb.: **l. bond**, one of the interest-bearing bonds of the 'Liberty' loans issued by the U.S. government in 1917–19; **l.-cap** = *cap of liberty* (see CAP *sb.*[1]); **-day** *Naut.*, a day on which part of a ship's crew are allowed to go ashore; so **-man**; **l. hall** (also with caps.), a place where one may do as one likes; **-party** *U.S. Hist.*, a political party which advocated the abolition of slavery; **-pole**, a tall mast or staff with a Phrygian cap or the like on the top; †**l. post**, a post marking the boundary of the Liberties of the City of London.

Hence **Li·berty** *v. trans.* to endow with liberties or privileges; to give liberty to. *Obs.* or *dial.*

Libethenite (libe·þĕnǝit)[1]. 1832. [f. *Libethen*, Czechoslovakia + -ITE.] *Min.* An olive-green phosphate of copper found in crystals and reniform masses.

L...occurs in quartz 1868.

†**Libi·dinist.** *rare.* 1628. [f. L. *libidin-*, *libidio* lust + -IST.] A lecher –1634.

Libidinous (libi·dinǝs), *a.* 1447. [ad. L. *libidinosus*, f. as prec.; see -OUS. Cf. F. *libidineux*.] **1.** Given to, full of, or characterized by lust; lustful, lecherous, lewd. †**2.** Provocative of lust. HOLLAND. Hence †**Libidino·sity**, lustfulness. **Libi·dinous-ly** *adv.*, **-ness.**

Libken. *Old Cant.* Also †**libkin.** 1567. [f. LIB *v.*[2] + KEN *sb.*[2]] A place to sleep in.

‖**Libra** (lǝi·bră). ME. [L. *libra* pound (12 ounces), balance, constellation so called. (In med.L. used for 'pound'; hence the abbrevs. £ = pound(s) sterling, lb. = pound weight.)] **1.** *Antiq.* A (Roman) pound. †**2.** Arm of a balance 1797. 3. *Astron.* (with capital L.) a. A zodiacal constellation, lying between Virgo and Scorpio. b. The seventh sign of the zodiac (♎), which the sun enters on the 23rd of September. ME.

Libral (ləi·brăl), *a.* 1656. [ad. L. *libralis* (see prec.).] Pertaining to a libra, or to Libra. *L. as*: the Roman 'as' weighing a pound.

Librarian (ləibrēə·riăn). 1670. [f. L. *librarius* concerned with books + -AN.] †1. A scribe, copyist -1725. 2. The custodian of a library 1713. †3. A dealer in books. NORTH. Hence **Libra·rianship.**

Library (ləi·brări). ME. [a. F. *librairie*, repr. Com. Rom. **libraria* (-*ia*, -Y [3]), f. L. *librarium* (F. *libraire* bookseller), subst. use of *librarius* adj., f. *libr-*, *liber* book, perh. a use of *liber* bark (see LIBER), an early writing material.] 1. A place set apart to contain books for reading, study, or reference. 2. The books contained in a library; 'a large collection of books, public or private' (J.) ME. b. Often a title for a series or set of books uniform in appearance and having something in common, as in 'The L. of Useful Knowledge', etc. 1692. c. *transf.* and *fig.*; esp. used to denote (*a*) a great mass of erudition; (*b*) the objects of study, the sources on which a person depends for instruction 1450. 3. *attrib.*, as *l.-book* 1727, *-door* 1609, *-stairs* 1598.

1. I there saw his l., i.e. the Room which once contained his Books 1779. *Free l.*, a municipal or other l. for the use of the public without payment. *Circulating l.*: a private commercial establishment for the lending of books. 2. Pisistratus .. is said to have been the first person in Greece who collected a l. THIRLWALL. c. Tostatus..who was a living l. TRAPP. Cards and men formed the l. of the Duchess of Marlborough J. HAWTHORNE.

Librate (ləi·brēit), *sb. Hist.* 1610. [ad. med.L. *librata* (sc. *terra*), f. *libra* pound; see -ATE [1].] A piece of land worth a pound a year.

Librate (ləi·brēit), *v.* 1623. [f. L. *librat-*, *librare*, f. *libra* balance.] †1. *trans.* To weigh; to poise, balance; to cause libration in -1806. 2. *intr.* To oscillate like the beam of a balance; to move from side to side or up and down 1694. 3. Of a bird, etc.; To poise, balance itself 1786.

2. He..is librating between vice and virtue 1822. 3. Made to flutter and l. like a kestrel over the place 1829.

Libration (ləibrē·ʃən). 1603. [ad. L. *librationem.*] 1. The action of librating; the state of being balanced or in equipoise. Also *transf.* and *fig.* 2. *Astron.* A real or apparent motion of an oscillating kind 1669. †3. Weighing (*lit.* and *fig.*) -1770.

1. Their pinions still, In loose l. stretched THOMSON. 2. *L. of the moon*: an apparent irregularity of the moon's motion which makes it appear to oscillate in such a manner that the parts near the edge of the disk are alternately visible and invisible. (There are three kinds, called *l. in latitude*, *l. in longitude*, and *diurnal* or *parallactic l.*) The moon..is liable to librations depending upon the position of the spectator MRS. SOMERVILLE. Hence **Libra·tional** *a.* pertaining to (the moon's) l.

Libratory (ləi·brătŏri), *a.* 1668. [f. L. *librat-*, *librare.*] Having a motion like that of the beam of a balance; oscillatory.

‖**Libretto** (libre·to). *Pl.* **-etti** (-e·ti). 1742. [It., 'little book', f. *libro* book.] The text or words of an opera or extended musical composition. Hence **Libre·ttist,** a writer of librettos.

Libriform (ləi·brifǫɹm), *a.* 1877. [f. L. *libr-*, *liber* bark; see -FORM.] *Bot.* Of the nature or character of liber.

Libyan (li·biăn). 1620. [f. L. *Libya* + -AN.] **A.** *adj.* Of or pertaining to ancient Libya. By some philologists applied to the Berber lang., or the group of mod. Hamitic langs. to which Berber belongs. **B.** *sb.* An inhabitant of Libya; the Libyan language. So **Libyo-**, comb. form = L. and —.

Lice, pl. of LOUSE.

Licence (ləi·sĕns), *sb.* Also **license.** ME. [a. F. *licence*, ad. L. *licentia*, f. *licere* to be lawful. The sp. *license* has no justification in the case of the sb. Cf. *advice* sb., *advise* vb., *practice* sb., *practise* vb., etc.] 1. Liberty (to do something), leave, permission. Now somewhat *rare.* †Also *occas.* exemption *from* (something). 2. A formal permission from a constituted authority to do something, e.g. to marry, preach, carry on some trade, etc.; a permit ME. b. The document embodying this 1598. c. In some Univs., a certificate of competency in some faculty 1727. 3. Liberty of action conceded or acknowledged; an instance of this ME. b. Excessive liberty; abuse of freedom; disregard of law or propriety 1450. c. Licentiousness, libertinism 1713. 4. Deviation from form or rule by a writer, an artist, etc. 1530. 5. *attrib.*, as *l.-duty*, etc. 1692.

1. And askeþ leue and lycence at londun to dwelle LANGL. Others would confine the license of disobedience to unjust laws MILL. 2. Phr. *L. of mortmain* (see MORTMAIN). (*To marry*) *by l.* in opposition to *by banns*. Licences to dealers in spirits and wine BURKE. 3. He..allowed great and public l. to his tongue 1868. b. They are for l., not for liberty SHEFFIELD. The intolerable l. with which the newspapers break..the rules of decorum BURKE. c. The license of the Restoration 1841. 4. A lycence poetycall 1530. The poem..allows a metrical l. KINGSLEY.

License, licence (ləi·sĕns), *v.* ME. [f. LICENCE *sb.*, q. v. for the spelling.] 1. *trans.* To give (a person) permission *to* (do something). Now *rare.* b. To permit (a thing) to be done; occas. with *dat.* of the person. Now *rare.* 1477. †2. [After F. *licencier.*] To give leave of departure to; to dismiss, set free *from*; to send away *to* -1814. 3. To grant (a person) a licence to do something, *e.g.* to practise a trade, hold a curacy, keep a dog, carry a gun, etc. Const. *for, to,* and *to* with *inf.* ME. b. To grant a licence permitting (a house, theatre, etc.) to be used for a specified purpose 1777. 4. To authorize the publication of (a book), the acting of (a play) 1628. 5. To allow liberty or scope to; to privilege, tolerate. *Obs.* exc. in *ppl. a.* 1605.

3. Judith Kent, widow, 'Licenced..to vend tea, coffee, tobacco, and snuff' MISS MITFORD. 4. This play was licensed on June 6th, 1634. 1858. Hence **Li·censable** *a.* **Licensee·**, one to whom a licence is granted.

Licensed (ləi·sĕnst), *ppl. a.* 1593. [f. LICENSE *v.* + -ED [1] or LICENCE *sb.* + -ED [2].] 1. Provided with a licence. Now often *spec.* (of a house, etc.) licensed for the sale of alcoholic liquor. *L. victualler*: see VICTUALLER. 1632. 2. Privileged, recognized, regular, tolerated 1593.

2. Clodius was a l. libertine FROUDE.

Licenser (ləi·sĕnsəɹ). 1644. [f. LICENSE *v.* + -ER [1].] One who licenses; esp. an official who authorizes the publication of books or papers (*l. of the press*), or the performance of plays (*l. of plays*), on being satisfied that law, public morals, or decency are not violated.

Licensure (ləi·sĕnsiuəɹ). *U.S.* 1846. [f. LICENSE *v.* + -URE.] A licensing; esp. to preach.

Licentiate (ləise·nʃiĕt), *sb.* ME. [ad. med. L. *licentiatus* (see below) used *absol.* as *sb.*] One who has obtained a licence to exercise some function; e.g. a. one who has received a formal attestation of professional competence or of proficiency in some art from some collegiate or other examining body; b. in the Presbyterian church: One who holds a licence to preach but as yet has no appointment; a probationer 1854.

a. *L. of the Royal College of Physicians* (abbrev. L.R.C.P.), *L. in Dental Surgery* (L.D.S.), *L. of the Royal Academy of Music* (L.R.A.M.), *L. of the College of Preceptors* (L.C.P.), etc.

†**Lice·ntiate,** *ppl. a.* 1424. [ad. med.L. *licentiatus*; see next.] 1. Allowed, licensed -1676. 2. Freed from rules; assuming licence, unrestrained, licentious 1593-1656.

Licentiate (ləise·nʃiēit), *v.* 1560. [f. med. L. *licentiat-*, *licentiare*, f. *licentia* LICENCE.] 1. *trans.* To give liberty to; to allow, permit (something) *to* (a person), (a person) *to* (do something), or *that* (etc.) ? *Obs.* 2. [After F. *licencier.*] To discharge (a servant). BYRON. Hence **Li:centia·tion,** the granting of a licence.

Licentious (ləise·nʃəs), *a.* 1535. [ad. med.L. *licentiosus*, f. *licentia* LICENCE; see -OUS.] Characterized by licence. 1. Disregarding accepted rules, esp. in matters of grammar or style 1589. 2. Unrestrained by law, decorum, or morality; lax. Now *rare.* 1535. 3. Libertine, lascivious, lewd. Now the prevailing sense. 1555.

1. Verse..somewhat l. in number of syllables HALLAM. 2. The lying and l. character of our newspapers JEFFERSON. 3. Whose l. morals all good men detested ROBERTSON. Hence **Lice·ntious-ly** *adv.*, **-ness.**

Lich (litʃ). *Obs.* exc. *arch.* and in *Comb.* Also **lych, lyke.** [OE. *lic* str. neut. :—OTeut. **likom* neut. Cf. Du. *lijk*, Ger. *leiche*, etc. Orig. sense prob. 'form, shape'.] = BODY. a. The living body. Also the trunk, as opp. to the limbs. b. A dead body; a corpse OE.

Comb.: †**l.-fowl** = LICH-OWL; **-house,** a mortuary; **-path** = *lich-way*; **-stone,** a stone to place the coffin on at the l.-gate; †**-wal, -wale,** a plant, the gromwell; †**-way,** a path along which a corpse has been carried to burial; †**-wort,** a plant, wall pellitory.

Lich, obs. f. LIKE.

Lichen (ləi·kĕn), *sb.* 1601. [a. L. *lichen*, ad. Gr. λειχήν. The pronunc. (li·tʃĕn) is now rare in educated use.] †1. = LIVERWORT -1759. 2. One of a class of small cryptogamic plants, often of a green, grey, or yellow tint, which grow on the surface of rocks, trees, etc. Also *collect.* 1715.

According to the modern theory a lichen consists of a fungus and an alga symbiotically united.

3. *Path.* A skin disease, characterized by an eruption of reddish solid papules over a limited area 1601. †4. After a L. use in Pliny: = CHESTNUT 4. -1661.

Hence **Li·chen** *v.* to cover with lichens 1859. **Li·chenal** *a.* of or pertaining to a lichen or lichens; also as *sb.* 1846. **Liche·nic** *a.* pertaining to or obtained from lichens 1836. **Li·chenin** *Chem.* a kind of starch obtained from Iceland moss and other lichens 1835. **Li·chenism,** the symbiosis of alga and fungus in a lichen 1887. **Li·chenist** = *lichenologist* 1833. **Li·chenize** = *lichen* vb. 1839. **Li·cheno·graphy,** description of lichens; hence *licheno·grapher*, *-o·graphist*; *lichenogra·phic*, *-al* a. 1824. **Li·chenoid** *a.* resembling a lichen or the disease lichen 1830. **Licheno·logy,** the science of lichens; hence *licheno·lo·gic*, *-al* a.; *licheno·logist*, one versed in lichenology 1830. **Li·chenose** *a.* = next (*a*) 1855. **Li·chenous** *a.* (*a*) pertaining to, consisting of, resembling, or overgrown with lichens; (*b*) pertaining to or of the nature of the disease lichen 1822. **Li·cheny** *a.* overgrown with lichens 1826.

Lich-gate, lych-gate (li·tʃgēit). *arch.* exc. *Arch.* 1482. [f. LICH corpse + GATE *sb.* [1]] The roofed gateway to a churchyard under which the corpse is set down at a funeral, to await the clergyman's arrival.

Lichi, var. of LITCHI.

Li·ch-owl. 1585. [f. LICH + OWL.] The screech-owl, so called because its cry was supposed to portend death in the house.

Licht, Sc. f. LIGHT.

Licit (li·sit), *a.* 1483. [ad. L. *licitus*, *licere* to be lawful.] Allowable, permitted, lawful.

The consumption of l. or duty-paid opium 1892. Hence **Li·cit-ly** *adv.*, **-ness.**

Licita·tion. *rare.* 1623. [ad. L. *licitationem*, f. *licitari* to bid at an auction.] Exposing for sale to the highest bidder.

Lick (lik), *sb.* 1579. [f. LICK *v.*] 1. An act of licking. Hence quasi-*concr.* a small quantity. 2. *U.S.* A spot to which animals resort to lick salt or salt earth. Also *buffalo-l.*, *salt-l.* 1751. 3. A smart blow. Also *transf.* and *fig.* 1678. 4. *dial.*, *U.S.* and *Austral.* A spurt, a spin; a spell of work 1837.

1. To have a l. at the Honey-pot DRYDEN. A l. of court white-wash GRAY. 3. We're used to a l. of a stick every day S. LOVER. *fig.* A l. at the Laureat CIBBER. 4. *Big licks* = hard work.

Lick (lik), *v.* [OE. *liccian* :—OTeut. **likkōn* (whence F. *lécher*, etc.), prob. cogn. w. Gr. λείχειν to lick, λίχνος dainty, L. *lingere*, etc.] 1. *trans.* To pass the tongue over (something), e.g. in order to taste, moisten the surface, etc. Also *absol.* With *off*: To remove by licking. With *up*: To take up by licking. †2. To lap with the tongue; to drink, sip. Also *intr.* constr. *of, on.* -1791. 3. *transf.* and *fig.* (from 1 and 2). a. Of persons and animals 1460. b. Of waves, flame, etc.: To lap, play lightly over, etc.; to take *up* (moisture, etc.) in passing over OE. 4. *To l.* (*a person* or *thing*) *into shape*: To give form to; to mould, make presentable, 'as a Bear doth her Whelps' (Burton) 1612. 5. *slang.* To beat, thrash. Also with *out of.* 1535. **b.** *slang.* To beat, get the better of; to excell 1800. **6.** *slang. intr.* To run or ride at full speed 1889.

1. The danger of licking adhesive stamps and envelopes 1885. Phr. *To l. one's fingers, to l. one's lips,* an action indicating relish or delighted anticipation of food. *To l. the ground, to l.* (another's) *shoe* or *spittle,* actions expressive of abject servility. How does thy honour? Let me licke thy shooe *Temp.* III. ii. 27. *To l. the dust,* †*the earth* [a Hebraism: Vulg. *terram lingere*], to fall prostrate, to suffer defeat. Betwixt them both, they lick't the platters clean RAY. **3. a.** †*To l. up* (an enemy's forces); to destroy, annihilate (after *Num.* xxii. 4); Yet sometyme thei wer slain, taken, and licked vp, or thei were ware HALL. **b.** The flames..licked up everything in their path 1893. **5.** Say you won't fag—they'll soon get tired of licking you HUGHES. **b.** Phr. *It licks me*: it is beyond my comprehension. *To l. into fits*: to defeat thoroughly.

Licker (li·kəɹ). 1440. [f. LICK *v.* + -ER[1].] One who or something which licks. Also *licker-up.*

Lickerish, liquorish (li·kəriʃ), *a.* 1500. [Altered f. LICKEROUS, with -ISH[1] for *-ous.*] †**1.** = LICKEROUS 1. Of a cook: Skilful in preparing dainties. -1728. **2.** = LICKEROUS 2, 2 b. 1500. **3.** = LICKEROUS 3. 1600. Hence **Li·ckerish-ly** *adv.*, **-ness.**

†**Li·ckerous,** *a.* ME. [a. AF. **likerous,* **lekerous,* repr. var. of OF. *lecheros* LECHEROUS.] **1.** Pleasing to the palate; *gen.* and *fig.* sweet, pleasant, delightful -1603. **2.** Of persons, etc.: Fond of delicious food. Const. *of, after.* -1653. **b.** *gen.* and *fig.* Eagerly desirous, longing, greedy for something pleasant. Const. *of*; also *to* do. -1632. **3.** Lecherous, lustful, wanton -1611.

3. And sikerly she hadde a likerous eye CHAUCER. Hence †**Li·ckerous-ly** *adv.*, †**-ness.**

Licking (li·kiŋ), *vbl. sb.* ME. [f. LICK *v.* + -ING[1].] **1.** The action of LICK *v.* **b.** *concr.* in pl. 1851. **2.** *colloq.* A beating, thrashing (*lit.* and *fig.*) 1756. **3.** *attrib.*, as **l.-place** *U.S.* = LICK *sb.* 2; etc. 1597.

2. The power to take a l. is better worth having than the power to administer one G. MEREDITH.

†**Li·ckpenny.** late ME. [f. LICK *v.*] One who or that which 'licks up the pennies', i. e. makes the money go -1824.

Law is a lick-penny, Mr. Tyrrel SCOTT.

†**Li·ck-spigot.** 1599. [f. LICK *v.* + SPIGOT.] One who licks the spigot; a tapster (*contemptuous*); also, a parasite -1700.

Li·ck-spittle. 1818. [f. LICK *v.* + SPITTLE.] An abject parasite; a toady. Also *attrib.* So †**Lick-spit** 1757.

attrib. A..l. awe of rank THACKERAY.

Licorice, alternative f. LIQUORICE.

Licorous, licourous, var. LICKEROUS.

Licour, -ish, obs. ff. LIQUOR, LICKERISH.

Lictor (li·ktǫɹ). ME. [L.; ? f. *lig-*, root of *ligare* to bind.] *Rom. Antiq.* An officer whose functions were to attend upon a magistrate, bearing the fasces before him, and to execute sentence of judgement upon offenders. Also *transf.*

Lid (lid). [OE. *hlid* neut. :—OTeut. **hliđom*, f. wk.-grade root of **hliđ-* to cover, in OE. *behlidan.*] **1.** That which covers the opening at the top of a vessel or closes the mouth of an aperture; the hinged upper part of a receptacle. **b.** The top crust of a pie (*dial.*) 1615. **2.** *Lid* (*of the eye*) = EYELID ME. **3.** Each of the covers of a book (*dial.*) 1459. **4.** *Bot.* and *Conch.* = OPERCULUM 1681. **5.** *attrib.*, as **l.-flower,** a tree or shrub of the genus *Calyptranthes* (N.O. *Myrtaceæ*), in which the upper part of the calyx forms a lid 1653.

1. Phr. (*slang* or *colloq.*) *To put the lid on*: to bring to a close or climax; so *with the lid off*, etc., with everything exposed to view.

Lidded (li·dėd), *ppl. a.* [OE. *gehlidod,* f. *hlid* (*gehlid*) LID. In mod. use, f. LID + -ED.] **1.** Having a lid; covered with or as with a lid. **2.** Of the eyes: Having lids, covered with lids; as *heavy-, high-lidded,* etc. 1818.

Lidless (li·dlės), *a.* 1522. [see -LESS.] Without a lid. **b.** Of the eyes: Having no lids. Chiefly *poet.* = 'ever-watchful'. 1796.

b. Her l. dragon-eyes COLERIDGE.

Lie (ləi), *sb.*[1] [OE. *lyge* str. masc. :—OTeut. **lugi-z,* f. **lug-*, wk. grade of **leug-*, OE. *léogan*; see LIE *v.*[2]] An act or instance of lying; a false statement made with intent to deceive; a criminal falsehood. **b.** *transf.* An imposture 1560.

It was perhaps a l. invented by political malignity FROUDE. *White l.*: a consciously untrue statement deemed venial or praiseworthy in view of its motive. **b.** Men of high degree are a l. *Ps.* lxii. 9. Phr. *To give the l.* (*to*): to accuse (a person) to his face of lying. Also *transf.* of facts, actions, etc. Hence occas. *the l.* is used for: The charge of falsehood; He abhors to take the Lye but not to tell it BERKELEY. *Comb.* **l.-tea,** said to be a transl. of the Chinese name for teas coloured for the European market.

Lie (ləi), *sb.*[2] 1697. [f. LIE *v.*[1]] **1.** Manner of lying; direction or position in which something lies; direction and amount of slope or inclination. Also *fig.* the position or aspect (of affairs, etc.). **b.** *Golf.* (*a*) The inclination of a club when grounded for a stroke. (*b*) The situation of a ball, good or bad. 1857. **2.** *concr.* A mass that lies; a stratum, layer 1728. **3.** The place where an animal, etc. is accustomed to lie. Also, room for lying. 1869. **4.** *Railways.* A siding into which trucks may be run for loading or unloading. (Also *lye.*) 1855.

1. The general l. and disposition of the boughs RUSKIN. Friedrich understands well enough..from the l. of matters, what his plan will be CARLYLE. **3.** A very favourite 'lie' for woodcock 1888.

Lie (ləi), *v.*[1] Pa. t. **lay** (lēɪ); pres. pple. **lying** (ləi·iŋ); pa. pple. **lain** (lēɪn). [Com. Teut. str. vb.: OE. *licgan,* f. (ult.) Teut. root **leg-* (: *lag-* : *lǣg-*) :—**legh-* (: *logh-* : *lēgh-*) to lie; cf. Gr. λέχος bed, ἄλοχος bedfellow, wife, λόχος lying in wait, L. *lectus* bed.]

I. 1. *intr.* Of persons or animals: To be in a prostrate or recumbent position. **b.** To be extended on a bier or the like; to be buried (in a specified place) OE. **c.** To be in one's bed for the purpose of sleeping or resting ME. **2.** To assume a recumbent or prostrate position ME. **3.** To be or remain in a specified position of subjection, helplessness, misery, degradation, or captivity; to be kept *in* prison; to continue *in* sin, etc. †Also *simply* = 'to l. in prison'; occas. idiomatically *to l. by it.* OE. **4.** To remain in a state of inactivity or concealment (not necessarily prone or reclining) ME. **b.** *Shooting.* Of game-birds: To remain crouching upon the ground. (Also *to l. dead.*) 1797. **5.** To dwell or sojourn; *esp.* to sleep or pass the night (in a place), to lodge temporarily. Now *rare* or *arch.* ME. **b.** *spec.* of a host or army (or its leader): To be encamped, to have or take up a position in a field ME. †**c.** To live under specified circumstances or engaged in some specified occupation -1719. **6.** Idiomatic uses (see below).

1. As he lay and read The Tuscan poets on the lawn TENNYSON. Phr. *To l. asleep, sick, dead, in a fever.* **b.** *To l. in state*: see STATE. Two of us in the churchyard l., My sister and my brother WORDSW. **c.** You must l. on the bed which you have made for yourself THACKERAY. Phr. *To l. with* (also †*by*): to have sexual intercourse with (somewhat *arch.*). **3.** Phr. *To l. by the heels* (arch.): see HEEL *sb.*[1] The defendant..was lying in prison as a debtor MACAULAY. Phr. *To l. under*: to be subject to. To l. under a Vow 1701, a delusion ADDISON, a disadvantage 1748. **4.** Phr. *To l. close, low, perdu,* etc., see those adjs. *To l. in ambush, in wait* (see the sbs.). *To l. at catch* or *upon the catch* (? arch. or dial.): to be captious, to seek to entrap a person. *To l. on* or *upon one's arms, to l. on one's oars* (see the sbs.). **b.** Phr. *To l. to the dogs, to the gun*: to permit the approach of a dog or the sportsman without rising. **5.** He lay that night at the deanery MACAULAY. **b.** †*To l. in leaguer*: see LEAGUER *sb.*[1] 1. †**c.** To l. at rack and manger MASSINGER. **6.** †*To l. at* or *upon*: to importune, urge -1737. †*To l. heavy upon*: to oppress, harass -1676. *To l.* †*at, to*: to apply oneself steadily to 1583. †(*With gerund*): To keep on or continue *doing* something (*rare*) -1692.

II. Said of things. **1.** Of material things: To be placed or set horizontally or lengthwise or at rest on the ground or other surface OE. **b.** To be deposited, remain permanently in a specified place ME. **c.** Of a building, etc.: To be overthrown or fallen ME. **2.** To remain unworked, unused, untouched, or undiscovered ME. †**3.** Of the wind, the tongue: To be at rest, subside -1689. **4.** To be situated (in space), to have a specified position OE. **b.** To be spread out to the view 1764. **c.** Of a road, way, journey, etc.: To extend OE. **d.** Of the wind: To remain in a specified quarter 1604. **5.** *Naut.* **a.** Of a ship: To be stationed in a berth or anchorage OE. **b.** To steer in a specified direction 1574. **6.** *fig.* Of immaterial things: To exist, be found, have place, reside (in some specified place or quarter); to be set, fixed, or arranged in some specified position or order ME. †**b.** Of thoughts, inclinations, etc.: To have a specified direction -1825. **c.** To rest or be imposed as a burden, charge, obligation, etc. *upon* a person; to press or weigh upon (one's mind or heart) ME. **d.** To be set *at stake*; to hang or depend *on* or *upon* a hazard, etc. 1590. **7.** (Chiefly in *Law.*) Of an action, charge, claim, etc.: To be admissible or sustainable ME.

1. Take as much as lies on a shilling of [etc.] WESLEY. **b.** A Petition from J. Macleod..was ordered to l. on the table 1804. Money lying in the bank (*mod.*). **c.** Phr. *To l. in ruin(s), in the dust.* How do thy towers in ruin l. KEBLE. *To l. heavy*: to be a heavy load *upon* (*lit.* and *fig.*: see HEAVY *a.*[1] I. 1). (Of food, etc.) *To l. heavy, cold,* etc. (†formerly, simply *to l.*) *on the stomach*: to be felt as oppressive. **2.** Phr. *To l. barren, fallow, hid, lea, waste*; also, *to l. on one's hands, at a stand.* Rarely within the living memory has so much of skill lain barren GLADSTONE. **4.** Within the manor of Collingham, where the lands lay CRUISE. **b.** What a future seemed to l. before him! J. PAYN. **c.** There lies your way SHAKS. **5. a.** The Zebra lay just off the pier 1851. **b.** The Success being to leeward, Captain Peard..lay across his hawse NELSON. *To l. the course* (quasi-*trans.*): (of a ship) to have her head in the direction wished. **6.** The fault lies at their own doors 1719. Their sympathies lay wholly with Gruffydd FREEMAN. Phr. *To l. in* (a person): to rest or centre in him; to depend upon him, be in his power (to do). (Now chiefly in phr. *as far as in* (*me,* etc.) *lies.*) *To l. in one's power, in* (or †*on*) *one's hands.* *To l. in*: to consist in, to have its ground or basis in; Pitt's strength lay in his character 1881. *To l. with*: to be the office or province of (some one) *to do* something. **b.** My humour lyes another way VILLIERS (Dk. Buckhm.). **c.** These Things..lay upon my Mind DE FOE. With those charges lying upon him BURKE. **d.** He persists As if his life lay on 't SHAKS. **7.** There doth lye an Appeal to the Bishop PRIDEAUX.

¶**III.** *trans.* Used causatively or by mistake for LAY *v.* Now *rare.* ME.

The cloth was lain 1809.

Comb. with advs. **Lie about.** To lie here and there, esp. in disorder. †**L. abroad.** To lodge out of one's own house or abode; to reside in a foreign country; An Embassadour is an honest man, sent to lie abroad for the good of his Countrey WALTON. **L. along. a.** To lie outstretched on the ground (now *arch.*); to extend along a surface. **b.** *Naut.* Of a ship: To incline to one side under pressure of a wind abeam. **L. by. a.** *Naut.* = *lie to*; see BY *adv.* **b.** To remain unused, be laid up in store. **c.** To keep quiet; to remain inactive, rest. **L. down. a.** See sense I. 2 and DOWN *adv.* †**b.** To be brought to bed *of* a child. **c.** (*colloq.*) *To take* (a beating, etc.) *lying down*; to receive it with abject submission. **L. in. a.** To be brought to bed *of,* †*with,* a child; to be confined. Also *fig.* †**b.** To cost, 'to stand (a person) in' so much. **L. off. a.** *Naut.* Of a ship or boat: To stand some distance away from the shore, etc. **b.** To cease work for a time. **L. out. a.** To sleep out, now *dial.* of cattle, to be left unhoused at night. **b.** *To l. out of one's money*: to remain unpaid. **L. over. a.** To be held over to a future occasion. **b.** To remain unpaid after the time when payment is due. **L. to.** *Naut.* Of a ship: To come almost to a standstill, with her head as near the wind as possible, by backing or shortening sail. **L. up. a.** To go into or remain in retirement or retreat; to take to one's bed or keep one's room as an invalid; (of a ship) to go into dock. **b.** *To l. up in lavender*: to be in safe keeping or custody.

Lie (ləi), *v.*[2] Infl. **lying** (ləi·iŋ), **lied** (ləid). [Com. Teut. str. vb.: OE. *léogan,* f. Teut. root **leug-* (: *laug-* : *lug-*), whence LIE *sb.*[1] Cf. Du. *liegen,* Ger. *lügen,* etc.] **1.** *intr.* To tell a lie or lies; to speak falsely. **2.** *fig.* Chiefly of inanimate objects: To convey a false impression; to be deceptive. ME. **3.** quasi-*trans.* with *adv.* or phr.: To take *away* by lying; to get (a person, etc.) *into* or *out of* by lying 1720.

1. He lies, and he knows he lies JOHNSON. Phr. *To l. of* (arch.), †*on,* †*upon*: to tell lies about. *To l. in one's teeth, throat, to l. like a trooper.* **2.** London's column, pointing at the skies, Like a tall bully, lifts the head, and lies POPE. **3.** Go on tamely to allow yourself to be lied into Party blindness 1884.

Lieberkühn (lī·bəɹkün). 1867. [f. the inventor J. N. *Lieberkühn* (1711-56), a Berlin anatomist.] *Optics.* A silver concave reflector fixed on the object-glass end of a microscope to bring the light to focus on an opaque object. Hence **Lie·berkühn·nian** *a.*, in *Lieberkühnian* *follicles* or *glands*, minute tubular cavities thickly distributed over the small intestines.

Liebig (lī·big). 1869. [f. Baron Justus von *Liebig* (1803–73).] More fully, *Liebig's extract* (*of beef*): A concentrated preparation of beef, containing the salts and extractive principles of the meat, without the albumen, gelatin, or fat.

Lief (līf), *a.* (*sb.*), and *adv.* [OE. *léof, líof* :—OTeut. **leubo-* :—pre-Teut. **leubho-*, f. Indo-Eur. root **leubh-* (: *loubh-* : *lubh-*, whence BELIEVE, LOVE).]

A. *adj.* **1.** Beloved, dear, agreeable, acceptable, precious. Also *l. and dear.* *Obs.* or *arch.* **b.** In various constructions with *have* (see HAVE *v.*, and cf. Ger. *lieb haben*): *I* (etc.) *had* (occas. *have*) *as l. as* (= 'would as willingly'), *I had liefer* (= 'would rather'), †*liefest*, with object a *sb.*, *inf.* phr. (with or without *to*), or clause ME. †**2.** Desirous, willing, glad. Const. *of, to* with *inf.* –1500. **3.** Antithetically to *loath*, in senses 1 and 2. Also *absol.* *Obs.* or *arch.* OE. †**4. a.** *absol.* = Sir! Sire! Lord! OE. and ME. †**b.** quasi-*sb.* A dear one; a friend, sweetheart, mistress; occas. a wife. So in compar., one who is dearer. –1633.

1. Our sov'reign prince and liefest liege SHENSTONE. Quickly go again As thou art l. and dear TENNYSON. b. I had as l. have let it alone 1766. 3. Now hence must I..be I loth or lief 1883.

B. *adv.* Dearly; gladly, willingly. Chiefly with *would*, pa. subj. Also in *as l.* (*as*), *the liefer*; *l. I were* = I would gladly be. (The advb. use is chiefly due to misinterpretation of the adj. use in *I had as l.*, *I had liefer*; see A. 1 b.)

I would as l. go there as anywhere THACKERAY.

Liege (līdʒ). ME. [a. OF. *lige, liege*; ? ad. OHG. *ledig* free.] **A.** *adj.* **1. a.** Of the superior: Entitled to feudal allegiance and service. Now rare exc. in *l. lord.* **b.** Of the vassal: Bound to render feudal allegiance and service ME. **2.** Of or pertaining to the bond between superior and vassal ME.

1. b. A right to call on every l. subject to render assistance SCOTT. 2. Homage l. and Feaute ME.

B. *sb.* **1.** = *liege lord* ME. **2.** A liege man. Hence, a loyal subject of the king. ME.

1. Nay, good my L., with patience hear ADDISON. 2. The emperor's lieges AUSTIN. Hence **Lie·gedom.** **Lie·geful** *a.*, **-ly** *adv.* **Lie·geless** *a.*

Liege man, lie·geman. ME. **1.** *Feudal Law.* A vassal sworn to the service and support of his superior lord. **2.** *transf.* and *fig.* A faithful follower or subject 1823.

2. Sworn liegemen of the Cross KEBLE.

Liegier, obs. f. LEDGER.

Lien (lī·ĕn, līn, ləi·ĕn). 1531. [a. F. *lien* :—L. *ligamen* bond. The usual pronunc. in England is (lī·ĕn), in U.S. (līn).] †**1.** *Anat.* A tendon. COPLAND. **2.** *Law.* A right to retain possession of property until a debt due to the person detaining it is satisfied 1531. Also *fig.* Hence **Lienee·**, an owner of property on which another holds a lien. **Li·enor**, one who holds a l.

Lienal (ləi,ī·năl), *a.* 1879. [f. L. *lien* spleen + -AL.] *Anat.* Of the spleen; splenic.

‖**Lienculus** (ləi,e·ŋkiŭlŏs). 1897. [mod.L., dim. of L. *lien* spleen.] *Anat.* One of the small masses of splenic tissue found in the neighbourhood of the spleen; an accessory spleen.

‖**Lienitis** (ləiĕnəi·tis). 1845. [mod.L., f. L. *lien* spleen + -ITIS.] *Path.* = SPLENITIS.

Lieno- (ləi,ī·no), comb. f. L. *lien* spleen, in adjs. signifying 'pertaining to the spleen and —', as **Lieno-gastric** *a.* pertaining to the spleen and the stomach; **Lieno-intestinal** *a.*

Lientery (ləi·ĕntĕri). 1547. [ad. F. *lienterie*, ad. mod.L. *lienteria*, ad. Gr. λειεντερία, f. λεῖος smooth + ἔντερα bowels.] *Path.* A form of diarrhœa, in which the food passes through the bowels partially or wholly undigested; an instance of this. var. **Lienteria.** Hence **Liente·ric** *a.* of or pertaining to l.

Lier (ləi·əɹ). 1583. [f. LIE *v.*[1] + -ER [1].] One who lies; see LIE *v.*[1]

There were liers in ambush against him *Joshua* viii. 14.

Lierne (li,ɔ̄·ɹn). Also †**leyrn.** 1466. [ad. F. *lierne*; etym. unkn.] *Arch.* In vaulting, a short rib which neither springs from an impost nor runs along the ridge, but connects the bosses and intersections of the principal ribs. Also *attrib.*, in *l.-vault*, etc.

Lieu (l[i]ū). ME. [a. F. *lieu* :—L. *locum*, accus. of *locus* place.] Place, stead.

Phr. *In* (*the*) *l. of*: in the place, room, or stead of; A quarter's rent in l. of notice 1891. *In l.* (used *absol.*) = INSTEAD 2 (*arch.*); A better in l. TUCKER.

Lieutenancy (lef-, lĕfte·nănsi). 1450. [f. LIEUTENANT; see -ANCY.] †**1.** Delegated authority. DONNE. **2.** The office of a lieutenant; e. g. that of deputy governor of a kingdom, etc., of Lord Lieutenant of a county; also, a lieutenant's commission in the army or navy 1450. **3.** The term of a lieutenant's office 1632. †**4.** The district or province governed by a lieutenant –1726. **5.** The body of deputy-lieutenants in a county. Also, in the city of London, the body of commissioners who perform the duties of a Lord Lieutenant with regard to the militia and volunteers 1679.

2. All your lordship can hope for, is only the l. of a county SWIFT.

Lieutenant (lef-, lĕfte·nănt, *U.S.* liute·nănt). ME. [a. F., f. *lieu* place + *tenant* holding (see TENANT). For the pronunc., cf. the rare OF. form *luef* for *lieu*, and the Sc. forms *luf-*, *lufftenand*. Thus the labial glide at the end of OF. *lieu* as the first element of a compound may sometimes have been apprehended by Englishmen as a *v* or *f*.] **1.** One who takes the place of another; usually, an officer, civil or military, who acts for a superior; a representative, substitute, vicegerent. †Also *fig.* †**b.** Used as = L. *legatus*, *proconsul*, *suffectus*, Gr. ἡγεμών –1741. **2.** *Mil.* and *Naval.* (Often abbrev. *Lieut.*, and in combs. *Lt.*) **a.** In the army: The officer next in rank below captain 1578. **b.** In the navy: The officer next in rank and power below the commander 1626.

1. They are his Liefetenants, his vicegerents in his Church STUBBES. *L. of the Tower* (of London), title of the acting commandant delegated by the Constable. *L. of Ireland, of a county*: see LORD LIEUTENANT.

Comb.: †**l.-captain,** the officer who commands the company under the captain or in his absence; **-colonel,** an army officer next in rank below a colonel, having the actual command of a regiment; hence **-colonelcy**; **-commander,** a naval officer, in rank next below a commander, and next above a lieutenant; **-governor,** the deputy of a governor, *esp.* (*a*) in the British colonies, the actual governor of a district or province in subordination to a governor-general; (*b*) in U.S., the deputy-governor of a state with certain independent duties and the right of succession to the governorship, in case of its becoming vacant; hence **-governorship,** the office, or the province, of a lieutenant-governor. Hence †**Lieute·nantry** 1552–1676 (chiefly *Sc.*). **Lieute·nantship** 1467 = LIEUTENANCY. Now *rare.*

Lieute·nant-ge·neral. 1483. [After F. *lieutenant général*, in which *général* was orig. an adj.] †**1.** *gen.* One who exercises a delegated rule or command; the vicegerent of a kingdom, etc. –1701. **2.** One who acts as deputy to a general. In the British army, an officer in rank next below a general, and next above a major-general. †Also *lieutenant-general of the ordnance.* (In the U.S. army the office is now in abeyance.) 1570.

Liever, var. of *liefer*, compar. of LIEF.

Lif, obs. f. LIEF.

Life (ləif), *sb.* [OE. *līf* str. neut. :—OTeut. **lībo*[m], f. Teut. root **līb-*, whence LIVE *v.*, OE. *belīfan* BELIVE *v.*, to remain. The general meaning of the root (Indo-Eur. **leip-, loip-, lip-*) is to continue, last, endure; cf. Gr. λιπαρής persistent.]

I. 1. a. Primarily, the condition, quality, or fact of being a living person or animal. **b.** More widely: The property which differentiates a living animal or plant, or a living portion of organic tissue, from dead or non-living matter; the assemblage of the functional activities by which the presence of this property is manifested. Often specialized, as in *animal, vegetable, psychical l.* 1567. **c.** Continuance of animate existence; opp. to *death* OE. **2.** *fig.* Used to designate a condition of power, activity, or happiness, in contrast to metaphorical 'death'. Chiefly in biblical and religious use: The condition of those who are 'alive unto righteousness'; the power or principle by which this condition is produced; also, the state of existence of the souls of the blessed departed. OE. **3.** Animate existence (esp. that of a human being) viewed as a possession of which one is deprived by death OE. **4.** Energy in action, thought, or expression; animation, vivacity, spirit 1583. **5.** The cause or source of living; the animating principle; one who or that which keeps a thing alive; soul; essence ME. **6.** *nonce-uses.* Vitality as embodied in an individual person or thing 1587. **b.** Living things in the aggregate 1728. **7.** (In early use commonly *the l.*) The living form or model; living semblance; life-size figure or presentation 1599.

1. a. The mouing creature that hath l. *Gen.* ii. 20. b. L. is a state of ceaseless change BURDON-SANDERSON. c. *Tree, water, elixir*, etc. *of l.*, see these sbs. (*A matter*, etc.) *of l. and death*: (something) on which it depends whether a person shall live or die; hence *fig.* (a matter) of vital importance. *Staff of l.*, see STAFF *sb.* *To come to l.*: to regain consciousness after a swoon. So *to bring to l.* 2. ȝour lyf is hid with Crist in God WYCLIF *Col.* iii. 3. 3. Phr. *To lose, save, lay down one's l.* *L. for l.*: a phrase expressing the *lex talionis.* [They] sold their lives very dearely EVELYN. Phr. *For* (*one's*) *l.*, *for dear l.*, etc., so as to save, or, as if to save, one's l. (*I cannot*) *for my l.*, *for the l. of me* (in trivial use). 4. His preaching was without much l. or learning BURNET. 5. Order, & distribution is the l. of dispatche BACON. *My l.*: my dearest (not now in familiar use). 6. b. The noise of l. begins again TENNYSON. 7. Phr. *After, from the l.*: (drawn) from the living model. *As large as l.*, life-size: hence *joc.* *To the l.*: with fidelity to the original.

II. 1. The period from birth to death OE. **b.** The term of duration of an inanimate thing 1703. **2.** In *Life assurance*: **a.** A person considered with regard to the probable future duration of his life. **b.** Any particular amount of expectation of life. **c.** An insurance on a person's life. 1692. **3.** *pl.* with reference to tenacity of life 1562. **4.** Transf. uses in games. *Cards* ('Commerce'). One of three counters, which each player has; so called because, when he has lost all of them, he falls out of the game. *Pool.* One of three chances which each player has. *Cricket.* The continuation of a batsman's innings after a chance of getting him out has been missed. 1806.

1. Phr. *All my* (*his*, etc.) *l.*: = in or during all my (etc.) l.; used advb. *For l.*: for all that remains of a person's l. *A lease, grant*, etc. *for* (*two, three*, etc.) *lives*: one which is to remain in force during the l. of the longest liver of (two, three, etc.) specified persons. Hence occas. the specified persons are called the *lives.* b. The average l. of the steel rails 1889. 2. a. *A good l.*: one who is likely to live at least to the term assigned as the average 'expectation' at his age. 3. A cat has nine lives *Prov.* 4. (*Cricket*) The captain..received a l...in the slips 1883.

III. 1. The series of actions and occurrences constituting the history of an individual from birth to death. In gen. sense, the course of human existence from birth to death. OE. **b.** A particular manner or course of living OE. **c.** In mod. use: The practical part of human existence; the business, active pleasures, or pursuits of the world. Often with reference to social gaieties or vicious pleasures; esp. in phr. *to see l.* 1771. **2.** A written account of a person's life; a biography ME.

1. (*Anything, nothing*) *in l.*: 'in the world', at all. Is L. worth living? MALLOCK. *This l.* (Vulg. *hæc vita*, Gr. ἡ ζωὴ αὕτη, 1 *Cor.* xv. 19), also *the* or *this present l.*: the earthly state of human existence, as dist. from *the future l.*, the state of existence after death. b. *A good, bad, happy, wretched*, etc. *l.* The l. of Sparta was the l. of a camp JOWETT. c. To see me happily settled in l. DASENT. 2. Few authors write their own lives JOHNSON.

IV. Phr. *On life, on live* = ALIVE. *Livesman*, etc.: see LIVE.

Comb. 1. General: as *l.-experience, -germ*, etc.; *l.-bringing, -saving, -working* adjs.; *l.-teeming* adj.; (with sense 'in, of, for, with, or as l.') *l.-bereft, -weary* adjs.; *l.-struggle*; (with sense 'lifelong; during one's whole l., for l.') *l.-annuity, -study*, etc.

2. Special: as **l.-arrow,** a barbed arrow with a line attached, which is fired from a gun to establish communication with a ship in distress; **-assurance** (see ASSURANCE 5); **-belt,** a belt of inflated india-rubber, of cork, or the like, used to support the body in the water; **-boat,** a boat specially constructed for saving l. at sea; **-breath,** the breath which supports l.; also *fig.*; **-buoy** (see BUOY *sb.* 1 b); **-cycle** *Biol.* = *life-history*; **-estate,** an estate held for a person's l.;

-force, vital energy; **-history** *Biol.*, the series of developments of an organism from the egg to the adult state; also, an account of these; **-hold,** property held for a l. or lives; **-insurance** (see INSURANCE 4); **-interest,** an interest or estate which determines on the falling of a l.; **-jacket** (cf. *l.-belt*); **-line,** a rope used for saving l., e.g. that attached to a life-buoy, etc.; also, the line of life (LINE *sb.*² I g); **-mortar,** a mortar for discharging a life-rocket; **-office,** an institution where life-insurances can be effected; **-peer,** a peer whose title lapses at his death; so *life-peerage*; **-raft,** a kind of raft for saving l. in a shipwreck; **-rate,** the rate at which a l. is insured; **-rocket** (cf. *life-arrow*); so **-shot**; **-spring,** the source of l.; **-string,** a string or nerve supposed to be essential to l.; *pl.* what is essential to the support of l.; **-table,** a statistical table exhibiting statistics as to the probability of life at different ages; **-tenant,** a tenant for life; **-work,** the work of a lifetime.

Li·fe-blood. 1590. **1.** The blood necessary to life. **2.** *transf.* and *fig.* The vital part or vitalizing influence 1596. **3.** (Also *live-blood.*) Popular name for an involuntary twitching of the lip or eyelid 1733.

2. A good Booke is the pretious life-blood of a master spirit MILT.

Lifeful (ləi·f,fŭl), *a. rare.* ME. [-FUL.] Full of life; having or giving life or vitality. Hence **Li·feful-ly** *adv.*, **-ness.**

Life-giver. 1598. One who or that which gives life. So **Life-giving** *sb.* and *a.* 1561.

Li·fe-guard. 1648. [Cf. Du. *lijfgarde* (obs.), G. *leibgarde* body-guard.] **1.** A body-guard of soldiers; now *pl.* (written *Life Guards*), in the British army, two regiments of the household cavalry. Also *attrib.* **2.** The guard or protection of a person's life; a protecting agent or influence. ? *Obs.* 1648. **3.** A device attached to the front of a locomotive for sweeping up small obstructions 1864. **4.** *U.S.* A person employed to save bathers, etc. from drowning 1896.

1. *attrib.* **Life-guard-man,** a member of a life-guard; also *Life Guardsman*, one of the Life Guards.

Lifeless (ləi·f,lės), *a.* [OE. *lífléas*, f. *líf* LIFE *sb.* + *-léas* -LESS.] Having no life; dead; insensible 1651; inanimate OE.; wanting vital quality or animation ME.; devoid of life or living beings 1728.

A l. carcass 1586. A livelesse image HEYWOOD. This market is lagging again.. Flax l. 1890. Treeless, herbless, l. mountain BROWNING. **Li·feless-ly** *adv.*, **-ness.**

Life-like, lifelike (ləi·f,ləik), *a.* 1514. **1.** Likely to live. Only in *phrase.* **2.** Resembling life; exactly like a real person or thing 1725. **3.** as *adv.* With animation or liveliness 1839. Hence **Li·felikeness.**

1. Here, mother.. I'm living and l., thank God 1881.

Lifelong (ləi·f,lǫŋ), *a.* 1757. [f LIFE *sb.* + LONG.] †**1.** = LIVELONG *a.* 1. **2.** Continuing for a lifetime 1855. **3.** as *adv.* LOWELL.

†**Lifen,** *v.* [f. LIFE *sb.* + -EN ⁵.] To make lifelike. MARSTON.

Life-preserver. 1638. **1.** One who preserves life. SIR T. HERBERT. **2.** A contrivance, e.g. a life-belt, or the like, used in saving life at sea 1804. **3.** A stick or bludgeon loaded with lead, for self-defence 1837.

Lifer (ləi·fəɹ). *slang.* 1830. [f. LIFE *sb.* + -ER ¹.] **1.** One sentenced to penal servitude (earlier, transportation) for life. **2.** A sentence for life 1832.

Liferent (ləi·f,rent). 1491. *Sc. Law.* A rent which one receives for life, usually for support; the right to use and enjoy property during one's life. Hence **Li·ferenter, Liferentrix.**

Life-size, *a.* 1841. (Of a picture or statue) equal in size to the original. **Life-sized** *a.*

Lifesome (ləi·fsǿm), *a. rare.* 1583. [f. LIFE *sb.* + -SOME.] †**1.** Fraught with life. T. WATSON. **2.** Full of animation, lively 1688. Hence **Li·fesome-ly** *adv.*, **-ness.**

Lifetime (ləi·ftəim). ME. The time that life continues.

Liflod(e, obs. f. LIVELIHOOD ¹.

Lift (lift), *sb.*¹ *Obs.* exc. *Sc.* and *poet.* [OE. *lyft* masc., neut., fem. Cf. Du. *lucht*, Ger. *luft*, ON. *lopt* neut. (see LOFT).] The sky, upper regions; †earlier also, the air, atmosphere. Also *pl.*, the (seven) heavens.

Lift (lift), *sb.*² ME. [f. LIFT *v.*]

I. 1. The action or an act of lifting (see also DEAD LIFT); a raising or rising; the distance through which anything is lifted and moved 1470. **b.** A help on the way given to a foot passenger by taking him into a vehicle 1712. **2.** *fig.* A 'rise'; promotion; a rise in price; an act of helping, or a circumstance that helps, to a better position 1622. †**b.** An emergency; = DEAD LIFT 2. –1632. **3.** An act of lifting or stealing; †a shift, trick. *Obs.* exc. *dial.* 1592. **4.** Elevated carriage (of the head, neck, etc.) 1835. **5.** *techn.* See below.

1. The Goat..gives the Fox a L., and so Out he Springs 1692. There was so much l. of sea 1857. **2.** The only l. to set him upon his legs PEPYS. A l. in the Navy BURKE. **5.** *Engineering.* The action of lifting a load through a vertical distance, or one of several successive distances. Hence *Coal-mining*, a series of workings being prosecuted to the rise at one time 1702. *Horology.* The amount of motion of a watch-balance produced by each impulse of vibration 1884. The extent to which anything rises, e.g. a safety-valve, the pestle of an ore stamp, the water in a canal lock 1829. *Aeronaut.* The upward pressure which the air exerts on a flying machine; the total weight which a flying machine can raise 1902.

†**II.** A person who lifts something; a thief (*slang*) –1630.

III. 1. *Naut.* pl. 'Ropes which reach from each mast-head to their respective yard-arms to steady and suspend the ends' (Smyth) 1485. **2.** *Shoemaking.* A layer of leather in the heel of a boot 1677. **3.** A hoist; = ELEVATOR 3 c. Also, the well or vertical opening in which this works. 1851. **4.** A set of pumps in a mine; also, the section of a shaft occupied by one set 1849.

IV. 1. The quantity or weight that can be lifted at one time. Also *Sc.* a large quantity. ME. **2.** *dial.* A gate without hinges, that must be lifted 1674. **3.** *dial.* A particular joint or cut of meat, usu. of beef 1688. **4.** A rising ground 1825.

attrib. and *Comb.*, as (sense I. 1) *l.-capstan, -pulley*, (sense III. 3) *l.-attendant, -railway, -shaft, -well*; also, **l.-bridge,** a bridge that may be raised to let a boat pass, e.g. on a canal; **-gate** = sense IV. 2; **-hammer** = *tilt-hammer*; **-latch,** one that rises and falls; **-lock,** a canal lock; **-pump,** any pump other than a force-pump; **-tenter,** in windmills, a governor for regulating the speed, by adjusting the sails, or for adjusting the action of grinding machinery.

Lift (lift), *v.* ME. [a. ON. *lypta* = MHG., mod.G. *lüften* :—OTeut. type **luftjan*, f. **luftus* (ON. *lopt* air, sky = LIFT *sb.*¹). Etymological sense, 'to move up into the air'. Pa. t. and pa. pple. formerly †**lift,** beside **lifted.**] **1.** *trans.* To raise into the air from the ground, or to a higher position; to elevate, heave, hoist. †Also, to erect (a building). Also with *up, aloft, away, off, out*, etc. **b.** *Sc.* To take up, pick up. Hence in *Golf*: To take up the ball. 1596. **c.** *colloq.* To bring (a constellation) above the horizon in sailing, etc. 1891. **2.** In immaterial sense and *fig.*: To elevate, raise. Also with *out, up*, etc. ME. **b.** To raise in dignity, rank, etc.; to exalt. Also with *up*, etc. Now *rare.* ME. **c.** Chiefly with *up*: To cheer, encourage. Also, to elate, puff up. 1450. **3.** *intr.* for *refl.* (also with *up*). To rise. Said *esp.* of a vessel riding on the waves. Also quasi-*pass.* (e.g. of a window): To admit of being raised. ME. **b.** Of clouds, fog, etc.: To rise and disperse. Also (*U.S.*) of rain: To cease temporarily. 1834. **c.** Of a floor, etc.: To swell or warp and rise 1793. †**4.** *To l. at*: **a.** To pull at (something) in trying to raise it (*lit.* and *fig.*). **b.** To rise in opposition to. –1704. **5.** *trans.* In various phrases, chiefly Hebraisms. See below. **6.** To bear or carry high 1671. **7.** To take up or collect (rents, etc.); to levy (contributions, fines, etc.); to draw (wages, profits, etc.). Now *dial.* ME. **8.** *slang.* To take up (a portable object) or drive away (cattle) with dishonest intentions; hence, to steal. Cf. *shop-lifting.* 1526. Also *transf.* †**9.** To carve (a swan). *techn.* 1500. **10.** *Cards. intr.* To cut (for deal). ? *Obs.* 1599. **11.** *trans.* To take up and remove; to drive (cattle) away or to market, to strike (a tent) 1670. **12.** To take up out of the ground; to dig up (potatoes) 1844. **13.** To hit (the ball) into the air; esp. in *Cricket* 1874.

1. He lifted his cane *in terrorem* SCOTT. **c.** She'll [a steamer] l. the Southern Cross in a week R. KIPLING. **2. b.** *absol.* The Lord..bringeth low, and lifteth vp 1 *Sam.* ii. 7. **c.** His heart was lifted vp to his destruction 2 *Chron.* xxvi. 16. **d.** To raise in price, value, or amount 1907. **5.** Phr. *To l.* (*up*) *one's eyes, brow, face, visage*: to look up (*lit.* and *fig.*). *To l.* (*up*) *the hand(s*, (occas. *one's arm*): (*a*) *gen.*; (*b*) in prayer, thanksgiving, etc.; (*c*) in taking an oath; (*d*) in hostility *against* (a person); (*e*) to do a stroke of work (*mod. slang*). *To l. up one's head*: (*a*) *literally*; (*b*) *fig.* to regain courage or energy; to rally; †*To l. up the head of* (a person): used in the Bible for: to bring out from prison. *To l. up one's heart, mind, soul*: to raise one's thoughts or desires; to exalt oneself (with pride). *To l.* (*up*) *a cry, one's voice*, etc.: to cry out loudly; also *fig.* *To l. up one's heel, horn* (see those sbs.). **8.** He took to his old courses, and lifted a purse here, and a watch there THACKERAY. **11.** Some hot-headed proposals were made, one being to l. tools at once 1896. **13.** W. G. lifted Spofforth (i.e. the ball bowled by him) round to the leg boundary 1882. Hence **Li·ftable** *a.*

Lifter (li·ftəɹ). 1535. [f. LIFT *v.* + -ER ¹.] **1.** One who lifts or raises. Also with *up.* **b.** A thief. Cf. *cattle-, shop-l.* 1592. **2.** Something which lifts or is used for lifting. Also with *up.* 1570. **b.** *Founding.* 'A tool for dressing the mould; also a contrivance attached to a cope to hold the sand together when the cope is lifted' (Webster) 1864.

Lifting (li·ftiŋ), *vbl. sb.* ME. [f. LIFT *v.* + -ING ¹.] The action of LIFT *v.* Also *lifting up.*

attrib. and *Comb.* **a.** *gen.*, as *l. power*, etc.; **b.** a contrivance or portion of a machine adapted for lifting, as *l.-bar, -crane, -gear*, etc.; **l.-cam,** a cam or projection by which a l. movement is effected, e.g. in firearms; **-dog,** (*a*) = *lifting-cam*; (*b*) a claw-hook for grasping a column of bore-rods while raising or lowering them; **-jack** (see JACK *sb.*¹ II. 4).

Lifting (li·ftiŋ), *ppl. a.* ME. [-ING ².] That lifts.

Comb.: **l.-bridge,** a bridge of which either a part or the whole may be drawn up at one end when needful; **-gate** = LIFT *sb.*² IV. 2; **-pump,** any pump other than a force-pump; **-sail,** a sail whose action tends to lift the bows out of the water; **-set,** the series of pumps by which water is raised from the bottom of a mine by successive lifts.

Lig, obs. and dial. f. LIE *v.*¹

Ligament (li·gămĕnt). ME. [ad. L. *ligamentum*, f. *ligare* to bind.] **1.** Anything used in binding or tying; a band, tie; *Surg.* a bandage, ligature. *Obs.* in lit. sense. –1753. **b.** *fig.* Chiefly, a tie, bond of union ME. **2.** *Anat.* Any short band of tough, flexible, fibrous tissue which binds two bones of the body together. Hence, any membranous fold which supports an organ and keeps it in position. ME. **b.** A similar part in lower organisms 1797. **c.** *spec.* in *Conch.* The elastic substance which holds together the valves of a bivalve shell 1816.

Hence **Ligame·ntal, Ligame·ntary, Ligame·ntous** *adjs.*, of the nature of a l.; composed of the tissue proper to ligaments; of or pertaining to a l. **Ligame·ntously** *adv* by ligaments.

Ligan, obs. f. LAGAN, wreckage.

Ligate (ləi·geⁱt), *v.* 1599. [f. L. *ligat-*, *ligare* to bind.] Chiefly *Surg.* To bind with a ligature or bandage; *spec.* to tie up (a bleeding artery, etc.).

Ligation (ləigēⁱ·ʃən). 1597. [ad. L. *ligationem.*] †**1.** The action or process of binding; the condition of being bound; suspension (of the faculties) –1684. **2.** The action of binding with a ligature; *esp.* in *Surg.*, the operation of tying up (a bleeding artery, etc.). Also, an instance of this. 1597. **3.** A ligature, bandage, bond, tie; also, the place of tying (*arch.*) 1597.

3. A bundle tied with tape, and sealed at each fold and l. with black wax SCOTT.

Ligature (li·gătiŭɹ), *sb.* ME. [ad. L. *ligatura*, f. *ligare.*] **1.** Anything used in binding or tying; a band, tie, etc. Chiefly *spec.* in *Surg.*, a thread or cord used to tie up a bleeding artery, etc. **b.** *fig.* A bond, tie 1627. **2.** = LIGAMENT 2. Not now in good use. ME. **3.** The action of tying; an instance of this. Also, a tie or the place of one 1541. **4.** *Mus.* A method of indicating the binding of notes into groups. In mod. notation: a TIE or SLUR. In *Counterpoint*: a SYNCOPATION. 1597. **5.** In *Writing* or *Printing*: A monogram. Also, a stroke connecting two letters. *In l.*, combined in one character or type. 1693.

†6. Binding quality; also *concr.* -1727. Hence **Li·gature** *v.* to bind with a l. or bandage; *spec.* in *Surg.* to tie up (an artery, etc.).

Lige, obs. f. LIE *v.*[1], LIEGE.

Ligeance (ləi·dʒăns, lī·dʒăns). ME. [a. OF. *ligeance, legiance*, etc., f. *lige* LIEGE; see -ANCE. Cf. ALLEGIANCE.] 1. = ALLEGIANCE 2. *arch.* 2. The sway of a sovereign over his subjects or lieges; the territories subject to a sovereign. Now only in legal use. ME. So †**Li·geancy.**

Ligge, obs. f. LIE *v.*[1]

Ligger (li·gəɪ), *sb. dial.* 1483. [f. *lig*, north. var. of LIE *v.*[1] + -ER[1]. Cf. LEDGER *sb.*, a doublet of this wd.] 1. A coverlet. †2. = LEDGER *sb.* 2. -1518. †3. The nether millstone. PEGGE. 4. A plank bridge 1840. 5. *Angling.* A line with a float and bait which is left in the water 1825. Hence **Li·gger** *v.* to fish with a l.

Light (ləit), *sb.* [OE. *lēoht* str. neut. (early ME. *līht*) :—OTeut. **leuhtom* :—pre-Teut. **leuktom*, f. Indo-Eur. root **leuk-* to shine, be white. (Not in ON.) The primary sense is possibly 'that which is bright'.] 1. The natural agent or influence which evokes the activity of the organ of sight. a. Viewed as the medium of visual perception. Also, the condition of space in which vision is possible. Opp. to *darkness.* b. Viewed as itself an object of perception. Also, an individual shining or appearance of light. OE. c. Viewed as residing in or emanating from a luminary OE. d. In scientific use (see below) 1704. e. The portion of light which illuminates a given space 1533. f. A gleam or sparkle in the eye, expressive of animation or the like 1593. g. In various fig. phrases (see below). h. *pl.* [after L. *lumina.*] Graces of style. ADDISON. 2. *spec.* The illumination which proceeds from the sun in day-time; daylight. Also, day-time, day-break. (Usu. *the l.*; also, *the l. of day.*) OE. 3. The state of being visible or exposed to view OE. 4. Power of vision, eyesight (now *poet.* or *rhet.*). Also *pl.* = the eyes (now only *slang*). OE. 5. A body from which illumination emanates; the sun or other heavenly body (after *Gen.* i. 6) OE.; an ignited candle, lamp, etc. OE.; *collect.* candles, etc. used to illuminate a particular place OE.; a signal-fire or beacon-lamp, e. g. on a ship or in a lighthouse; hence, the lighthouse 1604; †a linkman STEELE. 6. Used *fig.* with reference to mental illumination or elucidation. a. In phrases (see below) 1420. b. Illumination or enlightenment as possessed by the mind, or as derivable from a particular source ME. c. *pl.* (*a*) Facts, discoveries, or suggestions which explain a subject. (*b*) The natural or acquired information and powers of an individual intellect. 1526. d. A suggestion that helps to the solution of a problem. Now *spec.* in an acrostic, each of the words to be guessed, their initials (or initials and finals) forming the answer to the puzzle. 1894. 7. The brightness of Heaven, the illumination of the soul by divine truth, etc. OE. b. *spec.* Among Quakers, the inward revelation of Christ in the soul 1656. 8. *fig.* (from sense 5): One who is eminent or conspicuous; a luminary 1592. 9. *fig.* (from sense 1 e): A consideration which illuminates or points to a particular view of a subject. Hence, the aspect in which anything is viewed or judged. 1689. 10. A window or opening in a wall for the admission of light; *spec.* a perpendicular division of a mullioned window ME. b. *Gardening.* A glazed compartment in the side or roof of a greenhouse or the top of a frame 1733. 11. *Mech.* An aperture or clear space 1776. 12. *Painting.* Light or illuminated surface in a picture; any portion of a picture represented as lighted up 1622. Also *fig.* 13. *Law.* The light falling on the windows of a house from the sky, interference with which by neighbours is illegal. (*Ancient Lights*, an inscription often put on the face or side of a house, to give warning against obstruction of the access of light.) 1768. 14. A flame or spark serving to ignite any combustible substance; also, something used for igniting; e. g. a spill, taper, match 1684.

1. a. And God said, Let there be l.: and there was l. *Gen.* i. 3. b. The long l. shakes across the lakes TENNYSON. *Northern, Southern Lights* (= AURORA *Borealis, Australis*), *Zodiacal l.*: see the adjs. c. Phr. *To give l.* (said of a luminary). A goodly Bekon geuyng l. HALL. d. Senses in scientific use: (*a*) the thing (whether matter or energy) which is communicated from a luminous body to the body illuminated by it; The L. of the Sun 1704; (*b*) this thing regarded as producing sensation 1704; (*c*) the sensation produced 1800; (*d*) the process (variously conceived) by which the communication is made 1875; (*e*) certain characteristics of such processes (rays or waves) 1900; (*f*) physical energies and processes of the same type as those involved in the production of vision, but having possibly a different range of periods (e.g. Röntgen rays) 1865. e. The picture..is in a bad l. (i.e. imperfectly visible) 1797. Phr. *In l.*: lighted up. *One's l.*: the ordinary share of light which a person enjoys for seeing around him. *To stand in a person's l.* = to cut him off from this; hence *fig.* to prejudice his interests. So *to stand in one's own l.* f. Yet do I cease not to behold The love-light in her eye H. COLERIDGE. g. *To put out* or *quench* (one's) *l.*: to extinguish his 'vital spark'. Quench thou his l., Destruction dark! SCOTT. Phr. *L. of* one's *eye(s)*: applied to a loved object. *The l. of God's countenance* (*Ps.* iv. 6, etc.) = Divine favour. Hence, sarcastically, *the l. of (a person's) countenance*: (his) sanction, approving presence. 2. Phr. *To see the l.*: to be brought forth or published. 3. Phr. *To come to l.*: to be made visible or made known. The thing that is hid bringeth he foorth to l. *Job* xxviii. 11. 5. Make we heuen & erth..and lyghtys fayre to se 1460. *Wax lights* = wax candles for lighting (now *rare* in this use). Phr. *Fixed, flashing, intermittent, revolving l.* (in a lighthouse). As a harbour l. reveals the port 1894. 6. a. *To give* (*carry, bring*) *l.* (†*to* or *into* a subject). *To get, receive l.* Now usu. *to throw* (*cast, shed*) *l. upon.* b. *L. of nature*, the capacity of discerning divine truths without the help of revelation. The lycht of ressoun 1513. The men of England, the men, I mean, of l. and leading BURKE. c. He did his best; he worked according to his lights THACKERAY. *New light(s*: novel doctrines (esp. theol. and eccles.) the partisans of which lay claim to superior enlightenment 1650; hence *Old light(s*, the doctrines to which the 'new lights' are opposed; *Old Lights* (Sc. *Auld Lichts*) and *New Lights*, designations for persons holding the respective views: see N.E.D. He was afraid of Fox, for going after new lights SEWEL. 7. *Angel* (or *spirit*) *of l.*, one who dwells in Heaven. Diuels soonest tempt resembling spirits of l. SHAKS. 8. Joan of Arc, A l. of ancient France TENNYSON. 9. Phr. *To set in a* (certain) *light.* *In the l. of*: (*a*) with the help given by (some fact); (*b*) viewed as being (so and so). In the l. of all that has been said and done 1893. 12. The Italian masters universally make the horizon the chief l. of their picture RUSKIN. 14. Phr. *To strike a l.*, to produce a flame, etc. with a match, etc. (see STRIKE *v.*).

Comb.: **l.-ball** *Mil.*, a combustible fired from a mortar at night, to throw l. on the operations of the enemy; **-boat** = LIGHTSHIP; **-due, -duty**, a toll levied on ships for the upkeep of lights in lighthouses and lightships; **-head**, the top portion of a 'light' (sense 10); **-keeper**, one who has charge of the l. in a lighthouse, etc.; **-man**, (*a*) a light-keeper; (*b*) a linkman; hence **lightmanship**; **-money** = *light-due*; **-port**, 'a scuttle made for showing a l. through' (Smyth); **-tower**, a lighthouse; **-vessel** = LIGHTSHIP; **-year** *Astron.*, the distance l. travels in a year, i.e. about 63,000 times the distance of the earth from the sun, taken as the unit of stellar distance.

Light (ləit), *a.*[1] [OE. *lēoht, līht* :—OTeut. **lįҗhto-* (*-tjo-*), f. Teut. root **lįҗgw-* :—pre-Teut. **leŋghw*; cf. Skr. *laghu*, Gr. ἐλαφρός light, ἐλαχύς small, etc.; cf. also LUNG.]

I. 1. Of little weight, not heavy. b. Deficient in weight ('*too* light') 1589. 2. Of small specific gravity 1559. 3. Bearing a small load. Of a vessel: Having a small burden, or (usu.) unladen, without cargo. 1573. Also *fig.* 4. Chiefly *Mil.* Lightly armed or equipped. †Also, lightly clad. ME. 5. Of a vehicle or vessel: Constructed for light loads and for swift movement OE. 6. Of a building: Not looking heavy; graceful in form 1762. 7. Boxing. *L. heavy-weight*, a boxer from 12 st. 7 to 11 st. 6.

1. My yoke is easie, and my burden is l. *Matt.* xi. 30. Phr. *To lie l.* (cf. HEAVY *a.*[1] I. 1). *L. ice*, that which has but little depth in the water. *L. sails*, all above the topgallant sails; also the studding sails and flying jib. Wheat..l. in the ear BURKE. b. Clipt and L. Money 1700. 2. Hydrogen, the lightest gas LOCKYER. 3. He did for heavines that his Cart went l. MILT. *L. engine*: an engine alone, without a train. *L. railway*: a railway constructed for l. traffic. *L. porter.* *L. water-line*, the water-line of a ship when just launched, or quite unladen. 4. Phr. *In l. marching order*: i. e. carrying only arms and ammunition. 5. *L. cart* = 'spring cart' (see CART *sb.* 3). 6. Small l. spires 1850.

II. 1. Having little momentum or force; acting gently. Also *l. of touch.* OE. 2. Having little density or cohesive force. Of soil: Friable, porous, workable. Of a cloud: Fleecy, evanescent. 1523. b. Of bread, etc.: That has risen properly; not heavy 1460. 3. Of food or drink: Easy of digestion. Of wine, beer, etc.: Containing little alcohol. OE. 4. *L. in the mouth* (of a horse): sensitive to the bit 1727. 5. Of accent or syllables: Unemphatic. Hence, of rhythm, consisting of such syllables. 1575.

1. Waxe..yeelds at last to euerie l. impression SHAKS. His l. walk GEO. ELIOT. A l. breeze 1885. 2. There is a l. cloud by the moon BYRON.

III. 1. Of small consequence, not weighty; slight, trivial. Of a sin: Venial. OE. †b. Cheap. Of a price: Low. Also *l. cheap* = CHEAP *a.* and *adv.* -1647. †c. Of persons: Of small account -1548. 2. Characterized by levity, frivolous ME. b. Chiefly of women: Wanton, unchaste ME.

1. This is no l. matter *Junius Lett.* Phr. *To set l. by* or *of* (a person or thing): to despise, slight, undervalue. *To make l. of*: to treat as of small or no importance. The Natives make l. of such things as we call Colds FRYER. 2. That l. perpetual talk about him NEWMAN.

IV. 1. Moving readily; active, nimble, quick. *arch.* OE. 2. That moves or is moved easily; pliant, fickle, unsteady; facile (of belief, etc.). Const. *of, to* with *inf.* Now *rare.* ME.

1. Phr. *L. of foot, of person*; †*l.-fingers.* 2. Be not lyght of credence in no case SKELTON.

V. 1. Easy to bear or endure OE. 2. Easy to accomplish, requiring little exertion; now only qualifying *task, work*, etc. OE. 3. Of literature, plays, music, etc.: Requiring little mental effort; amusing 1597. 4. Of sleep: Not heavy; easily shaken off. Hence *l. sleeper.* OE.

1. How l. and portable my paine seemes now! *Lear* III. vi. 115. 2. The service will be l. and easy FRANKLIN. 3. Phr. *L. comedian*: an actor of l. comedy. 4. A man who at all times was a l. sleeper 1894.

VI. Free from the weight of care or sorrow; cheerful. *Obs.* exc. in *l. heart.* ME.

VII. Of the head: Dizzy, giddy. Also of persons: = LIGHT-HEADED 1590.

Is he not l. of Braine? *Oth.* IV. i. 280.

Light (ləit), *a.*[2] [OE. *lēoht* (Anglian *lēht*); see LIGHT *sb.*] 1. †a. Bright, shining, luminous -1760. b. Having plenty of light, not dark. †Earlier: Brightly illuminated; *fig.* enlightened mentally. OE. 2. Pale in hue. Also = *l.-coloured.* (Hyphened when prefixed to another adj. of colour used attrib.) ME.

1. a. *On* (*of, in*) *a l. fire*: in a blaze (common in 16–18th c.). All Sodome was of a l. fire WARREN. b. When the morning is l., they practise it [euill] *Micah* ii. 1. 2. A l. bob Periwig 1686. Light-drab cloth MISS BRADDON.

†**Light**, *ppl. a.* 1495. [pa. pple. of LIGHT *v.*[2]] Lighted -1632.

Light (ləit), *adv.*[1] [OE. *lēohte*, f. OTeut. **lįҗhto-* LIGHT *a.*[1]] 1. In a light manner; see LIGHT *a.*[1] 2. *Comb.* (with pres. and pa. pples.) as *l.-bounding, -harnessed*, etc. 1533.

†**Light**, *adv.*[2] [OE. *lēohte*, f. *lēoht* LIGHT *a.*[2]] Brightly, clearly -1710.

Light (ləit), *v.*[1] [OE. *līhtan* :—OTeut. type **līhtjan*, **lįҗhtjan*, f. **līhto-*, **lįҗhto-*, LIGHT *a.*[1]]

I. †1. *trans.* To make light, lessen the weight of. Also *fig.* -1600. 2. To relieve *of* a (material) load; to unload (a ship). Also, to 'relieve' (a person) *of* his property. ? *Obs.* ME. †3. To relieve (*of* pain, sorrow, etc.); to comfort, cheer -1597. †Also *intr.* †4. To make of less effect. FOTHERBY. 5. a. *Naut.* 'To move or lift anything along' (Smyth). *trans.* and *absol.* 1841. b. ? Hence *to l. out* (*U.S. slang*): to decamp 1884.

2. We must..l. this weary vessell of her lode SPENSER. 5. b. And so when I couldn't stand it no longer, I lit out MARK TWAIN.

II. To descend. Cf. ALIGHT *v.*[1] [App. an absol. use of the vb. in sense I. 2 ('to relieve a horse, etc. of one's weight').] 1. *intr.* To descend *from* a horse or vehicle; to dismount. †Sometimes conjugated with *to be.* OE. †2. Of persons: To descend. Occas. *refl.* -1533. 3. To fall and settle on a surface, as a bird, a snowflake, etc. Also with *down.* ME. 4. To have a particular place of incidence or arrival (see below) ME.

1. Stern Hassan..from his horse Disdains to l. BYRON. 3. Phr. *To l. on one's feet* or *legs* (fig.): to be fortunate or successful. I have made scores of new acquaintances and lighted on my legs as usual THACKERAY. 4. a. Of a blow or weapon: To fall and strike; to fall (short, etc.) (now *rare*); There flies my Dart, l. where it will 1604. †b. To arrive *at* a point; to fall *into* a condition; to 'land' in a particular place or position -1697. c. *To l. on, upon*: to fall or descend upon; to fall to the lot of; *occas.* conjugated with *to be*; The plague of Egypt l. vppon you all 1607. d. Of persons. *To l. on* or *upon*: to chance upon; to meet with or discover; to come across 1470. e. To come or fall *into* a person's hands; to chance *into* a person's company. (Now *rare* or *obs.*) 1562. f. To turn out (well, happily); also *simply*, to happen. (Now *dial.*) 1607.

Light (ləit), *v.*[2] Pa. t. and pple. **lighted, lit**; pa. pple. pseudo-*arch.* **litten.** [OE. *lihtan* :—OTeut. **liuhtjan*, f. **leuhto-* LIGHT *sb.* or *a.*[2]] †1. *intr.* To give light; to shine; to be alight or burning. Also, to lighten. -1774. †b. Of day, etc.: To grow light -1596. 2. *trans.* To set burning (a candle, etc., a fire, a combustible); to ignite. Also with *up.* OE. Also *transf.* and *fig.* b. *intr.* To take fire, be lighted; *transf.* to 'kindle' ME. 3. *trans.* To give light to (a room, etc.); to illuminate; *esp.* to furnish with means of illumination. (Rarely with *up.*) ME. b. *transf.* (Chiefly with *up.*) To cause (the eyes, features, etc.) to brighten with animation. Also, to brighten up (writing). Also *intr.* for *refl.* or *pass.* 1766. 4. To give light to (a person); hence, to show the way to (*lit.* and *fig.*). Also *absol.* ME. 5. To illumine spiritually or intellectually. ? *Obs.* or *arch.* ME.

1. b. 1 *Hen. IV*, III. ii. 138. 2. *transf.* Thine eyes were lit from other skies B. TAYLOR. absol. *To l. up*: to l. one's pipe, cigar, etc. (*colloq.*). 3. The Globe, that lights the lower world SHAKS. St. Andrew's church..is lighted with gas 1840. *absol.* (*colloq.*) Isn't it time to light up? Phr. *To l. up*: to furnish or fill with abundance of light; to illuminate in a special manner; to make prominent by means of light; Lit up by the rising moon W. IRVING. b. Her expressive features all lit up with Joy 1766. 4. Here comes a candle to l. you to bed 18.. Hence **Li·ghtable** *a.* that can be lighted.

Lightage (ləi·tėdʒ). 1606. [f. LIGHT *sb.*[2] + -AGE.] †1. A toll paid by a ship coming to a port where there is a lighthouse -1789. 2. Provision of (artificial) light 1862.

Light-armed, *a.* 1579. [LIGHT *a.*[1]] Bearing light armour or arms. Also *fig.*

Li·ght-bob. 1785. [BOB *sb.*[7]] A soldier of the light infantry.

Lighten (ləi·t'n), *v.*[1] ME. [f. LIGHT *a.*[1] + -EN[5]; also, in sense 5, an extension of LIGHT *v.*[1]] 1. *trans.* To reduce or remove the load of (a ship, etc.); to relieve *of* (a burden, etc.). Also *intr.* for *pass.* 2. To remove a burden from, relieve (the heart or mind); †to cheer. Now *rare.* b. *intr.* for *refl.* or *pass.* Somewhat *rare.* ME. 3. *trans.* To make lighter; to alleviate, mitigate 1483. †b. To lessen the pressure of -1797. c. To make nimble (*rare*) 1599. 4. *intr.* To grow lighter 1720. †5. To descend, alight; to light *upon* -1704.

1. To l. the cart..I descended and walked 1871. 2. To l. his conscience MACAULAY. 3. How we may light'n Each others burden in our share of woe MILT. b. Peraduenture hee will l. his hand from off you 1 *Sam.* vi. 5. c. *Much Ado* v. iv. 120. 5. O Lorde, let thy mercy l. upon us *Bk. Com. Prayer.*

Lighten (ləi·t'n), *v.*[2] ME. [f. LIGHT *a.*[2] + -EN[5].] 1. *trans.* To give light to; to make bright or luminous; to light up. Also *fig.* b. To cause (the countenance or looks) to light up. Also *intr.* for *pass.* of the face, eyes, etc. 1795. †2. In Biblical lang.: To restore sight to (the eyes) -1535. 3. To shed spiritual light upon (*arch.*) ME. †4. To kindle, ignite; = LIGHT *v.*[2] 2. -1645. 5. *intr.* To shine, flash, burn brightly; to glow with light ME. b. To shine like light *on.* CARY. 6. To emit flashes of lightning. Chiefly *impers.* 1440. 7. *trans.* To cause to flash *out* or *forth*; to send *down* as lightning (*lit.* and *fig.*) 1586.

1. God..l. his face on vs HAMPOLE *Ps.* lxvi. 1. b. His eye lightened 1890. 2. L. myne eyes, that I slepe not in death COVERDALE *Ps.* xii[i]. 3. 3. 2 *Hen. IV*, II. i. 208. 4. As one Taper lightneth another HOWELL. 5. His steely lance, that lighten'd as he pass'd POPE. 6. Like skies that rain and l. BYRON.

Lighter (ləi·təɹ), *sb.*[1] 1372. [f. LIGHT *v.*[1] (sense 2) + -ER[1], or ad. Du. *lichter.*] A boat, usu. a flat-bottomed barge, used in lightening or unloading (sometimes loading) ships that cannot be wharfed, and for transporting goods in harbour, etc. Also *attrib.*, as **Li·ghterman,** one employed on or owning a l. Hence **Li·ghterage,** transhipment or unloading of cargo by means of a l.; the charges for this.

Lighter (ləi·təɹ), *sb.*[2] 1553. [f. LIGHT *v.*[2]] One who or that which lights or kindles.

Lighter (ləi·təɹ), *v.* 1840. [f. LIGHTER *sb.*[1]] *trans.* To remove or transport (goods) in or as in a lighter. Also *absol.* or *intr.*

Li:ghter-than-ai·r, designating aircraft of the balloon type that rise in the air by reason of lesser specific gravity 1909.

Light-fingered, *a.* 1547. Having light and nimble fingers. a. *gen.* 1804. b. Thievish, dishonest 1547. †c. Prompt in striking; pugnacious -1607.

Lightfoot (ləi·tfut), *a.* ME. [LIGHT *a.*[1]] 1. *poet.* = LIGHT-FOOTED. (Common in 16th c.) 1440. †2. quasi-*sb.* A name for the hare and the deer -1815.

Light-footed, *a.* 1490. Having a light foot; treading lightly, active, nimble.

Lightful (ləi·tfŭl), *a.* ME. [f. LIGHT *sb.* + -FUL.] Full of light (*lit.* and *fig.*); luminous, bright.

Al thi body schal be liȝtful WYCLIF *Luke* xi. 34. Hence **Li·ghtfulness.**

Light-handed, *a.* 1440. a. Having a light touch (*lit.* and *fig.*). b. Carrying little. c. Of a vessel or factory: = SHORT-HANDED. Hence **Light-ha·ndedness.**

Li·ghthead. 1751. A light-headed person. Also quasi-*adj.* = next.

Light-headed, *a.* ? 1537. 1. Disordered in the head; giddy, delirious. 2. Frivolous, thoughtless; fickle 1579. †3. quasi-*adv.* FULLER.

2. The light-headed doings of the Queen Dowager BURTON. Hence **Light-hea·ded·ly** *adv.*, **-ness.**

Light-hearted, *a.* ME. 1. Having a light heart; cheerful, gay. 2. Proceeding from a light heart 1841. Hence **Light-hea·rted·ly** *adv.*, **-ness** 1611.

Light-heeled, *a.* 1590. 1. Brisk in walking or running; nimble. †2. Of a woman: Loose, unchaste -1796. †**Light-heels,** a loose woman.

Light horse. 1532. 1. †a. *collect. sing.* Light horsemen; a body of light cavalry. b. = LIGHT HORSEMAN. †2. A courtesan 1627.

Light horseman. 1548. 1. A light-armed cavalry soldier. 2. Slang name for one of a class of Thames thieves 1800. †3. 'The light boat, since called a gig' (Smyth) -1708. †4. A variety of fancy pigeons. R. HOLME. 5. †a. An Australian sea-fish, prob. the Sweep, *Scorpis æquipennis.* b. A W. Indian fish of the genus *Ephippus.* 1789.

Li·ghthouse. 1622. [f. LIGHT *sb.* + HOUSE *sb.*[1]] A tower or other structure, with a powerful light or lights (orig. a beacon) at the top, erected at some important or dangerous point on or near the sea-coast for the guidance of mariners; a *pharos.*

Lightless (ləi·tlės), *a.* [OE. *lēohtlēas*, f. *lēoht* LIGHT *sb.* + *-lēas* -LESS.] 1. Receiving no light; dark. Also *fig.* 2. Giving no light ME. Hence **Li·ghtlessness.**

Light-limbed, *a.* 1695. Having light limbs; agile.

The light-limbed Matadore BYRON.

Li·ghtly, *v.* Chiefly *Sc.* ME. [f. †*lightly* adj., contemptuous.] *trans.* To make light of, despise, disparage.

It's best no to l. them that have that character SCOTT.

Lightly (ləi·tli), *adv.* [OE. *lēohtlīce*, f. *lēoht* LIGHT *a.*[1] + -LY[2].] In a light manner. 1. With little weight; with little pressure, force, or violence; gently. 2. In no great quantity or thickness; to no great amount OE. †b. Slightly -1697. 3. Without depression; cheerfully, gaily ME. 4. Easily, readily. *Obs.* exc. *arch.* ME. 5. Nimbly. †In early use, swiftly; *occas.* at once. ME. †6. Probably, perhaps -1672. †b. As is apt to happen; commonly, often -1676. 7. a. Carelessly, indifferently. b. Slightingly. ME. 8. For a slight cause; without careful consideration OE. †9. 'Not chastely'. SWIFT.

1. At the first he l. afflicted the land of Zebulun *Isa.* ix. 1. I sleep l. enough 1852. 2. They are but l. rewarded SHAKS. L. clad 1875. 3. Try to bear l. what must needs be JOWETT. 4. Credulous people believe l. whatever they hear CHESTERF. L. come, l. go *Provb.* 5. L. vaulting off his saddle 1632. 7. Thinking l. of the possession of gold JOWETT. 8. These are opinions that I have not l. formed, or that I can l. quit BURKE.

Li·ghtmans. *Thieves' cant.* 1567. [f. LIGHT *a.*[2]; cf. DARKMANS.] The day.

Light-minded, *a.* 1611. Having a light mind; frivolous. Hence **Light-mi·ndedness.**

Lightness[1] (ləi·tnės). ME. [f. LIGHT *a.*[1] + -NESS.] The quality or fact of being light; see LIGHT *a.*[1]

Lightness[2] (ləi·tnės). [OE. *līhtnes*, f. *līht*, *lēoht* LIGHT *a.*[2] + -NESS.] †1. Brightness, light (*lit.* and *fig.*) -1824. 2. Illumination. Now only *lit.* ME.

1. An insane l. about the eyes SCOTT. 2. The l. of an apartment LYTTON.

Lightning (ləi·tniŋ). ME. [Spec. use of *lightening* vbl. sb. of LIGHTEN *v.*[2]; now differentiated in spelling.] 1. The visible discharge of electricity between groups of clouds, or between the clouds and the ground. Also, A flash of lightning (now *rare*). 2. *slang.* Gin 1781.

1. *Forked l., chain* or *chained l.*: designations of l. which assumes the form of a zigzag or divided line. *Sheet l.*: that which illuminates a wide surface at once. *Summer* or *heat l.*: sheet l. without audible thunder, the result of a distant storm. *Like l.*, with the speed of l. (hyperbolically for 'extremely swiftly'); This Notion ran like Lightening thro' the City DE FOE. Also, *like greased l.* (slang). *fig.* She..Makes wicked lightnings of her eyes TENNYSON. *attrib.* Her l. glance DISRAELI.

Comb.: **l.-arrester,** a device to protect telegraphic apparatus, etc. from l.; **-bone,** some kind of fossil bone; **-bug** = FIRE-FLY; **-conductor,** a metallic rod or wire fixed to an exposed point of a building, or the mast of a ship, to carry l. harmlessly into the earth or sea; **-discharger** = *lightning-arrester*; **-express** *U.S.*, name for certain very rapid trains; **-pains** *pl.*, sharp, shooting, momentary pains, felt by sufferers from locomotor ataxy; **-print,** an appearance sometimes found on the skin of men and animals and on clothing struck by l., pop. supposed to be photographs of surrounding objects; **-proof** *a.*, protected from l.; **-rod** = *lightning-conductor*; **-stone, -tube** = FULGURITE 1; **-strike,** a sudden strike (of workmen) without warning.

Light of love, light o' love. 1578. [See LIGHT *a.*[1] IV. 2.] 1. As predicative phr.: Inconstant in love 1579. 2. as *sb.* †a. Inconstancy in love. T. PROCTOR. b. A woman inconstant in love; also, a wanton, a harlot 1599. †3. Name of an old dance-tune -1612.

3. Best sing it to the tune of *Light O' Loue* SHAKS.

Lights (ləits), *sb. pl.* ME. [Subst. use of LIGHT *a.*[1] Cf. LUNG.] The lungs. Now only the lungs of sheep, pigs, bullocks, etc., used as food (esp. for cats and dogs).

Li·ghtship. 1837. [f. LIGHT *sb.*] A vessel bearing a light, *esp.* one moored where a lighthouse cannot be placed; a floating light.

Li·ght-skirts. 1597. A woman of light character. Also *attrib.* (in form *light-skirt*).

Lightsome (ləi·tsə̆m), *a.*[1] ME. [f. LIGHT *a.*[1] + -SOME.] 1. Having the effect or appearance of lightness; light, graceful, elegant. †Also, in early use, easy. Somewhat *rare.* 1440. 2. Light-hearted, cheerful; also, enlivening, entertaining ME. b. Flighty, frivolous 1533. 3. Moving lightly; lively, quick 1601.

1. The lofty tower, straight and l. as a lily 1877. 2. L. sangs SCOTT. 3. As l. as a bird WORDSW. Hence **Li·ghtsome·ly** *adv.*[1], **-ness**[1].

Li·ghtsome, *a.*[2] ME. [f. LIGHT *sb.* + -SOME.] 1. Light-giving, luminous 1440. Also *fig.* 2. Of an apartment, a building, etc.: Well-lighted, bright 1538. Also *fig.* 3. Clear, manifest. Now *rare.* 1532. †4. Light-hued -1674.

1. L. clouds and shining seas SHELLEY. 2. His.. Roomes, so Large and L. BACON. Hence **Li·ghtsome·ly** *adv.*[2], **-ness**[2].

Li·ght-weight, light weight. 1773. [f. LIGHT *a.*[1]] **A.** *sb. Sporting.* A man or animal under the average weight; also of motor-cycles; esp. in *Boxing*, a boxer from 9 st. 9 to 9 st. Also in *Racing* handicaps, a horse carrying light weights, or a jockey riding at a low weight. **B.** *adj.* Light in weight; said *esp.* of coins and cloth; cf. LIGHT *a.*[1] 1 b. Also *fig.* 1809.

Lightwood[1] (ləi·twud). 1685. [f. LIGHT *a.*[1]] A name for trees having light wood; in Australia esp. *Acacia Melanoxylon*.

Li·ghtwood[2]. *N. Amer.* and *W. Ind.* 1693. [f. LIGHT *sb.* (or LIGHT *v.*[2]).] **a.** Any wood used in lighting a fire; esp. resinous pine-wood. **b.** Any tree (e. g. *Amyris balsamifera*, candle-wood) the wood of which burns with a brilliant flame.

†**Li·ghty,** *a.* ME. [f. LIGHT *sb.* or *a.*[1] + -Y[1].] **1.** Full of light, bright. WYCLIF. **2.** Well-informed. TURNER.

Lign-aloes (ləin,æ·lo^u^z). ME. [ad. late L. *lignum aloēs* 'wood of the aloe'.] **a.** = ALOE 3. **b.** = ALOE 1. **c.** [= Sp. *linaloe*.] An aromatic wood obtained from a Mexican tree of the genus *Bursera*.

Ligneous (li·gnĭəs), *a.* 1626. [f. L. *ligneus* (f. *lignum* wood) + -OUS.] **1.** Of the nature of wood; woody; opp. to *herbaceous*. **2.** (A mod. use, chiefly *joc.*) Wooden. 1812.

1. That fossil, l. substance called peat 1792. 2. *L. marble*, wood treated so as to resemble marble.

Ligni- (li·gni), comb. f. L. *lignum* wood, as in **Ligniferous** (-i·ferəs) *a.*, bearing or producing wood. **Li·gniform** *a.*, of the form or appearance of wood. **Lignipe·rdous** [L. *perdere*] *a.*, wood-destroying. **Ligni·vorous** [L. *-vorus*] *a.*, wood-devouring.

Lignify (li·gnifəi), *v.* 1828. [f. L. *lignum* + -(I)FY.] To make or become ligneous. So **Lignifica·tion** 1808.

Lignin (li·gnin). Also **-ine.** 1822. [f. L. *lignum* + -IN[1].] *Chem.* An organic substance forming the essential part of woody fibre. *Comb.* **l.-dynamite,** wood-sawdust saturated with nitroglycerine, used as an explosive.

Lignite (li·gnəit). 1808. [a. F. *lignite*, f. L. *lignum*; see -ITE[1].] *Min.* A variety of brown coal bearing visible traces of its ligneous structure. **Ligni·tic** *a.* pertaining to, or of the nature of, l. **Ligniti·ferous** *a.* producing l.

Ligno- (li·gno), used as comb. f. L. *lignum* wood, as in **Lignoce·llulose,** lignin combined with cellulose. **Lignoce·ric** *a.*, in *lignoceric acid*, a fatty acid contained in paraffin and in beech-wood tar.

Lignose (li·gno^u^s). 1698. [ad. L. *lignosus*, f. *lignum*; see -OSE.] **A.** *adj.* = LIGNEOUS. **B.** *sb.* **a.** *Chem.* One of the constituents of lignin 1878. **b.** An explosive consisting of wood fibre and nitroglycerine 1884.

Li·gnous, *a. rare* or *Obs.* 1664. [ad. L. *lignosus*, f. *lignum*; see -OUS.] = LIGNEOUS.

‖**Lignum** (li·gnŏm). ME. [L., = 'wood'.] †**1.** *Bot.* Woody tissue 1826. **2. l. aloes** (†occas. *aloe*) = LIGN-ALOES; **l. vitæ** (vəi·tī) = GUAIACUM 1–3.

‖**Ligula** (li·giŭlă). 1760. [L., by-form of *lingula*, dim. of *lingua* tongue.] **a.** *Bot.* A ligule. **b.** *Zool.* A tongue-like structure forming part of the labium in insects, or of the parapodia in annelids. **c.** *Anat.* A band of white matter in the wall of the fourth ventricle of the brain.

Hence **Li·gular** *a.* pertaining to or like a l.

Ligulate (li·giŭlĕt), *a.* 1760. [f. LIGULA + -ATE[2].] **1.** *Bot.* Having the form of a ligula, strap-shaped, as the ray florets in composite flowers; furnished with a ligula, as a leaf. **2.** Of letters in an inscription: Connected by a band 1851.

1. The 5 segments that make up the l. floret of a Composita LINDLEY. So **Li·gulated** *a.* 1753.

Ligule (li·giul). 1862. [ad. L. LIGULA; cf. F. *ligule*.] *Bot.* A thin appendage at the base of the blade of a leaf, esp. in grasses; a ligulate corolla in composites.

Liguli- (li·giŭli), comb. f. LIGULA in botanical terms, as *liguliflorate*, *-florous* (L. *flor-*, *flos*), having ligulate florets.

Ligurian (ləigiū̆·riăn, lig-), *a.* and *sb.* 1601. [f. L. *Liguria* + -AN.] **A.** *adj.* Belonging to the country anciently called *Liguria* in Cisalpine Gaul, including Genoa, parts of Piedmont and Savoy, etc. Sometimes as epithet of a race of mankind of which the Ligurians are the supposed type. 1632. **B.** *sb.* An inhabitant or native of Liguria; a person belonging to the Ligurian race; also, a Ligurian bee.

A. *L. bee*: a kind of honey-bee, *Apis ligustrica*, indigenous in southern Europe.

Ligustrin (ligʊ·strin). 1865. [f. L. *ligustrum* privet + -IN[1].] *Chem.* The bitter principle of privet.

Likable: see LIKEABLE.

Like (ləik), *sb.*[1] ME. [f. LIKE *v.*] †**1.** (One's) good pleasure. (Also *pl.*) –1615. †**2.** A liking (for). Const. *of*. NASHE. **3.** In mod. use pl. *likes* (coupled with *dislikes*): Feelings of liking; predilections 1851.

3. Her odd likes and dislikes BLACK.

Like (ləik), *a.*, *adv.*, (*conj.*), and *sb.*[2] Comp. **liker**; superl. **likest.** [Early ME. *līch*, *līk* (? late OE. *līc*; cf. LIKENESS), shortened f. OE. *gelīc* :—OTeut. **galīko-*, f. pref. *ga-* (= L. *com-*) Y-*prefix* + **līko-* body, form. Cf. L. *conformis* CONFORM *a.* The inflected compar. and superl. are now usually *poet.* or *rhet.*]

A. *adj.* **1.** Having the same characteristics as some other person or thing; similar; resembling; analogous. Const. *to*, *unto* (arch.), now commonly with simple dative. **b.** With following regimen denoting a particular example of a class of which something is predicated 1627. **c.** Without construction: Resembling something already indicated or implied ME. **d.** Of two or more things: Mutually similar; in predicative use = alike (now *rare*) ME. **2.** In phraseological and proverbial expressions (see below). **3.** Of a portrait: Resembling the original. Now only *predicative*. 1561. **4.** *Math.* = *Similar*, exc. in *l. quantities* and *l. signs* (see below) 1557. **5.** *Golf.* (See quot.) 1887. **6.** †**a.** Apt, suitable, befitting. Chiefly predicative. –1592. **b.** Such as one might expect from 1667. **7.** *predicatively*, chiefly with the vbs. *feel*, *look*, *sound* 1654. **8.** In accordance with appearances, probable, likely. Now only *dial.* ME. **9.** *predicatively*, const. *to* with *inf.*: Likely *to*. *arch.* and *dial.* ME. **b.** (Now *colloq.* or *dial.*) Apparently on the point of 1560.

1. Wee also are men of l. passions with you *Acts* xiv. 15. Sweet sleep, were death l. to thee SHELLEY. Phr. *There is none* or *nothing l.* —, = 'so good or so wonderful as'; There is none like her, none TENNYSON. What we have The likest God within the soul TENNYSON. Phr. *What is he* (or *it*) *l.?* = 'What sort of a man is he?', 'What sort of a thing is it?' *To look l.* (occas. *to be l.*), = 'to have the appearance of being'; e.g. 'He looks l. a fool'. *L. that* (perh. = F. *comme cela*): of the nature, character, or habit indicated. **b.** A critic l. (= 'such as') you STEVENSON. **c.** *The l.*: such as have been mentioned. *In l. manner*, see MANNER; *in l. wise*, see LIKEWISE. **d.** Provb. *As l. as two peas*: see PEA *sb.* Things which seem to be l. may be different JEVONS. **2.** *L. case* (advb. phr.): in the same way (now only *dial.*) 1534. *L. master, l. man* (as the master, so the man) 1548. *Anything l.*, *nothing l.*, *something l.*: anything, nothing, something approaching (another thing) in size or quality. *Something l.* (ellipt.) = something l. what he, it (etc.) should be, or what is aimed at (*colloq.*, as an emphatic expression of satisfaction) 1547. (These latter phrases are also used *adverbially*.) **3.** I got your photograph at last: it is a beastly thing: not a bit l. E. FITZGERALD. **4.** *L. Quantities* (in Algebra), such as are expressed by the same Letters, equally repeated in each Quantity. *L. Signs*, are when both are Affirmative, or both Negative. PHILLIPS. **5.** When both parties have played the same number of strokes they are said to be *like* DONALDSON. **6. a.** The likest instruments to put a bad matter in execution 1592. **b.** That would be liker a Drunkard than a Gentleman 1703. **7.** The Forty Colonies..are all pretty like (= giving promise of) rebelling just now CARLYLE. *To feel l.* (orig. U.S.): to be in the humour for (*rec. colloq.*). **9.** My graue is l. to be my wedding bed *Rom. & Jul.* I. v. 137. **b.** After the treaty had been l. to have been broken off STRYPE. Phr. *Had l. to* (for *was l. to*), chiefly with perf. inf.: = 'had come near to, narrowly missed (—ing)'.

Comb., as *l.-minded* (whence *like-mindedness*), etc.

B. *adv.* (quasi-*prep.*, *conj.*). **1.** (Const. as in A. 1.) In or after the manner of; in the same manner or to the same extent as; as in the case of; in the manner characteristic of. *L. that*: in that manner (cf. A. 1 quots.). ME. **2.** = ALIKE; in a like degree; equally. Now *arch.* or *poet.* (qualifying adj. or adv.) ME. **3.** In the manner of one who (or that which) is —. *Obs.* exc. in *l. mad* (see MAD *a.*) 1500. †**4.** In accordance with –1586. **5.** *L. as.* **a.** Introducing a clause: In the same way as, even as; (just) as if. Also, *l. as if.* ME. *arch.* or *dial.* **b.** With ellipsis of the vb. in the clause. *Obs.* exc. *poet.* 1489. **6.** Used as *conj.*: = 'like as', as. Now considered vulgar or slovenly 1530. †**b.** As well as; as also –1663. **c.** †As if, 'like as'. Also (now *dial.*) *as l.* 1493. **7.** *dial.* and *vulgar.* = 'as it were', 'so to speak' 1801. **8.** Likely, probably. Rare exc. in phr. *l. enough*, *very l.*, (*as*) *l. as not* (colloq. or dial.) 1563.

1. Featur'd l. him, l. him with friends possest SHAKS. What was the use of his talking l. that? 1872. Phr. *l. anything*, *l. a shot*, *l. fun*, *blazes*, etc. **2.** L. warlike as the Wolfe *Cymb.* III. iii. 41. **5. a.** I held the letter in my hand l. as if I was stupid COLERIDGE. **6.** To act l. Judith did with Holofernes 1715. There is more of morning visiting, like in country life in England W. IRVING. **b.** *Rich. III*, III. v. 9. **8.** Most l. I did SHAKS.

C. *absol.* and *sb.* **1.** With qualifying poss. pron., etc.: Counterpart, equal, match, analogue. Occas. in *pl.* (*his*, etc.) *likes*. ME. **2.** An instance of similarity ME. **3.** *The l.*: the same kind of thing. (Now chiefly in neg. contexts.) 1553. †**b.** = *that* or *those* (followed by *of*). *rare.* –1654. **4.** *Golf.* (See quot.) 1863.

1. His lyke is not in al y^e^ world LD. BERNERS. **2.** Phr. *L.* (*will*) *to l.*, *l. draws to l.*, *l. begets l.*, etc.; *l. for l.*; *l. cures l.* **3.** Phr. *I never saw the l.* *And the l.*, *or the l.*: = 'and so forth'. See also SUCH-LIKE. *The like*(*s of* (rarely *to*): such a person or thing as; now often depreciatory (*colloq.*). **b.** His death was accompanied by the l. of Orange EARL MONM. **4.** If your opponent has played one stroke more than you—i.e. 'the odd', your next stroke will be 'the like' FORGAN.

Like (ləik), *v.*[1] [OE. *līcian* :—OTeut. **līkǣjan*, **līkōjan*, f. **līko-* body (orig. appearance, form): see LICH.] **1.** *intr.* To please, suit a person. Chiefly quasi-*trans.* with *dat.* Also *impers.*, as in *it likes me*. Now only *arch.* and *dial.* †**b.** *simply.* To be pleasing –1616. †**2.** *refl.* and *intr.* To please oneself, delight *in* (something) –1549. **3.** *intr.* To be pleased or glad ME. †**4.** To get on, do well, thrive. Chiefly with *well*, *better*, etc. –1681. **5.** To derive pleasure *of*, occas. *by*, *with* (a person or thing); to approve *of*, become fond *of*. Also with *well* or *ill*. *Obs.* exc. *dial.* ME. **6.** *trans.* (The current sense.) To find agreeable or congenial; to feel attracted to (a person); to have a taste or fancy for, take pleasure in (a thing, etc.). In early use *to l. well* (now *arch.*, though we say *to l. very well*), and *to l. ill* = to dislike. (Often contrasted with *love*, as expressing a weaker sentiment.) ME. Also *absol.* **b.** With inf. as obj.: To find it agreeable, feel inclined *to do* or *be* so and so ME. **c.** Often = *like to have* 1822. **d.** The neutral sense inferable from *to l. well* or *ill* (see below) survives in the interrog. use with *how*, as in 'How do you l. my new gown?', etc. 1596.

1. I rode sullenly Upon a certain path that liked me not ROSSETTI. **b.** If his Play doe not l., the Diuell is in't B. JONS. Phr. *To l. well* or *ill*. to be pleasing or the reverse; Where it liked her best she sought Her shelter WORDSW. **3.** Phr. *To l. ill*: to be displeased or sad (now only *Sc.*). **6.** I never lik'd thy talk MILT. *absol.* Looking [he] liked, and liking loved SCOTT. **b.** If you would l. to go, We'll visit him SHELLEY. Phr. *I should l.* (= F. *je voudrais bien*, G. *ich möchte gern*), often in conditional use, to express a desire; often derisively in *I should l. to see* (something not possible), *I should l. to know* (something unknowable). *To do as one likes* (ellipt.). **c.** Would you l. the armchair? (*mod.*). **d.** How l. you this old satire? TENNYSON.

Like, *v.*[2] ME. [f. LIKE *a.*] †**1.** *trans.* To fashion in a certain likeness; to compare *to*; to make a likeness of –1622. **2.** *intr.* (Const. *inf.*) †To seem, pretend; to look like or be near *to* doing (something) or *to* being treated (in a specified manner). Now *vulgar* and *dial.* ME.

1. If to gold I l. her Haire WITHER. **2.** Wee had likt to haue had our two noses snapt off with two old men without teeth *Much Ado* v. i. 115.

-like, *suffix*, forming adjs. and advs. These compounds of LIKE *a.* and *adv.* are entirely distinct from the derivs. formed with *-lik(e*, ME. dial. form of -LY[1], -LY[2]. Cf. ME. *gredilike* adv. (= greedily), and mod. Sc. *greedy-like*.

1. Appended to sbs. **a.** Forming adjs. with sense 'similar to —', 'befitting —'. Examples are *godlike, ladylike, clockworklike.* The hyphen is used in formations not generally current. late ME. **b.** Forming advs. with sense 'in or after the manner of —', 'so as to resemble —'. Examples are *gentlemanlike, bishoplike, Brutus-like*, etc. These advs. are now perh. archaistic or obs., recent examples being explicable as quasi-advb. uses of the adj. In this use *-like* is nearly always hyphened. 1530. **2.** Appended to adjs. **a.** Forming adjs. Common in Sc., but not in Eng.; the sense is usually 'resembling one that is —', as in *genteel-like.* 1470. **b.** Forming advs. with the sense 'like one that is —'. *Obs.* exc. in *Sc.* 1470.

Likeable, likable (ləi·kăb'l), *a.* 1730. [f. LIKE *v.*[1] + -ABLE.] Worthy of being liked; pleasing; agreeable; as, *l. people.* Hence **Likeabi·lity, Li·keableness,** l. quality.

†Li·kehood. [f. LIKE *a.* + -HOOD.] Likelihood, probability. G. HARVEY.

Li·kelihead. *arch.* ME. [f. LIKELY *a.* + -HEAD.] **1.** = next, 2. Chiefly in phr. *by* or *of l.* **2.** = next, 1. ME.

Likelihood (ləi·klihud). ME. [f. LIKELY *a.* + -HOOD.] **†1.** Likeness; resemblance. Also an instance of this. -1688. **2.** Probability; an instance of this 1449. **†3.** Something that is likely, a probability; hence, an indication, sign. Freq. in *pl.* -1656. **4.** Promise of success. Now only as an echo of Shaks. 1596.

1. There is no l. between pure light and black darkness RALEIGH. 2. There was a l. of rain JOHNSON. *The l.*: the probable fact, or probable amount. Now *rare* exc. *Sc.* 3. *Two Gent.* v. ii. 43. 4. A fellow of no marke, nor likelyhood SHAKS.

So **Li·keliness,** in all senses, in all senses. ME.

Likely (ləi·kli), *a.* and *adv.* ME. [a. ON. *líklig-r*, f. *lík-r* LIKE *a.* + *-lig-r* -LY[1]. (OE. had *gelîclic.*)]

A. *adj.* **†1.** Like, similar (*till, to*). Also, resembling the original. -1661. **2.** Having an appearance of truth or fact; seeming as if it would happen, or prove to be as stated; probable ME. **3.** Apparently suitable or qualified (*for* a purpose or an action); apparently able or fitted (*to do* or *to be* something) ME. **4.** (Now chiefly *U.S.*) **a.** Strong or capable looking. **b.** Giving promise of success or excellence; hopeful 1454. **5.** [? Infl. by LIKE *v.*[1]] Comely, handsome. ? Now *U.S.* and *dial.* 1470. **†6.** Seemly, appropriate -1742. **†7.** *Was l.*, also catachr. *had l.*: came near *to do* or *be* (etc.); = *was* or *had like* -1652.

2. No likelier cause can be alleg'd MILT. 'Tis very l. you will never receive this 1710. Phr. *He is l. to* (with inf.) = 'it is likely that he will'. 3. We are not yet come to a l. place WALTON. The likeliest place.. to meet with us 1748. 4. Tall, well-set, l. Fellows 1686. *Comb.*, as *l.-looking* adj.

B. *adv.* **†1. a.** Similarly. **b.** With close resemblance (in portraiture). -1600. **2.** Probably. (Now chiefly *most l., very l.*) ME. **†3.** In a fit manner, suitably, reasonably -1674.

2. You may be very l. right in that JOWETT.

Liken (ləi·k'n), *v.* ME. [f. LIKE *a.* + -EN[5].] **1.** *trans.* To represent as like; to compare (*to, unto, with*). Also, *to l. together.* **2.** To make like (*rare*) ME. **†3.** *intr.* To be, or become, like. Also *trans.* to symbolize, represent. -1838.

1. I likened him often..to sheet-lightning CARLYLE.

Likeness (ləi·knės). [OE. (Northumb.) *lícnes*, shortened f. *gelícness.*] **1.** Resemblance, similarity; an instance of this. Const. *to*; †formerly *of* (or gen. of pron.), *with.* **2.** That which resembles an object; a semblance. Hence *gen.* form, shape, esp. in phr. *in l. of.* †In OE. = figure, stature. OE. **3.** A copy, counterpart, image, portrait. Of persons: One who closely resembles another. OE. **†4.** A comparison; hence, a parable -ME.

1. It was a l. to her little boy that had affected me so pleasantly 1866. 2. An Enemy in the l. of a Friend 1692. 3. Here, take my L. with you, whilst 'tis so COWLEY. Phr. *To take a person's l.*: to make a portrait of him. 4. He seide to hem also a liknesse [Vulg. *similitudinem*] WYCLIF *Luke* v. 36.

Likerish, -ous: see LICKERISH, etc.

Likewalk: see LYKE-WAKE.

Likewise (ləi·kwəiz), *adv.* 1449. [abbrev. from *in like wise*; see LIKE *a.* and WISE *sb.*] **†1.** *In like wise*: in the same manner -1673. **2.** Similarly; = 1. *Obs.* exc. *arch.* in *to do l.* (after *Luke* x. 37). 1460. **3.** Also, as well, moreover, too 1509.

2. Looke on mee, and doe l. *Judg.* vii. 17. So **†Li·keways.**

‖Likin (lī·kīn). Also **lekin.** 1876. [Chin. *li-kin*, f. *li* LI[2] + *kin* money.] A Chinese provincial transit duty.

Liking (ləi·kiŋ), *vbl. sb.* [OE. *lícung*, f. *lícian*; see LIKE *v.*[1] and -ING[1].] **†1.** The fact of being to one's taste, or of being liked -1579. **†2.** Pleasure, enjoyment; an instance of this -1548. **3.** The bent of the will; (a person's) pleasure. Also *pl.* Now *rare.* ME. **4.** The condition of being fond of or not averse to (a person or thing); fancy for or inclination to (some object) ME. **†b.** Approval, consent 1607. **c.** *On* or *upon l.*: on approval or trial. Now *rare* in educated use. 1615. **†5.** An object liked; (one's) beloved -1667. **†6.** (Good or healthy) bodily condition -1774.

3. I leaue thee to thine own l. GREENE. Phr. *to* (rarely *after, in*) *one's l.*: to one's taste; A Gentleman, who would willingly marry, if he could find a Wife to his L. STEELE. 4. Friendships begin with l. GEO. ELIOT. c. After spending a few months on l., I was unanimously chosen 1834. 6. A bay Mare.., in good L. 1705.

†Liking, *ppl. a.* ME. [f. LIKE *v.*[1] + -ING[2].] **1.** Pleasant, agreeable, attractive; favourable. Const. *till, to.* -1610. **2.** 'In condition'; healthy, plump; (of a soil) rich -1656.

1. The wynd to hym was likyng HALL. 2. Normandie is enriched with a fat and l. soil HEYLIN. Hence **†Li·kingly** *adv.* in a pleasing manner; to one's liking.

Lilac (ləi·lăk). Also **laylock** (now chiefly *dial.* or *U.S.*). 1625. [a. F. *lilac* (Cotgr.; now *lilas*), app. (ult.) ad. Pers. *līlak*, var. of *nīlak* bluish, f. Pers. *nīl* blue, indigo (Skr. *nīla*, Hindī *līl*).] **1.** A shrub, *Syringa vulgaris*, with pale pinkish violet, or white, blossoms. Also, the flower of this shrub. Also *transf.* of other species of *Syringa* or plants of other genera. **2.** The colour of lilac blossom 1791. **b.** *attrib.* or *adj.* Of this colour 1801.

2. She brought us Academic silks, in hue The l. TENNYSON. b. L. ribbons 1801. *Comb.* **l.-moth,** a little chocolate-coloured moth (*Lazotænia ribeana*). Hence **Lilaceous** (ləilēⁱ·ʃəs) *a.*

Lilacin (ləi·lăsin). Also **-ine.** 1842. [f. LILAC + -IN[1].] *Chem.* = SYRINGIN.

Liliaceous (liliēⁱ·ʃəs), *a.* 1730. [f. L. *liliaceus*, f. *lilium*; see -ACEOUS.] Pertaining to or characteristic of the order *Liliaceæ*; lily-like.

Lilial (li·liăl). *Bot.* 1846. [ad. mod.L. *lilialis*, f. *lilium* LILY.] *adj.* Only in *L. alliance*: In Lindley's classification, the alliance which includes the *Liliaceæ.* *sb.* A member of this alliance.

Lilied (li·lid), *a.* 1614. [f. LILY + -ED[2].] **1.** Resembling a lily in hue. **2.** Covered with, or having many, lilies 1633; embellished with the heraldic lilies or fleur-de-lis 1795.

2. Dance no more By sandy Ladons Lillied banks MILT. The l. banner of France 1884.

†Lill, *v.* 1530. [Onomatopœic; cf. LOLL *v.*] *trans.* To loll or hang (the tongue) *out* (rarely *forth*); rarely *intr.* of the tongue. -1656.

Lillibullero (lilibŭlīə·ro). 1688. [Unmeaning.] Part of refrain (hence, name and tune) of a song ridiculing the Irish, popular about 1688. Hence **Lillibulle·ro** *v.* to sing l. over. STERNE.

Lilliput (li·lipɒt). An imaginary country in *Gulliver's Travels* (1726), peopled by pygmies six inches high. *attrib.* = diminutive 1867.

Lilliputian (lilipiū·ʃiăn). 1726. **A.** *sb.* An inhabitant of LILLIPUT; hence, a person of diminutive size, character, or mind.

Oh, Gemini! would I had been born a L.! FIELDING.

B. *adj.* Of or pertaining to Lilliput or its inhabitants; hence, diminutive; petty 1726.

The L. Statesmen rise To malice of gigantic size LLOYD.

Lilly-pilly. 1860. An Australian timber-tree, *Eugenia Smithii* (N.O. *Myrtaceæ*).

Lilt (lilt), *sb.* 1728. [f. LILT *v.*] **1.** A song or tune, *esp.* a cheerful one. Chiefly *Sc.* **2.** The swing of a tune or of verse. Chiefly *literary.* 1840. **3.** A springing action 1869.

1. Is't some words ye've learnt by rote, Or a l. o' dool and sorrow? *Jacobite Relics.* 2. The lines go with a l., and sing themselves to music of their own STEVENSON.

Lilt (lilt), *v.* *Sc.*, *n. dial.*, and *literary.* [ME. *lulte* (*ü*); perh. cogn. w. Du., LG. *lul*, pipe.] **†1.** *trans.* To sound (an alarum); to lift up (the voice) -1513. **2.** *trans.* and *intr.* To sing cheerfully or merrily; to sing with a lilt 1786. **3.** *n. dial.* 'To move with a lively action' 1834.

1. L. up your pipes RAMSAY. 2. Lilting a tune to supply the lack of conversation EMILY BRONTË. 3. Whether the bird flit here or there, O'er table *lilt*, or perch on chair WORDSW.

Lily (li·li). [OE. *lilie* wk. fem., ad. L. *lilium*, a. Gr. λείριον.] **1.** Any plant (or its flower) of the genus *Lilium* (N.O. *Liliaceæ*) of bulbous plants bearing large showy white, reddish, or purplish flowers (often spotted inside) at the top of a tall slender stem; *esp.* the White or Madonna Lily (*L. candidum*). **b.** With qualification, applied to other plants of the genus *Lilium* or N.O. *Liliaceæ*, and to certain allied plants 1555. **c.** Used in all versions of the Bible to render Heb. *shūshan, shōshan, shōshannāh*, LXX and NT. κρίνον. **2. L. of** (or **†in**) **the valley** or *vale* (now *poet.*), †*May l.*, *Convallaria majalis*, a spring-flowering plant having two largish leaves and racemes of white bell-shaped fragrant flowers 1538. **3.** *fig.* Applied to persons or things of exceptional whiteness, fairness, or purity; e.g. the white of a beautiful complexion (*sing.* and *pl.*; cf. *rose*) ME. **4.** A representation of the flower 1459; the heraldic fleur-de-lis, as in the arms of the old French monarchy; hence, the royal arms of France, the French (Bourbon) dynasty ME.; †the fleur-de-lis which marks the north on a compass -1661.

1. The wand-like l., which lifted up..its moonlight-coloured cup SHELLEY. b. *Flax, orange, panther, Persian, tiger, Turk's-cap l.* etc. (see the first element); also, belonging to N.O. *Amaryllidaceæ, belladonna, calla, Guernsey, Jacobean, lent, pond, sword l.*, etc. (see the first element). **African l.,** *Agapanthus umbellatus.* **Atamasco l.,** *Zephyranthes Atamasco.* **Yellow l.,** the daffodil (*dial.*). 2. That shy plant..the l. of the vale, That loves the ground WORDSW. 3. A Virgin, A most vnspotted Lilly *Hen. VIII*, v. v. 62. 4. Item, one box of silver ..chased with liliis 1464. Great Edward, with the lilies on his brow From haughty Gallia torn GRAY.

attrib. and *Comb.* **1.** General: as *l.-bank, -crown, -root*, etc.; *l.-clear, -whitening* adjs.; *l.-like* adj. and adv.; *l.-cradled, -crowned* adjs.

2. Special: as **l.-beetle,** the beetle *Crioceris merdigera*, which infests lilies; **-encrinite,** an encrinite resembling a l. in shape; **-iron,** a harpoon with a detachable head used in killing sword-fish; **-pad** *U.S.*, the broad floating leaf of the water-lily; **-star,** (*a*) = *feather-star*, a crinoid of the family *Comatulidæ*; (*b*) the star-like flower of the water-lily.

b. In plant-names (little used): **l. asphodel, daffodil,** names for the genus *Amaryllis*; **-bind, -bine** *dial.*, bindweed; **l. hyacinth,** **‑jacinth,** the genus *Scilla*, esp. *S. Liliohyacinthus*; **l. pink,** the genus *Aphyllanthes*; **l. thorn,** the genus *Catesbæa*; **-worts,** Lindley's name for the N.O. *Liliaceæ.*

B. as *adj.* **a.** White or fair as a lily; lily-white; lily-like 15.. **b.** Pale, colourless, bloodless 1590.

a. Elaine, the l. maid of Astolat TENNYSON. A l.-fingered idler 1873. b. These Lilly Lips SHAKS. Thou Lilly-liuer'd Boy *Macb.* v. iii. 15.

Li·ly-flower. ME. The flower of the (white) lily; *occas.* the heraldic fleur-de-lis.

Li·ly-pot. 1540. **1.** A flower-pot with a lily growing in it; frequent as a symbolic accessory in pictures of the Annunciation. **2.** An ornamental vase imitating this; †*spec.* a tobacco-jar 1610.

Lily-white, *a.* (Stress variable.) ME. White as a lily. Hence **Lily-whiteness.**

Lim, obs. f. LIMB *sb.*[1], LIME *sb.*[1]

Lima (lī·mă), name of the capital of Peru, used *attrib.* in: **L. bark,** the bark of some species of *Cinchona*; a kind of Peruvian bark; **L. bean,** *Phaseolus lunatus*; also, *P. perennis*; **L.-wood,** a kind of Brazil-wood.

†Limace. *rare.* 1491. [a. F., or ad. L. *limacem, limax* slug, snail.] A shell-snail -1592.

Limaceous (ləimēⁱ·ʃəs), *a.* 1656. [f. L. *limac-, limax* + -EOUS (cf. -ACEOUS).] Pertaining to slugs or snails; snail-like; now, pertaining to the genus *Limax* of slugs. So **Lima·ciform** *a.* having the form of a slug.

‖**Limaçon** (lĭmasoṅ). 1581. [Fr., = snail-shell, spiral staircase, etc., f. *limace* (see LIMACE).] †1. A kind of military manœuvre. [So in OFr.] –1591. 2. *Math.* Pascal's name for a certain curve of the fourth degree. 3. A metallic gimp 1893.

Limail, lemel (lī·mĕl) ME. [a. F. *limaille*, f. *limer*:—L. *limare* to file.] Metal filings.

An Ounce..Of siluer lemaille CHAUCER.

‖**Liman** (lĭmā·n). 1858. [Russian; = 'estuary'.] A shallow narrow marsh at the mouth of a river, where salt is made.

Limation (ləimē·ʃən). Now *rare.* 1612. [ad. late L. *limationem*, f. *limare*, f. *lima* file.] Filing; *fig.* 'polishing up'. †b. *Astron.* Correction of errors in calculation or observation. FLAMSTEED.

Limb (lim), *sb.*[1] [OE. *lim* str. neut.:—OTeut. type **limo-*; according to Kluge from a root **lĭ-* in OTeut. **lipu-* LITH *sb.*] 1. Any organ or part of the body. *Obs.* exc. *dial.* 2. A part of an animal body distinct from the head or the trunk, e.g. a leg, arm, wing OE. Also *fig.* b. = LEG. Now only (esp. U.S.) in prudish use. ME. 3. In uses originally *fig.* (cf. MEMBER). See below. OE. 4. Transf. senses. a. A main branch of a tree OE. b. A projecting section of a building; one of the four branches of a cross; a member or clause of a sentence, or the like; a spur of a mountain range; one of the pieces forming the lock of a gun 1577. †c. [tr. med.L. *membrum*.] An estate, etc. dependent on another –1647.

1. Þe lyme of syȝte [L. *organum visus*] ME. 2. Their weake limmes and failing ioyntes 1581. Phr. *Life and l.*, *l. and carcase*, *l. and wind*, i.e. all the bodily faculties employed in certain connexions. *To tear* or *pull (one) l. from l.* b. The poor brute [a horse]..fell..fracturing his l. *Pittsburg Chron.* 3. a. A member (e.g. of the church, of Christ, etc.); a branch or section; a component part. *Obs.* exc. in nonce-uses. OE. An army is but the l. of a nation KINGLAKE. b. *L. of the devil*, *of Satan*, *of hell*: an agent or scion of the evil one; hence, a mischievous wicked person (now *dial.*) OE. c. Hence, *limb* alone = a mischievous young rascal (*colloq.*) 1625. d. *L. of the law*: a lawyer, a police officer, or other legal functionary (*derisive*). †e. Applied to things, as *a lim of Idolatry* –1661. 4. A slender crosslet..The shaft and limbs were rods of yew SCOTT. In another l. of the same sentence KINGLAKE.

Limb (lim), *sb.*[2] 1450. [ad. L. *limbus* hem, border, edge, etc., or F. *limbe*. Cf. LIMBUS, LIMBO.] †1. *Sc.* = LIMBO 1. –1797. †2. An edging. DIGBY. 3. In scientific use: The edge or boundary of a surface; the graduated edge of a quadrant or the like 1593; the edge of the disk of the sun, moon, etc. 1677. b. *Bot.* The lamina of a monopetalous corolla, of a petal or sepal. Also, the blade of a leaf. 1735.

3. The sun's lower l. was just free of the hill T. HARDY.

Limb (lim), *v.* 1623. [f. LIMB *sb.*[1]] 1. *trans.* To pull limb from limb, dismember. Also with *up.* 1674. †2. *refl.* To provide oneself with limbs MILT.

Limbate (li·mbeᶦt), *a.* 1826. [ad. late L. *limbatus*, f. *limbus* LIMB *sb.*[2]] *Biol.* Of a part or organ: Having a limb or border; bordered; *Bot.* said of a flower having an edging of a different colour from the rest. Hence **Limba·tion**, the formation of a border; a border distinguished by colour or structure 1881.

Limbeck (li·mbek), *sb. arch.* ME. [aphet. f. ALEMBIC.] = ALEMBIC. Also *fig.*

†**Li·mbeck**, *v.* 1598. [f. the sb.] 1. *trans.* To treat as in an alembic; to distil. Chiefly *fig.*; esp. to rack (the brain) in the effort to extract ideas. –1661. 2. To distil or extract (an essence, etc.) as by an alembic –1657.

1. Wasting my wits, and Limbeking my braines MABBE.

Limbed (limd), *a.* ME. [f. LIMB *sb.*[1] + -ED[2].] Having limbs. Usu. in comb., as *well-*, *straight-l.*, etc.

Perfet formes, Limb'd and full grown MILT.

Limber (li·mbəɹ), *sb.*[1] 1480. [Earlier *lymor(e*, perh. corruption of a form *lymnar* in Gavin Douglas, ? ad. F. *limonière* the shafts and connected framework of a vehicle.] 1. The shaft of a cart or carriage. *Obs.* exc. *dial.* 2. *Mil.* (In early use *pl.*) The detachable fore part of a gun-carriage, consisting of two wheels and an axle, a pole for the horses, and a frame which holds one or two ammunition-chests 1497.

Comb.: l.-**box**, -**chest** *Mil.*, the ammunition box carried by a l.; -**hook**, the iron hook at the back of the l. to which the trail of the gun-carriage is attached; -**horse** *dial.*, the horse that is placed between the shafts; -**saddle**, a cart-saddle.

Limber (li·mbəɹ), *sb.*[2] 1626. [? a corruption of F. *lumière* hole, perforation (lit. 'light').] *Naut. pl.* Holes cut through the floor-timbers on each side of the keelson to form a passage for water to the pump-well.

Comb.: l.-**board**, one of the short removable boards in a ship's floor above the limbers; -**chain**, a chain used like a limber-rope; -**passage**, the passage or channel formed by the limber-strakes on each side of the keelson; -**rope**, a rope passing through the limber-holes, by which they may be cleared of dirt; -**strake** (or -**streak**), the first course of inside planking next the keelson; -**tar**, the bilge-water or refuse found in the hold of a ship that imports tar.

Limber (li·mbəɹ), *a.* 1565. [? a compound of LIMB *sb.*[1] Skeat suggests connexion with LIMP *a.*] 1. Easily bent; flexible, pliant, supple. b. Of persons, etc.: Lithe and nimble 1582. †c. Limp, flaccid, flabby –1747. 2. *fig.* 1602.

1. The Bargeman that doth rowe with long and l. Oare TURBERV. b. A little child, a l. elf COLERIDGE. c. A rabbit, if stale, will be l. and slimy; if new, white and stiff MRS. GLASSE. 2. Men of l. and pliable Consciences 1695. Hence **Li·mberness.**

Limber (li·mbəɹ), *v.*[1] 1748. [f. prec.] *trans.* To make limber, pliant, or supple.

Limber (li·mbəɹ), *v.*[2] 1843. [f. LIMBER *sb.*[1]] *Mil.* To attach the limber to (a gun); *absol.* to fasten together the two parts of a gun-carriage, in order to move away: usu. *to l. up.*

†**Li·mberha·m.** 1675. [f. LIMBER *a.* + HAM *sb.*[1]] a. One who has limber hams; *fig.* an obsequious person, lackey. b. A character like Dryden's '*Limberham*, a tame, foolish keeper' –1766.

Limbless (li·mlės), *a.* 1594. [f. LIMB *sb.*[1] + -LESS.] Having no limbs.

Limb-meal (li·m,mīl), *adv. Obs.* exc. *arch.* and *dial.* [OE. *limmǣlum*; see LIMB *sb.*[1] and -MEAL.] Limb from limb, limb by limb; piecemeal.

O that I had her heere, to teare her Limb-meale SHAKS.

Limbo (li·mbo͞u). ME. [L., abl. sing. of *limbus* (see LIMBUS). Cf. It. *limbo* and LIMB *sb.*[2]] 1. A region on the border of Hell, the abode of the just who died before Christ's coming, and of unbaptized infants. (More explicitly *limbo patrum*, *limbo infantum*; see LIMBUS.) Hence *gen.* †b. Hell, Hades –1637. 2. *transf.* and *fig.* a. Prison, durance 1590. b. Any unfavourable place or condition, likened to Limbo 1642.

1. 'Tis a just Idea of a L. of the Infants CLEVELAND. *gen.* A L. large and broad, since calld The Paradise of Fools MILT. 2. a. I haue some of 'em in *Limbo Patrum* SHAKS. b. L. of Lost Reputations MOORE (*title*). *Comb.* †l.-**lake**, the pit of Hell.

‖**Limbus** (li·mbŏs). 1440. [L., = edge, border; in med.L., a region on the border of Hell.] 1. Occas. = LIMBO 1. *L. patrum* = 'the limbo of the fathers', i.e. of the just who died before Christ's coming. *L. infantum* = 'the limbo of infants'. 2. Used *techn.* in lit. sense of 'border' or 'edge'; e.g. in *Bot.* = LIMB *sb.*[2] 3 b 1671.

2. Round the crater is the l., which is a decorated border of floral or other ornaments BIRCH.

Lime (ləim), *sb.*[1] [OE. *līm* str. masc.:—OTeut. **līmo-* = L. *līmus* mud, f. root *lī-* in L. *linere* to smear.] 1. = BIRD-LIME. Now only *poet.* (In OE. any adhesive substance.) 2. Usually coupled with *stone*: Mortar or cement used in building. Now *Sc.* OE. 3. The alkaline earth which is the chief constituent of mortar; calcium oxide (CaO). It is obtained by calcining limestone (carbonate of lime), the heat driving off the carbonic acid, and leaving a brittle white solid, which is pure lime (or QUICKLIME). It is powerfully caustic, and combines readily with water, evolving great heat in the process, and forming hydrate of lime (*slaked lime*). †4. a. The CALX of metals. b. Any alkaline earth. –1796.

1. Toils for Beasts, and L. for Birds were found DRYDEN. You must lay l. to tangle her desires By walefull Sonnets *Two Gent.* III. ii. 68. 3. You Rogue, heere 's L. in this Sacke too SHAKS. *L. and hair*: a kind of plasterer's cement which added hair binds closely together.

Comb.: l.-**ash** *dial.*, a composition of ashes and l. used as a rough kind of flooring for kitchens, etc.; -**ball** (*light*), limelight; also *attrib.*; -**rock**, limestone (? now *U.S.*); -**wash**, *sb.* a mixture of l. and water, used for coating walls, etc.; *vb.* to whitewash with this; -**work**, a place where l. is made (also *pl.*).

b. In names of minerals, denoting the presence of l. or calcium, e.g. *l.-marl*, *-slate*; l.-**feldspar**, triclinic feldspar containing calcium.

Lime (ləim), *sb.*[2] 1622. [a. F. *lime*, ad. Sp. *lima*, a. Arab. *līmaʰ*; see LEMON *sb.*[1]] The globular fruit of the tree *Citrus Medica*, var. *acida*, smaller and more acid than the lemon; *sour lime*. Its juice is much used as a drink. **Sweet L.**, *Citrus Medica*, var. *Limetta*.

Comb.: l.-**juice**, the juice of the l., used as a drink and as an antiscorbutic; -**punch**, punch made with lime-juice instead of lemon-juice; so -**squash**.

Lime (ləim), *sb.*[3] 1625. [app. altered f. *line* LIND.] 1. A tree of the genus *Tilia*, esp. *T. europæa*, an ornamental tree having heart-shaped leaves and small fragrant yellowish flowers. 2. The seed of the lime-tree. MRS. GLASSE.

Lime (ləim), *v.*[1] OE. [f. LIME *sb.*[1]] 1. *trans.* To cement. Chiefly *fig.* 2. To smear (twigs, etc.) with bird-lime, for catching birds ME. b. To smear with a sticky substance (*rare*) ME. 3. To catch with bird-lime. Often *fig.* ME. †4. To defile –1592. 5. To treat or dress with lime 1598. †b. To coat with lime-wash –1615.

1. I will not ruinate my Father's House, Who gaue his blood to lyme the stones together SHAKS. 2. My selfe haue lym'd a Bush for her SHAKS. 3. He was ..limed this time [matrimonially] 1870. 5. *Merry W.* I. iii. 15. Then l. and sow with oats 1799. b. Houses newly limed 1615.

†**Lime**, *v.*[2] 1555. [Origin unkn. Cf. LINE *v.*[3]] *trans.* To impregnate (a bitch). Also *pass.* and *intr.* to copulate *with*, be coupled *to*. –1682.

Lime (-hound): see LYAM (-HOUND).

Li·me-burner. ME. [LIME *sb.*[1]] One who makes lime by burning limestone.

Lime-kiln (ləi·mkiln, -kil). ME. A kiln in which lime is made by calcining limestone. Also *transf.* and *fig.*

Limelight (ləi·mləit). 1826. [f. LIME *sb.*[1]] The intense white light produced by heating a piece of lime in an oxyhydrogen flame. Called also DRUMMOND LIGHT.

Phr. *In the l.* (orig. Theatr.): in a very conspicuous position. Hence **Li·melight** *v.*, to illuminate by l.

‖**Limen** (ləi·men). 1895. [L., = 'threshold'; introduced as equiv. of G. *schwelle* (Herbart *Psychol.* 1824). Cf. SUBLIMINAL.] *Psychol.* The limit below which a given stimulus ceases to be perceptible; the minimum amount of nerve-excitation required to produce a sensation. Also called THRESHOLD.

Li·me-pit. 1440. [f. LIME *sb.*[1]] 1. a. A limestone quarry. b. A pit in which lime is burnt. 2. A pit in which tanners dress skins with lime 1591.

Li·mer[1]. *arch.* ME. [a. AF. *limer* = OF. *liemier* (mod.F. *limier*), f. OF. *liem* (F. *lien*) leash; see LIEN and LYAM.] A kind of hound; *prop.* a leash-hound; in early use (now *arch.*) a bloodhound; later, a mongrel.

Limer[2] (ləi·məɹ). 1611. [f. LIME *v.*[1] + -ER[1].] One who limes; one who snares with bird-lime; one who limewashes. Also, a brush for limewashing.

Limerick (li·mərik). 1898. [Said to be from a chorus 'Will you come up to Limerick?', following an extemporized 'nonsense-verse' sung by each member of a convivial party.] A form of nonsense-verse; erron. applied to that written by Lear.

†**Lime-rod.** ME. [f. LIME *sb.*[1]] = LIME-TWIG –1626.

Limestone (ləi·mstōᵘn). 1523. [f. LIME *sb.*[1] + STONE.] A rock which consists chiefly of carbonate of lime, and yields lime when burnt. (The crystalline variety is marble.)

Li·me-twig, *sb.* ME. [f. LIME *sb.*[1]] 1. A twig smeared with bird-lime for catching birds. †2. *attrib.* or *adj.* Ensnaring; pilfering

-1730. Hence †**Li·me-twig** *v. trans.* to catch as with a lime-twig; to entangle, ensnare.

Li·me-water. 1677. [f. LIME *sb.*[1]] A solution of lime in water, used medicinally and to clarify water.

Limicoline (ləimi·kǒləin, -in), *a.* 1872. [f. L. *limicola* (f. *limus* mud + *colere* to inhabit) + -INE [2].] Of or pertaining to the *Limicolæ*, a family of shore or wading birds.

Liminal (li·minăl), *a.* 1884. [f. L. *limin-*, *limen* LIMEN + -AL.] Of or pertaining to a limen, or (*gen.*) to the initial stage.

Limit (li·mit), *sb.* ME. [ad. F. *limite*, ad. L. *limitem*, *limes* boundary.] 1. A boundary, frontier; a landmark. Now only: A bounding line or terminal point; chiefly *pl.* bounds. 2. One of the fixed points or values between which the possible or permissible range of anything is confined; a bound beyond which something ceases to be possible or allowable ME. b. *Math.* (*a*) A finite quantity to which the sum of a converging series progressively approximates, but to which it cannot become equal in a finite number of terms; a fixed value to which a function similarly approximates. (*b*) Each of the two values of a variable between which a definite integral is taken. (*c*) The ultimate position of the point of intersection of two lines, which, by their relative motion, are tending to coalescence. 1753. c. Astron. *L. of a planet*: its greatest heliocentric latitude 1704. d. *gen.* Limitation, restriction within limits. Chiefly in phr. *without l.* 1599. ¶e. Prescribed time; period of repose after child-bearing. SHAKS. f. A thing (or person) having some (usu. objectionable) quality or attribute in the highest possible or tolerable degree (*colloq.*, orig. *U.S.*) 1906. †3. The tract or region defined by a boundary; *pl.* the bounds, territories -1792. †4. *Logic.* = TERM (med.L. *terminus*) BLUNDEVILLE.

1. Hence is the Water enforced to enlarge his limits 1625. A point may be the l. of a line BERKELEY. 2. Finding thy worth a limmit past my praise SHAKS. Nature has set limits to the pleasures of sense REID. e. *Rich. II*, I. iii. 151. *Wint. T.* III. ii. 107. f. Well, that's the limit! (*mod.*) 3. At length into the limits of the North They came MILT. *P. L.* v. 755.

Limit (li·mit), *v.* ME. [ad. F. *limiter*, ad. L. *limitare*, f. *limit-*, *limes* LIMIT.] 1. *trans.* To assign within limits; to appoint, fix definitely; to specify. Also with *away*, *over*. Const. *dat.*, or *to*, (*till*), *upon*, and *to* with *inf.* *Obs.* exc. in legal language. †b. To appoint (a person) to an office; to assign (a duty) to a person -1638. †c. To lot or plot *out*; to allot -1649. 2. To confine within limits (*rarely* in material sense); to bound, restrict. Const. *to*. b. To serve as a limit or boundary to; to mark off *from*. Also *to l. in*. Now *rare*. 1582. †3. *intr.* To beg within specified limits. [f. LIMITER (sense 1).] NORTHBROOKE.

1. At the daye before lymytted and assygned 1494. A power..to l. other uses CRUISE. 2. He thought a government limited by law was only a name BURNET. The commerce..was still mainly limited to the exportation of wool to Flanders GREEN. b. This rule thus fixed no tyme shall l., or hazard 1582. 3. They [Popishe friers] go ydelly a limiting abrode 1577. Hence **Li·mitable** *a.* that may be limited. **Li·mitableness.** **Li·miting** *ppl. a.*

Limitanean (limitēⁱ·niăn), *a.* 1839. [f. late L. *limitaneus* + -AN.] *Rom. Antiq.* Stationed on the border. So †**Li·mitany** *a.* 1611.

Limitarian (limitēᵊ·riăn), *a.* and *sb.* 1818. [f. LIMIT *sb.* + *-arian* as in *unitarian*, etc.] A dyslogistic term applied to theologians who hold the doctrine of 'limited redemption'.

Limitary (li·mitări), *a.* and *sb.* 1620. [ad. L. *limitaris*; see LIMIT and -ARY [2].] 1. Subject to limits; limited. b. Of a friar: Licensed to beg within certain limits. SCOTT. 2. Of or pertaining to a boundary; situate on the boundary 1650. 3. Serving as a boundary; limiting, confining, containing. Const. *of*. 1807. 4. *sb.* = LIMITER 1. Heylin.

1. The poor l. creature calling himself a man of the world DE QUINCEY. 2. This County (because a L.) did abound with Fortifications FULLER. 3. The horizon's l. line 1807.

Limitate (li·mitēⁱt), *pa. pple.* and *ppl. a.* 1581. [ad. L. *limitatus*, *limitare*.] †A. *pa. pple.* = LIMITED -1585. B. *ppl. a.* a. Of and: Parted off by boundaries (*rare*) 1853. b. *Bot.* Bounded by a distinct line 1871.

Limitation (limitēⁱ·ʃən). ME. [ad. L. *limitationem*, f. *limitare* to LIMIT.] 1. The action of limiting (see the vb.); an instance of this. †2. a. An allotted space; the district or circuit of an itinerant officer or preaching friar; the region belonging to a particular nation; *fig.* one's allotted sphere -1552. †b. An allotted time. *Cor.* II. iii. 146. 3. The condition of being limited 1597. 4. A point or respect in which something is limited; a limiting provision, rule, or circumstance 1523. 5. *Law.* a. The statutory specification of a period, or the period specified by statute, within which an action must be brought 1540. b. The specification of a period, or the period specified, for the continuance of an estate or the operation of a law 1767. c. The settlement of an estate by a special provision or with a special modification; the modification or provision itself 1767. 6. = LIMIT 1, 2. Also *pl.* bounds. 1523.

1. A fresh l. of the succession to the throne 1863. 3. The natural dulness and l. of our faculties BERKELEY. 4. Most of the provinces coupled their acquiescence with limitations which rendered it of little worth PRESCOTT. 6. She knew the limitations of her own powers too well to attempt [etc.] JANE AUSTEN.

Limitative (li·mitētiv). 1530. [ad. F. *limitatif*, *-ive*, ad. med.L. *limitativus*, f. L. *limitare*; see -ATIVE.] A. *adj.* 1. Limiting, restrictive. †2. Conditional. SCARLETT.

1. *L. judgement* (Logic): used by Kant to denote judgements of the type 'Every A is a not-B'; also *occas.* a judgement serving to limit or modify another.

B. *sb. Logic.* A limitative judgement. BOWEN.

Limited (li·mitĕd), *ppl. a.* 1551. [f. LIMIT *v.* + -ED [1].] 1. In senses of the vb. 2. quasi-*sb.* = *limited mail.* (*U.S. colloq.*) 1887.

1. *L. company*: short for *l. liability company* (see LIABILITY). *L. mail*: a mail train taking only a l. number of passengers. *L. monarchy*: one in which the functions of the monarch are exercised under constitutional restrictions; so *l. government*, *monarch*, *royalty*. Hence **Li·mited-ly** *adv.*, **-ness.**

Limiter (li·mitəɹ). Also **-or, -our.** ME. [f. LIMIT *v.* + -ER [1].] 1. (Also *friar l.*) A friar licensed to beg within certain limits. *Obs.* exc. *Hist.* 2. One who or that which limits (see the vb.) 1483.

1. A limitoure of the graye fryers, in the tyme of his limitation preached manye tymes and hadde but one Sermon LATIMER.

Limitless (li·mitlĕs), *a.* 1581. [f. LIMIT *sb.* + -LESS.] Having or admitting of no limits; illimitable; unbounded. Hence **Li·mitless-ly** *adv.*, **-ness.**

Limitor, -our, obs. ff. LIMITER.

Limitrophe (li·mitrōᵘf). 1589. [a. F., ad. late L. *limitrophus*, *limitotrophus* (a hybrid f. L. *limit-*, *limes* + Gr. -τροφος nourishing), applied to lands set apart for the support of troops on the frontier.]

A. *adj.* Situated on the frontier; bordering on, adjacent *to* (another country) 1826.

The policy of a l. frontier with Russia revived 1881.

†B. *sb.* A border-land -1598.

Limmer (li·məɹ). *Sc.* and *n. dial.* 1456. [? conn. w. LIMB *sb.*] A. *sb.* 1. A rogue, scoundrel. *arch.* 2. A light woman; in weaker sense, a jade, hussy, minx 1566. B. *adj.* Knavish, scoundrelly 1500.

Limn (lim), *v.* Now *literary* and *arch.* ME. [Altered f. LUMINE *v.*] †1. *trans.* To illuminate (letters, manuscripts, etc.). Also *absol.* -1588. †2. To embellish with gold or bright colour; to depict *in* (gold, etc.). Also (*rare*), to lay on (colour). -1653. 3. To paint (a picture); to portray, depict (a subject). †Formerly *spec.* to paint in water-colour or distemper. 1592. b. *transf.* and *fig.* 1593. †4. *absol.* or *intr.* To paint; *esp.* in water-colour or distemper -1678.

3. Where Apelles limb'd to life Loathed Vulcans louely wife WITHER. *fig.* The..picture of a great man..limned in words SMILES. Provb. *To l. the water, to l.* (something) *on water*: said of something transient or futile. Hence **Limner** (li·mnəɹ), an illuminator of manuscripts (*Hist.*); a (portrait) painter. **Li·mnery,** the work of a limner.

Limonin (li·mǒnin). Also **-ine.** 1845. [f. mod.L. *limonum* (F. *limon*) LEMON + -IN.] *Chem.* The bitter principle contained in the pips of oranges, lemons, etc.

Limonite (ləi·mǒnəit). 1823. [prob. f. Gr. λειμών meadow; cf. its earlier Ger. name *wiesenerz*, meadow-ore; see -ITE.] *Min. Orig.*, bog iron ore; *now*, extended to all forms of hydrous sesquioxide of iron.

Limous (ləi·məs), *a.* ? *Obs.* ME. [ad. L. *limosus*, f. *limus* mud.] Muddy; slimy.

Limousine (li·muzīn). 1902. [Fr.] A motor-car with a closed body and a roofed place for the driver.

Limp (limp), *sb.*[1] 1818. [f. LIMP *v.*] The action of limping; a limping gait or walk.

Limp (limp), *sb.*[2] 1596. *Mining.* An instrument for throwing off the refuse from the ore in the operation of jigging.

Limp (limp), *a.* 1706. [?] 1. Wanting in stiffness, flaccid; flexible, pliant. b. Used of a kind of binding without mill-board 1863. 2. *transf.* and *fig.* Wanting in firmness, strictness, nervous energy, etc. 1853.

1. His [Byron's] l. collars 1897. 2. Loose l. rhymes 1880. Hence **Li·mp-ly** *adv.*, **-ness.**

Limp (limp), *v.* ME. [cogn. w. MHG. *limphin* (rare) in same sense.] *intr.* To walk lamely, to halt. Occas. with cogn. obj. Also *fig.* Hence **Li·mper.** **Li·mpingly** *adv.*

Limpet (limp·ĕt). Also *Sc.* **lampit.** [OE. *lempedu*, a. late L. *lampreda* limpet, also LAMPREY.] A gasteropod mollusc of the genus *Patella* with a tent-shaped shell, adhering tightly to rocks. b. *fig.* A person, esp. a State employee, who clings to office 1905.

He..stuck like a lampit to a rock SCOTT.

Limpid (li·mpid), *a.* 1613. [ad. F. *limpide*, or L. *limpidus*, prob. conn. w. *lympha* clear liquid; see LYMPH.] Free from turbidity; pellucid, clear. Also *fig.*

L. waters DRYDEN, air COWPER, crystal 1834. A l. soprano 1847. *fig.* L. language GLADSTONE. So **Limpi·dity, Li·mpidness.** **Li·mpidly** *adv.*

Limuloid (li·miŭloid), *a.* (*sb.*) 1859. [f. mod.L. *Limulus* (see below) + -OID.] Of, pertaining to, or resembling the genus *Limulus* or king-crabs; also as *sb.*

Limy (ləi·mi), *a.* 1552. [f. LIME *sb.*[1] + -Y [1].] 1. Besmeared with bird-lime. 2. Consisting of or containing lime 1676. 3. Resembling lime 1775.

†**Lin,** *v.* [OE. *linnan* :—OTeut. **linnan* cogn. w. OE. *liðe* (:—**linþjo-*) gentle; see LITHE *a.*] 1. *intr.* To cease, leave off; desist *from*. Of the wind: To drop. As a command: 'Leave off!' 'Let go!' -1725. ¶b. Misused for: To fail, omit. PRIOR. 2. *trans.* To cease from, leave off -1643.

Lin, obs. var. of LINN [1], waterfall.

Linable, lineable (ləi·năb'l), *a.* 1698. [f. LINE *sb.*[2] or *v.*[2] + -ABLE.] Ranged in a straight line.

Linage (ləi·nĕdʒ). Also **lineage.** 1883. [f. LINE *sb.*[2] + -AGE.] a. Position (of figures) in line. b. Quantity of printed or written matter estimated in lines 1884. c. Payment at so much per line 1888.

c. An editor..offered him [Mr. Swinburne] 'l.' for a poem 1888.

Linage, obs. f. LINEAGE.

Linarite (ləi·nărəit). 1844. [f. *Linares*, Spain, where supposed to be found.] *Min.* Sulphate of lead and copper, found in brilliant blue crystals.

Linch (linʃ), *sb.*[1] *Obs.* exc. in *Comb.* [OE. *lynis* masc. = OS. *lunisa* fem. (Du. *luns*, *lens*, mod.G. *lünse*).] †1. = LINCH-PIN -1497. †2. *Naut.* ? A belaying-pin 1549.

Linch (linʃ), *sb.*[2] *dial.* 1591. [repr. OE. *hlinc*; see LINK *sb.*[1]] A rising ground; also = LINCHET (1 and 2).

Linch (linʃ), *v.* 1898. [f. LINCH *sb.*[1]] *trans.* To fasten with or as with a linch-pin.

Linchet (li·nʃĕt). Also **lynchet.** *dial.* 1674. [f. LINCH *sb.*[2]] 1. A strip of green land between two pieces of ploughed land. 2. A slope or terrace along the face of a chalk down 1797.

Li·nch-pin. ME. [f. LINCH *sb.*[1] + PIN.] A pin passed through the end of an axle-tree to keep the wheel in its place.

Lincoln (li·ŋkən). ME. [Name of the county town of Lincolnshire.] **1.** Used *attrib.* or *adj.*; esp. in **L. green,** a bright green stuff made at L. **2.** *ellipt.* as *sb.* in *pl.* A variety of sheep originally bred in Lincolnshire 1837.

Lincture (li·ŋktiŭɹ). 1621. [f. L. *lingere* to lick; see -URE.] = next.

Linctus (li·ŋktŏs). Pl. **linctuses.** 1681. [a. L. *linctus*, f. as prec.] A syrupy medicine to be licked up with the tongue.

†**Lind.** Also **lyne, line.** See also LINN [2]. [OE. *lind* str. fem. and *linde* wk. fem. (Du. *linde*) :—OTeut. **lendā*, perh. cogn. w. Gr. ἐλάτη silver fir.] = LINDEN *sb.* **1** -1796. Also *attrib.*, as *l.-grove*, etc. 1450.

Lindabrides (lindæ·bridīz). *arch.* 1640. The name of a lady in the 'Mirror of Knighthood' (1585), used allusively for: A lady-love, a mistress.

Linden (li·ndĕn), *sb.* 1577. [LINDEN *a.* used subst.] **1.** The lime-tree (see LIME *sb.*[3]). Also *attrib.* **2.** *Antiq.* Used to render OE. *lind*, shield of lime-tree wood 1855.

†**Li·nden,** *a.* [OE. *linden*, f. *lind*; see LIND.] Made of the wood of the lime-tree -ME.

Line (ləin), *sb.*[1] Now chiefly *dial.* [OE. *lín* neut. :—Com. Teut. type **līnom*, a. or cogn. w. L. *linum* flax (whence F. *lin*), cogn. w. Gr. λίνον.] **1.** = FLAX. †**a.** The fibre of flax. *Obs.* exc. as in b. **b.** In mod. techn. use, flax of a fine and long staple, which has been separated by the hackle from the tow 1835. **c.** The flax plant ME. **2.** Flax spun or woven; linen thread or cloth (now *rare* or *obs.*); †**a** napkin of linen; in *pl.* linen vestments OE. **3.** *attrib.*, as *l.-dresser, -spinner*, etc. ME.

2. Nor anie weauer, which his worke doth boast In dieper, in damaske, or in lyne SPENSER.

Line (ləin), *sb.*[2] [Two wds.: (1) OE. *line* wk. fem.; prob. an early Teut. adoption of L. *linea* (see below); (2) ME. *ligne, line*, a. F. *ligne* :—pop.L. **linja*, repr. cl. L. *līnea* (earlier *linia*), orig. 'linen thread', a subst. use of *līnea* fem. of *līneus* (**līnius*) adj., flaxen, f. *linum* flax = LINE *sb.*[1]]

I. Cord, etc. **1.** A rope, cord, string. *Obs.* in gen. sense; now chiefly *Naut.* or as short for *clothes-line*, etc. **b.** Cord, as a material 1797. †**c.** A 'cord' in the body (*rare*) -1780. **d.** Used of a spider's thread (*poet.*) 1732. **e.** A telegraph or telephone wire or cable. Also, a telegraph route, a telegraphic system. 1851. **f.** *pl.* Reins. *dial.* and *U.S.* 1852. †**g.** *L. of life*: the thread spun by the Fates, determining the length of a person's life -1681. **2.** A cord bearing a hook or hooks, for fishing. (Also *fishing-l.*) ME. †**3.** *pl.* Strings or cords laid for snaring birds -1753. **4.** A cord used by builders and others for taking measurements, or for making things level or straight ME. **b.** *pl.* Appointed lot in life; after *Ps.* xvi. 6; app. = land marked out for dwelling in 1611. †**5.** Rule, canon, precept; standard of life or practice (*rare*) -1611. **6.** *Hard lines* (colloq.): ill luck, bad fortune. (Prob. naut. in origin; often assoc. w. 4 b.) 1824.

1. And by her in a l. a milkewhite lambe she lad SPENSER. Shirts waving upon lines JOHNSON. **c.** COWPER *Table T.* 487. **e.** The American trans-Pacific l. 1854. **f.** He stepped into the carry-all and took the lines G. W. CABLE. **g.** Lo, thou a spanns length mad'st my living l. SIDNEY. **2.** *fig.* I am angling now, (Though you perceiue me not how I giue Lyne) SHAKS. It's policy to give 'em l. enough DICKENS. **4.** *L.-and-plummet* (attrib.): rigidly methodical. *fig.* This decencie is..the l. and leuell for al good makers to do their busines by PUTTENHAM. Phr. *By l., by l. and level, by rule and l.*, etc.: with methodical accuracy. **b.** The lines are fallen vnto mee in pleasant places; yea, I haue a goodly heritage *Ps.* xvi. 6. **5.** Their l. is gone out through all the earth, and their words to the end of the world *Ps.* xix. 4.

II. A thread-like mark. **1.** A long and narrow stroke or mark, traced with a pen, a tool, etc. upon a surface ME. Also *fig.* **b.** *Mus.* One of the parallel strokes forming the stave, or placed above or below it (*ledger lines*) 1602. **c.** *Fine Art.* Applied *spec.* to the lines employed in a picture; chiefly *collect.* or in generalized sense, character of draughtsmanship, method of rendering form. Also *pl.* the distinctive features of composition in a picture. Also with reference to engraving (see *line engraving* in Combs.). 1616. **d.** In tennis, football, etc., *the line* denotes a particular line which marks the limit of legitimate or successful play 1546. **2.** Anything resembling a traced mark; e. g. a thin band of colour; a suture, seam, furrow, ridge, etc. ME. **b.** A furrow or seam in the face or hands. In *Palmistry*: A mark on the palm of the hand supposed to indicate one's fate, etc. 1538. **c.** A narrow region in a spectrum, appearing to the eye as a fine straight black or shining stroke transverse to the length of the spectrum. Called collect. *Fraunhofer's lines.* 1831. **3.** *Math.* A continuous extent (whether straight or curved) of length without breadth or thickness; the limit of a surface; the trace of a moving point 1559. **4.** A circle of the terrestrial or celestial sphere; e. g. †*ecliptic, equinoctial,* †*tropic l.* Now *rare.* ME. **b.** *The l.*: the equinoctial line; the equator. (Occas. written with a capital.) 1568. **5.** Often used for 'straight line' (sense II. 3); esp. in *Physics* and *techn.* (see below) ME. **6.** A direction as traced by marks on a surface or as indicated by a row of persons or objects 1500. **7.** Contour, outline; lineament 1590. **8.** *pl.* The outlines, plan, or draught of a building or other structure; *spec.* in *Shipbuilding*, the outlines of a vessel as shown in its horizontal, vertical, and oblique sections. (Also *fig.*) 1673. **b.** *fig.* Plan of construction, of action, or procedure; now chiefly in phr. *on* (such and such) *lines* 1757. **9.** [After F. *ligne.*] The twelfth part of an inch 1665. **10.** A limit, boundary; more fully, *l. of demarcation.* †**11.** Degree, rank, station -1785.

1. An expression of forms only by simple lines 1821. *fig.* The lines of his character are..broad and clear 1878. Phr. *L. of lines, of numbers*, Gunter's l. *L. of shadows*; = QUADRAT **1. c.** Portraits..all beautifully engraved in l. 18.. Phr. *L. of beauty*: the curve (like a slender elongated S), which according to Hogarth is a necessary element in all beauty of form. **2.** Yon grey Lines, That fret the Clouds SHAKS. *Lines of growth* (Conch.): the eccentric striæ or lines, due to successive layers of shelly matter, by which the animal increases the shell. **b.** He does smile his face into more lynes, then is in the new Mappe SHAKS. Lines of premature age on the face 1895. Phr. *L. of life, of fortune, of the head, of the heart, of health* or *liver* (*hepatic l.*). **4. b.** Phr. *Under the l.*: on the equator; The straight of Malaca is vnder the l. 1588. **5.** Phr. *L. of fire*: the indefinite projection of the axis of the gun-barrel. *On the l.*: said of a picture in an exhibition so hung that its centre is about on a level with the eye. *As straight as a l., right as a* or *any l.*: straightforward; also, straightway. **6.** *To bring into* (*a*) *l.*: to align; *fig.* to make (persons) unanimous. The term *in l.* is applied to a battalion when its companies are deployed on the same alignment to their full extent, i.e. in two ranks. Columns are said to be *in l.* when their fronts are on the same alignment. VOYLE & STEVENSON. **b.** *To get a l. on* (U.S. colloq.): to acquire information about (a thing) 1903. **7.** The savage lines of his mouth MACAULAY. **10.** Phr. *To draw a* (or *the*) *line* (*fig.*): to determine the limit between two things; *mod. colloq.*, to lay down a definite limit of action beyond which one refuses to go. Also *to* †*lay, form a l.* *Mason and Dixon's l.*: the southern boundary of Pennsylvania, forming the line of demarcation between the free and the slave States. Named from the two astronomers who surveyed it. **11.** Women in the middle l. of life 1785.

III. Applied to things arranged along a (straight) line. **1.** A row or series of persons or things 1557. **2.** *Mil.* A trench or rampart; *pl.* (also *collect. sing.*) a connected series of field-works. Also, one of the rows of tents or huts in a camp, etc. 1645. **3.** *Mil.* and *Naut.* A row or rank of soldiers (dist. from a *column*); a row of ships in a certain order. Also occas. *collect. sing.* = ships of the line. 1704. **b.** *The l.*: in the British army, the regular and numbered troops as dist. from the guards and the auxiliary forces; in U.S., the regular fighting force of all arms 1802. **4.** A regular succession of public conveyances plying between certain places; e. g. the Cunard l. (of steamers), etc. 1848. **5.** A row of written or printed letters (see below) OE.

1. A l. of trading posts W. IRVING. The l. of festal light in Christ-Church hall M. ARNOLD. **2.** He took the French Lines without Bloodshed STEELE. **3.** Their L. consisted of 52 Ships and 24 Gallies 1704. *L. of battle*: see BATTLE *sb.* *Ship of the l.*: a l.-of-battle ship. *All along the l.*: at every point. **5. a.** *gen.* One row of letters in any piece of writing or letterpress; often, esp. in *pl.*, put for the contents of what is written or printed OE. Phr. *To read between the lines*: to discover a meaning or purpose not obvious or explicitly expressed in a piece of writing. **b.** *spec.* in *Printing.* A row of types or quads 1659. **c.** A few words in writing; a short letter 1647. Just a l. to say that all goes well MRS. CARLYLE. **d.** The portion of a metrical composition which is usually written in one line; a verse; *pl.* verses, poetry. Also *pl.*, (so many) lines of verse, etc. set to be written out as a school imposition. 1563. Marlowes mighty l. B. JONS. And ten low words oft creep in one dull line POPE. **e.** Short for *marriage lines*, certificate of marriage. Also *transf.* 1829. **f.** *pl.* The words of an actor's part 1882. **g.** *L. upon l.*: now taken as referring to reiteration of statements in successive lines (for the orig. meaning see I. 5) 1611.

IV. Serial succession. **1.** A continuous series of persons (rarely of things) in chronological succession. Chiefly with reference to family descent. ME. **2.** Lineage, stock, race. Somewhat *arch.* ME.

1. Purchases in the l. of the mother or grandmother CRUISE. Phr. *Male, female, direct l.* *Heir of l.* = *heir-at-law* (see HEIR *sb.* 1). †*By l.*: by lineal descent. **2.** The l. of Cyrus being extinct BANCROFT.

V. A direction. **1.** Track, course, direction; route ME. **b.** Short for *l. of rails, railway l., tram l.* 1825. **c.** *Hunting.* The straight course in the hunting field 1836. **2.** Course of action, procedure, life, thought, etc. ME. **3.** A department of activity; a branch of business, etc. 1638. †**4.** In *pl.*: = 'Goings on', caprices or fits of temper. (Cf. Warwickshire *on a l.* = in a rage.) SHAKS. **5.** *Comm.* An order for goods; the goods so ordered; also, the stock on hand of a particular class of goods 1882.

1. They ran on parallel lines that never met ZANGWILL. Phr. *L. of communication, of march, of operations.* **b.** A single track of rails, as in *the up l., the down l.*; a part of a railway system, as in *main l., branch l.*; an entire system, as in *the Midland l.* **c.** Phr. *To ride the l., to take, keep one's own l.* **2.** The Protectionists, as a party, have taken no l. in the matter LEWIS. **3.** Something in the l. of duty JOHNSON. Phr. *In* (or *out of*) *one's l.*: suited (or unsuited) to one's capacity, taste, etc. Her jokes aren't in my l. R. KIPLING. **4.** Your husband is in his olde lines (*Mod. edd.* lunes) againe *Merry W.* IV. ii. 22.

Combs. **1.** General: as *l. battalion, -guard, regiment, -room*, etc.; †in *Bot.* = *linear.*

2. Special: as **l.-bait,** bait used in line-fishing; **-boat,** a boat used for line-fishing; **-breeding** *U.S.*, breeding from stock of one strain or variety; **-coordinate** *Math.*, one of a set of quantities defining the position of a l.; **l. drawing,** a drawing done with a pen or pencil; **l. engraving,** the art of engraving 'in line', i.e. by lines incised on the plate, as dist. from etching and mezzotint; an engraving so executed; **-firing** *Mil.*, firing by a body of men in l.; **-hunter,** a hound which hunts by the l. of the scent alone; so **-hunting** *a.*; **-integral** *Math.*, the integral, taken along a l., of any differential that has a continuously varying value along that l.; **-integration,** the operation of finding a line-integral; **-rocket,** a small rocket attached to a l. or wire along which it is made to run; **-soldier,** a linesman; **-storm** *U.S.*, an equinoctial storm; **-wire** *Telegraphy*, the wire which connects the stations of a telegraph-line; **-work,** drawing or designing done with the pen or pencil (as opp. to wash, etc.).

Line (ləin), *v.*[1] ME. [f. LINE *sb.*[1]; with reference to frequent use of linen as lining material.] **1.** *trans.* To apply a second layer of (different) material to the inner side of (a garment; later, a box, culinary article, etc.); to cover on the inside. Also *transf.* and *fig.* †**2.** To reinforce, fortify. Also *fig.* -1761. **3.** To fill (one's purse, pocket, stomach, etc.); to cram, stuff 1514. **4.** To cover the outside of; to overlay, drape, pad (*lit.* and *fig.*); to face (a turf-slope). *Obs.* exc. *Naut.*, to add a layer of wood to. 1572. **5.** *techn.* (chiefly *to l. up*); see below. 1880. **6.** To serve as a lining for 1726.

1. A mode of lining culinary..articles with enamel YEATS. *transf.* Poplar that with silver lines his leaf COWPER. **2.** *Macb.* I. iii. 112. **3.** The Iustice, In faire round belly, with good Capon lin'd SHAKS. **5. a.** *Bookbinding.* To glue on the back of (a book) a paper covering continuous with the lining of the back of the cover. **b.** *Cabinet-making.* To put a moulding round (the top of a piece of furniture). **6.** These mortal lullabies of pain May bind a book, may l. a box TENNYSON.

Line (ləin), *v.*[2] ME. [f. LINE *sb.*[2]] **1.** *trans.* To tie with a line, string, or cord (*rare*). **2.** To measure or test with a line, to cut to a line; also *absol.* Occas. *fig.* to reach as with a measuring-line. *Obs.* exc. *techn.* ME. **3.** (*U.S.*) To angle with a hook and line (*rare*) 1833. **4.** To trace with, or as with, a line or lines; to delineate, sketch. Chiefly with advs.

1600. **5.** To mark with a line or lines; to cover with lines. Also with *off, out.* 1530. **6.** *U.S.* To follow the line of flight of (bees) 1827. **7. a.** *trans.* To bring (ships, soldiers, etc.) into a line or into line with others; also with *up.* Hence *U.S.* to assign (a person) *to* (certain work). 1796. **b.** *intr.* (*a*) To present to the eye a line of a specified kind 1794. (*b*) To form a (good) line with others; to fall into line; also with *out, up*; *fig.* to come *up to* a certain line 1790. (*c*) To run in line *with*; to border upon 1881. **8. a.** To arrange a line (orig. of troops) along (a hedge, road, etc.) 1647. **b.** To have or take one's place or to have a place in line along (a road, etc.) 1598.

4. Phr. *To l. in*: to put in with a hard pencil the permanent lines of (a freehand drawing); also, to insert (objects) in the outline of a picture. *To l. off*: to mark off by lines. *To l. out*: to trace the outlines of (something to be made); to forecast, adumbrate. 5. Selfish cares..had lined his narrow brow SHELLEY. Phr. *To l. through*: to draw a line *through* (an entry). 8. a. They having lined the hedges behind them with their reserve CLARENDON. b. The Streets were lin'd by the Militia 1707.

Line (ləin), *v.*[3] ME. [ad. F. *ligner.*] *trans.* Of a dog, wolf, etc.: To copulate with, cover.

Lineable, *a.*: see LINABLE.

Lineage (li·nĭ*e*dʒ). Now only *literary.* [ME. *li(g)nage,* a. OF. *lignage, linage*:—pop.L. **lineaticum* (see -AGE), f. *linea* LINE *sb.*[2] The sp. *lineage* is late 17th c.; the mod. pronunc. is infl. by *lineal* or L. *linea.*] **1.** Lineal descent from an ancestor; ancestry, pedigree. **2.** quasi-*concr.* (Chiefly *collect.*) †**a.** One's ancestors collectively. [So F. *lignage,* as opp. to *lignée* = descendants.] –1557. **b.** The descendants of a specified ancestor [= F. *lignée*] ME. †**c.** A tribe or clan –1604.

1. Norman l. was vulgarly regarded as the more honourable STUBBS. 2. b. Of this Mariage ensued a plenteous lignage, to witt, three Sonnes and foure Daughters 1623.

Lineal (li·nĭăl). ME. [a. F. *linéal,* f. late L. *linealis,* f. *linea* LINE *sb.*[2]]

A. *adj.* **1.** Of or pertaining to a line or lines; consisting of lines. Of writing: Arranged in regular lines. **b.** Of measures: = LINEAR *a.* 3. 1696. **2.** That is in the direct line; opp. to *collateral* ME. **b.** Pertaining to or transmitted by lineal descent 1486. **c.** Lineally descended (*rare*); †legitimate 1590.

1. Phr. *L. translation*: one made line for line (*rare*). *L. number, perspective*: see LINEAR. 2. I am the..lyneall heyre HALL. The Prime and Ancient Right of L. Succession LOCKE. b. As if they waged some l. feud with time BAILEY. c. For only you are l. to the throne DRYDEN.

†**B.** *sb.* One who is related in the direct line. FOOTE.

Hence **Linea·lity,** quality of being l.; uniformity of direction of writing. **Li·neally** *adv.* in a l. manner; *occas.* with regard to the lines or outline of anything; line for line.

Lineament (li·nĭămĕnt). ME. [a. F. *linéament,* ad. L. *lineamentum,* f. *lineare* (in unrecorded sense 'to trace lines'), f. *linea* LINE *sb.*[2]] †**1.** A line; a diagram, outline, sketch; *pl.* outlines, designs. *lit.* and *fig.* –1811. †**b.** A minute portion, a trace; *pl.* elements, rudiments –1811. †**2.** A portion of the body, considered with regard to its contour, a distinctive feature –1772. **b.** *fig.* in *pl.* Distinctive features or characteristics 1638. **3.** In narrower sense, a portion of the face viewed with respect to its outline; a feature 1513.

2. Man he seems In all his lineaments, though in his face The glimpses of his Fathers glory shine MILT. b. The principal lineaments of the law of contract STEPHEN. 3. A single fine l. cannot make a handsom face 1702. Hence **Li·neamenta·tion,** representation in form or l.

Linear (li·nĭăɹ), *a.* 1642. [ad. L. *linearis,* f. *linea* LINE *sb.*[2] Cf. F. *linéaire.*] **1.** Of or pertaining to a line or lines 1656. **2.** Consisting of, or involving the use of, lines 1840. **3.** Extended in a line or in length; *spec.* in *Math.* involving measurement in one dimension only 1706. **4.** Resembling a line; long, narrow, and of uniform breadth 1642; *spec.* in *Bot.* and *Zool.*, thread-like, narrow and elongated 1753.

1. *L. perspective*: that branch of perspective which is concerned with the apparent form, magnitude, and position of visual objects, as dist. from AERIAL *perspective.* 2. L. design RUSKIN. 3. *L. equation,* an equation of the first degree. 4. L. leaf 1753. L. feathers 1874. Hence **Li·nearly** *adv.* †**Li·neary** *a.* (in senses 2, 3) 1551–1664.

Lineate (li·nĭ*e*t), *ppl. a.* and *sb.* 1643. [ad. L. *lineatus,* f. *lineare* to reduce to a line, f. *linea.*] **a.** *ppl. a.* Marked with lines, *spec.* in *Bot.* †**b.** *sb.* A figure formed of lines 1674.

Lineate (li·nĭ*e*ᵢt), *v.* 1558. [f. L. *lineat-* (see prec.).] *trans.* **a.** To mark with lines. †**b.** To delineate, describe –1648. **Li·neated** *ppl. a.*

Lineation (linĭ*ē*ᵢ·ʃən). ME. [ad. L. *lineation-em,* f. *lineare* (see above).] **1.** The action of drawing lines or marking with lines; a marking or line on a surface; such lines collectively. **2.** A division into lines (of verse) 1853.

†**Li·neature.** 1603. [See LINEATE *v.* and -URE.] Something having an outline or shape; an outline; *Geom.* a periphery –1651.

Lineman (ləi·nmăn). 1858. [f. LINE *sb.*[2] + MAN.] **1.** A man employed to attend to a railway, telegraph, or telephone line. **2.** One who carries the line in surveying. SIMMONDS.

Linen (li·nėn). [OE. *linen, līnnen*:— OTeut. type **līnīno-,* f. **līnoᵐ* flax; see LINE *sb.*[1] and -EN[4].]

A. *adj.* Made of flax. In mod.Eng. felt as the sb. used attrib.: Made of linen.

Lappyng [it] in a clene lynnen clothe ME.

B. *sb.* **1.** Cloth woven from flax ME. **b.** *pl.* Kinds of linen; linen goods 1748. **2.** Something made of linen; a linen garment, etc. *Obs.* in *sing.*; the *pl.* is found in Sc. writers. 1566. **3.** *collect.* **a.** Garments, etc. made of linen, or, by extension, of calico, etc. Often *spec.* = undergarments, e. g. shirts; also = bed-, table-linen. ME. †**b.** Strips of linen, *esp.* for use as bandages; *pl.* graveclothes –1796.

1. Clothed in purple and fine linen *Luke* xvi. 19. 3. a. *To wash one's dirty l. at home*: to say nothing in public about family scandals, etc.

Comb.: **l.-decency,** (*nonce-use*), outward conformity to convention; **-draper,** a retail dealer in linens, calico's, etc.; **-fold, -pattern, -scroll,** a carved or moulded ornament for a panel, representing a fold or scroll of linen; **-panel,** one decorated with a linen-scroll; **-press,** a cupboard for linen.

Hence **Linene·tte,** an imitation l. 1894.

Linen-armourer. 1603. **a.** *Hist.* A maker of 'linen armour' (i. e. gambesons and similar adjuncts to armour). †**b.** *joc.* A tailor.

a. The Merchant-Taylors, then called Linnen-Armourers, were eminent not only in Peace, but War 1687.

†**Li·nener.** 1609. [f. LINEN *sb.* + -ER[1].] A linen-draper or shirt-maker –1625.

Lineolate (li·nĭŏlėt), *a.* 1852. [f. L. *lineola,* dim. of *linea* LINE *sb.*[2] + -ATE[2] 2.] *Bot.* and *Zool.* Marked with minute lines. So **Li·neolated** *a.* 1819.

Line-out. 1900. [f. *line out,* LINE *v.*[2] 7 b (*b*).] *Rugby Football.* The arrangement of forwards opposite to one another when the ball is about to be thrown in from touch.

Liner[1] (ləi·nəɹ). 1611. [f. LINE *v.*[1]] **1.** One who lines anything. **2.** *Mech.* Something which serves as a lining. **a.** An inside cylinder, or a vessel placed inside another 1886. **b.** A thin piece of metal, etc. placed between two parts to adjust them; a shim 1869. **c.** A slab on which pieces of marble, etc. are fastened for grinding or polishing 1875.

Liner[2] (ləi·nəɹ). ME. [f. LINE *sb.*[2] or *v.*[2]]

I. Of persons. **1.** *Sc.* One who traces the boundaries of properties in burghs. **2.** One who paints lines on the wheels, etc. of carriages. Also *l.-out.* 1819. **3.** A writer of items for the newspapers, which are paid for at so much per line. (Cf. PENNY-A-LINER.) 1861. **4.** = LINESMAN 1. 1870.

II. Of things. †**1.** A thin plate of iron or brass, for showing whether any piece of work to which it is applied is straight or not. MOXON. **2. a.** A steam-ship, or other vessel, belonging to a 'line' of packets 1838. **b.** A line-of-battle ship 1858. **3.** *Baseball.* A ball which, when struck, flies through the air in a nearly straight line not far from the ground 1874. **4.** *colloq.* A picture hung 'on the line' (see LINE *sb.*[2] II. 5) 1887.

Linesman (ləi·nzmăn). 1856. [f. *line's* (LINE *sb.*[2]) + MAN.] **1.** A soldier belonging to a regiment of the line. **2.** = LINEMAN 1. 1883. **3. a.** *Lawn Tennis.* An umpire posted near to one of the lines, to decide whether any particular ball falls within the court or not. **b.** *Association Football.* An official whose chief duty is to mark when and where the ball crosses the touch-line or the goal-line. 1890.

Line-up. 1889. [f. *line up,* LINE *v.*[2] 7 b (*b*).] An instance of bringing into line; the assembling of a number of persons in a line or file. Also *fig.*

Ling[1] (liŋ). [ME. *lenge, lienge,* later *ling(e.* Prob. conn. w. LONG *a.*] **1.** A long slender gadoid fish, *Molva molva,* of N. Europe. It is largely used for food (usu. either salted or dried). **2.** In America, New Zealand, etc., the burbot, the cultus cod, etc. 1850. **3.** *attrib.* 1489.

Ling[2] (liŋ). ME. [a. ON. *lyng*:—OTeut. type **lingwoᵐ.*] A name of kinds of Heather, esp. *Calluna vulgaris.* Also *attrib.*, as **l.-bird,** the meadow-pipit, *Anthus pratensis* 1814.

-ling (liŋ), *suffix*[1], forming sbs. A Com. Teut. formative, arising from the addition of *-iŋgo-z* -ING[3] to noun-stems formed with *-ilo-* (-EL[1], -LE 1).

1. In OE., and subseq. in ME. and mod.E., *-ling* added to sbs. forms sbs. with sense 'a person or thing belonging to or connected with (the primary sb.)', as *hȳrling* hireling, etc. The derivs. from adjs. have the sense 'a person or thing that has the quality denoted by the adj.', e.g. *déorling* darling, etc.; so from an adv., *underling* subordinate. The personal designations in *-ling* are now always contemptuous or unfavourable, as *courtling, earthling, worldling,* etc. A few words, e.g. *shaveling, starveling, stripling,* formed on vb.-stems, follow the analogy of *nursling,* where the first element is ambiguous. In these uses the suffix is no longer productive.

2. In ON. the suffix had a diminutive force. In Eng. this use appears first in *codling* (*c* 1314), *gosling* (15th c.), *duckling,* etc. Hence many new dim. formations, chiefly contemptuous personal designations, as *lordling,* etc. In this use the suffix is still a living formative.

-ling[2], **-lin(g)s** *suffix,* forming advs., now mostly *dial.* The Teut. root *liŋg-, laŋg-, luŋg-* to extend, appears in OE. (with or without advb. *-s*) added to sbs. forming advs. of direction or extent, as *on bæcling* backwards, *nihtlanges* for a night, *grundlunga, -linga* to the ground. ME. formations are *grufelyng* GROVELLING, *headling(s, noseling, sideling(s*; formations from adjs. denoting condition or position are more numerous later, as *darkling(s, flatling(s, hidlings.* (Cf. MLG. *sunderlingen, -es,* Du. *zonderling* adj., EFris. *sirlings* sidelong, WFris. *sidjlongs.*)

‖**Lingam** (li·ŋgăm), **linga** (li·ŋgă). 1719. [a. Skr. *liṅga,* nom. case *liṅgam.*] Among the Hindus, a phallus, worshipped as a symbol of the God Siva. Hence **Li·ngamism,** the worship of lingams.

Lingel, lingle[1] (li·ŋg'l). Now *dial.* 1440. [a. OF. *lignoel, ligneul*:—pop.L. **lineolum,* f. L. *linea* LINE *sb.*[2]] A shoemaker's waxed thread.

Lingel, lingle[2] (li·ŋg'l). Now *dial.* ME. [app. repr. AF. **lengle*:—L. *lingula* strap, etc.; dim. of *lingua* tongue.] †**1.** *collect. sing.* The leather straps, etc. of a horse's harness. Only ME. **2.** A thong or latchet 1538. †**3.** A flat blade or spoon, a spatula –1611.

†**Lingence.** [f. L. *lingere* to lick; see -ENCE.] A linctus. FULLER.

Linger (li·ŋgəɹ), *v.* [Northern ME. *lenger,* freq. of OE. *lęngan* v., cogn. w. LONG *a.*; see -ER[5].] †**1.** *intr.* To stay (in a place). Only ME. **2.** To stay behind, loiter; to stay on or hang about in a place, esp. from reluctance to leave it 1530. **b.** To proceed at a slow pace, loiter. Also *fig.* 1826. **3.** 'To remain long in languor and pain' (J.); to continue barely alive 1534. **4.** To be tardy in doing or beginning anything; to delay; to dawdle 1548. **5.** *fig.* **a.** To be slow to pass away or disappear 1764. **b.** To be slow in coming or accruing 1842. **c.** To be protracted, to drag on 1836. **6.** quasi-*trans.*, esp. with advb. compl.: To draw out, prolong, protract by lingering, tarrying, or dallying 1550. †**7.** *trans.* To cause to linger; to protract, draw out; also, to defer –1633. †**b.** To put off (a person) –1606. **8.** *intr.* To hanker. Const. *after*; occas. with *inf.* 1641.

2. Then l. not,..away, take horse SHAKS. b. *fig.* I l. round a subject STANLEY. 3. He lingered for nearly two years 1898. 4. Either Malcolm lingered

in his preparations, or [etc.] FREEMAN. 5. a. He has still a doubt lingering in his mind JOWETT. b. Knowledge comes, but wisdom lingers TENNYSON. 6. 2 *Hen. IV*, I. ii. 265. Far from gay cities, and the ways of men, I l. life POPE. Hence **Li·ngerer.** **Li·ngeringly** *adv.*

‖**Lingerie** (læ̃ŋʒrī). 1835. [Fr., f. *linge* linen.] Linen articles collectively; those in a woman's wardrobe or *trousseau*.

Linget, obs. f. LINGOT.

Lingism (li·ŋiz'm). 1879. [f. *Ling*, a Swedish physician + -ISM.] Ling's mode of treating certain diseases, as obesity, by gymnastics; kinesitherapy.

Lingo[1] (li·ŋgo). 1660. [? corrupt f. LINGUA (*franca*); cf. Pg. *lingoa*.] A contemptuous word for: Foreign speech or language; the vocabulary of a special subject or jargon of a class of persons.

Lingo[2], **lingoa.** 1800. [Moluccan *lenggoa*, dial. var. of Malay *lĭgūh*.] A large leguminous tree, *Pterocarpus indicus*, or its wood, also called *Burmese rosewood*, *Amboyna wood*, *Kyabuka*, etc.

Lingot (li·ŋgǫt). ? *Obs.* or *arch.* 1488. [a. F.; see INGOT.] = INGOT.

-lings: see -LING[2].

‖**Lingua** (li·ŋgwă). 1675. [L., = tongue; in sense 2 chiefly from It.] 1. The tongue or a tongue-like organ; *spec.* in *Entom.* (*a*) the ligula; (*b*) a tongue-like prolongation of the hypopharynx; (*c*) the proboscis of a butterfly or moth. 1826. 2. A language or 'lingo' 1675. b. **Lingua franca** [It., = 'Frankish tongue']: a mixed language or jargon used in the Levant, consisting largely of Italian words without their inflexions. Also *transf.* any mixed jargon used for intercourse between people speaking different languages.

2. b. Addressing himself to me..in a most fluent lingua-franca, half Italian and half Portuguese BECKFORD.

Linguadental: see LINGUO-.

Lingual (li·ŋgwăl). ME. [ad. med.L. *lingualis*, f. *lingua*.] A. *adj.* †1. Tongue-shaped. Only ME. 2. *Anat.*, *Zool.*, etc. Of or pertaining to the tongue, or to any tongue-like part (see LINGUA 1) 1650. 3. *Phonetics.* Of sounds: Formed by the tongue. ? *Obs.* exc. as = CEREBRAL (e. g. in Whitney's *Skr. Grammar*). 1668. 4. a. Pertaining to the tongue as the organ of speech. b. Pertaining to language or languages. 1774.

2. *L. nerve*, a tactile and sensory nerve, supplying the tongue. *L. ribbon*, in molluscs, = ODONTOPHORE. *L. teeth*, the chitinous band of teeth which is borne upon the odontophore.

B. *sb.* 1. A lingual sound (see A. 3) 1668. 2. *Anat.* The lingual nerve 1877.

Hence **Lingua·lity**, l. quality. **Li·ngualize** *v. trans.* to make l. **Li·ngually** *adv.*

Linguet, var. of LANGUET.

Linguiform (li·ŋgwifǭım), *a.* Also erron. lingua-, linguæ-. 1753. [f. LINGUA; see -FORM.] Shaped like the tongue.

Linguist (li·ŋgwist). 1588. [f. L. *lingua* + -IST.] 1. One skilled in other tongues besides his own. Often qualified, as a *good*, *bad*, *perfect l.*, etc. 1591. †2. A student of language; a philologist -1817. †3. An interpreter. (Formerly much used in the East.) -1882. †4. One who knows how to talk; a master of language -1691.

1. He was a l., a mathematician, and a poet MACAULAY. 4. He dispute with him. Hee's a rare l. WEBSTER. Hence **Li·nguistry** (*rare*), study of language.

Linguistic (liŋgwi·stik), *a.* and *sb.* 1837. [f. LINGUIST + -IC.] A. *adj.* Of or pertaining to the knowledge or study of languages. Also used *erron.* for: Of or pertaining to language or languages. 1856. B. *sb.* [-IC 2.] The science of languages; philology 1837; *pl.* **lingui·stics** 1855. So **Lingui·stical** *a.* 1823. Hence **Lingui·stically** *adv.*

Lingula (li·ŋgiŭlă). Pl. **-læ** (-lī). 1664. [L., dim. of *lingua*. Cf. LIGULA.] 1. A little tongue or tongue-like part. Now only *spec.* in *Anat.* 2. A genus of bivalve molluscs, including many fossil species; any shell of the genus 1836.

2. *L. flags*, micaceous flagstones and slates of N. Wales, containing the l. in large quantities. Hence **Li·ngular** *a. Anat.*, of or pertaining to a l.

Lingulate (li·ŋgiŭlᵉ't), *a.* 1849. [ad. L. *lingulatus*; see LINGULA and -ATE[2].] Tongue-shaped. So **Li·ngulated** 1797.

Linguo-, †**lingua-**, used as comb. f. L. *lingua* (the correct form would be *lingui-*), in **Linguo-**, †**linguade·ntal** *a.*, of or formed by tongue and teeth; also *sb.*, a sound so formed.

Liniment (li·niměnt). ME. [ad. L. *linimentum*, f. *linire* to smear.] †1. Something used for smearing or anointing -1691. 2. An embrocation usually made with oil 1543.

Lining (ləi·niŋ), *vbl. sb.*[1] ME. [f. LINE *v.*[1] + -ING[1].] 1. *concr.* The stuff with which garments are lined. Also *fig.* b. *pl.* Drawers; underclothing (*dial.*) 1614. 2. Any material occurring or placed next beneath the outside one 1713. 3. *fig.* Contents; that which is inside ME. 4. The action of LINE *v.*[1] Also *l. up*, in bookbinding and carpentry. 1839. 5. *attrib.*, as *l. paper*, etc. 1585.

2. I have found unvalued repositories of learning in the l. of bandboxes POPE. 3. The l. of his coffers shall make Coates To decke our souldiers for these Irish warres SHAKS.

Li·ning, *vbl. sb.*[2] 1478. [f. LINE *v.*[2]] Alignment; the use of a measuring line for alignment; the tracing of lines; etc. 1598. b. *Sc.* The authoritative fixing of the boundaries of burghal properties.

Link (liŋk), *sb.*[1] [OE. *hlinc*, ? a deriv., with *k* suffix, of *hlin-*, LEAN *v.*[1]] a. Rising ground; a ridge or bank. *Obs.* exc. *dial.* b. *pl.* (*Sc.* and *north.*) More or less level or gently undulating sandy ground near the sea-shore, covered with turf, coarse grass, etc. c. *pl.* The ground on which golf is played, often resembling that in b (also *a links* as sing.).

Link (liŋk), *sb.*[2] 1440. [a. ON. **hlenkr* (Icel. *hlekkr*):—OTeut. type **hlaŋkio-z*; cogn. w. OE. *hlęncan* pl., armour, OHG. *lancha* FLANK, mod.G. *gelenk* articulation, joint, etc.] 1. A single ring or loop of a chain. †Also, *pl.* chains, fetters. 1450. †b. *sing.* A chain. Also *transf.* and *fig.* -1730. c. One division, being a hundredth part, of the chain used in surveying (see CHAIN *sb.* II. 3); used as a measure of length. (In Gunter's chain the link is 7·92 inches.) 1661. d. Short for *sleeve-link* 1807. 2. Something looped, or forming part of a chain-like arrangement. a. A loop (in knitting); a segment of a cord, etc.; a lock of hair. In *Angling*, one of the segments of a hair-line. 1440. b. A division of a chain of sausages, etc. (Chiefly *pl.*) Now *dial.* 1440. c. *pl.* Windings of a stream; also, the ground lying along these. *Sc.* 1700. 3. A connecting part; a thing (*occas.* a person) that connects others; a member of a series; a means of connexion 1548. b. Any intermediate rod or piece transmitting motive power from one part of a machine to another. Also = *link-motion* (Dicts.). 1825. 4. A machine for linking or joining together the loops of fabrics 1892.

1. Linkes of Iron *Jul. C.* I. iii. 94. 2. Sir, a new linke to the Bucket must needes bee had SHAKS. c. The lairdship of the bonny Links of Forth 1700. 3. *Missing l.*: see MISSING *ppl. a.*

attrib. and *Comb.*, as *l.-belt*, *-chain*, etc.; **l.-block** *Steam-engine*, the block actuated by the link-motion and giving motion to a valve-stem; **-motion**, (*a*) *Steam-engine*, a valve-gear for reversing the motion of the engine, etc., consisting of two eccentrics and their rods, which give motion to a slide-valve by means of a 'link'; (*b*) *Geom.*, a linkage in which all the points describe definite curves in the same plane or in parallel planes; **-staff** *Surveying*, = *offset-staff* (see OFFSET *sb.*); **-structure** *Math.*, a linkage or linkwork; **-work**, (*a*) work composed of or arranged in links; (*b*) *Mech.*, that species of gearing by which motions are transmitted by links; (*c*) *Geom.*, a system of lines, pivoted together so as to rotate about one another; **-worming**, protection of a rope by worming it with chains.

Link (liŋk), *sb.*[3] 1526. [? a use of prec.; the material may have been made in strings and divided into links or segments.] 1. A torch made of tow and pitch, etc., formerly used for lighting people along the streets. b. A link-boy 1845. †2. ? The material of 'links' used as blacking 1596.

1. In the strong glare of the l. DICKENS. 2. There was no Linke to Colour Peters hat SHAKS.

Link (liŋk), *v.* ME. [f. LINK *sb.*[2]] 1. *trans.* To couple or join with or as with a link (*in* or *into* a chain, *in* amity, etc.). Also *absol.* a. things, persons *together*. b. one thing (*in*) *with* or (*on*) *to* another ME. c. To pass (one's arm) *through* or *in* another's 1843. 2. *intr.* To be coupled, joined, or connected (e. g. in friendship, etc.) 1540. 3. *To link up* (*trans.* and *intr.*): to connect, combine, etc. 1897.

1. Linked together by many promises and professions, and by an entire conjunction in guilt CLARENDON. b. Strong fetters l. him to the rock SOUTHEY. 2. No one generation could l. with the other BURKE. Hence **Li·nked** *ppl. a.*; *spec.* in *Mil.* of two infantry battalions (or regiments) which are coupled together to form a regimental district. **Li·nker**, one who or that which links or joins.

Linkage (li·ŋkědʒ). 1874. [f. LINK *sb.*[2] or *v.* + -AGE.] The condition or manner of being linked; a system of links.

Applied e.g. (*Chem.*) to the union of atoms or radicals in a molecule; (*Geom.*) to a system of straight lines, etc. pivoted together so as to rotate about one another.

Li·nk-boy. 1660. A boy employed to carry a link (LINK *sb.*[3] 1). So **Li·nkman** 1716.

Lin-lan-lone. A formation echoic of the sound of a chime of three bells. TENNYSON.

Linn[1] (lin). Chiefly *Sc.* [app. two words confused: OE. *hlynn* str. fem., torrent, and Gael. *linne* = Ir. *linn*, Welsh *llyn*, etc.] 1. A torrent running over rocks; a waterfall. 2. A pool, esp. one into which a cataract falls 1577. 3. A ravine with precipitous sides 1799.

Linn[2]. Now *dial.* 1475. [Altered f. LIND.] The linden or lime; also, the wood of this tree; *attrib.* in *l.-bark*, etc.

‖**Linnæa** (linī·ă). 1862. [mod.L.; after the Swedish naturalist C. F. *Linné* (latinized *Linnæus*).] *Bot.* A slender evergreen flowering plant (*L. borealis*) of the north temperate and frigid zones.

Linnæan, Linnean (linī·ăn). 1753. [f. *Linnæus* (see prec.) + -AN. The sp. *Linnæan* is usual, but the Linnean Society adopts the other form.] A. *adj.* Of or pertaining to Linnæus or his system; given or instituted by Linnæus; adhering to his system. B. *sb.* A follower of Linnæus or his system 1772.

Linnæite (linī·əit). 1849. [Named after *Linnæus*, who first described it; see -ITE.] *Min.* Sulphide of cobalt, containing some nickel and copper.

Linnet (li·nět). 1530. [a. OF. *linette*, *linot*, *linotte* (mod.F. *linotte*), f. *lin* flax, on the seeds of which it feeds]. 1. A song-bird, *Linota* (or *Linaria*) *cannabina*, of the family *Fringillidæ*. Its plumage is brown or warm grey; but in summer the breast and crown of the cock (when wild) become crimson or rose-colour. Allied species are the Mountain-Linnet or Twite (*Linota flavirostris* or *L. montium*) and the Lesser Redpoll (*L. rufescens*). 2. Applied, with qualifications, to birds of other genera 1868. 3. *Mining. pl.* Oxidized lead ores 1881.

2. *Green l.*, the greenfinch. *Pine l.*, a siskin of N. America, *Chrysomitris* (or *Spinus*) *pinus*.

Lino (ləi·no). Abbrev. of LINOLEUM, LINOTYPE.

Linocut (ləi·nŏkɒt). 1923. [f. LINO(LEUM + CUT *sb.*[2]] A design cut in relief on a block of linoleum; a print obtained from this.

Linoleic (linolī·ik), *a.* 1857. [f. L. *linum* + *oleum* + -IC.] *Chem. L. acid*: an acid found as a glyceride in linseed and other oils. Hence **Lino·leate**, a salt of l. acid.

Linoleum (linōᵘ·lĭŏm). Patented by F. Walton, 1860 and 1863. [f. L. *linum* flax + *oleum* oil.] A kind of floor-cloth of canvas coated with a preparation of oxidized linseed-oil.

Linotype (ləi·nŏtəip). 1888. [= *line o' type*.] *Printing.* a. A type-bar or -line. b. (= *l.-machine*) a machine for producing stereotyped lines or bars of words, etc., as a substitute for type-setting.

Linsang (li·nsæŋ). 1885. [a. Javanese *linsang*, *wlinsang*, erron. rendered 'otter' in Dicts.] A kind of civet cat, *Linsang* (or *Prionodon*) *gracilis*, of Borneo and Java.

Linseed (li·nsīd). Also **lintseed** (*n. dial.*). [OE. *līnsǣd* = LINE *sb.*[1] + SEED *sb.*] The seed of flax, well known as the source of linseed-oil, and as a medicament. †Occas. the flax-plant.

attrib. and *Comb.*, as l. **cake**, l. pressed into cakes in extracting the oil, used as food for cattle; **-meal**, l. ground in a mill; **-oil**, the oil expressed from l.; **l. poultice**, one made of l. or linseed-meal; **-tea**, an infusion of l., used as a demulcent.

Linsey (li·nzi). ME. [? f. LINE *sb.*[1] + SAY silk.] Orig., perh. some coarse linen fabric. Later, = next. Also *attrib.*

Linsey-woolsey (li·nzi wu·lzi). 1483. [f. prec. + WOOL, with jingling ending.] **1.** Orig., a textile material, of mixed wool and flax; now, a dress material of coarse inferior wool, woven upon a cotton warp. Also *pl.* pieces or kinds of this. **2.** *fig.*, etc., *esp.* a strange medley in talk or action; nonsense 1592. **3.** *attrib.* or *adj.* 1618. **b.** *fig.*: chiefly = 'neither one thing nor the other' 1565.

2. What linsie wolsy hast thou to speake to vs againe? *All 's Well* IV. i. 13. **3. b.** An asse in a rocket, a lince wolse bishop T. STAPLETON.

Linstock (li·nstǫk). *Obs.* exc. *Hist.* 1560. [In 16th c. *lint-*, *linestocke*, ad. Du. *lontstok*, f. *lont* match + *stok* stick.] A staff about three feet long, having a pointed foot to stick in the deck or ground, and a forked head to hold a match.

Their master gunner..confronts me with his linstock, readie to giue fire B. JONS.

Lint (lint). [ME. *linnet*; conn. w. LINE *sb.*[1]; perh. a. F. *linette*, f. *lin* LINE *sb.*[1]; see -ET.] **1.** (Now only *Sc.*) The flax-plant 1458. **2.** (Chiefly *Sc.*) Flax prepared for spinning. Also, flax refuse, used as a combustible. ME. **3.** A soft material for dressing wounds (formerly also burnt for tinder), prepared by ravelling or scraping linen cloth. †In *pl.*, pieces of this. ME. **b.** Fluff (*rare*) 1611. **4.** Now only *dial.* or *U.S.* Netting for fishing-nets 1615.

attrib. and *Comb.*, as **l.-doctor** *Calico-printing*, a sharp-edged ruler for removing fibres which may have come off the calico in the act of printing; **-scraper**, a person employed to scrape lint (for hospital use); also (*slang*) a young surgeon; **-white** *a.*, white as l.; flaxen. Hence **Li·nty** *a.*

Lintel (li·ntĕl). ME. [a. OF. *lintel* threshold (F. *linteau*) :—pop.L. **limitale* or **limitellum* (f. *limit-*, *limes* LIMIT *sb.*, confused with *limin-*, *limen* threshold).] **1.** A horizontal piece of timber, stone, etc. placed over a door, window, or other opening to discharge the superincumbent weight. **2.** *attrib.*, as *l.-piece*, etc. 1575. Hence **Li·ntelled** *a.* furnished with a l.

Linter (li·ntəɹ). *U.S.* 1890. [f. LINT + -ER[1].] A machine for removing short-staple cotton-fibre from cotton-seed after ginning; the fibre thus obtained, used in making mattresses, etc.

Lintie (li·nti). *Sc.* Also **linty.** 1795. [f. *lint* in LINTWHITE + dim. ending -IE (-Y[6]).] = LINNET.

Lintseed, -stock: see LINSEED, -STOCK.

Lintwhite (li·nt₍hwəit). Chiefly *Sc.* [OE. *linetwige*, perh. f. *lin* LINE *sb.*[1] + *-twige* (? cogn. w. OHG. *zwigôn* to pluck). Cf. TWITE *sb.*] = LINNET.

The l. and the throstlecock Have voices sweet and clear TENNYSON.

‖**Linum** (ləi·nɒ̆m). 1867. [mod.L. use of L. *linum* LINE *sb.*[1]] *Bot.* A genus of plants including flax, and various ornamental species.

Liny, liney (ləi·ni), *a.* 1807. [f. LINE *sb.*[2] + -Y[1].] **1.** Of the nature of or resembling a line, thin, meagre. **2.** Full of, or marked with, lines 1817.

2. The leaf being..rendered l. by bold markings of its ribs RUSKIN.

Lion (ləi·ən). [In OE. *léa*, *lío*, *léo*. The mod. form represents an adoption of AF. *liun* (F. *lion*), a Com. Rom. wd. :—L. *leonem*, nom. *leo*, a. Gr. λέων (stem λεοντ-). With the Gr. wd. cf. Heb. *lābī* lion.] **1.** A large carnivorous quadruped, *Panthera leo*, now found native only in Africa and southern Asia, of a tawny colour, and having a tufted tail, and in the male usu. a flowing shaggy mane. **b.** Extended to other animals of the genus *Felis*, as the *American mountain l.*, the puma or cougar 1630. **2.** *fig.* (chiefly after biblical usage; cf. *Rev.* v. 5; also *Ps.* xxxv. 17, lvii. 4, etc.). See quots. ME. **3.** *pl.* Things of note (in a town, etc.); sights worth seeing; esp. in phr. *to see* or *show the lions*. (This use is derived from the practice of taking visitors to see the lions formerly kept in the Tower of London.) 1590. **b.** Hence: A person of note who is much sought after 1715. **c.** *Oxford slang.* A visitor to Oxford 1785. **4.** An image or picture of a lion. (Often a sign for inns and taverns; usu. *Red*, *White*, etc. *L.*) ME. **5.** The constellation and zodiacal sign LEO. Also *Little L.*: Leo Minor. ME. †**6.** Alchemy. *Green l.*: a 'spirit' of great transmuting power; occas. identified with the philosophical mercury. *Red l.*: the tincture of gold. –1664. **7.** *attrib.* or *adj.* = 'lion-like' 1614.

1. The L. is (beyond dispute) Allow'd the most majestic brute GAY. Provbs. and phr. *A l. in the way* (or *path*): after *Prov.* xxvi. 13, applied to a danger or obstacle, esp. an imaginary one. *The lion's mouth*: a place of great peril. (Cf. *Ps.* xxii. 21, 2 *Tim.* iv. 17.) *The lion's share*: the largest or choicest portion. *The lion's skin* (with reference to the fable of the ass in the lion's skin; see also *Hen. V*, IV. iii. 93). *The lion's provider*: = JACKAL (*lit.* and *fig.*). *To twist the lion's tail*: frequent in (chiefly U.S.) journalistic use with reference to insults to or encroachments on the rights of Great Britain. †*Cotswold l.*: a sheep 1450. **2.** He, my Lyon, and my noble Lord SPENSER. A Lyon among sheepe and a sheepe among Lyons PUTTENHAM. *The L. of the North*, Gustavus Adolphus. **3.** The churches were the best lions we met with in our way MALKIN. †*To have seen the lions*: in early use, to have had experience of life (B. JONS. *Cynthia's Rev.* v. ii). **b.** The literary l. who likes to be petted LYTTON. **4.** Hark, countrymen! either renew the fight, Or tear the lions out of England's coat SHAKS. *British L.*, the l. as the national emblem of Great Britain; hence *fig.* the British nation. So *Scottish l.* **7.** Strong mother of a Lion-line TENNYSON.

Comb.: **l.-ant**, the same as ANT-LION; **-dog** [after F. *chien-lion* (Buffon)], a variety of dog having a flowing mane; **-dragon**, a heraldic beast having the fore part like a l. and the hind part like a wyvern; **-hunter**, one who hunts lions; one who is given to lionizing celebrities; so **-hunting** (*lit.* and *fig.*); **-lizard**, the basilisk, its crest being compared to a lion's mane; **-monkey**, the marikina or silky marmoset; **-tailed** *baboon*, *monkey*, the wanderoo (*Macacus silenus*); **-tamer** (1798).

Lion, Lion Herald, etc.: see LYON.

Lionced, leonced (ləi·ǫ̆nst), *a.* 1828. [irreg. f. LION.] *Her.* Adorned with lions' heads, as a cross, etc.

Lioncel (ləi·ǫnsel). 1610. [ad. OF. *lioncel*, dim. of *lion* LION.] A small or young lion; chiefly *Her.* var. ‖**Li·onceau** late ME.–1610.

†**Lion-drunk**, *a.* 1592. Said of a man in the second of the four stages of drunkenness, in which he becomes violent and quarrelsome.

Lionel (ləi·ŏnĕl). 1661. [a. F., dim. of *lion* LION.] *Her.* = LIONCEL.

Lioness (ləi·ŏnĕs). ME. [a. OF. *lion(n)esse*, *leonesse* (now repl. by *lionne*), f. *lion* LION.] **1.** The female of the lion. Also *fig.* of persons. **2.** A woman who is lionized; a lady visitor to Oxford (*slang*) 1808.

Li·onet. 1586. [See LION and -ET.] A young lion.

Li·on-heart. 1665. †**a.** A heart like that of a lion, i. e. courageous. **b.** A lion-hearted person; used as tr. *Cœur de Lion*.

b. What songs..The lion-heart, Plantagenet, Sang looking thro' his prison bars TENNYSON. So **Lion-hearted** *a.* courageous.

Li·onhood. 1833. [+ -HOOD.] The condition of being a 'lion'.

Lionism (ləi·ŏniz'm). 1835. [+ -ISM.] The practice of lionizing; the condition of being lionized.

Lionize (ləi·ŏnəiz), *v.* 1809. [f. LION + -IZE.] **1.** *trans.* To visit the 'lions' of (a place); to go over (a place of interest) 1838. **2. a.** To show the 'lions' to (a person). Also *absol.* **b.** To show the 'lions' of (a place). 1830. **3.** *intr.* To see the 'lions' of a place 1825. **4.** *trans.* To treat (a person) as a 'lion'; to make a 'lion' of 1809. **5.** *intr.* To be a 'lion' 1834.

3. We sallied forth to l...which is the Oxford term for gazing about, usually applied to strangers 1825.

Li·on-like, *a.* (*adv.*) 1556. **1.** Resembling a lion or what belongs to one. So **Li·only** *a.* (now *rare*). **2.** *adv.* 1610.

Lionne (lyǫn). ME. [F., fem. of *lion* LION.] †**1.** A lioness. Only ME. ‖**2.** A woman of the highest fashion 1846.

Lionship (ləi·ənʃip). 1769. [+ -SHIP.] The quality or condition of being a lion; also as a mock title.

Lip (lip), *sb.* [OE. *lippa* wk. masc. :— OTeut. type **lipjon-*, cogn. w. OS. *lepor*, OHG. *leffur*, *lefs*, etc. :—OTeut. **lepoz-*, **leps*, f. root **lep-*, pre-Teut. **leb-*; cf. L. *labium*, *labrum*, etc.]

I. 1. Either of the two fleshy structures which form the edges of the mouth. Dist. as *upper* and *lower*, also *under*. **2.** Chiefly *pl.* Considered as one of the organs of speech; often in fig. contexts OE. †**b.** *sing.* Language (*lit.* and *fig.*) –1695. **c.** *slang.* Impudent or saucy talk 1821.

1. When she drinkes, against her lips I bob SHAKS. Phr. (*Immersed*, *steeped*) *to the lips*. *To bite one's l.*, (*a*) to show vexation; (*b*) to repress emotion. *To carry* or *keep a stiff upper l.*, not to lose heart; in bad sense, to be hard or obstinate. *To curl one's l.*, to bend or raise the upper lip slightly on one side, as an expression of contempt or scorn. †*To hang the l.*, to look vexed. *To lick one's lips* (see LICK *v.* 1). *To smack one's lips*, to express relish for food, *fig.* to express delight. **2.** Atheisme is rather in the L., than in the Heart of Man BACON. Phr. *To escape* (a person's) *lips* (see ESCAPE *v.* 2 b). *To hang on* (a person's) *lips*: to listen with rapt attention to his words. **b.** Phr. *Of one l.* (a Hebraism); also, agreeing in one story.

II. 1. The margin of a cup, a bell, etc. 1592. **b.** The edge of an opening or cavity 1726. **c.** Any edge or rim, esp. one that projects 1608. **2.** In scientific and techn. uses. See below.

1. b. Every stream of lava descending from the lips of the crater LYELL. **c.** The l. of the hammer of a gun 1813. **2. a.** *Surg.* One of the edges of a wound ME. **b.** *Anat.* and *Zool.* = LABIUM or LABRUM 1597. **c.** *Bot.* (*a*) One of the two divisions of a bilabiate corolla or calyx. (*b*) = LABELLUM 1. 1776. **d.** *Conch.* One of the edges of the opening of a spiral shell 1681. **e.** *Mech.* The helical blade on the end of an auger 1884. **f.** *Organ-building.* One of the two edges above and below the mouth of an organ-pipe 1727.

attrib. and *Comb.* **1.** General: as *l.-favour*, *-smile*, etc.; (in sense 'not heartfelt', 'of the lips only') *l.-comfort*, *-comforter*, *-devotion*, *-homage*, *-love*, *-religion*, *-service*, *-wisdom*, *-worship*, etc.; *l.-born* adj.

2. Special: as **l.-auger**, one having pod and l., as dist. from the screw auger; **-bit**, a boring tool used in a brace, and having a cutting l. projecting beyond the end of the barrel; **-hook**, the upper hook of several on a line, which is put through the l. of a live bait; **-language**, (for the deaf and dumb) language communicated by movements of the lips; **-pipe** *Organ-building*, a flue-pipe; **-reading**, (in the case of the deaf and dumb) the apprehending of what another says by watching the movements of his lips; so **-speaking**; **-stick**, a stick of cosmetic for colouring the lips; **-tooth**, a tooth on the l. of a shell; **-vein**, a labial vein; **-work** = LIP-LABOUR.

Lip (lip), *v.*[1] 1604. [f. LIP *sb.*] **1.** *trans.* To touch with the lips, apply the lips to 1826. **b.** To kiss (*poet.*) 1604. **c.** *transf.* Of water: To kiss, to lap 1842. **2.** To pronounce with the lips only; to murmur softly; to utter (? *obs.*); (*slang*) to sing (a song) 1789. **3. a.** *trans.* To serve as a lip or margin to 1845. **b.** *Golf.* To hit the ball just to the lip or edge of (a hole) 1899.

1. Or the bubble on the wine, which breaks Before you l. the glass PRAED. **b.** A hand that Kings Haue lipt, and trembled kissing SHAKS. **3. a.** The margin ..lips the pool with gentleness 1880.

†**Lip**, *v.*[2] ME. [?: cf. LOP *v.*] *trans.* To cut off (the head of an animal); to prune (a root); to shear (a sheep) –1607.

Lipæmia: see LIPO-.

Liparite (li·părəit). 1865. [f. Gr. λιπαρός shining + -ITE[1].] *Min.* = FLUORITE.

Lipic (li·pik), *a.* 1838. [f. Gr. λίπος fat + -IC.] *Chem.* In *l. acid*: a crystallizable acid produced by the action of nitric acid upon a fatty acid.

Li·p-labour. 1538. Labour of the lips: empty talk; *esp.* vain repetition in prayer; †kissing –1665.

Liplet (li·plĕt). 1816. [f. LIP *sb.* + -LET.] A little lip or (*Entom.*) lip-like projection.

Lipo- (lipo) (bef. a vowel **lip-**), comb. f. Gr. λίπος fat; as in ‖**Li:pohæ·mia** (also *lipæmia*) [Gr. αἷμα blood], *Path.* prevalence of fatty matter in the circulation.

Lipogram (li·pǒgræm). 1711. [Back-formation f. Gr. λιπογράμματος *adj.*, wanting a letter, f. λιπ-, wk. stem of λείπειν to leave, be wanting + γραμματ-, γράμμα letter.] A composition from which all words that contain a certain letter or letters are omitted. Hence **Li:pogramma·tic** *a.*, of, pertaining to, or of the nature of a l. So **Lipogra·mmatist**, a writer of lipograms.

‖**Lipoma** (lipōu·mă). Pl. **-mata** (-mătă). 1830. [mod.L., f. Gr. λίπος fat + -ωμα.] *Path.* A fatty tumour. **Lipo·mato·sis**, excess of fat in a tissue. **Lipo·matoid, Lipo·matous** *adjs.* resembling, or of the nature of, a l.

Lipothymy (lipǫ·þimi), **lipothymia** (lipǫþəi·miă). 1603. [ad. and a. mod.L. *lipothymia*, ad. Gr. λιποθυμία, f. λιπ-, wk. stem of λείπειν to leave, fail, etc. + θυμός animation.] Fainting, swooning, syncope.

fig. When nature is in a lipothymie JER. TAYLOR. So **Lipothy·mial, Lipothy·mic** *adjs.* of or pertaining to l.: characterized by l.

Lipped (lipt), *ppl. a.* ME. [f. LIP *sb.* or *v.*[1] + -ED.] 1. Having or furnished with a lip or lips. Often qualified, as *blubber-, red-, thick-l.* 2. *Bot.* = LABIATE; also, having a labellum 1731.

Lippen (li·pĕn), *v.* Chiefly *Sc.* ME. [?] 1. *intr.* To confide, rely, trust. 2. *trans.* To entrust ME. 3. To expect confidently ME.

Lippitude (li·pitiud). Now *rare.* 1626. [ad. L. *lippitudo* (f. *lippus* blear-eyed).] Soreness of the eyes; blearedness.

Lipsalve (li·p,sāv). 1591. [f. LIP *sb.* + SALVE *sb.*] Salve or ointment for the lips; an example of this; *fig.* flattering speech.

Lipse, obs. var. of LISP *v.*

‖**Li·quable.** 1460. [ad. L. *liquabilis*; see LIQUATE *v.* and -ABLE.] **A.** *adj.* That can be liquefied. Also, soluble (in a liquid). –1768. **B.** *sb.* [sc. *substance.*] –1612.

Liquate (ləi·kwe¹t), *v.* 1669. [f. L. *liquat-, liquare* to melt, cogn. w. *liquor* LIQUOR.] †1. *trans.* To make liquid, cause to flow. Also *intr.*, to melt. –1728. 2. *Metall.* To separate metals or free them from impurities by liquefying. Also to *l. out.* 1864.

Liquation (likwē¹·ʃən). 1471. [ad. L. *liquationem*, f. *liquare*; see prec.] 1. The making or becoming liquid; the condition or capacity of being melted 1612. 2. *Metall.* The action of separating metals by fusion.

Liquefacient (likwĭfē¹·ʃĕnt). 1853. [ad. L. *liquefacientem*; see LIQUEFY and -FACIENT.]

A. *adj.* Making liquid 1889.

B. *sb.* Something which serves to liquefy; *spec.* in *Med.*, an agent (e.g. mercury and iodine) supposed to have the power of liquefying solid deposits 1853. Also, an agent which increases the amount of fluid secretions 1889.

Liquefaction (likwĭfæ·kʃən). Also †**liqui-.** late ME. [a. F. *liquéfaction*, ad. L. *liquefactionem.*] The action or process of liquefying, or the state of being liquefied; reduction to a liquid state. †Also *fig.* of the 'melting' of the soul –1711.

Liquefactive (likwĭfæ·ktiv), *a.* 1877. [f. L. *liquefacere* to LIQUEFY.] Having the effect of liquefying.

Liquefy (li·kwĭfəi), *v.* Also †**liquify.** 1483. [a. F. *liquéfier*, ad. L. *liquefacere* to make liquid, f. *liquere* to be liquid; see -FY.] 1. *trans.* To reduce (a solid, air, gas) into a liquid condition. †Formerly, to dissolve (in a liquid). 1547. 2. *fig.* To 'melt' with spiritual ardour. Also *intr.* for *pass.* 1483. 3. *intr.* To become liquid; †*rarely* to dissolve (in water) 1583.

3. The ice liquefying rapidly TYNDALL. Hence **Li·quefi·able** *a.* **Li·quefier.**

Liquescent (likwe·sĕnt), *a.* 1727. [ad. L. *liquescentem*; see -ESCENT.] In process of becoming liquid; apt to become liquid. Hence **Lique·scence** (*rare*).

‖**Liqueur** (lĭkōr; often likiūə·ɹ), *sb.* 1742. [F.; = LIQUOR *sb.*] 1. A strong alcoholic liquor sweetened and flavoured with aromatic substances. b. A mixture (of sugar and certain wines or alcohol) used to sweeten and flavour champagne 1872. 2. Short for *liqueur-glass.*

Comb.: **l. brandy**, a brandy of special bouquet, consumed in small quantities as a l.; **-glass**, a very small drinking glass used for liqueurs; **-wine** [= F. *vin de liqueur*], one of the strong and delicate-flavoured wines that have the character of liqueurs. Hence **Liqueu·r** *v.* to flavour (champagne) with a l.

Liquid (li·kwid). ME. [a. OF. *liquide*, ad. L. *liquidus*, f. *liquere* to be liquid; cf. LIQUATE *v.*, LIQUOR.] **A.** *adj.* I. Said of a material substance in that condition in which its particles move freely over each other (so that its masses have no determinate shape), but do not tend to separate as do those of a gas; not solid nor gaseous; resembling water, oil, alcohol, etc. in their normal condition. Hence, composed of a substance in this condition. b. Watery. *poet.* and *rhet.* 1606.

L. sap SPENSER, fire SHAKS. b. Behold The strong ribb'd Barke through l. Mountaines cut SHAKS.

II. Transf. and fig. senses. 1. Of light, fire, the air: Clear, transparent, bright 1590. 2. Of sounds: Flowing, pure and clear in tone; not harsh or grating. Also in *Phonetics*, Vowel-like (see B. 2). 1637. †3. Of proofs, exposition, etc.: Clear, manifest –1726. b. Of an account or debt: Undisputed 1660. 4. Not fixed or stable. Of movement: Facile, unconstrained. 1835. 5. Of assets, securities, etc.: Promptly convertible into cash 1818.

1. They That wing the l. Air, or swim the Sea DRYDEN. 2. The l. and gurgling notes of the bobolink 1879. 4. The l. nature, so to speak, of its technical terms. They mean anything and everything DEUTSCH.

B. *sb.* 1. A liquid substance (see A. I). In *pl.* often = *liquid food.* 1708. 2. *Phonetics.* A name applied to the sounds of *l, m, n, r,* or (by some writers) only to those of *l* and *r.* Cf. F. *mouillé* lit. 'wet'. 1530.

2. It [L] melteth in the sounding, and is therefore called a l., the tongue striking the root of the palate gently B. JONS.

Hence **Li·quidless** *a.* **Li·quid·ly** *adv.*, **-ness.** **Li·quidize** *v. trans.* to make l.

Liquidambar (likwidæ·mbəɹ). Also **liquid amber.** 1598. [a. mod.L. *liquidambar*, app. irreg. f. L. *liquidus* + med.L. *ambar* AMBER.] 1. A resinous gum which exudes from the bark of the tree *Liquidambar styraciflua.* Called also *copalm balsam.* 2. *Bot.* A genus of trees, N.O. *Hamamelideæ*, consisting of two species, *L. orientalis* of Asia Minor (which yields the balsam liquid storax), and *L. styraciflua*, the Sweet-gum tree of N. America; a tree of this genus 1843.

Li·quidate, *pa. pple.* and *ppl. a.* *Law.* 1574. [ad. late L. *liquidatus* (see next).] Ascertained and fixed in amount.

Liquidate (li·kwide¹t), *v.* 1575. [f. late L. *liquidat-, liquidare*, f. *liquidus.*] †1. *trans.* To make clear or plain; to render unambiguous; to settle (differences, etc.) –1780. b. To clear away (objections). *rare.* 1620. 2. To determine and apportion by agreement or by litigation; to set out clearly (accounts). Now *U.S.* 3. To clear off, pay (a debt). Also *absol.* in *U.S. slang.* 1755. 4. *Law* and *Comm.* a. *trans.* To ascertain and set out clearly the liabilities of (a company or firm) and to apportion the assets; to wind up. b. *intr.* To go into liquidation. 1870. 5. *trans.* To make liquid (*rare*) 1656.

1. Ere we l. our differences by the sword H. WALPOLE. 2. Agreed to pay the debt on its being liquidated 1798. 3. To l. the National Debt 1834. Hence **Li·quidator**, a person appointed to wind up a company.

Liquidation (likwidē¹·ʃən). 1575. [See prec.] 1. *Law.* The action or process of ascertaining and apportioning the amounts of a debt, etc. 2. The clearing off or settling (of a debt) 1786. 3. The action or process of winding up a company; the state or condition of being wound up; *esp.* in phr. *to go into l.* 1869. 4. *U.S. slang.* The taking of liquid refreshment. 1889.

2. The l. of Debt is a national duty LUBBOCK.

Liquidity (likwi·dĭti). 1620. [ad. L. *liquiditatem*, f. *liquidus* LIQUID; see -ITY.] The quality or condition of being liquid.

Liquor (li·kəɹ), *sb.* [ME. *licur(e, likour,* etc., a. OF. *licur, licour, likeur* (mod.F. *liqueur*), a. L. *liquor*; cf. LIQUATE, LIQUID. Assim. to the L. wd. in spelling, without change of pronunciation.] †1. A liquid; matter in a liquid state; *occas.* a fluid –1701. b. The liquid constituent of a secretion or the like; the liquid product of a chemical operation 1565. 2. A prepared solution used as a wash or bath, and in industrial processes, e.g. in *Tanning* 1583. b. *Brewing.* Water 1691. 3. Liquid for drinking. Now usu. *spec.* a drink produced by fermentation or distillation. ME. Also *fig.* b. *slang.* (Chiefly *U.S.*) A drink (of an intoxicating beverage). Also, *a liquor-up.* 1860. 4. The water in which meat has been boiled; the fat in which bacon, fish, etc. has been fried; the liquid contained in oysters ME. 5. The liquid produced by infusion (in testing tea) 1870. ‖6. The L. word, pronounced ləi·kwǫɹ and li·kwǫɹ, used (*a*) in *Pharmacy* and *Med.* in the names of solutions of specified medicinal substances in water; (*b*) in *Physiol.*, as *l. sanguinis*, the blood-plasma, etc. 1796.

1. b. Phr. *L. of flints* = *liquor silicum* (see below); *l. of the Hollanders*, the chloride of olefiant gas; *l. of Libavius*, bichloride of tin. 3. Neither shal he drinke any l. of grapes *Num.* vi. 3. *Malt l. Spirituous l. Vinous l.* Phr. *Disguised with l.* *To be* (*the*) *worse for l.*: to be overcome by drink. 6. (*a*) *Liquor ammoniæ*, strong solution of ammonia. *Liquor potassæ*, an aqueous solution of hydrate of potash. *Liquor silicum*, soluble glass. (*b*) *Liquor amnii*, the fluid contained in the sac of the amnion.

Comb.: **l.-pump**, a portable pump for emptying casks, etc.; **-thief**, a tube which is let down through the bung-hole of a cask in sampling spirits.

Liquor (li·kəɹ), *v.* 1502. [f. LIQUOR *sb.*] 1. *trans.* To cover or smear with a liquor; *esp.* to lubricate with grease or oil 1573. 2. *esp.* To dress (leather, boots, etc.) with oil or grease 1502. 3. To steep in or soak with a liquor; to steep (malt) in water 1743. 4. To supply with liquor to drink; to ply with liquor. Also *to l. up.* Now *slang.* 1560. 5. *intr.* (*slang.*) To drink alcoholic liquor. Also *to l. up.* 1839.

2. They would melt mee out of my fat drop by drop, and l. Fishermen's boots with me SHAKS.

Liquorice, licorice (li·kŏris). [ME. *licorys*, a. AF. *lycorys*, OF. **licorice*, ad. late L. *liquiritia*, corruptly a. Gr. γλυκύρριζα, f. γλυκύς sweet + ῥίζα root. Mod.F. *réglisse* is a metathetic form of the late L. wd.] 1. The rhizome (also called *liquorice-root*) of the plant *Glycyrrhiza glabra.* Also, a black substance (used medicinally and as a sweetmeat) prepared from the evaporated juice of this; also called *Spanish l., Spanish juice*, etc. 2. The plant itself. Also other species, esp. *G. echinata.* 1548. 3. With qualification, used of plants the roots of which resemble or are used as substitutes for the true liquorice, as *mountain, wild l.*, etc. 1548.

3. L., Wild, *Astragalus*; *Caperaria*; *Glycine* J. LEE. Wild L., *Abrus*; also an American name for *Galium circæzans* (Treas. Bot.).

Comb.: **l. vetch**, *Astragalus glycyphyllus*; **l. weed**, a tropical plant, *Scoparia dulcis.*

Liquorish (li·kəriʃ), *a.* 1789. [f. LIQUOR *sb.* + -ISH[1]. A sense-perversion of LICKERISH.] Fond of or indicating fondness for liquor. Hence **Li·quorish·ly** *adv.*, **-ness.**

Liquorist (li·kərist). 1839. [a. F. *liquoriste.*] A maker of liqueurs.

‖**Lira** (lī·ră). *Pl.* ‖**lire** (lī·re), *rarely* **liras.** 1617. [It. *lira*, contr. f. L. *libra* pound, see LIBRA.] An Italian silver coin, the unit of monetary value in Italy: equal in value to the French franc, and containing 100 centesimi.

Lire (ləiəɹ). *Obs.* exc. *Sc.* and *n. dial.* [OE. *līra* wk. masc.; etym. unkn.] Flesh, muscle, brawn. Hence **Li·ry** *a.* fleshy.

‖**Lirella** (lire·lă). 1839. [mod.L., = F. *lirelle*, dim. f. L. *lira* furrow.] *Bot.* The narrow shield or apothecium, with a furrow along the middle, found in some lichens. Hence **Lire·lliform** *a.* shaped like a l.

Li·ripipe, li·ripoop. *Obs.* exc. *Hist.* 1546. [ad. med.L. *liripipium, leropipium*, variously explained as 'tippet of a hood', 'cord', 'shoe-lace', etc. Etym. unkn.] 1. In early academical costume: The long tail of a graduate's hood 1737. †2. One's 'lesson', 'rôle', or 'part'; chiefly in phr. *to know* or *have* (one's) *liripoop, to teach* (a person) *his l.* –1633. †3. A silly person –17..

Lis (līs). *Pl.* **lis, lisses.** 1611. [a. F. *lis* lily.] *Her.* = FLEUR-DE-LIS 2.

Lisbon (li·zbən). 1767. [The capital of Portugal.] a. A white wine of the province of Estremadura. b. Clayed sugar. c. A kind of lemon 1897.

Lisle (ləil). 1851. Name of a French town (now *Lille*): *attrib.* in *L. glove*, a fine thread glove for summer wear; *L. thread*, a hard twisted cotton thread, orig. made at L.; etc.

Lisp (lisp), *sb.* 1625. [f. LISP *v.*] The action or an act of lisping; *transf.* rippling of water, rustling of leaves, etc.

A young lady of sixty-five..with an engaging l. DICKENS.

Lisp (lisp), *v.* Pa. t. and pple. **lisped** (lispt). [OE. **wlispian* (only in comb.), f. *wlisp, wlips* adj., lisping.] 1. *intr.* To substitute for s and z sounds approaching þ and ð in speaking; either from a defect in the organs of speech or as an affectation. Also, *loosely*, to speak with childlike utterance. 2. *trans.* To utter with a lisp (also with *out*); to utter with childlike, imperfect, or faltering articulation (also *fig.*) 1620.

1. He can carue too, and lispe SHAKS. As little children l., and tell of Heaven KEBLE. 2. To l. mysteries to those that would be deterred by any other way of expressing them BOYLE. *fig.* The light wave lisps 'Greece' BROWNING. Hence **Li·sper. Li·spingly** *adv.*

Lispound (li·spaund). 1502. [ad. MLG. *lispunt* = *livsch punt* 'Livonian pound'.] A unit of weight (12 to 30 lb.) used in the Baltic trade, and in Orkney and Shetland.

†**Liss.** [OE. *līðs, līss*, f. *līðe* gentle, soft, LITHE *a.*] 1. Release; mitigation; hence, cessation -1802. 2. Tranquillity, peace, rest; joy -ME.

Lissom (li·səm), *a.* Also **lissome.** 1800. [Contr. var. of LITHESOME.] Supple, limber; agile; lithesome.

Straight, but as lissome as a hazel wand TENNYSON. Hence **Li·ssomness.**

†**List**, *sb.*[1] [OE. *hlyst* masc. and fem.:—OTeut. **hlusti-z* :—OAryan **klusti-s*, f. root **klus-* (: *kleus-* : *klous-*), extended form of **klu-* (Teut. **hlū-*); see LOUD *a.*] 1. Hearing; the sense of hearing -ME. 2. The ear -1535.

List (list), *sb.*[2] [OE. *liste* wk. fem.; cf. Ger. *leiste.*]

I. Border, edging, strip. †1. *gen.* A border, hem, bordering strip -1696. †b. Applied to the lobe of the ear -1631. 2. *spec.* The selvage or border of a cloth, usu. of different material from the body. Also *fig.* ME. b. Such selvages collectively; the material of which the selvage of cloth consists 1567. c. *attrib.* (quasi-*adj.*) = Made of list, as *l. slippers*, etc. 1661. 3. A strip of cloth or other fabric ME. 4. A band or strip of any material; a line or band conspicuously marked on a surface. ? *Obs.* ME. b. One of the divisions of a head of hair, of a beard. [Cf. It. *lista.*] 1859. 5. A stripe of colour. 1496. 6. *Arch.* A small square moulding or ring encircling the foot of a column, between the torus below and the shaft above. Cf. LISTEL. 1663. 7. *Carpentry.* a. The upper rail of a railing. b. *Carpentry.* A strip cut from the edge of a plank. 8. *Tin-plating.* The wire of tin left on the under edge of a tinned plate, and removed by plunging the plate into the list-pot. 1688.

II. Boundary. †1. A limit, boundary. Often *pl.* -1645. 2. *spec.* in *pl.* The palisades or other barriers enclosing a space set apart for tilting; *hence*, a space so enclosed in which tournaments, etc. were held. Occas., the arena in which bulls fight or wrestlers contend, etc. ME. b. *transf.* and *fig.* A place of combat or contest. Phr. *To enter (the) lists.* 1579. †3. a. *sing.* and *pl.* A railed or staked enclosure. b. *pl.* The starting-place of a race (= L. *carceres*). Also *sing.* A race-course or exercising ground for horses. -1737.

1. I am bound to your Neece sir: I meane she is the l. of my voyage SHAKS. 2. Cambalo That faught in listes with the bretheren two For Canacee CHAUCER. When the Lists set wide, Gave room to the fierce Bulls DRYDEN. b. See, Chloris, how the clouds Tilt in the azure lists DRUMM. OF HAWTH.

Comb. **l.-pot**, a cast-iron trough containing a small quantity of melted tin, in which the tinned plates are plunged to remove the l. (sense I. 7 c).

List (list), *sb.*[3] ME. [f. LIST *v.*[1]] †1. Pleasure, joy, delight -1573. 2. Appetite, craving; desire; inclination. *arch.* ME. 3. (One's) desire or wish; (one's) good pleasure. Phr. *at (one's) l. arch.* ME.

2. I had little l. or leisure to write FULLER.

List (list), *sb.*[4] †Also (*Naut.*) **lust.** 1633. [? use of prec.] 1. *Naut.* The careening or inclination of a ship to one side. 2. *transf.* A leaning over (of a building, etc.) 1793.

1. The cargo shifted giving the ship a l. to port 1881.

List (list), *sb.*[5] 1602. [a. F. *liste*; prob. same as LIST *sb.*[2] 'strip' (e. g. of paper).] A catalogue or roll of names, figures, words, or the like. In early use, *esp.* a catalogue of the names of persons having the same duties; *spec.* a catalogue of the soldiers of an army or of a particular arm. b. *Racing slang.* Short for: The list of geldings in training. Hence *to put on the l.* = to castrate. 1890.

Active l., a l. of officers in the army or navy liable to be called upon for active service. *Free l.*, (*a*) a l. of persons admitted free to a theatre, etc.; (*b*) a l. of articles which are duty-free. *Army-l.*, CIVIL LIST, *retired l.*, *sick-l.*, etc. (see the first wds.).

List (list), *v.*[1] *arch.* [OE. *lystan* :—OTeut. **lustjan*, f. **lustuz* pleasure; see LUST *sb.*] 1. *impers. trans.* To be pleasing to: *Me list* (occas. *listeth*): I please, like, care, or desire. 2. With *personal* construction: To desire, like, wish, choose (with or without dependent inf.) ME. †3. *trans.* To desire or wish for (something) -1587.

1. The lestyth nat a louere be CHAUCER. To do as me listeth with myne awne TINDALE *Matt.* xx. 15. 2. If we l. to speake *Haml.* I. v. 177. The winde bloweth where it listeth *John* iii. 8.

List (list), *v.*[2] *arch.* [OE. *hlystan*, f. *hlyst* LIST *sb.*[1]] = LISTEN *v.* 1, 2.

L., l., I hear Som far off hallow break the silent Air MILT. *Comus* 480. Wilt then l. to me? COWPER. I l. no more the tuck of drum SCOTT.

List (list), *v.*[3] ME. [f. LIST *sb.*[2]; cf. OF. *lister* to put a list on (cloth); G. *leisten*, Du. *lijsten.*] †1. *trans.* To put a list, border, or edge round (an object); to border, edge. Also, to put as a list *upon.* -1703. b. To fix list upon the edge of (a door) 1860. †2. To enclose; to rail *in* -1565. †b. To bound. HOOKER. 3. *Carpentry.* To cut away the sappy edge of a board; to shape a block or stave by chopping 1635.

1. A Danish curtaxe, listed with gold or silver MILT. b. Monsieur Leclerc..listed the doors against approaching winter breezes 1881.

List (list), *v.*[4] 1614. [f. LIST *sb.*[5] In senses 3 and 4, now aphet. f. *enlist*, and often written *'list.*] 1. *trans.* To set down in a list; to catalogue, register. b. To set down in a special or official list (e. g. of cases for trial, of stocks, etc.) 1702. †2. To comprise in a list or catalogue; to enrol; to put in the same category *with* -1777. 3. To appoint formally (an officer); also in *pass.* to be appointed or gazetted as (captain, etc.). Later, only = ENLIST *v.* 1 1643. Also *transf.* and *fig.* 4. *refl.* and *intr.* (for *refl.*) = ENLIST *v.* 3. Phr. *To l. (oneself) a soldier* or *for a soldier.* 1643. Also *transf.* and *fig.*

1. About one hundred species of butterflies have been listed 1887. 3. He listed me when I was out of my senses SOUTHEY. *fig.* He that is born, is listed; life is war YOUNG. 4. He listed at last for a sodger STEVENSON. *transf.* Merely that they [M.P.'s] may l. under party banners STEPHEN.

List (list), *v.*[5] 1626. [f. LIST *sb.*[4]] *intr.* Of a ship: To careen, heel, or incline to one side. Also with *off.*

She listed to port and filled rapidly 1885.

Listel (li·stĕl). 1598. [a. F. *listel*, ad. It. *listello* (also used), dim. of *lista* = LIST *sb.*[2]] *Arch.* A small list or fillet.

Listen (li·s'n), *sb.* 1803. [f. next.] The action or an act of listening; a spell of listening. Chiefly in phr. *On* or *upon the l.*

Listen (li·s'n), *v.* [ONorthumb. *lysna*, f. (ult.) Teut. root **hlus-*; see LIST *sb.*[1] Cf. OE. *hlosnian*, from the same root.] 1. *trans.* To hear attentively; to give ear to; to pay attention to. Now *arch.* or *poet.* 2. *intr.* To make an effort to hear something; to give ear ME.

1. At which I ceas't, and listen'd them a while MILT. 2. They will be sure to l. if they find that you are a good speaker JOWETT. *To l. to (unto)*: to give ear to (= sense 1); also, to allow oneself to be persuaded by. List'n not to his Temptations MILT. *To l. for, †after*: to be eager or make an effort to catch the sound of. *To l. in*: to listen to concert performances, news, etc. transmitted by wireless. Hence **Li·stener**, one who listens; an attentive hearer. **Li·stening** *vbl. sb.*; *spec.* in **Listening gallery** *Fortif.*, a gallery run out under and beyond the glacis in the direction of the besiegers' works, to enable the besieged to hear and estimate the distance the besiegers have mined.

†**Lister**[1]. ME. [a. OF. *listre*, altered f. *litre* :—L. *lector* (see LECTOR).] A reader or lector -1555.

Lister[2] (li·stəɹ). 1678. [f. LIST *v.*[4] + -ER[1].] 1. An enlister. 2. One who makes out a list, *spec.* (*U.S.*) of taxable property.

Lister, var. of LEISTER.

Listerian (listī·riăn), *a.* 1880. Applied to the system of antiseptic surgery invented by Lord Lister. So **Listerine** (li·sterin), a proprietary antiseptic solution named after Lister 1889. **Li·sterism**, the system of antiseptic surgery originated by Lister 1880. **Li·sterize** *v.* to treat on Listerian methods 1902.

Listful (li·stfŭl), *a. arch.* 1595. [f. LIST *v.*[2] + -FUL.] Inclined to listen, attentive.

Listing (li·stiŋ), *sb.* ME. [f. LIST *sb.*[2] + -ING[1].] 1. Selvage; the material of which the list of cloth is composed. 2. *Naut.* A narrow strip cut out off the edge of a plank to show its condition, or in order to put in a new piece 1846. *Comb.* **l.-pot** = *list-pot*: see LIST *sb.*[2]

Listless (li·stlĕs), *a.* 1440. [f. LIST *sb.*[3] + -LESS.] †a. Destitute of relish or inclination for some object or pursuit; const. *of.* b. Unwilling to move, act, or make any exertion; languid, indifferent.

b. A dull discourse naturally produces a l. audience 1766. Hence **Li·stless-ly** *adv.*, **-ness.**

Lit, *sb. Obs.* exc. *dial.* [late OE., a. ON. *litr.*] Dye, dye-stuff. Hence **Lit** *v.*, to dye.

Lit (lit), *ppl. a.* 1820. [pa. pple. of LIGHT *v.*[2]] Lighted, illumined; also with *up.* (Also in *comb.*, as *sun-lit.*)

Lit, pa. t. of LIGHT *v.*[1] and [2].

Litany (li·tăni). ME. [ad. med.L. *litanīa*, *letanīa*, a. Gr. λιτανεία prayer, f. λιτανεύειν, f. λιτανός suppliant, f. λιτή supplication.] 1. *Eccl.* A form of public prayer, usually penitential, consisting of a series of petitions, in which the clergy lead and the people respond. A litany may be used either as part of a service or by itself, in the latter case often in procession. b. *The L.*: that form of 'general supplication' appointed for use in the Book of Common Prayer 1544. 2. *transf.* A form of supplication resembling a litany; also, a continuous repetition or long enumeration resembling those of litanies ME.

1. *attrib.*, as *l. desk.* 2. Lord deliver me from my self, is a part of my Letany SIR T. BROWNE. Hear them mumble Their l. of curses SHELLEY.

Litarge, -y, obs. ff. LITHARGE.

Litchi (lī·tʃī). 1588. [Chinese *li-chi.*] The fruit of the *Nephelium litchi* (N.O. *Sapindaceæ*), a tree introduced from China into Bengal.

Lite, *sb.*, *a.*, and *adv. Obs.* exc. *arch.* or *dial.* [Partly repr. OE. *lȳt* sb., adj., adv., and partly ON. *lítt* adv., contr. of *lítet*, neut. of *lítell*; see LITTLE.] A. *sb.* 1. Little, not much. 2. Few OE. B. *adj.* (Uninflected in OE.) 1. Few OE. 2. Little in amount ME. 3. Small ME. C. *adv.* Little: in a small degree OE.

-lite (= F. *-lite*, G. *-lith*, *-lit*), ending of names of minerals, repr. Gr. λίθος stone. The form *-lite*, instead of -LITH, is due to the example of the French geologists.

Liter, var. of LITRE.

Literacy (li·tĕrăsi). 1883. [f. LITERATE; see -ACY.] Quality or state of being literate.

‖**Literæ humaniores** (li·tərī hiumēniō·rīz). 1747. See HUMANE *a.* 2, LETTER *sb.*[1] II. 4; *spec.* the name of a School in the University of Oxford. (Abbrev. *Lit. Hum.*)

Literal (li·tĕrăl). ME. [a. OF. *literal* (F. *littéral*), ad. L. *litteralis*, f. *littera* LETTER *sb.*] A. *adj.* 1. Of or pertaining to letters of the alphabet; of or the nature of letters; expressed by letters. †Of a verse: ALLITERATIVE. b. Of a misprint, etc.: Affecting a letter 1606. 2. Of a translation, version, transcript, etc.: Representing the very words of the original; verbally exact 1599. 3. a. *Theol.* Pertaining to the 'letter' (of Scripture); in interpretation, applied to taking the words of a text, etc., in their natural and customary meaning, and using the ordinary rules of grammar; opp. to *mystical, allegorical*, etc. †Also *occas.* of a law, etc.: That is to be interpreted literally. ME. **b.** Hence, applied to taking words in their etymological or primary sense, or in the sense expressed by the actual wording of a passage, without recourse to any metaphorical or suggested meaning 1597. **c.** Of persons: Prosaic, matter-of-fact 1778. **4.** Used to denote that the accompanying sb. has its literal sense, without metaphor, exaggeration, or inaccuracy; literally so called 1646. †**5.** Epistolary –1657. †**6.** = LITERARY –1604.

1. The art of expressing their thoughts by l. characters 1733. The l. notation of numbers JOHNSON. b. 'Twas a l. fault in that Copy, which Casaubon used BENTLEY. 2. The common way..is not a l. Translation, but a kind of Paraphrase DRYDEN. 3. a. Where a litterall construction will stand, the farthest from the letter is commonly the worst HOOKER. b. I see very few people; and, in the l. sense of the word, I hear nothing CHESTERF.

B. *sb.* †**1.** A literal interpretation or meaning –1646. **2.** *Printing.* A literal misprint 1622.

Hence **Li·teralness,** quality of being l.

Literalism (li·tĕrăliz'm). 1644. [f. prec. + -ISM.] **1.** The disposition to take and interpret words in their literal sense. **2.** A peculiarity of expression due to literality (*mod.*). **3.** *Fine Arts.* The disposition to represent objects or interpret representations faithfully, without idealization 1863. So **Li·teralist,** one who adheres to the letter of a text or statement. Also, in art and literature, an exact copyist. **Literali·stic** *a.* pertaining to or characteristic of a literalist; having the character of l.

Literality (litĕræ·lĭti). 1643. [f. LITERAL + -ITY.] The quality or fact of being literal; literalness. †Also, a literal meaning.

Literalize (li·tĕrăləiz), *v.* 1826. [f. LITERAL + -IZE.] *trans* To represent or accept as literal.

To l. poetical allegory 1827, metaphors 1856. Hence **Literaliza·tion, Li·teralizer.**

Literally (li·tĕrăli), *adv.* 1533. [f. LITERAL + -LY [2].] **1.** In the very words, word for word. Also *transf.* 1646. **2.** In the literal sense 1533. **b.** Used to indicate that the following word or phrase must be taken in its literal (now often *erron.*, in its strongest admissible) sense 1687.

1. Which are l. thus translated SIR T. BROWNE. 2. It is found that the Act does not mean l. what it says 1895. b. The singular fate of dying l. of hunger HUME. Literally worn to a shadow 1825. For the last four years..I l. coined money 1863.

Literary (li·tĕrări), *a.* 1646. [ad. L. *litterarius*, f. *littera* letter.] †**1.** Pertaining to the letters of the alphabet –1793. †**2.** Carried on by letters; epistolary. SMOLLETT. **3.** Of or pertaining to, or of the nature of, literature, polite learning, or books and written compositions; pertaining to that kind of written composition which has value on account of its qualities of form 1749. **4.** Versed in literature; *spec.* engaged in literature as a profession. Of a society, etc.: Consisting of literary men. 1791.

3. *L. history* (e.g. of a legend, an event, etc.): the history of the treatment of, and references to, the subject in literature. *L. property*: (*a*) property which consists in written or printed compositions; (*b*) the exclusive right of publication as recognized and limited by law. A man of l. merit GOLDSM. A l. reputation JOHNSON, conflict MACAULAY. Hence **Li·terarily** *adv.* **Li·terariness. Li·teraryism,** addiction to l. forms; an instance of this.

‖**Literata** (litĕrē̆·tă). *Pl.* **-tæ.** [L. fem. of *litteratus*: see next.] A learned or literary lady. COLERIDGE.

Literate (li·tĕrĕt). ME. [ad. L. *litteratus*, f. *littera.*] **A.** *adj.* **1.** Acquainted with letters; educated, learned. In early use, const. *in.* **2.** Literary 1648.

1. A polite and l. Court CHESTERF. 2. To beguile, ..with some l. diversion, the tedious length of those days 1651. Hence †**Literated** *a.* learned.

B. *sb.* **1.** A liberally educated or learned person 1550. **2.** *spec.* In the Church of England, one admitted to holy orders without having a university degree 1824. **3.** One who can read and write. Opp. to *illiterate.* 1894.

1. Callista was a Greek; a l., or blue-stocking J. H. NEWMAN.

‖**Literati** (litĕrē̆·təi), *sb. pl.* Also †**litterati.** 1621. [L.: see LITERATE.] Men of letters; the learned class as a whole.

To be..examined & approued as the l. in China BURTON.

‖**Literatim** (litĕrē̆·tim), *adv.* 1643. [med.L. *lit(t)eratim*, f. L. *littera* LETTER.] Letter for letter; literally.

Literation (litĕrē̆·ʃən). [f. L. *littera* + -ATION.] The action or process of representing (sounds or words) by letters. (Mod. Dicts.)

‖**Literato** (litĕră·to). 1704. [It. *litterato*, ad. L. *litteratus.*] One of the literati; a man of letters; a learned man.

Literator (li·tĕrē̆tǫ̆ɹ). 1635. [a. L. *lit(t)erator*, f. *littera.*] †**1.** A pretender to learning, a sciolist –1641. **2.** A literary man; = LITTERATEUR 1791. **3.** †A bibliographer. Also, a grammarian, critic (*rare*) 1727.

2. [French] preceptors..a set of pert petulant literators BURKE.

Literature (li·tĕrătiŭɹ). ME. [ad. (? through F.) L. *litteratura*, f. *littera* a letter.] **1.** Acquaintance with 'letters' or books; literary culture. Now *rare* or *obsol.* **2.** Literary work or production; the activity or profession of a man of letters; the realm of letters 1779. **3.** Literary productions as a whole; the writings of a country or period, or of the world in general. Now also, less widely, writings esteemed for beauty of form or emotional effect. 1812. **b.** The body of books, etc. that treat of a subject 1860. **c.** *colloq.* Any printed matter 1895.

1. Another person of infinite l. [Selden] 1693. 2. L., the most seductive, the most deceiving, the most dangerous of professions MORLEY. 3. Their l., their works of art offer models that have never been excelled SIR H. DAVY. *Light l.*: see LIGHT *a.*[1] V. 3.

‖**Literatus** (litĕrē̆·tǫ̆s). *rare.* 1704. [L. *lit(t)eratus.*] One of the LITERATI.

Our bright ideal of a l. may chance to be married DE QUINCEY.

Lith (liþ), *sb. Obs.* exc. *arch.* or *dial.* [OE. *liþ* neut.:—OTeut. **liþu-* :—pre-Teut. **litu-* f. root **lī-*; see LIMB *sb.*[1]] **1.** A limb. **2.** A joint; freq. in *l. and limb* OE. **3.** *Sc.* A division (of an orange, etc.); one of the rings round the base of a cow's horn 1795.

Lith, obs. 3rd sing. pres. ind. of LIE.

-lith, terminal element repr. Gr. λίθος stone, used chiefly in *Biol.* and *Path.*, as *coccolith*, etc. In *Min.* -LITE is the usual form.

‖**Lithæmia** (liþī·miă). 1874. [mod.L., f. Gr. λίθος stone + αἷμα blood.] *Path.* The condition in which lithic or uric acid is in excess in the blood; formerly called *uricæmia.* Hence **Lithæ·mic** *a.*

Lithagogue (li·þăgǫg). 1844. [f. Gr. λίθος stone + ἀγωγός drawing forth.] *Path. adj.* and *sb.* (A medicine) having the power to expel calculi from the kidneys or bladder.

Lithanode (li·þănōud). 1887. [f. as prec. + ANODE.] *Electr.* A hard compact form of peroxide of lead, used in storage batteries.

Litharge (li·þāɹdʒ). ME. [a. or ad. OF. *litarge, litargire* (F. *litharge*), ad. L. *lithargyrus*, a. Gr., f. λίθος stone + ἄργυρος silver.] **1.** Monoxide of lead (PbO) prepared by exposing melted lead to a current of air. †**2.** = WHITE LEAD or RED LEAD –1800.

1. †*L. of gold*: l. when coloured red by mixture of red lead. †*L. of silver*: a name given to l. as being a by-product in the separation of silver from lead.

Lithate (li·þē̆t). 1821. [f. LITH-IC *a.*[1] + -ATE [1].] *Chem.* A salt of lithic acid.

Lithe (ləið), *a.* [OE. *līðe*, f. (ult.) Teut. and WAryan root **len-*, whence L. *lentus* slow, etc.] †**1.** Of persons, their actions, etc.: Gentle, meek –ME. **2.** Of things: Mild, soft; agreeable, mellow, pleasant. Of a medicine: Gentle in operation. *Obs.* exc. *dial.* OE. **3.** Easily bent; flexible, limber, pliant, supple. (The current sense.) ME.

3. Th' unwieldy Elephant..wreathd His L. Proboscis MILT. Hence **Li·the·ly** *adv.*, **-ness.**

†**Lithe,** *v.*[1] [OE. *līð-an*, wk. vb. f. *līðe* LITHE *a.*] *trans.* To render 'lithe', i.e. gentle or mild; to influence gently; to relax; to mitigate; to relieve; to render supple; to bend, subdue –1642.

Lithe (ləið), *v.*[2] *Obs.* exc. *arch.* and *dial.* ME. [a. ON. *hlýða*, f. *hljóð* neut., listening, sound, f. Teut. root **hleu-* to hear; see LIST *sb.*[1]] *intr.* To hearken, listen. Also, to hear *of* (a thing).

Lither (li·ðəɹ). [OE. *lýðre* :—prehist. **liuþrjo-*, the first element of MHG., G. *liederlich* lewd.] **A.** *adj.* †**1.** Of persons, etc.: Bad, wicked; base, rascally. Of an animal: Ill-tempered. –1546. †**2.** Of things: Bad (chiefly in physical senses). Of a part of the body: Withered, impotent. –1622. †**b.** Of the air: Pestilential. Only ME. **3.** Lazy, sluggish, spiritless. Now *dial.* 1460. **4.** Pliant, supple; (of the air, sky) yielding (*arch.*) 1565.

4. The l. Skie SHAKS. †**Li·ther·ly** *a.* and *adv.*, **-ness.**

†**B.** *adv.* Badly, wickedly; ill, poorly –ME.

Lithesome (ləi·ðsǫ̆m), *a.* 1768. [f. LITHE *a.* + -SOME.] = LISSOM.

Lithia [1] (li·þiă). 1818. [a. mod.L. *lithia*, altered f. *lithion*, mod.L. ad. Gr. λίθειον, neut. of λίθειος stony; after *soda, potassa.*] *Chem.* The oxide of lithium, LiO. Also *attrib.* **b.** *colloq.* Short for *lithia water* 1893.

Lithia water is..prescribed to gouty..persons 1878.

‖**Lithia** [2] (li·þiă). 1822. [mod.L., f. Gr. λίθος stone.] *Path.* The formation of sandy or stony concretions in the body, *esp.* in the Meibomian follicles of the eye. (Cf. next.)

‖**Lithiasis** (liþəi·ăsis). 1657. [mod.L., Gr. λιθίασις, f. λιθιᾶν, f. λίθος stone.] *Path.* The formation of stony concretions in the body, *esp.* in the urinary passages.

Lithic (li·þik), *a.*[1] 1797. [ad. Gr. λιθικός, f. λίθος.] **1.** *Chem.* and *Path.* Of or pertaining to 'stone' or calculi in the bladder. **2.** *gen.* Of, pertaining to, or consisting of stone 1862.

1. †*L. acid*: uric acid. The uric, or l., acid calculus 1876. 2. *L. age*, the 'stone age' of Archæology. L. ornaments J. FERGUSSON.

Lithic (li·þik), *a.*[2] 1839. [f. LITH-IUM + -IC.] *Chem.* Pertaining to lithium.

Lithiophilite (liþiǫ·filəit). 1878. [f. LITHI-UM + Gr. φίλος friend + -ITE.] *Min.* A mineral containing a large proportion of lithium.

Lithium (li·þiǫ̆m). 1818. [f. LITHIA [1]; see -IUM.] *Chem.* An alkali-metal occurring in small quantities in various minerals.

Litho (li·þo). 1890. Techn. abbrev. of LITHOGRAPH.

Litho- (liþo), bef. a vowel **lith-,** comb. f. Gr. λίθος stone; in various scientific and technical words, as **Litho·genous** [Gr. -γενής producing + -OUS] *a.*, stone-producing, applied to those animals which produce coral. **Litho·phagous** [Gr. -φάγος eating] *a.*, stone-eating, as certain molluscs which bore through stones. **Li·thophane** [Gr. -φανής appearing], a kind of ornamentation produced by impressing upon porcelain-glass in a soft state figures which are made visible by transmitted light; so **Lithopha·nic** *a.*; **Litho·phany,** the art of making this. **Li·thotint,** the art or process of printing tinted pictures from lithographic stones; a picture so printed.

Lithochromatic (li:þokromæ·tik). 1846. [f. LITHO- + Gr. χρωματ-, χρῶμα colour + -IC.] *adj.* Pertaining to lithochromatics. *sb. pl.* The art or process of applying oil colours to stone and taking impressions therefrom. So **Li·thochrome,** chromolithography 1854. **Litho·chromy,** painting on stone 1829; also, chromolithography 1885.

Lithoclast (li·þǫ̆klast). 1829. [f. LITHO- + Gr. -κλάστης breaker, f. κλᾶν to break.] †**1.** A stone-breaker. BURCKHARDT. **2.** *Surg.* An instrument for breaking up stone in the bladder 1847. Hence **Lithocla·stic** *a.*

Lithocyst (li·þǫ̆sist). 1859. [f. LITHO- + CYST.] **1.** *Zool.* One of the sacs containing mineral particles found in certain Medusæ, and supposed to be organs of hearing. **2.** *Bot.* A cell containing crystals of calcium carbonate in the leaves of certain plants. VINES.

Lithodomous (liþǫ·dŏməs), *a.* 1862. [f. mod.L. generic name *Lithodomus*, ad. Gr. λιθοδόμος mason + -OUS.] *Zool.* Boring in stone, as mussels of the genus *Lithodomus.*

Lithoglyph (li·þǫ̆glif). 1842. [f. LITHO- + Gr. γλύφειν to carve.] An incision or engraving on stone.

Lithograph (li·þǒgraf), *sb.* 1839. [f. LITHO- + -GRAPH (or from LITHOGRAPHY).] 1. A lithographic print. 2. An inscription on stone. WHITTIER.

Li·thograph, *v.* 1825. [f. as prec.] 1. *trans.* To print from stone; to produce by lithography. 2. To write or engrave on stone (*rare*) 1872. So **Litho·grapher,** †one who writes about stones 1685; one who practises lithography 1828. †**Litho·graphize** *v.*

Lithographic (liþǒgræ·fik), *a.* 1813. [f. LITHOGRAPHY + -IC.] 1. Pertaining to, employed in, or produced by lithography; engraved on or printed from stone. 2. Descriptive of stones or rocks (*rare*) 1820.

1. L. impressions from drawings 1813. L. chalk and l. ink 1839. *L. limestone, slate, stone*: a compact yellowish slaty limestone used in lithography. So **Lithogra·phical** *a.* pertaining to lithography (*rare*); lithological.

Lithography (liþǫ·grăfi). 1708. [See LITHO- and -GRAPHY.] †1. A description of stones or rocks. 2. The art or process of making a drawing, design, or writing on lithographic stone, so that impressions in ink can be taken from it 1813.

2. The process of l. consists essentially in the application of a greasy ink on to a damp stone 1879.

Lithoid (li·þoid), *a.* 1833. [ad. Gr. λιθοειδής, f. λίθος; see -OID.] Of the nature or structure of stone. So **Lithoi·dal** *a.* 1833.

Lithology (liþǫ·lŏdʒi). 1716. [See LITHO- and -LOGY.] 1. The science of the nature and composition of stones and rocks. 2. The department of medical science concerned with calculi in the human body. Also, a treatise on calculi. 1802.

Hence **Litholo·gic, -al** *a.* **Litholo·gically** *adv.* **Litho·logist,** one versed in l.

Lithomancy (li·þǒmænsi). 1646. [f. Gr. λίθος; see -MANCY.] Divination from stones.

Lithomarge (li·þǒmāɹdʒ). 1753. [ad. mod.L. *lithomarga* (also used), f. Gr. λίθος + L. *marga* marl.] *Geol.* 'An early name for several kinds of soft clay-like minerals, including kaolin' (A. H. Chester).

Lithontriptic (liþǫntri·ptik), **lithonthryptic** (-þri·ptik). 1646. [ad. F. *lithontriptique* or mod.L. *lithontripticus* (in 17th c. corrected to *-thrypticus*), repr. Gr. λίθων θρυπτικά '(drugs) comminutive of stones (in the kidneys)'. Cf. LITHOTRIPTIC.] *Med. adj.* and *sb.* (A medicine) having the property of breaking up stone in the bladder.

Lithophyte (li·þǒfəit). 1747. [f. Gr. λίθος + φυτόν plant.] 1. *Zool.* A polyp the substance of which is stony or calcareous, as some corals. 2. *Bot.* A plant growing on stone or rock 1895. **Lithophy·tic, -phy·tous** *adjs.*

Lithotome (li·þǒtoᵘm). 1758. [ad. Gr. λιθοτόμον adj. neut., stone-cutting, f. λίθος + -τομος cutting.] *Surg.* An instrument for cutting the bladder in lithotomy; prop. called a *cystotome.* Hence **Lithoto·mic, -al** *a.*

Lithotomy (liþǫ·tŏmi). 1721. [ad. late L. *lithotomia*, a. Gr., f. λίθος + -τομία cutting.] The operation, art, or process of cutting for stone in the bladder. So **Litho·tomist,** one who practises l. 1663; also, one who cuts inscriptions on stone 1713. **Litho·tomize** *v. trans.* to subject to l. 1836.

Lithotripsy (li·þǒtripsi). 1834. [f. LITHO- + Gr. τρῖψις rubbing.] The operation of rubbing down or crushing stone in the bladder. So **Lithotri·ptic** [refash. f. LITHONTRIPTIC, as if f. Gr. -τριπτικός, f. τρίβειν to rub] *a.* = LITHONTRIPTIC 1847. **Lithotri·ptor** 1847 (**lithon-** 1825) *Surg.* an instrument for lithotripsy.

Lithotritor (li·þǒtrəitǫɹ). 1828. [ad. F. *lithotriteur*, altered f. LITHOTRIPTOR, as if f. L. *tritor, terere* to rub.] *Surg.* = LITHOTRIPTOR. So **Li·thotrite,** a form of lithotriptor for crushing stone into minute particles which can be voided 1839. **Lithotri·tic** *a.* 1830. **Litho·tritist,** one who practises lithotrity 1836. **Litho·tritize** *v. trans.* to subject to lithotrity 1842. **Litho·trity,** lithotripsy, esp. by means of a lithotrite 1827.

Lithotype (li·þǒtəip), *sb.* 1875. [f. LITHO- + TYPE *sb.*] 1. A stereotype plate made with gum-shellac, sand, tar, and linseed-oil. 2. An etched stone surface for printing 1875. 3. A lithographed finger-print. CONAN DOYLE. So **Li·thotype** *v. trans.* to prepare for printing by lithotypy. **Lithoty·pic** *a.* **Litho·typy,** the process of making lithotypes (sense 1); also printing from etched stone.

Lithsman (li·þsˌmæ̆n). *Hist.* [OE. *liðsmann*, a. ON. *liðsmað-r* (accus. *-mann*), f. *liðs*, genit. of *lið* host + *maðr* MAN.] A sailor in the navy under the Danish kings of England.

Lithuanian (liþiuˌēⁱ·niăn), *a.* and *sb.* 1555. [f. *Lithuania* + -AN.] Belonging to (a native of) Lithuania, its people or language; *sb.* also, the Lithuanian language. So **Lithuanic** (liþiuˌæ·nik) 1841.

Lithy (li·ði), *a. dial.* [OE. *liðig*; cf. Du. and G. *ledig*. Etym. unkn.] Pliable, flexible, supple; soft, unresisting.

Litigable (li·tigăb'l), *a.* 1764. [See LITIGATE and -ABLE.] That may be litigated; disputable.

Litigant (li·tigănt). 1638. [ad. F. *litigant*, ad. L. *litigantem* (see next).] **A.** *adj.* Engaged in a lawsuit or in a dispute. Only in connexion with *party*. **B.** *sb.* A person engaged in a lawsuit or dispute 1659.

A. The parties l. are agreed that [etc.] CHILLINGW. B. Poverty is no bar to the l. 1885.

Litigate (li·tigeⁱt), *v.* 1615. [f. L. *litigat-*, *litigare*, f. *lit-*, *lis* lawsuit.] 1. *intr.* To be a party to a lawsuit; to go to law. Also †*gen.* to dispute. 2. *trans.* To contest at law; to plead for or against 1741. b. *gen.* To dispute, contest (a point, etc.) 1739.

2. My grandfather's estate is to be litigated with me 1748. Hence **Li·tigator,** one who litigates.

Litigation (litigēⁱ·ʃən). 1567. [ad. late L. *litigationem*; see prec.] 1. The action of carrying on a suit in law or equity; legal proceedings 1647. b. The practice of going to law 1785. 2. Disputation (now *rare*) 1567.

1. Phr. *In l.*: in process of investigation before a court of law. b. The spirit of l. TROLLOPE.

Litigious (liti·dʒəs), *a.* ME. [ad. F. *litigieux*, ad. L. *litigiosus*, f. *litigium* litigation; see -OUS.] 1. a. Fond of disputes, contentious (now *rare*). b. Fond of going to law. †2. Disputable, questionable; productive of contention -1648. b. Disputable at law; that is or is liable to become the subject of a lawsuit, esp. of a benefice 1568. 3. Of or pertaining to lawsuits 1589.

1. a. Socrates hade ii. l. and malicious wifes ME. b. They [Hindus] are very l... They will persevere in a law-suit till they are ruined ELPHINSTONE. 2. The time of his birth seemeth to him to be l. CROOKE. 3. Pleasing thoughts of l. terms, fat contentions, and flowing fees MILT. **Liti·gious-ly** *adv.*, **-ness.**

Litmus (li·tmǒs). 1502. [Altered from MDu. *leecmos*, *lijcmoes*, mod.Du. *lakmoes*, f. *lak* LAC¹ + *moes* pulp. Cf. ONorw. *litmosi.*] A blue colouring matter obtained from various lichens, esp. archil, *Roccella tinctoria.* (It is turned red by acids, and turned blue again by alkalis.) Also *attrib.*

L. blue, a blue pigment prepared from l.; **l. paper,** unsized paper stained blue with l., used as a test for acids; when reddened by an acid, it serves as a test for alkalis.

‖**Litotes** (ləi·tŏtīz, li·t-). 1657. [a. Gr. λιτότης, f. λιτός smooth, plain, small, etc.] *Rhet.* A figure, in which an affirmative is expressed by the negative of the contrary; an instance of this; e.g. *a citizen of no mean city.*

Litre (lī·təɹ, Fr. litr). Also *U.S.* **liter.** 1810. [a. F. *litre* (formed 1793); app. f. late L. *litra*, a. Gr. λίτρα pound.] The unit of capacity in the metric system, represented by a cube whose edge is the tenth of a metre, and = about 1¾ pints.

Li·tster. *Obs.* exc. *Hist.* ME. [f. LIT *v.* + -STER.] A dyer.

Litten (lit'n), *ppl. a.* 1849. [pseudo-arch. pple. of LIGHT *v.*²] Lighted; as, *red-l.*, etc.

Litter (li·təɹ), *sb.* ME. [ad. AF. *litere*, OF. *litiere*, F. *litière* :—med.L. *lectaria*, f. L. *lectus* (F. *lit*) bed.] †1. A bed -1481. b. In techn. use: A bed or substratum of various materials 1848. 2. a. A vehicle containing a couch shut in by curtains, and carried on men's shoulders or by animals. b. A framework supporting a bed or couch for transporting the sick and wounded. ME. 3. Straw, rushes, or the like, serving as bedding. †a. For human beings -1774. b. For animals. (Now also, the straw and dung together.) ME. c. Hence applied to straw, etc. †for plaster, †for thatch, or for the protection of plants 1453. 4. Odds and ends, miscellaneous rubbish; a state of untidiness; a disorderly accumulation of things lying about 1730. 5. The young brought forth at a birth 1486; also *transf.* and *fig.* (*contemptuous*) 1565; †an act of bringing forth young (said of animals only) -1794.

2. He ordeyned lyttyers for the wounded knyghtes MALORY. To keep himself close shut up in his l. 1734. 3. a. Phr. *To make l. of* (one's life): to sacrifice lavishly (= F. *faire litière de*). b. The l. of a farmyard gathered under the windows of his bed-chamber MACAULAY. 4. She was ashamed to be seen in such a pickle,.. her house was in such a l. FIELDING. 5. The l. is lyke to the syre and the damme HEYWOOD. Phr. *At a* or *one l.* Hence **Li·ttery** *a.* of or pertaining to l.; untidy.

Litter (li·təɹ), *v.* ME. [f. LITTER *sb.*] †1. *trans.* To carry in a litter. DARRELL. 2. To furnish (a horse, etc.) with litter or straw for his bed. Also *to l. down.* ME. 3. *intr.* To lie down on a bed or on litter (*rare*) 1634. 4. *trans.* To cover with litter. Also with *down.* 1700. 5. To cover as with litter, to strew *with* objects scattered in disorder. Also with *about, on, over* 1713. 6. Chiefly of animals: To bring forth (young). Also *absol.* or *intr.* 1484.

2. Tell them how they l. their Jades..in the House of God HACKET. 4. But, for his ease, well littered was the floor DRYDEN. 5. Dinner was over. The floor was littered with rushes and fragments of rolls and broken meat FROUDE. 6. Saue for the Son, that she did littour heere, A frekelld whelpe, hag-borne *Temp.* I. ii. 282.

‖**Littérateur** (literatör). 1806. [F., ad. L. *litterator*, f. *littera* letter.] A literary man, a writer of literary works. So ‖**Littératrice,** a literary woman, an authoress.

Little (li·t'l), *a.*, *adv.*, and *sb.* [OE. *lýtel*, *lytel* :—WGer. **luttilo-*, f. **lūt-* (prob. f. root of OE. *lútan* to bow down: see LOUT *v.*¹) represented in OE. *lýt*, *lyt*, etc.] **A.** *adj.* The opposite of *great* or *much.* Compar. LESS, LESSER; superl. LEAST. (In certain uses the adj. has no recognized mode of comparison; for these a synonym (as *smaller, smallest*) is used, or occas. the dial. or illiterate *littler*, *littlest.*)

I. Opp. to *great.* Often synonymous with *small*, but capable of emotional implications, which *small* is not. In mod. Eng. usu. in antithesis to *great* or *big*, not to *large.* 1. Small in size, not large or big; (of persons) short in stature. b. Used to designate the smaller or smallest of two or more species, countries, places, things, etc. bearing the same name ME. 2. Used *spec.* of young children or animals OE. 3. Used with an implication of endearment or depreciation, or of tender feeling on the part of the speaker 1567. 4. Of collective unities: Small in number OE. 5. Of immaterial things, in respect of their quantity, length in series, etc. ME. 6. Of dimension, distance, or time: Short OE.; †bare, scarcely complete (16–17th c.). 7. Of qualities, conditions, occurrences, etc.: Small in extent or degree ME. b. With sb. indicating occupation, etc.: That is such on a small scale 1440. c. Now often playful, indicating amusement on the speaker's part 1885. 8. Not important; trivial OE.; not distinguished (now *rare*) ME. 9. Paltry, contemptible; little-minded 1483.

1. My l. body is wearie of this great world SHAKS. b. L. Mouse-tail 1776. The L. Auk 1876. †*L. Britain*, Brittany. *L. Malvern. The L. Bear.* (With superl. meaning) *L. finger, toe.* 2. My l. sonne SHAKS. *L. one* (often pl.): child, young one. My wife! my l. ones! Destitute, helpless SHELLEY. *L. language*: Swift's name for the infantine dialect which he used in talk and correspondence with 'Stella'. 3. He [a dog] had the dearest l. ways (*mod.*). Bless your l. heart! (*mod.*). 4. Our Court shall be a l. Achademe SHAKS. What l. town by river or sea shore..Is emptied of this folk, this pious morn? KEATS. 5. I said thou hadst a fine wit: true saies she, a fine l. one SHAKS. 6. Our l. life Is rounded with a sleepe SHAKS. A l. half league broad 1697. 7. Where l. feares grow great, great loue growes there SHAKS. b. A much larger capital than any l.

farmer can possess A. YOUNG. **c.** So this is your l. game (*mod.*). I understand his l. ways (*mod.*). **8.** Constant attention in the littlest things DICKENS. No patronising condescension to l. people LYTTON. **9.** The l. cunning of l. minds COWDEN CLARKE.

II. Opp. to *much*. **1.** Not much; barely any. (Often *but l.* Also in phr. *l. or no* . . .) OE. **2.** *A l.*: a small quantity of; some, though not much. Prob. orig. *a l. of* (see B. II. 1 b), with ellipsis of *of*. †**b.** *Rarely* without *a* in this sense (SHAKS.). †**3.** With pl. and collect. sing.: = FEW -1660.

1. I haue l. wealth to loose SHAKS. God help me for my l. wit! WORDSW. 2. A litul stale ale 1450. A l. learning is a dang'rous thing POPE. **b.** O do not sweare, Hold l. faith, though thou hast too much feare *Twel. N.* v. i. 174.

Phr. **L. Englander,** one who advocates a 'little England', that is, desires to restrict the dimensions of the Empire. So **L. Englandism. L. giant,** 'a jointed iron nozzle used in hydraulic mining' (Raymond). **L. hours,** the 'hours' of prime, terce, sext, and none (F. *les petites heures*). **L. people,** fairies.

Comb.: **l.-endian** *a.* and *sb.*, the designation of the orthodox party in Lilliput on the question at which end an egg should be opened (Swift *Gulliver* iv); hence *allusively*; **-thrift,** a wastrel.

B. *absol.* and *sb.*

I. The adj. used *absol.* **1.** Chiefly with *the*: Those that are little OE. **2.** *The l.*: that which is little; the little qualities, aspects, etc. 1791. **3.** Not much; only a small amount: often *but l., very, rather l.* ME.

1. They came all to mete her, litle & greate COVERDALE *Judith* xiii. 13. 2. The great and l. of thy lot COWPER. 3. *L. or nothing*: hardly anything. *To make l. of* or *set l. by*, etc.: see the vbs. Man wants but l. here below, Nor wants that l. long GOLDSM. Of political sagacity he had very l. (*mod.*). The l. of his poems which remains GROTE.

II. *sb.* (With *a* or in *pl.*) **1.** A small quantity, piece, portion; a small thing; a trifle ME. **b.** Const. *of*. (In early use with *genitive*.) OE. **c.** Used advb.: To a slight extent; in a small degree; somewhat, rather ME. **2.** A short time or distance OE. **b.** Used *advb.* For or at a short time or distance ME. †**3.** *But a l.* = 'but little' (see I. 3) -1628.

1. When a man's being shaved, what a l. will make him laugh D. JERROLD. **b.** Let me recommend you a l. of this pike DISRAELI. **c.** *Not a l.*: a good deal, extremely. We are not a l. hungry, I can tell you MARRYAT. 2. Phr. *After a l., for a l., in a l.* We will go for a l. into the garden 1881. **b.** A l. onward lend thy guiding hand To these dark steps, a l. further on MILT. 3. *Tam. Shr.* I. ii. 61.

Phrases, chiefly with repetition of *little*, having the sense: By small degrees; a little at a time; gradually. **a.** *By l. and l.* †**b.** *L. and l.* **c.** *L. by l.* Also *In l.*: on a small scale; formerly esp. with reference to *Painting* = in miniature.

C. *adv.* **1.** To only a small extent; not much, not very OE. **b.** When preceding and qualifying the vbs. *know, think, care,* and the like, *little* becomes an emphatic negative, as in *he l. knows* = 'he is very far from knowing' ME. †**2.** A little time (before); for a little time -1604.

1. They liked us as l. as they did one another ADDISON. **b.** They l. know How dearly I abide that boast so vaine MILT. *P. L.* IV. 86.

†**Li·ttle,** *v.* [OE. *lӯtlian*, f. *lӯtel* LITTLE *a.*] To make or become little -1642.

Little-ease. Now *Hist.* or *arch.* 1529. A place of little ease for him who occupies it; *spec.* the name of a dungeon in the Tower of London, etc. Also, the pillory, stocks.

Worthy to be cast in bocardo or lytle ease LATIMER.

Little-go. 1795. [f. LITTLE *a.* + GO *sb.* Cf. GREAT-GO.] **1.** A private and illegal lottery. Now *Hist.* **2.** *Univ. colloq.* The popular name (still current at Cambridge) for the first examination for the B.A. degree 1820.

Little man. ME. **1.** The little finger. *Obs.* exc. *dial.* **2.** A small landowner or capitalist 1811. **3.** *pl.* Fairies, 'little folk' 1850.

Little master. ME. †**1.** A sub-master. WYCLIF. **2.** *pl.* A group of 16th c. German engravers, followers of Dürer, so called from the smallness of their prints 1837. **3.** A manufacturer in a small way of business, who works as a journeyman 1870.

Littleness (li·t'lnės). [OE. *lӯtelnes*; see LITTLE *a.* and -NESS.] The attribute of being little (see LITTLE *a.*). Also with *a* and *pl.*

I confess, I love L. almost in all things, A little convenient Estate, a little chearful House, a little Company, and a very little Feast COWLEY. L. of soul 1779. Vainglorious littlenesses H. WALPOLE.

Little-worth, *a.* (*sb.*) Now *arch.* and *Sc.* ME. Of little worth; esp. *Sc.* = of worthless character.

Littoral (li·tŏrăl). Also **litoral.** 1656. [ad. L. *littoralis*, better *litoralis*, f. *litor-*, *litus* (often *littus*) shore.] **A.** *adj.* Of or pertaining to the shore; existing, taking place upon, or adjacent to the shore. **b.** *Zool., Geol.*, etc.: Growing, living, or deposited on the 'littoral zone' (see quot. 1876) 1661.

The l. extent of Italy 1869. **b.** The Littoral [zone] lies between high and low water mark 1876.

B. *sb.* A littoral district; the region lying along the shore. [After It. *littorale*, F. *littoral*.] 1828.

The towns along the Mediterranean l. 1859.

Liturgic (litɒ·ɹdʒik). 1656. [ad. late L. *liturgicus*, a. Gr. λειτουργικός, f. λειτουργός; see LITURGY.] **A.** *adj.* = LITURGICAL. **b.** *Gr. Antiq.* (Cf. LITURGY 3.) 1849. **B.** *sb. pl.* †**1.** ? Liturgical books. BARROW. **2. a.** The study of liturgies, their form, origin, etc. **b.** That part of pastoral theology which deals with the conduct of public worship. 1855.

Liturgical (litɒ·ɹdʒikăl), *a.* 1641. [f. as prec. + -AL.] Pertaining to or connected with public worship; having to do with liturgies, or *spec.* with the Liturgy or Eucharistic service. Also, pertaining to liturgics.

L. day: a day on which mass was celebrated. **Litu·rgically** *adv.* from a l. point of view; in a liturgy.

Liturgiology (litɒɹdʒiǫ·lŏdʒi). 1863. [f. LITURGY + -OLOGY.] The science which treats of liturgies. Hence **Litu:rgiolo·gical** *a.* **Liturgio·logist,** one skilled in l.

Liturgist (li·tɒɹdʒist). 1649. [f. LITURGY + -IST.] **1.** One who uses or favours the use of a liturgy. **2.** An authority on liturgies; a compiler of a liturgy or liturgies 1657. **3.** One who celebrates divine worship 1848.

1. The lip-work of every Prelatical L. MILT.

Liturgy (li·tɒɹdʒi). 1560. [ad. med.L. *liturgia*, a. Gr. λειτουργία, f. λειτουργός public servant, minister; app. f. λεώς, λαός people + -εργος that works.] **1.** The service of the Holy Eucharist; prop. that of the Eastern Church. In liturgics, used *spec.* of the different types of Eucharistic service. **2.** A form of public worship; a collection of formularies for the conduct of this 1593. Also *fig.* **b.** Chiefly with *the*: The Book of Common Prayer 1629. **3.** *Gr. Antiq.* At Athens, a public office or duty discharged by the richer citizens at their own expense 1836.

2. *fig.* The Liturgie of Loue, *Ouid de arte amandi* B. JONS.

‖**Lituus** (li·tiu̯ɒs). 1611. [L.] **1.** *Rom. Antiq.* **a.** The crooked staff borne by an augur. **b.** A curved trumpet, a clarion. **2.** *Math.* A spiral represented by the polar equation $r^2\theta = a$. 1758.

Livable: see LIVEABLE.

Live (ləiv), *a.* 1542. [Attrib. use of *live* in *on live*, ALIVE.] **1.** That is alive; living, as opp. to 'dead'. **b.** *joc.*, esp. in 'a real live —' (*slang*) 1887. **2.** *transf.* and *fig.* Full of life or active power 1647; full of energy; up to date; of present interest and importance; not obsolete or exhausted (chiefly *U.S.*) 1877. **3.** Of combustibles: Flaming, glowing; also *transf.* and *fig.* 1611. **4.** Containing unexpended energy; (of a shell) unexploded; (of a rail, wire, etc.) charged with electricity; (of a cartridge) containing a bullet 1799. **5. a.** Of a mineral, a rock: Native, unwrought; = L. *vivus*. **b.** Of air: In its native state, pure. 1661. **6.** Said of machines or parts which either themselves move or impart motion to others 1825. **7.** Of or pertaining to a living being 1613.

1. The importation of l. cattle 1897. *L. hair, feathers*: hair or feathers pulled from a living animal. Phr. *A l. certainty*: put for *a dead certainty* THACKERAY. **b.** A real l. glass milk-jug 1887, philosopher 1890. 2. The l. murmur of a summer's day M. ARNOLD. A new type of 'live' newspaper BRYCE. A l. issue 1900. 3. L. coal 1611, embers BOWEN. 4. *L. wire* (*fig.*), a highly energetic person (orig. *U.S.*). 5. **b.** His essences turn'd the l. air sick TENNYSON. 6. *L. axle*, one communicating power, as dist. from a dead or blind axle KNIGHT. *L. ring*, a circular gang of wheels, as used in the turn-tables of draw-bridges, and in those for locomotives KNIGHT. 7. *L. weight*, the weight of an animal while living.

Combs., etc.: **l.-birth,** the fact of a child's being born alive; **-hole** *Brickmaking*, the flue; **l. load,** the load to which a structure (or vehicle) is subjected in addition to its own weight; **-matter** *Printing*, type in page or column ready for printing; **-steam,** (*a*) steam from the boiler at its full pressure; dist. from *dead-steam*; (*b*) steam from the boiler; dist. from *exhaust-steam*. **b.** In names of contrivances for holding living objects or for examining them microscopically, as *l.-box, -trap, -well*.

Live (liv), *v.* Pa. t. and pple. **lived** (livd). [Com. Teut. wk. vb.: OE. *libban* (WS.), *lifian, lifgan* (Anglian and poet.): f. Teut. root *lib-* (: *laib-*) to remain, continue, whence LIFE *sb.*, q. v.] **1.** *intr.* To be alive; to have life either as an animal or as a plant; to be capable of vital functions. (In this sense the compound present *is living*, not the simple present, is now usual.) **b.** *fig.* Of things: To exist, be found (*poet.*) 1593. **2.** To feed, subsist (†*by*, †*of*, *on, upon*, †*with*, rarely †*in* the actual food or the means of providing it) OE. Also *fig.* **3.** To procure oneself the means of subsistence (*by*, †*of*, *on* or *upon*, †*with*) OE. **4.** To pass life in a specified fashion, indicated by an adv. or advb. phr. (see below) OE. **5.** quasi-*trans.* with cognate *obj.* = 4. OE. **b.** *transf.* in *Hunting*. To keep up (the pace). Also *absol.* in phr. *to l. with hounds* 1840. **6.** quasi-*trans.* *To l. down*: †**a.** To outlive (*nonce-use*). **b.** To silence, wear out (prejudice, slander, etc.) by a blameless course of life. **c.** To lose hold of (a fancy) as life goes on. 1731. **7.** *trans.* To express in one's life 1542. **8.** To have life that deserves the name; to enjoy or use one's life abundantly 1606. **9.** To continue in life; to have one's life prolonged OE. **b.** *fig.* (*poet.* and *rhet.*) Of things: To survive, continue in operation 1768. **10.** Chiefly of a vessel: To escape destruction; to remain afloat. Also quasi-*trans.* of persons. 1601. **11.** To continue in the memory of men; to escape oblivion 1586. **12.** To dwell, reside. Also, to cohabit ME. Also *fig.*

1. And Ioseph said..Doeth my father yet liue? *Gen.* xlv. 3. **b.** No glory liues behinde the backe of such *Much Ado* III. i. 110. 2. A man lyueth not in breed aloon WYCLIF *Matt.* iv. 4. To liue vpon other mens labours STUBBES. To l. on one's means 1852. 3. Every one..must l. by his trade 1796. Phr. *To l. from* HAND TO MOUTH. *To l. by one's wits*: see WIT. Provb. *L. and let l.* 4. Wych tyme he lyuyd more vertusely STARKEY. We l. in quite a small way 1836. They saw no society; lived wholly to their work CARLYLE. Phr. *To l. in clover* (see CLOVER). *To l. fast* (see FAST *adv.*). *To l. well*: (*a*) to feed luxuriously; (*b*) to be well to do; (*c*) to live a virtuous life. *To l. in* (or *within*) *oneself*: to rely upon oneself for occupation and diversion, not upon 'society'. †*To l. up*: *fig.* to live on a high level (DRYDEN). *To l. up to*: not to fall below (principles, rules, etc.). Also, to push expenditure to the limits of (one's fortune). 5. This is no life for men at armes to liue MARLOWE & NASHE. 7. Our Minister lives Sermons FULLER. To l. a lie 1770. 8. He was living up to the last days of his life THACKERAY. 9. To the use of A. for 99 years, if he should so long l. CRUISE. While the tree lived, he in these fields lived on M. ARNOLD. Phr. *To l. out*: to complete (a term o. life); to survive the end of (a period). *To l. to* (be or do so and so). *Long l.* (formerly simply *l.*) *the king!* **b.** E'en in our Ashes l. their wonted Fires GRAY. 10. It was impossible for the Boat to l. any longer in that Sea NARBOROUGH. The savages in the boat never could l. out the storm DE FOE. 11. Mens euill manners, liue in Brasse, their Vertues We write in Water SHAKS. 12. It was admitted that they lived together 1891. Phr. *To l. in*: (of shop-assistants) to reside in the establishment; opp. to *to l. out*. *To l. in* (a room, etc.): to treat as one's ordinary abode. *To l. out* (U.S. colloq.): to be in domestic service.

Comb. **L. (for) ever,** (*a*) = LIVELONG *sb.* 1 and 2; (*b*) Everlasting Flower.

Liveable, livable (li·văb'l), *a.* 1664. [f. LIVE *v.* + -ABLE.] †**1.** Conducive to (comfortable) living. PEPYS. **2.** Of a house, room, locality: That may be lived in; suitable for living in 1814. **3.** Of life: That can be lived; supportable 1841. **4.** Of persons (also *liveable with*): That may be lived with; companionable 1860.

2. His rooms at the top of the Albany are very liveable 1849. Hence **Li·veableness,** l. quality.

Lived (ləivd), *a.* 1589. [f. LIFE *sb.* + -ED [2].] Having (such or so long) life.

†**Li·velihead.** 1412. [f. LIVELY + -HEAD.] 1. Liveliness; vivacity –1717. b. Living form. Also, condition of being alive. –1596. 2. Means of living; also, inheritance –1590.

Livelihood[1] (ləi·vlihud). [OE. *līflād*, f. *līf* life + *lād* course, way, also subsistence. Assim. in form to next.] †1. Lifetime; manner of life; conduct –1581. 2. Means of living, maintenance ME. †b. Food, victuals –1688. †Also *fig.* †3. Income, revenue, stipend; *pl.* emoluments –1621. †4. Property yielding an income; an estate, inheritance, patrimony –1627.

2. Phr. *To earn, gain, get, make, seek a l.* Fishermen who gain their l. on its waters HERSCHEL.

†**Li·velihood**[2]. 1566. [f. LIVELY *a.* + -HOOD.] Liveliness, in various senses –1646.

The tirrany of her sorrowes takes all liuelihood from her cheeke SHAKS.

Livelong, live-long (li·vlǫŋ), *sb.* 1578. [f. LIVE *v.* + LONG *adv.*] A name of plants. 1. *Sedum Telephium*, ORPINE. †2. American Cudweed, *Antennaria margaritacea* –1656.

Livelong (li·vlǫŋ), *a. poet.* and *rhet.* Also *Sc.* lee-lang. ME. [Orig. two wds. = LIEF *a.* and LONG *a.* Subseq. felt as if f. LIVE *v.* + LONG *a.*, and so spelt.] 1. Emotional intensive of *long*. Chiefly in *the l. day, night.* 2. *nonce-use.* That lives long; lasting 1630. ¶3. Taken as = LIFELONG 2 (prob. with pronunc. ləiv-) FREEMAN.

1. He watched there the lee-lang night HOGG. 2. Thou in our wonder and astonishment Hast built thy self a l. Monument MILT.

Lively (ləi·vli), *a.* [OE. *līflic*, f. *līf* LIFE + *-lic* -LY[1].] †1. = LIVE *a.* 1, LIVING –1638. †b. = LIVE *a.* 3, 5, LIVING –1632. †c. Of or pertaining to a living person. Of instruction, etc.: Imparted *viva voce*. –1709. †2. Necessary to life, vital –1640. 3. Of an image, picture, etc.: Life-like, animated, vivid. (Cf. 4.) ME. 4. Full of life; see quots. ME. 5. Of colour, light, etc.: Vivid, brilliant, fresh ME. 6. Gay, sprightly 1580. 7. *Naut.* Of a vessel: Capable of rising lightly to the sea 1697.

1. What shall I doe Now I behold thy liuely body so? SHAKS. c. This [*sc.* Moses] is he..who receiued the liuely oracles [λόγια ζῶντα], to giue vnto vs *Acts* vii. 38. 3. Full l. is the semblaunt, though the substance dead SPENSER. A l. description of [etc.] 1849. 4. A man..of l. parts LAW. A l. remembrance 1769, consciousness of the truth M. ARNOLD. A more l. combustion 1854. A pretty l. week 1887. *joc.* Things are getting l. (*mod.*). 5. Her liuelie colour kil'd with deadlie cares SHAKS. 6. An entertaining and l. Essay 1756. L. in conversation 1868. Hence **Li·velily** *adv.* **Li·veliness.**

Lively (ləi·vli), *adv.* Now *rare.* [OE. *līflīce*, f. *līf* LIFE + *-līce* -LY[2].] †1. (OE. only.) So as to impart life. †2. As a living person or thing –1590. 3. With animation, actively, briskly, vigorously ME. †4. In a life-like manner; vividly ME.; clearly, plainly –1673. †5. Of a vessel: (Floating) in a lively manner (see LIVELY *a.* 7). SMEATON.

3. You must act l.; do it without distraction CROMWELL. 4. Wel koude he peynten lifly that it wroghte CHAUCER.

Liven (ləi·v'n), *v. colloq.* 1884. [f. LIFE + -EN[5]. Cf. ENLIVEN.] To make or become lively; to brighten. Also with *up*.

Live-oak (ləi·v,ōu·k). 1610. [LIVE *a.*] An American evergreen tree (*Quercus virens*) growing in the southern Atlantic States. Applied to some other species in the Pacific States.

Liver[1] (li·vəɹ). [OE. *lifer* fem. :—OTeut. **librā*.] 1. A large glandular organ in vertebrate animals, serving to secrete bile and to purify the venous blood. Also, the flesh of this, *e.g.* used as food. (Its colour is usually dark reddish-brown.) b. Applied to analogous organs or tissues in invertebrates 1841. 2. *fig.* and *allusive.* a. As a vital organ of the body (coupled with *brain* and *heart*); also, as the supposed seat of love and violent passion. (Now only *arch.*) b. A *white l.* is spoken of as characterizing a coward; whence *white-livered*. ME. 3. Liver-complaint. Often qualified as *bronze, cirrhotic, hobnailed l.* 1805. 4. *Old Chem.* Applied (tr. L. *hepar*) to certain liver-coloured substances, e.g. metallic sulphides, and compounds of a metal or of sulphur with an 'alkali' 1664. 5. *Agric.* 'Livery' soil 1803. 6. *adj.* Liver-coloured 1868.

1. A fry'd l. and bacon GOLDSM. *Line of the l.*, also *l.-line* (Palmistry): the line which stretches from the wrist to the base of the little finger. 2. a. To quench the coale which in his liuer glowes SHAKS. *Lucr.* 47. To you (the Liuer, Heart, and Braine of Britaine) By whom (I grant) she liues *Cymb.* v. v. 15. b. How manie cowards..Who inward searcht, haue lyuers white as milke SHAKS. 3. Dyspeptic troubles..usually attributed to l. 1898. 4. *L. of antimony*, Antimony open'd by Salt-peter and Fire PHILLIPS.

attrib. and *Comb.*, as *l. abscess, attack, colour, disease, disorder*, etc.; *l.-coloured* adj.; **l.-brown** *a.*, dark brownish red; **-complaint**, disease of the l.; **l. fluke**, a trematoid worm infesting the l.; †**-grown** *a.*, having an enlarged l.; also, adherent as an enlarged l.; (*fig.* in MILT.); **-leaf** *U.S.* = LIVERWORT 2; **-pyrites**, hepatic pyrites; **-shark**, the basking shark (*Cetorhinus maximus*); **-spots**, yellowish brown patches or spots of chloasma; **-stone** = HEPATITE[1]; †**-vein**, the basilic vein; also *allusively*, 'the style and manner of men in love' (Schmidt); **-weed**, *Hepatica triloba*; **-wing**, the right wing of a fowl, etc., which, when dressed for cooking, has the l. tucked under it; hence *joc.*, the right arm.

Hence **Li·verish** *a.* resembling l.; having the symptoms of disordered l.

Liver[2] (li·vəɹ). ME. [f. LIVE *v.* + -ER[1].] 1. One who is alive; a living creature. Now *rare.* Also, an inhabitant (chiefly *U.S.*). b. One who lives (in a specified way, for a long time, etc.) ME. 2. One who lives a life of pleasure (= F. *viveur*). R. S. SURTEES.

1. A L. on Sasquehanna River 1747. b. The Queen ..will be no long l. SWIFT. A loose l. 1836. *Good l.*: (*a*) one who leads a good life; (*b*) one given to good living.

Liver[3] (ləi·vəɹ). 1668. [Back-formation from *Liverpool*.] A name arbitrarily given to the bird figured in the arms of the city of Liverpool. (It was orig. intended for the eagle of St. John the Evangelist.)

Liver, etc., aphetic f. DELIVER, etc.

Liveried (li·vəɹid), *a.* 1634. [f. LIVERY *sb.* + -ED[2].] Dressed in, furnished with, or wearing a livery.

Liverpudlian (livəɹpʊ·dliăn). 1833. [f. *Liverpool* (with joc. substitution of *puddle* for *pool*) + -IAN.] *adj.* Belonging to Liverpool. *sb.* A native or inhabitant of Liverpool.

Liverwort (li·vəɹwɒ̄ɹt). ME. [tr. med.L. HEPATICA (applied to plants having liver-shaped parts or used in liver diseases).] A name of various plants. 1. = HEPATICA 2. Sometimes called Stone L. 2. *Anemone* (*Hepatica*) *triloba*; = HEPATICA 1. Formerly called Noble L., Three-leaf L. (In U.S. *liver-leaf*.) 1578. †3. Agrimony –1617.

Livery (li·vəri), *sb.* ME. [a. AF. *liveré*, f. *livrée*, pa. pple. fem. of *livrer*; see -Y[5].] 1. a. The dispensing of food, provisions, or clothing to retainers or servants; hence *gen.* provision, allowance. b. The food or provisions so dispensed; a ration. Now *Hist.* c. Allowance of provender for horses. Now *rare* or *Obs.* exc. in LIVERY-STABLE. 1440. 2. A distinctive suit or badge bestowed by a person upon his retainers or servants; a distinctive badge or suit worn by a servant or official, a member of a company, etc.; the distinctive uniform style of dress worn by a person's servants, etc. (now only men-servants) ME. Also *transf.* and *fig.* †3. *collect. sing.* a. Retainers or servants in livery. ME. b. Following, faction –1613. c. = *livery company* or the liverymen of a company 1521. †4. Lodging; quarters –1525. 5. *Law.* a. The legal delivery of property into a person's possession. b. The writ by which possession is obtained from the court of wards. ME. †6. *gen.* The action of handing over; delivery (of goods, money, etc., of a writ) –1745. 7. A particular sort of wool, that which comes from the breech of the animal 1837. 8. *U.S.* A livery-stable.

1. There he made large lyueray, Bothe of ale and of wyne 1492. c. Phr. *At l.*: (of a horse) kept for the owner, and fed and groomed at a fixed charge. 2. Phr. *In l.*: wearing a particular l. *Out of l.*: (of a servant) not dressed in l.; wearing plain clothes. A Servant out of l. leaped from the box LYTTON. *fig.* Now.. Twilight gray Had in her sober Liverie all things clad MILT. 3. c. Phr. *To take up one's l.* (orig. in sense 2): to become a liveryman of a City company. 5. a. Phr. *To have, give, take l.* *To sue* (also *sue for, sue out*) *one's l.*: to institute a suit as heir in the court of wards to obtain possession of lands. *L. of seisin* (often erron. *l. and seisin*): the delivery of property into the corporal possession of a person; e.g. of a house, by giving him the key, or the like; of land, by handing him a twig or a piece of turf, etc. (Now virtually abolished by 8 & 9 Vict. cap. 106 § 2.)

attrib. and *Comb.*, esp. in sense 'kept at livery or for hire', as *l. horse, nag*; transf. *l. friend, mistress*, etc.; also **l. company**, one of the London City companies which had formerly a distinctive costume used on special occasions; **l. fine**, the payment due from those who become liverymen in a London company; **l. servant**, a servant who wears l.; †**l. table**, a table on which 'liveries' or rations were put; hence, a side table.

Hence †**Li·very** *v.* to array in or as in a l. SHAKS.

Livery (li·vəri), *a.* 1778. [f. LIVER[1] + -Y[1].] 1. Of the consistency or colour of liver; *dial.* (of soil) heavy, tenacious. 2. *colloq.* Liverish (*mod.*).

Li·very-man, li·veryman. 1682. †1. A liveried retainer or servant. 1693. 2. A freeman of the City of London entitled to wear the livery of his company, and to exercise other privileges 1682. 3. A keeper of or attendant at a livery-stable 1841.

2. All freemen or Liverymen of this city hath a Right to Choose their sherriffs C. FIENNES.

Livery-stable. 1705. A stable where horses are kept at livery, or are let out for hire. (Also *l. and bait stable.*)

†**Lives.** [OE. *līfes*, gen. sing. of *līf* LIFE *sb.*] a. *pred.* = alive; *occas.* as *sb.*, the living –ME. b. *attrib.* = live, living –1600.

b. No lyues creature Be it of fyssh, or bryd, or beest, or man CHAUCER.

Live stock, li·ve-stock. 1775. Domestic animals generally; any animals kept or dealt in for use or profit. Also *transf.*

Livid (li·vid), *a.* *a* 1500. [ad. F. *livide* or L. *lividus*, f. *livere* to be livid.] Of a bluish leaden colour; discoloured as by a bruise; black and blue.

There followed no Carbuncle, no purple or liuide Spots BACON. So **Livi·dity** (1477), **Li·vidness** (1656), l. quality or condition; a pale-bluish discoloration.

Living (li·viŋ), *vbl. sb.* ME. [f. LIVE *v.* + -ING[1].] 1. The action of LIVE *v.* in various senses. 2. The action, process, or method of gaining one's livelihood 1538. 3. The means of living; livelihood, maintenance; †also, an endowment ME. b. Food; †*pl.* victuals ME. †4. Property, esp. landed estate; *pl.* estates, possessions –1813. †b. A tenement –1819. 5. *Eccl.* A benefice. More fully *ecclesiastical, spiritual l.* ME.

1. There would be no l. for me in a cave DE FOE. Plain l. and high thinking are no more WORDSW. 2. To..fynd to them some honest lyvyngs 1538. 3. Phr. *To earn, get, make a l.* 4. Men whose liuing lieth together in one Shire BACON. 5. To take a l. only to get a l., is an horrid impiety 1703.

attrib. and *Comb.*, as *l.-room, -wagon*, etc.; *l.-broker*; **l.-wage**, a wage on which a worker can live; so *l. price*.

Living (li·viŋ), *ppl. a.* OE. [f. LIVE *v.* + -ING[2].] 1. *Predicatively*, or *attrib.* following the sb.: Alive, or when alive. 2. *attrib.* That lives or has life. a. Said of the Deity OE. b. of human beings, etc. In mod. use, 'now (or then) existing or living', 'contemporary' ME. c. *transf.* (*a*) In phrases of biblical origin. Of water: Constantly flowing; also, refreshing. (*b*) Of coals: Burning, flaming. Cf. LIVE *a.* 3. (*c*) Of rock, stone: Native. ME. d. Of a language: Still in vernacular use. (Cf. *dead language.*) 1706. e. *fig.* ME. 3. Of or pertaining to a living person or what is living 1676. 4. = LIVELY *a.* 4-6. 1718.

1. Where a testator..gives to his four children then l. JARMAN. 2. a. The Church of the liuing God 1 *Tim.* iii. 15. b. He was generally esteemed the greatest l. master of the art of war MACAULAY. Phr. *The l.* (absol.): those who are alive. *The land of the l.* (see *Ps.* xxvii. 13, lii. 5, etc.). *L. skeleton*: a person of very emaciated frame. c. In a spacious cave of l. stone DRYDEN. The fish ponds..were fed by a l. stream 1843. e. The l. question of the hour O. W. HOLMES. The l. fact 1871. Phr. *L. death*: a state of misery not fit to be called life. 3. Phr. *Within l. memory*: within the recollection of persons still alive. *L. force* = *Vis viva* (VIS *sb.*[2]). 4. A l. image of the man 1888. *L. gale* (Naut.): a tremendous gale. Hence **Li·ving-ly** *adv.*, **-ness.**

Livor (ləi·vǫɹ). 1607. [a. L.] 1. *Path.* Lividness, discoloration of the skin 1656. †2. Ill-will, malignity –1675.

‖**Livre** (lī·vr). 1553. [F. :—L. *libra* Roman pound.] An old French money of account, divided into 20 sols (or sous), and about equal to the present franc.

‖**Lixivium** (liksi·viǒm). *Pl.* **-ia.** 1612. [L., neut. of *lixivius* (also *lixivus*) adj., made into lye, f. *lix* ashes, lye.] Water impregnated with alkaline salts extracted from wood ashes (or other substances); lye. Hence **Lixi·vial** *a.* of or pertaining to l.; obtained by lixiviation; †also formerly, alkaline. †**Lixi·viate** *a.* obtained by lixiviation; of or pertaining to a l. or to lixivial salts; alkaline; *sb.* a l.; **Lixi·viate** *v. trans.* to impregnate with l.; to subject to lixiviation; **Lixivia·tion,** the action or process of separating a soluble from an insoluble substance by percolation of water, as salts from wood ashes. **Lixi·vious** *a.* = *lixivial.*

Lizard (li·zăɹd). ME. [a. OF. *lesard* masc., *lesarde* fem. (mod.F. *lézard, lézarde*), repr. L. *lacertus* masc., *lacerta* fem., lizard. The OF. ending was assim. to suffix -ARD.] **1.** A small reptile of the genus *Lacerta* or other genera of the order *Lacertilia,* having an elongated body, a long tail, four legs, and a scaly or granulated hide; in scientific use, any reptile of this order; sometimes extended to the larger saurians, as the crocodiles. **2.** A figure of a lizard; esp. in *Her.* 1455. **3.** A fancy variety of the canary. In full *l. canary.* 1865. **4.** *Naut.* A piece of rope having a thimble or block spliced into one or both ends 1794. **5.** A piece of timber with a forked end, used in dragging a heavy stone, etc. 1875.

attrib. and *Comb.*, as **l.-bird, dragon,** animals half l. and half bird or dragon; **l. canary** (see 3); †**l. fish,** (*a*) the horse-mackerel or scad; (*b*) a fish of the genus *Synodus*; **-green,** a colour like that of the green l. (*Lacerta viridis*); also as adj.; **-skin** *a.*, made of the skin of a l. **b.** with **lizard's,** as **lizard's tail,** a N. Amer. plant of the genus *Saururus*, with small white flowers in a slender spike; in the W. Indies, applied to *Heckeria peltata.*

'll (l; after a consonant 'l). 1576. Contr. f. WILL, after pronouns ending in a vowel; occas., colloq., after other words, as in *that'll do.* Formerly also 'le, as in *Ile* or *I'le*, etc.

LL. Contr. for L. *legum* of laws, in degrees, as LL.B. = *Legum Baccalaureus,* Bachelor of Laws, LL.D. = *Legum Doctor,* Doctor of Laws.

Llama (lā·mă, Sp. lya·ma). 1600. [a. Sp. *llama*; prob. Peruvian.] A S. Amer. ruminant quadruped, *Auchenia llama,* closely allied to the camel, but smaller, humpless, and woolly-haired; used as a beast of burden in the Andes. **b.** (Material made of) its wool 1882.

‖**Llano** (lā·no, Sp. lya·no). 1613. [Sp.:—L. *planum* PLAIN.] A level treeless plain or steppe in the northern parts of S. America.

Lloyd's (loidz). [f. the name of Edward *Lloyd* who opened a coffee-house in London in 1688, a resort of shipping underwriters.] The incorporated society of marine underwriters in London (1871).

L.s Register, an annual alphabetic list of ships assigned to various classes; see also A IV. 2.

Lo (lōu), *int. arch.* [Two wds.: (1) ME. *lō*:—OE. *lá,* an exclam. of surprise, grief, or joy, and also used with vocatives. (2) ME. *lo* with close *ō*, prob. short f. *lōke* (OE. *lóca*), imper. of LOOK *v.*] †**a.** In early use, a vague exclam. = mod. O! or Oh! **b.** = Look! See! Behold! Also freq. in mod. use, *Lo and behold.*

Lo! He comes with clouds descending WESLEY.

Loach (lōutʃ). ME. [a. F. *loche* loach, also *dial.* slug.] **1.** A small European freshwater fish, *Cobitis* (*Nemachilus*) *barbatula* (*-us*), esteemed for food; also, any fish of the family *Cobitidæ.* †**2.** *fig.* A simpleton –1620.

Load (lōud), *sb.* [OE. *lád* fem., way, course, journey, conveyance:—OTeut. **laiđā* (whence **laiđjan* to LEAD), related to **līþan* to go (OE. *līđan*). Infl. as to meaning by association with LADE *v.*] †**1.** Carriage. Also, an act of loading. –1523. **2.** That which is to be carried; a burden. Also, the amount usually carried; e. g. *cart-l., wagon-l.*, etc. ME. **b.** Hence, this customary quantity, taken as a unit of measure or weight for certain substances ME. **c.** The charge of a fire-arm 1692. **3.** A material object or a force, acting or conceived as a weight, clog, or the like 1593. **4.** *Mech.*, etc. **a.** Amount of pressure on a structure due either to its own weight or to a superimposed weight 1871. **b.** Amount of external resistance to be overcome by a machine or prime mover 1895. **c.** *Electr.* The amount of current supplied by a dynamo or generating station at any given time 1902. **5.** *fig.* A burden (of affliction, sin, responsibility, etc.) 1593. **6.** *Loads*: superabundance, 'heaps' (*colloq.*) 1606.

2. Æneas bare a liuing loade SHAKS. **b.** As a measure, a l. of wheat is usually 40 bushels, of lime 64 (in some districts 32) bushels, of timber 50 cubic feet, of hay 36 trusses (= 18 cwt.), etc. A l. of lead ore (in the Peak, Derbyshire) = 9 dishes (see DISH *sb.* 6 b). Wheat futures are usually dealt with in 'loads'. A l. is a thousand quarters 1898. **3.** *2 Hen. VI*, I. ii. 2. **5.** Our life's a l. DRYDEN.

attrib. and *Comb.*, as **l. displacement, draught,** the displacement or draught of a vessel when laden; **l. factor,** the ratio of the average to the maximum amount of work, power, etc., of consumption to production, etc.; **l.-line** = LOAD-WATER-LINE.

Load (lōud), *v.* Pa. pple. **loaded**; *dial.* **loaden.** 1495. [f. LOAD *sb.*] **1.** *trans.* To put a load on or in; to furnish with a burden, cargo, or lading; to charge *with* a load. Freq. in pa. pple. 1503. **2.** To place on or in a vehicle as a load for transport; to put on board as cargo 1495. **b.** *absol.* or *intr.* To take in one's load or cargo. Also with *up.* 1720. **3.** To add a weight to, to add to the weight of; to be a burden upon; to oppress *with* a material weight; to weight, *spec.* with lead; to increase the resistance in the working of (a machine) by the addition of a weight 1578. **b.** To adulterate with something to increase the weight or 'body' of 1860. **4.** To supply in excess or overwhelming abundance *with.* Chiefly in pa. pple. 1577. **5.** To put the charge into (a firearm); also *absol.* 1626. **6.** *fig.* To weigh down, burden, oppress (*with* something immaterial) 1526. **b.** To overwhelm *with* abuse, reproaches, etc. 1662. **7.** To pile *on* (*rare*) 1580. **b.** *Painting.* To lay (colour) on thickly in opaque masses 1859. **8.** *intr.* To collect into a heap; to become clogged 1806. **9.** *refl.* and *intr.* (*Stock-exchange.*) To buy heavily of stock. Also *To be loaded up*: to have large quantities of a thing in hand as security. 1885. **10.** *Life-insurance.* To increase (a premium) by adding a charge (called the 'loading') for contingencies, etc.; to charge (a life) with a 'loaded' premium 1867.

1. A large Dutch ship..loaden with tea 1775. **2.** We were to l. mahogany for home 1900. **3.** Trees loaden with fairest Fruit MILT. A bat loaded with lead 1802. A stomach loaded with food. A table loaded with delicacies (*mod.*). **b.** To l. paper, i. e. to adulterate it with clay or cheap fibres 1887. Loaded claret THACKERAY. **4.** *Loaded with*: charged, fraught, or heavily laden with; Loaded with Riches and Honours STEELE. **6.** Lest so stern a solitude should l. And break thy being J. H. NEWMAN.

Loaded (lōu·dĕd), *ppl. a.* 1661. [f. LOAD *v.* + -ED [1].] **1.** In senses of LOAD *v.* **b.** Weighted, esp. with lead, as a *l. stick, whip* 1771. ¶**c.** Charged with magnetism. [After LOADSTONE.] PRIOR. **2.** *techn.* Of wine: Adulterated so as to appear full-bodied. Of the tongue: Thickly furred. Of the liver: Charged with excess of bile. Of the urine: Surcharged with salts, etc. 1860. **3.** *U.S. slang.* Drunk 1890.

1. Where ease my l. Heart? OTWAY. **b.** *L. dice*: dice so weighted with lead as to fall oftenest with a particular face upwards.

Loaden (lōu·d'n), *v. Obs.* exc. *dial.* 1568. [f. LOAD *sb.* + -EN [5].] *trans.* = LOAD *v.*

Loader (lōu·dəɹ). 1476. [f. LOAD *v.* + -ER [1].] **1.** One who or that which loads. **b.** An attendant whose business it is to load guns for a man who is shooting game 1869. †**2.** App. a dicing term; a doublet. Also *fig.* DRYDEN. **3.** A gun which is loaded in a particular way, as in BREECH-LOADER, MUZZLE-*loader, single-loader* 1858.

Loading (lōu·diŋ), *vbl. sb.* 1494. [f. LOAD *v.* + -ING [1].] **1.** The action of LOAD *v.* 1523. **2.** *Life-insurance.* The practice of making an addition to the pure premium for expenses and contingencies. Hence, the difference between the premium payable by the assured and the net premium deducible from any table at the time in use. 1867. **3.** *concr.* A load, lading, cargo. Now *rare.* 1494.

1. Phr. †*Bill of l.* = bill of lading.

Loading (lōu·diŋ), *ppl. a.* 1625. [f. LOAD *v.* + -ING [2].] **1.** That loads; †*fig.* Burdensome, oppressive –1642. **2.** That is loaded in a specified way; as in *breech-loading* 1858.

Loadstar: see LODESTAR.

Loadstone, lodestone (lōu·dstoun). 1515. [f. *load,* LODE + STONE *sb.* Literally 'way-stone', from the use of the magnet in guiding mariners.] **1.** Magnetic oxide of iron; a piece of this used as a magnet. **2.** *fig.* Something which attracts 1577.

2. Load-star of love, and load-stone of all hearts 1649.

†**Loa·dum.** Also **lodam(e,** etc. 1591. [?] A game of cards; in one form, called *losing l.*, the loser won the game –1755.

Load-water-line. 1769. The line of floatation of a ship when she has her full cargo on board. (Called also *load-line, Plimsoll's mark,* etc.) Hence **Load-water-draught, -length. Load-water-section,** a horizontal section at the load-water-line in the ship-builder's draught.

Loaf (lōuf), *sb.*[1] Pl. **loaves** (lōuvz). [Com. Teut.: OE. *hláf* masc.:—OTeut. **hlaiƀo-z.*] **1.** Bread. *Obs.* exc. *dial.* **2.** A portion of bread baked in one mass; one of the portions, of uniform size and shape, into which a batch of bread is divided OE. **3.** A moulded conical mass of sugar; a sugar-loaf ME. †**4.** A mass or lump (of anything) –1694. **5.** A head (of a cabbage) 1585.

2. *Brown l.*, a l. of BROWN BREAD. *White l.*, one made of fine wheaten flour only. *Provb.* For better is halfe a lofe than no bread 1546. Phr. *Loaves and fishes* (fig. after John vi. 26): pecuniary benefit as a motive for religious profession (or, *occas.*, for a show of public spirit). *Comb.*: **l.-cake** *U.S.*, a plain cake made in the form of a loaf.

Loaf (lōuf), *v.*[1] 1578. [f. LOAF *sb.*[1] 5.] *intr.* To form a loaf or head.

Loaf (lōuf), *v.*[2] *slang.* 1838. [Obscure.] *intr.* To spend time idly. Also quasi-*trans.* To idle *away* (time). So **Loaf** *sb.*[2], the action of loafing 1855. **Loa·fer** 1835.

Loaf-sugar. 1440. Sugar refined and moulded into a loaf or conical mass.

Loam (lōum), *sb.* [OE. *lám* neut. = mod.G. *lehm* masc.; the OTeut. forms **laimo-, *laimon-* are from the root *lai-*: *lī-* to be sticky; see also LIME *sb.*[1]] †**1.** Clay, clayey earth, mud –1657. **b.** *loosely,* Earth, ground, soil (*arch.*) ME. **2.** Clay moistened with water so as to form a paste; *spec.* a composition of moistened clay and sand with chopped straw, etc., used in making bricks and casting-moulds, plastering walls, grafting, etc. 1395. **3.** A rich soil composed chiefly of clay and sand with an admixture of decomposed vegetable matter 1664. **4.** *attrib.* or *adj.* Made or consisting of loam 1536.

1. A House of Clay best fits a Guest of Lome AUSTIN. **2.** But we wash a wall of l.; we labour in vain HOOKER. **3.** The fruity district of deep l. T. HARDY. Hence **Loam** *v.* to cover, plaster, or dress with l. **Loa·my** *a.* of, pertaining to, consisting of, or resembling l.

Loan (lōun), *sb.*[1] ME. [a. ON. *lán* neut. = OE. *lǽn* fem.:—OTeut. **laihwniz-, -oz-,* neut., f. (ult.) Indo-Eur. root **loiq-* (: *leiq-*: *liq-*), represented in Gr. λείπειν to leave, OE. *lēon* to lend.] †**1.** A gift or grant from a superior –1470. **2.** A thing lent; *esp.* a sum of money lent for a time, to be returned in money or money's worth, and usually at interest ME. **b.** *fig.* Said, in recent use, of a word, a custom, etc. 'borrowed' or adopted by one people from another 1891. **3.** The action, or an act, of lending ME. **4.** *National finance.* **a.** A contribution of money, formerly often forced, from individuals or public bodies, towards the expenses of the state, acknowledged by the government as a debt 1439. **b.** An arrangement or contract by which a government receives upon its own credit advances of money on specified conditions, esp. the payment of a stipulated interest 1765.

2. Security for a pecuniary l. 1844. **3.** I am promis'd the l. of it [a book] HEARNE. **4. a.** Since Juarez triumphed, there have been no forced loans, no exactions G. DUFF. **b.** It had been thought necessary to offer..ten per cent. per annum, on a l. 1844.

Comb.: **l.-collection,** a collection of works of art,

curiosities, or the like, lent by their owners for exhibition; **-holder**, one who holds debentures or other acknowledgements of a l.; a mortgagee; **-money,** money payable as a contribution to a government loan; money advanced as a loan; **-monger,** a loan-contractor (*contemptuous*); **-society,** a body of persons who pay periodical subscriptions to form a fund from which loans may be made to members or others; **-word** [after G. *lehnwort* 1856], a word adopted from another language 1861.

Loan (lōun), *sb.*[2] Now only *Sc.* and *dial.* ME. [See LANE *sb.*] **1.** A lane, a by-road. **2.** = LOANING 2. 1715.

Loan (lōun), *v.* Now chiefly *U.S.* ME. [f. LOAN *sb.*[1]] *trans.* To grant the loan of; to lend. Also with *out.* Hence **Loa·nable** *a.* that may be loaned or lent; (of capital, etc.) available for use in loans.

Loaning (lōu·niŋ). *Sc.* and *n. dial.* ME. [f. LOAN *sb.*[2] + -ING [1].] **1.** = LOAN *sb.*[2] 1. **2.** An open uncultivated piece of ground near a farm-house or village, on which the cows are milked 1750.

2. But now they are moaning on ilka green l. MISS ELLIOT.

Loa·n-o:ffice. 1720. **1.** An office for lending money to private borrowers. **2.** An office for receiving subscriptions to a government loan 1777.

†**Loath,** *sb.* [OE. *láð*, orig. neut. of *láð* LOATH *a.* In sense 2 f. LOATHE *v.*] **1.** Something hateful or harmful -1460. **2.** Dislike, hatred, ill will; later, physical disgust, loathing -1728.

Loath, loth (lōuþ), *a.* [Com. Teut.: OE. *láð* (cf. Ger. *leider* unfortunately, which is prop. the compar. of the adj.):—OTeut. **laiþo-*, adopted in Rom. as F. *laid*, It. *laido* ugly.] †**1.** Hostile, angry, spiteful -ME. †**2.** Repulsive, hateful, loathsome -1592. †**3.** Ugly -1546. **4.** Averse, disinclined, unwilling. **b.** Sometimes quasi-*adv.* Phr. *Nothing l.*: not at all unwilling. ME.

4. She lyueth loþ of this lyf CHAUCER. The residue shewed themselues unwilling and loath to depart HAKLUYT. I..would be loth he should not do well PEPYS. **Loath to depart.** Orig. the tune of a song (prob. containing those words) expressive of regret for departure; *transf.* any tune played as a farewell. Hence **Loa·thness,** the quality or condition of being l.

Loathe (lōuð), *v.* [OE. *láðian*:—OTeut. type **laiþōjan*, f. **laiþo-* LOATH *a.*] †**1.** *intr.* To be hateful, displeasing, or offensive. Const. *dat.* or *to.* -1597. †**b.** *impers.* -1596. †**2.** To be or become disgusted, to feel disgust. Const. *at, for, of, with.* -1609. †**3.** *trans.* To excite loathing or disgust in (a person, etc.). Const. *of.* Also, to render loath *to* (do something) or averse *from* (something). -1661. **4.** To feel aversion or dislike for; to be reluctant *to* (do something). Now only: To have an intense aversion for; to regard with utter disgust. ME. **b.** To feel a disgust for (food, etc.) ME.

3. They are..good for nothing but to loath pious souls 1661. 4. In my soul I loath All affectation COWPER. Mother, I l. him HT. MARTINEAU. b. The full soule loatheth an honie combe *Prov.* xxvii. 7. Hence **Loa·ther. Loa·thingly** *adv.*

Loathful (lōu·ðfŭl), *a.* Also *Sc* **laithfu'.** 1450. [f. LOATH *sb.* + -FUL.] **1.** That is an object of loathing; hateful, loathsome. Now *rare.* **2.** Reluctant, bashful. Now *Sc.* 1561.

1. And lothefull idlenes he doth detest SPENSER. 2. But blate and laithfu', scarce can weel behave BURNS. Hence **Loa·thful-ly** *adv.*, **-ness.**

Loathing (lōu·ðiŋ), *vbl. sb.* ME. [f. LOATHE *v.* + -ING [1].] The action of LOATHE *v.*; abhorrence; strong distaste (for food).

L. of remuneration 1792, for venison 1901.

Loathly (lōu·ðli), *a.* [OE. *láðlic*, f. *láð* LOATH *a.* + *-lic* -LY [1].] Hateful, disgusting, loathsome, repulsive, hideous, horrible. Revived in 19th c. as a literary word.

Thou art so loothly, and so oold also CHAUCER. A l. worm BESANT. Hence **Loa·thliness** (now *rare*).

Loathly (lōu·ðli), *adv.* [OE. *láðlíce*, f. *láð* LOATH *a.* + *-líce* -LY [2].] †**1.** In a manner to cause loathing; foully, hideously -1600. †**b.** With detestation. *Lear* II. i. 51. **2.** Reluctantly, unwillingly. Now *rare.* 1547.

1. With dust and blood his locks were l. dight FAIRFAX. 2. The child goes, but l. 1880.

Loathsome (lōu·ðsŏm), *a.* ME. [f. LOATH *sb.* + -SOME.] **1.** Exciting disgust or loathing; noisome, sickening; odious, repulsive, shocking. †**2.** Affected with loathing or disgust. Const. *of.* -1579.

1. A Gouty scrofulous Substance, very loathsom to look upon 1703. Errors which make some of Rousseau's confessions l. L. STEPHEN. Hence **Loa·thsome-ly** *adv.*, **-ness.**

Loathy (lōu·ði), *a. arch.* 1481. [f. LOATH *sb.* + -Y [1].] = prec.

Lob (lǫb), *sb.*[1] ME. [Perh. onomatopœic.] †**1.** The pollack -1769. **2.** A country bumpkin; a lout. Now *dial.* 1533. **3.** Something pendulous, e. g. the wattles of a fowl, hanging ornaments, etc. (*rare*) 1688. **4.** A lump, a large piece; a nugget (of gold), etc. Chiefly *dial.* 1825. **5.** *Brewing.* A thick mixture. (Cf. LOBLOLLY, LOBSCOUSE.) 1839. **6.** *attrib.* or *adj.* Rustic; loutish; clumsy. Also *appos.* as quasi-proper name. 1508.

2. Farewell thou L. of spirits, Ile be gon SHAKS. This L. too was made principal Prolocutor 1658. 6. A Giant..that was cal'd Lob-lie-by-the-fire 1613.

Lob (lǫb), *sb.*[2] Also **lobb.** 1681. *Mining.* *pl.* Steps in a mine. Also applied to an irregular vein of ore resembling a flight of steps.

Lob (lǫb), *sb.*[3] 1875. [f. LOB *v.*] **1.** *Cricket.* A slow underhand ball. Also *attrib.* **2.** *Lawn-tennis.* A ball tossed high in the air, and, if possible, over the opponent's head. Also *attrib.* in *l.-volley.* 1890.

Lob (lǫb), *v.* Infl. **lobbed** (lǫbd), **lobbing.** 1596. [f. LOB *sb.*[1]] †**1.** *intr.* To behave like a lout. J. SMYTH. **2.** *trans.* To cause or allow to hang heavily; to droop. ? *Obs.* exc. *slang.* 1599. **3.** *intr.* To move heavily or clumsily (often with *along*). Of a cabman: To crawl or prowl in search of a fare. 1819. **4.** *trans.* To throw heavily or clumsily; to toss or bowl with a slow movement. In *Lawn-tennis*, to strike (a ball) well into the air so as to fall at the back of the opponent's court. 1847. **5.** *Brewing.* To add 'lob' to (see LOB *sb.*[1] 5) 1838. **6.** *Mining.* To break into small pieces, as ore preliminary to hand sorting 1875.

2. Their poore Iades L. downe their heads SHAKS. 3. The enemy's shells came lobbing into it [the trench] L. OLIPHANT.

Lobar (lōu·băɹ), *a.* 1856. [ad. mod.L. *lobaris*, f. L. *lobus* LOBE; see -AR [1].] Pertaining to a lobe.

Lobate (lōu·bēᵗt), *a.* 1760. [ad. mod.L. *lobatus*, f. L. *lobus* LOBE; see -ATE [2].] *Nat. Hist.* Having or characterized by lobes; lobed. So **Lo·bated** *a.* 1703. Hence **Lo·bately** *adv.* so as to form lobes. **Loba·tion,** the formation of lobes; the condition of being l.

Lobato- (loubē¹·to), comb. f. LOBATE with sense 'lobate and..', as *l.-digitate*, etc.

†**Lo·bbish,** *a.* 1567. [f. LOB *sb.*[1] + -ISH [1].] Like a lob; clownish -1586.

Lobby (lǫ·bi), *sb.* 1553. [ad. med.L. *lobium* or *lobia*; see LODGE *sb.* Orig. a monastic term.] †**1.** ? A covered walk, cloister (in a monastery). BECON. **2.** A passage or corridor; often used as a waiting-place or ante-room 1575. †**b.** *Naut.* An apartment or passage-way in the fore part of a cabin under the quarter-deck 1815-50. **c.** *Agric.* A small enclosure for cattle adjoining the farm-yard 1777. **3.** *spec.* In the House of Commons and other houses of legislature, a large entrance-hall open to the public, and chiefly used for interviews between members and non-members of the House; also (in full *division l.*), one of the two corridors to which members retire to vote 1640. **b.** *collect.* Those who frequent the lobbies of the House or who vote in a particular lobby; *U.S.* those who frequent the lobby in order to influence members of the legislature; the body of lobbyists 1859. **4.** *attrib.*, as *l.-correspondent*, etc. 1650.

2. The box l. of a theatre DICKENS. 3. If the hon. member divides, I shall go into the same l. with him BRIGHT. b. The l. and corruption are legitimate subjects for satire 1884. *Comb.* **l.-member,** a lobbyist.

Lobby (lǫ·bi), *v.* orig. *U.S.* 1832. [f. LOBBY *sb.*] **1.** *intr.* To frequent the lobby of a legislative assembly for the purpose of influencing members' votes; to solicit the votes of members. **2.** *trans.* To influence (members of a house of legislature) in the exercise of their functions by frequenting the lobby. Also, to get (a measure) *through* Congress by means of such influence. 1850.

Lobbyist (lǫ·bi,ist). Chiefly *U.S.* 1863. [f. LOBBY *sb.* + -IST.] One who frequents the lobbies of the House of Representatives in order to influence members in their votes. Also *occas.*, a journalist, etc., who frequents the lobby of the House of Commons. So **Lo·bbyism,** the system of lobbying.

Lobcock (lǫ·bkǫk). Now *dial.* 1553. [f. LOB *sb.*[1] + COCK *sb.*[1]] A country bumpkin; a clown; a blundering fool.

Lobe (lōub). 1541. [ad. late L. *lobus*, a. Gr. λοβός lobe of the ear or of the liver, pod, etc. :—pre-Hellenic **logw-*, cogn. w. **legw-* in L. *legumen* pod, *legula* lobe of the ear.] **1.** A roundish projecting part, usu. one of two or more separated by a fissure: *spec.* **a.** One of the divisions of the liver or lungs formed by the fissures. **b.** The lower soft pendulous part of the external ear 1719. **c.** *Bot.* and *Zool.* A rounded projection or part of a leaf or other organ 1671. **d.** One of the divisions of the brain 1672. **e.** The larger and projecting part of a cam-wheel 1855.

Comb.: **l.-foot,** a lobe-footed bird; **-footed** *a.*, having lobate feet, as some birds. Hence **Lobed** (lōubd) *a.*, having a lobe or lobes; lobate (chiefly *Nat. Hist.*) 1787. **Lobelet** (lōu·b,lėt), a small lobe, a lobule 1836.

Lobelia (lobī·liă). 1739. [Mod.L., f. Matthias de *Lobel* (1538-1616); see -IA.] A genus of herbaceous (rarely shrubby) plants, having blue, scarlet, or purple flowers, with deeply cleft spurless corolla; a plant of this genus, or its flower. **b.** *Pharmacy.* The herb *L. inflata* 1858.

Lobeliaceous (-ēᵗ·ʃəs), *a.* 1830. [f. mod.L. *Lobeliaceæ* (f. LOBELIA) + -OUS; see -ACEOUS.] *Bot.* Belonging to the N.O. *Lobeliaceæ.*

Lobeline (lōu·bīləin). Also **lobeli(i)n.** 1836. [f. LOBELIA + -INE [5].] *Chem.* An oily alkaloid with a pungent tobacco-like taste obtained from *Lobelia inflata* (Indian tobacco).

Loblolly (lǫ·blǫli). Now *dial.* 1597. [perh. onomatopœic; cf. dial. *lob*, to bubble in boiling, said esp. of porridge, *lolly* (obs. Devon), broth, etc. boiled in a pot.] **1.** Thick gruel or spoon-meat, as used by seamen, etc.; burgoo. **2.** A bumpkin, rustic, boor 1604.

Comb.: **l. bay,** an ornamental tree, *Gordonia Lasianthus*, of the southern U.S.; **l. boy,** a surgeon's attendant on shipboard; also *dial.* an errand boy, man of all work; **l. pine,** the tree *Pinus Tæda*, growing in swamps in the southern U.S.; **l. tree** = *loblolly wood*; **l. wood,** *Cupania glabra*; also *Pisonia cordata* (*Treas. Bot.*).

Lobose (lōu·bous), *a.* 1885. [ad. mod.L. *lobosus*, f. *lobus* LOBE.] Having many or large lobes; *spec.* pertaining to the order *Lobosa* of Rhizopods.

Lobscouse (lǫ·bskaus). *Naut.* and *dial.* 1706. [?] A sailor's dish of meat stewed with vegetables and ship's biscuit, or the like.

Lobsided, var. of LOP-SIDED.

Lob's pound. Now *dial.* 1597. [See LOB *sb.*[1] 2.] Prison; jail; the lock-up. Also *fig.*, an entanglement, difficulty.

Lobster (lǫ·bstəɹ). [OE. *lopustre*, etc., corruptly ad. L. *locusta* LOCUST (orig. lobster). The substitution of *p* for L. *c* is unexplained.] **1.** A large marine stalk-eyed ten-footed long-tailed crustacean of the genus *Homarus*, much used for food; it is greenish or bluish black when raw, and red when boiled; the first pair of feet form the characteristic 'claws'. **b.** The flesh of this, as food 1789. †**2.** An opprobrious name (? for a red-faced man) -1609. **3.** A contemptuous name for: A British soldier; orig. referring to the jointed plate-armour (called *lobster-tail*) worn by Roundhead cuirassiers; later, to the red coat. Also *boiled l.* 1643. **4.** Short for *lobster-caterpillar, -moth* 1869.

1. **Norway l.,** *Nephrops norvegicus.* **Spiny** or **thorny l.,** *Palinurus vulgaris* = CRAYFISH 3 b. Gauntlets..were..oftener of small plates of iron rivetted together, in imitation of the lobster's tail GROSE. 2. You whorson L. B. JONS. 3. *Raw* (or *unboiled*) *l.*: a policeman; so called on account of his blue uniform.

attrib. and *Comb.*, as *l.-fishery, -sauce*, etc.; **l.-box** *slang*, (*a*) a transport ship; (*b*) barracks; **-clad** *a.*, clad in jointed armour suggesting a lobster's shell; **-coated** *a.*, red-coated; **-crab,** a crustacean of the family *Porcellanidæ*; a porcelain-crab; **-creel** = *lobster-pot*; **-joint,** a joint in an instrument resembling a joint in a lobster's claws; **-louse,** a parasite of the l., *Nicothoe astaci*; **-moth,** the bombycid moth *Stauropus fagi*; **-pot,** a basket, etc., serving as a trap to catch lobsters; **-smack** *joc.*, a military transport; **-tail,** a piece of armour jointed after the manner of a lobster's tail; also *attrib.*; **-tailed** *a.*, wearing 'lobster-tail' armour.

Lobular (lǫ·biŭlăɹ), *a.* 1822. [f. LOBULE + -AR.] *Anat.*, etc. Pertaining to or having the form of a lobule or lobules. Of pneumonia: Affecting the lobules of the lungs.

Lobulate (lǫ·biŭlět), *a.* 1838. [f. LOBULE + -ATE².] Having or consisting of lobules. **Lo·bulated** *a.* 1783. **Lobula·tion,** the formation of lobules; a lobulated condition 1861. **Lobulato-,** comb. f. = 'lobulate and . .' 1846.

Lobule (lǫ·biul). 1682. [ad. mod.L. *lobulus* (also used in Eng.), dim. of *lobus* LOBE.] A small lobe. Chiefly *Anat.*

Lob-worm (lǫ·b,wɔ̄ɹm). 1651. [f. LOB *sb.*¹] **a.** A large earthworm used for bait by anglers. **b.** The lug-worm (see LUG *sb.*³) 1854.

‖**Local** (lokal), *sb.*¹ Commonly *erron.* **locale** (lokā·l), fem. 1772. [Fr., *local* adj. used absol.; see next.] A place or locality; esp. a place considered with reference to some particular event or particular operations.

Local (lōu·kăl), *a.* and *sb.*² ME. [a. F. *local*, ad. L. *localis*, f. *locus* place.]

A. *adj.* **1.** Pertaining to or concerned with place or position in space. Now chiefly in *l. situation.* 1485. †**b.** Having spatial position –1729. †**c.** *L. motion*, movement from place to place, locomotion –1707. **d.** *Grammar.* Relating to place or situation 1842. **2.** Belonging to, existing in, or peculiar to a particular place or places ME. **b.** Belonging to a town or other limited region, as dist. from the country as a whole 1688. **c.** In various specific collocations (see below) 1772. **3.** *Law.* (In renderings of AF. *chose local, trespas local*) 1598. **4.** Pertaining to a particular place in a system, series, etc., or to a particular portion of an object (see below). **5.** Pertaining to places (in the geographical sense) or to an individual place as such 1605. **6.** *Math.* Pertaining to a locus 1704.

1. c. Plants have no l. or progressive Motion 1707. **2.** *L. time*: the time of day or night reckoned from the instant of transit of the mean sun over the l. meridian. Truth is not l. COWPER. Mr. Yeo, the l. lawyer 1891. **b.** *L. government*, the administration of the affairs of a town, etc. by the inhabitants, as dist. from the state at large. *L. Government Board*: a former department of state acting as the central authority for Local Government in England and Wales. **c.** *L. examination*, one held in a number of different places under the direction of a central board at one of the Universities. *L. preacher* (among the Methodists), a layman authorized to preach in the district in which he resides. *L. rank*, the rank given to an officer in his Majesty's service serving in a foreign land with other troops, whereby he is equalized in rank with officers whose first commissions are of the same date, but who have been more fortunate in promotion. *L. veto*: the prohibition of the sale of liquors in a district, under the system of l. option. **Local option.** The principle of allowing localities to decide whether the trade in liquor, etc. shall be prohibited within the district 1868. **4. a.** Pertaining to, or affecting, a particular part or organ of the body 1541: I employed only l. means for their cure ABERNETHY. A l. inflammation 1899. **b.** Electr. and Magnetism. *L. action*, action between different parts of a plate in an electric battery, as dist. from the general action of the battery. *L. attraction*, the effect of the iron in a ship on her compasses. *L. battery*, the battery of a l. circuit. *L. circuit*, one which includes only the apparatus in the office, and is closed by a relay. 1841. **c. Local colour:** (*a*) In *Painting*, the colour natural to each object or part of a picture 1706. (*b*) Hence, in art and literature, the representation in vivid detail of the manners, dress, scenery, etc. of a particular period or country 1721. Hence **Lo·cally** *adv.* in a l. manner.

B. *sb.* (the adj. used *absol.*) **1.** A person attached by his occupation, etc. to, or an inhabitant of, a particular locality. Chiefly *pl.* 1835. **b.** *esp.* A local preacher 1824. **2.** Something local: an item of local news in a newspaper 1869; a postage-stamp of only local currency 1870; *Telegr.* a local battery or circuit 1875; a local train 1902; a local examination 1893.

Locale, erron. f. LOCAL *sb.*¹

Localism (lōu·kăliz'm). 1823. [f. LOCAL *a.* + -ISM.] Attachment to a locality; limitation of ideas, sympathies, and interests resulting from this; disposition to favour what is local 1843. **2.** A local idiom, custom, or the like.

2. All talk scandal, gossip, localisms 1858.

Localist (lōu·kălist). 1683. [f. LOCAL *a.* + -IST.] One who treats or regards things as local; a student of what is local; one who assigns a local origin to (diseases).

'Localists' attributed the epidemics to local conditions, atmospheric changes, [etc.] 1901. Hence **Locali·stic** *a.* (of a theory) attributing a local nature or origin.

Locality (lokæ·lĭti). 1628. [a. F. *localité*, ad. late L. *localitatem*, f. *localis* LOCAL.] **1.** The fact or quality of having a place, i.e. of having position in space. †**2.** The fact of being local. Also *pl.* local characteristics, feelings, or prejudices. –1802. **3.** *pl.* The features of a particular place. [So Fr.] 1828. **4. a.** The place in which an object (e.g. a plant, a mineral, etc.) is, or is to be found 1834. **b.** A district as the site occupied by certain persons or things, or as the scene of certain activities 1830. **5.** *Law.* Limitation to a county, district, or place. BLACKSTONE. **6.** *Phrenol.* The faculty of recognizing and remembering places 1815. **7.** *Psychol.* in phr. *sense of l.* 1888.

1. That the Soul and Angels..have nothing to do with grosser l., is generally opinion'd GLANVILL. **4. a.** A blind man..feeling all around him with his cane, so as to find out his l. HAWTHORNE. **5.** The l. of trial 1768. **7.** *L., sense of*, the faculty of distinguishing the part of a sensory surface to which a stimulus is applied (*Syd. Soc. Lex.*) 1888.

Localization (lōukăləizē¹·ʃən). 1816. [f. LOCALIZE *v.* + -ATION.] **1.** The action of localizing; the fact of being localized 1853. **b.** *Phys.* The process of fixing, or fact of being fixed, in some particular part or organ of the body 1855. **2.** Assignment to a particular place or locality. Also, the determination of the locality of an object. 1816.

1. Centralization or l. of administrative power 1853. **2.** The localisation of a bullet in a wound 1881.

Localize (lōu·kăləiz), *v.* 1600. [f. LOCAL *a.* + -IZE.] †**1.** *intr.* To act in accordance with the custom of the place. G. HARVEY. **2.** *trans.* To make local; to invest with local characteristics 1792. **3.** To fix in a particular place, or in a particular part of a whole or system. Usu.: To attach or restrict *to* a particular locality. 1798. **4.** To attribute to a particular place; to find a locality for, determine the locality of. Occas. constr. *to.* 1816.

4. The Romans appropriated and localised every tale and tradition H. COLERIDGE. **Lo·calizable** *a.*

‖**Locanda** (loka·nda). 1838. [It., ad. med.L. (*camera, domus*) *locanda* (room, house) to be let.] A lodging-house or inn.

Locate (lōu·keᶦt, lokē¹·t), *v.* 1652. [f. L. *locat-*, *locare* to place, let for hire, f. *locus.*] **1.** *trans.* To fix the situation or site of (lands granted, a building, etc.). Chiefly *U.S.* 1765. **2.** To survey and define the limits of; to lay out (a road); to enter on or take possession of (a land-claim, a gold-mine, etc.). *U.S.* 1739. **3.** To fix or establish in a place; to settle. Chiefly *U.S.* 1807. **b.** *pass.* Of a quality, faculty, etc.: To have its seat 1829. **4.** *intr.* for *refl.* To establish oneself in a place, to settle 1652. **5.** To allocate, allot, apportion 1816. **6.** To refer to a particular place; to state the locality of 1807. **7.** To discover the exact locality of (a person or thing) 1882. **8.** *Civil Law.* As tr. L. *locare*: To let out, hire out. MUIRHEAD.

2. He..located a valuable claim near the Pyramid Mountains 1885. **3.** The motives that led me to l. myself at Tunbridge R. CUMBERLAND. **6.** That large Philosophy which embraces and locates truth of every kind J. H. NEWMAN. **7.** The gunboats yesterday.. located the enemy's position at Kerreri 1898.

Location (lokē¹·ʃən). Now chiefly *U.S.* 1592. [ad. L. *locationem*, f. *locare* to LOCATE.] **1.** *Civil* and *Sc. Law.* The action of letting for hire (correl. w. CONDUCTION) 1592. **2.** The action of placing; the fact or condition of being placed; settlement in a place 1623. **3.** Local position, situation. Also, position in a series. 1597. **4.** The marking out or surveying of a tract of land (*esp.* of a claim) or a settlement; the laying out of a road or the like. *U.S.* 1718. **5.** *concr.* (*U.S.*) A tract of land marked out or surveyed; *spec.* a mining claim. Also, in the S. African colonies, the quarters set apart for natives. 1792. **b.** *Austral.* A farm or station 1828. **6.** Place of settlement or residence. Chiefly *U.S.* 1827.

1. Phr. *Contract of l.*: a contract by which the use of a chattel is agreed to be given, or by which a person agrees to give his services, for hire. **3.** The l. of the praetorium 1883. **5. b.** Rides about the l. 1863. **6.** They visited Windsor. Mr. Beck said that if he had such a l. he should always live there BESANT & RICE.

Locative (lǫ·kătiv). 1804. [f. L. *locat-*, *locare* to LOCATE; see -IVE.] **A.** *adj.* Pertaining to location. **1.** *Gram.* Name of the case-form denoting 'place where'; e.g. L. *domī* = at home. Also, pertaining to this case. 1841. **2.** Serving to locate the position of something 1817. **B.** *sb. Gram.* The locative case 1804.

Locator (lokē¹·tǫɹ). 1607. [a. L.] **1.** One who lets for hire; esp. in *Civil* and *Sc. Law.* **2.** *U.S.* One who or a thing which locates (see LOCATE *v.* 2) 1817.

Loch (lǫχ). *Sc.* ME. [Gael. (and Irish) *loch.*] A lake; also, an arm of the sea, *esp.* when narrow or partially landlocked.

Loch, var. of LOHOCH.

Lochaber (lǫχæ·bəɹ). 1618. [Name of a district in Inverness-shire.] *attrib.* in *L.-axe* (Antiq.): 'A sort of halbert of a large size, having a strong hook behind for laying hold of the object assaulted' (Jam.).

Lochage (lǫ·kēdʒ). Also quasi-L. ‖**lochagus** (lokē¹·gǒs). 1808. [ad. Gr. λοχαγός, f. λόχος LOCHUS + ἀγ-, ἄγειν to lead.] *Gr. Antiq.* The commander of a lochus.

Lochan (lǫ·χăn). *Sc.* 1789. [Gael., dim. of *loch.*] A small loch or lake.

Loche, var. of LOACH.

‖**Lochia** (lǫ·kiă). *pl.* 1685. [mod.L., ad. Gr. λόχια, neut. pl. of λόχιος adj., pertaining to childbirth, f. λόχος a lying-in. Cf. F. *lochies.*] *Path.* The discharge from the uterus and vagina which follows child-birth. Hence **Lo·chial** *a.* of or pertaining to the l.

‖**Lochus** (lǫ·kǒs). Pl. **lochi** (lǫ·kəi). 1832. [mod.L., ad. Gr. λόχος.] *Gr. Antiq.* A division of the army, in Sparta and other states.

Lock (lǫk), *sb.*¹ [OE. *loc* masc. :—OTeut. **lokko-z*, **lukko-z* :—pre-Teut. **lugno-s.*] **1.** One of the natural divisions of a head of hair, a beard, etc.; a tress. In *pl.* = the hair of the head. †**b.** A lovelock; also, a tress of artificial hair –1688. **c.** *transf.* and *fig.* (of foliage, etc.) 1567. **2.** A tuft or flock (of wool, cotton, etc.) ME. **3.** A (small) quantity of hay, straw, etc.; a handful, armful. Now *dial.* 1440.

1. With these..the Spirits Elect Bind thir resplendent locks MILT. **c.** The locks of the approaching storm SHELLEY. **2.** A l. of wooll falls without noise BP. HALL. **3.** A l. of bacon 1843, of straw T. HARDY.

Lock (lǫk), *sb.*² [OE. *loc* neut. :— OTeut. **lokoᵐ*, **lukoᵐ*, f. *luk-*, wk. grade of the root *lŭk-* (: *leuk-* : *louk-*) to close, enclose.]

I. A contrivance for fastening. **1.** An appliance for fastening a door, lid, etc., consisting of a bolt or bolts which can be propelled and withdrawn by means of a key or similar instrument. (In OE. applied to a bar, bolt, latch, or the like.) OE. **2.** A cotter, a forelock 1875. †**3.** A hobble or shackle for a horse's foot; a horse-lock 1486. **4.** A contrivance to keep a wheel from turning 1884. **5.** In fire-arms, the piece of mechanism by means of which the charge is exploded. (See also FIRELOCK, FLINT-LOCK, MATCHLOCK.) 1547. **6.** Short for ROWLOCK 1850.

1. *fig.* I kept a l. upon my lips CARLYLE. Phr. *L. and key*: a typical expression for appliances for fastening or securing. *Under l. and key*: securely locked up. **5.** Phr. *L., stock, and barrel* = the entirety of anything: The whole thing, l., stock, and barrel, isn't worth one big yellow sea-poppy R. KIPLING.

II. A barrier, an enclosure. †**1.** A barrier on a river, which can be opened or closed at will –1758. †**2.** The waterway between the piers of a bridge –1813. **3.** On a canal or river: A portion of the channel shut off above and below by folding gates provided with sluices to let the water out and in, and thus raise or lower boats from one level to another 1577. †**b.** A lift on a railway, for raising and lowering vehicles from one level to another –1825. **4.** *Engineering.* An antechamber giving access to a chamber in which work is carried on in compressed air; an *air-lock* 1874.

III. f. LOCK *v.* **1.** A locking together, interlocking; an assemblage of objects jammed together, now esp. a 'block', 'jam' of carriages in the streets 1550. †**2.** A grapple, grip, or trick in wrestling; hence *fig.* a dodge; a difficulty, dilemma 1608. **3.** The swerving (to right or left) of the wheels of the fore-carriage of a vehicle from the line of direction of the hind-wheels 1851. **4.** *Thieves' slang.* (App. short for *lock-all-fast.*) A receiver of stolen goods; also, a house where stolen goods are received 1700.

1. Stopped on the road from Epsom in a l. of carriages THACKERAY. 2. The Enemy is at his old l. CROMWELL.

IV. (More fully *Lock-hospital.*) A hospital for the treatment of venereal diseases. (Now usually with capital L.) 1700.

attrib. and *Comb.* **1.** General: as (sense I. 1) *l.-maker, -staple,* etc.; (sense I. 5) *l.-action,* etc.; (sense II. 3) *l.-bank, -duty, -house, -keeper,* etc.

2. Special: as **l.-bay,** the space of water between the gates of a canal-lock; **-chamber,** the space enclosed between the side-walls and gates of a l.; **-nut,** a nut screwed down upon another to prevent its breaking loose, a check-nut; **-pulley,** two pulleys that can be worked separately or together; **-rail,** in doors, the rail nearest the l.; **-spring,** the spring by means of which the case of a watch is opened or closed; **-step** *Mil.,* a step in which the heel of one man is brought nearly in contact with the joint of the great toe of another; hence *lock-step* adv. and vb.; **-stitch,** a sewing-machine stitch, in which two threads are locked firmly together; also *attrib.*

Lock (lǫk), *v.* Pa. t. and pple. **locked** (lǫkt). ME. [f. LOCK *sb.*[2]] **1.** *trans.* To fasten (a door, box, drawer, etc.) with a lock and key; occas. with *up.* Hence (chiefly with *up*), to secure (a chamber, building, enclosure) by locking the doors. **b.** *intr.* Of a door: To be locked; to admit of being locked 1590. **2.** *trans.* To shut up with a lock; to put under lock and key. Const. *in, into, within.* Also with advs. *in, up.* ME. **3.** *transf.* **a.** To enclose, hem in. Chiefly with *in.* ME. **b.** To keep securely, as if in a locked receptacle. Chiefly with *up.* 1562. **c.** Comm. and Finance. *To l. up*: To invest (capital) *in* something not easily convertible into money 1692. **d.** Of sleep, enchantment, etc.: To hold fast, overpower completely. Also with *up.* 1725. **4.** To shut off with or as with a lock *from* (a person); to preclude *from* (something) by or as by locking. Also with *up.* 1601. **5.** To fasten, make or set fast, fix; *techn.* to fasten or engage (one part of a machine) *to* another; in *pass.* (of a joint), to be rendered rigid 1670. **b.** To put a lock on the foot of (a horse); to fasten (a wheel) so as to keep it from turning 1694. **c.** *intr.* for *refl.* Of mechanism, a joint: To become fixed or set fast. †Of an animal's flanks: To draw together 1658. **6.** To fix or join firmly by interlacing or fitting of parts into each other. Also with *together, up.* 1592. Also *intr.* for *refl.* 1688. **b.** *Fencing.* To seize the adversary's sword-arm, by turning one's left arm round it, in order to disarm him 1782. **c.** *To l. horns*: (of cattle) to entangle horns with horns in fighting. Hence *fig.* U.S., to engage in combat *with* (some one). 1839. **d.** To embrace closely; also, to grapple in combat. Now only *passive. lit.* and *fig.* 1611. **7.** *Mil.* (*absol.* and *passive*) *To l. up,* to take the closest possible order in line or in file 1802. **8.** *intr.* Of a vehicle: To admit of the fore-wheels passing askew under the body of the carriage. Said also of the wheel. 1669. **9.** *Engineering* and *Navigation.* **a.** *intr.* Of a canal: To pass by a lock *into.* Also of the vessel: To pass *down, in,* or *out* through a lock. Of persons: To pass *out* through an air-lock. 1795. **b.** *trans.* To pass (a vessel) *down, in, out,* or *through* by means of a lock 1840. **c.** *trans.* To furnish (a canal) with locks; to shut *off* (a portion of a river) by means of a lock 1892.

1. Were not my doores lockt vp, and I shut out? SHAKS. *fig.* And David's Lips are lock't FITZGERALD. Phr. *To l. up* (absol.): to l. up the house, l. the doors. 2. To l. up wine POPE. 3. a. A still salt pool, lock'd in with bars of sand TENNYSON. b. Prudent men l. up their motives SHENSTONE. d. I lay fast locked in sleep for eight hours TYNDALL. 4. To locke it [*sc.* life] From Action and Adventure *Cymb.* IV. iv. 2. Phr. **L. out:** (*a*) to turn (a person) out and l. the door against him; (*b*) to keep out (persons) by locking the door; hence (of an employer) to refuse employment to (operatives) in an industrial dispute. 5. *To l. up a form* (Printing): to fix the types or pages in a metal frame so as to prepare them for press, etc. 6. Pray you, l. hand in hand SHAKS.

-lock, *suffix,* surviving in mod.Eng. only in WEDLOCK, repr. OE. *-lác* 'actions or proceedings, practice', which appears in about a dozen compounds, e.g. *brýdlác* nuptials, *feohtlác* warfare, *réaflác* robbery, *wedlác* pledge-giving, the first three of which survived into early ME., and the other into mod. Eng. with altered meaning.

Lockage (lǫ·kėdʒ). 1770. [f. LOCK *sb.*[2] and *v.* + -AGE.] †**1.** The means of locking (pieces of timber) together. PLOT. **2. a.** The amount of rise and fall effected by a lock or series of locks on a canal or river. **b.** The passage of a vessel through a lock; the toll paid for this 1771. **c.** The construction and working of locks; also, aggregate of locks constructed 1809. **3.** *attrib.,* as *l. water,* etc. 1816.

Locked (lǫkt), *ppl. a.* 1470. [f. LOCK *v.* + -ED[1].] In senses of LOCK *v.* Also with *up.*

Locked jaw: (*a*) a jaw set fast by spasmodic contraction of the muscles; (*b*) = LOCK-JAW, and occas. = JAW-FALL 2.

Locker (lǫ·kəɹ). ME. [f. LOCK *sb.*[2] or *v.* + -ER[1].] **1.** One who locks; *spec.* an officer at the Custom House, in charge of a locked-up warehouse, acting under the warehouse-keeper 1735. Also with *up, out.* **2.** *techn.* Something that locks or closes; e.g. a stop to a bell ME. **3.** A box or chest with a lock; also, a small cupboard, e.g. one placed under a window-seat 1440. **b.** *Naut.* A chest or compartment for containing clothes, stores, ammunition, etc. Often specified, as *chain-, shot-l.* 1626. **4.** A compartment in a pigeon-house, a pigeon-hole 1600. **b.** *Eccl.* A cupboard, recess, or niche in a wall, usually near an altar, fitted with a door and lock, for the reservation of the Sacrament, etc. 1517.

3. b. fig. phr. (*Not*) *a shot in the l.*: (no) money in one's pocket, (not) a chance left. *Laid in the lockers,* dead. *Davy Jones's l.*: see DAVY JONES.

Locket (lǫ·kėt). ME. [ad. OF. *locquet, loquet, luquet* (mod.F. *loquet* latch), dim. of *loc* latch, lock, cogn. w. LOCK *sb.*[2]] †**1.** One of the iron cross-bars of a window –1598. **2.** One of the metal plates or bands on a scabbard 1562. †**3.** A fastening or socket. BUTLER. †**4.** A group of small jewels set in a pattern –1706. **5.** †**a.** 'A small lock; any catch or spring to fasten a necklace or other ornament' (J.) –1765. Hence **b.** A small case of gold or silver, containing a miniature, a lock of hair, etc., and worn as an ornament 1679.

Lockfast (lǫ·kfɑst), *a.* 1453. [(1) f. LOCK *sb.*[2] + FAST *a.*; (2) f. LOCK *v.* + FAST *adv.*] **1.** Chiefly *Sc.* Fastened or secured by a lock. Also as quasi-*sb.* A safe. **2.** *Mech.* Adapted for locking something fast; fast-locking 1881.

Lockian (lǫ·kiǎn). 1858. [f. the name of the English philosopher John *Locke* (1632–1704) + -IAN.] *adj.* Of or pertaining to Locke or his followers. *sb.* A follower of Locke. Hence **Lo·ckianism,** the doctrines of Locke or his followers. So **Lo·ckist** *sb.* 1705.

Lo·ck-jaw. 1803. [Altered f. *locked jaw*: see LOCKED *ppl. a.*] Pop. name for trismus, or tonic spasm of the muscles of mastication; a variety of tetanus. Also = TETANUS. Hence **Lo·ck-jawed** *ppl. a.* having the jaws fixed; *fig.* unable to speak 1801.

Lockless (lǫ·klės), *a.* 1591. [f. LOCK *sb.*[2] + -LESS.] Having no lock.

Lockman (lǫ·kmæ̆n). Also **locksman.** 1470. [f. LOCK *sb.*[2] + MAN *sb.*] †**a.** In Scotland: A public executioner, hangman –1818. **b.** In the Isle of Man: A coroner's summoner 1863. **c.** A man employed at a canal or river lock 1846.

Lo·ck-out. Pl. **lock-outs** (*erron.* **locks-out**). 1860. [f. phr. *lock out*; see LOCK *v.* 4.] An act of locking out a body of operatives; *i.e.* a refusal on the part of an employer, or employers acting in concert, to furnish work to their operatives except on conditions to be accepted by the latter collectively.

Lockram (lǫ·krăm). *Obs.* exc. *Hist.* 1483. [ad. F. *locrenan,* f. *Locronan* (lit. 'cell of St. Ronan'), name of a village in Brittany, where formerly made. Cf. BUCKRAM.] A linen fabric of various qualities; an article made of this; *pl.,* pieces of this. Also *attrib.*

Locksmith (lǫ·ksmiþ). ME. [f. LOCK *sb.*[2] + SMITH.] An artificer whose occupation is to make or mend locks.

Lo·ck-up, *sb.* (*a.*) 1767. [f. LOCK *v.* + UP *adv.*] **1.** The action of locking up a school, etc. for the night; also, the time of this 1871; the action of locking up capital; also, an amount locked up 1822. **2.** (Short for *lock-up house* or *room.*) An apartment or building that can be locked up; *esp.* a house or room for the (temporary) detention of offenders 1859.

attrib. or *adj.,* with sense 'capable of being locked up'; as *lock-up coach-house, room,* etc.; **lock-up house,** a house of detention 1767; **lock-up shop,** a detached apartment used as a shop and locked up at night.

Locky (lǫ·ki), *a.* 1611. [f. LOCK *sb.*[1] + -Y[1].] Of or pertaining to locks (of hair); having locks in plenty.

Loco[1] (lōu·ko). *U.S.* 1883. [A use of Sp. *loco* insane.] One of several leguminous plants (chiefly species of *Astragalus*) found in the western and south-western U.S., which, when eaten by cattle, produce *loco-disease.* More fully *l.-plant, l.-weed.* **b.** = *loco-disease. Comb.* **l.-disease,** a disease in horses, affecting the brain, caused by eating l.

Loco[2]. 1896. Short for LOCOMOTIVE *sb.*

Lo:co-descri·ptive, *a.* 1815. [f. *loco-* (in LOCOMOTION) erron. taken as comb. form of L. *locus.*] Descriptive of local scenery, etc.

Loco-foco (lōu·koˌfōu·ko). *U.S.* 1834. [An invented word; said by some to be made up of *loco* in *locomotive,* imagined to mean 'self-moving', and *foco* for It. *fuoco* or Sp. *fuego* fire.] †**1.** 'A self-igniting cigar or match' (Bartlett). More fully *loco-foco cigar, match.* –1852. **2.** *U.S. Polit. Hist.* Used *attrib.* as the designation of the 'Equal Rights' section of the Democratic party (for the origin of the name see N.E.D.). Hence *absol.,* a member of this party. 1837. Hence **Lo:cofo·coism.**

Locomobile (lōukǒmōu·bil). 1889. [f. L. *loco,* abl. of *locus* place + *mobilis* MOBILE.] **a.** *adj.* Having the power to move about, as *a locomobile crane.* **b.** *sb.* A locomobile vehicle, engine, etc. 1902.

Locomote (lōu·kǒmōut), *v.* 1846. [Back-formation from next.] *intr.* To move about from place to place. (Orig. *slang*; now in biological use.)

Locomotion (lōukǒmōu·ʃən). 1646. [f. L. *loco* (see next) + *motionem* MOTION.] **1.** The action or power of moving from place to place; progressive motion of an animal. **2.** Movement from place to place, esp. by artificial means; travel; the means of travelling 1788. **3.** Progressive movement of an inanimate body 1851.

1. Movement..of the body as a whole..is termed l. HUXLEY. 2. I have no taste whatever for l., by earth, air, or sea MRS. CARLYLE.

Locomotive (lōu·kǒmōutiv, lōukǒmōu·tiv). 1612. [f. L. *loco,* abl. of *locus* place + *motivus* MOTIVE *a.* Suggested by the scholastic phr. *in loco moveri.*]

A. *adj.* **1.** Of or pertaining to locomotion, or (*joc.*) to travel. **2.** Having the power of locomotion 1657; *joc.* (of a person) given to locomotion 1732; (of a vehicle or piece of machinery) moving by its own power 1815. **3.** Adapted for or used in locomotion 1841.

1. *L. faculty, power,* the faculty or power of movement from place to place by an act of the will. In these l. days one is too apt to forget one's neighbours HELPS. 2. A caterpillar then may be regarded as a l. egg 1816. *L. tailor* (slang), a tramping workman FARMER. *L.* (*steam*) *engine*: an engine constructed for movement from place to place by its own power (as opp. to 'stationary' engine); *esp.* a steam-engine adapted to draw a train of carriages

along a railway; a railway-engine. Now generally shortened to *locomotive*.
B. *sb.* 1. = *Locomotive engine* (see above) 1829. b. *slang. pl.* The legs 1841. 2. An animal having powers of locomotion 1872.
Comb. l.-car *U.S.*, a l. and a car combined in one vehicle; a dummy engine (Webster).
Hence **Locomo·tive·ly** *adv.*, **-ness.** **Lo·comoti·vity,** the quality or fact of being l.

Locomotor (lōu·kǒmōutəɹ). 1822. [f. L. *loco*, abl. of *locus* + *motor*; see MOTOR. Cf. F. *locomoteur*, whence the adj. use.] A. *sb.* One who or that which has locomotive power. B. *adj.* (Chiefly *Phys.*) Of, pertaining to, or concerned with locomotion 1870.
L. ataxy: see ATAXY 2.

Locomotory (lōukǒmōu·tŏri), *a.* 1835. [f. as prec. + MOTORY.] Pertaining to, or having the power of, locomotion.

‖**Loculus** (lǫ·kiŭləs). *Pl.* **-li** (-ləi). 1858. [L., dim. of *locus.*] 1. A small chamber or cell in an ancient tomb for corpses or urns. 2. *Zool.*, *Anat.*, and *Bot.* One of a number of small cavities or cells separated by septa 1861.
So **Lo·culament** = LOCULUS 2. 1656. **Lo·cular** (1847), **Lo·culate** (1866), **Lo·culated** (1801) *adjs.* having or divided into loculi; **Locula·tion** (1819). **Lo·culicidal** *a.* of a carpel, etc., that dehisces through the back or dorsal suture of the loculus 1819. **Loculici·dally** *adv.* 1847. **Lo·culose** (1855), **Loculous** (1840) *adjs.* full of or divided into loculi.

‖**Locum tenens** (lōu·kǒm tī·nenz). 1641. [med.L., = 'one who holds the place (of another)'.] One filling an office temporarily in place of another, *esp.* a doctor or a clergyman; a deputy, substitute. Hence **Lo·cum-te·nency,** the position of being a *locum tenens*.

‖**Locus** (lōu·kǒs). *Pl.* **loci** (lōu·sai). 1715. [L., = 'place'.] 1. Place of something, locality. 2. A subject, head, topic. [So in L. writers, after Gr. τόπος.] 1753. 3. *Math.* The curve or figure constituted by all the points which satisfy a particular equation of relation between co-ordinates, or generated by a point, line, or surface moving in accordance with mathematically defined conditions 1727.
Latin phrases: **l. classicus**, a standard passage which is authoritative on a subject; **l. communis**, a COMMONPLACE; **l. in quo**, the locality of an event, etc.; in *Law*, the land on which trespass has been committed; **l. pœnitentiæ** (after Heb. xii. 17), a place of repentance; in *Law*, an opportunity allowed to a person to recede from some engagement, so long as some decisive step has not been taken; **l. standi**, lit. 'place of standing', recognized position; in *Law*, a right to appear in court. Also GENIUS *loci*.

Locust (lōu·kǒst), *sb.* ME. [a. OF. *locuste* or L. *locusta* locust, orig. LOBSTER.] 1. An orthopterous saltatorial insect of the family *Acridiidæ* (characterized by short horns), esp. *Œdipoda migratoria* (or *Pachytylus migratorius*), the Migratory Locust, well known for its ravages in Asia and Africa, where, migrating in myriads, it often eats up every green thing. In many countries used for food. 2. *fig.* A person of devouring or destructive propensities 1546. 3. a. The fruit of the carob-tree. b. A cassia-pod. 1615. 4. = LOCUST-TREE 1640.
1. The white ant can destroy fleets and cities, and the locusts erase a province DISRAELI. 2. Those locusts called middle-men COBBETT.
attrib. and *Comb.*, as *l.-swarm*, etc.; *l. fruit*, *timber*, etc.; **l.-bean,** the fruit of the carob-tree; **-beetle** = *locust-borer*; **-bird,** the rose-coloured starling, *Pastor roseus*, which devours locusts; **-borer,** a longicorn beetle, *Cyllene robiniæ*, whose larva destroys the locust-tree; **-eater,** a bird of the genus *Gryllivora*.
Hence **Locust** *v. intr.* to swarm and devour as locusts do (TENNYSON).

Lo·cust-tree. 1623. [In sense 1 f. LOCUST *sb.* In the other senses, ?.] 1. The carob-tree, *Ceratonia siliqua*. 2. = ACACIA [1] 2. 1640. 3. The COURBARIL of Guiana and the West Indies 1629. 4. A leguminous plant of New Zealand (*Sophora tetraptera*) 1872.
Bastard Locust-tree of the W. Indies, *Clethra tinifolia*. **Honey Locust-tree,** a N. Amer. ornamental tree, *Gleditschia triacanthos*. **Swamp** or **Water Locust-tree,** *G. monosperma*.

Locution (lokiū·ʃən). ME. [ad. L. *locutionem* (*loquu-*), f. *loqui* to speak.] †1. The act of speaking -1767. 2. Speech as the expression of thought; discourse; also, style of discourse, expression. Now *rare* or *Obs.* 1519. 3. A phrase, expression ME.
2. I hate these figures in l., These about phrases forc'd by ceremonie MARSTON. 3. A..figurative loqucion 1547.

Locutory (lǫ·kiŭtŏri). 1450. [ad. med.L. *locutorium* (also used in Eng.), neut. of **locutorius*, f. *locutor*; see -ORY.] An apartment in a monastery set apart for conversation, a parlour; *occas.* a grille at which conversation is allowed with those outside.

Lode (lōud). [OE. *lād* fem.; see LOAD *sb.*, of which *lode* is a var., now differentiated.] 1. †Way, journey; *dial.* a road. 2. A water-course; an aqueduct, channel; an open drain in fenny districts. Now *local.* 1572. †3. Leading, guidance. ME. only. 4. A loadstone 1509. 5. *Mining.* A vein of metal ore 1602.
2. Down that long dark l... he..skated home KINGSLEY. 4. As with the Loade The Steele we touch DRAYTON.

†**Lodeman.** [OE. *lādmann*, f. *lād* LODE + *mann* MAN *sb.*] In OE., a leader, guide; later, only *spec.* a pilot -1536. So †**Lo·des-man** ME.-1594.

Lodemanage (lōu·dmǎnėdʒ). *Obs.* or *Hist.* ME. [a. AF. *lodmanage*, f. OE. *lādmann*; see prec. and -AGE.] Pilotage.

Lodestar, loadstar (lōu·dstāɹ). ME. [f. *load*, LODE + STAR *sb.*] 1. A star that shows the way; *esp.* the pole-star. 2. *fig.* A guiding star; that on which one's attention or hopes are fixed ME.
2. Your eyes are loadstarres SHAKS. France [became] the lode-star of Continental democracy M. ARNOLD.

Lodestone: see LOADSTONE.

Lodge (lǫdʒ), *sb.* [ME. *loge*, *logge*, a. OF. *loge*, *loige* arbour, hut, etc. (F. *loge* hut, cottage, box at a theatre, etc.):—med.L. *laubia*, *lobia* (whence LOBBY), a. OHG. **laubja*, later *loubpea*, *lauba*, sheltered place, booth, hut; mod.G. *laube* arbour, summerhouse.] 1. A small dwelling; a hut or booth; a tent, arbour, or the like. Now *dial.* †b. A cell, prison -1704. c. An out-house (*dial.*) 1706. 2. A house in a forest or other wild place, e. g. in the Highlands of Scotland, occupied in the hunting or shooting season 1465. 3. A house or cottage at the entrance of a park or in the grounds belonging to a mansion, occupied by a caretaker, keeper, gardener, etc.; the room or 'box' occupied by the porter of a college, a factory, etc. 1500. 4. *gen.* A lodging, abode, esp. a temporary one; †formerly also *transf.* a place to hold something 1571. 5. The workshop of a body of 'freemasons' (see FREEMASON 1). *Obs.* exc. *Hist.* ME. 6. *Freemasonry*, etc. The place of meeting for members of a branch; hence, the members composing a branch; also, a meeting of a 'lodge' 1686. 7. The residence of the head of a college at Cambridge 1769. 8. The den or lair of an animal; now only of a beaver or an otter 1567. 9. The tent of a N. Amer. Indian; a wigwam. Also, the number usually occupying one tent, as a unit of enumeration, reckoned at from four to six. 1805. †10. A collection of objects lodged close together DE FOE. 11. †a. = LOGGIA -1813. b. = LOGE 2 (*rare*) 1730. 12. *Mining.* A room or flat adjoining the shaft, for discharging ore, etc. 1881.
1. So to the Silvan L. They came MILT. 2. As melancholy as a L. in a Warren SHAKS. 4. [A raven's] airy l. COWPER. 6. Phr. *Grand l.*, the governing body of the freemasons (and of other societies), presided over by the grand-master. *Orange l.* (see ORANGE *sb.*[2] 2). 10. The Maldives, a famous l. of islands 1720.
Comb.: **l.-book,** a book recording the doings of a masonic l.; **-gate,** the gate of a park, etc. at which there is a l.

Lodge (lǫdʒ), *v.* ME. [ad. OF. *logier* (mod.F. *loger*), f. *loge* LODGE *sb.*]
I. *trans.* †1. To place in tents or the like; to encamp, station (an army). Often *refl.* -1598. 2. To provide with temporary quarters; to receive into one's house for the night. Also, to provide with a habitation; to place as a resident *in* a building; also in *pass.*, to be (well or ill) accommodated with regard to house-room. ME. †Also *fig.* b. To serve as a lodging or habitation for. Often *transf.* and *fig.* of things: To contain; in *pass.*, to be contained *in* something. 1449. c. To have as a lodger 1741. 3. To place, deposit. See below. 4. To discover the lodge of (a buck) 1576. 5. To lay flat. Now only of wind or rain: To beat down (crops). 1593.
2. Be not forgetfull to l. straungers COVERDALE *Heb.* xiii. 2. You l. your horses more magnificently than yourself LYTTON. *fig. Rich. III.* II. i. 65. b. The Memory [can] l. a greater store of Images, than all the Senses can present at one time CHEYNE. 3. a. To put and leave in a place of custody or security 1666. To l. [a person] in..a state prison MAR. EDGEWORTH, money in the hands of a banker 1882. b. To deposit in court or with an official a formal statement of (an information, complaint, objection, etc.). Hence, *pop.*, to allege (an objection). 1708. The impeachment which the king had lodged against him HUME. c. To vest, cause to reside, *in* a person or thing, place (power, etc.) *with* or *in the hands of* a person 1670. The power of the Crown is always lodged in a single person HUME. d. To get (a thing) into the intended place 1611. Wounded..By a bullet lodged in the thorax SHERIDAN. e. To throw (something) so that it is caught in its fall; to cause to 'lodge' or be intercepted; (of a current, etc.) to deposit in passing 1606. To l. sand, clay, etc. in a crate filled with stone PIKE. †f. To set or fasten in a socket or the like -1825. 4. The deer is lodg'd. I've track'd her to her covert ADDISON.
II. *intr.* †1. To encamp -1603. 2. To dwell temporarily in a place; *esp.* to pass the night. Now *rare*. ME. b. To dwell, reside. Later, chiefly *transf.* and *fig.* of a thing = to have its seat, reside. Now *rare*. ME. c. *spec.* To be a lodger, to live in lodgings 1749. 3. To be arrested in fall or progress; to stick in a position 1611. 4. *Hunting.* Of a buck: *intr.* To betake himself to his lodge or lair. Also quasi-*pass.*, to be in his lodge. 1470. 5. Of corn: = *to be lodged* (see sense I. 5) 1630.
2. He lodged in the cottage of a peasant GIBBON. b. Sure something holy lodges in that brest MILT. *Comus* 246. 3. The ball lodged in the shoulder LYTTON. 5. As corn lodgeth by too great abundance 1630. Hence **Lo·dgeable** *a.* that may be lodged in; that may or can be lodged.

Lodged (lǫdʒd), *ppl. a.* 1580. [f. prec. + -ED [1].] In senses of LODGE *v.* 1596. b. *Her.* Of a buck, hart, etc.: Represented as lying on the ground.
b. Arms.—Sable, a buck l. Argent 1580.

Lodgement, lodgment (lǫ·dʒmĕnt). 1598. [a. F. *logement*, f. *loger* to LODGE; see -MENT.] 1. A place or building in which persons or things are lodged; a place of shelter or protection; in early use *Mil.*, quarters for soldiers. ? Now *rare* or *Obs.* b. A lodging-place; a lodging-house; lodgings. Now *rare.* 1703. c. *Gunnery.* 'The hollow or cavity in the under part of the bore, where the shot rests when rammed home' (Voyle) 1872. 2. *Mil.* A temporary defensive work made on a captured portion of the enemy's fortifications 1677. 3. a. The action of making good a position on an enemy's ground, or obtaining a foothold; hence, a stable position gained, a foothold. Also *transf.* and *fig.* 1702. b. The action of depositing (money, securities, etc.); *concr.* a deposit of money. Now only *legal.* 1760. c. The lodging of a thing or the accumulation of matter intercepted in fall or transit; *concr.* a mass of matter so lodged 1739. 4. Accommodation in a lodging-place; provision of lodgings; lodging (*rare*) 1805.
3. a. Phr. *To make* or *find a lodgement*. My friend, who had found a lodgment upon the edge of a rock TYNDALL. b. A decree for..lodgment in Court of a sum [etc.] 1884. c. Some [rain] finding lodgment in little hollows of the rock HUXLEY.

Lodger (lǫ·dʒəɹ). ME. [f. LODGE *v.* + -ER [1].] One who, or that which, lodges. b. *esp.* One who occupies hired rooms in another person's house 1596.
attrib. **l.-franchise,** a right to vote conferred by statute upon persons occupying lodgings.

Lodging (lǫ·dʒiŋ), *vbl. sb.* ME. [f. LODGE *v.* + -ING [1].] 1. The action of LODGE *v.* 1480. †2. Dwelling, abode -1611. 3. Accommodation for rest at night or for residence; now only, accommodation in hired rooms or in a lodging-house ME. †b. Material to lie or sleep upon -1691. 4. *concr.* A dwelling-place, abode; †military quarters, encampment. (In sense of 'hired rooms', the pl. *lodgings* is now usual.) ME. Also *transf.* and *fig.* †b. *Hunting.* The lair of a buck, stag, etc. -1610. 5. Specialized uses of the *plural*. See below. 1475.
2. They haue taken vp their l. at Geba *Isa.* x. 29.

3. My l. it is on the Cold ground DAVENANT. Phr. *Board and l.* 4. He lives in a L. of Ten Shillings a Week STEELE. *fig.* Christians..acknowledged their Bodies to be the L. of Christ SIR T. BROWNE. 5. †a. Military quarters -1677. Very cold Lodgings, hard Marches, Scarcity of Provisions HUBBARD. b. A room or rooms hired for residence in the house of another (*now*, not in an inn or hotel) 1640. Wits take lodgings in the sound of Bow POPE. c. An official residence 1661. The Provost's Lodgings (Queen's College, Oxford) 1827. *Judges' lodgings*: the house occupied by the judges (in some assize towns) during the assizes.

Comb.: **l.-house**, †(*a*) a dwelling-house; (*b*) a house, other than an inn or hotel, in which lodgings are let 1766; also *transf.* and *fig.*; **-money**, an allowance made by government to all officers and soldiers for whom there is no room in barracks (Voyle); **-room**, a sleeping apartment, bedroom (now *local*).

Lodicule (lǫ·dikiūl). 1864. [ad. L. *lodicula*, dim. of *lodix* coverlet.] *Bot.* The hypogynous scale of a grass.

Loess (lōu·es, Ger. lös). Also **löss**, *erron.* **loëss**. 1833. [a. Ger. dial. *löss*.] *Geol.* A deposit of fine yellowish-grey loam found in the Rhine and other river valleys.

Lof, Loff(e, obs. f. LUFF, LAUGH.

Loft (lǫft), *sb.* [Late OE. *loft*, a. ON. *loft* neut., air, sky, upper room, cogn. w. OE. *lyft*; see LIFT *sb.*[1]] †1. Air, sky, upper region -1590. 2. An upper chamber, an attic; any apartment ME. b. The apartment over a stable. (Cf. HAYLOFT.) 1530. c. A pigeon-house. Hence, a flock (of pigeons). 1735. 3. A gallery in a church or public room. (Cf. *organ-*, *rood-l.*) 1504. 4. A floor or story in a house 1465. *Obs.* exc. *U.S.* One of the upper floors of a warehouse or business building 1890. †5. A layer, stage, stratum. Also *transf.* of the lateral branches of trees. -1686. 6. *Golf.* In the head of a club: Slope backward from the vertical. Also, the action of lofting; a lofting stroke. 1887.

1. Phr. †*On, upon* (*the*) *l.*: (*a*) = ALOFT; (*b*) in a high voice, loudly. 2. I preached at five in a large l. WESLEY. 5. And hills of Snow and lofts of piled Thunder MILT. *Comb.* **l.-dried** *adj.*

†**Loft**, *a. rare.* ME. [app. aphetic f. ALOFT.] Elated, elevated -1590.

Loft (lǫft), *v.* 1518. [f. LOFT *sb.*] 1. *trans.* †To insert a layer of planks in (a building) so as to separate the lofts or stories -1646. Also, to furnish with an upper story or loft. †2. To store in a loft -1785. 3. *Golf.* To hit (a ball) into the air so as to clear an obstacle; to hit the ball over (an obstacle). 1857. Hence **Lo·fter**, a club for lofting the ball.

3. If there is a high face to l. SIR W. G. SIMPSON.

Lo·fting, *vbl. sb.* 1537. [f. LOFT *sb.* or *v.* + -ING [1].] A roofing, ceiling, or flooring.

Lofty (lǫ·fti), *a.* ME. [f. LOFT *sb.* (in *on loft*, *aloft*) + -Y [1].] 1. Of imposing altitude, towering (not said of persons); soaring 1590. 2. *fig.*, etc. a. Haughty, overweening, proud 1485. b. Exalted in rank, character, quality. Of aims, desires, etc.: Directed to high objects 1548. c. Of compositions, etc. (hence of writers or speakers): Elevated in style or sentiment 1565. d. Of majestic sound 1596.

1. Vpon a loftie and high mountaine hast thou set thy bed *Isa.* lvii. 7. Of loftiest stature COWPER. Birds of l. Wing WESLEY. 2. a. The eyes of the loftie shall be humbled *Isa.* v. 15. Inclined to treat every-body..with a sort of l. good humour BLACK. b. The High and loftie One that inhabiteth eternitie *Isa.* lvii. 15. c. He knew Himself to sing, and build the l. rhyme MILT. d. Sound all the l. Instruments of Warre SHAKS. Hence **Lo·ftily** *adv.* **Lo·ftiness.**

Log (lǫg), *sb.*[1] [Late ME. *logge*; perh. of symbolic origin (cf. Du. *log* clumsy, heavy).]

I. *gen.* 1. A bulky mass of wood; now usu. an unhewn portion of a felled tree, or a length cut off for firewood. b. *fig.* 1579. c. *Mining.* A balance weight, placed near the end of the pit-rope, to prevent its running back over the pulley 1860. †d. In Old St. Paul's, a block or bench on which serving-men sat -1639. 2. A heavy piece of wood, fastened to a man's or beast's leg, to impede his movements. †Also *fig.* 1589. b. A former military punishment. *Obs.* exc. *Hist.* 1830. 3. *pl. Austral. slang.* A jail or lock-up. (Formerly built of logs. Cf. *log-house.*) 1888.

1. Bring in great logs and let them lie, To make a solid core of heat TENNYSON. Phr. *In the l.*: in unhewn condition. b. [The ship] being no other then a logge in the sea HAWKINS. To sleep like a l. 1886. Phr. *To have a log to roll*: see LOG-ROLLING. 2. Here I am tied like a l. to you DICKENS. Phr. *King L.*: the l. which Jupiter in the fable made king over the frogs; used as the type of inertness on the part of rulers, as 'King Stork' typifies an excess of activity.

II. *Naut.*, etc. 1. An apparatus for ascertaining the rate of a ship's motion, consisting of a thin quadrant of wood, loaded so as to float upright, and fastened to a line wound on a reel. Said also of other appliances for the same purpose. 1574. 2. Short for LOG-BOOK 1825. b. *Mech.* The record of an engine, boiler, etc. in which a series of observations have been taken 1875. c. = LOG-BOOK 3. 1882. 3. *Tailoring.* A document fixing the number of hours to be credited to journeymen for making each description of garment; the scale of computation embodied in this 1861.

1. During the chace we ran per l. seventy miles SIR E. BERRY. Phr. *To heave, throw the l.*, (*to sail* or *calculate one's way*) *by the l.*

Combs.: **l.-board**, a hinged pair of boards on which the particulars of a ship's l. are noted for transcription into the log-book; **-cabin**, a small house built of rough logs (*U.S.*); **-canoe**, one hollowed out of a single tree; **-chip** = *log-ship*; **-house**, a house built of logs; in early use (*U.S.*), a prison; **-juice** *slang*, cheap port wine; **-knot** *Naut.*, a knot made in a log-line to indicate a specified length; **-line** *Naut.*, a line of 100 fathoms or more to which the l. is attached; also the sort of line used for this purpose; **-man**, †(*a*) one employed to carry logs; (*b*) one employed in cutting and carrying logs to a mill (*local U.S.*); **-perch**, a freshwater fish, *Percina caprodes*, of N. America; **-reel**, the reel on which the log-line is wound; **-ship**, also *log-chip*, a flat piece of wood in the form of a quadrant, which is loaded so as to keep upright in the water; **-slate**, a double slate used instead of the *log-board*; **-work**, (*a*) the arrangement of logs in the walls of a building; (*b*) the keeping of a l. or log-book.

‖**Log** (lǫg, lōug), *sb.*[2] 1530. [Heb. *lōg*.] A Hebrew measure for liquids, the twelfth part of a hin, = about ⅝ of a pint.

Log (lǫg), *v.*[1] 1622. [f. LOG *sb.*[1]] 1. *trans.* †To deprive (a tree) of branches; to cut (timber) into logs. Also *absol.* 1699. 2. *Naut.* To enter (esp. the distance run by a ship) in the log-book; hence *gen.*, to record 1823. b. Of a ship: To run (a certain distance) by log-measurements 1883. c. To enter the name of (a man as an offender) in a log-book, with a penalty attached. Hence, to fine. 1889.

2. b. This day we logged 160 miles E. F. KNIGHT.

Log (lǫg), *v.*[2] 1808. [? Onomatopœic.] *trans.* and *intr.* To rock, oscillate.

Log, abbrev. of LOGARITHM, LOGARITHMIC.

Loganberry (lōu·gănbe:ri). 1900. [f. Judge *Logan*, U.S.A., its first grower.] A fruit obtained by a cross between the raspberry and blackberry.

Logan-stone (lǫ·gănstōun). Also **loggan-stone, logan.** 1759. [f. *logan* logging (f. LOG *v.*[2]) + STONE.] A rocking-stone.

Logaœdic (lǫgăi̯·dik), *a.* 1844. [ad. late L. *logaœdicus*, ad. Gr. λογαοιδικός, f. λόγος discourse + ἀοιδή song (as standing in rhythm between prose and poetry).] *Prosody.* Composed of dactyls combined with trochees, or anapæsts with iambs. As *sb.*, a logaœdic verse.

Logarithm (lǫ·gărĭþ'm). 1615. [ad. mod.L. *logarithmus* (Napier, 1614), f. Gr. λόγος proportion, ratio + ἀριθμός number. *Logarithmus* is usu. taken to mean 'ratio-number'; but Napier may have taken λόγος as = 'reckoning', 'calculation' (cf. LOGISTIC).] *Math.* One of a class of arithmetical functions, invented by John Napier of Merchiston (died 1617), and tabulated for use in abridging calculation. Abbreviated *log* (no period).

The sum of the logarithms of any two or more numbers is the logarithm of their product; hence a table of logarithms enables one to substitute addition and subtraction for multiplication and division, and multiplication and division for involution and evolution. *Natural, hyperbolic*, or *Napierian logarithms*, those of which the base is the incommensurable quantity *e* (2·71828+), used in analytical investigations. *Common, decimal*, or *Briggsian logarithms* those in vented by Henry Briggs (died 1630), of which the base is 10, used in practical calculations. *Logistic logarithms*: see LOGISTIC.

Logarithmic (lǫgări·þmik), *a.* (and *sb.*) 1698. [f. LOGARITHM + -IC.] *Math.* 1. Of or pertaining to logarithms. Also = 'logarithm (increased by ten) of', as in *log sine, tangent, secant*, etc.; opp. to *natural.* b. Pertaining to the logarithmic curve 1875. 2. *sb.* = *logarithmic curve* or *line* 1753.

1. *L. curve* (or *line*), a curve having its ordinates in geometrical progression and its abscissas in arithmetical progression, so that the abscissas are the logarithms of the corresponding ordinates. *L. spiral*, a spiral which intersects all its radiants at the same angle. So **Logari·thmical** *a.* 1631. Hence **Logari·thmically** *adv.*

Lo·g-book. 1679. 1. *Naut.* A book in which the particulars of a ship's voyage (including her rate of progress as measured by the log) are entered daily from the log-board. Hence *transf.* and *fig.*, a journal of travel. 2. *Tailoring.* = LOG *sb.*[1] II. 3. 1869. 3. A kind of journal of proceedings to be kept by the master of a public elementary school 1872.

‖**Loge** (lōuʒ). 1749. [Fr.; see LODGE *sb.*] 1. A booth, stall. CHESTERF. 2. A box in a theatre or opera-house 1768.

-loger (lŏdʒəɹ), a word-ending repr. Gr. -λόγος (L. *-logus*); see -LOGUE, -LOGY. The oldest word with this ending is *astrologer* (14th c.); it may be either f. L. *astrologus* + -ER [1] (a type of derivation afterwards common), or f. *astrology* + -ER [1] (cf. *astronomyer, astronomer*). On the analogy of this word, *-loger* was applied in a few instances to form personal designations correlative with words in *-logy*, *-logic-al*, as in *chronologer, philologer*, etc.; but it is now superseded by -LOGIST.

Lo·ggat, lo·gget. *Obs.* exc. *Hist.* 1541. [app. f. LOG *sb.*[1]] 1. An old game, played by throwing pieces of wood at a stake fixed in the ground; the player who is nearest the stake wins. 2. A pole, heavy stake 1600.

1. *Haml.* v. i. 100. 2. Beating of fruit downe with long poales, loggets, or such like MARKHAM.

Logged (lǫgd), *ppl. a.* 1820. [f. LOG *v.*[1] + -ED [1].] a. Reduced to the condition of a log (*lit.* and *fig.*). Of water: Stagnant. Of a vessel: Water-logged. b. Of land: Cleared by hewing the timber into logs.

Logger (lǫ·gəɹ). *N. Amer.* 1734. [f. LOG *v.*[1] + -ER [1].] One who fells timber or cuts it into logs; a lumberman.

Loggerhead (lǫ·gəɹhed). 1588. [prob. f. dial. *logger* sb. = LOG *sb.*[1] I. 2.] 1. A block-head. 2. A head out of proportion to the body; a large or 'thick' head. Chiefly *fig.* 1598. 3. An iron instrument with a long handle and a ball or bulb at the end, used, when heated, for melting pitch, etc. 1687. 4. A stout wooden post, built into the stern of a whale-boat, for catching a turn of the line to. Also *transf.* 1840. 5. As pop. name of heavy-headed animals. a. (Also *l. turtle*, †*tortoise.*) A species of turtle, *Thalassochelys caretta* 1657. b. Applied to species of birds; *esp.* a N. American shrike, *Lanius ludovicianus* or *carolinensis* 1657. 6. *pl.* A plant of the genus *Centaurea* 1829.

1. A pitifull, sneaking, whining Puritan, related to yᵉ L. at Lambeth HEARNE. '*We three* loggerheads be': an inscription under a common public-house sign, in which two wooden heads are shown, the spectator being the third. See MALONE on *Twel. N.* II. iii. 17. 2. Let us retire, and lay our two logger-heads together RICHARDSON.

Phr. †*To fall, get, go to loggerheads*: to come to blows. *To be at loggerheads*: to be in contention about differences of opinion; also, rarely, *to come to l.*

Comb. **l.-sponge**, a W. Indian sponge of inferior quality; probably named from Loggerhead Key.

Hence **Lo·gger-headed** *a.* thick-headed, stupid; (of animals) having a large head.

‖**Loggia** (lǫ·dʒiă; It. lǭ·dʒa). *Pl.* **loggias**, It. loggie. 1742. [a. It. *loggia*; see LODGE *sb.*] A gallery or arcade having one or more of its sides open to the air.

Logging (lǫ·giŋ), *vbl. sb.* 1706. [f. LOG *v.*[1] + -ING [1].] The action of felling timber or hewing it into logs. Also *concr.* A quantity of timber felled. Also *attrib.*

-logian (lōu·dʒiăn), an ending occurring first in *astrologian* (-(*i*)*en* CHAUCER), a. OF. *astrologien*, f. *astrologie*: see -AN, -IAN, and hence in a few mod. wds. correlative to names of sciences in -LOGY. Now usu. repl. by -LOGIST.

Logic (lǫ·dʒik). ME. [a. F. *logique*, ad. med.L. *logica*, ad. Gr. λογική (ellipt. for ἡ λογικὴ τέχνη, med.L. *ars logica*), fem. of λογικός pertaining to reasoning, f. λόγος; see LOGOS.] 1. The branch of philosophy that treats of the forms of thinking in general, and esp. of inference and scientific method. b. *pl.* in the same sense. Not now in general use. 1637. c. Name of a class in Roman Catholic schools 1705. d. With reference to Hegel: The fundamental science of thought and its categories (including metaphysics or ontology) 1838. 2. A system of logic; a treatise on logic. Also, the science or art of reasoning as applied to a department of knowledge. ME. 3. Logical argumentation; a mode of argumentation viewed as good or bad according to its conformity or want of conformity to logical principles. Also, logical pertinence or propriety. 1601. b. *transf.* A means of convincing or proving 1682. 4. *attrib.* Of or pertaining to logic 1440.

1. L. may be most briefly defined as the Science of Reasoning JEVONS. 2. The logick of taste, if I may be allowed the expression BURKE. The empirical l. of Mill, the formal l. of Kant 1882. 3. England, as Mr. Disraeli once said, is not governed by l. 1891. To argue with more learning than l. (*mod.*). b. Bonner's Logick, Fire and Faggot 1682. 4. Questions ..deeper than any of our Logic-plummets hitherto will sound CARLYLE. *Comb.* †l.-fisted *a.*, having the hand clenched, like L. in personification (see Bacon *Adv. Learn.* II. xviii. § 5).

-logic (lǫ·dʒik), **-logical** (lǫ·dʒikăl), endings orig. repr. Gr. -λογικός in adjs. derived from adjs. and sbs. in -λογος, -λογον, having derivative nouns in -λογία, Eng. -LOGY. Such adjs. are commonly apprehended as if f. *-logy* + -IC. Hence, with few exceptions (e. g. *apology*), a sb. in *-logy* now implies a possible correlative adj. in *-logical*. See further -ICAL, and cf. GEOLOGIC.

Logical (lǫ·dʒikăl), *a.* (and *sb.*) 1500. [f. LOGIC *sb.* and L. *logicus* + -AL.] 1. Of or pertaining to logic; also, of the nature of formal argument. 2. That is in conformity with the laws of correct reasoning 1689. 3. That follows as a reasonable inference; that is in accordance with the logic of events, of human character, etc. 1860. 4. Of persons: Capable of reasoning correctly; also, reasoning correctly (in a particular case) 1664. 5. *nonce-use.* Rational 1652. 6. *sb. pl.* The subjects which are studied in a course of instruction in logic. *Obs.* exc. *Hist.* 1551.

1. L. Demonstrations 1707, writers WHATELY, generalizations 1851. 2. A process of l. reasoning D. STEWART. 3. In France accordingly feudal government runs its l. career STUBBS. 4. A clear and L. Head ADDISON. 6. *Little* or *small logicals*: certain minor questions treated in the *Parva Logicalia* of Petrus Hispanus and others. Hence **Logicality. Lo·gically** *adv.*

Logician (lǫdʒi·ʃăn). ME. [a. F. *logicien*, f. *logique*; see -ICIAN.] 1. A writer on logic; a student of logic. b. A member of the school class called Logic 1705. 2. One skilled in reasoning 1592. So †**Logi·cianer** 1548.

Logicize (lǫ·dʒisəiz), *v. rare.* 1835. [f. LOGIC or L. *logicus* + -IZE.] 1. *intr.* To employ logic. 2. *trans.* To turn into logic 1865.

Logie (lōᵘ·gi). 1860. [f. name of inventor.] *Theatr.* Ornament of zinc to simulate jewellery.

‖**Logion** (lǫ·giǫn). *Pl.* **logia** (lǫ·giă). 1875. [Gr. λόγιον oracle, f. λόγος speech.] A traditional maxim of a religious teacher or sage. Chiefly used with reference to sayings of Jesus not recorded in the Gospels.

-logist (lŏdʒist), f. -LOGY + -IST, forming sbs. 'one who is versed in—logy'. The only living formative with this function.

Logistic (lodʒi·stik). 1628. [ad. med.L. *logisticus*, ad. Gr. λογιστικός, f. λογίζεσθαι to reckon, reason; see LOGOS.]

A. *adj.* †1. ? Pertaining to reasoning -1644. 2. Pertaining to reckoning or calculation 1706. 3. *Math.* a. In *l. curve*, etc. = logarithmic. b. *L. logarithms*: logarithms of sexagesimal numbers, used in astronomical calculations. c. *L. numbers*: old name for ratios or fractions. 1727. So **Logi·stical** *a.* 1570.

B. *sb.* †1. A calculator. W. ROBINSON. 2. *Math.* A logistic curve 1727. 3. *pl.* (rarely *sing.*) a. The art of arithmetical calculation; the elementary processes of arithmetic 1656. b. Logistical or sexagesimal arithmetic 1801.

Logistics, *sb. pl.*[1]: see LOGISTIC B. 3.

Logistics (lodʒi·stiks), *sb. pl.*[2] 1879. [ad. F. *logistique*, f. *loger* to quarter, LODGE; see -ISTIC.] The art of moving and quartering troops (i.e. quarter-master's work), now esp. of organizing supplies.

Logocracy (lǫgǫ·krăsi). 1804. [f. Gr. λόγος + -CRACY.] A community or system of government in which words are the ruling powers.

†‖**Logodæ·dalus.** *Pl.* **-i.** Also **logodædale.** 1611. [mod.L., a. Gr. λογοδαίδαλος, f. λόγος + δαίδαλος cunning.] One who is cunning in words -1664. So **Logodæ·dalist** 1654. **Logodæ·daly** (*rare*), cunning in words.

Logogram (lǫ·gŏgræm). 1820. [f. Gr. λόγος + -GRAM.] 1. = LOGOGRIPH. 2. A sign or character representing a word; in *Phonography*, a word-letter; a single stroke which represents a word 1840.

Logograph (lǫ·gŏgraf), *sb.* 1797. [f. as prec. + -GRAPH.] ¶1. Used erron. for LOGOGRIPH. 2. *Phonography.* = LOGOGRAM 2. 1888. 3. = LOGOTYPE 1872. 4. = LOGOGRAPHER 2. 1862. 5. An instrument for giving a graphic representation of speech-sounds 1879. Hence **Lo·gograph** *v. trans.* to print with logotypes.

Logographer (lǫgǫ·grăfəɹ). 1656. [f. late L. *logographus* (a. Gr. λογογράφος) + -ER[1]; see -GRAPHER.] †1. A lawyer's clerk; an accountant -1735. 2. *Gr. Antiq.* A writer of traditional history in prose 1846. 3. *Gr. Antiq.* A professional speech-writer 1853. 4. One who practises logography 1860.

Logography (lǫgǫ·grăfi). 1783. [ad. Gr. λογογραφία, f. λόγος + -γραφία.] 1. A method of printing with entire words, instead of single letters. 2. A method of long-hand reporting in which several reporters were employed, each taking down a few words in succession 1842. Hence **Logogra·phic, -al** *a.* pertaining to l. (sense 1); consisting of characters or signs, each of which represents an entire word. **Logogra·phically** *adv.*

Logogriph (lǫ·gŏgrif). 1597. [ad. F. *logogriphe*, f. Gr. λόγος word + γρῖφος fishing-basket, riddle.] A kind of enigma, in which a certain word, and other words that can be formed out of all or any of its letters, are to be guessed from synonyms of them introduced into a set of verses. Occas.: Any anagram or puzzle involving anagrams. Hence **Logogri·phic** *a.* of or pertaining to logogriphs, of the nature of a l.

Logomachy (lǫgǫ·măki). 1569. [ad. Gr. λογομαχία, f. λόγος + -μαχία fighting.] 1. Contention about words; an instance of this. 2. ? *U.S.* A game of word-making (Webster).

1. This quarrel tending to vain logomachies..ended in confusion SEWEL. **Lo·gomach, Logoma·chic, -ical** *a.*, **Logo·machist, Logo·machize** *v.*

Logometric (lǫgŏme·trik), *a.* 1813. [f. Gr. λόγος ratio + μέτρον + -IC.] Indicating ratios by measurement. Applied by Wollaston to his 'scale' for chemical equivalents.

‖**Logos** (lǫ·gǫs). 1587. [Gr. λόγος word, speech, discourse, reason, f. λογ-, ablaut-var. of λεγ- in λέγειν to say.] A term used by Hellenistic and Neo-platonist philosophers in certain senses developed from its ordinary senses 'reason' and 'word'; in the N.T. rendered 'Word', as a designation of Jesus Christ; hence used by Christian theologians for the Second Person of the Trinity. By mod. writers used untranslated, esp. in discussions of the doctrine of the Trinity in its philosophical aspects.

Logothete (lǫ·gŏþīt). 1781. [ad. med.L. *logotheta*, ad. Gr. λογοθέτης, primarily 'one who audits accounts', f. λόγος account + θε-, stem of τιθέναι to set + agent-suffix -της.] Any of various functionaries under the Byzantine emperors; also a chancellor, esp. in Sicily.

Logotype (lǫ·gŏtəip). 1816. [f. Gr. λόγος word + TYPE.] *Printing.* A type containing a word, or two or more letters, cast in one piece. Hence **Lo·gotypy** = LOGOGRAPHY 1.

Lo·g-roll, *v.* 1835. [Back-formation from LOG-ROLLING.] a. *trans.* To procure the passing of (a bill) by log-rolling. b. *intr.* To engage in log-rolling.

The leading politicians who..log-roll the railway bills 1865. b. To log-roll with everybody who was willing to work with him 1879.

Lo·g-ro·ller. 1864. [f. LOG *sb.*[1] + ROLLER.] 1. One who engages in political or literary log-rolling. 2. *U.S.* A sawmill device for loading logs 1884.

Lo·g-ro·lling. 1823. [f. LOG *sb.*[1] + ROLLING *vbl. sb.*] 1. *U.S.* The action of rolling logs to any spot; a meeting for co-operation in doing this 1848. 2. *U.S. slang.* Combination for political or other co-operation. (Suggested by the phr. 'You roll my log and I'll roll yours'.) 1823. b. Mutual puffing in literary publications ? 1845.

2. Our log-rolling, our stumps and their politics.. are yet unsung EMERSON.

-logue (lǫg), repr. Gr. -λογος, -λογον in adapted wds. (mostly through Fr.), as *analogue, catalogue, dialogue.* The wds. with this ending which designate persons, e. g. *Assyriologue, ideologue*, are now little used, derivs. in *-loger, -logist*, or *-logian* being preferred.

Logwood (lǫ·gwud). 1581. [f. LOG *sb.*[1] + WOOD.] †1. Logs stored for fuel. PEPYS. 2. The heartwood of an American tree (*Hæmatoxylon Campechianum*); so called because imported in logs; also, the dye or drug extracted from this 1581. b. The tree itself 1652. 3. *attrib.*, as *l. red* 1752.

Logy (lōᵘ·gi), *a. U.S.* 1859. [Cf. Du. *log* heavy, dull.] Dull and heavy in motion or thought. b. as *sb.*: A heavy fish. R. KIPLING.

-logy (lŏdʒi), earlier *-logie*, an ending occurring orig. in wds. adapted from Gr. words in -λογία (the earliest, e. g. *theology*, through F. *-logie*, med.L. *-logia*). In some instances the terminal element is λόγος word, discourse (e. g. in τετραλογία tetralogy, τριλογία trilogy); more commonly it is the root λογ- (ablaut-var. of λεγ-, λέγειν to speak; cf. LOGOS). In this latter case, the sbs. in -λογία usually denote the character, action, or department of knowledge of a person described by an adj. or sb. in -λόγος, meaning either '(one) who speaks (in a certain way)', or '(one) who treats of (a certain subject)'. Hence (1) wds. anglicized as *brachylogy, cacology, eulogy, tautology*, etc.; and (2) names of sciences or departments of study, e. g. *theology, astrology*, etc. Words of the last-mentioned class, in which the first element is always a sb., have *o* for their combining vowel, following the Gr. analogy; exceptions are *petralogy* and *mineralogy*. All mod. formations in *-logy* may imply correlative formations in -LOGICAL and -LOGIST (or in the case of some of the older wds. -LOGER or -LOGIAN).

Lohoch (lōᵘ·hǫk). 1544. Also †**loch**, dial. **loach.** [a. obs. F. *loch, lohoc*, a. med.L. *lohoc, looch*, a. Arab.] *Med.* A linctus.

Loin (loin). ME. [ad. OF. *loigne, logne*, dial. var. of *longe* (mod.F. *longe* loin of veal):— med.L. **lumbea*, fem. of **lumbeus* adj., belonging to the loin, f. L. *lumbus*:—WAryan **londhwo-*: see LEND *sb.*[1]] 1. Chiefly *pl.* The part or parts of a human being or quadruped, situated on both sides of the vertebral column, between the false ribs and the hip-bone. b. As food; chiefly, the joint of meat which includes the vertebræ of the loins ME. 2. Chiefly *Biblical* and *poet.* This part of the body, a. as that about which the clothes are bound 1526. b. as the seat of strength and generative power. †Hence occas. = 'sire', 'offspring', 'descendants'. Also *fig.* 1535.

2. a. Phr. *To gird (up) the loins* (lit. and fig.), to prepare for strenuous exertion. b. Loe now, his strength is in his loynes *Job* xl. 16. A multitude, like which the populous North Pour'd never from her frozen loyns MILT. *attrib.* l. cloth 1859.

Loir (loi·ɹ). 1774. [a. F. *loir*:—pop.L. **glīrem*, for *glīrem, glis.*] The Fat Dormouse (*Myoxus glis*).

Loiter (loi·təɹ), *v.* ME. [a. MDu. *loteren* to wag about (like a loose tooth), Du. *leuteren.*] 1. *intr.* To idle. Now only: To linger indolently on one's way; to hang idly about a place; to dawdle over a task. **b.** To travel indolently and with frequent pauses. With advs. or advb. phrases. 1728. **2.** *trans.* **a.** To allow (time, etc.) to pass idly. Const. *away.* †**b.** To postpone getting or giving 1549.

1. Sir John, you loyter heere too long SHAKS. Officers..loitered in the hall, as if waiting for orders SCOTT. **b.** The Avon loiters past the churchyard HAWTHORNE. **2.** We loitered away the rest of the day (*mod.*). Hence **Loi·terer,** one who loiters; †a vagabond. **Loi·teringly** *adv.*

Loke (lōᵘk). *dial.* 1787. [repr. OE. *loca*, f. root of *louk* v. to shut, lock.] A lane; a 'cul-de-sac'; a grass road; a private lane or road.

Loll (lǫl), *sb.* 1582. [f. LOLL *v.*] **1.** The action or posture of lolling 1709. **2.** One who or that which lolls, e.g. a tongue 1582. **3.** A pet, a spoilt child 1728.

Loll (lǫl), *v.* ME. [app. symbolic of rocking or swinging; cf. LULL *v.*] **1.** *intr.* To hang down loosely; to droop, dangle. Also with *down.* *Obs.* or *arch.* †**2.** *trans.* To let droop or dangle –1650. **3.** To thrust, hang *out* (the tongue) 1611. **b.** *intr.* for *refl.* Of the tongue: To protrude. Usu. with *out.* 1801. **4.** *intr.* To lean idly; to recline or rest in a relaxed attitude, resting against something. Also with *about, back, out.* (The chief current sense.) ME. **b.** *trans.* To allow to rest idly (*rare*). Also, to pass *away* (time) in lolling about. 1696. †**5.** *intr.* To saunter (*rare*) –1678.

1. A great white feather lolling down 1849. **3.** Fierce Tigers couch'd around, and loll'd their fawning Tongues DRYDEN. **4.** And, among the rest, Duncomb, lolling, with his heels upon another chair PEPYS. Hence **Lo·ller** [1]. **Lo·llingly** *adv.*

Lollard (lǫ·lăɹd). Now *Hist.* ME. [a. MDu. *lollaerd*, lit. 'mumbler, mutterer', f. *lollen*; see -ARD.] **1.** A name of contempt given in the 14th c. to certain heretics, who were either followers of Wyclif or held opinions similar to his. ¶**2.** [Assoc. w. LOLL *v.*] One who lolls; an idler. *Obs. rare.* –1659.

1. *attrib.* Jack Sharp, l. rebel, was a weaver of Abingdon 1897. **2.** A pulpited divine..a l. indeed over his elbow-cushion MILT. Hence **Lo·llardist.** **Lo·llardism,** the tenets and practice of the Lollards. **Lo·llardry** (now *rare*), **Lo·llardy** *sbs.*, the tenets of the Lollards. **Lo·llardy** *a.* characteristic of the Lollards. var. †**Lo·ller** [2].

Lollipop (lǫ·lipǫp). *colloq.* 1796. [?] **a.** *dial.* A kind of sweetmeat, consisting chiefly of sugar or treacle, that dissolves easily in the mouth. **b.** *pl.* (formerly also *collect. sing.*) Sweetmeats in general. Also shortened **Lo·lly** *Austral.* and *dial.*

Lollop (lǫ·lǝp), *v. colloq.* 1745. [Onomatopœic extension of LOLL *v.*] **1.** *intr.* To lounge or sprawl; to go with a lounging gait. **2.** To bob up and down 1851. Hence **Lo·llop** *sb.* 1834.

2. To l. about in the trough of a heavy sea 1878.

Loll-shraub (lǫlˌʃrǭb). Also **-shrob.** 1816. ['Englishman's Hindustani *lāl-shrāb* red wine' (Yule).] 'The universal name for claret in India' (Yule).

Lombard (lǫ·mbăɹd, lʊ·mbăɹd), *sb.*[1] and *a.* ME. [a. F., ad. It. *lombardo*, contr. repr. late L. *Langobardus, Longobardus*, Teut. **Laŋgobarđo-z, -barđon-*; a compound of **laŋgo-* LONG *a.* and *Bardi*, L. form of the name of the people.]

A. *sb.* **1.** *a. Hist.* A person belonging to the Germanic people (L. *Langobardi*) who conquered Italy in the 6th c., whence the name of Lombardy. **b.** A native of Lombardy. 1480. †**2.** A native of Lombardy engaged as a banker, money-changer, or pawnbroker; hence *gen.* a banker, pawnbroker, etc. –1709. †**3.** A bank, money-changer's or money-lender's office; a pawnshop –1799.

2. They are fallen to the L., left at the Brokers GREENE. **3.** No sooner got I coine..But to the bancke or lumbard straight it went MARKHAM.

B. *adj.* **1.** Belonging to the Lombards or to Lombardy; Lombardic 1500. †**2.** *Cookery.* In **l. pie** (see LUMBER-PIE).

Hence †**Lombardee·r,** 'an usurer or broaker' (Blount); **Lombarde·sque** *a.*, resembling the L. school of painters; **Lo·mbardism,** a Lombardic idiom; **Lomba·rdo-,** comb. form with sense 'Lombardic combined with..'.

Lombard (lǫ·mbăɹd), *sb.*[2] *Hist.* 1838. [ad. obs. Sp. *lombarda.* Cf. late Gr. λουμπάρδα, app. synonymous with βουμβάρδα BOMBARD.] A military engine used in Spain in the 16th c.

Lombardic (lǫmbā·ɹdik), *a.* 1697. [ad. med.L. *lombardicus*; see LOMBARD *sb.*[1] and -IC.] Pertaining to Lombardy or the Lombards. Applied *spec.* to the architecture of northern Italy from the 7th to the 13th century; to a type of handwriting found in Italian MSS. during the same period; and to the school of painters, including Leonardo da Vinci, Mantegna, and Luini, which flourished in Lombardy during the 15th and 16th centuries. **b.** *absol.* Lombardic writing 1893.

Lo·mbard-street. 1598. Name of a street in London, orig. occupied by Lombard bankers, and still containing many banks. *fig.* The 'money market'; the body of financiers.

'It is Lombard Street to a China orange', quoth Uncle Jack LYTTON.

Loment (lōᵘ·ment). ME. [ad. L. *lomentum* bean-meal (orig. a wash made of bean-meal), f. *lo-, lavare* to wash.] †**1.** Bean-meal. Only ME. **2.** *Bot.* = LOMENTUM 1814.

‖**Lomentum** (lome·ntǝ̆m). *Pl.* **-ta.** 1836. [L.; see prec.] A legume which is contracted in the spaces between the seeds, breaking up when mature into one-seeded joints. Hence **Lomenta·ceous** *a.* of the nature of or resembling a l.; characterized by lomenta; belonging to the N.O. *Lomentaceæ*, a former sub-order of *Cruciferæ.*

Lomonite, early var. LAUMONTITE.

Lond(e, obs. f. LAND.

London (lʊ·ndǝn), name of the capital of England, used *attrib.*:

L. clay, a geological formation belonging to the lower division of the Eocene tertiary, in the southeast of England and esp. at and near London; **L. particular** *colloq.*, a L. fog; **L. paste,** a caustic composed of equal parts of quicklime and caustic soda mixed with alcohol; **L. rocket,** the plant *Sisymbrium Irio*, which sprang up abundantly on the ruins of the great fire of London in 1666.

Hence **Lo·ndoner,** a native (or inhabitant) of London 1460; †a ship belonging to London 1764. **Lo·ndonism,** a habit, manner, or peculiarity of speech belonging to Londoners 1803. **Lo·ndonize** *v. trans.* to make like London or Londoners 1778; *intr.* to visit or frequent London LAMB.

Lo·ndon pri·de. 1629. **a.** The Sweet William, *Dianthus barbatus.* Now *dial.* **b.** *Lychnis Chalcedonica.* Now *dial.* 1688. **c.** *Saxifraga umbrosa*, having pretty pink flowers on long stalks, commonly grown in towns; also called *none-so-pretty.*

Lone (lōᵘn), *a.* 1530. [Aphet. f. ALONE.] **1.** Having no companions; solitary. Chiefly *poet.* and *rhet.* **b.** Lonesome 1839. **2.** Unmarried; single or widowed. Now only of women, with mock-pathetic reference to sense 1. 1548. **3.** Standing apart from others of its kind; isolated. Formerly *esp.* in phr. *l. house.* 1667. **4.** *poet.* Of places: Lonely; unfrequented, uninhabited 1712.

1. As some l. miser, visiting his store GOLDSM. Phr. *To play, hold a l. hand*: in Quadrille and Euchre, to play against all the other players, or without help from one's partner. Hence *l. hand, l. player* = a person playing such a game. **2.** Queen Elizabeth being a l. woman, and having few friends, refusing to marry 1642. **3.** At some l. ale-house in the Berkshire moors M. ARNOLD. **4.** In l. Glenartney's hazel shade SCOTT. Hence **Lo·neness** (now *rare* or *dial.*).

Lonely (lōᵘ·nli), *a.* 1607. [f. LONE *a.* + -LY [1].] **1.** Having no companionship; solitary, lone. **2.** *poet.* = LONE 3. 1632. **3.** = LONE 4. 1629. **4.** Dejected at the consciousness of being alone; having a feeling of solitariness 1811. **b.** *poet.* Imparting a feeling of loneliness; dreary 1813.

1. To give due light To the misled and l. Travailer MILT. *Comus* 200. **2.** That l. tree against the western sky M. ARNOLD. **3.** An isle..the loneliest in a l. sea TENNYSON. Hence **Lo·nelihood** (*poet.*), loneliness. **Lo·nelily** *adv.* **Lo·neliness.**

Lonesome (lōᵘ·nsǝ̆m), *a.* 1647. [f. LONE *a.* + -SOME.] **1.** Of persons, etc.: Solitary, lonely. In later use: Feeling lonely or forlorn. **b.** *By* (or *on*) *one's lonesome*, all alone 1908. **2.** Of localities: Solitary, unfrequented, desolate; also, making one feel forlorn 1647.

1. The l. Bittern shall possess This fenny seat BLACKMORE. You must..not be l. because I'm not at home DICKENS. **2.** Like one that on a l. road Doth walk in fear and dread COLERIDGE.

Hence **Lo·nesome·ly** *adv.*, **-ness.**

Long (lǫŋ), *a.*[1] and *sb.* [Com. Teut.: OE. *lang, lǫng* :—OTeut. **laŋgo-* :—pre-Teut. **loŋgho-* (= L. *longus*); an alteration (according to some) of **dloŋgho-*, cogn. w. Gr. δολιχός, etc.]

A. *adj.* **I.** With reference to spatial measurement. **1.** Great in measurement from end to end. Opp. to *short.* **b.** Tall. Now *rare* exc. *joc.* OE. **c.** Qualifying a sb. denoting a measure of length, to indicate an extent greater than that expressed by the sb. 1619. **d.** Of action, vision, etc.: Extending to a great distance. (Cf. *l. sight*, below.) 1604. **2.** Having (more or less, or a specified) extension from end to end; often with adv. or advb. phr. OE. **3.** Elongated 1551.

1. A l. and large difference CHAUCER. The l. low line of the Dutch coast 1893. A l. distance, journey (*mod.*). Phr. *L. arm, hand*: used *transf.* and *fig.* of extent of reach; The l. arm of coincidence 1899. *A l. face* (colloq.): a dismal or solemn expression 1786. *A l. head*: one of more than normal length from back to front; *fig.* capacity for calculation and forethought. *To make a l. nose* (slang): to put the thumb to the nose in mockery. *A l. tongue* (fig.): loquacity. *L. litter*: long straw, etc. serving as bedding. *L. forage*: straw and green fodder, as dist. from hay, oats, etc. *A l. drink* (colloq.): *lit.* of liquor in a l. glass; hence, a large measure of liquor. **c.** A l. mile from Launceston 1697. **d.** Phr. *At l. weapons*: (fighting) at long range. So, *at l. bowls* or *balls*: said of ships exchanging shots at a distance. *L. train* = *l. distance train.* **2.** A mark 30 feet long by 20. 1854. Phr. *It's as l. as it's broad* (see BROAD *a.*). **3.** Phr. *L. square*: an oblong rectangle. *L. in the* TOOTH.

II. With reference to serial extent or duration. **1.** Of a series, enumeration, speech, sentence, word, etc.: Having a great extent from beginning to end OE. **b.** *colloq.* Of numbers, and of things numbered: Large. Chiefly in *l. family, odds, price.* 1746. **2.** Of a period of time, or a process, state, or action viewed with reference to time: Having a great extent in duration OE. **3.** Having (more or less, or a specified) extension serially or temporally ME. **4.** Continuing too long; lengthy, prolix, tedious ME. **5.** Qualifying a sb. denoting a period of time, a number, or quantity, to indicate an extent greater than that expressed by the sb.; also, to indicate that the time is felt by the speaker to be excessive or unusual in duration 1592. **6.** That has continued or will continue in action, operation, or obligation for a long period. Freq. applied to feelings, dispositions, etc.; hence also, to persons exhibiting these. ME. **7.** Of a point of time: Distant, remote. Now only in *l. date*, and in the legal phr. *a l. day.* ME. **b.** Of bills, promissory notes, etc.: Of long date, having a long time to run 1861. **8.** *Phonetics* and *Prosody.* Applied to a vowel (now also to a cons.) when its utterance has the greater of the two measures of duration recognized in speech-sounds. Also, in *Prosody*, of a syllable: Occupying a longer time (e.g. two time-units) in utterance than a *short* syllable. OE. **9.** *Comm.* Said of the market (e.g. in cotton) when consumers have made large contracts in advance against an anticipated scarcity 1859.

1. Phr. *L. bill*: one containing many items; hence, one in which the charges are excessive. *L. hour*: one indicated by many strokes; Before the l. hour of midnight all was hush 1827. **b.** Phr. *L. suit* (in Card games): one in which more than three cards are held; *fig.* (*colloq.*), a thing at which one excels. **2.** Enjoy ..Short pleasures, for l. woes are to succeed MILT. *L. of life* = 'of l. life' (now *rare*). *L. time, while*, etc.: often used advb. (now, exc. *poet.*, always with *a*) = LONG *adv.* **1.** *This l. time* or *while*: for a l. time down to the present. Similarly with preceding prep., *for, of* (*arch.* or *dial.*); now always with *a.* I have not seen him for a long time (*mod.*). **3.** *Mids. N.* v. i. 61. **4.** I cou'd be l. in Precepts DRYDEN. Phr. †*It were* (*too*) *l. to*, etc. *To think l.* (chiefly *Sc.*): to grow weary or impatient; Haue I thought l. to see this mornings face, And doth it giue me such a sight as this? SHAKS. **5.** Phr. *L. years*: = 'many years'. *At* (*the*) *l. last*: see LAST *a.* II. *L. dozen, hundred*: see the sbs. **6.** A l. farewell to all my Greatnesse SHAKS. His recollections..contained some..surprises to his longest friends T. MOZLEY. Phr. *L. memory*: one that remembers events for a l. period. *A l. word* (colloq.): one that indicates a l. time; 'Never' is a l. word 1883. **7. b.** Rates given for l. paper, as compared with those for bills on demand GOSCHEN. **8.** Phr. *L. mark*: the mark (‾) placed over a vowel letter to indicate l. quantity. In ordinary language 'the long *a, e, i, o, u*' denotes that sound of the letter which is used as its alphabetical name, while 'the short *a, e, i, o, u*' denotes the sound which the letter most commonly has in a stressed short syllable. N.E.D.

Comb., etc.: **l.-axed** *a.*, having a l. axis; **-bowls**, the game of ninepins; **-butt** *Billiards*, a cue for reaching a ball beyond the range of the half-butt; **l. card**, one of a suit remaining in one hand after the others of the suit are played; **l.-clothes**, the garments of a baby in arms; **-dated** *a.*, extending to a distant date; chiefly of an acceptance, falling due at a distant date; **l. division, home, jump** (see the sbs.); **l. firm** *slang*, a swindling business concern; **l. measure**, (*a*) lineal measure, the measure of length; (*b*) a table of lineal measures; (*c*) = next; **l. metre**, the metre of a hymn-stanza in iambic rhythm of four lines of eight syllables each; **l. nine** *U.S.*, a cheap cigar; **L. Parliament**, the Parliament which sat from Nov. 1640 to March 1653, and again for a short time in 1659, and was dissolved in 1660; †also, the second Parliament of Charles II (1661–1678); **l.-pig**, tr. cannibal's name for human flesh; **l. primer** *Printing* (see PRIMER); **l. service** *Mil.*, 'the maximum period a recruit can enlist for in any branch of the service, viz. for 12 years' (Voyle); **l. ship** *Hist.*, a ship of great length, built to accommodate a considerable number of rowers; a ship of war, a galley; = L. *navis longa*; **l.-shot**, (*a*) a shot fired at a distance; (*b*) a distant range; **l. sight**, power of seeing distant objects; also, the defect of sight by which only distant objects are seen distinctly; **l.-sixes**, long candles, six to the pound; **-staple** *a.* having a long fibre; applied to cotton of a superior grade; **l. stone**, a menhir; **l. sword** (see SWORD); **l.-threads**, warp; **L. Vacation**, summer vacation at the Law-Courts and Universities; **l.-wall, way**, used *attrib.* to imply a method of working in which all available coal is extracted at once; **l. wave** *Wireless*, a wave having a wave-length of (about) 800 metres and upwards; **whist** (see WHIST *sb.*); **l.-wool**, (*a*) a long-stapled wool, suitable for combing or carding; (*b*) a long-woolled sheep; **writ** = PREROGATIVE-*w.*

b. In names of animals, as **l.-bill**, a bird with a l. bill, *e.g.* a snipe; **l. clam**, (*a*) *Mya arenaria* (see CLAM *sb.*[2] 1 c); (*b*) the razor-clam, *Ensis americana*; **l.-horn**, (*a*) one of a breed of long-horned cattle; (*b*) the long-eared owl, *Otus vulgaris*; **-nose**, the Garfish; **-wing**, the swift.

c. In names of plants, etc., as **†l.-bean** = KIDNEY BEAN; **-flax**, flax to be spun its natural length without cutting; **-leek**, the ordinary leek (*Allium porrum*); **-pod**, a variety of broad bean which produces a very l. pod; **l. purples**, (*a*) the early purple orchis, *O. mascula* SHAKS.; (*b*) *Lythrum Salicaria*; (*c*) *Vicia Cracca* TENNYSON.

d. *Cricket*: **l. field (off, on)**, the position of a fieldsman who stands at a distance behind the bowler, either to his left or right; **l.-hop**, a ball that makes a long flight after pitching, before reaching the wicket; **l. off, on**, short for *long field off, on*; **l.-stop**, a fieldsman who stands behind the wicket-keeper to stop balls that pass him; hence *long-stop* vb., to field as long-stop. Also *long leg, long slip* (see the sbs.).

B. Quasi-*sb.* and *sb.* **I.** The adj. used *absol.* **1.** In various phrases with preps. See below. ME. **2.** Without prep.: Much time. Now chiefly in *to take l.* 1470. **b.** as the predicate of an impersonal clause (see below) OE. **3.** *The l. and the short of* (*it*, etc.): the sum total, substance, upshot 1500.

1. *Before l.* (short for †*before it be long*): soon. So *ere long*. Perhaps we may meet ere l. 1760. I'll be here again before l. TROLLOPE. *For l.*: throughout a l. period; also *predicatively*, destined or likely to continue l. The children..had been restless for l. 1895. *At* (*the*) *longest*: on the longest estimate. Short, at the longest, were the life of man PUSEY. 2. Phr. *That l.* (colloq.): that length of time. **b.** Phr. *It is* (*was, will be*, etc.) *l. before, since, to* (something); *it will be l. first; ere it be l.* 3. The l. and the short of it..is that you must pay me this money 1898.

II. As *sb.* (with *a* and *pl.*) **1.** *Mus.* A long note; *spec.* in the early notation, a note equivalent to two or three breves, according to the rhythm employed 1460. **2.** *Prosody.* A long syllable 1548. **3.** Building. *Longs and shorts*: long and short blocks placed alternately in a vertical line; the style of masonry to which this arrangement belongs 1845. **4.** (*colloq.*) = *Long Vacation* (see A. Combs.) 1885. **5.** *pl.* = *long-clothes* 1841. **6.** *Comm.* One who has bought in expectation of future demand 1881.

2. Phr. *Longs and shorts*: quantitative (esp. Latin or Greek) verses or versification. Hence **L.-and-short** *v.* to make Gr. or L. verses (BYRON). 6. Wheat fell off owing to longs unloading 1890.

Long (lǫŋ), *a.*[2] ME. [Aphet. f. ME. *ilong*, OE. *gelang* ALONG *a.*[1]] Phr. *L. of* (†*l. on*): attributable to, owing to, 'along of'. Now *arch.* and *dial.*

That all these Have fallen out profitless, 'tis l. of you SWINBURNE.

Long (lǫŋ), *adv.* Comp. **longer** (lǫ·ŋgəɹ), **longest** (lǫ·ŋgėst). [OE. *lange, lǫnge*:—OTeut. **laŋgô*, f. **laŋgo-* LONG *a.*[1]] **1.** For or during a long time. **2.** In expressions like *to be l. about one's work*, the adv. *long* becomes a quasi-adj. = 'occupying a long time', 'delaying long' ME. **3.** With an agent-noun, as *l.-liver.* Also *longer, longest liver*, in legal use for 'the survivor, the last survivor' 1485. **4.** Followed by *after, before, ere, since*, etc.: = At, from, or to a point of time far distant from the time indicated ME. **5.** The compar. (chiefly with *any, no, much*, etc.) has the sense: After the point of time indicated by the context (= L. *amplius*). *No longer*: not now as formerly. ME. **6.** Throughout the length of (a period specified). [Cf. G. *sein leben lang.*] ME. **†7.** At or to a great or a specified distance in space; far (*rare*) –1586.

1. Man wants but little here below, Nor wants that little l. GOLDSM. To cling to your profession as l. as you can THIRLWALL. *So* (or *as*) *l. as*: often = 'provided that', 'if only'. *So l.* (colloq.): good-bye, 'au revoir' 1834. 2. Ile not be l. before I call vpon thee SHAKS. I advise to be l. a chusing a kind of life 1671. The opportunity was not l. in coming 1894. Phr. *Not to be l. for this world*: to have only a short time to live. 4. Such is life—as Mrs. Harris l. since observed SWINBURNE. 5. There was no longer any room for doubt 1894. 6. He traveyled all night l. to Winchester warde 1568.

Long (lǫŋ), *v.*[1] [OE. *langian*:—OTeut. **laŋgôjan*, **laŋgæjan*, f. **laŋgo-* LONG *a.*[1]] **†1.** To lengthen. *trans.* and *intr.* –1500. **†2.** *impers.* with accus. *Me longs* (*longeth*): I have a yearning desire; I long –ME. **3.** *intr.* To have a yearning desire; to wish earnestly. Const. *for* (*after*), or *to* with inf. ME.

3. I haue longed after thy precepts *Ps.* cxix. 40. This man longed for her TROLLOPE.

Long (lǫŋ), *v.*[2] *arch.* ME. [f. *lang, long*, aphet. f. OE. *gelang* at hand, dependent on, ALONG *a.*[1] Now repl. by BELONG *v.*] **1.** *intr.* To be appropriate *to*; to refer or relate *to*; to be a part, appendage, or dependency; to belong. Now only *poet.* as a rare archaism (written *'long*). **†b.** To concern (a person); hence, to befit, beseem –1564. **†2.** (Const. *to, unto.*) = BELONG *v.* 3. –1608

1. b. She durste never seyn ne do But that thing that hir longed to CHAUCER.

Long, aphet. f. ALONG.

-long (lǫŋ), **†-longs** *suffix*, forming advs. The earliest instance, *endlong*, from ON. *endlangr* adj., 'extending from end to end', is prop. a compound of LONG *a.*[1]; but in Eng. it was used as an adv. with the sense 'endwise', 'end foremost'. The ending *-long* thus became a var. of -LING *suffix*[2].

†Long-acre. 1607. App. a proper name for a long narrow field containing an acre. (Still in use as the name of a London street.) *allusively*, One's estate or patrimony –1659.

Long-ago. 1834. Attrib. use of advb. phr. *long ago* (see AGO): That has long gone by; that belongs to the distant past. Also quasi-*sb.* and *sb.*, the distant past or its events.

Longan (lǫ·ŋgăn). 1732. [Chinese *lung-yen*, lit. 'dragon's eye', f. *lung* dragon + *yen* eye.] The fruit of an evergreen tree, *Nephelium Longanum*, cultivated in China and the E. Indies; also, the tree.

Longanimity (lǫŋgăni·mĭti). Now *rare.* 1450. [ad. late L. *longanimitatem*, f. *longanimus*, after Gr. *μακροθυμία*.] Long-suffering; forbearance or patience. So **Longa·nimous** *a.* 1620.

Lo·ng-boat. 1515. The largest boat belonging to a sailing vessel.

Long-bow (lǫ·ŋbōu). 1500. [See BOW *sb.*[1] 4.] The bow drawn by hand and discharging a long feathered arrow (cf. CROSS-BOW). †*occas.* A soldier armed with a long bow.

Phr. *To draw* or *pull the* (or *a*) *long-bow*: to make exaggerated statements (*colloq.*).

Long-breathed (-breþt), *a.* 1568. [See BREATHED II.] Long of breath (*lit.* and *fig.*).

Long cloth, lo·ng-cloth. 1545. A kind of cotton cloth or calico made in long pieces.

Long coat, lo·ng-coat. 1603. **a.** A coat reaching to the ankles; also in *pl.* = *long-clothes.* **b.** One who wears a long coat.

Long-drawn, *a.* 1646. **1.** Prolonged to a great or inordinate length. Also *long-drawn-out.* **2.** Having great longitudinal extension. Chiefly *poet.* 1750.

1. A longdrawn carol TENNYSON. 2. The long-drawn Isle and fretted Vault GRAY.

Longe: see LUNGE.

Long-eared, *a.* 1591. **1.** Having long ears; *spec.* in names of animals. **2.** Asinine 1605.

1. The long-eared owl 1831. 2. An evil, heavy-laden, long-eared age CARLYLE.

†Longee. 1678. = LUNGE *sb.*[2] BUTLER.

Longeval, longæval (lǫndʒī·văl), *a.* 1597. [f. L. *longævus* LONGEVOUS + -AL.] Long-lived, long-lasting. So **†Longe·ve, longæ·ve** *a.* 1673–8.

Longevity (lǫndʒe·vĭti). Also **†-ævitie**, etc. 1615. [ad. L. *longævitatem*, f. *longævus.*] Long life; long duration of existence.

Young men are careless of l. HAMERTON.

Longevous, -ævous (lǫndʒī·vəs), *a.* Now *rare.* 1680. [f. L. *longævus* (f. *longus* LONG *a*[1]. + *ævum* age) + -OUS.] Long-lived; living or having lived to a great age.

Lo·ng-hand, lo·nghand. 1666. Handwriting of the ordinary character, as dist. from shorthand.

Long-head. 1650. [f. LONG *a.*[1]] One who has a skull of more than average length; *spec.* one the breadth of whose head is less than four-fifths of its length; a dolichocephalic person.

Long-headed, *a.* 1700. **1.** Having a long head 1875. **2.** Of great discernment or foresight; shrewd.

1. Long-headed glands DARWIN, men 1888. 2. Long-headed customers, knowing dogs DICKENS. Hence **Long-hea·dedness.**

Longi- (lǫ·ndʒi), comb. f. L. *longus* LONG *a.*[1], in various terms, chiefly scientific, as **Lo·ngicorn** [mod.L. *longicornis*], *adj.* pertaining to the *Longicornes* or *Longicornia*, a group of beetles having very long antennæ; *sb.* one of these 1848. **†Longila·teral** *a.*, long-sided; of the form of a long parallelogram 1658.

Longiloquence (lǫndʒi·lŏkwĕns). *rare.* 1836. [f. L. *longus* + *loquentia* speaking.] Speaking at great length.

American l. in oratory F. HALL.

Longimanous (lǫndʒi·mănəs), *a.* *rare.* 1646. [f. late L. *longimanus* + -OUS.] Long-handed; *Zool.* applied to certain apes. †*fig.* Far-reaching.

Longimetry (lǫndʒi·mĭtri). *rare.* 1674. [f. L. *longus* + -METRY.] The measuring of distances. Hence **Longime·tric** *a.*

Longing (lǫ·ŋiŋ), *vbl. sb.* [OE. *langung*, f. *langian* LONG *v.*[1]] **1.** The action of LONG *v.*[1]; yearning desire. Const. *for, after*, or with *inf.* **2.** *Path.* The fanciful cravings incident to women during pregnancy. Chiefly *pl.* 1552.

1. Giue me my Robe, put on my Crowne, I haue Immortall longings in me *Ant. & Cl.* v. ii. 284.

Lo·nging, *ppl. a.* 1509. [f. LONG *v.*[1] + -ING[2].] That longs; characterized by yearning desire.

Nor cast one l. ling'ring Look behind! GRAY. Hence **Lo·nging-ly** *adv.*, **-ness.**

Longinquity (lǫndʒi·ŋkwĭti). Now *rare.* 1549. [ad. L. *longinquitas*, f. *longinquus*, f. *longus* LONG *a.*[1]] **1.** Long distance; remoteness. **2.** Remoteness or long continuance (of time) 1623.

Longish (lǫ·ŋiʃ), *a.*[1] 1611. [f. LONG *a.*[1] + -ISH[1].] Somewhat long.

Longitude (lǫ·ndʒitiūd). ME. [ad. L. *longitudo*, f. *longus.*] **1.** Length, longitudinal extent; *occas.* a length; a long figure. †Also, tallness. Now chiefly *joc.* **2.** Length (of time, etc.); long continuance. Now *rare.* 1607. **3.** *Geog.* **†a.** The extent lengthwise (i. e. from east to west) of the habitable world as known to the ancients. **b.** Distance east or west on the earth's surface, measured by the angle which the meridian of a particular place makes with a standard meridian, as that of Greenwich. It is reckoned to 180° east or west, and is expressed either in degrees, etc., or in time (15° being equivalent to 1 hour). Abbrev. *long.* ME. **4.** *Astron.* The distance of a heavenly body reckoned (in degrees, etc.) eastward on the ecliptic from the vernal equinoctial point to a circle at right angles to the ecliptic through that heavenly body. ME.

1. A petticoat, of scanty l. SCOTT. 3. *Circle of l.*: see CIRCLE *sb.* 2.

Comb. l. **star**, any of the fixed stars which have been selected for finding the l. by lunar observations.

Longitudinal (lǫndʒitiū·dinăl). 1541. [f. L. *longitudin-, longitudo* LONGITUDE + -AL.] A. *adj.* 1. Of or pertaining to length; (extent) in length 1765. 2. Extending or proceeding lengthwise 1715. b. *Acoustics.* Of vibrations: Produced in the direction of the vibrating body; also, executed in the direction in which the sound travels 1867. 3. Pertaining to longitude 1874. Hence **Longitu·dinally** *adv.*

B. *sb.* †1. *Anat.* A name for two muscles of the epigastrium 1541. 2. *Ship-building.* In iron and steel ships, a plate (nearly) parallel to the vertical keel 1869. 3. A railway sleeper lying parallel with the rail 1864.

Lo·ng-leg. 1585. †1. = BUPRESTIS 1. -1783. 2. **Long-legs.** a. The stilt; the 'long-legged plover' 1713. b. = DADDY-LONG-LEGS 1753. Hence **Long-legged** *a.* having long legs; *Naut.* of a ship, drawing much water.

Long-line. 1755. 1. A deep-sea fishing-line 1876. 2. *attrib.* a. Written or printed with long lines. b. Furnished with or using long-lines (sense 1). 1755. Hence **Long-lining,** fishing with long-lines.

Long-lived (-ləivd, -livd), *a.* ME. [f. LONG *a.*¹ + *live,* LIFE *sb.* + -ED ².] Having a long life or existence; lasting a long time; longeval.

The long-lived summer days JEFFERIES.

Longly (lǫ·ŋli), *adv.* ME. [f. LONG *a.*¹ + -LY ².] †1. = LONG *adv.* 1. -1605. 2. At considerable length. Now *Sc.* ME. 3. To a considerable length (in space). *rare.* 1662.

Long-necked, *a.* 1605. Having a long neck; used *spec.* in names of animals.

Longness (lǫ·ŋnės). Now *rare.* [OE. *langnes,* f. *lang* LONG *a.*¹ + *-nes* -NESS.] Length; †protractedness.

Long-nosed, *a.* 1552. Having a long nose; used *spec.* in names of animals.

Longobard (lǫ·ŋgŏbaɹd), *sb.* and *a.* 1598. [ad. L. *Longobardi* (see LOMBARD *sb.*¹).] = LOMBARD. So **Longoba·rdic** *a.* Lombardic.

Long robe. 1601. Put symbolically for: The legal profession; esp. in *gentlemen,* etc., *of the long robe* = lawyers, barristers. Also *occas.* = The priesthood or ministry. (Cf. GOWN *sb.*)

Long run, lo·ng-run. 1627. Phr. *in* (also †*at,* †*on,* †*upon*) *the long run*: in the end; when things have run their full course; as the outcome of many vicissitudes. (Cf. F. *à la longue.*)

Longshanks (lǫ·ŋʃæŋks). 1590. 1. A nickname given to Edward I of England on account of his long legs. 2. A stilt or long-legged plover 1817.

Lo·ng-shore, *attrib. phr.* 1822. [Aphet. f. ALONGSHORE.] Existing on or frequenting the shore; found or employed along the shore. Hence **Lo·ngshoreman,** a man employed in loading and unloading ships, or in fishing for oysters, etc. along the shore.

Long-sighted, *a.* 1790. 1. Having 'long sight' (see LONG *a.*¹); able to see objects distinctly at a distance but not close at hand; hypermetropic. 2. *fig.* Far-seeing 1791. Hence **Longsi·ghtedness.**

Longsome (lǫ·ŋsəm), *a.* Now chiefly *dial.* and *arch.* [OE. *langsum,* f. *lang* LONG *a.*¹ + *-sum* -SOME.] Long, lengthy; long-lasting; *esp.* tediously long; †dilatory.

The way there was a little l. STEVENSON.

Long standing. 1601. Continuance for a long time in a settled position, rank, etc. Chiefly in phr. *of long standing.* Also *attrib.*

Long sufferance. *arch.* ME. = next.

Long-suffering, *sb.* 1526 (Tindale). Patient endurance of provocation or trial; longanimity.

The riches of his goodnesse, and forbearance, and long suffering *Rom.* ii. 4. So **Long-suffering** *a.* 1535 (Coverdale).

Long sword. *Obs.* exc. *Hist.* 1593. A sword with a long cutting blade. Often *fig.* or *allusive.* Also cognomen (AF. *Longespei*) of William, son of Henry II and Fair Rosamond.

Lo·ng-tail. 1575. 1. A long-tailed animal; *spec.* a greyhound; formerly, a horse or dog with the tail uncut. 2. A nickname for: †a. A native of Kent -1701. b. A Chinaman 1867. 3. *attrib.* 1848.

1. *Cut and long-tail*: *lit.* horses and dogs with cut tails and long tails; *fig.* in sense 'riff-raff'. So **Long-tailed** *a.* having a long tail; (of words) having a long termination (*joc.*) 1500.

Long Tom. 1854. 1. *dial.* A name for the long-tailed titmouse, etc. 2. A kind of gold-washing cradle 1855. 3. A gun of large size and long range 1867.

Lo·ng-tongue. 1731. A person or animal with a long tongue, e.g. the wryneck (*dial.*). So **Long-tongued** *a.* chattering, babbling 1553.

Long-waisted, *a.* 1647. 1. Having a long waist, as a person, a ship, etc. 1653. †2. *fig.* Easy; loose -1658.

Longways (lǫ·ŋwēⁱz), *adv.* 1588. [f. LONG *a.*¹ + WAY *sb.* + advb. *s.*] Lengthways, longitudinally.

Long-winded, *a.* 1589. 1. Long-breathed 1596. Also *fig.* 2. Of persons: Tediously long in speech or dilatory in action. Of speech, etc.: Tediously long.

1. Men of endurance,—deep-chested, long-winded, tough EMERSON. 2. Such a long-winded Discourse 1652. Hence **Longwi·nded·ly** *adv.,* **-ness.**

Longwise (lǫ·ŋwəiz), *adv.* (*a.*) 1544. [f. LONG *a.*¹ + -WISE.] Lengthwise, longitudinally.

Loo (lū), *sb.*¹ 1675. [abbrev. f. LANTERLOO.] 1. A round card-game. In three-card loo the cards have the same value as in whist; in five-card loo the Jack of Clubs ('Pam') is the highest card. A player who fails to take a trick or breaks any of the laws of the game is 'looed', i.e. required to pay a certain sum or 'loo' to the pool. b. The fact of being looed. c. The sum added to the pool by a player who is looed. 2. A party playing at loo 1760. †3. Party, set -1774.

1. *Limited l.*: l. in which the l. or penalty is limited to a fixed sum. *Unlimited l.*: l. in which each player looed has to put in the amount there was in the pool. *Comb.* **l.-table,** a table for playing l. upon; now the trade name of a particular form of round table, orig. devised for this purpose.

Loo, *sb.*² *Obs.* exc. *Hist.* 1690. [F. *loup*; see LOUP.] A velvet mask partly covering the face, formerly worn by women to protect the complexion.

Loo (lū), *v.*¹ 1680. [f. LOO *sb.*¹] *trans.* To subject to a forfeit at loo. Also *transf.* and *fig.*

A flush..*loos the board,* i.e. the holder receives the amount of a loo from every one, and the hand is not played H. JONES.

Loo, *v.*² *Obs.* exc. *dial.* 1666. [aphet. f. HALLOO *v.*] *trans.* To urge on with shouts.

Loo (lū), *int.* 1605. [aphet. f. HALLOO *int.*] A cry to incite a dog to the chase; = HALLOO *int.* Also *l. in!* Also quasi-*sb.*

Loob (lūb). 1674. *Tin-mining.* 1. A pit or vessel into which the dross and earth is delivered by the trough. RAY. 2. *pl.* Slime containing ore 1778.

Looby (lū·bi). Now chiefly *dial.* ME. [Cf. LOB *sb.*¹, LUBBER, etc.] A lazy hulking fellow; a lout; a clown. Also *attrib.* Hence †**Loo·bily** *a.* looby-like.

Looch, var. of LOHOCH.

Loof (lūf), *sb.*¹ *Sc.* and *n. dial.* ME. [a. ON. *lófe* wk. masc.] The palm of the hand.

Loof, *sb.*² and *v.*: see LUFF *sb.* and *v.*

Loof (lūf), *sb.*³ 1865. [a. Arab. *lūf* (see next).] = next.

Loofah (lū·fă). 1887. [a. Egyptian Arab. *lūfaʰ*, a plant of this species.] The fibrous substance of the pod of the plant *Luffa ægyptiaca,* used as a sponge or flesh-brush. Also *attrib.,* as *l.-tree.*

Look (luk), *sb.* ME. [f. LOOK *v.*] 1. The action or an act of looking; a glance of the eyes; a particular direction of the eyes or face. 2. a. Appearance, aspect (of the countenance, of things) ME. b. *pl.* as sing. Occas. = good looks. 1564.

1. For lookes kill loue, and loue by lookes reuiueth SHAKS. Phr. *To have a look at* (colloq.): to look at for the purpose of examining; In the meantime I shall have a l. at Warsaw 1885. With sick and scornful looks averse TENNYSON. 2. a. A man may bee knowen by his looke *Ecclus.* xix. 29. b. Lean are their Looks DRYDEN. Catherine was in very good looks (= was looking well) JANE AUSTEN. *To have a l. of*: to resemble vaguely.

Comb., as *l.-back, -down, -forward, -on, -up,* corresponding to phrases under the vb.

Look (luk), *v.* [OE. *lōcian*:—OTeut. type *lōkōjan. Cf. OHG. *luogen,* G. dial. *lugen* to look, spy.]

I. To direct one's sight. 1. *intr.* To give a direction to one's sight; to apply one's power of vision; to direct one's eyes *at* (*on, upon* arch.). b. *occas.* To give a look of surprise, to stare. Now *colloq.* 1610. c. quasi-*trans.,* as in *to l.* (a person or thing) *in the face* ME. d. with cogn. obj. 1592. e. *trans.* with complement or prep.: To bring by one's looks into a certain place or condition. Now *rare.* 1611. f. To express by a look or glance, or by one's countenance 1727. 2. With indirect question: To apply one's sight to ascertain (*who, what, how, whether,* etc.). Now only when a single glance will give an answer. ME. 3. *fig.* a. 'To direct the intellectual eye' (J.); to turn or fix one's attention or regard. Now usu. const. *at*; formerly *on* or *upon.* 1548. b. To take care, make sure, see (*that* or *how* something is done; also with *that* omitted). Now *arch.* OE. c. To expect. Const. *to* with *inf.* 1513. †d. with indirect question: To consider, ascertain (*who, when, whether,* etc.); to try (*if* something can be done). Also *simply,* to consider the matter, make inquiry. -1692. 4. Idiomatic uses of the imperative. a. = 'see', 'behold', 'lo' OE. †b. Prefixed to interrog. pron. or adv., or relative conj., forming indef. relatives = *whoever, whatever, however,* etc. OE. -1625. 5. **Look sharp.** Orig. (with *sharp* as adv.) = 'keep strict watch'. In later use, 'lose no time' (with vb. in sense of branch III, and *sharp* as complementary adj.; now merely *colloq.*). 1711. 6. Trans. uses, chiefly = intr. uses with preps. See below. ME.

1. Looking neither to the right nor left 1797. She could not l. on the sweet heaven TENNYSON. Phr. (*Fair,* etc.) *to l. at,* †*on,* †*upon*: with respect to appearance. *To l. at him* (*me, it,* etc.): *colloq.* = judging from his (my, etc.) appearance. *Not to l. at* (†*on, upon*): often emphatically for 'not to touch, taste, meddle with'. Looke therfore ere thou leape 1550. Wherefore looke ye so sadly to-day? *Gen.* xl. 7. b. Yes, you may l.! (*mod.*). c. To l. death in the face SOUTH. An eye that looks one through and through 1891. Phr. *To look a gift horse in the mouth*: see HORSE *sb.* d. Such lookes as none could looke but beauties queen SHAKS. e. Thou shalt l. us out of pain G. HERBERT. f. She *look'd* a lecture, Each eye a sermon, and her brow a homily BYRON. Phr. *To l. daggers*: see DAGGER *sb.* 2. 2. I will l. what time the train starts (*mod.*). †*L. else*: see whether it be not so. *Go l.* = 'find it out'; a contemptuous refusal to say (now *dial.*). 3. a. He that made vs with such large discourse, Looking before and after *Haml.* IV. iv. 37 (1604 Qo.). Instead of reforming others.. let him l. at home BENTHAM. The whole mode and manner of looking at things varies with every age M. PATTISON. b. Look't be done *Oth.* IV. iii. 8. c. By whom we l. to be protected HOBBES. 4. a. *L. you* (mod. colloq.) = 'mind this'. *L. here,* a brusque preface to an order, expostulation, reprimand, etc. Now, l. here, my man..I'll have no feelings here DICKENS. 5. Glass of ale, young woman; and l. sharp, please! 1874. 6. a. To look at; to view, inspect, examine. Now *dial.* †*To l. babies*: to gaze at the reflection of one's face in another's eyes. ME. †b. To consult or refer to; to 'turn up'. In the imper. = VIDE. Also, to search for (a word, etc.) in a book of reference. (Cf. *l. up.*) -1813. L. Lord Bacon in his life FULLER. †c. To seek, search for; to *l. for.* Also, to seek or search out. -1821. He hath bin all this day to looke you SHAKS. †d. To expect, look for -1611. His fortune gives him more than he could looke DANIEL.

II. To face a certain way. 1. *intr.* To have a certain outlook; to face, front, or be turned *towards, into, on to,* etc. 1555. b. Of parts of the body, etc.: To face or turn 1648. 2. To show a tendency; to tend, point 1647. †b. To tend *to,* promise *to.* SHAKS.

1. Pisgah, which looketh toward Ieshimon *Num.* xxi. 20. b. The florets looking downwards 1776. 2. All the facts l. the other way 1881. b. *Cor.* III. iii. 29.

III. To have a certain appearance. [Cf. similar use in passive sense of *smell, taste, feel.*] 1. *intr.* To have the appearance of being; to seem ME. b. with adv. of manner:

To have a certain look or appearance ME. (Now *rare* exc. with *well, ill, badly*.) ME. **c.** Const. *inf.* To seem to the view (*lit.* and *fig.*) 1775. **d.** Quasi-*trans.* To have an appearance corresponding with (one's character, condition, etc.) 1828. **2. Look like. a.** To have the appearance of being 1440. **b.** with gerund, vbl. sb., or sb.: To give promise of, show a likelihood of 1593.

1. Phr. *To l. well, ill*, i.e. 'in good, bad health'. *To l. black, blue*, etc. (fig.): see the adjs. 'You made me l. rather a fool, Arminius', I began M. ARNOLD. **b.** The skies looke grimly SHAKS. **c.** A..hat that looked to be made of beaver 1890. Phr. *To l. as if*—: to have an appearance suggesting that—. Often *it looks* (or *things l.*) *as if*—. It looks as if there was going to be a free fight 1892. **d.** Phr. *To l. one's age*: to have the appearance of being as old as one is. *To l. oneself*: to appear to be in one's usual health. **2. a.** This looks like a lad of spirit GOLDSM. **b.** Later on ..he..looked like biting 1883. It looks like rain 1888.

Spec. uses with preps. **L. about —. a.** To make searches in various parts of (a room, etc.); to go about observing in (a country, town, etc.). **b.** *To l. about one*: to turn one's eyes to surrounding objects; to examine one's position and circumstances; to be apprehensive. **L. after —. a.** To follow with the eye. †Also, to observe the course of (a person). **†b.** To search for. **†c.** To anticipate; to look forward to. **d.** To seek for, demand (qualities). **e.** To busy oneself about; to consider. **f.** To attend to; to take care of; to 'see to'. **L. behind —.** With pron. used refl. *Not* or *never to l. behind one* (colloq.): to have an uninterrupted career of advancement. **L. for —. a.** To expect, hope for, be on the watch for. **b.** To seek, search for. **L. into —. a.** To direct one's sight to the interior of. Also, to consult (a book) in a cursory manner. **b.** To examine minutely, investigate. **c.** To enter (a house, etc.) for a moment in passing. **L. on —. a.** To pay regard to; to respect. Now *dial.* **b.** To regard *as.* **c.** To regard with a specified feeling. **L. over —. a.** To inspect cursorily; †to examine. **b.** To ignore. Now only, to overlook (a fault). **L. through —. a.** To direct one's sight through; also *fig.* **†b.** To be visible through (*Haml.* IV. vii. 152). **c.** To direct one's view over the whole of; to glance through. **L. to —. a.** To direct a look to. **b.** To direct one's attention to. In Bibl. use, *occas.* to regard with favour. **c.** To attend to, take care of; †to nurse. **d.** In the *imperative*, etc.: To direct one's solicitude to (something endangered). **e.** *To l. to it*: to beware. Often with *cl.*, to see *that.* **f.** To keep watch upon. **g.** To rely on (a person, etc.) *for* something. **h.** To look forward to; to count upon. **L. toward(s —.** See simple senses and TOWARD(S. **b.** *To l. towards a person*: to drink his health (now *joc.*). **L. unto —.** *arch.* = *Look to* (senses a–f). **L. upon —. †a.** = *look on* (sense a). **b.** = *look on* (senses b, c). †Also, *to l. upon it*: to be of opinion *that.*

Spec. uses with advs. **L. about.** *intr.* See simple senses and ABOUT *adv.*; *fig.* to be on the look-out. Also const. *for* (†*after*): to be in search of. **L. around.** *intr.* To l. in several directions; *fig.* to take a comprehensive view of things. **L. back.** *intr.* **a.** To turn and l. at something in the direction from which one is going. **b.** To think on the past. Const. *into, on, upon, to.* **†c.** *trans.* = *look back to.* (*Ant. & Cl.* III. xi. 53.) **d.** *colloq.* in neg. contexts: To show signs of interrupted progress. **L. down. a.** *intr.* See simple senses and DOWN *adv.* **b.** *fig.* *To l. down on, upon*: to scorn; to consider oneself superior to. **c.** To quell by one's looks. **L. downward.** *intr.* = *look down.* **L. forth.** *intr.* To l. out (of a window, etc., on to something). Now *arch.* and *poet.* **L. in. a.** See simple senses and IN *adv.* **b.** To enter a room, etc. to see something; hence, now, to make a call (*upon* a person); to 'drop in'. **L. on.** *intr.* To direct one's looks towards an object; often, to be a mere spectator. *To look on ahead*: to look forward into the future. **b.** colloq. *To l. on* (*with*): to read from a book, etc. at the same time (with another person). **L. out. a.** *intr.* To look from within to the outside; also, to put one's head out of a window, etc. **b.** To show itself. SHAKS. **c.** To be on the look out; to take care. **d.** *To l. out for*: to be on the look out for; to await vigilantly. **e.** To have or afford an outlook. **f.** *trans.* To find or choose out by looking. **L. over.** *trans.* To cast one's eyes over; to examine (papers, etc.). **L. round.** *intr.* **a.** To l. about in every direction. **b.** *fig.* To search about *for.* **L. through. a.** *trans.* To penetrate with a glance. **b.** To examine exhaustively. **†c.** *intr.* To become visible. SHAKS. **L. up. a.** To raise the eyes, turn the face upwards. **†b.** To take courage. SHAKS. **c.** *To l. up to*: (*a*) to direct the look up towards; to raise the eyes towards, in adoration, supplication, etc.; (*b*) *fig.* to respect or venerate. **d.** *slang.* To improve. Chiefly *Comm.* **e.** To search for (something) in a dictionary, among papers, or the like; to consult (books). **f.** To call on (a person) in order to see him. *colloq.* **g.** To search for. **h.** *To l.* (a person) *up and down*: to scrutinize his appearance from head to foot.

Loo·k-down. *U.S.* 1882. [f. phr. *look down.*] The Horse-head or Moon-fish, *Selene vomer.*

Looker (lu·kəɹ). ME. [f. LOOK *v.* + -ER^{1}.] 1. One who looks *at, on, to, upon*, etc. 2. One who looks after anything; a guardian, keeper, shepherd, farm-bailiff. Now *local.* ME. 3. A handsome person (esp. *U.S. colloq.*) 1904.

1. **Looker on, l.-on,** one who looks on; a beholder, spectator, eyewitness. Often, one who merely looks on. Cf. *onlooker.*

Look-in, *sb.* 1847. [f. LOOK *sb.* + IN *adv.*] 1. A hasty glance. Hence, a short visit. 2. *Sport. slang.* A chance of success 1870.

Looking (lu·kiŋ), *vbl. sb.* ME. [f. LOOK *v.* + -ING^{1}.] 1. The action of LOOK *v.* †2. Look, expression of countenance, appearance –1610. 3. *attrib.* 1519.

2. Wherefore this ghastly l.? *Temp.* II. i. 309.

Looking (lu·kiŋ), *ppl. a.* 1590. [f. as prec. + -ING^{2}.] 1. That looks or gazes (*rare*) 1649. 2. Forming combs., as *good-, ill-looking, westward-looking.*

Loo·king-gla·ss. 1526. [f. LOOKING *vbl. sb.* + GLASS.] 1. A glass to look in, in order to see one's own face or figure; a mirror made of glass coated with an amalgam of quicksilver. 2. Plate glass, or glass silvered for use as a mirror 1682. 3. *Lady's* or *Venus' l.*, the plant *Campanula Speculum.*

1. *fig.* The Eyes, the Looking-glasses of Nature 1658. *Comb.*: **l. plant,** an Asiatic tree, *Heritiera littoralis*; **l. writing,** writing done backwards, so as to be legible by means of a mirror.

Loo·k ou·t, look-out. *Pl.* **look-outs.** 1699. [f. phr. *look out.*] 1. The action of looking out (*lit.* and *fig.*). Orig. *Naut.* 1748. 2. *concr.*: see quots. 1699. 3. A more or less distant view 1779; a prospective condition, an outlook 1825. 4. with possessive sb. or pron., *That is —'s look-out* (colloq.): i.e. that concerns only his interest, he must see to that himself 1844. 5. *attrib.*, as *look-out man*, etc. 1781.

1. Phr. *To keep a* (*good*, etc.) *look-out*; *to be, place, put on* or *upon the look out*; const. *for, to*, or *to* with *inf.* The gamekeeper..was upon the look-out for poachers 1815. 2. The Look-out formerly built on Sullivan's Island 1700. One man on deck as a look-out R. H. DANA. Ere the channel was full enough for the look-outs (= look-out vessels) to intercept her 1841. 3. This leads to a little tower..The look-out charming 1779. It seemed a rather blue look-out 1889.

Look-see (lu·ksī). *slang.* 1883. [?Pidgin English.] An inspection, survey.

Loom (lūm), *sb.*^{1} [ME. *lome*, aphet. repr. OE. *gelóma* wk. masc., utensil, implement, f. *ge-* Y- + *lóma* as in *andlóman* pl., apparatus, furniture. Ult. etym. unkn.] 1. An implement or tool of any kind. *Obs.* exc. *Sc.* and *n. dial.* 2. An open vessel of any kind, as a bucket, tub, vat, etc. *Obs.* exc. *Sc.* ME. 3. A machine in which yarn or thread is woven into fabric by the crossing of threads called respectively the warp and weft ME. Also *fig.* **†b.** *transf.* Attributed to a spider or caterpillar: *occas.* (*poet.*) the web itself –1647. 4. The art, business, or process of weaving 1676.

3. The shaft of his speare was like a weauers lome (app. = beam of a l.) COVERDALE 1 *Sam.* xvii. 7. 4. In the L. unskill'd DRYDEN.

Loom (lūm), *sb.*^{2} 1694. [a. ON. *lómr.*] A name given to species of the Guillemot and the Diver, esp. *Alca bruennichi* and *Colymbus septentrionalis* (Red-throated Diver).

Loom (lūm), *sb.*^{3} 1697. Also **lum.** [Scand.: cf. Norw. *lom, lumm*, Icel. *hlumr, hlummr.*] The shaft of an oar; also, limited to the part between the rowlock and the hands in rowing; also, loosely, the handle.

Loom (lūm), *sb.*^{4} 1836. [f. LOOM *v.*^{2}] A seaman's term for the indistinct and exaggerated appearance of land on the horizon, an object seen through mist or darkness, etc.

Loom (lūm), *v.*^{1} *rare.* 1548. [f. LOOM *sb.*^{1}] 1. *trans.* To weave (a fabric). 2. *To l. the web*: to mount the warp on the loom 1827.

Loom (lūm), *v.*^{2} 1591. [Obscure: see N.E.D.] †1. Of a ship at sea: To move slowly up and down (*rare*) –1678. 2. *intr.* To appear indistinctly; to come into view in an exaggerated and indefinite form. Also with *up.* **b.** *fig.* of immaterial things 1591.

2. Men are magnified to giants, and brigs 'l. up'.. into ships of the line KANE. **b.** Cash affairs l. well in the offing SCOTT.

Loon^{1} (lūn). Chiefly *Sc.* and *n. dial.* 1450. [In 16th c. *lowen, lowne.* Etym. obscure.] 1. A rogue, scamp; an idler. **b.** A strumpet, concubine 1560. 2. A man of low condition; in phr. *lord and l.* Now only *arch.* 1535. 3. A boor, lout, clown 1619. 4. A boy, lad, youth 1560.

Loon^{2} (lūn). 1634. [App. altered f. LOOM *sb.*^{2}, perh. after prec.] A name for certain aquatic birds. 1. Any bird of the genus *Colymbus*, esp. *C. glacialis.* 2. The Great Crested Grebe; the Little Grebe or Dabchick 1678.

Loony, luny (lū·ni). *vulgar.* 1872. [Shortened f. LUNATIC + -Y^{1}.] *adj.* Lunatic, crazed, silly. *sb.* A lunatic.

Loop (lūp), *sb.*^{1} ME. [Obscure: see N.E.D.] 1. The doubling or return into itself of a portion of a string, cord, thong, or the like, so as to leave an aperture between the parts; the portion so doubled, usu. fastened at the ends. 2. A ring or curved piece of metal, etc., for the insertion of a bolt, ramrod, or rope, as a handle, etc.; *dial.* a door-hinge 1674. 3. Something in the form of a loop, e.g. a line traced on paper, a bend of a river, etc. 1668. 4. In specific applications: see below 1846.

1. There are rows of buttons and loops down the breast of the tunic 1815. We should speak of a *mesh* in netting, a *loop* in knitting 1880. 3. I wish..you would..open the loops of your l's SCOTT. 4. **a.** *Anat.* A looped vessel or fibre. *L. of Henle*, the looped part of a uriniferous tubule 1846. **b.** *Zool.* In brachiopods, the folding of the brachial appendages 1851. **c.** *Acoustics.* The portion of a vibrating string, column of air, etc. between two nodes 1878. **d.** *Railways* and *Telegraphy.* A line of rails or a telegraph wire diverging from, and afterwards returning to, the main line or circuit 1863. **e.** The circuit in a centrifugal railway, along the upper portion of which the passenger travels head downwards 1900. *To loop the l.*, to travel along such a circuit, or in a similar course through the air in an aeroplane. **f.** *Electr.* A complete electric circuit; a multiple or branch circuit.

Comb.: **l.-knot,** †(*a*) a reef-knot; (*b*) a single knot tied in a double cord, so as to leave a l. beyond the knot; **-lace,** (*a*) a series of loops as an ornament; (*b*) a kind of lace consisting of patterns worked on a ground of fine net; hence **-laced** *a.*; **-line,** see 4 d.; **-stitch,** a kind of fancy stitch consisting of loops.

Loop (lūp), *sb.*^{2} ME. [Prob. conn. w. MDu. *lûpen* (mod.Du. *luipen*) to peer.] = LOOP-HOLE.

Loop (lūp), *sb.*^{3} ME. [ad. F. *loupe.* Cf. G. *luppe.*] 1. *Metall.* A mass of iron in a pasty condition ready for the tilt-hammer or rolls; a bloom 1674. †2. A precious stone of imperfect brilliancy, *esp.* a sapphire –1548.

Loop (lūp), *v.*^{1} 1832. [f. LOOP *sb.*^{1} Cf. LOOPED *a.*^{1}, which is much earlier.] 1. *trans.* To form into a loop or loops; also with *round* 1856. 2. *intr.* To form a loop; *spec.* of certain larvæ 1832. 3. *trans.* To put or form loops upon 1894. 4. To enclose *in* or *with* something formed into a loop 1840. 5. Chiefly with *adv.* or *phr.*: To fasten (*back, up*) by forming into, or by means of, a loop; to connect by means of a loop or loops. Also *intr.* for *refl.* 1837. 6. *Electr.* To connect so as to form a loop. 7. Phr. *to l. the loop* (see LOOP *sb.*^{1} 4 e) 1904.

1. The other end is already looped, or as sailors would say, 'doubled in a bight' KANE. 5. She had an abundance of dark hair looped up BLACK.

†Loop, *v.*^{2} 1674. [f. LOOP *sb.*^{3}] *intr.* Of heated iron-ore: To form a loop (LOOP *sb.*^{3}).

Looped (lūpt), *a.*^{1} 1513. [f. LOOP *sb.*^{1} and *v.*^{1} + -ED.] 1. Coiled or wreathed in loops; †intertwined. †2. Having, or fastened with, a loop. Of a dart: Furnished with a thong for throwing. –1609. 3. Of lace: Wrought upon a ground of fine net 1698. 4. Held in a loop, held *up* by a loop 1869.

Looped (lūpt), *a.*^{2} 1605. [f. LOOP *sb.*^{2} + -ED^{2}.] Having loop-holes.

Your loopt and windowed raggednes SHAKS.

Looper (lū·pəɹ). 1731. [f. LOOP *v.*^{1} + -ER^{1}.] One who or that which makes loops. 1. The larva of any geometrid moth, which in crawling bends the middle of its body into a loop. 2. A contrivance in a machine for making loops or looping pieces together 1857.

Loop-hole, loophole (lū·phoul), *sb.* 1591. [f. LOOP *sb.*^{2} + HOLE *sb.*] 1. *Fortif.* A narrow vertical opening, usually widening inwards, cut in a wall, etc., for shooting through. †b.

Naut. A port-hole –1769. **2.** A similar opening to look through, or to admit light and air 1591. **3.** *fig.* An outlet or means of escape 1663.

2. *fig.* 'Tis pleasant through the loopholes of retreat To peep at such a world COWPER. **3.** The Test Act..left loopholes through which schismatics sometimes crept into civil employments MACAULAY.

Loo·p-hole, *v.* 1810. [f. prec.] *trans.* To cut loop-holes in the walls of; to provide with loop-holes.

Looping (lū·piŋ), *vbl. sb.* 1480. [f. LOOP *v.*[1] + -ING[1].] The action of LOOP *v.*[1] **b.** *concr.* Material formed into loops; loops as a trimming 1647.

Looping (lū·piŋ), *ppl. a.* 1854. [f. LOOP *v.*[1] + -ING[2].] That forms loops.

L. caterpillar = LOOPER 1. *L.-snail*, a snail of the genus *Truncatella*.

Loopy (lū·pi), *a.* 1824. [f. LOOP *sb.*[1] + -Y[1].] **1.** Full of or characterized by loops 1856. **2.** *Sc.* Deceitful, crafty. SCOTT.

Loord, var. of LOURD *Obs.*

Loos, obs. f. LOSE, LOSS.

Loose (lūs), *sb.* 1519. [f. LOOSE *v.* and *a.*] **1.** *Archery.* The act of discharging an arrow. **†2.** The close of a matter; the upshot, issue –1647. **3.** A condition of looseness, laxity, or unrestraint; hence, free indulgence; unrestrained action or feeling. *Obs.* exc. in phr. *to give a l.* (occas. *give l.*) *to*, to give full vent to; to free from restraint; *occas.*, to give (a horse) the rein. 1593. **†4.** Liberation, release –1734. **†5.** An impetuous course or rush –1737.

1. *fig.* To allow me a L. at the Crimes of the Guilty DE FOE. **2.** Phr. *At* (or *in*) *the* (*very*) *l.*: at the last moment (*L.L.L.* v. ii. 752). **3.** The little boy..gave a l. to his innocent tongue, and asked many questions THACKERAY. **4.** Phr. *To make a l. from*: to get away from the company of.

Loose (lūs), *a.* and *adv.* [ME. *lōs* (with close *ō*), a. ON. *lǫus-s*, *laus-s* = OE. *léas* LEASE *a.*, q. v.]

A. *adj.* **1.** Unbound, unattached. **a.** Free from bonds or physical restraint. Now used only in implied contrast. **b.** *transf.* and *fig.*, e. g. of the tongue: Not 'tied', free to speak. 1726. **c.** Freed from an obligation, etc.; at liberty. *Obs.* exc. *dial.* 1553. **†d.** Free *from* or *of*; released *from*; unattached *to* –1821. **†e.** Ungirt; naked –1709. **f.** Of an inanimate thing: Detached. Phr. *To come, get l.* 1728. **g.** Not joined to anything else. Of a chemical element: Free, uncombined 1828. **h.** Having an end or ends hanging free. (See also LOOSE END.) 1781. **i.** Not bound together; not tied up or secured 1488. **j.** Unconnected; rambling; detached, stray, random. Now *rare.* 1681. **k.** Free for disposal; unattached, unappropriated, unoccupied. *Obs.* exc. *joc.* 1479. **2.** Not rigidly fixed in place; ready to shift or come apart ME. **†b.** Of the eyes: Not fixed, roving –1751. **3.** Not tense or stretched; slack, relaxed 1460. **b.** Of clothes: Loosely fitting 1463. **4.** Not close or compact in arrangement or structure ME. **b.** *Bot.* = LAX *a.* 3 b. Also, 'of a soft cellular texture' (Lindley). 1776. **c.** Of handwriting: Straggling 1711. **d.** Applied to exercise or play in which the players, etc. act more independently 1802. **5.** Wanting in retentiveness or power of restraint ME. **b.** Of the bowels: Relaxed 1508. **6.** Of qualities, actions, statements, ideas, etc.: Not rigid, strict, correct, or careful; hence, inexact, indefinite, vague 1606. **†b.** Of conditions, undertakings, etc.: Lacking security, unsettled –1687. **c.** *Cricket.* Of bowling: Not accurate in pitch. Of fielding, etc.: Slack, careless. 1859. **7.** Of persons, etc.: Lax in principle, conduct, or speech; chiefly in narrower sense, unchaste, dissolute, immoral 1470. **8.** Applied to a stable in which animals are kept without being fastened up. So also *l. box* (see BOX *sb.*[2] II. 4) 1813.

1. a. You are afraid if you see the Beare l. SHAKS. He got one hand l. (*mod.*). **b.** Murder is l. 1879. **f.** Some of the pages have come l. (*mod.*). **h.** As to Logic, its chain of conclusions hangs l. at both ends J. H. NEWMAN. **i.** Her haire not l. nor ti'd in formall plat SHAKS. **j.** A good deal of l. information CARLYLE. **k.** I hope you read..at l. hours, other books JOHNSON. *L. card*: a card in a hand that is of no value, and consequently the properest to throw away (HOYLE). **2.** His bridge was only l. planks DE FOE. **3.** The labour'd Oxe In his l. traces MILT. My knees l. under me STEVENSON. Phr. *With a l. rein* (fig.): slackly, without rigour. **b.** Men in l. flannel jackets 1901. **4.** The Ashes with Aire between, lie looser BACON. The l. assault of the Mexicans 1777. **5.** A rash young fool; carries a l. tongue CARLYLE. **6.** L. and negligent curiosity MILT. L., exaggerated calculations HUME. L. tradition and reports PALEY. A l. construction 1872. L. thinkers and l. talkers 1875. **7.** A l. liuer 1591.

Spec. collocations: **l. box**, a stable in which a horse is allowed to move about freely; **l. fish** (*colloq.*), a person of irregular habits; **l.-leaf** *a.*, of a ledger, etc.: with each leaf separate and detachable; **l. pulley**, a pulley running loosely on the shaft on which it is journaled; also *fast and l. pulley* (see FAST *a.*).

Comb.: **l.-bodied** *a.*, (of a dress) loose-fitting; **-tongued** *a.*, blabbing.

B. quasi-*sb.* and *sb.* **1.** *absol.* **a.** *On the l.*: 'on the spree' 1849. **b.** *In the l.*: not made up or prepared 1898. **2.** *Rugby Football.* That part of the play in which the ball travels freely from player to player 1892.

C. *adv.* Loosely; with a loose hold 1591.

Phr. *To sit l.* (fig.): to be independent or indifferent; to hold loosely *to*, not to be enslaved *to*; *occas.* not to weigh heavily *upon*. *To hold l.*: to be indifferent. *To play fast and l.*: see FAST AND LOOSE b.

Hence **Loo·se-ly** *adv.*, **-ness. Loo·sish** *a.* somewhat l.

Loose (lūs), *v.* ME. [f. LOOSE *a.*] **1.** *trans.* To let loose, set free; to release from bonds or constraint. **2.** To undo, untie (fetters, a knot); to break (a seal). Now *dial.* or *poet.* ME. Also *fig.* **b.** To detach, cast loose, let go; chiefly *Naut.* ME. **3.** †*To l. the anchor*: to weigh anchor 1450. **b.** Hence *absol.* To weigh anchor; *occas.* with *up* 1526. **†4.** To let fly (an arrow); to let off (a gun). ME. Also *absol.* or *intr.* **b.** *trans.* (*transf.* and *fig.*) To give vent to, emit; to cause or allow to proceed from one 1508. **5.** = LOOSEN *v.* 3. Also *intr.* for *pass.* Now only *arch.* ME. **6.** To make loose or slack; †*pass.* (of nerves) to be unstrung. Now *arch.* exc. in *to l. hold* (colloq.): to let go. 1440. **†b.** *transf.* To relax or loosen (the bowels). Also *absol.* –1651. **†7.** [Cf. L. *solvere.*] To break up, dissolve, do away with. Chiefly *fig.* –1819. **†8.** To solve, explain –1660. **9.** *pass.* and *intr.* To finish working; (of a school, factory, etc.) to close, disperse, break up (*dial.*) 1813.

1. The captiue exile hasteneth that he may be loosed *Isa.* li. 14. The wine loosed the tongues of the guests 1902. **2. b.** She loosed the boat from its moorings GEO. ELIOT. **4. b.** L. now and then A scattred smile, and that Ile liue vpon *A. Y. L.* III. v. 103.

Loose end. 1546. An end of a string, etc., left hanging loose; *fig.* of something left disconnected, undecided, or unguarded. Chiefly *pl.*

Phr. *At* (*after, on*) *a loose end*: having no regular occupation; not knowing what to be at. Also (*to leave a matter*) *at a loose end*: unsettled. *colloq.*, orig. *dial.* 1851.

Loosen (lū·s'n), *v.* ME. [f. LOOSE *a.* + -EN[5].] To make loose or looser. **1.** *trans.* = LOOSE *v.* 1. **2.** To undo, unfasten (bonds, a knot, etc.). Now usu.: To render looser or less tight. ME. **3.** To weaken the adhesion or attachment of; to unfix, detach 1667. †Also *fig.* Also *intr.* for *refl.* or *pass.* **4.** *trans.* To make less coherent 1697. **5.** To relax (the bowels) 1587; to render (a cough) looser 1833. **6.** To relax in severity or strictness 1798.

1. *fig.* By degrees her tongue was loosened TROLLOPE. The fragrance of the valley was loosened 1893. **3.** From thir foundations loosning to and fro They pluckt the seated Hills MILT. Phr. *To l.* (a person's) *hide* (slang): to flog. **4.** He struck the snow with his baton to l. it TYNDALL. **6.** The men neither straggled nor loosened their discipline 1899. Hence **Loo·sener,** one who or that which loosens.

Loosestrife (lū·sˌstrəif). 1548. [f. LOOSE *v.* + STRIFE *sb.*, a mistransl. of late L. *lysimachia*, also *-machion*, taken as if directly f. the adj. λυσίμαχος 'loosing' (i. e. ending) strife (f. λυσι-, λύειν + μάχη), instead of as a. Gr. λυσιμάχιον, f. the personal name Λυσίμαχος Lysimachus, its discoverer.] The name of two tall upright plants growing in moist places: **a.** *Lysimachia vulgaris* (N.O. *Primulaceæ*), Golden or Yellow L., flowering in July, and bearing racemes of golden-yellow flowers. **b.** *Lythrum Salicaria* (N.O. *Lythraceæ*), Red, Purple, or Spiked L., blooming in summer, with a showy spike of purplish-red flowers. Also a book-name for the genera *Lysimachia* and *Lythrum*, and extended to plants of other genera.

b. When through the Wytham flats, Red l. and blond meadow-sweet among..We tracked the shy Thames shore M. ARNOLD.

Loot (lūt), *sb.* 1839. [a. Hindī *lūt*, referred by some to the Skr. root *lup* = *rup* to break; by others to Skr. *lunt* to rob.] Goods taken from an enemy, a captured city, etc. in time of war; also, something taken by force; booty, plunder, spoil; occas. *transf.*, illicit gains, 'pillage' (e. g. by a public servant). Also, the action of looting.

The talismanic gathering-word *Loot* (plunder) 1839.

Loot (lūt), *v.* 1842. [f. prec. sb.] *trans.* To plunder, sack (a city, building) 1845; to carry off as loot or booty 1847; also *absol.*

To l. a village 1845, cattle and grain 1887. Hence **Loo·ter.**

Loover, obs. f. LOUVER.

†Lop (lǫp), *sb.*[1] [OE. *loppe* wk. fem.; etym. unkn.] A spider –ME.

Lop (lǫp), *sb.*[2] Now *dial.* 1440. [prob. a. ON. **hloppa* wk. fem., f. root of *hlǫupa* (*hlaupa*) to LEAP.] A flea.

Lop (lǫp), *sb.*[3] ME. [Partly source, partly deriv. of LOP *v.*[1]] **1.** The smaller branches and twigs of trees; faggot-wood, loppings. Also, a branch lopped off. **†2.** A lopped tree or part –1656. **†3.** The action of lopping a tree or its boughs –1600.

1. Phr. *L. and top, l. and crop.*

Lop (lǫp), *sb.*[4] 1829. [Onomatopœic.] *Naut.* A state of the sea in which the waves are short and lumpy.

Lop (lǫp), *sb.*[5] 1868. [Short for *lop-rabbit*; see LOP *v.*[2]] A variety of rabbit with long drooping ears. Also *full-*, *half-l.*, etc.

Lop (lǫp), *v.*[1] 1480. [prob. f. LOP *sb.*[3]] **1.** *trans.* To cut off the branches, twigs, etc., *rarely* the top or 'head', of (a tree); to trim. **b.** *transf.* and *fig.* †Also with *away*, *off.* 1602. **2.** To cut off (the branches, twigs, etc.) from a tree; to shorten by cutting off the extremities. Now chiefly with *away*, *off.* 1593. **b.** *transf.* and *fig.* To cut off (a person's limbs or head). Also *gen.*, to cut off, reduce by cutting. Also with *away*, *down*, *off.* 1586. **c.** *absol.* or *intr.* 1588.

1. In the moneth of December..l. hedges and trees MARKHAM. **b.** When our grandsire great..Lop'd the French lillies DRAYTON. **2.** He lopped off the tops as they sprang up N. BACON. **b.** His leg was lopp'd CRABBE. To l. off part of a visit 1864.

Lop (lǫp), *v.*[2] 1578. [perh. onomatopœic; cf. LOB *v.*] **1.** *intr.* To hang loosely or limply; to droop; to sway limply about. **b.** *trans.* To droop (the ears) 1828. **2.** *intr.* To slouch; to hang idly about 1587. **3.** To move with short irregular bounds. Cf. LOPE *v.* 1895.

3. Lopping easily along, a fox crosses through the teazles C. J. CORNISH. *Comb.*: **l.-eaves,** eaves which hang down at the sides; **-rabbit** (see LOP *sb.*[5]).

Lop (lǫp), *v.*[3] 1897. [Cf. LOP *sb.*[4]] *intr.* Of water: To break in short lumpy waves.

Lope (lōup), *sb.* ME. [a. ON. *hlǫup*; see LEAP *sb.*[1] Cf. Du. *loop.*] **†1.** = LEAP *sb.*[1] –1734. **2.** A long bounding stride (chiefly of animals) 1846.

2. The easy l. of the 'rickshaw coolie R. KIPLING.

Lope (lōup), *v.* 1483. [a. ON. *hlǫupa*; see LEAP *v.*] **1.** *intr.* To leap, jump, spring. Also with *about*. *Obs.* exc. *dial.* **2.** *intr.* To run, run away. Now only *slang* and *dial.* 1572. **3.** To run with a long bounding stride. (Said chiefly of animals.) 1825.

3. The larger wolves..l. hungrily around 1848.

Lop-ear (lǫ·pˌīᵊɹ), *sb.* (and *a.*) 1692. [LOP *v.*[2]] **1.** *pl.* Ears that droop or hang down. **2.** A kind of rabbit with such ears. Also *attrib.* 1877. So **Lo·p-eared** *a.* having ears which hang loosely down 1687.

†Lo·peman. [a. Du. *loopman* (obs.), f. *loopen* to run + *man* MAN *sb.*] A runner. FLETCHER.

Loper (lōu·pəɹ). 1483. [f. LOPE *v.* + -ER[1].] **†1.** A leaper, dancer. **2.** *Ropemaking.* A swivel upon which yarns are hooked at one end while being twisted into cordage. [? a. Du. *looper* runner.] 1794.

Lopho- (lǫ·fǫ, lǫfǫ·), bef. a vowel **loph-**, comb. f. Gr. λόφος crest: in various scientific terms, as **Lo·phobranch** (-bræŋk), **-bra·nchiate** [Gr. βράγχια gills] *Ichthyol.* **a.** *adj.* having the gills disposed in tufts; **b.** *sb.* a l. fish 1834. **Lo·phophore** [Gr. -φόρος bearing] **a.** *Zool.* in Polyzoa, the oral disk at the free end of the polypide, bearing the tentacles 1850; **b.** a bird of the genus *Lophophorus*, with crested crown and brilliant plumage 1883.

Lophodont (lǫ·fodǫnt). 1887. [f. prec. + Gr. ὀδοντ- TOOTH.] Characterized by having ridges on the crowns of the molar teeth.

Lopped (lǫpt), *ppl. a.* 1570. [f. LOP *v.*[1] + -ED [1].] In senses of the vb. *Bot.* and *Zool.* Truncate. **b.** *Her.* Cut so as to show the thickness; snagged 1828.

Lopper (lǫ·pəɹ), *sb.* 1538. [f. LOP *v.*[1] + -ER [1].] One who lops (a tree).

Lopper (lǫ·pəɹ), *v.* Now only *Sc.* and *n. dial.* ME. [?f. ON. *hlaup* (*hlaup*) coagulation + -ER [5].] **1.** *intr.* Of milk: To curdle. **2.** 'To dabble, to besmear, or to cover so as to clot' (Jam.) 1818.

Lopping (lǫ·piŋ), *vbl. sb.* 1480. [f. LOP *v.*[1] + -ING [1].] **1.** The action of LOP *v.*[1] (The cant term of the Rye House conspirators for the killing of the King and the Duke of York.) **2.** Chiefly *pl.* Branches and shoots lopped from a tree. Also, material for lopping. 1589. **3.** *attrib.* 1659.

2. He shall gather vp the loppings to make fewell of SURFLET.

Lo·ppy, *a.* 1855. [f. LOP *v.*[2] + -Y [1].] That hangs loosely; limp.

Lopseed (lǫ·psīd). 1850. [f. LOP *v.*[2]] A North American perennial herb, *Phryma leptostachya*, with small purple flowers and spikes of strongly reflexed fruits.

Lop-sided, lopsided (lǫ:pˌsəi·dėd), *a.* 1711. [f. LOP *v.*[2] + SIDE *sb.* + -ED [2].] That lops or leans on or towards one side; having one side lower or smaller than the other. Orig. *Naut.* (of a ship): Disproportionately heavy on one side.

Loquacious (lǫkwēⁱ·ʃəs), *a.* 1667. [f. L. *loquaci-*, *loquax* (f. *loqui*) + -OUS.] **1.** Given to much talking; talkative. **2.** *transf.* Of birds, water, etc.: Chattering, babbling. Chiefly *poet.* 1697.

1. The chief Exercise of the Female l. Faculty STEELE. 2. L. Frogs DRYDEN. Hence **Loqua·cious·ly** *adv.*, **-ness.**

Loquacity (lǫkwæ·sĭti). 1596. [ad. F. *loquacité*, ad. L. *loquacitas*, f. *loquax* (see prec.).] The condition or quality of being loquacious; talkativeness.

The only limit to his l. was his strength BUCKLE.

Loquat (lō^u·kwæt). 1814. [a. Chinese *luh kwat*, lit. 'rush orange'.] The fruit of *Eriobotrya japonica*, a native of China and Japan, introduced into southern Europe, India, and Australia. Also, the tree itself. Also *l. tree.*

Lor', lor (lǭɹ), *int. vulgar.* 1835. A clipped form of LORD, used as an exclam.

Loral (lōᵊ·răl), *a.* (and *sb.*) 1874. [f. L. *lorum* LORE *sb.*[2] + -AL.] *Zool.* Pertaining to the lore. Hence as *sb.* = *l. shield* or *plate* (see LORE *sb.*[2]).

Lorate (lōᵊ·reⁱt), *a.* 1836. [f. as prec. + -ATE [2].] Strap-shaped.

Lorcha (lǭ·ɹtʃă), **lorch** (lǭɹtʃ). 1653. [a. Pg. *lorcha*; origin unkn.] A light Chinese sailing vessel with the hull after a European model, but a Chinese rig, usually carrying guns.

Lord (lǭɹd), *sb.* [OE. *hlāford*, once *hlāfweard*, repr. a prehistoric **hlaibward-*, f. **hlaib-* (OE. *hlāf*) LOAF + **ward-* (OE. *weard*) keeper (see WARD *sb.*). (Cf. OE. *hlāf-ǣta*, lit. 'bread-eater', a servant, and LADY.) Taken as the customary rendering of L. *dominus*, whence in part the sense-development.]

I. A master, ruler. †**1.** A master of servants; the male head of a household –1611. **2.** One to whom service and obedience are due; a master, chief, prince, sovereign. Now only *rhet.* Also *l. and master.* OE. **b.** *fig.* One who or something which has the mastery or pre-eminence ME. **c.** An owner, possessor, proprietor (of land, houses, etc.). Now only *poet.* or *rhet.* ME. **d.** A 'magnate' in some particular industry. (Cf. *King.*) 1823. **3.** *spec.* A feudal superior; the proprietor of a fee, manor, etc. OE. **4.** A husband. Now only *poet.* or *joc.* OE. **5.** [Cf. 2 b.] *Astrol.* The planet that has a dominant influence over an event, period, region, etc. ME. **6. The Lord** (vocatively **Lord**): God OE. **b.** As an exclam. of surprise. Now only in profane or trivial use. ME. **7.** As a title of Jesus Christ. Commonly *Our L.*; also *the L.* ME.

1. *Matt.* xxiv. 46. 2. Man over men He made not L. MILT. transf. *L. L. L.* IV. i. 38. **b.** *Lords of (the) creation*: mankind; now *joc.*, men as opp. to women. My bosomes L. sits lightly in his throne SHAKS. **c.** L. of few Acres, and those barren too DRYDEN. **d.** The cotton lords are not more popular than the landlords COBDEN. 3. *L. of the Manor* (see MANOR). *L. mesne, paramount* (see those wds.). 4. *Tam. Shr.* V. ii. 131. 6. The L. increase this businesse SHAKS. Phr. *(The) L. knows who, what, how,* etc.: a flippant expression of one's own ignorance of a matter. *L. have mercy (on us)*: (*a*) a prayer (chalked on house-doors in time of plague); (*b*) in trivial use (vulgarly *lord-a-mercy*, etc.), as an exclam. of astonishment. So (in trivial use only) *L. bless me.* **b.** O L. I must laugh SHAKS. 7. How loyal in the following of thy L.! TENNYSON. Phr. *(In) the year of our L.*, †*of our Lord's incarnation*: = ANNO DOMINI. *Comb.*, etc. **The Lord's Prayer** [= L. *oratio Dominica*], the prayer taught by Jesus to His disciples (see *Matt.* vi. 9–13); the paternoster. **The Lord's Supper** [= L. *cena Dominica*, Gr. τὸ κυριακὸν δεῖπνον 1 *Cor.* xi. 24], the Holy Communion. **The Lord's table** [= Gr. τραπέζα κυρίου 1 *Cor.* x. 21]: cf. ALTAR 2 b; hence, the Holy Communion.

II. As a designation of rank, etc. **1.** In early use employed vaguely for any man of exalted position, and in a narrower sense applied to barons (see BARON 1). Now, = NOBLEMAN: A peer of the realm, or one who by courtesy is entitled to the prefix Lord, or some higher title, as a part of his ordinary appellation ME. **2.** pl. *The Lords*: the lords of parliament, temporal and spiritual, as constituting one of the two bodies composing the legislature of the United Kingdom 1451. **3.** Applied, with defining word, to the individual members of a Board appointed to perform the duties of some high office of state that has been put in commission (see below) 1642. **4.** Forming part of various official titles (see below) 1598. **b.** In ceremonious use, prefixed to the titles of bishops, whether lords of parliament or not 1639. **5.** As a prefixed title, forming part of a person's customary appellation. Abbrev. Ld., Lo. 1455.

Now used as follows. In substitution for 'Marquis', 'Earl', or 'Viscount' (whether denoting a peer, or applied 'by courtesy' to the eldest son of a peer of higher rank); the word *of* being dropped. Thus 'Lord Hartington' may be used instead of 'The Marquis of Hartington', etc. A baron is always called 'Lord —', as 'Lord Tennyson'; the Christian name, if used, comes first, as 'Alfred, Lord Tennyson'. The younger sons of dukes and marquises have the courtesy title of 'Lord' followed by the Christian name and surname, as 'Lord John Russell'.

The Lord, the early form of the prefixed title, still survives in certain formal uses, and in the superscription of letters.

6. Jocular uses. See below. 1556. **b.** *slang.* A hunchback 1700. **7. My Lord** (usu. pronounced milǭ·ɹd). **a.** Prefixed to a name or title. (*a*) Formerly used where we now use simply 'Lord' (see II. 5), with or without *of.* (Now only *arch.*) (*b*) *My L. of* (*London*, etc.): a respectful mode of referring to a bishop (*obs.* or *arch.*). (*c*) Prefixed to a title of rank or office; now only *vocatively*; as in *my L. Mayor, my L. Duke*, etc. 1440. **b.** Used separately. (*a*) The usual polite and respectful form of address to a nobleman under the rank of a duke, and to a bishop; also in speaking of them. (*b*) In courts of law used in addressing a judge of the Supreme Court; in Scotland and Ireland in addressing a judge of any of the superior courts. (In affected pronunciation *my Lud, m'lud*: see LUD.) **c.** pl. *My lords*: (*a*) form of address to a number of noblemen or bishops, and to two or more of the superior judges sitting in court together; (*b*) in departmental correspondence, used as a collective designation for the ministers composing the department.

1. The Englishman of to-day still dearly loves a l. 1900. Phr. *To live like a l.*: to fare sumptuously. *To treat* (a person) *like a l.*: to entertain sumptuously, to treat with great deference. Phr. *Drunk as a l.*; *to swear like a l.* *Lord-in-waiting, L. of the Bedchamber*, any nobleman holding certain offices in attendance on the person of the sovereign, called 'in waiting' if the sovereign is a queen, 'of the bedchamber' if a king. 2. The Lords..suspended the sitting until eleven at night 1879. *The Lords Temporal*, the temporal or lay peers. *The Lords Spiritual*: the bishops who are lords of parliament, and, formerly, the mitred abbots. *House of Lords* (see HOUSE *sb.*[1] 4 d). 3. *Lords Commissioners* (now simply *Lords*) *of the Admiralty, of the Treasury*; *Lords Commissioners of the Great Seal.* Also *Lords Justices (of Ireland)*: the commissioners to whom, in the early 18th c., the viceregal authority was entrusted. *Civil L.*: the one civilian member (besides the First L.) of the Board of Admiralty, the others being *Naval Lords.* 4. *L. (High) Admiral, L. Chamberlain, L. (High) Chancellor, L. Chief Justice, L. High Commissioner, L. Deputy, L. Marshal, L. President, L. Privy Seal, L. Treasurer, L. Warden*, etc. **Lord-rector**, an honorary title for the elected chief in certain Scotch Universities; hence *Lord-rectorship.* 5. *The L. Harry*: see HARRY *sb.* 6. *L. of Misrule* (see MISRULE), etc. **b.** His pupil..was..on account of his hump, distinguished by the title of My Lord SMOLLETT.

Lord (lǭɹd), *v.* ME. [f. LORD *sb.*] **1.** *intr.* †**a.** To exercise lordship –1489. **b.** To play the lord (now usu. with *over*); to assume airs of grandeur; to rule tyrannically, domineer ME. **2.** *trans.* To be or act as lord of; to control, manage, rule (*rare*) 1586. **3.** To confer the title of lord upon 1610; to address as 'Lord' 1636.

1. *To l. it*; They..l. it as they list SPENSER.

Lording (lǭ·ɹdiŋ). [OE. *hlāfording*; see LORD *sb.*, -ING [3].] **1.** = LORD *sb.* I. 2. Rarely *sing.* = Sir! freq. in *pl.* = Sirs! Gentlemen! *Obs.* exc. *arch.* **2.** As dim. of LORD: A little lord, a petty lord; usu. *contemptuous* 1577. **3.** A kind of apple or pear 1664.

1. It was a Lordings daughter SHAKS. 2. When you were Boyes: You were pretty Lordings then? SHAKS.

Lo·rdkin. [-KIN.] A little or young lord. THACKERAY.

Lordless (lǭ·ɹdlės), *a.* [OE. *hlāfordlēas*, f. *hlāford* LORD *sb.* + *-lēas* -LESS.] Without a lord. Of a woman: Husbandless.

Lo·rd-lieute·nant. *Pl.* **lords-lieutenant(s, lord-lieutenants.** 1557. **a.** In Ireland (before the establishment of the Irish Free State in 1922): The Viceroy 1614. **b.** In a county: The chief executive authority and head of the magistracy, appointed by the sovereign by patent. Under him and of his appointing are deputy-lieutenants. 1557. Hence **Lo·rd-lieute·nancy.**

Lordlike (lǭ·ɹdləik). 1470. [-LIKE.] **a.** *adj.* Befitting or like a lord; lordly. Now *rare.* †**b.** *adv.* After the fashion of a lord; domineeringly; sumptuously –1727.

Lordling (lǭ·ɹdliŋ). ME. [-LING [1].] **1.** A little or puny lord; often *contemptuous.* Occas. = LORDING *sb.* 1. †**2.** A kind of apple 1727.

Lordly (lǭ·ɹdli). [OE. *hlāfordlic*, f. LORD *sb.* + -LY.]

A. *adj.* **1.** Of or pertaining to a lord; consisting of, or administered by, lords. Now *rare.* **2.** Having the character, attributes, appearance, or demeanour of a lord. Of actions: Befitting a lord; honourable. ME. **b.** Haughty, imperious, lofty, disdainful ME. **3.** Of things: Suitable for a lord; hence, grand, magnificent, noble 1535. **4.** *absol.* 1470.

1. A l. prelacy 1862. 2. A l. spectacle CARLYLE. **b.** The L. domineering of the English 1665. 3. I built my soul a l. pleasurehouse TENNYSON. Hence **Lo·rdlily** *adv.* **Lo·rdliness,** †the condition or state of a lord; l. disposition.

B. *adv.* After the manner of a lord; in a lordly manner ME.

Lord Mayor. 1554. A title, orig. of the mayors of London, York, and Dublin only, but now also of some other large towns.

Lord Mayor's Day, Nov. 9, when the Lord Mayor goes in procession with the city dignitaries to and from Westminster, where he receives from the Lord Chancellor the assent of the Crown to his election. *Lord Mayor's Show*, the procession on Lord Mayor's Day.

Lordolatry (lǫɹdǫ·lătri). *joc.* 1846. [f. LORD *sb.* + -(O)LATRY.] Worship of lords.

The..prevalence of L. in this country THACKERAY.

‖**Lordosis** (lǫɹdō^u·sis). 1704. [mod.L., a. Gr. λόρδωσις, f. λορδός bent backwards.] *Path.* Anterior curvature of the spine, producing convexity in front.

Lords and ladies. 1760. A popular name for the wild arum (*Arum maculatum*), in reference to the dark and light spadices.

Lord's day or **Day.** ME. [Prop., *The Lord's Day* = L. *dies Dominica*, Gr. ἡ κυριακὴ ἡμέρα Rev. i. 10.] A Christian appellation for Sunday.

Lord's day (without the article) is no longer used, except by some Nonconformists. *The Lord's day* is the form now current.

Lordship (lǭ·ɹdʃip). OE. [See LORD and -SHIP.] 1. The dignity and functions of a lord; dominion, rule; ownership *of* or dominion †*on, over*; rarely *pl.* 2. The land or territory of a lord; a domain, estate, manor, seignory ME. †b. A government, province, district –1578. 3. The personality of a lord, esp. with possess. prons. 1489. b. *joc.* (as a mock complimentary designation for ordinary persons or animals) 1892. 4. *Sc.* A royalty 1861.

1. Our first parent had L. over Sea, and Land, and Air MILT. 3. *Your lordship(s*: a form of address to noblemen (except archbishops and dukes), and to judges. b. His l. [the donkey] 1892.

Lore (lōᵊɹ), *sb.*[1] [OE. *lār* str. fem. :—OTeut. **laizā*, f. root *lais-*; cf. LEARN *v.*] 1. The act of teaching; the condition of being taught; instruction; a piece of instruction; a lesson. Now *arch.* and *dial.* 2. That which is taught; doctrine. Applied chiefly to religious doctrine. Now *poet.* or *arch.* OE. †b. *pl.* Doctrines, precepts, ordinances –1580. †c. A creed, religion –1550. †3. Advice, counsel; instruction, command, order –1667. 4. That which is learned; learning, scholarship, erudition. Now only *arch.* and *Sc.* Also, recently: The body of traditional facts or beliefs relating to some subject; as, *animal, bird, fairy, plant l.* ME.

1. She finish'd, and the suttle Fiend his l. Soon learnd MILT. 2. Her [Vertue's] l. MILT. The l. of Christ TRENCH. 4. Skill'd in legendary l. GOLDSM.

Lore (lōᵊɹ), *sb.*[2] 1621. [ad. L. *lorum* strap, thong.] †1. A strap, thong, rein (*rare*) –1636. 2. *Nat. Hist.* A strap-like appendage or part in certain insects, birds, and snakes 1817.

Lore, str. pa. t. and pple. of LEESE *v.*

Loreal (lōᵊ·rĭăl), *a.* and *sb.* 1849. [? irreg. f. LORE *sb.*[2] + -AL.] = LORAL.

†**Lorel.** [ME. *lorel*, f. *loren*, pa. pple. of LEESE *v.*, as LOSEL from the var. *losen*.] A worthless person, rogue, blackguard; = LOSEL. In 16th c. often opp. to *lord*.

Cock Lorel. See *Cocke Lorelles Bote* (printed by Wynkyn de Worde *c* 1515). *allusively*, Rogue, reprobate.

Loren, pa. pple. of LEESE *v.*

‖**Lorgnette** (lǭrnye·t). 1820. [Fr., f. *lorgner* to squint; see -ETTE.] a. A pair of eye-glasses held in the hand, usu. by a long handle. b. An opera-glass.

‖**Lorgnon** (lǭ·ɹnyon). 1846. [Fr.] a. A single or double eye-glass; a lorgnette. b. An opera-glass.

Lori, var. of LORIS.

‖**Lorica** (lŏrəi·kă). 1706. [L., f. *lorum* strap.] 1. *Rom. Antiq.* A cuirass or corslet of leather. 2. *Old Chem.* A kind of lute or paste for coating vessels before subjecting them to heat 1753. 3. *Zool.* The protective case or sheath of some infusorians and rotifers; also applied to the carapace of crustaceans 1856. 4. *Bot.* The integument of seeds. LINDLEY.

Loricate (lǭ·rikeᶦt). 1826. [ad. L. *loricatus*, f. LORICA; see -ATE[2].] *Zool.* A. *adj.* Covered with 'armour' or adjoining plates or scales; having a lorica. So **Lo·ricated** *a.* 1623. B. *sb. pl.* [repr. mod.L. *Loricati* or *Loricata*.] Applied to various groups of animals having such an integument, as those represented by the armadillos, crocodiles, and certain infusorians 1855.

Loricate (lǭ·rikeᶦt), *v.* 1623. [f. L. *loricat-*, *loricare*, f. LORICA.] *trans.* To enclose in or cover with a protective coating. Hence **Lorica·tion**, the action of loricating; *concr.* a defensive covering or casing 1706.

Lorikeet (lǭrikī·t). 1772. [f. LORY + *-keet* in PARRAKEET.] Name for small brightly-coloured parrots of the Malay Archipelago, comprehending the genera *Charmosyna, Loriculus,* and *Coriphilus*.

Lorimer, loriner (lǭ·rimǝɹ, lǭ·rinǝɹ). Now *Hist.* ME. [a. OF. *loremier, lorenier* (F. *lormier*), f. *lorain* thong.] A maker of bits and metal mountings for horses' bridles; also, a spurrier, and (generally) a maker of small iron ware, etc. (Now only in the title of a London livery company.)

†**Lo·ring,** *vbl. sb.* [f. LORE *sb.*[1] + -ING[1].] Teaching, instruction. SPENSER.

Loriot (lǭ·riǭt). 1601. [a. F. *loriot*, a corruption (due to the added article) of OF. *oriot*, altered f. *oriole* ORIOLE.] The Golden Oriole, *Oriolus galbula*.

Loris (lōᵊ·ris). Also *erron.* **lori, lory.** 1774. [a. F. *loris* (Buffon).] A small slender tailless nocturnal climbing lemur of Ceylon (*Loris gracilis*); also extended to the related genus *Nycticebus*.

Lorn (lǭɹn), *ppl. a.* ME. [pa. pple. of LEESE *v.*] †1. Lost, perished, ruined; doomed –1805. 2. = FORLORN 4, 5. 1475.

1. If thou readest, thou art l.! SCOTT. 2. Left lone and l. 1876.

Lorry, lurry (lǭ·ri, lɒ·ri). 1838. [prob. f. dial. *lurry, lorry* to pull, tug.] 1. A long flat wagon without sides, or with low sides, running on four low wheels. Also, a truck or wagon running on railways or tramways. 2. *Mining.* A running bridge over a pit 1883.

Lory (lōᵊ·ri). 1692. [a. Malay *lūrī*, dial. var. of *nūrī*. Cf. F. *lori*.] A parrot-like bird of the family *Loriinæ*, with brilliant plumage, from South-eastern Asia and Australia. Also the S. African touraco, *Turacus albicristatus*.

Losable, loseable (lū·zăb'l), *a.* 1611. [f. LOSE *v.* + -ABLE.] Capable of being lost.

Losang(e, obs. f. LOZENGE.

†**Lose,** *sb.* ME. [a. OF. *los, loz, loos* :—L. *laudes*, pl. of *laus* praise.] Praise, renown, fame. Also (good or bad) reputation; *occas.* ill fame. *Out of lose*: to one's dispraise. –1825.

Lose (lūz), *v.*[1] [OE. *losian*, f. *los* Loss, used mostly *intr.* (sense 1). Later, synonymous with the cognate LEESE *v.*, which it finally superseded.] †1. *intr.* To perish; to be lost –ME. †2. *trans.* To destroy, ruin; to be the ruin of –1628. b. To ruin in estimation (*rare*) 1605. c. *pass.* To be brought to destruction, ruin, or misery; to be killed; to be damned. Of a ship, etc.: To perish at sea. OE. 3. To incur the privation of (something that one possesses or has control of); to part with through negligence or misadventure; to be deprived of. See below. ME. 4. *absol.* or *intr.* To suffer loss; to cease to possess something; to be deprived of or part with some of one's or its possessions, attributes, or qualities; to become deteriorated or incur disadvantage ME. b. Of an immaterial thing: To be deprived of its power or force (*rare*) 1794. 5. To become unable to find; to cease to know the whereabouts of OE. b. To fail to keep in sight. Also, *to l. sight of.* Also *occas.*, to cease to hear (*poet.*); to fail to follow in argument (*obs.* or *arch.*) 1587. c. To draw away from; to leave hopelessly behind in a race 1704. †d. To fail to retain in the mind or memory; to forget –1712. e. To cease to follow (the right track); also, to cease to find (traces of a person, etc.). Chiefly in *to l. one's way* (lit. and fig.). 1530. 6. To spend unprofitably; to waste, get no return or result for (one's labour or efforts); to let slip (opportunities); to waste (time) ME. 7. To fail to obtain (e.g. a prize); *occas.* constr. *to.* Also, to fail to catch (a train, etc.). ME. b. To fail to apprehend; not to 'catch' (words, etc.) 1567. c. *Hunting.* To fail to catch (an animal) 1599. 8. To forfeit (a stake); to be defeated in (a game, battle, lawsuit); to fail to carry (a motion). In *Cricket*: To have (a wicket) taken. Const. *to.* 1440. 9. *causal.* To cause the loss of; often const. *dative* of the person suffering loss ME. 10. *refl.* (and corresponding *pass.*). a. To go astray. Also *fig.* 1535. b. To become merged (*in* something else). Also *fig.* 1604. c. To become engrossed (*in* thought, etc.); to be overwhelmed (*in* wonder); †to be distracted (from excitement, etc.) 1604. d. To become obscured (*in* clouds, etc.) 1697.

2. b. *Lear* I. i. 236. c. The Woman that Deliberates is lost ADDISON. 3. a. To l. lands, goods, a right, quality, a place, etc. ME. b. To l. a limb, faculty, one's life, etc. *To l. one's head*: see HEAD *sb.* *To l. heart*: to become discouraged. *To l. one's heart*: to fall in love. *To l. one's legs* (slang): to get drunk. c. To l. a relative, friend, servant, etc. by death, men in battle ME. To l. a patient 1882. d. *To l. patience, one's temper, to l. caste, hold, one's balance*, etc. *To l. ground*: to fail to keep one's position; esp. *fig.* to decline in reputation, favour, health, etc. e. To l. an ague 1677, one's fears 1742, a sense of misery 1859. f. To l. (a portion of itself, a quality, or appurtenance) ME. Til that the brighte sonne loste his hewe CHAUCER. Her household duties had lost their interest 1894. g. The *passive* is often used without any reference to a determinate person or thing as 'losing'; e.g. (of an art, etc.) to cease to be known or practised; (of a quality, etc.) to cease to be present 1667. 4. Both armies lost heavily (*mod.*). c. *To l. out* (*U.S.*): to be unsuccessful, to fail 1889. 5. Like a Schoole-boy that had lost his A.B.C. SHAKS. c. His great stride and iron legs..enabled him, in the language of the turf, to l. his antagonist 1886. d. Being ouerfull of selfe-affaires, My minde did l. it SHAKS. I am in great danger of losing my English 1718. 6. There is no time to be lost MARRYAT. *To be lost on* or *upon*: to have no effect upon; Your kindness is not lost upon me 1833. 7. Hee shall in no wise l. his reward *Matt.* x. 42. b. I did not l. a word of his speech (*mod.*). 8. If we loose the Field, We cannot keepe the Towne SHAKS. *absol.* A captiue victor that hath lost in gaine SHAKS. 9. The crimes of John lost him all the northern part of his French possessions FREEMAN. 10. a. I love to l. my selfe in a mystery SIR T. BROWNE. b. All surprise was shortly lost in other feelings JANE AUSTEN. c. I..l. myself in melancholy musings W. IRVING. d. Woody mountains half in vapours lost POPE.

†**Lose,** *v.*[2] [f. LOSE *sb.*, or perh. aphetic f. ALOSE *v.*] *trans.* To praise. Only in ME.

Losel (lōᵘ·zĕl). *arch.* and *dial.* ME. [app. f. *losen*, pa. pple. of LEESE *v.* Etym. sense 'one who is lost', 'a son of perdition'.] A. *sb.* A worthless person; a profligate, rake, scoundrel; in weaker sense, a ragamuffin, ne'er-do-well. B. *adj.* Good-for-nothing, worthless 1601. Hence **Lo·selry**, profligacy, debauchery, rascality (*rare*).

†**Losenger.** ME. [a. OF. *losengeour, -ere*, f. *losenge* :—(ult.) med.L. *laudēmia*, a deriv. of L. *laud-, laus* praise.] 1. A false flatterer, a lying rascal, a deceiver –1616. ¶2. *Sc.* A sluggard. DOUGLAS. †**Losengery,** flattery, deceit.

Loser (lū·zǝɹ). ME. [f. LOSE *v*[1] + -ER[1].] 1. One who loses (see LOSE *v.*[1]). b. A horse that loses in a race 1902. 2. *Billiards.* A losing hazard 1873. 3. *Tennis.* A losing stroke 1928. 4. *Bridge.* A losing card 1918.

Losing (lū·ziŋ), *vbl. sb.* OE. [f. LOSE *v.*[1] + -ING[1].] The action of LOSE *v.*[1]

attrib. in l.-money, a payment allowed to the loser in certain competitions.

Lo·sing, *ppl. a.* 1519. [f. LOSE *v.*[1] + -ING[2].] That loses, or results in loss.

L. game, (*a*) a game played with ill success (usu. *fig.*); (*b*) a game in which the loser wins the stakes. **L. hazard,** see the sb. **Lo·singly** *adv.*

Loss (lǭs), *sb.* [OE. and early ME. *los*, only in dat. *lose*, corresponds to ON. *los* neut., 'breaking up of the ranks of an army' (Vigfusson) :—OTeut. **losom*, f. **lus-*, wk. grade of the root **leus-*, **laus-*; see LEESE *v.*, LEASE *a.*, LOOSE *a.* The mod. form may have been a back-formation from the pa. pple. *lost*.] 1. The condition or fact of being lost, destroyed, or ruined. Now only with mixture of other senses. 2. The fact of losing. See senses of LOSE *v.*[1] Const. with *of* or objective genitive. ME. †3. *occas.* Cause or occasion of ruin or deprivation –1548. 4. An instance of losing. Also, a person, thing, or amount lost. ME. 5. Detriment or disadvantage resulting from deprivation or change of conditions; an instance of this. (Opp. to *gain*.) ME. 6. *Mil.* The losing of men by death, wounds, or capture; also (*sing.* and *pl.*) the number of men so lost ME. †7. Lack, default –1632. †8. *Tennis.* A lost chase (see CHASE *sb.*[1] 7) –1619.

1. Thou hast..quitted all to save A World from utter l. MILT. 2. The l. of power 1620, of sight MILT. The L. of a Mother STEELE. The battle's l. SHELLEY. The l. of an hour TYNDALL, of a train (*mod.*). *L. of life*: the being put to death (as a punishment). Also, the 'sacrifice' of human lives. 3. Womman was the los of al mankynde CHAUCER. 4. A rich fellow enough, goe to, and a fellow that hath had losses SHAKS. 5. L. and gain NEWMAN (*title*). He is no l. (*mod.*). Phr. *To have a great l. in* (or *of*): to suffer severely by

losing. 6. They were repulsed with l. GROTE. 7. Phr. *In the l. of question*: provided there is no dispute. *Meas. for M.* II. iv. 90.

Phrase. **At a loss, †at l.** Of a hound: Having lost the track or scent; at fault. Hence of persons: At fault; puzzled what to say or do. *At a l. for*: unable to discover or obtain (something needed).

Comb.: l.-leader *U.S.*, an article sold below cost for the purpose of attracting buyers.

†Lost, *sb.* ME. [app. f. *lost*, pa. pple. of LOSE *v.*[1]] = LOSS *sb.* -1671.

Lost (lǫst), *ppl. a.* 1500. [Pa. pple. of LOSE *v.*[1]] 1. That has perished or been destroyed; ruined, esp. morally or spiritually; (of the soul) damned 1533. 2. Not retained in possession; no longer to be found. Also, of a person or animal: Having gone astray, having lost his or its way 1526. 3. Of time, labour, space: Not used advantageously; spent in vain; †thence, vain. Of opportunities: Missed. 1500. 4. Of a battle, game: In which one has been defeated. Also *transf.* Of a person: Defeated (*poet.*). 1724.

1. A l. man BURNET, ship FALCONER. 2. The thought..of l. happiness MILT. The L. Leader BROWNING (*title*). A 'Lost Ball' 1849. *To give* (*over* or *up*) *for l.*, to consider, set down as lost. 3. It were l. sorrow to waile one that's l. SHAKS. To make up for l. time 1889. 4. In the l. battle, borne down by the flying SCOTT.

Phr. *To be l. to*: a. to have passed from the possession of; b. (of a person) to have no sense of (right, shame, etc.); also *rarely*, to have lost all interest in; †to be forgotten by, unknown to (the world).

Lot (lǫt), *sb.* [OE. *hlot* neut. (rendering L. *sors, portio*) :—OTeut. type **hluto-m*, f. wk. grade of root *hleut-* (: *hlaut-* : *hlūt-*) in OE. *hlēotan* to cast lots, obtain by lot. Prob. some Eng. uses are due to the influence of Fr. *lot*.] 1. An object (usu. a piece of wood) used in an ancient method of selection or decision by chance; a number of these being placed in a receptacle and shaken or drawn out. Nearly always in phr. *to cast* (arch.), *draw* (†*send*, †*throw*, etc.) *lots* (or †*lot*). b. In abstract sense: The use of this, or any equivalent process, to obtain a decision. Chiefly in phr. *by l.* ME. c. The choice resulting from a casting of lots ME. †d. *sing.* and *pl.* Applied to games of chance or to divinatory appeals to chance -1777. 2. What falls to a person by lot OE. b. *fig.* One's destiny, fortune, or portion in this life; condition (good or bad) in life ME. 3. A tax, due, custom; esp. in *scot and lot* (see SCOT *sb.*[2]). b. *Derbyshire Mines.* See quots. 1631. †4. A prize in a lottery -1711. Also in the card-game LOTTERY. 5. a. (Now chiefly *U.S.*) A plot or portion of land assigned by the state to a particular owner. Hence, any piece of land divided off, e.g. for building or pasture. b. One of the plots in which a tract of land is divided when offered for sale. 1450. 6. An article, or set of articles, offered separately at a general sale; *esp.* each of the items at a sale by auction 1704. b. *transf.* of a person (*colloq.*); chiefly in *a bad l.* 1862. 7. *gen.* A number or quantity of persons or things associated in some way; also, a quantity (of anything). Now only *colloq.*, exc. of goods, live stock, etc. Often slightly depreciatory. 1725. 8. *colloq.* A considerable number or quantity; a good deal, a great deal. Used in sing. (*a l.*) and pl.; also as quasi-adv. Often absol. Also with adj., as *a good l.*, *a great l.* 1812.

1. Phr. *To cast* (rarely *throw*) *in one's l. with*: to associate oneself with the fortunes of. b. Good Counsell comes not by L., nor by Inheritance HOBBES. c. Phr. *The l. falls on* (a person or thing). 2. Now cometh thy l. (= 'turn'), now comestow on the rynge CHAUCER. The lott is fallen vnto me in a fayre grounde COVERDALE *Ps.* xv[i]. 6. Phr. *To fall to the l. of. To have neither part nor l. in*, after Acts viii. 21. b. Bewailing His l. unfortunate in nuptial choice MILT. Phr. *The l. falls* (*to* a person), (*it*) *falls to the l. of* (a person), *it falls to* (him) *as his l.* (to have or to do something). 3. b. The Duty called L...shall be One Thirteenth Part of all Ore raised within the Jurisdiction of the Barmote Courts 1851. 4. *Great l., chief l.*, the highest prize. 6. L. after l. was disposed of..at..good prices 1859. 7. Two several lots of children 1854. A large l. of ore RAYMOND. Phr. *The l.* = the whole number or quantity. A shilling for the l. 1877. 8. I've lots to do 1891. I would give a l. to [etc.] 1901.

Comb.: **l.-mead, -meadow**, a common meadow, the shares in which are apportioned by l.; **-seller**, one who sells a variety of small articles, or 'a lot', all for 1*d.*; so **-selling.**

Lot (lǫt), *v.* 1449. [f. LOT *sb.* Cf. F. *lotir* to cast lots, etc.]

I. *intr.* 1. To cast lots. Const. interrog. cl., or *for. rare.* 1483. 2. *To l. upon*: to count upon, expect. Now *U.S.* 1642.

II. *trans.* 1. To assign *to* one as his portion; to assign as one's lot or destiny. Also with *out.* 1524. 2. To divide (land) into lots. Usu. with *out*: To portion out and allot (*to* a person or persons). 1449. 3. To divide or group into lots for sale. Also with *out.* 1709. 4. To cast lots for; to apportion or distribute by lot. Now *rare.* 1703. 5. To choose (pressed men) by lot for service. *Obs.* exc. *Hist.* 1758.

‖**Lota, lotah** (lōᵘ·tă). *Anglo-Ind.* Also lootah, loto. 1809. [Hindi *loṭa*.] A spheroidal water-pot, usu. of polished brass.

Lote (lōᵘt), *sb. arch.* 1510. Anglicized form of LOTUS, in various senses. So **Lote-tree**. *arch.* 1548.

†Lote, *v.* ME. only. [?OE. **lotian*, f. *lut-*, ablaut-var. of *lūt-* in OE. *lūtian*; cf. LOUT *v.*[1]] *intr.* To lurk, lie concealed. Hence **†Lo·teby**, a lover, a paramour ME.

Loth, alternative f. LOATH.

Lothario (lǫþēᵊ·ri,ǫ). 1756. [A character in Rowe's *Fair Penitent*.] A libertine, gay deceiver, rake. (With capital L.)

The gay L. dresses for the fight 1756.

Lotion (lōᵘ·ʃən). ME. [ad. L. *lotionem*, f. *lavare* (stem *laut-*, *lot-*) to wash; see LAVE *v.*[1]] †1. The action of washing (the body); washing with a medicinal preparation; *pl.* ritual ablutions -1797. †2. The washing of metals, medicines, etc. in water to cleanse them -1796. 3. *Pharm.* A liquid preparation used externally to heal wounds, relieve pain, beautify the skin, etc. ME. 4. *slang.* Alcoholic drink 1876.

Loto; see LOTA, LOTTO.

‖**Lotophagi** (lōᵘtǫ·fădʒəi), *sb. pl.* 1601. [L., a. Gr. Λωτοφάγοι, f. λωτός LOTUS + φαγεῖν to eat.] The lotus-eaters; a people in Greek legend who lived on the fruit of the lotus, which caused a dreamy forgetfulness in those who ate it. So **Loto·phagous** *a. rare*, lotus-eating, resembling the L. 1855.

Lottery (lǫ·təri). 1567. [ad. It. *lotteria* (whence F. *loterie*), f. *lotto* LOT *sb.*; see LOTTO.] 1. An arrangement for the distribution of prizes by chance among persons purchasing tickets. Slips or lots, bearing the same numbers as the tickets, and representing either prizes or blanks, are drawn from a wheel. Also *transf.* and *fig.* †2. Sortilege, appeal to the lot; also, chance, issue of events as determined by chance -1663. †3. Something which comes by lot or fortune. *Ant. & Cl.* II. ii. 248. 4. A round game at cards, in which certain cards carry prizes 1830.

Comb. **l.-wheel**, a vertical wheel bearing on its axis a drum by the revolution of which the numbered slips are shuffled before being drawn.

Lotto, loto (lǫ·to, lōᵘ·to). 1778. [a. F. *lot(t)o*, a. It. *lotto*, ad. Teut. word repr. by LOT *sb.*] A game played with cards divided into numbered and blank squares and numbered disks to be drawn on the principle of a lottery.

A disk is drawn from a bag, and its number called; a counter is placed on the square so numbered, the player whose card first gets one row covered being the winner.

Lotus (lōᵘ·tǫs), **lotos** (lōᵘ·tǫs). *Pl.* **lotuses.** 1540. [a. L. *lotus*, Gr. λωτός.] 1. The plant yielding the fruit eaten by the LOTOPHAGI; represented by Homer (*Od.* ix. 90 ff.) as producing a state of dreamy forgetfulness and loss of all desire to return home. (Identified by some with the jujube-tree, *Zizyphus Lotus*.) Hence *allusively*. 2. A tree mentioned by ancient writers, having hard, black wood; prob. the nettle-tree, *Celtis australis* 1551. 3. The water-lily of Egypt and Asia, *Nymphæa Lotus* (and other species), and *Nelumbium speciosum* 1584. b. *Arch.* An ornament repr. the Egyptian water-lily. 4. Some kind of clover or trefoil (in Homer, food for horses) 1562. 5. Name of a genus of leguminous plants, including the Bird's-foot Trefoil, *Lotus corniculatus* 1753.

1. Eating the Lotos day by day TENNYSON. 4. When with rush-grass tall, Lotus and all sweet herbage, every one Had pastured been SHELLEY.

Lotus-eater. Also **lotos-**. 1832. One of the LOTOPHAGI; *transf.* one who gives himself up to dreamy and luxurious ease. So **Lotus-eating** *vbl. sb.* and *ppl. a.* 1861.

‖**Louche** (lūʃ), *a. rare.* 1819. [F. *louche* squinting, OF. *lousche* :—L. *lusca*, fem. of *luscus* one-eyed.] Oblique, not straightforward.

Loud (laud), *a.* [Com. WGer.: OE. *hlūd*, :—Indo-Eur. **klūtó-*, pa. pple. f. root *kleu-* to hear (Teut. *hleu-*), whence Gr. κλύειν to hear, κλέος renown, L. *cluere* to be famed, *cliens* (pres. pple., lit. 'hearer'), etc.] 1. Of sounds or voices: Strongly audible; striking forcibly on the sense of hearing. Hence, with agent-n.: That speaks, sings, etc. with a loud voice. b. Giving a forcible sound, sonorous. c. Of a place, etc.: Full of noise, re-echoing 1595. 2. *fig.* a. Clamorous, noisy; emphatic, vehement in expression 1530. †b. Manifest, palpable, flagrant. Chiefly of a lie. -1700. 3. *transf.* Of smell or flavour: Powerful, offensive. Now chiefly *U.S. colloq.* 1641. 4. Of colours, dress, etc.: Vulgarly obtrusive. Opp. to *quiet.* 1849.

1. A l. halloo SCOTT, speaker 1855. b. L. wyndes ME., seas 1898. c. Streets and factories l. with life 1878. 3. The strong breath and l. stench of avarice MILT. 4. The l. pattern of his trousers 1878. *Comb.* **l. speaker** *Wireless Telephony*, any one of several similar instruments for converting electrical impulses into sounds loud enough to be heard at a distance. **Lou·dish** *a.* somewhat l. **Lou·d-ly** *adv.*, **-ness.**

Loud (laud), *adv.* [OE. *hlūde* :—OTeut. **hlūdō*, f. **hlūdo-* LOUD *a.*] 1. Loudly; aloud. 2. Of smell: Strongly, offensively 1871. *Comb.* **l.-spoken** *a.* given to loud speaking.

Louden (lau·d'n), *v.* 1848. [f. LOUD *a.* + -EN[5].] To become or make loud or louder.

†Lough[1]. [ME. *lough, loȝe*; perh. repr. ONorthumb. *luh*, ?a. Irish *loch* (see LOCH), or a. the original of Welsh *llwch* lake, pool.] A lake, pool. In ME. poetry *occas.*, Water, sea. -1829. *attrib.*, as **l.-diver, -plover,** names for the female smew 1678.

Lough[2] (lǫχ). ME. [a. Irish *loch* (see LOCH), with spelling of prec.] A lake or arm of the sea (in Ireland); = Sc. LOCH.

‖**Louis** (lū·i). *Hist.* Pl. **louis.** Also **†lewis**, *pl.* lewis('s. 1689. [F. *louis*, use of the Christian name of many French kings.] = LOUIS D'OR.

‖**Louis d'or** (lūidǭ·ɪ). *Hist.* 1689. [F., lit. 'gold louis'; see prec.] A gold coin issued in the reign of Louis XIII and subsequently till the time of Louis XVI. After the Restoration applied to the 20-franc piece or Napoleon.

‖**Louis Quatorze** (lūikætǭ·ɪz). 1842. Louis XIV, King of France, 1643–1715. Used as adj. to designate the styles in architecture, furniture, etc. of his reign. So **Louis Quinze** (-kæ̃nz), Louis XV, 1715–74. **Louis Seize** (-sēz), Louis XVI, 1774–93. **Louis Treize** (-trēz), Louis XIII, 1610–43.

Lounge (laundʒ), *sb.* 1775. [f. LOUNGE *v.*] 1. An act, spell, or course of lounging; a saunter, stroll; also, a lounging gait 1806. b. *slang* (Eton and Cambridge), 'a treat, a chief meal' 1844. 2. A place where one can lounge; esp. applied to a sitting-room for guests in a hotel, etc.; a gathering of loungers 1775. 3. A kind of sofa or easy chair on which one can lie at length 1852. 4. *attrib.* 1800.

2. But pray, Mr. Fag, what kind of a place is this Bath?..*Fag*...'tis a good l. SHERIDAN.

attrib. **l. lizard**, one who frequents hotel lounges, e.g. as a professional dancing partner.

Lounge (laundʒ), *v.* 1508. [perh. suggested by LUNGIS.] 1. *intr.* To move indolently, resting between-whiles, or the like. 2. To recline lazily, to loll 1746. 3. To idle 1671. 4. *trans.* To pass (time, etc.) *away* (rarely *out*) with lounging 1776. Hence **Lou·nger.**

4. To l. away whole months 1776.

attrib. **l. suit**, a suit comprising a short coat designed for ordinary wear.

Loup (laup), *sb.*[1] *Sc.* ME. [a. ON. *hlaup*.] = LEAP *sb.*[1] So **Loup** *v.* [a. ON. *hlaupa*].

‖**Loup** (lū), *sb.*[2] 1834. [a. F. *loup*, lit. 'wolf' :—L. *lupum*.] A light mask or half-mask of silk or velvet worn by women.

Loup, obs. f. Loop.

‖**Loup cervier** (lu sęrvye). 1725. [F., ad. L. *lupus cervarius* (Pliny) the lynx (*lupus* wolf, *cervarius* that hunts stags, f. *cervus*).] The Canada Lynx (*Lynx Canadensis*).

Lour, lower (lauəɹ, lau·əɹ), *sb.* ME. [f. Lour *v.*] **1.** A gloomy or sullen look; a scowl. **2.** Of the sky, etc.: Gloominess, threatening appearance 1596.

1. In one smile or lowre of thy sweet eye Consists my perpetuall day Drayton. 2. The tempest's lower J. Wilson. Hence **Lou·ry, low·ery** *a.* dull, gloomy 1648.

Lour, lower (lauəɹ, lau·əɹ), *v.* [ME. *louren*, ? repr. an OE. **lúrian*. Cf. Du. *loeren*, late MHG. and MLG. *lûren* to lie in wait (mod.G. *lauern*), etc.] **1.** *intr.* To frown, scowl; to look angry or sullen. **b.** quasi-*trans.* To express by frowning. Wesley. **2.** *transf.* and *fig.* Of the clouds, sky, etc.: To look dark and threatening 1450.

1. Nor from that right to part an hour, Smile she or lowre Milt. b. To lour defiance 1746. 2. A shadow lour'd on the fields M. Arnold. Hence **Lou·ringly, Low·eringly** *adv.* gloomily, threateningly.

†**Lourd.** ME. [a. F. *lourd* heavy.] **A.** *adj.* Sluggish, dull, sottish, stupid -1681. **B.** *sb.* A sottish fellow, a lout 1579-90.

Louse (laus), *sb.* Pl. **lice** (ləis). [Com. Teut.: OE. *lús* = Du. *luis*, Ger. *laus*, etc.] **1.** A parasitic insect of the genus *Pediculus*, infesting the human hair and skin. Applied also to other kinds of insects parasitic on mammals, birds, and plants, and to the degraded crustaceans which infest fishes; often differentiated, as *bird-, fish-, plant-, sea-l.* **2.** *transf.* Applied in scorn to human beings 1633.

1. 'Tis not that I value the money three skips of a l. Swift.

Comb.: **l.-disease**, Phthiriasis; **lousewort**, †(*a*) Stinking Hellebore, *Helleborus fœtidus*; (*b*) any plant of the genus *Pedicularis*, esp. *P. palustris* and *P. sylvatica*; (*c*) Yellow Rattle, *Rhinanthus Crista-galli*; (*d*) *Delphinium Staphisagria.*

Louse (lauz), *v.* 1440. [f. Louse *sb.*] **1.** *trans.* To clear (a person, oneself, a garment) of lice. Also *intr.* for *refl.* †**2.** *intr.* To be infested with lice. *Lear* III. ii. 29.

Lousy (lau·zi), *a.* ME. [f. Louse *sb.* + -y[1].] **1.** Full of lice, infested by lice. †**b.** Characterized by the presence of lice -1830. **2.** *fig.* Dirty, filthy, obscene. Also: Mean, sorry, scurvy, vile, contemptible. Now *slang.* ME.

1. I do not give to a l. Tibetan Kipling. b. †*L. disease, evil* = Phthiriasis. 2. A l. story 1893. Hence **Lou·sily** *adv.*, **Lou·siness.**

Lout (laut), *sb.* 1548. [? orig. dial., conn. w. Lout *v.*[1]] **1.** An awkward fellow; a bumpkin, clown. **2.** *Rugby School slang.* A common fellow, 'cad' 1857.

1. 'Tis no trusting to yond foolish Lowt Shaks. Hence **Lou·tish** *a.* like a l. **Lou·tish-ly** *adv.*, **-ness.**

Lout (laut), *v.*[1] Pa. t. and pple. **louted.** Now *arch.*, *poet.*, and *dial.* [Orig. a str. vb., OE. *lútan* = ON. *lúta*, f. Teut. root *leut-*, *laut-*: *lŭt-*.] *intr.* (occas. *refl.*) To bend, bow, make obeisance; to stoop; also with *down.* **b.** *fig.* To bow, stoop, submit (*to*) ME.

He faire the knight saluted, louting low Spenser.

Lout, *v.*[2] 1530. [? f. Lout *sb.*] **1.** *trans.* To treat with contumely, mock. (Cf. Flout *v.*) **2.** *intr.* To act as a lout; to loll about 1807.

1. 1 *Hen. VI*, IV. iii. 13.

Louver (lū·vəɹ). Also **louvre, luffer.** [ME. *luver, lover*, a. OF. *lover, lovier*, ? altered f. **loer*:—med.L. **lodarium* cogn. w. med.L. *lodium*. The form *louvre* is due to confusion with F. *Louvre.*] **1.** A domed turret-like erection on the hall-roof, etc. of a mediæval building, with lateral openings for the passage of smoke or light. (Cf. Lantern 3.) †**2.** A dovecote of this construction -1661. **3.** Chiefly *pl.* An arrangement of overlapping boards, laths, or slips of glass, admitting air, but excluding rain 1555.

1. Ne lightned was with window, nor with louer Spenser. *Comb.* **l.** (*luffer*) **boards** (see 3). Hence **Louvered** *ppl. a.* arranged like louvers, provided with a l. or louvers.

†‖**Louvre** (lūvr). 1729. [Fr.; from the *Louvre* at Paris.] Some kind of dance -1772.

Lovable, loveable (lv·văb'l), *a.* ME. (coined afresh in the 19th c.) [f. Love *v.*[1] + -able.] Deserving of being loved; amiable; attractive.

'She is..very loveable—that is the exact word.' 'I fear it is not English', said Miss Hauton 1814. Hence **Lov(e)abi·lity, Lo·v(e)ableness. Lo·v(e)ably** *adv.*

Lovage (lv·vėdʒ). [ME. *loveache*, altered (as if *love-ache*: see Ache *sb.*[2]) from OF. *levesche*:—late L. *levisticum*, ? a corruption of L. *ligusticum* adj. neut., Ligurian.] The umbelliferous herb *Levisticum officinale*, used as a domestic remedy; also applied, with or without defining word, to other umbellifers.

Love (lvv), *sb.* [OE. *lufu* str. fem. = OHG. *luba*:—Teut. type **lubā*, not found elsewhere; f. wk. grade of Teut. root *leub-*: *laub*: *lub-*:—Indo-Eur. *leubh-*: *loubh-*: *lubh-* (cf. L. *lubet* (*libet*), *lubido* (*libido*), Skr. *lubh* to desire, etc.).] **1.** That state of feeling with regard to a person which arises from recognition of attractive qualities, from sympathy, or from natural ties, and manifests itself in warm affection and attachment. **b.** An instance of affection. †Also, an act of kindness. OE. **2.** In religious use, applied to the paternal benevolence and affection of God, to the affectionate devotion due to God from His creatures, and to the affection of one created being to another thence arising OE. **3.** Strong predilection *for* or devotion *to* (something). OE. **4.** That feeling of attachment which is based upon difference of sex; the affection between lover and sweetheart OE. **b.** An instance of being in love. Also *collect. pl.* love-affairs 1589. **5.** (With capital.) The personification of sexual affection; usu. masculine, = Eros, Amor, or Cupid; formerly also = Venus ME. **b.** with *pl.* A Cupid; any one of the many nameless gods of love imagined by mythologists; a figure or representation of the god of love 1594. **6.** The sexual instinct and its gratification ME. **7.** A beloved person; *esp.* a sweetheart. (Often used as a term of endearment.) ME. Also *transf.* of animals. †**b.** A paramour (man or woman) -1613. **c.** The object of love; the beloved (of..) 1734. **d.** A charming or delightful person or thing; a 'duck' (*colloq.*) 1814. **8. a.** *For l.*: without stakes, for nothing 1678. **b.** In scoring in various games, as tennis, rackets, etc.: No score, nothing; *l. all*, no score on either side. 1742. **c.** A form of euchre 1886. †**9.** A game of guessing the number of fingers held up in a quick movement of the hand; = Mora[2] -1725. †**10.** 'A kind of thin silk stuff' (J.), formerly used when in mourning; a border of this. Also *love-hood*. 1650-1829. **11.** A name for Traveller's Joy, *Clematis Vitalba* 1640.

1. Thy loue hath bene more speciall vnto me, then the loue of wemen Coverdale 2 *Sam.* i. 26. Loue doth moue the mynde to mercie 1557. Phr. (*Give*) *my l. to..*, or *L. to..*: convey a message of affection to (a third person). Also *to send one's l.* b. What good loue may I performe for you? Shaks. 2. God is loue 1 *John* iv. 16. This is the loue of God, that we keepe his commandements *Ibid.* v. 3. 3. Blynde auarice and loue of money Hall. The l. of ease and the l. of occupation Fowler. 4. It is commonly a weak man who marries for l. Johnson. The greatest weakness of the play is in the scenes of l. Johnson. b. I suppose, the Colonel was cross'd in his first L. Swift. 5. In peace, L. tunes the shepherd's reed; In war, he mounts the warrior's steed Scott. b. The little Loves, that waited by, Bow'd Cowley. 6. Come, let vs take our fill of loue vntill the morning *Prov.* vii. 18. 7. Liue with me and be my Loue Marlowe. d. The tiniest teacups you ever beheld —perfect loves! 1864.

Phrases. *For the l. of*: for the sake of, on account of. Now chiefly in adjurations. †*For* or *of all* (*the*) *loves, of all l.*: a phr. of strong entreaty. *For l. or money*: at any price, by any means. (In neg. contexts.) *In l.* (*with*): enamoured (of); *transf.* very fond (of) or much addicted (to). *Out of l.* (*with*): the opposite of *in l.* (*with*); disgusted with. *To fall in l.*: to become enamoured; *transf.* to become very fond of. Const. *with. To make l.*: to pay amorous attention; with *to* = to court, woo.

b. Proverbs, etc. *L. is blind. Labour of l.*: work that one delights in, or work undertaken to benefit a person one loves. *L. in a cottage*: marriage with insufficient means. *There's no l. lost between them*: an ambiguous phrase, meaning: †(*a*) Their affection is mutual; (*b*) *now*, They have no l. for each other.

Combs. a. General: as *l.-adept*; *l.-inspiring*; *l.-stricken*; and many others, of obvious meaning.

b. Special: **l.-affair**, orig. *pl.* the experiences connected with being in l.; now *sing.* an amour; **-begotten** *a.*, illegitimate; **-call**, a call or note used as a means of amorous communication between the sexes; **-child**, a child born out of wedlock 1805; **-cup**, †(*a*) a philtre; (*b*) a loving-cup; **-dart**, an organ found in certain snails, the *spiculum amoris*; **-drink**, a drink to excite l., a philtre; **-favour** (see Favour *sb.* 6); †**-juice**, a juice which dropped on the eyes has the effect of a philtre; **-letter**, a letter of courtship; **-making**, amorous proposals or intercourse, courtship; **-match**, a marriage for l., not for money or convenience; **-mate**, one with whom one is mated in love, a lover or sweetheart; **-philtre**, = Philtre; **-potion**, a philtre; **-scene**, a scene, esp. in a story or play, consisting of an interview between lovers; **-song**, an amorous song ME.; **-story**, a story about the affection between lovers; **-token**, something given as a token of love OE.

In names of plants and animals: **l.-bind**, Traveller's Joy; **-entangle, -entangled** = *love-in-a-mist* (*a*); **-grass**, a grass of the genus *Eragrostis*; **l.-in-a-mist**, (*a*) the Fennel-flower, *Nigella damascena*; (*b*) a W. Indian plant, *Passiflora fœtida*; **l.-in-idleness** (also †**l.-in-idle**), the Heartsease, *Viola tricolor* (cf. Idle *sb.* 1, Idleness 1); **l.-lies-(a)-bleeding**, the garden-plant *Amaranthus caudatus*, having a long drooping purplish-red spike of bloom; **l.-parrakeet, -parrot** = Love-bird; **-tree**, the Judas-tree, *Cercis Siliquastrum*; also *tree of love*; **-vine**, the Dodder.

Love (lvv), *v.*[1] [OE. *lufian*, f. *lufu* Love *sb.*] **1.** *trans.* To bear love to; to entertain a great regard for; to hold dear. **2.** *absol.* and *intr.* To entertain a strong affection; *spec.* to be in love ME. **3.** *trans.* **a.** To be unwilling to part with (life, honour, etc.) OE. **b.** To be fond of; to be devoted or addicted to. In U.S. a frequent vulgarism for *like.* ME. **c.** To take pleasure in the existence of (a virtue, a practice, a state of things) ME. **4.** Of plants or animals: To tend to thrive in (a certain kind of situation) 1573. **5.** Const. *inf.* To have great pleasure in doing something; †with negative, not to like. †Also *rarely* of things (= L. *amare*, Gr. φιλεῖν) to be accustomed. ME. **6.** To caress, embrace affectionately. (A childish use.) 1877.

1. Whom forsothe the Lord loueth, he chastiseth Wyclif *Prov.* iii. 12. I neuer knew woman loue man so Shaks. L. me, l. my dog *Provb.* (*Lord*) *l. you* (or *your heart*), etc.: a vulgar ejaculation. *I l. my love with an A, with a B*, etc.: a formula used in games of forfeits. 2. One that lou'd not wisely, but too well Shaks. Loue (= l. one another), and be Friends *Jul. C.* IV. iii. 131. 3. a. No man styrre and he l. his lyfe 1530. b. Loue not sleepe, lest thou come to pouertie *Prov.* xx. 13. c. I l. firm government Burke. 4. The violet loves a sunny bank B. Taylor. 5. They don't l. to be told the Truth 1704.

†**Love**, *v.*[2] [OE. *lofian* = G. *loben.*] To praise -1596.

Lo·ve-apple. ? *Obs.* Also **apple of love.** 1578. [tr. F. *pomme d'amour*, G. *liebesapfel.*] The fruit of the Tomato, *Lycopersicum esculentum.* †Formerly also the Brinjal.

Lo·ve-bird. 1595. A very small bird of the parrot tribe, esp. the W. African Lovebird, *Agapornis pullarius*, remarkable for the affection it shows for its mate. Also applied to other species of parrot.

†**Lo·veday.** ME. [tr. med.L. *dies amoris.*] **1.** A day appointed for a meeting for the amicable settlement of a dispute; hence, an agreement entered into at such a meeting -1655. **2.** A day for love-making. Greene.

†**Love-drury.** ME. only. [f. Love *sb.* + Dru(e)ry.] = Druery 1, 2.

Lovee (lvvī·). *nonce-wd.* 1754 (Richardson). [f. Love *sb.* + -ee[1].] One who is loved.

Lo·ve-feast. 1580. **1.** *Eccl. Antiq.* Used as tr. Gr. ἀγάπη, Eccl. L. Agape. Among the early Christians, a meal partaken of in token of brotherly love; app. orig. in connexion with the Eucharist; *transf.* a parochial feast at a festival time. **2.** Among Methodists, etc. a religious service in imitation of this 1738.

Loveful (lv·vfŭl), *a.* ME. [f. Love *sb.* + -ful.] †**1.** Lovable -1596. **2.** Abounding in love (now *rare*) ME.

Lo·ve-knot. ME. A knot or bow of ribbon tied in a peculiar way, supposed to be a love token. Cf. *true-love knot.*

Loveless (lv·vlės), *a.* ME. [f. Love *sb.* + -less.] **1. a.** Not feeling love. **b.** Not loved. †**2.** Unlovely. Holland. Hence **Lo·veless-ly** *adv.*, **-ness.**

Lovelihead (lʋ·vlihed). *rare.* 1633. [f. LOVELY *a.* + -HEAD.] Loveliness.

Lovelock (lʋ·vlǫk). 1592. [f. LOVE *sb.* + LOCK *sb.*[1]] A particular curl worn by courtiers in the time of Elizabeth and James I; later, any curl or tress of a striking character.

Lo·ve-lorn, *a.* 1634. Forsaken by one's love; pining from love.
The love-lorn Nightingale MILT.

Lovely (lʋ·vli), *a.* [OE. *luflic*, f. *lufu* LOVE + *-lic* -LY[1].] †1. Loving, kind, affectionate -1602. †b. Amorous -1599. 2. Lovable; having qualities that attract love OE. 3. Lovable on account of beauty; beautiful. Now with emotional sense: Exquisitely beautiful. ME. b. with ref. to moral or spiritual beauty 1805. 4. *colloq.* Delightful, highly excellent 1614.
1. b. Sweet Cytherea..Did court the Lad with many a louely looke SHAKS. 2. Being beloued in all companies for his louely qualities SIDNEY. 3. Til the teares..Like enuious flouds ore-run her louely face SHAKS. The loveliest and best That Time and Fate of all their Vintage prest E. FITZGERALD. L. all times she [Oxford] lies, l. tonight M. ARNOLD. 4. Come my friend Coridon, this Trout looks l. WALTON. Hence **Lo·velily** *adv.* **Lo·veliness.**

†Lo·vely, *adv.* [OE. *luflīce*, f. *lufu* LOVE *sb.* + *-līce* -LY[2].] 1. Lovingly, affectionately -1596. 2. Lovably, beautifully -1811.
2. Oh thou weed: Who art so louely faire SHAKS.

Lover (lʋ·vəɹ). Also †**lovyer**(e, etc. ME. [f. LOVE *v.* + -ER[1].] One who loves. 1. A friend or wellwisher. Now *rare.* 2. One who is in love with or enamoured of a person of the other sex; now (exc. in *pl.*) usu. applied to the male ME. b. One who loves illicitly; a paramour 1611. 3. One who has an affection, a fancy, or liking for (something) ME.
1. Ionathas and Dauid are sworne louers 1535. L. of souls! great God! I look to Thee J. H. NEWMAN. 2. A louyer, and a lusty Bacheler CHAUCER. b. *Jer.* iii. 1. 3. He was a great l. of his country CLARENDON. Lovers of Liberty HUME, of Selborne 1901.

Lover, obs. f. LOUVER.

Loverly (lʋ·vəɹli). 1875. [f. LOVER + -LY.] A. *adj.* Like a lover. B. *adv.* In the manner of a lover. So **Lo·verwise** *adv.* in the manner of a lover.

Lovery, obs. f. LOUVER.

Lovesick (lʋ·vsik), *a.* 1530. [f. LOVE *sb.* + SICK *a.*] Languishing for or with love.
Purple the Sailes: and so purfumed that The Windes were Loue-sicke with them SHAKS. Where Nightingales their Love-sick Ditty sing DRYDEN. Hence **Lovesickness.**

Lovesome (lʋ·vsʋ̆m), *a.* Now *arch.* or *dial.* [OE. *lufsum*, f. *lufu* LOVE *sb.*; see -SOME.] = LOVELY *a.* in all senses. Hence **Lo·vesomeness.**

Loveworthy (lʋ·vwʋ̄:ɹðĭ), *a.* ME. [f. LOVE *sb.* + WORTHY *a.*] Worthy to be loved. Hence **Loveworthiness.**

Lovey (lʋ·vi). Also **lovy.** 1731. [f. LOVE *sb.* + -Y[6].] A term of affection: = 'Dear love', 'darling'. Also **Lo·vey-do·vey** *sb.* and *a.*
And what would Dovey do if Lovey were to die? *Punch* 1884.

Loving (lʋ·viŋ), *ppl. a.* OE. [f. LOVE *v.* + -ING[2].] 1. That loves; affectionate. 2. Manifesting love; proceeding from love 1450.
1. *Your l. friend* (in 16th c. an ordinary form of subscription for letters). *Our l. subjects* (a usual phrase in royal proclamations). 2. They continue that louing custome [widow burning] deuoutly to this day SIR T. HERBERT. **Loving cup,** a large drinking vessel, usu. of silver, passed from hand to hand, generally at the close of a banquet, for each guest to drink from in turn 1808. **Loving·ly** *adv.*, **-ness.**

Loving-kindness (lʋ·viŋ₁kəi·ndnės). 1535 (Coverdale). [f. LOVING *ppl. a.* + KINDNESS. Orig. two wds.] Affectionate and tender consideration. *Ps.* lxxxix. 33.

Low (lōᵘ), *sb.*[1] [OE. *hlāw*, *hlǣw* masc. :—OTeut. **hlaiwoz-*, *-iz-* neut. :—pre-Teut. **kloiwos-*, *-es-*, f. root *klei-* to slope; see LEAN *v.*[1] and cf. L. *clivus.*] 1. = LAW *sb.*[2] 1. *arch.* 2. A tumulus. ? *Obs.* OE.

Low, lowe (lōᵘ), *sb.*[2] Chiefly *Sc.* and *n. dial.* ME. [a. ON. *loge* wk. masc. (Da. *lue*) :—OTeut. type **logon-* (*lugon-*), pre-Teut. **lukón-*, f. (ult.) *luk-* wk. grade of the Indo-Eur. root *leuk-*; see LIGHT *sb.*] Flame; a flame, a blaze.

Low (lōᵘ), *sb.*[3] 1549. [f. LOW *v.*[3]] The action of LOW *v.*[3]; the ordinary sound uttered by an ox or cow.
Bull Ioue, sir, had an amiable l. SHAKS.

Low (lōᵘ), *a.* and *sb.*[4] [Early ME. *lāh* (*lāg-*), a. ON. *lágr* :—OTeut. **lǣgio-*, f. root of LIE *v.*[1]]

A. *adj.* (Usu. the opposite of *high.*) I. 1. Of small upward extent; not tall; little, short. (Now rarely of persons.) b. Rising but little from a surface. *L. relief* = BAS-RELIEF 1711. c. Of a woman's dress: Cut so as to leave the neck, etc. exposed. See also *l. neck.* 1857. 2. Not elevated in position. †Formerly, as in *Low Germany*, *L. Egypt* (*obs.*), denoting the part near the sea-shore (now only in the compar. LOWER). Also LOW-COUNTRY. ME. b. Of a heavenly body: Near the horizon 1676. c. Lying dead, or dead and buried. Now only *predicative.* ME. d. Of an obeisance: Profound, deep 1548. e. *Phonetics.* Of a vowel sound: Produced with the tongue or some part of it in a low position 1876. 3. Of a liquid: Less in vertical measurement than the normal; shallow. Hence: Containing or yielding less water than usual. *Low tide* = LOW WATER. (For *low ebb*, see EBB *sb.*) 1440.
1. Apes With foreheads villanous l. SHAKS. Of a l. stature 1724. L. buildings PARKER. 2. Trees growing in l. and shady places BERKELEY. b. There was a l. moon 1889. c. The last great Englishman is l. TENNYSON. 3. The Springs and Rivers are very l. 1695.

II. Transf. and fig. senses. 1. Of humble rank, position, or estimation. (Only in *compar.* and *superl.* exc. *contemptuously.*) ME. 2. Of inferior quality or style; wanting in elevation, commonplace, mean ME. b. Of style, words, expressions, a writer: The opposite of sublime; undignified 1672. c. Little advanced in civilization or organization 1859. 3. a. Abject, mean 1559. b. Degraded, dissolute 1599. c. Coarse, vulgar; not 'respectable' 1759. 4. Wanting in vigour; poorly nourished, weak ME. b. Dejected, dispirited, dull, esp. in phr. *l. spirits* 1737. c. Of diet: Not stimulating; poor 1715. 5. Not high in amount or degree of intensity. (Often with reference to position in a graduated scale.) ME. b. *Geog.* Of latitude: Denoted by a low number; not far from the equator 1748. c. Of things: Having a low value, price, or degree of some quality. Of a playing-card: Of small numerical value. 1727. d. Of condition: Not flourishing or advanced 1596. 6. a. Of musical sounds: Produced or characterized by slow vibrations; grave ME. b. Of the voice, a sound: Not loud 1440. 7. Humble, lowly, meek. Now *rare.* ME. 8. (Cf. sense I. 3.) Of one's pockets, money, etc.: Nearly empty or exhausted 1700. 9. Of an opinion, estimate: Depreciatory, disparaging (*mod.*). 10. Of a date: Recent. Chiefly in *compar.* and *superl.* (*mod.*). 11. Of religious doctrine: The opposite of *high* (see HIGH *a.* II. 11); often *colloq.* = LOW CHURCH 1854.
1. Men l. in the social scale DEUTSCH. 2. Much parliamentary ability of a l. kind MACAULAY. b. And ten l. words oft creep in one dull line POPE. c. Germs of bacteria and other l. organisms TYNDALL. 3. a. Flattery or fawning or other l. arts 1799. b. L. woomene 1599. c. She has evidently kept l. company MME. D'ARBLAY. 4. She..grew l. from loss of appetite 1783. c. Such l. diet as sour milk and potatoes BERKELEY. 5. The fever is kept l. 1789. Chinese workmen..work for l. wages 1885. c. In general a l. card is to be played second hand 1885. d. My Creditors grow cruell, my estate is very l. SHAKS. 6. b. Her voice was euer soft, Gentle, and l. SHAKS. 8. Phr. *To be l. in pocket.* 9. I have a l. opinion of his abilities (*mod.*).

Phrases. *To lay l.*: a. To lay flat; to overthrow, to stretch lifeless. b. To bury. c. *fig.* To abase, humble. *To lie l.*: a. *lit.* To lie in a l. position or on a l. level; also, to crouch. b. To lie on or in the ground, lie prostrate or dead; *fig.* to be humbled, abased. c. *Mod. slang.* To keep quiet, remain in hiding; to bide one's time. Also *To burn l.*: to burn feebly or with reduced flame; *to run l.*: to be nearly exhausted, to become scanty.

Combs. 1. General: in concord with sbs. forming combs. used attrib. or quasi-adj., as *l.-blast, -flash, -grade, -pressure,* etc.; *l.-arched, -priced, -rented* adjs.; **l.-necked,** (of a dress) cut l. in the neck or bosom; *l.-lying,* etc.

2. Special: as **l. celebration,** the administration of the Holy Communion without assistant ministers and choir; **l. comedian,** an actor of l. comedy; **l. comedy,** (*a*) comedy in which the subject and treatment border upon farce; (*b*) *Theatr. slang* = *low comedian*; **L. Dutch** (see DUTCH); hence *Low-Dutchman*; **L. German** (see GERMAN); **L. Latin** *a.* and *sb.* [= F. *bas-latin*], late Latin or mediæval Latin; hence **L.-Latinist,** a scholar in Low Latin; **l. mass** (see MASS *sb.*[1]); **l. milling** (see MILLING *vbl. sb.*); **l.-sail,** easy sail (EASY *a.* 5); **l. side window,** a small window lower than the other windows, found in some old churches, a leper window 1847; **l. tea,** *U.S.*, a plain tea; **L. Week,** the week following Easter week, beginning with Low SUNDAY.

B. quasi-*sb.* and *sb.* 1. What is low, a low position, place, or area ME. †2. With preps. *At, in, on l.*: down low, on the ground, below, on earth -1460. 3. (with *a* and *pl.*) a. A piece of low-lying land 1790. b. An area of low barometric pressure 1878. 4. In *All-fours*: The deuce of trumps, or the lowest trump dealt 1818. 5. *U.S.* A low level or figure 1911.

Low (lōᵘ), *adv.* [ME. *laȝe, lahe, loȝe*, f. the adj.] 1. In a low position; on or under the ground; little above some base ME. b. *fig.* Humbly; in a low condition or rank; on poor diet; at a low rate ME. 2. To a low point, position, or posture; along a low course, in a low direction ME. 3. In a low tone, gently, softly; at a low pitch, on low notes ME. 4. With reference to time: Far down, or to a point far down; late 1625.
1. The towne standeth lowe HALL. Ears hung l. COWPER. b. Live cool for a time, and rather l. CHESTERF. Phr. *To play l.*: to play for small stakes. 2. Thou shalt come downe very l. *Deut.* xxviii. 43. Party fights are won by aiming l. O. W. HOLMES. *fig.* Verse cannot stoop so l. as thy desert COWPER. 3. Your true loues coming, That can sing both high and l. SHAKS. He read his sermon..so brokenly and l., that nobody could hear at any distance PEPYS. 4. As l. as the restoration SWIFT.

Low (lōᵘ), *v.*[1] *Obs.* exc. *dial.* ME. [f. LOW *a.*] 1. *trans.* To make or bring low; to abase, humble, lower. 2. To diminish, lessen; to depreciate ME. 3. To lower; to lower the level of (ground) 1450.

Low (lōᵘ), *v.*[2] *Obs.* exc. *dial.* ME. [a. ON. *loga*, f. *loge* LOW *sb.*[2]] *intr.* To flame, blaze, glow; *fig.* to be on fire with passion, etc. Also with *up.*

Low (lōᵘ), *v.*[3] [Com. Teut.: OE. *hlōwan*; f. Teut. root *hlō-* :—WAryan *klā-*; cf. L. *clāmare*, Gr. κικλήσκειν to call.] 1. *intr.* Of cattle: To utter their cry; to moo. Also *transf.* 2. *trans.* To utter in a voice like that of cattle; to bellow *forth* 1547.
1. The sober herd that lowed to meet their young GOLDSM.

†Low·bell, low-bell, *sb.* 1578. [?f. LOW *a.* + BELL.] 1. A small bell, *esp.* a cow-bell or sheep-bell; *joc.*, any bell -1664. 2. A bell used in fowling at night. (The birds are stupefied with the noise of the bell and the sudden glare from lights in a tin-lined box, and a net is then thrown over them.) Also *fig.* -1821.
1. A bell hanged about sheepe or goates, a lowebell FLORIO. 2. Some he catches..with frights (as Black-birds with..a Low-Bell) BOYLE. Hence **Low·bell** *v.* †to catch (birds) by the use of a l.; *transf.* to scare as the lowbeller does birds 1581-1660; to deride by jangling of tins, etc. (*dial.*). **Low·beller,** one who does this.

Low-·born, *a.* ME. Born in a low station.

Low-bred, *a.* 1757. Brought up in a low, inferior, vulgar fashion; characterized by low breeding, conduct, or manners.

Low-·browed, *a.* 1632. [f. LOW *a.* + BROW *sb.*[1] + -ED[2].] 1. Having a low brow 1868. 2. *transf.* Of rocks: Beetling. Of a building, doorway, etc.: Having a low entrance; dark, gloomy. 3. Not being, or claiming to be, highly intellectual. Hence **Low·brow** *sb.* and *a.* 1913.
2. There under..low-brow'd Rocks..In dark Cimmerian desert ever dwell MILT.

Low Church. 1702. [app. from *Low-Churchman*, and used attrib. as in *Low Church party*, and then subst.] A. *adj.* or *attrib. phr.* Of, belonging to, or characteristic of Low-Churchmen, or their principles and practices 1710. B. *sb.* [orig. short for *L. C. party, L. C. principles.*] The party or principles of the Low-Churchmen. Hence **Low-Chu·rchism.**

Low-Churchman. 1702. [Cf. HIGH-CHURCHMAN.] A member of the Church of England holding opinions which give a low place to the authority and claims of the Episcopate and the priesthood, to the inherent grace of the sacraments, and to matters of eccl. organization, thus differing little from the opinions held by Protestant Nonconformists. (In later use, mostly = EVANGELICAL.)

Low-country. 1530. **1.** A region whose level is lower than that of the surrounding country. **2.** *pl.* **Low Countries,** the district now forming the kingdoms of Holland and Belgium, and the grand duchy of Luxemburg; the Netherlands in the wider sense 1548. **b.** *attrib.*, quasi-*adj.* Belonging to (†or having served in) the Low Countries 1625.

Low down, *a.* and *adv.* 1548. [f. LOW *a.* and *adv.* + DOWN *adv.*] **a.** Used as emphatic for the adj. in predicative use, and for the adv. **b.** In attrib. use (*low-down*); orig. *U.S.*, degraded, abject 1865. **c.** *sb.* (*U.S. slang.*) The actual facts; inside information 1926.

a. They had played it rather low down on the preacher 1890. b. A beautiful low-down catch 1882. So much better than he could have expected from his 'low-down' relative 1811. Hence **Low-downer** *U.S.* a 'poor white' of the southern States 1871.

Lower (lōᵘ·əɹ), *a.* (*sb.*) and *adv.* ME. [f. LOW *a.* + -ER[3].]

A. *adj.* **1.** The comparative of LOW *a.*, q. v. **2.** Used as the specific designation of an object, a class or group of objects, a part or parts of some whole (with reference either to local situation or to rank, dignity, or place in classification); occas. in partitive concord (= 'the lower part of'). Cf. UPPER, HIGHER. 1590. **3.** quasi-*sb.* One lower; an inferior ME.

1. And in the lowest deep a l. deep Still MILT. At a l. period than the apostolic age 1839. A l. class, l. pay MACAULAY. I feel l. and sadder than ever 1873. Keep that l. in tone 1895. 2. L. Syria SHAKS., Asia 1631. Every l. facultie Of sense MILT. The l. sort in the camp BURKE. Merchants from the L. Danube MACAULAY. The L. Cambrian, Silurian 1873.

Spec. collocations: **l. boy,** a boy in the *lower school* (see below); **l.-case** *Printing* (see CASE *sb.*[2] 6); **l. chamber** = *lower house*; **l. classes,** those below the middle rank in society; **l. criticism,** verbal or textual criticism; so **l. critic,** one occupied with this; **l. deck,** the deck immediately over the hold, orig. only of a ship with two decks; **L. Empire** [= F. *Bas-Empire*], the later Roman Empire; now usually, from the reign of Constantine; **l. fourth, fifth,** etc., the l. division of the fourth, fifth, etc. form in a public school; **l. house,** the inferior branch of a legislature consisting of two houses; also of the convocation of the Church of England; **l. †order** or **orders** = *lower classes*; **l. school,** in public schools, usually the forms below the fifth; (*the* or *this*) **l. world,** earth as opp. to heaven.

B. *adv.* Comparative of LOW *adv.* 1548.

Then he fell to play l. 1648. Still farther north [the snow line] reaches yet l. HUXLEY.

Lower (lōᵘ·əɹ), *v.* 1606. [f. LOWER *a.*] **1.** *trans.* To cause or allow to descend, to let down gradually (e.g. a boat, a drawbridge, etc.); to haul down (a sail, a flag). Also with *away* (Naut.), *down.* 1659. Also *absol.* **b.** To diminish the height of 1858. **c.** *Wood-engraving.* To remove by cutting or scraping, or to depress (the surface of a block) 1839. **2.** *intr.* To descend, sink (also *fig.*). Often with *down.* Also *Naut.* of a yard: To admit of being let down. 1606. **b.** To slope downwards 1813. **3. a.** *trans.* To diminish in amount, price, proportion, etc. 1690. **b.** *intr.* To become lower in price 1697. **4.** *trans.* To make lower in quality or degree; to lessen the intensity or elevation of 1780. Also *intr.* **†b.** To reduce the strength or quality of (a liquid, the air) –1844. **c.** *Mus.* To depress in pitch 1889. **5.** *trans.* To bring down in rank, station, or estimation; to degrade, dishonour 1771. Also *intr.* for *refl.* **6.** *trans.* To bring down to a lower position on a graduated scale 1860.

1. The workmen have to be lowered by ropes down the face of the cliff 1895. 2. Smoke lowering down from chimney-pots DICKENS. 3. a. They lowered the rents 1886. b. Meat will l. in price 1823. 4. The Mahratta government..might have been induced to l. its tone JAS. MILL. Lowering his voice 1834. 5. His letter has lowered him in my opinion 1771. 6. To l. the freezing point 1871.

Lower: see LOUR *sb.* and *v.*

Lowermost (lōᵘ·əɹmoᵘst), *a.* 1561. [f. LOWER *a.* + -MOST.] = LOWEST *a.*

Lowest (lōᵘ·ėst), *a.* (*sb.*) and *adv.* ME. [f. LOW *a.* + -EST.]

A. *adj.* The superlative of LOW *a.*, q.v.

You would sound mee from my lowest Note to the top of my Compasse SHAKS. Harsh Thunder, that the l. bottom shook Of Erebus MILT. At the l. ebb 1681, price 1780.

B. *absol.* or as *sb.* **1.** The lowest part, position, or pitch. *Obs.* exc. with *at.* ME. **2.** One who or that which is lowest 1785.

1. When taste was almost at its l. in England 1897.

C. *adv.* The superlative of LOW *adv.* ME.

The salary of our l.-paid Judges 1834.

Lowish (lōᵘ·iʃ), *a.* 1689. [-ISH[1].] Somewhat low.

Lowland (lōᵘ·lænd). 1508. [f. LOW *a.* + LAND.] **A.** *sb.* **1.** Low or level land; land lying lower than the surrounding country. Usu. *pl.* 1693. **2.** *spec.* (Now always *pl.*) The less mountainous part of Scotland, lying south and east of the Highlands 1631.

1. *sing.* The cities of the l. R.V. *Jer.* xxxiii. 13.

B. *attrib.* or *adj.* **1.** Of, pertaining to, or inhabiting low land or a level district 1567. **2.** *spec.* Of, belonging to, or characteristic of the Lowlands of Scotland 1508.

Hence **Low·lander,** an inhabitant of a low-lying country or district 1835; *spec.* a native of the Lowlands of Scotland 1692.

Lowlihead (lōᵘ·lihed). *arch.* ME. [f. LOWLY *a.* + -HEAD.] Humility, lowliness. So **Low·lihood** (*rare*).

Low-lived (lōᵘ·ləi·vd), *a.* Also **†low-lifed.** 1760. [f. LOW *a.* + *live-*, LIFE + -ED[2].] Of persons: Living a low life; vulgar, mean. Hence of actions, etc.

Lowly (lōᵘ·li), *a.* Somewhat *arch.* ME. [f. LOW *a.* + -LY[1].] **1.** Humble in feeling or demeanour; not proud or ambitious. **2.** Humble in condition or quality; modest, unpretending 1634. **3.** Low in situation or growth 1593. **b.** ?Lying low. 1 *Hen. VI*, III. iii. 47. **¶4.** *occas.* Low in character, mean 1741.

1. Take my yoke vpon you, and learne of me, for I am meeke and l. in heart *Matt.* xi. 29. 2. Courtesie ..is sooner found in l. sheds..then in tapstry Halls MILT. 3. L. Shrubs DRYDEN, Lands POPE. In lowliest depths of bosky dells 1852. Hence **Low·lily** *adv.* **Low·liness.**

Lowly (lōᵘ·li), *adv.* ME. [f. LOW *a.* + -LY[2].] **1.** In a lowly manner; humbly, reverently; modestly. **2.** In a low manner or degree ME.

1. L. they bow'd adoring MILT. 2. I will show my selfe highly fed, and l. taught SHAKS. Sadly and l. singing 1839.

Lo·wman, low man. 1592. [f. LOW *a.* + MAN.] Usu. *pl.* Dice loaded so as to turn up low numbers.

Lown(e, var. of LOON[1].

Lowness (lōᵘ·nės). ME. [f. LOW *a.* + -NESS.] **1.** The quality or condition of being LOW, q. v. **2.** As a mock title of dignity 1771.

Low-pitched, *ppl. a.* 1622. **1.** Pitched in a low key or tone (*lit.* and *fig.*); little elevated; of low quality. **2.** Of a roof: Having but a slight angular elevation. Hence of a room: Having a low ceiling. 1833.

1. Poor and low-pitched desires MILT.

Lowry (lauᵊ·ri). 1875. [Cf. LORRY.] *U.S. Railways.* An open box-car.

Low-spi·rited, *a.* 1588. Having low spirits. **†a.** Mean in spirit; abject, cowardly, paltry –1795. **b.** Wanting in animation; dejected, dispirited 1753. Hence **Low-spi·ritedness.**

Low Sunday. ME. The Sunday next after Easter Sunday.

Low water. late ME. The state of the tide when the water is lowest; the time of lowest ebb. Also, a low stage of the water in a river, lake, etc. **b.** *fig.* Chiefly in phr. *in low water*: 'hard up' 1785.

b. His lordship was in low water financially 1886.

Low-wa·ter mark. a. *lit.* The line on the shore reached by the tide or by a river at low water; a mark to indicate this 1526. **b.** *fig.* The lowest point reached in number, quantity, quality, etc. 1651.

b. My ink is at low water-mark for all my acquaintance H. WALPOLE.

Lowy. *Obs.* exc. *Hist.* 1389. [a. OF. *louee, lieuee* :—late L. *leucata*, f. *leuca* (F. *lieue*) LEAGUE *sb.*[1]] A liberty extending for about a league outside a town.

Loxodromic (lǫksodrǫ·mik). 1679. [f. Gr. λοξός oblique + δρόμος course + -IC.] **A.** *adj.* Pertaining to oblique sailing, or sailing by the rhumb 1702. **B.** *sb.* = *L. line, table* 1679. **b. Loxodromics**: the art of oblique sailing 1704.

L. chart, projection, another name for Mercator's projection. *L. curve, line, spiral,* a rhumb-line. *L. tables,* traverse tables.

Hence **Lo·xodrome** = *l. line* 1880. **Loxodro·mical** *a.* 1704, **-ly** *adv.* 1752. **Loxo·dromism,** the tracing of or moving in a loxodromic line or curve 1853. **Loxo·dromy,** a loxodromic line or course; also = *loxodromics* 1656.

Loy (loi). [a. Ir. *laighe.*] **a.** *Anglo-Ir.* A kind of spade used in Ireland 1763. **b.** *U.S.* A similar tool with a broad chisel point for making post-holes (*mod.*).

Loyal (loi·ăl), *a.* (*sb.*) 1531. [a. F. *loyal*, OF. *loial, leial*, semi-popular ad. L. *legalem* (see LEGAL *a.*), f. *leg-*, *lex* law. Cf. LEAL *a.*] **1.** True to obligations of duty, love, etc.; faithful to plighted troth 1604. **2.** Faithful in allegiance to the sovereign or constituted government. Also, *now,* enthusiastically devoted to the sovereign's person and family. 1531. **3.** Of things, actions, etc.: Exhibiting loyalty 1598. **†4.** = LEGAL. **a.** Of a child: Legitimate. **b.** Of money: Genuine. **c.** Of goods: Of the legal standard of quality. –1690. **5.** *sb. pl.* **†a.** Liege subjects 1540–1602. **b.** In recent use: Loyal, as opp. to disaffected, subjects 1885.

1. Your true and loyall wife *Oth.* IV. ii. 35. L. to his word TENNYSON. L. friendships 1871. 2. We [*sc.* French Canadians] are l. because we are free SIR W. LAURIER. 3. 'Loyal and patriotic' toasts DICKENS. Hence **Loy·alism,** the principles or actions of a loyalist; loyalty. **Loy·alist,** one who is l.; one who adheres to his sovereign or to constituted authority, *esp.* in times of revolt; one who supports the existing form of government. **Loy·alize** *v.* to make l.; to restore to faithful allegiance; to attach to the loyalist party. **Loy·al·ly** *adv.*, **-ness.**

Loyalty (loi·ălti). ME. [a. OF. *loialté* (mod. *loyauté*), f. *loyal* LOYAL *a.*; see -TY.] **1.** Faithful adherence to one's promise, oath, word, etc.; †conjugal fidelity. **2.** Faithful adherence to the sovereign or lawful government. Also, *now,* enthusiastic devotion to the sovereign's person and family. 1531. **†3.** Legality (of marriage). R. COKE.

1. And piety with wishes placed above, And steady l., and faithful love GOLDSM. 2. Under the rule of Elizabeth l. became more and more a passion GREEN.

†Loyn. ME. [a. OF. *loigne*: see LUNGE *sb.*[1]] A length (of cord); a leash for a hawk –1575.

Lozenge (lǫ·zėndʒ). ME. [a. OF. *losenge, losange*; perh. a deriv. of the word which appears as Prov. *lausa*, etc. slab, tombstone.] **1.** A plane rectilineal figure with four equal sides and two acute and two obtuse angles; a rhomb, 'diamond'. In *Her.*, such a figure used as a bearing (cf. FUSIL[1]), and placed with its longer axis vertical. **b.** A lozenge-shaped shield bearing the arms of a spinster or widow 1797. **c.** *Math.* = RHOMBUS. Now only in *spherical l.* 1551. **d.** A lozenge-shaped facet of a precious stone when cut 1750. **2.** A small cake or tablet, orig. diamond-shaped, of medicated or flavoured sugar, concentrated meat, etc., to be dissolved in the mouth 1530. **3.** A lozenge-shaped pane of glass in a casement 1656. **4.** *attrib.* or *adj.* Lozenge-shaped; composed of lozenges 1658.

4. Gravers are of two sorts, square and l. IMISON. L. brickwork BROWNING, ornament 1870. *L. moulding, L. fret,* a kind of moulding characterized by lozenge-shaped ornaments.

Comb.: **l.-coach,** a coach with the owner's coat of arms emblazoned on a l., a dowager's or widow's coach (H. Walpole). Hence **Lo·zenged** *a.* = LOZENGY *a.* 1523.

Lozengy (lǫ·zėndʒi), *a.* 1562. [a. OF. *losangié*, f. *losange* LOZENGE.] *Her.*, etc. Covered with lozenges of alternate tinctures; divided into lozenges; also, lozenge-shaped.

L. s. d., £. s. d. (e·lesdī·), abbrev. for 'pounds, shillings, and pence' (see the letters L, S, D); hence often = 'money'. Hence **L. S. Deism** (*joc.*), worship of money.

Lu, obs. f. LOO *sb.*[1]

Lubbard (lɒ·bǎɹd). *Obs.* exc. *Sc.* and *n. dial.* 1586. [Altered f. LUBBER; see -ARD.] = LUBBER *sb.* **b.** *attrib.* Lubberly 1679.

Lubber (lɒ·bəɹ), *sb.* ME. [?ad. OF. *lobeor*, f. *lober* to deceive, sponge upon, mock; but, if so, infl. by LOB *sb.*[1]] **1.** A big, clumsy, stupid fellow; esp. one who does nothing; a lout. Now *arch.* or *dial.* **b.** A sailor's term for: A clumsy seaman. (Cf. LAND-LUBBER.) 1579. †**c.** A drudge, scullion -1706. **2.** *attrib.* or *adj.* (In *l. lips* perh. a different wd.) 1530.

1. If you will measure your lubbers length againe, tarry SHAKS. b. He swore woundily at the lieutenant, and called him..swab and l. SMOLLETT. 2. Then narrow court and l. King, farewell! TENNYSON.

Comb.: **l.-grasshopper**, a name for two large-bodied clumsy insects of the U.S.; (*a*) *Brachystola magna*, of the western plains; (*b*) *Romalea microptera*, of the Gulf States; **-head**, a blockhead; **lubber's line, mark, point** *Naut.*, a vertical line inside a compass-case, indicating the direction of the ship's head.

Hence **Lu·bber** *v.* to behave like a l.; to navigate a boat like a l. 1530. **Lu·bberland**, an imaginary land of plenty without labour 1598.

Lubber fiend. 1632 (Milton). [Cf. LUBBER *sb.* 1 c.] A beneficent goblin who performs some of the drudgery of a household or farm during the night; a 'Lob-lie-by-the-fire'.

Lubberly (lʊ·bəɹli). 1573. [f. LUBBER *sb.* + -LY.] **A.** *adj.* **1.** Of the nature of a lubber; loutish; clumsy; lazy; stupid; sometimes *transf.* of animals and inanimate things. Also of things: Appropriate to or characteristic of a lubber. **2.** In naut. use: Resembling, pertaining to, or characteristic of a lubber; unseamanlike 1795.

1. Great l. Southdowns [sheep] 1847, l. barges 1862. A l., yellow-haired boy of twelve 1859. 2. A case of l. navigation 1884. Hence **Lu·bberliness.**

B. *adv.* In a lubberly manner; like a lubber; unskilfully, clumsily 1594.

Lubber's hole. Also †**lubber-hole.** 1772. *Naut.* A hole in the ship's top, close to the mast, affording an easier way of ascent or descent than by climbing the futtock shrouds.

Lubric (l¹ū·brik), *a.* 1490. [a. F. *lubrique*, or ad. L. *lubricus*, f. Aryan root **sleub-*; see SLIP *v.*[1]] **1.** Smooth and slippery. Now *rare.* †**2.** *fig.* Slippery, shifty; unsteady; prone to danger or error -1660. **3.** Lascivious 1490.

2. Lubrick is the estate of Favorites 1646. 3. This lubrique and adult'rate age DRYDEN. So **Lu·brical** *a.* 1601.

Lubricant (l¹ū·brikănt). 1822. [f. L. *lubricantem*, pr. pple. of *lubricare*, f. *lubricus*; see prec.] **A.** *adj.* Lubricating. **B.** *sb.* An oil, or other material, used to lubricate machinery. Hence *transf.* **a.** A fluid which makes motion or action smooth or removes friction. **b.** (*joc.*) Any oily or greasy substance. 1828.

Paraffin-oil..had been found the best of all anti-friction lubricants 1882.

Lubricate (l¹ū·brikeⁱt), *v.* 1623. [f. L. *lubricat-*, *lubricare*; see prec.] **1.** *trans.* To make slippery or smooth by applying a fluid or unguent. **b.** To apply oil or other unguent to (a machine) in order to minimize friction 1742. **c.** *gen.* To oil or grease 1791. **d.** *fig.* 1784. **2.** *absol.* or *intr.* To act as a lubricant 1726.

1. b. Man's..balmy bath, That supples, lubricates, and keeps in play, The various movements of this nice machine YOUNG. d. Here rills of oily eloquence in soft Meanders l. the course they take COWPER. Hence **Lu·bricating** *vbl. sb.* and *ppl. a.* (esp. in *l. oil*). **Lubrica·tion.**

Lubricator (l¹ū·brikeⁱtəɹ). 1756. [f. prec. + -OR.] **1.** One who or that which lubricates. Also *fig.* **2.** An oil-cup or other contrivance for lubricating a machine or instrument 183..

1. Water is..a great..l. of the fibres BURKE.

Lubricity (l¹ubri·sĭti). 1491. [ad. F. *lubricité* or L. *lubricitas.*] **1.** Slipperiness, smoothness; oiliness 1547. **2.** *fig.* Slipperiness, shiftiness; instability; elusiveness 1613. **3.** Lasciviousness, lewdness, wantonness 1491.

1. The scented l. of soap SYD. SMITH. 2. The l. of mundan greatnesse HOWELL. 3. Mens vaine pleasures and idle lubricities 1593.

Lubricous (l¹ū·brikəs), *a.* 1535. [f. L. *lubricus* LUBRIC + -OUS.] = LUBRIC. So **Lubri·cious** *a.* 1583.

Lubrify (l¹ū·brifəi), *v.* Now *rare.* 1611. [ad. F. *lubrifier*, irreg. f. L. *lubricus*; see -FY.] *trans.* To make slippery or smooth; to lubricate. So **Lubrifa·ction** (1542) [see -FACTION], **Lubrifica·tion** (1611), lubrication.

Lucan (l¹ū·kăn), *a.* Also **Lukan.** 1876. [f. L. *Lucas* Luke + -AN.] Pertaining to St. Luke.

Lucarne (l¹ukā·ɹn). 1548. [Earlier *lucane*, a. OF. *lucane*, mod.F. *lucarne*; origin unkn.] A skylight, a dormer or garret window. (Now only as F.) Also *l. window.*

Luce (l¹ūs). ME. [a. OF. *lus*, *luis*, repr. late L. *lucius.*] The pike (*Esox lucius*), *esp.* when full grown.

Lucent (l¹ū·sĕnt), *a.* 1500. [ad. L. *lucentem.*] **1.** Shining, bright, luminous. Also *fig.* **2.** Translucent; clear 1820.

1. The Sun's l. Orbe MILT. 2. L. syrops, tinct with cinnamon KEATS. Hence **Lu·cency**, luminosity 1656.

Lucern[1] (l¹usə̄·ɹn). *Obs.* exc. *Hist.* 1532. [Prob. a. early mod.G. *lüchsern* adj., pertaining to the lynx, f. *luchs* lynx; app. orig. a name for the fur; cf. MARTEN.] **1.** The lynx. **b.** The skin or fur of the lynx, formerly much valued. ¶**2.** A kind of hunting dog. CHAPMAN.

†**Lucern**[2]. [app. erron. f. LUCE, after prec.] The full-grown pike. MARKHAM.

Lucernal (l¹usə̄·ɹnăl), *a.* 1787. [f. L. *lucerna* lamp + -AL.] Pertaining to a lamp; *l. microscope*, a microscope in which the object is illuminated by a lamp or other artificial light.

Lucerne, lucern (l¹usə̄·ɹn). 1626. (In 17th and 18th c. agricultural books often *la lucerne*, with Fr. def. article.) [a. F. *luzerne*, ad. mod.Pr. *luzerno*; etym. unkn.] The leguminous plant *Medicago sativa*, resembling clover, cultivated for fodder; purple medick.

Lucian (l¹ū·ʃiăn). [repr. Gr. Λουκιανός, L *Lucianus.*] The name of a celebrated writer of Greek dialogues (*c* 160 A. D.); *allusively*, a witty scoffer (1750). Hence **Lucia·nic** (1820), †**-ical** (1561) *a.* pertaining to or like L. and his style; marked by a scoffing wit. **Lucia·nically** *adv.* 1592. †**Lucianist**, a disciple of L. 1585-92.

Lucid (l¹ū·sid), *a.* 1591. [ad. L. *lucidus*, f. *lucere* to shine. Cf. F. *lucide.*] **1.** Bright, shining, luminous, resplendent. Now *poet.* and *techn. Entom.* and *Bot.* = Smooth and shining. *Astr.* Of a star: Visible to the naked eye. **2.** Translucent, pellucid, clear 1620. **3.** **Lucid interval** [med.L. *lucida intervalla* (pl.), also in early use in English]: **a.** A period of temporary sanity occurring between attacks of lunacy. †Formerly also, an interval of apparent health between the periods of a malady. 1645. **b.** *transf.* and *fig.* A period of calm in the midst of tumult or confusion 1622. **c.** In etymol. sense: An interval of sunshine in a storm 1749. **4.** Clear in reasoning, expression, or arrangement; easily intelligible; also *transf.* of a person in reference to reasoning or statement 1786. **5.** Of persons: Clear in intellect; rational 1843.

1. The l. firmament SPENSER. 2. The l. wave POPE. 3. a. She had a l. interval, while making the will 1839. b. Which [dissensions] although they had had..l. intervals.., yet [etc.] BACON. 4. The sermon was long but l. 1876. A l. reasoner 1879. 5. Two apparently l. people 1859. **Luci·dity. Lu·cid-ly** *adv.*, **-ness.**

‖**Lucida** (l¹ū·sidă). 1727. [L. (sc. *stella* star).] *Astr.* The brightest star of the constellation, group, etc. mentioned.

Lucifer (l¹ū·sifəɹ). OE. [L. *lucifer* adj., light-bringing; used as proper name of the morning star; f. *luc(i)-*, *lux* light + *-fer* bringing. Cf. Gr. φωσφόρος.] **1.** The morning star; the planet Venus when she appears in the sky before sunrise. Now only *poet.* **2.** The rebel archangel whose fall from heaven was supposed to be referred to in Isa. xiv. 12; Satan, the Devil. Now chiefly in the phr. *As proud as L.* †**b.** *allusively.* One who seeks to dethrone God; *occas.* one who presumptuously rebels against an earthly sovereign -1618. **3.** (Orig. **lucifer match**) A friction match made usually of a splint of wood tipped with an inflammable substance ignited on a prepared surface 1831.

1. After that lucifere the day sterre hath chasyd awey the dirke nyht CHAUCER. 2. And when he falles, he falles like L., Neuer to hope againe SHAKS.

†**Luciferian** (l¹ūsifī³·riăn), *a.*[1] and *sb.*[1] 1570. [f. LUCIFER + -IAN.] **A.** *adj.* Of or pertaining to Lucifer; Satanic, devilish; as proud as Lucifer -1773. **B.** *sb.* A Luciferian or Satanic person. TRAPP. So †**Luciferine** *a.* 1546-88, †**Luciferous** *a.*[1] 1554-93.

Lucife·rian, *a.*[2] and *sb.*[2] 1550. [f. L. proper name *Lucifer* (see below) + -IAN.] Of or pertaining to (An adherent of) the sect founded by Lucifer, bishop of Cagliari in the fourth century, who separated from the Church because it was too lenient towards Arians who repented of their heresy 1607.

Luciferous (l¹usi·fĕrəs), *a.*[2] 1648. [f. L. *lucifer* light-bearing + -OUS.] **1.** That brings, conveys, or emits light. Now *rare.* 1656. **2.** *fig.* Luminous, illuminating.

2. So L. an Experiment BOYLE. Hence **Luci·ferous-ly** *adv.*, **-ness.**

Lucific (l¹usi·fik), *a.* 1701. [ad. late L. *lucificus*, f. *luci-*, *lux* light; see -FIC.] Light-producing.

Luciform (l¹ū·sifǭɹm), *a.* Now *rare.* 1668. [ad. L. **luciformis* (repr. Gr. αὐγοειδής); f. *luci-*, *lux*; see -FORM.] Having the character of light, luminous; applied *spec.* to the 'vehicle' of the soul (αὐγοειδὲς ὄχημα) imagined by the Neo-Platonists; *occas.* to the spiritual body of the Resurrection.

Lucifugous (l¹usi·fiŭgəs), *a.* 1654. [f. L. *lucifugus*, f. *luci-*, *lux* + *fugere*; see -OUS.] Shunning the light.

Bats and other such shy and l. creatures 1865.

Lucimeter (l¹usi·mĭtəɹ). 1825. [Hybrid f. L. *luci-*, *lux* + -METER.] **a.** An instrument for measuring the intensity of light; a photometer. **b.** An instrument for measuring the evaporative effect of sunlight 1890.

‖**Lucina** (l¹usəi·nă). ME. [L. fem. of *lucinus* adj., f. *luc-*, *lux* light; see -INE[1].] In Roman mythology, the goddess of childbirth, sometimes identified with Juno or with Diana; hence, a midwife. **b.** By identification with Diana: The moon (*poet.*) 1500.

Death must be the L. of life SIR T. BROWNE.

Luck (lʊk). late ME. [a. LG. *luk*, shortened f. *geluk* (= mod.G. *glück*). Ult. etym. unkn.] **1.** Fortune good or ill; the fortuitous happening of events affecting the interests of a person; a person's condition with regard to the favourable or unfavourable character of such events. Often with adj., as *bad, evil, good, hard l.*, ILL LUCK. Also, the fancied tendency of chance (esp. in gambling) to produce a run of favourable or unfavourable events; the disposition ascribed to chance at a particular time. 1481. **b.** Chance as a cause or bestower of success and failure. Occas. *personified.* 1534. **2.** Good fortune; success, prosperity or advantage coming by chance ME. **b.** *occas.* A name given to an object on which the prosperity of a family, etc. is supposed to depend 1800. †**3.** An omen -1600.

1. It hath beene my l. alwayes to beat the bush, while another kild the Hare 1602. Better l. next time 1791. The l. turns at last 1856. b. L., in the great game of war, is undoubtedly lord of all 1899. 2. No man can have lucke alwayes at playe 1583. Phr. *To have the l.*, to be so fortunate as (*to* be or do something). b. 'The L. of Eden Hall': an oriental glass goblet (of the 15th c. or earlier) in the possession of the Musgraves of Eden, Cumberland, so called with reference to the words, 'If this glass will break or fall, Farewell the l. of Eden-hall'.

Phrases. *Bad l. to* (a person or thing)*!*: a vulgar expression of ill will, disgust, or disappointment. *Down on* (occas. *in*) *one's l.*: in ill luck, in misfortune (*slang*). *For l.*: in order to bring good l. *In l.*: enjoying good l. *Out of l.*: having bad l., in misfortune. *To try one's l.*: see TRY *v.* *Worse l.*: unfortunately, 'more's the pity' (*colloq.*). *Run, stroke of l.*: see the sbs.

Comb. **l.-money, -penny**, a piece of money given or kept for l., esp. in the sale of live-stock.

Luckily (lʊ·kili), *adv.* 1482. [f. LUCKY *a.* + -LY[2].] **1.** In a lucky manner; successfully, prosperously, happily. Now *rare.* **2.** Qualifying the sentence as a whole, indicating that the fact or circumstance is a lucky one 1717.

2. Climbing a long snow-slope which was l. in fair order L. STEPHEN.

Luckiness (lʊ·kinĕs). 1561. [-NESS.] The quality or condition of being lucky.

Luckless (lʊ·klĕs), *a.* 1563. [f. LUCK + -LESS.] **1.** Having no luck or good fortune; unlucky, hapless, ill-starred, unfortunate. †**2.** Ominous of ill -1637.

1. I, and ten thousand in this lucklesse Realme SHAKS. 2. The shreikes of lucklesse Owles B. JONS. Hence **Lu·ckless-ly** *adv.*, **-ness.**

Lucky (lʊ·ki), *sb.*[1] *Sc.* Also **luckie.** 1717. [f. LUCKY *a.* 5.] A familiar name for an elderly woman; *spec.* a grandmother. Also applied, joc. or affectionately, to a woman of any age; a wife, mistress. **b.** *spec.* The mistress of an ale-house.

Lucky (lɒ·ki), *sb.*[2] *slang.* 1834. In phr. *To cut* or *make one's l.*: to escape, decamp.

Lucky (lɒ·ki), *a.* 1502. [f. LUCK + -Y[1].] **1.** Attended by good luck. In early use, Fortunate, successful, prosperous. Now: Favoured by chance. **b.** Of a literary composition: Having an unstudied felicity 1700. **2.** Of the nature of good luck; occurring by chance and producing happy results 1547. **3.** Presaging or likely to promote good luck; well-omened 1549. **4.** Occurring by chance; casual, fortuitous 1691. **5.** *Sc.* Used as a term or address of endearment, esp. to a woman. [Cf. Icel. *heill* good luck, used similarly.] 1555.

1. A dexterous and l. player MACAULAY. A l. guess CRABBE. b. Genius now and then produces a l. trifle JOHNSON. 2. L. legacies JOHNSON. 3. They say, a Fool's hansel is l. B. JONS. *L. penny, sixpence* (usu. one bent or perforated, carried as a charm). *L. stone* (often, one with a natural hole through it). *Comb.* **l.-proach** *Sc.* = FATHER-LASHER.

Lu·cky-bag. 1825. [f. prec. adj.] A bag, at fairs and bazaars, in which, on paying a small sum, one dips one's hand and draws an article of greater or less value. Often *fig.*

Lucrative (l[i]ū·krătiv), *a.* ME. [ad. L. *lucrativus*, f. *lucrari* to gain.] **1.** Yielding gain or profit; gainful. †**2.** Of persons, etc.: Bent upon or directed towards making of gain; avaricious, covetous –1797.

1. A l. contract warded off the blow for a time SCOTT. A l. traffic with the coast of Guinea 1874. Hence **Lu·crative·ly** *adv.*, **-ness.**

Lucre (l[i]ū·kəɹ). ME. [ad. (perh. through F. *lucre*) L. *lucrum*, f. root **lū-, leu-, lou-*, whence Gr. ἀπολαύειν to enjoy, G. *lohn* wages, etc.] **1.** Gain, profit, pecuniary advantage. Now only in bad sense: Gain viewed as a low motive for action; 'pelf'. **2.** Const. *of.* †**a.** Gain or profit derived from (something). **b.** Acquisition of (something profitable) (*arch.*) ME.

1. His sonnes..turned aside after l., and tooke bribes 1 *Sam.* viii. 3. *Filthy l.*: see FILTHY. 2. b. I am going to make a book for the l. of gain SOUTHEY.

Lucretian (l[i]ukrī·ʃiăn), *a.* (*sb.*) 1712. [f. *Lucretius*, Latin poet and Epicurean philosopher + -AN.] Pertaining to, characteristic of, or resembling Lucretius or his philosophy. As quasi-*sb.* A follower of Lucretius 1881.

The L. comfort is none to me TUCKER.

†**Lucta·tion.** 1651. [ad. L. *luctationem*, f. *luctari* to struggle.] Struggling, wrestling –1698. **b.** *transf.* Agitation due to chemical reaction. Also, a struggling for breath. –1693.

Lu·ctual, *a.* 1613. [f. L. *luctus* mourning + -AL.] Mournful –1655.

Lucubrate (l[i]ū·kiubreɪt), *v.* 1623. [f. L. *lucubrat-*, *lucubrare*, f. *luc-*, *lux* light.] **1.** *intr.* Literally, To work by artificial light. In mod. use, to produce lucubrations. **2.** *trans.* To produce (literary compositions) by laborious study. (Rec. Dicts.) Hence **Lu·cubrator,** a nocturnal student; one who produces lucubrations. †**Lucubratory** *a.* meditative; *sb.* (*joc.*) a 'thinking-shop'.

Lucubration (l[i]ūkiubrē·ʃən). 1595. [ad. L. *lucubrationem*; see prec.] **1.** The action of lucubrating; nocturnal study or meditation; study in general. **2.** quasi-*concr.* Usu. *pl.* The product of this; hence, a literary work showing signs of careful elaboration. Now suggesting something pedantic or over-elaborate. 1611.

1. The well-earned harvest of..many a midnight l. GIBBON. 2. Tons of dusty lucubration CARLYLE.

Luculent (l[i]ū·kiŭlĕnt), *a.* ME. [ad. L. *luculentus*, f. *luc-*, *lux* light.] **1.** Full of light; bright, shining. Now *rare.* **2.** †**a.** Of oratory, writings: Brilliant. Hence of a writer, etc. **b.** Of evidence, arguments: Clear, cogent. Of explanations: Lucid. 1548. **3.** Of persons: Brilliant, illustrious –1620.

1. L. along The purer rivers flow THOMSON. 2. b. The most l. testimonies that Christian Religion hath HOOKER. 3. Most debonaire, and L. Ladie B. JONS. Hence **Lu·culently** *adv.*

Lucullian, -ean (l[i]ukɒ·liăn, l[i]ūkɒlī·ăn), *a.* 1601. [ad. L. *Lucullianus*, or f. L. *Luculleus*, f. *Lucullus.*] Pertaining to or characteristic of L. Licinius Lucullus, a wealthy Roman famous for the luxury of his banquets.

†*Lucullean marble*: some kind of black marble.

‖**Lucumo** (l[i]ū·kiumo). Also **-on.** 1837. [L., an Etruscan title.] One of the Etruscan nobles, who were at once priests and princes.

Lud (lɒd). 1725. Minced form of LORD *sb.*

O l.! he has almost cracked my head GOLDSM. 'My Lud', said Mr. Caterham, 'my case is completed' 1898.

Luddite (lɒ·dəit). 1811. [Said (but without confirmation) to be f. Ned *Lud*, a lunatic living about 1779, who in a fit of rage smashed up two frames belonging to a Leicestershire 'stockinger'.] A member of an organized band of mechanics and their friends, who (1811–16) went about destroying machinery in the midlands and north of England.

Are you not near the Luddites? And down with all kings but King Ludd? BYRON. **Lu·ddism** 1812.

Ludibrious (l[i]udi·briəs), *a.* 1563. [ad. late L. *ludibriosus*, f. *ludibrium*, f. *ludere* to play.] †**1.** Apt to be a subject of jest or mockery –1675. **2.** Full of scorn; inclined to scoff; mocking. Now *rare.* 1641. So †**Lu·dibry,** derision 1637–1723.

Ludicro- (l[i]ū·dikro), used as comb. f. L. *ludicrus* LUDICROUS, in sense 'ludicrous and..', as *l.-pathetic*, etc.

Ludicrous (l[i]ū·dikrəs), *a.* 1619. [f. L. *ludicrus* + -OUS.] †**1.** Pertaining to play; sportive; jocular, derisive –1781. †**2.** Given to jesting; frivolous; also, witty, humorous –1827. **3.** Ridiculous; laughably absurd 1782.

3. The Duke was in a state of l. distress MACAULAY. Hence **Lu·dicrous·ly** *adv.*, **-ness.**

Ludification (l[i]ūdifikē·ʃən). Now *rare.* late ME. [ad. L. *ludificationem.*] A deception or mocking. So †**Ludificatory** *a.* deceptive. BARROW.

Ludo (l[i]ū·do). 1898. [a. L. *ludo* I play.] A game played with dice and counters on a special board.

‖**Lues** (l[i]ū·īz). 1634. [L., = 'plague'.] A plague or pestilence; a spreading disease, *esp.* syphilis (*L. venerea*); also, a contagious disease among cattle. Hence **Lue·tic** *a.* [badly formed], pertaining to, or affected with, l.

Luff (lɒf), *sb.* [Early ME. *lof*, *loof*, app. a. OF. *lof*, used in sense 1 below. Cf. Du. *loef*, etc. Ult. etym. uncertain.] *Naut.* †**1.** Some contrivance for altering the course of a ship; e. g. a rudder, a paddle, or some kind of machine for working on the sails –1485. †**2.** The weather-gauge, or part of a ship towards the wind –1622. **3.** The weather-part of a fore-and-aft sail, i. e. the side next the mast or stay 1513. **4.** The fullest part of a ship's bow, where the sides begin to curve in towards the stem 1624.

Phr. *To turn, wend the l.*: to change one's course; also *fig.* *L. a l.*: hugging the wind closely. *To keep one's l.*: to keep close to the wind; to keep to windward, keep one's distance. *To spring one's l.*: to bring the ship's head closer to the wind.

Comb., etc.: **l.-tackle,** a purchase composed of a double and a single block, used for various purposes; **l. upon l.,** a luff-tackle attached to the fall of another, to increase the purchase.

Luff (lɒf), *v.* ME. [f. LUFF *sb.*; cf. Du. *loeven*, F. *lofer.*] *Naut.* **1.** *intr.* To bring the head of a ship nearer to the wind; to steer or sail nearer the wind; to sail in a specified direction with the head kept close to the wind. **2.** *trans.* To bring the head of (a vessel) nearer to the wind. Also with *up.* 1606. **3.** In yacht-racing: To get the windward side of (an opponent). Also with *away.* 1894.

1. *To l. round* or *alee*: to make the excess of the movement of luffing, in order to throw the ship's head up in the wind, for the purpose of tacking her, etc. 2. *L. the helm*, the call or order to the steersman.

Luffer, var. of LOUVER.

Lug (lɒg), *sb.*[1] Now *dial.* ME. [?] **1.** A long stick or pole; the branch or limb of a tree. **2.** A measure **a.** of length; a pole or perch, varying locally; usu. of 16½ feet 1562; **b.** of surface: a square pole or perch 1602.

Lug (lɒg), *sb.*[2] Chiefly *Sc.* and *n. dial.* 1495. [Perh. Scandinavian, = 'something that can be pulled or laid hold of'.] **1.** One of the flaps or lappets of a cap or bonnet, covering the ears. **2.** = EAR *sb.*[1] 1 and 4. 1507. **3.** An object resembling the external ear: **a.** The handle of a pitcher, etc. Also *techn.*, an appendage by which an object may be lifted or suspended. 1624. **b.** The side-wall (of a fire-place or other recess); a (chimney) corner 1784. **c.** *Electr.* A fitting of copper or brass to which electrical wires are connected. **4.** *Comb.* **l.-mark** *sb.* and *v.* = EAR-MARK.

Lug (lɒg), *sb.*[3] Also **log.** 1602. [Cf. LURG.] A large marine worm (*Arenicola marina*) much used for bait. Also **l.-worm.**

Lug (lɒg), *sb.*[4] 1830. Short for LUGSAIL.

Lug, *sb.*[5] 1616. [f. LUG *v.*] The act of lugging; *concr.* (*U.S.*) that which is lugged.

Lug (lɒg), *v.* ME. [Prob. Scandinavian; cf. Sw. *lugga* to pull a person's hair, f. *lugg* forelock, etc.] **1.** *trans.* To pull, give a pull to; to tease, worry, bait (a bear, bull, etc.). *Obs.* exc. *dial.* **2.** *intr.* To pull, tug. Of a horse: To press heavily *on* (the bit or reins). ME. †**b.** To take a pull *at* (liquor, the breast). Also *trans.* To pull at (the breast). –1617. **c.** To move *about*, *along*, heavily and slowly; to drag. Now only *techn.* ME. **3.** *trans.* To drag, tug with violent effort ME. **b.** *colloq.* hyperbolically 1652. **4.** *fig.* To drag in forcibly or irrelevantly 1721.

3. I lugged this Money home to my Cave, and laid it up DE FOE. b. Boswell..succeeded in lugging him [Johnson] into the wilds of the Highlands L. STEPHEN. 4. Counsel..had lugged in every thing he could to prejudice the case 1901.

L. out. a. *trans.* See prec. senses and *out.* ME. **b.** *absol.* or *intr.* To draw one's sword; to pull out money or a purse *arch.* 1684.

Luge (l[i]ūdʒ), *sb.* 1907. [Fr.] A kind of toboggan used in Switzerland. Also *vb.*

Luggage (lɒ·gĕdʒ). 1596. [f. LUG *v.* + -AGE.] **1.** †In early use: What has to be lugged about; inconveniently heavy baggage. Also, the baggage of an army. Now, The baggage belonging to a traveller or passenger. **2.** †**a.** With *a.* An encumbrance –1693. **b.** *pl.* *nonce-use* = IMPEDIMENTA. Carlyle.

1. A Boy of the House, who rode after us with the L. SWIFT. *fig.* The cumbersome l. of riches LAMB.

Lugger (lɒ·gəɹ). 1795. [perh. f. *lug* in LUGSAIL; but cf. Du. *logger.*] A vessel carrying a lugsail or lugsails, with one, two, or three masts.

Lu·gsail. 1677. [? f. LUG *v.* or LUG *sb.*[2]] A four-cornered sail, bent upon a yard which is slung at about one-third or one-fourth of its length from one end, and so hangs obliquely.

Lugubrious (l[i]ugi[i]ū·briəs), *a.* 1601. [f. L. *lugubris* + -OUS.] Characterized by mourning; doleful, dismal, sorrowful. Hence **Lugu·brious·ly** *adv.*, **-ness.** var. †**Lugu·brous** 1632–1708.

Lug-worm: see LUG *sb.*[3]

Luke (l[i]ūk), *a.* *Obs.* exc. *dial.* [ME. *lheuc*, *leuk*, perh. f. OE. *hléow* LEW *a.*] = next.

Nine penn'orth o' brandy and water l. DICKENS.

Lukewarm (l[i]ū·k,wǭɹm), *a.* (*sb.*) ME. [f. LUKE *a.* + WARM *a.*] **1.** Moderately warm, tepid. **2.** Of persons, etc.: Having little warmth or depth of feeling, lacking zeal or enthusiasm, indifferent 1522. **3.** *sb.* A lukewarm person 1693.

1. Apply the Collyrium luke-warm 1658. 2. Our l. Temper 1718. L. advocate 1771, accents 1804. Hence **Lu·kewarm·ly** *adv.*, **-ness.** **Lu·kewarmth** (now *rare*) 1598.

Lull (lɒl), *sb.*[1] 1659. [f. LULL *v.*] **1.** That which lulls; a lulling sound, etc. 1719; †soothing drink, 'nepenthe' 1659. **2.** A lulled or stupefied condition 1822. **3.** A short intermission in a storm, etc. 1815.

Lull, *sb.*[2] 1820. [a. Du. *lul.*] *Whaling.* A tube to convey blubber into the hold.

Lull (lɒl), *v.* ME. [Imitative of (lu lu) or similar sounds in lullabies.] **1.** *trans.* To soothe with sounds or caresses; to induce to sleep or to pleasing quiescence. **2.** *fig.* To quiet (suspicion) by deception; to delude into a sense of security 1601. **3.** *trans.* To quiet (winds, sea, etc.) 1680. **4.** *intr.* Of the sea or wind: To become gradually diminished in force or power. Also *fig.* 1808.

1. The Virgin voyce That Babies l. a-sleepe SHAKS. 3. Lull'd like the depth of ocean when at rest BYRON. 4. The wind lulled, the rain came down in a deluge MARRYAT.

Lullaby (lʊ·lăbəi), *int.* and *sb.* 1560. [f. †*lulla*, onomatopœic + *-by* as in *by-by*, BYE-BYE [1].] 1. *int.* A soothing refrain, used to quiet an infant or esp. send it to sleep. Also *gen.* †b. Used for 'farewell', 'good-night'. SHAKS. 2. *sb.* A song sung to a child to put it to sleep. Also, any soothing song. 1588. b. *transf.* and *fig.* 1611.

1. L., oh, l.! The brat will never shut an eye HOOD. b. *Twel. N.* v. i. 48. 2. b. The bees have hummed their noontide l. ROGERS. Hence **Lu·llaby** *v.* to soothe with a l.; to sing to sleep. Also *absol.* or *intr.* 1592.

Lum (lʊm). *n. dial.* and *Sc.* 1507. [? an application of OF. *lum* light (:—L. *lumen*).] †1. ? A skylight. 2. A chimney; also, a chimney-top 1697.

Lumachella (liūmăke·lă). Also **lumachel(le**, etc. 1727. [a. It. *lumachella* little snail, f. *lumaca*.] *Min.* A dark-coloured compact limestone containing shells which frequently emit fire-like reflections; fire-marble.

Lumbago (lʊmbē·go), *sb.* 1693. [a. L. *lumbago*, f. *lumbus* loin.] *Med.* A rheumatic affection in the lumbar region of the body. So **Lumba·ginous** *a.* pertaining to, resembling, or afflicted with l. 1620. **Lumba·go** *v.* to afflict with l. 1796.

Lumbar (lʊ·mbăɹ). 1656. [ad. mod.L. *lumbaris*, f. L. *lumbus* loin.] A. *adj.* Of, belonging to, or situated in the loin; as *l. arteries, vein*, etc. B. *sb.* [The adj. used ellipt.] An artery, nerve, vein, or vertebra situated in the loin 1858. var. †**Lu·mbal** *a.* and *sb.* 1696.

Lumber (lʊ·mbəɹ), *sb.*[1] 1552. [Prob. f. LUMBER *v.*[1]; but at one time assoc. w. LUMBER *sb.*[2]] 1. Disused articles of furniture and the like, which only take up room; useless odds and ends. b. *fig.* Useless or cumbrous material 1649. 2. Superfluous fat, esp. in horses 1806. 3. *N. Amer.* Timber sawn into rough planks or otherwise roughly prepared for the market 1662.

1. Stands, dishes, formes, chaires, stoles, and other lumbar 1587. b. The bookful blockhead..With loads of learned l. in his head POPE.

Comb.: **l.-carrier**, a vessel employed in the lumber-trade; **-man**, one who works among l., esp. in felling and dressing rough timber in the forest; **-mill**, a sawmill for cutting up l.; **-room**, a room for l. or disused chattels; **-trade**, the trade in rough timber; **-wood**, a wood where l. is cut.

†**Lu·mber**, *sb.*[2] 1617. [var. of LOMBARD *sb.*[1]] 1. A pawnbroking establishment -1749. 2. Money due with respect to articles pawned. BUTLER.

1. Phr. *To put to l.*: to put in pawn. *To be in l.* (slang): to be imprisoned.

Lumber (lʊ·mbəɹ), *v.*[1] [ME. *lomere*, perh. f. *lome* LAME *a.*; or ? of direct imitative formation in Eng.] 1. *intr.* To move in a clumsy or blundering manner; now only, to move heavily by reason of bulk and mass. †2. To rumble. 1529-1621.

1. Hush! I hear him lumbering in! FOOTE.

Lumber (lʊ·mbəɹ), *v.*[2] 1642. [f. LUMBER *sb.*[1]] 1. *trans.* To cover, fill up, or obstruct with lumber; to encumber. Occas. with *over, up.* b. *intr.* To lie as lumber 1850. 2. *trans.* To heap or place together as lumber 1678. 3. *intr.* (*N. Amer.*) To cut forest timber and prepare it for the market. Occas. *trans.* 1809.

1. Empty bottles lumbered the bottom of every closet W. IRVING. Hence **Lu·mberer** (*N. Amer.*), one employed in the lumber or timber trade.

Lu·mber, *v.*[3] *slang.* 1812. [f. LUMBER *sb.*[2]] To deposit (property) in pawn; hence in *passive*, to be placed away privily, to be imprisoned.

†**Lumber-pie.** Also **lumbar-pie.** 1656. [See LOMBARD *a.* 2.] A savoury pie made of meat or fish and eggs.

Lumbo- (lʊ·mbo), used as comb. f. L. *lumbus* loin, as **l.-abdominal** *a.*, pertaining to the loins and the abdomen; so *l.-costal, -sacral*, etc.

Lumbrical (lʊmbrəi·kăl, lʊ·mbrikăl). 1694. [ad. mod.L. *lumbricalis*; see LUMBRICUS and -AL.] *Nat. Hist.* A. *adj.* Pertaining to or resembling a lumbricus or worm; *Anat.* applied to certain fusiform muscles in the hand and the foot which assist in flexing the digits. B. *sb.* Often in L. form **lumbricalis**, pl. **-es.** A lumbrical muscle 1706.

Lumbriciform (lʊmbr(ə)i·sifǭɹm), *a.* 1828. [See LUMBRICUS and -FORM.] Resembling a lumbricus; vermiform.

Lumbricoid (lʊmbrəi·koid, lʊ·mbrikoid). 1849. [ad. mod.L. *lumbricoides*; see LUMBRICUS and -OID.] *Zool.* A. *adj.* Resembling the lumbricus or earth-worm. B. *sb.* The round-worm.

‖**Lumbricus** (lʊmbrəi·kʊ̆s). *Pl.* **-ci** (-səi). ME. [L.] a. The earth-worm, *L. terrestris.* b. The round-worm which infests the intestines, *Ascaris lumbricoides.*

‖**Lumen** (liū·men). *Pl.* **lumina** (liū·mină). 1873. [L., = light; an opening.] 1. *Anat.*, *Bot.*, etc. A cavity or space enclosed by the walls of a tube, cell, or the like. 2. *Photom.* A unit of light flux.

Luminant (liū·minănt). 1884. [ad. late L. *luminantem*, pres. pple. of *luminare.*] A. *adj.* Illuminating, luminous 1891. B. *sb.* An illuminant. **Lu·minance**, luminousness 1880.

Luminarist (liū·minărist). 1888. [ad. F. *luminariste*, f. L. *lumin-, lumen* light.] A painter who treats light effectively, or whose colour is luminous. So **-ism.**

That..subtle l. Adrian van Ostade 1888.

Luminary (liū·minări), *sb.* 1450. [ad. OF. *luminarie*, F. *luminaire* masc., ad. med.L. *luminarium, luminare*, f. L. *lumin-, lumen*; cf. -ARY [1].] 1. A natural light-giving body, *esp.* the sun or the moon 1489. 2. An artificial light; †in 17th c. *pl.*, illuminations betokening rejoicing (so med.L. *luminaria*) 1483. 3. *fig.* A source of intellectual, moral, or spiritual light; a person of 'light and leading' 1450.

1. Where the great Luminarie..Dispenses Light from farr MILT. 2. There were extraordinary luminaries in all the windows in the publick streets LUTTRELL. 3. A late happy Discovery by two great Luminaries of this Island BENTLEY. So **Lu·minary** *a.* (*rare*), pertaining to light 1794.

Luminate (liū·mineit), *v.* *Obs.* or *arch.* 1623. [f. late L. *luminat-, luminare.*] *trans.* To light up, illuminate. Hence **Lumina·tion** (*rare*), a shedding or emission of light; †*concr.* an illumination 1654.

Lumine (liū·min), *v.* Now *rare* or *Obs.* ME. [a. OF. *lumine*, late L. *luminare.* Cf. LIMN *v.*, ILLUMINE *v.*] *trans.* To light up, illumine. †In early use, to illuminate (manuscripts, etc.). So †**Luminer**, illuminator.

Luminescent (liūmine·sĕnt), *a.* 1889. [f. L. *lumin-, lumen* + -ESCENT.] a. Emitting light otherwise than as a result of incandescence. b. Pertaining to luminescence. Hence **Lumine·sce** *v. intr.* to become l. **Lumine·scence**, l. condition or quality.

Luminiferous (liūmini·fĕrəs), *a.* 1801. [f. as prec. + -(I)FEROUS.] Producing or transmitting light; *esp.* in *l. ether* (see ETHER 5).

Luminist (liū·minist). *rare.* 1901. [f. as prec. + -IST.] = LUMINARIST. So **-ism.**

Luminous (liū·minəs), *a.* ME. [ad. L. *luminosus*, f. *lumin-, lumen* light.] 1. Full of light; emitting light; shining, bright. b. Of a room: Well lighted 1610. 2. *transf.* and *fig.*: esp. of writers, etc. 1450.

1. The phaenomenon of the l. sea 1792. Some of the cuttle-fishes are slightly l. 1851. *spec.* Applied to paint, etc. which shows up in the dark. b. The library ..is elegant and l. JOHNSON. 2. The l. page of Gibbon SHERIDAN. L. eloquence MACAULAY. Hence **Lumino·sity**, the quality or condition of being l.; also *concr.* 1634. **Lu·minous-ly** *adv.*, **-ness.**

Lummy (lʊ·mi), *a. slang.* 1838. First-rate.

Lump (lʊmp), *sb.*[1] [ME. *lump.* Cf. Da. (16th c.) *lump(e* lump, Norw. and Sw. dial. *lump* block, stump, log, etc. Ult. etym. unkn.] 1. A compact piece or mass with no particular shape; often with implication of excessive size, protuberant outline, or clumsiness. b. A great quantity; a 'lot', 'heap'. Also *pl.* 'lots', 'heaps'. *slang* or *dial.* 1523. 2. Applied *spec.* (chiefly *fig.* in Biblical use) to the mass of clay taken up by a potter or sculptor for one operation, and to the mass of dough intended for one baking 1526. †b. Hence, *allusively*, the whole mass or quantity of anything. Also, the 'mass', 'bulk', great majority. -1711. †3. An aggregate of units; a congeries, heap, clump, cluster; *occas.* a group (of persons) -1781. 4. A protuberance, swelling, or excrescence, *esp.* one caused by disease or injury in an animal body 1475. 5. Applied to persons. *colloq.* a. A heavy, dull person 1597. b. A big sturdy creature 1630. 6. *techn.* a. A bloom or loop of malleable iron 1686. b. A kind of thickish paving brick or tile 1787. c. A barge or lighter used in dockyards 1796. d. In firearms: (*a*) The nipple-seat on a gun-barrel; (*b*) a steel projection under the barrel on a break-joint breech-loader which descends into a recess in the action. 1844.

1. A l. of Sugar SWIFT, of lead, iron, etc. TYNDALL. *transf.* Thou lumpe of fowle Deformitie SHAKS. Phr. *A l. in one's throat*: (*a*) a swelling in the throat; (*b*) a feeling of tightness in the throat due to emotion (*popular*). *L. of clay*: the human body; a soulless person (*disparaging*). b. A l. of money 1869. 2. 1 *Cor.* v. 6. Before that sin turned..all our l. to leaven G. HERBERT. 3. Take a lumpe of figs 2 *Kings* xx. 7. Phrases. *By the l.* (rarely *by l.*): = *in the lump.* †*In a l.*: the whole together. *In the l.*: in the mass; in gross; wholesale. *All of a l.*: altogether, in a heap; also, swollen so as as appear one l.

Comb.: **l.-coal**, coal including the largest lumps as they come from the mine; **l. gold**, gold in nuggets; **l. sugar**, loaf sugar broken into lumps or cut into cubes 1623; **l. sum**, a sum which covers a number of items.

Lump (lʊmp), *sb.*[2] 1545. [= MLG. *lumpen*, MDu. *lompe*, G. *lump, lumpfisch*, F. *lompe*; hence mod.L. *lumpus* (specific name). The Du. and LG. forms are evidenced earlier than the Eng.] 1. An uncouth-looking spiny-finned fish of a leaden-blue colour, *Cyclopterus lumpus*, having a suctorial disk on its belly with which it adheres strongly to objects; the sea-owl. 2. *Comb.*: **l.-fish, l. sucker**, = 1.

Lump (lʊmp), *v.*[1] 1577. [Of symbolic sound: cf. *dump, hump, mump*, etc.] 1. *intr.* To look sulky or disagreeable. 2. *trans.* In antithesis with *like*: To be displeased at (something that must be endured). *colloq.* 1833.

2. If you don't like it you may l. it HALIBURTON.

Lump (lʊmp), *v.*[2] 1624. [f. LUMP *sb.*[1]] 1. *trans.* a. To melt down into a lump. b. To form or raise into lumps. c. To cover with lumps. 1797. 2. To put together in one lump, mass, sum, or group; to consider or deal with in the lump without regard for particulars or details 1624. 3. To lay the whole of (a particular sum of money) *on* a single object 1864. 4. *intr.* To collect *together* into a lump; to be formed or raised into lumps 1720. 5. To move heavily *along*; to drop *down* like a lump 1861.

2. They always l. the petty officers and common seamen MARRYAT. The premium and the principal are lumped in one sum SIR J. BACON. 3. He lumped it all upon an outsider *Derby Day* iii. 32. 4. The old one [cushion], which used to l. up all in a heap 1856.

Lumper (lʊ·mpəɹ), *sb.* 1785. [f. LUMP *v.* + -ER [1].] 1. A labourer employed in loading and unloading cargoes, esp. timber. 2. *slang.* A small contractor, sweater 1851. 3. One who lumps things together 1852. 4. *Ireland.* A coarse variety of potato 1837.

3. It is good to have hair-splitters and lumpers DARWIN.

Lu·mper, *v.* *Obs.* exc. *dial.* 1581. [Cf. LUMP *v.*[2] 5.] *intr.* To move clumsily; to blunder along.

Lump-fish: see LUMP *sb.*[2]

Lu·mping, *ppl. a.* ME. [f. LUMP *sb.*[1] or *v.*[2] + -ING [2].] †1. Coagulating. LAVINGTON. †2. Weighing heavy. ME. only. b. Hence *colloq.*: Great, big 1705. c. Of movement: Heavy, clumsy. Also of the noise so produced. 1884. 3. Characterized by taking things in a lump without regard for detail 1793.

2. b. *L. pennyworth* (now *dial.*) = 'plenty for one's money'. *L. weight*, good or full weight. 3. L. methods of cost-keeping 1896.

Lumpish (lʊ·mpiʃ), *a.* 1528. [f. LUMP *sb.*[1] (and in part LUMP *v.*[1]) + -ISH [1].] †1. Heavy and unwieldy. 1545. 2. Heavy and clumsy in appearance, shape, or movement 1555. 3. Stupidly dull or heavy; sluggishly inactive; unapprehensive 1528. †4. Low-spirited, dejected, melancholy -1741. 5. Of sound: Dull and heavy 1742. 6. In lumps, lumpy. *Obs.* (exc. as nonce-use). 1735.

4. She is l., heavy, mellancholly SHAKS. Hence **Lu·mpish-ly** *adv.*, **-ness.**

Lumpkin (lʊ·mᵖkin). *dial.* 1901. [f. LUMP *sb.*[1] + -KIN. (Cf. the character Tony Lumpkin in Goldsmith's *She Stoops to Conquer.*)] A clumsy, blundering person.

Lump sucker: see LUMP *sb.*[2]

Lumpy (lʊ·mpi), *a.* 1707. [f. LUMP *sb.*[1] + -Y[1].] 1. Full of lumps. b. Of water: Cut up by the wind into small waves 1857. 2. Having an outline or shape characterized by lumps 1708. 3. *slang.* Drunk 1810. Hence **Lu·mpily** *adv.*, **Lu·mpiness.**

‖**Luna** (liū·nă). ME. [L., = moon. (In senses 1 and 2 written with capital L as proper name.)] 1. The moon (personified) 1529. 2. †a. *Alch.* Silver. b. *Her.* A name for argent in blazoning the arms of sovereigns. ME. c. **L. cornea** = HORN-SILVER, chloride of silver fused. Also *Lunæ* (erron. *Luna*) *cornua.* 1706. 3. *Eccl.* A lunette. 4. In full *luna-moth*: A large moth of N. America, *Actias luna*, having crescent-shaped spots on the wings 1884.

1. And L. hides her selfe to pleasure vs KYD. 2. a. Sol gold is, and L. silver we threpe CHAUCER.

Lunacy (liū·năsi). 1541. [f. LUNATIC; see -ACY 3.] The condition of being a lunatic; intermittent insanity as formerly attributed to the changes of the moon; now *gen.* any form of insanity (idiocy usually excepted). In *Law*, such mental unsoundness as interferes with civil rights or transactions. †Also, an attack of this. b. *transf.* and *fig.* Mad folly 1588.

Commission of l., a commission, issuing from a court, authorizing inquiry into a person's sanity. *Commissioner in l.*, now, a member of a board inspecting asylums and granting licences to private persons who undertake the charge of lunatics. *Master in l.*, an officer who investigates cases of alleged lunacy and makes orders dealing with the persons and estates of lunatics.

This disease of lunacie, is a disease whose distemper followeth the course of the moon SWAN. *attrib.* The L. Acts 1881. b. The wicked lunacies of the gaming-table COLERIDGE.

Lunar (liū·năɹ). 1626. [ad. L. *lunaris*, f. *luna*; see -AR.] A. *adj.* 1. Of or belonging to the moon; situated in the moon; †influenced by or dependent on the moon, or supposed to be so. 2. *transf.* and *fig.* a. Monthly, menstrual (*rare*) 1683. b. Like the moon; not warmly bright; pale, pallid 1742. 3. Crescent-shaped, LUNATE. Also, marked with crescent-shaped spots, as *l. underwing.* 1635. 4. Of or containing silver 1800.

1. **L. cycle**: see CYCLE *sb.* 2 (quot.). **L. day**, the interval between two successive crossings of the meridian by the moon. **L. distance**, in *Naut. Astr.*, the distance of the moon from the sun, a planet, or a fixed star, which is used in calculating longitude at sea. **L. month**, the interval from one new moon to the next, about 29½ days; in pop. language, 28 days (four weeks). **L. rainbow**, one formed by the moon's rays. **L. tables**, tables for showing or calculating the true place of the moon at any time. **L. theory**, the deduction of the moon's motion from the law of gravitation. **L. year**, a period of 12 l. months (about 354⅓ days). 2. b. Even the lustre of Partridge [in *Tom Jones*] is pallid and l. beside the noontide glory of Micawber SWINBURNE. 3. *L. bone* (= medical L. *os lunare*): = B. 3. 4. **Lunar caustic**, nitrate of silver fused.

B. *sb.* †1. A moon-like body, a satellite 1651. 2. A l. distance or observation 1830. 3. A bone of the wrist, shaped like a half-moon. Also in L. form **lunare** (liunē·ri). 1854.

Lunarian (liunē·riăn). 1708. [f. L. *lunaris* + -IAN.] A. *adj.* Inhabiting the moon. LOCKYER. B. *sb.* 1. A dweller in the moon 1708. 2. One who observes or describes the moon; one who used the lunar method in finding longitude 1817.

Lunary (liū·nări), *sb.* †Also in L. form **lunaria.** ME. [ad. med.L. *lunaria*, f. L. *luna.*] a. The garden plant HONESTY, *Lunaria biennis.* b. The fern called MOONWORT, *Botrychium Lunaria.*

Lunary (liū·nări), *a.* 1561. [ad. F. *lunaire*, L. *lunaris*; see LUNAR and -ARY.] = LUNAR *a.*, in various senses.

Lunate (liū·nět), *a.* 1777. [ad. L. *lunatus*, f. *luna*; see -ATE[2].] Crescent-shaped. Chiefly *Nat. Hist.*

L. eyes 1828, leaves 1870. So **Lu·nated** *a.* (now *rare*) 1673.

Lunatic (liū·nătik). ME. [ad. late L. *lunaticus*, f. L. *luna*; see -ATIC.] A. *adj.* 1. Orig., affected with the intermittent insanity formerly attributed to the changes of the moon. In mod. use, = INSANE. Not now employed technically by physicians. b. Of things: Indicating lunacy; crazy 1605. c. *fig.* Madly foolish, idiotic, 'mad' 1571. †2. Influenced by the moon -1593. †b. *Farriery.* Moon-blind -1737.

1. He was..euery moneth once Lunaticke LYDG. The House of Castile..terminated in a l. girl 1889. c. No policy can be more l. than the policy of annexation BRIGHT. So **Luna·tical** *a.* (*rare*) 1599.

B. *sb.* A person of unsound mind; a madman ME. b. *fig.* A madly foolish person 1602.

The Lunaticke, the Louer, and the Poet, Are of imagination all compact SHAKS. *attrib.* **l. asylum** (also **l. hospital**, †**house**), a hospital for the reception and treatment of lunatics.

Lunation (liunē¹·ʃən). ME. [ad. med.L. *lunationem*, f. *luna*; see -ATION.] 1. The time from one new moon to the next, a lunar month (about 29½ days). †2. The time of full moon -1686. 3. A menstruation (*rare*) 1822.

Lunch (lʊnʃ), *sb.* 1591. [Perh. f. LUMP *sb.*[1], on the analogy of *hump, hunch, bump, bunch.*] †1. A piece, a thick piece; a hunch -1785. 2. Colloq. for LUNCHEON *sb.* 2. (Now the usual word exc. in formal use.) 1829.

2. *U.S.* A light repast taken at any time in the twenty-four hours. Hence **Lunch** *v. intr.* to take l. 1823; *trans.* (*colloq.*) to provide l. for 1892.

Luncheon (lʊ·nʃən), *sb.* 1580. [Perh. extended from *lunch*, after *punch, puncheon*, etc.] †1. = LUNCH *sb.* 1. -1824. 2. Orig., a slight repast taken between two meal-times, *esp.* in the morning. Still so applied by those who dine at midday; with others, *luncheon* denotes a less ceremonious midday meal than dinner. Now somewhat *formal.* 1652.

1. A large l. of brown bread H. BROOKE. 2. *U.S.* (cf. LUNCH *sb.* 2 quots.). *attrib.* A l. bar 1891. L.-baskets 1903. Hence **Lu·ncheon** *v. intr.* to lunch.

Lundyfoot (lʊ·ndifut). 1811. [f. *Lundy Foot*, a Dublin tobacconist.] A kind of snuff.

Lune[1] (liūn). 1470. [var. of LOYN.] *Hawking.* A leash for a hawk.

Lune[2] (liūn). *arch.* 1611. [ad. med.L. *luna* lit. 'moon', hence 'fit of lunacy', whence F. *lune*, G. *laune.*] *pl.* Fits of lunacy; mad freaks or tantrums.

Lune[3] (liūn). 1704. [a. F. *lune*:—L. *luna.*] 1. *Geom.* The figure formed on a sphere or on a plane by two arcs of circles that enclose a space. 2. Anything in the shape of a crescent or half-moon 1706.

Lunel (liune·l). 1770. [f. *Lunel* (Hérault) a town in France.] A sweet muscat wine. Also *l.-wine.*

Lunette (liune·t). †Also **lunet(t.** 1580. [a. F. *lunette*, dim. of *lune* moon.] †1. A little moon, a satellite. BP. HALL. †2. The figure of a crescent moon -1787. 3. *Farriery.* A horseshoe consisting of the front semicircular portion only. Also *l.-shoe.* 1580. 4. *Arch.* a. An arched aperture in a concave ceiling for the admission of light 1613. b. A crescent-shaped or semicircular space in a ceiling, dome, etc., decorated with paintings or sculptures; a piece of decoration filling this 1722. 5. *Fortif.* A work larger than a redan, consisting of two faces and two flanks 1704. 6. A blinker for a horse 1652. 7. †a. *pl.* Spectacles -1796. b. A kind of concavo-convex lens for spectacles 1855. 8. A watch-glass of flattened shape 1832. 9. In the guillotine, the circular hole for the victim's neck 1859. 10. *Glass-making.* A flue in the side of a furnace, to admit smoke and flame to the arch; a linnet-hole 1839. 11. A forked iron plate into which the stock of a field-gun carriage is inserted 1875. 12. *Eccl.* A circular crystal case to hold the consecrated Host 1890.

Lung (lʊŋ). [OE. *lungen* str. fem.; f. Teut. root **luŋg-* :—Indo-Eur. **lŋgh-* in Skr. *laghu-*, Gr. ἐλαφρός light; see LIGHT *a.*[1] (The lungs were so called because of their lightness; cf. LIGHTS.)] 1. Each of the two breathing organs in man and most vertebrates, placed within the cavity of the thorax, one on each side of the heart, and communicating with the trachea or windpipe. b. *transf.* and *fig.* 1651. 2. Applied to analogous organs in other animals 1889. †3. *pl.* One who blows the fire; a chemist's assistant -1663. 4. **Lungs of (the) oak, †oak-lungs** = LUNGWORT c. 1650.

1. Gentlemen,..of such sensible and nimble Lungs that they always vse to laugh at nothing SHAKS. b. *Lungs of* (*London*, etc.), open spaces within or adjacent to a city 1808.

Comb.: **l.-fever**, pneumonia; **-fish**, a fish having lungs as well as gills, a dipnoan; **-flower**, the Marsh Gentian (Gerarde); †**lung(s)-growing**, a disease in cattle, in which the lungs adhere to the side; so †**l.-grown** *a.*; **l. lichen** = LUNGWORT c; **-power**, power of voice; **-worm**, a parasite infesting the lungs of cattle.

Lunge, longe (lʊndʒ), *sb.*[1] 1607. [a. F. *longe* halter, var. of OF. *loigne* :—pop.L. **longea*, f. L. *longus* LONG *a.*] †1. *gen.* A thong, cord. TOPSELL. 2. A long rope used in training horses; it is fastened at one end to the horse's head and held at the other by the trainer, who causes the horse to canter in a circle 1720. 3. a. The use of the lunge in training horses. b. A circular exercising-ground in which the lunge is used. 1833.

Lunge (lʊndʒ), *sb.*[2] Also **lounge.** 1748. [Aphet. var. of ALLONGE[1].] 1. A thrust with a sword (spec. in *Fencing*) or other weapon. 2. A sudden forward movement; a plunge, rush 1873.

Lunge (lʊndʒ), *sb.*[3] *Amer.* Also **longe,** 'longe, 'lunge. 1882. [Short for *maskalonge*, etc., var. of MASKINONGE.] The Great Lake trout (*Salvelinus namaycush*).

Lunge (lʊndʒ), *v.*[1] Also **lounge.** 1735. [f. LUNGE *sb.*[2]] 1. *intr.* a. *Fencing.* To make a thrust with a foil or rapier. b. *Boxing.* To deliver a straightforward blow. 1809. c. quasi-*trans.* with cognate obj. To deliver (a kick, etc.); also with *out* 1735. 2. *trans.* To drive or thrust with or as with a lunge 1841. 3. *intr.* To move with a lunge; to make a sudden forward movement; to rush 1821.

1. c. The Mulligan..lunged out a kick THACKERAY.

Lunge, longe (lʊndʒ), *v.*[2] Also **lounge.** 1806. [f. LUNGE *sb.*[1]] 1. *trans.* To put (a horse) through his paces by the use of the lunge; to make a horse go round the lunge. 2. *intr.* Of the horse: To go round the lunge in a specified direction 1833.

Lunged (lʊŋd), *ppl. a.* 1693. [f. LUNG + -ED[2].] Having lungs, or something resembling lungs; as *small-, weak-l.*, etc.

Lungeous (lʊ·ndʒəs), *a.* *dial.* 1787. [f. LUNGE *sb.*[2] or *v.*[1] + -OUS.] Rough-mannered, violent (in play).

‖**Lungi** (lu·ngī). 1616. [Urdū (Pers.) *lungī*, f. *lung* of the same meaning.] A loin-cloth. Also, the material of this.

†**Lu·ngis.** 1560. [a. OF. *longis* :—L. *Longīnus*, apocryphal name of the centurion who pierced our Lord with a spear, pop. assoc. w. L. *longus* long.] a. A long, slim, awkward fellow; a lout. b. A laggard, a lingerer. -1706.

Lungwort (lʊ·ŋwɒɹt). [OE. *lungenwyrt*, f. *lungen* LUNG + *wyrt* WORT.] The Eng. name of various plants; *esp.* a. The boraginaceous plant *Pulmonaria officinalis* (Common Lungwort), having leaves with white spots (fancied to resemble the spots in a diseased lung) 1538. †b. The Great Mullein, *Verbascum Thapsus* -1706. c. A species of lichen (*Sticta pulmonacea* or *pulmonaria*), otherwise known as Lungs of Oak (see LUNG 4) and Tree Lungwort 1578.

Luniform (liū·nifǭɹm), *a.* 1826. [f. L. *luna* moon; see -FORM.] Moon-shaped; *spec.* in *Nat. Hist.*

Lunisolar (liū:ni,sōu·lăɹ), *a.* 1691. [f. L. *luna* + SOLAR.] *Astr.* Pertaining to the mutual relations of the sun and moon, or resulting from their combined action.

L. period: a cycle of 532 years (= 19×28, the numbers of years in the cycles of the moon and sun respectively). *L. year*: a year divided into lunar months, but whose average length is determined by the sun.

Lunistice (liū·nistis). 1650. [f. L. *luna* moon, after *solstice.*] *Astr.* The point or time at which the moon is furthest north or south in her monthly course.

Luniti·dal, *a.* 1851. [f. L. *luna* + TIDAL.] Pertaining to the movements of the tide dependent on the moon.

L. interval: the interval between the culmination of the moon and the time of high water.

Lunt (lɒnt), *sb. Sc.* 1550. [a. Du. *lont* a match.] 1. A slow match; also, a torch. 2. Smoke without flame, as that from a pipe. Also, hot vapour. 1785. Hence **Lunt** *v. intr.* to smoke, emit smoke; also, (of smoke) to curl; quasi-*trans.* to smoke (a pipe); *trans.* to kindle, light *up*.

‖**Lunula** (liū·niŭlă). 1571. [L., dim. of *luna*.] = LUNULE. Hence **Lu·nular** *a.* pertaining to or resembling a lunule, crescent-shaped 1727; †*sb.* a crescent-shaped figure 1570–1789. **Lu·nulate** (1760), **-ated** (1705) *adjs.* crescent-shaped; marked with crescent-shaped spots.

Lunule (liū·niul). 1737. [a. F., ad. L. *lunula*, dim. of *luna*.] *Nat. Hist.* and *Geom.* A crescent-shaped mark, body, or figure. So **Lu·nulet** *Nat. Hist.* a small lunule 1826.

Lunulite (liū·niŭləit). 1845. [ad. mod.L. *lunulites*; see LUNULA and -ITE [1].] *Geol.* A small fossil coral, more or less circular in shape.

Luny, var. of LOONY.

‖**Lupercal** (liū·pəɹkăl), *sb.* 1513. [L., subst. form of *lupercale*, neut. of *lupercalis* pertaining to Lupercus, the Roman Pan.] *Rom. Antiq.* 1. A grotto on the Palatine sacred to Lupercus. 2. A festival held annually in February in honour of Lupercus. Also *pl.* **Lupercalia.** 1600.

2. You all did see, that on the Lupercall, I thrice presented him a Kingly Crowne *Jul. C.* III. ii. 200. So †**Lupe·rcal** *a. rare*, pertaining to the Lupercal or Lupercalia 1607–56.

Lupine, lupin (liū·pin), *sb.* ME. [ad. L. *lupinus, lupinum*.] 1. Any plant of the leguminous genus *Lupinus*; in early use, chiefly *L. albus*, cultivated for the seed and for fodder; later, species of various colours cultivated in flower-gardens. 2. *pl.* The seed of this plant.

Lupine (liū·pəin), *a.* 1660. [ad. L. *lupinus*, f. *lupus* wolf.] Having the nature or qualities of a wolf.

Lupinin (liū·pinin). 1839. [ad. F. *lupinine*; see LUPINE *sb.* and -IN [1].] *Chem.* A bitter glucoside obtained from the seeds of *Lupinus albus*.

Lupulin (liū·piŭlin). 1826. [f. mod.L. *lupulus* hop + -IN [1].] 1. *Bot.* The resinous yellow powder found under the scales of the calyx of the hop. 2. *Chem.* The bitter principle obtained from this powder 1839. Hence **Lupuli·nic** *a.* relating to lupulin.

‖**Lupus** (liū·pɒs). 1590. [L., = wolf.] 1. *Med.* A disease of the skin, usually tubercular and ulcerous, eating into the substance and leaving deep scars. 2. *Astr.* The Wolf, a constellation south of Scorpio 1706. 3. The pike or luce 1706. Hence **Lu·pous** *a.* pertaining to or affected with l. 1883.

Lurch (lɒ̄ɹtʃ), *sb.*[1] 1533. [a. F. *lourche* (erron. *l'ourche*) a game like backgammon; also used as adj. in the phr. *demeurer lourche*.] †1. A game supposed to have resembled backgammon –1693. 2. Used in some games to denote a state of the score in which the winner is far ahead of the loser; often, a 'maiden set' or love-game; at cribbage, a game in which the winner scores 61 before the loser has scored 31; in whist, a treble. Now *rare* or *Obs.* 1570. 3. Discomfiture; disadvantage. *Obs.* exc. in phr. *to leave in the l.*, to leave in adverse circumstances without assistance. 1584. †4. [f. LURCH *v.*[1] 2] A cheat, swindle –1616.

2. Phr. *To save the l.*: in whist, to prevent one's adversary from scoring a treble. 3. Phr. †*To give* (a person) *the l.*: to get the better of.

Lurch (lɒ̄ɹtʃ), *sb.*[2] 1568. [f. LURCH *v.*[1]] 1. An act of lurching or getting the start in obtaining food, profit, etc. 2. phr. *To lie at* (*on, upon the*) *l.*: to lie concealed; to lie in wait 1578.

Lurch (lɒ̄ɹtʃ), *sb.*[3] 1819. [?] 1. (Orig. *Naut.*) A sudden leaning over to one side, as of a ship, a person staggering, etc. Also, a lurching gait. 2. *U.S.* A propensity, leaning 1854.

1. Here the ship gave a l., and he grew sea-sick BYRON.

Lurch (lɒ̄ɹtʃ), *v.*[1] ME. [app. a var. of LURK *v.*] †1. *intr.* To remain in or about a place furtively –1790. b. Of a greyhound: To run cunning, and let the opponent do the work 1824. 2. *trans.* To get the start of (a person) so as to prevent him from obtaining a fair share of food, profit, etc. Later, to defraud, cheat, rob. *arch.* 1530. †3. To be beforehand in securing (something); to engross, monopolize (commodities); later, to pilfer, filch, steal –1660. 4. To catch (rabbits) by means of lurchers 1727.

1. I my selfe..am faine to shuffle, to hedge, and to l. SHAKS. 2. You haue lurch'd your friends of the better halfe of the garland B. JONS. 3. *absol.* Wherein had he been a thiefe, if he had not..meant to l. out of the common Treasury? BP. HALL.

Lurch (lɒ̄ɹtʃ), *v.*[2] ME. [f. LURCH *sb.*[1]] 1. *trans.* To defeat by a lurch, as in cribbage, etc. (see LURCH *sb.*[1] 2). †b. *fig.* To defeat 1716–1829. †2. To leave in the lurch, disappoint, deceive 1651–1810.

Lurch (lɒ̄ɹtʃ), *v.*[3] (Orig. *Naut.*) 1833. [f. LURCH *sb.*[3]] 1. *intr.* Of a ship, etc.: To make a lurch; to lean suddenly over to one side; to move with lurches. 2. To move suddenly, unsteadily, and without purpose in any direction; to stagger 1851.

1. The boat lurched through the breakers like a log 1845. 2. Where the tipsy trainband-man is lurching against the post THACKERAY.

Lurcher (lɒ̄·ɹtʃəɹ). 1528. [f. LURCH *v.*[1] + -ER [1].] †1. One who forestalls others of their fair share of food; hence, a glutton –1616. 2. One who filches in a mean fashion; a petty thief, swindler, rogue 1528. 3. One who loiters or lies hidden in a suspicious manner; a spy 1706. 4. A cross-bred dog, properly between the collie and the greyhound; much used by poachers for catching hares and rabbits 1668. b. *slang.* A bumbailiff 1785.

Lurdan (lɒ̄·ɹdăn). *arch.* or *Sc.* and *dial.* ME. [a. OF. *lourdin*, f. *lourd* heavy; see LOURD.] A. *sb.* A term of abuse; a sluggard, vagabond, loafer. B. *adj.* Worthless, ill-bred, lazy ME.

Lure (liūᵊɹ), *sb.*[1] ME. [a. OF. *leurre, loerre, loire*, cogn. w. It. *logoro* bait; prob. of Teut. origin; cf. G. *luder* bait.] 1. An apparatus used by falconers to recall their hawks, being a bunch of feathers attached to a cord, within which, during its training, the hawk finds its food 1440. 2. *Her.* A representation of this, consisting of two birds' wings with the points downwards, and joined above by a ring attached to a cord 1572. 3. (orig. *fig.*) Something which allures, entices, or tempts ME. 4. A means of alluring animals to be captured; in *Angling* a more general term than *bait* 1700. ¶b. Erron.: A trap or snare (*fig.*) 1463. 5. The cry of a falconer recalling his hawk; *fig.* any alluring cry 1653.

1. As Faulcons to the l., away she flies SHAKS. Phr. *To alight on the l., to bring, call, come, stoop to* (*the* or *one's*) *l.* 3. How many have with a smile made small account Of beauty and her lures? MILT.

Lure (liūᵊɹ), *sb.*[2] *techn.* Also **lewer.** 1858. [Shortened from VELURE.] A pad of silk or velvet used by hatters for smoothing.

Lure (liūᵊɹ), *v.* ME. [f. LURE *sb.*[1]] 1. *trans.* To recall (a hawk) by casting the lure; to call (a hawk) to the lure. 2. *intr.* To call to a hawk while casting the lure 1530; †to call loudly –1626. 3. To allure, entice, tempt ME.

3. Lured into a snare by treachery 1855.

Lurg (lɒ̄ɹg). *local.* 1880. [Cf. LUG *sb.*[3]] A British marine worm used for bait; the white-rag worm.

Lurid (liūᵊ·rid), *a.* 1656. [ad. L. *luridus*.] 1. Pale and dismal in colour; wan; ghastly of hue. 2. Shining with a red glow or glare amid darkness 1727. 3. *fig.* (from 1 or 2), with connotation of 'terrible', 'ominous', 'ghostly', 'sensational'; also, marked by violent passion or crime 1850. 4. In scientific use: Of a dingy-brown or yellowish-brown colour 1767.

1. A leaden glare..makes the snow and ice more l. SYMONDS. 2. At night also the l. reflection of immense fires hung in the sky W. IRVING. A softness gathered over the l. fires of her eye 1852. 3. He adds one fact more which casts a l. light on the annals of the persecution 1879. Hence **Lu·rid·ly** *adv.*, **-ness.**

Lurk (lɒ̄ɹk), *sb.* 1829. [f. LURK *v.*] 1. The action of prowling about. In phr. *on the l.* 2. *slang.* A method of fraud 1851.

2. The 'bereavement lurk' is a lucrative one—(i.e.) the pretended loss of a wife [etc.] 1875.

Lurk (lɒ̄ɹk), *v.* Now *literary.* ME. [app. f. *lur-* LOUR *v.* with freq. suffix as in *tal-k*. Cf. LG. *lurken* to shuffle along, Norw. *lurka* to sneak away, etc.] 1. *intr.* To hide oneself; to lie in ambush. (Now only with indication of place.) †b. To shirk work; to idle –1792. 2. *transf.* and *fig.* Of things: To escape observation, to be concealed or latent ME. 3. To move about furtively; to steal *along, away, out.* Now *rare.* ME.

1. Shaftesbury..had left his house and secretly lurked in the city HUME. 2. The Vices that l. in the secret Corners of the Soul ADDISON.

Lurry (lɒ·ri). *Obs.* exc. *dial.* 1580. [Short f. LIRIPOOP.] 1. Something said by rote; a lesson, set speech, 'patter'; *fig.* a cant formula. 2. A confusion of voices; babel, hubbub 1649. 3. A confused assemblage (of persons) or mass (of things) 1607.

1. Then was the Priest set to con his motions, and his Postures, his Liturgies, and his Lurries MILT.

Lurry: see LORRY.

Luscious (lɒ·ʃəs), *a.* ME. [perh. aphetic f. DELICIOUS.] 1. Sweet and highly pleasant in taste or smell. 2. Sweet to excess, cloying, sickly 1530. 3. Of immaterial things, esp. of language, literary style, etc.: Sweet and highly pleasing to the eye, ear, or mind. Chiefly dyslogistic. 1651. †4. Of tales, talk, writing, etc.: Lascivious, voluptuous, wanton –1815.

1. L. woodbine SHAKS. The most l. fruits JOHNSON. *fig.* The l. sweets of sin BOYLE. 3. A l. Style stuffed with gawdy Metaphors and Fancy 1738. The groups of children,..l. in colour and faint in light RUSKIN. Hence **Lu·scious·ly** *adv.*, **-ness.**

Luser(a)n, var. of LUCERN [1].

Lush (lɒʃ), *sb. slang.* 1790. [? suggested by LUSH *a.*] Liquor, drink; a drinking bout. Hence **Lu·shy** *a.* drunk.

Lush (lɒʃ), *a.* 1440. [? altered f. LASH *a.*] 1. Lax, flaccid; soft, tender. *Obs.* exc. *dial.* 2. Of grass, etc.: Succulent and luxuriant in growth 1610. Also *fig.* b. Of a season: Of luxuriant vegetation 1818. ¶3. Erron. applied to colour (a misapprehension of Shakspere's use): Deep, not pale and faint 1744.

2. How l. and lusty the grasse lookes SHAKS. In the warm hedge grew l. eglantine SHELLEY. 3. The l. rose lingers late T. MARTIN.

Lush (lɒʃ), *v. slang.* 1811. [f. LUSH *sb.*] 1. *trans.* To ply with 'lush' or drink 1821. 2. *intr.* and *trans.* To drink 1811. Hence **Lush·ing** *vbl. sb.* (in *pl.* abundance; cf. *lashings*).

†**Lu·shburg.** ME. [Anglicized name of Luxemburg.] An imitation of the English silver penny, imported from Luxemburg in the reign of Edward III. Also *L. sterling.* –1716.

God woot no lussheburgh payen ye CHAUCER.

Lusitanian (liūsitēⁱ·niăn). 1607. [f. L. *Lusitania* (see below) + -AN.] A. *adj.* Of or belonging to Lusitania, an ancient name of the region roughly corresponding to modern Portugal; hence (usu. *poet.*), of or pertaining to Portugal 1720. B. *sb.* An inhabitant of Lusitania; hence, a Portuguese.

†**Lusk**, *sb.* ME. [f. LUSK *v.*] A lazy fellow; a sluggard –1694. Hence **Lusk** *a.* lazy, sluggish 1775. †**Lu·skish** *a.* 1530, **-ly** *adv.*, **-ness.**

†**Lusk**, *v.* ME. [Cf. OHG. *loscên*.] *intr.* To lie hid; to lie idly or at ease, skulk –1662.

Lusory (liū·səri), *a.* 1653. [ad. L. *lusorius* belonging to a player (f. *lusor*) + -OUS.] Used as a pastime; of the nature of play; written in a playful style.

A refined species of comic poetry,—l. yet elegant D'ISRAELI. So †**Luso·rious** *a.* 1613–1697.

Lust (lɒst), *sb.* Now *literary* [Com. Teut.: OE. *lust* masc.:—OTeut. **lustu-z.* Cf. Du., G. *lust.*] †1. Pleasure, delight; also, a source of pleasure –1607. †2. Desire, appetite, relish or inclination for something –1627. †b. (One's) desire or wish; (one's) good pleasure –1677. 3. *spec.* in Biblical and Theol. use: Sensuous appetite or desire, as sinful OE.

4. Sexual appetite or desire. Now only: Libidinous desire, degrading animal passion. (The chief current use.) OE. 5. In mod. rhet. use: Lawless and passionate desire *of* or *for* some object. In poetry occas.: Overmastering desire (esp. of battle). 1678. †6. Vigour, lustiness; fertility (of soil) –1682.

1. Litle leysure, and lesse l., either to heare Sermons or to read bookes FOXE. 3. Phr. *The lusts of the flesh, fleshly lusts.* 4. He never spared man in his anger, nor woman in his l. NAUNTON. 5. A l. of power 1786, of applause H. WALPOLE, of accumulation RUSKIN.

Lust (lvst), *v. literary* and *arch.* ME. [f. LUST *sb.*] †1. *trans.* To please, delight (also *absol.*). ME. only. †2. *intr.* To desire, choose, wish –1618. 3. To have a strong, excessive, or inordinate desire (*arch.*) 1530. b. *spec.* of sexual desire 1526.

3 If we be an hungred, we l. for bread 1563. b. Yet dost thou l. after the daughter of our despised race LYTTON. Hence **Lu·ster**, one who lusts. A l. after power C. BRONTË.

Luster, obs. and U.S. f. LUSTRE.

Lustful (lv·stfŭl), *a.* [OE. *lustfull*; see LUST *sb.* and -FUL.] 1. Having a strong or excessive desire (for something). Also with *of* or *to do. Obs.* or *arch.* 2. Vigorous, lusty (*arch.*) 1561. 3. Full of or characterized by lust; pertaining to or manifesting sensual desire; libidinous 1579. †4. Provocative of lust –1667.

2. This want of lustfull health 1561. 3. Bred..to the taste Of l. appetence MILT. 4. Not all the l. Shell-fish of the Sea [etc.] COWLEY. Hence **Lu·stful-ly** *adv.*, **-ness.**

†**Lu·stick**, *a.* and *adv.* Also **-ique.** 1601. [a. Du. *lustig.*] a. *adj.* Merry, jolly; chiefly with reference to drinking. b. *adv.* Merrily, jovially. –1691.

Lustihood (lv·stihud). *arch.* 1599. [f. LUSTY + -HOOD.] Lustiness, vigour of body; †lustfulness. So **Lu·stihead** [-HEAD] ME., now *arch.*

Lustily (lv·stili), *adv.* ME. [f. LUSTY + -LY [2].] In a lusty or vigorous manner; †lustfully –1589.

Lustiness (lv·stinės). ME. [f. LUSTY + -NESS.] †Pleasure, delight –1550; vigour ME.; †lustfulness, libidinousness –1619.

Lustless (lv·stlės), *a.* Now *rare* or *Obs.* ME. [-LESS.] †1. Without vigour or energy, listless –1612. †2. Joyless –1586. 3. Without lust or sexual appetite 1586.

Lustra, pl. of LUSTRUM.

Lustral (lv·străl), *a.* 1533. [ad. L. *lustralis*, f. *lustrum.*] 1. Pertaining to the Roman lustrum or purificatory sacrifice; hence, purificatory. 2. Quinquennial 1781.

1. The assistants were sprinkled with l. water GIBBON.

Lustrate (lv·strēɪt), *v.* 1623. [f. L. *lustrat-*, *lustrare* to purify by lustral rites, to go round, survey, etc., f. *lustrum*; see LUSTRUM.] 1. *trans.* To purify by a propitiatory offering; *gen.* to purify 1653. †2. a. *intr.* To pass or go *through* (a place). b. *trans.* To pass through or traverse. –1721. †3. *trans.* To view, survey –1648.

1. There was..a great Plague; the Oracle advis'd them to l. the City 1655. Hence **Lu·strative** *a.* pertaining to lustration, purification, or (*joc.*) washing. **Lu·stratory** *a.* (*rare*), lustral, expiatory.

Lustration (lvstrē·ʃən). 1614. [ad. L. *lustrationem.*] 1. The action of lustrating; the performance of an expiatory sacrifice or a purificatory rite. b. *gen.* Washing. Chiefly *joc.* 1825. 2. *fig.* Purification, *esp* spiritual or moral 1655. 3. The action of going round, viewing, or surveying a place; the review (of an army) 1614. Now *rare.* †4. An inspection, census. SIR T. BROWNE. *rare.* 5. = LUSTRE *sb.*[2] F. W. NEWMAN. *rare.*

1. Signatures of the cross, and lustrations by holy water TUCKER. 2. Let them [the prelates] perform a l.; let them purify..this country from this sin CHATHAM.

Lustre (lv·stəɪ), *sb.*[1] Formerly (still *U.S.*) luster. 1522. [a. F. *lustre* masc.; Com. Rom. sb. f. L. *lustrare* to illumine.] 1. The quality of shining by reflected light; sheen, refulgence; gloss. Often with adj., as *metallic, pearly, silky, waxy l.* b. rarely in *pl.* Appearances of lustre 1614. c. A composition used to impart a lustre to manufactured articles 1727. 2. Luminosity, brilliancy, bright light 1549; *concr.* a shining body or form 1742. 3. *transf.* Radiant beauty or splendour (of the countenance, of natural objects, etc.) 1602. 4. *fig.*, esp. Brilliance or splendour of renown; glory. Also, splendid beauty (of language, etc.). 1555. †b. Something that adds lustre; a glory –1647. †c. External splendour –1674. 5. a. One of the prismatic glass pendants attached to a chandelier, etc. b. A chandelier [the usual sense in Fr.]. 1716. 6. A thin light dress material having a cotton (formerly also silk or linen) warp and woollen weft and a lustrous surface 1831.

1. All stones of l. shoot their vivid ray GRAY. 2. And now the scorching Sun was mounted high, In all its l. ADDISON. 3. Virgins are like the fair flower in its l. GAY. 4. The pomp and l. of his language J. WARTON. Mythical l. illumined all the historic facts of Abraham's life 1874. c. Solemnizing Nativities and Deaths with equal L. SIR T. BROWNE.

Comb.: **l. mottling**, the peculiar mottling seen in pœcilitic rocks; **l. ware**, cheap pottery with surface ornamentation in bright metallic colours. Hence **Lu·streless** *a.*

Lustre (lv·stəɪ), *sb.*[2] Formerly (still *U.S.*) luster. ME. [Anglicized f. L. *lustrum.*] A period of five years.

Come eight more lustres, and your heads will be bald like mine THACKERAY.

†**Lu·stre**, *v.*[1] *rare.* 1541. [ad. L. *lustrare.*] = LUSTRATE *v.* 1, 3. –1645.

Lustre (lv·stəɪ), *v.*[2] 1582. [ad. L. *lustrare*; see LUSTRE *sb.*[1]] †1. *trans.* a. To render illustrious. b. To illustrate. c. To make specious or attractive. –1644. 2. *intr.* To be or become lustrous. Now *rare.* 1582. 3. *trans.* To put a lustre upon (cloth, pottery, etc.) 1883.

Lustring (lv·striŋ). *Obs.* exc. *arch.* (See also LUTESTRING [2].) 1697. [Alteration of F. *lustrine*, as if f. LUSTRE *sb.*[1] + -ING [1] or -ING [3].] A glossy silk fabric. var. **Lu·strine** 1851.

Lustrous (lv·strəs), *a.* 1601. [f. LUSTRE *sb.*[1] + -OUS.] Having lustre, sheen, or gloss.

Where beauty cannot keep her l. eyes KEATS. Hence **Lu·strous-ly** *adv.*, **-ness.**

‖**Lustrum.** *Pl.* **lustra, lustrums.** 1590. [L., prob. f. root of *luere* to wash.] 1. *Rom. Antiq.* A purificatory sacrifice made quinquennially, after the census had been taken 1598. 2. A period of five years 1590.

Lusty (lv·sti), *a.* Now *dial.* or *rare arch.* ME. [f. LUST *sb.* + -Y [1]. Cf. G. *lustig.*] †1. Joyful, merry; lively –1621. †2. Pleasing, pleasant. Of persons: Gaily dressed. -1610. †3. Full of desire, desirous –1657. †4. Full of sexual desire; lustful –1697. 5. Full of healthy vigour; strong ME. †6. Insolent, arrogant, self-confident –1674. †7. Of a fire, wine, poison, a disease, etc.: Strong, powerful –1692. †b. Of a ship: Sailing well –1669. 8. Of actions: Vigorous. Of a meal, etc.: Hearty, abundant. 1672. †9. Massive, substantial, large –1842. 10. Of persons: Massively built. Hence, corpulent, fat 1772.

5. A mery herte maketh a l. age COVERDALE *Prov.* xvii. 22. Like a l. flower in June's caress KEATS. *transf.* The l. young democracy BLACKIE. 8. The Turk..gave him two or three l. kicks on the seat of honour BURKE.

‖**Lusus naturæ** (l[i]ū·sŏs nē·tiū·rī). Also simply lusus. 1661. [L., = a sport of nature.] A sport or freak of nature; a markedly abnormal natural production.

Lutanist, lutenist (l[i]ū·tănist, -ĕnist). 1600. [ad. med.L. *lutanista*, f. *lutana* lute.] A lute-player.

†**Luta·rious**, *a.* [f. L. *lutarius* (f. *lutum* mud) + -OUS.] Inhabiting mud. GREW. So †**Lu·tary** *a.* (*rare*) 1661.

†**Luta·tion.** 1611. [f. L. *lutare* LUTE *v.*[2]] The process of luting; the material used in luting –1657.

Lute (l[i]ūt), *sb.*[1] ME. [a. OF. *lut* (now *luth*); a. Arab. *al-ʿūd*, where *al-* is the def. art. Cf. Pg. *alaude.*] A stringed musical instrument, formerly much in vogue, the strings of which were struck with the fingers of the right hand and stopped on the frets with the left. b. The name of a stop in some forms of the harpsichord 1879.

Comb.: **l.-backed** *a.*, having a back shaped like a l.; **-pin**, one of the pegs or screws for turning the strings of the l.

Lute (l[i]ūt), *sb.*[2] ME. [ad. OF. *lut* (F. *lut*) or med.L. (use of L. *lutum* mud).] 1. Tenacious clay or cement, used to stop an orifice, to make a joint air-tight, to coat a retort, etc., and to protect a graft. †2. Mud –1756. 3. A packing-ring of india-rubber for making jars airtight 1875.

Lute (l[i]ūt), *sb.*[3] *U.S.* 1875. [a. Du. *loet.*] *Brickmaking.* A straight-edged piece of wood for scraping off superfluous clay from a brick-mould.

Lute (l[i]ūt), *v.*[1] Now *rare.* ME. [f. LUTE *sb.*[1]] a. *intr.* To play on the lute; quasi-*trans.* to express by means of the lute. b. *intr.* To sound like a lute. KEATS.

a. Thanne luted Loue in a loude note, *Ecce quam bonum et quam iocundum, etc.* LANGL.

Lute (l[i]ūt), *v.*[2] late ME. [ad. L. *lutare* (F. *luter*), f. *lutum*; see LUTE *sb.*[2]] *trans.* To close, seal, or cover with lute; to fasten or fix with lute.

Before they distill, luting the Limbeck 1594. The lids were luted down 1879.

Luteic (l[i]utī·ik), *a.* 1892. [f. L. *luteus* yellow + -IC.] *Chem.* In *l. acid*: a yellow colouring matter prepared from the flowers of *Euphorbia Cyparissias.*

Lutein (l[i]ū·tīin). Also **-ine.** 1869. [f. L. *luteum* yolk of egg (neut. of *luteus* yellow) + -IN [1].] *Chem.* A substance of a deep yellow colour found in the yolk of eggs and the ovaries of animals.

Lutenist: see LUTANIST.

Luteo- (l[i]ū·tīo), used as comb. f. L. *luteus* LUTEOUS, signifying the presence of a yellow colour with some other. **Lu:teo-coba·ltic** *a.* *Chem.*, containing a compound of cobalt with a yellow colour. **Lu:teo-fu·lvous** *a.* *Bot.*, of a tawny yellow colour.

Luteolin (l[i]ū·tīŏlin). Also **-ine.** 1839. [ad. F. *lutéolin*, f. mod.L. (*reseda*) *luteola* weld.] *Chem.* The yellow colouring matter of weld (*Reseda luteola*).

Luteous (l[i]ū·tīəs), *a.* 1657. [f. L. *luteus* (f. *lutum* yellow weed) + -OUS.] *Nat. Hist.* Of a deep orange yellow colour.

Luter (l[i]ū·təɪ). *Obs.* exc. *Hist.* 1474. [f. LUTE *v.*[1] + -ER [1].] A lute-player.

Lutescent (l[i]ute·sĕnt), *a.* 1819. [f. L. *luteus* yellow + -ESCENT.] *Nat. Hist.* Inclining to yellow.

Lu·te-string [1]. 1530. [f. LUTE *sb.*[1] + STRING *sb.*] 1. A string of a lute. 2. A noctuid moth having lines resembling the strings of a lute on its wings 1819.

Lutestring [2] (l[i]ū·tstriŋ). 1471. [Origin obscure. Cf. LUSTRING.] A kind of glossy silk fabric; a dress or a ribbon of this.

Lutheran (l[i]ū·þərăn). 1521. [f. proper name *Luther* + -AN.] A. *adj.* Pertaining to Martin Luther (1483–1546), his opinions and followers. (In 16th c. used by Roman Catholics as coextensive with PROTESTANT. Now chiefly applied to doctrinal views peculiar to Luther, and to churches which accept the Augsburg Confession.) 1530. B. *sb.* A follower of Luther; an adherent of his doctrines; a member of the Lutheran church 1521.

B. I know her for A spleeny L. SHAKS. Hence **Lu·theranism**, the body of L. doctrine; the holding of L. opinions 1560. **Lu·theranize** *v.* to make or become L. 1845. var. †**Luthe·rian** *a.* and *sb.* 1526–89.

Lutherism (l[i]ū·þeriz'm). 1695. [f. *Luther* + -ISM.] a. = LUTHERANISM. b. Something characteristic of Luther, or done or said in imitation of him.

Luthern (l[i]ū·þəɪn). 1669. [? corrupt f. LUCARNE.] A dormer-window. Also *l.-light*, *-window.*

Lutist (l[i]ū·tist). 1627. [f. LUTE *sb.*[1] + -IST.] A lute-player. Also, a maker of lutes.

Lutose (l[i]ū·tōus), *a.* 1826. [ad. L. *lutosus*, f. *lutum* mud.] Covered with mud; miry. So **Luto·sity** 1650.

Lutulent (l[i]ū·tiŭlĕnt), *a. rare.* 1600. [ad. L. *lutulentus*, f. *lutum.*] Muddy, turbid. Hence **Lu·tulence** (*rare*), muddiness; mud, dirt 1727.

†**Lux**, *v.* 1708. [ad. F. *luxer*, ad. L. *luxare*; see LUXATE *v.*] = LUXATE *v.* –1775.

†**Lu·xate**, *ppl. a.* 1597. [ad. L. *luxatus*; see next.] Luxated –1661.

Luxate (lʊ·kseⁱt), *v.* 1623. [f. L. *luxat-*, *luxare*, f. *luxus* dislocated, a. Gr. λοξός.] *trans.* To dislocate, put out of joint. So **Luxa·tion** *Surg.*, dislocation 1552.

Luxe. 1558. [a. F., ad. L. *luxus*.] †1. Luxury –1746. ‖2. As Fr.: Luxuriousness, sumptuous elegance; esp. in *édition de luxe*, *train de luxe* 1819.

Luxuriance (lʊgziūᵊ·riǎns, -ʒū-, lʊksiūᵊ·riǎns). 1728. [f. LUXURIANT; see -ANCE.] The condition of being luxuriant; superabundant growth or development; exuberance. Also quasi-*concr.*

The faults which grow out of the l. of freedom BURKE. So **Luxu·riancy** (now *rare*) 1648.

Luxuriant (lʊgziūᵊ·riǎnt, -ʒū-, lʊksiūᵊ·riǎnt), *a.* 1540. [ad. L. *luxuriantem*, pres. pple. of *luxuriare*, f. *luxuria* luxury.] 1. Producing abundantly, prolific. Now *rare.* 2. Of plants, etc.: Growing profusely, exuberant, rank 1661. b. *spec.* in *Bot.* Applied where the organs of nutrition are more developed than those of fructification 1760. 3. Exuberantly productive, as genius, fancy, etc.; profuse, excessive, as speech, action, etc.; (of ornamentation) excessively rich 1625. ¶4. Misused for LUXURIOUS 1671.

1. The growth of the l. year POPE. 2. Wit's like a L. Vine COWLEY. 3. The irish jig, which they can dance with a most l. expression A. YOUNG. The l. (= excessively prosperous) great ones of the world GOLDSM. Hence **Luxu·riantly** *adv.*

Luxuriate (lʊgziūᵊ·rieⁱt, -ʒū-, lʊksiūᵊ·rieⁱt), *v.* 1621. [f. L. *luxuriat-*, *luxuriare*; see prec.] 1. *intr.* Of a plant: To grow rank. Now *rare.* Also *fig.* †Of a writer: To write at exuberant length. †b. *fig.* To grow or develop exuberantly *into* (error, folly, etc.) 1651–1808. 2. To indulge in luxury; to feast, enjoy oneself. Now only with *in*, *on.* 1621. b. To take great delight, revel *in* (something) 1650.

1. The vineyards hereabouts are..left to l. 1832. 2. A huge crocodile luxuriating in the slime 1832. b. The Oriental mind..luxuriates in dreams 1880. Hence **Luxuria·tion** 1839.

†**Luxuriety.** [f. LUXURIOUS, after *variety*, etc.] Luxuriance. STERNE.

Luxurious (lʊgziūᵊ·riəs, -ʒū-, lʊksiūᵊ·riəs), *a.* ME. [ad. OF. *luxurius* (mod.F. *luxurieux*), ad. L. *luxuriosus*; see LUXURY and -OUS.] †1. Lascivious, lecherous, unchaste –1697. †2. Outrageous, extravagant, excessive –1665. 3. a. Of persons, etc.: Given to luxury or self-indulgence 1606. b. Of things: Of or pertaining to luxury; characterized by luxury 1650. ¶4. = LUXURIANT 2. Now *rare.* 1644.

3. a. Corinth..was..excessively proud and l. 1691. b. L. wealth MILT., provisions 1879. 4. L. Vines 1653, grass 1801. Hence **Luxu·rious·ly** *adv.*, **-ness.**

Lu·xurist. *Obs.* or *arch.* 1689. [f. LUXURY + -IST.] One addicted to luxury.

Luxury (lʊ·kʃŭri, lʊ·ksiŭri). ME. [a. OF. *luxurie*, ad. L. *luxuria*, f. *luxus* abundance, etc.] †1. Lasciviousness, lust; *pl.* lusts –1812. †2. = LUXURIANCE 1611–1695. 3. Habitual use of what is choice or costly, whether food, dress, furniture, or appliances 1633. 4. *transf.* Refined and intense enjoyment 1715. 5. quasi-*concr.* Sumptuous and exquisite food or surroundings 1704. b. Something which conduces to enjoyment over and above the necessaries of life. Hence, now, something which is desirable but not indispensable. 1780. 6. *abstr.* Luxuriousness 1849.

1. Grov'lling in the sty..of shameless l. CRABBE. 3. I never knew or want or luxurie P. FLETCHER. 4. And learn the l. of doing good GOLDSM. 5. Tables covered with l. JOHNSON. 6. Necessaries come always before luxuries BENTHAM.

LXX. 1662. The Roman numeral symbol for Seventy; hence, abbrev. for SEPTUAGINT.

-ly, *suffix* [1], appended to sbs. to form adjs., represents OE. *-lĭc*:—OTeut. *-lĭko-*, from the sb. **lĭkom* appearance, form, body (see LICH). The primitive force of the suffix is therefore 'having the appearance or form indicated by the first element of the word'.

The most general senses of the suffix are 'having the qualities appropriate to', 'characteristic of', 'befitting'; e.g. *beastly*, *beggarly*, *cowardly*, *kingly*, *scholarly*, *soldierly*. Another use is to form adjs. denoting periodic recurrence, as *daily*, *hourly*, *yearly*, etc.

-ly, *suffix* [2], forming advs., represents OE. *-lĭce*, derived from *-lĭko-* (see -LY [1]) with an adverb-forming suffix *-ô*, repr. the ending of the abl. fem. (pre-Teut. *-ād*) or neut. (pre-Teut. *-ōd*); or, according to others, that of the instrumental neut. (pre-Teut. *-ōm*).

In OTeut. an adv. with this suffix must have implied the existence of an adj. with the suffix corresponding to -LY [1]. In OE., however, there are instances (e.g. *bealdlīce* boldly, *swētlīce* sweetly) in which an adv. has been formed from a simple adj. without the intervention of an adj. in *-lic*, and this became the regular mode of forming an adv. of manner. Down to the 17th c., *-ly* was frequently attached even to adjs. in *-ly*, as *godlily*, *kindlily*, *lowlily*, *statelily*; but these formations are now generally avoided by recourse to some periphrastic form of expression. In *daily*, *hourly*, etc., the adj. and the adv. are identical in form. *Partly* and *purposely* are examples of an adv. f. sb. + *-ly* [2] with no related adj. Advs. in *-ly* were in several cases app. formed in ME. in imitation of OF. adverbs in *-ment*, before the corresponding adjective existed in English. Since the 16th c. the suffix has been added to ordinal numerals to form advs. denoting serial position, as *firstly*, *secondly*, etc., after F. *premièrement*, etc.

When *-ly* is attached to a disyllabic or polysyllabic adj. in *-le*, the word is contracted, as *ably*, *simply*, etc.; monosyllables in *-le* retain the *e* in writing, as *solely*; *wholly* is peculiar. Adjs. of more than one syll. ending in *y* change *y* to *i* bef. *-ly*, as *merrily*; in formations from monosyllabic adjs. the usage varies, e.g. *slily*, *slyly*. In *duly*, *truly*, the *e* is dropped. Adjs. in *-ic* nearly always form advs. in -ICALLY.

Lyam (ləi·ăm), **lyme** (ləim). *Obs.* exc. *Hist.* ME. [a. OF. *liem* (mod.F. *lien*):—L. *ligamen*. Cf. LIEN.] 1. A leash for hounds, or (*Her.*) a representation of this. 2. Short for LYAM-HOUND 1486.

Lyam-hound, lyme-hound. *Obs.* exc. *Hist.* 1527. [f. LYAM + HOUND.] A blood-hound. Also *fig.*

Lyard, lyart, *a.* *Obs.* exc. *dial.* ME. [a. OF. *liart.*] Grey, silvery grey approaching white. Applied by Burns to the colour of withered leaves.

The bandsters are lyart and runkled and grey MISS ELLIOT.

Lycanthropy (ləikæ·nþrŏpi). 1594. [ad. Gr. λυκανθρωπία, f. λυκάνθρωπος lit. wolf-man, f. λύκος + ἄνθρωπος.] 1. A kind of insanity in which the patient imagines himself to be a wolf, or, loosely, a beast of any kind. 2. The kind of witchcraft in which human beings were supposed to assume the form and nature of wolves 1830.

Hence **Lycanthrope** (ləi·kænþrōᵘp, ləikæ·nþrəp), one afflicted with l. 1621; also used as a synonym of werewolf 1831. **Lycanthro·pic** *a.* of, belonging to, or suffering from l. 1829. **Lyca·nthropist**, a lycanthrope 1727.

‖**Lycée** (lise). 1865. [F., ad. L. *Lyceum* (see next).] In France, a secondary school maintained by the State, as dist. from a *collège* or secondary school maintained by a municipality.

Lyceum (ləisī·ŏm). Also *erron.* **Lycæum.** 1579. [a. L. *Lyceum*, ad. Gr. Λύκειον, neut. of Λύκειος epithet of Apollo, to whose temple the Lyceum was adjacent.] 1. (With cap. L.) Name of a garden with covered walks at Athens, in which Aristotle taught. Hence, the Aristotelian philosophy and its adherents. Also *transf.* 2. Adopted as the title of literary institutions, and of the buildings erected for them, usu. including lecture-rooms, class-rooms, and a library 18.. 3. = LYCÉE 1827. 4. *U.S.* An institution in which popular lectures are delivered on literary and scientific subjects 1820.

Lych(e, obs. f. LIKE.

Lychee, var. of LITCHI.

Lych-gate; see LICH-GATE.

‖**Lychnis** (li·knis). *Pl.* **lychnides** (li·knidīz). 1601. [L., a. Gr. λυχνίς some red flower, f. λύχνος lamp.] *Bot.* A genus of caryophyllaceous plants, including the Campion and the Ragged Robin.

Lychnoscope (li·knŏskōᵘp). 1843. [f. Gr. λύχνος lamp + -σκόπος -SCOPE.] *Arch.* A name given to the low side window (see LOW *a. Combs.* 2) on the supposition that its purpose was to allow lepers to see the altar lights.

†**Lycium.** 1597. [late L., a. Gr. λύκιον, orig. neut. sing. of Λύκιος Lycian.] The shrub Box-thorn (*L. barbarum*), its fruit, or the juice extracted from it –1839.

‖**Lycoperdon** (ləikŏpə·ɹdǫn). 1756. [mod.L.; irreg. f. Gr. λύκος wolf + πέρδεσθαι to break wind.] *Bot.* The fungus Puff-ball, *L. Bovista.*

Lycopodium (ləikŏpōᵘ·diŏm). 1706. [mod.L., f. Gr. λύκος wolf + ποδ-, πούς foot, from the claw-like shape of the root.] 1. *Bot.* A plant of the cryptogamous genus *Lycopodium*; a club-moss. 2. A fine inflammable powder, also called 'vegetable brimstone', consisting of the spores of *Lycopodium*, used in surgery as an absorbent, and in theatres for making stage lightning 1836.

Hence **Ly·copod**, a club-moss 1846. **Ly·copodia·ceous** *a.* pertaining to the N.O. *Lycopodiaceæ* 1852. **Lyco·podite**, a fossil l. 1839.

Lyddite (li·dəit). 1888. [f. *Lydd* in Kent, where first tested.] A high explosive, composed chiefly of picric acid; used in making explosive shells.

Lydian (li·diăn). 1545. [f. L. *Lydius*, Gr. Λύδιος + -AN.] A. *adj.* 1. Pertaining to the Lydians, a people of Asia Minor, or to Lydia 1584. 2. *spec.* in *Mus.* a. A mode in ancient Greek music of a soft and effeminate character. b. The third of the authentic ecclesiastical modes, having F for its 'final', and C for its 'dominant'. 1579.

2. a. Lap me in soft L. aires, Married to immortal verse MILT. *Comb.* **L.-stone** *Min.*, a black variety of jasper (basanite), used by jewellers as a touchstone for testing gold.

B. *sb.* An inhabitant of Lydia; also, the language of the Lydians 1545.

Lye (ləi), *sb.* [OE. *léag*:—OTeut. **laugâ*; prob. f. root **lau-* to wash (see LATHER) + suffix *-gâ*:—OAryan *-qā*.] 1. Alkalized water made by the lixiviation of vegetable ashes; also applied to any strong alkaline solution, esp. one used for washing. b. Any detergent; a cleansing substance. Also *fig.* ME. 2. Water impregnated with salts by decoction or lixiviation. Now *rare.* 1634. 3. *attrib.*, as *l.-ashes*, etc. 1601.

Lye, var. of LIE.

Lying (ləi·iŋ), *vbl. sb.*[1] ME. [f. LIE *v.*[1] + -ING [1].] 1. The action of LIE *v.*[1] 2. *concr.* With qualification (as *dry*, *soft*, etc. *l.*): Accommodation for repose 1853.

Lying (ləi·iŋ), *vbl. sb.*[2] ME. [f. LIE *v.*[2] + -ING [1].] The action of LIE *v.*[2]; the telling of lies.

Lying (ləi·iŋ), *ppl. a.*[1] OE. [f. LIE *v.*[1] + -ING [2].] That lies (see the vb.).

Comb.: **l.-dog**, a setter; **-panel**, †(*a*) one which occupies the lowest place in a series; (*b*) one whose largest dimension, or whose grain, lies horizontally; **-wall** *Mining* = *foot-wall* (FOOT *sb. Combs.* 2).

Lying (ləi·iŋ), *ppl. a.*[2] ME. [f. LIE *v.*[2] + -ING [2].] That lies; mendacious; deceitful, false. Hence **Ly·ingly** *adv.*

Ly·ing-i·n. ME. [LYING *vbl. sb.*[1]] The being in childbed; accouchement. Also *attrib.* as *l. hospital.*

Lyken, obs. f. LIKE *v.*

Ly·ke-wake, ly·kewake (ləi·k,wēⁱk). ME. [f. *lyke*, LICH + WAKE *sb.*] The watch kept at night over a dead body.

Lym, Lymail(le, obs. ff. LEAM *sb.*[1], LIMAIL.

Ly·me-grass. 1776. [?f. LIME *sb.*[1] with reference to its binding quality, the spelling being infl. by *Elymus*.] The name for grasses of the genus *Elymus*, esp. *E. arenarius*, which is planted on sand to keep it from shifting.

Lymph (limf). 1630. [ad. L. *lympha* (also used in Eng.), var. (due to association w. Gr.

νύμφη NYMPH) of *limpa (whence *limpidus* LIMPID).] 1. Pure water; water in general; a stream. Only *poet.* and *rhet.* Also *fig.* and *transf.* †2. *Bot.* The sap in plants –1830. 3. *Phys.* A colourless alkaline fluid, derived from various tissues and organs of the body, resembling blood but containing no red corpuscles 1725. 4. a. The exudation from a sore, etc. b. Now often *spec.* for *vaccine l.*, the matter taken from cow-pox vesicles, etc. to be used in vaccination; also extended to any morbid matter similarly used as a prophylactic. 1800. 5. *attrib.*, as *l.-cell, -corpuscle*; *l.-secretion*; *l.-forming* adj.; **l.-heart,** in some lower vertebrates, one of a number of contractile muscular sacs which pump the l. forward.

Lymphad (li·mfæd). Also †**lang-, lum-,** lime-. 1536. [Gael. *longfhada* (= *long* ship + *fada* long).] A one-masted galley propelled by oars. Now only *Hist.*, and *Sc. Her.*

‖**Lymphadenitis** (limfædĭnəi·tis). 1879. [mod.L., f. LYMPH + Gr. ἀδήν gland + -ITIS.] *Path.* Inflammation of the lymphatic glands. So **Lympha·denoid** *a.* resembling the tissue of a lymphatic gland 1877. ‖**Ly:mphadeno·ma,** a tumour consisting of lymphoid tissue 1873.

‖**Lymphangitis** (limfændʒəi·tis). 1861. [mod.L., f. L. *lympha* LYMPH + Gr. ἀγγεῖον vessel + -ITIS.] *Path.* Inflammation of the walls of the lymphatic vessels.

Lymphatic (limfæ·tik). 1649. [ad. L. *lymphaticus* mad, frenzied, f. *lympha* LYMPH. The cl.L. word may be due to association of *lympha* w. Gr. νύμφη; cf. νυμφιᾶν to be frenzy-stricken.] A. *adj.* †I. Frenzied, mad –1822. II. In senses conn. w. LYMPH. 1. a. *Phys.* and *Anat.* Pertaining to or concerned in the secretion or conveyance of lymph, as in *l. gland, vessel.* Also, of the nature of lymph, as *l. fluid, humour* (rare). 1649. †b. *Bot.* Containing or conveying sap –1836. 2. Having the characteristics (flabby muscles, pale skin, sluggishness) formerly attributed to an excess of lymph in the system 1834.

1. a. *L. system*, the l. vessels and glands collectively. *L. heart* = *lymph-heart.* 2. In..persons of a l. habit, the skin becomes white J. FORBES.

B. *sb.* †1. A lunatic, a madman –1763. 2. Chiefly *pl.* Vessels similar to veins, whose function is the conveyance of lymph. †Also applied to the sap-vessels in plants. 1667.

Lymphoid (li·mfoid), *a.* 1867. [f. LYMPH + -OID.] *Phys.* Resembling lymph, lymph-corpuscles, or the tissue of lymphatic glands.

‖**Lymphoma** (limfōᵘ·mă). *Pl.* **-mata.** 1873. [f. LYMPH, after *carcinoma*, etc.] *Path.* A tumour having the structure of a lymphatic gland. Hence **Lympho·matous** *a.*

Lymphous (li·mfəs), *a.* 1672. [f. LYMPH + -OUS.] *Phys.* Containing, of the nature of, or resembling lymph.

Lymphy (li·mfi), *a.* 1848. [f. LYMPH + -Y [1].] Of the nature of or resembling lymph.

Lyn, obs. f. LINN.

Lyncean (linsī·ăn), *a.* 1622. [f. L. *lynceus* (a. Gr. λύγκειος, f. λύγξ LYNX) + -AN. Occas. used with a reference to *Lynceus*, an Argonaut, famous for his sharp sight.] Lynx-like; sharp-sighted.

Lynch (linʃ), *v.* Orig. *U.S.* 1836. [f. *Lynch*; see LYNCH LAW.] *trans.* To condemn and punish by lynch law. Orig., to whip, tar and feather, or the like; now only, to inflict sentence of death by lynch law.

Lynchet, variant of LINCHET.

Lynch law. Orig. *U.S.* In early use **Lynch's (Linch's) law.** 1811. The practice of inflicting summary punishment upon an offender, by a self-constituted court without legal authority; now limited to the summary execution of one charged with a flagrant offence. (The capital L is still often used.)

The originator of Lynch law was Captain William Lynch of Pittsylvania in Virginia. According to A. Ellicott (*Life and Lett.*, 1908, 200) 'this self-created judicial tribunal was first organised in the state of Virginia about the year 1776'; another authority gives the date definitely as 1780.

Lynch law, however shocking it may seem to Europeans, is far removed from arbitrary violence BRYCE. **Judge Lynch,** the imaginary authority from whom the sentences of lynch law are said to proceed.

Lynn. Common U.S. var. of LINN [2].

Lynx (liŋks). ME. [a. L. *lynx, lyncem*, a. Gr. λύγξ (λυγκ-), cogn. w. OE. *lox*, G. *luchs.*] 1. Any animal of the sub-genus *Lynx* of the genus *Felis*, having a tufted ear-tip, short tail, and spotted fur. 2. The fur of the lynx 1839. 3. A northern constellation 1798.

1. A black l. snarled and pricked a tufted ear BROWNING. *Comb.* **l.-eye,** an eye as keen as that of a l.; so **-eyed** *a.*, having eyes like those of a l.; keen-sighted.

Lyon, short form, with early spelling, of *Lyon King of Arms* (see KING-OF-ARMS), the title of the chief herald in Scotland; so named from the lion on the royal shield. Also *Lyon Herald* (see HERALD *sb.*), *Lyon King.*

‖**Lyra** (ləiə·ră). 1586. [L., a. Gr. λύρα.] †1. A lyre –1724. 2. *Astr.* (With cap. L.) An ancient northern constellation; = HARP *sb.* 2. 1658. 3. *Anat.* A part of the under surface of the corpus callosum of the brain, marked with lines suggesting the strings of a lyre 1756.

Lyraid (ləiə·re,id), **Lyrid** (ləiə·rid). 1883. [f. LYRA + -ID [3].] *Astr.* One of a group of meteors apparently radiating from Lyra.

Lyrate (ləiə·reᵗt), *a.* 1760. [ad. mod.L. *lyratus*, f. *lyra* LYRE; see -ATE [2].] *Nat. Hist.* Shaped like a lyre. In *Bot.*, of a leaf: Pinnatifid, with the upper lobes much larger than the lower. So **Ly·rated** *a.* 1753. Hence **Ly·rately** *adv.* in a l. form.

Lyre (ləiəɹ). ME. [a. F. *lyre*, OF. *lire*, ad. L. *lyra*, a. Gr. λύρα.] 1. A stringed instrument of the harp kind, used by the Greeks for accompanying song and recitation. b. *fig.* esp. as the symbol of lyric poetry 1683. 2. *Astr.* = LYRA 2. 1868. 3. *Anat.* = LYRA 3. 1900.

1. b. Make me thy l. even as the forest is SHELLEY. *Comb.*: **l.-bat,** a species of bat, *Megaderma lyra*; **-bird,** an Australian bird, *Menura superba* or *M. novæ-hollandiæ*, resembling a pheasant, with a beautiful lyre-shaped tail; **-pheasant, -tail** = *lyre-bird*; **-turtle** *U.S.*, the leather-back or trunk-turtle, *Dermochelys coriaceus.*

Lyric (li·rik). 1581. [a. F. *lyrique*, or ad. L. *lyricus*, a. Gr., f. λύρα LYRE.]

A. *adj.* 1. Of or pertaining to the lyre; meant to be sung; pertaining to or characteristic of song. Now the name for short poems, usually divided into stanzas or strophes, and directly expressing the poet's own thoughts and sentiments. Hence, applied to the poet. 1589. 2. Of persons: Given to song, singing (*poet.*) 1814.

1. L. poetry is the expression by the poet of his own feelings RUSKIN. *L. drama, l. stage*, the opera.

B. *sb.* 1. *absol.* (with *the*): That which is lyrical; lyric style, verse, etc. 1586. †2. A lyric poet –1839. 3. A lyric poem. Also *pl.*, verses in lyric metre. 1581.

1. From the high l. down to the low rational BYRON. 3. An Eton boy follows..Horace in lyrics 1849.

Lyrical (li·rikăl), *a.* 1581. [f. as LYRIC *a.* + -AL.] 1. = LYRIC *a.* Also, having the qualities of lyric poetry. 2. Resembling what is found in lyric poetry 1817.

1. L. Ballads (*title*) 1798. Hence **Ly·rical·ly** *adv.*, **-ness.**

Lyricism (li·riciz'm). 1760. [f. LYRIC + -ISM.] Lyric character or style; the pursuit or eulogy of the same; (with *pl.*) a lyrical expression or characteristic. *Occas.* (after F. *lyrisme*), affectation of high-flown sentiment or poetic enthusiasm.

Lyrid: see LYRAID.

Lyriform (ləiə·rifǭɹm), *a.* 1856. [-FORM.] Lyre-shaped.

Lyrism (ləiə·riz'm, li·riz'm). 1859. [a. F. *lyrisme*, or ad. Gr. λυρισμός, f. λύρα LYRE.] = LYRICISM.

Lyrist (li·rist). 1656. [ad. L. *lyrista*, ad. Gr. λυριστής, f. λύρα LYRE.] 1. A player on the lyre, or a singer who accompanies himself on the lyre. 2. A lyric poet 1813.

2. From her wilds Ierne sent The sweetest l. of her saddest wrong SHELLEY.

‖**Lysis** (ləi·sis). 1822. [L., Gr. λύσις a loosening.] 1. *Arch.* 'A plinth or step above the cornice of the podium of ancient temples, which surrounded or embraced the stylobate' (Gwilt) 1842. 2. *Path.* An insensible or gradual solution or termination of a disease or disorder. Opp. to CRISIS 1. 3. *Med.* Dissolution of a cell by a **Ly·sin,** as in infection or immunization. Hence **Ly·tic** *a.* 1902.

-lysis, *suffix*, repr. Gr. λύσις loosening, used in various scientific terms, as *electrolysis*, etc. The corresp. adjs. end in **-lytic** [Gr. λυτικός].

Lysol (ləi·sǫl). 1891. [Trade name, f. Gr. λύσις (see prec.) + -OL.] A saponified mixture of creosol and oil, used as a disinfectant.

Lythe (ləið). *Sc.* 1769. The pollack.

M

M (em), the thirteenth letter of the modern and twelfth of the ancient Roman alphabet, represents historically Gr. *mū* and Semitic *mēm.* The Phœnician form of the letter is Ꮃ, whence the early Gr. and L. Ꮃ, Ꮇ, M. In Eng. it has always expressed what was doubtless its original sound, that of the bilabial nasal consonant. It is capable of being used as a sonant or vowel, denoted by ('m) in the notation here followed; but in Eng. this occurs only after (ð) and (z) at the end of words, as *rhythm, spasm, schism*, and the suffix *-ism*; in these words many speakers substitute (-əm). It is never silent, exc. initially bef. *n* in Gr. derivs., as *mnemonic.*

I. 1. The letter and its sound. b. **M roof:** a kind of roof formed by the junction of two ordinary gable roofs with a valley between them, making the section resembling the letter M. 2. *Printing.* = EM.

II. Symbolical uses. 1. Used to denote serial order; applied e. g. to the thirteenth, or more usually the twelfth (I or J being omitted) group or section, the twelfth sheet of a book, etc. 2. The Roman numeral symbol for: A thousand. (Now *rare*, exc. in dates.)

III. Abbrevs. M. = Mark, Margaret, etc.; = †Majesty, in ancient criminal proceedings; = Member, as in M.P. (q.v.), M.C., Member of Congress (*U.S.*), M.R.C.P., Member of the Royal College of Physicians; *Mus.* = metronome; *Math.* = modulus; (M. or m.) in astronomical tables, etc. = meridian or meridional; also (after *twelve*) = L. *meridies* noon; cf. A.M. (= *ante meridiem*) before noon, P.M. (= *post m.*) after noon; m. = mass, in *Mech.*; = molar, in dental formulæ; = minute, metre (mm. = millimetre); in log-books = mist; *Mus.* It. *mano* or F. *main* (as *mano destra, main droite*), *mezzo* (as *mf* = *mezzoforte*), in organ music, *manual.* See also M.B., M.D., MS.

b. Abbrev. for Master: †(*a*) generally, = the later MISTER, MR. (*b*) Used for *master* or L. *magister* in academical degrees, as M.A. or A.M. (*magister artium*), Master of Arts; M.Ch. (*magister chirurgiæ*), Master of Surgery; also in M.C., Master of the ceremonies; M.F.H., Master of fox-hounds.

‖c. = MONSIEUR (q.v.) as prefixed title.

-m, in I'M = I am; see BE *v.*

Ma (mā). 1829. Vulg. abbrev. of MAMMA.

Maad, obs. f. MADE.

Ma'am (mæm; usu. unstressed məm, 'm). Also written as vulgar **marm, mem, mim, mum, 'm.** 1668. A colloq. shortening of MADAM, now used only parenthetically or at the end of a sentence.

Formerly the ordinary respectful form of address to a (married) woman: now used at Court in addressing the Queen or a royal princess, and by servants to their mistresses. Hence **Ma'am** *v. trans.*, to address as 'ma'am' 1813.

Maat, obs. f. MATE.

†**Mab,** *sb.* 1557. [Cf. *map*, 17th c. form of MOP *sb.*[1]; also *Mab*, short for *Mabel.*] A slattern; a woman of loose character –1725. So †**Mab** *v. intr.* to dress untidily 1691–1829.

†**Mabble,** *v.* Also **mable.** [Cf. MOBLE *v.*] *trans.* To wrap or muffle up (the head). G. SANDYS.

Mac (mæk). Also *Mack.* 1500. [Ir. and Gael. *mac* :—OCeltic *makko-s, cogn. w. Welsh *mab* :—OWelsh *map* :—OCeltic *makwo-s.] The Gaelic word for 'son', occurring as a prefix in Sc. and Ir. names, and thus = Eng. *-son.* Hence, a person whose name contains the prefix *Mac*; †also contempt.: A Celtic Irishman.

Mac. Colloq. abbrev. of MACKINTOSH 2.

‖**Macabre** (makā·br), *a.* ME. [repr. F. *macabre*, an error for OF. *macabré*; perh. pop. corruption of OF. *Macabé* = Maccabæus.] 1.

Danse Macabre, also †*dance* (*of*) *Machabree*, *-bray* (obs.), *dance Macaber*: the Dance of Death (see DANCE *sb.*). **2.** Gruesome, like the *danse Macabre*; applied to literary or artistic productions 1889.

Macaco[1] (măkē·ko). 1771. [a. Pg. *macaco* monkey, ape; cited in 1648 (in the form *macaquo*) as the Congo name.] Orig., a S. African monkey described by Marcgrave (1648); now, any monkey of the genus *Macacus*; = MACAQUE.

Macaco[2] (măkē·ko). 1751. [a. F. (Buffon) *mococo*; origin unkn.] A name given to certain lemurs, *esp.* to the genus *Lemur*.

‖**Macacus** (măkē·kŏs). *Pl.* **-ci** (-səi). 1871. [mod.L., ad. F. *macaque*; see MACAQUE.] A genus of Old World catarrhine monkeys of the family *Cercopithecidæ*; now restricted to species resembling the bonnet macaque or toque; a monkey of this genus.

Macadam (mækæ·dăm). 1824. **1.** The name of John Loudon *McAdam* (1756–1836) used *attrib.* to designate a kind of roadway and of material advocated by him; see MACADAMIZE. **2.** The material of which a macadamized road is made 1826. Hence **Maca·damite** *sb.* one who practises or advocates this system of road-making; *adj.* pertaining to this system of road-making.

Macadamize (mækæ·dăməiz), *v.* 1825. [f. prec. + -IZE.] **1.** *trans.* To make or repair (a road) according to McAdam's system, by compacting into a solid mass successive layers of stone broken into pieces of nearly uniform size; hence extended to similar methods of road-making 1826. **b.** *fig.* To render level; to level, raze 1826. **2.** To convert into road-metal 1841. **b.** *transf.* and *fig.* To break up (something hard) *into* pieces. ? *Obs.* 1825.

Hence **Maca:damiza·tion**, the process, system, or practice of making macadamized roads; also, the converting of stone into road-metal. **Maca·damizer**, one who makes, or one who keeps to, macadamized roads.

†**Maca·o.** Also **makao.** 1778. [f. *Macao*, a Pg. settlement on the coast of China, noted for gambling.] A gambling game at cards resembling vingt-et-un.

Macao, obs. f. MACAW[1].

Macaque (măkā·k). 1698. [a. F., ad. Pg. *macaco*; see MACACO[1].] †**1.** Some Brazilian species of monkey. FROGER. **2.** A monkey of the genus MACACUS 1840.

Macarize (mæ·kărəiz), *v. rare.* Also **macarise, makarize.** 1816. [f. Gr. μακαρίζειν, f. μάκαρ happy; see -IZE.] *trans.* To account or call happy or blessed. So **Ma·carism** [Gr. μακαρισμός], an accounting happy; also, = BEATITUDE 2. 1818.

Macaroni (mækărō·ni). *Pl.* **-ies.** Also †**maccaroni**, etc. 1599. [a. It. *maccaroni*, earlier form of *maccheroni*, pl. of *maccherone*; ult. etym. unkn.] **1.** A kind of wheaten paste, of Italian origin, formed into long slender tubes and dried for use as food. **2. a.** *Hist.* One of a class of 18th c. exquisites, consisting of young men who had travelled and affected continental tastes and fashions. **b.** *dial.* A fop, dandy. 1764. **3.** A species of crested penguin, *Eudyptes chrysolophus*. In full *m. penguin*. 1838. **4.** A medley (such as a macaronic poem) 1884. **5.** = *macaroni tool* 1867.

2. You are a delicate Londoner; you are a maccaroni; you can't ride BOSWELL. *Comb.* **m. cheese**, a savoury of m. and cheese baked; **m. tool**, a square-cutting tool used in wood-carving. Hence †**Macaro·nian** *a.* = MACARONIC 1727–1788. **Macaro·nism**, dandyism 1775.

Macaronic (mækărǫ·nik). 1611. [ad. mod.L. *macaronicus*, f. (ult.) It. *maccheroni* MACARONI.] **A.** *adj.* **1.** Used to designate a form of verse containing vernacular words in a Latin context with Latin terminations and in Latin constructions. Also *transf.*; and applied *loosely* to any form of verse in which two or more langs. are jumbled together. Hence: Resembling the mixed jargon of macaronic poetry. 1638. †**2.** Of the nature of a medley –1816. **B.** *sb.* **1. a.** Macaronic language or composition. **b.** *pl.* Macaronic verses. 1668. †**2.** A medley. COTGR.

Macaroon (mækărū·n). 1611. [a. F. *macaron*, ad. It. *maccarone*; see MACARONI.] **1.** A small cake or biscuit made chiefly of ground almonds, white of egg, and sugar. †**2.** = MACARONI 1. –1753. †**3.** A buffoon; a dolt. Also *dial.* a fop. –1825.

Macartney (măkā·ɹtni). 1834. [The name of George, Earl *Macartney* (1737–1806).] A pheasant of the genus *Euplocamus*, esp. *E. ignitus*.

Macassar (măkæ·səɹ). 1666. [Name (= native *Mangkasara*) of a district in the island of Celebes.] **Macassar oil**, an unguent for the hair, said to consist of ingredients obtained from Macassar. Also applied commercially to other oils, etc. imported from the East.

Macauco, var. of MACACO.

Macaw[1] (măkǭ·). 1668. [a. Pg. *macao*, of obscure origin.] Any parrot of the genus *Ara*, inhabiting tropical and subtropical America and remarkable for their gaudy plumage.

Macaw[2] (măkǭ·). 1657. [prob. Carib.] W. Indian name for palms of the genus *Acrocomia*. Now only *attrib.* in *m.-berry*, *-palm*, *-tree*; also **m.-bush**, a W. Indian plant, *Solanum mammosum*.

Macco (mæ·ko). ? *Obs.* 1809. ? Var. of MACAO.

Maccoboy (mæ·kŏboi). Also **maccaboy, mackabaw**, etc. 1740. [f. *Macouba*, a district in Martinique.] A kind of snuff, usually scented with attar of roses.

Mace[1] (mēⁱs). ME. [a. OF. *masse*, *mace* :–L. type **mat(t)ea* (whence prob. *mat(t)eola* ? mallet).] **1.** A heavy staff or club, either all of metal or metal-headed, often spiked; formerly a weapon of war. †In early use also, any club. **2.** A staff of office resembling this, borne before certain officials. †Also formerly = the sceptre of sovereignty. 1440. **b.** A mace-bearer 1663. **3.** A stick with a flat square head, used in *Bagatelle*, and formerly in *Billiards*, for propelling the ball 1727. **4.** *Tanning.* A knobbed mallet used in dressing leather to make it supple 1839.

1. Then cam Treason with hir mas Hevy as a clobbe of leed LYDG. *fig.* O Murd'rous slumber! Layest thou thy Leaden M. vpon my Boy? SHAKS. **2. b.** And here upon a M. was sent to bring Cromwell into the Court 1663. *Comb.* **Ma·ce-bearer**, an official who carries a mace, as a symbol of authority, before some high functionary 1552.

Mace[2] (mēⁱs). [ME. *macis*, a. F. *macis*; origin unkn. *Macis* was in Eng. taken as a pl., whence *mace* sing.] A spice consisting of the dried outer covering of the nutmeg.

Mace[3] (mēⁱs). 1598. [a. Malay *mās*, f. Skr. *māsha* bean.] A weight and money of account equal to one-tenth of a tael.

‖**Macédoine** (mæsedwān). 1846. [Fr.] A dish of fruit or vegetables embedded in jelly.

Macedon (mæ·sǐdǫn). ME. [ad. L. *Macedonem* (*Macedo*), Gr. Μακεδόνα (-ών).] †**1.** One of the people (esp. Alexander the Great) that inhabited Macedonia –1700. †**b.** quasi-*adj.* Macedonian –1710. **2.** Macedonia 1584.

1. The valiant M... Lamented that there were no more [worlds] to conquer MASSINGER. **2.** Phillip of M. BACON.

Macedonian (mæsǐdōᵘ·niăn), *a.*[1] and *sb.*[1] 1556. [f. L. *Macedonius* (= Gr. Μακεδόνιος, f. Μακεδών; see prec.) + -AN.] Pertaining to (A native or inhabitant of) Macedonia.

Macedonian (mæsǐdōᵘ·niăn), *a.*[2] and *sb.*[2] 1449. [ad. Eccl.L. *Macedonianus*, f. *Macedonius*; see -AN.] Applied to the followers of Macedonius, a heretical Bishop of Constantinople in the 4th c. Hence **Macedo·nianism.**

Macer (mēⁱ·səɹ). ME. [a. OF. *maissier*, *massier*, f. *masse* MACE[1]; see -ER[2].] A mace-bearer; *spec.* in Scotland, an official who keeps order in courts of law. Hence **Ma·cership.**

Macerate (mæ·sĕrēⁱt), *v.* 1547. [f. L. *macerat-*, *macerare*, f. root *mac-*, perh. cogn. w. Gr. μάσσειν to knead.] **1.** *trans.* To soften by steeping in a liquid, with or without heat; to wear away or separate the soft parts of, by steeping 1563. **b.** *intr.* for *pass.* To undergo maceration 1610. **2.** *trans.* To cause (the body, flesh, etc.) to waste or wear away, esp. by fasting 1547. †**b.** *fig.* To oppress, crush –1640. †**3.** To fret, vex, worry –1761.

2. To..m. his body for his owne sinnes PURCHAS. **3.** A city so macerated with expectation STERNE. Hence **Macera·tion**, the action or process of macerating or condition of being macerated 1612. **Ma·cerator**, one who macerates; a vessel used for maceration 1891.

†**Machecoled**, *pa. pple.* ME. [a. OF. *machecollé*.] Machicolated –1500. Hence †**Machecoling** *vbl. sb.* machicolation 1491.

Machet(t)e, macheto, vars. of MATCHET.

Machiavel (mæ·kiăvel). 1570. [Anglicized name of Niccolò *Machiavelli*, a Florentine statesman and writer of the work *Del Principe*.] One who acts on the principles of Machiavelli; an intriguer, an unscrupulous schemer.

Am I subtle? Am I a Machiuell? SHAKS.

Machiavellian (mæ:kiăve·liăn). 1568. [f. prec. or *Machiavelli* + -(I)AN.] **A.** *adj.* Of, pertaining to, or characteristic of Machiavelli, or his alleged principles; preferring expediency to morality; practising duplicity, *esp.* in statecraft; astute, cunning, intriguing 1579.

Divide et regna is an old Matchiavilian maxime and trick 1637.

B. *sb.* A follower of Machiavelli; one who adopts his principles in statecraft or in general conduct.

Hence **Ma:chiave·llianism**, the principles and practice of Machiavelli or of the Machiavellians. So **Ma:chiave·llism**, Machiavellianism 1592. **Ma·chiave·llist**, a Machiavellian 1589.

Machicolation (mătʃikŏlē·ʃən). 1788. [f. ppl. stem of med.L. *machicol(l)are* = OF. *machecoller*; see -ATION.] *Arch.* An opening between the corbels which support a projecting parapet, or in the floor of a gallery or the roof of a portal, through which combustibles, molten lead, stones, etc., were dropped upon assailants. Also, a projecting structure containing such openings. So **Machi·colate** *v. trans.* to furnish with m.; chiefly in *pa. pple.* and *ppl. a.* 1773.

Machinate (mæ·kinēⁱt), *v.* 1600. [f. L. *machinat-*, *machinari*, f. *machina* machine.] **1.** *intr.* To lay plots; to intrigue, scheme. **2.** *trans.* To contrive, plan, plot. Now *rare.* 1602.

1. A Tyrant conspires, machinates, [etc.] 1689. Hence **Ma·chinator** 1611.

Machination (mækinē·ʃən). ME. [ad. L. *machinationem*, f. *machinari*.] **1.** The action or process of contriving or planning; contrivance, intrigue, plotting. Now *rare.* 1549. **2.** An instance of this; an intrigue, plot, scheme. Usu. in bad sense. 1477. †**3.** The use or construction of machinery –1711. †**4.** Something contrived or constructed, e.g. a weapon, a framework or apparatus –1680.

1. By secret m., or by confederacy with others HOBBES. **2.** This machinacion fayling, another.. was put on foote 1678.

Machine (măʃī·n), *sb.* 1549. [ad. F. *machine*, ad. L. *machina*, ad. Gr. μηχανή, f. μῆχος contrivance, cogn. w. Teut. **magan* to be able (see MAY *v.*[1]).] **1.** A structure of any kind, material or immaterial; a fabric, an erection. Now *rare.* **b.** *spec.* A vehicle of any kind (usu. wheeled). *Obs.* exc. *Sc.* 1687. **2.** A military engine, siege-tower, or the like. Now *rare.* (= L. *machina.*) 1656. †**3.** An apparatus, appliance, instrument –1741. **4.** An apparatus for applying mechanical power, consisting of a number of parts, each having a definite function 1673. **b.** Often short for *sewing-m.*, *printing-m.*, or any machine in question. Also, for a bicycle or tricycle. 1841. **c.** Applied to the human and animal frame as a combination of several parts 1602. **d.** A combination of parts moving mechanically, as contrasted with a being acting voluntarily. Hence applied to a person who acts mechanically, without intelligence, or to one whose actions exhibit a machine-like regularity 1692. **5.** *Mech.* Any instrument for transmitting force, or modifying its application 1704. **6.** *Theatr.* [= L. *machina.*] A contrivance for the production of stage effects. Also in *pl.* stage machinery. Now *rare.* 1658. **7.** Hence in literary use: A contrivance for dramatic presentation; a supernatural agency or personage introduced into a poem; the interposition of one of these 1678. 8. *Politics* (orig. *U.S.*). The controlling organization of a political party; often used disparagingly 1876.

1. b. Your very kind letter of the 15th, . . I received by the machine BURKE. 4. *fig.* The great state wheels in all the political machines of Europe FIELDING. c. Thine euermore most deere Lady, whilst this M. is to him SHAKS. d. The nearer the soldiers approach to machines, perhaps the better A. HAMILTON. 5. *Simple m.*: one in which there is no combination of parts, e.g. a lever. *Compound m.*: one whose efficiency depends on the combined action of two or more parts. 7. The episodes of Circe, of the Sirens, and of Polyphemus, are machines 1897.

attrib. and *Comb.*, as **m. bolt**, a machine screw; esp. a bolt with a square or hexagonal head and the upper portion of the shank not threaded; **-gun**, a mounted gun which is mechanically operated, delivering a continuous fire 1870; **-man**, one who manages a m.; **-minder** (*Print.*); **m. screw**, a screw adapted for screwing into metal rather than into wood; **-shop**, a workshop for making or repairing machines; **-tool**, a m. for cutting or shaping wood, metals, etc., by means of a tool, esp. one used in a machine-shop; **-twist** *U.S.*, a kind of silk twist, made especially for the sewing-m.; **-work**, †(*a*) poetic or dramatic 'machinery'; (*b*) work done by a m., as dist. from that done by hand.

Machine (măʃīˑn), *v.* 1450. [orig. a. F. *machiner*, ad. L. *machinari* (see MACHINATE); later, f. MACHINE *sb.*] †1. a. *trans.* To contrive, plot; also, to resolve *that*. b. *intr.* To plot (*against* a person). -1679. 2. *trans.* To form, make, or operate upon by means of a machine 1827. 3. *nonce-use. fig.* To work (a project, etc.) like a machine 1881. †4. *intr.* To appear, as a god, from a 'machine'; to serve as a poetic 'machine' 1697.

2. Making shirts, machining men's coats [etc.] 1886.

Machiner (măʃīˑnəɹ). 1798. [f. MACHINE *sb.* + -ER¹.] 1. A horse employed to draw a 'machine' or vehicle. 2. One who works a machine 1827.

Machinery (măʃīˑnĕri). 1687. [f. MACHINE *sb.* + -ERY.] 1. *Theatr.* and *literary.* †a. Stage appliances and contrivances. (Cf. MACHINE *sb.* 6.) b. The assemblage of machines (MACHINE *sb.* 7) employed in a poem. 2. Machines, or their parts, taken collectively; the mechanism or works of a machine or machines 1731. b. A system or kind of machinery (*lit.* and *fig.*) 1849.

1. The M., Madam, is a term invented by the Critics, to signify that part which the Deities, Angels, or Dæmons, are made to act in a Poem POPE. 2. *fig.* The whole m. of government was out of joint 1855.

Machinist (măʃīˑnist). 1706. [orig., ad. F. *machiniste*, f. *machine*; later, f. MACHINE *sb.* + -IST.] 1. One who invents, makes, or controls machines; an engineer. b. *Theatr.* One who makes or manages the stage machinery. Now *rare.* 1739. 2. One who works a machine, esp. a sewing-machine 1879. 3. *U.S.* A supporter of machinism in politics; a member of a political machine 1883. So **Machiˑnism**, management of parties by political machines.

-machy, in actual use **-omachy** (ǫˑmăki), repr. Gr. -μαχία, the ending of certain Gr. sbs. with the general sense 'fighting, warfare', from adjs. in -μάχος 'that fights'. Eng. examples are *logomachy*, *angelomachy*, etc.

Macilent (mæˑsilĕnt), *a.* Now *rare.* 1535. [ad. L. *macilentus* lean.] Lean, shrivelled, thin; *fig.* of verses: Jejune, poor. Hence **Maˑcilency** (now *rare*), leanness 1632.

Macintosh: see MACKINTOSH.

Mack. Colloq. abbrev. MACKINTOSH 2.

Mackerel¹ (mæˑkərel). ME. [a. OF. *makerel* (F. *maquereau*) of unkn. origin.] 1. A sea-fish, *Scomber scombrus*, marked on the back with dark stripes; much used for food. Also applied with qualifying word to other fishes of the same genus or family; esp. **Spanish m.**, the tunny, *S. colias.* 2. *Angling.* Short for *mackerel-fly* 1799.

1. Bad fortunes are like m. at midsummer 1623.

attrib. and *Comb.*: **m.-back**, **-backed** *adjs.*, †(*a*) *slang*, long-backed; (*b*) said of clouds, sky (see *mackerel-sky*); **-bird**, local name for the wryneck and the young kittiwake; so called because they usually appear about the same time as the m.; **-breeze**, **-gale**, a (strong) breeze that ruffles the water, so as to favour the catching of m.; **-clouds** (see *mackerel-sky*); **-cock**, the Manx Shearwater (*local*); **-fly** *Angling*, a species of May-fly, also an artificial fly imitating this; **-guide**, the garfish (*local*); **-gull**, U.S. name for the tern; **-midge**, the young of the rockling (*Motella*); **-plough**, a knife used for creasing the sides of lean m. in order to improve their appearance; **-shark**, the porbeagle; **-sky**, a sky dappled with small white fleecy clouds 1669.

†**Maˑckerel**². ME. [ad. OF. *makerel*, *-elle* (F. *maquereau*, *maquerelle*) of unkn. origin.] A procurer or procuress -1700.

Mackinaw (mæˑkinǭ). 1841. The name (also written *Mackinac*) of an island in the strait between Lakes Huron and Michigan.

Comb.: **M. blanket**, also simply **M.**, a thick blanket, such as used to be distributed to the Indians of the North-west by the U.S. government. **M.** (**boat**), a large flat-bottomed sharp-ended boat, used on the Great Lakes. **M. trout**, the lake trout.

Mackintosh (mæˑkintǫʃ). Also **macintosh.** 1835. 1. The name of Charles *Macintosh* (1766–1843), used *attrib.* (or in genitive) to designate garments made of the waterproof material patented by him, consisting of layers of cloth cemented with india-rubber. Now taken as an attrib. use of 3, and written with a small initial. 2. Short for *M. cloak*, *coat*, etc. 1836. (Colloq. abbrev. *mack.*) 3. The material of which 'Mackintosh' garments are made; now any cloth made waterproof by a coating of india-rubber. Also *attrib.* 1880.

Mackle, macle (mæˑk'l), *sb.* 1706. [ad. F. *macule*, ad. L. *macula* spot.] *Printing.* A blur in printing; a doubling of the impression; also, a blurred sheet. So **Maˑckle, maˑcle** *v.* to blur or become blurred; now usu. *trans.* to print (a page) blurred or double 1594.

Macle (mæˑk'l). 1680. [a. F. *macle*, ad. L. *macula* spot, mesh.] 1. *Cryst.* A twin crystal. Also *attrib.* 1801. 2. *Min.* A dark spot in certain minerals 1839. 3. = CHIASTOLITE 1821. 4. *Her.* = MASCLE 2. 1680. Hence **Maˑcled, maˑckled** *ppl. a.* (of a crystal) twin; marked like chiastolite; *Her.* mascled.

Macramé (măkrāˑme). Also **-mi.** 1869. [app. a. Turk. *maqrama* towel, napkin, handkerchief, a. Arab.] A fringe or trimming of knotted thread or cord; knotted-work; the art of making this. Also *attrib.*

Macro- (mæˑkro), bef. a vowel **macr-**, repr. Gr. μακρο-, comb. f. μακρός long, large, in various scientific uses.

a. *Anat.* and *Path.* in sbs. denoting excessive development of some part, as *macrocheilia* (of the lips), *-glossia* (of the tongue), *-melia* (of a limb); also MACROCEPHALY.

b. In sbs. (chiefly in antithesis with *micro-*) indicating either an individual of unusual size, or one containing a number of smaller individuals; as *macro-cyst*, etc.

c. *Cryst.* **Maːcrodiaˑgonal** *sb.* the longer of the diagonals of a rhombic prism; *adj.* pertaining to this diagonal. **Maˑcrodome**, a dome (see DOME *sb.* 5 b) parallel to the macrodiagonal. **Macropiˑnacoid**, a pinacoid parallel to the vertical and macrodiagonal axes. **Maˑcroprism**, a prism of an orthorhombic crystal between the macropinacoid and the unit prism. **Maːcropyˑramid**, a pyramid corresponding to the macroprism.

d. in adjs., with sense 'containing or possessed of some object in a largely developed form', as **Macrodaˑctyl, -dactyˑlic, -daˑctylous** [Gr. δάκτυλος] *adjs.*, having long fingers or toes. **Maˑcrodont** [Gr. ὀδοντ-, ὀδούς] *a.*, having long teeth. **Macrognaˑthic, Macroˑgnathous** [Gr. γνάθος] *adjs.*, having long or protruding jaws. **Maːcropleuˑral** [Gr. πλευρά rib, side] *a.*, having long pleuræ. **Maːcrostyˑlous** *a.*, *Bot.* having a long style.

Macrobiotic (mæːkrobəiǫˑtik). 1797. [f. Gr. μακροβίοτος (f. μακρός + βίοτος) + -IC.] A. *adj.* Inclined or tending to prolong life; relating to the prolongation of life. B. *sb. pl.* The science of prolonging life.

Macrocephalic (mæːkro͵sĭfæˑlik), *a.* 1851. [f. Gr. μακροκέφαλος (f. μακρός + κεφαλή) + -IC.] Having a long or large head; also said of the head or skull. So **Macroceˑphalous** *a.* long-headed; in *Bot.* said of dicotyledonous embryos whose cotyledons are consolidated 1835. **Macroceˑphaly**, excessive length or size of the head 1889.

Macrocosm (mæˑkrokǫz'm). 1600. [ad. F. *macrocosme*, ad. med.L. *macrocosmus*, repr. Gr. *μακρὸς κόσμος.] The 'great world' or universe, as dist. from the 'little world' or MICROCOSM, i.e. from man as an epitome of the universe. Also *transf.*

The microcosm repeats the m. HUXLEY. Hence **Maːcrocoˑsmic** *a.* of or pertaining to the m.

Macrology (măkrǫˑlŏdʒi). 1616. [ad. L. *macrologia*, a. Gr., f. μακρός + -λόγος.] *Rhet.* The use of redundant words or phrases. *gen.* Prolixity of speech.

Macromere (mæˑkromīᵊɹ). 1877. [f. Gr. μακρός long + μέρος part.] *Embryol.* The larger of the two masses into which the vitellus of the developing ovum of *Lamellibranchiata* divides; cf. MICROMERE. Hence **Macromeˑral, Macromeˑric** *adjs.*

Macrometer (mækrǫˑmĭtəɹ). 1825. [f. MACRO- + -METER.] An instrument for measuring distant or inaccessible objects.

‖**Macron** (mæˑkrǫn, mēˑkrǫn). 1851. [a. Gr. μακρόν, neut. of μακρός long.] A straight horizontal line (¯) placed over a vowel to indicate that it is 'long'.

Macropod (mæˑkrǫ́pǫd). 1864. [a. Gr. μακροποδ-, μακρόπους long-footed, f. μακρός + ποδ-, πούς.] *adj.* Long-footed. *sb.* A long-footed animal, e.g. a spider-crab. **Macroˑpodal** (1830), **-ous** (1852) *adjs. Bot.*, of a monocotyledonous embryo: Having the radicle large in proportion to the cotyledon. **Macropoˑdian** *Zool.*, one of a tribe of brachyurous decapod crustaceans 1839.

Macroscopic (mæːkro͵skǫˑpik), *a.* 1872. [f. MACRO- + -SCOPIC.] Visible to the naked eye; opp. to MICROSCOPIC. So **Maːcroscoˑpical** *a.*, **-ly** *adv.*

Macrospore (mæˑkrospōᵊɹ). 1859. [f. MACRO- + SPORE.] *Bot.* and *Zool.* One of the larger spores in certain flowerless plants and unicellular animals; opp. to MICROSPORE. So **Maːcrosporaˑnge, -aˑngium** *Bot.* the sporange containing macrospores 1875.

Macrurous, macrourous (măkrūᵊˑrəs), *a.* 1826. [f. mod.L. *macrura* neut. pl. (f. Gr. μακρός + οὐρά tail) + -OUS.] *Zool.* Belonging to the *Macrura* or long-tailed tribe of Decapod Crustacea (lobsters, etc.). So **Macruˑral, -ouˑral, Macruˑran, -ouˑran** *adjs.* and *sbs.*

Mactation (mæktēⁱˑʃən). 1640. [ad. L. *mactationem*, f. *mactare* to slay.] The action of killing a sacrificial victim.

‖**Macula** (mæˑkiŭlă). *Pl.* **-æ.** ME. [L.] A spot or stain: *Astron.* a dark spot in the sun; *Min.* a spot in a mineral due to the presence of particles of some other mineral; *Path.* a spot or stain in the skin, *esp.* a permanent one. Hence **Maˑcular** *a.* of, pertaining to, or marked by the presence of maculæ 1822.

Maculate (mæˑkiŭlĕt), *ppl. a.* 1490. [ad. L. *maculatus*, *maculare.*] Maculated. Now only in antithesis to *immaculate.*

Maculate (mæˑkiŭleⁱt), *v.* ME. [f. L. *maculat-*, *maculare*, f. *macula.*] *trans.* To spot, stain, soil, defile, pollute. Hence **Maˑculated** *ppl. a.* spotted, stained; also, marked with maculæ. So **Maculaˑtion**, the action of spotting or staining or the condition of being spotted or stained ME.; also, the state of being marked with, or a particular arrangement of, maculæ 1826.

Macule (mæˑkiul), *sb.* 1483. [f. L. *macula.*] A blemish, spot. *Obs.* in gen. sense. b. *Path.* = MACULA 1863. c. *Printing.* = MACKLE *sb.* 1841. So **Macule** [F. *maculer*] *v. trans.* †To spot, stain ME.; *Printing.* = MACKLE *v.* 1841.

Maculose (mæˑkiŭlōus), *a.* 1727. [ad. L. *maculosus.*] Full of spots; spotted. So **Maˑculous** *a.* 1688.

†**Mad**, *sb.* 1573. [var. of MATHE.] 1. A maggot or grub; *esp.* the larva of the blow-fly, which causes a disease in sheep. Also *pl.*, the disease so caused. -1688. 2. An earthworm -1691.

Mad (mæd), *a.* [Aphet. f. OE. *gemǣd(e)d*, pa. pple. of **gemǣdan* to render insane:— OTeut. **gamaiđo-*, f. *ga-* prefix (Y-) + **maiđo-*, f. (ult.) Indo-European root **mei-* to change (cf. L. *mutare*).] 1. Suffering from mental disease; out of one's mind; insane, lunatic. In mod. use chiefly: Maniacal, frenzied. †b. Causing madness (*rare*) -1676. 2. Foolish, unwise. Now only: Wildly foolish; ruinously imprudent. OE. 3. Carried away by enthusiasm or desire; wildly excited; infatuated ME. b. Wildly desirous *to* do something (now *rare*) 1627. 4. Beside oneself with anger; furious. Now only *colloq.* (In many dialects and in U.S. the ordinary word for 'angry'.) ME. 5. Of an animal: Rabid 1538. 6. Uncontrolled by reason; extravagant in gaiety; wild 1597. b. *transf.* of storm, wind 1836.

1. And then to hear a dead man chatter Is enough to drive one m. TENNYSON. Phr. *To go, run m. Like m.*: lit., in the manner of one who is m.; hence, furiously, violently. b. It's [new Wine's] m. Fumes DRYDEN. 2. A Mad World my Masters MIDDLETON. The chief justice..was not m. enough to risk a quarrel on such a subject MACAULAY. 3. The World is running m. after Farce DRYDEN. We are now m. about tar-water H. WALPOLE. b. All m. to speak, and none to hearken SWIFT. 4. They that are m. against me, are sworne against me *Ps.* cii. 8. 5. The dog, to gain some private ends, Went m., and bit the man GOLDSM. 6. In m. spirits 1777.

Provbs. *As m. as a buck, a hatter, a March hare.*

Mad (mæd), *v.* ME. [f. MAD *a.*] 1. *trans.* To make mad (see MAD *a.*). Now *rare* exc. *U.S. colloq.*, to exasperate. 2. *intr.* To be or to become mad; to act like a madman. Now *rare.* ME. †b. To become infatuated –1624.

1. Sin..Mads the ill-counsell'd heart 1850. 2. Far from the madding crowd's ignoble strife GRAY.

Madagass. Also **Madegass.** 1793. [var. of MALAGASH.] 1. A native or inhabitant of Madagascar. 2. A light-complexioned negro of Jamaica 1873.

Madam (mæ·dəm), *sb.* ME. [a. OF. *ma dame* (in mod.F. MADAME), lit. 'my lady'. Generally written *madam* when used as English, otherwise MADAME. Pl. MESDAMES; the Eng. pl. (exc. in sense 2) being obs.] 1. A form of polite address to a woman (substituted for the name), orig. used by servants in speaking to their mistress, and the like, and by people generally in speaking to a lady. In oral use now chiefly employed by salesmen and saleswomen in addressing adult female customers or by those in the position of servants to the public. From the 17th c., the title normally used in beginning or subscribing a letter to a woman of any station, except where the use of the name (as in 'Dear Mrs. A.', etc.) is permitted. (Corresponding to SIR.)

As a prefixed title. †a. Prefixed to a first or sole name –1749. b. Prefixed to a surname: (*a*) Now in U.S., and perh. formerly in England, the style of a woman who has a married son (whose wife is styled 'Mrs.'). (*b*) *dial.* The style of a married woman of position, e.g. the squire's wife.

2. (with *pl.*) A woman who is addressed as 'madam'. †a. A lady of rank or station. Also *fig.* –1632. b. (*a*) An affected fine lady 1598. †(*b*) A kept mistress, a prostitute –1761. (*c*) A hussy, minx 1802.

‖**Madame** (madam; often mădā·m, or anglicized mæ·dəm). Also **madam.** Pl. MESDAMES. 1599. [Fr.; see prec.] 1. The title prefixed to the surname of a French married woman (=Eng. 'Mrs.', 'Lady', etc.). Abbrev. *Mme.* (In Eng. use often assumed (instead of Mrs.) by singers or musicians, dressmakers, etc.) †2. The title given to female members of the French royal family; a French princess; *spec.* the eldest daughter of the French king or of the dauphin; in the reign of Louis XIV, the wife of MONSIEUR, the king's only brother –1798. †3. A French married woman; a Frenchman's wife –1765.

1. Mrs. Skelton, daughter to Madam Orfeur LUTTRELL.

Madapollam (mædăpǫ·lăm). 1832. [The name of a suburb of Narsapur, Madras presidency.] A kind of cotton cloth, orig. manufactured at Madapollam.

Ma·d-apple. 1597. [tr. L. *malum insanum*, a corruption of an oriental word (cf. BRINJAL).] The fruit of the EGG-PLANT.

Mad-brained, *a.* 1577. Having a mad brain; hot-headed, uncontrolled. So **Ma·d-brain,** a mad-brained person; also *attrib.* or *adj.* 1570.

Madcap (mæ·dkæp). 1588. [f. MAD *a.* + CAP *sb.*] A. *sb.* †a. A madman, maniac (*rare*). b. One who acts like a maniac; a reckless, wildly impulsive person. Often applied playfully to young women. 1589. B. *attrib.* or *adj.* Mad; reckless, wildly impulsive.

A. Come-on you mad-cap: Ile to the Ale-house with you SHAKS. B. That last is Beroune, the mery mad-cap Lord SHAKS.

Madden (mæ·d'n), *v.* 1735. [f. MAD *a.* + -EN [5].] To become or make mad.

My fierce steed maddens to be gone 1811. Fierce spirits..maddened by fanaticism MACAULAY. Hence **Ma·ddeningly** *adv.*

Madder (mæ·dəɹ), *sb.* [OE. *mædere* wk. fem. corresp. to ON. *maðra* in place-names; app. conn. w. MDu., MLG. *mêde* madder.] 1. A herbaceous climbing plant, *Rubia tinctorum*, with rough hairy stems and small yellowish flowers; cultivated for the dye obtained from it. With qualifying words applied to plants allied to or resembling this. 2. The root of this plant, used medicinally and as a source of dye-stuff; the dye-stuff or pigment prepared from this ME. 3. The colour obtained from madder dyes or pigments, as *crimson m.*, etc. 1861. Hence **Ma·dder** *v. trans.* to dye or treat with madder 1461.

Maddish (mæ·diʃ), *a.* 1573. [f. MAD *a.* + -ISH [1].] Somewhat mad.

Ma·d-do·ctor. 1703. [f. MAD *a.* used *absol.*] A physician who treats mental diseases; an alienist.

Made (mēɪd), *ppl. a.* ME. [pa. pple. of MAKE *v.*] 1. Produced or obtained by 'making'. 2. Of which the making has taken place ME.

1. Phr. *M. earth, ground*: solid ground that has been 'made' by filling up a marsh, embanking a river, etc. *M. dish* (Cookery): a dish composed of several ingredients. *M. gravy*: a gravy artificially compounded. *M. mast* (Naut.): one composed of several pieces of timber. *M. block*: a pulley-block composed of several parts joined together. *M. wines*: name for 'British wines' (as currant, gooseberry, etc. wine). 2. None but m. soldiers..would be employed 1796. Teach a boy arithmetic thoroughly, and he is a m. man SMILES.

Comb. **made-up,** †(*a*) consummate, accomplished; (*b*) put together; composed of parts from various sources; (*c*) artificially contrived or prepared, esp. in order to deceive; (*d*) of a person's mind', resolved, decided; (*e*) of articles of trade, ready-made.

†**Ma·defy,** *v.* ME. [a. F. *madéfier*, ad. L. *madefacere*, f. *madere* to be wet; see -FY.] *trans.* To make wet; to moisten –1671. So **Madefa·ction** [F. *madéfaction*], a wetting or moistening (now *rare*) 1581.

Madeira (mădī°·ră). 1585. [a. Pg.; so called because formerly thickly wooded (Pg. *madeira* = Sp. *madera* timber :—L. *materia* MATTER *sb.*).] 1. (With capital M.) An island in the Atlantic Ocean. Used *attrib.* in names of things produced in or connected with the island, as *M. lace*; **M. chair,** a kind of cane chair; **M. nut** *U.S.*, the common European walnut; **M. wine** = sense 2. 1664. 2. A white wine produced in the island of Madeira 1585.

Comb. **m. cake,** a kind of sponge-cake.

‖**Mademoiselle** (madəmwazẹl; often anglicized mædəmŏze·l). 1450. [Fr.; orig. *ma* my, *demoiselle* DAMSEL.] 1. The title applied to an unmarried Frenchwoman. In English often used *absol.* as the designation of a French governess or the French teacher in a girls' school. Abbrev. *Mlle.* Pl. **mesdemoiselles** (medəmwazẹl), abbrev. *Mlles.* 1696. 2. *Fr. Hist.* The title (as a substitute for the name) of the eldest daughter of 'Monsieur', the eldest brother of the king. Subseq. applied to the eldest daughter of the king, or, if he had none, to the first princess of the blood, while unmarried 1679. 3. *occas.* A person usually referred to as 'mademoiselle', an unmarried Frenchwoman; *spec.* a French governess 1642. 4. *U.S.* A sea fish, *Sciæna punctata* 1882.

Madge (mædʒ). 1591. [prop., pet-name for *Margaret*.] 1. The Barn-Owl, *Aluco flammeus.* Also *m.-owl.* 2. The Common Magpie, *Pica caudata* 1823.

Mad-headed, *a.* 1567. = MAD-BRAINED.

Madhouse (mæ·dhaus). Now *rhet.* or *derisive.* 1687. [f. MAD *a.* used *absol.*] A house for the reception and detention of the insane; a lunatic asylum.

‖**Madia** (mē̆·diă). 1839. [a. mod.L. *madia*, a. Chilian *madi.*] A composite plant, *Madia sativa*, native in Chili; cultivated for the oil (*m. oil*) obtained from its seeds.

Madid (mæ·did), *a.* Now *rare.* 1615. [ad. L. *madidus.*] Wet, moist.

Madly (mæ·dli), *adv.* ME. [f. MAD *a.* + -LY [2].] In an insane or foolish manner.

Madman (mæ·dmăn). ME. [Orig. two words.] One who is insane; a lunatic. Also, one who behaves like a lunatic, a wildly foolish person.

I have been a m. and a fool BETHUNE.

†**Ma·dnep.** Also **-nip.** 1597. [f. MAD *a.* + *nep, nip*, NEEP.] The Cow Parsnip, *Heracleum Sphondylium* –1712.

Madness (mæ·dnės). ME. [f. MAD *a.* + -NESS.] 1. Mental disease, insanity; mania. Also (in animals) rabies. 2. Extravagant folly ME. 3. Ungovernable anger, rage, fury 1665. 4. Extravagant excitement; ecstasy 1596.

2. To advance towards London would have been m. MACAULAY. 3. The m. of the people soon subsided GIBBON. 4. Such a hare is m. the youth, to skip ore the meshes of good counsaile the cripple SHAKS.

Madonna (mădǫ·nă). 1584. [a. It. *madonna*, orig. two words (*ma* OIt. f. *mia* fem., my; *donna* = F. *dame* :—L. *domina* lady). Cf. MADAM.] ‖1. †a. As an Italian form of address or title: My lady, madam –1827. †b. An Italian lady –1639. 2. a. An Italian designation of the Virgin Mary; usu. with *the.* b. A picture or statue of the Virgin Mary. 1644.

2. A faire Madonna of Pietro Perugino, painted on the wall EVELYN. 'Ave Mary' was her moan, 'M., sad is night and morn' TENNYSON.

attrib. and *Comb.*, as **M.-braided** *a.*, (of the hair) braided on each side of the face, after the manner of the M. in Italian representations; **M. lily,** the White Lily, *Lilium candidum*, as in pictures of the M.

Madras (mădra·s). 1833. 1. Name of a city and province of India; used *attrib.* in the names of things produced there or originally connected therewith: **Madras (net) muslin,** a handsome, but coarse make of muslin, produced in several varieties; **M. work,** the work executed upon M. handkerchiefs; etc. 1864. 2. In full *M. handkerchief*: a bright-coloured handkerchief of silk and cotton worn by the negroes of the W. Indies as a head-dress, 'formerly exported from Madras' (Yule).

‖**Madrasah** (mădræ·sa), **medresseh** (medre·se). 1630. [Different pronunciations of Arab. *madrasah*, f. *darasa* to study.] A Mohammedan college.

Madre-perl. *rare.* [ad. It. *madreperla*, f. *madre* mother + *perla* PEARL.] Mother-of-pearl. LONGF.

Madrepore (mæ·drĭpo°ɹ). 1751. [ad. mod.L. *madrepora* or F. *madrépore*, ad. It. *madrepora*, app. f. *madre* mother + *poro* (ad. L. *porus* PORE *sb.*; or ?ad. late L. *porus*, a. Gr. πῶρος stalactite).] Formerly, any perforate coral; now usually, a polypidom of the genus *Madrepora* or family *Madreporidæ*; also, the animal producing this.

Hence **Madrepo·ric** *a.* pertaining or related to, consisting or characteristic of, madrepore coral; resembling madrepore coral, as certain structures in echinoderms 1817. **Ma·drepo·riform** *a.* having the form or characters of madrepore coral 1840. **Madrepo·rite,** †(*a*) *Palæont.* fossil madrepore –1843; (*b*) *Min.* a calcareous rock resembling madrepore 1802; (*c*) *Zool.* a madreporic body in echinoderms 1877.

‖**Madrier** (mæ·driəɹ). 1704. [Fr.] *Fortif.* A thick plank used for various purposes, as to receive the mouth of a petard, to support the earth in mines or fortifications, etc.

Madrigal (mæ·drigăl). 1588. [ad. It. *madrigale*; ? f. L. *mandra*, a. Gr. μάνδρα fold, thus orig. a 'pastoral song'.] 1. A short lyrical poem of amatory character. 2. *Mus.* An old style of contrapuntal unaccompanied part-song for several voices; also *loosely*, applied to other part-songs 1588. 3. *transf.* and *fig.* A song, ditty 1589.

1. He [Clément Marot] was..the restorer of the m. WARTON. 2. And who shall silence all the airs and madrigals, that whisper softnes in chambers? MILT. 3. By shallow Rivers, to whose fals Melodious birds sing Madrigals MARLOWE. Hence **Madriga·lian** *a.* pertaining to, consisting or characteristic of, or dealing with madrigals 1848. **Ma·drigalist,** a writer or composer of madrigals 1789.

||**Madroño** (madrō·nʸo). Also **madrona**, madrone. 1850. [Sp.] A handsome evergreen tree of western N. America, *Arbutus Menziesii*, having a very hard wood and bearing yellow berries.

Madwort (mæ·d,wɒɹt). 1597. [? tr. L. *alyssum*, a. Gr. ἄλυσσον, f. ἀ- (priv.) + λύσσα rabies.] 1. A herb of the genus *Alyssum*. 2. The Trailing Catchweed, *Asperugo procumbens*. (Also called *German m.*) 1760.

Mæcenas (mīsī·næs). *Pl.* **Mæcenases**, †**Mæcenates** (-ī·tīz). 1561. A Roman knight, the patron of Horace and Virgil. Hence: A generous patron of literature or art; occas. *gen.* a patron.

Maelstrom (mēⁱ·lstrǒm). 1682. [a. early mod.Du. *maelstrom* (now *maalstroom*) whirlpool, f. *malen* to grind, also to whirl round + *stroom* stream.] A famous whirlpool on the west coast of Norway, formerly supposed to suck in and destroy all vessels within a long radius. Also *transf.* a great whirlpool. Also *fig.*

Mænad (mī·næd). 1579. [ad. L. *Mænad-*, *Mænas*, a. Gr. Μαιναδ-, Μαινάς, f. μαίνεσθαι to rave.] A Bacchante. Hence **Mæna·dic** *a.* characteristic of a M.; infuriated.

||**Maestoso** (maęstō·so). 1724. [It., = majestic.] *Mus.* A direction: To be executed majestically.

||**Maestro** (maę·stro). 1797. [It., = master.] A master in music; a great composer, teacher, or conductor.

†**Maffick** (mæ·fik), *v.* 1900 (no longer used). [Back-formation from *mafficking* (= the place-name *Ma·feking* treated joc. as a pres. pple.).] *intr.* A journalistic word, used to designate the extravagant behaviour of the London crowds on the relief of Mafeking (17 May, 1900); also *transf.*

Maffle (mæ·f'l), *v.* *Obs.* exc. *dial.* ME. [Cf. early mod.Du. *maffelen* to move the jaws.] 1. *intr.* To stammer; to mumble. 2. To bungle; to delay, waste time 1781. 3. *trans.* To confuse, bewilder, muddle 1820. Hence **Ma·ffler.** **Ma·fflingly** *adv.*

||**Mafia** (mafī·a). Also **maffia.** 1875. [Sicilian.] In Sicily, the spirit of hostility to law and its ministers, often manifesting itself in vindictive crimes. Also, the body of those who share in this spirit.

Mag (mæg), *sb.*¹ ME. [Short for *Margaret.*] Used as a personal name in various prov. phr.; also, as a proper name for a magpie, hence = MAGPIE.

Mag (mæg), *sb.*² *slang.* Also **meg.** 1781. [?] A halfpenny.

Mag (mæg), *sb.*³ 1801. Abbrev. of MAGAZINE (sense 5 b). So **Maga** (mæ·gă), abbrev. for Blackwood's Magazine 1825.

Mag, *sb.*⁴ 1920. Abbrev. of MAGNETO.

Mag (mæg), *v.* Also **meg.** 1810. [? back-formation from MAGPIE.] *intr.* To chatter. So Mag *sb.*⁵ chatter, talk; a chatterbox 1778.

Magazine (mægăzī·n), *sb.* 1583. [a. F. *magasin* (OF. *magazin*), a. Arab. *makhāzin*, pl. of *makhzan* storehouse, f. *khazana* to store up.] 1. A storehouse or repository for goods or merchandise; a warehouse, depot. Now *rare.* Also *fig.* b. *transf.* of a country or district 1596. c. A portable receptacle for articles of value. Now *rare.* 1768. 2. *Mil.* a. *gen.* A building in which are stored arms, ammunition, and provisions for an army. b. *spec.* A powder magazine. 1596. Also *fig.* 3. a. *Mil.* The contents of a magazine; a store. Also *collect. pl.* Stores, provisions, munitions of war; armament, military equipment 1589. Also *fig.* b. *gen.* A store, heap; †a wardrobe 1615. Also *fig.* †4. A victualling ship; more fully *magazine(s ship* 1624. 5. †a. Used in the titles of books, with sense: A storehouse of information -1802. b. A periodical publication containing articles by various writers, intended chiefly for the general reader 1731. 6. a. A chamber in a repeating rifle, machine-gun, etc., containing a supply of cartridges which are fed automatically to the breech 1867. b. A case for carrying a supply of cartridges 1892. c. A reservoir or supply-chamber in a machine, stove, battery, etc. 1873.

1. b. Constantinople..Aleppo..and grand Cayro.. are the three Maggezzines of the whole Empire LITHGOW. 2. Here Irish wit is seen! When nothing's left that's worth defence, We build a m. SWIFT. 3. a. A corps of 5000 men..had carried away a m. of arms WELLINGTON. b. A..m. of flesh, milk, butter, and cheese DE FOE.

attrib. and *Comb.*, as *m. article*, *-editor*; *m. rifle*; **m. gun,** a gun (i.e. either a cannon or a rifle, etc.) provided with a 'magazine' (sense 6 a); **-stove,** one having a fuel-chamber which supplies coal to the fire by some self-feeding process. Hence **Magazi·ne** *v.* (now *rare*) *trans.* to lay up in or as in a magazine 1643; *intr.* to conduct a magazine 1763. **Magazi·ner** (1758), **-i·nist** (1821) one who writes for magazines. **Magazi·nish** *a.* 1794.

Magdalen, Magdalene (mæ·gdălěn, -lǐn). ME. [ad. Eccl.L. (*Maria*) *Magdalena*, *-lene*, a. Gr. (Μαρία ἡ) Μαγδαληνή (Mary) of Magdala (on the sea of Galilee). The vernacular form of the word (adopted through Fr.) is MAUDLIN; whence the pronunciation (mǭ·dlin) in the names of Magdalen and Magdalene Colleges.] 1. a. *The Magdalen(e*: a disciple of Christ named Mary (Luke viii. 2), commonly identified with the 'sinner' of Luke vii. 37, and therefore appearing in Western hagiology as a repentant harlot elevated to saintship. b. A picture of Mary Magdalen 1661. 2. *transf.* One whose history resembles that of the Magdalen; *spec.* a reformed prostitute 1693. 3. [Short for *M. hospital.*] A home for the reformation of prostitutes 1766. 4. A kind of peach 1706.

Comb.: **M. day,** the feast of St. Mary Magdalen, 22 July; **M. asylum, charity, home, hospital, house** = sense 3.

†**Magdaleon.** 1450. [ad. med.L. *magdaleonem*, *magdaleo*, also *magdalium*, f. Gr. μαγδαλιά dough or bread-crumb (Galen).] *Pharmacy.* A cylindrical roll of plaster, salve, or any medicinal substance.

Mage (mēⁱdʒ), *arch.* ME. [Eng. form of MAGUS.] 1. A magician; *transf.* a person of wisdom and learning. 2. *pl.* The Magi 1584.

Magellan (măge·lăn). 1638. Eng. form of the name of Fernão de *Magalhães* (? 1470–1521), the Portuguese navigator who first passed through the Straits of M. into the Pacific Ocean; used *attrib.* (or in possessive) = MAGELLANIC. Hence **Magella·nic** *a.* [mod.L. *Magellanicus*] pertaining to or named after Magellan 1602.

M. clouds, two large globular cloudy spots formed of nebulæ and clusters of stars, visible in the southern hemisphere.

Magenta (mădʒe·ntă). 1860. Name of a brilliant crimson aniline dye, discovered shortly after the date, 1859, of the battle of Magenta, in Northern Italy. Also *attrib.* or *adj.*

Magged (mægd), *a.* 1867. *Naut.* Worn, fretted; as, a *m. brace.*

Maggot (mæ·gǫt). ME. [? conn. w. ME. *maðek*, *maddock.*] 1. A worm or grub; chiefly applied to the larva of the cheese-fly and the flesh-fly or blue-bottle. Also *fig.* 2. A whimsical fancy; a crotchet 1625. 3. A whimsical or capricious person 1681.

1. *Red m.*: the larva of the wheat-midge. 2. She's got some m. in her head about being loved for her own sake 1898. Hence **Ma·ggoty** *a.* full of maggots.

Ma·ggot-pie. *Obs.* exc. *dial.* 1573. [f. ME. *Magote*, a. F. *Margot*, pet name for *Marguerite* Margaret + PIE.] A magpie.

Magi (mēⁱ·dʒəi), *sb. pl.*: see MAGUS.

Magian (mēⁱ·dʒiăn). 1578. [f. L. MAGUS + -IAN.] A. *sb.* One of the Magi; a follower of or believer in the Magi; a magician, wizard. B. *adj.* Of or pertaining to the Magi 1716; magical (KEATS). Hence **Ma·gianism,** the tenets or doctrines of the Magi 1716.

Magic (mæ·dʒik), *sb.* ME. [ad. OF. *magique*, ad. late L. *magica* (sc. *ars*).] 1. The pretended art of influencing the course of events by compelling the agency of spiritual beings, or by bringing into operation some occult controlling principle of nature; sorcery, witchcraft. Also, the practice of this art. †b. A magical procedure or rite; also *concr.* a charm, fetish -1814. 2. *fig.* A secret and overmastering influence resembling magic in its effects 1611. 3. *transf.* The art of producing (by legerdemain, optical illusion, etc.) surprising phenomena resembling the results of 'magic'; conjuring 1831.

1. M., which means the unnatural interference with nature 1884. *Black m.* [= F. *magie noire*]: modern name for the kind of m. that involved the invocation of devils; opp. to *white m.* [= F. *magie blanche*]. *Natural m.*: that which did not involve recourse to the agency of personal spirits. 2. Oh Royall Peece: There's Magick in thy Maiestie SHAKS.

Magic (mæ·dʒik), *a.* ME. [a. F. *magique*, ad. L. *magicus*, ad. Gr. μαγικός, lit. pertaining to the Magi, f. μάγος; see MAGUS.] 1. Of or pertaining to magic. Also, working or produced by enchantment. Not used predicatively. b. Of a material object, a diagram, etc.: Employed in magic rites, endued with magic powers, enchanted 1697. 2. Producing appearances or results like those of sorcery 1696.

1. To magike artes against my will I bend SURREY. b. *M. glass*, *mirror*: one in which the spectator is supposed to see the representation of future events or distant scenes; often *fig.* 2. Longings..that..the m. curtain [would] once more arise SCOTT.

Phr. *M. square*: a square divided into smaller squares, each containing a number, so arranged that the sum of the figures in a row, vertical, horizontal, or diagonal, is always the same. *M. circle*: an arrangement of numbers in concentric circles with radial divisions, with arithmetical properties similar to those of the magic square.

So **Ma·gical** *a.* magic; resembling magic in action or effect; produced as by magic 1555. **Ma·gically** *adv.*

Magician (mădʒi·ʃăn). ME. [a. F. *magicien*, f. L. *magica* MAGIC *sb.*] One skilled in magic; a necromancer, wizard. Also *occas.*, a conjuror.

fig. The M. of the North [i.e. Walter Scott] 1877.

Ma·gic la·ntern. 1696. [tr. mod.L. *laterna magica.*] An optical instrument by means of which a magnified image of a picture on glass is thrown upon a white screen or wall in a darkened room.

Magilp, var. of MEGILP.

Magism (mēⁱ·dʒiz'm). 1844. [f. L. *magus* + -ISM.] The beliefs, principles, and practices of the Magi.

||**Magister** (mădʒi·stəɹ). 1756. A mediæval and mod.L. title of academic rank, usu. rendered by MASTER, but occas. employed *Hist.* or in speaking of foreign universities.

Magisterial (mædʒistīᵊ·riăl), *a.* 1632. [ad. med.L. *magisterialis*, f. late L. *magisterius*, f. L. *magister* MASTER *sb.*] Of or pertaining to a master or a magistrate. †1. Of or pertaining to a master-workman; displaying a master's skill -1683. 2. Of or pertaining to one qualified to speak with authority; authoritative. Of persons: Having the bearing or authority of a master; *occas.*, dictatorial. 1632. 3. Of, pertaining to, or proper to a magistrateor magistrates. Of persons: Holding the office of a magistrate. Of an inquiry: Conducted by magistrates. 1660. †4. *Alch.* and *Med.* = MAGISTRAL 2. -1722. †5. quasi-*sb.* or *sb.* = MAGISTERY 3. -1662.

2. These M. Propositions don't Dispute for Belief, but demand it COLLIER. A M. Air and too much Heat and Passion appear in their Writings BENTLEY. 3. The m. inquiry into the charge of arson 1885. Hence †**Magisteriality,** mastership, authoritative position. **Ma·giste·rial·ly** *adv.*, †**-ness.**

||**Magisterium** (mædʒistīᵊ·riǔm). 1593. [L., = next.] †1. *Alch.* = MAGISTERY 3 a. -1675. 2. *R. C. Theol.* The teaching function of the Church 183..

Magistery (mæ·dʒistĕri). *Obs.* exc. *Hist.* 1566. [ad. L. *magisterium* the office of a master; in med.L. the philosopher's stone; f. *magister* MASTER *sb.*] †1. = MAGISTRACY 2, 3. -1585. †2. The quality or functions of a master; mastership, authoritative appearance. b. The office of a (Grand) Master. -1706. 3. *Alch.*, *Med.*, etc. a. A master principle of nature; a potent transmuting or curative quality or agency; a substance that has this quality, e.g. the philosopher's stone 1594. b. A product or result of transmutation 1605. c. The concentrated essence of a substance 1641. d. The residuum obtained by precipitation from an acid solution, e.g. *m. of bismuth*, etc.; a precipitate 1602. e. A specific 1669.

Magistracy (mæ·dʒistrăsi). 1577. [f. MAGISTRATE; see -ACY.] †1. The condition of being a magistrate -1693. **2.** The office of a magistrate; *occas.* conduct in office as a magistrate. Now *rare.* 1577. **3.** Magistrates collectively 1601.

Magistral (mădʒi·străl). 1572. [a. F., or ad. L. *magistralis*, f. *magister.*] **A.** *adj.* **1.** Of, pertaining to, or befitting a master; authoritative, dogmatic. Now *rare.* 1605. **2.** *Pharmacy.* Of a remedy, a formula: Devised by a physician for a particular case; opp. to OFFICINAL 1605. †**b.** By some writers taken to mean: Sovereign, supremely effective -1678. **3.** *Fortif.* Leading, principal, master -1828. **4.** *occas.*, Having the title of 'Master'; of or pertaining to a master or masters 1837.

1. Your assertion..is more Magistrall, then true 1641. **2.** Some Magistrall Opiate 1638. **3.** *M. line*: in field fortifications, the interior crest line; in permanent fortifications, usually the line of the top of the escarp of each work. **4.** The men are rebuked, in the m. homilies, for their ingratitude in striking RUSKIN.

B. *sb.* †**1.** *Pharmacy.* A magistral preparation or formula -1670. **2.** *Fortif.* = *Magistral line.* (See A. 3.) 1853. ‖**3.** *Metallurgy.* [Sp. (maχistra·l).] Roasted copper pyrites used in the reduction of silver ore 1839.

Hence †**Magistra·lity,** the quality or condition of being m.; quasi-*concr.* a dogmatic utterance; in *Med.* a special prescription. †**Magi·strally** *adv.*

Magistrand (mæ·dʒistrænd). *Sc.* 1642. [ad. med.L. *magistrandus*, gerund. pple. of *magistrari* to become a Master (of Arts).] Orig., in Scottish Universities, an Arts student in the fourth, or highest, class; later, one in the fourth year. Now, in official use, only at Aberdeen.

Magistrate (mæ·dʒistrēt). ME. [ad. L. *magistratus*, f. *magister* (see -ATE[1] 1 a).] †**1.** The office and dignity of a magistrate -1530. **2.** A civil officer charged with the administration of the laws, a member of the executive government ME. **3.** *spec.* A 'justice of the peace' (see JUSTICE *sb.* III. 3); also applied to salaried officials having criminal jurisdiction of the first instance; as, *police, stipendiary*, and, in Ireland, *resident m.* 1688.

2. The king was too eminent a m. to be trusted with discretionary power HUME. *Chief m., first m.*: in a monarchy, the sovereign; in a republic, usually the president. Hence **Ma·gistrateship.** †**Magistra·tic, Magistra·tical** *a.* of, pertaining to, or befitting a m. or magistrates. **Magistra·tically** *adv.*

Magistrature (mæ·dʒistrētiŭı). 1672. [a. F., f. *magistrat* MAGISTRATE.] **1.** The dignity or office of a magistrate; *occas.* the exercise of the office; with *a* and *pl.* an individual office. **b.** The term of a magistrate's office 1720. **2.** *collect.* = MAGISTRACY 3. 1679.

Magma (mæ·gmă). ME. [a. L. *magma* (sense 1), Gr. μάγμα, f. root of μάσσειν to knead.] †**1.** The dregs that remain from a semi-liquid substance after the liquid part has been removed by pressure or evaporation -1856. **2.** Any crude mixture of mineral or organic matters in the state of a thin paste 1681. **3.** *Geol.* **a.** One of two or more supposed strata of fluid or semi-fluid matter lying beneath the earth's crust. **b.** The amorphous basis of certain porphyritic rocks. 1804. Hence **Magma·tic** *a.*

Magna Charta, Magna Carta (mæ·gnă kā·ɹtă). 1568. [med.L., = 'great charter'.] The Great Charter of English personal and political liberty, obtained from King John in 1215. Also *transf.* and *fig.*

†‖**Magna·le,** *pl.* **-alia.** 1623. [as if L. **magnale*, sing. of *magnalia* (in L. only *magnalia* neut. pl.), f. *magnus* great.] A great or wonderful thing -1702; *pl.* wonders 1645-81.

†**Magna·lity.** [f. prec. + -ITY.] A great or wonderful thing. SIR T. BROWNE.

Magnanimity (mægnăni·miti). ME. [a. F. *magnanimité*, ad. L. *magnanimitatem.*] †**1.** The (vague) name of a virtue in mediæval ethics -1526. †**2.** Lofty courage; fortitude -1801. **3.** As tr. Aristotle's μεγαλοψυχία 'greatness of soul' (see *Eth. N.* iv. 3). Also, loftiness of thought or purpose. Now *rare.* 1598. **4.** Nobility of feeling; superiority to petty resentment or jealousy 1771. **b.** *pl.* Instances of this 1639. †**5.** Magnificence. SIR T. BROWNE.

4. It may be m. in Lord Mansfield to despise attacks made upon himself BURKE.

Magnanimous (mægnæ·niməs), *a.* Also †**-ious.** 1584. [f. L. *magnanimus* (f. *magnus* + *animus*; repr. Gr. μεγαλόψυχος) + -OUS.] **1.** Great in courage; nobly valiant. Also, proceeding from or manifesting high courage. ? *Obs.* **2.** High-souled; lofty of purpose; noble in feeling or conduct. Now esp.: Superior to petty resentment or jealousy. 1598.

1. The incouragement, that the magnanimious Cesar gaue vnto his souldiours 1584. **2.** Pitch thy behaviour low, thy projects high; So shalt thou humble and m. be G. HERBERT. They knew..what strength was, that would not bend But in m. meekness WORDSW. Hence **Magna·nimous-ly** *adv.*, **-ness** (*rare*).

Magnate (mæ·gnēt). Chiefly *pl.* ME. [ad. late L. *magnat-*, *magnas*, f. *magnus* great.] **1.** A great man; a noble; a person of great influence or eminence in any sphere; now *spec.* one prominent in the management of a large industry or enterprise, as, an *oil magnate* (U.S.). **2.** In Hungary, and formerly in Poland, a member of the Upper House in the Diet 1797.

Magne- (mæ·gnĭ), irreg. comb. form for MAGNETO-, as in **Ma·gne-cry·stal,** a crystal acted upon by magnetism; etc. 1831.

†**Magnes.** ME. [L., = Gr. ὁ Μάγνης λίθος, the Magnesian stone, MAGNET.] A magnet, loadstone -1750. Also *m.-stone.* **b.** *transf.* Magnetic virtue. EVELYN.

Magnesia (mægnī·ʃă). ME. [a. med.L. *magnesia*, a. Gr. ἡ Μαγνησία λίθος, 'the Magnesian stone', (1) the loadstone; (2) a shining stone, perh. talc.] †**1.** *Alch.* A mineral said to be an ingredient of the philosopher's stone -1610. †**2.** = MANGANESE 1. Also *black m.* (opp. to †*white m.* = mod.L. *magnesia alba* = 3) -1797. **3. a.** Orig., and still pop., applied to hydrated magnesium carbonate, a white earthy powder, used as an antacid and cathartic. **b.** In mod. *Chemistry*, an alkaline earth, now recognized as the oxide of magnesium (MgO). 1755. Hence **Magne·sian** *a.* of, pertaining to, or containing m.; in M. limestone *Geol.* = DOLOMITE.

Magnesic (mægnī·sik), *a.* 1877. [f. MAGNESIA and MAGNESIUM + -IC.] **a.** Containing magnesia. **b.** Of, pertaining to, or containing magnesium.

Magnesite (mæ·gnĭsəit). 1815. [f. MAGNESIA + -ITE[1].] *Min.* Carbonate of magnesium, occurring commonly in compact white masses, but occas. crystalline.

Magnesium (mægnī·ziŏm, -ī·ʃiŏm). 1808. [f. MAGNESIA; see -UM, -IUM.] *Chem.* †**1.** = MANGANESE 1. Sir H. Davy. **2.** A chemical element, one of the 'metals of the alkaline earths', being the base of magnesia. Symbol Mg. Found only in composition. 1812.

Comb.: **m. light,** a brilliant light produced by the combustion of m.; **m. ribbon, thread, wire,** a thin strip or wire of m. prepared for burning.

Magnet (mæ·gnėt). 1440. [a. OF. *magnete*, or ad. L. *magneta*, accus. of *magnes*; see MAGNES.] **1.** *Min.* = LOADSTONE; a variety of magnetite (proto-sesquioxide of iron) having the power of attracting iron and steel, and other properties. **2.** A piece of loadstone; also, a piece of iron or steel to which the characteristic properties of loadstone have been imparted by contact, by induction, or by means of an electric current. When a magnet is suspended freely, one of its poles (hence called the north pole) points approximately north, and the other (the south pole) approximately south. 1625. **b.** Any body possessing the properties characteristic of a magnet 1797. **3.** *fig.* Something which attracts 1655.

1. In midst of this white City stands a Castle built of M. MILT. **2.** *Bar m.*, a polarized rod of iron, now much used in the construction of electro-magnetic apparatus. *Natural m.*: one consisting of loadstone; opp. to *artificial m.* **3.** Two magnets, heaven and earth, allure to bliss, The larger loadstone that, the nearer this DRYDEN.

attrib. and *Comb.*, as **m. core,** the rod or bar of soft magnetized iron placed in the middle of an electro-magnet; **m. helix,** a coil of wire such as surrounds the core of an electro-magnet.

Magnetic (mægne·tik). 1632. [ad. mod.L. *magneticus*, f. *magnet-*; see MAGNET and -IC.] **A.** *adj.* **1.** Having the properties of a magnet; pertaining to a magnet or to magnetism; producing, caused by, or operating by means of magnetism 1634. **2.** *fig.* Having powers of attraction; very seductive. Now often with a tinge of sense 4. 1632. **3.** Applied to all bodies which are acted upon by the loadstone; also, = PARAMAGNETIC 1837. **4.** Pertaining to animal magnetism; mesmeric 1800.

2. That m. influence which irresistibly draws our feet to spots on which our imagination has long fed M. PATTISON. **4.** As if he had been in a m. slumber DICKENS.

B. *sb.* †**1.** = MAGNET -1671. **2. a.** Any metal which is acted upon by the loadstone 1847. **b.** A paramagnetic body 1890. **3.** **Magnetics**: the science of magnetism 1786. So **Magne·tical** *a.*; **-ly** *adv.*, †**-ness.**

Magnetico- (mægne·tiko), used (*rarely*) as comb. form of MAGNETIC = 'magnetic and..'.

Magneti·ferous, *a.* 1832. [f. MAGNET + -IFEROUS.] Producing or conducting magnetism.

Magnetism (mæ·gnėtiz'm). 1616. [See MAGNET and -ISM.] **1.** The characteristic properties of the magnet; magnetic phenomena and their laws. Also, the natural agency concerned in producing these phenomena; now regarded as a modification of energy. **b.** *fig.* Attractive power, esp. personal charm or ascendancy; *occas.* with a tinge of sense 3. 1655. **2.** The science which treats of magnetic phenomena 1828. **3.** Short for *animal magnetism* (see ANIMAL) = MESMERISM 1785.

1. *Terrestrial m.*: the magnetic properties of the earth, considered as a whole. **b.** Now, m. is among the highest qualities which an American popular leader can possess BRYCE.

Magnetist (mæ·gnėtist). 1761. [f. MAGNET + -IST.] **1.** One skilled in the science of magnetism. **2.** One who practises animal magnetism; a mesmerist. Also *animal m.* 1802.

Magnetite (mæ·gnėtəit). 1851. [ad. G. *magnetit*; see MAGNET and -ITE[1] 2 b.] *Min.* Proto-sesquioxide of iron, which is readily attracted by the magnet; magnetic oxide of iron.

Magnetizable (mæ·gnėtəizăb'l), *a.* 1797. [f. MAGNETIZE + -ABLE.] Capable of being magnetized. Hence **Ma:gnetizabi·lity.**

Magnetize (mæ·gnėtəiz), *v.* 1785. [f. MAGNET + -IZE.] **1.** *trans.* To charge with magnetic properties 1801. **2.** *intr.* To become magnetic. (Dicts.) **3.** *trans.* To attract as a magnet does. Chiefly *fig.* (with mixture of sense 4), to subdue or win by personal charm. 1836. **4.** To influence by animal magnetism; to mesmerize. Also *fig.* 1785.

1. To m. a steel bar 1801. **3.** External Nature is.. an enchantress who magnetises the human spirit MOZLEY. Hence **Ma:gnetiza·tion,** the action of magnetizing or condition of being magnetized. **Ma·gnetizer,** one who or that which magnetizes; *esp.* a mesmerist.

Magneto (mægnī·to), *sb.* 1882. Colloq. abbrev. for *magneto-electric machine*; *spec.* the ignition apparatus of internal combustion engines.

Magneto- (mægnī·to-), repr. comb. form of Gr. μάγνητ-, μάγνης MAGNET, denoting processes carried on by magnetic means, or the application of magnetism to departments of art or industry; as in **m.-therapy,** the treatment of disease by the external application of metal plates inducing magnetic electricity; etc.

Magne:to-ele·ctric, *a.* 1831. Pertaining to electric phenomena involving electric currents induced in conductors by the relative motion of these conductors with respect to either permanent magnets or electro-magnets; as, *magneto-electric induction.*

Magneto-electric machine: first used by Faraday, in 1831, to denote a machine generating currents by magneto-electric induction; by later writers employed in various limited senses, and in recent times commonly limited to the machines with permanent steel magnets; see N.E.D. So **Magne:to-ele·ctrical** *a.*

Magne:to-electri·city. 1832. Electricity generated by the relative movement of electric conductors and magnets of any kind.

Magne·togram. 1884. [f. MAGNETO- + -GRAM.] The automatic record of magnetic needles.

Magnetograph (mægnī·togrαf). 1847. [f. MAGNETO- + -GRAPH.] 1. An instrument recording automatically the movements of the magnetometer. Also *attrib.* 2. = MAGNETOGRAM. (U.S. Dicts.)

Magnetometer (mægnĭtǫ·mĭtəɹ). 1827. [ad. F. *magnétomètre*; see MAGNETO- and -METER.] An instrument for measuring magnetic forces, esp. terrestrial magnetism. Hence **Magne:to·me·tric, -al** *a.* of, pertaining to, or measured by the m. **Magneto·metry,** measurement by means of the m.

Magne:tomo·tor. 1823. [f. MAGNETO- + MOTOR.] A voltaic series of large plates producing a great quantity of electricity of low intensity, adapted to the exhibition of electro-magnetic phenomena.

Magnifiable (mæ·gnifəi,ăb'l), *a.* [f. MAGNIFY + -ABLE.] Capable of being magnified. SIR T. BROWNE.

Magnific (mægni·fik), *a.* Now *literary* and *arch.* Also †**magnifique.** 1490. [a. F. *magnifique*, ad. L. *magnificus*, f. *magnus*; see -FIC.] †1. Renowned, glorious –1669. †2. = MAGNIFICENT 2. –1655. 3. = MAGNIFICENT 3, 4. 1490. 4. Imposing by vastness or dignity. Of language, etc.: Exalted, sublime; *occas.* in derisive sense, grandiloquent. 1558. †5. Of compositions, titles, etc.: Serving to magnify or extol –1667.

3. The pillared dome m. heaved Its ample roof THOMSON. 4. Power..God's gift m. BROWNING.

Magnifical (mægni·fikăl), *a.* 1538. [f. as prec. + -AL.] = MAGNIFIC. Hence **Magni·fically** *adv.* (*arch.*).

‖**Magnificat** (mægni·fikæt). ME. [L., 3rd pers. sing. pres. ind. of *magnificare* to MAGNIFY.] 1. The hymn of the Virgin Mary in *Luke* i. 46–55 (in the Vulgate beginning *Magnificat anima mea Dominum*), used as a canticle. 2. *transf.* A song of praise; a pæan 1614.

†**Magni·ficate,** *v.* 1598. [f. ppl. stem of L. *magnificare* to MAGNIFY.] *trans.* = MAGNIFY *v.* –1672.

Magnification (mæ:gnifikēⁱ·ʃən). 1625. [ad. L. *magnificationem*; see MAGNIFY and -ATION.] The action of magnifying or condition of being magnified; laudation; enlargement. Also quasi-*concr.* a magnified reproduction.

Magnificence (mægni·fisĕns). ME. [a. F., ad. L. *magnificentia*; see MAGNIFICENT and -ENCE.] 1. The name of one of the Aristotelian and scholastic 'virtues', repr. Gr. μεγαλοπρέπεια, liberality of expenditure combined with good taste. †2. Sovereign bounty or munificence –1647. †3. Glory; greatness of nature or reputation –1667. 4. Sumptuousness or splendour of surroundings or appointments ME. †b. An instance of this; a splendid ceremony –1674. 5. Grandeur or imposing beauty of appearance. †Also *pl.* features of magnificence. ME. 6. A title of honour, applied to kings and other distinguished persons. *Obs.* exc. *Hist.* or as a foreign title. ME.

1. Thanne comth M., that is to seyn, whan a man dooth and perfourneth grete werkes of goodnesse CHAUCER. 4. Nor doth this grandeur and majestic show Of luxury, though call'd m.,..allure mine eye MILT. 5. Not Babilon, Nor great Alcairo such m. Equal'd in all thir glories MILT. So **Magni·ficency;** also with *a* and *pl.*

Magnificent (mægni·fisĕnt), *a.* 1513. [a. OF. *magnificent*, f. L. *magnificent-*, altered stem of *magnificus*, lit. doing great deeds, f. *magnus*; see -FIC.] 1. Characterized by greatness of achievement or by conduct befitting lofty position. *Obs.* exc. as a titular epithet, e. g. in Lorenzo the M., etc. 2. Royally lavish or munificent (now *rare*) 1579. 3. Splendid, stately; living in splendour and pomp 1526. 4. Sumptuously constructed or adorned; also, imposingly beautiful 1540. 5. Of immaterial things: Imposing, exalted 1639. 6. Used to express admiration 1704.

2. A Prince is neuer so m., As when hee's sparing to inrich a few With th' iniuries of many MASSINGER. 4. That m. Temple of Salomon 1540. 6. The day was m. 1860. Hence **Magni·ficently** *adv.*

‖**Magnifico** (mægni·fiko). 1573. [It., = MAGNIFIC.] Title bestowed upon the magnates of Venice; also *transf.*

Magnifier (mæ·gnifəiəɹ). 1550. [f. MAGNIFY *v.* + -ER[1].] One who or that which magnifies. Also *fig.*

Magnify (mæ·gnifəi), *v.* ME. [ad. L. *magnificare*, f. *magnificus.* Sense 4 is Eng. only.] 1. *trans.* To speak or act for the glory of (a person or thing); to laud, extol (*arch.*). 2. To make greater in size, status, importance, or qualities; to enlarge, augment. Now *rare.* ME. 3. *trans.* To represent as great or greater; to exaggerate 1759. 4. To increase the apparent size of an object by artificial means. Also *absol.* 1665. 5. *intr.* 'A cant word for *to have effect*' (J.); to signify. Now *dial.* 1712.

1. If the invention of the ship was thought so noble ..how much more are letters to be magnified, which as ships pass through the vast seas of time BACON. 4. *fig.* The effects of fogs upon our estimation of dimension..are well known: men are magnified to giants KANE.

Magnifying glass, a glass lens, or combination of lenses, used to increase the apparent size of any object seen through it 1665.

Magniloquence (mægni·lǒkwĕns). 1623. [f. next; see -ENCE.] The quality of being magniloquent.

Magniloquent (mægni·lǒkwĕnt), *a.* 1656. [f. L. *magniloquus*, f. *magnus* great + *-loquus* speaking + -ENT.] Lofty or ambitious in expression, grandiloquent. Also, *occas.*, talking big, boastful. Hence **Magni·loquently** *adv.* So †**Magni·loquous** *a.*

Magnitude (mæ·gnitiŭd). ME. [ad. L. *magnitudo*, f. *magnus*, cogn. w. Gr. μέγας, OTeut. **mikilo-*; see MUCH.] 1. = GREATNESS, in various senses; see quots. 2. Size, whether great or small; in *Geom.*, the measure or extent of a line, area, volume, or angle 1570. 3. A class in a system of classification determined by size: *esp.* each of the classes into which the fixed stars have been arranged according to their degree of brilliancy 1641. b. *Of the first m.* (fig.): of the utmost greatness or importance 1693.

1. [Boadicea's] orations..wherein is expressed all m. of a spirit, breathing to the libertie and redemption of her Countrie B. JONS. The height, and strength, and m. of their building DE FOE. The m. of his crimes *Junius Lett.* 2. quasi-*concr.* A long m., we terme a Line 1570. 3. The stars 'of the first m.' are the most brilliant; the 'sixth m.' includes those that are barely visible to the naked eye; the seventh and lower magnitudes are telescopic only. The classification into 'magnitudes',..is now a matter of photometric measurement. N.E.D.

Magnolia (mægnōᵘ·liă). 1748. [a. mod.L. *magnolia*, f. name of Pierre *Magnol* (latinized *Magnolius*), professor of botany at Montpellier, 1638–1715.] A genus of large (rarely shrubby) trees (the typical genus of the N.O. *Magnoliaceæ*) cultivated for their foliage and flowers. Hence **Magnolia·ceous** *a.* of or belonging to the N.O. *Magnoliaceæ*.

Magnum (mæ·gnǒm). 1788. [neut. sing. of L. *magnus* used subst.] A bottle containing two quarts of wine or spirits; also, as a measure of liquor. b. A large glass (of spirits). DICKENS.

A..partiality for..magnums of old port 1893.

Magnum bonum (mæ·gnǒm bōᵘ·nǒm). 1721. [neut. sing. of L. *magnus* and *bonus.*] 1. A kind of large yellow cooking-plum. Also *magnum bonum plum.* 2. = MAGNUM. 1800. 3. A kind of potato 1882. 4. A large-barrelled steel pen 1851.

‖**Magnum opus.** See OPUS.

‖**Magot** (mæ·gǫt, mago). 1607. [Fr.] 1. A species of ape (*Macacus inuus*); the tailless Barbary Ape. 2. A small grotesque figure of porcelain, ivory, etc. of Chinese or Japanese workmanship 1844.

Magpie (mæ·gpəi). 1605. [f. MAG *sb.*[1] + PIE *sb.*[1]] 1. A common European bird, *Pica caudata*, of the family *Corvidæ*, with a long pointed tail and black-and-white plumage; distinguished for its chattering voice and thievish habits. b. *Austral.* Applied to the black-and-white Crow-shrike (*Gymnorrhina*); also, in Tasmania, to the genus *Strepera* 1859. 2. *transf.* An idle or impertinent chatterer 1632. 3. †a. A derisive term for an Anglican bishop, from his black chimere and white rochet. b. Now, a joc. name for this episcopal costume. 1704. 4. a. = *magpie moth* 1749. b. A kind of potato 1794. c. A variety of the domestic pigeon 1868. 5. *slang.* A halfpenny. DICKENS. 6. *Mil. slang.* A shot from a rifle that strikes the outermost division but one of a target, and is signalled by a black and white flag 1884.

1. And only hear the M. gossip Garrulous under a roof of pine TENNYSON.

attrib. and *Comb.*, as **m. diver,** (*a*) the Golden-eye Duck, *Clangula glaucion*; (*b*) the Smew, *Merganser albellus*; **m. lark,** a small Australian bird, *Grallina picata*; **m. moth,** a white moth, patched with black and some yellow spots, *Abraxas grossulariata.*

Ma·gsman. *slang.* 1838. [f. MAG *sb.*[5]] A street swindler, 'confidence man'.

‖**Maguari** (măgwā·ri). 1678. [Tupi *mbaguári.*] A S. American Stork, *Euxenura maguari*, with a forked tail.

‖**Maguey** (mæ·gweⁱ; Sp. magē·y). 1555. [Sp., a. Haytian.] The American aloe, *Agave americana.*

‖**Magus** (mēⁱ·gǒs). *Pl.* **Magi** (mēⁱ·dʒəi). ME. [L., a. Gr. μάγος, a. OPers. *magus.*] 1. *Hist.* A member of the ancient Persian priestly caste. Hence, one skilled in Oriental magic and astrology, an ancient magician or sorcerer. b. Applied to the heathen sorcerers who opposed St. Patrick 1822. 2. *spec. The (three) Magi*: the three 'wise men' who came from the East (see WISE MAN 3) ME.

Magyar (ma·dʸar, mæ·gyar). 1797. [Native name.] A. *sb.* 1. A member of the Mongoloid race, now forming the predominant section of the inhabitants of Hungary. 2. The language of the Magyars; Hungarian 1828. B. *adj.* Of or pertaining to the Magyars, or to their language 1828. b. Applied recently to a type of female dress in which bodice and sleeves are cut in one piece. Hence **Ma·gyarize** *v. trans.* to assimilate to the M. type; to translate (names) into M.

‖**Mahal** (măhā·l). *Indian.* 1623 (**mawle**). [Urdū (Arab.) *mahall*, f. Arab. root *halla* to lodge.] 1. Private apartments or lodgings. 2. A summer house or palace 1625. 3. A territorial division in India; a ward of a town. Also, a division of an estate or tract of land for farming, hunting, etc. 1793.

Mahaleb (mā·hăleb). 1558. [a. F. *mahaleb*, a. Arab. *mahlab.*] A kind of cherry, *Prunus Mahaleb*, the kernels of which are used by perfumers.

‖**Maharaj** (maharā·dʒ). 1826. [Hindī *mahārāj*, f. *mahā* great + *rāj* sovereignty, sovereign.] = next.

‖**Maharaja(h)** (maharā·dʒa). 1698. [Hindī *mahārājā*, f. *mahā* great + *rājā* RAJA(H.)] The title of certain Indian princes. So ‖**Maharanee** (maharā·nī) [Hindī *mahārānī*, see RANEE], the wife of a maharajah 1862.

Mahatma (măhæ·tmă). 1884. [ad. Skr. *mahātman* 'great-souled', f. *mahā* great + *ātman* soul.] In Esoteric Buddhism, one of a class of persons with preternatural powers, supposed to exist in India and Tibet.

‖**Mahdi** (mā·di). 1792. [Arab. *mahdīy*, lit. 'he who is guided aright', pass. pple. of *hadā* to lead in the right way.] A spiritual and temporal leader expected by the Mohammedans to appear in the latter days. Applied from about 1880 to insurrectionary leaders in the Soudan, who claimed to be the expected Mahdi. Hence **Ma·hd(i)ism,** the rebel movements in the Soudan about 1880. **Ma·hd(i)ist.**

Mah Jong (mā dʒǫ·ŋ). 1923. [Chinese, lit. sparrows.] An old Chinese game, played usu. by four persons with 136 or 144 'tiles'.

Mahlstick, var. of MAULSTICK.

Mahoe (măhōᵘ·). 1666. [Carib. *mahou*; in Fr. *mahot* (also used in Eng.).] The name of several trees. (Also *m.-tree.*) a. A sterculiaceous tree or large shrub (*Sterculia caribæa*), a native of the W. Indies. b. A malvaceous shrub or tree (*Paritium tiliaceum* and *P. elatum*), found in many tropical countries. c.

Applied with qualifications to species of *Hibiscus, Ochroma*, etc.

Mahogany (măhǫ·găni). 1671. [Written *mohogeney* in 1671; of unkn. origin.] **1.** The wood of *Swietenia Mahagoni* (N.O. *Cedrelaceæ*), a tree indigenous to the tropical parts of America. Its colour varies from yellow to a rich red brown, it is very hard and fine-grained, and takes a high polish. Also differentiated as *Baywood, Cuba, Honduras, Jamaica, Spanish m.* **b.** The tree itself 1759. **2.** *transf.* Applied to woods resembling mahogany, and to the trees producing them. In Australia mainly used for species of *Eucalyptus*, esp. the Jarrah (*E. marginata*). 1842. **3.** *colloq.* A table, esp. a dining-table 1840. **4.** *dial.* A Cornish beverage compounded of gin and treacle 1791. **5.** *attrib.* and quasi-*adj.* **a.** Made of mahogany 1730. **b.** Of the colour of mahogany, polished reddish-brown 1737.

3. Other families did not welcome us to their m. THACKERAY.

Mahomet (măhǫ·mėt; in verse occas. mē̆·homet). See also MAUMET. ME. [Cf. F. *Mahomet*, med.L. *Mah-, Machometus*.] **1.** The pop. rendering of Arabic *Muḥammad*, MOHAMMED (now the lit. form). †**2.** An idol –1553. †**3.** = MAHOMETAN –1747. **4.** A kind of pigeon. ? *Obs.* 1735.

1. If the Hill will not come to M., M. wil go to the hil BACON.

Mahometan (măhǫ·mėtăn), *a.* and *sb.* 1529. [ad. med.L. *Ma(c)hometanus*, f. *Ma(c)hometus* = MOHAMMEDAN. Hence **Maho·metanism** = MOHAMMEDANISM; so †**Maho·metism** 1597; also †**Maho·metist**, a MOHAMMEDAN 1553.

Mahometry (măhǫ·mėtri). *Obs.* exc. *arch.* 1481. [f. MAHOMET + -RY.] = MOHAMMEDANISM. In 16th c. misused for 'idolatry'.

†‖**Mahone.** 1572. [Occurs as F. *mahonne*, Turk. *māwuna*.] A flat-bottomed sailing vessel formerly used by the Turks –1658.

Mahound (măhū·nd, măhau·nd). [Early ME. *Mahun, -um*, a. OF. *Mahun, -um, -om*, short f. *Mahomet*. Cf. MAUMET.] **1.** The 'false prophet' Mohammed. Now only *arch.* †**2.** *gen.* A false god; an idol. (Cf. MAUMET.) ME. only. **3.** *Sc.* A name for the devil. Also *transf. Obs.* (? exc. *dial.*) ME. †**4.** *attrib.* Mohammedan, heathen. FLETCHER.

1. The Carle..by Turmagant and M. swore SPENSER. 4. Who's this? my Mauhound cousin? 1624.

‖**Mahout** (măhau·t). *Indian.* 1662. [Hindī *mahāut, mahāwat*.] An elephant-driver.

Mahratta, Mahratti: see MARATHA, MARATHI.

‖**Mahseer** (mā·siəɹ). 1854. [Hindī *mahāsir*.] A large Indian freshwater cyprinoid fish, *Barbus tor*, resembling the barbel.

†**Ma·hu.** 1603. [? suggested by MAHOUND.] Used as the name of a devil. *Lear* III. iv. 149.

‖**Mahwa** (mā·wa). 1687. [Hindī *mahwa*, repr. Skr. *madhūka*, f. *madhu* sweet.] **1.** An E. Indian timber tree, *Bassia latifolia*; also *B. butyracea*. **2.** An ardent spirit distilled from the flowers of the Mahwa tree 1810; also *m. arrack*.

Maid (mēd). ME. [Shortened from MAIDEN; not identical w. OE. *mæȝeð* = G. *magd*.] **1.** A girl; a young (unmarried) woman. Now only (exc. *dial.*) *arch.* or *playful*. **2.** A virgin; *spec.* of the Virgin Mary. *Obs.* or *arch.* ME. **b.** *Hist.* As a title of Joan of Arc, *The M.* (*of God, of Orleans*), tr. F. *la Pucelle* 1548. †**c.** *transf.* A man that has never had sexual intercourse. (Cf. Gr. παρθένος.) –1710. **3.** An unmarried woman, spinster. (Now *rare* exc. in OLD MAID.) 1603. **4.** A MAIDSERVANT; often differentiated as *bar-, chamber-, house-, nurse-, servant-m.*, etc., q.v.; *lady's maid* (see LADY) ME. **5.** *dial.* **a.** = MAIDEN *sb.* 5. 1677. **b.** A clothes-horse 1795. **6.** A name for the Skate and Thornback (*Raia batis* and *R. clavata*) when young, and the Twait Shad, *Alosa finta* 1579.

1. Faire and fresh of hewe, As a mayde in hir beaute LYDG. 2. Who serueth our lord, And the mayde marye CAXTON. c. He Dy'd a *Maid* 1710 3 A m. almost a hundred yeare old 1648. 4. We kept no m.:—and I had much to do 1835. *M.-of-all-work*, a female servant who does all kinds of housework.

‖**Maidan** (məidā·n). *Indian.* 1625. [Pers.] An open space in or near a town; an esplanade or parade-ground.

Maiden (mē̆·d'n), *sb.* and *a.* [OE. *mæȝden* str. neut. :—OTeut. **magadīnom*, dim. f. Teut. word repr. by OE. *mæȝð*, f. root **mag-* to have power. Related to pre-Teut. **moghus* boy, young man, whence OE. *magu*. Cf. MAY *sb.*[1]] **A.** *sb.* **1.** = MAID 1. (Not now in colloq. use exc. *dial.*) **2.** = MAID 2. Now *rare*. OE. †**b.** *transf.* = MAID 2 c. –1497. **3.** = MAID 3. *Obs.* exc. *dial.* 1775. **4.** A maidservant, a female attendant (*arch.* and *dial.*) OE. **5.** The instrument, similar to a guillotine, formerly used in Edinburgh for beheading criminals 1581. **6.** *dial.* A clothes-horse 1859. **7.** Short for *maiden horse, over, race, tree* (see B).

1. A m. of our century, yet most meek TENNYSON. 2. Why then you are no m. SHAKS. 4. As the eyes of a m. [looke] vnto the hand of her mistresse *Ps.* cxxiii. 2. *Comb.* **m. plum** (**tree**), a name of the W. Indian trees, (*a*) *Comocladia integrifolia*; (*b*) *Chrysobalanus*.

B. *adj.* (the sb. in appositive and attrib. uses). **I.** Literal uses. **1.** Unmarried; as, *m. aunt, lady, sister* ME. **2.** Of or pertaining to a maiden, or to maidenhood; befitting, or having the qualities of, a maiden 1591. **3.** Of female animals: Uncoupled, unmated 1840.

1. M. aunts with small fortunes JOHNSON. 2. *M. name*: the surname of a married woman before marriage.

II. Fig. uses. **1.** That has yielded no results. **a.** Of an assize, circuit, session: Formerly, one at which no prisoner was condemned to death; now, one at which there are no cases for trial. **b.** Of a game, esp. *Cricket*, of an over: One in which no runs are scored. **c.** Of a tide: One on which no vessels enter or leave the dock. **d.** Of a horse, etc.: That has never won a prize. Hence of a prize or a race: Open to maiden horses, etc. 1760. **2.** That has not been conquered, tried, worked, etc.; *esp.* **a.** Of a town, castle, fortress, etc.: That has never been taken 1593; **b.** Of a plant or tree: That has grown from seed, not from a stock 1649; **c.** Of a soldier, a weapon, etc.: Untried 1603. **3.** That is the first of its kind; made, used, etc. for the first time. Occas. in sense *early, earliest*. 1555.

1. b. An occasional 'maiden over' 1893. 2. a. She was a m. City, bright and free WORDSW. c. A m. knight—to me is given Such hope, I know not fear TENNYSON. 3. A m. trip 1884, m. speech (= the first delivered in the House by a member of parliament).

†**Maiden** (mē̆·d'n), *v.* 1597. [f. MAIDEN *sb.*] In phr. *To m. it*: to act like a maiden, be coy. BP. HALL.

Maidenhair (mē̆·d'n,hēəɹ). ME. [f. MAIDEN *sb.* + HAIR.] The name of certain ferns having fine hair-like stalks and delicate fronds: **a.** *Adiantum Capillus-veneris*, or True M., formerly much used in medicine 1450; **b.** *Asplenium Trichomanes*, or Common or English M. ME.; **c.** *Asplenium Ruta-muraria*, or White M. 1597.

Comb.: **m. grass**, *Briza media*; **-tree**, the ginkgo.

Maidenhead (mē̆·d'nhed). *arch.* ME. [f. MAIDEN *sb.* + -HEAD.] **1.** The condition of a maiden; virginity; said occas. of a man. †**2.** *transf.* and *fig.*, *esp.* the first stage or first-fruits of anything; the first example, proof, trial, or use –1775.

2. The maiden head of my industrie I yeelded to a noble Mecenas (renoumed Lecester) FLORIO.

Maidenhood (mē̆·d'nhud). [OE. *mæȝdenhād*, see MAIDEN and -HOOD.] The condition of being a maiden; the time of life during which one is a maiden. Formerly also = MAIDENHEAD 2.

Mai·denlike. 15... [f. MAIDEN *sb.* + -LIKE.] **a.** *adj.* Such as is usual with maidens; befitting a maiden. **b.** *adv.* After the manner of a maiden.

Maidenly (mē̆·d'nli), *a.* and *adv.* 1450. [f. as prec. + -LY.] **A.** *adj.* **1.** Of or pertaining to a maiden or to maidenhood. †**2.** Resembling a maiden in action or bearing; gentle, modest, timid –1672. **3.** Proper to, or characteristic of a maiden 1532.

1. Her m. bloom fresh-glowing R. ELLIS. 2. 2 *Hen. IV*, II. ii. 82. 3. M. reserve 1748, modesty 1849.

B. *adv.* In a maidenly manner 1596. Hence **Mai·denliness**, m. quality.

Maiden's blush. 1648. Used as a name for a delicate pink colour. Hence, a rose of this colour.

Mai·denship. 1602. [f. MAIDEN *sb.* + -SHIP.] The personality of a maiden; chiefly in *Your M.*, as a playful form of address.

Maidhood (mē̆·d,hud). ME. [-HOOD.] = MAIDENHOOD.

Maid Marian. 1525. A female personage in the May-game and morris-dance. In the later forms of the story of Robin Hood, the companion of the outlaw.

Maid of honour. 1586. **1.** An unmarried lady who attends upon a queen or princess. **2.** A kind of cheesecake 1769. **3.** The principal bridesmaid at a wedding (*U.S.*) 1906.

Mai·dse:rvant. 1526. A female servant, usu. a domestic servant.

Maieutic (mē̆iū·tik), *a.* (*sb.*) 1655. [ad. Gr. μαιευτικός (*lit.* 'obstetric'; used *fig.* by Socrates), f. μαιεύεσθαι, f. μαῖα midwife.] Pertaining to (intellectual) midwifery, *i. e.* to the Socratic process of helping a person to bring into full consciousness conceptions previously latent in his mind. **b.** *sb. pl.* The maieutic art 1885. So †**Maieutical** *a.* CUDWORTH.

Maigre (mē̆·gəɹ), *sb.* Also **meagre.** 1835. [a. F. *maigre*.] A large fish, *Sciæna aquila*, common in the Mediterranean.

‖**Maigre** (mę̄gr, mē̆·gəɹ), *a.* 1683. [F., lit. lean; see MEAGRE *a.*] **1.** Of soup, etc.: Not containing flesh or its juices; proper for 'maigre' days 1787. **2.** Applied to those days on which, according to ecclesiastical rule, flesh may not be eaten 1683. †**3.** *To eat, keep, live m.*: to live on maigre diet –1778.

1. A common m. dish 1787.

Mail (mē̆l), *sb.*[1] ME. [a. F. *maille* :—L. *macula* spot, mesh of a net.] †**1.** One of the metal rings or plates of which mail-armour was composed –1706. **2.** *collect.* Armour composed of interlaced rings or chain-work or of overlapping plates fastened upon a groundwork ME. †**b.** A piece of mail-armour –1617. **c.** *transf.* of the protective shell or scales of some animals 1714. **d.** *fig.* 1813. **3.** *Hawking.* The breast-feathers of a hawk when the feathers are full-grown. Occas. applied to the plumage of other birds. 1486. **4.** *Rope-making.* A kind of steel chain-work, flat, and fastened upon leather, for rubbing off the loose hemp that remains on white cordage 1750.

2. *Coat of m.*: see COAT *sb.* Also CHAIN-*mail*, RING-*mail*. c. Where the sea-snakes coil and twine, Dry their m. and bask in the brine M. ARNOLD. d. She was clad in the m. of endurance 1866.

attrib. and *Comb.*, as *m.-armour, -plate, -shirt*, etc.; *m.-clad* adj.; **m.-shell**, a name for the genus *Chiton*.

Mail (mē̆l), *sb.*[2] Now only *Sc.* [Late OE. *māl*, a. ON. *mál* neut., speech, agreement = OE. (poet.) *mǣl* speech.] Payment, tax, tribute, rent. (Cf. BLACK MAIL.)

Phr. *Mails and duties*: the rents of an estate, whether in money or grain.

Mail (mē̆l), *sb.*[3] [ME. *male*, a. OF. *male* (F. *malle*); of Teut. origin; cf. MDu. *male* (Du. *maal*), etc.] **1.** A bag, pack, or wallet; a travelling bag. Now only *Sc.* and *U.S.* in *pl.* = baggage. **2.** A bag or packet of letters or dispatches for conveyance by post, more fully *m. of letters* 1654. **b.** orig. *U.S.* (A person's) batch of letters 1890. **3.** The person, vehicle, or train that carries the mail or postal matter; often short for *m.-coach, m.-train*, etc. Hence, the system of transmission of letters by post; the POST. (So now in *U.S.* In England the word signifies only the dispatch of letters abroad, as the *Indian m.*, etc., or is short for mail-train, as the *night m.*, etc.) 1654.

1. A male tweyfold on his croper lay CHAUCER. 2. The arrival and distribution of a m. of letters 1893. *The m.*, all the postal matter conveyed on one occasion. b. That official was opening his m. 1890.

attrib. and *Comb.*: **m.-bag**, a large bag in which the m. is carried; **-box**, (*a*) a box in which the mail-bags were placed on a mail-coach; (*b*) *U.S.*, a letter-box; **-cart**, (*a*) a vehicle in which the m. is carried by road; (*b*) a light vehicle to carry children, pushed or pulled by hand; **-catcher** *U.S.*, a contrivance attached to a railroad car for catching a mail-bag while the train is in motion; **m. contractor,** one who contracts with the government for the conveyance of the mails; **-guard,** the guard of a mail-coach; **-phaeton,** a high two-seated phaeton drawn by a pair of horses; **-stage** *U.S.* = MAIL-COACH; **-train,** a fast train which carries the mails.

†**Mail,** *sb.*[4] *Obs.* exc. as alien (mày). Also maill(e; and see MALL. 1670. [a. F. *mail* :—L. *malleus* hammer.] The game of pall-mall; a place where it was played; hence (from the 'Mail' at Paris), a public promenade bordered by trees. *The Mail* (in St. James's Park, London): now the MALL.

Mail (mēɪl), *v.*[1] 1795. [f. MAIL *sb.*[1]] *trans.* To clothe or arm with or as with mail.

Mail (mēɪl), *v.*[2] 1570. [?] †1. *trans.* To tie (*up*), wrap up (goods, a parcel, etc.); to envelop. Also *fig.* –1660. 2. *spec.* in *Hawking.* To wrap (a hawk) up in a handkerchief, either to tame her, or to keep her quiet during an operation 1575.

Mail (mēɪl), *v.*[3] *U.S.* 1828. [f. MAIL *sb.*[3]] *trans.* To send by post, to post. Hence **Mai·lable** *a.* that may be sent by post; **-bi·lity.**

Mai·l-coach. 1787. [MAIL *sb.*[3] 2.] 1. A stage-coach used primarily for the conveyance of the mail. Later, a coach employed by the Post Office for carrying parcels by road. 2. A railway carriage carrying the mail 1838.

Mailed (mēɪld), *a.* ME. [f. MAIL *sb.*[1] + -ED[2].] †1. Covered with or composed of mail –1856. 2. Mail-clad. Of a vessel: Ironclad. 1596. Also *fig.* 3. *transf.* of animals, etc.: Having a skin or outer covering resembling mail-armour 1681. 4. Of a hawk: Having breast-feathers (of a specified colour) 1575.

2. The mayled Mars shall on his Altar sit Vp to the eares in blood SHAKS. Phr. *The m. fist* [tr. G. *die gepanzerte faust*], (symbolically) armed force.

Mailing (mēɪ·liŋ). *Sc.* 1452. [f. MAIL *sb.*[2] + -ING[1].] 1. A rented farm. 2. The rent paid for a farm 1725.

2. Let the creatures stay at a moderate m. SCOTT.

Maim (mēɪm), *sb.* *Obs.* or *arch.* [ME. *maheym, mayne,* a. OF. *mayhem, mahaing, main,* etc.; vbl. sb. related to *mahaignier* MAIM *v.*] An injury to the body which causes the loss of a limb, or of the use of it; loss or permanent disablement of a limb; *transf.* and *fig.* mutilation or disablement; hence, any injury or hurt 1543.

Your Father's sicknesse is a mayme to vs SHAKS. They are so eminent in their generations, that their omission would make a m. in history FULLER.

Maim (mēɪm), *a. rare.* 1475. [Related to prec.] Maimed.

His own life being m. R. L. STEVENSON.

Maim (mēɪm), *v.* [ME. *maynhe, mayn,* etc., a. OF. *mahaignier, mayner,* etc. Ult. origin unkn.] *trans.* To deprive of the use of some member; to mutilate, cripple. †Earlier, to disable, hurt, wound, disfigure. b. *fig.* To mutilate, cripple, render powerless or essentially incomplete; †to deprive *of* ME.

By the antient law of England he that maimed any man, whereby he lost any part of his body, was sentenced to lose the like part BLACKSTONE. b. Thereby is England main'd And faine to go with a staffe SHAKS. Hence **Mai·med-ly** *adv.*, **-ness.**

Main (mēɪn), *sb.*[1] [OE. *mægen,* f. root **mag-*; see MAY *v.*[1], MIGHT *sb.*]

I. Physical strength, force, or power. *Obs.* exc. in phr. *with might and m.* †Also *fig.*

He gan aduaunce With huge force and insupportable mayne SPENSER.

II. Absol. uses of MAIN *a.* 1. *ellipt.* for *main land,* MAINLAND (*arch.*) 1555. b. Short for SPANISH *Main,* q. v. 1890. 2. *ellipt.* for MAIN SEA: The high sea, the ocean. Now *poet.* 1579. †b. *transf.* A broad expanse –1667. 3. The most important part; the chief matter or principal thing in hand 1602. b. Const. *of.* The principal part (*of* some whole); the important or essential point 1595. †4. The object aimed at; end, purpose –1657. 5. (for *main drain,* etc.) A principal channel, duct, or conductor for conveying water, sewage, gas, or electricity, e. g. along the street of a town 1727. 6. Short for *mainmast* 1894. 7. *techn.* A main line of railway 1892.

1. The island..was separated from the m. by a channel half a mile broad THIRLWALL. b. Drake.. sailed once more for the M. CORBETT. 2. To gaze O'er land and m. TENNYSON. b. Natiuity once in the maine of light, Crawles to maturity SHAKS. 3. We let the M. go, while we grasp at the accessories 1702. Phr. *In the m.,* in all essential points; mainly. b. The m. of life is composed of small incidents JOHNSON. 6. The German flag flying at the main 1894.

Main (mēɪn), *sb.*[2] 1567. [?] 1. In the game of hazard, a number (from 5 to 9 inclusive) called by the caster before the dice are thrown 1575. †b. *fig.* esp. coupled with or opp. to *by* (see BY *sb.*[2]) –1781. 2. A match fought between cocks; also *locally,* a match at bowls, etc. 1760 (cf. *main match* 1716, opp. to *by-battle*).

1. Diceplayers, that gaine more by the bye then by the maine 1598. He likes to throw a m. of an evening THACKERAY. *fig. 1 Hen. IV,* IV. i. 47. 2. My lord would ride twenty miles..to see a m. fought THACKERAY.

Main (mēɪn), *a.* [Partly repr. OE. *mægen-* or ON. *megen-* (MAIN *sb.*[1]) in compounds; partly ad. ON. *megenn, megn* adj., strong, powerful.] 1. Strong, vigorous, mighty; manifesting, or exerting, great physical strength or force. †2. Of an army, host, etc.: Great in numbers; 'mighty'; powerful in arms; †completely equipped ME. 3. Of great size or bulk. *Obs.* exc. *dial.* ME. 4. Said of a continuous stretch of land or water; occas. also of void space 1548. †b. Of earth, rock: Forming the principal mass; solid –1647. †5. Highly important. Rarely const. *to.* –1671. 6. Very great (in degree, value, etc.); highly remarkable; very considerable of its kind. *Obs.* exc. *dial.* ME. 7. Chief in size or extent; constituting the bulk; the chief part of (what is denoted by the sb.) 1584. †b. General –1638. 8. Of pre-eminent importance; principal, chief, leading 1476. †9. *Main flood*: a. High water. b. A large or full-flowing body of water. Also *m. tide.* c. The ocean or MAIN SEA. –1605. 10. *Naut.* Pertaining to, connected with, or near the mainmast or mainsail 1485.

1. That Maine, which by maine force Warwicke did winne SHAKS. It was a maine (= violent) storme DIGBY. Soaring on m. wing MILT. Phr. *By* (†*with*) *m. force*: by force exerted to the full. †*A m. pace* or *speed* = at full speed. 2. *M. battle*: a pitched battle, opp. to skirmishing. 3. On thir heads M. Promontories flung MILT. 4. Over all the face of Earth M. Ocean flow'd MILT. 5. That, which thou aright Beleivst so m. to our success MILT. 6. It's a m. untruth SCOTT. A m. fool 1860. 7. *M. body,* †*battle*: the body of troops which form the bulk of an armed force, marching between the vanguard and the rear. b. Which is no further, Then the maine voyce of Denmarke goes withall SHAKS. 8. The statements may be grouped under two m. heads FREEMAN. *M. drain, pipe, stream, root, line* (of a railway), etc.

Special collocations: **m. centre,** in side-lever engines, the strong shaft upon which the side-levers vibrate; **m. couple** *Arch.,* the principal truss in a roof; **m. earth,** the chief earth in which the fox kennels; **m. keel,** the principal keel of a ship, as dist. from the false keel and the kelson; **m. piece** *Shipbuilding,* the principal timber in certain parts of a wooden ship, like the rudder, windlass, etc.

Main (mēɪn), *adv.* Now *dial.* 1632. [f. MAIN *a.* Cf. *mighty* adv.] Very, exceedingly.

I was m. stupid indeed, and much disposed to sleep SCOTT.

Mai·n-brace[1]. 1487. [MAIN *a.,* BRACE *sb.*[3]] *Naut.* The brace attached to the main-yard.

Phr. *To splice the main-brace* (*Naut. slang*): to serve out grog; hence, to drink freely 1805.

Mai·n-brace[2]. 1794. [MAIN *a.,* BRACE *sb.*[2]] A principal brace; *Mech.* in a system of braces, that which resists the main strain.

Main chance. 1579. [MAIN *a.*] †1. = MAIN *sb.*[2] 1; usu. *fig.* or *allusive.* a. The likeliest course to obtain success. b. The general probability as to a future event or the success of an undertaking. c. The most important point at stake; also, the general outcome of a series of events; the whole fortunes of a person, a nation, etc. –1703. 2. That which is of principal importance in life; now *esp.* one's own interests 1584.

1. a. Phr. *To look, have an eye,* etc., *to the main chance*: to be solicitous (for some object). 2. Be careful still of the main Chance, my Son DRYDEN.

Main-course. 1515. [MAIN *a.,* COURSE *sb.* 20.] *Naut.* The mainsail (of a square-rigged ship).

Main-deck. 1748. [MAIN *a.,* DECK *sb.* 2.] a. In a man-of-war, the deck next below the spar-deck. b. In a merchantman, that part of the upper deck which lies between the poop and the forecastle. Also *fig.*

Main-guard. 1653. 1. *Fortif.* The keep of a castle; also, the building within a fortress in which the 'main-guard' (sense 2 b) is lodged. 2. *Mil.* a. A guard of cavalry posted on the wings of a camp towards the enemy. b. In fortresses, a guard having the custody of all disturbers of the peace, drunkards, etc. 1706.

Mainland (mēɪ·nlǣnd). ME. [MAIN *a.* 4.] A continuous body of land; dist. from *island* or *peninsula.* †Formerly *occas.* = land as opp. to sea, *terra firma.* b. Applied to the largest island of the Shetlands, also of the Orkneys (Pomona) 1596. Also *attrib.*

Pillars of chalk have thus been separated from the m. HUXLEY. Hence **Mai·nlander** 1860.

Mainly (mēɪ·nli), *adv.* ME. [f. MAIN *a.* + -LY[2].] †1. With force, vigour, or violence; mightily –1656. †2. In a great degree; greatly, very much, a great deal. Also *occas.* entirely, perfectly. –1800. b. Used as an intensive with adjs. and advs. = MAIN *adv.* Now *dial.* 1670. 3. For the most part; chiefly, principally 1667.

2. I think we should suit one another m. LAMB.

Mainmast (mēɪ·nmɑst, -məst). 15.. [f. MAIN *a.* (sense 10) + MAST *sb.*[1]] The principal mast in a ship. Also *attrib.*

Mai·nour, ma·nner. *Obs.* exc. *Hist.* or *arch.* 1472. [a. AF. *meinoure, mainoure, -oevere* = OF. *maneuvre,* lit. 'hand-work'; see MANŒUVRE.] 1. *Law.* The stolen thing which is found in a thief's possession when arrested; chiefly in phr. *taken, found with the m.* 2. *With* (later *in*) *the mainour* (usu. *manner*): in the act of doing something unlawful, 'in flagrante delicto' 1530.

2. If..there be no witnesse against her, neither she be taken with the maner *Num.* v. 13.

Mainpernor. *Obs.* exc. *Hist.* or *arch.* ME. [a. AF. *mainpernour* = OF. **mainprenor, -eur,* f. *mainprendre*; see next.] *Law.* A surety for a prisoner's appearance in court on a specified day; one who gives mainprize for another.

So †**Mainpernable** *a.,* capable of being mainprized 1456–1772.

Mainprize (mēɪ·nprəiz), *sb.* *Obs.* exc. *Hist.* ME. [a. AF., OF. *mein-, mainprise,* f. *mainprendre* (f. *main* hand + *prendre* to take; see PRIZE *sb.*), = med.L. *manucapere,* lit. 'to take in the hand', hence 'to assume responsibility'.] 1. *gen.* Suretyship 1447. 2. *spec.* The action of procuring the release of a prisoner by becoming surety ('mainpernor') for his appearance in court at a specified time ME. Also *fig.* 3. *concr.* One's mainpernor or mainpernors ME.

2. *Writ of m.*: a writ directed to the sheriff, commanding him to take sureties for the prisoner's appearance, usually called mainpernors, and to set him at large (Blackstone). 3. Resolv'd to leave the Squire for Bail And M. for him to the Goal BUTLER. Hence †**Mai·nprize** *v.* to procure or grant the release of (a prisoner) by m.; to accept mainpernors for the appearance of. Often *fig.* ME. –1681.

Mains (mēɪnz), *sb. pl.* *Sc.* and *n.* 1479. [Aphet. f. pl. of DOMAIN, DEMESNE.] The farm attached to a mansion house; a home farm. (Retained in Scotland in the names of farms, e. g. the Mains of Forthar.)

Mainsail (mēɪ·nsēɪl, -s'l). 1485. [See MAIN *a.* 10.] The principal sail of a ship: in square-rigged vessels, that bent to the main-yard; in fore-and-aft rigged vessels, that set on the after part of the mainmast.

They..hoysed vppe the mayne sayle to the wynde TINDALE *Acts* xxvii. 40.

Main sea. *arch.* 1526. [See MAIN *a.* 4.] The high sea. Also *fig.*

Main-sheet, mai·nsheet. 1485. *Naut.* The rope which secures the mainsail when set.

Mainspring (mēɪ·nspriŋ). 1591. [MAIN *a.* 8.] 1. A principal spring in a piece of mechanism. a. In a gun-lock, the spring which drives the hammer 1616. b. The principal coiled spring of a watch, clock, etc. 1591. 2. *fig.* The chief motive power or incentive 1695.

Mainstay (mēɪ·nstēɪ). 1485. [See MAIN *a.* 8, 10.] 1. *Naut.* The stay which extends from the maintop to the foot of the foremast. Also *attrib.* 2. Chief support 1787.

1. *attrib.* **mainstaysail**, a storm-sail set on the m. 2. Direct record is the m. of History TYLOR.

Mainswear, obs. f. MANSWEAR.

Maintain (mē¹n-, mĕntē¹·n), *v.* [ME. *maintene, -teine*, a. F. *maintenir* :—L. phr. *manu tenere*, lit. 'to hold in one's hand'.] †1. *trans.* To practise habitually (an action, etc.); to observe (a rule, custom) –1611. 2. †a. *gen.* To continue, persevere in –1545. b. To carry on, keep up; to have ground for sustaining (an action) ME. c. To continue in, preserve, retain (a condition, position, attitude, etc.) 1837. 3. To keep in being; to preserve unimpaired (a cause, right, state of things, etc.) ME. 4. To cause (a person) to continue *in* a state, relation, position, possession of property, etc. ME. b. *Comm.* To keep (stock) from declining in price 1881. †5. To keep in good order, to rule (a people, country); to preserve *in* (a state of peace, etc.) –1602. 6. To support (one's state in life) by expenditure, etc.; to sustain (life) by nourishment ME. †b. To afford –1605. 7. To provide with means of subsistence or necessaries of life. †Also, to keep *in* (clothing). ME. 8. To pay or furnish the means for the keeping up of; to keep supplied or equipped (e. g. a ship, a garrison); to keep (a road, a building) in repair ME. 9. To back up (a cause, one's side or interest, a party, etc.); to support or uphold *in* (an action) ME. †b. In bad sense: To aid or abet *in* (wrong-doing); to back up *in* (error, etc.) –1552. c. *Law.* To give support to (a suitor) in an action in which one is not concerned 1716. 10. To hold (a place, position, possession) against hostility or attack ME. 11. To uphold, defend (an opinion, statement, tenet, etc.); to assert to be true or right ME.

1. *Titus* iii. 14. 2. b. To m. the doubtful combat DRYDEN, correspondence HEARNE., an action at law CRUISE. c. Pitt maintained a stately..reserve 1898. 3. The necessity of justice to m. peace and order HUME. He had a reputation to m. JOWETT. 4. The limb was maintained in this state of tension for several seconds 1874. 6. Sufficeth, that I haue maintaines my state SHAKS. b. *Tam. Shr.* v. i. 79. 7. A time.. When every rood of ground maintained its man GOLDSM. 8. Tenne talents yeerely, to maintaine the burnt offerings vpon the Altar euery day 1 *Esdras* iv. 52. 9. Who single hast maintaind Against revolted multitudes the Cause Of Truth MILT. c. Where one maintains one Side, to have Part of the Thing in Suit, which is called Champerty 1716. 10. Phr. *To m. one's ground* (often *fig.*). 11. And he ones saye a thyng, he will mayntayne it to dye for it PALSGR. He..Maintains the Multitude can never err DRYDEN. Hence **Maintai·nable** *a.* **Maintai·ner.**

Maintenance (mē¹·ntĕnăns). ME. [a. F., f. *maintenir*; see prec. and -ANCE.] †1. Bearing, deportment, behaviour –1596. 2. The action of maintaining; the state or fact of being maintained; means of sustentation ME. 3. The action of wrongfully aiding and abetting litigation; *spec.* sustentation of a suit or suitor at law by a party who has no interest in the proceedings or who acts from any improper motive ME. 4. *Cap* (or †*hat*) *of m.*: a kind of hat or cap formerly worn as a symbol of official dignity or high rank, or carried before a sovereign or a high dignitary in processions 1485.

1. She had so stedfaste countenaunce, So noble porte and meyntenaunce CHAUCER. 2. For the maintenaunce of theyr authoritie SIR T. MORE. M. of troops BURKE, of opinions 1875. A comfortable m. LAW. Phr. *Separate m.*: support given by a husband to a wife when the parties are separated. 3. Actions for m. are in modern times rare though possible 1901. 4. *Her.* Applied to a cap with two horn-like points behind, borne as a charge or in place of a wreath.

‖**Maintenon** (mæ̃ntənoṅ). 1805. The name of the Marquise de Maintenon, secretly married to Louis XIV in 1685; used *attrib.* in *M. bonnet, chop, cutlet*, etc.

Main-top (mē¹·nˌtǫp). 1485. [See MAIN *a.* 10.] *Naut.* The TOP of the mainmast; a platform just above the head of the lower mainmast. Often = *main-topgallant-masthead.* Also *attrib.*, as *main-top bowline, -man.*

Main-topgallant (mē¹·nˌtǫpgæ·lănt). 1626. [See MAIN *a.* 10.] *Naut.* Used *attrib.* in **main-topgallant-mast**, the mast above the main-topmast; so *main-topgallant-mast-head, -sail (-yard), -yard*, etc. Similarly **Main-top-mast** (mē¹nˌtǫ·pmast, -məst), the mast next above the lower mainmast; also *attrib.* 1495; **Main-topsail** (mē¹nˌtǫ·psē¹l, -s'l), the sail above the mainsail; also *attrib.* 1618.

Main-yard (mē¹·nˌyāɹd). 1485. [See MAIN *a.* 10.] *Naut.* The yard on which the mainsail is extended.

‖**Maison(n)ette** (mē¹zǫne·t). 1818. [Fr. (*-nn-*), dim. of *maison.*] A small house; in recent use, a portion of a house used as a self-contained dwelling.

Maister, -ery, var. of MASTER, -ERY.

Maistres(se, obs. f. MISTRESS.

‖**Maître d'hôtel** (mē̆tr' dotĕl). 1540. [Fr., = 'house-master'.] A major-domo, a steward or butler. b. A hotel manager 1891.

Maize (mē¹z). 1565. [a. Sp. *maiz*, †*mahiz*, of Cuban origin.] 1. An American graminaceous plant (*Zea Mays*) or the grain produced by it; = INDIAN CORN. 2. = *m.-yellow* 1890.

Comb.: **m.-bird, -thief**, an American blackbird of the subfamily *Agelæinæ*, so called from its fondness for m.; **-eater**, a S. American maize-bird; **-sugar**, glucose; **-yellow**, a yellow like that of m. Hence **Maize·na**, maize-starch prepared for food 1862.

Majestatic (mædʒĕstæ·tik), *a.* Now *rare.* 1659. [ad. med.L. *majestaticus*, f. *majestat-* MAJESTY.] Pertaining to the majesty of God. So †**Majesta·tical** *a.* 1694.

Majestic (mădʒe·stik), *a.* 1601. [f. MAJESTY + -IC.] Possessing or characterized by majesty; of imposing dignity or grandeur.

He was grave and m., and carried it something like a king DE FOE. Virgil's great majestick lines 1704. So **Maje·stical** *a.* majestic 1579; **-ly** *adv.*

Majesty (mæ·dʒĕsti). ME. [a. F. *majesté*, ad. L. *majestatem*, f. **majes-*, ablaut-var. of **majos-* (*majus, majorem* greater: see MAJOR) + *-tat-* -TY.] 1. The dignity or greatness of a sovereign; sovereign power, sovereignty. Also, the person or personality of a sovereign. b. *spec.* The greatness and glory of God. (The earliest use) ME. c. *transf.* of other beings. d. *Rom. Hist.* As tr. L. *majestas*: The sovereign power and dignity of the Roman people, *esp.* considered with reference to offences against it 1565. (Cf. LESE-MAJESTY.) 2. Preceded by a poss., *Your, His, Her, the King's, the Queen's*: used as an honorific title in speaking to or of a king, queen, emperor, or empress. ME. †3. The external magnificence befitting a sovereign –1667. 4. Kingly or queenly dignity of look, bearing, or appearance 1531. b. *transf.* of natural objects, etc. 1555. 5. Impressive stateliness of character, expression, or action 1597. 6. *Religious Art.* A figure of the Father or the Son (occas. the Virgin Mary) represented in glory within a nimbus [1485], 1847.

1. A man who..was known to have free access to m. MACAULAY. b. That far-beaming blaze of M. MILT. 2. *Your M.*, a respectful substitute for *you. His, Her M.* (abbrev. H.M.) may be either prefixed to *the King, the Queen, King George V*, etc., or substituted for them; so *Their Majesties*, when more than one is meant. (In the syntax of this word, as of *highness, grace*, etc., the neut. pronouns *it, its, which*, cannot be used with reference to a foregoing (*Your, His, Her*) *Majesty*; either the titular form is repeated, or the pronoun is the same as if 'you', or 'the king', 'the queen' had been used instead of the periphrastic form.) 4. Some great Potentate..such Majestie Invests him coming MILT. b. The Moon Rising in clouded Majestie MILT.

Majolica, maiolica (mădʒǫ·likă, măyǫ·likă). 1555. [a. It. *maiolica*, prob. f. *Majorca* (called *Majolica* in 14th c.).] Orig., a name for a fine kind of Italian pottery coated with an opaque white enamel ornamented with metallic colours; later, applied to all kinds of glazed Italian ware. Also, a modern imitation ware. Also *attrib.*

Major (mē¹·dʒəɹ), *sb.*¹ 1643. [a. F. *major*, short for *sergent-major*, SERGEANT-MAJOR, orig. a much higher grade than now.] 1. In the army: An officer next below the rank of a lieutenant-colonel and above that of a captain. 2. A full wig tied back in one curl. *Obs.* exc. *Hist.* 1753. 3. *Angling.* An artificial salmon-fly 1867.

Major (mē¹·dʒəɹ), *a.* and *sb.*² ME. [a. L. *major*, used as compar. of *magnus* great. F. *majeur, major* is perh. the proximate source of some senses. (See also MAYOR.)] A. *adj.* I. = GREATER (but not followed by *than*). 1. Distinctive epithet of the greater of two things, species, etc., that have a common designation; also applied to those members of a class that form a subdivision on the ground of being greater than the rest; opp. to *minor.* 2. *Mus.* a. Applied to intervals greater by a chromatic semitone than those called *minor*, i. e. to the normal or perfect intervals; as *m. third, sixth, seventh* (and, occas. in recent use, *m. fourth* and *fifth*). Hence also applied to the note distant by a major interval from a given note. b. Applied to a common chord or triad containing a major third between the root and the second note; hence to a cadence ending on such a chord. c. Denoting those keys, or that mode, in which the scale has a major third (and also a major sixth and seventh). (In naming a key, *major* follows the letter, as *C major.*) 1694. 3. That constitutes the majority; now only with *part, portion*, or the like. †Also, preponderating in quantity. 1594. †4. Paramount to all other claims. *Tr. & Cr.* v. i. 49. 5. Following the sb. qualified (see below) 1616. 6. Of full age, out of (one's) minority 1646.

1. *M. excommunication* (= greater e.), *orders, prophets.* †*M. Fellow* (Cambridge): a senior Fellow. *M. epilepsy*: epilepsy proper, as dist. from the 'petit mal'. *M. point* (Football): a goal (opp. to a *minor point*, i. e. a try). *M. alcaics*, etc.: the longer of the two types of alcaics, etc. *M. term* (Logic): the term which enters into the predicate of the conclusion of a syllogism. *M. premiss, proposition*: that premiss which contains the major term. *M. axis* (Math.): the axis (of a conic section) which passes through the foci; also called *transverse axis.* †*M. circle* (Astron.) = great circle (see CIRCLE *sb.* 2). 3. When they are the m. part of a general assembly HOOKER. 5. a. *Quart, Quint, Tierce m.*: see QUART *sb.*², QUINT *sb.*², TIERCE; also DRUM-MAJOR, SERGEANT-MAJOR, etc. b. *Bob-m.* (Bell-ringing): a bob (BOB *sb.*⁵) rung upon eight bells. c. In boys' schools, appended to a surname to distinguish the elder or senior of two boys of the same surname. Brown m. had a trick of bringing up unpleasant topics 1866.

B. *sb.* 1. A 'major' individual of a specified class 1626. 2. *Logic.* The major premiss in a syllogism 1530. 3. Short for *major key, mode*, etc. (see A. 2) 1667. 4. One who has 'come of age' 1616.

5. *U.S.* A subject to which special attention is given during a certain period of study 1890. Hence **Ma·jor** *v. intr.* (*U.S.*), to take, or qualify *in*, a m. 1927.

‖**Majorat** (maʒora). 1827. [Fr. and Ger., ad. med.L. *majoratus*, f. L. *majorem* MAJOR *a.* (= 'elder'); see -ATE¹.] *Continental Law.* The right of primogeniture; also, an estate going with this right.

†**Majorate**, *v. rare.* 1656. [f. med.L. *majorat-, majorare*, f. L. *majorem*; see MAJOR *a.*] To make greater; to cause to increase or develop –1660. So †**Majora·tion** 1626–73.

Major-domo (mē¹·dʒəɹˌdōᵘ·mo). 1589. [ad. Sp. *mayordomo*, It. *maggiordomo*, ad. med.L. *major domûs* 'chief of the house', the title of the highest official of the royal household under the Merovingians, commonly rendered 'mayor of the palace' (see MAYOR).] In early use, the chief official of an Italian or Spanish princely household, often having some functions of a minister of state; later, applied to the head servant of a wealthy household in foreign countries, and (joc.) to an English house-steward or butler.

Ma·jor-ge·neral. 1642. [a. F. *major général*, where *major* is the sb.] 1. An officer of the lowest grade of general officers, ranking below a lieutenant-general. 2. *Hist.* One of the officers placed in command of an administrative district under Cromwell's system of military government (1655–1657).

Majority (mădʒǫ·rīti). 1552. [a. F. *majorité*, ad. med.L. *majoritatem*, f. L. *majorem* MAJOR *a.*] †1. The state or fact of being greater; superiority; pre-eminence –1741. 2. The state of being 'major' or of age 1565. 3. The greater number or part; more than half; *spec.* the larger party voting together in a deliberative assembly or electoral body 1691. 4. The number by which, in voting, the votes cast on one side exceed those cast on the other 1743. †5. Ancestry. [After L. *majores* ancestors.] SIR T. BROWNE. 6. [Prop. a distinct word; see MAJOR *sb.*[1]] The rank or office of a major 1760.

2. The M. of Mr. C. L. A...has been celebrated [etc.] 1867. 3. In a House of Commons all things are determin'd by a M. POPE. *Absolute m.*: a majority that includes more than half of the votes cast or of the possible voters. *The m.*: the dead. *To join, go,* or *pass over to the m.* [After L. phr. *abiit ad plures.*] 4. Carried by a very small m. THIRLWALL. 6. Promoted to a half-pay m. 1900.

Majorize (mē¹·dʒəraiz), *v.* [f. MAJOR *sb.*[2] + -IZE.] *Rugby Football.* To convert a try into a goal, i. e. to increase the points from three to five.

Majorship (mē¹·dʒəɹʃip). 1717. [f. MAJOR *sb.*[1] + -SHIP.] The office or rank of a major; majority.

Majuscule (mădʒʊ·skiul). 1727. [a. F., ad. L. *majuscula* (sc. *littera*), fem. of *majusculus* somewhat larger, dim. of *major* (neut. *majus*); see MAJOR *a.*] **A.** *adj.* †**a.** *Printing.* Of a letter: Capital. **b.** *Palæogr.* Of a letter: Large (whether capital or uncial). Also, written in majuscules. **B.** *sb.* †**a.** *Printing.* A large or capital letter. **b.** *Palæogr.* A large letter, whether capital or uncial. 1825.

Hence **Maju·scular** *a.* of the nature of **a m.**; composed of majuscules.

Make (mē¹k), *sb.*[1] *Obs.* exc. *dial.* [OE. *ʒemaca* wk. masc. :—OTeut. type **gamakon-*, subst. form of **gamako-* adj. (OE. *ʒemæc* equal, well-matched), f. **ga-* Y- *prefix* + **mako-*, app. 'fit, suitable', whence prob. **makōjan* MAKE *v.*] **1.** An (or one's) equal, peer, match; one's like. **2.** A mate, companion. (*occas.* The opponent with whom a fighter is matched.) ME. **3.** Of animals, esp. birds: A mate (male or female) OE. **4.** Of human beings: A mate, consort; a husband or wife, lover or mistress ME.

4. Like a widdow hauing lost her m. SIDNEY.

Make (mē¹k), *sb.*[2] ME. [f. MAKE *v.*] †**1.** Doing, action -1535. **2.** The manner in which a thing is made. **a.** Style of construction, kind of composition ME. **b.** Form or composition, structure, constitution. Often of the body: Build. ME. **c.** Of immaterial things: Form, fashion; hence, sort, character, nature 1660. **3.** Mental or moral constitution, disposition, or character 1674. **4.** Kind, sort, species (*dial.*) 1740. **5.** The action or process of making or manufacture. Now *rare* exc. *techn.* 1743. **6.** Amount manufactured; quantity produced 1865. **7.** *Electr.* The action of making contact in an electric circuit; the position in which contact is made (in phr. *at m.*) 1875.

2. a. The caps and bonnets were of quite a new m. 1833. A slow m. of bromide paper 1889. b. A huge man, with the m. and muscles of a prize-fighter MRS. H. WARD. 3. Deeming there were more in the World of my m. 1674. 5. Qualified by poss. denoting the manufacturer, with implication of style or quality. Are these shoes your own m.? Phr. *On the m.*: intent on profit or advancement. *slang.* (orig. *U.S.*)

Make (mē¹k), *v.* Pa. t. and pple. **made** (mē¹d). [Com. WGer.: OE. *macian*, app. f. **mako-* fit, suitable (see MAKE *sb.*[1]).]

I. 1. *trans.* To produce by combination of parts, or by giving a certain form to a portion of matter; to construct, frame, fashion, bring into existence. Also *absol.*, esp. in phr. *m. or mend.* **2.** To compose, write as the author (a book, poem, verses, poetry, etc.) ME. †Also *absol.* or *intr.* **b.** To draw up (a legal document) ME. **3.** To put together materials for (a fire) and light them ME. **4.** To set apart and prepare the site for (a garden, park, road, etc.) late ME.

1. The beaver makes its hole, the bee makes its cell 1852. That dress, made full..suits you 1865. An Indian can m. almost anything out of bamboo 1859. Let me m. the tea DICKENS. Do you know who made you? MRS. STOWE. She..said..that you were made (= naturally fitted) for your vocation 1870. The drums were made of metal 1892. 2. Would you.. have me marry a woman that makes verses? 1803. *absol.* I m. to please my selfe, and not for them WITHER. b. He may..have time to make a written will 1797. 4. How changed is here each spot man makes or fills! M. ARNOLD.

II. 1. To cause to exist; to produce by action, bring about ME. †**b.** Const. dat. of the person, or with *to, unto*: To cause to happen to; to cause to experience; to bring into a person's possession or power -1725. **2.** To give rise to; to have as a result or consequence ME. **3.** *Gram.* Of a word: To form (a case, tense, etc.) in a specified manner; to change into (a specified form) when inflected OE. **4.** To establish (a rule, etc.); to enact (a law); to impose (a rate); †to institute (a religious order, etc.) OE. †**b.** To arrange (a match) -1752. **5. a.** To appoint (an officer), ordain (a minister) ME. **b.** *Naut.* To promote in rank 1795. **c.** *gen.* To cause to become (what is specified by the object) 1594. **d.** To fix (a price). Now only *Comm.* 1567. **6.** To provide (a meal, feast), give (a dinner, etc.). *Obs.* exc. *arch.* OE. **7.** To form by collection of individuals (see below) ME. **8.** To bring forth; to have as a product ME. **9.** Used with const. *of* or *out of* to designate the action of causing what is denoted by the regimen of the prep. to become what is denoted by the object of the verb ME.

1. He makes a solitude, and calls it—peace! BYRON. To m. a corner in rice 1897. *To m. melody, mintrelsy*; *to m. a note*, etc.; *to m. ado*, (*a*) *commotion, fun, a fuss, game, an impression, a row, a sensation, sport, a stir*, etc.; *to m. room, way*: see the substantives. *To m. peace*: (*a*) to bring about a condition of peace (*b*) to conclude a treaty of peace. 2. One Fool makes many SWIFT. *To m. a difference. To m. work*: to occasion the necessity for work to be done; to give trouble. 4. A receiving order is 'made' on the day it is pronounced, not when it is drawn up 1898. 5. a. The fourme and maner of makynge and consecratynge, Bishoppes, Priestes and Deacons 1552. He [Rich. II] then made nine Knights, and created four Earls 1641. b. Frank is made. He was yesterday raised to the rank of Commander JANE AUSTEN. c. He was..a man to make both friends and enemies J. H. NEWMAN. 6. He made a feast, drank fierce and fast [etc.] M. ARNOLD. 7. The greatest strength and power that he can m. SHAKS. *To make a head* (see HEAD *sb.*). *To m. a House*: to ensure the presence of the number (now 40) of members required to constitute a sitting of the House (of Commons). So *to m. a quorum. To m. a bag* (Sporting): to kill a number of game. *To m. the bag*: to contribute most of the total of the game killed. *To m. a book* (Betting): to arrange a series of bets on the same race or event, with odds calculated with a view to a gain on the whole transaction. 8. *To m. water*, †*urine*: see the sbs. 9. He is going to m. a night of it 1809. *To m. a business, practice, trade of*; *to m. an example, a fool of*; *to m. an ass, a beast, an exhibition of oneself*: see the sbs. *To m.* (much, little, something, nothing, etc.) *of*: to turn to (much or little) account. *To m. the best, the most of*: see BEST *sb.*, MOST *sb.* *To m. a hash, mess, muddle of*: to bungle (a business).

III. 1. To entertain (doubt, scruple, question, etc.) in the mind; to formulate mentally; to form (a judgement) ME. **b.** To recognize in classification (a certain number of kinds, species, etc.) 1562. **c.** *legal.* To formulate, set out (a case, title) 1883. **2.** Used with const. as in II. 9 in idiomatic expressions relating to questions of estimation, calculation, or meaning: see below ME. **3.** *Naut.* To descry or discern; to come in sight of 1565.

1. I m. no doubt every one..has practised similar stratagems 1844. *To m.* (*great*, etc.) *account of*: to have a high opinion of. b. Our School-men..m. nine kinds of bad Spirits BURTON. c. To m. a good title 1891. 2. *To m. head or tail* (also *top or tail*) *of, to m. sense of*: see the sbs. *To m.* (much, little, nothing, etc.) *of*: to have a (high, low, etc.) opinion of; to value at a (high, low, etc.) rate; to treat with (much, no, etc.) consideration. *To m. much of*: often, to treat with marked courtesy and show of affection. *To m. nothing of* (doing something): to find no difficulty in or feel no scruples at. *To m. light of*: see LIGHT *a.*[1] III. 1. *To m. of* (intr.): = *to m. much of.* (*Obs.* exc. *dial.*) *What do you m. of that?*: what do you understand to be the meaning of that? 3. We..made the Coast of Galway, in Ireland, the 10th DE FOE.

IV. Said of constituent parts or material. **1.** To amount to. Also, of the latest item added, to bring up the sum to (a certain amount). ME. **2.** To be sufficient to constitute ME. **3.** To amount to, signify (much, little, nothing, etc.) in relation to the question in point. Const. *for, to.* Now *rare.* 1456. †**b.** Of arguments or evidence: To avail (much, little, etc.) *for, against* -1690. **4.** To count as, form, be (a part or unit in an aggregate, a particular member in a series) ME. **5.** To be the material or components of; to be made or admit of being made into ME. **6.** To become by development or training 1572.

1. Nine Taylors m. but one man 1672. Twice one makes two 1892. 2. One swalowe maketh not sommer HEYWOOD. Worth makes the man POPE. 3. The course which he intended made much for the glory of God A. V. *Transl. Pref.* ¶ 3. *To m. no matter* (somewhat *arch.*): not to matter. 4. You came in and made the fourteenth 1892. *To m. one* (*of*): often, to take part in a combined action, be present at a meeting, etc.; also, to assimilate oneself to one's company. 5. She was fit to have made a Spouse for Jupiter himself 1699. They [frogs] m. a good soup 1787. 6. She will make him a good wife 1885.

V. 1. To gain, acquire, or earn (money, reputation, etc.) by labour, business, or the like. Const. *of, out of.* ME. **b.** To fetch (a certain price) 1868. **2.** *Cards.* To win (a trick); to play (a card) to advantage. Also *intr.* of a card: to take a trick. 1608. **b.** In games: To secure (a certain score); to score (a point in the game); to perform (a stroke) successfully 1680. **3.** To gain, put on (weight). Also of a tree, to produce a growth of (timber). *To m. water* (Naut.): to take in water by a leak. 1832.

1. *To m. a* (or *one's*) *fortune, capital out of, a living, a name* (for oneself): see the sbs. 2. In the third round you m. your Queen HOYLE. His partner ..has his last trump drawn, and the ace and king of diamonds m. CAVENDISH. b. He made ten fours, six threes, and two twos 1890.

VI. †**1.** To bring *to* a specified condition, reduce *to* -1692. **2.** *intr.* To attempt or 'offer' (*to do* something) 1880. **3.** With ellipsis of verb of motion: To prepare to go; to proceed in a certain direction 1488. **4.** To prepare (a bed) for sleeping in ME. **5.** To shut, close, bar (a door). Now *arch.* and *dial.* ME. **6.** *Cards.* To shuffle 1876. **7.** Naut. *To m. sail*: (*a*) to spread a sail or sails; hence, to set sail, to sail; (*b*) to spread additional sails 1450. **8.** To train (a hawk, dog, horse) ME. **9.** To secure the advancement of; to 'be the making of'; chiefly, to set up (*esp.* in *pass.*) ME.

1. Phr. †*To m. to death*; †*to m. away, out of the way, hence* = make away with. 2. He makes to follow, then stops 1900. 3. I made steadily but slowly towards them STEVENSON. 5. M. the doores vpon a womans wit, and it will out at the casement SHAKS. 8. A Setting-dog that he has *made* himself ADDISON. 9. Bismarck has made Germany 1890. Phr. *To m. or mar* (occas. *to m. or break*): to cause either the complete success or ruin of (a person or thing). Also *absol.*

VII. 1. To cause to be, render OE. Also *absol.* **2.** With sb. as complement. **a.** To cause (a person or thing) to be or become (what is denoted by the complement) OE. **b.** *spec.* To appoint to the office of; to raise to the dignity of; to create (a person) a noble, etc. ME. **c.** To determine (a thing, occas. a person) to be (what is expressed by the complement); to set down as (a law, penalty, etc.) 1500. **d.** To transform into something else. Chiefly in *pass.*, after L. *fieri.* ME. **3.** To convert *into* 1583. **4.** To regard as, consider or compute to be; to represent as (so-and-so); to cause to appear as ME. **b.** *Naut.* To announce or indicate (a particular time) by sounding a bell or otherwise; often in the order *make it so* 1835.

1. His generosity made him courted by many dependents JOHNSON. I wish you had made (= arranged so as to pass through) London in your way LAMB. *To m. English*: to translate into English. *To m. even, fast, good, ready, sure, unready, void, waste*; *to m. it hot, warm, m. things lively*; *to m. oneself scarce, to m. ready, sure*: see the adjs. 2. a. It's pity that fellow was not made a soldier 1603. b. She made Marlborough a duke 1890. c. I made it my pride to keep aloof STEVENSON. d. I will make the riuers Ilands *Isa.* xlii. 15. 3. Fresh curds newly pressed, and made into little cheeses MORYSON. 4. What time may you m. it, Mr. Twemlow? DICKENS. What do you make the time? I make it half-past five (*mod.*). Macbeth is not half so bad as the play makes him 1879. b. Noon was made; the captain dined R. L. STEVENSON.

VIII. Causative uses. **1.** To cause (something to happen); to bring it about *that. Obs.* exc. *arch.* OE. **2.** With obj. and inf.: To cause a person or thing to do something; to have something done to a person or thing (inf. without *to* when both *make* and the dependent verb are in the active voice; otherwise *arch.*) ME. **3.** To constrain *to do* something; to compel, force (now always without *to* bef. the inf. when *make* is active) 1592. **b.** with ellipsis of inf. (*colloq.*) 1888. **4.** To consider, represent, or allege *to* be or do something 1594.

2. I wonder what makes these Bells ring SWIFT.

The two statements can hardly be made to agree (*mod.*). Phr. *To m. both ends meet* (END *sb.* Phrases 2), *one's hair stand on end*, etc. *To m. believe*: †(*a*) [after F. *faire croire*] to cause people to believe; (*b*) in mod. use (often with hyphen, *make-believe*), to pretend *to do* something; to simulate a belief *that*. 3. He made me stay and sup with him 1662. b. The enemy will not play the game..and there are none to m. him (*mod.*). 4. What do you m. that bird to be? 1825. Most of the Chronicles m. Richard die in 1026 FREEMAN.

IX. 1. †a. To work (a miracle); to commit (a crime, sin, fault), tell (a lie); to do (justice, mercy); to give (alms) –1715. **b.** To wage (WAR) ME. **c.** To perform (a bodily movement or gesture) ME. **d.** To enter into, conclude (a bargain, contract). So, *to m. a marriage* (now only *legal*). ME. **e.** *Eccl.*, in *to m. one's confession, one's communion.* Also, †to do (penance). ME. **f.** With reference to locomotion or travel (see below) ME. **g.** To deliver orally (a speech, an oration). **2.** In questions introduced by *what*, e.g. *What m. you here?* = What are you doing here? What is your business, right, or purpose? Now *arch.* ME. **3.** With sbs. expressing the action of vbs., *make* forms phrases equivalent to those vbs. (see exx. below) ME. **4.** To eat (a meal) 1542. **5.** To offer, present, render. Const. *to* or *dative.* ME. **b.** *Law.* Of a court, a judge: To render, give (a decision, judgement). Still *U.S.* 1804. **6.** To put forth (an effort) 1456. **7.** To incur, suffer (something undesirable) 1453. **8.** To accomplish (a distance) by travelling, etc. 1564. **b.** orig. *Naut.* To reach, arrive at (a place); *slang*, to catch (a train, etc.) 1624. **9.** In phrases like *to m. long hours* (i.e. to work many hours a day). Also, *to m. good time*: to accomplish a distance in a short time. 1887.

1. b. To m. the campaign was the dearest wish of Harry's life THACKERAY. c. *To m. a* (or *one's*) *bow, m. a curtsy, m. a face* (*at*), *m. a leg, m.* (*an*) *obeisance, a salaam*, etc.: see the sbs. f. *To m. an excursion, an expedition, a journey, a tour, a trip, a voyage, to m. one's way, to m. a circuit*: see the sbs. 3. *To m.* (*one's*) *abode, an acquisition, an assertion, an award, a blunder,* (*an*) *excuse, a motion,* (*an*) *oath, a promise,* (*a*) *reply, a slip, a start, a venture, a vow*, etc. 4. He made his simple morning meal 1890. 5. *To m. amends, love, satisfaction*: see the sbs. *To m. head*: see HEAD *sb.* 7. *To m. shipwreck* (arch.), *a loss.* 8. I must m. the distance on foot 1899.

X. 1. *intr.* (the obj. *it* being omitted); in OE. with adv.; later with adj., in *to m. bold, free, merry*, etc. (see the adjs.). **2.** *To m. as if, as though* (arch. *as*): to behave as if; to pretend that ME. **3.** To have to do *with* (a person or thing); to interfere *in* (a matter). *dial.* 1564. **4.** *Naut.* Of the flood or ebb tide: To begin to flow or ebb; also, to be in progress. Hence of the tide: To flow towards the land; also, to flow in a specified direction. 1651. **5.** Of arguments, evidences, influences: To 'tell' (on one side or the other). Chiefly with *for, with, against.* 1892.

2. He..beckons, and makes as he would speak LONGF. 3. And so, Sir, pray don't meddle or m. with the maids 1756. 4. The tide made to the westward DE FOE. The ebb was now making 1883. 5. He had the highest opinion of..precedents—when they made in his own favour 1892.

In specialized senses with preps. **Make after —.** To pursue, follow (*arch.*). **M. against —. a.** To 'tell' against. **†b.** To go to attack. **M. at —.** To make a hostile movement towards. Now somewhat *arch.* **M. for —. a.** To operate in favour of; to favour, further, aid. **b.** To go in the direction of; also, to 'go for'. **M. to —. †a.** To tend to support; to be conducive to. **†b.** To be pertinent to. **†c.** To proceed towards. **M. with —. †a.** To side with. Of things: To tell in favour of. **†b.** To select as one's adversary.

With adverbs. **M. away.** (Now repl. in trans. senses by *make away with.*) **†a.** *trans.* To put out of the way, put to death; also, to put an end to (a person's life). **†b.** To destroy. **†c.** To alienate; to dispose of, get rid of. **d.** *intr.* To run away; = *make off* (c). **M. away** *with.* **a.** = prec. a. **b.** To remove from its rightful place or ownership; to get rid of; to squander; to destroy fraudulently. **M. in.** *intr.* To go in; to intervene; to join in a fray; in *Hawking*, (of the falconer), to go up to a hawk after it has killed. **M. off. †a.** *trans.* To dispose of. **b.** *Farming.* To fatten (lambs) for the market. **c.** *intr.* To depart suddenly, often with a disparaging implication; to hasten away; to decamp. **d.** *To m. off with*: to decamp with (something) in one's possession. **M. on.** *intr.* To proceed; to hasten on. **M. out. a.** To draw up (a list, a document, etc.); to make a draft of; to write out (a bill, cheque, etc.). **b.** (*a*) To succeed in accomplishing; to effect. Now *Sc.* (*b*) To manage, make shift *to do* something. Also *absol.* to get along; to get on (well, badly). Also *to m. it out.* Chiefly *U.S.* **c.** †To compensate; to eke out. Also *intr.* to make up, compensate *for.* **d.** To make complete; to get together with difficulty. **e.** To fill up (the time). ?*Obs.* **f.** To represent clearly or in detail; now only in *Art.* **g.** To demonstrate, prove. Also *colloq.* **h.** To represent, pretend. **i.** To arrive at an understanding of; to decipher. Also (with clause or obj. and inf.) to discover, find out. **j.** To succeed in perceiving or identifying. **k.** To start forth; to get away. ? Now only *dial.* **M. over. a.** *trans.* To transfer (*prop.* by a formal agreement) the possession of (a thing) *to* another. **b.** To remake, refashion. Now only *U.S.* **M. up. †a.** To build up; to repair by filling up gaps. **b.** (*a*) To make complete. Also, to raise (a sum) *to* a larger sum. (*b*) To make good; to supply (a deficiency). (*c*) *intr.* To compensate *for*, atone *for.* **c.** To fill up (a gap, etc.); to stop up (a passage, etc.); to shut up (a door, a house). Now chiefly *dial.* **d.** To wrap up (an article); to put together (a parcel) *of* goods. **e.** To put together into a particular form; to fit together (pieces) to form a garment; to make (cloth) into clothing; also quasi-*pass.* to admit of being made up; *trans.* to compound (medicines, etc.); to mix (dough); to get together (a company, a sum); *Printing*, to arrange into columns or pages; to add fuel to (a fire) so as to keep it up. **f.** To compile (a list, etc.); to concoct (a story, lie); to improvise (verses). **g.** Of component parts: To compose (a sum, total, or whole). **h.** To prepare (an actor) for his part by dressing him, giving him false hair, etc. Also *intr.* for *refl.* To prepare (a bed) for a particular occasion. Also, to 'do up' (a room) (? *local*). **i.** To set out the items of (an account) in order; to add up and balance (an account). **j.** *To m. up one's mind*: to come to a decision or conclusion. Hence, *to m. up one's mind for, to*, or *to do* (something): to be reconciled to the thought of, to be prepared for. **k.** To arrange (a marriage, a treaty, etc.); to settle (a dispute, etc.); *intr.* (also often *to m. it up*) to be reconciled after a dispute. **l.** *intr.* (*a*) To advance in a certain direction; now only in *to m. up to*, to draw near to. (*b*) *To m. up to* (fig.): to make advances to; to pay court or make love to.

Make-, the stem of MAKE *v.* in comb., as in **m.-play** = MAKE-SPORT; **-rime,** a phrase introduced merely for rime; **-talk,** something said for the sake of talking; **-way,** an event which leads up to another; etc.

Makebate (mē̆ⁱ·kbē̆ⁱt). 1529. [f. MAKE *v.* + BATE *sb.*[1]] One who or that which creates contention; a breeder of strife. †Also *attrib.*

Ma·ke-belie:f. *rare.* 1833. Substituted for next on the erron. assumption that *make-believe* is incorrect.

Ma·ke-belie:ve. 1811. [The phr. *make believe* used subst.] **1.** Pretence. Also with *a* and *pl.* **2.** One who makes believe or pretends 1863. **3.** *attrib.* or *adj.* Of the nature of make-believe 1824.

1. Her mourning is all make-believe 1811. 3. Here again I am met with a make-believe reply GLADSTONE.

†Ma·ke-game. 1762. = MAKE-SPORT. –1817.

Ma·keless, *a.* *Obs.* exc. *dial.* ME. [f. MAKE *sb.*[1] + -LESS.] **1.** Matchless, peerless. **2.** Mateless ME.

Ma·ke-peace. 1516. [See MAKE *v.* II. 1.] A peace-maker.

Maker (mē̆ⁱ·kəɹ). ME. [f. MAKE *v.* + -ER[1].] **1.** One who makes, fashions, constructs, prepares for use, etc.; a manufacturer. **2.** Qualified by *the*, or an attrib. phr.: Applied to God as the Creator of the universe. (Now with capital M.) ME. **3.** One who brings about a condition, effect, state of mind, etc. ME. **4.** A poet. *Obs.* exc. *arch.* (Cf. Gr. ποιητής.) ME. **5.** 'The person who signs a promissory note' (Wharton).

2. Let vs knele before the Lorde oure m. COVERDALE *Ps.* xciv. [xcv.] 6. †*To receive* or *take one's M.*: to make one's communion.

Make-ready. 1887. [f. phr. *make ready.*] *Printing.* The operation of making a form ready to be printed; the form so made ready, or the sheet or sheets used to effect this.

Makeshift (mē̆ⁱ·kˌʃift). 1565. [f. phr. *to make shift.*] **†1.** One given to making shifts; a shifty person, a rogue –1608. **2.** That with which one makes shift; a temporary and inferior substitute 1802. **3.** The action of making shift 1870. **4.** *attrib.* or *adj.* With which one makes shift 1683. **b.** *transf.* Characterized by makeshifts 1824.

2. The cottage was a sorry antediluvian make-shift of a building LAMB. 4. A make-shift dinner 1809.

†Make-sport. 1582. [See MAKE *v.* II. 1.] One who or that which provides sport for others; a laughing-stock –1661.

Ma·ke-up. 1821. [f. phr. *make up* (see MAKE *v.*).] **1.** The way in which anything is put together; composition, constitution. **2.** Chiefly *Theatr.* An appearance of face, dress, etc. assumed in impersonating a character 1858. **3.** *Printing.* The process of making up type into columns and pages; the matter so made up. Also, an editor's selection of articles to form a number of a periodical. 1852. **4.** A made-up story 1844. **5.** *attrib.* (sense 2) 1885.

1. Something in the..make-up of their clothes H. SPENCER.

Make-weight, makeweight (mē̆ⁱ·kˌwē̆ⁱt). 1695. [See MAKE *v.* IV. 1.] **1.** A small quantity added to make up a certain weight; *spec.* a small candle. **2.** *fig.* A person or thing of little account thrown in to make up a deficiency or fill a gap 1776. **3.** A counterpoise 1787. **4.** *attrib.* Serving as a make-weight 1701.

2. The mines..are now thrown in as a make-weight in the scale BURKE.

Maki (mē̆ⁱ·ki, mæ·ki). 1774. [repr. Malagasy *maka.*] French name of the LEMUR.

Making (mē̆ⁱ·kiŋ), *vbl. sb.* [OE. *macung*, f. *macian*; see MAKE *v.* and -ING[1].] **1.** The action of MAKE *v.*; fabrication, production, preparation; institution, appointment; doing, performance (of an action); conversion into something; etc. Also occas., the process of being made. **2.** *spec.* in techn. uses: The training or bringing to the required condition (of an animal); the preparation (of hay); the curing (of fish) ME. **†3.** Poetical composition. Also *pl.* = poems. –1614. **4.** Advancement, success. *Obs.* exc. in *to be the m. of*: to be what ensures the success of. 1470. **†5.** The way in which a thing is made; 'make' –1669. **6.** *concr.* Something that has been made; a product of manufacture. Also, the quantity made at one time. ME. **b.** *pl.* Earnings, profits (*colloq.*) 1837. **7.** The material out of which something may be made; the potentiality of becoming something; in phr. *to have* or *to be the making(s of* 1613.

1. The m. of the world 1842, of a codicil 1891, of several engineers 1897. Phr. *Of* (so-and-so's) *m.* = made by (so-and-so); A poet of Nature's own m. CARLYLE. *In the m.*: used adjectively, to designate something as existing in an undeveloped state; Opinion in good men is but knowledge in the m. MILT. 7. She had all the Royall makings of a Queene SHAKS.

Comb. **m.-iron,** a kind of grooved chisel used by caulkers to finish off seams.

Making-up. 1593. In the senses of *make up* (see MAKE *v.*); completion; compounding; reconciliation; dressing up for the impersonation of a character; the balancing of accounts at the end of a period. Also *attrib.*

Mal- (mæl), *prefix*, formerly often written **male-** (but pronounced as one syllable), repr. F. *mal* adv.:—L. *male* ill, badly. It occurs orig. in adoptions from Fr., as *maltreat, malfeasance*; also, *maladroit, malcontent* (= the reverse of *adroit, content*), etc. In English formations it conveys the sense 'ill', 'wrong', 'improper(ly', as in *malpractice, malformation, malodorous*, etc.

Malabar (mæ·lăbāɹ), name of a sea-board district in the S.W. of India, used attrib.; as in **M. nut,** an acanthaceous plant, *Justicia Adhatoda*; **M.-oil,** an oil obtained from the livers of various fishes found on the M. coast.

Malacaton, -catoon, var. ff. MELOCOTON.

Malacca (mălæ·kă). 1611. Name of a town and district on the Malay peninsula in the S.E. of Asia; used attrib.; as in **M. apple** = *Malay apple* (see MALAY *a.*); **M. cane** (also simply *Malacca*), a walking-cane of a rich brown colour, often clouded or mottled, made of the stem of the palm *Calamus Scipionum.*

Malachite (mæ·lăkəit). 1567. [a. OF. *melochite*, F. *malachite*, ad. L. **malachites, molochites*, Gr. *μαλαχίτης, *μολοχίτης, a stone resembling the leaf of the mallow in colour, f. μαλάχη, μολόχη the mallow.] Hydrous carbonate of copper, occurring as a mineral of a green colour, susceptible of a high polish. Also, a specimen of this. **b.** *Blue m.* = AZURITE 1821. *Comb.* **M.-green**, (*a*) = malachite; (*b*) a dye of the colour of m.

Malaco- (mæ·lăko), comb. f. Gr. μαλακός soft, in many scientific terms, as: **Ma·lacoderm** [Gr. δέρμα skin] *Nat. Hist.* *a.* having a soft skin; *sb.* a soft-skinned animal, esp. of the *Malacodermata* (*-derma*, *-dermi*), a division in old classification of reptiles, of beetles, and of *Anthozoa* 1835; hence **Malacode·rmatous** *a.* **Ma·lacolite** [-LITE] *Min.* = DIOPSIDE 1823. **Malaco·logy** [F. *malacologie*], that branch of zoology which treats of molluscs 1836; hence **Malacolo·gical** *a.*; **Malaco·logist**, one versed in m. **Ma·lacoptery·gian** [Gr. πτέρυξ wing] *a.* of or pertaining to the *Malacopterygii* or soft-finned fishes; *sb.* one of these; so **Ma·lacoptery·gious** *a.* ‖**Malaco·steon** [Gr. ὀστέον bone] *Path.* = OSTEOMALACIA 1801. **Malaco·stomous** [mod.L. *malacostomus*; Gr. στόμα mouth] *a.* of fishes: having a soft mouth (i. e. toothless jaws) 1753. **Malaco·stracan** [Gr. μαλακόστρακα; ὄστρακον shell] *a.* of or belonging to the *Malacostraca*, an order of *Crustacea*; *sb.* one of these 1835; so **Malaco·stracous** *a.* **Malacozo·ic** [Gr. ζῷον animal] *a.* applied by Huxley to the series of animals from the *Polyzoa* to the *Mollusca* 1877.

Ma·ladapta·tion. 1877. [MAL- *prefix.*] Faulty adaptation.

Maladive (mæ·lădiv), *a. rare.* 1481. [a. F. *maladif, -ive*, f. *malade*; see MALADY.] Sickly.

Maladju·stment. 1833. [MAL- *prefix.*] Faulty adjustment.

Maladminister (mælædmi·nistəɹ), *v.* 1705. [MAL- *prefix.*] To administer inefficiently or badly.

Maladministration (mæ:lædministrēⁱ·ʃən). Also †**male-**. 1644. [MAL- *prefix.*] Faulty administration; inefficient or improper management of affairs, esp. public affairs.

‖**Maladresse** (mælădre·s). Also **maladdress.** 1804. [a. F., noun of quality to next.] Want of dexterity or tact; awkwardness.

Maladroit (mæ·lădroit), *a.* 1685. [a. F.; see MAL- and ADROIT *a.*] Wanting in adroitness; awkward, bungling. Hence **Ma·ladroit-ly** *adv.*, **-ness.**

Malady (mæ·lădi). ME. [a. F. *maladie*, f. *malade* = Pr. *malapte* :—late L. *male habitus.*] **1.** †Ill health, disease; an ailment, a disease. **2.** *fig.* A morbid or depraved condition; something that calls for a remedy ME.

1. Abstinence ingenders maladies SHAKS. 2. Astrology is another m. of weak minds 1786.

‖**Mala fide** (mēⁱ·le fəi·dĭ). 1681. [L., = 'in bad faith'. Cf. BONA FIDE.] *adv.* In bad faith. *adj.* Chiefly with agent-nouns: Acting in bad faith; pretended, sham. So **Ma·la fi·des** *Law*, bad faith, intent to deceive 1681.

Malaga (mæ·lăgă). 1608. Name of a seaport in the south of Spain. Used *attrib.* in *M. raisins, sack, wine.* Also as sb. (short for *M. wine*), a white wine exported from M.

Ma·lagash. 1711. [Cf. F. *Malgache.*] Var. of next.

Malagasy (mælăgæ·si). 1835. [Used in the native lang., but prob. an altered form of a foreign word represented by *Madagass*, etc., whence *Madagascar.*] *adj.* and *sb.* Of or pertaining to, a native of, Madagascar. **b.** The language spoken there.

Malaguetta (mælăge·tă). 1568. [?] The capsules or seeds of *Amomum Meliguetta* of W. Africa, used as a spice and in medicine; also known as *Grains of Paradise* and *Guinea Grains.* Also *attrib.*, as *m. pepper.*

‖**Malaise** (mæ·lēⁱz, Fr. malɛ̄z). 1768. [F., f. OF. *mal* bad, ill + *aise* EASE *sb.*] A condition of bodily discomfort, *esp.* a condition of lassitude, without the development of specific disease. Also *fig.*

Malander, mallender (mæ·lĕndəɹ). Now only *pl.* late ME. [a. F. *malandre* a sore in a horse's knee, ad. L. *malandria* (neut. pl. and fem. sing.).] A dry scabby eruption behind the knee in horses.

Malapert (mæ·lăpɔ̄rt). *Obs.* exc. *arch.* late ME. [a. OF. *malapert*, the contrary of *appert* = *espert* clever, able (:—L. *expertus*). The Eng. sense points rather to *mal* 'improperly' + *apert* bold (see APERT *a.*).] **A.** *adj.* Presumptuous, impudent, saucy. **B.** *sb.* A presumptuous or saucy person 1622.

His malepert boldnes might peraduenture be punished SIR T. MORE. Hence **Ma·lapert-ly** *adv.*, **-ness.**

Malaprop (mæ·lăprǫp). 1823. [f. Mrs. *Malaprop* (after MALAPROPOS), in Sheridan's play, *The Rivals* (1775).] *sb.* = MALAPROPISM. *adj.* = MALAPROPIAN. So **Malapropian** (mælăprǫ·piăn), *a.* of the nature of, or given to, malapropisms 1860. **Malapropism** (mæ·lăprǫpiz'm), ludicrous misuse of words; an instance of this 1849.

Mr. Lewes is sending what a Malapropian friend once called a 'missile' to Sara GEO. ELIOT.

Malapropos (malaprọpo, mælæprǒpōᵘ·), *adv.*, *a.*, and *sb.* Also written **mal à propos, mal-a-propos, mal apropos**, etc. 1668. [F. *mal à propos*, f. *mal* ill + *à* to + *propos* purpose; see MAL- and APROPOS.] **A.** *adv.* In an inopportune or awkward manner; unseasonably, inappropriately. **B.** *adj.* Inopportune, inappropriate 1711. **C.** *sb.* Something inopportune or inappropriate 1868. Hence **Malapropo·ism** = MALAPROPISM 1834.

Malar (mēⁱ·lăɹ), *a.* (and *sb.*) 1782. [ad. mod.L. *malaris*, f. L. *mala* jaw, cheek-bone, cheek.] **1.** Of or belonging to the cheek. **2.** *sb.* (or *absol.* = *m. bone*) The cheek-bone 1866.

Malaria (mălēᵊ·riă). 1740. [a. It. *mal'aria* for *mala aria*, lit. 'bad air'.] **a.** The unwholesome atmosphere which results from the exhalations of marshy districts. **b.** (= *m. fever*) A febrile disease (formerly attributed to this) caused by a blood-parasite (*m. parasite*), conveyed by the bite of a mosquito. Also *transf.* and *fig.*

Ma·lassimila·tion. 1865. [MAL-.] Imperfect assimilation; *esp.* in *Path.* imperfect absorption of nutriment into the system.

Malate (mēⁱ·lēⁱt). 1794. [f. MALIC *a.* + -ATE[4].] *Chem.* A salt of malic acid.

†**Malax**, *v.* late ME. [ad. L. *malaxare*; see MALAXATE.] *trans.* To rub or knead (a plaster, etc.) to softness; *gen.* to soften –1764.

Malaxate (mæ·lækseⁱt), *v.* 1657. [f. L. *malaxat-*, *malaxare*, ad. Gr. μαλάσσειν, related to μαλακός soft; see -ATE[3].] *trans.* To soften by kneading or mixing, or by means of an emollient. Hence **Malaxa·tion**, the action of reducing to a soft mass by kneading or rolling. **Ma·laxator**, a mixing-mill.

Malay (mălēⁱ·). 1598. [repr. the native name *malāyu.*] **A.** *sb.* **1.** One of a race predominating in Malacca and the Eastern Archipelago, a Malayan. **2.** The Malay language 1598. **3.** Short for *M. fowl* 1830.

1. In person the Malays are short, squat, and robust 1840.

B. *adj.* Of, pertaining to, or characteristic of the Malays or their country 1779. **b.** In names of plants, animals, etc., e. g. **M. apple**, a myrtaceous tree, *Jambosa* (*Eugenia*) *malaccensis*, with an edible fruit; **M. fowl**, a large variety of domestic fowl introduced from the Malay Peninsula; etc. 1820.

Hence **Mala·yan** *a.* and *sb.*, in same senses.

Malayalam (mælăyā·læm). [Native name.] Name of a cultivated Dravidian dialect, closely related to Tamil.

Malaysian (mălēⁱ·siăn), *a.* 1883. [f. *Malaysia*, i. e. the Malay archipelago + -AN.] Of or belonging to Malaysia.

Malco·nduct. Also †**male-**. 1741. [MAL-.] Improper conduct; *esp.* improper or dishonest administration of an office, business, etc.

Ma·lco·nforma·tion. 1776. [MAL-.] Bad or faulty conformation.

Malcontent (mæ·lkǫntent). Also †**male-**. 1581. [a. OF.; see MAL- and CONTENT *a.*] **A.** *adj.* Discontented, dissatisfied. Now chiefly in political use: Inclined to rebellion or mutiny; restless and disaffected 1586.

You stand pensiue, as halfe malecontent SHAKS.

B. *sb.* **1.** A malcontent person (see A.) 1581. †**2.** The state of being discontented. [Really a distinct word; see CONTENT *sb.*] –1663.

2. A necessity of sadnesse and malecontent MILT. Hence †**Malconte·nted** *a.*, †**-ly** *adv.*, †**-ness.**

Male (mēⁱl). [ME. *masle*, a. OF. *male*, *masle* (mod.F. *mâle*) :—L. *masculus* (f. *mas* male person), whence MASCULINE *a.*] **A.** *adj.* **I. 1.** Of or belonging to the sex which begets offspring, or performs the fecundating function. Used: **a.** of persons ME. **b.** of animals ME. **c.** of certain plants (of dioecious species) the flowers of which contain only the fecundating organs ME. **d.** of certain plants to which sex was formerly attributed on account of some peculiarity of habit, colour, etc. 1562. **2.** Of or pertaining to a man or men, or to male animals; peculiar to men; composed or consisting of men 1631. **b.** Adapted to or meant for the use of a man 1788. †**3.** *transf.* **a.** Said of precious stones, on account of depth, brilliance, or other accident of colour; also of other stones, with reference to their hardness or other esteemed qualities. [Gr. ἄρρην, L. *masculus.*] –1855. †**b.** Used to distinguish the harder and more compact kind of sand or gravel 1601–1813. †**4. Male incense.** [So in L. and Fr.] A superior quality of incense, known by the greater size of the 'tears' in which it is collected; frankincense 1598–1727. **5.** Of rime: see under MASCULINE *a.* 3. 1581. **6.** Said of the external layer of bark on a tree 1884.

1. a. Caine, the first male-childe SHAKS. Phr. *Heir, issue, line, tail m.* (Law). **b.** There is no more mercy in him, then there is milke in a male-Tyger SHAKS. **c.** The catkins which appear in January are the m. parts of a nut-tree 1791. **d. M. fern**, *Asplenium* (*Nephrodium*) *Filix-mas.* 2. They keep as good female company as I do m. SWIFT. **b.** M. Hospital 1828. 3. Lordly male-sapphires BROWNING.

II. A distinctive epithet for that part of an instrument or contrivance which is adapted to penetrate or fill the corresponding female part 1669.

Phr. *M. gauge*: the outer gauge or screw of a printing-press. *M. screw*: the spiral pin or rod which fits the spirally bored circular socket of the female screw.

B. *sb.* **1.** A male animal ME. **2.** A male person; a boy or man. Only in expressed or implied antithesis with *female* ME.; *occas.* a male plant 1548. **3.** *Comb.* **m. impersonator**, a female who personates a male on the stage.

Male, obs. f. MAIL.

Male-: see MAL-.

Maledicent (mælĭdəi·sĕnt). Now *rare.* 1599. [ad. L. *maledicentem*, *-dicere.*] **A.** *adj.* Given to evil-speaking; of the nature of evil-speaking, slanderous. **B.** *sb.* One who speaks evil of another 1657. Hence †**Maledi·cency**, the practice of speaking evil 1653.

Maledict (mæ·lĭdikt), *a.* (*sb.*) *arch.* 1550. [ad. L. *maledictus*; see prec.] Accursed. Also as *sb.*

Malediction (mælĭdi·kʃən). 1447. [ad. L. *maledictionem.*] **1.** The utterance of a curse; the being under a ban or curse. **2.** Reviling, slander; the condition of being reviled or slandered 1526.

1. I..loaded him with maledictions SCOTT.

Malefa·ction. 1602. [ad. L. *malefactionem.*] Evil-doing; an instance of this.

Malefactor (mæ·lĭfæktəɹ). 1440. [a. L., f. *malefacere.*] **1.** One guilty of a heinous offence against the law; a felon, a criminal. Also *transf.* **2.** An evil-doer; one who does ill towards another; opp. to *benefactor* 1483. So **Ma·lefactress**, a female m. 1647.

Malefeazance: see MALFEASANCE.

Malefic (măle·fik). 1652. [ad. L. *maleficus*, f. *male* ill; see -FIC.] **A.** *adj.* Productive of disaster or evil; baleful. Said esp. of stellar influences and magical practices. **B.** *sb.* **a.** *Astrol.* A malefic aspect or body. †**b.** A malefic doer; a malign wizard. 1652. So †**Male·fical** *a.* 1615–1652, **-ly** *adv.*

Malefice (mæ·lĭfis). late ME. [ad. L. *maleficium*, f. *maleficus*; see prec.] **1.** A wicked enchantment; sorcery (*arch.*). **2.** An evil deed; mischief. *Obs.* or *arch.* 1591. †**3.** *Astrol.* Malefic character. GAULE.

Maleficent (măle·fisĕnt), *a.* 1678. [f. L. *maleficent-*, altered stem of *maleficus* MALEFIC *a.*] 1. Of things, etc.: Working harm, hurtful, malefic. Const. *to.* 2. Of persons, etc.: Wrong-doing, criminal 1760.

†**Malefi·cial,** *a.* 1601. [f. L. *maleficium* + -AL.] Malefic, maleficent -1831.

†**Malefi·ciate,** *v.* 1621. [f. med.L. *maleficiat-*, *maleficiare*, f. L. *maleficium.*] *trans.* To bewitch; *spec.* to render impotent by spells -1693. Hence †**Maleficia·tion.**

Maleic (mălī·ik), *a.* 1838. [ad. F. *maléique*; formed by altering *malique* MALIC.] *Chem.* In *m. acid*: a product of the dry distillation of malic acid.

†**Malengin.** late ME. [a. OF., f. *mal* evil (see MAL-) + *engin* contrivance.] Evil machination, ill intent; fraud, deceit, guile -1726.

‖**Mal-entendu** (malantandü). 1780. [Fr., f. *mal* ill + *entendu* understood.] A misunderstanding.

‖**Maleo** (mæ·lĭ,o). 1869. [Native name.] A megapode bird, *Megacephalon maleo*, inhabiting Celebes.

Maletolt. *Obs.* exc. *Hist.* Also **-tot**(e, etc. 1514. [a. AF. *maletoute*, OF. *maltolte* (mod.F. *maltôte*), repr. med.L. *mala tolta* (*mala* adj. fem. + *tolta* tax, f. med.L. *tolt-*, ppl. stem of L. *tollere*).] *Law.* An unjust or burdensome tax.

Malevolence (măle·vŏlĕns). 1489. [a. OF. *mali-*, *malevolence*, ad. L. *mali-*, *malevolentia*; see MALEVOLENT.] The attribute of being malevolent; ill-will. So †**Malevolency.**

Malevolent (măle·vŏlĕnt), *a.* (*sb.*) 1509. [a. OF. *malivolent*, ad. L. *mali-*, *malevolentem*, f. *male* ill + *volentem*, *velle* to wish.] 1. Of persons, etc.: Desirous of evil to others; indicative of ill-will; disposed or addicted to ill-will. †b. *transf.* 1719. †2. *Astrol.* Exercising a baleful influence. Also *transf.* and *fig.* -1696. †3. *sb.* A person of evil wishes or designs -1670.

1. b. To secure plants from m. winds 1719. Hence **Male·volently** *adv.* So †**Male·volous** *a.* (in sense 1) 1536-1727.

Malfeasance (mælfī·zăns). Also †**male-.** 1696. [a. AF. **malfaisance*, f. OF. *malfaisant* (MAL-, F. *faire* to do).] 1. *Law.* Evil-doing; *spec.* official misconduct in public affairs. 2. *gen.* Wrong-doing; an instance of this 1856. So **Malfea·sant,** a malefactor 1882.

Malforma·tion. 1800. [MAL-.] Faulty or anomalous formation or structure of parts. Also *fig.* So **Malfo·rmed** *a.* badly formed; marked by m.; also *transf.* and *fig.* 1817.

‖**Malgré** (malgre), *prep.* 1608. [Fr.; see MAUGRE.] In spite of, notwithstanding. Also †‖**Malgra·do** [It.] 1590.

Malic (mē¹·lik), *a.* 1797. [a. F. *malique*, f. L. *malum* apple.] *Chem.* In *m. acid*: an acid, $C_4H_6O_5$, derived from the apple, the berries of the mountain-ash, and other fruits.

Malice (mæ·lis), *sb.* ME. [a. F. *malice*, ad. L. *malitia*, f. *malus* bad.] †1. Badness; wickedness -1605. †2. Harmfulness; harmful action or effect. Of a disease, poison, etc.: Virulence. -1685. 3. Active ill-will or hatred. In mod. use occas.: Desire to tease (cf. F. *malice*). ME. b. *fig.* Attributed to fortune, or impersonal agencies 1660. †4. Malicious conduct; a malicious act or device -1669. 5. *Law.* Wrongful intention; *esp.* that kind of evil intent which aggravates the guilt of certain offences (esp. of murder) 1547.

1. It seemeth the children of time do take after the nature and m. of the father BACON. 2. Our Cannons m. vainly shall be spent SHAKS. 3. God forbid any M. should preuayle SHAKS. Phr. *To bear m.*: to feel ill-will; now usually, to keep alive revengeful feelings on account of some injury. 4. *Cor.* II. ii. 36. 5. In the best known definitions of m. it is scarcely distinguishable from intention MARKBY. *M. aforethought*: = *malice prepense* (see PREPENSE *a*).

†**Ma·lice,** *v.* 1547. [f. prec.] 1. *trans.* To regard with malice -1694. 2. *intr.* To entertain malice -1592.

Malicious (măli·ʃəs), *a.* ME. [a. OF. *malicius* (mod.F. *malicieux*), ad. L. *malitiosus*, f. *malitia*; see MALICE *sb.* and -OUS.] 1. Given to malice; addicted to sentiments or acts of ill-will. Now occas.: Inclined to tease. Also *absol.* 2. Proceeding from or characterized by malice. Earlier often: †Evil, wicked. Now occas.: 'Mischievous'. ME. 3. *Law.* Characterized by 'malice prepense', as in *m. damage, prosecution, waste,* etc. 1530. †4. *Med.* Malignant, virulent -1720. †5. Artful -1590.

1. Either you must Confesse your selues wondrous M., Or be accus'd of Folly SHAKS. 2. The private whisper of a m. groundlesse lye 1651. Hence **Mali·cious·ly** *adv.*, **-ness.**

Malign (măləi·n), *a.* ME. [a. OF. *maligne*, *malin* (mod.F. *malin*), ad. L. *malignus* evil-disposed, f. *malus.* Cf. BENIGN *a.*] 1. Characterized by ill-will; desiring, or rejoicing in, the suffering of others; malignant, malevolent. Now *rare.* 1450. 2. Of things: Baleful ME. 3. Of diseases: Malignant 1541. 4. *Astrol.* Having a baleful influence. Also *transf.* 1605.

1. Some tempers are so m., that they wish ill to all, and believe ill of all 1674. 2. A struggle between two forces, the one beneficent, the other m. BRYCE. 3. Old and maligne vlcers T. GALE. 4. Saturn which is a planet Maligne BACON. **Mali·gn·ly** *adv.*

Malign (mălǝi·n), *v.* late ME. [a. OF. *malignier*, *maliner* to plot, deceive, ad. L. *malignare* to do or contrive maliciously, f. *malignus* MALIGN *a.*] †1. *intr.* To speak evil, entertain malice, plot, contrive (*against*). †2. *trans.* To regard with hatred. Also, to resent, take amiss. -1667. †3. To regard with envy; to begrudge -1706. 4. To speak ill of (one), to traduce, slander 1647.

3. Strangers conspired together against him, and maligned him in the wildernesse *Ecclus.* xlv. 18. The envious Gods Maligne our happinesse 1638. 4. No religion was ever so maligned, age after age 1758.

Mali·gnance. 1641. [See -ANCE.] = next.

Malignancy (măli·gnănsi). 1601. [f. MALIGNANT *a.*; see -ANCY.] The quality of being malignant. 1. Disaffection to rightful authority. *Obs.* exc. *Hist.* (Cf. MALIGNANT B.) 1644. 2. *Path.* Of a disease, tumour, etc. 1685. 3. Baleful character; unpropitiousness; noxiousness 1601. 4. Malignant disposition; intense malevolence; desire to inflict injury or suffering 1640. 5. An instance of malignancy 1652.

1. The m., which at that time began to appear in people MAY. 3. My starres shine darkely ouer me; the malignancie of my fate, might perhaps distemper yours SHAKS. 4. Penetration gives her more artifice and m. 1706.

Malignant (măli·gnănt), *a.* and *sb.* 1542. [ad. late L. *malignantem*, *malignare*, *-ari* (see MALIGN *v.*).] A. *adj.* †1. Disposed to rebel; disaffected, malcontent -1659. Also *absol.* b. *spec.* Applied between 1641 and 1660 by the supporters of the Parliament and the Commonwealth to their adversaries 1641. 2. Of a disease: Virulent; exceptionally contagious or infectious. Now used to differentiate a definite variety of a disease, as *m. cholera, m. small-pox,* etc. 1568. 3. Having an evil influence. Chiefly *Astrol.*, etc. = MALIGN. Formerly also: Poisonous, deleterious. 1591. 4. Characterized by malignity; keenly desirous of the misfortune of another, or of others generally 1592.

1. In Aleppo once, Where a m., and a Turbond-Turke Beate a Venetian SHAKS. *The church m.*: applied to the followers of antichrist, and by early Protestants to the Church of Rome. 2. *M. growth, tumour*: in mod. use one which tends to spread and recur and so prove fatal. 3. O m. and ill-boading Starres SHAKS. A witch..charged with having..a m. touch 1765. 4. So shall the Worlde goe on, To good m., to bad men benigne MILT.

B. *sb.* A malcontent 1597. b. Used by opponents as a designation for a supporter of Charles I against the Parliament; a Royalist, Cavalier. Also, applied by Puritans and Covenanters to their eccl. opponents. Now *Hist.* 1642.

Hence **Mali·gnantly** *adv.* in a m. manner.

Maligner (mălǝi·nəɹ). late ME. [f. MALIGN *v.* + -ER [1].] One who maligns; a traducer, a slanderer.

Malignify (măli·gnifəi), *v. rare.* 1613. [f. L. *malignus* + *-ficare*; see -FY.] *trans.* To render malign.

Malignity (măli·gnĭti). late ME. [a. OF. *malignité*, ad. L. *malignitas*, f. *malignus* MALIGN *a.*; see -ITY.] 1. Deep-rooted ill-will; persistent desire to cause suffering to another person; propensity to this feeling. b. *pl.* Malignant feelings or actions 1529. 2. Wickedness, heinousness (*arch.*) 1534. 3. Noxiousness (*arch.*) 1605. 4. Of diseases, etc.: Malignant character 1646.

1. Thanne comth malignitee thurgh which a man anoyeth his neighebor priuely CHAUCER. 3. The m. of the atmosphere 1858.

Malinger (măli·ŋgəɹ), *v.* 1820. [prob. back-formation f. next.] *intr.* To pretend illness, or to produce or protract disease, in order to escape duty; said esp. of soldiers and sailors.

Malingerer (măli·ŋgərəɹ). 1768 (in form maligner), 1785 (malingeror). [? irreg. f. F. *malingre* sickly (of unkn. origin) + -ER [1].] One who malingers.

Malison (mæ·lisən). *arch.* and *dial.* ME. [a. OF. *maleison*:—L. *maledictionem.*] A curse, malediction.

Malkin, mawkin (mǭ·kin). *Obs.* exc. *dial.* ME. [dim. of *Matilda, Maud* (ME. *Maalde, Malde*); see -KIN.] †1. A female personal name; applied typically to a woman of the lower classes -1670. †b. Proper name of a female spectre or demon -1605. 2. A slut, slattern; *occas.* a lewd woman 1586. 3. A mop; a bundle of rags fastened to the end of a stick ME. b. *Naut.* 'A joint-staff sponge, for cleaning out a piece of ordnance' (Smyth). 4. A scarecrow (also *fig.*); a guy 1633. 5. A designation, or quasi-proper name for: a. a cat (*dial.*) 1673; b. a hare (*Sc.* and *n. dial.*) 1724.

Mall [1] (mǫl). †Also **mell, maul.** 1662. [A use of *mall*, MAUL *sb.*[1], in certain 17th c. senses of F. *mail.* Cf. PALL-MALL.] 1. The mallet used in the game of 'mall' or 'pall-mall'; = PALL-MALL 1. 2. The game; = PALL-MALL 2. 1675. 3. The alley in which the game was played; = PALL-MALL 3. 1687. 4. *The Mall* (mæl): a walk bordered by trees in St. James's Park, London, which was orig. a 'mall' in sense 3. 1674. b. *transf.* A sheltered walk serving as a promenade 1737.

Mall [2]: see MAUL, MAW.

Mallard (mæ·lăɹd). ME. [a. OF. *malart*, *mallart* wild drake; of obscure origin.] 1. The male of the wild duck (*Anas boscas*). †Formerly also = DRAKE [2]. 2. Used for either sex ME. b. The flesh of this bird 1440. 3. *The M.*: a festival celebrated on the 14th Jan. at All Souls College, Oxford 1632.

Malleable (mæ·lĭ,ăb'l), *a.* late ME. [a. OF., ad. L. **malleabilis*, f. L. *malleare* to MALLEATE; see -ABLE.] 1. That can be deprived of form by hammering or pressure, without a tendency to return to it, or to fracture; applied to metals, etc. 2. *transf.* and *fig.* Capable of being fashioned or adapted 1612.

1. *M. iron*: iron which has been decarburized by oxidation under prolonged heat and rendered capable of being malleated in a slight degree. Hence **Ma·lleabi·lity, Ma·lleableness,** the property of being m. **Ma·lleableize, ma·lleablize** *v. trans.* to render m.

Mallear (mæ·lĭ,ăɹ), *a.* 1889. [ad. mod.L. *mallearis*, f. MALLEUS.] Pertaining to the malleus.

Malleate (mæ·lĭ,ĕt), *a.* 1884. [ad. mod.L. *malleatus*, f. *malleus.*] *Zool.* Furnished with a malleus.

Malleate (mæ·lĭ,eᶦt), *v.* Now *rare.* 1597. [f. L. *malleat-*, *malleare*, f. *malleus.*] *trans.* To beat with a hammer; *spec.* to beat (metal) thin or flat.

Malleation (mælĭ,ē¹·ʃən). 1596. [ad. late L. *malleationem*, f. *malleare*; see prec.] 1. The action of malleating or condition of being malleated. Now *rare.* Also *fig.* 2. *Path.* A convulsive disorder characterized by the hammering one part of the body against another; occurring as a symptom in chorea and insanity 1822.

Mallecho: see MICHING MALICHO.

‖**Mallee** [1] (mǭ·lĭ). *Anglo-Ind.* 1759. [Hindi *mālī.*] One of the gardener caste in India; hence, any native gardener.

Mallee [2] (mæ·lĭ). 1848. [Native Austral.] Any one of several scrubby species of eucalyptus; esp. *Eucalyptus dumosa* and *E. oleosa.* **M. bird, fowl, hen,** an Australian mound-bird, *Leipoa ocellata.*

Mallein (mæ·lɪ̆ˌin). Also **-ine.** 1892. [f. L. *malleus* glanders + -IN.[1]] A sterilized culture of the bacillus of glanders, used for inoculation.

‖**Mallemuck.** Also **mallemoke, -mock,** etc. 1694. [a. Du. *mallemok*, f. *mal* foolish + *mok* gull.] The fulmar, *Fulmarus glacialis*; also applied to similar or related birds.

Mallender, var. f. MALANDER.

‖**Malleolus** (mælɪ̄·ŏlǒs). *Pl.* **-i.** 1693. [L., dim. of *malleus* hammer.] **1.** *Anat.* Either of the two bony eminences of the leg bone at the ankle. (The *internal m.* belongs to the tibia, the *external m.* to the fibula.) **2.** *Hort.* A layer which when separated from the parent stem presents a hammer-shape 1706.

Mallet (mæ·lėt), *sb.*[1] late ME. [a. F. *maillet* wooden hammer, dim. of *mail* MAUL *sb.*[1]] A kind of hammer, usually of wood, smaller than a maul or beetle. **b.** *Games.* The wooden hammer used for striking the balls in croquet or polo; also *transf.* the player who uses this 1868. †**c.** *fig.* A person or agency that smites, beats down, or crushes. [After L. *malleus.*] –1823.

c. Sometimes like a m., to strike the Israelites 1561. *Comb.* **m.-shoot,** a hammer-shaped slip of a tree for planting.

†**Ma·llet,** *sb.*[2] *rare.* 1612 (Shelton). [ad. Sp. *maleta.*] A little portmanteau.

Mallet (mæ·lėt), *v. Obs.* exc. *arch.* 1594. [f. MALLET *sb.*[1]] *trans.* To beat, hammer.

‖**Malleus** (mæ·lɪ̆ˌǒs). *Pl.* **-ei** (-ɪ̆ˌəi). 1669. [L., lit. 'hammer'.] *Anat.* **1.** The outermost of the three small bones (*malleus, incus,* and *stapes*) in the ear of mammals, which transmits the vibrations of the tympanum to the incus or 'anvil'. **2.** One of two organs of the trophi or mouth-apparatus in *Rotifera,* which work upon the incus 1850.

Mallophagous (mælǫ·făgəs), *a.* 1890. [f. mod.L. *mallophagus* (f. Gr. μαλλός lock of wool + -φάγος eating) + -OUS.] *Entom.* Of an insect: Devouring wool, hair, feathers, etc.; applied to the *Mallophaga*, a group of apodous parasitic insects.

Mallow (mæ·lo^u^). [OE. *mealuwe* wk. fem., a. L. *malva*; prob. conn. w. Gr. μαλάχη, μολόχη.] **1.** (Also *pl.* const. as *sing.*) A common wild plant, *Malva sylvestris* (N.O. *Malvaceæ*), with hairy stems and leaves and red-dish-purple flowers; it is very mucilaginous. Called also *Common, Field, Wild m.* Hence extended to other plants of the genus *Malva* or N.O. *Malvaceæ.* **2.** = MARSH MALLOW, *Althæa officinalis.* Called also *Water, White M.* ME. **3.** The Syrian Mallow, *Hibiscus syriacus* ME. **4.** *Garden* or *Rose M.*, the hollyhock, *Althæa rosea* 1577. **5.** The leaf or fibre of the mallow used for writing upon. COWLEY.

1. Indian m., (*a*) *Abutilon Avicennæ,* (*b*) any plant of the genera *Urena* or *Sida.* **Jews' m.,** *Corchorus olitorius.* Also MARSH MALLOW, q.v. **Tree m.,** *Lavatera arborea.* **Yellow m.** = *Indian mallow.*

‖**Mallum** (mæ·lǒm), **mallus** (mæ·lǒs). 1844. [med.L., ad. OFrankish **mall-*, contr. f. OTeut. **maþlo-* (OE. *mæðel* meeting, discussion, etc.).] *Hist.* The hundred-court among the Franks.

Malm (mām), *sb.* [OE. *mealm-*, in comb. *mealmstān* (see 3); cogn. w. ON. *malm-r* ore, metal, Goth. *malma* masc., sand, f. root **mel-*, *mal-* to grind; see MEAL *sb.*[1]] **1. a.** A soft friable rock, consisting largely of chalky material. **b.** The light loamy soil formed by the disintegration of this. 1477. **2.** Short for *malm-brick* 1858. **3.** *attrib.*: **m.-brick,** the best kind of brick; **-rock** *Geol.* = GREENSAND 1 c; **-stone** = sense 1 a. OE. Hence **Ma·lmy** *a.* of a loamy character.

Malm (mām), *v.* 1619. [f. prec.] *trans.* †**a.** To treat (land) with malm. **b.** To convert (clay) into artificial malm for brickmaking; to cover (brick-earth) with artificial malm.

‖**Malmag** (mæ·lmæg). 1838. [repr. *malmay* in Sp. dialect of the Philippines.] The Spectre, *Tarsius spectrum*, a small lemuroid animal, native of Borneo and the Philippines.

Malmaison (mælmē·zǫn). 1892. [Short for *Souvenirs de Malmaison* (Fr. 'recollections of Malmaison', the palace of the empress Josephine).] *Hort.* A variety of the carnation.

Malmsey (mā·mzi). late ME. [ad. med.L. *malmasia*, a corruption of Gr. Μονεμβασία (Monemvasia).] **1.** A strong sweet wine, orig. from Monemvasia (Napoli di Malvasia) in the Morea; but now also from Spain, the Azores, etc. Also *attrib.* **2.** A kind of grape, from which this wine was originally made 1511.

Malnutrition (mælniutri·ʃən). 1862. [MAL-.] Insufficient nutrition.

Mal-observa·tion. 1886. Defective observation.

Malodorous (mælō^u^·dŏrəs), *a.* 1850. [MAL-.] Evil-smelling. Hence **Malo·dorously** *adv.*, **-ness.**

Malodour (mælō^u^·dəɹ). 1825. [MAL-.] An evil smell, a stench.

Malpighian (mælpi·giăn), *a.* 1847. [f. name of Marcello *Malpighi*, an Italian physician (1628–94) + -AN.] **1.** *Anat.* Distinctive epithet of certain structures (esp. in the substance of the kidneys) discovered by Malpighi, and of others connected with these. **2.** *Bot.* In *M. cells*: those which compose the outer layer of the seed in *Malpighiaceæ* 1900.

Malposi·tion. 1836. [MAL-.] Misplacement 1862. **b.** *spec.* in *Obstetrics.* Faulty position of a part or organ, esp. of the fœtus in the uterus.

Malpra·ctice. 1671. [MAL-.] **1.** *Law.* **a.** Improper treatment or culpable neglect of a patient by a physician. **b.** Illegal action by which a person seeks a benefit for himself, while in a position of trust 1758. **2.** *gen.* A criminal or overtly mischievous action; wrong-doing 1772.

1. b. Malpractices begin with the prospectus and continue till liquidation 1895. So **Malpra·xis.**

Malt (mǭlt), *sb.* [Com. Teut.: OE. *mealt* :—OTeut. **maltos-* neut.; f. the root of MELT, SMELT *vbs.*] **1.** Barley or other grain prepared for brewing or distilling by steeping, germinating, and kiln-drying, or by gelatinization, etc. **2.** *transf.* Used for: Malt liquor (*slang* or *colloq.*) 1718.

1. *Extract of m.*, a preparation of m. used as food for invalids. Provb. *The m. is above the meal,* said of a person under the influence of drink.

attrib. and *Comb.*, as *m.-spirits*; *m-cellar, -meal,* etc.; **m. extract,** a saccharine and mucilaginous substance obtained from wort; also = *extract of m.*; **-floor,** (*a*) a floor on which the malt is spread to germinate; (*b*) a perforated floor in the malt-kiln, through which heat ascends from a furnace below to dry the barley laid upon it; **-kiln,** a kiln in which the m. is dried after steeping and couching; **m. liquor,** liquor made from m. by fermentation, as ale, beer, stout, etc.; **-sugar** = MALTOSE; **-tax,** a tax on m., now replaced by the beer-duty; **m. vinegar,** vinegar made from the fermentation of m.

Malt (mǭlt), *v.* 1440. [f. MALT *sb.*] **1.** *trans.* To convert (grain) into malt. Also *absol.* **b.** *intr.* To admit of being malted 1766. **2.** *transf.* (*pass.* and *intr.*) Of seeds: To come to the condition of malt owing to germination being checked by drought 1733. **3.** *trans.* To make (liquor) with malt 1605. **4.** *intr.* To drink malt liquor (*vulgar*) 1813.

3. A man of worship, whose beere was better hopped than maulted CAMDEN.

Malta (mǭ·ltă). 1651. Name of an island in the Mediterranean; used *attrib.*, as †**M. cross** = *Maltese cross*; **M. fever,** a complicated fever of long duration, common in M.

†**Ma·ltalent.** ME. [a. OF., f. *mal* evil + *talent* disposition, temper (see TALENT).] Ill-will, malevolence –1828.

Malt-dust. 1512. The refuse which falls from the grain in malting.

Maltese (mǭltī·z), *a.* and *sb. sing.* and *pl.* 1615. [f. MALTA + -ESE.] **A.** *adj.* Of or pertaining to Malta and its inhabitants, or to the Knights of Malta 1797.

M. cat, a short-haired blue-coloured variety of the domestic cat; **M. cross,** see CROSS *sb.* 13; **M. dog,** a small kind of spaniel, with a roundish muzzle, and long, silky, generally white hair; **M. lace,** a lace having arabesque or geometric patterns, said to have been orig. made in Malta; **M. orange,** the 'blood' orange, much grown in southern Italy.

B. *sb.* **1. a.** A native or an inhabitant of Malta. **b.** A Knight of Malta. 1615. **2.** The language of the natives of Malta, a corrupt Arabic 1828. **3.** Short for *Maltese lace* 1900.

Maltha (mæ·lþă). late ME. (**malthe**). 1601. [a. L., a Gr. μάλθα, μάλθη mixture of wax and pitch.] **1.** A kind of cement made by mixing pitch and wax, or lime and sand, with other ingredients. **2.** The name anciently given to some viscid form of bitumen; applied variously to asphaltum, to mineral tar, and to ozocerite (Kirwan's 'mineral tallow') 1601.

†**Ma·lt-horse.** 1561. A heavy kind of horse used by maltsters; occas., as a term of abuse –1616.

Mome, M., Capon, Coxcombe, Idiot SHAKS.

Malt-house (mǭ·ltˌhaus). OE. A building in which malt is prepared and stored; a malting.

Malthusian (mælþiū·ziăn). 1812. [f. T. R. *Malthus* + -IAN.] **A.** *adj.* Pertaining to T. R. Malthus (1766–1835) or his teaching 1821. **B.** *sb.* A follower or supporter of T. R. Malthus in his views on population. Hence **Malthusianism** (mælþiū·ziănizm), the teaching of Malthus and his followers, who held that, as population increases faster than the means of subsistence, its increase should be checked, mainly by moral restraint: popularly viewed as a proposal to check marriage 1833.

Maltine (mǭ·ltīn). 1889. [f. MALT *sb.* + -INE [5].] Commercial name for various preparations of malt.

Malting (mǭ·ltiŋ), *vbl. sb.* 1440. [f. MALT *v.* + -ING [1].] **1.** In senses of MALT *v.* **2.** A MALT-HOUSE 1846. **3.** *attrib.*, as **m.-floor, -kiln,** etc. = *malt-floor, -kiln,* etc. 1467.

Maltman (mǭ·ltmæ̆n). ME. A maltster.

Maltose (mǭ·ltō^u^s). 1862. [a. F., f. MALT *sb.*; see -OSE.] *Chem.* Sugar produced from starch-paste as by the action of malt.

Maltreat (mæltrī·t), *v.* 1708. [a. F. *maltraiter*; see MAL- and TREAT *v.*] *trans.* To abuse, ill-use; to handle roughly or rudely. Hence **Maltrea·tment** 1721.

Maltster (mǭ·ltstəɹ). ME. [f. MALT *sb.* + -STER.] One whose occupation is to make malt.

Ma·lt-worm. 1440. †**1.** A weevil which infests malt. **2.** *transf.* A toper 1550.

Malty (mǭ·lti), *a.* 1819. [f. MALT *sb.* + -Y [1].] Addicted to, affected by, or containing malt (liquor). Also *slang*, drunk. **b.** Of the nature of or resembling malt 1830.

Malvaceous (mælvē^i^·ʃəs), *a.* 1699. [f. late L. *malvaceus* (whence mod.L. *Malvaceæ*), f. *malva* mallow; see -ACEOUS.] *Bot.* Pertaining to the genus *Malva* (the Mallow), or to the N.O. *Malvaceæ.*

Malval (mæ·lvăl), *a.* 1836. [f. L. *malva* MALLOW + -AL.] *Bot.* Only in *M. alliance, exogens*: an alliance embracing the N.O. *Malvaceæ* and other orders (Lindley).

Malversation (mælvəɹsē^i^·ʃən). 1549. [a. F., f. *malverser*, ad. L. *male versari* to conduct oneself wrongly.] Corrupt behaviour in a position of trust; an instance of this. **b.** Corrupt administration *of* something 1706.

b. Cardonnel was turned out of the House of Commons..for m. of public money THACKERAY.

Malvoisie (mæ·lvoizi). *Obs.* exc. *arch.* †Also **-esie,** etc. late ME. [a. OF. *malvesie*, ad. It. *malvasia*, corruption of Gr. Μονεμβασία (cf. MALMSEY).] **1.** = MALMSEY **1.** **2.** = MALMSEY **2.** 1517.

Mam (mæm). *colloq.* 1500. [See MAMMA [1].] A childish word for mother; corresp. to DAD.

Mama, var. of MAMMA [1].

‖**Mamamouchi.** 1672. A mock-Turkish title, from Molière's play *Le Bourgeois Gentilhomme* IV. iii. Hence occas.: A pompous-sounding title; also, one assuming such a title.

This ridiculous M. [The Duke of Newcastle] H. WALPOLE.

Mamelon (mæ·mĕlǫn). 1830. [a. F. *mamelon* nipple, f. *mamelle* :—L. *mamilla*, dim. of *mamma* breast.] **1.** A rounded eminence or hummock. **2.** A small hemispherical tubercle 1872. Hence **Ma·melonated** *a.* covered with rounded protuberances.

‖**Mameluco** (mæmĕlū·ko). 1863. [Pg., lit. a mameluke; see next.] A cross-breed between a white and a Brazilian Indian.

Mameluke (mæ·mĕlūk). *Obs.* exc. *Hist.* 1511. [Ult. a. Arab. *mamlūk* slave, f. *malaka* to possess. The Turkish pronunc. is (memlūk).] 1. A member of the military body, originally composed of Circassian slaves, which seized the throne of Egypt in 1254, and continued to form the ruling class in that country until exterminated by Mohammed Ali in 1811. 2. A slave (in Mohammedan countries) 1600. 3. *fig.* A 'fighting slave' of the Pope, etc. 1531.

3. The Assumptionists are mere mamelukes of the Vatican 1902.

‖**Mamilla** (mæmi·lă). Also **mammilla.** 1693. [L., dim. of *mamma.*] 1. The nipple of the female breast; also, the male mamma. 2. *transf.* (*Anat.*, *Bot.*, etc.) Any nipple-shaped organ or protuberance; a papilla 1818. Hence **Ma·m(m)illar** *a.* = MAMILLARY 2. **Mami·lliform, Ma·milloid** *adjs.* resembling a m.

Mamillary (mæ·milări), *a.* Also **mamm-.** 1615. [f. L. *mamillaris*, f. *mamilla*; see prec. and -ARY [2].] 1. Of or pertaining to the breast; †having mammæ 1669. 2. Of the form of a mamma 1615. b. Having mammiform protuberances 1813.

2. *M. brooch* (Antiq.): one consisting of two cup-shaped pieces connected by a handle 1862.

Ma·millate, *a.* Also **mamm-.** 1826. [ad. L. *mamillatus*, f. *mamilla* + -ATE [1].] = next.

Mamillated (mæ·mileᶦtĕd), *ppl. a.* Also **mamm-.** 1741. [f. prec. + -ED [1].] 1. Having rounded protuberances; covered with mammiform excrescences. *spec.* in *Path.*, *Geol.*, and *Min.* 2. Having a nipple-shaped process or part 1839.

Mamillation (mæmilēᶦ·ʃən). Also **mamm-.** 1856. [f. MAMILLA + -ATION.] 1. The condition of being mamillated. 2. *concr.* in *pl.* Rounded bosses 1863.

Mamma [1] (mămā·). Also **mama.** 1579. [A reduplication of *ma*, an instinctive infantine utterance. The spelling *mama* is now rare. In U.S. commonly stressed *ma·mma*; in educated Eng. use always on the last syllable.] = Mother; used chiefly in the vocative, or with a possess. pronoun (as 'my mamma'); also without article in the manner of a proper name (e.g. 'Mamma is well').

‖**Mamma** [2] (mæ·mă). *Pl.* **-æ.** OE. [L.] The milk-secreting organ of the female in mammalia. Also the corresponding structure in males. Hence **Ma·mmary** *a.* of or belonging to the m.; having the form of a m. **Mammi·ferous** *a.* mammalian; (of a part of the body) bearing the mammæ. **Ma·mmiform** *a.*, also *erron.* **mammæform,** having the form of a m.

Mammal (mæ·măl). 1826. [First used in pl. as an anglicized form of MAMMALIA.] An animal of the class mammalia. Also *attrib.*

‖**Mammalia** (mămē̆ᶦ·liă), *sb. pl.* 1773. [mod. L. (Linn.), neut. pl. of late L. *mammalis* adj., f. *mamma*; see MAMMA [2].] A class of animals characterized by the possession of mammæ in which milk is secreted for the nourishment of their young.

The *Mammalia* are divided into the *placental* and the *implacental* mammalia (see the adjs.), the latter comprising only the marsupials and the monotremes. Except the monotremes, all mammalia are viviparous.

Hence **Mammali·ferous** *a. Geol.* containing mammalian remains.

Mammalian (mămēᶦ·liăn). 1835. [f. prec. + -AN.] A. *adj.* Of or belonging to the mammalia. B. *sb.* One of the mammalia.

Mammalogy (mămæ·lŏdʒi). 1833. [irreg. f. MAMMALIA + -LOGY.] The science of mammals. Hence **Mammalo·gical** *a.* pertaining to m. **Mamma·logist,** one versed in m.

Mammee (mæmī·). 1572. [In Sp. *mamey*, from Haytian.] A large tree (*Mammea americana*, N.O. *Guttiferæ*) of tropical America which bears a large fruit with a yellow pulp of pleasant taste. Also, the fruit of this tree; also called **mammee-apple.**

†**Ma·mmer,** *v.* late ME. [Imitative.] *intr.* To stammer, mutter; also, to vacillate -1842.

Mammet, var. of MAUMET.

Mammifer (mæ·mifəɹ). Now *rare.* 1832. [a. F. *mammifère.*] = MAMMAL.

‖**Mammifera** (mămi·fĕră). *rare.* 1827. [mod.L. neut. pl. of **mammifer* adj., f. L. *mamma* + *-fer* bearing.] = MAMMALIA.

Mammock (mæ·mək), *sb. arch.* and *dial.* 1529. [?] A scrap, shred, broken or torn piece. Also *fig.* Hence **Ma·mmock** *v. trans.* to break, cut, or tear into fragments or shreds.

Mammodi (mæ·mŏdi). 1828. [ad. F. *mamoudi*, f. Urdū (Pers.) *maḥmūdī* a sort of fine muslin.] A kind of muslin or fine linen.

Mammon (mæ·mən). late ME. [a. late L. *ma(m)mona* masc. (Vulg.), a. Gr. (N.T.) μαμωνᾶς (late texts μαμμωνᾶς), a. Aramaic *māmōn, māmōnā* riches, gain.] A term of opprobrium for wealth regarded as an idol or evil influence. Usu. more or less personified.

Ye cannot serue God and M. *Matt.* vi. 24. Hence **Ma·mmonish** *a.* influenced by or devoted to m. **Ma·mmonism,** devotion to the pursuit of riches. **Ma·mmonist, Ma·mmonite,** a worshipper of m. **Ma·mmonitish** *a.* mammon-like. **Ma·mmonize** *v. rare*, to influence through m.; whence **Ma·mmoniza·tion.**

Mammose (mæ·mōᵘs), *a.* 1856. [ad. L. *mammosus*; see MAMMA [2] and -OSE.] Having breast-like protuberances.

Mammoth (mæ·mǫþ), *sb.* (*a.*) 1706. [a. Russian *mammot* (now *mamant*) of unkn. origin.] 1. A large extinct species of elephant (*Elephas primigenius*) formerly native in Europe and northern Asia; its remains are often found in the alluvial deposits in Siberia. Also *fig.* b. *U.S.* Often applied to the fossil mastodon 1816. 2. *adj.* Resembling the mammoth in size; huge 1814.

†**Mammothrept.** 1599. [ad. late L. *mammothreptus*, a. Gr. μαμμόθρεπτος, f. μάμμη grandmother + θρεπτός vbl. adj., f. τρέφειν to bring up.] A spoilt child; a nursling -1651.

You are a meere m. in judgement B. JONS.

Mammy (mæ·mi). 1523. [dim. of MAM.] 1. A child's word for mother. 2. In southern U.S.: A coloured woman having the care of white children 1859.

Mamsell (mæmze·l). *colloq.* [a. F. *mam'selle*, contr. of MADEMOISELLE.] = MADEMOISELLE 3. Thackeray.

†**Mamzer.** 1562. [a. late L. *mamzer*, a Heb. word adopted by the Vulgate in Deut. xxiii. 2.] A bastard -1865.

Man (mæn), *sb. Pl.* **men.** [Com. Teut.: OE. *man(n, mǫn(n* (pl. *mę̄n(n*). Ult. origin uncertain.]

I. 1. A human being; = L. *homo.* OE. and occas. later. Now surviving in general or indef. applications in the sense 'person' (e.g. with *every, any, no*, and in the pl. with *all, any, some*, etc.). 2. In generic sense, without article: The human creature regarded abstractly; hence, the human race or species, mankind. In *Zool.*: The human creature or race viewed as a genus of animals (*Homo*: in the present classification consisting of only one species, *H. sapiens*). OE. 3. In biblical, etc. use, with *inner, inward, outer, outward*: The spiritual and material parts (respectively) of a human person; hence applied *joc.* to parts of the physical frame of man. b. With *old, new*: used to denote the spiritual condition of the unregenerate and the regenerate. OE.

1. He deserueth it as lytell as euer dyd man 1530. The Lord had but one paire of men in Paradise 1597. Measuring other mens actions and consciences SANDERSON. Phr. *To be, become, be made m.*: to have or assume human nature. 2. Man is said to live without food for seven days GOLDSM. Men are weak, but M. is strong LOWELL. 3. To clothe the outer man; to refresh the inner man (*mod.*).

II. 1. An adult male person OE. b. generically (without article). The male human being. Also *predicatively.* 1591. c. with special ref. to adult age. (Sometimes, A male who has attained his majority) ME. d. without express contrast ME. e. In the vocative, usually implying contempt or impatience. late ME. f. Phrases (see below). ¶2. Applied to beings other than human, e.g. God, the Devil, Death -17.. 3. In pregnant sense: An adult male eminently endowed with manly qualities. late ME. †b. Manliness, courage -1605. 4. A person of position, importance, or note 1541. 5. A husband. Now only *Sc.* and *dial.*, exc. in phr. *m. and wife.* ME. 6. A LIEGEMAN or vassal. Now *Hist.* †Also *fig.* OE. 7. A manservant; a valet ME. b. As correl. of *master.* Now commonly applied (chiefly in *pl.*) to workmen as dist. from their employers. late ME. 8. Applied (chiefly in *pl.*) to members of a fighting force; now esp. to the common soldiers as dist. from the officers ME. 9. In universities, etc.: An undergraduate or student 1803.

1. They speake..here the Hebrew tongue, man, woman and child 1632. b. Woman is not undevelopt m., But diverse TENNYSON. c. The Child is father of the M. WORDSW. *M. and boy*: †(*a*) one and all; (*b*) (advb. phr.): from boyhood upwards. †*To write m.*: to be entitled by years to call oneself a m. †(*To grow up*, etc.) *to m.*: to adult age. d. [He] was hand and glove with some of the best men in town THACKERAY. *The m.*: occas. used for 'he', with a tinge of depreciation, sympathy, or the like: so *the good m.*, *the poor m.*, etc. The late earl was not much liked; the present m. is more popular (*mod.*). e. Here, read it, read it, m. DISRAELI. f. *Little m.*: a term (now joc. or affectionate) for a young male child. *A m.* = 'one' or 'any one', but implies a reference to the male sex only. So †*a man's self, a man's own.* In *M. by m.*, *between m. and m.*, *m. for m.*, *per m.*, *as one m.* (app. orig. a Hebraism = with one accord, †altogether), *to a m.* (= without exception), *man* = 'individual (male) person'. *As a m.*: (considered) in regard to his personal character exclusively. So *The m.*: what one is merely 'as a m.' *The* (*very*) *m.* (ellipt. in predicative use): the man most suitable *for* or *to do* something. *The m. for me* (colloq. *for my money*; see MONEY): the man whom I should choose to employ or support. *My, your*, etc. *m.*: the person one needs, or with whom one has to do. *To be one's own m.*: (*a*) to be in full possession of one's senses, faculties, or powers; (*b*) to be at one's own disposal. (*Every, not a*) *m. Jack*: see JACK *sb.*[1] 2. *University, Oxford, Cambridge*, etc. *m.*: one who is or has been a member of a (particular) university, public school, etc. *Best m., handy m., reading m.*, etc., see the adjs. 2. But was the Diuell a proper m., Gossip? B. JONS. 3. He [Cromwell] was a m. MORLEY. Pym, the m. of men BROWNING. Phr. *To play the m.* b. Hauing more m. then wit about me SHAKS. 4. [To] set him upon his legs, and make him a m. for ever SANDERSON. 7. a. Find out..who's master, who's m. SWIFT. *M. Friday*: a servile follower; a factotum. (After Robinson Crusoe's 'man Friday'.) b. The masters had locked out the men..from seventeen factories 1860. 8. The English had lost more than 2,400 officers and men 1880.

III. Transf. uses. 1. One of the pieces in chess, draughts, and backgammon. late ME. 2. With qualification: A ship 1473. 3. Applied to any representation of a man 1636. *M. of straw* (fig.): see STRAW *sb.* 4. In Cumberland, Westmorland, and Lonsdale: A cairn marking a summit or prominent point of a mountain; cf. *Low Man, High M.* as local names for particular cairns 1800.

1. The cheste-bourde and men 1562. 2. They chased a Barbadoes and a Jamaica m. into Limrick 1665.

Phrases and combs. a. Phrases. **M. of Belial,** a worthless or wicked m. (cf. 1 *Sam.* xxv. 25); **m. of blood** (Hebraism), one who is laden with blood-guiltiness; **m. in blue** *slang*, a policeman; **m. of God** (Hebraism), (*a*) a saint, (*b*) an ecclesiastic; **m. of Kent,** one of the inhabitants of Kent east of the river Medway (cf. KENTISH *man*); †**m. of Rome,** the Pope.

b. Obvious combs., as *m.-famine*, etc.; *m.* (='male') *cook, m. nurse*, etc.; *one-man* (show), etc.; *m.-stealer*; *m.-stealing*; *m.-worthy* adj.; *m.-made* ppl. adj.; *m.-fashion* adv.

c. Special combs.: **m.-ape,** an anthropoid ape; **-engine,** a kind of lift for lowering and raising men in a shaft, consisting essentially of a reciprocating vertical rod with platforms at intervals; **-machine** = *man-engine*; **-mountain,** the name given to Gulliver by the Lilliputians; **-power,** (*a*) the power exerted by a man; as a unit, one-eighth of a horse-power; (*b*) the amount of men available for state or other services; **-rope,** a rope on either side of a gangway or ladder, used in ascending and descending a ship's side, etc.

Man (mæn), *v.* [OE. *mannian*, f. *mann* MAN *sb.*] 1. *trans.* (*Mil.* and *Naut.*) To furnish (a fort, ship, etc.) with men. Said also of the men. b. *Naut.* To place men at or on (a particular part of a ship), as at the capstan to heave anchor, or on the yards to salute a distinguished person. Said also of the men; hence *transf.* to exert force upon (a rope, etc.). 1697. †c. To equip and send (a boat, occas. an army) with its complement of men *out, forth,* etc. -1774. **2.** To supply with a man, men, or inhabitants. late ME. †**3.** To escort (esp. a woman) -1688. **4.** To make manly or manlike 1615. **5.** *Falconry.* To accustom (a hawk, etc.) to the presence of men. Hence (*transf.* and *gen.*) to make tame or tractable 1575.

1. M. the Pinnace, and get her by the Ship's Side 1694. b. Manned Ship and cheered Sir John Jervis 1796. 2. To be mand with one bare Page CHAPMAN. The pulpits were manned with seditious preachers SOUTHEY. 4. My Soul's up in Arms, And Mans each part about me DRYDEN.

Manace, obs. f. MENACE *sb.* and *v.*

Manacle (mæ·năk'l), *sb.* [ME. *manicle*, a. OF. *manicle* handcuff, ad. L. *manicula*, dim. of *manus* hand.] A fetter for the hand; usu. *pl.* **b.** Chiefly *pl.*, bonds, restraints 1587.

1. Wee'le put you..in Manacles, Then reason safely with you SHAKS. b. The Manacles Of the all-building-Law SHAKS. Hence **Ma·nacle** *v. trans.* to fetter or confine (the hands); *loosely*, to fetter; to fasten, secure. Also *fig.*

Manage (mæ·nėdʒ), *sb.* Also (in senses 1-3) MANÈGE. 1577. [ad. It. *maneggio* (F. *manège*), vbl. sb. f. *maneggiare*; see MANAGE *v.*] **1.** The training of a horse in its paces. *Obs.* exc. *arch.* (Now usually MANÈGE.) Also *transf.* and *fig.* 1586. **2.** The action and paces of a trained horse; *spec.* a short gallop at full speed. *Obs.* exc. *arch.* 1577. **3.** A riding-school 1655. **4.** The skilful handling of (a weapon) 1611. †**5.** Management; conduct (of affairs); administration, direction, control 1581. †**6.** Treatment -1626.

1. Speake tearmes of m. to thy bounding Steed SHAKS. 2. His horses..are taught their mannage SHAKS. 5. Young men in the conduct and mannage of Actions, embrace more then they can hold BACON. 6. Quick-silver will not endure the Mannage of the Fire BACON.

Manage (mæ·nėdʒ), *v.* 1561. [ad. It. *maneggiare* to handle = F. *manier* :—pop.L. **manidiare*, f. L. *manus* hand.] **1.** *trans.* To train (a horse) in his paces; to put through the exercises of the manège. Now merged in senses 2 and 7. †**b.** *intr.* Of a horse: To perform the exercises of the manège -1719. **2.** *trans.* To handle, wield (a weapon, tool, etc.). Now only, to make (a weapon, instrument, etc.) serve one's purpose (well or ill). 1586. **b.** To handle, work (a ship or boat) 1600. **3.** To conduct (a war, an undertaking, etc.). Now, To carry on successfully or otherwise; to control the course of (affairs) by one's own action. 1579. Also *absol.* **4.** *trans.* To control the affairs of (a household, institution, state, etc.); to take charge of (cattle, etc.) 1609. **5.** To administer (finances, provisions, etc.) 1649. **6.** To deal with carefully; to husband. ? *Obs.* 1649. †**b.** To treat (persons) with indulgence or consideration. Also *absol.* -1796. **7.** To cause (persons, animals, etc.) to submit to one's control 1594. **8.** To bring over to one's wishes by artifice, flattery, etc. 1706. **9.** To operate upon; to treat (land) 1655. **10.** To bring to pass by contrivance; hence, to succeed in accomplishing. Also, with *inf.* as obj.; often ironically, to be so unskilful or unlucky as *to do* something. 1722. **b.** *absol.* To contrive to get along or pull through (under disadvantages). *colloq.* 1899.

2. Put vp thy Sword, Or m. it to part these men with me SHAKS. 3. So you see,..they m. these things better in France LADY MORGAN. *absol.* If I had not managed very cleverly 1791. Her father.. Hadn't a head to m. TENNYSON. 6. I am obliged to m. my health, and I have many things to do BERKELEY. 8. Managing mankind, by studying their tempers and humouring their weaknesses DISRAELI. 10. I managed to lose..£2,500 MACREADY.

Manageable (mæ·nėdʒăb'l), *a.* 1598. [f. prec. + -ABLE.] That can be managed; tractable; workable; capable of being accomplished by contrivance; etc.

A meek and m. child MRS. BROWNING. Hence **Manageabi·lity, Ma·nageableness,** the condition or quality of being m. **Ma·nageably** *adv.*

Management (mæ·nėdʒmĕnt). 1598. [f. MANAGE *v.* + -MENT.] **1.** The action or manner of managing (see the vb.). †In early use sometimes in pl. **b.** *spec.* The working (of land); hence *dial.* manuring; *concr.* manure. †**c.** An instance of managing -1676. **2.** The use of contrivance for effecting some purpose; often in bad sense, implying deceit or trickery 1666. †Also with *a* and *pl.* †**3.** A negotiation -1715. **4.** Power of managing; administrative skill; also, †tact, ingenuity 1715. †**5.** Indulgence or consideration shown towards a person; politic moderation; an instance of this. [= F. *ménagement.*] -1818. **6.** *collect.* A governing body, e.g. a board of directors, a board of governors, etc. 1739. **7.** *attrib.*, as *m. expenses*, etc. 1903.

1. In contracts and m. of State affaires HOLLAND. 2. Talent for intrigue or 'management' BRYCE. 3. He [the Duke of Savoy] had great Managements with several Ecclesiasticks before he turn'd Hermite ADDISON. 5. When I have any thing to object to persons in power,..I use no sort of m. towards them BURKE.

Manager (mæ·nėdʒəɪ). 1588. [f. MANAGE *v.* + -ER[1].] **1.** One who manages (something specified). Now *rare* in general sense. **2.** One skilled in managing affairs, money, etc. 1670. **3.** One who manages a business, an institution, etc. 1705. **4.** One of several members of either house of parliament appointed for the performance of some duty in which both houses are concerned 1667. **5.** *Law.* A person appointed, usu. by a court of chancery, to manage a business for the benefit of creditors or others; usu. *receiver and m.* 1793.

2. She is not what is called a good m. 1806. 4. The conference [between Lords and Commons] is conducted by 'Managers' for both houses 1840. Hence **Ma·nageress,** a woman m., e.g. of a theatre or hotel. **Manage·rial** *a.* of, pertaining to, or characteristic of a m. **Ma·nagership,** the office, or the control, of a m.

†**Ma·nagery.** 1633. [f. MANAGE *sb.* or *v.* + -ERY; but often infl. by F. *ménagerie.*] **1.** Domestic or agricultural administration -1734. **b.** Economy -1705. **2.** The art of managing (weapons, implements) 1654-93. **3.** Managership; an administrative office 1643-1734. **4.** Cunning or adroit management; an instance of this -1734. **5.** = MANAGE *sb.* 1, 3. -1782.

Ma·naging, *ppl. a.* 1715. [-ING[2].] That manages. **1.** Addicted to scheming or to assuming the direction of affairs. **2.** Economical 1754. **3.** Having executive control 1766.

1. That brisk, m., lively, imperious woman THACKERAY. 3. You want a firstrate m. man DISRAELI.

Manakin (mæ·năkin). Also **-ikin.** 1743. [Var. of MANIKIN.] One of the small gaily-coloured birds of the passerine family *Pipridæ*, inhabiting tropical America.

Man-at-arms. Orig. †**man-of-arms.** late ME. [tr. OF. *homme d'armes, homme a armes.*] A soldier; *esp.* a heavy-armed soldier on horseback.

Manatee (mænătī·). Also **manati, manatin.** 1555. [a. Sp. *manatí*, a. Carib *manattouï.*] *Zool.* A large aquatic herbivorous cetacean of the genus *Manatus* (order *Sirenia*), esp. *M. americanus*; it inhabits the shallow waters of rivers and estuaries on the Atlantic shores within the tropics. Also LAMANTIN.

Comb. **m.-grass,** a marine plant of the W. Indies, *Thalassia testudinum.*

†**Mana·tion.** 1656. [ad. L. *manationem*, f. *manare.*] The action of flowing out -1814.

Manav(i)lins (mănæ·v(i)linz), *sb. pl. slang.* Now *rare.* 1865. [?] Odds and ends.

Manbote (mæ·nbōᵘt). *Obs.* exc. *Hist.* [OE. *mannbót*: see MAN *sb.*, BOOT *sb.*[1]] A fine paid to an overlord for the loss of a man.

Manche, maunche (mānʃ). late ME. [a. F. *manche* :—L. *manica*, f. *manus* hand.] **1.** A sleeve. *Obs.* exc. as used by antiquaries. **2.** *Her.* A sleeve used as a charge, esp. the hanging sleeve of the 14th c. 1486.

Manchester (mæ·ntʃėstəɪ). 1552. Name of a city in Lancashire, the chief seat of the cotton manufacture. **1.** Used *attrib.* or as *adj.* in *M. cottons*, etc. **M. wares,** cotton goods manufactured at M.; hence *M. warehouse, warehouseman.* **2.** *M. School*: a name first applied by Disraeli to Cobden and Bright and their followers, who, before the repeal of the Corn Laws, held their meetings at M. and advocated free trade. Also, in *M. policy*, etc., used to designate a policy of laissez-faire and self-interest 1848.

Manchet (mæ·ntʃėt). *Obs.* exc. *dial.* or *Hist.* late ME. [?] †**1.** The finest kind of wheaten bread -1791. **2.** A small loaf or roll of this. Now only *arch.* or *dial.* 1481. **b.** *Her.* 1640. **3.** *attrib.*, as *m. bread*, etc.

Ma·n-child. *Pl.* **men-children.** late ME. A male child.

Manchineel (mæntʃinī·l). 1630. [a. F. *mancenille*, a. Sp. *manzanilla*, dim. of *manzana* apple, altered f. OSp. *mazana* :—L. *matiana* (neut. pl., sc. *poma, mala*) a kind of apple, named from the Roman gens *Matia.*] A W. Indian tree, *Hippomane Mancinella*, having a poisonous and caustic milky sap, and acrid fruit resembling an apple. Also *m. tree.*

Bastard m., a W. Indian tree, *Cameraria latifolia.*

Manchu (mæntʃū·). 1736. [lit. 'pure'.] (One) of the native Mongolian race of Manchuria which formed the ruling class in China from 1644 to 1912.

†**Ma·ncipate,** *ppl. a.* 1502. [ad. L. *mancipatus*; see next.] Made subject (*to*) -1687.

Mancipate (mæ·nsipeⁱt), *v.* 1574. [f. L. *mancipat-, mancipare*, f. *manus* + root of *capere.*] **1.** *Roman Law.* (*trans.*) To hand over by MANCIPATION 1656. †**2.** To make subject, enslave (*to, unto*) -1756. Hence **Ma·ncipatory** *a.* pertaining to or involving mancipation. So **Ma·ncipable** *a.* 1875.

Mancipation (mænsipēⁱ·ʃən). 1577. [ad. L. *mancipationem*; see prec.] **1.** The ceremonial process by which certain kinds of property (called *res mancipi*) were transferred 1656. **2.** *gen.* The action of enslaving; the state of being enslaved.

1. M. .. is performed by recital of certain words of style, in presence of a balance-holder and five witnesses MUIRHEAD.

Manciple (mæ·nsip'l). ME. [a. OF. *manciple, mancipe*, ad. L. *mancipium*, f. *manus* + root of *capere.*] **1.** An officer or servant who buys provisions for a college, an inn of court, a monastery, etc. †**2.** A bondslave, servant. [= L. *mancipium.*] -1587.

Mancus (mæ·ŋkŏs). *Obs.* exc. *Hist.* [OE. *mancus* masc. = OS. *mancus* (glossing *bazanticum, aureus*), etc.] An OE. money of account of the value of thirty pence.

-mancy, a terminal element, repr. OF. *-mancie*, late L. *-mantia*, Gr. *μαντεία* divination; as *chiromancy, necromancy, hydromancy*, etc. The related adjs. end in -MANTIC.

Mandæan (mændī·ăn), *a.* and *sb.* 1875. [f. Mandæan Aramaic *mandayyā* (rendering Gr. *γνωστικοί* Gnostics; f. *mandā* knowledge) + -AN.] The designation of a Gnostic sect still surviving in Mesopotamia, and of the Aramaic dialect of their sacred books.

‖**Mandamus** (mændēⁱ·mŏs). 1535. [L., = 'we command'.] *Law.* A term applied orig. to writs, letters missive, or mandates issued by the sovereign directing the performance of certain acts, but subseq. restricted to the judicial writ issued in the king's name from the Court of King's Bench (now, from the Crown side of the King's Bench Division of the High Court of Justice) and directed to an inferior court, a corporation, an officer, etc., commanding some specified thing to be done.

'Its general object is to enforce the performance of some public duty in respect of which there is no specific legal remedy' (G. H. B. Kenrick).

Mandarin[1] (mæ·ndărin). 1589 (**mandeline**). [a. Pg. *mandarim*, a. Malay *mantrī*, a. Hindī *mantrī* :—Skr. *mantrin* counsellor, f. (ult.) root *man* to think.] **1.** A generic name for all grades of Chinese officials, of which there were nine, each distinguished by a particular kind of button. (The Chinese name is *Kwan.*) †Formerly extended to other Asiatic officials. **b.** A grotesque toy figure in Chinese costume, that goes on nodding after it is shaken 1781. **2.** The language spoken in China by officials and educated people 1727. **3.** Short for *mandarin porcelain* 1873.

1. c. *transf.* A pedantic official, bureaucrat.

Combs., etc.: **m. duck,** a duck of bright and gay plumage, *Aix galericulata*, native to China; **m. jar,** a jar of m. porcelain; **m. porcelain,** Japanese porcelain decorated with figures of mandarins; **m. vase,** a vase of m. porcelain. Hence **Ma·ndarinate,** the office of a m.; mandarins as a body; government by mandarins. **Mandari·nic** *a.* pertaining to a m. **Ma·ndarinism,** the m. system, government by mandarins. **Ma·ndarinship.**

Mandarin [2], **mandarine** (mæ·ndărin, -īn). 1816. [= F. *mandarine*; perh. f. prec., with reference to the colour of the yellow silk robes of mandarins.] **1.** A small flattened deep-coloured orange, with sweet pulp and thin easily-separable rind. Also *m. orange*. Also *attrib.* **2.** A colour (obtained from coal-tar) resembling that of the mandarin orange. Also *m.-orange, -yellow*. 1883. **3.** A liqueur 1882. Hence **Ma·ndarining** *vbl. sb.* the process of giving an orange colour to silk or wool by the action of nitric acid 1839.

Mandatary (mæ·ndătəri). 1611. [ad. L. *mandatarius*, f. *mandatum*; see -ARY [1].] †**1.** One who is appointed to a benefice by a papal mandate –1726. **2.** = MANDATORY *sb.* 1656.

Mandate (mæ·ndĕt), *sb.* 1552. [ad. L. *mandatum*, neut. pa. pple. of *mandare*. Cf. F. *mandat*.] **1.** *gen.* A command, order, injunction. Now *poet.* and *rhet.* 1576. **2.** *spec.* A judicial or legal command from a superior to an inferior 1552. **b.** A papal rescript, esp. with reference to preferment to a benefice 1611. **c.** A command from the sovereign to elect a fellow of a college or to confer a degree (*Hist.*) 1617. †**d.** A pastoral letter –1824. **3. a.** *Rom. Law.* A commission by which one person requested another to act for him gratuitously, undertaking to indemnify him against loss 1756. **b.** *Scots Law.* A contract by which one person employs another to act for him in his affairs 1681. **c.** A contract of gratuitous bailment 1781. **4.** *Politics.* [After F. *mandat*.] The instruction as to policy supposed to be given by the electors to a parliament or a member of parliament. Also *transf.* 1774. **5.** A commission from the League of Nations to a power (*the mandatory*) to administer, etc. a territory 1919. **6.** †*attrib.* = MAUNDY 1546.

2. b. Mandates for deposing sovereigns BURKE.

Mandate (mæ·ndeⁱt), *v.* 1724. [f. L. *mandat-*, ppl. stem of *mandare*.] **1.** To commit (a sermon) to memory *Sc.* **2.** To hand over (a territory) to a mandatory (chiefly *pa. pple.*) 1922.

Mandative (mæ·ndătiv), *a. rare.* 1651. [ad. late L. *mandativus*, f. *mandare*; see prec. and -ATIVE.] Pertaining to command.

‖**Mandator** (mændē·tǫɹ). 1681. [L., f. *mandare* (see MANDATE).] One who gives a mandate, esp. in the legal senses.

Mandatory (mæ·ndătəri). 1576. [ad. late L. *mandatorius*, f. *mandator*; see prec.] **A.** *adj.* Of the nature of, pertaining to, or conveying a command or mandate. **b.** Of actions: Obligatory, esp. in consequence of a command 1818. **c.** Concerning which the League of Nations has issued a mandate 1921. **B.** *sb.* One to whom a mandate is given (esp. in *Law*) 1661; see also MANDATE *sb.* 5.

‖**Manda·tum.** 1547. [L.] = MANDATE.

Mandelic (mænde·lik), *a.* 1844. [f. G. *mandel* almond + -IC.] *Chem.* In *m. acid* (G. *mandelsäure*): an acid formed by the action of hydrochloric acid upon amygdalin.

Manderelle, -il, obs. ff. MANDREL.

Mandible (mæ·ndib'l). Now only *Anat.* and *Zool.* 1548. [ad. late L. *mandibula* (also used), *-ulum*, f. *mandĕre* to masticate.] A jaw or jawbone; *esp.* the lower jaw (in mammals and fishes). **b.** In birds, (usually) either part, upper or lower, of the beak 1686. **c.** In insects, either half of the upper or anterior pair of jaws 1826. So **Mandi·bular, -ary** *adjs.* belonging to or connected with a m. **Mandi·buliform** *a. Entom.* shaped like a m.

Mandibulate (mændi·biŭleⁱt), *a.* (*sb.*) 1826. [ad. mod.L. *mandibulatus*, f. late L. *mandibula*; see -ATE [2].] **1.** Provided with mandibles; applied to a group of insects (the *Mandibulata*) which have the organs of the mouth adapted for mastication. **b.** *sb.* One of these. **2.** Of organs: Adapted for mastication 1835. So **Mandi·bulated** *a.*

Mandibulo- (mændi·biŭlo), irreg. comb. form of late L. *mandibula* MANDIBLE, used with sense 'pertaining to the mandible and ...', as *m.-hyoid*, etc.

Mandil (mæ·ndil). 1662. [Arab. *mindīl*, *mandīl* sash, turban-cloth, handkerchief, ad. L. *mantile* (see MANTLE *sb.*).] A turban.

Mandilion (mændi·liǝn). *Obs.* exc. *Hist.* 1577. [a. F. *mandillon*, ad. It. *mandiglione*, augm. f. *mandiglia*.] A loose coat or cassock, in later times sleeveless, formerly worn as a kind of overcoat.

Mandioca, var. MANIOC.

†**Mandment.** ME. [a. OF. *mandement*:— late L. *mandamentum*, f. *mandare*.] A commandment; that which is commanded. Also, command, rule. –1567.

Mandola (mændō̆u·lă), **mandora** (mændō̆ᵊ·ră). 1758. [a. It. *mandola, mandora*.] A larger variety of the mandolin.

Mandolin, -ine (mæ·ndǝlin). 1707. [ad. F. *mandoline*, ad. It. *mandolino* (also used), dim. of prec.] An instrument of the lute kind having four to six metal strings stretched upon a deeply-rounded body. Hence **Ma·ndolinist,** a performer on the m.

Mandore (mændōᵊ·ɹ). 1823. [ad. F., ad. It. *mandora*.] = MANDOLA.

Mandragora (mændræ·gŏră). OE. [late L., a. Gr. μανδραγόρας.] **1. a.** The plant MANDRAKE. Now only *Hist.* **b.** *Bot.* The genus to which this plant belongs. **c.** As the type of a narcotic (Shaks.). †**2.** *Chinese mandragoras*: ginseng –1741.

1. c. *Oth.* III. iii. 330. I haue..drunke Lethe and M. to forget you CHAPMAN. Hence **Mandra·gorite,** one who is habitually under the influence of m.

Mandrake (mæ·ndreⁱk). [ME. *mandrag(g)e*, short form of MANDRAGORA.] **1.** Any plant of the genus *Mandragora*, having very short stems, thick, fleshy, often forked, roots, and fetid lance-shaped leaves.

The mandrake is poisonous, having emetic and narcotic properties. Its forked root was thought to resemble the human form, and was fabled to shriek when plucked up from the ground.

†**b.** In allusive and fig. uses –1676. **2.** The root of White Bryony 1585. **3.** *U.S.* The May-apple, *Podophyllum peltatum* 1845. **4.** *attrib.* 1563.

1. And shrikes like Mandrakes torne out of the earth SHAKS. **b.** Thou horson M. SHAKS. He stands as if his Legs had taken root; A very M.! DAVENANT. **4. M. apple,** the fruit of the m.

Mandrel, mandril (mæ·ndrĕl, -ĭl). 1516. [?] **1.** A miner's pick. **2.** In a lathe, an arbor or axis to which work is secured while it is being turned. Also, a similar part in a circular saw or cutter. 1665. **3.** A cylindrical rod, core, or axis round which metal or other material is forged, cast, moulded, or shaped 1790. **4.** *attrib.* 1825.

4. *M.-lathe,* a lathe adapted for turning hollow work, which is clasped by a chuck on the end of the mandrel in the head-stock (KNIGHT).

Mandrill (mæ·ndril). Also **-il.** 1744. [app. f. MAN *sb.* + DRILL *sb.*[3]] The largest, most hideous, and most ferocious of the baboons, *Cynocephalus maimon* or *mormon*, of W. Africa.

Manducable (mæ·ndiŭkăb'l), *a. Obs.* or *arch.* 1614. [ad. L. type **manducabilis*; see next and -ABLE.] Capable of being manducated; eatable.

Manducate (mæ·ndiŭkeⁱt), *v.* 1623. [f. ppl. stem of L. *manducare* to chew; see -ATE [3].] *trans.* To chew, eat. So **Manduca·tion,** the action of eating (chiefly *Theol.*, as *carnal, literal, spiritual m.*, etc.); the action of chewing 1551. **Ma·nducatory** *a.* (chiefly *Phys.*), pertaining to or fitted for manducation.

Mane (mēⁱn). [OE. *manu* str. fem. :—O Teut. **manō* (primary sense prob. 'neck').] **1.** The long hair on the back of the neck and the shoulders of various animals, esp. the horse and the lion. Also *fig.* and *transf.* †**2.** The hackles of a game-cock 1614–1727. **3.** *Agric.* A ridge or tuft of grass or stubble, left by the mowers 1523. Hence **Maned** *ppl. a.* having a m.; in *Her.* = CRINED.

-mane (mēⁱn), the ending of some words adopted from Fr., as *Anglomane*, etc. Viewed as a Gallicism; the Eng. *-maniac* is preferred.

Ma·n-ea:ter. 1600. [MAN *sb.*] **1.** A cannibal. **2.** An animal that eats or has a propensity for eating men; e. g. a shark (esp. *Carcharodon rondeleti*) 1837; a tiger, lion, hyena 1862. So **Ma·n-ea:ting** *vbl. sb.* and *ppl. a.*

‖**Manège, manege** (manẹ̄ʒ). 1644. [Fr. form of MANAGE *sb.*] **1.** A riding-school. **2.** The movements proper to a trained horse; the art or practice of training horses; horsemanship 1776.

‖**Maneh** (mā·ne). 1611. [Heb. *mānèʰ*; see MINA [1].] *Heb. Antiq.* A Heb. coin and weight, equal to from sixty to one hundred shekels.

Maneless (mēⁱ·n,lės), *a.* 1828. [f. MANE + -LESS.] Without or destitute of a mane.

Manequin(e, obs. f. MANIKIN.

Manerial (mănīᵊ·riăl), *a.* 1765. [f. med.L. *manerium* MANOR + -AL.] = MANORIAL *a.*

‖**Manes** (mēⁱ·nīz), *sb. pl.* late ME. [L. *manes* pl.] The deified souls of departed ancestors (as beneficent spirits). Also, the shade of a departed person, as an object of reverence, or as demanding to be propitiated by vengeance.

The m. of my son shall smile this day, While I, in blood, my vows of vengeance pay DRYDEN.

Manful (mæ·nfŭl), *a.* late ME. [f. MAN *sb.* + -FUL.] **1.** = MANLY *a.* **2.** †**2.** *occas.* = MANLY *a.* 3. FULLER.

1. A stoute and m. minde 1576. Hence **Ma·nfully** *adv.*, **-ness.**

Mangabey (mæ·ngăbeⁱ). 1774. [Name of a region of Madagascar. The erron. application is due to Buffon.] A monkey of the African genus *Cercocebus*; esp. the Sooty M., *C. fuliginosus.*

Mangan-, repr. MANGANESE (G. *mangan*) in compound names of minerals, as **m.-amphibole** = RHODONITE; etc.

Manganate (mæ·ŋgănĕt). 1839. [f. MANGAN-IC + -ATE [1].] *Chem.* A salt of manganic acid. So †**Mangane·sate** 1819.

Manganese (mæ·ŋgănīz). 1676. [a. F. *manganèse*, a. It. *manganese*, corrupt form of L. *magnesia*; see MAGNESIA 2.] **1.** A black mineral (now recognized as an oxide of a metal; see sense 2) used in glass-making and other processes. Also called **black m.** **2.** *Chem.* The metallic element (symbol Mn) of which 'black manganese' is the oxide 1783. (Also called †**Manganes(i)um.**)

1. The black m. of commerce is usually a mixture of various oxides, but the term is applied esp. to m. dioxide, MnO_2, which is the valuable ingredient in the mixture (N.E.D.).

attrib. and *Comb.*, as **m. bronze,** (*a*) a bronze dye, (*b*) an alloy of copper and zinc with m.; **m. green,** an unstable green dye derived from manganate of barium; **m. steel,** a malleable mixture of iron and m.

Manganesian (mæŋgănī·ziăn), *a.* 1795. [f. prec. + -IAN.] Pertaining to manganese, or characterized by its presence. So †**Mangane·sic** *a. m. acid* = manganic acid 1819; **Mangane·s(e)ous** *acid*, manganous acid.

Manganic (mæŋgæ·nik), *a.* 1836. [f. MANGAN-ESE + -IC.] *Chem.* Applied to compounds containing manganese in its higher valency.

M. acid: an acid (H_2MnO_4) not known exc. in comb. with alkalis, with which it forms *manganates*.

Manganiferous (mæŋgăni·fĕrəs), *a.* 1851. [f. MANGANESE + -(I)FEROUS.] *Min.* Containing or yielding manganese. So **Manganin** (mæ·ŋgănin) [-IN [1]], *Metall.* an alloy of copper, manganese, and nickel, much used in the construction of standard resistance coils 1902. **Manganite** (mæ·ŋganəit), [-ITE [1]], *Min.* a hydrated sesquioxide of manganese, occurring massive and in pseudo-crystals; grey manganese ore 1827; *Chem.* a salt of manganous acid 1865. ‖**Manganium** (mæŋgēⁱ·niǝm) [mod.L.] *Chem.* = MANGANESE 2. 1850.

Manganous (mæ·ŋgănəs), *a.* 1823. [f. MANGAN-ESE + -OUS.] **a.** Of the nature of, or containing, manganese. **b.** *Chem.* Containing manganese in its lower valency.

Mange (mēⁱndʒ). [Late ME. *manjewe*, a. OF. *manjue, mangeue* itch, vbl. sb. f. *manjuer* = *mangier* (mod.F. *manger*) to eat.] A cutaneous disease occurring in many hairy and woolly animals, caused by an arachnidan parasite. Also *loosely*, a dirty, scabby or scurfy condition of the skin. †**b.** *fig.* A restless desire, an itch to do something –1790.

b. If yet thy head possess the M. of Writing WOLCOT.

Mangel (mæ·ŋg'l), **mangold** (mæ·ŋgǭld). 1856. Short for next.

Mangel - wurzel, mangold - wurzel (mæ·ŋg'l-, mæ·ŋgǭld₁wǭ·ɹz'l). 1779. [a. G. *mangold-wurzel* (corruptly *mangelwurzel*), f. *mangold* beet (of unkn. origin) + *wurzel* root.] A variety of beet, with a root larger than that of the garden beet; cultivated as a food for cattle. By some considered as a hybrid between the red and the white beet. Also *attrib.*

Manger (mē̆·ndʒəɹ). ME. [a. F. *mangeoire* :—pop. L. **manducatoria*, f. *manducare* (F. *manger*) to eat.] 1. A box or trough in a stable or cowhouse, from which horses and cattle eat. 2. *Naut.* A small berthing in the bows of a ship, intended to keep the water entering the hawse-holes from flooding the deck 1627.

Mangle (mæ·ŋg'l), *sb.*¹ 1613. [a. Sp. *mangle*; see MANGROVE.] = MANGROVE.

Mangle (mæ·ŋg'l), *sb.*² 1774. [a. Du. *mangel* masc. (= G. *mangel* fem.), app. short for *mangelstok*, f. stem of *mangelen* to mangle. The Du. and G. word is (ult.) f. Gr. μάγγανον (see MANGONEL).] A machine for rolling and pressing linen and cotton clothing, etc. after washing; now consisting of two or more cylinders working one upon another.

Comb.: **m.-wheel,** a wheel which, by an ingenious adjustment of rack and pinion, causes the movable part of a m. to travel backwards and forwards, while the wheel itself rotates in only one direction; applied also to a similar wheel in textile machines; similarly **m. pinion, rack.**

Mangle (mæ·ŋg'l), *v.*¹ late ME. [ad. AF. *mangler*, *mahangler*, app. frequent. of *mahaignier* MAIM *v.*] 1. *trans.* To hack, cut, or lacerate by repeated blows; to reduce thus to a more or less unrecognizable condition. Also *transf.* and *fig.* 2. To cut or hack (a thing) roughly, so as to damage and disfigure 1530. 3. *fig.* Now chiefly: To make (words) unrecognizable by mispronunciation; to spoil (a quotation, text, etc.) by gross blundering or falsification. Formerly often: To mutilate, deprive of essential parts. 1533.

1. A human head was found severed from the body ..and so frightfully mangled that no feature could be recognised MACAULAY. 2. The bench.., Though mangled, hacked, and hewed, not yet destroyed COWPER. 3. Remember how they m. our Brittish names abroad MILT.

Mangle (mæ·ŋg'l), *v.*² 1775. [f. MANGLE *sb.*²] 1. *trans.* To press smooth with a mangle. 2. To beat (lead) flat on a roller 1880.

Mango (mæ·ŋgo^u), *sb.*¹ *Pl.* **mangoes, -gos** (mæ·ŋgo^uz). 1582. [a. Pg. *manga*, a. Malay *maŋgā*, a. Tamil *mān-kāy* (*mān* = mango-tree + *kāy* = fruit).] 1. The fruit of *Mangifera indica* (N.O. *Anacardiaceæ*); it is a fleshy drupe, having in the wild state a turpentine flavour; the best kinds are eaten ripe; the green fruit is used for pickles and conserves. 2. The tree 1678. 3. *Cookery.* A pickle, esp. of melons or cucumbers, resembling that made of green mangoes 1699. 4. Short for *mango-bird*, *m.-fish* 1819.

Comb.: **m.-bird,** (*a*) an oriole (*Oriolus kundoo*), native of India; (*b*) a humming-bird (*Lampornis mango*), native of Jamaica; **-fish,** a golden-coloured fish, *Polynemus paradiseus* or *risua*, inhabiting the tropical seas between India and the Malay archipelago; **m. (tree) trick,** an Indian juggling trick in which a mango-tree appears to spring up and bear fruit within an hour or two.

†**Ma·ngo,** *sb.*² [a. L. *mango*.] A slave-dealer. B. JONS.

Mangold (-wurzel): see MANGEL (-WURZEL).

Mangonel (mæ·ŋgǫnel). *Obs.* exc. *Hist.* ME. [a. OF. *mangonel*, *-elle* f. (mod.F. *mangonneau*), dim. f. late L. *mangona*, *mangonum*, ad. Gr. μάγγανον an engine of war, a pulley, etc.] A military engine for casting stones, etc.

†**Ma·ngonism.** 1656. [a. F. *mangonisme*, f. L. *mangon-*, *mango* broker, etc.; see -ISM.] 1. The craft of setting out saleable things to advantage. BLOUNT. 2. A method of treating plants contrary to nature, in order to produce changes in their growth -1722. So †**Ma·ngonist,** one who furbishes up inferior wares for sale 1605-98. †**Ma:ngoniza·tion,** the action of tricking out for sale 1660-78. †**Ma·ngonize** *v. trans.* to furbish up (inferior wares) for sale 1623; *intr.* to traffic in slaves 1601.

Mangosteen (mæ·ŋgǫstīn). Also **-stan,** etc. 1598. [a. Malay *mangustan*.] 1. The fruit of the E. Indian tree *Garcinia Mangostana* (N.O. *Guttiferæ*). It is about the size of an apple, with a thick reddish-brown rind, and a white juicy pulp of delicious flavour. 2. The tree 1734. 3. **Wild m. (tree),** *Embryopteris glutinifera* 1753.

Mangrove (mæ·ŋgrǭuv). 1613. [Cf. Pg. *mangue*, Sp. *mangle*; the second syll. is due to assoc. with GROVE.] 1. Any tree or shrub of the genus *Rhizophora*, or the allied genus *Bruguiera*; esp. the Common M., *R. Mangle*.

The species are all tropical, growing in the mud on the sea-shore down to low-water-mark; they have large masses of interlacing roots above ground, which intercept mud and weeds, and thus cause the land to encroach on the sea.

2. Applied to plants of similar habit and appearance; *esp.* the White Mangrove (*Avicennia officinalis*) found in Brazil and Australia, and the Black or Olive Mangrove (*A. nitida*) of tropical America and Africa 1683. 3. *attrib.*, as *m. jungle*, *root*, *swamp*, *tree*, etc. 1672.

‖**Mangue** (mæŋg). 1840. [a. F.] The KUSIMANSE (*Crossarchus obscurus*).

Mangy (mē̆·ndʒi), *a.* late ME. [f. MANGE + -Y¹.] 1. Having the mange; of the nature of or caused by the mange. †Also formerly: Scabby. 2. Squalid, shabby 1529. 3. Beggarly, mean, 'lousy'. Common in 17th c. 1538. Hence **Ma·ngily** *adv.* **Ma·nginess.**

Manhad(d)en, var. of MENHADEN.

Man-ha·ndle, *v.* 1457. [f. MAN *sb.* + HANDLE *v.*] †1. *trans.* To handle a tool. 2. *Naut.*, etc. 'To move by force of men, without levers or tackles' (Smyth) 1867. 3. *slang.* To handle roughly; to pull or hustle about 1865.

†**Ma·nhead.** ME. [f. MAN *sb.* + -HEAD.] = MANHOOD, in various senses -1588.

Ma·n-hole. 1793. A hole or opening in a floor, pavement, boiler, sewer, etc., through which a man may pass. Also, a recess in a wall, etc., used as a place of refuge, e. g. to avoid passing trains.

Manhood (mæ·nhud). ME. [See -HOOD.] 1. The state or condition of being human; human nature. 2. The state of being a man, as opp. to childhood or to womanhood ME. 3. The qualities eminently becoming a man; manliness, courage, valour (*arch.*) ME. †4. Humanity, humaneness -1571. 5. Men collectively 1588. 6. *attrib.* 1873.

2. Children, as they grow to m. FROUDE. 3. Peace hath higher tests of m. Than battle ever knew WHITTIER. 5. The whole m. of Greece fought the battell of Salamis HOLLAND. 6. **M. suffrage:** suffrage granted to all male citizens of lawful age not disqualified by crime, insanity, etc.

Ma·n-hu:nter. 1555. A hunter of men; usually a contemptuous term for cannibals, slave-dealers, brigands, etc.

Mania (mē̆·niă). late ME. [a. L., a. Gr. μανία, related to μαίνεσθαι to be mad, f. wk. grade of Indo-Eur. root **men-* (see MIND *sb.*). Cf. F. *manie* (also formerly used in Engl.).] 1. *Nosology.* Mental derangement characterized by excitement, hallucinations, and, in its acute stage, by great violence. 2. Chiefly with *a* or *the*: A vehement passion or desire; also (after F. *manie*), a craze, a rage. Const. *for*, *of*. Also a period of excitement affecting a body of persons. 1689.

2. The m. of land speculation 1807. The tulip m. in Holland 1777 Hence **Manic** (mæ·nik) *a.*

-mania, a terminal element, repr. Gr. μανία MANIA in composition, with the general sense 'a certain kind of madness', as *kleptomania*, *megalomania*; or 'the state of being mad after some object', as *bibliomania*, *Anglomania*, etc. The sbs. in *-mania* have, or may have, correlative sbs. in *-maniac*; the words in -MANE are few, and are viewed as Gallicisms.

†**Ma·niable,** *a.* 1483. [a. OF., f. *manier* to handle, f. L. *manus* hand.] 1. Easy to handle; manageable -1727. 2. That may be handled, palpable -1686.

Maniac (mē̆·niæ̆k). 1604. [ad. late L. *maniacus*, f. (ult.) Gr. μανία MANIA.] A. *adj.* 1. Affected with mania. 2. Of, pertaining to, or characterized by mania; characteristic of a maniac 1727. b. Frantic 1809.

2. b. The performance of a m. hornpipe DICKENS.

B. *sb.* One who is affected with mania 1763. So **Mani·acal** *a.* 1678, **-ly** *adv.*

-maniac: see -MANIA.

Manicate (mæ·nikeᵗt), *a.* 1832. [ad. L. *manicatus* furnished with sleeves.] *Bot.* Covered with hairs interwoven into a mass that can be easily separated from the surface.

Manichæan, Manichean (mænikī·ăn). 1556. [f. L. *Manichæus* MANICHEE + -AN.] *adj.* Of or pertaining to the Manichees or their doctrine; characteristic of a Manichee. *sb.* = MANICHEE. Also *transf.* So **Ma·nichæism, Ma·nicheism,** the doctrine or principles of the Manichees. **Ma·nichæist** = MANICHEE.

Manichee (mænikī·). late ME. [ad. late L. *Manichæus*, late Gr. Μανιχαῖος, from *Manes* or *Manichæus*, the founder of the sect, who lived in Persia in the 3rd century after Christ.] An adherent of a religious system widely accepted from the 3rd to the 5th century, composed of Gnostic Christian, Mazdean, and pagan elements, and representing Satan as co-eternal with God.

Leo said that the Devil reigned in all other heresies, but had rais'd his very throne in that of the Manichees ECHARD.

Manichord (mæ·nikǭɹd). *Obs.* exc. *Hist.* 1668. [a. F. *manicorde*, *manichordion*, corruptly a. med.L. **monochordium*, *monocordum*, a. late Gr. μονοχόρδιον, Gr. μονόχορδον MONOCHORD; perh. assoc. w. L. *manus* hand.] = CLAVICHORD.

†**Ma·nicon.** [a. L. *manicon*, Gr. μανικόν, f. μανία MANIA.] A kind of nightshade, supposed to cause madness *Hudibras* III. i. 324.

Manicure (mæ·nikiuᵊɹ), *sb.* 1880. [a. F., f. L. *manus* hand + *cura* care. Cf. PEDICURE.] 1. One who undertakes professionally the treatment of the hands and finger-nails. 2. The treatment of the hands and finger-nails 1887. Hence **Ma·nicure** *v. trans.* and *intr.* to apply m. treatment (to). **Ma·nicurist** = sense 1.

†**Manie.** late ME. [a. F., ad. L. *mania*.] = MANIA -1623.

Manifest (mæ·nifest), *sb.* 1561. [a. F. *manifeste* vbl. sb., f. *manifester*.] 1. *gen.* A manifestation, indication. Now *rare.* 2. A public declaration; an open statement; a manifesto. *Obs.* exc. as gallicism. 3. The list of a ship's cargo, signed by the master, for the use of officers of customs 1706.

Manifest (mæ·nifest), *a.* late ME. [ad. L. *manifestus*, earlier *manufestus*, ?f. *manus* hand + **festus* struck, f. root found in *offendere*, *defendere*. Thus primarily 'palpable'.] 1. Evident to the eye, mind, or judgement; obvious. †2. Having evident signs *of*; evidently possessed *of* or guilty *of*. [Const. after L.] -1725.

1. That the works of God should be made m. in him *John* ix. 3. 2. Calisto there stood m. of shame DRYDEN. Hence **Ma·nifest-ly** *adv.*, **-ness.**

Manifest (mæ·nifest), *v.* late ME. [ad. F. *manifester*, or L. *manifestare*, f. *manifestus* (see prec.).] 1. *trans.* To make evident to the eye or to the mind; to show plainly. b. Of things: To be evidence of, prove 1508. †2. To clear up (a matter) -1669. 3. a. To display (a quality, condition, feeling, etc.); to reveal the presence of, evince 1567. b. *refl.* Of a thing: To reveal itself as existing or operative 1808. 4. To record in a ship's manifest 1541. 5. *intr.* To make a public expression of opinion 1898. 6. *Spiritualism.* Of a ghost (*refl.* or *intr.*): To reveal its presence, appear 1858. 7. *Hist.* In Spanish law, to protect by a MANIFESTATION (sense 4) 1818.

1. [He] manifested forth his glory *John* ii. 11. b. Thy Life did m., thou lou'dst me not SHAKS. 3. b. No tendency, in general, to dysentery, manifested itself at this time 1808.

Manifestation (mænifestē̆·ʃən). late ME. [ad. late L. *manifestationem*; see prec.] 1. The action of manifesting or the fact of being manifested. b. An instance of this; hence, that by which something is manifested 1785. 2. A public act on the part of a government intended as a display of its power and determination to enforce some demand; also, a collective action (e. g. a procession, public meeting, etc.) undertaken by a political party, etc., in order to call attention to its views 1844. 3. *Spiritualism.* A phenomenon by which the presence of a spirit is supposed to be rendered perceptible 1853. 4. *Hist.* In Spanish law, a process by which an accused person might be protected from the action of judges and removed to a special prison out of their reach. Also, this prison (= Sp. *carcel de los manifestados*). 1769.

1. The matter..requireth more wordes for the m. thereof than I may now affoorde 1570. b. The first m. of thought is speech MAX MÜLLER.

Manifesto (mænife·sto), *sb.* 1644. [a. It. *manifesto.*] †1. A proof, a piece of evidence –1686. 2. A public declaration by a sovereign prince or state, or by an individual or body of individuals whose proceedings are of public importance, making known past actions and explaining the motives for actions announced as forthcoming.

2. The manifestoes of modern agrarianism 1839. Hence **Manife·sto** *v. rare*, to issue a m. or manifestoes.

Manifold (mæ·nifōuld), *a.*, *adv.*, and *sb.*[1] Now *literary.* [Com. Teut.: OE. *manigfeald*; see MANY *a.* and -FOLD.] A. *adj.* 1. Having various forms, features, relations, applications, etc.; †complex. b. Qualifying a personal designation: That is such in many ways or in many relations ME. 2. Qualifying pl. sb.: Numerous and varied. †Formerly simply: Numerous. OE.

1. They..m. in sin, deserv'd to fall MILT. b. The m. Linguist, and the army-potent souldier SHAKS. 2. Overwhelmed by m. vexations 1849.

†B. *adv.* In many ways, modes, degrees, etc. –1593. †b. In the proportion of many to one. *Luke* xviii. 30.

C. *absol.* and *sb.* †1. Phr. *By* (rarely *on*) *m.*: many times over –1596. 2. That which is manifold. a. *spec.* In the Kantian philosophy, the sum of the particulars furnished by sense before they have been unified by the understanding 1855. b. *gen.* 1856. 3. *Math.* A general conception of which time and space are particular varieties 1890. 4. A copy made by a manifold writer 1884. 5. *Mech.* A pipe or chamber with several outlets or valves forming connexions with other pipes, etc. 1891.

2. b. The picturesque m. of life 1902.

D. *Comb.*: **m.-paper**, carbonized paper used in making several copies of a writing at one time; **m. writer**, an apparatus fitted with carbonized paper for doing this; so **m. writing.**

Ma·nifold, *sb.*[2] *dial.* Also **manifolds.** ME. [f. MANY *a.* + FOLD *sb.*[2]] The intestines or bowels; *spec.* the manyplies or third stomach of a ruminant.

Manifold (mæ·nifōuld), *v.* [OE. *manigfealdian*, f. the adj.; see MANIFOLD *a.* Recently re-coined.] *trans.* To make manifold, multiply. *rare* exc. as in b. b. *spec.* To make copies (of), as by a manifold writer 1865.

b. The Home Secretary received such precise and timely information that he was enabled to have it manifolded 1881.

Ma·nifoldly, *adv.* Now only *literary.* OE. [See MANIFOLD *a.* and -LY[2].] In manifold ways; †*occas.* in the proportion of many to one.

Manifoldness (mæ·nifōuldnės). OE. [See MANIFOLD *a.* and -NESS.] 1. The quality or condition of being manifold; varied character; multiplicity. 2. *Math.* = MANIFOLD C. 3. [A transl. of G. *mannigfaltigkeit.*] 1873.

Maniform (mæ·nifǭɹm), *a.* 1826. [ad. mod.L. *maniformis*, f. L. *manus*; see -FORM.] Having the form of a hand; *Entom.* chelate.

Manihot, var. of MANIOC.

Manikin (mæ·nikin). 1570. [a. Du. *manneken*, dim. of *man* MAN *sb.*; see -KIN.] 1. A little man (often *contemptuous*); a dwarf, pygmy. Also *fig.* 1601. 2. a. An artist's lay figure 1570. b. A model of the human body used for exhibiting the anatomical structure or for demonstrating surgical operations 1831. 3. *attrib.* or *adj.* Dwarf, pygmy, undersized; puny 1840.

2. Thus, of a Manneken (as the Dutch painters terme it) in the same Symmetrie, may a Giant be made 1570. 3. The m. grasp of the English ministry DISRAELI.

Manikin, var. of MANAKIN.

Manilio, var. of next, and of MANILLE.

Manilla[1] (mǎni·lǎ). 1556. [Sp.; ? a dim. of L. *manus* hand; or ? f. L. *monilia*, pl. of *monile* collar, necklace.] A ring of metal worn on the arm or wrist by some African tribes and used as a medium of exchange.

Manillas..are regularly manufactured at Birmingham for the African traders 1851.

Manilla[2], **Manila** (mani·lǎ). 1697. [Native name; the form *Manila* is correct, but rare.] 1. Name of the capital of the Philippine Islands, used attrib. in *M. copal, grass, tobacco*, etc., products of those islands. 2. (In full *M. hemp.*) A fibrous material, obtained from the leaves of *Musa textilis* (see ABACA), for ropes, matting, textile fabrics, paper, etc. Hence *M. cable, hat, paper, rope*, etc. 1814. 3. (In full *M. cheroot.*) A kind of cheroot manufactured in Manila 1839.

Manille (mǎni·l). 1674. [Corruptly a. Sp. *malilla*, dim. of *mala* (prob. fem. of *malo* bad).] *Cards.* In quadrille and ombre, the second best trump.

Man in the moon. ME. 1. The fancied semblance of a man (or a man's face) in the disk of the moon. 2. Referred to as the type of an imaginary person (e.g. the person who supplies money for illicit expenditure at elections) 1596.

1. Which he knows no more then the Man in the Moon MARVELL.

Manioc (mæ·niǫk). Also **mandioc**, etc. 1568. [repr. Tupi *mandioca*, Guarani *mandio*, which denotes the root of the plant. The bot. L. form *manihot* is app. a Fr. spelling with silent *t.*] = CASSAVA 1, 2.

Maniple (mæ·nip'l). ME. [a. OF. *maniple* (mod.F. *manipule*), ad. L. *manipulus* handful, f. *manus* + **pl-*, wk. form of root **plē-* to fill (as in *plēnus*).] †1. A handful (*lit.* and *fig.*) 1632–1829. 2. *Rom. Antiq.* A subdivision of the Roman legion, of which a cohort contained three, numbering 120 men each among the *hastati* and *principes*, and 60 each among the *triarii* 1533. †b. In mod. warfare, a small band of soldiers of more or less definite number –1644. 3. *Eccl.* In the Western Church, one of the Eucharistic vestments, consisting now of a strip of stuff two to four feet in length worn hanging from the left arm; said to have been orig. a napkin ME.

Manipular (mǎni·piŭlǎɹ), *a.* (*sb.*) 1623. [ad. L. *manipularis*, f. *manipulus.*] 1. Pertaining to the MANIPLE (sense 2); characterized by formation in maniples. 2. = MANIPULATIVE. [Not a justifiable sense.] 1831. 3. *sb.* A soldier of a maniple 1862.

2. An unequivocal m. token of resentment 1831.

Manipulate (mǎni·piŭlēit), *v.* 1827. [App. a back-formation from MANIPULATION.] 1. *trans.* To handle, esp. with dexterity; to treat by manual (and, hence, any mechanical) means 1831. b. *absol.* or *intr.* in *Chem.* 1827. 2. To handle or treat (questions, artistic matter, resources, etc.) with skill 1856. 3. To manage by dexterous (esp. unfair) contrivance or influence 1864.

1. To m. guillotines CARLYLE. 2. The art of manipulating money FROUDE. 3. It will be possible for firms to m. their books 1893. Hence **Mani·pulative, Mani·pulatory** *adjs.* pertaining to or involving manipulation. **Mani·pulator,** one who or that which manipulates or facilitates manipulation.

Manipulation (mǎnipiŭlē·ʃən). 1727. [a. F., ad. mod.L. type **manipulationem*, f. **manipulare*, f. L. *manipulus* MANIPLE.] †1. The method of digging silver ore. (Only in Dicts.) 2. *Chem.* The method of handling apparatus, etc. in experiments. In *Pharmacy*, 'the preparation of drugs' (Webster 1828). 1796. 3. *gen.* The handling of objects for a particular purpose; in *Surgery*, the manual examination of a part of the body. Also, manual action. 1826. 4. Dexterous (esp. unfair) management of persons or things 1828.

2. The various sources of inaccuracy to which chemical manipulations are liable 1805. 3. The m. of a musket GREENER. 4. The third estate..was only too susceptible of royal m. STUBBS.

‖**Manis** (mē·nis). 1770. [mod.L. (Linn.), assumed sing. of MANES.] *Zool.* The typical genus of the family *Manidæ* (scaly ant-eaters); any one of these, a pangolin.

‖**Manitou** (mæ·nitu). Also **manito, manitu** (-ido), **moneto.** 1671. [Algonquin *manito, manitu*; said to be from a vb. meaning 'to surpass'.] Among some American Indians, a spirit (of good or of evil) which is an object of religious awe; also, anything having supernatural power, as a fetish.

Manitrunk (mæ·nitrɒŋk). 1826. [f. L. *manus* taken as 'fore-leg' + *truncus* trunk.] *Entom.* The anterior segment of the thorax.

Ma·n-keen, *a.* Now *dial.* 1568. [f. MAN *sb.* + KEEN *a.*] Of animals (*rarely* of persons): Inclined to attack men; fierce, savage.

Mankin. 1820. [f. MAN *sb.* + -KIN.] A manikin.

Mankind, *sb.* and *a.*[1] ME. [f. MAN *sb.* + KIND *sb.*] A. *sb.* I. (Now mænkəi·nd.) 1. The human species. Now only *collect.* and with pl. concord. †2. Human nature –1567. †b. Humanity. B. JONS.

1. M. never suffer any work to be lost which tends to make them more wise or happy GOLDSM.

II. (Now mæ·nkəind.) The male sex; persons of the male sex 1526.

The..silliness of m. and womankind at large 1874.

B. *adj.* †1. Human. R. SCOT. †2. Male –1638. †3. Of women: Masculine, viragolike –1635.

†**Ma·nkind,** *a.*[2] 1519. [?] = MAN-KEEN –1672.

Manks, obs. f. MANX.

Manless (mæ·nlės), *a.* OE. [f. MAN *sb.* + -LESS.] 1. Having no men. †2. Unmanly –1653; inhuman 1611. Hence †**Ma·nless·ly** *adv.*, **-ness.**

Ma·nlihood. *rare.* 1641. [f. MANLY *a.* + -HOOD.] Manliness.

Manlike (mæ·nləik), *a.* (*adv.*) 1450. [f. MAN *sb.* + LIKE *a.*] 1. Having the qualities proper to a man. Of women: Having masculine qualities; mannish. b. Befitting a man 1561. 2. Resembling a man 1590. 3. *adv.* = MANFULLY 1560.

1. That m. nation 1579. The m. Amazons POPE. b. Glaring Chloe's m. Taste and Mien SHENSTONE. 2. The M. apes HUXLEY. 3. M. let him turn and face it [the danger] EMERSON. Hence **Ma·nlike·ly** *adv.*, **-ness.**

Manling (mæ·nliŋ). 1575. [-LING[1].] A little man; sometimes *depreciatory.*

Manly (mæ·nli), *a.* ME. [f. MAN *sb.* + LY[1].] †1. Belonging to human beings; human –1625. 2. Possessing the virtues proper to a man; chiefly, courageous, independent, frank, upright ME. b. Of a woman: Possessing qualities characteristic of a man 1511. c. *transf.* and *fig.* 1697. 3. Befitting or belonging to a man ME. †4. Grown up; adult, mature –1691.

2. Be stronge now and m. ye Philistynes..Be m. and fighte COVERDALE 1 *Sam.* iv. 9. 3. I saw the wound,..here on his m. brest SHAKS. M. sports 1851. Hence **Ma·nlily** *adv.* **Ma·nliness.**

Manly (mæ·nli), *adv.* [OE. *mannlīce*; see MAN *sb.* and -LY[2].] †1. In a manly manner; manfully; courageously, with valour or energy. †2. Like a human being; humanely. b. Like fallen man; unregenerately. –1547. †3. Excellently, 'bravely'. *Macb.* IV. iii. 235.

1. Our Souldiers..stood m. to it LITHGOW.

Ma·n-mi·dwife. Now *rare.* Pl. **men-midwives.** 1625. An accoucheur.

Ma·n-mi·lliner. *Pl.* **men-, man-milliners.** 1792. A man who makes or vends millinery; in contemptuous use, a man who occupies himself excessively with embellishments of dress or ornaments. So **Ma·n-mi·llinery**, a contemptuous term for clothing or apparel (e.g. uniforms, vestments) to which men devote too much attention.

Manna (mæ·nǎ). OE. [a. late L. *manna* neut. indecl., a. Hellenistic Gr. μάννα neut. indecl., ad. Heb. *mān*, perh. repr. Arab. *mann*, the exudation of *Tamarix gallica*. In Exod. xvi. 15 the word is represented as arising from the question (in Aramaic) *man hū?* 'what is it?', which admits of being interpreted 'It is *mān*'.]

I. Biblical, etc. uses. 1. The substance miraculously supplied to the Israelites during their progress through the Wilderness. (See *Exod.* xvi.) Also *transf.* and *fig.* 2. Spiritual nourishment; food divinely supplied, *esp.* the Holy Communion. late ME.

1. *fig.* His Tongue Dropt M., and could make the worse appear The better reason MILT.

II. In *Pharmacy*, etc. 1. A sweet pale yellow or whitish concrete juice obtained from incisions in the bark of the Manna ash, *Fraxinus Ornus*, chiefly in Calabria and Sicily; used as a gentle laxative. Also, any similar exudation. 1533. †2. In early *Chem.*: A white powder –1706. 3. = *manna seeds* 1785. 4. A species of grass, *Setaria* (*Panicum*) *italica*, better known as Italian or Hungarian millet 1897. †5. A grain (of frankincense); frankincense in grains. [Strictly another wd.] –1753.

1. **Australian m.**, a secretion of certain species of Eucalyptus, esp. *E. viminalis*. **Briançon m.**, a substance secreted by the common larch. **Hebrew, Jews', Mount Sinai, Persian m.**, the product of *Alhaga maurorum* or of *Tamarix gallica*, var. *mannifera*.

attrib. and *Comb.*, as **m. ash (tree)**, the tree *Fraxinus Ornus*; **m.-grass**, †(*a*) = DEW-GRASS; (*b*) the aquatic grass *Glyceria fluitans*; **m. seeds**, the seeds of manna-grass, *Glyceria fluitans*; **m. sugar** = MANNITE; **m. tree** = *manna ash.*

Manna-croup (mæ·năkrū·p). 1843. [ad. Russ. *mánnaya krupá* lit. groats of manna.] a. A coarse granular meal consisting of the large hard grains of wheat-flour not ground into fine flour by the mill-stones; used for making puddings, soups, etc. b. A similar meal made from the seeds of the manna-grass.

Mannequin (mæ·nĕkwin, -kin). 1902. [F.] A dressmaker's live model for exhibiting new fashions.

Mannequin, var. of MANIKIN.

Manner (mæ·nəɹ), *sb.*[1] ME. [a. AF. *manere* (OF. *maniere*, mod.F. *manière*), repr. pop.L. **man*(*u*)*aria*, app. fem. of L. *manuarius* used subst., f. *manus* hand; thus primarily = 'mode of handling'. Used as tr. L. *modus* and *mos*, and assim. in meaning to both words.] 1. The way in which something is done or takes place; mode of action or procedure. 2. Customary mode of acting or behaviour; habitual practice; usage, custom, fashion. Now only *literary* or *arch.* ME. 3. *collect. pl.* †a. A person's habitual behaviour or conduct; moral character, morals –1794. †b. Conduct in its moral aspect; also, morality as a subject of study; the moral code embodied in general custom or sentiment –1776. c. The modes of life, rules of behaviour, conditions of society, prevailing in a people ME. d. Good customs or way of living 1579. †e. *Literary criticism.* Character, distinctive varieties of disposition and temperament, as portrayed in epic or dramatic poetry; the portraiture of character, as an element of poetic art. (After Aristotle's use of ἤθη.) –1780. †f. Habits (of animals). Cf. F. *mœurs*. –1831. 4. Outward bearing. With reference to a speaker: Characteristic style of attitude, gesture, and utterance. ME. b. A distinguished or fashionable air 1694. 5. *pl.* (†formerly also *sing.*) External behaviour in social intercourse. late ME. 6. Polite behaviour or deportment; habits indicating good breeding. Usu. in *pl.* late ME. b. Forms of politeness or respect. *Obs.* exc. *arch.* or *dial.* in *To do* or *make one's manners*. 1596. 7. a. Method or style of execution in art or literature 1662. b. *spec.* The method or style characteristic of a particular artist, etc.; often = mannerism 1706. 8. Species, kind, sort. Now only *arch.* in *What m.* (*of*) . . . ? ME. b. *sing.* with pl. construction, qualified by *all*, *many*, *these*, or a numeral. Now only in *all m. of* = all sorts of. ME. †9. [= L. *modus*.] Measure, moderation. *In m.*: in due measure. –1502.

1. God spake at sondrie tymes & in diuers maners in the olde tyme to our fathers by the Prophetes N.T. (Geneva) *Heb.* i. 1. Phr. *In like m.* *M. of speaking* [cf. F. *manière de parler*]: form of expression. *In a m. of speaking*: so to speak. *Adverb of m.* (Gram.): one which answers, or asks, the question *how?* †*In* (*the*) *m. of*: after the fashion of, in the guise of. *In a m.* (formerly †*in m.*): in some way, so to speak, as it were. 2. Here Ctesippus, as his m. was, burst into a roar of laughter JOWETT. Phr. *To the m. born*: in *Haml.* I. iv. 15, destined by birth to be subject to the custom; later often: Naturally fitted for some position or employment. 3. a. Euell speakinges corruppe good maners COVERDALE 1 *Cor.* xv. 33. b. The rule of faith and manners TILLOTSON. c. To study the manners of the age D'ISRAELI. d. Oh! raise us up, return to us again; And give us manners, virtue, freedom, power WORDSW. 4. Something in the boy's m. attracted the banker's interest FROUDE. 5. Hugh..was in manners and bearing an Englishman GREEN. 6. We could not, in manners, refuse him 1760. 7. a. M. is all in all, whatever is writ, The substitute for genius, sense, and wit COWPER. b. A picture of Raphael in his first m. H. WALPOLE. 8. What m. of Fellow was hee that robb'd you? SHAKS. b. These externall m. of Laments SHAKS. Phr. *No* (or *any*) *m. of* . . : periphrastic for 'no, any (person or thing) whatever'. (†*Of* formerly omitted.) *By no* (or *any*) *m. of means*: see MEANS.

Comb. **manners-bit** *dial.*, a portion of a dish left by the guests that the host may not think he has provided too little.

Manner, *sb.*[2] (*taken with the m.*): see MAINOUR.

Mannered (mæ·nəɹd), *a.* late ME. [f. MANNER *sb.*[1] + -ED[2].] 1. Having manners of a specified kind (as *evil-*, *gentle-*, *rough-m.*, etc.). †b. Of a literary work, etc.: Exhibiting manners or character. (Cf. Horace, *A.P.* 319 *morataque recte fabula*.) –1789. 2. Marked by manner or mannerism, esp. in art or literature 1801.

1. Giue her Princely training, that she may be manere'd as she is borne SHAKS. 2. That Spohr was too doctrinaire and m. [etc.] 1884.

Mannerism (mæ·nəriz'm). 1803. [f. MANNER *sb.*[1] + -ISM.] Excessive or affected addiction to a distinctive manner, esp. in art and literature. b. An instance of this; a trick of manner 1819.

Mr. Stewart's style..has character without m., or eccentricity 1803. So **Ma·nnerist** [orig. after F. *manièriste*], one who is addicted to m. 1695. **Manneri·stic, -al** *a.* marked by m. 1830.

Ma·nnerless, *a.* 1460. [-LESS.] Without manners.

Mannerly (mæ·nəɹli), *a.* ME. [f. MANNER *sb.*[1] + -LY[1].] †1. Seemly, respectable –1697. †2. Moral, well-conducted –1549. 3. Well-mannered; polite 1529.

3. Criticism must be truthful, but it may also be m. 1887. Hence **Ma·nnerliness**, m. quality.

Ma·nnerly, *adv.* ME. [f. MANNER *sb.*[1] + -LY[2].] †1. In a seemly manner, properly –1647. †2. Politely, courteously 1519.

2. Eate the thinge that is set before the, manerly COVERDALE *Ecclus.* xxxi. 16.

Mannide (mæ·nəid). 1862. [f. MANNA + -IDE.] *Chem.* A syrupy substance obtained by heating mannite with butyric acid.

Mannish (mæ·niʃ), *a.* [OE. *męnnisc* :— OTeut. **mannisko-*, f. **mann-* MAN *sb.* + *-isko-* -ISH[1]. In many uses re-coined f. MAN *sb.* + -ISH[1].] †1. Of or belonging to mankind; human –1674. 2. Of a woman, etc.: Masculine. Chiefly *contemptuous.* ME. 3. Pertaining to or characteristic of a grown man (often opp. to *childish*); aping manhood 1530. 4. Characteristic of a man as dist. from a woman 1748. †5. quasi-*adv.* Like a man. CHAUCER.

2. A woman impudent and m. growne, Is not more loth'd, then an effeminate man SHAKS. 3. Why must every thing smack of man and m.? Is the world all grown up? LAMB. 4. Oh! what a m. room 1884. Hence **Ma·nnish-ly** *adv.*, **-ness.**

Mannite (mæ·nəit). 1830. [f. MANNA + -ITE[1].] *Chem.* A substance, $C_6H_{14}O_6$, obtained chiefly from manna; = manna sugar. Hence **Manni·tic** *a.* derived from m.; as *mannitic acid*, $C_6H_{12}O_7$.

Manœuvre (mănū·vəɹ), *sb.* Also *U.S.* **manœuver, -euver.** 1479. [a. F. *manœuvre* :—late L. *manopera*, f. *manoperare*; see MANŒUVRE *v.*] †1. Hand-labour (*rare*). 2. *Mil.* and *Naval.* The planned movement or evolution of troops or vessels of war; a device in navigation; exercise or a movement in military or naval tactics 1758. b. Skilful management *of* 1834. 3. A deceptive or elusive movement made by a person, animal, etc. 1774. 4. *transf.* and *fig.* An artful plan; an adroit move; also, management of affairs by scheming 1774. †5. A method of working –1789.

4. These Acts of Parliament and ministerial manœuvres will injure me 1774. 5. I do not understand the m. of sugar H. WALPOLE.

Manœuvre (mănū·vəɹ), *v.* Forms: see prec. sb. 1777. [ad. F. *manœuvrer* :—late L. *manoperare* for L. *manu operari* to work with the hand.] 1. *intr. Mil.* and *Naval.* To perform manœuvres; to make changes of position in the disposition of troops, vessels, etc. Also *to m. it.* b. *transf.* and *fig.*, esp.: To manage by artifice, to scheme 1809. c. To drive (a person) *into* or *out of* by manœuvring 1817. 2. *trans. Mil.* and *Naval.* To cause (troops or vessels) to perform manœuvres; to handle (a boat) 1777. b. *transf.* and *fig.* To manipulate adroitly. Also *occas.* to effect by stratagem. 1815.

1. b. I remember her manœuvring to gain a husband, and then manœuvring to manage him MAR. EDGEWORTH. c. When she had manœuvred him into a fever of passionate love, she often felt and always assumed indifference PEACOCK. Hence **Manœu·vrer.**

Man of the world. ME. †a. A secular person. b. A worldly or irreligious person (after Ps. xvii. 14). c. A man versed in the ways of the world and prepared to accept its conventions.

c. A true, fashionable, unprincipled man of the world 1778.

Man-of-war (mæ:nəvwǭ·ɹ). *Pl.* **men-of-war.** late ME. [In sense 1 app. after F. *homme de guerre*; for sense 2 cf. MAN *sb.* III. 2.] 1. A fighting man; a soldier. *Obs.* exc. *arch.* or *joc.* 2. A vessel equipped for warfare; an armed ship belonging to the recognized navy of a country. Also *attrib.* 1484. †3. (In full *man-of-war bird* or *hawk.*) The frigate-bird, *Fregata aquila.* Also applied to the albatross and occas. to species of skua (Newton). –1885.

1. The Lord is a man of warre *Exod.* xv. 3. 2. *Man-of-war's man*: a sailor serving on a man-of-war. Phr. *Portuguese man-of-war*: A marine hydrozoan of the genus *Physalia*; so called from its floating on the sea with a sail-like crest displayed.

Manometer (mănǫ·mĭtəɹ). 1730. [ad. F. *manomètre*, f. Gr. μανός thin, rare + μέτρον measure.] An instrument for ascertaining the elastic force of gases or vapours. Hence **Manome·tric** (1873), **Manome·trical** (1777) *a.*

Manometric flame, a flame arranged to pulsate under the influence of sound-waves, used in an apparatus for analysing sounds.

Manor (mæ·nəɹ). ME. [a. OF. *manoir* dwelling, subst. use of *manoir* inf., to dwell :— L. *manere.*] †1. A mansion, habitation; the principal house of an estate –1610. †Also *fig.* †2. The mansion of a lord with the land belonging to it; hence, a landed possession –1600. 3. A unit of English territorial organization, orig. of the nature of a feudal lordship. It now consists of the lord's demesne (if any) and of lands from the holders of which he has the right to exact certain fees and fines, and within which he has certain privileges. 1538. b. Applied to certain districts in the U.S. which were manors in colonial times 1639. 4. *attrib.*, as *m.-court*, etc. 1667.

3. By an ancient custom of this m. [Mansfield], the heirs were declared of age as soon as born 1797. *Lord of the m.*, the person or corporation having the seignorial rights of a m.

Hence **Mano·rial** *a.* of or pertaining to a m. or manors; incidental to a m. 1785.

Manor-house (mæ·nəɹ,haus). 1575. [f. MANOR + HOUSE *sb.*[1]] The mansion of the lord of a manor. So **Ma·nor-place** 1426.

‖**Manqué** (mañke). 1841. [F., pa. pple. of *manquer* to fall short (of).] That might have been but is not.

Manqueller (mæ·nkweləɹ). *Obs.* exc. *arch.* ME. [f. MAN *sb.* + QUELLER.] A murderer.

†**Ma·nred.** [OE. *mannrǽden*, f. *mann* MAN *sb.* + *-rǽden* -RED.] 1. Homage –1679. 2. Vassals collectively; the men whom a lord can call upon in time of war; a supply of men for warfare –1630. 3. The 'conduct' (of an army) –1581. So **Manrent.** *Sc.* Now *Hist.*

Mansard (mæ·nsăɹd). 1734. [a. F. *mansarde* (*toit en mansarde*), f. name of François *Mansard*, French architect, 1598–1666.] *Arch.* A form of curb-roof, in which each face of the roof has two slopes, the lower one steeper than the other. Usu. *m. roof.*

Manse (mæns). 1490. [ad. med.L. *mansus*, *mansum*, *mansa* dwelling, etc., f. L. *mans-*, *manere* to dwell, remain.] †1. A mansion-house or 'capital messuage' –1781. 2. A measure of land regarded as sufficient for the support of a family. *Obs.* exc. *Hist.* 1597. 3.

An ecclesiastical residence; now *esp.* the house of the minister of a parish in Scotland 1534.
2. A monastery founded at Ripon and endowed with xxx manses of land MILMAN. 3. The castle of St. Andrews..had been the Bishop of St. Andrews his manse 1683.

Ma·n-se·rvant. *Pl.* **men-servants.** 1551. A male servant.

Mansion (mæ·nʃən), *sb.* ME. [a. OF. *mansion*, ad. L. *mansionem*, f. *manere* to dwell.] †1. The action of remaining, dwelling, or staying in a place. Also, continuance in a position or state. –1722. 2. A place of abode, an abiding-place. Now *arch.* ME. Also *transf.* and *fig.* †b. Chiefly *pl.* A separate dwelling-place or apartment in a large house or enclosure –1697. 3. †a. *gen.* A house, tent, etc. –1781. b. In early use: The chief residence of a lord; a manor-house. Hence, later, a large and stately residence. 1512. c. *fig.* (e. g. of the body as enclosing the soul) 1526. d. Used in *pl.* of large buildings divided into flats 1901. †4. A halting-place in a journey; a stage –1737. 5. *Astrol.* a. = HOUSE *sb.*[1] 8. b. Each of the twenty-eight divisions of the ecliptic, which are occupied by the moon on successive days. ME. †6. Used as tr. med.L. *mansa, mansus* a hide of land; see MANSE 2. –1809. 7. *attrib.* †*m.-place* = senses 3 b, c, 4. 1473.
1. Phr. *To have, keep, make, take* (one's) *m.* = to abide, dwell. These poets near our Princes sleep, And in one grave their m. keep DENHAM. 2. Where the bleak Swiss their stormy m. tread GOLDSM. *fig.* When thy mind Shall be a m. for all lovely forms WORDSW. b. In my fathers housse are many mansions TINDALE *John* xiv. 2. Hell it self will pass away, And leave her dolorous mansions to the peering day MILT. 3. b. The lordly M. of its pride Is stripped WORDSW.
Hence †**Ma·nsion** *v. rare*, to reside 1638–1711.

Ma·nsion-house. 1533. †a. A house in which a person resides –1755. b. The house of the lord of a manor, the chief residence of a landed proprietor; hence (now only U.S.) a great house 1641. c. An official residence. Now *spec.* the official residence of the Lord Mayor of London. 1546.
a. He took his present Lodging in St. John Street, at the Mansion-House of a Taylor's Widow STEELE.

Mansionry (mæ·nʃənri). *rare.* 1605. [f. MANSION *sb.* + -RY.] ? Mansions collectively. In *Macb.* I. vi. 5 perh. mispr. for *masonry*.

Manslaughter (mæ·nslǭtəɹ). ME. [f. MAN *sb.* + SLAUGHTER. The earlier word was *manslaught* (OE. *mannslæht*).] 1. †a. Homicide; chiefly criminal homicide, *esp.* murder –1611. b. The 'slaughtering' of human beings 1450. 2. *Law.* Criminal homicide without malice aforethought 1447.
2. In this there are also degrees of guilt, which divide the offence into m., and murder BLACKSTONE.

Manslayer (mæ·nslēⁱ,əɹ). ME. One who kills a man; a homicide; *occas.* one who commits manslaughter. So **Ma·n-slaying** *vbl. sb.*

Mansuete (mænswī·t, mæ·nswīt), *a. Obs.* or *arch.* late ME. [ad. L. *mansuetus*, *mansuescere* to tame, f. *manus* hand + *suescere* to accustom, become accustomed.] Gentle, mild; tame, not wild or fierce.

Mansuetude (mæ·nswĭtiud). *arch.* late ME. [ad. L. *mansuetudo*; see prec. and -TUDE.] Gentleness, meekness.

Manswear (mæ·nsweəɹ), *v. Obs.* exc. *arch.* and *dial.* Pa. t. **-swore**, pa. pple. **-sworn.** [OE. *mánswęrian*, f. *mán* wickedness + *swęrian* to SWEAR.] 1. *intr.* To swear falsely. 2. *refl.* To perjure oneself ME. †3. To swear falsely by (a god) –1567.

Mansworn (mæ·nswǭɹn), *ppl. a. Obs.* exc. *Sc.* and *n. dial.* ME. [pa. pple. of prec.] Forsworn, perjured.

Manteau. *Obs.* exc. *Hist.* 1671. [a. F. :—L. *mantellum*; see MANTLE *sb.*] A loose upper garment formerly worn by women; also, a mantle or cloak.

Mantel (mæ·nt'l). 1489. [var. of MANTLE *sb.*] †1. = MANTELET 2 a –1578. 2. a. = MANTEL-TREE 1. ? *Obs.* 1519. b. = MANTELPIECE 1. 1532. c. = MANTELSHELF 1742. d. *attrib.* **m.-board**, a wooden shelf, usu. draped, fixed upon a mantelshelf.

Mantelet, mantlet (mæ·ntlėt). late ME. [a. OF. *mantelet*, dim. of *mantel* (F. *manteau*) MANTLE, MANTEL.] 1. A kind of short, loose, sleeveless mantle covering the shoulders. †b. A woollen covering for a horse –1548. 2. a. *Mil.* A movable shelter for men-at-arms when attacking a fortified place. *Obs.* exc. *Hist.* 1524. b. A screen, now usually of rope, to protect men working a gun 1859. c. A bullet-proof shelter from which firing results can be observed and signalled 1874.

Ma·ntelpiece. 1686. [f. MANTEL + PIECE *sb.*] 1. The ornamental structure of wood, marble, etc. above and around a fireplace. 2. = MANTELSHELF.

Ma·ntelshelf. 1828. [f. MANTEL + SHELF.] That projecting part of a mantelpiece which serves as a shelf.

Ma·ntel-tree. 1482. [f. MANTEL + TREE.] 1. A beam across the opening of a fireplace, supporting the masonry above; in later use, a stone or arch serving the same purpose. 2. = MANTELPIECE 1, 2. 1634.

Mantic (mæ·ntik), *a.* 1850. [ad. Gr. μαντικός, f. μάντις soothsayer, f. root *man-*; see MANIA.] Pertaining to divination.
Revelation knows nothing of this m. fury TRENCH.

-mantic, repr. Gr. μαντικός (see prec.) in comb., is the ending of adjs. related to sbs. in -MANCY, as in *geomantic*, etc.

Manticore (mæ·ntikoəɹ). *Obs.* exc. *Hist.* Also **mantiger.** ME. [ad. L. *manticora*, repr. Gr. μαντιχώρας, a corrupt reading in Aristotle *Hist. Anim.* II. i. 53 for μαρτιχόρας, app. an OPers. word for 'man-eater'.] 1. A fabulous monster having the body of a lion, the head of a man, porcupine's quills, and the tail or sting of a scorpion. 2. *Her.* A monster figured with the body of a beast of prey, the head of a man with spiral or curved horns, and sometimes the feet of a dragon 1562.

Mantilla (mænti·lă). 1717. [a. Sp. *mantilla*, dim. of *manta* mantle.] 1. A large veil worn by women over the head and the shoulders. 2. A small cape or mantle 1859.

‖**Mantis** (mæ·ntis). 1658. [mod.L., a. Gr. μάντις prophet (also, some insect); see MANTIC *a.*] *Entom.* An orthopterous insect of the genus *Mantis* or family *Mantidæ*; *esp.* the Praying Mantis, *M. religiosa*, which holds its forelegs in a position suggesting hands folded in prayer. b. *attrib.*, as **m.-crab, -shrimp,** a stomatopodous crustacean, *Squilla mantis* and other species.

Mantissa (mænti·să). 1641. [a. L., = 'makeweight'; said to be of Etruscan origin.] †1. An addition of trivial importance, esp. to a discourse –1671. 2. *Math.* The decimal part of a logarithm 1865.

Mantle (mæ·nt'l), *sb.* [From two sources. (1) OE. *męntel* masc.:—prehistoric **mantilo-z*, ad. L. *mantellum, mantelum* cloak. (2) In the 12th c., taken up again in the OF. form *mantel* (mod.F. *manteau*; see MANTEAU).] 1. A loose sleeveless cloak of varying length. b. Used allusively with reference to the descent of Elijah's mantle (2 Kings ii. 13) 1660. c. *Her.* = MANTLING *vbl. sb.* 2. 1577. 2. *transf.* and *fig.* A covering ME. †b. *spec.* The foam that covers the surface of liquor; the green vegetable coating on standing water –1605. †3. A kind of woollen cloth; a blanket of this –1582. †4. A measure of quantity of furs, containing from 30 to 100 skins according to size –1662. 5. *Mech.* A covering, envelope, or shade employed in various mechanical contrivances (see below) 1609. 6. *Zool., Bot.*, etc. Applied to various coverings or envelopes, as that enclosing the viscera in molluscs (see quots.) 1460; *Ornith.* the plumage of the back and folded wings when distinct in colour, etc. from the rest. (So F. *manteau.*) 1840.
1. As she fled, her m. she did fall SHAKS. b. On Heine..the largest portion of Goethe's m. fell M. ARNOLD. c. The m. upon the panels [of Mr. Glossin's coach] only bore a plain cipher of G. G. 1815. 2. Well couer'd with the Nights black M. SHAKS. Ruins, over which vegetation had thrown a wild m. of ivy SCOTT. b. *Lear* III. iv. 139. 5. a. A linen cloth employed in the swarming of bees 1609. b. The leather hood of an open carriage 1794. c. An enclosed chute which leads the water from a fore-bay to a water-wheel 1875. d. The outer wall and casing of an iron blast furnace, above the hearth 1881. e. A fragile lace-like tube, which, fixed around a burning gas jet, becomes incandescent and gives a brilliant light 1887. 6. An Ascidian consists ..of an external membranous bag or 'mantle', within which is a Muscular envelope 1874. Each one of the inner layers..of this m. has its initial group above the apex of the pterome 1884. 7. *Comb.* **m.-knot**, a clasp, composed of a number of precious stones [cf. F. *nœud de diamants*].

Mantle (mæ·nt'l), *v.* late ME. [f. prec. sb.] 1. *trans.* To clothe or wrap in or as in a mantle. Also with *up, over.* 1450. b. Said of wings. MILT. *P. L.* v. 279. 2. *transf.* and *fig.* To cover or conceal; to envelop; †to cloak (a fault) late ME. 3. *Falconry. refl.* and *intr.* To spread first one wing and then the other over the corresponding outstretched leg for exercise, as a perched hawk does. *Obs.* exc. *Hist.* 1486. 4. *intr.* Of liquids: To be or become covered with a coating or scum; to form a 'head' or froth; to cream. Also *transf.* and *fig.* 1596. 5. Of the blood: To suffuse the cheeks with a blush. Said also of a blush, etc. (rarely *trans.*). Of the face: To flush. 1707. 6. *intr.* To form a mantle or covering; to spread over a surface 1634.
1. The mourning-stole no more Mantled her form M. ARNOLD. 2. The ignorant fumes that m. Their clearer reason SHAKS. Mountains..mantled and capped with snow 1890. 3. *fig.* There my fraile fancy, fed with full delight, Doth bath in blisse, and mantleth most at Ease SPENSER. 4. *fig.* There are a sort of men, whose visages Do creame and m. like a standing pond SHAKS. 5. Her rich face mantling with emotion DISRAELI.

Mantlet, var. of MANTELET.

Mantling (mæ·ntliŋ), *vbl. sb.* 1507. [f. MANTLE *sb.* or *v.* + -ING[1].] †1. The action of making a mantle. 2. *Her.* The ornamental accessory of drapery or scroll-work frequently depicted behind and around an achievement; a lambrequin 1591. 3. What serves the purpose of a mantle; a covering, envelope, etc. 1652. 4. The action of the vb. (senses 3–5) 1652.

‖**Manto** (mæ·ntǫ). 1679. [It. or Sp.] A (Spanish, etc.) cloak or mantle.

†**Manto·logy.** *rare.* 1774. [Badly f. Gr. μάντις + -OLOGY.] The art or practice of divination. Hence **Manto·logist**, a diviner 1864.

Manton (mæ·ntən). 1816. A fowling-piece made by Joseph *Manton* (?1766–1835), a noted gunsmith. Also *Joe Manton.*

‖**Mantra** (mæ·ntră). *Indian.* 1808. [Skr. *mantra*, lit. 'instrument of thought', f. *man* to think.] A sacred text or passage, esp. one from the Vedas used as a prayer or incantation.

Ma·n-trap. 1788. A trap for catching men, esp. trespassers in private grounds.

Mantua (mæ·ntiuă). *Obs.* exc. *Hist.* 1678. [Corruption of MANTEAU, infl. by the place-name *Mantua.*] 1. = MANTEAU. †2. = *mantua silk* –1787. 3. *attrib.*, as *m. gown, petticoat, silk.* So **Ma·ntua-ma·ker**, one who makes mantuas; later, a dress-maker 1694.

Mantuan (mæ·ntiuăn). 1588. [ad. L. *Mantuanus*, f. *Mantua*; see -AN.] **A.** *adj.* Of or belonging to Mantua in northern Italy, where Virgil was born; hence, Virgilian 1709. **B.** *sb.* A native or inhabitant of Mantua.
The m., the M. Muse, Swan, Virgil.

Manual (mæ·niuăl). late ME. [ad. (through F.) L. *manualis*, f. *manus* hand.] **A.** *adj.* 1. Of, pertaining to, or done with the hands. Now esp. of (physical) labour. b. Of a signature, etc.: Autograph. Chiefly in SIGN MANUAL. 1476. c. Of a weapon, tool, etc.: That is used or worked with the hands. Now *rare* exc. in *m.* (*fire*) *engine* as dist. from *steam* (*fire*) *engine.* 1591. 2. *Law.* Of occupation, possession: Actual, not merely prospective 1538. 3. That works with the hands (*arch.*) 1658. †4. Furnished with hands. SIR T. BROWNE. 5. Of a book, etc.: Of the nature of a manual 1881.
1. Patron of industry and m. arts POPE. I expressed my ideas by m. signs TYLOR. Phr. *M. exercise* (*Mil.*), drill in handling a rifle. *M. alphabet*, the finger alphabet. Hence **Ma·nually** *adv.*
B. *sb.* 1. A small book for handy use. a. In the mediæval Church, a book containing the forms to be observed in administration of the sacraments. late ME. b. A handbook 1533. 2.

Short for *manual exercise* 1762. 3. Short for *manual fire-engine* 1872. 4. A key-board of an organ played with the hands, as dist. from the *pedals* 1852.

2. The corporal went through his *manual* with exactness STERNE.

Ma·nualist. 1592. [f. prec. + -IST.] †1. One who labours with the hands. 2. One who favours the manual method of teaching the deaf 1883.

Manuary (mæ·niuări). 1576. [ad. L. *manuarius*, f. *manus* hand; see -ARY [1].] A. *adj.* 1. = MANUAL *a.* 1. *Obs.* exc. in affected use. †2. = MANUAL *a.* 3. -1678. B. *sb.* †1. One who works with his hands -1656. †2. Manual work -1616.

‖**Manubrium** (măniū·briŏm). *Pl.* **-ia, -iums.** 1660. [L., = 'a haft'.] †1. A handle or haft. 2. *Anat.* and *Zool.* A handle-like part. a. The broad upper division of the sternum of mammals, with which the two first ribs articulate. b. The handle-like bony process of the malleus of the ear in man and many mammals. c. A small process, often bifurcate, at the root of the keel of the sternum in birds. d. The lower part of the malleus in rotifers. e. A peduncle which depends from the roof of the gonocalyx of hydroids or of the swimming-bell of medusæ. 1848. 3. *Bot.* A process projecting from each of the shields forming the inner wall of the antheridium in characeous plants 1875. Hence **Manubrial** *a.* 1835.

Manucaption (mæniukæ·pʃən). *Obs.* exc. *Hist.* 1588. [ad. med.L. *manucaptionem*, f. *manu capere*, lit. to 'take by the hand'.] *Law.* a. = MAINPRIZE. b. A writ directing the bringing in of a person charged with a felony. So **Manuca·ptor** = MAINPERNOR 1581.

Manucode (mæ·niukōud). 1835. [a. F. (Buffon), short f. mod.L. *manucodiata*; see next.] †a. = next. b. Any bird of either of the genera *Manucodia* and *Phonygama*, inhabiting the Papuan region, and formerly classed with the birds of paradise.

†‖**Manucodiata.** 1555. [a. mod.L. *manucodiata*, ad. Malay *mānuq dēwāta* 'bird of the gods'.] A bird of paradise -1691.

Manuduction (mæniudv·kʃən). 1502. [ad. med.L. *manuductionem*, f. *manu ducere* to lead by the hand.] 1. Guidance, introduction, direction. 2. Means or instrument of guidance; a guide or introduction 1624. So †**Manuductor**, a guide, director 1657-1677; the conductor of a band or choir -1852.

†**Manufactor.** 1649. [f. L. *manu facere*.] A manufacturer or artificer -1812.

Manufactory (mæniufæ·ktŏri), *sb.* and *a.* 1618. [ad. L. types **manufactorius, -a, -um*, f. as prec.; see -ORY [1, 2].] A. *sb.* †1. = MANUFACTURE *sb.* 2 -1786. †2. MANUFACTURE 1 b. -1846. 3. A factory or workshop, as a *cotton m.* 1692. B. *adj.* Pertaining to, of the nature of, or engaged in manufacture -1741.

Manufacture (mæniufæ·ktiŭɹ), *sb.* 1567. [a. F., ad. med.L. **manufactura*, f. *manu facere* to make by hand.] 1. †a. The action or process of making by hand. BACON. b. The making of articles or material (now, on a large scale) by physical labour or mechanical power 1622. c. A branch of productive industry 1683. d. In depreciatory sense, production of a merely mechanical kind. Also *fig.* applied, e.g. to literary work, or to the fabrication of false statements on a large scale for the market. 1829. 2. *concr.* †a. A person's handiwork. Also *fig.* -1726. b. A product of physical labour or machinery 1611. †3. Working with the hands; a manual occupation, handicraft -1699. †4. A manufacturing establishment or business -1783.

1. b. A single article, either of domestic or foreign growth or m. MCCULLOCH. 1. c. *Linen, woollen, worsted m.* 2. b. Colchester baize, a coarse rug-like m. DE FOE. Hence **Manufa·ctural** *a.* pertaining to m.

Manufacture (mæniufæ·ktiŭɹ), *v.* 1683. [f. prec.] 1. *trans.* To work up (material) into forms suitable for use. 2. To produce by labour (now esp. on a large scale) 1755. b. *transf.* Said of natural agencies 1876. 3. *fig.* In disparaging sense: To fabricate, invent; also, to produce (literary work) mechanically 1762. 4. To admit of being manufactured 1763.

2. b. Poisons manufactured within the system 1899. 3. The speech is evidently manufactured by the historian GIBBON. Hence **Manufa·cturer**, †an operative in a manufactory; the owner of a manufactory; also *transf.* and *fig.* **Manufa·cturing** *ppl. a.* engaged or concerned in manufacture.

†**Manumise, manumiss,** *v.* 1523. [f. L. *manumiss-*, *manumittere* to MANUMIT.] = MANUMIT *v.* -1819.

Manumission (mæniumi·ʃən). *Obs.* exc. *Hist.* late ME. [a. F., ad. L. *manumissionem*, f. *manumittere*; see MANUMIT *v.*] The action of manumitting, or the fact of being manumitted; an act or instance of this. Also *transf.* and *fig.*

M. is properly when the Lord makes a deed to his villeine to enfranchise him by this word (*Manumittere*) which is the same as to put him out of the hands and power of another COKE.

Manumit (mæniumi·t), *v.* late ME. [ad. L. *manumittere*, ante-cl. *manu emittere*, lit. 'to send forth from one's hand', i.e. from one's control.] *trans.* To release from slavery; to liberate from bondage or servitude; to set free. Also *transf.* and *fig.* Also *absol.*

Christian masters were not bound to m. their slaves JER. TAYLOR.

Manurable (măniū·răb'l), *a.* 1628. [f. MANURE *v.* + -ABLE.] †1. *Law.* Admitting of being held in corporeal possession -1767. †2. Of land: That can be worked or cultivated -1756. 3. That can be manured 1828.

Manurance (măniū·răns). 1468. [f. MANURE *v.* + -ANCE.] 1. Tenure, occupation (of land, etc.); control, management. Now only in *Law*. 2. †Cultivation (of land), †tillage; manuring 1572. †b. *fig.* Cultivation (of the character or faculties) -1615.

2. b. The culture and m. of minds in youth BACON.

Manure (măniū·ɹ), *sb.* 1549. [f. MANURE *v.* Formerly *ma·nure*, and so still in Cowper (1784); and still *dial.* (mæ·nəɹ).] 1. Dung or compost spread over or mixed with soil to fertilize it. †2. Manuring; cultivation -1696. 3. *attrib.*, as *m.-heap*, etc. 1766.

Manure (măniū·ɹ), *v.* late ME. [a. AF. *maynoverer* to work with the hands; see MANŒUVRE *v.*] †1. *trans.* To hold, occupy (land, etc.); to administer, manage -1645. †2. To till, cultivate (land) -1774. †b. To cultivate, train (a plant, the body or mind, etc.) -1797. 3. [f. MANURE *sb.* 1] To enrich (land) with fertilizing material; to apply manure to 1599. †4. To work up -1575; to manœuvre (a ship) 1569.

1. That which is manually occupied, manured and possessed COKE. 2. A barren Sand, not capable of being manur'd by either Spade or Plow 1700. b. Who like a nut tree must be manured by beating FULLER. 3. The Corps of half her Senate M. the Fields of Thessaly ADDISON. Hence **Manu·rer.**

†**Manurement.** 1639. [f. MANURE *v.* + -MENT.] Cultivation (*lit.* and *fig.*) -1707.

Manurial (măniū·riăl), *a.* 1861. [irreg. f. MANURE *sb.* + -IAL.] Pertaining to, or of the nature of manure.

Manuring (măniū·riŋ), *vbl. sb.* late ME. [f. MANURE *v.* + -ING [1].] †a. Occupation, tenure. †b. Cultivation, tillage. c. Fertilization by means of manure; †occas. *concr.* = manure.

‖**Manus** (mē·nŏs). 1826. [L., 'hand'.] 1. *Anat.* The terminal or distal segment of the fore limb of a vertebrate animal. Also, the claw of a crustacean; *Entom.* the tarsus of the anterior leg; *Ichth.* the pectoral fin. 2. *Rom. Law.* The power or authority of a husband over his wife 1854. †3. *Manus Christi* [= 'hand of Christ'], a cordial 1516-1706.

Manuscript (mæ·niuˌskript). 1597. Abbrev. MS. (*pl.* MSS.). [ad. med.L. *manuscriptus*, f. L. *manu-* abl., by hand + *scriptus*, pa. pple. of *scribere* to write.] A. *adj.* Written by hand, not printed.

Manvscript Poems of great Antiquitie 1597.

B. *sb.* 1. A book, document, or the like, written by hand; a writing of any kind, as dist. from printed matter. Also *transf.* and *fig.* 1600. 2. Writing (as opp. to print); also, (a person's) handwriting 1849.

1. John Mill..borrowed the m. [of the 'French Revolution'] as it was thrown off, that he might make notes and suggestions FROUDE. *fig.* Alas,.. That Youth's sweet-scented M. should close! FITZGERALD. *attrib.* Special Assistant in the MS. Department. Hence **Manuscri·ptal** *a. rare*, of or pertaining to a m. or manuscripts; found or occurring in a m. So **Manuscri·ption** *rare*, the action of writing by hand; a written inscription LAMB.

†**Manutenency.** 1633. [ad. med.L. *manutenentia* (= F. *maintenance*), f. L. *manu tenere*; see MAINTAIN *v.*] Support, maintenance -1699. So †**Manute·ntion** 1603-57.

Manward (mæ·nwǫɹd). late ME. [See -WARD.] A. *adv.* (In early use *to m.*, also *to menward.*) a. Towards man, in the direction of man. b. In relation to man. B. *adj.* Tending or directed towards man 1867.

Manx (mæŋks). 1572. [Metathetic a. ON. **mansk-r*, f. *Man-* (nom. *Mǫn* :—**Manu*, a. OIr. *Manu*), the Isle of Man.] A. *adj.* Of or pertaining to the Isle of Man, its inhabitants, language, etc. B. *sb.* 1. (As *pl.*) The people of the Isle of Man 1688. 2. The Celtic language spoken in the Isle of Man 1672. Hence **Ma·nxman**, a native of the Isle of Man.

M. cat: a tailless variety of cat, indigenous to the Isle of Man. *M. penny*: a coin stamped with the device of three legs.

Many (me·ni), *a.* and *sb.* [Com. Teut.: OE. *maniȝ, mǫniȝ* :—OTeut. **manago-* :—Indo-Eur. **monogho-*.] A. *adj.* The adjectival designation of great indefinite number. 1. Used *distributively* with a *sing.* (Formerly sometimes with pl. vb.) 2. With *pl. sb.* OE. 3. *ellipt.* and *absol.* in pl. sense: Many individuals of the kind specified (often *many of*); also (as quasi-pron.), many persons OE. 4. With As, How, So, Too (q. v.), the adj. only expresses the notion of number in the abstract. With *pl. sb.*; also *ellipt.* and *absol.* = '(as, etc.) many persons'. OE.

1. To m. a youth, and m. a maid MILT. M. a more unlikely thing has happened 1809. *M. a(n) one*: = 'many a person'. Now chiefly *colloq.* 2. We must drink m. happy returns to her DICKENS. *M. times, m. ways, (on) m. wise*, advb. phr.; see the sbs. 3. I see, one Fool makes m. SWIFT. M. of his ideas..did not belong to him peculiarly MORLEY. Phr. *The m.* (= Gr. οἱ πολλοί): the great body of people; the multitude. 4. As m. words as make an even line CRABBE. *As m. as*: idiomatic for 'all who'. *As m.*: the same number of. *One too m.*: used predicatively of something not wanted. *Too m. for*: more than a match for 1692. (Prop. with a pl. subject, but said *joc.* of a single person or thing 1708.)

Comb. a. parasynthetic (unlimited in number), as *m.-acred, -fountained, -voiced*, etc. b. *poet.* with pples. in quasi-advb. sense = 'in many ways, many times, much', as *m.-beaming, -blossoming*, etc.

B. quasi-*sb.* and *sb.* 1. quasi-*sb.* On the analogy of *a few* (see FEW *a.* 2), *a many* has from the 16th c. been followed by a pl. sb. or used *absol.* in pl. sense. Without adj. now *arch.*; formerly with various adjs., now only *a good many, a great many.* In such collocations *many* may be interpreted as a sb., meaning 'a great number'. (Cf. MEINIE.) a. with pl. sb. (or *people*) immediately following 1590. b. Const. *of*; now only followed by a definite sb. or pron. 1525. c. *ellipt.* and *absol.* SHAKS. †2. By confusion with MEINIE: Company, host, flock; (one's) retinue or following -1700. 3. *Philos.* A multitude, plurality. Opp. to *one.* 1619.

1. a. A m. such miracles H. MORE. b. He..had invited a m. of his kindred and friends 1652. c. A good m. died of hardship and fatigue 1875. 2. The manie begins to march along; thronging one another for haste 1609. 3. One idea, throughout all manys, wrapt up in one T. TAYLOR. Hence **Ma·nyness** plurality (*rare*) 1609.

Many-: see MANI-.

Many-headed, *a.* (Stress variable.) 1586. Having many heads.

Keep nothing sacred; 'tis but just The many-headed beast (= the people) should know TENNYSON.

Manyplies (me·niplaiz), *sb. pl.* Chiefly *dial.* 1774. [f. MANY + *plies*, pl. of PLY, fold.] The omasum or third stomach of a ruminant.

Many-sided, *a.* (Stress variable.) 1660. 1. Having many sides; multilateral. 2. *fig.* Having many aspects, capacities, or possibilities 1843.

2. Raleigh was..a many-sided man; soldier, sailor, statesman, historian, and poet GARDINER. Hence **Manysi·dedness.**

Manyways *adv.*: see WAY.

Manywise *adv.*: see WISE *sb.*

‖**Manzanilla** (mænzäni·lă, Sp. manþani·lʸa). 1843. [Sp., f. *manzanilla* camomile.] A dry light sherry with a bitterish flavour.

‖**Manzanita** (mænzănī·tă, Sp. manþanī·ta). 1872. [Sp., dim. of *manzana* apple.] One of the berry-bearing shrubs of the genus *Arctostaphylos* found in the U.S.; the bearberry.

Maori (ma·ŏri, mau·ri), *sb.* (*a.*) *Pl.* **Maori, Maori(e)s.** 1843. [Native name; said to mean 'of the usual kind' (Morris).] **1.** An individual of the brown race inhabiting New Zealand. Also *attrib.* or *adj.* pertaining to this race or their language; *absol.* the language. **2.** A New South Wales fish, *Coris lineolatus* 1882.

Map (mæp), *sb.* 1527. [ad. L. *mappa*, in class.L. 'table-cloth, napkin', but in med.L. used *transf.* in *mappa mundi* MAPPEMONDE.] **1.** A representation of the earth's surface or a part of it, its physical and political features, etc., or of the heavens, delineated on a flat surface of paper, etc., according to a definite scale or projection. Also *transf.* **2.** *fig.* A detailed representation in epitome; a circumstantial account of a state of things. Now *rare* or *Obs.* 1586. †**b.** The very picture (*of* a virtue, vice, character, etc.). (So Sp. *mapa.*) –1698.

1. Colloq. phr. *Off the map*: of no account, obsolete. *On the map*: of some account or importance. **2.** I don't know the m. of their situation BURKE. **b.** What were man if he were once left to himselfe? A m. of misery 1591.

Comb.: **m. lichen**, a lichen, *Lecidea geographica*, the thallus of which has markings resembling a m.

Map (mæp), *v.* Infl. **mapped** (mæpt), **mapping.** 1586. [f. MAP *sb.*] **1.** *trans.* To make a map of; to represent on a map 1602. Also *transf.* and *fig.* **2. M. out. a.** To represent in detail on a map 1656. **b.** *fig.* †To record minutely 1619; to plan out (a course of conduct, one's time, etc.) 1883. **c.** To divide (a country) *into* districts, as by lines on a map 1860.

1. *transf.* I am neere to th' place where they should meet, if Pisanio haue mapp'd it truely SHAKS. **2. c.** The Continent was not then mapped out with tourists' routes 1870. Hence **Mapping** *vbl. sb.* (also *attrib.* as **m. pen**).

Maple (mē·p'l). [OE. **mapel*, **mapul*, only in *mapeltrēow* maple-tree, and in *mapulder*; cf. OS. *mapulder*, MLG. *mapeldorn.*] **1.** Any tree or shrub of the genus *Acer*, many of which are grown for shade or ornament, for their wood, or for a sugar product. The Common Maple is *Acer campestre*. The fruit of these trees is a double-winged samara or 'key'. **2.** The light, hard, close-grained wood of any of these trees. late ME.

1. Bird's-eye M. = *sugar maple*. **Red, Scarlet,** or **Swamp M.**, *A. rubrum*. **Silver, Silver-leaved,** or **White M.**, *A. dasycarpum*, of eastern North America. **Sugar M.**, *A. saccharinum* of North America, which yields maple-sugar. **Sycamore M.**, *A. pseudo platanus* (see SYCAMORE).

attrib. and *Comb.*, as *m. leaf*, etc.; **m.-honey** *U.S.*, the uncrystallized part of the sap of the sugar m.; **m. molasses, syrup** *U.S.*, a syrup obtained by evaporating maple sap or dissolving maple sugar; **m. sugar**, the sugar obtained by evaporation from the sap of certain maples.

Mappemonde (mæpmōu·nd). Now only *Hist.* late ME. [a. F. *mappemonde*, ad. med.L. *mappa mundi.*] The map of the world; in early use, the world itself.

‖**Maqui** (ma·kī). 1704. [Chilian Sp.] The Chilian shrub *Aristotelia Maqui* (N.O. *Tiliaceæ*), yielding a valuable fibre, and producing berries used in the adulteration of wine.

Mar (māɹ), *sb.* ME. [f. MAR *v.*] †**1.** A hindrance; an impediment in speech –1824. **2.** Something that mars; a drawback *to*. In early use, †a fault. 1551.

Mar (māɹ), *v.* [Com. Teut.: OE. *męrran*, f. Teut. root **marz-*, whence also OE. *mearrian* to go astray, err.] **1.** *trans.* To hinder, interrupt, or stop (a person, event, or thing). *Obs.* exc. *Sc.* **2.** To spoil, impair OE. **3.** *trans.* To harm, injure (a person, etc.); to disfigure (now *arch.*); †to ruin; to damage morally ME.

2. Striuing to better, oft we marre what's well SHAKS. The wine is spilled, and the bottles will bee marred *Mark* ii. 22. Phr. *To make or m.* (see MAKE *v.* VI. 9). **3.** Mend your speach..lest it m. your fortunes SHAKS. Digby Lord Gerard..was utterly mar'd by keeping company with base lewd fellowes WOOD.

Mar, north. and Sc. f. MORE.

Mar-, *vbl. stem*, prefixed to sbs., with sense 'one who or something which mars', and *adjs.*, with sense 'that mars'; as *mar-all* sb. and adj., *mar-feast*, etc. **b.** *esp.* in **mar-prelate**, first used in the pseudonym 'Martin Marprelate', the writer of certain tracts issued in 1588–9; hence *attrib.*

Marabou (mæ·răbū). Also **marabout, marabu.** 1823. [a. F. *marabou(t*, app. repr. a vulgar Arabic use of *murābiṭ* hermit, MARABOUT.] **1.** A large stork or heron, *Leptoptilus marabou* or *crumenifer*, a native of Western Africa. Now applied also to the adjutant-bird of India, *L. dubius* or *argala*. 1826. **2.** In full *m. feather, plume*. A tuft or plume of down from under the wings and tail of these birds, used for trimming hats and dresses; *collect. sing.* trimming made of these feathers 1823. **3.** An exceptionally white kind of raw silk which can be dyed without first removing the natural gum 1835.

2. A m. feather which she wears in her turban THACKERAY.

‖**Marabout** (mæ·răbūt). 1623. [repr. Arab. *murābiṭ* hermit. The mod.Eng. form is from Fr.] **1.** A Mohammedan hermit or monk, esp. amongst the Moors and Berbers of N. Africa. **2.** A shrine marking the burial-place of a marabout 1859.

‖**Marah** (mā·ră). late ME. [Heb. *mārāh*, fem. of *mar* bitter.] The Heb. word for 'bitter' or 'bitterness', used as a proper name (Exod. xv and Ruth i); hence allusively.

Never had any writer so vast a command of the whole eloquence of scorn, misanthropy, and despair. That M. was never dry MACAULAY.

Maranatha (mæränæ·þă). late ME. [Aramaic *māran ăthā* 'Our Lord has come', or *maranā 'thā* 'O our Lord, come thou'.] An Aramaic phrase occurring in 1 Cor. xvi. 22; see ANATHEMA MARANATHA. As an abbrev. of this formula used subst. for: A terrible curse.

‖**Marasca** (măræ·skă). 1864. [It., aphetic f. *amarasca*, f. *amaro* bitter.] A small black cherry, *Prunus avium*, grown in Dalmatia.

‖**Maraschino** (mæräskī·no). 1791. [It., f. *marasca*; see prec. Cf. F. *marasquin.*] A liqueur distilled from the marasca cherry.

‖**Marasmus** (măræ·zmŏs). 1656. [mod.L., a. Gr. μαρασμός, f. μαραίνειν to waste.] Wasting of the body. Hence **Mara·smic** *a.*

‖**Maratha, Mahratta** (mără·tă, măræ·tă). 1758. [Held to be f. Sk. *mahā rāshtra* great country.] **1.** One of a warlike Hindu race occupying the central and south-western parts of India 1763. **2.** *attrib.* or *adj.* Pertaining to the Marathas 1758.

‖**Marathi** (mără·tī). 1698 (**Moratty**). [f. *Maratha*; see prec.] The language of the Marathas.

Marathon (mæ·răþŏn). 1896. [Name of Greek city, the scene of a victory of the Athenians over the Persians (490 B.C.), the news of which was conveyed by a runner to Athens, a distance of about 20 miles.] *attrib.* in *m.-race*, etc., a long-distance race.

Maraud (mărǭ·d), *v.* 1708. [a. F. *marauder*, f. *maraud* rogue, vagabond.] **1.** *intr.* To make a raid for the purpose of plundering. **2.** *trans.* To plunder; to harry 1829.

1. They met with a Party of French that had been Marauding ADDISON. Hence **Marau·d** *sb.* the act of marauding. **Marau·der** 1698.

Maravedi (mæravē·di). *Obs.* exc. *Hist.* late ME. [a. Sp. *maravedí*, a deriv. of Arab. *Murābiṭīn* (pl. of *murābiṭ*; see MARABOUT), name of a Moorish dynasty at Cordova.] **1.** An old Spanish gold coin, weighing about 60 grains and worth fourteen shillings 1643. **2.** A former Spanish copper coin and money of account, valued at about ⅙ of a penny sterling.

2. I will strip thee of every m. thou hast in the world SCOTT.

Marble (mā·ɹb'l), *sb.* [ME. *marbre, marble*, a. F. *marbre*:—L. *marmor*, ad. or cogn. w. Gr. μάρμαρος shining stone, marble (whence μαρμαίρειν to sparkle).] **I. 1.** Limestone in a crystalline (or, less strictly, also a granular) state and capable of taking a polish; occurring in many varieties; much used in sculpture and architecture. **b.** A kind or variety of marble 1640. **c.** As a type of something hard, inflexible, durable, or smooth 1586. **d.** As the material of which a tomb or tombstone is made (*poet.*) 1613. **2.** A piece, block, or slab of marble; a marble monument. Also *fig.* ME. †**b.** A marble tomb or tombstone –1730. **c.** *Antiq.* (*pl.*) Applied to certain collections of sculptures, etc. 1667. **3.** A small ball, orig. of marble, now of baked clay, porcelain, etc., used in a children's game; hence in *pl.* the game itself. Also a small ball of glass, etc., used in other games. 1694. **4.** *Bookbinding.* The marbled pattern or paper used in ornamenting books 1699.

1. *Black, fibrous, green, grey, red, variegated, white m.*; *Carrara, Egyptian, English, Genoese, Italian,* PARIAN, *Pentelican, Purbeck m.* Also RUIN, VERD ANTIQUE *m.*, etc. **c.** Writing all injuries in m. PURCHAS. **d.** When I am forgotten..And sleepe in dull cold M. SHAKS. **2.** An Inscription on a M. LEONI. **c.** *Arundel, Arundelian,* or *Oxford marbles*, a collection of sculptures, etc. made by the Earl of Arundel (died 1646) and presented to the University of Oxford. *Elgin marbles*, a collection (now in the British Museum) of ancient sculptures from the Parthenon, which was sold by Lord Elgin to the nation in 1816.

II. *attrib.* or *adj.* **a.** Made or consisting of marble. Also, like that of marble. ME. **b.** White, hard, cold, or rigid like marble. (Rarely used *predicatively.*) 1591. **c.** Enduring as marble, or as if carved in marble 1596. **d.** *poet.* Smooth as marble 1557. **e.** Of a variegated or mottled colour; marbled. late ME.

a. A m. Madona like a Colosse EVELYN. **b.** His M., obdurate Heart SOUTH. Her m. brow, and eager lips SHELLEY. **d.** Through the pure m. Air MILT. **e.** Countless m.-covered octavos HAN. MORE. Phr. †*m. colours*: used *fig.* by Drummond to express ostentatious splendour. Hence **Ma·rbly** *a.* resembling marble 1439.

Marble (mā·ɹb'l), *v.* 1628. [f. prec. sb. Cf. F. *marbrer.*] **1.** *trans.* To stain or colour (paper, edges of books, soap, etc.) so as to make them look like variegated marble. **2.** To make white like marble (*rare*) 1791.

2. Features, marbled by the moon B. TAYLOR. Hence **Ma·rbling** *vbl. sb.* the action of the vb.; also *concr.* 1686.

Marbled (mā·ɹb'ld), *ppl. a.* 1599. [f. MARBLE *sb.* and *v.* + -ED.] **1.** In occas. uses: Portrayed in marble; having buildings, etc. of marble; turned into marble (*fig.*); decorated or covered with marble. **2. a.** Coloured or stained with variegated patterns like those of marble 1671. **b.** Veined, mottled, or dappled (*with* markings of various colours). Chiefly *Nat. Hist.* and *Path.* 1694. **c.** Of meat: Having the lean streaked with thin layers of fat. (A sign of the best quality.) 1770. **3.** Used as the specific designation of various animals and plants having mottled or dappled markings 1699.

1. Sunium's m. steep BYRON. **2. a.** Common m. paper 1699. **b.** The m. Sky 1719. **3. M. beauty**, the moth *Bryophila perla*.

Marbleize (mā·ɹb'ləiz), *v.* *U.S.* 1875. [f. MARBLE *sb.* + -IZE.] *trans.* To colour in imitation of marble.

Marbler (mā·ɹbləɹ). 1402. [f. MARBLE *sb.* and *v.* + -ER [1].] †**1.** A hewer of marble –1538. †**2.** One who carves, or works in, marble –1720. **3.** One who marbles paper, etc.; an instrument for marbling paper 1835.

Marc (māɹk). 1601. [a. F. *marc*; explained as a vbl. noun f. *marcher* in the sense 'to tread'.] The refuse which remains after the pressure of grapes or other fruits.

Marc, obs. f. MARK, MARQUE.

†**Marcantant.** [Corruption of It. *mercatante.*] A merchant. *Tam. Shr.* IV. ii. 63.

Marcasite (mā·ɹkăsəit). 1471. [ad. med.L. *marcasita*, app. f. with suffix L. *-ita*, Gr. -ίτης, -ITE [1].] *Min.* **1.** Pyrites, *esp.* the crystallized forms of iron pyrites used in the 18th c. for ornaments; by some restricted to the arsenical varieties; in recent use, white iron pyrites (iron disulphide). **2.** A specimen of

marcasite; an ornament made of crystallized iron pyrites 1555.
The 'marcasites' of gold and silver were app. specimens of copper and iron pyrites with the lustre of gold and silver N.E.D. 2. Half the ladies of our acquaintance .. carry their jewels to town, and bring nothing but paste and marcasites back GOLDSM. Hence **Marcasi·tical** *a.* pertaining to or containing m.

‖**Marcassin** (maɹkæ·sin). 1727. [Fr.] *Her.* A young wild boar, used as a charge.

Marcel (maɹse·l). 1906. [f. name of Paris hairdresser.] Applied to a method of waving the hair; as *m.-wave, -waved*, adj. Also as vb.

‖**Marcelline** (mā·ɹsĕlin). 1835. [Fr.] A silk fabric used for linings.

Marcella, marsella (maɹse·lă). 1812. [*Marsella*, Cat. and Sp. f. MARSEILLES.] A kind of twilled cotton or linen cloth used for waistcoats, etc.

Marcescent (maɹse·sĕnt), *a.* (*sb.*) 1727. [ad. L. *marcescentem, marcescere*, inceptive of *marcēre* to be faint or languid.] *Bot.* Of parts of a plant: withering but not falling off. b. *sb.* A plant having marcescent parts 1859. Hence **Marce·scence**, m. condition.

Marcgrave: see MARGRAVE.

†**March**, *sb.*1 [OE. *merece* str. masc.] Smallage or wild celery, *Apium graveolens* –1632.

March (māɹtʃ), *sb.*2 [Early ME. *march*, a. AF. *marche*, OF. *march(e*, var. of *marz, mars* (mod.F. *mars*) :—L. *Martium* (nom. *Martius* sc. *mensis*, lit. month of Mars).] The third month of the year in the Julian and Gregorian calendar. Abbrev. Mar.
The Ides of M. are come SHAKS. Hair More black than ashbuds in the front of M. TENNYSON. *attrib.* One bushell of m. dust is worth a kynges raunsome HEYWOOD.
Comb.: **M. ale, beer**, a strong ale or beer brewed in M.; **M. brown**, a fly used in angling; **M. hare**, a proverbial type of madness; †**M. mad** = mad as a M. hare; **M. violet**, the garden violet, *Viola odorata*.

March (māɹtʃ), *sb.*3 ME. [a. F. *marche* fem., Com. Rom., ad. Teut. **markā* (OE. *mearc*); see MARK *sb.*1] 1. Boundary, frontier, border. a. The border of a country. Hence, a tract of land on the border of a country, or a tract of debatable land separating two countries. Often *collect. pl.*, esp. with ref. to the borderland of England and Scotland, and England and Wales. Now *Hist.* b. The boundary of an estate. Chiefly *Sc.* 1540. 2. Country, territory. *Obs.* exc. in ref. to continental names, as It. *Marca* (cf. MARK *sb.*1 I. 3).
1. The lord Hunsdon lord warden of the east marches, and gouernor of Berwike HOLINSHED. Granted in fief..as a m. or border territory FREEMAN. 2. The olde marche of Brandenburg 1758. The Marches comprise the M. of Ancona .. and the M. of Fermo.
attrib. and *Comb.*, as (sense 1 b) *m.-balk, -dike, -ditch*, etc.; (sense 1 a) *m.-law, -treason* (arch.), etc.

March (māɹtʃ), *sb.*4 1572. [a. F. *marche*, vbl. n. from *marcher*; see MARCH *v.*2] 1. *Mil.* The action of marching; the regular forward movement together and in time of a body of troops. Also, any orderly forward movement. 1590. b. Steady progression on a long journey; a long and toilsome walk 1691. 2. *transf.* and *fig.* Advance, forward movement, progress, e. g. of time, events, population, knowledge, etc. 1625. 3. *Mil.* The distance covered by troops in a single day 1594. 4. The regular and uniform step of a body of men, esp. of troops. Also qualified, as *double, quick, slow m.* 1773. b. *fig.* Of verse: Rhythmic movement 1635. 5. *Mil.* A beating of the drum in a particular rhythm as an accompaniment to the marching of troops 1572. 6. *Mus.* A tune or composition of marked rhythm (usu. including the rhythmical drum-beats, sense 5), designed to accompany the marching of troops, etc.; also any similar composition; usually in common time, and with a subsidiary intermediate section or 'trio'. So also *m. past.* 1603. 7. *Games.* a. *Euchre.* A taking of all five tricks 1886. b. *Chess*, etc. The move of a 'man' 1672.
1. Two mightier Troopes..Which ioyn'd with him, and made their m. for Burdeaux SHAKS. Phr. *Column of m.*, a formation assumed by troops on the line of m. *Line of m.*: direction or route of marching; *transf.* way. *M. past*, the marching past of a body of men, esp. in review. 2. The regular m. of history H. WALPOLE. And drill the raw world for the m. of mind, Till crowds at length be sane and crowns be just TENNYSON. 3. The army are .. within two or three marches of the Ebro WELLINGTON. Phr. *To gain, get a m. on* or *upon*: to get ahead of to the extent of a m. *To steal a m.* (*on* or *upon*): to gain a m. by stealth; often *fig.* 6. Each regiment in the British service has its special m. for marching past 1876. *Dead m.*: see DEAD *Combs.* 2; also *funeral m.* *Rogue's m., wedding m.* (see ROGUE, WEDDING).

March (māɹtʃ), *v.*1 ME. [a. OF. *marchir*, f. *marche* MARCH *sb.*3] *intr.* To border *upon, on*; to have a common frontier *with* (*to*, †*unto*). Said of countries, estates, etc., and hence of their rulers, owners, or inhabitants.
The frontiers of Dakota, Montana, and Washington m. with the Canadian Dominion 1889.

March (māɹtʃ), *v.*2 1515. [a. F. *marcher*, orig. to tread, trample, hence, to walk.] 1. *intr.* To walk in a military manner with regular and measured tread; to walk in step. Also, to begin to walk in step (esp. in commands, as *Quick march!*), to set out from quarters. Freq. with advs., as *away, forth, off, on, out, past.* b. quasi-*trans.* To go upon (a warfare); to traverse (a distance) in marching 1619. 2. To walk, proceed *off, on, out*, in a steady and deliberate manner 1572. 3. *transf.* and *fig.* See quots. 1600. 4. *trans.* (causatively). To cause to march or move in military order 1595; to force (a person) to go; to *march off* 1884.
1. Men that in battle array,..M. with banner and bugle and fife, To the death for their native land TENNYSON. The word *March*, given singly, at all times denotes that 'slow time' is to be taken 1833. 2. Miss Ophelia marched straight to her own chamber MRS. STOWE. 3. Without a strain the great ship marches by CLOUGH. It was the president who made the enterprise m. SKRINE. 4. I should be glad to m. you to the gate 1896.

Marcher1 (mā·ɹtʃəɹ). *Obs.* exc. *Hist.* 1440. [f. MARCH *sb.*3 + -ER 1.] †1. One whose territory adjoins that of another. ME. only. 2. An inhabitant of a march or border district 1470.
2. *Lord M.* (pl. *Lords Marchers*), a lord who enjoyed royal liberties and had exclusive jurisdiction over territory in the marches which he obtained by border warfare. Hence *Lordship M.*, territory so obtained and held.

Marcher2 (mā·ɹtʃəɹ). 1611. [f. MARCH *v.*2 + -ER 1.] One who marches or walks.

‖**Marchese** (markē·ze). 1517. [It.; see MARQUIS.] In Italy: A marquis. So ‖**Marchesa** (markē·za), a marchioness 1797.

Marchet, obs. f. MARKET.

Marching (mā·ɹtʃiŋ), *vbl. sb.* 1560. [f. MARCH *v.*2 + -ING 1.] The action of MARCH *v.*2
attrib. and *Comb.*: **m. money**, the additional pay received by officers and soldiers when marching from one place to another; **m. order**, equipment for marching; *pl.* orders to march. So **Ma·rching** *ppl. a.*, esp. in *m. regiment*, one which had not any permanent quarters, but was liable to be sent anywhere 1667.

Marchioness (mā·ɹʃənĕs). 15... [ad. med. L. *marchionissa*, f. *marchionem*, f. *marca* MARK *sb.*1, MARCH *sb.*3] 1. The wife or widow of a marquis, or a lady holding in her own right the position equal to that of marquis. b. *allusive.* A maid-of-all-work. (See DICKENS *Old C. Shop* lvii.) 1883. 2. A kind of pear 1706. 3. A size of slate, 22 inches by 11, or 20 by 12. 1878.

Ma·rch-land. 1536. [f. MARCH *sb.*3 + LAND *sb.* OE. had *mearc-land*.] A border territory; border-land, frontier-land.

Ma·rch-man. *Obs.* exc. *Hist.* late ME. [f. MARCH *sb.*3 + MAN *sb.*] An inhabitant of the marches or borders.

Marchpane (mā·ɹtʃpeɪn). Superseded by MARZIPAN. 1494. [Occurs as F. *massepain*, It. *marzapane*, Sp. *mazapan*, G. *marzipan*. Etym. unkn. Various adoptions of continental form are recorded.] 1. A paste of pounded almonds, sugar, etc., made up into cakes, etc.; a cake or fancy form of this. †b. *fig.* –1652. 2. *attrib.* 1587. †b. quasi-*adj.* Dainty, superfine –1649.

†**Ma·rcid**, *a.* 1656. [ad. L. *marcidus*, f. *marcēre* to wither.] 1. a. Withered, wasted, decayed. b. Weak, exhausted. –1822. 2. *M. fever*: a fever that causes wasting –1684.

Marcionite (mā·ɹʃiŏnəit). 1540. [ad. late L. *Marcionita*, f. *Marcion*; see -ITE 1.] An adherent of the sect founded at Rome by Marcion of Sinope, an ascetic gnostic of the 2nd c. Also †**Ma·rcionist** 1449.
Marcion accepted as sacred books ten of St. Paul's epistles and a garbled form of the gospel of St. Luke, and regarded the creation of the world and the revelation of the Old Testament as the work of a finite and imperfect God, whose authority is abrogated by the manifestation of the supreme God in Jesus Christ.

Marconi (maɹkōu·ni). 1897. Name of the inventor (born 1874) of a system of wireless telegraphy; used *attrib.* of this system, and of things connected with it. Hence **Marconi** *v.*, to send a marconigram (*intr.* and *trans.*) 1919. **Marco·nigram**, a wireless telegram 1902. **Marco·nigraph**, the apparatus used for transmitting marconigrams 1903; also as vb.

Marcor (mā·ɹkǫɹ). 1646. [a. L., f. *marcēre*; see MARCID.] †a. *gen.* Decay. b. *Path.* Emaciation of the body.

Marcosian (maɹkōu·ziăn). 1587. [f. Eccl. Gr. Μαρκώσιος (app. f. Syriac *Marqūs* Marcus) + -AN.] *Hist.* An adherent of a Gnostic system founded by one Marcus in the 2nd c. Also *adj.*

‖**Mardi gras** (mardi gra). 1848. [Fr. 'fat Tuesday'.] Shrove Tuesday; *U.S.* as observed in New Orleans.

Mare1 (mēᵊɹ). [OE. *mēre* wk. fem. (:— OTeut. **marhjō(n)*-, f. **marho-z* horse, OE. *mearh*) gave *mere, meare* (16th c.); the present form dates from 12th c. and presumably repr. oblique ff. of OE. *mærh, mearh* horse (cf. *fare*, dial. var. of *farrow* :—OE. *færh, fearh*) perh. infl. by MARE 2.] 1. The female of any equine animal, esp. of the domestic horse (*Equus caballus*). 2. *transf.*, chiefly with implication of 'riding' 1568. 3. A throw in wrestling. Also *flying m.* 1602.
1. *Grey m.* (see GREY *a.* 4). 2. The two or three-legg'd M. (= 'the gallows') 1694. See also SHANK.

†**Mare**2. [OE. *mare* wk. fem. :—OTeut. **maron-, -ōn-*, whence OF. *mare* in *cauchemar* nightmare, f. *cauchier* to trample.] 1. = NIGHTMARE. 2. A spectre, hag –1529.
1. The Incubus, which we call the M. BACON.

†**Marechal.** 1676. [app. an application of F. *maréchal* or *maréchale*.] A scent or perfume; a hair powder scented with it –1852.

‖**Maréchal Niel** (mareʃal nīl). 1867. Also anglicized **Marshal Niel** (ma·ɹʃăl nīl). [F., named after Adolphe *Niel* (1802–69), Marshal of France.] A yellow climbing rose.

‖**Maremma** (măre·mă). *Pl.* **maremme.** 1832. [a. It. *maremma* :—L. *maritima*, fem. of *maritimus* MARITIME.] Low marshy insalubrious country by the sea shore.

Mareschal, obs. f. MARSHAL.

Mare's nest. 1619. [MARE 1.] Orig. in phr. *to have found a mare's nest*; to imagine that one has discovered something wonderful.

Mare's tail, mares-tail (mēᵊ·ɹztēɪl). 1762. 1. A book-name for aquatic or marsh plants of the N.O. *Halorageæ*, esp. *Hippuris vulgaris*. 2. *pl.* Long straight streaks of cirrus, supposed to foretoken bad weather 1775.

Margaret (mā·ɹgărĕt). ME. [a. OF. *Margarete, -ite* (mod.F. *Marguerite*), ad. late L. *Margarita*, an application of L. *margarita* pearl: see MARGARITE 1.] 1. A female name. †2. A daisy; called also *herb M.* –1640. 3. A variety of apple, and also of pear 1664.

Margaric (maɹgæ·rik), *a.* 1819. [ad. F. *margarique*, f. Gr. μάργαρον = μαργαρίτης pearl + *-ique*, -IC, in reference to the pearly lustre of the crystals or scales.] *Chem.* In **Margaric acid**: †a. orig. the name given by Chevreul to one of the three fatty acids (*oleic, margaric, stearic*), the glyceryl derivs. of which were thought to form the chief constituents of animal fats. So *m. ether*.
It was shown by Heintz in 1852 that the three fatty acids of animal fat are the oleic, palmitic, and stearic, and that the 'margaric' of Chevreul was really a mixture of palmitic and stearic acid.
b. Now, applied to an acid of composition $C_{17}H_{34}O_2$, artificially prepared 1865. Hence **Ma·rgarate**, a salt of m. acid.

Margarin (mā·ɹgărin). Also **-ine.** 1836. [ad. F. *margarine*, f. *margarique* MARGARIC; see -IN [1].] *Chem.* The margarate of glyceryl or glyceride of margaric acid. †**a.** Orig. applied to a fatty substance in certain animal and vegetable oils, supposed to be the glyceride of the 'margaric acid' of Chevreul, really a mixture of stearin and palmitin. **b.** Now, the glyceride of margaric acid in its later application (see prec. b).

Margarine (mā·ɹgărīn, *pop.* māɹdʒərī·n). 1873. [a. F. *margarine*, a misapplication of the chemical term: see prec.] The legal name (by Act 50 and 51 Vict. c. 29) for any substitute for butter made from OLEOMARGARINE (q. v.), and for all substances made in imitation of butter, and offered for sale.

Margaritaceous (māɹgăritēⁱ·ʃəs), *a.* 1826. [f. mod.L. *margaritaceus*, f. *margarita*; see -ACEOUS.] *Nat. Hist.* Pearly.

Margarite [1] (mā·ɹgărəit). *Obs.* exc. *arch.* ME. [a. OF. *margarite* (mod.F. *marguerite*), ad. L. *margarita*, ad. Gr. μαργαρίτης, f. μάργαρον pearl, μάργαρος pearl-oyster + -ίτης; see -ITE [1]. Prob. from some oriental lang.] **1.** A pearl. †**2.** = MARGARET 2.

Margarite [2] (mā·ɹgărəit). 1823. [f. Gr. μάργαρον pearl + -ITE [1].] *Min.* 'Pearl mica', a hydrous silicate found in scales having a pearly lustre.

Margaritic (māɹgări·tik), *a.* 1819. [f. L. *margarita* pearl + -IC.] *Chem. M. acid*: †**a.** used for Chevreul's 'margaric acid' (MARGARIC a); **b.** the name given to one of the fatty acids resulting from the saponification of castor oil.

Margaritiferous (māɹgăriti·fĕrəs), *a.* 1656. [f. L. *margaritifer* (Pliny), f. *margarita*; see -FEROUS.] Producing pearls.

Margarodite (mā·ɹgărŏdəit). 1849. [ad. G. *margarodit*, f. late Gr. μαργαρώδης pearly, f. μάργαρον; see -ITE [1] 2 b.] *Min.* A variety of potash mica having a pearly lustre.

‖ **Margaux** (mā·ɹgōu, Fr. margo). Also †**margose.** 1705. Claret produced in the commune of Margaux (Gironde), France.

Margay (mā·ɹgeⁱ). 1781. [a. F. *margay* (Buffon), altered from *margaia*, repr. inexactly Tupi *mbaracaïa*.] A S. American tiger cat, *Felis tigrina*.

Marge (māɹdʒ), *sb.* Now *poet.* or *rhet.* 1551. [ad. F. *marge*:—L. *marginem* MARGIN.] = MARGIN *sb.* 1, 3.

In-il'd on mighty Neptune's m. DRAYTON.

Margent (mā·ɹdʒĕnt), *sb.* Now *arch.* and *poet.* 1485. [Altered f. MARGIN *sb.*] **1.** = MARGIN *sb.* 1. 1538. **2.** = MARGIN *sb.* 3. 1485. †**b.** The margin of a book as being the place for a commentary or summary; hence the commentary or summary itself 1579–1733. **4.** quasi-*adj.* = marginal 1555.

1. By slow Meander's m. green MILT. 2. b. And what obscur'd in this faire volume lies, Find written in the M. of his eyes SHAKS. Hence †**Margent** *v. trans.* to insert as a marginal note, to add marginal notes to 1610–63.

Margin (mā·ɹdʒin), *sb.* ME. [ad. L. *marginem* (nom. *margo*), cogn. w. MARK *sb.*[1]] **1.** That part of a surface which lies immediately within its boundary; also, the space immediately adjacent to a well, a river, or piece of water; an edge, border, or brink. **b.** *Nat. Hist.* The contour or boundary line of a body, or a distinct border differing in texture, etc. from the main body 1760. **2.** *fig.* **a.** The limit below or beyond which something ceases to be possible or desirable 1863. **b.** An amount (of space, time, money, material, etc.) in addition to what is strictly necessary, serving as a provision for contingencies, or the like 1852. **c.** *Stockbroking* and *Comm.* A certain sum deposited with a broker to cover the risk of loss on a transaction on account 1882. **d.** *Life-insurance.* = LOADING *vbl. sb.* 2. 1881. **3.** The space on a page between the extreme edge and the main body of written or printed matter. Often restricted to the margins at the sides of the page ('inner' and 'outer' margins). ME. **4. a.** *Joinery.* The flat part of the stiles and rails of framed work. **b.** *Building*, etc. That part of a course of slates, plates, etc. which is not covered by the next course 1678.

1. On the M. of a Lake, close to the Edge of the Water 1774. 2. a. No tax can be levied from those who are on the m. of bare subsistence ROGERS. b. The narrow m. of profit ROGERS. *Comb.* **m. draft, draught** = DRAFT *sb.* 6 a.

Margin (mā·ɹdʒin), *v.* 1607. [f. prec. sb. Cf. F. *marginer.*] **1.** *trans.* To furnish with marginal notes. **2.** To specify in the margin of a page 1640. **3.** To provide with a margin, edge, or border 1715. **4.** *Stockbroking.* To deposit a margin upon (stock) 1889.

Marginal (mā·ɹdʒinăl). 1576. [ad. mod.L. *marginalis*, f. *margin-*, *margo*, MARGIN *sb.*] **A.** *adj.* **1.** Written or printed in the margin of a page, as *m. note, reference*; also, having marginal notes. **2.** Pertaining to an edge, border, or boundary; situated at the extreme edge (of an area, etc.) 1658. **3.** That is on the margin below or beyond which something ceases to be possible or desirable 1887.

1. †*M. finger*: a finger or hand set in the margin to call attention to something; hence *fig.* 2. A m. growth of willow and flag BLACK. 3. M. prices 1887.

B. *sb.* A marginal note, reference, or decoration. Now *rare.* 1602. Hence **Ma·rginal** *v. trans.* = MARGENT *v.* **Ma·rginally** *adv.*

‖ **Marginalia** (māɹdʒinēⁱ·liă), *sb. pl.* 1832. [L. neut. pl. of *marginalis* MARGINAL.] Marginal notes.

Marginate (mā·ɹdʒinĕt), *a.* 1777. [ad. L. *marginatus*, *marginare.*] *Nat. Hist.* and *Path.* Having a distinct margin. So **Ma·rginated** *ppl. a.* 1727.

Marginate (mā·ɹdʒineⁱt), *v.* 1609. [f. L. *marginat-*, *marginare.*] †**1.** *trans.* To annotate with marginal notes. **2.** To furnish with a margin or border 1623. Hence **Margina·tion**, a marginated appearance or marking.

Margined (mā·ɹdʒind), *a.* 1826. [f. MARGIN *sb.* or *v.* + -ED.] Chiefly *Nat. Hist.* and *Bot.* Having a margin; marginate. (Often as pple. followed by 'with'.)

Marginicidal (māɹdʒinisəi·dăl), *a.* 1889. [f. L. *margin(i)-*, *margo* + *-cīd-* to cut + -AL.] *Bot.* Dehiscent by the disjunction of the united margins of the carpels.

‖ **Margosa** (maɹgōu·să). 1813. [Short for Pg. *amargosa*, fem. of *amargoso* bitter.] An E. Indian tree, *Melia Azadirachta*, yielding a bitter oil.

Margravate (mā·ɹgrĕvĕt). 1802. [f. next + -ATE [1].] = MARGRAVIATE.

Margrave (mā·ɹgreⁱv). *Hist.* Also **markgrave, mar(k)graf**, etc. 1551. [a. MDu. *markgrave* (mod.Du. *markgraaf*), lit. 'count of a mark or border territory'; see MARK *sb.*[1] and GRAVE *sb.*[3]] A German title, orig. of a military governor of a border province; subseq. the hereditary title of certain princes of the Holy Roman Empire.

Margraviate (māɹgrēⁱ·viˌĕt). 1702. [ad. med.L. **margraviatus*, f. *margravius* MARGRAVE.] The territory ruled by a margrave.

Margravine (mā·ɹgrĕvin). 1692. [a. Du. *markgravin*, fem. of *markgraaf* MARGRAVE.] The wife of a margrave.

Marguerite (mā·ɹgĕrīt). 1866. [a. F. *marguerite* (see MARGARET).] The Ox-eye Daisy, *Chrysanthemum Leucanthemum*; also *C. frutescens* or Paris Daisy. **Blue M.**, *Agathæa* (*Detris*) *cælestis*.

Marian (mēə·riăn), *sb.*[1] 1567. A female name. See also MAID MARIAN.

Marian (mēə·riăn), *a.* and *sb.*[2] 1608. [f. L. *Maria* Mary + -AN.] **A.** *adj.* **1.** Pertaining to the Virgin Mary 1701. **2.** Pertaining to Mary Queen of England or her time (1553–8) 1608. **3.** Relating to Mary Queen of Scots (1542–87) 1902. **B.** *sb.* **1.** A worshipper of the Virgin Mary 1635. **2.** An adherent of Mary Queen of Scots 1893. **3.** An English Roman Catholic of Queen Mary's reign 1899.

A. 2. The M. persecution in England 1608.

Marie, obs. f. MARRY.

†**Mariet.** 1597. [a. F. *Mariette*, f. *Marie* Mary.] The Canterbury Bell, *Campanula Medium* –1658.

Marigenous (mări·dʒĭnəs), *a.* 1599. [f. L. *mare* sea + -GEN + -OUS.] Produced in or by the sea.

Marigold (mæ·rigōuld). ME. [f. MARY (prob. the Virgin Mary) + *gold*, obs. name of the flower.] **1.** The name of several plants having golden or bright yellow flowers. **a.** A plant of the genus *Calendula* (N.O. *Compositæ*), esp. *C. officinalis*, common in country gardens. **b.** Any plant of the genus *Tagetes*, native to S. America and Mexico, and much cultivated in gardens. **African m.**, *T. erecta*; **French m.**, *T. patula*. 1548. **c.** *Chrysanthemum segetum*; usu. CORN-*m.*, also *field, wild, yellow m.* 1578. **d.** *Fig m.* (see FIG *sb.*[1]). Also MARSH MARIGOLD. **2.** A variety of apple (in full *m. apple*). ? *Obs.* 1577.

Comb.: **m. apple** (see 2); **m. bird, finch,** the golden-crested wren or kinglet, *Regulus cristatus*; **m. window** *Arch.*, a rose window.

‖**Marikina** (mærikī·nă). 1774. [repr. Tupi *miriquinā.*] The silky tamarin, *Midas rosalia*.

‖ **Marimba** (mări·mbă). 1704. [Congo.] A kind of xylophone, used by natives in Africa.

‖ **Marimonda** (mærimǫ·ndă). 1758. [Amer. Sp.] A spider-monkey of tropical America, *Ateles belzebuth*.

‖ **Marina** (mărī·nă). Also *erron.* **-o.** 1805. [It. and Sp.] A promenade or esplanade by the sea.

Marinade (mærinēⁱ·d), *sb.* 1704. [a. F. *marinade*, ad. Sp. *marinada*, f. *marinar* to pickle in brine, f. *marino* MARINE *a.*] A pickle, generally composed of wine and vinegar, with herbs and spices, in which fish or meat is steeped; also, the fish or meat thus pickled. So **Ma·rinade** *v.* to steep in m.; to marinate 1682.

Marinate (mæ·rineⁱt), *v.* 1645. [f. prec.: see -ATE [3].] *trans.* To pickle (fish, etc.) with marinade.

Marine (mărī·n). ME. [a. F. *marin* (fem. *-ine*):—L. *marinus*, f. *mare* sea.] **A.** *adj.* **1.** Of or belonging to, found in, or produced by the sea; *Zool.* inhabiting the deep sea, pelagic. †**b.** Of sculptured figures, etc.: Representing sea-gods, fishes, sea-shells, etc. –1741. **c.** Of a painter: That depicts sea subjects 1883. †**2.** Belonging to, or situated at, the sea-side; maritime –1728. **3.** Connected with the sea; pertaining to shipping, a navy, or naval force; relating to naval matters 1551. **4.** Of soldiers: Serving on board ship, as *m. force* 1690. **5.** Used or for use at sea 1704.

1. M. denudation is not equally active at all depths of the sea HUXLEY. *M. rainbow*: a rainbow formed on sea-spray. †*M. acid* (Old Chem.): the acid obtained from m. salt, hydrochloric acid. 3. *M. board*: an establishment at a port for carrying into effect the provisions of the Merchant Shipping Act. *M. insurance*, insurance against perils at sea. 5. *M. barometer, chronometer, galvanometer, watch.* **M. glue**, an adhesive composition used in ship carpentry.

B. *sb.* †**1.** [= F. *marine.*] The sea-coast; a promenade by the sea; also, the country or district near the coast –1703. **2.** [= F. *marine.*] The shipping, fleet, navy, or naval service of a country; sea-going vessels collectively, esp. with reference to nationality or class, as *mercantile m.* (now the chief use) 1669. ‖**3.** The continental counterpart of the English Admiralty (as a department of the government) 1784. **4.** One who serves on board ship. †**a.** A mariner –1634. **b.** A soldier who serves on board a man-of-war; one of a body of troops enlisted to do military service on board ship, at dockyards, etc.; also in *pl.* used collectively 1672. **5.** *Painting.* A sea piece 1846.

1. In the summer time every evening the m. is full with all sorts of people with musick, singing, and dancing 1687. 2. France knew that America had the largest mercantile m. COBDEN. 4. b. *Royal Marines*, troops who serve on British men-of-war. Phr. *Tell that to the marines*: a colloq. expression of disbelief. 5. One of the marines of Salvator RUSKIN.

Marined (mărī·nd), *a.* 1823. [f. MARINE *a.* + -ED.] *Her.* An epithet for an animal that has the lower part of the body like a fish.

Mariner (mæ·rinəɹ). ME. [a. AF. *mariner* = F. *marinier*, f. L. *marinus* MARINE *a.*] **1.** A sailor, seaman; in law, any person employed on a ship. †**2.** = MARINE *sb.* 4 b. 1642–1699.

1. *Master m.*: †a captain of a merchant vessel;

a skilled seaman certified as competent to command a merchant vessel. *Comb.* **mariner's compass, needle** (see these words). Hence †**Ma·rinership,** seamanship 1542–1613.

Marine store(s. 1831. **1.** *pl.* Old ship's materials as an object of merchandise 1831. **2.** *sing.* A shop where such old odds and ends (old iron, bottles, etc.) are sold 1837.

attrib. as *marine store dealer.*

Mariolatry (mēᵊriǫ·lătri). 1612. [f. Gr. Μαρία Mary + λατρεία (see LATRIA, -LATRY), after IDOLATRY.] The idolatrous worship of the Virgin Mary. Hence **Mario·later,** one who practises Mariolatry. **Mario·latrous** *a.* characterized by Mariolatry.

Marionette (mæriǒne·t). 1620. [a. F. *marionnette*, f. *Marion*, dim. of *Marie* MARY; see -ETTE.] **1.** A puppet actuated by strings and used to represent persons (or animals) in action. Also *fig.* **2.** The buffle-headed duck, *Bucephala albeola* 1838. **3.** *attrib.* 1856.

3. The m.-players will please the children JOWETT.

Mariposa lily (mæripǒu·să,li:li). 1882. [f. Sp. *mariposa* butterfly.] A plant of the genus *Calochortus*, native to California and Mexico.

Marish (mæ·riʃ). *poet.* and *dial.* [ME. *mareis, mares*, a. (O)F. *marais* :— med.L. *mariscus*, a. OTeut. **marisko-* MARSH *sb.*] **A.** *sb.* = MARSH. **B.** *adj.* Marshy; such as is produced in a marsh 1543.

A. As Ev'ning Mist Ris'n from a River o're the m. glides MILT. B. ¶App. associated with L. *mare* sea, and hence = salt. Her cheekes o'reflowne With m. teares QUARLES.

Marist (mēᵊ·rist). 1877. [a. F. *Mariste*, f. *Marie* Mary; see -IST.] A member of the Roman Catholic Society of Mary, devoted to the work of foreign missions and to teaching.

Marital (mæ·rităl), *a.* 1603. [ad. L. *maritalis*, f. *maritus* husband; see -AL.] **1.** Pertaining or relating to a husband; husbandly 1616. **2.** Of or pertaining to marriage; matrimonial. Hence **Marita·lity,** excessive affection of a wife for her husband. **Ma·ritally** *adv.* as if married.

Maritime (mæ·ritəim). Also †**-ayne, -an(e, -in(e** (after OF. variant forms). 1550. [ad. L. *maritimus*, f. *mari-*, *mare* sea + suffix *-timus* (as in *finitimus, intimus*, etc.).] **A.** *adj.* **1.** Bordering on the sea; living near the sea-coast 1598. **b.** Living or found near the sea 1608. **2.** Connected with the sea; relating to or dealing with matters of commerce or navigation on the sea 1591. **3.** Of a fighting force: Intended for service at sea 1550. **4.** Of, pertaining to, arising from, or existing in, the sea. Now *rare* or *Obs.* 1624. **5.** Nautical 1743.

1. Brittany (a marittime part of France) SIR T. HERBERT. A m. people 1854. **b.** The coarse m. cabbage 1856. **2. M. insurance** = *marine insurance.* **M. interest,** premium or interest on a bottomry bond. **5.** He was far from having a m. appearance DICKENS.

B. *sb.* †**1.** The sea-coast; a country or district adjoining the sea –1657. †**2.** A person living near the sea 1655.

Marjoram (mā·ɹdʒərəm). late ME. [a. OF. *majorane*, **marjoraine*. Ult. etym. unkn.] Any plant of the genus *Origanum* (N.O. *Labiatæ*); esp. the Wild M., *O. vulgare*, and the Sweet M., *O. Majorana*, an aromatic herb used in cookery.

Mark (māɹk), *sb.*[1] [OE. *mearc*, Anglian *merc*, str. fem., boundary, landmark, sign :—OTeut. **markā*, cogn. w. L. *margo* MARGIN. Early adopted into Romanic (F. *marque*, It. etc. *marca*). Prim. sense prob. 'boundary'.]

I. Boundary. **1.** A boundary, frontier, limit; rarely in *pl.* †territories. *Obs.* exc. *Hist.* or *arch.* **2.** *Hist.* Name in mediæval Germany for the tract of land held in common by a village community. Hence applied to tracts of land similarly held in primitive Teut. times. Also *attrib.*, as in *m.-system*, etc. 1848. **3.** Used to represent G. *Mark* as the name of certain principalities, esp. the Mark of Brandenburg 1726.

2. Each community occupied a territory or m., which was divided into three, or rather four portions 1876.

II. Sign of a boundary, position, etc. †**1.** = LANDMARK **1.** –1697. †**2.** A stone or other monument set up or standing as a memorial, or as a guide –1591. **3.** A target, butt, or other object set up to be aimed at. Hence *transf.* the thing that is aimed at in shooting or throwing. ME. †**b.** The quarry of a hawk, etc. –1691. **c.** *Boxing slang.* The pit of the stomach, the 'wind' 1747. **d.** *fig.* 1549. **e.** *Bowls.* The jack. Also, a proper bowling distance or a position allowed for the jack. 1630. **4.** A post, etc. placed to indicate the terminal point of a race; a goal. Often *fig.*, an object desired. ME. **5.** An object on shore or at sea serving as a guide to travellers, *esp.* a LANDMARK, *leading-mark*, SEA-MARK. Also *fig.* late ME.

1. COVERDALE *Deut.* xxvii. 17. **3.** Do not look from the m. to the arrow and back again 'STONEHENGE'. **d.** A m. to wrath, and hate, and wrong assign'd 1586. Phr. *Easy m.* (colloq.): a thing easily attained. *Beside, far from, near, short of, wide of the m.*; *to hit, miss the m.*, to attain or miss some desired object or end. **4.** Let this be our perpetual marke, to aide all men faithfully 1561. **5.** Men that have past by a Rock at Sea, set up some m., thereby to remember their former danger, and avoid it HOBBES.

III. A sign, indication. **1.** A sign, token, symptom (*of* something) OE. **b.** A characteristic property; a criterion 1522. **c.** *spec.* A depression caused by a fold in the enamel of a horse's incisor tooth, which gives some indication of the age of the animal. Also *m. of mouth.* Also *fig.* late ME. **2.** A sign affixed or impressed for distinction. **a.** A device, stamp, seal, label, brand, inscription, written character, or the like, indicating ownership, quality, etc. ME. **b.** A badge, brand, etc., assumed by or imposed on a person; *occas.* in *pl.* †insignia ME. **c.** A cross, or the like, used by illiterate persons in place of a signature OE. **d.** A written symbol 1737. **e.** (*a*) *Good, bad m.*: a written character used to indicate an instance of good or bad conduct respectively; hence *fig.* a point noted to a person's credit or discredit. (*b*) The unit of the numerical award given by a teacher or examiner to a candidate in a competitive examination, etc. 1829. †**f.** In schools, a badge worn by the pupil who had last committed some particular fault 1832–55. **g.** *Her.* A small charge added to a coat of arms as a sign of distinction; esp. in *m. of* CADENCY 1702. **h.** *Freemasonry.* Used *attrib.* (with reference to sense III. 2 a), to designate a degree, grade, or rank immediately superior to that of a free and accepted mason (see *Combs.*). **3.** A line, dot, object, etc. intended to record or indicate position 1460. **b.** *Naut.* A measured notification on a hand lead-line, indicated by a piece of white, blue, or red bunting, a piece of leather, or a knot 1769. **c.** *fig.* 1765. **d.** *Rugby Football.* The heel-mark on the ground, made by a player who has obtained a fair catch 1867. **4.** A visible trace or impression diversifying a surface, as a line, dot, stain, discoloration, scar, or the like ME. **5.** That which is signified by a mark. †**a.** Those who bear a particular mark or stamp (*fig.*); a person's race, sect, etc. –1555. **b.** A particular brand, make, quality, or size of an article 1488. **c.** *vulgar.* That which suits one's taste 1760. **6.** (*God*) *bless* (or *save*) *the m.*: an exclam., prob. originally a formula to avert an evil omen, and hence used by way of apology for mentioning anything horrible, disgusting, or profane. In mod. literary use (after Shaks.), an expression of impatient scorn. 1591. **7.** A die or stamp for impressing a manufacturer's mark on goods 1797.

1. Is it not a great Marque of Honor? GALE. Marks of Truth, of Falsehood WATTS. **2. a.** The first of these [Hall-marks] was the *King's mark*—a leopard's or lion's head crowned 1885. EAR-, HALL-, TRADE-MARK, q.v. **b.** *God's m., m. of clergy, of holy church*: the tonsure. *M. of the Beast*: see *Rev.* xvi. 2 and BEAST *sb.* 5. **d.** A m. of interrogation (?) 1862. **3.** *Plimsoll's m.*: a load-line required by the Merchant Shipping Act, 1876, to be placed upon the hull of a British vessel. *To be above, beneath, near, under, up to, within the m.*: to be above (etc.) a fixed or recognized standard. *Athletics.* A line indicating the starting-point. **4.** *To leave, make a m.*: to leave or make a permanent, important, or obvious impression. *To make one's m.*: to attain distinction. **5. a.** Moore wikkednesse Than all the m. of Adam may redresse CHAUCER.

IV. Remark, notice. †**1.** Attention, notice –1823. **2.** *Of m.*: noteworthy, important, conspicuous. Also *of great, little*, etc. *m.* 1590.

2. A fellow of no marke, nor likelyhood SHAKS.

V. *attrib.* and *Comb.*: **m.-boat,** a boat moored at a particular spot as a sea-mark; **m.-book,** a book for recording marks; **-lodge,** a lodge of mark masons; **m. man, m. mason, m. master** (mason), a freemason holding a certain rank in mark masonry (cf. III. 2 h); **m. tooth,** the tooth of a horse containing the m. (cf. III. 1 c); **-vessel** = *mark-boat.*

Mark (māɹk), *sb.*[2] [Found in all Teut. and Rom. langs.; late OE. *marc* neut.] **1.** A denomination of weight (chiefly for gold and silver); usu. regarded as = 8 ounces. Now used only to represent its continental equivalent. **2.** A money of account, orig. representing the value of a mark weight of pure silver. **a.** In England, = 13*s.* 4*d.* or ⅔ of the £ sterling. *Obs.* exc. *Hist.* OE. **b.** In Scotland, = 13*s.* 4*d.* Scots, = 13⅓*d.* English. 1480. **c.** Repr. the continental word in its various forms, as a name of foreign moneys of account 1475. **3.** As the name of a coin. **a.** In Scotland, a coin worth 13*s.* 4*d.* Scots. *Obs.* exc. *Hist.* 1480. **b.** Used as the name of various coins on the Continent, *esp.* a silver coin of the German Empire first issued in 1875, and formerly worth slightly less than the Eng. shilling 1727.

Mark (māɹk), *v.* [OE. *mearcian* :—OTeut. **markōjan*, f. **markā* MARK *sb.*[1] Some senses are due to F. *marquer.*]

I. To put a mark upon. **1.** *trans.* To trace out boundaries for; to plot out (ground); to set out the ground plan of (a building); *fig.* to plan out, design. Also with *out.* **2.** To make a mark or marks on (anything) OE. Also *absol.* **b.** *spec.* To put an identifying mark on linen, etc. 1530. **c.** *Comm.* To attach to (an article) figures or signs indicating the price 1894. **d.** *pass.* To have or bear natural marks. Also *fig.* ME. **3.** To form or portray by making marks ME. **4.** *fig.* To designate as if by placing a mark upon; to destine. †Also with complement, to designate as being (so and so). OE. Also with *out.* **b.** To separate *from* something else as by a line or distinctive mark. Now chiefly with *off.* 1703. **5.** To express or indicate by marks or signs OE. **b.** In games: To record (the points gained by the players). Chiefly *absol.*, and in phr. *to m. the game.* 1816. **c.** Of a graduated instrument: To show, register (so many degrees, etc.) 1882. **6.** In immaterial sense: **a.** To make perceptible by some indication 1904. **b.** To manifest (one's approval, displeasure, etc.) by some act, or by reward or punishment 1791. **7.** To be a mark of or upon 1687. **b.** *pass.* Of lines, features, etc.: To be (more or less) strikingly noticeable 1824. **c.** To be a distinguishing mark or feature of. Often *pass.*, to be characterized, distinguished, or made remarkable (now only const. *by*) 1661. **8.** *Mil.* **a.** To indicate the pivots, formations, etc. in military evolutions 1796. **b.** *To m. time*: to move the feet as in marching, but without advancing. Also *transf.* and *fig.* 1833.

2. My bodie's mark'd With Roman Swords SHAKS. I can get no pen that will m. SHELLEY. **c.** Phr. *To m. down*: to label (goods) with a lower figure; to reduce the indicated price of. So *To m. up*: to mark at a higher price. **4.** If we are markt to die SHAKS. Melancholy mark'd him for her own GRAY. **5.** He draws the chart and marks the sunken reefs 1879. **b.** One large round one [counter] that marks 500 'CAVENDISH'. Phr. *To m. up* (colloq.): to add (an item) to an existing tavern score; hence, to give credit for. **6. a.** To m. the..accent by a..prolongation of the first note of the bar 1904. **7.** Wolf's coming to Halle in 1783..marks an era [etc.] M. ARNOLD. **c.** No triumph—no exultation..marks her manner COWDEN CLARKE.

II. †**1.** To direct (one's way). Also *refl.* and *intr.* to proceed, advance. –1596. †**2.** To aim a blow or missile at; to strike, hit –1529.

III. 1. To notice or keep the eye upon; to observe. Now *poet.* and *rhet.* ME. **2.** To consider; to give heed or attention to. Often with *well.* ME. **3.** *Sport.* **a.** *trans.* To note and keep in mind the spot to which (the game) has retired after being 'put up'. Also *to m. down.* 1450. **b.** *Football.* To keep close to (an opponent) in order to hamper him if he receives the ball 1887. **4.** *absol.* or *intr.* To take notice; to fix (one's) attention; to consider. Occas.: To ascertain by observation (*what, whether*, etc.). 1526.

1. So near that..I could m. him well, Myself unseen

WORDSW. She quickened her pace to m. him in the glory of the battle MEREDITH. 2. Marke the perfect man, and behold the vpright: for the end of that man is peace *Ps.* xxxvii. 37. 4. Marke, I pray you, and see how this man seeketh mischiefe 1 *Kings* xx. 7.

Marked (mā·ɹkt), *ppl. a.* OE. [f. MARK *sb.*[1] and *v.* + -ED.] 1. Having a visible mark. Also, affixed as a mark; expressed by a mark. 2. *Marked man*: one whose doings are watched with suspicion or hostility 1833. 3. Easy to distinguish or recognize 1795.

m. bar, a particular form of pig-iron; **m. iron** = *marked bar*; **m. proof**, an impression of an engraving in which some detail is left unfinished as a mark of an early state of the plate. Hence **Markedly** (mā·ɹkėdli) *adv.*, **-ness.**

Marker (ma·ɹkəɹ). 1486. [f. MARK *v.* + -ER[1].] 1. One who marks (see MARK *v.*). a. One who marks game. b. One who records the score in games, esp. billiards, or at target practice 1532. 2. An implement for marking 1725. 3. A book-marker 1852. 4. *U.S.* A tablet or other permanent memorial 1906.

Market (mā·ɹkėt), *sb.* [Late OE. *market*, a. ONF. *market*:—L. *mercatus*, f. *mercari* to trade; see MERCANTILE. Early adopted into Teut. langs.] 1. The meeting together of people for the purchase and sale of provisions or live stock, publicly exposed, at a fixed time and place; the time of this; also, the company assembled. 2. *Law.* The privilege granted to the lord of a manor, a municipality or other body, to establish a meeting of persons to buy and sell OE. 3. An open space or covered building in which cattle, provisions, etc. are exposed for sale; a market-place, market-house ME. 4. The action or business of buying and selling; a purchase or sale; a (good or bad) bargain (*lit.* and *fig.*). *Obs.* exc. as in phrases (see below). 1525. †b. The marketing *of* (a commodity) -1680. 5. Sale as controlled by supply and demand; hence, demand 1689. 6. Opportunity of buying or selling 1684. 7. Price in the market, market value. Also *fig.* 1535. 8. A place or seat of trade; a country, district, etc. in which there is a demand for articles of trade; hence, the trade of such a country, etc. 1615.

1. †*High m.*: the time when the m. is busiest. *fig.* Sell when you can, you are not for all markets SHAKS. Phr. *To bring to m.*: to offer for sale (*lit.* and *fig.*). *To bring one's eggs* (or *one's hogs*) *to a bad m.*: to fail in one's schemes. *M. overt* (in *Law*): open m.; the exposal of vendible goods in an open place so that any one who passes by may see them. 4. The Juncto ..willing to make the best of a bad m., prepare for war 1660. *To make a* or *one's market of* (something): to make (it) an object of bargaining or profit. *To mar another's*, or *one's own m.*: to spoil his or one's own trade (*lit.* and *fig.*). *To mend one's m.*: to improve one's bargain. b. *Haml.* IV. iv. 34 (Qo. 2). 5. The extra quantity can only find a m., by calling forth an additional demand equal to itself MILL. Phr. *To make a m.* (Stock Exchange): to induce active dealing in a stock or shares, by being both a buyer and a seller at about the same price; to bring an enterprise to the notice of the public by interesting dealers in it (by means of options or otherwise) 1899. 6. Phr. *To lose one's m.*: to miss one's chance of doing business. *To overstand one's m.*: to stand out about terms till the opportunity is lost. *The m.*: the particular trade or traffic in the commodity specified in the context. Chiefly *in* or *on the m.* *To be in the m.*: (of a person) to be a buyer; (of a possession) to be offered for sale (so *to come into the m.*). *To engross the m.*: to buy up the stock of any commodity in order to sell it again at an enhanced price. 7. These lands at present would sell at a low m. BURKE. 8. Wars for a m. 1891.

Comb.: **m. bell**, a bell rung to announce the commencement of a m.; **m. cross**, a cross erected in a m.-place; **-custom**, the dues levied on goods brought to m.; **-garden**, a piece of land on which vegetables are grown for the m.; hence *m.-gardener*; **m. man**, one who deals in a m.; **-place, square**, a square or wide open space where a m. is held; **-rate**, the current value of a commodity; **-stead** *arch.* = *market-place*; **m. town**, a town which has the privilege of holding a m.; **-value**, saleable value.

Market (mā·ɹkėt), *v.* 1455. [f. prec. sb.] 1. *trans.* To sell; also, to bring or send to market. 2. *intr.* To buy and sell in a market; to go to market with produce; to purchase provisions 1635.

1. The Treasurer..for a Price Mercates his Maister, to extend his Purse G. DANIEL.

Marketable (mā·ɹkėtăb'l), *a.* 1600. [f. prec. + -ABLE.] 1. Capable of being marketed; that finds a ready market; saleable. 2. Concerned with trade. Of price, value: That may be obtained in buying or selling. 1602.

1. One of them Is a plaine Fish, and no doubt m. SHAKS. Unpossessed of any m. talent 1851. 2. To enlarge the m. area by [etc.] 1872.

Marketeer (mārkėtīᵊ·ɹ). *U.S.* 1832. [See -EER.] One who sells in a market.

Marketer (mā·ɹkėtəɹ). *U.S.* 1787. [f. MARKET *v.* + -ER[1].] One who goes to market; one who buys or sells in a market.

Marketing (mā·ɹkėtiŋ), *vbl. sb.* 1561. [f. MARKET *v.* + -ING[1].] 1. The action of MARKET *v.* 2. a. Something bought in the market 1701. b. Produce to be sold in the market; also, a consignment of such produce 1886.

‖ **Markhor(e** (mā·ɹkǫɹ). Also **markhoor.** 1867. [Pers. *mārkhōr*, lit. 'serpent-eater'.] A large wild goat (*Capra falconeri*), of N. India.

Marking (mā·ɹkiŋ), *vbl. sb.* ME. [f. MARK *v.* + -ING[1].] 1. The action of MARK *v.* 2. *concr.* A mark or pattern of marks ME.

1. I doe confesse much of the hearing of it, but little of the m. of it SHAKS.

attrib. and *Comb.*: **m. board**, (*a*) a board for registering the score in certain games; (*b*) a board in the Stock Exchange upon which transactions are posted; **m. ink**, (*a*) an indelible ink for marking linen, etc.; (*b*) a mixture for marking packing-cases with a stencil, etc.; **m. iron**, a branding iron; **m.-nut**, the fruit of the tree *Semecarpus Anacardium*, the juice of which makes an indelible black stain on linen, etc.

Markis, etc., obs. var. of MARQUIS, etc.

Marksman (mā·ɹksmæ̆n). 1660. [f. *mark's*, genitive of MARK *sb.*[1] + MAN *sb.*] 1. One skilled or practised in aiming at a mark; *spec.* one who reaches a certain recognized degree of proficiency in rifle practice. 2. One who makes a mark in place of a signature 1777. Earlier †**Ma·rkman** 1577–1654.

2. The..drover who signed the contract was a m. 1885. Hence **Ma·rksmanship**, the function, quality, or art of a m.

Ma·rkworthy, *a.* 1827. [f. MARK *sb.*[1] + WORTHY *a.*, after G. *merkwürdig*.] Worthy of note.

Marl (māɹl), *sb.* late ME. [a. OF. *marle* (in mod.F. repl. by *marne*):—late L. *margila*, dim. of L. *marga*, said by Pliny to be a Gaulish wd.] 1. A kind of soil consisting principally of clay mixed with carbonate of lime, valuable as a fertilizer. 2. *poet.* Used generically for: Earth 1590.

1. **Red m.**: (*a*) m. of a red colour; (*b*) reddle; (*c*) *Geol.* the New Red Sandstone. *Burning m.*: used symbolically, after Milton, in ref. to the torments of hell (*P. L.* I. 296).

Comb.: **m.-grass**, Zigzag Clover, *Trifolium medium*; also Red Clover, *T. pratense*; **-stone** *Geol.*, argillaceous and ferruginous limestone, which lies between the upper and lower Lias of England.

Hence **Marla·ceous, Ma·rly** *adjs.* resembling, composed of, or abounding in m.

Marl (māɹl), *v.*[1] late ME. [f. MARL *sb.* Cf. F. *marner*.] To apply marl to (ground); to fertilize with marl.

fig. Marl'd with bleaching bones H. COLERIDGE.

Marl (māɹl), *v.*[2] 1425. [a. Du. and LG. *marlen*, app. a frequent. f. MDu. *merren* to tie.] *Naut.* To fasten with marline; to secure *together* by a succession of half-hitches; to wind marline or other small stuff round (a rope), securing it with a hitch at each turn. Orig. in **Ma·rling** *vbl. sb.* used *attrib.* in *m.-cord, -line, -twine* = MARLINE.

Marled (māɹld), *ppl. a.* 1603. Chiefly *Sc.* Also **merled.** [Cf. OF. *merellé*.] Marbled, spotted, streaked. So **Marl** *a.*

Marline (mā·ɹlin). Also **marling**, etc. 1417. [a. Du. *marlijn* (f. *marren* to bind + *lijn* LINE *sb.*[2]).] *Naut.* Small line of two strands, used for seizings.

Marline-spike, marlinspike (mā·ɹlinspəik). 1626. [orig. app. *marling-spike*, f. *marling* vbl. sb. (f. MARL *v.*[2]) + SPIKE *sb.*] 1. *Naut.* An iron tool tapering to a point, used to separate the strands of rope in splicing, as a lever in marling, etc. 2. A sailor's name for a tropic bird (*Phaethon*) and a jäger or skua-gull (*Stercorarius*), in allusion to the two long pointed tail-feathers 1867.

Marlite (mā·ɹləit). Also **-yte.** 1794. [f. MARL *sb.* + -ITE[2].] *Min.* A variety of marl which resists the action of the air. Hence **Marli·tic** *a.*

Marl-pit (mā·ɹlpit). late ME. [f. MARL *sb.*] A pit from which marl is dug.

Marmalade (mā·ɹmălėᵗd). 1480. [a. F. *marmelade*, a. Pg. *marmelada*, f. *marmelo* quince, repr. L. *melimelum*, a. Gr., f. μέλι honey + μῆλον apple.] 1. A preserve made by boiling fruits (orig. quinces, now usu. Seville oranges) with sugar. 2. The fruit of *Lucuma mammosa*; also, the tree itself. Also called *natural m.* 1797.

attrib. **m.-tree**, the mammee-sapota (see sense 2).

Marmarosis (māɹmărōᵘ·sis). 1882. [f. Gr. μάρμαρος marble + -OSIS.] *Geol.* The conversion of limestone into marble by metamorphism. So **Ma·rmarize** *v.* to subject to m. 1893.

Marmolite (mā·ɹmŏləit). 1822. [Referred to Gr. μαρμαίρειν to shine; see -LITE.] *Min.* A laminated serpentine, of a pearly lustre and pale green colour.

Marmoraceous (māɹmŏrēᵗ·ʃəs), *a.* 1822. [f. L. *marmor* MARBLE; see -ACEOUS.] Pertaining to, or like, marble.

Marmorate (mā·ɹmŏrēᵗt), *a.* 1537. [ad. L. *marmoratus*, *marmorare*, f. *marmor*.] †1. Overlaid with marble. 2. *Nat. Hist.* Variegated or veined like marble 1826.

Marmoreal (maɹmōᵊ·rĭăl), *a.* *poet.* and *rhet.* 1798. [f. L. *marmoreus* (f. *marmor*) + -AL.] 1. Resembling marble or a marble statue. 2. Made of marble 1825.

2. Minaret And terrace and m. spire 1880.

Marmorize, *v.* 1897. [f. L. *marmor* + -IZE.] = MARMARIZE.

Marmose (mā·ɹmoᵘs). 1774. [a. F. *marmose* (Buffon), perh. from colonial Du.] One of several species of small S. Amer. opossums which have only a rudimentary pouch and carry their young on their back.

Marmoset (mā·ɹmŏzet). late ME. [a. OF. *marmouset* grotesque image; origin obscure.] †1. A grotesque figure -1736. 2. †a. In early use: Any small monkey. b. Now restricted to the tropical Amer. monkeys of the family *Hapalidæ* (or *Mididæ*), comprising two genera, *Hapale* (the true marmosets) and *Midas* (the tamarins). †3. Applied: a. to a woman or child; cf. *monkey* -1754. b. to a man, as a term of abuse or contempt; cf. *ape*. Occas. (as in OF.) a favourite. -1825.

2. I have seen her..as changeful as a marmozet SCOTT.

Marmot (mā·ɹmǫt). 1607. [ad. F. *marmotte* fem., prob. an altered form of Romansch *murmont*:—L. **murem montis* 'mountain mouse'.] A rodent of the genus *Arctomys* or subfamily *Arctomyinæ* of the squirrel family, esp. *A. marmotta*, sometimes called the Alpine marmot. Also applied (with qualification) to other animals of the same or allied genera.

‖ **Marocain** (mæ·rŏkēᵗn). 1922. [F. *marocain*, f. *Maroc* Morocco.] A dress fabric of wool, silk, or cotton, having a wavy texture.

Maronite (mæ·rŏnəit). 1511. [ad. late L. *Maronita*, f. *Maron* name of the Syrian founder of the sect (4th c.); see -ITE[1].] One of a sect of Syrian Christians, dwelling in Lebanon and Anti-Lebanon; orig. Monothelites, but subseq. united with the Roman Church.

Maroon (mărū·n), *sb.*[1] and *a.* 1594. [a. F. *marron*, ad. It. *marrone*.] A. *sb.* †1. A large kind of sweet chestnut native to Southern Europe; also, the tree bearing this -1699. 2. [= F. *marron*.] A particular kind of brownish-crimson or claret colour 1791. 3. A firework composed of a small cubical box of pasteboard, wrapped round with twine and filled with gunpowder; it explodes with a report like that of a cannon 1749. B. *adj.* Of the colour described in A. 2. 1843.

Maroon (mărū·n), *sb.*[2] 1666. [a. F. *marron*, said to be a corruption of Sp. *cimarrón* wild, untamed.] 1. One of a class of negroes, orig. fugitive slaves, living in the mountains and forests of Dutch Guiana and the West Indies. 2. A person who is marooned 1883.

Maroon (mărū·n), *v.* 1699. [f. prec.] †1. *pass.* or *intr.* To be lost in the wilds. DAMPIER.

2. *trans.* To put (a person) ashore and leave him on a desolate island or coast (as was done by the buccaneers) by way of punishment 1724. **3.** *transf.* To leave in a position from which one cannot get away: said e.g. of floods 1910. **4.** *Southern U.S.* To camp out for several days on a pleasure party 1777. **5.** To 'hang about' 1808.

4. Marooning differs from pic-nicing in this—the former continues several days, the other lasts but one HALIBURTON. Hence **Maroo·ner**, a pirate; one who is marooned (sense 2); one who goes marooning (sense 4).

†**Maroquin**, *a.* and *sb.* 1511. [a. F. *maroquin*, orig. an adj. 'pertaining to Morocco', f. *Maroc* Morocco.] **a.** *adj.* (in *m. skins, leather*; also with sense 'made of morocco') = MOROCCO *a.* **b.** *sb.* Morocco leather. -1823.

Marplot (mā·ɹ₁plǫt). 1708. [See MAR-.] **a.** *sb.* One who mars or defeats a plot or design by officious interference. Said also of things. **b.** *adj.* That mars or defeats a plot or design 1850.

Marprelate: see MAR-.

Marque (māɹk). 1419. [a. F. *marque*, ad. Pr. *marca*, vbl. sb. f. *marcar* (med.L. *marcare*) to seize as a pledge.] †**1.** Reprisals; occas. = *letter of m.* (see 2) -1614. **2. Letter of marque. a.** Usu. pl., *letters of m.* (*and reprisal*). Orig., a licence granted by a sovereign to a subject, authorizing him to make reprisals on the subjects of a hostile state for injuries done to him by the enemy's army. Hence, later, a licence to fit out an armed vessel or privateer and employ it in the capture of the merchant shipping of the enemy's subjects, the holder of letters of marque being entitled by international law to commit against the hostile nation acts which would otherwise have been condemned as piracy. (Abolished in European nations by the Congress of Paris in 1856) 1447. **b.** A ship carrying letters of marque; a privateer 1800.

Marquee (maɹkī·). 1690. [f. F. *marquise*, apprehended as pl.; cf. MARQUISE 3.] A large tent, as an officer's field-tent, or one used at an entertainment, or the like. Also *attrib.*, as *m. tent*, etc.

Marquetry, marqueterie (mā·ɹkĕtri). 1563. [a. F. *marqueterie*, f. *marqueter* to variegate, f. *marque* MARK *sb.*[1]] Inlaid work, esp. as used for the decoration of furniture.

Marquis, marquess (mā·ɹkwis, -ĕs). ME. [a. OF. *marchis*, later *marquis*; f. Com. Rom. **marca* (see MARCH *sb.*[3], MARK *sb.*[1]) frontier, frontier territory + -ESE. The wd. is thus orig. an adj. qualifying a sb. repr. by Eng. COUNT, so that the title = MARGRAVE. The med.L. form was *marchionem* (*marchio*); cf. *marchioness*.] **1.** Orig., the title of the ruler of certain territories ('marches' or frontier districts) in various European countries. Later, in Romanic-speaking countries, a mere title indicating rank immediately below that of duke and above that of count. **2.** As an English title it designates a specific degree of the peerage, between those of duke and earl. When a duke is also a marquis, his second title is given by courtesy to his eldest son; thus the eldest son of the Duke of Devonshire is called 'the Marquis of Hartington'. late ME.

Marquisate (mā·ɹkwisět). 15... [f. MARQUIS + -ATE[1], after F. *marquisat*, etc.] **1.** The dignity or status of a marquis. Also, †a place from which the title is taken. **2.** In various European countries: The territorial lordship or possessions of a marquis or margrave 1591. So †**Ma·rquisdom**, †**Ma·rquisship**.

‖**Marquise** (maɹkī·z, Fr. markīz). 1706. [F., fem. of *marquis*.] **1.** = MARCHIONESS. Only as a title of foreign nobility. 1894. **2.** A kind of pear 1706. **3.** = MARQUEE 1783. **4.** In full *m. ring*: A finger-ring set with a pointed oval cluster of gems 1885.

Marquois (mā·ɹkwoiz). 1788. [f. name of inventor.] Used *attrib.* in *m. scale* (*and triangle*), an apparatus for drawing equidistant parallel lines with speed and accuracy. Sometimes written *Marquoi's*, *Marquois's*.

Marram (mæ·rəm). *local.* 1640. [a. ON. *maralm-r*, f. *mar-r* sea + *halm-r* HAULM.] **1.** The Sea Reed or Bent Grass (*Psamma arenaria*), which binds together the sands on the shores of N. Europe. Also *m.-grass*, *sea-m.* **2.** A sand-hill grown over with this grass 1834.

Marrer (mā·rəɹ). late ME. [f. MAR *v.* + -ER[1].] One who mars; a destroyer, injurer, spoiler.

Marriable (mæ·riăb'l), *a.* Now *rare.* 1440. [a. OF. *mariable*, f. *marier*.] That may be married; in early use = MARRIAGEABLE.

Marriage (mæ·rĕdʒ). [ME. *mariage*, a. F. :—pop. L. **maritaticum*, f. *maritus*; see MARITAL *a.* and -AGE.] **1.** The relation between married persons; wedlock. **2.** The action, or an act, of marrying; the ceremony by which two persons are made husband and wife ME. **b.** A wedding feast. *Obs.* or *arch.* ME. **3.** A particular matrimonial union 1473. †**b.** *concr.* A person viewed as a prospective husband or wife; a (good or bad) match -1621. **4.** *transf.* and *fig.* Intimate union. late ME. †**5.** A dowry -1587. **6.** *Cards.* In bezique, etc., the declaration of a king and queen of the same suit 1861.

1. Nor does he dishonour M. that praises Virginity DONNE. Phr. *In m.* (now arch.): in the matrimonial state. *To give, take in m.*: to give, take as husband or wife. *Communal m.* (Anthropol.): the system by which within a small community all the men are regarded as married to all the women; sometimes called *group m.* *Plural m.*: polygamy. 2. *Civil m.*: a m. performed by an officer of the state, without religious ceremony. *Fleet m.*: see FLEET *sb.*[2] *Scotch m.*: a marriage by a mutual declaration before witnesses, without other formality. b. Iesus was called also and his disciples vnto the mariage TINDALE *John* ii. 2. 3. *Cross m.*: the m. of a man to the sister of his sister's husband. 4. The m. of verse and tune T. HARDY.

attrib. and *Comb.*: **M. Act**, any of the Acts of Parliament regulating marriages, e.g. 4 Geo. IV. c. 76, 6 & 7 Will. IV. c. 85, etc.; **m. articles**, an antenuptial agreement by the parties with respect to rights of property and succession; **m. brokage, brokerage**, consideration given for bringing about a m. (contracts for which are void by English law); **m. licence**, an official permission to marry (in England, a document granted by the ordinary or his surrogate, authorizing a couple to be married without the proclamation of banns); **m. lines**, a certificate of m.; **m. portion**, a portion or dowry, etc., given to a bride at her m.; **m. settlement**, an arrangement made by deed in consideration of an intended m., whereby certain property is secured for the wife, and sometimes also for the children.

Marriageable (mæ·rĕdʒăb'l), *a.* 1555. [f. prec. + -ABLE.] Of persons: Fit for marriage, of an age to marry. **b.** *transf.*, esp. of the vine 1663. **c.** Of age, etc.: Befitting marriage or the married state 1597.

Marriage-bed. 1590. The bed used by a married couple; hence *transf.* marital intercourse, with its rights and duties.

To defile, violate the m.: to commit adultery.

Married (mæ·rid), *ppl. a.* ME. [f. MARRY *v.* + -ED[1].] **1.** United in wedlock; also *fig.* **2.** Pertaining to persons so united or to matrimony 1588.

1. What says the m. woman? SHAKS. 2. M. Life; a comedy BUCKSTONE (*title*).

Marrier (mæ·ri₁əɹ). 1589. [f. MARRY *v.* + -ER[1].] One who marries (in various senses).

Marron, var. of MAROON *sb.*[1]

‖**Marron glacé** (ma·roṅ gla·se). [F., = iced chestnut.] A sweetmeat consisting of a chestnut coated with icing sugar.

Marrow[1] (mæ·rou). [Com. Teut.: OE. *mearg*, *mearh* neut. :—OTeut. **mazgo-*.] **1.** The soft vascular fatty substance usually contained in the cavities of bones. **b.** The substance forming the spinal cord. Now always *spinal m.* late ME. †**c.** Used (chiefly after L. *medulla*) for: The pith (of a plant); the pulp (of a fruit). Also *m. of wheat* = *medulla tritici* (Vulg.), the finest flour. -1793. **2.** *fig.* **a.** As the type of rich food. late ME. **b.** As the seat of vitality and strength. late ME. **c.** The inmost part. late ME. **d.** The vital part; the essence; the 'goodness'. Often *pith and m.* 1530. **3. Vegetable m.**: **a.** A kind of gourd, the fruit of *Cucurbita ovifera* 1816. **b.** The fruit of the avocado 1763. **4.** A marrow-fat pea 1882.

1. The very m. in my bones is cold DICKENS. 2. a. My soule shall be satisfied as with m. and fatnesse *Ps.* lxiii. 5. b. The pith and m. of manhood 1848. d. The very M., Life and Sum of all their Teaching BUNYAN.

attrib. and *Comb.*, as **m. pea** = *marrowfat pea*; **m.-spoon**, a spoon for extracting the m. from bones. Hence **Ma·rrowless** *a.* having no m. (*lit.* and *fig.*). **Ma·rrowy** *a.* of the nature of, or full of, m.

Marrow[2] (mæ·rou). *Obs.* exc. *dial.* 1440. [?] **1.** A companion, partner, mate. **2.** A husband or wife 1578. **3.** One's equal or like; one's match in a contest 1548. **4.** A thing which makes a pair with another 1674.

2. Busk ye, busk ye, my bony bony bride, Busk ye, busk ye, my winsome m. 1724.

Marrowbone (mæ·roubōun). late ME. [f. MARROW[1].] **1.** A bone containing edible marrow. Also *fig.* **2.** *pl.* Jocularly: The knees. (Rarely *sing.*) 1532. **3.** *pl.* = CROSS-BONES 1832. **4.** *pl.* (*slang.*) Fists as weapons; pugilists 1625. **5.** *attrib.*, as *m.-pie*, etc.

Marrowfat (mæ·roufæt). 1733. [f. MARROW[1] + FAT *sb.*[2]] (More fully *m. pea.*) A kind of large rich pea.

Marrowsky (mărau·ski). 1863. [f. proper name.] A deformed language in which the initial consonants of contiguous words are transposed.

Marry (mæ·ri), *v.* ME. [a. F. *marier* :—L. *maritare*, f. *maritus* ppl. adj., married, f. *mari-* (*mas*) man, male.] **I.** *trans.* **1.** To join in wedlock; to constitute as man and wife according to the laws and customs of a nation. Const. *to*; also *together*. **b.** Said of the priest or functionary who performs the rite. Also *absol.* 1530. **2.** To give in marriage. Said esp. of a parent or guardian. ME. **3.** Said of either contracting party: To take in marriage. (Now the familiar use.) late ME. †**4.** *refl.* and *reciprocal.* -1818. **5.** *transf.* and *fig.* To unite intimately 1526. **b.** *Naut.* To fasten (two ropes) end to end, in such a way that the joining may not prevent their being drawn through a block 1815. Also, to place (two ropes) together so that they may be hauled on at the same time 1867. **c.** *Cards.* In bezique, etc. Of the king or queen, *To be married*: to be declared as held in the same hand with the queen or king of the same suit 1870.

1. The King was maried secreetlie at Chelsey..to one Jane Seymor 1536. b. Come sister, you shall be the Priest, and marrie vs SHAKS. 2. Good mother, do not m. me to yond foole SHAKS. 3. He married a Woman of great Beauty and Fortune ADDISON. 4. Ah me! when shall I m. me? Lovers are plenty; but fail to relieve me GOLDSM. 5. Soft Lydian Aires, Married to immortal verse MILT.

II. *intr.* **a.** To wed; to take a husband or wife. Const. *with*; occas. *to.* ME. **b.** *transf.* and *fig.* To enter into intimate union; to join, so as to form one 1508.

a. Marrying in hast, and Repenting at leisure 1614. b. By that old bridge..where the waters m. TENNYSON.

Marry (mæ·ri), *int.* *Obs.* exc. *arch.* or *dial.* ME. [Orig., the name of the Virgin MARY used as an oath or an ejaculation.] An exclam. of asseveration, surprise, indignation, etc. **a.** Simply. (Often in answering a question: = 'why, to be sure'.) **b.** With interjection or exclamatory phrase 1590.

a. M., hang the idiot..to bring me such stuff GOLDSM. b. *M. come up*: used to express indignant or amused surprise or contempt: = 'hoity-toity' 1592. Marrie come vp I trow, Is this the Poultis for my aking bones? SHAKS.

Mars (māɹz). late ME. [a. L. *Mars* (stem *Mart-*), app. reduced f. *Mavors* (*Mavort-*).] **1.** The Roman god of war. Often used for: Warfare, warlike prowess, fortune in war. **b.** *allusively.* A great warrior 1569. **2.** *Astron.* The fourth planet in the order of distance from the sun, revolving in an orbit lying between that of the Earth and Jupiter. late ME. †**b.** *Old Chem.* The name of the metal iron -1758. †**c.** *Her.* The name for the tincture gules in blazoning by the names of the heavenly bodies 1572. **d.** = *Mars yellow*: see below 1899.

1. An eye like M., to threaten or command SHAKS. *Mars' hill, hill of M.*, the Areopagus at Athens. b. *Rich. II*, II. iii. 101. *Comb.* **M. colours**, as *brown, red, violet, yellow*, pigments prepared from earths, and coloured with iron oxide.

‖**Marsala** (maɹsā·lă). 1806. [Name of a town in Sicily.] (More fully *M. wine.*) A class of white wines resembling a light sherry, exported from Marsala.

‖ **Marseillais** (marseyę), *a.* (*sb.*) 1686. [Fr., f. *Marseille* Marseilles; see -ESE.] Of or pertaining to (Inhabitants of) Marseilles.

‖ **Marseillaise** (marseyę̄z, maɹsėlē·z). 1826. [Fr., fem. of prec.] The national song of the French Republic, composed by Rouget de l'Isle in 1792; so named from having been first sung in Paris by Marseilles 'patriots'.

†**Marseilles** (mąɹsē·lz). 1762. [English name of *Marseille*, a seaport in southern France.] A stiff cotton fabric, similar to piqué. Also *M. quilting*.

Marsh (māɹʃ). [OE. *męrsc, męrisc* masc.; repr. W.Ger. **marisk-* (whence med.L. *mariscus*), f. OTeut. **mari-* sea, lake, MERE *sb.*[1]; see -ISH.[1] See also MARISH.] A tract of low-lying land, usually flooded in winter and more or less watery at all times.

There were meruaylouse great marshes and daungerous passages LD. BERNERS.

attrib. and *Comb.* 1. General: *m.-ground, -miasmata*, etc.; *m.-birds, -flies, -herbs*, etc.; *m.-dweller, -dwelling* adj.

2. Special: **m. fever**, malaria fever; **m.-fire, -light**, a will-o'-the-wisp; †**-wall**, a dike.

b. In names of animals inhabiting marshes, as **m. blackbird**, the American red-winged starling, *Agelæus phœniceus*; **m. deer**, a S. American deer, *Cariacus paludosus*; **m. diver**, ? the Water Rail, *Rallus aquaticus*; **-goose**, the greylag goose, *Anser cinereus*; **m. harrier**, the moor buzzard, *Circus æruginosus*; **m. hawk**, the American marsh harrier, *C. hudsonius*; **m. hen**, the moor-hen, *Gallinula chloropus*; *U.S.* applied to other rails, esp. *Rallus elegans* and *R. crepitans*; **m. hog** *Palæont.*, a variety of the pig of which the remains are found in the Swiss lake-villages; **m. quail** *U.S.*, the meadow lark, *Sturnella magna*; **m. worm**, a worm used in angling, called also *blue-head*.

c. In names of plants that grow in marshes, as **m. asphodel**, *Narthecium ossifragum*; **m. bent** (grass), *Agrostis vulgaris*; **m. grass**, any grass that grows in marshy land, *spec.* one of the genus *Spartina*; **m. trefoil** [tr. L. *Trifolium palustre*], the buckbean, *Menyanthes trifoliata*.

Marshal (māɹʃăl), *sb.* ME. [a. OF. *mareschal, marescal* (mod.F. *maréchal*):—Frankish L. *mariscalcus*:—OTeut. type **marhoskalko-z*, f. **marho-z* horse + **skalko-z* servant (G. *schalk* rogue).] †1. One who tends horses; *esp.* a farrier; a shoeing smith –1720. 2. One of the chief functionaries of a royal household or court; *spec.* a high officer of state in England; now EARL MARSHAL, q. v. ME. 3. As a title of military rank. †a. Orig., A commander, general. Subseq., an officer of a definite rank, which varied according to period and country. –1696. b. An officer of the highest rank in certain foreign armies. Often as prefixed title. 1475. †4. An officer of a court of law answerable for the charge and custody of prisoners and for the keeping of order, and frequently having the charge of a prison. Also †*M. of the Exchequer, of the King's* (or *Queen's*) *Bench*. (So named as deputies of the M. of England; see 2.) ME. 5. An officer charged with the arrangement of ceremonies, esp. with the ordering of guests at a banquet, etc. ME. b. (More fully *City M.*) An officer of the corporation of the City of London 1632. 6. **Knight marshal.** †a. A military officer with the functions of a quartermaster. b. *Hist.* An officer of the English royal household, who had judicial cognizance of transgressions 'within the king's house and verge', i.e. within a radius of twelve miles from the king's palace. (Abolished in 1846.) 1556. †7. = PROVOST-MARSHAL –1633. 8. a. *Oxford.* The chief of the proctors' 'bull-dogs' 1810. b. *Cambridge.* Each of two officials who act as the Vice-Chancellor's messengers, summon meetings, etc. 1800. 9. *U.S.* 'In America, a civil officer, appointed by the President and a Senate of the United States, in each judicial district, answering to the sheriff of a county. His duty is to execute all precepts directed to him, issued under the authority of the United States' (Webster) 1793. ¶10. For *m. court, law*, etc., see MARTIAL *a.*, COURT MARTIAL.

1. Alle maner of werkmen; as goldsmythes, marchallis, smythes of alle forges CAXTON. 4. *M. of the Admiralty*: an officer of the Court of Admiralty. *Judge's m.*: an official (now usually a barrister) who accompanies a judge on circuit, and is charged with secretarial and other duties. 5. †*M. of the King's* (or *Queen's*) *house*: = Knight marshal (see 6 b). 9. *M.-at-Arms*: an official of the House of Representatives corresponding to the English sergeant-at-arms. Hence **Ma·rshalship**, the office of m.

Marshal (māɹʃăl), *v.* late ME. [f. MARSHAL *sb.*] †1. *trans.* To tend (horses) as a farrier –1506. 2. To arrange in proper order at a feast, table, etc. 1450. 3. *Her.* To combine (two or more coats of arms) in one escutcheon, so as to form a single composition 1572. 4. To arrange or draw up (soldiers) in order for fighting, exercise, or review; to arrange (competitors) for a race, etc. 1587. Also *transf.* and *fig.* b. *refl.* and *intr.* To take up positions in or as in a military array or a procession 1687. 5. *trans.* To dispose (things, material or immaterial) in methodical order 1550. b. *Comm.* To arrange (assets or securities) in the order in which they are available to meet various kinds of claims 1773. 6. To usher, guide (a person) on his way; to conduct ceremoniously 1586.

4. To commaund the men to be marshalled into the order that shall bee appointed BARRET. b. The procession was marshalling A. DUNCAN. 5. So to the office in the evening to marshall my papers PEPYS. 6. Thou marshall'st me the way that I was going SHAKS.

Marshalcy (māɹʃălsi). [ME. a. AF. *mareschalcie*:—Frankish L. *mariscalcia*, f. *mariscalcus* MARSHAL *sb.* As used now, prob. f. MARSHAL *sb.* + -CY, after *captaincy*, etc.] †1. Farriery –1720. 2. The office, rank, or position of a marshal ME. †3. The military force under the command of a marshal –1748.

Marshalman. Orig. **marshal's man.** 1638. One of a number of men belonging to the royal household and going before the king in processions; also, a similar officer under the marshal of the City of London.

Marshalsea (māɹʃălsī). *Hist.* late ME. [The same wd. as MARSHALCY.] A court (abolished in 1849) formerly held by or for the knight marshal, orig. for the purpose of hearing cases between the king's servants. Also, a prison in Southwark under the control of the knight marshal (abolished in 1842).

Marshbanker, etc.: see MOSSBUNKER.

Marsh gas. 1848. Light carburetted hydrogen, CH_4, found in coal-mines and about stagnant pools.

Marshland (māɹʃ,lænd). [OE. *męrsclǫnd*; see MARSH, LAND *sb.*] Marshy country.

Marsh-mallow. [OE. *męrscmealwe.*] (Also *pl.*, const. as *sing.*) A shrubby herb, *Althæa officinalis* (N.O. *Malvaceæ*), which grows near salt marshes, having ovate leaves, pale rose-coloured flowers, and a mucilaginous root. Also, a confection made from this root.

Marsh marigold. 1578. A ranunculaceous plant, *Caltha palustris*, growing in moist meadows and bearing showy golden flowers.

Marshy (māɹʃi), *a.* late ME. [f. MARSH + -Y.[1]] Pertaining to or of the nature of a marsh; consisting of or containing marshes or marshland. b. Produced in marshland 1697. Hence **Ma·rshiness.**

Marsipobranch (māɹsipobræŋk). 1872. [Anglicized f. mod.L. *Marsipobranchii*, f. Gr. μάρσιπος pouch (see MARSUPIUM) + βράγχια gills.] One of the *Marsipobranchii*, a class of vertebrates having gills in the form of pouches, and comprising the lampreys and hags. So **Ma:rsipobra·nchiate** *a.* and *sb.*

Marsupial (maɹsiū·piăl). 1696. [ad. mod. L. *marsupialis*, f. L. *marsupium* pouch, purse (see MARSUPIUM).] **A.** *adj.* 1. Pertaining to or resembling a marsupium or pouch. 2. A designation of mammals (including the kangaroos, opossums, etc.) of the family *Marsupialia*, characterized by having a pouch in which to carry their young, which are born imperfect; of or pertaining to this family 1825. b. Connected with this pouch 1819. **B.** *sb.* A marsupial animal 1835. So **Marsu·pian, Marsu·piate** *adjs.* and *sbs.*

‖ **Marsupium** (maɹsiū·piŏm). 1698. [L., ad. Gr. μαρσύπιον, -σίπιον, dim. of μάρσιπος purse.] A bag or pouch, or something resembling a pouch. *Zool.* a. The bag or pouch of a marsupial. b. A pouch for similar use in certain crustaceans, marsipobranchs, etc. 1843. c. The pecten of the eye of a bird or reptile 1795.

Mart (māɹt), *sb.*[1] 1713. [The second element of FOUMART, q.v.] The marten.

†**Mart**, *sb.*[2] late ME. [ad. L. *Martem*; see MARS.] = MARS 1, 2. –1636.

Mart (māɹt), *sb.*[3] late ME. [a. Du. *markt* (commonly pronounced *mart*); see MARKET *sb.*] 1. A fair. *Obs.* or *arch.* †b. *spec.* The German booksellers' fair, held at Easter, orig. at Frankfurt, later at Leipzig –1655. 2. A market-place, market hall, etc. Now *poet.* or *rhet.*, exc. as = 'auction room', and as a tradesman's name for shop. 1590. 3. More widely: A city, region, or locality where things are bought and sold; an emporium. Also *transf.* and *fig.* 1581. †4. Buying and selling; bargaining. Also, a bargain. –1637. †5. *attrib.* as in *m.-time, -town*, etc. –1761.

2. The crowded m., the cultivated plain GOLDSM. 3. She is a m. of nations *Isa.* xxiii. 3. 4. They.. maken a M. of their good name SPENSER.

†**Mart**, *sb.*[4] 1587. [Alteration of MARQUE, app. infl. by prec.] = MARQUE; in phr. *letter(s*, etc. *of m.* Also *attrib.* –1753.

†**Mart** (māɹt), *v.* 1553. [f. MART *sb.*[3]; cf. Du. *markten.*] 1. *intr.* To do business at a mart; to chaffer, bargain –1628. 2. *trans.* To traffic in –1788.

2. To sell, and M. your Offices for Gold SHAKS.

‖ **Martaban** (māɹtăbæn). 1622. Name of a town in Pegu, used *attrib.* (esp. in *M. jar*) to designate a kind of glazed pottery made there. Hence as *sb.*

Martagon (māɹtăgən). 1477. [a. F. *martagon*, a. Turk. *martagān* 'a special form of turban adopted by Sultan Muhammed I; hence the martagon lily' (Redhouse).] The Turk's-cap lily, *Lilium Martagon*. Also *Scarlet m.*: the Scarlet Turk's-cap, *L. chalcedonicum*.

Martel (māɹtĕl), *sb.* 1474. [a. OF. *martel* (mod.F. *marteau*):—pop.L. **martellum*.] A hammer; esp. one used in war. Also ‖**M.-de-fer** [Fr. = 'iron hammer'], a weapon which had at one end a pick and at the other a hammer. *Obs.* exc. *Antiq.* Hence †**Ma·rtel** *v. intr.* (*rare*), to hammer SPENSER.

Marteline (maɹtĕlin). 1875. [a. F., f. OF. *martel*; see prec.] A small hammer, pointed at one end, used by sculptors and marble-workers.

Martello (maɹte·lo). 1803. [Corruption of the name of Cape *Mortella* in Corsica, where there was a tower of this kind which the English fleet captured in 1794.] *M. tower* (occas. *m.*): a small circular fort with massive walls; usually erected on a coast to prevent the landing of enemies.

Marten (māɹtĕn). [Late ME. *martren*, a. OF. *martrine* (sc. *peau* skin), f. *martre*, app. an extended form of OTeut. **marþuz* (OE. *mearð*; cf. FOUMART).] †1. The skins or fur of the marten. Often in *pl.* –1696. 2. An animal of any one of certain species of *Mustela*, yielding a valuable fur. Often differentiated, as **beech-m., stone-m.,** *M. foina*; **pine** (or †**fir**) **m.,** *M. martes*; **American pine m.,** *M. americana*.

Martial (māɹʃăl), *a.* late ME. [a. F. *martial*, ad. L. *martialis* of or belonging to Mars, f. *Mart(i)-* MARS.] 1. Of or pertaining to war or battle. b. Of sports, exercises, etc.: Serving as training for warfare. late ME. c. Of music: Appropriate to warfare 1662. 2. Of or pertaining to 'the Army', or the military profession. *Obs.* exc. in COURT MARTIAL. 1470. 3. Warlike; brave; valiant; given to fighting. late ME. 4. Characteristic of a warrior 1592. 5. Resembling that of the god Mars. *Cymb.* IV. ii. 310. 6. Of or belonging to the planet Mars 1621. 7. In early *Chem.*: Of or pertaining to iron; containing iron 1684.

1. M. equipage MILT. M. virtues 1872. c. Sonorous mettal blowing M. sounds MILT. 3. Wake the m. spirit in their breasts BRYANT. 4. Go, write it in a m. hand, be curst and briefe SHAKS.

Phr. **Martial law.** a. Military government, by which the ordinary law is suspended, and the military authorities are empowered to arrest and punish offenders at their discretion. †b. = *military law* (MILITARY *a.*). Hence **Ma·rtialism,** warlike qualities. **Ma·rtialize** *v. rare*, to make m. **Ma·rtially** *adv.*

Martialist (mā·ɹʃălist). 1569. [f. MARTIAL *a.* + -IST.] †1. *Astrol.* A person born under the influence of the planet Mars -1686. 2. A military man; one skilled in warfare. Now *rare.* 1576. 3. A Martian. PROCTOR.

Martian (mā·ɹʃăn). late ME. [f. L. *Martius* (f. *Martem* MARS) + -AN.] A. *adj.* 1. †a. Having the temperament due to the influence of the planet Mars. b. Of or pertaining to Mars or its supposed inhabitants. †2. Of or pertaining to war or battle -1596. 3. Of or pertaining to the month of March 1623.

3. Gay are the M. Kalends MACAULAY.

B. *sb.* An inhabitant of Mars 1892.

†**Ma·rtiloge.** ME. [ad. med.L. *martilogium*, contr. f. *martyrologium.*] A martyrology -1548.

Martin[1] (mā·ɹtin). Also **marten**, etc. 1450. [a. F. *Martin*, ad. L. *Martinus* the Christian name.] 1. A bird of the swallow family, *Chelidon urbica.* It builds a mud nest on the walls of houses, etc.; hence called **house-martin.** The **sand-m.** or **bank-m.** is *Cotile riparia*; the **purple m.** of N. America is *Progne subis* or *purpurea.* **Bee-m.**, the American king-bird, *Tyrannus carolinensis.* †2. A dupe. [? a different wd.] 1591-1621.

Martin[2] (mā·ɹtin). 1533. The name of St. Martin bishop of Tours (4th c.) used *attrib.* and in *Comb.* †1. **M. chain,** a sham gold chain. (Cf. 3 b.) BECON. So †*St. M.'s ring.* 2. More fully †**M. dry,** also [Fr.] ‖**M. sec**: a kind of pear, ripe at Martinmas 1664. 3. †a. **St. M.**: St. Martin's day, Martinmas 1533. †b. **St. Martin's**: the parish of St. Martin-le-Grand, London, at one time the resort of dealers in sham jewellery -1618. c. **St. Martin's day,** the 11th of November, Martinmas; (St.) **Martin's eve,** the eve of St. Martin's day, 10th November; **St. Martin's Summer,** a season of fine mild weather occurring about Martinmas (SHAKS.).

†**Ma·rtinet**[1]. 1460. [a. F. *martinet*, dim. of proper name *Martin*; see MARTIN[1].] A name for the martin and the swift -1833.

Martinet[2] (mā·ɹtinėt). 1523. [a. F.] 1. A military engine for throwing large stones. *Hist.* 2. *Naut.* One of the leech-lines of a sail 1582.

Martinet[3] (māɹtine·t). 1676. [f. General *Martinet*, a French drill-master of the reign of Louis XIV.] †1. The system of drill invented by Martinet. WYCHERLEY. 2. A military or naval officer who is a stickler for strict discipline; hence, any rigid disciplinarian 1779. 3. *attrib.* or *adj.* 1814.

3. A sort of m. attention to the minutiæ and technicalities of discipline SCOTT. Hence **Martine·tism,** the spirit or action of a m. **Martine·t(t)ish** *a.* having the characteristics of a m.

Martingale (mā·ɹtiŋgēl). 1589. [a. F., etym. unkn.] 1. A strap or straps fastened at one end to the noseband, bit, or reins, and at the other to the girth, to prevent a horse from rearing or throwing back his head. 2. *Naut.* A rope for guying down the jib-boom to the dolphin-striker; also called *m.-guy*, *-stay* 1794. b. A dolphin-striker (see DOLPHIN) 1794. 3. A system in gambling which consists in doubling the stake when losing in order to recoup oneself 1815.

3. You have not played as yet? Do not do so; above all avoid a m. if you do THACKERAY.

Martini (maɹtī·ni). 1870. Short for **Martini-Henry** (rifle) [f. the names of Frederic *Martini*, Swiss inventor (1832-97), and A. *Henry*, Scottish gunmaker (died 1894)]: a rifle which combines Henry's seven-grooved barrel with Martini's block-action breech mechanism.

Martinmas (mā·ɹtinmăs). Also †**Martlemas,** etc. ME. [f. MARTIN[2] + MASS *sb.*[1]] 1. The feast of St. Martin, 11 Nov. †2. Used as a derisive appellation. 2 *Hen. IV*, II. ii. 110.

Martlet (mā·ɹtlėt). 1538. [a. F. *martelet*, app. an altered form of *martinet.*] 1. The swift, *Cypselus apus*, formerly often confused with the swallow and the house-martin. 2. *Her.* An imaginary bird without feet, borne as a charge. Used as a mark of cadency for a fourth son 1550.

Martyr (mā·ɹtəɹ), *sb.* [OE. *martyr*, ad. Eccl.L. *martyr*, a. Gr. *μάρτυρ*, late Gr. form of *μάρτυς* (stem *μαρτυρ-*) witness.] 1 *Eccl.* A designation of honour (connoting the highest degree of saintship) for: One who voluntarily undergoes the penalty of death for refusing to renounce the Christian faith or for obedience to any law or command of the Church. †b. Used sarcastically for: One who suffers death in an evil cause -1841. c. Used in the etymological sense of: Witness 1642. 2. One who undergoes death (or great suffering) on behalf of any belief or cause, or through devotion to some object. Const. *to.* 1597. 3. *hyperbolically.* A constant sufferer. Const. *to* (an ailment, etc.) 1560. 4. *attrib.*, as *m.-king*, etc. 1532.

1. It was necessary to resist unto blood, to acquire the glorious Privilege of a M. NELSON. c. The elect Martyrs and witnesses of their Redeemer MILT. 2. A M. to Science (*heading*) 1863. 3. She is a m. to dyspepsia and bad cooking FR. A. KEMBLE. Phr. *To make a m. of*: to subject to inconvenience. *To make a m. of oneself* (joc.): to sacrifice one's inclinations for the sake of gaining credit for doing so.

Martyr (mā·ɹtəɹ), *v.* OE. [f. prec. sb.] 1. *trans.* To put to death as a martyr. †2. To kill, esp. by a cruel death -1794. 3. To cause suffering or misery to (*arch.*) ME. †4. To mutilate, spoil -1658. 5. To represent as a martyr. MILT.

1. Tyndale was martyr'd at Fylford HEARNE. 3. Rack'd with Sciatics, martyr'd with the Stone POPE. To m. anyone with jests 1860. 4. Time hath so martyred the Records, that [etc.] SIR T. BROWNE.

Martyrdom (mā·ɹtəɹdəm). [OE. *martyrdōm*; see MARTYR *sb.* and -DOM.] 1. The sufferings and death of a martyr. Also, the act of becoming or condition of being a martyr. 2. Torment, torture; extreme suffering. late ME.

1. The palm of martirdom for to receyue CHAUCER. *transf.* Social martyrdoms place no saints upon the calendar HELPS.

Martyrize (mā·ɹtĭrəiz), *v.* 1450. [ad. med.L. *martyrizare* (cf. F. *martyriser*), f. *martyr*; see MARTYR *sb.* and -IZE.] 1. *trans.* To make a martyr of; to martyr. 2. *intr.* To be or become a martyr (*rare*) 1524. Hence **Ma·rtyriza·tion.**

Martyrly (mā·ɹtəɹli), *a. rare.* 1659. [f. MARTYR *sb.* + -LY[1].] Martyr-like. So **Ma·rtyrly** *adv.*

†**Martyrologe.** 1500. [a. F., ad. med.L. *martyrologium.*] = next -1721.

Martyrology (māɹtĭrǫ·lŏdʒi). 1599. [ad. med.L. *martyrologium*, a. late Gr. *μαρτυρολόγιον*, f. *μάρτυρ* MARTYR *sb.* + *λόγος* account.] 1. A list or register of martyrs; a history of martyrs. 2. The histories of martyrs collectively 1801. Hence **Ma·rtyrolo·gic, -al** *a.* **Martyro·logist,** a writer of m.; one versed in the history of martyrs.

Martyry (mā·ɹtĭri). ME. [ad. med.L. *martyrium*, a. Gr. *μαρτύριον*, f. *μάρτυρ* MARTYR *sb.*] †1. Martyrdom; suffering (*rare*) -1677. 2. A shrine, oratory, or church erected in memory of a martyr; an erection marking the place of a martyrdom or the spot where a martyr's relics lie 1708.

Marvel (mā·ɹvĕl), *sb.* ME. [a. OF. *merveille* fem., repr. Com. Rom. *mirabilia*, neut. pl. taken as fem. sing. of L. *mirabilis* adj., f. *mirari* to wonder at.] †1. = MIRACLE 1. -1600. 2. A wonderful or astonishing thing; a wonder ME. b. A wonderful example *of* (some quality) 1873. †3. A wonderful story -1484. 4. Astonishment, wonder ME.

2. Marvels still the vulgar love SCOTT. b. The house was a m. of neatness and comfort BLACK. 4. Use lessens m., it is said SCOTT.

Phr. *What m., no m.*: = what wonder, no wonder (*arch.*). **M. of Peru, of the World** = FOUR O'CLOCK 1.

Marvel (mā·ɹvĕl), *v.* Now only *literary.* ME. [a. OF. *merveillier*, f. *merveille*; see prec. sb.] 1. *intr.* (in *obs.* or *arch.* use also *refl.*, *impers.*, and *pass.*) To be filled with wonder or astonishment. (In mod. use, stronger than *wonder.*) Const. *at*, †*of*, †*on*, †*upon*; *inf.*; also with clause, expressing the object of wonder. 2. To ask oneself wonderingly. Const. interrog. clause. late ME. †3. *trans.* To wonder or be astonished at -1819. †4. To cause to wonder -1567.

1. To m. at the inequalities of human destiny TROLLOPE. 2. I cannot but marvaile from what Sibyl or Oracle they stole the Prophesie of the worlds destruction by fire SIR T. BROWNE. 3. Let it not be Maruelled, if sometimes they proue Excellent Persons BACON.

Marvellous (mā·ɹvĕləs), *a.* and *adv.* Also (now *U.S.*) marvelous. ME. [a. OF. *merveillos* (mod.F. *merveilleux*), f. *merveille*; see MARVEL *sb.* and -OUS.] A. *adj.* Such as to excite wonder; astonishing, surprising. b. *spec.* Of poetic material: Concerned with the supernatural 1715. c. *The m.*: that which is extravagantly improbable 1749.

Lyke to the Raynbow mervelose unto syght 1471. c. The prodigies and the m. of Bible-religion M. ARNOLD.

†B. *adv.* In a m. manner or degree -1777. Hence **Ma·rvellous·ly** *adv.*, **-ness.**

Marver (mā·ɹvəɹ), *sb.* 1832. [Corruptly a. F. *marbre* MARBLE.] A polished slab of marble or iron upon which glass-blowers roll and shape the plastic glass while still on the blow-pipe. Hence **Ma·rver** *v.*

Marxian (mā·ɹksiăn), *a.* and *sb.* 1896. Pertaining to or characteristic of, an adherent of, the doctrines of the German Socialist Karl Marx (1818-83). Also **Ma·rxism, Ma·rxist.**

Mary (mēᵊ·ri). [OE. *Maria*, *Marie*, a. L. *María*, a. Gr. *Μαρία*, *Μαριάμ*, ad. Heb. *Miryām*, Miriam.] 1. A female Christian name. The mother of Jesus Christ, commonly called the (Blessed) Virgin Mary, or Saint Mary. Used in asseverations (cf. MARRY *int.*). 2. *Australian slang.* A native woman 1884.

Comb.: **m.-bud** (*obs.* exc. in echoes of Shaks.), the bud of a marigold. **Mary-lily,** the Madonna lily.

Mary, obs. f. MARROW[1], MARRY.

Marzipan (mā·ɹzipæ·n). 1891. [Ger.] (See MARCHPANE for etym. and def.)

Mas. Also **mass, mess.** 1575. [Shortened f. MASTER *sb.*[1]] †1. Vulgar shortening of *master*, usually followed by a proper name or official title -1722. 2. **Mas John,** applied joc. or contemptuously to a Scottish Presbyterian minister (*arch.*) 1661.

2. These new Mess-Johns in robes and coronets BURKE.

-mas: see MASS *sb.*[1]

Mascagnine (mæskæ·nyəin). Also **-ite.** 1836. [f. Prof. *Mascagni*, its discoverer; see -INE[5].] *Min.* 'Sulphate of ammonium, occurring in crusts and stalactitic forms near volcanoes' (Chester).

Mascle (mɑ·sk'l). ME. [Cf. F. *macle*, ad. L. *macula.*] †1. = MESH of a net -1696. 2. *Her.* A charge in the form of a lozenge with a lozenge-shaped opening through which the 'field' appears 1486. 3. *Antiq.* One of the perforated lozenge-shaped plates of metal coating the military tunic of the 13th c. 1822. Hence **Ma·scled** *a.* covered with mascles.

‖**Mascot** (mæ·skǫt). Also **mascotte.** 1884. [ad. provincial F. *mascotte.* Taken up from E. Audran's opera 'La Mascotte', played in 1880.] A person or thing supposed to bring luck. Hence **Ma·scotism Ma·scotry.**

Masculine (mæ·skiŭlin). late ME. [a. F. *masculin*, *-ine*, ad. L. *masculinus*, f. *masculus*; see MALE *a.* and -INE[1].] A. *adj.* 1. Of the male sex; male. Now *rare.* †2. Said of inanimate objects to which the male sex was attributed on the ground of some quality, e.g. relative superiority, strength, etc. 1590. 3. *Gram.* Of or pertaining to the gender to which appellations of males normally belong. late ME. 4. Pertaining to the male sex; consisting of males 1601. 5. Having the appropriate excellences of the male sex; virile; vigorous, powerful. Usu. of attributes, actions, or productions 1629. †b. Of material things, etc.: Powerful in action -1728. 6. Of a woman: Having the qualities proper to man 1617.

2. Phr. †*M. hour* (Astrol.): one ruled by a m. planet. †*M. frankincense, gum* = *male incense* (see MALE *a.* 4). 3. *M. rime* (Pros.): in French versification, a rime between lines ending in stressed syllables, as opp. to the feminine rime ending in *e* mute. Hence *gen.* a 'single' rime on a stressed syllable. 4. M attyre *Twel. N.* v. i. 257. Hee was soone after slain in Ireland, and his whole M. race RALEIGH. 5. He proved a stout and m. Prince 1678. 6. The m. women of the Low Countries vse to make voyages for trafficke 1617.

B. *sb.* 1. That which is of the male sex 1550. 2. A person of the male sex 1652. 3. *Gram.* The masculine gender; a word or form of the masculine gender 1530. **Ma·sculine·ly** *adv.*, **-ness. Masculi·nity,** m. quality or condition; that which is m. **Masculiniza·tion, -ize** *v.*

Masculo- (mæ·skiŭlo), comb. f. L. *masculus* male, as **m.-feminine** *a.* partly masculine and partly feminine, etc.

†Maselin. ME. only. [a. OF. *maselin*, also *mazerin*, etc., f. *mazre, madre*, bowl of maple-wood.] = MAZER 2.

Mash (mæʃ), *sb.*[1] [OE. *másc-, máx-*, corresp. to late MHG., mod.G. *meisch* masc., crushed grapes for wine-making, infused malt for beer; perh. related by ablaut to OE. *miscian* to MIX.] 1. *Brewing.* Malt mixed with hot water to form wort. 2. A mixture of boiled grain, bran or meal, etc., given warm as food to horses and cattle. Also qualified, as *bran-m.* (BRAN[1]). 1577. 3. *gen.* Something reduced to a soft pulp, by beating or crushing, by steeping in water, etc. 1598. b. *fig.* A confused mixture; a muddle 1598. c. (without article.) Mashed state (*lit.* and *fig.*) 1630.

3. The streets are one m. of snow 1880. b. I haue made a faire m. on't B. JONS. c. The paper is boiled to m. 1751.

Comb.: **m.-tub, -tun, -vat,** a tub in which malt is mashed; **-wort** (OE. *mǽscwyrt*), wort, infused malt.

Mash (mæʃ), *sb.*[2] *slang.* 1882. [f. MASH *v.*[2]] 1. A person on whom one of the opposite sex is 'mashed'. Also, a 'swell'. 2. The action of MASH *v.*[2], in *on the m.* 1888.

Mash (mæʃ), *sb.*[3] 1825. [Either f. next, or ad. F. *masse* MACE[1].] A hammer for breaking stones. So **Mash** *v.*[3] 1762.

Mash (mæʃ), *v.*[1] ME. [f. MASH *sb.*[1]] 1. *Brewing. trans.* To mix (malt) with hot water to form wort. (Also with *up.*) b. *dial.* To infuse (tea). Also *intr.* of the tea: To draw. 1845. 2. To crush, pound, or smash to a pulp. Also with *up.* ME. 3. To reduce (fruit, potatoes, etc.) to a homogeneous mass by crushing, beating, or stirring 1615. Also *fig.*

3. No cold mutton to hash,..not even potatoes to m. HOOD. Hence **Mashed** (mæʃt) *ppl. a.* (*m. potatoes* 1747).

Mash (mæʃ), *v.*[2] *slang.* (orig. *U.S.*) 1879. [?] 1. *trans.* To excite sentimental admiration in (one of the opposite sex). 2. pass. *To be mashed on*: to have such admiration for, to be 'gone' on. Also *intr.* 1883.

Masher[1] (mæ·ʃəɹ). 1500. [f. MASH *v.*[1] + -ER[1].] †1. One who mashes (malt) or mixes (wine) -1611. 2. A machine or vessel for mashing malt, fruit, etc. 1878.

Masher[2] (mæ·ʃəɹ). *slang.* 1882. [f. MASH *v.*[2] + -ER[1].] A fop of affected manners and 'loud' style of dress who frequented music-halls, etc., and posed as a lady-killer. b. *U.S.* A man who thrusts himself on women.

Mashie, mashy (mæ·ʃi). 1881. [?] *Golf.* A golf-club having an iron head with straight sole and face, slightly more lofted than the iron.

Mashlin, dial. f. MASLIN[2].

Mashy (mæ·ʃi), *a.* 1730. [f. MASH *sb.*[1] + -Y[1].] Of the nature of a mash.

‖**Masjid** (mɒ·sdʒid). 1646 (**mesgid**). [a. Arab. *masjid*; see MOSQUE.] A mosque.

Mask, *sb.*[1] *Obs.* exc. *dial.* [? repr. OE. **mǽsc* (by metathesis *max*) net.] A mesh.

Mask (mɑsk), *sb.*[2] 1534. [a. F. *masque*, of disputed origin; cf. Sp. *máscara*, It. *maschera*, and med.L. *mascus, masca.* See N.E.D. Cf. MASQUE.] 1. a. A covering, usually of velvet or silk (with eye-holes), worn to conceal the face at balls, masquerades, etc. b. A screen of wire, gauze, etc. worn on the face for protection 1591. c. *Antiq.* The hollow figure of a human head worn by ancient Greek and Roman actors 1705. d. A likeness of a person's face in clay, wax, etc.; esp. one made by taking a mould from the face itself. Also *death-m.* 1780. e. A grotesque representation of a face worn on festive and other occasions, to produce a humorous or terrifying effect 1837. 2. *fig.* a. A cloak, disguise, pretence 1577. b. Something which covers or hides from view 1752. 3. A masked person 1580. 4. In techn. uses (see below) 1731.

1. One of the ladies would, and did sit with her m. on PEPYS. b. *Mask*,..a face protection to be worn in glass-works or foundries, to protect against radiant heat (Knight). Also = GAS-*mask*. 2. a. Phr. *Under the m. of, to put on, assume, throw* or *pull off*, or *drop the m.* (*of*), etc. b. The new soft-fallen m. Of snow upon the mountains KEATS. 3. A Masque, armed cap-a-pie DE QUINCEY. 4. a. *Arch.*, etc. A (grotesque) head or face in stone, used in panels, keystones of arches, etc.; also, in metal on a shield. Also, a kind of corbel the shadow of which is like a man's profile. 1731. b. *Hunting.* The face or head of a fox (or otter). 1828. In recent use, the head-skin of any 'big game'. c. *Fortif.* A screen to protect men working, to conceal a battery, etc.; also, a casemated redoubt serving as a counter-guard to the caponier 1802. d. *Entom.* The enlarged labium of the larval and pupal dragon-fly. Also *Zool.* a formation of the head resembling a mask. 1797. e. *Photogr.* A piece of opaque paper used to cover any part of a negative, lantern-slide, or print which it is desired to obscure or shade 1876. f. *Surg.* A piece of linen, with holes for the eyes, nose, and mouth, used for applications to the face 1890.

Comb.: **m.-crab,** a crab of the family *Corystidæ*, with mask-like markings on the carapace.

Mask, *v.*[1] *Obs.* exc. *dial.* late ME. [f. MASK *sb.*[1]] *trans.* To mesh, enmesh (*lit.* and *fig.*).

Mask (mɑsk), *v.*[2] *Sc.* 1480. North. var. of MASH *v.*[1]

Mask (mɑsk), *v.*[3] Also **masque.** 1562. [f. MASK *sb.*[2] Cf. F. *masquer.*] 1. *trans.* To cover (the face) with a mask. Chiefly *pass.* To wear a mask. 1588. b. *gen.* To disguise 1847. 2. *transf.* To conceal from view by interposing something 1583. b. *Mil.* and *Fortif.* (*a*) To conceal (a battery, a force, etc.) from the enemy's view. (*b*) To hinder (a fortress, an army, etc.) from action by watching it with a sufficient force. (*c*) To hinder the action of a friendly force by standing in the line of its fire. 1706. 3. *fig.* To disguise (feelings, etc.); to conceal the real nature, intent, or meaning of 1588. †4. *intr.* To take part in a masque or masquerade. Also *to m. it.* -1731. †5. *intr.* To be or go in disguise. Often *fig.* -1649.

1. The Trompet sounds, be maskt, the maskers come SHAKS. 2. Masking the Businesse from the common Eye SHAKS. 3. He has been obliged to m. his pretensions SHERIDAN.

Masked (mɑskt), *ppl. a.* 1585. [f. MASK *sb.*[2] or *v.*[3] + -ED.] 1. Having or wearing a mask 1637. b. Used (often repr. L. *larvatus, personatus*) as the specific name of animals having some formation or marking resembling a mask 1840. c. *Bot.* Of a corolla: = PERSONATE 1793. 2. *transf.* and *fig.* Having the real features or character disguised. Also *occas.* Concealed from view. 1585. b. *Nosology.* Of diseases, esp. intermittent fevers: not recognizable by the usual criteria 1833. 3. *Mil.* and *Fortif.* Chiefly in *m. battery*; see MASK *v.*[3] 2 b. 1759.

1. *M. ball* [F. *bal masqué*]: a ball at which those taking part wear masks. b. The Japan, or M. Pig (*Sus pliciceps* Gray). The M. Crab [= *mask-crab*, MASK *sb.*[2]]. 2. The m. hypocrisie of this olde foxe 1585.

Masker, masquer (mɑ·skəɹ), *sb.* 1533. [f. MASK *v.*[3] + -ER[1].] One who takes part in a masquerade or masque; a masquerader.

Masker (mɑ·skəɹ), *v. Obs.* exc. *dial.* [OE. **malscrian*, implied in *malscrung* vbl. sb.; app. cogn. w. Goth. **malsks* in *untila-malsks* precipitate.] a. *trans.* To bewilder, confuse. b. *pass.* To be bewildered.

†Ma·skery, ma·squery. 1548. [a. F. *masquerie*, f. *masque* MASK *sb.*[2]; see -ERY.] Masking, wearing of masks; a masquerade. Also, masquerader's attire. -1655.

Maskinonge (mæskinǫ·ndʒ, -ǫ·ndʒī). Also **muskallunge,** etc. 1796. [Odjibwa.] A large pike, *Esox nobilior*, inhabiting the Great Lakes of N. America, valued as a food-fish.

Maslin[1] (mæ·zlin). Now *dial.* [OE. *mæs(t)ling, mæslen* neut., app. f. **mæs* (cogn. w. MHG. *mess(e* neut., brass) + -LING[2]. See N.E.D.] 1. A kind of brass. Now only *attrib.* 2. A vessel made of maslin; now (*dial.*) = *m. kettle* (see 3) OE. 3. *attrib.* or *adj.* = Made of maslin. Now chiefly in **m. kettle,** a large pan for boiling fruit for preserve.

Maslin[2] (mæ·zlin). ME. (For the numerous variant spellings see N.E.D.) [a. OF. *mesteillon*:—late L. *mistilionem*, f. **mistilium*, f. L. *mistus*, pa. pple. of *miscere* to mix.] Mixed grain, *esp.* rye mixed with wheat. Also, bread made of mixed corn. †b. *fig.* A mixture, medley -1855. c. *attrib.*, as *m. bread, corn*; also as *adj.* (*fig.*) mixed, mingled 1544.

Masochism (mæ·zǫkiz'm). 1893. [f. the name of Leopold von Sacher-*Masoch* (1835-95), Austrian novelist, who described it + -ISM.] A form of sexual perversion in which one finds pleasure in abuse and cruelty from his or her associate (cf. SADISM). **Ma·sochist, -i·stic** *a.*

Mason (mē̆ⁱ·s'n), *sb.* ME. [a. OF. *masson, maçon* (mod.F. *maçon*):—pop.L. type **mācionem* (*mācio*) or **mattionem* (*mattio*). Etym. obscure.] 1. A builder and worker in stone. 2. = FREEMASON 1, 2. 1483.

Comb.: **m.-work,** stone-work, masonry; also in names of insects, etc., which build a nest of sand, mud, or the like; as *m.-ant* (= F. *fourmi maçonne*); **m.-bee** (= F. *abeille maçonne*), an insect of the genera *Osmia, Chalcidoma,* and *Anthophora*; **-spider,** a trap-door spider (*Mygale*); **(free)mason-wasp,** a solitary wasp, *Odynerus murarius.* Also **m.-shell,** a carrier-shell. Hence **Maso·nic** *a.* of or pertaining to masons or masonry (see MASONRY).

Mason (mē̆ⁱ·s'n), *v.* late ME. [ad. F. *maçonner*, f. *maçon* MASON *sb.*] *trans.* To build of stone (or brick, etc.); to build up or strengthen with masonry. Also with *together, out.* †b. To build *in* or *into* a wall -1596. Hence **Ma·soned** *ppl. a.*; *spec.* in *Her.* marked with lines representing the joints or divisions between blocks of stone. Also *gen.*

Masonry (mē̆ⁱ·s'nri), *sb.* late ME. [a. F. *maçonnerie*, f. *maçon* MASON *sb.*; see -ERY, -RY.] 1. The occupation of a mason; the art or work of building in stone. Now *rare.* 2. *concr.* Work executed by a mason; stone-work. late ME. 3. = FREEMASONRY 1, 2. 1686. 4. *attrib.* Composed or built of masonry 1875. Hence **Ma·sonry** *v. trans.* to build or strengthen with m.

Masoola: see MASSOOLA(H.

‖**Masora(h, Massora(h** (măsō°·ră). 1613. [More correctly *Masoreth*, repr. Heb. *masōreth* 'bond (of the covenant)', occurring in Ezek. xx. 37.] The body of traditional information relating to the text of the Hebrew Bible; the collection of critical notes in which this information is preserved.

Masorete, Massorete (mæ·sŏrīt). 1587. [Orig. a misapplication of *Masoreth*, better form of MASORA.] One of the Jewish scholars who contributed to the Masora. Hence **Mas(s)ore·tic, -al,** *a.* var. **Ma·sorite.**

Masque (mɑsk). 1514. [Orig. the same wd. as MASK *sb.*[2]; now differentiated.] 1. A masquerade, masked ball. [So in Fr.] Now *rare.* 2. A form of amateur histrionic entertainment, originally consisting of dancing and acting in dumb show, the performers being masked; afterwards including dialogue and song 1562. Also *transf.* and *fig.* 3. A dramatic composition for this kind of entertainment 1605. †4. A set of masquers -1625.

2. *fig.* The M. of Anarchy SHELLEY (*title*). 3. A Maske presented at Ludlow Castle MILT. (*title of Comus*).

Masque, Masquer, etc.: see MASK, etc.

Masquerade (mɑskĕrē̆ⁱ·d), *sb.* 1587. [ad. Sp. *mascarada*, f. *máscara* mask; usually taken as a. Arab. *maskharah* laughing-stock, f. root *sakhira* to ridicule.] 1. A masked ball 1597. b. *transf.* and *fig.* usually with reference to the fantastic or motley character of a masquerade 1587. 2. Masquerade dress 1668. 3. Acting or living under false pretences; false outward show; pretence 1674. b. *concr.* A travesty. DISRAELI. †4. One who takes part in a masquerade -1727. †5. A name for one or more textile fabrics -1714.

3. The smooth tongue's habitual m. CRABBE. 5. [*Masquerade*, a shot silk of various tints FAIRHOLT.]

Masquerade (mɑskĕrē̆ⁱ·d), *v.* 1654. [f. prec. sb.] †1. *trans.* To disguise as at a masquerade (*rare*) -1717. 2. *intr.* To appear or go about in disguise; to pass oneself off under a false character 1692.

Hence **Masquera·der** (*lit.* and *fig.*).

Mass (mæs, mās), *sb.*[1] [OE. *mæsse* wk. fem., a. pop.L. *messa* :—Eccl. L. *missa*, vbl. sb. f. L. *mittere* to dismiss. Some explain that *missa* at first denoted the solemn dimissory formula at the conclusion of a service, *Ite, missa est*, and hence came to be applied to the service itself. The sense 'feast-day' of OE. survives in names of church festivals in *-mas*.] **1.** The Eucharistic service; in post-Reformation use, chiefly that of the R. C. Church. Also, a celebration of the Eucharist having a particular object or intention. **2.** In pre-Reformation use, the sacrament of the Eucharist; subseq., the Eucharist as administered and doctrinally viewed by Roman Catholics OE. **b.** The form of liturgy used in the celebration of the Eucharist. late ME. **3.** A musical setting of those parts of the mass which are usually sung 1597. **4.** Used in oaths. late ME.

1. Suitable masses said for the benefit of his soul SCOTT. Freq. without article, as in phr. *At m.*, (*to go*) *to m.*; *to say, sing, hear, attend m.* Phr. †*Neither m. nor matins*: nothing of very serious import. **High** (or **solemn** or †**great**) **m.**, m. celebrated with the assistance of deacon and subdeacon, with incense and music. **Low** (or †**little**) **m.**, m. said without note and with the minimum of ceremony. 2. Admitting a real presence in the m. 1853. 4. Phr. *By the m.*; also simply *mass* (often *mess*).

Comb.: **m.-bell**, (*a*) a bell that calls people to m.; (*b*) a bell that is rung during m., a sacring-bell; **-money**, (*a*) offerings of money made at m.; (*b*) money paid to a priest for saying m.

Mass (mæs), *sb.*[2] late ME. [a. F. *masse*, ad. L. *massa*, prob. a. Gr. μᾶζα barley-cake, perh. cogn. w. Gr. μάσσειν to knead.] **1.** A coherent body of matter (as dough, clay, metal), not yet shaped; a lump of raw material for moulding, casting, sculpture, etc. Now merged in sense 2. **b.** An amorphous quantity of material used in or remaining after a chemical or other operation; in *Pharmacy*, the substance from which pills are made 1562. †**c.** A plastic substance –1700. **2.** In wider sense: A solid physical object of relatively large bulk. In mod. *Physics*, often contrasted with *molecule* or *atom*. 1440. **b.** *Mining.* A mineral deposit of irregular shape, dist. from a *bed* or *vein* 1855. **3.** A dense aggregation of objects apparently forming a continuous body 1609. **4.** *transf.* and *fig.* **a.** A large quantity, amount, or number 1585. **b.** Applied to an extensive unbroken expanse (of colour, light, shadow, etc.). Also, in *Fine Art*, one of the several main portions distinguishable in a composition. 1662. **c.** A volume or body of sound, esp. when produced by many instruments or voices of the same character 1879. **5.** Of human beings: A compact body; an aggregate in which individuality is lost 1713. **b.** *Mil.* A formation of troops in which the battalions, etc. are arranged one behind another. Opp. to *line*. 1889. **6.** *abstr.* **a.** Solid bulk, massiveness 1602. **b.** *Physics.* The quantity of matter which a body contains; in strict use dist. from *weight* 1704.

1. Of Gold in Masse eight thousand.. Cichars HOOKER. 2. The mighty m. of the Finsteraarhorn TYNDALL. 3. There were masses of camellias and azaleas OUIDA. 4. I remember a masse of things, but nothing distinctly SHAKS. Great Masses of Treasure BACON. A m. of evidence TYLOR. Phr. *The (great) m. of*: the greater part or majority of. *The m.*: the generality; the main body. *In the m.*: without distinction of parts or individuals. *To be a* (or *one*) *m. of bruises, faults*, etc. b. The effect producible by *masses* of light and shade 1797. 5. Away with this hurrah of masses, and let us have the considerate vote of single men EMERSON. *The masses*: the lower orders. 6. a. Gathering m. as it travelled KANE. b. Phr. *Centre of m.*: see CENTRE.

attrib. and *Comb.* **a.** *Arch.* 'Arranged in large masses', as *m.-pier*. **b.** *Mil.*, etc. 'Involving masses of people', as *m. drill, vote*. **c.** *Physics*, as *m.-attraction, -moment*. **d.** *Spec.*: **m. meeting**, a large public meeting, usually political (orig. *U.S.*); **m. production**, the production of manufactured articles in large quantities by a standardized process; **m. suggestion**, the influencing of the minds of a large body of people by the suggestion of an idea of general application.

Mass, *v.*[1] Now *rare* or *Obs.* [OE. *mæssian*, f. *mæsse* MASS *sb.*[1]] **1.** *intr.* To celebrate mass; to sing or say mass. **2.** *trans.* To pass *away* (time) at mass 1784.

Mass (mæs), *v.*[2] 1563. [a. F. *masser*, f. *masse* MASS *sb.*[2]] **1.** *trans.* To form or gather into a mass; to arrange, or bring together, in masses. Also with *up*. 1604. **b.** *Mil.*; also, to concentrate (troops) in a particular place 1861. **2.** *refl.* and *intr.* To collect, or come together in masses 1563.

1. Who mass'd, round that slight brow, these clouds of doom? M. ARNOLD. b. Austria is massing troops in Herzegovina 1885.

Massa (mæ·sə). Also **Mas'r.** 1774. Negro corruption of *master*.

Massacre (mæ·săkəɹ), *sb.* 1586. [a. F. *massacre* masc., in OF. *maçacre*, etc., shambles, also butchery; ult. etym. unkn. Spenser stresses *massa·cre*, Shaks. and Marlowe *ma·ssacre*.] **1.** A general slaughter (of human beings; also occas., of wild animals). Also *fig.* †**2.** A cruel or peculiarly atrocious murder –1608.

1. On the late Massacher in Piemont MILT. (*title*). *M. of St. Bartholomew* (earlier †*m. of Paris*): the m. of the Huguenots of France on the 24th of August 1572. *M. of Glencoe*: the m. of the Macdonalds of Glencoe on Feb. 13th, 1692, by the Campbells, under authority from William III. *M. of the Innocents*: see INNOCENT B. 2. 2. *Rich. III*, IV. iii. 2.

Massacre (mæ·săkəɹ), *v.* 1581. [a. F. *massacrer*, f. *massacre*; see prec.] **1.** *trans.* To kill indiscriminately (a number of human beings, occas. animals). Also occas. *absol.* **2.** To murder cruelly or violently 1601. †**3.** To mutilate, mangle –1651.

1. These are the Guisians, That seeke to m. our guiltles liues MARLOWE. 2. Caesar..was masakred with 23. wounds 1606.

Massage (mæsā·ʒ), *sb.* 1876. [a. F., f. *masser* to apply massage to (the body); ? a. Pg. *amassar* to knead, f. *massa* dough (= MASS *sb.*[2]).] The application of friction, kneading, etc. to the muscles and joints of the body, in order to stimulate their action and increase their suppleness. Hence **Massa·ge** *v.*

‖**Massasauga** (mæsăsǭ·gă). 1842. [Amer. Indian. Cf. Natick *massa* great, *sahsauag* rattling, *seseka* rattlesnake.] A small N. Amer. rattlesnake of the genus *Crotalophorus* (or *Caudisona*).

Ma·ss-book. OE. [f. MASS *sb.*[1] + BOOK *sb.*] = MISSAL *sb.*[1]

‖**Massé** (mæ·se, mase), *a.* and *sb.* 1873. [Fr., pa. pple. of *masser* to make this stroke, f. *masse* MACE[1].] *Billiards.* Applied to a stroke made with the cue held perpendicular.

†**Ma·sser.** [OE. *mæssere*, f. *mæssian* MASS *v.*[1]; see -ER[1].] A priest who celebrates mass; also, one who attends mass. (After OE. only as a term of derision.) –1579.

Masseter (mæsī·təɹ). 1666. [a. mod.L. *masseter*, a. Gr. μασητήρ, f. μασᾶσθαι to chew.] *Anat.* (Usu. *m. muscle.*) The masticatory muscle which passes from the malar bone and zygomatic arch to the ramus of the lower jaw. Hence **Massete·ric** *a.* of or pertaining to the m.; *sb.* a masseteric nerve, muscle, artery, etc.

‖**Masseur** (masör). 1876. [Fr.; f. *masser*; see MASSAGE *sb.*] A man who practises massage. So ‖**Masseuse** (masöz), a woman who practises massage.

Ma·ss-house. *Obs.* exc. *Hist.* 1644. [MASS *sb.*[1]] In 17–18th c. a Protestant term for a Roman Catholic place of worship.

Massicot (mæ·sikǫt). 1472 (*masticot*). [a. F. *massicot*, †*mast-*, ad. It. *marzacotto*, ad. Sp. *mazacote* sort of mortar.] Yellow monoxide of lead used as a pigment (cf. LITHARGE).

‖**Massif** (mæ·sif). Also †**-ife.** 1524. [Fr.; subst. use of *massif* MASSIVE *a.*] †**a.** A block or mass of stone. **b.** A large mountain-mass; the central mass of a mountain; a compact portion of a range 1885.

†**Ma·ssily**, *adv.* late ME. [f. MASSY + -LY[2].] Massively –1668. So †**Ma·ssiness.**

Massive (mæ·siv), *a.* late ME. [ad. F. *massif*, f. *masse* MASS *sb.*[2]; see -IVE.] **1.** Forming a large mass; large and heavy or solid. **b.** Of articles of gold or silver: Solid, not hollow or plated. **c.** Of architectural or artistic style: Presenting great masses, solid 1841. **d.** Of the features, head, etc.: Largely moulded or modelled 1843. **2.** *transf.* and *fig.* **a.** Solid, substantial; imposing in scale 1581. **b.** *Psych.* Of a sensation, a state of consciousness: Having large volume or magnitude 1855. **c.** *Path.* Of a disease, etc.: Affecting a large continuous portion of tissue 1897. **3.** Forming a solid or continuous mass; compact, dense, or (sometimes, merely) uniform in internal structure; existing in compact continuous masses. Now esp. *Min.* applied to minerals not definitely crystalline, and *Geol.* to rocks or formations presenting no structural divisions. 1558.

1. Its ceilings..heavy with m. beams DICKENS. Hence **Ma·ssive·ly** *adv.*, **-ness.** **Massi·vity.**

Ma·ss-mo:nger. *arch.* 1550. [MASS *sb.*[1]] A contemptuous term for a Roman Catholic. So †**Mass-monging** *vbl. sb.* and *ppl. a.*

‖**Massoola(h** (mæsū·lă). Also **musoola**, etc. 1685. [app. f. Arab. *mawṣūl* joined, united.] A large surf-boat used on the Coromandel coast. Often *m.-boat*.

Ma·ss-penny. *arch.* late ME. [MASS *sb.*[1]] An offering of money made at mass.

Ma·ss-priest. *arch.* OE. [MASS *sb.*[1]] A (Christian) priest.

From the 16th c. chiefly a hostile term for a Roman Catholic priest.

Massy (mæ·si), *a.* Now *rhet.* or *arch.* late ME. [f. MASS *sb.*[2] + -Y[1].] **1.** Full of substance or mass. **a.** Solid and weighty. Said esp. of the precious metals: Occurring in mass; wrought in solid pieces. †**b.** Having three dimensions –1645. †**c.** Close, compact, dense –1814. **2.** Consisting of a large mass or masses 1587. **b.** Of architecture: Presenting great masses 1819. **3.** Spreading in a mass or in masses 1672. **b.** Of persons and animals: Bulky, large-bodied. late ME. **4.** *transf.* and *fig.* 1588.

1. As a massee vessel of gold WYCLIF *Ecclus.* l. 10. M. old plate SHERIDAN. c. The massiest air 1814. 2. A m. oaken table SCOTT. 3. Infantry in m. columns ALISON. 4. A grosse and m. paradox MILT. *Comb.* *m.-proof* adj. With antick Pillars m. proof MILT.

Mast (mɑst), *sb.*[1] [Com. Teut.: OE. *mæst* masc. :—OTeut. **mastoz* :—W. Indo-Eur. type **mazdos*, whence L. *malus*.] **1.** A long pole or spar of timber, iron, or steel set upright on a ship's keel, to support the sails. **b.** A piece of timber suitable for a mast 1496. **2.** The tall upright pole of a derrick or similar machine; a climbing pole in a gymnasium; a structure to support a wireless aerial; etc. 1646.

1. The larger masts are composed of several lengths, called *lower m.*, TOPMAST, TOPGALLANT *mast*, and ROYAL *mast*. N.E.D. The tallest Pine Hewn on Norwegian hills, to be the M. Of some great Ammiral MILT. Phr. *Before the m.*: see BEFORE B. 2. *At the m.*: on deck by the mainmast. *To nail one's colours to the m.*, to adopt an unyielding attitude. *To spring, step a m.*: see SPRING, STEP *vbs.*

Comb.: **m.-buoy**, one which carries a m.; **-tree**, a name given to certain tall erect trees.

Mast (mɑst), *sb.*[2] [Com. WGer.: OE. *mæst* masc. :—OTeut. **mastoz*, prob. f. (ult.) root *med-* (see MEAT *sb.*).] **1.** The fruit of the beech, oak, chestnut, and other forest-trees, esp. as food for swine. Rare in *pl.* †**2.** The condition of feeding on mast. Only in phr. *to lie at m.*, *to put to m.* –1664.

1. The Oakes beare M., the Briars Scarlet Heps SHAKS.

Mast (mɑst), *v.* 1627. [f. MAST *sb.*[1]] *trans.* To furnish with masts.

Mastage (mɑ·stėdʒ). *Obs.* exc. *Hist.* 1610. [f. MAST *sb.*[2] + -AGE.] = MAST *sb.*[2] 1. Also, the right of feeding animals on mast.

‖**Mastax** (mæ·stæks). 1855. [mod.L., f. Gr. μάσταξ mouth.] The pharynx of a rotifer.

Masted (mɑ·stėd), *ppl. a.* 1627. [f. MAST *v.* or *sb.*[1] + -ED.] **1.** Furnished with a mast or masts. **2.** Thronged with masts 1757.

Master (mā·stəɹ), *sb.*[1] [Partly OE. *mægester*, *magister* (ME. *meister, -tre, maister, -tre*), a. L. *magister, magistrum*; partly a. OF. *maistre* (mod.F. *maître*) :—L. *magistrum, magister*, related to *magis* adv., more.]

I. A man having control or authority. †**1.** *gen.* A director, leader, chief, commander; a ruler, governor –1596. Also *transf.* (chiefly of animals). **2.** *spec.* (*Naut.*) **a.** The captain of a merchant vessel; called also †*m.* MARINER. **b.** The officer (ranking next below a lieutenant) entrusted with the navigation of a ship of war. Now styled *navigating officer*. †**c.** *M. and commander*: since 1814 repl. by COMMANDER ME. **3.** An employer; correl. w. *servant, man*; also with *apprentice*. late ME. **b.** Applied to a sovereign in relation to his ministers or officers. Now chiefly *Hist.* 1470. **4.** The owner of a dog, horse, slave, etc. late ME. **5.** The male head of a house or household 1536. **b.** With poss. adj.: (One's) husband (*dial.*) late ME. **6.** A possessor, owner. Now *rare*, exc. in phr. *to be m. of*: to possess; also, occas., to have a mastery of (a subject). late ME. **7.** One who has the control, use, or disposition of something at will. Chiefly *predicative.* ME. **b.** *transf.* of things. late ME. **8.** One who overcomes another, a victor ME. **9.** *Bowls.* = JACK *sb.*¹ II. 11.

2. b. *Master's mate*, an officer subordinate to but working with the m. of a ship of war. **3.** Who 's m., who 's man SWIFT. Provb. *Like m., like man.* **4.** An Asse [knoweth] his masters stall COVERDALE *Isa.* i. 3. **5.** The m. of the house begins first LANE. **6.** I was m. of more than twenty pounds 1785. **7.** The person who really commands the army is your m. BURKE. **b.** Loue is your m. SHAKS.

II. A teacher. **1.** A tutor, preceptor; in later use chiefly a teacher in a school; also, a teacher of an art, a language, etc. OE. **2.** He whose disciple one is in religion, philosophy, art, etc. ME. **†3.** A scholar of authority –1597. **4.** In academic sense, = med.L. *magister*: The holder of a specific degree, originally conveying authority to teach in the university. In Eng. use (until recently) confined to the Faculty of Arts: the full title is in L. *artium magister*, in Eng. *master of arts* (abbrev. M.A. or, now rarely, A.M.). Latterly the degrees of *Master of Science* (M.Sc.), *Master in* or *of Surgery* (*Magister Chirurgiæ*, M.Ch.), have been given in Oxford, etc. late ME. **5.** A workman who is in business on his own account, as dist. from a journeyman; a workman of approved skill; also *transf.* and *fig.* late ME. **6.** An artist of distinguished skill, one who is regarded as a model of excellence in his art 1533. **b.** A work by a master. Now only in *old m.*, and occas. *modern m.* 1752.

1. The village m. taught his little school GOLDSM. French in a fortnight without a M. (*title*) 1856. **2.** My maister Chaucer LYDG. *The* (*our, his, my*) *M.*: often applied to Christ. **3.** *M. of the sentences* (*magister sententiarum*), the name given to Peter Lombard, Bishop of Paris in the 12th c., from his book *Sententiarum libri quatuor*, a collection of patristic comments on passages of Scripture. **5.** It is a stroke of a maister CAXTON. **6.** *Old Master*, a master who lived between the 13th and the 16th or 17th century. The pictures of the Tuscan and Venetian masters EMERSON. **b.** As a picture-dealer stares at an alleged old m. 1851.

III. As a title of office. **1.** The head of certain colleges (in Oxford, Cambridge, etc.), guilds, corporations, livery companies, hospitals, etc. Formerly also used for GRAND MASTER, *Great master*, the title of the head of a military order. Also as in *master-general*, *m. provincial*, titles of dignitaries of monastic and other religious organizations. **2.** In the designations of certain legal functionaries (see below). late ME. **3. a.** In designations of officials having duties of control, superintendence, or safe-keeping. late ME. **b.** *Mil.* in various titles of command. late ME. **†4.** Great master. = GRAND MASTER 1, 2. –1685.

1. *M. of the Temple*: (*a*) *Hist.* the grand master of the Knights Templar; (*b*) the principal clergyman of the Temple Church, London. He was made M. of Balliol Coll. WOOD. **2.** *M. of the* (or *in*) *Chancery*, (*a*) until 1852, one of the twelve assistants to the Lord Chancellor, the chief of whom was M. of the Rolls; (*b*) since 1897 any one of four chief clerks of the Chancery Division of the Supreme Court. *M. of the Court* (*of Common Pleas, of the King's Bench, of the Exchequer*), any one of five officers in each of those courts (now, in the corresponding division of the Supreme Court) charged with the duty of recording the proceedings. *M. of* (*the*) *Faculties*, the chief officer of the Court of Faculties (cf. FACULTY III. b). *M. in Lunacy*, see LUNACY. *M. of the Requests*, see REQUEST. *M. of the Wards* (*and Liveries*), see WARD. **3.** *M. of the* (*King's, Queen's*) *Household*, an officer under the Steward of the Royal Household. *M. of the Jewel-house*, the keeper of the Crown Jewels in the Tower of London. *M. of the* (*King's*) *Music*, an officer of the Royal Household, the conductor of the King's band. *M. of the Robes, of the Wardrobe*, the keeper of the 'great' wardrobe of the King, Queen, or other exalted personage. *M. of* (*the*) *Works* or (now dial.) *Work*, an official who superintends building operations. For *M. of Ceremonies, of the Mint, of Misrule, of the Revels, of the Rolls*, see the second sbs. *M. of the Horse*: (*a*) in England, the title of the third official of the royal household; also rarely *transf.* in joc. use, a head groom or stableman; (*b*) *Antiq.* used as tr. L. *magister equitum*, master of the 'knights', under the Roman republic the title of the commander of the cavalry appointed by a dictator. *M. of the Buckhounds*, the fourth great officer of the household. *M. of hounds*: one who owns, or has the control of, a pack of hounds; usually, the leading member of a hunt who is elected to the office; chiefly = *M. of foxhounds* (abbrev. M.F.H.). Also *m. of beagles, harriers, staghounds*, etc. **b.** *M.* (*General*) *of the Ordnance*, the controller of the Ordnance and Artillery (now, the head of the Board of Ordnance).

IV. As a title of rank or compliment. **1. a.** *sing.* = Sir. Now only in uneducated use. **b.** *pl.* (in later times always *my masters*) = Sirs, gentlemen. Now *arch.* or *rhet.*, chiefly ironical or derisive. ME. **2.** Prefixed to the name or designation of a man. In ordinary use now only *dial.*, but in literature occas. *arch.* or *Hist.*; otherwise repl. by MR. (mi·stəɹ). ME. **3.** Prefixed (esp. by servants and inferiors) to the name of boys and young men not old enough for 'Mr.'. **4.** The heir-apparent to a Scottish peerage (below the rank of earl; formerly, below that of marquis) is often known as **The M. of ——**; the specific designation being usu. identical with the baronial title of the family 1489.

1. Y'are welcome Masters, welcome all SHAKS. **2.** Maister Latymer encouraged Maister Ridley when both were at the stake FOXE. And yet m. Parson must not be called couetous 1625. **3.** Maids, misses, and little m...in a third [coach] SWIFT. Phr. *masters and misses* = young people. **4.** The M. of Ravenswood led the way SCOTT.

V. Attrib. uses. **1.** Used appositively or as *adj.* in the sense 'that is a master'. **a.** As prefixed to designations of persons, now *rhet.*, with implication of imposing greatness ME. **b.** *spec.* denoting (*a*) the leader of a herd of animals, (*b*) the official who has command over others so designated, (*c*) one who is a master, as opp. to an apprentice or journeyman, hence = supremely skilled. **2.** Applied *transf.* as a qualification of things, with the sense 'main', 'principal', 'controlling' ME.

1. a. The master-deuil, Belsabub 1575. The Choice and M. Spirits of this Age SHAKS. **b.** A M.-Pike, that for his Bulk, Beauty, and Strength, was look'd upon to be the Prince of the River R. L'ESTRANGE. A Master-Printer 1683. The king's m. butcher J. GRANT. The French consider the English the master-colonists of the world 1900. **2.** A main Pillar and Master-branch in Englands Grandeur 1667. The lord of irony,—that master-spell BYRON.

Comb.: **m. attendant**, 'an officer in the royal dockyards appointed to assist in the fitting or dismantling, removing or securing vessels of war, etc.' (Smyth); **m. fault** *Geol.*, a fault which governs the configuration of the surrounding area; **m. hand**, (*a*) the hand of a m., the agency of one highly skilled or one possessing commanding power; (*b*) a highly skilled worker; **m. joint** *Geol.*, a principal joint in a rock mass; **m. mariner** (see MARINER); **m. sinew**, a main sinew; *esp.* the tendon in the hock of a quadruped, corresponding to the tendon of Achilles in man; **m. workman**, a workman thoroughly conversant with his trade; one who employs workmen; also *fig.*

Master (mɑ·stəɹ), *sb.*² 1880. [f. MAST *sb.*¹ + -ER¹ 1.] A ship having (so many) masts, as *three-m.*, etc.

Master (mā·stəɹ), *v.* ME. [f. MASTER *sb.*¹ Cf. OF. *maistrier.*] **1.** *trans.* To get the better of; to overcome or defeat. **2.** To reduce to subjection; to break, tame (an animal). late ME. **3.** *techn.* To temper or season; to modify. Now only in *Dyeing*, to season or age (dye stuffs), and in *Tanning*, to subject (skins) to the action of an astringent lye. late ME. **4.** To make oneself master of; to acquire complete understanding of (a fact, a proposition), or complete facility in using (an instrument, etc.) 1740. **5.** To rule as a master; to be the master of (a servant, scholar, house, etc.) 1611. **†6.** *trans.* To own, possess –1638. **7.** To address by the style of 'master'. STUBBES.

1. Kings nor authority can m. fate FLETCHER. **2.** The Zebra..could never be entirely mastered GOLDSM. **4.** To m. the difference between 'would' and 'should' 1901. **6.** The wealth That the world masters SHAKS.

Ma·ster-at-a·rms. 1748. *Naut.* Formerly a warrant-officer in the navy who instructed the officers and crew of a ship of war in the exercise of small arms, and acted as principal police officer on board, but now a first-class petty officer doing duty in the latter capacity only. Also *transf.*, the principal police officer on board a ship of the mercantile marine.

Ma·ster-bui·lder. 1557. [MASTER *sb.*¹ II.] **1.** One who is skilled in the art of building, an architect. Chiefly in rhet. use or fig. context. **2.** One who employs workmen in building 1714. **3.** *Naut.* A petty officer formerly employed on the construction of ships 1799.

Masterdom (mā·stəɹdəm). OE. [f. MASTER *sb.*¹ + -DOM.] **†1.** The office of a teacher; the degree of master (of divinity) –ME. **2.** Dominion, supremacy; †victory in battle 1475. **†3.** = MASTERSHIP 3 –1601.

Masterful (mā·stəɹfŭl), *a.* ME. [f. MASTER *sb.*¹ + -FUL.] **1.** Addicted to acting the part of master; imperious, self-willed. Of actions: High-handed, arbitrary. **†b.** *Law.* (chiefly *Sc.*) Of beggars, etc.: Using violence or threats 1474–1754. **2.** Having the capacities of a master; qualified to command. late ME. **b.** Of language, looks, etc.: Indicative of mastery 1824. **3.** = MASTERLY 2. 1613.

1. Yonder m. cuckoo Crowds every egg out of the nest EMERSON. **2. b.** His m., pale face MRS. BROWNING. **3.** Whether pleasing or displeasing to your taste they are entirely m. RUSKIN. Hence **Ma·sterful·ly** *adv.*, **-ness.**

Masterhood (mā·stəɹhu·d). 1454. [f. MASTER *sb.*¹ + -HOOD.] The condition or quality of being a master.

Master-key. 1576. A key that will open a number of different locks.

Masterless (mā·stəɹlės), *a.* late ME. [f. MASTER *sb.*¹ and (sense 2) *v.* + -LESS.] **1.** Having no master. **b.** Vagrant, vagabond. *Obs.* exc. *Hist.* 1471. **†2.** That cannot be mastered; ungovernable –1767.

†Ma·sterlike, *a.* and *adv.* 1500. [f. MASTER *sb.*¹ + -LIKE.] **a.** *adj.* Despotic, autocratic, sovereign; authoritative, magisterial; exhibiting masterly ability. **b.** *adv.* In a masterlike manner –1666.

a. I begin to doubt the picture..is not of his making, it is so m. PEPYS.

Masterly (mā·stəɹli), *a.* 1531. [f. MASTER *sb.*¹ + -LY¹.] **†1.** Belonging to, or characteristic of, a master or lord; usu. in bad sense, arbitrary, despotic; imperious, overbearing –1766. **2.** Worthy of a master or skilled workman; skilfully performed 1666.

2. How m. are the strokes of Virgil! DRYDEN. A small but m. work 1804. M. speeches 1880. Hence **Ma·sterliness.** So **Ma·sterly** *adv.* late ME.

Master-mason. late ME. **1.** A mason who designs and carries out building in stone or who employs workmen to shape and fit stonework. **2.** A fully qualified freemason, who has passed the third degree 1723.

Masterpiece (mā·stəɹpīs). 1605. [f. MASTER *sb.*¹ + PIECE *sb.*; prob. after Du. *meesterstuk* or G. *meisterstück*, the piece of work by which a craftsman gained the rank of 'master'.] **1.** A production surpassing in excellence all others by the same hand; also, a production of masterly skill; a consummate example 1610. **†b.** An action of masterly ability –1715. **†2.** The most important feature, or the chief excellence, of a person or thing –1697.

1. Man is heav'n's Master-piece QUARLES. A m. of assurance FIELDING, of policy FREEMAN. **b.** Confusion now has made his Master-peece SHAKS. **2.** His learning in the law being his m. CLARENDON.

Mastership (mā·stəɹʃip). late ME. [Cf. G. *meisterschaft.*] **1.** The condition of being a master or ruler; dominion, rule, control. **†b.** 'Upper hand', mastery 1573–1829. **2.** The office, function, dignity, or term of office of a 'master' 1455. **b.** The position of a master in or of a school 1806. **†3.** With poss. pron.: The personality of a master. Often abbrev. M. –1622. **4.** The skill or knowledge constituting a master 1607. **b.** The status or degree of a master (in a craft, a university, etc.) 1688. **5.** The existence of masters or employers as the characteristic form of industrial organization 1868.

2. The M. of the Rolls 1873. **3.** How now Signior Launce? what newes with your M.? SHAKS. **4.** M. in tongue-fence; this is the quality of qualities CARLYLE.

Master-singer (mā·stəɹsi·ŋəɹ). Now *rare.* 1810. Anglicization of MEISTERSINGER.

Master-stroke (mā·stəɹstrōuk). 1679. [Cf. G. *meisterstreich.*] **1.** A masterly line or touch (in painting, etc.). Also *transf.* **2.** A surpassingly skilful act (of cunning, policy, etc.); one's cleverest move or device 1711.

2. The steeple..is a master-stroke of absurdity H. WALPOLE.

†**Master-vein.** late ME. [MASTER *sb.*[1] V. 2.] One of the great veins or arteries of the body; *spec.* applied to the saphena –1683.

Master-work (mā·stəɹwɒɹk). 1606. [MASTER *sb.*[1] V. 2. Cf. G. *meisterwerk*, F. *chef-d'œuvre*.] 1. An action or procedure of supreme importance. 2. A masterpiece 1617. †3. A main drain or channel –1789.

Masterwort (mā·stəɹwɒɹt). 1548. [f. MASTER *sb.*[1] + WORT *sb.*, after G. *meisterwurz*.] The umbelliferous plant *Peucedanum (Imperatoria) Ostruthium*, formerly cultivated as a pot-herb, and used in medicine.

Also applied to other genera, as *Astrantia* (Black M.); the goutweed, *Ægopodium Podagraria* (English or Wild M.); and the U.S. plants *Angelica atropurpurea* and *Heracleum lanatum*.

Mastery (mā·stəri). ME. [a. OF. *maistrie*, f. *maistre* MASTER *sb.*[1]] 1. The state or condition of being master; authority, sway, dominion; an instance of this. †b. Predominance; prevailing character –1642. 2. 'Upper-hand'; victory. Now only: Victory resulting in the subjection of the vanquished (cf. sense 1). ME. †3. Superior force or power –1818. 4. The skill or knowledge which constitutes a master. *Obs.* or *arch.* exc. with mixture of sense 7. ME. †5. An exercise or work of skill or power –1667. †6. A competitive feat of strength or skill; esp. in phr. *to try masteries*, to 'try conclusions' –1697. 7. (*transf.* from 1.) Intellectual command over (a subject of study) 1668. b. The action of mastering (a subject) 1797.

1. The Priesthood was not a Maistry, but a Ministry HOBBES. 2. Four Champions fierce Strive here for Maistrie MILT. 4. Use maketh Masterie NORTON. 5. *To do, make, work*, etc. (*a*) *m.* or *masteries*: to perform a wonderful feat or trick. Ye shul wel seen at eye, That I wol doon a maistrie er I go CHAUCER. *It is great, little, no m.*: it is hard or easy (to do something). 6. This is but to try Masteries with Fortune BACON. 7. His m. of English was supreme 1880.

Mast-head, *sb.* (Stress variable.) 1748. [MAST *sb.*[1]] 1. The head or highest part of a mast, esp. of the lower mast. 2. A sailor stationed at the mast-head. 3. *attrib.* as *m.-light*, etc. 1822.

Mast-head, *v.* 1829. [f. the sb.] 1. *trans.* To send (a sailor) to the mast-head as a punishment. Also *transf.* and *fig.* 2. To raise (a sail, yard, etc.) to its position on the mast or at the mast-head 1840.

Mastic (mæ·stik). late ME. [a. F. *mastic* masc., ad. late L. *mastichum* (also *mastix*), altered f. L. *masticha, mastiche*, a. Gr. μαστίχη. Ult. etym. obscure.] 1. A gum or resin which exudes from the bark of *Pistacia Lentiscus* and some other trees. Now used chiefly in making varnish. 2. (In full *m. tree.*) An evergreen shrub yielding mastic gum, *Pistacia Lentiscus* of the Levant. Applied also to other species of *Pistacia*, and to the W. Indian *Bursera gummifera* and Peruvian *Schinus Molle*. late ME. 3. A timber tree of the W. Indies and Florida, *Sideroxylon Mastichodendron* 1657. †4. (In full **Herb Mastic.**) The plant *Thymus Mastichina* –1836. 5. A resinous or bituminous cement; also, a lime cement used by builders 1706. 6. A liquor flavoured with mastic used in Turkey and Greece. 7. The colour of mastic; a shade of pale yellow 1890.

attrib. and *Comb.*, as *m. gum*, etc.; **m. varnish**, a fine varnish used for varnishing pictures.

Masticate (mæ·stikeit), *v.* 1649. [f. late L. *masticat-*, ppl. stem of *masticare* to chew.] 1. *trans.* To grind (food) to a pulp with the teeth; to chew. 2. To crush or knead (rubber) to a pulp 1849. So **Mastica·tion** 1565. **Ma·sticator** (also *attrib.* as *m. muscle*).

Masticatory (mæ·stikătəri). 1611. [ad. mod.L. *masticatorius, -orium*, f. *masticare*; see -ORY[1] and [2].] a. *adj.* Of, pertaining to, or concerned with mastication; affecting the organs of mastication. b. *sb.* A medicinal substance to be chewed 1611.

Masticic (mæsti·sik), **mastichic** (mæsti·kik), *a.* 1845. [f. MASTIC + -IC.] *Chem.* In *m. acid*: an acid resin; the portion (about 90 per cent.) of mastic soluble in alcohol. So **Ma·sticin**, the insoluble residue of mastic 1844.

Masticot, early form of MASSICOT.

Mastiff (mɑ·stif). *Pl.* **mastiffs.** (Also †**mastis,** †**mastie, -y.**) ME. [repr. OF. *mastin* (mod.F. *mâtin*) :—pop.L. **mansuetinus*, f. L. *mansuetus* tame. More or less confused with OF. *mestif* mongrel. The form of the Eng. word is unexplained.] A large, powerful dog with a large head, drooping ears and pendulous lips, valuable as a watch-dog.

Comb. **m. bat**, a name for bats of the genus *Molossus*.

Masting (mɑ·stiŋ), *vbl. sb.* 1627. [f. MAST *v.*[1] + -ING[1].] 1. The action or process of fitting with masts. b. Masts collectively 1702. 2. *attrib.*, as *m.-sheers*, etc. 1760.

Comb.: **m.-house**, (*a*) a place where masts are made and stored; (*b*) a building furnished with apparatus for fixing masts; **m. pine**, *Pinus Strobus*.

‖**Mastitis** (mæstəi·tis). 1842. [mod.L., f. Gr. μαστός + -ITIS.] *Med.* Inflammation of the breast.

-mastix (mæ·stiks), repr. Gr. μάστιξ scourge, freq. used in the 17th c. (rarely later), and designating persons violently hostile to some person or class, as *Episcopo-mastix*, etc. Also in titles of books attacking some person, class, institution, etc., as *Histriomastix* [L. *histrio* actor], *Satiromastix*, etc.

Mastless (mɑ·stlės), *a.*[1] 1593. [f. MAST *sb.*[1] + -LESS.] Without a mast or masts.

Mastless (mɑ·stlės), *a.*[2] [f. MAST *sb.*[2] + -LESS.] Without mast or acorns. DRYDEN.

Masto- (mæ·sto), used (*Anat.* and *Path.*) a. to represent MASTOID *sb.*, in combs. with sense 'pertaining jointly to the mastoid process or bone and some other part of the skull', as *m.-parietal* adj., etc.; b. as comb. f. Gr. μαστός breast, in names of diseases of the female breast, as *mastodynia, -dyny*, neuralgia of the female breast, etc.

Mastodon (mæ·stŏdǫn). 1813. [mod.L., f. Gr. μαστός breast + ὀδοντ-, ὀδούς tooth. Cf. F. *mastodonte* (Cuvier, 1806).] *Palæont.* A large extinct mammal resembling the elephant, characterized by having nipple-shaped tubercles in pairs on the crowns of the molar teeth. Also **Ma·stodont** *sb.* (1826) and *a.*; hence **Mastodo·ntic** *a.*

Mastoid (mæ·stoid). 1732. [ad. mod.L. *mastoides*, f. Gr. μαστός; see -OID.] A. *adj.* Shaped like a female breast.

M. process (Anat.), a nipple-shaped, conical prominence of the temporal bone. *M. bone*, a bone of the skull, in fishes and reptiles, homologous with the m. process. *M. cancer* (Path.), a kind of firm carcinomatous growth, the section of which is thought to resemble the boiled udder of the cow 1857.

B. *absol.* as *sb.* = *m. process* or *bone* 1842. b. *attrib.* = 'of or pertaining to the m. process', as *m. cell, muscle* 1800. Hence **Mastoi·dal** *a.*

Mastoidean (mæstoi·dĭan), *a.* 1841. [f. mod.L. *mastoideus* (f. *mastoides* MASTOID) + -AN.] Of or belonging to the mastoid.

Mastras, -es(s(e, obs. ff. MISTRESS.

Masturbate (mæ·stɒɹbeit), *v.* 1857. [f. L. *masturbat-, masturbari*; etym. unkn.] *intr.* and *refl.* To practise self-abuse. So **Masturba·tion** 1766. **Ma·sturbator.**

†**Ma·sty**, *a.* late ME. [f. MAST *sb.*[2] + -Y[1].] 1. Producing mast –1630. 2. Of a swine: Fattened. CHAUCER. 3. Burly, big-bodied –1886.

Mat (mæt), *sb.*[1] [OE. *matt, meatt, meatte*, ad. late L. *matta*.] 1. A piece of a coarse fabric of plaited rushes, sedge, straw, bast, etc., used to lie, sit, or kneel upon, to cover floors, walls, plants, etc., and in packing furniture. 2. a. An article (orig. of this material) placed near a door for persons entering to wipe their shoes upon (= DOOR-*mat*), or similar to those so used 1665. b. A thin flat article (orig. made of plaited straw), placed under a dish, plate, or vessel in order to protect the table from heat, etc. Also applied to other similar articles. 1875. 3. *transf.* A thick tangled mass 1835. 4. *Naut.* A thick web of rope yarn used to protect the standing rigging from the friction of other ropes 1497. 5. *Engineering.* = MATTRESS 3. 1884. 6. *attrib.* 1530.

2. *On the m.* (slang), up for trial, 'in for it'.

Comb.: **m.-grass**, (*a*) *Nardus stricta*, (*b*) *Psamma arenaria*, the marram grass; **-rush**, the bulrush, *Scirpus lacustris*; also = *matweed*; **matweed**, a name for various rush-like grasses.

Mat (mæt), *sb.*[2] Also **matt.** 1845. [a. F. *mat*, subst. use of *mat*, MAT *a.*] 1. *Glass-painting.* A layer of colour 'matted' on the glass (see MAT *v.*[2] b) 1881. 2. a. *Gilding.* The effect of 'mat' or unburnished gold. b. *Metal-work.* A roughened, frosted, or figured groundwork. 1866. 3. A border of dead gold round a framed picture 1845. 4. A matting-punch 1890.

Mat (mæt), *sb.*[3] 1766. = MATADOR 2.

Mat (mæt), *a.* Also †**matte, matt.** 1648. [a. F. *mat*; see MATE *a.*] Of colours, surfaces: Without lustre, dull, 'dead'.

Mat (mæt), *v.*[1] 1549. [f. MAT *sb.*[1]] 1. *trans.* To cover or furnish with mats or matting. 2. *transf.* To cover with an entangled mass 1577. 3. To entangle *together* in a thick mass 1577; to make by interlacing 1824. 4. *intr.* To become entangled *together* 1742.

2. A temple..matted with ivy 1849. 3. And o'er his eyebrows hung his matted hair DRYDEN.

Mat (mæt), *v.*[2] 1602. [a. F. *mater*, f. *mat*; see MAT, MATE *adjs.*] *trans.* To make (colours, etc.) dull; to give a mat appearance to (gilding, metal, etc.); to frost (glass). b. *Glass-painting.* To cover (glass) with a softened layer of colour 1885.

Matachin (mætăʃī·n). *Obs.* exc. *Antiq.* 1578. [a. F. *matachin*, conjectured to be a. Arab. *mutawajjihīn*, pres. pple. pl. of *tawajjaha* to assume a mask.] 1. A kind of sword-dancer in a fantastic dress. †2. A dance performed by matachins. Also *transf.* and *fig.* –1677. 3. *attrib.*, as *m. dance*, etc. 1584.

2. *fig.* He was taken into seruice..to a base office in his Kitchin; so that (in a kind of Mattacina of humane fortune) Hee turned a Broach, that had worne a Crowne BACON.

Mataco (mæ·tăko). 1834. [prob. S. Amer.] The small three-banded armadillo, *Tolypeutes tricinctus*, which rolls itself up into a ball.

Matador (mæ·tădǭɹ). In senses 2 and 3 usu. -ore. 1674 [a. Sp. *matador* :—L. *mactatorem*, f. *mactare* to kill.] 1. In Spanish bull-fights, the man appointed to kill the bull 1681. 2. *Cards.* In quadrille and ombre, any of the three best trumps 1674. 3. *Dominoes.* Any of certain pieces (viz. those whose numbers make up seven, and the double blank) which in a particular form of the game (the *matador game*) can be played at any time 1865.

Matæology (mætĭ,ǫ·lŏdʒi). 1656. [f. Gr. μάταιος vain + -λογία discourse.] Vain or unprofitable discourse. So †**Matæolo·gian** 1653.

†**Matæotechny.** 1576. [f. as prec. + τέχνη art.] An unprofitable science –1675.

Match (mætʃ), *sb.*[1] [OE. *gemæcca, gemecca* :—OTeut. **gamakjon-*, related to **gamakon-*, OE. *gemaca*, MAKE *sb.*[1]]

I. One of a pair. †1. A husband or wife, a mate, consort, a lover. Also of animals. –1658. †2. One's equal; one's fellow, companion –1571. 3. †a. An antagonist, rival –1593. b. A person (occas. a number of persons, a thing) able to contend with another as an equal ME. 4. A person or thing that equals another in some quality 1470. 5. A person or thing that exactly corresponds to or forms a pair with another 1474. †Formerly often *pl.*

2. Marry thy m. 1547. 3. a. M. to m. I haue encountred him SHAKS. b. Phr. *To find, meet one's m.*; *to be, prove oneself, a m. for*. *More than a m. for*: able to overcome. His followers..were no m. for regular soldiers MACAULAY. 4. I neuer found their matches 1632. 5. You might by..looking through any Star on the Globe see its M. in Heaven 1674. Extraordinary matches for carriages have sold at 400 dollars per pair 1808.

II. The action of matching. †1. A matching of adversaries against each other; a contest viewed with regard to the equality or inequality of the parties –1628. 2. A competitive trial of skill in which two or more persons or sides are matched against each other; an arrangement for such a contest. Also applied to a contest of animals. 1545. †3. A suitable pairing –1748. b. A (well or ill) matched pair (or set); two (or more) things which accord (well or ill) in colour, size, etc. 1542. 4. A matrimonial compact or alliance; esp. one viewed as more or less advantageous 1547. †b. The action of marrying; relationship by marriage -1655. c. A person viewed with regard to eligibility as a partner in marriage 1586. †5. An agreement, an appointment; a compact, bargain -1768.

1. This was a mache vn-mete. late ME. 2. [He] leaves it a drawn m. 1651. 3. b. These ribbons are a bad match (*mod.*). 4. It seems to me a very good m. for her 1866. b. *By m.*: in consequence of a marriage; By m., it came to Tremenet RISDON. c. He 's the great m. of the county MEREDITH. 5. Phr. *It is a m.* (or, *A m.!*): = 'Agreed', 'Done'. A m., 'tis done SHAKS.

Comb.: **m.-game**, a game (esp. of chess) forming part of a m.; also U.S. = sense II. 2; **-play**, the play in a m.; also in *Golf*, play in which holes, not strokes, are counted; so *m.-player*; **-rifle**, one used in firing competitions: **-rifling** *Gun-making*, a method of rifling guns to adapt them for long-range shooting in matches; **m. wagon**, a railway wagon run in connexion with a break-down crane.

Match (mætʃ), *sb.*[2] late ME. [a. OF. *mesche, meiche* (mod.F. *mèche*):—pop. L. **micca*, **miccia*. Ult. etym. obscure.] †1. The wick of a candle or lamp -1646. 2. A wick, cord, or rope of hemp, tow, cotton, etc., so prepared that when lighted at the end it is not easily extinguished, and burns at a uniform rate; used for firing cannon, etc. Also in *Mining*. 1549. b. The material of which matches consist; cord, etc., prepared for ignition 1572. 3. A piece of cord, cloth, paper, wood, etc., dipped in melted sulphur, so as to be readily ignited by the use of a tinder-box, and serving to light a candle, etc. *Obs.* exc. *Hist.* 1519. b. A similar article used for fumigation 1703. 4. A short slender piece of wood, wax taper, etc., tipped with some composition that bursts into flame when rubbed on a rough or specially prepared surface 1831.

4. Phr. *To strike a m.*: to ignite a m. by friction (the verb is borrowed from *to strike a light*). *Paraffin m.*: one having the splints dipped in paraffin. *Safety m.*: one which can be ignited only by striking on a specially prepared surface.

attrib. and *Comb.*, as *m.-box*, *-girl*, *-seller*; **m.-paper**, touch-paper; **-paste**, that used for making the heads of matches; **m.-splint**, **-stick**, the wood of a m.; **-thread**, the thread used as m. for firing guns, etc.; **matchwood**, †(*a*) touchwood; (*b*) wood suitable for match-sticks; (*c*) in phr. (*to break*, etc.) *into matchwood*, into minute splinters.

Match (mætʃ), *a.* 1483. [f. MATCH *sb.*[1]] That matches; corresponding. *Obs.* exc. *techn.* in certain special collocations, in most of which *match-* may be interpreted as an attrib. use of MATCH *v.*[1], as *m.-gearing*, *-plane*, *-plate*.

Match (mætʃ), *v.*[1] late ME. [f. MATCH *sb.*[1]] 1. *trans.* To join in marriage; to procure a match for. Also *rarely*, †to couple (animals). Const. *to*, †*unto*, *with*. b. *intr.* for *refl.* To ally oneself in marriage. Now *rare* exc. *dial.* 1568. †2. *trans.* To associate; to put together so as to form a pair or set *with* (another person or thing) -1645. 3. To encounter as an adversary. Now, to prove a match for. late ME. †b. *intr.* To meet in combat *with* -1595. 4. *trans.* To array or place in opposition *with*; to pit *against* another. Chiefly *refl.* and *pass.* late ME. 5. To arrange in a suitable or equal pair or set; to provide with an adversary of equal power. Often in *pass.*, *to be well*, *ill matched*. 1530. b. To make to correspond *to* or *with* 1680. c. To furnish (boards) with a tongue and a groove, at the edges 1833. 6. To compare in respect of superiority 1581. †7. To regard or treat as equal -1606. 8. To be equal to, to equal; to be the match or counterpart of. Also *absol.* of two things: To be mutually equal. 1592. b. *intr.* To be equal *with*; to correspond, be suitable *to*. Also (*rarely*), to fit *into*. 1567. 9. *trans.* To furnish with a match 1596. b. To compare so as to select one suitable *to*. POPE. †10. To procure as a match *Merch. V.* III. i. 81.

1. An idle king..Match'd with an aged wife TENNYSON. b. He matched into a most noble and martial family 1647. 2. *Much Ado* II. i. 111. 3. b. Strength matcht with strength, and power confronted power SHAKS. 4. To m. a bauble against the Pantheon DE QUINCEY. 5. Hounds..match'd in mouth like bels SHAKS. b. God doth m. His gifts to man's believing M. ARNOLD. 8. The event..cannot..m. the expectation C. BRONTË. Phr. *To m.* (used quasi-adv. or quasi-adj. after a sb.): corresponding in number, size, etc. with what has been mentioned. 9. I can m. this nonsense JOHNSON. Can you m. me this piece of yellow silk? 1861. Hence **Ma·tchable** *a.* that can be matched; †comparable; †well-suited. †**Ma·tchableness.**

Match (mætʃ), *v.*[2] 1703. [f. MATCH *sb.*[2]] *trans.* To fumigate (wines or liquors, or casks) by burning sulphur matches; now chiefly in *Cider-making*.

Match-board (mæ·tʃbōᵊɹd), *sb.* 1858. [f. MATCH *a.*] *Joinery.* A board which has a tongue cut along one edge and a groove in the opposite edge, so as to admit of being fitted into other similar boards to form one piece with them. Also *collect.* = *match-boarding*.

Hence **Ma·tch-board** *v.* to cover or supply with match-boards. **Ma·tch-boarding**, match-boards fitted together for use.

Matchcoat (mæ·tʃkōut). *Obs.* exc. *Hist.* 1642. [Orig. *matchco*, prob. Amer. Indian; afterwards corrupted, as if f. MATCH *sb.*[1] or *v.*[1] + COAT *sb.*] A kind of mantle worn by Amer. Indians, orig. made of fur skins, later of coarse woollen cloth called *match-cloth*.

Matcher (mæ·tʃəɹ). 1611. [f. MATCH *v.*[1] + -ER[1].] 1. One who matches. 2. A matching-machine (MATCH *v.*[1] 5 c) 1897.

Matchet (mæ·tʃét). Also **machet(t)e**, †**macheto.** 1598. [ad. Sp. *machete.*] A broad and heavy knife or cutlass, used, esp. in Central America and the West Indies, both as a tool and a weapon.

Matchless (mæ·tʃlės), *a.* 1530. [f. MATCH *sb.*[1] + -LESS.] 1. Without an equal, peerless. b. Used as *adv.* 1871. †2. That are not a match. SPENSER. Hence **Ma·tchless-ly** *adv.*

Matchlock (mæ·tʃlǫk). 1698. [f. MATCH *sb.*[2] + LOCK *sb.*[2]] 1. An old form of gun-lock in which a match (MATCH *sb.*[2] 2) is placed for igniting the powder. 2. A musket having a matchlock 1698. b. *attrib.*, as **matchlock-man**, a soldier armed with a matchlock 1782.

Ma·tch-maker[1]. 1639. [f. MATCH *sb.*[1] + MAKER.] 1. One who brings about a match; one who schemes to bring about marriages. 2. *Sporting.* One who enters into or arranges a match 1704. So **Ma·tch-making** *vbl. sb.*[1]

Ma·tch-maker[2]. 1643. [f. MATCH *sb.*[2] + MAKER.] One who makes match for guns, or lucifer matches. So **Ma·tch-making** *vbl. sb.*[2]

Mate (mēⁱt), *sb.*[1] [ME. *mat*, a. OF. *mat* in *eschec mat* CHECKMATE *sb.*] = CHECKMATE *sb.* 1.

Mate (mēⁱt), *sb.*[2] [ME. (late 14th c.) *mate*, app. a. MLG. *mate* or MDu. **mate* (mod. Du. *maat*), aphetic form of *gemate*:—OTeut. **gamaton-* companion, lit. 'mess-mate', f. *ga-* (see Y-) implying conjunction + *mat-* (see MEAT *sb.*).] 1. A habitual companion; a fellow-worker or partner. Now only in working-class use. b. Used as a form of address by sailors, labourers, etc. 1450. 2. A suitable associate; an equal. Now only *arch.* 1563. 3. One of a pair; now *esp.* a suitable partner in marriage 1549. 4. *Naut.* a. An officer (now only on a merchant ship) who sees to the execution of the master's commands, and in his absence takes charge of the ship. Formerly called *master's mate*. 1496. b. An assistant to some functionary on board ship, as *boatswain's*, *cook's*, *gunner's m.*, etc. 1610. †c. In the navy (in full *surgeon's m.*), an assistant to a ship's doctor; in the army, an assistant who acts as dispenser and dresser 1612-1811. d. *U.S. Navy.* A subordinate officer having no rank, but taking precedence of all other enlisted men 1890.

2. Ye knew me once no m. For you, there sitting where ye durst not soare MILT. 3. There shall the vultures also be gathered, euery one with her m. *Isa.* xxxiv. 15. 4. b. The Gunner, and his M. SHAKS.

†**Mate**, *a.* ME. [a. OF. *mat* mated at chess, etc. (mod.F. *mat*) = med.L. *mattus* 'tristis'. The Rom. word is a. Pers. *māt* at a loss, helpless (used in *shāh māt* 'the king is helpless', CHECKMATE).] 1. Mated at chess -1600. 2. Overcome, worsted, confounded -1513. 3. Exhausted, faint -1536. 4. Downcast, sorrowful -1560.

Mate (mēⁱt), *v.*[1] ME. [a. F. *mater*, f. *mat* MATE *a.*] 1. *trans.* (*Chess.*) To checkmate. Also *absol.* †2. *trans.* To overcome, subdue -1590. Also *transf.* †3. To nonplus, baffle (a person); to render nugatory (a design) -1670. †4. To put out of countenance; to render helpless; to daunt, abash; to stupefy -1827. †5. To exhaust, weary; to dull (passion) -1693.

2. *transf.* There is no passion in the minde of man, so weake, but it Mates, and Masters, the Feare of Death BACON. 3. They mated the Saxons in all their designes SPEED.

Mate (mēⁱt), *v.*[2] 1509. [f. MATE *sb.*[2]] 1. *trans.* To equal; to vie or cope with; to be a match for. Now *rare.* b. *intr.* To claim equality *with* (*arch.*) 1692. 2. *trans.* To match; to join in marriage; to take or give in marriage 1607. Also *intr.* for *refl.* 3. *trans.* To pair (animals, esp. birds) for breeding purposes 1601. Also *intr.* 4. *trans.* To join suitably *with*; to associate, treat as comparable *with* 1593. 5. *intr.* To keep company *with* 1832.

1. My euer Roiall Master, Dare m. a sounder man then Surrie can be SHAKS. 2. Thou art mated with a clown TENNYSON. 3. Pigeons can be mated for life DARWIN. *intr.* These birds do not m. BURROUGHS. 4. On a night, mated to his design DRYDEN.

‖**Maté** (mæ·te). 1717. [Sp. *mate*, a. Quichua *mati*, 'vessel or dish made of calabash'.] 1. A gourd, calabash, etc., in which the leaves of maté (see 2) are infused; also *maté-cup*. 2. An infusion of the leaves of the shrub *Ilex paraguayensis*; Paraguay-tea; also, the shrub itself, and its leaves prepared for infusion 1758. b. *attrib.*, as *m. wood*, etc. 1879.

‖**Matelassé** (matəlase). 1882. [Fr., pa. pple. of *matelasser* to quilt, f. *matelas* MATTRESS.] A French dress goods of silk, or silk and wool, having a raised design. Also *attrib.* or *adj.* having a raised pattern like quilting.

Mateless (mēⁱ·tlės), *a.* 1570. [f. MATE *sb.*[2] + -LESS.] Without a mate, or †peer.

‖**Matelote** (matəlot), *sb.* 1730. [Fr., f. *matelot* sailor.] A dish of fish served in a sauce of wine, onions, mushrooms, etc.; also, a dish of viands similarly dressed. Hence **Matelote** *v. trans.* to make into a m.

Mateo-: see MATÆO-.

‖**Mater** (mēⁱ·təɹ). 1594. [L. = MOTHER.] †1. The thickest plate of the astrolabe. BLUNDEVIL. 2. *Anat.* See DURA MATER, PIA MATER. 3. *Boys'* and *girls' slang.* Used familiarly for *mother.* (Cf. *pater.*) 1864.

‖**Materfamilias** (mēⁱ·təɹfămi·liǎs). 1756. [L., f. *mater* + *familias*, old gen. of *familia.*] The mother of a household.

Material (mătīᵊ·riăl). ME. [ad. late L. *materialis*, f. *materia* MATTER *sb.*: see -AL.]

A. *adj.* 1. *Scholastic Philosophy* and *Theol.* (Opp. to FORMAL.) a. Pertaining to matter as opp. to form. †Of number: Concrete. b. That is (so and so) merely so far as its 'matter' is concerned 1656. 2. *Logic.* Concerned with the matter, as dist. from the form, of reasoning. (Opp. to *formal.*) 1628. 3. Of, pertaining to, or consisting of matter; corporeal ME. 4. Concerned with or involving matter, its presence, use, or agency 1649. b. Usu. coupled with *gross*: Unspiritual 1588. c. Relating to the physical aspect of things; concerned with physical progress, bodily comfort, or the like 1843. 5. Of much consequence; important 1529. b. Pertinent, germane, or essential *to* 1603. c. *Law*, etc. Of such significance as to be likely to influence the determination of a cause, to alter the character of an instrument, etc. 1581. †6. Full of matter, sound information, or sense -1685. †7. Bulky, massive, solid -1735.

1. a. *M. cause*: see CAUSE *sb.* 4. b. *M. sin*: a wrong action apart from the evil intention necessary to constitute it a sin in the full sense; so *m. heresy*, *schism*, etc. *M. righteousness*: righteousness as definable by conduct, without regard to its motive. 2. The m. truth of the Conclusion depends upon the m. truth of the Premises BOWEN. 3. The m. world BUTLER. 4. *M. theory* (of heat): the theory that heat is a m. substance ('caloric'). b. His gross m. soul DRYDEN. c. France..is the country where m. well-being is most widely spread M. ARNOLD. 5. He would put that which was most Materiall in the Post-script BACON. c. A m. witness was wanting 1799. 6. A materiall foole SHAKS.

B. *sb.* †1. *pl.* Things that are material -1605. 2. The matter from which anything is made.

Chiefly *collect. pl.* or *sing.* 1556. b. The elements, constituent parts, or substance of something 1642. 3. Something that can be worked up or elaborated, *esp.* documents, etc. for historical composition; evidence from which a conclusion may be framed 1624. 4. Tools, apparatus, etc. for performing an action. Now only in *writing materials* (= pen, ink, paper) 1731.

2. Gunpowder..with other materials for kindling fire DE FOE. The raw m. out of which a good army may be formed MACAULAY. 3. Their books are m., not literature HOWELLS.

†**Mate·rial**, *v.* 1643. [f. MATERIAL *a.* and *sb.*] 1. *trans.* To bring into material form. SIR T. BROWNE. 2. To furnish material for. GLANVILL.

Materialism (mătī°riăliz'm). 1748. [ad. mod.L. *materialismus*, f. L. *materialis* MATERIAL *a.*; see -ISM.] 1. *Philos.* The doctrine that nothing exists except matter and its movements and modifications; also, that the phenomena of consciousness and will are wholly due to the operation of material agencies. 2. Hence in transf. uses: *esp.* applied to (*a*) theological views supposed to imply a defective sense of the reality of things purely spiritual 1850; (*b*) devotion to material needs or desires; a way of life, opinion, or tendency based entirely upon material interests 1851. ¶3. *concr.* The system of material things; the material universe 1817.

2. I fear..you will never rise beyond the grossest everyday m. 1903.

Materialist (mătī°riălist). 1668. [ad. mod. L. *materialista*; see prec. and -IST.] 1. An adherent of the philosophical system known as materialism. 2. Applied by Berkeley to believers in the objective existence of matter 1705. 3. One who takes a material view of things 1853. 4. *attrib.* or *adj.* = MATERIALISTIC.

1. The materialists, who conjoin all thought with extension HUME. *fig.* Those who hold that poetry is an acquirable art,—the materialists of fine literature SOUTHEY. Hence **Mate·riali·stic** *a.* pertaining to, characterized by, or addicted to materialism. **Materiali·stically** *adv.*

Materiality (mătī°riæ·lĭti). 1529. [ad. mod.L. *materialitas*; see MATERIAL *a.* and -ITY.] †1. That which constitutes the 'matter' of something; opp. to *formality* –1660. 2. The quality of being material 1570; that which is material; *pl.* things material 1811. 3. Material aspect or character; mere externality 1599. 4. The quality of being important for the purpose in hand. Now *legal.* 1644.

2. The decomposition of the rays of light proves their m. G. ADAMS. 4. Rules which tend to secure the m. of the issue H. J. STEPHEN.

Materialize (mătī°riăləiz), *v.* 1710. [f. MATERIAL *a.* + -IZE.] 1. *trans.* To make or represent as material; to invest with material attributes. 2. *Spiritualism.* To cause (a spirit, etc.) to appear in bodily form 1880. b. *intr.* To assume a bodily form 1884. c. *transf.* To become actual fact; to 'come off' (orig. *U.S.*) 1885. 3. *trans.* To make materialistic. Also *intr.* to favour materialistic views. 1820.

2. c. Year after year passed and these promises failed to materialise 1891. 3. The system..tends to m. our upper class, vulgarize our middle class, brutalize our lower class M. ARNOLD. Hence **Materializa·tion**, the giving a material form to; in *Spiritualism*, the appearance of a spirit in bodily form.

Materially (mătī°riăli), *adv.* 1502. [f. MATERIAL *a.* + -LY².] 1. Chiefly *Philos.* and *Logic.* With regard to matter as opp. to form. Also, with regard to constituent matter; in respect of material cause. 2. In, by, with, or in respect of material substance; 'in the state of matter' (J.) 1594. †3. Of speaking or writing: Soundly; to the point –1749. 4. In a material degree; substantially 1654. 5. In respect of material interests 1871.

1. What is formally correct may be m. false BOWEN. 2. As he created all Men out of the same matter, they are m. equal 1717. 4. Short cuts, by..which the road was m. shortened 1890. So **Mate·rialness.**

‖ **Materia medica** (mătī°riă me·dikă). 1699. [med.L., tr. Gr. ὕλη ἰατρική (Galen) = medical material.] The remedial substances used in medicine; that branch of medical science which treats of these 1811.

fig. What I may call the m. m. of morality TUCKER.

†**Materia·rian**, *a.* and *sb.* [f. late L. *materiarius* (f. *materia*) + -AN.] Applied to ancient heretics who believed in the eternity of matter. CUDWORTH.

†**Mate·riate**, *a.* 1588. [ad. L. *materiatus*, f. *materia*; see -ATE.²] 1. Composed or consisting of matter; solid, dense –1694. 2. Involved in matter; said of persons and things 1626–47.

Materiate (mătī°riēⁱt), *v.* Now *rare* or *Obs.* 1653. [f. L. *materiat-*, *materiare*, f. *materia.*] *trans.* In scholastic use. a. To supply or be the matter or material part of; in *pass.*, to be constituted materially *by* something 1680. b. To render (a 'form') inherent in a particular 'matter' 1653. So †**Materia·tion** 1646.

‖ **Matériel** (materiel). 1814. [Fr.; see MATERIAL *a.* and *sb.*] 1. a. The mechanical or material portion of an art; technique. *rare.* b. The 'stock-in-trade' for carrying on any business or undertaking. 2. A collective term for the articles, supplies, machinery, etc. used in an army, navy, or business, as dist. from the *personnel* or body of persons employed 1827.

Maternal (mătɔ̄·ɹnăl), *a.* (*sb.*) 1481. [ad. F. *maternel*, f. L. *maternus*, f. *mater* MOTHER *sb.*; see -AL.] 1. Of or pertaining to a mother or mothers, motherly 1492. b. (One's) mother's 1605. 2. a. That is a mother, or one's mother. Now *rare.* 1513. b. Having the instincts of motherhood, motherly 1784. 3. Inherited or derived from a mother; related through a mother 1656. 4. Of benevolent organizations: Providing for the requirements of maternity 1856. 5. *Phys.* Of parts of the placenta: Uterine (opp. to *fœtal*) 1816.

1. Ah! that m. smile! COWPER. b. The embrace m., the paternal smack 1894. *M. language*: mother tongue. Now *rare.* 2. b. M. earth, who doth her sweet smiles shed For all SHELLEY. 3. Alongside of him stood his m. uncle FREEMAN. Hence **Mate·rnally** *adv.*

Maternalize (mătɔ̄·ɹnăləiz), *v. rare.* 1877. [f. MATERNAL *a.* + -IZE.] *trans.* To make maternal; *absol.* to employ maternal methods.

Maternity (mătɔ̄·ɹnĭti). 1611. [ad. F. *maternité* = med.L. *maternitas*; see MATERNAL and -ITY.] 1. The quality or condition of being a mother; motherhood. b. Short for *maternity hospital* 1889. 2. Motherliness 1804. 3. *attrib.*: m. hospital, a hospital for the reception of women during confinement; so *m. nurse, ward*, etc. 1881.

Mateship (mēⁱ·tɪʃip). 1593. [f. MATE *sb.*² + -SHIP.] The condition of being a mate; companionship; †equality.

Matey (mēⁱ·ti), *sb.* 1833. Hypocoristic f. MATE *sb.*² (see -Y⁶).

Ma·tey, *a.* 1915. [f. MATE *sb.*² + -Y¹.] Friendly (*with*); sociable. **Ma·teyness.**

Matfellon (mæ·tfelən). *Obs.* exc. *dial.* late ME. [a. OF. *matefelon*, app. f. *mater* MATE *v.*¹ + *felon* FELON²; named from supposed curative properties.] = KNAPWEED.

Math (mɑþ). *Obs.* exc. *dial.* and in AFTERMATH. [OE. *mǽþ*, f. OTeut. *mǣ-* to Mow.] A mowing; the amount of a crop mowed. (See also LATTERMATH.)

†**Mathe.** [OE. *maþa* wk. masc., *maþu* str. fem.:—OTeut. **maþon-*, **maþā*, of obscure origin.] A maggot, grub, worm -1585.

Mathematic (mæþĭmæ·tik). late ME. [The adj. is ad. F. *mathématique*, or L. *mathematicus*, a. Gr., f. μαθηματ-, μάθημα something learned, science, f. root of μανθάνειν. The subst. uses represent different ellipt. or absol. uses of the Gr.-L. adj.] A. *adj.* = MATHEMATICAL *a.* Now *rare.* 1549. B. *sb.* 1. = MATHEMATICS. Now *rare.* late ME. †2. A mathematician; often, An astrologer –1688.

Mathematical (mæþĭmæ·tikăl). 1522. [f. L. *mathematicus*: see prec. and -ICAL.]

A. *adj.* 1. Of or pertaining to, relating to, or of the nature of mathematics 1530. b. Being what the name imports in mathematics. Chiefly in *m. point.* 1547. c. Learned or skilled in, studying or teaching, mathematics 1522. d. Used in mathematical operations 1625. 2. *transf.* Of proofs, certitude, etc.: Resembling what is found in mathematics; rigorously exact 1662. b. Constructed with mathematical regularity 1776. †3. Astrological –1674. †4. GEOMETRICAL –1656.

1. M. Truths LOCKE. c. A m. lecturer 1622, student 1839. d. *M. instruments*: now usually, the instruments used in drawing geometrical figures. 2. It will follow with certitude plainly M. H. MORE. b. Straight paths and m. grass-plots 1881. Hence **Mathema·tically** *adv.*

B. *sb.* 1. *pl.* Mathematical objects (*rare*) 1555. †2. *pl.* Mathematics; astrology –1619. †3. A mathematician or astrologer –1587.

Mathematician (mæ:þĭmăti·ʃăn). late ME. [ad. F. *mathématicien*, f. L. *mathematicus*, *mathematica* MATHEMATIC *sb.* 1 and 2; see -IAN.] One who is versed in mathematics. †b. An astrologer. Chiefly *Hist.* –1710.

Mathema·tico-, comb. f. L. *mathematicus*, with sense 'partly mathematical, partly ——'.

Mathematics (mæþĭmæ·tiks), *sb. pl.* 1581. [pl. of MATHEMATIC B. 1. Cf. F. *les mathématiques.*] Orig., the collective name for geometry, arithmetic, and certain sciences involving geometrical reasoning, as astronomy and optics. In mod. use, (*a*) the abstract science of quantity, including geometry, arithmetic, algebra, etc. (*pure m.*); (*b*) in a wider sense, those branches of research which consist in the application of this abstract science to concrete data (*applied* or *mixed m.*). Abbrev. **Maths.**

In early use construed as a plural, usu. with *the.* In recent use *the* is commonly dropped, and the sb. construed as a sing., exc. in (*the*) *higher m.*

‖ **Mathesis** (mæþī·sis). *arch.* late ME. [Gr., f. root of μανθάνειν to learn. Formerly often stressed *ma·thesis.*] Mental discipline; learning or science, *esp.* mathematical science.

Mad *Mathesis* alone was unconfin'd POPE.

Mathetic (mæþe·tik), *a.* 1816. [ad. Gr. μαθητικός; cogn. w. prec.] Pertaining to learning or scientific knowledge. Also (Bentham) in comb. form **mathetico-.**

Mathurin (mæ·þiurin). Also **Mat(h)urine.** 1611. [From the chapel of St. *Mathurin* at Paris.] A member of the order of regular canons founded (A.D. 1198) by St. John of Matha for the redemption of Christian captives. Also as *adj.*

‖ **Matico** (mătī·kǫ). 1838. [Sp. *yerba Matico* (*yerba* herb; *Matico* dim. of *Mateo* Matthew); named from a Spanish soldier who discovered its styptic properties.] A Peruvian shrub, *Piper angustifolium*; also its leaves.

Matie (mēⁱ·ti). 1858. [a. Du. *maatjes* (*haring*), earlier *maetgens-*, f. *maagd* MAID + *-ken* -KIN.] A herring at its best, i.e. when the roe or milt is not fully developed.

Matin (mæ·tin). *Pl.* **matins**; also **mattins.** [Early ME. *matines*, a. F. *matines* fem. pl. :—eccl. L. *matutinas* (nom. *matutinæ*), fem. pl. of *matutinus* pertaining to the morning.] I. In the pl. form. 1. *Eccl.* a. One of the canonical hours of the breviary; properly a midnight office, but occas. recited at daybreak, and followed immediately by lauds. †b. Often a term for the whole of the public service preceding the first mass on Sunday –1549. c. The order for public morning prayer in the Church of England since the Reformation 1548. 2. *fig.*, etc. a. Chiefly of birds: *To sing* (etc.) *matins*, to sing their morning song (*poet.*) 1530. b. A morning duty or performance 1641.

II. †1. A morning (*rare*) –1845. 2. A morning call or song (of birds). *poet.* 1632.

III. *attrib.* and *Comb.* a. with *matin*: (*a*) 'pertaining to or used at the time of matins' ME.; (*b*) 'belonging to the early morning, matinal' 1643. b. with *matins*: as *matins book, time*, etc. ME.

‖ **Mâtin** (matæ̃). 1774. [Fr.; see MASTIFF.] A large French watch-dog.

Matinal (mæ·tinăl), *a.* Now *rare.* 1803. [ad. F. *matinal*, f. *matin* morning; see MATIN and -AL.] Belonging to the morning; early. Also, early-rising, matutinal.

‖ **Matinée** (mæ·tineⁱ, Fr. matine). 1880. [Fr. *matinée* morning, what occupies a morning, f. *matin.*] A 'morning' (i.e. afternoon) theatrical or musical performance. *attrib.*, as *m. hat.*

Matlo(w (mæ·tlo). *slang.* 1904. [ad. F. *matelot.*] A sailor.

Matrass (mæ·træs). 1605. [a. F. *matras* = Sp. *matraz*, pharmaceutical L. *matracium.*]

A glass vessel with a round or oval body and a long neck, used by chemists for digesting and distilling.

Matriarch (mēⁱ·triāɹk). 1606. [f. L. *matr(i)-*, *mater* mother, after PATRIARCH (apprehended as if f. *pater*).] A woman having the status corresponding to that of a patriarch. Now usu. *joc.* Hence **Matria·rchal** *a.* of or pertaining to a m. or to maternal rule; pertaining to, based on, or of the nature of matriarchy. **Matria·rchate**, a matriarchal community or system.

Matriarchy (mēⁱ·triāɹki). 1885. [f. MATRIARCH, after PATRIARCHY.] That form of social organization in which the mother is the head of the family, and in which descent and relationship are reckoned through mothers.

Matrical (mæ·trikăl, mătrəi·kăl), *a.* 1611. [ad. late L. *matricalis*, f. *matric-* MATRIX; see -AL.] †1. Pertaining to the matrix or womb -1651. 2. Pertaining to the matrix of algæ 1882.

Matrice (mēⁱ·tris, mæ·tris). late ME. [ad. L. *matricem* MATRIX.] †1. = MATRIX 1. -1774. †b. *transf.* and *fig.* -1698. 2. *Type-founding.* = MATRIX 4. Now *rare.* 1587. 3. = MATRIX 3. *rare.* 1855.

Matricidal (mēⁱ·trisəi·dal, mæ·tri-), *a.* 1846. [f. MATRICIDE¹ and ² + -AL.] That kills his or her mother.

Matricide¹ (mēⁱ·trisəid, mæ·tri-). 1632. [ad. L. *matricida*; see -CIDE 1.] One who kills his or her mother.

Matricide² (mēⁱ·trisəid, mæ·tri-). 1594. [ad. L. *matricidium*; see -CIDE 2.] The action of killing one's mother.

‖**Matricula** (mătri·kiŭlă). 1555. [Late L., dim. of L. *matrix* (see MATRIX).] 1. A list or register of persons belonging to an order, society, or the like. Also, a certificate of enrolment in this. 2. *spec.* In the Holy Roman (and the German) Empire: A list of the contingents, in men and money, which the several States were bound to furnish to the empire 1845. *Obs.* exc. *Hist.*

Matricular (mătri·kiŭlăɹ), *a.* 1575. [ad. med.L. *matricularius* and *-aris*, f. *matricula*; see MATRICULA and -AR¹.] 1. Pertaining to, or of the nature of, a 'matricula' or official register of persons belonging to a university, an association, etc. b. (With reference to Germany): Pertaining to the 'matricula' (see prec. 2) 1762. 2. [as if f. MATRIX; see -ULAR.] Of or belonging to the matrix or womb 1896.

Matriculate (mătri·kiŭlēt). 1487. [ad. med.L. *matriculatus*, *matriculare*; see next.] A. *ppl. a.* Matriculated. B. *sb.* One who has been matriculated 1712.

Matriculate (mătri·kiŭleⁱt), *v.* 1577. [f. med.L. **matriculat-*, **matriculare*, f. MATRICULA, q. v.] †1. *trans.* To insert (a name) in a register or official list; usually, to admit or incorporate into a society or body of persons by inserting the name in a register; to enrol (soldiers). †Also *transf.* and *fig.* -1782. †b. *occas.* To adopt as a child; to adopt or naturalize (an alien, a foreign custom, book, etc.) -1704. 2. *spec.* To admit (a student) to a university or college by enrolling his name in the register 1579. b. *intr.* To be thus admitted 1851. 3. *Her.* To record (arms) in an official register 1586.

2. Bentley was matriculated at St. John's College, Cambridge DE QUINCEY. 3. The Ensigns Armorial ..are matriculated in the public registers of the Lyon Office 1809.

Matriculation (mătrikiŭlēⁱ·ʃən). 1588. [f. prec. + -ATION.] 1. The action of matriculating (see the vb.). Now chiefly in academic use, formal admission into a university or college. Occas. used for *m. examination.* 2. *Her.* A registration of armorial bearings 1810.

Matrimonial (mætrimōᵘ·niăl), *a.* 1532. [a. F., ad. late L. *matrimonialis* of or pertaining to matrimony, f. *matrimonium*; see MATRIMONY and -AL.] 1. Of or pertaining to matrimony. 2. Derived from marriage 1577. 3. Calculated to promote matrimony 1730.

1. He lugged about the m. load 1675. 3. M. charms FIELDING. Hence **Matrimo·nially** *adv.* according to the manner or laws of matrimony; by right of marriage. So †**Matrimo·nious** *a.* pertaining to marriage MILT.; -ly *adv.*

Matrimony (mæ·trimŏni). ME. [a. OF. *matremoine*, a. L. *matrimonium*, f. *matrem* mother; see -MONY.] 1. The rite of marriage; the action of marrying. †b. A marriage; an alliance by marriage -1756. †c. The marriage service -1724. 2. The state or condition of being husband and wife ME. 3. A game played with a full pack of cards and resembling Pope Joan. Also, the combination of king and queen of trumps in this and other card games 1801. 4. *slang* and *dial.* A mixture of two comestibles or beverages 1813.

1. Teaching that M. is a Sacrament, giveth to the Clergy the Judging of the lawfulnesse of Marriages HOBBES. *Comb.* **m. vine**, a name for *Lycium barbarum* or *L. vulgare.*

Matrix (mēⁱ·triks). *Pl.* **matrixes, matrices** (mēⁱ·-, mæ·trisīz). 1526. [a. L. *matrix*, *matric-*; app. f. *mater*, by change of the ending into the suffix of fem. agent-nouns. Cf. MATRICE.] 1. The uterus or womb. Also occas. used for OVARY. 2. A place or medium in which something is bred, produced, or developed 1555. b. A place or point of origin and growth 1605. c. The formative part of an animal organ, e.g. the pulp and capsule of the mammalian tooth 1835. d. *Bot.* The body on which a fungus or a lichen grows 1857. 3. An embedding or enclosing mass; *esp.* the rock-mass surrounding metal (see GANGUE), fossils, gems, and the like 1641. b. *Biol.* The substance situated between animal or vegetable cells 1802. 4. *Type-founding.* A piece of metal, usu. copper, by means of which the face of a type is cast, having the letter stamped on it in intaglio with a punch. Also in stereotyping, the mould of plaster, etc. into which stereotypers' metal is cast. 1626. b. *Antiq.* The bed in a slab in which a monumental brass is fixed 1861. 5. *Math.* A rectangular arrangement of quantities or symbols 1858. 6. *attrib.* 1598.

1. Every man chylde that fyrst openeth the m. shalbe called holy to the lorde TINDALE *Luke* ii. 23.

Matron (mēⁱ·trən). late ME. [a. F. *matrone*, ad. L. *matrona*, f. *matrem*, *mater* mother.] 1. A married woman, usually with the accessory idea of rank or dignity. b. *Eccl.* A married female saint 1519. 2. *spec.* A married woman considered as having expert knowledge in matters of pregnancy, etc.; now only in *jury of matrons* 1491. 3. A (married or unmarried) woman who has official charge of the domestic arrangements of a hospital, school, prison, etc. 1557. 4. *attrib.* quasi-*adj.* 1667.

1. When Adam and first M. Eve Had ended now their Orisons MILT. 3. The m. of the Chartreux is about to resign her place JOHNSON. 4. M. airs 1836. Hence **Ma·tronal** *a.* of, pertaining to, or appropriate to a m.; having the characteristics of a m. 1609. **Ma·tronhood**, the state or condition of being a m. 1836. **Ma·tronly** *a.* like a m.; suitable to a m. 1656. Also as *adv.*

Matronage (mēⁱ·trŏnĕdʒ). 1771. [f. prec. + -AGE.] 1. A body of matrons; matrons collectively. 2. Guardianship by a matron 1771. 3. The state of being a matron 1870.

1. His exemplary Queen, at the head of the m. of this land BURKE. 2. Under the m. of the housekeeper 1878.

Matronize (mēⁱ·trŏnəiz), *v.* 1754. [f. MATRON + -IZE.] 1. *trans.* To render matronly. 2. *intr.* To become or be made a matron 1802. 3. *trans.* To act as matron to; to chaperon 1807.

Ma·tron-like, *a.* 1575. [See -LIKE.] Like or befitting a matron; matronly.

Matronship (mēⁱ·trənʃip). 1550. [See -SHIP.] 1. The condition of being a matron. 2. The personality of a matron. In *your*, *her m.*, used joc. as a title 1591. 2. The office of matron in a hospital, workhouse, etc. 1843.

Matronymic (mætrŏni·mik), *a.* and *sb.* 1794. [Hybrid f. L. *matr-*, *mater* mother, after PATRONYMIC.] = METRONYMIC *a.* and *sb.*

Matross (mătrǫ·s). *Obs.* exc. *Hist.* 1639. [a. Du. *matroos* sailor, app. a corruption of F. *matelot*.] A soldier next in rank below the gunner in a train of artillery, who acted as a kind of assistant or mate.

Matt, freq. var. of MAT *a.*

‖**Mattamore** (mætămōᵊ·ɹ). 1695. [a. F. *matamore* (St. Olan, 1695), a. Arab. *maṭmūraʰ*, f. *ṭamara* to store up.] A subterranean habitation, storehouse, or granary.

Matte (mæt). 1839. [a. F. *matte*.] *Metallurgy.* An impure and unfinished metallic product of the smelting of various ores, esp. those of copper.

Matted (mæ·tĕd), *ppl. a.*¹ 1823. [f. MAT *v.*².] Dulled, deprived of lustre or gloss.

Matted (mæ·tĕd), *ppl. a.*² 1607. [f. MAT *v.*¹ + -ED¹.] 1. Laid or spread with matting or mats. b. Made of plaited rushes; of chairs, etc., rush-bottomed 1692. 2. Of vegetable growths, hair, etc.: Tangled and interlaced, or covered with tangle 1613. b. Compressed into the likeness of a mat 1825. c. Covered with a dense growth 1791. 3. Enclosed or wrapt in matting. Also with *up*. 1738.

1. A m. passage 1883. b. The ordinary m. chairs DE FOE. 2. The m. underwood and the rank green grass BLACK. c. The m. sward BRYANT.

Matter (mæ·təɹ), *sb.* [ME. *materie*, *matere*, *matiere*, a. OF. *matere*, *matiere* (mod.F. *matière*), ad. L. *materia* (also *materies*).]

I. In purely physical applications. 1. The substance, or substances, of which a physical object is made; constituent material. Now only with implication of sense 2 or 4. 2. Any physical substance not definitely particularized. Often qualified, as in *colouring*, *fæcal*, etc. *m.* late ME. 3. *spec.* (= *corrupt m.*) Purulent discharge, pus. late ME. 4. Physical or corporeal substance in general, as dist. from spirit, soul, mind, etc., and from qualities, actions, or conditions 1626.

1. The m. of the Heavens NEWTON, of the globe MILL. 2. Milk..deficient in fatty m. 1891. *Grey m.*, *white m.* (of the brain): see the adjs. 4. M. and Motion cannot think BENTLEY. †*Subtile m.* [tr. L. *materia subtilis*]: Descartes' name for a fluid which he supposed to fill the whole of space.

II. Contrasted with *form*. 1. *Philos.* In Aristotelian and scholastic use: That component of the essence of any thing or being which has bare existence, but which requires the addition of a particular 'form' (see FORM *sb.* 4 a) to constitute it as determinately existent. late ME. †b. = Chaos. BACON. c. In Kantian use, applied to that element of knowledge that is supplied by sensation, regarded apart from the 'form' which it receives from the categories of the understanding 1838. 2. *Theol.* A sacrament is said to have *matter* (as the water in baptism, the bread and wine in the Eucharist) and *form*, which is furnished by certain formulary words ME. 3. *Logic.* The particular content of a proposition or syllogism, as dist. from its form 1697.

1. Matere is neuer seen wythout fourme TREVISA. *First m.* (= L. *materia prima*, Gr. ἡ πρώτη ὕλη): mere possibility of being. b. First he breathed Light vpon the Face of the M. or Chaos BACON.

III. Material of thought, speech, or action. 1. Material for expression; something to say or write ME. †2. A theme, topic, subject of exposition -1704. 3. The substance of a book, speech, or the like; often opp. to the 'manner' in which it is presented. late ME. †b. Sense, substance. SHAKS. 4. That with which a science, art, law, etc. has to do; the subject-matter of a study -1594. 5. Ground, reason, or cause for doing or being something ME. †6. Material cause; that of which something consists or out of which it is developed -1825. 7. In vague sense, = 'things', 'something'; esp. with qualifying words, things or something of a specified kind, involving or related to a specified thing 1449. b. *spec.* in *Law.* Something which is to be tried or proved; statements which come under the consideration of the court 1532. 8. a. Things printed or written, as *manuscript*, etc. *m.* In *Printing* applied *techn.* to (*a*) the body of a printed work, as dist. from the headings, etc.; in newspapers, the general contents as dist. from the advertisements; (*b*) type set up; (*c*) 'copy'. 1683. b. (*Postal*) *m.*: whatever may be sent by post 1891.

1. For I am full of m., the spirit within me constraineth me *Job* xxxii. 18. 2. Thee, O Queene! the m. of my song SPENSER. 3. Was euer booke containing such vile m. So fairely bound? SHAKS. b. I was borne to speake all mirth, and no m. SHAKS. †*There is m. in it*: it is important. 5. Phr. †*To seek m.*: to

seek a pretext or occasion. 7. This is rather m. of fact then of Law 1651. b. *M. of record*, that which may be proved by some record. *Nude m.*, a naked allegation of a thing done, to be proved only by witnesses. Phr. *It makes* (later *is*) *no m.* = It is of no consequence; now often shortened to *No m.*, also *What m.?*

IV. A thing, affair, concern; corresp. to L. *res*. 1. A subject, affair, business ME. b. (One's) cause, concern, or affair. *Obs.* or *rare.* ME. c. *pl.* Events, affairs, circumstances, etc., understood to refer to a particular occasion, but not further specified 1570. †d. *pl.* Occas. used vaguely of concrete things –1826. 2. *contextually.* A subject of contention, dispute, litigation, or the like. late ME. 3. With qualification (attribute, or *of* and sb.): A thing, affair, subject, etc. of the kind indicated by the qualification. late ME. 4. Used as an indeterminate sb. to which to attach an epithet. late ME. †5. With qualifying adj., usu. *small*: A (certain) quantity or amount (*of*) –1772.

1. They order, said I, this m. better in France STERNE. b. Manage your matters well T. HOOK. c. This seems to be carrying matters too far BLACKSTONE. d. She [the landlady]..left the stranger to enjoy in quiet the excellent matters which she had placed before him SCOTT. 3. *Laughing, money m.*, see the first element. See also MATTER OF COURSE, MATTER OF FACT. *A m. of*: a 'case' of. 4. Instinct is a great m. SHAKS. Phr. *It is no such m.*, *another m. For that m.*: = 'for the m. of that'. 5. I..sent a small m. to his wife FIELDING. Phr. *A small m.*, occas. *a m.*, used advb. = Somewhat, slightly. Phr. *A m. of*: used to qualify a numeral, indicating that it is not literally exact; He had had, as he phrased it, a m. of four wives JOHNSON.

Phr. **The matter**: †a. That which is contemplated, intended, or desired. *To the m.*: to the point, relevant(ly); = L. *ad rem*. So *From the m. Much about the m.*: not far from the point. b. What actually involves or concerns some person or thing, esp. a circumstance which calls for remedy or explanation; chiefly in *What is the m.?* and the like. *What is the m. with..?* (colloq.) = What is amiss with..? hence (*joc.*) What is the objection to..? c. *In the m. of* (= law L. *in re*): in relation to, with regard to; chiefly in *Law*. d. *For the m. of that*: as far as that goes.

Matter (mæ·tǝɹ), *v.* 1530. [f. prec. sb.] 1. *intr.* To discharge matter or pus; to suppurate. 2. To be of importance; to signify; chiefly in interrog. and neg. sentences. (Freq. *impersonal.*) Const. *to*; also (*poet. rare*) with *dat.* 1581. 3. With a neg.: To be concerned about, care for, heed, mind. *Obs.* exc. *dial.* in sense: To approve of, like. 1649. †b. *absol.* or *intr.* To care, mind –1729.

2. Nor does it matter a straw whether [etc.] LANDOR. 3. If it had been out of doors I had not mattered it so much FIELDING.

Matterless (mæ·tǝɹlės), *a.* 1548. [-LESS.] 1. Not embodied in matter; immaterial. Now *rare.* †2. Devoid of matter, sense, or meaning –1767. 3. Immaterial, of no importance. Chiefly *dial.* 1650.

1. M. forms H. COLERIDGE. 2. M. words 1612.

Matter of course. 1739. Something which is to be expected in the natural course of things. b. *attrib.* or as *adj.* (written with hyphens): To be expected. Freq. of persons, etc.: Taking things as a matter of course. 1840.

b. The cool matter-of-course manner of this reply DICKENS.

Matter of fact (mæ:tǝrǝvfæ·kt). 1581. [See MATTER III. 7, IV. 3 and FACT 5.] A. *sb.* a. *Law.* That portion of a subject of enquiry which is concerned with the truth or falsehood of alleged facts; a particular issue of this nature; opp. to *matter of law*. b. What pertains to the sphere of fact as opp. to opinion, probability, or inference; something which is of the nature of a fact.

It is either a beleefe of Historie (as the Lawyers speeke, matter of fact:) or else of matter of art and opinion BACON. Phr. *As a m. of fact, in m. of fact*: in point of fact, really.

B. *attrib.* or *adj.* (Usu. hyphened.) Pertaining to, having regard to, or depending upon actual fact; unimaginative, prosaic 1712.

The more Callicles is irritated, the more provoking and matter of fact does Socrates become JOWETT

Mattery (mæ·tǝri), *a.* late ME. [f. MATTER *sb.* + -Y [1].] 1. Full of, forming, or discharging matter; purulent. Now *rare* †2. Full of matter or sense. B. JONS.

Mattins, variant of MATINS.

Matting (mæ·tiŋ), *vbl. sb.*[1] 1682. [f. MAT *v.*[1] and *sb.*[1]] 1. In various senses of MAT *v.*[1] 2. *concr.* A fabric of some coarse material, e.g. coir, bast, hemp, grass, etc., used as a covering for floors or roofs, or as material for packing, for tying plants, etc. Also *Naut.* = MAT *sb.*[1] 4. 1748. b. Materials for mats 1847. 3. *attrib.* 1688.

Matting (mæ·tiŋ), *vbl. sb.*[2] 1688. [f. MAT *v.*[2] + -ING [1].] 1. The production of a mat surface, in *Chasing, Gilding*, etc. Also, the mat surface itself. 2. The furnishing (of a picture) with a mat; *concr.* = MAT *sb.*[2] 3. 1864. 3. *Comb.*, as *m.-punch, -tool* 1877.

Mattock (mæ·tǝk), *sb.* [OE. *mattuc, mettuc* masc.; origin unkn.] An agricultural tool used for loosening hard ground, grubbing up trees, etc. It has a socketed steel head, having on one side an adze-shaped blade, and sometimes on the other a kind of pick.

attrib. Born To labour and the mattock-harden'd hand TENNYSON. Hence **Ma·ttock** *v.* to turn *up* with the m.

Mattress (mæ·trės). ME. [a. OF. *materas* (mod.F. *matelas*), ad. It. *materasso*, identified with Sp. and Pg. *almadraque*, ad. Arab. *al-maṭraḥ* place where something is thrown, mat, cushion, f. root *ṭaraḥa* to throw.] 1. A case of canvas or other coarse material, stuffed with hair, flocks, straw, or the like, used as a bed or (more commonly) as a support for a bed. Also, any similar appliance, esp. one consisting of wire cloth stretched upon a frame. †2. = MAT *sb.*[1] 1. –1706. 3. *Engineering.* A strong mat of brushwood bound or twisted together, used in layers in the construction of dikes, piers, etc. 1875.

†**Maturant,** *a.* and *sb.* 1661. [ad. L. *maturantem*, pr. pple. of *maturare*; see MATURE *v.*] = MATURATIVE *a.* and *sb.* –1856.

Maturate (mæ·tiureᶦt), *v.* 1541. [f. L. *maturat-, maturare*, f. *maturus*; see MATURE *a.*] 1. *trans.* (*Med.*) To cause (matter, a boil, etc.) to ripen or suppurate; to 'bring to a head'. Also *absol.* to cause suppuration. Now *rare* or *Obs.* †2. To mature, ripen (fruits, liquors, etc.). Also *fig.* –1756. †3. To mature, develop (men, hopes, etc.) –1791. †4. a. *Alchemy.* To purify and digest (a metal) by maturation; also with *into*. b. *Metall.* To bring (an ore) into the metallic state. –1758. †5. *intr.* Of fruit: To mature –1756. 6. Of a pustule: To suppurate 1746.

3. Yeares must m. men to such Functions 1622.

Maturation (mætiurēᶦ·ʃǝn). late ME. [a. F., ad. L. *maturationem*; see prec. and MATURE *v.*] 1. *Med.* The ripening of morbific matter; suppuration; the action of causing this. †2. *Alchemy.* The action of converting a baser metal into gold –1671. †3. *Physics.* The (supposed) natural ripening or development of material substances by the operation of heat and motion –1753. 4. Of fruits, juices, etc.: Development to ripeness; also, an instance of this 1621. b. Of liquors, etc.: The action of maturing; the process of becoming matured 1605. 5. The action of coming to full growth and development 1616. b. *transf.* and *fig.* (of a plan, work, etc.) 1655. †6. The forwarding (of a business, etc.) –1655.

5. b. The germination and m. of some truth J. H. NEWMAN.

Maturative (mătiūǝ·rătiv). late ME. [a. F. *maturatif, -ive*, ad. L. *maturativus*, f. *maturare.*] A. *adj.* 1. *Med.* That causes MATURATION (sense 1); pertaining to or characterized by maturation. †2. Having the power or function of maturing (fruits, etc.); of or pertaining to maturation –1685.

1. The m. or suppurative stage [of small-pox] 1858. B. *sb.* A maturative remedy. late ME.

Mature (mătiūǝ·ɹ), *a.* 1454. [ad. L. *maturus* ripe, early.] 1. Complete in natural development or growth; ripe; full grown; †ready *for* 1599. 2. Of a person: Fully developed in body and mind. Of qualities, etc.: Fully developed. 1600. b. Of or pertaining to maturity or manhood. *Wint. T.* I. i. 27. 3. (The earliest use.) Of thought or deliberation: Duly prolonged and careful. Of plans, etc.: Formed after due deliberation. 1454. †4. Prompt –1672. †5. Of an event: Occurring when the time is ripe. Of time: Due. (The opposite of 'premature'.) –1667. 6. *Med.* In a state of suppuration; ripe 1828.

1. *fig.* For now is love m. in ear TENNYSON. 2. The yongest Sonne of Priam;..Not yet m., yet matchlesse SHAKS. M. In wisdom COWPER. 3. Till his plans for revolt were m. 1839. No time for m. and careful reflection 1848. 5. *Lear* IV. vi. 282. Hence **Matu·re-ly** *adv.*, **-ness.**

Mature (mătiūǝ·ɹ), *v.* late ME. [Partly ad. obs. F. *maturer*, ad. L. *maturare*; partly f. MATURE *a.*] 1. *trans.* (*Med.*) = MATURATE *v.* 1. 2. To bring to maturity; to ripen; to bring to full growth. Also *pass.* = 6. 1626. 3. *transf.* To cause to develop fully; to perfect the development of (a person) mentally and physically 1660. 4. *fig.* To make ripe or ready; to perfect (a plan, etc.); to bring to a head 1667. †5. To forward duly. MARVELL. 6. *intr.* To come to maturity or perfect development; to grow ripe 1626. Also *transf.* and *fig.* 7. *Comm.* Of a bill, sum of money, etc.: To become due 1861.

3. His prudence was matured by experience GIBBON. 4. But these thoughts Full Counsel must m. MILT. 7. In March as much as 980,000*l.* will m. 1892.

Maturity (mătiūǝ·rĭti). late ME. [ad. F. *maturité*, or L. *maturitas*; see MATURE *a.* and -ITY.] †1. Deliberateness of action; mature consideration –1734. †2. Due promptness –1670. 3. The state of being mature; fullness or perfection of development or growth. late ME. 4. Of immaterial things: The state of being complete, perfect, or ready 1625. 5. *Comm.* The state of becoming due for payment; the time at which a bill becomes due; also, the bill itself 1815. 6. The state of an abscess in which the pus is fully formed 1676.

3. Thy full maturitie Of yeares and wisdome DANIEL. A single spreading oak, grown to m. HOGARTH. 4. Measures..brought to m. 1844. 5. The period of the date of m. of bills at or after sight 1860. Short-dated maturities 1923.

Matutinal (mætiu̇tǝi·năl, mătiū·tĭnăl), *a.* 1656. [ad. L. *matutinalis*, f. *matutinus*; see MATUTINE.] Of or pertaining to the morning, early. Also *rarely*, rising early.

Matutine (mæ·tiu̇tǝin), *a.* (and *sb.*) 1445. [ad. L. *matutinus*, f. *Matuta* (proper name of the goddess of dawn), allied to *maturus* MATURE *a.*] 1. Of or pertaining to the morning; occurring in the morning. b. Of a star; *spec.* in *Astron.* and *Astrol.*: That rises or is above the horizon before sunrise 1500. †2. *sb. pl.* Matins. FULLER. Hence **Ma·tutinely** *adv.* in the morning.

Maty (mēᶦ·ti), **mate** (mēᶦ·t). *Anglo-Ind.* 1810. [Origin obscure.] A native servant, *esp.* an assistant or under-servant.

Maucauco, obs. f. MACACO.[2]

Maud (mǭd). 1787. [?] A grey striped plaid worn by shepherds in the South of Scotland; also a travelling wrap resembling a maud.

Maudle (mǭ·d'l), *v. rare.* 1706. [Back-formation f. MAUDLIN *a.*, taken as pr. pple.] a. *trans.* To make maudlin. b. *intr.* To talk maudlinly.

Maudlin (mǭ·dlin), *sb.* ME. [a. OF. *Madelaine*, semi-pop. ad. L. *Magdalena*, MAGDALEN(E).] †1. As proper name: = MAGDALEN 1. –1573. †b. *transf.* A penitent resembling Mary Magdalen –1631. 2. †a. = COSTMARY. b. The herb *Achillea Ageratum.* (Also *sweet m.*) 1460. †3. A kind of peach (= MAGDALEN 4); also a kind of pear –1707. 4. [From the adj.] What is maudlin; weak or mawkish sentiment 1838.

Comb.: †m. **daisy,** the ox-eye daisy; **-wort** (*dial.*) = *m. daisy*.

Maudlin (mǭ·dlin), *a.* 1607. [f. prec. used attrib., in allusion to pictures of the Magdalen weeping.] 1. Weeping, lachrymose. *Obs.* or *arch.* 2. Mawkishly emotional; tearfully sentimental 1631. 3. (First in *maudlin-drunk.*) Used of that stage of drunkenness which is tearful and effusively affectionate 1616.

1. Heraclitus the M. Philosopher BUTLER. 2. A thousand m. oaths of friendship T. BROWN. 3. His potations had rendered him somewhat m. 1860.

Comb. **m.-drunk,** in the m. stage of intoxication. Hence **Mau·dlinism,** the state of being maudlin-drunk. **Mau·dlinly** *adv.* in a m. manner.

Maugrabee (mǭ·grăbī). 1704. [a. Arab. *maγrabīy* western.] An African Moor. So **Mau·grabin,** in same sense. Also *attrib.*

Maugre (mǭ·gəɹ), *sb.* and *prep.* ME. [a. OF. *maugré, malgré*, f. *mal* bad, evil + *gré* (see GREE *sb.*²).] †A. *sb.* 1. Ill-will, spite –1542. 2. The state of being regarded with ill-will. Also, an instance of this. –1560.

Phr. *In (the) m. of*: in spite of, notwithstanding.

B. *adv.* and *prep.* In spite of, notwithstanding; notwithstanding the power of ME. ¶Used by Spenser for: A curse upon . . !

Phr. *M.* (a person's) *teeth, head*: in spite of (his) resistance, notwithstanding all (he) can do.

†**Mau·gre**, *v.* 1597. [a. F. *maugréer*, f. *maugré* MAUGRE *sb.*] *trans.* To show ill-will to; to defy –1632.

Maukin, var. of MALKIN.

Maul, mall (mǭl), *sb.*¹ ME. [a. F. *mail* :—L. *malleum* (nom. *malleus*) hammer.] 1. = MACE¹ 1. Also, a wooden club. *Obs.* exc. *arch.* and *Hist.* 2. In early use, a massive hammer of any kind. Now, applied to special kinds of heavy hammers or beetles, commonly of wood, used (e.g.) in pile-driving, shipbuilding, etc. late ME. †Also *transf.* and *fig.* after L. *malleus* –1752. †3. [f. MAUL *v.*] A heavy blow. BUTLER. †4. *Rugby Football.* A mauling or tackling 1867.

Maul (mǭl), *sb.*² *dial.* late ME. Var. of MALLOW. (Cf. MAW *sb.*²)

Maul (mǭl), *v.* ME. [f. MAUL *sb.*¹] †1. *trans.* To beat or strike (with or as with a hammer); to hammer, batter –1633. b. *U.S.* To split (rails) with a maul and wedge 1686. †2. To strike (a person or animal) with a heavy weapon ME. 3. To beat and bruise; to maltreat; to knock about 1610. 4. *transf.* To damage seriously; to shatter, mangle 1692. 5. *fig.* To injure by criticizing, 'pull to pieces' 1593. 6. To handle roughly or carelessly 1781. †7. *Rugby Football. trans.* To hold (the player holding the ball) and endeavour to wrest it from him 1856.

3. It was proposed..that we should..m. the watch SMOLLETT. 4. Her larboard side is most terribly mauled 1758. 5. To vex and m. a ministerial race CRABBE. 6. He is a man that mauls every truth of God 1847.

Maulstick (mǭ·lstik). Also **mahlstick**, etc. 1658. [ad. Du. *maalstok*, f. *malen* to paint + *stok* stick.] A light stick with a soft leather ball at the upper end, held by painters in the left hand as a support for the right.

Maumet (mǭ·mėt). *Obs.* exc. *arch.* and *dial.* Also mammet, etc. ME. [a. OF. *mahumet* idol; a use of *Mahumet* MAHOMET, due to the mediæval notion that Mohammed was worshipped as a god.] †1. A false god; an idol –1647. 2. A doll, puppet; also, a 'guy'. Now only *dial.* 1494. †Also *fig.* 3. Applied to a person as a term of abuse. Now *dial.* 1529. †4. A kind of pigeon –1835.

2. This is no world To play with Mammets SHAKS. 3. A whining mammet SHAKS.

Maumetry (mǭ·mėtri). *Obs.* exc. *arch.* Also †mammitrie, etc. ME. [f. prec. + -RY.] 1. The worship of images; idolatry. Also, heathenism. †2. Idols collectively –1567. 3. Mohammedanism; = MAHOMETRY. late ME.

Maun (mǫn, mǭn), *v.* (*pres. ind.*) *Sc.* late ME. [a. ON. *man*.] Must; = MUN *v.*

Maunche: see MANCHE, MUNCH.

Maund (mǭnd), *sb.*¹ Now *local.* [OE. *mand, mǫnd* fem. The forms *maund(e* represent the OF. *mande*, adopted from Du. and LG.] 1. A wicker or other woven basket having a handle or handles. b. The contents of a maund 1869. 2. A measure of capacity varying locally 1545.

‖**Maund** (mǭnd), *sb.*² 1584. [English pron. of Hindi and Pers. *man*, cogn. w. Gr. *μνᾶ*, L. *mina*, Heb. *maneh*.] A denomination of weight current in India and Western Asia, varying greatly in value locally. The standard maund of the Indian empire is now = 100 lbs. troy, or 82⅔ lbs. avoirdupois.

†**Maund**, *v. Cant.* 1567. [?] To beg –1823.

†**Mau·nder**, *sb.*¹ *Cant.* 1609. [f. prec. + -ER¹.] A beggar –1829. So as vb. = prec. 1611.

Maunder (mǭ·ndəɹ), *sb.*² 1880. [f. MAUNDER *v.*] Idle incoherent talk or writing.

Maunder (mǭ·ndəɹ), *v.* 1621. [? imitative.] †1. *intr.* 'To grumble, mutter, or growl' –1848. 2. To move or act in a dreamy, idle, or inconsequent manner 1746. 3. To ramble or wander in one's talk. Also *trans.* To utter (something) in this manner 1831.

3. Mumbling and maundering the merest commonplaces CARLYLE. Hence **Mau·nderer**, a twaddler.

Maundy (mǭ·ndi). ME. [a. OF. *mandé*, ad. L. *mandatum* commandment, MANDATE *sb.* See John xiii. 34 ('Mandatum novum do vobis', the first words of the first antiphon at the ceremony of the pedilavium).] 1. The ceremony of washing the feet of the poor, performed by royal or other eminent persons on the Thursday before Easter, and commonly followed by the distribution of clothing, food, or money. In England, surviving in the distribution of 'maundy money'. b. The dole made at the ceremony 1850. †c. *fig.* Almsgiving, largesse –1647. †2. The Last Supper –1640. †3. A feast. *To make one's m.*: to feast. –1646.

attrib. and *Comb.*, as *m. ale, bread, cup*, things distributed at a m., or *m. man, people, woman*, people receiving them; also, **m. money**, silver money distributed by the royal almoner to poor people on Maundy Thursday at Whitehall; so *m. coin*; **m.-supper** = sense 2; **M.-week**, Holy Week.

Maundy Thursday. 1530. [See prec.] The Thursday next before Easter.

Mauquahog, obs. f. MOHAWK.

Mauresque, var. of MORESQUE.

Maurist (mǭ·rist). 1800. [f. (St.) *Maur* + -IST.] A French Benedictine monk belonging to the congregation of St. Maur, founded in 1618.

Mauser (mau·zəɹ). 1880. [f. the inventor's name.] (More fully *M. rifle.*) A repeating rifle having an interlocking bolt-head and box magazine.

Mausolean (mǭsǒlī·ăn), *a.* 1557. [f. next + -AN.] †1. *M. sepulchre, tomb* = MAUSOLEUM. Also *transf.* and *fig.* 2. Pertaining to, or resembling, mausoleums 1785.

Mausoleum (mǭsǒlī·ǒm). *Pl.* **-lea** (-lī·ă), **-leums**. 1546. [a. L. *mausoleum*, ad. Gr. *μαυσώλειον*, f. *Μαύσωλος* Mausolus.] 1. The magnificent tomb of Mausolus, King of Caria, erected in the middle of the 4th c. B.C. at Halicarnassus by his queen Artemisia. 2. A stately burial-place erected for or by a person of distinction 1600. ¶b. *loosely.* A stately tomb 1688. †3. = CATAFALQUE 1. –1752.

2. *fig.* The dead, Whose names are mausoleums of the Muse BYRON.

Mauther (mǭ·ðəɹ). *dial.* 1440. [?] A young girl; *locally*, a 'great awkward girl'.

‖**Mauvaise honte** (movęz oṅt). 1721. [Fr., lit. = 'ill shame'.] False shame; painful diffidence.

‖**Mauvais sujet** (movę süʒę). 1847. [Fr., = 'bad subject'.] A worthless fellow, a 'bad lot'.

Mauve (mōuv). 1859. [a. F. *mauve* :—L. *malva* MALLOW.] *sb.* A bright but delicate purple dye obtained from coal-tar aniline; the colour of this. *adj.* Of the colour of mauve.

Mauveine (mōu·vin). 1863. [f. F. *mauve* mallow + -INE⁵.] *Chem.* The base of the purple aniline dyes.

Maverick (mæ·vərik). 1872. [f. the name of Samuel A. *Maverick*, a civil engineer, who accidentally owned unbranded cattle in Texas from 1845 to 1856.] 1. *U.S.* In the cattle-breeding districts, a calf or yearling found without an owner's brand. 2. *transf.* A masterless person; one who is roving and casual 1892.

Mavis (mē¹·vis). Now *poet.* and *dial.* late ME. [a. F. *mauvis* masc. = Sp. *malviz* (? from Fr.); etym. unkn.] The song-thrush, *Turdus musicus.*

‖**Mavourneen** (măvū·rnīn). Also **-in.** 1800. [Irish *mo mhurnín.*] My darling.

Maw¹ (mǭ). [Com. Teut.: OE. *maga* wk. masc. :—OTeut. **magon-*.] 1. The stomach; the cavity of the stomach. Now only (exc. *joc.*) the stomach of animals; *spec.* the last of the four stomachs of a ruminant. Also *transf.* and *fig.* 2. Applied also to: †a. The crop of a granivorous bird –1731. b. The swim-bladder or sound of a fish. late ME. 3. The throat, gullet; now chiefly, the jaws or mouth 1530. †4. Used (like *stomach*) for: Appetite, inclination –1704.

1. Luckless landsmen's sea-sick maws BYRON. 3. The hungry m. of a pike 1873. 4. I have no great M. to that Business, methinks CIBBER.

Maw². Now *dial.* late ME. Var. of MAUL *sb.*²

Maw³ (mǭ). *Obs.* exc. *dial.* 1450. [a. ON. *má-r* = OE. *mǽw*; see MEW *sb.*¹] A gull, esp. the Common gull, *Larus canus.*

Maw⁴ (mǭ). *Obs.* exc. *Hist.* 1548. [?] An old game at cards, played with a piquet pack of thirty-six cards, by any number of persons from two to six.

Mawk (mǭk). *Obs.* exc. *dial.* late ME. [ad. ON. *maðk-r* earthworm.] = MAGGOT.

Mawkin, obs. f. MALKIN.

Maw·kingly, *a. Obs.* exc. *dial.* 1656. [f. *mawking*, MALKIN + -LY¹.] Slovenly.

Mawkish (mǭ·kiʃ), *a.* 1668. [f. MAWK + -ISH¹.] †1. Inclined to sickness; without appetite –1836. 2. Having a nauseating taste; now, having a faint, sickly flavour with little definite taste 1697. 3. *fig.* Imbued with sickly or false sentiment; lacking in robustness 1702.

1. The dean who us'd to dine at one, Is maukish, and his stomach gone SWIFT. 3. A m. popularity KEATS. Hence **Maw·kish-ly** *adv.*, **-ness.**

Mawky (mǭ·ki), *a. dial.* 1790. [f. MAWK + -Y¹.] 1. Maggoty; also, crotchety. 2. = MAWKISH 1830.

Mawseed (mǭ·sīd). 1730. [Half-translated ad. Ger. dial. *mahsaat, mohsamen*, f. *mah, moh* poppy + *saat, samen* seed.] The seed of the opium poppy, *Papaver somniferum.*

Mawworm¹ (mǭ·wǒɹm). 1607. [f. MAW¹ + WORM.] Any worm infesting the stomach or intestines of man and other mammals.

Mawworm² (mǭ·wǒɹm). 1850. (Prop. with initial capital.) A man who resembles *Mawworm*, a character in Bickerstaffe's play *The Hypocrite*, 1769; a hypocritical pretender to sanctity.

Something of the Maworm spirit, 'I like to be despised' 1850.

‖**Maxilla** (mæksi·lă). *Pl.* **-læ** (-lī). 1676. [L. *maxilla* jaw.] 1. A jaw or jaw-bone, *esp.* the upper jaw in mammals and most vertebrate animals. 2. One of the anterior limbs of insects and other arthropods, so modified as to serve the purpose of mastication 1798. Hence †**Maxillar** *a.* = next 1656–1720.

Maxillary (mæksi·lări, mæ·ksilări). 1626. [f. MAXILLA + -ARY¹. Cf. F. *maxillaire.*] A. *adj.* 1. Belonging to, connected with, or forming part of the jaw or jaw-bone, esp. of the upper jaw of vertebrate animals. 2. Belonging to, connected with, or forming part of the maxillæ of arthropods 1826. B. *sb.* = *maxillary bone.*

M. system: the system of classification of insects based on the form of the maxillæ.

Maxilliform (mæksi·lifǭɹm), *a.* 1835. [f. MAXILLA + -(I)FORM.] Formed like a maxilla.

Maxilliped, -pede (mæksi·liped, -pīd). 1846. [f. MAXILLA + L. *pedem, pes* foot.] *Zool.* A 'foot-jaw' (see FOOT *sb.*).

Maxillo-, comb. f. MAXILLA in sense 'pertaining to the maxilla and . . .'; so *m.-mandibular, -palatine, -pharyngeal, -turbinal*, etc.

Maxim¹ (mæ·ksim). late ME. [a. F. *maxime*, ad. L. *maxima* adj. fem. sing., used ellipt. (sc. *propositio*), in the sense of 'axiom' (= L. *dignitas*, Gr. *ἀξίωμα*).] †1. An axiom; a self-evident proposition assumed as a premiss –1692. 2. A proposition (esp. in aphoristic or sententious form) expressing some general truth of science or of experience 1594. b. *esp.* in *Law* 1567. 3. A rule or principle of conduct 1579. 4. *attrib.* 1806.

1. It is urged as an universal M., That Nothing can procede from Nothing BENTLEY. 2. The m. that knowledge is power 1874. b. The m., 'a man's house is his castle' 1893. 3. Her m. was, that it was time enough to come when she was called HT. MARTINEAU.

Maxim² (mæ·ksim). 1885. [f. Sir Hiram S. *Maxim*, the inventor.] In full *M.* (*machine*) *gun*: A single-barrelled quick-firing water-cooled machine-gun. Also *M.-Nordenfelt gun*, a modification of this.

†‖**Ma·xima.** 1565. [L., fem. sing. of *maximus*, used *ellipt.* for *maxima propositio, nota.*] 1. = MAXIM [1] -1594. 2. *Mus.* = LARGE C. 2.

Maxima, pl. of MAXIMUM.

Maximal (mæ·ksimăl), *a.* 1882. [f. MAXIMUM + -AL.] Consisting of, or relating to, a maximum; greatest possible.

Maximalist (mæ·ksimălist). 1909. [f. as prec. + -IST.] Used as an etymological equivalent of BOLSHEVIK, taken as connoting 'extremist'.

Maximite (mæ·ksiməit). 1897. [f. Hudson *Maxim*, the inventor.] A smokeless gunpowder composed of gun-cotton, nitroglycerine, and castor oil.

Maximize (mæ·ksimaiz), *v.* 1802. [f. L. *maximus* + -IZE.] 1. *trans.* a. To increase to the highest possible degree. b. To magnify to the utmost (in estimation or representation). 2. *intr.* To maintain the most rigorous or comprehensive interpretation possible of a doctrine or an obligation. Chiefly *Theol.* 1875. So **Ma·ximizer** 1868.

1. a. By this means, appropriate moral aptitude may be maximized BENTHAM. Hence **Maximiza·tion.**

Maximum (mæ·ksimŏm). *Pl.* **maxima**, *rarely* **-ums.** 1740. [a. L. *maximum*, neut. of *maximus*, superl. of *magnus* great.] 1. *Math.* The greatest of all the values of which a variable or a function is capable; the value of a continuously varying quantity at the point at which it ceases to increase and begins to decrease 1743. 2. *gen.* The highest attainable magnitude or quantity (of something); a superior limit 1740. 3. The highest amount (of temperature, barometric pressure, etc.) attained or recorded within a specified period 1850. 4. A superior limit imposed by authority; esp. in *Fr. Hist.*, a limit of price for corn 1821. 5. *attrib.* a. quasi-*adj.* or *adj.* That is a maximum, or that stands at the maximum; greatest 1834. b. Pertaining to a maximum or maxima, as *m. period*; **m. thermometer**, one which records automatically the highest temperature within a given period 1852.

2. The art of conducting a nation to the m. of happiness and the minimum of misery COLQUHOUN. 5. a. The m. density of average sea-water MAURY.

May (mēⁱ), *sb.*[1] *poet.* (*arch.*) OE. a. ON. *møyj-*, accus. (also as nom.) *mey*, Goth. *mawi* :— OTeut. **maujā-*, fem. f. **magu-z* : cf. MAIDEN.] A maiden, virgin.

Thow glorie of wommanhede, thow faire m. CHAUCER.

May (mēⁱ), *sb.*[2] [ME. a. F. *mai* :—L. *Maium* (nom. *Maius*, sc. *mensis*). Etym. obscure; connected by some with the goddess *Maia.*] 1. The fifth month of the year in the Julian and Gregorian calendar. b. *fig.* Bloom, prime, heyday (*poet.*) 1586. 2. The festivities of May-day 1506. 3. Blossoms of the hawthorn (*Cratægus Oxyacantha*); hence occas., the tree itself: so called because it blooms in May 1548. 4. *Cambridge Univ.* a. (*sing.* or *pl.*) = *May examination*; b. (*pl.*) = *May races* 1852.

1. While the jolly hours lead on propitious M. MILT. *personified.* She came adorned hither like sweet M. SHAKS. b. A Prince, In the mid might and flourish of his M. TENNYSON. *May and January*, or *December*: used to describe the marriage of a young woman to an old man. 2. *Queen of the M., Lady of the M.* (cf. MAY-LADY): a girl chosen to be queen of the games on May-day, being gaily dressed and crowned with flowers. 3. With blossoms red and white of fallen M. M. ARNOLD.

attrib. and *Comb.*, as *m.-blossom, M.-born, M. moon*, etc.; **M.-drink** [= G. *maitrank*, Du. *meidrank*], white wine medicated with woodruff, drunk in Belgium and northern Germany; **M. examination**, a college examination held at the end of the Easter term at Cambridge; **M. meetings**, meetings of religious and philanthropic societies formerly held annually in M. in Exeter Hall, London, etc.; **M. queen**, the Queen of the M. (see 2); **M. races**, intercollegiate boat-races held in the Easter term at Cambridge (now in June); **M.-term**, Easter term at Cambridge (*colloq.*); **-week**, the week of the M. races at Cambridge.

b. **M. beetle**, the cockchafer; **M. bird**, the whimbrel, *Numenius phæopus*; *U.S.* the bobolink; **M. fish**, the twait shad, as entering the rivers in M.; *U.S.* a killifish, *Fundulus majalis*; **M. parr, peal**, local names for salmon at certain stages of growth; etc.

c. †**M.-blossom**, lily of the valley; **-pop** *U.S.*, the fruit of the passion-flower; also the plant itself; **-rose**, any rose flowering in M.; also the guelder rose, *Viburnum Opulus*: **-thorn, -tree**, the hawthorn; **-wort**, *Galium cruciatum*.

May (mēⁱ; unstressed meⁱ, mĕ), *v.*[1] *Pa. t.* might (məit); mought (mǭt) now *dial.*, freq. in 16th and 17th c. literary use. [A Com. Teut. vb.: OE. *mæg, magon, meahte* (later *mihte*, also *muhte*). Primary sense, to be strong or able, to have power; the root OTeut. **mag-*, Indo-Eur. **magh-*, appears in MIGHT *sb.*, Gr. μῆχος contrivance, μηχανή MACHINE, etc.] †I. As a vb. of complete predication. *intr.* To be strong; to have power or influence; to prevail (*over*) -late ME.

Phr. *If I m.*: if I have any power in the matter.

II. As an auxiliary of predication. 1. = CAN *v.*[1] II. 2. *Obs.* exc. *arch.* OE. 2. = CAN *v.*[1] II. 3. OE. b. In poetry, *might* sometimes = 'used to', 'would'. KEATS. c. *Might* (subj.) is often used *colloq.* (*a*) with pres. inf. to convey a suggestion of action, or a complaint that some action is neglected; (*b*) with perf. inf. to express a complaint that some not difficult act or duty has been omitted 1805. 3. Expressing permission or sanction: To be allowed (to do something) OE. ¶b. *Law.* In the interpretation of statutes, *may* = *shall* or *must* 1728. 4. Expressing subjective possibility, i.e. the admissibility of a supposition (see quots.) ME. 5. Uses of the pa. t. subj. in the statement of a rejected hypothesis (or a future contingency deemed improbable) and its consequences (see quots.) OE. 6. In questions, *may* (or *might*) with inf. is used to render a question less abrupt or pointed 15... 7. As an auxiliary of the subj. mood. a. *May* with inf. serves as a periphrastic subj.: (*a*) in final clauses OE.; (*b*) in rel. clauses with final meaning; (*c*) in clauses depending on *wish, fear* vb. and sb., and the like OE. b. In expressions of wish, *may* with inf. has replaced (exc. *poet.* and *rhet.*) the simple pres. subj. 1586. c. *Might* is also used to express a wish, esp. one which can hardly be realized. late ME. d. *May* with inf. is used to emphasize the uncertainty of what is referred to OE. 8. With ellipsis of the inf. (see quots.) OE. 9. For *may well, may as well*, see WELL *adv.* †10. In advb. phr. = MAYHAP: **may chance, may-fortune** -1581.

1. We..have endured Sunshine and rain as we might M. ARNOLD. 2. A soldier may be anything, if brave COWPER. But the reign of Stilicho drew towards its end; and the proud minister might (= 'had opportunity to') perceive the symptoms of his approaching disgrace GIBBON. c. 'They might have offered to help us..' said Aunt Ecclesia, pettishly 1894. 3. May we take your coach to town? I saw it in the hangar THACKERAY. Also with *might* in deferential questions, e.g.: Might I trouble you for the pickles? (*mod.*). b. For *may* in the Case of a publick Officer is tantamount to *shall* 1728. 4. Stick to that truth, and it may (= 'perhaps will) chance to save thee FLETCHER. I dare say, my friend, that you may be (= 'perhaps are') right JOWETT. 5. Might we (= 'if we might') haue that happinesse.. we should [etc.] SHAKS. A Fault which easie Pardon might (= 'would perhaps') receive, Were Lovers Judges DRYDEN. The book is very much what might have been expected from the author 1891. 7. a. Lest my appearance might draw too many compliments JOHNSON. (*b*) Would I might But euer see that man SHAKS. Be not highminded, but fear..least thou also maist be cut off 1651. b. Long may he reigne 1611. d. And than he demaunded of his seruauntes what it might be LD. BERNERS. Come what come may SHAKS. 8. Things must be as they may SHAKS. The Moone shines faire, You may away by Night SHAKS. He that may not as he will, must do as he may 1721.

May (mēⁱ), *v.*[2] Now chiefly in vbl. sb. 1470. [f. MAY *sb.*[2]] *intr.* To take part in the festivities of May-day; to gather flowers in May.

‖**Maya** (mā·yă). 1823. [Skr.] Illusion: a prominent term of Hindu philosophy.

May·-apple. *U.S.* 1733. [MAY *sb.*[2]] 1. An American herbaceous plant, *Podophyllum peltatum*, bearing a yellowish, egg-shaped fruit, which appears in May.

Maybe, may-be (mēⁱ·bi), *adv., sb.*, and *a.* late ME. [Shortened from *it may be*; cf. F. *peut-être.*] 1. *adv.* Possibly, perhaps. Occas. used as conj. with *that* (cf. F. *peut-être que*). 2. *sb.* What may be; a possibility 1586. 3. *adj.* Which are possibly to come 1687.

1. This, may be, was the reason some imagin'd Hell there GLANVILL. 2. May be is a doubt, but what is must be regarded N. BRETON. 3. Those may-be years thou hast to live DRYDEN.

May·-bug. 1698. [MAY *sb.*[2]] The cockchafer.

May·-bush. 1579. [MAY *sb.*[2]] a. A branch of hawthorn. b. The hawthorn or may-tree.

May·-butter. 1584. [MAY *sb.*[2]; cf. F. *beurre de mai.*] Unsalted butter preserved in May for medicinal use. Also *fig.*

Maycock (mēⁱ·kǫk). *U.S.* 1588. [Algonquin (Powhattan dialect) *mahcawq.*] A kind of melon.

May·-day. late ME. [MAY *sb.*[2]] The first day of May.

May·-dew. late ME. [MAY *sb.*[2]] Dew gathered in May, supposed to have medicinal and cosmetic properties.

May duke, mayduke (mēⁱ·diūk). 1718. [Cf. *May cherry* and *Duke cherry* (Evelyn 1664).] A variety of sour cherry.

Mayflower (mēⁱ·flauəɹ). 1626. [f. MAY *sb.*[2] + FLOWER *sb.*] 1. A flower that blooms in May; used locally for the Cowslip (*Primula veris*), the Lady's Smock (*Cardamine pratensis*), etc. 2. A variety of apple. EVELYN. 3. *N. America.* a. *Azalea nudiflora.* b. The trailing arbutus, *Epigæa repens.* 1838.

May·-fly. 1651. [f. MAY *sb.*[2] + FLY *sb.*[1]] 1. An insect of the family *Ephemeridæ*; esp. as an angler's name for *Ephemera vulgata* and *E. dania* or either of the corresponding artificial flies. 2. An insect of the family *Phryganeidæ* or *Sianidæ*; the caddis-fly 1816.

May·-game. 1549. [MAY *sb.*[2]] 1. a. *pl.* The merrymakings associated with the first of May. b. *sing.* A set entertainment in the May-day festivities. 2. *transf.* and *gen.* Merrymaking, sport, frolic; foolery 1571. 3. A laughing-stock 1569. 4. *attrib.*; also as adj. with the sense 'trivial' 1586.

3. What is man but..the spoil of time, the may-game of fortune? QUARLES.

Mayhap (meⁱhæ·p, mēⁱ·hæp), *adv.* Now *arch., rhet.* and *dial.* 1536. [Shortened from (*it*) *may hap.*] Perhaps, perchance. So **May-happen** *adv.* now *arch.* and *dial.*

Mayhem (mēⁱ·hem), *sb.* 1472. [a. AF. *mahem, mahaym*, etc.; see MAIM *sb.*] *Old Law.* The crime of maiming a person so as to make him less able to defend himself or annoy his adversary. Also *fig.* Hence **Mayhem** *v. trans.* to inflict m. on 1534.

Maying (mēⁱ·iŋ), *vbl. sb.* 1470. [f. MAY *v.*[2]] The celebration of May-day or the month of May.

May·-lady. *Obs.* exc. *Hist.* 1560. [MAY *sb.*[2]] A Queen of the May. Also, a puppet in a May-day game.

May·-lord. 1599. [f. MAY *sb.*[2] + LORD *sb.*] A young man chosen to preside over the festivities of May-day; *transf.* one whose authority is flouted.

‖**Mayonnaise** (meⁱǒnēⁱ·z, Fr. mayonēz). 1841. [Fr.; etym. unkn.] A sauce consisting of yolk of egg beaten up with oil and vinegar, and seasoned with salt, etc., used as a dressing for salad, cold meat, or fish; also, a dish (of meat, etc.) having this dressing.

Mayor (mēəɹ). [Early ME. *mair, mer*, later *maier, mayer*, a. F. *maire* :—L. *major* nom., properly adj., greater (see MAJOR).] The head or chief officer of the municipal corporation of a city or borough.

M. of the Staple: see STAPLE *sb.*[2] *M. of the Palace* (Hist.): = F. *maire du palais*, a mod. transl. of med.L. *major domus* (occas. *m. palatii*), the title borne by the prime ministers of the Frankish kingdoms. Hence **May·oral** *a.* pertaining to a m. or mayoralty. **May·oress**, the wife of a m., or a lady who fulfils the duties belonging to a mayor's wife. **May·orship**, the office, position, or dignity of a m.

‖**Mayoral** (mayora·l), *sb.* 1598. [Sp., f. *mayor* greater.] A conductor in charge of a train of beasts of burden; also, a head shepherd; *occas.* the conductor of a diligence.

Mayoralty (mēə·rălti). late ME. [ad. OF. *mairalté*, f. *maire* MAYOR.] 1. The office of a mayor. 2. The period during which a mayor holds office 1494. 3. *attrib.* 1573.

Maypole (mēⁱ·pōul). 1554. [f. MAY *sb.*[2] + POLE *sb.*[1]] A high pole, painted with spiral stripes of different colours and decked with flowers, set up on an open space, for the merrymakers to dance round on May-day. *transf.* A lean m. of a man 1871.

Mayweed (mē·wīd). 1551. [For **maytheweed*, f. *maythe*, old name of the plant.] Stinking Camomile, *Anthemis Cotula*. Applied also to other plants resembling this.

Mazame (mäzē·m, masā·me). Also **mazama.** 1791. [a. F. *mazame* (Buffon), a. Mexican *maçame*, pl. of *maçatl* deer, mistaken for a sing.] 1. A name for various American species of deer; also for the Prong-horn. 2. The antilopine Rocky Mountain goat, *Oreamnus* or *Haplocerus montanus* 1852.

Mazard (mæ·zäɹd), *sb.*[1] 1601. [app. altered from MAZER, by association of -ER with -ARD.] †1. A mazer. 2. *joc.* (*arch.*) a. The head 1602. b. The face, 'phiz' 1762. 3. *slang.* (*Anglo-Irish.*) The 'head' of a coin 1802.

2. a. Knockt about the M. with a Sextons Spade SHAKS. Hence †**Mazard** *v. trans.* to knock on the head B. JONSON.

Mazard (mæ·zäɹd), *sb.*[2] *dial.* 1578. [? a use of prec.] A kind of small black cherry; also *attrib.*, as *m. cherry*.

†**Mazarine**, *sb.*[1] 1673. [? attrib. use of the name of Cardinal *Mazarin* (died 1662), or of the Duchesse de Mazarin (died 1699).] In early use also *m. dish, plate*: A deep plate, usually of metal –1773.

Mazarine (mæzărī·n), *sb.*[2] and *a.* 1684. [? as prec.] 1. In full *m. blue*: A deep rich blue 1686. 2. A stuff or a garment of this colour 1694. b. A London common-councilman; so called from the colour of his gown 1761. 3. *adj.* Of a mazarine blue colour.

Mazdaism (mæ·zdē,iz'm). Also **Mazdeism.** 1871. [f. Avestic *mazda*, name of the good principle (Ahura-mazda, Ormuzd) of ancient Persian theology.] The ancient Persian religion as taught in the Avesta; Zoroastrianism. So Mazde·an, -æ·an *a.* pertaining to the religion of the Avesta.

Maze (mēⁱz), *sb.* ME. [See MAZE *v.*] †1. **The maze.** Delirium, delusion; disappointment. ME. only. †2. a. A delusive fancy. b. A trick, deception. ME. only. 3. A state of bewilderment. *Obs.* exc. *dial.* late ME. 4. A confusing and baffling network of winding and intercommunicating paths; a labyrinth; *occas.* in *pl.*, the windings of a labyrinth. late ME. b. A winding movement, esp. in a dance 1610.

3. At this I was put to an exceeding M. BUNYAN. 4. They walke round about as it were in a round mase SIR T. MORE. *fig.* To lose us in this m. of error SIR T. BROWNE. Phr. *To tread a m.*

Maze (mēⁱz), *v.* ME. [Aphetic f. AMAZE (OE. *āmasian*).] 1. *trans.* To stupefy, daze; to put out of one's wits; †to craze. Chiefly in *pass.* Now *arch.* and *dial.* ME. †2. *intr.* To be stupefied or delirious; to wander in mind –1568. 3. *trans.* To bewilder, perplex, confuse 1482. 4. *intr.* To move in a mazy track 1591. †b. *trans.* To involve in a maze; to form mazes upon –1654.

1. Then said the King, 'The man is mazed with fear' MORRIS.

Mazeful (mēⁱ·zfŭl), *a.* *Obs.* exc. *arch.* 1595. [f. MAZE *sb.* + -FUL.] Bewildering, confounding.

Mazement (mēⁱ·zmĕnt). 1580. [f. MAZE *v.* + -MENT.] A state of stupor or trance. Also = AMAZEMENT.

Mazer (mēⁱ·zəɹ), *sb.* *Obs.* exc. *Hist.* ME. [a. OF. *masere, masre*; of Teut. origin; cf. OHG. *masar* (glossing L. *tuber, nodus*), MHG. *maser* excrescence on a tree, maple, drinking-cup, etc.] 1. A hard wood (? prop. maple) used as a material for drinking-cups. †b. The tree yielding this (*rare*) –1547. 2. A bowl, drinking-cup, or goblet without a foot, orig. made of mazer wood. Often applied to bowls entirely of metal, etc. ME. †3. = MAZARD *sb.*[1] 2. –1652. b. *transf.* A helmet. SYLVESTER.

2. One of his Shepherds describes a Bowl, or M., curiously Carv'd DRYDEN.

attrib. and *Comb.*; **m. bowl, cup, -dish** = 2; **m. wood** = 1. Hence †**Mazer** *v.* = MAZARD *v.*

Mazurka (măzʊ̄·ɹkă, măzūᵊ·ɹkă). 1818. [a. Polish *mazurka* woman of the Polish province Mazovia.] 1. A lively Polish dance resembling the polka; the music is in triple time. 2. A piece of music composed in the rhythm of this 1854.

Mazy (mēⁱ·zi), *a.* 1579. [f. MAZE *sb.* + -Y[1].] 1. Resembling or of the nature of a maze; full of windings and turnings. b. Moving in a maze-like course 1725. c. as *sb. joc.* Short for 'the mazy dance' 1840. 2. *spec.* (*Min.*) Having convoluted markings 1811.

1. Five miles meandering with a m. motion..the sacred river ran COLERIDGE. b. The m. leveret POPE. Hence **Ma·zily** *adv.* **Ma·ziness.**

M.B. (em bī). 1853. [Abbrev. of 'Mark of the Beast' (see MARK *sb.*[1] III. 2 b, and BEAST *sb.* 5), used joc. with reference to the popular view that this garment was a badge of 'Popery'.] *M.B. waistcoat*: a kind of waistcoat with no opening in front, worn by Anglican clergymen (originally, *c* 1840, only by Tractarians).

M.B. (em bī), abbrev. of L. *Medicinæ Baccalaureus* bachelor of medicine.

M.D. (em dī), abbrev. of L. *Medicinæ Doctor* doctor of medicine. Often used *colloq.* for: One holding the M.D. degree, a physician.

Me (mī, mi, mĭ), *pers. pron.*, *1st pers. sing.*, *acc.* and *dat.* [OE. *mē* accus. represents, like L. *me*, Gr. ἐμέ, με, etc., the bare stem, Indo-Eur. **eme-*, **me-*, of the pronoun. OE. had also *mec* (lost before ME.) :—pre-Teut. **mege* (= Gr. ἐμέγε), in which a limiting particle **ge* (= Gr. γε, 'at least') is added to the simple acc. The OE. *mē* dat. corresponds to mod.G. *mir*, Goth. *mis* :—pre-Teut. **mes* (with unexplained *s*).] The accus. and dat. form of the pronoun of the first person *I*. 1. *Accusative*, as direct object. 2. *Dative.* a. As indirect obj.; also (now *rare* exc. *arch.*) in dependence on certain impers. vbs. (cf. MESEEMS, METHINKS, etc.), adjs., and advs. OE. b. As dat. of interest (= *for me*), chiefly in commands (*arch.*) OE. c. Used expletively in narrative. (The so-called ethical dative.) *arch.* ME. 3. *Reflexive* (= myself, to or for myself.) Now chiefly *arch.* and *poet.* OE. 4. For the *nominative* (see quots.) 1500. 5. In various exclam. uses, without syntactical relation to the context (see quots.) 1589. 6. quasi-*sb.* Individuality; EGO 1828.

1. Call me not Naomi, call mee Marah *Ruth* i. 20. 2. a. Will you lend it me? 1898. b. Prick me the fellow from the path! M. ARNOLD. c. He enters me his name in the book LAMB. 3. And I awoke, and found me here KEATS. 4. Oh, the dogge is me, and I am my selfe SHAKS. Is she as tall as me? SHAKS. 5. Phr. *Ah me! Ay me! Dear me!* Me miserable! (= L. *me miserum!*) MILT. 'Don't you dance?' he said. 'Me?' cried she, embarrassed, 'yes, I believe so' MISS BURNEY. *And me*.. (vulgar) = 'especially considering that I am..'; And me a widow 1812. 6. Haunted and blinded by some shadow of his own little Me CARLYLE.

Meach, obs. f. MICHE.

†**Mea·cock.** 1526. [?] 1. An effeminate person; a coward, weakling –1834. 2. *attrib.* or *adj.* Effeminate; cowardly –1639.

Mead[1] (mīd). [Com. Teut. and Indo-Eur.: OE. *meodu* str. masc. :—OTeut. **meduz* :—Indo-Eur. **medhus* (cf. Skr. *mádhu* neut., honey, sweet drink, Gr. μέθυ wine, Welsh *medd*).] An alcoholic liquor made by fermenting a mixture of honey and water; also called *metheglin*. b. *transf.* esp. U.S., a beverage charged with carbonic acid gas, and flavoured with syrup of sarsaparilla 1890.

attrib. and *Comb.*, chiefly *arch.* or *Hist.*, as *m.-horn*; **m.-bench** (OE. *medubenc*), a seat at a feast when m. was drunk; **-hall** (OE. *meduheall*), a banqueting hall; **-wine**, a home-made 'wine' prepared from m.

Mead[2] (mīd). Now *poet.* and *dial.* [OE. *mǣd* str. fem. :—OTeut. **mǣdwā*; see next.] = MEADOW 1. †b. Meadow-land –1670.

As it were a mede Al ful of fresshe floures, whyte and rede CHAUCER. Riuers sweete along the meedes TUSSER. *Comb.* **m. grass**, meadow grass.

Meadow (me·dou), *sb.* [repr. OE. *mǣdw-*, obl. stem of *mǣd* str. fem., MEAD[2], f. (ult.) root **me-* (whence MOW *v.*).] 1. Orig., a piece of land permanently covered with grass which is mown for use as hay. In later use extended to include any piece of grass land; and locally applied esp. to a tract of low well-watered ground, usually near a river. b. Land used for meadows; meadow land OE. 2. *N. America.* a. A low level tract of uncultivated grass land, esp. along a river or in marshy regions near the sea 1670. b. *Beaver m.*: the rich fertile tract of land left dry above a demolished beaver dam 1784. 3. A feeding ground for fish 1890.

1. Ladie-smockes all siluer white, Do paint the Meadowes with delight SHAKS.

attrib. and *Comb.*, a. *m.-croft, -field, -flower*, etc.

b. Prefixed to names of animals as denizens of m. land; as **m. ant**, the small British ant, *Lasias flavus*; **m. chicken**, a name given in N. America to species of Rail or Coot; **m. crake, drake** = CORN-CRAKE; **m. fly**, an American fire-fly; **m. hen** = *meadow chicken*; **m. lark**, (*a*) = TITLARK; (*b*) *U.S.* the grackle, *Sturnella magna*; **m. mouse**, any field vole; **m. mussel**, a mussel found in American salt meadows, *Modiola plicatula*; **m. pipit** = TITLARK; **m. snipe**, (*a*) = *grass-bird* (see GRASS); (*b*) *U.S.* the common American snipe, *Gallinago Wilsoni*; **m. vole** = *meadow mouse*.

c. Prefixed to names of plants, to denote varieties or species growing in meadows; often in book-names as tr. L. *pratensis, -ense*, as in *m. barley, clover, trefoil*, etc.; also in **m. beauty**, U.S. name for *Rhexia*; called also *deergrass*; **m. campion, pink**, the Ragged Robin, *Lychnis Flos-cuculi*; **m. crocus, saffron**, *Colchicum autumnale*; **m. grass**, any grass of the genus *Poa*, esp. *P. pratensis*; **m. mushroom**, *Agaricus campestris*; **m. rhubarb, rue**, *Thalictrum flavum*. See also PARSNIP, SAXIFRAGE.

d. **m. green**, lively green, in which the yellow predominates; **m. ground**, (*a*) ground laid down in m.; (*b*) prairie land; **m. ore**, bog iron ore (cf. LIMONITE); **m. thatch**, coarse grass or rush used for thatching.

Hence **Mea·dow** *v.* to devote (land) to the production of grass. **Mea·dowy** *a.* resembling a m.

Meadow-sweet (me·douswīt). 1530. [f. MEADOW *sb.* + SWEET *sb.*] The rosaceous plant *Spiræa Ulmaria*, common in moist meadows and along the banks of streams, growing with erect, rigid stems to a height of about two feet, with dense heads of creamy white and highly fragrant flowers. In the U.S., *S. salicifolia*.

†**Mea·dsweet.** late ME. [f. MEAD[2] + SWEET *sb.*] = prec. –1782.

†**Mea·dwort.** [OE. *medowyrt*, f. *medo* MEAD[1] + *wyrt* WORT, plant; possibly the flowers were used for flavouring mead.] = MEADOW-SWEET –1783.

Meagre (mī·gəɹ), *a.* (*sb.*) (*U.S.* **meager.**) [ME. *megre*, a. OF. *megre* (mod.F. *maigre*) :—L. *macrum* (*macer*), cogn. w. Gr. μακρός long, μακεδνός tall, slender, μῆκος length.] 1. Of persons, animals, etc.: Lean, thin, emaciated. 2. Poor, scanty 1501. b. Of literary composition or material, ideas, resources, etc.: Wanting in fullness or elaboration 1539. 3. = MAIGRE *a.* 1705. b. *absol.* as *sb.* 'Maigre' diet.

1. Thou art so leane and m. waxen late SPENSER. 2. Very Maigre, Hungry Soil CHETHAM. The m. banquet LAMB. b. The continuation of a m. chronicle D'ISRAELI. A m. and imperfect form of faith J. MARTINEAU. 3. Phr. *Soup m.*, tr. F. *soupe maigre*. b. We make m. on Fridays always THACKERAY. Hence **Mea·gre·ly** *adv.*, **-ness.**

†**Meagre** (mī·gəɹ), *v.* 1563. [f. MEAGRE *a.*] *trans.* To make meagre or lean –1807.

Meagre, var. of MAIGRE *sb.*

Meak (mīk). *dial.* 1478. An implement with a long handle and crooked iron or blade used to cut down or pull up peas, bracken, etc.

Meaking (mī·kiŋ), *vbl. sb.* 1867. [? f. MEAK + -ING[1].] Only in *m. iron*: The tool used by caulkers to pick old oakum out of a vessel's seams.

Meal (mīl), *sb.*[1] [Com. Teut.: OE. *melo, melw-* str. neut. :—OTeut. **melwo*ᵐ, f. root **mel-, mal-, mul-*, whence Com. Teut. **malan* to grind, cogn. w. L. *molere, molina*, Gr. μύλη, μύλος, etc.] 1. The edible part of any grain or pulse (usu. exc. wheat) ground to a powder. Also *spec.* in Scotland and Ireland = OATMEAL; in U.S. = *Indian meal* (see INDIAN *a.* 3). *Whole m.*: see WHOLE. b. The finer part of the ground grain, in contrast with *bran*. Often *fig.* 1579. 2. *transf.* A powder produced by grinding (e. g. in *linseed m.*); a powdery substance resembling flour 1549.

Comb.: **m.-beetle**, a coleopterous insect (*Tenebrio molitor*), which infests granaries, etc., and is injurious to flour; **-mite**, the *Acarus farinæ*; **-moth**, either of two species of moth, *Asopia farinalis* and *Pyralis farinalis*, the larvæ of which feed on m. or flour;

-worm, the larva of the meal-beetle; **-worm beetle** = *meal-beetle*.

Meal (mīl), *sb.*[2] [Com. Teut.: OE. *mǽl* neut., mark, sign, measure, fixed time, occasion, meal:—OTeut. **mǣlo*m, f. Indo-Eur. root **me-* (Skr. *ma-*) to measure.] †1. A measure -ME. 2. Any of the customary occasions of taking food at regular times of the day, as a breakfast, dinner, supper, etc. OE. b. An occasion of taking food, a repast. Also, the material of a repast. ME. 3. The quantity of milk given by a cow at one milking; also, the time of milking 1613.

2. Meals, then, ought to be early or late in proportion to the habits of the individual COMBE. b. The blackbird, picking food, Sees thee, nor stops his m. M. ARNOLD.

Meal (mīl), *v.*[1] Somewhat *rare*. 1611. [f. MEAL *sb.*[1]] 1. *trans.* To cover or powder with meal. 2. a. *trans.* To grind into meal; to reduce to powder. b. *intr.* To become reduced to meal or powder. 1669. 3. *intr.* To yield meal 1799.

Meal (mīl), *v.*[2] 1827. [f. MEAL *sb.*[2]] *intr.* To make a meal; to feed.

†**Meal**, *v.*[3] [= OE. *mǽlan*, f. *mál* spot, stain, MOLE *sb.*[1]] *trans.* To spot, stain. *Meas. for M.* IV. ii. 86.

-meal, *suffix*, forming advs. (all obs. exc. *piecemeal*), repr. ME. *-mele* (occas. *-melum*), OE. *-mǽlum*, with the sense expressed in Latin by *-atim*, *-tim*, and in mod. Eng. by the repetition of the sb. preceded by *by*.

Mealie (mī·li). Also (from *pl.*) **milice.** 1853. [a. Cape Du. *milje* (pronounced mī·li), a. Pg. *milho* MILLET, used also for maize.] A S. Afr. name for maize; used chiefly in the *pl.*

Mealing (mī·liŋ), *vbl. sb.* 14... [f. MEAL *sb.*[1] or *v.*[1] + -ING[1].] The action of grinding meal; also, that of finely pulverizing gunpowder. Chiefly *attrib.*

M. stone, a stone used for grinding meal; **m. table**, a slab for mealing gunpowder upon.

†**Mea·lmouth**, *sb.* and *a.* 1546. [f. MEAL *sb.*[1] + MOUTH.] (A) mealy-mouthed (person) -1700. †**Mea·l-mouthed** *ppl. a.* 1570-1686.

Mealy (mī·li), *a.* 1533. [f. MEAL *sb.*[1] + -Y[1].] 1. Like meal, powdery. Of potatoes when boiled: Forming a dry and powdery mass (opp. to *waxy*). 2. Containing meal; farinaceous 1591. 3. Covered with flour 1704. 4. Covered with or as if with a fine dust or powder. Chiefly in *Bot.* and *Ent.* 1567. 5. Of colour: Spotty, uneven 1675. 6. Of complexion: Floury, pale 1838. 7. Soft-spoken, given to mince matters; mealy-mouthed 1600.

3. The wealthy miller's m. face TENNYSON. 4. Men like butter-flies, Shew not their mealie wings, but to the Summer SHAKS. **M. bug**, an insect which infests vines and hot-house plants. 5. A m. bay cob WHYTE MELVILLE. M. prints 1890. 6. I only know two sorts of boys. M. boys, and beef-faced boys DICKENS. 7. Bless its m. mouth! CARLYLE. **Mea·liness.**

Mealy-mouthed (mī·li,mauᵈðd), *a.* 1572. [Cf. MEALY *a.* 7.] Soft-spoken; not outspoken; afraid to speak one's mind or to use plain terms.

Mealy-mouth'd philanthropies TENNYSON. Hence **Mealy-mouthed-ly** *adv.*, **-ness.**

Mean (mīn), *sb.* ME. [Partly MEAN *a.*[2] used absol.; partly after the similar OF. use.]

I. That which is in the middle. 1. A condition, quality, disposition, course, etc., that is equally removed from two opposite (usu., blamable) extremes; a medium. †b. Moderation, measure -1718. †2. *Mus.* †a. A middle part, esp. the tenor or alto. Also, a person performing that part or the instrument on which it is played. Also *fig.* -1698. †b. A name for the second and the third string of a viol or lute. CHAPPELL. †3. *Logic.* The middle term of a syllogism. BACON. †4. Something interposed or intervening -1593. 5. *Math.* [= F. *moyenne*, ellipt. for *quantité moyenne.*] The term (or, in pl., the terms) intermediate between the first and last terms (called the extremes) of a progression of any kind (*arithmetic(al, geometric(al, harmonic(al m.*) 1571. b. An average amount or value; used for *m. pressure, temperature*, etc. 1803.

1. There is a m. in all things SWIFT. b. *In a m.*: with moderation; But to speake in a Meane BACON. *To use a m.*: to exercise moderation; Use a m. in sleep and waking CULPEPPER. 4. Phr. *By means*: through intermediate links (of descent). *Without any m.* (= F. *sans moyen*): directly, immediately, unconditionally. *In the m.*: in the meantime.

II. An intermediary agent or instrument. †1. A mediator, a 'go-between'. Also in pl. form, with sing. sense and constr. -1612. 2. That by which some object is or may be attained, or which is concerned in bringing about some result. Often contrasted with *end*. ME. †3. An opportunity; in early use *pl.* conditions, terms (of peace) -1613. 4. *pl.* [= F. *moyens.*] (One's) resources; chiefly, (a person's) pecuniary resources; sometimes more explicitly, *means of living, of subsistence*. In absol. sense also = 'money', 'wealth' 1603. †b. Formerly construed as sing.; a livelihood (*rare*) -1642. 5. †a. Mediation, intercession; instigation. late ME. b. Instrumentality; operation as an instrument, method, or proximate cause. (See below.) late ME.

1. He woweth hire by meenes and brocage CHAUCER. 2. Yet Nature is made better by no meane, But Nature makes the Meane SHAKS. Phr. *To be the means* (or †*the m.*) *of.* I was the means of this being done 1863. *By fair means*: see FAIR *a.* IV. 3. See also WAYS AND MEANS. *To find (the) means* (or †*m.*): to find out a way, contrive (now only const. *inf.*). *Means of grace* (Theol.): the sacraments, etc. viewed as the means by which divine grace is imparted to the soul; in Evangelical use often = 'public worship'. *Under the means of grace*: subject to the operation of the means of grace. 4. Let her haue needfull, but not lauish meanes SHAKS. My means were somewhat broken into TENNYSON. 5. a. Our Brother is imprison'd by your meanes SHAKS. b. Phr. *By all (manner of) means*: (*a*) in every possible way; (*b*) at any cost, without fail; (*c*) = 'certainly'. *By any (manner of) means* (or †*m.*): (*a*) in any way, anyhow, at all; †(*b*) by all means. *By no means* (or †*m.*), *by no manner of means* (or †*m.*): (*a*) in no way, not at all; (*b*) on no account. *By this* or *that means* (or †*m.*): (*a*) by means of this or that; in this or that way; thus; (*b*) in consequence, consequently. *By* or *through* (†*the*) *means* (or †*m.*) *of*: (*a*) by the instrumentality of (a person or thing); (*b*) in consequence of, owing to. †*By* (*the*) *means* (*that*): for the reason that, because.

Mean (mīn), *a.*[1] and *adv.*[1] ME. [App. repr. OE. *gemǽne* = G. *gemein*:—OTeut. **gamaini-*, f. *ga-* (= L. *com-*) Y- + **maini-*:—pre-Teut. **moini-* in L. *communis* (:—**commoinis*) COMMON *a.* Prim. sense 'possessed jointly'.]

I. Common to two or more; possessed jointly. *Obs.* exc. *dial.*

Phr. *In m.*: in common. *To go m.*: to share.

II. Inferior. †1. Of persons, etc.: Undistinguished; of low degree; often opp. to *noble* or *gentle*. Also *transf.* -1827. †b. Poor, badly off -1776. c. Poor in ability, learning, etc. *Obs.* exc. in phr. (*to*) *the meanest understanding*, etc., and as in 3. ME. d. (See below). 2. Of things: †Of little value; inferior -1770; petty; inconsiderable (now *rare*) 1585; low ME.; the reverse of imposing, shabby 1600. 3. *No m.* —: often = 'no contemptible', applied eulogistically to a person or thing 1596. 4. Of persons: Ignoble, small-minded 1665. 5. Penurious, stingy 1755.

1. He bears a lofty spirit in a m. condition BACON. b. Thou shalt not steal, though thou be very m. BUNYAN. c. Very m. Divines 1738. d. Phr. *M. white*: a term of contempt applied to the poor and landless white men in the Southern U.S., who in the days of slavery were regarded by the negroes as inferior to themselves. e. *U.S. colloq.* In low spirits or health; poorly, 'seedy' 1848. 2. The meanest flowret of the vale GRAY. A city of m. streets (*mod.*). Of things in general: poor in quality or condition 1817. 3. A citizen of no meane citie *Acts* xxi. 39. 4. Phr. *To feel m.* (*U.S.*): to feel ashamed of one's conduct. 5. He is not m. about money GEO. ELIOT. *Comb.*, as *m.-spirited* (1694).

†B. *adv.* = MEANLY -1719.

Mean (mīn), *a.*[2] and *adv.*[2] ME. [a. OF. *men, meen, moien*, etc. (mod.F. *moyen*):—late L. *medianus* that is in the middle, f. *medius*; see MID *a.*] A. *adj.* †1. Occupying a middle or an intermediate place. *M. term* (Logic) = 'middle term'. -1822. b. *Mus.* Applied to the tenor and alto parts and the tenor clef, as intermediate between the bass and treble -1721. 2. Intermediate in time; intervening. Now only in *in the m. time, while*. Also MEANTIME, MEANWHILE *advs.* 1464. 3. *Law.* Intermediate, either in time or status. Usu. spelt MESNE. ME. †4. Intermediary -1615. 5. Intermediate in kind, quality, or degree. Now *rare*. ME. 6. Not far above or below the average ME. 7. *Math.* a. Of an amount or value: That is an arithmetical mean. Hence used (as in *m. motion, diameter, distance, temperature*, etc.) in concord with a designation of variable concrete quantity, to express the mean value of this. b. *M. proportional*: the middle one of three quantities, of which the first has the same ratio to the second as the second has to the third. (Orig. *mean* was the sb.) 1571.

3. The king shal haue the meane issues 1548. M. Lords 1670. 4. To be m. intercessors and helpers to God *Homilies*. 5. The meane opinion betweene these is the best 1610. †*M. way* [= L. *via media*]: a middle course (as an escape from a dilemma). 6. Their Noses of a m. bigness DAMPIER. 7. a. *M. sun*: a fictitious sun, supposed for purposes of calculation to move in the celestial equator at the mean rate of the real sun. *M.* (*solar*) *time*: the time of day as it would be shown by the 'mean sun' (the time shown by an ordinary correctly regulated clock); so *m. noon*, etc. b. *Extreme and m. ratio*: see EXTREME *a.* 1.

B. *adv.* †1. Moderately; also, comparatively less -1612. 2. Intermediately 1548.

Mean (mīn), *v.*[1] Pa. t. and pple. **meant** (ment). [Com. WGer.: OE. *mǽnan*; perh. f. root **men-* to think (see MIND *sb.*).] 1. *trans.* To have in mind as a purpose; to purpose, design. Chiefly with *inf.* as obj. †b. To aim at (*rare*) -1706. c. To intend (a remark, etc.) to have a particular reference. Also †absol. *to m. by* = to intend to refer to. 1513. d. *intr.* To be (*well, ill*, etc.) intentioned or disposed. Const. *to, by*, or *dat.* ME. 2. *trans.* To intend to indicate (a certain object), or to convey (a certain sense). Occas. with cl. as obj. OE. 3. Of things, words, etc.: To have a certain signification; to import; to portend OE. b. Of a person: To be of importance *to* (another) 1888.

1. These cut-throates..meant presently to returne MORYSON. Phr. *To m. business*: see the sb. b. Who aimeth at the sky Shoots higher much than he that means a tree G. HERBERT. c. Did he m. it of any one in particular? (*mod.*). d. You seem to m. honestly DE FOE. 2. The Act does not m. literally what it says KEKEWICH. In indignant questions, as *What do you m. by that?* 3. Neither did hee know what a Disaster meant BACON.

†**Mean**, *v.*[2] Chiefly *Sc.* [OE. *mǽnan*: see MOAN *sb.*] To complain (of) -1800.

Meander (mi,æ·ndəɹ), *sb.* 1576. [a. L. *mæander*, Gr. *μαίανδρος*, appellative use of the name of a winding river in Phrygia.] 1. *pl.* Sinuous windings; flexuosities. Rarely in *sing.*, the action of winding; one of such windings. Also *transf.* and *fig.* 2. *pl.* Crooked or winding paths; windings, convolutions 1598. †Also *fig.* †b. *sing.* A winding course or plan; a labyrinth, maze (*lit.* and *fig.*) -1796. 3. A circuitous journey or movement; chiefly *pl.* 1631. 4. *Art.* An ornamental pattern of lines winding in and out or crossing one another rectangularly 1706.

1. The stream loses itself in a distant m. 1796. 2. *fig.* The meanders of the Law ARBUTHNOT. 3. So swarming bees..In airy rings, and wild meanders play YOUNG.

Meander (mi,æ·ndəɹ), *v.* 1612. [f. prec. sb.] 1. *intr.* Of a stream, etc.: To wind about in its course. 2. Of a person: To wander deviously or aimlessly 1831.

1. When you shall see in a beautiful Quarto Page, how a neat rivulet of Text shall m. thro' a meadow of margin SHERIDAN.

Meandrine (mi,æ·ndrin), *a.* 1846. [ad. mod.L. **mæandrinus*, f. L. *mæander* MEANDER *sb.*] Characterized by windings; said esp. of corals of the genus *Meandrina*, in allusion to the winding convolutions of the surface.

Meandrous (mi,æ·ndrəs), *a.* 1656. [f. MEANDER + -OUS.] Full of windings and turnings; esp. of a river. So †**Mea·ndrian** 1608, **Mea·ndric** 1658, †**Mea·ndry** 1614-19.

Meaning (mī·niŋ), *vbl. sb.* ME. [f. MEAN *v.*[1] + -ING[1].] 1. Intention, purpose (*arch.*). 2. That which is intended to be or actually is expressed or indicated; the signification, sense, import. ME. b. The intended sense of a person's words. ME. c. In generalized use: Significance 1690.

1. Be ye perfecte in one mynde, and one meanynge TINDALE 1 *Cor.* i. 10. 2. Difficulties may be raised about the m., as well as the truth, of the assertion BUTLER. What is the m. of all this parade? 1828. The Greeks had sought out the m. of their myths CLODD. b. Do not misunderstand my m. 1878. c. A look so full of m. KINGSLEY.

Meaning (mī·niŋ), *ppl. a.* 1581. [f. MEAN *v.*[1] + -ING [2].] 1. Having intention or purpose, as *well m.* 2. Expressive, significant 1728.

2. 'Had done business with him', said Mr. Barney with a m. look DICKENS. **Mea·ningly** *adv.* late ME.

Meaningless (mī·niŋlės), *a.* 1797. [f. MEANING *vbl. sb.* + -LESS.] Without signification; without purpose. Hence **Mea·ningless-ly** *adv.*, **-ness.**

Meanly (mī·nli), *adv.*[1] 1587. [f. MEAN *a.*[1] + -LY [2].] In a mean manner; poorly; basely, lowlily; shabbily; stingily, illiberally.

To think m. of: to have a mean estimate of.

†**Meanly,** *adv.*[2] late ME. [f. MEAN *a.*[2] + -LY [2].] 1. In the mean or middling degree or manner; moderately -1763. 2. Only moderately; hence, indifferently -1707.

Meanness (mī·n,nės). 1556. [f. MEAN *a.*[1] + -NESS.] The condition or quality of being mean; lowliness, insignificance 1583; inferiority; slightness; smallness (also *pl.*) 1556; littleness of character or mind 1660; poorness of appearance or equipment; poverty of execution, design, etc. 1656; niggardliness 1755.

I doubt however whether this Figure be not of a later Date..by the M. of the Workmanship ADDISON.

Meant (ment), *ppl. a.* 1470. [pa. pple. of MEAN *v.*[1]] In senses of the vb. (q. v.).

Mean time, mea·ntime. ME. [Prop. two wds. (see MEAN *a.*[2] 2 and TIME *sb.*), and still often so written in the phrases.]

A. *sb.* 1. *In the mean time.* a. During or within the time which intervenes. b. Used in adversative or concessive sense: While this is true; still, nevertheless 1633. †2. Without prep. = 1 a -1700. 3. *For the mean time*: so long as the interval lasts. Also predicatively: Intended to serve for the interim. 1480. 4. *attrib.* BROWNING.

2. The meane time Lady, Ile raise the preparation of a Warre SHAKS. 3. This order was for the meantime 1897.

B. *adv.* 1. = *In the mean time*, A. 1 a. 1588. †2. = *In the mean time*, A. 1 b. -1681.

Mean while, mea·nwhile. ME. [Prop. two wds. (see MEAN *a.*[2] 2 and WHILE *sb.*), and still often so written.] A. *sb.* 1. *In the mean while*: = MEAN TIME A. 1 a. b. In adversative or concessive use; cf. MEAN TIME 1 b. 1597. †2. *The mean while* = 'in the mean while' -1658. 3. *For the mean while* = 'for the mean time'; see MEAN TIME A. 3. CHAUCER.

B. *adv.* 1. = *In the mean while*, A. 1 a. 1440. 2. = *n the mean while*, A. 1 b. 1597.

Meany: see MANY, MEINIE

Mear(e, var. MARE, MERE *sb.*, *a.*, *v.*

Mease (mīz). ME. [a. OF. *meise*, *maise* barrel for herrings; of Teut. origin.] A measure for herrings, equal to five 'hundreds' (usu. 'long hundreds').

Measle (mī·z'l), *sb.* [ME. *maseles* pl., f. Teut. root **mas-*, **mæs-*, expressing the notion of 'spot' or 'excrescence'; cf. MAZER.] 1. *pl.* (†in 15th c. also *sing.*). An infectious disease of man (in medical L. called *Rubeola* and *Morbilli*), marked by an eruption of rose-coloured papulæ in irregular circles and crescents, preceded and accompanied by catarrhal and febrile symptoms. The pl. form is now usu. construed as a *sing.* b. *pl.* The pustules which mark this disease. late ME. 2. *pl.* (†formerly also *sing.*) A disease in swine, produced by the scolex of the tapeworm; in later use, a similar disease in other animals. (Due to a misinterpretation of the adj. *mesel* 'leprous' (see next) as used of swine thus affected.) 1587. b. The scolex or cysticercus which produces this disease 1863.

1. *German* (formerly also *false*, *French*, *hybrid*) *measles*: a contagious disease (*Roseola epidemica* or *Rubella*) distinct from measles, but like it in some of its symptoms.

†**Mea·sle,** *a.* late ME. [a use of MESEL *a.*, leprous; infl. in spelling by MEASLE *sb.*] Of swine, their flesh: Affected with measles, measly -1652.

Measle (mī·z'l), *v.* 1611. [f. MEASLE *sb.*] 1. *trans.* To infect with measles. 2. *transf.* To cover as with measles or spots 1638. 3. *intr.* To develop the eruption of measles (*colloq.*).

Measled (mī·z'ld), *ppl. a.* ME. [f. MEASLE *sb.*, *a.*, and *v.* + -ED.] 1. Infected with measles. 2. Spotted 1634. †3. *fig.* Poor, 'scurvy'. NASHE.

Measly (mī·zli), *a.* 1687. [f. MEASLE *sb.* + -Y [1].] 1. Of, pertaining to, or resembling measles 1782. 2. = MEASLE *a.* 1687. 3. Spotty 1876. 4. *slang.* Poor, of little value 1872.

Measurable (me·ʒ'ŭrăb'l), *a.* [ME. a. F. *mesurable*:—late L. *mensurabilis*, f. *mensurare*. In sense 3 f. MEASURE *v.*] †1. Of persons, etc.: Moderate, temperate; *occas.* modest -1608. 2. Of moderate size, quantity, duration, or speed. *Obs.* exc. as implied in 3. ME. 3. That can be measured; of such dimensions as to admit of being measured; *spec.* (of rainfall) not less than $\frac{1}{100}$ inch 1599. †4. Characterized by due measure or proportion 1563. †5. Regular in movement; metrical, rhythmical -1597. b. *Mus.* = MENSURABLE 3. 1614.

1. Of his diete mesurable was he CHAUCER. 3. Phr. *To come within a m. distance of* [etc.]. 4. According to the m. distribution of the Holy Ghost *Homilies*. Hence **Mea·surably** *adv.* (late ME.), †moderately; proportionably; in a measure (*U.S.*); to a m. extent.

Measure (me·ʒ'ŭı), *sb.* ME. [a. F. *mesure* :—L. *mensura*, f. *mens-*, *metiri* to measure.]

I. 1. The action or process of measuring, measurement. Now *rare.* 2. Size or quantity ascertained or ascertainable by measuring. Now chiefly in phr. (*made*) *to m.* (said of garments, etc.; as dist. from *ready-made*) ME. b. *techn.* The width of a printed page; the width of an organ pipe 1683. c. *Fencing.* The distance of one fencer from another as determined by the length of his reach when lunging or thrusting. Also, in military drill. 1591. †d. Duration (of time, of a musical note) -1706. 3. *fig.* See below. 1650. 4. An instrument for measuring. a. A vessel of standard capacity for dealing out fixed quantities of grain, liquids, some vegetables, coal, etc. ME. 3. A graduated rod, line, tape, etc. 1555. 5. A unit or denomination of measurement 1535. b. Used for some specific unit of capacity (†or of length) understood from context or usage. Also, such a quantity as is indicated by this unit. ME. c. *Chem.* A unit of volume, e. g. of a gas or liquid, usu. indicated by graduations on a tube, etc. Also, the quantity measured by such a unit. 1807. d. In mixtures or compositions: A 'part' as estimated by measurement 1837. 6. A system of measuring, as *linear*, *liquid*, *dry*, *London m.*, etc. ME. 7. That by which anything is computed or estimated. Chiefly in phr. *to be the m. of.* 1580. b. A standard; a criterion, test. Now *rare.* 1641. 8. *Math.* A quantity which is contained in another some number of times without remainder; a submultiple 1570. 9. [? *concr.* of sense 2.] A stratum or bed of mineral; now only *pl.* (*Geol.*) in *coal-measures*, *culm m.* 1665.

1. *By m.*: as determined by measuring (not weighing or counting). 2. Phr. *To know the m. of* (a person's) *foot*: see FOOT *sb.* Phrases c. *Full*, *good*, *short*, etc. *m.* (see the adjs.). Also *fig.* *To take measures*: to ascertain the different dimensions of a body. So, *to take the m. of* a person for clothes, etc. He that makes Coates for the Moone, had need take m. every noone 1647. c. *fig.* Come not within the m. of my wrath SHAKS. 3. Phr. *To take the m. of*, formerly *to take m. of*: to form an estimate of; now *esp.* to gauge the abilities or character of (a person). 5. The common m. for tiling is a square of 10 feet GWILT. b. Anon wee'l drinke a M. The Table round SHAKS. 7. b. Man is the m. of all truth Unto himself TENNYSON. 8. *Common m.* = common divisor (see DIVISOR). Also *fig.* *Greatest common m.* (abbrev. G.C.M.): the greatest quantity that divides each of a number of quantities exactly.

II. Prescribed extent or quantity. †1. What is adequate; satisfaction (of appetite, desire, need) -1607. 2. Proportion; due proportion, symmetry ME. 3. A limit. Now only in certain phrases, as *to set measures to*, *to know no m.*, etc. ME. †4. Moderation, temperance -1667. 5. A quantity, degree, or proportion (of something), esp. as granted to or bestowed upon a person 1610. 6. Treatment (of a certain kind) 'meted out' to a person. *Obs.* or *arch.* exc. in *hard m.* 1593.

1. Till either death hath clos'd these eyes of mine, Or Fortune giuen me m. of Reuenge SHAKS. 2. Phr. *In m. as*: in proportion as. [A Gallicism.] †*To hold m. with*: to be proportionate to. 3. What measures [can we set] to that anguish? PEARSON. Phr. *Beyond*, *above m.*, also *out of* (*all*) *m.* (arch.): beyond all bounds, excessively. *To keep* or *observe measure*(*s*: to be restrained in action. †*To keep measures with*: to use consideration towards (a person). *By m.*, *in m.*: to a limited extent, in part. *To fill up the m. of*: to add what is wanting to the completeness of. 5. Critias..begs that a larger m. of indulgence may be conceded to him JOWETT. Phr. *In a great* or *large m.*: largely. *In some* or *a m.*: in some degree, somewhat. *In the same m.*: to the same extent. 6. This is hard and vndeserued m. SHAKS.

III. 'Measured' sound or movement. 1. Poetical rhythm, as measured by quantity or accent; = METRE. Now only *literary.* 1450. 2. An air, tune, melody. Now *poet.* ME. 3. *Mus.* a. The relation between the time-values of a note of one denomination and a note of the next, determining the kind of rhythm (duple, triple, etc.); hence, the time of a piece of music. (Also called MODE.) 1597. b. A group of notes beginning with a main accent, and commonly included between two vertical lines or bars 1667. ¶c. Used erron. for L. *modus* as tr. Gr. τρόπος, ἁρμονία; see MODE 1635. 3. Rhythmical motion, esp. as regulated by music; the rhythm of a movement 1576. 4. A (grave or stately) dance (*arch.*) 1509.

1. Chaucer's verse seems to consist generally of five measures A. J. ELLIS. *Long m.* (in hymns): see LONG *a.*[1] 2. a. The triplex, sir, is a good tripping m. SHAKS. c. The Lydian m. was appropriated to.. songs of sorrow BURNEY. 3. Phr. *To keep m.*: to observe exact time. 4. Where fair Semiramis..Hath trod the measures MARLOWE.

IV. 1. A plan or course of action intended to attain some object 1698. 2. *spec.* A legislative enactment proposed or adopted 1759.

1. Phr. *To take*, *adopt*, *pursue* (certain) *measures.* Before..any measure of prevention..could be taken 1833. 2. Measures, and not men, is the common cant of affected moderation *Junius Lett.*

Measure (me·ʒ'ŭı), *v.* ME. [a. F. *mesurer*, f. *mesure.*] †1. *trans.* To regulate, moderate, restrain -1574. 2. To ascertain the spatial magnitude or quantity of (something); *properly*, by comparison with some fixed unit ME. b. To take (a person's) measure *for* clothes 1836. c. *fig.* 1747. d. With dimensions or amounts as obj. ME. e. *absol.* or *intr.* To take measurements; to use a measuring instrument 1611. f. *intr.* (in *pass.* sense). To admit of measurement 1765. 3. *trans.* Chiefly with *out*: To delimit (*poet.*) 1513. 4. To have a measurement of (so much) 1671. 5. To estimate the amount, duration, value, etc. of (an immaterial thing) by comparison with some standard 1667. 6. To appraise by a certain standard or rule, or by comparison with something else ME. 7. To be the measure of, or a means of measuring 1590. b. *Math.* Of a quantity: To be a measure or submultiple of (another quantity); also †*refl.* †Also *absol.* 1570. 8. To apportion by measure; to mete *out.* (Also *absol.* or *intr.*) *arch.* ME. 9. To proportion, adjust (something) *to* an object, or by a standard 1590. †b. To be commensurate with -1633. 10. To bring into competition or comparison *with.* Also *refl.* to try one's strength *against.* 1715. 11. To travel over, traverse (a certain distance, etc.). Chiefly *poet.* ME. †12. To turn into metre -1774.

2. Go, m. earth, weigh air, and state the tides POPE. I..endeavoured to m. some of the undulations TYNDALL. Phr. *To m.* (†*out*) *one's length*: to fall prostrate. *To m. swords*: *lit.* of adversaries in a duel, to ascertain that their swords are of equal length. Hence, to contend in battle, try one's strength *with.* d. He measured sixe measures of barley, and laide it on her *Ruth* iii. 15. 4. *P.R.* I. 210. Phr. *To m. up to* (or *with*): to be comparable *with*; to have necessary or fitting qualifications (chiefly *U.S.*) 1712. 8. Sermons were measured out with no grudging hand L. STEPHEN. 9. M. your desires by your fortune JER. TAYLOR. 11. For we must m. twentie miles to day SHAKS. Phr. *To m. back*: to retrace (one's steps, etc.). Now *rare.*

Measured (me·ʒ'ŭıd), *ppl. a.* ME. [f. MEASURE *sb.* and *v.* + -ED.] 1. In senses of MEASURE *v.* 2. Consisting of 'measures' or metrical groups; written in metre; metrical 1581. b. *gen.* Rhythmical; regular in movement 1633. c. *Mus.* = MENSURABLE 3. 1782. 3. Of language, etc.: Carefully weighed; restrained 1802.

1. Phr. *M. work*, piece-work. 2. b. Music..timely echo'd back the m. oar BYRON. A m. tread 1855. 3. Choice word and m. phrase WORDSW.

Measureless (me·ʒ'ŭɹlės), *a.* ME. [f. MEASURE *sb.* + -LESS.] Having no bounds; immeasurable. **Mea·sureless-ly** *adv.*, **-ness.**

Measurement (me·ʒ'ŭɹmėnt). 1751. [f. MEASURE *v.* + -MENT.] 1. The action or an act of measuring; mensuration. 2. A dimension ascertained by measuring; size or extent measured by a standard 1756. 3. A system of measuring or of measures 1867.

2. Iron vessels, within the m. allowed by law 1823.

Measurer (me·ʒ'ŭrəɹ). 1552. [f. MEASURE *v.* + -ER 1.] 1. One who measures or takes measurements; *esp.* one whose duty it is to see that goods or commodities are of the proper measure. Also *fig.* 2. An instrument for measuring, as a rain-gauge, an hour-glass 1764. 3. A measuring-worm; = GEOMETER 2.

Measuring (me·ʒ'ŭriŋ), *vbl. sb.* ME. [-ING 1.] The action of MEASURE *v.*

attrib. esp. in the names of vessels and instruments graduated for purposes of measurement, as *m.-chain, -glass, -rod* (also *fig.*), *-tape*, etc.; **m.-wheel**, (1) = HODOMETER; (2) = CIRCUMFERENTOR 2. Phr. **M. cast**: (*a*) *lit.* in the sport of throwing the bar, a throw so nearly equal to another that measurement is required to decide between them (? *Obs.*); (*b*) *fig.* a nice question, a ticklish point; a 'toss-up' (*arch.*).

Mea·suring, *ppl. a.* 1570. [-ING 2.] That measures.

M. worm: the larva of a geometrid moth; a geometer or looper 1859.

Meat (mīt), *sb.* [OE. *męte* :—**matiz*, perh. f. (ult.) root **mēd-* to be fat; see MAST *sb.*2] 1. Food in general; usually, solid food, in contradistinction to *drink*. Now *arch.* and *dial.* Also *fig.* b. The edible part of fruits, nuts, eggs, etc.: the pulp, kernel, yolk and white, etc. Now only *U.S.* exc. in proverbial phrase (see quot.). Also, the animal substance of a shell-fish. ME. †2. A kind of food, an article of food, a 'dish' -1726. 3. The flesh of animals used for food; now chiefly = BUTCHER'S MEAT, excluding fish and poultry ME. b. *pl.* Kinds of meat 1693. c. In mod. hunting use (*U.S.*), one's quarry or prey 1851. 4. A meal. Occas. used for dinner. *Obs.* exc. in phrases (see below) ME.

1. *Green m.*: grass or green vegetables used for food or fodder. Thy mete shall be mylk, honye, & wyne ME. *fig.* It is m. and drinke (= a source of intense enjoyment) to me to see a Clowne SHAKS. b. Thy head is as full of quarrels, as an egge is full of m. SHAKS. 4. Phr. *At m.*, †*at m. and meal*: at table, at one's meals. So *after m.*, *before m.* Your Soldiers vse him as the Grace 'fore meate, Their talke at Table, and their Thankes at End SHAKS.

attrib. and *Comb.*, as *m.-broth, -eater, -supper*, etc.; **m.-biscuit**, a biscuit made with concentrated m.; **-earth** *dial.*, good and fertile soil; **-fly**, a bluebottle fly; **m. lozenge**, a lozenge made with concentrated m.; **m. maggot**, the larva of the meat-fly; **-offering**, a sacrifice consisting of food; used in versions of the Bible as tr. Heb. *minḥah*, an offering of fine flour or parched corn and oil (R.V. 'meal-offering'); **m. tea**, a tea at which m. is served.

Meat (mīt), *v.* Now *dial.* late ME. [f. prec.] 1. *trans.* To supply with food or provender 1568. 2. *intr.* To partake of food.

1. Haste then, and meate your men CHAPMAN.

Meatal (mi͵ē·tăl), *a.* 1868. [irreg. f. MEATUS + -AL.] Of or pertaining to a meatus.

Meated (mī·tėd), *a.* 1573. [f. MEAT *sb.* + -ED 2.] In Comb. **well-m.**, (*a*) of animals, having plenty of flesh; (*b*) of cheese, rich in nutriment; **open-m.**, of cheese, juicy.

Meath(e, obs. ff. MEAD 1.

Meatless (mī·tlės), *a.* OE. 1. Having no food (*arch.*). 2. Without meat 1845. b. Of food: Containing no butcher's meat 1909.

Meato-, used as comb. f. MEATUS, in names of surgical instruments, etc. **Mea·to-scope** [-SCOPE], a speculum for examining the urethra near the meatus. **Mea·totome** [Gr. -τόμος], a spring knife for the cutting of a contracted meatus urinarius. **Meato·tomy** [Gr. -τομία], section of the meatus urinarius to make a larger opening.

‖**Meatus** (mi͵ē·tŏs). *Pl.* **meatus** (mi͵ē·tiŭs), meatuses. 1665. [L., f. *meare* to flow, run.] †1. A channel or tubular passage -1698. 2. *spec.* in *Anat.* †a. = PORE. b. With qualification, applied to certain passages in the body. 1665.

2. b. *Auditory m.* (L. *m. auditorius*): the channel of the ear. *Nasal* or *olfactory m.*: the passage of the nose. *Urinary m.*: the external orifice of the urethra.

Meaty (mī·ti), *a.* 1787. [f. MEAT *sb.* + -Y 1.] 1. Full of meat; fleshy. Also *fig.* (chiefly *U.S.*). 2. Of or pertaining to meat; having the flavour of meat 1864. Hence **Mea·tiness.**

Meaul, meawl(e, vars. of MIAUL.

Meaw(e, vars. of MIAOW.

Meazle, var. of MESEL (leper).

Mecca (me·kă). 1823. [repr. Arab. *Makkah*, birthplace of Mohammed, and place of pilgrimage of the Mohammedans.] 1. Any place which one holds supremely sacred, or which it is the aspiration of one's life to visit. 2. *attrib.*, in *M. balm, balsam* 1823.

1. Stratford..is the M. of American pilgrims 1887. Hence **Me·ccan** *a.* and *sb.*

Meccano (mĭkā·no). 1908. Trade name of a set of miniature parts from which engineering models can be constructed.

Mechanic (mĭkæ·nik). late ME. [ad. L. *mechanicus*, a. Gr., f. μηχανή MACHINE.]

A. *adj.* 1. Pertaining to or involving manual labour or skill. Now *rare.* 1549. 2. Of persons: Having a manual occupation 1549. †3. Vulgar, low, base -1762. 4. Of the nature of, or pertaining to, a machine or machines; worked by machinery. Now *poet.* or *rhet.* 1625. 5. Worked or working like a machine; acting mechanically. Somewhat *arch.* 1697. †b. Involuntary, automatic -1741. 6. = MECHANICAL *a.* 5. Now *rare* or *Obs.* 1664. †7. = MECHANICAL *a.* 6. -1790. †8. Skilled in mechanical contrivance -1748.

2. Are the m. and farming classes satisfied? 1837. 3. *Ant. & Cl.* IV. iv. 32. 4. *M. powers* or †*faculties*: = *mechanical powers* (see MECHANICAL *a.* 3). 5. The sad m. exercise, Like dull narcotics TENNYSON.

B. *sb.* †1. Manual labour or operation -1605. †b. A mechanical art -1691. †c. Mechanism. BACON. 2. A handicraftsman. Formerly often *contemptuous*: A low fellow. Now *rare.* 1562. 3. A skilled workman, esp. one who makes or uses machinery 1662.

1. c. The fault being in the very frame and Mechanicke of the parts BACON. 2. *Mechanics' institute* or *institution*: one of a class of societies, established (first in 1823) to afford their members facilities for self-education by classes and lectures. 3. What is here said of Chymists is applicable to all other Mechaniques HOBBES. The apprentice clings to his foot-rule, a practised m. will measure by his thumb EMERSON.

Mechanical (mĭkæ·nikăl). late ME. [f. late L. *mechanicus*; see prec. and -ICAL.]

A. *adj.* 1. Of arts, trades, occupations: Concerned with machines or tools. Hence, a. Concerned with the contrivance and making of machines or mechanism. b. Concerned with manual operations 1450. †c. *transf.* Pertaining to the mere technicalities of a profession or art -1763. 2. Of persons: Engaged in manual labour; of the artisan class. †Hence, mean, vulgar 1589. †b. Practical as opp. to speculative -1633. 3. †a. Of the nature of a machine or machines. b. Now: Acting, worked, or produced by a machine or mechanism. 1567. 4. Of persons, etc.: Resembling (inanimate) machines or their operations; lacking spontaneity or originality; machine-like; automatic 1607. 5. Of agencies, principles, etc.: Such as belong to the subject-matter of mechanics (now often opp. to *chemical*) 1626. b. *Geol.* Applied to formations in which the ingredients have undergone no chemical change 1833. 6. Of theories and theorists: Explaining phenomena by mechanical action 1692. 7. Concerned with or involving material objects or physical conditions 1664. 8. Pertaining to mechanics as a science 1648; having to do with machinery 1793. 9. *Math.* Applied to curves not expressible by equations of finite and rational algebraical form; = TRANSCENDENTAL 1727.

1. a. Machine-making..belongs to a high order of m. art 1872. b. Handie-crafte called Arte Mechanicall 1477. 2. Of mean m. parentage EARL MONM. 3. b. The m. pianoforte player 1902. Phr. *M. powers* or †*faculties*: the six 'simple machines' (see MACHINE *sb.* 5), the balance, lever, wheel, pulley, wedge, and screw. *M. drawing*: drawing performed with compasses, rulers, etc. *M. construction* (of curves): construction by the use of some apparatus, as dist. from tracing by calculation of successive points. *M. transport* (abbrev. M.T.), the motor branch of the R.A.S.C. 4. Versification is a thing in a great degree m. HAZLITT. 5. *M. mixture*, a mixture only separable into its component parts by m. means. 6. The M. Atheist BENTLEY. The m. theory of slaty cleavage TYNDALL. 8. M. Engineer 1881.

B. *sb.* 1. = MECHANIC B. 2. *arch.* 1590. 2. *pl.* †a. The science which relates to the construction of machines. BACON. b. Details of mechanical construction (*rare*) 1821.

1. A crew of patches, rude Mechanicals, That worke for bread vpon Athenian stals SHAKS.

Hence **Mecha·nicalism**, the doctrine that phenomena are mechanically caused; m. procedure. **Mecha·nicalize** *v.* **Mecha·nical-ly** *adv.*, **-ness.**

Mechanician (mekăni·ʃən). 1570. [f. MECHANIC + -IAN. Cf. F. *mécanicien.*] a. A mechanic, artisan. Now *rare.* b. One skilled in the construction of machinery.

Mecha·nico-, used as comb. f. L. *mechanicus*, with sense 'partly mechanical and partly . . .', as **m.-chemical** *a.*, comprising mechanics and chemistry; (of phenomena) pertaining partly to mechanics and partly to chemistry; **-corpuscular** *a.* epithet of the philosophy which explains all phenomena, material and spiritual, by the movement of atoms according to mechanical laws.

Mechanics (mĭkæ·niks). 1648. [In form a pl. of MECHANIC; see -IC 2.] a. Orig. (and still in pop. use): That body of theoretical and practical knowledge which is concerned with the invention and construction of machines, the explanation of their operation, and the calculation of their efficiency. b. That department of applied mathematics which treats of motion and tendencies to motion: comprising *kinematics*, the science of abstract motion, and *dynamics* (including *statics* and *kinetics*), the science of the action of forces in producing motion or equilibrium.

Analytical m.: mechanics treated by the differential and integral calculus. *Animal m.*: m. as applied to the study of the movements of animals.

Mechanism (me·kăniz'm). 1662. [ad. mod.L. *mechanismus*, f. Gr. μηχανή MACHINE; see -ISM.] 1. The structure, or mutual adaptation of parts, in a machine or anything comparable to a machine. 2. *concr.* A system of mutually adapted parts working together; a piece of machinery; the machinery (*lit.* or *fig.*) of some effect 1677. †3. Mechanical action -1794. 4. *Art.* The mechanical execution of a painting, sculpture, piece of music, etc.; technique. (Opp. to *style* or *expression.*) 1843.

1. The m. of society 1833, of movement in the animal frame BAIN, of a door 1867. 2. The m. of a watch 1822, of a flute 1871, of perception and memory 1885. 3. The M. or Necessity of human Actions HARTLEY.

Mechanist (me·kănist). 1606. [f. MECHANIC + -IST.] 1. †A mechanic; also, a machinist. 2. One versed in mechanics; a mechanician 1704. 3. One who holds a mechanical theory of the universe (now *rare*) 1668. Hence **Mechanis·tic** *a.* pertaining to mechanics or mechanism. Also, pertaining to mechanical theories in biology or philosophy.

Mechanize (me·kănəiz), *v.* 1678. [f. as prec. + -IZE.] *trans.* To make or render mechanical; to work out the mechanical details of (a design, idea, etc.); *spec.* to substitute mechanical power for man or horse power in (an army, etc.). **Me:chaniza·tion. Me·chanizer** = MECHANIST 3.

‖**Méchant** (meʃaṅ), *a.* Also fem. **-ante** (-āṅt). 1813. [Fr.] Malicious, spiteful.

Mr. Pendennis was wicked, *méchant*, perfectly abominable THACKERAY.

Mechlin (me·klin), *a.* and *sb.* 1483. [Name of a town in Belgium.] †1. *M. black*: a black cloth made at Mechlin. 2. In full *M. lace*: lace produced at Mechlin 1699.

Mechoacan (metʃo͡u·ăkăn). 1577. [Name of a Mexican province. Often written with a capital M.] 1. The root of a Mexican species of bindweed, *Ipomæa* (*Batatas*) *Jalapa*, formerly used as a purgative; also, the plant itself. Also called *white m.* †2. A purgative drug obtained from the roots of *Ipomæa* (*Batatas*) *Jalapa* and other similar plants -1768. 3. *attrib.*, as *m. root*, etc. 1632.

Meconic (mĭkǫ·nik), *a.* 1819. [f. Gr. μήκων poppy + -IC.] (*Chem.*) *M. acid*: a white crystalline acid obtained from opium. So *m. ether*. Hence **Meconate** (mī·kŏnĕt), a salt of m. acid 1836. So **Meconidine** (mĭkǫ·nidəin), an amorphous alkaloid found in opium 1871. **Meconin** (mī·kŏnin), a white crystalline neutral compound existing in opium, regarded as an anhydride of meconic acid 1833.

‖**Meconium** (mĭkōu·niŏm). 1601. [L., a. Gr. μηκώνιον, f. μήκων poppy.] †1. The inspissated juice of the poppy; opium –1804. 2. The dark excrementitious substance in the large intestines of the fœtus; hence, the first fæces of a new-born infant 1706.

Medal (me·dăl), *sb.* 1586. [a. F. *médaille*, ad. It. *medaglia* :—Com. Rom. **medallia* (whence F. *maille*):—pop.L. **metallea*, f. *metallum* METAL *sb.*] †1. A metal disk bearing a figure or an inscription, used as a charm or trinket –1674. 2. A piece of metal, usu. in the form of a coin, with an inscription, or device or figure to commemorate a person, action, or event; also as a distinction awarded to a soldier, a student, etc., for a heroic action, for merit, or for proficiency or skill in any art or subject. In collectors' use, extended to include coins. 1611. †3. *fig.* An image, representation (cf. MODEL *sb.*); something beyond the common run (as a medal compared with current coin) –1844. 4. *attrib.* 1658.

1. *Wint. T.* I. ii. 307. 2. Phr. *The reverse of the m.*: the other side of the question. 3. This little Meddal of God, the Soul of Man H. MORE.

Comb. **m.-play** *Golf*, play in which the score is reckoned by counting the number of strokes taken for the round by each player.

Medal (me·dăl), *v.* 1822. [f. prec.] *trans.* To decorate or honour with a medal.

Irving went home medalled by the King THACKERAY.

Medalet (me·dălĕt). Also **medallet**. 1789. [f. MEDAL *sb.* + -ET.] A small medal.

Medallic (mĭdæ·lik), *a.* 1702. [f. MEDAL *sb.* + -IC.] Of, pertaining to, or resembling a medal; represented on a medal.

Medallion (mĭdæ·lyən). 1658. [a. F. *médaillon*, ad. It. *medaglione*, augm. of *medaglia* MEDAL *sb.*] 1. A large medal. 2. Anything resembling this; e.g. in decorative work, an oval or circular panel or tablet; a portrait; a decorative design resembling a panel or tablet, as in a carpet, a window, etc. 1762.

2. A medalion of him in marble H. WALPOLE.

Medallist (me·dălist). Also **medalist**. 1682. [f. MEDAL *sb.* + -IST.] 1. One skilled in medals. 2. An engraver, designer, or maker of medals 1756. 3. A recipient of a medal awarded for merit 1797.

3. The Gold Medallists of the year (*mod.*).

Meddle (me·d'l), *v.* ME. [a. OF. *medler*, *mesdler*, var. of OF. *mesler* :—pop. L. **misculare*, f. L. *miscere* to mix. Cf. MELL *v.*] †1. *trans.* To mix, mingle; to combine, blend, intersperse. Const. *with*, *together*; also, *among*, *in*, *to*. –1658. †2. *intr.* for *refl.* To mingle, combine. Also *refl.* –1610. †3. To have sexual intercourse (*with*). Also *refl.* –1655. †4. To mingle in fight; to contend –1601. †5. *refl.* To busy oneself –1562. 6. *intr.* To concern oneself; to take part *in*. Now always, to busy oneself or take part interferingly. ME.

2. More to know Did neuer medle with my thoughts SHAKS. 4. *Twel. N.* III. iv. 275. 6. Happie that State wherein the Cobler meddles with his last 1622. Wholly unacquainted with the world in which they are so fond of meddling BURKE. Phr. *Neither make nor m.*: see MAKE *v.* Hence **Me·ddler**, one who meddles. **Me·ddlesome** *a.* given to interfering; -ly *adv.*; -ness. **Me·ddlingly** *adv.*

Mede (mīd). late ME. [ad. L. *Medus*, a. Gr. Μῆδος.] A native or inhabitant of Media.

The law of the Medes and Persians: see LAW *sb.*[1] I. 1.

Mede, obs. f. MEAD, MEED.

‖**Media** (mī·diă). *Pl.* (in sense 1) **mediæ** (mī·dĭī). 1841. [L. (sc. *litera*, *tunica*, etc.).] 1. *Phonetics.* A voiced or 'soft' mute; = MEDIAL *sb.* 2. 2. *Anat.* The middle tunic or membrane of an artery or vessel 1876.

Media (mī·diă), pl. of MEDIUM.

Mediacy (mī·diăsi). 1853. [f. MEDIATE *a.*; see -ACY.] *Logic* and *Philos.* Mediate state or quality.

Mediæval, medieval (medi,ī·văl, mīdi,ī·văl). 1827. [f. mod. L. *medium ævum* middle age + -AL.] A. *adj.* Of, pertaining to or characteristic of the Middle Ages. Of Art, Religion, etc.: Resembling or imitative of that of the Middle Ages. B. *sb.* One who lived in the Middle Ages. **Mediæ·-, medie·-vally** *adv.*

Mediævalism, medievalism (medi-, mīdi,ī·văliz'm). 1853. [f. prec. + -ISM.] The system of belief and practice characteristic of the Middle Ages; mediæval thought, religion, art, etc.; the adoption of or devotion to mediæval ideals or usages; *occas.* an instance of this. So **Mediæ·-, medie·valist**, one skilled in mediæval history or affairs; one who practises m. in art, religion, etc.

Mediævalize, medievalize (medi-, mīdi,ī·văləiz), *v.* 1854. [f. MEDIÆVAL + -IZE.] *trans.* To make mediæval in character; *intr.* to favour mediæval ideas or usages.

Medial (mī·diăl). 1570. [ad. late L. *medialis*, f. *medius*, cogn. with MID *a.* Cf. F. *médial*.]

A. *adj.* 1. Occupying a middle or intermediate position; middle; (of a letter, etc.) occurring in the middle of a word 1721. 2. Pertaining to a mathematical mean or average 1570. 3. Of average dimensions; *occas.* of ordinary attainments 1778. 4. *Mus.* See below. 1809. †5. *Phonetics.* (See B. 2.) 1833.

1. M. and paired fins GÜNTHER. *M. to*: situated in the middle of. 4. **M. accent**, the fall of a minor third from the dominant or reciting note (Helmore). **M. cadence**, in the eccl. modes, a cadence closing with the mediant of a mode. **M. consonances**, the major sixth and the major third.

B. *sb.* 1. †a. A letter of ordinary height, i.e. having no ascending or descending strokes 1620. b. A medial letter; a form of a letter used in the middle of a word 1776. †2. *Phonetics.* A voiced mute –1880.

2. Three medials, as they are called, *b*, *g*, *d* GUEST. Hence **Me·dially** *adv.*

Median (mī·diăn), *a.*[1] and *sb.*[1] 1541. [ad. L. *medianus*, f. *medius*; see -AN.]

A. *adj.* 1. Situated in the middle 1645. 2. Special scientific uses. See below. 1592. 3. *Statistics.* Used to designate that quantity which is so related to the quantities occurring in a given set of instances that exactly as many exceed as fall short of it 1894.

1. Lower and m. latitudes 1877. 2. *M. artery, nerve, vein* (Anat.): now applied to certain structures in the arm. *M. line*: (*a*) any line in the m. plane; (*b*) (*Bot.*) the midrib of a symmetric leaf; (*c*) (*Geog.*) the line along the middle of the calm belt between the north and south trade winds. *M. lithotomy* (Surg.): the method in which the incision is made through the m. line of the perinæum (opp. to *lateral*). *M. plane*: the plane which divides any body into two equal and symmetrical parts. *M. zone*: a zone along the sea-bottom between 50 and 100 fathoms in depth. 3. The average age of the population of the United States..is twenty-five years; the m. age is twenty-one years 1900.

B. *sb.* 1. *Anat.* The m. vein, nerve, etc. 1541. 2. *Math.* Each of the three lines drawn from the angles of a triangle to the middle points of the opposite sides, and meeting in a point within it 1888. 3. *Statistics.* A median quantity (see A. 3) 1902.

Median (mī·diăn), *a.*[2] and *sb.*[2] 1601. [f. *Media* + -AN.] A. *adj.* Of or belonging to the ancient kingdom of Media, or the Medes. B. *sb.* A Mede 1601.

Mediant (mī·diănt). 1753. [ad. It. *mediante*, repr. late L. *mediantem*, pr. pple. of *mediare* to be in the middle, f. *medius*; see MEDIUM. Cf. F. *médiant*.] *Mus.* a. In eccl. music: One of the 'regular modulations' of a mode. b. In mod. music, the third of any scale, lying midway between the tonic and the dominant. Also *attrib.*

‖**Mediastinum** (mīdiæstəi·nŏm). *Pl.* **-a**. 1541. (Also anglicized **-tine**, 1631–1732). [mod. L., neut. of med.L. *mediastinus* medial, f. *medius*, after cl. L. *mediastinus* sb., inferior servant.] *Anat.* A membranous middle septum or partition between two cavities of the body; esp. that formed by the two inner walls of the pleura, separating the right and left lungs. **Mediasti·nal** *a.* **Mediasti·no-**, comb. form.

Mediate (mī·diĕt), *a.* late ME. [ad. late L. *mediatus*, *mediare*; see MEDIATE *v.*] 1. Intermediate in position, rank, quality, time, etc. Now *rare*. †b. Of a person: Intermediary 1495–1660. c. Serving as a means to an end 1502. 2. Acting or related through an intermediate person or thing; opp. to *immediate*. See below. 1454.

1. After many m. preferments..at last he became Arch-bishop of Canterbury FULLER. 2. *Feudal Law.* Said of a superior and of a tenant or vassal, when the latter holds of the former through a mesne lord. Also *gen.* *M. inference* (Logic): an inference reached through a middle term. *M. knowledge*: knowledge obtained, not by intuition, but by means of inference or testimony. *M. testimony* (Law): secondary evidence. *M. auscultation* (Med.): auscultation performed with the interposition of some object, e.g. a stethoscope, between the body and the ear.

Hence **Me·diate-ly** *adv.* 1526, **-ness** 1704.

Mediate (mī·dieit), *v.* 1542. [f. late L. *mediat-*, *mediare*, f. *medius* middle; see MEDIUM.] †1. *trans.* To divide into two equal parts –1610. 2. *intr.* To be between; usu., to form a connecting link or a transitional stage between 1642. 3. To act as an intermediary; to intervene for the purpose of reconciling 1616. 4. *trans.* 'To effect by mediation' (J.); to procure by intercession 1592. b. To settle (a dispute) by mediation 1623. 5. To be the medium for bringing about (a result) or conveying (a gift, etc.); *pass.* to be communicated or imparted mediately 1630.

2. To m. between the old and the new STANLEY. 3. Bacon attempted to m. between his friend [the Earl of Essex] and the Queen MACAULAY. 4. To m. ..a suspension of armes BLOUNT. 5. A country which, like England, mediates the transactions of many others GOSCHEN.

Mediation (mīdiē^i·ʃən). late ME. [a. OF. *mediacion*, ad. late L. *mediationem*, f. *mediare*; see MEDIATE *v.*] †1. Halving, bisection –1727. 2. Agency or action as a mediator; the action of mediating between parties at variance; intercession on behalf of another. late ME. 3. Agency as an intermediary; instrumentality. late ME. 4. *Mus.* That part of a plainsong or an Anglican chant which lies between the two reciting notes 1845.

2. His [Gregory's] m. appeased the tumult of arms GIBBON. 3. To seek for peace..through the m. of a vigorous war BURKE.

Mediative (mī·diĕtiv), *a. rare.* 1813. [f. MEDIATE *v.* + -IVE.] That has the quality of mediating; pertaining to mediation.

Mediatize (mī·diătəiz), *v.* 1818. [ad. F. *médiatiser*, f. *médiat*; see MEDIATE *a.* and -IZE.] 1. *trans. Hist.* In Germany under the Holy Roman Empire: To reduce (a prince or state) from the position of an immediate vassal of the Empire to that of a mediate vassal. Hence, later: To annex (a principality) to another state, leaving to its former sovereign his title, and (usually) some rights of government. Also *fig.* 2. *intr.* To mediate (*mod.*).

1. His Highness has the misfortune of being a mediatised prince DISRAELI. Hence **Me·diatiza·tion**.

Mediator (mī·dieitəɹ). ME. [a. F. *médiateur*, ad. late L. *mediatorem*.] 1. One who mediates (see MEDIATE *v.*). 2. *Theol.* One who mediates between God and Man; *esp.* Jesus Christ ME. †3. A go-between; a messenger or agent –1697. 4. *Path.* Applied to those constituents of a serum which actively produce hæmolysis 1903. 5. A variation in the games of ombre and quadrille 1902.

2. For there is one God, and one Mediatour betweene God and men, the man Christ Iesus 1 *Tim.* ii. 5. Hence **Me·diato·rial**, †**Mediato·rian** *adjs.* of, pertaining to, resembling, or characteristic of a m. or mediation. **Me·diatorship**, the office of a m. **Me·diatory** *a.* having the function of mediating; pertaining to mediation.

Mediatrix (mīdiē^i·triks). *Pl.* **mediatrices** (mīdiĕtrəi·sīz). 1462. [a. L., fem. of *mediator*.] A female mediator. (Often applied to the Virgin Mary.) So **Me·diatress** 1616, **Me·diatrice** a. [F. *médiatrice*] late ME

Medic (me·dik). 1659. [ad. L. *medicus* adj. and sb., f. root of *mederi* to heal.] A. *adj.* = MEDICAL. Only *poet.* 1700. B. *sb.* A physician, medical man. *rare* exc. *U.S.* college slang for 'medical student'.

†**Me·dica.** 1577. = MEDICK –1753.

Medicable (me·dikăb'l), *a.* 1616. [ad. L. *medicabilis*; see MEDICATE *v.* and -ABLE.] 1. Admitting of cure or remedial treatment. †2. Possessing medicinal properties -1666.

Medical (me·dikăl), *a.* (*sb.*) 1646. [a. F. *médical*, ad. late L. *medicalis*, f. *medicus*; see MEDIC.] 1. Pertaining to the healing art or its professors; also, pertaining to 'medicine', as dist. from obstetrics, surgery, etc. b. Of diseases: Requiring medical as dist. from surgical treatment or diagnosis 1885. 2. Curative, medicinal (*rare*) 1646. 3. *sb.* A student or practitioner of medicine (*colloq.*) 1823.

1. M. Electricity 1778, practice 1799. †**M. finger,** the finger next to the little finger. **M. garden,** a garden for the cultivation of medicinal plants; a 'physic-garden'. *M. man*: a general term, including 'physician' and 'surgeon'. Hence **Me·dically** *adv.*

Medicament (mǐ-, medi·kămĕnt, me·dikămĕnt), *sb.* 1541. [a. F. *médicament*, ad. L. *medicamentum*; see MEDICATE *v.*, -MENT.] A substance used in curative treatment. Also *transf.* and *fig.* Hence **Medi·cament** *v.* to administer medicaments to. **Me:dicame·ntal** *a.* (now *rare*), of the nature of a m.; medicinal. **Me:dicame·ntally** *adv.* **Me:dicame·ntary** *a.* curative; treating of medicaments.

Medicaster (me·dikæstəɹ). 1602. [See MEDIC and -ASTER.] A pretender to medical skill; a quack, charlatan.

Medicate (me·dikeɪt), *v.* 1623. [f. L. *medicat-*, *medicare*, *-ari*, f. *medicus*.] 1. *trans.* To treat medically. †b. To treat (a thing) with drugs, etc. for any purpose -1775. 2. To impregnate with a medicinal substance 1707. †b. To 'doctor' (liquors, etc.) -1791.

2. The inhalation of steam medicated with terebene 1898. Hence **Medica·tion,** the action of medicating; *concr.* something used for this. **Me·dicative** *a.* curative.

Medicean (medisǐ·ăn, -tʃǐ·ăn), *a.* 1610. [f. mod.L. *Mediceus* (f. It. *Medici*, surname) + -AN.] Pertaining to the Medici, a family who ruled Florence during the 15th c. Used as the designation of the library at Florence (otherwise called Laurentian) founded by Lorenzo de' Medici, and of MSS. there preserved; also, of works of art in the Florentine collections.

Medicinable (me·dsĭnăb'l), *a.* late ME. [a. OF. *medecinable*, f. *medeciner*; see MEDICINE *v.* and -ABLE.] 1. = MEDICINAL. *Obs.* exc. *poet.* or *arch.* Also *fig.* †2. Of or belonging to medicine -1607.

Medicinal (mĭdi·sinăl), *a.* (*sb.*) ME. [ad. L. *medicinalis*; see MEDICINE and -AL.] 1. Having healing properties or attributes; adapted to medical uses. Const. *against*, *for*. Also *fig.* †2. Of or relating to the science or the practice of medicine -1804. b. Resembling medicine 1824. 3. *sb.* A medicinal substance; also, †*pl.* matters pertaining to medical science. late ME.

1. Dire inflammation which no cooling herb Or medcinal liquor can asswage MILT. 2. b. A m. taste 1824. Hence **Medi·cinally** *adv.*

Medicine (me·ds'n, me·disin, -s'n), *sb.*[1] ME. [a. OF. *medecine*, *-icine* (mod.F. *médecine*), ad. L. *medicina*, f. *medicus*; see MEDIC. The trisyllabic pronunc. is chiefly Sc. and U.S.] 1. The science and art concerned with the cure, alleviation, and prevention of disease, and with the restoration and preservation of health. Also, *less widely*, that branch which is the province of the physician; the art of restoring and preserving health by means of remedial substances and the regulation of diet, habits, etc.; dist. from *surgery* and *obstetrics*. 2. A medicament, esp. one taken internally; also, medicaments generally, 'physic' ME. b. *fig.* ME. †3. Applied to the philosopher's stone or elixir, to cosmetics, philtres, etc. -1615. 4. Used to represent the terms applied by Amer. Indians and other savages to any magical object or ceremony; a spell, charm, fetish; occas. = MANITOU 1805. b. = *medicine-man* 1817.

2. b. The miserable haue no other m. But onely hope SHAKS. c. *To take one's m.* (U.S.): to submit to something disagreeable 1894. 3. 1 *Hen. IV*, II. ii. 19. *Comb.*: (in sense 2), **m. ball,** a stuffed leather ball used for exercise; **m. seal, stamp,** a name for small cubical or oblong stones with inscriptions in intaglio, found among Roman remains, which seem to have been used by physicians for marking their drugs; **m. tree,** the horse-radish tree; (in sense 4), **m. man,** a magician among the Amer. Indians and other savages.

†**Me·dicine,** *sb.*[2] 1450. [a. F. *médecin*, ad. late L. *medicinus* adj. used *absol.*] A medical practitioner -1632.

I haue seen a m. That's able to breath life into a stone SHAKS.

Medicine (me·ds'n, me·disin, -s'n), *v.* 1450. [a. OF. *medeciner*, f. *medecine* MEDICINE *sb.*[1]] 1. *trans.* To cure by means of medicine; to give medicine to. b. To bring by medicinal virtue *to*. SHAKS. 2. *transf.* and *fig.* 1593.

1. b. Not Poppy, nor Mandragora..Shall euer m. thee to that sweete sleepe Which thou owd'st yesterday SHAKS. 2. Great greefes I see med'cine the lesse SHAKS. So **Mediciner** (*arch.*), a physician, medical man, leech; (*nonce-use*) as tr. Gr. φαρμακεύς poisoner.

Medick (mī·dik). late ME. [ad. L. *medica*, ad. Gr. Μηδική (πόα), lit. 'Median grass'.] Any plant of the genus *Medicago*, esp. *M. sativa*, Purple medick or LUCERNE.

Medico (me·diko). 1689. [a. It. *medico*.] A medical practitioner; also, a medical student. Now *slang* or *joc.*

Medico- (mediko), used as comb. f. L. *medicus* in combs. denoting the application of medical science to various subjects of research, as *m.-botanic(al*, *-electric*, *-legal*, *-psychological*, *-statistical*, etc.

Medicommissure (mīdikǫ·misiūɹ). Also **medio-**. 1882. [f. L. *medius* + COMMISSURE.] *Anat.* The middle commissure of the brain.

†**Me·dics,** *sb. pl.* 1663. [pl. of MEDIC; see -IC 2.] The science of medicine -1737.

Mediety (mĭdəi·ěti). late ME. [ad. L. *medietas*, f. *medius*; see -TY.] 1. †a. *gen.* A half -1686. b. *spec.* in *Law.* = MOIETY 1661. †2. Middle state, position, or quality -1651. †3. *Math.* The quality of being a mean between two quantities -1694.

Medieval, etc.: see MEDIÆVAL, etc.

‖ **Medine** (medī·n). 1583. [a. F. *medin*, a. Arab., f. the name *Mu'ayyad*.] An Egyptian coin corresp. to the Turkish PARA.

Medio- (mī·dio), used as comb. f. L. *medius*, with the sense either 'relating to the middle of' (an organ or part), as in *m.-carpal*, *-dorsal*, *-frontal*, etc., or 'in the middle', as in *m.-perforate*; also in **m.-inferior, -posterior** = 'lower middle', 'posterior-middle' (margin).

Mediocre (mī·diōᵘkəɹ), *a.* (*sb.*) 1586. [a. F. *médiocre*, ad. L. *mediocris*, f. *medius*.] 1. Of middling quality; neither bad nor good; indifferent. Also *absol.* 2. *sb.* Only *pl.* Mediocre persons (*rare*) 1834.

1. It is thus that m. people seek to lower great men CARLYLE. So **Me·diocrist,** a person of middling ability 1787.

Mediocrity (mīdiǫ·krĭti). 1450. [a. F. *médiocrité*, ad. L. *mediocritas*; see prec. and -ITY.] 1. Mean state or condition, mediety. Also, a mean. (Chiefly quasi-techn., with reference to the Aristotelian theory of 'the mean'. Now *rare*.) 1531. †2. A middle course in action; moderation, temperance -1774. †3. Moderate degree or rate, average quality or amount; tempered condition -1753. †4. Moderate fortune or condition in life -1816. 5. The quality or condition of being mediocre. Now chiefly *disparaging*. 1588. 6. *concr.* A person of mediocre ability 1694.

1. †*Golden m.* = *golden mean*. 5. The most important offices in the state were bestowed on decorous and laborious m. MACAULAY. 6. He is too much a m. CONGREVE.

Medism (mī·diz'm). 1849. [ad. L. *mēdismus*, Gr. μηδισμός, f. μηδίζειν to MEDIZE.] a. *Gr. Hist.* Sympathy with the Medes. b. A word or idiom belonging to the language of the Medes.

†**Meditance.** *rare.* 1612. [f. next; see -ANCE.] Meditation.

Meditant (me·ditănt). *rare.* 1614. [ad. L. *meditantem*, *meditari*.] a. *adj.* Meditating. b. *sb.* One who meditates.

Meditate (me·diteɪt), *v.* 1560. [f. L. *meditat-*, *meditari*, freq. f. root *mĕd-*, whence Gr. μέδεσθαι, μήδεσθαι, L. *mederi*, etc.] 1. *trans.* To reflect upon; to study, ponder. Now *rare.* 1580. b. To observe with intentness 1700. 2. To plan by revolving in the mind; to design mentally 1591. †3. To think -1609. 4. *intr.* To exercise the mind in (esp. devotional) thought or contemplation 1560.

1. Him [Rousseau] they study; him they m. BURKE. Phr. *To m. the Muse* (after L. *Musam meditari*, Virg. *Ecl.* i. 2): to occupy oneself in song or poetry. b. Like a lion..With inward rage he meditates his prey DRYDEN. 2. A creature meditating mischief GOLDSM. 4. And Isaac went out, to m. in the field, at the euentide *Gen.* xxiv. 63. **Me·ditatingly** *adv.*

Meditation (meditēɪ·ʃən). ME. [a. F. *méditation*, or ad. L. *meditationem*.] 1. The action, or an act, of meditating; serious and sustained reflection or mental contemplation. 2. *spec.* in religious use: The continuous application of the mind to the contemplation of some religious truth, mystery, or object of reverence, as a devotional exercise ME. b. The theme of one's meditation *Ps.* cxix. 97. 3. A discourse, written or spoken, of a meditative character ME.

1. The imperiall Votresse passed on, In maiden m., fancy free SHAKS. 2. In m. we converse with ourselves; in prayer we converse with God M. HENRY. 3. A m. upon a broom-stick SWIFT (*title*).

Meditative (me·ditĕtiv, -ētiv), *a.* (*sb.*) 1612. [See MEDITATE *v.* and -IVE.] 1. Inclined or accustomed to meditation 1656. b. Inclined to meditate (something specified). Const. *of*. 1876. 2. Accompanied by, or indicative of, meditation 1756. 3. Conducive to meditation 1868. †4. *Gram.* = DESIDERATIVE 1755. †5. *sb.* A desiderative word -1845.

1. His musing m. mind 1683. 2. M. walks 1756, pulls of a pipe 1903. **Me·ditative-ly** *adv.*, **-ness.**

Meditator (me·diteɪtəɹ). Also **-er.** 1665. [f. MEDITATE *v.* + -OR.] One who meditates.

†**Mediterrane,** *a.* and *sb.* late ME. [ad. OF. *mediterrain*, *-an*, ad. L. *mediterraneus* (see next).] = next -1662.

Mediterranean (meditĕrēɪ·nĭăn), *a.* and *sb.* 1594. [f. L. *mediterraneus* (f. *medius* + *terra*) + -AN.] A. *adj.* 1. Of land: Midland, inland, remote from the coast; opp. to *maritime*. Also, intermediate (between two areas). 1601. 2. Of water surfaces: Nearly or entirely surrounded by dry land; land-locked 1594.

1. The more m. parts of Russia BOYLE. 2. *M. Sea*: proper name of the sea which separates Europe from Africa. var. †**Mediterraneous** *a.*

B. *sb.* 1. An inland sea or lake; *spec.* the Mediterranean Sea 1652. b. *attrib.* or *adj.* Pertaining to the Mediterranean Sea 1599. †2. An inhabitant of an inland part 1654.

1. b. *M. fever* = *Malta fever* (see MALTA).

Medium (mī·diŏm). *Pl.* **media, -iums.** 1551. [a. L., neut. of *medius*.]

A. *sb.* 1. A middle quality, degree, or condition. Formerly also, †something intermediate in nature or degree. 1593. †b. Moderation -1780. †c. A middle course. DE FOE. †2. *Logic.* The middle term of a syllogism; hence, a ground of proof -1817. †3. A (geometrical or arithmetical) mean; an average 1551-1817. 4. Any intervening substance through which a force acts on objects at a distance or through which impressions are conveyed to the senses, e.g. air, the ether, etc. Often *fig.* 1595. b. Hence, Pervading or enveloping substance; the 'element' in which an organism lives; hence *fig.* one's environment, conditions of life 1865. 5. An intermediate agency, means, instrument, or channel. Also, intermediation, instrumentality. 1605. 6. *Painting.* Any liquid vehicle (as oil, water, etc.) with which pigments are mixed for use. Also, any of the varieties of painting as determined by the nature of the vehicle. 1854. 7. *Theatr.* A screen fixed in front of a gas-jet in order to throw a coloured light upon the stage 1859. 8. Applied to a person. a. *gen.* An agent, mediator 1817. b. *Spiritualism.* A person supposed to be the organ of communications from departed spirits 1853.

1. Poesy between the best and worst No m. knows BYRON. 3. I have reckoned upon a m., that a child just born will weigh 12 pounds SWIFT. 4. The air, which is the m. of musick and of all sounds 1643. b. You cannot thus abstract any man from the social m. by which he is surrounded GROTE. 5. The proposition is peace. Not peace through the m. of war BURKE. *M. of circulation* or *exchange*, *circulating m.*: something which serves as the ordinary representative of commercial value, and as the instrument

of exchange; usually coins or written promises or orders for the delivery of coins. 8. b. Attempts to pry by the help of 'mediums' into the book of Fate BRYCE.

B. *attrib.* or *adj.* 1. Intermediate between two degrees, amounts, qualities, or classes 1796. b. A size of paper between royal and demy 1711. †2. Average, mean -1800.

1. M. wave *Wireless*, a wave having a wave-length between 100 and 800 metres.

Comb., as *m.-grade*, *-pace*; *m.-coloured*, *-sized*, adjs.

Medius (mī·diǒs). 1565. [a. L.] *Mus.* †1. = MEAN *sb.* 2. -1758. 2. In eccl. music = MEDIANT 1782.

Medize (mī·dəiz), *v.* 1629. [ad. Gr. Μηδίζειν, f. Μῆδοι the Medes; see -IZE.] *intr.* To be a Mede in manners, language, and dress; to side with the Medes. Also *trans.* To make like a Mede.

‖**Medjidie** (medʒī·die). 1856. [Turkish (Arab.) *mejīdie*, f. *Abdu'l Majīd*.] 1. *The M.*: a Turkish order instituted in 1851 by the Sultan Abdul-Medjid. 2. A Turkish silver coin first minted by the Sultan Abdul-Medjid in 1844, equal to 20 piastres 1882.

Medlar (me·dləɹ). late ME. [a. OF. *medler*, f. **medle* (var. of *mesle*, whence earlier ME. *medle*).] 1. The fruit-tree *Mespilus germanica*. b. Applied to other trees 1718. 2. The fruit of the medlar tree, resembling a small brown-skinned apple, with a large cup-shaped eye between the persistent calyx-lobes. It is eaten only when decayed. late ME.

1. b. *Neapolitan* or *Oriental M.*, the AZAROLE, *Cratægus Azarolus*. *Japan M.*, the LOQUAT. 2. You'l be rotten ere you bee halfe ripe, and that's the right vertue of the Medler SHAKS. *Comb.* m. tree = 1.

Medle, obs. f. MEDDLE.

Medley (me·dli), *sb.* and *a.* ME. [a. OF. *medlee*, var. of *meslee* (mod.F. *mêlée*) :—pop. L. **misculata*, f. **misculare* to mix, MEDDLE *v.*]

A. *sb.* 1. Combat, conflict; fighting, *esp.* hand-to-hand fighting between two parties of combatants. Now only *arch.* 2. A combination, mixture; *esp.* a heterogeneous mixture; a mixed company 1440. 3. A cloth woven with wools of different colours or shades. late ME. †4. = MASLIN[1] 1 (*rare*) 1601. 5. A musical composition consisting of parts or subjects of an incongruous character 1626. 6. As the title of a literary miscellany 1630.

1. *fig.* In the press and m. of such extremities BURKE. 2. A wretched M. betwixt Priest and Layman 1683.

B. *adj.* †1. Of a mixed colour; motley -1681. 2. Composed of incongruous parts or elements; mixed, motley 1594. b. in CHANCE-MEDLEY.

1. He rood but hoomly in a medlee cote CHAUCER. *M. cloth* = A. 3. Hence Medley *v.* to make a m. of; to intermix.

Médoc, Medoc (medǫ·k). 1833. [a. F., from *Médoc* in S.W. France.] A name for the red wines produced in Médoc.

‖**Medulla** (mīdʊ·lă). 1643. [L., prob. cogn. w. *medius* middle.] 1. *Anat.* The marrow of bones; also, the spinal marrow. Also, †the substance of the brain. 1651. b. (More fully *m. oblongata*: lit. 'prolonged marrow'.) The hindmost segment of the brain 1676. c. The central parts of certain organs (esp. the kidney) 1878. d. The soft fatty substance which forms the sheath of a nerve 1839. e. The pith of mammalian hair. Also, the soft fibrous substance which occupies the axis of the capsule of a growing feather. 1826. f. The endosarc of protozoa 1888. 2. *Bot.* The soft internal tissue of plants 1651. †3. *fig.* The 'pith' or 'marrow' of a subject. Often used for: A compendium, abridgement, summary. -1769.

Medullary (mīdʊ·lări, me·dʊ̆lări), *a.* 1620. [ad. late L. *medullaris*: see prec. and -ARY[2].] 1. *Anat.* Of, pertaining to, of the nature of, or resembling marrow. Also, pertaining to the medulla of an organ or part (e. g. *the m. rays in the kidney*, *the m. sheath of a nerve*); *occas.* pertaining to the *medulla oblongata*. 1677. b. *Path.* An alternative epithet for encephaloid or soft cancer or sarcoma 1804. 2. †a. Pertaining to the soft internal substance or pulp (of plants). b. *Bot.* Of, relating to, or connected with the pith of plants. 1620.

2. b. *M. ray*: each of the processes in a woody stem connecting the pith with the bark. *M. sheath*: the sheath immediately surrounding the pith. So Medu·llar (1541), Medu·llous (1578) *adjs.*

Medullated (mī·dʊlēˈtėd), *ppl. a.* 1867. [f. late L. *medullatus* having a marrow; see -ED[1].] Having a medulla.

Medusa (mīdiū·să, -ză). late ME. [a. L., a. Gr. Μέδουσα.] 1. *Gr. Myth.* One of the three Gorgons, whose head, with snakes for hair, turned him who looked upon it into stone. 2. *Zool.* (Pl. *medusæ*, *-as.*) a. A soft gelatinous hydrozoan; a jelly-fish. b. One of the two types of reproductive zooids in hydrozoans; opp. to *hydroid*. 1758. c. *attrib.*, as *m.-bud*, etc. 1846. Hence Medu·sal *a.* (*Zool.*), pertaining to, or of the nature of, a m. Medu·san, Medu·sian *adjs.* of or pertaining to the medusæ or to medusoid animals; *sbs.* a medusan animal.

Medusa's head. Also, when used attrib., Medusa head. 1706. 1. *Astr.* A cluster of stars, including the bright star Algol, in the constellation Perseus. 2. a. An ophiuran echinoderm of either of the genera *Astrophyton* and *Euryale*; a basket-fish or sea-basket. b. A species of crinoid, *Pentacrinus caput-medusæ*. 1784. 3. a. A kind of spurge, *Euphorbia Caput-Medusæ*. b. A species of orchid, *Cirrhopetalum Medusæ*. c. A species of agaric, *Hydnum Caput-Medusæ*. 1760.

Medusiform (mīdiū·sifǫɹm), *a.* 1848. [f. MEDUSA + -(I)FORM.] *Zool.* = next, A.

Medusoid (mīdiū·soid). 1848. [f. MEDUSA + -OID.] A. *adj.* Medusa-like. B. *sb.* 1. The medusa-like generative bud of a fixed hydrozoan 1848. 2. A medusa or medusa-like animal 1882.

Meech, etc., var. f. MICHE, etc.

Meed (mīd), *sb.* [OE. *mēd* fem. :—WGer. *mēda* str. fem., cogn. w. OE. *meord* fem., reward, pay, Gr. μισθός, Skr. *mīdhá* prize, contest :—Indo-Eur. **mizdho-*, *-dha-*.] 1. In early use: Wages, hire; recompense, reward. Now only *poet.* or *rhet.* in sense: A reward, guerdon; one's merited portion *of* (praise, honour, etc.). †b. A gift. SHAKS. ¶c. Adjudged character or title (*rare*) 1833. †2. Corrupt gain; bribery. ME. only. †3. Merit, excellence, worth -1714.

1. He must not flote upon his watry bear..Without the m. of som melodious tear MILT. b. *Timon* I. i. 288. c. Pallas and Aphrodite, claiming each This m. of fairest TENNYSON. 2. He toke mede and money of the Scottis LD. BERNERS.

†**Meed**, *v.* ME. [f. MEED *sb.*] 1. *trans.* To reward; also, to bribe -1542. 2. To deserve HEYWOOD.

†**Mee·dful**, *a.* ME. [f. MEED *sb.* + -FUL.] Deserving of reward -1573. †Meedfully *adv.*

Meek (mīk), *a.* [Early ME. *meoc*, a. ON. *mjúk-r* soft, pliant, gentle.] 1. †a. Gentle, courteous, kind; merciful, indulgent -1609. b. (= Vulgate *mansuetus*): Free from self-will; piously humble and submissive; patient and unresentful ME. c. Submissive, humble; also, easily 'put upon' ME. †d. as *adv.* = *meekly* -1605. 2. Of animals: Tame, not fierce ME. 3. In physical applications: Not violent or strong; gentle. *Obs.* or *arch.* ME.

1. a. *Jul. C.* III. i. 255. b. In the blest Kingdoms m. of joy and love MILT. *absol.* Blessed are the meeke: for they shall inherit the earth *Matt.* v. 5. Phr. *As m. as a lamb, a maid*, etc., *as Moses*. d. *Macb.* I. vii. 17. 3. *M. mother* (tr. PIA MATER): see MOTHER *sb.*[1] Hence Mee·k-ly *adv.*, -ness.

†**Meek**, *v.* ME. [f. MEEK *a.*] 1. *trans.* To make meek in spirit, to humble; *occas.* to appease, mollify -1680. b. *refl.* To humble or abase oneself -1583. 2. *trans.* To tame (an animal) -1653. 3. *intr.* To become or be meek ME.

Meeken (mī·k'n), *v.* Now *rare*. late ME. [f. MEEK *a.* + -EN[5].] 1. *trans.* To make meek; to humble, soften, tame; †to mitigate; to bring low, abase. 2. *intr.* To become meek; to submit meekly (*to* something) 1844.

Meer(e: vars. of MARE[1], MAYOR, MERE, MORE.

Meered: see MERED.

Meerkat (mīə·ɹkæt). 1481. [a. Du. *meerkat* monkey, app. f. *meer* sea + *kat* cat.] †1. A monkey -1559. 2. A S. Afr. name for two small mammals: a. *Cynictis penicillata*, allied to the ichneumon. b. The suricate, *Suricata tetradactyla*, which is tamed as a pet. 1801.

Meerschaum (mīə·ɹʃǫm, -ʃəm). 1784. [a. G. *meerschaum*, lit. 'sea-foam' (tr. Pers. *kef-i-daryā*), in allusion to its frothy appearance.] 1. A hydrous silicate of magnesium occurring in soft white clay-like masses. A popular synonym for sepiolite. 2. (In full *m. pipe.*) A tobacco-pipe with a meerschaum bowl 1799.

Meet (mīt), *sb.* 1831. [f. MEET *v.*] The meeting of hounds and men for a hunt. Also, by extension, a meeting of cyclists, etc.

Meet (mīt), *a.* and *adv.* Now *arch.* [ME. *mēte*; prob. repr. OE. **gemǣte* with loss of prefix. OE. (WS.) *gemǣte* :—OTeut. **gamǣtjo-*, f. **ga-* (Y-) prefix = L. *com-* + **mǣtā* measure, f. **mǣt-*, ablaut-var. of **met-* (see METE *v.*[1]). Thus the etym. sense is 'commensurate'.]

A. *adj.* †1. Of proper dimensions; made to fit. Later: Close-fitting, barely large enough. †2. Equal *to*, on the same level -1687. 3. Suitable, fit, proper. Const. *for*, *to*, also *to* with *inf.* b. Predicatively: Fitting, becoming, proper. Chiefly in *it is m. that..*, *as* (or *than*) *is m.* ME. †4. Mild, gentle -1598.

2. Phr. *To be m. with*: to be even or quits with; You taxe Signior Benedicke too much, but hee'l be m. with you SHAKS. 3. Not here, O Apollo! Are haunts m. for thee M. ARNOLD. b. It is mete and right so to do *Bk. Com. Prayer.*

†B. *adv.* In a meet, fit, or proper manner; sufficiently. Also, exactly (in a certain position). -1688.

Meet (mīt), *v.* Infl. **met.** [OE. *mētan* :—OTeut. *(*ga*)*mōtjan*, f. **mōtom* MOOT *sb.*[1]]

I. *trans.* 1. To come upon, fall in with, find. Now only *dial.* exc. with person as obj.; otherwise repl. by *m. with*. 2. To come face to face with or into the company of (a person arriving at the same point from a different direction) ME. b. To go to a place at which (a person) arrives, in order e. g. to welcome, communicate with, accompany, or convey (him). Similarly, *to m. a coach, a train*, etc. ME. c. *transf.* With inanimate things as subj. or obj.: To come into contact, association, or junction with ME. d. Of an object of attention: To present itself before, to come under the observation of 1632. e. *To m.* a person's *eye, gaze*, etc.: to perceive that he is looking at one; also, to submit oneself to his look without turning away 1670. 3. To encounter or oppose in battle. Also (after F. *rencontrer*), to fight a duel with. ME. †b. To be even with. FLETCHER. c. To oppose, cope or grapple with (something impersonal) 1745. 4. To come by accident or design into the company of; to come across (a person) in society or business ME. 5. To encounter, experience (a certain fortune or destiny); to receive (reward, punishment, etc.). Now *rare* or *poet.*, repl. by *m. with*. 1440. 6. To come into conformity with (a person's wishes, etc.) 1694. 7. To satisfy (a demand or need). *To m. a bill* (Comm.): to pay it at maturity. 1833.

2. b. I'll m. the seven o'clock train DOYLE. Phr. *To m. half-way*: †to forestall; to respond to the friendly advances of; to make concessions to (a person) in consideration of equal concessions on his part; to come to a compromise with. *To m. trouble half-way*: to distress oneself with anticipations of what may happen. c. The gibbet was set up where King Street meets Cheapside MACAULAY. d. Phr. *To m. the eye* (*sight, view*), *the ear*: to be visible; audible. *To m. the eye of*: to happen to be seen by. 3. I only with an Oaken staff will m. thee MILT. c. The threats of Charles were met by Offa with defiance GREEN. 4. I loathe..the faces that one meets TENNYSON. His medical colleagues refuse to m. him in consultation (*mod.*). Phr. *To be well, happily*, etc., *met*. Also *ellipt.*, *Well met!* (as an expression of welcome). 5. This generous appeal met no response M. PATTISON. 6. I will do my best to m. you in the matter (*mod.*). 7. A remedy which exactly meets the necessities of the case SIR E. E. KAY.

II. *intr.* 1. Of two or more persons: To come face to face, so as to be in each other's presence or company. Often with *together*. Sometimes conjugated with *be*. ME. b. Of a society, etc.: To assemble for purposes of conference, business, worship, or the like 1530. †c. To keep an appointment -1717. d. To arrive at agreement 1851. 2. To come together in the shock of battle (*arch.*). late ME. 3. Of inanimate objects: To come into contact ME. **b.** Said of qualities, etc., uniting in the same person, etc. 1581. †**c.** To agree or tally (*rare*) –1823.

1. When shall we three m. againe? SHAKS. b. The Parliament will certainly m. on Friday next SWIFT. 3. Oh, East is East, and West is West, and never the twain shall m. KIPLING. b. Thou, the latest-left of all my knights, In whom should m. the offices of all TENNYSON.

Comb. **Meet with. a.** = senses I. 1, 5, which it has superseded in common use. †**b.** in various senses (I. 2, 2 c, 3, 3 b, 3 c), most of which are now expressed by *meet*.

Meeten (mī·t'n), *v.* 1807. [f. MEET *a.* + -EN [5].] *trans.* To make meet or fit (*for*).

Meeter (mī·təɹ). 1646. [f. MEET *v.* + -ER [1].] One who attends or takes part in a meeting.

Meeth: var. MEAD [1] (the drink).

Meeting (mī·tiŋ), *vbl. sb.* ME. [f. MEET *v.* + -ING [1]. OE. had *gemēting* in sense 3.] **1.** In senses of MEET *v.* **2.** Used *euphem.* for a duel 1812. **3.** An assembly of a number of people for entertainment, discussion, or the like 1513. **b.** An assembly of people, in England, of nonconformists, for purposes of worship; now *rare* exc. with reference to the Society of Friends (who apply it also to certain periodical assemblies for discussion and business); also, a dissenting chapel, a meeting-house (surviving in names of buildings as *Old, New M.*) 1593. †**4.** = MEETING-PLACE (*poet.*) –1801. **5.** *attrib.* **m.-folks**, dissenters.

1 At Peter's firste metinge with our Savyour Christe 1559. The meetings of the waters 1606. 3. He was no longer summoned to any m. of the board MACAULAY. b. We went to m. at Wells 1774. 4. 1 *Hen. IV*, III. ii. 174.

Mee·ting-house. 1636. †**1.** A (private) house used for a meeting. WOOD. **2.** A place of worship; in the gen. sense, now only *U.S.* In England, a dissenting place of worship, a conventicle; now usu. disparaging, exc. with reference to Quakers.

Mee·ting-place. 1553. A place in which a meeting occurs or is held; †**a** meeting-house.

†**Mee·tly,** *a.* ME. [f. MEET *a.* + -LY [1].] **1.** Moderate; of moderate size or quantity –1620. **2.** Fitting, proper, suitable, meet –1633.

Meetly (mī·tli), *adv.* late ME. [f. MEET *a.* + -LY [2].] **1.** Moderately, fairly. (Common in 16th c.) **2.** Fitly, suitably; as is meet 1502.

Meetness (mī·tnės). 1449. [f. MEET *a.* + -NESS.] The condition of being meet; fitness, suitableness.

Meg [1] (meg). 1538. [var. of MAG *sb.* [1]] Pet form of *Margaret*, used *dial.* to indicate a hoyden, coarse woman, etc. **b.** The great 15th c. gun in Edinburgh Castle was called *Mons Meg, Muckle* or *Great Meg, Roaring Meg* 1575.

Meg [2] (meg). *slang* and *dial.* 1688. [?] †**1.** A guinea –1742. **2.** A halfpenny (cf. MAG *sb.* [2]) 1781.

Mega- (me·gă), bef. a vowel **meg-**, repr. Gr. μεγα-, comb. f. μέγας great, as in: **Megacepha·lic** [Gr. κεφαλή] *a.* large-headed; *spec.* of a skull exceeding 1,450 cubic centimetres. **Me·gadont** [badly f. Gr. ὀδούς, ὀδοντ-] *a.* having large teeth. **Megagame·te,** the larger (or female) of two gametes or conjugating cells. **Me·gaseme** [Gr. σῆμα sign] *a.* having a large orbital index; *spec.* one over 89; *sb.* a m. skull. **Me·gasporange,** ||**-spora·ngium** (pl. **-ia**), a sporangium containing megaspores. **Me·gaspore** = MACROSPORE. **b.** Prefixed to names of units of measurement, force, etc., with sense 'a million times'; e.g. *megadyne, meg(a)erg, megavolt, megohm*, etc.

Megacosm (me·găkǫz'm). 1617. [f. Gr. μέγας + κόσμος COSMOS.] = MACROCOSM.

Megalithic (megăli·þik), *a.* 1839. [f. Gr. μέγας + λίθος stone + -IC.] *Antiq.* Consisting or constructed of large stones; *transf.* of a period, a people, etc. Hence **Me·galith,** a stone of great size used in construction or as a monument 1853.

Megalo- (me·gălo), bef. a vowel **megal-**, a. Gr. μεγαλο-, comb. f. μέγας great (cf. MEGA-), as in: **Me·galerg** *Physics* = *megerg* (see MEGA- b). **Me·galoblast, -cyte,** a large nucleated red blood-corpuscle occurring in anæmia.

Megalomania (megălomēⁱ·niă). 1890. [f. MEGALO- + MANIA.] *Nosology.* The insanity of self-exaltation; the passion for big things. Often *transf.* Hence **Megaloma·niac** *a.* and *sb.* **Megalomani·acal** *a.*

Megalophonous (megălǫ·fŏnəs), *a.* 1819. [f. Gr. μεγαλόφωνος, f. μεγαλο- + φωνή voice, sound; see -OUS.] Grand-sounding. SHELLEY.

||**Megalops** (me·gălǫps). 1855. [mod.L., f. Gr. μεγαλωπός, f. μεγαλο- MEGALO- + ὠπ-, ὤψ eye.] *Zool.* A larval stage in the development of crabs (formerly supposed to be a distinct genus), characterized by very large eyes. Also **Megalo·pa** 1815.

Megalosaur (me·gălosǭɹ). 1841. [f. Gr. μεγαλο- MEGALO- + σαῦρος lizard.] An animal of the extinct genus *Megalosaurus* (1824) of gigantic lizards. **Megalosau·rian** *a.* and *sb.*

Megaphone (me·găfōun). 1878. [f. Gr. μέγας + φωνή.] **1.** An instrument for carrying sound a long distance, invented by T. A. Edison. **2.** A large speaking-trumpet 1896.

Megapode (me·găpōud), **-pod** (-pǫd). 1857. [ad. mod.L. *Megapodius*, f. Gr. μέγας + ποδ-, πούς.] *Ornith.* Any bird of the genus *Megapodius* or family *Megapodiidæ*, a mound-building bird, native of Australia and the Malay Archipelago. **Mega·podan** *a.* and *sb.*

Megarian, -ean (megēᵊ·riăn). 1603. [(1) f. L. *Megara*, Gr. Μέγαρα (neut. pl.), a city in Greece + -IAN; (2) f. L. *Megareus* + -AN.] **A.** *adj.* Pertaining to the school of philosophy founded *c* 400 B.C. by Euclides of Megara. **B.** *sb.* One of this school. **Mega·ric** *a.* and *sb.*

Megascope (me·găskoup). 1831. [f. MEGA- + -SCOPE.] A kind of camera obscura or magic lantern for throwing a magnified image upon a screen.

Megascopic (megăskǫ·pik), *a.* 1879. [f. as prec. + -IC.] **1.** = MACROSCOPIC. **2.** Pertaining to a megascope; magnified, as an image 1902.

||**Megass** (megæ·s). Also **-asse.** 1847. [?] The fibrous residue after the expression of sugar from the cane. Cf. BAGASSE.

Megatherium (megăþīᵊ·riŏm). *Pl.* **-ia.** 1826. [mod.L. (Cuvier), as if Gr. μέγα θηρίον 'great beast'; see MEGA-.] An extinct genus of huge herbivorous edentates resembling the sloths; one of these. Also *transf.* applied to something huge 1850. Also anglicized **Me·gathere** 1839. Hence **Megathe·rial** *a.* resembling a m.; huge 1894. **Megathe·rian** *a.* of or pertaining to megatheria; *sb.* a m. or kindred animal 1842. **Megathe·rioid** *a.* resembling a m.; *sb.* a megatherioid animal 1839.

Megilp (mĭgi·lp), *sb.* (Many variant spellings.) 1768. [?] **1.** A mixture of linseed oil with turpentine or mastic varnish, or the like, employed as a vehicle for oil colours. **2.** A composition used by grainers 1827. Hence **Megi·lp** *v. trans.* to varnish with m.; to give to (oil colours) the quality imparted by m.

Megohm; see MEGA- b.

Megrim [1] (mī·grim). late ME. [a. F. *migraine*, semi-pop. ad. late L. *hemicrania*; see HEMICRANIA.] **1.** Hemicrania; a form of severe headache usually confined to one side of the head; nervous or sick headache; an attack of this. **b.** = VERTIGO 1595. **2.** A whim, fancy, fad 1593. **3.** *pl.* 'Vapours'; low spirits 1633. **4.** *pl.* The staggers 1639.

2. Hee is troubled with a perpetuall migrim; at sea hee wisheth to bee on land, and on land at sea 1631.

Megrim [2] (mī·grim). *dial.* Also **-in.** 1836. The scald-fish, *Arnoglossus laterna.*

Meibomian (məibōu·miăn), *a.* 1813. [f. *Meibomius* + -AN.] *Anat.* Distinguishing epithet of certain sebaceous glands in the human eyelid, discovered by H. Meibom (Meibomius) of Helmstadt (died 1700).

Meinie (mēⁱ·ni). *Obs.* exc. *arch.* ME. [a. OF. *meyné, mesnie*:—pop.L. **mansionata*, f. L. *mansionem* (whence F. *maison*). In Eng. partly confused with MANY *sb.*] **1.** A family, household. **2.** A body of retainers, dependents, etc.; a retinue, suite, train ME. †**3.** A company of persons having a common object of association; an army, ship's crew, congregation, etc. –1598. †**4.** The collection of pieces or 'men' used in the game of chess ME. only. **5.** A multitude of persons; chiefly disparaging, a 'crew', 'set'. Also, the masses. ME. †**6.** Of animals: A herd, drove, flock, etc.; a multitude –1556.

2. They summon'd vp their meiney, straight tooke Horse, Commanded me to follow SHAKS.

Meiocene, var. of MIOCENE.

||**Meiosis** (məi,ōu·sis). Also †**miosis.** 1577. [Gr., f. μειοῦν to lessen, f. μείων less.] *Rhet.* †**a.** A figure by which the impression is intentionally conveyed that a thing is less in size, importance, etc., than it really is. **b.** = LITOTES 1642.

b. The Words are a *Meiosis*, and import much more than they express SOUTH. Hence **Meio·tic** *a.* 1915.

Meiostemonous (məi,ostī·mŏnəs), *a.* Also **mio-.** 1832. [irreg. f. Gr. μείων + στημον-, στήμων stamen + -OUS.] *Bot.* Having fewer stamens than petals.

||**Meistersinger** (məi·stəɹsi:ŋəɹ). 1886. [G., = master-singer.] A member of one of the German artisan guilds of minstrels (14th–16th cent.).

Meith (mīþ). *Sc.* 1513. [app. a. ON. *mið* mark.] A landmark, sea-mark, boundary.

Mekhitarist (me·kitărist). Also **mech-.** 1834. [f. *Mekhitar* + -IST.] **A.** *sb.* One of a congregation of Armenian monks of the R. C. Church originally founded at Constantinople in 1701 by Mekhitar, an Armenian. **B.** *adj.* Of or belonging to these 1874.

Mekometer (mĭkǫ·mĭtəɹ). 1894. [f. Gr. μῆκος length + -METER.] An instrument for finding the range for infantry fire.

Melaconite (mĭlæ·kŏnəit). 1850. [Altered from †*melaconise* (1839), a. mod.F. *mélaconise*, f. Gr. μέλας black + κόνις dust; see -ITE [1].] *Min.* An earthy black oxide of copper.

||**Melada** (melā·dă). 1875. [Sp., f. *melar* to boil sugar a second time, f. *miel* honey.] The sugar and molasses obtained when cane-juice is boiled down to sugar-point.

||**Melæna** (mĭlī·nă). 1800. [mod.L., a. Gr. μέλαινα, fem. of μέλας black.] *Path.* A disease or (in mod. use) symptoms of a disease characterized by the evacuation and vomiting of dark bloody matter. **b.** *concr.* The matter thus discharged 1858.

Melam (me·læm). 1835. [Arbitrary coinage (Liebig 1834).] *Chem.* A buff-coloured, insoluble amorphous substance obtained by the distillation of sulphocyanide of ammonium.

Melamine (me·lăməin). Also **-in.** 1835. [Named by Liebig (1834); f. MEL(AM) + AMINE.] *Chem.* A crystalline substance obtained by boiling melam with potassic hydrate, or by heating cyanamide to 302° F.; called also *cyanuramide.*

†**Melampod.** Also **-pode.** 1579. [ad. L. *melampodium, -ion*, a. Gr. μελαμπόδιον black hellebore, f. μελαν-, μέλας black + ποδ-, πούς foot.] Black Hellebore, *Helleborus officinalis* –1656.

||**Melanæmia** (melănī·miă). 1860. [mod.L., f. Gr. μελαν-, μέλας + αἷμα blood.] *Path.* A morbid condition, associated with severe forms of malarial fever, in which the blood contains granules and flakes of black or brown pigment. Hence **Melanæ·mic** *a.* 1878.

||**Melancholia** (melănkōu·liă). *Pl.* **-iæ.** 1814. [Late L.; see MELANCHOLY.] A functional mental disease characterized by extreme depression of spirits. **Melancho·liac** *a.* affected with m.; *sb.* one so affected 1863.

†**Melancho·lian.** ME. [f. MELANCHOLY + -AN.] **A.** *adj.* Having the atrabilious temperament; addicted to 'melancholy' or irascibility. **B.** *sb.* One of an atrabilious temperament or affected with melancholy –1695.

Melancholic (melănkǫ·lik). late ME. [ad. late L. *melancholicus*, a. Gr., f. μελαν- black + χολή bile; see MELANCHOLY and -IC.] **A.** *adj.* †**1.** Pertaining to or containing 'melancholy' or 'black bile'; atrabilious. Of food, atmospheric or planetary influences, etc.: Tending to produce melancholy or atrabilious disorder. –1631. **2.** Of persons, etc. †**a.** Having the atrabiliar temperament or constitution. **b.** Constitutionally liable to (or †affected with) depression of spirits; gloomy, melancholy. ME. †**3.** Causing depression of spirits; saddening –1812. †**4.** Expressive of melancholy or sadness –1757. **5.** In mod. use: Pertaining to, or affected with, melancholia 1866.

2. b. Oliver was of the m. temperament MORLEY.

B. *sb.* **1.** †**a.** One who is affected with mental depression. **b.** One suffering from melancholia. 1586. †**2.** Used by Clarendon for: Depression of spirits.

Melancholily (me·lănkǫlili), *adv.* 1536. [f. MELANCHOLY *a.* + -LY [2].] In a melancholy manner. †**Me·lancholiness** 1528–1715.

Melancholious (melănkōᵘ·liəs), *a.* Now *rare.* late ME. [a. OF. *melancolieus*, f. *melancolie*; see -OUS.] **1.** Constitutionally inclined to melancholy; †atrabilious in constitution; gloomy. Also, of sounds, etc.: Expressive of melancholy. †**2.** Tending to cause, or of the nature of, atrabilious disorder –1562.

1. This pope.. was a fumisshe man and malincolyous 1523.

Melancholist (me·lănkǫ̆list). Now *rare* or *Obs.* 1599. [f. MELANCHOLY + -IST.] †One of a 'melancholic' constitution; one affected with melancholia.

Melancholize (me·lănkǒləiz), *v.* Now *rare* or *Obs.* 1597. [f. as prec. + -IZE.] To be or become or make melancholy.

Melancholy (me·lănkǫ̆li), *sb.* ME. [a. OF. *melancolie, malencolie*, etc. (mod. F. *mélancolie*), ad. L. *melancholia*, a. Gr., f. μελαν-, μέλας black + χολή bile.] †**1.** The condition of having too much 'black bile'; the disease supposed to result from this condition. From the 17th c. onwards used as the name of the mental disease now called technically MELANCHOLIA. –1866. †**b.** *concr.* The 'black bile' itself; one of the four chief fluids or cardinal humours of obsolete physiology –1653. †**2.** Irascibility, sullenness –1595. **3.** Sadness and depression of spirits; gloom or dejection, esp. when constitutional. Often *personified.* ME. †**b.** A vexation –1644. **c.** A state or †(often in *pl.*) mood of melancholy 1586. **d.** A tender or pensive sadness 1614.

2. *John* III. iii. 42. **3.** My minde was troubled with deepe Melancholly SHAKS. Hence loathed M., Of Cerberus and blackest midnight born MILT. **d.** But hail thou Goddes, sage and holy, Hail divinest M. MILT. *Comb.*, as *m.-mad, -sick* adjs., etc.

Melancholy (me·lănkǫ̆li), *a.* 1526. [From attrib. use of the sb.] †**1.** Affected with the disease of melancholy –1732. †**b.** Of or affected by the melancholy 'humour' –1667. †**2.** Irascible; sullen –1604. **3.** Of persons, etc.: Depressed in spirits; sad, gloomy, dejected; *esp.* of a constitutionally gloomy temperament 1579. Also *transf.* (of animals) 1593. **b.** Pensive; sadly meditative 1632. **4.** Suggestive or expressive of sadness, depressing, dismal 1592. **5.** Of a fact, state of things, etc.: Saddening, lamentable, deplorable 1710.

3. There is no more m. creature in existence than a mountebank off duty W. IRVING. *transf.* The mellancholy Owle, (Deaths ordinary messenger) NASHE. **b.** Sweet Bird.., Most musicall, most m.! MILT. **4.** M. Bells *Rom. & Jul.* IV. v. 86.

†**Me·lancholy**, *v.* 1491. [ad. OF. *melancolier.*] *trans.* To make melancholy –1657.

Melanchthonian (melăŋkþōᵘ·niăn). 1755. [f. Philipp *Melanchthon* (Gr. transl. of G. *schwarzerd* 'black earth'), a German reformer (1497–1560) + -IAN.] **A.** *adj.* Of or pertaining to Melanchthon or his opinions. **B.** *sb.* A follower of Melanchthon. †**Mela·nchthonist** 1564.

Melanesian (melănī·ʃiăn). 1849. [f. *Melanesia* (in sense 'the regions of islands inhabited by blacks'), f. Gr. μέλας black + νῆσος island + -AN.] **A.** *adj.* Of or pertaining to Melanesia (a group of islands in the western Pacific), its inhabitants, language, etc. **B.** *sb.* A native of Melanesia; the language of the Melanesians.

‖**Mélange, mel-** (melãnʒ), *sb.* 1653. [F., f. *mêler* MEDDLE *v.*] **1.** A mixture; usu. a heterogeneous collection, a medley. **2. a.** A dress fabric of cotton chain and woollen weft. **b.** A kind of woollen yarn of mingled colours. So **Melange** *v.* to mix (wool of different colours) 1880; also †**Mela·ngery**, a mixture 1733.

Melanian (mĭlēᵉ·niăn), *a.* 1861. [ad. F. *mélanien*, f. Gr. μελαν-, μέλας black; see -IAN.] *Ethn.* = next **1.**

Melanic (mĭlæ·nik), *a.* 1826. [f. as prec. + -IC.] **1.** *Ethn.* Having black hair and a dark complexion. **2.** Distinctive epithet of the black pigment occurring in melanosis; hence, affected with melanosis 1847.

Melanin (me·lănin). 1843. [f. Gr. μελαν-, μέλας + -IN [1].] *Chem.* and *Phys.* The black pigment of melanism; also that of melanosis.

Melanism (me·lăniz'm). 1843. [f. Gr. μελαν-, μέλας + -ISM.] Darkness of colour resulting from an abnormal development of black pigment in the epidermis, hair, feathers, etc. of animals; opp. to *albinism.* **b.** A melanic variety (of some species) 1863. Hence **Melani·stic** *a.* affected by m. 1874.

Melano- (me·lăno), a. Gr. μελανο-, comb. f. μέλας black, as in ‖**Melanode·rma, -de·rmia** [Gr. δέρμα skin; see -IA], *Path.* = MELASMA.

‖**Melanochroi** (melănǫ·krǫ,əi), *sb. pl.* 1866. [mod.L.; formed by Huxley to represent an assumed Gr. μελάνωχροι, f. μελαν-, μέλας black + ὠχρός pale.] *Anthrop.* In Huxley's classification: A subdivision of the *Leiotrichi* or smooth-haired class of mankind, having dark hair and pale complexion. **Melanochro·ic, Melano·chroid, Melano·chrous** *adjs.* pertaining to or resembling the *Melanochroi.*

Melanocomous (melănǫ·kŏməs), *a.* 1836. [f. Gr. μελανοκόμης (f. μελανο-, μέλας + κόμη hair) + -OUS.] Black-haired.

‖**Melanoi**, *sb. pl.* 1866. [Gr. μελανοί, pl. of μελανός = μέλας black.] *Anthrop.* Huxley's name for the black-haired and dark-complexioned division of the LEIOTRICHI.

Melanoid (me·lănoid), *a.* 1854. [f. Gr. μελανοειδής, f. μελανο-, μέλας + εἶδος form.] *Path.* Characterized by the presence of black pigment.

‖**Melanoma** (melănōᵘ·mă). *Pl.* **-mata.** *c* 1830. [mod.L., a. Gr. type μελάνωμα, f. μελανοῦσθαι to become black.] *Path.* A melanotic growth.

Melanose (me·lănōᵘs), *a.* 1823. [f. Gr. μελαν-, μέλας + -OSE; but app. suggested by next.] *Path.* Containing, or of the nature of, the black pigment contained in melanosis.

‖**Melanosis** (melănōᵘ·sis). *Pl.* **-oses** (-ōᵘ·sīz). 1823. [mod.L., a. late Gr. μελάνωσις, f. μελανοῦσθαι (see above).] *Path.* **1.** Abnormal development of a black pigment in some tissue. **2.** Black cancer 1834.

Melanotic (melănǫ·tik), *a.* 1829. [See MELANOSIS and -OTIC.] **1.** *Path.* Characterized by, or of the nature of, melanosis. **2.** *Zool.* = MELANISTIC 1872.

Melanotype (mĭlæ·nŏtəip). 1864. [f. MELANO- + -TYPE.] A kind of FERROTYPE.

Melanous (me·lănəs), *a.* 1836. [f. Gr. μελαν-, μέλας + -OUS.] *Anthrop.* With ref. to hair and complexion: Blackish, dark; *spec.* belonging to the MELANOI.

‖**Melanuria** (melăniūᵊ·riă). 1890. [mod.L., f. Gr. μελαν-, μέλας + οὖρον urine; see -IA.] *Path.* A condition in which the urine assumes a black or dark blue colour. Hence **Melanu·ric** *a.* [1] 1881.

Melanuric (melăniūᵊ·rik), *a.* [2] 1852. [Based on Ger. *melanurensäure* (Liebig), f. *mellan* mellone + *uren* a supposed base of urea + *säure* acid.] *Chem.* In *m. acid*, a white chalky powder, obtained by heating urea.

Melaphyre (me·lăfəiᵊr). 1841. [a. F. *mélaphyre*, f. Gr. μέλας + (*por*)*phyre* PORPHYRY.] *Petrology.* A species of black or dark-coloured porphyry.

‖**Melasma** (mĭlæ·zmă). 1817. [mod.L., a. Gr. μέλασμα black spot or dye, ult. f. μέλας black.] *Path.* Excess of black pigment in the skin. Hence **Mela·smic** *a.* 1865.

Melasses, obs. f. MOLASSES.

Melchite (me·lkəit). 1619. [ad. L. *Melchita* = 'royalists' (i.e. of the party of the Roman emperor), f. (ult.) Syr. *malkā* king.] Orig., the designation applied to those Eastern Christians who adhered to the orthodox faith as defined by the councils of Ephesus (A.D. 431) and Chalcedon (A.D. 451). Later, applied to those orthodox Eastern Christians who use an Arabic version of the Greek ritual, and esp. to those who have become Uniats.

Meld (meld), *v.* 1897. [app. ad. G. *melden* to announce.] *Cards.* In pinocle: = DECLARE (*vb.* 8) in bezique; also *sb.* a group of cards to be melded.

‖**Mêlée** (me·leᵢ, mẹle). 1648. [Fr.; see MEDLEY, MELLAY.] A mixed fight between two parties of combatants, a skirmish. Also *transf.* a lively debate.

Melene (me·līn). 1848. [f. Gr. μέλισσα bee + -ENE.] *Chem.* An olefine obtained by the distillation of beeswax. Called also **Melissylene.**

Melic (me·lik), *sb.* 1787. [ad. mod.L. *melica*, f. It. *melica, meliga* sorghum.] A grass belonging or allied to the genus *Melica.*

Melic (me·lik), *a.* 1699. [ad. Gr. μελικός, f. μέλος song.] Of poetry (esp. Gr. strophic odes): Intended to be sung.

‖**Meliceris** (melisīᵊ·ris). *Pl.* **-cerides** (-se·ridīz). 1562. [mod.L., a. Gr. μελικηρίς some eruptive disease, f. μελίκηρον honeycomb, f. μέλι honey + κηρός wax.] *Path.* An encysted tumour containing matter which resembles honey. **2.** An affection marked by exudation of viscid honeylike matter 1870. Hence **Melice·ric, Melice·rous** *adjs.* pertaining to a m.

Melicoton(ie, -y, var. ff. MELOCOTON.

†**Me·licrate.** 1563. [ad. late L. *melicrātum*, ad. Gr. μελίκρατον, f. μέλι + κρᾰ-, κεραννύναι to mix.] A drink made with honey and water –1775.

Melilite (me·liləit). Also **mell-**. 1796. [a. F. *mélilite*, mod.L. *melilithus*, f. Gr. μέλι honey + λίθος stone; see -LITE.] *Min.* A silicate of calcium, aluminium, and other bases, found in honey-yellow crystals 1821. **2.** = MELLITE (Kirwan).

Melilot (me·lilǫt). late ME. [a. OF. *melilot* (mod. F. *mélilot*), ad. late L. *melilotos*, a. Gr., a sweet kind of clover, f. μέλι honey + λωτός LOTUS.] A plant of the leguminous genus *Melilotus*, esp. *M. officinalis* or Yellow M., the dried flowers of which were formerly much used in making plasters, poultices, etc.

Melinite (me·linəit). 1886. [a. F. *mélinite*, f. Gr. μήλινος, f. μῆλον apple, quince.] A French explosive, said to be composed of picric acid, gun-cotton, and gum arabic.

Meliorate (mī·liŏreᵢt), *v.* 1552. [f. late L. *meliorat-, meliorare*, f. L. *melior* better.] **1.** *trans.* = AMELIORATE *v.* **1.** **2.** *intr.* = AMELIORATE *v.* **2.** 1654.

1. Religion is to m. the condition of a people JER. TAYLOR. *absol.* Instead of meliorating, it [chastisement *sine causa*] pejorates SEDLEY. Hence **Meliora·tion**, amelioration, improvement. **Me·liorative** *a.* tending to m. **Me·liorator, -er**, one who or that which meliorates.

Meliorism (mī·liŏriz'm). 1877. [f. L. *melior* + -ISM.] The doctrine, intermediate between optimism and pessimism, which affirms that the world may be made better by human effort. So **Me·liorist**, one who believes in m. 1858. **Meliori·stic** *a.* 1888.

Meliority (mīliǫ·rĭti). 1578. [ad. med.L. *melioritas*, f. L. *melior*; see -ITY.] The quality of being better; superiority.

Meliphagous (meli·fāgəs), *a.* 1826. [f. mod.L. *Meliphaga* (f. Gr. μέλι honey + -φαγος eating) + -OUS.] *Ornith.* Belonging to the *Meliphagidæ* or honey-eating birds.

‖**Melisma** (mĭli·zmă). 1880. [a. Gr. μέλισμα.] *Mus.* A song, air, or melody, as opp. to recitative or declamatory music.

Melitose (me·litōᵘs). 1861. [f. Gr. μελιτ-, μέλι honey + -OSE.] *Chem.* A kind of sugar obtained from the manna of Eucalyptus.

‖**Melituria** (melitiū°·riă). 1863. [mod.L., f. as prec. + οὖρον urine + -IA [1].] *Path.* = GLYCOSURIA.

Mell (mel), *sb.*[1] Now only *Sc.* and *dial.* ME. [North. var. of *mall*, MAUL *sb.*[1]] A heavy hammer or beetle of metal or wood; †a mace or club; also, a chairman's hammer.

†**Mell** (mel), *sb.*[2] 1575. [a. L. *mell-*, *mel*, = Gr. μελιτ-, μέλι.] Honey -1864.

Mell (mel), *v.* Now *arch.* and *dial.* ME. [a. OF. *meller*, var. of *mesler*; see MEDDLE *v.*] **1.** *trans.* To mix, mingle. Also with *together*, *up*. **2.** *intr.* for *refl.* To mix, have intercourse *with*, associate ME. †**3.** To copulate -1641. **4.** To mingle in combat ME. **5.** To concern or busy oneself; to deal, treat; to interfere, meddle. Const. *in*, †*of*, *with*. late ME.

Mellay (me·lē). ME. [a. OF. *mellée* MÊLÉE.] **1.** †Contention, fight; *spec.* a close hand to hand fight of two parties or combatants (*arch.*). †**2.** A cloth of a mixture of colours or shades; also, a mixed colour -1593.

1. He rode the m., lord of the ringing lists TENNYSON.

Mellic (me·lik), *a.* 1837. [Shortened from MELLITIC.] In *m. acid* = MELLITIC *acid*.

Melliferous (meli·fĕrəs), *a.* 1656. [f. L. *mellifer* (f. *mell(i)-*, *mel* honey + *-fer* bearing) + -OUS.] Yielding or producing honey.

Mellifluent (meli·fl*i*uĕnt), *a.* 1601. [ad. late L. *mellifluentem* (see next).] = MELLIFLUOUS. Hence **Melli·fluence.**

Mellifluous (meli·fluəs), *a.* late ME. [f. L. *mellifluus* (f. *mell-*, *mel* honey + *fluere* to flow) + -OUS.] **1.** Flowing with honey, honey-dropping; sweetened with or as with honey. Now *rare.* 1485. **2.** *fig.* Sweetly flowing, sweet as honey.

2. Saynt Bernard the mellifluous doctor CAXTON. M. and hony-tongued Shakespeare 1598. A m. voyce, as I am true knight SHAKS. Hence **Melli·fluous-ly** *adv.*, **-ness.**

Mellisonant (meli·sŏnănt), *a. arch.* 1634. [f. L. *mell(i)-*, *mel* honey + *sonantem.*] Sweet-sounding.

Mellite (me·ləit). 1801. [ad. mod.L. *mellites* (1793), f. L. *mell-*, *mel*; see -ITE [1].] *Min.* Native mellitate of aluminium, occurring in honey-yellow octahedral crystals. So **Mellitic** (meli·tik) *a.* in *m. acid*, the peculiar acid of mellite 1794; hence **Me·llitate**, a salt of this (formerly *mellate*) 1828.

Mellone (me·lōun). Also **mel(l)on.** 1835. [f. *mel-* (as in MELAM) + -ONE.] *Chem.* A compound of carbon and nitrogen obtained as a yellow powder by the action of heat on certain cyanogen-compounds. Hence **Me·llonide**, a compound of mellone with a metal 1845.

Mellow (me·lo^u), *a.* 1440. [perh. attrib. use of OE. *melo* (stem *melw-*), ME. *melowe*, MEAL *sb.*[1]] **1.** Of fruit: Soft, sweet, and juicy with ripeness. **b.** Of landscape, seasons, etc.: Characterized by ripeness 1819. **c.** Of wines, etc.: Well-matured; free from acidity or harshness 1700. **2.** *transf.* Soft; soft and smooth to the touch; orig. and esp. of earth, loamy, rich 1531. **3.** *fig.* Mature, ripe in age. Now chiefly, softened or sweetened by age or experience. 1592. **4.** Of sound, colour, light, etc.: Rich and soft; full and pure without harshness 1668. **5.** Good-humoured, genial, jovial 1711. **6.** Partly intoxicated 1611.

1. M. apples 1806, nuts SCOTT. b. Season of mists and m. fruitfulness KEATS. 2. Hoary Frosts..will rot the M. Soil DRYDEN. 3. The m. glory of the Attic Stage M. ARNOLD. 4. The m. bullfinch THOMSON. The golden harvest, of a m. brown COWPER. 6. The hateful fellow That's crabbed when he's m. SHERIDAN. Hence **Me·llow-ly** *adv.*, **-ness. Me·llowy** *a.* mellow.

Mellow (me·lo^u), *v.* 1572. [f. MELLOW *a.*] **1.** *trans.* To render mellow. **2.** *intr.* To become mellow 1594.

1. Wind, Sun and Dews, all..m. the Land 1707. Age..Mellows and makes the speech more fit for use COWPER. 2. His character mellowed and toned down in his later years 1861.

†**Melocoton.** Also †**malacato(o)n, -co-.** 1611. [a. Sp. *melocoton*, ad. It. *melocotogno*, ad. med.L. *melum cotoneum*, ad. Gr. μῆλον κυδώνιον 'Cydonian apple'; see COYN, QUINCE.] A peach grafted on a quince -1745.

Melodeon, melodion (mĭlōu·diən). 1858. [In sense 1, quasi-Gr. var. of MELODIUM; in sense 2, perh. f. MELODY after ACCORDION.] **1.** A wind instrument with a key-board, the bellows being moved by pedals worked by the feet; an earlier form of the 'American organ'. **2.** A kind of accordion 1880.

Melodic (mĭlǫ·dik), *a.* 1823. [ad. F. *mélodique*, ad. late L. *melodicus*, a. Gr., f. μελῳδία; see MELODY and -IC.] Of or pertaining to melody. Hence **Melo·dically** *adv.* So **Melo·dial** *a.*, **Melo·dially** *adv.* 1818.

Melo·dics. 1864. [See prec. and -IC 2.] The branch of musical science concerned with melody.

Melodious (mĭlōu·diəs), *a.* late ME. [ad. OF. *melodieus* (mod.F. *mélodieux*), f. L. *melodia*; see MELODY and -OUS.] **1.** Characterized by melody; sweet-sounding, tuneful. **2.** Producing melody 1588. **3.** Having a melody 1727.

1. Man..forges the subtile..air into wise and m. words EMERSON. 2. Where like a sweet mellodius bird it sung SHAKS. **Melo·dious-ly** *adv.*, **-ness.**

Melodist (me·lǫdist). 1789. [f. MELODY + -IST.] **1.** A singer. **2.** A composer of melodies; one skilled in melody 1826.

Melodium (mĭlōu·diŏm). 1847. [quasi-L. f. MELODY; cf. *harmonium.*] = MELODEON 1.

Melodize (me·lŏdəiz), *v.* 1662. [f. MELODY + -IZE.] **1.** *intr.* To make melody; occas. *joc.*, to play (*on* an instrument). **b.** *transf.* To blend harmoniously *with* 1811. **2.** *trans.* To make melodious 1759. **3.** To compose a melody for (a song) 1881.

Melodrama (me·lŏdrāmă, melŏdrā·mă). 1809. [Alteration of MELODRAME, after DRAMA.] **1.** In early use, a stage-play in which songs were interspersed, and in which orchestral music accompanied the action. Now, a dramatic piece characterized by sensational incident and violent appeals to the emotions, but with a happy ending. **b.** This species of dramatic composition or representation 1814. **2.** *transf.* Incidents, or a story, resembling a melodrama; also, melodramatic behaviour, occurrences, etc. 1814.

1. *attrib.* A m. kitchen, suitable for bandits or noblemen in disguise STEVENSON. 2. My idea of heaven is that there is no m. in it at all EMERSON. Hence **Melodrama·tic** *a.* having the characteristics of m.; characterized by sensationalism and spurious pathos. **Melodrama·tically** *adv.* **Melodra·matist**, a writer of melodramas. **Melodra·matize** *v.* to make melodramatic; also, to convert the story of (a novel) into a m.

†**Melodrame** (me·lŏdræm). Also **-dram.** 1802. [a. F. *mélodrame*, f. Gr. μέλος song, music + F. *drame* DRAMA.] = prec.

Melody (me·lŏdi), *sb.* ME. [a. OF. *melodie* (mod.F. *mélodie*), ad. late L. *melodia*, a. Gr. μελῳδία, f. μελῳδός, f. μέλος song + ᾠδ- contr. of ἀοιδ-, ablaut-var. of ἀείδειν to sing.] **1.** Sweet music; beautiful arrangement of musical sounds; beauty of musical sounds, tunefulness. **b.** *transf.* Musical quality in the arrangement of words 1789. **2.** A series of single notes arranged in musically expressive succession; a tune: = AIR *sb.* III. 1. 1609. **b.** The principal part in a harmonized piece of music. **c.** *transf.* Applied to poems written to be sung to particular melodies 1807. **d.** Applied to pictorial combinations of colour 1830. **3.** That element of musical form which consists in the arrangement of single notes in musical succession; dist. from *harmony* 1727.

1. Whilst all the winds with m. are ringing SHELLEY. Phr. *To make m.* (now *arch.*). 2. Heard melodies are sweet, but those unheard Are sweeter KEATS. d. Studied melodies of exquisite colour RUSKIN. Hence **Me·lody** *v. rare*, to make m., to sing.

Melologue (me·lǫlǫg). TOM MOORE. [f. Gr. μέλος song + λόγος speech (see -LOGUE). Cf. F. *mélologue* (Berlioz).] A musical composition in which some of the verses are sung and others recited.

Melon (me·lən). late ME. [a. F. *melon*, ad. late L. *melonem*, *melo*, prob. short for L. *melopepo*, a. Gr. μηλοπέπων, f. μῆλον apple + πέπων a gourd (orig. an ellipt. use of πέπων ripe).] **1.** A name for several kinds of gourds bearing sweet fruit, *esp.* the MUSK M., *Cucumis Melo*, and WATER M., *Citrullus vulgaris.* (Applied both to fruit and plant.) **2.** *Conch.* The shell of a mollusc of the genus *Melo.* Also *m.-shell*, *-volute.* 1840. **3.** A rounded mass of blubber taken from the top of the head of certain cetaceans 1887. **4.** *U.S. slang.* A large surplus of profits available for distribution to several people; phr. *to cut a m.* 1909.

Comb.: **m.-beetle**, a beetle of the genus *Diabrotica*, injurious to melons; **-cactus**, any plant of the genus *Melocactus*, so called from the melonlike ridged stems; **-pumpkin**, *Cucurbita maxima* or *C. Melopepo*; **-thistle** = *m.-cactus.*

Melophone (me·lofōun). 1859. [f. Gr. μέλος song + φωνή sound.] A kind of accordion. **Me·lophonist**, a melodist. THACKERAY.

Meloplasty (me·lǫplæsti). 1883. [f. Gr. μῆλον apple, *poet.* cheek + -πλαστος moulded + -Y [3].] *Surg.* The plastic restoration of a cheek. So **Melopla·stic** *a.* 1848.

‖**Melopœia** (melǫpī·iă). 1759. [a. Gr. μελοποιία, f. μελοποιός maker of songs, f. μέλος + ποι-, ποιεῖν.] *Antiq.* The art of composing melodies; the part of dramatic art concerned with music.

Melt (melt), *sb.* 1854. [f. MELT *v.*] **1.** The act or operation of melting 1897. **2.** Metal, etc., in a melted condition; the quantity melted at one time.

Melt (melt), *v.* Pa. t. **melted.** Pa. pple. **melted**; **molten** (mōu·lt'n). [Orig. two vbs.: (1) intr. strong vb. OE. *meltan*, pa. pple. *gemolten*; (2) wk. vb., normally trans., OE. *meltan* (WS. *mieltan*), pa. pple. *gemelted* :—**maltjan.*]

I. *intr.* **1.** To become liquefied by heat. **b.** *joc.* To perspire excessively 1787. **2.** To be dissolved, e.g. by the agency of moisture OE. **b.** Of clouds, vapour: To dissolve; to break *into* rain ME. **c.** To disappear 1611. **3.** Of a person, his heart, feelings, etc. †**a.** To be overwhelmed with dismay or grief -1611. **b.** To become softened by compassion or love; to dissolve *in* or *into* tears ME. **4.** To dwindle *away* ME. **5.** To filter in, become absorbed *into* ME. **6.** Of sound: To be soft and liquid 1626. **7.** To pass imperceptibly *into* something else 1781.

1. When the snow melts from the Mountaines MORYSON. Phr. *To m. away*: to be destroyed or wasted by being melted. b. [Our chariot-horse with heat Must seem to m. CHAPMAN]. 2. Phr. *To m. in the mouth*: said of food that is extremely tender. c. With shriekes She melted into Ayre SHAKS. 3. a. My soule melteth awaye for very heuynesse COVERDALE *Ps.* cxviii[i]. 28. b. She melted into a Flood of Tears STEELE. 4. The body of his party is melting away very fast BURKE. 7. Downs..That m. and fade into the distant sky COWPER.

II. *trans.* **1.** To reduce to a liquid condition by heat OE. †**b.** To form of molten material. late ME. **2.** To dissolve. late ME. **3.** To make tender, touch the feelings of. late ME. †**4.** To weaken, enervate SHAKS. **5.** To spend, squander (money); to cash (a cheque or bank-note) *slang* 1700. **6.** To blend *with* or *into* 1605.

1. The soring clouds into sad showres ymolt SPENSER. Phr. *To m. down* (also U.S. *up*): to melt (coin, etc.) in order that the metal may be used as raw material. b. *Isa.* xl. 19. 3. Her noble heart was molten in her breast TENNYSON. 4. *Timon* IV. iii. 256. 5. I had him arrested before he had time to m. the notes READE. 6. A grey mist..melted whole mountains into a soft dull grey BLACK.

Melting (me·ltiŋ), *vbl. sb.* late ME. [f. MELT *v.* + -ING [1].] **1.** The action of MELT *v.*; an instance of this. **2.** *concr. pl.* That which has been melted; a substance produced by melting 1558. **3.** *attrib.*, as *m.-furnace*, etc. late ME.

1. †*Surveyor of the Meltings*: the former designation of a certain officer of the mint; hence *the Meltings*, his office.

Comb.; **m.-heat**, the degree of heat required to melt a given substance; **-point**, that point of the thermometer which indicates the melting-heat of any particular solid: **-pot**, a vessel in which metals, etc., are melted; often *fig.* with ref. to remodelling of institutions, etc.

Me·lting, *ppl. a.* late ME. [-ING [2].] That melts; yielding to emotion, tender; (of sound, colour) liquid and soft; that 'melts in the mouth' (esp. of certain pears).

Like unto..m. wax 1577. M. Charitie 2 *Hen. IV*, IV. iv. 32. Albeit vn-vsed to the m. moode *Oth.* V. ii. 349. The m. voice through mazes running MILT. A first-rate m. pear DARWIN. **Me·lting-ly** *adv.*, **-ness.**

Melton (me·ltən). 1823. Name of a town in Leicestershire (more fully Melton Mowbray), a famous hunting centre. Used *attrib.*, esp. in *M. cloth* (also simply melton), a stout smooth cloth having the nap cut very close and the face finished without pressing or glossing. Hence **Melto·nian** *a.* pertaining to Melton Mowbray; *sb.* one who hunts at Melton Mowbray, an adept at hunting 1825.

Mem. Abbrev. of MEMORANDUM 1.

Mem, vulgar var. of MA'AM.

Member (me·mbəɹ), *sb.* [ME. *membre*, a. F. *membre* :—L. *membrum* limb.] 1. A part or organ of the body; chiefly, a limb, etc. (as opp. to the trunk). *arch.* †b. *spec.* (after L.): = 'privy member' –1728. c. *Biol.* Any part of a plant or animal viewed with regard to its form and position 1875. 2. *fig.* chiefly in *m. of Christ, of Satan* ME. 3. *transf.* Each constituent part of a complex structure. late ME. b. *Arch.* 'Any part of an edifice, or any moulding in a collection of mouldings, as those in a cornice, capital, base, etc.' (Gwilt) 1679. 4. Each individual belonging to a society or assembly. Also formerly, †an inhabitant or native (of a country or city). ME. b. *absol.* A person. Now *slang* and *dial.* 1525. †c. One who takes part in anything –1604. 5. One formally elected to take part in the proceedings of a parliament: in full *M. of Parliament* (abbrev. M.P.), in U.S. *M. of Congress* (M.C.) 1454. 6. A component part, branch, of a political body. late ME. †7. A branch (of a trade, art, profession); a branch, species, subdivision of a class –1614. 8. A section or district of an estate, manor, parish, or the like 1450. 9. *Math.* a. A group of figures or symbols forming part of a numerical expression or formula 1608. b. *Alg.* Either side of an equation 1702. 10. A division or clause of a sentence; a head of a discourse; a branch of a disjunctive proposition 1534. 11. Each of the items forming a series 1851.

1. *Privy m.* or *members*, †*carnal m.*: the secret part or parts. *The unruly m.* (after *James* iii. 5–8): the tongue. 2. Wherein I was made a m. of Christe *Bk. Com. Prayer.* 3. b. In later Gothic the pinnacle became gradually a decorative m. RUSKIN. 4. Here comes a m. of the common-wealth SHAKS. c. All members of our Cause SHAKS. 6. By estates of the realm they meant members, or necessary parts, of the parliament HALLAM. Hence **Me·mbral** *a.* pertaining to a m.; *Anat.* and *Zool.*, appendicular 1603.

†Me·mber, *v.* late ME. [a. OF. *membrer* :—L. *memorare.*] *trans.* = MEMORATE. –1589.

Membered (me·mbəɹd), *a.* ME. [f. MEMBER *sb.* + -ED².] Having members (of a specified kind or number); divided into members; †consisting of links or segments. b. *spec.* in *Her.* Said of a bird, when the legs are of a different tincture from the body 1530.

Membership (me·mbəɹʃip). 1647. [f. MEMBER *sb.* + -SHIP.] 1. The condition or status of being a member of a society, etc. 2. The number of members in a particular body 1850.

Membranaceous (membrănēⁱ·ʃəs), *a.* 1678. [f. late L. *membranaceus*, f. *membrana*; see next and -ACEOUS.] *Nat. Hist.* Membranous. In *Bot.* thin and semi-transparent, like a fine membrane.

Membrane (me·mbreⁱn). 1519. [ad. L. *membrana*, f. *membrum* MEMBER *sb.* The etym. sense is app. 'that which covers the members of the body'.] 1. A thin pliable sheet-like tissue (usually fibrous), serving to connect other structures or to line a part or organ. Also *collect. sing.* = membranous structure. 1615. b. *Path.* A morbid formation in certain diseases 1765. 2. †Parchment; a skin of parchment forming part of a roll 1519.

1. The m. of the nose 1788. The organic basis [of vegetable tissues] is simple m. and fibre 1846. *attrib.* **m.-bone** *Ichthyol.*, a bone originating in membranous tissue. 2. The third m. of this Roll 1890. Hence **Membra·neous** *a.* = MEMBRANOUS. **Membra·niform** *a.* [-FORM]. **Membra·no-**, comb. form.

Membranous (me·mbrănəs), *a.* 1597. [ad. F. *membraneux*, f. *membrane* MEMBRANE.] Consisting of, resembling, or of the nature of membrane. In *Bot.*, thin and more or less translucent. b. Of diseases: Pertaining to or involving the formation of a membrane 1875.

‖**Membranula** (membrēⁱ·niŭlă). Also **-ule.** 1821. [L., dim. of *membrana.*] A little membrane.

Memento (mĭme·ntǫ). *Pl.* **-oes, -os.** late ME. [Imper. of L. *meminisse* to remember, redupl. f. root **men-*; see MIND *sb.*] 1. *Liturg.* Either of two prayers beginning with *Memento* in the Canon of the Mass, in which the living and the dead are commemorated. 2. A reminder, warning, or hint as to conduct or with regard to future events 1582. b. *concr.* An object serving to remind or warn 1580. 3. Something to remind one of some person or event 1768. ¶4. Joc. misused for: a. A reverie; hence, a doze; b. (One's) memory 1587.

2. Phr. **M. mori** (mōᵊ·rəi). [L. = 'remember that you have to die'.] A warning or (*concr.*) a reminder of death, e.g. a skull 1596. b. Rings, deaths heads, and such mementoes FLETCHER.

Memnonian (memnōᵘ·niăn), *a.* 1614. [f. L. *Memnonius* (a. Gr. Μεμνόνειος, f. Μέμνων) + -AN.] a. Pertaining to the demigod Memnon, said to have erected the palace at Susa; hence, an epithet of Susa or Persia generally. b. Having the property of the statue of Memnon at Thebes in Egypt, said to give forth a musical sound when touched by the dawn.

Xerxes,..From Susa his M. Palace..Came MILT.

Memo. (me·mo). 1889. Abbrev. of MEMORANDUM; *colloq.* treated as a word. Cf. MEM.

Memoir (me·mwǭɹ). 1567. [a. F. *mémoire* masc., a spec. use of *mémoire* fem., MEMORY.] 1. A note, memorandum; a record –1755. †2. In diplomatic and official use: = MEMORANDUM (*rare*). Also *pl.* official reports of business done. –1829. 3. *collect. pl.* a. A record of events, a history treating of matters from the personal knowledge of the writer or with reference to particular sources of information 1659. b. An autobiographical record 1673. 4. A biography, or biographical notice 1826. 5. An essay on a learned subject on which the writer has made particular observations. Hence *pl.* the record of the transactions of a learned society. 1680.

3. The following memoirs of my Uncle Toby's courtship STERNE. Hence **Memoirist** (me·mwǭrist), a writer of memoirs, or of a m. **Me·moirism**, the practice of writing memoirs.

‖**Memorabilia** (me:mŏrăbi·liă). 1806. [neut. pl. of L. *memorabilis.*] Memorable or noteworthy things.

Memorable (me·mŏrăb'l), *a.* (*sb.*) 1483. [ad. L. *memorabilis*, f. *memorare*; see MEMORATE *v.* and -ABLE.] 1. Worth remembering; not to be forgotten. 2. Easy to be remembered 1599. 3. *sb. pl.* = MEMORABILIA 1611.

1. He nothing common did or mean, Upon that m. scene MARVELL. 2. *Hen. V*, II. iv. 53. 3. Recorded ..as one of the chiefe memorables in his raigne 1613. Hence **Memorabi·lity**, **Me·morableness**, m. quality; also, a person or thing worth remembering. **Me·morably** *adv.* so as to be remembered.

Memorandum (memŏræ·ndŏm), *sb.* *Pl.* **-anda** (-æ·ndă), **-andums** (-æ·ndŏmz). late ME. [L., neut. sing. of *memorandus*, gerundive of *memorare* (see MEMORATE *v.*).] 1. '(It is) to be remembered': placed at the head of a note of something to be remembered. Now only *legal.* 2. 'A note to help the memory' (J.); hence, a record of events, or of observations, esp. for future use 1542. b. *spec.* A record of a pecuniary transaction 1607. c. *Law.* The writing in which the terms of a transaction or contract are embodied 1591. d. *Diplomacy.* A summary of the grounds for or against an action, the state of a question, etc. 1658. †3. An injunction to remember something –1643. †4. A reminder; also, a memento, souvenir –1847. 5. *Comm.* An informal communication, esp. one on paper headed with the word 'Memorandum' and the name and address of the sender. 6. *attrib.* 1710.

2. c. *Marine Insurance.* A clause in a policy enumerating the articles in respect of which underwriters have no liability. *M. of association*, a document required by law for the registration of a joint-stock company, containing the name of the company, its object, capital, etc. d. These deliberations..resulted in the preparation of the so-called Berlin M. 1885. 6. **m. cheque**, a cheque given as an acknowledgement of indebtedness, but which is not to be presented for payment until a day agreed upon between the drawer and drawee. Hence **Memora·ndum** *v. trans.* to make a m. of 1805.

†Me·morate, *v.* 1623. [f. L. *memorat-*, *memorare*, f. *memor* mindful; see MEMORY.] *trans.* To bring to mind; to mention, recount, relate –1686. So **†Memora·tion**, mention; commemoration 1553–1627.

Memorative (me·mŏrătiv), *a.* (*sb.*) 1448. 1. Reminding one of something; commemorative. Now *rare.* †2. Of or pertaining to the memory, esp. in *m. faculty, power, virtue* 1481–1706. †3. Having a good memory; retentive 1481–1695. †4. *sb.* Something to put one in mind of a thing; a memorial 1597–1690.

4. Short sentences and memoratiues, as *Know thy selfe*..and the like J. KING.

Memorial (mĭmōᵊ·riăl). late ME. [a. OF. *memorial* (mod.F. *mémorial*), ad. L. *memorialis* adj., f. *memoria* MEMORY.] A. *adj.* 1. Preserving the memory of a person or thing, as a statue, a festival, etc. †2. Remembered; memorable –1631. 3. a. Of or pertaining to memory. †b. Mnemonic. †c. Done from memory. late ME.

1. M. windows 1866. A m. ring 1877. 3. b. Your Minutes or m. Aids 1745.

B. *sb.* †1. = MEMORY. late ME. 2. A memorial act; *spec.* (*Eccl.*) = COMMEMORATION 2 b. 1468. 3. Something to preserve the memory of a person, thing, or event, as a statue, a custom, etc. late ME. †4. A note or memorandum –1817. b. *Law.* An abstract of the particulars of a deed, etc., for registration 1813. c. *Scots Law.* A statement of facts drawn up for counsel's opinion. Also, an advocate's brief. 1752. 5. A record, chronicle, or memoir; now chiefly *pl.*, a record, often containing personal reminiscences 1513. 6. In diplomatic use: A general designation for various classes of informal state papers 1536. 7. A statement of facts forming the basis of or expressed in the form of a petition to a person in authority, a government, etc. 1713.

1. The sweet M. of the Just Shall flourish when he sleeps in dust TATE & BRADY. 3. This also that she hath done, shall be spoken of for a memoriall of her *Mark* xiv. 9. 5. Though of their Names in heav'nly Records now Be no m. MILT. **M. Day** *U.S.* the day set apart for honouring the memory of those who fell in the civil war of 1861–5. Hence **Memo·rialist**, one who presents a m. or writes memorials.

Memorial (mĭmōᵊ·riăl), *v.* 1764. [f. MEMORIAL *sb.*] 1. *trans.* = MEMORIALIZE 2. 1768. 2. *intr.* To draw up a memorial; to petition *for* 1764. 3. *Law.* To enter in a memorandum 1824.

Memorialize (mĭmōᵊ·riăləiz), *v.* 1798. [f. MEMORIAL *sb.* + -IZE.] 1. *trans.* To commemorate. 2. To address a memorial to.

‖**Memoria technica** (mĭmōᵊ·riă te·knikă). 1730. [L. = 'artificial memory'.] A system of mnemonics; a mnemonic contrivance.

Memorious, *a.* *Obs.* or *arch.* *rare.* 1599. [ad. med.L. *memoriosus*, f. *memoria*; see -OUS.] †1. Having a good memory; mindful *of* –1656. 2. Memorable 1883.

Memorist (me·mŏrist). *rare.* 1682. [f. MEMORY or MEMORIZE *v.*; see -IST.] †1. One who prompts the memory. SIR T. BROWNE. 2. *U.S.* One having a good memory 1872.

‖**Memoriter** (mĭmǫ·ritəɹ), *adv.* 1612. [L., f. *memor.*] From memory, by heart. b. as *adj.* Spoken or speaking 'memoriter' 1802.

Memorize (me·mŏrəiz), *v.* 1591. [f. MEMORY + -IZE.] 1. *trans.* To cause to be remembered, make memorable; also, to preserve the memory of in writing, record. Now *rare.* 1591. 2. To commit to memory 1856.

1. Except they meane to..m. another Golgotha SHAKS. A Cenotaph to memorise our grave 1822. The R.A. here memorised, was George Daw LAMB.

Memory (me·mŏri). ME. [a. OF. *memorie*, *memoire* (mod.F. *mémoire*), ad. L. *memoria*, f. *memor*, redupl. f. root **mer-*, Indo-Eur. **smer-* (Skr. *smar-*) to remember.] 1. The faculty by which things are remembered. 2. This faculty considered as residing in a particular individual. late ME. 3. Recollection, remembrance. late ME. b. An act or instance of remembrance; a recollection 1817. c. A person or thing held in remembrance 1842. 4. The fact or condition of being remembered; 'exemption from oblivion' (J.). late ME. 5. (Good or bad) posthumous repute 1450. **6.** The length of time over which memory extends 1530. **7.** *Liturg.* A commemoration, esp. of the departed. *Obs.* exc. *Hist.* ME. †**8.** A memorial writing; a record; a history -1730. †**9.** A memorial; a memento -1624. †**10.** A memorial tomb, shrine, chapel, or the like -1691. **11.** *attrib.*, as *m.-picture*, etc. 1642.

1. By the m. it [an idea] can be made an actual perception again LOCKE. Phr. *To commit to m.*: to learn by heart. *Art of m., artificial m.*: mnemonics, a mnemonic system. 2. I should haue a verie good wit, for I haue but a bad memorie MORLEY. Phr. *Of †good, sane, sound* (etc.) *m.* He was yet in memorie and alyve CHAUCER. 3. Phr. *From m.*; *to come to* (a person's) *m.*; *to bear, have, keep in m.* *To draw* or *take into* or *to m.*: to recollect. †*Out of m.*: forgotten. b. You put strange memories in my head TENNYSON. 4. That euer-liuing man of Memorie, Henrie the fift SHAKS. *In m. of, to the m. of*: so as to keep alive the remembrance of. 5. The memorie of the iust is blessed *Prov.* x. 7. Phr. *Of blessed, happy, famous* (etc.) *m.*: a formula used after the names of deceased sovereigns, princes, etc. 6. Phr. *Beyond, within the m.* (*of man*). †*Through all m.*: for all time (MILT.). Law. *Time of* (*legal*) *m.*; Time of m. hath been long ago ascertained by the law to commence from the reign of Richard the first BLACKSTONE. 9. These weedes are memories of those worser houres SHAKS. Hence **Me·moried** *a.* having a m. (of a specified kind) 1573; fraught with memories 1851.

Memphian (me·mfiăn). 1591. [f. *Memphis* + -AN.] **A.** *adj.* Pertaining to Memphis, a city of ancient Egypt; used vaguely for 'Egyptian'. **B.** *sb.* An inhabitant or native of Memphis; an Egyptian.

Busiris and his M. Chivalrie MILT. So **Memphi·tic** *a.* pertaining to Memphis, or to the dialect of Coptic spoken there 1450. †**Memphi·tical** *a.* 1581.

‖**Mem-sahib** (me·msāˌib). 1857. [f. *mem* = MA'AM + SAHIB.] Used by the natives of India in addressing European women.

Men, pl. of MAN *sb.*

Menace (me·năs), *sb.* [ME. *manasce, manace*, a. OF. *manace* (mod.F. *menace*), a Com. Rom. wd. :—L. *minacia*, f. *minac-, -ax* adj., f. *minari* to threaten.] A declaration or indication of hostile intention, or of a probable evil or catastrophe; a threat. **b.** The action of threatening ME. **c.** Said of a state of things, etc., which threatens danger, etc. 1857.

That M. of committing men to Hell-fire 1664. b. The voice of m. and complaint was silent GIBBON. The m. of the skies 1871.

Menace (me·năs), *v.* ME. [a. F. *menacer* :—pop. L. **minaciare*, f. *minacia* MENACE *sb.*] **1.** *trans.* To hold out menaces against; to threaten. **2.** *intr.* To utter menaces; to be threatening ME. **3.** *trans.* To threaten to inflict ME. †**4.** To use threateningly. MILT.

1. Your eyes do m. me: why looke you pale? SHAKS. Her life was menaced MACAULAY. 2. Earth below shook; heaven above menaced BURKE. 3. Such as m. warre 1621. Hence **Me·naceful** *a.* **Me·nacement. Me·nacer. Me·nacingly** *adv.*

Menad, -ic, var. MÆNAD, -IC.

Ménage, menage (menā·ʒ). Now only as Fr. ME. [a. OF. *manaige, menaige* (mod.F. *ménage*) :—pop. L. **mansionaticum*, f. L. *mansionem* MANSION, whence F. *maison*.] †**1.** The members of a household; a man's 'meinie' -1490. **2.** The management of a household, housekeeping; hence, a domestic establishment (often semi-*concr.*) 1698.

2. Nothing tended to make ladies so..inefficient in the m. as the study of the dead languages HAN. MORE.

Menage, etc.: see MANAGE, etc.

Menagerie (mĕnæ·dʒĕri). Also †**-ery.** 1712. [a. F. *ménagerie*, f. *ménage*; see MÉNAGE and -ERY.] **1.** A collection of wild animals in cages or enclosures, esp. one kept for exhibition. Also, the place where they are kept. †**2.** An aviary -1830.

1. *transf.* An old quack doctor named Levett.. completed this strange m. MACAULAY.

Menald (me·năld), *a.* Also †**menild, mennal.** 1611. [?] Of animals: Spotted, speckled. Of a deer: Of a dappled chestnut. Also *sb.* a deer of this colour.

Mend (mend), *sb.* ME. [Partly aphet. f. *amend* (see AMENDS); partly f. MEND *v.*] †**1.** Recompense, reparation; also, something given as compensation. Usu. *pl.* in form, construed as *sing.* -1816. †**2.** Remedy -1655. **3.** Phr. *On the m.*: recovering; (of affairs, etc.) improving in condition 1802. **4.** An act of mending, a repair; a repaired hole, etc. 1888.

Mend, *v.* ME. [aphet. f. AMEND *v.*]

I. To remove or atone for defects. **1.** *trans.* To free (a person, etc.) from sin or fault; to reform; *occas.* to cure *of* (a fault). Now *arch.* or *dial.* exc. in phr. *to m. one's manners, ways.* **b.** *intr.* for *refl.* Now *rare* exc. in provb. *It is never too late to m.* ME. **2.** To remove the defects of (a thing); to correct (what is faulty). Now only *occas.* as transf. of 5. ME. **b.** *intr.* To become less faulty. Of conditions: To improve. ME. **3.** *trans.* To rectify, remedy, remove (an evil); to put right (anything amiss) ME. **b.** *intr.* Of a fault: To undergo rectification. POPE. **4.** *trans.* To make amends or atone for (a misdeed, an injury); also *absol.* *Obs.* exc. in *Least said soonest mended.* ME. **5.** To restore to a complete or sound condition (a road, clothes, furniture, tools, fences, etc.); to repair. Also, to make good (the defective part). Now the prevailing sense. ME. **b.** To adjust, set right. *Obs.* exc. *Naut.* 1515. **6.** *trans.* To restore to health, cure, heal (*arch.*) ME. **b.** *intr.* To recover from sickness 1500. **c.** Of a wound, etc.: To heal. Of a malady: To abate. Now *dial.* 1607.

2. Never think of mending what you write. Let it go COBBETT. b. I hope the times will m. HOWELL. 3. She wolde come, and mende al that was mis CHAUCER. 5. As they were in the shyppe mendynge their nettes COVERDALE *Mark* i. 19. Phr. †*To m. the lights*: to trim the lamps, or snuff the candles. *To m. a fire*: to add fuel to it. *To m. a pen*: to cut a worn quill pen so as to make it write properly. b. Phr. *To m. sails*, to loose and skin them afresh on the yards. 6. b. The Queen is slowly mending of her gout SWIFT.

II. Without distinct reference to defect. **1.** *trans.* To improve the condition or fortune of. Now *rare* or *Obs.* exc. *refl.*, to better oneself. ME. †**2.** To improve by additions (*e.g.* wages, prices) -1697. **b.** *intr.* To improve in amount or price 1602. †**c.** *trans.* To supplement -1711. **3.** To improve in quality; to ameliorate (conditions, etc.). Now *rare.* 1603. †**b.** *intr.* To improve -1712. **4.** *trans.* To improve upon, surpass, better. Now only *colloq.* to produce something better than. ME.

2. And we will m. thy wages SHAKS. c. Wee'll m. our dinner here SHAKS. 4. In Vshering M. him who can SHAKS.

Phrases, etc. †*God m. all*, a pious wish. *To m. or end*: to improve or put an end to; in early use chiefly = 'to kill or cure'. *To m. the matter, to m. matters*: to improve the state of affairs concerning a person or thing. Often used *ironically*. *To m.* (*one's*) *pace*: to travel faster. †*To m. one's hand*: to improve one's work or conduct. Hence **Me·ndable** *a.* capable of improvement. **Me·nder.**

Mendacious (mendēⁱ·ʃəs), *a.* 1616. [f. L. *mendac-, -ax* (:—**mentnax*, f. root of *mentiri* to lie) + -IOUS.] Lying; untruthful; false.

A m. Legend 1616. [The Pagan ages] were not m. and distracted, but in their own poor way true and sane! CARLYLE. **Menda·cious·ly** *adv.*, **-ness.**

Mendacity (mendæ·sĭti). 1646. [ad. late L. *mendacitas*, f. *mendac-*; see prec. and -ITY.] The quality of being mendacious; habitual lying or deceiving; also, a lie or falsehood.

If wee call to minde the m. of Greece SIR T. BROWNE.

Mendelian (mendī·liăn), *a.* 1901. [f. Gregor Johann *Mendel* (1822–84) + -IAN.] *Biol.* Of or pertaining to Mendel, or following his law or theory of heredity. So **Mende·lianism, Mendelism** (me·ndĕliz'm), Mendel's theory of heredity. **Me·ndelist. Me·ndelize** *v. intr.* to exhibit Mendelian characters.

†**Mendiant,** *sb.* and *a.* 1483. [a. F. *mendiant*;—L. *mendicantem*: see next.] = next -1535.

Mendicant (me·ndikănt). 1474. [ad. L. *mendicantem*, f. *mendicare*, f. *mendicus* beggar.] **A.** *adj.* Begging; given to begging. Also, characteristic of a beggar. 1613. **b.** *spec.* Applied to those religious orders who lived entirely on alms 1547. **B.** *sb.* A beggar; one who lives by begging 1474. **b.** A begging friar 1530. **c.** Applied to Brahmin, Buddhist, etc. priests who beg for food 1613.

A. M. prophets go to rich men's doors JOWETT. B. There is surely a Physiognomy, which those.. Master Mendicants observe, whereby they instantly discover a merciful aspect SIR T. BROWNE.

Mendicate (me·ndikeⁱt), *v. rare.* 1618. [f. ppl. stem of L. *mendicare*; see prec.] **1.** *trans.* To ask for like a beggar. **2.** *intr.* To beg (*rare*). Dicts. Hence **Mendica·tion,** begging.

Mendicity (mendi·sĭti). late ME. [a. F. *mendicité*, ad. L. *mendicitas*, f. *mendicus*; see MENDICANT and -ITY.] **1.** The state or condition of a mendicant; beggary. Also, now usually, the existence or numbers of the mendicant class. **2.** The practice of begging 1801. **3.** *attrib.*, as *m. society* 1819.

Me·nding, *vbl. sb.* ME. [-ING[1].] Amendment (phr. †*on* or *in the m. hand*, see HAND *sb.* I. 4); repair; *colloq.* articles to be repaired, materials (*m. wool*) for repairing.

Mendment (me·ndmĕnt). ME. [aphet. f. AMENDMENT.] **1.** = AMENDMENT; improvement, etc. **2.** Improvement of the soil; *concr.* manure. Now *dial.* 1644.

Mendole (me·ndoᵘl). 1854. [a. It. (Venetian) *mendole*.] = CACKEREL 1.

Menevian (mĕnī·viăn), *a.* and *sb.* 1865. [f. *Menevia*, med.L. name of St. David's in Wales + -AN.] *Geol.* Name of a very ancient group of rocks found near St. David's, etc.

Me·n-folk(s. 1802. [See MAN *sb.*] **1.** The male sex. **2.** Human beings. MORRIS.

Meng, *v. Obs.* exc. *dial.* [OE. *męngan* (the normal development of which was *menge, minge*) :—OTeut. **maŋgjan*, f. root of OE. *gemang* AMONG. The forms *meng, ming* are app. due to ON. *mengja*.] **1.** *trans.* To mix (*lit.* and *fig.*). **2.** To produce by mixing. late ME. **3.** To stir up; to disturb, trouble, confound. Also *intr.* for *pass.* OE. **4. a.** *trans.* To bring (living creatures) together -ME. **b.** *refl.*, *pass.*, and *intr.* To be mingled *together*, or *with*, *among* others; to be joined in battle; to have sexual intercourse; to be united by marriage -1590. **5.** *intr.* Of things: To be or become mixed OE.

Menhaden (menhēⁱ·dən). Also **manhad(d)en.** 1792. [Corrupted f. Narragansett Indian *munnawhatteaûg*.] A U.S. fish of the herring family, *Brevoortia tyrannus*, much used for manure and producing a valuable oil.

Menhir (me·nhiəɹ). 1840. [Breton (*men* stone, *hir* long).] *Archæol.* A tall upright monumental stone, of varying antiquity, found in parts of Europe, and in Africa and Asia.

Menial (mī·niăl), *a.* (*sb.*) late ME. [a. AF. *meignal, menial*, f. *meiniee* MEINIE.] †**1.** Pertaining to the household, domestic. Also *transf.* -1709. **2.** Of a servant: Forming one of the household; domestic. Now only *contemptuous.* late ME. **3.** Of service: Proper to a menial; servile, degrading 1673. Of temper, spirit, occupations: Sordid 1837. **4.** *sb.* A 'menial' servant (see 2). Now chiefly *contemptuous.* late ME.

2. The labour of a m. servant..adds to the value of nothing ADAM SMITH. 3. Two other servants for m. offices SWIFT. 4. A hot m. in a red waistcoat THACKERAY. Hence **Me·nially** *adv.*

Meningeal (mĭni·ndʒiăl), *a.* 1829. [f. mod.L. *meningeus* (f. *mening-*, MENINX) + -AL.] *Anat.* and *Path.* Of or pertaining to the meninges.

M. artery: one of the arteries supplying the dura mater of the brain. So **Meni·ngic** *a.* 1822. **Men·ingism,** tendency to meningitis 1901.

Meninges, pl. of MENINX.

‖**Meningitis** (menindʒəi·tis). 1828. [mod. L., f. *mening-* MENINX + -ITIS.] *Path.* Inflammation of the membranes of the brain or spinal cord. Hence **Meningi·tic** *a.*

Meningo- (mĭni·ŋgo), comb. f. Gr. μῆνιγξ MENINX = pertaining to the meninx (and another part), as *m.-myelitis.*

‖**Meninx** (mī·niŋks). Chiefly *pl.* **meninges** (mĭni·ndʒīz). 1616. [mod.L., a. Gr. μῆνιγξ membrane.] Any of the three membranes enveloping the brain and spinal cord (*viz.* the dura mater, arachnoid, and pia mater).

‖**Meniscus** (mĭni·skŭs). *Pl.* **menisci** (mĭni·səi); also †**meniscusses.** 1693. [mod.L., a. Gr. μηνίσκος crescent, dim. of μήνη moon.] A crescent-shaped body. **1.** A crescent moon (*rare*) 1706. **2.** *Optics.* A lens convex on one side and concave on the other, esp. when of true crescent-shaped section (*converging m.*) 1693. **3.** *Physics.* The convex or concave upper surface of a liquid column, caused by capillarity 1812. 4. *Math.* A figure of the form of a crescent 1885. 5. *Anat.* A disk-like interarticular fibrocartilage situated in the interior of some joints to adapt the articular surfaces to each other, as in the wrist- and knee-joints 1830. 6. *attrib.*, as *m. lens*, etc. 1704. Hence **Meni·scal, -ate, -oid, -oidal** *adjs.* resembling a meniscus in form.

Meniver(e; see MINIVER.

Mennonist (me·nǒnist). Also †**Menon-.** 1645. [f. as next + -IST.] = next. So **Me·nnonism** 1684.

Mennonite (me·nǒnəit). 1565. [f. *Menno* + -ITE[1].] *Eccl.* A member of a sect of Christians which was founded in Friesland by *Menno* Simons (1492–1559). They are opposed to infant baptism, the taking of oaths, military service, and the holding of civic offices.

Meno- (meno), comb. f. Gr. μήν, μηνο- month, used = menses, as in **Me·nopause** (final cessation of the menses) 1872. ‖**Meno·rrha·gia** (excess) 1776. ‖**Meno·stasis** 1839, **Menosta·tion** 1822 (suppression).

Menology (mīnǫ·lŏdʒi). Also **menologium.** 1610. [ad. mod.L. *mēnologium*, ad. late Gr. μηνολόγιον, f. μηνο-, μήν month + λόγος account; see LOGOS.] 1. A calendar, esp. of the Greek church, with biographies of the saints. ¶2. The part of knowledge relating to the months 1807. So †**Menologe** 1626.

Menow(e, obs. ff. MINNOW.

‖**Mensa** (me·nsă). 1693. [L., = 'table'.] 1. *Eccl.* The top, or the top slab, of an altar 1848. 2. The grinding surface of a molar tooth.

Mensal (me·nsăl), *a.*[1] (*sb.*[1]) 1440. [ad. late L. *mensalis*, f. *mensa* table; see -AL.] 1. Pertaining to or used at the table; table-. 2. *Sc.* and *Irish Hist.* Applied to land, a church, benefice, etc., set aside for the maintenance of the table: now only with ref. to the R.C.Ch. in Ireland. Also as *sb.* A mensal church or benefice; †the provision of the royal table. 1605. 3. *Palmistry. M. line*, the 'line of fortune', the table-line 1602.

1. Conversation either mental or m. RICHARDSON.

Mensal (me·nsăl), *a.*[2] and *sb.*[2] 1483. [f. L. *mensis* month + -AL.] A. *adj.* Monthly 1860. †B. *sb.* A monthly account –1526.

Mense (mens), *sb. Obs.* exc. *Sc.* and *n. dial.* 1500. [Sc. pronunc. of MENSK.] Propriety, decorum; neatness, tidiness. So **Mense** *v. trans.* to grace; to be a credit to 1535. Hence **Me·nseful** *a.* proper, decorous; neat; discreet. **Me·nseless** *a.* destitute of decorum, neatness, or propriety.

‖**Menses** (me·nsīz), *sb. pl.* 1597. [L., pl. of *mensis* month.] *Path.* The discharge of blood from the uterus, occurring normally at intervals of a lunar month.

Menshevik (me·nʃěvik). 1920. [Russ. (f. *menshe* less), orig. applied to the minority section of the Russian Social Democratic Party in 1902.] A Russian socialist of the moderate party. Also **Me·nshevism, -ist.**

†**Mensk**, *sb.* ME. [a. ON. *mennska* humanity, corresp. to OE. *menniscu* :—OTeut. **manniskīn-*, wk. fem. of **mannisko-* (see MANNISH *a.*).] 1. Humanity, kindness; graciousness. ME. only. 2. Honour, dignity, reverence; *pl.* honours, dignities –1509. So †**Mensk** *v.* to reverence or honour; to grace; to adorn ME. –1470.

Menstrual (me·nstrŭăl). late ME. [a. F. *menstruel*, ad. L. *menstrualis*, f. *menstruus*, *menstruum*; see MENSTRUUM and -AL.] A. *adj.* 1. Monthly; happening once in a month, varying in monthly periods. Now only *Astr.* 1594. 2. Of or pertaining to the menses. late ME. †3. Pertaining to, or of the nature of, a menstruum 1471. †4. Of parts of the body: Produced from the menstrual blood of the mother; opp. to *spermatical*. BACON. B. *sb.* †1. *pl.* = MENSES –1599. †2. *Alch.* The 'menstrual' element (see A. 3, and cf. A. 4) supposed to be added to metal in its conversion into gold –1477.

†**Menstruant**, *a.* [ad. L. *menstruantem*, *menstruare* to menstruate.] Subject to menstruation. SIR T. BROWNE.

†**Menstruate**, *a.* late ME. only. [ad. late L. *menstruatus*, f. *menstruum*; see MENSTRUUM.] Menstruous.

Menstruate (me·nstrueˡt), *v.* 1658. [f. L. *menstruat-*, *menstruare*, f. *menstrua*; see MENSTRUUM and -ATE[3].] 1. *intr.* To discharge the menses 1800. 2. *trans.* To pollute as with menstrual blood. CLEVELAND. Hence **Menstrua·tion**, the process of menstruating 1776.

†**Menstrue.** late ME. [a. F. *menstrue*, ad. L. *menstruum*.] = MENSTRUUM –1684.

Menstruous, *a.* late ME. [ad. OF. *menstrueus*, ad. L. type **menstruosus*; see MENSTRUUM and -OUS.] 1. Discharging the menses. 2. Pertaining to the menses 1599. †b. Produced from menstrual blood. BACON. †3. Defiled with or as with menstrual blood. Hence, in 17th c. often: Horribly filthy or polluted. –1685.

3. All our Righteousnesses are as m. Rags BUNYAN.

†**Menstruo·sity**, the menstrual discharge 1506.

‖**Menstruum** (me·nstruǒm). *Pl.* **menstrua** (me·nstruă). late ME. [L., neut. of *menstruus* adj., monthly, f. *mens-*, *mensis*. In classical L. the sb. occurs only in the pl. *menstrua*.] †1. The menstrual discharge or menses –1726. 2. A solvent; any liquid agent by which a solid substance may be dissolved 1612.

In alchemy the base metal undergoing transmutation was compared to the seed within the womb in relation to the menstrual blood; hence sense 2.

2. Powerfull menstruums are made for its emolition [*sc.* of crystal] SIR T. BROWNE. *fig.* Paradoxes..are menstruums of friendship, they disintegrate regard 1890.

Mensurable (me·nsiŭrăb'l, me·nʃŭr-), *a.* 1604. [a. F. *mensurable*, ad. late L. *mensurabilis*, f. *mensurare*, f. *mensura* MEASURE *sb.*; see -ABLE.] 1. Capable of being measured; hence, having assigned limits. †2. Just, fair 1633. 3. *Mus.* Having 'measure' and fixed rhythm, with definite duration of notes and rests 1782. Hence **Mensurabi·lity, Me·nsurableness**, m. quality.

Mensural (me·nsiŭrăl, me·nʃŭrăl), *a.* 1609. [ad. med.L. *mensuralis*, f. L. *mensura* MEASURE *sb.*; see -AL.] 1. Pertaining to measure 1651. 2. *Mus.* = MENSURABLE 3.

Mensurate (me·nsiŭreˡt, me·nʃŭr-), *v. rare.* 1653. [ad. L. *mensuratus*, *mensurare*, f. *mensura* MEASURE *sb.*; see -ATE[3].] *trans.* To measure.

Mensuration (mensiŭrē·ʃən, menʃŭrē·ʃən). 1571. [ad. late L. *mensurationem*, f. L. *mensurare*; see prec.] 1. The action, or an act, of measuring. †b. Size as measured. COCKER. 2. *Math.* That branch which gives the rules for finding the lengths of lines, the areas of surfaces, and the volumes of solids 1704. Hence **Mensura·tional** *a.* concerned with m.

-ment (mĕnt), *suffix*, forming sbs. Originally occurring in adopted Fr. words in *-ment*, either repr. L. sbs. in *-mentum*, or formed on the analogy of these by the addition of the suffix to vb.-stems. The resulting sbs. expressed either the result or product of the action of the verb, the means or instrument of the action, or, in late pop.L., and hence in Fr., an act or process. Instances of the two former are *fragmentum* fragment, *alimentum* aliment, *ornamentum* ornament, etc. Many of the Eng. formations are hybrid; e.g. *acknowledgement*, *atonement*, *betterment*, *wonderment*, etc. The suffix has rarely been appended to any other part of speech than a verb, as in *funniment*, *merriment*, *oddment*. The letter *y* (after a cons.) ending a verb is changed to *i* bef. the suffix, as in *accompaniment*.

Ment, pa. pple. of MENG *v.*

Mental (me·ntăl), *a.*[1] late ME. [a. F., ad. late L. *mentalis*, f. *ment-*, *mens* mind; see -AL.] 1. Of or pertaining to the mind. 2. Carried on or performed by the mind 1526. 3. Concerned with the phenomena of mind 1820.

1. *spec.* Pertaining to, or characterized by, a disordered mind; also as *sb.* 2. *M. arithmetic*: the art of performing arithmetical operations within the mind, without the aid of written figures, etc. *M. reservation*: see RESERVATION. 3. M. Science 1860.

Hence **Me·ntally** *adv.* in or as regards the mind.

Mental (me·ntăl), *a.*[2] 1727. [a. F. *mental*, f. L. *mentum* chin; see -AL.] Pertaining to the chin or the mentum.

The second hole in the lower jaw..is named the m. hole BELL.

Mentality (mentæ·lĭti). 1691. [f. MENTAL *a.*[1] + -ITY.] 1. That which is of the nature of mind or of mental action. 2. Mental quality, intellectuality 1856. b. *loosely.* Mental disposition, outlook 1931.

2. Hudibras has the same hard m. EMERSON.

Mentation (mentē·ʃən). 1850. [f. L. *ment-*, *mens* + -ATION.] Mental action, esp. as attributed to the agency of the brain, etc.; also, a product of this, a state of mind.

Menthene (me·nþīn). 1838. [a. Ger. *menthen*, F. *menthène*, f. L. *mentha* mint; see -ENE.] *Chem.* A liquid hydro-carbon obtained from peppermint oil.

Menthol (me·nþǫl). 1876. [a. Ger. *menthol* (1861), f. L. *mentha* mint; see -OL.] *Chem.* A crystalline camphor-like substance obtained by cooling various mint-oils.

M. cone or *pencil*: a conical piece of mixed m. and spermaceti, for the relief of facial neuralgia.

Menticulture (me·ntikɒltiŭı). 1830. [f. L. *menti-*, *mens* + *cultura*, after *agriculture*.] Cultivation of the mind. **Me:nticu·ltural** *a.*

Mention (me·nʃən), *sb.* ME. [a. F., ad. L. *mentionem*, *mentio*, f. root *men-* of *menti-*, *mens* mind, etc.] †1. Bearing in mind, consideration. ME. only. 2. In early use, the action of commemorating in speech or writing. Now, the action, or an act, of incidentally referring to or remarking upon (a person or thing) in spoken or written discourse. ME. †3. Indication, evidence; a vestige, trace, remnant –1633.

2. He grows peevish at any m. of business JOHNSON. Phr. *To make m. of* (= Fr. *faire mention de*), now somewhat *arch.* or *literary*, exc. in neg. contexts. I will make m. of thy righteousnesse, euen of thine onely *Ps.* lxxi. 16. *Honourable m.* (rarely, after F. use, *m.* simply): a distinction awarded to exhibited works of art, etc. or to examination candidates that are of exceptional merit, but are not entitled to a prize. 3. Where he moves in the sea he causeth a m. of his way in the waters BP. HALL.

Mention (me·nʃən), *v.* 1530. [a. F. *mentionner*, f. *mention*; see prec.] 1. *trans.* To make mention of; to refer to incidentally; to specify by name or otherwise. b. To state incidentally (*that*, etc.) 1617. †2. *intr.* To speak or make mention *of* –1792.

1. Phr. *Not to m.*: used parenthetically to suggest that the speaker refrains from presenting the full strength of his case. Not to m. several others, Carracio is said to have assisted Aretine ADDISON. *Don't m. it*: a colloq. phr. used in deprecating thanks or apology. Hence **Me·ntionable** *a.*

Mento- (me·nto), used as comb. f. L. *mentum* chin, as in **Me:nto-Mecke·lian** *a.*, in *mento-Meckelian bone* or *element*, a small bone formed by the ossification of parts of Meckel's cartilage and the lower labial cartilage.

Mentor (me·ntǫı). 1750. [a. F. *mentor*, appellative use of *Mentor*, Gr. Μέντωρ (app. f. root **men-* (: *mon-*) to remember, think, counsel).] With capital M: Name of the guide and adviser of the young Telemachus; *allusively*, one who fulfils a similar office. Hence, as common noun: An experienced and trusted counsellor.

1. The deep..The only M. of his youth BYRON.

‖**Mentum** (me·ntǒm). 1826. [L., = 'chin'.] 1. *Anat.* The chin 1855. 2. *Entom.* A term variously applied to different parts of the labium, esp. the median portion 1826. 3. *Bot.* A basal projection in certain orchids 1866.

‖**Menu** (me·niu, mənü). 1837. [F. *menu* adj. (:—L. *minutus* MINUTE *a.*), used as sb. with the sense of detailed list, etc.] A bill of fare; also, the dishes served.

M. card, the card on which a m. is written.

Mephistopheles (mefistǫ·fĕlīz, -fəl-). Also †**-is, -us.** 1598. [G.; of unkn. origin.] The evil spirit to whom Faust (in the German legend) sold his soul. Also allusively.

That M. of diplomacy, Talleyrand 1818. Hence **Mephistophelean, -elian** (me:fistǫfī·liăn) *adjs.* pertaining to or resembling M. or his actions.

‖**Mephitis** (mĭfəi·tis). 1706. [L. *mephitis* noxious vapour.] A noxious or pestilential emanation, esp. from the earth; a noisome or poisonous stench. So **Mephitic** (mĭfi·tik) *a.* of, pertaining to, or due to m.; offensive to the smell 1623. **Mephitism** (me·fitiz'm), mephitic poisoning of the air 1801. †**Me·phitized** *ppl. a.* charged with m. 1794.

Mer-, used in combs. (chiefly nonce-words) formed after MERMAID, as *mer-child, -folk, -wife*, etc.

Mercantile (mɔ̄·ɹkăntəil), *a.* 1642. [a. F., ad. It. *mercantile*, f. *mercante* MERCHANT.] **1.** Of or belonging to merchants or their trade; commercial. **b.** That deals with commercial affairs 1841. **2.** Engaged in trade or commerce 1645. **3.** Mercenary; also, simply, disposed for bargaining 1756.

1. The Expedition of the Argonauts..was partly m., partly military ARBUTHNOT. Phr. *M. system* (also *m. doctrine, theory*), the system of economic doctrine and legislative policy based on the principle that money alone is wealth. b. Leaders of opinion on m. questions MILL. 2. *M. marine*, the shipping collectively employed in commerce. 3. The m. bard [*sc.* Dryden] WARTON. Hence **Me·rcantilism**, the m. spirit; commercialism; in *Pol. Econ.* the principles of the m. system. **Me·rcantilist** *sb.* an advocate of the m. system; *adj.* of or pertaining to mercantilism or the m. system.

Mercaptan (mɔ̄ɹkæ·ptăn). 1835. [G. (Zeise), f. L. *mercurium captans* 'catching mercury'.] *Chem.* A sulphur alcohol; any one of a series of compounds resembling the alcohols, but containing sulphur, not oxygen. Hence **Merca·ptal**, a compound of a mercaptan with an aldehyde 1892. **Merca·ptide**, a compound formed by the substitution of a metal for hydrogen in a mercaptan 1835.

Mercat(e, obs. ff. MARKET.

Mercatorial (mɔ̄ɹkătō·riăl), *a.* Now *rare.* 1700. [f. L. *mercatorius* (f. *mercator*, f. *mercari* to trade) + -AL.] Of or pertaining to merchants or merchandise; mercantile. So †**Mercatory** *a.* FULLER.

†**Mercature.** 1620. [ad. L. *mercatura*, f. *mercari.*] Trading, commerce –1755.

†**Merce**, *v.* 1483. Aphet. f. AMERCE –1661. So †**Me·rcement**, = AMERCEMENT; also, doom, adjudged punishment ME.–1598.

Mercenarian (mɔ̄ɹsǐnē·riăn). *rare.* 1598. [See next and -IAN.] = next A. 2, B. 2.

Mercenary (mɔ̄·ɹsǐnări). late ME. [ad. L. *mercenarius*, f. *merced-, merces* (see MERCY).] **A.** *adj.* **1.** Working merely for monetary or other reward; actuated by self-interest 1532. **b.** Of conduct, etc.: Having the love of lucre for its motive 1532. **2.** Hired; serving for hire. Now only of soldiers serving in a foreign army. 1589. †**b.** Of services, an office, etc.: Salaried, stipendiary. Of a profession, etc.: Carried on for the sake of gain –1782.

1. Such wretches are kept in pay by some m. bookseller GOLDSM. b. M. marriages 1837. 2. They.. began..to go ouer to serue as mercenarie soldiers in the Low Countries SIR J. SMYTH.

B. *sb.* †**1.** One who labours merely for hire; a hireling. late ME. –1844. **2.** One who receives payment for his services; now only, a professional soldier serving a foreign power 1523.

2. *fig.* Literary mercenaries, ready to serve under friend or foe 1861.

Mercer (mɔ̄·ɹsəɹ). ME. [a. F. *mercier* :– pop.L. **merciarius*, f. L. *merci-, merx* merchandise.] A dealer in textile fabrics, esp. silks and other costly materials (in full *silk-m.*). Also *occas.* a small-ware dealer. Hence †**Me·rcership** (*rare*), the trade of a m.

Mercerize (mɔ̄·ɹsəɹəiz), *v.* 1859. [f. the name John *Mercer* of Accrington, alleged inventor of the process in 1844 + -IZE.] *trans.* To prepare (cotton goods) for dyeing by treating with a solution of caustic potash or soda, or certain other chemicals.

Mercery (mɔ̄·ɹsəri). [ME. *mercerie*, a. F., f. *mercier* MERCER.] **1.** *collect. sing.* (rarely *pl.*) The wares sold by a mercer. †**2.** *The M.*: The Mercers' Company. Also, the trade in mercery-ware; the part where it is carried on. –1662. **3.** *attrib.* as *m.-ware.* late ME.

2. At the Sign of the Cock, in the M. 1651.

Merchandise (mɔ̄·ɹtʃăndəiz), *sb.* ME. [a. F. *marchandise*, f. *marchand* MERCHANT.] †**1.** The action or business of buying and selling commodities for profit; trading; traffic. Also *fig.* **2.** The commodities of commerce; movables which may be bought and sold ME. †**b.** A saleable commodity, an article of commerce –1853.

1. Phr. *To be of good m.*, to be easily marketable. *To make* (*a* or *one's*) *m.*, †to carry on a bargain; also (*arch.*) const. *of* = to traffic in (usu. in bad sense). There [at Rome] Where gainful merchandize is made of Christ CARY. 2. *Ant. & Cl.* II. v. 104.

Merchandise (mɔ̄·ɹtʃăndəiz), *v. arch.* late ME. [f. prec.] **1.** *intr.* To trade, traffic; †also, to make merchandise *of.* **2.** *trans.* To buy and sell; to barter; to traffic in 1538.

2. As Roman priests [merchandize] their pardons ROWE. Hence **Me·rchandiser**, a dealer in commodities; one who traffics 1597.

Merchandry (mɔ̄·ɹtʃăndri). *Obs.* exc. *arch.* late ME. [prob. a. AF. **marchanderie*, f. *marchand*; see -ERY, -RY.] = MERCHANTRY **1.** Earlier †**Merchandise, -dy.**

Merchant (mɔ̄·ɹtʃănt), *sb.* and *a.* ME. [a. OF. *marchand*, earlier *marchëant* (mod.F. *marchand*) = It. *mercatante*:—pop.L. **mercatantem*, f.**mercatare*, freq. of *mercari* to trade, f. *merc-, merx* merchandise.] **A.** *sb.* **1.** One who buys and sells commodities for profit; orig. *gen.*; but early restricted to wholesale traders, esp. those dealing with foreign countries. **b.** A shopkeeper. Now only *Sc.*, *n. dial.*, and *U.S.* late ME. **c.** *slang.* One who practises or specializes in some activity (cf. SPEED-*m.*) 1886. †**2.** A supercargo –1681. †**3.** A fellow, 'chap' –1610. †**4.** A trading vessel, merchantman –1740.

1. A wise Marchant neuer aduentureth all his goodes in one ship MORE. *fig.* These wee call Merchants of Light BACON. Phr. †*To play the m. with*: to cheat, get the better of. †*To have* or *put on m.'s ears*: to affect not to hear. 4. *Temp.* II. i. 5.

attrib. and *Comb.*: **m.** (formerly †**m.'s**) **iron**, bar iron in a form suitable for the market, made by heating together and rolling pieces of puddled iron; hence *m. bar, -rolls, train* (= train of rolls); **m. prince** (prob. after *Isa.* xxiii. 8), a m. of princely wealth.

B. *adj.* **1.** Having relation to merchandise; relating to trade or commerce, esp. in *law-, statute-m.* late ME. **2.** Of a ship: Serving for the transport of merchandise. Hence, of or pertaining to the mercantile marine, as in *m. seaman, service.* (Often hyphened.) late ME. **3.** Of a town: Occupied in commerce. Also, consisting of merchants, as in *guild-m., m.-guild.* 1467.

3. M. citie *Isa.* xxiii. 11.

Merchant (mɔ̄·ɹtʃănt), *v.* Now *rare.* late ME. [a. OF., F. *marchander*, f. *marchand.*] **1.** *intr.* To trade as a merchant. †Also, to negotiate; in bad sense, to haggle. **2.** *trans.* To deal in; to buy and sell 1511.

1. I held it not fit, we should m. with our Sovereign 1614. Hence **Me·rchantable** *a.* fit for market; saleable; †of or pertaining to trade; commercial.

Me·rchant-adve·nturer. *Obs.* exc. *Hist.* 1496. = MERCHANT-VENTURER.

†**Me·rchantly**, *a.* 1599. [f. MERCHANT *sb.* + -LY [1].] **a.** Of or pertaining to a merchant. **b.** Huckstering. –1736.

Me·rchantman. 1449. [f. MERCHANT *a.* + MAN.] **1.** = MERCHANT *sb.* **1.** *arch.* **2.** A vessel of the mercantile marine 1627.

Merchantry (mɔ̄·ɹtʃăntri). 1789. [f. MERCHANT *sb.* + -RY.] **1.** The business of a merchant; trade, commercial dealings. **2.** Merchants collectively. CARLYLE.

Me·rchant-tai·lor. *Obs.* exc. (with arch. spelling) in 'Company of Merchant Taylors' and the 'Merchant Taylors' School' (London). 1504. [f. MERCHANT + TAILOR.] A tailor who supplies the materials of which his goods are made; a member of the Company of Merchant Taylors. **b.** One educated at Merchant Taylors' School 1877.

Me·rchant-ve·nturer. *Obs.* exc. *Hist.* 1533. A merchant engaged in the dispatch of trading expeditions over sea, and the establishment of factories and trading stations in foreign countries. Hence, a member of an incorporated association of such merchants.

Me·rchet. *Obs.* exc. *Hist.* ME. [AF. *merchet* = ONF. *market* MARKET *sb.*] A fine paid by a tenant or bondsman to his overlord for liberty to give his daughter in marriage.

†**Merciable**, *a.* ME. [a. OF. *merciable*, f. *merci* MERCY.] Merciful –1579.

Mercian (mɔ̄·ɹʃiăn, mɔ̄·ɹsiăn). 1513. [f. *Mercia* (f. OE. *Myrce*, f. *mearc* MARK *sb.*[1]) + -AN.] **A.** *adj.* Of or belonging to the Old English kingdom of Mercia or its language 1655. **B.** *sb.* **1.** A native or inhabitant of Mercia 1513. **2.** The dialect of Old English spoken in Mercia 1887.

Merciful (mɔ̄·ɹsiful), *a.* ME. [f. MERCY + -FUL.] Having or exercising mercy; characterized by mercy.

Blessed be mercyful men, for thei shuln gete mercye WYCLIF *Matt.* v. 7. **Me·rciful-ly** *adv.*, **-ness.**

†**Me·rcify**, *v. rare.* 1596. [f. MERCY + -(I)FY.] *trans.* To pity, compassionate –1733.

Merciless (mɔ̄·ɹsilės), *a.* late ME. [f. MERCY + -LESS.] Devoid of mercy; showing no mercy; pitiless, unrelenting.

A stern prince, m. in his exactions PRESCOTT. *transf.* M. ridicule L. STEPHEN. **Me·rciless-ly** *adv.*, **-ness.**

Mercurial (məɹkiū·riăl), *a.* and *sb.* late ME. [a. F. *mercuriel, mercurial*, ad. L. *mercurialis*, f. *Mercurius* MERCURY; see -AL.] **A.** *adj.* **1.** Of or pertaining to the god Mercury; resembling what pertains to Mercury. Now *rare.* 1599. **2.** Pertaining to (†influenced by) the planet Mercury. late ME. **3.** Of persons: Born under the planet Mercury; having the qualities of such a nativity, as eloquence, ingenuity, aptitude for commerce 1593. **4.** (Hence) Volatile, sprightly, ready-witted. (Now taken as alluding to the properties of the metal mercury) 1647. **5.** Of or pertaining to, consisting of or containing, mercury or quicksilver; (of diseases, etc.) produced by the administration of mercury; (of an organ) showing mercurial symptoms 1657.

1. His Foote Mercuriall: his martiall Thigh, The brawns of Hercules SHAKS. 2. *M. finger*: the little finger. 4. The gay, gallant, m. Frenchman DISRAELI.

B. *sb.* †**1.** The plant mercury 1607–1626. †**2.** A person born under the planet Mercury (see A. 3); a lively or sprightly person; also, one addicted to cheating and thieving 1598–1696. **3.** A preparation of mercury used as a drug 1676.

2. The Mercurials with their swiftnesse rush over all things 1650. 3. The Cure is perform'd by Mercurials outwardly and inwardly 1735. Hence **Mercu·rialism** *Path.*, the condition induced by the absorption of mercury into the body. **Mercuria·lity**, m. condition; †the m. part (of something). **Mercu·rial-ly** *adv.*, **-ness.** So **Mercu·rian** †*a.* and *sb.* = MERCURIAL.

Mercurialist (məɹkiūə·riălist). 1566. [f. prec. + -IST.] †**1.** One under the influence of the planet Mercury –1651; an eloquent or ingenious person; a trader; *occas.* a sharper, a thief –1655. **2.** A medical man who makes free use of mercury 1835.

Mercurialize (məɹkiūə·riăləiz), *v.* 1611. [f. as prec. + -IZE.] †**1.** *intr.* To play the part of a mercurial person –1656. **2.** *trans.* To render mercurial in temper 1862. **3.** To subject to the action of mercury 1843. Hence **Mercu:rializa·tion**, subjection to treatment by mercury; a mercurial process used in the development of photographs.

Mercuric (məɹkiūə·rik), *a.* 1828. [f. MERCURY + -IC.] *Chem.* Said of compounds in which mercury has a valency of two.

M. chloride = CORROSIVE SUBLIMATE; *M. sulphide* = VERMILION.

Mercu·rify, *v.* 1680. [f. MERCURY + -FY.] **1.** *trans.* **a.** *Alch.* To change (a portion of a metallic mass) into the form of mercury. **b.** To extract mercury from (metallic ore). **2.** To combine, treat, or mingle with mercury 1846. Hence **Mercurifica·tion.**

Mercurous (mɔ̄·ɹkiŭrəs), *a.* 1865. [f. MERCURY + -OUS.] *Chem.* Said of compounds in which mercury has a valency of one.

Mercury (mɔ̄·ɹkiŭri), *sb.* ME. [ad. L. *Mercurius*, prob. f. *merc-, merx* merchandise. The use as a plant-name is Eng. only, suggested by L. (*herba*) *mercurialis* (MERCURIAL B. 1).] **I.** The god (and derived senses). **1.** A Roman deity, early identified with the Greek Hermes, the god of eloquence, skill, trading and thieving, the presider over roads, the conductor of departed souls to the Lower World, and the messenger of the gods; represented as a young man with winged sandals and a winged hat, and bearing the caduceus. **2.** A statue or image of Mercury; *spec.* = HERMA; hence, †a sign-post 1644. 3. *transf.* a. A messenger or news-bearer 1594. b. A guide or conductor 1592. †c. A dexterous thief. B. JONS. †d. A hawker of pamphlets, etc. –1721. 4. The title of certain journals. †Formerly also *gen.* = newspaper. 1643.

1. Now M. indue thee with leasing SHAKS. 3. a. *Rich. III*, II. i. 88. But what saies shee to mee? be briefe my good shee-Mercurie SHAKS. 4. Mercuries of furthest Regions BUTLER.

II. The planet. 1. *Astr.* The planet nearest to the sun, and the smallest of the major planets. late ME. 2. *Her.* The name for the tincture purpure in blazoning by the names of the heavenly bodies 1562.

III. The metal, etc. 1. The heavy silver-white liquid metal otherwise called QUICK-SILVER. It absorbs other metals, forming amalgams, and is commonly obtained by sublimation from cinnabar, its most important ore. Chem. symbol Hg (*hydrargyrum*). By alchemists represented by the sign of the planet Mercury (☿). late ME. b. A preparation of the metal or of one of its compounds (e. g. *m. sublimate*) used in medicine 1699. c. The column of mercury in a barometer or thermometer. Also *fig.* 1704. 2. *Old Chem.* a. One of the five elementary 'principles' of which all material substances were supposed to be compounded; also called *spirit* 1471. †3. *fig.* as an emblem of sprightliness, volatility, inconstancy, wittiness, etc. –1797.

3. He [Buckingham] was so full of m. that he could not fix long in any friendship or to any design BURNET.

IV. As a plant-name. 1. a. The pot-herb ALLGOOD, *Chenopodium Bonus-Henricus* (English, False M.). late ME. b. Any plant of the genus *Mercurialis*, esp. *M. perennis* (Dog's M.) 1548.

Hence †**Me·rcury** *v. trans.* to wash with a preparation of mercury B. JONS.

Mercy (mɜ̄·ɹsi). [ME. *merci*, a. F. *merci*, earlier *mercit* :—L. *mercedem* (nom. *merces*) reward, fee, (in Christian L.) pity, etc.] 1. Forbearance and compassion shown by one person to another who is in his power and who has no claim to receive kindness. b. *spec.* God's pitiful forbearance towards His creatures ME. 2. Disposition to forgive; mercifulness ME. 3. The clemency or forbearance of a conqueror, which he can extend or not as he thinks fit ME. 4. An act of mercy; esp. one vouchsafed by God to His creatures; a gift of God, a blessing ME. †5. = AMERCEMENT –1768. †6. Thanks (*rare*) –1500.

1. Phr. *To have m. on, upon, †of; to take m. on, show m.*, etc. *In m. (to)*, in the exercise of m. In m. to him, let us drop the subject *Junius Lett.* b. Lorde haue mercie vpon vs *Bk. Com. Prayer.* 2. Phr. *Of* (or *†for*) *one's m.* The taste whereof, God of his mercy giue You patience to indure SHAKS. †*To cry (one) m.*: to beg for pardon or forgiveness. Hence = 'to beg (one's) pardon'; often *colloq.* with 'I' omitted. Oh, cry you m., sir, I haue mistooke SHAKS. *Mercy* (ellipt.) = 'may God have m.!' Also *m. on us! for m.'s sake! lord-a-m.! m. me!* 3. Phr. †*To take to* (or *into*) *m.*: to extend pardon to (one who yields at discretion); to give quarter to. †(*To yield*) *to* or *upon m.*, (to surrender) at discretion. †*At m.*: (that has surrendered) at discretion; at the disposal of a victor or superior; on sufferance, liable to interference. The linen of the North, a trade casual, corrupted, and at m. SWIFT. *At the m. of (a person)*: liable to any treatment he may choose to employ. So †*in the m. of*; (*to leave* or *trust*) *to the m.* iron. *the tender mercies, of.* Leaving the civil service at the m. of a partisan chief BRYCE. 4. What a m. it was that I held the ace of spades! 1811.

Phr. *Works of m.* (also †*deeds*, †*duties of m.*, and simply †*mercies*): acts of compassion towards suffering fellow-creatures. *Sisters of M.*, title of a R. C. sisterhood founded at Dublin in 1827; *pop.*, the members of any nursing sisterhood. *House of M.*, a penitentiary or house of refuge.

Comb.: †m.-stool, -table = MERCY-SEAT (*fig.*); †-stroke, a *coup de grâce*.

Mercy-seat. 1530 (Tindale, *Ex.* xxv. 17, after Luther's *Gnadenstuhle*). The golden covering placed upon the Ark of the Covenant and regarded as the resting-place of God. Hence applied to the throne of God in heaven, and to Christ as 'the propitiation for our sins'.

†**Merd.** 1477. [a. F. *merde* :—L. *merda* dung.] Dung, excrement –1621.

Mere (mɪəɹ), *sb.*[1] [OE. *mere* str. masc., sea :—OTeut. **mari-* :—**mori-* or **məri-*, repr. in L. *mare* neut., etc.] †1. The sea –ME. 2. A sheet of standing water; a lake, pond. Now chiefly *poet.* and *dial.* OE. †3. An arm of the sea –1676. 4. A marsh, a fen. Now *dial.* ME.

2. Sometimes on lonely mountain-meres I find a magic bark TENNYSON.

Mere, mear (mɪəɹ), *sb.*[2] *arch.* and *dial.* Also meer(e. [OE. (*ge*)*mǣre*, str. neut. :—OTeut. *(*ga*)*mairjom*, cogn. w. L. *murus* (:—**moiros*) wall.] 1. A boundary; also, a landmark. b. *spec.* A green balk or road, serving as a boundary 1607. 2. *Derbysh. Lead-mining.* A measure of land containing lead-ore 1653.

Mere (mɪəɹ), *a.* and *adv.* late ME. [ad. L. *merus.*] A. *adj.* 1. Pure, unmixed, undiluted. 2. Performed or exercised by a person or persons specified without the help of any one else; sole. Chiefly *Law*, in *m. motion*, etc. 1444. 3. *Law. M. right*: right as dist. from possession 1559. †4. That is what it is in the full sense of the term; nothing less than; absolute, entire, sheer, perfect, etc. –1775. 5. That is barely or only what it is said to be; nothing more than 1581.

1. Meere wine ful of the grape HOLLAND. 2. We were wrong if of our m. motion we..fought with you, and ravaged your land JOWETT. 4. *Oth.* II. ii. 3. 5. Decorum's turn'd to m. civility GRAY. The merest nobody 1868.

†B. *adv.* = MERELY –1635.

Mere, mear (mɪəɹ), *v. Obs.* exc. *dial.* OE. [f. MERE *sb.*[2]] 1. *trans.* To mark *out* (land) by meres or boundaries. †2. *intr.* To abut *upon*; to be bounded *by* –1713.

1. This purchase will..meare and bounde his owne [property] EARL OF CORK.

Mere, obs. var. of MARE.

†**Mered,** *ppl. a.* Also **meered.** 1606. [perh. corrupt.] *The m. question*: either (*a*) the sole (MERE *a.*) ground of dispute; or (*b*) the matter to which the dispute is limited (MERE *v.*). *Ant. & Cl.* III. xiii. 10.

Merel (me·rəl). late ME. [a. OF. *merel* (F. *méreau*).] One of the counters used in the game called *merels*, which is played by two persons (cf. MORRIS *sb.*[2]).

Merely (mɪə·ɹli), *adv.* 1546. [f. MERE *a.* + -LY[2].] †1. Without admixture or qualification –1645. †2. Absolutely; altogether –1788; †actually –1601. 3. Only (what is referred to) and nothing more. Often after *not* 1580.

1. Such things as are not m., but mixedly Divine 1637. 3. The multitudes who read m. for the sake of talking JOS. BUTLER.

‖ **Merenchyma** (mĕre·ŋkimă). 1839. [mod. L., f. Gr. μέρος part + *-enchyma* in PARENCHYMA.] *Bot.* Tissue consisting of ellipsoidal and spheroidal cells. **Merenchy·matous** *a.*

Meresman (mɪə·ɹzmæ̆n). *Obs.* exc. *dial.* 1867. [f. *mere's*, gen. of MERE *sb.*[2] + MAN.] A man appointed to find out the exact boundaries of a parish, etc.

Merestone (mɪə·ɹstōun). *arch.* and *dial.* OE. [f. MERE *sb.*[2] + STONE.] A stone set up as a landmark.

Meretricious (merĭtri·ʃəs), *a.* 1626. [f. L. *meretricius* (f. *meretric-*, *-trix* harlot, f. *mereri* to serve for hire) + -OUS.] 1. Of, pertaining to, befitting, or of the character of a harlot. 2. Alluring by false show; showily attractive 1633.

2. The style he aims at is gaudy and m. 1846. Hence **Meretri·cious-ly** *adv.*, **-ness.**

‖ **Meretrix** (me·rĭtriks). *Pl.* **meretrices** (merĭtrəi·sīz). [L.] A prostitute, harlot.

Merganser (məɹgæ·nsəɹ). 1752. [mod.L., f. L. *mergus* diving-bird + *anser* goose.] Any bird of the genus *Mergus* or subfamily *Merginæ*, fish-eating ducks of great diving powers, with long narrow serrated bill hooked at the tip, inhabiting the northern parts of the Old World and N. America; esp. *M. merganser*, the common m. or GOOSANDER.

Merge (mɜ̄ɹdʒ), *v.* 1636. [ad. L. *mergere* to dip, plunge. Senses 2 and 3 come through Law Fr. *merger*, earlier translated 'drown'.] †1. *trans.* To plunge or sink *in* a (specified) activity, environment, etc.; to immerse –1751. 2. *Law.* To sink (a lesser estate, title, etc.) in a greater one. Hence *gen.*, to cause (something) to lose its own character or identity in something else. 1728. 3. *intr.* In *Law*, to be sunk in a greater title, estate, etc. Hence *gen.*, to sink and disappear by absorption *in* or *into* something else. 1726.

2. Their object is to m. all natural and all social sentiment in inordinate vanity BURKE. 3. Serfdom had merged..into free servitude FROUDE. Hence **Me·rgence**, the action of merging or condition of being merged.

Merger (mɜ̄·ɹdʒəɹ). 1728. [Law Fr.; see MERGE *v.* and -ER[4].] 1. *Law.* Extinguishment of a right, estate, contract, action, etc. by absorption in another. b. *U.S.* The consolidation of one firm or trading company with another 1889. 2. *gen.* An act of merging; the fact of being merged 1881.

Mericarp (me·rikāɹp). 1832. [a. F. *méricarpe*, irreg. f. Gr. μέρος part + καρπός fruit.] *Bot.* A portion of a fruit which splits away as a perfect fruit; *esp.* each of the two one-seeded carpels which constitute the fruit in umbelliferous plants.

Meridian (mĕri·diăn), *sb.* late ME. [MERIDIAN *a.* used ellipt.] 1. Midday, noon. *Obs.* exc. *joc.* b. *Hist.* A midday rest or siesta. [tr. med.L. *meridiana.*] 1798. c. *Sc.* A midday dram 1818. 2. The point at which the sun or a star attains its highest altitude 1450. b. *fig.* Culmination, full splendour 1613. c. The middle period of a man's life; his prime 1645. †3. The south –1601. 4. [Ellipt. for *m. circle* or *line.*] a. *Astr.* (More fully *celestial m.*) The great circle (of the celestial sphere) which passes through the celestial poles and the zenith of any place on the earth's surface. b. (More fully *terrestrial m.*) The great circle (of the earth) which lies in the plane of the celestial m. of a place, and which passes through the place and the poles; also often applied to that half of this circle that extends from pole to pole through the place. late ME.

So named because the sun crosses it at noon. A globe or map has usually a number of meridians drawn upon it at certain intervals on a parallel from the *first m.*, i.e. the m. (in British maps the m. of Greenwich) conventionally determined to be of longitude 0°.

c. *transf.* (*a*) Occas. applied to any great circle of a sphere that passes through the poles, or to a line, on a surface of revolution, that is in a plane with its axis 1721. (*b*) *Magnetic m.*: the great circle of the earth that passes through any point on its surface and the magnetic poles 1704. d. A graduated ring or semicircle of brass in which an artificial globe is suspended 1633. e. *attrib.* 1849. 5. *transf.* and *fig.* A locality or situation having its own particular character; the special character or circumstances of one place, person, etc. as dist. from others. Chiefly in fig. uses of astronomical phr. (see below). 1589.

2. b. I haue touch'd the highest point of all my Greatnesse, And from that full M. of my Glory, I haste now to my Setting SHAKS. c. As for her Age, I believe she was near upon the M. 1703. 4. e. *M. circle*, an astronomical instrument consisting of a telescope carrying a large graduated circle, by which the right ascension and declination of a star may be determined; a transit-circle; **m.-mark**, a mark fixed at some distance due north or south of an astronomical instrument, by pointing at which the instrument is set in the m. 5. A course of anecdotes..such as suited the m. of the..servants' hall W. IRVING. Phr. *Calculated to* or *for the m. of* = suited to the tastes, habits, capacities, etc. of.

Meridian (mĕri·diăn), *a.* late ME. [a. OF. *meridien*, or ad. L. *meridianus*, f. *meridies* midday, noon, dissimilated f. *medidies* (Varro), f. *medii-*, *medius* middle + *dies* day.] 1. Of or pertaining to midday or noon. Now *rare* exc. as in 2. 2. *esp.* Pertaining to the station, aspect, or power of the sun at midday. late ME. b. *fig.* Pertaining to the period of greatest elevation or splendour (of a person, state, etc.) 1672. †c. Consummate –1734. 3. Pertaining to a meridian. Chiefly in collocations orig. referable to sense 2. late ME. b. Passing along a meridian SIR T. BROWNE. 4. Southern, meridional (*rare*) late ME.

1. *M. ring*, a ring so marked within the hoop as to serve the purpose of a sun-dial. 2. Care veils in clouds the sun's m. beam CRABBE. b. The year 1713, when Swift was in his m. altitude EARL ORRERY. c. M. merit 1728. A M. Villain NORTH. 3. *M. circle* = MERIDIAN *sb.* 4. *M. line*: orig. = MERIDIAN *sb.* 4; now usually, a line (on a map, etc.) representing a meridian; also, a line traced on the earth's surface,

indicating the course of a portion of a meridian as ascertained by astronomical observations. *M altitude*: the angular distance between the horizon and the sun at noon, or (in later use) any heavenly body when crossing the meridian. 4. A stranger..Born far beyond the mountains; but his blood Is all m., as if never fann'd By the black wind that chills the polar flood BYRON.

†**Meridie.** [ad. L.] Noon. CHAUCER.

Meridional (mĕri·diŏnăl). late ME. [a. F., ad. late L. *meridionalis*, irreg. f. *meridies*; see MERIDIAN *a.*] **A.** *adj.* **1.** Southern, southerly. **b.** Characteristic of the inhabitants of the south (of Europe) 1847. †**2.** Pertaining to the noontide position of the sun. *M. line* = MERIDIAN *sb.* 4. -1834. **3.** Pertaining to or characteristic of noonday; chiefly *fig.* Now *rare* or *Obs.* 1624. **4.** Of or pertaining to a meridian 1555. **b.** Applied to designate markings on a roundish body that lie in a plane with its axis 1658. **B.** *sb.* An inhabitant of the south; esp. of the south of France 1591.

A. 1. The M. people are, for the most part, black and curled 1653. **b.** A dark, m. physiognomy MOTLEY. **3.** This abbey, when in its m. glory 1762.

Hence **Meri:diona·lity**, the state of being m. or on the meridian; aspect towards the south. **Meri·dionally** *adv.* north and south; also, in the direction of the poles (of a magnet).

‖ **Meringue** (mərǽŋg). 1706. [a. F. *meringue*; etym. unkn.] A delicate confection made of pounded sugar and whites of eggs; *esp.* a small cake made of this. Hence **Meringued** (-æ·ŋgd) *a.*, iced with m.

Merino (mĕrī·no). 1781. [a. Sp. *merino* distinctive name of a breed of sheep which is pastured in winter in Estremadura and in summer in 'la montaña'; cf. *merino* sb. overseer of cattle pastures :—med.L. *majorinus* governor, chief justiciary, f. *major* (cf. MAYOR).] **1.** In full *m. sheep*: A variety of sheep prized for its fine wool, orig. bred in Spain. Also *attrib.* as *m. breed, fleece, wool*, etc. **2.** A soft woollen material like fine French cashmere, orig. of merino wool 1823. **3.** A fine woollen yarn used for hosiery 1886.

Merismatic (merizmæ·tik), *a.* 1849. [f. mod.L. *merisma*, a. Gr., f. μερίζειν to divide into parts; see -ATIC.] *Biol.* Of cells or tissues Having the property of dividing into portions by the formation of internal partitions. Of processes: Involving such division.

Meristem (me·ristem). 1874. [irreg. f. Gr. μεριστός divided, divisible, f. μερίζειν, f. μέρος; cf. PHLOEM, XYLEM.] *Bot.* The unformed growing cellular tissue of the younger parts of plants; merismatic tissue.

Merit (me·rit), *sb.* ME. [a. OF. *merite* (mod.F. *mérite*), ad. L. *meritum*, f. *merere*, *-i*; perh. cogn. w. Gr. μείρεσθαι to receive a share, μέρος share, part.] †**1.** That which is deserved; due reward or punishment -1706. **2.** The condition or fact of deserving; 'character with respect to desert of either good or evil' (T.). Also *pl.* in same sense. Now *rare*. ME. **3.** The quality of deserving well, or of being entitled to reward or gratitude ME. **b.** *spec.* in *Theol.*, the quality, in actions or persons, of being entitled to reward from God ME. **4.** Excellence, worth. late ME. **5.** Something which entitles to reward or gratitude. Chiefly *pl.*; *spec.* in *Theol.*, good works as entitling to reward from God; also, the righteousness and sacrifice (of Christ) as 'imputed' to sinners ME. **6.** An excellence 1700.

1. Heere men may seen how synne hath his merite! CHAUCER. **2.** Phr. *The merits*, rarely †*the m.* (of a case, question, etc.): chiefly in *Law*, the intrinsic rights and wrongs of the matter. Hence, *to discuss, judge* (a proposal, etc.) *on its merits*, i.e. with regard only to its intrinsic excellences or defects. **3.** The principle of promotion by m. 1881. **4.** A Woman of Merit STEELE. **5.** MILT. *P. L.* III. 290. **6.** Would you ask for his merits? Alas! he had none GOLDSM. Phr. *To make a m. of*: to represent (some action of one's own) as meritorious.

Merit (me·rit), *v.* 1484. [a. F. *mériter*, f. *mérite* MERIT *sb.*] †**1.** *trans.* To reward, recompense -1611. **2.** = DESERVE *v.* 1 and 2. 1526. **3.** *absol.* or *intr.* To be deserving of good or evil 1599. **4.** *trans.* To earn by meritorious action; *spec.* in *Theol.*, to become entitled to (reward) at the hands of God; also, of Christ, to obtain by his merits (spiritual blessings) for mankind 1543. **5.** *intr.* To acquire merit; to become entitled to reward, gratitude, or commendation. *Obs.* exc. *Theol.* 1526.

2. To do aught may m. praise MILT. He merited ..to be trusted DE FOE. The thing merited confirmation TUCKER. **3.** Die! as thy frailties m. BOWEN. Phr. *To m. well* (*of* a person). **5.** I..am resolved that none shall m. at my Expence SWIFT. So **Me·ritable** *a.* = MERITORIOUS (now *rare*). **Me·ritedly** *adv.*

Me·rit-mo:nger. *contemptuous.* 1552. One who trades in merits; one who seeks to merit salvation or eternal reward by good works.

Meritorious (meritō^ə·riəs), *a.* late ME. [f. L. *meritorius* (f. *merere*, *-eri* to earn, deserve; see MERIT *sb.* and -ORY [2]) + -OUS.] **1.** Of actions: Productive of merit; serving to earn reward; esp. in *Theol.*, said of good works, penance, etc. †**2.** Of an action or agent: That earns or deserves some specified good or evil. Const. *of.* -1758. **3.** Deserving of reward or gratitude. Now usually: Well-deserving; having merit. (In literary criticism, a term of limited praise.) 1494. †**4.** Merited -1632.

2. *M. cause*: an action or agent that causes by meriting (some good or evil result). His Blood..is the m. cause of mans redemption BUNYAN. **3.** His patience had been most m. HT. MARTINEAU. Hence **Merito·rious-ly** *adv.*, **-ness.**

†**Meritory**, *a.* ME. [a. OF. *meritoire*, ad. L. *meritorius*.] = MERITORIOUS -1523.

Merk(*e*, var. ff. MARK, MIRK.

Merle (mǝ̄ɹl). 1450. [a. F. *merle* :—L. *merulus*, *merula* blackbird or ousel (also sea-carp).] The blackbird, *Turdus merula*. *arch.*

The m., in his noontide bow'r, Makes woodland echoes ring BURNS.

Merlin [1] (mǝ̄·ɹlin). ME. [a. AF. *merilun*, aphet. f. OF. *esmerillon* (mod.F. *émerillon*); an augm. f. Com. Rom. **smerillo*, perh. of Teut. origin.] A small European falcon, *Falco æsalon.*

Merlin [2]. 1644. The name of the soothsayer of the Arthurian legend; used as a title of almanacs, etc.

England's propheticall Merline 1644 (*title*).

†**Me·rling.** ME. [ad. OF. *merlanc* (F. *-an*), f. *merle* :—L. *merula*.] The whiting -1736.

Merlion, marlion (mǝ̄·ɹ-, mā·ɹliən). 1553. [Perh. var. of MERLIN [1].] *Her.* A bird, identical with MARTLET 2, or with the *merlette* of French heraldry.

Merlon (mǝ̄·ɹlən). 1704. [a. F., ad. It. *merlone*, augm. of *merlo* battlement.] The part of an embattled parapet between two embrasures; †a similar structure on a battleship.

Mermaid (mǝ̄·ɹmē^ɪd). late ME. [f. MERE *sb.*[1] + MAID.] **1.** An imaginary species of beings, supposed to inhabit the sea, and to have the head and trunk of a woman, ending in the tail of a fish or cetacean. †In early use often the SIREN of mythology. **2.** A representation of this, esp. *Her.* 1464. **b.** A shop or inn sign. late ME. **3.** *transf.* †**a.** A siren; in 16-17th c. applied to a prostitute. **b.** *joc.* A woman who is at home in the water 1880.

1. Half-hidden, like a m. in sea-weed KEATS. **2. b.** What things have we seen Done at the M.? BEAUMONT. **3.** *Com. Err.* III. ii. 45.

attrib. and *Comb.*: **m.-fish**, the monk-fish or angel-fish, *Rhina squatina*; **m.'s glove**, (*a*) a British sponge, *Halichondria palmata*, somewhat resembling a glove; (*b*) *pl.* = DEAD-MAN'S FINGERS 2; **m.'s head**, one of the small rounded sea-urchins, as *Spatangus cordatus*; **m.'s purse**, the horny egg-case of a skate, ray, or shark, a sea-purse.

Mermaiden (mǝ̄·ɹmē̆d'n). Now *rare*. late ME. = prec. 1, 2.

The cold strange eyes of a little M. M. ARNOLD.

Merman (mǝ̄·ɹmæ̆n). 1601. [f. MERE *sb.*[1] + MAN *sb.*, after MERMAID.] The male of the mermaid.

In *Her.*, the m. (also called *triton* or *Neptune*) is depicted as holding in the right hand a trident, and in the left a conch-shell trumpet.

Mero- [1] (me·ro), bef. a vowel **mer-**, comb. f. Gr. μέρος 'part, fraction', in various technical terms; occas. opp. to HOLO-. **Me·roblast** [Gr. βλαστός, -BLAST], *Biol.* an ovum which is only partly germinal; so **Merobla·stic** *a.* undergoing partial segmentation, as an ovum. **Merohe·dral** [Gr. ἕδρα seat, base], **Me:rosymme·trical, Me:rosystema·tic** *adjs.*, *Cryst.* (of a crystal) having less than the full number of faces of the type of symmetry to which it belongs; so **Merohe·dric** *a.*, **Merohe·drism, Merosy·mmetry. Me·rostome** [Gr. στόμα mouth], *Zool.* an arthropod of the order *Merostomata*; so **Merosto·matous, -o·stomous** *adjs.*

Mero- [2] (mī^ə·ro, mi^ə·rǫ·), comb. f. Gr. μηρός 'thigh', occurring in certain mod. scientific terms. **Me·rocele**, *Path.* femoral hernia; hence **Meroce·lic** *a.* **Merocerite** (-ǫ·sĕrəit) [Gr. κέρας horn], *Zool.* the fourth segment of the antenna of a crustacean; hence **Merocerí·tic** *a.* **Meropodite** (-ǫ·pŏdəit) [Gr. ποδ-, πούς foot], *Zool.* the fourth segment (from the base) of certain limbs of crustaceans; hence **Meropodi·tic** *a.*

‖ **Meros** (mī^ə·rǫs). Also **-us.** 1823. [mod.L., a. Gr. μηρός thigh.] **1.** *Arch.* The plane face between the channels in Doric triglyphs. **2.** *Zool.* A meropodite 1855.

-merous, the ending of the adjs. *dimerous*, etc., used *Bot.* = 'having (a specified number of) parts'. Often written *2-merous*, *five-merous*.

Merovingian (merǒvi·ndʒiăn). 1694. [ad. F. *Mérovingien*, f. med.L. *Merovingi* pl., f. (ult.) the name (in L. form *Meroveus*) of the reputed ancestor of the family.] **A.** *adj.* Pertaining to the line of Frankish kings founded by Clovis, and to the kingdoms reigned over by them in Gaul and Germany from A. D. 500 to A. D. 751-2. In *Palæogr.*, applied to the style of handwriting peculiar to that period. **B.** *sb.* A king or other member of this royal line. In *Palæogr.* = Merovingian script.

Merrily (me·rili), *adv.* late ME. [f. MERRY *a.* + -LY [2].] **1.** In early use: Pleasantly, cheerfully, happily. Now: Joyously, mirthfully, hilariously. †**2.** Jocularly, wittily -1704. **3.** With alacrity; briskly. Somewhat *arch.* 1530.

1. Full m. the humble Bee doth sing SHAKS. M. danced the Quaker's wife, And m. danced the Quaker 17... **3.** The hare..worked very m., and..beat a great favourite 1876.

Merriment (me·rimĕnt). 1576. [f. MERRY *a.* + -MENT.] †**1.** Something that makes mirth; a jest; a piece of fooling; *spec.* a brief comic dramatic entertainment -1632. †**b.** Applied as a title to comic pamphlets or the like -1824. **2.** The action (or †an act) of merry-making, or of making merry over something; jocularity; mirth, fun; †a festivity 1588. †**b.** Entertainment. *Mids. N.* III. ii. 146.

1. Your talke replenished with pleasant meriments 1576. **2.** Your flashes of M. that were wont to set the Table on a Rore SHAKS.

Merriness (me·rinĕs). Now *rare*. ME. [f. MERRY *a.* + -NESS.] The quality or condition of being merry.

Merry (me·ri), *sb.* 1595. [f. F. *merise* apprehended as a pl.] A kind of black cherry.

Merry (me·ri), *a.* and *adv.* [OE. *myr*(*i*)*ge* (:—OTeut. type **murgjo-*), whence *myrgð* MIRTH. Perh. identical with OTeut. **murgjo-* short, and cogn. w. Gr. βραχύς. The mod. form represents a south-eastern dial. variant.] **A.** *adj.* **1.** Of things: Pleasing, agreeable. **b.** Of a saying, jest, etc.: Amusing, diverting. *Obs.* or *arch.*, with mixture of sense 3. 1470. **2.** Of looks or appearance: †Agreeable, bright; hence, expressive of cheerfulness, mirthful (in mod. use merged in sense 3) ME. **3.** Of persons, etc.: Full of animated enjoyment; mirthful, hilarious. Also of disposition: Given to mirth. ME. †**b.** Happy -1634. **c.** Pleasantly amused; hence, facetious. Const. *with, on, upon* (a person). *Obs.* or *arch.* 1607. **d.** Slightly tipsy 1575. **4.** Of times or seasons: Characterized by festivity 1596.

1. Let others then..Extole the merrie Month of May 1567. It was neuer merrie worlde in England, since Gentlemen came vp SHAKS. To mery London, my most kyndly Nurse SPENSER. At the next mery wind tooke shipping HAKLUYT. Phr. *A m. mean*: a happy medium. **b.** The very merriest Passage in the whole Story 1728. **2.** Dark hair, and a m. brown eye HUGHES. **3.** He is melancholy without cause, and m. against the haire SHAKS. Phr. *To make m.* (refl. and intr.): to be festive, to indulge in jollity. *To make m.* (*over*, †*with*): to make fun (of). *The M. Monarch*: Charles II. **c.** I know his Lordship is but m. with

me SHAKS. 4. I wish you a very m. Christmas 1667.
M. dancers, Greek: see the sbs.
Comb., as *m.-conceited, -hearted, m.-mad* adjs.
B. *adv.* = MERRILY ME.

Merry-andrew, Merry-Andrew (meːriˌæ·ndrʊ). 1673. [app. f. MERRY *a.* + *Andrew* proper name.] A buffoon; a clown; prop. (in early use) a mountebank's assistant.

Me·rry-go-round. 1729. 1. A revolving machine carrying wooden horses or cars, on or in which people ride; a roundabout. 2. *fig.* A whirl 1856. Hence **Merry-go-rounder**, a 'lark'. DICKENS.

Merry-make (me·rimeᶦk), *sb. arch.* 1579. [f. vbl. phr. *make merry*, with inversion.] = MERRY-MAKING.

Me·rry-make, *v. rare.* 1714. [f. as prec.] *intr.* To make merry; to be festive. So **Me·rry-maker.**

Me·rry-making, *vbl. sb.* 1714. [f. MERRY *a.* + MAKING *vbl. sb.*] The action of making merry; conviviality; also, a convivial entertainment.

Merry man, me·rryman. late ME. 1. *pl. Merry men*: the companions in arms of a knight, an outlaw chief, etc. 2. (Chiefly *Mr. Merryman.*) A jester or buffoon 1785.
1. Robyn and his mery men 1510.

Merry-meeting. 1653. A convivial gathering.

Merrythought (me·riþǭt). 1607. [f. MERRY *a.* + THOUGHT *sb.*] The FURCULA or forked bone between the neck and breast of a bird; also called the wishbone.
The name has reference to the custom of two persons pulling the furcula of a fowl until it breaks; the notion being that the one who gets the longer piece will either be married first, or will get any wish he may form at the moment.

Me·rry-totter. *dial.* 1440. [f. MERRY *a.* + TOTTER *sb.*] A see-saw; a swing.

Merse (mers). *Sc.* 1810. [Sc. repr. OE. *mersc* MARSH.] Low flat land, usually beside a river or the sea; marsh.
The Merse is the district between the Lammermoors and the Tweed.

Mersion (mɔ̄·ɹʃən). *Obs.* or *rare.* 1659. [a. F., ad. L. *mersionem*, f. *mers-, mergere* to dip, MERGE.] The action, or act, of dipping; *spec.* with reference to baptism.

Merv (mɔ̄ɪv). 1887. [Short for F. (*satin*) *merveilleux.*] A silk material for ladies' dresses and dress-trimmings.

Mervail(e, -veil(l(e, obs. ff. MARVEL.

‖ **Merveilleux, -euse** (mɛrvɛyö, -öz). 1892. [Fr.; see MARVELLOUS.] Names for the extravagantly dressed French fops and fine ladies of the period of the Directory, who affected a revival of the classical costume of ancient Greece.

Merwoman (mɔ̄·ɹwumăn). 1809. [See MER- and cf. G. *meerweib.*] A MERMAID when older or married.

Mes-, comb. f. MESO- before a vowel.

‖ **Mesa** (mē·să). *South. U.S.* 1775. [Sp., lit. 'table':—L. *mensa.*] A high table-land.

Mesaconic (mesăkǫ·nik), *a.* 1854. [f. Gr. μεσός middle + (IT)ACONIC; this acid being intermediate between the itaconic and citraconic acids.] In *m. acid*: an acid, isomeric with itaconic acid, obtained by boiling a weak solution of citraconic acid with nitric acid. Hence **Mesa·conate**, a salt of m. acid.

Mesad (me·sæd), *adv.* 1882. [f. Gr. μέσος + *-ad* as in DEXTRAD.] = MESIAD.

Mesal (me·săl), *a.* 1882. [f. Gr. μέσος + -AL.] = MESIAL. Hence **Me·sally** *adv.*

‖ **Mésalliance** (mezalyāns). 1782. [F., f. *més-* MIS- + *alliance.* Cf. MISALLIANCE.] A marriage with a person of inferior social position.

Mesaraic (mesărē·ik). late ME. [ad. med.L. *mesaraïcus*, a. Gr., f. μεσάραιον, f. μέσον middle + ἀραιά flank, belly.] *Anat.* a. *adj.* = MESENTERIC. b. *sb.* One of the mesaraic veins 1528.

Mesaticephalic (me·sătiˌsĭfæ·lik), *a.* 1878. [f. Gr. μέσατος (superl. of μέσος) + κεφαλή head + -IC.] = MESOCEPHALIC. So **Me·saticephalism, Me·saticephaly**, the condition of being m. **Me·saticephalous** *a.* = MESATICEPHALIC.

‖ **Mescal** (meska·l). Also **mex(i)cal, mezcal.** 1828. [Sp. *mezcal*, a. Mexican *mexcalli.*] A strong intoxicant distilled from the fermented juice of the American aloe.

‖ **Mesdames** (medam). 1573. [F., pl. of MADAME.] 1. The plural of MADAME. 2. Used as pl. of Eng. MRS. 1792.

Meseems (mĭsī·mz), *impers. v. arch.* Also meseemeth. *Pa. t.* meseemed. late ME. [Orig. two words, *me* dative and *seems* 3rd pers. sing. of SEEM *v.* Cf. METHINKS.] It seems to me. (Used with dependent clause or parenthetically.)

†**Me·sel.** ME. [a. OF. *mesel* leprous, leper :—L. *misellus*, dim. of *miser* wretched.] A. *adj.* Leprous –1607. B. *sb.* 1. A leper –1550; *fig.* a foul person –1746. 2. Leprosy; *transf.* an affliction –1530. So †**Me·seled** *ppl. a.* †**Me·selry**, leprosy.

‖ **Mesembryanthemum** (mése·mbriæ·nþĭmŏm, méz-). 1825. [mod.L., miswritten for **mesembrianthemum*, f. (ult.) Gr. μεσημβρία noon + ἄνθεμον flower.] *Bot.* The typical genus of the N.O. *Mesembryaceæ*; a plant of this genus; a fig-marigold. (The flowers open only for a short time at midday; hence the name.)

‖ **Mesencephalon** (mesense·fălǫn). 1846. [mod.L., f. Gr. μέσος + ἐγκέφαλον ENCEPHALON.] *Anat.* The mid-brain. Hence **Mesencepha·lic** *a.*

‖ **Mesenchyma** (mese·ŋkimă). Also **-chyme** (me·seŋkəim). 1888. [mod.L., f. Gr. μέσος + ἔγχυμα infusion.] *Biol.* The cellular tissue which, arising from the hypoblast or the epiblast, constitutes, in some low forms of animal life, the mesoblast. Hence **Mese·nchymal, Mesenchy·matous** *adjs.*

Mesenteric (mesente·rik, mez-), *a.* 1656. [ad. mod.L. *mesentericus*, f. *mesenterium* MESENTERY; see -IC.] Pertaining to, connected with, or affecting the mesentery. So **Mesente·rial** *a.* 1605.

‖ **Mesenteron** (mése·ntĕrǫn, méz-). 1877. [mod.L., f. Gr. μέσος + ἔντερον gut, bowel.] The digestive portion of the primitive alimentary canal.

Mesentery (me·sĕntĕri, me·z-). 1547. [ad. med.L. *mesenterium*, a. Gr., f. μέσος + ἔντερον intestine.] 1. *Anat.* A fold of peritonæum which attaches some part of the intestinal canal to the posterior wall of the abdomen 1547. 2. *Zool.* (*pl.*) The vertical plates which divide the body cavity in actinozoa 1861. vars. **Mesenterium, Mesenterion** (†**Mezentereon**).

Meseraic, -ai(c)k, etc., obs. ff. MESARAIC.

Mesethmoid (mese·þmoid). 1875. [f. Gr. μέσος + ETHMOID.] *Anat.* The middle ethmoid bone. Also *attrib.* in *m. cartilage.*

Mesh (meʃ), *sb.* 1540. [Cogn. w. OE. *max* neut., net, and ON. *mǫskve* (see MASK *sb.*[1]).] 1. One of the open spaces or interstices of a net. Also, the similar space in any network, as a sieve. 1558. b. *pl.* The threads or cords which bound these; hence, network, netting 1602. 2. *fig.* Snare, etc. 1540. 3. *transf.* Network, interlaced structure 1712. 4. *Machinery.* [f. MESH *v.*] Engagement, or working contact, of the teeth of wheels with each other or with the rack; chiefly in *in* (*into*) *mesh* 1875.
2. Here in her haires The Painter plaies the Spider, and hath wouen A golden m. t'intrap the hearts of men SHAKS. The meshes of diplomacy 1897. *Comb.* **m.-connexion,** a method of arranging the coils in a dynamo; **m.-stick,** a stick used to form the m. of nets; **m.-work,** meshes collectively, network. Hence **Me·shy** *a.* consisting of meshes.

Mesh (meʃ), *v.* 1532. [f. MESH *sb.*] 1. *trans.* To catch in the meshes of a net 1547. 2. *transf.* and *fig.* To entangle, involve inextricably 1532. 3. *refl.* and *intr.* (for *refl.* or *pass.*) To become enmeshed or entangled 1589. b. *intr.* (*Machinery.*) Of the teeth of a wheel, etc.: To be engaged *with* another piece of machinery or with another toothed wheel 1875.
2. The Flyes by chance mesht in her hayre DRAYTON.

Mesh, var. of MASH.

Meshed (meʃt), *a.* 1664. [f. MESH *sb.* + -ED[2].] 1. Resembling meshes or network; tangled, intricate; intricately marked. 2. Having meshes.

Mesiad (mī·ziæd, me·siæd), *adv.* 1803. [f. MESI-AL + *-ad* toward. Cf. MESAD.] Towards the median line of a body.

Mesial (mī·ziăl, me·siăl), *a.* 1803. [irreg. f. Gr. μέσος middle + -IAL.] = MEDIAN *a.*[1] 2. Also, situated mesially with respect *to.* Hence **Me·sially** *adv.* in a m. position or direction.

Mesityl (me·sitil). 1838. [f. mod.L. *mesita, mesitēs*, a. Gr. μεσίτης go-between + -YL.] *Chem.* The hypothetical radical of acetone. Hence **Mesitylene** (mĕsi·tilīn), 'a hydrocarbon, isomeric with cumene, produced by the action of sulphuric acid upon acetone' (Watts). **Mesityle·nic** *a.* derived from mesitylene. **Mesity·lic** *a.* derived from or containing m. **Mesi·tylol** = MESITYLENE.

Meslen, etc.: see MASLIN[2].

Mesmerism (me·zmĕriz'm). 1802. [f. F. A. *Mesmer*, an Austrian physician (1734–1815) + -ISM.] The doctrine or system according to which a hypnotic state, usu. accompanied by insensibility to pain and muscular rigidity, can be induced by an influence (orig. known as 'animal magnetism') exercised by an operator over the will and nervous system of the patient; the process or practice of inducing this state, the state so induced, or the influence supposed to operate.
So **Mesme·ric, -ical** *a.* pertaining to, characteristic of, producing, or produced by m. 1829. **Me·smerist,** one who practises m.; *occas.* a believer in m. 1840. **Me·smerize** *v. trans.* to subject to the influence of m. 1829; hence **Me·smeriza·tion, Me·smerizer.**

†**Mesnage,** *sb.* [a. obs. F. *mesnage*, var. of *ménage.*] Economical management. JER. TAYLOR. So †**Mesnage** *v.* to 'husband'; to control, manage –1695.

Mesnalty (mī·nălti). 1542. [a. Law F. *menalte, mesnalte*, f. OF. *mene, mesne* MESNE *a.*, after AF. *comunalte* COMMONALTY.] *Law.* The estate or condition of a mesne lord.

Mesne (mīn), *a.*, *sb.*, and *adv.* late ME. [a. Law F. *mesne*, altered sp. of AF. *meen* MEAN *a.*] A. *adj.* 1. *Feudalism.* a. *M. lord*: a lord who holds an estate of a superior lord 1614. ¶b. *M. tenant*: erron. used for one who holds of a mesne lord 1853. 2. Occurring or performed at a time intermediate between two dates 1548. b. *M. process*: that part of a suit which intervenes between the primary and the final process 1625. 3. Intermediate, intervening: applied to persons 1810.
2. *M. encumbrance*: an encumbrance with a right of priority intermediate between the dates of two other encumbrances. *M. profits*: the profits of an estate received by a tenant in wrongful possession between two dates. 3. M. vendors 1810, lessees 1884.
†B. *sb.* 1. = MEAN *sb.* I. 1, II. 2. –1822. 2. = *M. lord* (see A. 1) –1704.
2. *Writ of m.*: 'an ancient..writ, which lay when the lord paramount distrained on the tenant paravail; the latter had a writ of m. against the m. lord' (Wharton).
†C. *adv.* At a time intermediate (*between* two other times). late ME.–1642.

Meso- (me·so), bef. a vowel occas. **mes-**, comb. form of Gr. μέσος middle, used in scientific terms, many of which have correlates with PRO-, or PROTO-, and META-. **Me·soblast** [-BLAST] *Biol.*, the middle germ-layer of the embryo; hence **Mesobla·stic** *a.* **Mesobra·nchial** *a.* applied to the middle lobe of the branchial region of the carapace of a crab. ‖**Mesocæ·cum** *Anat.* a fold of peritoneum attached to the cæcum. **Me·socarp** [Gr. καρπός fruit] *Bot.* the middle layer of a pericarp. **Mesocepha·lic** [Gr. κεφαλή head] *a.* (*a*) pertaining to the middle region of the head; (*b*) having the cranial cavity of medium capacity or a head of medium proportion; hence **Mesoce·phalism, -ce·phaly.** ‖**Mesoco·lon** *Anat.* a fold of peritoneum attached to the colon; hence **Mesoco·lic** *a.* **Me·soderm** [Gr. δέρμα skin] *Biol.* = *mesoblast*; hence **Mesode·rmal, -de·rmic** *adjs.* **Me·sodont** [Gr. ὀδοντ-, ὀδούς tooth] *a.* *Anthrop.* and *Entom.* having the teeth of medium size. ‖**Mesoga·ster** [Gr. γαστήρ stomach] *Anat.* = *mesogastrium* (*a*). ‖**Mesoga·strium** *Anat.* (*a*) a fold of peritoneum which attaches the stomach to the dorsal wall of the abdomen; (*b*) the umbilical region; hence **Mesoga·stric** *a. Anat.* pertaining to the mesogastrium; also *Zool.* pertaining to the middle gastric lobe of the carapace of a crab. **Mesogna·thic, -gnathous** [Gr. γνάθος jaw] *adjs., Anthrop.* having the jaws slightly projecting; having a gnathic index between 98 and 103. **Mesoli·thic** [Gr. λίθος stone] *a., Archæol.* belonging to a part of the prehistoric 'stone age' between the Palæolithic and the Neolithic. **Mesona·sal** [see NASAL] *a., Anat.* belonging or relating to the middle of the nose. ‖**Mesono·tum** [Gr. νῶτον back] *Entom.* the dorsal portion of the mesothorax; hence **Meso-no·tal** *a.* **Me·sophyll** [Gr. φύλλον leaf] *Bot.* the parenchyma between the epidermal layers of a leaf; hence **Mesophy·llic** *a.* **Me·soplast** [Gr. πλαστός moulded] *Biol.* the nucleus of a cell; hence **Mesopla·stic** *a.* ‖**Mesopo·dium** (also **me·sopod(e)** [Gr. πούς, ποδ- foot] *Zool.* the median region of the foot in molluscs; *Bot.* the intermediate portion of the axis of a phyllopodium; hence **Mesopo·dial** *a.* **Me·sor(r)hine, Mesor(r)hi·nian** [Gr. ῥιν-, ῥίς nose] *Anthrop., a.* having a somewhat broad but long nose, or a nasal index from 45 to 53; *sb.* a m. person. **Mesosei·smal** [Gr. σεισμός earthquake] *a.* pertaining to the centre of intensity of an earthquake. **Me·soseme** [Gr. σῆμα sign, 'index'] *a., Anthrop.* of skulls: having an orbital index from 84 to 89. ‖**Mesoste·rnum** *Entom.* the ventral piece of the middle segment of the thorax in insects; *Anat.* the middle portion of the sternum; hence **Meso-ste·rnal** *a.* and *sb.* **Mesosysto·lic** *a., Path.* occurring in the middle of the systole. **Me·sotherm** [Gr. θερμός hot] *Bot.* a plant requiring a moderately warm temperature. **Mesotho·rax** *Entom.* the middle ring or segment of the thorax of an insect; hence **Mesothora·cic** *a.*

Mesode (me·sǫud). 1850. [ad. Gr. μεσῳδός, f. μεσο- + ᾠδή ODE.] *Gr. Pros.* A portion of a choral ode, coming between the strophe and antistrophe, without anything to correspond with it. Hence **Meso·dic** *a.*

Mesolabe (me·sǫlē¹b). 1579. [ad. L. *mesolabium*, f. Gr. μεσόλαβος (or -ον), f. μέσος middle, mean + λαβ-, λαμβάνειν to take.] An ancient instrument used for ascertaining mean proportionals between two given lines, and for finding roots of quantities geometrically.

Mesology (mesǫ·lŏdʒi). 1811. [f. Gr. μέσον (taken as = 'medium') + -LOGY.] **1.** The science of means (of attaining happiness). Only in Bentham. **2.** The science of the relations between organisms and their environment 1883.

Mesophragm (me·sǒfræm). 1826. [ad. mod.L. *mesophragma* (also used in Eng.), f. Gr. μέσος + φράγμα partition.] *Zool.* **a.** *Entom.* The partition that separates the mesothorax from the metathorax. **b.** In Crustacea, the inner prolongation of the capital of an endosternite 1880.

Mesopotamia (mesǒpǒtē¹·miă). 1854. [a. Gr. μεσοποταμία (sc. χώρα country), f. μέσος middle + ποταμός river.] Name of the tract between the Tigris and the Euphrates. Hence *allusively* of any tract between rivers.

Mesothesis (mesǫ·þ*ĭ*sis). *rare.* 1812. [f. Gr. μέσος + θέσις THESIS.] Something interposed, serving to connect or reconcile antagonistic agencies or principles. So **Mesothe·tic, -ical** *a.* occupying a middle position.

Mesoxalic (mesǫksæ·lik), *a.* 1838. [f. MESO- + OXALIC *a.*] *Chem.* In *m. acid*: a dibasic acid obtained from alloxan. Hence **Meso·xalate**, a salt of m. acid.

‖**Mesozoa** (mesozō̆u·ă), *sb. pl.* 1877. [mod. L., f. Gr. μέσος + ζῷα animals.] *Zool.* Name for forms intermediate in structure between the Protozoa and the Metazoa. Also *sing.* **Meso-zo·on**, one of these.

Mesozoic (mesozō̆u·ik), *a.* 1840. [f. Gr. μέσος + ζωή life + -IC.] *Geol.* Name for the secondary period, intermediate between the Palæozoic and the Cainozoic.

Mesprise, obs. f. MISPRIZE *v.*¹

‖**Mesquin** (mẹskæ̃n), *a.* 1706. [Fr.] Mean, sordid.

†**Mesquita, mesquit**¹. 1477. [a. Sp. *mezquita* and It. *meschita*, ad. African Arab. *masgid*, dial. pronunc. of MASJID.] = MOSQUE -1665.

Mesquite, mesquit² (me·skīt, meskī·t). Also **muskeet**, etc. 1851. [a. Mexican Sp. *mezquite.*] **1.** Either of two leguminous trees growing in S.W. North America, *Prosopis juliflora* (honey mesquite), and *P. pubescens* (screw-pod mesquite). **2.** In full *mesquite-grass*: Any grass growing in the neighbourhood of the mesquite tree, esp. the genera *Bouteloua* and *Buchloe* 1851. **3.** *attrib.*, as **m. bean**, the pod of the mesquite tree, etc. 1854.

Mess (mes), *sb.* ME. [a. OF. *mes* (mod.F. *mets* viand, dish) :—late L. *missum*, neut. pa. pple. of L. *mittere* to send.] **I.** Portion of food, etc. **1.** A serving of food; a course of dishes; a prepared dish. Now only *arch.* exc. as in **2. b.** A quantity (of meat, etc.) sufficient to make a dish. (Now *dial.* and *U.S.*). Also, the quantity of milk given by a cow at one milking 1513. **2.** Applied to a made dish, or to a portion or a kind of liquid, or pulpy food, e. g. milk, broth, porridge, etc. late ME. **b.** A quantity of liquid or mixed food for an animal; a kind of such food 1738. **c.** A concoction, jumble, medley 1828. **3.** A state of confusion or muddle; a condition of embarrassment or trouble 1834. **b.** A dirty or untidy state of things 1851.

1. b. To borrow a messe of Vinegar SHAKS. **2.** *A m. of pottage* (cf. Gen. xxv. 29–34). Som for a messe of potage, with Esau, careth nat to sell the euerlastyng inheritaunce of heuen 1526. **3.** Phr. *To get into a m. To make a m. of*: to bungle (an undertaking).

II. Company of persons eating together. **1.** Orig., each group of four persons (sitting together and helped from the same dishes), into which the company at a banquet was commonly divided. Now only in the Inns of Court, a party of four benchers or four students. Hence, a company of persons who regularly take their meals together. late ME. **b.** In the Army and Navy: Each of the several parties into which a regiment or ship's company is divided, each party taking their meals together 1536. **c.** Without article: The taking of such a meal 1778. **d.** *gen.* = 'Table' (esp. in the sense 'provision of food') 1861. †**2.** *transf.* A set of four persons or things -1661.

1. b. Phr. *To lose the number of one's m.*: to die, be killed. **2.** You three fooles, lackt mee foole, to make vp the messe SHAKS.

Mess (mes), *v.* late ME. [f. MESS *sb.*] **1.** *trans.* To serve up (food); to divide (food) into messes or portions. *Obs.* exc. *dial.* †**2.** To divide (a ship's company) into messes -1690. **3.** *intr.* To take one's meals, esp. as one of a mess; also *rarely* to feed *upon* 1701. **b.** *trans.* To supply with meals 1811. **4.** *intr.* To make a mess; to dabble in water, mud, etc. Also, to 'potter' (const. *about* or with advs. *about, away*). 1853. **5.** *trans.* To make a mess of; to dirty, soil (a thing); to muddle (a business). Also with *up.* 1823.

4. I m. about my flowers and read snatches of French MRS. LYNN LINTON. **5.** Lank told him that he had messed the whole business 1901.

Mess, obs. f. MASS *sb.*¹

Message (me·sĕdʒ), *sb.* ME. [a. F. *message* :—pop.L. *missaticum, f. L. *miss-, mittere* to send.] **1.** An oral or written communication sent from one person to another; also, †intelligence, tidings, news. ¶Often applied to a communication sent by telegraph; hence *transf.* **b.** A divinely inspired communication by a prophet. Also *transf.* 1546. **c.** An official communication from the Sovereign to Parliament, or the like 1625. **2.** The business entrusted to a messenger; a mission, an errand ME. †**3.** One or more messengers or envoys, an embassage -1475.

1. Sometimes from her eyes I did receiue faire speechlesse messages SHAKS. Messages can pass through the brain and the nerves every moment J. TAIT. **b.** Byron and Burns..had a message to deliver 1828. Isaiah's m. is twofold; first ruin and then redemption 1902. **c.** The President, in his m. of the year..referred [etc.] J. M. LUDLOW. **2.** I..ran messages 1840.

Comb.: **m. stick**, a stick carved with significant marks, used, esp. by Australian aborigines, as a means of communication.

Message (me·sĕdʒ), *v.* 1583. [f. MESSAGE *sb.*] **1.** *trans.* To send as a message; to send by messenger; *spec.* to transmit (a sketch, plan, etc.) by means of signalling, telegraphing, etc. **2.** *intr.* To carry a message. DICKENS.

Messageer, -er(e, obs. ff. MESSENGER.

Messalian (mesē¹·liăn), **Massalian** (mæsē¹·liăn). 1591. [ad. late Gr. Μεσσαλιανός, Μασσαλιανός, ad. Syr.; the Gr. writers render the Syrian word εὐχίτης and εὐχόμενος one who prays.] **A.** *sb.* One of an ancient heretical sect, variously identified with the Euchites and with the Hesychasts. **B.** *adj.* Of or pertaining to the Messalians.

Messan (me·săn). *Sc.* Also **-in.** 1500. [a. Gael. *measan.*] A lap-dog; also applied to a person as a term of abuse. Also *m.-dog*, etc.

Messenger (me·sĕndʒəɹ). [ME. *messager, -ier*, a. F. *messager*, f. *message*; see MESSAGE *sb.* For the inserted *n*, cf. *passenger*, etc.] **1.** One who carries a message or goes on an errand; †an envoy, ambassador. **b.** The bearer *of* (a specified message) ME. **c.** *fig.* late ME. †**2.** *esp.* A forerunner, precursor, harbinger. Also *fig.* -1601. **3.** A government official employed to carry dispatches, and, formerly, to apprehend state prisoners; esp. one employed by the Secretaries of State 1535. **4.** An endless rope or chain passing from the capstan to the cable to haul it in. Also, a similar contrivance for hauling in a dredge. 1633. **5.** (In full *m.-bird.*) The secretary-bird 1793.

1. *God's m.*: (*a*) used for ANGEL, q. v.; (*b*) applied to a prophet, or to a clergyman, as charged with a message from God to mankind. **b.** Messengers of Warre SHAKS. **2.** *fig.* Yon grey Lines, That fret the Clouds, are Messengers of Day SHAKS. **3.** *King's* or *Queen's m.*, one who conveys dispatches to or from the Sovereign.

Messet (me·sĕt). *dial.* 1631. [Altered f. MESSAN.] A lap-dog. Also *attrib.*

Messiah (mĕsəi·ă, məs-). Also **Messias**, etc. [ME. *Messie*, a. F. *Messie*, ad. L. (Vulg.) *Messias*, a. Gr. Μεσσίας, ad. Aramaic *m'shīhā*, Heb. *māshīªh* anointed, f. *māshah* to anoint. The form *Messias* was used in John i. 41 and iv. 25 by Wyclif after the Vulgate, and by later translators. The form *Messiah*, invented by the Geneva translators of 1560, as looking more Hebraic than *Messias*, eventually became the only current form.] The Hebrew title (= 'anointed') applied in the O.T. to a promised deliverer of the Jewish nation, and hence to Jesus of Nazareth as such deliverer. Hence *transf.* an expected liberator of an oppressed people or country. (Written with capital M.)

Against the Lord and his M. dear MILT. Hence **Messi·ahship**, the character or office of the or a M.

Messianic (mesiæ·nik), *a.* 1834. [ad. mod.L. *Messianicus*, f. *Messias*; see prec. and -IC.] Of, pertaining to, or relating to the Messiah. Hence **Messia·nically** *adv.* as referring to the Messiah. **Messi·anism**, belief in a coming Messiah.

[Psalm lxxxvii] seems clearly Messianic COLERIDGE.

‖**Messidor** (mẹsidǫr). 1838. [Fr.; f. L. *messis* harvest + Gr. δῶρον gift.] The tenth month of the French revolutionary calendar.

Messieurs, *sb. pl.* 1624. [a. F., pl. of MONSIEUR.] **1.** (mẹsyö) The pl. of MONSIEUR. (As a prefixed title, now usu. abbrev. *MM.*, as in Fr.) **2.** (me·səɪz, me·syəɪz). See MESSRS.

‖**Messire** (mesīr). Now only *Hist.* 1477. [Fr.; repr. the nom. (L. *meus senior*), while *monsieur* represents the accus. (L. *meum seniorem*).] A title of honour (= Sir) prefixed to the name of a French noble of high rank, and later to the names of persons of quality, and members of the learned professions; also used as a form of address.

Mess-John: see *Mas John* (MAS 2).

Messmate (me·smē¹t). 1746. [f. MESS *sb.* + MATE *sb.*] A companion at meals; one of a mess, esp. of a ship's mess.

Messrs. (me·səɪz). 1779. Abbrev. of MESSIEURS used as pl. of MR.

Messuage (me·swĕdʒ). late ME. [a. AF. *messuage, mesuage*, prob. orig. misreading of *mesnage* MENAGE.] Orig., the portion of land intended as a site for a dwelling-house and its appurtenances. In mod. legal use, a dwelling-house with its outbuildings and curtilage and the adjacent land assigned to its use. *Capital m.*: that occupied by the owner of a property containing several messuages.

They wedded her to sixty thousand pounds, To lands in Kent and messuages in York TENNYSON.

Messy (me·si), *a.* 1843. [f. MESS *sb.* + -Y[1].] Of the nature of a mess; untidy. Hence **Me·ssiness.**

Mest(e, obs. ff. MOST.

Mestee: see MUSTEE.

Mester, obs. var. of MISTER *sb.*[1]

‖**Mestizo** (mestī·zo). 1588. [Sp. *mestizo*, Pg. *mestiço*:—pop.L. **mixticius*, f. L. *mixtum*, *miscere* to mix.] A Spanish or Portuguese half-caste; now chiefly, the offspring of a Spaniard and an American Indian. **b.** *attrib.*, as **m.-wool**, S. American wool from mixed breeds of sheep. So ‖**Mesti·za**, a woman of the mestizo race 1582.

Mestlen, -lin(g, -lyon, obs. ff. MASLIN 1, 2.

Met (met), *sb. Obs.* exc. *dial.* [OE. *ge-met* neut.:—OTeut. **ga-metom*, f. root **met-* METE *v.*] = MEASURE *sb.*

†**Met**, *ppl. a.* late ME. [See METE *v.*[1]] Measured -1460.

Met, pa. t. and pple. of MEET *v.*

‖**Meta** (mī·tă). *Pl.* **metæ** (mī·tī). 1577. [L.] *Rom. Antiq.* One of the conical columns set in the ground at each end of the Circus, to mark the turning-place in a race. Hence *transf.* A boundary.

Meta- (me·tă), *prefix*, bef. a vowel normally **met-** (also bef. *h*, the resulting *meth-* being pronounced meþ), repr. Gr. μετα-, μετ- (μεθ-), occurring separately as the prep. μετά with, after. Its chief senses are: sharing, action in common; pursuit or quest; and *esp.* change (of place, order, condition, or nature), corresp. to L. *trans-*. Occas. it has the sense 'after' or 'behind', as in *metaphrenon* (see 3 below).

1. In supposed analogy to METAPHYSICS (misapprehended as meaning 'the science of that which transcends the physical'), *meta-* has been prefixed to the name of a science, to form a designation for a higher science of the same nature but dealing with ulterior problems. Examples are **Metabiolo·gical** *a.*, **Meta-che·mistry, Metalo·gic, Metalo·gical** *a.*, **Metamathema·tics, Metapheno·menal** *a.*, **Metaphysio·logy.**

2. *Path.* Used to form adjs. applicable to diseases or symptoms, with the sense 'arising subsequently to'; e.g. **Meta-arthri·tic,** following on gout, **Metapneumo·nic**; etc.

3. *Anat.* and *Zool.* Used to express the notion of 'behind'; also often that of 'hinder', 'hindmost', 'situated at the back'; sometimes correlated with PRO- and MESO-. **Metabra·nchial** [Gr. βράγχια gills], *a.* applied to a division of the carapace of a crab situated behind and to one side of the mesobranchial lobe. ‖**Metacro·mion,** a process of the spine of the scapula behind the acromion in some mammals 1868. ‖**Metane·phron, -ne·phros** [Gk. νεφρός kidney], the hinder division of the typical segmental organ in vertebrates, from which are developed the kidney and the ureter 1877. ‖**Metano·tum** [Gk. νῶτον back], *Entom.* the dorsal part of the metathorax in insects 1836. **Me·taphragm** [Gk. φράγμα partition], *Entom.* the wall that separates the abdomen from the thorax in insects 1826. ‖**Meta·phrenon, -phrenum** [Gk. φρήν midriff], the part of the back that is behind the diaphragm 1621. **Metapneu·stic** [Gr. πνευστικός relating to breathing] *a.*, *Entom.* having a single pair of spiracles situated at the posterior end of the abdomen. ‖**Metapo·physis,** *pl.* **-ses** [APOPHYSIS], a small vertebral prominence 1866. **Me·tapore** [PORE], an orifice in the pia mater covering the fourth ventricle of the brain. ‖**Metaptery·gium,** *Ichth.* the hindmost section of the pterygium in certain fishes 1866. ‖**Metatho·rax,** *Entom.* the hindmost segment of the thorax in insects 1816; so **Metathora·cic** *a.*

4. *Bot.* and *Zool.* Used with the sense 'later', 'subsequent', 'more developed'. **Me·taphase, Meta·phasis,** the separation of the daughter chromosomes in nuclear division. **Me·taphyte,** ‖**Meta·phyton,** a multicellular plant; hence **Metaphy·tic** *a.*

5. *Geol.* In imitation of METAMORPHISM, used irreg. to form words referring to certain specific varieties of metamorphic processes, as **Metache·mic** *a.* applied to chemical metamorphism; etc.

6. In *Chemistry.* **a.** Used to designate compounds derived from, metameric with, or resembling in composition those to the names of which it is prefixed. **Metacre·sol,** one of the three modifications of cresol (*ortho-*, *meta-*, and *paracresol*). **Metage·latin,** a form of gelatin that remains fluid, used in photography. **Metalbu·min, -men,** a form of albumin found in dropsical fluids, etc. 1854. **Meta·ldehyde,** a solid isomeric with aldehyde 1841. **Metape·ctin,** an isomeric form of pectin produced by boiling with dilute acids. More systematically, *meta-* is used to distinguish one class of acids and their corresponding salts from another class (the ORTHO- acids) consisting of the same elements in different proportions, the *meta-* acids containing one, two, or three molecules of water less than the *ortho-* acids: as *metantimonic*, *metapectic*, *metaphosphoric*, *metasilicic*, *metatitanic* acids.

b. In the names of isomeric benzene di-derivatives, *meta-* denotes those compounds in which the two radicals that replace hydrogen in the benzene-ring are regarded as attached to alternate carbon atoms. The number of these is unlimited.

7. *Min.* **a.** Used to designate a mineral that is found along with another or is closely related to it, as in *metabrushite* (a calcium phosphate allied to brushite), etc. **b.** Proposed by Dana to designate minerals produced by metamorphism of sediments, as *metasyenite*, etc.

‖**Metabasis** (metæ·băsis). 1577. [mod.L., a. Gr. μετάβασις, related to μεταβαίνειν, f. μετα- META- + βαίνειν to go. Cf. BASIS.] A transition, *spec.* in *Rhet.*, from one subject or point to another, in *Med.*, from one remedy, etc. to another. So **Metaba·tic** *a.*, *Rhet.* pertaining to m.

‖**Metabola** (metæ·bŏlă), *sb. pl.* Formerly metabolia. 1817. [mod.L., neut. pl. of μεταβόλος changeable.] *Entom.* A division of insects comprising those which undergo complete metamorphosis.

Metabolic (metăbǫ·lik), *a.* 1743. [ad. Gr. μεταβολικός changeable.] **1.** Pertaining to or involving transition. **2.** *Biol.* and *Chem.* Pertaining to, involving, characterized or produced by, metabolism 1845. **3.** *Entom.* = METABOLOUS 1882. So **Metabo·lical** *a.*

Metabolism (metæ·bŏliz'm). 1878. [f. Gr. μεταβολή change + -ISM.] *Biol.* and *Chem.* The process, in an organism or a single cell, by which nutritive material is built up into living matter (*constructive m.*, *anabolism*), or by which protoplasm is broken down into simpler substances to perform special functions (*destructive m.*, *katabolism*). Hence **Meta·bolite,** a product of m. **Meta·bolize** *v.* to affect by m.

Metabolous (metæ·bŏləs), *a.* 1861. [f. Gr. μεταβόλος + -OUS.] *Entom.* Undergoing complete metamorphosis; belonging to the division METABOLA of insects.

Metacarpal (metăkā·ɹpăl). 1739. [f. next + -AL.] **a.** *adj.* Of or belonging to the metacarpus. **b.** *sb.* A metacarpal bone 1854.

‖**Metacarpus** (metăkā·ɹpŏs). Also †**Metacarp.** 1676. [mod.L., altered f. Gr. μετακάρπιον.] *Anat.* That part of the hand which is situated between the wrist and the fingers: in vertebrates generally, that part of the manus which is situated between the carpus and the phalanges.

Metacentre (me·tăsentəɹ). 1794. [ad. F. *métacentre*, f. *méta-* META- + *centre* CENTRE.] *Hydrostatics* and *Shipbuilding.* The limiting position of the point of intersection between the vertical line passing through the centre of gravity of a floating body when in equilibrium and the vertical line drawn through the centre of buoyancy when the body is slightly displaced; the *shifting centre.* To ensure stable equilibrium this point must be above the centre of gravity. **Metace·ntral, Metace·ntric** *adjs.*

Metacetone (metæ·sītōun). 1838. [a. F. *métacétone*; see META- 6 and ACETONE.] *Chem.* A colourless oil obtained by the distillation of sugar or starch with quicklime.

Metachromatism (metăkrōu·mătiz'm). 1876. [f. META- + Gr. χρωματ-, χρῶμα colour + -ISM.] Change or variation of colour.

Metachronism (metæ·krŏniz'm). 1617. [ad. med.L. *metachronismus*, abnormally f. Gr. μετάχρονος, -χρόνιος happening later, f. μετα- META- + χρόνος time.] An error in chronology consisting in placing an event later than its real date. (Cf. PARACHRONISM.)

Metacism (me·tăsiz'm). 1844. [ad. late L. *metacismus*, corruptly ad. late Gr. μυτακισμός fondness for the letter μ, f. μῦ name of the letter. Cf. ITACISM.] The placing of a word with final *m* before a word beginning with a vowel; regarded as a fault in Latin prose composition.

‖**Metacrasis** (metăkrē·sis). 1886. [f. META- + CRASIS.] *Geol.* Recombination, denoting changes such as the conversion of mud into a mass of mica, quartz, and other silicates.

Metagastric (metăgæ·strik), *a.* 1877. [f. META- + Gr. γαστήρ belly + -IC.] *Zool.* Applied to portions of the carapace in brachyurous crustaceans situated towards the hinder part of the gastrohepatic area.

Metage (mī·tėdʒ). 1527. [f. METE *v.*[1] + -AGE.] **1.** The action of measuring officially the content or weight of a load of grain, coal, etc.; the duty paid for this.

Metagenesis (metădʒe·nĭsis). 1849. [mod. L.; see META- and GENESIS.] *Biol.* Alternation of generations; alternation between sexual and asexual reproduction. So **Me:tagene·tic** *a. Zool.*, pertaining to, characterized by, or involving m. **Metagene·tically** *adv.*

Metageo·metry. 1882. [See META-.] The geometry of non-Euclidean space. So **Metageo·meter, -me·trical** *a.*

Metagnathous (metæ·gnăþəs), *a.* 1872. [f. Gr. μετά META- + γνάθος jaw + -OUS.] Having the tips of the mandibles crossed.

†**Metagra·mmatism.** 1605. [ad. Gr. μεταγραμματισμός (Galen), f. μετα- META- + γραμματ-, γράμμα letter; see -ISM.] The transposition of letters in a word or phrase; anagrammatism.

Metagraphy (metæ·grăfi). 1872. [f. Gr. μετα- META- + -γραφία writing.] Transliteration. Hence **Metagra·phic** *a.*

Metagrobolize (metăgrǫ·bŏləiz), *v.* 1653. [ad. obs. F. *metagraboulizer* (Rabelais).] **a.** To puzzle, mystify. **b.** To puzzle out.

‖**Métairie** (metęrī). 1817. [Fr., f. *métayer.*] A farm held on the MÉTAYER system.

Metal (me·tăl, me·t'l), *sb.* (and *a.*) Also †mettle, etc. ME. [a. OF. *metal*, *metail* (mod.F. *métal*), ad. L. *metallum*, ad. Gr. μέταλλον mine; app. conn. w. μεταλλᾶν to seek after.] **1.** Any member of the class of substances represented by gold, silver, copper, iron, lead, and tin, and orig. confined to these bodies together with certain alloys. In *Chem.* the 'metals' are a division of the 'elements' or simple substances. Of these some possess all the properties, such as high specific gravity and density, fusibility, malleability, etc., formerly viewed as characteristic of a metal, while others possess hardly any of them, the metallic lustre being perhaps the most constant. In pop. lang. not applied when the identity of the element is disguised in combination. **b.** Metallic substance ME. **c.** *pregnantly* for: Precious metal, gold. SHAKS. **d.** *spec.* = CAST-IRON 1794. **e.** *fig.*, *esp.* the 'stuff' of which a man is made 1552. **2.** *Her.* Either of the tinctures or and argent 1450. **3.** = ORE (after Spanish) 1604. †**4.** A mine. JER. TAYLOR. **5.** With qualification: A specific alloy of two or more metals used in an art or trade. Also as short for any of these. 1729. **6.** An object made of metal (see below) 1574. **7.** *Gunnery.* The metal composing the barrel of a gun 1644. **b.** The aggregate number or effective power of the guns on a ship of war 1757. **8.** Material, matter, substance, *esp.* earthy matter 1570. **9.** The material used for making glass, in a molten state 1589. **10.** Hardened clay, shale 1708. **11.** Broken stone used for macadamizing roads or as ballast for a railway. Also *road m.* 1838.

1. †*Noble* or *perfect metals*: gold and silver, as being the only metals that were known to endure any ordinary fire without being 'destroyed'; opp. to *base* or *imperfect metals.* **b.** The hammer breaks mettall, and the fire melts it 1649. **e.** We are.. Mettall, Marcus, steele to the very backe SHAKS. **4.** †Phr. *To condemn to metals* [L. *condemnare ad metalla*]. **5.** *Bath, Britannia, Dutch, white, yellow,* etc. *m.*: see these words. Also BELL-METAL, GUN-METAL, PRINCE'S *metal.* **6.** †**a.** A reflector of a telescope; A very distinct and perfect two-foot m. 1777. **b.** *pl.*

The rails of a railway, tramway, etc.; He found the deceased lying on the road, between the 'metals' 1841. 7. *Line of m.*: an imaginary line drawn along the surface of the m. between the two sights. So *over, undermetal.* b. *Heavy m.*: see HEAVY *a.*[1] 5. *attrib.* and *Comb.*, as *m.-broker*, *-bearing* adj., *-yield*; also, **m. bath,** a bath (of mercury, lead, fusible alloys, etc.) used in chemical operations requiring a higher temperature than a water bath can give; **m. bed,** the bed of broken stone in a macadamized road; **m. polish,** a polish used for brightening metals; **m. value,** value (of coin) merely as m.; **-work,** (artistic) work in m.

Metal, *v.* 1617. [f. the sb.] **1.** *trans.* To furnish or fit with metal. **2.** To make or mend (a road) with 'metal' 1806.

‖ **Metalepsis** (metăle·psis). 1577. [a. L., Gr. μετάληψις, f. μεταλαμβάνειν to substitute, f. μετα- META- + λαμβάνειν to take.] *Rhet.* A figure mentioned by Quintilian, consisting in the metonymical substitution of one word for another which is itself figurative.

Metaleptic (metăle·ptik), *a.* 1656. [ad. mod.L. *metalepticus*, a. Gr., f. μεταλαμβάνειν; see METALEPSIS.] **a.** Participating or acting with: *spec.* applied to muscles. **b.** Pertaining to metalepsis. Hence **Metale·ptically** *adv.* by metalepsis 1655.

Metallic (mĭtæ·lik), *a.* (*sb.*) 1567. [ad. L. *metallicus*, a. Gr., f. μέταλλον METAL *sb.*] **1.** Of, pertaining to, or containing a metal or metals; of the nature of or resembling a metal. **b.** Involving coin as dist. from paper money 1790. **2.** Having the form or outward characters of a metal 1797. **3.** Of a quality: Such as is characteristic of metals (see quots.) 1794. **4.** Yielding or producing metal 1689. †**5.** Connected with mining or metallurgy -1834. **6.** *sb. pl.* Articles or substances made of or containing metal 1612; *U.S.* powdered metal for lining the bearings of machine shafts 1894.

1. *M. pencil*: one with a tip made of lead or alloy, for writing indelibly on paper with a prepared surface. So *m. book, paper.* **3.** *M. lustre*, the peculiar sheen characteristic of metals. Their deep m. voices (i.e. voices of a harsh unmusical timbre) W. IRVING. M. (i.e. 'coppery') taste 1803. *fig.* With m. beliefs and regimental devotions CLOUGH. So †**Meta·llical** *a.*, **Meta·llically** *adv.*

Metalliferous (metăli·ferəs), *a.* 1656. [f. L. *metallifer* (f. *metallum* + *-fer* bearing): see -FEROUS.] Bearing or producing metal.

Metalline (me·tăləin), *a.* 1471. [ad. F. *métallin*, f. *métal* METAL *sb.*; see -INE[1].] **1.** = METALLIC **1. b.** Impregnated with metallic substances. Also, of vapours, arising from or produced by metals. 1626. **c.** Made of metal 1575. **2.** Resembling metal in appearance, lustre, etc. 1596. **3.** Metalliferous 1620.

1. The m. salts 1804. **2.** The rocks of a blew metaline colour, like vnto the best steele ore RALEIGH.

Metalling (me·tăliŋ), *vbl. sb.* 1819. [f. METAL *v.* (or *sb.*) + -ING[1].] **1.** The process of making or mending roads with metal. Also *concr.* = METAL *sb.* **11. 2.** Metal-work (*rare*). C. T. NEWTON.

Metallist (me·tălist). 1646. [f. METAL *sb.* + -IST.] **1.** One who is skilled in or works in metals. Now *rare.* **2.** An advocate of the use of a particular metal as currency 1886.

Metallize (me·tăləiz), *v.* 1594. [f. METAL *sb.* + -IZE.] **1.** *trans.* To render metallic; to impart a metallic form or appearance to. **2.** To vulcanize 1895. **Metalliza·tion.**

Metallo-, bef. a vowel **metall-**, comb. f. Gr. μέταλλον METAL *sb.*: **Metallochrome** (me·tălokrōᵘm) [Gr. χρῶμα colour], a prismatic tinting imparted to polished steel plates by depositing on them a film of lead oxide. **Metalloscopy** (metălǫ·skŏpi) [-SCOPY], the art of determining by external application what metals or metallic substances act most easily and favourably upon a given person. **Metallothe·rapy** [Gr. θεραπεία], the use of metals in healing or preventing diseases.

Metallography (metălǫ·grăfi). 1721. [ad. mod.L. *metallographia*, a. Gr., f. μέταλλον + -γραφία -GRAPHY.] **1.** 'A treatise or description of metals' (Bailey). **2.** The science relating to the internal structure of metals 1871. **3.** A printing process akin to lithography, in which metal plates are used instead of stones 1875. Hence **Meta·llograph,** a print produced by m. **Meta·llogra·phic** *a.*

Metalloid (me·tăloid), *a.* (*sb.*) 1832. [f. METAL *sb.* + -OID.] **1.** Having the form or appearance of a metal. Also, of or pertaining to metalloids. **2.** *sb. Chem.* †**a.** The metallic base of a fixed alkali or alkaline earth. **b.** A non-metallic element. So **Metalloi·dal** *a.*

Metallurgy (me·tălɒ̄ɹdʒi). 1704. [ad. mod.L. *metallurgia*, a. Gr., f. μεταλλουργός, f. μέταλλον METAL *sb.* + -εργος working, worker.] The art of working metals, comprising the separation of them from other matters in the ore, smelting, and refining; often, in a narrower sense, the process of extracting metals from their ores. Hence **Metallu·rgic, -al** *a.* of, pertaining to, or connected with m. **Me·tallurgist,** one who is skilled in m.; a worker in metal 1670.

Metamere (me·tămīᵊɹ). Also **metameron** (mĭtæ·mĕrǫn), *pl.* **-mera.** 1877. [f. Gr. μετα- META- + μέρος part.] *Zool.* One of the several similar segments of which certain bodies, e. g. the crayfish, consist.

Metameric (metăme·rik), *a.* 1847. [f. as prec. + -IC.] **1.** *Chem.* Characterized by metamerism. **2.** *Zool.* Of or pertaining to metameres 1875. Hence **Me·tamer,** *Chem.* a compound which is m. with something else.

Metamerism (metæ·mĕriz'm). 1848. [f. as prec.; see -ISM.] **1.** *Chem.* The condition of those isomeric compounds which, although of the same composition and molecular weight, have different chemical properties. **2.** *Zool.* Metameric segmentation 1877.

Metamorphic (metămǭ·ɹfik), *a.* 1816. [irreg. f. Gr. μετα- META- + μορφή form + -IC; after *metamorphosis.*] **1.** Characterized by metamorphosis or change of form. **2.** *Geol.* Pertaining to, characterized by, or formed by metamorphism. Of a rock or rock-formation: That has undergone transformation by means of heat, pressure, or natural agencies. 1833. **3.** That causes metamorphism or metamorphosis 1853.

2. It is usual to restrict the term 'M. System' to those crystalline schists—Gneiss, Quartz-rock, Mica-schist, and Clay-slate—which underlie all the fossiliferous strata PAGE.

Metamorphism (metămǭ·ɹfiz'm). 1845. [f. as prec. + -ISM.] **1.** *Geol.* The process of change of form or structure produced in a rock by various natural agencies. **2.** The process of metamorphosis (of an insect) 1866.

†**Metamorphize,** *v.* 1591. [f. as prec. + -IZE.] = METAMORPHOSE *v.* -1748.

Metamorphose (metămǭ·ɹfoᵘs, -fǭs), *sb.* 1608. [Anglicized form of METAMORPHOSIS.] = METAMORPHOSIS. Now *rare.*

Metamorphose (metămǭ·ɹfoᵘz, -fǭs), *v.* Also †**-oze.** 1576. [a. F. *métamorphoser*; see METAMORPHOSIS.] **1.** *trans.* To change in form; to turn *to* or *into* something else by enchantment or other supernatural means. **2.** *gen.* To change the form or character of; to transform. Const. *to, into.* 1576. **3.** To subject to METAMORPHOSIS OR METAMORPHISM 1664.

2. Never were a people so metamorphosed. The plain farmer and even the plain quaker is become a soldier BURKE. Hence **Metamo·rphoser.**

Metamorphosis (metămǭ·ɹfŏsis, -mǫɹfōᵘ·sis). *Pl.* **-ses** (-sīz). 1533. [a. L., a. Gr. μεταμόρφωσις, f. μεταμορφοῦν to transform, f. μετα- META- + μορφή form.] **1.** The action or process of changing in form or substance, esp. by magic or witchcraft. **b.** A metamorphosed form 1589. **2.** *transf.* A complete change in the appearance, condition, character of a person, of affairs, etc. 1548. **3. a.** *Physiology.* Change of form in animals and plants, or their parts, during life; esp. in a metabolous insect 1665. **b.** *Morphology.* The modification of organs or structures in form or function (including teratology) 1836. **c.** *Evolution.* Secular change of form 1847. **d.** *Histol.* The change of form which goes on in the elements of living organic structures 1839. **e.** *Chem.* The change of a compound to a new form 1853.

2. His visage changed as from a mask to a face... I know not that I have ever seen in any other human face an equal m. C. BRONTË. **3. a.** A perfect m., such as that of Sphinx, with three well-marked stages, larva, pupa, and imago 1888. var. †**Metamo·rphosy** 1530-1698. Hence **Metamorpho·tic** *a.* pertaining to, based on, or causing m. 1816.

Metaphor (me·tăfǫɹ). 1533. [a. F. *métaphore*, ad. L. *metaphora*, a. Gr., f. μεταφέρειν to transfer, f. μετα- META- + φέρειν (root φερ- : φορ-) to carry.] The figure of speech in which a name or descriptive term is transferred to some object to which it is not properly applicable; an instance of this.

Those beautiful Metaphors in Scripture, where Life is termed a Pilgrimage ADDISON. We should avoid making two inconsistent metaphors meet on one object. This is what is called *mixed metaphor* L. MURRAY. Hence **Metapho·ric, -al** *a.* **Metapho·rically** *adv.* **Me·taphorist** (*rare*), one who deals in metaphors. **Me·taphorize** *v. trans.* to change metaphorically *into*; to ply with m.

Metaphrase (me·tăfrēˈz), *sb.* 1607. [ad. mod.L. *metaphrasis* (also used), ad. Gr., f. μεταφράζειν to translate, etc.; see META- and PHRASE *sb.*] †**1.** A metrical translation -1767. **2.** A translation; later, a word-for-word translation as dist. from a paraphrase 1640. Hence **Me·taphrase** *v.* †to translate, esp. in verse 1608-1649; to render into other words 1868.

Metaphrast (me·tăfræst). 1610. [ad. Gr. μεταφράστης, f. μεταφράζειν to translate, f. μετα- META- + φράζειν to speak.] One who renders a composition into a different literary form; also, †a translator.

Metaphrastic (metăfræ·stik), *a.* (*sb.*) 1778. [ad. Gr. μεταφραστικός; see prec. and -IC.] **1.** Of the nature of metaphrase. **2.** *sb. pl.* The art of translation or interpretation 1895. So **Metaphra·stically** *adv.* 1577.

Metaphysic (metăfi·zik), *sb.*[1] late ME. [ad. scholastic L. *metaphysica* fem. sing. substituted for the older *metaphysica* neut. pl.; see METAPHYSICS.] **1.** = METAPHYSICS **1, 1 b.** ¶**2.** Something visionary. WARNER.

Metaphysic (metăfi·zik), *a.* and *sb.*[2] 1528. [ad. scholastic L. *metaphysicus* adj., developed from *metaphysica* sb. pl.; see METAPHYSICS.] **A.** *adj.* = METAPHYSICAL. Now *rare.* †**B.** *sb.* A metaphysician -1623.

Metaphysical (metăfi·zikăl), *a.* late ME. [f. METAPHYSIC + -AL.] **1.** Of, belonging to, or of the nature of, metaphysics; such as is recognized by metaphysics. **b.** Applied with reproach to over-subtle or too abstract reasoning, ideas, etc. 1646. **2.** Based on abstract general reasoning 1647. **3. a.** Applied to what is immaterial, incorporeal, or supersensible 1577. **b.** Supernatural 1590. **4.** Addicted to or fitted for the study of metaphysics 1628. **5.** Of some 17th c. poets: Addicted to witty conceits and far-fetched imagery 1744. **6.** Fantastic 1727.

1. A popular expression, which will not stand a Metaphysicall and strict examination SIR T. BROWNE. **2.** Wars have been waged for points of m. right SCOTT. **4.** The more m. and contemplative East KINGSLEY. **5.** The m. poets were men of learning, and to shew their learning was their whole endeavour JOHNSON. Hence **Metaphy·sically** *adv.* in a m. manner or sense; †supernaturally; †preternaturally.

Metaphysician (metăfizi·ʃăn). 1597. [a. F. *métaphysicien*, f. METAPHYSIC; see -ICIAN.] One versed in metaphysics.

Metaphysicize (metăfi·zisəiz), *v.* 1793. [f. METAPHYSIC + -IZE.] **1.** *intr.* To think, talk, or write metaphysically. Also quasi-*trans.* with *away.* **2.** *trans.* To treat metaphysically 1830.

1. He was everlastingly metaphysicising against metaphysics DE QUINCEY. I have metaphysicized away all my senses SOUTHEY.

Metaphysico- (metăfi·ziko), comb. f. METAPHYSIC *a.*, with sense 'partly metaphysical, partly . . .'.

Metaphysics (metăfi·ziks), *sb. pl.* 1569. [pl. of METAPHYSIC *sb.*[1], repr. med.L. *metaphysica* neut. pl., med.Gr. (τὰ) μεταφυσικά, 'the (works of Aristotle) after the Physics' (cf. META- and PHYSICS). From an early period, the word was used as a name for the branch of study, viz. ontology, treated in these works, and hence came to be misinterpreted as meaning 'the science of things transcending what is physical or natural'.] **1.** That branch of speculation which deals with the first principles of things, including such concepts as being, substance, essence, time, space, cause, identity, etc.; theoretical philosophy as the ultimate science of Being and Knowing. (Formerly often *The m.*) **b.** With *of*: The theoretical principles of some particular branch of knowledge 1845. **c.** In inaccurate or extended uses (see quots.) 1727. †**2.** In Marlowe: Occult or magical lore 1590.

1. If such Metaphysiques..be not Vain Philosophy, there was never any HOBBES. **b.** The m. of practical politics 1845. **c.** M. or pneumatics ADAM SMITH. The Philosophy of Mind—Psychology or M., in the widest signification of the terms SIR W. HAMILTON.

Metaplasm[1] (me·tăplæz'm). 1617. [ad. L. *metaplasmus* (in Quintilian 'rhetorical figure'), Gr. μεταπλασμός (see L. and Sc.), f. μεταπλάσσειν, f. μετα- META- + πλάσσειν to mould.] **a.** *Rhet.* The transposition of words from their usual or natural order. **b.** *Gram.* The alteration of a word by addition, removal, or transposition of letters or syllables. Also, the formation of oblique cases from a stem other than that of the nominative.

Me·taplasm[2]. 1875. [f. META- after *protoplasm.*] *Biol.* That part of protoplasm which contains the formative material.

Me·taplast. 1864. [f. Gr. μεταπλάσσειν; cf. METAPLASM[1].] *Gram.* A noun of which the cases are formed from different stems.

Metapodial (metăpōu·diăl). 1882. [ad. mod.L. *metapodialis*, f. next.] One of the ‖Metapodialia *sb. pl.*, the bones of the metacarpus and metatarsus taken together.

‖**Metapodium** (metăpōu·diŏm). 1853. [mod.L., f. Gr. μετα- META- + ποδ-, πούς foot.] **1.** *Anat.* = METATARSUS 1856. **2.** The posterior lobe of the foot in molluscs.

Metapolitics (metăpǫ·litiks), *sb. pl.* 1784. [META- 1.] Theoretical political science (often *contempt.*). So **Me:tapoli·tical** *a.* **Me:tapoli·ti·cian**, an adherent of metapolitical theories.

Metapsychics (metăsəi·kiks), *sb.pl.* 1905. [f. META- + PSYCHICS.] The science or study of certain phenomena which are 'beyond the scheme of orthodox psychology'. **Metapsy·chic, -ical** *adjs.* **Metapsy·chism, -ist.**

Metargon (metā·ɪgǫn). 1898. [f. META- + ARGON.] *Chem.* Sir W. Ramsay's name for a supposed gaseous element.

‖**Metasoma** (metăsōu·mă). Also **me·ta·some.** 1872. [mod.L., f. Gr. μετα- META- + σῶμα body.] *Zool.* The hinder part of the body in molluscs, or of the abdomen in arthropods. **Me:tasoma·tic** *a.* pertaining to the m.; *Geol.* pertaining to METASOMATOSIS.

‖**Metasomatosis** (me:tăsōumătōu·sis). 1886. [mod.L., f. META- + Gr. σωματ-, σῶμα body + -OSIS.] *Geol.* The transformation of one rock into another of an entirely different kind. Also **Metaso·matism.**

Metastable (me·tăstēi·b'l), *a.* 1899. [f. META- + STABLE.] *Physics.* Of a state of unstable equilibrium.

‖ **Metastasis** (metæ·stăsis). *Pl.* **-ses** (-sīz). 1577. [late L., a. Gr., f. μεθιστάναι to remove, change; see META- and STASIS.] **1.** *Rhet.* A rapid transition from one point to another. **2. a.** *Phys.* and *Path.* The transference of a bodily function, of a pain or a disease, of morbific matter, etc. from one part or organ to another 1663. **b.** *Biol.* The transformation of chemical compounds into other compounds in the process of assimilation by an organism 1875. **3.** *gen.* Transformation (*rare*) 1831.

3. The lamp and oil man, just then beginning, by a not unnatural m., to bloom into a lighthouse-engineer STEVENSON. Hence **Metasta·tic** *a.*

‖ **Metasternum** (metăstǝ·ɪnŏm). 1826. [mod.L., f. META- + STERNUM.] **1.** *Entom.* The median ventral piece of the metathorax in insects. **2.** *Anat.* The xiphisternum 1868. Hence **Metaste·rnal** *a.* and *sb.*

‖**Metastoma** (metæ·stŏmă). Also **me·ta·stome.** 1859. [mod.L., f. Gr. μετα- META- + στόμα mouth.] = LABIUM 2.

‖**Metatarsus** (metătā·ɪsŏs). *Pl.* **-si** (-səi). 1676. [mod.L.; see META- and TARSUS.] *Anat.* The group of five long bones of the foot lying between the tarsus and the toes. In birds, the bone which corresponds to tarsus and metatarsus together. **b.** *Entom.* (*a*) The proximal joint of the tarsus. (*b*) The entire tarsus of the hind foot. 1816. Hence **Meta·ta·rsal** *a.* of or belonging to the m.; *sb.* any bone of the m.

‖ **Metatheria** (metaþīə·riă), *sb. pl.* 1880. [mod.L., f. Gr. μετα- META- + θηρίον beast.] *Zool.* Huxley's term for the Marsupials. Hence **Metathe·rian** *a.* belonging to the M.; *sb.* one of these.

Metathesis (metæ·þĭsis). *Pl.* **-ses** (-sīz). 1577. [a. late L. (in sense 1), a. Gr. μετάθεσις, f. μετατιθέναι to transpose, change; see META- and THESIS.] **1.** †**a.** *Rhet.* The transposition of words. **b.** *Gram.* The interchange of position between sounds or letters in a word; the result of this. †**2.** *Path.* **a.** = METASTASIS 2 a. **b.** The transposition of a solid morbific substance from one part to another where it will be less injurious. -1832. **3.** *gen.* Change or reversal of condition 1705. **4.** *Chem.* The interchange of atoms or groups of atoms between two molecules, the structure of the molecules being not otherwise altered 1872.

1. The Assyrian Nipur, which is Nipru, with a mere m. of the two final letters RAWLINSON. So **Meta·the·tic, -ical** *a.*

‖ **Métayage** (metęyāʒ). 1877. [Fr.; irreg. f. *métayer*; see next.] A system of land tenure in Western Europe and U.S., in which the farmer pays a proportion (usu. half) of the produce (as rent) to the owner, who furnishes the stock and seed or a part thereof.

‖ **Métayer** (metęye). 1776. [F. *métayer* :— med.L. *medietarius*, f. *medietas* half; see MEDIETY, MOIETY.] A farmer who holds land on the *métayage* system. Also *attrib.*, as in *m. system, tenancy.*

‖**Metazoa** (metăzōu·ă), *sb. pl.* 1874. [f. Gr. μετα- META- 4 + ζῷα pl. of ζῷον animal.] Haeckel's term for one of the two great divisions (the other being PROTOZOA) of the animal kingdom, comprising those animals whose bodies consist of many cells. Also sing. **Metazo·on**, one of the m. Hence **Metazo·an** *a.* belonging to or characteristic of the M.; *sb.* one of the M. So **Metazo·ic** *a.*

Mete (mīt), *sb.*[1] late ME. [a. OF. *mete*, ad. L. *meta* goal, boundary.] †**1.** A goal -1480. **2.** A boundary, limit; a boundary stone or mark; *esp.* in phr. *metes and bounds*, common in legal use 1471.

Mete (mīt), *sb.*[2] 1768. [f. METE *v.*[1] Cf. MET *sb.*] Measure.

Mete (mīt), *v.*[1] Infl. **meted, meting.** [Com. Teut.: OE. *metan* :—OTeut. **met-* (: *mat-* : *mǣt-*) :—pre-Teut. **med-* (: *mod-* : *mēd-*) cogn. w. Gr. μέδιμνος corn-measure, L. *modius* bushel.] **1.** *trans.* = MEASURE *v.* 2. Now only *poet.* and *dial.* exc. in allusions to Matt. vii. 2. **2.** *absol.* or *intr.*; also, to aim at -1649. †**3.** *trans.* = MEASURE *v.* 3. -1819. **4.** = MEASURE *v.* 6 (*arch.*) OE. †**5.** To traverse (a distance). Also *absol.* or *intr.* (and *refl.*) To go, proceed. -1697. **6.** (Often with *out.*) To apportion by measure; to deal out; *esp.* to allot (punishment, reward, etc.) ME.

1. She..Metes the thin air and weighs the flying sound CRABBE. 2. *L. L. L.* IV. i. 134. 4. 2 *Hen. IV*, IV. iv. 77. 6. I m. and dole Unequal laws unto a savage race TENNYSON.

†**Mete**, *v.*[2] [OE. *mǣtan* wk. vb.; only Eng.] **1.** *impers. Me mette*: it occurred to me in a dream; I dreamt. Also with *sb.*, as *me mette sweven*, I dreamt a dream. -1643. **2.** *trans.* To dream -1570. **3.** *intr.* To dream (*of*). ME.

Mete, var. of MEAT, MEET, MET.

†**Metecorn.** [OE., f. *męte* MEAT *sb.* + CORN *sb.*[1]] An allowance (prop. of corn) made to servants, to inmates of a hospital, etc. -1523.

Metel (mī·tĕl). 1528. [a. mod.L. *methel*, a. Arab. *jauz* (= nut) *māþil.*] †**a.** *Methel nut*: a narcotic seed described by Avicenna, prob. *Datura Stramonium*, the Thorn-apple -1753. **b.** The specific name of the Hairy Thorn-apple, *Datura M.*, used as a name for the plant.

Metely, obs. f. MEETLY *a.* and *adv.*

Metempiric (metempi·rik). 1874. [f. META- + EMPIRIC.] **1.** (Also **Metempirics** constr. as sing.) The philosophy of things outside the sphere of knowledge derived from experience. **2.** One who believes in metempirical philosophy 1881. Hence **Metempi·ricism**, metempirical philosophy. **Metempi·ricist.**

Metempirical (metempi·rikăl), *a.* 1874. [f. META- + EMPIRICAL.] Pertaining to matters outside the range of knowledge derived from experience. Also: Maintaining the validity of concepts and opinions based otherwise than on experience.

If then the Empirical designates the province we include within the range of Science, the province we exclude may fitly be styled the M. LEWES. Hence **Metempi·rically** *adv.*

Metempsychose (mete·mpsikōuz), *v.* 1594. [f. next.] *trans.* To transfer or translate (a soul) from one body to another. So **Metempsycho·size** *v.*

Metempsychosis (mete:mpsikōu·sis). *Pl.* **-oses** (-ōu·sīz). 1590. [late L., a. Gr. μετεμψύχωσις, f. μετα- META- + ἐν in + ψυχή soul. Formerly often stressed *metempsy·chosis.*] Transmigration of the soul; *chiefly*, passage of the soul of a human being or animal at or after death into a new body of the same or a different species, a tenet of the Pythagoreans, the Buddhists, etc. Also *transf.* and *fig.*

fig. Departed empire has a m., if nothing else has LOWELL. Hence **Metempsycho·sist**, one who believes in m.

‖ **Metemptosis** (metemptōu·sis). 1727. [mod.L., f. Gr. μετά after + ἔμπτωσις, f. ἐμπίπτειν to fall in or upon.] The solar equation necessary to prevent the calendar new moon from happening a day too late. (Opp. to *proemptosis.*)

‖**Metencephalon** (metense·fălǫn). 1871. [mod.L., f. Gr. μετά after + ἐγκέφαλος brain, f. ἐν in + κεφαλή head.] **a.** In Huxley's use: The cerebellum with the pons Varolii. **b.** The after-brain, the last encephalic segment, called *Myelencephalon* by Huxley 1876. Hence **Metencepha·lic** *a.*

‖ **Metensomatosis** (metensōumătōu·sis). 1630. [mod.L., a. Gr., f. μετα- (denoting change) + ἐνσωμάτωσις (f. ἐν + σωματ-, σῶμα body); see -OSIS.] Re-embodiment (of the soul); a change of bodily elements.

Meteor (mī·tĭǫɪ). 1471. [ad. mod.L. *meteorum*, a. Gr. μετέωρον in pl. = atmospheric phenomena, subst. use of μετέωρος raised, lofty, f. μετα- META- + ἐωρ- ablaut var. of root of ἀείρειν to lift up.] **1.** Any atmospheric phenomenon. Now chiefly *techn.* **2.** *spec.* **a.** A small mass of matter from celestial space, rendered luminous by the heat engendered by collision with the earth's atmosphere; a fire-ball, a shooting star (in 17th c. also †a comet) 1593. **b.** Applied to the aurora borealis, the ignis fatuus, etc. 1592. **c.** *transf.* and *fig.* 1590. **3.** Passing into *adj.* 1711.

1. Atmospheric phenomena were formerly often classed as *aerial* or *airy meteors* (winds), *aqueous* or *watery meteors* (rain, snow, hail, dew, etc.), *luminous meteors* (the aurora, rainbow, halo, etc.), and *igneous* or *fiery meteors* (lightning, shooting stars, etc.). N. E. D. 2. And Meteors fright the fixed Starres of Heauen SHAKS. **c.** I have seen the Meteors of fashion rise and fall JOHNSON. 3. The m. flag of England CAMPBELL. Bothwell's m. course LANG.

Comb.: **m.-dust**, matter in a state of fine division, supposed to be diffused through interstellar space; **-powder**, a powdered-up alloy which is mixed with steel to form *meteor-steel*; **-steel**, an alloyed steel with a wavy appearance, resembling Damascus steel; **-stone** = *meteoric stone*; also *fig.*; **-stream**, the stream of meteors moving together in the same orbit; **-swarm, -system**, an aggregation of meteoroids pursuing the same orbit.

Meteoric (mītĭǫ·rik), *a.* 1631. [Partly ad. med.L. *meteoricus*, f. Gr. μετέωρος (see prec.); partly f. METEOR + -IC.] †**1.** Pertaining to the region of mid-air. DONNE. **2.** Meteorological, atmospherical 1830. **b.** *Bot.* Dependent upon atmospheric conditions 1789. **3.** Of, pertaining to, or derived from meteors; consisting of meteors 1812. **4.** *fig.* Transiently brilliant, flashing or dazzling like a meteor; also rapid, swift 1836.

2. M. agents, rain, wind, frost, etc. HERSCHEL.

3. *M. stone* = METEORITE. *M. paper* = 'natural flannel' (a fibrous texture often found covering meadows after an inundation). *M. steel* = meteor steel. 4. [Kean's] m. talent 1836. So †**Meteo·rical** *a.* Hence **Meteo·rically** *adv.*

Meteorism (mī·tĭ,ǒriz'm). 1843. [ad. medical L. *meteorismus* (also used), a. Gr. μετεωρισμός elevation, f. μετεωρίζειν.] *Path.* Flatulent distension of the abdomen with gas in the alimentary canal.

Meteorite (mī·tĭ,ǒrəi:t). 1834. [f. METEOR + -ITE [1].] A fallen meteor; a mass of stone or iron that has fallen from the sky upon the earth; a meteoric stone. Also (*loosely*), a meteor or meteoroid.

Meteorites, the so-called falling stars,..follow a perfectly definite track in space TAIT. Hence **Me·teori·tal, Meteori·tic** *adjs.*

Meteorize, *v. Obs.* or *arch.* 1657. [ad. Gr. μετεωρίζειν to elevate, f. μετέωρος; see METEOR and -IZE.] 1. *trans.* To vaporize, convert into vapour. Also *intr.* Only in Evelyn. 2. *intr.* To resemble a meteor; to flash, sparkle 1828.

Meteorograph (mī·tĭ,ǒrǒgrɑf). 1780. [a. F. *météorographe*; see METEOR and -GRAPH.] An apparatus for recording automatically several different kinds of meteorological phenomena at the same time. So **Me·teorogram.**

Meteorography (mī:tĭ,ǒrǫ·grăfi). 1736. [f. Gr. μετεωρο- METEOR + -γραφία -GRAPHY.] The descriptive science of meteors, or of meteorological phenomena. Hence **Meteorogra·phic, -al** *a.* pertaining to m.

Meteoroid (mī·tĭ,ǒroid). 1865. [f. METEOR + -OID.] a. *sb.* A body moving through space, of the same nature as those which when passing through the atmosphere became visible as meteors. b. *adj.* Of the nature of a m. Hence **Meteoroi·dal** *a.*

Meteorolite (mī·tĭ,ǒrǒləit). 1802. [ad. F. *météorolithe*, f. Gr. μετεωρο- METEOR + λίθος stone; see -LITE.] = METEORITE.

Meteorologist (mī:tĭ,ǒrǫ·lŏdʒist). 1621. [f. Gr. μετεωρολόγος; see -LOGIST.] One who is skilled in meteorology. So †**Meteoro·loger** 1683, †**Meteorolo·gian** 1614, †**Meteorologi·cian** 1580.

Meteorology (mī:tĭ,ǒrǫ·lŏdʒi). 1620. [ad. Gr. μετεωρολογία; see METEOR and -LOGY.] 1. The study of, or the science that treats of, the motions and phenomena of the atmosphere, esp. with a view to forecasting the weather. 2. The character, as regards weather, etc., *of* a particular region 1684.

1. In sundry Animals we deny not a kind of natural M., or innate presention both of wind and weather SIR T. BROWNE. 2. The Climate and M. of Madeira 1850. So **Meteorolo·gic** (1760), **-logical** (1570) *a.* pertaining to or connected with the science of m.; also, pertaining to atmospheric phenomena. **Me·teorolo·gically** *adv.*

Meteoroscopy (mī:tĭ,ǒrǫ·skŏpi). *rare.* 1658. [f. Gr. μετεωρο- METEOR + -SCOPY.] Observation of the stars.

Meteorous (mī·tĭ,ǒrəs, also *poet.* mītī·ǒrəs), *a.* 1667. [f. Gr. μετέωρος raised on high, μετέωρα neut. pl. METEOR + -OUS.] = METEORIC.

Meter (mī·təɹ), *sb.*[1] late ME. [f. METE *v.*[1] + -ER [1].] One who measures; a measurer, esp. of land, coal, and other commodities.

Meter (mī·təɹ), *sb.*[2] 1815. [First used in *gas-meter*; prob. a use of METER [1], after words in -METER.] 1. a. (In full *gas-meter.*) An apparatus for automatically measuring and recording the volume of gas supplied.

Usually, the gas is made to pass through receptacles of known capacity, each filling and discharge of one of these being registered by the movement of an index. b. Any apparatus for automatically measuring and recording the quantity of a fluid or the like flowing through it 1832. c. *fig.* A 'gauge', self-acting measure of the fluctuations of anything 1860. 2. *attrib.*, as *m. box, inspector, rent*, etc. 1882.

1. a. *Dry m.*: one in which no water is used; dist. from the earlier *wet m.* b. *Water-m., electric light m.*; also, *ampere-m., voltmeter, watt-m.*, etc. 2. **m. mailing machine,** a machine for franking an envelope, etc. (in lieu of the usual postage stamp), and registering the amount (1923); so **m.-mail, (postage) stamp.** Hence **Me·ter** *v. trans.*, to measure by means of a m. *Metered mail* (cf. *meter-mail* above).

Meter: see METRE.

-meter, in use commonly *-o·meter*, and occas. *-i·meter*, a terminal element in names of instruments for automatically measuring something. Early (17th c.) examples are *barometer, hygrometer, thermometer*, repr. mod.L. forms in *-metrum.* In these the ending was intended to represent the Gr. μέτρον measure (see METRE [1]); the formation is irregular, as the Gr. word does not occur in comb. with sbs., and would not correctly express 'instrument that measures'. Later, hybrid formations were introduced, some of them imitating the form of Gr. compounds, as *gasometer, galvanometer*, etc., while in others the combining-vowel of the L. first element is retained, as in *calorimeter*, etc. In late formations, as *voltameter, ammeter*, etc., no attempt is made to assimilate the form of the first element to that of a Gr. or L. combining form.

Meterage (mī·tərėdʒ). 1882. [f. METER *sb.*[1] + -AGE.] Measurement, or the price paid for it.

Metewand (mī·twǫnd). 1440. [f. METE *v.*[1] + WAND *sb.*] A measuring-rod. Now *dial. fig.* A true tochstone, a sure metwand lieth before both their eyes ASCHAM.

Meteyard (mī·tyāɹd). OE. [f. METE *v.*[1] + YARD *sb.*[2]] = prec. Now *dial.* Also *fig.*

Meth, obs. f. MEAD [1].

Methæmoglobin (meþī·moglōu·bin). 1870. [See META- and HÆMOGLOBIN.] *Chem.* A derivative of hæmoglobin obtained by the exposure of an aqueous solution of oxyhæmoglobin to the air.

Methane (me·þeⁱn). Also **-an.** 1868. [f. METH(YL) + -ANE.] *Chem.* Methyl hydride or MARSH-GAS, a colourless odourless gas emanating from stagnant pools, etc., and esp. coal-seams, in which, mixed with air, it forms FIRE-DAMP.

Metheglin (mĭþe·glin). *Obs.* exc. *Hist.* and *dial.* 1533. [a. Welsh *meddyglyn*, f. *meddyg* healing (ad. L. *medicus*) + *llyn* liquor.] A spiced or medicated form of mead, orig. peculiar to Wales.

Methene (me·þīn). 1885. [f. METH(YL) + -ENE.] *Chem.* = METHYLENE. Hence **Methenyl** (me·þĭnil), the hypothetical hydrocarbon radical CH 1868. So **Methide** (me·þəid), a combination of methyl with a metal 1868.

Methinks (miþi·ŋks), *impers. v.* Now *arch.* and *poet.* Pa. t. **methought** (miþǭ·t). [OE. *mē þyncþ* (pa. t. *mē þūhte*), where *mē* is dative, and *þyncþ* 3rd pers. sing. of *þyncan* to seem, THINK *v.*[1]] It seems to me. (Used with dependent clause or parenthetically.)

Methinkes you are sadder SHAKS. M. a strait canal is as rational at least as a mæandring bridge HOR. WALPOLE.

Methionic (meþiǫ·nik), *a.* 1842. [f. ME(THYL) + Gr. θεῖον sulphur; see -IC.] *Chem.* In *m. acid*: a disulpho-acid obtained from aniline. Hence **Methionate** (meþəi·ŏneⁱt), a salt of this.

Method (me·þǒd). 1541. [a. F. *méthode*, or ad. L. *methodus*, a. Gr., f. μετα- META- + ὁδός way.] I. Procedure for attaining an object. †1. *Med.* The regular systematic treatment proper for the cure of a given disease –1716. b. *Hist.* The system of medicine of the 'methodics' or 'methodists' –1790. 2. A special form of procedure adopted in any branch of mental activity, whether for exposition or for investigation 1586. 3. A way of doing anything, esp. according to a regular plan 1590. b. The methods of procedure in teaching, etc., considered as the object of a branch of study 1848.

2. It is a distinct property of the Comparative Method of investigation to abate national prejudices MAINE. 3. This is the usual m., but not mine—My way is to begin with the beginning BYRON. b. A Manual of M. for Pupil-Teachers (*title*) 1879.

II. Systematic arrangement. 1. A branch of Logic or Rhetoric which teaches how to arrange thoughts and topics for investigation, exposition, or literary composition 1551. 2. Orderly arrangement of ideas and topics; orderliness and sequence of thought or expression 1559. 3. The order and arrangement of a particular discourse, etc. 1591. †b. A methodical exposition –1829. †c. A summary of the contents of a book –1652. 4. Orderliness and regularity in doing anything 1611. †5. A disposition of things according to a regular plan –1754. 6. *Nat. Hist.* A system; scheme of classification 1826.

2. Though this be madnesse, Yet there is M. in't SHAKS. 3. *Verbatim* to rehearse the Methode of my Penne SHAKS. c. In what chapter of his bosome? To answer by the m. in the first of his hart SHAKS. 4. Early hours, and m., and ease, without hurry, will do everything 1754. 6. *Method* and *System*..have often been..used indifferently to signify the same thing KIRBY and SP.

Methodic (mĭþǫ·dik). *Obs.* exc. *Hist.* 1541. [ad. late L. *methodicus*, a. Gr., f. μέθοδος METHOD; see -IC.] A. *adj.* †1. Epithet of an ancient school of physicians holding views intermediate between those of the Dogmatic and the Empiric school –1751. 2. = METHODICAL *a.* 1620. B. *sb.* = METHODIST 1. 1541.

Methodical (mĭþǫ·dikăl), *a.* 1570. [See prec. and -ICAL.] 1. *Hist.* = METHODIC *a.* 1. 1597. 2. Characterized by method or order; arranged or disposed with order or regularity 1570. 3. Of persons, etc.: Acting with or observant of method or order 1664.

3. I find him a most exact and methodicall man PEPYS. Hence **Metho·dical-ly** *adv.*, **-ness.**

Methodism (me·þǒdiz'm). 1739. [f. METHOD + -ISM.] 1. The system of doctrine, practice, and organization characteristic of the Methodists. 2. Excessive regard for methods 1856.

2. The Somerset House gentlemen usually introduce their official m. at home 1856.

Methodist (me·þǒdist). 1593. [ad. mod.L. *methodista*; see METHOD and -IST.] 1. *Hist.* A physician of the methodic school. In the 17th c. sometimes applied to the regular practitioners of the day. 1598. 2. One who is skilled in, or attaches importance to, method; one who follows a (specified) method. Now *rare.* 1593. b. *Nat. Hist.* One who classifies according to a particular scheme. Also, in Kirby's use, one who prefers an artificial to a natural method of classification. 1753. 3. *Eccl.* The name given in the 17th c. to a class of Roman Catholic apologists 1686. 4. a. Orig., a member of the 'Holy Club', established at Oxford in 1729 by John and Charles Wesley and others; later, any of those who sympathized with the evangelistic movement led by the Wesleys and George Whitefield. b. In subseq. use, a member of any one of a number of religious bodies which originated from the labours of the Wesleys and Whitefield. 1733. c. *transf.* A person of strict religious views (*contempt.*) 1758. 5. *attrib.* or *adj.* Pertaining to Methodists or Methodism 1751.

4. b. He combines the manners of a Marquis with the morals of a M. W. S. GILBERT. 5. A M. Preacher WESLEY. Hence **Methodi·stic, -al** *a.* characteristic of or pertaining to Methodism or the Methodists: often *disparaging.* **Methodi·stically** *adv.*

Methodize (me·þǒdəiz), *v.* 1589. [f. METHOD + -IZE.] 1. *trans.* To reduce to order; to arrange in a methodical manner. b. To render (a person) methodical. MME D'ARBLAY. 2. *intr.* To talk methodistically. SMOLLETT.

1. He should be taught..to order and methodise his ideas BERKELEY. Hence **Methodiza·tion.**

Methodless (me·þǒdlės), *a.* 1609. [f. METHOD + -LESS.] Devoid of method or order; lacking the habit of order.

Methodology (meþǒdǫ·lŏdʒi). 1800. [ad. mod.L. *methodologia*, or F. *méthodologie*; see METHOD and -LOGY.] The science of method; a treatise or dissertation on method. Also *Nat. Hist.* Systematic classification. So **Methodolo·gical** *a.*, **-ly** *adv.* **Methodo·logist,** one who treats method as a science.

Methol (me·þǫl). 1842. [ad. F. *méthol*, f. *méthyle* METHYL; see -OL 1.] *Chem.* A colourless liquid, produced in the distillation of wood.

Methought, pa. t. of METHINKS.

Methoxyl (meþǫ·ksil). 1866. [f. METH(YL) + OX(YGEN) + -YL.] *Chem.* A hypothetical radical, CH_3O, analogous to hydroxyl.

Methuselah (mǐþiū·zělă). Also *corruptly* **Methusalem**, etc. late ME. [Heb.] The name of one of the pre-Noachian patriarchs, stated to have lived 969 years (*Gen.* v. 27); hence used as a type of longevity.

Methyl (me·þil). Formerly also **-ule, -yle.** 1844. [a. F. *méthyle*, G. *methyl*, back-formation f. F. *méthylène*, G. *methylen*, METHYLENE.] *Chem.* The hypothetical radical of the monocarbon series (CH_3), the base of pyroxylic or wood spirit or pyroligneous naphtha, of formic acid, and of a large series of organic compounds.

attrib. and *Comb.*, as *m. compound; m. bromide*, etc. Also prefixed (often without hyphen) to the name of an organic compound to express the addition of m. to its composition, or the replacement of hydrogen atoms by equivalents of m., as in *methylaniline*. *Spec. combs.*: **m. alcohol**, pyroxylic spirit; **m. green**, a green dye obtained by heating Paris violet with m. chloride; **m. mercaptan**, m. hydrosulphide, CH_3HS; **m. violet**, Paris violet, a reddish-blue coal-tar dye obtained from dimethylaniline.

Methylal (me·þilæl). 1838. [ad. F. *méthylal*, f. *méthyle* METHYL + *al(cool)* ALCOHOL.] *Chem.* A mobile aromatic liquid obtained by heating methyl alcohol with manganese dioxide and sulphuric acid; occas. used as an anæsthetic.

Methylamine (me·þilăməin). 1850. [f. METHYL + AMINE.] *Chem.* A compound in which one atom of the hydrogen in ammonia has been replaced by methyl.

Methylate (me·þilᵉ¹t), *sb.* 1835. [f. as METHYLIC; see -ATE¹.] *Chem.* A salt formed by the union of methyl with oxygen and a metallic base.

Methylate (me·þilᵉ¹t), *v.* 1865. [f. METHYL + -ATE.³] *trans.* To mix or impregnate with methyl; usu. to mix (spirit of wine) with pyroxylic spirit, etc., to render it unfit for drinking, and exempt it from the duties imposed on alcohol.

Methylated spirit, containing about ten per cent. of pyroxylic spirit, is the form in which alcohol is most used for industrial purposes.

Methylene (me·þilīn). 1835. [ad. F. *méthylène*, irreg. f. Gr. μέθυ wine + ὕλη wood.] *Chem.* A hypothetical radical of the hydrocarbons (CH_2); unknown in the free state, but occurring in many compounds, as *m. hydrate*, etc.

M.-azure, an oxidation product of m. blue; **m.-blue**, a coal-tar colour used in dyeing, and as a bacterioscopic reagent; **m.-violet** = *methyl violet*.

Methylic (mǐþi·lik), *a.* 1835. [Orig. f. METHYL(ENE + -IC; later, f. METHYL + -IC.] *Chem.* Of or pertaining to methyl. Chiefly in names of compounds, in which *methyl* is more commonly used attrib.

Metic (me·tik). 1808. [irreg. ad. Gr. μέτοικος, f. μετα- (denoting change) + -οικος dwelling, οἰκεῖν to dwell.] *Gr. Antiq.* A resident alien in a Greek city, having some of the privileges of citizenship.

Meticulous (mǐti·kiŭləs), *a.* 1535. [ad. L. *meticulosus*, f. *metus* fear.] †1. Timid -1674. 2. Over-careful about minute details 1827.

1. Melancholy and m. heads SIR T. BROWNE. 2. A stringent and m. discipline 1904. **Meti·culously** *adv.*

‖ **Métier** (metye). 1674. [Fr.:—pop.L. *misterium, altered f. L. *ministerium* (see MINISTRY), prob. influenced by *mysterium* MYSTERY.] A trade or profession; in Eng. use chiefly *transf.*, a person's 'line'.

Heretic-burning—in fact, 'tis his *m.* BARHAM.

‖ **Metif** (mē·tif). 1808. [F. *métif*, OF. *mestif* mongrel; cf. next.] The offspring of a white and a quadroon.

Metis (mē·tis). 1839. [a. F. *métis* :—late L. *misticius*, whence also MESTIZO.] The offspring of a white and an American Indian, esp. in Canada.

Metol (me·tǫl). 1893. [a. G. *metol*, an arbitrary name.] *Photogr.* A whitish soluble powder (sulphate of methylparamidometacresol) used as a developer.

Metonic (mǐtǫ·nik), *a.* 1696. [ad. mod.L. *Metonicus*, f. *Meton*, Gr. Μέτων, name of the Athenian who discovered the cycle.] *M. cycle, period, †year*: the cycle of 19 Julian years (about 235 lunations) in which the moon returns (nearly) to the same apparent position with regard to the sun, so that the new and full moons occur at the same dates in the corresponding year of each cycle.

Metonym (me·tŏnim). 1826. [ad. assumed Gr. *μετώνυμον; cf. *paronym*.] A word used in a transferred sense.

Metonymy (mǐtǫ·nĭmi). 1562. [ad. late L. *metonymia* (also used), a. Gr. μετωνυμία, lit. 'change of name', f. μέτ(α)- META- + -ωνυμ- = ὄνομα name.] *Rhet.* A figure in which the name of an attribute or adjunct is substituted for that of the thing meant, e. g. *sceptre* for *authority*. So **Metony·mical** *a.* pertaining to or involving m. 1579. **Metony·mically** *adv.* by m. 1574.

Metope¹ (me·tŏpi). 1563. [ad. L. *metopa*, a. Gr. μετόπη, f. μετά between + ὀπαί holes in a frieze to receive the beam-ends.] *Arch.* A square space between the triglyphs in a Doric frieze. *Demi-, Semi-m.*, the half-space between the corner and the triglyph next the corner.

Metope² (me·toup). 1880. [a. Gr. μέτωπον forehead.] *Zool.* Applied to the face of a crab. HUXLEY. So **Meto·pic** *a.* of or pertaining to the forehead; (of a skull) having the metopic suture persisting 1878. **Me·topism**, persistence of the frontal suture 1879.

Metoposcopy (metopǫ·skŏpi). 1569. [ad. mod.L. *metoposcopia*, f. *metoposcopus*, a. Gr.; see prec. and -SCOPY.] 1. The art of judging character or of telling a fortune by the forehead or face. 2. The physiognomical characters of a person's face 1653. Hence **Metoposco·pic, -al** *a.* **Metopo·scopist.**

‖**Metosteon** (metǫ·stĭ₁ǫn). 1868. [mod.L., f. Gr. μετά behind + ὀστέον bone.] *Ornith.* The centre of ossification for the posterior lateral processes of the sternum, behind the pleurosteon. Hence **Meto·steal** *a.*

Metre (mī·təɪ), *sb.*¹ [OE. *meter*, ad. L. *metrum*, a. Gr. μέτρον, f. Indo-Eur. root *mē̆- to measure; in the 14th c. adopted afresh from OF. *metre* (mod.F. *mètre*).] 1. Any form of poetic rhythm, its kind being determined by the character and number of the feet or groups of syllables of which it consists. 2. Metrical arrangement or method ME. 3. a. Composition in metre; verse. †b. A verse or poem; *occas.* a metrical version. ME. 4. *Pros.* A metrical group or measure; *spec.* a dipody in iambic, trochaic, and anapæstic rhythms 1880. 5. *attrib.* as *m. psalm* 1596.

1. Composed in a m. of Catullus TENNYSON. *Common, long, particular, short m.*: see these words. *Peculiar m., proper m.*, a metre used only in a particular hymn, or having no recognized name. 2. Then arrange this [prose] again into m. WHATELY. 3. A meter of iiii verses in the Utopian tongue 1556. Those luckless brains That..Indite much m. with much pains COWPER.

Metre (mī·təɪ), *sb.*² Also *U.S.* **meter.** 1797. [ad. F. *mètre*, ad. Gr. μέτρον measure.] The unit of length of the metric system, = 39·37 inches. b. *attrib.*, as *m. gauge* 1868.

b. **m.-gramme, -ton**, etc., the amount of work required to raise a gramme, a ton, etc. one m. in one second.

Metre (mī·təɪ), *v.* late ME. [f. METRE *sb.*¹] 1. To compose in or put into metre 1447. 2. *intr.* To versify. late ME. Hence **Me·tred** *ppl. a.* metrical; also *loosely*, rhythmical.

Metric (me·trik), *a.*¹ and *sb.* 1760. [ad. L. *metricus*, a. Gr., f. μέτρον METRE *sb.*¹] A. *adj.* = METRICAL *a.*¹ BLACKIE. B. *sb. sing.* and *pl.* The science or art that deals with metre.

Metric (me·trik), *a.*² 1864. [ad. F. *métrique*, f. *mètre* METRE *sb.*²] Pertaining to that system of weights and measures of which the metre is the unit.

The system is decimal throughout, and the unit in each of its branches has a definite relation to the metre; e.g. the gramme, the unit of weight, represents the weight of a cubic centimetre of water.

Metrical (me·trikăl), *a.*¹ late ME. [f. late L. *metricus* relating (1) to measuring, (2) to metre; see METRIC *a.*¹ and -ICAL.] 1. Pertaining or relating to metre or versification; consisting of or composed in metre; having the characteristics of metre. 2. Relating to, involving, used in, or determined by measurement 1650.

1. The old m. romances WARTON. 2. *M. geometry*: the science which deals with the comparison and relations of spatial magnitudes. **Me·trically** *adv.*

Metrical (me·trikăl), *a.*² 1797. [f. F. *métrique* METRIC *a.*²; see -ICAL.] 1. = METRIC *a.*² (which is now more usual). 2. Of lenses or their measurement: Pertaining to the system of which the unit is the 'dioptric', i.e. a focal length of one metre 1879.

Metrician (mǐtri·ʃən). late ME. [f. L. *metricus* METRIC *a.*¹, after *physician*.] †1. One who writes in metre -1548. 2. One who studies or is learned in metre 1835.

Metrification (me:trifikē¹·ʃən). 1861. [f. med.L. *metrificare*, f. *metrum* METRE *sb.*¹] The construction of a metrical composition; also, metrical structure.

Metrify (me·trifəi), *v.* 1523. [ad. F. *métrifier*, ad. L. *metrificare*; see -FY.] *trans.* To put into metre. Also *intr.* to make verses.

Metrist (me·trist). 1535. [ad. med.L. *metrista*, f. *metrum* METRE *sb.*¹; see -IST.] A metrical writer; one skilled in the handling of metre.

Metrology (metrǫ·lŏdʒi). 1816. [f. Gr. μέτρον measure + -LOGY.] a. A system of weights and measures. b. The science of weights and measures. **Metrolo·gical** *a.*

Metromania (metromē¹·niă). 1794. [f. Gr. μέτρον METRE *sb.*¹ + -MANIA; after F. *métromanie*.] A mania for writing verses. Hence **Metroma·niac.**

Metronome (me·trŏnōᵘm). 1816. [f. Gr. μέτρον METRE *sb.*¹ + νόμος law, rule.] An instrument used in music for marking the time by means of a graduated inverted pendulum with a sliding weight which can be regulated. Hence **Metrono·mic, -al** *a.* **Metrono·mically** *adv.* **Metro·nomy.**

Metronymic (mītrŏni·mik). 1868. [ad. Gr. μητρωνυμικός, f. μητρ-, μήτηρ mother + ὄνυμα, ὄνομα name.] A. *adj.* Derived from the name of a mother or other female ancestor, esp. by the addition of a suffix or prefix indicating descent. Also said of such a suffix or prefix. B. *sb.* A m. name.

Metropole (me·trŏpōᵘl). late ME. [a. OF., ad. L. *metropolis*; see METROPOLIS.] †1. A chief town -1685. 2. *Eccl.* The see of a metropolitan 1862. So †**Metropolie** 1633-65.

Metropolis (mǐtrǫ·pŏlis). *Pl.* **-polises.** 1535. [a. L., a. Gr. μητρόπολις, f. μητρο-, μήτηρ mother + πόλις city.] 1. The see of a metropolitan bishop. 2. The chief town or city of a country; a capital 1590. b. A chief centre of some form of activity 1675. c. *Nat. Hist.* The district in which a species, group, etc., is most represented 1826. 3. *Greek Hist.* The parent-state of a colony. Hence *transf.* 1568.

1. Irenaeus was the bishop of Lyons, the m. of Gaul LINGARD. 2. *The m.*, London as a whole, as dist. from *the City*. b. Our m. of law, by which I mean Edinburgh SCOTT.

Metropolitan (metrǫpǫ·lităn), *a.* and *sb.* late ME. [ad. late L. *metropolitanus*, f. Gr. μητροπολίτης, f. μητρόπολις.] A. *adj.* 1. Belonging to an ecclesiastical metropolis. Also, pertaining to or characteristic of a metropolitan. 1490. 2. Of, pertaining to, or constituting a metropolis. Also, belonging to or characteristic of 'the metropolis' (London). 1555. 3. Belonging to or constituting the mother country 1806. †4. *fig.* (from 1 and 2). Principal, chief -1686.

1. *M. bishop* = B. 1. 2. *M. city* or *town* = METROPOLIS. *M. police*: police pertaining to London as a whole.

B. *sb.* 1. *Eccl.* [In Gr. μητροπολίτης, in L. *metropolitanus*.] A bishop having the oversight of the bishops of a province; in the West equivalent to *archbishop*; in the Greek church ranking above an archbishop and below a patriarch ME. 2. A chief town or metropolis 1549. †3. *fig.* = METROPOLIS 2 b. -1704. 4. One who lives in a metropolis; one who has metropolitan ideas 1795. 5. A citizen of the mother-city of a colony. GROTE.

Hence **Metropo·litanate**, the office or see of a m. bishop.

Metropolite (mĭtrǫ·pǒləit). 1578. [ad. late L. *metropolita*, a. Gr. μητροπολίτης, f. μητρόπολις.] 1. = METROPOLITAN B. 1. †2. A metropolis -1635.

Metropolitical (metrǒpǒli·tikăl), *a.* 1541. [f. med.L. *metropoliticus*, f. *metropolita*; see prec. and -AL.] 1. *Eccl.* = METROPOLITAN A. 1. 2. = METROPOLITAN A. 2. 1603. Hence **Metropoli·tically** *adv.*

‖**Metrorrhagia** (mītrorē̆·dʒiă). 1856. [mod. L., f. Gr. μήτρα womb + -ραγία breaking forth.] *Path.* Uterine hæmorrhage.

Metroscope (mī·trǒskōup). 1855. [ad. F. *métroscope*, f. Gr. μήτρα womb; see -SCOPE.] a. An instrument for examining the uterus. b. An instrument for listening to the sounds of the heart of the fœtus during gestation.

Metrotome (mī·trǒtōum). 1856. [f. Gr. μήτρα womb + -τόμος cutter.] A cutting instrument used in operating on the womb.

-metry (repr. Gr. -μετρία action or process of measuring, f. -μέτρης measurer, μέτρον measure), a terminal element of sbs. correlative to sbs. in -METER, denoting *spec.* the process of measuring by the instrument '—meter'. A few such sbs. represent actual Greek words, as *geometry*, etc., or are formed on the analogy of these, as *aerometry*, etc.; many others, e. g. *calorimetry*, etc., are hybrid formations.

Mettle (me·t'l), *sb.* (and *a.*) Also †**metal.** 1581. [Orig. a var. of METAL *sb.*] 1. Quality of disposition or temperament 1584. 2. Of a horse, etc.: Natural vigour and ardour; spirit 1596. 3. Of persons: Ardent or spirited temperament; courage 1581. 4. *attrib.* or *adj.* Spirited, mettlesome, 'game'. Now *arch.* and *Sc.* 1592.

1. To try the spirit of men, of what m. they are made of ROGERS. 2. Her [a falcon's] m. makes her careless of danger WALTON. 3. A Corinthian, a lad of m. SHAKS. Phrases. *To be on* or *upon one's m.*: to be incited to do one's best. *To put* or *set* (a person) *on* or *upon his m.*, *to put to his m.*, *to try* (a person's) *m.*: to test his powers of endurance or resistance.

Hence **Me·ttled, Me·ttlesome** *adjs.* full of m.

Meum (mī·ǒm). 1594. [L., neut. of *meus.*] In phr. **Meum and tuum**: 'mine and thine'; what is one's own and what is another's: a pop. phrase used to express the rights of property. Also *meum, tuum*; *m. or tuum.*

‖**Meurtrière** (mörtrīḗr). 1802. [Fr.; fem. of *meurtrier* murderer, murderous, f. *meurtre.*] A small loophole, large enough to admit the barrel of a rifle, gun, or musket, through which a soldier may fire, under cover.

Meuse, muse (miūs, miūz), *sb.* Now *dial.* 1523. [a. OF. *muce, musse, mouce*, mod. dial. *muche* hiding-place, etc., f. *musser, muchier* to hide (whence MICHE *v.*).] 1. A gap in a fence or hedge through which hares, etc. habitually pass, and through which they run, when hunted, for relief. b. *transf.* and *fig.* A loophole or means of escape 1529. 2. The 'form' of a hare 1611. **Meuse** *v.* to go through a m.

Meuse, Meute, obs. ff. MEWS, MUTE *sbs.*[2,3]

Mew (miū), *sb.*[1] [OE. *mǣw* str. masc.; cf. mod.G. *möwe*; Du. *meeuw* fem.] A gull, *esp.* the common gull, *Larus canus*; a sea-mew.

Mew (miū), *sb.*[2] ME. [a. F. *mue* fem., vbl. sb. f. *muer* MEW *v.*[1]] 1. A cage for hawks, esp. while 'mewing' or moulting. 2. †a. A coop or cage in which fowls, etc. were confined for fattening. b. Now *dial.*, a breeding-cage. late ME. 3. †a. A place of confinement -1622. b. A secret place; a den. Now *rare.* late ME.

1. They make of the churche, for theyre hawkes a mewe BARCLAY. Phr. *In m.* (rarely *in the m.*): in process of moulting; also *fig.* 3. Phr. †*In m.*: in hiding or confinement, cooped up.

Mew, *sb.*[3]: see MEW *int.*

Mew (miū), *v.*[1] late ME. [a. F. *muer* to moult :—L. *mutare* to change.] 1. a. *trans.* Of a hawk, etc.: To moult, shed, or change (its feathers). Also in *passive* with the bird as subject. Now only *arch.* †Also *transf.* and *fig.* b. *absol.* and *intr.* To moult 1532. †2. *trans.* Of a stag: To cast (his horns) ME.

1. His feathers he [Cupid] meweth DRAYTON. As an Eagle muing (? = renewing by the process of moulting) her mighty youth MILTON. b. *transf.* One only suit to his backe which now is mewing FLETCHER. 2. *intr.* When they [deer] cast their heads, they are said to *mew* GOLDSM.

Mew (miū), *v.*[2] late ME. [f. MEW *sb.*[2]] 1. *trans.* To put a hawk in a mew at moulting time; to keep up 1533. †2. To coop *up* (poultry, etc.) for fattening (*rare*) -1639. 3. To shut up, confine, enclose; to hide, conceal 1450.

1. Merlins, which sometimes she mewed in her own chamber 1640. 2. *transf. Rich. III*, I. i. 132. 3. They keep me mew'd up here as they m. mad folkes FLETCHER.

Mew (miū), *v.*[3] ME. [Echoic; see next. Cf. MIAOW *v.*] *intr.* Of a cat, sea-birds, etc.: To utter the sound represented by 'mew'. Also *transf.* of a person. b. *trans.* To express by mewing 1900.

I heard the white-winged gulls mewing 1902.

Mew (miū), *int.* and *sb.*[3] 1596. [Echoic; cf. MIAOW.] 1. *int.* Used to represent the cry of a cat. Also *sb.* as a name for this. †2. Used as a derisive exclamation -1633.

1. I had rather be a Kitten, and cry m. [etc.] SHAKS.

Me-ward(s, orig. *to me ward(s* = towards me: see -WARD and TOWARD, TOWARDS.

Mewl (miūl), *v.* Also †**mule.** 1600. [Echoic; cf. MIAUL *v.*] *intr.* a. To cry feebly like an infant; to make a whining noise. Also *trans.* with *out.* b. To mew like a cat.

Mews (miūz). late ME. [Pl. of MEW *sb.*[2]; now construed as sing.] 1. The royal stables at Charing Cross in London, built on the site where the royal hawks were formerly mewed. Now *Hist.* 2. A set of stabling grouped round an open yard or alley. Also as *pl.* 1631.

2. Mr. Turveydrop's great room, which was built into a m. at the back DICKENS.

Mexican (me·ksikăn). 1604. [ad. Sp. *Mexicano* (now written *Mejicano*), f. *Mexico*; see -AN.] A. *adj.* Of or pertaining to Mexico.

In various names of natural and artificial products, etc. as **M. coca**, an American herb, yielding a nutritious fodder. **M. poppy**, *Argemone mexicana.*

B. *sb.* 1. A native or inhabitant of Mexico 1604. 2. = *Mexican dollar* (see DOLLAR 4) 1890.

Mezentian (mĭze·nʃăn), *a.* 1837. [f. *Mezentius* + -AN.] Comparable to the action of Mezentius, a mythical Etruscan king, who bound living men to corpses, and left them to die of starvation (Virg. *Æn.* viii. 485-8).

‖**Mezereon, -eum** (mĭzīᵊ·riǫ̆n, -ǒm). 1477. [med.L. *mezereon*, ad. Arab. *māzaryūn.*] 1. The low shrub *Daphne Mezereon*; also called †*Dutch m.* 2. *Pharm.* The dried bark of the root of this plant, used in liniments 1789. 3. *attrib.*, as *m. root*, etc. 1626.

‖**Mezuza(h** (mězū·ză). *Pl.* **mezuzoth** (mězū·zōþ). 1650. [Heb.; = 'door-post' (Deut. vi. 9, etc.).] Among the Jews, a piece of parchment inscribed on one side with the texts Deut. vi. 4-9 and xi. 13-21 and on the other with the divine name Shaddai, enclosed in a case and attached to the door-post.

Mezzanine (me·zănīn). 1711. [a. F., ad. It. *Mezzanino*, dim. of *mezzano* middle :—L. *medianus* MEDIAN.] 1. A low story between two higher ones, usually between the ground floor and the story above. Cf. ENTRESOL. Also *attrib.* in *m. floor, story.* b. *Theatr.* A floor beneath the stage. Also *m. floor.* 1859. 2. A small window, less in height than breadth, occurring in entresols and attics, etc. Also *m. window.* 1731.

‖**Mezza voce** (me·dza,vō·tʃe), *adv.* 1775. [It. *mezza* moderate, half + *voce* VOICE.] *Mus.* Prop. *a mezza voce*: With a medium volume of sound.

‖**Mezzo** (me·dzo, -tso), *sb.*[1] 1832. Short for MEZZO-SOPRANO, also *attrib.* as *m. voice.*

Me·zzo, *sb.*[2] 1886. Short for MEZZOTINT.

‖**Me·zzo**, *a.* 1811. [It. :—L. *medius*; see MEDIUM.] *Mus.* In *m. forte* rather loud, *m. piano* rather soft.

‖**Mezzo-rilievo** (me·dzo rīlie·vo). *Pl.* **-os.** 1598. [It. *mezzo* half + *rilievo* RELIEF *sb.*] 1. Half-relief; relief in which the figures project half their true proportions. 2. *concr.* A sculpture or carving in half-relief 1665.

‖**Mezzo-soprano** (me·dzo soprā·no, me·tso), *sb.* and *a.* 1753. [It.; see MEZZO *a.* and SOPRANO.] *Mus.* a. The part intermediate in compass between the soprano and contralto; b. a voice of this compass; c. a person having such a voice.

Mezzotint (me·tsotint, me·(d)zo-), *sb.* 1738. [Anglicized f. MEZZOTINTO.] 1. = MEZZOTINTO 1. *Obs.* or *arch.* 2. A method of engraving on copper or steel, in which the surface of the plate is first roughened uniformly, the lights and half-lights being then produced by scraping away the 'nap' thus formed, and the untouched parts giving the deepest shadows. Also, a print produced by this process. 1800. Hence **Me·zzotint** *v.* to engrave in mezzotint 1827; **Me·zzotinter** 1763.

‖**Mezzotinto** (medzoti·nto, -ts-), *sb.* and *a.* 1660. [It.; *mezzo* half, *tinto* tint.] †1. A half-tint -1788. 2. = MEZZOTINT *sb.* 2. 1661.

2. Prince Rupert first shewed me how to grave in Mezzo Tinto EVELYN.

Mho (mōu). 1883. [OHM spelt backwards; proposed by Lord Kelvin.] *Electr.* The unit of conductivity, being the conductivity of a body whose resistance is one ohm. So **Mhometer** (mǫ·mītəɹ), an instrument for measuring electrical conductivities.

Mhorr (mǭɹ). Also **m'horr, moh(o)r.** 1833. [Morocco Arabic.] A West African gazelle, having annulated horns. It produces bezoar stones.

Mi (mī). 1529. [Orig. the first syllable of L. *mira*; see GAMUT and UT.] The third note in Guido's hexachords, retained in solmization as the third note of the octave. (In Tonic Sol-fa often written *me.*)

M. I. = Mounted Infantry.

Miaow (miau), *int.* and *sb.* 1634. [Echoic. Cf. F. *miaou.*] The cry of a cat, or an imitation of it. Hence **Miaow** *v. intr.* 1632.

Miargyrite (məi,ā·ɹdʒirəit). 1836. [ad. G. *miargyrit*, f. Gr. μείων less + ἄργυρος silver + -ITE[1] 2 b.] *Min.* A black sulph-antimonide of silver, which contains less silver than red silver ore.

‖**Mias** (məi·ăs). *sing.* and *pl.* 1840. [Dayak *maias.*] The orang-outang, *Simia satyrus.*

Miascite (məi·ăskəit). Also **-cyte, -kite.** 1854. [ad. G. *miaszit*, f. *Miask*, in the Ural Mountains: see -ITE[1] 2 b.] *Petrology.* A rock essentially composed of orthoclase, elæolite, and dark mica.

Miasm (məi·æz'm). 1650. [a. F. *miasme.*] = next.

‖**Miasma** (məi,æ·zmă). *Pl.* **mia·smata, mia·smas.** 1665. [mod.L., a. Gr. μίασμα pollution, f. μιαίνειν to pollute.] Infectious or noxious exhalations from putrescent organic matter; poisonous germs floating in the atmosphere; noxious emanations, *esp.* malaria. Also *fig.* Hence **Mia·smal** *a.* containing miasmatic effluvia or germs. **Miasma·tic, Mia·smic, Mia·smous** *adjs.* having the nature of miasma, malarial.

Miaul (mi,ǭ·l), *v.* 1632. [ad. F. *miauler*, echoic.] 1. *intr.* To call or cry as a cat. 2. *trans.* To sing with a voice like that of a cat 1862. Hence **Miau·ler.**

Mica (məi·kă). 1684. [a. L. *mica* grain, crumb; perh. erron. assoc. w. *micare* to shine.] *Min.* †1. A small plate of talc, selenite, or the like, found in the structure of a rock. In pl. *micæ.* -1803. 2. Any one of a group of minerals composed essentially of silicate of aluminium combined with the silicates of other bases, e. g. soda, potash, and magnesia, and occurring in small glittering scales in granite, etc., or in crystals characterized by their perfect basal cleavage and their consequent separability into thin, transparent, and usually flexible laminæ 1778.

Comb.: **m.-powder**, a form of dynamite in which the siliceous earth is replaced by m. in fine scales; **-schist, -slate**, a slaty metamorphic rock composed of quartz and m. Hence **Mica·ceous** *a.* containing or resembling m.; pertaining to or of the nature of m.

Mice (məis), pl. of MOUSE.

‖**Micella** (mise·lă). *Pl.* **micellæ** (-ī). 1882. [mod.L., dim. of L. *mica* crumb.] *Biol.* The hypothetical solid molecular aggregate of which Nägeli considered the organized structures of plants to consist. Hence **Mice·llar** *a.*

Michael (məi·kəl). OE. [repr. Heb. *Mīkhāēl*, lit. 'who is like God?' Gr. Μιχαήλ, L. *Michael.*] 1. The name of one of the archangels. †2. = MICHAELMAS. -1622. 3. As a common Christian name of men ME.

1. *The feast of St. M., St. Michael's day*: Michaelmas. *Order of St. M. and St. George*: an English civil order of knighthood instituted in 1818, now a reward for distinguished services in the colonies and abroad.

Michaelmas (mi·kəlmăs). [OE. *Sanct Micheles mæsse*, ME. *michel masse*: see prec. and MASS *sb.*[1]] The feast of St. Michael, 29 Sept., an English quarter-day. Also *attrib.*

Comb.: *M. goose*, *rent*; **M. daisy**, a sea-starwort, (*a*) wild aster (*Aster Tripolium*); (*b*) one of several garden asters bearing masses of purplish flowers; **M. day** = Michaelmas; **M. eve**, the evening before M.; **M. term**, a term or session (beginning soon after M.) of the High Court of Justice in England; and also of Oxford, Cambridge, and other universities. **Old M. day**: the day that was 29 Sept. before the New Style was adopted; from 1900 onwards this has been 12 Oct.

Miche (mitʃ), *v.* Now *dial.* late ME. [app. a. OF. *muchier*, *mucier* to hide, also intr. to skulk.] †1. *trans.* To pilfer -1570. 2. *intr.* To shrink or retire from view; to skulk. Also const. *off.* 1558. b. To play truant 1580. So **Mi·cher**, †a secret or petty thief ME.-1823; †one who skulks about for improper or dishonest purposes -1630; a truant (now *dial.*) 1530. †**Mi·chery**, pilfering, thievishness; cheating.

†**Miching malicho.** 1603. Usu. explained as 'skulking mischief' (MICHE *v.*, Sp. *malhecho* misdeed); but form, origin, and meaning are uncertain.

Marry this is Myching Mallico, that meanes Mischeefe *Haml.* III. ii. 146 (1st Qo.).

Mickle (mi·k'l), **muckle** (mɒ·k'l), *a.*, *sb.*, and *adv.* *Obs.* exc. *dial.* and *arch.* [Com. Teut.: OE. *micel* (also *mycel*):—OTeut. **mikilo-*, corresp. to Gr. μεγαλο-, lengthened stem of μέγας great. For the phonology see N.E.D.] A. *adj.* 1. = GREAT *a.* 2. A great quantity or amount of; = MUCH *a.* OE. B. *absol.* and *sb.* 1. The adj. used *absol.* A great quantity or amount; much OE. †2. *sb.* Size, stature; bigness -1622. 3. A large sum or amount. Chiefly in proverb, *Many a little* (or *pickle*) *makes a mickle*. 1599. C. *adv.* Greatly; by far OE.

Micklemote, -gemote (mi·k'lmōᵘt, -gəmōᵘt). [repr. OE. *micel gemót*; see MICKLE *a.* and MOOT *sb.*[1]] *OE. Hist.* The great council or parliamentary assembly under the Anglo-Saxon kings.

Micracoustic (məikrăkau·stik). 1683. [a. F. *micracoustique*, f. Gr. μικρός small + ἀκουστικός ACOUSTIC *a.*] A. *adj.* Making weak sounds audible 1855. †B. *sb.* An instrument which magnifies small sounds -1704.

Micro- (məi·kro), bef. a vowel **micr-**, repr. Gr. μικρο-, comb. f. μικρός small.

1. Prefixed to a sb. to indicate relatively small size or extent, as *microbacillus*, *-bacterium*, *-gamete*, etc. **Mi·croblast** [-BLAST], *Biol.* = *microcyte.* ‖**Micro·co·ccus**, *pl.* **-cocci** (-kǫ·ksəi), [Gk. κόκκος berry], *Biol.* any one of a large genus of non-ciliated bacteria. **Mi·crocyte** [-CYTE], *Path.* a minute red blood-corpuscle. **Microfe·lsite**, *Geol.* and *Min.* a form of felsite incapable of resolution under the microscope. ‖**Microlepido·ptera**, *sb. pl.* *Entom.* a collector's term for certain small moths. **Mi·crolite, Mi·crolith** [Gr. λίθος stone], *Petrology*, the microscopic acicular particles contained in the glassy portions of felspar, hornblende, etc. **Micro-o·rganism**, *Biol.* a microbe. **Mi·crophyte** [Gr. φυτόν plant], a microscopic plant, *esp.* a bacterium. **Mi·crosome** [Gr. σῶμα body], a name for certain small granules which abound in vegetating cells of protoplasm. **Microzo·ospore**, *Bot.* a minute motile spore.

2. Prefixed to sbs. and derived adjs. to denote 'microscopic' in the sense 'with the microscope', 'revealed by the microscope'; as, a. *micro-chemistry* (hence *-chemic* adj., etc.), *-crystallography*, *-geology* (hence *-geological* adj., *-geologist*), etc., branches of research carried on by means of microscopic examination; b. *micro-foliation*, *-structure*, properties revealed by the microscope; so *micro-crystalline*, *-granite*; c. *micro-section*, *-slide*, objects prepared for study with the microscope.

3. *Phys.* and *Path.*, in sbs. of mod.L. form in *-ia*, compounded with Gr. names for different parts or functions of the body, and signifying arrested development of the part or function in question, as ‖**Microphtha·lmia** (also **Mi·crophthalmy**) [Gr. ὀφθαλμός], 'a Disease in the Eyes, the having little Eyes' (Bailey); hence **Microphtha·lmic** *a.* ‖**Micro·psia** [Gr. -οψία kind of vision], the state of vision in which objects appear smaller than natural.

4. Forming adjs. with sense 'containing or possessed of some object or constituent in minute form, quantity, or degree', as **Mi·crodont** [Gr. ὀδοντ-, ὀδούς], *Anat.* having small or short teeth. **Microphy·llous** [Gr. φύλλον], *Bot.* having small leaves. **Micro·podal, -ic, -ous** [Gr. ποδ-, πούς foot] small-footed. **Mi·croseme** [Gr. σῆμα sign], (of a skull) having an orbital index below 83. **Microsty·lous** *a.*, *Bot.* having a short style.

5. a. *Physics.* Prefixed to the name of a unit to form a name for one-millionth part of that unit, as *micro-ampere*, *-coulomb*, *-farad*, *-gramme*, *-litre*, *-millimetre*, *-ohm*, *-volt*, *-weber*. b. *Micro-millimetre*, (*a*) one-millionth of a millimetre; (*b*) *Bot.* one-thousandth of a millimetre.

6. Prefixed to names of instruments, as: **Microtasimeter**, an instrument for measuring infinitesimal pressure. **Micro-telephone**, a telephone constructed to render audible very weak sounds.

Microbe (məi·krōᵘb). 1881. Also ‖**micro·bion**, *pl.* **-ia** 1883. [a. F. *microbe* (Sédillot, 1878), f. Gr. μικρός small + βίος life.] *Biol.* An extremely minute living being, whether plant or animal; chiefly applied to the bacteria causing diseases and fermentation. Hence **Micro·bial, Micro·bian, Micro·bic** *adjs.* of or pertaining to microbes; due to microbes.

Microbicide (məikrōᵘ·bisəid). 1885. [f. MICROBE + -(I)CIDE[1].] *Biol.* A. *sb.* Something that kills microbes 1887. B. *adj.* Microbicidal. Hence **Micro·bicidal** *a.* pertaining to the killing of microbes.

Microbiology (məikrobəi,ǫ·lŏdʒi). 1885. [MICRO- 1.] *Biol.* The science which treats of micro-organisms. Hence **Microbiolo·gical** *a.* **Microbio·logist.**

‖**Microcephalic** (məikrosĭfæ·lik), *a.* 1856. [ult. f. Gr. μικρός small + κεφαλή head.] *Path.* and *Anthropol.* Having an abnormally small head. So **Microce·phalous,** *a.* 1840. **Microce·phaly** 1863.

Microcline (məi·krokləin). 1849. [ad. G. *mikroklin*, f. Gr. μικρός + κλίνειν to incline, as indicating that the angle between its cleavage plane differs a little from 90 degrees.] *Min.* A green and blue variety of felspar.

Microcosm (məi·krŏkǫz'm). ME. [ad. F. *microcosme*, ad. med.L. *microcosmus*, ad. late Gr. μικρὸς κόσμος.] 1. The 'little world' of human nature; man as an epitome of the 'great world' or universe. 2. Hence, any community or other complex unity, viewed as an epitome of the world 1562. b. A 'miniature' representation *of* 1808. †3. *Alch.* The philosopher's stone 1477.

1. The doctrine of a constant analogy between universal nature, or the macrocosm, and that of man, or the m. HALLAM. Hence †**Microco·smal** *a.*

Microcosmic (məikrokǫ·smik), *a.* 1783. [f. MICROCOSM + -IC.] 1. Of, pertaining to, or of the nature of a microcosm 1816. 2. *M. salt* [= L. *sal microcosmicus* (Bergmann)]: a phosphate of soda and ammonia, orig. derived from human urine, and much used as a blow-pipe flux. So **Microco·smical** *a.* 1570.

†**Mi·crocosmo·graphy.** 1606. [f. MICROCOSM + -(O)GRAPHY.] The description of the 'microcosm' or man -1628.

Micrography (məikrǫ·grăfi). 1658. [f. MICRO- 2 + -GRAPHY.] 1. The description or delineation of microscopic objects. 2. a. The art or practice of writing in microscopic characters. b. *Path.* Abnormally small handwriting, as a symptom of nervous disorder. 1899. Hence **Micro·grapher**, one addicted to m. **Microgra·phic** *a.* of or pertaining to m.; minutely written (as symptomatic of nervous disorder).

Microlithic (məikroli·þik), *a.* 1872. [f. Gr. μικρός + λίθος stone; see -IC.] *Antiq.* Consisting or constructed of small stones; *transf.* of a period, a people, etc. (opp. to MEGALITHIC).

Micrological (məikrolǫ·dʒikăl), *a.* 1847. [f. MICROLOGY + -ICAL.] 1. Characterized by minuteness of investigation or discussion 1879. 2. Of or pertaining to the study of minute objects; belonging to MICROLOGY 2. Hence **Microlo·gically** *adv.*

Micrology (məikrǫ·lŏdʒi). 1656. [ad. Gr. μικρολογία, f. μικρός small + -λογία; see -LOGY.] 1. The discussion or investigation of petty affairs; 'hair-splitting'. 2. (After MICROSCOPE.) That part of science which relates to the examination of minute objects; a treatise on microscopic objects 1849. So **Micro·logist,** one versed in m. (sense 2).

Micromere (məi·kromīᵊɪ). 1877. [f. MICRO- 1 + Gr. μέρος part.] *Embryology.* The smaller of the two masses into which the vitellus of the developing ovum of *Lamellibranchiata* divides (cf. MACROMERE). Hence **Microme·ral, Microme·ric** *adjs.* of or pertaining to the m.

Micrometer (məikrǫ·mĭtəɪ). 1670. [ad. F. *micromètre*, f. Gr. μικρός + μέτρον; see -METER.] An instrument for measuring minute objects or differences of dimension. 1. An astronomical instrument applied to telescopes for measuring very small angular distances. 2. An instrument applied to the microscope for measuring small objects 1790. 3. An instrument used in machine-construction, watchmaking, etc., for obtaining extreme accuracy in measurement; also *m. calliper(s, gauge* 1884.

attrib. and *Comb.*, as *m. cell*, *eye-piece*, etc.; **m. balance**, a balance for ascertaining minute weights, esp. in weighing coins; **m.-microscope**, an apparatus for reading and subdividing the divisions of large astronomical and geodetical instruments; **m. screw**, a screw attached to optical and other instruments for the exact measurement of very small angles. Hence **Microme·tric, -al** *a.* pertaining to or of the nature of a m.; carried on by or resulting from the use of a m. **Microme·trically** *adv.* **Micro·metry**, the measurement of minute objects; the use of the m.

Micron, mikron (məi·krǫn). 1892. [ad. Gr. μικρόν adj. neut.] The one-millionth part of a metre; denoted by the symbol μ.

¶**Micronesian** (məikronī·ʃiăn). 1896. [f. *Micronesia* (intended to mean 'the region of small islands'), f. Gr. μικρός + νῆσος + -AN.] A. *adj.* Of or pertaining to Micronesia (a group of small islands in the western region of the North Pacific, including the Caroline, Ladrone, Marshall and Gilbert Islands, etc.), its inhabitants, language, etc. B. *sb.* A native of Micronesia; the language of the Micronesians.

Microphone (məi·krŏfōᵘn). 1683. [f. Gr. μικρός + φωνή sound.] 1. An instrument by which small sounds can be intensified. 2. *spec.* An instrument by means of which the telephone is made to reproduce faint sounds with added intensity 1878. Hence **Micropho·nic** *a.*; *sb. pl.* the science of magnifying sounds. **Micro·phonous** *a.* having the property of augmenting weak sounds.

Microphonograph (məi:krofōᵘ·nŏgrɑf). 1897. [f. as prec. + PHONOGRAPH.] An instrument combining the principles of the microphone and the phonograph, designed for rendering sound audible to deaf-mutes.

Microphotograph (məi:krofōᵘ·tŏgrɑf). 1858. [MICRO- 1.] 1. A photograph reduced to microscopic size. 2. = PHOTOMICROGRAPH 1860. Hence **Microphotogra·phic** *a.* **Microphotogra·phically** *adv.*

Microphotography (məi:krofŏtǫ·grăfi). 1858. [f. MICRO- + PHOTOGRAPHY.] 1. The art or process of making microphotographs. 2. = PHOTOMICROGRAPHY 1858.

Micropyle (məi·kropəil). 1821. [a. F., f. Gr. μικρός + πύλη gate.] 1. *Bot.* The foramen in the integument of an ovule, by which the pollen penetrates to the apex of the nucleus or radicle. Also, the corresponding external aperture in the mature seed. 2. *Zool.* A special opening in a female cell for the entrance of the fertilizing cell 1859. Hence **Micropy·lar** *a.*

Microscope (məi·krŏskōᵘp). 1656. [ad. mod. L. *microscopium*, f. Gr. μικρός + σκοπεῖν to look; see -SCOPE.] 1. An optical instrument, consisting of a lens or a combination of lenses (or, rarely, also of mirrors) by which objects are so magnified that details invisible to the naked eye are clearly revealed. Also *transf.* and *fig.* **2.** *Astron.* (Also **Microsco·pium.**) A constellation south of Capricorn 1752.

1. *Lucernal, solar, oxy-hydrogen microscopes*: instruments of the nature of the magic lantern, illuminated by a lamp, the sun, and an oxy-hydrogen limelight respectively. *fig.* The critic Eye, that m. of Wit, Sees hairs and pores POPE. Hence **Micro·scopist**, one skilled in the use of the m. **Micro·scopy**, the art or practice of using the m.; the science of the microscopist.

Microscopic (məikrǫ̆skǫ·pik), *a.* 1680. [ad. mod.L. *microscopicus*; see MICROSCOPE and -IC.] **1.** = MICROSCOPICAL *a.* 1. Now *rare* exc. *fig.* 1779. **2.** Possessing or exercising the functions of a microscope 1680. **3.** So minute as to be invisible or indistinct without the use of a microscope *c* 1760.

1. *fig.* A m. self-examination 1850. **2.** Why has not Man a m. eye? For this plain reason, Man is not a Fly POPE. **3.** *fig.* Turner's m. touch RUSKIN.

Microscopical (məikrǫ̆skǫ·pikăl), *a.* 1664. [f. as prec. + -AL.] **1.** Pertaining to the microscope or its use; resembling what pertains to a microscope. **2.** = MICROSCOPIC 3. Now *rare*. 1665. Hence **Microsco·pically** *adv.*

Microseism (məikrosəi·z'm). 1887. [f. Gr. μικρός + σεισμός shaking.] A faint earthquake tremor. So **Microsei·smic, -al** *a.* 1877. **Microsei·smograph**, an instrument for recording microseisms 1881. **Microseismo·logy, -o·metry.**

Microspe·ctroscope. 1867. [f. MICRO- + SPECTROSCOPE.] A combination of the microscope and spectroscope devised for the examination of the absorptive spectrum of very minute quantities of substances.

Microspore (məi·krospōᵊɹ). 1856. [MICRO- 1.] **1.** *Bot.* and *Path.* A parasitic fungus which has small spores, characteristic of ringworm. **2.** *Bot.* One of the small (quasi-male) spores of certain cryptogams; opp. to MACROSPORE 1858. **3.** *Zool.* A spore-like form in Protozoa 1882. So ‖ **Micro·sporon** (in sense 1) 1876. **Mi:crospora·nge, -a·ngium** *Bot.* a capsule containing microspores 1881.

Microtome (məi·krǒtōᵘm). 1856. [f. Gr. μικρός + -τόμος that cuts, f. τομ-, τεμ-, root of τέμνειν.] An instrument for cutting extremely thin sections for microscopic work. **Micro·to·mic, -al** *a.*, **Micro·tomist, Micro·tomy.**

‖ **Microzoa** (məikrozōᵘ·ă), *sb. pl.* In sing. **-zoon** (-zōᵘ·ǫn). 1862. [mod.L., f. Gr. μικρός + ζῷον animal.] *Zool.* A general name for infusoria, rotifers, etc. Hence **Microzo·al, Microzo·ic** *adjs.* of the nature of, containing, or consisting of m.

Microzyme (məi·krozəim). Also **microzyma** (məikrozəi·mă). 1870. [f. MICRO- 1 + Gr. ζύμη yeast.] *Biol.* A zymotic microbe, to whose presence are attributed epidemic and other zymotic diseases.

Micturition (miktiŭri·ʃən). 1725. [f. L. *micturire*, desiderative vb. f. *mict-, minct-, mingere*.] The desire to make water; a morbid frequency in the voiding of urine. Often erron.: The action of making water.

Mid (mid), *a.*, *sb.*¹, and *adv.* [Com. Teut. and Indo-Eur.: OE. *midd* :—OTeut. **medjo-* :—Indo-Eur. **medhyo-*, whence Skr. *madhya*, Gr. μέσ(σ)ος, L. *medius*.] **A.** *adj.* **1.** Expressing adjectively the sense: (The) middle or midst of. (Now usu. hyphened.) **2.** Occupying a central, medial, or intermediate position. Now usu. superseded by MIDDLE *a.* late ME. **3.** *Phonetics.* Of a vowel-sound: Produced with the tongue or part of it in a middle position, between high and low 1876. **B.** *sb.*¹ *Obs.* exc. *dial.* The adj. used *absol.* = MIDDLE *sb.* ME. †**C.** *adv.* In the middle –1576.

A. 1. The plough was in m.-furrow stayed SCOTT. *Comb.*: *m.-career, -channel, -ocean, -season*, etc. **M.-brain**, the middle segment of the brain: = MESENCEPHALON; **-breast** *Entom.*, the underside of the mesothorax; **-totality** *Astr.*, the middle of the duration of the totality of an eclipse; **-wicket** in *Cricket*, the fieldsman or his position on the off-side; also *m.-wicket off, on* = MID-OFF, MID-ON. The M.-Victorian style of domestic architecture 1902. **2.** In the m.-days of autumn KEATS. *Comb.*: **m.-gut**, the mesenteron; **-iron** *Golf*, an iron with medium loft; also a stroke made with this; **-spoon** *Golf*, a spoon of medium size; **-watch**, the middle watch; **-workings**, workings with other workings above and below in the same mine or colliery.

Mid, *sb.*² 1797. Joc. shortening of MIDSHIPMAN.

†**Mid**, *prep.*¹ (*adv.*). [Com. Teut.: OE. *mid*, cogn. w. Gr. μετά (see META-). In 14th c. superseded by WITH.] = WITH in all senses, except that of 'against' (as in *to fight with*) –ME.

Mid, 'mid (mid), *prep.*² 1808. Poet. aphesis of AMID.

†**Mid-age.** 1440. [f. MID *a.* + AGE *sb.*] = MIDDLE AGE –1757.

Mid air. 1667 (Milton). The tract between the clouds and the part of the atmosphere near the ground: chiefly in phr. *in mid air.*

Midas (məi·dæs). 1568. [a. L., Gr. Μίδας.] **1.** The name of a fabled king of Phrygia, whose touch turned everything (including his food) into gold. Apollo gave him ass's ears for being dull to the charm of his lyre. Hence *allusively*. Also *attrib.* **2.** *Midas's ear*: the shell of a gastropod, *Auricula Midæ* 1713.

1. Thou gaudie gold, Hard food for M. SHAKS. The M. finger of the State COWPER.

Mid-course. 1513. [f. MID *a.* + COURSE.] The middle of one's or its course.

Midday (mi·dˌdēⁱ; stress variable). [OE. *middæg* (MID *a.*, DAY *sb.*).] **1.** The middle of the day; noon. †**2.** The South –1604.

1. Ere mid-day arriv'd In Eden MILT. *attrib.* and *Comb.*, as *m.-devotions, -dinner, -post, -splendour*, etc. Also †**m. devil, fiend**, transl. of Vulg. *dæmonium meridianum* Ps. xc[i]. 6, for which the Eng. Bible has 'the destruction that wasteth at noonday'.

Midden (mi·d'n). Now *dial.* (rarely *arch.*). ME. [Of Scand. origin; cf. Da. *mødding*, altered f. *møgdynge*, f. *møg* (see MUCK *sb.*¹) + *dynge* heap.] **1.** A dunghill. Also *fig.* **2.** Short for KITCHEN-MIDDEN 1866.

Middenstead (mi·d'nsted). 1607. [f. MIDDEN + STEAD.] The place where a dunghill is formed; a laystall.

Middest (mi·dėst), *a.* *superl.* 1590. [f. MID *a.* + -EST.] Most central; in the middle.

Middle (mi·d'l). [OE. *middel*, *midl-* adj. :—WGer. **middil-*, f. **middi-* :—OTeut. **medjo-* MID *a.*] **A.** *adj.* Not in predicative use. **1.** (Orig. in *superl.*) Used of that member of a group or sequence, or that part of a whole, which has the same number of members or parts on each side of it. **b.** Of a point or line: Equidistant from the extremities. late ME. †**c.** Average, mean –1790. **2.** Intermediate, intervening (see quots.) ME. **3.** In partitive concord: = '(The) middle or middle part of; mid.' Now *rare*. OE. **4.** *Philology.* **a.** *Gram.* Intermediate between active and passive: primarily (after Gr. μέση διάθεσις, μέσον ῥῆμα), the designation of a voice of Gr. verbs expressing reflexive or reciprocal action or intrans. conditions. **b.** Prefixed (after G. *mittel-*) to the name of a language, to denote a period in its history intermediate between those called *Old* and *New* or *Modern*, as in *Middle-English* (see ENGLISH *sb.*¹ 1 b), etc. **5.** *Geol.* Prefixed to the designation of a formation or period, to denote a subdivision intermediate between two others called 'Upper' and 'Lower' 1838.

1. That m. time of life which is happily tempered with the warmth of youth GOLDSM. *M. brother, sister, son*, etc. (*legal*): the second in age of three brothers, etc. *M. price* (Stock Exchange): the price intermediate between a jobber's buying and selling prices. **2.** They..speed the race, And spurring see decrease the m. space DRYDEN. Men of a m. condition SOUTH. A m. opinion 1782. A man of m. stature SCOTT. **3.** Neuer since the m. Summers spring Met we SHAKS. **5.** M. lias shale 1838.

Special collocations. **m. C** *Mus.*, the note on the first ledger line below the treble stave or above the bass stave; **m. deck**, the deck between the upper and lower decks; **m. distance** (see DISTANCE); **m. ear**, the tympanum; **M. Empire** = *Middle Kingdom*; **m. finger**, the second finger; **m. ground** *Naut.*, a shallow place, formerly a bank or bar; *Painting* = *middle distance*; **M. Kingdom**, a name for the 18 provinces of China proper, or the whole Chinese Empire; **m. line** (*a*) *Naut.*, a line dividing the ship exactly in the middle; (*b*) *Croquet*, the line of hoops placed in the m. of the lawn; **m. passage**, the m. portion (i.e. the part consisting of sea travel) of the journey of a slave carried from Africa to America; **m. pointed** *a.* *Arch.*, a name for Decorated Gothic; **m. post**, in *Carpentry* = KING-POST; **m. space** *Printing*, a space intermediate in size between 'thick' and 'thin'; **M. States**, the States which originally formed the m. part of the United States, intermediate between New England and the Southern States, namely, New York, New Jersey, Pennsylvania, and Delaware; **M. Temple** (see TEMPLE); **m. term** *Logic*, the term which is common to the premisses of a syllogism, and disappears in the conclusion; **m. tint** *Painting*, 'a mixed tint in which bright colours never predominate' (Fairholt); **m. wall**, a partition wall; **m. watch** *Naut.*, the watch from midnight to 4 a.m.; **m.-weight**, a man of average weight, *esp.* a boxer whose weight is from 11 st. 6 to 10 st. 7; **m. wicket** = *mid-wicket* (see MID *a.*).

B. *sb.* **1.** The middle point or part OE. **2.** = MIDST *sb.* 2. Now only in relation to an action, etc. OE. **3.** The middle part of the human body; the waist OE. **4.** A mean between two extremes ME. †**5.** Something intermediate –1667. **6.** *ellipt.* for various terms, as *middle term, voice* 1818. **7.** *Naut.* = *middle ground* 1702. **8.** *Football.* A return of the ball from one of the wings to mid-field in front of the goal 1899. **9.** (Orig. *m. article.*) A newspaper article on some social, ethical, or literary subject, such as is in some journals placed between the leading articles and the reviews 1862.

1. Canst thou..Murther thy breath in m. of a word? SHAKS. See, there come people downe by the m. of the land *Judg.* ix. 37. **2.** I have often been stopped in the middle of a speech JOWETT. **3.** A long Wigg that reaches down to his M. ADDISON. **4.** The rights of men are in a sort of m. BURKE.

Middle (mi·d'l), *v.* 1841. [f. MIDDLE *sb.*] **1.** *Naut.* (*trans.*) To fold or double in the middle. **2.** *techn.* To place in the middle 1883. **3.** *trans.* in *Football.* To return (the ball) from one of the wings to mid-field in front of goal; to centre. Also *absol.* 1871.

Middle age, *sb.* late ME. **1.** The period between youth and old age. **2.** *The M. Age* (1621), now usu. *the M. Ages* (1722): the period intermediate between 'ancient' and 'modern' times; in early use, from *c* 500 to *c* 1500; now loosely, the four centuries after A.D. 1000. **3.** *attrib.*, quasi-*adj.* (with hyphen). Belonging to the Middle Ages; mediæval 1753. So **Middle-aged** *a.* of middle age; characteristic of middle-aged people 1676; †mediæval 1710–1845.

Middle class, *sb.* 1812. The class of society between the 'upper' and the 'lower' class. Now usu. *pl.* Also *attrib.* (with hyphen). **b.** Used as *adj.* Characteristic of the middle classes; having the characteristics of the middle classes. (Depreciative.) 1893.

attrib., as in *m. education, life*, etc.; **m. examination**, an early name of the 'local examination' (LOCAL *a.* 2 c); **m. schools**, schools for the middle classes, intermediate between primary schools and the great public schools.

Middle earth. ME. **1.** [Perversion of ME. *middelerd*, alteration of *middenerd* (OE. *middangeard*).] The earth as placed between heaven and hell. Now only *arch.*, occas. applied to the real world as dist. from fairyland. †**2.** *Sea of middle earth, middle earth sea*, the Mediterranean –1613.

1. That maid is born of middle earth, And may of man be won SCOTT.

Middleman (mi·d'lmæ̆n). 1616. [f. MIDDLE *a.* + MAN *sb.*] †**1.** *Mil.* One of the soldiers in the fifth or sixth rank in a file of 10 deep –1696. **2.** One who takes a middle course 1741. **3.** (Orig. two words.) A person standing in intermediate relation to two parties concerned in some matter of business; usu. in an unfavourable sense. Chiefly applied to traders as intermediate between producers and consumers. 1795. **b.** In Ireland, one who leases land, and sub-lets it again at an advanced rate 1802.

3. The Metcalfes..were middlemen between the vendors and the vendees 1805.

Middlemost (mi·d'lmōᵘst), *a.* Now somewhat *rare*. ME. [f. MIDDLE *a.* + -MOST.] That is in the very middle, or nearest the middle. Now only with ref. to position.

Middler (mi·d'ləɹ). 1531. [f. MIDDLE *a.* + -ER¹.] †**1.** An intermediary, mediator –1675. **2.** The workman who performs the middle one of three operations in the preparation of flax 1847.

Middle way. ME. **1.** A course between two extremes. Cf. mod.L. *via media.* **2.** The middle of the way 1633. **b.** Used *advb.* Half-way, on the way 1568.

Middling (mi·dliŋ), *sb.* 1543. [Prob. orig. f. MID *a.* + -LING[1]; now the adj. used absol. or ellipt.] †**1.** Something intermediate; a middle term –1620. **2.** *pl.* Pins of medium size 1543. **3.** *pl.* Used as a trade name for the middle one of three grades of goods; e. g. *U.S.* of cotton 1793; of flour or meal 1842. **4.** *U.S.* The portion of a hog between the ham and the shoulder 1859.

Middling (mi·d'liŋ), *a.* and *adv.* 1456. [App. of Sc. origin; prob. f. MID *a.* or MIDDLE *a.* + -LING[2].] **A.** *adj.* †**1.** Intermediate between two things; forming a mean –1767. **2.** Of medium size; moderately large. Now *colloq.* or *vulgar.* 1596. †**b.** Average. HUME. **3.** *Comm.* Used to designate the second of three grades of goods 1550. **b.** Moderately good, mediocre 1652. **4.** Belonging to the middle classes 1692.

3. b. The abundant consumption of m. literature M. ARNOLD. 4. The m. classes SCOTT. The m. strata of society 1897.

B. *adv.* (Now chiefly *colloq.*) **1.** Moderately, fairly, tolerably 1719. **2.** Fairly well; chiefly *predicatively*, not very well in health 1810.

1. A m. good Anvil DE FOE. 2. 'How de do?' 'Middling' replies Mr. George DICKENS. Hence **Mi·ddlingly** *adv.*

Middy (mi·di). *colloq.* 1833. [f. MID *sb.*[2] + -Y[6].] A midshipman.

Mid-earth. 1559. = MIDDLE EARTH.

Mid-feather. 1748. **1.** *Salt-making.* A partition in a furnace dividing the flue into two chambers. **2.** *Mining.* A support for the centre of a tunnel 1897.

Mid-field. late ME. The middle of the field. Now chiefly in *Football.*

Midge (midʒ). [OE. *mycg* masc., *mycge* wk. fem.:—OTeut. *mugjo-z, *mugjōn-.] **1.** A popular name given to many small gnat-like insects; by some restricted to the *Chironomidæ.* **b.** A diminutive person 1796. **2.** The fry of various fishes 1832.

Midget (mi·dʒėt). 1865. [f. MIDGE + -ET.] An extremely small person; *spec.* such a person exhibited as a curiosity; *transf.* anything very small of its kind; also *attrib.* So **Mi·dgety** *a.* very small. JANE AUSTEN.

A little m. of a man MRS. H. B. STOWE.

Mid-heaven. 1594. **1.** *Astron.* and *Astrol.* **1.** The meridian; the point of the ecliptic on the meridian. **2.** The midst of the heavens 1612.

2. Or how the Sun shall in mid Heav'n stand still MILT.

‖**Midinette** (midine·t). 1909. [F., f. *midi* mid-day + *dînette* light dinner.] A Parisian shop-girl, *esp.* a milliner's assistant.

Midland (mi·dlănd). 1555. [f. MID *a.* + LAND.] **A.** *sb.* The middle part of a country. Also *pl.* the middle counties of England. **B.** *adj.* **1.** Situated inland; remote from the sea 1601. **b.** Belonging to the Midlands 1837. **2.** = MEDITERRANEAN *a.* 2. 1579.

1. *M. counties* (of England): the counties south of the Humber and Mersey and north of the Thames, except Norfolk, Suffolk, Essex, Middlesex, Hertfordshire, Gloucestershire, and the counties bordering on Wales. **b. M. dialect,** the dialect spoken in the m. counties. S. Lancashire, the Welsh border, Lincolnshire, and E. Anglia. 2. *M. sea,* the Mediterranean Sea. O'er the blue M. waters with the gale, Betwixt the Syrtes and soft Sicily MATT. ARNOLD.

Mid leg. 1590. [MID *a.*] **1.** The middle of the leg. **b.** *advb.* To the middle of the leg 1829. **2.** *Entom.* One of the intermediate or second pair of legs of an insect 1826.

Mid-lent. 1450. *M.* (*Sunday*), the 4th Sunday in Lent.

Midmost (mi·dmōust). [OE. *midmest,* formed with suffix -EST on WGer. *middjumo, OTeut. *midjumo-, superl. of *medjo- MID *a.* From 17th c. assim. to *-most.*] **A.** *adj.* **1.** That is in the very middle. **b.** *absol.* The midmost part. late ME. **2.** In partitive concord: The middle or midst of 1807. **3.** Most intimate. HAWTHORNE.

1. b. From the m. of Ida SWINBURNE. 2. High in the m. city the horse pours forth from its side Warriors armed BOWEN.

B. *adv.* In the middle or midst 1700. **b.** *prep.* In the middle or midst of 1867.

b. M. the beating of the steely sea MORRIS.

Midnight (mi·dnəit). [OE. *midniht,* f. MID *a.* + NIGHT.] **1.** The middle of the night; 12 o'clock at night. **2.** *transf.* and *fig.* Intense darkness; a period of intense darkness 1593. **3.** *attrib.* Of or pertaining to midnight, occurring at midnight, meeting at midnight. late ME.; dark as midnight 1601.

1. 'Tis now dead m. SHAKS. 2. The dark m. of papacy 1665. 3. Survey this M. Scene YOUNG. The m. train from Liverpool-street to Norwich 1905.

attrib. and *Comb.*, as **m. oil,** used *fig.* in phr. *to burn* (etc.) *the m. oil,* to sit up or work after m.; **m. sun,** the sun as seen in the Arctic regions at m.

Wee spend our mid-day sweat, our mid-night oyle QUARLES.

Midnoon (midnūn; stress variable). Now *rare* or *Obs.* 1580. [f. MID *a.* + NOON, after *midday, midnight,* to corresp. to *afternoon, forenoon.*] Midday; noon.

Gentlewoemen..who begin their morning at midnoone LYLY.

Mid-o·ff. 1881. [Short for *mid-wicket off*: see MID *a.*] *Cricket.* A fieldsman on the off-side, in front of the batsman and near the bowler. Also the place where he stands.

Mid-o·n. 1881. [Cf. prec.] *Cricket.* A fieldsman on the on-side, in front of the batsman and near the bowler. Also the place where he stands.

‖**Midrash** (mi·dræʃ). *Pl.* **midrashim** (midrā·ʃim). 1613. [Heb.; = 'commentary' (2 Chron. xxiv. 27, R. V.).] An ancient Jewish homiletic commentary on some portion of the Hebrew scriptures, in which allegory and legendary illustration were freely used. Hence **Midra·shic** *a.*

Midrib (mi·drib). 1696. [f. MID *a.* + RIB.] †**1.** In phr. *m. deep,* up to the middle of the ribs (of a horse) –1807. **2.** *Bot.* A principal rib continuous with the petiole extending through the middle of the blade of a leaf 1776. Hence **Mi·dribbed** *ppl. a.*

Midriff (mi·drif). [OE. *midhrif,* f. *midd* MID *a.* + *hrif* belly.] **1.** The diaphragm. †**2.** *transf.* A partition –1766.

1. *To shake, tickle the m.*: said of what causes laughter. A sight to shake The m. of despair with laughter TENNYSON.

Mids. [ME. *middes,* evolved from the advs. *in-middes, on-middes* (cf. IN MID, AMIDST; also *to-mids*).] **A.** *sb.* **1.** The middle; the midst. *Obs.* exc. *Sc.* †**2.** A means –1710. **3.** A mean; a middle course, a compromise. *Obs.* exc. *Sc.* 1553. †**B.** *prep.* In the middle of –1611.

Mid-sea. late ME. The open sea.

Mid-season. 1610. †**1.** Noon. SHAKS. **2.** The middle of the season. Also *attrib.* 1882.

Midship (mi·dʃip). 1555. [f. MID *a.* + SHIP.] The middle part of a ship or boat.

Comb.: **m. beam,** the longest beam of a ship, lodged in the m. frame; **m. bend, frame,** that timber or frame in a ship which has the greatest breadth; **m. port,** a porthole in the middle part of a ship.

Midshipman (mi·dʃipmăn). 1601. [f. prec. + MAN. So called because stationed 'amidships' when on duty.] In the navy, a rank intermediate between that of naval cadet and that of sub-lieutenant or in the U.S. navy that of ensign. Hence **Mi·dshipmanship.** COWPER.

Midshipmite (mi·dʃipməit). 1833. A sailor's perversion of MIDSHIPMAN.

Midships (mi·dʃips). 1626. [Aphet. f. AMIDSHIPS.] **1.** *sb.* The middle part of a ship. **2.** *adv.* = AMIDSHIPS 1838.

Midst (midst), *sb., adv.,* and *prep.* late ME. [Prob. two formations: (1) an extended form of *middes* MIDS, with excrescent *t* as in *amongst,* etc.; (2) MIDDEST *a.* used absol.] **A.** *sb.* **1.** The middle point or part; the centre, middle. *Obs.* or *arch.* **2.** *In the m. of*: Among, amid, surrounded by (a number of things or persons); also, 'in the thick of' (troubles, etc.); during the continuance of (an action, etc.) 1500. **b.** (*In*) *our, your, their m.*: among us, you, etc. 1586 (rare before 19th c.). †**3.** A middle course or term, mean. *Sc.* –1786.

2. In the myddest of lyfe we be in death *Bk. Com. Prayer.* In the m. of an adventure JOHNSON, of peace MACAULAY.

B. *adv.* **1.** In the middle place. Only in Milton's phrase. 1667. **2.** = 'In the midst'. Const. *of. poet. rare.* 1675.

1. Ioyn..to extoll Him first, him last, him m., and without end MILT.

C. *prep.* In the midst of. Commonly written *'midst,* as if aphet. for AMIDST. 1591.

M. others of less note, came one frail Form SHELLEY.

Midstream (mi·dstrīm). ME. The middle of the stream.

Midsummer (mi·dsʌmər). [OE. *midsumor*; see MID *a.* and SUMMER.] **1.** The middle of summer; the period of the summer solstice, about June 21st. **2.** = *M. Day* 1530.

attrib. and *Comb.*, as **m. daisy,** *Chrysanthemum Leucanthemum*; **M. Day,** the 24th of June, an English quarter-day; **m. madness,** the height of madness; †**m. moon,** the lunar month in which M. Day comes; a time when lunacy is supposed to be prevalent.

Mid-water. 1653. The middle portion of the water vertically.

Red-spotted trout poised in m. HOLMAN HUNT.

Midway (mi·dwēi·, *adj.* mi·dwēi). OE. **A.** *sb.* †**1.** The middle of the way or distance –1770. †**2.** A medium; a middle course, *via media* 1599–1677. **B.** *adj.* **1.** Situated in the middle of the way (*rare* exc. *poet.*) 1605. †**2.** Medium, moderate –1675. **C.** *adv.* In the middle of the way or distance; half-way ME. **D.** *prep.* In the middle of (*rare*) *c* 1798.

A. 3. *U.S.* The entertainment section of an exhibition or fair 1901. (From the inclusion of the 'Midway Plaisance' of Chicago in the grounds of the exposition of 1893.)

Mid-week. 1706. [f. MID *a.* + WEEK. Cf. G. *Mittwoch,* Wednesday.] The middle of the week. In Quaker use, a synonym for Fourth-day or Wednesday.

Midwife (mi·dwəif, *rare colloq.* mi·dif), *sb.* ME. [f. MID *prep.*[1] (*adv.*) + WIFE (= woman).] **1.** A woman who assists other women in childbirth; a female accoucheur. †**2.** = MAN-MIDWIFE –1770. **3.** *fig.* One who or that which helps to produce or bring anything to birth 1593.

1. She [Queen Mab] is the Fairies M. SHAKS. 3. And M. Time the ripen'd Plot to Murder brought DRYDEN.

Midwife (mi·dwəif), *v.* Now *rare.* 1638. [f. prec.] **1.** *trans.* To act as midwife to 1674. **2.** To help in bringing (a child) to the birth by acting the part of a midwife 1638. Also *fig.*

Midwifery (mi·dwifri, *rarely* mi·difri). 1483. [f. MIDWIFE *sb.* + -ERY.] The art or practice of assisting women in childbirth; the department of medical knowledge relating to this; obstetrics.

Midwinter (midwintər; stress variable). OE. [f. MID *a.* + WINTER.] The middle of the winter; *spec.* the winter solstice, Dec. 21st. Also formerly applied to Christmas. **b.** quasi-*adj.* (*fig.*), cold as midwinter 1870. Hence **Midwintry,** *a.*

Mien (mīn). Only *literary.* 1513. [Prob. aphet. f. DEMEAN *sb.*, assim. later to F. *mine.*] The air, bearing, or manner of a person, as expressing character or mood. †Also *transf.* of a thing. †**b.** Expression (of the face) = F. *mine du visage. rare.* 1680–99.

See..Fops at all corners, lady-like in m. COWPER.

Miff (mif), *sb. colloq.* and *dial.* 1623. [Perh. imitative; cf. early mod.G. *muff* int. and sb., a manifestation of disgust.] A petty quarrel; a huff, tiff. Hence **Miff** *a. rare,* out of humour (*with*). **Mi·ffy** *a.* easily offended. Also *transf.* of delicate plants.

Miff (mif), *v.* 1797. [f. MIFF *sb.*] **1.** *trans.* To take offence *with* or *at.* Also *transf.* of a plant, *to m. off,* to go off, fade. **2.** *trans.* To put out of humour 1824.

Might (məit). [OE. *miht* fem.:—OTeut. *mahti-z, f. root *mag- to be able or powerful; see MAY *v.*[1] In senses 1–3 often strengthened by collocation with MAIN *sb.*[1] I.] **1.** The quality of being able (to do, etc.); operative power. Const. *inf. Obs.* exc. *poet.* **b.** Power, efficacy, virtue (of impersonal agents). *Obs.* exc. *poet.* OE. †**2.** Bodily strength (great or small) –1611. **3.** Great or transcendent power or strength. Now somewhat *rhet.* OE. **4.** Power to enforce one's will. Chiefly in contrast with *right.* ME. †5. *pl.* The fifth of the nine orders of angels := VIRTUE 1 b. -1652.

1. For to be wise and loue, Exceedes man's m. SHAKS. Phr. *With all one's m.*, with all one's powers, b. Dead Shepheard, now I find thy saw of m. SHAKS. Phr. †*The fivefold mights*: the five senses. 2. Their m. hath failed, they became as women *Jer.* li. 30. 3. Divinest Shakespeare's m. SHELLEY. The m. Of the whole world's good wishes WORDSW. The whole m. of England 1857. 4. They went to war, preferring m. to right JOWETT.

Might, pa. t. of MAY *v.*[1]

Mightful (məi·tfŭl), *a. arch.* ME. [See -FUL.] Mighty; †efficacious.

Might-have-been. 1848. That which might have been; a person who might have been greater or more eminent.

Mightily (məi·tili), *adv.* OE. [f. MIGHTY *a.* + -LY [2].] 1. With great power or strength; with powerful effect; †also, with great effort, vehemently. 2. In a great degree, to a great extent; greatly 1593 (common 17th–18th c.).

1. Let man and beast..cry m. vnto God *Jonah* iii. 8. 2. I sat m. behind, and could see but little PEPYS.

Mi·ghtiness. late ME. [f. MIGHTY *a.* + -NESS.] The state or condition of being mighty. Also as a title of dignity.

Thinke you see them Great..: Then, in a moment, see How soone this Mightinesse meets Misery SHAKS. *High M.*, a title of dignity; esp. *pl.* = Du. *hoogmogendheden*, the members of the States-General of the United Provinces of the Netherlands; hence *gen.* in ironical use.

Mightless (məi·tlės), *a.* Now *arch.* ME. [-LESS.] Powerless.

†**Mi·ghtly,** *adv.* [OE. *mihtelīce*, var. of *mihtiglīce.*] = MIGHTILY -1744.

Mighty (məi·ti), *a.* and *adv.* [OE. *mihtig*; see MIGHT and -Y [1].] A. *adj.* 1. Possessing might or power; potent, strong. Now only *rhet.*, connoting greatness of power. 2. Of huge proportions; massive, bulky. late ME. 3. Of things, actions, events, agent-nouns: Very great in amount, extent, or degree. In later use chiefly *colloq.* 1586. 4. quasi-*sb.* (with *pl.*) A mighty person. Chiefly *pl.* late ME.

1. Fear not, isle of blowing woodland,..thou shalt be the m. one yet! TENNYSON. *M. works*, in biblical use (= Gr. δυνάμεις): miracles. 2. The lone wood and m. hill SCOTT. 3. A m. flux of blood CULPEPPER. A m. Favourite with the Captain 1743.

B. *adv.* (Qualifying an adj. or adv.) In a great degree; greatly; exceedingly; very. Formerly common *colloq.* (now chiefly ironical and U.S.). ME.

That is all m. fine DICKENS.

†**Migniard,** *a.* and *sb.* 1599. [a. F. *mignard*; related to MIGNON.] A. *adj.* Dainty; mincing; caressing -1653. B. *sb.* A courtesan, mistress -1652. So †Migniardise, caressing treatment; affected delicacy 1603-89. †Migniardize *v.* to make (language) affected in character; to treat (a person) caressingly 1598-1670.

‖**Mignon** (minʸon), *a.* Also -onne fem. 1556. [F.] Small and delicately formed.

Mignonette (minyənet). 1721. [a. F. *mignonnette* fem., dim. of *mignon*; see prec.] 1. A plant (*Reseda odorata*) having fragrant blossoms 1798. b. The colour of these; greyish green or greenish white 1885. 2. (More fully *m. lace.*) A light fine kind of lace. *Hist.*

Comb. m. pepper, coarsely ground pepper.

‖**Migraine** (mīgrėn). 1777. [F.; see MEGRIM [1].] = MEGRIM [1] 1. Hence Migrai·nous *a.*

Migrant (məi·grănt), *a.* and *sb.* 1672. [ad. L. *migrantem*: see next.] A. *adj.* Migrating; given to migration. B. *sb.* A migratory bird or other animal; a person who migrates 1760.

Migrate (məi·greᵗt), *v.* 1697. [f. L. *migrat-*, *migrare.*] 1. *intr.* To pass from one place to another. Also *trans.* in *pass.* To be transported. 2. *intr.* To move from one place of abode to another; *esp.* to leave one's country to settle in another; to remove to another country, town, college, university, etc. 1770. b. *Nat. Hist.* Of some animals: To go from one habitat to another; *spec.* of some birds and fishes, to come and go regularly with the seasons 1753. c. *fig.* Of inanimate objects: To undergo removal from one place to another 1929.

2. The agricultural labourer is tempted..to m. to a manufacturing town SIR B. BRODIE. b. Birds which m. in autumn 1889. Hence Mi·grative *a.* migratory.

Migra·tor, one who migrates; *spec.* a migratory bird.

Migration (məigrēⁱ·ʃən). 1611. [ad. L. *migrationem.*] The action, an act, of migrating.

Comb. m.-station, a fixed place for the regular observation of the m. of birds.

Migratory (məi·grătəri), *a.* 1753. [f. L. *migrat-*, *migrare.*] 1. Characterized by migration; given to migrating; *esp.* of animals, given to periodical migration 1753. b. Of a bodily organ, a disease, etc.: Characterized by movement from its normal position; *esp.* in *Histology* of a cell: Given to migration from the blood-vessels to the tissues 1876. 2. Of or pertaining to migration 1757.

2. The m. passages of the reindeer KANE.

‖**Mikado** (mikā·do). 1727. [Jap. *mi* august + *kado* door; cf. 'Sublime Porte'.] The title of the emperor of Japan.

Mike. Colloq. abbrev. of MICROPHONE.

Mil (mil). 1721. [ad. L. *mille* thousand; in senses 2 and 3 short for L. *millesimum* thousandth.] 1. *Per mil*: per thousand. 2. A unit of length used in measuring the diameter of wire, = $\frac{1}{1000}$ of an inch 1891. 3. *Pharm.* = MILLILITRE 1904.

‖**Milady** (milēⁱ·di). Also **miladi.** 1839. [F.; cf. MILORD.] A continental rendering of 'my lady', used in speaking to or of an English gentlewoman.

Milan (mi·lăn, milæ·n). 1464. [ad. It. *Milano.*] Name of the chief city of Lombardy; used *attrib.* in **M. point,** a fine hand-made lace; **M. steel** (*Hist.*), steel used by the armourers of M. for coats-of-mail, swords, etc. (so *M. hauberk, knife, mail*).

Milanese (milănī·z). 1484. [ad. It. *Milanese*; see -ESE.] A. *adj.* Of or pertaining to Milan, its inhabitants, manufactures, etc. 1756. B. *absol.* or as *sb.* 1. A native or inhabitant of Milan. (Unchanged for pl.) 1484. 2. *The M.*: the territory of the old duchy of Milan 1715.

Milch (miltʃ), *a.* [ME. *mielch*, *milche*, repr. OE. **milce* :—OTeut. **melukjo-*, f. *meluk-* MILK *sb.*] Of domestic mammals: Giving milk, kept for milking. †b. Applied to a wet-nurse, etc. -1709. †c. Applied *transf.* to the eyes when weeping (*Haml.* II. ii. 540).

Mi·lch-cow. late ME. [f. prec.] 1. A cow giving milk or kept for milking. 2. *fig.* A source of regularly-accruing profit; *esp.* a person from whom money is easily drawn 1601.

Milched (miltʃt), *ppl. a. local.* 1648. [f. MILCH *a.* + -ED.] In milk; in comb. *new-*, *old-m.* So Mi·lcher, a milch beast 1823.

Mild (məild), *a.* [Com. Teut.: OE. *milde* :—OTeut. **mildjo-*, *mildi-*, f. Indo-Eur. **meldh-* (: *moldh-* : *mldh-*), whence Gr. μαλθακός soft, mild, etc.] 1. Of persons, their disposition, etc. a. Kind, considerate, gracious, merciful; not harsh or severe. Now *rare* or *Obs.* b. Applied to God, Christ, and the Virgin Mary. *Obs.* exc. in traditional collocations. c. Gentle and conciliatory; not rough or fierce in manners OE. d. of rule, punishment, etc. Now chiefly in *comp.*: Less severe 1577. 2. Of an animal: Tame, gentle; not wild or fierce ME. 3. Of weather: Calm, fine, and moderately warm. late ME. 4. Of light, etc.: Softly radiant 1645. 5. Of a medicine: Operating gently. Of food, tobacco, etc.: Not rough or sharp or strong in taste or odour, not over-stimulating. late ME. b. Of ale or beer: Orig., not sour or stale; now, not strongly flavoured with hops (opp. to *bitter*). Also *absol.* = mild ale. 1550. c. Of a disease: Not severe or acute 1744. 6. Of exercise: Gentle, easy 1831. b. Used sarcastically to connote tameness or feebleness (in persons or their actions) 1885. 7. Soft, easy to work (*dial.*) 1852. ¶8. Of a slope: Gentle. Of a wood: Not thorny. BYRON. 9. Used *poet.* = MILDLY 1667.

1. a. So m. a master POPE. b. Ave Maria! maiden m.! SCOTT. c. The mildest man alive SPENSER. His m. eye beams benevolence no more SHELLEY. d. But ..why not adopt milder measures? MACAULAY. Phr. *As m. as a dove, as May, as milk*, etc. 2. Among wild Beasts: they at his sight grew m. MILT. 3. A m. September afternoon 1892. 4. M. as a star in water KEATS. 7. Phr. *M. steel*, steel containing only a little carbon, and not readily tempered or hardened. 9. And thus the Godlike Angel answerd milde MILT.

Hence Mi·ld·ly *adv.*, -ness.

Milden (məi·ld'n), *v.* 1603. [f. MILD *a.* + -EN [5].] To make or become mild or milder.

Mildew (mi·ldiū), *sb.* [OE. *mildēaw*, *mele-*, f. OTeut. **meliþ* honey + **đawwo-* DEW *sb.*] †1. = HONEY-DEW 1. -1658. 2. A morbid destructive growth of minute whitish fungi on plants. Also, a similar growth on paper, leather, wood, etc., when exposed to damp. Usu. *collect. sing.*; also with *a* and *pl.* ME.

2. *fig.* Neither the blasts of arbitrary power could break them off, nor the m. of servile opinion cause them to wither HALLAM. Hence Mi·ldewy *a.*

Mildew (mi·ldiū), *v.* 1552. [f. the sb.] To taint or become tainted with mildew.

Hee..Mildewes the white Wheate SHAKS.

Mile (məil). [OE. *mīl* fem. :—WGer. **milja*, a. L. *mil(l)ia*, pl. of *mil(l)e* thousand.] 1. Orig., the Roman lineal measure of 1,000 paces, about 1,618 yards. Hence, the British unit of measure derived from this, which has varied considerably at different times and in different localities. The legal mile in the British Empire and the U.S. is now 1,760 yards. (The use of the sing. form with a pl. numeral is now only vulgar or dial.) b. A race, or a portion of a race, extending over a mile's length of the course 1901. c. *transf.* and *fig.* Chiefly *adv.* in *pl.*, implying a great distance or interval 1588. 2. Used for its etymol. equivalent in other European languages. late ME. 3. *attrib.* 1610.

1. c. Villaine and he, be many Miles assunder SHAKS. Phr. *Geographical, geometrical, †maritime, nautic(al m.*: one minute of a great circle of the earth. The British Admiralty fixes it at 6,080 feet. 2. In Italy, Spain, and Portugal, the 'mile' ranges between ⅞ and 1¼ English miles. In Germany, Austria, Holland, and the Scandinavian countries, on the other hand, its values range from about 3¼ to over 6 English miles. N.E.D.

Comb. m.-mark, a milestone or other object placed to indicate the distance of a m. from the starting-point or from another mark.

Mileage (məi·lėdʒ). Also **milage.** 1754. [f. MILE + -AGE.] 1. A travelling allowance at a fixed rate per mile. 2. The aggregate number of miles of way made, used, or travelled over. Also, rate of travel in miles.

Miler (məi·lər). 1891. [f. MILE + -ER [1].] *Sporting slang.* A man or horse specially qualified or trained to run a mile.

Milesian (məilī·ʃăn, mi-, -ʒăn), *a.*[1] and *sb.*[1] 1596. [f. L. *Milesius* (Gr. Μιλήσιος) + -AN.] Of or pertaining to (an inhabitant of) Miletus in Asia Minor.

M. tales: a class of short erotic stories current in the 1st century B. C.

Milesian (məilī·ʃăn, mi-, -ʒăn), *a.*[2] and *sb.*[2] 1705. [f. *Milesius* (Miledh), a fabulous Spanish king whose sons are said to have conquered Ireland about 1300 B. C.] A. *adj.* Of or pertaining to King Milesius or his people; Irish. B. *sb.* A descendant of the companions of Milesius. Hence, an Irishman.

Mi·lestone. 1746. A pillar set up on a road or course to mark the miles. Hence Mi·lestone *v.*, to mark by or as by milestones.

Milfoil (mi·lfoil). [ME. *milfoil*, a. OF. :— L. *millefolium*, f. *mille* thousand + *folium* leaf. The leaves are many and finely divided; hence the name.] The common yarrow, *Achillea Millefolium.*

Water m., (*a*) the genus *Myriophyllum*; (*b*) the water violet, *Hottonia palustris.*

‖**Miliaria** (mili,ēᵊ·riă). 1807. [mod.L. use of L. *miliaria*, fem. of *miliarius*; see next.] *Path.* Miliary fever.

Miliary (mi·li,ări), *a.* (*sb.*) 1685. [ad. L. *miliarius* pertaining to millet, f. *milium* MILLET; see -ARY [1].] 1. *Phys.* and *Path.* Resembling a millet-seed or an aggregation of millet-seeds. 2. *Path.* Attended by spots or vesicles resembling millet-seeds or an aggregation of millet-seeds 1737. 3. *Nat. Hist.* Having numerous small granulations or projections 1760. 4. *sb. Zool.* A very small tubercle on the integument of some animals 1897.

1. *M. gland*: one of the sebaceous glands of the skin. *M. tubercle*: a greyish-white spherical body

about the size of a millet-seed, common in diseased tissues of the lungs, etc. **2.** *M. fever*: a fever marked by the presence of a rash resembling measles, with minute vesicles of the form of millet-seed.

‖**Milieu** (m*ī*lyö). 1877. [F., f. *mi* :—L. *medium* (see MEDIUM) + *lieu* place.] A medium, environment, surroundings.

‖**Miliola** (miləi·ŏlă). *Pl.* **-æ.** 1836. [mod. L., dim. of L. *milium* millet.] *Zool.* A genus of imperforate foraminifera; one of these. So **Mi·lioline** 1873, **Mi·liolite** 1833 *adjs.* and *sbs.*

Militancy (mi·litănsi). 1648 [f. next: see -ANCY.] The condition of being militant.

Militant (mi·litănt). late ME. [a. F., a. L. *militantem*, *militare* to MILITATE, f. *milit-*, *miles* soldier.] **A.** *adj.* **1.** Engaged in warfare, warring. **2.** Combative 1603.

1. *Church m.*: see CHURCH *sb.* II. 1. The chirche m., that laboureth here in erthe. late ME. **2.** The expenses of the m. Presbyterians 1903. Hence **Mi·litant-ly** *adv.*, **-ness.**

B. *sb.* One engaged in war or strife 1610.

†**Militar(e**, *a.* 1533. [ad. L. *militaris*; see -AR [2].] Military, martial -1640.

In Militar Commanders and Soldiers, Vaine-Glory is an Essential Point BACON.

Militarism (mi·lităriz'm). 1864. [a. F. *militarisme*, f. *militaire*; see MILITARY and -ISM.] The spirit and tendencies of the professional soldier; the prevalence of military sentiment and ideals among a people; the tendency to regard military efficiency as the paramount interest of the state. So **Mi·litarize** *v.*

Militarist (mi·litărist). 1601. [f. MILITARY + -IST.] †A soldier (SHAKS.); one who studies military science; now chiefly, one dominated by military ideas, an exponent of militarism.

Military (mi·litări). 1585. [ad. F. *militaire*, ad. L. *militaris*, f. *milit-*, *miles* soldier.] **A.** *adj.* **1.** Pertaining to soldiers; used or done by soldiers; befitting a soldier. **2.** Of or belonging to an army 1597. **b.** Soldierly 1588. **3.** Having reference to armed forces or to the army; connected with a state of war; dist. from *civil, ecclesiastical*, etc. 1590.

1. The M. profession 1591. M. rules SHAKS., m. obedience MILT., m. music BURNEY. A m. revolution 1843. **2.** The Throngs of Militarie men SHAKS. **b.** He was a man too m. to be warlike KINGLAKE. **3.** The public ecclesiastical, military, and maritime jurisdictions BLACKSTONE. Hence **Mi·litarily** *adv.* **Mi·litariness.**

Special collocations. **m. board,** a board dealing with the affairs of the army; **m. chest,** the treasury of an army; **m. engineering,** the art of constructing fortifications, bridges, etc. and the laying and destruction of mines; **m. fever,** enteric or typhus fever; **m. law,** the body of enactments and rules for the government of an army; also, one of these; **m. offence,** one cognizable by a m. court; **m. service** (*Feudalism*), the service in war due from a vassal to his superior; **m. tenure,** a feudal tenure under which a vassal owed his superior certain services in war.

B. *sb.* **1.** Soldiery; soldiers generally. Chiefly, *the m.*; now with pl. vb. 1757. †**2.** A military man -1837.

Militate (mi·lite̍t), *v.* 1625. [f. L. *militat-*, *militare*, f. *milit-*, *miles* soldier; see -ATE [3].] **1.** *intr.* To serve as a soldier; to take part in warfare. †Also *transf.* and *fig.* **2.** Of things. †**a.** To conflict *with*; also (of speech or action), to be directed *against*. **b.** Of evidence, facts, etc.: To tell *against* (rarely †*for*, *in favour of*) some conclusion or result 1642. †**3.** *trans.* To fight out (a question) -1762.

1. Men who m. merely for pay K. DIGBY. *fig.* The invisible powers of heaven..seemed to m. on the side of the pious emperor GIBBON. **2. a.** Something which militates with any rational plan BURKE. **b.** Everything may m. for, and nothing m. against, its authenticity 1838.

Militia (mili·ʃă). 1590. [a. L., f. *milit-*, *miles* soldier.] †**1.** A system of military discipline, organization, and tactics; the arts of war -1678. †**b.** Military service; warfare -1685. †**2.** The control and administration of the military and naval forces of a country -1647. **3.** A military force; in later use (= F. *milice*) a 'citizen army' as dist. from a body of professional soldiers 1590. Also *transf.* and *fig.* **4.** *spec.* A branch of the British military service, forming a part of 'the auxiliary forces' as dist. from the regular army. Also, a similar force raised in British North America. (Constr. either as *sing.* or *pl.*) 1659. **b.** *U.S.* The whole body of men legally amenable to military service 1777. **5.** *attrib.*, as *m. act*, etc. 1655.

1. The Normans had a peculiar M., or Fight, with Bowes and Arrowes RALEIGH. **2.** That the m., both by sea and land, might be settled by a bill CLARENDON. **3.** A good m., that is, a certain portion of the people called out in turn to learn the use of arms LD. BROUGHAM. Hence **Mili·tiaman.**

Milk (milk), *sb.* [Com. Teut.: OMercian *milc* (rare) = WS. *meol(u)c* fem. (whence southern ME. *melk*) :—OTeut. **meluk-s* fem., f. **melk-* to milk :—pre-Teut. **melg-*, cogn. w. Gr. ἀμέλγειν, L. *mulgere*, etc.] **1.** An opaque white fluid secreted by the mammary glands of female mammals for the nourishment of their young. †**b.** Milk considered as in process of secretion; hence, lactation -1697. **2.** *fig.* **a.** As the food of infancy; often (after 1 *Cor.* iii. 2, etc.) contrasted with '(strong) meat'. late ME. **b.** As a type of what is pleasant and nourishing 1592. **3.** A milk-like juice or sap secreted by certain plants. Cf. LATEX 2. late ME. **4.** A culinary, pharmaceutical, or other preparation of herbs, drugs, or the like, more or less resembling milk. late ME. **5.** The spat of an oyster before its discharge 1858.

1. They'l take suggestion, as a Cat laps milke SHAKS. Phr. *As like as m. to m.* (a Latinism). *In m.*, in a condition to yield m. **2. b.** Aduersities sweete milke, Philosophie SHAKS. Phr. *M. and honey*: (*a*) in the Bible phrase 'flowing with m. and honey' (*Num.* xvi. 13), hence (*b*) used to express abundance and prosperity. *M. of human kindness* (after Shaks.): compassion characteristic of humane persons. *Spilt m.*: irrecoverable loss or error. **3. b.** *The m. in the cocoa-nut*: a puzzling fact or circumstance, or the explanation of this (*colloq.*, orig. *U.S.*). **4.** *M. of almonds* = ALMOND-MILK. *M. of lime*: hydrate of lime mixed in water. *M. of sulphur*: precipitated sulphur.

attrib. and *Comb.* **1.** General: as *m.-diet, -fat, -porridge*, etc.; *m.-bowl, -cart, -cooler*, etc.; *m.-boy*, etc.; *m.-molar, -tusk*, etc.; *m.-carrier, -seller*, etc.; *m.-faced, -fed*, etc.

2. Special: **m.-abscess,** an abscess occurring in the breasts of women during lactation; **-brother,** a foster-brother; **-cell** *Bot.*, the cell in which the latex of plants is contained; **m. escutcheon,** an area covered by a reversed arrangement of the direction of the hair on the udder and thighs of a milch-cow; **m. factory,** one in which cream is extracted from m.; **-farm,** a dairy-farm; **-fever,** a slight feverish attack which sometimes occurs in women two or three days after childbirth; a similar complaint in milch-cows; **-glass,** an opalescent glass made from cryolite; **-leg,** 'white swelling', a painful swelling of the lower extremities, common after parturition; **-quartz,** an opaque white variety of quartz; **-sickness** *U.S.*, an endemic disease in cattle peculiar to the Western States of America, and sometimes communicated to man through infected meat; **-spot,** a white spot or rash in certain diseases; **-sugar,** sugar of m., lactose; **-thrush** = APHTHA; **-tube** *Bot.*, a laticiferous tube; **-vessel,** (*a*) a dairy utensil for holding m.; (*b*) the udder of a cow; (*c*) *Bot.* one of many tubes in which a milky fluid is secreted; **-walk,** a milkman's round. **b.** Prefixed to names of plants, usu. in the sense 'containing milk', as **m.-grass** = CORN-SALAD; **-parsley,** *Peucedanum palustre*; **m. pea, plant,** a prostrate leguminous plant of the genus *Galactia*, native of the warmer parts of N. America; **-tree,** (*a*) a shrub, *Euphorbia Tirucalli*, native of Africa, and naturalized in parts of India; (*b*) any tree yielding a wholesome milky juice, esp. the COW-TREE; (*c*) an apocynaceous tree, *Tanghinia venenifera*, native of Madagascar; **-vetch,** a plant of the leguminous genus *Astragalus.*

Milk (milk), *v.* [OE. *milcian*, f. *milc*, MILK *sb.*] **I. 1.** *trans.* To extract milk by handling from the teats of (a cow, goat, ewe, etc.). **b.** To draw (milk). Chiefly *pass.* late ME. †**c.** To obtain milk from by sucking. SHAKS. **2.** *intr.* To yield milk. Now only of cattle. OE. †**3.** *trans.* To suckle -1573.

1. Inprimis She can milke SHAKS. Phr. *To m. the ram, the bull*: *fig.* to engage in an impossible enterprise. **3.** *Macb.* I. vii. 55.

II. *transf.* and *fig.* **1.** *trans.* To drain away the contents of; to 'bleed' pecuniarily; to exploit, turn into a source of (illicit) profit 1526. **2.** To elicit, draw *out* 1628; to drain *away*, *out of* 1652. **3.** To extract juice, virus, etc. from 1746. **4.** To manipulate as one does the teat 1642. †**5.** To instil with the mother's milk DRYDEN & LEE.

1. He would m. her Purse and fill his own large Pockets 1695. Phr. *To m. the market, street* (U.S. slang): to hold stock in hand so as to make it fluctuate at will, and so yield any financial result desired. *To m. a wire*, to steal the message from it; *to m. a telegram*, to intercept it. **5.** You..milk'd slow Arts Of Womanish Tameness in my infant Mouth 1682.

Milk-and-water. 1511. Milk diluted with water. †**1.** The colour of milk and water -1571. **2.** Feeble or insipid discourse or mawkish sentiment 1819. **3.** *attrib.* or *adj.* Wishy-washy; insipid, feeble, mawkish 1783.

3. My rascals are no milk-and-water rascals THACKERAY. Hence **Milk-and-wa·terish, -wa·tery** *adjs.*

Milken (mi·lk'n), *a.* Now *rare* or *Obs.* 1570. [f. MILK *sb.* + -EN [4].] **1.** Consisting of milk. **2.** Milk-white 1586.

M. way, race = MILKY WAY; The way of fortune is like the m. way in the skie BACON.

Milker (mi·lkəɹ). 1475. [f. MILK *v.* I. + -ER [1].] **1.** One who or that which milks. **2.** An animal that yields milk, *esp.* a milch-cow. Chiefly with adj., *good, bad*, etc. 1807.

Milkiness (mi·lkinės). 1692. [f. MILKY *a.* + -NESS.] The state of being milky. **b.** Of sidereal and meteorological phenomena: Cloudy whiteness 1791.

fig. Softness and m. of temper TUCKER.

Milk-livered, *a.* 1605. Cowardly, white-livered.

Milk-Liuer'd man, That bear'st a cheeke for blowes SHAKS.

Mi·lkmaid. 1552. [f. MILK *sb.* + MAID.] A woman that milks or is employed in a dairy.

Milkman (mi·lkmæ̆n). 1589. [f. MILK *sb.* + MAN.] A man who sells milk.

Mi·lk-pu·nch. 1704. A drink made of spirits mixed with milk, etc.

Mi·lksop. late ME. [f. MILK *sb.* + SOP *sb.*] †**1.** A piece of bread soaked in milk. †Also *fig.* in *pl.* -1577. **2.** *fig.* An effeminate or spiritless man or youth. late ME.

2. To wedden a Milksope or a coward ape CHAUCER.

Mi·lkstone. 1705. A name for various white stones.

Mi·lk-tooth. 1727. One of a temporary set of teeth in young mammals.

Milkweed (mi·lkwīd). 1706. [f. MILK *sb.* + WEED *sb.*] A name for plants with milky juice.

e.g. the sow-thistle, *Sonchus oleraceus*; the brimstone-wort, *Peucedanum palustre*; the sun-spurge, *Euphorbia Helioscopia*; and plants of the N. Amer. genus *Asclepias*.

Mi·lk-white, *a.* OE. White as milk, pure white. †*M. girdle, way*, the Milky Way.

Milkwort (mi·lkwɒɹt). 1578. [f. MILK *sb.* + WORT.] **1.** Any plant of the genus *Polygala*, formerly supposed to increase the milk of nurses; esp. *Polygala vulgaris*. **2.** A primulaceous plant, *Glaux maritima*, common on the sea-coast and in salt marshes 1578. **3.** Any plant of the genus *Euphorbia* 1640.

Milky (mi·lki), *a.* late ME. [f. MILK *sb.* + -Y [1].] **1.** Having the appearance of milk, or of milk and water. Also (chiefly *poet.*) milk-white. **2.** Of or consisting of milk (*rare*) 1552. **3.** Containing, abounding in, or yielding milk 1641. **b.** *Bot.* Yielding milk-like juice 1861. **4.** *transf.* and *fig.* Of persons, etc.: Soft, gentle; in bad sense, timorous, effeminate, weakly amiable 1602.

1. With Fleeces m. white (= MILK-WHITE) DRYDEN. The *latex*, or m. fluid 1855. **3.** The milkie fruitfulnesse of the Cow 1641. **4.** Has friendship such a faint and milkie heart, It turnes in lesse then two nights? SHAKS. They made..me (the milkiest of men) a satirist BYRON.

Milky Way. late ME. [f. MILKY *a.* + WAY *sb.*, tr. L. *via lactea.*] **1.** = GALAXY 1. **2.** *fig.* **a.** A path brilliant in appearance, or leading to heaven 1649. †**b.** *poet.* The region of a woman's breast -1730.

Mill (mil), *sb.*[1] [OE. *mylen* masc. and fem. :—**mulino-*, **mulina*, a. late L. *molinum*, *molina*, f. *mola* mill, f. *mol-* root of *molere* to grind; see MEAL *sb.*[1] For the loss of the *n* cf. pron. (kil) of *kiln*; the form *miln* remains dial. and is the surname *Milne.*] **1.** A building fitted with machinery for grinding corn. Often in *Comb.*, as *water-, wind-, flour-m.* **b.** A mechanical apparatus for grinding corn 1535. **2.** A machine or apparatus for grinding to powder or pulp some solid substance. Also a building fitted with such machinery. Often in comb., as *coffee-, pepper-, paper-m.*, etc.

1560. **b.** An instrument for expressing juices by grinding or crushing; as *cane, cider m.* 1676. **c.** *Sc.* (also in form *mull*) A snuff-box, orig. one in which the tobacco was ground. **3.** Extended to any machine worked by wind or water power in the manner of a corn-mill, though not used for grinding. Subseq. applied to machines for performing certain operations upon material in the process of manufacture: as in *flatting-, fulling-, rolling-, saw-, stamping-m.* late ME. **b.** A machine invented in the 16th c. for the stamping of gold and silver coins. SHAKS. (*m.-sixpence*). **c.** *Calico* and *Bank-note printing*: A steel roller having upon it a pattern which is transferred by pressure to the printing plate 1839. **4.** A building or works fitted with machinery in which a (specific) manufacture is carried on (*cotton-, silk-, silver-m.*, etc.) 1502. **5.** A machine which does its work by rotary motion, esp. a lapidary's mill 1839. **6.** *slang.* Short for TREADMILL 1842. **7.** A pugilistic encounter 1825.

2. *fig.* Gods M. grinds slow; but sure G. HERBERT. Phr. *To draw water to (one's) m.*: to seize every advantage. *To put through the m.*: to cause to pass through a course of labour or experience, esp. an arduous or painful one; so *to go, to have been through the m.*

1. *attrib.* and *Comb.* as *m.-house, -wall.*

2. *Special Comb.*: **m.-bar (iron)**, rough bar iron as drawn out by the puddlers' rolls; **-hand**, one employed in a m. or factory; **-head,** (*a*) that part of a horse-mill from which the driving-gear is suspended; (*b*) the head of water which is to turn a m.; **m. ore** *Mining*, metallic ore fit for stamping or crushing; **-run,** (*a*) *Gold Mining*, the work of an amalgamating mill between two 'clean-ups'; (*b*) a mill-race; (*c*) *Mining*, a test of a given quantity of ore by treatment in a m.; **-shaft,** (*a*) a metal shaft used for driving machinery in a m.; (*b*) the tall chimney of a m.; **-stream,** a mill-race; also *fig.*; **-work,** (*a*) the machinery used in mills or factories; (*b*) the designing or erecting of this.

Mill (mil), *sb.*[2] 1791. [Short for L. *millesimum* thousandth part, after CENT. Cf. MIL.] A U.S. money of account, being one-thousandth of a dollar (one-tenth of a cent).

Mill (mil), *v.*[1] 1552. [f. MILL *sb.*[1]] **I. 1.** *trans.* To subject to the operation of a mill; to pass (cloth, etc.) through a fulling-mill; to thicken (cloth, etc.) by fulling; to grind (corn), produce (flour) by grinding, etc. Also, to produce or yield by milling; *intr.* to undergo milling. **2. a.** To stamp (coins) by means of the mill and press 1687. **b.** To flute the edge of (a coin or any piece of flat metal) 1724. **3.** To beat (chocolate, etc.) to a froth *Hist.* 1662.

1. This oval box, well filled With best tobacco finely milled COWPER. 3. M. the cream till it is all of a thick froth MRS. GLASSE. A second milled and frothed the chocolate DICKENS.

II. *slang.* To beat, strike; to fight, overcome; to smash, break open. Also *intr.* or *absol.* to box. 1700.

Tug.. milled away—one, two, right and left THACKERAY.

III. 1. *intr.* Of cattle (in U.S. also of persons): To keep moving round and round in a mass; also, to move in a circle 1888. **2.** *intr.* Of a whale: To turn suddenly round 1840.

Mill (mil), *v.*[2] 1567. [Perh. a use of prec.] *slang. trans.* To rob, steal.

Mi·llard. *dial.* Also †**mil(le)warde.** [OE. *myle(n)weard*, f. *mylen* MILL *sb.*[1] + *weard* WARD *sb.*, keeper. Cf. the surnames *Millard, Milward.*] = MILLER 1.

Mi·llboard. 1712. [Altered f. *milled board*: see MILLED *ppl. a.*] A kind of stout pasteboard, rolled with high pressure, used for binding, etc.; a piece of this. **b.** A specially prepared 'board' for sketching 1854.

Mi·ll-dam. ME. [f. MILL *sb.*[1]] A dam constructed across a stream to raise its level and make it available for turning a mill-wheel. Also, the entire area covered by the water held in check by the dam.

Milled (mild), *ppl. a.* 1622. [f. MILL *v.*[1] + -ED[1].] Having been subjected to the action of MILL *v.*[1]

Mill'd sixpences (cf. *mill-sixpence*, MILL *sb.*[1] 3 b) 1650. *M. board* = MILLBOARD 1707.

‖**Millefiori** (milĭfiō·ri). 1849. [It. *millefiori*, f. *mille* thousand + *fiori* flowers.] A kind of ornamental glass made by fusing together a number of glass rods of different sizes and colours, and cutting the mass into sections; usu. embedded in transparent glass to make paper-weights, etc.

‖**Millefleurs** (mīlflör). 1849. [F. *eau de millefleurs*, lit. 'water of a thousand flowers'.] A perfume distilled from flowers of different kinds.

Millenarian (milĭnēᵊ·riăn). 1631. [f. L. *millenarius* + -AN.] **A.** *adj.* Of or pertaining to the millennium; holding the doctrine of the millennium. **B.** *sb.* A believer in the millennium (in sense 2) 1674. Hence **Millena·rianism,** the doctrine of or belief in the coming of the millennium 1849.

Millenary (mi·lĭnări). 1550. [ad. L. *millenarius* consisting of or containing a thousand, f. *milleni* a thousand each, f. *mille.*] **A.** *adj.* **1.** Consisting of or pertaining to a thousand (esp. years) 1641. **b.** Commanding one thousand men 1608. **2.** Of or pertaining to the millennium, or those believing in the millennium 1577. Also *transf.* and *fig.*

B. *sb.* **1.** An aggregate of one thousand; *esp.* one thousand years; ten centuries 1550. **2.** An officer in command of a thousand men 1555. **3.** = MILLENARIAN *sb.* 1561.

1. He conceaveth the Elementall frame shall end in the seventh or Sabbaticall m. SIR T. BROWNE.

Millennial (mile·niăl), *a.* 1664. [f. MILLENNIUM + -AL.] **1.** Of a thousand years 1807. **2.** Of or pertaining to the millennium 1664.

1. The bloody scroll of our m. wrongs BYRON.

Millennian (mile·niăn), *a.* and *sb.* 1657. [f. as prec. + -AN.] = MILLENARIAN.

†**Millen(n)ist.** 1664. [f. MILLENNIUM + -IST.] A millenarian –1795.

Millennium (mile·niᵊm). *Pl.* **-iums,** *occas.* **-ia.** 1638. [a. mod.L. *millennium, f. L. *mille* thousand + *annus* year, after *biennium*, etc.] **1.** A period of one thousand years. Also, a thousandth anniversary. 1711. **2.** The period of one thousand years during which (*Rev.* xx. 1–5) Christ will reign in person on earth 1638. **3.** *fig.* A period of happiness and benign government 1820.

1. Let Thy feet, millenniums hence, be set In midst of knowledge TENNYSON.

Millepede (mi·lĭpīd). 1601. [ad. L. *millepeda* woodlouse, f. *mille* thousand + *ped-, pes* foot. Cf. F. *mille-pieds.*] *Zool.* **1.** Any one of the chilognathan myriapods, with numerous legs usu. placed on each of the segments in double pairs. **2.** Any one of several terrestrial isopod crustaceans, *esp.* the common woodlouse, *Oniscus asellus*; the armadillo, *Armadillo vulgaris*; and the slater, *Porcellio scaber* 1651. **3.** = CENTIPEDE 1705.

Millepore (mi·lĭpōᵊɹ). 1751. [ad. mod.L. *millepora*, f. *mille* thousand + *porus* passage, PORE *sb.*, or ad. F.] *Zool.* Any one of the *Hydromedusæ* of the genus *Millepora* or of the family *Milleporidæ*, in which the coral-like skeleton is covered with minute pores. Hence **Mi·lleporite,** a fossil m.

Miller (mi·ləɹ). late ME. [f. ME. *myll, myln* MILL *sb.*[1] + -ER[1]. Cf. the surnames *Miller, Milner.*] **1.** The proprietor or tenant of a corn-mill. **b.** One who works a mill of any kind 1839. **2.** Applied to certain white or white-powdered insects, as the cockchafer, etc., and to certain hairy caterpillars 1668. **3.** *slang.* A pugilist 1812.

1. A myller dusty-poll than dyde come 1515. Prov. *An honest m. hath a thumb of gold*: app. = there are no honest millers; a prov. alluded to by Chaucer and Gascoigne, a thumb of gold being taken to mean one that brings profit to the owner. *Too much water drowned the m.*: = one can have too much of a good thing.

Comb.: **m.-moth,** a white or 'mealy-scaled' moth; so **m.'s soul.**

Millerite[1] (mi·lərəit). *U.S.* 1846. [f. William *Miller* + -ITE[1].] A believer in the doctrines of William Miller (died 1849), an American preacher who taught that the coming of Christ and the end of the world were at hand.

Millerite[2] (mi·lərəit). 1854. [ad. G. *millerit*; named after W. H. *Miller*, professor of mineralogy at Cambridge, 1832–1870; see -ITE[1].] *Min.* Native sulphide of nickel, usu. occurring in brassy or bronze crystals; capillary pyrites.

Miller's thumb. 1440. [The head of the fish has some resemblance to a thumb. Cf. Prov. s. v. MILLER.] **1.** A small freshwater fish, *Cottus gobio*; the bullhead. **2.** Applied also to: **a.** the whiting-pout, *Gadus luscus*; **b.** *U.S.*, any freshwater sculpin of the genus *Uranidea*; **c.** the Black Goby, *Gobius niger* 1838. **3.** Applied locally to certain small birds, e. g. the Willow Wren 1838.

Millesimal (mile·simăl), *a.* and *sb.* 1719. [f. L. *millesimus* thousandth + -AL.] **A.** *adj.* Thousandth; consisting of thousandth parts. Also, of or belonging to a thousand, dealing with thousandths 1741. **B.** *sb.* A thousandth (part).

Millet (mi·lėt). late ME. [a. F. *millet*, dim. of *mil.*] **1.** A graminaceous plant, *Panicum miliaceum*, native of India, growing three or four feet high, and bearing a large crop of minute nutritious seeds; the seed itself. **2.** Applied to other graminaceous plants, esp. *Sorghum vulgare* (African, Black, Indian, Turkey M.) and *Setaria italica* (Italian or German M.) 1548.

M.-rash, miliary fever; **m.-grass,** the genus *Milium*, esp. *M. effusum*; **m.-seed,** the seed or grain of m.

Milli- (mi·li), comb. f. L. *mille* thousand, used esp. in the metric system to denote the thousandth part of the unit, as *milliampere*; *milliare*, $\frac{1}{1000}$ of an are (154·07 square inches), etc.; †*milli-millesm* (1650), *millistere, millivolt, milliweber*; **millibar,** $\frac{1}{1000}$ of a bar (unit of barometric pressure) 1912.

Milliard (mi·liăɹd). 1823. [a. F., f. *mille.*] A thousand millions.

Milliary (mi·liări). Also **miliary.** 1610. [ad. L. *milliarius*, f. *mille*: see MILE.] **A.** *adj.* Pertaining to the ancient Roman mile of a thousand paces; marking a mile 1700. **B.** *sb.* An ancient Roman milestone 1610.

The miliary column, set up as a centre from which to measure distances 1860.

Milligramme, -gram (mi·ligræm). 1810. [F.; see MILLI- and GRAMME.] In the metric system, a weight equal to $\frac{1}{1000}$ of a gramme, or ·0154 of an English grain.

Millilitre (mi·lilītəɹ). 1810. [F.; see MILLI- and LITRE.] In the metric system, a measure of capacity equal to $\frac{1}{1000}$ of a litre, or ·061 of a cubic inch.

Millimetre (mi·limītəɹ). 1807. [F.; see MILLI- and METRE.] In the metric system, a measure of length equal to $\frac{1}{1000}$ of a metre, or ·0393 inch. Also *attrib.* as *m. scale.* Abbrev. *mm.*

Milliner (mi·linəɹ). 1529. [f. MILAN + -ER[1].] **1.** A native or inhabitant of Milan. **2.** †**a.** A vendor of fancy wares and articles of apparel, esp. of those orig. made at Milan, e.g. Milan bonnets, ribbons, gloves, cutlery. **b.** Now, a person (usu. a woman) who makes or deals in women's hats and trimmings (and, formerly, drapery).

No M. can so fit his customers with Gloues SHAKS. A little French M. SHERIDAN.

Millinery (mi·linəri). 1679. [f. prec.; see -ERY.] The articles made or sold by milliners.

Milling (mi·liŋ), *vbl. sb.* 1466. [f. MILL *v.*[1] + -ING[1].] **1.** The action or process of subjecting something to the operation of a mill, as corn, etc. **b.** The treatment of a substance or material in any kind of mill; e. g. the operation of fulling cloth, rolling metals, crushing minerals, etc. 1617. **2.** *Coining.* The operation of producing a crenation or series of transverse lines on the edge of a coin as a protection against clipping. Now only *concr.* the crenation itself. 1817.

1. *High m.*, milling in which the wheat grain is reduced to flour by successive crackings, or slight and partial crushings, alternating with siftings and sortings of the product, resulting in a flour of extreme whiteness and nutritive quality. *Low m.*, milling in which the corn is reduced to flour by a system of mashing, repeated scraping and squeezing, usually attended with some heating of the product, and a single bolting.

Million (mi·lyən). late ME. [a. F., ad. It. †*millione*, f. *mille* thousand + *-one* augm.

suffix.] 1. The cardinal number equal to a thousand thousands. (Often used for an enormous number.) b. As adj. or quasi-adj. (in prose use, always with *a* or prefixed multiplier), followed immediately by a pl. (or collective) noun 1843. c. Also used as an ordinal when followed by other numbers, the last of which alone takes the ordinal form 1866. 2. *ellipt.* a. A million coins or units of money of account, *esp.* (in British use) a million pounds or (in the U.S.) dollars. late ME. b. *The million*: the multitude; the bulk of the population 1602.

1. Oh, 'giue ye-good-e'vn: heer's a m. of manners SHAKS. He could count his soldiers by the m. 1885. b. The roar of a m. cannon BORROW. 2. Increasing the national debt to near eighty millions Sterling 1790. b. The Play I remember pleas'd not the M. SHAKS. *attrib.* m. act, an act of parliament authorizing a lottery to be held in 1694 and succeeding years, by which a million pounds was to be raised.

Millionaire (milyənēə·ɹ). 1826. [a. F. *millionnaire* (formerly also in Engl.), f. *million*; see prec.] A person possessed of a 'million of money', as a million pounds, dollars, francs, etc.; a person of great wealth. So **Millionai·ress**, a female m.

Millionary (mi·lyənări), *a.* and *sb. rare.* 1816. [f. MILLION + -ARY[1].] A. *adj.* Possessing millions (of money). B. *sb.* = MILLIONAIRE 1834.

Millioned (mi·lyənd), *a.* (? 1600) 1747. [f. MILLION + -ED[2].] 1. Numbered by the million. 2. Possessed of millions (of money).

Millionth (mi·lyənþ), *a.* (*sb.*) 1673. [f. MILLION, after HUNDREDTH.] The ordinal number belonging to the cardinal MILLION. Also *absol.*, *attrib.*, and quasi-*sb.*

M. part, one of a million equal parts into which a whole is, or may be, divided.

Milliped, var. of MILLEPEDE.

Mi·ll-lead. 1609. [LEAD *sb.*[2]] = next.

Mi·ll-leat. 1609. An artificial channel for the conveyance of water to a mill.

Mi·ll-pond. 1697. The water retained above a mill-dam for driving a mill.

It was quite calm, and the Sea as smooth as a M. 1697. So **Mi·ll-pool** OE.

Mi·ll-post. ME. The post on which a windmill was formerly often supported. Often as a type of something thick and massive; hence *joc.* a massive leg.

Mi·ll-race. 1478. The current of water that drives a mill-wheel; also, the channel in which it runs.

Mill-rind (mi·lrəind). 1542. The iron which supports the upper millstone of a corn-mill, and carries the eye which rests upon the end of the mill spindle. b. *Her.* A conventional representation of this.

Mi·ll-round. 1851. The circular path travelled by a mill-horse. Also *fig.*

Millstone (mi·lstōun). OE. 1. One of a pair of circular stones used for grinding corn in a mill; *Her.* a representation of this. b. Stone used or suitable for this 1610. 2. *fig.* a. A heavy burden (cf. *Matt.* xviii. 6); b. a grinding or crushing instrument 1720.

1. *Nether m.*: see NETHER *a.* Phr. *To see far in* (*into, through*) *a m.*: to be extraordinarily acute (chiefly ironical). 2. a. The mill-stone intended for the necks of those vermin..the dealers in corn, was found to fall upon the heads of the consumers BENTHAM. **M. grit** (*Geol.*), a hard siliceous rock belonging to the carboniferous series, and found immediately below the coal-measures.

Mi·ll-wheel. OE. A wheel (esp. a water-wheel) used to drive a mill. b. *Her.* A figure of this 1688.

Mi·llwright. 1481. One who designs or sets up mills or mill machinery.

‖**Milor(d** (mĭlō·r). 1824. [F. *milord*, a. Eng. *my lord*.] The French designation for an English gentleman.

Milreis (mi·lrēⁱs). 1589. [a. Pg., f. *mil* thousand + REIS.] A Pg. gold coin and money of account, = 1,000 REIS. Also, a Brazilian silver coin of about half the value, in 1942 replaced by the cruzeiro.

Milt (milt), *sb.* [OE. *milte* str. masc., also wk. fem., spleen :—OTeut. **meltjo-*, **meltjōn-*, perh. f. root of MELT *v.*] 1. The spleen in mammals; also, an analogous organ in other vertebrates. Also *transf.* 2. The roe or spawn of the male fish; the soft roe of fishes 1483. Hence **Milt** *v.* 'to impregnate the roe or spawn of the female fish' (J.). **Mi·lter**, a male fish, esp. in spawning time; also = sense 2.

Miltonian (miltōu·niăn), *a.* 1708. [f. John *Milton* + -IAN.] Of or relating to Milton, or resembling his style or imagery.

Miltonic (miltǫ·nik), *a.* (and *sb.*) 1708. [f. as prec. + -IC.] A. *adj.* = prec. B. *sb. pl.* Verses of Milton. COWPER. Hence **Milto·nically** *adv.*

Miltonist (mi·ltənist). 1649. [f. *Milton* + -IST.] A follower of Milton in his views on divorce.

Miltwaste (mi·ltwēⁱst). 1578. [f. MILT *sb.* + WASTE.] The finger-fern, one of the spleenworts, *Asplenium Ceterach.*

Mim (mim), *a. Sc.* and *dial.* 1679. [Imitative of the action of pursing up the mouth.] Demure, primly silent or quiet.

Mime (məim), *sb.* 1616. [ad. L. *mimus*, a. Gr. *μῖμος*.] 1. *Antiq.* A performer in the dramatic pieces described in sense 4. 1784. 2. A buffoon; a pantomimist 1616. 3. *transf.* and *fig.* An imitator 1677. 4. *Antiq.* A kind of simple farcical drama among the Greeks and Romans, characterized by mimicry; a dialogue written for this. Also *transf.* of modern performances of this kind. 1642.

Mime (məim), *v.* 1616. [f. prec. sb.] 1. *intr.* To play a part with mimic gesture and action, usu. without words. Also *transf.* and *fig.* 2. *trans.* To imitate, mimic 1733. Hence **Mi·mer**, a mime, a buffoon.

Mimeograph (mi·mĭˌograf), *sb.* 1889. [irreg. f. Gr. *μιμέομαι* I imitate + -GRAPH.] An apparatus, invented by Edison, for producing stencils of written pages, from which many copies may be obtained. Hence **Mi·meograph** *v. trans.* to reproduce by means of a m.

‖**Mimesis** (məimī·sis). 1577. [Gr., = 'imitation'; cf. prec.] 1. *Rhet.* A figure of speech, whereby the words or actions of another are imitated. 2. *Biol.* = MIMICRY 2. 1845.

Mimetic (məime·tik), *a.* 1637. [ad. Gr. *μιμητικός*, f. *μιμεῖσθαι* to imitate.] 1. Addicted to or having an aptitude for mimicry or imitation; pertaining to imitation. 2. Characterized by imitation 1669. 3. = MIMIC *a.* 3. 1756. 4. *Biol.* Of animals, etc.: Characterized by mimicry or resemblance in appearance to some other animal or plant, or to some inorganic object. Of appearances or processes: Of the nature of mimicry. 1851. So †**Mime·tical** *a.* (in sense 2) 1617–1764. **Mime·tically** *adv.* 1647.

‖**Mimiambi** (mimiæ·mbəi, məi-), *sb. pl.* 1706. [L., a. Gr. *μιμίαμβοι* pl., f. *μῖμος* MIME *sb.* + *ἴαμβος* IAMBUS.] Mimes written in iambic or scazontic verse. So **Mimia·mbic** *a.* 1700; also *sb. pl.* = M. 1845.

Mimic (mi·mik). 1590. [ad. L. *mimicus*, ad. Gr. *μιμικός*, f. *μῖμος*; see MIME *sb.* and -IC.] A. *adj.* 1. †a. Exercising the profession of a mime; resembling a mime. b. Imitative. 1598. 2. Of actions, etc. †a. Histrionic; hence, hypocritical. b. Pertaining to, or of the nature of, mimicry or imitation. 1602. 3. Imitative as opposed to real. (The word does not now imply any deceptive intention or effect.) 1625.

1. b. Aristotle saith, that Man is the most Mimick of all Animals 1726. 2. The m. warfare of the opera stage ALISON.

B. *sb.* †A mime, burlesque actor 1590; one who is skilled in mimicry or ludicrous imitation 1599. b. 'A mean or servile imitator' (J.); also, something that mimics 1624.

Waited on By mimiques, jesters B. JONS. b. Cunning is only the Mimick of Discretion ADDISON.

Mimic (mi·mik), *v.* 1687. [f. MIMIC *sb.*] 1. *trans.* To ridicule by imitating (a person, his manner, etc.) 1697. 2. To copy with minute accuracy in externals. Chiefly contemptuous. 1687. 3. To represent imitatively, as by painting, etc. Of things: To resemble closely. 1770. 4. *Path.* Of a disease: To simulate (another disease) 1744. 5. *Biol.* To have a mimetic resemblance to (something else) in form or colour 1861.

1. He mocks and mimics all he sees and hears SHELLEY. 2. Just in the way that monkies m. man 1761. Vice has learned..to mimick Virtue STEELE. 3. He could m. marble on paper READE.

Mimical (mi·mikăl), *a.* 1603. [f. as MIMIC *a.* + -AL.] †1. = MIMIC *a.* 1. –1693. 2. †Befitting a mime; pertaining to, characterized by, or of the nature of mimicry 1610. †3. = MIMIC *a.* 3. –1693. Hence **Mi·mically** *adv.*

Mimicry (mi·mikri). 1687. [f. MIMIC *sb.* + -RY.] 1. The action or practice of mimicking; close imitation, either in sport or otherwise, of externals 1709. b. An act, instance, or mode of mimicking. Also *concr.* that by which something is mimicked. 1687. 2. *Biol.* A close external resemblance which a living creature, etc. bears to a different one, or to some inanimate object 1861.

1. As if in mimickry of insect play SOUTHEY. b. An Imitation and Mimickry of Good-nature ADDISON.

Mi·miny-pi·miny, *a.* 1815. [Imitative; cf. MIM; also NIMINY-PIMINY.] Ridiculously affected; finicking. Also *sb.* HAZLITT.

Mimographer (məimǫ·grăfəɹ). 1638. [f. L. *mimographus* (a. Gr., f. *μῖμος*); see -GRAPHER.] A writer of mimes.

‖**Mimosa** (mimōu·ză, mimōu·să). *Pl.* **-as**, also L. **-æ.** 1731. [mod.L.; app. f. L. *mimus* MIME *sb.* + *-osa* fem. suffix; see -OSE[1].] 1. *Bot.* (A plant of) the genus *Mimosa* of leguminous plants, including the common Sensitive Plant, *M. pudica*: chiefly applied to the latter and to certain trees of the genus *Acacia*, esp. the Australian Wattle-trees. 2. The bark of these Australian species, used in tanning 1852. 3. *attrib.*, as **m. gum**, gum arabic (see ARABIC *a.*).

Mimotannic (mimotæ·nik), *a.* 1857. [f. MIMO(SA) + TANNIC *a.*] *Chem.* In *M. acid*: a variety of tannic acid found in the mimosa.

‖**Mina**[1] (məi·nă, mi·nă). *Pl.* **-næ** (-nī), **-nas** (-năz). 1579. [L., ad. Gr. *μνᾶ* (see MNA); prob. Babylonian.] 1. A unit of weight anciently used in Greece, Egypt, etc.; about 1 lb. avoirdupois 1603. 2. A denomination of money in ancient Greece = 100 drachmas, or about £4. (Rendered 'pound' in the N. T.) 1579. 3. = MANEH 1737.

‖**Mina**[2] (məi·nă). 1769. Also **myna**, **miner**, **-or**, etc. [Hindī *mainā*.] Any of several birds of the starling family found in south-eastern Asia, esp. *Acridotheres tristis*, and *Eulabes religiosa*, the common talking starling of India. In Australia applied to species of the genera *Manorhina* and *Myzantha*.

Minacious (minēⁱ·ʃəs), *a.* 1660. [f. L. *minaci-*, *minax* + -OUS.] Menacing, threatening; full of threats or menaces. Hence **Mina·ciously** *adv.*, **-ness.**

Minacity (minæ·siti). 1656. [See prec. and -ITY.] 'Disposition to use threats' (J.); denunciation.

Minaret (mi·nărĕt). 1682. [a. Arab. *manārah*, *manārat* (Turk. *minàre*), f. root of *nār* fire.] A tall slender tower or turret, connected with a mosque, surrounded by one or more projecting balconies from which the muezzin calls the people to prayer. Also *transf.* (e. g. *m. of ice*).

Minatory (mi·nătŏri), *a.* and *sb.* 1532. [ad. late L. *minatorius*, f. *minari* to threaten.] A. *adj.* Threatening, menacing. †B. *sb.* A threat, a menace (*rare*) –1686. Hence **Mi·natorily** *adv.* So **Minato·rial** *a.*, **-ly** *adv.* 1847.

‖**Minauderie** (minōdri). 1763. [F., f. *minauder*, f. *mine*; see MIEN.] Coquettish airs.

The minauderies of the young ladies in the ballrooms THACKERAY.

Mince (mins), *sb.* 1850. [f. MINCE *v.*] Minced meat, esp. as forming a dish.

Mince (mins), *v.* [late ME. *mynce*, *mynsh*, ad. OF. *mincier*, *minchier*, accentual var. of *menuisier* :—pop.L. **minutiare*: see MINUTIA.] 1. *trans.* To cut (meat, etc.) small or into little pieces; b. to chop up or grind small with a knife or mincing-machine and cook (*mod.*). c. *transf.* To cut (a person) in small pieces 1602. 2. *transf.* and *fig.* To cut up, subdivide minutely. Also with *up*. 1450. 3. To make little of, minimize; to disparage; to palliate, extenuate (faults). Now *rare*. 1591. †Also *absol.* b. †To report (expressions) euphemistically; to moderate or restrain (one's language) 1599. 4. a. *trans.* To pronounce with affected elegance, clip (one's words). b. *absol.* or *intr.* To speak with affected elegance of pronunciation. 1545. 5. *intr.* To walk with short steps or with affected nicety; to walk in an affected manner 1562. b. *trans.* To perform or express mincingly 1603.

1. The Wife minced a bit of Meat SWIFT. c. *Haml.* II. ii. 537. 3. Wee m. our sins as though they needed no forgivenesse H. SMITH. Phr. *To m. the matter*: in early use, to extenuate it. Now only in neg. contexts, to express oneself delicately or politely; so *to m. matters*. b. I know no wayes to m. it in loue, but directly to say, I loue you SHAKS. 5. b. Behold yond simpring Dame,..that minces Vertue & do's shake the head to heare of pleasures name SHAKS. Hence **Mi·ncer**, one who or that which minces.

Minced (minst), *ppl. a.* late ME. [f. MINCE *v.* + -ED[1].] 1. Of meat, etc.: Cut up very small. Also *fig.* †2. Diminished; mutilated –1707.

Minced meat. 1578. 1. a. Meat chopped up very small. b. = MINCEMEAT 1 b. *rare* or *Obs.* 1762. 2. *fig.* Anything cut up very small 1649.

Minced-pie. 1607. Now only *U.S.* (*rare*). = MINCE-PIE.

Mi·ncemeat. 1663. [Altered from MINCED MEAT.] 1. †a. = MINCED MEAT 1 a –1747. b. A mixture of currants, raisins, sugar, suet, etc., and sometimes meat, chopped small; used in mince-pies 1845. 2. *To make m. of* (a person): to cut him up into very small pieces; to annihilate 1663.

Mince-pie·. 1600. [Altered from MINCED-PIE.] A pie containing mincemeat.

Mi·ncing, *vbl. sb.* 1533. [f. MINCE *v.* + -ING[1].] In senses of the vb.

m.-machine, a machine for mincing meat, etc.

Mi·ncing, *ppl. a.* 1530. [f. MINCE *v.* + -ING[2].] That minces; esp. of persons, their speech, gait, etc. Characterized by an affectedly dainty or elegant manner.

Ile..turne two minsing steps Into a manly stride SHAKS. [She] frightened a m. curate out of his life 1887. Hence **Mi·ncingly** *adv.*

Mind (məind), *sb.* [ME. *mynd*, repr. OE. *gemynd* fem. (also neut.):—OTeut. *gamundi-z, f. *ga- Y- + *mun-, wk.-grade of the Indo-Eur. root *men-*, *mon-*, *mn-* to think, remember, intend (cf. Gr. μέ-μονα, L. *monēre*, *mens*).] I. Memory. †1. The faculty of memory –ME. 2. The state of being remembered; remembrance OE. †3. That which is remembered *of* (a person or thing); the memory or record *of* –1489. †4. The action or an act of commemorating; a commemoration, a memorial OE. †b. *spec.* The commemoration of a departed soul, esp. by a requiem said or sung on the day of the funeral in any month or year following –1660. †5. Mention, record –1530.

2. Phr. *To have, bear, keep in m.*: to retain in memory; now only, to keep one's attention fixed upon. *To bring, call to m.*: to summon to remembrance. *To be* (*go, pass*) *out of m.*: to be forgotten. (*Obs.* exc. in 'Out of sight, out of m.', etc.) *Time out of m.*, used as adv. phr. = from time immemorial. *To put* (a person) *in m.*: to remind. 4. b. Upon the Anniversary, or the monthly, or weekly minds JER. TAYLOR.

II. Thought; purpose, intention. †1. The thought *of* (an object) –1589. 2. That which a person thinks about any subject or question; one's view or opinion. late ME. 3. Purpose or intention; desire or wish. *Obs.* exc. in phrases. ME. 4. Bent or direction of thoughts, desires, inclinations, etc. late ME. 5. Way of thinking and feeling; moral disposition 1500. 6. State of thought and feeling as to dejection, fortitude, firmness, etc. 1500.

2. Phr. *To speak one's m.* (*out*): to express one's opinion candidly, to speak plainly. So *to tell* (a person) *one's m.*, *to let* (a person) *know one's m.* *A piece* or *bit of one's m.*: see PIECE *sb.*, BIT *sb.*[2] 4. *To be of a* (specified) *m.*: to hold an opinion. *To be of* (another's) *m.*: to be of his way of thinking. *In my m.*: in my opinion. So *to my m.* *To be of one* or *a m.*: to be unanimous. 3. Sudden m. arose In Adam, not to let th' occasion pass MILT. Phr. *To know one's own m.*: to form and adhere to a decision. *To make up one's m.*: see MAKE *v.* †*To be of many minds*: to chop and change. *To be in two minds*: to vacillate between two intentions. *To change one's m.*, to alter one's purpose, opinion, disposition, etc. *To have a m.*: to wish, desire, be disposed *to do* something. So, *to have a great, good*, etc., *m.*, *to have no m.*; *to have half a m.*, now = to be strongly disposed or inclined *to do* something. They.. thought they could deal as they had a m. to with his property 1895. 4. Phr. *To set* (*have, keep*) *one's m. on*: to desire to attain or accomplish. *To give one's m. to*: to bend one's energies towards. *To one's m.*: as one would have it to be. Also, *after one's m.* 5. *Frame of m.*: see FRAME *sb.* II. 5. I would I knew his minde SHAKS. 6. A turne or two Ile walke To still my beating minde SHAKS.

III. 1. The seat of consciousness, thoughts, volitions, and feelings; also, the incorporeal subject of the psychical faculties; the soul as dist. from the body ME. b. Used of God. c. Mental or psychical being: opp. to *matter* 1759. d. A person regarded abstractly as the embodiment of mental qualities 1580. 2. In restricted sense: The intellectual powers, as dist. from the will and emotions. Often contrasted with *heart*. ME. b. Intellectual quality, mental power 1586. 3. The normal condition of the mental faculties; one's 'reason', 'wits'. late ME.

1. No Proposition can be said to be in the M... which it was never yet conscious of LOCKE. M. is the mysterious something which feels and thinks MILL. Phr. *On one's m.*: occupying one's (anxious) thoughts. *One's mind's eye*: mental vision, remembrance. b. Haunted for ever by the eternal m. WORDSW. d. Mindes innocent and quiet take That for an Hermitage LOVELACE. The religious m. of Europe 1883. 2. ABSENCE, PRESENCE *of m.*: see those wds. b. The days of advance, the works of the men of m. TENNYSON. 3. Phr. (*To be, go*) *out of one's m.*; *to lose one's m.*; *to be in one's right m.*, etc. *Of sound* (or *unsound*) *m.*

Comb. **m.-cure,** the curing of a disease by the influence of the healer's m. upon the patient's; so **-healing**; **-reader,** a thought-reader.

Mind (məind), *v.* ME. [f. MIND *sb.*] I. *trans.* To put in mind *of* something; to remind. Now *rare.* 2. To remember; to think of (a past or present object). Now *arch.* and *dial.* late ME. Also *absol.* b. In *imper.* To bear in mind. late ME. c. *intr.* with *of*, *on*, *upon*: To remember. Now *dial.* Also quasi-*refl.* in *I m. me*, etc. (*arch.*). late ME. 3. To perceive, notice; to have one's attention caught by. *Obs.* exc. *dial.* 1489. 4. To attend to, give heed to 1559. b. *absol.* or *intr.* Chiefly *colloq.* in *imper.* 1806. †5. *trans.* To have a mind to; to intend (doing something); also, to plan, provide for (something external to oneself) –1691. b. With *inf.* as obj.: To have a mind *to do* something. *Obs.* exc. *dial.* 1513. 6. To direct or apply oneself to; to practise diligently. late ME. †b. To care for –1748. 7. In neg., interrog., and conditional sentences: (Not) to care for. Hence: (Not) to object to, dislike. 1608. b. *absol.* or *intr.* 1786. 8. To remember and take care *to do* (something), *that* something is done 1641. 9. To take care of; to take heed (what one does) 1737. b. To look out for (something to be avoided). Now only in the imperative, or the like. 1690. Also *absol.* 10. *trans.* To look after; to have the care of 1694.

1. They m. us of the time When we made bricks in Egypt TENNYSON. 2. b. Mind to-morrow's early meeting BROWNING. 3. My Lord you nod, you do not minde the play SHAKS. 4. Let us take his advice, though he be one only, and not m. the others JOWETT. b. So I bar Latin, m. 1806. 5. What he [the King] minded, he compassed BACON. 6. Phr. *To m. his book* (colloq.; now obs. or arch.), of a schoolboy, to be diligent in his studies. *To m. one's business*: to prosecute it diligently; hence, *to m. one's own business*: to attend to one's own affairs and leave other people's alone. 7. Phr. *I should not m.* (something) = I should rather like to have it or do it; *do you* or *would you m.* (doing something)? = be so kind as to do it; *if you don't m.*, if you have no objection. b. Phr. *Never m.* = don't let it trouble you, it does not matter; also = it is none of your business. 8. M. you write DISRAELI. 9. *M. your eye*, look out, keep your eyes about you. *To m. one's P's and Q's*: see P. b. Phr. *If you don't m.* (absol.) = if you are not careful (to avoid something). 10. Let me m. your pigeons 1884.

Minded (məi·ndėd), *ppl. a.* 1503. [f. MIND *sb.* + -ED[2].] 1. Having a mind *to do* something; disposed. †2. Having a (favourable or hostile) disposition towards a person or thing –1677. 3. Having a mind of a specified character, as *healthy-*, *high-*, etc., *m.* 1503.

Minder (məi·ndəɹ). 1650. [f. MIND *sb.* and *v.* + -ER[1].] 1. One who minds; *esp.* one whose business is to attend to something, as *cattle-*, *engine-m.* 2. A child taken care of at a 'minding-school' 1865.

Mindful (məi·ndful), *a.* ME. [f. MIND *sb.* + -FUL.] 1. a. Taking thought or care *of*. b. Having remembrance *of*. TENNYSON. †2. Minded, inclined *to do* something –1681.

1. a. What thing is man, that thou art myndeful of him? WYCLIF *Heb.* ii. 6. 2. M. to rest 1681. Hence **Mi·ndful·ly** *adv.*, **-ness.**

Minding (məi·ndiŋ), *vbl. sb.* 1449. [f. MIND *v.* + -ING[1].] 1. The action of MIND *v.* 2. *dial.* A reminder 1601.

Comb. †**m.-school,** a dame-school for keeping children out of mischief.

Mindless (məi·ndlės), *a.* OE. [f. MIND *sb.* + -LESS.] 1. Destitute of mind; unintelligent. Also, †stupefied, insane. 2. Unmindful, thoughtless, heedless, careless *of* 1547.

1. M. rubbish 1866. 2. M. of others *Lives* DRYDEN. Hence **Mi·ndless·ly** *adv.*, **-ness.**

Mine (məin), *sb.* ME. [a. F. *mine.*] 1. An excavation made in the earth for the purpose of digging out metallic ores, or coal, salt, precious stones, etc. Also, the place yielding these. b. *fig.* An abundant source of supply 1541. 2. What is mined; mineral or ore. Now only used for iron ore. late ME. 3. *Mil.* Formerly, a subterranean passage excavated under the wall of a besieged fortress, for the purpose either of getting entrance, or of causing the wall to fall. Now, a subterranean gallery in which gunpowder is placed, for blowing up the enemy's fortifications; the charge of gunpowder so placed. Also, in recent naval warfare, a receptacle filled with dynamite or the like, moored beneath, or floating on or near, the surface of the water to destroy an enemy's vessel. 1483. Also *fig.*

1. b. Her memory was a m.; she knew by heart All Calderon and greater part of Lopé BYRON. 2. *All-mine*, designating the best quality of pig-iron, made from ore only; *part-m.*, designating that made from ore mixed with cinder.

Comb.: **m. adventure,** a speculation in mines; **m.-adventurer,** one who takes part in a m. adventure; **-dial** (cf. DIAL *sb.* 5); **-dragging,** the operation of dragging a body of water in order to remove submarine or floating mines; **m. field,** a portion of the sea or land in which mines have been laid; **m.-iron, -pig,** pig-iron made from m. or ore, as dist. from *cinder-pig*; **-layer,** a vessel used for laying mines; **-laying,** the operation of laying mines; **-stone, -stuff,** ore, *esp.* ironstone; **-sweeper,** a vessel used for mine-sweeping; **-sweeping** = *mine-dragging*; **-thrower** [tr. G. *minenwerfer*], a trench-mortar; **m. tin,** tin worked out of the lode; **-work,** (*a*) *Mil. pl.* subterranean passages of the nature of mines; (*b*) a system of workings belonging to a m; **wo·rker.**

Mine (məin), *poss. pron.* and *a.* [Com. Teut.: OE. *mīn*:—OTeut. *mīno-, f. *me-; see ME *pers. pron.*] The possessive pronoun of the first person sing. 1. Qualifying a following sb. Now only *arch.* or *poet.* before a vowel or *h*; otherwise repl. by MY, q. v. 2. Placed after the sb. Now only *arch.* in vocative. ME. 3. As predicative adj.: Belonging to me OE. 4. *ellipt.* = MY with the sb. supplied from the context ME. 5. *absol.* a. Those who are mine; chiefly, my family, my kindred OE. †b. That which is mine; my property –1596. c. *Of m.*: belonging to me: see OF *prep.*

1. Shall I not take m. ease in m. Inne? SHAKS. His, and m. lou'd darling SHAKS. 2. There, reader m.! 1852. 3. My doctryne is not myne, but his that hath sent me COVERDALE *John* vii. 16. 4. Your wylle & myne be one 1500. 5. a. Both I and m. alas would starve 1683. b. *Tam. Shrew* II. i. 385.

Mine (məin), *v.* ME. [ad. F. *miner*; related to MINE *sb.* Origin obscure.] 1. *intr.* To dig in the earth; *esp.* in a military sense, to dig under the foundations of a wall, etc. Also, to make subterranean passages. 2. *trans.* To dig or burrow in (the earth); also, to make (a hole, passage, etc.) underground. late ME. b. To make subterranean passages under 1820. 3. To dig away the foundations of (a wall, fort, etc.); to undermine. Now *rare.* late ME. 4. In modern warfare; To lay mines (see MINE *sb.* 3) under, for the purpose of destruction 1630. **5.** To obtain (metals, etc.) from a mine. late ME. **6.** *intr.* To dig for minerals, etc.; to make a mine; to work in a mine. late ME. **7.** *trans.* To dig in or penetrate for ore, metals, etc. 1839.

1. The Enemie mined; and they countermined RALEIGH. *fig.* To search and m. into that which is not reuealed BACON. **2.** *fig.* He may be said to m. his way into a subject, like a mole HAZLITT. **3.** *fig.* Hee..mines my gentility with my education SHAKS. **4.** The ground is mined and the train is laid 1851. **5.** Lignite..is mined near Brousa 1878. **7.** Lead veins have been traced even further down,..but they have not been mined 1839. Hence **Mi·neable** *a.* capable of being mined.

Miner (məi·nəɹ). [ME. *mynur, minour*, a. OF. *minëor, minour* (mod.F. *mineur*), f. *miner* to MINE; see -OR 2 b.] **1.** One who excavates the ground, or makes subterranean passages; *esp.* one who undermines a fortress, etc.; now *Mil.* a soldier whose work is the laying of mines. *Sappers and Miners*: see SAPPER. **2.** One who works in a mine ME. **3.** A name applied to various burrowing insects or larvæ. (See also LEAF-*miner*.) 1816. **4.** A vessel used for laying mines 1898.

1. *transf.* The mole, the m. of the soil COWPER.

Comb. **m. ant**, see sense 3; **miner's friend**, a name for the Davy safety-lamp; **miner's inch**, see INCH *sb.*[1] 1; also in names of diseases contracted by miners, as *miner's anæmia, elbow, worm*, etc.

Mineral (mi·nĕrăl), *sb.* late ME. [a. med.L. *minerale*, neut. of *mineralis* MINERAL *a.* Cf. OF. *mineral*.] **1.** Any substance which is obtained by mining. In early and in mod. techn. use, the ore (of a metal). †**2.** A mine –1602. **3.** Any natural substance that is neither animal nor vegetable 1602. †**b.** A mineral medicine or poison –1730. **c.** *pl.* = MINERAL WATER(S) 1903. **4.** In mod. scientific use, each of the species or kinds of natural inorganic substances 1813.

2. Like some Oare Among a Minerall of Mettels base SHAKS. **b.** *Cymb.* v. v. 50. *attrib.* **m. right**, the right or title to the minerals under a given surface, usu. including the right to mine them.

Mineral (mi·nĕrăl), *a.* 1477. [a. F. *minéral*, ad. med.L. *mineralis* pertaining to mines, f. med.L. *minera* mine, f. (ult.) pop.L. **mina, minare* to lead, drive.] †**1.** Pertaining to mines or mining; (of persons) skilled in mining matters –1706. **2.** Having the nature of a mineral (MINERAL *sb.* 1); obtained by mining 1581. **b.** Impregnated with mineral substances. (See MINERAL WATER.) 1562. **3.** Of material substances: Neither animal nor vegetable; inorganic 1599. **b.** Pertaining to inorganic matter 1876.

Special collocations: **m. candle**, a candle made of paraffin; **m. caoutchouc** = ELATERITE; **m. chameleon** (see CHAMELEON); **m. charcoal**, a charcoal-like substance, often found between layers of coal; **m. coal**, pit-coal, as dist. from charcoal; **m. cotton** = *m. wool*; **m. jelly**, vaseline; **m. kingdom** (see KINGDOM 5); **m. oil**, a general name for petroleum and the oils distilled from it; **m. pitch** = ASPHALT 1; **m. tallow, wax** = OZOCERITE; **m. tar**, a black viscid substance intermediate between petroleum and asphalt; **m. wool**, a fibrous wool-like material made by blowing a jet of air or steam through a stream of liquid slag; slag-wool.

b. in names of various pigments, as *m. black, blue, green, grey, purple, white, yellow*, etc.

†**Mi·neralist.** 1631. [See -IST.] A mineralogist –1796.

Mineralize (mi·nĕrăləiz), *v.* Also **-ise.** 1655. [f. MINERAL *sb.* and *a.* + -IZE.] **1.** *trans.* To transform (a metal) into an ore. **2.** To convert into a mineral substance 1799. **b.** *intr.* for *refl.* To become mineralized 1845. **3.** *trans.* To impregnate with mineral matters 1789. **4.** *intr.* To mineralogize 1792. **5.** *passive.* To be stocked with ore 1890.

2. The bones found in caverns are never mineralised BUCKLAND. **5.** A great quantity of stone, well mineralised, in the level 1890. Hence **Minerali·za·tion.**

Mineralizer (mi·nĕrăləizəɹ). 1795. [f. prec. + -ER [1].] **1.** A substance that combines with a metal to form an ore, as sulphur, arsenic, etc. **2.** The mineral with which a water is impregnated 1799.

Mineralogy (minĕræ·lŏdʒi). 1690. [f. MINERAL *sb.* + -LOGY.] The science which treats of minerals. Hence **Mineralo·gical** *a.* of or pertaining to m.; used in the study of minerals. **Mineralo·gically** *adv.* **Minera·logize** *v. intr.* to look for or study minerals. So **Minera·logist**, one versed in m. 1646; *Zool.* a carrier-shell 1851.

Mineral water. 1562. **a.** Orig., any natural water impregnated with some mineral substance. Also (with *a* and *pl.*) a kind of such water. **b.** Later, applied also to artificial imitations of such waters, and other effervescent drinks, e. g. soda-water, lemonade, ginger-beer, etc.

Minerva (minɔ̄·ɹvă). late ME. [a. L. *Minerva*, earlier *Menerva*:—pre-L. **menes-wā* (cf. Skr. *manasvin* 'full of mind or sense'), f. **menes-* = Skr. *manas* mind, Gr. μένος courage, fury, f. root **men-*; see MIND *sb.*] The Roman goddess of wisdom, anciently identified with the Greek Pallas Athene. †**b.** *fig.* Used for: Wisdom, ability. Also with allusion to the myth that Minerva was born from the head of Jupiter. –1734.

†*In spite of M.* (tr. L. *invitâ Minervâ*): contrary to one's natural bent. *Comb.* **M. (machine)** *Printing*, a small platen jobbing machine. **M. press**, a printing-press formerly existing in London; hence, the series of ultra-sentimental novels issued from it *c* 1800.

Minerval (minɔ̄·ɹvăl). 1603. [a. L., f. *Minerva*; see prec.] A gift given in gratitude by a scholar to a master.

Minery (məi·nəri). 1554. [ad. med.L. *mineria*, f. *minare* to MINE.] Mining; a place where mining operations are carried on.

Minever, Ming(e, var. MINIVER, MENG.

Mingle (mi·ŋg'l), *sb.* Now *rare.* 1548. [f. MINGLE *v.*] The action of mingling, the state of being mingled; mixture. Also *concr.* a mixture.

Mingle (mi·ŋg'l), *v.* [late ME. *mengel*, freq. of MENG *v.*; see -LE 3.] **1.** *trans.* To mix; to combine in a mixture, to blend. **b.** *poet.* To put in as an ingredient. TENNYSON. **2.** To bring together, intersperse (*with* or *among* others), to unite or join in company. Also with *up.* 1450. †**b.** To join (conversation, friendship, etc.) *with* another person. Also *to m. eyes*, look into each other's eyes. –1650. **3.** To concoct, compound 1611. **4.** *intr.* Of things: To join together (or *with* another); to mix, blend 1530. **5.** Of a person: To mix *with* others; to move about *among* or *in* a gathering. Also, to take part with others *in* some action, etc. 1605.

1. I..mengle my drynke with wepynge COVERDALE *Ps.* ci. 9. **b.** Fill the cup, and fill the can! M. madness, m. scorn! 1842. **2.** Both they and their sonnes haue mengled them selues with the daughters of them COVERDALE 1 *Esdras* viii. 70. **b.** *Wint. T.* IV. iv. 471. **3.** To m. strong drinke *Isa.* v. 22. **4.** I heard the rack As Earth and Skie would m. MILT. **5.** To m. in society 1870.

Mingle-mangle (mi·ŋg'lˌmæ·ŋg'l). 1549. [Redupl. of MINGLE *sb.*] A mixture; chiefly, a confused medley (of things or persons). Also *attrib.* or as *adj.* So **Mi·ngle-mangle** *v.*

Mi·nglement. 1674. [See -MENT.] The action of mingling; a mixture.

Mingy (mi·ndʒi), *a. colloq.* 1928. [Perh. f. M(EAN *a.* + ST)INGY *a.*] Mean, stingy.

Miniaceous (miniēⁱ·ʃəs), *a.* 1688. [f. L. *miniaceus*, f. *minium* native cinnabar, also, red lead; see -ACEOUS.] = MINIATE *a.*

Miniard, -ize: see MIGNIARD, -IZE.

Miniate (mi·niĕt), *a. rare.* 1890. [ad. L. *miniatus*, pa. pple. of *miniare* to MINIATE.] Of the colour of minium or red lead; vermilion-coloured. So **Minia·tous** *a.* 1826.

Miniate (mi·nieⁱt), *v.* 1657. [f. L. *miniat-*, ppl. stem of *miniare* (f. *minium*; see MINIUM) + -ATE [3].] *trans.* To colour or paint with vermilion; to rubricate or (more widely) to illuminate (a manuscript). Also *transf.* Hence **Mi·niator**, a rubricator, an illuminator.

Miniature (mi·niătiŭɹ, mi·nitiŭɹ, -tʃəɹ), *sb.* and *a.* 1586. [ad. It. *miniatura*, a. med.L. *miniatura*, f. *miniare* to rubricate, illuminate; see MINIATE *v.* Prob. infl. by the L. *min-* expressing smallness (in *minor, minimus*, etc.).] **A.** *sb.* †**1.** The action or process of miniating (see MINIATE *v.*) –1700. **2.** *concr.* An illumination; also, illuminated work in general 1700. **3.** The painting of 'miniatures' (in sense 4 below). Chiefly in phrase *in m.* 1656. **4.** *concr.* A portrait 'in miniature'; a portrait painted on a small scale and with minute finish, usu. on ivory or vellum 1716. **5.** *transf.* and *fig.* A reduced image or representation. Also *occas.* a minutely finished production. 1586. ¶**6.** A lineament. MASSINGER.

5. *In m.*: on a small scale; in brief; That which is correct in m. will be true in the large 1813. *Comb.* **m.-initial**, an ornamental initial having a m. picture painted within it.

B. *adj.* Represented on a small scale 1714. Hence **Mi·niature** *v. trans.* to embellish with miniatures; to represent or describe in m. **Mi·niaturist**, a miniator; one who paints m. pictures or portraits.

Minié (mi·nie). 1853. [See below.]

M. ball, bullet, an elongated bullet invented by Capt. C. E. Minié of Vincennes, which, when fired, was expanded by the powder contained in an iron cup inserted in a cavity at its base. *M. rifle*, a rifle for firing this bullet.

Minify (mi·nifəi), *v.* 1676. [Incorrectly f. L. *minor, minimus*, after *magnify*.] **1.** *trans.* To diminish in importance; to regard or represent (something) as smaller than it is. **2.** To lessen in actual size or importance 1866.

Minikin (mi·nikin), *sb.* and *a.* 1541. [ad. early mod.Du. *minneken*, f. *minne* love + *-kijn* -KIN.] **A.** *sb.* **1.** A playful or endearing term for a woman or girl. *Obs.* exc. *dial.* †**2.** A thin string of gut used for the treble string of the lute or viol. Also *attrib.*, as *m. string.* –1721. **3.** *transf.* and *fig.* A small or insignificant thing; a diminutive person 1761. **4.** A small kind of pin 1574. **5.** *Printing.* A size of type smaller than 'brilliant' 1890. **B.** *adj.* **1.** Dainty, elegant, sprightly. Now contemptuously: Affected, mincing. 1545. †**2.** Of a voice: Shrill –1608. **3.** Of a thing: Miniature; tiny 1589.

2. For one blast of thy m. mouth, thy sheepe shall take no harme SHAKS.

Minim (mi·nim). late ME. [As sb. repr. various ellipt. uses in med.L. of L. *minimus* smallest; as adj. ad. L. *minimus.*] **A.** *sb.* **1.** *Mus.* The character for a note half the value of a semibreve and double that of a crotchet (now with an open rounded head and a tail); a note of this value. Also *attrib.*, as *m. rest.* **2.** *Calligraphy.* A single down stroke of the pen 1603. **3.** The least possible portion (of something), a jot; †an atom, minute particle 1592. **4.** A creature or thing of the least size or importance 1590. **5.** A friar of the mendicant order (*Ordo Minimorum Eremitarum*) founded by St. Francis of Paula (*c* 1416–1507) 1546. †**6.** *Printing.* ? = MINION *sb.*[1] 3. –1818. **7.** The smallest fluid measure, about a drop; the sixtieth part of a fluid drachm. Also, a unit equal to a grain. *attrib.*, as *m.-measure.* 1809.

4. Phr. *M. of nature*, one of the smallest forms of animal life.

B. *adj.* Smallest, extremely small; †atomic 1670.

For man, a m. jot in time and space R. BRIDGES.

So **Mi·nimal** *a.* extremely minute in size; that is the least possible 1666.

Minimalist (mi·nimălist). 1918. [f. MINIMAL + -IST.] Used as an etymological equivalent of MENSHEVIK.

Miniment, obs. f. MUNIMENT.

Minimism (mi·nimiz'm). 1820. [f. L. *minimus* + -ISM.] **1.** Absorption in minute details. COLERIDGE. **2.** *Theol.* The minimizing view of what is involved in a dogma, esp. that of papal infallibility.

Minimize (mi·niməiz), *v.* 1802. [f. L. *minimus* + -IZE.] **1.** *trans.* **a.** To reduce to the smallest possible amount, extent, or degree. **b.** To estimate at the smallest possible amount. **2.** *intr.* To take the most moderate view possible of what is involved in a dogma 1875. Hence **Minimiza·tion, Mi·nimizer.**

Minimum (mi·nimɒ̆m). *Pl.* **minima** (mi·nimă). 1663. [a. L. *minimum*, neut. of *minimus* least.] **A.** *sb.* †**1.** *Nat. Philos.* The smallest portion into which matter is divisible; an atom. Also, the smallest possible portion of time or space. –1739. **2.** The least amount attainable, allowable, usual, etc. 1676. **3.** *Math.* = *minimum value*: see B. 1743. **4.**

The lowest amount or degree of variation (of temperature, a spectrum, etc.) attained or recorded 1823. 5. *attrib.*, as *m. period* 1860.

1. The imagination reaches a *minimum*, and may raise up to itself an idea, of which it cannot conceive any sub-division HUME. 5. **Minimum thermometer,** one which records automatically the lowest temperature since its last adjustment.

B. *adj.* [The sb. used appositively.] That is a minimum 1810.

M. value (of a variable quantity) *Math.*, a value at which it ceases to decrease and begins to increase.

Minimus (mi·nimŏs). *Pl.* **minimi** (mi·niməi). 1590. [a. L. *minimus.*] A. *sb.* 1. A creature of the smallest size. 2. *Anat.* The fifth digit; the little finger or toe 1881.

1. Get you gone you dwarfe, You *minimus* SHAKS.

B. *adj.* In some schools, appended to the surname of the youngest of several boys having the same. Abbrev. *min.*, *mini.*, or *mins.*

Mining (məi·niŋ), *vbl. sb.* 1523. [f. MINE *v.* + -ING[1].] 1. The action of MINE *v.* 2. *attrib.*, as *m.-camp*, etc. 1555.

Comb.: **m.-hole**, a hole bored to receive a blasting-charge in mining; **-ship**, one that carries and lays down submarine mines.

Minion (mi·nyən), *sb.*[1] and *a.* 1500. [a. F. *mignon* (also fem. *mignonne*) sb. and adj. Ult. etym. dubious.] A. *sb.* 1. A beloved object, darling, favourite. a. A lover or lady-love; also, a mistress or paramour (*obs.* or *rare*). b. One specially esteemed or favoured; a favourite, 'idol'; often *fig.* (now *contempt.*) 1566. c. *esp.* A favourite of a sovereign, etc.; an obsequious or servile dependant; a 'creature'; often (now *arch.*) as a form of address 1501. †2. A small kind of ordnance of about 3-inch calibre –1894. 3. *Printing.* (In full *m. type* or *letter.*) A size of type between 'nonpareil' and 'brevier' 1659. 4. *attrib.* a. (sense 1) as *m. maintainer*, etc. 1599. †b. (sense 2), as *m.-bore, gun*, etc. –1727.

1. a. What will not a fond lover undertake..for his m.? BARROW. c. The king is loue-sicke for his m. MARLOWE. It is no wonder if he helps himself from the city treasury and allows his minions to do so BRYCE.

B. *adj.* Now *rare.* 1. Dainty, elegant, pretty, neat 1528. 2. Dearly loved, favourite, pet 1716.

Hence †**Mi·nionize** *v. trans.* to raise to the position of a m.; *intr.* to play the wanton 1604–16. †**Mi·nionly** *adv.* delicately, elegantly 1539–1633. †**Mi·nionship,** the position of a m. 1645.

Minion (mi·nyən), *sb.*[2] 1621. [a. F. *minion* (Cotgr.), f. L. *minium.*] †1. = MINIUM –1654. 2. Calcined or sifted iron ore 1793.

Minionette (minyəne·t), *sb. U.S.* 1871. [f. MINION *sb.*[1] + -ETTE.] *Printing.* A size of type between nonpareil and minion, used in ornamental borders, etc.

†**Minione·tte,** *a.* 1749. [ad. F. *mignonnette* fem., after *minion.*] Small and pretty. H. WALPOLE.

†**Mi·nious,** *a.* [f. L. *minium* + -OUS.] Of the colour of minium, red. SIR T. BROWNE.

Minish (mi·niʃ), *v.* Now only *arch.* [late ME. *menuse*, ad. OF. *menusier, menuisier* :— pop.L. **minutiare*, f. *minutus* MINUTE *a.* Cf. MINCE *v.*] 1. *trans.* To make fewer or less; to reduce in power, influence, etc. 2. To remove, withdraw (a portion *of* or *from* something) 1483. Also *absol.* 3. To depreciate, belittle. late ME. 4. *intr.* To become less in quantity, number, size, etc. late ME.

1. When they are minished & brought lowe thorow oppression COVERDALE *Ps.* cvi[i]. 39. Hence †**Mi·nishment** 1533–1664.

Minister (mi·nistəɹ), *sb.* ME. [a. OF. *ministre*, a. L. *minister* servant, f. **minis-*, *minus* less; cf. *magister* MASTER *sb.*, f. *magis* more.] †1. A servant, attendant –1781. 2. One who acts as the agent or representative of a superior. Now *rare.* Also with *of.* ME. †b. An officer entrusted with the administration of the law, or attached to a court of justice –1723. †c. An underling –1625. 3. A high officer of state. a. One entrusted with the administration of a department of state 1625. b. A political agent accredited by one sovereign state to another 1709. 4. *Eccl.* a. In the rubrics of the Book of Common Prayer, the clergyman, or any of a number of clergymen, engaged in conducting worship on a particular occasion 1549. b. A person officially charged with spiritual functions in the Christian Church. Now rarely applied to an Anglican clergyman, and chiefly associated with Low Church views; but still usual in non-episcopal communions. ME. c. Applied to non-Christian religious functionaries. *Obs.* exc. *occas.* with reference to Jews. late ME. d. The title of the superior of certain religious orders; also *m. general* 1450. In the Society of Jesus, each of the five assistants of the general 1593.

1. When the seruant [*marg.* minister] of the man of God was risen early 2 *Kings* vi. 15. *transf.* My tonge..As Ministre of my wit CHAUCER. 3. What do Ministers (= the Ministry) mean to do? DICKENS. Phr. *M. for, of war, m. for foreign affairs*, etc. 4. b. Renan's appearance is something between the Catholic priest and the dissenting m. GEO. ELIOT. Phr. *M. of religion*, a clergyman of any denomination. Hence **Mi·nistership** 1565.

Minister (mi·nistəɹ), *v.* ME. [a. OF. *ministrer*, ad. L. *ministrare*, f. as prec.] I. *trans.* †1. To serve (food or drink) –1662. 2. To furnish, supply, impart (help, etc.). Now only (*arch.* or *literary*) with immaterial obj. late ME. †b. To prompt, suggest. *Meas. for M.* IV. v. 6. †3. To dispense, administer (a sacrament, the elements, etc.) –1816. †4. To apply or administer (something healing); also *absol.* and *fig.* late ME.–1680. †5. To execute or dispense (justice, law); to administer (punishment) –1596. †6. *Law.* To administer (an oath, etc.) –1722. †7. To manage (affairs, etc.) –1541.

2. They m. a singuler helpe and preseruatiue against vnbeleefe and error BACON.

II. *intr.* 1. To serve, wait at table; to render aid or tendance. late ME. 2. To serve or officiate in worship; to act as a minister of the Church ME. 3. To be helpful; also, to be conducive *to* something 1696.

1. The Sonne of man came not to bee ministred vnto, but to m. *Mark* x. 45. 3. To m. to his Necessities 1696. Hence **Mi·nistering** *vbl. sb.* and *ppl. a.* Or ministery, let vs wait on our ministring *Rom.* xii. 7. Are they not all mynistrynge spretes? COVERDALE *Heb.* i. 14. When pain and anguish wring the brow, A m. angel thou! SCOTT.

Ministerial (ministīə·riăl), *a.* (and *sb.*) 1561. [ad. F. *ministériel*, ad. med.L. *ministerialis*, f. L. *ministerium* MINISTRY. But felt as a deriv. of MINISTER *sb.*] 1. Pertaining to, or entrusted with, the execution of the law, or of the commands of a superior 1577. 2. Subsidiary, instrumental 1607. 3. Pertaining to the office, function, or character of a minister of religion 1561. 4. Of or pertaining to a minister of state; siding with or supporting the Ministry as against the Opposition 1655. 5. *sb. Hist.* An executive household officer under the feudal system 1818.

1. Phr. *M. act*: an act which is a necessary part of an official's duty, so that the agent is exempt from responsibility for its consequences. 2. Inferior and ministeriall Arts 1619. 4. M. cries of 'Oh' 1889. Hence **Ministe·rialist,** a supporter of the Ministry in office. **Ministe·rially** *adv.* in a m. manner or capacity; as a minister.

†**Ministral,** *a. rare.* 1727. [a. F.; see MINISTER *sb.* and -AL.] Pertaining to a minister or agent –1851.

Ministrant (mi·nistrănt). 1667. [ad. L. *ministrantem*, pr. pple. of *ministrare* to MINISTER.] A. *adj.* That ministers. Const. *to.* B. *sb.* One who ministers 1818.

A. Thrones and Powers, Princedoms, and Dominations m. MILT.

†**Mi·nistrate,** *v.* 1533. [f. L. *ministrat-*, ppl. stem of *ministrare.*] 1. *trans.* To administer –1727. 2. *intr.* To minister *to.* BROWNING.

Ministration (ministrēⁱ·ʃən). ME. [ad. L. *ministrationem.*] 1. The action (*occas.* an act) of ministering or serving. †b. Administration or exercise of (official) functions –1651. †c. Instrumentality –1555. 2. *spec.* Service as a priest or minister; *pl.* the services of ministers of religion 1535. 3. Administration of the sacraments, justice, law, an estate or revenue, etc.; *occas.* executorship (*arch.*). 4. The action of supplying, providing, or giving (something). Const. *of.* 1460.

1. b. Content with the nomination of Magistrates, and publique Ministers, that is to say, with the authority without the m. 1651.

Ministrative (mi·nistrĕtiv), *a.* 1833. [f. L. *ministrare*; see MINISTER *v.* and -IVE.] Pertaining to or of the nature of ministration; affording assistance.

Ministrator (mi·nistrēⁱtəɹ). *rare.* 1523. [a. L.] One who ministers or administers; †a testamentary executor.

Ministress (mi·nistrĕs). 1600. [f. MINISTER *sb.* + -ESS.] A woman who ministers or serves. Also *transf.* and *fig.*

Ministry (mi·nistri). [late ME. *ministerie*, ad. L. *ministerium*; see MINISTER *sb.*] 1. The action of ministering; the rendering of service. Now only in religious use. †2. A mode or kind of service; a function, office –1644. 3. The functions, or any specific function, pertaining to a minister of religion. late ME. b. The ministration of a particular minister 1623. c. The office of minister of the church, or of a religious body or congregation 1824. d. Christian ministers collectively, the clergy (now *rare*) 1561. 4. Agency, instrumentality. Now only with religious colouring. 1581. 5. The body of ministers charged with the administration of a country or state 1710. b. With reference to foreign countries: A ministerial department of government; a minister and his subordinates. Also, the building belonging to such a department. 1877. c. Administration of a minister of state; ministerial term.

1. The perpetual m. of one soul to another TENNYSON. 3. A certain Priest..was suspended from his m. at the Altar 1635. c. To educate a man for the m. SCOTT. 5. The Cabal M. were in power 1865. c. During Pitt's ministry (*mod.*).

Minium (mi·niŏm). *Obs.* exc. *Hist.* late ME. [a. L. = native cinnabar, red lead.] 1. = VERMILION. Also *attrib.* 2. = RED LEAD. Also, † its colour. 1650.

Miniver (mi·nivəɹ). ME. [a. F. *menu vair*, lit. 'little vair' (*menu* :—L. *minutus*, and *vair*: see VAIR *sb.*).] 1. A kind of fur used as a lining and trimming in ceremonial costume. In 1688 explained as 'plain white fur', and used recently in this sense. 2. †a. The animal from which the fur was supposed to be obtained. b. *dial.* The ermine in its white winter coat. 1665. 3. *attrib.*, as *m. cap*, etc. 1589.

Minivet (mi·nivet). 1862. [?] Any bird of the genus *Pericrocotus* of India.

Mink (miŋk). 1466. [Cf. Sw. *mänk, menk*, 'a stinking animal in Finland'.] 1. The skins or fur of the animals mentioned in sense 2. 2. A small semi-aquatic stoat-like animal of the genus *Putorius*; orig., the European species *P. lutreola*; now oftener the American *P. vison*, also called *mink-otter* 1624. 3. *attrib.*, as *m.-skin*, etc. 1812.

‖**Minnesinger** (mi·nĕsiŋəɹ). 1825. [Ger., f. *minne* love + *singer* SINGER.] One of the German lyrical poets and singers of the 12–14th centuries, who chiefly sang of love.

Minnow (mi·noᵘ). late ME. [Prob. repr. OE. **mynwe* wk. fem. = OHG. *munewa*, glossing L. *capedo*, i. e. *capito*, a fish with a large head. Perh. infl. by association with F. *menuise* small fry.] 1. A small cyprinoid freshwater fish, *Leuciscus phoxinus* or *Phoxinus lævis*, common in European streams, ponds, etc. Often loosely applied to any small fish; esp. the stickleback (*Gastrosteus*). In the U.S. it is applied similarly, chiefly to cyprinoids; and in Australia to fishes of the genus *Galaxias.* b. *transf.* and *fig.* as a type of smallness 1588. 2. *Angling.* A minnow, real or artificial, used as a bait 1615.

1. b. Phr. *A Triton of* or *among the minnows*: one who appears great from the insignificance of all those around him; Heare you this Triton of the Minnowes? SHAKS. *Comb.* **m.-tansy,** a dish of fried minnows seasoned with tansy.

Mino, obs. f. MINA[2].

Minoan (minōᵘ·ăn), *a.* and *sb.* 1894. [f. *Minos*, a famous king of Crete + -AN.] Of or pertaining to the prehistoric civilization of Crete (B.C. *c* 3000–1400). Also *sb.*

Minor (məi·nəɹ), *a.* and *sb.* ME. [a. L., f. Indo-Eur. root **min-* small; cf. L. *minuere*,

Gr. μινύθειν, etc.] A. *adj.* I. *Friar M.*, †*M. Friar*: a Franciscan.

Transl. of med.L. *Fratres Minores*, lit. 'lesser brethren', so named by St. Francis to express the humility he desired them to cultivate. The pl. is now *Friars Minor*.

II. 1. = LESSER (but not followed by *than*). Opp. to MAJOR. 1654. b. Comparatively small or unimportant. (Not now used with reference to physical magnitude, exc. as this involves importance.) 1623. 2. *Math.* See below 1850. 3. *Logic.* See below 1551. 4. That constitutes the minority. Also rarely in predicative use: In a minority. 1642. 5. *Mus.* a. Applied to intervals smaller by a chromatic semitone than those called *major*; a *m. third*, etc. Hence also to the note distant by a minor interval from a given note. b. Applied to a common chord or triad containing a minor third between the root and the second note; hence to a cadence ending on such a chord. c. Denoting those keys, or that mode, in which the scale has a minor third (and also a minor sixth and seventh). (In naming a key, *minor* follows the letter, as *A minor.*) 1694. d. Minor chords and keys are usually mournful or pathetic; hence various fig. allusions 1869. 6. Following the sb. qualified (see below) 1791.

1. *M. canon, excommunication* (= lesser e.) *orders, prophets.* †*M. Fellow* (Cambridge): a junior Fellow. *M. planet*: one of the asteroids or small planets between Mars and Jupiter. b. The base and m. sort of people SIR T. BROWNE. The m. critic, who hunts for blemishes *Junius Lett.* *M. operations* (Surg.): those which do not involve danger to life. *M. point* (Football): a try (in the Rugby game). 2. *M. axis* (of an ellipse): the diameter perpendicular to the major or transverse axis. *M. determinant*: a determinant whose matrix is formed from that of another determinant by erasing one or more rows and columns. 3. *M. term*: the subject of the conclusion of a syllogism. *M. premiss, proposition*: that premiss of a syllogism which contains the m. term. 5. d. His conversation was pitched in a m. key BURNAND. 6. *Quint, tierce m.*: see QUINT *sb.*[2], TIERCE. *Bob-m.* (Bell-ringing): a bob (BOB *sb.*[3]) rung upon six bells. In boys' schools, appended to a surname to distinguish the younger of two boys of the same surname (abbrev. *mi.*). A member of the fifth form, Green minor by name 1852.

III. Under age; below the age of majority. Now *rare.* 1579.

B. *sb.* 1. A Franciscan friar ME. 2. *Logic.* The minor premiss in a syllogism. late ME. 3. = INFANT *sb.*[1] 2. 1612. 4. *Mus.* Short for *m. key, mode*, etc. 1797. Also *fig.* (See A. II. 5 c, d.) 5. *Football.* A minor point 1890. 6. In boys' schools: cf. A. II. 6. 1863.

7. *U.S.* A subsidiary subject of study to which less time is devoted than to a major 1891.

†Mi·norate, *v.* 1534. [f. med.L. *minorat-*, ppl. stem of *minorare* to diminish, f. L. *minorem*.] *trans.* To diminish, depreciate –1727. So **†Minora·tion**, a lessening, diminution; mild purgation 1607–1696. **†Mi·norative** *a.* and *sb.* (a) gently laxative (medicine) –1747.

Minorca (minǭ·ɹkă). 1848. [Sp. *Menorca.*] Name of the second in size of the Balearic islands. Used *attrib.*, as *M.-fowl* (also *M.*), a black variety of the domestic fowl introduced from Spain; etc. Hence **Mino·rcan** *a.* of or belonging to M.; *sb.* an inhabitant of M.; also, the language of the Minorcans.

Minoress (məi·nŏrĕs). *Obs.* exc. *Hist.* [late ME. *menouresse*, a. OF., f. *menour* MINOR *sb.* 1; see -ESS.] A nun of the second order of St. Francis, known as Poor Clares, whose house outside Aldgate gave its name to the *Minories*, a street in the City of London.

Minorite (məi·nŏrəit). 1537. [f. MINOR + -ITE[1].] A. *sb.* 1. A friar minor or Franciscan. 2. †a. A person of minor rank –1670. b. One busied about minor matters. SOUTHEY. B. *adj.* Of the order of Friars Minor 1563.

A. 1. Malachias, the minorit or greie frier HOLINSHED.

Minority (məi-, minǫ·rĭti). 1533. [ad. F. *minorité* or med.L. *minoritas*, f. L. *minorem* MINOR; see -ITY.] †1. The condition or fact of being smaller, inferior, or subordinate –1751. 2. The state of being minor or under age; nonage 1547. Also *transf.* and *fig.* (now *rare*). 3. The smaller number or part; *spec.* the smaller party voting together against a majority 1736. 4. In voting, the number of votes cast for or by the smaller party 1774.

3. We are a m.; but then we are a very large m. BURKE. 4. The m. did not reach to more than 39 or 40 BURKE.

Comb.: **m. report**, a separate report made by those members of a committee, etc., who are unable to agree with the majority; **m. teller**, one who counts for a m.

Minotaur (mi·nǒtǭɹ). late ME. [ad. Gr. Μινώταυρος, f. Μίνως Minos + ταῦρος bull.] *Gr. Myth.* A fabulous monster, half bull and half man, the son of Pasiphaë, wife of Minos king of Crete, and a bull; he was fed on human flesh. Hence *allusively.*

The Imperial Minotaur [*sc.* Napoleon] 1900.

Minow, obs. f. MINNOW.

Minster (mi·nstəɹ). [OE. *mynster* :— **munistrjo-*, a. pop.L. **monisterium* = Eccl. L. *monasterium* MONASTERY.] †1. A monastery; a Christian religious house –1513. 2. The church of a monastery; also *gen.* any large church, *esp.* a collegiate or cathedral church OE. †b. *transf.* A temple –1581.

Minstrel (mi·nstrĕl), *sb.* ME. [a. OF. *ministrel* (F. *ménestrel*) :—late L. *ministerialem*, f. *ministerium*; see MINISTRY.] †1. *gen.* A servant having a special function. ME. only. 2. In early use: Any one whose profession was to entertain his patrons with music, story-telling, buffoonery, etc. In mod. use: A mediæval singer or musician, esp. one who sang or recited heroic or lyric poetry composed by himself or others. ME. 3. *transf.* Used *poet.* or *rhet.* for a musician, singer, or poet 1718. 4. Chiefly in *pl.* The designation of certain bands of public entertainers with blacked faces and grotesque costumes, who perform interludes, with songs and music ostensibly of negro origin 1864.

2. The Lay of the Last M. SCOTT (*title*). 3. I stood,..with Thee, Great M. of the Border! WORDSW. Hence **Mi·nstrel** *v.* to sing of, celebrate in song.

Minstrelsy (mi·nstrĕlsi). ME. [a. OF. *menestralies*; see MINSTREL.] 1. The art or occupation of a minstrel; the practice of playing and singing; now only *poet.* or *rhet.* 2. A body of minstrels ME. †3. *collect.* Musical instruments. Also, a kind of musical instrument. –1523. 4. Minstrel poetry; *occas.* a body of this 1802.

2. Toforn hym gooth the loude Mynstralcye CHAUCER.

Mint (mint), *sb.*[1] [OE. *mynet* neut., repr. WGer. **munita* fem., a. L. *moneta*; see MONEY.] †1. A piece of money; money. From 16th c. only *slang.* –1848. 2. A place where money is coined under public authority. late ME. b. A set of machines for coining 1592. 3. *transf.* and *fig.* A source of invention or fabrication 1555. †4. Coinage –1622. 5. A vast sum (of money); rarely *transf.* a vast amount (of something costly) 1655.

2. *Master of the m.*: the chief officer and custodian of the m. 3. A man..That hath a m. of phrases in his braine SHAKS. 5. He must have lost a m. of money 1833.

Comb.: **m.-bill**, a bill or promissory note issued by the officers of the m. against bullion deposited for coining; **m. condition**, (of a book, picture, etc.) fresh and perfect state as if only just produced; †**m. man**, one engaged or skilled in coining; **m.-mark**, a mark placed upon a coin to indicate the mint at which it was struck; **m.-master**, the master or manager of the mint; **m. price**, the price of bullion as recognized at the m.; so **m. value.**

Mint (mint), *sb.*[2] [OE. *minte* wk. fem. :— WGer. **minta*, a. L. *menta*, *mentha*, Gr. μίνθη (also μίνθος).] 1. Any aromatic labiate plant of the genus *Mentha*, esp. *M. viridis*, Garden Mint or SPEARMINT. 2. Applied with defining word to plants of allied genera, e.g. *Calamintha* 1548.

Comb.: **m. julep** (see JULEP 2); **-sauce**, a sauce made of finely chopped m., vinegar, and sugar; usually eaten with roast lamb; **-water**, a cordial distilled from m.

Mint (mint), *v.* 1546. [f. MINT *sb.*[1]] 1. *trans.* To make (coin) by stamping metal. b. *fig.* To coin or invent (a word or phrase); in contemptuous use, to invent, fabricate (something counterfeit) 1593. 2. To convert (bullion) into coin or money. Now *rare.* 1569. b. *fig.* To impress (something) with a stamp or character. Also with *out*, *upon.* Also, to stamp (an impress) *upon.* 1664.

1. b. One Happy Phrase, newly minted by the Dr. C. BOYLE.

Mintage (mi·ntĕdʒ). 1570. [f. MINT *v.* or *sb.*[1] + -AGE.] 1. The action or process (*occas.* the privilege) of coining money; coinage. Also *transf.* and *fig.* (cf. MINT *v.* 1 b). 2. *concr.* The product of a (particular) mint. Also *transf.* and *fig.* 1638. 3. The charge or duty for coining 1645. 4. The stamp impressed on a coin 1634.

1. Coins of Roman m. 1853. A new word of German m. DE QUINCEY.

Minter (mi·ntəɹ). [OE. *mynetere*, a. L. *monetarius*, f. *moneta*; see MONEY.] One who coins or stamps money. Also *fig.*

Minuend (mi·niuend). 1706. [ad. L. *minuendus* (sc. *numerus*), f. *minuere* to diminish.] *Arith.* The number or quantity from which another is to be subtracted.

Minuet (miniue·t). 1673. [ad. F. *menuet* adj. used subst., dim. of *menu* small; see MENU, etc.] 1. A slow, stately dance, in triple measure, for two dancers. 2. The music used to accompany this dance. Hence, a piece of music in the same rhythm and style, often forming one of the movements of a suite or sonata 1686.

1. I am fit for Nothing but low dancing now, a Corant, a Boreè, Or a Minnuét ETHEREDGE. *attrib.* You should do everything, said Lord Chesterfield, in m. time BAGEHOT.

Minum(e, obs. ff. MINIM.

Minunet, obs. f. MIGNONETTE.

Minus (məi·nɒs). 1481. [a. L. *minus* neut. of *minor* less; see MINOR *a.* The quasi-prep. use (sense 1), from which all the other Eng. uses are derived, probably originated in the commercial language of the Middle Ages. See N.E.D.] 1. quasi-*prep.* With the deduction of, exclusive of. Cf. LESS *a.* 4, F. *moins*, G. *weniger.* b. *predicatively* in colloq. use: Short of, without. Hence *occas.* as *adj.* 1813. 2. As the oral equivalent of the symbol (–), as helping to form a negative quantity, e.g. in '–3', '–*x*', which are read as *minus* 3, *minus x* 1579. b. Hence *attrib.* in *minus quantity*, a negative quantity; pop. misused for 'something non-existent' 1863. c. *adj.* Of the nature of a minus quantity; also *colloq.* non-existent 1800. d. *adv.* and *adj.* Negatively (electrified) 1747. 3. *sb.* a. *Math.* The symbol (–); also *minus sign.* b. A subtraction, a quantity subtracted; a loss, deficiency. c. A negative quantity. 1654.

1. If all mankind m. one, were of one opinion MILL. b. The Englishman got back to civilization m. his left arm 1903. 3. a. A slatefull of plusses, minusses, *x*, *y*, *z*'s 1836.

Minuscule (minɒ·skiul). 1705. [a. F., ad. L. *minuscula* (sc. *littera*), fem. of *minusculus* rather less, dim. of *minus.*] A. *adj.* †a. *Printing.* Of a letter: Small, lower-case. b. *Palæogr.* Of a letter: Small (see B. b). Also, written in minuscules. 1727. 2. *gen.* Very small 1893. B. *sb.* †a. *Printing.* A small or lower-case letter as opp. to a capital. b. *Palæogr.* A small letter as opp. to a capital or uncial; the small cursive script developed from the uncial; also, a manuscript in this writing. 1705.

b. The m. arose in the 7th century as a cursive monastic script I. TAYLOR.

†Mi·nutary, *a.* [f. MINUTE *sb.* + -ARY[1].] Consisting of minutes (of time). FULLER.

Minute (mi·nit), *sb.* late ME. [In branches I and III a. F. *minute* fem., ad. L. *minuta* adj. fem. used subst.; in branch II ad. L. *minutum* adj. neut. used subst.] I. A sixtieth (or other definite part) of a unit. 1. The sixtieth part of an hour (divided into sixty seconds). Also, one of the lines upon a dial marking the minute spaces. b. Vaguely: A short space of time; also, an instant, moment. late ME. c. A particular moment; occas. the appointed moment 1598. 2. *Geom.* The sixtieth part of a degree. (Marked thus ′; as in 5° 12′.) late ME. 3. *Arch.* The sixtieth or occas. some other part of the MODULE 1696.

1. For the lachesse Of half a Minut of an houre GOWER. b. The train will be starting in a m. (*mod.*).

c. Phr. *The m.* (*that*)..: as soon as. Hence **Mi·nutely** *a.* and *adv.*[1] (happening) every m.

II. Something small. †1. A coin of little value; a mite –1589. †2. Something minute; as *pl.* 'small fry'; a detail; something of small value 1515–1670.

2. Let me heare from thee euery m. of Newes B. JONS.

III. A rough draft; a memorandum; a brief summary of events or transactions, esp. (usu. *pl.*) the record of the proceedings of an assembly, committee, etc. 1502. b. An official memorandum authorizing or recommending a course, as a *Treasury m.* 1564.

Comb.: **m. bell**, the tolling of a bell at intervals of a m.; **-book**, a book in which minutes are recorded; **-glass**, a sand-glass that runs for a m.; **-gun**, one fired at intervals of a m.; used as a sign of mourning or distress; **-hand**, the longer hand of a time-piece, which indicates the minutes **-man**, a militiaman, during the American revolutionary period, who was ready to march at a minute's notice (*Hist.*); **-repeater**, a watch which 'repeats' the minutes.

Minute (məiniū·t, miniū·t), *a.* late ME. [ad. L. *minutus*, pa. pple. of *minuere* to make small.] †1. Chopped small. late ME. only. †2. Of imposts, etc.: Lesser; esp. in *m. tithes* = 'small tithes' –1696. 3. Very small in size, amount, or degree 1626. 4. Trifling, petty 1650. 5. Of investigations, etc.: Very detailed; very precise; very accurate *c* 1680.

3. Very m. changes of temperature GEIKIE. 4. These m. philosophers..are a sort of pirates who plunder all that come in their way BERKELEY. 5. M. regulations are apt to be transgressed JOWETT. Hence **Minu·tely** *adv.*[2], **-ness.**

Minute (mi·nit), *v.* 1605. [f. MINUTE *sb.*] 1. *trans.* To time to the minute. 2. To draft (a document or scheme); to record in a minute or memorandum; to make a minute of the contents of (a document) 1648.

1. To m. the speed of a train SMILES. 2. Phr. *To m. down*: to make a note of.

‖**Minutia** (məi-, miniū·ʃiă). *Pl.* **-iæ** (-iī). 1751. [a. L. *minutia* smallness, pl. *minutiæ* trifles, f. *minutus* MINUTE *a.*] A precise detail; a trivial matter or object. Usu. *pl.* So †**Minu·tial** *a.* pertaining to details 1612–1796. **Minu·tiose, -ous** *adjs.* attentive to minutiæ 1819.

Minx (miŋks). 1542. [?] †1. A pet dog. UDALL. 2. A pert girl, hussy. Now often playful. 1592. †b. A lewd woman –1728.

2. b. This is some Minxes token SHAKS.

Minx, obs. f. MINK.

Miny (məi·ni), *a. rare.* 1611. [f. MINE *sb.* + -Y[1].] 1. Pertaining to a mine; mineral. 2. Subterraneous. THOMSON.

Miocene (məi·ŏsīn), *a.* Also **mei-.** 1833. [irreg. f. Gr. μείων less + καινός new, recent.] *Geol.* Epithet of the middle division of the Tertiary strata, and the geological period it represents. Also quasi-*sb.* **Mioce·nic** *a.*

Miquelet (mi·kĕlĕt). 1670. [a. F., ad. Sp. *miquelete*, *miguelete*, f. Cat. *Miquel*, Sp. *Miguel* Michael.] a. In the 17th c., a member of a body of Catalonian banditti who infested the Pyrenees. b. Later, a Spanish guerrilla soldier during the Peninsular War; also, a member of a corps of French irregulars raised for service against the Spaniards. c. In mod. Spain, a soldier of certain local regiments, chiefly employed on escort duties.

‖**Mir** (mīr). 1877. A Russian village community.

Mirabelle (mirăbe·l). 1706. [a. F.] A variety of plum.

†**Mira·bilis.** 1673. = AQUA MIRABILIS –1687.

Mirabilite (miræ·biləit). 1854. [a. G. *mirabilit*, f. mod.L. (*sal*) *mirabilis*, Glauber's name for his salt; see -ITE[1].] *Min.* Native sodium sulphate (GLAUBER'S SALT).

†**Mi·rable**, *a.* and *sb.* 1450. [ad. L. *mirabilis*; see -ABLE.] A. *adj.* Wonderful, marvellous –1606. B. *sb.* Something wonderful –1653.

Miracle (mi·răk'l), *sb.* late OE. [a. OF., ad. L. *miraculum* object of wonder, f. *mirari* to wonder, f. *mirus* wonderful.] 1. A marvellous event exceeding the known powers of nature, and therefore supposed to be due to the special intervention of the Deity or of some supernatural agency; chiefly, an act (e.g. of healing) exhibiting control over the laws of nature, and serving as evidence that the agent is either divine or is specially favoured by God. 2. *transf.*, *esp.* as applied hyperbolically to an unusual achievement or event. late ME. b. *concr.* A wonderful object, a marvel. late ME. †3. A miraculous story; a legend. CHAUCER. 4. = *Miracle play* ME.

1. This is againe the second m. that Iesus did *John* iv. 54. 2. O M.! He blushes! DRYDEN. The radium 'miracle' 1903. Phr. *To a m.*: marvellously well 1643. b. A m. of worth DANIEL, of rare device COLERIDGE, of ingenuity (*mod.*). 3. CHAUCER *Sir Thopas* Prol. 1.

attrib. and *Comb.*, as *m.-monger*, etc.; **m. play**, one of the mediæval dramatic representations based on the life of Our Lord and the legends of the Saints 1602; **m. player, -playing** [from sense 4] late ME.

Miracle (mi·răk'l), *v.* 1611. [f. the sb.] a. *refl.* ? To be revealed by miracle. *Cymb.* IV. ii. 29. b. *intr.* To work miracles.

Miraculize (miræ·kiŭləiz), *v.* 1711. [f. L. *miraculum* + -IZE.] *trans.* To consider as miraculous.

Miraculous (miræ·kiŭləs), *a.* 1502. [ad. F. *miraculeux*, ad. med.L. *miraculosus*, f. *miraculum*; see -OUS.] 1. Of the nature of a miracle; beyond the agency of natural laws; supernatural. †b. Concerned with miracles –1845. 2. *transf.*, etc. Resembling a miracle; extraordinary; marvellous; astonishing 1573. 3. Of things (formerly also of persons): Having the power to work miracles; wonder-working 1596.

1. This strength M. yet remaining in those locks MILT. *Sams.* 587. 3. His word is more then the m. Harpe SHAKS. Hence **Mira·culous-ly** *adv.*, **-ness.**

‖**Mirador** (mīradǭ·ɹ). Also **-dore.** 1670. [Sp., f. *mirar* to look.] A watch-tower; also, a belvedere on the top of a Spanish house.

Mirage (mirā·ʒ). 1812. [a. F., f. (*se*) *mirer* to look at oneself in a mirror, to be reflected.] An optical illusion, common in hot countries, and esp. in sandy deserts, arising from the reflection of an object at some distance, often giving the false appearance of a sheet of water.

fig. A moist m. in desert eyes TENNYSON.

Mirbane (mǝ̄·ɹbeⁱn). 1857. [?; so in Fr.] *Essence, oil of m.*, nitrobenzol used in perfumery.

Mire (məiəɹ), *sb.* [ME. *mire*, a. ON. *mýr-r* fem.:—OTeut. *miuzjā:—*meuzjā, f. *meus-, ablaut-var. of *mus-; see MOSS.] 1. A piece of wet, swampy ground; a boggy place. Also *gen.* swampy ground, bog. 2. Wet or soft mud, slush, dirt. (Cf. 2 *Pet.* ii. 22.) ME. b. A mass of dirt 1871.

1. Fig. phr. *To bring, drag, lay, leave, stick in the m.*; *to find oneself in the m.* Honest water, which nere left man i' th' m. SHAKS. 2. b. Until a stumble, and the man's one m.! BROWNING. *Comb.* **m.-crow**, the laughing gull, *Larus ridibundus.*

†**Mire**, *a.* late ME. [f. prec.] Miry –1656.

Now that the Fields are dank, and ways are m. MILT.

Mire (məiəɹ), *v.* late ME. [f. MIRE *sb.*] I. *trans.* 1. To plunge or set fast in the mire. (Chiefly *pass.*) 1559. b. *fig.* To involve in difficulties. late ME. 2. To bespatter with mire or filth; to defile (*lit.* and *fig.*) 1508.

1. Some of them were mired in it [a slough] 1752. 2. Smeer'd thus and mir'd with infamie SHAKS.

II. *intr.* To sink in the mire, be bogged 1607.

Paint till a horse may myre upon your face SHAKS.

Mirific (məiri·fik), *a. rare.* 1490. [a. F. *mirifique*, ad. L. *mirificus*, f. *mirus* wonderful + *-ficus* (see -FIC).] Doing wonders; exciting astonishment; marvellous. So †**Miri·fical** *a.* 1603–1829. **Miri·fically** *adv.*

Miriness (məiə·rinĕs). 1608. [f. MIRY *a.* + -NESS.] Miry condition or quality.

Mirk, Mirky, etc., var. ff. MURK, etc.

Mirror (mi·rəɹ), *sb.* [ME. *mirour*, a. OF. *mir(e)our* (mod.F. *miroir*):—pop.L. *miratorium, f. *mirare to look at (cl. L. *mirari* to wonder): see -ORY.] I. Literal uses, etc. 1. A polished surface, now usu. of glass coated with tin amalgam or silver, which reflects images of objects; a looking-glass. b. *transf.* Applied to water (chiefly *poet.*) 1595. 2. *spec.* a. A magic glass or crystal ME. †b. A small glass formerly worn in the hat by men and at the girdle by women. B. JONS. 3. *Optics.* A polished surface, either *plane*, *convex*, or *concave*, that reflects rays of light; a speculum 1728.

1. And in her hand she held a mirrhour bright SPENSER. *fig.* To hold as 'twer the Mirrour up to Nature SHAKS. 3. *Burning m.*: a concave m. which concentrates the sun's rays at a focus, and causes them to set fire to objects.

II. Fig. uses. 1. That which gives a faithful reflection of anything. late ME. b. Used of a person (*poet.*) 1563. 2. That which exhibits something to be imitated; an exemplar. Now *rare.* ME. †b. Hence of persons: A paragon –1785. †c. A warning –1633.

1. The stage..the mirrour of life JOHNSON. b. Mirrour of Poets, Mirrour of our Age WALLER. 2. Sir Tristram..the m. of chivalry 1801. b. Our m. of ministers of finance BURKE.

III. a. *Arch.* A small oval ornament resembling a mirror in shape 1847. b. *Ornith.* The speculum of a bird's wing.

attrib. and *Comb.*, as *m.-silverer*, *-surface*, etc.; also **m. carp**, the looking-glass carp, *Cyprinus carpio*; **-plate**, a plate of glass suitable for a m.; **-writing**, writing which appears as though viewed in a m., reversed writing (a characteristic of aphasia).

Mirror (mi·rəɹ), *v.* 1820. [f. prec. sb.] *trans.* To reflect in the manner of a mirror.

Mirth (mǝ̄ɹþ). [OE. *myr(i)gþ* str. fem., f. (ult.) OTeut. *murgjo- MERRY *a.*] †1. Pleasurable feeling; joy, happiness –1696. 2. Rejoicing, *esp.* manifested rejoicing; merry-making; jollity ME. †3. A diversion, sport, entertainment –1606. 4. Merriment, hilarity; in early use, fun, ridicule. late ME. †b. Put for: The object of one's mirth –1708.

2. Be large in m., anon wee'l drinke a Measure The Table round SHAKS. 3. To giue a Kingdome for a M. SHAKS. 4. I was borne to speake all m., and no matter SHAKS. b. He's all my Exercise, my M., my Matter SHAKS.

Mirthful (mǝ̄·ɹþfŭl), *a.* ME. [f. MIRTH + -FUL.] 1. Full of mirth; gladsome, hilarious; expressive of mirth. b. Of places, seasons, etc.: Characterized by rejoicing 1450. 2. Of things: Amusing. SHAKS.

1. Each m. lout The ale-house seeks CLARE. A m. jest CRABBE. b. M. bower or hall KEBLE. Hence **Mi·rthful-ly** *adv.*, **-ness.**

Mirthless (mǝ̄·ɹþlĕs), *a.* late ME. [f. MIRTH + -LESS.] Joyless; sad, dismal. Hence **Mi·rthless-ly** *adv.*, **-ness.**

Miry (məiə·ri), *a.* late ME. [f. MIRE *sb.* + -Y[1].] 1. Of the nature of mire, swampy. 2. Abounding in mire, muddy 1440. 3. Covered with mud or mire 1496. 4. *fig.* Dirty; despicable 1532.

1. Marishes and myrie bogs SPENSER. 2. M. roads 1833. 4. A m. business 1877.

‖**Mirza** (mī·ɹzā). 1613. [Pers., short for *mirzād*, f. *mīr* (a. Arab. *amīr*: see AMEER) a prince + *zād* born.] In Persia: a. A royal prince; as a title, placed after the name. b. Title of honour prefixed to the name of an official or a man of learning.

†**Mis**, *a.* ME. [Partly the prefix MIS-[1] (4) used as a separate word; partly a reduced form of AMISS.] Bad; wrong; wicked. In predicative use: Amiss. –1556. So †**Mis** *adv.* wrongly; badly; amiss.

Mis- (mis), *prefix*[1], repr. OE. *mis-*:—OTeut. *misso- (whence *missjan MISS *v.*). The adj. *misso- had app. two senses: (1) divergent, astray, (2) mutual, alternate.

The hyphen is now employed chiefly in new or rarely used formations, and in words like *mis-say*, *mis-cite*, etc.

The predominant meaning of the prefix is that of 'amiss', 'wrong(ly)', 'bad(ly)', 'improper(ly)', 'mistaken(ly)'.

In early ME. many new compounds were made, some of which appear to have been suggested by French formations with *mes-* (see MIS-[2]); a word like *misjudge* has prob. a double origin, being partly of native formation, and partly an adaptation of OF. *mesjuger.* The most prolific period for the formation of *mis-* compounds was the 17th c., when writers such as Bacon, Donne, and Bp. Hall employed them largely.

In OE. *mis-* was prefixed to vbs., active and passive pples., nouns of action and condition, and adjs. In ME. its composition with agent-nouns and adverbs followed as a matter of course.

1. Prefixed to verbs, with the meaning 'amiss', 'badly', 'wrongly', 'perversely', 'mistakenly'; as †*misact*, MISDO, MISLEAD, MISLIKE, etc. b. In the 14th–16th c., in some words, as MISDEEM, etc., *mis-* took the force of 'unfavourably', and in MISBODE, MISDOUBT, etc., it intensified the notion of uneasy

feeling contained in the vb. These new senses and combs., however, are now *arch.* or *dial.*
2. Prefixed to pples. and ppl. adjs. with the same meaning as in 1; as *misbound, misbuilt.*
3. Similarly prefixed to vbl. sbs., as *misaccenting.*
4. Prefixed to nouns of action, condition, and quality, with the meaning 'bad', 'wrong', 'erroneous', 'perverse', 'misdirected'; as *misaccentuation, misappraisement, misattribution, misproposal.*
5. Prefixed to agent-nouns; as *misprofessor.*
6. Prefixed to adjs. with the sense of 'wrongly', 'erroneously', 'perversely'; as *misconvenient.*
7. Expressing negation (of something good or desirable); = DIS-, IN-, or UN-; as *misadvertence.*
8. Prefixed to words denoting something wrong or bad, serving as an intensive; as *misdemeriting.*
9. *Mis-* was often substituted for *dis-* (and even *des-*); hence the dial. *misdain* (after *disdain*), *miscry* for *descry.*

Mis- (mis), *prefix* [2], in compounds adopted from French represents OF. *mes-* (mod.F. *més-, mes-, mé-*):—Com. Rom. *minus-*, with the sense 'bad(ly)', 'wrong(ly)', 'amiss', and with neg. force, in comb. with verbs, adjs., and nouns. Examples are MISADVENTURE, MISCHANCE, MISCHIEF, MISCREANT, etc.

†**Misaccou·nt,** *v.* late ME. [MIS- [1] 1.] *trans.* To misreckon, misjudge –1655.

Misaddre·ss, *v.* 1648. [MIS- [1] 1.] *trans.* To address wrongly or impertinently.

Misadventure (misædve·ntiŭr, -tʃəɹ). ME. [a. OF. *mesaventure*, f. *mesavenir* to turn out badly, after *aventure*; see MIS- [2].] 1. Ill-luck, bad fortune. Usu.: A piece of bad fortune; a mishap. 2. *Law.* Homicide committed accidentally by a person in doing a lawful act, without intention of hurt; now chiefly in phr. *homicide* or *death by m.* 1509. Hence †**Misadve·ntured** *a.* unfortunate. SHAKS.

Misadve·nturous, *a.* Now *rare.* late ME. [Orig. a. OF. *mesaventureux*; later, f. MISADVENTURE + -OUS.] Unfortunate.

Misadvi·ce. 1632. [MIS- [1] 4.] Wrong advice.

Misadvi·se, *v.* late ME. [MIS- [1] 1.] †1. *refl.* To take a wrong counsel; to act unadvisedly –1602. 2. *trans.* To advise wrongly 1548. So †**Mis·advi·sed** *ppl. a.* ill-advised; injudicious.

†**Misaffe·ct,** *v.* 1586. [MIS- [1] 1, 7.] 1. *trans.* To affect injuriously –1650. 2. To dislike –1641.

†**Misaffe·cted,** *ppl. a.* 1621. [Partly f. prec. + -ED [1], partly f. MIS- [1] 2 + AFFECTED.] 1. Affected by illness or disease –1694. 2. Ill-disposed, disaffected –1645.

Misaffe·ction. Now *rare* or *Obs.* 1621. [MIS- [1] 4.] 1. Perverted affection; disaffection. 2. Physical disorder; disease 1673.

†**Misalle·ge,** *v.* 1559. [MIS- [1] 1.] *trans.* To cite falsely as supporting one's contention –1684. So †**Misallega·tion** 1633–47.

Misalli·ance. 1738. [f. MIS- [1] 4 + ALLIANCE, after F.] An improper alliance, association, or union; *esp.* a MÉSALLIANCE.

Misanthrope (mi·sænþrōup). 1683. (In 16–17th c. misant(h)ropos, *pl.* -pi.) [ad. Gr. μισάνθρωπος (adj.), f. μισ(ο)- (μισεῖν to hate) + ἄνθρωπος.] A man-hater; one who distrusts men and avoids them. b. as *adj.* = next 1757.

So **Misanthro·pic** (1762), **-al** (1621) *a.* characterized by misanthropy; man-hating. **Misanthro·pically** *adv.* **Misa·nthropist** = MISANTHROPE 1656. **Misa·nthropize** *v. intr.* to be a misanthrope; to hate mankind 1846. **Misa·nthropy,** hatred of mankind; the condition of a misanthrope 1656.

Misapply (misăplai·), *v.* 1571. [MIS- [1] 1.] *trans.* To make a wrong application of. So **Misapplica·tion** 1607.

Misappre·ciate, *v.* 1828. [MIS- [1] 1.] *trans.* To fail to appreciate rightly; to make a wrong estimate of. So **Misapprecia·tion.**

Mi:sapprehe·nd, *v.* 1646. [MIS- [1] 1.] *trans.* To apprehend wrongly; to misunderstand. So **Mi:sapprehe·nsion** 1629. **Mi:sapprehe·nsive** *a.* 1646.

Misappro·priate, *v.* 1857. [MIS- [1] 1.] *trans.* To appropriate to wrong uses; chiefly, to apply dishonestly to one's own use. So **Mi:sappropria·tion** 1794.

Misarra·nged, *pa. pple.* and *ppl. a.* 1848. [MIS- [1] 2.] Wrongly arranged. So **Misarra·ngement** 1784.

Misarray·. [MIS- [1] 4.] Disarray. SCOTT.

Misaventeur, -ur(e, etc.: obs. ff. MISADVENTURE.

Misbapti·ze, *v.* 1610. [MIS- [1] 1.] 1. *trans.* To misname. 2. To baptize wrongly. KEATS.

†**Misbea·r,** *v.* ME. [f. MIS- [1] 1 + BEAR *v.* [1]] *refl.* To misconduct oneself –1502.

Misbecome (misbĭkɒ·m), *v.* 1530. [MIS- [1] 1.] *trans.* To fail to become; to suit ill. So **Misbeco·ming** *ppl. a.* unbecoming, unsuitable. **Misbeco·ming·ly** *adv.*, **-ness.**

†**Misbe·de,** *v.* [OE. *misbēodan*, f. *mis-* MIS- [1] 1 + *bēodan* (see BID *v.* A).] *trans.* To ill-use; to injure, abuse. Also *intr.* const. *till.* –1496.
Or who hath yow misboden, or offended? CHAUCER.

Misbege·t, *v.* *rare.* ME. [MIS- [1] 1.] *trans.* To beget unlawfully.

Misbego·tten, *ppl. a.* and *sb.* Also **misbegot.** 1546. [MIS- [1] 2.] A. *adj.* 1. Unlawfully begotten; illegitimate; bastard 1554. Also *transf.* and *fig.* 2. Used as a term of opprobrium 1571. B. *sb.* A bastard; also, as a term of abuse (cf. A. 2). Now only *dial.*, in form *misbegot.* 1546.
A. 1. That m. diuell Falconbridge SHAKS. 2. Such a m. beast SOUTHEY.

Misbeha·ve, *v.* 1451. [MIS- [1] 1.] *refl.* and (later) *intr.* To conduct oneself improperly; to behave wrongly. So **Misbeha·ved** *ppl. a.* ill-behaved. SHAKS. **Misbeha·viour,** bad behaviour 1486.

Misbelief (misbĭlī·f). ME. [MIS- [1] 4, 7.] 1. Erroneous religious belief. 2. *gen.* False opinion or notion. late ME. †3. Want of belief; incredulity –1653. Hence †**Misbelieved** *a.* infidel, heathen; incredulous.

Misbelie·ve, *v.* late ME. [MIS- [1] 1, 7.] 1. *intr.* To believe amiss; to hold an erroneous belief. †2. *trans.* Not to believe; to disbelieve –1728. Hence **Misbelie·ver,** a heretic or infidel. **Misbelie·ving** *ppl. a.* heretical.

Misbesee·m, *v.* 1598. [MIS- [1] 1.] = MISBECOME.

Misbestow·, *v.* 1532. [MIS- [1] 1.] *trans.* To bestow wrongly or improperly. So **Misbestow·al,** wrong bestowal.

Misbi·rth. *rare.* 1648. [MIS- [1] 4.] = ABORTION.

Misbo·de, *v.* *rare.* 1626. [MIS- [1] 1.] *trans.* To forebode (something evil). So **Misbo·ding** *vbl. sb.* and *ppl. a.*

Misboden, pa. pple. of MISBEDE.

Misborn (misbǭ·ɹn), *ppl. a.* Now *rare.* OE. [MIS- [1] 2.] 1. Prematurely born; abortive. Hence, mis-shapen. 2. Born out of wedlock; hence, base-born 1590.

Misca·lculate, *v.* 1697. [MIS- [1] 1.] *trans.* To calculate or reckon wrongly. Also *absol.* or *intr.* Hence **Miscalcula·tion.**

Miscall (mis,kǭ·l), *v.* late ME. [MIS- [1] 1.] 1. *trans.* To call by a wrong name. 2. To call by a bad name; to call (a person) names; to revile. Now *dial.* 1449.
2. By opprobrious Epithets we m. each other SIR T. BROWNE.

Miscarriage (mis,kæ·rėdʒ). 1614. [MIS- [1] 4.] †1. Misbehaviour –1682. †b. An instance of this –1829. 2. Mismanagement (of a business); failure (of an enterprise, etc.). Now *rare.* 1651. b. An instance of this; a failure; a mistake. Now *rare*, exc. in *m. of justice.* 1614. †c. Mishap, disaster –1776. †d. An unfortunate lapse *into.* H. WALPOLE. 3. Untimely delivery (of a woman): usu. taken as synonymous with *abortion* 1662. 4. The failure (of a letter, etc.) to reach its destination 1650.
2. The m. of the late King's counsels BURNET. c. If I should meet with any..m. in the voyage DE FOE.

Miscarry (mis,kæ·ri), *v.* ME. [MIS- [1] 1.] †1. *intr.* To come to harm, misfortune, or destruction; to perish –1749. †b. *pass.* in same sense –1666. †2. *intr.* and *refl.* To go wrong or astray; to behave amiss –1732. 3. *intr.* Of a person: To fail in one's purpose or object 1612. 4. Of a business, design, etc.: To go wrong; to be a failure. †Also *pass.* 1607. †b. Of plants, seeds, etc.: To be abortive; to fail. Also *transf.* –1740. 5. To be delivered prematurely *of* a child 1527. †b. Said of the child. SHAKS. 6. *intr.* Of a letter, etc.: To fail to reach its proper destination 1613. †7. *trans.* To cause (a person) to go wrong; to lead astray –1700.
1. The great ships bringing corne from Siria and Egipt..doe seldome miscarrie 1601. 4. When a great action miscarrieth, the blame must be laid on some FULLER. 6. The Cardinals Letters to the Pope miscarried SHAKS.

†**Misca·st.** *sb.* [MIS- [1] 4.] Miscalculation. SANDYS.

Misca·st, *v.* *Obs.* exc. *dial.* late ME. [MIS- [1] 1.] 1. *trans.* To cast with evil intent. 2. To miscalculate. Also *absol.* 1598. 3. To mislay. HOLLAND.

Miscegenation (mi:sĭdʒĭnē·ʃən). 1864. [irreg. f. L. *miscere* to mix + *genus* race + -ATION.] Mixture of races; *esp.* the sexual union of whites with negroes.

†**Miscellana·rian.** [f. MISCELLANY + -ARIAN.] A writer of miscellanies. SHAFTESBURY.

†**Miscellane,** *a.* and *sb.* 1600. [ad. L. *miscellaneus* (see below).] A. *adj.* Mixed; miscellaneous –1658. B. *sb.* A mixture, medley, miscellany. (Cf. MASLIN [2].) –1664.

‖**Miscellanea** (misĕlē·niă). 1571. [neut. pl. of L. *miscellaneus* (see next).] A collection of miscellaneous literary compositions, notes, etc.; a literary miscellany.

Miscellaneous (misĕlē·niəs), *a.* 1637. [f. L. *miscellaneus*, f. *miscellus* mixed (f. *miscere*); see -EOUS.] 1. With sing. sb.: Of mixed composition or character. With pl. sb.: Of various kinds. 2. Of persons: Having various qualities or aspects: many-sided. †Also, general (as opp. to *technical*). 1646.
1. A m. rabble, who extol Things vulgar MILT. My second boy..received a sort of m. education GOLDSM. M. volumes of Manuscripts 1899. 2. A M. Writer SHAFTESB. Hence **Miscella·neous·ly** *adv.*, **-ness.**

Miscellany (mi·sĕlăni, mise·lăni), *sb.* 1599. [app. ad. F. *miscellanées* fem. pl. (ad. L. *miscellanea* neut. pl.: see MISCELLANEA), only in sense 2.] 1. A mixture, medley. †*M. madam*: a female dealer in miscellaneous articles. B. JONS. 2. *pl.* Miscellaneous pieces brought together to form a volume 1615. 3. The volume containing such miscellaneous pieces 1638.
3. The Bible, in fact, is a 'miscellany'—a very various one H. ROGERS. Hence **Misce·llanist,** a writer of miscellanies. So †**Miscellany** *a.* = MISCELLANEOUS 1629–1804.

Mischance (mis,tʃɑ·ns), *sb.* ME. [a. OF. *mesch(e)ance*, etc.; see MIS- [2] and CHANCE *sb.*] 1. Ill-luck, ill-success. In early use, disaster. 2. A piece of bad luck, a mishap; †*spec.* an accidental mutilation ME.
1. Beholding all his own m., Mute TENNYSON. 2. Phr. *By m.*: by an unlucky accident. Hence **Mischa·nceful** *a.* unlucky.

Mischa·nce, *v.* *Obs.* or *arch.* 1542. [MIS- [1] 1.] 1. *intr.* To happen unfortunately 1552. 2. *pass.* To be unfortunate.

Mischa·rge, *v.* Now *rare.* 1571. [MIS- [1] 1.] *trans.* To charge wrongly or falsely. So **Mischa·rge** *sb.* a mistake in charging, as in an account 1828.

Mischief (mi·stʃif), *sb.* ME. [a. OF. *meschief, -chef* (mod. *méchef*), vbl. sb. f. *meschever* (see MISCHIEVE).] †1. Evil plight; misfortune; distress; in ME. often, need, poverty –1679. †Also with *a* and *pl.* 2. Harm or evil as wrought by a person or a particular cause 1480. b. An injury so wrought. Now only in *collect. pl.* = 'evil consequences', and in phr. *to do oneself a m.* late ME. 3. *Law.* A condition in which a person suffers a wrong or is under some disability 1596. 4. †a. A disease or ailment. b. In medical parlance, a morbid condition not further defined. 1552. 5. Hurtful character or influence. Now *rare* or *Obs.* 1646. †6. Evil-doing –1611. 7. A cause or source of harm or evil; a worker of mischief; also, one who acts in a vexatious or annoying manner 1586. 8. Vexatious or annoying action or conduct. Also, a tendency to or disposition for such conduct. 1784.
2. The devil is seldom out of call when he is wanted for any m. DE FOE. Phr. *To make m.*: to create discord, e.g. by talebearing. b. Thy tongue deuiseth

mischiefes *Ps.* lii. 2. 3. Hee tooke his graunt subiect to that mischiefe BACON. Better a m., then an inconvenience 1670. 4. b. When the m. is confined to the lung 1899. 5. The m. of the precedent 1803. Phr. *The m.* (*of*..) *is* (*that*): the most unfortunate or vexatious part of the matter. 6. O full of all subtilty and all mischiefe *Acts* xiii. 10. 8. He..had more m. than ill-will in his composition W. IRVING.

Phrases, chiefly expletive and imprecatory. *A m. on..! A m. take..! To play the m.* (='the devil') (*with*). So in *What* (*how*, etc.) *the m...?* Also *to go to the m.*

Mischief (mi·stʃif), *v. arch.* 1440. [f. MISCHIEF *sb.*] = MISCHIEVE *v.* 1, 3, 3 b.

Mischiefful (mi·stʃif,fŭl), *a.* Now *dial.* ME. [f. as prec. + -FUL.] †1. Disastrous –1470. 2. Full of mischief; mischievous 1541.

Mi·schief-ma:ker. 1710. One who makes mischief, esp. by talebearing. So **Mi·schief-ma:king** *vbl. sb.* and *ppl. a.*

Mischieve (mistʃī·v), *v.* Now *dial.* or *arch.* ME. [a. OF. *meschever*, f. *mes-* MIS-[2] + *chever* CHEVE *v.*] †1. *intr.* To suffer harm or injury; to come to grief, miscarry –1604. 2. *trans.* To bring to destruction or ruin. late ME. 3. To inflict injury or loss upon 1475. b. To do physical harm to. late ME. †4. To abuse, slander –1785.

Mischievous (mi·stʃivəs), *a.* ME. [a. AF. *meschevous*, f. OF. *meschever* MISCHIEVE *v.* or *meschef*; see -OUS. Till 1700, stressing on the second syllable was common.] †1. Unfortunate, disastrous; *occas.* of persons, miserable, poverty-stricken –1583. 2. Of persons and animals, or their dispositions: Producing or designing mischief or harm. Now *rare.* 1473. 3. Of things, events, actions: Fraught with mischief or harm; having harmful effects. late ME. 4. Of persons, etc.: Characterized by acts of playful malice or petty annoyance 1676.

2. *Jul. C.* II. i. 33. 3. A m. fallacy LOWELL. 4. M. de Voltaire had..a big Ape, of excessively m. turn; who used to throw stones at the passers-by CARLYLE. Hence **Mi·schievous-ly** *adv.*, **-ness.**

Mischoi·ce. 1684. [MIS-[1] 4.] Wrong choice.

Mischoo·se, *v.* ME. [MIS-[1] 1.] *trans.* and *intr.* To choose wrongly.

†**Mischri·sten,** *v.* [MIS-[1] 1.] = MISBAPTIZE 1. DONNE.

Miscible (mi·sib'l), *a.* (*sb.*) 1570. [f. L. *miscere* to mix; see -IBLE.] Capable of being mixed (*with* something). †b. *sb.* A substance that will mix with another –1678. **Miscibi·lity.**

Mis-cite (mis,səi·t), *v.* 1591. [MIS-[1] 1.] *trans.* To cite incorrectly. **Mis-cita·tion** 1634.

Misco·lour, *v.* 1809. [MIS-[1] 1.] *trans.* To give a wrong colour to (facts, etc.); to misrepresent.

†**Misco·mfort,** *sb.* ME. [MIS-[1] 7.] = DISCOMFORT *sb.* 2. –1526. So †**Misco·mfort** *v.* to trouble, distress –1483.

Mi:scomprehe·nd, *v.* 1813. [MIS-[1] 1.] *trans.* To misunderstand. So **Mi:scomprehe·nsion.**

Mi:scomputa·tion. 1647. [MIS-[1] 4.] Misreckoning. So †**Miscompute** *sb.* SIR T. BROWNE; *v.* 1672.

Misconcei·t, *sb. arch.* 1576. [MIS-[1] 4.] = MISCONCEPTION. So **Misconcei·t** *v.* to have a false idea of; to think erroneously (that ...) 1595.

Misconcei·ve, *v.* late ME. [MIS-[1] 1.] 1. *intr.* To have a false conception or entertain wrong notions (*of*). Also with clause, †to suspect. 2. *trans.* To mistake the meaning of 1597.

2. To yeeld them..reasonable causes of those things, which, for want of due consideration heretofore, they misconceiued HOOKER. Hence **Misconcei·ver.**

Misconce·ption. 1665. [MIS-[1] 4.] The action or an act of misconceiving; a notion resulting from misconceiving.

Misco·nduct, *sb.* 1710. [MIS-[1] 4.] 1. Bad management; mismanagement. Often quasi-*spec.*, malfeasance. 2. Improper conduct. Often *spec.* in the sense of 'adultery'. 1729. †b. *pl.* Instances of misconduct –1857.

Misconduc·t, *v.* 1755. [MIS-[1] 1.] 1. *trans.* To mismanage. 2. *refl.* To misbehave oneself 1883.

Misconje·cture, *sb. rare.* 1646. [MIS-[1] 4.] Erroneous conjecture. So **Misconje·cture** *v.* (*rare*) 1626.

Misco·nsecrated, *ppl. a.* 1634. [MIS-[1] 2.] Consecrated to a wrong purpose; improperly consecrated. So **Misconsecra·tion** 1664.

Misconstru·ct, *v.* 1637. [MIS-[1] 1.] †1. Chiefly *Sc.* = MISCONSTRUE –1795. 2. To construct badly. DE QUINCEY.

Misconstru·ction. 1513. [MIS-[1] 4.] 1. The putting of a wrong construction on words or actions. 2. Faulty or bad construction (*rare*) 1819.

Misconstrue (-kǫ·nstru, -kǫnstrū·), *v.* late ME. [MIS-[1] 1.] 1. *trans.* To put a wrong construction on (words or actions); to mistake the meaning of (a person). 2. To infer wrongly. SCOTT.

1. Thou misconstrewest al the good which the bountifull prouidence of God doth vnto thee 1587. Hence **Misconstruable** *a.* **Misconstruer.**

Misconte·nt, *a. arch.* and *dial.* 1489. [MIS-[1] 6, 7.] Not content; dissatisfied; ill-pleased. So †**Misconte·nted** *a.* **Misconte·ntment** (*arch.*).

†**Misconti·nuance.** 1540. [AF.; see MIS-[2].] *Law.* Continuance by unlawful process –1771.

Misco·py, *sb.* 1881. [MIS-[1] 4.] An error in copying. So **Misco·py** *v.* to copy incorrectly 1825.

Miscorre·ct, *v.* 1697. [MIS-[1] 1.] *trans.* To correct wrongly. So **Miscorre·ction** 1685.

Miscou·nsel, *sb.* 1496. [MIS-[1] 4.] Wrong advice. So **Miscou·nsel** *v.* to counsel wrongly 1389.

Miscou·nt, *v.* late ME. [MIS-[1] 1.] 1. *trans.* To misreckon 1548. 2. *intr.* To make a wrong calculation. 3. To regard erroneously (*as*). TENNYSON. So **Miscou·nt** *sb.* a wrong reckoning 1586.

Miscreance (mi·skrĭ,ăns). Now *arch.* late ME. [a. OF. *mescreance* (mod.F. *mécréance*); see MIS-[2] and CREANCE.] False belief or faith; misbelief. So **Mi·screancy** in same sense; also villainy, depravity (cf. MISCREANT 2).

Miscreant (mi·skrĭ,ănt). ME. [a. OF. *mescreant* :—pop.L. **minuscredentem*; see MIS-[2] and CREANT *a.*[1]] A. *adj.* 1. Misbelieving; unbelieving, infidel. Now *arch.* 2. Depraved, villainous, base 1593.

1. Al m. Painyms, al false Jewes, al false heretikes MORE. 2. The..miscreantest rakehells in Italy 1593.

B. *sb.* 1. A misbeliever; an unbeliever, infidel. late ME. 2. A vile wretch; a villain, rascal 1590.

Miscrea·te, *v. rare.* 1603. [MIS-[1] 1.] *trans.* To create amiss. So **Mi·screate, Miscrea·ted** *pa. pples.* and *ppl. adjs.* created or formed unnaturally or improperly; mis-shapen (also as an abusive epithet) 1585. **Miscrea·tion** 1852. **Miscrea·tive** *a.* 1819.

Miscre·dit, *v.* 1554. [MIS-[1] 7.] To disbelieve.

Miscree·d. *poet.* 1821. [MIS-[1] 4.] A mistaken creed.

Mis-cue·, *sb.* 1873 (**miss cue**). [f. MIS-[1] 4 (or stem of MISS *v.*) + CUE *sb.*[3]] *Billiards.* A failure to strike the ball properly with the cue. So **Mis-cue·** *v.* to make a m.

Misda·te, *v.* 1586. [MIS-[1] 1.] *trans.* To affix a wrong date to; to date wrong. So **Misda·te** *sb.* a wrong date 1858.

Misdea·l, *v.* 1481. [f. MIS-[1] 1 + DEAL *v.*] †1. *intr.* To distribute unfairly. CAXTON. 2. To act improperly 1561. 3. *Cards.* To make a mistake in dealing; usu. *intr.*, but occas. *trans.* 1850. So **Misdea·l** *sb.* (*Cards*) an error in dealing 1850. **Misdea·ling** *vbl. sb.*

Misdeed (misdī·d). [OE. *misdǣd*; see MIS-[1] 4 and DEED *sb.*] An evil deed; a wrong action; a crime. †In ME. *collect.* = misdoings.

He was woundid for oure mysdede CHAUCER.

Misdee·m, *v.* Now chiefly *arch.* and *poet.* ME. [MIS-[1] 1.] †1. *trans.* To judge unfavourably, think evil of –1767. †2. *intr.* To think ill (*of*) –1671. 3. To be mistaken in one's view of. late ME. b. *trans.* To suppose (a person or thing) erroneously to be (something else); to mistake *for* 1667. 4. To form a wrong judgement (*of*); to hold a mistaken opinion ME. b. To suppose mistakenly 1596. †5. *trans.* To have a suspicion or inkling of –1607. †6. *intr.* To suspect something evil (or that ...) –1600.

2. What but thy malice mov'd thee to m. A righteous Job? MILT.

Misdeli·ver, *v.* 1858. [MIS-[1] 1.] To deliver wrongly; to hand down improperly. So **Misdeli·very,** wrong delivery.

Misdemea·n, *v.* 1494. [f. MIS-[1] 1 + DEMEAN *v.*[1]] 1. *refl.* To misconduct oneself. †2. *trans.* To misuse. SIR H. FINCH.

Misdemeanant (misdǐmī·nănt). 1819. [f. prec. + -ANT.] A person convicted of a misdemeanour. b. *transf.* A person guilty of misconduct 1886.

Misdemea·nour, -or. 1487. [MIS-[1] 4.] 1. Evil behaviour, misconduct. Now *rare.* 1494. b. An instance of this; a misdeed, offence 1494. 2. *Law.* One of a class of indictable offences deemed less heinous than felonies 1487. †3. A misdemeanant –1812.

2. This general definition comprehends both crimes and misdemesnors; which, properly speaking, are mere synonymous terms BLACKSTONE. Phr. *High m.*: a crime of a heinous nature, next to high treason.

†**Misdepa·rt,** *v.* [MIS-[1] 1.] *trans.* To distribute unfairly. CHAUCER.

Misderi·ve, *v.* 1649. [MIS-[1] 1.] †1. *trans.* To divert into a wrong channel. BP. HALL. 2. To assign a wrong derivation to 1817.

Misdescri·be, *v.* 1827. [MIS-[1] 1.] *trans.* To describe inaccurately. **Misdescri·ption.**

Misdese·rt. *Obs.* or *arch.* 1596. [MIS-[1] 4.] Ill-desert.

Misdevo·tion. 1612. [MIS-[1] 4.] Wrong or misdirected devotion.

†**Misdi·ght,** *pa. pple.* late ME. [MIS-[1] 2.] Ill-clothed; badly furnished or prepared; ill-treated –1607.

Misdire·ct, *v.* 1603. [MIS-[1] 1.] *trans.* To give a wrong direction to (a jury, a blow, etc.).

In the hurry of a trial the ablest judge may mistake the law, and misdirect the jury BLACKSTONE.

Misdire·ction. 1768. [MIS-[1] 4.] 1. The action of misdirecting or the condition of being misdirected; direction to a wrong address. 2. A wrong direction or course 1861.

Misdo (misdū·), *v.* [OE. *misdōn*; see MIS-[1] 1 and DO *v.*] 1. *intr.* To do evil or wrong. Now *rare* or *Obs.* 2. *trans.* To do amiss OE. †3. To harm, injure, wrong –1597. †4. To put out of existence. Also *refl.* –1619.

1. I have misdone; and I endure the Smart DRYDEN. 2. All is forgyuen that was mysse done 1440. Hence **Misdo·er,** a wrong-doer, evil-doer.

Misdo·ing, *vbl. sb.* ME. [MIS-[1] 3.] Wrong-doing, evil-doing; also *Law*, improper performance of an act. b. A misdeed. Chiefly in *pl.* 1543.

Forgyve thou all my mysdoynge COVERDALE.

Misdou·bt, *sb.* Now *arch.* and *dial.* 1592. [MIS-[1] 4.] Apprehension of evil; hence *gen.* mistrust, suspicion.

Change m. to resolution SHAKS.

Misdou·bt, *v.* Now chiefly *dial.* or *arch.* 1540. [f. MIS-[1] 1 + DOUBT *v.*] 1. *trans.* To have doubts as to the existence, truth, or reality of. b. with clause: To doubt (*but*) *that* ...; to have doubts as to *how* ... 1640. 2. To have doubts about the character, honesty, etc. of (a person) 1585. 3. To have misgivings in regard to, be suspicious about 1563. 4. To fear or suspect the existence or occurrence of (something evil) 1540. 5. To fear or suspect (that something is or will be the case) 1596. b. *refl.* and *intr.* To suspect; to have suspicions *of.* *Obs.* or *arch.* 1637.

1. I will never m. the piety of this nation LAUD. 2. I doe not m. my wife SHAKS. 3. The Bird that hath bin limed in a bush, With trembling wings misdoubteth euery bush SHAKS. 5. I m. the ladies won't like it 1885.

†**Misdou·btful,** *a.* 1575. [MIS-[1] 6.] Suspicious –1596.

†**Misdrea·d,** *sb.* [MIS-[1] 4.] Dread of evil. SHAKS.

Mise (mīz, məiz), *sb.* 1450. [a. AF., OF. *mise* action of placing or setting, expenses, etc., fem. abstract noun f. *mettre* (pa. pple. *mis*) to place.] †1. *pl.* Expenses or costs –1492. 2. A grant, payment, or tribute made to secure a liberty or immunity, as (*a*) by the people of Wales to a new Lord Marcher, king, or prince, (*b*) by the inhabitants of the County Palatine of Chester on a change of earl 1500. 3. A settlement by agreement; as the *M. of Amiens* and *M. of Lewes*, between Henry III and his barons 1700. 4. *Law.* The issue in a writ of right 1544. Hence **Mise** *v. trans.* to rate for the m. 1673.

Misease (misī·z), *sb. arch.* ME. [a. OF. *mesaise*, f. *mes-* MIS-[2] + *aise* EASE.] 1. Distress; misery; extreme suffering or discomfort. †2. Lack of the means of living; poverty, destitution –1490. Hence †**Misea·se(d)** *a.* in want; troubled, distressed –1553.

Mise·ducate, *v.* 1827. [MIS-[1] 1.] *trans.* To educate wrongly. So **Miseduca·tion** 1624.

‖**Mise-en-scène** (mīzansēn). [Fr.: see MISE, SCENE.] Staging of a play; also *fig.*

Misemploy·, *v.* 1609. [MIS-[1] 1.] *trans.* To employ amiss. So **Misemploy·ment** 1597.

†**Mise·nter**, *v.* 1551. [MIS-[1] 1.] *trans.* To enter erroneously. So **Mise·ntry** 1602.

†**Misentrea·t, -intrea·t**, *v.* 1450. [MIS-[1] 1.] *trans.* To treat badly; to ill-use –1583.

Miser (məi·zəɪ), *a.* and *sb.* 1542. [a. L.] A. *adj.* †1. Wretched –1612. 2. [attrib. use of B. 2.] Miserly; avaricious. *arch.* or *dial.* 1598.

2. The m.-spirit eyes the spendthrift heir SAVAGE.

B. *sb.* 1. A miserable or wretched person; a wretch. *Obs.* (*arch.* in Scott.) 1542. 2. One who lives miserably in order to hoard wealth. Also, an avaricious person, a niggard. 1560.

2. As some lone m., visiting his store, Bends at his treasure, counts, recounts it o'er GOLDSM.

Miserable (mi·zĕrăb'l), *a.* and *sb.* 1484. [a. F. *misérable*, ad. L. *miserabilis*, f. *miserari*, f. *miser* wretched.] A. *adj.* 1. Of persons: Wretchedly unhappy. Now often in somewhat trivial sense: Wretchedly uncomfortable. 1526. 2. Needy; wretchedly poor. *Obs.* exc. as merged in 1. 1585. 3. Of events, etc.: Fraught with misery; causing wretchedness 1500. 4. Of things: Pitiable; despicable; paltry, sorry, poor 1500. 5. Miserly, mean, stingy. Now *dial.* 1484. †6. Compassionate –1630.

1. O m. Mankind, to what fall Degraded! MILT. 3. I haue past a m. night, So full of fearefull Dreames SHAKS. 4. M. geuers of comforte are ye COVERDALE *Job* xvi. 2. M. tea 1900.

B. *sb.* A miserable person; one who is in extreme unhappiness or great want 1534. Hence **Mi·serableness.** So **Mi·serably** *adv.* late ME.

†**Misera·tion.** late ME. [ad. L. *miserationem*, f. *miserari.*] Pity, compassion, mercy –1638.

‖ **Misère** (mizē·ɪ, Fr. mizēr). 1830. [Fr. = MISERY.] *Cards.* A declaration by which the caller undertakes not to take a trick.

‖ **Miserere** (mizĕrī·ri). ME. [imper. sing. of L. *misereri* to have mercy.] 1. The fifty-first Psalm (fiftieth in the Vulgate), beginning *Miserere mei Deus* ('Have mercy upon me, O God'), being one of the Penitential Psalms. b. A musical setting of this 1776. 2. *transf.* A cry for mercy 1616. †3. In full *M. mei* (mī·əi): a name for the 'iliac passion' (see ILEUS 1) –1783. ¶4. = MISERICORD 2 c. 1798.

1. b. The 'Miserere' of Allegri 1845.

Misericord (mize·rikǭɪd). ME. [a. OF., ad. L. *misericordia*, f. *misericors*, f. *miseri-*, stem of *misereri* + *cord-*, *cor* heart.] †1. Compassion, pity. Also as *int.* –1705. 2. *Hist.* and *Antiq.* a. An indulgence or relaxation of a monastic rule 1802. b. An apartment in a monastery in which such indulgences, esp. as to food and drink, were permitted 1529. c. A shelving projection on the under side of a hinged seat in a choir stall, which, when turned up, gave support to one standing in the stall 1515. 3. A dagger with which the *coup de grâce* was given. late ME. Hence †**Miserico·rdious** *a.* compassionate, merciful.

Miserly (məi·zəɪli), *a.* 1593. [f. MISER *sb.* + -LY[1].] Niggardly, stingy. **Mi·serliness.**

Misery (mi·zĕri). late ME. [a. OF. *miserie*, ad. L. *miseria*, f. *miser.*] 1. Wretchedness of outward circumstances; distress caused by privation or poverty. Also with †*a* and *pl.* 2. Miserable or wretched state of mind; a condition of extreme unhappiness 1535. †3. Miserliness –1624. 4. = MISÈRE (*colloq.*).

1. The m. of unaided poverty RUSKIN. *personified*, He gave to Mis'ry all he had, a tear GOLDSM. The miseries of fallen greatness MACAULAY. 2. Thou art so full of m., Were it not better not to be? TENNYSON.

Misestee·m, *v.* 1611. [MIS-[1] 1.] *trans.* = MISESTIMATE *v.* So **Misestee·m** *sb.* want of esteem or respect 1850.

Mise·stimate, *v.* 1841. [MIS-[1] 1.] *trans.* To estimate erroneously. So **Mise·stimate** *sb.* 1852. **Misestima·tion** 1809.

Mise·xecute, *v.* 1647. [MIS-[1] 1.] *trans.* To carry out improperly. **Misexecu·tion** 1535.

Misexplai·n, *v.* 1674. [MIS-[1] 1.] *trans.* To explain incorrectly.

Misexposi·tion. 1524. [MIS-[1] 4.] Incorrect exposition.

Misexpre·ss, *v.* 1718. [MIS-[1] 1.] *refl.* To express oneself faultily. So **Misexpre·ssion** 1651. **Misexpre·ssive** *a.* expressing a wrong meaning 1816.

Misfai·th. late ME. [MIS-[1] 4.] Disbelief; mistrust.

Some sudden turn of anger born Of your m. TENNYSON.

†**Misfa·ll**, *v.* ME. [MIS-[1] 1.] 1. *intr.* To come to grief. ME. only. 2. *impers.* or said of the event: To fall out amiss. *It misfell me*: misfortune befell me. –1615.

†**Misfa·re**, *v.* [OE. *misfaran*; see MIS-[1] 1 and FARE *v.*[1]] 1. *intr.* To fare ill, come to grief –1633. 2. To go wrong; to transgress –1487. So †**Misfa·re** *sb.* going wrong; misfortune –1596.

†**Misfa·shion**, *v.* 1570. [MIS-[1] 1.] *trans.* To put out of shape; to make of a wrong shape –1647. So **Misfa·shioned** *ppl. a.* badly formed, mis-shapen 1500. **Misfa·shioning** *vbl. sb.* disfigurement, deformity 1469.

Misfeasance (misfī·zăns). 1596. [a. OF. *mesfaisance*, f. *mesfaisant*, pres. pple. of *mesfaire*, *méfaire* to misdo; see MIS-[2] and FEASANCE.] *Law.* A transgression, trespass; *spec.* the improper performance of a lawful act. So **Misfea·sor**, one who commits a m. 1631.

Misfea·ture. 1821. [MIS-[1] 4.] A distorted feature; a bad feature or trait.

†**Misfei·gn**, *v.* [MIS-[1] 1.] *intr.* To feign with a wrong intention. SPENSER.

Misfire (misfəi·ɪ), *v.* 1752. [MIS-[1] 1.] *intr.* Of a gun or its charge: To fail to be discharged. b. Said of an internal-combustion engine when its charge fails to ignite or ignites at the wrong time 1905. Hence **Misfi·re** *sb.* a failure to discharge 1839.

Misfit (misfi·t), *sb.* 1823. [f. MIS-[1] 4 + FIT *sb.*[3]] A garment, etc., which does not fit the person it is made for.

[The] shoemaker.. would occasionally have a m. or two on his hands KNIGHT. *transf.* Her mouth.. was an obvious m. for the set of teeth it contained 1862.

Misfi·t, *v.* 1885. [f. MIS-[1] 1 + FIT *v.*[1] or f. prec.] *trans.* and *intr.* To fit badly.

†**Misforgi·ve**, *v.* [MIS-[1] 1.] *trans.* = MISGIVE 1. Chaucer.

Misfo·rm, *v.* late ME. [MIS-[1] 1.] *trans.* To form amiss; to mis-shape. So **Misforma·tion**, malformation 1822.

Misfo·rtunate, *a.* Now chiefly *Sc.* and *U.S.* 1530. [MIS-[1] 6.] Unfortunate.

Misfortune (misfǭ·ɪtʃən), *sb.* 1502. [f. MIS-[1] 4 + FORTUNE *sb.*] 1. Bad fortune; ill-luck; also, an instance of this. 2. *dial.* and *colloq.* The bearing of an illegitimate child; hence, an illegitimate child 1801.

1. They come in no m. like other folke COVERDALE *Ps.* lxxii. 5. Misfortunes seldome come alone 1622. 2. Phr. *To have* or *meet with a m.* Hence **Misfo·rtuned** *a.* unfortunate 1578.

†**Misfo·rtune**, *v.* 1466. [MIS-[1] 1.] a. *impers.*, etc.: To happen unfortunately. b. *intr.* To happen by mischance *to do* something. c. To come to grief. –1615.

Misgive (misgi·v), *v.* 1513. [MIS-[1] 1, 7.] 1. *trans.* Of one's heart, mind, etc.: To cause (one) to be apprehensive (*that*); to incline to suspicion or foreboding. (The personal obj. was orig. a dat.) b. *absol.* or *intr.* To have misgivings 1604. 2. *intr.* To fail; to go wrong. Of a gun: To miss fire. Chiefly *Sc.* 1579. 3. *trans.* To bestow amiss; to cite wrongly 1611.

1. So doth my heart mis-giue me, in these Conflicts, What may befall him SHAKS. b. *Oth.* III. iv. 89.

Misgi·ving, *vbl. sb.* 1601. [f. prec. + -ING[1].] The action of MISGIVE *v.*; a feeling of mistrust, apprehension, or loss of confidence.

And my misgiuing still Falles shrewdly to the purpose SHAKS.

Misgo (misgōu·), *v.* Now *dial.* Pa. t. -went, pa. pple. -gone. ME. [MIS-[1] 1.] *intr.* To go wrong or astray; to err; to miscarry.

Misgo·tten, *pa. pple.* and *ppl. a.* late ME. [MIS-[1] 2.] 1. Wrongly acquired; ill-gotten. 2. = MISBEGOTTEN. late ME.

Misgo·vern, *v.* 1440. [MIS-[1] 1.] †1. *trans.* To mismanage, misdirect, misconduct –1621. 2. *trans.* To mismanage the government of (a state, etc.) 1587.

Misgo·vernance. *Obs.* exc. *arch.* late ME. [MIS-[1] 4.] †1. Misconduct, misbehaviour –1627. †2. Mismanagement, misuse –1678. 3. Bad government of a country or state 1447.

Misgo·verned, *ppl. a.* late ME. [MIS-[1] 2.] †1. Ill-conducted; immoral –1611. †2. Unruly; misdirected –1639. 3. Mismanaged 1834.

2. Rude mis-gouern'd hands SHAKS.

Misgo·vernment. late ME. [MIS-[1] 4.] †1. Unruly behaviour; misconduct –1665. †2. Mismanagement –1777. 3. Bad government of a country or state; maladministration. Hence, disorder, anarchy (cf. *misrule*) 1592.

†**Misgra·ffed**, *pa. pple.* [MIS-[1] 2.] Grafted amiss; *fig.* badly matched *Mids. N.* I. i. 137.

Misgra·fted, *ppl. a.* [MIS-[1] 2.] Grafted wrongly or unsuitably WARBURTON.

Misgrou·nded, *ppl. a.* 1598. [MIS-[1] 2.] Falsely grounded; ill-founded.

Misgrow·th. 1647. [MIS-[1] 4.] A distorted or abortive growth.

Misgui·dance. 1640. [MIS-[1] 4.] Misdirection. So †**Misgui·de** *sb.* 1596.

Misgui·de, *v.* late ME. [MIS-[1] 1.] †1. *refl.* To go astray; to conduct oneself or manage one's affairs badly –1651. 2. *trans.* To mismanage, misgovern. Hence (mod. *Sc.*) to treat badly; to injure, spoil 1494. 3. To misdirect 1509.

3. To.. m. the mind POPE. *absol.* The nobles.. have nearly ceased either to guide or m. CARLYLE. Hence **Misgui·dingly** *adv.* in a way to mislead.

Misgui·ded, *ppl. a.* 1490. [MIS-[1] 2.] †1. Ill-conducted, immoral –1523. 2. Misdirected in action or thought; hence, having a wrong purpose or intention 1659.

2. The m. and abus'd multitude MILT.

†**Misgye·**, *v.* late ME. [f. MIS-[1] 1 + *gye*, GUY *v.*[1]] *trans.* To misguide; *refl.* to misbehave –1500.

Mishandle (mishæ·nd'l), *v.* 1530. [MIS-[1] 1.] *trans.* To handle badly or improperly; to maltreat, ill-treat.

Mishap (mishæ·p), *sb.* ME. [f. MIS-[1] 4 + HAP *sb.*[1]] 1. Evil hap; bad luck. Now *rare.* 2. An unlucky accident ME.

2. Secure from worldly chaunces and mishaps SHAKS.

†**Misha·p**, *v.* ME. [MIS-[1] 1.] 1. *intr.* Of a person: To meet with mishap. Also, to have the misfortune *to do* something. –1533. 2. To happen unfortunately –1647. So †**Misha·ppen** *v.* in same senses ME.–1611.

Mishear (mishī·ɪ), *v.* ME. [MIS-[1] 1.] To hear incorrectly or imperfectly.

Mish-mash (mi·ʃmæʃ). 1450. [Redupl. of MASH *sb.*[1]] A medley, hodge-podge, jumble.

‖ **Mishnah, mishna** (mi·ʃnă). Also †**mischna.** 1610. [post-Biblical Heb. *mishnāh* (1) repetition, (2) instruction.] The collection of binding precepts or *halakhoth* (see HALACHAH) which forms the basis of the Talmud and embodies the contents of the oral law. Also, a paragraph of the mishnah. Hence **Mi·shnic, -al** *a.* pertaining to or characteristic of the m.

Misima·gine, *v.* 1625. [Mis-1 1.] *trans.* To imagine wrongly. **Misimagina·tion** 1618.

Misimpre·ssion. 1670. [Mis-1 4.] A wrong impression.

Misimpro·ve, *v.* Now *rare.* 1658. [Mis-1 7.] **1.** *trans.* To employ wrongly; to abuse, use ill. *Obs.* or *U.S.* **2.** To improve injudiciously 1847. So †**Misimpro·vement,** failure to employ properly, misuse 1644.

Misincli·ne, *v.* [Mis-1 1.] To incline in a wrong direction. BP. HALL. So **Misinclina·tion. Misincli·ned** *ppl. a.* wrongly inclined; disinclined 1716.

Misinfo·rm, *v.* late ME. [Mis-1 1.] *trans.* To inform amiss; to give misleading information (to). So **Misinfo·rmant, -fo·rmer. Misinforma·tion,** the action of misinforming; incorrect information 1587.

Misinstru·ct, *v.* 1547. [Mis-1 1.] *trans.* To instruct amiss. So **Misinstru·ction** 1642.

Misinte·lligence. 1639. [Mis-1 4.] **1.** Misunderstanding; disagreement. Now *rare* or *Obs.* **2.** Wrong impression as to facts 1779. **3.** Lack of intelligence (*rare*) 1848.

Misinte·rpret, *v.* 1589. [Mis-1 1.] *trans.* To give a wrong interpretation to. So **Mis·interpreta·tion** 1576.

Misjoi·n, *v.* 1540. [Mis-1 1.] *trans.* To join wrongly, inappropriately, or unsuitably; *spec.* in *Law* (cf. next).

Misjoi·nder. 1852. [Mis-1 4.] *Law.* Improper joinder of parties in an action or of causes of action in a suit.

Misju·dge, *v.* 1526. [Mis-1 1.] *trans.* To judge wrongly; to have false opinions of. So **Misju·dg(e)ment** 1526.

‖**Miskal** (mi·skăl). 1555. [Arab. *miṯqāl,* f. *ṯaqala* to weigh.] **1.** An Arabian measure of weight, equivalent to 24 carats or about 1½ dirhems. **2.** In Morocco, a money of account 1695.

†**Miskee·p,** *v.* ME. [Mis-1 1.] *trans.* To keep, guard, or observe badly –1649.

Misken (miske·n), *v.* *Sc.* and *n. dial.* ME. [f. Mis-1 1, 7 + Ken *v.*] = Misknow.

Were I you, Ranald, I would be for miskenning Sir Duncan SCOTT.

Mi·skin, dial. var. Mixen.

Misknow·, *v.* late ME. [Mis-1 1, 7.] †**1.** *trans.* Not to know; to be ignorant of –1632. **2.** To know badly; to misapprehend, misunderstand 1535. **3.** To fail to recognize, mistake the identity of (a person). late ME. **4.** To refuse to recognize 1483. So **Misknow·ledge,** †failure to recognize; also, spurious knowledge 1533.

Mislay (mislē·), *v.* late ME. [Mis-1 1.] **1.** *trans.* To place wrongly; to misplace; to err in placing (a thing). Now *rare.* **2.** To lay (a thing) by accident where it cannot readily be found 1614. †**3.** To allege incorrectly BACON.

1. The Fault is generally mislaid upon Nature LOCKE. **2.** I cannot conceive what possesses me..to m. papers SCOTT.

Mislead (mislī·d), *v.* *Pa. t.* and *pple.* misled. [OE. *mislǣdan*; see Mis-1 1 and Lead *v.*1] **1.** *trans.* To lead astray in conduct; to lead into error. †**b.** *refl.* To misconduct oneself. ME. only. †**2.** To mismanage –1494. **3.** To lead in the wrong direction 1575.

1. By ambition far misled SCOTT. *absol.* What can they teach, and not m.? MILT. **3.** Are you not hee, That..misleade night-wanderers? SHAKS.

Mislea·rn, *v.* 1678. [Mis-1 1.] *trans.* To learn badly.

Mislen, var. of Maslin 2.

Misli·ke, *sb.* ME. [f. Mislike *v.*] †**1.** The opposite of pleasure; discomfort; unhappiness. ME. only. **2.** Dislike (*of*), distaste (*for*), objection (*to*). Now *rare.* Also with *a* and *pl.* 1557. †**3.** Disaffection, disagreement –1654. †**4.** Wasting in animals or plants; sickliness, disease –1622.

2. Julian's m. of the rising faith TRENCH.

Misli·ke, *v.* Now chiefly *literary* or *dial.* [OE. *mislīcian*; see Mis-1 1 and Like *v.*1] **1.** *trans.* To displease. †**2.** *intr.* To be displeased; in ME. also, to be uneasy –1642. **3.** *trans.* To be displeased at; to dislike 1513. †**4.** *intr.* To grow sickly; to waste away –1606.

1. *absol.* That pleaseth well, and This as much mislikes DRAYTON. **3.** 'Tis not my speeches that you do m.: But 'tis my presence that doth trouble ye SHAKS. Hence **Misli·king** *vbl. sb.* = Mislike *sb.*

Mislin, var. of Maslin 2, Mistletoe.

†**Misli·ve,** *v.* OE. [Mis-1 1.] *intr.* To live a bad life –1579. Hence **Misli·ver** (*rare* or *Obs.*), an evil liver 1436.

Mislo·dge, *v.* 1676. [Mis-1 1.] *trans.* To lodge in a wrong place; †to mislay.

Mislu·ck, *sb.* Chiefly *Sc.* 1623. [Mis-1 4.] Misfortune. **Mislu·ck** *v.* to meet with misfortune.

Misly, obs. f. Mizzly.

Misma·ke, *v.* Now *Sc.* late ME. [Mis-1 1.] **a.** *trans.* To make badly. †**b.** To unmake, depose. **c.** *refl.* To disturb oneself.

Misma·nage, *v.* 1690. [Mis-1 1.] *trans.* and *intr.* To manage badly or wrongly. So **Misma·nagement** 1668. **Misma·nager** 1683.

Misma·rk, *v.* 1535. [Mis-1 1.] *trans.* To mark wrongly. Also in pa. pple., having wrong markings.

Misma·rry, *v.* 1892. [Mis-1 1.] *trans.* To marry unsuitably (*lit.* and *fig.*). So **Misma·rriage** 1817.

Misma·tch, *v.* 1599. [Mis-1 1.] *trans.* To match badly, esp. in marriage; *pass.* to be ill-mated. So **Misma·tch** *sb.* a bad match 1606.

Misma;ted, *pa. pple.* and *ppl. a.* 1825. [Mis-1 2.] Ill-matched, unsuitably allied.

Mismea·sure, *v.* 1742. [Mis-1 1.] *trans.* To measure or estimate incorrectly. So **Mismea·surement.**

Misme·tre, *v.* late ME. [Mis-1 1.] *trans.* To spoil the metre of.

Misna·me, *v.* 1500. [Mis-1 1.] **1.** = Miscall 1. 1537. †**2.** = Miscall 2. –1632.

Misnomer (misnōu·mər), *sb.* 1455. [a. AF., OF. *mesnom(m)er* inf. used subst., f. *mes-* Mis-2 + *nommer*:—L. *nominare* to name.] **1.** *Law.* A mistake in naming a person or place. **2.** *gen.* The use of a wrong name or term 1635. **3.** A wrong name or designation 1657.

2. The City which, by a m., is called the Metropolis 1882. **3.** My name of Epic's no m. BYRON. Hence **Misno·mer** *v. trans.* to misname 1740.

Misnu·mber, *v.* 1614. [Mis-1 1.] *trans.* To number incorrectly.

Miso- (məiso, miso), bef. a vowel usu. **mis-,** repr. Gr. μισο- (μισ-), comb. f. root of μισεῖν to hate, μῖσος hatred. Cf. Philo-.

Miso·gamy [Gr. γάμος marriage], hatred of marriage 1656; so **Misoga·mic** *a.,* **Miso·gamist. Miso·gynist** [Gr. γυνή woman], a woman-hater 1620; so **Mi·sogyne** = m.; **Misogy·nic, -ous, -istic, -istical** *adjs.*; **Miso·gynism, Miso·gyny. Miso·logy** [-logy], hatred of discussion or knowledge 1833; so **Miso·logist, Mi·sologue. Misone·ism** [Gr. νέος new], hatred of novelty 1886; hence **Misone·ist**; **Misonei·stic** *a.* **Misothe·ism** [Gr. θεός god], hatred of God or gods 1846; so **Misothe·ist, Misothei·stic** *a.*

Misobse·rvance. *rare.* 1496. [Mis-1 4.] Failure to observe rules or conditions properly. So **Misobse·rve** *v.*

†**Misopi·nion.** 1545. [Mis-1 4.] An erroneous opinion –1680.

Miso·rder, *sb.* Now *rare.* late ME. [Mis-1 4.] = Disorder *sb.*

†**Miso·rder,** *v.* 1494. [Mis-1 1.] **1.** *trans.* To put into disorder; to disturb, confuse –1597. **2.** To ill-treat, ill-use –1575. **3.** *refl.* To misbehave –1740.

1. 2 *Hen. IV*, IV. ii. 33.

Mispay·, *v.* ME. [a. OF. *mespaier*; see Mis-2 and Pay *v.*1] †**1.** *trans.* To displease, dissatisfy –1493. **2.** To pay by mistake 1698.

Misperfo·rm, *v.* 1656. [Mis-1 1.] *trans.* To perform improperly. So **Misperfo·rmance.**

Mispersua·de, *v.* Now *rare* or *Obs.* 1597. [Mis-1 1.] *trans.* To persuade wrongly or into error. So **Mispersua·sion** 1594.

Mispickel (mi·spikĕl). 1683. [a. G.] *Min.* Arsenopyrite.

Mispla·ce, *v.* 1551. [Mis-1 1.] **1.** *trans.* To put in a wrong place or in wrong hands 1594. †**b.** *absol.* To misplace one's words. SHAKS. **2.** To set (one's affections) on a wrong object; to place (one's confidence) amiss; †to spend (time) unprofitably 1638.

1. b. *Meas. for M.* II. i. 90. **2.** Munificence misplaced COWPER. So **Mispla·cement** 1655.

Misplaced (misplē·st), *ppl. a.* 1595. [Mis-1 2.] Put in a wrong place; devoted to a wrong object; out-of-place, ill-timed.

M. acts of foolery LAMB.

Misplea·d, *v.* *rare.* 1676. [Mis-1 1.] *trans.* To plead wrongly or falsely. So **Misplea·ding** *vbl. sb.* a mistake in pleading 1532.

Mispoi·nt, *v.* Now *rare* or *Obs.* 1542. [Mis-1 1.] †**a.** To point with the wrong finger. **b.** To punctuate wrongly; to mispunctuate.

Misprai·se, *v.* Now *rare.* ME. [Mis-1 1, 7.] **1.** *trans.* To dispraise, blame. **2.** To praise amiss 1631.

Mispri·nt, *v.* 1494. [Mis-1 1.] *trans.* To print incorrectly. So **Mi·spri·nt** *sb.* 1818.

Misprisal (misprəi·zăl). *rare.* 1620. [f. Misprize *v.*1 + -al 2.] Contempt, disdain, scorn.

Misprision1 (mispri·ʒən). late ME. [a. AF. *mesprisioun* = OF. *mesprison, -prision*:— pop. L. **minusprœhensionem,* f. **minusprœhendere*; see Mis-2 and Prehension *v.*] **1.** *Law.* A wrong action or omission; *spec.* a misdemeanour or neglect of duty on the part of a public official. **2.** The mistaking one thing, etc., for another; a mistake (*arch.*) 1588.

1. *M. of treason, of felony*: orig., an offence or misdemeanor akin to treason or felony, but not liable to the capital penalty. Later misunderstood as meaning only concealment of a person's knowledge of treasonable actions or designs. Also *transf.* in pop. use. **2.** The m. of this passage has aided in fostering the delusive notion J. C. HARE.

Misprision2 (mispri·ʒən). *arch.* 1586. [f. Misprize *v.*1 after prec.] **a.** Contempt, scorn. **b.** Failure to appreciate or recognize as valuable.

That dost in vile m. shackle vp My loue SHAKS.

Misprize (misprəi·z), *v.*1 1481. [a. OF. *mesprisier, -priser* (mod.F. *mépriser*):—L. **minuspretiare*; see Mis-2 and Prize *v.*] *trans.* **a.** To despise, contemn, scorn. **b.** To fail to appreciate.

a. *Much Ado* III. i. 52. **b.** It sorrows me that you misprise my love HEYWOOD. Hence **Mispri·ze** *sb.*1 = Misprision2 (*rare*) 1590.

†**Mispri·ze,** *v.*2 1485. [f. OF. *mespris,* pa. pple. of *mesprendre* to commit a crime (mod. F. *méprendre*).] **1.** *intr.* To commit an offence –1500. **2.** *trans.* To mistake, misunderstand –1657.

2. Monsieur Gaspar..misprise me not B. JONS. Hence †**Mispri·ze** *sb.*2 mistake SPENSER.

Mispronou·nce, *v.* 1593. [Mis-1 1.] *trans.* To pronounce incorrectly.

They mispronounc't and I mislik't MILT. So **Mispronuncia·tion** 1539.

Mispropo·rtioned, *ppl. a.* 1552. [Mis-1 2.] Badly or wrongly proportioned. So **Mispropo·rtion** *sb.* lack of proportion 1825. **Mispropo·rtion** *v. trans.* 'to join without due proportion' (J.).

Misproud (misprau·d), *a.* *arch.* ME. [Mis-1 6.] Wrongly or wickedly proud; arrogant.

Mispu·nctuate, *v.* 1849. [Mis-1 1.] To punctuate incorrectly. **Mispunctua·tion** 1807.

Misquo·te, *v.* 1596. [Mis-1 1.] *trans.* To quote incorrectly.

Looke how we can, or sad or merrily, Interpretation will m. our lookes SHAKS. So **Misquota·tion,** inaccuracy in quoting; an incorrect quotation 1773.

Misra·te, *v.* Now *rare.* 1624. [Mis-1 1.] *trans.* To estimate wrongly.

Misrea·d, *v.* 1809. [Mis-1 1.] *trans.* To read or interpret wrongly.

Misreci·te, *v.* 1572. [Mis-1 1.] *trans.* To recite incorrectly; to give a wrong account of. So **Misreci·tal** 1539.

Misre·ckon, *v.* 1524. [Mis-1 1.] **1.** To reckon incorrectly; to miscalculate, miscount. †**2.** *trans.* To present an incorrect account to –1654. So **Misre·ckoning** *vbl. sb.* 1540.

Misrela·te, *v.* 1621. [Mis-1 1.] *trans.* To relate or recount incorrectly. So **Misrela·tion**; also **Misrela·ted** *ppl. a.* wrongly related or connected.

Misreli·gion. *rare.* 1623. [MIS-¹ 4.] False religion.

Misreme·mber, *v.* 1533. [MIS-¹ 1.] *trans.* To remember wrongly; to have an imperfect recollection of. Now chiefly *dial.* to forget. So **Misreme·mbrance** (*rare*) 1542.

Misre·nder, *v.* 1661. [MIS-¹ 1.] *trans.* To render or interpret incorrectly.

Misrepo·rt, *sb.* ME. [MIS-¹ 4.] †1. Evil report; ill repute -1697. 2. False or erroneous report, as of the actions, etc., of a person 1530.

Misrepo·rt, *v.* late ME. [MIS-¹ 1.] 1. *trans.* To report erroneously; to give a false account of the statements or opinions of. †2. To speak ill of; to slander -1625.

Mi·srepresе·nt, *v.* 1647. [MIS-¹ 1.] *trans.* To represent improperly or imperfectly; to give a false account of. So **Mi·srepresenta·tion** 1647. **Mi·srepresе·ntative** *a.* not properly representative (*of*) 1736.

Misru·le, *sb.* late ME. [MIS-¹ 4.] †1. Disorderly conduct; ill-regulated life; excess -1613. 2. Bad government (of a state, etc.); misgovernment; a state of disorder, anarchy, or rebellion. late ME.

Lord (also *Abbot, Master*) *of M.*: one chosen to preside over the Christmas games and revels in a great man's house (*Hist.*); also *transf.* and *fig.*

Misru·le, *v.* ME. [MIS-¹ 1.] †1. *trans.* To manage or control badly -1530. 2. To rule (a country, etc.) badly. late ME.

†Misru·ly, *a.* late ME. [MIS-¹ 6.] Disorderly; unruly -1598.

Miss (mis), *sb.*¹ ME. [Mainly f. MISS *v.*; but perh. in early uses = OE. *miss or ON. *missir, missa.*] I. Loss, lack. (Cf. MISS *v.* IV.) 1. The fact or condition of missing or being without; loss, lack, privation. Const. *of* or *genitive.* 1470. †b. Observable lack -1722. 2. Disadvantage or regret occasioned by loss, absence, or privation *of* a person or thing ME.

1. At Carthage, the misse of so great a person was diuersly construed RALEIGH. 2. Phr. *To feel the m. of; there is no (great) m. of.* Now *dial.* or *vulgar.*

II. Wrong, mistake. (Cf. MISS *v.* V.) †1. Wrong; offence, injury; a wrong, misdeed -1616. †2. Error, mistake. ASCHAM.

2. Without any great misse in the hardest pointes of Grammer 1568.

III. Failure to hit or attain. (Cf. MISS *v.* I.) 1. Failure to hit something aimed at 1555. 2. Failure to obtain or achieve something. Now *rare.* 1609. 3. *Printing.* The omitting to lay on a sheet in feeding a printing-machine 1888.

1. Provb.: *A m. is as good as a mile*: failure by however little is still failure. *To give a m.* (Billiards): to avoid hitting the object ball, esp. in playing for safety. The opponent is said *to score a m.*

Miss (mis), *sb.*² 1666. [Abbrev. of MISTRESS.] 1. A kept mistress. Less commonly, a whore. *Obs.* exc. *dial.* 1675. 2. As a title of an unmarried woman or girl 1666. 3. With ellipsis of the proper name. Not now in educated use. 1667. 4. A young unmarried woman; a girl, *esp.* a schoolgirl; in mod. use, often connoting squeamishness or sentimentality. (In literary English use now only playful or contemptuous.) 1667.

2. *The Misses Smith, the Miss Smiths*: alternative forms of the pl., of which the former is grammatically the more proper. *Miss Smith*: normally the eldest (unmarried) daughter of the family. 3. Is it m. or the cash of mamma you pursue? BYRON. 'I beg your pardon, Miss', said she [a maidservant] 1850. 4. Under the tyranny of some small m. of two or three 1885. Hence **Mi·ssish** *a.* like a m.; hence, affected, prim, squeamish, or sentimental. **Mi·ssishness.**

Miss (mis), *sb.*³ 1767. [? a use of prec., or of MISS *sb.*¹] *Cards.* An extra hand for which any of the players may discard his own.

Miss (mis), *v.* [OE. *missan*:—OTeut. **missjan*, f. ppl. stem **misso-*; see MIS-¹.] I. *trans.* To fail to hit, meet, or light upon. 1. To fail to hit (something aimed at). b. Occas., of a missile, a blow, etc.: To pass by without touching 1749. 2. Not to hit upon (the right path) 1547. 3. To fail to obtain footing on (a step, plank, etc.) 1550. 4. To fail to meet (a person). Also occas. *intr.* for *reciprocal.* 1589.

1. Mark like this Was Bertram never known to m. SCOTT. †*To m. the cushion*: to miss the mark; to make a mistake, err. *To m. one's aim, one's* (or *the*) *mark* (fig.): see MARK *sb.*¹ II. 3 d. absol. *Hit or m.*: see HIT *v.* 2. *To m. one's way.* 3. Blind with rage she miss'd the plank, and rolled In the river TENNYSON. 4. I wonder how I missed you NASHE. Then we missed: now we meet MEREDITH.

Phrases. **To m. fire.** Of firearms: To fail to go off. Hence *fig.* to be unsuccessful. **To m. stays** (*Naut.*): To fail in an attempt to go about from one tack to another. Also *fig.*

II. *trans.* To fail to attain. 1. To fail to get; to come short of, go without ME. b. Not to have the satisfaction of hearing, seeing, or witnessing (something) 1841. 2. To fail to do, achieve, or accomplish (something). late ME. 3. To escape, avoid. Now only *dial.*, exc. with adv. 1526. 4. To let slip (an opportunity, etc.) 1628; to fail to catch (a train, etc.) 1823. 5. To fail to see; to fail to 'catch' or understand 1588.

1. Since the time I missed the solicitor's place BACON. b. I would not have missed the speech..for a great deal JOWETT. 2. To m. a stroke at billiards 1888. 5. I sat so high and far off that I missed most of the words PEPYS.

III. *trans.* To omit. 1. To omit, leave out. Also with *out.* 1530. 2. To omit the performance of; to fail to keep (an appointment); to omit to be present at 1598.

1. To m. one of the responses SCOTT. 2. I never missed chapel RUSKIN.

IV. *trans.* To be without; lack; want. †1. To be without, lack; to cease to have, lose. Also with *away.* -1677. †b. Contextually, to do without -1637. 2. To discover the absence of ME. 3. To feel the want of 1470.

1. b. We cannot misse him; he do's make our fire [etc.] SHAKS. 2. One morn I missed him on the custom'd hill GRAY. 3. Milton was too busy to much m. his wife JOHNSON.

V. *intr.* †1. To go wrong, make a mistake, err -1754. †2. To be lacking -1828. †3. To come to an end, give out, fail -1529. 4. To be unsuccessful. Now *arch.* or *Obs.* 1592. 5. Of crops, etc.: To be abortive (*dial.*) 1615.

1. Starres are poore books, and oftentimes do misse G. HERBERT. 2. 1 *Sam.* xxv. 7. 3. Til the day gan misse CHAUCER.

Miss of —. Chiefly *Obs.* or *arch.* = senses I. 1, 4, 5; II. 1-4; IV. 1. **M. on —.** To fail to hit upon. LAMB.

Miss, obs. f. MASS *sb.*¹

Missal (mi·săl), *sb.*¹ ME. [ad. eccl.L. *missale*, neut. sing. of *missalis* (see next).] The book containing the service of the Mass for the whole year; a mass-book. ¶b. Vaguely: A Roman Catholic book of prayers, esp. when illuminated 1651.

attrib., etc., as **m. caps** (*Printing*), a style of fancy letter, used sometimes as initials to Old English or Black letter.

Missal (mi·săl), *a.* (*sb.*²) 1466. [ad. eccl. L. *missalis*, f. *missa* MASS *sb.*¹] Of or pertaining to the Mass; mass-.

Mis-say (mis,sē¹·), *v. arch.* Pa. t. and pple. **mis-said** (mis,se·d). [MIS-¹ 1.] 1. *trans.* To speak evil of or against; to slander, vilify. Now *arch.* and *poet.* †b. To say with evil intent -1614. †2. *intr.* To speak evil -1596. 3. *trans.* To say wrongly. Now *rare.* late ME. b. *intr.* To say something wrong or amiss. late ME.

1. Far liefer had I fight a score of times Than hear thee so m. me and revile TENNYSON.

Mis-see, *v.* 1591. [MIS-¹ 1.] To see imperfectly; to take a wrong view of.

Mis-see·m, *v.* Now *rare.* late ME. [MIS-¹ 1.] *trans.* To misbecome.

Missel (mi·sĕl). [OE. *mistel*, (1) basil, (2) mistletoe; of unkn. origin.] †1. Mistletoe -1670. 2. Short for MISSEL-BIRD, -THRUSH. 1845.

Mi·ssel-bird. Now *dial.* 1626. [f. prec.] = MISSEL-THRUSH.

Misseldin(e, obs. ff. MISTLETOE.

Mi·ssel-thrush. 1774. [f. MISSEL.] A species of thrush, *Turdus viscivorus*, which feeds on the berries of the mistletoe.

Mis-se·nd, *v.* late ME. [MIS-¹ 1.] *trans.* To send to a wrong place or person.

Mis-se·rve, *v.* Now *rare.* ME. [Orig., a. OF. *messervir*; later f. MIS-¹ 1 + SERVE *v.*] 1. *trans.* To serve badly or unfaithfully. †2. *intr.* To miss fire -1685.

Mis-set (mis,se·t), *v.* ME. [MIS-¹ 1.] 1. *trans.* To misplace. †2. To put out of humour, 'upset' (*Sc.*) -1818.

Miss-fi·re. 1811. [f. phr. *to miss fire.*] = MISFIRE *sb.*

Mis-shape (misʃē¹·p), *sb.* Now *rare.* 1465. [MIS-¹ 4.] A bad or deformed shape or figure; deformity. Also, a mis-shapen body or person.

Mis-shape (misʃē¹·p), *v.* 1450. [MIS-¹ 1.] *trans.* To shape ill; to give a bad form to; to deform. *lit.* and *fig.*

Figures monstrous and mis-shap'd POPE.

Mis-shapen (misʃē¹·p'n), *ppl. a.* late ME. [f. MIS-¹ 2 + *shapen* pa. pple.] Having a bad or ugly shape; ill-shaped; deformed.

The m. hairy Scandinavian troll EMERSON. *fig.* Crooked and m. minds FLORIO. Hence **Mis-sha·pen-ly** *adv.*, **-ness.**

Mis-shea·thed, *ppl. a.* [MIS-¹ 2.] Sheathed by mistake. *Rom. & Jul.* v. iii. 205.

Missible (mi·sib'l), *a. rare.* 1789. [f. L. *miss-*, *mittere* + -IBLE.] Capable of being sent.

†Missi·ficate, *v.* 1641. [f. eccl. L. *missificat-*, *missificare*, f. *missa* MASS *sb.*¹] *intr.* To perform Mass -1694. So **†Missifica·tion** [see -FICATION] 1641.

Missile (mi·səil, mi·sil), *a.* and *sb.* 1606. [ad. L. *missilis* (neut. sing. *missile* as sb.), f. *miss-*, *mittere* to send; see -ILE.] A. *adj.* Capable of being thrown; adapted to be discharged from the hand or from a machine or engine; chiefly in *m. weapon* 1611. b. Applied to weapons that discharge arrows, bullets, etc. 1819.

We bend the bow, or wing the m. dart POPE. b. Their long-bows, slings, and other m. weapons SCOTT.

B. *sb.* 1. A missile object or weapon, as a stone, an arrow, a bullet 1656. 2. *pl.* = L. *missilia, res missiles*, largess (i. e. sweets, perfumes, etc.) thrown by the Roman emperors to the people 1606.

Mi·ssing, *ppl. a.* 1530. [f. MISS *v.* + -ING ².] 1. Not present; not found; absent; gone. 2. That fails to hit 1586.

1. Moses was in the Mount, and m. long MILT. The ship is what is called a m. ship, i.e. has been so long on the voyage that the owner has reason to suspect that she has met with some casualty ARNOULD.

Special collocations: **m. link,** (*a*) something lacking to complete a series; (*b*) *Zool.* a hypothetical type assumed to connect two related types; *esp.* a hypothetical intermediate form between the anthropoid apes and man; also applied to an animal (or person) supposed to resemble this.

Mission (mi·ʃən), *sb.* 1598. [ad. L. *missionem*, f. *mittere* (*miss-*) to send.] †1. The action or an act of sending -1698. 2. A sending or being sent to perform some function or service; *Theol.* the sending of the Second or Third Person of the Trinity by the First, or of the Third by the Second, for the production of a temporal effect 1609. 3. *Eccl.* The action of sending men forth with authority to preach the faith and administer the sacraments; hence, authority given by God or the Church to preach 1613. 4. A body of persons sent to a foreign country to conduct negotiations, watch over interests, etc. 1626. 5. A body of persons sent out by a religious community to convert the heathen; also, to spiritualize various classes of people 1622. 6. A permanent establishment of missionaries in a country; a particular field of missionary activity; a missionary post or station 1769. b. *transf.* An organization in a particular district for the conversion of the people 1800. 7. A special course of religious services, sermons, etc., organized in connexion with a particular church or parish for this purpose 1772. 8. The commission of a messenger, envoy, or agent; now *esp.* the errand of a political mission 1671. 9. (A person's) vocation or work in life. Also *transf.* attributed to things. Occas. *trivial* or *contempt.* 1805. 10. *attrib.*, as *m. church, house, work*, etc. 1792.

1. *Tr. & Cr.* III. iii. 189. 2. The M. of the Comforter 1846. 3. Christ..in the M. first of his Twelve, and after of his Seventy 1641. Men..who, so far from having any Orders or M., had not so much as Baptism CHALLONER. 5. Like zealous Missions, they did care pretend Of souls in show, but made the gold their end DRYDEN. *Home, city, police-court m.* 6. They..To the nearest m. sped and ask'd the Jesuit's aid SOUTHEY.

8. How to accomplish best His end of being on Earth, and m. high MILT. A M. to the King of Dahomey 1863. 10. b. *U.S.* Denoting a style of architecture, furniture, etc. characteristic of the Spanish Roman Catholic missions in California.

Mission (mi·ʃən), *v.* 1692. [f. prec. sb.] 1. *trans.* To send on a mission; to give (a person) a mission to perform. Chiefly in *pass.* 2. To conduct a religious mission among (a people) or in (a district) 1772. Also *intr.*

Missionary (mi·ʃənări), *a.* and *sb.* 1644. [ad. mod.L. *missionarius*, f. *mission-* MISSION + *-arius* -ARY^1.] A. *adj.* 1. Of or pertaining to missions; engaged in a mission; proper to one sent on a mission; occupied in or characterized by mission-work. 2. That is sent out or forth. Now *Obs.* or *poet.* 1691.

1. *M. box*: a box for contributions towards the funds of a m. society.

B. *sb.* 1. A person who carries on missionary work, esp. among the heathen 1656. 2. An agent or emissary; esp. one sent on a political mission. Now *rare* or *Obs.* 1693. †3. A missionary establishment –1761.

1. Phr. *Home m.*: a person (usu. a layman) employed to labour in the spiritual instruction of the poor. *City m.*: one so employed amongst the poor of a city; so *town m.* *Police-court m.*: a person employed to attend a police-court, and to work for the spiritual and moral benefit of those brought before it. *transf.* The fanatic missionaries of sedition GIBBON.

Missioner (mi·ʃənəɹ). 1654. [f. MISSION + -ER^1.] One sent on a mission, a missionary. In mod. use chiefly, one who conducts a parochial mission.

The pope enjoined his m. to remove the pagan idols GOLDSM. *fig.* A m. of peace and order in every parish BURKE.

Missionize (mi·ʃənəiz), *v.* 1826. [f. MISSION *sb.* + -IZE.] *intr.* To do missionary work. Also *trans.*

Missis, missus (mi·sis, -iz, mi·sŏs). *dial.* and *vulgar.* 1837. [Corruption of MISTRESS. The oral equivalent of MRS. (q. v.).] 1. Wife 1839. 2. Used by servants (usu. without article) in speaking of their mistresses.

1. *The missis*: used by a man in speaking of his own or of another man's wife. Hence **Mi·ssis** *v.* to address as 'Mrs.' DICKENS.

Missish (mi·siʃ), *a.* 1795. [f. MISS *sb.*^{2} + -ISH^1.] Characteristic of a miss; affected or sentimental.

Missive (mi·siv), *a.* and *sb.* 1466. [ad. F. *missive* fem., or med.L. *missivus*, f. *miss-*, *mittere* to send; see -IVE.] A. *adj.* 1. *Letter m., m. letter.* Usu. pl. *letters m.* or †*missives.* †a. *gen.* An epistle sent from one person to another –1710. b. A letter or letters sent by a superior authority to a particular person or body of persons, conveying a command, recommendation, or permission. Now chiefly, a letter from the sovereign to a dean and chapter nominating a person to be elected bishop. (See CONGÉ D'ÉLIRE.) 1466. †2. = MISSILE *a.* –1809. †3. That is sent –1830.

1. b. A letter missiue Vnder the Kynges signett 1487. 2. Not with their m. weapons onely..but with their drawne swords KNOLLES.

B. *sb.* 1. A written message; a letter. Occas. *spec.* = A. 1. Now usu., an official letter, or high-flown for 'letter'. late ME. 2. *Scots Law.* A document in the form of a letter interchanged by the parties to a contract 1561. †3. A messenger (*rare*) –1649. †4. Something hurled or thrown; *esp.* a missile weapon –1809.

1. Mysterious missives, sealed with red 1885. 3. Missiues from the King, who all-hail'd me Thane of Cawdor SHAKS.

Mis-so·rt, *v.* 1581. [MIS-^{1} 1.] *trans.* To sort badly.

Mis-sou·nd, *v.* 1500. [MIS-^{1} 1.] 1. *intr.* To sound amiss. 2. *trans.* To mispronounce.

Mis-spea·k, *v.* ME. [MIS-^{1} 1.] †1. *intr.* To speak wrongly or improperly; to speak evil –1613. †2. *trans.* To speak evil of –1584. 3. To speak incorrectly or improperly (*rare*) 1593. So **Mis-spee·ch**, †evil-speaking; incorrect speaking ME.

Mis-spe·ll, *v.* 1655. [MIS-^{1} 1.] *trans.* To spell incorrectly. Hence **Mis-spe·ll, -spe·lling** *sbs.* a bad spelling.

Mis-spe·nd, *v.* late ME. [MIS-^{1} 1.] *trans.* To spend amiss or wastefully. So †**Mis-spe·nse, -e·nce**, improper or wasteful expenditure 1591–1788. **Mis-spent** *ppl. a.* ill-spent, wasted 1500.

Mis-sta·te, *v.* 1650. [MIS-^{1} 1.] *trans.* To state erroneously. So **Mis-sta·tement** 1790.

Misstay·, *v.* 1885. [f. phr. *to miss stays* (see MISS *v.* I. *Phrases*).] *intr.* Of a ship: To miss stays. Also *sb.* 1878.

†**Mis-ste·p**, *v.* late ME. [MIS-^{1} 1.] *intr.* To take a wrong step; to go astray –1598. So **Mis-ste·p** *sb.* a wrong step; a FAUX PAS 1855.

Mis-sty·le, *v.* *rare.* 1604. [MIS-^{1} 1.] *trans.* To style or term incorrectly.

†**Mis-succee·ding**, *vbl. sb.* 1661. [MIS-^{1} 3.] Ill-success FULLER. †**Mis-succe·ss** 1656.

Mis-sui·t, *v.* 1618. [MIS-^{1} 1.] *trans.* To suit ill.

Mis-swo·rn, *ppl. a.* 1506. [MIS-^{1} 2.] a. Forsworn. b. Whose name has been taken in vain.

Missy (mi·si), *sb.* 1676. [f. MISS *sb.*^{2} + -Y^6.] An affectionate or playful form of MISS. Occas. *contempt.*

Missy, var. of MISY. *Obs.*

Mist (mist), *sb.*^{1} [OE. *mist* str. masc. :— OTeut. *mihstoz, f. *mīg- :—pre-Teut. *migh-, *meigh-*, as in Gr. ὀμίχλη, etc.] 1. Vapour of water precipitated in very fine droplets, smaller and more densely aggregated than those of rain. b. *transf.* A cloud (of small particles) resembling a mist; a haze or haziness; hence *fig.* of time, etc. 1785. 2. Dimness of eyesight; a filmy appearance before the eyes caused by disorders of the body or by tears OE. 3. Applied to immaterial things conceived as dimming, obscuring, or blurring OE. †4. An atmosphere of doubt –1715.

1. Whan the moysture of the dewe stryketh upwarde agayne, it maketh a myste 1530. *Scotch m.*: a thick, soaking mist characteristic of the Scottish hills. b. Times..half shrouded in the m. of legend FREEMAN. 2. O'er her meek eyes came a happy m. TENNYSON. 3. The mists Of despondency and gloom M. ARNOLD. Phr. *Mists of death, deathly mists.*

Comb.: **m.-bow**, a fog-bow (FOG *sb.*^{2}); **-flower**, a plant of the tropical American genus *Conoclinium.*

†**Mist**, *sb.*^{2} late ME. [Perh. a use of prec. infl. by *mystic.*] Things spiritual or mystical. *In m.*: mystically. –1667 (MILT. *P. L.* v. 435).

Mist (mist), *v.* [OE. *mistian*, f. *mist* MIST *sb.*^{1}] 1. *intr.* To be or become misty; (of the eyes, outlines, etc.) to become dim, obscure, or blurred. 2. *trans.* To cover or obscure with or as with mist; to bedim (the eyes) with tears. late ME.

1. When thy gold breath is misting in the west KEATS. 2. He sits Misted with darknes like a smoaky roome 1598.

Mistakable (mistē^1·kăb'l), *a.* 1646. [f. MISTAKE *v.* + -ABLE.] Capable of being mistaken, misapprehended, or misunderstood. Hence **Mista·kableness. Mista·kably** *adv.*

Mistake (mistē^1·k), *sb.* 1638. [f. next.] *prop.* A misconception of the meaning of something; *hence*, an error or fault in thought or action.

The great m. of expecting too much of life 1856. *gen.* Infallibility is an absolute security of the understanding from all possibility of m. in what it believes TILLOTSON. Phr. †*A m. of*: a misconception as to. †*Under a m.*: under a misapprehension. *By m.*: mistakenly. *And no m.*: undoubtedly; used *colloq.* to emphasize a preceding statement. Also used attrib., (*and-*) *no-m.* = undoubted. The real old original and-no-mistake nobility THACKERAY.

Mistake (mistē^1·k), *v.* ME. [a. ON. *mistaka* to take by mistake, refl. to miscarry, f. *mis-* = MIS-^{1} + *taka* to TAKE.] †1. *trans.* To take wrongfully, wrongly, or in error –1631. †2. *intr.* To transgress, offend –1822. 3. To err in the choice of. late ME. 4. *trans.* To misunderstand the meaning or †character of (a person). late ME. 5. To take (an opinion, statement, action, purpose, etc.) in a wrong sense 1496. 6. *intr.* To make a mistake; to be in error; to take a wrong view 1581. †7. *trans.* To suppose erroneously to be or to do . . . –1736. 8. *To mistake* (a person or thing) *for* (another): to suppose erroneously the former to be the latter 1611. 9. To take to be somebody or something else 1590. †10. To commit an error in regard to (a date, etc.); to perform (an action) at a wrong time –1734.

3. Phr. *To m. the* or *one's road* (*way*); *to m. one's mark.* 4. Why, thou whorson Asse, thou mistak'st me SHAKS. 5. The judge may m. the law *Junius Lett.* 6. Oh, cry you mercy sir, I haue mistooke SHAKS. You're mistaken I dare say DICKENS. 7. Lest I should be mistaken to vilify Reason 1736. 8. She [a hen] mistakes a Piece of Chalk for an Egg, and sits upon it in the same manner ADDISON. 9. Phr. *There's no mistaking* = it is impossible not to recognize. There was no mistaking the fact DICKENS. Hence **Mista·kingly** *adv.*

Mistaken (mistē^1·k'n), *ppl. a.* 1597. [pa. pple. of prec. vb.] †1. Wrongly supposed to be so. 2. Of persons: Taking a wrong view 1601. 3. *transf.* of their opinions, actions, etc.: Wrongly conceived or carried out; erroneous 1676.

2. I think him honest, though m. *Junius Lett.* 3. A m. feeling of loyalty FREEMAN. Hence **Mista·ken-ly** *adv.*, **-ness.**

Misteach (mistī·tʃ), *v.* [OE. *mistǣcan*; see MIS-^{1} 1 and TEACH *v.*] *trans.* To teach or instruct badly or wrongly. So **Mistaught** (mistǭ·t), *ppl. a.* 1552.

Mistell (miste·l), *v.* late ME. [MIS-^{1} 1.] †1. To miscount –1647. 2. To relate incorrectly; †to misinform 1565.

†**Miste·mper**, *v.* 1547. [f. MIS-^{1} 1 + TEMPER *v.*] *trans.* To disturb or disorder –1642.

Miste·mpered, *ppl. a.* *Obs.* or *arch.* 1506. [MIS-^{1} 2.] 1. Badly mixed. 2. Disordered, deranged 1541. 3. Of weapons: Tempered for an evil purpose. *Rom. & Jul.* I. i. 94.

Mister (mi·stəɹ), *sb.*^{1} *Obs.* exc. *arch.* or *dial.* ME. [a. OF. *mestier, mester*, mod.F. *métier* :—pop. L. *misterium for L. *ministerium*; see MINISTRY and cf. MÉTIER.] †1. Handicraft, trade; profession, craft –1613. †2. Office, business, function. ME. only. †3. Occupation. ME. only. †4. Need –1768.

Comb. †**m. man, misters** (genitive) **man**: a craftsman. Phr. like *all mister* (*men*), *what mister* (*man*) were subsequently misapprehended as = 'of all (what, etc.) class(es, kind(s'; hence *arch.* and *dial.*

Mister (mi·stəɹ), *sb.*^{2} 1551. [Weakened form of MASTER *sb.*^{1}] 1. Title of courtesy prefixed to the surname or Christian name of a man, and to designations of office or occupation. The oral equivalent of MR. (q. v.). b. The word 'mister' (Mr.) as a prefix or title 1758. 2. = SIR (or less respectful than that title). Now only *vulgar.* 1760.

1. b. They never spoke to us without putting M. to our Names GOLDSM. 2. 'Good morning, mister', said Dominicus HAWTHORNE.

†**Mi·ster**, *v.*^{1} Chiefly *Sc.* ME. [f. MISTER *sb.*^{1}] 1. *intr.* To be necessary or needful –1715. 2. *trans.* To have need of, require –1722. 3. *intr.* To have need (*of*) –1572.

1. As for my name, it mistreth not to tell SPENSER.

Mi·ster, *v.*^{2} 1742. [f. MISTER *sb.*^{2}] *trans.* To address or speak of as 'Mr.'

'Pray, don't m. such fellows to me', cries the Lady FIELDING.

Miste·rm, *v.* 1579. [MIS-^{1} 1.] *trans.* To apply a wrong term or name to.

Mistery: see MYSTERY ^{2}.

Mistful (mi·stfŭl), *a.* 1599. [f. MIST *sb.*^{1} + -FUL.] Full of mist; obscured by or as by mist.

Misthi·nk, *v.* ME. [f. MIS-^{1} 1 + THINK *v.*^{2}] †1. *intr.* To have sinful thoughts –1615. 2. To think mistakenly 1530. 3. *trans.* To have a bad opinion of. Also *intr.* const. *of.* 1593. 4. With cogn. obj.: To think bad thoughts 1618. So **Misthou·ght**, erroneous thought or notion; mistaken opinion 1596.

Misthrive (misþrəi·v), *v.* 1567. [MIS-^{1} 7.] *intr.* To be unsuccessful; not to thrive.

‖**Mistico** (mi·stiko). 1801. [Sp., taken to be a. Arab. *misteḥ* (lit. flat surface).] A Mediterranean coasting vessel having two sails.

†**Misti·de**, *v.* [OE. *mistīdan*; see MIS-^{1} 1 and TIDE *v.*] 1. *intr.* To happen amiss or unfortunately –ME. 2. To have misfortune. CHAUCER.

Mistigris (mi·stigris). 1882. [ad. F. *mistigri* knave of spades.] The name of the blank card in a variety of draw poker; hence, the game in which it is used.

†**Mistime** (mistəi·m), *v.* [OE. *mistīmian*; see MIS-^{1} 1 and TIME *v.*] †1. *intr.* Of the event: To happen amiss. Of the person: To

come to grief. –late ME. **2.** To time wrongly or improperly; to do or perform at a wrong time; to miscalculate the time of. late ME.

†**Mi·stion.** 1612. [ad. L. *mistionem.* Cf. MIXTION.] Mixtion, mixture –1680.

Mistitle (mistəi·t'l), *v.* 1618. [MIS-[1] 1.] *trans.* To give a wrong title or name to.

Mistle, obs. f. MISSEL, MIZZLE.

Mistletoe (mi·z'ltoᵘ, mi·s'ltoᵘ). [OE. *mistiltān,* f. *mistil, -el* (see MISSEL) + *tān* twig.] A parasitic plant of Europe, *Viscum album,* growing, in Britain, on the apple-tree, rarely on the oak, and bearing a whitish berry, from which a birdlime is prepared. It was held in veneration by the Druids, esp. when found growing on the oak. Also applied to various allied plants.

The m. is still hung up in farm-houses and kitchens at Christmas; and the young men have the privilege of kissing the girls under it W. IRVING. *Comb.* **m. thrush,** the missel-thrush, *Turdus viscivorus.*

Mistral (mi·străl, mistrā·l). 1604. [a. F., a. Pr. *mistral*:—L. *magistralis* MAGISTRAL; *lit.* 'master-wind'.] A violent cold north-east wind experienced in the Mediterranean provinces of France, etc.

Mistransla·te, *v.* 1532. [MIS-[1] 1.] *trans.* To translate incorrectly. **Mistransla·tion** 1694.

†**Mistrea·ding,** *vbl. sb.* 1596. [MIS-[1] 3.] A mis-step; a misdeed –1772.

Mistreat (mistrī·t), *v.* 1453. [MIS-[1] 1.] *trans.* To treat badly or wrongly; to ill-treat, maltreat. So **Mistrea·tment** 1716.

Mistress (mi·strĕs). ME. [a. OF. *maistresse,* mod.F. *maîtresse,* f. *maistre, maître* MASTER *sb.*[1] + *-esse,* -ESS.] **I. 1.** A woman who has the care of or authority over servants or attendants, and, in early use, of children or young women. **2.** The female head of a household or of an establishment of any kind. late ME. **3.** A woman who has power to control or dispose *of* something. Now *rare* exc. in *one's own m., m. of the situation,* etc. late ME. †**4.** The female governor of a state, etc. –1785. **b.** Also of countries, etc. late ME. †**5.** A woman, a goddess, a virtue, passion, etc., having dominion over a person or regarded as a protecting or guiding influence –1677. †**6.** A woman, or personified thing, regarded as the authoress, creatress, or patroness of an art, religion, a state of life, etc. –1708. **7.** A female possessor or owner 1551. **8.** A woman who has mastered any art, craft, or subject 1484. **9.** A woman who is loved and courted by a man. (Now only in unequivocal contexts.) 1509. **10.** A woman who illicitly occupies the place of wife. late ME.

1. As the eyes of a maiden [look] vnto the hand of her mistresse *Ps.* cxxiii. 2. **2.** The m. of a family must be ever watchful MRS. CHAPONE. **3.** You are your own m. 1794. **b.** *transf.* Such a lord is Love, And Beauty such a m. of the world TENNYSON. **4. b.** Rome now is m. of the whole World, sea and land, to either pole B. JONS. **7.** Phr. *To be m. of*: to have in her possession or at her disposal; also, to be perfectly acquainted with (a subject). **9.** I giue thee this For thy sweet Mistris sake, because thou lou'st her SHAKS.

II. A female teacher, instructress; now only, one engaged in a school, or teaching a special subject, as music, etc. late ME.

III. As a title. **1.** Used vocatively; = MADAM, MA'AM. *Obs.* exc. *arch.* late ME. **2.** As a title of courtesy. Now *Obs.* or *dial.* 1461. **b.** *transf.* and *joc.* 1577. **3.** In the title of certain Court offices 1710.

1. Studies my Ladie? Mistresse, looke on me SHAKS. **2.** So, here is m. Stella again SWIFT. M. Gilpin (careful soul!) COWPER. **b.** Mistris line, is not this my Ierkin? SHAKS. **3.** *M. of the Robes*: a lady of high rank, charged with the care of the Queen's wardrobe.

IV. Techn. **1.** *Bowls.* = JACK *sb.*[1] II. 11. Often *fig.* 1586. **2.** A lantern used in coal-mines 1851.

1. So, so, rub on, and kisse the mistresse SHAKS.

Mistressly (mi·strĕsli), *a.* 1748. [-LY[1].] **1.** Belonging to the mistress of a household. RICHARDSON. **2.** [after MASTERLY 2.] Like one who is a mistress in her art 1786.

2. I did see the new bust of Mrs. Siddons, and a very m. performance it is indeed H. WALPOLE.

Mi·stress-piece. Now *rare.* 1648. [f. MISTRESS after *masterpiece.*] A feminine masterpiece.

Mi·stress-ship. 1460. [f. MISTRESS + -SHIP.] **1.** Authority of one in the position of a mistress 1581. †**2.** A style of address; always in *your m.* –1632. **3.** The post of mistress in a school 1891.

Mistrial (mistrəi·ăl). 1628. [MIS-[1] 4.] A trial vitiated by some error. Also, *U.S.,* an inconclusive trial, as where the jury cannot agree.

Mistri·st, *sb.* and *v. Obs.* or *dial.* late ME. = MISTRUST.

†**Mistrow·,** *v. north.* ME. [ad. ON. *mistrúa,* f. *mis-* MIS-[1] + *trúa* (see TROW *v.*).] = MISTRUST *v.* –1480. So †**Mistrow·** *sb.* ME.

Mistrust (mistrʊ·st), *sb.* late ME. [MIS-[1] 7.] Lack of trust or confidence; suspicion, distrust. **Mistru·stless** *a.* unsuspecting 1586.

Mistrust (mistrʊ·st), *v.* late ME. [f. MIS-[1] 7 + TRUST *v.*] **1.** *trans.* Not to trust (a person); to suspect the actions, intentions, motives, etc. of. Also *refl.* **2.** To have doubts about (a thing); to doubt the truth, validity, or genuineness of. late ME. †**3.** To suspect the existence or anticipate the occurrence of (something evil) –1728. **b.** To suspect *that* something has happened or will happen (now *rare*). late ME. **4.** *intr.* To be distrustful, suspicious, or without confidence. late ME.

1. I will neuer m. my wife againe SHAKS. **2.** For my part I am ever ready to m. a promising title GOLDSM. **3.** They were all asleepe mistrusting no harme FLORIO. Hence **Mistru·stingly** *adv.*

Mistru·stful, *a.* 1529. [f. MISTRUST *sb.* + -FUL.] Full of mistrust; wanting in confidence; distrustful, suspicious. Const. *of.* †**b.** *transf.* Causing mistrust 1592.

b. Or stonish'd as night-wanderers often are, Their light blown out in some m. wood SHAKS. Hence **Mistru·stful·ly** *adv.,* **-ness.**

Mistry·st, *v. Sc.* and *north.* 1816. [MIS-[1] 1, 7.] **1.** *trans.* To fail to keep an engagement with. **2.** *pass.* To be perplexed.

Mistu·ne, *v.* 1504. [MIS-[1] 1.] *trans.* To tune wrongly; to make discordant; to perform (music) out of tune.

Misturn (mistʊ̄·ɹn), *v.* ME. [MIS-[1] 1.] *trans.* and *intr.* To turn in a wrong direction.

Mistu·tored, *ppl. a.* 1757. [MIS-[1] 2.] Badly instructed or brought up.

Misty (mi·sti), *a.*[1] [OE. *mistig,* f. *mist* MIST *sb.*[1] + -Y[1].] **1.** Covered with mist; accompanied or characterized by mist; consisting of mist. **b.** Clouded, blinded, or blurred as if by mist 1590. **2.** *fig.* Obscure; vague, indistinct. late ME. **b.** Of persons: Clouded in intellect 1822.

1. And Iocond day Stands tipto on the mistie Mountaines tops SHAKS. **2.** The Philosopher..is so hard of vtterance, and so mistie to bee conceiued, [etc.] SIDNEY. A m. recollection TYLOR. Hence **Mi·stily** *adv.,* **-ness.**

†**Mi·sty,** *a.*[2] late ME. [A use of prec. for L. *mysticus.*] Mystical, spiritual –1570.

Mi:sundersta·nd, *v.* ME. [MIS-[1] 1.] Not to understand rightly; to take in a wrong sense; to misinterpret the actions, etc. of (a person).

To be great is to be misunderstood EMERSON.

Mi:sundersta·nding, *vbl. sb.* 1449. [MIS-[1] 3.] **1.** Failure to understand; misconception, misinterpretation. **2.** Dissension, disagreement 1642.

2. Some little pique or m. between them GEO. ELIOT.

Misusage (misyū·sĕdʒ). Now *rare.* 1532. [MIS-[1] 4.] †**1.** Misconduct –1579. **2.** Ill-usage; maltreatment 1554. **3.** Wrong use, misuse 1567.

Misuse (misyū·s), *sb.* late ME. [MIS-[1] 4.] **1.** Wrong or improper use; misapplication. †**2.** Ill-usage. SHAKS. †**3.** Evil custom or conduct –1604.

1. Artful m. of the confidence of others 1866. **2.** *1 Hen. IV,* I. i. 43. **3.** *Oth.* IV. ii. 109.

Misuse (misyū·z), *v.* late ME. [MIS-[1] 1. Cf. OF. *mesuser.*] **1.** *trans.* To use or employ wrongly or improperly; to misapply. **2.** To maltreat, ill-use 1540. †**b.** To violate –1540. †**3.** *refl.* To misconduct oneself 1532–81. †**4.** To speak evil of; to revile, deride –1633. †**5.** To deceive –1601.

1. I haue misvs'd the Kings Presse damnably SHAKS. **2.** Who misuses a dog would m. a child TENNYSON. **5.** Proofe enough, to m. the Prince, to vexe Claudio SHAKS. Hence **Misu·ser**[1], one who misuses 1548.

Misuser[2] (misyū·zəɹ). 1625. [a. OF. *mesuser,* inf. as sb.; see -ER[4].] *Law.* Unlawful use of a liberty or benefit such as may lead to its forfeiture.

Misva·lue, *v.* 1626. [MIS-[1] 1.] *trans.* To value falsely or wrongly; to misesteem. So **Misvalua·tion.**

Ignored or misvalued during his life 1900.

Misve·nture. Now *arch.* 1563. [MIS-[1] 4.] An unfortunate venture; a misadventure.

Misvou·ched, *pa. pple.* and *ppl. a.* 1626. [MIS-[1] 2.] **1.** Alleged wrongly. BACON. **2.** Not well vouched for 1876.

†**Miswa·ndered,** *ppl. a.* 1590. [MIS-[1] 2.] In which one has gone astray –1620. †**Miswa·ndering** *ppl. a.* going astray. late ME. –1645.

†**Misway·.** [MIS-[1] 4.] A wrong path. CHAUCER.

Miswe·dded, *a.* [MIS-[1] 2.] Unsuitably married; *transf.* of a marriage MILT.

†**Miswee·n,** *v.* 1590. [MIS-[1] 1.] **1.** *intr.* To have a wrong opinion –1640. **2.** *trans.* To think wrongly of –1749.

†**Miswe·nd,** *v.* ME. [MIS-[1] 1.] To lead or go astray (*lit.* and *fig.*) –1723.

Misword (miswʊ̄·ɹd), *sb.* Now *dial.* ME. [MIS-[1] 4.] A harsh, angry, or cross word.

Mis-wo·rd, *v.* 1883. [MIS-[1] 1.] *trans.* To word incorrectly. So **Mis-wo·rding** *vbl. sb.* wrong wording 1680.

Miswo·rship, *sb.* 1626. [MIS-[1] 4.] Wrong or false worship. So **Miswo·rship** *v. trans.* to worship amiss. **Miswo·rshipper.**

Miswrite (misrəi·t), *v.* OE. [MIS-[1] 1.] *trans.* To write incorrectly.

†**Miswrou·ght,** *pa. pple.* ME. [MIS-[1] 2.] Done amiss; manufactured badly –1626.

†**Mi·sy.** 1601. [a. L. *misy* (Pliny), a. Gr. μίσυ.] **1.** A kind of mushroom or truffle. HOLLAND. **2.** *Min.* Copiapite, or some related species –1775.

Misyoke (misyōᵘ·k), *v.* 1645. [MIS-[1] 1.] *trans.* To yoke (in marriage) unsuitably. Also *intr.*

Miszea·lous, *a.* 1617. [MIS-[1] 6.] Wrongly zealous.

Mitch-board (mi·tʃboᵊɹd). 1883. [?] *Naut.* A support for a boom, yard, etc., when not in use.

Mite[1] (məit). [OE. *mīte* wk. fem. :—OTeut. **mītōn-*. Cf. F. *mite,* of Teut. origin.] In early use, any minute insect or arachnid. Now usually restricted to certain genera of the order *Acarida* of arachnids, and chiefly applied to the cheese-mite, *Tyroglyphus* (formerly *Acarus*) *domesticus.*

Mite[2] (məit). ME. [a. MDu. *mīte* fem. :—OTeut. **mītōn-*; prob. identical with prec. Cf. early mod.G. *meite,* something very small.] **1.** Orig., a Flemish copper coin of very small value. From the 14th c., used as tr. L. *minutum* (Vulg.), Gr. λεπτόν in Mark xii. 43, where two 'mites' are stated to make a 'farthing' (Gr. κοδράντης, L. *quadrans*); hence pop. = 'half-farthing'. **b.** *fig.* An immaterial contribution, but the best one can do, to some object or cause (see *Mark* xii. 43) 1650. †**2.** A small weight: *spec.* one twentieth of a grain troy –1738. **3.** A minute particle or portion; a tiny fragment. Now *colloq.* or *vulgar.* 1608. **4.** *fig.* A jot, whit. Now *colloq.* late ME. **5.** A very small object; often, a tiny child 1594.

1. And there came a poore wyddowe, and put in two mytes, which make a farthinge COVERDALE *Mark* xii. 43. **b.** It may not be amiss to contribute my m. of advice BERKELEY. **5.** A m. of a boy DICKENS.

Miter: see MITRE.

Mithras (mi·þræs), **Mithra** (mi·þrǎ). 1585. [L. *Mithras, Mithres* = Gr. Μίθρας, a. OPers. *Mithra,* = Skr. *Mitra,* one of the gods of the Vedic pantheon.] A god of the ancient Persians, in later times often identified with the sun. Hence **Mithra·ic** *a.* of or connected with M. or his worship. **Mi·thraism. Mi·thraist.**

Mithridate (mi·þridĕⁱt). Also †‖**Mithrida·tum.** 1528. [ad. med.L. *mithridatum,* altered from late L. *mithridatium*, orig. neut. of *Mithridatius* adj., pertaining to Mithridates, f. L. *Mithri-, Mithradates*, Gr. Μιθρι-, Μιθραδάτης.] 1. *Old Pharmacy.* A composition in the form of an electuary, regarded as a universal antidote against poison and infectious disease. Hence any similar antidote. Also *transf.* and *fig.* 2. In full *m. mustard*, a name for the plants *Lepidium campestre* and *Thlaspi arvense.* Also *Bastard m. mustard*: candytuft. 1597. Hence, **Mi·thridatism**, immunity from a poison induced by administering gradually increased doses of it 1851. **Mi·thridatize,** *v. trans.* to produce mithridatism in 1866.

Mithridatic (miþridæ·tik), *a.* 1649. [ad. L. *mithridaticus*, a. Gr., f. Μιθριδάτης; see -IC.] 1. Of or pertaining to Mithridates VI, king of Pontus. 2. Of or pertaining to mithridate 1847. 3. a. Resembling Mithridates or his alleged immunity from poisons; pertaining to mithridatism 1868.

Mitigable (mi·tigăb'l), *a.* 1677. [f. L. *mitigare* to MITIGATE.] Capable of being mitigated.

Mitigant (mi·tigănt), *a.* and *sb. rare.* 1541. [ad. L. *mitigantem*, pr. pple. of *mitigare*; see -ANT[1].] A. *adj.* Mitigating, lenitive. B. *sb.* A lenitive 1865.

Mitigate (mi·tigeⁱt), *v.* late ME. [f. L. *mitigat-, mitigare*, f. *mitis* mild.] 1. *trans.* To render (a person, etc.) milder; to appease, mollify. Now *rare.* 2. To render (anger, etc.) less violent; to appease 1494. 3. To alleviate (a disease, an evil). late ME. 4. To abate the rigour of (a law) 1532. 5. To reduce the severity of (a punishment, etc.) 1533. b. To render (a custom, etc.) more humane 1835. 6. To moderate (heat, cold, etc.) 1611. 7. To palliate (an offence) 1719. 8. With a quality as obj.: To moderate (the severity, rigour, etc., *of* something) 1571. 9. *intr.* To become mitigated; to grow milder or less severe (*rare*) 1633.

2. To m. the king's anger PRESCOTT. 3. The swelling of his woundes to m. SPENSER. 5. Those hard censures.. are to be mitigated BURTON. b. Christianity first mitigated, and then abolished slavery 1835. 8. We could greatly wish that the rigor of this their opinion were alayed and mitigated HOOKER. Hence **Mi·tigative** *a.* lenitive; *sb.* a soothing remedy. **Mi·tigator.** **Mi·tigatory** *a.* tending or serving to m.; *sb.* something which serves to m.

Mitigation (mitigēⁱ·ʃən). late ME. [ad. L. *mitigationem.*] 1. The action of mitigating or the state of being mitigated. b. quasi-*concr.* A circumstance that mitigates 1729. †2. A qualification (of words or statements) -1709.

1. Without any m. or remorce of voice SHAKS. In m. of damages BLACKSTONE.

†**Mi·ting.** 1440. [f. MITE[2] + -ING[3].] A diminutive creature. Used in endearment or contempt -1585.

Mitis (mī·tis). 1885. [app. f. L. *mitis* mild, in the sense of *mild steel* (see MILD *a.* 7).] *Metall.* In *m. casting*: a method of increasing the fluidity of molten iron by adding a minute quantity of aluminium to the charge in the crucible; also, a casting produced by this process. So *m.-metal, process*, etc.

‖**Mitosis** (mitōᵘ·sis). *Pl.* **-oses** (-ōᵘ·sīz). 1888. [mod.L., f. Gr. μίτος thread; see -OSIS.] *Biol.* The process of division of the nucleus of a cell into minute threads. Hence **Mito·tic** *a.* pertaining to, characterized by, or exhibiting m.

‖**Mitraille** (mītray, mitrēⁱ·l), *sb.* 1868. [F. *mitraille*, OF. *mi(s)traille* small money, pieces of metal; a var. of OF. *mitaille*, f. *mite*; cf. MITE[2].] Fragments of iron, heads of nails, etc. shot in masses from a cannon; now *spec.* small shot fired from a mitrailleuse. So **Mitrai·lle** *v.* to assail with m. (*rare*) 1844.

‖**Mitrailleur** (mītrayör). 1869. [F., f. *mitrailler* to fire mitraille.] = MITRAILLEUSE.

‖**Mitrailleuse** (mītrayȫz). 1870. [Fr., f. as prec.] A breech-loading machine-gun with a number of barrels fitted together, so arranged that it can discharge small missiles simultaneously or in rapid succession.

Mitral (məi·trăl), *a.* and *sb.* 1610. [a. F., ad. mod.L. *mitralis*, f. L. *mitra*; see MITRE *sb.*[1] and -AL.] A. *adj.* 1. Of, pertaining to, or resembling a mitre. 2. *Anat.* **M. valve**: the left auriculo-ventricular valve of the heart, so called from its shape. Also called *bicuspid valve.* 1705. b. *Anat.* and *Path.* Of or pertaining to the m. valve 1853. B. *sb.* = *M. valve* 1835.

Mitre (məi·təɹ), *sb.*[1] Also (now *U.S.*) miter. late ME. [ad. F. *mitre*, ad. L. *mitra*, a. Gr. μίτρα belt, turban, etc.] 1. a. *Antiq.* As tr. Gr. μίτρα, L. *mitra*: A headband worn by ancient Greek women; also, a kind of head-dress common among Asiatics, considered by the Romans a mark of effeminacy when worn by men. ¶Used by Chapman and Pope as tr. Homeric μίτρη, a belt or girdle 1611. †b. Applied by travellers to the turban worn by certain Asiatic peoples, and the like 1585-1638. 2. A sacerdotal head-dress. a. *Heb. Antiq.* The ceremonial turban of the high priest. late ME. b. *Eccl.* A bishop's tall cap, deeply cleft at the top, the outline of the front and back having the shape of a pointed arch: part of the insignia of a bishop in the Western Church, and worn also by certain abbots, etc. late ME. c. Used as the symbol of the episcopal office or dignity. late ME. d. *Her.* The representation of a mitre 1610. 3. A name of taverns and hotels 1608. 4. *Conch.* A mitre-shell 1840.

2. c. Learning being..reckon'd a very ordinary Qualification for yᵉ M. HEARNE. 3. *attrib.* A right Miter supper MIDDLETON.

attrib. and *Comb.*: **m.-mushroom,** an edible mushroom (*Helvella crispa*), so called from the shape of the pileus; **-shell,** any species of marine univalve shells of the genus *Mitra.*

Mitre (məi·təɹ), *sb.*[2] Also (now *U.S.*) miter. 1678. [Perh. transf. use of prec.] 1. In Joinery, etc.: A joint (also *m.-joint*) in which the line of junction bisects the angle (usu. a right angle) between the two pieces. 2. Short for *mitre square* 1678. 3. Short for *mitre-wheel* 1844. 3. = GUSSET 2. 1882.

1. *Keyed m.*: a mitre-joint strengthened by the insertion of keys (see KEY *sb.*[1] III. 1). *Lapped m.*: a combination of the lap and m. joints.

Comb.: **m.-arch,** the curve formed by the m. or junction of two curved surfaces, as in groining, etc.; **-bevel** = *mitre square*; **-block, -board,** (*a*) a joiner's mitre box; (*b*) = *mitre shooting-board*; **m. box,** a joiner's templet with kerfs or guides for the saw in cutting mitre-joints; **-dovetail, dovetailing,** a combination of the m. and dovetail joints; **-gauge,** a gauge for determining the angle of a mitre; **-joint** (see sense 1); **m. shooting-board,** a shooting-board used in chamfering the edges of wood; **m. square,** a square with the blade set at an angle of 45° for striking lines on something to be mitred; **-valve,** a puppet value having its face and seat inclined 45° to its axis; **-wheel,** each of a pair of bevelled cog-wheels, the axes of which are at right angles, and which have their teeth set at an angle of 45°.

Mitre (məi·təɹ), *v.*[1] late ME. [f. MITRE *sb.*[1]] *trans.* To confer a mitre upon. Chiefly in pa. pple. *mitred*, invested *with* something by way of mitre.

Mitre (məi·təɹ), *v.*[2] Also (now *U.S.*) miter. 1731. [f. MITRE *sb.*[2]] 1. *trans.* To join with a mitre-joint; to cut or shape to a mitre. Also with *away, up.* b. *intr.* To meet in a mitre-joint 1820. 2. *Needlework.* To make an angle in (a straight strip or band, etc.) by cutting out a three-cornered piece and uniting the resulting edges 1880.

1. *To m. the square*: to bisect the angle of a joint.

Mitred (məi·təɹd), *ppl. a.* late ME. [f. MITRE *sb.*[1] and *v.*[1] + -ED.] 1. Entitled or privileged to wear a mitre. 2. Wearing or adorned with a mitre. late ME. 3. Formed like a mitre; having a mitre-shaped apex; *Nat. Hist.* in specific names (= mod.L. *mitratus*) 1547.

1. *M. abbot* (= med.L. *abbas mitratus*): an abbot invested by the pope with the privilege of wearing a mitre; *m. abbey*, an abbey ruled by a mitred abbot.

Mitre-wort (məi·təɹwɒɹt). 1845. [f. MITRE *sb.*[1] + WORT.] Any plant of the genus *Mitella.*

False mitre-wort: a plant of the genus *Tiarella.*

Mitriform (məi·trifǭɹm), *a.* 1824. [ad. mod.L. *mitriformis*, f. *mitra* MITRE *sb.*[1]; see -FORM.] a. *Bot.* Shaped like a mitre: applied to the calyptra of mosses, etc. b. *Conch.* Shaped like a mitre-shell.

Mitring (məi·t'riŋ), *vbl. sb.* 1731. [f. MITRE *v.*[2] + -ING[1].] The action of MITRE *v.*[2]; also *concr.* the shaped end of a piece prepared to be mitred with another.

Comb. **m.-machine,** any machine for mitring neatly and accurately.

Mitt (mit). Also **mit.** Chiefly in *pl.* 1765. Shortened form of MITTEN.

Mitten (mi·tən). late ME. [a. F. *mitaine*, of unkn. etym.] 1. A covering for the hand, differing from a glove in having no fingers, but only a thumb; worn either for warmth or protection. Also (now *dial.*) applied to a thick winter glove. 2. A sort of glove of lace or knitted work covering the forearm, wrist, and part of the hand 1755.

1. Phr. *To handle without mittens*: to treat unmercifully. 2. Phr. *To get the m.*: of a lover, to be dismissed; hence, to be dismissed from any office or position. Hence **Mi·ttened** *a.* furnished with, or wearing, mittens.

†**Mi·ttent,** *a.* 1661. [ad. L. *mittentem*, pr. pple. of *mittere* to send.] *Path.* Said of the organ or part supposed to send peccant 'humours' to another -1684.

‖**Mittimus** (mi·timɒ̆s), *sb.* 1443. [L., = 'we send', the first word of the writ in Latin.] †1. *Law.* A writ for removing records from one court to another -1559. 2. *Law.* A warrant directed to the keeper of a prison, ordering him to receive into custody and hold in safe-keeping, until delivered in due course of law, the person sent and specified in the warrant 1591. 3. *colloq.* A dismissal from office; a notice to quit (*dial.*) 1596. 4. *joc.* A magistrate 1630.

2. No words, Sir; a Wife, or a M. 1728. 3. Phr. *To get one's m.*: to be dismissed; also, to get one's 'quietus'. 4. Nay, 'tis but what old M. commanded SHERIDAN. Hence **Mi·ttimus** *v.* to commit to jail by a warrant.

Mity (məi·ti), *a.* 1681. [f. MITE[1] + -Y[1].] Full of or abounding in mites; said esp. of cheese.

Mix (miks), *sb.* 1586. [f. MIX *v.*] Chiefly *colloq.*: A muddle, mess also, a state of being mixed or confused.

Mix (miks), *v.* Pa. t. and pple. **mixed** (mikst). 1480. [Back-formation from *mixt* (see MIXED *ppl. a.*). Cf. MIXT *v.*] 1. *trans.* To put together (two or more substances, groups, or classes) so that the particles or members of each are more or less evenly diffused among those of the rest; to mingle, blend. Also with *with.* b. With immaterial obj. 1597. †c. To put in as an ingredient, to intersperse. Const. *to.* -1742. d. To prepare (a compound) by putting ingredients together 1592. e. *hyperbolically.* To confound 1667. 2. *intr.* = to be mixed. Also, to admit of being mixed; to go (well or badly) along with 1632. 3. *trans.* To unite (persons) in dealings or acquaintance. Chiefly *refl.* and *pass.* Now *rare.* 1535. 4. *intr.* To have intercourse *with* (occas. *among*); to take part *in* 1667. b. To have sexual intercourse *with* 1615. c. To join battle. DRYDEN. 5. *trans.* and *intr.* To cross in breeding 1737.

1. Aufidius, myxt heddy wyne, and honey all in one 1566. Oxygen gas and sulphurous acid gas probably combine when simply mixed together 1811. b. Brothers, you mixe your Sadnesse with some Feare SHAKS. d. Had'st thou no poyson mixt? SHAKS. e. MILT. *P.L.* VII. 215. 2. Her dear idea mixes with every scene of pleasure GOLDSM. 4. To m. in the best society 1872.

Mix up. a. *trans.* To m. intimately, to m. *with* something else. b. In immaterial applications. Now only: To m. irrelevantly or unsuitably; to confuse. c. To associate *with* (inferior or bad company); to connect *with*, involve *in* (something 'shady'). Chiefly *refl.* and *pass.*

Mixed, †**mixt** (mikst), *ppl. a.* 1448. [Orig. *mixt*, a. F. *mixte*, ad. L. *mixtus*, pa. pple. of *miscere.* *Mixt* being taken as an Eng. pple. in *-t*, was alternatively spelt with *-ed*, whence the vb. MIX.] 1. *Law.* Formerly applied to an action which partook of the nature both of a real and of a personal action. 2. In senses of MIX *v.* 1530. 3. Of a company of persons: Not select, containing persons of doubtful character or status 1611. 4. Of sciences: Involving matter; not pure or simply theoretical. Now *rare* exc. in *m. mathematics.* 1641. 5. Comprising both sexes 1644. 6.

colloq. Muddled; *esp.* muzzy with drink 1872. 7. *Phonetics.* Of a vowel sound: Intermediate between *high* and *low*; pronounced with the tongue in a flattened position 1867.

2. Unbounded liberty of the press..is one of the evils attending..mixt forms of Government HUME. 5. *M. school*, one in which boys and girls are taught together. *M. bathing*.

Spec. collocations: †**m. angle,** a mixtilinear angle; **m. marriage,** a marriage between persons of different races or religions; **m. metal,** an alloy; **m. metaphor,** the combination of inconsistent metaphors in one figure; **m. number,** the sum of an integer and a fraction; **m. train,** a railway train made up of both passenger-carriages and goods-wagons; formerly also a train carrying different classes of passengers. Hence **Mi·xed-ly** *adv.*, **-ness.**

Mixen (mi·ksən). Now *dial.* or *arch.* [OE. *mixen* :—**mihsinnja*, f. **mihso-*, f. wk. grade of Teut. root **mĭgh-*.] 1. A dunghill; also, a compost-heap used for manure. 2. A term of abuse for a woman (*dial.*) 1764.

Mi·xer. 1611. One who or that which mixes. b. orig. *U.S.* A person in respect of his capacity for mixing with others; esp. *a good m.* 1896.

Mix-Hellene (mikshelī·n) 1856. [ad. Gr. μιξέλλην: see MIXO- and HELLENE.] A person of mixed Greek and barbarian blood.

Mixo- (mi·kso), repr. Gr. μιξο-, f. root of μιγνύναι, with the sense 'mixed', as **Mixo·gamous** [Gr. γάμος] *a.*, *Ichth.* (of fishes) given to promiscuous pairing; **Mixo·gamy,** the condition of being mixogamous; etc.

Mixolydian (miksoli·diăn), *a.* 1589. [f. Gr. μιξο-λύδιος half-Lydian; see MIXO- and LYDIAN.] *Mus.* a. The highest in pitch of the modes in ancient Greek music. b. The fourth of the 'authentic' ecclesiaetical modes, having G for its final and D for its dominant.

†**Mixt,** *sb.* 1589. [ad. L. *mixtum*, neut. of *mixtus*; see MIXED *ppl. a.*] 1. A substance consisting of different elements mixed together; esp. in *Old Chem.*, a compound -1805. 2. In immaterial applications: A compound -1647.

†**Mixt,** *v.* 1526. [Inferred from the pa. pple *mixt* (see MIXED *ppl. a.*).] = MIX *v.* -1609.

Mixtilinear (mikstili·niăɹ), *a.* 1702. [f. L. *mixtus*, after *rectilinear*.] Formed or bounded partly by straight, partly by curved lines. So **Mixtili·neal** *a.*

†**Mi·xtion.** late ME. [a. F., ad. L. *mixtionem*, f. *miscere* (*mixt-*); see MIXED *ppl. a.*] = MIXTURE 1, 2, 3, 5. -1757.

Mixture (mi·kstiŭɹ, -tʃəɹ). 1460. [ad. L. *mixtura*, f. *mixt-* (see prec.).] 1. The action, process, or fact of mixing or becoming mixed; also, an instance of this 1530. b. Mixed state or condition 1597. 2. *concr.* A product of mixing 1460. 3. *spec.* a. A medicinal preparation of two or more ingredients mixed together. In *Pharmacy*, now applied to potions or liquid medicines. 1592. b. A cloth of variegated fabric, as *Heather, Oxford m.* 1722. c. A blend of tea, tobacco, snuff, etc. 1840. d. Gas or vaporized oil mixed with air, forming the explosive charge in an internal-combustion engine 1894. 4. The mechanical mixing of two substances as dist. from (*chemical*) *combination*; also *concr.* the product of such a mixing, as dist. from a *compound* 1797. b. A fluid containing some foreign substance in suspension; opp. to *solution* 1765. 5. The action or an act of adding as an ingredient; the presence of a foreign element in the composition of something; quasi-*concr.* an amount or proportion of something foreign that has been added; admixture. *Without m.*: unmixed, pure. 1526. 6. *Mus.* In full *m.-stop*: An organ-stop comprising several ranks of pipes, used in combination with the foundation-stops 1688.

1. b. There was a m. of company SWIFT. 2. A fatal m. of weakness and temerity 1732. 3. a. What if this m. do not worke at all? SHAKS. 5. The same shall drinke of the wine of the wrath of God, which is powred out without m. into the cup of his indignation *Rev.* xiv. 10.

Mizen, mizzen (mi·z'n). 1465. [a. F. *misaine*, said to be ad. It. *mezzana* mizen-sail; the It. word is fem. of *mezzano* middle.] *Naut.* 1. (Also **mizen-sail.**) A fore-and-aft sail set on the after side of the mizen-mast. Often synonymous with SPANKER. 2. = MIZEN-MAST. Now *rare.* 1583. 3. *attrib.*, as *m.-boom* 1485.

Mi·zen-mast. 1420. The aftermost mast of a three-masted ship. So **Mi·zen-to·p,** the 'top' of a mizen-mast; a platform just above the head of the lower mizen-mast 1667. **Mi·zen-topga·llant-mast,** the mast above the mizen-topmast 1864. **Mi·zen-to·pmast,** the mast next above the lower mizen-mast 1626. **Mi·zen-to·psail,** the sail set on the mizen-topmast 1626. **Mi·zen-yard,** the yard on which the mizen-sail is extended 1485.

Mizmaze (mi·zmeⁱz). 1547. [Redupl. of MAZE *sb.*] †1. A labyrinth or maze. Chiefly *fig.* -1794. 2. Mystification. Chiefly *dial.* 1604.

Mizzle (mi·z'l), *sb. Obs.* or *dial.* 1490. [f. MIZZLE *v.*[1]] Slight or drizzling rain, drizzle.

Mizzle (mi·z'l), *v.*[1] *dial.* 1483. [Cogn. w. Du. dial. *miezelen*, LG. *miseln*, etc.; see -LE 3.] 1. *intr.* (*impers.*) To drizzle. †2. *trans.* Of a cloud (also *impers.*): To send down in a drizzling shower -1592. **Mi·zzly** *a.* 1566.

Mizzle (mi·z'l), *v.*[2] *slang.* 1781. [?] *intr.* To disappear suddenly; *imper.* = be off!

Mizzy (mi·zi). *dial.* [ME. *misy*; cf. OE. *mēos* moss, bog.] A quagmire.

‖**Mna.** 1603. [Gr. μνᾶ.] = MINA [1].

‖**Mneme** (nī·mi). 1913. [Gr. 'memory'.] *Psychol.* Capacity for retaining after-effects of experience or stimulation.

Mnemonic (nīmǫ·nik). 1753. [ad. Gr. μνημονικός, f. μνημον-, μνήμων mindful, f. μνα-, μνᾶσθαι to remember.] A. *adj.* 1. Intended to aid the memory; pertaining to mnemonics. 2. Of or pertaining to memory 1825.

2. The m. power of the late Professor Porson 1825.

B. *sb.* a. A mnemonic device. b. = MNEMONICS. 1858. So **Mnemo·nical** *a.* = A. 1. **Mnemo·nically** *adv.* **Mnemoni·cian, Mne·monist,** one versed in mnemonics. **Mnemo·nics** *sb. pl.* [see *-ics*, -IC 2], the art of assisting the memory, esp. by artificial aids; a system of precepts intended to aid the memory 1721. Also **Mne·motechny** (-te:kni), mnemonics 1845.

Mo (mōᵘ), *adv.*, quasi-*sb.*, and *a.* †Also moe. *Obs.* exc. *Sc.* and *n.* (mae). [Com. Teut.: OE. *mā*:—OTeut. **maiz*.] †A. *adv.* 1. In or to a greater degree, extent, or quantity -ME. 2. Longer, further, again. Chiefly qualified by *any, no, none*; *ever, never.* -1812. B. quasi-*sb.* †1. A greater number; more of the kind specified -1684. 2. Others of the kind specified OE. C. *adj.* = MORE *a.* OE.

A. 2. Gent'lest fair, mourne, mourne no moe FLETCHER. B. 2. And besides which axioms, there are divers moe BACON.

Mo (mōᵘ). 1896. Colloq. abbrev. of MOMENT.

‖**Moa** (mōᵘ·ă). 1842. [Maori.] A giant extinct flightless bird of New Zealand, *Dinornis gigantea*, allied to the kiwi.

Moabite (mōᵘ·ăbəit), *sb.* and *a.* late ME. [ad. L. *Moabita* (Gr. Μωαβίτης, repr. Heb. *mōābī*), f. *Moab* + -ITE [1].] A. *sb.* One of the people of Moab, which bordered on the territory of the trans-Jordanic Israelites. In 16–17th c. applied opprobriously to Roman Catholics. B. *adj.* Pertaining to Moab or the Moabites 1870.

The M. stone, a monument erected by Mesha king of Moab *c* 850 B.C., furnishing the earliest known inscription in the Phoenician alphabet.

Hence **Mo·abitish** *a.*

Moan (mōᵘn), *sb.* ME. [app. repr. OE. **mān* :—**main-*, whence OE. *mǣnan* to mourn.] 1. Complaint, lamentation; a complaint, lament. Now apprehended as a transf. use of 2. †b. A state of grief or lamentation -1631. 2. In mod. use: A low mournful murmur (less deep than a groan) indicative of physical or mental suffering 1673. b. *transf.* of the plaintive sound produced by the wind, water, etc. 1813.

1. A carpenter..made such pitiful m. to be taken in DE FOE. b. Thy mirth shall turne to moane SHAKS. 2. M. of an enemy massacred TENNYSON. b. The brooklet's m. SCOTT. The m. of the adjacent pines TYNDALL.

Moan (mōᵘn), *v.* 1548 (earlier possible exx. are doubtful). [f. prec.] 1. *trans.* To complain of, lament; to bewail 1548. †b. *refl.* To bewail one's lot -1642. †2. To condole with (a person) -1669. 3. *intr.* To make complaint or lamentation. Const. *of, for.* Now *arch.* or *poet.* 1593. 4. *intr.* To utter a moan or moans 1724. b. *transf.* of inanimate things 1805. 5. *trans.* To utter moaningly.

1. This man was greatly moaned of the people STOW. 3. And what is life, that we should m.? TENNYSON. 4. In bed she moaning lay WORDSW. b. Though the harbour bar be moaning KINGSLEY. 5. Fair Madeline began to weep And m. forth witless words KEATS. Hence **Moa·ningly** *adv.*

Moanful (mōᵘ·nfŭl), *a.* 1573. [f. MOAN *sb.* + -FUL.] 1. Full of moaning; expressing lamentation or grief. Now somewhat *rare.* 1586. †2. Causing lamentation -1662. Hence **Moa·nfully** *adv.*

Moat (mōᵘt), *sb.* [ME. *mote, mot*, app. identical w. MOTE *sb.*[2] mound, etc., a. OF. *mote, motte.*] 1. *Fortif.* A deep and wide ditch surrounding a town, castle, etc., usually filled with water. 2. A pond, lake; *esp.* a fish-pond. *Obs.* exc. *dial.* 1463.

1. The siluer sea, Which serues it in the office of a wall, Or as a Moate defensiue to a house SHAKS.

Moat (mōᵘt), *v.* late ME. [f. MOAT *sb.*] *trans.* To surround with or as with a moat, ditch, or trench. Also with *about, in, round.*

The torrent broke down the quays...We were moated into our house all day H. WALPOLE.

Mob (mǫb), *sb.*[1] 1688. [Abbrev. of MOBILE *sb.*[2]] 1. The disorderly and riotous part of the population, the rabble; a tumultuous crowd bent on lawlessness. 2. The lower orders; the uncultured or illiterate as a class; the masses 1691. †3. Without *the* -1789. 4. A promiscuous assemblage of people. In Australian use, without disparaging implication, a crowd. 1688. b. *transf.* and *fig.* of things, etc. *Obs.* exc. *Austral.* 1728. 5. *slang.* A gang of thieves or pickpockets working together 1843.

1. When mobs were roaring themselves hoarse for 'Wilkes and liberty' GREEN. 2. The m. of the great cities..is hostile to us DUFF. 3. I saw the street..full of m. DE FOE. 4. The M. of Gentlemen who wrote with Ease POPE. A m. of steady men 1890. b. She sees a M. of Metaphors advance POPE. 5. *Swell m.*, a class of pickpockets who dress stylishly.

Comb. **m. law,** 'law' imposed and enforced by a m.

Mob (mǫb), *sb.*[2] *Obs.* exc. *Hist.* 1665. [Cf. MOB *v.*[1] and MAB.] †1. *Cant.* A strumpet -1697. †2. A négligé attire -1712. 3. = MOB-CAP 1748.

†**Mob,** *v.*[1] 1664. [Cf. prec. and MOBLE *v.*] *trans.* To muffle the head of (a person); to dress untidily -1837.

To m. (it), to go a-mobbing: to go in disguise to the unfashionable part of a theatre, etc. Hence, to frequent low company.

Mob (mǫb), *v.*[2] 1709. [f. MOB *sb.*[1]] 1. *trans.* To attack in a mob; to crowd round and molest; to throng. Also, to force *into* something by such action. 2. *intr.* To congregate in a mob; also *to m. it* 1711. 3. *trans.* To mix *up* with a mob. TENNYSON.

Mobbish (mǫ·biʃ), *a.* 1695. [f. MOB *sb.*[1] + -ISH [1].] Resembling a mob; disorderly, tumultuous. Also, †appealing to the mob; vulgar, clap-trap.

His m. fallacious way of arguing 1711. An irregular and m. appearance SCOTT.

Mobble: see MOBLE.

Mob-cap. 1812. [f. MOB *sb.*[2]] An indoor cap worn by women in the 18th and early 19th c.

A mob-cap; I mean a cap,..with side-pieces fastening under the chin DICKENS.

Mobile (mōᵘ·bil), *sb.*[1] 1549. [a. F. *mobile* (in *premier mobile*, etc.), a. L. *mobile* adj. neut.; see MOBILE *a.*] †1. *First, grand, great, principal m.*, anglicized forms of PRIMUM MOBILE (*lit.* and *fig.*) -1797. 2. *Metaph.* A body in motion or capable of movement. Now *rare.* 1676.

Mobile (mōᵘ·bilĭ), *sb.*[2] *arch.* 1676. [Short for L. *mobile vulgus* the excitable crowd.] The populace, rabble, MOB.

Yᵉ mobele was very rud to yᵉ Dutch Imbasidor 1679.

Mobile (mōᵘ·bəil, -il), *a.* 1490. [a. F., ad. L. *mobilis*, f. *mo-*, *movere* to MOVE.] 1. Capable of movement; movable 1490. b. Of a limb, etc.; Movable; not fixed, free 1828. c. Of a fluid: That has its particles capable of free movement. d. Of a cell, molecule, etc.: Free; not adnate or fixed 1871. 2. Characterized by facility of movement. a. Of features: Easily changing in expression 1851. b. Of persons: Wanting in stability; also, versatile 1855. 3. *Mil.* Of troops: That may be rapidly moved from place to place 1879.

1. †*M. spirits*, the 'spirits' by which the motor impulses were supposed to be transmitted to the muscles. 2. a. The thin m. lips..picture the inner soul of the man GREEN. b. Women's minds are by nature more m. than those of men, less capable of persisting long in the same continuous effort MILL.

Mobiliary (mobi·liări), *a.* 1682. [ad.F. *mobiliaire*, f. L. *mobilis* movable; see -ARY[1].] 1. In the Channel Islands: Relating to movable property. 2. *Mil.* Pertaining to mobilization 1888.

Mobility[1] (mobi·lĭti). 1490. [a. F. *mobilité*, ad. L. *mobilitas*, f. *mobilis*; see MOBILE and -ITY.] The quality or condition of being mobile.

Nature not having given that m. to the eyes of flies BOYLE. To promote the m. of labour and capital 1889.

Mobility[2] (mobi·lĭti). 1690. [f. MOBILE *sb.*[2], MOB *sb.*[1], after *nobility*.] The mob; the lower classes.

Mobilization (mōu:biləizē·ʃən). 1799. [a. F. *mobilisation*, f. *mobiliser*; see next and -ATION.] The action or process of mobilizing. 1. *Law.* The conversion of real or immovable property into personal or movable property. 2. *Mil.* and *Naval.* The mobilizing (an army, a fleet, etc.) 1866.

Mobilize (mōu·biləiz), *v.* 1838. [ad. F. *mobiliser*, f. *mobile*; see MOBILE *a.*] 1. *trans.* To render movable or capable of movement; to bring into circulation. 2. *Mil.* To prepare (an army or fleet) for active service 1853. b. *intr.* (for *pass.*) To undergo mobilization 1878.

Moble, mobble (mǫ·b'l), *v.* *Obs.* exc. *dial.* 1603. [frequent. f. MOB *v.*[1] Cf. MABBLE *v.*] *trans.* To muffle (one's) head or face. Chiefly with *up*.

But who, O who had seene the mobled Queene? *Haml.* (Qos.) II. ii. 524.

Mobocracy (mǫbǫ·krăsi). 1754. [f. MOB *sb.*[1]: see -CRACY.] 1. Government by a mob. 2. The mob as a ruling body 1754.

2. The shopocracy in the pit, and the m. in the gallery 1856. So **Mo·bocrat**, a demagogue 1798. **Mobocra·tic** *a.* 1775.

Mobsman (mǫ·bzmăen). 1851. [f. *mob's*, genitive of MOB *sb.*[1]] 1. One of a mob 1868. 2. (In full *swell m.*) A member of the swell mob (see MOB *sb.*[1] 5).

Moccasin (mǫ·kăsin). 1612. [a. Powhatan *mo·ckasin*, Odjibwa *ma·kisin*, Narragansett *moku·ssin*, etc.] 1. A kind of foot-gear made of deerskin or other soft leather, worn by N. Amer. Indians, trappers, backwoodsmen, etc. 2. [Perh. a distinct word.] In full **M. snake**: a venomous crotaline snake, *Ancistrodon piscivorus*, of the Southern U.S. *Highland* or *Upland M.*, the Cottonmouth, *A. atrofuscus*, a similar snake inhabiting the dry land and mountainous regions. 1791.

M. flower, plant, U.S. name for the genus *Cypripedium* (Lady's Slipper); **yellow m.**, *C. pubescens*. Hence **Mo·cassined** *a.*

Mocha[1] (mōu·kă). 1679. [Prob. identical with the place-name MOCHA[2]. Now written with capital M.] 1. (Also *M. stone, pebble.*) A variety of chalcedony resembling or identical with moss-agate. 2. One of several geometrid moths, esp. of the genus *Ephyra* 1775.

Mocha[2] (mōu·kă). 1773. [Name of an Arabian port at the entrance of the Red Sea.] In full, *M. coffee*: a fine quality of coffee; orig. that produced in the Yemen province, in which Mocha is situated.

Moche, obs. f. MUCH *sb.*, *a.*, and *adv.*

Mochel(l, -il(l, obs. ff. MICKLE.

Mock (mǫk), *sb.* Now *rare* or *arch.* 1440. [f. MOCK *v.*] 1. An act of mocking or derision. b. Mockery 1568. 2. Something deserving of scorn 1489. 3. The action of mocking or imitating; *concr.* an imitation, a counterfeit 1646.

1. He..called me boye, and gave me many a mocke 1509. Phr. *To make a m. of*: to bring into contempt.

Mock (mǫk), *a.* (Not used predicatively.) 1548. [Partly f. prec., partly f. stem of MOCK *v.* in comb. with an object. The hyphen is still often used in the collocations of the adj. with sbs.] Prefixed to a sb.; = sham, counterfeit, imitation, pretended.

I feare me some be rather mocke gospellers then faythful ploughmen LATIMER. That superior Greatness and Mock-Majesty, which is ascribed to the Prince of the fallen Angels ADDISON. A m. trial in which their enemies were judges THIRLWALL.

Spec. collocations (usu. hyphened): **m. auction**, a Dutch auction (see AUCTION *sb.* 3); also, a fraudulent auction, in which confederates bid briskly in order to elicit genuine bids; **-lead** = BLENDE; **-moon** = PARASELENE; **-rainbow**, a secondary rainbow (see RAINBOW); **-sun** = PARHELION. Also in names of culinary preparations, as **m.-duck, -goose**, a piece of pork from which the crackling has been removed, baked with a stuffing of sage and onions (*colloq.*); **-venison**, leg of mutton long hung, cooked after the manner of venison. b. In names of plants, as **m.-orange**, (*a*) the common syringa, *Philadelphus coronarius*; (*b*) the Carolina cherry-laurel, *Prunus caroliniana*; (*c*) the Australian native laurel, *Pittosporum undulatum*. c. In names of birds, as **m.-nightingale**, the Blackcap, the Sedge-warbler.

Comb. a. with adjs. and advs. with sense 'counterfeitly'. Chiefly implying humorous or ludicrous simulation, as in MOCK-HEROIC. b. With a vb., with joc. sense 'pretendingly', as *mock-knight*.

Mock (mǫk), *v.* [ME. *mokken*, *mocque*, ad. OF. *mocquer* (F. *moquer*) to deride, jeer = Pr. *mocar*; cf. Pg. *moca.*] 1. *trans.* To hold up to ridicule; to deride 1450. b. To defy; to set at nought 1558. c. *fig.* of impersonal things 1667. 2. *intr.* To act or speak in derision; to jeer, scoff; to flout. Const. *at*, †*with*. 1450. †b. To jest -1611. 3. *trans.* To impose upon; to befool; to tantalize 1470. 4. To ridicule by imitation of speech or action. (The current colloq. use.) Hence, to mimic, counterfeit. 1595. †b. To simulate, make a false pretence of. SHAKS.

1. M. not a Cobler for his black thumbes FULLER. b. Let's mocke the midnight Bell SHAKS. c. A perishing That mocks the gladness of the Spring WORDSW. 2. I wil mocke when your feare commeth *Prov.* i. 26. b. *Gen.* xix. 14. 3. Behold, thou hast mocked me, and told mee lies *Judg.* xvi. 10. 4. Prepare To see the Life as liuely mock'd, as euer Still Sleepe mock'd Death SHAKS. He mocks and mimics all he sees and hears 1822. b. 3 *Hen. VI*, III. iii. 255. Hence **Mo·ckable** *a.*

†**Mockado** (mǫkā·do). 1543. [app. a corruption of It. *mocaiardo* mohair.] A kind of cloth much used for clothing in the 16th and 17th centuries. Also *attrib.*, as *m. doublet*, etc. -1660. b. *fig.* as the type of an inferior material. Also *attrib.* or *adj.*: Trumpery, inferior. -1741.

b. Fustian, or m. Eloquence 1621.

†**Mo·ckage.** 1470. [f. MOCK *v.* + -AGE.] (Very common in 16th and 17th c.) = MOCKERY 1 and 2. -1686.

Mo·ck-bird. 1649. [f. MOCK *sb.* + BIRD *sb.*] = MOCKING-BIRD.

Mocker (mǫ·kəɹ). 1477. [f. MOCK *v.* + -ER[1].] One who or that which mocks or scoffs. b. A mocking-bird 1773.

Mockery (mǫ·kəri). late ME. [a. F. *moquerie*, f. *moquer* to MOCK.] 1. Derision; a derisive utterance or action. b. A subject or occasion of derision 1560. 2. Mimicry; a counterfeit representation; an unreal appearance. Now only, an impudent simulation. 1599. 3. Ludicrously or insultingly futile action 1602. 4. *attrib.*, as *m. King* 1593.

1. Wherefore was I to this keene m. borne? SHAKS. b. Genius will have become a m., and virtue an empty shade HAZLITT. 2. Hence horrible shadow, Vnreal mock'ry hence SHAKS. The m. of a trial 1872. 3. It is as the Ayre, invulnerable, And our vaine blowes, malicious M. SHAKS.

Mo·ck-hero·ic, *a.* and *sb.* 1711. [f. MOCK *a.*] A. *adj.* Imitating in a burlesque manner the heroic style. B. *sb.* A burlesque imitation of the heroic style 1728.

Mo·cking-bird. 1676. [f. *mocking* ppl. a.] 1. An Amer. passerine song-bird of the genus *Mimus*, esp. *M. polyglottus*, characterized by its habit of mimicking the notes of other birds. 2. Applied to other birds having a similar aptitude; esp. the Sedge-warbler and the Blackcap 1779.

Mockingly (mǫ·kiŋli), *adv.* 1545. [f. *mocking* ppl. a. + -LY[2].] In a mocking manner.

†**Mo·cking-stock.** 1526. [f. *mocking* vbl. sb. + STOCK.] A laughing-stock -1833.

Mock turtle. 1763. [MOCK *a.*] 1. Calf's head dressed with sauces and condiments so as to resemble turtle. 2. (In full, *Mock turtle soup.*) A soup made (usu. of calf's head) in imitation of turtle soup 1783.

‖**Moco** (mōu·ko). 1834. [Tupi *mocó.*] The rock cavy, *Cavia rupestris*.

Mod., abbrev. for MODERN, MODERATO.

Modal (mōu·dăl), *a.* (*sb.*) 1569. [ad. med.L. *modalis*, f. L. *modus*; see MODE and -AL.] 1. Pertaining to mode or form as opp. to substance 1625. 2. *Law.* Of a legacy, contract, etc.: Containing provisions defining the manner in which it is to take effect 1590. 3. *Mus.* Pertaining to mode 1597. 4. *Logic.* Of a proposition: Involving the affirmation of possibility, impossibility, necessity, or contingency; or, according to others, a proposition in which the predicate is affirmed or denied of the subject with any kind of qualification. Of a syllogism: Containing a modal proposition as a premiss. 1569. 5. *Gram.* a. Of or pertaining to mood; performing the function of a mood. b. Of a particle: Denoting manner or modality. 1798. 6. *sb.* A modal proposition (see sense 4) 1725. Hence **Mo·dally** *adv.*, with ref. to mode or manner.

Modalism (mōu·dăliz'm). 1859. [f. prec. + -ISM.] The Sabellian doctrine that the distinction in the Trinity is 'modal' only, i.e. that the Father, the Son, and the Holy Spirit are merely three different modes of manifestation of the Divine nature. So **Mo·dalist** 1832. **Modali·stic** *a.*

Modality (modæ·lĭti). 1545. [ad. med.L. *modalitas*, f. *modalis*; see MODAL and -ITY.] 1. The quality or fact of being modal; state or condition in respect of mode or manner. Now *rare*. 2. *Logic.* a. In the scholastic logic, the fact of being a modal proposition or syllogism. Also, the modal qualification. 1628. b. In Kant, etc., that feature of a judgement which causes it to be classed as problematic, assertory, or apodictic 1836.

Mode (mōud). late ME. [In branch I, ad. L. *modus* measure, etc., f. W. Indo-Eur. **mod-* (: **med-*; see METE *v.*[1]). In branch II, a. F. *mode* fem., ad. L. *modus* (with change of gender due to final *e*); the Fr. word (= fashion) was adopted into Eng. in the 17th c.] I. 1. *Mus.* †a. A tune, air. b. A kind or form of scale; a particular scheme or system of sounds. (*a*) In ancient Greek music: Each of the scales (Dorian, Phrygian, Lydian, etc.), according to one or other of which a piece of music in the diatonic style was composed 1674. (*b*) In mediæval church music: Each of the scales in which PLAINSONG was composed; beginning on different notes of the natural scale, and thus having the intervals (tones and semitones) differently arranged 1721. (*c*) In mod. music: Each of the two classes (*major* and *minor*) of keys, having the intervals differently arranged. Formerly sometimes = KEY *sb.*[1] II. 5 b. 1721. †2. *Gram.* = MOOD *sb.*[2] 2. 1520–1843. 3. *Logic.* [= med.L. *modus*, tr. Gr. τρόπος.] a. = MOOD *sb.*[2] 1. 1532. b. The character of a modal proposition; each of the four kinds into which modal propositions are divided (see MODAL 4) 1852. 4. A way or manner of doing or being; a method of procedure 1667. 5. A form, manner, or variety. Now *rare* exc. in *m. of life* and similar uses. 1661. 6. *Philos.* a. A manner or state of being of a thing; a thing considered as possessing certain non-essential attributes. b. An attribute or quality of a substance 1677. 7. *Mus.* In mensurable music, the proportion (3 or 2) of a long to a large or a breve to a long, determining the rhythm of a piece. Now *Hist.* 1667.

4. A regular m. of bringing to an amicable adjustment..any questions which might hereafter arise WELLINGTON. 5. Every m. of life has its conveniences JOHNSON. The m. of superstition which prevailed in their own times GIBBON. Heat considered as a M. of Motion TYNDALL (*title*). 6. a. That a Spirit is not an Accident or M. of Substance, all in a manner profess GLANVILL. *Mixed m.*: a mode formed by the combination of different simple ideas.

II. 1. A prevailing fashion or custom, practice or style 1645. 2. Conventional usage in dress, manners, habit of life, etc., esp. among persons of fashion 1692. **3.** *The m.*: the fashion for the time being (*arch.*) 1649. †**4.** = ALAMODE 4. 1751-(*Hist.*).

1. Larding of meat after the m. of France HOWELL. 3. The m. she fixes by the gown she wears YOUNG. What do you take to be the most fashionable age about town? Some time ago, forty was all the m. GOLDSM.

Model (mǫ·dĕl), *sb.* 1575. [a. OF. *modelle* (mod.F. *modèle*), ad. It. *modello*, dim. of *modo*, ad. L. *modus* MODE.] **I.** Representation of structure. †**1.** An architect's set of designs for a projected building; hence, a similar set of drawings representing an existing building. Also occas. a delineation of a ground-plan. -1714. †**b.** *transf.* A summary, epitome, or abstract -1772. **2.** A representation in three dimensions of some projected or existing structure, or of some material object, showing the proportions and arrangement of its parts 1610. **b.** *fig.* Something that accurately resembles something else. *Obs.* exc. *dial.* in *the* (*very*) *model of.* 1593. †**3.** A mould; something that envelops closely. SHAKS. †**4.** A small portrait. Hence confused with MEDAL. -1658. **5.** An object or figure made in clay, wax, etc., and intended to be reproduced in more durable material 1686.

1. When we meane to build, We first surųey the Plot, then draw the Modell SHAKS. 2. *Working m.*, one so constructed as to imitate the movements of the machine represented.

II. Type of design. **1.** Design; style of structure or form; pattern, build, make 1593. †**2.** Scale of construction; allotted measure; the measure of a person's ability -1675. **3.** Of a violin, viol, etc.: Curvature of surface 1836.

1. *The* (*New*) *M.* (Hist.): the plan for the reorganization of the Parliamentary army, passed in 1644-5. b. In dressmaking, etc., any article made by a recognized designer; any copy of such an article; also, a motor car, etc. of a particular design. 2. Thus much (considering the modell of the whole worke) is sufficient HOBBES.

III. An object of imitation. **1.** A person, or work, that is proposed or adopted for imitation 1639. **2.** A person who poses for artists and art-students 1691. **b.** A mannequin. **3.** A perfect exemplar *of* some excellence 1700.

1. I then resolved some m. to pursue, Perused French critics, and began anew GAY. 3. Mr. Gray thought the narrative of Thucydides the m. of history 1805.

attrib. and *Comb.* Serving as, or suited to be, a model, exemplary; as *m. lodging-house, m. dwellings. Spec.* **m.-drawing**, in art-teaching, drawing in perspective from solid figures; **-room**, a room for the storage or exhibition of models of machinery, etc.

Model (mǫ·dĕl), *v.* 1604. [f. prec. sb.] †**1.** *trans.* To present as in an outline; to portray in detail -1667. **2.** To produce in clay, wax, or the like (a figure or imitation of anything) 1665. **3.** To give shape to (a document, argument, etc.) 1625. **b.** To form after a particular model. Usu. const. *after, on, upon.* 1730. †**4.** To organize (a community, a government, etc.) -1842. †**5.** To train or mould (a person) to a mode of life; also, to make a tool of -1734. **6.** To act or pose as a model (III. 2, b) 1927.

1. Cease dreames,..To modell forth the passions of to morrow DRUMM. OF HAWTH. MILT. *P. L.* VIII. 79. 3. Budgets..modelled too much on..free-trade principles 1885. b. He modelled his court on that of Nádir Sháh ELPHINSTONE. Hence **Mo·deller** 1603.

†**Mo·delize,** *v.* 1599. [f. MODEL *sb.* + -IZE.] *trans.* To model -1810. Hence **Mo·delizing** *ppl. a.* formative.

Modelling (mǫ·dĕliŋ), *vbl. sb.* 1799. [f. MODEL *v.* + -ING[1].] The action or art of making models; the art of making a model in clay or wax to be copied in more durable materials by the sculptor or founder; the representation of solid form in sculpture, or of material relief and solidity in painting.

attrib., as *m.-clay, -stick, -tool, -wax.*

Modena (mǫ·dĭnă). 1822. [Name of an Italian city.] A deep purple colour.

Moder, obs. f. MOTHER.

Moderantism (mǫ·dĕrăntiz'm). *Obs.* exc. *Hist.* 1793. [a. F. *modérantisme*, f. *modérant*, pr. pple. of *modérer*, ad. L. *moderari*: see below.] In France, during the Revolution, and later, the doctrines and spirit of the Moderate party in politics. So **Mo·derantist.**

Moderate (mǫ·dĕrĕt), *a.* and *sb.* late ME. [ad. L. *moderatus*, pa. pple. of *moderari*; see next.] **A.** *adj.* **1.** Exhibiting moderation; avoiding extremes; temperate in conduct or expression. **2.** Not strongly partisan 1644. **b.** Hence (now usu. with initial capital) used as the designation of various parties and their views: see B. below 1753. **3.** Fairly large or good; tolerable. Now, mediocre, scanty. late ME. **b.** Of physical processes, etc.: Not intense, violent, or rigorous. Of the voice: Neither loud nor low. late ME. Of prices, charges: Not high 1904.

1. Sound sleepe commeth of m. eating *Ecclus.* xxxi. 20. 2. The temptation to a Prime Minister is to appoint only 'moderate' men 1889. b. The M. clergy..were very unpopular 1848. 3. There's not so much left to furnish out a m. Table SHAKS. The rest are very m. productions PUSEY. b. Winde that is m. and not contraryouse to Shypmen. late ME. Bake them in a m. oven 1769. **Mo·derate·ly** *adv.*, **-ness.**

B. *sb.* One who holds moderate opinions in politics, religion, etc. Hence (now usu. with initial capital), a member of any party customarily called 'Moderate'; e. g. in the French Revolution, applied to the Girondins. 1794. **b.** In the Church of Scotland in the 18th and early 19th c., a member of that party which held lax views on doctrine and discipline. **c.** In recent municipal politics (opp. to *Progressive*): A member of the party hostile to undertakings involving large expenditure 1894.

Moderate (mǫ·dĕreit), *v.* late ME. [f. L. *moderat-, moderari*, f. **moder-* :—**modes-* (whence *modestus* MODEST), a noun-stem parallel with *modo-, modus* measure, MODE.] **1.** *trans.* To render less violent, intense, rigorous, or burdensome; †to reduce (a fine, charge, etc.). **b.** *intr.* for *refl.* To become less violent, etc. Now *rare.* 1678. †**2.** *trans.* To regulate, restrain, control, rule -1808. †**b.** To adjust, arrange; to modify -1630. **3.** In academic and Eccl. use: To preside over (a deliberative body) or at (a debate, etc.) 1577. **b.** *intr.* To act as moderator; to preside 1581. †**4.** *trans.* To settle as an arbitrator -1744. †Also *absol.* or *intr.* To act as mediator or arbitrator -1756.

1. I..advise you to m. your demands 1732. b. Fortunately the weather moderated 1897. 2. The woman was ordayned..to gouerne and m. the house at home 1615. 3. b. Phr. *To moderate* (*in*) *a call*; in the Scottish Presbyterian churches, to preside over a meeting of a congregation for signing a call to a minister-elect; hence, to sign such a call. 4. It passeth mine abilitie to m. the question CAREW. Endeavouring to m. between the rival Powers SWIFT.

Moderation (mǫdĕrēɪ·ʃən). late ME. [a. F. *modération*, ad. L. *moderationem*; see prec. and -ATION.] **1.** The action or an act of moderating (see prec.). Now *rare* or *Obs.* **2.** The quality of being moderate; now *esp.*: avoidance of extremes; self-control, temperance; occas. clemency. late ME. **3.** *pl.* In the Univ. of Oxford, the 'First Public Examination' for the degree of B.A., conducted by the Moderators (see MODERATOR 4 a). Colloq. abbrev. MODS. 1858.

1. What is all Virtue but a M. of Excesses? SOUTH. 2. Can you write with sufficient m., as 'tis called, when one suppresses the one half of what one feels or could say on a subject? LAMB. Phr. *In m.*: in a moderate manner or proportion.

Moderatism (mǫ·dĕrătiz'm). 1795. [f. MODERATE *a.* and *sb.* + -ISM.] The doctrines or policy of any of the parties known as 'Moderate'; addiction to moderate views or courses of action. So **Mo·deratist** 1716.

‖**Moderato** (mǫdĕrā·to). 1724. [It.; cf. MODERATE.] *Mus.* A direction: At a moderate pace or tempo. Abbrev. *Mod.*

Moderator (mǫ·dĕreitəɹ). late ME. [a. F. *modérateur*, a. L. *moderator*, f. *moderari*; see MODERATE *v.*] †**1.** A ruler, governor, director -1867. **2.** An arbiter, umpire, judge; a mediator 1560. **3.** A presiding officer or president, *esp.* (U.S.) one elected to preside over a 'town meeting' 1573. **4.** In academic use: **a.** A public officer formerly appointed to preside over the disputations prescribed in the University schools for candidates for degrees. Now (*a*) at Cambridge, one of the officers who preside over the examination for the Mathematical Tripos; (*b*) at Oxford, an examiner for Moderations. 1573. **b.** At Dublin, a candidate for the degree of B.A. who passes out first (Senior) or second (Junior) in honours 1838. **5.** In the Presbyterian churches: A minister elected to preside over any one of the eccl. bodies, *e. g.* the congregation, the presbytery, etc. 1563. **6.** One who or that which makes moderate 1621. **b.** (Occas. *modérateur.*). A mechanical contrivance for regulating something, esp. the supply of oil to the wick in a lamp; also short for *m.-lamp* 1851.

4. a. As he was abroad in the schooles, so wuld neds seme a m. at home too in the haul G. HARVEY. 6. Hope, that sweet m. of passions as Simonides calls it BURTON.

attrib., in names of certain structures exercising a regulating action, as *m.-band, -ligament.* **M.-lamp,** a lamp with a moderator (sense 6 b). Hence **Mo·deratorship,** the function, office, or position of a m. †**Moderatress,** †**Moderatrix,** a female m.

Modern (mǫ·dəɹn), *a.* and *sb.* 1500. [ad. late L. *modernus*, f. *modo* just now (after *hodiernus* that is of to-day, f. *hodie*).] **A.** *adj.* †**1.** Now existing -1752. **2.** Of or pertaining to the present and recent times; originating in the current age or period 1585. **b.** *Geol.* and *Zool.* Belonging to a comparatively recent period in the life-history of the world 1823. **c.** Prefixed to the name of a language to designate that form of the language that is now in use, in contrast to any earlier form. **d.** *M. languages*: (the study of) the better-known living literary languages of Europe (sometimes merely French and German) 1838. **e.** Applied (in contradistinction to *classical*) to subjects of school instruction other than the ancient languages and literature 1862. **3.** Characteristic of the present and recent times; not antiquated or obsolete 1590. †**4.** Every-day, ordinary, commonplace. (Freq. in Shaks.) 1591-1610.

2. *M. History*: history of the times subsequent to the Middle Ages. c. *M. English*: see ENGLISH *sb.* 1 b. e. Phr. *M. school, m. side*: a school or part of a school in which m. subjects are chiefly or exclusively taught. *Modern Greats* (colloq.): the honour school of philosophy, politics, and economics at the University of Oxford. 3. He is indeed the Pattern of m. Foppery 1676. 4. The Justice,..Full of wise sawes and moderne instances SHAKS.

B. *sb.* (Chiefly *pl.*) **1.** One who belongs to the present time or a modern epoch 1585. **2.** One whose tastes or opinions are modern 1897.

1. Some in ancient books delight; Others prefer what moderns write PRIOR. So **Mode·rnity. Mo·dern·ly** *adv.*; **-ness.**

Modernism (mǫ·dəɹniz'm). 1737. [f. MODERN *a.* + -ISM.] **1.** A usage, expression, or peculiarity of style, etc., characteristic of modern times. **2.** Modern quality of thought, expression, workmanship, etc.; sympathy with what is modern 1830. **3.** A mode of theological inquiry according to which the Bible and the doctrines of the Church are examined in the light of 'modern thought' 1907. (Cf. MODERNIST 3.)

1. ['Its'] is a comparative m. in the language EARLE.

Modernist (mǫ·dəɹnist). 1588. [f. as prec. + -IST.] †**1.** A modern -1592. **2.** A supporter or follower of modern ways or methods; in the 18th c., a maintainer of the superiority of modern over ancient literature 1704. **3.** An adherent of modernism (in sense 3) 1907.

3. Applied orig. to members of the R.C.Ch. whose opinions were condemned in the encyclical *Pascendi gregis* of Pope Pius X 'de modernistarum doctrinis', 8 Sept. 1907.

Modernize (mǫ·dəɹnəiz), *v.* 1741. [ad. F. *moderniser*, f. *moderne*; see MODERN *a.* and -IZE.] **1.** *trans.* To make or render modern; to give a modern character or appearance to. **2.** *intr.* To adopt modern customs, habits, etc. (*rare*) 1753.

1. I have taken the liberty to m. the language FIELDING. The King has decided to have Windsor Castle thoroughly modernised 1901. Hence **Mo·derniza·tion** 1770. **Mo·dernizer** 1732.

Modest (mǫ·dĕst), *a.* 1565. [ad. F. *modeste*, ad. L. *modestus* keeping measure, moderate, modest, f. **modes-*; see MODE.] †**1.** Well-conducted, orderly; not domineering -1652. **2.** Having a humble estimate of one's own merits; unobtrusive, retiring, bashful; (of actions, etc.) proceeding from or indicating these qualities 1565. **3.** Of women: Decorous in manner and conduct; not forward or lewd; 'shamefast'. Hence (in later use also of men), scrupulously chaste. 1591. **4.** Of demands, statements, estimates: Not excessive

æ (man). ɑ (pass). ɑu (loud). ʌ (cut). ɛ (Fr. chef). ə (ever). əi (*I, eye*). ə (Fr. eau de vie). i (s*i*t). *i* (Psych*e*). ǫ (wh*a*t). ǫ (g*o*t).

1601. **5.** Of things: Unpretentious in appearance, style, amount, etc. 1770.

2. You are so m., that me thinks I may promise to grant it before it is asked WALTON. *fig.* Wee, m., crimson-tipped flow'r BURNS. **3.** The m. matron, and the blushing maid GOLDSM. **4.** By a m. Computation [etc.] ADDISON. **5.** The village preacher's m. mansion GOLDSM. Hence **Mo·dest-ly** *adv.* 1548, **-ness** 1546.

Modesty (mǫ·dėsti). 1531. [a. F. *modestie* or ad. L. *modestia*, f. *modestus* MODEST *a.*] †**1.** Moderation; freedom from excess; self-control; clemency –1781. **2.** The quality of being modest (see MODEST *a.*) 1553. **3.** Womanly propriety of behaviour; scrupulous chastity of thought, speech, and conduct 1565. **b.** A kind of veil to cover the bosom. In full *m.-bit, -piece.* 1713. **4.** Unpretentious character (of things) 1906.

1. *Jul. C.* III. i. 213. **2.** An Excess of M. obstructs the Tongue ADDISON. **3.** By my modestie (the iewell in my dower) SHAKS. **4.** The m. of their homes 1906.

Modicum (mǫ·dikǒm). 1470. [a. L., neut. sing. of *modicus*, f. *modus* measure; see MODE.] **1.** A small quantity or portion (of food, money, etc.). †**2.** Applied joc. to a person of small size; also, to a woman (cf. *piece, bit*). –1632.

1. A small M. of good Wine 1725. *gen. Tr. & Cr.* II. i. 74.

Modifiable (mǫ·difəi,ăb'l), *a.* 1611. [f. MODIFY *v.* + -ABLE.] That can be modified. Hence **Mo:difiabi·lity, Mo·difiableness.**

Modification (mǫdifikē¹·ʃən). 1502. [a. F., or ad. L. *modificationem*, n. of action f. *modificare, -ari* to MODIFY.] **1.** The action of modifying; a limitation, restriction, qualification 1603. †**2.** *Philos.* Determination of a substance into a particular mode or modes of being. (Merged in 3.) –1837. †**b.** One of the particular forms into which a substance or entity is differentiated –1841. **3.** The action of making changes in an object without altering its essential nature; the state of being thus changed; partial alteration 1774. **4.** The result of such alteration; a modified form or variety 1669. **5.** *Scots Law.* Assessment, etc. (see MODIFY *v.* 5) 1485. **6.** *Gram.* **a.** Qualification of the sense of one word, phrase, etc. by another; an instance of this 1727. **b.** Alteration of a vowel by umlaut; an instance of this 1845.

3. Sir, a partial repeal, or..a *m.*, would have satisfied a timid, unsystematic, procrastinating Ministry BURKE. **4.** All the parts of a plant..are mere modifications of a leaf 1867.

Modificative (mǫ·difikeᶦtiv), *a.* and *sb.* 1661. [ad. med.L. *modificativus*; see MODIFY and -ATIVE.] **A.** *adj.* That modifies. **B.** *sb.* Something that modifies; a modifying word or clause.

Modificatory (mǫ·difikeᶦtŏri), *a.* 1824. [f. L. *modificator*; see -ORY².] Modifying; tending to modify.

Modify (mǫ·difəi), *v.* late ME. [a. F. *modifier*, ad. L. *modificare, -ari* to limit, moderate, f. *modus*; see -FY.] †**1.** To limit, restrain; to assuage –1546. **2.** To make less severe, rigorous, or decided; to tone down. late ME. **3. a.** *Philos.* To give (an object) its particular modality or form of being 1643. †**b.** *gen.* To distinguish by investing with specific characteristics. (Merged in 4.) –1777. **4.** To make partial changes in; to alter without radical transformation 1780. **5.** *Scots Law.* To assess, award (a payment); *esp.* to determine the amount of (a parish minister's stipend) 1457. **6.** *Gram.* **a.** To qualify the sense of (a word, phrase, etc.) 1727. **b.** To change (a vowel) by umlaut 1845.

2. I..prayed hym..that he wold..modefyen his vengeaunce, and to with-drawe his Iugement 1426. Upon the whole I conceive that it would be best for the court to m. their sentence WELLINGTON. **4.** The Crown must either assent to or reject bills in Parliament, but cannot m. them 1863. **Mo·difier** 1583.

Modillion (modi·lyən). 1563. [ad. It. *modiglione*; ult. etym. unkn.] *Arch.* A projecting bracket placed in series under the corona of the cornice in Corinthian, Composite, and Roman Ionic orders.

‖ **Modiolus** (modəi·ŏlǒs). 1823. [L. *modiolus* nave of a wheel, dim. of MODIUS.] *Anat.* The conical axis around which the cochlea of the ear winds. Hence **Modi·olar** *a.*

Modish (mōᵘ·diʃ), *a.* 1660. [f. MODE + -ISH¹.] **1.** Of persons: Following the mode or prevailing fashion (usu. with a suggestion of disparagement). **2.** Of things: Conforming to the mode; also, fashionable 1663.

Very common in 17th–18th c.; now somewhat *arch.*

1. The m. Hypocrite endeavours to appear more vicious than he really is, the other kind of Hypocrite more virtuous ADDISON. **2.** A good velvet cloak.. and other things m. PEPYS. Hence **Mo·dish-ly** *adv.* 1665, **-ness** 1676.

‖ **Modiste** (modi̇·st). 1852. [Fr., f. *mode* fashion: see MODE.] One who makes or deals in articles of fashion; a milliner, dressmaker.

‖ **Modius** (mōᵘ·diǒs). *Pl.* **-ii** (-iəi). late ME. [L. *modius*, whence F. *muid.*] *Antiq.* **1.** A Roman corn-measure, equal to about a peck. Also, in the Middle Ages, a measure of capacity of varying size. **2.** A tall cylindrical head-dress with which certain deities are represented in ancient art 1800.

Mods (mǫdz). 1858. Colloq. abbrev. of *Moderations*; see MODERATION 4.

Modular (mǫ·diŭlăɹ), *a.* 1798. [ad. mod. L. *modularis*; see MODULUS and -AR¹.] Of or pertaining to a module or modulus.

Modulate (mǫ·diŭleᶦt), *v.* 1557. [f. L. *modulat-, modulari* to measure, etc., f. *modulus*; see MODULE.] **1.** *trans.* To set or regulate; to adjust; to soften, temper, tone down 1623. **2.** *spec.* To attune (the voice, sounds, etc.) to a certain pitch or key; to vary in tone; to give tune or melody to. Const. *to*, †*unto.* 1615. **3. a.** To sing, intone (a song). **b.** *intr.* To play (*on* an instrument). *rare.* 1557. **4.** *Mus. intr.* To pass from one key *to* or *into* another. (Also said of the key.) 1721.

2. Is it credible that any person could m. her voice so artfully as to resemble so many voices? BROOME. *fig.* He [Bentley] would not stop to m. a tuneless sentence DE QUINCEY.

Modulation (mǫdiŭlē¹·ʃən). late ME. [a. F., or ad. L. *modulationem.*] **1.** The action of regulating, toning down, etc. (see prec. 1) 1531. **2.** The action of inflecting the voice or an instrument musically 1543. **3.** The action of singing or making music; an air or melody. Now *rare.* late ME. **4.** *Mus.* †**a.** Management of melody and harmony in a particular mode or key. Also a chord or succession of notes, an air or melody. –1797. **b.** In mod. use: The action of passing from one key to another; a change of key 1696. **5.** *transf.* Harmonious use of language in writing 1759. **6.** *Arch.* The proportioning of the parts of an order by the module 1665.

2. With the same gentle m. of voice as when he spoke to Seth GEO. ELIOT. **3.** The profaner but more lively m. of *Voulez vous danser, Mademoiselle* T. L. PEACOCK. **5.** The regulation of figures, the selection of words, the m. of periods JOHNSON.

Modulator (mǫ·diŭleᶦtəɹ). 1500. [a. L., agent-n. f. *modulari* to MODULATE.] **1.** One who or that which modulates. **2.** A chart used in the tonic sol-fa system, showing the relations of tones and scales 1862.

Module (mǫ·diul). 1586. [a. F. *module*, or ad. L. *modulus*, dim. of *modus* measure; see MODE. The earliest senses show confusion of the word with MODEL.] †**1.** = MODEL *sb.* II. 2. –1681. **2.** †**a.** The plan in little of some large work. Cf. MODEL *sb.* I. 1. –1695. †**b.** = MODEL *sb.* I. 2. –1661. †**c.** *poet.* A mere image –1608. †**d.** *poet.* = MODEL *sb.* III. 1. –1598. **3.** A standard or unit for measuring 1628. **4.** *Arch.* In the classic orders, the unit of length by which the proportions of the parts are expressed; usu. the semidiameter of the column at the base of the shaft 1664.

2. c. Come, bring forth this counterfet m. SHAKS. **3.** Not made..by measure or m. 1712.

‖ **Modulus** (mǫ·diŭlǒs). *Pl.* **-li** (-ləi), **-luses.** 1563. [L.; see MODULE.] †**1.** *Arch.* = MODULE *sb.* 4. **2.** *Math.* **a.** A number by which Napierian logarithms must be multiplied in order to obtain the corresponding logarithms in another system (usu. that with base 10) 1753. **b.** A constant multiplier, coefficient, or parameter involved in a given function of a variable 1843. **c.** A measure of a quantity which depends upon two or more other quantities. In rec. use chiefly, the absolute value of a complex quantity. 1845. **3.** *Physics* and *Mech.* A constant indicating the relation between the amount of a physical effect and that of the force producing it 1807.

‖ **Modus** (mōᵘ·dǒs). *Pl.* (*rare*) **modi** (mōᵘ·dəi); (in sense 3) **moduses.** 1618. [L.; see MODE.] **1.** Mode or manner of operation 1648. †**2.** *Philos.* (*m. essendi* or *existendi*) = MODE I. 6. –1679. **3.** (*m. decimandi*) A money payment in lieu of tithe 1618.

3. The spiritual person who still took his tithe-pig or his *modus* GEO. ELIOT.

Phr. (mod.L.): **m. agendi,** the mode in which a thing acts or operates; **m. operandi,** the way in which a thing, cause, etc., operates; the way in which a person goes to work; **m. vivendi,** a mode of living; i.e. a working arrangement between contending parties, pending settlement of matters in dispute.

†**Mo·dy,** *a.* 1701. [f. MODE + -Y¹.] Modish –1771.

Moe, var. MO more; obs. f. MOW.

Moeble, obs. f. MOBILE; var. MOBLE.

Mœso-Goth (mī·sogǫþ). 1818. [ad. late L. *Mœsogothi* pl., f. L. *Mœsi* the people of *Mœsia* (= mod. Bulgaria and Serbia) + *Gothi*; see GOTH.] A member of the Gothic tribe that inhabited Mœsia in the 4th–5th c. A.D. So **Mœso-Gothic** (mīsogǫ·þik). [late L. *Mœsogothicus*] *a.* pertaining to the Mœso-Goths or their language; *sb.* the M. language.

Moët (moᵢę). 1841. [f. *Moët et Chandon* of Rheims.] The name of a kind of champagne.

‖ **Mofette** (mofe·t). 1822. [F., ad. It. (Naples) *mofetta* = Sp. *mofeta.*] An exhalation of mephitic gas escaping from a fissure; also, a fissure from which such exhalations escape.

‖ **Mofussil** (mofʊ·sil). *Anglo-Ind.* 1781. [Hindustāni *mufaççil*, ad. Arab. *mufaççal*, pa. pple. of *faççala* to divide, separate.] **1.** In India, the country as dist. from the 'Presidency'; the rural localities as dist. from the chief station. **2.** *attrib.* Rural, provincial 1836.

1. Thus if, in Calcutta, one talks of the M., he means anywhere in Bengal out of Calcutta 1886.

Mogul (mogʊ·l, mōᵘ·gʊl). 1588. [a. Pers. and Arab. *muγal, muγul*, a mispronunc. of MONGOL.] **A.** *sb.* **1.** A Mongol or Mongolian; *spec.* in *Hist.* (*a*) A follower of Baber, who founded the Mongol empire in Hindustan in 1526; (*b*) a follower of Jenghis Khan in the 13th c. 1601. **2.** *The Great* or *Grand M.*, also *the M.*: designation among Europeans of the emperor of Delhi, whose empire at one time included most of Hindustan; the last nominal emperor was dethroned in 1857. 1588. **b.** *transf.* A great personage; an autocratic ruler 1678. **3.** *pl.* Playing cards of the best quality; so called from the picture of the Great Mogul on the wrappers 1842.

2. b. I don't deny your sister comes the M. over us DICKENS. **3.** [A case in which the plaintiff applied for an injunction to restrain the defendant from using the Great Mogul as a stamp upon his cards, was decided in 1742.]

B. *adj.* Of, pertaining or relating to, the Moguls, or the Mongol empire in India 1617.

Moguntine (mogʊ·ntin), *a.* 1641. [f. L. *Moguntia*, ancient name of Mainz, where printing was invented by Gutenberg.] Of or pertaining to Mainz in Germany; also, belonging to the art of printing.

Mohair (mōᵘ·hēᵊɹ). 1619 (earlier **mocayare** 1570). [ult. a. Arab. *muχayyar* cloth of goats' hair (lit. 'select, choice', pa. pple. of *χayyara* to choose). Cf. MOIRE.] **1.** Prop., a kind of fine camlet made from the hair of the Angora goat, sometimes watered. Also, yarn made from this hair. Now often, an imitation of true mohair, made usu. of a mixture of wool and cotton. 1570. **2.** A garment made of such material 1673. **3.** The hair of the Angora goat 1753. †**4.** *slang.* A soldier's nickname for a civilian 1785. **5.** *attrib.*, as *m.* (*boot*) *laces.*

Mohammed (mohæ·mėd). 1615. The name (repr. Arab. *Muḥammad*) of the founder of the Moslem religion. (See MAHOMET.)

Mohammedan (mohæ·mėdăn). 1681. [f. prec. + -AN. Now more usual for older MAHOMETAN.] **A.** *adj.* Of or relating to Mohammed, or to his doctrine. **B.** *sb.* A follower of Mohammed; a believer in his doctrine 1777.

Hence **Moha·mmedanism** 1815, †**Moha·mmedism**, the M. religion 1614–1850.

‖ **Moharram, mu-** (mohæ·rǫm). 1861. [Arab. *muharram* (lit. 'sacred').] **a.** The first month of the Mohammedan year, containing thirty days. **b.** A Shiite festival held during the first 10 days of this month.

Mohawk (mōu·hǫk). Also †**Mohock**, etc. 1638. [N. Amer. Indian.] **1.** One of a tribe of N. Amer. Indians, formerly supposed to be cannibals. **2.** The language of the Mohawks 1754. **3.** *Skating.* A step or stroke from any edge in one direction to the same edge on the other foot in an opposite direction 1880.

Mohican (mōu·ikăn, mohī·kăn). Also **-egan.** 1766. [From the native name.] **A.** *adj.* Of or pertaining to the Mohicans. **B.** *sb.* One of a warlike tribe of N. Amer. Indians of the Algonquin stock, formerly occupying the western part of Connecticut and Massachusetts. Also, the language of this tribe.

‖ **Moho** (mōu·ho). 1848. [Maori.] An extinct ralline bird, *Notornis Mantelli*, of New Zealand.

Mohock (mōu·hǫk). Also **-awk,** etc. 1711. [transf. use of *mohock* MOHAWK; now differentiated in spelling.] One of a class of aristocratic ruffians who infested the streets of London by night in the 18th c.

Mohoohoo. 1849. [Native name.] The white rhinoceros of Bechuanaland.

‖ **Mohur** (mōu·hǝɹ). 1621. [Pers. *muhr* seal, cogn. w. Skr. *mudrā* seal.] The chief gold coin of British India, worth 15 rupees.

Moider: see MOITHER.

Moidore (moi·dōǝɹ). 1711. [Corruptly a. Pg. *moeda d'ouro* (*moeda* MONEY, *ouro* :—L. *aurum* gold).] A gold coin of Portugal, formerly current in England. Later, used as a name for the sum of 27*s.*, its value.

Moiety (moi·ĕti, -ĭti). 1444. [late ME. *moite, moitie*, a. OF. *moité, moitié* :—L. *medietatem*, f. *medius* middle. Cf. MEDIETY.] **1.** A half; esp. in legal or quasi-legal use. **2.** *loosely.* One of two (or more) parts into which something is divided; †one's share 1596. †**b.** *Contextually.* A small part –1650. **3.** *joc.* One's 'better half', i.e. a wife (rarely, a husband). (So F. *moitié.*) 1737.

1. The moitie or half pairte of the mannor 1545. 2. The Southern and greater M. of this Island FULLER. 3. The Lady with a skeleton m. in the old print LAMB.

Moil (moil), *sb.*[1] *arch.* and *dial.* 1612. [f. MOIL *v.*] **1.** Toil, drudgery; freq. in *toil and m.* **2.** Turmoil, confusion 1855.

1. This night his weekly m. is at an end BURNS.

Moil, *sb.*[2] 1871. [?] *Mining.* A tool for cutting ground accurately.

Moil (moil), *v.* late ME. [a. OF. *moillier* (:—pop. L. **molliare*, f. L. *mollis* soft) to moisten, also *intr.* to paddle in mud (mod.F. *mouiller* to wet).] **1.** *trans.* To wet, moisten; to soil, bedaub. *Obs.* exc. *dial.* and *arch.* †**2.** *intr.* To make oneself wet and muddy; to wallow in mire –1599. **3.** To toil, drudge; esp. in *to toil and m.* 1548. †**4.** *trans.* To weary; to harass, worry. Chiefly *pass.* –1869.

1. *fig.* Thou..doest thy mynd in durty pleasures moyle SPENSER. 3. To toyle and moyle for worldly drosse 1580. 4. *refl.* But 'e tued an' moil'd 'issén deäd TENNYSON.

Moile, var. of MULE [1] and [2].

‖ **Moire** (mwār, m(w)ōǝɹ). 1660. [F. *moire*, an adoption of some form of Eng. MOHAIR.] Orig., a kind of watered mohair; later, any watered fabric; *esp.* a watered or clouded silk. Also **M. antique.**

‖ **Moiré** (mware, m(w)ōǝ·rē). 1818. [Fr., pa. pple. of *moirer* to give the appearance of moire to.] **A.** *adj.* Of silk: Watered. Of metals: Having a watered or clouded appearance. 1823. **B.** *sb.* **1.** A variegated or clouded appearance like that of watered silk; esp. on metals. ¶**2.** Used erron. for MOIRE 1851.

Moist (moist), *a.* (and *sb.*) late ME. [a. OF. *moiste* (mod.F. *moite*); ult. etym. dubious.] **1.** Slightly wet; damp, humid. **b.** Of a season, climate, etc.: Wet; rainy 1481. †**2.** Of plants, fruits, etc.: 'Juicy, succulent' (J.); fresh as opp. to dried –1611. †**b.** New, not stale or worn. CHAUCER. †**3.** Yielding moisture; that brings rain or moisture; containing water, etc. –1704. †**4.** Liquid; watery –1611. **5.** Associated or connected with liquid or tears. *spec.* Of diseases, etc.: Marked by a discharge of matter, phlegm, etc. 1562. **b.** *Med.* Of sounds heard in auscultation: Suggesting the presence of liquid 1843. †**6.** *absol.* or *sb.* That which is moist; moisture. Also, moist quality. –1742.

1. Haue you not a m. eye? a dry hand?.. a white beard?..and wil you cal your selfe yong? SHAKS. Like the red-rose bud m. with morning-dew THOMSON. **b.** One somer is softe and moyste, And another is drye and wyndy CAXTON. 2. Nor [shall he] eate m. grapes, or dried *Num.* vi. 3. **b.** A draughte of moyste and corny Ale CHAUCER. 3. Ere twice..M. Hesperus hath quench'd her sleepy Lampe SHAKS. 4. The m. waies of the sea they saild CHAPMAN. 6. Who..Bear his swift errands over m. and dry MILT. Hence **Moi·stful** *a. rare.* 1591. **Moi·stless** *a.* 1592. **Moi·stly** *adv.* **Moi·stness.**

Moist, *v. Obs.* exc. *dial.* late ME. [f. prec.] *trans.* = MOISTEN *v.*

Now no more The iuyce of Egypts Grape shall moyst this lip SHAKS.

Moisten (moi·s'n), *v.* 1580. [f. MOIST *a.* + -EN [5].] *trans.* and *intr.* To make or become moist.

Phr. *To m. the lips, throat*, etc., with ref. to quenching thirst. *To m. one's clay* (see CLAY *sb.*). *fig.* It moistened [= softened] not his executioner's heart with any pity FULLER. Hence **Moi·stener.**

Moisture (moi·stiŭɹ, moi·stʃǝɹ), *sb.* late ME. [a. OF. *moistour* (mod.F. *moiteur*), f. *moiste* MOIST *a.*] †**1.** Moistness; the quality or state of being moist or damp –1794. **2.** Water or other liquid diffused in small quantity through air as vapour, or through a solid substance, or condensed upon a surface. late ME. †**b.** The liquid part of a body. In mediæval philosophy, the 'humours'. –1732. †**3.** Liquid in general –1741.

2. Some fell vpon a rocke, and assoone as it was sprung vp, it withered away, because it lacked m. *Luke* viii. 6. Snow is not the only solid form in which atmospheric m. is precipitated HUXLEY. **b.** I cannot weepe: for all my bodies moysture Scarce serues to quench my Furnace-burning hart SHAKS. Hence †**Moi·sture** *v.* to moisten; to make wet or damp; also *intr.* 1471–1610. **Moi·stureless** *a.* 1828.

Moisty (moi·sti), *a.* late ME. [f. MOIST *a.* + -Y [1].] †**1.** Of ale: New. CHAUCER. **2.** Moist, damp: usu. coupled with *misty.*

Moither (moi·ðǝɹ), *v. dial.* Also **moider.** 1674. [Obscure.] **1.** *trans.* To worry, bother, fatigue. Chiefly *pass.* and *refl.* **2.** *intr.* To talk incoherently; to wander in one's mind 1839. **3.** *intr.* To labour hard 1828.

Mokado(u)r, vars. of MUCKENDER.

Moke [1] (mōuk). *dial.* 1604. [Assumed sing. of *mokes* :—OE. *māx* net; see MESH.] A mesh of a net. Also *pl.* wicker-work.

Moke [2] (mōuk). *slang* and *dial.* 1848. [?] A donkey. Also *transf.* = DONKEY 2.

‖ **Mola** (mōu·lă). 1601. [L.] A fleshy mass occurring in the womb; a false conception.

Molar (mōu·lăɹ), *a.*[1] and *sb.* 1541. [ad. L. *molaris*, f. *mola* a millstone; see -AR [1].] **A.** *adj.* **1.** Grinding, serving to grind; applied *spec.* to the back teeth of mammals 1626. **2.** Of or pertaining to a molar tooth 1831. **B.** *sb.* A molar or grinding tooth; a grinder 1541.

True m., a m. tooth in the adult which is not preceded by a deciduous or milk-molar. *False m.*, a m. tooth which has replaced a milk-tooth. So **Mo·lary** *a.* = A. 1. 1826.

Molar (mōu·lăɹ), *a.*[2] 1862. [f. L. *moles* mass; see -AR [1].] Pertaining to mass; acting on or by means of large masses of matter. Often opp. to *molecular.*

‖ **Molasse** (molas). 1796. [F.] *Geol.* A soft coherent greenish sandstone of Miocene age, esp. that found between the Alps and the Jura.

Molasses (molæ·sėz). (Properly *pl.*, construed as *sing.*) 1570. [a. Pg. *melaço* :—late L. *mellaceum* must, f. *mell-, mel* honey.] The thick viscid syrup drained from raw sugar in the process of manufacture. In U.S. used promiscuously with *treacle.*

Our lading, which was Sugar, Dates, Almonds, and Malassos or sugar Syrrope HAKLUYT.

Mold, Mold-: see MOULD, MOULD-.

Mole (mōul), *sb.*[1] [OE. *māl.*] †**1.** A discoloured spot, esp. on cloth, linen, etc. –1825. **2.** *spec.* A spot or blemish on the human skin; in mod. use, an abnormal pigmented prominence on the skin, sometimes hairy. late ME. †**b.** *fig.* A fault; a distinguishing mark –1743.

2. My father had a moale vpon his brow SHAKS.

Mole (mōul), *sb.*[2] [late ME. *mulle, molle*, corresp. to MDu. *mol, moll(e*, etc., of obscure origin.] **1.** Any one of the small mammals of the family *Talpidæ*; *esp.* the common mole, *Talpa europæa*, a small animal having a velvety fur, usu. blackish, very small but not blind eyes, and very short strong fore-limbs for burrowing and excavating. **2.** *transf.* and *fig.* One who works in darkness 1601. **b.** One who sees imperfectly 1610. **3.** The borer of a mole-plough 1805. **4.** *pl.* Moleskin trousers. Also *m. trousers.* 1890. **5.** The colour of moleskin 1908.

1. While Moles the crumbled Earth in Hillocks raise GAY. As blind as a m. BENTLEY. 2. Well said old M., can'st worke i' th' ground so fast? SHAKS.

attrib. and *Comb.*: as *m.-catcher*; **m.-cast,** a mole-hill; **-cricket,** any fossorial orthopterous insect of the genus *Gryllotalpa*; **-plough,** a plough in which a pointed iron shoe makes an underground channel resembling the track of a mole, to serve as a drain; **-rat,** (*a*) any myomorphic rodent of the family *Spalacidæ*; (*b*) *dial.* the common m.

Mole (mōul), *sb.*[3] 1548. [In sense 1, ad. L. *moles* fem., mass. In senses 2 and 3, a. F. *môle* masc., ad. L. *moles.*] †**1.** A great mass; the collective mass of any object –1711. **2.** A massive structure, esp. of stone, serving as a pier or breakwater, or joining two places separated by water. Hence, the water-area within the mole; an artificial harbour. 1548. †**3.** *Antiq.* A Roman form of mausoleum –1818.

3. The m. of Adrian. GWILT.

†**Mole,** *sb.*[4] 1547. [ad. L. *mola* (Gr. μύλη).] *Antiq.* A cake made of grains of spelt coarsely ground and mixed with salt (*mola salsa*), strewn on the victims at sacrifices –1697.

Mole, *sb.*[5] 1611. [a. F. *môle* = MOLA.]

†**Mole,** *v.* Chiefly *dial.* late ME. [f. MOLE *sb.*[1]] *trans.* To spot, stain, discolour –1818.

†**Mo·lebut.** *rare.* 1598. [a. F. *molebout.*] The sun-fish, *Orthagoriscus mola* –1736.

Molecular (mole·kiŭlăɹ), *a.* 1823. [f. mod.L. *molecula* (see MOLECULE) + -AR [1].] Pertaining to, consisting of, or concerned with molecules; acting or inherent in the molecules of a substance. *M. heat, weight*: see the sbs. Hence **Molecula·rity, Mole·cularly** *adv.*

Molecule (mǫ·lĭkiŭl, mōu·lĭkiŭl). 1794 (earlier in L. form, 1678–1800). [a. F. *molécule*, ad. mod.L. *molecula*, dim. of L. *moles* mass.] **1.** *Physics* and *Chem.* One of the minute discrete particles of which material substances are conceived to consist. In modern chemistry the molecules of any element or compound are assumed to be of uniform size and mass, representing the smallest portions into which the substance can be divided without losing its chemical identity. **2.** In pop. use: A small particle 1799.

1. A group of atoms drawn and held together by what chemists term affinity, is called a m. TYNDALL.

Mole-head. 1585. [f. MOLE *sb.*[3] + HEAD *sb.*] = PIER-HEAD.

Mo·le-hill, molehill. late ME. [f. MOLE *sb.*[2]] A small mound, or occas. a ridge, of earth thrown up by moles in burrowing.

Phr. *To make a mountain (out) of a mole-hill*: to make too much of a small difficulty or grievance.

Molendinar. 1820. [ad. med.L. *molendinarius*, f. *molendinum* mill. (In Glasgow pron. molĕndī·năr.)] **A.** *adj.* Of or concerning a mill or miller. **B.** *sb.* A molar tooth. SCOTT. So **Mole·ndinary** *a.* and *sb.*

Moleskin (mōu·lskin). 1668. [f. MOLE *sb.*[2] + SKIN.] **1.** The skin of the mole used as a fur. **2.** A strong, soft, fine-piled cotton fustian, the surface of which is shaved before dyeing 1803. **3.** *pl.* Trousers, etc., made of moleskin (in sense 2) 1836.

Mole·st, *sb. Obs.* exc. *arch.* ME. [a. OF. *moleste*, ad. L. *molestia* trouble, f. *molestus*; see next.] Trouble, injury.

Molest (mole·st), *v.* late ME. [a. OF. *molester*, ad. L. *molestare* to trouble, annoy, f. *molestus*, f. **moles-*, perh. cogn. w. *moles* mass, burden.] †**1.** *trans.* To cause trouble to; to vex, annoy, put to inconvenience -1726. †b. Of disease: To afflict -1696. 2. To meddle with (a person) injuriously or with hostile intent 1494.

2. No protestant..ought..to be forc'd or molested for religion MILT. Hence **Mole·ster.**

Molestation (mǭlèstē·ʃən, mǫl-). late ME. [a. OF., ad. L. *molestationem*, f. *molestare*; see prec.] 1. The action of molesting or condition of being molested; annoyance, disturbance; †vexation. 2. With *a* and *pl.*: A trouble, annoyance, vexation; *concr.* a cause of annoyance. Now *rare.* late ME.

Molestful (mǫle·stfŭl), *a.* Now *rare.* 1596. [f. MOLEST *sb.* or *v.* + -FUL.] Troublesome.

Molewarp, obs. f. MOULDWARP.

‖ **Molimen** (mǫləi·men). *Pl.* **molimina** (mǫli·mină). 1865. [L., f. *moliri* to make an effort.] *Phys.* and *Path.* An effort by which the system endeavours to perform any natural function, esp. *menstrual m.*, the straining to bring about the catamenia.

Molinary (mǭu·linări), *a. rare.* 1774. [f. late L. *molinarius*, f. *molina* mill; see -ARY [1].] Of or pertaining to the grinding of corn.

Moline (mǫləi·n). 1562. [Cf. AF. *moliné*, f. *molin* (mod.F. *moulin*) mill; see MILL *sb.*[1] and -EE.] *Her.* **A.** *adj.* Of or resembling the expanded and curved extremities of a mill-rind. **B.** *sb.* = *Cross moline* 1777.

Cross m., a cross each of the arms of which terminates in two expanded and curved branches resembling the extremities of a mill-rind.

Molinism [1] (mǫ·liniz'm). 1669. [f. Luis *Molina*, a Spanish Jesuit (1535-1600) + -ISM.] The doctrine of Molina that the efficacy of grace depends simply on the will which freely accepts it. So **Mo·linist** [1] 1655.

Molinism [2] (mǫ·liniz'm). 1720. [f. Miguel de *Molinos*, a Spanish priest (1627-96).] Quietism. Hence **Mo·linist** [2] 1868.

Moll (mǫl), *sb.* 1567. [Familiar dim. of *Mary.* Cf. MOLLY.] 1. A female personal name. 2. A prostitute 1604.

†**Moll,** *a. rare.* 1474. [a. OF. *mol* (mod.F. *mou, mol*):—L. *mollem, mollis* soft.] 1. Soft. CAXTON. 2. *Mus.* In *B moll*, ♭ *moll* = flat. (Also BEMOL.) -1667.

Molla(h, var. of MULLAH.

Molleton (mǫ·létǫn). 1858. [a. F. *molleton.*] = SWANSKIN.

Mollify (mǫ·lifəi), *v.* late ME. [ad. F. *mollifier*, ad. L. *mollificare*, f. *mollis*; see -FY.] 1. *trans.* To render soft or supple. Now *rare.* 2. To soften in temper or disposition; to appease. late ME. †b. *intr.* To become softened; to relent -1823. †3. To abate the violence of (passions; also heat, cold, etc.); to relieve (care) -1833. 4. To lessen the harshness of (laws, etc.); to abate the rigour of (demands); also, to euphemize. Now *rare.* 1523.

2. I must m. him with money 1667. 4. Now mince the Sin, And mollifie Damnation with a Phrase DRYDEN. Hence **Mo·llifiable** *a.* 1611. **Mollifica·tion.** late ME. **Mo·llifier** 1592.

‖ **Mollities** (mǫli·ʃi,īz). 1604. [L., f. *mollis.*] †a. *fig.* Effeminacy. b. *Med.* Softening 1835.

Mollitious (mǫli·ʃəs), *a. rare.* 1646. [f. prec. + -OUS.] Luxurious, sensuous.

Mollusc, mollusk (mǫ·lŏsk). 1783. [ad. F. *mollusque*, ad. mod.L. *molluscum*, neut. of *molluscus*: see next.] *Nat. Hist.* An animal belonging to the Mollusca.

‖ **Mollusca** (mǫ̆lʊ·skă), *sb. pl.* 1783. [mod. L. (1650), neut. pl. of L. *molluscus*, f. *mollis* soft: used orig. as a rendering of Aristotle's τὰ μαλάκια (cuttlefish).] *Zool.* a. Applied by Linnæus to a heterogeneous group of invertebrates, comprising the Echinoderms, Hydroids, Annelids, and naked Mollusca. b. Now (mainly after Cuvier), a phylum, comprising soft-bodied unsegmented animals (usu. having a hard shell) of the five classes Amphineura (chitons), Gastropoda (limpets, snails, etc.), Scaphopoda (tooth-shells), Cephalopoda (cuttlefish, etc.), and Lamellibranchia (oysters, mussels, etc.). Hence **Mollu·scan** *a.* **Mollu·scoid** *a.*; *sb.* one of the **Molluscoi·dea,** also **-oida,** a division (now discarded) comprising the Polyzoa, Brachiopoda, and Tunicata.

Molluscous (mǫ̆lʊ·skəs), *a.* 1813. [f. L. *molluscus* + -OUS.] Of or belonging to the Mollusca; *fig.* flabby, invertebrate.

Molly (mǫ·li). 1719. [f. MOLL *sb.* 1 + -Y [6].] 1. (With capital M.) A familiar pet-form of *Mary*; occas. applied to a prostitute. 2. An effeminate man or boy; a milksop. Also *Miss Molly.* 1754.

Comb. **M. cotton-tail** *U.S.* = *cotton-tail.*

Molly-coddle (mǫ·likǫd'l), *sb.* 1833. [f. MOLLY + CODDLE *v.*[2]] One who coddles himself or is coddled; an effeminate man. **Mo·lly-coddle** *v.* to coddle or cocker up 1867.

Molly Maguire (mǫ·limăgwəiᵊ·ɹ). 1867 [See MOLLY; *Maguire* is a common Irish surname.] A member of a secret society formed in Ireland in 1843 for the purpose of resisting the payment of rent. Also *transf.* A similar society formed in the mining districts of Pennsylvania.

Moloch (mǭu·lǫk). 1661. [a. L. *Moloch* (Vulg.), Gr. Μόλοχ, Μολόχ (LXX), repr. Heb. *mō·lek.* See N.E.D.] 1. The name of a Canaanite idol, to whom children were sacrificed as burnt offerings (*Lev.* xviii. 21); in Milton, one of the devils. Hence, an object to which horrible sacrifices are made. 1667. 2. The Australian thorn-lizard or thorn-devil, *Moloch horridus*, one of the most grotesque and hideous of reptiles 1845. 3. A Brazilian monkey, *Callithrix moloch* 1875.

1. M., horrid King besmear'd with blood Of human sacrifice, and parents tears MILT. Hence **Mo·lochize** *v.* to sacrifice as to M. TENNYSON.

Molosses, obs. f. MOLASSES.

Molossian (mǫ̆lǫ·siăn). *Hist.* 1592. [f. L. *Molossia* (= Gr. Μολοσσία), f. Gr. Μολοσσός MOLOSSUS; see -(I)AN.] **A.** *adj.* Of or pertaining to Molossia, a country in Epirus; esp. *M. dog, hound*, a kind of mastiff 1649. **B.** *sb.* An inhabitant of Molossia.

‖ **Molossus** (mǫ̆lǫ·sǫ̆s). Also **molo·ss** (1731). 1586. [L., = Gr. Μολοσσός: see prec.] *Prosody.* A foot of three long syllables.

Molt: see MELT *v.*; obs. f. MOULT.

Molten (mǭu·lt'n), *ppl. a.* ME. [strong pa. pple. of MELT *v.*] 1. Liquefied by heat. (Now only of bodies that require great heat to melt them; not, e.g., of wax or ice.) 2. a. Of metal, etc.: That has been melted (and again solidified). b. Of an image, etc.: Produced by melting and running into a mould.

1. I am as hot as m. Lead SHAKS. *fig.* The m. passion of Burke 1884. 2. b. They made a m. calf COVERDALE *Exod.* xxxii. 4. Hence **Mo·ltenly** *adv.* like what is m.

Molucca (mǫ̆lʊ·kă). 1681. The name (*the Moluccas, the M. Islands*) of a group of islands (also called the Spice Islands) situated in the Eastern Archipelago; used *attrib.* in **M. bean,** the fruit of a species of BONDUC, *Guilandina Bonducella*; etc.

Moly (mǭu·li). 1567. [a. L., a. Gr. μῶλυ.] 1. *Myth.* A fabulous plant having a white flower and a black root, endowed with magic properties, said by Homer to have been given by Hermes to Odysseus as a charm against the sorceries of Circe. 2. Applied to various plants supposed to be identical with the moly of Homer; *esp.* the wild garlic, *Allium Moly* 1597.

Molybdate (mǫli·bdět). 1794. [f. as MOLYBDIC *a.*; see -ATE [1].] *Chem.* A salt of molybdic acid.

†**Molybdena** (mǫlibdī·nă). 1693. [a. L. *molybdæna*, a. Gr. μολύβδαινα, f. μόλυβδος lead.] a. Applied vaguely to various salts or ores of lead. b. An older name for MOLYBDENITE. c. From *c* 1790 to *c* 1820 occas. used for MOLYBDENUM.

Molybdenite (mǫli·bdĕnəit). 1796. [f. prec. + -ITE [1].] †a. *Chem.* An artificial sulphide of molybdenum. b. *Min.* Disulphide of molybdenum occurring in tabular bluish-grey crystals.

Molybdenum (mǫlibdī·nŏm, mǫli·bdĭnŏm). 1816. [mod.L., alteration of MOLYBDENA.] *Chem.* A metallic element (symbol Mo) occurring in combination, as in molybdenite, wulfenite, etc. When separated it is a brittle, almost infusible silver-white metal, permanent at ordinary temperatures, but rapidly oxidized by heat.

Molybdic (mǫli·bdik), *a.* 1796. [f. MOLYBDENA + -IC.] a. *Min.* Containing or derived from molybdenum. b. *Chem.* Applied to compounds containing molybdenum in its higher valency; esp. in *m. acid.*

Molybdite (mǫli·bdəit). 1868. [f. MOLYBDENA + -ITE [1].] *Min.* Trioxide of molybdenum occurring in yellow capillary crystals or incrustations.

Molybdous (mǫli·bdəs), *a.* 1796. [f. MOLYBDENA + -OUS.] *Chem.* Applied to compounds into which molybdenum enters in its lower valency, as opp. to MOLYBDIC.

Mom. *U.S.* 1911. Shortened f. MOMMA.

Mome [1] (mǭum). *Obs.* exc. *arch.* 1553. [?] A blockhead, dolt, fool.

Mome [2]. 1563. Anglicized f. MOMUS.

Moment (mǭu·mĕnt), *sb.* ME. [ad. L. *momentum*, f. *mo-, movere* to move.] 1. A point of time, an instant. †2. In the 17-18th c. occas. used for SECOND -1767. †3. A small particle -1754. †b. *Math.* An infinitesimal increment or decrement of a varying quantity -1743. 4. Importance, weight. Now only in *of (great, little,* etc.) *m.* 1522. †5. Cause or motive of action; determining influence or consideration -1691. 6. A definite stage or turning-point in a course of events 1666. 7. *Mech.* Applied, with qualifying words, to certain functions serving as the measure of some mechanical effect depending on two different factors 1830. 8. One of the elements of a complex conceptual entity. (After Ger. use.) 1863.

1. We shall all be chaunged and that in a m. and in the twincklynge of an eye TINDALE 1 *Cor.* xv. 52. Phr. *The m.*: occas. in pregnant sense, the fitting or favourable m. *For the m.*: so far as the near future is concerned; also, during the brief space referred to. *One m.*: ellipt. for 'wait' or 'listen one m.' *On the spur of the m.*: see SPUR. *The m.*: ellipt. for 'the m. when' or 'that'. *This m.*: used advb. for (*a*) immediately; (*b*) hardly a m. ago. *To the m.*: with exact punctuality; also, for the exact time required. 3. *To the m.*: to the smallest detail. 4. Things which appear at first view of little m. BURKE. 7. *The m. of a force* or *a velocity* about a point, the product of the length of the directed line representing the force or the velocity, multiplied by the length of the perpendicular from the point. *M. of a couple*, the product of either of the two equal forces into the length of the arm. *M. of inertia* of a body about any axis, the sum of the products of the mass of each particle of the body into the square of its least distance from the axis. *M. of momentum* of a rotating body, the product of momentum into the distance from the axis. 8. Being and not-Being are the elements or moments of Becoming FERRIER. *Comb.* **m.-axis** *Physics*, a line indicating by its length and direction respectively the m. and the direction of a couple. Hence †**Moment** *v.* to time precisely. FULLER.

Momental (mome·ntăl), *a.* 1606. [a. F., ad. late L. **momentalis*, f. *momentum*; see prec. and -AL.] †1. Momentary -1646. 2. *Math.* Of or pertaining to momentum, as *m. ellipse*, etc. 1877.

1. Not one momentall minute doth she swerue BRETON. Hence †**Mome·ntally** *adv.* from moment to moment; for a moment 1612-1646.

†**Momenta·neous,** *a.* 1610. [f. L. *momentaneus* + -OUS.] 1. Momentary -1801. 2. Instantaneous -1793. 3. Pertaining to an infinitesimal division of time 1708.

†**Momentany,** *a.* 1508. [ad. F. *momentané*, ad. L. *momentaneus.*] Pertaining to the moment; transitory; evanescent -1726.

Momentary (mǭu·mĕntări), *a.* 1526. [ad. L. *momentarius*, f. *momentum*; see MOMENT *sb.* and -ARY [2].] 1. Lasting but for a moment; transitory. 2. Short-lived; ephemeral 1587. 3. Recurring at every moment. Now *rare.* 1745. †4. Instantaneous -1847. †5. *Math.* Pertaining to an infinitesimal portion of time -1833. 6. quasi-*adv.* POPE.

1. His Griefs are M., and his Joys Immortal STEELE. 2. Born like a m. fly, To flutter, buzz about, and die 1762. 3. A dealer in the fine arts in m. fear of a spunging-house 1799. Hence **Mo·mentarily** *adv.* for a moment; at every moment; †instantly 1654.

Momently (mǭu·mĕntli), *adv.* 1676. [f. MOMENT *sb.* + -LY [2].] 1. Every moment. 2. At any moment; on the instant 1775. 3. For a single moment 1868.

Momentous (moᵘme·ntəs), *a.* 1652. [f. MOMENT *sb.* + -OUS.] †1. Having motive force. 2. Of moment; important, weighty 1656. 3. Of persons: Having influence or importance. Now *rare.* 1667.

2. There remaineth a second objection, which is the more m. 1656. Hence **Mome·ntous·ly** *adv.*, **-ness.**

Momentum (moᵘme·ntŏm). *Pl.* **-ta.** 1699. [a. L.; see MOMENT *sb.*] †1. = MOMENT *sb.* 3 b. 1735. †2. 'Impulsive weight' (J.); force of movement –1817. †3. *Mech.* = MOMENT *sb.* 7. 1839. 4. *Mech.* The 'quantity of motion' of a moving body, measured by the product of the mass into the velocity 1699. Hence, in pop. use, impetus gained by movement 1860. 5. = MOMENT *sb.* 8. 1829.

4. *fig.* That m. of ignorance,..presumption, and lust of plunder, which nothing has been able to resist BURKE.

Mo·mma. *U.S. colloq.* 1895. = MAMMA [1].

Mommer, etc., var. of MUMMER, etc.

‖**Momus** (mōᵘ·mŏs). Occas. *pl.* **Momi, Momusses, Momus's.** 1563. [L. *Momus*, Gr. Μῶμος, personification of μῶμος ridicule.] A Greek divinity, the god of ridicule; hence, a fault-finder, a captious critic. *A daughter, disciple, son of M.*, a wag, buffoon.

Mona (mōᵘ·nă). 1774. [a. Sp., Pg., It. *mona* monkey (whence mod.L. specific name).] A small, long-tailed African monkey, *Cercopithecus mona.*

Monachal, monacal (mɒ·năkăl), *a.* 1587. [ad. eccl. L. *monachalis*, f. *monachus* MONK.] Of or pertaining to a monk or monastic life; monastic; monkish.

Monachism (mɒ·năkiz'm). 1577. [f. L. *monachus* + -ISM.] 1. The monastic system or principle; monasticism. †2. A monkish characteristic. MILT. So **Mo·nachist** *a.* favouring m.

Monacid (mɒnæ·sid), *a.* 1862. [MONO- 2.] *Chem.* Having the power of saturating one molecule of a monobasic acid.

Monad (mɒ·næd). Also †**-ade.** 1615. [ad. L. *monad-*, *monas*, ad. Gr. μονάς unit, f. μόνος alone.] 1. The number one, unity; an arithmetical unit. Now only *Hist.* with reference to the Pythagorean or other Greek philosophies. b. Applied to the Deity 1642. 2. An ultimate unit of being; an absolutely simple entity 1748.

Chiefly used with reference to the philosophy of Leibnitz (1646–1716), according to which the universe of existence consists of entities without parts, extension, or figure, and possessing, in infinitely varied degrees, the power of perception.

3. *Biol.* A hypothetical simple organism, assumed as the first term in the genealogy of living beings 1835. 4. *Zool.* A protozoon of the genus *Monas*, or, more widely, of the order *Monadidea* or the class *Flagellata* 1836. 5. *Chem.* An element or radical which has the combining power of one atom of hydrogen 1865. 6. quasi-*adj.* = MONADIC 1846.

Comb. **m.-deme** (DEME [2] 2); *m. atom, element*, etc.

‖**Monadelphia** (mɒnăde·lfiă). 1753. [mod. L. (Linn.), f. Gr. μόνος one + ἀδελφός brother + -IA [1].] *Bot.* The sixteenth class in the Linnæan Sexual System, comprising plants with hermaphrodite flowers having the stamens united in one bundle. Hence **Mo·nadelph,** a plant of this class. **Monade·lphian, Monade·lphous** *adjs.*

Monadic (mɒnæ·dik), *a.* 1788. [ad. Gr. μοναδικός composed of units, f. μοναδ-, μονάς MONAD.] 1. Composed of monads or units; pertaining to or of the nature of a monad; existing singly. Also quasi-*sb.*, that which is so composed. 2. *Chem.* Of the nature of a monad; univalent 1872. 3. Relating to monadism 1862. **Mona·dical** *a.* in sense 1. 1642.

Monadiform (mɒnæ·difɔɹm), *a.* 1862. [f. MONAD; see -FORM.] *Biol.* Having the form of a monad.

Monadism (mɒ·nădiz'm). 1875. [f. MONAD + -ISM.] The theory of the monadic nature of matter or of substance generally; the doctrine of monads, esp. that of Leibnitz.

Monadology (mɒnădɒ·lŏdʒi). 1732. [a. F. *monadologie* (Leibnitz); see MONAD and -LOGY.] The doctrine of monads.

Monal: see MONAUL.

Monamide (mɒ·nămәid). 1861. [f. MON(O)- + AMIDE.] *Chem.* An amide formed by the displacement of one of the three hydrogen atoms of ammonia.

Monamine (mɒ·nămәin). 1859. [f. as prec. + AMINE.] *Chem.* An amine formed by the exchange of one of the three hydrogen atoms of ammonia for a basic radical.

‖**Monandria** (mɒnæ·ndriă). 1753. [mod.L. (Linn.), f. Gr. μόνανδρος having one husband (f. μόνος + ἀνδρ- male, taken in the sense 'stamen').] *Bot.* The first class in the Linnæan Sexual System, comprising all plants having hermaphrodite flowers with but one stamen or male organ. Hence **Mona·ndrous** *a.* 1806.

Monandry (mɒnæ·ndri). 1855. [ad. Gr. *μονανδρία; see MONANDRIA and -Y [3].] The custom of having only one husband at a time.

Monarch (mɒ·năɹk), *sb.* 1450. [ad. L. *monarcha*, ad. Gr. μονάρχης (usu. μόναρχος), f. μόνος single + ἄρχειν to rule.] 1. Orig., a sole and absolute ruler of a state. In mod. use, a sovereign bearing the title of king, queen, emperor, or empress, or the like. (Now more or less rhet., exc. in techn. use.) b. *transf.* and *fig.* 1581. 2. A very large red and black butterfly 1893.

1. He is reputed as absolute a monark as any other in India SIR T. HERBERT. b. Come thou M. of the Vine, Plumpie Bacchus SHAKS. Mont Blanc is the m. of mountains BYRON. Hence **Mo·narch** *v. intr.* to act the m.: also *to m. it.*

Monarch (mɒ·naɹk), *a.* 1884. [f. Gr. μόνος single + ἀρχή beginning; cf. DIARCH.] *Bot.* Arising from only one point of origin, as the woody tissue of a root.

Monarchal (mɒ̆nā·ɹkăl), *a.* 1586. [f. MONARCH *sb.* + -AL.] 1. Of, belonging to, or befitting a monarch 1592. 2. Having the status or exercising the functions of a monarch 1586. 3. Ruled by a monarch; monarchical. Now *rare* or *Obs.* 1586.

1. Satan, whom now transcendent glory rais'd Above his fellows, with M. pride..thus spake MILT. 3. Nations m. and aristocratical LANDOR.

Monarchess (mɒ·năɹkės). Now *rare.* 1595. [f. MONARCH *sb.* + -ESS.] A female monarch.

Monarchial (mɒ̆nā·ɹkiăl), *a.* 1600. [f. L. *monarchia* + -AL.] = MONARCHAL *a.*

Monarchian (mɒ̆nā·ɹkiăn). 1765. [ad. late L. *monarchiani* pl., f. *monarchia*; see MONARCHY and -AN.] A. *sb.* One of those heretics in the 2nd and 3rd centuries who denied the doctrine of the Trinity, interpreting ἡ μοναρχία τοῦ Θεοῦ, 'the monarchy of God' (a current designation for monotheism), as implying this. B. *adj.* Of or belonging to the Monarchians or to Monarchianism 1847. Hence **Mona·rchianism,** the anti-trinitarian doctrine of the Monarchians.

Monarchic (mɒ̆nā·ɹkik), *a.* 1612. [a. F. *monarchique*, ad. Gr. μοναρχικός, f. μόναρχος; see -IC.] 1. Of a government: Having the characteristics of monarchy. Now usu. MONARCHICAL. 1624. 2. Of or belonging to a monarchy; favouring monarchy 1647. 3. Of or pertaining to a monarch or monarchs. Now *rare* or *Obs.* 1612.

Monarchical (mɒ̆nā·ɹkikăl), *a.* 1576. [f. as prec.; see -ICAL.] 1. Of the nature of a monarchy; *esp.* of government, vested in a monarch 1589. 2. = MONARCHIC *a.* 2. 1628. 3. = MONARCHIC *a.* 3. 1576. 4. Having undivided rule; †autocratic 1618. Hence **Mona·rchically** *adv.*

Monarchism (mɒ·năɹkiz'm). 1838. [a. F. *monarchisme*, f. *monarchie*; see -ISM.] The principles of monarchical government; attachment to monarchy. So **Mo·narchist,** an advocate of monarchy 1647.

Monarchize (mɒ·năɹkəiz), *v.* 1592. [f. MONARCH *sb.* + -IZE.] 1. *intr.* To perform the office of monarch; to rule absolutely. Also *to m. it.* 2. *trans.* †a. To rule over as a monarch –1621. b. To make a monarchy of 1660.

1. Allowing him a breath, a little Scene, To M., be fear'd, and kill with lookes SHAKS.

†**Mona·rcho.** 1588. [repr. It. *monarca* MONARCH.] 1. The title assumed by an insane Italian who fancied himself emperor of the world; hence *transf.* –1634. 2. Used derisively for MONARCH. Marston.

Monarchy (mɒ·năɹki). late ME. [a. F. *monarchie*, ad. L. *monarchia*, Gr. μοναρχία rule of one, f. μόναρχος MONARCH.] †1. Undivided rule by a single person; absolute power –1876. 2. A state ruled by a monarch; also, the rule or government exercised by a monarch. late ME. 3. Monarchical rule 1638. †4. The territory of a monarch (*rare*) –1699.

1. Gregory VII..claimed the m. of the world 1876. 2. *Absolute* or *despotic m.*, government in which the will of the monarch is absolute. *Constitutional m.* (see CONSTITUTIONAL *a.* 4). *Elective m.*, one in which the monarch is elected. *Hereditary m.*, one in which the monarch succeeds by heredity. *Limited m.* (see LIMITED). 3. The very institution of m. was repulsive to them BUCKLE. *fig.* The M. of right Reason STEELE.

‖**Monas** (mɒ·næs). *Pl.* **monades** (mɒ·nădīz). 1568. [Gr. μονάς; see MONAD.] = MONAD.

Monasterial (mɒnăstīᵊ·riăl), *a.* late ME. [f. L. *monasterium* (see MONASTERY) + -AL.] Belonging to or of the nature of a monastery. Hence **Monaste·rially** *adv.* like a monk.

Monastery (mɒ·năstəri). late ME. [ad. eccl. L. *monasterium*, a. late Gr. μοναστήριον, f. μονάζειν to live alone, f. μόνος.] A place of residence of a community (now almost exclusively, of monks) living secluded from the world under religious vows.

Monastic (mɒ̆næ·stik), *a.* (and *sb.*) 1600. [ad. med.L. *monasticus*, a. late Gr. μοναστικός, f. μονάζειν; see prec.] 1. Pertaining to or characteristic of monks, nuns, friars, and the like, or monasteries. 2. *Bookbinding.* Epithet of a method of finishing by tooling without gold; = 'antique' 1880. 3. *sb.* A member of a monastic order; a monk 1632.

1. To forsweare the ful stream of yᵉ world, and to liue in a nooke meerly Monastick SHAKS. So **Mona·stical** *a.* pertaining to m. life. late ME.; **-ly** *adv.*

Monasticism (mɒ̆næ·stisiz'm). 1795. [f. MONASTIC + -ISM.] The monastic system.

Monatomic (mɒnătɒ·mik), *a.* 1848. [f. MON(O)- + ATOM + -IC.] *Chem.* Containing one atom; consisting of molecules each containing one atom. Also used for: Univalent. So **Mona·tomism,** m. quality or condition.

Monaul (mɒnǭ·l). Also **monal, minaul,** etc. 1769. [Hind. *munāl* or *monāl*.] Anglo-Indian name for the Impeyan pheasant.

Monaxial (mɒnæ·ksiăl), *a.* 1880. [f. MON(O)- + L. *axis* + -AL, after AXIAL.] *Bot.* and *Zool.* Having only one axis; developing along a single line.

Monazite (mɒ·năzəit). 1836. [a. Ger. *monazit*, f. Gr. μονάζειν to be solitary, on account of its rarity.] *Min.* Phosphate of the cerium metals, found in reddish or brownish crystals.

‖**Mondaine** (moṅdēn). 1908. [Fr.; cf. MUNDANE.] A woman belonging to the world of fashion.

Monday (mɒ·ndeⁱ, -di). [OE. *Mōnandæg*, f. *mōnan*, gen. of *mōna* MOON *sb.* + *dæg* DAY; tr. late L. *Lunæ dies.*] The second day of the week.

But soft, What day is this? M., my Lord SHAKS. **Black M.,** (*a*) a name for Easter M.; (*b*) *school slang*, the first school-day after a vacation. **Saint M.,** used with reference to the practice among workmen of being idle on M., as a consequence of drunkenness on Sunday; chiefly in *to keep Saint M.* 1753. Hence **Mo·ndayish** *a.* affected with the indisposition, often felt by clergymen on Monday, resulting from Sunday's work 1804.

‖**Monde** (moṅd). 1765. [Fr., = 'world'. Cf. BEAU-MONDE.] The world of fashionable people; society. Also, the set in which one moves.

Mondial (mɒ·ndiăl), *a.* 1918. [ad. F. *mondial*, ad. late L. *mundialis*, f. *mundus* world.] World-wide.

Mone, obs. f. MOAN, MOON.

Monest, obs. f. MONISH *v.*

Monetary (mɒ·nĭtări, mɒ·n-), *a.* 1802. [ad. L. *monetarius* of or belonging to the mint, f. *moneta* mint.] 1. Of or pertaining to the coinage or currency. 2. Pertaining to or concerned with money, pecuniary 1860.

1. *M. unit*, the standard unit of value of a country's coinage. 2. Deep in great m. transactions 1865.

Moneth(e, obs. ff. MONTH.

Monetize (mv·nĭtəiz, mǫ·n-), *v.* 1880. [f. L. *moneta* + -IZE.] *trans.* To give a standard value to (a metal) in the coinage of a country; to put into circulation as money. So **Monetiza·tion** 1864.

Money (mv·ni), *sb.* *Pl.* **moneys** (mv·niz). ME. [a. OF. *moneie* (mod.F. *monnaie*) :— L. *moneta* : orig. the name of a goddess in whose temple at Rome money was coined, hence, a mint, money. The pl. **monies** is now used chiefly in sense 4.] 1. Current coin; metal stamped in pieces as a medium of exchange and measure of value. **b.** Hence, anything serving the same purposes as coin. late ME. **c.** In mod. use applied indifferently to coin and to such promissory documents representing coin (esp. bank-notes) as are currently accepted as a medium of exchange. See PAPER MONEY. 1819. 2. (With *pl.*) A particular coin or coinage. Also, a denomination of value representing a fraction or a multiple of the value of some coin; in full, *money of account*. late ME. 3. Coin in reference to its purchasing power; hence, possessions or property viewed as convertible into money ME. **b.** as a commodity in the market 1687. 4. *pl.* Prop. = 'sums of money', but often = the sing. (sense 3). Now chiefly in legal or quasi-legal use, or as an archaism. late ME.

1. I will giue thee the worth of it in m. 1 *Kings* xxi. 2. *fig.* Words are wise mens counters, they do but reckon by them: but they are the mony of fooles HOBBES. †*White m.*: standard silver coin. **c.** In international commerce..a good bill [*sc.* of exchange] is good m. 1903. 3. Wealth and m...are, in common language, considered as in every respect synonymous ADAM SMITH. **b.** The value of m. must be judged, like every thing else, from it's rate at market BURKE. 4. You come to me, and you say, Shylocke, we would haue moneyes SHAKS. From Shaks. onwards the use of the pl. for the sing. has been attributed to Jews, whose pronunc. is sometimes ridiculed by the spelling 'monish'.

Phrases. *M. makes the mare to go*; *m. is the sinews of war*; *time is m.*; etc. *For love or m.*: see LOVE *sb.* (*So and so*) *for my m.* (colloq.) = 'is what I desire or like', 'is my choice', 'give me..'. *To make m.*: to acquire or earn m. *To coin m.*: to make m. rapidly. (*It is*) *not everybody's* or *every man's m.*: not what everybody would find worth its price. *There is m. in* (*something*): m. can be made out of it.

attrib. and *Comb.*: **m.-bill**, a bill in Parliament for granting supplies; **-broker**, a money-dealer; **-clause**, a clause (in a parliamentary bill) for granting supplies; **-column**, (*a*) a portion of a page marked off by vertically ruled lines for figures denoting sums of money; (*b*) the column of a newspaper devoted to the money-market; **-dealer**, one who deals in m. in the way of exchange, banking, lending, etc.; so **-dealing** *vbl. sb.*; **-jobber**, a dealer in m. or coin; **-market**, the sphere of operation of the dealers in loans, stocks, and shares; **-monger**, a dealer in money, esp. in the way of lending it; hence **-mongering**, **†-monging** *vbl. sb.* and *ppl. a.*; **-order**, an order for payment of a specified sum, issued at one post-office and payable at another (in British use restricted to what is pop. called a *post-office order*, as dist. from a *postal order*); **†-scrivener**, one whose business it is to raise loans, put money out at interest, etc., on behalf of his clients; **-spider** = next (*a*); also, a spider of the genus *Salticus*; **-spinner**, (*a*) a small spider, *Aranea scenica*, supposed to bring good luck in money or other matters to the person over whom it crawls; (*b*) one who makes great sums by speculation or usury.

Money (mv·ni), *v.* late ME. [In sense 1, ad. F. *monnayer*; in other senses, f. MONEY *sb.*] 1. *trans.* To coin or mint (money). *rare.* †2. To supply with money; hence, to bribe -1625. 3. To dispose of for money (*rare*) 1611.

Mo·neyage. *Hist.* 1747. [a. OF. *monneage* (mod. F. *monnayage*) mint, tax upon money, f. *monnayer* MONEY *v.*] 'A payment by the moneyers for the privilege of coining; otherwise explained as a payment by the subjects to prevent loss by the depreciation or change of coinage' (Stubbs).

Mo·ney-bag. 1565. 1. A bag for holding money. In pl. often joc. for 'wealth'. 2. *transf. pl.* A person notable as having or loving money 1818.

Mo·ney-bound, *a.* *joc.* 1825. [after *weather-bound.*] Detained by want of money.

Mo·ney-box. 1585. A box for money; *esp.* a closed box into which coin is dropped through a slit.

Mo·ney-cha·nger. late ME. One whose business it is to change money at a fixed rate.

Moneyed (mv·nid), *a.* Also **monied.** 1457. [f. MONEY *sb.* + -ED [2].] 1. Having money, rich in money. *M. man* often *spec.* = CAPITALIST. 2. Consisting of money, derived from money 1790. 3. *M. interest*: interest in money as a possession; a class of persons having such interest. (Cf. *landed interest.*) 1711. 4. *U.S.* Of a company, etc.: Having power to deal in money 1872.

1. The monied men and leaders of commerce RUSKIN. 2. The monied resources of the State 1835.

Moneyer (mv·niəɹ). ME. [a. OF. *mon(n)ier*, *mon(n)oier* :—L. *monetarius* minter.] †1. **a.** A money-changer. ME. only. **b.** A money-dealer, banker, capitalist 1706. 2. One who coins money; a minter. Now chiefly *Hist.* late ME.

2. The Provost and Company of Moneyers 1668.

Mo·ney-grub. 1768. [Cf. GRUB *sb.*] One who is sordidly intent on amassing money. So **Mo·ney-gru:bber. Mo·ney-gru:bbing** *vbl. sb.* and *ppl. a.*

Mo·ney-lender. *c* 1780. One whose business is lending money at interest. So **Mo·ney-lending** *vbl. sb.* and *ppl. a.*

Moneyless (mv·niléṡ), *a.* ME. [-LESS.] Without money.

Mo·ney-ma·ker. late ME. †1. A minter, moneyer -1523. 2. One who gains and accumulates money; one intent on getting money 1864. So **Mo·ney-making** *vbl. sb.* acquisition of wealth; *ppl. a.* occupied in, or intent on, acquiring wealth; also (of things) lucrative.

Money matter. 1552. [MATTER *sb.* IV. 3.] An affair turning upon money. Chiefly *pl.*, the financial side of things.

Money's-worth. 1588. [WORTH *sb.*] 1. Something recognized as worth money or equivalent to money 1604. 2. Full value for money paid or to be paid. (Now chiefly with poss. pron.)

Mo·ney-wort. 1578. [After the old L. name *Nummularia.*] The plant *Lysimachia Nummularia* or Herb Twopence, which has roundish glossy leaves. Also, a book-name for *Anagallis tenella* and other plants.

Mongcorn (mv·ŋkǫɹn). *Obs.* exc. *dial.* ME. [f. ME. *mong* mixture + CORN *sb.*[1]] 'Mixed corn' = MASLIN [2].

Monger (mv·ŋgəɹ). [OE. *mangere*, f. *mangian* to traffic (*with*), to barter, f. L. *mango* trader.] A dealer, trader, trafficker. Now *rare*, exc. as the second element in compounds, as *cheesemonger*, *fishmonger*, *ironmonger*. Since 16th c., chiefly, one who carries on a petty or disreputable traffic, as *fashion-m.*, *mass-m.*, *news-m.*, *scandal-m.*, etc.

Mongering (mv·ŋgəriŋ), *vbl. sb.* 1846. [f. MONGER + -ING [1].] Trading, trafficking. Chiefly used as a second element in compounds. So **Mo·ngering** *ppl. a.*, **Mo·ngery.**

Mongol (mǫ·ŋgǫl). 1738. [Native name, said to be f. *mong* 'brave'. Cf. MOGUL.] **A.** *sb.* One of an Asiatic race now chiefly inhabiting Mongolia, between China proper and Siberia; also more widely, a Mongolian. **B.** *adj.* Pertaining to or characteristic of the Mongols, their country, or language; Mongolian 1763.

Mongolian (mǫŋgōu·liăn). 1738. [f. MONGOL + -IAN.] **A.** *adj.* 1. = MONGOL *a.* 2. *Anthropology.* Belonging to the yellow-skinned straight-haired type of mankind 1828. 3. Applied to a type of idiots resembling the Mongolians in physiognomy 1892. **B.** *sb.* A native of Mongolia; the language of the Mongols; one of the Mongolian race of mankind (see A. 2) 1846. So **Mongo·lic** *a.* and *sb.* 1834.

Mongoloid (mǫ·ŋgǫloid), *a.* (and *sb.*) 1868. [f. MONGOL + -OID.] 1. Belonging to that one of the five principal races of mankind which prevails over the vast region lying east of a line drawn from Lapland to Siam. HUXLEY. 2. = MONGOLIAN *a.* 3. 1899. 3. *sb.* One of the Mongoloid race 1868.

Mongoose, mungoose (mǫ·ngūs, mv·ŋgūs). 1698. [a. Marathi *mangūs.*] 1. An ichneumon, *Herpestes griseus*, common in India, and able to kill venomous snakes unharmed. Also applied to other ichneumons (subfamily *Herpestinæ*). 2. A species of lemur or maki, *Lemur mongoz* 1758.

Mongrel (mv·ŋgrĕl), *sb.* and *a.* 1486 (mengrell). [app. f. root *meng-*, *mang-*, *mong-* to mix (see MENG *v.*) + -REL.] **A.** *sb.* 1. A dog of no definable breed, resulting from various crossings. †**b.** Applied to persons as a term of contempt. (Cf. *cur.*) -1764. 2. An animal or plant resulting from the crossing of different breeds or kinds; restricted by some to the result of the crossing of varieties (opp. to *hybrid*) 1677. 3. A person not of pure race. Chiefly *disparaging.* 1542.

2. The parents of mongrels are varieties, and mostly domestic varieties DARWIN. *fig.* Though his two faculties of Serving-man and Sollíciter, should compound into one m. MILT.

B. *adj.* (the sb. used attrib. and appositively). 1. Of dogs: That is a mongrel 1576. **b.** As an abusive epithet for a person 1605. 2. In wider use, of animals and plants 1635. 3. Of persons: Of mixed race. Chiefly *disparaging.* 1606. 4. *transf.* That is 'neither one thing nor the other'. Chiefly *contempt.* 1581. **b.** Applied to a word or a dialect 1610.

1. **b.** A Knaue, a Rascall,..and the Sonne and Heire of a Mungrill Bitch SHAKS. 4. These Mungrell Pamphlets (part true, part false) FULLER. Hence **Mo·ngrelism**, the condition of being m. or hybrid. **Mo·ngrelize** *trans.* to make m. in race, etc.

'Mongst (mvŋst), *prep. poet.* 1590. Aphet. f. AMONGST.

Monial (mōu·niăl). ME. [a. OF. *moinel*, *moynel*, *monial* (mod.F. *meneau*), of unkn. origin.] *Arch.* Now *Antiq.* A mullion.

Monied, var. of MONEYED.

Monilated (mǫ·nileitĕd), *ppl. a.* 1877. [f. L. *monile* necklace + -ATE [2] + -ED [1].] *Anat.* = next.

Moniliform (mǫni·lifǭɹm), *a.* 1802. [a. F. *moniliforme*, or ad. mod.L. *moniliformis*, f. *monile* necklace; see -FORM.] Of the form of a necklace; having contractions at regular intervals; consisting of protuberances suggesting a string of beads.

Moniment, obs. f. MONUMENT.

Monish (mǫ·niʃ), *v.* ME. Now *rare.* [a. OF. *monester* :—pop.L. **monestare* : see ADMONISH.] To admonish. Hence **Mo·nisher**, **Mo·nishment** (*arch.*).

Monism (mǫ·niz'm). 1862. [ad. mod.L. *monismus*, f. Gr. μόνος single; see -ISM.] *Philos.* **a.** The doctrine that only one being exists. **b.** A general name for those theories which deny the duality (i.e. the existence as two ultimate kinds of substance) of matter and mind 1876. **c.** The doctrine that there is only one Supreme Being, as opp. to the belief in a Good and an Evil Principle as co-ordinate powers 1872.

b. Thus materialism and idealism or spiritualism are both species of m.; the name, however, is often applied specifically to a third variety, viz. the doctrine that physical and psychical phenomena are alike manifestations of a reality which cannot be identified with either matter or mind. N.E.D. So **Mo·nist**, one who holds a doctrine of m. (in any sense) 1836. **Moni·stic** *a.*, **Moni·stically** *adv.*

Monition (mŏni·ʃən). late ME. [a. OF., or ad. L. *monitionem*, f. *monit-*, *monere.*] 1. †**a.** Instruction. **b.** Warning. Also, a warning. 2. A warning of the presence or imminence of something (now only, of some impending danger). late ME. 3. An official or legal intimation or notice 1460. **b.** A formal notice from a bishop or an eccl. court admonishing a person to refrain from a specified offence 1509. **c.** In those courts which use the civil law process, a process in the nature of a summons 1840.

1. Sage monitions from his friends His talents to employ for nobler ends SWIFT. 2. The first monitions of the impending catastrophe occurred in 63 A.D. 1906. Hence **Moni·tion** *v.* *Eccl. Law.*, to warn by a m.

Monitor (mǫ·nitǫ̆ɹ), *sb.* 1546. [a. L., f. *monere*; see -OR.] 1. One who (or that which) admonishes another as to his conduct. Now somewhat *arch.* †Also (*rare*), an instigator. 1596. 2. A senior pupil in a school, with special duties, esp. that of keeping order, and occas. of acting as teacher to a junior class 1546. 3. Something that reminds or gives warning 1655. †4. = BACK-BOARD 4. -1831. 5. A lizard of the family *Monitoridæ* or *Varanidæ*, inhabiting Africa and Australia, supposed to give warning of the vicinity of crocodiles 1826. 6. An ironclad having a very low free-board and one or more revolving turrets containing great guns; so called from the name given by Captain Ericsson, its inventor, to the first vessel of the sort 1862. 7. *U.S.* (In full *m. roof* or *top.*) A raised part of a roof (e. g. in a railway-carriage), with openings for light and ventilation. Hence *m.-car.* 1871. 8. A jointed nozzle used in hydraulic mining, which may be turned in any direction 1881.

1. In this [*sc.* religion] you need not be a M. to the King BACON. Conscience, this once able m.,—placed on high as a judge within us STERNE. Hence **Mo·nitor** *v. trans.* to guide as a m. KEATS. **Monito·rial** *a.* monitory; of, pertaining to, or performed by monitors in schools. **Monito·rially** *adv.* **Mo·nitorship.** **Mo·nitress,** a female m.

Monitory (mɒ·nitəri). 1450. [ad. L. *monitorius*; see prec. and -ORY.] **A.** *adj.* 1. Giving or conveying a warning; admonitory. **b.** *M. letter* = B. 2. 1696. 2. *M. lizard* = MONITOR *sb.* 5. 1810. **B.** *sb.* †1. An admonition -1677. 2. A letter containing an admonition or warning, esp. one issued by a bishop or pope 1624.

A. 1. He heard the m. growl [of a mastiff] WORDSW.

Monk (mɒŋk). [OE. *munuc* :—**muniko-*, ad. pop. L. **monicus* for *monachus*, a. late Gr. μοναχός adj., single, solitary, f. μόνος alone. The word orig. meant a religious hermit or solitary.] 1. A member of a community of men living apart from the world under vows of poverty, chastity, and obedience, according to a rule. (Cf. *friar.*) 2. As the name of certain animals, esp. with reference to the cowl or hood of a monk; see also SEA-MONK 1713. 3. As the name of various objects in certain arts and crafts 1683.

1. **Black m.,** a Benedictine; also, a Black or Augustinian canon; **†gray m., white m.,** a Cistercian m. But all Hoods, make not Monkes SHAKS. The object of a m. was to make a good man of himself, the object of a friar was to do a good work among others 1889. 2. *Tropidorhynchus Corniculatus*. Its bare head and neck have also suggested the names of 'Friar Bird', 'Monk', 'Leather Head', etc. J. GOULD. 3. The Sheet Printed on has a black blotch on it: Which Blotch is called a M. MOXON. A round-faced pestle, called a M. 1763. The piece of agarick used to communicate the fire to the powder is called the m. 1834.

Comb.: **m.-bat,** the *Molossus nasutus* of Jamaica, etc.; **M.-Latin,** the corrupt Latin used by monks; **m.-seal,** a white-bellied seal inhabiting the Mediterranean; **m.'s rhubarb,** a species of dock, esp. *Rumex Patientia* and *R. alpinus.*

Monkdom (mɒ·ŋkdəm). 1862. [f. prec. + -DOM.] The condition of a monk; monks collectively; the domain of monks.

Monkery (mɒ·ŋkəri). Chiefly *contempt.* 1536. [f. MONK + -ERY.] 1. The state, condition, or profession of monks; monastic life, monasticism. 2. **a.** A body of monks; a monastery 1549. **b.** Monks collectively; also, the monks (of a particular place) 1552. 3. *pl.* Monkish practices or paraphernalia 1624. 4. Conduct or practice characteristic of monks (esp. in the Middle Ages) 1649.

1. You quote not one line from any Father in the third century, in favour of m. WESLEY. 2. **a.** A long residence..in courts, monkeries, and barracks 1852.

Monkey (mɒ·ŋki), *sb. Pl.* **†monkies, monkeys.** 1530. [Of obscure origin. Possibly MLG. **moneke*, dim. of Romanic **monna* (F. †*monne*, It. *monna*, etc. female ape) of unknown etym.] **I.** 1. An animal of any species of the group of mammals closely allied to and resembling man, and ranging from the anthropoid apes to the marmosets; any animal of the order *Primates* except man and the lemurs. In a more restricted sense, the term is taken to exclude the anthropoid apes and the baboons. 2. *transf.* **a.** One who resembles a monkey; *esp.* a mimic 1589. **b.** A term of playful contempt, chiefly of young people 1604. 3. **a.** A young hare. *dial.* **b.** A sheep. *Australian.* 1881.

1. His Monkie..tore his Principall Note-Booke all to pieces, when by chance it lay forth BACON. *Howling m.*, a m. of the genus *Mycetes*. 2. **b.** Well, little monkeys mine, I must go write; and so good-night SWIFT.

II. †1. A kind of gun or cannon -1663. 2. A machine consisting of a heavy hammer or ram working vertically in a groove and used in pile-driving, etc. Also, the ram itself and the hook by which it is raised. 1750. 3. Applied to various receptacles for liquor; *esp.* a globular earthenware water-vessel with a straight upright neck 1834. 4. *Betting-slang.* £500; in America, $500. 1832.

Phrases (colloq. and slang). *To suck* (or *sup*) *the m.*: (*a*) to drink from the bottle; hence, to tipple; (*b*) to drink out of a cocoa-nut emptied of milk and filled with spirit; (*c*) to drink spirits from a cask through a straw or tube inserted in a small hole. *My monkey's up*: I am angry or enraged. So *to get one's m. up, to put* (a person's) *m. up.*

attrib. and *Comb.*: **m.-block,** 'a small single block strapped with a swivel; also, those nailed on the topsail-yards of some merchantmen, to lead the bunt-lines through' (Smyth); **-board,** a footboard at the back of a vehicle for a footman or conductor to stand on; **-boat,** (*a*) a small boat used in docks and on the Thames; **-engine,** a pile-driver having a ram moving in a wooden frame; **-gaff** *U.S.*, a small gaff on some large merchant-vessels, placed above the spanker-gaff; **-jacket,** a short close-fitting jacket, such as is worn by sailors; **-rail,** a supplementary rail above the quarter-rail; **-shines** *pl.*, *U.S. slang*, monkey-like tricks or antics; **monkey('s)-tail,** a short iron bar used in training naval guns; a lanyard attached to the end of a lever; **m. tricks,** mischievous tricks 1780; **-wrench,** a wrench or spanner having a movable jaw.

b. m.-bread, the fruit of the baobab tree; also, the tree; **-cup,** the pitcher-plant, genus *Nepenthes*; **-flower,** the genus *Mimulus*; **m. nut,** a name for the pea-nut, *Arachis hypogæa*; **-puzzle,** the puzzle-monkey, *Araucaria imbricata.*

Mo·nkey, *v.* 1859. [f. prec.] 1. *trans.* **a.** To ape the manners of, mimic. **b.** To mock, make a jest of. 2. *intr.* To play mischievous or foolish tricks 1886.

Mo·nkey-face. 1598. A (human) face like a monkey's. So **Mo·nkey-faced** *a.*

Monkeyfy (mɒ·ŋkifəi), *v.* Also **†monkify.** 1761. [f. MONKEY *sb.* + -FY.] To make like a monkey; to make ridiculous-looking.

Monkeyish (mɒ·ŋki,iʃ), *a.* 1621. [f. MONKEY *sb.* + -ISH [1].] Like a monkey in imitativeness or mischievousness. **Mo·nkeyishness.**

Mo·nkeyism. 1845. [f. MONKEY *sb.* + -ISM.] Monkey-like character or behaviour.

Mo·nkey-pot. Also **monkey's pot.** 1. The woody seed-vessel of the Brazilian tree *Lecythis ollaria*; the tree itself. 2. A vessel used in tropical countries for cooling water 1897.

†Monkeyro·ny. 1773. Alteration of MACARONI (sense 2) -1786.

Mo·nk-fish. 1610. [f. MONK.] 1. The Angel-fish, *Squatina angelus.* 2. The Angler, *Lophius piscatorius* 1666.

Monkhood (mɒ·ŋkhud). OE. [f. MONK + -HOOD.] The state or profession of a monk; monasticism; monks collectively.

Monkish (mɒ·ŋkiʃ), *a.* 1546. [f. MONK + -ISH [1].] 1. Of or belonging to monks; monastic. **b.** That is a monk 1697. **c.** Used or done by monks 1612. 2. Resembling a monk or what pertains to a monk 1577. 3. Characteristic of monks or the monastic system. Chiefly *depreciatory.* 1570.

1. **b.** An old M. author 1697. **c.** M. Latin 1761. 2. A thinne lippe, and a little m. eye 1602. Hence **Mo·nkishness.**

Monkly (mɒ·ŋkli), *a.* Now *rare.* OE. [f. MONK + -LY [1].] Of or pertaining to a monk or monks; monastic.

Monkship (mɒ·ŋkʃip). 1620. [f. MONK + -SHIP.] The monastic system; monks collectively. With *poss. pron.* The personality of a monk.

Monk's-hood, monkshood (mɒ·ŋkshud). 1578. [From likeness of form.] 1. A plant of the genus *Aconitum*, esp. *A. Napellus.* 2. Applied to species of the genus *Delphinium* (Larkspur) and to *Dielytra Cucullaria* 1597.

Monmouth (mɒ·n-, mɒ·nməþ). *Hist.* 1599. The name of an English county town (formerly regarded as part of Wales), used *attrib.* 1. *M. cap*: a flat round cap formerly worn by soldiers and sailors. 2. *M. cock*: a military 'cock' of the hat 1711-69.

1. The Welchmen..wearing Leekes in their M. caps SHAKS.

Mono- (mɒno, mŏnɒ·), bef. a vowel often **mon-**, repr. Gr. μονο-, comb. f. μόνος alone, only, single, occurring in a number of words adopted from existing Greek compounds (as MONARCH, MONOGAMY, MONOPOLY), and hence used to form words independently of a Greek original. In recent formations *mono-* is often combined (instead of UNI-) with a Latin element, and occas. prefixed to an English word. Many of these words have correlatives in DI- *pref.*[2], TRI-, POLY-, etc.

1. General words: **Monoca·rdian** [Gr. καρδία] *a.*, having a single auricle and ventricle to the heart, as fishes and reptiles. **Monoci·liate**(d *adjs.*, *Zool.* having a single cilium. **Monoco·ndylar, -condy·lian, -condy·lic** [Gr. μονοκόνδυλος] *adjs.*, *Zool.* having one occipital condyle, as the skull of birds and reptiles. **Monocro·tic, Mono·crotous** [Gr. κρότος beat] *adjs.*, *Phys.* of a pulse, having a single beat, not DICROTIC. **Mo·nocyst** *Path.* a tumour consisting of a single cyst. **Monoda·ctyl(e, Monoda·ctylous** [Gr. δάκτυλος finger] *adjs.*, *Zool.* having only one finger, toe, or claw; in Crustacea = SUBCHELATE. **Monoga·stric** [Gr. γαστήρ stomach] *a.*, *Anat.* having only one stomach or digestive cavity. **Mo·noïde·ism,** concentration of the mind upon one idea; esp. as a form of monomania. **Mono·latry,** worship of one out of many gods. **Monomeni·scous** *a.*, applied to those eyes, in invertebrates, that have only one lens. **Mono·merous** [Gr. μέρος part] *a.*, *Entom.* consisting of only one member or joint; *Bot.* applied to flowers having one member in each whorl. **Monope·talous** *a.*, of a flower, having the corolla in one piece or the petals united so as to form a tube. **Mo·nophase** *a.*, *Electr.* exhibiting a single phase. **Monophyle·tic** [Gr. φυλετικός, f. φυλέτης tribesman] *a.*, pertaining to one family or race or to descent from a single prototypal form. **Monophy·llous** [Gr. φύλλον leaf] *a.*, of a calyx, consisting of one leaf. **Monophy·odont** [Gr. φύειν to generate + ὀδοντ-, ὀδούς tooth] *a.*, having only one set of teeth. **Mo·noplast -plastid** [Gr. πλαστός formed], *Biol.* a single o. simple cell; an organism or stage of an organism consisting of such; hence **Monopla·stic** *a.* ‖**Monople·gia** [Gr. πληγή stroke], *Path.* paralysis of one part or limb only; hence **Monople·gic** *a.* **Mono·pody** [Gr. ποδ-, πούς foot], *Pros.* a measure consisting of a single foot. **Monopo·lylogue** [POLY- + -LOGUE], an entertainment in which one actor sustains many characters. **Monopsy·chism** [Gr. ψυχή soul], the theory that all souls are one; the unity of souls thus asserted. **Monopyre·nous** [Gr. πυρήν fruit-stone] *a.*, *Bot.* having but one stone or kernel; said of fruits. **Mo·norail,** a railway with carriages running on a single rail. **Monose·palous** *a.*, *Bot.* prop., having one lateral sepal only; but misused for *gamosepalous.* **Monosi·phonous** *a.*, *Bot.* having a single siphon; applied to certain Algæ. **Monospe·rmous** [Gr. σπέρμα] *a.*, *Bot.* having only one seed. **Mono·stichous** [Gr. στίχος row] *a.*, *Zool.* consisting of a single layer or row. **Mo·nostyle** [Gr. στῦλος pillar], *Arch.* having or consisting of a single shaft, pillar, or column; so **Monosty·lar** *a.* **Monosymme·trical** *a.*, *Bot.* of flowers, fruits, etc.: divisible into exactly similar halves in one plane only. **Monothe·cal** [Gr. θήκη case, box] *a.*, *Bot.* having only one loculament or cell; applied to anthers. **Mono·tomous** [Gr. τομή cutting] *a.*, *Min.* having a cleavage distinct only in a certain direction. **Monozo·ic** [Gr. ζῷον animal] *a.*, *Zool.* applied to a spore which produces one sporozoite.

2. *Chem.* Used in the names of compounds to signify the presence of a single atom or combining equivalent of the element or radical indicated by the word to which *mono-* is prefixed; as in **Monoba·sic** [BASE *sb.*[1]] *a.*, having one base, or one atom of a base; of an acid, containing one atom of replaceable hydrogen. **Monoca·rbon** *a.*, containing or derived from one atom of carbon. **Monoste·arin,** that species of stearin formed from glycerin by the replacement by stearyl of one only of the three OH groups.

Monocarpellary (mɒ:nokā·ɹpělări), *a.* 1863. [MONO-.] *Bot.* Having or consisting of a single carpel.

Monocarpic (mɒnokā·ɹpik), *a.* 1849. [f. as next + -IC.] *Bot.* Of a plant: Bearing fruit only once (and then dying). So **Mo·nocarp,** a m. plant 1846.

Monocarpous (mɒnokā·ɹpəs), *a.* 1731. [f. mod.L. *monocarpus*, f. Gr. μόνος MONO- + καρπός fruit; see -OUS.] 1. *Bot.* = MONOCARPELLARY. 2. *Bot.* = MONOCARPIC 1830.

Monocephalous (mɒnose·făləs), *a.* 1845. [f. mod.L. *monocephalus*, Gr. μονοκέφαλος one-headed + -OUS.] Having only one head. Applied **a.** to a fruit or ovary which has but one head or summit; b. to a plant which has its flowers disposed in a single head or umbel.

†**Monoceros** (mǫnǫ·sĕrǫs). ME. [a. OF. *monoceros*, a. L., a. Gr. μονόκερως, f. μόνος MONO- + κέρας horn.] 1. The UNICORN -1749. 2. A fish having one horn, as the saw-fish, sword-fish, or narwhal -1825.

Monochlamydeous (mǫnǫklămi·dĭəs), *a.* 1830. [f. mod.L. *Monochlamydeæ*, f. Gr. μόνος MONO- + χλαμυδ-, χλαμύς cloak; see -EOUS.] *Bot.* Having only one floral envelope; having a single perianth; belonging to the division *Monochlamydeæ*.

Monochloro- (mǫnǫklō°ro). Also **mo-nochlor-.** 1855. [See MONO- 2 and CHLORO-.] *Chem.* Comb. form, expressing the presence in a compound of one equivalent of chlorine, as *monochloracetic acid*, etc.

Monochord (mǫ·nǫ̆kǫɹd). late ME. [a. F. *monocorde*, ad. med.L. *monochordos, -on*, a. Gr. μονόχορδον adj. neut., f. μόνος MONO- + χορδή string (see CHORD *sb.*).] 1. A musical instrument composed of a sound-board with a single string; used for the mathematical determination of musical intervals. 2. A mediæval musical instrument with several strings and bridges for the production of a combination of sounds. *Obs.* exc. *Hist.* late ME. 3. A harmonious combination of sound; hence *fig.* harmony, agreement. Now *rare*. late ME.

Monochromatic (mǫnǫ̆kromæ·tik), *a.* 1822. [f. Gr. μόνος MONO- + χρωματικός CHROMATIC.] 1. Of or presenting one colour only; applied *spec.* to light of one wave-length. 2. Executed in monochrome 1823.

1. *M. lamp*, a lamp which produces a m. light. Hence **Monochroma·tically** *adv.*

Monochrome (mǫ·nokrōᵘm), *sb.* (and *a.*). 1662. [In sense 1, ad. med.L. *monochroma, -chromat-*; in other uses a. F. or ad. Gr. μονόχρωμος, -ον, a by-form of μονοχρώματος.] 1. A painting executed in different tints of one colour. 2. Representation in one colour; esp. in phr. (to paint, etc.) *in m.* Hence occas., the being in one colour, a tract of one colour. 1851. 3. *adj.* Having only one colour; executed in one colour 1849.

2. One cold monotonous m. of gray FERGUSSON. Hence **Monochro·mic, -al** *a.* = MONOCHROME *a.* **Mo·nochro·mist,** a painter in m. **Monochro·mous** *a.* **Mo·nochro·my,** the art of painting in m.

Monocle (mǫ·nǫ̆k'l). 1858. [a. F., ad. L. MONOCULUS.] A single eye-glass.

Monoclinal (mǫnokləi·năl), *a.* 1858. [f. Gr. μόνος MONO- + κλίνειν to bend + -AL.] *Geol.* Applied to strata that dip in one and the same direction. So **Mo·nocline,** a m. fold 1879.

Monoclinic (mǫnokli·nik), *a.* 1868. [f. as prec. + -IC.] *Cryst.* Having one of the axial intersections oblique.

Monoclinous (mǫnǫklǝi·nǝs), *a.* 1828. [f. F. *monocline*, or mod.L. *monoclinus*, f. Gr. μόνος MONO- + κλίνη bed; see -OUS.] 1. *Bot.* Having both stamens and pistils in the same flower; hermaphrodite. 2. *Geol.* = MONOCLINAL 1882.

Monocotyledon (mǫ:nokǫtilī·dǫ̆n). 1727. [ad. mod.L. *monocotyledon*, f. Gr. μόνος MONO- + κοτυληδών; see COTYLEDON.] *Bot.* A flowering plant having one cotyledon or seed-leaf. The Monocotyledons, or Endogens, constitute one of the two great classes of flowering plants. Hence **Monocotyle·donous** *a.*, having a single cotyledon; belonging to the class of Monocotyledons 1770.

Monocracy (mǫ̆nǫ·krăsi). 1651. [See next and -CRACY.] Government by a single person, autocracy.

Monocrat (mǫ·nǫ̆kræt). 1792. [ad. Gr. μονοκρατής, f. μόνος MONO- + κρατεῖν to rule; see -CRAT.] *U.S. Hist.* A partisan of monocracy; a nickname given *c* 1790 by Jefferson to members of the Federalist party, because they sided with England against France. Hence **Monocra·tic** *a.*

Monocular (mǫ̆nǫ·kiŭlaɹ), *a.* 1640. [f. late L. *monoculus* (see MONOCULUS) + -AR.] 1. Having only one eye, or the use of only one. Now *rare*. 2. Of or pertaining to one eye only; adapted to one eye 1858.

1. He had..catch'd M. Trouts 1696. 2. M. vision 1858. Hence **Monocula·rity,** m. condition. **Mo-no·cularly** *adv.* with the use of one eye only.

Monocule (mǫ·nokiŭl). *rare.* 1771. [a. F., or ad. L. *monoculus*.] A creature with one eye only (e.g. the Cyclops). Also, a member of the Linnæan genus MONOCULUS.

Monoculous (mǫ̆nǫ·kiŭləs), *a.* 1656. [f. L. *monoculus* (see next) + -OUS.] One-eyed.

‖ **Monoculus** (mǫ̆nǫ·kiŭlŭs). 1440. [late L., irreg. f. Gr. μόνος MON(O)- + L. *oculus*.] 1. A one-eyed being. 2. A Linnæan genus of minute crustaceans; a member of this genus 1752.

Monocycle (mǫ·nǫ̆səik'l). 1869. [f. Gr. μόνος MONO- + κύκλος wheel, CYCLE.] A velocipede having only one wheel.

Monocyclic (mǫnosi·klik, -səi·klik), *a.* 1882. [f. as prec. + -IC.] *Bot.* and *Zool.* Having or consisting of a single circle or whorl of parts.

Monodelph (mǫ·nǫ̆delf). 1842. [ad. F. *Monodelphe*, f. mod.L. *Monodelphia*, f. μόνος MONO- + δελφύς womb.] *Zool.* A mammal of the subclass *Monodelphia*, characterized by a single uterus and vagina, and comprising all mammals except the monotremes and marsupials. So **Monode·lphian, Monode·l-phic, Monode·lphous** *adjs.*

Monodic (mǫ̆nǫ·dik), *a.* 1818. [ad. Gr. μονῳδικός, f. μονῳδός; see MONODY and -IC.] Pertaining to or of the nature of monody. In *Music*, characterized by the predominance of one part or melody, to which the other parts merely furnish harmonies.

Monodist (mǫ·nǫ̆dist). 1751. [f. MONODY + -IST.] One who writes or sings a monody. So **Mo·nodize** *v. trans.* to make the subject of a monody. COLERIDGE.

Monodrama (mǫ·nodrāmă). Also †**-dram(e.** 1793. [f. MONO- + DRAMA.] A dramatic piece for a single performer. Hence **Mo:no-drama·tic** *a.*

Monody (mǫ·nǫ̆di). 1623. [ad. L. *monodia*, a. Gr. μονῳδία solo, lament, f. μονῳδός, f. μόνος + ᾠδός, contr. f. ἀοιδ-, ablaut-var. of ἀείδειν to sing. Cf. ᾠδή ODE.] 1. In Greek literature: a. A lyric ode sung by a single voice; an ode sung by one of the actors in a tragedy (as dist. from the chorus); hence, a mournful song or dirge. b. A funeral oration. GIBBON. 2. A poem in which the mourner bewails some one's death 1637. 3. Monotonous sound POE.

2. In this M. the Author bewails a learned Friend, unfortunately drown'd MILT.

‖ **Monœcia** (mǫnī·ʃiă). 1753. [mod.L. (Linn.), f. Gr. μόνος MONO- + οἶκος house; cf. DIŒCIA.] *Bot.* The twenty-first class in the Sexual System of Linnæus, comprising plants which have the stamens and pistils in separate flowers, but on the same plant.

Monœcious (mǫnī·ʃəs), *a.* 1761. [f. prec. + -OUS.] 1. *Bot.* a. Of phanerogams: Having unisexual male and female flowers on the same plant; belonging to the class MONŒCIA. b. Of cryptogams: Having both male and female organs on the same individual 1861. 2. *Zool.* Having the two sexes in one individual; hermaphrodite 1826. So **Monœ·cism** 1875.

‖ **Monogamia** (mǫnogē·miă, -gæ·miă). 1760. [mod.L. (Linn.) use of late L. *monogamia* 'single marriage', MONOGAMY.] *Bot.* The sixth order in the nineteenth class (*Syngenesia*) of the Linnæan Sexual System, containing species which bear solitary flowers in which the anthers are united. Hence **Mo·nogam,** a plant of this order 1828.

Monogamist (mǫ̆nǫ·gămist). 1651. [f. Gr. μονόγαμος marrying only once (f. μόνος MONO- + γάμος marriage) + -IST.] 1. 'One who disallows second marriages' (J.); also, one who is debarred from second marriage after the death of the first spouse; opp. to *digamist*. 2. One who practises or favours monogamy (sense 2), as opp. to *bigamist* or *polygamist* 1731. 3. quasi-*adj.* 1875.

Monogamy (mǫ̆nǫ·gămi). 1612. [ad. F. *monogamie*, ad. eccl. L. *monogamia*, Gr. μονογαμία, f. μονόγαμος (see prec.).] 1. The practice or principle of marrying only once; opp. to *digamy*. Now *rare*. 2. The condition, rule, or custom of being married to only one person at a time (opp. to *bigamy* or *polygamy*) 1708. 3. *Zool.* The habit of living in pairs, or having only one mate 1785. Hence **Mono-ga·mian, Monoga·mic** *adjs.* of or pertaining to m.; monogamous. **Mono·gamous** *a.* practising m.; of or pertaining to m.

Monogenesis (mǫnodʒe·nĭsis). 1864. [a. mod.L.; see MONO- and GENESIS.] *Biol.* a. Development of all living things from a single cell, or of all human beings from a single pair. b. Asexual reproduction. **Monogene·tic** *a.* 1873.

Monogenic (mǫnodʒe·nik), *a.* 1893. [f. Gr. μόνος MONO- + γένος kind, origin (see -GEN) + -IC.] 1. Math. *M. function*: a function which has a single differential coefficient. 2. *Biol.* Of or pertaining to monogenesis; monogenetic 1897. **Mono·genous** *a.* 1866.

Monogenism (mǫ̆nǫ·dʒĕniz'm). 1865. [f. MONO- + -GEN + -ISM.] The doctrine of MONOGENY. So **Mono·genist,** one who maintains this doctrine 1857.

Monogeny (mǫ̆nǫ·dʒĕni). 1865. [f. MONO- + -GENY.] The (theoretical) origination of mankind from one common pair of ancestors; also, *loosely*, monogenism.

Monoglot (mǫ·nǫ̆glǫt). 1830. [ad. Gr. μονόγλωττος, f. μόνος + γλῶττα, γλῶσσα tongue.] A. *adj.* 1. That speaks, writes, or understands only one language. 2. Written in only one language 1890. B. *sb.* One who knows only one language 1894.

Monogony (mǫ̆nǫ·gŏni). 1873. [f. Gr. μόνος MONO- + -γονία begetting.] *Biol.* Asexual propagation: opp. to *amphigony*.

Monogram (mǫ·nǫ̆græm). 1610. [Two formations. (1) In sense 1, ad. L. *monogrammus* adj., a. Gr. *μονόγραμμος, f. μόνος single + γραμμή line. (2) In sense 2, ad. late L. *monogramma* neut., irreg. f. late Gr. μονόγραμμον, neut. of μονόγραμμος, f. μόνος single + γράμμα letter.] †1. A picture drawn in lines without shading or colour; a sketch -1843. 2. A character composed of two or more letters interwoven together, the letters being usually the initials of a person's name 1696.

2. *The Christian m.* or *m. of Christ*, the combination (☧) of the first two letters of Χριστός (Christ). Hence **Mo·nogramma·tic, -al** *a.* of, pertaining to, or in the style of, a m.

Monograph (mǫ·nǫ̆graf), *sb.* 1821. [f. MONO- + -GRAPH.] 1. Orig., a separate treatise on a single species, genus, or larger group of plants, animals, or minerals. (Often with const. *of.*) Hence *gen.* a separate treatise on a single object or class of objects. ¶2. Misused for MONOGRAM 2. 1849.

1. A M. of Fossil Crustacea 1876, on Poe 1880. Hence **Mo·nograph** *v.* to write a m. on; to discuss in a m. **Mono·grapher,** a writer of a m.

Monography (mǫ̆nǫ·grăfi). 1773. [f. Gr. μόνος + γράφειν; see -GRAPHY.] = MONOGRAPH 1.

‖ **Monogynia** (mǫnodʒi·niă). 1760. [mod.L. (Linn.), f. *monogynus* (f. Gr. μόνος + γυνή, used for 'pistil'): see -IA [1].] *Bot.* The first order in each of the first thirteen classes of the Linnæan Sexual System, comprising plants having flowers with only one pistil. Hence **Monogyn** (mǫ·nodʒin). **Monogy·nian, Monog-y·nic, Mono·gynous** *adjs.* having only one pistil; belonging to the order *Monogynia*.

Monogyny (mǫ̆nǫ·dʒini). 1876. [f. MONO- + Gr. γυνή.] The practice of mating with only one female, or marrying only one wife. (Cf. MONANDRY.)

Monoicous (mǫ̆noi·kəs), *a.* 1822. [f. mod. L. *monoicus*, F. *monoïque*, irreg. ad. Gr. *μόνοικος (see MONŒCIA) + -OUS.] *Bot.* a. = MONŒCIOUS 1. Now *rare* or *Obs.* b. Applied by Darwin to those polygamous plants which have the three sexual varieties together on the same individual; opp. to *trioicous*.

Monoline (mǫ·nǫ̆ləin). 189.. [f. MONO- + LINE *sb.*[2]] 1. Name for one of the printing machines which cast a line at a time. Cf.

LINOTYPE. **2.** = *monorail* (see MONO- 1) 1903.

Monolith (mǫ·nŏliþ). 1848. [a. F. *monolithe* adj. and sb., a. Gr. μονόλιθος made out of one stone, f. μόνος + λίθος.] **A.** *sb.* A single block of stone, esp. one shaped into a pillar or monument. **B.** *adj.* Of the nature of a monolith 1850. Hence **Mo·nolithal** (*rare*), **Monoli·thic** *adjs.* formed of a single block of stone; consisting of or relating to monoliths.

Monologist (mǫ̆nǫ·lŏdʒist). 1625. [f. Gr. μονόλογος (see MONOLOGUE) + -IST.] †**1.** One who repeats the same word. **2.** One who soliloquizes; also, one who monopolizes the conversation 1711. So **Mono·logize** *v. intr.* to talk in monologue.

Monologue (mǫ·nŏlǫg), *sb.* 1668. [a. F. *monologue*, 'one that loues to heare himselfe talke' (Cotgr.), ad. Gr. μονόλογος speaking alone. See -LOGUE.] **1.** 'A scene in which a person of the drama speaks by himself' (J.); contrasted with *chorus* and *dialogue*. Also, in mod. use, a dramatic composition for a single performer. **b.** *gen.* Literary composition of this nature 1668. **2.** Talk or discourse of the nature of a soliloquy 1859.

1. The m. in Hamlet 1872. **b.** He also gives you an account of himself..in m. DRYDEN. So **Mono·lo·gic, -al** *a.* **Mo·nologue** *v. intr.* **Mo·nologuist,** also **-logueist,** one who talks or performs in m. **Mo·nologuize** *v.* to monologize.

Monology (mǫ̆nǫ·lŏdʒi). 1608. [ad. Gr. μονολογία.] †**a.** A monologue. **b.** The habit of monologizing.

b. Coleridge persisted in m. through his whole life DE QUINCEY.

Monomachy (mǫ̆nǫ·măki). 1582. [a. F., or ad. L. *monomachia* (also used), a. Gr., f. μόνος + μαχ-, μάχεσθαι to fight.] A single combat; a duel. So **Mono·machist,** one who fights in single combat. DE QUINCEY.

Monomania (mǫnomē¹·niă). 1823. [a. mod.L. *monomania*, f. Gr. μόνος + μανία MANIA.] Insanity on one subject only.

b. I call it quite my m., it is such a subject of mine DICKENS. Hence **Monoma·niac** *sb.* one who suffers from m.; also *adj.* **Mo:nomani·acal** *a.*

Monomark (mǫ·nomāɹk). 1925. [f. MONO- + MARK *sb.*¹] One of a system of registered marks (letters and figures) identifying articles, goods, addresses, etc.

Monometallic (mǫnomĭtæ·lik), *a.* 1877. [f. MONO- + METALLIC, after *bimetallic*.] Pertaining to, involving, or using a standard of currency based upon one metal. Hence **Monome·tallism,** the m. system or standard of currency. **Monome·tallist,** one who advocates monometallism.

Monometer (mǫ̆nǫ·mĭtəɹ). 1847. [a. L., a. Gr. μονόμετρος, f. μόνος MONO- + μέτρον.] *Pros.* A line consisting of one metre.

Monometric (mǫnome·trik), *a.* 1837. [f. Gr. μόνος MONO- + μέτρον METRE + -IC.] *Cryst.* = ISOMETRIC 3.

Monomial (mǫ̆nōᵘ·miăl). 1706. [irreg. f. MONO- after *binomial*.] *Alg.* (An expression) consisting of one term only.

Monomorphous (mǫnomǭ·ɹfəs), *a.* 1839. [f. Gr. μόνος MONO- + μορφή form + -OUS.] Having only one form throughout development. So **Monomo·rphic** *a.* 1880.

Monomyary (mǫnomai·ări), *a.* and *sb.* 1835. [f. mod.L. *Monomyaria* n. pl. (f. Gr. μόνος MONO- + μῦς muscle) + -ARY¹.] **A.** *adj.* Belonging to the group *Monomyaria* of bivalves, having only one adductor muscle. **B.** *sb.* A bivalve of this group 1842. So **Monomya·rian** *a.* and *sb.* 1837.

Mononomial (mǫnonōᵘ·miăl), *a.* and *sb.* 1844. A more correct form of MONOMIAL.

Monophthong (mǫ·nǫ̆fþǫŋ). 1620. [ad. Gr. μονόφθογγος adj., f. μόνος MONO- + φθόγγος sound.] A single vowel sound. **Monophtho·ngal** *a.* consisting of a m. **Monophtho·ngize** *v. trans.* to convert into a m.

Monophysite (mǫ̆nǫ·fisəit), *sb.* (*a.*) 1698. [ad. eccl. L. *Monophysita*, a. eccl. Gr. Μονοφυσίτης, f. μόνος MONO- + φύσις nature; see -ITE¹ 1.] *Eccl. Hist.* A heretic who believes that there is only one nature in the person of Jesus Christ. Hence **Monophysi·tic, -al** *a.* pertaining to the Monophysites or their heresy. **Mono·physitism.**

Monoplane (mǫ·noplein). 1910. [f. MONO- + PLANE *sb.*³] An aeroplane having one plane.

Monopode (mǫ·nopōᵘd). 1816. [ad. L. *monopodius*, a. Gr. *μονοπόδιος = μονόπους (-ποδ-), f. μόνος MONO- + πούς foot.] **1.** A creature having only one foot; *spec.* one of a race of men fabled to have only one foot, with which they shaded themselves from the heat of the sun (see Pliny *Nat. Hist.* VII. ii). **2.** = MONOPODIUM 1890.

‖ **Monopodium** (mǫnopōᵘ·diŏm). 1875. [mod.L., f. as prec.] *Bot.* A single axis which extends at the apex, producing in succession lateral structures beneath it. **Monopo·dial** *a.*

Monopolism (mǫ̆nǫ·pŏliz'm). 1881. [f. MONOPOLY + -ISM.] The system of monopolies.

Monopolist (mǫ̆nǫ·pŏlist). 1601. [f. as prec. + -IST.] One who monopolizes or possesses a monopoly; one who favours monopoly.

transf. The monopolists of political power BRIGHT. Hence **Monopoli·stic** *a.*

Monopolize (mǫ̆nǫ·pŏləiz), *v.* 1611. [f. as prec. + -IZE.] **1.** *trans.* To get into one's hands the whole stock of (a commodity); to gain or hold exclusive possession of (a trade); to engross. **2.** *transf.* and *fig.* To obtain exclusive possession or control of 1628.

2. This fellow, Hawk, is monopolising your niece DICKENS. Hence **Mono:poliza·tion** 1727. **Mono·polizer** 1629.

Monopoly (mǫ̆nǫ·pŏli). 1534. [ad. late L. *monopolium*, a. Gr. μονοπώλιον, f. μόνος MONO- + πωλεῖν to sell.] **1.** Exclusive possession of the trade in some commodity. **2.** An exclusive privilege (conferred by the sovereign or the state) of selling some commodity or trading with a particular place or country 1596. **3.** *transf.* and *fig.* Exclusive possession, control, or exercise of something 1643. **4.** A thing which is the subject of a monopoly 1838. **5.** A trading company that has a monopoly 1871. **6.** *attrib.*, as *m. price*, etc. 1625.

1. Suffer not thies ryche men to bye vp all,..and with theyr monopolye to kepe the market alone as please them 1551. **2.** The m. of the right to print the Bible in England is still possessed by the Universities of Oxford and Cambridge, and her Majesty's printer for England 1875. **3.** Neither side has a m. of right or..wrong FREEMAN. **4.** The culture..of tobacco was made a Crown m. G. DUFF.

‖ **Monopteros** (mǫ̆nǫ·ptĕrǫs). Also †**-on.** 1706. [subst. use of late L. *monopteros* adj. (Vitruvius), a. Gr. *μονόπτερος having one wing, f. μόνος MONO- + πτερόν wing.] *Arch.* A temple consisting of a single circle of columns supporting a roof. Hence **Mono·pteral** *a.* 1823.

Monoptote (mǫ·nǫ̆ptoᵘt). 1612. [ad. late L. *monoptotus*, a. late Gr., f. Gr. μόνος + πτωτός falling, cogn. w. πτῶσις case, f. πίπτειν to fall.] A noun occurring in a single oblique case (as L. *astu*).

Monorhine (mǫ·norəin), *a.* Also **monorrhine.** 1890. [f. mod.L. *Monorhina*, f. Gr. μόνος + ῥιν-, ῥίς nose.] *Zool.* Having a single nasal passage; belonging to the group *Monorhina* of vertebrates, comprising the lampreys and hags. Also **Mo·norhinal, Mo·norhinous** *adjs.*

Monorime, -rhyme (mǫ·norəim). 1731. [a. F. *monorime*, f. Gr. μόνος MONO- + *rime* RIME, RHYME.] **A.** *sb.* A poetical composition or passage in which all the lines have the same rime. **b.** *pl.* Lines forming a 'tirade' with one rime. **B.** *adj.* Having a single rime 1833.

Monostich (mǫ·nostik). 1577. [ad. late L. *monostichum*, a. Gr. μονόστιχον adj. neut., f. μόνος MONO- + στίχος row, line, or verse.] *Pros.* A poem or epigram consisting of but one metrical line.

Monostrophic (mǫnostrǫ·fik), *a.* (and *sb.*) 1671. [ad. Gr. μονοστροφικός, f. μονόστροφος adj., f. μόνος MONO- + στροφή recurring metrical scheme, STROPHE.] *Pros.* Consisting of repetitions of one and the same strophic arrangement; *sb. pl.* monostrophic verses.

Monosyllabic (mǫ:nosilæ·bik), *a.* 1824. [ad. med.L. *monosyllabicus*, f. late L. *monosyllabus* = Gr. μονοσύλλαβος adj., f. μόνος MONO- + συλλαβή syllable.] **1.** Of a word: Consisting of one syllable 1828. **2.** Consisting of monosyllables or of a monosyllable 1824. **3.** Of a person: Uttering only monosyllables 1870.

2. The Chinese, and other m. tongues 1824. Throwing out a m. hint to his cattle GEO. ELIOT. So †**Monosylla·bical** *a.* 1686–1776, **-ly** *adv.*

Monosyllabism (mǫnosi·lăbiz'm). 1804. [f. F. *monosyllabe* + -ISM.] Addiction to the use of monosyllables; the quality of being monosyllabic.

Monosyllable (mǫnosi·lăb'l). 1533. [ad. late L. *monosyllabus* after SYLLABLE.] **A.** *sb.* A word of one syllable. **B.** *adj.* = MONOSYLLABIC *a.* 1, 2. *rare.* 1589.

Phr. *To speak* (*answer*, etc.) *in monosyllables*: to speak with intentional curtness; to answer little but 'yes' or 'no'.

‖**Monotessaron** (mǫnote·sărǫ̆n). 1831. [med. L., f. (erron. after *diatessaron*) Gr. μόνος single + τέσσαρες four.] = DIATESSARON 3.

Monothalamic (mǫnoþălæ·mik), *a.* 1870. [f. as next + -IC.] *Bot.* Of a fruit: Formed from one pistil or flower.

Monothalamous (mǫnoþæ·lăməs), *a.* 1816. [f. Gr. μόνος MONO- + θάλαμος (see THALAMUS) + -OUS.] *Bot.* and *Zool.* Having only one chamber; unilocular: as the chambered shells of foraminiferous and gasteropodous molluscs.

Monotheism (mǫ·noþī,iz'm). 1660. [f. Gr. μόνος + θεός + -ISM.] The doctrine that there is only one God. So **Mo·notheist,** an adherent of m. **Mo:nothei·stic, -al** *a.* **Mo:nothei·stically** *adv.*

Monothelete (mǫ̆nǫ·þĭlīt). 1850. *Theol.* A more correct form of MONOTHELITE. So **Mo:nothele·tian** *a.*, etc.

Monothelism (mǫ̆nǫ·þĭliz'm). *rare.* 1685. [f. next + -ISM.] = MONOTHELITISM.

Monothelite (mǫ̆nǫ·þĭləit). late ME. [ad. med.L. *monothelita*, ad. late Gr. μονοθελήτης, f. Gr. μόνος + θελητής, agent-n. f. θέλειν to will. Cf. F. *monothélite*.] **A.** *sb.* An adherent of the 7th c. heretical sect which maintained that Christ has only one will. **B.** *adj.* Of or pertaining to the Monothelites or their doctrine 1619. Hence **Monotheli·tic** *a.* **Mono·thelitism.**

Monotint (mǫ·notint). 1886. [f. MONO- + TINT.] Representation in a single colour; also, a picture in only one colour. Chiefly in phr. *in m.*

Monotone (mǫ·notoᵘn). 1644. [ad. mod.L. *monotonus*, a. late Gr., f. Gr. μόνος + τόνος TONE. The sb. use is Eng. only.] **A.** *adj.* = MONOTONOUS *a.* 1 (rarely 2) 1769.

As lulling as the m. waves KINGLAKE.

B. *sb.* **1.** The utterance of a number of successive syllables without change of tone 1644. **2.** Sameness of style in writing; something composed in such a style 1871. **3.** *fig.* A monotonous continuance or recurrence *of* something 1856.

1. *transf.* Tolling, tolling, tolling In that muffled m. POE. Hence **Mo·notone** *v.* to recite, sing, speak in one unvaried tone. **Monoto·nic, -al** *a.* relating to or uttered in a m.; **-ly** *adv.* **Mono·tonist,** one who speaks monotonously; one who harps on one subject; one who loves monotony.

Monotonous (mǫ̆nǫ·tŏnəs), *a.* 1778. [f. Gr. μονότονος (see prec.) + -OUS.] **1. a.** Of sound or utterance: Having little or no variation in tone or cadence. **b.** Producing but one tone or note; as the drum, etc. 1811. **2.** *transf.* and *fig.* Lacking in variety; wearisome through continued sameness 1791.

2. The m. smoothness of Byron's versification MACAULAY. Dull straight streets of m. houses GREEN. Hence **Mono·tonous-ly** *adv.*, **-ness.**

Monotony (mǫ̆nǫ·tŏni). 1706. [f. late Gr. μονοτονία, f. μονότονος MONOTONE *a.*] The quality of being monotonous. **1.** Sameness of tone or pitch; want of variety in cadence or inflexion; occas. quasi-*concr.* a monotone 1724. **2.** *transf.* and *fig.* Wearisome sameness of effect; lack of interesting variety.

2. At sea, everything that breaks the m. of the surrounding expanse, attracts attention W. IRVING.

‖ **Monotremata** (mǫnotrī·mătă), *sb. pl.* 1833. [mod.L., neut. pl. of *monotrematus* adj., f. Gr. μόνος MONO- + τρηματ-, τρῆμα perforation, hole, f. τρα- root of τετραίνειν to perforate.] *Zool.* The lowest Order of Mammalia, having only one opening or vent for the genital, urinary, and digestive organs.

The Order comprises the duck-billed platypus (*Ornithorhynchus paradoxus*) and several species of spiny ant-eaters. Hence **Monotre·matous** *a.* **Mo·notreme** *a.* and *sb.* 1835.

Monotriglyph (mǫnǫtrəi·glif), *a.* 1706. [ad. late L. *monotriglyphos*, a. Gr., f. μόνος MONO- + τρίγλυφος TRIGLYPH.] *Arch.* Having only one triglyph in the space over an intercolumniation, as the entablature in the Doric order.

Monotype (mǫ·nǫtəip). 1882. [f. MONO- + TYPE.] 1. A print from a metal plate on which a picture is painted. Also, the process of producing such prints. 2. Name given by the inventor, Tolbert Lanston, to a composing-machine which first casts, and then sets up the type by means of a perforated paper roll which has been previously produced on another part of the machine. (Cf. LINOTYPE, MONOLINE.) 1895.

Monotypic (mǫnoti·pik), *a.* 1874. [f. mod. L. *monotypus* (f. Gr. μόνος + τύπος) + -IC.] Having or containing only one type or representative. So **Mono·typous** *a.* 1856.

Monoxide (mǫnǫ·ksəid). 1869. [f. MONO- 2 + OXIDE.] *Chem.* An oxide containing one equivalent of oxygen.

Monoxy-, monox-. 1863. [f. MONO- 2 + OXY(GEN).] *Chem.* Comb. form, expressing the presence in a compound of one equivalent of oxygen.

‖ **Monoxylon** (mǫnǫ·ksilǫn). *Pl.* **-la.** Also in mod.Gr. form †**monoxylo.** 1555. [a. Gr. μονόξυλον, neut. of μονόξυλος; see next.] A canoe or boat made from one piece of timber. Also **Mono·xyl(e.**

Monoxylous (mǫnǫ·ksiləs), *a.* 1863. [f. L. *monoxylus* (a. Gr., f. μόνος + ξύλον wood, timber) + -OUS.] Made out of a single piece of wood; also, using one piece of wood to make a boat or coffin, etc. So **Monoxy·lic** *a.*

Monroeism (mǒnrōu·iz'm). 1896. [f. James *Monroe*, president of the U.S. 1817–1825.] The 'Monroe doctrine' (see DOCTRINE). So **Monroe·ist**, a supporter of this.

‖**Monseigneur** (moṅsẹnyör). *Pl.* **messeigneurs** (mẹsẹnyör). 1600. [F., f. *mon* my + *seigneur* lord.] 1. A French title given to persons of eminence, esp. to princes, cardinals, archbishops, and bishops. Abbrev. *Mgr.* †The title conferred since the time of Louis XIV upon the Dauphin of France. 1610. †2. Used for MONSIGNOR –1660.

‖ **Monsieur** (məsyö, məsyö). 1500. [F., orig. two words, *mon* my, *sieur* lord.] 1. The title of courtesy prefixed to the name, surname, or nobiliary title of a Frenchman; now = Eng. 'Mr.', except that it is also applied to any title of rank. In English often used in speaking of Europeans other than Frenchmen. Abbrev. *M.* (the forms *Mons.*, *Monsr*. are not now in use in France). See also the pl. MESSIEURS. 1512. 2. Used (*a*) in speaking to or of a Frenchman; (*b*) in literal renderings of French speech 1588. 3. *Hist.* A title of the second son or next younger brother of the King of France 1572. 4. A Frenchman generally. Now *rare* or *Obs.* 1500.

1. *transf.* Mounsieur Cobweb, good Mounsier get your weapons in your hand SHAKS. 4. Now I would pray our Monsieurs To thinke an English Courtier may be wise, And neuer see the Louure SHAKS. Hence †**Monsieurship** 1579–1673.

‖**Monsignor, -ore** (mǫnsī·nyǭr, -nyǭ·re). *Pl.* monsignori (-nyǭ·ri). 1635. [It. *Monsignore* (shortened *-signor*), formed after F. MONSEIGNEUR; see SIGNOR.] An honorific title bestowed upon prelates, officers of the Papal court and household, etc.

Monsoon (mǫnsū·n). 1584. [a. early mod. Du. *monssoen*, *-soyn*, a. Pg. *monção*, perh. a. Arab. *mausim*, lit. season, hence monsoon, f. *wasama* to mark.] 1. A seasonal wind prevailing in southern Asia, blowing approximately from the south-west in summer (*wet* or *rainy m.*), and in winter from the north-east (*dry m.*). b. The rainy season which accompanies the south-west monsoon 1747. 2. *transf.* Any wind which has periodic alternations. Cf. TRADE-WIND. 1691.

Monster (mǫ·nstəɹ), *sb.* ME. [a. OF. *monstre*, ad. L. *monstrum*; orig. a divine portent or warning, f. *monere* to warn.] A. *sb.* †1. A prodigy, a marvel –1710. 2. A malformed animal or plant; a misshapen birth, an abortion. Cf. MONSTROSITY. ME. 3. An imaginary animal, either partly brute and partly human, or compounded of elements from two or more animal forms; e. g. the centaur, sphinx, minotaur, wyvern. late ME. 4. A person of inhuman cruelty or wickedness; a monstrous example *of* (some particular vice) 1556. 5. An animal of huge size; hence, anything of vast proportions 1530.

2. The princes keep favourite dwarfs. The Emperor and Empress have two of these little Monsters LADY M. W. MONTAGU. *fig.* The non-Christian religions are not to the wise man mere monsters M. ARNOLD. 3. *transf.* You'l draw A faultless M. which the world ne're saw 1682. 4. These monsters of inhumanity ADDISON. 5. I condempne thee to be ·xxviii· yeres a m. in ye see 1533.

B. *adj.* Of extraordinary size; gigantic, huge, monstrous 1839.

The phrase 'monster meeting' was due to me F. ROGERS (*c* 1842).

Mo·nster, *v. rare.* 1605. [f. prec. sb.] 1. *trans.* To make a monster of. 2. To exhibit as a monster, or as something wonderful 1607.

1. *Lear* I. i. 223. 2. I had rather haue one scratch my Head i' th' Sun,..then idly sit To heare my Nothings monster'd SHAKS.

Monstrance (mǫ·nstrăns). ME. [a. OF. *monstrance*, ad. med.L. *monstrantia*, f. L. *monstrantem*, *monstrare*; see -ANCE.] †1. Demonstration, proof. ME. only. 2. *R. C. Ch.* a. An open or transparent vessel of gold or silver in which the host is exposed 1506. b. A receptacle for the exhibition of relics 1522. So †**Monstral,** †**Monstrant,** †**Mo·nstre** *sbs.* (in sense 2).

Monstrosity (mǫnstrǫ·siti). 1555. [ad. late L. *monstrositas*, f. *monstrosus* MONSTROUS; see -ITY.] 1. An abnormality of growth; *concr.* a part or organ that is such; also occas. = MONSTER *sb.* 2. 2. = MONSTER *sb.* 3. 1643. 3. The condition or fact of being monstrous 1656. Also *transf.* and *fig.*

2. *fig.* The Multitude..confused together, make but one great beast, and a m. more prodigious then Hydra SIR T. BROWNE.

Monstrous (mǫ·nstrəs), *a.* 1460. [ad. OF. *monstreux*, *-tereux*, ad. late L. *monstrosus*, f. L. *monstrum*; see -OUS.] †1. Deviating from the natural order; unnatural –1736. 2. Abnormally formed; malformed 1597. 3. Having the nature or appearance of a monster (see MONSTER *sb.* 3) 1540. b. Abounding in monsters. *poet.* 1637. 4. Of unnaturally huge dimensions; gigantic, enormous 1500. 5. Outrageously wrong or absurd 1573. 6. Atrocious, horrible 1560. †7. As an exclam. = 'astounding' –1693. †8. As a colloq. or affected intensive –1825. b. quasi-*adv.* 'Mighty'. Now *rare* or *Obs.* 1587.

1. An atheist, a man in my opinion m. LYLY. More m. Tales have oft amus'd the Vulgar 1701. 2. A man in shape, immane, and monsterous CHAPMAN. 3. Their m. Idol DE FOE. b. Where thou..under the whelming tide Visit'st the bottom of the m. world MILT. 4. In bulk as huge As whom the Fables name of m. size, Titanian,..Briarios..or that Sea-beast Leviathan MILT. 5. Wilt thou tell a m. lie? SHAKS. 6. Thou m. slanderer of heauen and earth SHAKS. 7. O m.! eleuen Buckrom men growne out of two? SHAKS. 8. A m. favourite of George's 1782. b. She's a m. shocking dresser MISS BURNEY. Hence **Mo·nstrous·ly** *adv.*, **-ness.** So †**Mo·nstruous.** late ME.–1727; †**Monstruo·sity,** †**Mo·nstruous·ly** *adv.*, †**-ness.**

Mont, obs. f. MOUNT.

‖ **Montagnard** (moṅtan^yar). 1879. [F., f. *montagne*; see MOUNTAIN and -ARD.] *Hist.* A member of the MOUNTAIN (sense 5).

Monta(i)gne, obs. ff. MOUNTAIN.

‖ **Montaña** (mǫnta·n^yă). 1840. [Sp., mountain.] In Spanish-American countries: A forest of considerable extent; *spec.* the name of the part of Peru east of the Andes.

Montane (mǫ·ntein), *a.* 1863. [ad. L. *montanus*, f. *mons* MOUNT *sb.*[1]] = MOUNTAIN II. a, b.

Montanism (mǫ·ntăniz'm). 1597. [f. *Montanus* (see below) + -ISM.] The tenets of a heretical Christian sect, founded in Phrygia by Montanus in the 2nd century.

Montanus claimed for himself and two female associates prophetic inspiration. The tenets of the sect were millenarian and severely ascetic. So **Mo·ntanist,** a believer in M. 1449; as *adj.* = **Montani·stic,** †**-al** *a.* of or relating to M. **Mo·ntanize** *v. intr.* to follow the doctrines of the Montanists.

†**Montant.** *rare.* Also **montanto.** 1598. [a. F. *montant* 'an upright blow, or thrust' (Cotgr.).] A 'downright' blow or thrust. *Merry W.* II. iii. 27.

Montant, early form of MUNTIN.

‖**Montbretia** (mǫntbrī·ʃiă). 1899. [mod.L., after A. F. E. Coquebert de *Montbret*, a French botanist (1780–1801).] A genus of iridaceous plants, bearing bright orange-coloured flowers; a plant of this genus.

Monte (mǫ·nte). Also **monty.** 1850. [a. Sp. *monte* mountain; heap of cards left after each player has his share.] A Spanish game of chance, played with a pack of forty-five cards.

Three-card m., a game of Mexican origin, played with three cards only, of which one is usu. a court-card.

Monteith (mǫntī·þ). Also †**monteigh,** †**-éff, -eth.** 1683. [Named, according to Anthony Wood, after a certain 'Monsieur Monteigh'.] *Antiq.* A punch-bowl with a scalloped brim, also used for cooling and carrying glasses.

Montem (mǫ·ntem). *Obs.* exc. *Hist.* 1743. [From L. *ad montem*, 'to the Hill'.] A festival (orig. annual, later triennial) formerly celebrated by the scholars of Eton, who went in fancy costumes to 'Salt Hill', a mound near Slough, and there collected money from the bystanders, to support at King's College, Cambridge, the senior colleger of the school.

‖ **Montero** (mǫntēə·ro). Also **montera,** etc. 1611. [Sp. *montera*, f. *montero* hunter, lit. 'mountaineer', f. *monte*; see MOUNT *sb.*[1]] A Spanish hunter's cap with a spherical crown and a flap. Also *m. cap.*

Montgolfier (mǫntgǫ·lfiəɹ; Fr. moṅgǫlfye). 1784. [Named after the brothers J. M. and J. E. *Montgolfier* of Annonay, France, its inventors.] A balloon raised by heated air instead of gas; a fire-balloon. (In full *M. balloon.*)

Month (mʌnþ). [Com. Teut.: OE. *mónað* masc. :—OTeut. **mǣnoþ-*, related to **mǣnon-* MOON *sb.* In the 16–17th c. the spelling *moneth* was almost universal.] A measure of time corresponding to the period of revolution of the moon. 1. Any one of the twelve portions into which the conventional year is divided. More explicitly *calendar m.* 2. *Astr.* a. (In full *Lunar m.*) The period in which the moon makes a complete revolution relatively to some point, either fixed or movable OE. b. *Solar m.*: the twelfth part of the solar year; the time occupied by the sun in passing through one of the signs of the zodiac OE. 3. A space of time, either (*a*) extending from any day to the corresponding day of the next calendar month (called 'a calendar month'), or (*b*) containing 28 days (often miscalled a 'lunar month') OE. b. Used as an indefinite measure of time, esp. in *pl.*, a long while 1601. †4. *pl.* = MENSES –1694.

2. a. Usually the term denotes the *synodical month*, i. e. the period from one new moon to the next, the length of which is 29 days, 12 hours, 44 minutes, 2·7 seconds. The other kinds of lunar month (the lengths of which are all between 27 and 28 days) are the *anomalistic*, *sidereal*, *tropical*, and *nodical months*: see those adjs. N.E.D. 3. A m. in law is a lunar m., or twenty-eight days, unless otherwise expressed BLACKSTONE. The Word 'Month' to mean Calendar Month, unless words be added showing Lunar Month to be intended *Act* 13–14 *Vict.* c. 21. b. 'Dead', he answered. 'When?' 'Months back.' MEREDITH.

Phrases. *M. by m.*: in each successive m. *M. after m.*: each m. as a sequel to the preceding (without suggestion of continuity). *From m. to m.*: continuously from one m. to the next. *M. of Sun-*

days (colloq.): an indefinite period. *This day m.*: at a time a m. after the day indicated.

Monthly (mʊ·nþli), *a.* and *sb.* 1572. [f. MONTH + -LY[1].] **A.** *adj.* **1.** Done or recurring once a month or every month 1647. **b.** = MENSTRUAL *a.* 2. 1612. **2.** Pertaining to a month; payable every month 1572. **3.** Continued for a month. Now *rare.* 1589.

1. The m. parcel from London LYTTON. 2. A m. salary 1843. 3. Minutes ioyes are monthlie woes GREENE.

Spec. collocations. †**m. mind** = MONTH'S MIND; **m. nurse,** one who attends a woman during the first month after child-birth; **m. rose (tree),** the Indian or China rose, supposed to flower every month.

B. *sb.* **1.** *pl.* = MENSES (*vulgar*). 1872. **2.** A magazine, etc. published once a month 1856.

Monthly (mʊ·nþli), *adv.* 1533. [-LY[2].] Once a month; in each or every month; month by month.

Month's mind. 1466. **1.** *Eccl.* The commemoration of a deceased person by the celebration of masses, etc., on a day one month from the date of his death. **2.** An inclination, a fancy, a liking. Also (rarely) *To be in a month's mind,* to have a strong expectation. *Obs.* exc. *dial.* 1580.

Monticle (mǫ·ntik'l). 1490. [ad. F. *monticule*; see next.] A small mountain or hill.

Monticule (mǫ·ntikiul). 1799. [a. F., ad. late L. *monticulus,* dim. of *monti-, mons* mountain; see -CULE.] **1.** = MONTICLE. **b.** *spec.* A small conical mound produced by a volcanic eruption 1833. **2.** *Anat.* and *Zool.* A minute eminence (on an animal, etc.) 1874.

‖ **Monton** (mǫ·ntǫn). 1858. [Sp., = 'heap', f. *monte* MOUNT *sb.*[1]] *Mining.* A heap of ore; a batch under the process of amalgamation.

Montross, obs. f. MATROSS.

Monture (mǫ·ntiūɹ). 1831. [a. F., f. *monter* to MOUNT; see -URE.] A mounting or setting; the manner in which anything is set or mounted.

Monture: see MOUNTURE.

Monument (mǫ·niument), *sb.* ME. [ad. L. *monu-, monimentum,* f. *monere* to remind; see -MENT.] †**1.** A sepulchre, place of sepulture -1658. **2.** A written document, record; a legal instrument. (Occas. confused with *muniment.*) 1440. †**b.** A piece of information given in writing -1650. **3.** An indication, evidence, or token (of some fact). Now *rare.* 1605. †**b.** A mark, indication; a portent -1657. **c.** *U.S. Law.* Any object fixed permanently in the soil and used as a means of ascertaining the location of a tract or a boundary 1828. **4.** Anything that by its survival commemorates a person, action, period, or event 1530. **b.** An enduring evidence or example 1675. **5.** A structure, edifice, or erection intended to commemorate a notable person, action, or event 1602. **b.** A structure of stone or other material erected over the grave or in church, etc., in memory of the dead 1588. †**c.** A carved figure, effigy SHAKS.

1. In that dim M. where Tybalt lies SHAKS. 2. This discourse..I have transcribed from the original, and put it among the monuments in the end of the book 1709. 3. b. *Tam. Shr.* III. ii. 97. 4. b. It may be considered as a m. of the taste and skill of the authors HAZLITT. 5. *The M.*: a Doric column 202 feet high in the City of London, built to commemorate the great fire of London 1666. b. Honours shall gather round his m. *Junius Lett.* c. You are no Maiden but a m. SHAKS. Hence **Mo·nument** *v. trans.* to cause to be perpetually remembered; to record on, or furnish with, a m. (*nonce-uses*) 1606.

Monumental (mǫniume·ntăl), *a.* 1601. [ad. late L. *monumentalis,* f. L. *monumentum*; see prec. and -AL.] **1.** Pertaining to a monument, or to monuments in general 1604. **2.** Serving as a monument, or †as a memento 1601. **3.** Like a monument 1606. **4.** *transf.* Of literary works, etc.: Massive and permanent. Also, *loosely,* vast, stupendous. 1658. **5.** Historically prominent; remaining conspicuous 1844.

1. Press'd with a Load of M. Clay! POPE. 2. Hee hath giuen her his monumentall Ring SHAKS. 3. Pine, or m. Oake MILT. 4. His m. obtuseness GEO. ELIOT. A truly m. work 1894. 5. That gallery of m. men SWINBURNE. Hence **Monume·ntally** *adv.* by way of a monument; in a m. degree.

-mony, *suffix,* occurring only in sbs. adopted from Latin; repr. L. *-monia* in *acrimony, ceremony,* etc., and L. *-monium* in *matrimony, parsimony,* etc.

Moo (mū), *v.* 1549. [Echoic.] *intr.* Of a cow, etc.: To low. Of a person: To make the sound 'moo'. Hence **Moo** *sb.* 1789.

Moo, obs. f. MO, more.

Mooch, mouch (mūtʃ), *v.* Now *slang* and *dial.* 1460. [perh. ult. from the same source as MICHE *v.*, q. v.] †**1.** *intr.* ? To pretend poverty. **2.** To play truant 1622. **3.** *intr.* To loaf, skulk, or hang *about*; to slouch *along* 1851. **4.** *trans.* To pilfer, steal 1862. Hence **Mooch, mouch** *sb.* (esp. *on the m.*), **Moo·cher, mou·cher.**

Mood[1] (mūd). [Com. Teut.: OE. *mōd* neut.:—OTeut. **mōdo-*, f. pre-Teut. root **mō-* : *mē* : *mə* (in Gr. μα-τεύειν to seek, in Doric Gr. μῶσθαι to seek after).] †**1.** Mind, heart, thought, feeling -late ME. †**2.** *spec.* Courage, anger 1600. **3.** A frame of mind or state of feelings OE. **b.** *pl.* Fits of variable or unaccountable temper 1859.

2. Who, in my moode, I stab'd vnto the heart SHAKS. 3. Fortune is merry, And in this m. will giue vs any thing SHAKS. Phr. *In a m.* (*for* something), *in the m.* (*to do* something) disposed.

Mood[2] (mūd). 1569. [var. of MODE, assoc. w. prec.] **1.** *Logic.* Any one of the classes into which each of the four figures of valid categorical syllogisms is subdivided with reference to the quality and quantity of the constituent propositions. **2.** *Gram.* Any one of the groups of forms in the conjugation of a verb which serve to indicate the function in which the verb is used; i. e. whether it expresses a predication, a command, a wish, or the like; that quality of a verb which depends on the question to which of these groups its form belongs 1573. **3.** *Mus.* †**a.** = MODE 7. -1782. †**b.** = MODE 1 b. -1844.

3. b. Anon they move In perfect Phalanx to the Dorian m. Of Flutes and soft Recorders MILT. *transf.* That strain I heard was of a higher m. MILT.

Mooder, obs. f. MOTHER *sb.*[1]

Moody (mū·di), *a.* [OE. *mōdig,* f. **mōdo-* MOOD[1].] †**1.** Brave, bold, proud, high-spirited -1755. †**2.** Proud, haughty; head-strong, stubborn, wilful -1460. †**3.** Angry, wrathful -1697. **4.** Subject to moods; ill-humoured, gloomy, sullen, melancholy 1593. **b.** Applied to humour, thought, action, etc. 1593. **c.** Expressive of ill humour 1596.

3. Angry Jove..the m. sire DRYDEN. 4. The Iews, a headstrong, m.. murmuring race DRYDEN. b. M. Madness laughing wild GRAY. c. Maiestie might neuer yet endure The m. Frontier of a seruant brow SHAKS. Hence **Moo·dily** *adv.* **Moo·diness.**

Mool(l)**a**(h, obs. ff. MULLAH.

‖ **Moolvee** (mū·lvi). 1625. [Urdū *mulvī,* a. Arab., prop. an adj., judicial, but used as sb., = *maulā* MULLAH, of which it is a deriv.] A Mohammedan doctor of the law; in India, a complimentary term among Mohammedans for a teacher of Arabic, or any learned man.

Moon (mūn), *sb.* [Com. Teut.: OE. *mōna* wk. masc.:—OTeut. **mēnon-*, usu. taken to be f. root **mē-* to measure.] **1.** The satellite of the earth; a secondary planet, whose light, derived from the sun, is reflected to the earth, and serves to dispel the darkness of the night. **b.** Since the disappearance of OE. grammatical genders, the moon has been treated as feminine; in poetry it is sometimes, after classical example, identified with various goddesses. **2.** The moon as visible during one (lunar) month, spoken of as a distinct object from that of another month. Similarly, with qualifying words: The moon as shining at a particular time or place, etc. See also FULL MOON, NEW MOON, etc. OE. **3.** With ref. to the moon's position above the earth, etc.; often quasi-personified ME. **4.** An appearance in the sky resembling a moon OE. **5.** A figure or representation of the moon, either crescent-shaped or circular; a moon-shaped marking, ornament, or vessel. late ME. **6.** The satellite of a planet 1665. **7.** *poet.* = MOONLIGHT. late ME. **8.** The period from one new moon to the next; a lunation, lunar month; *gen.* a month. late ME. †**9.** *The m.* **a.** *Alch.* Silver. **b.** *Her.* Argent. -1651. †**10.** = LUNE 2. -1642.

1. To wexe and wane..As dooth the faire whyte mone CHAUCER. The minde of men chaungeth as the mone HAWES. *Mean m.* (Astr.): an imaginary m., supposed to move uniformly in the ecliptic, completing its circuit in the same time as the actual m. *Calendar, ecclesiastical m.*: an imaginary m. used in determining the date of Easter. Provb. *To believe that the m. is made of green cheese*: to believe an absurdity. *Minion of the m.* = MOON-MAN 1. 2. Phr. *There is a* (*no*) *m.* = the m. is visible (not visible) at the time and in the place referred to. *The old m. in the new moon's arms* (or *lap*): the appearance of the m. during the first quarter in which the dark portion of the orb is made more or less luminous by earth-light. 3. 'Tis like the howling of Irish Wolues against the Moone SHAKS. While over head the M. Sits Arbitress MILT. He was a mere child in the world, but he didn't cry for the m. DICKENS. Phr. *To shoot the m.* (slang): to make a moonlight flitting. 4. *John* IV. ii. 182. 5. Precious oils In hollow'd moons of gems TENNYSON. 6. And other Suns..With thir attendant Moons MILT. 7. White in the m. the long road lies A. E. HOUSMAN. 8. This is the m. of roses, The lovely and flowerful time HENLEY.

attrib. and *Comb.*: **m.-blink,** a temporary evening blindness caused by sleeping in the moonshine in tropical climates; **-bow,** a lunar rainbow; **-culminating** *ppl. a.*, applied to such stars (used in calculating longitude) as culminate with the m. and are near its parallel of declination; **-daisy,** the ox-eye daisy, *Chrysanthemum Leucanthemum*; **-dog,** a dog that bays the m.; **-glade** *U.S.*, the track made by moonlight on water; **-madness,** lunacy; **-month,** a lunar month; **-rainbow,** a lunar rainbow; **-trefoil,** *Medicago arborea.*

Moon (mūn), *v.* 1601. [f. prec.] **1. a.** *trans.* To expose to the rays of the moon. **b.** *intr.* To shine as a moon; to move as a satellite. **2.** *intr.* To move or look listlessly or aimlessly *about, along, around,* etc., as if moonstruck. *colloq.* 1848. **b.** *trans.* To pass away (the time) in a listless manner 1876. **3.** To hunt by moonlight 1898.

1. *refl.* The huge man..not sunning, but mooning himself—apricating himself in the occasional moonbeams DE QUINCEY. 2. I mooned up and down the High-street T. HUGHES.

Moo·nbeam. 1590. A ray of moonlight.

Moo·n-blind, *a.* 1668. **1.** Of horses: Suffering from moon-eye. †**2.** *fig.* Purblind -1757. **3.** Suffering from blindness brought on by sleeping exposed to the moon's rays 1830. Hence **Moo·n-blindness.**

Moo·n-calf. 1565. †**1.** An abortive shapeless fleshy mass in the womb; a false conception (regarded as produced by the influence of the moon) -1658. **b.** A misshapen birth. *Obs.* or *arch.* 1610. **c.** A congenital idiot; a born fool 1620. **2.** A mooning, absent-minded person 1613.

Moo·n-dial. 1686. A dial for showing the hours of the night by the moon.

Mooned (mūnd, *poet.* mū·nėd), *ppl. a.* 1550. †**1.** Lunatic. CHEKE. **2.** Crescent-shaped; also, having moon-shaped markings 1607. **3.** Attended by or associated with the moon 1629. **4.** Moonlit. LYTTON.

2. Th' Angelic Squadron..sharpning in m. hornes Thir Phalanx MILT. 3. M. Ashtaroth MILT.

Mooner (mū·nəɹ). 1576. [f. MOON *sb.* or *v.* + -ER[1].] †**1.** A kind of watch-dog -1688. **2.** One who moons about 1848.

Moo·n-eye. 1607. [f. MOON *sb.* + EYE *sb.*; in sense 1 tr. L. *oculus lunaticus* (Vegetius).] **1.** *Farriery.* (Usu. *pl.*) An eye affected with intermittent blindness (attributed to the moon's influence); also, moon-blindness. **2.** The cisco 1884.

Moo·n-eyed, *ppl. a.* 1610. [f. prec. + -ED[2].] **1.** *Farriery.* Affected with the disease of moon-eye; moon-blind. †**b.** Purblind; squint-eyed -1785. †**2.** Having eyes that see well at night -1817. **3.** Having round, wide-open eyes, as a terrified person 1790.

Moo·n-fern. 1671. = LUNARY *sb.* b.

Moo·n-fish. 1646. A name for various fishes resembling, or having parts that resemble, the moon; e. g. the sunfish (*Orthagoriscus mola*), the opah.

Moo·n-flower. 1787. **1.** The moon-daisy. **2.** A tropical plant, *Ipomœa Bona-nox,* that blooms at night, having large fragrant white flowers. *U.S.*

Moong, mung (mūŋ, mʊŋ). 1800. [Hindī *mūng.*] A species of vetch, *Phaseolus Mungo,* common in India; also, its fibre, of which mats are made.

Moonish (mū·niʃ), *a. Obs.* or *arch.* late ME. [f. MOON *sb.* + -ISH [1].] Resembling or characteristic of the moon; influenced by the moon; changeable, fickle.

At which time would I, being but a m. youth, greeue, be effeminate, changeable SHAKS.

Moonless (mū·nlės), *a.* 1508. [+ -LESS.] Without a moon; not lit up by the moon.

Moonlight (mū·nləit), *sb.* and *a.* late ME. [f. MOON *sb.* + LIGHT *sb.*] **A.** *sb.* **1.** The light of the moon. †**2.** A moonlight landscape -1778. †**3.** = MOONSHINE 3. -1829. **B.** *attrib.* or *adj.* Accompanied by, bathed in, moonlight; moonlit; done by moonlight 1584.

B. *M. flit, flitting*: the removal of household goods by night to avoid paying rent.

Moonlight (mū·nləit), *v.* 1887. [f. MOONLIGHTER.] **a.** *pass.* To be attacked by moonlighters. **b.** *intr.* To engage in moonlighting.

Moonlighter (mū·nləitəɹ). 1882. [f. MOONLIGHT *sb.* + -ER [1].] One who engages in moonlighting or commits a moonlighting outrage.

Moonlighting (mū·nləitiŋ), *vbl. sb.* 1881. [f. as prec. + -ING [1].] **1.** The performance by night of an expedition, or of an illicit action. **2.** *spec.* In Ireland, the perpetration by night of outrages on tenants who incurred the hostility of the Land League 1882.

Moonlit (mū·nlit), *a.* 1817. [f. MOON *sb.* + LIT *ppl. a.*] Lit up by the moon; flooded with moonlight. So **Moo·n-litten** *a. poet.*

†**Moo·n-man.** 1608. **1.** A night-walker; one who robs by night 1632. **2.** A gipsy -1700. **3.** A dweller in the moon -1847.

Moonraker (mū·nrēkəɹ). 1787. [RAKER.] **1.** A native of Wiltshire. (See quot.) **2.** *Naut.* A sail above the sky-sail 1867.

1. Wiltshire Moonrakers. Some Wiltshire rustics, ..seeing the figure of the moon in a pond, attempted to rake it out GROSE. Hence **Moo·n-raking** *vbl. sb. fig.* pursuing vain thoughts, woolgathering.

Moo·nrise. 1728. [f. MOON *sb.* + RISE *sb.*] The rise of the moon. Also, The East.

Moo·nseed. 1739. [f. MOON *sb.* + SEED *sb.*, after mod.L. *menispermum.*] A plant of the genus *Menispermum* (having lunate seeds).

Moo·nset. *poet.* 1845. [f. MOON *sb.*, after *sunset.*] The setting of the moon.

‖ **Moonshee, munshi** (mū·nʃī). 1622. [Urdū *munshī*, a. Arab.] A native secretary or language-teacher in India.

Moonshine (mū·nʃəin). late ME. [f. MOON *sb.* + SHINE *sb.*] **1.** = MOONLIGHT *sb.* 1. Now *rare* or *poet.* †**b.** *transf.* (*joc.*). A month. *Lear* I. ii. 5. **2.** Foolish or visionary talk, ideas, plans, etc. 1468. **3.** Smuggled or illicit spirit. *dial.* 1785. †**4.** as *adj.* Moonlit; (of persons) active by moonlight or at night -1831.

2. As for all this talk about Federalism, it is m. 1887. **Moo·nshiner** *U.S.*, a distiller of m. (sense 3).

Moonshiny (mū·nʃəini), *a.* 1602. [f. prec. + -Y [1].] **1.** = MOONLIGHT *a.* **2.** White as moonlight 1825. **3.** Of the nature of moonshine; vain, unreal 1880.

3. Unsubstantial emptinesses and m. illusions 1884.

‖ **Moonsiff, munsif** (mū·nsif). 1812. [Urdū, a. Arab. *munçif* just, honest.] A native judge in India.

Moonstone (mū·nstōun). 1632. [f. MOON *sb.* + STONE *sb.*, after L. *selenites*, Gr. σεληνίτης (λίθος) SELENITE.] A translucent stone (a variety of feldspar) having a pearly lustre, used as a gem.

Moonstruck (mū·nstrʋk), *ppl. a.* 1674. [f. MOON *sb.* + STRUCK.] **1.** Mentally affected or deranged (through the supposed influence of the moon); in early use = lunatic; now, distracted or dazed. **2.** = MOON-BLIND 3; also, made unsuitable for food, as fish, by the moon's influence 1846.

1. And Moon struck madness, pining Atrophie MILT. So **Moo·n-stricken** *ppl. a.*

Moonwort (mū·nwʋɹt). 1578. [f. MOON *sb.* + WORT, after med.L. *lunaria.*] = LUNARY *sb.*

Moony (mū·ni), *a.* 1586. [f. MOON *sb.* and *v.* + -Y [1].] **1.** Of or belonging to the moon; like the moon; like that of the moon. **2.** Moon-shaped; †lunate; hence, bearing a crescent as an emblem or ensign; circular 1591. **3.** Illuminated by the moon; resembling moonlight 1648. **4.** Given to mooning; stupidly dreamy 1848.

2. The M. Standards of proud Ottoman 1591. 4. Casting upon the reflection of his white neckcloth a pleased m. smile THACKERAY.

Moor (mūəɹ, mōəɹ), *sb.* [1] [OE. *mōr*:—OTeut. **mōro-*; prim. sense perh. 'dead' or barren land.] **1.** A tract of unenclosed waste ground; now usu., a heath. Also, a tract of ground preserved for shooting. †**2.** A marsh -1787. **3.** *dial.* The soil of which moorland consists; peat 1596. **4.** *Cornwall.* **a.** A moor or waste land where tin is found; hence *m.-house, -tin, -works.* **b.** A quantity of ore in a particular part of a lode, as a 'moor' of tin. 1602.

1. Could you on this faire Mountaine leaue to feed, And batten on this Moore? SHAKS. The moors thrown on the market for the year hung heavily on hand at first 1886.

attrib. and *Comb.*, as *m.-dike, -keeper*; *m.-bred* adj.; **m.-ball**, a sponge-like ball formed by the threads of a freshwater alga, *Conferva ægagropila*; **-band**, a hard substratum of the soil found in moorland, consisting of clay, iron ore, and small stones, and impervious to moisture; called also **m.-band pan**; **-coal**, a friable variety of lignite; **-evil**, a kind of dysentery in sheep and cattle; **-hag** = *peat-hag* (see PEAT [1]); **-pan** = *moor-band*; **-sickness** = *moor-evil.* **b.** In names of plants: **m.-berry**, any plant of the genus *Vaccinium*; **m. myrtle**, bog myrtle, *Myrica Gale*; **-palm**, any of several cotton-grasses or sedges growing on moors, or their flower-heads; the catkin of the dwarf sallow; **-wort**, *Andromeda polifolia.* **c.** In names of animals: **m.-bird** (esp. the grouse); **m. buzzard, harrier, hawk**, the marsh harrier, *Circus æruginosus*; **m. coot**, the common gallinule or water-hen, *Gallinula chloropus*; **m. game**, the red grouse, *Lagopus scoticus*; also rarely, the black grouse, *Tetrao tetrix*; **m.-tetter, -tit, -titling**, (*a*) the stone-chat, *Pratincola rubicola*; (*b*) the meadow-pipit, *Anthus pratensis.*

Moor (mūəɹ, mōəɹ), *sb.* [2] [late ME. *More*, a. F. *More, Maure*, ad. L. *Maurus*, Gr. Μαῦρος. Possibly from some ancient N. Afr. word.] **1.** In *Ancient History*, a native of Mauretania, a region corresponding to parts of Morocco and Algeria. Later, one belonging to the people of mixed Berber and Arab race, Mohammedan in religion, who in the 8th c. conquered Spain. As late as the 17th c., the Moors were supposed to be mostly black or very swarthy (though 'white Moors' were known), and hence the word was often used for 'negro'. **2.** A Mohammedan, esp. one living in India 1588.

1. Ethiopes, which we nowe caule Moores, Moorens, or Negros 1555.

Moor (mūəɹ, mōəɹ), *sb.* [3] 1750. [f. MOOR *v.*] An act of mooring.

Moor (mūəɹ, mōəɹ), *v.* [late ME. *more*; prob. repr. OE. **mārian* :—WG. **mairōjan.* The word passed into Fr. as *amarrer.*] **1.** *trans.* To secure (a ship, boat, etc.) in a particular place by means of chains or ropes, either fastened to the shore or to anchors. **2.** *absol.* and *intr.* **a.** To anchor 1627. **b.** Of a ship: To be made secure by means of anchors 1697.

1. A ship may be either moored by the head..or by the head and stern FALCONER. 2. **a.** Two cables is the least, and foure cables the best to more by CAPT. SMITH. **b.** At length on Oozy ground his Gallies m. DRYDEN. Hence **Moo·rage**, the action of mooring; the condition of being moored; a place for mooring; also, money paid for the use of moorings 1648.

Moo·r-cock. ME. [f. MOOR *sb.* [1] + COCK *sb.* [1]] The male of the red grouse. Also occas. the blackcock.

Mooress (mūə·rės, mōə·rės). 1611. [f. MOOR *sb.* [2] + -ESS.] A female Moor.

Moo·r-fowl. 1506. [f. MOOR *sb.* [1] + FOWL.] **1.** *Sc.* The red grouse, *Lagopus scoticus.* **2.** *South Carolina.* The ruffed grouse 1791.

Moo·r-hen. ME. [f. MOOR *sb.* [1] + HEN.] **1.** The Water-hen, *Gallinula chloropus.* **2.** The female of the red grouse, *Lagopus scoticus.*

Mooring (mūə·riŋ, mōə·riŋ), *vbl. sb.* late ME. [f. MOOR *v.* + -ING [1].] **1.** The action of MOOR *v.* **2.** *concr.* (Usu. *pl.*) The rope, chain, etc. by which a floating object is made fast; also the object to which it is moored 1744. **3.** *pl.* The place where a vessel can be moored 1758. **4.** *attrib.*, as *m.-mast* (for an airship).

2. *fig.* The tempest which had driven him from his domestic m. was followed by a fitful calm 1854.

Moorish (mūə·riʃ, mōə·riʃ), *a.* [1] late ME. [f. MOOR *sb.* [1] + -ISH [1].] †**1.** Of soil: Boggy, swampy -1820. †**b.** Of water: Such as is found in bogs -1640. **2.** Of or pertaining to a moor; abounding in moors or moorland; having the characteristics of a moor 1546. **3.** Growing on moors 1612.

2. M. Skiddaw and far-sweeping Saddleback RUSKIN.

Moorish (mūə·riʃ, mōə·riʃ), *a.* [2] late ME. [f. MOOR *sb.* [2] + -ISH [1].] **1.** Of or pertaining to the Moors. **2.** Mohammedan. Now only *colloq.* in Southern India and Ceylon. 1613.

1. The greatest peculiarity in the M. architecture is the horse-shoe arch. (Cf. MORESQUE.) 1797.

Moorland (mūə·ɹlǣnd, mōə·ɹ-). OE. [f. MOOR *sb.* [1] + LAND *sb.*] **1.** Uncultivated land; in mod. use, land abounding in heather; a moor. **2.** *attrib.* or *adj.* Of the nature of or pertaining to moorland; inhabiting moorland 1612. Hence **Moo·rlander**, one who lives in a m.; *spec.* one who lives in the Moorlands of Staffordshire 1646.

Moorman [1] (mūə·ɹ-, mōə·ɹmǣn). 1687. [MOOR *sb.* [1]] **1.** One who lives on a moor 1790. **2.** An official who has charge of a moor.

Moorman [2]. 1698. [f. MOOR *sb.* [2] + MAN *sb.*] = MOOR *sb.* [2]; in India, a Mohammedan.

Moor-pout (mūə·ɹpaut, mōə·ɹ-). 1506. [f. MOOR *sb.* [1] + *pout*; see POULT *sb.*] A young grouse.

†**Moors,** *a.* and *sb. Anglo-Ind.* 1767. [a. Du. *Moorsch*, MOORISH.] Urdū or Hindustānī -1840.

Moorstone (mūə·ɹ-, mōə·ɹstōun). 1600. [MOOR *sb.* [1]] **1.** A kind of granite found chiefly in Cornwall. **2.** A slab of this 1698.

‖ **Mooruk** (mūə·ruk). 1860. [From its cry.] A kind of cassowary, *Casuarius Bennetti.*

‖ **Moory** (mūə·ri), *sb.* 1605. [prob. native adj. formation from *Moor* = Mohammedan (see MOOR *sb.* [2]).] A kind of Indian cloth.

Moory (mūə·ri, mōə·ri), *a.* late ME. [f. MOOR *sb.* [1] + -Y [1].] **1.** Marshy, fenny; growing in a marsh or fen. **2.** Of, pertaining to, or like a moor; abounding in heath 1794.

1. With winged course ore Hill or moarie Dale MILT.

Moose (mūs). 1613. [a. Narragansett *moos.*] A cervine animal native to N. America closely allied to, or identical with, the European Elk (*Alces malchis*). Also *m. deer.*

attrib. and *Comb.*, as *m.-flesh, -track, -trail*, etc.: **m. bird** *U.S.*, the Canada jay, *Garrulus canadensis*; **m. call**, a trumpet of birch bark used by hunters in calling moose; **m.-wood**, (*a*) striped maple, *Acer Pennsylvanicum*; (*b*) leatherwood; **m. yard**, an area in which the snow is trodden down by moose, where they remain together in winter.

Moot, *sb.* [Early ME. *mōt, imōt*, repr. OE. *mōt* neut. and *gemōt* neut., cogn. w. MEET *v.*] †**1.** *gen.* Meeting, encounter -1470. **2.** An assembly of people, esp. one forming a court of judicature; a meeting, also the place where a meeting is held. *Obs.* exc. *Hist.* OE. †**3.** Litigation; an action at law; a plea; accusation -1609. †**4.** Argument; disputation; talking -1676. **5.** *Law.* The discussion of a hypothetical case by students at the Inns of Court for practice; also, a case of this kind. Now only at Gray's Inn. 1531.

2. In the Anglo-Saxon moots may be discerned the first germs of popular government in England 1885. 5. A m. was held last night in the hall of Gray's-inn on the following question 1876.

Comb.: **m. court**, a court at which students argue imaginary cases for practice; **m.-stow** *Hist.*, the place where a m. was held.

Moot (mūt), *a.* 1577. [f. attrib. use of MOOT *sb.*] That can be argued; debatable; not decided, doubtful.

M. case, primarily, a case for discussion in a 'moot'; hence, a doubtful case. Those who are..quite prepared to discuss m. and difficult points 1899.

Moot (mūt), *v.* [OE. *mōtian*, f. *mōt* MOOT *sb.*] †**1. a.** *intr.* To speak, to converse -1644. †**b.** *trans.* To say, to utter -1585. †**2. a.** *intr.* To argue, to plead, to discuss, esp. in a law case. In later use, *esp.* to debate an imaginary case of law (see MOOT *sb.* [1] 5) -1652. †**b.** *trans.* To argue (a point, case, etc.) -1796. **3.** *trans.* To raise (a point, subject, etc.) for discussion 1685.

2. a. He talkes Statutes as fiercely, as if he had mooted seuen yeers in the Inns of Court 1628. Hence **Moo·table** *a.* **Moo·ted** *ppl.a.* brought forward for discussion; also *U.S.* = MOOT *a.* **Moo·ter,** †one who discusses a m. case –1827; one who proposes a question, etc. 1844.

Moot, obs. f. MOTE *sb.* and *v.*

Moot hall. late ME. [f. MOOT *sb.* + HALL.] A hall in which a moot is held.

The hall in which the assizes are held at Carlisle, still goes by the name of the mote, or moot-hall 1794.

Moo·t-hill. 1609. [f. MOOT *sb.* + HILL *sb.*] *Antiq.* A hill on which moots or assemblies were held.

†**Moo·t-house.** [OE. *mōthūs.*] = MOOT HALL –1677.

†**Moo·tman.** 1602. [f. MOOT *v.* + MAN *sb.*] A law student of an Inn of Court; a student who argues a moot case –1797.

Mop (mǫp), *sb.*[1] 1496. [Late 15th c. *mappe*, perh. ad. L. *mappa* napkin.] **1.** A bundle of coarse yarn or cloth fastened at the end of a stick, used in cleaning floors, etc. **2.** *transf.* Applied to instruments resembling a mop 1869. **3.** A thick mass (of hair, etc.) 1616.

1. Now Moll had whirl'd her M. with dext'rous Airs SWIFT.

attrib. and *Comb.*, as **m.-brush,** a round paint-brush with a short thick head; **-head,** (*a*) the head of a m.; (*b*) a thick head of hair resembling a m.; also, a person having a m. of hair.

Mop (mǫp), *sb.*[2] 1581. [f. MOP *v.*[1]] A grimace, esp. one made by a monkey. Chiefly in *mops and mows.*

†**Mop,** *sb.*[3] 1589. [?] In *whiting-m., gurnard-m.*, a young whiting or gurnard. Also *fig.* –1758.

Mop (mǫp), *sb.*[4] *dial.* 1677. [Perh. short for *mop-fair*, a hiring fair, at which the maids carried mops or brooms in token of the capacity in which they wished to engage.] A local name for the annual gathering at which servants are hired; a statute fair.

Mop (mǫp), *v.*[1] 1567. [Perh. imitative of the movement of the lips; cf. Du. *moppen* to pout.] *intr.* To make a grimace. Chiefly in phr. *to mop and mow.*

Mop (mǫp), *v.*[2] 1709. [f. MOP *sb.*[1]] **1.** *trans.* To rub with a mop; to wipe with or as with a mop. Also with *out.* **2.** To wipe sweat, tears, etc., from (the face, brow, etc.). Also *rarely* with *up.* 1840.

1. *To m. the floor with* (slang): said of a combatant in whose hands his opponent is helpless.

M. up: to absorb, wipe up, with or as with a mop; to absorb, get hold of (profits, etc.); to make an end of, slaughter.

Mope (mōup), *sb.* 1540. [Related to MOPE *v.*] †**1.** A fool –1788. **2.** One who mopes; a gloomy, listless person 1693. **3.** *pl. The mopes*: depression of spirits 1825.

Mope (mōup), *v.* 1568. [?] **1.** *intr.* To be in a state of bewilderment; to go about or act aimlessly. *Obs.* exc *dial.* **2.** To be dull, dejected, and spiritless 1590. Also quasi-*trans.* with *away* 1791. **3.** *trans.* To make dull, dejected, or melancholy. Now only *refl.* and in *pass.* 1602.

1. *Hen. V*, III. vii. 143. **2.** Here I sit moping all the live-long Night STEELE. **3.** My father is moped to death for want of you both 1803.

Mope-eyed (mōu·pˌəi·d), *a.* 1606. [f. stem of MOPE *v.* (see sense 1).] Purblind, short-sighted.

Mopish (mōu·piʃ), *a.* 1621. [f. MOPE *v.* + -ISH[1].] Given to moping; causing moping; dejected. Hence **Mo·pish-ly** *adv.*, **-ness** 1598.

Moplah (mǫ·plă). *Anglo-Ind.* 1787. [a. Malayālam *māppila.*] One of the Mohammedan inhabitants of Malabar, descended from Moors and Arabs who have settled on that coast, and married Malabar women.

Mopoke (mōu·pōuk), **morepork** (mōə·ɹpōəɹk). 1827. [Imitative of the bird's note.] Name in New Zealand of an owl, the *Spiloglaux novæ-zealandiæ*, in Tasmania of the night-jar, *Podargus cuvieri*, and in Australia of various birds. Also, the note of the bird.

Moppet (mǫ·pėt). 1601. [f. late ME. *mop(p)* baby, rag doll + -ET.] **1.** An endearing term for a baby, a girl, etc.; a darling. Also, a gaily dressed woman (*contempt.*). †**2.** A rag doll (*rare*) 1755.

Moppy (mǫ·pi), *a.* 1725. [f. MOP *sb.*[1] + -Y[1].] Resembling (as thick as) a mop.

†**Mops.** 1565. [Cf. MOPPET.] A term of endearment for a young girl –1654.

Mopstick (mǫ·pstik). 1710. [f. MOP *sb.*[1] + STICK.] The handle of a mop.

Mopus[1] (mōu·pǒs). *Obs.* exc. *dial.* 1700. [f. MOPE *sb.*] A mope; a dull stupid person.

Mo·pus[2]. *slang.* 1769. Usu. in *pl.* Money.

Mopy (mōu·pi), *a.* 1827. [f. MOPE *v.* + -Y[1].] Given to or causing moping.

Moquette (mǫke·t). 1762 (**mocketto**). [a. F. *moquette*; corruption of *mocade* MOCKADO (Hatz.-Darm.).] A fabric with a velvety pile, used for carpeting and upholstery.

‖ **Mora**[1] (mōə·ră). 1569. [L. *mora* delay.] **1.** *Sc. Law.* Negligent delay. †**2.** A delay (*rare*) –1677. **3.** (Pl. *moræ.*) A unit of metrical time equal to a short syllable 1832.

‖ **Mora**[2], **morra** (mǫ·ră). 1706. [It. *mora*; origin unkn.] A popular game in Italy in which one player guesses the number of fingers held up simultaneously by another player. A similar game in China. (Cf. LOVE *sb.* 9.)

‖**Mora**[3] (mōə·ră). *Pl.* **moras.** 1838. [a. Gr. μόρα, f. μορ-, μερ- to divide.] *Gr. Hist.* One of the (orig. six) divisions of which the Spartan army consisted.

‖ **Mora**[4] (mōə·ră). 1826. [Shortened from Tupi *moiratinga*, f. *moira* tree + *tinga* white.] A lofty tree, *Mora excelsa*, found in British Guiana and Trinidad.

Moraine (mǒrēɪ·n). 1789. [a. F.] An accumulation of débris from the mountains carried down and deposited by a glacier.

Lateral, terminal m. a deposit at the side or at the end of a glacier respectively. *Medial m.*, a deposit between two conjoining glaciers. **b.** In rock-gardening, a raised border or ridge of stones, etc. on which plants are grown. **Morai·nal, Morai·nic** *adjs.*

Moral (mǫ·răl), *sb.* late ME. [Subst. use of MORAL *a.*; but also infl. by late L. *morale* neut. sing., *moralia* neut. pl., F. *moral, morale* (see MORALE).] **1.** *pl.* (earlier †*sing.*) Used as tr. L. *Moralia* pl. as the title of writings by St. Gregory the Great, Plutarch, Seneca, etc. **2.** The moral teaching (of a fable, an occurrence, etc.); also in phr. *to point a m.* 1500. **b.** That part of a fable, etc., which points the moral meaning 1560. †**c.** Meaning, import –1841. †**3.** A symbolical figure –1599. ¶**b.** Vulgarly confused with *model.* Counterpart, double. Chiefly in *the very m. of* ... 1757. **4.** = MORALITY 4 b. *Obs.* exc. *Hist.* 1578. †**5.** (A person's) moral principles or practice –1820. ‖**b.** The condition (of troops, etc.) as to discipline and confidence. [Fr.; pronounced (mǫral).] 1883. **6.** *pl.* In early use: †(A person's) moral qualities or endowments. Now, Moral habits or conduct; also *spec.*, sexual conduct. 1613. **7.** *pl.* Moral science; ethics. Chiefly construed as *sing.* Now *rare.* 1651. **8.** *slang.* A moral certainty 1861.

2. To point a m., or adorn a tale JOHNSON. **c.** *Tam. Shr.* IV. iv. 79. **3.** *Hen. V*, III. vi. 40. **b.** He 's the very m. (as the old women call it) of Sir John 1850. **6.** The morals of Sedley were such as, even in that age, gave great scandal MACAULAY. **7.** In morals the action is judged by the intention SWINBURNE.

Moral (mǫ·răl), *a.* ME. [ad. L. *moralis* (Cicero, *De Fato* II. i, rendering Gr. ἠθικός ETHIC *a.*), f. *mor-, mos* custom (pl. *mores* manners, morals, character); see -AL.] **1.** Of or pertaining to character or disposition; of or pertaining to the distinction between right and wrong, or good and evil, in relation to actions, volitions, or character; ethical. **b.** Of knowledge, opinions, judgements, etc.: Relating to the nature and application of the distinction between right and wrong 1500. **c.** *Moral sense*: the power of apprehending the difference between right and wrong, esp. when viewed as an innate faculty of the human mind. So *m. faculty.* 1699. **d.** Of feelings: Arising from the contemplation of an action, character, etc., as good or bad 1768. **e.** Of concepts or terms: Involving ethical praise or blame 1845. **2.** Concerned with virtue and vice, or the rules of right conduct, as a subject of study. late ME. **3.** †**a.** Of a writer, etc.: That enunciates moral precepts –1742. **b.** Of a literary, pictorial, or dramatic work: That deals with the ruling of conduct; that conveys a moral; also, †allegorical, emblematical. late ME. **c.** Of a literary work: Good in moral effect 1671. **4.** *Moral law*: the body of requirements in conformity to which virtuous action consists; one of these requirements. Opp. to 'positive' or 'instituted' laws. late ME. **5.** Of rights, obligations, etc.: Founded on the moral law. Opp. to *legal.* 1690. **6. a.** Of actions: Subject to the moral law; having the property of being right or wrong 1594. **b.** Of an agent, etc.: Capable of moral action 1736. **7.** Pertaining to or operating on the character or conduct of human beings; acting through or upon the moral sense 1597. **b.** Applied to the indirect effect of some action or event (e. g. a victory or defeat) in producing confidence or discouragement, and the like 1835. **8.** Of, pertaining to, or concerned with the morals (of a person or a community) 1794. **9.** Of persons, etc.: Conforming to the rules of morality; morally good 1638. **b.** Virtuous with regard to sexual conduct 1803. **c.** Of a tale, etc.: Not ribald or vicious. late ME. **10.** Used to designate that kind of probable evidence which rests on a knowledge of character and of the general tendencies of human nature; often more loosely applied to all evidence which is merely probable 1646.

1. *M. virtue*: tr. L. *virtus moralis*, Gr. ἀρετὴ ἠθική (Aristotle), (an) excellence of character or disposition, as dist. from *intellectual virtue* (ἀρετὴ διανοητική). *M. virtue* is occas. restricted to such virtues as may be attained without the aid of religion. **b.** A correct m. judgment GEO. ELIOT. **2.** *M. philosophy*: the part of philosophy which treats of the virtues and vices, the criteria of right and wrong, the formation of virtuous character, and the like; ethical philosophy, ethics. Formerly used more widely, including psychology and metaphysics. So, in recent use, *m. science.* At Cambridge, etc. *m. sciences* is used as a comprehensive name for all that is now commonly understood by 'philosophy'. Also *attrib.*, as in *m. sciences tripos.* *M. theology*: the practical part of ethics treated as a branch of theology; the part of theological learning which is concerned with cases of conscience. **3. a.** O m. Gower this boke I directe To the CHAUCER. **b.** *Moral play* (*Obs.* exc. *Hist.*) = MORALITY 4 b. **4.** The m. law must be the law of the perfect man H. SPENCER. **5.** The sense of m. responsibility in connexion with the use of capital MORLEY. **6. b.** Every creature possessing mind is a m. agent 1868. **7.** I wonder that thou..goest about to apply a morall medicine to a mortifying mischiefe SHAKS. There is now very little m. hold which the latter [the clergy] possess COBBETT. The moral-force men and the physical-force men 1851. *M. courage*: courage to encounter odium, disapproval, or contempt, rather than depart from what is right; dist. from *physical courage.* **b.** *M. victory*: a defeat or an indecisive result claimed as a victory on account of its moral effects. **8.** The m. interests of society 1848. **9.** A m., sensible, and well-bred man COWPER. **10.** In Matters of Faith, an exceeding great Probability is called a m. Certainty WATTS.

Phr. *M. sense* or *interpretation*: orig., interpretation of events recorded in Holy Scripture as typical of something in the life of the Christian soul; †hence *transf.* applied to the moral of a fable, etc.

Moral (mǫ·răl), *v. rare.* 1600. [f. prec.] = MORALIZE *v.*

‖ **Morale** (mǒrā·l; as Fr. moral). 1752. [F., fem. of *moral* adj.; see MORAL *a.*] **1.** Morality, morals: moral principles or practice; moral teaching 1812; moral aspect 1834. **2.** Moral condition; conduct, behaviour; esp. with regard to confidence, discipline, etc. Said of a body of troops, etc. 1831.

2. The *morale* of the troops is excellent 1870.

Moralism (mǫ·răliz'm). 1828. [f. MORAL + -ISM.] **1.** Addiction to moralizing; (with *pl.*) an act of moralizing. **2.** The practice of a natural system of morality; morality not spiritualized 1850.

Moralist (mǫ·rălist). 1621. [f. MORAL + -IST.] **1.** One who practises morality. **2.** A teacher of morals; a moral philosopher 1639. **3.** A merely moral man. (Cf. MORALISM 2.) 1649.

1. And many a holy text around she strews, That teach the rustic m. to die GRAY. **Morali·stic** *a.*

Morality (mǒræ·lĭti). late ME. [a. F. *moralité*, ad. L. *moralitas*, f. *moralis*; see MORAL *a.* and -ITY.] †**1.** Knowledge of moral science. late ME. only. **2.** *pl.* Moral qualities or endowments. late ME. **3.** Moral discourse or instruction; a moral exhortation. Now chiefly in disparaging sense, moralizing. late ME. †b. Moral sense or interpretation (see MORAL *a.*); also, the moral (of a fable, etc.) –1623. †4. A literary or artistic production inculcating a moral lesson; a moralizing commentary; a moral allegory –1649. b. *Hist.* Name for the species of drama (popular in the 16th c.) in which some moral or spiritual lesson was inculcated, and in which the chief characters were personifications of abstract qualities 1765. 5. Moral science 1449. b. *pl.* Points of ethics, moral principles or rules 1605. c. A particular system of morals 1680. d. Ethical aspect (of a question) 1869. 6. The quality or fact of being moral 1592. 7. Moral conduct; usu. good moral conduct 1609. b. A mock-title for one who assumes airs of virtue 1672.

1. Of moralitee he [*sc.* Seneca] was the flour CHAUCER. 2. A saint..in her moralities BYRON. 3. Quaint monkish moralities and scriptural quotations 1877. 5. I am bold to think, that m. is capable of demonstration, as well as mathematicks LOCKE. c. The m. of the Gospel had a direct influence upon the politics of the age FREEMAN. 6. Instances..of genius and m. united in a lawyer..are distinguished by their singularity *Junius Lett.* 7. We do not look in great cities for our best m. JANE AUSTEN.

Moralize (mǫ·răləiz), *v.* 1450. [a. F. *moraliser*, ad. late L. *moralizare*, f. *moralis*; see MORAL *a.* and -IZE.] 1. *trans.* To interpret morally or symbolically; to point the moral of; to make (an event, etc.) the subject of moral reflection. †2. Of an event: To exemplify the moral of (a fable, etc.) –1611. †b. To supply (a poem) with a moral –1754. 3. *intr.* To indulge in moral reflection; to found a moral (*on* or *upon* an event, etc.) 1525. b. *trans.* To change the condition or aspect of (a person or thing) by moral discourse or reflection. Const. *into, out of.* 1722. 4. To make moral; to affect the moral quality of (actions, feelings) 1592. 5. To improve the morals of 1633.

1. But what said Iaques? Did he not m. this spectacle? SHAKS. 2. I speake..onely to shewe how it doth m. this Prouerbe, That where the Body is, the Eagles will Resort 1601. 3. No one can m. better after a misfortune has taken place W. IRVING. b. To m. Affliction into Use 1722. 4. Good and bad Stars m. not our Actions SIR T. BROWNE. 5. To M. the Stage 1723. Hence **Moraliza·tion, Mo·ralizer. Mo·ralizingly** *adv.*

Morally (mǫ·răli), *adv.* late ME. [f. MORAL *a.* + -LY [2].] †1. In a moral sense –1509. 2. In respect of moral conduct; from the point of view of ethics; with reference to moral responsibility 1449. 3. Virtuously 1540. 4. On grounds of moral evidence; according to the normal human judgement, or to reason and probability (cf. VIRTUALLY 1 b) 1615.

2. A government is m. bound to keep itself in existence KINGSLEY. 3. To live m. DRYDEN. 4. It being m. sure, that the Earl of Essex would put himself in their way CLARENDON.

Morass (mŏræ·s). 1655. Now *literary* exc. in the West Indies (pron. mǫ·rəs). [a. Du. *moeras*, a. (ult.) OF. *maresc, marais*; see MARISH.] A wet swampy tract, a bog, marsh; *occas.*, boggy land.

attrib. and *Comb.*, as **m. ore**, bog iron ore; **m.-weed** *West Ind.*, the aquatic plant hornwort, *Ceratophyllum demersum.* Hence **Mora·ssy** *a.*

Morat (mōᵊ·ræt). 1807. [ad. med.L. *moratum*, f. L. *morus* mulberry; see -ATE [1].] *Antiq.* A drink made of honey and flavoured with mulberries.

Moration (morē·ʃən). *rare.* 1650. [ad. L. *morationem, morari.*] Delay, tarrying.

‖**Moratorium** (mǫrătōᵊ·riŏm). 1875. [mod. L., neut. of late L. *moratorius*, f. *morari.*] *Law.* A legal authorization to a debtor to postpone payment for a certain time. So **Mo·ratory** *a.* authorizing delay in payment.

Moravian (mŏrē·viăn), *sb.*[1] and *a.*[1] 1577. [f. med.L. *Moravia* Moray (ad. Gael. *Muireibh*) + -AN.] A. *sb.* An inhabitant of Moray, in Scotland. B. *adj.* Of or pertaining to Moray 1897.

Moravian (mŏrē·viăn), *sb.*[2] and *a.*[2] 1616. [f. *Moravia* (med.L., f. *Morava* the river March), part of the Austro-Hungarian empire, Ger. *Mähren*; see -AN.] A. *sb.* 1. An inhabitant of Moravia. GIBBON. 2. A member of a Protestant sect, founded in Saxony by emigrants from Moravia, and holding Hussite doctrines 1746. B. *adj.* 1. Of or pertaining to Moravia 1616. 2. Of or belonging to the sect of the Moravians 1745. Hence **Mora·vianism.**

Moray (mōᵊ·rē¹, mŏrē·). *U.S.* 1624. [a. Pg. *moreia* :—L. *muræna.*] Any tropical species of eel of the family *Murænidæ.*

Morbid (mǭ·ɹbid), *a.* 1656. [ad. L. *morbidus*, f. *morbus* disease, f. root of *mori* to die.] 1. Of the nature of or indicative of disease; also, †morbific. †b. Of persons or animals, their parts, etc.: Diseased, unhealthy –1846. 2. Of mind, ideas, etc.: Unwholesome, sickly. Hence of persons: Given to morbid feelings or fancies. 1834.

1. Of m. hue his features THOMSON. b. *M. anatomy*: the anatomy of diseased organs or structures. 2. The m. German fancies which proved so fatal to Carlyle RUSKIN. Hence **Mo·rbid·ly** *adv.*, **-ness** 1668.

‖**Morbidezza** (mǫrbide·tsa). 1624. [It., f. *morbido* morbid.] *Painting.* Life-like delicacy in flesh-tints.

Morbidity (mǫɹbi·dĭti). 1721. [f. MORBID *a.* + -ITY.] 1. The quality or condition of being morbid; a morbid state or symptom; *pl.* morbid characteristics. 2. *Med.* Prevalence of disease; the sick rate in a district 1882.

Morbific (mǫɹbi·fik), *a.* 1652. [ad. F. *morbifique* or mod.L. *morbificus*, f. *morbus*; see -FIC.] Causing disease. ¶b. Occas. misused for: Caused by disease 1658. So †**Morbi·fical** *a.* 1620–1694. **Morbi·fically** *adv.*

Morbillous (mǫɹbi·ləs), *a.* 1775. [ad. med. L. *morbillosus*, f. *morbillus*, dim. of L. *morbus.*] *Path.* Of or pertaining to measles.

‖**Morbleu** (morblö̆). 1664. [Fr.; a perversion of *mort Dieu* God's death.] A comic oath; usu. attributed to French speakers.

†**Morbo·se**, *a.* 1691. [ad. L. *morbosus*, f. *morbus*; see -OSE.] Proceeding from disease, causing disease, unhealthy –1765. Hence †**Morbo·sity** 1646–1689. So †**Mo·rbous** *a.* 1651–1684.

‖**Morbus** (mǭ·ɹbŏs). L., = disease, as in CHOLERA *m.*

‖**Morceau** (morsø). 1751. [F.; see MORSEL *sb.*] A short literary or musical piece.

‖**Morcellement** (morsęlmaṅ). 1848. [Fr., f. *morceler* to break in pieces, f. OF. *morcel* MORSEL: see -MENT.] Division (*spec.* of land or property) into small portions.

Mordacious (mǫɹdē·ʃəs), *a.* Now *rare.* 1650. [f. L. *mordac-, -ax* (f. *mordere* to bite) + -IOUS.] 1. Biting; given to biting 1777. †2. Of substances: Pungent, caustic –1684. 3. Of sarcasm, etc.: Biting, keen 1650. Hence **Morda·ciously** *adv.*

Mordacity (mǫrdæ·sĭti). 1601. [ad. F. *mordacité*, ad. L. *mordacitas*; see prec. and -ITY.] 1. Propensity to biting 1677. 2. 'Biting' or mordant quality.

2. He ieasteth, but without mordacitie *c* 1630.

Mordant (mǭ·ɹdănt), *sb.* late ME. [a. OF., subst. use of *mordant* adj.; see next.] †1. An instrument that bites or holds fast; e.g. a tag of metal at the end of the pendant of a girdle –1500. 2. *Dyeing.* A substance used for fixing colouring matters on stuffs 1791. b. *Gilding.* An adhesive compound for fixing gold-leaf 1825. 3. *Etching.* The fluid used to 'bite in' the lines on the plate 1878.

Mordant (mǭ·ɹdănt), *a.* 1474. [a. F. *mordant*, pres. pple. of *mordre* to bite:—pop. L. **mordēre* (= class. L. *mordēre*).] Biting. 1. Of sarcasm (hence of speakers, etc.): Caustic, incisive. 2. Corrosive. Now *rare.* 1601. 3. That causes pain or smart. Of pain: acute, burning. 1845. 4. Serving to fix colouring matter or gold-leaf 1825. Hence **Mo·rdancy,** sarcastic force; incisiveness 1656.

Mordant (mǭ·ɹdănt), *v.* 1836. [f. MORDANT *sb.*] *Dyeing.* To impregnate with a mordant.

Mordent (mǭ·ɹdĕnt). Also **mordente** (mǫɹde·nte). 1806. [a. G. *mordent*, or ad. It. *mordente*, pr. pple. of *mordere* to bite.] *Mus.* A grace consisting in the rapid alternation of a note with the one immediately below it. Also applied to other graces.

†**Mo·rdicant,** *a.* 1597. [ad. L. *mordicantem, mordicare*, f. *mordere* to bite.] Biting, sharp, pungent –1834. Hence †**Mo·rdicancy,** m. quality; also, a biting irritation 1693–9.

†**Mordica·tion.** late ME. [ad. L. *mordicationem.*] A biting, burning, or gnawing sensation or pain –1684. So †**Mordicative** *a.*, biting, sharp, pungent. late ME.–1634.

†**Mordishee·n.** *Anglo-Ind.* 1598. [a. Pg. *mordexim*, a. Marathi *modachi.*] Cholera –1787.

More, *sb.*[1] *Obs.* exc. *dial.* [OE. *more, moru* wk. fem.:—OTeut. **murhōn-.*] A root; a tree-stump; †*fig.* 'root', origin. †b. A plant. SPENSER.

More (mōᵊɹ), *a.* (*sb.*[2]) and *adv.* [The adj. is Com. Teut.: OE. *māra* :—OTeut. **maizon-*, f. **maiz* adv., which is represented by OE. *mā.* The use of the neut. adj. as quasi-sb. and adv. occurs in OE., but rarely, as *mā* (see MO) was the ordinary word in both applications.] A. *adj.* 1. Greater. 2. [Modelled on the older use of MO with partitive genitive.] Existing in greater quantity, amount, or degree; a greater quantity or amount of. late ME. 3. (With sb. in *pl.*) A greater number of .. 1584; existing in greater numbers, more numerous (now only in pred. use) 1565. (Not in A.V. or Shaks.) 4. Additional to the quantity or number expressed or implied; further. Now *rare* exc. as preceded by an indef. or num. adj., e.g. *any more, two more*, etc.; and in arch. phrases like *without more ado.* ME.

1. Hit semed moche m. Then I had any Egle seyne CHAUCER. Lets flye to some strong Cittadell, For our m. safety 1632. Phr. *The m. part.* (*The*) *more's the pity. The m. fool you.* 2. Perchance my Lord, I shew m. craft then loue SHAKS. 3. M. things are wrought by prayer Than this world dreams of TENNYSON. They that be with us are m. than they that be with them R.V. 2 *Kings* vi. 16. 4. Oliver..basin and spoon in hand, said..'Please, sir, I want some m.' DICKENS.

B. *absol.* and quasi-*sb.* †1. Used *absol.* in the sense 'greater' –1646. 2. Something that is more; a greater quantity, amount, degree, etc. OE. b. Used predicatively: Something of greater importance or magnitude 1484. 3. (With pl. construction.) A greater number *of* the class specified; also, a greater number of persons 1629. 4. An additional quantity, amount, or number ME.

1. Phr. †*M. and less* = persons of all ranks (*Macb.* v. iv. 12). 2. Where m. is meant then meets the ear MILT. The m. I saw of my guide the m. I liked him TYNDALL. 91 acres, m. or less (= approximately) of excellent..land 1798. b. Phr. *To be m.*: to count for m.; The individual withers, and the world is m. and m. TENNYSON. 4. This Answer Proteus gave, nor m. he said DRYDEN. Hints haunt me ever of a m. beyond CLOUGH. Phr. *Of which m. anon.* Now *arch.* or *joc. And m.*: indicating an indefinite addition to what has been mentioned.

C. *adv.* 1. In a greater degree, to a greater extent ME. b. Forming the comparative of most adjs. and advs. of more than one syllable and of all of more than two syllables ME. c. Formerly prefixed pleonastically to the comparative of the adj. or adv. *Obs.* exc. *arch.* ME. 2. Phr. *M. or less*: in a greater or less degree; to a greater or less extent. Hence with negative: (Not) at all. ME. 3. Qualifying a predicate or a predicative adjunct as being applicable in a greater degree *than* another ME. 4. Additionally, in addition. a. In neg., interrog., or hypothetical contexts: Further, longer, again OE. b. Besides, moreover ME. 5. *More than* before adjs., advs., vbs., and descriptive sbs., indicates that the word thus qualified is inadequate to the intended meaning 1553. b. *Neither m. nor less than*: exactly, precisely, (that) and nothing else 1460. 6. Used conjunctionally to introduce a clause or sentence of the nature of an important addition. Now only *arch.* chiefly in *nay m.*, rarely (*and*) *m.* late ME. †7. quasi-*prep.* = PLUS 1. –1706.

1. The m. he explains, the m. I am puzzled BERKELEY. b. He finds Rest m. agreeable than Motion STEELE. c. But Paris was to me M. lovelier than all the world beside TENNYSON. Phr. *The m.* = the rather, the more so (*because*, etc.). 2. Lawyers..that are m. or less passionate according as they are paid for it ADDISON. 3. M. dead than alive 1834. 4. a. Hee..sent forth the doue, which returned not againe

vnto him any m. *Gen.* viii. 12. **b.** Ile not offend thee with a vaine teare m. B. JONS. **5.** My much m. than disrespect for the Jamaica Committee RUSKIN. **6.** We are betroathd: nay m., our mariage howre.. Determin'd of SHAKS. Phr. *M. by token*: see TOKEN *sb.* 7. That Number m. one 1706.

†**More,** *v.* ME. [f. MORE *a.*] *trans.* and *intr.* To increase –1483.

More, var. MOHUR; obs. f. MOOR.

-more (mōᵊɹ), *suffix*, forming advs. of place (rarely of time) in the comparative degree. Chiefly appended to advs. having already the comparative ending *-er*, as in *furthermore*, etc.

Moreen (mŏrī·n). 1691. [Perh. f. MOIRE.] A stout woollen or woollen and cotton material either plain or watered, used for curtains, etc.

Morel[1] (more·l). ME. [a. OF. *morele* (mod. F. *-elle*), prob. fem. of *morel* dark-coloured.] A name for kinds of NIGHTSHADE; chiefly the Black Nightshade (*petty m.*).

Morel[2] (more·l). 1611. [app. a. F. *morelle.*] A morello cherry.

Morel[3] (more·l). 1672. [a. F. *morille*; etym. obscure.] An edible fungus of the genus *Morchella*, esp. *M. esculenta.*

Morello (mŏre·lo). Also †**a.** 1648. [Etym. obscure. Cf. It. *morello* blackish.] A dark-coloured kind of cherry with a bitter taste.

‖**More·na.** [Sp., fem. of *moreno* dark-complexioned.] A brunette. PEPYS.

†**Mo·reness.** late ME. [f. MORE *a.* + -NESS.] **1.** The condition of being greater than another. late ME. only. **2.** Plurality –1674.

Moreover (mōᵊrōᵘ·vəɹ), *adv.* Now only *literary.* late ME. [f. MORE *adv.* + OVER *adv.*] †**1.** In the phr. *And yet more over* = 'that is not all' –1526. **2.** Introducing an additional statement: Besides, further. (Often following *and*, occas. *but.*) late ME. †**b.** Governing a clause: Besides *that. Haml.* II. ii. 2.

2. More ouer there was no water for the multitude TINDALE *Num.* xx. 2.

Morepork, var. of MOPOKE.

Moresco (more·sko). 1551. [a. It. *moresco*, f. *Moro* MOOR *sb.*[2]; see -ESQUE.] **A.** *adj.* Of or pertaining to the Moors; Moorish. **B.** *sb.* **1.** A Moor 1577. †**2.** The Moorish language –1678. **3.** A morris-dance 1625.

Moresque (more·sk). 1611. [a. F. *moresque*, ad. It. *moresco*; see prec. and -ESQUE.] **A.** *adj.* Moorish in style or ornamental design. **B.** *sb.* **1.** Arabesque ornament 1727. **2.** A Moorish woman 1895.

†**Morfound,** *v.* late ME. [ad. F. *morfondre*, f. *morve* mucus + *fondre* to melt, FOUND *v.*[2]] *intr.* and *pass.* Of horses, etc.: To take a thorough chill, to be benumbed with cold –1720. Hence †**Morfound** *sb.* 1523–1725.

Morganatic (mǭɹgănæ·tik), *a.* 1727. [ad. mod. L. *morganaticus*, evolved from the med.L. phrase *matrimonium ad morganaticam*, a marriage by which the wife and children, if any, are entitled to no share in the husband's possessions beyond the 'morning-gift'. *Morganatica* is prob. synonymous with *morganaticum* MORNING-GIFT, f. OHG. *morgan* (= MORN) in **morgangeba.*] Epithet of a kind of marriage between a man of exalted rank and a woman of lower station in which it is provided that neither the wife nor her children shall share the dignities or inherit the possessions of her husband; also, occas., used of the marriage of a woman of superior rank to a man of inferior station. Hence **Morgana·tically** *adv.*

Morgay (mǭ·ɹgē¹). Also **-ghi.** 1672. [a. Cornish *morgi*, f. *môr* sea + *ci* dog.] The Dog-fish, esp. the lesser spotted Dog-fish.

‖**Morgen** (mǭ·ɹgən). 1674. [Du. and G. *morgen*, app. = 'area of land that can be ploughed in one morning'.] A measure of land in Holland and the Dutch colonies, equal to about two acres. Also in Prussia, Norway, and Denmark, a measure of land now equal to about two-thirds of an acre.

Morgenstern (mǭ·ɹgənstɜ̄ɹn). 1637. [a. Ger., lit. 'morning star'.] *Antiq.* A club with a head set with spikes (cf. MORNING STAR 2).

†**Morglay.** ME. [perh. a. W. *mawrgleddyf* (or a cogn. form), f. *mawr* great + *cleddyf* sword. Cf. CLAYMORE.] The sword belonging to Sir Bevis; hence, a sword (1582–1647).

‖**Morgue**[1] (mǭɹg, morg). 1599. [Fr.; origin unkn.] A haughty demeanour, haughty superiority, pride.

An amiable family, and with nothing at all of the English *morgue* M. ARNOLD.

‖**Morgue**[2] (mǭɹg, morg). 1821. [Fr.] Name of a building in Paris, in which the bodies of persons found dead are exposed for identification. Hence (esp. in U.S.), any building used for the same purpose.

†**Mo·rian.** 1500. [Early mod.E. *Morien*, a. OF. *Morien*, f. *More*, MOOR *sb.*[2]; see -IAN.] **A.** *adj.* Moorish; hence, black, dark –1597. **B.** *sb.* A Moor, blackamoor, negro –1657.

Moribund (mǫ·ribʊnd). 1721. [ad. L. *moribundus*, f. *mori* to die.] **A.** *adj.* At the point of death; in a dying state. **B.** *sb.* A dying person 1835.

A. *fig.* The wail of a m. world CARLYLE. Hence **Moribu·ndity.**

Morice, obs. f. MORRIS *sb.*[1] and *v.*

Morigerate (mori·dʒĕrĕt), *a. rare.* 1533. [ad. late L. *morigeratus*, *morigerari*: see next.] Complying, obedient. So **Morigera·tion,** obedience, compliance 1605.

Morigerous (mori·dʒĕrəs), *a.* 1600. [f. L. *morigerus* (f. *mor-*, *mos* custom, humour + *gerere*; after phr. *morem gerere* to humour a person) + -OUS.] Obedient, compliant, submissive. Const. *to.*

Morillon[1] (mori·lən). 1664. [a. F., related to *morel* dark-coloured: see MOREL[1].] A variety of vine; also, its fruit.

Morillon[2] (mori·lən). 1678. [a. F.] The female or young of the Golden-Eye (*Clangula glaucion*).

Morin (mōᵊ·rin). 1837. [a. F. *morine*, f. L. *morus* (in mod.L. name of a genus formerly including the fustic-tree); see -IN.[1]] *Chem.* A yellow colouring matter obtained from fustic.

Morindin (mori·ndin). 1848. [f. mod.L. *Morinda* (f. L. *morus* mulberry-tree + *Indus* Indian), a cinchonaceous genus of plants, the bark of which yields red and yellow dyes + -IN.[1]] *Chem.* A yellow crystalline colouring matter.

‖**Moringa** (mori·ŋgă). 1753. [mod.L.] The ben-nut tree (BEN *sb.*[3]).

Morion[1] (mǫ·riən). 1554. [a. F. *morion*, Sp. *morrion*, or It. *morione*; perh. orig. Sp., f. *morra* crown of the head.] *Antiq.* A kind of helmet, without beaver or visor, worn in the 16th and 17th c.

The soldiers of the guard With musquet, pike, and m. SCOTT.

Morion[2] (mǫ·riən). 1748. [a. F., a. corrupt L. *morion* (for *mormorion*).] *Min.* Black smoky quartz.

Morisco (mori·sko). 1550. [a. Sp. *Morisco*, f. *Moro* MOOR *sb.*[2] Cf. MORESCO.] **A.** *adj.* Of or pertaining to the Moors; Moorish. **B.** *sb.* **1.** A Moor, *esp.* one of the Moors in Spain 1550. **2.** Arabesque ornament 1727. **3.** A morris-dance 1561. †**b.** A morris-dancer. 2 *Hen. VI*, III. i. 365. So †**Morisk** *a.* and *sb.*

Morkin (mǭ·ɹkin). [Late ME. *mortkyn* = AF. *mortekine*, altered f. OF. *mortecine*, ad. L. *morticina* carrion, f. *mort-*, *mors* death.] A beast that dies by disease or accident.

Morling (mǭ·ɹliŋ). Also **mortling.** 1448. [App. formed after MORKIN by substituting -LING for -KIN.] **1.** Wool taken from the skin of a dead sheep. (*Obs.* exc. in schedules to Acts of Parliament.) Opp. to *shorling.* †**2.** = MORKIN –1753.

†**Mo·rmal.** late ME. (Chaucer). [a. OF. *mortmal*, f. *mort* dead + *mal* evil.] An inflamed sore, esp. on the leg –1685.

‖**Mormaor** (mǫɹmē·ǒɹ). Also **maormor.** 1807. [a. Gael. *mormaer*, mod. *mòrmhaor*, app. f. *mòr* great + *maor* bailiff, steward.] In ancient Scotland, a high steward of a province.

†**Mo·rmo.** 1605. [a. Gr. μορμώ, a hideous she-monster.] A hobgoblin, bugbear –1738.

Mormon (mǭ·ɹmən). 1837. [f. *Mormon*, the alleged author of 'The Book of Mormon'.] **1.** A member of a religious body, calling itself 'The Church of Jesus Christ of the Latter-day Saints', having its head-quarters at Salt Lake City, Utah, U.S.A., and founded in 1830 at Manchester, New York, by Joseph Smith on the basis of supposed divine revelations contained in 'The Book of Mormon'.

The best known feature of the sect is the practice of polygamy; but this is not countenanced by the Book of Mormon or the law of the U.S.

Hence **Mo·rmondom,** Mormons collectively, their territory, or their usages. **Mo·rmonism,** the religious doctrines of the Mormons 1834. **Mo·rmonite** *sb.* a M. 1833, *adj.* of or pertaining to the Mormons.

Morn (mǭɹn). [Com. Teut.: OE. *morgen*:—OTeut. **murganoz*, prob. cogn. w. W. *bore*, OW. *more* morning, Skr. *máricih* ray of light.] **1.** Dawn, sunrise. Only *poet.* **b.** The east 1642. **2.** The early part of the day; morning. Now chiefly *poet.* OE. **3.** The next morning. Hence = MORROW 2. OE.

1. While the still m. went out with Sandals gray MILT. Phr. *Northern m.*: the aurora borealis TENNYSON. **2.** One m. I miss'd him on the custom'd hill GRAY. **3.** He wad be glad if I wad eat a reisted haddock..at breakfast wi' him the m. SCOTT.

Morne (mǭɹn), *sb.* 1494. [a. F. *morne*, f. OF. *morner* to blunt (a lance), f. *morne* blunted.] *Antiq.* The rebated head of a tilting lance.

‖**Morne** (mǫrn), *a.* 1844. [Fr.; perh. f. Teut. root of MOURN *v.*] Dismal, dreary.

A silence m. and drear AYTOUN.

‖**Morné** (mǫrne), *a.* 1722. [Fr.; pa. pple. of *morner* to blunt.] *Her.* Said of a lion rampant represented as having no tongue, teeth, or claws.

Morning (mǭ·ɹniŋ), *sb.* (and *a.*) [ME. *morwening*, *morning*, f. *morwen* MORN + -ING[1], after EVENING.] **I. 1.** Orig., the time of the approach or beginning of morn. In mod. use: The early part of the day-time, ending at noon or at the hour of the midday meal. **b.** The portion of the day extending to the fashionable dinner time 1745. Now *Obs.* or *arch.* **c.** *fig.* The beginning, or early part 1595. **2.** With qualifying adj. denoting the kind of weather, etc., prevailing, or the pleasure, etc., experienced during the morning. late ME. **3.** *poet.* The dawn, daybreak; the light of dawn. Often *personified.* 1593. **4.** A morning draught, taken before breakfast. Chiefly *Sc.* 1718. **b.** 'A slight repast taken at rising' (Jam.). *dial.* 1818.

1. The m. weares, 'tis time we were at Church SHAKS. *In the morning*, appended to an hour-date, means between midnight and noon; = *a.m.* **c.** In the m. of my victories 1595. **2.** In a Frosty M. 1678. *Good m.*: see GOOD *a.* III. 1. *M., noon, and night* = all the day, incessantly. *All (the) m.* (*Of* or *on*) *mornings*, *in* or *of a m.* (*dial.*): habitually in the m. *This m.*: the m. of to-day. **3.** See how the M. opes her golden Gates SHAKS. *Northern m.*: the aurora borealis 1836.

II. *attrib.* (and quasi-*adj.*) Existing, prevailing, or taking place in the morning 1535. **b.** In poetry, *morning* adj. often connotes vaguely the attributes possessed in the morning, or the fact that morning is the time referred to 1590. **c.** Of things intended to be worn in the morning 1620.

Your loue is like a mornynge cloude, & like a dew yᵗ goeth early awaye COVERDALE *Hosea* vi. 4. **b.** The m. Larke SHAKS. The Schoole-boy with his.. shining m. face SHAKS. **c.** A loose Morning-dress 1700. A man's m. suit 1896.

Comb.: **m. call,** a visit paid during the 'morning' (*i.e.* afternoon); **m.-gun,** a gun fired from the admiral's ship, or at a military post or camp, to announce day-break; **-land,** the East, the Orient; **-office,** morning prayer; **m. prayer,** (*a*) a prayer said in the m.; (*b*) the Anglican service of matins; **-room,** a room used as a sitting-room during the early part of the day; **-sickness,** nausea occurring in the morning, one of the earlier symptoms of pregnancy.

Mo·rning-gift. 1597. *Antiq.* A mod. rendering of OE. *morgengifu* or its equivalents = a gift made by the husband to the wife on the morning after the consummation of the marriage.

Mo·rning-glory. 1836. [f. MORNING + GLORY *sb.*] An American convolvulaceous plant, *Ipomœa purpurea*; also applied to other species of *Ipomœa*, and allied plants.

Morning star. 1535. **1.** = LUCIFER 1. Also *gen.* a star or planet that is visible in the morning. **b.** *fig.* Applied (after *Rev.* xxii. 16) to Christ; also, to any person who is regarded as the precursor of a figurative 'dawn' 1567. **2.** *Antiq.* = MORGENSTERN 1684.

1. The bright morning Star, Dayes harbinger MILT. b. John Wickliffe, the morning star of the Reformation 1732.

Mo·rning-tide. Now *poet.* 1530. [f. MORNING + TIDE.] The morning, or early part of the day.

Morning-watch. 1535 (Coverdale). [f. MORNING + WATCH *sb.*] **1.** The last of the (three or four) watches into which the night was divided by the Jews and Romans. **2.** *Naut.* The watch between 4 and 8 a.m.; the men on duty at that time 1840.

Mo·rnward(s, *adv. poet. rare.* 1850. [f. MORN + -WARD(S.] Towards the morning; eastward.

‖**Moro** (mō·ro). 1886. [Sp., = MOOR *sb.*[2]] A Mohammedan Malay of the southern Philippine Islands.

Moroccan (mŏrǫ·kăn), *a.* and *sb.* 1860. [f. next + -AN.] Of or pertaining to (an inhabitant of) Morocco.

Morocco (mŏrǫ·ko). Formerly also **Marocco**, etc. 1634. [The European name (= It. *Marocco*, Sp. *Marruecos*, F. *Maroc*) of the sultanate called in Arabic *Maγrib-al-Aqçā* 'Extreme West'. comprising the north-western part of Africa. The native form of the name is *Marrākesh*.] **1.** Used *attrib.* in the sense 'of or pertaining to or made in Morocco'; as in *M. cherry, gum,* etc. 1664. **b.** *M. leather*: see **2.** So *M. hides, skins.* 1716. **2.** (In full *morocco-leather.*) Leather made (orig. in Morocco and the Barbary States, and now in Europe) from goatskins tanned with sumac. Also, a leather in imitation of this, made from sheepskins and lambskins, etc., used chiefly in shoemaking. 1634. **b.** *attrib.*, as *m. bindings* 1817.

2. **French m.**, an inferior Levant m., having a smaller and less prominent grain. **Levant m.**, a high-grade m., with a large grain, properly made from the skin of the Angora goat. **Persian m.**, see PERSIAN *a.*

†**Morology** (morǫ·lŏdʒi). 1596. [ad. Gr. μωρολογία, f. μωρός foolish: see -LOGY.] Foolish talking -1656.

Moron (mōᵊ·ɹǫn). 1913. [a. Gr. μωρόν, neut. of μωρός foolish.] A person whose intellectual development is arrested.

Morone, incorrect var. MAROON *sb.*[1], *a.*

Morose (mŏrōᵘ·s), *a.*[1] 1565. [ad. L. *morosus* peevish, etc., f. *mor-, mos* manner; see MORAL *a.* and -OSE.] **1.** Sour-tempered, sullen, gloomy, and unsocial. †**2.** Scrupulous, fastidious -1696.

1. He was a man of very m. manners, and a very sowr aspect CLARENDON. *transf.* The m. climate A. LANG. 2. He was a very m. interpreter 1695. Hence **Moro·se-ly** *adv.*, **-ness** 1653.

Morose (mŏrōᵘ·s), *a.*[2] *rare.* 1644. [ad. late L. *morosus*, f. *mora* delay: see -OSE.] **1.** *Casuistry.* Chiefly in the phr. *m. delectation*, the habit of dwelling with enjoyment on evil thoughts. So *m. thoughts.* **2.** *Civil Law.* Chargeable with negligent delay 1875.

Morosity (morǫ·sĭti). Now *rare.* 1534. [ad. F. *morosité*, ad. L. *morositas*, f. *morosus*; see -ITY.] Moroseness.

Morosoph (mōᵘ·rŏsǫf). 1693. [a. F. *morosophe* (Rabelais), ad. Gr. μωρόσοφος, f. μωρός foolish + σοφός wise.] †**a.** In Rabelais: A 'wise fool', jester. **b.** A foolish pedant.

Moroxite (morǫ·ksait). 1814. [a. G. *Moroxit*, f. Gr. μόροξος a kind of pipeclay; see -ITE[1] 2 b.] *Min.* A crystallized form of apatite, found in Norway and Finland.

Morphean (mǭɹfĭ·ăn, mǭ·ɹfĭăn), *a.* 1694. [f. MORPHEUS + -AN.] Of or pertaining to MORPHEUS; sleepy, drowsy.

‖**Morpheus** (mǭ·rfiūs). late ME. [L.; Ovid's name for the god of dreams, the son of Sleep, as if a. Gr. *Μορφεύς, f. μορφή form.] The god of dreams (or, pop., of sleep). Hence (irreg.) **Morphe·tic** *a.* pertaining to sleep. MME. D'ARBLAY.

†**Morphew** (mǭ·ɹfiu). late ME. [ad. med.L. *morphea*, a. It. *morfea*; origin unkn.] A leprous or scurfy eruption -1835. Also *fig.*

Morphia (mǭ·ɹfiă). 1818. [mod.L., f. MORPHEUS; see -IA[1].] *Chem.* = MORPHINE.

Morphic (mǭ·ɹfik), *a.* 1868. [f. Gr. μορφή; see -IC.] *Biol.* Of or pertaining to form; morphological.

Morphine (mǭ·ɹfin), *sb.* Also **-in.** 1828. [a. G. *morphin*, f. MORPHEUS; see -INE[5].] *Chem.* The most important alkaloid narcotic principle of opium, largely used in medicine to alleviate pain. **b.** *attrib.*, as *m. habit*, etc.

Hence **Mo·rphine** *v. trans.*, to drug with m. **Mo·rphinism,** the effect of m. on the human system; the practice of injecting m. into the system. **Mo·rphinist,** one who takes m. to excess.

Morphinomania (mǭ:ɹfinomē·niă). 1887. [f. prec.: see -MANIA.] *Nosology.* Uncontrollable craving for morphine or opium. Hence **Morphinoma·niac,** one affected with m. Also **Morphioma·nia** 1882, **-ma·niac.**

‖**Morphoge·nesis.** 1890. [mod.L., f. Gr. μορφή form + γένεσις origin.] *Biol.* The origination of morphological characters. So **Morphogene·tic** *a.* 1880, **Morpho·geny** 1879.

Morphography (mǭɹfǫ·grăfi). 1856. [f. Gr. μορφή + -GRAPHY.] The scientific description of form; descriptive morphology; also, the phenomena which this deals with. Hence **Morpho·grapher. Morphogra·phic, -al** *a.*

Morphology (mǭɹfǫ·lŏdʒi). 1830. [f. Gr. μορφή + -LOGY.] The science of form. **1.** *Biol.* That branch of biology which deals with the form of animals and plants, and the structures, homologies, and metamorphoses which govern or influence that form. **2.** *Philol.* That branch of grammar which is concerned with inflexion and word-formation 1869. **3.** *gen.* 1885. Hence **Morpholo·gic, -al** *a.* of, pertaining to, or derived from m.; of or pertaining to the history of form 1830. **Morpholo·gically** *adv.* **Morpho·logist** 1845.

Morphon (mǭ·ɹfǫn). Also **-one.** *Pl.* (badly formed) **-ontes.** 1873. [a. G. *morphon* (pl. *-onten*), explained by Haeckel as f. Gr. μορφή form + ὄν being.] *Biol.* A morphological individual, element, or factor.

Morphosis (mǭɹfōᵘ·sis). *Pl.* **-ses** (-sīz). 1675. [mod.L., a Gr. μόρφωσις a shaping, f. μορφοῦν to shape, f. μορφή.] †**1.** Form, figure, configuration -1676. **2.** *Bot.* The manner or order of development of an organ or organism 1857. So **Morpho·tic** *a.* formative; contributory to organic structure 1876.

Morra, var. of MORA[2].

Morrice, obs. f. MORRIS.

Morricer (mǫ·risəɹ). [f. *morrice* MORRIS *sb.*[1] + -ER.[1]] A morris-dancer. SCOTT.

Morris (mǫ·ris), *sb.*[1] 1500. [Subst. use of *morys*, obs. var. of MOORISH *a.*[2]] **1.** = MORRIS-DANCE 1512. **2.** A body of morris-dancers 1500. **3.** *transf.* and *fig.* 1547. **4.** *attrib.*, as *m. feast*, etc. **m. bell,** one of the small metal bells attached to the clothing of morris-dancers. 1560.

1. Footing the M. about a May pole 1589. 3. Gulls in an aëry morrice Gleam and vanish and gleam HENLEY.

Morris (mǫ·ris), *sb.*[2] *Obs.* exc. *Hist.* 1590. [Corruption of *merels*; see MEREL.] The game of 'merels'. Chiefly *nine men's (peg) m.*

Morris (mǫ·ris), *sb.*[3] 1769. [f. William *Morris* of Holyhead.] An elongated flat eel-like fish formerly named *Leptocephalus morrisii*, but now taken to be the immature young of the conger-eel. Also *Anglesea m.*

Morris, morrice (mǫ·ris), *v.* 1725. [f. MORRIS *sb.*[1]] **1.** *intr.* To dance. †**2.** *slang.* To decamp. Also with *off.* -1838.

2. I think the Welshman must *morris* COWPER.

Mo·rris-dance. 1458. [f. MORRIS *sb.*[1] + DANCE *sb.*] A grotesque dance performed by persons in fancy costume, usu. representing characters from the Robin Hood legend. Hence, any similar mumming performance. Also, a representation of this dance. Hence **Mo·rris-dancer** 1507.

Morris-pike (mǫ·risˌpaik). *Obs.* exc. *Hist.* 1487. [f. *morys*, obs. var. of MOORISH *a.*[2]] A form of pike supposed to be of Moorish origin.

Morris tube. 1884. [f. Richard *Morris*, the inventor.] A small-bore rifle barrel capable of being inserted in a large-bore rifle for shooting practice.

Morrow (mǫ·rou), *sb.* Now only *literary* and *dial.* [ME. *morwe, moru*, shortened var. of *morwen* MORN.] **1.** = MORN 1, MORNING 1; occas. = GOOD MORROW 1. *Obs.* exc. *dial.* **2.** The day next after the present, or any specified day ME. **3.** *transf.* and *fig.*, esp.: The time immediately following a particular event 1586. **4.** *attrib.* (now only *poet.*), as *m. day*, (*a*) the next day; (*b*) daybreak ME.

1. Wel loved he by the morwe a sop in wyn CHAUCER. 2. Care not then for the morow, for the morow shall care for it self COVERDALE *Matt.* vi. 34. *The m.*, freq. used advb. = on the following day. 3. Let them sleepe on, Till this stormy night be gone, And th' eternall m. dawne CRASHAW. Hence **Mo·rrow** *v. intr.* to dawn.

†**Mo·rrow-mass.** 1440. The first mass of the day -1635.

†**Mo·rrow-tide.** ME. = MORNING-TIDE -1520.

Morse (mǭɹs), *sb.*[1] late ME. [a. OF. *mors*:—L. *morsus* bite, catch of a buckle.] The clasp or fastening of a cope.

Morse (mǭɹs), *sb.*[2] 1475. [a. Lapp. *morsa, morssa.*] The sea-horse or walrus, *Trichechus rosmarus.*

Morse (mǭɹs), *sb.*[3] The name of the American electrician S. F. B. *Morse* (1791-1872), the inventor (1837) of the recording telegraph, and of the alphabet (in which the letters are expressed by dots and dashes) used for sending messages by this instrument: used *attrib.*, as in *M. Code*, etc. 1860; also *ellipt.* as *sb.* = 'M. telegraph'.

Morsel (mǭ·ɹsĕl), *sb.* ME. [a. OF. *morsel* (mod.F. *morceau*), dim. of OF. *mors*:—L. *morsum* bite, f. pa. ppl. stem of *mordere* to bite.] **1.** A bite; a mouthful; now, a small piece of food (cf. 2). **b.** A small meal; a snack 1470. **c.** *transf.* and *fig.* late ME. **2.** A small piece (of anything); a fragment ME.

1. She eat of the Fruit, and made her Husband likewise to eat of it, whence it ensued that they were both of them by that unhappy M. subjected to the pains of Death 1663. c. That revenge was no unpleasing m. to him MILT. 2. A m. of territory MOTLEY. Hence **Mo·rsel** *v.* to divide into morsels 1598; (with *out*) to distribute in small quantities 1855.

Mo·rsing, *vbl. sb. Sc. Obs.* exc. *Hist.* 1552. [f. (ult.) F. *amorcer* to prime (a gun).] The action of priming (a gun). Also *attrib.*, as *m.-horn, -powder*; *m.-hole*, touch-hole.

†**Mo·rsure.** late ME. [a. F., ad. L. *morsura*, f. *mors-, mordere* to bite.] The action of biting; a bite -1819.

Mort (mǭɹt), *sb.*[1] ME. [Partly a. F. *mort*:—L. *mortem*; partly a. F. *mort* (fem. *morte*), adj.:—pop. L. **mortum* for L. *mortuum* dead.] †**1.** Death, slaughter -1590. **2.** *Hunting.* The note sounded on a horn at the death of the deer 1500. **b.** The death, the kill (*arch.*). KINGSLEY. **3.** The skin of a sheep or lamb that has died a natural death. Also *m. skin* (*dial.*) 1495.

2. And then to sigh, as 'twere The M. o' th' Deere SHAKS. *Comb.*: **m.-cloth** *Sc.*, a funeral pall; also, fees paid for the use of it; **m. safe** *Sc.*, an iron frame placed over a coffin or at the entrance to a grave as a protection against resurrectionists; †**m. stone,** a stone on which the bearers of a dead body rested the coffin.

Mort, *sb.*[2] *local.* 1530. [?] The salmon in its third year.

Mort (mǭɹt), *sb.*[3] *Cant.* Also **mot.** 1561. [?] **a.** A girl or woman, as KINCHIN-, *walking m.*, etc. **b.** A harlot, loose woman 1567.

Mort (mǭɹt), *sb.*[4] 1694. [? dial. corruption of *mortal* used as an intensive (e.g. with *deal*).] A great quantity or number; a great deal. Usu. const. *of*; rarely *absol.* Also *pl.*

Here's a m. o' merrymaking, hey? SHERIDAN.

†**Mort,** *a.* late ME. [a. F.] Dead -1658.

Mortal (mǭ·ɹtăl), *sb.* 1526 (Tindale). [f. MORTAL *a.*] **1.** Mortal thing or substance. 1 *Cor.* xv. 53. **2.** One who is mortal 1567. **b.** Used playfully for 'person'. In neg. contexts emphatic for '(any) one', '(no) one'. 1718.

2. Lord, what fooles these mortals be! SHAKS. b. She dared not trust such a treasure to m. READE.

Mortal (mǭ·ɹtăl), *a.* late ME. [a. OF. *mortel*, or ad. L. *mortalis*, f. *mort-*, *mors*.] **1.** Subject to death, destined to die. **2.** Causing death, deadly, fatal. Const. *to*. Now only of diseases, wounds, and blows. late ME. †**b.** Of a season or region: Characterized by many deaths –1803. **3. a.** Of war, a battle, etc.: Fought to the death. late ME. **b.** Of an enemy: Implacable. late ME. **c.** Of enmity, hatred, etc.: Pursued to the death, unappeasable; deadly. late ME. **4.** Of pain, grief, fear, etc.: Deadly in its effects. Often used hyperbolically. late ME. **5.** Of sin: = DEADLY *a.* 5. Opp. to *venial*. late ME. **6.** Pertaining to or accompanying death 1542. **7.** *transf.* (from sense 1.) Of or pertaining to man as a creature destined to die; relating to humanity. late ME. **8.** In colloq. or slang uses. **a.** Extremely great 1716. **b.** As an emphatic expletive (with *any*, *every*, or a neg.) 1609. **c.** *slang*. Long and tedious 1820. **9.** *adv.* = MORTALLY. Extremely, excessively (*dial.* and *vulgar*) late ME.

1. For what wears out the life of m. men? M. ARNOLD. 2. A m. wound SCOTT. *fig.* A m. defect in their constitution PALEY. 3. **a.** The shocking Squadrons meet in m. Fight DRYDEN. **b.** *fig.* The mortallest enemy unto knowledge SIR T. BROWNE. **c.** *fig.* A Tribe of Egotists for whom I have always had a m. Aversion ADDISON. 4. The marriage gave m. offence to his father M. ARNOLD. 5. Mans m. crime MILT. 6. This Fellow has a good m. Look—place him near the Corps STEELE. 7. When we haue shuffel'd off this mortall coile SHAKS. 8. **a.** I was a m. sight younger then DICKENS. **b.** We may eat any m. thing we like 1892. **c.** For three m. hours SCOTT. 9. Missis was m. angry THACKERAY. †**Mo·rtalness** 1530.

Mortality (mǫɹtæ·lĭti). ME. [ad. F. *mortalité*, ad. L. *mortalitatem*, f. *mortalis*; see MORTAL *a.* and -ITY.] **1.** The condition of being mortal or subject to death; mortal nature or existence. **b.** Mortals collectively. Now *rare* or *Obs.* 1601. **2.** Loss of life on a large scale, as by war or pestilence; †*spec.* a visitation of deadly plague. late ME. **b.** The number of deaths in a given area or period, from a particular disease, etc.; death-rate 1645. †**c.** Death (of individuals) –1772. **d.** Mortal remains 1827. **3.** Of a sin: The quality of being mortal 1532. **4.** *attrib.*, as *m. bill*, *returns*, *table* 1665.

1. Never did man put off m. with a braver courage 1644. 2. Years of dearth..are generally among the common people years of sickness and m. ADAM SMITH. **b.** *Bill of mortality*: see BILL *sb.*[3] **c.** 1 *Hen. VI*, IV. v. 32.

Mortalize (mǭ·ɹtăləiz), *v.* 1633. [f. MORTAL + -IZE.] *trans.* To make mortal.

Mortally (mǭ·ɹtăli), *adv.* late ME. [f. MORTAL *a.* + -LY.[2]] **1.** So as to cause death; †(to fight) to the death. **2.** In reference to hatred, jealousy, fear, etc.: Bitterly, intensely. late ME. **3.** In the way of mortal sin (see MORTAL *a.* 5) 1526. **4.** *colloq.* Extremely, exceedingly. (Cf. MORTAL *a.* 8, 9.) 1759.

Mortancestry (mǫɹtæ·nsĕstri). 1471. *Scots Law.* Corrupt Sc. form of MORT D'ANCESTOR.

Mortar (mǭ·ɹtəɹ), *sb.*[1] [partly repr. OE. *mortere* masc., a. L. *mortarium*, of unkn. etym.; later, a. F. *mortier*. Senses 2, 3, 4 were taken from Fr.] **1.** A vessel of a hard material (e.g. marble), having a cup-shaped cavity, in which ingredients are pounded with a pestle. Also *transf.* **2.** A bowl of wax or oil with a floating wick, and later a kind of thick candle, used esp. as a night-light. *Obs.* exc. *Hist.* ME. **3.** orig. †*m.-piece*: A short piece of ordnance with a large bore and with trunnions on its breech for throwing shells at high angles 1558. **b.** *transf.* A contrivance for firing pyrotechnic shells or bombs and for throwing a life-line 1669. †**4.** = MORTIER 1604–86.

2. For, by this morter which that I see brenne, Knowe I ful wel that day is not far henne CHAUCER. 3. **b.** The rocket and m. apparatus..has frequently done good service where a lifeboat would have been useless 1873.

Comb.: **m.-bed,** (*a*) see BED *sb.* II. 5 a; (*b*) the bed on which the ore is crushed in a stamp-mill; †**-piece** (see 3); **m. vessel,** a class of gun-boat for mounting sea-service mortars.

Mortar (mǭ·ɹtəɹ), *sb.*[2] [ME. *morter*, *mortier*, a. F. *mortier*:—L. *mortarium* product of trituration.] A mixture of cement (or lime), sand, and water, used to make the joints between stones and bricks in building; also for plastering, etc.

Phr. *Bricks and m.*, (*a*) the essential materials used in building; (*b*) used colloq. for 'houses' or 'house property'. *fig.* A trowel or two of biographic m. CARLYLE.

Comb.: **m.-bed,** the layer of m. between courses of brickwork or masonry; **-liquid** = GROUT *sb.*[2]. Hence **Mo·rtary** *a.*

Mortar (mǭ·ɹtəɹ), *v.* late ME. [f. prec.] *trans.* To plaster with mortar; to fix or join with or as with mortar.

Mo·rtar-board. 1854. [f. MORTAR *sb.*[2] + BOARD *sb.*] **1.** A board for holding mortar 1876. **2.** A pop. name for the academic or college cap with its projecting square top 1854.

Mort d'ancestor (mǫɹdæ·nsĕstəɹ). ME. [a. AF. *mordancestre*, *mort d'auncestre* 'ancestor's death'.] *Old Law.* The term applied to an assize brought by the right heir against one who wrongfully took possession of his inheritance on the death of his ancestor.

Mortgage (mǭ·ɹgĕdʒ), *sb.* late ME. [a. OF. *mortgage*, lit. 'dead pledge' (see MORT *a.* and GAGE *sb.*[1]); whence med.L. *mortuum vadium* and *mor(t)gagium*.] *Law.* The conveyance of real or personal property by a debtor (called the *mortgagor*) to a creditor (called the *mortgagee*) as security for a money debt, with the proviso that the property shall be reconveyed upon payment to the mortgagee of the sum secured within a certain period. Also applied to the deed effecting this, the rights conferred on the mortgagee, and the condition of being mortgaged.

'The general object of mortgage is to secure a money debt by making it a charge on land, so that, if the debt be not paid by a time agreed upon between the parties, the creditor may sell the land and pay himself out of the proceeds' (*Encycl. Brit.* s.v.). For the etymological meaning formerly current see COKE *On Litt.* 205.

fig. They will purchase the hollow happiness of the next five minutes, by a m. on the independance and comfort of years HAZLITT. Phrases. †*In m.*: mortgaged. *To lend on m.*: to advance (money) on the security of property, esp. land or houses.

b. *attrib.*, as *m. debt*, *deed*, *money*, *term*, etc.

Mortgage (mǭ·ɹgĕdʒ), *v.* 1467. [a. OF. *mor(t)gager*, or from prec. sb.] *trans.* To make over (property, esp. land or houses) as security for a money debt, on condition that if the debt be discharged the grant shall be void. **b.** *fig.* To pledge; to make liable; *esp.* to establish a claim in advance upon (an income or the like); hence *pass.* to be attached or pledged (*to* something) in advance 1588.

b. Mortgaging their lives to Covetise SPENSER. And I my selfe am morgag'd to thy will SHAKS. Hence **Mo·rtgageable** *a.* **Mortgagee** (mǭɹgĕdʒī·) 1584, **Mo·rtgager, Mortgago·r** (mǭɹgĕdʒǭ·ɹ) 1559. (See MORTGAGE *sb.*)

Mortice, variant of MORTISE.

‖**Mortier** (mortye). 1727. [Fr.: see MORTAR *sb.*[1]] A cap formerly worn by high officials in France.

Mortiferous (mǫɹti·fĕrəs), *a.* Now *rare.* 1535. [f. L. *mortifer*, *-ferus*; see MORT *sb.*[1] and -FEROUS.] Bringing or producing death; deadly. **b.** *transf.* Bringing spiritual death 1542. Hence **Morti·ferous·ly** *adv.*, **-ness.**

Mortific (mǫɹti·fik), *a. rare.* 1651. [ad. eccl. L. *mortificus*; see MORT *sb.*[1] and -FIC.] Death-producing; deadly.

Mortification (mǫɹtifikē·ʃən). late ME. [a. F., or ad. eccl. L. *mortificationem*.] **1.** In religious use: The action of mortifying the flesh or its lusts by the practice of austere living, esp. by the self-infliction of bodily pain or discomfort. **2.** *Path.* The death of a part of the body while the rest is living; gangrene, necrosis 1555. †**3.** Destruction of vital or active qualities; devitalization –1770. †**4.** *Old Chem.* Alteration of the form of metals, etc.; destruction or neutralization of the active qualities of chemical substances –1678. **5.** *Sc. Law.* The act of disposing of property for religious, or, since the Reformation, for charitable or public purposes. Also, property so given. (Cf. MORTMAIN.) 1471. **6.** The feeling of humiliation caused by a disappointment, a slight, or an untoward accident. Also, an instance of this; a cause or source of such humiliation. 1692.

1. He destroyed his health by his austerity and mortifications 1848. Phr. *M. of the body*, *of sin*, etc. 5. Thomas Moodie's m. for building a kirk in Edinburgh 1685. 6. He continued to offer his advice daily, and had the m. to find it daily rejected MACAULAY.

Mortify (mǭ·ɹtifəi), *v.* late ME. [a. F. *mortifier*, ad. L. *mortificare*, f. *morti-*, *mors* MORT *sb.*[1]; see -FY.] †**1.** *trans.* To deprive of life; to kill. Also, to make as if dead; to render insensible. –1692. †**b.** *intr.* for *pass.* To lose vitality –1707. †**2.** *trans.* To kill (in transf. and fig. senses); to destroy the vitality, vigour, or activity of; to neutralize; to deaden; to dull, etc. –1711. †**3.** *Old Chem.* To alter or destroy the outward form of; to hinder the operation of (spirits) by mixing with other things –1704. **4.** To bring into subjection (the body, etc.) by self-denial, abstinence, or bodily discipline. late ME. †**b.** To render dead to the world and the flesh –1581. †**c.** *absol.* or *intr.* To practise mortification; to be an ascetic –1842. **5.** *trans. Sc. Law.* To dispose of (property) by mortification 1498. †**6.** *Cookery.* To make (raw meat, game, etc.) tender by hanging, keeping, etc. Also *intr.* for *pass.* –1790. **7.** *pass.* and *intr. Path.* To become mortified or gangrenous. Also (rarely) *trans.*, to render mortified. late ME. **8.** *trans.* To cause to feel humiliated; to cause (a person) mortification (freq. in *pass.*) 1691.

1. The Lord mortifieth, and quykeneth WYCLIF 1 *Sam.* ii. 6. 2. The knowledge of future evils mortifies present felicities SIR T. BROWNE. 3. This quik-silver wol I mortifye CHAUCER. 4. Mortifie therfore youre members which are on the erth TINDALE *Col.* iii. 5. **c.** Imagine him mortifying with his barrel of oysters in dreary solitude JANE AUSTEN. 7. The wound..began to mortifie and grow blacke 1603. 8. I could easily forgive his pride, if he had not mortified mine JANE AUSTEN. Hence **Mo·rtified** *ppl. a.* **Mo·rtified·ly** *adv.*, **-ness. Mo·rtifier. Mo·rtifyingly** *adv.*

Mortise, mortice (mǭ·ɹtis), *sb.* late ME. [a. F. *mortaise*, of unkn. origin.] **1.** A cavity or hole into which the end of some other part of a framework or structure is fitted so as to form a joint; also, a groove or slot for the reception of a rope, an adjustable pin, etc. **2.** *spec.* in *Carpentry*, etc. The counterpart of a TENON; a cavity, usu. rectangular in shape, cut in the surface of a piece of timber, etc., to receive the shaped end or tenon of another piece 1440. **3.** *nonce-use* [from the vb.] State of being mortised. TENNYSON.

2. *M. and tenon*, *tenon and m.*, as the component parts of a particular kind of joint; hence, a joint composed of a m. and tenon. Also *collect.* as a method of joining material.

attrib. and *Comb.*: **m. clamp,** a clamp mortised at the ends; **m. gauge,** a carpenter's tool for scribing parallel lines for mortises; **m.-hole** = sense 1; *fig.* an obscure place; **-joint,** a m. and tenon joint; **m. lock,** one made for insertion in a m. cut in the edge of the lock-rail of a door; **m. wheel,** a cast-iron wheel having cogs of wood set into mortises.

Mortise, mortice (mǭ·ɹtis), *v.* 1440. [f. prec. sb.] **1.** *trans.* To fasten or join securely; *spec.* in *Carpentry*, etc., to join with a mortise; to fasten *into* or *to* by means of mortise and tenon; to secure (a tenon) with a mortise. Also *intr.* for *pass.* **2.** To cut a mortise in; also with *through* 1703.

1. Maiestie..is a massie wheele..To whose huge Spoakes, ten thousand lesser things Are mortiz'd and adioyn'd SHAKS.

Mortlake (mǭ·ɹtlēˈk). *Obs.* exc. *Hist.* 1682. Name of the Surrey town used *attrib.* in *M. hangings*, *tapestry*, a kind of tapestry woven there in the reigns of James I and Charles I.

Mortling, var. of MORLING.

Mortmain (mǭ·ɹtmēˈn). 1450. [a. AF. *morte mayn*, OF. *mortemain*, ad. med.L. *mortua manus*, *manus mortua* 'dead hand' (in Eng. legal use, prob. a metaphorical expression for impersonal ownership).] *Law.* The condition of lands or tenements held inalienably by an ecclesiastical or other corporation. **b.** A licence of mortmain 1567. **c.** *transf.* and *fig.*

The M. Act: the statute 9 Geo. II, cap. 36, passed in 1736, imposing restrictions on the devising of property to charitable uses; also, the title of various later statutes. *Licence of M.*: an instrument conveying the permission of the king to alienate property in m. **b.** A Mortmaine to found a Colledge 1655.

†**Mo·rtress.** late ME. [a. OF. *mortreux*, pl. of *morterel*, kind of milk soup.] A kind of soup

or pottage, made either of bread and milk or of various kinds of meat -1626.

Mortuary (mǭ·ɹtiuˌări). late ME. [ad. L. *mortuarius* adj. (med.L. *mortuarium* neut., used as sb.), f. *mortuus*; see -ARY¹.] **A.** *sb.* **1.** A customary gift formerly claimed by the incumbent of a parish from the estate of a deceased parishioner. late ME. †**b.** A fine payable to certain ecclesiastical dignitaries on the death of a priest within their respective jurisdictions -1778. †**2.** A funeral; obsequies -1613. **3.** A dead-house. Also, a place specially prepared for the temporary reception of a corpse. 1865.

1. *attrib.* Tithe-Pig, and m. Guinea POPE.

B. *adj.* **1.** Of or belonging to the burial of the dead 1514. **2.** Of, concerned with, or depending upon death; reminiscent of death 1540.

1. He carried me with him as often as he could to these m. ceremonies SCOTT. 2. A m. ring 1855.

‖**Morula** (mǭ·rŭlă). 1874. [mod.L., dim. of L. *morum* mulberry.] *Embryol.* Haeckel's term for that stage of development of an ovum in which it has become completely segmented.

Morw(e, Morwening(e, obs. ff. MORROW, MORNING.

Mosaic (mǒzē·ik), *sb.* and *a.*¹ late ME. [a. F. *mosaïque* adj., used subst. in masc., ad. med.L. *mosaicus, musaicus,* as if a. Gr. *μουσαϊκός, f. *μουσαῖος, by-form of μούσειος, f. μοῦσα MUSE *sb.*¹] **A.** *sb.* **1.** The process of producing pictures or patterns by cementing together small pieces of stone, glass, etc. of various colours; pictures or patterns thus produced; the constructive or decorative material of these. late ME. **b.** Applied to work analogous to mosaic or resembling it, as *wood, wool m.*, etc. 1727. **2.** A piece of mosaic work 1678. **3.** *transf.* and *fig.* in certain scientific uses 1877.

1. *transf.* MILT. *P. L.* IV. 700. 2. *fig.* He [Pitt in 1766] made an administration, so checkered..; a cabinet so variously inlaid; such a piece of diversified M.;..that it was indeed a very curious show BURKE.

B. *adj.* **1.** Pertaining to that form of art described in A. 1; produced by this method 1585. **2. M. vision:** the manner of vision of the compound eye of an arthropod 1880; so *m. theory.* **3.** *Biol.* Pertaining to or exhibiting alternative characters of both parents.

1. *fig.* Let the m. brain of old Burton give forth the workings of this strange union CARLYLE. *M. wool-work*: a kind of work used in rugs, carpets, etc., in which coloured threads are arranged side by side so that the cross-section shows a pattern resembling that of mosaic. So *m. carpet*, etc.

Hence **Mosa·icist,** a worker, or dealer, in m. 1847. **Mosa·icked** *a.*, also **mosaiced,** ornamented with, or composed of, m. work 1849.

Mosaic (mǒzē·ik), *a.*² 1662. [ad. mod.L. *Mosaicus,* f. L. *Moses.*] Of, pertaining, or relating to Moses the lawgiver of the Hebrews, or the writings, etc. attributed to him.

M. law, the ancient law of the Hebrews, contained in the Pentateuch.

Mosa·ic, *v. rare.* 1839. [f. MOSAIC *sb.*] **1.** *trans.* To adorn with mosaics. **2.** To combine as if into a mosaic; also, to produce by so doing 1841.

†**Mosa·ical,** *a.*¹ 1586. [f. as MOSAIC *a.*¹; see -ICAL.] = MOSAIC *a.*¹ -1687. Hence **Mosa·ically** *adv. rare.* 1614.

Mosaical (mǒzē·ikăl), *a.*² 1563. [f. as MOSAIC *a.*²: see -ICAL.] **1.** Pertaining to or resembling what is Mosaic. †Formerly also often = MOSAIC *a.*² †**2.** *M. rod*: a divining rod -1778.

Mosaic gold. 1746. [f. MOSAIC *a.*¹ and *sb.*] **1.** [tr. late L. *aurum musivum.*] A disulphide of tin. **2.** = ORMOLU 1839.

Mosaic work. Now *rare.* 1606. **1.** = MOSAIC *sb.* 1. **2.** = MOSAIC *sb.* 2. 1687.

Mosaism (mōᵘ·zeˌiz'm). 1845. [ad. mod.L. *Mosaismus,* f. *Moses*; see -ISM.] The religious system, laws, and ceremonies prescribed by Moses; adherence to these.

‖**Mosasaurus** (mōᵘsăsǭ·rɒs). Also **Moso-, Mosæ-.** *Pl.* -i. 1830. [mod.L., f. L. *Mosa* the river Meuse + Gr. σαῦρος lizard.] *Palæont.* A genus of large extinct marine reptiles, combining the characters of a saurian reptile with those of a snake. First discovered near Maestricht (on the Meuse) in 1780. Hence **Mo·sasaur,** a reptile of the genus *Mosasaurus.* **Mosasau·rian** *a.* of or pertaining to the m.; belonging to the sub-order *Mosasauria*; *sb.* a reptile of this sub-order. **Mosasau·roid** *a.*

Moschatel (mǫskăte·l). 1732. [a. F. *moscatelle,* ad. It. *moscatella,* f. *moscato* musk.] *Bot.* A small herb (*Adoxa Moschatellina*), having pale-green flowers with a musky smell, found in shady places: freq. *tuberous m.*

Mosel(l, obs. ff. MUZZLE.

Moselle (moze·l). 1687. [Fr. name (= G. *Mosel*) of a river which joins the Rhine at Coblentz.] In full *M. wine*: a dry white wine, produced near the Moselle.

Moses (mōᵘ·zĭz). 1528. [a. L. *Moses,* Gr. Μωσῆς, ad. Heb. *Mōshéh.*] **1.** Applied allusively to some one resembling Moses, esp. as lawgiver or leader. **b.** Used as an oath or expletive 1855. †**2. a.** A kind of boat used in the West Indies. **b.** *M. boat*: a kind of boat used in Massachusetts 1706-1775.

Comb. **Moses' rod,** a divining-rod.

Mosk, var. of MOSQUE; obs. f. MUSK.

Moslem, Muslim (mǫ·zlĕm, mǫ·s-, mɒ·zlim), *sb.* and *a.* 1615. [a. Arab. *muslim,* active pple. of *aslama,* of which the noun of action is *islām*; see ISLAM.] **A.** *sb.* One who professes Islam; a Mohammedan. (Pl. **Moslems,** occas. **Moslemin, Moslem.**) **B.** *adj.* Of or pertaining to the Moslems; Mohammedan 1777. Hence **Mo·slemize** *v.* 1845.

Mosque (mǫsk). late ME. [In 16th c. *mosquee* (later shortened to *mosque*), a. F. *mosquée,* a. It. *moschea,* a. Arab. *masgid,* f. *sagada* to worship.] A Mohammedan temple or place of worship.

The m.: those who worship in mosques; the body of Mohammedans.

Mosquito (mǫskī·to). 1583. [a. Sp. and Pg. *mosquito,* dim. of *mosca* (:—L. *musca*) fly.] **1.** A gnat of several different species of the genus *Culex* (esp. *C. mosquito*) and allied genera, the female of which punctures the skins of animals, and sucks their blood, by means of a long proboscis. **2.** *attrib.*, as *m.-bite* 1805.

1. Howbeit the Muskitto or Gnats pestered us extreamly 1665.

Comb.: **m.-bar** *U.S.*, a kind of m.-net; **-blight,** a plant-bug of the East Indian genus *Helopeltis*; **-fly, -gnat** (= sense 1); **-hawk** *U.S.*, any dragon-fly which preys upon mosquitoes; **-net,** a net (of lace, gauze, etc.) to keep off mosquitoes; so **-netting**; so **m.-canopy, -curtain.**

b. M. craft, small light vessels adapted for rapid manœuvring. So **m. fleet,** a fleet of such vessels; **m.-built** *a.*, said of a light vessel adapted for being rapidly manœuvred.

Moss (mǫs), *sb.* [OE. *mos* neut., bog :—OTeut. **muso*ᵐ, related to OE. *mēos* moss = ON. *mýrr* MIRE *sb.* (f. *meus-*), and L. *muscus* moss.] **I.** A bog, swamp, or morass; a peat-bog. (Chiefly *Sc.* and *n. dial.*) **b.** Wet spongy soil: bog 1596. **II.** The plant. **1.** Any of the small herbaceous cryptogamous plants constituting the class *Musci,* some characteristic of bogs, others growing in crowded masses on the surface of the ground, or on stones, trees, etc. In pop. language often extended to small cryptogams of other orders, esp. lichens and lycopods, etc. ME. **b.** With *a* and *pl.*: A species or kind of moss 1562. **2.** With defining word 1597. **3.** *transf.* An excrescence or incrustation resembling moss; *esp.* the mossy covering of the stalk and calyx of the moss rose 1607. **4.** Short for Moss ROSE 1837.

II. 1. Hence, ancle-deep in m. and flow'ry thyme, We mount again COWPER. Provb. *A rolling stone gathers no m.*: i.e. a man who is constantly changing from place to place or calling to calling will never grow rich. **b.** On high Ben-more green mosses grow SCOTT. **2. American m.,** the dried stems of Florida m., used in upholstery; **black m.** = *Florida moss*; **Canary m.,** *Parmelia perlata,* a lichen used for dyeing; **Florida m.,** *Tillandsia usneoides*; **snake m.,** club-moss, *Lycopodium clavatum*; **white m.,** a name for various lichens. Also BOG-*moss,* CLUB-MOSS, ICELAND *moss,* etc., q. v.

Comb. **1.** In sense I. **a.** In names of plants growing in bogs: as **m.-berry,** the cranberry, *Vaccinium Oxycoccos*; **-corn,** the silverweed, *Potentilla anserina*; **-rush,** goose-corn, *Juncus squarrosus*; **-whin,** *Genista anglica.*

b. Spec. comb.: **m.-earth,** earth composed of, or largely mixed with, peat; **-flow,** a semi-fluid part of a bog or morass; **-oak,** oak-wood preserved in a black state in peat-bogs, etc., bog-oak; also, a seat made of this.

2. In sense II. 1. Spec. comb.: **m.-agate,** a variety of agate containing brown or black moss-like dendritic forms; **-animal, -animalcule,** a bryozoon or polyzoon; **m. campion,** a dwarf, perennial, tufted moss-like plant (*Silene acaulis*) with purple flowers, growing in northern latitudes; **-carder,** also **-carder bee,** *Bombus muscorum,* a variety of humble-bee; **-coral** = *moss-animalcule* (see above); **m. pink,** a species of phlox (*Phlox subulata*), with dark purple flowers, growing on rocky hills and sandy soils in the central U.S.; **-starch** = LICHENIN.

Moss (mǫs), *v.* late ME. [f. MOSS *sb.*] †**1.** *intr.* To become mossy -1654. **2.** To gather moss (chiefly in gerund *mossing*) 1700. **3.** *trans.* **a.** To cover with a growth of moss 1600. †**b.** To roof with moss -1722.

2. Sam. Stocks came a mossing 1700. 3. **a.** An old Oake, whose bows were moss'd with age SHAKS.

Mo·ss-back. *U.S.* 1872. [f. MOSS *sb.* + BACK *sb.*¹; perh. orig. a perversion of next.] **1.** = next. **2.** *slang.* **a.** During the U.S. civil war, one who hid himself to avoid conscription for the Southern army 1872. **b.** One 'behind the times'; an extreme conservative 1885.

Mossbunker (mǫ·sbɒŋkəɹ). Also **moss-banker,** etc. 1792. [a. Du. *marsbanker* (formerly also *masbank*), of unkn. etym.] The menhaden.

Mo·ss-grown, *a.* late ME. [f. MOSS *sb.* + GROWN.] Overgrown with moss. **b.** *fig.* Antiquated.

Mo·ss-hag. *Sc.* 1816. [f. MOSS *sb.* + HAG *sb.*⁴] A pit or hole from which peat has been dug.

Moss rose. 1731. [MOSS *sb.*] A garden variety of the cabbage rose, *Rosa centifolia*; so called from the moss-like growth on its calyx and stalk.

Mo·ss-trooper. 1651. [MOSS *sb.* I.] One of the freebooters who infested the mosses of the Scottish Border, in the middle of the 17th c. **b.** *transf.* A bandit or raider 1701.

Mossy (mǫ·si), *a.* 1558. [Alteration of obs. or dial. *mosy* (= OE., ME. *mos* + *-y*), after MOSS *sb.*] **I.** *Sc.* and *dial.* Marshy, boggy, peaty 1596. **II. 1.** Overgrown or covered with moss, abounding in moss. Also of a fountain, spring, etc.: Encircled with moss; issuing from a moss-grown rock, etc. 1565. **2.** As if covered with moss; downy, velvety 15... **3.** Resembling moss; as down, etc. 1558.

II. 1. And every bird lulled on its m. bough SHELLEY. Where thou sittest by thy m. spring R. BRIDGES. 3. A mossie beard 1585. Hence **Mo·ssiness.**

Most (mōᵘst), *a.* (*sb.*) and *adv.* [Com. Teut.: OE. *mǣst, mást,* ME. *mest, mast, moost,* f. the root of **maiz* MO *adv.* + *-isto-* (see -EST).] **A.** *adj.* **I. 1.** = GREATEST *a.* in various applications. *Obs.* exc. in phr. *for the m. part*: usually; in the main. **2.** With *sb.* in *pl.*: The greatest number of; the majority of OE. **3.** Existing in the greatest quantity, amount, or degree; the greatest amount or quantity of. late ME.

1. The m. noumber shall have the choice and election 1579. The sence of death is m. in apprehension SHAKS. †*M. master*: ruler, commander; also, one who is 'master' in a contest, etc. 2. Party loyalty is strong enough, with m. people BRYCE. 3. Have not I the m. Reason to complain? SWIFT.

II. *absol.* (quasi-*sb.*) **1.** Absol. uses of sense I. 1. The greatest persons (or, rarely, things). Usu. assoc. w. *least.* Now only *poet.* in *m. and least* = 'all without exception'. ME. **2.** The greatest amount or quantity OE. **3.** (Construed as *pl.*) The greatest number. Now usu. without the article. 1470.

1. Enuenoming the hearts of m. and least 1600. 2. This is really the m. that I can concede (*mod.*). Phr. *To make the m. of*: (*a*) To employ to the best advantage; (*b*) To treat with the greatest consideration; (*c*) To exhibit at the best or worst. **At most, at the m.** A qualifying phr., indicating that the attached amount, number, or quantity is the largest admissible; or that a statement expresses not less, but probably more, than the truth. 3. Portraits, m. of them of persons now dead BURKE. A gentleman.. who felt the infirmities of age at an earlier period than m. do 1791.

B. *adv.* **1.** As a superl. of comparison: In the greatest degree; to the greatest extent OE. **2.** As an intensive superlative qualifying adjs. and advs.: In the greatest possible degree 1508. †**3.** Mostly; for the most part -1734. **4.** Almost, nearly. Now *dial.* and *U.S.* 1584.

1. He..thought it m. for his honor & profite 1548. The m. dogged of fighters 1892. My m. extremest time of misery (now only *poet.*) 1881. 2. Oh horrible, Oh horrible, m. horrible SHAKS. *M. Christian, M. Honourable*, etc., see the adjs. 3. He took m. to silence,..yet, when he did speak, it was much to the purpose NORTH. 4. M. everybody's here THACKERAY.
Comb.: †**mostwhat** *adv.*, for the most part, also quasi-*adj.*, the greater part of; †**mostwhen** *adv.*, on m. occasions; †**mostwhere** *adv.*, in most places.

-most (mōᵘst, mǒst, məst), *suffix*, forming adjs. in the superl. degree, is an altered form of OE. *-mest*, a combination of two distinct OTeut. superl. suffixes, *-mo-* and *-isto-* -EST. The OE. superlatives in *-mest* descended from OTeut., except *midmest* MIDMOST, are formed not on adjs. but on prepositional or demonstrative stems; e.g. *æftemest* (see AFTERMOST), *formest* or *fyrmest* FOREMOST, *inmest* INMOST, *ūtmest* or *ȳtmest* UTMOST, etc. On the analogy of these older words, *-mest* was in OE. used to form the superlatives of several adjs. of local and temporal meaning, as *lætmest*, *ēastmest*, etc. In late OE. the adjs. in *-mest* were regarded as compounds of *mǣst* MOST, and were often spelt *-mæst*. In the 15th and 16th c. the suffix *-most* (taken as = MOST *a.*) was added to many comparatives in *-er*, as in *furthermost*, *hindermost*, etc. In subsequent formations, with the single exception of *bettermost*, the application of the suffix has been restricted to words denoting position in place, time, or serial order, as in OE.

Moste, obs. f. MUST *sb.* and *v.*, MOIST *a.*

Mostic(k, obs. vars. of MAULSTICK.

Mostly (mōᵘ·stli), *adv.* 1594. [f. MOST *a.* + -LY.^{2}] 1. For the most part. †2. In the greatest degree; most -1768.

†**Mot** ^{1}. 1586. [a. F. *mot* word, saying = It. *motto* (see MOTTO) :—pop.L. **mottum*, altered f. *muttum* uttered sound, cogn. w. *muttire* to murmur.] A motto -1659.
And Tarqvins eye maie read the m. a farre, 'How he in peace is wounded not in warre' SHAKS.

‖**Mot** ^{2} (mo). 1813. [Fr.; see prec.] A witty saying. **M. juste**, the precise expression for the meaning intended.

Mot: see MORT *sb.*^{3}

Mote (mōᵘt), *sb.*^{1} [OE. *mot* neut. (dat. *mote*), perh. cogn. w. Du. *mot*, LG. *mut* dust, grit.] 1. A particle of dust; *esp.* one of the specks seen floating in the sunbeam; an irritating particle in the eye or throat. †b. A minute particle, an atom; a trifle -1725. †c. = ATOM 2. -1601. †2. A spot, a blemish -1711.
1. As the gay motes that people the Sun Beams MILT. b. Phr. †(*Not*) *a m.*: (not) a jot. 2. *Hen. V*, IV. i. 189.

Mote (mōᵘt), *sb.*^{2} *Obs.* exc. *Hist.* [ME. *mote*, a. OF. *mote*, *motte* clod, hillock, mound, castle, etc. (mod.F. *motte* clod, mound). See MOAT *sb.*, prob. orig. the same word.] 1. A mound, eminence, hill, esp. as the seat of a camp, city, castle, fort, etc.; also, an embankment. 2. A barrow, tumulus 1513.

Mote, moot, *sb.*^{3} *Obs.* exc. *arch.* ME. [a. F. *mot* (see MOT^1), similarly used.] *Hunting.* A note of a horn or bugle.

Mote (mōᵘt), *v. arch.* [A WGer. and Gothic preterite-present verb: OE. *mōt* :—OTeut. **mōtā*; the pa. t. is MUST.] 1. = MAY *v.*^{1} II. 1–4. ¶b. Used as pa. t. (esp. by confusion in the 16th c. with *mought*, pa. t. of MAY *v.*^{1}) = *might, could* -1765. c. In wishes, forming a periphrastic subj.: = MAY *v.*^{1} II. 7 b. ME. 2. = MUST *v.*^{1} II. 1. OE. ¶b. Used erron. as pa. t. 1596.
1. Nor m. my shell awake the weary Nine BYRON. b. SPENSER *F.Q.* IV. ii. 8. c. *Amen.* So m. it be 1775. 2. I merueylle moche of thy wordes that I m. dye in bataille MALORY. b. Sith he mought needs sail by Judaea H. MORE.

Mo·ted, *a.* 1821. [f. MOTE *sb.*^{1} + -ED^2.] Full of motes.

Mo·te-hill. 1682. *Antiq.* = MOTE *sb.*^{2} 1.

Motet (mote·t). late ME. [a. F., dim. of *mot* word (see MOT^1).] *Mus.* †a. A melody. b. A vocal composition in harmony, set usually to words from Scripture, for church use 1597.
The boy and I again to the singing of Mr. Porter's mottets PEPYS.

Moth (mǫþ), *sb.* [OE. *moþþe*, *mohðe* wk. fem.: perh. conn. w. Teut. root **mug-* as in MIDGE.] 1. A small nocturnal lepidopterous insect of the genus *Tinea*, which breeds in cloth, furs, etc., on which its larva feeds; a clothes-moth. In early use applied to the larva. From the 16th c. taken to denote primarily the insect in its winged state, and applied to any nocturnal lepidopterous insect of similar appearance. b. *fig.* Something that eats away, gnaws, or wastes silently and gradually 1577. c. In allusion to the insignificance of the moth, or to its liability to be attracted by the flame of a candle to its own destruction 1596. †d. Applied vaguely to various kinds of 'vermin', as lice, bugs, cockroaches -1748. e. (Also with cap.) Trade name of a type of light aeroplane 1926. 2. *Entom.* Any insect of that one of the two great divisions of the *Lepidoptera* which includes the 'moths' in the older sense 1753.
1. The Moath breedeth upon Cloth;..It delighteth to be about the Flame of a Candle BACON. b. The Corruptions and Mothes of Historie, which are Epitomes BACON. 2. CODLING-*m.*, HAWK-M., etc. q.v.
attrib. and *Comb.*: **m.-blight**, various species of homopterous insects of the genus *Aleurodes*, which are destructive to plants; **-gnat**, a dipterous insect of the family *Psychodidæ*; **-hunter**, (*a*) one who hunts for moths; (*b*) the Nightjar; **-worm**, the larva of a m. Hence **Moth** *v. intr.* to hunt for moths (chiefly in gerund *mothing*).

Mo·th-eaten, *pa. pple.* and *a.* late ME. Eaten away or destroyed by moths. Often *fig.*

Mother (mʊ·ðəɹ), *sb.*^{1} [Com. Teut. and Indo-Eur.: OE. *mōdor* :—OTeut. **mōđar-* :—pre-Teut. **mātē·r-*, cogn. with Gr. μήτηρ, L. *mater*.] I. 1. A woman who has given birth to a child; *gen.* a female parent. 2. *fig.* Applied to things regarded as giving birth, or standing in the relation of a mother, e.g. a condition that gives rise to another, the Church, Nature, one's native country, one's university OE. 3. A woman who exercises control like that of a mother, or who is looked up to as a mother, late ME. 4. A term of address for, or a prefix to the surname of, an elderly woman of the lower class. late ME.
1. Cybele, M. of a hundred gods MILT. *transf.* All my m. came into my eyes, And gaue me vp to teares SHAKS. 2. Ydelnes, moder of all vyces 1463. Earth all-bearing M. MILT. The Good of M. Church 1726. Scotland, my auld, respected Mither! BURNS. Nature, a m. kind alike to all GOLDSM. Aqueous vapour is the great m. of clouds 1868. 3. The glorius Virgine, the Mothir 1563. They call me Lady Abbess, or M. at the least, who address me SCOTT. 4. *M. Carey's Chicken, Goose*: see CHICKEN, GOOSE. *M. Hubbard*: a kind of cloak (named after the person in the nursery rime). *M. Shipton*: a legendary 'prophetess' of the 16th c.; also, a moth, *Euclidea mi* (the *Shipton moth*).
II. Techn. uses. †1. After L. *mater*. *Anat. Hard m.* = DURA MATER; *godly, meek, mild, soft m.* = PIA MATER -1615. 2. = *mother-liquor, -water* 1611. 3. (More fully, *artificial m.*) An apparatus for rearing chickens artificially 1807. III. †1. The womb -1706. 2. Hysteria. Also *fits of the m.* *Obs.* or *arch.* late ME. IV. Quasi-adj. 1. Used *appos.* = 'that is a mother' ME. 2. a. Simple attrib. (more or less *rhet.*): as *m. arms*, etc. late ME. b. with the sense 'inherited or learned from one's mother', 'native', as in MOTHER TONGUE, and the like 1603.
IV. 1. The M. Cow DRYDEN. The Mother-goddess Cybele 1904. O dear Britain! O my M. Isle! COLERIDGE. A 'primary' or 'mother-vesicle' 1885.
Comb.: **m.-city** = METROPOLIS in various senses; †**m. fit** = 'fit of the mother' (sense III. 2); **m. idea** [= F. *idée mère*], the fundamental idea (e.g. of a literary work, etc.); **m. liquid, liquor** = the liquid left after crystallization, e.g. of sea-salt; **-lye**, the mother liquor of an alkali; **m. maid, maiden**, the Virgin Mary; **m.'s mark**, a nævus; **mothers' meeting**, a (periodical) meeting of mothers connected with a parish or congregation, for instruction and counsel; **m. queen** = QUEEN-MOTHER; also applied to a queen-bee; **m. right**, (*a*) = MATRIARCHY; (*b*) the custom by which dynastic succession passes only through the female line; **m. ship**, a ship having charge of one or more torpedo boats; **m. stone**, the matrix of a mineral; also, a stone from which other minerals are derived by structural or chemical change; **-water** = *mother liquor*.

Mother (mʊ·ðəɹ), *sb.*^{2} 1538. [Prob. an application of MOTHER *sb.*^{1}; cf. It., Sp. *madre* scum, F. *mère* (*de vinaigre*).] †1. Dregs, scum -1870. 2. *spec.* (In full *m. of vinegar.*) A ropy mucilaginous substance produced in vinegar during acetous fermentation by a mould-fungus called *Mycoderma aceti* 1601. †3. *M. of grapes*: = MARC -1725.

Mother (mʊ·ðəɹ), *v.*^{1} 1542. [f. MOTHER *sb.*^{1}] 1. *trans.* To be the mother of, give birth to (*lit.* and *fig.*) 1548. 2. To take care of as a mother 1863. 3. To acknowledge the maternity of (a child) 1622. 4. Const. *on*, *upon*. To attribute the maternity of (a child) to (a woman) 1542. 5. To find a mother for (a lamb or calf). Also const. *upon*. 1844.
3. That the Queen, to have put lady Elizabeth besides the Crown, would have mothered another bodies Child; but King Philip scorn'd to father it 1679. 4. *fig.* Many venerable repartees were mothered on her 1907.

Mother (mʊ·ðəɹ), *v.*^{2} 1718. [f. MOTHER *sb.*^{2}] *intr.* To become mothery.

Mother-church. ME. 1. †a. A parish church, as dist. from a chapel of ease -1688. b. The principal or original church of a country, region, or city. late ME. 2. A church (i.e. body of Christians) of which another church is an offshoot; also, the original church from which all others have sprung 1574.
1. b. The mother church of the whole land, the church of Christ at Canterbury FREEMAN. ¶See also MOTHER *sb.*^{1} I. 2 quot. 1726.

Mother country. 1587. 1. A country in relation to its colonies. 2. One's native country 1595.

Mothercraft (mʊ·ðəɹkraft). 1914. [f. MOTHER *sb.*^{1} + CRAFT.] The craft or art of caring for young children as a mother.

Mother earth. 1586. The earth as the mother of its productions and inhabitants; also (in somewhat joc. use), the ground.
He..With bloudy mouth his mother earth did kis SPENSER.

Motherhood (mʊ·ðəɹhud). 1473. [-HOOD.] 1. The condition or fact of being a mother; the status of a mother. b. The feeling or love of a mother 1593. 2. Mothers collectively 1835.

Mothering (mʊ·ðəriŋ), *vbl. sb.* 1648. [f. MOTHER *v.*^{1} and *sb.*^{1} + -ING^1.] 1. Motherly care and supervision 1868. 2. The custom of visiting parents and giving or receiving presents on Mid-lent Sunday, hence called *M. Sunday*.
2. Ile to thee a Simnell bring, 'Gainst thou go'st a m. HERRICK.

Mo·ther-in-law. 1440. [See -IN-LAW.] 1. The mother of one's husband or wife. 2. = STEPMOTHER. Now incorrect. 1482.
1. The everlasting Din of Mothers-in-law 1688.

Motherland (mʊ·ðəɹlænd, -lănd). 1711. [f. MOTHER *sb.*^{1} + LAND *sb.*] a. A country as the producer of anything. b. One's native country.

Motherless (mʊ·ðəɹlės), *a.* OE. [-LESS.] Having no mother.

Mo·therlike, *a.* and *adv.* 1530. [f. MOTHER *sb.*^{1} + -LIKE.] Like a mother.

Motherly (mʊ·ðəɹli), *a.* [OE. *mōdorlic*; see MOTHER *sb.*^{1} and -LY^1.] 1. Of or pertaining to a mother (*rare*). 2. Befitting a mother ME. 3. Resembling a mother 1530.
3. A brisk, wholesome, m. body 1882. Hence **Mo·therliness**. **Mo·therly** *adv.* in a m. manner.

Mo·ther na·ked, *a.* late ME. As naked as at birth.

Mother of pearl. 1510. [Cf. F. †*mère perle*, It. *madreperla*.] = NACRE.

Mother of thyme. 1597. Wild thyme.

Mother's son. ME. A man. Chiefly in phr., *every mother's son*.

Mother tongue. late ME. [In sense 1, *mother* was orig. the uninflected genitive.] 1. One's native language. 2. An original language from which others spring 1645.

Mother wit. 1529. [Earlier *mederis wytte*, 1440.] Native or natural wit; common sense.

Mo·therwort. late ME. [f. MOTHER *sb.*^{1} (sense III. 1) + WORT.] A name for plants formerly supposed to be valuable in diseases of the womb; now chiefly *Leonurus Cardiaca*; formerly also the mugwort, *Artemisia vulgaris*.

Mothery (mʊ·ðəri), *a.* 1709. [f. MOTHER *sb.*^{2} + -Y^1.] Mouldy, feculent.

Moth mullein. 1578. [After mod.L. *blattaria*, f. *blatta* moth.] The plant *Verbascum Blattaria*.

Mothy (mǫ·þi), *a.* 1596. [f. MOTH *sb.* + -Y[1].] Infested by moths.

‖ **Motif** (motī·f). 1848. [Fr.; see MOTIVE.] **1.** In art and literature, a distinctive feature or element of a design or composition; a particular type of subject; also, the dominant idea of a work; *Mus.* a leading figure or short phrase, a subject or theme; see also LEITMOTIV. **2.** *Dress-making.* An ornament of lace, braid, or the like, sewn separately on a dress 1882. ¶**3.** Often used instead of MOTIVE, in order to avoid the suggestion of volition associated with the Eng. word 1874.

Motific (moᵘti·fik), *a.* 1822. [f. L. *motus* + -FIC.] Producing motion.

Motile (mōᵘ·til), *a.* 1864. [ad. L. *motilis, f. *mot-, movere* to move; see -ILE.] *Biol.* Exhibiting, or capable of, motion. So **Moti·lity** 1834.

Motion (mōᵘ·ʃən), *sb.* late ME. [a. F., ad. L. *motionem*, f. *movere* to MOVE.] **1.** The process of moving; the condition of a body (point, line, etc.) when at each successive instant it occupies a different position in space. Also, An instance, kind, or variety of this process or condition. **b.** *Philos.* (now only *Hist.*) *Motion* (Gr. κίνησις) was formerly applied to all kinds of change, the term *local motion* being used to distinguish change of place 1678. **2.** Change of place in an animate body or its parts; an instance of this, a movement 1588. **b.** Capability of moving (as the property of an animate body) 1603. **c.** The action of moving the body in walking, running, etc. Also, gait, carriage. 1598. †**d.** Bodily exertion (tending to fatigue); *pl.* = bodily exercises –1695. **3.** An act of moving the body (or its members); a change of posture; a gesture; †a grimace, antic 1608. **b.** A step, gesture, or other movement acquired by drill and training (e.g. in *Fencing*) 1601. **c.** *Mil.* Each of the several successive actions of a prescribed exercise of arms 1635. **4.** Commotion, agitated condition (e.g. of water); shaking, oscillation (of a ship, a vehicle). †Also, a political commotion; agitation (of the mind or feelings). late ME. **5.** *pl.* Movements on the part of a person or body of persons, when pursuing an affair; *esp.* the movements of an army in the field. Now *rare.* 1674. **6.** The action of moving, prompting, or urging (a person to do something, etc.); a proposal, suggestion; an instigation, prompting, or bidding. *Obs.* in general sense. late ME. **7.** *spec.* **a.** A proposition formally made in a deliberative assembly 1579. **b.** *Law.* An application made to a court or judge by a party to an action or his counsel, to obtain some rule or order of court necessary to the progress of the action 1726. †**8.** An inward prompting or impulse; a desire or inclination (*to* or *towards*). Also, an emotion. –1726. †**b.** *spec.* A working of God in the soul –1772. **9.** The involuntary action of the intestines, leading to discharge of their contents; an evacuation of the bowels. Also, chiefly in *pl.*, that which is evacuated; the fæces. 1598. **10.** *Mus.* †**a.** Movement (quick or slow); tempo –1752. **b.** (*a*) The melodic progression of a voice or voice-part: dist. as *conjunct* and *disjunct.* (*b*) The progression of two or more parts with relation to each other: dist. as *similar, parallel, contrary, oblique*, and *mixed.* 1731. †**11. a.** A puppet-show –1678. **b.** A puppet. Also applied contempt. to a person. –1689. **12.** A piece of mechanism which itself moves, or which sets other pieces moving or modifies their motion; †the MOVEMENT of a watch 1605.

1. *M. of* ROTATION, *of* TRANSLATION; see those words. *Laws of M.*: see LAW *sb.*[1] III. 1. Diogenes confuted him who denyed there was any m., by saying nothing but walking before his eyes FULLER. 2. To retard the m. of the heart and circulating fluids 1799. b. Devoid of sense and m. MILT. d. His violent m. going up Shotover Hill on foot WOOD. 3. Speaking or mute all comliness and grace Attends thee, and each word, each m. formes MILT. Phr. *To make a m.* or *motions*: to beckon, invite by gestures (*to do* something). 4. But in a minute she 'gan stir, With a short uneasy m. COLERIDGE. 5. Phr. *To make a m.*: to begin to move in some particular direction or with some specified purpose; About an Hour after they made a M. to attack us again DE FOE. 7. a. The M. being made, and the Question being put STEELE. 8. Phr. *Of* (†*upon*) *one's own* (or †*proper*) *m.* = of one's own accord. Now *arch.* 9. Shall I loose my Doctor? No, hee giues me the Potions and the Motions SHAKS. 11. a. Then hee compast a M. of the Prodigall sonne SHAKS.

Phrase. **In motion.** **a.** *lit.* In a state of moving or of being moved. Opp. to *at rest.* Phr. *To put* (*set*) *in m.* **b.** *fig.* In a state of activity, excitement, commotion, or the like.

Comb.: **m.-bar**, a guide-bar in a steam-engine; **-block**, the guide which forms a connexion between the piston-rod and connecting-rod; **m. picture** = MOVING *picture.* **-work**, the mechanism for moving the hands of a watch or clock.

Motion (mōᵘ·ʃən), *v.* 1476. [f. MOTION *sb.*] †**1.** *trans.* To propose, move, bring forward –1823. †**b.** To propose or recommend (a person) for employment, or as a partner in marriage –1694. †**c.** To petition or suggest to (a person) –1544. †**2.** *intr.* or *absol.* To make a proposal, bring forward a motion, offer a plan (*rare*) –1839. **3.** *trans.* To direct or guide by a gesture or movement 1787. **4.** *intr.* †**a.** To make a movement as if *to do* something 1747–1803. **b.** To make a movement or gesture in order to direct or guide 1788.

2. MILT. *P. L.* IX. 229. 3. She motioned him..to be silent L. HUNT. 4. a. She..motioned to depart 1803. b. She..motioned to him to stand by her side 1897. Hence †**Mo·tioner**, one who motions, proposes, or instigates; also *transf.* of things –1665.

Motionless (mōᵘ·ʃənlės), *a.* 1599. [f. MOTION *sb.* + -LESS.] Having no movement; incapable of motion. **Mo·tionlessness** 1817.

Motitation (mōᵘtitēⁱ·ʃən). *rare.* 1641. [f. L. *motitare*, frequent. of *mot-, movere*; see -ATION.] A quivering movement.

Motive (mōᵘ·tiv), *sb.* late ME. [a. F. *motif* masc., subst. use of OF. *motif* MOTIVE *a.* Cf. It. *motivo.*] †**1.** Something moved; a motion, proposition; esp. in *to move* (or *make*) *a m.* –1652. **2.** That which moves or induces a person to act in a certain way; a desire, fear, reason, etc., which influences a person's volition: also often applied to a result or object which is desired. late ME. †**b.** A moving or exciting cause –1727. †**3.** A mover, instigator, promoter –1681. †**4.** A moving limb or organ. (Only in Shaks.) **5.** In art and literature: = MOTIF 1. 1851.

2. By M., I mean the whole of that which moves, excites, or invites the Mind to Volition 1754. b. *Oth.* IV. ii. 42. 4. The slauish motiue of recanting feare [i.e. the tongue] SHAKS. 5. A great composition always has a leading emotional purpose, technically called its m., to which all its lines and forms have some relation RUSKIN. *Leading m.*: see LEADING *ppl. a.* Hence **Mo·tiveless** *a.* having no m.

Motive (mōᵘ·tiv), *a.* 1502. [ad. OF. *motif* or med.L. *motivus*, f. *mot-, movere* to MOVE; see -IVE.] **1.** That moves or tends to move a person to a course of action. Now somewhat *rare.* **2.** Having the quality of initiating movement; productive of physical or mechanical motion; *spec.* in Physics, etc. 1578. **b.** Of nerves = MOTOR *a.* 2. 1668. **3.** Concerned with or having the quality of initiating action 1569. †**4.** Of the limbs: Concerned with the faculty of motion or locomotion 1541–1835.

1. Those..whose m. principles are selfish 1858. 2. *M. energy*: see ENERGY 6. *M. power*, moving or impelling power (so also *m. force*); also, the mechanical energy (as steam, electricity, air, etc.) used to drive machinery. 3. Public reputation is a m. power DISRAELI. 4. The m. parts of animals SIR T. BROWNE. Hence **Moti·vity**, the power of initiating motion; in *Dynamics*, kinetic energy.

Motive (mōᵘ·tiv), *v.* 1650. [f. MOTIVE *sb.*] **1.** *trans.* To give or supply a motive to; to be the motive of; also *pass.*, to be prompted by (something) as a motive. **2.** In *pass.*, of incidents in a drama, etc.: To be provided with a motive to render them credible 1858.

2. His malice must be motived in some satisfactory way 1858.

‖**Motivo** (motī·vo). 1789. [It.; see MOTIVE *sb.*] *Mus.* = MOTIF (by which it has now been superseded).

Motley (mǫ·tli), *a.* and *sb.* late ME. [Etym. dub. Perh. related to MOTE *sb.*[1], as if = speckly.] **A.** *adj.* **1.** Diversified in colour; variegated; parti-coloured; chequered. **b.** esp. of a fool's dress. Hence *m. fool.* 1600. **2.** *transf.* and *fig.* Composed of elements of diverse or varied character 1687. †**3.** Varying in character or mood; changeable in form –1755.

1. M. dresses of black and white 1851. b. I met a foole i' th Forrest, A m. Foole SHAKS. 2. M. images POPE. A motly crew 1748.

B. *sb.* †**1.** A cloth of a mixed colour; a mixture –1617. **2. a.** A variegated, chequered, or mixed colour; also *transf.* and *fig.* an incongruous mixture 1440. **3.** A parti-coloured dress worn by the professional fool or jester, freq. in phr. *to wear m.*; hence, allusively, foolery, nonsense. *A piece of m.*, a fool. *Obs.* exc. *Hist.* 1600. **b.** A fool, jester 1600.

1. *transf.* The fresshe hawethorn In whyte motle, that so swote doth smelle LYDG. 3. A worthy foole: Motley's the onely weare SHAKS. b. I haue..made my selfe a m. to the view SHAKS. Hence **Mo·tley** *v. trans.* to make m. or parti-coloured in hue; to diversify in character; to mix incongruously. **Mo·tleyness**, m. condition or quality 1819.

Motmot (mǫ·t,mǫt). 1837. [mod.L.; app. echoic of the bird's note.] A bird of the family *Momotidæ*, native of Mexico and S. America.

Moto-, irreg. repr. L. *mot-* (as in MOTION, etc.): used *Anat.* as in **m.-sensitive** *a.*, composed of motor and sensitive nerve-fibres; and in combs. as †*motocycle* = MOTOR *c.*, etc.

Motograph (mōᵘ·tǒgrɑf). 1877. [f. MOTO- + -GRAPH.] A receiver for an electric telegraph or telephone, invented by Edison.

Motor (mōᵘ·tə). 1586. [a. L. *motor*, f. *movere.*] **A.** *sb.* **1.** One who or something which imparts motion; an agent or force that produces mechanical motion. **2. a.** *Anat.* A muscle which moves a particular part of the animal frame. **b.** A nerve whose function it is to excite muscular activity in a particular part of the animal body. 1808. **3.** An apparatus for employing some natural agent or force for the impulsion of machinery; a machine that supplies the motive power for the propulsion of a carriage or vessel. In recent use also in a narrower sense excluding steam engines. 1856. **b.** Short for MOTOR CAR. 1900. **4.** *Math.* An operator or quantity which represents the displacement of a rigid body 1873. **5.** *attrib.*, designating a vehicle driven by a motor, as *m. bicycle, boat, cab, cycle* 1894; connected with a motor car or motoring, as *m.-coat, -horn, -road*, etc. 1902; **m.-bandit**, a thief who uses a motor car in his depredations.

1. †*First* or *prime m.* [= med.L. *primus motor*] = PRIMUM MOBILE 1; (*b*) applied (allusively) to God, as the cause of the motion of the heavens; (*c*) the first instigator, or the chief director, e.g. of a plot, etc.; (*d*) the part that initiates motion in a piece of mechanism, etc.

B. *adj.* [After F. *moteur, motrice.*] **1.** Giving, imparting, or producing motion 1872. **2.** *Phys.* Of nerves (opp. to *sensory*), muscles, etc.: Conveying or imparting an impulse which results or tends to result in motion. So *m. area* (*region, zone*): that part of the cortex of the brain from which motor impulses are directed to the various parts of the animal body. 1824. **3.** Of or pertaining to motor nerves 1878. Hence **Mo·tor** *v. trans.*, to convey in a motor car; *intr.* to travel in a motor car 1896.

Mo·tor car. 1895. [MOTOR *sb.* 5.] **1.** A carriage propelled by a motor, for use on ordinary roads. **2.** *U.S.* A motor-driven car on an electric railroad.

Motorial (motōᵊ·riăl), *a.* 1843. [f. L. *motorius* (see MOTORY) + -AL.] Of or pertaining to motion; *spec.* of or pertaining to a motor nerve; motor.

Motorist (mōᵘ·tərist). 1896. [f. MOTOR *sb.* + -IST.] One who motors, esp. habitually.

Mo·torize, *v.* 1918. [f. MOTOR + -IZE.] *trans.* To provide with motor vehicles or traffic; to convert into a motor-driven vehicle.

Mo·tor-man. 1890. [f. MOTOR *sb.*] The driver of a motor vehicle; *spec.* the hired driver of a public motor-driven conveyance.

Motory (mōᵘ·təri), *a.* 1691. [ad. late L. *motorius*, f. *motor.*] **1.** *Phys.* = MOTOR *a.* 2, 3. **2.** *gen.* That causes motion 1799.

1. The m. Muscles RAY.

Motte (mǫt). *U.S.* Also **mot(t.** 1844. [app. a use of F. *motte* mound.] A clump of trees in a prairie.

‖**Mottetto** (mǫte·to), *pl.* **-ti.** 1644. [It.; see MOTET.] = MOTET b.

Mottle (mǫ·t'l), *sb.* 1676. [Prob. a back-formation from MOTLEY *a.*] **1.** One of a number of spots or blotches by which a surface is variegated. **2.** The arrangement of such spots or blotches forming a mottled surface 1858. **b.** A woollen yarn of variegated colour 1887. So **Mo·ttle** *a.* mottled, now only in Combs. e.g. *m.-faced* (Dickens).

Mottle (mǫ·t'l), *v.* 1676. [f. as MOTTLE *sb.*] *trans.* To mark or cover with spots or blotches; *spec.* in *Soap-making*, to impart a mottled appearance to white soap by the addition of chemicals. Hence **Mo·ttled** *ppl. a.* dappled with spots or blotches; marked with spots, streaks, or patches of different colour.

Mo·ttler. 1839. [f. prec. + -ER [1].] **a.** A workman who mottles soap. **b.** A house-painter's brush for mottling.

Motto (mǫ·to). *Pl.* **-os, -oes.** 1589. [a. It. *motto* = F. *mot*; see MOT [1].] **1.** Orig., a word, sentence, or phrase attached as a legend to an 'impresa' or emblematical design. Hence, more widely, a short sentence or phrase inscribed on some object, and expressing an appropriate reflection or sentiment; also, a proverbial or pithy maxim adopted by a person as his rule of conduct. **b.** *spec.* in *Her.* A significant word or sentence usually placed upon a scroll, occas. having some reference to the name or exploits of the bearer, to the charges upon the shield or to the crest, but more often expressing merely a pious aspiration or exalted sentiment 1600. **c.** The poetical lines contained in a motto-kiss or paper cracker. Also U.S. = *m.-kiss.* **3.** A short quotation (or original passage) prefixed to a literary work or to one of its parts, and expressing some idea appropriate to its contents 1711. **4.** *Mus.* A recurrent phrase 1891.

1. 'Nitor in adversum' is the m. for a man like me BURKE. b. *Festina Lente*—'Hasten slowly', or 'On slow', is the M. of the Onslow family CUSSANS. *Comb.* **m.-kiss,** a sweetmeat wrapped in fancy paper, having a m. or scrap of poetry enclosed with it. Hence **Mo·ttoed** *a.* inscribed with a m. †or legend 1608.

Motty (mǫ·ti), *a. Sc.* 1599. [f. *mot*, Sc. pronunc. of MOTE *sb.*[1] + -Y [1].] Containing motes.

‖**Motu proprio** (mōu·tiu prǫ·prio). 1847. [L., = of one's own motion.] A papal rescript of which the provisions are decided on by the pope personally.

Mouch, variant of MOOCH.

‖**Moucharaby** (muʃa·răbi). 1884. [Fr.; corruptly a. mod. Arab.] In northern Africa, an external balcony enclosed with latticework.

Mouchoir (muʃwar). 1690. [Fr.] A handkerchief.

‖**Moue** (mū). 1850. [Fr.; see MOW *sb.*[2]] A pout.

Mouedhin, var. of MUEZZIN.

Moufflon (mū·flǫn). 1774. [a. F. *mouflon*, ad. early Sard. **mofrone* :—late L. *mufron.*] A wild sheep, esp. *Ovis musimon*, native of the mountainous regions of southern Europe.

Mought(e, obs. pa. t. of MAY *v.*[1]

‖**Mouillé** (muye). 1833. [pa. pple. of F. *mouiller* to wet, moisten.] *Romance Philol.* Of a consonant, chiefly *l*, also *n*, *r*: Palatalized or 'fronted', changed into (ly *and hence* y, ny, ry).

‖**Moujik, muzhik** (mū·ʒik). 1568. [Russ., 'peasant'.] **1.** A Russian peasant. **2.** (In full *m. blouse, coat.*) A loose fur cape for ladies' wear 1897.

Moul, *v. Obs.* or *dial.* [a. or cogn. w. ON. **mugla*, f. Teut. root **mug-*.] To grow or make mouldy.

Mould (mōuld), *sb.*[1] Also (now *U. S.*) **mold.** [OE. *molde* :—OTeut. **moldā*, *muldā*, root of **mul-* (: *mel-* : *mal-*) to pulverize, grind; see MEAL *sb.*[1]] **1.** Loose, broken, or friable earth; hence, the surface soil, which is easily broken up. Also *pl.* (now only *dial.*) lumps or clods of earth. **2.** The earth of the grave. Also *pl.* Now only *poet.* or *dial.* OE. **3.** The upper soil of cultivated land; garden-soil; *spec.* soil rich in organic matter and suitable for the cultivation of plants ME. **4.** Earth as the material of the human body. *Obs.* or *poet.* ME. **†5.** The ground regarded as a surface or as a solid stratum –1624. **6.** The world on which we dwell. Also, the land of a particular region. *Obs.* or *poet.* OE.

2. When Spring with dewy fingers cold Returns to deck their hallowed mold COLLINS. 3. *Leaf-m.*, *vegetable m.* (see these words). 4. *Man of m.*: a mortal man. Be mercifull great Duke to men of m. SHAKS. (Occas. misunderstood as 'men of parts or distinction', and so used by some mod. writers.) 6. The fairest knight on Scottish mold SCOTT.

Mould (mōuld), *sb.*[2] Now *dial.* [OE. *molda* or *-e* = MDu. *moude* 'fonticulus'.] The top or dome of the head; also the fontanelle in an infant's head.

Mould (mōuld), *sb.*[3] Also (now *U.S.*) **mold.** [ME. *mold(e*, app. metathetic alteration of OF. *modle* (mod.F. *moule*) :—L. *modulum* (see MODULE).] **I. 1.** A pattern by which something is shaped; e.g. the templet used by a shipbuilder, mason, bricklayer, or plasterer. **2.** A hollow form or matrix into which fluid or plastic material is cast or pressed and allowed to cool or harden so as to take a particular shape or pattern. late ME. **b.** *gen.* A modelled surface from which an impression can be taken 1530. **3.** *spec.* in *Cookery.* A hollow utensil of metal or earthenware used to give a shape to puddings, jelly, etc. Also, a pudding, etc., shaped in a mould. 1573. **4.** *transf.* and *fig.* 1557. **†b.** Said of the body with reference to its clothes –1639. **†5.** A model, a pattern –1618. **6.** A frame or body on or round which a manufactured article is made; e.g. the frame on which a sheet of paper, a basket, a hurdle (etc.) is made 1655. **7.** A package of leaves of gold-beater's skin between which gold-leaf is placed for beating 1727. **8.** *Photo-engraving.* The gelatine which receives the impression from the negative and from which the copper plate is taken; also, the metal plate itself 1875.

2. The liquid Ore he dreined Into fit moulds prepar'd MILT. Phr. *To break the m.*: *fig.* to render impossible the repetition of a certain type of creation. 4. Phr. *To be cast in a* (certain) *m.*: to have a certain form or character. b. *Macb.* I. iii. 145. 5. The glasse of Fashion, and the m. of Forme SHAKS.

II. Imparted form or make; result of moulding. **1.** Distinctive nature as indicative of origin; esp. of persons, native constitution or character ME. **2.** The form or shape of an animal body, or (less usually) of something inanimate. Now *techn.* (among cattle- or stud-breeders); otherwise *rhet.* 15.. **b.** *concr.* Bodily form, body. Chiefly *poet.* 1579. **†3.** The form or structural type or model of a building or ship –1774. **†4.** Style, fashion, mode –1656. **5.** That which is moulded or fashioned (*rare*) 1667. **6.** *Arch.* A moulding or group of mouldings belonging to a particular member of a building 1480. **7.** *Geol.* An impression made in earth by the convex side of a fossil shell 1748. **8.** = *m. candle* 1797.

1. Merchants.., That trade in mettall of the purest m. MARLOWE. A character of a finer m. JOWETT. 2. b. Whom doth she behold?..His vital presence? his corporeal m.? WORDSW.

Comb. **m. candle,** a candle made in a m. (as dist. from a dip-candle); **m.-loft** *Shipbuilding*, a room on the floor of which the plans of a ship are drawn at full size.

Mould (mōuld), *sb.*[4] Also (now *U. S.*) **mold.** late ME. [Perh. from MOULD *a.*] A woolly or furry growth (consisting of minute fungi) which forms on substances that lie for some time in moist warm air. As a disease of the hop plant = FEN *sb.*[2]

A man that hates cheese must call me fool for loving blue mold MANDEVILLE. *fig.* The m. of time 1829.

Mould (mōuld), *a.* (orig. *ppl.*) *Obs.* exc. *dial.* ME. [f. MOUL *v.* + -ED [1].] Mouldy.

Mould (mōuld), *v.*[1] Also (now *U.S.*) **mold.** 1530. [f. MOULD *sb.*[1]] **1.** *trans.* †To bury; to cover (plants) with mould; to earth *up.* **†2.** *To m. away*: to moulder, crumble away –1633.

Mould (mōuld), *v.*[2] late ME. Also (now *U.S.*) **mold.** [f. MOULD *sb.*[3]] **1.** *trans.* To mix or knead (dough, bread); now *techn.*: To shape into loaves. **†2.** To mix (ingredients) to form a paste –1652. **†b.** *fig.* To mix *up* (*with*) –1855. **3.** To shape; to fashion, form, model. Chiefly *poet.* 1475. **4.** To shape (fluid or plastic matter) in or as in a mould 1573. **5.** *transf.* and *fig.* To create, produce, or form *out of* certain elements or material, or *upon* a certain pattern; also, to plan, design. Also with *up.* 1603. **6.** To bring into a particular shape or form; to shape or model the character or style of. Const. *into*, *to.* 1605. **7.** *intr.* and *refl.* (now *rare*). To assume a certain form; to shape itself (*into*) 1612. **8.** *trans. Shipbuilding.* To give a particular mould to (a vessel); to shape timbers with moulds 1570.

3. Two louely berries molded on one stem SHAKS. 4. In harden'd orbs the school-boy moulds the snow GAY. 5. They say best men are moulded out of faults SHAKS. 6. Logic was beginning to m. human thought JOWETT. Hence **Mou·ldable** *a.* 1626.

Mould (mōuld), *v.*[3] Also (now *U.S.*) **mold.** 1460. [f. MOULD *sb.*[4]] **1.** *trans.* †**a.** To allow to become mouldy. **b.** To cause to contract mould. **2.** *intr.* To become mouldy or covered with mould 1530. **b.** *transf.* and *fig.* of things that lie unused 1547.

2. b. The Grecians..were not wont to suffer bookes of worth to lye moulding in Kings Libraries BIBLE *Transl. Pref.* ¶ 6.

Mould-board (mōu·ldbōəɹd). 1508. Also (now *U.S.*) **mold-.** [f. MOULD *sb.*[1] + BOARD *sb.*; replacing earlier *moldbred* (BRED *sb.*).] The board or metal plate in a plough, which turns over the furrow-slice.

Moulder (mōu·ldəɹ), *sb.* Also (now *U.S.*) **molder.** 1440. [f. MOULD *v.*[2] + -ER [1].] **1.** One who moulds dough or bread. **2. a.** One who makes moulds for casting. **b.** One who moulds clay into bricks. 1535. **†3.** An instrument for moulding –1823.

Moulder (mōu·ldəɹ), *v.* 1531. Also (now *U.S.*) **molder.** [f. MOULD *sb.*[1] + -ER [5].] **1.** *intr.* To turn to dust by natural decay; to waste away; to crumble. Also with *away*, *down.* **2.** *transf.* To dwindle. Said chiefly of armies. Also with *away.* Now *rare* or *Obs.* 1674. **3.** *trans.* To cause to crumble, fall to pieces, or decay. Also with *away*, *down.* Now *rare* or *dial.* 1649.

1. When statues m., and when arches fall PRIOR. *fig.* Never man, I think, So moulder'd in a sinecure as he TENNYSON. 2. If he had sat still the other great army would have mouldered to nothing CLARENDON. 3. *transf.* How many men have we seene Molder and crumble away great Estates DONNE. Hence **Mou·ldery** *a.* crumbly 1600.

Mouldiness (mōu·ldinės). 1577. [f. MOULDY *a.* + -NESS.] The condition of being mouldy; often *concr.* mould.

Mou·lding, *vbl. sb.*[1] 1699. [f. MOULD *v.*[1] + -ING [1].] The earthing-*up* of plants.

Mou·lding, *vbl. sb.*[2] ME. [f. MOULD *v.*[2] + -ING [1].] **1.** The action of MOULD *v.*[2] **b.** Bodily form. SCOTT. **2.** *concr.* A moulded object 1727. **3.** *spec.* (*Arch.*, etc.) An ornamental variety of contour given to stone-, wood-, or metal-work, effected by means of carving or the application of pieces in relief; material shaped and prepared in this way.

Moulding-board. ME. [f. prec.] *Baking.* A board on which dough or paste is kneaded and shaped.

Mouldwarp (mōu·ldwǫɹp). Now chiefly *n. dial.* [ME. *moldwarp*, *molwarp*, *-werp*, repr. OE. **moldweorp*, lit. 'earth-thrower', f. **moldā* MOULD *sb.*[1] + **werp-* to throw] = MOLE *sb.*[2]

Mouldy (mōu·ldi), *a.* late ME. Also (now *U.S.*) **moldy.** [f. MOULD *sb.*[4] + -Y [1].] Overgrown or covered with mould; hence, mouldering or mouldered. **b.** Of, consisting of, or resembling mould (*rare*) 1579.

Hee liues vpon mouldie stew'd Pruines SHAKS. *fig.* Away you mouldie Rogue, away SHAKS. Pretty m. health STEVENSON.

‖**Moulin** (mulæ̃n). 1860. [F., *lit.* a mill.] A nearly vertical well or shaft in a glacier, formed by the surface water falling through a crack in the ice, and gradually scooping out a deep chasm.

Moulinet (mū·line·t). 1662. [a. F., dim. of *moulin* mill; see -ET.] **1.** A winch. **2.** *Fencing.* A circular swing of a sword or sabre 1875.

Moult (mōult), *sb.* Also (now *U.S.*) **molt.** 1815. [f. MOULT *v.*] The action of moulting in birds, or (*transf.*) in reptiles, crustacea, etc.

Moult (mōult), *v.* [ME. *mouten* :—OE. **mūtian*, a Com. WGer. adoption of L. *mutare* to change. The *l* is on the analogy of *fault*, etc., and the mod. pronunc. is based on the new spelling.] †1. *intr.* Of feathers: To be shed in the process of change of plumage. Also with *off.* Hence loosely of hair. -1647. 2. Of birds: To shed or cast feathers in changing plumage 1440; also *trans.* with feathers as obj. 1530.

2. *transf.* The youthful crayfish 'moult', or shed their shells 8 times in their first twelvemonth of life 1902; *trans. Ham.* II. ii. 306; *fig.* I moulted my stick to-day H. WALPOLE.

†Mou·lten, *ppl. a.* [irreg. strong pa. pple. of prec.] Having moulted. SHAKS.

A moulten Rauen 1 *Hen. IV*, III. i. 152.

Moulten, obs. f. MOLTEN.

Moun, obs. f. MAY *v.*[1], MOUNT *sb.*[2]

Mound (maund), *sb.*[1] ME. [a. F. *monde* :—L. *mundus* world.] †1. The world; the earth as man's abode. ME. only. 2. An orb or ball of gold, etc., repr. the globe of the earth; often surmounting a crown, or forming part of the insignia of royalty. Also *Her.* a figure of this, as a bearing; often used as including the cross which commonly surmounts it.

Mound (maund), *sb.*[2] 1551. [Etym. obsc. Perh. from the vb., which appears somewhat earlier.] 1. A hedge or other fence bounding a field or garden. Now only *dial.* †b. *fig.* A boundary -1742. 2. *Mil.* = MOUNT *sb.*[1] 2a. Hence *gen.* an embankment, a dam. Now *rare.* 1558. 3. An artificial elevation of earth or stones; *esp.* the earth heaped up upon a grave 1726. b. A natural elevation resembling a heap or pile of earth; a hillock 1810. 4. *spec.* a. A pile of fuel for roasting ores. b. The heap of earth, dead leaves, etc., built by megapodes for their eggs. c. *Archæol.* An elevation produced upon a land surface by the natural burial of an abandoned city. d. A kind of earthwork formerly constructed by natives of parts of N. America. e. = KITCHEN-MIDDEN. 1839.

1. This great gardin, compast with a m. SPENSER. 2. The mounds and dykes of the low fat Bedford level BURKE. 3. A church-yard's dreary mounds CLARE.

attrib. and *Comb.*: m.-bird = next (*b*); -builder, (*a*) one of a prehistoric race of American Indians, who erected immense burial and fortification mounds 1841; (*b*) any of the megapode birds which deposit their eggs in a mound 1880; -burial *Archæol.*, the practice of burying beneath a m. or cairn; -dweller, a primitive man who dwelt in a rudely erected m.; so -dwelling.

Mound (maund), *v.* 1515. [Cf. prec.] 1. *trans.* To enclose or bound with a fence. Also *absol.* or *intr.*, to make fences. *Obs.* exc. *dial.* 2. To enclose, bound, or fortify with an embankment 1600. 3. To heap up in a mound or hillock 1859.

Mounseer (maunsīə·ɹ). *arch.* 1641. An illiterate or derisive anglicized pronunciation of MONSIEUR.

Mount (maunt), *sb.*[1] [OE. *munt* masc., ad. L. *montem, mons.* Blended in 12th c. with F. *mont.*] I. 1. In early use, a mountain, lofty hill; from 17th c. in prose use *esp.* a more or less conical hill of moderate height rising from a plain; a hillock. Now chiefly *poet.* exc. in proper names of mountains or hills, and in *the Sermon on the M.* When prefixed abbrev. *Mt.* 2. *Mil.* a. A substantial work of earth or other material, thrown up to resist an attack or to advance an assault. *Obs.* exc. *Hist.* 1558. †b. = CAVALIER *sb.* 4. Also *fig.* -1721. †3. An artificial mound of earth, stones, etc.; *esp.* a raised piece of ground, or walk, in a garden -1813. Also *transf.*

1. *fig.* I have a m. of mischiefe clogs my soule 1602. 2. I..will lay siege against thee with a m., and I will raise forts against thee *Isa.* xxix. 3. 3. At the End of both the Side Grounds, I would haue a M. of some Pretty Height..to looke abroad into the Fields BACON.

II. In transf. uses. †1. [After It. *monte.*] A bank -1765. 2. *Palmistry.* One of the fleshy prominences on the palm of the hand by the development of which palmists profess to ascertain the degree of influence exercised by a particular planet 1644.

1. †Mount of piety, mount piety, a rendering of It. *monte di pietà*, Fr. *mont-de-piété*, in Italy and France, a pawnbroking establishment instituted and carried on by the State for the purpose of affording loans to the poor at low interest.

Mount (maunt), *sb.*[2] ME. [f. MOUNT *v.* Cf. F. *monte* fem.] †1. = AMOUNT *sb.* -1651. 2. An act of mounting (*rare*); a manner of mounting 1486. 3. That in or on which anything is mounted, fitted, supported, or placed; a mounting, fitting, or setting; *spec.* (*a*) the margin surrounding a picture, or the cardboard on which a drawing is mounted; (*b*) *pl.* the metal ornaments serving as borders, edges, or guards to the angles and prominent parts of 18th c. furniture, etc.; (*c*) the glass slip with its adjuncts used to preserve objects for examination under the microscope. 1739. b. Of a fan: (*a*) The pieces of wood, ivory, etc. forming the frame or support. (*b*) The silk, paper, etc. forming the surface of the fan. 1811. 4. *colloq.* A horse, etc., provided for a person's riding 1856. 5. An opportunity or occasion of riding; hence, an undertaking to ride or an act of riding (a horse) in a race 1856.

4. A good high-bred dromedary is as comfortable a m. as can be desired 1885.

Mount (maunt), *v.* [ME., a. OF. *monter* :—Com. Rom. **montare*, f. *mont-, mons* MOUNT *sb.*[1]] I. *intr.* 1. To go upwards, ascend. Also with *up.* b. Of the blood: To rise into the cheeks. Also, of the effects of wine: To go to the head. 1625. 2. *fig.* a. To ascend to a higher level in rank, estimation, power, excellence, completeness, etc. late ME. b. To ascend or go back in date (*arch.*) 1796. 3. To get upon the back of a horse, etc., for the purpose of riding. Const. *on, upon,* †*to.* 1509. 4. To get up *on* something; e.g. a platform, a stage 1642. 5. To rise in amount; to increase by addition. Chiefly with *up.* late ME. †6. To amount *to* a certain sum, number, or quantity -1738. 7. *slang.* To swear or give false evidence for payment 1789.

1. Doth the Aegle mounte vp..at thy commaundement? COVERDALE *Job* xxxix. 27. They causyd the mynstrell to m. vp on y[e] ladder LD. BERNERS. [The chamois] always m. or descend in an oblique direction GOLDSM. 2. b. For the antiquity of which [method] we must m. up to Celsus 1803. 3. Wel father in Gods name, m. on my shoulder, I pray you 1582. 5. The debts of the Crown mounted to four times its annual income GREEN.

II. *trans.* 1. To ascend or climb up (a hill, etc.); to ascend (a river, stair) 1500. 2. To get upon the back of (a horse, etc.) for the purpose of riding 1599. 3. To get upon, for copulation. Now only *colloq.* of animals. 1592. 4. To get upon or into, from below 1698.

1. Phr. *To m. a breach*: to ascend it for the purpose of assault or attack. The stayres That m. the Capitoll SHAKS. 4. The Boy accordingly mounted the Pulpit ADDISON.

III. *trans.* in causative uses. †1. To cause to ascend or rise: to raise. Also with *up.* -1766. †2. In various *fig.* or non-material uses (see quots.) -1796. 3. To set or place upon an elevation. Now only with *on, upon.* 1567. 4. To set on horseback; to help into the saddle; also, to furnish with a saddle-horse. In *pass.*, to be seated on horseback. 1603. 5. *Mil.* a. To raise (guns) into position 1539. b. Of a fort, a ship: To have (cannon) in position 1748. c. *pass.* To be provided *with* cannon 1662. d. To raise the muzzle of (a gun) 1545. e. To post for defence or observation. Hence *to m.* (†*the*) *guard*: to go on duty as a guard. Also *transf.* 1687. 6. To put in position for use or exhibition; *spec.* to fix on a mount; occas. to stage (a play) 1712. 7. To put on, assume, display oneself as wearing (some special article of costume). *arch.* 1812.

1. Hedg-hogs, which..m. Their pricks at my footfall SHAKS. 2. What power is it, which mounts my loue so hye? SHAKS. Who mounts the meeke, and beates the lofty downe QUARLES. Some have mounted his ordinarie yearly in-come to eight millions of gold FULLER. 3. No wonder we see more than the ancients, because we are mounted upon their shoulders J. H. NEWMAN. 4. He was..excellently well mounted, on a very gallant horse 1662. 6. The paste used for 'mounting' water-colour paintings 1859. He mounted his rod, and tried casting in shallow water 1895. b. In theatrical parlance..'The piece was excellently mounted' 1874. 7. I expect he has mounted a pair of leather breeches W. IRVING.

Mountain (mau·ntėn). ME. [a. OF. *montaigne* :—pop.L. **montania*, *-*ea*, perh. fem. (sc. *regio, terra*) mountain region, f. *montem, mons.*] I. 1. A natural elevation of the earth's surface, rising notably above the surrounding level. See also HILL *sb.* 1. b. *poet.* Used in *pl.* as the type of a region remote from civilization 1601. 2. *transf.* A huge heap or pile; a towering mass 1450. 3. *fig.* A quantity or amount of impressive proportions 1592. 4. (In full *m. wine.*) A variety of Malaga wine, made from grapes grown on the mountains 1710. 5. *The Mountain* [Fr. *la Montagne*]: an extreme party led by Robespierre and Danton in the first French Revolution, so called because it occupied the most elevated position in the chamber of assembly 1799.

1. That chain of majestic mountains [*sc.* the Sussex Downs] G. WHITE. Mountains formed in the volcanic way are almost always conical GEIKIE. Phr. *To run* (etc.) *mountains high*, said hyperbolically of high seas DE FOE; cf. *mountain-high* adj. 1693. b. *Twel. N.* IV. i. 52. 2. †*M. of ice* = ICEBERG.

II. *attrib.* passing into *adj.* a. Of or belonging to mountains; situated in or on mountains; consisting of mountains. late ME. b. Born in or inhabiting mountains; having one's abode in mountains; coming from the mountains 1591. c. Used in the mountains 1848. d. Resembling a mountain; huge, enormous 1656.

a. Your m. air is sweet 1865. b. The m.-boar on battle set SCOTT. c. M.-chaises 1897. d. Me all thy M. Waves have press'd TATE & BRADY.

Comb.: m. artillery, m. battery, (a battery of) light guns for use in mountainous countries; so m.-gun, -howitzer; m. chain (CHAIN *sb.* 4); m. cure, the cure of disease (esp. tuberculous) by residence at high elevations; m. dew, Scotch whisky; m. railway; m. range; m. sickness, a malady caused by breathing the rarefied air of m. heights; m. wine (see I. 4 above).

b. In the names of minerals, etc. [chiefly after G. compounds of *berg-*]: m. cork, flesh, leather, paper, wood, descriptive names for varieties of asbestos; m. crystal = ROCK-CRYSTAL; m. flour, meal, (*a*) a recent freshwater deposit consisting of the siliceous frustules of diatoms; (*b*) a white cottonlike variety of calcite occurring as an efflorescence on rocks; m. limestone *Geol.*, a thick massive limestone belonging to the carboniferous series; m. milk, a soft spongy variety of carbonate of lime.

c. Prefixed to the names of many animals found in upland districts: as, m. cat, a catamount or catamountain; m. eagle, the golden eagle, *Aquila chrysaëtus*; m. hare, the alpine hare, *Lepus variabilis*, native of the northern parts of both hemispheres; m. lion = PUMA; m. panther, (*a*) = OUNCE *sb.*[2] 2; (*b*) = PUMA.

d. In names of plants, etc., growing in elevated situations: as, m. cowslip, a herbaceous plant, *Primula Auricula*, native of the Swiss Alps; m. ebony, a leguminous tree of the genus *Bauhinia*, having dark-coloured and hard wood; also, the wood; m. mint, †(*a*) calamint, (*b*) the U.S. genus *Pycnanthemum*; m. pine, a dwarf alpine pine, *Pinus Pumilio*, native of Europe; m. rose, the rhododendron.

Mountain ash. 1597. The tree *Pyrus* (formerly *Sorbus*) *Aucuparia*, characterized by its delicate pinnate leaves and masses of bright scarlet berries; the rowan-tree. In N. America applied to the native species, *Pyrus americana* and *P. sambucifolia.*

Mountaineer (mauntėnīə·ɹ), *sb.* 1610. [f. MOUNTAIN + -EER.] 1. A native of or dweller among mountains. 2. A member of the 'Mountain' (see MOUNTAIN I. 5) 1802. 3. A mountain-climber 1860. Hence **Mountainee·r** *v. intr.* to be a mountain-climber; usu. in *vbl. sb.* and *ppl. a.*

†Mountainer. 1598. [f. as prec. + -ER [1].] = prec. sb. 1. -1744.

Mountainet, -ette (mauntėne·t). 1586. [a. F. *montagnette*, dim. of *montagne.*] A small mountain; a hillock, mound.

Mountain flax. 1718. 1. Purging flax, *Linum catharticum.* 2. = AMIANTHUS 1. 1807.

Mountain-green. 1727. [After G. *berggrün.*] †1. *Min.* = MALACHITE -1841. 2. Name of a colour 1796.

Mountainous (mau·ntėnəs), *a.* 1601. [a. F. *montagneux* :—pop.L. **montaniosus*, f. **montania* MOUNTAIN; see -OUS.] 1. Characterized by, abounding in, or of the nature of mountains. 2. Mountain-like; huge, enormous. Now *rare.* 1607. †3. Inhabiting mountains; hence, barbarous -1703. †4. Derived from mountains -1801.

2. The two m. cheek-bones of the house-keeper FIELDING. 3. Ignorant and Mountanous People BACON. Hence **Mou·ntainous-ly** *adv.*, **-ness.**

Mountainy (mau·ntėni), *a.* Now *dial.* 1613. [f. MOUNTAIN + Y[1].] Having or belonging to mountains.

Mountant (mau·ntănt), *sb.* 1886. [f. MOUNT *v.* + -ANT[1], after F. *montant.*] An adhesive paste for mounting photographs, etc.

†**Mountant**, *a.* 1525. [a. F. *montant*, f. *monter.*] Mounting, rising –1812.

Mountebank (mau·ntĭbæŋk), *sb.* 1577. [ad. It. *montambanco, montimbanco*, contr. f. *monta in banco*, lit. 'mount-on-bench'. Cf. SALTIMBANCO.] **1.** An itinerant quack who from a platform appealed to his audience by means of stories, tricks, juggling, and the like, often with the assistance of a professional clown. **2.** *fig.* An impudent charlatan 1589. **3.** *appos.* (quasi-*adj.*) That is a mountebank; characteristic of a mountebank 1603.

1. Men..will often preferre a Mountabanke or Witch, before a learned Phisitian BACON. 2. The Mountebanks and Zanies of Patriotism COLERIDGE. Hence **Mou·ntebankery**, action, or an act, which bespeaks a m. **Mou·ntebankish** *a.*

Mou·ntebank, *v.* 1602. [f. prec.] †**1.** *trans.* To prevail over (a person) by mountebank persuasion –1702. †**2.** To transform by mountebank trickery. DE FOE. **3.** *intr.* To play the mountebank. Usu. with *it.* 1602.

Mounted (mau·ntėd), *ppl. a.* 1582. [f. MOUNT *v.* + -ED[1].] **1.** Elevated (*lit.* and *fig.*). **2.** Seated or appointed to serve on horseback 1598. **3.** Set up for use, as cannon. Of a fort, ship, etc.: Furnished (*with* cannon). 1639.

2. While M. Infantry are footmen trained for purposes of mobility to ride a horse or bicycle, M. Rifles are horsemen trained to fight on foot 1901.

Mounter (mau·ntəɹ). 1609. [f. MOUNT *v.* + -ER[1].] **1.** *gen.* One who ascends. **2.** One whose business it is to mount, fit, or set (anything) in order 1747.

Mounting (mau·ntiŋ), *vbl. sb.* late ME. [f. MOUNT *v.* + -ING[1].] **1.** The action of MOUNT *v.* **2.** *concr.* **a.** Something that serves as a mount, support, or setting to anything 1618. †**b.** *sing.* and *pl. Mil.* A soldier's outfit or kit –1722.

1. *attrib.* **m.-block**, a block of stone from which to mount on horseback. 2. a. *Hilt*, the head or m. of a sword 1767.

†**Mou·nture.** ME. [a. OF. *monture*, f. *monter* to MOUNT.] **1.** A horse, etc., for riding –1600. **2.** = MOUNTING 2. –1575. †**3.** *Mil.* The angle at which a gun is elevated –1692.

†**Mou·nty.** 1586. [a. F. *montée*, f. *monter* to MOUNT.] *Falconry.* The action, or an act, of rising in pursuit of the quarry –1657.

Mourn (mōəɹn), *v.* [Com. Teut.: OE. *murnan*, f. Teut. root **mur-*, prob. f. Indo-Eur. **smer-* to remember, whence Gr. μέριμνα care, sorrow.] **I.** *intr.* **1.** To feel sorrow, grief, or regret; to sorrow, grieve, lament. †**b.** Of animals: To pine –1784. **c.** *fig.* Of a plant or flower. †Also, to droop, hang down. 1626. **2.** *esp.* To lament the death of some one. Const. *for.* ME. **b.** To show the conventional signs of grief for a period following a person's death; *esp.* to put on mourning 1530. **3.** Of a dove: = MOAN *v.* 4. 1535.

1. In all euyll thou mayst fynde cause to mourne and sorowe 1526. I mourned for the iniquitie 1 *Esdras* viii. 72. 2. A widow bird sate mourning for her love SHELLEY. b. We mourne in black, why m. we not in blood? SHAKS. 3. The dove mourned in the pine SHELLEY.

II. *trans.* **1.** To grieve or sorrow for (something); to lament, deplore, bewail OE. **2.** To lament, grieve, or sorrow for, to express grief for (some one dead) 1526. **3.** To utter in a sorrowful manner 1607.

1. Mourning, in others, our own miseries 1586. 2. Here comes his Body, mourn'd by Marke Antony SHAKS. 3. Where the love-lorn Nightingale Nightly to thee her sad Song mourneth well MILT.

Mourner (mōə·ɹnəɹ). late ME. [f. prec. + -ER[1].] **1.** One who mourns or grieves; *spec.* one who mourns the death of a friend, etc.; one who attends a funeral out of respect or affection for the deceased. †**b.** One employed or hired to attend funerals –1741. **2.** *Indian m.*: the sad-tree 1597.

1. *Chief m.*: the nearest relative present at a funeral. When..the mourners go aboute the stretes COVERDALE *Eccl.* xii. 2.

Mournful (mōə·ɹnfŭl), *a.* 1542. [f. MOURN *v.* + -FUL.] **1.** Denoting, exhibiting, or expressive of mourning or deep sorrow. **2.** Feeling or oppressed with deep sorrow 1579.

1. He shook his head with an intensely m. air DICKENS. 2. Thou wilt the m. Spirit chear WESLEY. Hence **Mou·rnful-ly** *adv.*, **-ness.**

Mourning (mōə·ɹniŋ), *vbl. sb.* ME. [f. MOURN *v.* + -ING[1].] **1.** The action of MOURN *v.* Also with *a* and *pl.* **2.** *spec.* The feeling or the expression of sorrow for a death; also, a lament ME. **3.** The wearing of black clothes, etc., as a manifestation of sorrow for the death of a friend. Also, the period during which they are worn. 1532. **b.** An instance of this. Now *rare.* 1611. **4.** The dress (now usu. black) worn by mourners. Also occas. applied to the black draperies placed on buildings, etc. on occasions of mourning. 1654.

1. The mournynges of soch as be in captiuyte COVERDALE *Ps.* ci[i]. 20. 2. The noise of the m. of a mighty nation TENNYSON. 3. b. And he made a m. for his father seuen days *Gen.* l. 10. 4. Pray desire Mrs. Taylor to inform me what m. I should buy for my mother and Miss Porter JOHNSON. *Deep m.*: complete or full m.; so HALF-M. (†*second m.*). *In m.* (as adjectival phr.): wearing the garments indicative of grief. So *To go* or *put into m.*; *to be out of m.*, etc.

attrib. and *Comb.*: **m.-band**, a strip of black cloth or crape worn round the sleeve of a coat or round the hat in token of bereavement; **m. border**, a black border on note-paper, envelopes, etc., used by persons who are in m.; **m. coach**, (*a*) a black coach, usually draped in black, used by a person in mourning *Hist.*; (*b*) a closed carriage used by mourners at a funeral; **-paper**, note-paper with a black edge; **-ring**, a ring worn as a memorial of a deceased person.

Mou·rning, *ppl. a.* OE. [f. MOURN *v.* + -ING[2].] That mourns; sorrowing, lamenting; characterized by or expressive of grief.

Spec. collocations: **m. bride**, a pop. name for the sweet scabious, *Scabiosa atropurpurea*; **m. dove**, the common American or Carolina turtle-dove, *Zenaidura carolinensis*; **m. warbler**, an American warbler, *Geothlypis philadelphia*; **m. widow**, a European geranium, *Geranium phæum*. Hence **Mou·rningly** *adv.* 1519.

Mournival (mōə·ɹnivăl). Now only *Hist.* 1530. [a. F. *mornifle*, of unkn. origin.] *Cards.* **1.** A set of four aces, kings, queens, or knaves, in one hand. †**2.** *transf.* A set of four (things or persons) –1711.

Mouse (maus), *sb. Pl.* **mice** (məis). [Com. Teut.: OE. *mūs* :—Indo-Eur. **mūs-* (L. *mus*, Gr. μῦς, Skr. *mūṣ*).] **I. 1.** An animal of any of the smaller species of the genus *Mus* of rodents; e.g. the house mouse, *M. musculus*, the field or wood mouse, *M. sylvaticus*, the harvest mouse, *M. minutus*. **b.** Popularly applied to animals of other genera having some resemblance to mice, esp. the shrews (*Sorex*) and the voles (*Arvicola*) OE. **2.** As a type of something small or insignificant. Chiefly after Horace. 1584. †**3.** As a playful term of endearment –1798. **4.** *techn.* Applied to things resembling a mouse in shape, etc. **a.** *Naut.* (*a*) A kind of ball or knob, wrought on the collars of stays by means of spun-yarn, to prevent the running eye from slipping. (*b*) = MOUSING *vbl. sb.* 2 a (*concr.*). 1750. **b.** A match used in firing a mine or a gun 1867. **5.** *slang.* A lump or discoloured bruise, *esp.* a black eye 1854.

1. Phr. *Drunk, mum, mute, quiet, still*, etc., *as a m.* (†*in a cheese*). *M. and man*, every living thing. 2. The mountains travail'd, and brought forth A scorned m.! B. JONS. tr. *Horace, Art P.* 199. 3. *Haml.* III. iv. 183.

II. †**1.** A muscle. *Obs.* in gen. sense. –1561. **2.** *spec.* Applied variously to certain muscular parts of meat. Now only *dial.* 1584.

attrib. and *Comb.*: **m.-bird**, any bird of the African genus *Colius*; **-hawk**, (*a*) a hawk that devours mice; (*b*) the short-eared owl or hawk-owl, *Asio brachyotus*; **m. lemur**, any small Madagascan lemur of the genus *Chirogaleus*; **-mark**, a birth-mark resembling a mouse.

Mouse (mauz), *v.* ME. [f. MOUSE *sb.*] **1.** *intr.* To hunt for or catch mice; said esp. of a cat or an owl. **2.** *transf.* and *fig.* To hunt or search industriously or captiously: to go or move *about* softly in search of something, to prowl. Also with *around, along.* 1575. **b.** *trans.* To hunt for patiently and carefully. Also with *out. U.S.* 1864. †**3.** *trans.* To handle as a cat does a mouse; to tear, bite –1647. †**b.** To pull about good-naturedly but roughly –1691. **4.** *Naut.* To put a mouse (see MOUSE *sb.* I. 4 a) on (a stay); to secure (a hook) with a mouse 1769.

2. Mousing for faults 1778. Phr. *To m. over* (a book): to study eagerly. *U.S.* 3. *John* II. i. 354.

Mou·se-colour, *sb.* (*a.*). 1606. **1.** A colour like that of the common mouse; a dark grey with a yellowish tinge. **2.** *attrib.* or *adj.* Mouse-coloured 1716. **Mouse-coloured** *a.* 1687.

Mou·se-deer. Also **moose-.** 1836. [Both forms are app. corruptions of *musk-deer.*] The Chevrotain (*Tragulus meminna*), native of Ceylon and Java.

Mouse-dun. late ME. **a.** *adj.* Mouse-coloured. **b.** *sb.* Mouse-colour.

Mou·se-ear. ME. [tr. med.L. *auricula muris*, Gr. μυὸς ὠτίς; see MYOSOTE.] A name for various plants mostly with soft hairy leaves, as *Hieracium Pilosella* (also *m. hawkweed*), various species of *Cerastium* (also *m. chickweed*), and of *Myosotis* (as the forget-me-not), and *Sisymbrium Thaliana* (also *m. cress*). So **Mouse-eared** *a.* having leaves resembling a mouse's ear: *spec.* in *m. chickweed, hawkweed* (see above) 1789.

Mou·se-hole. late ME. A hole used by a mouse for passage or abode; a hole only big enough to admit a mouse.

Mou·se-hunt[1]. *Obs.* exc. *dial.* 1481. [a. MDu. *muushont* weasel, f. *muus* mouse + *hont* dog (see HOUND *sb.*[1]).] A weasel, also *gen.* an animal that hunts mice.

Mouse-hunt[2]. *rare.* 1828. [HUNT *sb.*[2]] A hunt for mice.

Mou·se-pea. *Obs.* exc. *dial.* [OE. *mūs-pise.*] The Heath-pea (*Lathyrus macrorrhizus*); also the Meadow Vetchling (*L. pratensis*).

Mouser (mau·zəɹ, -səɹ). late ME. [f. MOUSE *v.* or *sb.* + -ER[1].] An animal that catches mice, e.g. a cat, an owl. Also *fig.*

Mou·setail. 1548. [f. MOUSE *sb.* + TAIL *sb.*[1]] †**1.** The stonecrop, *Sedum acre* –1611. **2.** A plant of the genus *Myosurus*, esp. *M. minimus*, from the shape of its seed receptacle 1578.

Mousetrap (mau·sˌtræp). *Pl.* **mouse-traps**, also †**mice-traps.** 1475. [f. MOUSE *sb.* + TRAP *sb.*[1]] A trap for catching mice.

transf. The house..is too small, a mere mouse-trap 1839. *Comb.* **m.-switch** *Electr.*, an automatic switch moved by a spring which is released when the current through a controlling magnet falls below a certain limit.

Mousing (mau·ziŋ), *vbl. sb.* 1832. [f. MOUSE *v.* + -ING[1].] **1.** The action of MOUSE *v.* 1856. **2.** *Naut.* **a.** The action of fastening spun-yarn or rope, etc., round the point and shank of a hook; *concr.* the rope or yarn so fastened; **b.** The action of making a mouse on a rope; *concr.* the mouse so made 1832. **3.** *attrib.*, as *m. hook*, etc. 1856.

Mousing (mau·ziŋ), *ppl. a.* 1605. [f. as prec. + -ING[2].] That hunts or catches mice. **b.** *transf.* Prying, prowling, rapacious, inquisitive 1692.

Mousle (mau·z'l), *v. arch.* Also **mouzle.** 1662. [freq. of MOUSE *v.* after *tousle.*] *trans.* To pull about roughly.

‖**Mousquetaire** (muskətǭr). 1706. [Fr.; cf. MUSKETEER.] **1.** *Fr. Hist.* Orig. a foot-soldier armed with a musket; in the 17th and 18th c. a member of either the Grey or White and the Black Mousquetaires (so called from the colour of their horses), which formed part of the king's household troops. They were all of noble birth, and were famous as dandies. **2.** Applied *attrib.* to certain styles of articles of female attire, as in *m. cloak, cuff*, etc. Also short for *m. glove* [1850 *à la m.*], 1883.

‖**Mousse** (mūs). 1892. [Fr., = moss.] *Cookery.* A sweet made of whipped cream frozen.

‖**Mousseline** (muslīn). 1696. [Fr.; see MUSLIN.] **1.** French muslin; also, a dress of this. (Often short for *m. de laine.*) **b. M. de laine** ('muslin of wool'), a dress-material, orig. all wool, but later of wool and cotton, printed with various patterns. **c. M. de soie** ('muslin of silk'), a thin silk fabric resembling muslin 1850. **2.** A thin blown glass-ware with ornamentation resembling muslin or lace. Also, a wine-glass of this. 1862.

Moustache (mustɑ·ʃ, mʊ̆s-). Also (now *U.S.*) **mustache.** 1585. [a. F. *moustache* fem., ad. It. *mostaccio, mostacchio*; see MUSTACHIO.] **1.** The hair which grows upon the upper lip of men: either (*a*) that on both sides, or (*b*) that on one side of the lip, as a single moustache, or as a 'pair of moustaches'. **2.** *Zool.* Hair or bristles, resembling a moustache, round the mouth of certain animals 1605.

1. And he twirl'd his m. with so charming an air,—His moustaches I should say, because he'd a pair BARHAM. *Old m.* [tr. F. *vieille moustache*]: an old soldier.

Comb.: **m.-cup**, a cup with an arrangement to protect the m. when drinking; **m. monkey**, a W. African monkey, *Cercopithecus cephus*. Hence **Mousta·ched** *a.*

Mousy (mau·si), *sb.* Also **-ie.** 1693. [f. MOUSE *sb.* + -Y[6].] Playful dim. of *mouse.*

Mousy (mau·si), *a.* Also **-ey.** 1812. [f. MOUSE *sb.* + -Y[1].] **1.** Resembling a mouse, its colour, smell, etc. 1859. **2.** As quiet as a mouse 1812. **3.** Infested with mice 1871.

Mouth (mauþ), *sb.* [Com. Teut.: OE. *múþ*:—OTeut. **munþo-z*:—pre-Teut. **mn̥to-s*, corresp. to L. *mentum* chin.] **I. 1.** The external orifice in an animal body which serves for the ingestion of food, together with the cavity to which this leads, containing the apparatus of mastication and the organs of vocal utterance. **b.** In expressions like *a good, bad, hard*, etc. *m.*, used with ref. to a horse's readiness to feel and obey the pressure of the bit. Hence *abstr.* of a horse: Capability of being guided by the bit. 1727. **2.** As the receptacle of food, or with ref. to swallowing, devouring, taste, etc. OE. **b.** A person viewed only as a consumer of food 1550. **3.** As the instrument of speech or voice. (In this use *tongue* is more usual.) OE. **4.** The orifice of the mouth considered as part of the face OE.

1. He was thrust in the m. with a Speare SHAKS. Mouths that gaped TENNYSON. Phr. †*To draw one's m.*: to extract a tooth. PEPYS. **b.** A horse that has no m. 1791. **2.** Phr. *The m. waters* (*after, at* something), (it) *makes* (*one's*) *m. water*, referring to the flow of saliva caused by the anticipation of appetizing food; also *fig.* *To open one's m. wide*, to ask a high price. See also HAND TO MOUTH. **b.** *Useless m.*, one who does no work but has to be fed. **3.** You must borrow me Gargantuas m. first: 'tis a Word too great for any m. of this Ages size SHAKS. I had the relation from his own m. DE FOE. Phr. *By word of m.*: orally; often opp. to 'by writing'. (*To condemn a person*) *out of his own m.* (Luke xix. 22): by the evidence of his own words. *With one m.*, with one voice; unanimously. (A Hebraism.) Now *rare.* *To open one's m.*: to begin speaking. *To close, shut one's m.*: to refrain from speaking. *To stop* (a person's) *m.*: to keep (him) from talking. *To put words into another's m.* = to tell him what to say. *To put* (a speech) *into a person's m.*: to represent him as having uttered it. *To take the words out of* another's *m.*: to say what he was about to say. *To make a poor m.*, to plead poverty. *To give m.*: (of a hound) to bark or bay vehemently, also *transf.* of a person. **4.** Hir m. ful smal, and ther-to softe and reed CHAUCER. Phr. *Down in the m.*, having the corners of the m. turned downwards, as a sign of dissatisfaction; dejected, dispirited. *To laugh* (*on*) *the wrong side of one's m.*, in early use to laugh in a forced manner; now, to lament instead of laughing. *To make a* (*wry, ugly, hard*, etc.) *m.*, or *mouths*: to express disapproval, derision, etc., by putting awry one's m.; of an animal, to menace with the m.; also *fig.* to refuse to believe or accept. Const. *at, upon.*

II. Transf. applications to persons. **1.** A spokesman. *Obs.* exc. in renderings of foreign modes of speech. 1563. **†2.** *slang.* A silly person; a dupe –1823.

1. I was but the m. of the rest, and spoke what they have dictated to me PEPYS.

III. Applied to things resembling a mouth. **1.** The opening of anything, e.g. a bottle, a furnace, a beehive, a cave, etc.; also *fig.* of the pit of Hell ME. **2.** The outfall of a river; the entrance to a haven, valley, etc. OE. **3.** The opening out of a tube, passage, drain, burrow, and the like; the hole or aperture of various natural or artificial structures 1582. **4.** The fork between the open jaws of scissors, pincers, or a vice; the working edge of a tool 1576. **†5.** A mouthpiece –1821.

attrib. and *Comb.*: with the meaning 'coming from the m. only and not from the heart', as *m.-charity, -friend, -honour*; also **m.-filling** *a. fig.* (of an oath, compliment, etc.), that fills the m., bombastic, inflated; **-footed** *a.*, having a foot-jaw (see FOOT *sb.*); **m. pipe** *Organ-building*, an organ pipe having an oblong opening, called the *mouth*, at the junction of the body with the foot, a flue-pipe; **m.-wash**, a therapeutic wash for the m.

Mouth (mauð), *v.* ME. [f. prec.] **1.** *trans.* To pronounce, speak; to give utterance to. *Obs.* exc. *arch.* **2.** *trans.* To utter in a pompously oratorical style, or with great distinctness of articulation; to declaim. Also with *out.* 1602. **3.** *intr.* To use a pompous or affected style of utterance; to declaim. Also *to m. it.* 1602. **4.** *trans.* To put or take (something) in the mouth; to seize with the mouth; to press (a thing) with the mouth or lips. late ME. **5.** To train the mouth of (a horse); to accustom to the use of the bit 1533. **†6.** *intr.* (*contempt.*) To join lips (*with*); to kiss –1693. **7.** To make mouths; to grimace 1827. **8.** Of a river: To disembogue (*in, into*) 1598.

1. He that knows not how to m. a curse QUARLES. **2.** He.. mouths a sentence, as curs m. a bone CHURCHILL. **3.** Nay, and thoul't m., Ile rant as well as thou SHAKS. **4.** *Haml.* IV. ii. 20. **6.** *Meas. for M.* III. ii. 194.

Mouthed (mauðd), *a.* ME. [f. MOUTH *sb.* + -ED[2].] **1.** Having a mouth, or such-and-such a mouth or mouths. **†2.** Gaping, open-mouthed –1649.

1. A many-m. chorus 1905.

Mouther (mau·ðəɹ). 1822. [f. MOUTH *v.* + -ER[1].] One who mouths; a boastful or declamatory speaker.

Mouthful (mau·þful). 1530. [-FUL.] A quantity that fills the mouth; as much as a mouth can take in at one time; hence, a small quantity. Also *transf.* said esp. *colloq.* of a long name which 'fills' the mouth when uttered.

Mouth glue. 1573. Glue (orig. a preparation of isinglass) to be used by moistening with the tongue.

Mouthless (mau·þlės), *a.* OE. [-LESS.] Having no mouth.

Mouth-organ. 1668. **1.** A musical instrument operated by the mouth; e.g. a pan-pipe, a jews'-harp. **2.** *Zool.* One of the appendages forming the mouth (of an insect, crustacean, etc.) 1863.

Mou·th(-)piece. 1683. **1.** A piece placed at or forming the mouth (of a receptacle, organ-pipe, etc.). **2.** Something to put in the mouth: e.g. the part of a musical instrument, a pipe, etc., which is placed between the lips. Also, that part of a bit which crosses the horse's mouth. 1727. **3.** One who speaks on behalf of another or others 1805.

3. The thing called the Cabinet is nothing more than the mouth-piece of the Boroughmongers COBBETT.

Mouthy (mau·ði), *a.* 1589. [f. MOUTH *sb.* + -Y[1].] Characterized by railing, ranting, or the use of bombastic language.

He..was prone to be m. and magniloquent W. IRVING.

Mouton. late ME. [a. OF. *mouton*, lit. 'sheep' (see MUTTON).] **1.** (mū·tǫn) A French gold coin of the 14th–15th c., bearing the figure of the Lamb of God (whence the name). *Hist.* **2.** (mutoṅ) A spy quartered with an accused person to obtain evidence against him 1804.

‖**Moutonnée** (mutone), *a.* 1872. [Fr. (in *roche moutonnée*), fem. pa. pple. of *moutonner*, f. *mouton* sheep; see MUTTON.] *Geol.* Rounded like a sheep's back; said of rocks shaped by glacial action.

Movable, moveable (mū·văb'l). late ME. [a. OF. *movable*, f. *movoir* to MOVE; see -ABLE.] **A.** *adj.* **†1.** Apt or disposed to movement –1705. **†2.** *fig.* Changeable, fickle, inconstant –1682. **3.** Capable of being moved; not fixed in one place or posture. late ME. **4.** Of property: Admitting of being removed or displaced; applied to 'personal' as opp. to 'real' property. In *Sc. Law*, opp. to HERITABLE *a.* late ME. **5.** Changing from one date to another every year. late ME. **6.** *Semitic Gram.* Of certain letters, etc.: Pronounced; not 'quiescent' 1837.

2. The moeuable poeple [orig. *mobile vulgus*] CHAUCER. **3.** This moveable structure of shelves COWPER. The clinical history of the movable (= FLOATING) kidney 1878. **5.** *M. feast*: an eccl. festival which, being always on the same day of the week, varies in date from year to year; also *transf.* and *joc.* Breakfast is a m. feast with us (*mod.*).

B. *sb.* **†1.** In the Ptolemaic astronomy: Any of the nine concentric revolving spheres of the heavens. Chiefly in *First* or *highest m.* = PRIMUM MOBILE. late ME. **2.** *pl.* Personal property; property that is capable of being moved, as dist. from real or fixed property (as land, houses, etc.). In *Sc.* and *Civil Law*, opp. to 'heritable' property. 1440. **3.** An article of furniture that may be removed from the building in which it is placed; opp. to *fixture.* Now chiefly in *pl.* 1523. **†4.** Something capable of being set in motion; *spec.* any part of the works of a watch –1779. **†5.** A person given to movement or change –1658.

2. *Rich. III*, III. i. 195. **3.** I wrote to you..for my movables BYRON. Hence **Movabi·lity, Mo·vableness, Mo·vably** *adv.*

Move (mūv), *sb.* 1439. [f. MOVE *v.*] **†1.** A proposal; motion (*rare*). **2.** *Chess*, etc. The moving or changing of position of a piece in the regular course of the game; the manner in which a piece is allowed to be moved; (a player's) turn to move 1656. **b.** *fig.* A device, trick; an action calculated to secure some end 1812. **3.** An act of moving from a stationary position; a beginning of movement or departure; esp. in phr. *to make a m.* 1827. **4.** A change of house or place of sojourn 1853.

2. *The m.*: the right to make the first move in the game (so in *pawn and m.* in chess, with reference to odds). **b.** *A* (*good, bad*, etc.) *m.*: a (prudent, etc.) step or proceeding. *To be up to every m. on the board*: to be cunning, smart, wide-awake, experienced. **3.** Directly there was a m., the ladies went to bed 1856. *On the m.*: travelling, moving about. *To get a m. on* (orig. *U.S.*), to hurry up.

Move (mūv), *v.* [ME. *move*, a. AF. *mover*, OF. *movoir*:—L. *movere.*] **I.** *trans.* **1.** To change the position of; to shift, remove; *occas.* to dislodge or displace (something fixed). Also *to m. away, along*, etc. **b.** *Chess*, etc. To change the position of (a piece) in course of play 1474. **c.** To bring or apply (something) *to* –1611. **†d.** To raise (one's hat, cap) or bow as a gesture of salutation –1825. Cf. II. 2 c below. **2.** To put or keep in motion; to shake, stir, or disturb. late ME. **3.** To change the position or posture of (one's body or any member). late ME. **†4.** To put forth, utter (sound) –1674. **5.** *Med.* To cause (the bowels) to act; also *absol.* Also *intr.* of the bowels = to be moved, to act. 1700. **6.** To stir up or excite (an emotion, appetite, etc.) in a person; to provoke (laughter, contradiction). late ME. **7.** To stir up, commence (strife, war, etc.). Now *rare* or *Obs.* ME. **8.** To affect with emotion; to excite *to* (laughter or tears). Often *spec.* to affect with tender or compassionate emotion. ME. **9.** To prompt, actuate, or incline *to* (an action) or *to do* (something) ME. **†10.** To urge (a person) *to* (an action) or *to do* (something); to apply or appeal to. late ME. **11.** To make a formal application, suit, or request to (the sovereign, a court, Parliament, etc.). Const. *for.* Cf. MOTION *sb.* 7 b. 1683. **†12.** To propose or suggest (something to be done); to prefer (a request); to lodge (a complaint); to propound (a question, etc.), mention (a matter). Const. *to* (a person). late ME. **13.** *spec.* **†a.** To plead (a cause) etc.) in a court; to bring (an action at law) –1641. **b.** To propose (a resolution, etc.) formally in a deliberative assembly. Also with *clause.* 1452.

1. But none myght stere the swerd nor meue hit MALORY. **b.** My liege, I m. my bishop TENNYSON. **c.** *Deut.* xxiii. 25. **2.** *To m. heaven and earth*: to make unheard-of efforts (*to do* something). **3.** She moved her lips..but could not speak T. HARDY. **6.** To moue wilde laughter in the throate of death? SHAKS. **8.** And Iesus mooued with compassion, put foorth his hand, and touched him *Mark* i. 41. Phr. *To m. to anger, wrath*, etc. **9.** What reason shou'd thy Mind to Marriage move? DRYDEN. *absol.* I feare these stubborn lines lack power to moue SHAKS. Phr. *The spirit moves me*: a phrase orig. in Quaker use, referring to the Holy Spirit; now = 'I feel impelled or in the humour (*to do* something)'. **11.** The Bank now moved the Court..for..a reversal of the verdict 1885. **13. b.** Your Lordship would undertake to m. the Address PITT. I moved first that the L. Chancellor be brought to the barre 1621.

II. *intr.* **1.** To go, advance, proceed, pass from one place to another, esp. deliberately. Also with advs., as *about, away,* etc. ME. **b.** Of an army, etc.: To go forward, march. Also, to quit one's position. ME. **c.** *transf.* late ME. **d.** *Chess,* etc. (*a*) Of a piece: To be transferred from one position to another in the course of the game; (*b*) Of a player: To make a move 1474. **e.** To change one's abode 1707. **f.** Of goods: To change hands, find buyers 1759. **2.** Of living beings: To change position or posture, to exhibit motion. Freq. with neg. = not to stir. ME. **b.** To dance. Also with cogn. obj. Now *rare.* 1594. **c.** To raise the hat, bow in salutation (now *provincial*) 1594. **3.** Of inanimate objects: To suffer change of position or posture; to be stirred. late ME. **b.** Of a piece of machinery: To turn, work, revolve. late ME. **4.** Of animate beings: To live, 'have one's being', esp. *in* a particular sphere. Also *transf.* and *fig.* of things. ME. **5.** To take action, proceed (*in* an affair). Also with cogn. obj. (fig.) *to m. a step.* late ME. †**6.** To proceed, originate *from* –1676. **7.** *To m. for*: to make a request, proposal, or application for (something) 1638.

1. Katie never ran: she moved To meet me TENNYSON. Phr. *M. on*: a policeman's order to a person who stands too long in one place; also *trans.* to order to move on. **b.** Anon they m. In perfect Phalanx to the Dorian mood MILT. **c.** Then the tale Shall m. on soberly KEATS. **e.** *To m. about,* etc., to keep changing one's abode. *To m. in,* to take possession of a new domicile. **2.** He heareth not, he stirreth not, he moueth not SHAKS. Nor would his lips M. HENLEY. **c.** At least we m. when we meet one another DICKENS. **3.** Then m. the trees, the copses nod TENNYSON. **4.** The little world in which she moved DISRAELI. **5.** God moves in a mysterious way His wonders to perform COWPER. I would urge parents to m. in the matter LUBBOCK. **7.** I moved for a physician to be sent to her from Oxford 1707. Hence **Mo·veless** *a.* having no movement; immovable, fixed 1578. **Mo·veless-ly** *adv.,* **-ness.**

Movement (mū·vmĕnt). late ME. [a. OF. *movement* (mod.F. *mouvement*), ad. med.L. *movimentum,* f. *movere*; see MOVE *v.* and -MENT. Rare between 14th and 18th c.; not in Shaks., A.V., or Milton's poetry.] **1.** The action or process of moving (see MOVE *v.*). Also, a particular act or manner of moving. **b.** *Mil.* and *Nav.* A tactical or strategical change of position 1784. **c.** Chiefly *pl.*: Actions, activities, doings of a person or body of persons 1833. **2.** *concr.* (*Mech.*) (*a*) The moving mechanism of a watch or clock; (*b*) a particular part or group of parts in a mechanism serving some special purpose 1678. **3. a.** A moving (of the mind) towards or from some object; an impulse of desire or aversion, an act of volition. Now *rare.* 1456. **b.** In a poem or narrative: Progress of incidents, development of plot; the quality of having plenty of incident, or of carrying on the interest of the reader 1838. **c.** *Fine Art.* In a painting, etc., the quality of suggesting that the figures represented are moving. Also, in *Arch.,* harmonious variety in the lines and ornamentation of a building. 1773. **4. a.** *Mus.* (*a*) The manner in which a piece or a passage moves; variously applied to melodic progression (now usu. MOTION *sb.* 10 b), 'tempo', and rhythm. (*b*) A principal division of a musical work, as a sonata or symphony, having a distinctive structure of its own. 1771. **b.** *Prosody.* Rhythmical or accentual character 1871. **5.** A series of actions and endeavours by a body of persons, tending more or less continuously towards some special end; as *the Oxford m.* (see OXFORD), *the Labour m.* 1828. **b.** *The m.* = *m. party* 1831. **c.** The way in which things are moving at a particular time or in a particular field 1846. **6.** *Comm.* Activity in the market for some commodity. Also, a rise or fall in price. 1886.

1. There was a general m. toward the door 1894. **c.** The police watched the movements of the mob (*mod.*). **3. a.** I blush'd in my turn; but from what movements I leave to the few who feel to analyse STERNE. **4. b.** The orderly and majestic m. of the Roman hexameter 1887. **5.** Oxford is the home they say of movements, and Cambridge of men 1885. Phr. *In the m.* [after F. *dans le mouvement*]: 'in the swim', in the prevalent direction or tendency of things. **6.** An upward m. in stocks 1895.

attrib. and *Comb.,* as **m. cure** = *kinesipathy* (see KINESI-); **m. party** [after F. *le parti du mouvement*], the 'liberal' or innovating party in the first half of the 19th c.

Mover (mū·vəɹ). late ME. [f. MOVE *v.* + -ER [1].] **1.** One who moves or sets in motion. Applied *esp.* to God; also *First M.* **2.** Something which sets in motion or actuates 1586. **b.** A machine or mechanical agency which imparts motion 1654. **3.** One who incites to action; one who promotes or originates (an action, etc.) 1497. **b.** One who moves a proposal in a deliberative assembly 1737. **4.** A person or thing that moves or is in motion. Now chiefly of an animal. 1592. **5.** *Chess.* With prefixed numeral, denoting a problem in which the king is to be mated in the specified number of moves 1900.

1. Oh thou eternall mouer of the heauens SHAKS. **2.** Phr. *First m.,* in mediæval astronomy = *first motor,* PRIMUM MOBILE. **b.** *First* or *prime m.*: an initial source, natural or mechanical, of motive power. **3.** Providence, which I humbly recognize as the first m. of your thoughts in my favour DE FOE. **4.** Though elegant in form, this buck is but a poor m. 1895.

Movie (mū·vi). orig. *U.S.* 1913. [f. MOV(ING *picture* + -IE, -Y [6].] A cinematograph picture: usu. *pl.* cinema pictures, 'the cinema'. *Comb.* **mo·vietone,** a form of sound-film.

Moving (mū·viŋ), *ppl. a.* late ME. [f. MOVE *v.* + -ING [2].] **a.** That moves. **b.** That originates or actuates 1489. **c.** That touches the feelings or affects the mind 1591.

a. M. picture, a cinematograph picture or film 1899. **M. plant,** the Indian plant, *Meibomia gyrans,* the leaflets of which are in constant motion. **M. staircase, stairway,** an escalator. **b.** He was a m. spirit in fun and mischief 1902. **c.** The gentle spirit of mouing words SHAKS. I..begged, by all that was m., to be delivered out of the Dungeon SWIFT. Hence **Mo·vingly** *adv.,* **-ness.**

Mow (mau), *sb.*[1] Now chiefly *dial.* or *U.S.* [OE. *mūga,* corresp. to ON. *múge* swath.] **1.** A stack of hay, corn, beans, peas, etc.; also, a heap of grain or hay in a barn. Cf. HAY-MOW. **2.** A place in a barn where hay or corn is heaped up 1755. †**3.** A heap or pile; also, a mound, hillock –1681.

Mow (mau, mōᵘ), *sb.*[2] Now *literary* or *dial.*; in Scot. pron. (mau). ME. [a. OF. *moe, moue* mouth, lip, pout (mod.F. *moue*).] A grimace; *esp.,* a derisive grimace.

Phr. *Mops and mows* (see MOP *sb.*[2]), *mocks and mows, mows and mocks.*

Mow (mōᵘ), *v.*[1] *Pa. t.* **mowed;** *pa. pple.* **mowed, mown.** [Com. WGer. vb.: OE. *māwan.* The root, OTeut. *mǣ-, pre-Teut. *mē-, occurs in MEAD, MEADOW, and in Gr. ἀμᾶν to reap.] **1.** *trans.* To cut down grass, corn, etc. in a field, etc. with a scythe or a machine: with (*a*) corn, etc. or (*b*) field, etc. as obj. **b.** *absol.* or *intr.* **2.** *transf.* and *fig.* To sweep down in battle; to destroy or kill indiscriminately or in great numbers; now usu. with *down*; also with cognate obj. ME.

1. The hay of our town is almost fit to be mowed SWIFT. **b.** Like an ill Mower, that mowes on still, and neuer whets his Syth BACON. **2.** To m. whole Troops, and make whole Armies fly POPE. The rifle mowed them down as they approached 1884.

Mow (mau), *v.*[2] Now *dial.* late ME. [f. MOW *sb.*[1]] *trans.* To put in mows. Also with *up.*

Mow (mau, mōᵘ), *v.*[3] late ME. [f. MOW *sb.*[2]] *intr.* To make mouths or grimaces.

Mowburn (mōᵘ·bɒɹn), *v.* 1707. [Back-formation from next.] *intr.* Of hay, corn, etc.: To heat and ferment through being stacked too green.

Mow·burnt, *a.* 1548. [f. MOW *sb.*[1] + BURNT *ppl. a.*] Of hay, corn, etc.: Spoilt by becoming overheated in the mow.

Mowe, obs. f. MAY *v.*[1], MEW *sb.*[2], MOVE *v.,* MOW.

Mower (mōᵘ·əɹ). late ME. [f. MOW *v.*[1] + -ER [1].] **1.** One who cuts grass, etc. with a scythe. **2.** A mowing-machine 1852.

Mowing (mōᵘ·iŋ), *vbl. sb.* 1494. [f. MOW *v.*[1] + -ING [1].] **1.** The action of MOW *v.*[1] **b.** *concr.* The quantity of grass cut at one time; also *pl.* grass removed by mowing 1764. **2.** *U.S.* Land on which grass is grown for hay 1786.

attrib. and *Comb.,* as *m.-machine,* etc.; **m. grass,** grass reserved for mowing.

Mown (mōᵘn), *ppl. a.* OE. [pa. pple. of MOW *v.*[1]] Cut down with a scythe or mowing-machine. Cf. NEW-MOWN.

Moxa (mǫ·ksă). 1677. [a. Jap. *mokusa* (phonetically mǫ·ksa), contr. f. *moe kusa* burning herb.] **1.** The downy covering of the dried leaves of *Artemisia Moxa*; esp. as prepared for burning on the skin as a counter-irritant for gout, etc. Also, the plant. **2.** Any substance used like moxa for burning on the skin 1833.

‖**Moya** (mōᵘ·ya). 1830. [Name of a former mountain near Quito.] *Geol.* Volcanic mud.

Moyen (moi·ĕn), *sb.* and *a.* *Obs.* exc. *Sc.* 1440. [a. OF. *moyen,* var. *meien* MEAN *a.*[2]] **A.** *sb.* A means; means, resources; mediation; instrumentality. †**B.** *adj.* Middle 1481–1550.

Moyl(e: see MOIL, MULE.

Mozarab (mozæ·răb). Also **Mozarabe, Muzarab.** 1753. [a. Sp. *Mozárabe,* corrupt form of an Arabic word meaning 'would-be Arab'.] *Hist.* In Spain under Moorish rule: One of those Christians who, on condition of owning allegiance to the Moorish king, and conforming to certain Moorish customs, were allowed the exercise of their own religion. So †**Mozarabite** 1537. **Moza·rabic** *a.* 1706.

Moze (mōᵘz), *v.* 1505. [?] = GIG *v.*[3]

Mozzetta, mozetta (moze·tă, ‖ mǫtse̜tta). 1774. [It. *mozzetta,* dim. of *mozza*; see AMICE [2].] *Eccl.* A cape with a small hood, worn by the Pope and other dignitaries of the R. C. Ch.

M.P. 1809. Abbrev. for 'Member of Parliament'. Pl. *M.P.'s,* occas. *M.P.s.*

Mr. 1447. [Orig. an abbrev. of MASTER.] †**1.** In the 16th and 17th c. used for MASTER –1674. **2.** As a prefixed title, now pronounced (mi·stəɹ), or (mistəɹ, m'stəɹ). The regular abbrev. of MISTER *sb.*[2] 1, which is now used only occas. (chiefly *joc.*). For pl. *Messrs.,* MESSIEURS 2, is used. 1447. **b.** Prefixed to a foreign name. Now *rare.* 1601.

1. I refused the Title of Mr. of Arts 1674. **2.** All the lettres of M[r]. Secretary 1524. 'Mr. Justice —', the style of a Judge of the Supreme Court. Mr. Chairman, Mr. President, Mr. Mayor, etc., forms used now only vocatively.

Mrs. 1582. [Orig. an abbrev. of MISTRESS.] †**1.** In the 17th c. often written for MISTRESS –1679. **2.** As a prefixed title of courtesy. Now pronounced (mi·sis, mi·siz); cf. MISSIS. **a.** Prefixed to the surname of a married woman who has no superior title 1582. †**b.** In the 17th and 18th c. prefixed to the name of an unmarried lady or girl –1791.

MS., abbrev. of L. *manu scriptum* MANUSCRIPT.

Often pron. (em es), e.g. [He] drew forth an MS. (Byron).

MSS., used (1) as pl. of prec., and (2) as adj. in concord with a pl. sb.; (3) erron. for MS.

Mt., abbrev. of MOUNT *sb.*[1]

Mucate (miū·kĕt). 1815. [see -ATE [1] 1 c.] *Chem.* A salt of mucic acid.

Mucedin (miū·sidin, miusī·din). 1871. [f. L. *mucedo* mucus (in mod.L. 'mould') + -IN [1].] *Chem.* A nitrogenous substance, one of the constituents of gluten. So **Mucedinous** (-se·d-) *a. Bot.* having the character of mould or mildew 1857.

Much (mɒtʃ), *a.,* quasi-*sb.,* and *adv.* [Early ME. *muche, moche, meche, miche,* shortened from *muchel, mochel, mechel, michel*; see MICKLE.] **A.** *adj.* †**1.** = GREAT *a.,* in various applications –1697. **2.** A great quantity or amount of, existing or present in great quantity ME. **3.** With agent-noun: that is much in the habit of performing the action 1711.

1. *M. Burstead, M. Wenlock,* names of English villages. †*M. deal*: a great part; also *advb.* largely. **2.** There is m. truth in that remark of yours JOWETT. A pale yellow sun..showed the m. dirt of the place KIPLING. Phr. *M.* (ironically, = *no*) *good may it do you. Too m.*: see TOO. **3.** Your long and m. talkers hated him LAMB.

B. *absol.* and quasi-*sb.* †**1.** Used *absol.* in the sense 'great'. Only in *m. and lite, m. and little* = all (people) without exception. ME. only. **2.** A great deal, a great quantity. Provb. *M. will have more.* ME.

2. He who drinks m. is a Slave to himself 1710.

There was room for m. of thoughtful consultation FREEMAN. Phr. *By m.*: by a great deal. *To think m. of*: see THINK *v.* *To make m. of*: see MAKE *v.* II. 9, III. 2. *To be m.*: chiefly neg., (not) to be important or conspicuous, esp. in a specified relation. It was also m., that one that was so great a Louer of Peace should bee so happy in Warre BACON. *Not to be m. to look at*: to be of unattractive appearance. You are not m. to look at DICKENS. *To think (it) m.* (with *inf.*): to regard as important or onerous; to be shy of (doing something).

C. *adv.* **1.** In a great degree; to a great extent; greatly ME. **b.** = VERY. *Obs.* exc. with *like*. 1449. **c.** Used ironically for 'not at all' 1590. **d.** *Not much*: not likely, certainly not (*colloq.*). **2.** Pretty nearly 1560. **3.** For a large part of one's time 1755.

1. For my part, I don't m. like it GOLDSM. 2. *M. as, m. of an age, of a muchness, of a size, of a piece.* All of them left the World m. as they found it TEMPLE. It was m. about that time 1704.

Muchel(e, etc.: see MICKLE, etc.

Muchly (mɒ·tʃli), *adv.* Now *joc.* 1621. [f. MUCH *a.* + -LY².] Much, exceedingly.

Muchness (mɒ·tʃnĕs). late ME. [f. MUCH *a.* + -NESS.] †**1.** Large size or bulk; also, size, magnitude (large or small) –1631. **2.** Greatness in quantity, number, or degree. late ME.

Phr. *Much of a m.*: much of the same importance or value; very much alike (*colloq.*).

†**Mu·chwhat**, *sb.* and *adv.* ME. [f. MUCH *adv.* + WHAT *pron.*] **a.** *sb.* Many matters. **b.** *adv.* Greatly; nearly, almost; just; pretty much, pretty well –1701 (very common in 17th c.).

b. Much-what in like manner as before GLANVILL.

Mucic (miū·sik), *a.* 1809. [a. F. *mucique*, f. L. *mucus*; see MUCUS and -IC.] *Chem.* In *m. acid*: an acid formed by the action of dilute nitric acid upon various kinds of gum. *M. ether*, an ether obtained from *m. acid*.

Mucid (miū·sid), *a. rare.* 1656. [ad. L. *mucidus*, f. *mucere* to be mouldy.] Mouldy, musty. So **Mu·cidous** *a.* 1866.

Muciferous (miusi·fĕrəs), *a.* 1842. [f. L. *mucus* + *-fer* bearing + -OUS; see -FEROUS.] Secreting or conveying mucus. So **Muci·fic** *a.* producing mucus 1848. **Mu·ciform** *a.* resembling mucus 1848.

Mucigen (miū·sidʒĕn). 1876. [f. L. *mucus* + -GEN.] *Chem.* The substance of the granules forming a mucous cell.

Mucigenous (miusi·dʒĕnəs), *a.* 1886. [f. as prec. + -OUS.] **a.** Producing mucus. **b.** Of the nature of mucigen.

Mucilage (miū·silĕdʒ). late ME. [a. F. *mucilage*, ad. late L. *mucilago* musty juice, f. L. *mucus*.] **1.** A viscous substance obtained from the roots, seeds, etc., of plants by maceration in water. Also *pl.* in same sense. **b.** *transf.* A viscous mass, a pulp 1657. **c.** *spec.* Chiefly *U.S.* The adhesive in England commonly called 'gum' 1880. **2.** A viscous lubricating fluid (e.g. mucus, synovia) in animal bodies 1600. **3.** *Bot.* A gummy secretion present in various parts of vegetable organisms 1677. **Mu·cilage** *v.* to stick with or as with m.

Mucilaginous (miūsilæ·dʒinəs), *a.* 1646. [See MUCILAGE and -OUS.] **1.** Having the nature or properties of mucilage; soft, moist, and viscous. Also, pertaining to or characteristic of mucilage. **2.** Containing or secreting mucilage 1689.

2. *M. glands*: the fringed vascular folds of the synovial membrane. **Mucila·ginous·ly** *adv.*, **-ness.**

Mucin (miū·sin). Also **-ine.** 1846. [a. F. *mucine*, f. L. *mucus* MUCUS; see -IN¹.] *Phys.* The nitrogenous principle of mucus. Hence **Mu·cinous** *a.*

Mucinogen (miusi·nŏdʒĕn). 1886. [f. MUCIN + -(O)GEN.] *Phys.* = MUCIGEN.

Muciparous (miusi·părəs), *a.* 1835. [See MUCUS and -PAROUS.] Producing mucus.

Muck (mɒk), *sb.*¹ [ME. *muk*, prob. of Scand. origin. Cf. ON. vb. *moka*: see MUCK *v.*] **1.** Farmyard manure. Now chiefly *dial.* †**2.** *fig.* Contemptuously applied to money –1710. **3.** Unclean and soiling matter; dirt, filth; also, anything disgusting. Now *colloq.* late ME. **4.** *dial.* or *colloq.* An uncleanly or untidy condition 1766. **5.** *attrib.*, as *m. cart*, etc.

2. Moyling for mucke and trash 1633. 3. The m. doctors give you 1899. *fig.* You rank stark M. o' th' World DRYDEN.

Comb.: **m.-bar**, iron roughly shaped into bars by being passed once through the rolls; **-iron**, crude puddled iron ready for squeezing or rolling; **-wet** *a.* wet as m.

Muck (mɒk), *sb.*² 1687. [The second syllable of AMUCK taken erron. as a sb.] In *to run a m.* = 'to run AMUCK'. Hence, an act of running amuck.

Muck, *v.* late ME. [f. MUCK *sb.*¹ Cf. ON. *moka* to shovel (manure).] **1.** *trans.* To free from muck. **2.** To dress with muck, to manure 1440. **3.** *trans.* To make dirty; to soil. Now *vulgar.* 1832. **b.** *fig. slang.* To make a 'mess' of 1899.

Phr. *To m. about*: to go aimlessly about (*colloq.*).

Muckender (mɒ·kĕndəɹ). *Obs.* exc. *dial.* late ME. [In 15th c. *mokedore*, prob. an Occitanian dial. equivalent of F. *mouchoir*.] A handkerchief. †Also, a table-napkin; a bib.

†**Mu·cker**, *sb.*¹ 1483. [f. MUCK *v.* + -ER¹.] **1.** A scavenger –1790. **2.** A money-grubber –1584.

Mucker (mɒ·kəɹ), *sb.*² *slang.* 1852. [f. MUCK *sb.*¹ + -ER¹.] A heavy fall, as in the muck: a 'cropper'.

To come, go a m.: chiefly *fig.*, to come to grief.

Mucker (mɒ·kəɹ), *sb.*³ *U.S. slang.* 1890. [Prob. a. G. *mucker* sulky person, etc.] **a.** A fanatic or hypocrite. **b.** A rough, coarse person.

Mucker (mɒ·kəɹ), *v.*¹ *Obs.* exc. *dial.* ME. [?f. MUCK *sb.*¹ + -ER⁵.] *trans.* To hoard (money, goods). Hence **Mu·ckerer.**

Mucker (mɒ·kəɹ), *v.*² *slang.* 1861. [f. MUCKER *sb.*²] **a.** *intr.* To 'come a mucker'; to come to grief. **b.** *trans.* To ruin (one's chances).

†**Mu·ckibus.** *vulgar.* [Joc. formation from MUCK *sb.*¹] Tipsy, fuddled. H. WALPOLE.

Muckle, dial. var. of MICKLE.

Mu·ckna. 1780. [Hindustani.] A male elephant without, or with only rudimentary tusks.

Mu·ck-rake, *sb.* 1684. A rake for collecting muck. In literary use only *fig.* (after Bunyan *Pilgr.*). **Mu·ck-rake** *v. intr.*, **-raker.**

Mucksy (mɒ·ksi), *a. dial.* 1666. [f. MUCK *sb.*¹ + -SY (cf. *tricksy*, etc.).] Mucky, dirty.

Mu·ckworm. 1598. [f. MUCK *sb.*¹ + WORM.] **1.** A worm or grub that lives in muck. **2.** *fig.* in various applications; *esp.* **a.** a money-grubber 1598; **b.** = GUTTER-SNIPE 2 b. 1859.

Mucky (mɒ·ki), *a.* 1538. [f. MUCK *sb.*¹ + -Y¹.] **1.** Dirty, filthy, muddy. †**b.** *fig.* Applied to money, also to a miserly person –1652. **2.** Consisting of or resembling muck 1570.

1. b. Mynded to prefer oure muckye monie.. before the ioyse of heauen LATIMER. Hence **Mu·ckiness.**

Muco- (miū·ko), used as comb. f. MUCUS, to indicate the presence of mucous matter. **Mu·cocele** *Path.*, a mucous dilatation of the lachrymal gland or of the vermiform appendix. **Muco·pu·rulent** *a.*, of the nature of, characterized by the presence of, both mucus and pus.

Mucoid (miū·koid), *a.* 1849. [f. MUCUS + -OID.] Resembling mucus.

M. degeneration: transformation of cells or intercellular substance into a substance containing mucin.

‖**Mucor** (miū·kɒɹ). 1818. [L., f. *mucere* to be mouldy.] *Bot.* A plant belonging or allied to the genus *Mucor* of fungi, orig. including all the mould-plants.

Mucoso- (miukōᵘ·so), comb. f. L. *mucosus* mucous in adjs. with sense 'partly mucus and partly —', as **m.-calca·reous** *a.*, consisting of mucus and lime; etc.

Mucous (miū·kəs), *a.* 1646. [ad. L. *mucosus*, f. *mucus*; see -OUS.] **1.** Containing, consisting of, or resembling mucus; slimy. **2.** Characterized by the presence of mucus 1825. **3.** *Bot.* Covered with a viscous secretion or with a coat readily soluble in water 1839.

2. *M. râle*, a sound indicating a m. condition of the lungs.

Spec. collocations: **M. membrane**, the lining membrane of those cavities of the body which communicate with the exterior, continuous with the skin and secreting a fluid containing mucus. **M. tissue**, gelatinous connective tissue. **Muco·sity** 1684.

‖**Mucro** (miū·kro). *Pl.* **mucrones** (miukrōᵘ·nīz), **mucros.** 1646. [L. *mucro* point.] *Zool.* and *Bot.* A sharp point or process, as of a leaf or shell.

Mucronate (miū·krŏnĕt), *a.* 1776. [ad. L. *mucronatus*, f. *mucronem* MUCRO; see -ATE².] Terminating in a point; esp. *Bot.* abruptly terminated by a hard short point. So **Mu·cronated** *a.* 1657. Hence **Mu·cronately** *adv.*

Mucronulate (miukrɒ·niŭlĕt), *a.* 1829. [ad. mod.L. *mucronulatus*, f. *mucronula*, f. L. *mucron-* MUCRO.] Having a small sharp point. **Mucro·nulated, Mucro·nulatous** *adjs.*

Muculent (miū·kiŭlĕnt), *a.* 1656. [ad. L. *muculentus*, f. *mucus* MUCUS; see -ULENT.] Slimy, mucous.

Mucus (miū·kɒs). 1661. [a. L. *mucus* mucus of the nose, cogn. w. Gr. μύσσεσθαι, μυκτήρ nose, nostril; cf. L. *emungere*.] **1.** A viscid or slimy substance not miscible with water, secreted by the mucous membrane of animals. **2.** *Bot.* A gummy or glutinous substance soluble in water; found in all plants 1839. **3.** A viscid substance exuded by certain animals, esp. the slime of fishes 1835. **4.** *attrib.*, as *m. duct*, etc. 1835.

Mud (mɒd), *sb.*¹ [ME. *mode*, *mudde*, cogn. w. MLG., LG. *mudde*.] **1.** Wet and soft soil or earthy matter; mire, sludge. **b.** *pl.* Tracts of mud on the margin of a tidal river 1883. **c.** *Geol.* A mixture of finely comminuted particles of rock with water, of varying consistency; usu. either deposited from suspension in water, or ejected from volcanoes. Also *pl.* kinds of mud. 1878. **2.** *fig.* **a.** As a type of what is worthless or polluting 1563. †**b.** The lowest or worst part of anything; the lowest stratum; the dregs –1856.

1. b. Herons—which feed on the muds left by the tide 1897. 2. b. Defoe said in his wrath, 'the Englishman was the m. of all races' EMERSON. Phr. *As clear as m.*: said in mockery of something by no means clear. *To fling* or *throw m.*: to make disgraceful imputations. *To stick in the m.*: see STICK *v.*¹

attrib. and *Comb.* **1.** General: as, *m. colour*; *m.-exhausted*, etc., adjs.; *m.-slinging*, *-throwing*.

2. Special: **m.-bath**, a medicinal bath of heated m.; **-boat**, (*a*) a board with sides, used for crossing tidal m. for the purpose of shooting sea-birds; (*b*) a barge for carrying away m. dredged from a river or bar; **-drum**, a cylindrical chamber attached to a boiler to collect the sediment and mud in the water for removal; **-flat**, a stretch of muddy land left uncovered at low tide; **mudguard**, a guard over the wheel of a cycle or other vehicle, serving as a protection against m.; **-lava**, volcanic m. (= MOYA); **m. pie**, m. or wet earth formed by children in the shape of a pie; **-quake** *joc.*, an earthquake in Holland (H. WALPOLE); **-scow**, a flat mud-boat; **m. sill**, the lowest sill of a structure, usually embedded in the soil; hence *fig.* (*U.S.*) a person of the lowest class of society; **-stone** *Geol.* shale readily reduced to mud by the action of frost; **m. volcano**, a volcano which discharges m. instead of lava.

b. In names of animals: **m. bass**, a small freshwater sun-fish (*Acantharchus pomotis*) of U.S.; **m.-cat, catfish** *U.S.*, names given to several species of catfish; **m. crab**, a crab of the genus *Panopæus*; **m. dab**, the winter flounder, *Pseudopleuronectes americanus*; **-dauber**, a wasp of the genus *Pelopæus* that builds its nest of m.; **-devil** = HELLBENDER 1; **m. eel** = *mud iguana*; **-hen**, a moor-hen, rail, gallinule, or coot; **m. iguana**, the siren, *Siren lacertina*; **m. minnow**, any fish of the family *Umbridæ*; **m. puppy** *U.S.*, the axolotl, the hellbender, and other salamanders; **-terrapin, -tortoise, -turtle** *U.S.*, a turtle which lives in the m. or muddy water, esp. species of *Trionychidæ* and *Emydidæ*; **-worm**, a worm that lives in the m., *esp.* one of the *Limicolæ*; also *fig.* applied contemptuously to a person.

c. In names of plants: **m.-rush, -sedge**, various cyperaceous plants; **-wort**, any herb of the genus *Limosella*, esp. *L. aquatica*.

Mud (mɒd), *sb.*² 1477. [a. Du. *mudde*, *mud*; see MODIUS.] A Du. measure of capacity, a hectolitre.

Mud (mɒd), *v.* Now *rare.* 1593. [f. MUD *sb.*¹] **1.** *trans.* To make (water, liquor) turbid by stirring up the mud or sediment at the bottom. Also *fig.* **2.** To cover or plaster with mud 1632. **3.** To bury in mud. SHAKS. **4.** *intr.* Of eels, etc.: To lie dormant in the mud 1606.

Mudar, madar (mɒdā·ɹ). 1819. [a. Hindī *madār*.] **a.** E. Indian name for shrubs of the genus *Calotropis*, esp. *C. gigantea*, the root-bark of which yields a diaphoretic medicine and the inner bark of the stem a strong silky fibre known as yercum. **b.** The medicinal product of the root. Hence **Mu·darine**, a bitter principle obtained from the root-bark of the m.

Muddle (mɒ·d'l), *sb.* 1818. [f. MUDDLE *v.*] **1.** A muddled condition; confusion; intellectual bewilderment. Also, a bungle, mess. **2.** A confused assemblage 1865.

1. *To make a m. of*: to bungle.

Muddle (mɒ·d'l), *v.* 1596. [f. MUD *sb.*[1] or *v.*; see -LE.] **1.** *intr.* To bathe or wallow in mud or muddy water. *Obs.* exc. *arch.* 1607. **b.** To grub in the soil; to do dirty work; also †*fig.* (*rare*) 1756. **2.** *trans.* To make muddy. Now *rare.* 1624. **b.** *transf.* To destroy the clearness of (colours) 1596. **3.** To confuse, bewilder, esp. with drink. Also, to render (speech) confused or indistinct. 1687. **4.** To mix up blunderingly, to confuse *together* 1836. **b.** To bungle, mismanage (an affair); also, to render (accounts) unintelligible by want of method 1885. **5.** *intr.* To busy oneself in a confused, unmethodical, and ineffective manner 1806. **6.** *trans.* with *away.* To waste, get rid of (money, time, etc.) without clearly knowing how 1827.

2. Where they mudled the Water and Fished after MARVELL. 3. Their old Master seems to have had his Brains so muddled BENTLEY. 4. My Critic has muddled it together in a most extraordinary manner J. H. NEWMAN. 5. He meddled or rather muddled with literature W. IRVING.

Phr. *To m. about*: to potter about, busy oneself aimlessly. *To m. on*: to get along in a haphazard way through makeshifts. *To m. through*: to attain one's end in spite of blunder upon blunder. Hence **Mu·ddler** 1884.

Mu·ddle-hea·ded, *a.* 1759. [f. MUDDLE *sb.* or *v.*] Having a muddled head; characteristic of one with a muddled head; stupid, confused. So **Mu·ddle-head**, a m. person. **Muddlehea·dedness.**

Muddy (mɒ·di), *a.* late ME. [f. MUD *sb.*[1] + -Y[1].] **1.** Abounding in mud; turbid or foul with mud; covered or bespattered with mud 1526; resembling mud 1737. **2.** Living or growing in mud 1598. **3.** Of a liquid: Not clear, thick, turbid 1618. **4.** *transf.* **a.** Not clear in colour. Of light: Dull, smoky. 1590. **b.** Of the voice: Thick 1841. **5.** Not clear in mind; muddled 1611. **6.** Of style, thought, etc.: Obscure, vague, confused 1611. **7.** Morally impure or dirty. Now *rare.* late ME.

1. M. marysshes 1555. 2. M. weeds SHELLEY. 3. M. coffee and scorched toast MRS. CARLYLE. 5. Cold hearts and m. understandings BURKE. 6. The present m. French transcendentalism THACKERAY. 7. She is a muddie queane, a filthy beast 1603. Hence **Mu·ddily** *adv.* **Mu·ddiness.**

Muddy (mɒ·di), *v.* 1601. [f. MUDDY *a.*] To make or become muddy.

Mu·d-fish. 1502. Any of several fishes which frequent muddy water or burrow in the mud; *esp.* the common European loach, bowfin, lepidosiren, and mud minnow.

‖**Mudir** (mudīə·ɪ). 1864. [Turk. use of Arab. *mudīr*, active pple. of *adāra* to govern.] In Turkey, the governor of a village or canton; in Egypt, the governor of a province.

Hence **Mudi·rate**, ‖**Mudi·rieh**, the territory, also the official head-quarters, of a m.

Mudlark (mɒ·dlāɹk). 1796. [f. MUD *sb.*[1] + LARK *sb.*[1]] **1.** *colloq.* One who dabbles, works, or lives in mud; *esp.* a gutter-child, street arab. **2.** A pipit (*local*) 1882.

‖**Muezzin** (mu,e·zin). Also **mueddin**, etc. 1585. [Arab. *mu'aððin*, active pple. of *aððana*, freq. of *aðana* to proclaim, f. *uðn* ear.] In Mohammedan countries, a public crier who proclaims the regular hours of prayer (cf. MINARET).

†**Muff**, *sb.*[1] 1590. [a. Du. *mof*, contempt. name for a Westphalian.] A depreciative term for a German or Swiss -1656.

Muff (mɒf), *sb.*[2] 1599. [Prob. a. Du. *mof*, a. F. *moufle*; cf. MUFFLE *sb.*[1]] **1.** A covering (usu. of fur and of cylindrical shape) into which both hands are thrust from opposite ends to keep them warm. A similar covering for the feet (*foot-m.*). †**2.** = MITTEN 2. -1749. **3.** A tuft of feathers on the head of some domestic fowls 1809. **4.** *techn.* **a.** *Glass-manuf.* A cylinder of blown glass for flattening out into a plate 1875. **b.** *Mech.* A short hollow cylinder surrounding an object, or used to connect two adjoining pipes 1875.

Muff (mɒf), *sb.*[3] *colloq.* 1837. [?] **1.** Orig., one who is awkward or stupid in some athletic sport. Hence = DUFFER *sb.*[2] 1. **2.** [Prob. from MUFF *v.*[1]] A failure; anything bungled; *spec.* in any game at ball, failure to hold a ball that comes into one's hands 1871.

1. A tremendous m. in the hunting-field 1880. Hence **Mu·ffish** *a.* **Mu·ffism.**

Muff (mɒf), *sb.*[4] *dial.* 1831. [Perh. a use of MUFF *sb.*[2]] The whitethroat, *Sylvia cinerea.*

Muff, *v.*[1] *colloq.* and *slang.* 1841. [f. MUFF *sb.*[3]] *trans.* To make a muddle or mess of, to bungle; to miss (a catch or ball) at cricket, etc. Also *intr.*, to miss catches, to act bunglingly.

Muff, *v.*[2] 1868. *trans.* = MUFFLE *v.* 5.

Muffetee (mɒfĕtī·). 1706. [app. irreg. f. MUFF *sb.*[2]] **1.** A muffler worn round the neck. *Obs.* exc. *dial.* **2.** A worsted cuff worn on the wrist 1808.

Muffin (mɒ·fin). 1703. [?] **1.** A light, flat, circular, spongy cake, eaten toasted and buttered at breakfast or tea. Formerly (now *dial.*) applied to other kinds of tea-cake. **2.** A kind of flat earthenware or china plate 1864.

Comb.: **m.-bell**, the bell rung by a muffin-man; **-face** *slang*, an expressionless countenance; **-man**, a man who sells muffins. Hence **Muffinee·r**, a small castor with a perforated top for sprinkling sugar or salt on muffins; also, a covered dish to keep muffins hot 1806.

Muffle (mɒ·f'l), *sb.*[1] 1570. [In branch I. app. f. MUFFLE *v.*; in II. and III. a. F. *moufle.*] **I. 1.** = MUFFLER 1 a. *rare.* **2.** Something that muffles or deadens sound 1734. **3.** Muffling effect; muffled sound 1886. **II.** A receptacle, placed within a furnace, for heating substances without exposure to the direct action of the fire; spec. in *Chem.*, *Metall.*, and *Ceramics* 1644. **III. 1.** = MUFFLER 2 a. 1747. **2.** = MITTEN 1 and 2. 1808.

Mu·ffle, *sb.*[2] 1601. [a. F. *mufle*, of unkn. origin.] The thick part of the upper lip and nose of ruminants and rodents.

Muffle (mɒ·f'l), *v.* late ME. [app. aphetic a. OF. *emmoufler*, f. *en-* + *moufle* thick glove, MUFFLE *sb.*[1]] **1.** *trans.* To wrap or cover up or enfold esp. so as to conceal, also for warmth and protection from the weather. †**2.** To prevent from seeing by covering up the head (or eyes); to blindfold; also *fig.* -1700. **3.** To restrain (a person) from speaking by wrapping up his head 1570. **4.** To wrap up (oars, a drum, bell, etc.) so as to deaden the sound 1761. **b.** To deaden (a sound). Chiefly in *passive.* 1832. **5.** To render (glass) semi-opaque by giving it a crinkled surface 1908.

1. The Duke of Suffolk, muffled vp in ragges? SHAKS. *fig.* M. your false loue with some shew of blindnesse SHAKS. 4. The drums were muffled with black cloth 1806. **b.** The panther's roar came muffled TENNYSON.

Muffler (mɒ·flər). 1535. [f. prec. + -ER[1].] **1. a.** A sort of kerchief or scarf formerly worn by women to cover part of the face and the neck. *Obs.* exc. *Hist.* †**b.** A bandage for blindfolding a person -1621. **c.** A wrap or scarf (usu. of wool or silk) worn round the neck for warmth 1594. **d.** *fig.* Something that muffles or disguises 1633. **2. a.** A boxing-glove 1755. **b.** A glove or mitten 1824. **c.** A leather glove for lunatics who tear up their clothes. DICKENS. **3.** Something to deaden sound; *spec.* a piece of mechanism to deaden the noise of escaping gases, etc., a silencer; in a pianoforte, a felt strip which is inserted between the hammers and strings by depressing the soft pedal 1856.

1. Mufflers.., which they call Masks 1694. **b.** *Hen. V*, III. vi. 33. **c.** Very unwell. Went to meeting with my m. 1787.

‖ **Mufti**[1] (mɒ·fti). 1586. [Arab. *muftī*, active pple. of *aftā* to give a FETWA or decision on a point of law.] A Mohammedan priest or expounder of the law; in Turkey restricted to the official head of the religion of the state (formerly often †*Grand M.*) and his deputies.

Mufti[2] (mɒ·fti). 1816. [perh. facetious use of prec.] **1.** Plain clothes worn by any one who has a right to wear a uniform; esp. *in m.* **2.** A civilian; one who wears mufti 1833.

Mug (mɒg), *sb.*[1] 1570. [cf. Sw. *mugg*, Norw. *mugge, mugga.*] **1.** *dial.* Any (large) earthenware vessel or bowl; also, a pot, jug, or ewer. **2.** A drinking-vessel, usu. cylindrical, with or without a handle 1664. **b.** A mug with its contents; the liquid in a mug 1682. **3.** A cooling drink 1633.

Mug (mɒg), *sb.*[2] *slang.* 1708. [perh. a use of prec.] The face or mouth.

Mug (mɒg), *sb.*[3] *slang.* 1859. A stupid person; a muff, duffer; a card-sharper's dupe.

Mug (mɒg), *sb.*[4] *slang.* 1853. [f. MUG *v.*[3]] **1.** An examination. **2.** One who mugs or reads hard 1888.

Mug, *v.*[1] *dial.* ME. [Cf. Norw. *mugga.*] To drizzle.

Mug, *v.*[2] *slang.* 1855. [f. MUG *sb.*[2]] *Theatr.* **a.** *intr.* To 'make a face'; to grimace. **b.** *To m. up*: to paint one's face; to make up.

Mug, *v.*[3] *slang.* 1848. *intr.* To read hard, to 'grind'; *trans.* to get *up* (a subject).

‖**Mugger** (mɒ·gəɹ). Also **-ur, -ar.** 1844. [Hindī *magar.*] The broad-nosed crocodile of India.

Mugget (mɒ·gĕt). *Obs.* exc. *dial.* 1481. [?] The intestines of a calf or sheep, as an article of food; †a dish made of these -1677.

Muggins (mɒ·ginz). 1865. [perh. the surname *Muggins*, with allusion to MUG *sb.*[3]] **1.** *slang.* A fool, simpleton 1873. **2. a.** A children's game of cards 1865. **b.** A game of dominoes in which the players count by fives 1881.

Mu·ggish, *a. rare.* 1655. [cf. MUG *v.*[1]] Damp, musty.

Muggletonian (mɒg'l,tōu·niăn). 1670. [f. *Muggleton* + -IAN.] **A.** *sb.* A member of the sect founded *c* 1651 by Lodowicke Muggleton and John Reeve, who claimed to be the 'two witnesses' of Rev. xi. 3–6. **B.** *adj.* Belonging to this sect.

Muggy (mɒ·gi), *a.* 1731. [f. MUG *v.*[1] + -Y[1].] **1.** Mouldy, moist, damp, wet. *Obs.* exc. *dial.* **2.** Of weather, a day, etc.: Damp, close and warm 1746. **b.** Stifling 1820.

2. Weather quite m. MISS BURNEY. **b.** The 'muggy' smell so generally noticeable in lodging-houses and barrack-rooms 1906. Hence **Mu·gginess.**

Mu·g-house. 1685. [MUG *sb.*[1]] An ale-house, beer-house.

Mugient (miū·dʒiĕnt), *a. rare.* 1646. [ad. L. *mugientem.*] Lowing, bellowing. Hence †**Mu·giency**, a bellowing 1646.

Mugweed (mɒ·gwīd). *dial.* late ME. [f. *mug-* (in MUGWORT) + WEED.] **a.** Mugwort, *Artemisia vulgaris.* **b.** Crosswort, *Galium Cruciata*; also *golden m.*

Mugwort (mɒ·gwɒɹt). [OE. *mu(c)gwyrt* repr. WGer. **muggiwurti*, f. **mugjo-* fly, MIDGE + **wurti-* plant, WORT.] **1.** The plant *Artemisia vulgaris*, formerly also called *motherwort.* Also applied to wormwood, *A. Absinthium*, etc. **2.** = MUGWEED **b.** 1796.

Mugwump (mɒ·gwɒmp), *sb. U.S.* 1832. [a. Natick *mugquomp* great chief.] **1.** *joc.* A great man, a 'boss'. **2.** An Independent in politics; *spec.* a Republican who refused to support the nominee of the party for president in the 1884 election. Hence **Mu·gwump** *v. intr.* to play the part of a m. **Mu·gwumpery, Mu·gwumpism. Mu·gwumpish** *a.*

Muhammad, etc.: var. MOHAMMED, etc.

Muir, Sc. var. of MOOR *sb.*[1]

Mulatto (miulæ·to). 1595. [a. Sp. (and Pg.) *mulato* young mule, hence, one of a mixed race, obscurely f. *mulo* MULE[1].] **A.** *sb.* One who is the offspring of a European and a Negro; hence, any half-breed resembling a mulatto. **B.** *adj.* Belonging to the class of mulattos; of the colour of a m.; tawny 1622. So †**Mula·tta** [a. Sp. *mulata*] 1622–1828. **Mula·tress** [ad. F. *mulâtresse*], a female m. 1845.

Mulberry (mɒ·lbĕri). [late ME. *mulberie*, earlier *murberie*, OE. *mōrberige*, corresp. to OHG. *môr-*, *mûrberi*, *mûlberia* (G. *maulbeere*); f. L. *morum* mulberry + BERRY *sb.*[1]] **1.** The fruit of any tree of the genus *Morus*, *esp.* the

Black Mulberry, *M. nigra*; also, the tree. **2.** Applied to plants or trees of other genera; e.g. the Blackberry. Also PAPER-*m.* 1672. **3.** A dark purple colour like that of mulberries. Also as *adj.* = m.-coloured. 1837.

3. If ever there was a wolf in a m. suit, that ere Job Trotter 's him DICKENS.

Comb.: *m.-faced*, etc.; also **m. bush,** a children's game, with a ditty 'Here we go round the mulberry-bush'; **m. germ, mass** = MORULA; **m. rash,** a name given to the rash of typhus fever.

Mulch (mɒlʃ), *sb.* 1657. [cf. G. dial. *molsch* soft, beginning to decay.] Half-rotten straw; in *Gardening*, a mixture of wet straw, leaves, loose earth, etc., spread on the ground to protect the roots of newly planted trees, etc. Hence **Mulch** *v. trans.* to cover with m. 1802.

Mulct (mɒlkt), *sb.* 1591. [ad. L. *mulcta, multa.*] **1.** A fine imposed for an offence. Also *occas.* a compulsory payment. **2.** A penalty of any kind 1619. Hence †**Mu·lctary** *a.* of the nature of a fine 1695. †**Mu·lctuary** *a.* that punishes by a fine; punishable by a fine 1613–89.

Mulct (mɒlkt), *v.* 1483. [ad. L. *mulctare, multare*, f. *mulcta, multa* MULCT *sb.*] **1.** *trans.* To punish (a person, †an offence) by a fine. †Also *occas.* to subject to a penalty of any kind. **2.** To deprive or divest *of* 1748.

Mule[1] (miūl). [In OE. *mūl* masc., ad. L. *mulus*; later, ad. OF. *mul* masc., *mule* fem. :—L. *mulus* masc., *mula* fem.] **1.** The offspring of a he-ass and a mare. Also, pop., the offspring of a she-ass and a stallion (techn. called a HINNY). (Without good grounds, the mule is a proverbial type of obstinacy.) **2.** *transf.* **a.** A stupid or obstinate person 1470. **b.** One who is 'neither one thing nor the other' B. JONS. **3.** A hybrid plant or animal; *esp.* a mule canary 1727. **4.** *techn.* **a.** A kind of spinning jenny invented by S. Crompton 1797. **b.** *Numism.* A coin presenting two obverse types, or two reverse types, or types which do not correspond 1884. **c.** An electric tractor for drawing vessels through canals.

1. She was as obstinate as a m. on that point 1809.

attrib. and *Comb.*: **m. armadillo,** *Dasypus septemcinctus* or *hybridus*; **m.-bird, m. canary,** a cross between a canary and another finch, esp. the goldfinch; **m. deer,** *Cariacus macrotis*, on account of its mule-like ears; **m. jenny** = sense 4 a; **m. twist, yarn,** yarn spun on a m.

Mule[2] (miūl). late ME. [a. F. *mule* fem., slipper, *mules* pl., chilblains.] †**1.** A chilblain on the heel; also, later, a sore on a horse's heel –1720. **2.** A kind of slipper or shoe 1562.

Muleteer (miūlĕtīə·ɪ). 1538. [a. F. *muletier*, f. *mulet*, dim. of OF. *mul*; see MULE[1] and -EER.] A mule-driver.

Muley (miū·li). Also **mulley.** 1573. [var. of Sc. and Anglo-Ir. *moiley*.] **A.** *sb.* **1.** Name for a hornless cow. (Now common in U.S.) Also used for any cow (*dial.*). **2.** *U.S.* A muley saw (see B. 2) 1864. **B.** *adj.* **1.** Of cattle: Hornless 1885. **2.** *U.S.* (*Mech.*) In **m. axle,** a car axle having no collars at the ends of the journals; **m. saw,** a stiff long saw which is not stretched in a gate or sash but has guide-carriages called *m.-heads* 1872.

Muliebrity (miūli,e·briti). *rare.* 1592. [ad. L. *muliebritas*, f. *muliebris* (f. *mulier* woman).] Womanhood; the characteristics or qualities of a woman.

†**Mulier** (miū·liəɪ). late ME. [repr. AF. *mulieré*, Law Lat. *mulieratus*, f. AF. *mulier*, OF. *moiller* wife, ad. L. *mulier* woman.] **A.** *adj.* Of a child: Born in wedlock, legitimate; also in *Eccl. Law*, legitimized by marriage –1642. **B.** *sb.* A legitimate child; a child born in wedlock –1766. Hence †**Mu·lierly** *adv.* (begotten or born) in wedlock; legitimately 1506–86. †**Mu·lierty,** the condition of being a legitimate issue 1628. var. †**Muliery** –1572.

Mulierose (miū·liĕrōᵘs), *a. rare.* 1721. [ad. L. *mulierosus*.] Fond of women. So **Mu:liero·sity** 1656.

Mulish (miū·liʃ), *a.* 1751. [f. MULE[1] + -ISH[1].] Characteristic of, or resembling, a mule; intractable, stubborn. Hence **Mu·lishly** *adv.*, **-ness.**

Mull (mɒl), *sb.*[1] *Obs.* exc. *dial.* [ME. *mol, mul*, cogn. w. OE. *myl*; f. Teut. root **mul-* (: *mal-, mel-*); see MEAL *sb.*[1]] Something reduced to small particles; dust, ashes, mould, rubbish.

Mull (mɒl), *sb.*[2] *Sc.* late ME. [In Gael. *maol*; in Icel. *múli* (perh. identical with *múli* snout).] In Scotland, a promontory or headland.

Mull (mɒl), *sb.*[3] 1640. [a. Du. *mul*.] The lowest of the four qualities of Dutch madder. Also **m.-madder.**

Mull (mɒl), *sb.*[4] *Sc.* 1771. See MILL *sb.*[1] 2 c.

Mull (mɒl), *sb.*[5] 1798. Shortened f. MULMULL.

Mull (mɒl), *sb.*[6] *colloq.* or *slang.* 1821. [Cf. MUFF *sb.*[3] 2, *v.*[1]] A muddle, mess. Chiefly in phr. *to make a m. of.*

Mull (mɒl), *v.*[1] *Obs.* exc. *dial.* late ME. [f. MULL *sb.*[1]] *trans.* To grind to powder, pulverize; to crumble.

†**Mull,** *v.*[2] *rare.* 1607. [?] *trans.* To dull, stupefy –1687.

Mull (mɒl), *v.*[3] 1607. [?] *trans.* To make (wine, beer, etc.) into a hot drink with the addition of sugar, spices, beaten yolk of egg, etc.

Mull (mɒl), *v.*[4] 1862. [f. MULL *sb.*[6]] **1.** *trans.* (*Athletics.*) To make a failure of. **2.** *intr.* To work (*over*) mentally; to cogitate, ruminate, ponder. *colloq. U.S.* 1879.

Mullah (mɒ·lă). 1613. [a. Pers., Turk., and Urdū *mullā*, corrupt pronunc. of Arab. *maulā*.] A Mohammedan title for one learned in theology and sacred law.

Mullein (mɒ·lĕn, -in). late ME. [a. AF. *moleine* (F. *moulaine* Cotgr.; *molène* Littré), perh. f. F. *mol* soft.] **1.** Common name of various species of the genus *Verbascum*, herbaceous plants with woolly leaves and an erect woolly raceme of yellow flowers; esp. *V. Thapsus*, Common or Great (Torch) M. **2.** Short for *mullein moth* 1868.

attrib. and *Comb.*: **m. foxglove,** a wild plant of the U.S., *Seymeria macrophylla*; **m. moth, shark,** a moth, *Cucullia Verbasci*, whose larva feeds upon the m. plant; **m. tea,** an infusion of m. leaves.

Muller (mɒ·ləɪ), *sb.* late ME. [perh. a. AF. **moloir*, f. *mol-*, *moldre* (mod.F. *moudre* to grind).] A stone with a flat base or grinding surface, used, in conjunction with a grinding stone or slab, in grinding painters' colours, apothecaries' powders, etc. Also **m.-stone. b.** Applied to mechanical contrivances for grinding or crushing 1858. Hence **Mu·ller** *v. trans.* to grind with a m.

Müllerian (mülīə·riăn), *a.* 1875. [f. Joh. *Müller* (1801–58), a German physiologist + -IAN.] In *M. duct*, each of a pair of ducts in a vertebrate embryo, which in the female become oviducts or Fallopian tubes.

Mullet[1] (mɒ·lĕt). 1440. [ME. *molet, mulet*, a. OF. *mulet*, dim. f. L. *mullus* red mullet.] **1.** A name for any fish of **a.** the genus *Mullus*, family *Mullidæ*, of which the Red mullet (*M. barbatus*) is the type; **b.** the genus *Mugil*, family *Mugilidæ*, of which the Grey mullet (*M. capito*) is the best-known species. **2.** Applied to fish of other genera, as Black m., *Menticirrus nebulosus*, the American king-fish, etc. 1880.

1. Mullets, Sous'd in high-countrey wines B. JONS.

Mullet[2] (mɒ·lĕt). late ME. [a. OF. *molette* rowel, mullet (mod.F. *molette* rowel).] *Her.* A figure of a star, having five (or more) straight points. Given as a mark of cadency for a third son.

†**Mu·llet**[3]. late ME. [a. F. *molet*.] *pl.* A kind of pincers or tweezers –1634. Hence †**Mu·llet** *v.* to treat with these 1649.

Mulley, var. of MULEY.

Mulligatawny (mɒ:ligătǭ·ni). 1784. [a. Tamil *milagu-tannīr* 'pepper-water' (Yule).] An East Indian highly seasoned soup. Also *m. soup.* **b.** *M. paste*, a curry paste used for flavouring this soup 1858.

Mulligrubs (mɒ·ligrɒbz), *sb. pl.* 1599. [Arbitrary.] A state of depression of spirits; a fit of megrims or spleen; in early use in phr. (*in*) *her, his*, etc. *mulligrubs*; hence joc., stomach-ache or colic.

Whose dog lyes sicke o' th m.? FLETCHER.

Mullion (mɒ·lyən). 1567. [Prob. metathetic var. of *muniall*, MONIAL.] *Arch.* A vertical bar dividing the lights in a window, esp. in Gothic architecture; also, a similar bar in screen-work.

attrib. and *Comb.* **m. window** = mullioned window. Hence **Mu·llioned** *a.*

Mullock (mɒ·lək). late ME. [f. MULL *sb.*[1] + -OCK.] **1.** Rubbish, refuse matter. Now only *dial.* **2.** *Austral.* Rock which does not contain gold; also, the refuse from which gold has been extracted 1864.

Mulmull (mɒ·lmɒl). 1619. [a. Hindī *malmal.*] A thin variety of muslin. Cf. MULL *sb.*[5]

†**Mulse.** 1533. [ad. L. *mulsum*, neut. pa. pple. of *mulcere* to sweeten.] A liquor made of honey mixed with water or wine; hydromel, mead. Also *m.-water.* –1661.

Multangular (mɒltæ·ŋgiŭlaɪ), *a.* (*sb.*). Also **multi-.** 1677. [ad. mod.L. *multangularis*; see MULTI- and ANGULAR.] **A.** *adj.* Having many angles; polygonal. **B.** *sb. rare.* A polygon 1766. **Multa·ngularly** *adv.*, **-ness.** So †**Multa·ngulous** *a.* 1659–80.

Multa·nimous, *a. rare.* 1854. [f. L. *multus* MULTI- + *animus* + -OUS.] Having a many-sided mind.

Multarti·culate, *a. rare.* Also **multi-.** 1681. [See MULTI-.] *Zool.* Having many articulations or joints.

Multeity (mɒltī·iti). 1814. [f. L *multus*.] The quality of being many; manifoldness.

Multi- (mɒ·lti), occas. bef. a vowel **mult-,** comb. f. L. *multus* much, many. (The L. compounds were chiefly parasynthetic, as *multicaulis* many-stalked.)

1. Forming parasynthetic adjs. with the sense 'having many..', having sometimes corresponding forms in POLY-. **a.** In scientific and technical use: as *multia·xial*, having many axes or lines of growth, *-camerate* (chambers), *-capsular*, *-carinate(d* (keels), *-cellular* (cells), *-central*, *-cipital* (heads), *-costate* (ribs), *-cuspid(ate* (cusps) *-dentate* (teeth), *-digitate* (fingers), *-dimensional*, *-floral*, *-florous* (flowers), *-foliate* (leaves), *-jugate*, *-jugous* (pairs of leaflets), *-lineal*, *-linear*, *-lobar*, *-lobate*, *-lobed*, *-locular*, *-loculate(d* (cells), *-nodal*, *-nodate*, *-nodous*, *-nuclear*, *-nucleate(d*, *-polar*, *-radiate(d* (rays), *-ramose*, *-ramous* (branches), *-septate* (septa or partitions), *-siliquose* (pods), *-striate* (striæ or streaks), *-tubercular*, *-ate* (tubercles), *-tubular* (tubes). **Multise·rial, -se·riate,** arranged in many series or rows. **Multivo·ltine** [It. *volta* time, turn], (of a silkworm) producing several broods a year.

b. In general use (mostly nonce-wds.): as *multifaced.* **Multiflu·vian** [L. *fluvius*], having many rivers flowing into it. **Multili·ngual,** using, characterized by, or written in, many languages. **Multino·minal,** †**-no·minous,** having many names. **Multiti·tular,** having many titles.

2. Prefixed to a sb. either with adjectival sense = 'multiple, manifold', or with adverbial sense = 'in many ways or directions'. **Mu·lticycle,** (*a*) a cycle having more than three wheels; (*b*) a cycle for two or more riders. **Mu·ltifoil,** a foil (in a window) of more than five divisions. **Multiloca·tion,** location in many places at the same time. **Mu:ltimillionai·re,** one who is worth two or more millions of money.

3. Prefixed to a sb. forming a compound used attrib. with the force of a parasynthetic adj. **Mu·lticharge,** (of a gun) capable of containing several charges. **Mu·lticoil,** possessing more than one coil. **Mu·lticy·linder,** (of an engine) having three or more cylinders. **Mu·ltispeed,** (of a motor) of several (usu. definite) speeds.

Mu·lti-colour, *sb.* and *a.* 1849. [MULTI- 2, 3. Cf. L. *multicolor* adj.] **1. a.** The condition of being many-coloured. **b.** *pl.* Many or various colours 1901. **2. a.** *attrib.* Applied to printing in many colours or a machine for such printing 1884. **b.** *adj.* Many-coloured 1881. **Multi-coloured** *a.*, of many colours 1845.

Multifarious (mɒltifēᵊ·riəs), *a.* (*sb.*). 1593. [f. late L. *multifarius* (cl. L. *multifariam* adv.) + -OUS.] **1.** Having great variety; (with pl. sb.) many and various. **b.** *Bot.* Arranged in many rows, as leaves (*rare*) 1838. **2.** *Law.* 'Improperly joining in one bill distinct matters, and thereby confounding them' (Story) 1838. **3.** *sb.* In Kantian philosophy = MANIFOLD *sb.*[1] 2 a. 1819.

1. That m. thing called a state BURKE. Hence **Multifa·riously** *adv.*, **-ness.**

Multiferous (mɒlti·fĕrəs), *a. rare.* 1656. [See MULTI- and -FEROUS.] Bearing much or many; fruitful.

Multifid (mɒ·ltifid), *a.* 1731. [ad. L. *multifidus*, f. *multus* MULTI- + *fid-, findere* to cleave.] *Bot.* and *Zool.* Having many divisions; cleft into many parts.

A simple, bifid, or m. fold of the integument HUXLEY. So **Multi·fidous** *a.*, said esp. of feet 1646.

Mu·ltifold, *a.* 1806. [f. MULTI- + -FOLD.] Manifold.

Multiform (mɒ·ltifǫɹm), *a.* and *sb.* 1603. [ad. F. *multiforme* or L. *multiformis*: see MULTI- and -FORM.] **A.** *adj.* Having many forms, shapes, or appearances; of many and various forms or kinds. **B.** *sb.* That which is multiform. Also, multiform character, multiformity 1849.

A. The m. brogue, which salutes the ears of a traveller in..New-York 1817. So **Multifo·rmity,** diversity or variety of form 1589. **Multifo·rmous** *a.* multiform 1670.

Multila·teral, *a.* 1696. [MULTI- 1] = MANY-SIDED 1, 2.

Multi·loquy. 1542. [ad. L. *multiloquium*, f. *multi-* much + *loqui* to speak.] Much speaking, talkativeness.

So **Multi·loquence** 1760; **Multi·loquent** (1656), **-lo·quious** (1640), **-loquous** (1664) *adjs.*, given to much talking.

Multinomial (mɒltinō^u·miăl), *a.* and *sb.* 1608. [f. MULTI- 1, after *binomial.*] *Alg.* **A.** *adj.* Of an expression: Consisting of many (i.e. more than two) terms connected by the signs + or −. **B.** *sb.* A m. expression 1674.

Multi·parous, *a.* 1646. [f. mod.L. *multiparus*: see MULTI- and -PAROUS.] **1.** Bringing forth many young at a birth; characterized by such parturition. **2.** Of or pertaining to, or that is, a **Multi·para** (a woman who has borne more than one child) 1860. **3.** *Bot.* Applied to a cyme that has many axes 1880. So **Multipa·rient** *a.* (in sense 1). 1822. Hence **Multipa·rity** 1890.

Multipartite (mɒltipā·ɹtəit), *a.* 1721. [ad. L. *multipartitus*: see MULTI- and PARTITE *a.*] Divided into many parts; having many divisions.

Multiped, -pede (mɒ·ltiped, -pīd), *sb.* and *a.* Now *rare.* 1601. [ad. L. *multiped-, -pes* sb. and adj., *-peda* sb., f. *multus* MULTI- + *pes* foot.] **A.** *sb.* A many-footed creature; †*spec.* a woodlouse. **B.** *adj.* Many-footed 1736.

Multiple (mɒ·ltip'l), *a.* and *sb.* 1647. [a. F., ad. late L. *multiplus* = L. *multiplex* (see MULTIPLEX).] **A.** *adj.* **1.** *Math.* That is a multiple (see B. 1); †that is some multiple *of* 1714. **2.** Consisting of or characterized by many parts, elements, or individual components; manifold. With pl. sb.: Many and various. 1647. **3.** In techn. use; esp.

a. *Astron. M. star*: a cluster of stars forming apparently one system 1850. **b.** *Electr. M. arc*: a compound electric circuit. *M. telegraphy*: a system by which many messages may be sent over the same wire 1873. **c.** In the Kantian philosophy: That is a manifold (*rare*) 1839.

1. *M. proportion, ratio*: the proportion or ratio existing between a quantity and some multiple of it, or between several multiples of it. *Law of m. proportions* (Chem.): the generalization that whenever elements combine together in several proportions, the proportions in which the one element unites with the other invariably bear a simple relation to one another. Thus 1 part by weight of hydrogen unites with 8 parts by weight of oxygen, forming water, and with 16 or 8×2 parts of oxygen, forming peroxide of hydrogen. **2. M. shop, store**: one of several shops of the same kind under one and the same management, situated in different localities.

B. *sb.* **1.** *Math.* A quantity which contains another quantity some number of times without remainder. Thus 4 is a multiple of 2; 6 of 2 and of 3. 1685. Also *fig.* **2.** In the Kantian philosophy: = MANIFOLD *sb.*[1] 2 a. 1839.

1. *Least common m.* (L.C.M.): the least quantity that contains two or more quantities some number of times without remainder; e.g. 12 is the L.C.M. of 2, 3, and 4.

Mu·ltiplepoi·nding (pi·ndiŋ). 1693. [See POIND *v.*] *Sc. Law.* An action raised by the holder of a fund or property to which there are several claimants, who are thereby required to come together and settle their claims in court.

Multiplex (mɒ·ltipleks), *a.* and *sb.* 1557. [a. L., f. *multus* MULTI- + *-plex* = -FOLD.] **A.** *adj.* †**1.** *Math.* **a.** *M. to, of*: that is some multiple of –1690. †**b.** *M. proportion*, multiple proportion –1788. **2.** = MANIFOLD *a.* 1, 2; MULTIPLE *a.* 2, 3. 1676. **B.** *sb.* †**1.** *Math.* = MULTIPLE *sb.* 1. –1695. **2.** = MULTIPLE *sb.* 2. 1836.

Mu·ltipliable, *a.* 1625. [f. MULTIPLY *v.* + -ABLE.] Capable of being multiplied.

Multiplicable (mɒ·ltiplikăb'l), *a.* 1471. [ad. L. *multiplicabilis*, f. *multiplicare*.] = prec. Hence **Mu·ltiplicabi·lity** 1677.

Multiplicand (mɒ:ltiplikæ·nd, mɒ·ltiplikænd). 1594. [ad. L. *multiplicandus*, gerund. of *multiplicare*.] *Math.* The quantity to be multiplied; correl. to *multiplier*.

Multiplicate (mɒ·ltiplikĕ^t, mɒlti·plikĕ^t), *a.* and *sb.* Now *rare.* late ME. [ad. L. *multiplicatus*, pa. pple. of *multiplicare*.] **A.** *adj.* †Multiplied, increased; manifold; multiplex. **B.** *sb.* **a.** *In m.*: in many exactly corresponding copies or reproductions. **b.** One of such copies. 1858. So †**Mu·ltiplicated** *pa. pple.* folded many times 1638.

Multiplication (mɒ·ltiplikē^i·ʃən). late ME. [a. F., ad. L. *multiplicationem*.] **1.** The act or process of multiplying; the state of being multiplied. Now *rare* exc. as coloured by sense 3. **2.** Propagation of animals and plants. late ME. **3.** *Math.* The process of finding the quantity produced (see PRODUCT) by taking a given quantity (the *multiplicand*) as many times as there are units in another given quantity (the *multiplier*); or, in the case of a fractional multiplier, of finding the same fraction of the multiplicand as the multiplier is of unity. late ME. **b.** In *Higher Algebra*: The successive application of operators 1843. †**4.** *Alch.* The art of 'multiplying' –1696. **5.** *Bot.* Increase in the number of whorls or of organs in a whorl 1849.

1. M. of words in the body of the Law, is m. of ambiguity HOBBES. One of the peculiarities which distinguish the present age is the m. of books JOHNSON. Repeated transcription involves m. of error 1881. **2.** Multiplicacioun and encrese of men and children in þe norþ TREVISA.

attrib.: **m. table,** a table of products of factors taken in pairs, usually beginning 'twice one are two' (2×1 = 2) and going up to some assumed limit. Also †*table of m.*

Multiplicative (mɒ·ltiplikĕ^itiv), *a.* and *sb.* 1653. [ad. med. L. *multiplicativus*, f. *multiplicat-, multiplicare*; see -IVE.] Tending, or having the power, to multiply or increase. **b.** *Gram.* Applied to numerals that express 'so many times'. Also *sb.*, a m. numeral. 1727.

Multiplicator (mɒ·ltiplikē^itǫɹ). 1542. [a. late L.] **1.** *Math.* = MULTIPLIER 2. Now *rare* or *obs.* **2.** *Elect.* and *Magn.* = MULTIPLIER 4. 1823. **b.** In a galvanometer, a flat coil of conducting wire for multiplying the effect of the current 1884.

†**Multipli·cious,** *a.* 1617. [f. L. *multiplici-, -plex*; see -OUS.] Multiplex –1713. Hence †**Multipli·ciously** *adv.*

Multiplicity (mɒltipli·sĭti). 1587. [ad. L. *multiplicitas*.] **1.** Multiplex quality or condition; manifold variety. **b.** In the Kantian philosophy = MANIFOLD *sb.*[1] 2 a. 1839. **2.** *The m. of*: the great number of. So *a, such (a), this*, etc. *m. of.* 1598.

2. Such m. of words he hath 1598.

Multiplier (mɒ·ltipləi,əɹ). late ME. [f. MULTIPLY *v.* + -ER[1].] **1.** One who or a thing which multiplies something 1470. **2.** *Math.* The quantity by which another (the *multiplicand*) is multiplied 1542. †**3.** One who performs the alchemical process of multiplication; hence, a false coiner –1560. **4.** *Electr.* and *Magn.* An instrument used for multiplying or increasing by repetition the intensity of a force, current, etc. so as to make it appreciable or mensurable 1823. **5.** *Angling.* A kind of reel by which the speed at which the fishing-line is gathered in at each turn of the handle is accelerated; also *multiplying-reel* 1867. **6.** An arithmometer for multiplying 1875.

Multiply (mɒ·ltipləi), *v.* ME. [a. OF. (mod.F.) *multiplier*, ad. L. *multiplicare*, f. *multiplic-* MULTIPLEX.] **1.** *trans.* To cause to become much, many, or more; to make many or manifold. Now *rare* exc. as coloured by sense 5. **b.** To adduce a large number of (instances, etc.) 1716. †**c.** To increase the intensity of; *occas.* to magnify optically –1651. **2.** *intr.* To become of great number or quantity; to be increased by accumulation or repetition ME. **3.** *trans.* To increase (a family, etc.) by procreation (freq. in *pass.*); †to cause (the earth) to become populous. *Obs.* or *arch.* –1784. **b.** To breed (animals); to propagate (plants) 1471. **4.** *intr.* To increase in number by natural generation ME. **5.** *trans.* (*Math.*) To operate upon (a *multiplicand*) with a *multiplier* so as to produce a *product* having the same ratio to the multiplicand as the multiplier has to unity. In *Higher Algebra*, to apply an operator to (an operand). late ME. **b.** *intr.* To perform the process of multiplication 1579. †**6.** *Alch.* (*trans.* and *intr.*) To increase the precious metals, as by transmutation of the baser metals. Also *intr.* (for *pass.*), said of the precious metals. late ME.

1. Swete wordes multiplien & encressen frendes CHAUCER. Phr. *To m. words*: †(*a*) to be loquacious; (*b*) to be verbose. *To m. evil upon evil*: to add evil to evil. **c.** Wee M. Smells, which may seeme strange BACON. **2.** The flame increased—multiplied—at one point after another KINGSLEY. **4.** As for my Cats, they multiply'd DE FOE. **5.** Phr. *To m.* (one quantity) *into*, †*in* (another); *to m.* (two quantities) *together*: to find the product of the two quantities. **6.** Upon Nature thei falsely lye For Mettalls doe not Multiplie 1477.

Multiply (mɒ·ltipli), *adv.* 1881. [f. MULTIPLE + -LY[2].] In a multiple manner; *spec.* in *Math.*

Mu·ltiplying-glass. 1628. †**1.** A magnifying-glass –1680. **2.** A toy consisting of a concave glass or lens, the surface of which is cut into numerous facets so as to give as many reflections of the object observed 1671.

Multipotent (mɒlti·pŏtent), *a. rare.* 1606. [ad. L. *multipotent-, -ens*; see MULTI- and POTENT.] Having much power.

Multipre·sence. 1614. [ad. mod.L. *multipræsentia*: see MULTI- and PRESENCE.] The fact or faculty of being present in many places at once. So **Multipre·sent** *a.*

The multi-presence of Christ's body BP. HALL.

Multisect (mɒ·ltisekt), *a.* 1826. [ad. mod.L. *multisectus*, f. *multus* MULTI- + *sectus*, pa. pple. of *secare* to cut.] *Entom.* Of an insect: Divided into numerous segments. So **Mu·ltisect** *v.* 1862.

Multisonant (mɒlti·sŏnănt), *a. rare.* 1656. [f. L. *multison-us*: see MULTI- and SONANT.] Having many sounds; sounding much. So **Multi·sonous** *a.*

Multitude (mɒ·ltitiūd). ME. [a. F., or ad. L. *multitudo, -tudin-*, f. *multus*; see -TUDE.] **1.** Numerousness; great number. Also, number whether great or small. **2.** A great number, a host, a crowd (*of* persons or things). Often *ellipt.* = m. of men, etc. in question. ME. **b.** *pl.* Great numbers, hosts, crowds 1596. †**c.** A great quantity (*of* something) –1777. **3.** A large gathering of people; a throng. late ME. **4.** With *the*: 'The many', the populace, the common people 1535.

1. Euen as the sand that is vpon the Sea-shore in m. *Josh.* xi. 4. **2.** A m. of actions done by a m. of men HOBBES. **b.** Multitudes of words bring much error 1683. **c.** All this..m. of misery CHATHAM. **3.** A Multitude 's a Bulky Coward 1682. **4.** The many-headed M. SHAKS.

Multitudinous (mɒltitiū·dinəs), *a.* 1605. [f. L. *multitudin-, multitudo* + -OUS.] **1. a.** with pl. sb.: Existing in multitudes; very numerous 1629. **b.** with collect. sb.: Consisting of a multitude 1606. **c.** with sing. sb.: Existing in a multitude of forms; having many elements or features; arising from or involving a multitude 1656. **d.** Said of the ocean or any mass of water with reference to its great bulk or to its innumerable ripples 1605. **e.** Crowded (*with*). *poet.* 1820. **2.** Of or pertaining to the multitude. *Cor.* III. i. 156.

1. a. The m. Pagans and Idolaters 1650. **b.** A more m. brood of sectaries HALLAM. **c.** The m. moan and wail of the lost spirits KINGSLEY. **d.** This my Hand will rather The m. Seas incarnardine SHAKS. **e.** To live In a home m. with herds BROWNING. So **Multitu·dinary** *a.* (*rare*) 1846. **Multitu·dinism,** the principle which places the interests of multitudes before those of individuals, esp. in religion 1860. Hence **Multitu·dinous·ly** *adv.*, **-ness.**

Multivalent (mɒltivǣlĕnt), *a.* 1872. [See MULTI- 1.] *Chem.* Having many degrees of valency. Hence **Multi·valence, -ency.**

Multivalve (mɒ·ltivælv), *a.* and *sb.* 1753. [ad. mod.L. *multivalvis*; see MULTI- and VALVE.] *Zool.* and *Bot.* Having many valves; *sb.* a m. shell or animal having such a shell. Hence **Mu·ltivalved, Multiva·lvular** *adjs.*

Multivarious (mɒltivēᵊ·riəs), *a.* Now *rare.* 1620. [f. MULTI- + L. *varius*, as tr. Gr. πολυποίκιλος much-variegated.] Manifold and diverse.

Multivious (mɒlti·viəs), *a.* 1656. [f. L. *multivius* (f. *multus* + *via*) + -OUS.] Having many ways; going in many directions.

Multivocal (mɒlti·vǒkăl), *a.* and *sb.* 1810. [f. L. *multus* MULTI- + *vocare* to call, after *univocal*, etc.] Susceptible of many meanings; *sb.* a m. word.

An ambiguous or m. word COLERIDGE.

Multocular (mɒltǫ·kiŭlăɹ), *a.* 1713. [f. L. *multus* MULT(I- + *oculus* + -AR [1].] Having many eyes.

‖**Multum** (mɒ·ltɒm), 1820. [perh. a use of L. *multum* much.] *Brewing.* An extract of quassia and liquorice, used by brewers as an adulterant. *Hard m.*, a preparation of *Cocculus indicus*, similarly used.

‖**Multum in parvo** (mɒ·ltǒm in pā·ɹvo). 1732. [L., = 'much in little'.] A great deal in a small compass. Also *attrib.*, as 'm.-in-p. pocket-knife'.

Multungulate (mɒltɒ·ŋgiŭlět), *a.* and *sb.* 1839. [ad. mod.L. *multungulatus*, f. L. *multus* MULT(I- + *ungula* hoof; see -ATE [2].] Having more than two hoofs; *sb.* a m. animal.

Multure (mɒ·ltiŭɹ, -tʃəɹ). ME. [a. OF. *molture, moulture*, mod.F. *mouture* :—med.L. *molitura*, f. *molit-, molere* to grind.] A toll in kind paid to the miller for grinding corn; the right to exact this. Hence **Mu·lturer,** one who pays toll for the grinding of his corn at a mill.

Mum (mɒm), *sb.*[1], *int.*, and *a.* late ME. [Echoic; cf. Ger. *mumm.*] **A.** *sb.* †1. An inarticulate sound made with closed lips. Also, in neg. or hypothetical context = '(not) the slightest word'. -1651. 2. Refusal to speak, silence (*colloq.*) 1562. †3. A silent person -1808. **B.** *int.* = 'Hush!' 'silence!' 'not a word!' Also in *m.'s the word*, late ME. **C.** *adj.* Strictly silent or secret. Sometimes quasi-*adv.*, as *to stand m.*, etc. (*colloq.*). 1521.

B. No more woords, but m. & stand a while aside 1568.

Mum (mɒm), *sb.*[2] Now chiefly *Hist.* 1640. [a. G. *mumme.*] A kind of beer originally brewed in Brunswick.

I thinke you'r drunk With Lubecks beere or Brunswicks M. 1640.

Mum (mɒm), *sb.*[3] 1823. [Shortened f. MUMMY *sb.*[2]] A pet name for 'mother'.

Mum (mɒm), *v.* late ME. [f. MUM *int.* or *sb.*[1]] †1. *trans.* To silence; to put to silence -1654. †2. *intr.* To make an inarticulate sound with closed lips; hence, to keep silence -1637. †3. To whisper -1680. 4. To act in dumb show; to play as a mummer 1530.

4. When a whole People goes mumming and miming CARLYLE.

Mum, vulgar var. of MA'AM.

Mumble (mɒ·mb'l), *v.* [ME. *momele*, freq. formation on MUM *int.*; cf. Du. *mummelen*, G. *mummeln*, etc.] 1. *intr.* To speak indistinctly or with the lips partly closed; to mutter. 2. *trans.* To utter in low or indistinct tones 1440. 3. *intr.* and *trans.* To chew or bite softly, as with toothless gums (now *rare*) ME. †4. To maul, maltreat. Also, to bungle. -1753.

1. So tottered, muttered, mumbled he, till he died BROWNING. 2. By one meanes or other, he learned to m. a Masse 1626. 3. Sitting..alone, mumblyng on a crust 1561. And Gums unarm'd to m. Meat in vain DRYDEN. 4. Mr. Fox mumbled the Chancellor and his lawyers H. WALPOLE.

Comb.: †**m.-matins,** a Romish priest; †**m.-news,** a tale-bearer. Hence **Mu·mble** *sb.* an act of mumbling. **Mu·mbler. Mu·mblingly** *adv.*

Mumbo Jumbo (mɒ·mbo₁dʒɒ·mbo). 1738. [?] 1. A grotesque idol said to have been worshipped by certain tribes of negroes. 2. *transf.* An object of senseless veneration 1847.

†**Mu·mbu·dget.** 1564. = MUM *int.*, *a.*, and *sb.*[1] -1663.

(Quoth she) Mum budget BUTLER *Hud.* I. iii. 208.

Mumchance (mɒ·mtʃɑns), *sb.* and *a.* 1528. [a. MLG. *mummenschanze, -kanze*, a certain game of dice, also, a masked serenade, f. *mummen* MUM *v.* + *schanz* a. F. *chance*; see CHANCE *sb.*] **A.** *sb.* †1. A dicing game resembling hazard -1656. †2. Masquerade; mumming -1591. 3. In similative phrases: One who acts in dumb show. Hence, one who has nothing to say; a dummy. 1694. **B.** *adj.* Silent; tongue-tied (*arch.* and *dial.*) 1681.

A. Phr. †*To play m.*: *fig.* or *allusively*, to preserve a dogged silence. B. Poor Twenty Ninth of February that had sate all this while m. at the sideboard LAMB.

Mummer (mɒ·məɹ). 1440. [a.OF. *momeur, -eor*, f. *momer* (prob. of Teut. origin) = MUM *v.*] †1. One who mutters or murmurs -1548. 2. †An actor in a dumb show; one who takes part in a mumming 1502. **b.** *slang*, etc. A 'play-actor' 1840.

2. Grave mummers! sleeveless some, and shirtless others POPE.

Mummery (mɒ·məri). 1530. [a. OF *mommerie*, F. *momerie*; see prec. and -Y [3].] 1. A performance of mummers. 2. *transf.* 'Play-acting'. Often applied contempt. to religious ritual. 1549.

1. Your Fathers..Disdain'd the M. of Foreign Strollers 1719. 2. Those rags of Popish mummeries 1864.

Mummify (mɒ·mifəi), *v.* 1628. [ad. F. *momifier*, f. *momie* MUMMY; see -FY.] 1. *trans.* To make into a mummy; to preserve by embalming and drying. Also, to dry into the semblance of a mummy. Also *transf.* and *fig.* 3. *Path.* (chiefly in pa. pple.) To shrivel or dry up (tissues, etc.) 1857. **Mummifica·tion** 1800.

Mumming (mɒ·miŋ), *vbl. sb.* 1465. [f. MUM *v.* + -ING [1].] The action of disguising oneself; *spec.* the action of taking part in the representation of a mummers' play. Chiefly in phr. *to go a mumming*. Also, a performance of mummers. **b.** *transf.* and *fig.* Often with contempt. ref. to religious ceremonial 1528.

Mummy (mɒ·mi), *sb.*[1] late ME. [a. F. *momie*, †*mumie*, ad. med.L. *mumia*, a. Arab. *mūmiyā* an embalmed body, a mummy, f. *mūm* wax.] 1. A medicinal preparation of the substance of mummies (see 3); hence, an unctuous liquid or gum used medicinally. *Obs.* exc. *Hist.* (formerly also in med.L. form). †**b.** *joc.* Dead flesh -1622. **c.** A pulpy substance or mass. Chiefly in *to beat*, etc. *to a m.* (earlier, *to m.*). 1601. 2. In transf., etc., uses. †**a.** A sovereign remedy -1671. **b.** A medicinal bituminous drug obtained from the East 1601. †**c.** *Gardening.* A kind of wax used in grafting, etc. -1789. **d.** A rich brown bituminous pigment 1854. 3. A dead body embalmed (according to the ancient Egyptian or other method) as a preparation for burial 1615. **b.** A human or animal body desiccated by exposure to sun or air. Also applied to a frozen carcase found in prehistoric ice. 1727. **c.** *Stock Exchange slang*: *pl.* Egyptian securities 1903.

1. *fig.* This universal medicine made of church m. is to cure all the evils of the time BURKE. b. *Merry W.* III. v. 18. 3. *fig.* The old theological dogmas had become mere mummies 1876.

Comb.: **m.-case,** the case of wood, etc. (usu. decorated with hieroglyphics) in which Egyptian mummies were enclosed; **-pits** *pl.*, the catacombs in which the Egyptian mummies were interred; **-wheat,** a variety of wheat cultivated in Egypt, and said to have been grown from grains found in mummy-cases. **Mu·mmiform** *a.* 1856. **Mu·mmy** *v.* to mummify 1620.

Mummy (mɒ·mi), *sb.*[2] 1839. [Childish var. of MAMMY.] A child's word for mother.

Mu·mmy-cloth. 1843. 1. The cloth in which Egyptian mummies were wrapped. 2. *U.S.* A trade name for certain modern fabrics more or less resembling the material of mummy-cloths. Also *momie-cloth*. 1886.

Mump, *sb.* 1592. [Symbolic of the movements of the lips in making a 'mouth'.] †1. A grimace -1635. 2. *pl.* See MUMPS *sb. pl.*

Mump (mɒmp), *v.*[1] 1586. [Related to MUMP *sb.*] †1. *trans.* To utter imperfectly; to mumble, mutter. Also with *out*, -1773. 2. *intr.* †**a.** To grimace with the lips; to grin. Also *transf.* and *fig.* -1754. **b.** To assume a demure or miserable aspect of countenance; to be silent or sullen; to sulk, mope (*arch.*) 1610. 3. **a.** *intr.* To mumble with the gums; to move the jaws as if munching food; to munch, nibble. *Obs.* exc. *dial.* 1596. †**b.** *trans.* To chew with toothless gums -1838.

1. Old men,..Who m. their passion GOLDSM. 2. b. It is better to enjoy a novel than to m. STEVENSON. 3. When he mumped or spoke, they [*sc.* his nose and chin] approached one another like a pair of nut-crackers SMOLLETT.

Mump (mɒmp), *v.*[2] *colloq.* (orig. *slang*). 1651. [prob. a. Du. *mompen* to cheat. Sense 2 may belong to prec.] †1. *trans.* To overreach, cheat. Const. *of, out of.* -1734. 2. **a.** *intr.* To beg; †to sponge on others. **b.** *trans.* To obtain by begging or sponging. **c.** To visit (a house) in the course of a begging round. 1673.

2. One prince came mumping to them annually with a lamentable story about his distresses MACAULAY. Hence **Mu·mper,** a beggar.

Mumpish (mɒ·mpiʃ), *a.* 1721. [f. MUMP *sb.* or *v.*[1] + -ISH [1].] Sullenly angry; depressed.

†**Mumps,** *sb.* 1598. [? short for MUMPSIMUS 1 b.] A term of contempt or mock endearment for a woman -1695.

Mumps (mɒmps), *sb. pl.* 1598. [Plural of MUMP *sb.*] 1. (const. as *sing.*). An acute specific contagious disease characterized by inflammation and swelling of the parotid and salivary glands. 2. A fit of melancholy or ill temper; sulks 1599.

Mumpsimus (mɒ·mpsimɒ̆s). 1530. [An illiterate alteration of *sumpsimus* in the Mass: see N.E.D.] †1. One who obstinately adheres to old ways; an ignorant and bigoted opponent of reform -1553. ¶**b.** As a vague term of contempt: An old fogey -1815. 2. A traditional custom, etc., obstinately adhered to however unreasonable it may be 1545. 3. *attrib.*, quasi-*adj.* Stupidly conservative 1680.

3. The m., and 'well as we are' people SYD. SMITH.

Mun, *v. north.* and *midl.* ME. [a. ON. *monu, munu*, preterite-pres. vb. used as auxiliary of fut. (cf. MAUN).] Const. inf. without *to*: Must; †formerly occas. = shall.

Munch (mɒnʃ), *v.* late ME. [app. onomatopœic.] 1. *trans.* To eat with noticeable action of the jaws, as cattle chewing fodder, etc. Also with *up*. 2. *intr.* and *absol.* Also with *away*. 1530. **b.** To work the jaws up and down, as old toothless people do in talking. DICKENS.

1. I could m. your good dry Oates SHAKS. 2. *Macb.* I. iii. 5. Hence **Munch** *sb.* an act of munching.

Munchausen (mɒn₁tʃǭ·zən). The name of Baron Munchausen, the hero of a narrative of extravagant adventures, written in English by the German Rudolf Erich Raspe (1785); hence, an extravagantly mendacious story of adventure. Hence **Munchau·senism** 1850.

Mundane (mɒ·ndeⁱn), *a.* 1475. [a. F. *mondain*, ad. L. *mundanus*, f. *mundus* world.] 1. Belonging to this world (i.e. the earth); worldly; earthly. **b.** Belonging to the world as dist. from the church; secular (*rare*) 1848. 2. Pertaining to the universe; cosmic 1642. 3. *Astrol.* Pertaining to the horizon and not to the ecliptic or zodiac; chiefly in *m. aspect, parallel* 1687. 4. *Nat. Hist.* Found in all parts of the world. DARWIN.

1. Entangled with the birdlime of fleshly passions and m. vanity 1652. 2. *M. soul, spirit*: the *anima mundi* of the Platonists 1642. *M. era*, an era reckoned from the time of the creation of the world 1838. Hence **Mu·ndane·ly** *adv.*, **-ness. Mundanity** (-æ·n-), worldliness (now *rare*).

†**Munda·tion.** 1633. [ad. L. *mundationem*, f. *mundare*, f. *mundus* clean.] The action of cleansing; cleansed state -1755. So **Mu·ndatory** *a.*, cleansing (*rare*) 1706; *sb.* a means or implement of cleansing; a purificator 1674.

Mundic (mɒ·ndik). 1671. [prob. Celtic Cornish.] Cornish miners' name for pyrites.

Mundify (mɒ·ndifəi), *v.* Now *rare* or *Obs.* late ME. [ad. L. *mundificare*, f. *mundus* clean; see -FY.] 1. *trans.* To cleanse, purify (*lit.* and *fig.*) 1504. 2. *trans.* In medical use: To free (the body, blood, etc.) from noxious matter; to cleanse, deterge. late ME. Hence **Mundifica·tion** 1543. †**Mundificative** *a.* and *sb.* late ME.-1727. †**Mu·ndifier** 1603-1727.

Mundil, var. of MANDIL, turban.

Mundu·ngus. 1637. [Joc. use of Sp. *mondongo* tripe, etc.] †1. Offal, refuse (*rare*) –1834. 2. Bad-smelling tobacco 1641.

2. Clouds of vile m. vapour SCOTT.

‖**Munga** (mʊ·ŋgă). 1843. The bonnet monkey.

Mungcorn(e, var. ff. MONGCORN.

Mungo[1] (mʊ·ŋgo). 1738. [var. of MONGOOSE.] †1. = MONGOOSE 1 –1845. 2. *M.-root* (also *mungo*): the plant *Ophiorrhiza Mungos*, a supposed antidote against the poison of snakes 1738.

†**Mu·ngo**[2]. 1769. [Name of a negro in Bickerstaffe's *The Padlock* (1768).] A typical name for a black slave. Hence, a negro. –1839.

Mungo[3] (mʊ·ŋgo). Also **mongoe.** 1857. [?] Cloth made from devilled woollen rags; like shoddy, but of a better quality.

Mungoos(e, Mungos, var. ff. MONGOOSE, MUNGO[1].

Mungrel(l, -il(l, obs. ff. MONGREL.

Municipal (miuni·sipăl), *a.* and *sb.* 1540. [ad. L. *municipalis*, f. *municip-*, *municeps* member of a MUNICIPIUM, f. *munia* civic offices + root of *capere* to take.] A. *adj.* 1. Pertaining to the internal affairs of a state as dist. from its foreign relations (now *rare*). b. *transf.* Belonging to one place only; having narrow limits 1631. 2. Pertaining to the local self-government or corporate government of a city or town 1600. 3. *Roman Hist.* Of or pertaining to a MUNICIPIUM; hence, contempt., provincial 1618.

1. M. or civil law; that is, the rule by which particular districts, communities, or nations are governed BLACKSTONE. Phr. *M. rights, jurisdiction*, etc. 2. M. charters 1864. A m. tramway 1898.

B. *sb.* 1. *Roman Hist.* An inhabitant of a municipium (tr. L. *municeps*) 1727. ‖2. [Fr.; short for *garde municipale*.] A member of the Municipal Guard, a body of soldiers under the control of the municipality of Paris 1837. Hence **Muni·cipalism**, m. or local patriotism; m. institutions generally; also, preference for the m. principle in local government. **Muni·cipalist**, an advocate of m. action or control; also, one skilled in m. administration. **Muni·cipally** *adv.* with regard to a municipality or to m. affairs.

Municipality (miunisipæ·lĭti). 1790. [a. F. *municipalité*, f. *municipal*; see prec.] 1. A town, city, or district possessed of privileges of local self-government, also applied to its inhabitants collectively. 2. The governing body of such a town or district 1795. 3. A MUNICIPIUM 1805. 4. Government on municipal principles. E. A. FREEMAN.

4. Here [in Italy] was m. on its grandest scale 187..

Municipalize (miuni·sipăləiz), *v.* 1880. [f. MUNICIPAL *a.* + -IZE.] *trans.* To bring under municipal ownership or control; to endow with municipal institutions. Hence **Municipaliza·tion.**

‖**Municipium** (miŭnisi·piŏm). *Pl.* **municipia.** 1720. [L., f. *municip-*, *municeps*; see MUNICIPAL *a.*] *Roman Antiq.* A city whose citizens had the privileges of Roman citizens. var. †**Muni·cipy** (*rare*) 1579.

†**Muni·fic**, *a.* 1754. [ad. L. *munificus*, f. *munus* gift; see -FIC.] = MUNIFICENT. So †**Munifi·cal** *a.* 1603.

Munificence (miuni·fisĕns). 1555. [a. F., ad. L. *munificentia*, f. *munificent-* MUNIFICENT *a.*] The quality of being munificent; splendid or princely generosity. So †**Muni·ficency** 1504–1651.

Munificent (miuni·fisĕnt), *a.* 1583. [ad. L. *munificent-*, altered stem of *munificus* MUNIFIC *a.*] Splendidly generous in giving; (of actions, gifts) characterized by splendid generosity.

Think it not enough to be Liberal, but M. SIR T. BROWNE. Hence **Muni·ficently** *adv.*

†**Munifience.** 1596. [Badly f. MUNIFY + -ENCE.] Fortification, defence. SPENSER.

†**Mu·nify**, *v.* 1603. [irreg. f. L. *munio* (*munire*) + -FY.] To fortify; to provide with defences –1635.

Muniment (miŭ·niměnt). late ME. [a. OF., ad. L. *munimentum* fortification (in med.L. title-deed, etc.), f. *munire*; see -MENT.] 1. A document, e.g. a title-deed, etc., preserved as evidence of rights or privileges. Chiefly in *collect. pl.* 2. Anything serving as a means of defence or protection. Now *rare.* 1546. †b. *pl.* Things with which a person or place is provided; furnishings –1852. 3. *attrib.*, as *m.-room*, etc.; also m. deed, a title-deed 1656.

2. We cannot spare the coarsest m. of virtue EMERSON.

Muni·te, *v.* *Obs.* exc. *Hist.* *Pa. pple.* †**munyte**, †**munite.** late ME. [f. L. *munit-*, *munire*, earlier *mœnire*, f. *mœnia* pl., walls, ramparts.] *trans.* To fortify, strengthen, protect.

Munition (miuni·ʃən), *sb.* 1533. [a. F., ad. L. *munitionem*, f. *munire*; see prec.] †1. a. The action of fortifying or defending, fortification (*lit.* and *fig.*). b. *concr.* Anything that serves as a defence or protection 1533. 2. *sing.* and *pl.* = AMMUNITION *sb.* 1. Often *munition(s of war.* 1533.

1. With what m. he did fortifie His heart DANIEL. Hence **Muni·tion** *v.* to supply with munitions of war 1578; to furnish (a room) *rare* 1877; to work in a munition-factory 1916. **Muni·tioner**, one who has the custody of ammunition; (also **Munitionee·r**) a worker in a munition-factory.

Munity (miŭ·niti). Now *rare.* 1467. [App. alteration of IMMUNITY, as if f. L. *munire* to fortify.] A granted right or privilege.

‖**Munjeet** (mʊndʒī·t). 1813. [Bengālī *manjīṭh*.] The Bengal Madder, *Rubia cordifolia* (formerly *Munjista*); the roots of this plant used in dyeing.

Munjistin (mʊndʒi·stin). 1863. [f. mod.L. *Munjista* (see prec.) + -IN[1].] *Chem.* An orange colouring matter contained in munjeet.

Munnion (mʊ·nyən). 1593. [Alteration of *munial* MONIAL.] *Arch.* = MULLION.

Munsif: see MOONSIFF.

Muntin (mʊ·ntin). Also **-ing.** 1611 (**mountan**). [Earlier *mountaunt*, a. F. *montant*, subst. use of pres. pple. of *monter* to MOUNT.] *Building.* A central vertical piece between two panels, the side pieces being called *stiles*.

Muntjak (mʊ·ntdʒæk). 1798. [a. Sunda *minchek*.] A small Asiatic deer of the genus *Cervulus*, esp. *C. muntjak* of Java.

Muntz (mʊnts). [Patented 1832; name of G. F. *Muntz*, of Birmingham, inventor.] *M. metal*: an alloy of copper and zinc used esp. for sheathing the bottoms of ships.

Muræna, murena (miurī·nă). 1555. [a. L. *muræna*, *murena* sea-eel, lamprey, a. Gr. μύραινα, also σμύραινα, a fem. formation on μῦρος, σμῦρος sea-eel.] In early use, a kind of eel mentioned by ancient writers. Now usually, a fish of the genus *Muræna*, the type of the family *Murænidæ* or Eels. Hence **Muræ·noid** *a.* belonging to the family *Murænidæ* of fishes; *sb.* a m. fish 1803.

Murage (miūº·rėdʒ). Now *Hist.* late ME. [a. OF. *murage*, in med.L. *muragium*, f. F. *mur* MURE; see -AGE.] A toll or tax levied for the building or repairing of the walls of a town. Also the right of levying such a toll.

Mu·ral, *sb.* 1471. [a. F. *muraille*:—Com. Rom. **muralia*, repr. neut. pl. of *muralis* taken as fem. sing.; see -AL 2.] 1. A wall –1555. 2. [f. next.] *U.S.* A mural decoration.

Mural (miūº·răl), *a.* 1546. [a. F. *mural*, ad. L. *muralis*, f. *murus* wall; see MURE and -AL 1.] 1. Of, pertaining to, or resembling a wall 1586. 2. Placed, fixed, or executed on a wall 1561. †b. Of a fruit-tree: Growing against, and fastened to, a wall. Also of the fruit. –1731. 3. *Phys.* and *Path.* Belonging to or connected with the wall of the body or of any of its cavities. Cf. PARIETAL. 1884.

1. And soon repaird Her m. breach MILT. Lofty unbroken m. precipices 1880. **M. crown** (*Roman Antiq.*): an embattled crown, conferred upon the soldier who first scaled the wall of a besieged town. So *m. coronet, garland, wreath*, etc. Hence, any embattled crown. 2. The m. tablets to the memory of departed rectors 1837. *M. arch* (Astr.): a wall or arch to which is attached an instrument (*m. arc, circle, quadrant*, etc.) for observing meridian altitudes.

Murder (mɒ̄·ɹdəɹ), *sb.* Also (now *dial.* and *Hist.* or *arch.*) **murther.** [OE. *morðor* neut. :—OTeut. **murþrom* :—pre-Teut. **mrtro-m*, f. root **mer-* : *mor-* : *mr-* to die, whence L. *mori, mors* (*morti-*) death, Gr. μορτός, βροτός, etc., mortal. The change of OE. *ð* to *d* before *r* is exceptional.] 1. The most heinous kind of criminal homicide; an instance of this. In *Eng. Law*, defined as the unlawful killing of a human being with malice aforethought; often *wilful m.* b. Often applied to a death-sentence, killing of men in war, or any action causing destruction of human life, which is regarded as morally wicked, whether legal or not. *Judicial m.*: see JUDICIAL *a.* 1. 1551. †2. Without moral reprobation: Terrible destruction of life –1590. 3. As a cry or exclam. of real or pretended alarm 1470.

1. There was..one called Barrabas, which in the vproure had committed murthur COVERDALE *Mark* xv. 7. *M. in the first degree* (U.S.): i.e. where there are no extenuating circumstances; opp. to *m. in the second degree.* Provb. *M. will out*: i.e. cannot be hidden. *The m. is out*: said when something is suddenly revealed or explained. b. Condemn them for the Murther of Socrates STILLINGFL. 3. *To cry blue m.* (slang): to make an extravagant outcry.

Murder (mɒ̄·ɹdəɹ), *v.* Also (now *dial.*) **murther.** [prob. not a survival of OE. (*á-*, *for-*, *of-*)*myrðrian* (:—OTeut. **murþrjan*, f. **murþro-* MURDER *sb.*) but a new formation on the sb., partly suggested by OF. *mordrir* (mod.F. *meurtrir* to bruise).] 1. *trans.* To kill (a human being) unlawfully with malice aforethought; to kill wickedly, inhumanly, or barbarously ME. b. To slaughter in a terrible manner, to massacre ME. c. *absol.* To commit murder. Now *rare.* 1535. 2. To spoil by bad execution, representation, pronunciation, etc. 1644. 3. To consume (time) unprofitably 1712.

1. Hamilton murdered the old man in cold blood MACAULAY. *fig.* Macbeth does murther Sleepe, the innocent Sleepe SHAKS. 2. The Sense too oft is murder'd by the Sound 1693. 3. It kills time, or rather murders it, this company-keeping SCOTT.

Murderer (mɒ̄·ɹdərəɹ). ME. [Partly f. prec. + -ER[1]; partly a. AF. *mordreour*, *murdreour*, agent-n. f. *mordrer* = prec.] 1. One who murders or is guilty of a murder. †2. A small cannon or mortar used to clear the decks when an enemy boards a ship; a *murdering piece* 1497–1704. Hence **Mu·rderess** 1588.

Murderous (mɒ̄·ɹdərəs), *a.* 1535. [f. MURDER *sb.* + -OUS.] 1. Of persons: †Guilty of murder; capable of or bent on murder. Also *transf.* of weapons, physical agents, etc. 2. Of the nature of, characteristic of, or involving murder 1593.

1. Stay murtherous villaines SHAKS. The Murd'rous King MILT. 2. A murd'rous deede SHAKS. Where ..the brown Indian marks with m. aim GOLDSM. Hence **Mu·rderous·ly** *adv.*, **-ness.**

†**Mure**, *sb.* 1471. [a. F. *mur* :—L. *murum* (*murus*).] A wall –1651.

Mure (miūºɹ), *v.* late ME. [a. F. *murer* :—L. *murare*, f. *murus*.] *trans.* = IMMURE *v.* 1, 2; also, to block *up*, or build up (a door, gate, etc.) with bricks and mortar, stones, etc.

The fiue Kings are mured in a caue *Josh.* x. *heading.*

†**Mu·renger.** Also **muringer.** 1506. [Orig. *murager*, f. MURAGE; cf. *passenger*, etc.] An officer whose duty it was to keep the walls of a city in repair –1815.

Murex (miūº·reks). *Pl.* **murices** (miūº·risīz), also **murexes.** 1589. [a. L., prob. cogn. w. Gr. μύαξ sea-mussel.] A kind of shell-fish, which yields a purple dye. Hence **Mu·rexan** *Chem.* purpuric acid 1838. **Mu·rexide**, purpurate of ammonia 1838.

Muriate (miūº·riĕt), *sb.* 1790. [a. F. *muriate*, f. *muriatique* MURIATIC. See -ATE[1] 1 c.] *Chem.* Old name, still current *Comm.*, for CHLORIDE.

Muriate (miūº·rieⁱt), *v.* *rare.* 1699. [f. L. *muria* + -ATE[3].] *trans.* To pickle in brine.

Muriated (miūº·riĕⁱtėd) *ppl. a.* 1789. [f. MURIATE *sb.* or *v.* + -ED.] †a. *Chem.* Combined with chlorine. *M. iron, lead*, etc. = chloride of iron, etc. b. Impregnated with a chloride or chlorides.

Muriatic (miūºriæ·tik), *a.* 1675. [ad. L. *muriaticus* pickled in brine, f. *muria* brine.] †1. Pertaining to, of the nature of, consisting of, or containing brine 1830. 2. *Chem.* Applied to substances obtained from the sea, as in *m.*

acid, hydrochloric acid (now *Comm.*): †*m. salt*, a chloride; †*m. ether*, chloric ether.

Muricate (miūᵊ·rikět), *a.* 1661. [ad. L. *muricatus* shaped like the murex, f. *muric-* MUREX.] *Bot.* and *Zool.* Furnished with sharp points, studded with short hard excrescences. So Mu·ricated *a.* 1707.

Muricoid (miūᵊ·rikoid), *a.* 1890. [f. L. *muric-*, *murex* + -OID.] *Zool.* Resembling a murex or some part of a murex.

Mu·riform, *a.* 1832. [ad. mod.L. *muriformis*, f. L. *murus* wall: see -FORM.] *Bot.* Applied to cellular tissue suggesting resemblance to courses of bricks in a wall.

Murine (miūᵊ·rəin, -rin). 1607. [ad. L. *murinus*, f. *mur-*, *mus* mouse.] **A.** *adj.* Resembling a mouse; of or belonging to the family *Muridæ* or the sub-family *Murinæ*. **B.** *sb.* A member of this family or sub-family 1879.

Murk, mirk (mɒ̄ɹk), *sb.*[1] [OE. *mirce*, related to MURK *a.*] **1.** Darkness (*lit.* and *fig.*). Now chiefly *Sc.* **2.** Thick or murky air or vapour ME.

1. Ere twice in murke and occidentall dampe Moist Hesperus hath quench'd her sleepy Lampe SHAKS.

Murk (mɒ̄ɹk), *sb.*[2] 1676. = MARC.

Murk, mirk (mɒ̄ɹk), *a.* Now *dial.* (*Sc.*) and *poet.* or *arch.* [OE. *mirce* :—OTeut. **merkwjo-*, **merkwi-*. The Sc. spelling *mirk* is favoured in mod. poetic use.] Deficient in light, dark; dark in colour.

M. Monday *Sc.*, the day of the great solar eclipse of 29 Mar. (= 8 April N.S.) 1652. *fig.* Mirk despair Made me think life was little worth RAMSAY. Hence Mu·rkness, mi·rkness.

Murk, mirk (mɒ̄ɹk), *v.* ME. [f. MURK *a.*] †**1.** *intr.* To grow dark –1633. **2.** *trans.* To darken, obscure (*lit.* and *fig.*) ME.

Murky (mɒ̄·ɹki), *a.* *rare* bef. 17th c. ME. [f. MURK *sb.*[1] + -Y[1]] **1.** Of places: Dark and gloomy. **2.** Of darkness, the atmosphere: Thick and heavy. **3.** Sullen, 'dark'.

1. Hell is m. SHAKS. 2. So sented the grim Feature, and upturn'd His Nostril wide into the murkie Air MILT. Hence Mu·rkily *adv.* Mu·rkiness.

Murmur (mɒ̄·ɹmɒ̆ɹ), *sb.* late ME. [a. F. *murmure* masc., f. *murmurer* to MURMUR.] **1.** Subdued continuous sound; an instance of this. Now *rare* exc. in *the m. of* (a brook, the waves, etc.). **b.** *Path.* A sound of this kind heard in auscultation 1833. **2.** †**a.** Muttered or indistinct complaint, grumbling, or repining. **b.** An instance of this. late ME. †**3.** Rumour. *In m.*: 'whispered about'. –1772. **4.** A softly spoken word or sentence; subdued or nearly inarticulate speech 1674. **b.** *Phonetics.* Applied to the utterance of voiced sounds 1669.

1. All the live m. of a summer's day M. ARNOLD. 2. Some discontents there are; some idle murmurs DRYDEN. 4. What billing, exchanging stolen glances, and broken murmurs? GOLDSM. b. *m.-vowel*, the vowel (ə). Hence Mu·rmurous *a.* accompanied by m.; abounding in or characterized by murmurs; †complaining. Mu·rmurous·ly *adv.*, -ness.

Murmur (mɒ̄·ɹmɒ̆ɹ), *v.* late ME. [a. F. *murmurer*, ad. L. *murmurare*, f. *murmur*.] **1.** *intr.* To produce or emit a low continuous sound. **2.** To complain in low muttered tones; to grumble. Often with *at*, *against*. 1474. **3.** *trans.* To utter (sounds, words) in a low voice and indistinctly 1535.

1. They murmureden as dooth a swarm of Been CHAUCER. 2. The peple m. and ryse agayn theyr lord CAXTON. 3. The Pharisees heard that the people murmured such things concerning him *John* vii. 32. Hence †Murmura·tion, murmuring. late ME. –1687. Mu·rmurer 1526. Mu·rmuringly *adv.* 1611.

Murphy (mɒ̄·ɹfi). 1811. *slang.* [Use of a common Irish surname.] A potato.

Murphy('s) button. *Surg.* 1895. A device invented by J. B. Murphy, an American surgeon, for reuniting the parts of an intestine after complete severance.

†**Murr.** late ME. [Prob. of symbolic origin.] A severe form of catarrh –1756.

‖**Murra** (mɒ·ră). Also **murrha, myrrha.** 1598. [L. *murra* = late Gr. μόρρια.] *Rom. Antiq.* A substance of which precious vases and other vessels are made.

Murrain (mɒ·rěn), *sb.* and *a.* ME. [a. F. *morine* = Sp. *morriña* cattle plague, perh. a deriv. of L. *mori* to die.] **A.** *sb.* †**1.** Plague, pestilence –1613. **2.** An infectious disease in cattle. late ME. †**3.** Flesh of animals that have died of disease; also, dead flesh, carrion –1610. †**4.** Mortality (usu., by pestilence); *occas.* slaughter –1632. **5.** *attrib.*, as *m. cattle*, etc. 1490. †**B.** *adj.* Ill-conditioned, 'plaguy'. Also quasi-*adv.* 'confoundedly'. –1728.

A. 1. Phr. †*A m. of* (*it*), *m. meet them*, *m. on* (*one*), may a m. or pestilence fall on (some one). *With a m.*, *what a* (*the*) *m.*, etc.: exclamations of anger. 2. *transf.* The m. among bees is very rare 1657.

Murre (mɒ̄ɹ). 1602. [?] **a.** Any of several guillemots; **b.** the razor-billed auk. So **Murrelet** (mɒ·ɹlět), a small species of auk.

Murrey (mɒ·ri), *sb.* and *a.* Now *Hist.* or *arch.* late ME. [a. OF. *moré* adj. and sb., *morée* fem. sb., murrey colour, murrey-coloured cloth, ad. med.L. *moratus*, *morata*, f. L. *morum* mulberry.] (Of) the colour of the mulberry; purple-red; also, cloth of this colour.

M. and blue were the colours of the house of York 1834.

Murrhine (mɒ·rin, -əin), *a.* and *sb.* Also my-. 1579. [ad. L. *murr(h)inus*, f. *murra* (see MURRA); cf. late Gk. μόρρινος.] Made of or pertaining to murra. *M. glass*: a mod. fancy name for a delicate ware brought from the East, and made of fluor-spar. *sb.* A m. vase.

Murrion, Murry, Murther, Murza: see MORION[1], MURRAIN, MORAY, MURDER, MIRZA.

Mus, obs. f. MOUSE.

‖**Musa** (miū·ză). *Pl.* **-æ, -as.** Also 16–17th c. **muse.** 1578 (musa, mose). [mod.L., f. Arab. *mauzaʰ*.] In early use, the plantain or banana tree. Now only *Bot.*, a plant of the genus including the plantain tree (*M. paradisiaca*), the banana.

Hence Musa·ceous *a.* pertaining to the N.O. *Musaceæ* (typical genus *Musa*) 1852.

Musang (miusæ·ŋ). 1783. [a. Malay *musang* wild cat.] An E. Indian palm-civet (*Paradoxurus hermaphroditus*).

Mus.B., Mus.Bac. Abbrev. of mod.L. *Musicæ Baccalaureus* 'bachelor of music'.

Muscadel, var. of MUSCATEL.

‖**Muscadin** (müskadæ̃n). 1794. [Fr.; *muscadin* musk-comfit used transf.] A Parisian term for: A dandy, exquisite. Hence applied in contempt to the members of a moderate party in the French Revolution (about 1794–6), composed chiefly of young men of the upper middle class.

Muscadine (mɒ·skădəin, -in). 1517. [perh. Eng. formation on Pr. *muscat*, fem. *muscade* (see MUSCATEL) + -INE[4].] **1.** In full *m.-wine*. = MUSCATEL **1.** *Obs.* exc. *Hist.* **2.** In full *m. grape*. The name of varieties of grape having the flavour or odour of musk; also, a vine bearing a variety of this grape 1611.

‖**Muscæ** (mɒ·sī). 1753. [L., nom. pl. of *musca* fly.] Specks which appear to float before the eyes; in full *muscæ volitantes* (vǫlitæ·ntīz).

Muscal(l)onge, var. ff. MASKINONGE.

Muscardine (mɒskā·ɹdin). 1846. [a. F.] A disease of silkworms, caused by a vegetable parasite or fungus. Hence Mu·scardined *a.*

‖**Muscari** (mɒskēᵊ·ri, -rəi). 1597. [mod.L.] A genus of plants of the hyacinth tribe of *Liliaceæ*; a plant of this genus, esp. *M. botryoides*, the grape hyacinth.

Muscat (mɒ·skæt). 1578. [a. F. *muscat* adj., a. Pr. *muscat* adj. = It. *moscato* having the flavour of musk :—late L. **muscatus*, f. *muscus* MUSK *sb.*] **1.** In full *m. wine*. = MUSCATEL **1.** **2.** In full *m. grape*. = MUSCADINE **2.** 1655. †**3.** A kind of peach; also, a kind of pear –1741. **4.** A fungus, *Agaricus albellus* 1887.

Comb. **m. rose** [F. *rose muscate*], the musk-rose.

Muscatel, muscadel (mɒskăte·l, -de·l). late ME. [a. OF. *muscadel*, *muscatel*, a. Pr. **muscadel*, dim. of *muscat*; see prec.] **1.** A strong sweet wine made from the muscat or similar grape. **2.** = MUSCADINE **2.** 1517. **3.** *pl.* In full *m. raisins*. Raisins prepared from the muscatel grape, Malaga raisins 1652.

‖**Muschelkalk** (mu·ʃělkalk). 1833. [Ger., f. *muschel* mussel + *kalk* lime.] *Geol.* A limestone bed belonging to the red sandstone formation of Germany.

Muscid (mɒ·sid), *a.* (*sb.*). 1895. [f. mod.L. *Muscidæ*, f. *musca* fly; see -ID[3].] *Entom.* Of or pertaining to the dipterous family *Muscidæ*, or flesh-flies; *sb.* one of these.

Muscle (mɒ·s'l). 1533. [a. F., or ad. L. *musculus*, dim. of *mus* mouse, from the fancied similarity of the form of some muscles.] **1.** *Anat.* and *Phys.* Any one of the contractile fibrous bands or bundles, having the function of producing movement in the animal body. **2.** *collect.* The muscles collectively; muscular substance or tissue 1781. **b.** Used in ref. to the exercise of the muscles, esp. as opposed to the mind 1850.

1. *Not to move a m.*: to be perfectly motionless.

Comb.: **m. sensation, m. sense** = *muscular sensation, sense* (see MUSCULAR *a.* 1). Hence **Mu·scle** *v.*, *to m. in(to* (U.S.): to force one's way in(to. Mu·scled *a.* (chiefly with adj. or adv. prefixed). **Muscly** (mɒ·s'li), *a.* composed of muscle, exhibiting great muscular development (*rare*) 1594.

†**Muscle**: see MUSSEL.

†**Mu·scling.** 1709. [f. MUSCLE + -ING[1].] The delineation or representation of the muscles in Painting or Sculpture –1720.

Muscology (mɒskǫ·lŏdʒi). 1818. [ad. mod.L. *muscologia*, f. L. *muscus* moss; see -OLOGY.] = BRYOLOGY. So **Musco·logist.**

Muscose (mɒ·skōus), *a.* 1707. [ad. L. *muscosus*, f. *muscus*; see -OSE.] Moss-like.

Muscovado (mɒskŏvā·do). 1619. [a. Sp. *mascabado* adj. = Pg. *mascavado* (sugar) of lowest quality.] In full *m. sugar*: Raw or unrefined sugar obtained from the juice of the sugar-cane by evaporation and draining of the molasses.

Muscovite (mɒ·skŏvəit), *sb.*[1] and *a.* Now *Hist.* or *arch.* 1537. [ad. mod.L. *Muscovita*, f. *Muscovia* MUSCOVY; see -ITE[1] 1.] **A.** *sb.* A native or inhabitant of Muscovy; a Russian. **B.** *adj.* Of or pertaining to Muscovy or its inhabitants, Russian 1601. Also †**Musco·vian** 1555–1691.

Muscovite (mɒ·skŏvəit), *sb.*[2] 1862. [f. the name *Muscovy* (*glass*); see -ITE[1] 2 b.] *Min.* Common mica.

Muscovy (mɒ·skŏvi). 1573. [a. F. *Muscovie*, later *Moscovie*, ad. mod.L. *Moscovia*, f. Russian name of Moscow.] The name of the principality of Moscow, applied to Russia generally. **I.** Used attrib. or quasi-*adj.* in the name of things belonging to, produced in, or obtained from Muscovy, as **M. hide, leather,** Russia leather; †**M. glass,** common mica; also, occas., = TALC. **II.** Uses due to misinterpretation or perversion of designations connected with MUSK *sb.* **1.** A species of Crane's-bill or Geranium, *Erodium moschatum* 1688. **2.** = MUSK-RAT **1.** 1693. **3. Muscovy duck.** = MUSK-DUCK **1.** 1657.

Muscular (mɒ·skiŭlăɹ), *a.* 1681. [ad. mod.L. **muscularis*, f. *musculus* MUSCLE.] **1.** Of or belonging to muscle or the muscles 1685. **2.** Composed of or of the nature of muscle 1681. **3.** Characterized by muscle, having well-developed muscles 1736.

1. *M. feeling, sensation*: feeling or sensation which accompanies the action of the muscles. *M. sense*: the faculty of m. sensation, popularly regarded as a particular application of the sense of 'touch'. M. sound, or the resonance attending sudden m. contraction [of the heart] 1837. M. rheumatism 1896. 3. The spreading Shoulders, m., and broad THOMSON. Phr. *M. Christianity*: applied since about 1857 to a variety of Christian opinion and practice (associated with the writings of Charles Kingsley) which lays stress upon the importance of a healthy condition of body as conducive to morality and true religion. So **Muscula·rity**, the quality or state of being m. 1681. **Mu·scularize** *v.* to make m. **Mu·scularly** *adv.*

Musculation (mɒskiulē·ʃən). 1857. [a. F., f. L. *musculus*; see MUSCLE and -ATION.] **a.** The function of muscular movement. **b.** The disposition or arrangement of muscles.

Musculature (mɒ·skiŭlătiūɹ). 1875. [a. F., f. L. *musculus*.] The muscular system of the whole body or of one of its organs.

Muscule, obs. f. MUSCLE, MUSSEL.

Musculo- (mɒ·skiŭlo), comb. f. L. *musculus* MUSCLE, usu. in sense 'pertaining to muscle and . . .', as *m.-arterial, -cutaneous, -ligamentous, -tendinous* adjs.

†**Mu·sculous,** *a.* 1541. [ad. L. *musculosus*, f. *musculus*; see MUSCLE and -OUS.] = MUSCULAR -1775.

Mus.D., Mus.Doc. 1786. Abbrev. of mod.L. *Musicæ Doctor*, doctor of music.

Muse (miūz), *sb.*[1] late ME. [a. F., ad. L. *musa*, a. Gr. μοῦσα :—pre-Hellenic **montya*, f. Indo-Eur. *mon-* (: *men* : *mn-*) to think, remember; see MIND *sb.*] **1.** *Myth.* (Now usu. w. capital.) One of nine sister-goddesses, the offspring of Zeus and Mnemosyne (Memory), regarded as the inspirers of learning and the arts, esp. of poetry and music, and represented as young and beautiful virgins. **b.** In classical poetry *the muse* is often invoked as if there were only one 1629. **2.** (With or without capital.) **a.** Chiefly with possessive: The inspiring goddess of a particular poet. Hence, his particular genius, style, or spirit. late ME. **b.** *The M.*: poetry personified, as an object of devotion. So *the Muses*: the liberal arts, polite literature. 1755. **c.** *transf.* One under the guidance of a Muse, a poet 1615.

1. In modern use Clio is the Muse of history, Thalia of Comedy, Melpomene of tragedy, Euterpe of music, Terpsichore of dancing, and Urania of astronomy. The other names, Erato, Polyhymnia, and Calliope, are not so frequently mentioned in modern literature. So songe the myghty M., she That cleped ys caliope CHAUCER. 2. a. As though my muze were mute and durst not sing GASCOIGNE. Foole saide My m. to mee, looke in thy heart and write SIDNEY. b. And strictly meditate the thankles M. MILT. The votaries of the northern muses JOHNSON. c. That attenuated but majestic m. Mrs. Montagu 1905.

Muse (miūz), *sb.*[2] *arch.* 1475. [f. MUSE *v.*] †**a.** The action of musing; profound abstraction. **b.** A fit of abstraction; now only in *sing.* †**c.** *To be at a m.*: to 'wonder' (*whether*, etc.).

a. He..was fill'd With admiration, and deep M. to heare Of things so high and strange MILT.

†**Muse,** *sb.*[3] See MUSA.

Muse (miūz), *v.* ME. Now *literary.* [a. F. *muser* to waste time, also to meditate = Pr. *musar*, It. *musare* to stare about, idle, loiter.] **1.** *intr.* To be absorbed in thought; to ponder; also *trans.* (now *rare*) to ponder over, reflect upon, contemplate. **2.** *intr.* With dependent question: To be at a loss to discover, wonder *what, how*, etc. Now *rare.* late ME. **3.** To be astonished, wonder, marvel (now *rare, poet.*) ME.; †also *trans.* to marvel at 1567–1610. **4.** *intr.* To gaze meditatively *on, upon.* ME. †**5.** To mutter (discontentedly); to grumble, complain. late ME.–1598; also *trans.* late ME. only. **b.** *trans.* To say or murmur meditatively 1834.

1. Whyle I was thus musynge, the fyre kyndled COVERDALE *Ps.* xxxviii. 3. 2. Whyle men mused what the matter ment MORE. 3. Do not m. at me my most worthy Friends SHAKS. I m. my Lord of Gloster is not come SHAKS. I cannot too much m. Such shapes SHAKS. 4. The mind..Is left to m. upon the solemn scene WORDSW. 5. *Merry W.* v. v. 253. Hence **Mu·ser.** **Mu·singly** *adv.*

Muse: see MEUSE.

Museful (miū·zfŭl), *a.* 1618. [f. MUSE *sb.*[2] + -FUL.] Absorbed in thought; pensive.

Full of m. Mopings DRYDEN. Hence **Mu·sefully** *adv.* 1885.

Mu·seless, *a. pedantic.* 1644. [f. MUSE *sb.*[1] + -LESS, after Gr. ἄμουσος.] Without learning; uncultured.

The m. cry of the multitude RUSKIN.

Musellim (muse·lim). 1687. [Arab. *musallim*, lit. paymaster.] A Turkish officer, the lieutenant of a pasha.

Muset (miū·zėt). *Obs.* exc. *dial.* (**mussit**). 1592. [a. OF. *mucette, mussette*; see MEUSE.] = MEUSE *sb.* 1.

Musette (miuze·t). late ME. [a. F., dim. of OF. *muse.*] **1.** A kind of bagpipe. **2.** A soft pastoral air imitating the sound of the bagpipe; a dance for this music 1726. **3.** A reed stop on an organ 1825. **4.** A small kind of oboe 1880.

Museum (miuzī·ʌm). Also †**musæum.** 1615. [a. L., ad. Gr. μουσεῖον, μουσαῖον seat of the muses, f. μοῦσα MUSE *sb.*[1].] **1. a.** *Hist* (with capital M.) The university building erected at Alexandria by Ptolemy Soter. †**b.** *gen.* A building or apartment dedicated to the pursuit of learning or the arts; a study; a library -1760. **2.** A building used for storing and exhibiting objects illustrative of antiquities, natural history, art, etc. 1683.

2. The *Museum* or *Ashmole's Museum*, a neat Building in the City of Oxford 1706. *fig.* Miss Blanche.. had quite a little m. of locks of hair in her treasure-chest THACKERAY. *attrib.* **m.-piece,** a piece worthy of exhibition in a m.; a very fine example; also, in derogatory sense, an antiquated or outdated specimen.

Mush (mʌʃ), *sb.*[1] 1671. [App. a var. of MASH *sb.*[1]] **1.** *N. Amer.* A kind of porridge made with meal (chiefly of maize) boiled in water or milk. **2.** Anything soft and pulpy 1824.

2. *fig.* Stewed into m., hearing a popular preacher 1856.

Mush (mʌʃ), *sb.*[2] *slang.* 1821. [Shortened f. MUSHROOM *sb.*] **1.** An umbrella. **2.** A small cab-proprietor 1887.

Mush (mʌʃ), *v.* *Sc.* 1578. [Perh. a. OF. *moucher* to cut.] *trans.* 'To cut out with a stamp, to nick or notch' (Jam.).

Musha (mʌ·ʃă), *int.* 1831. [a. Ir. *maiseadh*, lit. 'if it is so'.] An exclam. of strong feeling used by Irish speakers.

Mushroom (mʌ·ʃrʊm), *sb.* late ME. [a. F. *mousseron*, usu. held to be f. *mousse* moss.] **1.** In early use, a fungus of any of the larger 'umbrella-shaped' species. Now, the common edible fungus, *Psalliota* (*Agaricus*) *campestris*, and closely resembling species. Some apply *mushroom* to the edible fungi, and *toadstool* to the poisonous. The mushroom is a proverbial type of rapid growth. **2.** *fig.* **a.** A person or family that has suddenly sprung into notice; an upstart. Also applied to a city, institution, etc. 1593. †**b.** A contemptible person -1769. **3. a.** *slang* (disused). An umbrella 1856. **b.** *colloq.* A low-crowned circular hat, *esp.* a lady's straw hat with down-curving brim 1865. **4.** = *mushroom-colour* 1884. **5.** *attrib.* or quasi-*adj.*, esp. with sense 'upstart', 'ephemeral' 1599.

2. a. Sheffield is an old oak; Birmingham is a m. BENTHAM. 5. A Mushrome Love sprung from a transitory View SAVAGE.

Comb.: **m. anchor,** a mooring anchor having a saucer-shaped head upon a central shaft; **m.-colour,** a pale pinkish colour resembling that of a m.; **m.-**†**coral, -stone** = FUNGITE; **-ring** = FAIRY-RING; **m. spawn,** the vegetative mycelium of mushrooms, usu. embedded in an earthy matrix.

Mushroom (mʌ·ʃrʊm), *v.* 1893. [f. prec.] *intr.* Of rifle-bullets: To expand and flatten (*out*). **b.** *U.S.* Of fire: To spread outwards 1903. **c.** *trans.* To cause (a bullet) to 'mushroom'.

Mu·shrooming, *gerund* and *pr. pple.* 1894. [f. prec. sb.] Gathering mushrooms.

Mushy (mʌ·ʃi), *a. colloq.* 1876. [f. MUSH *sb.*[1] + -Y[1].] Soft, pulpy; also *fig.* Hence **Mu·shiness.**

Music (miū·zik). ME. [a. F. *musique*, ad. L. *musica*, ad. Gr. μουσική (sc. τέχνη) lit. 'the art of the Muse' (fem. of μουσικός, f. μοῦσα MUSE *sb.*[1]).] **1.** That one of the fine arts which is concerned with the combination of sounds with a view to beauty of form and the expression of thought or feeling; also, the science of the laws or principles by which this art is regulated. **2.** Sounds in melodic or harmonic combination, whether produced by voice or instruments. late ME. **b.** *transf.* Applied, e.g., to the song of birds the murmur of running water, etc., *spec.* the cry of hounds on seeing the chase. Also in ironical collocations. 1590. **3.** Musical composition 1607. †**4.** A piece of music composed or performed -1674. **5.** A company of musicians; the company of musicians attached to a military force; a 'band of music' (see BAND *sb.*[3] 4). [Cf. F. *musique.*] *Obs.* exc. in military or court use. 1586. **6.** Musical instruments (now *dial.*) 1661. **7.** The written or printed score of a musical composition; such scores collectively; musical composition as represented by graphic symbols 1770. **8.** *U.S. colloq.* Liveliness; excited wrangling; diversion; sport 1859.

1. Considered as an art, music has two distinct branches, the art of the composer and that of the executant. The word is often used with special ref. to the executive branch, and to instrumental execution rather than vocal N.E.D. 2. Musick has Charms to sooth a savage Breast CONGREVE. *fig.* I shall now be kil'd, Even with the musick of her voice DAVENANT. He murmurs near the running brooks A m. sweeter than their own WORDSW. Phr. *Rough m.*: noisy uproar; *esp.* a din produced by knocking together pots, pans, kettles, etc. for purposes of annoyance 1708. b. Clashing of swords was then daily musicke in every street 1617. 3. Phr. *To set to m.*: to provide (a poem, etc.) with m. to which it may be sung. 4. *Cymb.* II. iii. 44. 5. He says many of the musique are ready to starve PEPYS. 6. She plays the M. without one sensation but the feel of the ivory at her fingers KEATS.

Phr. (*colloq.*). *To face the m.*, to face boldly the consequences of one's actions 1850.

attrib. and *Comb.*, as *m.-desk, -lesson, -master, -rack, -room, -stand*, etc.; **m.-book,** a book containing music-scores; **-box,** †(*a*) a barrel-organ; (*b*) = *musical box* (see MUSICAL *a.*); (*c*) *joc.*, a pianoforte; **-demy,** a white thick soft paper, used by music publishers for printing music, 21 by 14½ inches; **m. gallery,** a gallery in a church or hall for the accommodation of the musicians; **-hall,** a hall used for musical performances *spec.* (since about 1885) a hall licensed for singing, dancing, and other entertainments exclusive of dramatic performances; also *attrib.*; **-loft,** a gallery for musicians; *spec.* an organ-loft; **-paper,** paper ruled for writing m. upon; **-pen,** a pen having five points for drawing at one time the five lines of the musical stave; †**-shell,** one of several species of gasteropodous molluscs of the family *Volutidæ*, having markings on the shell resembling written music; **m.-stool,** a stool (usu. with adjustable seat) for one who plays on the piano. Hence **Mu·sicless** *a.*

Musical (miū·zikăl), *a.* (and *sb.*) late ME. [a. F., ad. med.L. *musicalis*, f. L. *musica* MUSIC.] **A.** *adj.* **1.** Of or belonging to music. **2.** Having the nature of music; tuneful, melodious, harmonious; pleasing in sound, euphonious. Of sounds: Having the nature of 'tones', as dist. from mere 'noises'. late ME. **3.** Fond of or skilled in music. late ME. **4.** Set to or accompanied by music 1685.

2. The musicall confusion Of hounds and eccho in coniunction SHAKS.

Spec. collocations: **m. box,** a mechanical m. instrument consisting of a revolving toothed cylinder working upon a resonant comb-like metal plate; **m. chairs,** a game in which a number of players march to music round a smaller number of chairs and each try to secure a seat when the music stops; **m. chime,** a set of bells arranged to play a tune, a carillon; **m. clock,** a clock which produces short tunes at regular intervals; **m. glasses** = HARMONICA 1 a, b; **m. ride,** a kind of equestrian dance executed by the Life or Horse Guards to the accompaniment of music; **m. shell** = *music-shell*; **m. snuff-box,** a snuff-box containing a small m. instrument worked by machinery.

B. *sb.* A musical party 1823. Also in Fr. form **musicale.** *U.S.* 1883. Hence **Musica·lity,** m. quality or character. **Mu·sical-ly** *adv.*, **-ness.**

Musician (miuzi·ʃăn). late ME. [a. F. *musicien*, f. L. *musica* MUSIC.] **1.** One skilled in the science or practice of music. **2.** A professional performer of (esp. instrumental) music. Also *transf.* and *fig.* 1450.

Musicens (whiche encludeth singing and plaieng) 1555. Hence **Musi·cianly** *a.* characteristic or worthy of a skilled m. 1864.

Musicianer (miuzi·ʃănəɹ). Now chiefly *Irish.* 1540. [f. prec. + -ER[1].] = MUSICIAN.

Musico- (miū·ziko), comb. f. L. *musicus*, as in *m.-dramatic* adj., etc.

Musimon, obs. f. MUSMON.

Musit, var. of MUSET.

†**Mu·sive,** *a.* and *sb.* 1506. [a. F. *musif, -ive*, ad. late L. *musivus*, in *opus musivum* mosaic work.] **A.** *adj.* = MOSAIC *a.*[1] **1.** -1813. **B.** *sb.* = MOSAIC *sb.* 1. -1658.

Musk (mʌsk), *sb.* late ME. [a. F. *musc*, ad. late L. *muscus*, med.L. *mos(c)hus*, late Gr. μόσκος, μόσχος.] **1.** An odoriferous reddish-brown substance secreted in a gland or sac by the male musk-deer. It is used as the basis of many perfumes, and in medicine as a stimulant and antispasmodic. Also applied occas. to substances of similar odour secreted by certain other animals. **b.** An artificial preparation imitating musk 1658. **2.** An animal which produces 'musk', now usu. the MUSK-DEER, sometimes called *Tibet* (or *pouched*) *m.*; also applied to other animals resembling this or possessing a musky smell 1470. **3.** A name for plants having a musky odour, esp. *musk-plant* (*b*) 1731. **b.** Short for *m. apple, pear* 1708.

1. They lefte a very sweete sauour behynde them sweeter then muske 1555. **b.** Animall-musk, seems to excell the vegetable SIR T. BROWNE. **2.** In the m. the fur is thick and elastic, fit for a cold country 1879. **3.** Close in a bower of hyacinth and m. KEATS.

attrib. and *Comb.* **a.** In names for the receptacle in the musk-deer, etc., which contains the musk, as *m.-bag, -gland, -pod, -sac.*

b. In the names of plants having a musky odour, as **m. carnation,** the clove-gillyflower; **m. cranes-bill, geranium,** *Erodium moschatum*; **m. crow-foot, root,** *Adoxa Moschatellina*; **m.-flower** = *musk-plant* (*b*); **-hyacinth,** one of the grape-hyacinths, *Muscari moschatum*; **-mallow,** (*a*) *Malva moschata*; (*b*) = *musk-plant* (*a*); **m. orchis,** *Herminium Monorchis*; **m.-plant,** †(*a*) *Hibiscus Abelmoschus*; (*b*) *Mimulus moschatus*; (*c*) = *musk-mallow* (*a*); **-rose,** a rambling rose, *Rosa moschata*, having fragrant white flowers; **-seed,** the seed of *Hibiscus Abelmoschus*; **m. thistle,** the thistle *Carduus nutans.*

c. In the names of varieties of fruits having a musky smell or taste, as *m. apple, pear,* etc.

d. In the names of animals having a musky odour, as †**m.-beaver** = MUSK-RAT 1; **-beetle,** a longicorn beetle, *Callichroma moschata*; **-bison, -buffalo** = *m.-ox*; **-kangaroo,** a very small, rat-like, arboreal kangaroo, *Hypsiprymnodon moschatus*; **-mole,** a Mongolian mole, *Scaptochirus moschatus*; **-ox,** a ruminant of Arctic America, *Ovibos moschatus*; **-shrew,** the Indian musk-rat (see MUSK-RAT 2); **-tortoise, -turtle,** a small American fresh-water turtle, *Aromochelys odorata*; **-weasel,** any viverrine carnivore.

Musk, *v. rare.* 1632. [f. MUSK *sb.*] *trans.* To perfume with or as with musk.

Muskadel(l, Muskalinge, etc., **Muskat,** var. MUSCATEL, MASKINONGE, MUSK-CAT.

†**Mu·sk-cat.** Also †**musket, -at,** etc. 1551. The animal from which musk is got; usu., the MUSK-DEER. Cf. CIVET-CAT. -1794. **b.** *transf.* applied as a term of reproach to a fop; also to a courtesan 1566–1777.

†**Mu·sk-cod.** 1599. [COD *sb.*[1]] **1.** The bag or gland containing musk 1672–1721. **2.** *transf.* A scented fop -1634.

Mu·sk-deer. 1681. A small hornless ruminant (*Moschus moschiferus*) of Central Asia, the male of which yields the perfume called 'musk' (see MUSK *sb.* 1). Also, a chevrotain.

Mu·sk-duck. 1774. **1.** A tropical American duck, *Cairina moschata*, erron. called the *Muscovy* and *Barbary duck.* **2.** An Australian duck, *Biziura lobata*, so called from the musky odour of the male 1834.

Musked (mɒskt), *a.* Now *rare.* 1576. [f. MUSK *sb.* or *v.* + -ED.] Flavoured or perfumed with musk; tasting like musk. (Often in names of plants and fruits, transl. mod.L. *moschatus.*)

Musket[1] (mɒ·skėt). *Obs.* exc. *Hist.* late ME. [a. ONF. *musket, mousquet*, dim. of Com. Rom. **mosca* :—L. *musca* fly.] The male of the sparrowhawk.

Musket[2] (mɒ·skėt). 1587. [a. F. *mousquet*, ad. It. *moschetto*, orig. a kind of sparrow-hawk (see prec.). Cf. *falcon, falconet*, etc.] A hand-gun carried by infantry soldiers. (Orig. applied to the matchlock gun, and now usu. restricted to obsolete kinds of infantry gun, as dist. from the rifle.)

Muskettes and calleevers and holebertes shall be provided for this company 1587.

Comb.: **m.-arrow,** a short arrow discharged from a m.; **-rest,** a forked staff to support the heavy m. formerly in use; **m. shot,** (*a*) shot fired from a musket, a musket-ball, (*b*) the range of a musket; **-slit,** a slit in a wall through which a m. may be fired. Hence **Musketee·r** *Hist.*, a soldier armed with a m. 1590.

Musketo(e, obs. ff. MOSQUITO.

Musketoon (mɒskėtū·n). *Obs.* exc. *Hist.* 1638. [a. F. *mousqueton*, ad. It. *moschettone*, f. *moschetto* MUSKET[2]; see -OON.] A kind of musket, short and with a large bore; a soldier armed with this.

Musketry (mɒ·skėtri). 1646. [ad. F. *mousqueterie*, f. *mousquet*; see MUSKET[2] and -ERY, -RY.] **1.** Muskets collectively. **2.** The fire of muskets 1756. **3.** The art or science of manipulating small arms 1854. **4.** Musketeers 1772.

Musk melon. 1573. [f. MUSK *sb.*] The MELON, *Cucumis Melo.* (Applied both to fruit and plant.)

Mu·sk-rat. 1620. **1.** A large aquatic rodent, *Fiber zibethicus*, common throughout N. America, so called from its musky smell. Also called MUSQUASH. **b.** The fur or skin of the musk-rat 1879. **2.** Applied to other rat-like animals having a musky odour; as the musk-kangaroo, the musk-shrew, the DESMAN, etc. 1681.

Mu·sk-root. 1844. Any of several plants having strong-scented roots, as moschatel, spikenard, sumbul; also, a drug obtained from the root of sumbul.

Mu·sk-tree. 1848. Any of several Australian trees or shrubs having a musky smell, as *Marlea vitiensis, Olearia argophylla* (Silver-leaved M.), and *O. viscosa* (Dwarf M.).

Mu·sk-wood. 1725. Any of several trees having a musky smell, as *Trichilia moschata* and *Guarea trichilioides* of the West Indies, and the Australian silver-leaved musk-tree; the wood of any of these.

Musky (mɒ·ski), *a.* 1610. [f. MUSK *sb.* + -Y[1].] Smelling or tasting of musk, or somewhat like musk; scented with musk. Hence **Mu·skiness.**

Muslim: see MOSLEM.

Muslin (mɒ·zlin). 1609. [a. F. *mousseline*, ad. It. *mussolina, -ino*, f. *Mussolo*, the town of Mosul in Mesopotamia, where muslin was formerly made.] **1.** General name for the most delicately woven cotton fabrics, used for ladies' dresses, curtains, hangings, etc. Also, a garment of this. **b.** *U.S.* Any of various coarser and heavier cotton goods, used for shirts, bedding, etc. 1872. **2.** *slang.* 'The fair sex'. *A bit of m.*, a woman or girl. 1823. **3.** *Naut. slang.* 'Canvas', sails 1822. **4.** *attrib.* or *adj.* Made or consisting of muslin 1684.

Muslinet (mɒzline·t). Also **-ette.** 1787. [f. MUSLIN + -ET.] A thick variety of muslin; used for infants' clothing, etc.

Musmon (mɒ·smǫn). Also †**musi-.** 1601. [a. L. *musimon-* (Pliny), late Gr. μούσμων (Strabo).] = MOUFFLON.

‖**Musnud** (mɒ·snɒd). 1763. [Urdū *masnad*, a. Arab. *misnad*, f. *sanada* to lean against.] A seat made of cushions, esp. one used as a throne by native princes of India.

Musquash (mɒ·skwǫʃ). 1624. [a. Abnaki *muskwessu* or other Algonkin equivalent.] The musk-rat, or its fur (1884).

attrib. and *Comb.*, as **m. root,** Water Hemlock, *Cicuta maculata.*

Musquaw (mɒ·skwǭ). 1861. [Cree Indian.] An American name for the Black Bear.

Musque(e)to, etc., **Musquet,** var. MOSQUITO, MUSKET.

†**Mu·srol.** 1551. [a. F. *muserolle*, ad. It. *museruola*, f. *muso* muzzle.] The nose-band of a bridle -1833.

Muss (mɒs), *sb.*[1] *Obs.* exc. *dial.* 1591. [?] A game in which small objects are thrown down to be scrambled for.

Muss (mɒs), *sb.*[2] *dial.* and *U.S.* 1843. [app. var. of MESS *sb.*] **1.** A disturbance, row 1848. **2.** A state of untidiness; a muddle, mess. Hence **Muss** *v. trans.* to make untidy; to crumple, ruffle; to smear, mess; to entangle, confuse 1850.

Mussel (mɒ·s'l). [OE. *muscle*, etc., wk. fem., a. late L. *muscula*, altered form of L. *musculus*, dim. of *mus* mouse.] **1.** A bivalve mollusc belonging to either of the two families *Mytilacea* (Sea Mussels) and *Unionacea* (Fresh-water Mussels). **2.** A fossil bivalve shell found in ironstone bands in coal 1834.

attrib. and *Comb.*, as **m. band** *Geol.*, a bed of clay ironstone containing fossil bivalve shells, anthracosia, etc.; **m.-bank, -bed,** a layer of mussels at the bottom of the sea; **m. digger** *U.S.*, a name for the California grey whale; **m. plum,** a dark purple variety of plum; **m. scale,** an insect having the shape of a small mussel-shell, which attacks the bark of apple-trees.

Mu·ssel-shell. OE. The shell of a mussel. **b.** One who gapes like a mussel-shell. *Merry W.* IV. v. 29.

†**Mu·ssitate,** *v.* 1626. [f. L. *mussitat-*, ppl. stem of *mussitare*, freq. of *mussare* to mutter.] *intr.* To mutter -1721. So †**Mussita·tion** 1649–1891.

‖**Mussuck** (mɒ·sɒ̆k). *Anglo-Ind.* 1610. [Hindī *maşak.*] A leather water-bag.

Mussulman (mɒ·sʊ̆lmæ̆n), *sb.* and *a. Pl.* **-mans.** *Catachr. pl.* **-men.** 1563. [a. Pers. *musulmān*, primarily an adj. f. Pers. (a. Arab.) *muslim*; see MOSLEM.] (A) Mohammedan. Hence **Mussulmanic,** †**Mu·ssulmanish** *adjs.* = M.; **Mu·ssulmanism** (now *rare*), Mohammedanism; ‖**Mussulmanlik,** the M. faith, Islam; †**Mu·ssulmans** *Anglo-Ind.*, the Urdū language. So **Mu·ssulwoman,** a female M. (*joc.*) 1668.

Mussy (mɒ·si), *a. U.S.* 1859. [f. MUSS *sb.*[2] + -Y[1].] Untidy, rumpled, tousled. Hence **Mu·ssiness.**

Must (mɒst), *sb.*[1] OE. [ad. L. *mustum*, orig. neut. (sc. *vinum*) of *mustus* adj., new, fresh.] **1.** New wine; grape-juice unfermented or before fermentation is complete. Also *new m.* †**b.** *In (the) m., on the m.*: said of wine in process of fermentation 1533–1700. **2.** †**a.** Any juice or liquor undergoing or prepared for undergoing alcoholic fermentation. late ME.–1708. **b.** The pulp of apples or pears after the juice has been pressed out in making cider or perry (*dial.*) 1670. †**3.** A variety of cider-apple 1664–1707.

1. Will put newe muste into old bottelles UDALL. *fig.* Els the Jewes might haue..preferred the old wine of Moses lawe, aboue the new m. of the doctrine of Christ 1563.

Must (mɒst), *sb.*[2] 1602. [perh. back-formation f. MUSTY *a.*] Mustiness; mould.

Must, *sb.*[3] 1603. The verb MUST used as a noun.

Must is for kings, And low obedience for low underlings DEKKER.

Must (mɒst), *a.* and *sb.*[4] Also **musth.** 1871. [a. Urdū *mast*, a. Pers. *mast*, lit. 'intoxicated'.] **A.** *adj.* Applied to male animals, as elephants and camels, in a state of dangerous frenzy to which they are subject at irregular intervals. Phr. *To go m.* **B.** *sb.* The condition or state of being 'must'; an elephant in must 1878.

Must (mɒst), *v.*[1] [OE. *mōste*, pa. t. of *mōt* pret.-pres., MOTE *v.*] †**I.** The pa. t. of MOTE *v.*, in senses 1 and 2. -1471. **II.** Used as a pres. tense, and hence (under certain conditions) as a pa. tense corresponding to this. **1.** Expressing necessity: Am (is, are) obliged or required to; have (has) to; it is necessary that (I, you, he, it, etc.) should: = MOTE *v.* 2. ME. **b.** Used to express a fixed or certain futurity. *I m.* = I am fated or certain to..., I shall certainly or inevitably... late ME. **c.** In expressions like *I m. say* = I cannot help saying. Also in explanatory clauses, as *you m. know* or *understand* = you ought to be informed, I would have you know. 1563. **d.** As a pa. tense: Was obliged, had to; it was necessary that (I, he, it, etc.) should. (Now only in oblique narration, and when the speaker has in his mind what might have been said or thought at the time.) 1691. **e.** As a pa. or historical pres. tense with ref. to some foolish or annoying action or some untoward event. Now *colloq.* late ME. **2.** In the 1st pers., *must* often expresses an insistent demand or a firm resolve on the part of the speaker. Hence also in the 2nd and 3rd persons, rendering sentiments imputed to others. late ME. **3.** As *must* has no pa. pple., the need of a past conditional is supplied by placing the principal verb in the perfect infinitive; as, *I m. have seen (done) it* 1460. **4.** Expressing the inferred or presumed certainty of a fact; either (with present inf.) relating to the present time, as in *you m. be aware of this* = I cannot doubt that you are aware of this; or (with perf. inf.) relating to the past, as in *he m. have done it* = it is to be concluded that he did it 1652. **5.** In *m. not* the negative has the same effect as if it belonged to the following infinitive 1583. **6.** Elliptical uses. **a.** With ellipsis of a verb of motion (now *arch.*) late ME. **b.** With ellipsis of infinitive to be supplied from the context ME.

1. Tom, you m. go with us to [etc.] SWIFT. **b.** He m. increace: and I muste decreace TINDALE *John* iii. 30. **c.** I m. beg to be absolved from the promise JOWETT. **d.** He could not bear to be idle..he m. always be doing something 1894. **e.** Just when I was busiest, that bore C. m. come in and waste three hours (*mod.*). 2. I m., and will go DRYDEN. Let us leave this room, if you m. laugh 1798. 3. If he had looked he m. have seen the light of the approaching train 1896. 4. This m. have been a sad shock to the poor disconsolate parent GOLDSM. 5. You m. not meruaile Helen at my course SHAKS. 6. a. His work is done, the minister m. out SWIFT. b. I have not spoken to the king One word; and one I m. Farewell! TENNYSON.

Must, *v.*² *Obs.* exc. *dial.* 1530. [f. as MUST *sb.*²] *intr.* and *trans.* To become, or make, musty or mouldy.

Mustache: see MOUSTACHE.

Mustachio (mustɑ·ʃo, mɒ̆s-). *Pl.* **mustachios** (-ʃoz). 1551. [Partly from Sp. *mostacho*, and partly from It. *mostaccio* MOUSTACHE, a deriv. of Gr. *μυστακ-*, *μύσταξ* masc. moustache, said to be a var. of *μάσταξ* fem., mouth, jaws. Obs. in sing., but the pl. *mustachios* is largely used.] = MOUSTACHE 1, 2; *transf.* esp. †the whiskers of a cat; †the awn or bristles of certain grasses 1591–1790. Hence **Mustachioed** *a.* moustached.

Mustang (mɒ·stæŋ). 1808. [app. f. older Sp. *mestengo*, f. *mesta*, an association of graziers.] 1. The wild or half-wild horse of Mexico, California, etc. Also *m. pony*. 2. In full *M. grape*: A small red grape, *Vitis candicans*, of Texas 1854.

Mustard (mɒ·stăɹd). ME. [a. OF. *mo(u)starde* (mod.F. *moutarde*), f. Com. Rom. **mosto* MUST *sb.*¹ The name etymologically belongs to the condiment as orig. prepared from the ground seeds mixed with must.] 1. The seeds of the plant mustard (see 2) ground or pounded to a powder, sometimes called *flour of m.*; also, this substance as made into a paste, and used as a condiment, or applied to the skin as a poultice or plaster. 2. Any of the cruciferous plants yielding these seeds, forming the Linnæan genus *Sinapis*, but now included in the genus *Brassica*; esp. *B. nigra*, the black (or brown) mustard, and *B. alba*, the white mustard ME. b. Applied with defining word to various other (chiefly cruciferous) plants resembling mustard in appearance, taste, etc. 1597.

2. *M. and cress*, the plants white mustard and cress (*Lepidium sativum*) used in the seed-leaf as a salad-herb. b. **Poor man's m.**, hedge-garlic. **Wild m.**, (*a*) charlock, *Brassica arvensis*; (*b*) *Raphanus Raphanistrum*.

Comb.: **m. beetle**, a small black beetle (*Phædon armoraciæ*) destructive to mustard plants; †**m.-bowl**, a wooden bowl in which mustard seed was pounded, proverbially referred to as the instrument for producing stage thunder; **-gas**, a variety of poison gas; **-oil**, an oil obtained from mustard seed; **-pot**, a pot or cruet for holding table m.; **m.-shrub**, a West Indian shrub, *Capparis ferruginea*, the berries of which have a pungent flavour; **-tree**, the m. of the N.T., described as a 'tree' (see next 1).

Mustard seed. late ME. 1. The seed of mustard.

The 'mustard seed' (κόκκος σινάπεως) of the N.T., spoken of as producing a 'tree' (*Matt.* xiii. 31), is prob. the seed of the black mustard (*Brassica nigra*), which in Palestine grows to a great height.

†2. = MUSTARD 2. –1681. 3. *U.S.* A very fine shot used in shooting birds to minimize injury to the plumage 1884.

Mustee (mɒstī·), **mestee** (mestī·). 1699. [Corruptly a. Sp. *mestizo* (pronounced mestī·þo); see MESTIZO.] The offspring of a white and a quadroon; also, loosely, a half-caste.

Musteline (mɒ·stĭləin). 1656. [ad. L. *mustelinus* of or belonging to a weasel, f. *mustela* weasel.] A. *adj.* Of, pertaining to, or characteristic of the subfamily *Mustelinæ* of weasels; *spec.* of the brown tawny colour of the summer fur of the weasel. B. *sb.* A m. animal 1891.

Muster (mɒ·stəɹ), *sb.*¹ late ME. [a. OF. *mo(u)stre* (later *monstre*, now *montre*) repr. Com. Rom. verbal noun f. **mostrare* to show :—L. *monstrare*.] †1. The action, or an act, of showing; manifestation; exhibition, display –1661. 2. A pattern, specimen, example. Now only *Comm.*, a pattern, sample. late ME. 3. An act of mustering soldiers, sailors, etc.; an assembling of men for inspection, ascertainment of numbers, introduction into service, exercise, or the like. Phr. *To make, take a m.* late ME. 4. The number of persons or things mustered or assembled on a particular occasion; an assembly, collection. late ME. 5. A muster-roll 1565. 6. *Muster out*: the action of 'mustering out'; discharge from service. *U.S.* 1892.

1. They begin to make some m. and shew of their learning 1581. 2. In mod. use confined to certain particular branches of commerce or particular localities (used, e.g. in the Sheffield cutlery trade, and by British merchants in Asia) N. E. D. A few musters of new Teas have been shewn 1879. 3. They took a m. and found their Army amounted to four thousand Foot, and six hundred Horse 1726. Phr. *To pass m.*: orig. *Mil.* to undergo m. or review without censure; hence *transf.* and *fig.* to bear examination or inspection, to come up to the required standard, to be above, or go free from, censure; to succeed, be accepted (*as* or *for* the possessor of certain qualities). *False m.*: a fraudulent presentation at a m., or a fraudulent inclusion in a muster-roll, of men who are not available for service. Formerly often *fig.* 4. A tolerable m. of amateurs and boxing gentry 1810. 5. I..got put down upon the m. DICKENS.

attrib. and *Comb.*: **m.-book**, a book in which muster-rolls are transcribed 1587; **m.-master**, an officer who was responsible for the accuracy of the muster-roll (now *Hist.*) 1579; **m.-roll**, a register of the officers and men in an army or ship's company (also *fig.*) 1605.

†**Muster**, *sb.*² 1466. Short for MUSTERDEVILLERS –1549.

Muster (mɒ·stəɹ), *v.* ME. [a. OF. *mo(u)strer* :—L. *monstrare* to show.] †1. *trans.* To show, display, exhibit; to show up, report, tell, explain –1622. †b. *intr.* for *refl.* To show, to appear, to be displayed; to make a (good, bad, etc.) appearance –1597. 2. *trans.* To collect or assemble (*primarily* soldiers) for ascertainment of numbers, inspection, exercise, display, or introduction into service. late ME. b. *intr.* for *refl.* Of an army, etc.: To come together for inspection, exercise, or preparation for service 1450. †c. *trans.* To enlist, enroll –1748. d. To call the roll of. Now chiefly *Naut.* 1670. e. Of an army, etc.: To comprise, to number 1837. 3. To collect, bring together (persons or things); *esp.* to bring forward from one's own stores 1586. b. *fig.* To summon, gather up (one's thoughts, courage, strength, etc.) 1588. 4. *intr.* To assemble, gather together in a body 1603. 5. *trans.* To 'take stock of' 1625. 6. *intr.* To pass muster *for*. LAMB.

2. How busy he was in mustering, how diligent in setting forward HALL. I then in London,..Muster'd my Soldiers SHAKS. b. *fig.* A field of fancies musterd in my mynd 1611. c. We being not knowne, not muster'd Among the Bands SHAKS. d. Phr. *To m. in* (U.S.): to m. (a watch) at the time of duty. *To m. in (into) (the) service* (U.S.): to enroll as recruits. *To m. out (of service)* U.S.: to summon together in order to discharge from service; to pay off (soldiers). 3. All the Hands we could m...were but twelve 1743. b. Muster your Wits, stand in your owne defence SHAKS. Mustring all her wiles MILT. 4. Oh, heauens Why doe's my bloud thus m. to my heart? SHAKS. 5. Mustering cattle 1875.

Phr. **Muster up.** a. To bring together (troops) for battle, etc. b. *fig.* To summon up, gather up, marshal.

a. In Oxfordshire shalt m. vp thy friends SHAKS. b. She had mustered up courage to speak to him 1893.

†**Musterdevillers.** (Many variant spellings.) 1400. [f. *Mouster(de)villers*, old form of the name of Montivilliers, Normandy.] A grey woollen cloth –1564.

Musty (mɒ·sti), *a.* (and *sb.*) 1530. [perh. cogn. w. MOIST *a.*] 1. a. Spoiled with damp; moist and fetid. b. Having the rank odour or taste of mouldy substances 1530. 2. *fig.* a. Spoiled with age; stale; antiquated 1592. b. Of persons: Dull, 'mouldy', antiquated 1637. 3. Ill-humoured, peevish, sullen. *Obs.* exc. *dial.* 1620. †4. *sb.* A kind of snuff having a musty flavour. STEELE.

1. Old m. papers 1693. Unsavoury smells of m. hay DICKENS. b. Do not all Houses and Places grow m...if the Air be any way prevented by Window-shutters..? 1683. Sour milk and m. eggs 1891. 2. a. Some old m. laws 1683. b. A m. moralist FIELDING. Hence **Mu·stily** *adv.* **Mu·stiness.** †**Mu·sty** *v.* to become or make m. or mouldy 1631–1707.

Mutable (miū·tăb'l), *a.* and *sb.* late ME. [ad. L. *mutabilis*, f. *mutare*; see -ABLE.] A. *adj.* 1. Inconstant in mind, will, or disposition; fickle; unsettled, variable. Now *rare*. 2. Liable or subject to change or alteration. b. *Gram.* Subject to mutation 1707.

1. The m. mynde of quene Elyzabeth 1548. 2. The Use of Clothes continues, though the Fashion of them has been m. STEELE.

B. *sb.* A mutable consonant 1821.

[Letters] capable of aspiration, or mutables 1843. Hence **Mutabi·lity**, **Mu·tableness** (now *rare*). **Mu·tably** *adv.*

Mutage (miū·tĕdʒ). 1839. [a. F., f. *muter*; see MUTE *v.*⁴] The process of muting wine.

Mutant (miū·tănt), *a.* and *sb.* 1901. [ad. L. *mutant-*, pr. pple. of *mutare* MUTATE.] *Biol.* (A form) resulting from mutation.

Mutate (miutēⁱ·t), *v.* 1818. [f. L. *mutat-*, ppl. stem of *mutare* (:—older **moitare*, f. root **moi-* to change); see -ATE ³.] a. *intr.* To undergo change; *Gram.* to undergo mutation. b. *trans.* (*Gram.*) To cause mutation of.

Mutation (miutēⁱ·ʃən). late ME. [a. F. *mutacion*, *-ation*, ad. L. *mutationem*; see MUTATE and -ATION.] 1. The action or process of changing; alteration, change. 2. *Mus.* In mediæval solmization: The change from one hexachord to another involving a change of the syllable applied to a given note 1597. 3. *Philol.* a. In the Celtic langs., a change of an initial consonant, depending on the character of the preceding word 1843. b. In Germanic langs., modification of an accented vowel under the influence of a following vowel (*i, u, a/o*) or consonants *j* (= *y*), *w*; umlaut. 1875. 4. *Biol.* Used (in contrast to *variation*) for the kind of change which results in the production of a new species. Hence quasi-*concr.* a species resulting from this process. 1894.

1. O world! But that thy strange mutations make vs hate thee Life would not yeelde to age SHAKS.

attrib. **Mutation stop**, an organ-stop whose pipes produce tones a fifth or a major third above the proper pitch of the key struck, or above one of its octaves.

‖**Muta·tis muta·ndis**, *adv. phr.* 1498. [L.] 'Things being changed that have to be changed', i.e. with the necessary changes.

Mutative (miū·tătiv), *a.* 1743. [a. OF. *mutatif*, a. med. L. *mutativ-us*, f. *mutat-*; see MUTATE *v.* and -ATIVE.] Of, pertaining to, or characterized by mutation or sudden variation.

Mutch (mɒtʃ). *dial.* and *Sc.* 1473. [a. MDu. *mutse* (mod.Du. *muts*) = MHG., mod. G. *mütze*; cf. AMICE ².] †1. *Sc.* A night covering for the head –1831. 2. A cap or coif, usu. of linen, worn by women and young children 1634.

Mutchkin (mɒ·tʃkin). *Sc.* late ME. [a. early mod.Du. *mudseken* (now *mutsje*), app. a dim. of *mud(de* MUD *sb.*²] A measure of capacity for liquids, etc.; the fourth part of the old Scots pint, or about three-quarters of an imperial pint.

Mute (miūt), *a.* and *sb.*¹ [late ME. *muet*, a. F. :—pop.L. **mutettus* dim. of L. *mutus*. In 16th c. assim. to L. *mutus*.] A. *adj.* 1. Not emitting articulate sound; silent. 2. Destitute of the faculty of speech; dumb. late ME. b. Applied to the lower animals 1667. 3. Temporarily bereft of the power of speech 1483. 4. Of things or action: Not characterized by speech or vocal utterance 1599. 5. *Gram.* and *Phonetics*. a. Of a consonant: Produced by an entire interruption of the passage of breath, or by the complete closure of the organs of the mouth; 'stopped' 1589. b. Of a letter: Not pronounced, silent 1638. 6. *Sporting.* Not giving tongue (said of hounds while hunting) 1677. 7. Said of metals that do not ring when struck 1806.

1. Phr. *To stand m.* (*of malice*): in *Law*, to refuse deliberately to plead. Some m. inglorious Milton here may rest GRAY. *transf.* The groves are still and m.! SCOTT. *M. swan*: the common swan, *Cygnus olor*. 2. b. Oaths..seem to be considered as the only language the m. creation can comprehend 1845. 3. M. with wonder I stood 1887. 4. M. solemn Sorrow, free from Female Noise DRYDEN. *transf.* The jurisdiction of the magistrate was m. and impotent GIBBON. 6. Phr. *To run m.*: to follow the chase without giving tongue. Hence **Mu·te-ly** *adv.*, **-ness.**

B. *sb.*¹ 1. *Phonetics.* An element of speech formed by a position of the vocal organs such as stops the breath, or entirely interrupts the sound; a stopped consonant, a 'stop' 1530. 2. A person precluded by nature, mutilation, or employment from the exercise of speech. **a.** A person dumb by nature or as a result of mutilation. **b.** An actor on the stage whose part is performed only in dumb show 1579. **c.** In oriental countries: A dumb house-servant or janitor 1599. †**d.** *Law.* One who refuses to plead to an indictment -1738. **e.** A professional attendant at a funeral 1762. **3.** *Mus.* **a.** A clip of metal, wood, or ivory that can be placed over the bridge of a violin or the like to deaden the resonance without affecting the vibration of the strings 1811. **b.** A pad that can be inserted into the bell of a metal wind-instrument to muffle the sound 1841.

1. Mutes (*mutæ*), these letters *b, c, d, g, h, k, p, q, t,* are so called, because they have no sound, without the assistance of a vowel BLOUNT. 3. **c.** Our graue Like Turkish m., shall haue a tonguelesse mouth SHAKS. *Comb.* **m.-closure** (*Phonetics*), closure of the oral passage so as to form a m.

†**Mute,** *sb.*[2] 1575. [f. MUTE *v.*[1] Cf. F. *émeut.*] The action of 'muting'; *concr.* (*sing.* and *pl.*) dung (of birds) -1820.

†**Mute,** *sb.*[3] ME. [a. OF. *muete, meute* (mod.F. *meute*):—pop.L. **movita,* f. L. *movere* to MOVE.] A pack of hounds -1688; also, the cry of hounds working (ME.).

Mute (miūt), *sb.*[4] *dial.* 1843. A kind of mule.

Mute (miūt), *v.*[1] *Obs.* exc. *dial.* 1450. [a. OF. *meutir,* aphet. f. *esmeutir,* f. Teut. *smelt-* (MDu. *smelt*) 'stercus'.] Of a bird, esp. a hawk: **a.** *intr.* To void the fæces. **b.** *trans.* To discharge as fæces. Hence **Mu·ting** *vbl. sb.*, also *concr.* 'droppings'.

†**Mute,** *v.*[2] 1570. [perh. a. L. *mutire.*] *intr.* To murmur -1655.

Mute (miūt), *v.*[3] 1861. [f. MUTE *a.*] *trans.* To deaden or subdue the sound of; *spec.* in *Mus.*, to muffle the sound of (a musical instrument).

Mute (miūt), *v.*[4] 1839. [f. F. *muter,* f. L. *mutus* dumb.] *trans.* To check the fermentation of (must).

Mutic (miū·tik), *a.* 1777. [ad. L. *muticus* awnless.] = MUTILATE *a.* 2. **a.** *Bot.* Without a point or beard. **b.** *Entom.* Wanting spines. So **Mu·ticous** *a.* 1856.

Mutilate (miū·tileᶦt), *a.* 1532. [ad. L. *mutilatus,* pa. pple. of *mutilare* to MUTILATE.] **1.** Of a human body, a limb, and other things: Mutilated (in senses 1 and 2 of next). *Obs.* exc. *poet.* **2.** *Nat. Hist.* Deficient in some part common to the species or to closely related species, or possessing it only in an imperfect or modified form 1760.

Mutilate (miū·tileᶦt), *v.* 1534. [f. L. *mutilat-,* ppl. stem of *mutilare* to lop off; f. *mutilus* maimed (cf. Gr. μύτιλος hornless); see -ATE[3].] **1.** *trans.* To deprive (a person or animal) of a limb or organ of the body; to cut off or otherwise destroy the use of (a limb or organ) 1562. **2.** To render (a thing, e.g. a record, etc.) imperfect by cutting off or destroying a part 1534.

1. The Greeks..mutilated the slain THIRLWALL. 2. I wil not in any worde wyllinglye mangle or mutulate that honourable mans worke MORE. Hence **Mu·tilator,** also †**-er,** one who mutilates.

Mutilation (miūtilēᶦ·ʃən). 1525. [ad. L. *mutilationem.*] The action of mutilating; deprivation of a limb or of an essential part. **b.** *spec.* Castration 1727.

†**Mutilous,** *a.* 1649. [f. L. *mutilus* (see MUTILATE *v.*) + -OUS.] Of things: Mutilated, imperfect -1707.

†**Mutine,** *sb.* and *a.*[1] 1560. [a. F. *mutin* adj.:—Rom. **movitino,* f. pop. L. **movita*; see MUTE *sb.*[3]] **1.** Popular tumult; rebellion, mutiny -1600. **2.** A mutineer -1604. **3.** *adj.* Mutinous -1598.

‖**Mutine** (mütin), *a.*[2] 1870. [Fr., fem. of *mutin* adj.; see prec.] Of a girl's or woman's looks: Rebellious, unsubmissive.

†**Mutine,** *v.* 1555. [a. F. *mutiner,* f. *mutin*; see MUTINE *sb.*] **1.** *intr.* To rebel, mutiny -1692. Also *fig.* **2.** *trans.* To incite to revolt -1613. Hence †**Mutiner** = next 1569.

Mutineer (miūtinīᵊ·ɪ), *sb.* 1610. [a. F. *mutinier* (16th c.), f. *mutin*; see MUTINE *sb.*] One who mutinies. **Mutinee·r** *v.* to mutiny.

Mutinize (miū·tinəiz), *v.* Now *arch.* 1605. [f. MUTINE *sb.* + -IZE.] †**a.** *intr.* To mutiny. **b.** *trans.* To cause mutiny in.

Mutinous (miū·tinəs), *a.* 1578. [f. MUTINE *sb.* + -OUS.] **1.** Given to mutiny, rebellious; †turbulent -1621. **b.** *transf.* and *fig.* of the elements, passions, etc. 1610. **2.** Of the nature of or proceeding from mutiny; characterized by or expressing mutiny 1592. **3.** = MUTINE *a.*[2] 1882.

1. The m. humour of the Camp SIR T. HERBERT. **b.** I haue..call'd forth the mutenous windes SHAKS. 2. For the late license of printing all m. and seditious discourses was not yet in fashion 1647. Hence **Mu·tinous-ly** *adv.*, **-ness.**

Mutiny (miū·tini), *sb.* 1567. [f. MUTINE *v.* or *sb.* + -Y[4].] **1.** Open revolt against constituted authority; now chiefly *spec.* revolt of soldiers or sailors against their officers; behaviour subversive of discipline 1579. **b.** A mutinous revolt 1581. **c.** In attrib. uses; now often with sense 'that took part in or was present during the Indian Mutiny' 1731. †**2.** Discord, contention; a state of discord, a dispute, quarrel -1667.

1. Hear a rumour of the Goorkha corps..in open m., and refusing to march 1857. **b.** *The Indian M.,* a revolt of the native troops of Bengal in 1857-8. **c.** *M. Act,* an Act, passed annually from 1689 to 1879, dealing with offences against discipline in the military and naval forces, etc., now embodied in the Army Act, 1881. I was a M. baby, as they call it KIPLING. 2. *Rom. & Jul.* I. v. 82.

Mutiny (miū·tini), *v.* 1584. [f. prec.] **1.** *intr.* To commit the offence of mutiny; to rise in revolt *against* (rarely †*upon*); to refuse submission to discipline or obedience to the lawful command of a superior, esp. in the military and naval services. †**b.** To contend (*with*); to quarrel -1603. †**2.** *trans.* To cause to mutiny or rebel *against* -1648.

1. *fig.* The powers of pleasure m. for employment JOHNSON. **b.** My very haires do m.: for the white Reproue the browne for rashnesse, and they them For feare SHAKS.

Mutism (miū·tiz'm). 1824. [ad. F. *mutisme,* f. L. *mutus*; see MUTE *a.* and -ISM.] The state or condition of being mute or a mute.

Muto- (miū·to), used as comb. form of L. *mutare* to change: **Mu·tograph,** an apparatus for taking a series of photographs of objects in motion; hence **Mu·tograph** *v. trans.* **Mu·toscope,** an apparatus for exhibiting a scene recorded by the mutograph; hence **Mutosco·pic** *a.*

Mutt (mʋt). *slang* (orig. *U.S.*). 1910. [Abbrev. of *mutton-head.*] An ignorant blunderer; a blockhead; *contempt.* a small dog.

Mutter (mʋ·təɪ), *v.* late ME. [Prob. imitative, with freq. suffix -ER [5].] **1.** *intr.* To speak in low and barely audible tones, with the mouth nearly closed. **b.** *esp.* To murmur, complain, grumble (*against, at*) 1548. **c.** *transf.* To make a low rumbling sound, as thunder 1797. **2.** *trans.* To utter with imperfect articulation and in a low tone. Also *fig.* to express or say in secret. late ME.

1. Seeke..vnto wizards that peepe and that m. *Isa.* viii. 19. **b.** The worthie magistrate Moses was muttered against ABP. SANDYS. 2. There are a kinde of men, So loose of Soule, that in their sleepes will m. Their Affayres SHAKS. Hence **Mu·tter** *sb.*, the act of muttering. **Mu·tterer, Mu·tteringly** *adv.*

Mutton (mʋ·t'n). [ME. *motoun, moton* (rarely *moltoun*), a. OF. *moton,* rarely *molton* (mod.F. *mouton*):—med.L. *multonem,* prob. f. Gaulish **multos* (OIr. *molt* ram, Welsh *mollt*).] **1.** The flesh of sheep, as food. **2.** A sheep, esp. one intended to be eaten. Now only *joc.* ME. **b.** The carcase of a sheep. *Obs.* or *arch.* 1607. **3.** *slang.* Food for lust; loose women, prostitutes. Also *laced m.* (see LACED *ppl. a.*[1]) late ME. †**4.** Short for *mutton-candle* (see below) -1859.

1. They..had a breast of m. and a pint of wine SWIFT. 2. Pious men, Like muttons in a pen THACKERAY. Phr. *As dead as m.*: quite dead. *To take* (or *eat*) *a bit of* (or *one's*) *m. with*: to dine with. *To return to one's muttons* (*joc.*), to return to the matter in hand (after F. *revenons à nos moutons*).

Comb.: **m.-bird,** any of several petrels and shearwaters of the genera *Œstrelata* and *Puffinus* of the South Seas; **-broth**; **-candle,** a candle made of mutton-fat; **-fist** *slang,* a large red coarse hand, or a person having such a hand; **-ham,** a leg of mutton cured like a ham; **-head** *colloq.*, a dull, stupid person; hence **-headed** *a.*; †**-monger** *slang,* a whoremonger; a great eater of mutton; a sheep-stealer; **-wood,** a composite tree (*Olearia Colensoi*) of New Zealand; so called because it grows on islands frequented by mutton-birds.

Mu·tton-cho·p. 1720. A piece of mutton (usually one rib with the end chopped off, together with half the vertebra to which it is attached) for broiling or frying.

Mutton-chop (*whisker*): a side whisker shaped like a mutton-chop, i.e. roundish at one end and narrow and prolonged at the other.

Mu·tton-fish. 1735. **1.** A name for various American and W. Indian sea-fish, esp. the eel-like *Zoarces anguillaris.* **2.** *Austral.* An ormer 1882.

Muttony (mʋ·t'ni), *a.* 1858. [f. MUTTON + -Y[1].] Having the qualities of mutton.

Mutual (miū·tiuăl), *a.* 1477. [a. F. *mutuel,* f. L. *mutuus* borrowed, reciprocal:—**moitwos,* f. root *moi-* to change (cf. MUTATE).] **1.** Of relations, feelings, actions: Possessed, entertained, or done by each towards or with regard to the other; reciprocal. **b.** Qualifying personal designations of relationship, friendship, or hostility 1562. **c.** *transf.* Pertaining to or characterized by some (implied) mutual action or relation 1848. **2.** Respective; belonging to each respectively 1548. †**3.** Of intercourse: Intimate -1749. **4.** Pertaining to both parties; common. (Now regarded as incorrect.) 1591. †**5.** Responsive -1850.

1. M. fear is the only solid basis of alliance JOWETT. Phr. *M. admiration society*: a coterie of persons who over-estimate each other's merits 1858. **b.** Kings And subjects, m. foes SHELLEY. **c.** *M. terms, principles*: name for a business arrangement in which exchange of services takes the place of money payments 1848. 2. The time would not allow them to enter into minute details of their m. adventures 1796. 4. Mr. Hobhouse was desirous that I should express our m. opinion of Pope BYRON. Our m. friend Mr. Wright SCOTT. 5. Who then could guess If ever more should meet those m. eyes! BYRON. Hence **Mu·tual-ly** *adv.*, **-ness.**

Mutualism (miū·tiuăliz'm). 1863. [f. MUTUAL *a.* + -ISM.] **1.** The doctrine that individual and collective well-being is attainable only by mutual dependence. **2.** *Biol.* A condition of symbiosis in which two associated organisms contribute mutually to the well-being of each other 1876. So **Mu·tualist,** an advocate of m. 1892; *Biol.* one of two organisms which mutually live on each other 1876.

Mutuality (miūtiu,æ·lĭti). 1586. [f. MUTUAL *a.* + -ITY.] **1.** The quality or condition of being mutual; reciprocity. **b.** *Law.* A condition of things under which two parties are mutually bound to perform certain reciprocal duties 1845. **2.** Interchange of acts of goodwill; intimacy 1604. **3.** *Biol.* The rendering of mutual service by organisms in the condition of symbiosis 1876.

Mutualize (miū·tiuăləiz), *v.* 1812. [f. MUTUAL *a.* + -IZE.] *trans.* and *intr.* To make or become mutual. Hence **Mutualiza·tion.**

Mutuary (miū·tiu,ări). 1839. [ad. L. *mutuarius,* f. *mutuus* borrowed; see -ARY[1].] *Civil Law.* The borrower in a contract of mutuum.

†**Mu·tuate,** *v.* 1548. [f. L. *mutuat-, mutuari* to borrow, f. *mutuus*; see MUTUAL *a.* and -ATE[3].] *trans.* To borrow -1716. So †**Mutua·tion** 1604-1827. †**Mutuati·tious** *a.* borrowed 1625-1813.

Mutule (miū·tiul). 1563. [a. F. (It. *mutulo*), ad. L. *mutulus* modillion.] *Arch.* A block projecting under the corona of the Doric cornice, corresp. to the modillion of other orders.

†**Mu·tuum.** 1486. [a. L., neut. of *mutuus* borrowed.] *Civil Law.* A contract under which such things are lent as are consumed in the use, on condition that they are restored in kind and of the same quantity and quality -1839.

Muzarab(ic, var. ff. MOZARAB(IC.

Muzhik, var. of MOUJIK.

Muzz (mʋz), *sb. slang.* Also **muz.** 1788. [Cf. next.] One who 'muzzes' over books.

Muzz (mʋz), *v. slang.* 1775. [?] **1.** *intr.* To study intently; to 'mug'. Const. *over.*

2. *trans.* To render 'muzzy'; to fuddle (cf. MUZZLE *v.*²) 1787.

Muzzle (mɒ·z'l), *sb.* late ME. [a. OF. *musel, muzel, muisel,* mod.F. *museau* :—med. L. *musellum,* dim. of med.L. *musus, musum*; origin unkn.] **I. 1.** The projecting part of an animal's head which includes the nose and mouth. **2.** That end of a fire-arm from which the shot is discharged; *spec.* in a cannon, the part extending from the astragal to the extreme end mouldings 1566. **†3.** The nozzle of a pair of bellows. SWIFT. **4.** *Agric.* The clevis or bridle of a plough 1765.

1. *transf.* Of a black m., and long beard, beware DRYDEN. 2. *Charged (crammed) to the m.*: loaded, filled, or stuffed *with*. The boy..crammed to the m. with lies MEREDITH.

II. An arrangement of straps or wires, put over an animal's mouth to prevent it from biting, eating, or rooting. late ME. **b.** An ornamental piece of armour covering a horse's nose 1860.

A moosle that letteth dogges to bite 1556. *fig.* So to enure Rome to the snaffle, and break the Senate to the musle 1644.

Comb.: **m.-loader,** a gun that is loaded at the m. (opp. to *breech-loader*); so **-loading** *ppl. a.*; **-sight,** a sight placed at or near the m. of a gun; **m. velocity,** the velocity at which a projectile leaves the muzzle of a gun.

Mu·zzle, *v.*¹ late ME. [f. MUZZLE *sb.*] **1.** *intr.* To thrust out the muzzle or nose; to feel, smell, or root about with the muzzle 1489. **2.** *trans.* To bring the muzzle or snout close to 1600. **†b.** To root about or amongst -1733. **†c.** 'To fondle with the mouth close. A low word' (J.). -1708. **3.** To put a muzzle on (an animal or its mouth) 1470. **†4.** *transf.* To muffle. late ME.; *Sc.* to veil, mask (the face) 1457-1590. **5.** To restrain from speaking 1531. **6.** *Naut.* **†a.** *To lie muzzled*: (of a ship) to remain inactive. **b.** In yachting use: To take in (a sail). 1697.

1. If we euer be like swine, muzling in the ground HIERON. 2. The Bear comes directly up to Him, Muzzles, and Smells to him R. L'ESTRANGE. 3. Thou shalt not mosell the mouth of the oxe TINDALE 1 *Cor.* ix. 9. *fig.* My dagger muzzel'd SHAKS. 5. What establishment can m. its fools and lunatics SYD. SMITH.

Mu·zzle, *v.*² *dial.* 1796. [app. connected with MUZZ *v.* and MUZZY.] **a.** *trans.* To make 'muzzy'; to fuddle. **b.** *intr.* To drink to excess 1828.

Muzzy (mɒ·zi), *a. colloq.* and *dial.* 1727. [perh. a later form of obs. slang *mossy* stupid, dull (1597-1602).] **1.** Dull, stupid, spiritless, gloomy; also, mentally hazy. Of times, places: Dully, gloomy. **b.** *transf.* Blurred 1832. **2.** Stupid with excess of liquor 1775.

1. A damn'd m. dinner at Boodle's 1770. His view of the past will be rather m. THACKERAY. **b.** The execution..is vague and m. 1867. 2. His m., whiskified brain THACKERAY. Hence **Mu·zzily** *adv.* **Mu·zziness.**

My (məi, *unstressed* mi), *poss. adj.* [Early ME. *mī*, reduced form of *mīn* (see MINE *poss. pron.*), used orig. bef. consonants except *h*, and becoming later the poss. adj. of the 1st pers. sing. in prose use.] **1.** Of or belonging to me. The poss. genitive of I *pron.* **b.** Used with vague application. Also with ethical force in certain idiomatic collocations. 1592. **2. a.** Prefixed affectionately, compassionately, or familiarly, to certain terms of address, as *my boy, my friend, my man, my good fellow,* also *my son, my daughter* (but, as a rule, not to other terms of relationship, as *father, mother,* etc., used vocatively) ME. **b.** *esp.* in *my dear* (*dearest*), *my love,* etc. 1807. **c.** Prefixed to the name of the person addressed 1732. **3.** In ejaculations, as *my eye! my word!* etc. (see these words); *my God!* used to express strong feeling or excitement; whence (ellipt.) *My!* or *Oh, my!* which is common (esp. *U.S.*) as a mild exclam. of surprise; also *Oh-my* vb., to say 'Oh, my!' 1707.

1. My time will now be my own GIBBON. **b.** I brought down my bird every shot 1808. 2. **c.** Awake, my St. John! POPE. 3. My, what a race I've had! 'MARK TWAIN'. The servant maids..were listening and..oh-mying over the bargains 1893.

Myal (məi·ăl). 1774. [Perh. of W. Afr. origin.] Only in attrib. use denoting persons or things associated with the practice of **My·alism** (1843), a kind of sorcery practised esp. by the natives of the W. Indies. Hence **My·alist** 1851.

‖**Myalgia** (məi,æ·ldʒiă). 1860. [mod.L., f. Gr. μῦς muscle + -αλγία, ἄλγος pain.] *Path.* Pain in the muscles; muscular rheumatism. Hence **Mya·lgic** *a.*

Myall¹ (məi·ăl). 1835. [Native name.] A wild aboriginal of Australia.

Myall² (məi·ăl). 1845. [Native name.] An Australian acacia or its wood, esp. *Acacia pendula* or *A. homalophylla* (which yields a useful hard scented wood).

‖**Myasthenia** (məi,ăsþī·niă). 1856. [mod.L., f. Gr. μῦς muscle + ἀσθένεια weakness.] Muscular weakness. Hence **Myasthe·nic** *a.*

‖**Mycelium** (məisī·liɒ̆m). 1836. [mod.L., f. Gr. μύκης mushroom, after *epithelium.*] *Bot.* The vegetative part of the thallus of fungi, consisting of white filamentous tubes (hyphæ); the spawn of mushrooms. Hence **Myce·lial, Myce·lian** *adjs.* consisting of or characterized by m. **Myce·lioid** *a.* resembling or having the structure of m.

Mycenæan (məisīnī·ăn). 1797. [f. L. *Mycenæus* (f. *Mycenæ*) + -AN.] **A.** *adj.* Of or belonging to Mycenæ, an ancient Greek city in the Argive plain, and esp. its civilization, culture, art, etc. **B.** *sb.* A native or inhabitant of Mycenæ.

‖**Mycetes** (məisī·tīz), *sb. pl.* 1876. [mod.L., ad. Gr. μύκητες, pl. of μύκης mushroom, fungus.] *Biol.* The group of organisms known as microbes. Hence **Myce·tic** *a.*

Myceto- (məisī·to, məisītǫ·), bef. a vowel **mycet-**, comb. f. Gr μύκης mushroom. **Myceto·logy,** the science of fungi. ‖**Mycetozo·a,** a group of fungoid organisms, consisting chiefly of the Myxomycetes; also **Mycetozo·an,** ‖**-zo·on,** a member of this group.

‖**Mycetoma** (məisītōᵘ·mă). 1874. [mod.L., f. Gr. μυκητ-, μύκης + -ωμα (cf. *sarcoma*).] *Path.* A fungoid disease of the foot (or hand). Hence **Myceto·matous** *a.*

Myco- (məi·ko), irreg. comb. form (for MYCETO-) of Gr. μύκης mushroom, as in **mycodextrin, -inulin, -protein,** substances occurring in certain fungi; also **Myco·logy,** that branch of botany which treats of fungi; hence **Mycolo·gic, -al** *a.*, **-ly** *adv.*, **Myco·logist**; **Myco·phagy,** the eating of fungi or mushrooms; hence **Myco·phagist.**

‖**Mycoderma** (məikodə̄·mă). Also **my·coderm.** 1846. [mod.L.; see MYCO- and DERMA.] The pellicle which forms on the surface of liquors during alcoholic fermentation ('mother of vinegar'); hence as the name of a genus of fermentation-fungi. Hence **Mycode·rmatoid, -de·rmatous, -de·rmic** *adjs.*

‖**Mycosis** (məikōᵘ·sis). 1876. [f. Gr. μύκης mushroom + -OSIS.] *Path.* A disease caused by parasitic fungi in any part of the body. Hence **Myco·tic** *a.*

Mycterism (mi·ktěriz'm). *rare.* 1593. [ad. Gr. μυκτηρισμός, f. μυκτηρίζειν to sneer at, f. μυκτήρ nose.] A gibe or scoff.

Mydaleine (məidǣ·līˌin). 1887. [fr. Gr. μυδαλέος dripping, wet + -INE⁵.] *Physiol. Chem.* A poisonous ptomaine obtained from putrid flesh and herring brines.

‖**Mydriasis** (midriǝ̄·sis). 1805. [late L., a. Gr. μυδρίασις.] *Path.* Excessive dilatation of the pupil of the eye. Hence **Mydria·tic** *a.*

‖**Myelencephalon** (məi·ělense·fălǫn). 1866. [f. Gr. μυελός, -όν marrow + ENCEPHALON.] *Anat.* **a.** The cerebro-spinal axis or system (Owen). **b.** The medulla oblongata (Huxley). So **Myelencepha·lic** *a.* pertaining to or connected with the m. 1866.

Myelin, -ine (məi·ělin). 1867. [a. G. *myelin*, f. Gr. μυελός marrow; see -IN¹, -INE⁵.] **1.** *Chem.* Virchow's term for a fatty substance obtainable from various animal tissues (e.g. brain-substance, yolk of egg), and also from some vegetable tissues. **2.** *Anat.* The medullary sheath of nerve-fibres, or white substance of Schwann 1873.

Myelitis (məi,ělǝi·tis). 1835. [mod.L., f. Gr. μυελός, marrow + -ITIS.] Inflammation of the spinal cord. Hence **Myeli·tic** *a.*

Myelo- (məi·ělo, məi,ělǫ·), bef. a vowel **Myel-**, comb. f. Gr. μυελός, -όν marrow. **My·elocœle** [Gr. κοῖλος hollow], the cavity of the myelon or spinal cord. **Myeloge·nic** *a.* originating in the bone marrow. **Myelo·pathy,** disease of the spinal cord; hence **Myelopa·thic** *a.*

Myeloid (məi·ěloid), *a.* 1857. [f. Gr. μυελός marrow + -OID.] Resembling or pertaining to marrow.

‖**Myiasis** (məi,iǝ̄·sis). 1837. [mod.L., f. Gr. μυῖα fly + -ASIS.] *Path.* Injury inflicted by dipterous larvæ on the human body.

‖**Mylodon** (məi·lǒdǫn). 1839. [mod.L., f. Gr. μύλη, μύλος molar + ὀδοντ-, ὀδούς tooth.] A genus of gigantic extinct sloths from the Pleistocene, having teeth more or less cylindrical. So **My·lodont** *sb.* and *a.*

Mylohyoid (məiloˌhəi·oid), *a.* and *sb.* 1838. [ad. mod.L. *mylohyoideus* (also used earlier), f. Gr. μύλη, -ος (see prec.) + ὑοειδής HYOID.] Applied to a flat triangular muscle extending from the lower jaw to the hyoid bone.

Myna: see MINA².

‖**Mynheer** (mainhē·r, mənē·r). 1652. [Du. *mijnheer*, f. *mijn* my + *heer* lord, master.] The Dutch equivalent of 'sir', 'Mr.'; hence, a Dutchman.

Myo- (məi·o), comb. f. Gr. μῦς (gen. μυός) muscle. ‖**Myoco·mma** (pl. **-co·mmata, -co·mmas**) [Gr. κόμμα segment], one of the divisions of the muscular system of lower vertebrates. **Myodyna·mics** *sb. pl.*, that branch of physiology which treats of muscular contraction. ‖**Myofibro·ma,** a tumour consisting of muscular and fibrous tissue. **Myoge·nic** *a.* produced by or arising in the muscles. **Myo·pathy** [-PATHY], any affection of the muscles. **Myophy·sics,** the physics of muscular action. **Myopo·lar** *a.* relating to muscular polarity. **Myosarco·ma,** a sarcoma partly composed of muscular tissue. **My·oscope** [-SCOPE], an instrument for observing muscular contraction.

‖**Myocardium** (məi,okā·ɹdiɒ̆m). 1866. [mod.L., f. Gr. μυο- MYO- + καρδία heart.] The muscular substance of the heart. Hence **Myoca·rdial** *a.* Also **My:ocardi·tis,** inflammation of the m.; whence **My:ocardi·tic** *a.*

Myograph (məi·ǒgrɑf). 1867. [f. MYO- + -GRAPH.] An instrument for taking tracings of muscular contractions and relaxations. Hence **Myogra·phic, -al** *a.* So **My·ogram,** a tracing made by a m. 1890.

Myology (məi,ǫ·lǒdʒi). 1649. [ad. mod.L. *myologia*; see MYO- and -LOGY.] That branch of anatomy which treats of muscles. **b.** A myological description; the myological features of an animal. Hence **Myolo·gic, -al** *a.* **Myo·logist.**

‖**Myoma** (məi,ōᵘ·mă). 1875. [mod.L., f. Gr. μῦς muscle + -ωμα (after *sarcoma*).] *Path.* A tumour composed of muscular tissue. Hence **Myo·matous** *a.*

Myomorph (məi·ǒmǫɹf). 1887. [ad. mod. L. *Myomorpha*, f. Gr. μυ(ο)-, μῦς mouse + μορφή shape.] *Zool.* A rodent of the division *Myomorpha* (including mice, rats, dormice, etc.). So **Myomo·rphic** 1880, **-mo·rphine** 1898 *adjs.*

Myope (məi·ōᵘp). 1728. [a. F., ad. late L. *myop-, myops*, a. Gr. μυωπ-, μύωψ.] A short-sighted person. So ‖**Myo·pia, My·opy,** short-sightedness. Hence **Myopic** (məi,ǫ·pik) *a.*; **My·opism,** myopia.

Myosin (məi·ǒsin). Also **-ine.** 1869. [f. Gr. μῦς muscle + -OSE² + -IN¹.] *Chem.* The chief ingredient of the clot formed on coagulation of muscle-plasma.

‖**Myosis** (məi,ōᵘ·sis). 1819. [f. Gr. μύειν to shut the eyes + -OSIS.] *Path.* Contraction of the pupil of the eye. Hence **Myotic** (məi,ǫ·tik) *a.* pertaining to or causing m.; *sb.* an agent which causes m.

Myosote (məi·ǒsōᵘt). 1879. [ad. L. *myosotis*, a. Gr. μυοσωτίς, f. μυός-, gen. of μῦς + ὠτ-, οὖς ear.] The forget-me-not, *Myosotis palustris.*

Myotome (məi·ǒtōᵘm). 1846. [f. MYO- ; see -TOME.] **1.** *Anat.* A muscular segment or metamere 1856. **2.** *Surg.* An instrument for dividing muscle. So **Myoto·mic** *a.* pertaining to myotomy or a m. 1856.

Myotomy (məiǫ·tŏmi). 1676. [ad. mod. L. *myotomia*, f. Gr. μυ(ο)-, μῦς muscle + τομή, -τομία cutting.] Dissection, anatomy, or surgical division of muscles.

Myria- (mi·riă), rarely **myrio-**, bef. a vowel **myri-**, comb. f. Gr. μυριάς MYRIAD (or μυρίοι countless, μύριοι 10,000). **1.** With the meaning 'ten thousand', in names of weights and measures of the metric system: **My·riagram(me, -litre, -metre, My·riare** = 10,000 grammes, litres, metres, ares. 1804. **2.** With the meaning 'very numerous': **Myriaca·nthous** *a.* [Gr. ἄκανθος thorn], having very many spines; etc. 1856.

Myriad (mi·riăd). 1555. [ad. med.L. *myriad-*, *myrias*, a. Gr. μυριαδ-, μυριάς, f. μυρίοι countless, μύριοι ten thousand. Cf. F. *myriade.*] **A.** *sb.* **1.** As a numeral: Ten thousand. **2.** *transf.* (*pl.*) Countless numbers, hosts (*of*) 1555. **b.** *sing.* in same sense 1850. **3.** *absol.* Countless numbers of men, animals, or inanimate things (indicated contextually) 1559. **b.** *sing.* in same sense 1718.

2. Their myriads of horse WELLINGTON. **3.** Who.. Cloth'd with transcendent brightness didst outshine Myriads though bright MILT.

B. *adj.* Existing in myriads; countless. Chiefly *poet.* 1800. **b.** with *sing. sb.* Consisting of myriads. Also, having a myriad phases. 1817.

The City's moonlit spires and m. lamps SHELLEY. **b.** The m. mind of Shakspeare 1854. *Comb.*, as *m.-handed, -minded* adjs. Hence **My·riadfold** *a.* countless in number or aspects; *sb.* only advb., with indef. article: *A m.*, an infinite amount. **My·riadth** *a.* that is a very minute part of a whole.

Myriapod (mi·riăpǫd). Also **myrio-**. 1826. [ad. mod.L. *Myriapoda*, f. Gr. μυριάς MYRIAD + ποδ-, πούς foot.] **A.** *adj.* Having very numerous legs; *spec.* pertaining to or having the characteristics of the class *Myriapoda* of arthropodous animals, comprising the centipedes and millipedes. **B.** *sb.* One of these.

Hence **Myria·podan, Myria·podous** *adjs.* = MYRIAPOD *a.*

‖ **Myrica** (mirəi·kă). 1706. [L., a. Gr. μυρίκη.] **1.** The tamarisk. **2.** A Linnæan genus of shrubs including the bog myrtle, *M. Gale* 1797.

Comb. **m.-tallow, -wax** = myrtle wax.

Myricin (mirəi·sin, mi·-, məi·risin). Also **-ine.** 1821. [f. prec. + -IN [1].] *Chem.* That part of bees-wax which is insoluble in boiling alcohol.

Myrio-: see MYRIA-.

Myriologue (mi·riǒlǫg). 1824. [ad. mod. Gr. μυριολόγιον, corrupt f. μοιρολόγιον, f. μοῖρα fate + λόγος speech.] An extemporaneous funeral song, composed and sung by a woman. Hence **Myriolo·gical** *a.* So **Myrio·logist**, one who sings or composes a m.

Myriorama (miriǒræ·mă, -ā·mă). 1824. [f. Gr. μυρίος countless + ὅραμα view.] A picture made of a number of separate sections which are capable of being combined in numerous ways so as to form different scenes. **b.** An entertainment consisting of a series of views 1901.

Myristic (məi-, miri·stik), *a.* 1848. [f. med.L. (*nux*) *myristica*, Linnæan generic name of the nutmeg-tree, f. Gr. μυρίζειν to anoint.] *Chem.* In *m. acid*: a fatty acid found in nutmeg-oil and other vegetable and animal fats. Hence **Myri·state**, a salt of m. acid. **Myri·stin**, the glyceride of m. acid. **Myri·stone**, a crystalline substance obtained by the distillation of calcium myristate.

Myrmeco- (mɔ̄·ɹmǐko, -kǫ·, məɹmī·ko), comb. form of Gr. μυρμηκ-, μύρμηξ ant; as in: **Myrmecolo·gical** *a.*, pertaining to myrmecology. **Myrmeco·logy**, the scientific study of ants; whence **Myrmeco·logist**. **Myrmeco·phagous** *a.* ant-eating. **Myrmeco·philous** *a.* applied to insects that live in ant-hills or to plants that are cross-fertilized by ants.

Myrmecoid (mɔ̄·ɹmǐkoid), *a. rare.* 1861. [ad. Gr. μυρμηκοειδής, f. μύρμηξ ant.] Antlike.

Myrmicine (mə·ɹmisəin), *a.* 1881. [ad. mod. L. *Myrmicinæ*, f. *Myrmica*: see -INE [1].] *Entom.* Of or belonging to the sub-family *Myrmicinæ* of stinging ants.

Myrmidon (mɔ̄·ɹmidən). late ME. [ad. L. *Myrmidones* pl., a. Gr. Μυρμιδόνες.] **1.** (With capital M.) One of a warlike race of men inhabiting Thessaly, who followed Achilles to the siege of Troy (*Il.* ii. 684). **b.** Used of Achilles himself. *Tr. & Cr.* I. iii. 378. **2.** *transf.* A faithful follower or servant. Now chiefly *joc.* 1610. **3.** In derogatory sense: An unscrupulously faithful attendant or hireling; a hired ruffian 1649.

2. Now, my myrmidons, fall on 1698. **3.** *M. of the law, of justice*: applied contempt. to a policeman, bailiff, or other inferior administrative officer of the law. Bow-street myrmidons BYRON. Hence **Myrmido·nian** *a.* 1624.

Myrobalan (məirǫ·bălăn). late ME. [a. F. *myrobolan*, or L. *myrobalanum*, a. Gr. μυροβάλανος, f. μύρον unguent, balsam + βάλανος acorn, date, ben-nut.] **1.** The astringent plum-like fruit of species of *Terminalia*, e. g. *T. Bellerica* (see BELLERIC), *T. Chebula* (see CHEBULE), *T. citrina*; formerly used medicinally, but now chiefly in dyeing, tanning, and ink-making. **2.** A variety of plum 1664.

Myronic (məirǫ·nik), *a.* 1840. [ad. F. *myronique*, f. Gr. μύρον unguent.] In *m. acid*, an acid obtained from black mustard. Hence **My·ronate**, a salt of m. acid.

Myrosin (məiᵊrǒ·sin). Also **-ine, -yne.** 1840. [ad. F. *myrosyne*, f. Gr. μύρον unguent + *-yne* (= -IN [1], -INE [5]), with inserted *s.*] *Chem.* A nitrogenous ferment contained in the seeds of black mustard.

Myrrh [1] (mɔ̄ɹ). [OE. *myrra*, *-e* :—L. *myrrha*, a. Gr. μύρρα, of Semitic origin (Arab. *murr*, Heb. *mōr*).] **1.** A gum-resin produced by several species of *Commiphora* (*Balsamodendron*), esp. *C. Myrrha* (see 2); used for perfumery and as an ingredient in incense. Also *Med.* the tincture made from this. †**2.** Any shrub or tree that yields the gum-resin, esp. *Commiphora* (*Balsamodendron*) *Myrrha* -1634.

1. Often with ref. to *Matt.* ii. 11. **2.** With Groves of myrrhe, and cinnamon MILT.

Comb.: **m. resin**, a resin obtained from m. by alcohol **m.-seed**, a book-name for *Myrospermum pubescens*. Hence **Myrrhed** (mɔ̄ɹd) *ppl. a.* mixed or sprinkled with m. (*rare*) 1450. **My·rrhy** *a.* smelling like m. 1842.

Myrrh [2] (mɔ̄ɹ). 1597. [ad. late L. *myrrhis*, *murris*, a. Gr. μυρρίς.] Sweet Cicely, *Myrrhis odorata.*

Myrrhine: see MURRHINE.

My·rrh-tree. late ME. [MYRRH [1].] = MYRRH [1] 2.

†**Myrt.** late ME. [ad. L. *myrt-us*, a. Gr. μύρτος. Cf. F. *myrte.*] = MYRTLE -1615.

Myrtaceous (məɹtēⁱ·ʃəs), *a. Bot.* [f. mod. L. *Myrtace-æ*, f. *myrtus* MYRT.] Belonging to the N.O. *Myrtaceæ*, of which the myrtle is the type.

Myrtiform (mɔ̄·ɹtifǫɹm), *a.* 1840. [ad. mod.L. *myrtiformis*, f. *myrtus.*] Of the shape of a myrtle-berry; in *m. caruncle, fossa.*

Myrtle (mɔ̄·ɹt'l). late ME. [a. OF. *mirt-*, *myrtille*, *-il*, (1) myrtle-berry, (2) bilberry, whortleberry, ad. pop.L. **myrtilla*, *-us*, dim. of L. *myrta*, *-us.*] †**1.** The fruit or berry of the myrtle tree -1732. **2.** A plant of the genus *Myrtus*, esp. *M. communis*, the Common Myrtle, a shrub having shiny evergreen leaves and white sweet-scented flowers, now used chiefly in perfumery. The myrtle was held sacred to Venus and is used as an emblem of love. Also applied with qualifying word to allied or similar plants, esp. of the genus *Myrica*, as *bog m.*, *Dutch m.*, Sweet Gale, *Myrica Gale.* 1562. **3.** Short for *myrtle-green* 1884.

2. I will plant in the wildernes..the M., and the Oyle tree *Isa.* xli. 19. The Sweet Gale or Bog M., ..the badge of the Campbells 1866.

attrib. and *Comb.*, as *m. wreath*, etc.; **m. bird** (U.S.), *Dendroica* (*Silvicola*) *coronata*, which feeds on the berries of the candleberry m.; **m. green**, a shade of green like that of m. leaves; **m. wax**, wax produced by the candleberry m.

My·rtle-berry. 1579. **a.** The fruit of the myrtle (*Myrtus*). **b.** The bilberry or whortleberry. **c.** *Myrtle-berry wax* = myrtle wax.

Myself (məise·lf, mise·lf), *pron.* OE. [orig. ME *acc.-dat. pron.* + SELF, q. v. The transition from *meself* to *miself*, *myself* was prob. due, partly to unstressing of the vowel of *me*, partly to the analogy of *herself*, in which *her* was felt as a possessive genitive.] **I.** Emphatic uses. **1.** In apposition with *I*: In my own person; for my part. **2.** By ellipsis of *I*, *myself* comes to be used as a nominative. (As simple subject, now only *poet.*) ME. **3.** Substituted for ME as the object of a verb or governed by a prep. ME. **4.** (passing into *sb.*) My being or personality; my own or very self 1526.

1. I my selff will fight agaynst you COVERDALE *Jer.* xxi. 5. **2.** Ther was also a Reve and a Millere,..A Maunciple, and m. CHAUCER. M. when young did eagerly frequent Doctor and Saint FITZGERALD. One of our party and m. started on an expedition 1866. **3.** To m., mountains are the beginning and the end of all natural scenery RUSKIN. **4.** †*Another m.* [after L. *alter ego*]: a second self. *To be m., to feel like m.*: to be, or feel as if I were, in my normal condition of body or mind.

II. Reflexive uses. As direct or indirect obj., in acc. and inf. const., or in dependence on a prep. (Orig. only emphatic refl., but now in gen. use, repl. the refl. *me*, which is now only *arch.*) OE.

I very often walk by m. in Westminster Abbey ADDISON.

Mystacal (mi·stăkăl), *a.* 1888. [f. Gr. μυστακ-, μύσταξ (see MOUSTACHE) + -AL.] Resembling a moustache. So **Mysta·cial** *a.* 1782.

Mystagogue (mi·stăgǫg). 1550. [ad. L. *mystagogus*, a. Gr., f. μύστης (see MYSTIC) + ἀγωγός leading, ἄγειν to lead.] A teacher of mystical doctrines; *orig.*, to candidates for initiation into the Eleusinian or other mysteries. Hence **Mystagogic** (-gǫ·dʒik), **-al** *a.* pertaining to a m. or mystagogy; **-ly** *adv.* **My·stagogy**, interpretation of mysteries; initiation, or instruction preparatory to initiation, in mysteries.

Mysterial (mistīᵊ·riăl), *a.* Now *rare.* 1529. [ad. late L. *mysterialis*, f. *mysterium* MYSTERY [1].] Mysterious; †mystical. So †**Myste·rially** *adv.* late ME. only.

Mysteriarch (mistīᵊ·riāɹk). 1656. [ad. eccl. L. *mysteriarches*, a. Gr., f. μυστήριον MYSTERY [1] + -άρχης ruling, ἄρχειν to rule.] One who presides over mysteries.

Mysterious (mistīᵊ·riəs), *a.* 1616. [f. L. *mysterium* MYSTERY [1] + -OUS.] **1.** Full of, or wrapt in, mystery; of obscure origin, nature, or purpose. **2.** Of persons: †**a.** Dealing with or versed in mysteries; using occult arts. **b.** Whose movements are full of mystery; delighting in mystery 1620. **3.** That is due to a mystery. MILT. *P. L.* viii. 599.

1. God moves in a m. way His wonders to perform COWPER. A few m. words having been exchanged 1797. It is a m. sea, that has baffled for centuries the research of navigators 1853. **2. b.** Sheila..is romantic and m., and believes in..dreams 1874. Hence **Myste·rious·ly** *adv.*, **-ness.**

Mysterize (mi·stərəiz), *v. rare.* 1650. [f. MYSTERY [1] + -IZE.] **a.** *trans.* To interpret mystically. SIR T. BROWNE. **b.** *intr.* To make mysteries of things 1845.

Mystery [1] (mi·stəri). [ME. *mist-*, *mysterye*, *-ie*, etc., a. AF. **misterie* (OF. *mistere*, mod.F. *mystère*), ad. L. *mysterium*, a. Gr. μυστήριον, f. root of μύειν to close (the lips or eyes).] **I.** Theological uses. †**1.** *In* (*his*) *m.*: mystically -1628. **2.** A religious truth known only by divine revelation; usu. a doctrine of the faith involving difficulties which human reason is incapable of solving. late ME. **3.** A religious ordinance or rite, *esp.* a sacramental rite of the Christian religion; *spec.* (*pl.*) the Eucharist; *occas.* the consecrated elements 1506. **4.** An incident in the life of our Lord or of the Saints regarded as having a mystical significance. Hence, each of the fifteen divisions of the rosary corresponding to the 'mysteries of redemption' 1655.

2. By the misterye of thy holy incarnacion,..Good Lorde deliuer vs 1549.

II. Other uses. 1. A hidden or secret thing; something beyond human knowledge or comprehension; an enigma ME. †b. A personal secret –1617. c. A political or diplomatic secret; a secret of state. *Obs.* exc. as a use of the gen. sense. 1618. 2. In generalized sense. a. The condition of being secret or obscure; mysteriousness. Also, mysteries collectively. 1601. b. The behaviour or attitude of mind of one who makes a secret of things (often intrinsically unimportant) 1692. †3. Mysterious reason; mystic meaning –1687. 4. An action or practice about which there is some secrecy; a trade or other secret. Now often *trivial.* 1594. 5. Chiefly *pl.* In ancient religious systems, certain secret rites to which only the initiated were admitted 1643. b. The secrets of freemasonry 1738. 6. Used (after F. *mystère*, med.L. *mysterium*) as a name for the miracle-play. (Often erron. referred to MYSTERY² on the ground that the miracle-plays were often acted by the trade guilds.) 17.. 7. a. A kind of fly for salmon fishing 1867. b. A kind of cake or pudding 1889.

1. The M. of Edwin Drood DICKENS (*title*). b. *Haml.* III. ii. 382. Phr. *To make a m. of*: to treat as a secret in order to make an impression. 2. a. A Science without m. is unknown; a Religion without m. is absurd H. DRUMMOND. Phr. *Wrapped in m.*

Comb.: **m.-man**, a conjuror, a medicine-man; **-play** = sense II. 6; **-ship**, an armed and camouflaged merchantman used to decoy submarines in the war of 1914–18; = Q-BOAT.

Mystery² (mi·stəri). late ME. [ad. med.L. *misterium*, var. of *ministerium* (MISTER *sb.*¹), by confusion with *mysterium* MYSTERY¹.] †1. Service, occupation; office, ministry –1533. 2. Handicraft; craft, art; (one's) trade or calling (*arch.*) late ME. †b. Skill, art –1661. 3. A trade guild or company (*arch.* or *Hist.*). late ME.

2. That noble Science or M. of the healing mans body 1612. Phr. *Art and m.*: a formula in indentures of apprenticeship to a trade. 3. President of the m. of the workers in iron SCOTT.

Mystic (mi·stik). late ME. [a. OF., F. *mystique*, ad. L. *mysticus*, a. Gr. μυστικός, f. μύστης one initiated into mysteries (see MYSTERY¹ II. 5).] A. *adj.* 1. Spiritually allegorical or symbolical. Also = MYSTICAL *a.* 1, but now somewhat rhet. 2. Pertaining to the ancient religious mysteries, etc.; occult, esoteric 1615. †3. Secret, concealed –1697. 4. Pertaining to or connected with that branch of theology which relates to the direct communion of the soul with God. Now *rare.* 1639. 5. Of hidden meaning or nature; enigmatical 1631. b. In recent use: Inspiring an awed sense of mystery 1842.

1. The m. Dove Hovering His gracious brow above KEBLE. 2. The m. rites of Demeter 1835. 5. Foole, thou didst not understand The mystique language of the eye nor hand DONNE. b. An arm Clothed in white samite, m., wonderful TENNYSON.

B. *sb.* †1. Mystical meaning or representation. Only ME. 2. Orig., a 'mystic doctor', an exponent of mystical theology; also, one who maintains the importance of this. Hence: One who seeks by contemplation and self-surrender to obtain union with or absorption into the Deity, or who believes in the spiritual apprehension of truths inaccessible to the understanding 1679. 3. *occas.* One initiated into mysteries 1859.

2. Those mysticks who would discard the passions of hope and fear 1714. 3. This was the meaning of the founders of the mysteries when they said, 'Many are the wand bearers but few are the mystics' JOWETT.

Mystical (mi·stikăl), *a.* 1471. [f. as prec.; see -ICAL.] 1. Having a certain spiritual character or import by virtue of a connexion or union with God transcending human comprehension: said esp. with ref. to the Church as the Body of Christ, and to sacramental ordinances 1529. b. (Spiritually) allegorical or symbolical 1500. 2. Of dark import, obscure meaning, or occult influence. Now *rare* or *Obs.* 1500. †b. Of a person: Obscure in speech or style –1626. 3. Connected with occult rites or practices 1577. †4. = MYSTIC *a.* 3. –1687. 5. = MYSTIC *a.* 4. Also, pertaining to mystics or mysticism. 1613.

1. The churches mysticall repast G. HERBERT. b. The m. horseman in the Apocalypse 1861. 2. That m. needle which mariners talk of SCOTT. 3. 'Tis the sunset of life gives me m. lore, And coming events cast their shadows before CAMPBELL. 5. With my ascetick course of life I joined the reading all the Misticall Authors I could find BURNET. Hence **My·stical-ly** *adv.*, **-ness.**

Mysticete (mi·stisīt). 1801. [ad. mod.L. *mysticetus*, a. Gr. μυστίκητος (in old edd. of Aristotle *Hist. Anim.* III. xii, where mod. edd. read ὁ μῦς τὸ κῆτος).] 1. The Arctic Right Whale, *Balæna mysticetus.* 2. A whalebone whale 1876.

Mysticism (mi·stisiz'm). 1736. [f. MYSTIC + -ISM.] 1. The opinions, mental tendencies, or habits of thought and feeling, characteristic of mystics; belief in the possibility of union with the Divine nature by means of ecstatic contemplation; reliance on spiritual intuition as the means of acquiring knowledge of mysteries inaccessible to the understanding. 2. As a term of reproach. a. Applied loosely to any religious belief associated with self-delusion and dreamy confusion of thought. b. Sometimes applied to philosophical or scientific theories which assume occult qualities or mysterious agencies of which no rational account can be given. 1763.

Mysticize (mi·stisəiz), *v.* 1680. [f. MYSTIC *a.* + -IZE.] *trans.* To render mystical; to give a mystic meaning to.

My·stico-, comb. f. Gr. μυστικός MYSTIC, with sense 'partly mystical and partly ——', or 'mystically', as *mystico-religious* adj.

Mystification (mi:stifikē¹·ʃən). 1815. [ad. F., f. *mystifier* MYSTIFY *v.*²] The action of mystifying a person; an instance of this; the condition or fact of being mystified.

Special pleading of advocates, whose main talent is quibbling and m. 1826. So **My·stificator** [ad. F. *mystificateur*] *rare.* 1823.

Mystify (mi·stifəi), *v.*¹ *rare.* Also †**mist-.** 1734. [f. MIST *sb.*¹ or MISTY *a.*¹ + -FY.] Only in pa. pple.: Beclouded; befogged (*lit.* and *fig.*).

Mystify (mi·stifəi), *v.*² Also **mist-.** 1814. [ad. F. *mystifier*, irreg. f. *mystère* MYSTERY¹ or *mystique* MYSTIC; see -FY. Cf. prec.] 1. To bewilder; to play on the credulity of; to hoax, humbug. 2. To wrap up or involve in mystery; to make mystical; to interpret mystically 1829. 3. To involve in obscurity; to obscure the meaning or character of 1827.

1. Puebla was to choose his words—to hint at dark intrigues—to m. the council 1873. 2. The fabulous age, in which vulgar fact becomes mystified, and tinted up with delectable fiction W. IRVING. 3. We abhor those who m. it [*sc.* the Gospel] SPURGEON.

Myth (miþ). Also †**mythe.** 1830. [ad. mod.L. MYTHUS. (Cf. F. *mythe.*) Still occas. pron. (məiþ).] 1. A purely fictitious narrative usually involving supernatural persons, actions, or events, and embodying some popular idea concerning natural or historical phenomena. Often used vaguely to include any narrative having fictitious elements. 2. A fictitious or imaginary person or object 1849.

1. It is chronicled in an old Armenian m. that the wise men of the East were none other than the three sons of Noe 1899. 2. Parliamentary control was a m. 1888.

Mythic, -al (mi·þik, -ăl), *a.* 1669. [ad. or f. late L. *mythicus*, a. Gr. μυθικός, f. μῦθος MYTH; see -IC, -ICAL.] 1. Of the nature of, consisting of, or based on a myth or myths. b. *transf.* Having no foundation in fact 1870. 2. Existing only in myth 1678. 3. Of writers, their methods: Dealing with or involving the use of myths 1874.

1. A tradition, perhaps true, perhaps mythical, grew up, of Homer's blindness GLADSTONE. To reject the Gospels themselves as mythic 1881. b. Her influence is mythical DISRAELI. 3. The grave Thucydides, least mythical of historians 1888.

Hence **My·thically** *adv.* in a mythical manner; by means of myths 1847. **My·thicism,** the principle of attributing a mythical character to narratives of supernatural events 1840. **My·thicist,** an exponent of mythicism or mythical theories 1871. **My·thicize** *v. trans.* to turn into myth; to interpret mythically 1840.

My·thico-, comb. f. Gr. μυθικός MYTHIC, with sense 'mythical and —'.

Mythism (mi·þiz'm). 1848. [f. MYTH *sb.* + -ISM.] = MYTHICISM. So **My·thist** 1840. **My·thize** *v.* 1851.

Mytho- (məi·þo, mi·þo, miþǫ·, məiþǫ·), comb. f. Gr. μῦθος MYTH. **Mythoge·nesis,** the production of myths. **Mytho·gony** [Gr. -γονία creation], the study of the origin of myths. **Mytho·grapher,** a writer or narrator of myths. **Mytho·graphy,** representation or expression of myths. **Mythopœ·ic, -poe·tic,** [Gr. ποιεῖν to make] *adjs.* myth-making or relating to the making of myths. **Mythopo·em,** a mythical poem; **Mythopo·etry,** mythological poetry; so **Mythopo·et.**

Mythologer (miþǫ·lŏdʒəɹ). 1610. [f. L. *mythologus*, a. Gr.; see MYTHO- and -LOGER.] A mythologist. So **Mytholo·gian** (*rare*) 1613.

Mythologic, -ical (miþŏlǫ·dʒik, -ăl), *a.* 1614. [ad. or f. late L. *mythologicus*, a. Gr., f. μυθολογία MYTHOLOGY; see -IC, -ICAL.] Of or belonging to mythology or myths; mythical. Hence **Mytholo·gically** *adv.*

Mythologist (miþǫ·lŏdʒist). 1631. [f. L. *mythologus*, a. Gr.; see -LOGUE and -IST.] 1. A writer of myths 1642. 2. One versed in myths or mythology.

Mythologize (miþǫ·lŏdʒəiz), *v.* 1603. [ad. F. *mythologiser*; see next and -IZE.] †1. *trans.* To interpret (a story, fable) with regard to its mythological features –1727. 2. *intr.* To relate a myth or myths; to construct a mythology 1609. b. *trans.* To relate (something fictitious) (*rare*) 1851. 3. To represent or express mythologically (*rare*) 1678. 4. To make mythical; to convert into myth or mythology 1847.

1. This Parable was immediately mythologised. The Whale was interpreted to be Hobbes's *Leviathan* SWIFT. Hence **Mytho·logizer** (*rare*).

Mythology (miþǫ·lŏdʒi). late ME. [a. F. *mythologie* or ad. late L. *mythologia*; see MYTHO- and -LOGY.] †1. The exposition of myths –1656. †b. Symbolical meaning (of a fable, etc.) –1734. 2. A mythical story (*rare*). †Formerly: A parable, allegory. 1603. b. *gen.* without article 1646. 3. A body of myths, esp. that belonging to the religious literature or tradition of a country or people 1781. 4. That department of knowledge which deals with myths 1836.

1. b. Those [*sc. Whig* and *Tory*] were the Appellatives; but the M. was Seditious and Loyal NORTH. 2. b. The Heathen Religion is mostly couched under M. SWIFT. 3. The M...of the Iliad 1830. 4. The science of comparative m. 1864.

‖**Mythus** (məi·þŏs). 1825. Also in form mythos (1753). [mod.L., = late L. *mythos*, a. Gr. μῦθος.] = MYTH 1.

‖**Mytilus** (mi·tilŏs). 1817. [L.] A genus of bivalves, now comprising the marine mussels. Hence **My·tiloid** *a.* mussel-like; belonging to the family *Mytilidæ*; *sb.* a member of this family; a mussel 1847.

Myxinoid (mi·ksinoid), *a.* (*sb.*) 1846. [f. mod.L. *Myxine* (f. Gr. μύξα slime) + -OID.] Pertaining to (a fish of) the family *Myxinidæ* (typical genus *Myxine*) of cyclostomous fishes.

Myxo- (mi·kso), bef. a vowel **myx-**, comb. f. Gr. μύξα slime, mucus: as in ‖**Myxœde·ma,** a disease characterized by swelling due to infiltration of gelatinous fluid into the tissues; hence **Myxœde·matous, -œde·mic** *adjs.* ‖**Myxomyce·tes** *sb. pl.*, the slime-moulds or slime-fungi; hence **Myxomyce·tous** *a.* **My·xopod** [Gr. ποδ-, πούς foot], a protozoan possessing pseudopodia.

‖**Myxoma** (miksō·mă). *Pl.* **myxo·mata.** 1870. [mod.L., f. Gr. μύξα mucus, after *sarcoma.*] *Path.* A tumour consisting of mucous or gelatinous tissue. Hence **Myxo·matous** *a.*

Myzont (məi·zǫnt), *a.* and *sb.* 1882. [ad. Gr. μυζοντ-, pres. ppl. stem of μύζειν to suck.] *Zool.* = MARSIPOBRANCH, MARSIPOBRANCHIATE *a.* and *sb.*

‖**Myzostoma** (məizǫ·stŏmă). Also anglicized **myzostome.** 1876. [mod. L., f. Gr. μύζειν to suck + στόμα mouth.] *Zool.* One of an order of small parasitic worms, having disk-like bodies provided with suckers. Hence **Myzosto·matous, Myzo·stomous** *adjs.*

N

N (en), the fourteenth letter of the modern, and thirteenth of the ancient Roman alphabet, represents historically, and is in form derived from, the Greek *nū* and the Semitic *nun*. It usually denotes a voiced nasal consonant with front closure (the point of the tongue touching the teeth or the fore part of the palate). The sound is in certain positions a sonant or vowel, here denoted by ('n), as in *bidden* (bi·d'n). It is silent only in a few cases at the end of syllables after *l* and *m*, as *kiln*, *damn*, *hymn*, *column*, etc.

Before (g) and (k), *n* may also represent a nasal with back tongue-closure, here denoted by (ŋ), as in *finger* (fi·ŋgəɹ), *think* (þiŋk). When not followed by these sounds this back-nasal is expressed by the digraph *ng* as in *hang* (hæŋ), etc.

In ME. the *n* of the indef. article *an* is often transferred to a following word beginning with a vowel, as in *newt*, *nickname*. A similar transference takes place with the *n* of *mīn*, *myn* my, and *þīn*, *thyn* thy: see NAIN, NAUNT, etc.

I. 1. The letter used to represent the sound OE. **b.** In *Printing* used as a unit of measurement (often *en*; cf. EM); also *n.-quadrat* 1683. **2.** Used to indicate that the name of a person is to be inserted by the speaker or reader OE. **3.** Used to denote one of a series of things, a point in a diagram, etc. 1677. **4.** In *Math.* used to indicate an indefinite number. *To the* n^{th} *(power)*, to any required power; hence *fig.* to any extent 1852. **5.** *n-declension*, the 'weak' declension of Teut. nouns and adjs., in which the stem ends in *n*; so *n-stem*, *n-plural* 1843. **6.** *N-rays* (orig. *n-rays*), N^1*-rays* (orig. n_1*-rays*), forms of radiation having opposite effects; named from the initial letter of Nancy, at which University the *N-rays* were discovered 1903.

II. Abbrevs. **a.** Miscellaneous. N. = various proper names, as Nicholas, Naomi, etc.; N (*Chem.*) = nitrogen; n. (*Gram.*) = noun, neuter, nominative; n.b. = no ball. n.d. = no date; NF. = Norman French; N.O. = Natural Order; n.p. = (*a*) new paragraph; (*b*) no place; N.S. (*Banking*) = not sufficient. **b.** N. = North; in points of the compass and London postal districts, as N.E., NE. = North-east, etc.; N.B. = North Britain (Scotland), North British; N.C. = North Carolina. **c.** N. = New, as in N.B. = New Brunswick; N.E.D. = (A) New English Dictionary (on Historical Principles); N.J. = New Jersey; N.S. = New Style; N.T. = New Testament. **d.** N. = National, as in N.S.P.C.A. = National Society for the Prevention of Cruelty to Animals; N.U.R. = National Union of Railwaymen; N.U.T. = National Union of Teachers. See also N.B.

n-, in OE. and ME., the negative particle *ne* in combination with a word beginning with a vowel, *h*, or *w*, as *nam*, am not, *nis*, is not, etc.

†**Na**, *adv.*[1] and *conj.* [OE. *ná* = *ne* NE + *á* ever, A *adv.*] Not; nor -1786.

Na (nā), *adv.*[2] *Sc.* and *n. dial.* ME. [repr. OE. *ná* (see prec.), and corresp. to the midland and southern No.] No, in answer to a question, to express dissent, etc.

Na (nă), *adv.*[3] *Sc.* and *n. dial.* 1714. [Enclitic form of No *adv.* 'not', often affixed.] Not. Used chiefly with auxiliary verbs, as *canna*, *dinna* (= don't), *hasna*, etc.

Naam (nām). [OE. *naam*, *nám*, a. ON. *nám*, related to *niman* to take, NIM.] *Hist. Law.* The act of taking another's goods by way of distraint; the goods thus taken.

Nab (næb), *sb.*[1] Chiefly *n.* and *Sc.* late ME. [a. ON. *nabbr* and *nabbi* projecting peak or knoll.] **1.** A jutting out part of a hill or rock; a peak or promontory; a summit. **2.** A projection or spur on the bolt of a lock 1677.

†**Nab**, *sb.*[2] *Obs. Cant.* 1673. [perh. a use of prec. Cf. the later NOB.] A hat -1754.

Nab (næb), *v. slang.* or *colloq.* 1686. [Cf. NAP *v.*[3]] **1.** *trans.* To catch and take into custody; to apprehend, arrest. **2.** To snatch or seize (a thing); to steal 1814.

Nabal (nē¹·băl). 1604. [See 1 Sam. xxv. 3 ff.] A churlish or miserly person.

Nabob (nē¹·bǫb). 1612. [ad. Urdū *nawwāb* deputy governor; see NAWAB.] **1.** Title of certain Mohammedan officials, who acted as deputy governors of provinces or districts in the Mogul Empire; an official thus designated; a governor of a town or district in India. **2.** *transf.* A person of great wealth; *spec.* one who has returned from India with a large fortune 1764.

2. Dawdling, like a bilious old n. at a watering place MACAULAY. Hence **Na·bobess**, a female n. 1767. **Na·bobship**, the office or rank of a n.; a district governed by a n. 1753.

Nabs (næbz). 1790. [Obscure; cf. NIBS, and 16th c. *my nobs* = my darling.] *His nabs*, he; *my nabs*, my friend; myself.

‖**Nacelle** (năse·l). 1909. [F. :—late L. *navicella*, dim. of *navis* ship.] The framework of an aeroplane or dirigible containing the engine, controlling gear, and propellers.

†**Nache.** ME. (**nage**); 1523 (**nache**). [a. OF. *nache* :—pop.L. **natica*, f. *natis* buttock. Cf. AITCH-BONE.] The point of the rump in an ox or cow; the rump.

Nacre (nē¹·kəɹ). 1598. [a. F. *nacre*, prob. of Oriental origin.] **1.** The pinna or sea-pen, or other shell-fish yielding mother-of-pearl. **2.** A smooth, shining, iridescent substance forming the inner layer in many shells; mother-of-pearl 1689. Hence **Na·cred** *a.* faced with, having the hues of, n. 1755. **Na·creous** *a.* consisting of n.; resembling n. in substance or in hues 1819.

†**Nad(de**, had not; see NE and HAVE *v.* -1480.

Nadder, Naddre, etc., obs. ff. ADDER.

Nadir (nē¹·dəɹ). late ME. [ad. (ult.) Arab. *naḍīr* opposite to, over against (also as *sb.*). In sense 2 used ellipt. for *naḍīr as-samt* 'opposite to the zenith'.] *Astron.* †**1.** A point in the heavens diametrically opposite to some other point, esp. to the sun. Const. *of* and *to*. -1738. **2.** The point of the heavens diametrically opposite to the zenith; the point directly under the observer 1495. **3.** *transf.* The lowest point (*of* anything); the place or time of greatest depression or degradation 1793.

3. The seventh century is the *nadir* of the human mind in Europe HALLAM. **Na·diral** *a. rare* 1891.

Nae(-), Sc. var. of NA(-) = NO(-).

‖**Nævus** (nī·vǒs). *Pl.* **nævi** (nī·vəi). 1835. Also (17th c.) anglicized **næve.** [L.] *Path.* A hypertrophied state of the blood-vessels of the skin, forming spots or elevations of a red or purplish colour, usu. congenital; a mole. Hence **Næ·void** *a.* of the nature of a n.

Nag (næg), *sb.*[1] late ME. [?] A small riding horse or pony. †**b.** *transf.* as a term of abuse -1606.

Nag (næg), *sb.*[2] 1894. [f. next.] The act of nagging.

Nag (næg), *v.* 1828. [Orig. a dial. word, and prob. of Scand. origin.] **1.** To be persistently worrying or irritating by continued fault-finding, scolding, or urging. **2.** *trans.* To assail or annoy (a person) in this manner. 1840. Also **nagnag.**

1. It's no good my mother nagging at me TROLLOPE. **2.** Is it pleasant..to have your wife nagnagging you because she has not been invited..? THACKERAY. Hence **Na·gging** *vbl. sb.* and *ppl. a.*

‖**Nagari** (nā·gărī). 1776. = DEVANAGARI.

Naggy (næ·gi), *a.* 1697 (**knaggie**). [f. NAG *v.* + -Y[1].] Given to nagging.

Nagor (nē¹·gǫɹ). 1780. [Arbitrary alteration by Buffon of *nanguer*, a species of antelope formerly recognized.] The Senegal antelope, *Cervicapra redunca.*

Nagualism (næ·gwăliz'm, næ·wăl-). 1883. [f. Quiché *naual* wizard + -ISM.] A system of superstition practised by a secret sect formerly existing in Central America.

Naiad (nəi·æd, nē¹·æd). 1610. [ad. L. *Naïas*, *Naïad-*, Gr. Ναϊάς, Ναϊαδ-, related to νάειν to flow, νᾶμα running water.] *Myth.* One of a number of beautiful young nymphs imagined as living in, and being the tutelary spirits of, rivers and springs; a river nymph. Also **Naïd** (nē¹·id) [L. *Naïs*, Gr. Ναΐς] -1717.

You Nimphs cald Nayades of yᵉ windring brooks SHAKS. Also **Naiades** (nəi·ădīz, nē¹·ădīz), *sb. pl.* ME. The flowry-kirtl'd Naiades MILT.

Naiant (nē¹·ănt), *a.* 1562. [a. AF. **naiant* = OF. *noiant*, pr. pple. of *noier* :—L. *natare* to swim.] *Her.* Swimming.

‖**Naib** (nā·ib, nē¹·ib). 1682. [Arab. *nā'ib* deputy; cf. NAWAB.] A deputy governor; a deputy.

‖**Naïf** (naïf), *a.* Now *rare.* 1598. [F. :—L. *nativum*; see NAÏVE.] = NAÏVE.

‖**Naik** (nā·ik, nē¹·ik). 1588. [Urdū *nāik*, Hindī *nāyak* :—Skr. *nāyaka* leader.] **1.** An Indian title of authority; a governor. **2.** A military officer; in later use, a corporal of native infantry 1787.

Nail (nē¹l), *sb.* [OE. *næg(e)l*, from a root **nag-* obscurely represented in L. *unguis*, Gr. ὄνυξ, ὄνυχος, etc.] **I. 1.** A hard, oval-shaped, protective covering of modified epidermis, formed upon the upper tip of the fingers and toes in Man and the Quadrumana, and answering to the claws and hoofs of other animals and birds. **b.** A similar growth on the toes of beasts and birds; a claw or talon OE. **2.** Anything resembling a nail in shape or colour; *esp.* a nail-like excrescence, situated on the upper mandible of certain soft-billed birds. late ME.

1. A scoldyng woman, whose weapon is onely her toungue and her nayles HALL.

Phrases. *A n.* or *nail's breadth* (cf. L. *transversum unguem*), the smallest amount. *To bite, blow, pare one's nails.* *From the tender n.* (tr. L. *de tenero ungui*, Hor. *Odes* III. vi. 24), from early youth. *To the* or *a n.* (tr. L. *ad unguem*, Hor. *Sat.* I. v. 32), to a nicety, to perfection. *Tooth and n.*: see TOOTH.

II. A small spike or piece of metal (gen. with a point and a broadened head, so as to be easily driven in by a hammer), used to fix one thing firmly to another, or as a peg, or occas. as an ornament; rarely, a wooden peg (cf. *tree-n.*) OE.

As a nayle, the moo knockes it hath the more sure it is fixed 1526. *fig.* The countless nails that rivet the chains of habit LAMB. Provb. *One n. drives out another.* The nails of the Cross..were converted by the emperor into a helmet LECKY.

Phrases. *To hit the (right) n. on the head*, to hit the mark, to say or do exactly the right thing. *To drive the n. home*, to push a matter to a conclusion. *A n. in one's (its) coffin*, something that contributes to the end of the person or thing referred to. *On the n.* (cf. SUPERNACULUM), on the spot, at once. Chiefly of making money payments. *Hard as nails*, in perfect condition. *Right as nails*, quite right.

III. 1. = CLOVE *sb.*[3]; †also, a measure of land. Now only *south. dial.* late ME. **2.** A measure of length for cloth; 2¼ inches, or the sixteenth part of a yard 1465.

attrib. and *Comb.*, as *n.-brush*, *-scissors*, etc.; **n. rod**, a strip or rod of iron from which nails are cut. Hence **Nai·lless** *a.* destitute of nails.

Nail (nē¹l), *v.* [OE. *nægl(i)an*, f. **nagl-* NAIL *sb.*] **I. 1.** *trans.* To fix or fasten (a person or thing) with nails *on* or *to* something else. **2. a.** To pierce or drive through with a nail or nails. Now *rare* or *Obs.* **b.** To fix or fasten with nails. Also with *about*, *in*, *together*, etc. ME. **c.** To stud with (or as with) nails; to mark by driving in a nail (*rare*) late ME. †**d.** *Mil.* To spike (a cannon) -1781. **3.** *Nail up*: **a.** To close up firmly by fixing with nails 1530. **b.** To affix at some height by means of nails; to fasten with nails to a wall, etc. 1630. †**c.** *Mil.* = 2 d. -1781. **4.** *Nail down*, to fix down with nails; to fix down the lid of (a box) in this way 1669.

1. He was nailed to the tre ME. The royal anathema was nailed on the Episcopal gate at London D'ISRAELI. He called to his coachman..to wait as if nailed to the spot MEREDITH. Phr. *To n. one's colours to the mast*, to adopt an unyielding attitude. *To n. to the counter*, to expose as false or spurious (as shopkeepers deal with bad coin). *To n. to the barndoor*, to exhibit after the manner of dead vermin. **2. b.** He is now deed, and nayled in his chest CHAUCER. **c.** Those Stars which n. Heav'ns pavement 1648.

II. 1. To fix, make fast, as by means of nails; to secure. Now *rare* or *Obs.* late ME. **2.** To fix (a person or thing) firmly *to* something; e. g. *to* or *on* the ground, etc., with a weapon 1590. **b.** To fix, or keep (one) fixed, *to* or in a certain place, position or occupation 1611. **c.** To fix or fasten (the eyes, mind, etc.) *to* or *on* the object of one's attention 1591. **3.** To fix or pin one *down* to something 1615. **4.** *slang.* **a.** To secure; to succeed in catching or getting hold of (a person or thing); to steal 1760. **b.** To catch (one) in some fix 1766.

2. To whose Fingers their Money is as it were glued and nailed 1691. **b.** Those Whose headaches n. them to a noonday bed COWPER. **c.** I cannot n. my mind to one subject of contemplation SCOTT. 4. a. [He] insisted on nailing me for dinner before he would leave me THACKERAY. Hence **Nai·ler,** a nail-maker; one who drives in nails 1440; *slang*, a marvellously good specimen; a very skilful hand *at* something 1818. **Nai·ling** *ppl. a.* fixing like a nail; *slang*, excellent, splendid 1883.

Nailery (nē·ləri). 1798. [f. NAILER: see -ERY.] A place or workshop where nails are made.

Nai·l-head. 1683. [f. NAIL *sb.* + HEAD *sb.* II. 1.] 1. The head of a nail. 2. An ornament shaped like the head of a nail 1836. b. *attrib.*, with *moulding, ornament, pattern* 1845.

2. The n. being an ornament easily cut, was much used in almost all periods of Norman work PARKER.

So **Nai·l-headed** *a.* 1801.

Nain (nēn), *a. Sc.* ME. [See OWN *a.*] (One's) own. Hence **Nainse·l',** **-se·ll,** (one's) own self; *her nainsel'*, a phr. supposed to be used by Highlanders in place of the 1st pers. pron.

‖**Nainsook** (nē·nsuk). 1804. [Urdū (Hindī) *nainsukh*, f. *nain* eye + *sukh* pleasure.] A cotton fabric, a kind of muslin or jaconet, of Indian origin.

‖ **Naïs** (nē·is). *Pl.* **naïdes** (nē·idīz). 1697. [L. *Naïs*, Gr. Ναΐς.] 1. *Mythol.* = NAIAD. 2. *Zool.* A small fresh-water worm allied to the earthworm 1835.

Naissant (nē·sănt), *a.* 1572. [a. F. *naissant*, pr. pple. of *naître* :—Rom. **nascere* for L. *nasci* to be born; cf. NASCENT.] 1. *Her.* Of animals: Issuing from the middle of the fess or other ordinary. 2. That is in the act of springing up, coming into existence, or being produced (*rare*) 1885.

Naïve (na,ī·v, nā·īv, nē·īv), *a.* Also **naive.** 1654. [F., fem. of NAÏF :—L. *nativum* NATIVE *a.*] Characterized by unsophisticated or unconventional simplicity or artlessness. Hence **Nai·vely** *adv.* 1705.

‖**Naïveté** (naīvte, nē·īvti). 1673. Also **naïvety** (1708). [F.; see prec. and -TY.] The condition or quality of being naïve; a naïve remark, etc.

He had a sort of n. and openness of demeanour SCOTT.

‖**Naja** (nē·dʒă, nē·yă). 1753. [mod.L., f. Hindī *nāg* snake.] A genus of highly venomous snakes, comprising the species *N. tripudians* of India and *N. haje* of Africa; the Indian or African cobra; a snake of either of these species.

Naked (nē·kėd), *a.* and *sb.* [OE. *nacod*, f. stem **naq-* :—**nogʷ-*, which appears in Skr. *nagnás*, L. *nudus*, etc.] A. *adj.* I. 1. Unclothed; stripped to the skin. b. Of a horse or ass: Unsaddled, bare-backed OE. 2. Of parts of the body: Not covered by clothing; bare, exposed ME. 3. Destitute of clothing (implying wretchedness). Also *occas.* of animals: Stripped of the usual warm covering. OE. b. Bare of means (*rare*) 1625. †4. Without weapons (or armour); unarmed -1787. b. Defenceless, unprotected; open *to* assault or injury 1560.

1. To bed he goes; and Jemy euer used to lye n., as is the use of a number 1608. b. A n. man on a n. horse is a fine spectacle DARWIN. 2. There is my Dagger, And heere my n. Breast SHAKS. *transf.* He..Had gazed on Nature's n. loveliness SHELLEY. Phr. *N. bed*, orig. a bed in which the occupant slept entirely n.; later used with ref. to the removal of the ordinary wearing apparel. Now *arch.* 3. Poore n. wretches..That bide the pelting of this pittilesse storme SHAKS. 4. b. Left n. to infinite temptations 1688.

II. 1. Of a sword, etc.: Not covered by a sheath OE. 2. Free from concealment or reserve; straightforward. Now *rare.* ME. 3. Uncovered, stripped of all disguise or concealment. late ME. b. Plain, obvious, clear 1589.

1. In her right hand a n. poniard 1634. 2. By this n. confession of my life 1652. *The n. truth*, the plain truth, without concealment or addition. 3. Nakid is helle beforn hym WYCLIF *Job* xxvi. 6. b. Chamberlayne laid his plan, in all its n. absurdity, before the Commons MACAULAY.

III. †1. Bare, destitute, or devoid *of* something; unoccupied, blank -1822. 2. Of physical objects or features: Lacking some natural or ordinary covering, as vegetation, foliage 1549. 3. Lacking the usual furniture or ornament. late ME. 4. Unprotected, exposed 1607. 5. *Bot.* a. Of parts of a plant: Having no covering, leaves, hairs, etc. 1578. 6. *Zool.* Destitute of hair or scales; not defended by a shell 1769.

1. The maritine Townes..being left halfe n. of defence 1632. 2. Sea-beaten rocks and n. shores COWPER. Let birds be silent on the n. spray SPENSER. Huge precipices of n. stone MACAULAY. Phr. *N. fallow*, a bare fallow, one on which no crop at all is grown. *transf.* Wild swans struggling with the n. storm SHELLEY. 3. Some forlorne and n. Hermitage SHAKS. *N. flooring*, the timbers which support the flooring boards. 4. I always felt it on the n. nerve BURKE. *N. light*, one not placed within a case. *N. fire*, one not closed in any contrivance.

IV. 1. Left without any addition; not overlaid with remarks or comments OE. b. Not otherwise supported or confirmed; (chiefly in legal use) not supported by proof or evidence. late ME. 2. *N. eye*, the eye unassisted by any aid to vision. So *n. sight.* 1664.

1. He chooses to suppose..a n. possibility BURKE. The n. facts BLACKSTONE. b. A n. and bare promise of affiance 1555. For the evidence of these designs, Mr. Hastings presents his own n. assertion 1817.

B. *sb.* †1. *Art. The n.*: the nude 1735-1815. b. The face or plain surface (of a wall, etc.) 1726. †2. *Art.* A nude figure 1622-1675. Hence **Na·ked·ly** *adv.*, **-ness.**

Naker (nē·kəɪ). Current in 14th c.; now *Hist.* ME. [a. OF. *nacre*, ad. (ult.) Arab., Pers. *naqāra(h).*] A kettle-drum.

Pypes, trompes, nakers, and clariounes CHAUCER.

†**Nale,** in phr. *at* (*the*) or *atte nale* (= at the ale): see ALE 2.

†**Nam,** am not: see NE, BE *v.* OE. -1576.

Namaycush (næ·mėkɒʃ). 1785. [Amer. Indian.] The great lake trout (*Cristivomer namaycush*) of N. America.

Namby-pamby (næ·mbi,pæ·mbi), *a.* and *sb.* 1745. [Formed fancifully on the name of *Ambrose* Philips (died 1749), who wrote pastorals ridiculed by Carey (in *Namby Pamby* 1726) and Pope (*Dunc.* iii. 319).] A. *adj.* 1. Of style, actions, etc.: Weakly sentimental, insipidly pretty. 2. Of persons: Inclined to affected daintiness, of a weak or trifling character 1774.

2. She was a namby-pamby milk-and-water affected creature THACKERAY.

B. *sb.* 1. That which is marked by affected prettiness and feeble sentimentality 1764. 2. A namby-pamby person 1885. Hence **Na·mby-pa·mbyism** 1834.

Name (nēm), *sb.* [OE. *nama*, with cognates in all Indo-Eur. langs., as Skr. *nāman*, Gr. ὄνομα, L. *nomen.*] I. 1. The particular combination of vocal sounds employed as the individual designation of a single person, animal, place, or thing. 2. The specific word or words (term) used to denote a member of a particular class of beings or objects OE.

1. Peter Simple, you say your n. is? SHAKS. God needeth not to distinguish his Celestiall servants by names HOBBES. Phr. *To keep one's n. on, take one's n. off, the books of a college or hall*: (in Oxford and Cambridge use) to continue to be, cease to be, an actual member of the college or hall. 2. Now foloys the naamys of all maner of hawkys 1486. There is a Fault, which, tho' common, wants a N. STEELE. *To call names*: see CALL *v.* III.

II. In pregnant senses, chiefly of biblical origin. 1. The name (sense 1) of God or Christ, regarded as symbolizing the divine nature or power OE. 2. a. The name of a person as implying his individual characteristics. late ME. b. The name (sense 1) of a person or group of persons, as implying all the individuals that bear it; those having a certain name; hence, a family, clan, people. late ME. 3. The name (sense 1) of a person as mentioned by others with admiration or commendation; hence, the fame or reputation involved in a well-known name ME. b. One whose name is well known (*rare*) 1611. 4. The reputation *of* some character or attribute ME. b. With *a* and *adj.* late ME. c. (Usu. in phr. *to get* or *make* (*oneself*) *a n.*) A distinguished name. late ME. 5. Without article: Repute, fame, distinction. Now *rare.* late ME. 6. One's repute or reputation, etc.; esp. *one's* (*good*) *n.* ME. 7. The mere appellation in contrast to the person or thing; reputation without correspondence in fact. late ME.

1. Thee we adore Eternal N. WESLEY. 2. a. By the hand Of that black N., Edward, black Prince of Wales SHAKS. b. All the clans hostile to the n. of Campbell were set in motion MACAULAY. 3. Some to the fascination of a n. Surrender judgment hoodwinked COWPER. Phr. *Of no n., without* (*a*) *n.*, implying obscurity. b. I am become a n.; For always roaming..Much have I seen and known TENNYSON. 4. b. A good N., for good and faire dealing BACON. 5. Phr. *Of* (*great*, etc.) *n.*, noted, distinguished, famous. Authors of illustrious n...Are sadly prone to quarrel COWPER. 6. I love you so well that your good n. is mine TENNYSON. 7. Christian in n., and infidel in heart COWPER.

Phrases. **By name. a.** Used with verbs of naming or calling, or, later, simply added to the proper appellation of a person, as *a spy, John Jones by n.* **b.** With vbs. of summoning, or mentioning, or in enumeration of individuals. **c.** With *know.* (*a*) Individually. (*b*) By repute only; not personally. **In** one's **n., in the n. of** one. **a.** Used in phr. expressing invocation of or devotion to the persons of the Godhead. This, in the N. of Heauen, I promise thee SHAKS. **b.** In adjurations, orig. solemn, but latterly freq. trivial; What in the n. of fortune have they been doing to you? 1861. **c.** Denoting that one acts as deputy for another; or implying that the action is done on account of or on behalf of some other person or persons. Hence, by contrast, *in one's own n.* †**d.** = Under the character or designation of, as. **e.** Indicating the assigned ownership of a thing, as *consols standing in the n. of A. B., deceased.* **By the n. of,** called or known by, having, the n. of. Now *colloq.* and *U.S.* So *of the n. of.* **To** one's **n.** (colloq.), belonging to one.

attrib. and *Comb.*, as *n.-giver*; 'bearing a name', as *n.-card, -plate*, etc.; 'named after, or giving a n. to, one', as *n.-saint, -sire*, etc.; **n.-part,** the part in a play from which it takes its n.

Name (nēm), *v.* [OE. (*ge*)*namian*, f. *nama* NAME *sb.*] I. 1. *trans.* To give a name or names to; to call by some name. 2. To call by some title or epithet OE. †b. To allege or declare (a person or thing) *to be* something -1647. 3. To call (a person or thing) by the right name 1450.

1. Then one of them shal n. the childe, and dippe him in the water *Bk. Com. Prayer.* A Son..Whom she brought up and Comus nam'd MILT. 2. Ye shalbe named the prestes of the Lorde COVERDALE *Isa.* lxi. 6. 3. *Temp.* I. ii. 335. I'm sure I've seen that bonie face, But yet I canna n. ye BURNS.

II. 1. To nominate, assign, or appoint (a person) to some office, duty, or position OE. 2. To mention or specify (a person or persons, etc.) by name OE. b. Of the Speaker of the House of Commons: To indicate (a member) by name as guilty of disorderly conduct or disobedience to the chair 1792. c. *Name!* Used in parliamentary practice, etc., to demand that a member be 'named', or that the name of some person alluded to by a speaker shall be given 1817. 3. To mention, speak of, or specify (a thing) by its name or usual designation. late ME. b. To make mention of, to speak about (a fact, etc.); to cite as an instance; to give particulars of 1542. 4. With cogn. obj. late ME. 5. To mention or specify as something desired or decided upon; to appoint or fix (a sum, time, etc.) 1593.

1. Such persons, as shalbe named to be iustices of peace 1542. 2. Now n. the rest of the Players SHAKS. Phr. *To n. on* (or *in*) *the same day* or *in the same breath* (*with*), to bring into comparison or connexion. Only in neg. and interrog. sentences. c. Loud cries of hear, hear, name, name, order *Parl. Deb.* 279. 1817. 3. N. not Religion, for thou lou'st the Flesh SHAKS. b. The measures we have named were only part of Henry's legislation GREEN. He names the price for ev'ry office paid POPE. 4. When tongues speak sweetly, then they n. her name SHAKS. 5. Phr. *To n. the day*, of a woman, to fix her wedding day 1748.

Nameable (nē·măb'l), *a.* 1840. [f. prec. + -ABLE.] That admits of being named.

Na·me-child. 1845. [f. NAME *sb.* + CHILD.] One called after, or named out of regard for, another.

Name-day (nē·m,dē). Also **name's-day.** 1721. [f. NAME *sb.* + DAY *sb.*] 1. The day of the saint whose name one bears. (Used chiefly with ref. to continental sovereigns.) 2. *London Stock Exch.* The day before the account-day, on which the buyers of shares or stock pass to the sellers tickets setting forth the names into which they are to be transferred 1902.

Nameless (nē·mlės), *a.* ME. [f. NAME *sb.* + -LESS. Senses 5-8 are chiefly *poet.* or *rhet.*] 1. Not possessed of a (distinguished) name; unknown by name; obscure, inglorious. b. Not mentioned by name 1535. 2. Left unnamed in order to avoid giving offence, or the like. late ME. †3. Of a book, letter, etc.: Anonymous –1822. 4. Of a person: Anonymous, unknown 1591. 5. Bearing no legitimate name 1593. b. Having no name 1638. 6. Of tombs, etc.: Bearing no name or inscription 1655. 7. Inexpressible, indefinable 1591. 8. Unutterable; horrible, abominable 1611.

1. To be namelesse in worthy deeds exceeds an infamous history SIR T. BROWNE. b. N. in dark oblivion let them dwell MILT. 2. On the authority of one who shall be n. JOWETT. 4. A certain n. Socinian was the Author of them STILLINGFL. 5. Blur'd with namelesse bastardie SHAKS. b. Iles for the greatest part namelesse and numberlesse 1638. 7. A n. sense of fear SHELLEY. 8. A flood of n. sensualities LIDDON. Hence **Na·meless-ly** *adv.*, **-ness** 1847.

Namely (nēⁱ·mli), *adv.* ME. [f. NAME *sb.* + -LY², after OF. *nommeement* or L. *nominatim.*] †1. Particularly –1700. 2. To wit; that is to say; videlicet 1450. †b. With *as.* For example –1653.

1. Returning thanks..for many blessings and favors ..And, n., for the enjoyment of the Gospel 1700. 2. That thou hast not prayed for, haue I geuen the also, n., ryches, and honoure COVERDALE 1 *Kings* iii. 13. b. Almost all things, as namelie butter, cheese, fagots 1583.

Namer (nēⁱ·məɹ). 1627. [f. NAME *v.* + -ER¹.] One who, or that which, gives a name or names.

Namesake (nēⁱ·msēⁱk). 1646. [Prob. orig. in phr. *for the name's sake.*] A person or thing having the same name as another.

Nammo(re, Na-mo(re, obs. ff. NO MO, NO MORE.

Nandu (næ·ndu). Also **-dou.** 1835. [ad. Brazilian *nhandú.*] A variety of ostrich (*Rhea Americana*) peculiar to S. America.

Nankeen (nænkī·n), *sb.* (and *a.*) Also **-kin.** 1755. [f. *Nankin* or *Nanking*, 'southern capital', in the province of Kiangsu in China.] 1. A kind of cotton cloth, orig. made at Nanking from a yellow variety of cotton, but now from ordinary cotton dyed yellow. b. With *pl.* A kind of this cloth 1781. 2. *attrib.* or *adj.* Made of nankeen 1774. b. *pl.* Trousers made of nankeen 1806. 3. A yellow or pale buff; the colour of nankeen. Also *attrib.* 1775. 4. A kind of Chinese porcelain 1781.

1. *N. cotton*, the variety of cotton from which nankeen cloth was originally made. 3. *N. bird, crane*, or *night-hawk, n. hawk*: names of Australian birds.

Nanny. 1912. [As next.] Child's name for a nurse.

Nanny-goat (næ·ni,gōᵘt). 1788. [f. fem. name *Nanny* = Ann; cf. BILLY-GOAT.] A she-goat (*colloq.*). Also ellipt. **Nanny.**

Nantz (nænts), *sb.* (and *a.*) Now *arch.* 1684. [From *Nantes* in France, where made.] (Often *right N.*) Brandy.

‖ **Naos** (nēⁱ·ǫs). 1775. [Gr.] A temple; the inner cell or sanctuary of a temple.

Nap (næp), *sb.*¹ ME. [f. NAP *v.*¹] A short light sleep, *esp.* during the day. Phr. *To take a n.*

Nap (næp), *sb.*² late ME. [a. MDu. or MLG. *noppe*, sb. related to *noppen* NAP *v.*²] 1. orig. The rough layer of projecting threads or fibres on the surface of a textile fabric, requiring to be smoothed by shearing; in later use, the surface given to cloth by artificial raising of the short fibres, with subsequent cutting and smoothing; the pile. b. With *pl.* A cloth having a nap on it 1771. 2. *transf.* A surface resembling the nap of cloth 1591. 3. The smooth and glossy surface of a beaver, felt, or silk hat 1727.

1. *fig.* To dresse the Common-wealth, and turne it, and set a new n. vpon it SHAKS.

Nap (næp), *sb.*³ 1820. [Abbrev. of *Napoleon.*] 1. = NAPOLEON 1. 2. A card game, in which each player receives five cards, and calls the number of tricks he expects to win; one who calls five is said to *go N.*, and to *make his N.* if he wins them all 1879. b. *To go n.*, to stake all one can, to speculate heavily 1884.

Nap (næp), *v.*¹ [OE. *hnappian*, app. related to OHG. (*h*)*naffizan* 'dormitare'.] *intr.* To sleep lightly for a brief time.

Phr. *To take* or *catch* (*one*) *napping*, to find (one) asleep; also *fig.* to take unawares or off one's guard.

Nap (næp), *v.*² 1483. [a. MDu. or MLG. *noppen*, of uncertain origin.] †1. *trans.* To trim (cloth) by shearing the nap –1582. 2. To furnish with a nap; to raise a nap on 1620.

Nap, *v.*³ *Cant* and *slang.* 1673. = NAB *v.*

Napæa (năpī·ă). *rare.* 1612. [a. L., ad. Gr. Ναπαία, fem. of ναπαῖος, f. νάπη a wooded dell.] A nymph haunting wooded dells.

Nape (nēⁱp). ME. [?] The back of the neck; that part which contains the first cervical vertebra. b. esp. in phr. *the n. of the neck* ME.

‖ **Napellus** (năpe·lǫs). 1626. [med.L., f. *napus* turnip.] *Bot.* The common aconite; monks'-hood, wolf's-bane.

Naperer (nēⁱ·pərəɹ). *Obs.* exc. *Hist.* 1450. [f. NAPERY + -ER¹.] The person having charge of the royal table linen.

Napery (nēⁱ·pəri). ME. [a. obs. F. *naperie*, f. *nape* (*nappe*) :—L. *mappa*; see NAPKIN.] 1. Household linen, esp. table linen. †2. The charge of the royal linen; the office of naperer –1628. †3. The making up or manufacture of personal or household linen (*rare*) –1650.

Naphtha (næ·fþă, næ·pþă). 1572. [a. L., a. Gr. νάφθα, perh. of Oriental origin. Anglicized as *napta* in late ME.] A name orig. applied to an inflammable volatile liquid (a constituent of asphalt and bitumen) issuing from the earth in certain localities; now applied to most of the inflammable oils obtained by dry distillation of organic substances, esp. coal, shale, and petroleum. Also *attrib.*, as *n.-fuel, -lamp.* Hence **Na·phthous** *a.*

Naphthalene (næ·fþălīn). Also **-in(e.** 1821. [f. NAPHTHA + *-l-* + -ENE; named by Kidd.] *Chem.* A white crystalline substance, of peculiar smell and pungent taste, usually obtained as a product in the distillation of coal-tar. Also *attrib.* with names of colours. So **Naphtha·lic** 1837.

Naphthalize (næ·fþăləiz), *v.* 1842. [f. as prec. + -IZE.] *trans.* To mingle, saturate, or impregnate with naphtha.

Naphthol (næ·fþǫl). 1849. [f. NAPHTHA + -OL.] *Chem.* One of two phenols of naphthaline, distinguished as α (*or* alpha) and β (*or* beta) naphthol; the latter is employed in the cure of skin-diseases, etc.

Na·phthyl. 1866. [f. as prec. + -YL.] *Chem.* The monatomic radical of naphthylamine.

Naphthy·lamine. Also **-in.** 1857. [f. as prec. + AMINE.] *Chem.* A crystalline substance produced by the action of ammonium sulphide, or acetic acid, on an alcoholic solution of nitro-naphthaline.

Napierian (nēⁱpiə·riăn), *a.* 1816. [f. John *Napier* (see next) + -IAN.] Invented by Napier (see LOGARITHM).

Napier's bones. 1658. Narrow slips of bone, ivory, wood, etc., divided into compartments marked with certain digits, and used to facilitate the variations of multiplication and division according to a method invented by John Napier of Merchiston (1550–1617). Also occas. called *Napier's rods.*

Napiform (nēⁱ·pifǭɹm), *a.* 1846. [f. L. *napus* turnip + -FORM.] Having the shape or appearance of a turnip; esp. *Bot.* of roots.

Napkin (næ·pkin). late ME. [app. f. F. *nappe* (see NAPERY) + -KIN.] 1. A square piece of linen, used at meals to wipe the fingers or lips, or to serve certain dishes on; a serviette. b. A small towel 1687. 2. A (pocket-)handkerchief. Now only *Sc.* and *n. dial.* 1530. 3. An infant's diaper.

2. *To hide, lay up, wrap up*, etc. *in a n.*, in allusion to Luke xix. 20. *Comb.* **n.-ring**, a ring placed on a table-napkin when rolled up to distinguish it. Hence †**Na·pkin** *v.* to wrap *up* or hide in or as in a n. –1680.

Naples (nēⁱ·pl'z). 1507. The name of a city in Southern Italy, used to designate various things in some way associated with it. †1. As an epithet of venereal disease (cf. NEAPOLITAN *a.*) –1656. 2. **N. yellow,** a yellow pigment in the form of a fine powder, prepared from antimony, and orig. manufactured at Naples; also, the colour of this 1738.

Napless (næ·plės), *a.* 1596. [f. NAP *sb.*² + -LESS.] Having no nap; worn threadbare. The Naples Vesture of Humilitie SHAKS.

Napoleon (năpōᵘ·liŏn). 1814. [a. F. *napoléon*, f. Christian name of certain Emperors of the French, esp. *Napoleon I* (1769–1821).] 1. A gold coin issued by Napoleon I, of the value of twenty francs. 2. A make of long or high boot 1853. 3. = NAP *sb.*³ 2. 1876. Hence **Napoleo·nic** *a.* connected with or characteristic of Napoleon. **Napoleo·nically** *adv.* **Napo·leonist**, an adherent of N. or of the Napoleonic dynasty; also *attrib.* = Napoleonic. **Napo·leonize** *v.* to govern in the style of N.

Napoo (napū·). 1915 (orig. army slang). [ad. F. *il n'y en a plus* there's nothing left.] There is or was nothing to be done; no good!

‖**Nappe** (næp). 1906. [Fr. 'table-cloth'.] 1. The sheet of water falling over a weir, etc. 2. *Geol.* A recumbent fold or anticline 1927.

Nappy (næ·pi), *a.*¹ Now *rare.* 1499. [ad. MDu. *noppigh*, or MLG. *noppich*, f. *noppe* NAP *sb.*²] Having a nap; downy, shaggy.

Nappy (næ·pi), *a.*² 1529. [prob. transf. use of prec.] 1. Of ale, etc.: Having a head, foaming; heady, strong. 2. Slightly exhilarated by drink 1721. Hence **Na·ppy** *sb.* ale.

Napu (nā·pu). 1820. [a. Malay.] The musk-deer of Java and Sumatra.

Nar, *a. Obs.* exc. *n. dial.* [Partly OE. *nēarra*, comp. of *nēah* NIGH; partly a. ON. *nærri.*] Nearer. Also *adv.* [a. ON.], nearer, near.

Narceine (nā·ɹsī,in, -əin). Also **-in.** 1834. [a. F. *narcéine*, f. Gr. νάρκη numbness; see -INE⁵.] *Chem.* A bitter crystalline alkaloid obtained from opium, sometimes used in medicine instead of morphia. var. **Narceia** (-ĭ·ă).

Narciss (naɹsi·s). 1586. [ad. L. *Narcissus* or a. F.] = NARCISSUS.

Narcissism (naɹsi·siz'm). 1921. [f. *Narcissus*, name of a beautiful youth who fell in love with his own reflexion and pined away.] A morbid self-love or self-admiration.

Narcissus (naɹsi·sǫs). *Pl.* **narcissi, -cissuses.** 1548. [a. L., ad. Gr. νάρκισσος, said to be f. νάρκη numbness, in ref. to the narcotic effects produced by it.] *Bot.* A genus of the order *Amaryllidaceæ*, containing many species; a plant of this genus; now esp. *Narcissus poeticus*, a bulbous plant, bearing a heavily scented single white flower with an undivided corona edged with crimson and yellow.

Narcosis (naɹkōᵘ·sis). 1693. [a. Gr. νάρκωσις, f. ναρκοῦν to benumb.] *Path.* The production of a narcotic state; the operation or effects of narcotics upon the system; a state of insensibility.

Narcotic (naɹkǫ·tik), *sb.* late ME. [ad. F. *narcotique*, or med.L. *narcoticum*, Gr. ναρκωτικόν adj. neut.; see next.] *Med.* A substance which when swallowed, inhaled, or injected into the system induces drowsiness, sleep, stupefaction, or insensibility, according to its strength and the amount taken.

Narcotic (naɹkǫ·tik), *a.* 1601. [ad. med.L. *narcoticus* or Gr. ναρκωτικός, f. ναρκοῦν to benumb, stupefy; see NARCOSIS and -IC.] 1. Of substances, etc.: Having the effect of inducing stupor, sleep, or insensibility. b. *transf.* of persons, actions, etc.: Producing sleep or dullness 1751. 2. Of the nature of narcosis 1661.

1. b. Silly and n. lecturers 1888. So **Narco·tical** *a.* soporific 1587; **-ly** *adv.* 1654.

Narco·tico-a·crid, *a.* and *sb.* 1829. [f. *narcotico*, as comb. form of f. NARCOTIC *a.*] *Med.* (A poison) possessing both narcotic and acrid properties.

Narcotine (nā·ɹkǒtin, -əin). 1823. [f. NARCOTIC *a.* + -INE⁵, or a. F.] *Chem.* A bitter crystalline alkaloid derived from opium, sometimes used in medicine.

Narcotism (nā·ɹkǒtiz'm). 1831. [f. as prec. + -ISM.] 1. The condition produced by narcotics; a state of somnolence or insensibility. b. The method of producing insensibility by narcotics 1843. 2. A morbid inclination to sleep 1843. 3. *transf.* The narcotic influence *of* something 1867. So **Na·rcotist,** one addicted to the use of narcotics.

Narcotize (nā·ɹkǒtəiz), *v.* 1843. [f. NARCOT-IC *a.*] 1. *trans.* To drug or render insensible with a narcotic. **2.** *transf.* To dull or deaden 1864. Hence **Narcotiza·tion.**

Nard (nāɹd). late ME. [= OF. *narde* (mod.F. *nard*), ad. L. *nardus*, ad. Gr. *νάρδος*, of Oriental origin.] **1.** An aromatic balsam used by the ancients, derived from the plant of the same name (see sense 2 and cf. SPIKENARD). **2.** An aromatic plant, esp. that yielding the ointment used by the ancients (supposed to be *Nardostachys Jatamansi*) 1591.

1. Marie took a pound of oynement spikenard, or trewe nard, precious WYCLIF *John* xii. 3.

Nardoo (naɹdū·, nā·ɹdū). Also **-du.** 1861. [Native Australian.] **1.** The sporocarp of the plant *Marsilea quadrifolia*, used as food by the Australian aborigines; the flour made from this. **2.** The plant itself, also called *clover-fern* 1864.

‖ **Nardus** (nā·ɹdɒs). Now *rare.* OE. [L.; see NARD.] Nard, spikenard (the ointment and plant).

Nare (nēᵊɹ). Now only *arch.* late ME. [ad. L. *naris* (usu. in pl. *nares*; see next).] A nostril –1663; *spec.* of a hawk 1486.

‖ **Nares** (nēᵊ·rīz). 1693. [L., pl. of *naris* (see prec.), related to OE. *nasu* nose.] *Anat. pl.* The nostrils or nasal passages. Hence **Na·rial** *a.* 1870.

Narghile, nargileh (nā·ɹgile). Also **-gilly.** 1839. [= F. *narghileh*, ad. Pers. (or Turk.) *nārgīleh*, f. Pers. *nārgīl* cocoa-nut, of which the bowl was originally made.] An Oriental tobacco-pipe in which the smoke passes through water before reaching the mouth; a HOOKAH.

Narrate (nærēⁱ·t), *v.* [First recorded in 1656; stigmatized as Sc. by S. Richardson and Johnson; not in gen. Engl. use before the 19th c.; f. L. *narrat-*, *narrare*, prob. for **gnarare*, related to *gnarus* knowing, and thus ult. to KNOW *v.*] *trans.* To relate, recount, give an account of. Also *absol.*

In narrating interesting facts, his comments.. often fatigue by their plenitude 1788. So **Narra·tor** 1611. **Na·rratory** *a.* of a narrative nature 1586. **Narra·tress, -trix** 1798.

Narration (nærēⁱ·ʃən). late ME. [a. F., or ad. L. *narrationem*; see prec. and -ATION.] **1.** The action of relating or recounting, or the fact of being recounted; an instance of this. In early use esp. in phr. *to make n.* **b.** That which is narrated; a story, narrative, account. late ME. **2. a.** *Rhet.* That part of an oration in which the facts of the matter are stated 1509. †**b.** The narrative part of a poem; a narrative passage in a drama 1586–1783.

1. [Dante] the great master of laconic n. LOWELL. **b.** The following N. is a sufficient Testimony of the Truth of this Observation STEELE.

Narrative (næ·rătiv), *sb.* 1561. [f. as next.] **1.** *Sc. Law.* That part of a deed or document which narrates the relevant or essential facts. **2.** An account or narration; a tale, recital (of facts, etc.) 1566. **3.** (Without article.) The practice or act of narrating; something to narrate 1748.

2 He shall find me ready to maintain the truth of my n. *Junius Lett.* 3. To have frequent recourse to n betrays great want of imagination CHESTERF.

Narrative (næ·rătiv), *a.* 1605. [ad. L. *narrativus*, f. *narrat-*; see NARRATE *v.* and -IVE.] **1.** That narrates; occupied or concerned with, having the character of, narration. †**2.** Garrulous, talkative –1826.

1. The *Paradise Lost* is an Epic or N. Poem ADDISON. 2. Mr. John Smith (called Narrative Smith) 1681. Hence **Na·rratively** *adv.*

Narrow (næ·roᵘ), *a.* and *sb.* [OE. *nearu* = OS. *naru*; etym. unkn.] **A.** *adj.* **1.** Having little breadth or width in comparison with the length. **b.** *Phonetics.* Of vowels, in contrast to *wide* or *open* 1844. **2.** Of restricted extent or size. *N. house*, the grave. OE. **b.** Lying or pressing close OE. **3.** Limited or restricted in range or scope or amount; of slight dimensions or extent 1523. **b.** Of time, brief (*rare*) 1611. **4.** Parsimonious, mean (now *dial.*); lacking in sympathy; narrow-minded, illiberal ME. **5.** Characterized by close or exact scrutiny ME. **b.** *transf.* of the eyes, etc. partly with ref. to near-sightedness 1577. **6.** Involving or marked by close approximation to something expressed or implied; near, close; (of an escape) barely effected 1551. **7.** *Comb.* as *n.-hearted, -leaved, -necked, -shouldered, -sighted, -souled, -spirited* adjs.

1. The streets are for the most part n. and winding 1756. Phr. *The n. way*; Strait is the gate, and n. is the way, which leadeth unto life *Matt.* vii. 14. *N. cloth*, cloth under 52 inches wide. *N. front* (Mil.): a battalion, &c. is said to assume a n. front, when it goes from line into column 1802. *N. goods*, braid, ribbons, and the like. *N. work*, excavations 3 yards in width and under. **b.** Each of the vowels..is either *n.* or *wide*, according as the tongue and uvula are tense..or relaxed SWEET. 2. The place where we dwell..is to narow for vs COVERDALE 2 *Kings* vi. 1. **b.** Life, within a n. ring Of giddy joys comprised COWPER. 3. The question is yet driuen to a narrower issue HOOKER. Let me rather have a n. estate and wide soul 1688. 4. Archibald..was n. in his ordinary expenses JOHNSON in *Boswell.* I daily find more Instances of this n. Party-Humour ADDISON. The days of cold hearts and n. minds MACAULAY. A n. oligarchy MACAULAY. 5. Seeking to make a narrower inquiry SMOLLETT. **b.** Looking into her eyes with his n. gaze GEO. ELIOT. 6. What's a n. squeak, a close shave, to such as I am? 1860.

B. *sb.* **1.** A narrow place, or thing; the narrow part of something. Now *rare.* ME. **2.** *spec.* Chiefly in *pl.* **a.** A narrow part of a strait or river, a pass or valley (chiefly *U.S.*); a street 1633. **b.** *Mining.* A narrow gallery 1850.

1. *fig.* When it came to the n. of any question he would still profess himself conquered by Mr. Hooker's reason 1702.

Na·rrow, *adv.* Now *rare.* [OE. *nearwe*, f. *nearu* NARROW *a.*] †**1.** Closely, strictly –1460. †**2.** Carefully, keenly –1596. **3.** Narrowly, in various senses ME.

3. Phr. *To fall n.*, to fall short. *To go n.*, of a horse, to keep the legs too close together.

Narrow (næ·roᵘ), *v.* [OE. *nearwian*, f. *nearu* NARROW *a.*; but, later, f. the adj.] **1.** *intr.* To become narrower; to diminish, contract. **2.** *trans.* To make narrower; †also *fig.* to constrict, constrain OE. **b.** To contract, reduce 1674. **c.** To drive into a narrow space, press closely 1814.

1. Following up The river as it narrow'd to the hills TENNYSON. 2. She narrowed her lids slightly O. W. HOLMES. **b.** He has here pretty well narrowed the field of taxation BURKE. **c.** Tho' the gathering enemy n. thee TENNYSON. Hence **Na·rrower.** **Na·rrowing** *vbl. sb.* the action of the vb.; a narrowed place or part.

Narrow-eyed, *a.* 1599. [NARROW *a.* 1 and 5.] Having narrow eyes.

Narrow gauge. 1841. A gauge of less than 4 ft. 8½ in. (as opp. to the BROAD GAUGE); formerly, the gauge of 4 ft. 8½ in.

Narrowly (næ·roᵘli), *adv.* [OE. *nearulīce*, f. *nearu* NARROW *a.* + *-līce*, -LY²; but, later, f. the adj.] **1.** With close attention or scrutiny. **2.** In a contracted or confined manner OE. †**3.** †**a.** Barely, scarcely. ME. only. **b.** Only just (escape, miss) 1560. †**4.** Closely –1707. **5.** Illiberally; strictly 1708.

1. I watched him n. for Six and Thirty Years 1709. 3. **b.** One [arrow] very n. missed my left eye SWIFT.

Narrow-minded, *a.* 1625. [NARROW *a.* 4.] Lacking in breadth of mind; incapable of or not given to broad views or wide sympathy. Hence **Narrow-mi·nded·ly** *adv.*, **-ness.**

Narrowness (næ·roᵘnės). 1530. [f. NARROW *a.* Cf. OE. *nearunes.*] The fact or quality of being narrow.

Narrow seas. late ME. [NARROW *a.* 1.] The channels separating Great Britain from the Continent and from Ireland.

Sterne Falconbridge commands the Narrow Seas SHAKS.

Narthex (nā·ɹþeks). 1673. [a. Gr. *νάρθηξ*, prop. the name of a tall umbelliferous plant with a hollow stalk.] *Archæol.* A vestibule or portico stretching across the western end of some early Christian churches, divided from the nave by a wall, screen, or railing, and set apart for women, catechumens, etc.

Narw(e, obs. ff. NARROW.

Narwhal (nā·ɹhwăl). 1658. [ad. Da. or Sw. *narhval* (f. *hval* WHALE), related obscurely to ON. *náhvalr* (f. *ná-r* corpse, with ref. to the colour of the skin).] A delphinoid cetacean (*Monodon monoceros*) inhabiting the Arctic seas, having only two teeth, one (or both) of which develops into a spirally-twisted straight horn; the sea-unicorn.

Nary (nēᵊ·ri), *a.* 1836. *U.S.* and *dial.* [var. of NE'ER A.] Neither; no; not a.

Nasal (nēⁱ·zăl), *sb.* 1480. [In sense 1, a. OF. *nasal*, *nasel*; otherwise a subst. use of next.] **1.** A nose-piece on a helmet. **2.** A nasal letter or sound 1669. **3.** *Anat.* A nasal bone 1854.

Nasal (nēⁱ·zăl), *a.* 1656. [ad. med.L. **nasalis*, f. *nasus* nose; see -AL.] **1.** Of or pertaining to the nose; used in connexion with the nose (1875). **2.** Of speech-sounds: Produced, more or less, by means of the nose 1669. **b.** Characterized by the presence of sounds so produced 1669.

1. Phr. *N. artery, bone, cartilage*, etc., *n. douche speculum*, etc. 2. In n. sounds, such as *m*, the passage of the nose is left open SWEET. **b.** Odious as a n. twang Heard at conventicle COWPER. Hence **Nasa·lity,** the quality of being n.; an instance of this. **Na·sally** *adv.*

Nasalize (nēⁱ·zăləiz), *v.* 1846. [f. NASAL *a.* + -IZE.] **a.** *intr.* To speak through the nose. **b.** *trans.* To utter with a nasal sound. Hence **Na:saliza·tion.**

Nascency (næ·sĕnsi). 1682. [ad. L. *nascentia*; see next and -ENCY.] The process or fact of being brought into existence; birth.

Nascent (næ·sĕnt), *a.* 1624. [ad. L. *nascent-*, *nascens*, *nasci* to be born.] **1.** In the act of being born or brought forth. **2.** *transf.* In the act or condition of coming into existence; just beginning to form, grow, develop, etc. 1706.

1. Food for the n. larvæ 1816. 2. Imagination.. reigns in all n. societies of men GRAY. That cartilage in truth is only n. or imperfect bone PALEY. Phr. *N. state*, the state of coming into existence, beginning to form, etc.; *Chem.* the condition of an element at the moment of liberation from a compound.

Naseberry (nēⁱ·zbĕri). 1698. [Corruptly ad. Sp. or Pg. *néspera* medlar (Sp. *níspero* medlar tree).] A W. Indian tree (*Sapota Achras*) which yields an edible fruit called the Sapodilla plum.

Nash-gab, -gob. *Sc.* and *n. dial.* 1816. [f. dial. *nash* impertinence + GAB *sb.*] Impertinent talk; a pert or gossiping person.

Nasiform (nēⁱ·zifǫɹm), *a. rare.* 1752. [f. L. *nasus* + -FORM.] Nose-shaped.

Naso- (nēⁱ·zo), mod. comb. form of L. *nasus* nose, used **a.** in terms relating to the nose in conjunction with some other part, as *n.-frontal, -lachrymal, -palatal, -pharyngeal*, adjs.; also *n.-pharyngitis, -pharynx*, etc. †**b.** in terms denoting nasal sounds, as *n.-guttural.*

Nasturtium (năstɒ̄·ɹʃɒ̆m). Also (corruptly) **-tian** (-ʃən). 1570. [a. L., named, acc. to Pliny, from its pungency ('nomen accepit a narium tormento').] **1.** A genus of cruciferous plants having a pungent taste, including the Watercress (*N. officinale*); also, a plant belonging to this genus. Now only *Bot.* **2.** A trailing plant of the S. American genus *Tropæolum*, cultivated in gardens for its showy orange-coloured flowers; Indian Cress. (Now usu. denoting the larger species *Tropæolum majus*, but at first applied to *T. minus*, both introduced from Peru.) 1704.

Nasty (nɑ·sti), *a.* late ME. [Origin unkn.] **1.** Foul, filthy, dirty, unclean, esp. to a disgusting degree; offensive through filth or dirt. Also, morally filthy, obscene 1601. **2.** Offensive to smell or taste; nauseous 1548. **3.** Disagreeable, unpleasant 1634. **b.** Difficult to deal with, dangerous; rather serious 1828. **4.** Ill-natured, 'disagreeable' (*to* another) 1825.

1. The nastie filthinesse of the nation in generall MORYSON. The greatest heap of n. language that perhaps ever was put together 1731. 2. For one good smell by the river's side, there be ten n. ones MARRYAT. 3. It is a cursed n. morning FIELDING. **b.** This is a n. ditch we are coming to 1875. A n. blow on the finger 1883. 4. 'He's a n. stuck-up monkey,..' said Mrs. Squeers DICKENS. Lest the headstrong William might turn n. 1874. N. little tricks 1888. *absol.* The cheap and n. 1884. Hence **Na·stily** *adv.* **Na·stiness** 1611.

Nasute (nēⁱ·siūt, năsiū·t), *a.* 1653. [ad. L. *nasutus*, f. *nasus* nose.] †**1.** Keen-scented, sagacious –1707. **2.** *Zool.* Nose-shaped. Having a large nose or prominent nostrils 1884.

Natal (nēⁱ·tăl), *a.* late ME. [ad. L. *natalis*, f. *nat-*, *nasci* to be born + *-alis*; see -AL.] †**1.** Presiding over nativities. CHAUCER. **2.**

Of places: Native. Chiefly *poet.* late ME. 3. Of or pertaining to (one's) birth; connected with one's birth 1447.

2. He sought his n. mountain-peaks divine SHELLEY. 3. *N. hour* or *day*, the hour or day of one's birth.

†**Natali·tial**, *a.* 1611. [f. L. *natalitius* (f. *natalis* NATAL) + -AL.] Belonging to or connected with one's birth or birthday –1679. So †**Natali·tious** *a.* 1646–1669.

Natality (nătæ·lĭti). 1483. [f. NATAL *a.* + -ITY. In recent use ad. F. *natalité*.] 1. Birth (*rare*). 2. Birth-rate 1888.

Natant (nēⁱ·tănt), *a.* 1707. [ad. L. *natantem, natare* to swim.] Swimming, floating.

Natation (nătēⁱ·ʃən). 1542. [ad. L. *natationem*, f. *natare* to swim.] The action or art of swimming; also, †that which swims or floats. Hence **Nata·tional** *a.*, **Nata·tionist**.

‖ **Natatores** (nēⁱtătōᵊ·rīz). 1823. [L., pl. of *natator*, f. *natare* to swim.] *Ornith. pl.* An order of birds adapted for swimming, including ducks, geese, swans and pelicans.

Natatorial (nēⁱtătōᵊ·riăl), *a.* 1816. [f. as next + -AL.] 1. Of or belonging to swimming. b. Of organs: Adapted for swimming 1823. 2. Characterized by swimming; *esp.* in *Ornith.* of the *Natatores* 1839.

Natatory (nēⁱ·tătəri), *a.* 1799. [ad. late L. *natatorius*; see NATATION and -ORY.] 1. Of organs: Adapted for swimming or floating. 2. Of or belonging to swimming 1836. 3. Characterized by swimming 1887.

3. Nereus.. With his n. daughters 1895.

Natch-bone. *rare.* 1613. [var. of NACHE.] = AITCH-BONE.

Nates (nēⁱ·tīz), *sb. pl.* 1681. [a. L. *nates*, pl. of *natis* rump, buttock.] *Anat.* and *Med.* 1. The buttocks, haunches 1706. 2. The anterior and larger pair of the optic lobes (*corpora quadrigemina*) of the brain 1681.

Natheless, nathless (nēⁱ·þlĕs, næ·þlĕs), *adv.* (and *prep.*). Now only *arch.* [f. OE. *ná* never + *þe* THE *adv.* + *læs* LESS *adv.*] Nevertheless. b. *prep.* In spite of, notwithstanding (*rare*) 1567.

†**Nathemo(re**, *adv.* OE. [f. as prec. + MO(RE.] Never the more –1596.

‖ **Natica** (næ·tikă). 1840. [mod.L., perh. f. med.L. *natica* buttock, f. L. *natis*; see NATES.] *Zool.* A genus of carnivorous seasnails; a snail of this genus.

Nation (nēⁱ·ʃən), *sb.* ME. [a. F., ad. L. *nationem*, f. *nat-*, *nasci* to be born.] I. 1. A distinct race or people, characterized by common descent, language, or history, usu. organized as a separate political state and occupying a definite territory. †b. People of a particular nation –1818. c. In mediæval universities, a body of students belonging to a particular district, country, or group of countries; still retained in the universities of Glasgow and Aberdeen in connexion with the election of the Rector 1664. †d. A country, kingdom (*rare*) –1668. †2. Without article: Nationality –1641. 3. *The n.*, the whole people of a country 1602.

1. In Switzerland four languages are spoken; yet the Swiss certainly make one n. FREEMAN. *transf.* The famous Nations of the dead SIR T. BROWNE. b. It being express in his orders not to permit any n... to come on shore and stay there DE FOE. 2. Though he were a Fleming by Nation, yet was hee not separated from the interest of France 1641.

The nations: a. *biblical*, the heathen nations, the Gentiles. b. *poet.*, the peoples of the earth collectively. *Law of nations*: see LAW *sb.*[1] 4. *League of Nations*: see LEAGUE *sb.*[2] 1 b.

II. 1. †a. A family, kindred, clan –1584. b. A tribe of N. American Indians 1763. †2. A particular class, kind, or race of persons or of animals –1781.

1. b. The sachems and warriors of the Six Nations 1775. 2. All the barbarous n. of scholemen ASCHAM. The scaly Nations of the Sea profound DRYDEN.

Nation (nēⁱ·ʃən), *adv.*, *a.*, *int. dial.* and *U.S.* 1785. Euphemistic abbrev. of DAMNATION 3.

National (næ·ʃənăl), *a.* and *sb.* 1597. [ad. F. *national*; see NATION *sb.* and -AL.] A. *adj.* 1. Of or belonging to a or the nation; affecting or shared by the nation as a whole. b. Of troops: Maintained by a nation 1842. c. Of or belonging to the French Government during the time of the first Republic 1793. 2. Characteristic or distinctive of a nation 1625. 3. Strongly upholding one's own nation or countrymen 1711. b. Devoted to the interests of the nation as a whole 1801.

1. N. corruption must be purged by n. calamities BOLINGBROKE. 2. That an unsavoury odour is gentilitious or n. unto the Jews SIR T. BROWNE. It is of great consequence to preserve a n. character 1778. 3. He is intensely n... He believes that the Scots are the finest race in the world 1871.

Spec. collocations: **n. council, debt** (see the sbs.); **n. anthem**, a hymn adopted by a people and used (esp. on public occasions) as an expression of national and patriotic sentiment (in the British Empire, 'God save the King'); **N. Assembly**, an assembly consisting of representatives of a nation; spec. †(*a*) = *General Assembly* (see ASSEMBLY); (*b*) a synod of the Church in a particular nation; (*c*) the first of the revolutionary assemblies of France, in session 1789–91; also applied at various times to the popular assembly, and now to the two houses, the Senate and the Chamber of Deputies, when in joint session; (*d*) the deliberative and legislative body created by the Church of England Assembly (Powers) Act, 1919; **n. bank**, a bank associated with the national finances; *U.S.* one whose circulating notes are secured by U.S. bonds deposited with the government; **n. church**, (*a*) a church consisting of a nation; (*b*) a church established by law in a particular nation; **n. guard**, an armed force existing in France at various times between 1789 and 1871; **n. insurance**, a scheme organized by the state for the compulsory insurance of employed persons against sickness or unemployment; **N. Republicans**, *U.S.*, an early name for the Whig party; **n. school**, one of the schools established by the **National Society**, founded in 1811 to promote the education of the poor.

B. *sb.* †1. One who supports national, not party, interests –1768. 2. *pl.* (after F. *nationaux*): Persons belonging to the same nation; (one's) fellow-countrymen 1887. Hence **Na·tional-ly** *adv.*, **ness**.

Nationalism (næ·ʃənăliz'm). 1844. [f. NATIONAL *a.* + -ISM.] 1. Devotion to one's nation; a policy of national independence. b. *spec.* The programme of the Irish Nationalist party 1885. 2. A form of socialism, based on the nationalizing of all industry 1892.

Nationalist (næ·ʃənălist). 1715. [f. as prec. + -IST.] An adherent or supporter of nationalism; an advocate of national rights, etc. b. *spec.* One who advocates the claims of Ireland to be an independent nation 1846. Hence **Nationali·stic** *a.*

b. The Nationalists, in short, are to call the tune and the people of this country to pay the piper 1893.

Nationality (næʃənæ·lĭti). 1691. [f. as prec. + -ITY.] 1. National quality or character. 2. National feeling 1772. 3. The fact of belonging to a particular nation 1828. 4. Separate existence as a nation; national independence or consolidation 1832. 5. A nation 1832.

1. Ancient British n. received into itself a Roman n. 1854. I have little faith in that quality in literature which is commonly called n. LOWELL. 2. He could not but see in them that n. which I should think no liberal minded Scotsman will deny BOSWELL.

Nationalize (næ·ʃənăləiz), *v.* Also **-ise.** 1800. [f. NATIONAL *a.* + -IZE, or ad. F. *nationaliser*.] 1. *trans.* To render national in character. 2. To naturalize; to admit into, or make part of, a nation 1809. b. *intr.* To become naturalized 1891. 3. To bring under the control of, to make the property of, the nation 1869.

1. He took what may be called cosmopolitan traditions,.. and nationalized them LOWELL. 3. It is a perfectly intelligible proposition that all the land in the kingdom ought to be 'nationalized' 1881. Hence **Na·tionaliza·tion.**

Nationalty (næ·ʃənălti). 1812. [f. NATIONAL *a.* + -TY, after *personalty*, etc.] National property.

Nationhood (nēⁱ·ʃənhud). 1850. [f. NATION *sb.* + -HOOD.] The state or fact of being a nation.

Native (nēⁱ·tiv), *sb.* 1450. [ad. med.L. *nativus*, sb. use of L. *nativus* adj. (see next).] 1. One born in bondage; a born thrall. Now only *Hist.* 2. *Astrol.* One born under a particular planet or sign 1509. 3. One born in a place; or, *legally*, one whose parents have their domicile in a place 1535. b. In Australia, a white person born in the country 1861. 4. One of the original or indigenous inhabitants of a country; now *esp.* one belonging to a non-European or uncivilized race 1603. 5. An animal or plant (†or mineral) indigenous to a locality 1690. b. An oyster altogether or partially reared in British waters; now *spec.* those reared in artificial beds 1818. †6. *pl.* Fellow-countrymen –1655. 7. Native place (or country). Now only *dial.* 1604.

2. Nebulous Stars.. being joyn'd with the Luminaries to afflict a N. with blindness 1679. 3. He speaks English like a n. LYTTON. 4. Columbus. continued to interrogate all the natives 1777. 5. b. A newly-opened oyster-shop,.. with natives laid one deep in circular marble basins in the windows DICKENS.

Native (nēⁱ·tiv), *a.* late ME. [Not gen. current before the 16th c. Mainly ad. L. *nativus* (f. *nat-*, *nasci* to be born + *-ivus* -IVE), but infl. by F. *natif*.] I. 1. Belonging to, or connected with, a person or thing by nature; inherent, innate. b. Natural *to* a person or thing 1533. c. Natural. Now *rare.* 1509. 2. Left in a natural state; *esp.* untouched by art; unadorned, simple 1560. 3. That was the place or scene of one's birth. Also const. *to.* 1500. b. Original, parent 1590. 4. Belonging to, or natural to, one by reason of the circumstances of one's birth.

1. So angelik was her natyf beute, That lyke thing immortal seemyd she CHAUCER. b. If there is a thing specially n. to religion, it is peace and union M. ARNOLD. 2. If.. sweetest Shakespear.. Warble his n. Wood-notes wild MILT. Mere Words,.. used only as they serve to betray those who understand them in their n. sense STEELE. 3. Say.. the cause Why thou departedst from thy natiue home? SHAKS. b. Is this the way I must return to n. dust? MILT. 4. The Language I haue learn'd these forty yeares (My natiue English) now I must forgo SHAKS. A.. people, tenacious of their n. liberty 1801.

II. 1. Connected with one by birth or race; closely related. Now *rare.* 1470. †2. Being what one is by right of birth; natural, rightful –1593. 3. Of metals, etc.: Occurring naturally in a pure or uncombined state; also used to describe a mineral occurring in nature, as opp. to a similar substance formed artificially. So *n. rock.* 1695. b. *transf.* Applied to the state or form of such substances 1753.

2. The Head is not more Natiue to the Heart.. Then is the Throne of Denmark to thy Father SHAKS. 3. *Rich. II*, III. ii. 25. b. Substances.. found in the bowels of the earth, in their n. state GOLDSM.

III. 1. Born in a particular place or country; belonging to a particular race, district, etc., by birth. In mod. use, *spec.* with connotation of non-European (cf. NATIVE *sb.* 4). 1470. 2. Of indigenous origin, production, or growth 1555. 3. Of or belonging to the native of a particular place 1796.

1. Be caus I am a natyff Scottis man 1470. Are you natiue of this place? SHAKS. 2. Trade is twofold, viz. N., and Forein 1670. It is rather a difficult matter to define what is a n. oyster 1865. *N. bear* (the KOOLAH), *bustard, cat, dog* (= DINGO-), *hen, rabbit, turkey*: names of Australian animals and birds. *N. bread*, an underground fungus (*Mylitta australis*) eaten by Australian aborigines. 3. Living in the n. houses 1897. Hence **Na·tive-ly** *adv.*, **-ness.**

Native-born, *a.* 1500. [f. prec. + BORN *ppl. a.*] Belonging to a particular place or country by birth; sometimes *spec.* applied to persons of immigrant race born in a colony.

Nativism (nēⁱ·tiviz'm). 1856. [f. as prec. + -ISM; with sense 2 cf. F. *nativisme*.] 1. (Chiefly *U.S.*) Prejudice in favour of natives against strangers; the practice or policy of giving effect to this. 2. *Philos.* The doctrine of innate ideas 1887. So **Na·tivist**, one who favours n. in either sense.

Nativity (năti·vĭti). ME. [a. F. *nativité*, ad. L. *nativitatem*; see NATIVE *a.* and -ITY. (Early ME. *nativiteð* repr. OF. *nativited*.)] 1. The birth of Christ, of the Virgin Mary, or of St. John Baptist. Also, a picture representing the Nativity. 2. The festival of the birth of Christ; Christmas. Also, that of the birth of the Virgin Mary, Sept. 8, or of St. John Baptist, June 24. ME. 3. Birth. late ME. 4. A horoscope. late ME. 5. Birth as determining nationality 1592. Now *rare.*

1. At the time of his n... there was peace amongst all nations ABP. SANDYS. 3. I haue serued him from the houre of my Natiuitie to this instant SHAKS. *fig.* Plagiary had not its N. with Printing SIR T. BROWNE. 5. He owed this to his Scotch n. 1821.

Natrolite (næ·trələit, nēⁱ·-). 1805. [f. NATRON + -LITE.] *Min.* A hydrous silicate of aluminium and sodium.

Natron (nēⁱ·trŏn). 1684. [a. F. and Sp., ad. Arab. *naṭrūn, niṭrūn*, ad. Gr. *νίτρον*

NITRE. Cf. ANATRON.] Native sesquicarbonate of soda, occurring in solution or as a deposit (mixed with other substances) in various parts of the world. **b.** *attrib.* in *n. lake* 1821.

Na·tter, *v. dial.* 1829. *intr.* To fret, nag.

Natterjack (næ·tədʒæk). 1769. [?] A British species of toad (*Bufo calamita*), having a light yellow stripe down the back.

Nattier (næ·tiəɹ). 1918. [The name of a French painter, Jean Marc *Nattier* (1685–1766).] *N. blue:* a variety of blue.

Natty (næ·ti), *a.* 1785. [perh. a deriv. of NEAT *a.*] Neatly smart; spruce, trim; exhibiting dainty tidiness, taste, or skill.

A n. spark of eighteen 1806. His uncle used to ..arrange the n. curl on his forehead THACKERAY. Hence **Na·ttily** *adv.* **Na·ttiness.**

Natural (see next), *sb.* 1509. [Subst. use of next, after F. *naturel*, L. *naturalis*, etc.] **I.** †**1.** A native of a place or country –1657. **2.** *arch.* One naturally deficient in intellect 1533.

2. She..is not quite a n., that is, not an absolute idiot MME. D'ARBLAY.

II. †**1.** *pl.* Natural gifts or powers of mind (or body) –1678. †**2.** *In* one's *pure naturals* (after med.L. *in puris naturalibus*): not altered or improved in any way; also, in a perfectly naked state –1737. †**3.** *pl.* Natural things or objects –1738. **4.** *Mus.* **a.** A natural note 1609. **b.** The sign ♮ used to cancel a preceding sharp or flat, and give a note its 'natural' value 1797. **c.** One of the white keys on a pianoforte, etc. 1880. **5.** In the card-game of vingt-et-un, an ace and a ten dealt in the first instance, making exactly 21. 1849.

Natural (næ·tʃŭrăl, næ·tiŭrăl), *a.* ME. [a. OF. *natural*, or ad. L. *naturalis*, f. *natura* NATURE *sb.* + -AL.] **I. 1.** Of law and justice: Based upon the innate moral feeling of mankind; instinctively felt to be right and fair. **2.** Constituted by nature. late ME. **b.** *Bot.* Applied spec. to Jussieu's arrangement of plants according to the likeness they bear to each other, in contrast with the sexual system of Linnæus, and to the orders, families, etc. resulting from this arrangement 1803. **3.** Taking place or operating in accordance with the ordinary course of nature 1477. **4.** In a state of nature, without spiritual enlightenment 1526. **5.** Having a real or physical existence, as opp. to what is spiritual, intellectual or fictitious; pertaining to the physical (as opp. to the spiritual) world 1526. **6.** Existing in, or formed by, nature; not artificial 1568. **b.** Of vegetation: Self-sown or planted. Also of land: Not cultivated. 1526. **7.** Life-like 1581. **b.** Simple, unaffected, easy 1607. **c.** Not disfigured or disguised 1800.

1. Man, yf he be brought vp in corrupt opynyon, hath no perceyuance of thys n. law 1538. N. justice required that the loss..should be recouped by the other party 1883. **2.** *N. day*, i.e. twenty-four hours. *N. year*, the period occupied by the earth in making its revolution round the sun; the solar year. *N. number*, one without fractions; also, an actual number as dist. from a logarithm. *N. note, key*, etc. (*Mus.*): opp. to *sharp* or *flat*. *N. scale*, the scale of C major, so called as having no accidentals. **3.** It was no naturall eclypse CAXTON. We were come into a more convenient and naturall temperature 1604. So likewise yong men..die by naturall death as well as old men doe 1576. **4.** For the naturall man perceaveth not the thyngs off the sprete off god TINDALE 1 *Cor.* ii. 14. *N. religion*, 'the Things knowable concerning God and our Duty by the Light of Nature' (Watts). *N. theology*, a theology based upon human reasoning, apart from revelation. **5.** Which is the naturall man, And which the spirit? SHAKS. **6.** A fertile plain, watered by the n. and artificial channels of the Tigris GIBBON. 'Natural' sticks—that is, those cut from the stem with the bark on 1878. *N. wig*, one made of human hair. **7. b.** Just put all thought of yourself aside and be n. 1863.

II. 1. Present by nature; innate; not acquired or assumed. late ME. **2.** Normally connected with, or pertaining to, a person or thing; consonant with the nature or character of the person or thing. late ME. **b.** Coming easily or spontaneously *to* one 1589. **c.** Naturally arising from the circumstances of the case 1667. **3.** Standing in a specified relationship to another person or thing by reason of the nature of things or the force of circumstances 1516. †**b.** Natural-born –1656. †**4.** Native (country or language) –1661. †**5.** *N. parts* or *places*, the genitals –1754.

1. The n. love of life SWIFT. †*N. parts*, native ability, apart from learning –1771. **2.** The n. recoil of superstition is scepticism 1850. *N. life*, used chiefly (and now only) with ref. to the duration of this life. **b.** Phr. *To come n. to*, to be a n. action for (one). **c.** Som n. tears they drop'd, but wip'd them soon MILT. **3.** My naturall enemy death 1516. **b.** Whom should hee follow, but his naturall King? SHAKS.

III. †**1.** Of children: Legitimate –1741. †**b.** Similarly *n. father, brother*, etc. –1641. **c.** In later use, that is such by nature only; hence, illegitimate, bastard 1586. **2.** Having a specified character by nature; esp. in *n. fool*, †*idiot*. late ME. †**3.** Native-born –1665. **4.** Having natural feeling; kindly. Now *rare* 1470.

1. Not one of his naturall children, yet brought up with his other children 1599. **b.** My selfe..They take for Naturall Father SHAKS. **c.** He was never married, but had n. daughters 1817. **2.** Thou [art] a naturall Coward, without instinct SHAKS. **3.** Good and naturall English words 1579. **4.** I pray you to be a good and naturall modre unto hyr 1530.

IV. Dealing or concerned with, relating to, nature as an object of study or research, as *n. science*. late ME.

Some N. Observations made..in Shropshire 1707. The three branches of the N. Sciences 1840. *N. philosophy*, the study of n. bodies as such and of the phenomena connected with them; physics. So *N. philosopher*, a physicist. Hence **Na·turally** *adv.* in a n. manner. **Na·turalness.**

Na·tural-born, *a.* 1583. [f. prec. + BORN *ppl. a.*] Having a specified position or character by birth; esp. with *subject*.

Na·tural Hi·story. 1555. [HISTORY *sb.* 4.] **1.** A work dealing with the properties of natural objects, plants, or animals; a scientific account *of* any subject on similar lines. **2.** The aggregate of facts relating to the natural objects *of* a place, or the characteristics *of* a class of persons or things. Also *transf.* 1593. **3.** orig., The systematic study of all natural objects, animal, vegetable, and mineral; now restricted to the study of animal life, usu. in a popular manner 1662.

1. That Natural History, which he wrote of all plants BACON. **2.** Another incident in natural history ..is..Toads eat larks! 1816.

Naturalism (næ·tʃŭrăliz'm, næ·tiŭ-). 1641. [f. NATURAL *a.* + -ISM. Cf. F. *naturalisme.*] **1.** Action arising from, or based on, natural instincts (†also with *pl.*); a system of morality or religion having a purely natural basis. **2.** *Philos.* A view of the world, and of man's relation to it, in which only the operation of natural (as opp. to supernatural or spiritual) laws and forces is assumed 1750. **3.** A style or method, in literature and art, characterized by close adherence to nature 1850. **4.** Adherence to what is natural 1865.

3. The Gothic n. advancing gradually from the Byzantine severity RUSKIN. **4.** Goethe's profound, imperturbable n. M. ARNOLD.

Naturalist (næ·tʃŭrălist, næ·tiŭ-). 1587. [ad. F. *naturaliste*; or f. NATURAL *a.* + -IST.] **1.** One who studies natural, in contrast to spiritual, things; an adherent of, or believer in, naturalism. **b.** One who follows the light of nature, as contrasted with revelation 1608. **2.** One who studies, or is versed in, natural science; a physicist. Now *rare* or *Obs.* 1587. **b.** *spec.* One who makes a special study of animals or plants. (A less precise term than *zoologist, botanist*, etc.) 1600. **c.** A dealer in cage animals, dogs, etc.; also, a taxidermist 1863. **3.** A representative of naturalism in art or literature 1784. **4.** *adj.* Naturalistic 1830.

2. b. A lion; of whom the n. writeth [etc.] 1600.

Naturalistic (nætʃŭrăli·stik, nætiŭ-), *a.* 1840. [f. prec. + -IC.] **1.** In accordance with the doctrine of naturalism; of the nature of, characterized by, naturalism 1860. **2.** Aiming at a faithful representation of nature in art or literature 1849. **3.** Of or belonging to natural history 1859. **Naturali·stically** *adv.*

Naturality (nætʃŭræ·lĭti, nætiŭ-). Now *rare*. 1533. [ad. F. *naturalité* or late L. *naturalitatem*; see NATURAL *a.* and -ITY.] †**1.** Natural character or quality –1651. †**2.** Naturalness –1678. **3.** Natural feeling or conduct. In later use *Sc.* 1628. **4.** An illustration drawn from natural things 1649.

Naturalize (næ·tʃŭrăləiz, næ·tiŭ-), *v.* 1571. [ad. F. *naturaliser*; see NATURAL *a.* and -IZE.] **I. 1.** *trans.* To admit (an alien) to the position and rights of citizenship; to invest with the privileges of a native-born subject. **2.** To introduce (a word, practice, thing, etc.) into a country or into common use 1593. **3.** To introduce (animals or plants) to places where they are not indigenous, but in which they may flourish under the same conditions as those which are native 1708. **4.** *intr.* (or *refl.*) To become naturalized; to settle down in a natural manner 1660.

1. By their naturalizing Men of all Countries, they have laid the beginnings of many great advantages 1667. *fig.* Persons..not naturalized by conversion.. from another religion to this DONNE. **2.** The yard was naturalized as an English measure 1866. **3.** Our Melons, our Peaches..are Strangers among us,.. naturalized in our English Gardens ADDISON.

II. †**1.** *trans.* To make natural or familiar (*to*); occas. to familiarize –1742. **2. a.** To free from conventionality 1603. **b.** To free from the supernatural or miraculous 1647. **3.** To pursue the studies of a naturalist 1787.

1. *All's Well* I. i. 223. Custom has naturalized his Labour to him SOUTH. **2. a.** Were I of the trade I would n. Arte, as much as they Artize nature FLORIO. So **Na·turaliza·tion,** the action of naturalizing; the fact of being naturalized 1578.

Nature (nē̆·tʃŭɹ, nē̆·tiŭɹ), *sb.* ME. [a. F. *nature*, ad. L. *natura* birth, course of things, etc., f. *nat-*, *nasci* to be born. Cf. KIND *sb.*] **I. 1.** The essential qualities of a thing; the inherent and inseparable combination of properties essentially pertaining to anything and giving it its fundamental character. **2.** The inherent and innate disposition or character of a person (or animal) ME. **b.** The general inherent character or disposition of mankind. More fully *human n.* 1526. **3.** With *a* and *pl.* An individual character, disposition, etc., considered as a kind of entity in itself; hence, a person or thing of a particular quality or character. late ME. **b.** *Artillery.* A class or size of guns or shot 1813.

1. The Passion of Love in its N. has been thought to resemble Fire ADDISON. You have twice had warning of the fleeting n. of riches 1832. **2.** Men may change their Climate, but they cannot their N. STEELE. GOOD NATURE, ILL NATURE, SECOND NATURE: see those phrases. **b.** A just and lively image of human n. DRYDEN. Men have a physical as well as a spiritual n. 1878. *Mod.* It's only human n. to do that. **3.** There are some Natures in the World who never can proceed sincerely in Business TEMPLE.

Phr. *Of* (a certain) *n.*; A plan of this n. 1765. *Of* or *in the n. of*; A Peace is of the n. of a Conquest SHAKS. *In the n. of things, of the case*; It is, in the n. of the case, probable that [etc.] PALEY. *By n.*, in virtue of the very character or essence of the thing or person; He..ordained thy will By n. free, not over-rul'd by Fate MILT.

II. 1. The vital or physical powers *of* man; the strength or substance *of* a thing ME. †**2. a.** Semen. **b.** The menses. –1607. †**3.** The female pudendum, esp. that of a mare –1750.

III. 1. The inherent dominating power or impulse (in men or animals) by which action or character is determined, directed, or controlled. (Sometimes personified.) late ME. **b.** Natural feeling or affection. Now *dial.* 1605. **2.** The inherent power or force by which the physical and mental activities of man are sustained. (Sometimes personified.) late ME. **b.** The vital functions as requiring to be supported by nourishment, etc. 1460.

1. 'Twas N., sir, whose strong behest Impelled me to the deed COWPER. *Law of N.*: see LAW *sb.*[1] I. 9 c. *Light of N.*: see LIGHT *sb.* 6 b. *Against n.*, contrary to what n. prompts, unnatural, immoral, vicious. **b.** Stop vp th' accesse, and passage to Remorse, That no compunctious visitings of N. Shake my fell purpose SHAKS. **2.** Tir'd nature's sweet restorer, balmy sleep! YOUNG. **b.** When with meats & drinks they had suffic'd Not burd'nd N. MILT.

IV. 1. The creative and regulative physical power which is conceived of as operating in the physical world and as the immediate cause of all its phenomena. late ME. **b.** Personified as a female being. (Usu. with capital.) late ME. **c.** Contrasted with medical skill or treatment in the cure of wounds or diseases 1597. **d.** Contrasted with art (see ART *sb.* I. 2.). Also, naturalness. 1704. **2.** The material world, or its collective objects or phenomena, the features and products of the earth itself, as contrasted with those of human civilization 1662.

1. That common saying, that God and N. the minister of God doe nothing without cause 1594. b. Flowres which only Dame N. trauels with SIR T. HERBERT. c. N., in desperate diseases, frequently does most when she is left entirely to herself BURKE. *Against*, or *contrary to*, *n. Debt of n.*, etc.: see DEBT *sb. Course of n.*: see COURSE *sb.* 13. *Law(s) of n.*: see LAW *sb.*[1] III. 1. *In n.*, in the actual system of things, in real fact. 2. To enjoy cool n. in a country seat COWPER. *In n.*, anywhere; at all. *The* or *a state of n.*: (*a*) the moral state natural to man, as opp. to a state of grace; (*b*) the condition of man before the organization of society; (*c*) an uncultivated or undomesticated condition; (*d*) physical nakedness.

attrib. and *Comb.*, as *n.-cure*, *-study*, *-worship*; **n.-god**, one of the powers or phenomena of n. personified as a god; so **-being, deity**; **-people**, people in a primitive state of culture; **-spirit**, a spirit supposed to reside in some natural element or object.

†Na·ture, *v.* late ME. [ad. med.L. *naturare*, f. *natura* NATURE *sb.*] *intr.* in pres. pple. or ppl. a. *naturing* [after med.L. *natura naturans*]: Creative, and giving to each thing its specific nature –1694.

Natured (nēi·tſŭd, nēi·tiŭd), *ppl. a.* 1577. [f. NATURE *sb.* + -ED [2].] Having a (good, ill, etc.) nature or disposition.

Nature-printing. 1855. [Cf. G. *natur(selbst)druck.*] The method or process of producing a print of a leaf, etc., by means of the mark made by the object itself, under pressure, on a prepared plate. **Nature-print** *v.* and *sb.*

Na·turize, *v. rare.* 1607. [f. NATURE *sb.* + -IZE. Cf. NATURE *v.*] *trans.* To invest with a specific nature.

†Nau·frage. 1480. [a. F., ad. L. *naufragium* for **navifragium*, f. *navis* + *frag-*, *frangere* to break.] Shipwreck (*lit.* and *fig.*) –1755.

Naught (nǭt), *sb.*, *a.*, and *adv.* [OE. *nāwiht*, f. *ne* NE + *āwiht* AUGHT. Cf. NOUGHT.] A. *sb.* 1. Nothing, nought. (Now *arch.*) †2. Wickedness, evil, moral wrong, mischief –1656. †b. That which is wrong in method –1658. 3. With *a* and *pl. Arith.* A cipher, a nought 1649. b. (From B. 2.) One who is bad 1657.

1. God made them and mans generacion of n. *2 Macc.* vii. 28. Phr. *To bring, come, go to n. To set at n., set n. by*: see SET *v.* †*To call all to n.*, to abuse or decry vehemently. *To be n.*, to efface oneself, to keep quiet or withdraw. Usu. in imper. 2. Phr. *To do n.*

B. *adj.* [Orig. the sb. in predic. use.] 1. Of no worth or value; good for nothing; worthless, bad, poor OE. †b. Of no legal value; invalid –1660. †c. Bad in condition or quality –1813. †2. Morally bad; wicked –1740. †b. Immoral; vicious –1693. †3. Injurious, hurtful; unlucky –1658. †4. Lost, ruined –1826.

1. Tom sings well; but his Luck 's n. SWIFT. b. The election is..n. and voide 1632. c. Which [figges] can not be eaten because they are n. *Bible* (Douay) Jer. xxiv. 3. 2. But if thine eye be n.; thy whole body shall be darksome N.T. (Rhem.) *Matt.* vi. 23. 4. Be gone, away, All will be n. else SHAKS.

C. *adv.* †1. [Orig. the accus. of the sb. used advb.] Not. OE.–late ME. †2. [From B.] Badly, wrongly –1625.

Naughty (nǭ·ti), *a.* late ME. [f. NAUGHT *sb.* + -Y [1].] †1. Having or possessing naught; poor, needy. late ME. only. 2. †a. Of persons: Morally bad, wicked –1699. b. Of children: Given to doing wrong, esp. through waywardness or disobedience. Also used playfully of older persons. 1633. 3. Of actions, places, things, etc.: Characterized by moral badness or wickedness; bad, wrong, blameworthy, improper. In mod. use applied playfully. 1536. †4. Bad, inferior, not up to the usual standard or quality –1799.

2. b. Go, get you gone, you n. girl, you are well enough SWIFT. 3. Naughtie and Pestilent bokes should be burned 1560. This naughtie world 1620. It was very n. of her, she felt aware 1871. 4. 'Tis a naughtie night to swimme in SHAKS. Hence **Nau·ghtily** 1552. **Nau·ghtiness** 1541.

Naughty pack. *Obs.* exc. *dial.* 1530. [PACK *sb.*[1] 4.] †A woman (or man) of bad character –1743. b. *dial.* A naughty child 1828.

‖ **Naumachia** (nǫmēi·kiă). *Pl.* **-iæ, -ias.** 1596. [L., a. Gr. ναυμαχία, f. ναῦς ship + μάχη fight.] 1. A mimic sea-fight. 2. A place specially constructed for the exhibition of mock sea-fights 1617.

Naunt (nānt). Now *dial.* or *arch.* 1621. [var. of AUNT, with *n* transferred from *myn* 'mine'; see N.] Aunt.

‖ **Nauplius** (nǭ·pliŭs). *Pl.* **-plii** (-pliəi). 1836. [L. *nauplius* kind of shellfish, or *Nauplius*, a. Gr. Ναύπλιος, a son of Poseidon.] †a. O. F. Müller's name for a supposed genus of crustaceans. b. A larval stage of development in some of the lower crustaceans 1869.

Nausea (nǭ·sĭă, nǭ·ʃĭă). 1569. [a. L., a. Gr. ναυσία, ναυτία, f. ναῦς ship.] 1. A feeling of sickness, with loathing of food and inclination to vomit. b. Sea-sickness. (The orig. sense.) 1771. 2. *transf.* A strong feeling of disgust or loathing 1619. 3. That which causes sickness or loathing 1654.

2. Sated to n. as we have been with the doctrines of Sentimentality CARLYLE.

Nau·seant. 1846. [ad. L. *nauseant-*, pr. pple. of *nauseare* to NAUSEATE.] *Med.* A substance which produces nausea. *adj.* Producing nausea 1864.

Nauseate (nǭ·sĭ,eit, nǭ·ʃĭ,eit), *v.* 1640. [f. L. *nauseat-*, *nauseare*, f. *nausea*, after Gr. ναυσιᾶν (cf. NAUSEA).] 1. *trans.* To reject (food, etc.) with loathing or nausea 1646. 2. To affect with nausea; to create a loathing in 1654. 3. *intr.* To become affected with nausea, to feel sick (*at* something) 1640.

1. *fig.* The Prince began to n. the match, and to meditate all honourable evasions 1654. 2. It nauseated their very Stomachs, made them sick when they thought of it DE FOE. 3. *fig.* He cannot but hate that in himself, which he nauseates at in another 1657. Hence **Nau·seatingly** *adv.* 1883. **Nausea·tion**, the action of nauseating, or state of being nauseated 1628.

Nauseous (nǭ·sĭəs, nǭ·ʃəs), *a.* 1604. [f. NAUSEA + -OUS.] †1. Inclined to nausea; fastidious (*rare*) –1678. 2. Causing nausea or squeamishness; also, later, highly unpleasant to the taste or smell 1612. 3. *fig.* Loathsome, disgusting; highly offensive 1663.

2. Cured by remedies in themselves very n. and unpalatable DICKENS. 3. All affectation of talking piously is quite n. 1751. **Nau·seous-ly** *adv.*, **-ness.**

Nautch (nǭtʃ), *sb.* Also **notch, na(t)ch.** 1796. [a. Urdū (Hindī) *nāch*, Prakrit *nachcha*, Skr. *nṛitya*, f. *nṛit-* to dance.] 1. An East Indian exhibition of dancing, performed by professional dancing-girls. b. A nautch girl. BROWNING. 2. *attrib.*, as *n. dancer, girl* 1809.

Nautic (nǭ·tik), *a.* 1613. [ad. F. *nautique*, or L. *nauticus*, ad. Gr. ναυτικός, f. ναύτης sailor, f. ναῦς ship.] *adj.* Nautical. (Chiefly in poetic or dignified use.)

Nautical (nǭ·tikăl), *a.* 1552.] f. as prec. + -AL.] 1. Pertaining to seamen or to the art of navigation. b. In special applications, as *n. almanac, day, distance, mile*, etc. (see quots. and the various sbs.) 1765. 2. *absol.* A nautical person or writer 1840.

1. My n. enthusiasm fairly got the better of me 1834. b. *N. almanac*, a year-book containing information for the use of mariners. *N. Day.* This day commences at noon, twelve hours before the civil day SMYTH. The rhumb-line intercepted between any two places through which it passes, is called their *n. distance* OGILVIE. **Nau·tically** *adv.* 1835.

Nautilus (nǭ·tilŭs). *Pl.* **-i** (-əi); also **-uses.** 1601. [a. L., ad. Gr. ναυτίλος sailor, f. ναύτης seaman, f. ναῦς ship.] a. In full, *Paper Nautilus*, the argonaut, a small dibranchiate cephalopod, the female of which is protected by a very thin, single-chambered, detached shell, and has webbed dorsal arms which it was formerly believed to use as sails. b. In full, *Pearly Nautilus*, a tetrabranchiate cephalopod (*N. pompilius*) found in the Indian and Pacific Oceans, having a beautiful chambered shell with nacreous septa; also, any related fossil species.

a. Learn of the little N. to sail, Spread the thin oar, and catch the driving gale POPE. The paper-shelled n. 1753. b. *attrib.* A fairy cup made out of a N. shell SCOTT. Hence **Nau·tilite** (*Palæont.*), a fossil n. 1748. **Nau·tiloid** *a.* resembling the n. in form; *sb.* a nautiloid mollusc 1847.

Naval (nēi·văl), *a.* 1593. [ad. L. *navalis*, f. *navis* ship; see -AL. Cf. F. *naval.*] 1. *N. crown*: (*a*) the crown or garland given by the Romans to one who had distinguished himself in a sea-fight; (*b*) the form of crown used as a badge in the navy. 2. Of or pertaining to, connected with, characteristic of, used in, the navy (†or shipping); (of persons) serving in the navy 1602. 3. Fought, gained, sustained, carried out, etc. by means of ships or a navy 1606. b. Consisting of, or based on the possession of ships of war 1617.

2. *N. officer*: (*a*) an officer in the navy (see OFFICER *sb.*); (*b*) *U.S.*, an officer whose duty it is to receive copies of all manifests and entries in the Custom House. *N. stores*, all those articles or materials made use of in shipping or in the navy; also *spec.*, the different resinous products of trade. *Royal N.* (*Volunteer*) *Reserve* (see RESERVE *sb.*); abbrev. R.N.(V.)R. 3. Lest..the Seamen should be forgetful and unfitting for n. warfare 1660. Beaks of ships in n. triumph borne 1700. b. The N. Strength of this Realm 1720. The n. power of Carthage 1869. Hence **Na·vally** *adv.* 1816.

Nave (nēiv), *sb.*[1] [OE. *nafu*:—OTeut. **nabō*, related to Skr. *nābhi*, *nābha* nave, navel.] The central part or block of a wheel, into which the end of the axle-tree is inserted, and from which the spokes radiate; = HUB.

Nave (nēiv), *sb.*[2] 1649. [ad. L. *navem*, acc. of *navis* ship; so It., Sp. *nave*; see also NEF.] The body of a church, from the inner door to the choir or chancel, usually separated from the aisles by pillars.

Navel (nēi·v'l), *sb.* [OE. *nafela*:—OTeut. **nabalon-*, related to Skr. *nābhīla*, and more obscurely to Gr. ὀμφαλός, L. *umbilicus*. Cf. NAVE *sb.*[1]] 1. A rounded depression, with a raised centre, situated on the abdomen at the point where the umbilical cord was originally attached; the umbilicus. 2. The centre or central point of anything, e. g. of a country, sea, forest, etc. late ME. †3. The nave of a wheel (*rare*) –1624.

1. Launcelot..smote hym on the sholder and clafe hym to the nauel MALORY. 2. Within the navil of this hideous Wood..a Sorcerer dwels MILT.

attrib. and *Comb.*, as *n.-knot*, *-vein*, etc.; **n.-gall**, a gall in the middle of a horse's back; **n. orange**, a large variety of orange, having a navel-like formation at the top; **-point** *Her.*, the point next below the fesse point; **n.-string**, the umbilical cord; **n.-wort**, various plants, esp. *Cotyledon umbilicus*. Hence **Navel** *v.* in *pa. pple.* situated in the middle 1818.

Navew (nēi·viu). Now *rare.* 1533. [a. F. **naveu*, obs. var. of *naveau*, earlier *navel*:—pop. L. **napellum*, f. **napum*, L. *napus* (see NEEP).] The rape (*Brassica napus*) or cole-seed (*B. campestris*).

‖ **Navicula** (nāvi·kiŭlă). 1853. [L., dim. of *navis* ship.] *Eccl.* An incense-boat.

Navicular (năvi·kiŭlăɹ), *a.* and *sb.* 1541. [ad. late L. *navicularis*; see prec. and -AR.] A. *adj.* 1. *N. bone*, the scaphoid bone of the hand (*rare*), or the corresponding bone in the foot lying between the astragalus and cuneiform bones. b. *Farriery.* Connected with the navicular bone of a horse's foot, esp. *n. joint, disease* 1828. 2. Pertaining to, connected with, boats –1721. 3. Having the form of a (small) boat 1774. 4. *N. fossa*, (*a*) the depression between the helix and anthelix of the ear; (*b*) the anterior portion of the urethra 1816.

3. The name of this, and of all the n. shrines was Baris J. BRYANT. The n. goddess of Egypt was called Isis 1816. Glumes n., entire 1806.

B. *ellipt.* passing into *sb.* = Navicular bone (1816), disease (1888): see above.

Navigable (næ·vigăb'l), *a.* 1527. [a. F., or ad. L. *navigabilis*, f. *navigare*; see NAVIGATE *v.*] 1. Admitting of being navigated, affording passage for ships or boats. 2. Of ships: Capable of navigation; seaworthy (*rare*) 1535. b. Of balloons: Dirigible 1903.

1. Yf the North sea were not nauigable by reason of extreme cold and Ise 1553. An incomparable great iland..nauigable round about 1625. At Lechlade..the Thames ceases to be n. 1878. Hence **Navigabi·lity** 1846, **Na·vigableness** 1720.

Navigate (næ·vigeit), *v.* 1588. [f. L. *navigat-*, *navigare*, f. *navis* ship + *agere* to drive, guide.] †1. *intr.* To go from one place to another in a ship or ships, to sail. 2. *trans.* To sail over, on, or through (the sea, a river, etc.) 1646. 3. To sail, direct, or manage (a ship) 1670. 4. Of vessels (now *rare*): a. *intr.* To sail; to ply 1758. b. *trans.* To sail on or over (the sea, etc.) 1858. 5. To manage, direct the course of (aircraft) 1784.

1. In the Summer you may n. as you please CHESTERF. 2. Drusus..was the first who navigated

the Northern Ocean 1705. *fig.* The number of vehicles which n. the streets 1845. 3. Want of hands to n. his ships 1758. 4. b. Ships destined to n. the icy seas 1878.

Navigation (nævigēˈʃən). 1527. [a. F., or ad. L. *navigationem*, f. *navigare*; see prec.] 1. The action of navigating; the action or practice of passing on water in ships or other vessels 1533. 2. The art or science of directing the movements of vessels on the sea, including more esp. the methods of determining a ship's position and course by the principles of geometry and nautical astronomy 1559. 3. An expedition or journey by water. Now *rare.* 1527. †4. *concr.* The means of navigation; shipping. In later use *U.S.* -1850. †5. Shipping business -1720. 6. †a. A passage or course by which one may sail -1654. b. A canal or other waterway (now *dial.*) 1720.

1. Phr. *Aerial n.*, the science, art, or practice of sailing or floating in the air; aeronautics. *Inland n.*, communication by means of canals and navigable rivers. 2. My Father now and then sending me small Sums of Money, I laid them out in learning N. SWIFT. 3. Their N. was short, and favoured with gentle windes 1632. 4. *Macb.* IV. i. 54.

attrib., as *n. season*; **n. act** or **law**, a legal enactment regulating n. or shipping; **n. coal**, steam coal. Hence **Naviga·tional** *a.*

Navigator (næ·vigeitəɹ). 1590. [a. L., f. *navigare*; see NAVIGATE *v.* and -OR.] 1. One who navigates; a sailor or seaman, esp. one skilled in the art of navigation; one who conducts explorations by sea. 2. A labourer employed in the work of excavating and constructing a canal (cf. NAVIGATION 6 b), or, in later use, any similar kind of earthwork. Now usu. NAVVY. 1775.

2. Seven old navigators (as canal-men are called in the midland counties) SOUTHEY.

Navvy (næ·vi), *sb.* 1832. [abbrev. of prec. 2.] 1. A labourer employed in the excavation and construction of earthworks, such as canals, railways, drains, etc. 2. A machine for excavating earth; a *steam n.* 1877.

Hence **Na·vvy** *v.*, to do navvy's work.

Navy (nē·vi). ME. [a. OF. *navie* fleet:— Rom. **navia*, f. L. *navis* ship; see -Y [3].] †1. (Without article.) Ships or shipping -1473. 2. A fleet; a number of ships collected together, esp. for purposes of war. Now *poet.* and *rhet.* ME. 3. The whole of the ships of war belonging to a nation or ruler considered collectively, with all the organization necessary for their command and maintenance; a regularly organized and maintained naval force 1540. b. The officers and men serving in a particular navy 1648. 4. *ellipt.* Navy blue 1884.

2. The nauee of Yram, the which bare gold of Oofer WYCLIF 1 *Kings* x. 11. 3. Alfred the Great was the founder of the English n. 1840. Phr. *The king's* (*queen's*) *n.*, *the Royal n.*, †*n. royal.* b. The Indian n. now consists of 150 officers 1845.

attrib. and *Comb.*, as *n. man, revolver, surgeon*, etc.; **n. agent**, one who manages the business affairs of naval officers; **n. bill**, a bill issued by the Admiralty in place of ready-money payment, or drawn by a naval officer on the Admiralty; **n. blue**, a dark blue, the colour of the British naval uniform; **N. Board**, a former name for the Admiralty; **N. League**, a body founded in 1895 with the object of arousing national interest in the British N.; **N. List**, an official publication containing a list of the officers of the Navy, and other nautical information; †**N. Office**, the Admiralty building; **n. register**, *U.S.* = *Navy List*; **n. yard**, a government dockyard (now *U.S.*).

‖**Nawab** (nǎwǭ·b). 1758. [Urdū *nawwāb*, var. of *nuwwāb*, pl. of (Arab.) *nā'ib* deputy.] = NABOB.

†**Nawle**, obs. f. AWL.

Nay (nē), *v.* *Obs.* exc. *arch.* late ME. [a. OF. *neier*, var. *noier*, *nier*:—L. *negare*, or, later, f. NAY *adv.*] 1. †To refuse (ME. only); to give a refusal to (a person) 1592. †2. a. To deny (a matter) -1560; †b. *intr.* To say nay -1680.

Nay (nē), *adv.* and *sb.* ME. [a. ON. *nei*, f. *ne* NE + *ei* ever = OE. *á*; cf. NA *adv.*[1] and [2].] A. *adv.* 1. A word used to express negation, dissent, denial, or refusal, in answer to some statement, question, command, etc. (In older use *nay* (like *yea*) was usu. employed when the preceding statement, etc., contained no negative; otherwise *no.*) Now *arch.* or *dial.* 2. Used to introduce a more precise or forcible term or statement than that which precedes 1585.

1. Phr. *To say n.*: (*a*) To make denial or refusal. (*b*) To deny or refuse (one); to forbid, prohibit. Also, to refuse (a thing) *to* one. (*c*) To express dissent or contradiction. 2. I have weighty, nay unanswerable reasons MISS BURNEY.

B. *sb.* An utterance of the word 'nay'; a negative reply or vote; a denial, refusal, or prohibition ME.

He would have no n. at God's hands 1643. Phr. †*It* (*there*, etc.) *is no n.* = 'It cannot be denied'. Also simply *no n.* †*Without n.*, beyond doubt, assuredly.

Nay-say, *sb.* 1631. [f. NAY *adv.* + SAY *sb.*] Refusal, denial. So **Nay·say** *v.* to refuse (one). *dial.* and *arch.* 1773.

†**Nay·ward.** *rare.* [f. NAY *sb.* + -WARD.] *To the n.*, towards denial or unbelief. *Wint. T.* II. i. 64.

Nayword (nē·wɔ̄ɹd). 1598. [?] 1. A watchword or catchword (*rare*) 2. A byword, a proverb 1601. Now *dial.*

1. *Merry W.* II. ii. 131. 2. *Twel. N.* II. iii. 146.

Nazarene (næzărī·n). ME. [ad. L. *Nazarenus*, ad. Gr. Ναζαρηνός (Mark i. 24), f. Ναζαρέτ Nazareth.] A. *adj.* 1. Of or belonging to Nazareth (*rare*). 2. Belonging to the sect of the Nazarenes 1689. B. *sb.* 1. A native of Nazareth 1611. b. A follower of Jesus of Nazareth; a Christian. (So called esp. by Jews and Mohammedans.) late ME. 2. *pl.* An early Jewish-Christian sect, allied to the Ebionites. var. **Nazare·an.** 1689.

B. 1. He shalbe called a N. *Matt.* ii. 23. b. The very name of N. Was wormwood to his Paynim spleen BYRON.

Nazarite [1] (næ·zărəit). 1535. [f. L. *Nazaræus* (ad. Gr. Ναζωραῖος) + -ITE [1].] = prec. sb.

Nazarite [2] (næ·zărəit). Also **-irite.** 1560. [f. L. *Nazaræus*, f. Heb. *nāzar* to separate oneself, to refrain from anything.] Among the ancient Hebrews, one who took certain vows of abstinence (see Numbers vi).

To drinke wine..was a pollution both of the Nazarites and Priestes 1585. Hence **Na·zariteship, Nazari·tic** *a.*, **Na·zaritish** *a.*, **Na·zaritism.**

Naze (nēz). 1774. [app. inferred from place-names.] A promontory or headland.

‖**Nazi** (nā·tsi, nā·zi). 1930. [Ger., f. *nationalsozialist.*] A member of the German National Socialist party.

N.B. (en bī), abbrev. of NOTA BENE.

N.C.O., = NON-COMMISSIONED *officer.*

Ne, *adv.* and *conj.* *arch.* [OE. *ne* = L. *ne*- (*nefas*, etc.), Skr. *na*, rel. to Goth. *ne*, L. *ne*, Gr. νη-, Skr. *nā*.] = NOT *adv.* †Also as *n*- comb. w. a vb., as *nadde* had not, *nam* am not.

1. A youth Who ne in virtue's ways did take delight BYRON. Phr. †*Ne were, ne had..been*, were it not, had it not been (for). 2. They nentende nyght nor day But vnto merthe LYDG.

B. *conj.* = NOR. *arch.* or *Obs.* OE. †b. = Nor, and . . not, neither -1618.

1. *Ne..ne* (sometimes) = neither..nor. Now only *arch.* Ne could we laugh, ne wail COLERIDGE.

Neaf, obs. f. NIEVE, fist.

Neal (nīl), *v.* *Obs.* exc. *dial.* 1538. [Aphet. f. ANNEAL *v.*] *trans.* = ANNEAL *v.* 2, 4. Also †*intr.* to undergo the process of annealing -1684.

Neanderthaloid (nĭæ·ndəɹtā·loid), *a.* 1887. [See def. and -OID.] Having the characteristics of a skull of very low type found at Neanderthal in Rhenish Prussia in 1857; characterized by this type of skull. So **Nea·nderthal** *man*, etc.

Neap (nīp), *sb.*[1] *n. dial.* and *U.S.* 1553. [perh. of Scand. origin; cf. Norw. dial. *neip* a forked pole, etc.] 1. The pole or tongue of a cart. (Now *U.S.*) 2. A three-legged rest, used to support the shaft of a vehicle 1691.

Neap (nīp), *a.* and *sb.*[2] [OE. *nēp* (obscure) in *nēpflōd.*] 1. *N. tide*, a tide occurring shortly after the first and third quarters of the moon, in which the high-water level stands at its lowest point. 2. *absol.* A neap tide 1584.

1. *N. season*, the time of n. tide. 2. High springs and dead Neapes 1627.

Neap (nīp), *v.* 1652. [f. prec.] 1. *intr.* Of tides: To become lower, to tend towards the neap. Also *pass.* 2. *To be neaped*, of a vessel: to be left aground on the height of a spring-tide 1704.

Neapolitan (nĭæpǫ·lităn). late ME. [ad. L. *Neapolitanus*, f. *Neapolites* (see -ITE), f. *Neapolis* (Gr. Νεάπολις 'new town'), Naples.] A. *adj.* Belonging or native to, distinctive or characteristic of, connected with, Naples 1592.

†*N. disease*: see NAPLES 1. *N. ice*, one made in layers of different flavours. *N. violet*, a double sweet-scented variety of viola. *N. yellow*, Naples yellow.

B. *sb.* An inhabitant or native of Naples. ME.

A blood-bespotted Neopolitan SHAKS.

Near (nīəɹ), *a.* ME. [f. NEAR *adv.*[2]] 1. Closely related by blood or kinship. 2. Close, intimate, familiar 1523. 3. With ref. to animals or vehicles: Left (as opp. to †*far, off*, = right): horses, etc., being usu. mounted, led, or approached from the left side 1453. 4. Close at hand; not distant 1565. 5. Of a road: Short, direct. (Chiefly in *compar.* and *superl.*) 1579. 6. Close, narrow 1548. 7. Closely affecting or touching one 1605. 8. Niggardly, mean 1616.

1. They are her neere kinsewomen *Lev.* xviii. 17. 2. Your neere friends and familiar companions 1576. 3. The track of the left or n. wheel 1842. 4. When we look at a n. object with both eyes BERKELEY. *N. distance*, the part of a scene between foreground and background. *N. point*, a point, at a distance of about 4 or 5 inches from the eye, within which clear vision is no longer possible without optical assistance. *N. work*, work involving proximity of the eye to the object. b. That resembles (what is denoted), as *n. beer.* 6. It was a n. race 1856. 7. Euery minute of his being thrusts Against my neer'st of Life SHAKS. 8. A good-natured man, but reckoned n. 1753. **Nea·rness.**

Near (nīəɹ), *v.* 1513. [f. NEAR *adv.*[2] or *a.*] 1. *intr.* To draw or come near, to approach. 2. *trans.* To draw near to, to approach. †Also, to be near. 1610.

1. Still it ner'd and ner'd COLERIDGE. 2. Keep off, I charge thee neere me not HEYWOOD.

Near (nīəɹ), *adv.*[1] (and *prep.*). *Obs.* exc. *dial.* [OE. *nēar*, etc., comp. of *nēah* NIGH *adv.*] †I. In advb. (or prepositional) use. With verbs of motion. Nearer or closer (to a place, point, or person). Freq. governing a noun in the dative -1596.

Pardon me, I will come no n. 1596. *No n.!* (or *n.!*) Naut.: a command to the helmsman to come no closer to the wind.

II. In predic. use after the subst. vb. (Freq. with dative or *to.*) 1. Nearer in space or time, †in relationship OE. 2. Nearer to one's end or purpose. (Only in neg. and interrog. clauses; *dial.*) late ME.

1. The nere to the churche, the ferther from God 1562. The neere in blood, the neerer bloody SHAKS. 2. Phr. *Never the n.* (common 1560–1625).

Near (nīəɹ), *adv.*[2] (and *prep.*) ME. [a. ON. *nǽr*, prop. compar. of *ná-* = OE. *nēah* NIGH, but also used as a positive.] I. Used absol. (without *to* or dependent sb.). **Denoting proximity.* 1. To, within, or at a short distance; to, or in, close proximity. b. *Naut.* Close to the wind 1634. 2. Of time: Close at hand ME. 3. Closely connected with one by kinship or intimacy. late ME.

1. Things n. seem further off; farst off, the nearst at hand H. MORE. N. is my shirt, but nearer is my skin! 1890. Phr. *Far and n.* (see FAR *adv.*), properly meaning 'farther (off) and nearer (at hand)'. b. *No Nearer!* = *No near* (see NEAR *adv.*[1]). 2. My heart failed me as the time drew n. MRS. CARLYLE. Phr. *N. upon*, close upon a particular time. 3. In company with one 'n. and dear' 1826. Phr. *N. akin* or *of kin* (see AKIN *adv.* and KIN).

***Denoting approximation in degree or amount.* 4. Within a (very) little, almost. (Now usu. expressed by NEARLY.) ME. 5. With negatives: (Not) by a great deal or a long way, (not) anything like, (not) nearly. Usu. followed by *so.* 1447. 6. Closely, esp. in respect of pressure or touching, of resemblance, connexion, scrutiny, etc. Now *rare.* 1456. 7. In phr. *as n. as* (one can, etc.) 1538. †8. Narrowly, only by a little (*rare*) -1819.

4. They appear to have been pretty n. of an Age 1696. It cost us n. a Fortnight's Time DE FOE. I am n. upon eighty years of age LANDOR. 5. He is nothing neere so much delighted 1638. 6. His Majesty had another Exception against the Duke, which touched him as n. CLARENDON. The nearer it [tragedy] approaches the reality,..the more perfect is its power BURKE.

****Denoting manner.* 9. Thriftily; parsimoniously, meanly 1625. 10. With the legs close together 1710.

10. A Horse that goes wide before, and n. behind 1737.

II. Followed by *to* (or †*unto*). 1. Close *to* a place, thing, or person, in respect of space, or *to* a point in time ME. **2.** Closely related *to* one by kinship, etc., esp. in *n. and dear* 1450. **3.** Close *to* something in respect of likeness or correspondence 1548. **4.** *To go n. to* (with inf.), to be on the point of, almost to succeed in (doing something). Also const. gerund. 1593.

1. Neere vnto the said plaine are diuers woods and forrests 1600. Phr. †*To come* or *go n. to*, to touch closely. **3.** The case that comes nearest to this of those I have seen NORTH. **4.** It would go n. to break her heart 1889.

III. Governing a sb. (passing into *prep.*). **1.** Close to or upon (a place, person, thing, point of time, state or condition) ME. †**2.** Intimate with (one) –1660. **3.** Close to (a thing or person) in point of similarity or achievement 1585. Latterly chiefly *U.S.*, as in *n. beer.*

1. Our Coffee-house is n. one of the Inns of Court STEELE. I must have gone very n. convincing him 1825. The time draws n. the birth of Christ TENNYSON. The hope was n. fulfilment 1902. *fig.* I thinke we came neere you when wee saide you loued LYLY. Phr. *To lie, come,* or *go n.* (one, the heart, etc.), to touch or affect deeply. **2.** 2 *Hen. IV*, v. i. 81. **3.** Their language..is nearer the Latine, then the Italian 1632.

Near by, *adv.* and *a.* late ME. [NEAR *adv.*[2] and BY *adv.*] **A.** *adv.* **1.** Close at hand. **2.** Nearly, almost. *Sc.* 1456. **B.** *adj.* (*near-by, nearby*) Neighbouring. orig. *U.S.* 1858.

Nearctic (nɪ,ā·ɹktik), *a.* 1858. [NEO-.] *Zool.* Comprising, or pertaining to, the temperate and arctic parts of N. America, in respect of the distribution of birds, etc.

Near East. 1869. [NEAR *a.* 4.] The south-eastern part of Europe; the Balkan States together with Asia Minor. Hence **Near-Ea·stern** *a.*, **-Ea·sterly** *adv.*

Near hand, *adv., prep.*, and *a.* Now only *Sc.* and *dial.* ME. [NEAR *adv.*[2] and HAND *sb.*] **A.** *adv.* **1.** Close at hand, close by. †**b.** At close quarters (*rare*) –1670. **2.** Nearly, almost ME. **B.** *prep.* Near to, close to. ME.

Nearly (nīə·ɹli), *adv.* 1540. [-LY [2].] **1.** In a near manner; closely; intimately. **2.** Particularly 1562. **3.** Almost, all but 1683.

1. To be n. acquainted with the people of different countries can happen to very few JOHNSON. **2.** This ..I only mention, because it so n. touches myself SWIFT. **3.** I languished here for n. three weeks GOLDSM. Phr. *Not..n.*, nothing like.

Near-sighted, *a.* 1686. Short-sighted. Hence **Near-si·ghtedness** 1811.

Neat (nīt), *sb.* [OE. *nēat* :—OTeut. **nautom*, f. *naut-*, ablaut-var. of *neut-* to enjoy or possess.] **1.** *sing.* An animal of the ox-kind; an ox or bullock, a cow or heifer. Now *rare* or *arch.* **2.** (†*pl.* or) *collect.* Cattle OE.

1. A savage Bull.., he was a gallant-looking n. MORRIS. **2.** The Steere, the Heyefer, and the Calfe, Are all call'd N. SHAKS. *appos.* Every kind of n. cattle 1805.

Neat (nīt), *a.* and *adv.* 1542. [ad. AF. *neit, net*, F. *net* :—L. *nitidum*, f. *nitere* to shine] **A.** *adj.* **I.** †**1.** Clean. Also const. *from*, –1632. †**2.** Clear, bright –1797. **3.** Of liquors: Pure; *spec.* undiluted 1579. **b.** Of other substances (*rare*) 1651. **4.** Free from any reductions; clear, net. (Now usu. NET.) 1599. **b.** Exact, precise. Now *dial.* 1682.

2. Fresh springing wells, as christall neate SPENSER. **3.** I was obliged to drink rum it wouldn't ha done to ha drunk the water n. 1851. **4.** A n. sum, to cover all expenses 1817.

II. †**1.** Of persons: Inclined to refinement or elegance; trim or smart in apparel –1656. **2.** Characterized by elegance of form without unnecessary embellishment; of agreeable but simple appearance; nicely made or proportioned 1549. **3.** Of language, style, etc.: Well expressed; *esp.* brief, clear, and to the point; cleverly or smartly put or phrased 1586. **b.** Of preparations, cookery, etc.: Dainty, elegant, tasteful. Now *rare.* 1611. **c.** Cleverly done 1598. **4.** Inclined to tidiness 1577; skilful and precise 1612. **5.** Put or kept in good order, tidy 1596.

1. Still to be n., still to be drest, As you were going to a feast B. JONS. **2.** Many n. houses and pleasant seats there be in the country FULLER. The furniture was n. 1888. **3.** A n. speech by one Pym 1621. **b.** A very n. and curious Banquet SIR T. HERBERT. **c.** A n. and happy turn to give the subject DICKENS. **4.** He was n. and methodical in all small matters 1885. **5.** A tradesman's books should always be kept clear and n. 1745.

B. *adv.* Neatly 1665. Hence **Nea·tly** *adv.* in a n. manner or style. **Nea·tness.**

Neaten (nī·t'n), *v.* 1898. [f. NEAT *a.* + -EN.] *trans.* To make neat, *esp.* in needlework.

Neath, 'neath (nīþ), *prep. dial.* and *poet.* 1787. [Aphetic f. ANEATH.] Beneath.

Neat-handed, *a.* 1632. [NEAT *a.*] Deft in handling things; dexterous. Hence **Neat-ha·ndedness** 1839.

Neatherd (nī·t,hōɹd). late ME. [f. NEAT *sb.* + HERD *sb.*[2]] One who has the care of neat cattle, a cowherd.

Nea·t-house. Also **neats'.** 1440. [f. NEAT *sb.*] **1.** A house or shed in which cattle are kept. **2.** A locality near Chelsea Bridge, where there was a celebrated market garden. Also *pl.* 1632.

Neatify (nī·tifəi), *v.* Now *rare* or *Obs.* 1601. [f. NEAT *a.* + -IFY.] *trans.* To make neat, to purify.

Neat's foot. 1579. [f. NEAT *sb.*] The foot of an ox, used as an article of food 1595. **b.** *attrib.* in **neat's-foot oil,** an oil obtained from the feet of neat cattle.

Neat's leather. 1530. [f. NEAT *sb.*] Leather made from the hides of neat cattle.

Neat's tongue. 1596. [f. NEAT *sb.*] An ox-tongue, used as an article of food.

Silence is onely commendable In a neats tongue dri'd SHAKS.

Neb (neb). Now chiefly *north.* and *Sc.* [OE. *nebb* (:—**nebj-*) neut. = ON. *nef* (stem *nefj-*; Norw. *nev*, *næv*, Sw. *näf*).] **1.** The beak or bill of a bird. **b.** The mouth (of a person) 1611. **2.** The nose; the snout of an animal OE. **3.** The point or nib of a pen (or pencil) 1599. **b.** Any projecting part or point; a peak, tip, spout, etc. 1584.

‖**Ne·bbuk.** Also **nabk.** 1846. [Arab. *nebq*, *nebeq*.] The Christ's Thorn, *Zizyphus Spina-Christi*, or its fruit.

‖**Nebula** (ne·biŭlă). *Pl.* **-æ** (-ī). 1661. [L., related to Gr. νεφέλη.] **1. a.** A film upon, or covering, the eye; *spec.* a clouded speck or spot on the cornea causing defective vision. **b.** A cloudy or flocculent appearance 1805. **2.** *Astron.* An indistinct cloud-like cluster of distant stars, or a luminous patch of supposed gaseous or stellar matter lying beyond the limits of the solar system 1727. **3.** Mist 1894.

Nebular (ne·biŭlăɹ), *a.* 1837. [f. prec. + -AR [1].] **1.** *N. hypothesis* or *theory*, the theory, propounded by Kant and elaborated by Herschel and Laplace, which supposes a nebula to be the first state of the solar and stellar systems. **2.** Consisting of, concerned with, or relating to a nebula or nebulæ 1856.

Nebule [1] (ne·biul). late ME. [Anglicized f. NEBULA.] **1.** A cloud; a mist or fog. **2.** *Astron.* A nebula 1830.

Nebule [2] (ne·biul). 1823. [app. due to misapprehension of next.] *Arch.* A moulding of a wavy or serpentine form.

Nebulé (ne·biulė), **nebuly** (ne·biuli), *a.* Also **-ée.** 1550. [a. F. *nébulé*, ad. med.L. *nebulatus, nebulare.*] **1.** *Her.* Of a wavy or serpentine form, like the edges of conventional clouds; represented in the form of a cloud. **2.** *Arch.* Of mouldings: see NEBULE [2] 1842.

Nebulium (nĭbiū·liŏm). 1898. orig. **nebulum.** [f. NEBULA + -IUM.] *Chem.* An element the existence of which is inferred from certain green lines in the spectra of gaseous nebulæ.

Nebulize (ne·biŭləiz), *v. rare.* 1872. [f. NEBULA.] **1.** *trans.* To reduce to a mist or spray. **2.** *intr.* To become nebulous or indefinite 1891. Hence **Ne·bulizer,** an instrument for converting a liquid into a fine spray, esp. for medical purposes 1874.

Nebulose (ne·biŭlōus), *a.* late ME. [ad. L. *nebulosus*; see NEBULA and -OSE.] Cloudy, misty, indistinct (*lit.* and *fig.*). **b.** Clouded, cloudlike 1826.

Nebulosity (nebiŭlǫ·sĭti). 1761. [a. F. *nébulosité*; see next and -ITY.] **1.** Nebulous or indistinctly luminous appearance; a faintly luminous patch or mass. **b.** Nebulous state or form; nebulous matter 1833. **2.** Cloudiness; indistinctness 1809.

1. b. *fig.* He had been a mere n. whom she had never distinctly outlined T. HARDY.

Nebulous (ne·biŭləs), *a.* late ME. [ad. L. *nebulosus*; see NEBULA and -OUS.] **1.** Cloudy, foggy, misty, dank (*rare*). **2.** *Astron.* **a.** *N. star*, a small cluster of indistinct stars, or a star which is surrounded by a luminous haze 1679. **b.** Of the nature of a nebula or nebulæ; consisting of, abounding in, nebulæ 1784. **3.** Cloud-like 1805. **b.** *fig.* Hazy, vague, formless 1831. **4.** Clouded in colour; turbid 1820.

3. b. N. disquisitions on Religion CARLYLE. Hence **Ne·bulous-ly** *adv.*, **-ness.**

Necessarian (nesėsēə·riăn). 1777. [f. NECESSARY + -IAN.] A believer in necessity; a necessitarian. **b.** *attrib.* or as *adj.* 1795. Hence **Necessa·rianism,** necessitarianism 1840.

Necessarily (ne·sėsărili), *adv.* 1488. [-LY [2].] †**1.** (Senses now merged in 3.) Unavoidably –1710; indispensably –1748. **2.** As a necessary result or consequence 1509. **3.** Of necessity; inevitably 1562. So **Ne·cessariness,** indispensability (now *rare*) 1551.

Necessary (ne·sėsări), *a.* and *sb.* late ME. [ad. L. *necessarius*, f. *necesse* needful; see -ARY.] **A.** *adj.* **I. 1.** Indispensable, requisite, needful; that cannot be done without. Also const. *to* or *for* (a person or thing) and with *inf.* †**b.** Commodious, convenient (*rare*) –1548. **2.** Of servants, etc.: Rendering (certain) necessary or useful services, as *n. woman. Hist.* **3.** Of actions: Needful to be done 1601.

1. Which wife is not..called an impediment or n. evil 1577. Since light so n. is to life MILT. Phr. *N. house*, a privy. So *n. place, stool, vault.* Now *dial.* **3.** Still doubting if that deed Be just which is most n. SHELLEY.

II. 1. Inevitably determined or fixed by predestination or natural laws; happening or existing by an inherent necessity. late ME. **b.** Of mental concepts or processes: Inevitably resulting from the constitution of things or of the mind itself 1551. **c.** Inevitably produced by a previous condition of things 1860. **2.** Of actions: Determined by force of nature or circumstances. late ME. **b.** Enforced by another; compulsory 1655. **3.** Of agents: Impelled by the action of circumstances upon the will; having no independent volition 1690.

1. b. The ideas of space and time are called in philosophy n. ideas 1878. **2.** The n. action, where all the motives are on one side 1855. **3.** They all agree, that man is not a free but a n. agent WESLEY.

B. *sb.* **1.** A necessary thing; an essential or requisite ME. **2.** A necessary house (*dial.*) 1756. **3.** With *the.* That which is needful; *spec.* the necessary funds or money *colloq.* 1772.

1. She denied herself every n. MME. D'ARBLAY. The money to buy the necessaries of their household 1875.

Necessitarian (nĭsesitēə·riăn). 1798. [f. NECESSITY + -ARIAN; cf. NECESSARIAN.] One who maintains that all human action is necessarily determined by antecedent causes, as opposed to one who believes in the freedom of the will. Hence **Necessita·rianism** 1854.

Necessitate (nĭse·sitėit), *v.* 1628. [f. med. L. *necessitat-*, *necessitare*, f. *necessitas* NECESSITY; cf. F. *nécessiter.*] **1.** *trans.* To bring (a person) under some necessity; to compel, oblige, or force. (Chiefly in *pass.*) Now *rare* (freq. in 17th c.). **2.** To render necessary; *esp.* to demand, require, or involve as a necessary condition or result 1628. †**3.** To reduce (a person) to want or necessity –1700.

1. Each boy is necessitated to decide and act for himself 1779. Necessitated by weak health to the regularity and the quiet of a monk PATER. **2.** Assumptions..such as the received theology necessitates M. ARNOLD. **3.** The King..being necessitated for Money 1700. Hence **Necessita·tion,** the action of necessitating; the result of this 1652.

Necessitous (nĭse·sitəs), *a.* 1611. [ad. F. *nécessiteux*, or f. NECESSITY + -OUS.] **1.** Placed or living in a condition of necessity; poor, needy. **2.** Characterized by necessity or poverty 1639.

1. A greedy and n. publick BURKE. *absol.* The ambitious hoped for kingdoms; the greedy and the n. for plunder CHESTERF. **2.** In n. circumstances 1885. Hence **Nece·ssitous-ly** *adv.*, **-ness.**

Necessitude (nĭse·sitiūd). Now *rare.* 1612. [ad. L. *necessitudo*, f. *necesse* necessary; see

-TUDE.] †1. A relation or connexion between persons -1653. 2. Necessity, need 1677.

1. Between Parents and their children there is so great a necessitude JER. TAYLOR.

Necessity (nǐse·sǐti). late ME. [a. F. *nécessité*, ad. L. *necessitatem*, f. *necesse* necessary; see -ITY.] I. †1. a. The fact of being inevitably fixed or determined -1568. †b. The constraining power *of* something -1533. 2. Constraint or compulsion having its basis in the natural constitution of things; *esp.* such constraint conceived as a law prevailing throughout the material universe and within the sphere of human action. late ME. b. Differentiated as *absolute, conditional, logical, moral, natural, philosophical, physical* 1587. 3. The constraining power of circumstances; a condition of things compelling to a certain course of action. late ME. †4. A necessary piece of business; a necessary act -1676. †b. Something unavoidable. SHAKS. 5. a. An unavoidable compulsion or obligation of doing something. Also with *inf.* Now *rare.* 1630. b. An imperative need *for* or †*of* something 1673. 6. The fact of being indispensable; the indispensableness *of* some act or thing 1597.

2. Who can..breake the chayne of strong necessitee SPENSER. b. Physical n. has its origin in the established order and laws of the material universe 1840. 3. I know the rigour of political n.; but I see here, as little of n...as of propriety BURKE. Phr. *Work of n.*, something which cannot possibly or naturally be left undone. *Of n.*: Necessarily. *Phrases and proverbs.* To maken vertu of necessite CHAUCER. N... hath no law 1614. N. is the Mother of Invention 1658. 4. b. 2 *Hen. IV*, III. i. 92. 5. b. He..produced a n. of private conversation JOHNSON. 6. The n. of adopting some measures to subsist their armies WELLINGTON.

II. 1. †a. What is necessarily required; necessaries -1650. b. A necessary thing 1481. 2. The condition of being necessitous; want, poverty 1475. 3. A situation of hardship or difficulty; a pressing need or want. (Chiefly in *pl.*) 1450. †4. Want *of* a thing -1754.

2. Necessities sharpe pinch SHAKS. They will not ask whether his n. be a sufficient title HOBBES. 3. The necessities of the mother country 1775.

Neck (nek), *sb.*[1] [OE. *hnecca* (rare) = MDu. *necke*, MHG. *nacke*, etc.] I. 1. That portion of the body lying between the head and shoulders; †in early use the nape of the neck. b. The cervical vertebræ. Chiefly in phr. *to break the n.* ME. 2. a. The flesh of the neck of an animal, esp. of beef or mutton 1603. b. That part of a garment which covers, or lies next to, the neck 1530.

1. He would..make two Fellows who hated, embrace and fall upon each other's N. STEELE. b. I had as liefe thou didst breake his necke as his finger SHAKS. Without regard for the safety of their own necks 1893. 2. a. Eight to a n. of mutton—is not that your commons 1603.

II. In fig. or allusive expressions, implying subjugation, submission, resistance, †the imposition of a burden or charge; or with allusion to hanging or beheading. late ME.

Wilt thou set thy foot o' my necke SHAKS. Let his N. answere for it SHAKS. *Oth.* v. ii. 170. Sturdiest Oaks Bow'd thir Stiff necks MILT.

Phrases. *In, on,* or *upon the n. of*, on the top of. Now only *dial.* *To break the n. of*, to counteract the chief force or main effect of; to finish the main part of. *N. and heels* = neck and crop. Now *dial.* *N. and crop*, bodily, altogether. *N. or nothing* (occ. *nought*), expressing determination and readiness to take all risks; also *attrib.* of persons or actions. *N. and n.*, of horses, etc.: keeping abreast; also *fig.*; *attrib.* close, near. *To get it in the n.* (slang), to sustain a severe blow, as of defeat, reprimand, etc.

III. In transf. uses. 1. The narrow part *of* some passage, cavity, or vessel, *esp.* the part of a bottle next the mouth ME. 2. Of natural formations, or artificial structures: A pass between hills or mountains; the narrow part *of* a mountain pass; a narrow channel or inlet; the narrow part *of* a sound; *Fortif.* The narrow part *of* a bastion or embrasure; an isthmus or narrow promontory; a narrow stretch of wood, ice, etc. 1555. 3. A narrow or constricted part in any manufactured article; a connecting part between two portions of a thing 1598. b. The part of a violin, etc., connecting the head and the body 1611. c. *Arch.* The lower part of a capital, lying immediately above the astragal terminating the shaft of the column 1624. d. In cannon, (*a*) the narrow part connecting the cascabel with the breech; (*b*) the part immediately behind the swell of the muzzle 1753. 4. a. *Bot.* A neck-like part in plants 1672. b. Excessive elongation of stem or stalk 1882. 5. *Anat.* a. The small circular depression where the base of a tooth ends and the roots begin 1732. b. A constricted part in a bone 1726.

Combs.: n.-cell *Bot.*, a cell forming (part of) the n. in the archegonium of ferns or bryophytes; -fillet, in cannon, a fillet on the breech, next to the n. of the cascabel; -mould(ing) *Arch.*, a moulding on the n. of a capital; -twister *U.S. slang*, a kind of drink; -wear, collars and ties.

Neck, *sb.*[2] *s.w. dial.* late ME. [?] The last handful or sheaf of corn cut at harvest-time.

Neck (nek), *v.* Now only *techn.* or *dial.* 1450. [f. NECK *sb.*[1]] 1. *trans.* To strike on the neck, esp. so as to stun or kill; to behead; to pull the neck of (a fowl). b. *intr.* (*U.S.*) To indulge in intimate hugging and kissing. 2. To make or clear the neck of (a drain) 1844. 3. *pass.* or *intr.* To break off at the head 1828. 4. To reduce the diameter of, by planing, etc. 1873.

Ne·ck-band. 1446. [f. NECK *sb.*[1]] 1. A band for the neck. 2. The part of a garment encircling the neck 1591.

†Ne·ck-beef. 1662. [f. NECK *sb.*[1]] Beef from the necks of cattle, which is of poor quality. Hence *transf.* of anything inferior and cheap. -1812.

Ne·ck-bone. ME. [f. NECK *sb.*[1]] The bone (or †nape) of the neck; a cervical vertebra.

Ne·ckcloth. 1639. [f. NECK *sb.*[1]] A cloth worn round the neck; a cravat. Now *rare.* b. *transf.* The hangman's rope 1836.

Necked (nekt), *a.* late ME. [f. NECK *sb.*[1]] 1. Having a neck *like* something specified, or of a specified kind. 2. Having a neck 1841.

Neckerchief (ne·kəɹtʃif). late ME. [f. NECK *sb.*[1] + KERCHIEF.] A kerchief worn about the neck. So **Ne·ckercher** (now *dial.*). So **Neck-ha·ndkerchief** 1642.

Necking (ne·kiŋ), *sb.* 1804. [f. NECK *sb.*[1] + -ING[1].] *Arch.* The part of a column lying between the capital and the shaft.

Necklace (ne·klės), *sb.* 1590. [f. NECK *sb.*[1] + LACE *sb.*] 1. An ornament of precious stones, precious metal, beads, etc. worn round the neck. †b. A lace or ribbon for the neck; a neck-tie -1740. 2. *transf.* A noose or halter 1616. 3. *Naut.* A chain or strop round a mast 1860. 4. *attrib.* applied to certain plants or woods having features resembling strings of beads, as *n.-tree.*

Necklace (ne·klės), *v.* 1702. [f. prec.] 1. *trans.* and *intr.* To form into a necklace. 2. *trans.* To surround with, or as with, a necklace 1763.

Necklet (ne·klėt). 1865. [f. NECK *sb.*[1] + -LET.] A closely fitting ornamental band for the neck.

Ne·ck-piece. 1611. [f. NECK *sb.*[1]] 1. The part of a garment next the neck. b. A piece of armour, cloth, etc., covering the neck 1752. 2. Of meat: The part of the carcass between the shoulder and the head 1818.

Ne·ck-tie. 1838. [f. NECK *sb.*[1]] A narrow band of woven or knitted material placed round the neck and tied or knotted in front.

Ne·ck-verse. 1450. [f. NECK *sb.*[1]] A Latin verse printed in black-letter (usu. the beginning of *Ps.* li) formerly set before one claiming benefit of clergy (see CLERGY), by reading which he might save his neck. Now only *Hist.* †Also in *transf.* or *fig.* uses -1659.

Ne·ckweed. 1562. [f. NECK *sb.*[1]] †1. The plant hemp (with ref. to the use of hempen rope for hanging persons) -1681. 2. *U.S.* An American weed, *Veronica peregrina* or Purslane Speedwell, formerly supposed to be of service in scrofulous affections, whence the name 1846.

Necro- (nekro), *occas.* **necr-**, comb. f. Gr. νεκρός dead body or person, occurring in compounds either of Gr. origin, as NECROPOLIS, etc., or of modern formation, as NECROBIOSIS, etc.; also **necro·latry**, worship of the dead; **necro·phagous**, feeding on dead bodies or carrion; **ne·crophore**, a burying-beetle, one belonging to the genus *Necrophorus*; **necro·scopy**, examination of bodies after death; **necro·tomy**, the dissection of dead bodies; the excision of dead bone or tissue.

‖**Necrobiosis** (nekrobəiōᵘ·sis). 1880. [mod. L., f. NECRO- + Gr. βίος life; see -OSIS.] *Path.* The process of decay or death in tissues of the body; the gradual degeneration and death of a part through suspended or imperfect nutrition; an instance of this. So **Necrobio·tic** *a.* 1875.

Necrology (nekrǫ·lŏdʒi). 1727. [See NECRO- and -LOGY.] 1. An ecclesiastical or monastic register containing entries of the deaths of persons connected with, or commemorated by, the church, monastery, etc. b. A death-roll 1854. 2. An obituary notice 1799. Hence **Necrolo·gic**, **-al** *a.* obituary; **-ally** *adv.* **Necro·logist**, one who writes an obituary notice. **Ne·crologue**, an obituary notice.

Necromancer (ne·kromænsəɹ). ME. Earlier nigro-. [a. OF. *nigromansere*; see next and -ER[1].] One who practises necromancy; more generally, a wizard, magician.

Necromancy (ne·kromænsi). ME. Earlier nigro-. [a. OF. *nygromancie* (more usu. *-mance*) = med.L. *nigromantia*, an alteration, by association with L. *niger, nigr-*, black (cf. BLACK ART), of L. *necromantia*, ad. Gr. νεκρομαντεία, f. νεκρο- NECRO- + μαντεία divination.] 1. The pretended art of revealing future events, etc., by means of communication with the dead; more generally, magic, enchantment, conjuration. Also with *a* and *pl.* 2. Applied, after Gr. and L. use, to the part of the Odyssey describing Ulysses' visit to Hades 1601.

1. You by your N. have disturb'd him, and rais'd his Ghost MARVELL. Love, with all his necromancies, fled 1849.

Necromantic (nekromæ·ntik), *a.* and *sb.* 1574. [ad. late L. *necromanticus* or med.L. *negro-*; see prec. and -MANTIC.] A. *adj.* 1. Given to the practice of necromancy. 2. Of, belonging to, or used in necromancy or magic; performed by necromancy 1590. b. *transf.* Magical, wonderful 1630. B. *sb.* A necromancer -1652. †**Necromantical** *a.*, **-ly** *adv.*

Ne·cronite. 1819. [f. NECRO- + (N)ITE.] *Min.* A variety of orthoclase, giving out a fetid smell when broken or struck.

Necropolis (nekrǫ·polis). *Pl.* **-ises.** 1819. [a. Gr. νεκρόπολις, f. νεκρός corpse + πόλις city.] A cemetery; freq. used as the name of cemeteries in or near cities. b. An old or prehistoric burying-place 1850.

Necropsy (nekrǫ·psi). 1856. [ad. Gr. *νεκροψία, f. νεκρός corpse + ὄψις sight.] 1. A post-mortem examination, an autopsy. 2. Surgical investigation of a dead body 1881.

Necrose (nekrōᵘ·s, ne·krous), *v.* 1873. [f. NECROSIS.] *Path. intr.* To mortify; to become affected with necrosis.

Necrosed (nekrōᵘ·st, ne·kroust), *ppl. a.* 1830. [f. NECROS-IS + -ED; cf. F. *nécrosé.*] *Path.* Mortified, affected by necrosis.

‖**Necrosis** (nekrōᵘ·sis). 1665. [mod.L., a. Gr. νέκρωσις, f. νεκροῦν to kill, mortify, f. νεκρός; see -OSIS.] 1. *Path.* The death of a circumscribed piece of tissue; mortification, esp. of the bones. 2. *Bot.* Canker; a drying and dying of the branch of a tree, beginning with the bark and eating inwards 1866. So **Necro·tic** *a.* **Ne·crotize** *v. intr.* to become affected with n.

Nectar (ne·ktăɹ). 1555. [a. L., a. Gr. νέκταρ; etym. unkn.] 1. *Class. Myth.* The drink of the gods. Cf. AMBROSIA. Also *fig.* 2. *transf.* a. Any delicious wine or other drink 1583. b. The sweet fluid or honey produced by plants, esp. as collected by bees 1609.

1. But might I of Jove's n. sup, I would not change for thine B. JONS. Hence **Necta·rean** *a.* **Ne·ctared** *a.* filled, flavoured, or impregnated with n.; deliciously sweet or fragrant (*lit.* and *fig.*). **Necta·reous** *a.* consisting of n. **Necta·reous·ly** *adv.*, **-ness.** **Nectari·ferous** *a.* bearing or producing n. **Ne·ctarous** *a.* resembling n.

Nectarine (ne·ktărin, -īn), *sb.* 1616. [app. a sb. use of next.] A variety of the common peach, with a thinner and downless skin and a firmer pulp.

Nectarine (ne·ktărin), *a.* 1611. [f. NECTAR + -INE [2].] Of the nature of, sweet as, nectar.

‖ **Nectarium** (nektē·riŏm). Pl. **-ia.** 1753. [mod.L.] = NECTARY 2.

Nectary (ne·ktări). 1759. [f. NECTAR, or ad. mod.L. *nectarium*; see -ARY.] 1. *Bot.* The organ or part of a flower or plant which secretes honey. 2. *Entom.* A wart-like tube on the body of an aphis, from which 'honey-dew' is exuded 1890.

Nectocalyx (nektǫ̆kē̆·liks). *Pl.* **-calyces.** 1859. [mod.L., f. Gr. νηκτός swimming (f. νήχειν) + CALYX.] *Zool.* The swimming-bell which forms the natatory organ in many hydrozoans. So **Ne·ctosac,** the interior of a n. (also called *nectocyst*); **Ne·ctosome,** the upper portion of a siphonophore, bearing the natatory organs. **Ne·ctostem,** the axis of a series of nectocalyces. Hence **Nectoca·lycine** *a.* of the nature of, resembling or pertaining to, a n.

Nedder, obs. f. ADDER.

Neddy (ne·di). 1790. [Dim. of *Ned*, abbrev. of *Edward*; see -Y [6].] 1. A donkey. 2. *Cant.* A life-preserver 1864.

‖ **Née** (nē̆), *ppl. a.* 1835. [F., pa. pple. fem. of *naître*.] Born; used in adding a married woman's maiden name, as, Madame de Staël, *née* Necker.

Need (nīd), *sb.* [Com. Teut.: OE. *nēd*, *nīed* :—OTeut. **naudi-*; also *nēod* :—**neud-* (see NEED *v.*).] I. †1. Violence, constraint or compulsion, exercised upon or by persons –ME. 2. Necessity arising from the facts and circumstances of a case. Chiefly in phr. *if* (etc.) *n. require*, *if n. be* (or *were*), *there is no n.* OE. 3. In predic. use: Necessary, needful. Now *rare.* OE. 4. Imperative call or demand for the presence, possession, etc., *of* something OE. 5. A condition of affairs placing one in difficulty or distress; a time of difficulty or trouble OE. 6. A condition marked by the lack or want of some necessary thing, or requiring some extraneous aid or addition OE. b. A state of extreme want or destitution ME.

2. Repeat this if N. be WESLEY. There was no n. of you to confess it 1845. *To have n. to*, to be under a necessity to do something, to require to. †Also with omission of *to*, and with *that*. *Had n. to*, would require to, ought to. So with omission of *to*; The Portuguese had n. have the stomachs of ostriches BECKFORD. 3. Some Reformed Churches..have.. made themselves much poorer than was n. 1849. 4. The n. of further securities against the royal power GREEN. Phr. *To have n. of* (†*to*, †*unto*) the thing required. †Const. with direct object: To need, require; Here he had n. All circumspection MILT. Phr. *To have n.*, to be in straits or in want. Now *rare* or *Obs.* 5. I thank you for lending me a hand at my n. BUNYAN. Phr. *At n.*; Sir William of Deloraine, good at n. SCOTT. 6. The great n. of her heart compelled her to [etc.] GEO. ELIOT. *Prov.* A friend in n. is a friend indeed. b. When n. crept in, love walked out 1847.

II. †1. A matter requiring action to be taken; a piece of necessary business. In later use chiefly *pl.* Also *good n.*, good service –1508. †b. Chiefly *pl.* One's errands or business –1550. 2. A particular point or respect in which some necessity or want is present or is felt OE.

2. Servile subjection to daily needs 1874. †*At a n.*, in an emergency or crisis. So †*in a n.* †*For a n.*, in an emergency.

Need (nīd), *v.* [OE. *nēodian* (rare), f. *nēod* NEED *sb.*] I. *intr.* †1. *It needs*, it is needful or necessary. Usu. const. with *that* or inf., and occas. without *it.* –1765. 2. *There needs*, there is need for (some thing or person) 1440. †b. *What needs . . ?* What need is there for (something)? –1662. c. *It needs*, it requires 1839. 3. *impers.* Of things: To be needful or necessary 1526.

2. There needes no such Apologie SHAKS. c. It needs heaven-sent moments for this skill M. ARNOLD. 3. But little learning needs in noble blood DRYDEN.

II. †1. To be needful or necessary *to* a person, or *to* some end or purpose –1496. †2. Impersonally: a. To be necessary for (one) *to* do something –1590. †b. So *What need(s . . ?* Why should (one)? –1597.

2. b. What nedeth me then to laboure eny more for wyszdome? COVERDALE *Eccl.* ii. 15.

III. †1. To have need *of* (also *to*) a thing –1598. 2. *trans.* To stand in need of, to require. late ME. b. *intr.* To be in need or want. late ME. 3. To be under a necessity or obligation *to* do something. late ME. b. With omission of *to*, when the clause has the forms *it* (*he*, *I*, etc.) *need not*, (*why*) *need* (*it*, etc.)? 1470.

2. Pickwick needed no second invitation DICKENS. b. Betere is to dyen, than to neden WYCLIF *Ecclus.* xl. 29. 3. Vice..to be hated, needs but to be seen POPE. b. I n. hardly ask again JOWETT. Hence **Nee·ded** *ppl. a.* required. **Nee·der.**

†**Need,** *adv.* [OE. *nēde*, etc., orig. the instrumental case of *nēd* NEED *sb.*] Of necessity, necessarily, etc. –1732.

Nee·dfire. 1535. [prob. OE. **nēdfȳr* (NEED *sb.*, FIRE *sb.*)] †1. *Sc.* Spontaneous combustion. Only in phr. *to take n.* –1669. 2. Fire obtained from dry wood by means of violent friction, formerly used as a means of curing disease among cattle 1633. 3. A beacon or bonfire 1805.

Needful (nī·dfŭl), *a.* (and *sb.*) ME. [f. NEED *sb.* + -FUL.] 1. Of persons: Needy, necessitous. Now *rare.* 2. Of circumstances, occasions, etc.: Characterized by need or necessity. Now *rare.* ME. 3. Requisite, necessary. Also const. *to* or *for* the person or thing concerned. ME. 4. *The n.*, what is necessary or requisite 1709. b. *colloq.* The necessary funds; money, cash 1774. 5. *sb.* A necessary thing 1856.

2. Why..hydest [thou] thy face in that neadeful tyme of trouble *Bible* (Cranmer) *Ps.* x. 1. 3. We myght doo any nedeful busynesse upon the Sunday 1545. Phr. *It is n. that* or *to* (with inf.). 4. To live I must have 'the n.' C. BRONTË. Hence **Nee·dful-ly** *adv.*, **-ness.**

†**Nee·dham.** 1573. Name of a small town (Needham Market) near Ipswich in Suffolk, used punningly with allusion to NEED *sb.*; hence, need, poverty, beggary –1661.

They are said to be in the high way to N. who do hasten to poverty FULLER.

Needle (nī·d'l), *sb.* [OE. *nǣdl* fem. :—pre-Teut. **nētlā*, f. the root **nē-* to sew, which appears prob. in L. *nēre* to spin, Gr. νῆσις spinning, νῆμα thread. The ME. metathetic form *neld(e* is still represented dial.] I. 1. A small and slender piece of polished steel having a fine point at one end and at the other a hole or eye (see EYE *sb.*) for thread; used in sewing. b. *transf.* A needlewoman (*rare*) 1834. 2. a. A piece of magnetized steel (orig. a needle in sense 1) used as an indicator of direction (in later use as a part of the COMPASS), or in connexion with magnetic or electric apparatus, e. g. the telegraph. late ME. Also *ellipt.* = needle telegraph. b. A small strip of gold or silver of known fineness used with a touchstone in testing the purity of other pieces of those metals 1469. c. The tongue of a balance 1589. 3. a. A pointed instrument used in engraving or etching 1662. b. *Surg.* A long slender pointed instrument used in operations; the end of a hypodermic or other syringe; a pointed electrode used in surgical electrolysis 1727. c. In breech-loading fire-arms, a slender steel pin which ignites the cartridge by impact 1853. 4. a. A knitting or netting pin 1719. b. One of the parallel pieces of wire in a stocking frame or in the Jacquard loom 1839. 5. *Mining.* A sharp-pointed copper or brass rod with which a small hole is made through the stemming to the cartridge in blasting operations 1839.

1. *Sharp as a n.*: see the adj. *Pins and needles*: see PIN *sb.* *fig.* Catherine ran infinite pins and needles of speech into them READE. Phr. *To look for*, or *seek*, *a n. in a meadow*, *haystack*, *bottle* (*truss* or *bundle*) *of hay*, to attempt a hopeless task. *Needle's eye*, denoting the smallest possible opening or space, chiefly with ref. to *Matt.* xix. 24, etc. 2. a. *Magnetic n.*, a magnetized rod turning on a pivot, as in a mariner's compass; so *mariner's n.* 3. d. The thin pointed piece of metal, wood, etc., that receives and transmits the vibrations set up by a revolving gramophone disk 1902.

II. 1. A pillar or obelisk. late ME. 2. A sharp-pointed mass of rock; *esp.* in *pl.* as the name of those to the west of the Isle of Wight. late ME. 3. A beam of wood, *esp.* one used as a temporary support for a wall during underpinning 1471. 4. *Chem.* and *Min.* A crystal or spicule resembling a needle in shape 1712. 5. One of the leaves of the fir and pine trees 1798. 6. *slang. The n.*, a fit of irritation or nervousness 1887.

Comb.: **n.-bath,** a shower-bath with a very fine and strong spray; **-bolt,** the bolt which carries the n. in a needle-gun; **-book,** a needle-case shaped like a book; **-case,** a case in which needles are kept; **-dial,** a dial bearing a n. in an electrical apparatus; **-furze** or **gorse,** *Genista anglica*; **-lace,** lace made with the n., as opp. to bobbin-lace; **-syringe,** a sharp-pointed hypodermic syringe; **-telegraph,** a telegraph in which the n. is employed as an indicator; **-worm,** a small worm parasitic in horses.

Needle (nī·d'l), *v.* 1715. [f. prec.] 1. *trans.* To sew or pierce with (or as with) a needle. b. To penetrate; to pierce or thread (one's way); to underpin with needle-beams, etc. 1820. 2. *intr.* a. To form acicular crystals. b. To pass through, or in and out, like a needle. c. To use the needle, to sew. 1780.

Nee·dle-fish. 1601. [NEEDLE *sb.* I. 1.] A name for various fishes; esp. the pipe-fish or gar-fish.

Nee·dleful. 1611. [NEEDLE *sb.* I. 1.] The amount of thread which is put into a needle at one time.

Nee·dle-gun. 1865. [NEEDLE *sb.* I. 3 c.] A gun in which the cartridge is exploded by the impact of a needle.

Nee·dle-point. 1700. [NEEDLE *sb.* I. 1.] 1. The point of a needle; also *transf.* 2. Point-lace made with the needle 1869. So **Nee·dle-pointed** *a.* 1599. Chiefly *fig.*

Needler (nī·dləɹ). ME. [f. NEEDLE *sb.* + -ER [1].] A needle-maker.

Needless (nī·dlĕs), *a.* ME. [f. NEED *sb.* + -LESS.] †1. In quasi-advb. use: Without any compulsion or necessity; needlessly –1475. 2. Not needed; unnecessary, useless ME. (Common from *c* 1570.) †3. Having no want; not in need –1668.

2. The message was n. MACAULAY. Beware of.. questions which raise n. doubts 1880. 3. *A. Y. L.* II. i. 46. Hence **Nee·dless-ly** *adv.*, **-ness.**

Nee·dlestone. 1820. [ad. G. *nadelstein.*] *Min.* A name formerly given to minerals having needle-like crystals, as natrolite and scolecite.

Nee·dlewoman. 1611. [NEEDLE *sb.* I. 1.] A woman who works with the needle; a sempstress. Also with qualification, as *good*, *bad.*

Nee·dlework. late ME. [f. NEEDLE *sb.* I. 1.] 1. Work done with the needle; sewing, embroidery, or fancy work. †b. *pl.* Pieces or kinds of this –1748. So **Nee·dleworker** 1611.

Needly (nī·dli), *a. rare.* 1671. [f. NEEDLE *sb.* + -Y [1].] Resembling a needle or needles.

†**Nee·dly,** *adv.* ME. [f. NEED *sb.* + -LY [2].] Necessarily; of necessity –1647.

Needment (nī·dmĕnt). 1590. [f. NEED *sb.* or *v.*] 1. *pl.* Things needed; *esp.* personal necessaries carried as luggage. 2. *pl.* Needs, requirements 1603.

1. Carrying each his needments tied up in a pocket-handkerchief WORDSW.

Needs (nīdz), *adv.* [OE. *nēdes*; see NEED *sb.* and -S.] Of necessity, necessarily. Now chiefly with *must* (colloq. often iron. implying foolish or perverse insistence).

Stooping down as n. he must Who cannot sit upright COWPER. The Squire must n. have something of the old ceremonies observed on the occasion W. IRVING. She shall go, if n. must BROWNING.

†**Nee·dsly,** *adv.* 1449. [f. as prec. + -LY [2].] Of necessity. (Usu. with *must.*) –1656.

Needy (nī·di), *a.* ME. [f. NEED *sb.* + -Y [1].] 1. Of persons: Poor, necessitous. †b. In need *of* a thing (*rare*) –1601. 2. Of circumstances: Characterized by poverty or need 1574. †3. Needful, necessary –1608.

1. What time the pore and nedye are releved 1560. The n. Cheat, The poor and friendless Villain POPE. 2. In his needie shop a Tortoyrs hung SHAKS. 3. *Per.* I. iv. 95. Hence †**Nee·dily** *adv.* **Nee·diness.**

Neeld, obs. and dial. f. NEEDLE.

Neem (nīm). 1824. [a. Hindī *nīm*, Skr. *nimba.*] An E. Indian tree, the margosa.

Neep (nīp). *Sc.* and *n. dial.* [OE. *nǣp*, ad. L. *nāpus.*] A turnip.

Neer, obs. f. NEAR.

Ne'er (nēᵊɹ), *adv. dial.* or *poet.* ME. Contr. f. NEVER, as *e'er* for *ever.*] 1. Never. b. *Sc.* Euphem. for *deil*, devil. SCOTT. 2. *Ne'er the less* = NEVERTHELESS ME.

Ne'er a, *adj. phr. dial.* or *poet.* Also **narrow a, narra.** late ME. [f. prec. + A *adj.*[2]] Never a, not a, no.

Ne'er-do-well, *sb.* and *a.* Also *Sc.* and *n.* -weel. 1737. **A.** *sb.* One who never does, and never will do, well; a good-for-nothing. **B.** *adj.* Good-for-nothing, worthless 1773.

Neeze (nīz), *v.* Now *Sc.* and *n. dial.* [ME. *nēsen*, prob. ad. ON. *hnjósa*; prob. imitative. Cf. FNESE.] To sneeze. Hence **Nee·zing** *vbl. sb.* (*n.-powder*).

‖**Nef** (nef, nęf). 1687. [F., ship, etc. :—L. *navem*; cf. NAVE *sb.*[2]] †**1.** The nave of a church -1775. **2.** An incense-boat 1867.

Nefandous (nĭfæ·ndəs), *a.* *Obs.* or *arch.* 1640. f.] L. *nefandus*, f. *ne* not + *fandus*, gerundive of *fari* to speak.] Not to be spoken of; unmentionable, abominable.

Many n. crimes 1640. A most n. error 1827.

Nefarious (nĭfē³·riəs), *a.* 1604. [f. L. *nefarius*, f. *nefas* wrong, impiety; see -OUS.] Wicked, iniquitous, villainous. So **Nefa·riously** *adv.* 1599.

Negate (nĭgē¹·t), *v.* 1623. [f. L. *negat-*, *negare.*] *trans.* To deny, negative; to deny the existence of; to destroy, nullify, render ineffective. (Freq. in recent use.)

Negation (nĭgē¹·ʃən). 1530. [a. F., or ad. L. *negationem.*] **1.** The action of denying or of making a statement involving the use of 'no', 'not', 'never', etc. Also const. *of.* **b.** An instance of this; a refusal or contradiction; a denial 1576. **c.** *Logic.* Opp. to AFFIRMATION 3. 1570. **2.** The absence or opposite of something which is actual, positive, or affirmative 1642. **3.** A negative or unreal thing, a nonentity; a thing whose essence consists in the absence of something positive 1707.

1. This is the n. of God erected into a system of Government GLADSTONE. **2.** Death is nothing more than the n. of life FIELDING. Hence **Nega·tional** *a.* negative, using or involving n. 1865. **Nega·tionist**, one who denies accepted beliefs without advancing anything positive in their place 1856.

Negative (ne·gătiv), *sb.* late ME. [f. next, or a. F. *négative.*] **1.** †**a.** A negative command, a prohibition -1581. **b.** A negative statement or proposition; a negative mode of stating anything 1567. **c.** A negative reply; †a denial or refusal 1571. **2.** A negative word or particle; a negative term 1567. †**3.** A right of veto -1796. †**b.** A negative or adverse vote -1743. **4.** *Photogr.* A print made on prepared glass or other transparent substance by the direct action of light, in which the lights and shadows of nature are reversed, and from which positive prints are made 1853.

1. a. The text Deut. 6 hath the negative, Thou shalt serue no strange gods 1581. **b.** I am not bound to prove a n. *Junius Lett.* xliv. (1788) 252. **c.** Dreading a n. COWPER. **2.** If your foure negatiues make your two affirmatiues, why then the worse for my friends SHAKS. Phr. *The negative*: The side, position, or aspect of a question which is opposed to the affirmative or positive. *In the n.*: †(*a*) In the face of, in opposition to, something. †(*b*) On the negative side of a question. (*c*) In favour of or with the effect of rejecting a proposal or suggestion. (*d*) With denial or negation; negatively; of a negative character.

Negative (ne·gătiv), *a.* late ME. [ad. F. *négatif, -ive*, or late L. *negativus*; see NEGATE *v.* and -IVE.] **I.** †**1.** Of persons: Making denial of something -1736. **2.** Expressing, conveying, or implying negation or denial 1509. **b.** *spec.* in *Logic*, of propositions, etc., or names 1551. **3. a.** Of commands, etc.: Prohibitory 1526. **b.** Expressing refusal; refusing consent to a proposal or motion 1535. **c.** Able to impose a veto (now *rare*) 1648.

1. *Wint. T.* I. ii. 274. **2.** There are two n. conclusions which seeme necessary 1649. **b.** Names, called N., which are notes to signifie that a word is not the name of the thing in question HOBBES. A n. proposition..asserts a difference or discrepancy JEVONS. **3. b.** They..yealded to his request, notwithstanding my negatiue voyce 1576. **c.** Denying me any power of a N. voice as King *Eikon Bas.* vi (1662) 20.

II. 1. Characterized by the absence of distinguishing features; devoid of positive attributes 1565. **2.** In *Algebra*, denoting quantities which are to be subtracted from other quantities, or from zero; marked by the sign —. 1673. **b.** *N. sign*, the sign — used to mark a negative quantity 1704. **3.** Applied to the kind of electricity produced by friction upon resin, wax, gutta-percha, etc., as dist. from that produced by rubbed glass, which is called *positive* 1755. **b.** Characterized by the presence or production of negative electricity 1799. **4.** Extending or reckoned on the other side of the point from which the positive is measured, or in an opposite direction to that regarded as positive 1802. **5.** *Photogr.* Characterized by a reversal of the lights and shadows of the object, scene, etc. 1840.

1. A man who..was thought to be made choice of only for his n. qualities CLARENDON.

Comb.: **n. crystal**, (*a*) a crystal in which the index of refraction is greater for the ordinary than the extraordinary ray; (*b*) a crystalliform cavity in a mineral mass; **n. eye-piece**, one consisting of two plano-convex lenses, the convex sides of both being turned towards the object-glass. Hence **Ne·gatively** *adv.*, **-ness**. **Negati·vity**, the fact or quality of being n. 1860.

Negative (ne·gătiv), *v.* 1706. [f. prec.] **1.** *trans.* **a.** *U.S.* To reject (a person proposed for some office). **b.** *U.S.* To veto (a bill, etc.) 1749. **2.** To reject, set aside (a proposal, motion, etc.); to refuse to entertain or countenance 1778. **3.** To disprove; to show to be false 1790; to deny, contradict 1812. **4.** To neutralize 1837.

2. Resolutions..were negatived without a division 1812. Taxation..implies compact, and negatives any right to plunder COLERIDGE. **3.** All our reasonings seemed to be negatived by the results 1853.

Negatory (ne·gătŏri), *a.* 1580. [ad. F. *négatoire.*] Of the nature of negation.

Neger (nī·gəɹ). *Sc.* and *n. dial.* 1568. [ad. F. *nègre*, ad. Sp. *negro* NEGRO.] A negro.

Neglect (nĭgle·kt), *sb.* 1588. [ad. L. *neglectus* (rare), f. *neglect-*, ppl. stem of *neglegere*; see next.] **1.** The fact of disregarding, slighting, or paying no attention to, a person, etc.; the fact or condition of being so treated; †a slight. **b.** Disregard *of*, or with respect to, something; †indifference 1597. **2.** Want of attention to what ought to be done; negligence. Also const. *of.* 1591. **b.** An omission or oversight (now *rare*) 1638.

1. Rescue my poor remains from vile n. PRIOR. **2.** Everybody fancies that his own n. will do no harm JOWETT. **b.** A province..gradually recovering from the effects of Mahratta ravages and neglects 1845. **Negle·ctful** *a.* careless; **-ly** *adv.*; **-ness** 1644.

Neglect (nĭgle·kt), *v.* 1529. [f. L. *neglect-*, *neglegere*, f. *neg-* not + *legere* to pick up.] **1.** *trans.* To disregard; to pay little or no respect or attention to; to slight. **2.** To fail to bestow proper attention or care upon 1538. **3.** To fail to perform, render, discharge (a duty), or take (a precaution) 1533. **4.** With *inf.* To omit through carelessness *to do* something 1548.

1. That noble discourse had been neglected by the generation to which it was addressed MACAULAY. **2.** Their own education..has been neglected JOWETT. **4.** If they n. To punish crime SHELLEY. Hence **Negle·ctable** *a.* **Negle·ctedly** *adv.* **Negle·cter, -or.** †**Negle·ctingly** *adv.* †**Negle·ction**, negligence, neglect. †**Negle·ctive** *a.* (common in 17th c.), neglectful, inattentive.

‖**Négligé** (ne·glizeⁱ, neglize). 1835. [F., pa. pple. of *négliger* to neglect.] Free and easy attire as worn by women, esp. before 'dressing'; also, a loose gown worn by women on certain informal occasions.

Negligee. *Obs.* or *Hist.* 1756. [ad. F. *négligé*; see prec. In sense 1 pron. (neglidʒi).] **1.** A kind of loose gown worn by women in the 18th c. **2.** A necklace of irregular beads 1841.

Negligence (ne·glidʒĕns). ME. [a. OF., or ad. L. *negligentia, -legentia*, f. *negligere*, to NEGLECT.] **1.** Want of attention to what ought to be done or looked after; lack of proper care in doing something. †**b.** Neglect -1778. **2.** An instance or act of inattention or careless behaviour. late ME. **3.** A careless indifference, as in appearance or costume, or in literary or artistic style; in later use esp. with suggestion of an agreeable absence of artificiality or restraint. late ME.

1. The deceased was also guilty of n. or of want of reasonable care contributing to the accident 1884. **b.** *Haml.* IV. v. 134. **2.** Our synnes, negligences, and ignoraunces 1549. **3.** Nothing is so modish as an agreeable N. ADDISON.

Negligent (ne·glidʒĕnt), *a.* late ME. [a. OF., or ad. L. *negligent-*, *negligens*, pres. pple. of *negligere* to neglect.] **1.** Of persons: Inattentive to what ought to be done; neglectful. Also const. *of.* **b.** Indifferent 1440. **2.** Of actions, conduct, etc.: Characterized by or displaying negligence or carelessness 1500.

1. To better him if he be n., to be like him if he be diligent 1581. **2.** O n. and heedlesse Discipline SHAKS. Hence **Ne·gligently** *adv.*

Negligible (ne·glidʒib'l), *a.* 1829. [a. L. *negligere* + -IBLE.] Capable of being neglected or disregarded.

Negotiable (nĭgōᵘ·ʃiăb'l), *a.* 1758. [f. NEGOTIATE *v.* + -ABLE.] **1.** Of bills, drafts, cheques, etc.: Capable of being negotiated; transferable or assignable in the course of business from one person to another. **2.** Admitting of being crossed, ascended, etc. 1880.

1. The funds and other n. securities MILL. **2.** That this [path] was n. was evident 1880. Hence **Negotiabi·lity**, n. quality 1828.

Negotiate (nĭgōᵘ·ʃieⁱt), *v.* 1599. [f. ppl. stem of L. *negotiare*, f. *negotium*, f. *neg-* not + *otium* ease.] **1.** *intr.* To confer (*with* another) for the purpose of arranging some matter by mutual agreement; to discuss a matter with a view to a settlement or compromise. †**b.** To traffic -1759. **2.** *trans.* To deal with, manage, or conduct (a matter, etc., requiring skill or consideration) 1619. **b.** To arrange for, bring about (something) by means of negotiation 1721. **3.** To transfer or assign (a bill, etc.) to another in return for something of equal value, to convert into cash or notes; to get or give value for (bills, cheques, etc.) in money 1682. **b.** To carry out, as a business or monetary transaction 1809. **4.** (Orig. *Hunting.*) To clear (a hedge or fence); to succeed in getting round, over, or through (an obstacle, etc.) 1862.

1. Both parties were now willing to n. with the view of gaining time BUCKLE. **2.** To n. this affair we sent a Turk 1703. **b.** It was impossible..to n. a sale of their effects PRESCOTT. **3.** When I paid it by these securities, you pledged yourself not to n. them LEVER. **4.** The first fence I negotiated successfully 1862. Hence **Nego·tiant**, **Nego·tiator**, †a trader; one who negotiates (a matter, bills, loans, etc.). **Nego·tiatress, -trix**, a female negotiator.

Negotiation (nĭgōᵘʃiē¹·ʃən). Also **-oci-**. 1579. [ad. L. *negotiationem*; see prec. and -ATION.] **1.** †**a.** A business transaction -1662. †**b.** Trading, traffic -1669. **2.** A course of treaty with another (or others) to bring about some result, esp. in affairs of state. Freq. in *pl.* 1579. **3.** The action or business of negotiating with others 1597. **4.** The action of getting over or round some obstacle by skilful manœuvring 1885.

1. b. The Phenicians..possessed themselves of the sea coasts, the better to carry on their n. 1669. **2.** The long n. of a political marriage was terminated by a war 1828. **3.** The established channels of peaceable n. WELLINGTON.

†**Nego·tious**, *a.* *rare.* 1603. [ad. L. *negotiosus*, f. *negotium*; see -OUS.] Involving, or given to, occupation or business -1656.

Negress (nī·grės). 1786. [ad. F. *négresse*; see NEGRO and -ESS.] A female negro.

Negrillo (nĭgri·lo). 1853. [a. Sp., dim. of NEGRO.] **a.** A little negro. **b.** One of a race of dwarfish negroes living in Central or Southern Africa 1866.

Negrito (nĭgrī·to). 1840. [a. Sp., dim. of NEGRO.] One of a diminutive negroid race existing in the Malayo-Polynesian region; esp. one of the Aëtas in the Philippine Islands.

Negro (nī·gro). 1555. [a. Sp. or Pg. *negro* :—L. *nigrum, niger* black. Cf. NEGER, NIGGER.] **I.** An individual (esp. a male) belonging to the African race of mankind, which is distinguished by a black skin, black woolly hair, flat nose, and thick protruding lips. Also *transf.* in various uses.

Phr. †*To wash a n.*, to attempt an impossible task (*rare*, chiefly 17th c.). *Comb.* **negro's head**, the Ivory Palm.

II. *attrib.* (passing into *adj.*). **1.** With names of persons: Belonging to the race of negroes; black-skinned 1594. **2.** Consisting of, inhabited by, of or belonging to, a negro or negroes 1652.

1. I bought me a N. Slave DE FOE. *N. minstrels*: a troupe of comic entertainers, having blackened hands and faces, who sing plantation songs in the manner of American negroes. **2.** A N. School 1740. Abyssinia and the N. countries 1841.

In spec. uses, as **n. ant**, a blackish ant; **n. corn**,

the Turkish millet or dhurra; **n. monkey,** a black monkey of the Malay Peninsula, Java, etc. (*Semnopithecus maurus*).

Negro-head. 1839. 1. A strong black plug tobacco. 2. An inferior quality of india-rubber 1881.

Negroid (nī·groid). 1859. [f. NEGRO; see -OID.] A. *adj.* Of a negro type. B. *sb.* A person of a negro type 1859. Hence **Negroi·dal** *a.*

Negrophil (nī·grofil). Also **-phile.** 1803. [f. NEGRO + -PHIL or a. F. *négrophile.*] A friend of the negroes; one who favours the advancement of negro interests or rights. So **Negro·philism** 1865. **Negro·philist** 1842.

Negrophobia (nīgrofōu·biă). 1833. [f. NEGRO + -PHOBIA.] Intense dislike of the negro. **Negropho·biac** *a.* **Negro·phobist.**

‖**Negus**[1] (nī·gʊs). 1594. [Amharic *negus* or *n'gus* kinged, king.] Title of the supreme ruler of Abyssinia.

Negus[2] (nī·gʊs). 1743. [Inventor's name, Col. Francis *Negus* (died 1732).] Wine (esp. port or sherry) and hot water, sweetened, and flavoured with lemon and spice.

Neif (nīf). Now only *Hist.* 1532. [a. AF. :—L. *nativum* NATIVE.] One born in a state of bondage; occas. *spec.* a female serf.

Neigh (nēi), *sb.* 1513. [f. next.] The natural cry or call of the horse.

Neigh (nēi), *v.* [OE. *hnǣgan* (imitative).] 1. *intr.* Of a horse: To utter its characteristic cry. 2. *trans.* To utter in or as in neighing 1623.

1. *transf.* Adultery neighing at his neighbour's door COWPER.

Neighbour (nēi·bəɹ), *sb.* [OE. *nēahgebūr* (f. *nēah* NIGH *a.* + *gebūr*; see BOOR).] 1. One who lives near or next to another; e.g. in an adjoining house, or in the same street or village. b. More widely, in echoes of Biblical passages (as Luke x. 27) ME. 2. a. (Chiefly *pl.*) One who dwells in an adjacent town, district, or land. Also applied to the rulers of adjacent countries. OE. b. A person or thing which is in close proximity to another 1567. 3. In *attrib.* use, passing into *adj.* Living or situate near or close to some other person or thing. Now *rare* with names of persons and abstract sbs. 1530.

1. Come, neighbours, we must wag COWPER. Near neighbors are seldom good ones 1790. b. The name of n. containeth..also those whom we know not, yea, and our enemies 1570. 2. a. Nowe that he possesseth Lorayne, he shall be their nere n. 1560. b. *fig. Rich. III*, IV. ii. 43. 3. Our Neighbour-Shepheard's Sonne SHAKS. The Neighbor roome SHAKS. All our Neighbour-States 1668.

Neighbour (nēi·bəɹ), *v.* 1586. [f. prec.] I. *intr.* 1. Of persons: To live near or close *to* a person, place, etc.; to border *upon.* Also freq. with *near.* Now *arch.* 2. Of things or places: To lie near or close (*to* or *upon* something else); to be contiguous *with* 1592. 3. To be on neighbourly terms with others 1820.

1. Let us..beare affection..unto such as N. at any time neere unto us 1615. 2. A copse that neighbours by SHAKS. 3. The Welsh won't n. with them BORROW.

II. *trans.* 1. To lie next or close to, border upon 1586. b. To approach 1859. 2. a. To bring near *to* something 1662. b. To place in conjunction *with* something 1791.

1. He seemed..to suck in fresh vigour from the soil which he neighboured LAMB. *Neighboured by* or *with*, (*a*) having (some person or thing) as near neighbour or close at hand; (*b*) brought or placed near *to* some person or thing. 2. a. The barbarous Scythian ..shall to my bosome Be as well neighbour'd SHAKS.

Neighboured (nēi·bəɹd), *ppl. a.* 1562. [f. NEIGHBOUR *sb.* or *v.* + -ED.] Having neighbours or surroundings (of a specified kind).

Neighbourhood (nēi·bəɹhud). 1449. [f. NEIGHBOUR *sb.* + -HOOD.] 1. Friendly relations between neighbours; neighbourly feeling or conduct. 2. The quality, condition, or fact of being neighbours or lying near to something; nearness 1567. 3. The vicinity, or near situation, *of* something 1577. 4. Resort or haunt of persons near one; company; neighbours 1596. 5. A community; a certain number of people who live close together 1625. 6. The people living near to a certain place 1686. b. A district, freq. considered in ref. to the character or circumstances of its inhabitants 1697.

1. There is a Law of N. which does not leave a man perfect master on his own ground BURKE. Phr. The rules of *good n.* 2. Then the prison and the palace were in awful n. LYTTON. 3. Phr. *In the n. of*, somewhere about. 4. Immediate n. I have none, save one family 1800. 6. b. The back slums of his ferocious n. DISRAELI. 7. *attrib.*, as *n. meeting, party, school.*

Nei·ghbouring, *ppl. a.* 1601. [f. NEIGHBOUR *v.* + -ING[2].] That neighbours; lying or living near, adjacent.

The n. monarchies BURKE. A n. bush 1863.

Neighbourly (nēi·bəɹli), *a.* 1558. [f. NEIGHBOUR *sb.* + -LY[1].] 1. Characteristic of a neighbour or neighbours; friendly, kindly. 2. Of persons: Inclined to act as neighbours; situated as neighbours 1612.

1. He hath a n. charitie in him SHAKS. 2. Farmers as a rule are n. 1886. Hence **Nei·ghbourliness.** So **Nei·ghbourly** *adv.* after the manner of neighbours 1525.

Nei·ghbourship. 1456. [f. as prec. + -SHIP.] 1. The state or fact of being a neighbour; nearness, propinquity. Also *pl.* 2. Neighbourly relations 1456.

Neither (nəi·ðəɹ, nī·ðəɹ), *adv.* (*conj.*) and *a.* [Early ME. *naiðer, neyþer*, etc., alterations of *na*(*u*)*ther*, NO(U)THER, on analogy of EITHER.] A. *adv.* (*conj.*) 1. Introducing the mention of alternatives or different things, about each of which a negative statement is to be made. See quots. 2. = Nor, nor yet; and not, also not. Now used only when the alternatives are expressed in clauses or sentences. 1462. 3. Used to strengthen a preceding negative; = Either 1551. †b. Without a preceding negative –1742.

1. *Neither..nor.* Quarter was to be n. taken nor given MACAULAY. Phr. *N. here nor there*: see HERE *adv.* With another neg., usu. preceding. Now *rare.* Christianity abrogated no duty..neither for Jew nor Gentile 1849. With two sing. subjects and pl. vb. N. search nor labour are necessary JOHNSON. *Neither ..or.* Engaging to spare n. trouble or expence 1786. †*Neither..neither.* N. alwaies, n. to euery one, n. of euery sort 1620. 2. If there are no teachers, n. are there disciples JOWETT. 3. There were no books n. DISRAELI. b. *Com. Err.* v. i. 94.

B. 1. *adj.* Not the one or the other. late ME. 2. *absol.* as *pron.* ME. †b. *N. of both, of either* –1633. †c. Not any one, none (of more than two) –1846. d. With pl. vb. 1611.

1. Nothing n. way SHAKS. 2. N. of his visitors saw him 1870. b. *L.L.L.* v. ii. 459. c. Matter, Form, and Accidents; n. of which can be the Aristotelick Nature CUDWORTH. d. N. of us are the proper judges 1781.

‖**Nek.** *S. Afr.* 1834. [Du.] A neck between two hills.

Nekton (ne·ktǫn). 1895. [G.; ad. Gr. νηκτόν neut.: see NECTOCALYX.] Free-swimming organic life: opp. to *benthos* and *plankton.*

Nelly (ne·li). 1823. [perh. the feminine name.] A large sea-bird (*Ossifraga gigantea*) of the petrel group.

Nelson (ne·lsən). 1889. In *double, half, quarter n.*, etc., designations of holds in *Wrestling.*

‖**Nelumbium** (nīlʊ·mbiŏm). 1857. [mod. L., f. Singhalese *nelumbu* or *nelum.*] *Bot.* A genus of water-beans (also called *Nelumbo*), to which the lotus of Egypt and Asia belongs.

‖**Nemathecium** (nemăþī·ʃiŏm). *Pl.* **-ia.** 1830. [mod.L., f. Gr. νῆμα thread + θήκη box, sheath, etc.] *Bot.* A warty protuberance developed in some of the florideous algæ, usu. containing tetraspores. Hence **Nemathe·cial** *a.*

Nemathelminth (nemăþe·lminþ). 1890. [f. Gr. νήματ-, νῆμα thread + ἑλμινθ-, ἕλμινς worm.] *Zool.* One of that class of worms which includes the nematodes and related forms.

Nemato- (ne·mătǫ), comb. form of Gr. νῆμα, νήματος thread; as in **Ne·matoblast,** *Biol.* a blastema which develops into a spermatozoon. **Ne:matoca·lyx,** *Zool.* a calyx containing nematocysts, occurring in some *Hydromedusæ*; hence **Ne:matoca·lycine** *a.* **Ne:matoce·ratous** [Gr. κέρας horn] *a.*, *Entom.* having filiform antennæ. **Ne·matocyst,** *Zool.* a small cell in the external layer of jelly-fishes and other cœlenterates, containing a thread capable of being ejected and of producing a stinging sensation; a lasso-cell or thread-cell. **Ne·matogen,** *Biol.*, in Dicyemids, the form which produces a filiform embryo; hence **Ne:matoge·nic, Nemato·genous** *adjs.* **Ne·matognath** [Gr. γνάθος jaw], *Zool.* a fish of the sub-order *Nematognathi*; a catfish; also **Ne:mato·gnathous** *a.* **Ne·matophore,** *Zool.* a special cup-shaped process of the cœnosarc in certain hydrozoans, having nematocysts at the extremity; hence **Nemato·phorous** *a.*

Nematode (ne·mătōud), *a.* and *sb.* 1861. [See NEMATO- and -ODE.] 1. *adj.* Of worms: Pertaining to the class *Nematoda* or *Nematoidea*, comprising those of a cylindrical or slender thread-like form (chiefly parasitic in animals and plants), such as the common round-worm, maw-worm, etc. 2. [Partly *attrib.* uses of 3.] Pertaining to, or characteristic of worms of this class 1866. 3. *sb.* A nematode worm 1865. **Ne·matoid** *a.* and *sb.*

Nem. con. 1588. Abbrev. of L. phr. *nemine contradicente* 'no one dissenting or opposing', without a dissentient voice.

Nemean (nīmī·ăn, nī·miăn), *a.* 1588. [f. L. *Nem*(*e*)*æus, Nemēus*, ad. Gr. Νεμεαῖος, Νέμεος, f. Νεμέα.] Of or belonging to Nemea, a wooded district near Argos in Greece. 1. *N. lion*, a lion killed by Hercules at Nemea. 2. *N. games* or *festival*, a Greek festival, held at Nemea in the second and fourth years of each Olympiad 1656.

Nemertean (nīmə·ɹtiăn), *sb.* and *a.* 1861. [f. mod.L. *Nemertes*, a. Gr. Νημερτής name of a sea-nymph.] = NEMERTINE *sb.* and *a.*

Neme·rtid. 1870. [f. as prec. + -ID.] A nemertean form. Also *attrib.* or as *adj.*

Nemertine (nīmə·ɹtəin). 1851. [f. as prec. + -INE.] A. *adj.* Belonging to the class of flat-worms (chiefly marine) known as *Nemertina, Nemertida*, or *Nemertea*, usu. having an elongated, very contractile body, and often brilliantly coloured. B. *sb.* A flat-worm of the class *Nemertina*; a ribbon-worm 1875.

Nemesia (nīmī·ʒiă). 1886. [mod. L. (1803).] A plant of a S. African genus of flowering plants, a few species of which are cultivated as hardy annuals.

Nemesis (ne·mĭsis). 1553. [a. Gr. νέμεσις (f. νέμειν to give what is due), righteous indignation, also personified as 'the goddess of Retribution'.] 1. The goddess of retribution; hence, one who avenges or punishes. 2. Retributive justice; an instance of this 1597.

2. Guilt..produces a fear of the divine N. 1733.

‖**Nemophila** (nīmǫ·filă). Also *erron.* **-phyl(l)a.** 1838. [mod.L., f. Gr. νέμος glade + -φιλος -PHIL.] *Bot.* A genus of ornamental herbaceous annuals (N.O. *Hydrophyllaceæ*), esp. *N. insignis*; a plant of this genus.

Nemoral (ne·mŏrăl), *a. rare.* 1656. [ad. L. *nemoralis*, f. *nemor-*, *nemus* grove.] Of, living in, or frequenting groves or woods.

Nenuphar (ne·niufāɹ). 1425. [a. med.L., ad. Arab.-Pers. *nīnūfar, nīlūfar*, ad. Skr. *nīlōtpala* blue lotus, f. *nīl* blue + *utpala* lotus, water-lily.] A water-lily, esp. the common white or yellow species.

Neo- (nī·o), comb. form of Gr. νέος new (as in νεόγαμος newly married), common in recent use as a prefix to adjs. and sbs.

1. a. In combs. denoting a new or modern form of some doctrine, belief, practice, language, etc., or designating those who advocate, adopt, or use it, as *N.-Anglican, -Christian, -Darwinian*, etc.; *N.-Anglicanism, -Christianity, -Darwinianism*, etc. b. *Chem.* designating certain more recently discovered varieties of isomeric hydrocarbons, as *n.-paraffins.* c. *Geol.* denoting the most recent division of a period, as *N.-cambrian, -devonian*, etc. d. In terms denoting sciences or scientists that deal with recent forms of animals and plants, as *neo-botany, -botanist.* 2. In misc. combs., as **Neoa·rctic** *a.* = NEARCTIC. **Ne·ocene** *a. Geol.* belonging to the later Tertiary (Miocene and Pliocene). **Neoco·smic** *a.* (see PALÆOCOSMIC). **Neogæan, -gean** (nī,ǫdʒī·ăn) *a.*, of or pertaining to the New World or western hemisphere. **Neogra·phic** *a.*, of the nature of, pertaining to, a new system of writing or spelling. **Neomo·rphism,** the process of change into a new form.

Neocomian (nī,okōu·miăn), *a.* and *sb.* 1843. [ad. F. *Néocomien*, f. *Neocomium* (f. Gr. νέος new + κώμη village), latinized form of *Neuchâtel.*] Belonging to or characteristic of the series of lower cretaceous rocks found at Neuchâtel in Switzerland; *sb.* the Neocomian series or period 1888.

Neodamode (nīˌǫ·dămōᵘd). 1808. [ad. Gr. νεοδαμώδης, f. νέος new + δᾶμος, δῆμος people.] *Gr. Antiq.* Among the ancient Spartans, an enfranchised Helot. Chiefly *attrib.*

Neodymium (nī·odi·mi*ǒ*m). 1886. [f. NEO- and DIDYMIUM.] *Chem.* A rare metallic element separated from praseodymium in 1885 by Auer von Welsbach.

Neolithic (nīˌoli·þik), *a.* 1865. [f. Gr. νέος new + λίθος stone.] *Archæol.* Of or belonging to the later stone age, characterized by the use of ground or polished stone implements and weapons.

Neologian (nīˌolōᵘ·dʒiăn). 1831. [f. NEOLOGY + -AN.] **A.** *adj.* **1.** Inclined towards theological neologism 1833. **2.** Of the nature of, marked by, neologism (sense 2) 1831.

2. The n. article about German divinity MACAULAY.

B. *sb.* A neologist (sense 2) 1846.

Neolo·gic, -al, *a.* 1754. [See NEOLOGY and -IC, -ICAL.] Of the nature of, characterized by, neologism (sense 2) 1827.

Neologism (niˌǫ·lŏdʒiz'm). 1800. [ad. F. *néologisme*; see NEOLOGY and -ISM.] **1.** The use of, or the practice of using, new words. **b.** A new word or expression 1803. **2.** Tendency to, adoption of, novel (rationalistic) views in theology or matters of religion 1827.

1. b. Scotticisms, neologisms..dance through each page 1803.

Neologist (niˌǫ·lŏdʒist). 1785. [= F. *néologiste*; see NEOLOGY and -IST.] **1.** One who invents or uses new words or forms. **2.** One who rationalizes in theology or religious matters 1827.

2. The Neologists of the present day deny that the miracles took place in the manner related in the sacred record J. H. NEWMAN.

Neologize (niˌǫ·lŏdʒəiz), *v.* 1846. [ad. F. *néologiser*: see NEOLOGY and -IZE.] **1.** *intr.* To invent or use new words or phrases. **2.** To introduce or accept new theological doctrines 1882.

Neology (niˌǫ·lŏdʒi). 1797. [ad. F. *néologie*, f. *néo-* NEO- + *-logie*, Gr. -λογία; see -LOGY.] = NEOLOGISM 1 and 2.

‖**Neomenia** (nīˌomī·niă). late ME. [eccl. L., a. Gr. νεομηνία, f. νέος new NEO- + μήνη moon.] In Gr. and Jewish antiq., the time of the new moon, the beginning of the lunar month; also, the festival held at that time.

Neon (nī·ǫn). 1898. [Gr. νέον, neut. of νέος new.] *Chem.* An atmospheric gas discovered in 1898.

Neonomian (nīˌonōᵘ·miăn). 1692. [f. Gr. νέος NEO- + νόμος law, after ANTINOMIAN.] *sb.* One who maintains that the Gospel is a new law taking the place of the old or Mosaic law. *adj.* Pertaining to the assertion of a new law. Hence **Neono·mianism.**

Neophyte (nī·ŏfəit). Also **-phite.** 1451. [ad. F., or eccl. L. *neophytus*, ad. Gr. νεόφυτος (1 Tim. iii. 6), lit. 'newly planted', f. νέος NEO- + φυτόν plant, φυτεύειν to plant. Not in gen. use bef. the 19th c.] **1.** A new convert, esp. with ref. to the primitive Christian Church. **2.** One who is newly initiated into anything; a novice 1599.

2. *attrib.* A certain neophite and girlish trepidation 1883. **Ne·ophytic, -phytish** *adjs.* **Ne·ophytism.**

Neoplasm (nī·oplæz'm). 1864. [f. NEO- + Gr. πλάσμα formation.] *Path.* A new formation of tissue in some part of the body; a tumour. So **Neopla·sma** (*pl.* -ata). **Neopla·stic** *a.*

Neoplatonic (nīˌoplăt*ǫ*·nik), *a.* 1836. [f. NEO- + PLATONIC *a.*] Of or pertaining to Neoplatonism or the Neoplatonists. Hence **Neoplato·nically** *adv.* So **Neoplatoni·cian** *a.* Neoplatonic 1831; *sb.* a Neoplatonist 1842.

Neoplatonism (nīˌoplē¹·tŏniz'm). 1845. [f. NEO- + PLATONISM.] A philosophical and religious system, chiefly consisting of a mixture of Platonic ideas with Oriental mysticism, which originated at Alexandria in the 3rd c., and is esp. represented in the writings of Plotinus, Porphyry, and Proclus. **Neopla·tonist** 1837.

Neossine (niˌǫ·səin). 1849. [f. Gr. νεοσσός a young bird + -INE⁵.] The substance of which the edible birds' nests of the East are made, being a mucus secreted by the salivary glands of a genus of swifts (*Collocalia*). Hence **Neo·ssidine.**

Neoteric (nīˌote·rik). 1577. [ad. late L. *neotericus* adj. and sb., ad. Gr. νεωτερικός, f. νεώτερος, compar. of νέος new.] **A.** *adj.* Recent, new, modern. **B.** *sb.* A modern; esp. a modern writer or author 1598.

A. Our n. sages 1876. The n. fashion of spending a honeymoon on the railway MEREDITH. B. A landscape of a justly admired n. LAMB.

Neoterism (niˌǫ·tĕriz'm). 1851. [ad. Gr. νεωτερισμός, f. νεωτερίζειν to make innovations.] The use of new words or phrases; a new term or expression. So **Neo·terist; Neoteri·stic** *a.*; **Neo·terize** *v.*

Neotro·pical, *a.* 1858. [f. NEO- + TROPICAL *a.*] Including, belonging to, or characteristic of, Tropical and South America as a zoogeographical region.

‖**Neoza** (niˌōᵘ·ză). 1832. [Bhutanese.] *N. pine*, a Himalayan pine (*Pinus Gerardiana*), the cones of which contain edible seeds.

Neozoic (nīˌozōᵘ·ik), *a.* 1854. [f. NEO- 1 c, after PALÆOZOIC.] *Geol.* **1.** Post-palæozoic (comprising both Mesozoic and Cainozoic). **2.** = CAINOZOIC 1873.

‖**Nepenthe** (nīpe·nþī). 1596. [var. of next.] **1.** = NEPENTHES 1. **b.** *Med.* A drink possessing sedative properties 1681. **2.** The plant supposed to supply the drug 1623.

1. A crystal glass, Mantling with bright N. SHELLEY.

‖**Nepenthes** (nīpe·nþīz). 1580. [L., a. Gr. νηπενθές (*Odyss.* iv. 221, qualifying φάρμακον), adj. neut., f. νη- not (see NE) + πένθος grief.] **1.** A drug of Egyptian origin mentioned in the Odyssey as capable of banishing grief or trouble from the mind; hence, any drug or potion having this power; also, occas. the plant supposed to yield the drug. **2.** A genus of plants (chiefly East Indian) in which the leaves have the form of pitchers; the Pitcher-plant 1747.

1. Where is..that herbe N. that procureth all delights? LYLY.

Nephalism (ne·făliz'm). *rare.* 1861. [ad. late Gr. νηφαλισμός, f. νηφάλιος sober.] Teetotalism. So **Ne·phalist.**

Nepheline (ne·fēlin). Also **-in.** 1814. [a. F. *néphéline*, f. Gr. νεφέλη cloud, because its fragments are rendered cloudy by immersion in nitric acid.] *Min.* A double silicate of aluminium and sodium, occurring chiefly in volcanic deposits in Italy. var. **Ne·phelite.**

Nephelo-, comb. form of Gr. νεφέλη; as in **Ne:phelodo·meter,** an instrument for ascertaining the distances of the clouds. **Nephelo·meter,** an instrument to register the comparative cloudiness of the sky.

Nephew (ne·viu, ne·fiu). ME. [a. OF. *neveu*:—L. *nepotem*, acc. of *nepos* grandson, nephew, descendant.] **1.** A brother's or sister's son; also, the son of a brother- or sister-in-law. **b.** *euphem.* The illegitimate son of an ecclesiastic 1587. †**2.** A niece –1585. †**3.** A grandson –1699. †**4.** A descendant –1676.

1. 'Mr. Jones your nephew, sir!'..'He is indeed.. my own sister's son' FIELDING. b. More papal 'nephews' had been stalled and mitred in the English Church DIXON. 3. Ye had your nevewes, sonnes of your chyldren, maryed LD. BERNERS. 4. Thy children's children & nephews to come 1597. Hence **Ne·phewship** 1647.

Nephology (nefǫ·lŏdʒi). 1890. [f. Gr. νέφος cloud + -LOGY.] That department of meteorology which treats of clouds.

Nephoscope (ne·fŏskōᵘp). 1881. [f. Gr. νέφος + -SCOPE.] An instrument used to determine the altitude, velocity, and direction of clouds.

‖**Nephralgia** (nĕfræ·ldʒiă). 1800. [mod.L., f. Gr. νεφρός kidney + -αλγία, f. ἄλγος pain.] *Path.* Pain in, or neuralgia of, the kidneys. Hence **Nephra·lgic** *a.*

Nephridium (nĕfri·di*ǒ*m). *Pl.* **-dia.** 1877. [mod.L., ad. Gr. *νεφρίδιον, dim. of νεφρός; cf. *gonidium*, etc.] *Zool.* A primitive excretory organ in the lower invertebrates, analogous in function to the kidney, but also, in some forms of Mollusca, used in reproduction. Hence **Nephri·dial** *a.* 1884.

Nephrite (ne·frəit). 1794. [a. G. *nephrit*, f. Gr. νεφρός, in allusion to its supposed efficacy in kidney disease; cf. JADE *sb.*²] *Min.* The mineral jade.

Nephritic (nĕfri·tik), *a.* 1580. [ad. late L. *nephriticus*, ad. Gr. νεφριτικός, f. νεφρῖτις NEPHRITIS.] **1.** Of pains, etc.: Affecting, having their seat or origin in, the kidneys; renal. †**2.** Of medicines, etc.: Helping to cure affections of the kidneys –1799. **3.** Affected with pain or disease in the kidneys 1656.

1. Chronic n. disease 1859. 2. Garlick is..Nephritick 1710. †*N. wood*, a wood of which the infusion (*n. tincture*) was formerly used as a remedy in diseases of the kidney. †*N. stone*, jade, nephrite –1811. 3. N. patients 1834.

Nephritis (nĕfrəi·tis). 1580. [ad. late L. *nephritis*, a. Gr., f. νεφρός kidney.] *Path.* Inflammation of the kidneys.

Nephro- (ne·fro, nĕfrǫ·), comb. form of Gr. νεφρός kidney; as in **Nephrodi·nic** *a.*, of molluscs, discharging the genital products by means of nephridia. **Nephrolithi·asis,** disease caused by the presence of renal calculi. **Nephroli·thic** *a.*, pertaining to calculi in the kidney. **Nephro·logy,** the scientific study of the kidneys and their diseases. **Nephro·rrhaphy,** the suturation of a displaced kidney in its normal place. **Nephro·stoma, Ne·phrostome,** a funnel-shaped ciliated aperture in a primitive kidney.

Nephrotomy (nĕfrǫ·tŏmi). 1696. [ad. mod.L. *nephrotomia*, f. Gr. νεφρός kidney + -τομία, τομή cutting.] *Surg.* Incision of the kidney, esp. for renal calculus. So **Nephro·tomize** *v.* 1825.

‖**Ne plus ultra** (nī pl*ɒ*s *ɒ*·ltră). †Also **ne plus.** 1638. [L. '(let there) not (be) more (sailing) beyond', alleged to have been inscribed on the Pillars of Hercules.] **1.** A command to go no further; also, an impassable obstacle or limitation 1661. **2.** The furthest point reached or capable of being reached 1638. **b.** *esp.* The point of highest attainment; the highest pitch *of* some quality, etc.; the acme, culmination 1696.

2. b. The populace..have arrived at their *ne plus ultra* of insolence 1760.

Nepotal (ne·pŏtăl), *a.* 1837. [f. L. *nepot-*, *nepos* nephew + -AL.] Of the nature of, belonging or pertaining to, a nephew or nephews.

Nepotic (nĕpǫ·tik), *a.* 1847. [f. as prec. + -IC.] **a.** Inclined to, of the nature of, nepotism. **b.** Holding the position of a nephew.

To set bounds..to the personal or n. ambition of the ruling pontiff MILMAN.

Nepotism (ne·pŏtiz'm). 1670. [ad. F. *népotisme* or It. *nepotismo*, f. *nepote* nephew; see -ISM.] The practice, on the part of the Popes or other ecclesiastics (and hence of other persons), of showing special favour to nephews (or other relatives) in conferring offices; unfair preferment of nephews, etc., to other qualified persons.

This n. of the Bishop who made a maintenance for his kinsfolk out of the estates of the Church FREEMAN. So **Ne·potist,** one given to n. 1837.

Neptune (ne·ptiūn). late ME. [a. F., or ad. L. *Neptunus.*] **1.** *Rom. Myth.* The god of the sea, corresponding to the Greek *Poseidon*; also *transf.* the sea or ocean. **2.** The most remote planet of the solar system, discovered by Galle in 1846. **3.** A large brass or copper pan used in trade with African natives 1833.

1. *Neptune's cup* (or *goblet*): a. A species of coral; b. A kind of sponge (*Thalassema Neptuni*).

Neptunian (neptiū·niăn). 1656. [f. L. *Neptunius*, f. *Neptunus* + -AN. Cf. F. *Neptunien.*] **A.** *adj.* **1.** Pertaining to the sea-god Neptune, or to the sea (*rare*). **2.** *Geol.* Resulting from, produced by, the action of water. (Opp. to *volcanic* or *plutonic.*) 1794. **b.** Based upon the view that certain geological formations are due to the action of water 1802. **3.** Of or belonging to the planet Neptune 1849. **B.** *sb.* = NEPTUNIST 2. 1799.

Neptunist (ne·ptiunist). 1593. [f. NEPTUNE + -IST.] †**1.** A nautical person (*rare*) –1597. **2.** An asserter of the Neptunian origin of certain geological formations 1802.

†**Nere,** were not; see NE and BE *v.* –1600.

Nereid (nīᵊ·rīˌid). Also erron. **Neread.** 1513. [ad. L. *Nereïs, Nereïd-*, a. Gr. Νηρηΐς,

Νηρεΐς, -ιδ-, f. Νηρεύς name of an ancient sea-god]. **1.** *Myth.* A daughter of Nereus; a sea-nymph. **2.** *Zool.* An errant annelid of the family *Nereidæ*; a sea-centipede 1840.

1. Behold the Nereids under the green sea SHELLEY.

Nere·idean. *rare.* 1835. [f. mod.L. *Nereidæ*, f. L. *Nereid-*, NEREID; see -EAN.] *Zool.* A nereid or similar marine annelid.

‖**Nereides** (nĭrī·idīz, nīə·rĭ͵idīz), *sb. pl.* late ME. [L., pl. of *Nereïs* NEREID.] Nereids.

Nere·idous, *a.* 1839. [f. NEREID + -OUS.] *Zool.* Resembling a nereid; belonging to the *Nereidæ*.

‖**Nereis** (nīə·rĭ͵is). 1752. [L.; see NEREID.] *Zool.* †**1.** A medusid (*rare*) –1813. **2.** The typical genus of the *Nereidæ*; the sea-centipede 1797.

‖**Nerita** (nĭrəi·tă). *Pl.* -æ, also -as. 1748. [L., ad. Gr. νηρίτης sea-mussel, f. Νηρεύς; see NEREID.] *Zool.* A genus of gasteropod molluscs; a mollusc of this genus. So **Nerite** (nīə·rəit), 1708.

Nerka (nɔ̄·ɹkă). 1764. [?] The blueback salmon (*Oncorhynchus nerka*) of Alaska and Kamchatka.

Neroli (nīə·rŏli). 1676. [ad. F. *néroli*, It. *neroli*, from the name of an Italian princess.] An essential oil distilled from the flowers of the bitter orange. Also *n. oil, oil of n.*

Neronian (nĭrōu·niăn), *a.* 1598. [ad. L. *Neronianus*, f. C. Claudius *Nero*, Roman Emperor A.D. 54–68.] **1.** Characteristic of, resembling that (or those) of, Nero; exhibiting his tyranny, cruelty, or depravity. **2.** Of, pertaining to, or connected with, the emperor Nero or his times 1650. So **Nero·nic** *a.*

Nerval (nɔ̄·ɹvăl), *a.* 1636. [a. F., or ad. L. *nervalis*; see NERVE *sb.* and -AL.] Of, relating to, or affecting the nerves; neural.

†**Ne·rvate,** *v.* 1682. [f. L. **nervat-*, **nervare*, f. *nervus* NERVE *sb.*] *trans.* To nerve, support, strengthen –1792.

Nervation (nəɹvē·ʃən). 1841. [ad.F.] *Bot.* The disposition of the nerves in leaves, insects' wings, etc. So **Ne·rvature** 1866.

Nerve (nɔ̄ɹv), *sb.* late ME. [ad. L. *nervus* sinew, tendon, bow-string, etc.; cf. Gr. νεῦρον.] **I. 1.** A sinew or tendon. Now *poet.*, exc. in phr. *to strain every n.*, to make the utmost exertion. **2.** *fig.* in *pl.* Those things, parts, or elements, which constitute the main strength or vigour *of* something. Also *sing.* in same sense. 1603. **3.** Strength, vigour, energy 1605. **4.** A sinew or tendon used for some practical purpose, esp. *poet.* [after L. use], a bow-string 1674. **5. a.** *Bot.* One of the ribs of fibro-vascular matter extending through the parenchyma of a leaf; esp. the midrib 1585. **b.** *Entom.* = NERVURE 1833.

2. Agamemnon, Thou..Nerue and Bone of Greece SHAKS. Money, which is the N. and Sinew of War 1726. Prosperity had relaxed the nerves of discipline GIBBON. 3. Mightiest deeds Above the n. of mortal arm MILT.

II. 1. A fibre or bundle of fibres arising from the brain, spinal cord, or other ganglionic organ, capable of stimulation by various means, and serving to convey impulses (esp. of sensation and motion) between the brain, etc., and some other part of the body 1606. **b.** In non-scientific use, with ref. to feeling, courage, etc. 1601. **c.** A disordered nervous system; nervousness 1890. **2.** Nervous fibre 1839. **3.** Courage or coolness in danger 1809. **b.** *colloq.* Impudent boldness or assurance 1899.

1. b. We soldiers need nerves of steel! BROWNING. **d.** Phr. *To get on one's nerves*: to be a worry or annoyance to one. 3. O iron n. to true occasion true! TENNYSON. *attrib.* and *Comb.*: **n.-canal, -cavity,** the pulp-cavity of a tooth; **-cell,** one of the cells composing the cellular element of nervous tissue; **-centre,** a group of ganglion-cells closely connected with one another and associated in performing some function; **-deafness,** deafness due to disorder of the acoustic nerve; **-fibre,** the fibrous matter composing the nervous system, or one of the thread-like units of this; **-knot,** a ganglion.

Nerve (nɔ̄ɹv), *v.* 1749. [f. prec.] **1.** *trans.* To give strength or vigour to (the arm, etc.). **2.** To imbue with courage, to embolden 1810.

2. *refl.* He hath nerved himself, And now defies them BYRON.

Nerved (nɔ̄ɹvd), *ppl. a.* 1800. [f. NERVE *sb.* + -ED[2].] **1.** *Bot.* Of leaves: Having a nerve or nerves; ribbed. **2.** In *Comb.* Having nerves of a specified kind or number, as *five-, full-, weak-n.*

Nerveless (nɔ̄·ɹvlĕs), *a.* 1735. [-LESS.] **1.** Wanting nerve, incapable of effort, weak, inert 1742. **2.** Characterized by lack of vigour or energy 1735. **3. a.** *Bot.* and *Entom.* Having no nervures 1796. **b.** *Anat.* and *Zool.* Having no nerves 1862.

1. His old right hand lay n., listless, dead KEATS. 2. Sad o'er all, profound dejection sat, And n. fear 1735. Lord Byron retains the same n. and pointless kind of blank verse 1822. Hence **Ne·rveless-ly** *adv.*, **-ness.**

Nervine (nɔ̄·ɹvəin). 1661. [ad. mod.L. *nervinus*, f. *nervus* NERVE.] **A.** *adj.* †**1.** Used for the sinews. **2.** Having the quality of acting on the nerves, relieving nervous disorders 1718. **B.** *sb.* A medicine that acts upon the nerves; a nerve-tonic 1730.

Nervo-, comb. f. L. *nervus* NERVE, as in **n.-muscular** *a.*, concerned with both nerves and muscles; etc.

Nervose (nɔ̄·ɹvōus), *a.* late ME. [ad. L. *nervosus*; see NERVE *sb.* and -OSE.] **1.** Pertaining to or affecting the nerves († or sinews). *rare.* **2.** *Bot.* = NERVED **1.** 1753. Hence **Nervo·sity** 1611.

Nervous (nɔ̄·ɹvəs), *a.* late ME. [ad. L. *nervosus*; see prec. and -OUS.] †**1.** Affecting the sinews. ME. only. **2.** Sinewy, muscular; vigorous, strong. late ME. **3.** Of writings, arguments, speakers, etc.: Vigorous, forcible; free from weakness and diffuseness 1637. †**4.** Sinewy, tendinous –1796; †resembling a sinew in texture; strong –1762. †**5.** *Bot.* Nerved –1776. **6.** Full of nerves 1659. **7.** Of or belonging to the nerves 1665. **b.** Affecting the nerves; characterized by a disordered state of the nerves 1734. **c.** Pertaining to the nerves 1804. **8.** Of medicines, etc.: Acting upon the nerves or nervous system 1718. **9.** Of persons: Suffering from disorder of the nerves; also, excitable, easily agitated, timid 1740. **10.** Characterized by agitation of the nerves 1775.

2. The n. strength and weight of one of the muscular armourer's [hands] SCOTT. 3. Whatever is short should be n., masculine, and compact COWPER. 6. The retina, or the n. coat of the eye 1855. 7. The brain and spinal cord are termed the n. centres 1848. *N. system*, the complex of nerves and nerve-centres. 1665. **b.** A severe n. fever ensued 1869. **c.** Modern n. physiology 1877. 8. The gentle fair on n. tea relies CRABBE. 9. The ladies were too narvous to venture further than the entrance to the cavern 1763. 10. With all the eagerness of the most n. irritability JANE AUSTEN. Hence **Ne·rvous-ly** *adv.*, **-ness.**

Nervure (nɔ̄·ɹviŭɹ). 1816. [a. F., f. L. *nervus*; see -URE.] **1.** *Entom.* One of the slender hollow tubes forming the framework of the wings of insects. **2.** *Bot.* A principal vein of a leaf 1842.

Nervy (nɔ̄·ɹvi), *a.* 1607. [f. NERVE *sb.* + -Y[1].] **1.** Vigorous, sinewy, full of strength. Now *poet.* **2.** Boldly courageous. (*rare*). 1882. **b.** *slang.* Coolly or impudently confident 1897. **3.** *colloq.* Having disordered nerves; easily excitable, hysterical, 'jumpy' 1906.

1. Death, that darke Spirit, in 's neruie Arme doth lye SHAKS.

Nescience (ne·ʃiĕns, nĭ·-). 1612. [ad. late L. *nescientia*, f. *nesciens*; see next.] Absence of knowledge, ignorance.

The ignorance and involuntary n. of men JER. TAYLOR. There was in Adam a n. of many things MANNING.

Nescient (ne·ʃiĕnt, nĭ·-). 1626. [ad. L. *nescientem*, *nescire*, f. *ne* not and *scire* to know.] **A.** *adj.* Ignorant. Chiefly const. *of.* **b.** Agnostic 1876. **B.** *sb.* An agnostic 1872.

Nese. Now only *Sc.* [ME.] The nose.

Nesh (neʃ), *a.* (and *adv.*). Now *dial.* [OE. *hnesce*: ult. etym. unkn.] **1.** Soft in texture or consistency; in later use, tender, succulent, juicy. **2. a.** Slack, negligent OE. **b.** Timid; faint-hearted. late ME. †**3.** Tender, mild, kind –1530. **4.** Delicate, weak; unable to endure fatigue or exposure; sensitive to cold. (Prevailing mod. dial. use.) OE. **Ne·shness.**

Ness (nes). [OE. *næs* related to OE. *nasu* nose. In ME. only in place-names, whence the present gen. use.] A promontory.

-ness, *suffix*, repr. OE. *-nes(s)*, *-nis(s)*, *nys(s)*, fem.; orig. compounded of the *n* of *n*-stems and the suffix *-assus*, related to wk. vbs. in *-atjan*. **1.** In OE. *-nes* is most usu. attached to adjs. and pa. pples. to form sbs. expressing a state or condition, as *biternes*. The same formation is frequent in all periods of the language. Formations from compound adjs. are also common, as *selfconceitedness*, etc.; and even from adjectival phrases, as *used-upness*, *up-to-dateness*. The latter, however, and also formations on pronouns, adverbs, etc., as *I-ness*, *everydayness*, etc., are seldom in serious use. **b.** Used absol. in *pl.* 1775. **2.** In particularized use compounds in *-ness* are often concr. in sense; similarly in titles of dignity as *highness*, *holiness*, and in WILDERNESS, WITNESS.

1. b. Cleverness and contentedness, and all the other good nesses LOWELL.

Nesslerize (ne·slĕrəiz), *v.* 1881. [f. the name *Nessler* + -IZE.] *Chem. intr.* To employ Nessler's reagent as a test for ammonia in water.

Nest (nest), *sb.* [OE. *nest*, related to L. *nidus*, Skr. *nīḍá*:—**nizdo-*, f. *ni-* down (see NETHER) and *sed-* to sit.] **1.** The structure made, or the place selected, by a bird for laying and incubating its eggs and sheltering its unfledged young. **b.** A place or structure used by animals or insects as an abode or lair or as a spawning or breeding place. late ME. **2.** A place in which a person (or personified thing) finds rest or has residence; a lodging, home, bed, etc.; a secluded or snug retreat OE. **b.** A receptacle 1589. **3.** A place of habitual residence or resort of thieves, robbers, pirates, etc. late ME. **b.** A haunt *of* crime, vice, etc. 1576. **4.** A brood, swarm, colony of birds, insects, or other animals 1470. **b.** A collection of people, esp. of the same class or frequenting a common resort 1589. **5.** A collection of similar objects; also *fig.* of immaterial things 1642. **6.** A set or series of similar objects, *esp.* of such as are contained in the same receptacle, or fit one within the other according to size 1521. **7.** *Min.* An isolated deposit of a mineral or metal occurring in the midst of other formations 1725.

1. The mery foulis in thair n. DUNBAR. The proverbe sayes, 'That it is an evill birde, will file its owne n.' 1599. **b.** Fore-warning winde Did seeme to say, seeke not a Scorpions N. SHAKS. 2. Like some poore man's n. SPENSER. The lightest wind was in its n. SHELLEY. 3. The hill-fortress became a mere n. of robbers FREEMAN. **b.** Gold, which is..The neast of strife 1576. 4. That n. of Hornets POPE. **b.** Should I call the whole university of Oxford a n. of fools 1721. [The Americans] are a sad n. GEO. III. 5. Born and bred in some hideous n. of alleys 1875. 6. One N. of Drawers 1704. *attrib.* **nest-box,** (*a*) a box containing others of graduated sizes packed in a n.; (*b*) a box provided for a domestic fowl or other bird to lay its eggs in.

Nest (nest), *v.* ME. [f. prec.] **1.** *intr.* Of birds, etc.: To make or have a nest or abode in a particular place. **b.** To engage in nest-building 1774. **2.** To settle or lodge as in a nest 1591. **3.** In *pa. pple.* Settled, established, in or as in a nest 1599. **b.** Packed one inside another 1870. **c.** Used for making nests *in* 1883. **4.** *intr.* To go bird's-nesting 1896.

1. I have..seen them nesting in the Borough 1773. 2. Where better could her love then here have nested? 1633. *refl.* A Rabble of Pirats n. themselves in Salla 1652. 3. The side hills are well wooded, and nested among them are some delightful country-houses 1834. **c.** Chestnuts nested in by song birds STEVENSON.

Ne·st-egg. 1606. [f. NEST *sb.* + EGG *sb.*] **1.** A real or artificial egg left in a nest to induce the hen to go on laying there. **2.** Something serving as an inducement or decoy 1678. **3.** A sum of money put by as a reserve or serving as the nucleus of a fund 1700.

2. Books and money laid for shew, Like nest-eggs to make clients lay BUTLER. 3. A nice little n. of five hundred pounds in the bank RUSKIN.

Ne·stful. 1598. [f. NEST *sb.* + -FUL.] The quantity (of eggs or young) that a nest can contain.

Nestle (ne·s'l), *v.* [OE. *nestlian*, f. *nest* NEST *sb.*: see -LE 3.] **1.** *intr.* = NEST *v.* **1.** **b.** To lodge or settle as in a nest. late ME. †**2.** To take up one's abode, to settle or squat in a place –1797. Also *refl.* (now *rare*) 1547.

3. Of persons: To settle down comfortably, as in a nest 1687. **b.** To draw or press *close*, or near, *to* a thing or person, esp. in an affectionate manner 1709. **4.** Of things or qualities: To lie half hidden or embedded in some place or thing 1788. **b.** Of dwellings, etc.: To lie snugly in some situation 1842. **5.** *trans.* To push *in*, to press, rest, or settle (one's head, etc.) in a snug or affectionate manner 1696. **6.** To place in, or as in, a nest; to provide with a nesting-place; to set in a secure place *lit.* and *fig.* 1548.

1. The birdes nestled in hir branches 1545. 2. If they can n. in the country for any time..they cannot fail of profiting of the discontents BURKE. A gentleman..who had nestled himself in an English borough 1826. 3. She nestled luxuriously among the cushions 1883. Nestling closer to him in the dark corner 1863. 4. b. Large groves of palm trees, among which nestled small hamlets 1884. 6. Trees..which serve to n. and pearch all sorts of birds EVELYN. The words had nestled their venomous life in her GEO. ELIOT.

Nestle-cock. Now only *dial.* 1626. [f. NESTLE *v.* + COCK *sb.*[1]] The last-hatched bird, or weakling of a brood; hence, a mother's pet; a spoilt or delicate child.

Nestling (ne·s(t)liŋ). late ME. [f. NEST *sb.* + -LING[1], or NESTLE *v.* + -ING[3].] A young bird which is not yet old enough to leave the nest.

Nestor (ne·stǫɹ). 1588. [a. Gr. Νέστωρ.] Name of a Homeric hero famous for his age and wisdom, applied allusively to an old man.

Nestorian (nestōᵊ·riăn), *a.* and *sb.* 1449. [ad. L. *Nestorianus*, f. *Nestorius*; see next.] Pertaining to, characteristic of or professing, an adherent of, Nestorianism.

Nesto·rianism. 1612. [f. NESTORIAN + -ISM.] *Theol.* The doctrine of Nestorius (patriarch of Constantinople, deposed in 431) according to which distinct divine and human persons are to be attributed to Christ.

Net (net), *sb.*[1] [Com. Teut.: OE. *net(t.)*] **1.** An open-work fabric of twine or strong cord, forming meshes of a suitable size, used for catching fish, birds, etc. Freq. specialized, as *bag-, beach-, cast(ing)-, dip-, dredge-, drift-, fishing-, trawl-n.*, etc.; *herring-, mackerel-, rabbit-, sparrow-n.*, etc. **b.** *fig.* A moral or mental snare, trap, or entanglement OE. **c.** *transf.* A spider's web OE. **2.** An open-work fabric of mesh-work, of various materials, used for covering, protecting, confining, holding, etc. OE. **3.** A piece of fine mesh-work used as a veil, or to confine the hair 1483. **b.** A kind of machine-made lace composed of small meshes. 1832. **4.** Something resembling a net; a reticulation or network; in recent *Math.*, a system of intersections of lines, curves, etc. 1594.

1. b. Skill'd to..draw Hearts after them tangl'd in Amorous Nets MILT. Not only was the town..a mere n. of peril for their lives STEVENSON. 2. *At the nets* (Cricket): on a pitch enclosed by nets which prevent the escape of balls, used for practice in batting. Their wickets at the nets were as a rule very poor 1889. 3. b. Her mob-cap was of spotted n. 1862. *attrib.* **net-ball**, a girls' game in which the object is to score by throwing a ball through a hoop from which a network depends.

Net, *sb.*[2] Now *rare.* [OE. *nette* fem., a deriv. of prec.] The omentum.

Net (net), *a.* Also **nett.** ME. [a. F. *net, nette* (see NEAT *a.*).] **1.** †**a.** Of persons: Trim, smart, esp. in dress (*rare*) –1562. **b.** Of things: Neat, smart (*rare*) 1637. **2.** †Clean; bright, clear –1609. **b.** Pure, unadulterated, unmixed (*rare*) 1713. **3.** Of amounts: Free from, or not subject to, any deduction 1500. **b.** Sold at, based upon, net prices 1893.

2. Her brest all naked, as nett yvory SPENSER. b. N. Natural French Wine 1713. 3. The 'n. effective power'..of an engine 1840. b. A book sold at 12s. becomes under the n. system 10s. n. 1894.

Net (net), *v.*[1] 1593. [f. NET *sb.*[1]] **1.** *trans.* **a.** To cover with, to hem *in*, close *round*, as with a net 1607. **b.** To pen in by means of nets 1847. **2. a.** To take, catch, or capture (people, fish, birds, etc.) with or as with a net 1801. **b.** To fish (a river, etc.) with a net; to set nets in 1843. **3.** *intr.* To make nets or network; to occupy oneself with netting 1674. **b.** *trans.* To make (a thing) by the process of producing network 1789. **4.** *trans.* and *absol.* In games: To send (a ball) into the net 1906.

1. a. To leave his favourite tree..after..netting it to keep off the birds MISS EDGEWORTH. 2. a. One or two of Plutarch's touches..had netted her fancy MEREDITH. 3. I often..see you..sitting netting in your parlour 1789. b. I had more purses netted then Than I could hope to fill HOOD.

Net, *v.*[2] 1758. [f. NET *a.* 3.] **1.** *trans.* To gain as a net sum or as clear profit. **2.** To bring in as a profit or net sum 1786.

1. By the new plan..he can n. a full profit of £4 per acre 1862.

Nether (ne·ðəɹ), *a.* [Com. Teut.: OE. *neoþera, niþera*, f. *niþer* adv., down.] Lower, under (in contrast to *higher, over,* or *upper*).

The hornéd Moon, with one bright star Within the n. tip COLERIDGE. The great reservoirs of melted matter..in the n. regions 1830. His n. person was rendered conspicuous by a pair of dingy small-clothes 1835. An uneasy gnawing of the n. lip LYTTON. *N. millstone* (or *stone*), now only in fig. or allusive use. His heart is as strong as a stone and as hard as the n. milstone BIBLE (Genev.) *Job* xli. 14.

Ne·therlander. 1610. [ad. Du. *Nederlander*, f. *Nederland*; see -ER[1].] An inhabitant or native of the Netherlands (formerly including Flanders and Belgium). So **Ne·therlandian** (*rare*), **Ne·therlandish** *adjs.* 1600.

Ne·thermore, *a.* and *adv.* *Obs.* or *arch.* late ME. [f. NETHER *a.* + -MORE.] *adj.* Nether, lower, inferior.

Ne·thermost, *a.* ME. [f. as prec. + -MOST.] Lowest, undermost, furthest down.

From the n. fire..Thy servant deliver J. H. NEWMAN.

Ne·therstock. *Obs.* exc. *Hist.* 1565. [f. as prec. + STOCK.] A stocking.

‖**Netsuke** (ne·tsukē). Also **-ké.** 1883. [Japanese.] A small piece of ivory, wood, etc., carved or decorated, worn by the Japanese as a bob or button on the cord by which articles are suspended from the girdle.

Ne·tting, *sb.* 1567. [f. NET *sb.*[1] or *v.*[1] + -ING[1].] **1.** *Naut.* A coarse network of small ropes used for various purposes, as to prevent boarding, stow hammocks or sails in, etc. **2.** Nets or network used for various purposes 1846.

2. Cover the beds..with n. to keep off the birds.

Ne·tting, *vbl. sb.* 1801. [f. NET *v.*[1] + -ING[1].] **1.** The making of a net or nets, *spec.* a kind of fancy work in which a network fabric is made with needles. **2.** The action or the right of fishing with a net 1875.

Nettle (ne·t'l), *sb.* [Com. Teut.: OE. *net(e)le* (and *netel*):—OTeut. **natilōn-*, a deriv. (see -LE 1) from a stem **nat-* as in OHG. *nazza.*] A plant of the genus *Urtica*, of which the species *U. dioica*, the Common or Great Nettle, and *U. urens*, the Small Nettle, grow profusely on waste ground, waysides, etc., and are covered with stinging hairs. **b.** attrib., *n.-bed, -beer*, etc.

1. The Greek, Italian, or Roman Nettle is *U. pilulifera*. With distinctive epithets the name of *nettle* is also given to a number of plants belonging to other genera, as *blind, dead, deaf, red, white nettle*; *bee-, hedge-, hemp-, wood-nettle*.

In groping flowers wyth Nettels stong we are 1563. *fig.* Out of this N., Danger; we plucke this Flower, Safety SHAKS.

Comb.: **n. battery**, one of the stinging organs of a hydrozoon; **-bird, -creeper,** the Whitethroat and the Golden Warbler, which nest among nettles; **-rash**, an exanthematous eruption on the skin, appearing in patches like those produced by the 'sting' of a n.; **-wort**, (*a*) a spurgewort of the genus *Acalypha*; (*b*) a plant of the n. family.

Nettle (ne·t'l), *v.* late ME. [f. NETTLE *sb.*] **1.** *trans.* To beat or 'sting' with nettles. **b.** (Also *absol.*) To 'sting' as a nettle does 1858. **2.** To irritate, vex, pique 1562. **b.** In *pa. pple.* Const. *at, by, with*, etc. late ME. **3.** To prick or stir up; to incite 1592.

1. 1 *Hen. IV*, I. iii. 240. 2. This last discourse nettled me DE FOE. b. He beyng netteled with these uncurteous..prickes and thornes HALL. Hence **Ne·ttler** (Milton), **Ne·ttling** *vbl. sb.* and *ppl. a.*

Nettle. Var. of *Knettle*, KNITTLE.

†**Ne·ttle-cloth.** 1539. [f. NETTLE *sb.* Cf. G. *nesseltuch.*] Cloth made of nettle-fibres –1626.

Ne·ttle-tree. 1548. **1.** A tree of the genus *Celtis*, belonging to the natural order *Ulmaceæ*, esp. *C. australis*, the European, and *C. occidentalis*, the N. American species. **2.** An Australian tree of the genus *Laportea*, esp. the Giant Nettle (*L. gigas*) and Small-leaved Nettle (*L. photiniphylla*) 1849.

Netty (ne·ti), *a.* Now *rare.* 1628. [f. NET *sb.*[1] + -Y[1].] Net-like; made of net.

Network (ne·twɒɹk). 1560. [f. NET *sb.*[1] + WORK *sb.*] **1.** Work in which threads, wires, or the like, are arranged in the form of a net; *esp.* a light fabric made of netted threads. **2.** (With *a* and *pl.*) A piece of work having this form 1590. **b.** *transf.* Of structures in animals and plants 1658. **c.** A complex system of rivers, canals, railways, wireless transmitting stations, etc. 1839. **3.** *attrib.* Made of or resembling network 1601.

1. I do give to my said aunte one suyte of networke 1575. 2. *fig.* Their law is a n. of fictions EMERSON. c. The Northmen..had surrounded their whole camp with a n. of trenches FREEMAN. 3. A Gold and Silk Net-work purse JOHNSON.

‖**Neuma** (niū·mă). *Pl.* **neu·mata, neu·mæ.** 1776. [med.L.] *Mus.* = next.

Neume, neum (niūm). 1440. [a. F. *neume*, ad. med.L. NEUMA, ad. Gr. πνεῦμα breath; see PNEUMA.] *Mus.* **1.** In plainsong, a prolonged pause or group of notes sung to a single syllable, esp. at the end of a melody. **2.** One of a set of signs orig. employed to indicate the structure of a melody 1843.

Neur-, var. of NEURO-, used bef. vowels (and *h*), as in **Neuradyna·mia,** nervous debility, neurasthenia. **Neurarthro·pathy,** disease of the joints in which the nerves are affected. **Neura·xis,** the nervous axis of the body; the brain and spinal column. **Neurypno·logy,** that branch of science which deals with the phenomena of hypnotism.

Neural (niūᵊ·răl), *a.* 1839. [f. Gr. νεῦρον nerve + -AL.] **1.** *Anat.* Pertaining or relating to, or connected with, the nerves; *spec.* pertaining to the cerebro-spinal system of vertebrates (as opp. to *hæmal*). Freq. in *n. arch, canal, cavity, spine, tube*, etc. **b.** Situated on, or inclining to, that side of the body in which the central nervous axis lies 1861. **2.** *Phys.* Relating to, or occurring in the nerves as organs which convey sensation or impulse 1864. **3.** *Path.* Affecting the nerve-tissues or nervous system; nervous 1883.

Neuralgia (niuræ·ldʒiă). 1822. [a. mod.L. f. Gr. νεῦρον nerve + ἄλγος pain.] *Path.* An affection of one or more nerves (esp. of the head or face), causing pain which is intermittent but frequently intense; an instance of this. Hence **Neura·lgic** (niuræ·ldʒik) *a.*

Neurapophysis (niūᵊrăpǫ·fisis). *Pl.* **-physes** (-fisīz). 1839. [f. NEUR- + APOPHYSIS.] *Anat.* **1.** (Chiefly in *pl.*) One or other of the two processes of a vertebra which form the neural arch. **2.** The spinous process arising from the bony elements which compose the neural arch; the neural spine 1870. Hence **Neurapophy·sial** *a.*

Neurasthenia (niūᵊræsþī·niă). 1856. [f. as prec. + ASTHENIA.] *Path.* An atonic condition of the nervous system; functional nervous weakness; nervous debility. Hence **Neurasthenic** (-þe·nik), *a.* caused by, affected with, symptomatic of, neurasthenia; *sb.* a person suffering from this 1884.

Neuration (niurēⁱ·ʃən). 1826. [f. Gr. νεῦρον nerve + -ATION] = NERVATION.

Neurectomy (niure·ktŏmi). 1856. [f. NEUR- + Gr. ἐκτομή; see -TOMY.] *Surg.* The operation of excising a nerve.

Neurenteric (niūᵊrente·rik), *a.* 1884. [f. NEUR- + ENTERIC.] *Anat.* Connected with the nervous and intestinal systems. *N. canal*, a prolongation of the neural canal behind the notochord into the archenteron in some vertebrate embryos.

Neuridine (niūᵊ·ridəin). Also **-in.** 1887. [f. Gr. νεῦρον nerve = -ID + -INE[5].] *Chem.* A non-poisonous ptomaine of a gelatinous nature, chiefly occurring as a product of putrefaction.

Neurilema (niūᵊrilī·mă), **neurilemma** (-le·mă). 1825. [orig. f. Gr. νεῦρον nerve + εἴλημα covering; subseq. taken as f. Gr. λέμμα husk, skin.] *Anat.* **a.** The delicate membranous outer sheath of a nerve. **b.** The sheath of a nerve-funiculus, the perineurium.

Neurility (niuri·lĭti). 1860. [f. NEUR- + -ILITY.] The power of a nerve to transmit impulse or sensation.

Neurine (niū·rəin). Also **-in.** 1839. [f. NEUR- + -INE [5].] **1.** *Anat.* Nerve-substance or tissue; the matter contained in the nerve-tubes. **2.** *Chem.* **a.** A poisonous alkaloid or ptomaine, derived from putrefying flesh, etc.; choline. **b.** An alkaloid produced with the former, and differing very slightly from it in chemical composition, but more actively poisonous. 1869.

Neuritis (niurəi·tis). 1840. [a. Gr. *νευρῖτις, f. νεῦρον nerve; see -ITIS.] *Path.* Inflammation of a nerve or nerves. Hence **Neuri·tic** *a.*

Neuro- (niūə·ro), comb. form of Gr. νεῦρον nerve, used chiefly in *Anat.* and *Path.* terms as in **Neu·roblast**, an embryonic nucleated cell from which the nerve-fibres originate. **Neuro·ce·ntral** *a.*, connected with the centrum and neural arch of a vertebra, esp. in *neurocentral suture.* **Neu·rocœle** (-sīl), the central cavity of the cerebro-spinal system. **Neuro·graphy,** scientific description of the nerves. **Neuroke·ratin,** a substance closely resembling keratin, found in certain nerve-tissues. **Neurole·mma** = NEURILEMA. **Neu·romere,** a part or segment of the nervous system; hence **Neuro·merous** *a.*, characterized by a segmented nervous system. **Neuromu·scular** *a.*, relating or belonging to both nerve(s) and muscle(s). **Neu·ropath,** a person subject to, or affected by, nervous disease. **Neuropatho·logy,** the study of nervous diseases and their treatment; hence **Neuropatholo·gical** *a.* **Neurophysio·logy,** the physiology of the nervous system. **Neu·ropore,** an exterior orifice in the neural canal of some embryos. **Neuropsy·chic** *a.*, pertaining to the nervous and psychic functions. **Neuropsycholo·gical** *a.*, dealing with psychology in relation to the nerves. **Neuroske·leton,** *Anat.* the endoskeleton; so **Neuroske·letal** *a.* **Neuroto·xin,** a substance having a poisonous effect on the nerves; so **Neuroto·xic** *a.* **Neurova·scular** *a.*, having both a nervous and a vascular character.

Neuroglia (niurǫ·gliă). 1873. [f. NEURO- + late Gr. γλία glue; named by Virchow.] *Anat.* The delicate connective tissue found in the great nerve-centres, and in the retina; the reticular or sustentacular tissue.

Neurolite (niūə·rŏləit). *Min.* 1836. [f. NEURO- + -LITE.] A variety of pinite with fibrous texture.

Neurology (niurǫ·lŏdʒi). 1681. [ad. mod.L. *neurologia*, ad. mod.Gr. νευρολογία; see NEURO- and -LOGY.] The scientific study or knowledge of the anatomy, functions, and diseases of the nerves and the nervous system. Hence **Neurolo·gical** *a.* **Neuro·logist** 1832.

Neuroma (niurōu·mă). *Pl.* **-mata.** 1839. [f. Gr. νεῦρον nerve + -OMA.] *Path.* A tumour growing upon a nerve or in nerve-tissue. Hence **Neuro·matous** *a.*

‖ **Neuron** (niūə·rǫn). Also **-one.** 1884. [a. Gr. νεῦρον sinew, cord, nerve.] **1.** The cerebro-spinal axis. **2.** A process of a nerve-cell 1896. **3.** A nerve-cell with its appendages 1896. Hence **Neuro·nic** *a.*

Neuropathy (niurǫ·păþi). 1857. [f. NEURO- + -PATHY.] Nervous disease; a case of this. Hence **Neuropa·thic** *a.*, relating to, caused or distinguished by nervous disease or functional weakness of the nervous system. **Neuro·pathist,** one who makes a special study of nervous diseases.

Neuropod (niūə·rŏpǫd). 1856. [f. NEURO- + -POD.] *Zool.* An annulose or invertebrate animal, in which the limbs or motor organs are on the neural aspect of the body. Hence **Neuro·podous** *a.*

Neuropodium (niūərǫpōu·diŭm). 1870. [mod.L., f. NEURO- + Gr. πόδιον, dim. of πούς foot.] *Zool.* The lower, ventral, or neural branch of a parapodium. Hence **Neuropo·dial** *a.*

‖ **Neuroptera** (niurǫ·ptĕră), *sb. pl.* 1752. [mod.L., f. NEURO- + Gr. πτέρον wing.] *Entom.* An order of insects, having four membranous transparent wings, with reticulate neuration. Hence **Neuro·pter,** an insect of this order. **Neuro·pterous** *a.*

Neurosis (niurōu·sis). *Pl.* **-ses.** 1776. [ad. late Gr. νεύρωσις, f. νεῦρον nerve; see -OSIS.] **1.** *Path.* A functional derangement arising from disorders of the nervous system, esp. such as are unaccompanied by organic change. **2.** *Psychol.* A change in the nerve-cells of the brain resulting in morbid psychic activity 1871.

Neurotic (niurǫ·tik), *sb.* 1661. [See next.] **1.** *Med.* A drug having a (bracing) effect upon the nervous system. **2.** A neurotic person 1896.

Neurotic (niurǫ·tik), *a.* 1775. [f. Gr. νεῦρον nerve + -OTIC.] **1.** Acting upon, or stimulating, the nerves. **2.** Of the nature of, marked by, neurosis or nervous disorder 1873. **3.** Of persons: Affected by neurosis; having disordered nerves 1887.

3. The n. woman is sensitive, zealous, managing 1887.

Neurotomy (niurǫ·tŏmi). 1704. [ad. mod.L. *neurotomia*; see NEURO- and -TOMY.] *Surg.* The section of a nerve, for the purpose of producing sensory paralysis. So **Neuro·tomist,** one who practises or studies n.; *fig.* a dissector of feelings or emotions.

Neuter (niū·təɹ), *a.* and *sb.* late ME. [a. F. *neutre* or L. *neuter* neither, f. *ne-* not (see NE) + *uter* either (of two).] **A.** *adj.* **1.** *Gram.* **a.** Of gender: Neither masculine nor feminine. Hence also, later, of parts of speech, etc. **b.** Of a verb: Neither active nor passive; intransitive 1530. **c.** *N. passive*, semi-deponent 1530. **2.** = NEUTRAL *a.* Now *rare* or *arch.* Phr. *To stand n.* 1525. **3.** Belonging to neither of two specified or usual categories 1591. **4. a.** *Bot.* Having neither pistils nor stamens; asexual 1785. **b.** *Entom.* Sexually undeveloped, sterile 1816.

1. The n., or feigned gender: whose notion conceives neither sex B. JONS. 2. It was a n. town indifferent to both 1560. As to these matters I shall be impartial, though I cannot be n. STEELE.

B. *sb.* **1.** *Gram.* **a.** A neuter verb 1530. **b.** A neuter noun or adjective 1611. **2.** A neutral thing (*rare*) 1522. **3.** One who holds himself neutral 1556. **4. a.** *Entom.* A sexually undeveloped female insect; a mature worker 1797. **b.** A castrated animal 1900.

3. Must we stand dubious and neuters between both BENTLEY. Which knows no n., owns but friends or foes BYRON. Hence **Neu·ter** *v. trans.* to castrate.

Neutral (niū·trăl), *sb.* and *a.* 1449. [a. obs. F. *neutral*, or ad.L. *neutralis*; see prec. and -AL.] **A.** *sb.* **1.** One who remains neutral between two parties or sides; a subject of a neutral state, etc. **2.** A neutral salt 1822.

1. b. A position of the parts in a gear mechanism in which no power is transmitted 1914. Hence **Neu·tralism,** maintenance of neutrality. **Neu·tralist,** one who maintains a neutral attitude 1623.

B. *adj.* **1.** Of rulers, states, etc.: Not assisting either party in the case of a war between other states 1549. **b.** Belonging to a power which remains inactive during hostilities; exempted or excluded from the sphere of warlike operations 1711. **2.** Taking neither side in a dispute; indifferent 1551. **b.** Belonging to neither party or side 1564. **3.** Belonging to neither of two specified or implied categories; occupying a middle position between two extremes 1567. **b.** Undefined, vague 1805. **c.** Having no decided colour; of a bluish or greyish appearance 1821. **4. a.** *Chem.* Neither acid nor basic; not distinguished by either acid or alkaline reaction 1661. **b.** *Optics.* Having or indicating none of the phenomena of polarization 1813. **c.** *Electr.* Neither positive nor negative 1837. **d.** *Mech.* Lying at the point where the forces of extension and compression meet and are in equilibrium 1845. **5.** = NEUTER *a.* 4. 1747.

1. b. N. goods..are not liable to capture under enemy's flag 1878. 2. While sagely n. sits thy silent friend SMOLLETT. 3. b. Miss Merry was elderly and altogether n. in expression GEO. ELIOT. c. The most remote distance becomes a mass of n. colour 1821. 4. c. *N. temperature*, that at which no current is produced by two metals arranged to exhibit thermo-electric force. *N. point*, the point of temperature at which a given pair of metals have the same thermo-electric power. Hence **Neu·trally** *adv.*

Neutrality (niutræ·lĭti). 1480. [ad. F. *neutralité*, or med.L. *neutralitas*, f. *neutralis* NEUTER *a.*; see -ITY.] **1.** (With *the.*) The neutral party or powers in a dispute or war. Now only *Hist.* **2.** A neutral attitude between contending parties or powers; abstention from taking any part in a war between other states 1494. **b.** The condition of being inclined neither way; absence of decided views, feeling, or expression; indifference 1561. **3.** An intermediate state or condition 1570. **b.** *Chem.* The fact or state of being neutral 1880.

1. The association of the Northern States in 1780, known by the name of the armed N. SCOTT. 2. England set aside the balanced n. of Elizabeth GREEN. The n. of the port of Lisbon WELLINGTON. b. Those Readers that can iudge of the truth of a historie and the newtrallitie of the writer 1600.

Neutralize (niū·trăləiz), *v.* 1665. [ad. F. *neutraliser*; see NEUTRAL *a.* and -IZE.] †**1.** *intr.* To remain neutral (*rare*). **2.** *trans.* **a.** *Chem.* To render neutral. Also refl. 1759. **b.** *Electr.* To render electrically inert 1837. **3.** To counterbalance; to render ineffective by an opposite force or effect 1795. **4.** To exempt or exclude (a place) from the sphere of warlike operations 1856.

2. a. The solution was..neutralized by sulphuric acid FARADAY. 3. The very nature of our academic institutions..neutralizes a taste for the productions of native genius HAZLITT. 4. The Black Sea is neutralised 1856. Hence **Neutraliza·tion** (in senses 2–4) 1808. **Neu·tralizer** 1843.

Neutral-tinted, *a.* 1879. Of a neutral tint (see NEUTRAL *a.* 3c).

Neutro- (niū·tro), comb. form of NEUTRAL *a.*, as in **Neu·trophil(e** *a.*, that can be stained with neutral solutions; *sb.* a cell that may be so stained. **Neu·tro-sa·line** *a.*, *Chem.* that possesses the properties of a neutral salt.

Neutron (niū·trǫn). 1921. [f. NEUTRAL *a.* 4c: after ELECTRON [2] and PROTON.] *Physics.* An electrically neutral particle consisting of an electron and a proton in close association.

‖ **Névé** (neve). 1853. [F., ad. Alpine dial. *nevé*:—Rom. **nivatum*, f. *niv-*, *nix* snow.] **1.** = FIRN. **2.** A field or bed of frozen snow 1884.

†**Ne·ven,** *v.* ME. [a. ON. *nefna*, also *nemna*, f. *nafn*, *namn*; see NAME *sb.*] **1.** *trans.* To name –1513. **2.** To mention, give an account of –1529. **3.** With cognate obj.: To utter –1520.

Never (ne·vəɹ), *adv.* [OE. *nǽfre*, f. *ne* NE + *ǽfre* EVER.] **I. 1.** At no time, on no occasion. (Formerly often with *ne, no, none*, etc.) **b.** With *after, before, since, yet*, etc. OE. **c.** Repeated for emphasis 1605. **d.** In emphatic denial, or expressing surprise 1836. **2.** Not at all, in no way. late ME. **3.** *Never a*: not a, no ... at all ME. **4.** *Never so*, in conditional clauses, denoting an unlimited degree or amount OE. **5.** *Never the*, followed by a comparative: None the, not at all the (better, etc.) ME.

1. Serpent like,..That bowes the Grasse, but neuer makes no path 1632. A braver n. drew a sword; A wiser n. SCOTT. Provb. *N. is a long word* (or *day*). b. The fact was n. before observed TYNDALL. c. *Lear* v. iii. 308. d. This almost caused Jemima to faint with terror. 'Well, I n.', said she THACKERAY. 2. Phr. *N. you fear* (or *mind*). *N. mind. N. any* or *one*, no one, none at all. 3. You have n. a shirt on DE FOE. Phr. †*N. a deal*, not a bit; see DEAL *sb.*[1] So *n. a whit*; see WHIT. *N. a one*, not (a single) one. 4. Sufficient for a whole host, be it neuer so great BIBLE *Transl. Pref.* 5. I am n. the wiser, nor the more able to account for Temple's letter GRAY. Phr. *N. the less, nevertheless*, no less, not in any way less, by no means less. So *N. the more, neverthemore.*

II. In attrib. phrases, formed with inf., or with pa. pples. and pres. pples. (hyphened) as *n. enough to be admired, n. to be forgotten*; *n.-ended, -satisfied*; *n.-ceasing, -dying, -ending, -fading.* Also *Never Never* (*Land* or *Country*), in Australia, the unpopulated northern part of Queensland; the desert country of the interior.

Nevermo·re, *adv.* ME. [f. NEVER + MORE *adv.*] Never again, at no future time.

He never more henceforth will dare set foot In Paradise MILT. Weep now or n. 1845.

†**Never the lat(t)er,** *adv.* ME. [See NEVER 5 and LATER, LATTER *advs.*] = next –1652.

Ne·verthele·ss, *adv.* ME. [See NEVER 5, LESS *adv.*] Notwithstanding; none the less.

They, knowing them to be evil, n. indulge in them JOWETT.

New (niū), *a.* and *sb.* [Com. Teut.: OE. *nīwe, nēowe*:—OTeut. **niujoz*, f. Indo-Eur. stem **new(j)-*, appearing in Gr. νέος, L. *novus*, W. *newydd*.] **A.** *adj.* **I. 1.** Not existing before;

now made, or brought into existence, for the first time. **b.** Of a novel kind ME. **2.** Not previously known; now known for the first time OE. **b.** Strange, unfamiliar (*to* one) 1595. **3.** Starting anew OE.; fresh, further, additional 1576; restored after demolition, decay, disappearance, etc. OE. **4.** Other than the former or old; different, changed OE. **5.** Used with *the* as a distinguishing epithet, implying some difference or change of nature or character OE.

1. To morow is a new day 1520. N. Discov'ries DRYDEN. **b.** Newe-fashiond cloathes I loue to weare, Newe tires, newe ruffes 1611. 2. We..curious are to hear, What happ'ns n. MILT. Seeking n. countries DE FOE. Tell not as n. what everybody knows COWPER. The n. acquaintance soon became a guest COWPER. **b.** Alacke, how n. Is husband in my mouth SHAKS. 3. As the Sun is daily n. and old SHAKS. A motion for a n. trial 1818. A n. cause of displeasure MACAULAY. 4. For in Christ Iesu nether circumcision auayleth eny thinge at all nor vncircumcision; but a n. creature TINDALE *Gal.* vi. 15. He must turne the leafe, and take out a n. lesson 1577. N. Lords, n. lawes CAPT. SMITH. Fresh Woods, and Pastures n. MILT. A n. classification of birds 1849. 5. The olde doctryne and ye newe COVERDALE. According to the newe fashion 1590. It was in New-France 1687. From N. Orleans to the mouth of the Missouri 1833. The 'n. diplomacy' 1898. *New woman*, a woman who has 'advanced' ideas on women's rights 1894. *N. learning, Testament, World*, etc.; see the sbs.

II. 1. Of recent origin or growth; †young; freshly made, produced, or grown; not yet used or worn. Also (now *rare*) of events or points of time: Recent, not long ago. OE. **2.** Having or retaining the qualities of a fresh or recent thing; showing no decline or decay. In later use esp. *ever n.* ME. **3.** Having but recently come into a certain state, position, or relationship OE. **b.** Fresh *from* some place, state, or operation 1700. **4.** That has just recently risen to notice; not belonging to a noted family 1611.

1. She semede lyk a rose newe Of colour CHAUCER. As with n. Wine intoxicated both They swim in mirth MILT. The n. red sandstone 1845. Provb. *N. brooms sweep clean. New rich* (tr. F. *nouveau riche*): one who has recently attained to wealth: usu. with connotation of ostentation or vulgar show. Similarly, since the war of 1914–18, *n. poor*. 2. Heav'ns last best gift, my ever n. delight MILT. 3. Newe soldiers and nouices of warre 1590. The Government was n. to office 1884. **b.** N. from her sickness 1700. 4. A n. man, as I am styled in Rome 1611. Hence **New·ness**, the state, fact, or quality of being new.

B. *absol.* or as *sb.* **1.** That which is new OE. **2.** *The n. of the moon*, the time at which the moon is n. (see NEW MOON). Now *rare* or *obs.* late ME. **3. Of new.** †**a.** Of late; newly –1728. †**b.** Afresh, over again –1865. †**c.** By new arrangement, appointment, etc. –1658.

1. As in the arts, so also in politics, the n. must always prevail over the old JOWETT. 2. Shooe him in the n. of the moone 1610.

†New, *v.* [OE. *nīwian*, f. *nīwe* NEW *a.*] To make or become new; to renew (itself) –1569.

New (niū), *adv.* [OE. *nīwe*, f. the adj.] †**I.** In ordinary advb. uses. **1.** Newly, recently –1610. **2.** Anew, afresh –1615.

1. Euen before this truce, but n. before SHAKS. 2. I Richards body haue interred n. SHAKS. Phr. *N. and n.*, ever anew, over and over.

II. Preceding, and in later use hyphened with the qualified word. **1.** Newly, recently, freshly ME. **2.** With pa. pples. used predicatively in the sense of 'Anew, afresh'. (Also in Cotgr. to render Fr. pa. pples. in *re-*.) ME. **b.** Placed after a noun or pronoun 1593. **3.** With active forms of trans. vbs., in the same sense. (Also in Cotgr. to render Fr. vbs. in *re-*.) 1442. **4.** With pres. pples. of intr. vbs. used attrib., as *n.-appearing*, etc. 1594.

1. The new-gathered Mulberries 1620. New-departed Souls KEN. As sullen as a beast new-caged TENNYSON. 2. Some [verses]..I have entirely new express'd POPE. **b.** Me thinkes I am a Prophet n. inspir'd SHAKS. 3. She had new-whitened the house all below stairs PEPYS.

New-blown, *ppl. a.* 1667. [NEW *adv.* II. 1.] Of flowers: Newly opened.

fig. Converting the sweet Flow'r of new blown Hope To deadly Night-Shade 1740.

New-born, *ppl. a.* ME. [NEW *adv.* II. 1.] **1.** Just born. **2.** Born anew; regenerated.

1. Where is the new borne kynge of the Iues? COVERDALE *Matt.* ii. 2. *fig.* His newborn virtues COWPER. 2. *fig.* The number of the new-born increased WESLEY.

New-coined, *ppl. a.* 1598. [NEW *adv.* II. 1.] Freshly coined; newly made or invented; as, *new-coined words*.

New-come, *ppl. a.* and *sb.* OE. [NEW *adv.* II. 1.] **A.** *ppl. a.* Newly arrived; but lately come. **B.** *sb.* A new or recent arrival; a novice. Now *rare* or *arch.* 1577. So **New·co:mer,** a new arrival 1592.

New-create, *v.* 1604. [NEW *adv.* II. 3.] *trans.* To create anew.

Newel (niū·ĕl). 1611. [a. OF. *nouel* (mod.F. *noyau*), kernel, stone, newel, etc. :— Rom. **nucale*, f. L. *nuc-*, *nux* nut.] **1.** *Arch.* The pillar forming the centre from which the steps of a winding stair radiate; †one of the stones forming this. **2.** The post at the head or foot of a stair supporting the hand-rail 1833. **3.** *attrib.*, as *n.-staircase*, etc. 1798.

1. *Open* or *hollow n.*, a central open space or well in a winding stair. Hence **New·elled** *a.* 1677.

New E·nglander. 1637. [f. *New England* (so named by Capt. John Smith in 1616) + -ER [1].] An inhabitant or native of New England, comprising the six north-eastern states of the U.S. So **New E·nglish,** of or pertaining to New England.

New-fallen, *a.* 1592. [NEW *adv.* II. 1.] **1.** Newly or recently fallen. †**2.** Newly fallen to one –1600. **3.** Newly dropped; new-born 1684.

1. As apt as new-fall'n snow takes any dint SHAKS. 2. *A. Y. L.* v. iv. 182.

Newfangle (niūfæ·ŋg'l), *a.* and *sb.* Now *dial.* [ME. *newefangel*, f. *newe*, NEW *a.* + *-fangel*, repr. OE. **fangol* 'inclined to take', from the stem *fang-* FANG *v.*[1]] *adj.* = NEWFANGLED. *sb.* A new thing or fashion; a novelty 1520. Hence **Newfa·ngle** *v.* to make newfangled. **Newfa·ngleness** (*rare* or *Obs.*).

Newfangled (niūfæ·ŋg'ld), *a.* 1470. [f. prec.] **1.** Very fond of novelty or new things. **2.** New-fashioned, novel (*depreciatory*) 1533.

1. These new fangled Christians 1659. 2. Gorgeous apparell and new fangled fashions 1598. Hence **Newfa·ngledness** 1549.

New-fashioned, *ppl. a.* 1611. [NEW *adv.* II. 1.] Made after a new fashion; of a new type or of recent invention.

New-found, *a.* 1496. [NEW *adv.* II. 1.] Newly found or invented; recently discovered. **b.** Of lands, islands, etc., esp. with ref. to America or certain parts of it (as in next) 1509.

Newfoundland (niufau·ndlænd, niū·fəndlænd, niu:faundlæ·nd). 1585. The name of a large island at the mouth of the river St. Lawrence used attrib., esp. in *N. dog.*, a large breed of dog, noted for its sagacity, good temper, strength, and swimming powers. *N. fish*, codfish.

Newfoundlander (niufau·ndlændəɹ). 1611. [Cf. prec. and -ER [1].] **1.** A native or inhabitant of Newfoundland. **2.** A ship belonging to Newfoundland 1801. **3.** A Newfoundland dog 1806.

New-furnish, *v.* 1611. [NEW *adv.* II. 3.] *trans.* To refurnish.

Newgate (niū·gĕt). 1596. Name of a celebrated London prison (pulled down in 1902), used attrib. as **N. fashion,** etc.; also **N. bird,** a gaol-bird; **N. Calendar,** a former publication containing accounts of prisoners in N.; **N. frill** (or **fringe,** a fringe of beard worn under the chin; **N. knocker,** a lock of hair twisted back from the temple to the ear, worn by costermongers, etc. Hence **New·gatory** *a.* belonging to N. (with pun on *nugatory*).

Newish (niū·iʃ), *a.* 1570. [f. NEW *a.* + -ISH [1].] Somewhat new.

New-laid, *ppl. a.* 1528. [NEW *adv.* II. 1.] Of eggs: Newly or freshly laid.

New light: see LIGHT *sb.* 6 c, quots.

Newly (niū·li), *adv.* OE. [f. NEW *a.* + -LY [2].] **1.** Very recently or lately. **2.** Anew, afresh OE. **3.** In a new fashion 1553.

1. The Infante Cardinal..being dead but n. EVELYN. A Ladies head newly dress'd for a Ball 1676. 2. She was n. planked inside and out 1876. 3. A word n. or fancifully applied 1885.

Newmanism (niū·măniz'm). 1838. [f. John Henry *Newman* (1801–90) + -ISM.] The views on theological and ecclesiastical matters put forward by Newman while a member of the Anglican Church; the principles involved in Newman's teaching. So **New·manite,** a follower of Newman 1837.

Newmarket (niū·maɹkėt, niū·māɹkėt). 1685. Name of a town (east of Cambridge) famous for its horse-races, used *attrib.* or *ellipt.* **1.** *attrib.* with *condition, cut, tail*; also **N. coat,** a long, close-fitting coat, orig. worn for riding; **N. greyhound,** a greyhound of a speedy, yet stout, breed. **2.** *ellipt.* A Newmarket coat 1843. **3.** A card-game in which the object is to play the same cards as certain duplicates which are exhibited and on which stakes are laid 1840.

New moon. OE. [NEW *a.* I. 3.] **1.** The moon when first seen as a slender crescent shortly after its conjunction with the sun. **2.** The time when the new moon appears; also *Astron.* the time at which the moon is in conjunction with the sun. **b.** = NEOMENIA. OE.

1. The new moone..Wi' the auld moone in hir arme 17.. 2. A few hours after 'new moon', the moon appears a little to the east of the sun as a thin crescent 1864.

New-mown, *ppl. a.* 1470. [NEW *adv.* II. 1, 2.] Freshly cut, just mown, as, *n. hay*.

News (niūz), *sb.* (*pl.*) late ME. [pl. of NEW *a.*, after OF. *noveles* (mod.F. *nouvelles*), or med.L. *nova*, pl. of *novum* a new thing.] †**1.** New things, novelties –1565. **2.** Tidings; new information of recent events; new occurrences as a subject of report or talk. late ME. **b.** Construed as *sing.* 1566. **3.** The newspaper(s); a newspaper. Now *rare.* 1738.

1. Not for a vayne and curious desiere to see newes 1551. 2. There are bad n. from Palermo SHELLEY. **b.** The next n. was that I was in the water 1897. Provb. *No n., good n. Ill n. fly fast.* †*No n.*, nothing new. *In the n.*, in the public eye.

attrib. and *Comb.*: **n.-agent,** a regular dealer in newspapers and periodicals; **-boat,** a boat which puts out to passing vessels to receive and communicate news; †**-book,** a small newspaper; **-boy,** a boy who sells newspapers in the streets, or delivers them; **-editor,** on a daily newspaper, the editor in charge of the telegraphic news; **-print,** (*a*) newspapers; (*b*) printing-paper for newspapers; **-reel,** a cinema film giving the news of the day; **-room,** a reading-room set apart for newspapers; **-sheet,** = SHEET *sb.*[1] 6 d; **-stand,** a stall for the sale of newspapers; **newsvendor,** a newspaper seller. Hence **News** *v. trans.* to tell or spread as n. Now *dial.* **New·sless** *a.* devoid of n.

New-set, *v.* 1709. [NEW *adv.* II. 3.] *trans.* To set afresh or in a new fashion. So New-set, *ppl. a.* 1553.

New·s-le:tter. *Hist.* 1674. A letter specially written to communicate the news of the day, common in the late 17th and early 18th c.; also, a printed account of the news (sometimes with blanks left for private additions).

New·s-man. 1596. **1.** A bearer or collector of news; a news-writer. Now *arch.* **2.** A man who sells or delivers newspapers 1796.

New·smo:nger. 1592. One who collects and retails news.

Newspaper (niū·spe:pəɹ). 1670. [f. NEWS *sb.*] A printed, now usu. daily or weekly, publication containing the news, advertisements, literary matter, and other items of public interest.

New·s-wri:ter. 1700. One who writes up the news for the information of others; in early use, a writer of news-letters.

Newsy (niū·zi), *a.* 1832. [f. NEWS + -Y [1].] Full of news; given to retailing news. Hence **New·siness.**

Newt (niūt). late ME. [For *ewt* (with *n-* from *an*: see N), var. of *evet* EFT *sb.*] Any of certain aquatic salamanders (*Triton* or *Triturus*).

Newtonian (niutōu·niăn). 1713. [f. Sir Isaac *Newton* (1642–1727) + -IAN.] **A.** *adj.* **1.** Devised, discovered, or suggested by Newton; pertaining to, or arising from, the theory of the universe propounded by Newton. **2.** Resembling, characteristic of, accepting the views of, Newton 1742. **3.** Of telescopes, their parts, etc.: Of the kind devised by Newton 1761.

1. The N. theory of gravitation 1830. 2. Men of N. capacity MORLEY. 3. An excellent N. reflector 1872.

B. *sb.* A follower of Newton; one who accepts the N. system 1741. Hence **Newto·nianism,** the N. system.

New-Year. Also **New year, Newyear.** ME. [f. NEW *a.* + YEAR.] 1. The coming year; the commencement of another year; the first few days of a year. 2. *attrib.* as *New-year day*, etc. late ME.

1. Phr. *New-year's day* (in U.S. also with ellipse of *day*), the first day of the year. So *New-year's eve, morn, morrow, tide.*

New Yo·rker. 1796. [-ER[1].] A native or inhabitant of the state or city of New York.

New Zea·lander. 1791. [-ER[1].] **a.** One of the aborigines of New Zealand; a Maori. **b.** A European settler in New Zealand.

Nexal (ne·ksăl), *a. Rom. Law.* 1886. [f. L. *nexus* or *nexum*, bond, obligation + -AL.] Characterized by the imposition of servitude as a penalty on a defaulting debtor.

Next (nekst), *a., sb.*, and *adv.* [OE. *nehst, next* (WS. *niẓhst*), superl. of *néah* NIGH.] A. *adj.* and *sb.* I. In attrib. use, or absol. as *sb.* †1. Lying nearest in place or position –1710. 2. Of persons: Living nearest to one; happening to be nearest at a particular time. Now *rare* or *Obs.* OE. 3. Nearest in relationship or kinship. Also *absol.* in *the n. of* (one's) *blood, kin*, etc. OE. †4. Closest to hand, most convenient –1679; of ends, causes, etc., least remote –1754. 5. Of periods of time: Immediately following or preceding. Also const. *after*. OE. **b.** Of persons, things, occasions, etc.: Coming directly after another in point of time. late ME. **c.** *ellipt.* with omission of *letter, number*, etc. 1629. 6. Immediately succeeding or preceding in respect of position, order, arrangement, value, birth, etc. OE.

1. †*The n. way*, the shortest, most convenient or direct way. *fig.* I speake the truth the n. waie SHAKS. 3. Thou art the nexte kynsman COVERDALE *Ruth* iii. 9. The widow, or n. of kin BLACKSTONE. *N. friend*, nearest friend or relative; *spec.* in Law, one who represents any person who is not able to appear *sui juris*, in a suit at law. 4. Extremity makes the n. the best remedy FULLER. 5. The n. morning of the skirmish of the Boyn 1711. What is written on public affairs in one week may be..obsolete..the n. 1859. **b.** Have him peach'd the n. Sessions GAY. **c.** To be continued in our n. 1893. 6. When Gabriel to his n. in power thus spake MILT. In the n. place, the chairs should be dusted 1756. *N. best*, second-best.

II. In predic. use or following the sb. 1. Nearest in place or position OE. †**b.** *transf.* of help, accidents, etc. –1568. 2. Of days, etc.: Immediately following; coming directly after (the time in question) ME. 3. Immediately following (or going *before*) in order or succession ME. 4. Nearest in respect of kinship, intimacy, or other such relationship ME. **b.** Nearest *after* or *to* (another) in rank or excellence 1535. 5. **Next to,** the nearest approach to; very nearly, almost 1656.

1. In the parish n. adjoining 1765. [She] drew a chair n. to her MISS BURNEY. 2. The end of February n. CARLYLE. 3. Thammuz came n. behind MILT. *What n.?* an exclam. of surprise. 4. **b.** Phr. *N. after, n. to*, used in loose apposition to the person or thing spoken of; He was, n. after Lucy,..by far the best news-gatherer of the country side MISS MITFORD. 5. Phr. *To get n. to* (U.S.): to become acquainted with. So *To put n. to*: to acquaint (one) with. 1896.

III. Governing a sb. (orig. in dative). Nearest to in respect of situation, rank, condition, character, etc. OE. **b.** In loose apposition ME.

One n. himself in power, and n. in crime MILT. All of them..wear Drawers n. their Skin 1687. **b.** The thing that..I loue best, n. my wyfe and children 1568.

B. *adv.* †1. Last, on the last occasion. –ME. 2. In the next place; immediately thereafter ME. 3. On the first future or subsequent occasion 1536.

2. Hippias the sage spoke n. JOWETT. 3. When he n. doth ride abroad May I be there to see COWPER.

Next door. 1485. [NEXT *a.* I. 1.] 1. The (door of the) nearest or adjoining house. 2. In advb. use. **a.** Very close or near *to* (a state, condition, etc.); almost amounting *to* (something) 1529. **b.** In or at the next house (*to* a person or place) 1579. 3. *attrib.* as *ne·xt-door neighbour* 1749.

1. The girl from next door but one DICKENS. 2. **a.** To be next Door to Starving DE FOE. **b.** The Armenian lady next door 1863.

Ne·xtly, *adv.* Now *rare.* 1584. [-LY[2].] In the next place; next.

‖ **Nexus** (ne·ksɒ̆s). 1663. [L., f. *nex-, nectere* to bind.] 1. A bond or link; a means of connexion. 2. A connected group or series 1858.

1. Cash Payment..the universal sole n. of man to man CARLYLE. *Causal n.*, the necessary connexion between cause and effect.

Niagara (nəiˌæ·gără). 1799. [Name of a N. American river, on which there is a famous waterfall.] A cataract, torrent, deluge. Hence **Niaga·rean, -ian** *adjs.* resembling N.

‖ **Niaiserie** (niˌē·zəri). 1657. Now *rare.* [F., f. *niais* simple.] Foolish or silly simplicity; an instance of this.

Niata (niā·tă). 1868. [Native name.] A dwarf variety of cattle bred in S. America. Hence **Niatism** (nəi·ătiz'm), dwarfed condition.

Nib (nib), *sb.* 1585. [Prob. a var. of NEB.] 1. = NEB 1, 2. 2. = NEB 3. 1611. **b.** A separate pen-point, for fitting into a penholder 1837. **c.** Each of the divisions of a pen-point 1840. 3. = NEB 3b. 1713. 4. *dial.* **a.** *pl.* The two short handles projecting from the shaft or sned of a scythe 1673. **b.** The pole or draught-tree of an ox-cart or timber-carriage 1808. 5. *pl.* Pieces of crushed cocoa-beans 1842. 6. A lump or knot in wool or raw silk 1879.

Nib, *v.*[1] *Obs.* exc. *dial.* 1558. [App. related to NIBBLE *v.*] †1. *trans.* To peck, pick, prick –1645. 2. *intr.* and *trans.* To nibble. Now *dial.* 1613.

Nib, *v.*[2] 1757. [f. NIB *sb.*] *trans.* To mend the nib of (a pen).

Nibble (ni·b'l), *sb.* 1658. [f. next.] The act or fact of nibbling; an instance of this, esp. of a fish at a bait. 2. A quantity (of grass) sufficient for a nibble 1838.

Nibble (ni·b'l), *v.* 1460. [Source obscure. Cf. LG. (*k*)*nibbelen* and KNABBLE *v.*] 1. *trans.* To take little bites of (a thing); to bite away little by little. 2. *intr.* To take little bites; to eat or feed in this fashion 1582. **b.** To carp (*at* something), to make trifling criticisms 1591. 3. *slang.* To catch, nab; to pilfer 1608.

1. Some, clambring..N. the bushie shrubs SPENSER. All my baits nibbled off, And not the fish caught 1617. 2. To let them play and n. with the bait a while MILT. Hence **Ni·bbler. Ni·bblingly** *adv.*

Nibbling (ni·bliŋ), *vbl. sb.* 1590. [f. prec. + -ING[1].] 1. The action of the verb; an instance of this; a portion nibbled. 2. *techn.* The gradual reduction of the edge of a piece of glass to a circular form before it is ground for a lens 1850.

Ni·blick. 1862. [Orig. obscure.] A golf club, with a stiff shaft and a round heavy head, used to take the ball out of a bad lie.

Nibs. *slang.* 1821. [Orig. obscure.] = NABS.

Nicæan (nəisī·ăn), *a.* and *sb.* 1706. [f. *Nicæa* (see NICENE) + -AN.] = NICENE *a.* and *sb.*

Nicaragua (nikăræ·giuă). 1703. [Name of a republic in Central America.] *N. wood*, a red dye-wood similar to Brazil wood, obtained from species of *Cæsalpinia*; peach-wood.

Niccolite (ni·kŏləit). 1868. [f. mod.L. *niccolum* NICKEL + -ITE[1] 4.] *Min.* Native arsenide of nickel; copper-nickel, nickeline.

Nice (nəis), *a.* ME. [a. OF. *nice*:—L. *nescius* ignorant, f. *nescire*, f. *ne-* not (see NE) and *scire* to know.] †1. Foolish, stupid –1560. †2. Wanton, lascivious –1606. †3. Strange, rare –1555. †4. Tender, delicate, over-refined –1720. †5. Coy, (affectedly) modest; shy, reluctant –1676. 6. Difficult to please or satisfy; fastidiously careful, precise, or punctilious; 'particular'. Now *rare* or *arch.* 1551. 7. Requiring or involving great precision, accuracy, or minuteness 1513. 8. Not readily apprehended, difficult to decide, determine, or distinguish; minutely or delicately precise 1513. †9. Slender, thin; unimportant, trivial –1604. 10. †**a.** Critical, doubtful –1710. **b.** Delicate, needing tactful handling 1617. 11. Able to discriminate in a high degree, finely discriminative 1586. **b.** Delicate in manipulation 1711. 12. Minutely or carefully accurate; finely poised or adjusted 1599. 13. Of food: Dainty, appetizing 1712. 14. *colloq.* Agreeable; delightful 1769. **b.** *To look n.*, to have an agreeable, attractive, or pretty appearance 1793. **c.** Kind, considerate, or pleasant (to others) 1830. **d.** In ironical use. Also *n. and* 1846. **e.** In negative contexts: Refined, in good taste *c* 1860.

2. *L. L. L.* III. i. 24. *Ant. & Cl.* III. xiii. 180. 4. He ..was of so n. and tender a composition, that a little rain or wind would disorder him CLARENDON. 5. Ere ..The n. Morn on th' Indian steep From her cabin'd loop hole peep MILT. †Phr. *To make it n.*, to display reluctance, make a scruple –1677. *John* III. iv. 138. 6. The Parliament is alwayes very n. and curious on this point 1661. Some people are more n. than wise COWPER. I should..not be too n. about the means 1887. 7. N. philosophical experiments 1822. 8. One of the nicest problems for a man to solve 1847. The nicer shades of meaning 1870. 9. *Oth.* III. iii. 15. *Jul. C.* IV. iii. 8. 10. 1 *Hen. IV*, IV. i. 48. **b.** The nicest political negociations 1777. 11. A n. observer of mens actions and manners 1617. A n. pallate in good liquor had made my landlord a favourite companion 1755. A n. sense of elegance and form 1845. 12. Despight his n. fence, and his actiue practise SHAKS. Weigh arguments in the nicest intellectual scales 1875. 13. You must give us something very nice, for we are used to live well JANE AUSTEN. 14. The n. long letter which I have..received from you JANE AUSTEN. How n. it must be to be able to get about in cars, omnibuses and railway trains again! 1897. **c.** 'Not n. of Master Enoch', said Dick T. HARDY. **d.** You'll be n. and ill in the morning D. JERROLD. Hence **Ni·cely** *adv.* **Ni·ceness.**

Nicene (nəi·sīn, nəisī·n), *a.* late ME. [ad. late L. *Nicenus, Nicænus*, f. *Nicea, Nicæa*, Gr. Νίκαια, name of a town in Bithynia.] 1. *N. Council*, one or other of two Church Councils held at Nicæa, the first in the year 325 to deal with the Arian controversy, and the second in 787 to consider the question of images. 2. *N. Creed*, the creed used in the Eucharistic services of the Eastern and the Western Church, being that received at Constantinople in A.D. 381 (except for the Western addition of the FILIOQUE, q.v.), which is an expanded form of the formula set forth by the Council of Nicæa, A.D. 325. 1567. 3. Connected with, originating from, relating to, the Nicene Council(s) 1597. Hence **Nice·nian, Nice·nist.**

Nicety (nəi·sĕti). ME. [a. OF. *niceté*; see NICE *a.* and -TY.] I. †1. Foolish conduct; wantonness –1483. †2. Reserve, shyness, coyness –1757. †3. Excessive refinement or elegance in dress or manner of living –1652. 4. Scrupulosity, punctiliousness 1693; fastidiousness 1723. 5. Precision, accuracy, minuteness 1660. 6. The quality of requiring consideration or management; delicacy, difficulty, subtlety 1707. **b.** The point in which precision is required or which is difficult to hit 1727.

2. Pride and Ignorance..preferring nicity before health 1652. N. and affectation; which is no more but modesty depraved into a vice DRYDEN. 4. Such as had a N. in their Sense of Honour STEELE. Those who can distinguish with the utmost n. the boundaries of vice and virtue JOHNSON. My own n., and the n. of my friends, have made me..an idle, helpless being JANE AUSTEN. 6. The question..is one of considerable n. and difficulty 1845.

II. 1. Something choice, elegant, or dainty, *esp.* something to eat (now *rare* or *Obs.*) late ME. 2. A nice or minute distinction; a subtle point in theory or practice 1589. **b.** A minute point or detail 1649.

1. Niceties do little towards filling the bellies of a hungry family 1793. Clean linen and other niceties of apparel HAWTHORNE. 2. Theological niceties 1880. **b.** Young women..do not know the niceties of legal proof 1875.

Niche (nitʃ), *sb.* 1611. [a. F., ad. It. *nicchia* of uncertain etym.] 1. A shallow, ornamental recess or hollow in a wall, to contain a statue or other decorative object. 2. A small vaulted recess or chamber made in the thickness of a wall, or in the ground 1662. 3. *fig.* **a.** A place or position adapted to the character, or suited to the merits, of a person or thing 1726. **b.** A place of retreat or retirement 1725.

1. You have the blessed Virgin and a Child sitting in a Nitch STEELE. 3. **a.** The work fills a n. of its own and is without competitor 1869.

Niche (nitʃ), *v.* 1752. [f. prec. or ad. F. *nicher* to nest, nestle:—pop. L. **nidicare*, f. *nidus* nest.] 1. *trans.* (in *pass.*) To place (an image, etc.) in a niche or similar recess 1757. 2. To place in some recess or nook; to ensconce 1752. 3. *refl.* To settle or ensconce (oneself) quietly or comfortably 1824.

1. A waxen Virgin niched in a little box against the wall 'MARK TWAIN'. 2. Niched between two bouncing

lasses, he had commenced acquaintance with them 1847. 3. Here Dolly loved to retreat and n. herself down in a quiet corner 1878.

Nichil, early form of NIHIL.

Nicholas (ni·kŏlăs). [Name of an early Christian saint (died A.D. 326), bishop of Myra in Lycia, patron of scholars, esp. of schoolboys.] †1. *St. Nicholas' bishop*, a boy-bishop elected by choir-boys or scholars on St. Nicholas' Eve (Dec. 5) 1501–5. 2. *St. Nicholas' clerks*: †a. Poor scholars 1489–1581. b. Highwaymen (now only *arch.*) 1570.

2. b. If they meete not with S. Nicolas Clarks, Ile giue thee this necke SHAKS.

Nick (nik), *sb.*¹ 1483. [Orig. obscure.] I. 1. A notch, groove, or slit in something; an incision, indentation. b. *Printing.* A notch made on one side of the shank of a type, serving as a guide to the compositor in setting 1683. 2. A notch used as a means of keeping a score: hence †reckoning, account 1483. 3. A gap in a range of hills 1793. 4. A cut; the act of cutting 1816.

1. *spec.* The Notch or N., in the Arrow for the Bowstring to go in 1688. A n. is the mark cut in the mandible of a swan to distinguish its ownership 1842. 2. He lou'd her out of all nicke SHAKS.

II. †1. A pun –1589. 2. In the game of hazard: A throw which is either the same as the main, or has a fixed correspondence to it 1635.

III. 1. *The* (*very*) *n.*: a. The critical moment. Chiefly used in phr. *in* (†*at, upon*) *the n.* 1577. Now *in the* (*very*) *n. of time* 1643. †b. The exact point aimed at; the mark –1656. 2. The precise moment or time of some occurrence or event 1645. 3. (With *a* and *pl.*) A critical point or moment. Now *rare.* 1628.

1. a. Married..they would have been, if I had not come just in the n. 1774. He had changed sides at the very n. of time DICKENS. 2. In the very n. Of giving up BROWNING.

Nick (nik), *sb.*² 1643. [Prob. abbrev. of *Nicholas.*] The devil. Usu. *Old N.*

You..made us laugh with your conceit, being always conceited as Old N. 1886.

Nick (nik), *v.* 1523. [Origin obscure.] I. 1. *trans.* To make a nick or notch in; to cut in nicks or notches; to indent 1530. b. To score by means of a notch or notches on a stick or tally. Also with *up, down*, and in fig. use. 1523. 2. To cut into or through; to cut short 1592. b. To fashion or mark out by cutting 1605. 3. To make an incision at the root of (a horse's tail) in order to make him carry it higher; also with *horse* as obj. 1737.

1. b. I'll get a knife and n. it down, that Mr. Neverout came to our House SWIFT. 3. Prosecuted..for 'nicking' two hackneys and a chestnut mare 1896.

II. †1. To tally with, resemble, suit exactly –1702. †2. To hit off or fit *with* (or *in*) an appropriate name –1693. b. To nickname. *Obs.* exc. as *nonce-wd.* 1605. 3. a. *To n. it*, to make a hit; to guess rightly 1624. b. To hit, arrive at with precision; to hit *off* neatly or precisely 1673. 4. To hit (the proper time, season, etc. for something) 1664. b. To catch (a boat, train, etc.) 1841. 5. *slang.* To catch, take unawares; to nab, nail. Now *spec.* of the police. 1622. b. To steal 1869.

2. I have so nickt his Character in a Name as will make you split 1687. b. Goodith.., by which name King Henry the first was nicked in contempt CAMDEN. 3. a. Have I not nick'd it, tutor? MASSINGER. b. You just nicked my palate LAMB. 4. I had nicked my time, and..I embarked 1843. 5. All my pals got nicked, and I chucked it 1893.

III. †1. In the game of hazard: To win against (the others) by casting a nick –1684. 2. To make (a winning cast) at hazard; to get as a nick; to throw the nick of (a certain number) 1598. †3. To trick, cheat; to defraud *of*, do out *of* –1818. 4. *intr.* In hunting, racing, etc.: To cut in. Also with past, up, etc. 1852.

3. He was nick'd of three pieces of cambrick GAY. 4. [He is] always nicking and skirting SURTEES.

IV. Of breeding stocks: To unite, couple 1865.

Nickar, early form of NICKER *sb.*³

Nickel (ni·k'l), *sb.* 1775. [Abbrev. of G. *kupfernickel*, mining name of the copper-coloured ore (niccolite) from which nickel was first obtained by A. F. von Cronstedt in 1751. The second element is G. *nickel* dwarf, mischievous demon, the name being given to the ore because it yielded no copper in spite of its appearance.] 1. A hard, silvery-white lustrous metal, usu. occurring in combination with arsenic or sulphur and associated with cobalt; it is malleable and ductile, and resistant to oxidation, and is used principally in alloys. 2. *U.S. colloq.* †a. A one-cent piece partly made of nickel –1858. b. A five-cent piece (containing one part of nickel to three of copper) 1883.

attrib., in **n. bloom, green, ochre** = ANNABERGITE; **n. silver**, an alloy similar to German silver; **n. steel**, an alloy of iron with n. Hence **Ni·ckel, Ni·ckelize** *vbs. trans.*, to coat with n. **Ni·ckelic** *a.* pertaining to, or containing, n. **Ni·ckeli·ferous** *a.* containing or yielding n. **Ni·ckeline** *sb.* = NICCOLITE; *a.* consisting of n. **Ni·ckelous** *a.* containing n.

Nicker, *sb.*¹ 1669. [f. NICK *v.*] †1. One who cheats at play –1714. †2. One who fits a thing neatly MARVELL. 3. One who hits in throwing; *spec.* early in the 18th c., one of the disorderly youths who made a practice of breaking windows by throwing coppers at them 1716. 4. One who, or that which, nicks or cuts 1810; *spec.* that part of a centre-bit which cuts the circle of the hole made by the tool 1846.

Nicker (ni·kəɹ), *sb.*² 1675. = KNICKER¹.

Nicker (ni·kəɹ), *sb.*³ Also **-ar.** 1696. [perh. native name.] The hard seed of the bonduc tree; also = NICKER-TREE.

Ni·cker, *v.* Chiefly *Sc.* and *north. dial.* 1774. [Imitative.] 1. *intr.* To neigh. 2. To laugh loudly or shrilly. Also *trans.*

Ni·cker-tree. 1707. [See NICKER *sb.*³] = BONDUC.

Nicking (ni·kiŋ), *vbl. sb.* 1551. [f. NICK *v.* + -ING¹.] 1. The action of notching or cutting. b. A notch or indentation; a cutting or set of cuts 1844. 2. The action of hitting (upon) or striking 1668.

1. b. *Nicking*, the cutting made by the hewer at the side of the face. *Nickings* is the small coal produced in making the n. 1881.

Nick-nack. 1692. Var. of KNICK-KNACK.

Nickname (ni·knēⁱm), *sb.* 1440. [For EKE-NAME, with *n* from *an* (see N).] A name added to, or substituted for, the proper name of a person, place, etc., usu. in ridicule or pleasantry. b. A familiar form of a Christian name 1605.

He unfortunately got the N. of the Squeaking Doctor ADDISON. b. A wery good name it [*sc.* Job] is; only one, I know, that ain't got a n. to it DICKENS.

Ni·ckname, *v.* 1536. [f. the sb.] 1. *trans.* To call by an incorrect name; to misname. †b. To mention by mistake (*rare*) –1665. 2. To give a nickname to (one); to call by a nickname 1567.

1. You lispe, and n. Gods creatures SHAKS. b. *L.L.L.* v. ii. 349. 2. They were soon nicknamed Methodists WESLEY.

Nicol (ni·kəl). 1838. [f. William *Nicol*, its inventor (died 1851).] *Opt.* A prism of Iceland spar, so constructed as to transmit only the extraordinary ray of doubly refracted light. (Also freq. *Nicol's prism.*)

Nicolaitan (nikŏlēⁱ·tăn). 1526. [f. Gr. Νικολαΐτης, f. personal name Νικόλαος + -AN.] *sb.* A member of an early Christian party or sect mentioned in Rev. ii. 6, 15, the precise nature of which is uncertain. *adj.* Held by the Nicolaitans 1864. So †**Nicolaite** *sb.* –1586.

‖**Nicotia** (nikōᵘ·ʃiă). 1830. [mod.L. f. *nicot-* (see NICOTIANA) + -IA¹.] a. Nicotianin. b. Nicotine.

†**Nico·tian**, *sb.*¹ 1577. [ad. F. *nicotiane* or mod.L. *nicotiana* (see below).] The tobacco-plant –1673.

Nicotian (nikōᵘ·ʃiăn), *a.* and *sb.*² 1825. [f. *nicot-* (see next) + -IAN.] A. *adj.* Of or pertaining to tobacco; arising from the use of tobacco. B. *sb.* 1. = NICOTIANIN 1840. 2. A tobacco-smoker O. W. HOLMES.

‖**Nicotiana** (nikōᵘʃiē·nă, -tiā·nă). 1600. [mod. L. (sc. *herba*), f. Jacques *Nicot*, who introduced tobacco into France in 1560.] 1. The tobacco-plant. 2. A genus of plants (chiefly American) of the nightshade family, to which the tobacco-plant (*N. Tabacum*) belongs 1846.

Nicotianin (nikōᵘ·ʃiănin). Also **-ine.** 1838. [f. prec. + -IN¹.] *Chem.* A camphorous bitter substance, extracted from tobacco.

Nicotic (nikǫ·tik), *a.* 1857. [f. *nicot-* (see NICOTIANA) + -IC.] *Chem.* Of or pertaining to nicotine, esp. in *N. acid.*

Nicotina (nikŏtəi·nă). 1838. [f. *nicot-* (see NICOTIANA) + -INA.] *Chem.* = next.

Nicotine (ni·kŏtīn, ni·kŏtīn). Also **-in.** 1819. [a. F.; see NICOTIANA and -INE⁵.] A poisonous alkaloid forming the essential principle of tobacco, from which it is obtained as an oily liquid. Hence **Nicoti·nian** *a.* = NICOTIAN *a.* **Ni·cotinism**, a diseased condition produced by the excessive use of tobacco. **Ni·cotinize, Ni·cotize**, *vbs. trans.* to drug or saturate with n.

Nictate (ni·ktēⁱt), *v.* 1691. [f. L. *nictat-*, *nictare.*] *intr.* To wink. Only in *nictating membrane*; see NICTITATE *v.* Hence **Nicta·tion.**

Nictitate (ni·ktitēⁱt), *v.* 1822. [f. med.L. *nictitat-*, *nictitare*, freq. of *nictare*; see prec.] *intr.* Of the eyelids: To wink (*rare*). Hence **Ni·ctitating** *ppl. a.*, in *nictitating membrane*, a third or inner eyelid present in many animals, serving to protect the eye from dust, etc., and to keep it moist 1713. So **Nictita·tion** 1784.

Nidamental (nəidăme·ntăl), *a.* 1835. [f. L. *nidamentum* + -AL.] 1. *Zool.* Serving as a receptacle for the ova of molluscs or other marine animals; forming a collection of ova. 2. Serving as a nest or nests 1879.

Ni·ddering, *sb.* and *a.* Also **nider-.** 1596. [erron. form of NITHING.] *sb.* A base coward or wretch. *adj.* Base, cowardly, vile 1848.

Nide (nəid). 1679. [ad. F. *nid* or L. *nidus.*] A brood or nest of pheasants. Also *transf.* of geese. Now only *arch.*

Nidificate (ni·difikēⁱt), *v.* 1816. [f. L. *nidificat-*, *nidificare*, f. *nidus.*] *intr.* To make a nest.

All the Birds of Prey..n. in lofty situations 1835. So **Nidifica·tion**, the operation of nest-building; the manner in which this is done 1658.

Nidify (ni·difəi), *v.* 1656. [ad. L. *nidificare*; see prec.] *intr.* To build a nest or nests.

Nid-nod, *v.* 1787. [Redupl. f. NOD *v.*] To nod repeatedly.

Nidor (nəi·dǭɹ). Now *rare.* 1619. [a. L.] The smell of animal substances when burned, roasted, or boiled; †a strong odour of any kind.

Nidorous (nəi·dŏrəs), *a.* Now *rare.* 1626. [f. prec. + -OUS.] Of smells: Resembling that of cooked or burnt animal substances; strong and unpleasant. b. Applied to stomachic eructations 1651.

Nidulant (ni·diŭlănt), *a.* Now *rare.* 1797. [f. L. *nidulant*, *nidulari*, f. *nidus.*] Nestling; embedded in pulp or cotton, or in a berry.

‖**Nidus** (nəi·dŏs). *Pl.* **nidi** (nəi·dəi), **niduses** (nəi·dŏsĕz). 1742. [L.: see NEST *sb.*] 1. a. *Zool.* A nest or place in which insects, snails, etc., deposit their eggs. b. *Bot.* A place or substance in which spores or seeds develop 1796. c. *Phys.* and *Path.* A place of origin or development *for* some state or substance 1804. d. *fig.* A source or place of origin 1807. 2. A place in which something is formed, deposited, settled, or located 1778. 3. A collection *of* eggs, tubercles, etc. 1822.

1. c. The mammary gland seems to be the n. for this diseased action ABERNETHY. d. The Sorbonne, formerly the n. of pedantry 1817.

Niece (nīs). ME. [a. F. *nièce*:—pop. L. *neptia*, for L. *neptis.*] 1. †a. A grand-daughter, or more remote female descendant (Common down to *c* 1600). b. A daughter of one's brother (brother-in-law) or sister (sister-in-law). †2. A female relative –1508.

1. b. His neece by the sister's side 1673.

Niellated (ni·elēⁱtĕd), *ppl. a.* 1886. [ad. It. *niellato*, pa. pple. of *niellare*, f. NIELLO.] Inlaid in niello.

‖**Niello** (ni,e·lo), *sb.* *Pl.* **-i, -os.** 1816. [It. *niello*:—pop. L. **nigellum*, neut. of *nigellus*, dim. of *niger* black.] 1. A black composition, consisting of metallic alloys, for filling in engraved designs on silver or other metals. b. Ornamental work in niello 1842. 2. A specimen of niello work 1840. 3. An impression on paper of the design which is to be filled with niello 1854. Hence **Nie·llist**, a worker or artist in n. **Nie·llo** *v.* inlay with n. **Nie·lloed** *ppl. a.*

Nietzschean (nī·tʃiăn), *a.* and *sb.* 1914. [f. the name of the German philosopher Friedrich Wilhelm *Nietzsche* (1844–1900) + -AN.] Pertaining to or characteristic of Nietzsche or his philosophy of the *Übermensch* (see SUPERMAN). So **Nie·tzscheanism, Nie·tzscheism.**

Nieve (nīv), **nief** (nīf). Now *dial.* or *arch.* [ME. *neve, nefe*, ad. ON. *hnefi, nefi.*] A clenched hand, a fist.

Giue me your neafe, Mounsieur Mustardseed SHAKS.

Nifle (nəi·f'l). Now *dial.* late ME. [perh. ad. med.L. NICHIL, infl. by *trifle*, with which it is often combined.] A trifle; †a trifling or fictitious tale. (Common *c* 1550–1650.)

‖ **Nigella** (nəidʒe·lă). late ME. [L., fem. of *nigellus*; see NIELLO.] *Bot.* A genus of ranunculaceous plants, having numerous black seeds, esp. the Fennel-flower (*N. sativa*) and Love-in-a-mist (*N. damascena*); also, the seeds of this used for medicinal purposes.

Niggard (ni·găɹd), *sb.* and *a.* late ME. [prob. AF. deriv., with -ARD, of earlier *nig* or *nigon*, perh. of Scand. origin (cf. *niggle*).] **A.** *sb.* **1.** A mean, stingy, or parsimonious person; a miser. **2.** *dial.* A false bottom for a grate, to economize fuel. Also *n. iron.* 1688.

1. The negard then saith to his money.., my god arte thou 1510. Be niggards of advice on no pretence, For the worst avarice is that of sense POPE.

B. *adj.* **1.** Miserly, parsimonious, mean; unwilling to give or spend anything. late ME. **2.** Of actions and qualities: Niggardly, ungenerous 1672. **3.** Scanty 1751.

1. N. with pence and lavish with millions BENTHAM. Hence **†Ni·ggardise**, niggardliness. **Ni·ggardly** *adv.* in a n. manner; **-ness.**

Niggardly (ni·găɹdli), *a.* 1561. [f. prec. *sb.* + -LY [1].] **1.** Having a niggard's nature; close-fisted, stingy; sparing 1571. **2.** Of actions, qualities, etc.: Characteristic of a niggard; mean, miserly 1561. **3.** Such as a niggard would give; meanly small; scanty 1599.

1. The Israelites..were perpetually slack or n. in the service of Jehovah M. ARNOLD. 3. The niggardliest mouse of biefe will cost him sixpence 1599. Hence **Ni·ggardliness.**

Nigger (ni·gəɹ). 1786. [Alteration of NEGER.] **1.** A negro. (Colloq. and usu. contempt.) Also *transf.* of members of other dark-skinned races. **2.** The black caterpillar of the turnip saw-fly 1840. **3.** *attrib.* (or *adj.*). **a.** Belonging to the negro race; black-skinned. Also *n.-minstrel*; see NEGRO. 1836. **b.** Of, or belonging to, occupied by, negroes. Also *transf.* 1834. **c.** The name of a colour 1914.

1. A similar error has turned Othello..into a rank, woolly-pated, thick-lipped n. H. COLERIDGE. 3. a. The real n. baby is known under the name of pickaninny 1872. Hence **Ni·ggerdom, Ni·ggerish** *a.*

Ni·ggerhead. 1859. [f. prec. + HEAD *sb.*] Applied to various black or dark-coloured roundish objects. (Cf. NEGRO-HEAD.)

A clump or tussock of vegetation (*U.S.*), the black or rough head of some plants (*Austral.*); *Min.* a dark-coloured nodule or boulder; = NEGRO-HEAD 1.

Niggle (ni·g'l), *v.* 1599. [app. of Scand. origin.] **1.** *intr.* To work, or do anything, in a fiddling way; to trifle (†*with* a thing); to spend time unnecessarily on petty details; to keep moving *along*, in a fiddling or ineffective manner. **†2.** Of girls: To be restless or fidgety from wantonness –1809.

1. Take heed, daughter, You n. not with your conscience MASSINGER. When I have nobody at all at my place but workmen;..I n. after them up and down MME. D'ARBLAY. Hence **Ni·ggled** *ppl. a.* over-elaborated 1884. **Ni·ggler** 1862. **Ni·ggling** *ppl. a.*, trifling, petty, finicking. **Ni·ggly** *a.*

Nigh (nəi), *adv.*, *a.*, and *sb.* [Com. Teut.: OE. *nēah, nēh.*] Orig. compared, as an adv., *nēar*, NEAR *adv.*, as an adj., *nēarra*, ME. *ner*, NAR *a.* The relationship of these forms to the positive becoming obscured, they were replaced by *nigher, nighest.*] = NEAR *adv.* and *a.* (which in all senses has taken the place of *nigh* exc. in arch. or dial. use.) **Denoting proximity in place, time*, etc. **I.** *adv.* With dependent dative (passing into *prep.*), or followed by *to.*

There came other shippes..nye vnto yᵉ place COVERDALE. Neuer harme,..Come our louely Lady nye SHAKS. A Ship..N. Rivers Mouth or Foreland MILT.

II. *adv.* Used absol. as complement or predicate (passing into *adj.*) OE.

Now is your husband nie SHAKS. So saying, he drew n. MILT. The hour is n. 1866. Phr. *N. at hand* (see HAND *sb.*). †*N. and far* (cf. FAR *adv.*).

III. *adj.* In attrib. use.

Is there any nigher way to lead unto damnation? 1547. Signe of n. battail, or got victory SPENSER. The n. trace-chain of the n. horse 1844.

***Denoting approximation in degree or amount.* **IV.** *adv.* **1.** Nearly, almost, all but OE. **†2.** Nearly, closely –1587. **3.** Near or close (to), in respect of attainment, resemblance, †likelihood, etc. ME. **4.** as *adj.* Close, near; parsimonious 1555.

1. Thenne the quene was nyghe oute of her wytte MALORY. I gave nie five times five assaultes 1559. 2. For I am shave as nye as is a frere CHAUCER. 3. Her sarcasms and self-will..go n. to confirm it L. HUNT.

Nigh (nəi), *v.* Now *rare.* ME. [f. NIGH *adv.*] **1.** *trans.* To go, come, or draw near to; to approach closely. **2.** *It nighs*: It draws *to* or *towards* a time. *Obs.* or *arch.* ME. **3.** *intr.* To draw or come near *toward* or *to* a person, place, etc. ME. **4.** To go, come, or draw near; to approach ME.

2. When it nigh'd to Christmas tide 1821. 4. Now day is doen, and night is nighing fast SPENSER.

Nigh by, *adv.* (and *a.*) late ME. [f. NIGH *adv.* + BY; cf. NEAR BY.] **†1.** *adv.* Nearly, almost (*rare*) –1448. **2.** Near to; near at hand 1500.

Nigh hand, *adv.* OE. [f. NIGH *adv.* + HAND *sb.*; cf. NEAR HAND.] **1.** Near or close at hand; close by. **b.** Governing a *sb.* Near, close to ME. **2.** Almost, nearly ME.

2. Wasn't it enough for you to nigh-hand kill one of my horses? 1842.

Nighly (nəi·li), *adv.* [OE. *nēahlīce*; see NIGH *adv.* and -LY [2].] **1.** Nearly, almost. **†2.** Nearly, closely –1691. **†3.** Niggardly –1579.

Nighness (nəi·nės). late ME. [f. NIGH *a.* + -NESS.] The quality or state of being NIGH.

The nighnes of blood which they be of unto hym 1471.

Night (nəit), *sb.* [Com. Teut. and Indo-Eur.: OE. *niht*, f. pre-Teut. stem **nokt-*, represented by L. *noct-*, *nox*, Gr. νυκτ-, νύξ, Skr. *nákta, nákti*, Lith. *naktis*, etc.] **1.** The period of darkness between day and day; that part of the natural day (of 24 hours) during which no light is received from the sun; the time between sunset and sunrise or dusk and dawn. **b.** The darkness which prevails during this time; the dark 1855. **2.** The close of daylight ME. **3.** With *a* and *pl.* One of the intervals of darkness between two days OE. **4.** With possessive pronouns: The particular night on which a person performs some duty (†receives visitors, etc.). Also *n. out*, the evening on which a domestic servant is free to go out. 1525. **b.** The kind of night one has had, or usually has 1667.

1. Yᵉ nyghte..gyueth triews to alle labours, and by slepyng maketh swete alle peynes and traueylles CAXTON. Phr. *As black, dark*, etc., *as n. Personified* (*as a female being*). They must for aye consort with blacke browd n. SHAKS. *fig.* Yet hath my n. of life some memorie SHAKS. Dido..clos'd her Lids at last, in endless N. DRYDEN. b. I heard The shrill-edged shriek..divide the shuddering n. TENNYSON. 2. *Mids. N.* III. ii. 275. 3. Now will he lie ten nights awake caruing the fashion of a new dublet SHAKS. A Crown ..Brings sleepless nights MILT. The missing of an Opera the first N. ADDISON. *Christmas, first, Midsummer, wedding n.*, etc.; see these words. Phr. *To make* (or *have*) *a n. of it*, to spend the n. in enjoyment or revelling. *A n. out*: a night spent away from home, esp. in amusement. 4. Her annual n. (= benefit n.) DICKENS. b. My nights are very restless and tiresome JOHNSON.

Phrases. **a.** Adverbial. *N. and day*, always, continually. *N.* (*n*)*or day*, by n. or by day. *All*, or *the whole, n.* (*long*), throughout the n. **b.** Prepositional. *By n.*, during the n., in the night-time. *By n. and day*, always, at any time. *At n.*, at nightfall, in the evening. Also designating the hours of darkness, esp. up to midnight. †*On nights*, by n. (habitually). Also A-NIGHTS, *o'* and *in nights.* So *At nights, of nights. On* (*upon*), *in*, or *of the n.*, by n., during the n. Now only with *in.*

attrib. and *Comb.* **1.** General: as *n.-bringing*, etc.; *n.-clad, -enshrouded*, etc.; *n.-black, -swift*, etc.; in sense of 'by n.', 'during the n.', as *n.-blowing, -warbling*, etc.; *n.-angling*, etc.; *n.-fallen, -scented*, etc.; in senses 'of n.', 'existing, prevailing, taking place, etc., during the n.', as *n.-air, -attack, -brawl, -fears*; with sense '(intended to be) worn or used during the n.', as *n.-attire, -bell*; with sense 'acting, or on duty or abroad, during the n.', as *n.-attendant, -brawler, -nurse, -porter*; so *n. duty.* Also with names of animals, birds, plants, etc., as *n.-dog, -moth, -warbler, -weed, -willow-herb.*

2. Spec.: as **n.-bag**, a travelling bag containing necessaries for the n.; **-blue**, a dyestuff giving a blue which retains its colour under artificial light; **-boat**, a passenger-boat which travels by n.; **-cart**, a cart for removing night-soil; **-chair**, a commode for use by n.; **-cloud**, the form of cloud known as *stratus*; **-club**, a club frequented during the night hours, esp. for drinking and dancing; **-eyed** *a.*, capable of seeing in the night-time; **-fire**, a fire kindled at, or for the n.; **-line**, a line with baited hooks set to catch fish by n.; **-rider**, one who rides on horseback by night, esp. *U.S.* one who damaged tobacco plantations; **-school**, a school held in the evening, esp. for those who have ceased to attend a day-school; **-sight**, = NYCTALOPIA; **-singer**, a bird that sings by n.; *spec.* the sedge-warbler; **-soil**, excrementitious matter removed by night from cesspools, etc.; **-stick**, *U.S.* a strong stick carried by a policeman at night; **-sweat**, profuse perspiration occurring during the n., symptomatic of certain diseases; **-wanderer**, one who or that which wanders by n.; one who is travelling by n. (SHAKS. and MILT.); so **-wandering**, *ppl. a.*; **-water**, water which collects or is stored during the n.

Night (nəit), *v.* ME. [f. the sb.] **1.** *intr.* To spend or pass the night; to remain or lodge for the night. Now *rare.* **†2.** *impers.* To grow dark –1520. **†3.** *pass.* To be overtaken by night –1641.

Ni·ght-bird. 1546. **1.** A bird of nocturnal habits; *esp.* the owl or the nightingale 1608. **2.** *transf.* One who goes about at night, *esp.* a night-thief.

Ni·ght-bli·ndness. 1754. *Path.* = NYCTALOPIA. So **Ni·ght-blind** *a.* 1898.

Ni·ght-cap. late ME. [f. NIGHT *sb.* + CAP *sb.*[1]] **1.** A covering for the head, worn esp. in bed. **2.** An alcoholic drink taken immediately before going to bed to induce sleep 1818.

1. *transf.* They say in Wales, When certain Hills have their Night-caps on, they mean mischief BACON.

Ni·ght-ce·llar. 1743. [f. NIGHT *sb.* + CELLAR *sb.*] A cellar serving as a low-class tavern or place of resort during the night.

Ni·ght-clothes. 1602. **1.** Such garments as are worn in bed. **†2.** Négligé or informal dress worn in the evening –1751.

2. My Lady Castlemaine, who looked prettily in her night-clothes PEPYS.

Ni·ght-crow. Now *arch.* ME. [f. NIGHT *sb.* + CROW *sb.*[1]] A bird supposed to croak or cry in the night and to be of ill omen; prob. an owl or a nightjar. Also *transf.* of persons.

Ni·ght-dress. 1712. A night-gown or other dress worn in bed.

Ni·ghted, *ppl. a.* 1604. [f. NIGHT *v.* + -ED [1].] **1.** Made dark or black as night SHAKS. **2.** Benighted 1640.

†Ni·ghtertale. Chiefly *north.* and *Sc.* ME. [prob. a. ON. *náttarþel* (f. *náttar*, gen. of *nátt* NIGHT *sb.* + *þel* groundwork, stuff, etc.) with assimilation to *tale* reckoning.] Night-time, the night. Only in phr. *by, on, a* (etc.) *n.* –1670.

Ni·ghtfall. 1611. **1.** The coming on of night; the time of dusk 1700. **2.** That which falls at night (*rare*) 1611.

Ni·ght-glass. 1779. *Naut.* A short refracting telescope for use at night.

Ni·ght-gown. late ME. **1.** A dressing-gown. Now only *Hist.* **†2.** A kind of gown worn by ladies in the 18th c., orig. as an evening dress –1778. **3.** A long, loose, light garment worn by women or children in bed 1822.

Ni·ght-hag. Now *rare.* 1666. [f. NIGHT *sb.* + HAG *sb.*[1]] A female demon supposed to ride the air by night; the nightmare.

Ni·ght-hawk. 1611. [f. NIGHT *sb.* + HAWK *sb.*[1]] **1.** A name for various birds; esp. the Nightjar or Goatsucker. **2.** *fig.* One who seeks his prey by night 1818.

Nightingale (nəi·tiŋgēl). [ME. *niȝtingale*, alteration of OE. *nihtegala*, f. *niht* NIGHT *sb.* + *galan* GALE *v.*[1]] A small reddish-brown or tawny migratory bird, *Daulias* (*Luscinia*) *luscinia*, celebrated for the sweet song of the male heard by night during the breeding season. Applied with qualification to other sweet-singing birds. **b.** *Dutch n.*, a frog 1769.

1. The lorn n. Mourns not her mate with such melodious pain SHELLEY. *transf.* His voice .. was so naturally musical, that..honest Tom Southerne used always to call him [Pope] The little n. 1751.

Ni·ghtjar. 1630. [f. NIGHT *sb.* + JAR *sb.*[1]] A name for the GOATSUCKER, from the peculiar whirring noise which the male makes during the period of incubation. Also applied to other birds of the genus *Caprimulgus* 1712.

Ni·ghtless, *a.* 1613. [-LESS.] Having no night.

Ni·ght-light. 1648. 1. The faint light which is perceptible in the night. 2. A light which burns or shines during the night 1839. b. A short thick candle, a wick, etc., designed to burn during the night, e.g. in sick-rooms, etc. 1844.

Ni·ght-long, *a.* and *adv.* 1850. [f. NIGHT *sb.* + LONG *a.*] 1. *adj.* That lasts or has lasted the whole night. 2. *adv.* During the whole night 1870.

Nightly (nəi·tli), *a.* [OE. *nihtlic*: see NIGHT *sb.* and -LY [1].] 1. Coming or happening by night; done by night. b. Happening every night 1705. 2. Of or pertaining to the night; used by night; acting by night ME. b. Dark as, or with, night; resembling night 1602.

2. Some pilgrim..With many a tale repays the n. bed GOLDSM. b. Good Hamlet cast thy n. colour off SHAKS.

Nightly (nəi·tli), *adv.* 1457. [f. NIGHT *sb.* + -LY [2].] 1. Every night. 2. At or by night; during the night 1592.

1. The clamorous Owle that n. hoots SHAKS. 2. When the blue wave rolls n. on deep Galilee BYRON.

Ni·ghtman. 1606. [f. NIGHT *sb.* + MAN *sb.*] A man employed during the night to empty cesspools, etc., and to remove night-soil.

Nightmare (nəi·tmēəɹ), *sb.* ME. [f. NIGHT *sb.* + MARE *sb.*[2]] 1. A female monster supposed to settle upon people and animals in their sleep producing a feeling of suffocation. 2. A feeling of suffocation or great distress felt during sleep, from which the sleeper vainly tries to free himself; a bad dream producing these or similar sensations 1562.

1. *fig.* For weeks past this n. of war has been riding us THACKERAY. 2. A good remedy agaynst the stranglyng of the nyght mare 1562. *attrib.* A n. sleep CARLYLE. *fig.* Quilp..was a perpetual nightmare to the child DICKENS. Hence **Ni·ghtmare** *v. trans.* to beset as by a n. Also *fig.*

Ni·ght-owl. 1513. An owl which flies especially by night.

Ni·ght-piece. 1605. A painting or picture representing a night-scene.

Ni·ght-rail. Now only *Hist.* or *dial.* 1552. [f. NIGHT *sb.* + RAIL *sb.*[1]] A loose wrap, dressing-gown, or negligee.

Ni·ght-ra·ven. Now only *poet.* [OE. *nihthræfn*: see NIGHT *sb.* and RAVEN *sb.*] A nocturnal bird, variously identified as a night-owl, night-heron, or night-jar, or imagined as a distinct species.

Where brooding darkness spreads his jealous wings, And the night-Raven sings MILT.

Ni·ght-sea·son. *arch.* 1535. Night-time.

Nightshade (nəi·tʃēᵻd). [OE. *nihtscada*; app. f. NIGHT *sb.* + SHADE *sb.*, perh. with allusion to the poisonous properties of the berries.] 1. a. A plant of the genus *Solanum*, esp. *S. nigrum* (Black N.), with white flowers, and black poisonous berries, or *S. Dulcamara* (Woody N.), with purple flowers, and bright red berries. b. A plant of the genus *Atropa*, Deadly N. or BELLADONNA. 2. Used with specific names to denote species of *Solanum, Atropa*, etc. 1839.

2. **Enchanter's N.** (see ENCHANTER). **Sleeping** or **Sleepy N.** = *Deadly N.* **Stinking N.**, Henbane. **Three-leaved N.**, a N. Amer. plant (*Trillium*), having simple stems with three leaves at the top.

Ni·ght-shift. 1710. †1. A shift worn by women at night –1727. 2. A shift, or gang of workmen, employed during the night 1839; the time the shift lasts 1860.

Ni·ght-shirt. 1857. A long shirt worn by men or boys in bed.

Ni·ght-spell. late ME. †1. A spell used against harm by night –1674. 2. A spell used to cause harm by night 1589.

Ni·ght-tide. late ME. 1. Night-time. 2. A tide of the sea occurring at night 1795.

Ni·ght-time. late ME. The time between evening and morning; the time of night or darkness.

Ni·ght-wa·lker. 1447. 1. One who walks about by night, esp. with criminal intentions; a bully or thief. Now *rare.* (Common in 17th c.) †b. A prostitute –1825. 2. An animal that moves about by night 1686. So **Ni·ght-walking** *vbl. sb.* and *ppl. a.*

Ni·ght-watch. OE. 1. A watch or guard kept during the night; the time such a watch is kept. 2. The person or persons keeping such a watch. late ME. 3. One of the (three or four) watches into which the night was divided by the Jews and Romans; hence, any similar period. Usu. in *pl.* ME.

3. I..meditate on thee in the night-watches *Ps.* lxiii. 6. So **Ni·ght-watcher**; **-watching** *vbl. sb.* and *ppl. a.*

Ni·ght-wa·tchman. 1874. A watchman who is on duty by night.

Ni·ght-work, *sb.* 1594. Work done, or to be done, during the night.

Nighty (nəi·ti). 1895. [f. NIGHT-DRESS or NIGHT-GOWN + -Y [6].] A familiar (orig. nursery) name for a night-gown or night-dress.

Nigrescent (nəigre·sĕnt, nig-), *a.* 1755. [ad. L. *nigrescentem, nigrescere*, f. *niger* black.] Blackish, somewhat black. So **Nigre·scence**, the process of becoming black; blackness; *spec.* darkness of hair, eyes, or complexion 1856.

Nigrify (ni·grifəi), *v.* 1656. [ad. L. *nigrificare*, f. *niger* black; see -FY.] *trans.* To blacken.

Nigrine (ni·grəin). Also **-in.** 1805. [f. L. *nigr-* black + -INE [5].] *Min.* A black ferruginous variety of rutile.

Nigritian (nigri·ʃiăn). 1733. [f. *Nigritia* (see def.) + -AN.] A. *adj.* Of or belonging to Nigritia, a region nearly co-extensive with the Sudan, the home of the most pronounced types of the negro race; of or belonging to the negro race. B. *sb.* An inhabitant of Nigritia 1881.

Nigritude (ni·gritiud). 1651. [ad. L. *nigritudo*, f. *nigr-, niger* black; see -TUDE.] Black; *concr.* a black thing.

Nigromancer, -mancy, etc.; see NECRO-.

Nigrosine (ni·grǒsin). Also **-in.** 1892. [f. L. *nigr-* black + -OSE + -INE [5].] *Chem.* A blue-grey or blue-black colouring matter derived from aniline hydro-chlorate.

‖ **Nigua** (ni·gwă). 1622. [Sp.] The chigoe or jigger.

‖ **Nihil** (nəi·hil). 1579. Earlier **Nichil** (1500). [L., 'nothing'.] 1. A thing of no worth or value (*rare*). 2. *Law.* The return made by the sheriff to the exchequer in cases where the party named in the writ had no goods on which a levy could be made 1629.

Nihilism (nəi·(h)iliz'm). 1817. [f. L. *nihil* nothing + -ISM. Cf. F. *nihilisme*, etc.] 1. Negative doctrines in religion or morals; total rejection of current religious beliefs or moral principles. 2. *Philos.* A form of scepticism, involving the denial of all existence 1836. 3. The doctrines or principles of the Russian Nihilists 1868.

Nihilist (nəi·(h)ilist). 1836. [f. as prec. + -IST.] 1. One who professes nihilism in philosophy or religion. 2. A member of a Russian revolutionary party professing extreme anti-social principles 1871. Hence **Nihili·stic** *a.*

Nihility (nəihi·lĭti). 1678. [ad. med.L. *nihilitas*, f. *nihil*; see -ITY.] The quality or state of being nothing; non-existence, nullity. b. With *a* and *pl.* A mere nothing; a non-existent thing 1765.

Nil [1]. Now *rare* or *Obs.* 1597. [a. Arab. and Pers. *nil*; see ANIL.] 1. The indigo plant; indigo dye 1598. 2. A species of convolvulus with blue flowers.

‖ **Nil** [2]. 1833. [L., contr. f. NIHIL.] Nothing.

Nilgai (nī·lgai). 1882. [a. Hindī, f. *nīl* blue + *gāi* cow.] = NYLGHAU.

Nill (nil), *v.* Now *arch.* [OE. (pres.t.) *nylle*, f. *ne* NE 2 + *wille* WILL *v.*[1]] 1. *intr.* To be unwilling, not to will. b. In the phrases *n. he, will he*; *nilling, willing*, etc. ME. 2. *trans.* Not to will (a thing); to refuse; to negative, etc. OE.

1. If I may rest, I nill live in sorrowe SPENSER. b. Nylle he wille he, he shalle put forthe his honde 1440. 2. So as to will what he wills..and to n. what he nills 1708. Hence †**Nill** *sb.* a disinclination or aversion to something –1677.

Nilometer (nəilǫ·mĭtəɹ). 1707. [ad. Gr. Νειλομέτριον, after words in -METER.] A graduated pillar or the like, to show the height to which the Nile rises during its annual floods.

Nilot (nəi·lǫt). 1893. [ad. Gr. Νειλώτης.] A native inhabitant of the banks of the Upper Nile.

Nilotic (nəilǫ·tik), *a.* 1653. [ad. L. *Niloticus*, a. Gr. Νειλωτικός, f. Νεῖλος the Nile; see -IC.] Of or pertaining to the Nile, the Nile region, or its inhabitants or languages.

Nim, *v.* Now only *arch.* [Com. Teut.: OE. *niman*, f. root *nem-*, perh. occurring in Gr. νέμειν to deal out, etc.] †1. *trans.* To take, in various senses –1566. †2. *intr.* To betake oneself, to go –1430. 3. *trans.* To steal, filch, pilfer 1606. Also *intr.* (Common in 17th c.)

3. The thieuing knaue the purse he nimbly nims 1630.

Nimb (nimb). 1849. [ad. L. NIMBUS.] A nimbus or halo. Hence **Nimbed** *a.*

Nimble (ni·mb'l), *a.* (and *adv.*) [Two forms: OE *nǽmel*, f. **nǽm-*, ablaut-var. of the stem (**nem-*) of *niman* to take, NIM *v.* + -EL, -LE 1; OE. *numol, -ul, -el*, f. ppl. stem *num-* of the same verb.] †1. Quick at comprehending or learning; hence wise –1483. 2. Quick and light in movement or action; agile, active, swift ME. 3. Of the mental faculties, etc.: Quick in devising, designing, etc.; acute, alert 1589. b. Of persons: Quick or ready-witted 1604. c. Cleverly or smartly contrived 1602. 4. Quick or ready *at* or *in* (or *to* do) something 1591. †5. Quasi-*adv.* Nimbly 1568.

2. Now see him mounted once again Upon his n. steed COWPER. The 'n. ninepence' being considered 'better than the slow shilling' 1851. 3. b. A n. dialectician 1893.

Comb.: *n.-fingered, -footed, -witted* adjs.; also **n.-come-quick** *a.*, of rapid growth. Hence **Ni·mble** *v.* †*trans.* to make n.; *intr.* to move nimbly. Now *rare* or *Obs.* **Ni·mbling** *vbl. sb.* and *ppl. a.* **Ni·mbleness. Ni·mbly** *adv.*

Nimbus (ni·mbŏs). *Pl.* **nimbi** (*rare*). 1616. [a. L., = a cloud, etc., perh. related to *nebula, nubes.*] 1. A bright cloud, or cloudlike splendour, imagined as investing deities when they appeared on earth. 2. *Art.* A bright or golden disk surrounding the head, esp. of a saint. Cf. AUREOLE 2, HALO *sb.* 2. 1727. 3. *Meteorol.* A rain-cloud 1803.

1. *transf.* The romantic old castle surrounded by the n. of both history and romance 1881. 2. At Venice, one only knows a fisherman by his net, and a saint by his n. RUSKIN. 3. A rainy southwester.. was now spreading with its black n. over the bay 1856. Hence **Ni·mbused** *a.* 1852.

Nimiety (nimǝi·ĕti). 1564. [ad. late L. *nimietas*, f. *nimis* too much.] Excess, redundancy; an instance of this.

Ni·miny-pi·miny. 1801. [Imitative of a mincing utterance.] Mincing, affected; lacking in force or spirit.

A n. creature, afraid of a petticoat and a bottle STEVENSON.

Nimious (ni·miəs), *a.* 1485. [f. L. *nimius*, f. *nimis* too much; see -OUS.] Overmuch, excessive. Now chiefly as a Sc. legal term.

Nimmer (ni·məɹ). ME. [f. NIM *v.* + -ER [1].] One who takes. b. A pilferer, a thief 1608.

Nimrod (ni·mrǫd). 1545. [See Gen. x. 8–9.] †1. A tyrant –1697. 2. A great hunter 1712.

Nincom, -cum, abbrev. ff. NINCOMPOOP.

Nincompoop (ni·nkǫ̆mpūp). 1676. [Etym. unkn.; prob. fanciful.] A fool, blockhead, simpleton, ninny.

An old Ninny hammer, a Dotard, a N. 1713.

Nine (nəin), *a.* and *sb.* [OE. *nigon*, etc. :—**nigun*, a var. of OTeut. **niwun*. The Indo-Eur. **newn̥* is represented in all the cognate langs., as Skr. *náva*, Gr. ἐννέα, L. *novem*, etc.] The cardinal number next after eight; symbols 9 or ix. A. *adj.* 1. In concord with sb. expressed. (Also coupled with a higher cardinal numeral, as *n. and twenty.*) 2. With sb. unexpressed OE. b. Of the hour of the day 1548.

1. When I was crown'd, I was but n. moneths old SHAKS. 2. Fancies..too greene and idle For Girles of n. SHAKS. N. of the strongest men of his band SCOTT. I started at n. next morning BORROW. *The N.*, the

nine Muses. **b.** *N. o'clock*, attrib. with ref. to the left-hand position of the hour hand at that time. It was a '9 o'clock wind'..It blew from the left side of the rifleman 1894.

Phrases. *A n. days' wonder*, in ref. to the time a novelty is said to hold attention; also applied to an event of temporary interest. *N. times* (etc.) *out of ten*, in the great majority of cases. *Possession is n. points of the law*: see POSSESSION.

Comb., as *n.-feet, -foot, -hole, -pound*, etc.; *n.-year-old* sb. and adj.; *n.-lived, -tailed*, etc.; *n.-pounder*; also **n.-bark**, an Amer. shrub, *Spiræa opulifolia*, having many layers of bark; **nine-men's morris**; see MORRIS *sb.*[2]

B. *sb.* **1.** The number nine; the figure or symbol representing this. late ME. **2. a.** *Cards.* A card marked with nine pips 1599. **b.** A set of nine persons, players, etc. 1860. **3.** *Long n.*: **a.** A nine-pounder gun 1799. **b.** *U.S.* A kind of cigar 1837. **4.** (*Up*) *to the nines* (rarely *nine*), to perfection 1787.

4. When she's dressed up to the nines for some grand party T. HARDY.

Nine-eyed (nəi·n,əid), *a.* 1694. Having nine eyes. †**1.** As an opprobrious epithet (*rare*) –1703. **2.** *Nine-eyed eel*, the lamprey. Sc. 1810. So **Nine-eyes** (*dial.*) 1841.

Ninefold (nəi·nfōuld). OE. [f. NINE + -FOLD.] **A.** *adj.* **1.** Nine times as great or numerous. **2.** Consisting of nine folds or parts. Also (with sb. in *pl.*): Nine in number 1594. **B.** *sb.* An attendant company of nine 1605.

A. 1. A n. woe remains behind HOOD. **2.** N. harmony MILT. **B.** *Lear* III. iv. 126.

C. *adv.* To nine times the number 1849.

Nine-holes. 1573. **a.** A game in which the players endeavour to roll small balls into nine holes made in the ground, each hole having a separate scoring value. **b.** A similar game played with a board having nine holes or arches.

Ni·ne-ki·ller. 1801. [Transl. Du. *negendooder* or G. *neuntöter*.] The butcher bird or shrike (*Lanius excubitor* or *L. borealis*).

Ninepence (nəi·npĕns). 1606. **1.** The sum of nine pence. **2.** A coin of the value of nine pence. (In former English use applied to the Irish shilling. In U.S. a name for the Sp. real = 12½ cents.) 1663.

1. Phr. *As right as n.* 1890. **2.** *Nimble n.*: see NIMBLE *a.*

Ninepenny (nəi·npĕni), *sb.* and *a.* 1826. **A.** *sb.* A coin equal in value to nine pennies 1830. **B.** *adj.* **1.** Of the value of ninepence 1894. **2.** *N. marl* = Nine men's morris 1826.

Ninepins (nəi·npinz), *sb. pl.* 1580. [PIN *sb.*[1]] **1.** A game in which nine 'pins' are set up to be knocked down by a ball or bowl thrown at them. **2.** The pins with which this game is played; also sing. one of these 1664. **3.** *attrib.* as *n. alley, yard* 1756.

Nineteen (nəintī·n, nəi·ntīn), *a.* (and *sb.*) [OE. *nigontiene*; see NINE and TEN.] The cardinal number composed of nine and ten; symbols 19 or xix. **1.** In concord with sb. expressed. **2.** With sb. understood ME. †**3.** = Nineteenth –1523.

2. Phr. *To talk* (*run*) *n. to the dozen*: to talk, or run on, at a great rate.

Nineteenth (nəintī·nþ, nəi·ntīnþ), *a.* and *sb.* [ME. *nintenthe*, superseding older *nintethe*, OE. *nigontēoða*; see prec. and -TH.] The ordinal numeral corresponding to the cardinal NINETEEN. **A.** *adj.* In concord with sb. expressed or understood.

1. *The n. hole*: the convivial gathering place of golfers after play on the course.

B. *sb.* **a.** A nineteenth part. **b.** *Mus.* An interval of two octaves and a fifth. 1597. **Ninetee·nthly** *adv.* in the n. place; also as *sb.*

Nine-tenths. 1812. Nine parts out of ten; also *loosely*, nearly the whole of any number or amount.

Ninetieth (nəi·ntieþ), *a.* (*sb.*) OE. [f. next + *-eth*, -TH.] The ordinal number corresponding to the cardinal NINETY.

Ninety (nəi·nti), *a.* and *sb.* [OE. *nigontig*; see NINE and -TY.] **1.** The cardinal number equal to nine tens, represented by 90 or xc. Also with omission of sb., and in comb. with numbers below ten (ordinal and cardinal), as *ninety-one, ninety-first*, etc. **2.** *The nineties*: The numbers between n. and a hundred; *esp.* the years between n. and a hundred in a particular century or in a person's life 1883.

Ninevite (ni·nĭvəit). 1550. [ad. L. *Ninivita*, f. *Ninive* Nineveh; see -ITE.] An inhabitant of Nineveh.

Ninny (ni·ni). 1593. [perh. abbrev. of *innocent* with prefixed *n* (see N 2).] A simpleton; a fool.

Ni·nny-ha·mmer. 1592. [app. f. prec.] A simpleton.

‖**Ninon** (nī·non). 1913. [F.; pet form of *Anne.*] A light semi-transparent silk material.

Ninth (nəinþ), *a.* and *sb.* [late OE. *nigonða*, superseding earlier *nigoða*; see NINE and -TH.] The ordinal numeral corresponding to the cardinal NINE. **A.** *adj.* **1.** With sb. expressed or understood. **b.** The ninth day (*of* a month) 1596. **2.** *N. part* or *deal*, one of the nine equal parts into which a thing may be divided OE.

B. *sb.* **1.** = Ninth part ME. **2.** *Mus.* The interval of an octave and a second; a tone at this interval 1591. **b.** (Also *n. chord*) A chord of the dominant seventh with the ninth added.

1. Find one n...of £57. 15*s.* 1870. Hence **Ni·nthly** *adv.* in the n. place; *sb.* the n. head of a sermon.

Niobate (nəi·ŏbeᵗt). 1845. [f. NIOBIUM + -ATE [1].] *Chem.* A salt of niobic acid.

Niobe (nəi·ŏbī). 1589. [a. Gr. Νιόβη.] In Greek myth., the name of the daughter of Tantalus, who was changed into stone while weeping for her children; hence *transf.* and *fig.* *Haml.* I. ii. 149. Hence **Niobe·an** *a.* 1847.

Niobic (nəiōu·bik), *a.* 1845. [f. NIOBIUM + -IC 1 b.] *Chem.* Of or pertaining to, derived from, niobium; esp. in *n. acid, oxide.*

Niobite (nəi·ŏbəit). 1854. [f. next + -ITE [1].] **1.** *Min.* = COLUMBITE. **2.** *Chem.* A niobic salt 1866.

Niobium (nəiōu·biŭm). 1845. [f. NIOBE, daughter of Tantalus + -IUM; named by H. Rose, who rediscovered it in the tantalites of Bavaria.] *Chem.* A metallic element, occurring in tantalite and other minerals. Symbol Nb. Hence **Nio·bous** *a.* derived from n. (denoting a lower degree of oxidation than *niobic*).

Nip, *sb.*[1] 1549. [f. NIP *v.*[1]] **I. 1.** The act of nipping; a pinch; a sharp bite 1551. **b.** *Naut.* Pressure exerted by ice on the sides of a vessel; the crushing effect of this 1850. **c.** *Naut.* The grip of a rope where it is twisted round something; the part of a rope held fast in this way 1841. **2.** A sharp saying, or comment; a slight rebuke, or sarcasm. Now somewhat *rare.* 1549. **3.** A check to vegetation caused by cold; the quality in wind or weather which produces this 1614. **4.** *N. and tuck* (U.S.), neck and neck, a close thing 1832.

1. b. On the following morning we sustained a slight 'n.', caused by the ice setting rapidly in towards us 1878. **2.** Many a shrewd n. has he in old days given to the Philistines, this editor M. ARNOLD.

II. †**1.** A cutpurse or pickpocket –1700. **2.** In wool- or silk-combing apparatus, a piece of mechanism which catches and carries forward the material 1884. **III.** A small piece pinched off something; a fragment, little bit 1606.

Nip, *sb.*[2] 1796. [app. abbrev. of NIPPERKIN.] †**a.** A half-pint of ale –1824. **b.** A small quantity of spirits, usu. less than a glass 1869.

Nip, *v.*[1] late ME. [Etym. uncertain. Cf. obs. Sc. *gnip* and *knip.*] **I.** *trans.* **1.** To compress or catch between two surfaces or points; to pinch, squeeze sharply. †**b.** To close up (a glass vessel) by pressing together the heated end of the neck or tube –1665. **c.** *Naut.* Of ice: To squeeze or crush (the sides of a vessel) 1853. **2.** To pinch *off.* late ME. **3.** To check the growth or development of (something), as by pinching off the buds or shoots of a plant 1581. **4.** Of cold: To affect painfully or injuriously 1548. †**5.** To censure –1720. **6.** To touch (one) closely; to vex. Now *rare.* 1553. **7.** To snatch or seize smartly. Chiefly *dial.* or *slang.* 1560. **b.** *slang.* To arrest 1566.

1. They doe bite and with their teeth n. one another 1585. **2.** The small shoots..must be nipt off 1707. Phr. *To n. in the bud*, to arrest or check at the very beginning. **4.** The wind blew keenly, nipping the features DICKENS. **6.** Not a word can bee spoke, but nips him somewhere 1633. **7.** Phr. *To n. a bung* (slang), to cut a purse.

II. *intr.* **1.** To give a nip or pinch; to cause or produce pinching 1460. †**2.** *Cant.* To pick pockets, to steal –1634. **3.** *slang.* To move rapidly or nimbly 1825. Const. with *in, out, up*, etc.

3. 'N. in, sir', said the driver 1889.

Nip, *v.*[2] 1887. [f. NIP *sb.*[2]] **1.** *intr.* To take nips of liquor. **2.** *trans.* To take (liquor) in nips 1897.

Nipa (nī·pă, nəi·pă). 1588. [Sp., Pg., a. Malay *nīpah.*] †**1.** A kind of toddy obtained from the spadix of the nipa palm (see 2) –1616. **2.** A kind of palm (*Nipa fruticans*), native to the coasts and islands of the Indian seas; also, the foliage of this plant 1839.

Nipper (ni·pəɹ), *sb.* 1535. [f. NIP *v.*[1] + -ER [1].] **I. 1.** One who nips (see NIP *v.*[1]) **b.** *U.S.* The Cunner, and the Bluefish 1888. †**2.** *Cant.* A thief or pickpocket –1785. **3.** A boy who assists a costermonger, carter, or workman 1851. **b.** *slang.* A boy, lad 1872.

1. I offre my backe vnto yᵉ smyters, and my chekes to the nyppers COVERDALE *Isa.* l. 5. **3. b.** The mind of the East End 'nipper' is equal to most emergencies 1892.

II. 1. *pl.* An instrument, usu. made of iron or steel, having two jaws by which a thing may be seized and held firmly, or cut through, by pressure on the handles; forceps, pincers, pliers. Freq. *a pair of nippers.* 1541. **b.** *slang.* Pince-nez 1876. **2.** (Usu. in *pl.*) **a.** One of the incisors of a horse 1621. **b.** One of the great claws or chelæ of the Crustacea 1769. **3.** *Naut.* **a.** A piece of braided cordage used to prevent a cable from slipping 1627. **b.** A thick woollen mitten or glove used by codfishers to protect their wrists and hands 1897.

Nipper (ni·pəɹ), *v.* 1794. [f. NIPPER *sb.*] *Naut.* To secure (a rope) by means of cross-turns; to fasten with nippers.

Nipperkin (ni·pəɹkin). Now *rare.* 1671. [Perh. of Du. or LG. origin.] **1.** A measure or vessel for liquors, containing half a pint or less 1694. **2.** The quantity contained in such a measure; a small quantity of wine, ale, or spirits. In later use chiefly *Sc.* 1671.

Nipping, *ppl. a.* 1547. [f. NIP *v.*[1] + -ING [2].] That nips; sharp, biting; checking growth, blighting. So **Ni·ppingly** *adv.* 1542.

†**Nippitate,** *sb.* Also **-ato, -atum, -aty.** 1575. [Of obscure origin.] Good ale or other liquor of prime quality and strength –1693. Hence †**Nippitate** *a.* strong, good –1634.

Nipple (ni·p'l), *sb.* 1530. [Etym. unkn.] **1.** The small prominence in which the ducts of the mammary gland terminate externally in nearly all mammals of both sexes; esp. that of a woman's breast; a teat. **b.** *transf.* A cover to protect the nipple while a child is sucking; also, the teat of a nursing-bottle 1661. **2.** Something resembling a nipple in function and form 1573. **b.** A prominence such as marks the outlet of any secretory gland 1713. **c.** A projection of any kind having the appearance of a nipple 1839. **3.** A short perforated piece made upon, or screwed into, the breech of a muzzle-loading gun, on which the percussion cap is fixed and exploded 1822.

1. *fig.* He infected the Universitie, from which he suck'd no milk but poysoned her nipples FULLER.

Comb. **ni·pplewort**, a common wayside annual (*Lapsana communis*). Hence **Nipple** *v.* to furnish with or as with a n. or nipples 1882.

Nippy (ni·pi), *a.* (*sb.*) 1575. [f. NIP *v.*[1] + -Y [1].] **1.** Of a nipping nature or disposition: see the vb. **2.** *slang.* Sharp, quick, nimble 1853. **B.** *sb.* [Registered trade-mark of Messrs. J. Lyons & Co., Ltd.] A waitress in a Lyons restaurant 1924.

‖**Nirvana** (nəɹvā·nă). Also **-wana.** 1836. [a. Skr. *nirvāṇa*, blowing out, extinction, etc., f. *nirvā* to be extinguished, f. *nis* out + *vā* to blow.] In Buddhist theology, the extinction of individual existence, or the extinction of all desires and passions and attainment of perfect beatitude.

†**Nis,** is not; see NE and BE *v.* –1586.

‖**Nisi** (nəi·səi). 1817. [L., 'unless'.] *Law.* A limiting term added to such words as *decree, order*, or *rule*, to indicate that these are not absolute or final, but are to be valid or take effect unless some cause is shown, or reason arises, to prevent this.

‖ **Nisi prius** (nəi·səi prəi·ɒ̆s). 1468. [L., 'unless previously'.] *Law.* A writ directed to a sheriff commanding him to provide a jury at the Court of Westminster on a certain day, unless the judges of assize previously come to the county from which the jury is to be returned 1495. **b.** The clause in such a writ beginning with these words 1543. **c.** The authority or commission to try causes conferred by this clause on judges of assize 1596. **2.** An action tried under a writ of this kind 1468. **3.** The trial or hearing of civil causes by judges of assize; court-business of this kind. Hence *Cause, Court, Justice*, etc., of *Nisi Prius*. 1543. **4.** *attrib.* as *Nisi Prius Court, sitting* 1734.

†**Nist**, for *ne wist*, knew not; see NE and WIT *v.* –1447.

‖ **Nisus** (nəi·sɒ̆s). 1699. [L., f. *niti* to endeavour.] Effort, endeavour, impulse.

This *Nisus* of the Mind to free the Body 1741.

Nit. [OE. *hnitu* = Du. *neet*, G. *niss*; related to Gr. κονιδ-, κονίς dust.] **1.** The egg of a louse or other insect parasitic on man or animals; the insect itself in a young state. †**2.** Applied to persons in contempt or jest –1632.

2. Thou Flea, thou N., thou winter cricket thou SHAKS. Phr. *As dead as a n.*

Ni·t-grass. 1847. [f. prec.] *Bot.* A species of grass, so called from its small nit-like flowers.

Nithing (nəi·ðiŋ). Now only *arch.* or *Hist.* OE. [a. ON. *níðing-r*, f. *níð* envy, hatred, malice.] **1.** A vile coward; an abject wretch; a villain of the lowest type. **2.** *N.-post* or *stake*, a post or stake set up as a form of insult to a person 1847.

Nitid (ni·tid), *a.* 1656. [ad. L. *nitidus*, f. *nitere* to shine.] Bright, shining, glossy (*lit.* and *fig.*).

Nitraniline (nəitræ·niləin). 1846. [f. NITRE *sb.* + ANILINE.] *Chem.* Nitro-aniline.

Nitrate (nəi·tre̥t), *sb.* 1794. [f. NITRE + -ATE¹ or ad. F.] *Chem.* **1.** A salt produced by the combination of nitric acid with a base, or a compound formed by the interaction of nitric acid and an alcohol. **2.** *ellipt.* Potassium nitrate or sodium nitrate used as a fertilizer 1846. **3.** *attrib.*, as *n. deposit*; *n. bath, Photogr.* the solution of n. of silver into which the plate to be developed is placed.

Nitrate (nəi·treit), *v.* 1872. [See NITRE and -ATE³.] *Chem.* To treat, combine, or impregnate with nitric acid.

Nitrated (nəi·treited), *ppl. a.* 1694. [Cf. prec.] **1.** Chemically treated with nitric acid (†or nitre). **2.** Impregnated with nitre 1799. **3.** Manured with nitrate of soda or potash 1841.

Nitratine (nəi·trătin). 1849. [f. NITRATE *sb.* + -INE⁵.] *Min.* Native sodium nitrate.

Nitre (nəi·tər). late ME. [a. F., ad. L. *nitrum*, ad. Gr. νίτρον, perh. of Oriental origin. Cf. NATRON.] **1.** †**a.** Natron. **b.** Potassium nitrate; saltpetre. †**c.** A supposed nitrous element in the air or in plants –1796. **2.** Used allus.: **a.** In sense 1 a, in echoes of Jer. ii. 22. 1587. **b.** In sense 1 b, with ref. to the use of saltpetre in gunpowder. 1649. **3.** *Cubic n.*, sodium nitrate 1782. **4.** *attrib.* as *n.-bed, -pit*, etc.

2. a. Let them take much snow and n., yet of themselues can they neuer be cleane 1612. **b.** Som tumultuous cloud Instinct with Fire and N. MILT. **4.** **N.-bush**, a species of *Nitraria*, a genus of plants so named because first noticed near Siberian nitre-works. (*Sweet*) *spirits of n.*; see SPIRIT.

Ni·triary, *rare.* 1839. [ad. F. *nitrière*; see NITRE and -ARY¹.] An artificial nitre-bed.

Nitric (nəi·trik), *a.* 1794. [ad. F. *nitrique*; see NITRE and -IC.] Of, pertaining to, derived from, nitre. (In *Chem.* dist. from NITROUS; see -IC 1 b.)

N. acid, a highly corrosive and caustic acid (HNO_3), which is usu. obtained by treating potassium nitrate or sodium nitrate with sulphuric acid, and in its pure state is a clear colourless liquid with an acrid taste; as used in the arts for dissolving metals, etc., it is known as *aquafortis*. *N. oxide*, a colourless gas (formerly also called *nitrous gas* or *air*) obtained by the action of nitric acid on metals, esp. copper. *N. ether*, a compound obtained by the interaction of ethyl alcohol and nitric acid, also called *ethyl nitrate*.

Nitride (nəi·trəid). 1850. [f. NITRE + -IDE.] *Chem.* A compound of nitrogen with another element or radical.

Nitrify (nəi·trifəi), *v.* 1828. [ad. F. *nitrifier*; see NITRE and -FY.] **1.** *trans.* To convert into, impregnate with, nitre; to make nitrous. **2.** *intr.* To turn to nitre; to become nitrous 1884. Hence **Ni·trifi:able** *a.* capable of being nitrified. **Ni·trifica·tion**, the process of nitrifying; the process of impregnating with nitric acid.

Nitrile (nəi·tril). Also **-yle, -il.** 1848. [f. NITRE + -ILE.] *Chem.* A cyanogen compound of an alcohol radical, in which the alkyl grouping is directly attached to carbon and in which the nitrogen atom may be regarded as trivalent.

Nitrite (nəi·trəit). 1800. [f. NITRE + -ITE¹.] *Chem.* A compound produced by the combination of a base or an alcohol with nitrous acid.

Nitro- (nəi·tro), comb. form. of Gr. νίτρον (as in νιτροποιός making nitre).

a. In names of acids, denoting the combination of nitric with an organic acid, as **nitromuria·tic acid,** nitrohydrochloric acid, *n.-trityric, -sulphuric*.

b. In names of chemical compounds or groupings, denoting the presence of the nitro-grouping NO_2 in place of hydrogen, as *n.-aniline, -benzoate*; **nitromu·riate,** a compound (*of* a base) produced by treatment with nitromuriatic acid. **nitropru·sside,** one of a series of salts obtained by the action of nitric acid upon ferrocyanides. **nitrosu·lphate,** a compound (*of* a base) produced by the action of nitrosulphuric acid.

c. In certain names of minerals, as **nitrocalcite,** native calcium nitrate; **nitroglau·berite,** a compound of sodium nitrate and sodium sulphate; **nitroma·gnesite,** native magnesium nitrate.

d. In miscellaneous combs., as **n.-a·cid,** a compound of nitric with an organic acid; **-be·nzide, -be·nzol** = NITROBENZENE; **-ce·llulose,** a compound of nitric acid and cellulose; **-co·mpound,** a compound substance resulting from the action of nitric acid; **-explo·sive,** an explosive prepared by means of nitric acid; **-pow·der,** a gunpowder prepared by means of nitric acid; **-su·bstitute,** a compound in which nitrogen peroxide is substituted for hydrogen.

Nitrobenzene (nəitrobe·nzīn). 1868. [NITRO- b.] *Chem.* A poisonous yellowish liquid, smelling like oil of bitter almonds, which is used in the preparation of aniline.

Ni·troform. 1866. [f. NITRO- d + -FORM.] *Chem.* A colourless crystallizable substance, with a bitter taste and unpleasant smell, which readily inflames and detonates.

Nitrogen (nəi·trŏdʒĕn). 1794. [ad. F. *nitrogène* (Chaptal 1790); see NITRO- and -GEN 1.] *Chem.* A 'permanent' gas (symbol N), without colour, taste, or smell, which forms about four-fifths of the atmosphere. Hence **Nitro·genize** *v. trans.* to combine with n. 1897. **Nitro·genized** *ppl. a.*, combined or furnished with n. 1843. **Nitro·genous** *a.* containing, having the nature of, n. 1828.

Nitroglu·cose. 1858. [NITRO- b.] A compound produced by the action of nitrosulphuric acid on cane or grape sugar, used esp. in photography.

Nitroglycerine, -in (nəitrogli·sĕrin). 1857. [NITRO- d.] A violently explosive substance obtained by adding glycerine to a mixture of nitric and sulphuric acids.

Nitrohydrochlo·ric, *a.* 1836. [NITRO- a.] *Chem.* In *n. acid*, a mixture of nitric and hydrochloric acids, forming a powerful solvent, also called *nitromuriatic acid* and *aqua regia*.

Nitrolic (nəitrǫ·lik), *a.* 1892. [f. NITRE + -OL + -IC.] *Chem.* In *n. acids*, acids formed by the action of nitrous acid on any of the sodium derivatives of primary nitro-paraffins.

Nitrolim (nəi·trŏlim). Also **-lime.** 1909. [NITRO- + LIME.] Cyanamide of calcium, used with other constituents, as a fertilizer.

Nitroma·nnite. 1857. [f. NITRO- d.] An explosive crystalline substance, obtained by treating mannite with nitric and sulphuric acids.

Nitrometer (nəitrǫ·mĭtər). 1828. [f. NITRO- d + -METER.] An instrument for determining the amount of nitrogen or some of its compounds in a substance.

Nitroso- (nəitrōu·so), *Chem.*, used as comb. form to indicate the presence of a nitrosyl (NO), as in *n.-compound, -derivative, -substitution*, and in specific names such as *n.-naphthaline (-ene), -phenol*.

Nitrosyl (nəi·trŏsil). 1866. [See prec. and -YL.] *Chem.* The grouping NO.

Nitrous (nəi·trəs), *a.* 1601. [ad. L. *nitrosus*; see NITRE and -OUS.] Having the nature or qualities of nitre; impregnated with nitre. **b.** Mixed or impregnated with nitre so as to form an explosive compound 1667. †**c.** As an epithet applied to the air, on the supposition that it was charged with particles of nitre –1784.

N. acid, an acid having n. properties; in later use *spec.* an acid (HNO_2) which contains less oxygen than *nitric acid*. *N. gas*, a mixture of oxides of nitrogen, such as is obtained when most metals are acted on by nitric acid in the presence of air. *N. oxide*, a colourless gas (nitrogen protoxide, N_2O), which when inhaled produces exhilaration (hence called *laughing gas*) or anæsthesia. *N. salt*, a salt containing nitre.

Nitroxyl (nəitrǫ·ksil). 1869. [f. NITRO- + OX(IDE + -YL.] *Chem.* The grouping NO_2.

Ni·tta. 1797. [Native name.] *Bot.* A West African tree (*Parkia africana* or *biglandula*), bearing pods which contain edible pulp and seeds.

Nitty (ni·ti), *a.* Now *rare.* 1570. [f. NIT + -Y¹.] Full of, abounding or infested with, nits.

Niveous (ni·vĭ̦əs), *a.* 1623. [ad. L. *niveus*, f. *niv-, nix* snow.] Snowy, resembling snow.

Nix. 1833. [a. G. *nix* masc.] A water-elf. (Cf. next.)

Nixie (ni·ksi). 1816. [ad. G. *nixe* fem.; see prec.] A female water-elf; a water-nymph.

‖ **Nizam** (nizā·m). 1768. [Urdū and Turk. *nizām*, ad. Arab. *nidām* order, arrangement; in sense 1, short for *nizām-al-mulk* 'governor of the empire'.] **1.** The hereditary title of the rulers of Hyderabad belonging to the dynasty founded by Asaf Jāh, Subahdar of the Deccan, 1713–48. **2.** The Turkish regular army; the men, or one of the men, composing this 1840.

No., Nº. 1583. Abbrev. of L. *numero* in number, abl. sing. of *numerus* = NUMBER *sb.* I. 4 and read as *number*. Also pl. *Nos.* 'numbers'.

No (nōu), *a.* ME. [Reduced form of *nān, nōn* NONE *a.*, orig. used only bef. consonants.] **I. 1.** Not any. **2.** Qualifying a noun and adj. in close connexion, usu. implying that an adj. of an opposite meaning would be more appropriate ME. **b.** Preceded by *the* or personal pronoun. Now only with *no small* or *little*. 1559. **3.** Qualifying a sb. in the predicate: Not (a). late ME. **b.** *hyperbolically*. Hardly any 1837. **4.** Qualifying a verbal sb. or gerund in the predicate, denoting the impossibility of the action specified 1560.

1. There is no neede of any such redresse SHAKS. Provb., No news, good news. *No one*, nobody. (See ONE.) **2.** This one prayer yet remains,..No long petition MILT. **b.** Falsifinge..the scriptures, to the no small admiration of all the learned readers 1559. **3.** He chose a wife..who..was no chicken SMOLLETT. **b.** The mare will get there in no time (*mod.*). **4.** There 's no accounting for tastes, sir THACKERAY.

II. In combination with sbs. or adjs. **1. a.** Denoting that the thing (or person) in question cannot properly be called by that name, as *no-faith, no-marriage*, etc. 1565. **b.** Denoting entire absence of the thing named 1603. **2.** In attrib. phrases: **a.** Denoting objection or opposition to the thing in question, as *no-popery man*, etc. 1825. **b.** Denoting absence of the thing named, as *no-confidence vote* 1832. **3.** In parasynthetic combs., as *no-coloured, -shaped*, etc. 1836; *no-trumper*, a hand at bridge on which one declares 'no trumps'.

1. Frightened with certain no-persons called ghosts FIELDING. **b.** Walking in the Middle Temple..to get them a Stomach to their No-dinners 1700. **2. a.** Just in his..'no-nonsense' style L. HUNT. **b.** A real, genuine, no-mistake Osiris O. W. HOLMES. **3.** He was a brown-whiskered, white-hatted, no-coated cabman DICKENS.

No (nōu), *adv.*¹ [Two forms: (1) repr. OE. *nó*, f. *ne* NE + *ó* always, var. of *á*, A *adv.*, O *adv.* (2) Southern and midl. representatives of OE. *ná*, NA *adv.*¹] = NOT. **1.** In ordinary uses. Now only *Sc.* **2.** Expressing the negative in an alternative choice, possibility, etc. (Usu. *whether..or no.*) late ME.

1. Alas! it 's no thy neebor sweet, The bonie Lark BURNS. **2.** I am uncertain whether or no to notice.. some of his previous exploits 1813.

No (nōu), *adv.*² [OE. *ná*, identical with NA *adv.*¹] With comparatives: Not any, not at all (better, etc.). See also No LESS, No MO(RE.

They now no longer enjoyed the Ease of Mind..in which they were formerly happy STEELE.

No (nōu), *adv.*³ and *sb.* ME. [Southern and midl. form of NA *adv.*²] A. *adv.* 1. A word used to express a negative reply to a question, request, etc., or to introduce a correction of an erroneous opinion or assumption. (Cf. NAY *adv.*) 2. Repeated for the sake of emphasis or earnestness 1500. 3. Introducing a more emphatic or comprehensive statement, followed by *not*, or *nor*. late ME. b. Introducing a correction or contradiction 1616.

1. Art thou the Prophet? And he answered: No COVERDALE *John* i. 21. *ellipt.* Then I propose the question in Parliamentary form, 'Aye or no' GLADSTONE. 2. I answered..'No, no, Sir; that will not do' BOSWELL. 3. Who spake no slander, no, nor listened to it TENNYSON. b. That class of persons was composed of men—no, he could not call them men..—of individuals 1825.

B. *sb.* 1. An utterance of the word *no*; an instance of its use; a denial 1575. b. A negative vote or decision 1589. 2. *pl.* Those who vote on the negative side in a division 1657.

1. Russet yeas, and honest kersie noes SHAKS. The Everlasting No CARLYLE. 2. The ayes proved 138 and the noes 129 1669.

Noachian (noˌēi·kiăn), *a.* 1678. [f. *Noach* = *Noah* + -IAN.] Of or relating to the patriarch Noah or his time, esp. *N. deluge*, the Flood. So **Noa·chic** *a.* 1722.

Noah's Ark (nōu·əzˌā·ɹk). 1611. [See *Gen.* vi. 14, etc.] 1. The ark in which Noah and his family, with the animals prescribed, were saved from the Flood. b. A toy consisting of an ark-shaped box, filled with figures of Noah, his family, and the animals 1846. 2. Anything suggestive of the Ark in respect of size, shape, etc., *esp.* a large, cumbrous, or old-fashioned trunk or vehicle 1829. 3. A small bivalve mollusc (*Arca Noæ*) 1713. 4. A cloud-formation somewhat resembling the outline of a ship's hull 1787.

1 b. Noah's Arks, in which Birds and Beasts were an uncommonly tight fit DICKENS. 2. The barouche will hold us all. It is a regular Noah's Ark MISS BRADDON. *Noah's nightcap*, the eschscholtzia.

Nob (nǫb), *sb.*¹ *slang.* 1700. [perh. a var. of KNOB *sb.*] 1. The head. 2. In *Cribbage*, the knave of the same suit as the turn-up card, counting one to the holder; esp. in phr. *one for his n.* 1821.

Nob (nǫb), *sb.*² *slang.* Also *Sc.* **knabb, nab.** 1755. [Origin obscure; app. not an abbrev. of *nobleman.*] A person of some wealth or social distinction.

Nob, *sb.*³ 1774. Var. of KNOB *sb.*

Nob, *v.* *Boxing slang.* 1812. [f. NOB *sb.*¹ 1.] 1. *trans.* To strike (one) on the head. 2. *intr.* To deliver blows on the head 1812.

No ball, no-ball, *sb.* 17.. [f. No *a.* + BALL *sb.*¹] 1. The words used by an umpire at cricket to signify that the ball has not been bowled in accordance with the rules of the game. 2. A ball not bowled in accordance with the rules 1884. Hence **No-ball** *v. trans.* to condemn as a no-ball; to declare a bowler to have delivered a no-ball.

Nobble (nǫ·b'l), *v. slang.* 1847. [Origin. obscure.] 1. *trans.* To tamper with (a horse) as by drugging or laming it, in order to prevent it from winning a race. b. To secure (a person, etc.) to one's own side or interest by bribery or other underhand methods 1865. 2. To steal 1854. 3. To seize, catch 1877. Hence **No·bbler**, one who nobbles horses 1854.

Nobby (nǫ·bi), *a. slang.* 1810. [f. NOB *sb.*² + -Y¹.] Belonging to, or characteristic of, the 'nobs'; extremely smart or elegant. Hence **No·bbily** *adv.*

Nobiliary (nobi·liări), *a.* 1762. [ad. F. *nobiliaire*, L. **nobiliarius*; see NOBLE *a.* and -ARY.] Of or pertaining to the nobility.

N. particle, the preposition (as F. *de*, G. *von*) forming part of a noble title. He was frankly proud of.. n. rank 1889.

†**Nobilitate** (nobi·liteit), *v.* 1538. [f. ppl. stem of L. *nobilitare*, f. *nobilis* NOBLE.] = ENNOBLE *v.* in various senses –1699. b. To raise (one) to noble rank –1763. Hence †**Nobilita·tion**, the action of ennobling –1775.

Nobility (nobi·lĭti). late ME. [ad. F. *nobilité* or L. *nobilitas*, f. *nobilis* NOBLE; see -ITY.] 1. The quality of being noble in respect of excellence, value, or importance. Now *rare.* b. Nobleness or dignity of mind or character 1595. 2. The quality, state, or condition of being noble in respect of rank or birth 1440. 3. (With *the.*) The body of persons forming the noble class in any country or state 1530. 4. (With *a.*) A noble class; a body of nobles 1612.

1. b. They say base men being in Loue, haue then a Nobilitie in their Natures, more then is natiue to them SHAKS. 2. Their Merchants who are grown rich..buy their N. ADDISON. 3. A street where many of the n. reside JOHNSON. 4. A great..Nobilite addeth maiesty to a Monarch, but diminisheth power BACON.

Noble (nōu·b'l), *a.* and *sb.* ME. [a. F. *noble*, ad. L. *nobilis*, f. **gnō-* to KNOW; see -BLE.] A. *adj.* 1. Illustrious or distinguished by position, character, or exploits. (Now merged in 2 and 3.) b. Of actions: Illustrious, great 1470. 2. Illustrious by rank, title, or birth; belonging to, or forming, the nobility of a country or state ME. b. Pertaining to, connected with, a person or persons of high rank. late ME. 3. Having high moral qualities or ideals; of a great or lofty character; proceeding from, characteristic of, indicating or displaying, greatness of character or moral superiority 1503.

1. b. What poore an Instrument May do a N. deede SHAKS. 2. More faire and famous it is to be made, then to be borne N. 1631. b. At your n. pleasure SHAKS. 3. This was the Noblest Roman of them all SHAKS. Whether 'tis Nobler in the minde to suffer The Slings and Arrowes of outragious Fortune SHAKS. A zeal worthy of a nobler cause 1831.

II. 1. Distinguished by splendour, magnificence, or stateliness of appearance; of impressive proportions or size ME. 2. Having qualities or properties of a very high or admirable kind ME. b. Of precious stones, metals, or minerals. late ME. c. Of parts of the body, *spec.* of those without which life cannot be maintained, as the heart, lungs, etc. late ME. d. Of hawks. (See IGNOBLE *a.*) 1614. 3. Splendid, admirable ME. 4. *The n. science (of defence), the n. art*, the art of (†fencing, or) boxing 1588.

1. Being past Rochester, this n. riuer goeth to Chatham 1577. 2. Highly dangerous it is for those, that have been us'd to the most generous Wines, suddenly to abandon those N. liquors 1725. b. The three first [Gold, Platina, Silver] and Quicksilver commonly called N. and Perfect metals 1796. 3. See that there be a n. supper provided SHERIDAN. *Comb.*, as *n.-couraged, -hearted, -looking* adjs.

B. *sb.* 1. A member of the nobility ME. 2. A former English gold coin, first minted by Edward III, having the current value of 6*s.* 8*d.* (or 10*s.*). Also *Angel, George, Rose, Thistle n.*, for which see these words. Hence †**No·ble** *v.* to ennoble –1621.

Nobleman (nōu·b'lmæ̆n). 1526. 1. One of the nobility; a peer. b. Formerly, a nobleman's son as a member of the University of Oxford or Cambridge 1682. 2. *pl.* The superior pieces in the game of chess 1680. Hence **No·blemanly** *a.* 1809.

Noble-minded, *a.* 1586. [f. NOBLE *a.* + MIND *sb.*] Possessed of or characterized by a noble mind, magnanimous. So **Noblemi·ndedness** 1583.

Nobleness (nōu·b'lnės). late ME. [-NESS.] 1. The state or quality of being NOBLE. †b. With personal pronouns as a title –1772.

1. We must prove the n. of the delights, and thence the n. of the animal RUSKIN.

Noblesse (noble·s). ME. [a. OF. :—Rom. **nobilitia*; see NOBLE *a.* and -ESS².] (Frequent down to the 17th cent., later re-adopted from F.) 1. Noble birth or condition. 2. The nobility; persons of noble rank 1598.

1. The n. of his Ancestours is forgotten JER. TAYLOR. 2. That advantage..which the n. of France would never suffer in their peasants DRYDEN.

Noblewoman (nōu·b'lwumăn). 1575. [Cf. NOBLEMAN.] A woman of noble birth or rank.

Nobly (nōu·bli), *adv.* ME. [f. NOBLE *a.* + -LY².] 1. With noble courage or spirit; gallantly, bravely. 2. Splendidly, magnificently ME. 3. In the condition or status of a noble; as or like a noble; esp. *n. born* 1591.

1. Patriots have toiled, and in their country's cause Bled n. COWPER. 2. There I was stopped and dined mighty n. at a good table PEPYS. 3. Thinking it better to be n. remembered than n. born RUSKIN.

Nobody (nōu·bǫdi). ME. [f. No *a.* + BODY *sb.* III. 2. Written as two words from the 14th to the 18th c., and with hyphen in the 17th and 18th.] 1. No person; no one. b. Followed by *they, their*, or *them* 1548. 2. A person, or persons, of no importance, authority, or position 1581. b. So with *a* and *pl.* 1583.

1. And whan they came to the vttemost ende of yᵉ tentes, beholde, there was no body COVERDALE 2 *Kings* vii. 5. b. N. ever put so much of themselves into their work 1874. 2. b. Which exasperates somebodies who feel they are treated as nobodies 1899.

Nocake (nōu·kēik). *U.S.* 1634. [Narragansett *nokehick*, Natick *noohkik* maize.] Indian corn parched and pounded into meal.

Nocent (nōu·sĕnt), *a.* and *sb.* Now *rare* or *arch.* late ME. [ad. L. *nocent-*, *nocens*, f. *nocere* to hurt.] A. *adj.* 1. Harmful, injurious, hurtful 1485. 2. Guilty; criminal 1566. B. *sb.* A guilty person 1447.

A. 2. The innocent and the n. 1678. Hence **No·cently** *adv.*

Nock (nǫk), *sb.*¹ late ME. [perh. same word as next.] 1. *Archery.* a. orig., One of the small tips of horn fixed at each end of a bow and provided with a notch for holding the string (*obs.*); in later use, the notch cut in this or in the bow itself. b. A small piece of horn fixed in the butt-end of an arrow, provided with a notch for receiving the bowstring; also, the notch itself 1530. Hence **Nock** *v.* to provide (a bow or arrow) with a n.; to fit (the arrow) to the bowstring.

Nock (nǫk), *sb.*² 1794. [a. Du., Flem., and Fris. *nok* or LG. *nokk.*] *Naut.* In sails: The foremost upper corner of boomsails, and of staysails cut with a square tack.

Noct-, comb. form of L. *nox, noct-*, night, used in words based on L. *ambulare* to walk, as **Nocta·mbulant** *a.*, night-walking. **Nocta·mbulation, Nocta·mbulism**, somnambulism. **Nocta·mbulist**, a somnambulist; hence **Nocta·mbulistic** *a.* **Nocta·mbulous** *a.*, given to night-walking.

Nocti-, comb. form of L. *nox, noct-*, night, as in **Nocti·dial** [L. *dies* day] *a.*, comprising a night and a day.

‖ **Noctiluca** (nǫktilʼū·kă). *Pl.* **-lucæ** (-lʼū·sī). 1680. [ad. L., moon, lantern, f. *nocti-*, *nox* night + *lucere* to shine.] †1. A species of phosphorus –1738. 2. *Zool.* A marine animalcule, of a nearly spherical shape, which produces a phosphorescent appearance in the sea 1855. Hence **Noctilu·cin(e**, the light-giving substance in phosphorescent animalcules. **Noctilu·cous**, *a.* (*rare*) phosphorescent.

Noctivagant (nǫkti·văgănt), *a.* (and *sb.*). 1620. [f. NOCTI- + VAGANT *a.*] Wandering by night. Also **Nocti·vagous** 1801. So †**Noctivaga·tion**, wandering by night, esp. as an unlawful practice subject to a fine –1678.

No·ctograph. 1864. [irreg. f. L. *noct-*, *nox* night + -GRAPH.] A writing-frame for a blind person.

‖ **Noctua** (nǫ·ktiuă). 1840. [a. L., night-owl.] *Entom.* A moth of the genus *Noctua.*

Noctuid (nǫ·ktiuˌid). 1880. [f. mod.L. *Noctuidæ*; see prec. and -ID.] *Entom.* a. *adj.* Belonging to the family of moths named *Noctuidæ.* b. *sb.* A noctuid moth.

Noctule (nǫ·ktiul). 1771. [a. F. (Buffon), ad. It. *nottola* bat; hence mod.L. *noctula.*] *Zool.* The largest British species of bat (*Vesperugo noctula*); the great bat.

Nocturn (nǫ·ktɒn). ME. [a. F. *nocturne*, ad. late or med.L. *nocturna* adj. fem. sing.] *Eccl.* 1. One of the divisions, usu. three, of the office of matins. †2. Any of the seven portions into which the Psalms were divided for recitation 1549.

Nocturnal (nǫktɒ̄·măl), *a.* and *sb.* 1485. [ad. late L. *nocturnalis*, f. *nocturnus*, f. *noct-*, *nox* night.] A. *adj.* 1. Of or pertaining to the night; done, held, or occurring by night. 2. *Zool.* a. Active during the night 1726. b. Capable of vision by night 1840.

1. In this dismal gloom of n. peregrination JOHNSON. 2. a. The hedge hog is a n. animal PENNANT.

B. *sb.* 1. An astronomical instrument for taking observations by which to ascertain the hour of the night, etc. 1627. 2. A night-walker; a night-hag (*arch.*) 1693. Hence **Noctu·rnally** *adv.*

Nocturne (nǫ·ktɒɹn). 1862. [a. F.; cf. NOCTURN.] 1. *Mus.* An instrumental composition of a dreamy character, expressive of sentiment appropriate to evening or night. 2. *Painting.* A night-piece, night-scene 1880.

2. I can't thank you too much for the name 'Nocturne' as the title for my moonlights WHISTLER.

Nocuous (nǫ·kiu,əs), *a.* 1635. [a. L. *nocuus*, f. *nocere*; cf. *innocuous.*] Noxious, hurtful; venomous, poisonous.

Nod (nǫd), *sb.* 1540. [f. next.] 1. A short, quick inclination of the head used as a sign, esp. of salutation, assent, or to direct attention to something. **b.** A sign of this kind conveying a command, or expressive of absolute power 1567. 2. An involuntary forward movement of the head in one who has fallen asleep or is drowsy; hence, a nap 1610.

1. A Look or a N. only ought to correct them, when they do amiss LOCKE. [The] smirk..was converted into a familiar n. MISS BURNEY. **b.** In Turkey, where the sole n. of the despot is death 1787. 2. *transf.* Even Homer had his nods now and then 1793. *The land of Nod*, sleep. [A pun on the place-name, *Gen.* iv. 16.]

Nod (nǫd), *v.* late ME. [Origin obscure.] I. 1. *intr.* To make a quick inclination of the head, esp. in salutation, assent, or command. 2. To let the head fall forward with a quick, short, involuntary motion when drowsy or asleep 1562. **b.** To be momentarily inattentive; to make a slip or mistake. In echoes of Horace *Ars Poet.* 359 (*dormitat Homerus*). 1677. 3. To swing or sway from the perpendicular, as if about to fall 1582. 4. To bend or incline downward or forward with a swaying movement 1606.

1. N. to him, Elues, and doe him Curtesies SHAKS. 2. She would be seen..to n. a little way forward, and stop with a jerk DICKENS. **b.** Homer nods; and the duke of Bedford may dream BURKE. 3. If ancient Fabricks n., and threat to fall DRYDEN. *fig.* A later Empire nods in its decay SHELLEY. 4. Green hazels o'er his basnet n. SCOTT.

II. 1. *trans.* To incline (the head) 1553. 2. To signify by, to say with, a nod 1713. 3. To invite, send, or bring, by a nod 1606. 4. To cause to bend or sway KEATS.

1. Some noddes their hedde at euery sentence 1553. 2. He nodded assent GEO. ELIOT. 3. Cleopatra Hath nodded him to her SHAKS.

Nodal (nōu·dăl), *a.* 1831. [f. NODE + -AL.] Pertaining to, of the nature of, a node or nodes, in various senses.

N. line or *point*, a line or point of absolute or comparative rest in a vibrating body or surface; cf. NODE 5 a. *N. point*, a stopping- or starting-point; a point constituting a node of any kind.

Nodated, *ppl. a. rare* or *Obs.* 1710. [f. L. *nodatus, nodare* to knot + -ED[1].] Knotted.

Nodding (nǫ·diŋ), *vbl. sb.* 1495. [-ING[1].] The action of the verb NOD, esp. in *n. acquaintance*, a slight acquaintance (*with* a person), extending no further than recognition by a nod 1711.

Nodding (nǫ·diŋ), *ppl. a.* 1590. [-ING[2].] 1. That nods. 2. *Bot.* (and *Entom.*) Bent or curved downward 1776.

1. The n. Violet SHAKS. The n. promontories SHELLEY.

Noddle (nǫ·d'l), *sb.* late ME. [Origin obscure.] 1. †**a.** The back *of* the head -1676. **b.** The back *of* the neck. Now *dial.* 1564. 2. *absol.* †**a.** The back of the head. **b.** The head or pate. (Colloq. or joc.) late ME. 3. The head as the seat of mind or thought. (Colloq., and usu. playful or contempt.) 1579.

2. **b.** Many a sharp rap with the rolling-pin have I had over my n. THACKERAY. 3. Slatternly girls, without an idea inside their noddles! TROLLOPE.

Noddle (nǫ·d'l), *v.* 1733. [freq. of NOD *v.*; see -LE.] 1. *trans.* To nod (the head) quickly or slightly. 2. *intr.* To nod or shake the head. (Now *dial.*) 1734.

1. The bishop..noddling his head, and beating time with his foot T. L. PEACOCK.

Noddy (nǫ·di), *sb.*[1] 1530. Formerly also **noddypeak, noddypoll.** [perh. f. NOD *v.*] 1. A fool, simpleton, noodle. 2. A soot-coloured sea-bird (*Anous stolidus*) of tropical regions, having the figure of a tern, but with shorter wings and tail less forked 1578.

Noddy (nǫ·di), *sb.*[2] 1589. [Origin obscure.] 1. A card-game resembling cribbage. Also *n.-fifteen.* Now *rare.* †2. The knave in various card-games. Also *knave n.* -1799.

Noddy (nǫ·di), *sb.*[3] 1639. [perh. f. NOD *v.*] 1. A light two-wheeled hackney-carriage, formerly used in Ireland and Scotland. 2. An inverted pendulum fitted with a spring which tends to restore it to a vertical position 1846.

Node (nōud). 1572. [ad. L. NODUS.] I. A knot or complication; an entanglement. 2. A knot, knob, or protuberance on a root, branch, etc. 1582. **b.** *Bot.* The point of a stem from which the leaves spring 1835. 3. **a.** *Path.* A hard tumour; a knotty swelling or concretion, esp. on a joint affected by gout or rheumatism 1610. **b.** Any knot, lump, or knotty formation 1753. 4. *Astr.* One of the two points at which the orbit of a planet intersects the ecliptic, or in which two great circles of the celestial sphere intersect each other 1665. 5. **a.** A point or line of absolute or comparative rest in a vibrating body 1831. Cf. NODAL *a.* **b.** A central point in any complex or system 1869. 6. *Geom.* A point at which a curve crosses itself; a double or multiple point 1850.

4. *Ascending* and *descending n.*: see the adjs. Hence **No·dous** *a.* full of knots, knotty.

Nodi-, comb. form of L. *nodus* knot, NODE, as in **Nodi·ferous** *a.*, bearing nodes.

Nodical (nōu·dikăl), *a.* 1839. [f. NODE 4 + -ICAL.] *Astr.* Of or pertaining to the nodes. *N. month*: the mean time of revolution from ascending node to ascending node.

Nodosarian (nōu·dosē̆·riăn). 1858. [f. mod.L. *Nodosaria* (see def.) + -AN.] **a.** *adj.* Belonging to a family (*Nodosaria*) of vitreous-shelled foraminifera, the individuals of which are composed of a rectilinear succession of similar chambers. **b.** *sb.* An individual of this family. So **Nodo·sarine** *a.* and *sb.*

Nodose (nodōu·s), *a.* 1721. [ad. L. *nodosus*; see NODE and -OSE.] Knotty; furnished with, or characterized by, knot-like swellings.

Nodosity (nodǫ·sĭti). 1601. [ad. L. *nodositas*, f. *nodosus*; see prec. and -ITY.] 1. The state or quality of being nodose or knotty 1611. 2. A knotty swelling or protuberance.

Nodular (nǫ·diŭlăɹ), *a.* 1794. [f. NODULE + -AR.] 1. *Min.* and *Geol.* Having the form of, occurring in, nodules. 2. Of zoophytes: Having nodes on the stem 1846. 3. *Path.* Of the nature of, characterized by, knotty tumours 1872.

Nodulated (nǫ·diŭlē̆tĕd), *a.* 1835. [ad. L. **nodulatus* (f. *nodulus* NODULE) + -ED[1].] Furnished with, characterized by, nodular growths. So **Nodula·tion,** the process of becoming n., or the result of this.

Nodule (nǫ·diul). 1600. [ad. L. *nodulus*, dim. of *nodus* knot; see -ULE.] †1. A small quantity of some medicinal substance tied up in a bag -1756. 2. *Min.* and *Geol.* A small rounded lump of some mineral or earthy substance 1695. 3. *Bot.* A small node or knot in the stem or other part of a plant 1796. 4. *Anat.* **a.** The anterior segment of the inferior vermis of the cerebellum in the fourth ventricle 1839. **b.** A small knot or knotty tumour in some part of the body 1845. Hence **Nodulo·se, no·dulous,** *adjs.* Having little knots or knobs 1828.

‖**Nodus** (nōu·dɒ̆s). *Pl.* **nodi.** late ME. [L.] †1. *Path.* = NODE 3a. -1706. 2. A knotty point, a difficulty or complication 1727.

2. The whole n. may be more of a logical cobweb, than any actual material perplexity CARLYLE.

‖**Noel** (nōuˌe·l). Also **noël.** 1811. [F.] = NOWEL.

Noesis (no,ī·sis). 1881. [a. Gr. νόησις, f. νοεῖν, f. νόος mind, thought.] **a.** The sum-total of the mental action of a rational animal. MIVART. **b.** An intellectual view of the moral and physical world 1905.

Noetian (no,ī·ʃiăn), *sb.* and *a.* 1585. [ad. L. **Noetianus*, f. *Noetus*, a native of Smyrna and presbyter of the church in Asia Minor (*c* A.D. 230.)] **A.** *sb.* A follower of Noetus in acknowledging only one person (the Father) in the Godhead. **B.** *adj.* Of, pertaining or relating to, Noetus or Noetianism 1719. Hence **Noe·tianism,** the heresy of Noetus 1874.

Noetic (no,e·tik), *a.* and *sb.* 1644. [ad. Gr. νοητικός, f. νόησις NOESIS.] **A.** *adj.* 1. Of or pertaining to the mind or intellect; characterized by, or consisting in, intellectual activity. 2. Originating or existing in the mind or intellect; purely intellectual or abstract 1810. 3. Given to intellectual speculation 1882.

1. The n. faculty, intellect proper, or place of principles SIR W. HAMILTON. 3. The new Oriel sect was declared to be N., whatever that may mean MOZLEY.

B. *sb.* 1. A science of the intellect. Also *pl.* 1825. 2. That which has a purely intellectual existence or basis 1854. 3. A member of the noetic school (see A. 3) 1882.

3. The Noetics knew nothing of the philosophical movement which was taking place on the continent M. PATTISON.

Nog (nǫg), *sb.*[1] 1611. [Origin obscure.] A peg, pin, or small block of wood serving for various purposes; chiefly *techn.* Also, a knag or stump on a tree or branch.

Nogs, the same as Wood Bricks...The term is chiefly used in the north of England GWILT. *Nog*, square bits of wood piled to support the roof of coal mines 1856.

Nog (nǫg), *sb.*[2] 1693. [Origin obscure.] A kind of strong beer brewed, in East Anglia.

Nog, *v.* 1711. [f. NOG *sb.*[1]] 1. *trans.* To secure by nogs or pegs. 2. To build with timber-framing and brick 1805.

Noggin (nǫ·gin). 1630. [Origin obscure.] 1. A small drinking vessel; a mug or cup. 2. A small quantity of liquor, usu. a quarter of a pint 1693. 3. *attrib.*, as *n.-bottle, -stave* 1663.

Nogging (nǫ·giŋ). Also **-in.** 1825. [f. NOG *sb.*[1] or *v.* + -ING[1].] (Usu. *brick-n.*) Brickwork built up between wooden quarters or framing. **b.** *N.-pieces*, horizontal pieces of wood nailed to the quarters to strengthen the work in brick-nogging.

No-go. Also **no go.** 1870. [The phr. *no go* used subst.; see GO *sb.*] An impracticable situation; an impasse; an indecisive contest.

No·how, *adv.* 1775. [f. NO *a.* + HOW *adv.*] 1. In no manner, by no means; not at all. **b.** In uneducated speech freq. with another negative. 2. In no particular manner or condition; with no distinctive appearance or character 1779.

1. **b.** That don't dovetail n. READE.

Noil (noil). 1623. [Origin obscure.] *pl.* and *sing.* The short pieces and knots of wool combed out of the long staple.

Noint, 'noint, aphetic forms of ANOINT *v.*

Noise (noiz), *sb.* ME. [a. F. (11th c.), of unkn. origin.] 1. Loud outcry, clamour, or shouting; din or disturbance. †2. Common talk, rumour; also, evil report, scandal -1734. 3. A loud or harsh sound of any kind; a din ME. **b.** Sounds of this kind collectively 1450. 4. In neutral sense, a sound of any kind (defined by the context). late ME. 5. An agreeable or melodious sound. Now *rare.* ME. †**b.** A company or band of musicians -1668.

1. Who is that at the doore yt keeps all this n. SHAKS. I wish you'd hold your n.! DICKENS. Phr. *Without n.*, in a quiet manner; without display, privately. 2. All agree in the n. of more plotts 1655. 3. I never heard any one make such a n. on a piano MISS BRADDON. **b.** Preferring quiet and solitude to the n. of a great town BERKELEY. 5. A n. like of a hidden brook In the leafy month of June COLERIDGE. **b.** A whole n. of fiddles at his heels DRYDEN.

Phr. *To make* (or †*keep*) *a n.* (in other than literal senses): **a.** To talk much or loudly *about* a thing. **b.** To be much talked of (*arch.*). **c.** *To make a n. in the world*, to attain to notoriety or renown. *The* (or *a*) *big n.*: a person of importance (orig. *U.S.*).

Noise (noiz), *v.* late ME. [f. prec., or ad. OF. *noisier, noiser*, to make a noise, to quarrel, wrangle.] 1. *trans.* To report, rumour, spread (*abroad*). Now somewhat *rare.* †2. To spread a report concerning (a person, etc.); *esp.* to speak ill of -1530. 3. *intr.* **a.** To talk loudly or much *of* a thing. late ME. **b.** To make a noise or outcry. late ME.

1. Hit is noysed that ye loue quene Gueneuer MALORY. They have noyzed and bruted abrode most shameful sklaunders 1555. 3. **a.** A plan, much noised of in those days CARLYLE. **b.** Noising loud and threatening high MILT. Hence **Noi·seful** *a.* full of noise; noisy.

Noiseless (noi·zlės), *a.* 1601. Silent, quiet; making no stir or commotion.

Th' inaudible, and noiseless foot of time SHAKS. Hence Noi·seless-ly *adv.*, -ness.

Noisette[1] (nwaze·t). 1837. [f. Philippe *Noisette*, who first introduced it.] A variety of rose, being a cross between a common China rose and a musk-rose.

Noisette[2] (nwaze·t). 1891. [Fr. = nut.] A small piece of meat rolled up and filled with stuffing.

Noisome (noi·sǒm), *a.* late ME. [f. NOY *sb.* or *v.* + -SOME.] 1. Harmful, injurious, noxious. 2. Ill-smelling 1577. 3. Disagreeable, offensive 1440.

1. He shall deliuer thee from the snare of the fouler: and from the n. pestilence BIBLE *Ps.* xci. 3. 2. Nasty streets, noisom Ditches 1678. 3. Such a n. thing as a collection of postage stamps 1899. Hence Noi·some-ly *adv.* (*rare*), -ness.

Noisy (noi·zi), *a.* 1693. [f. NOISE *sb.* + -Y[1].] 1. Making, or given to making, a loud noise; clamorous, turbulent. 2. Full of, characterized by, noise 1693.

1. A n. crowd DRYDEN. 2. A filthy and n. market MACAULAY. Hence Noi·sily *adv.* Noi·siness.

Nold(e, would not, see NILL *v.*

‖**Nolens volens** (nō̆u·lenz vō̆u·lenz). 1593. [L. pr. pples. of *nolle* and *velle.*] Willing or unwilling, willy-nilly.

No less, *adv.* and *a.* ME. [NO *adv.*[2] + LESS *a.*] Not less, as much, in various uses.

‖**Noli me tangere** (nō̆u·ləi mī tæ·ndʒěrī). late ME. [L., 'touch me not', occurring in the Vulgate, *John* xx. 17; cf. sense 5.] 1. *Path.* Any of several ulcerous cutaneous diseases of the face, esp. lupus and rodent ulcer. 2. *Bot.* A species of balsam, so called from the forcible expulsion of its ripe seeds (see TOUCH-ME-NOT). Now only as part of the full botanical name, *Impatiens Noli (me) tangere.* 1563. 3. A person or thing that must not be touched or interfered with 1475. 4. A warning or prohibition against meddling or interference, etc. 1634. 5. A painting representing the appearance of Christ to Mary Magdalen 1680.

3. Mr. Wormwood, the *noli-me-tangere* of literary lions LYTTON. 4. Every dish,..carrying a 'noli me tangere' on the face of it 1806. *attrib.* A sort of *noli me tangere* manner DE QUINCEY.

Noll (nō̆ul). Now *dial.* [OE. *hnoll.*] 1. The top or crown of the head; the head generally; the noddle. †b. *transf.* A (dull, drunken, etc.) person -1600. †2. The nape of the neck; the back of the head -1720.

1. The nappy Ale makes many a drunken N. 1626.

‖**Nolle prosequi** (nǫ·lī prǫ·sěkwəi). 1681. [L., 'to be unwilling to pursue'.] *Law.* An entry made upon the record of a court, when the plaintiff or prosecutor abandons part, or all, of his suit or prosecution against a defendant. Abbrev. Nol(le pros; also Nolle *sb.* and *v. U.S.*

Nolt (nō̆ult, nǫlt). *Sc.* 1470. [Graphic var. of NOWT.] = NEAT *sb.* 2, NOWT 1.

‖**Nom** (noṅ). 1679. [Fr., 'name'.] Used in expressions denoting a pseudonym, a false or assumed name; esp. a. *Nom de guerre* (noṅ də gęr), lit. 'war-name', a name assumed by, or assigned to, a person engaged in some action or enterprise. b. *Nom de plume* (noṅ də plüm), lit. 'pen-name', a name assumed by a writer.

‖**Noma** (nō̆u·mă). 1834. [L., a. Gr. νομή, f. νομ-, νέμειν to feed.] *Path.* A gangrenous ulceration of the cheek or vulva, occurring mainly in young children.

Nomad (nǫ·mæd, nō̆u·mæd), *sb.* and *a.* 1587. [ad. L. *Nomad-*, *Nomas*, a. Gr. νομαδ-, νομάς, f. νομ-, νέμειν to pasture.] 1. One of a race or tribe which moves from place to place to find pasture; hence, one who lives a wandering life. 2. *attrib.* or *adj.* a. Living as a nomad; nomadic 1798. b. Belonging to or characteristic of nomads 1835. Hence No·madism, the practice, fact, or state of living a wandering life 1841. No·madize *v. intr.* to live, or roam about, as nomads 1799.

Nomade (nǫ·mēd, nō̆u·mēd), *sb.* and *a.* 1775. [var. of prec.; in later use prob. after F.] = NOMAD 1. 1775. 2. *attrib.* or *adj.* a. = NOMAD 2 a. 1817. b. = NOMAD 2 b. 1819.

Nomades (nǫ·mădīz), *sb. pl.* Now *rare.* 1555. [a. L., ad. Gr. Νομάδες, pl. of νομάς; see NOMAD.] a. The nomad tribes or peoples mentioned by ancient writers. b. Such tribes as move about from place to place.

Nomadic (nomæ·dik), *a.* 1799. [ad. Gr. νομαδικός, f. νομαδ- NOMAD; see -IC.] 1. Characterized by, or leading, a wandering life. 2. Peculiar to, distinctive of, a wandering people or manner of life 1825. So Noma·dical *a.*, -ly *adv.*

No man. OE. [f. *none*, NO *a.* + MAN *sb.*] No one, nobody.

No man's land: a piece of waste, or unowned, land; in early use as the name of a plot of ground, lying outside the north wall of London, and used as a place of execution. Also *Naut.*, a space amidships used to contain any blocks, ropes, tackles, etc. necessary on the forecastle; *Mil.*, an unoccupied space between fronts of opposing forces.

Nomarch (nǫ·maɹk). 1656. [ad. Gr. νομάρχης or νόμαρχος, f. νομός NOME *sb.*[1] + ἄρχειν; cf. *monarch*, etc.] †1. A local ruler or governor (*rare*) -1678. 2. The governor of an ancient Egyptian nome 1846. 3. The governor of a modern Greek nomarchy 1880.

Nomarchy (nǫ·maɹki). 1863. [ad. Gr. νομαρχία; see prec. and cf. *monarchy.*] One of the provinces into which modern Greece is divided.

‖**No·mbril.** 1562. [F., = the navel.] *Her.* That point on an escutcheon which lies midway between the true centre (or fesse point) and the base point. Occas. vaguely alluded to as the centre of the escutcheon.

Nome (nō̆um), *sb.*[1] 1727. [ad. Gr. νομός, f. νέμειν to divide.] One of the thirty-six territorial divisions of Ancient Egypt.

Nome (nō̆um), *sb.*[2] 1753. [ad. Gr. νομός; see prec.] An ancient Greek form of musical composition.

†**Nome,** *sb.*[3] 1665. [a. F. *nôme*, second element in *binôme*, etc.] *Math.* A member of a compound quantity -1738.

Nomenclate (nō̆u·měnklēit), *v. rare.* 1801. [Back-formation from NOMENCLATURE.] *trans.* To assign a name or names to; to call by a certain name.

Nomenclator (nō̆u·měnklēitǫɹ). 1585. [a. L., f. *nomen* + *calare* to call.] †1. Used as the title of books containing list of words; hence, a vocabulary -1707. 2. *Rom. Antiq.* a. A servant or dependent who had to inform his master or patron of the names of persons, esp. when canvassing for office. b. A steward or usher who assigned or indicated the places at a banquet 1601. 3. One who announces, or communicates to another the names of persons or guests 1599. 4. One who gives or invents names for things; *esp.* in a classification of natural objects 1644.

Nomenclature (nō̆u·měnklētiuɹ, nome·nklětiuɹ, -tʃəɹ), *sb.* 1610. [ad. L. *nomenclatura* (Pliny); see prec. and -URE.] 1. A name, appellation, designation. Now *rare.* 2. A list or collection of names or particulars; a catalogue, a register 1635. †b. A glossary, a vocabulary -1745. 3. The system or set of names for things, etc., commonly employed by a person or community 1664. b. The terminology of a science 1789. c. The collective names given (or to be given) to places in a district or region 1828. 4. (Without article.) Names or designations forming a set or system 1785. 5. (With *a* and *pl.*) A particular set or system of names or designations 1809.

2. He rank't in the N. of Fooles 1635. 3. c. The n. of the frozen regions 1828. Hence Nomencla·tural *a.* relating to, or concerned with, n. Nomenclature *v.* to name or designate 1803.

Nomic (nǫ·mik), *a.* 1727. [f. Gr. νόμος NOME *sb.*[2]] Pertaining to, having the character of, Greek musical nomes.

Nominal (nǫ·minăl), *a.* and *sb.* late ME. [ad. L. *nominalis*, f. *nomin-*, *nomen* name. So F. *nominal.*] A. *adj.* 1. *Gram.* Of the nature of, or pertaining to, a noun or nouns (*rare*). 2. Belonging or pertaining to the nominalists; holding views akin to these (*rare*) 1528. 3. Of the nature of, consisting in, pertaining or relating to, a name or names (as opp. to things) 1620. 4. Existing in name only, as dist. from *real* or *actual*; merely named, stated, or expressed, without ref. to reality or fact 1624. 5. a. Consisting of, containing, or giving names 1802. b. Assigned to a person by name 1882.

3. *N. definition*, a statement of all the marks which are connoted in the name of the concept. 4. Thus.. blindly adopting n. pleasures, I lost real one's CHESTERF. An action for mere n. damages 1799. 5. a. A n. list of the officers and crew of the gunboat Wasp 1884. b. The shares are still n., and the original subscribers, as well as subsequent holders are liable on them 1882. Hence No·minally *adv.*, by name; in name, as opp. to *really*.

B. *sb.* 1. A nominalist. Now *rare* or *Obs.* 1519. 2. *Mus.* A note giving its name to a scale 1811.

Nominalism (nǫ·minăliz'm). 1836. [ad. F. *nominalisme*; see NOMINAL B. 1 and -ISM.] The view which regards universals or abstract concepts as mere names without any corresponding realities.

Nominalist (nǫ·minălist). 1654. [f. NOMINAL A. 2 + -IST.] One who maintains or accepts the doctrine of nominalism. Hence Nominali·stic *a.* 1863.

Nominate (nǫ·minět), *pa. pple.* and *ppl. a.* 1485. A. *pa. pple.* †1. Named, entitled -1567. †2. Nominated, appointed -1648. B. *ppl. a.* 1. a. Having a special name. b. Mentioning a particular name. 1818. 2. Nominated to an office. Chiefly *Sc. Law.* 1681.

Nominate (nǫ·mineit). *v.* 1545. [f. L. *nominat-*, *nominare* to name, f. *nomin-*, *nomen.*] 1. *trans.* To call by the name of; to call, name, designate. Now somewhat *rare.* †b. To provide with a name -1697. 2. To mention or specify by name. Now somewhat *rare.* 1593. 3. To name, fix, appoint, specify. Now *rare.* 1564. 4. To appoint (a person) by name to some office or duty 1560. b. To enter or put up the name of (one) as a proper person or candidate for election 1601.

1. Those animals whom we are pleased to n. 'the lower creation' 1868. 3. Let the forfeite Be nominated for an equall pound Of your faire flesh SHAKS. 4. b. We are thinking to augment our Club, and I am desirous of nominating you JOHNSON.

Nomination (nǫminēi·ʃən). late ME. [a. OF. *nominacion*, *-ation*, or ad. L. *nominationem*, f. *nominare.*] †1. The action of mentioning by name -1665. †b. The action of appointing or the fact of being appointed (*rare*) -1753. 2. The action (or right) of appointing a person by name to some office or duty 1454. b. The action of proposing as a candidate, or as a suitable person to be elected 1601. 3. The fact or position of being nominated; freq. in phr. *to put in n.*, to nominate 1494. †4. Name, designation, denomination -1794. 5. Assignation of a name or names 1552; designation by a certain name 1865.

2. He had absolute power over every n. to an English benefice FROUDE. b. The n. of a member for South Lancashire 1861. 3. The commons yesterday, after they expelled Mr. Wollaston, had in n. some others 1699.

Nominative (nǫ·minătiv), *a.* and *sb.* late ME. [a. F. *nominatif*, *-ive*, or ad. L. *nominativus (casus)*; see NOMINATE *v.* and -IVE.] A. *adj.* 1. Gram. *N. case*, that case which belongs to the subject of a finite verb (or of a participle in the absolute construction) or to a word referring thereto. b. Of or pertaining to the (or a) nominative case 1824. 2. Nominated; appointed by nomination 1660. 3. Bearing the name of a person 1872. B. *sb.* 1. The nominative case 1620. *N. of address*, the vocative. 2. A word in the nominative case; a form which is the nominative case of a word 1668. b. A subject (*to* a verb) 1824. Hence Nominati·val *a.* of or pertaining to the n. case 1843.

Nominator (nǫ·mineitǫɹ). 1659. [ad. late L.; see -ATOR.] One who nominates to office or for election.

Nominee (nǫminī·). 1688. [f. NOMINATE *v.* + -EE[1].] 1. The person who is named in connexion with, or as the recipient of, an annuity, grant, etc. 1697. 2. One who is nominated for some office.

†**No mo,** *sb.* and *a.* [f. OE. *nā* NO *adv.*[2] + *mā* MO *sb.* and *a.*] No more (in number) -1813.

Nomo-, ad. Gr. νομο-, comb. form of νόμος law, as in Nomo·cracy, a system of government based on a legal code; the rule of law in a community. **Nomo·grapher** [Gr. νομογράφος], (*a*) a writer of laws, a legislator; (*b*) one skilled in nomography. **Nomo·graphy** (*a*) a treatise on laws; (*b*) the logic of the will (Bentham); (*c*) the expression of law in a written form. **Nomo·logy,** (*a*) the science of the laws of mind; (*b*) that part of Botany which relates to the laws which govern the variations of organs; (*c*) the inductive science of law.

No more, *sb., a.,* and *adv.* [f. OE. *ná* No *adv.*[2] + MORE *sb.*[2] Cf. NO LESS.] **A.** *sb.* Nothing more or further. **B.** *adj.* Not any more; no further. late ME. **C.** *adv.* **1.** No longer. (Passing into 2.) ME. **b.** As predicate: No longer existent; departed, dead 1601. **2.** Never again; nevermore ME. **3.** To no greater extent; in no greater degree. **4.** Just as little; neither.

1. b. Cassius is no more SHAKS. 3. Eche of them ..spared no thynge, no more than yf the Kynge of Englande had bene there in proper persone LD. BERNERS. 4. You are not yong, no more am I SHAKS.

†No·mothete. *rare.* 1586. [ad. Gr. νομοθέτης.] A lawgiver or legislator -1641. Hence **Nomothe·tic, -al** *a.* law-giving; legislative 1619.

-nomy, a second element in compounds, repr. Gr. -νομία (related to νόμος law, νέμειν to distribute) as in *autonomy, economy,* etc.; also in words formed after these, as *geonomy, zoonomy,* etc.

‖**Non** (nǫn). 1551. [L., 'not'.] The first word in many Latin phrases; see Main words.

Non- (nǫn), *prefix*, formerly often written separate, used to express negation. The earlier formations were either directly adopted from, or modelled upon, AF. compounds in *noun-* = OF. *non-, nom-* (mod.F. *non-*):—L. *non* 'not' used as a prefix. It appears first in English towards the end of the 14th c. in *non-power* (Chaucer, Langland, Wyclif), and *non-residence, nonsuit* (Wyclif). In the majority of the compounds of *non-* the hyphen is usu. retained; but it is commonly omitted in a few, such as *nonconformist, nonentity, nonsense,* in which the etymological meaning has been lost sight of. Normally the prefix receives only secondary stress, but it has the main stress in *nonage, nonchalant, nondescript, nonsense.*

1. Prefixed to nouns of action, condition, or quality, as *non-acquaintance* = want of acquaintance, *non-adherence* = the condition or quality of not being adherent, *non-attendance* = failure or neglect to attend, *non-compliance* = failure or refusal to comply. 2. Prefixed to agent-nouns and designations of persons and objects, as *non-abstainer* = one who is not an abstainer or does not abstain, *non-accent* = absence or lack of accent. 3. Prefixed to adjectives, as *non-absorbable* = not absorbable, that cannot be absorbed. 4. Prefixed to a sb. (or vbl. sb.) forming a phrase used attrib., as *non-church* people. 5. Prefixed to an infinitive, as *non-act* = not to act, to refuse, neglect, or omit to act; also in attrib. phr., as *non-skid* tyre, *non-stop* train. 6. Prefixed to ppl. adjs., as *non-articulated* = not articulated, *non-budding* = not budding, that does not bud. b. Prefixed to combs. formed with ppl. adjs., as *non-slave-grown* commodities. 7. Prefixed to gerunds and vbl. sbs., as *non-accompanying* = failure or neglect to accompany. 8. Prefixed to adverbs, as *non-contentiously* = not contentiously. See also Main words.

Non-abi·lity. 1477. [NON- 1.] Inability, incapacity; *spec.* inability to commence a suit at law.

Non-a·ccess. 1799. [NON- 1.] *Law.* Impossibility of access for sexual intercourse, as in the case of a husband being abroad or at sea.

Nonage (nōu·nědʒ). late ME. [a. AF. *nounage* = OF. *nonage*, f. *non-* (see NON-) + *age* AGE *sb.*] **1.** The condition of being under age; the period of legal infancy; minority. **2.** *fig.* The period of immaturity 1584.

1. He had passed a riotous n. STEVENSON. 2. Nations outgrew their spiritual n. FARRAR.

Nonagenarian (nǫnădʒĭnēᵊ·riăn). 1804. [f. L. *nonagenarius* (f. *nonageni* ninety each); see -IAN.] **A.** *adj.* Ninety years old, or between ninety and a hundred. **B.** *sb.* A person of such age.

Nonagesimal (nǫnădʒe·simăl). 1704. [f. L. *nonagesimus*, ordinal of *nonaginta* ninety; see -AL.] **1.** *adj.* In *n. degree, point*: that point of the ecliptic which is highest above the horizon at any given time, being 90° above the point at which the ecliptic intersects the horizon. **2.** *sb.* The nonagesimal degree 1789.

Nonagon (nǫ·năgǫn). 1688. [irreg. f. L. *nonus* ninth, after *hexagon*.] *Geom.* A figure having nine angles; an enneagon.

Nonane (nōu·neⁱn). 1868. [f. L. *nonus* ninth + -ANE 2.] *Chem.* A hydrocarbon(C_9H_{20}), being the ninth of the methane series.

Non-appea·rance. 1475. [NON- 1.] Failure or neglect to appear, *esp.* in a court of law, as a party to a suit or as a witness.

Non-a·rcking, *ppl. a.* Also **-arcing.** 1895. [f. NON- 6 + ARC 5.] *Electr.* Of a metal: That does not form a voltaic arc or allow it to be formed.

Nonary (nōu·nări), *a.* 1666. [ad. L. *nonarius*, f. *nonus* ninth.] *Arith. N. scale*: a scale of notation having nine as its basis 1870.

‖**Non-assumpsit** (nǫn ăsɒ·mpsit). 1631. [L., 'he did not undertake'.] *Law.* A plea in an action of assumpsit by which the defendant denies that he made any promise or undertaking.

‖**Non avenu** (nonavnü). 1840. [F.] Not having happened.

Nonce (nǫns). [orig. in ME. phrases **for þan ane*, **for þan anes*, the latter of which was altered by wrong division (see N) to *for þe nanes, nones*, lit. = for the one (thing, occasion, etc.). **1. For the nonce: a.** For the particular purpose; expressly. *Obs.* exc. *dial.* ME. **b.** In ME. poetry used as a metrical tag, with no special meaning. **c.** For the occasion; hence, for the time being; temporarily 1589. **2.** *At the very n.*: at the very moment 1855. **3.** *attrib.* **nonce-word,** a word apparently used only for the nonce (see N.E.D. vol. I, p. xx); so *nonce-use*, etc.

1. A Cook they hadde with hem for the nones, To boille the chiknes with the mary-bones CHAUCER. c. I therefore made a virtue of necessity, and was a good Catholic for the n. 1859.

Nonchalance (nǫ·nʃălăns; as F., noṅʃalāṅs). 1678. [a. F., f. *nonchalant*; see next.] The condition of being nonchalant.

Nonchalant (nǫ·nʃălănt; as F., noṅʃalaṅ), *a.* 1734. [a. F., f. *nonchaloir*, f. *non-* + *chaloir* (:—L. *calere*) to be warm.] Wanting in warmth of feeling; lacking in enthusiasm or interest; indifferent. Hence **No·nchalant-ly** *adv.*, **-ness.**

No·n-claim. 1488. [a. AF. *nounclaim*; see NON- 1 and CLAIM *sb.*] *Law.* Failure or neglect to make a claim within the time limited by law.

Non-coll. *colloq.* Short for next.

Non-colle·giate. 1683. [NON- 2, 3.] **A.** *adj.* Not belonging to a college; belonging to the body of students (in certain universities) not attached to any college or hall (*scholares nulli collegio vel aulæ ascripti*). Also, occas. of a university. Not having a collegiate system. 1874. **B.** *sb.* One not educated or trained in a college; one of a non-collegiate body.

Non-com. 1883. Colloq. abbrev. of *non-commissioned officer.*

Non-co·mbatant. 1811. [NON- 2.] One who is not a combatant, as a civilian in time of war; *spec.* in the army and navy, one whose duties do not include that of fighting, as a surgeon, purser, or chaplain.

Non-commi·ssioned, *a.* 1703. [NON- 6.] **1.** Of officers of the army (†and navy): Not holding a commission. **2.** Of a ship: Not put in commission 1868.

Non-commi·ttal, *sb.* (*a.*) 1836. [NON- 1.] Refusal to commit oneself to a particular view or course of action. (orig. *U.S.*) **b.** *attrib.* or *adj.* Characterized by such refusal; (*esp.* of words and actions) implying neither consent nor dissent 1851. Hence **Non-commi·ttally** *adv.* 1885.

Non-commu·nicant, *sb.* (*a.*) 1598. [NON- 2.] One who is not a communicant or does not communicate (e. g. at a particular service); in the 17th c. often *spec.*, one who did not communicate according to the rites of the Church of England. So **Non-commu·nicating** *vbl. sb.* and *ppl. a.*

‖**Non compos mentis** (nǫn kǫ·mpǫs me·ntis). 1607. [L., 'not master of one's mind'.] Not *compos mentis*; not in one's right mind. Also as *sb.* Abbrev. **Non co·mpos** 1628.

Non-compou·nder. 1651. [NON- 2.] One who does not compound; *spec. Hist.* one of that section of the Jacobites which desired the restoration of James II without imposing any conditions on him.

Non-con. 1681. Abbrev. of NONCONFORMIST.

Non-conde·nsing, *ppl. a.* 1841. [NON- 6.] Applied to a kind of steam-engine in which the steam on leaving the cylinder is not condensed in a condenser but is discharged into the atmosphere.

Non-condu·ctor. 1759. [NON- 2.] *Physics.* A substance or medium that does not permit the passage of any form of energy (as heat or electricity). Hence **Non-conductibi·lity,** the quality or condition of being a non-conductor 1844. **Non-condu·cting** *ppl. a.* that is a non-conductor 1771. **Non-condu·ction** 1828.

Nonconfo·rming, *ppl. a.* 1646. [NON- 6.] = NONCONFORMIST *attrib.*

Nonconformist (nǫnkǫ̆nfǭ·ɹmist). 1619. [NON- 2.] **1. a.** (Usu. with capital N.) Orig., one who, while adhering to the doctrine of the Church of England, refused to conform to its discipline and practice. Now *Hist.* **b.** Later, a member of a religious body which is separated from the Church of England; in mod. use, usu. = Protestant Dissenter. **c.** *gen.* One who does not conform to the doctrine or discipline of an established church 1672. **†2.** One who does not conform to a particular practice or course of action -1685. **3.** *attrib.* or *adj.* 1641.

1. b. I suppose the Nonconformists value themselves tho upon their Conscience and not their numbers 1672. 3. The minimum demand of the great N. party is the..abdication of Mr. Parnell 1890. *N. conscience*, the views held to be characteristic of Nonconformists esp. as affecting their attitude on public affairs.

Nonconformity (nǫnkǫ̆nfǭ·ɹmĭti). 1618. [NON- 1.] **1.** Refusal to conform to the doctrine, discipline, or polity of an established church, orig. and now *esp.* of the Church of England; the principles and practice of Nonconformists; in mod. use, usu. = Protestant dissent. Also, Nonconformists as a body. (Usu. with capital N.) **2.** Want of conformity or refusal to conform to a rule, practice, or requirement. Const. *to, with* 1682. **3.** Want of correspondence, agreement, or adaptability between persons or things 1672.

2. The..sufferings caused by n. to the laws of life 1879.

Non-conta·gion. 1808. [NON- 1.] *Med.* The condition or property of being non-contagious. So **Non-conta·gious** *a.*

No·n-content. 1778. [NON- 2. See CONTENT *a.* 3 c.] **a.** In the House of Lords, one who votes 'Not content'. **b.** One who is not content 1860.

Non-contradi·ction. 1836. [NON- 1.] The absence of contradiction; in Logic, *principle* or *law* of *non-contradiction* = 'principle of contradiction' (see CONTRADICTION 4, quot.).

Nonda (nǫ·ndă). 1847. [Native name.] A rosaceous tree, *Parinarium Nonda*, of north-eastern Australia, yielding an edible fruit.

Nondescript (nǫ·ndĭskript). 1683. [NON- 3.] **A.** *adj.* **†1.** *Nat. Hist.* Of a species, etc.: Not hitherto described. Also *transf.* -1820. **2.** Not easily described or classified; that is neither one thing nor another 1806.

2. Those n. animals that are neither boys nor young men 1876.

B. *sb.* **†1.** *Nat. Hist.* A species, etc., that has not been hitherto described. Also *transf.* -1817. **2.** A person or thing that is of no particular class or kind 1811.

1. *transf.* A valuable addition of nondescripts to the ..known classes, genera and species, which..beautify the *hortus siccus* of dissent BURKE.

Nondo (nǫ·ndo). 1860. A tall, umbelliferous plant, *Ligusticum actæifolium*, found in North America.

None (nōᵘn), *sb.* 1656. [a. F., or ad. L. *nona*; see NOON and NONES.] **†1.** *N. of the day*: the third quarter of the day, from 3.0 p.m. to 6.0 p.m. **2.** = NONES 2. 1845.

None (nɒn), *pron., a.,* and *adv.* [OE. *nán*, f. *ne* NE + *án* ONE *a.*] **A.** *pron.* **1.** No one, not any (one), of a number of persons or things. Also, neither *of* two (now *dial.*). **2.** No one, no person, nobody. Also *n. other*, no other person (now *arch.*). OE. **b.** *pl.* No persons. (Now the commoner usage.) OE. †**c.** *N. other*, no other thing (or course); nothing else -1645. **3.** *ellipt.* Not any (such thing or person as that mentioned) OE. **b.** In predicative use, denoting lack of the essential qualities of the thing or person mentioned OE. **c.** *N. of*, not in the least 1571. **4.** No part or amount of some thing, quality, etc. ME.

1. N. of these however are known to us GOLDSM. He was n. of your hesitating half story-tellers LAMB. His understanding was n. of the clearest 1888. 2. There is n. like her, n. TENNYSON. b. N. have all; all must have some 1641. c. Sir, this is n. other but the hand of God CROMWELL. 3. It seems to be a much greater Affront..to have an ill opinion of him, than to have n. at all 1718. c. It was n. of my business DE FOE. 4. Of that there 's n., or little SHAKS.

B. *adj.* Not any; = No *a.* 1. Now *arch.* (In later use only bef. vowels and *h*, and after 1600 usu. repl. by *no.*) OE. **b.** Followed by *other.* Now *arch.* OE. **c.** Placed after (or separated from) the noun OE.

To render grants of n. effect 1801. b. I have n. other disease, than a swelling in my legs SWIFT. c. Remedy there was n. HOBBES.

C. *adv.* **1.** With comparatives: †**a.** = No *adv.*² (*rare*) -1691. **b.** With *the*: In no way, to no extent 1799. †**2.** *Or n.*, or no, or not. (Common in Chaucer). -1452. **3.** By no means, not at all. Now usu. followed by *so* or *too.* 1651.

1. b. The children n. the less knew their love RUSKIN. 3. Their merits are n. too liberally recognised 1885.

None, obs. var. of OWN (see N) -1679.

Non-effe·ctive. 1756. [NON- 3.] **A.** *adj.* **1.** Producing no effect 1862. **2.** Of soldiers and sailors: Not fit or qualified for active service 1802. **3.** [attrib. use of B.] Pertaining to, consisting of, connected with non-effectives or their maintenance 1756. **B.** *sb.* A soldier or sailor who is not fit or qualified for active service 1800.

Non-effi·cient, *a.* (*sb.*) 1863. [NON- 3.] Of volunteers: Not efficient; not having acquired a certificate of efficiency. Also *sb.*

Non-ego (nǫnī·go, -e·go). 1829. [NON- 2.] *Metaph.* All that is not the ego or conscious self; the object as opp. to the subject. Hence **Non-egoi·stical** *a.*

Non-ele·ct, *a.* 1674. [NON- 3.] Not elect (chiefly in the theological sense). Usu. *absol.* So **Non-ele·ction** 1651.

†**Non-ele·ctric.** 1739. [NON- 3.] **a.** *adj.* Not electric; incapable of developing electricity when excited by friction -1797. **b.** *sb.* A non-electric substance -1832.

†‖**Non-ens** (nǫne·nz). *Pl.* **nonentia** (-e·nʃiă). 1603. [mod.L., f. *non* not + *ens* (see ENS).] Something which has no existence; a nonentity -1803.

Nonentity (nǫne·ntĭti). 1600. [NON- 1.] **1.** The quality or condition of not being or existing; non-being, non-existence 1643. **2.** A non-existent thing; hence, a thing existing in the imagination only; a figment, a nothing 1600. **b.** What does not exist 1655. **3.** A person or thing of no consequence or importance 1710.

3. He was an atom, a n., a very worm, and no man LYTTON.

Nones (nōᵘnz). late ME. [In sense 1, a. F., or ad. L. *nonæ* (acc. *nonas*), fem. pl. of *nonus* ninth. In sense 2, pl. of NONE *sb.*] **1.** *Rom. Antiq.* The ninth day (by inclusive reckoning) before the Ides of each month, being thus the 7th of March, May, July, and October, and the 5th of all other months. **2.** *Eccl.* A daily office, orig. said at the ninth hour of the day (about 3 p.m.), but in later use sometimes earlier 1709.

Non-esse·ntial. 1751. [NON- 3.] **a.** *adj.* Not essential (in various senses). **b.** *sb.* A thing that is not essential or of the utmost consequence 1806.

‖**Non est** (nǫn e·st). 1870. = next.

‖**Non est inventus** (nǫn est inve·ntŭs). 1475. [L., 'he was not found'.] *Law.* The answer made by the sheriff in the return of the writ when the defendant is not to be found in his bailiwick. In 16-17th c. often allusively.

Nonesuch (nʊ·nsʊtʃ). 1590. [f. NONE *pron.* and *a.* + SUCH *a.* See also NONSUCH, now the usual form.] **I. 1.** An unmatched or unrivalled thing 1590. **b.** A person who has no equal; a paragon 1647. †**2.** The most eminent person or thing *of* some class, kind, place, etc. -1670. †**3.** *adj.* Unequalled, incomparable -1715.

1. The Scripture itself..presenteth Solomon's [temple] as a N., or peerless structure FULLER.

II. *spec.* **1.** The Scarlet Lychnis. 1597. **2.** = NONSUCH II. 1. 1762.

Nonet (nōᵘne·t). 1865. [ad. It. *nonetto* (also used), f. *nono* ninth; see -ET.] *Mus.* A composition for nine instruments or voices.

Non-Eucli·dean, -ian, *a.* 1874. [NON- 3.] Not Euclidean or in accordance with the principles of Euclid.

Non-Euclidean geometry: a system involving the study of the consequences which follow from denying (or merely dispensing with) any of the assumptions on which the Euclidean system is founded. *Non-Euclidean space*: the kind of space with which this geometry deals.

Non-exi·stence. 1646. [NON- 1.] **1.** The condition of being non-existent; non-being, nonentity. **2.** A non-existent thing. Also (indefinitely) that which has no existence.

1. Some I never heard of; tho' that is no Argument of their Non-Existence 1728.

Non-exi·stent. 1658. [NON- 3.] **a.** *adj.* Not existent or having existence 1682. **b.** *sb.* A person or thing that does not exist.

Non-feasance (nǫnfī·zăns). 1596. [NON- 1.] Omission of some act which ought to have been done. (Dist. from MALFEASANCE, MISFEASANCE.)

Non-gre·mial. 1841. [NON- 2.] A non-resident member (of the university of Cambridge). Also in *n. examinations*, an early name for the 'local' examinations -1865.

Nonillion (nǫni·lyən). 1690. [a. F., f. L. *nonus* ninth, after *million*.] The ninth power of a million, denoted by 1 followed by 54 ciphers. In American use, an octillion multiplied by 1000, denoted by 1 followed by 30 ciphers.

Non-importa·tion. 1770. [NON- 1.] Neglect or refusal to import. **b.** *attrib.* in *non-importation agreement* or *act*, applied to various agreements or acts made by the American colonial governments (from 1768 to 1774) to prevent the importation of goods from Great Britain and her colonies.

Non-i·ntercourse. 1809. [NON- 1.] Want of intercourse. **b.** *attrib.* in *non-intercourse act*, in *U.S. Hist.*, an Act of 1809 prohibiting ships from France and Great Britain from entering American ports.

Non-interfe·rence. 1830. [NON- 1.] Failure or refusal to interfere, *esp.* in politics.

Non-interve·ntion. 1831. [NON- 1. So in F.] Absence of intervention; in international politics, systematic non-interference by a nation in the affairs of other nations except where its own interests are directly involved.

Non-intru·sion. 1840. [NON- 1.] Absence of intrusion; *spec.* in the Church of Scotland, applied to the principle of resisting the intrusion by patrons of unacceptable ministers upon objecting congregations.

Nonius (nōᵘ·niŏs). 1750. [mod.L. name of Pedro *Nunes*, a Portuguese mathematician (1492-1577).] A contrivance for the graduation of mathematical instruments, invented by Nuñez and described by him in his work *De Crepusculis* (A.D. 1542). Often erron. used for the VERNIER, which is an improved form of the Nuñez instrument.

Non-joi·nder. 1833. [NON- 1.] *Law.* The omission to join, as a party to a suit.

Non-ju·rant. 1696. [f. NON-JUROR; see -ANT and cf. JURANT.] *Hist.* **A.** *adj.* That is a non-juror; belonging to or characteristic of non-jurors. **B.** *sb.* = NON-JUROR 1702. Hence **Non-ju·rancy**, the condition of being a non-juror; the principles of the non-jurors 1715.

Non-ju·ring, *ppl. a.* 1691. [f. NON-JUROR; see -ING.²] *Hist.* Refusing the oath of allegiance; belonging to the party of non-jurors.

Non-juror, nonjuror (nǫn,dʒūᵊ·rəɹ). 1691. [NON- 2.] *Hist.* One of the beneficed clergy who refused to take the oath of allegiance in 1689 to William and Mary.

Non-jury. 1897. [NON- 4.] *attrib.* in *non-jury action, case*, an action or case not requiring a jury.

‖**Non liquet** (nǫn ləi·kwėt). 1605. [L., 'it is not clear'.] A condition of uncertainty as to whether a thing is so or not; *spec.* in *Law*, a verdict given by a jury in a doubtful case, deferring the matter to another day for trial.

Non-me·mber. 1650. [NON- 2.] One who is not a member. So **Non-me·mbership.**

Non-me·tal. 1866. [NON- 2.] *Chem.* A non-metallic element. So **Non-meta·llic** *a.* not metallic; *Chem.* that is not a metallic element 1815.

Non-mo·ral, *a.* 1866. [NON- 3.] Not moral; having no moral standard; wanting in moral instinct or sense.

Keats,..the most absolutely non-moral of all serious writers SWINBURNE. So **Non-mora·lity.**

Non-na·tural. 1621. [NON- 3.] **A.** *adj.* †**1.** *Non-natural things* [medical L. *res non-naturales*] = 'non-naturals' (see B) -1738. **2.** Not belonging to the natural order of things; not according to or dependent upon nature 1826. **3.** Not in accordance with the natural meaning 1844.

3. The word 'wife' is taken in a non-natural sense 1884.

B. *sb. pl. Old Med.* The six things necessary to health, but liable, by abuse or accident, to become the cause of disease, *viz.* air, meat and drink, sleep and waking, motion and rest, excretion and retention, the affections of the mind 1708.

Non-nece·ssity. 1594. [NON- 1.] The condition of being unnecessary; absence of necessity.

‖**Non nobis** (nǫn nōᵘ·bis). 1475. The first words of the psalm (part of cxiii in the Vulgate) beginning *Non nobis, Domine, non nobis* 'Not unto us, O Lord, not unto us', used as an expression of gratitude or thanksgiving for mercies vouchsafed.

Nonny-nonny (nǫ·ni,nǫ·ni). *Obs.* exc. *arch.* 1533. A meaningless refrain, formerly often used to cover indelicate allusions.

Non-obe·dience. 1582. [NON- 1.] Neglect of obedience; failure to obey.

‖**Non obstante** (nǫnǫbstæ·ntī). late ME. [mod.L., 'not being in the way', orig. agreeing with a sb. in the abl. absol. construction, e. g. *non obstante veredicto* 'notwithstanding the verdict'.] †**1.** as *adv.* or *prep.* Notwithstanding -1653. **2.** as *sb.* (*Law.*) The first two words of a clause formerly used in statutes and letters patent, which conveyed a licence from the king to do a thing notwithstanding any statute to the contrary (*non obstante aliquo statuto in contrarium*); hence, a clause of this nature. Now *Hist.* 1444. †**3.** *transf.* and *gen.* **a.** A dispensation from or relaxation of a law or rule. Const. *on, of, to.* **b.** An exception to a rule -1742. †**c.** *With a non obstante to*: notwithstanding -1710.

2. King Henry the 3, though he at first detested.. these..*Non-obstantes* in Popes Bulls..yet at last he began to imitate them PRYNNE.

Nonoic (nonōᵘ·ik), *a.* 1891. [f. L. *nonus* ninth, after *octoic.*] *Chem.* The ninth in the series of fatty acids.

Nonpareil (nǫnpăre·l). 1477. [a. F.; see NON- and PAREIL *a.* and *sb.*] **A.** *adj.* Having no equal; peerless. **B.** *sb.* **1.** A person or thing having no equal; something unique 1479. **2.** *Printing.* A size of type intermediate between emerald and ruby (in America between minion and agate) 1647.

This line is printed in nonpareil type.

3. A kind of comfit 1697. **4.** A kind of apple 1731. **5. a.** A small beautifully coloured finch of the southern U.S., *Cyanospiza* (*Emberiza*) *ciris.* **b.** The rose parrakeet, *Platycercus eximius.* 1758. **6.** A name for several moths 1778.

Non-pay·ment. late ME. [NON- 1.] Failure or neglect to pay; the condition of not being paid.

Non-perfo·rmance. 1509. [NON- 1.] Failure or neglect to perform or fulfil a condition, promise, etc.; the condition of not being performed.

‖ **Non placet, non-placet** (nǫn plēⁱ·sėt). 1589. [L.; see NON and PLACET.] The Latin for 'it does not please' (*scil.* me, us), being the formula used in university and ecclesiastical assemblies in giving a negative vote; hence, as *sb.*, a negative vote in such an assembly, and †*gen.* an expression of dissent or disapproval. Hence **Non-pla·cet** *v. trans.* to vote *non placet* upon (a proposition); to throw out (a measure).

Nonplus (nǫ·nplɒs). 1582. [f. L. phr. *non plus* not more, no further. Cf. obs. F. *mettre à non-plus* to nonplus.] **A.** *sb.* A state in which no more can be said or done; inability to proceed; a state of perplexity or puzzle. Usu. in phr. *to be at* (rarely *in*) *a n.* = to be nonplussed; *to put, bring, drive, reduce to a n.* = NONPLUS *v.* **b.** *At a n.*: unprepared (*rare*) 1803.

1. I have done! any man, that can, go further! I confess myself at a non-plus BEAUM. & FL. b. He can never find our larder at a n. MAR. EDGEWORTH.

†**B.** *adj.* [app. short for *at a n.*] At a nonplus; perplexed, embarrassed –1631.

No·nplus, *v.* 1591. [f. prec.] *trans.* To bring to a nonplus or standstill; to perplex. **b.** With a thing as obj.: To render ineffective or inoperative 1640.

In which [*sc.* wrangling] his Parts were so accomplisht, That right, or wrong, he ne'r was non-plust BUTLER. Hence **No·nplussed** *ppl. a.*

‖ **Non plus ultra** (nǫn plɒs ɒ·ltrǎ). 1678. [L., 'not more beyond'.] = NE PLUS ULTRA 2 b.

‖ **Non possumus** (nǫn pǫ·siumɒ̆s). 1883. [L., 'we can not'.] A statement or answer expressing inability to move in a matter.

Non-profi·ciency. 1592. [NON- 1.] Failure to make progress or improve. So **Non-profi·cient** [NON- 2], one who fails to make progress or improve.

Non-pros (nǫnprǫ·s). 1675. *Law.* Abbrev. of next. Hence **Non-prossed** (nǫnprǫ·st) *pa. pple.* (said of the suit or of the plaintiff).

Non-prosequitur (nǫnprǫse·kwitɒ̆ɹ). 1768. [L., 'he does not prosecute'.] *Law.* A judgement entered against a plaintiff in a suit in which he does not appear to prosecute.

Non-re·gent. Now *Hist.* 1504. [NON- 2.] A master of arts whose regency has ceased. Also *attrib.* or as *adj.*

Non-regula·tion. 1845. [NON- 4.] Applied to provinces in India in which the ordinary laws are not in force.

Non-re·sidence. late ME. [NON- 1.] **1.** Systematic absence of a clergyman from his benefice or charge. **2.** *transf.* and *gen.* The fact of not residing in a particular place 1583. So †**Non-re·sidency** –1696.

Non-re·sident, *a.* 1530. [NON- 3.] **1.** Of a clergyman: Not residing where his official duties require him to reside; culpably absent from his benefice or charge. **2.** *transf.* and *gen.* Not residing on one's estate; not resident in a particular place 1540.

1. The non-resident and plurality-gaping Prelats MILT. So **Non-re·sident** *sb.* one who is n. (in both senses) 1583.

Non-reside·ntial, *a.* 1898. [NON- 3.] Not residential, as a college or university.

Non-resi·stance. 1643. [NON- 1.] The practice or principle of not resisting authority, even when it is unjustly exercised. Now only *Hist.* with ref. to the *doctrine of non-resistance* as held in England in the 17th c. (Cf. *passive obedience.*) Also *gen.* (const. *to*).

Non-resi·stant. 1702. [NON- 2, 3.] **a.** *adj.* Not resistant; †pertaining to or involving the doctrine of non-resistance. **b.** *sb.* One who does not resist authority or force (occas. = NON-COMBATANT); one who holds or practises the doctrine of non-resistance 1850. So **Non-resi·sting** *ppl. a.* (= sense a).

Nonsense (nǫ·nsěns), *sb.* 1614. [f. NON- 2 + SENSE *sb.* Cf. F. *nonsens.*] **1.** That which is not sense; words which make no sense or convey absurd ideas; also, absurd or senseless action. (Often used exclamatorily.) **2.** Absurdity, nonsensicalness 1630. **3.** Unsubstantial or worthless stuff or things 1638. **4.** A meaning that makes no sense 1650.

1. For learned N. has a deeper Sound, Than easy Sense, and goes for more profound BUTLER. 'It's all stuff and n.,' said the little lady 1894. *No n.*: no foolish or extravagant conduct; no humbug. Chiefly in phr. *stand no n.* (also used as adj.). 4. How easy it is to a Caviller to give a new Sense, or a new N. to any thing POPE.

attrib. and *Comb.*, as **n.-book,** a book of n. or nonsense verses; **n. verses,** verses consisting of words and phrases arranged without regard to the sense 1822. **b.** That is n.; full of n.; †formerly often used as *adj.* = Nonsensical; as *a n. sculpture*, etc.

Nonsensical (nǫnse·nsikăl). 1655. [f. prec. + -ICAL.] **A.** *adj.* That is nonsense; of the nature of, or full of, nonsense; absurd. Also of persons. **B.** *sb.* A nonsensical, absurd, or trifling thing 1842. Hence **Nonse·nsical-ly** *adv.*, **-ness.**

‖ **Non sequitur** (nǫn se·kwitɒ̆ɹ). 1533. [L., 'it does not follow'.] An inference or conclusion which does not follow from the premisses. Also *transf.* and *fig.*

Non-soci·ety. 1851. [NON- 4.] *attrib.* Not belonging to a society; *spec.* (now *rare*) applied to non-union workmen or establishments.

Non-subscri·ber. Now *Hist.* 1599. [NON- 2.] **1.** One who refuses to subscribe to an undertaking, a creed, etc. **2.** One who does not pay a subscription 1713. So **Non-subscri·ption,** refusal or failure to subscribe (e. g. to a religious creed) 1736.

Non-substa·ntial, *a.* 1836. [NON- 3.] *Philos.* Not substantial. Hence **Non-substa·ntialism,** the theory that there is no substance underlying phenomena; = NIHILISM 2. Also **Non-substa·ntialist,** one who holds the doctrine of non-substantialism; = NIHILIST 1.

Nonsuch (nǫ·nsɒtʃ). 1620. [var. of NONESUCH, and now the usual form.] **I.** = NONESUCH I. 1–3. **II. 1.** A species of Lucern, *Medicago lupulina*. Also called *black n.* 1668. **2.** A variety of apple (†and pear) 1676.

Nonsuit (nǫ·nsiūt), *sb.* late ME. [a. AF. *no(u)nsute*; see NON- 1 and SUIT *sb.*] *Law.* orig., The cessation of a suit resulting from the voluntary withdrawal of the plaintiff; in mod. use, the stoppage of a suit by the judge, when, in his opinion, the plaintiff fails to make out a legal cause of action or to bring sufficient evidence.

†**No-nsuit,** *a.* 1476. [app. a pa. pple. formed after words like *execute.*] *Law.* Nonsuited –1817.

No·nsuit, *v.* 1531. [f. NONSUIT *sb.* or *a.*] *Law. trans.* To subject to a nonsuit. †Also *transf.* and *fig.* –1714.

Non-te·nure. 1574. [a. AF. *nountenure*; see NON- 1 and TENURE.] *Old Law.* A plea in bar to a real action, in which the defendant said that he did not hold the land.

†**Non-term.** 1607. [NON- 1.] The time of vacation between two terms; the cessation of term; hence *gen.*, a period of inaction –1824.

Nontronite (nǫ·ntrǒnəit). 1832. [ad. F., f. *Nontron* (in France), its locality.] *Min.* A pale-yellow variety of chloropal.

†**Non u·ltra.** 1672. [L., 'not beyond'.] = NE PLUS ULTRA 2, 2 b. –1704.

Non-u·nion, *a.* 1863. [NON- 4.] Not belonging to a trade-union; also, manufactured by non-union men. So **Non-u·nionist,** one who does not belong to a trade-union 1861. **Non-u·nionism,** the principles of non-unionists.

Non-u·ser. 1565. [NON- 1.] *Law.* Neglect to use a right, by which it may become void.

Non-va·scular, *a.* 1857. [NON- 3.] *Anat.* Destitute of vessels for the circulation of fluids.

Nonyl (nǫ·nil). 1866. [f. L. *nonus* ninth + -YL.] *Chem.* The ninth in the series of alcohol radicals of the general formula C_nH_{2n+1}. So **No·nylene,** a hydrocarbon produced in the decomposition of lime soap; whence **Nonyle·nic** *a.* **Nony·lic** *a.*, pertaining to or derived from n.

Noodle (nū·d'l), *sb.*[1] 1753. [Origin obscure.] A simpleton. Hence **Noo·dledom,** noodles collectively; foolishness; an instance of this.

Noodle, *sb.*[2] 1779. [a. G. *nudel*, of unkn. etym.] A strip or ball of dough made with wheat, flour, and eggs, and served in soup. Also *attrib.* in **n.-soup.**

Nook (nuk), *sb.* [ME. *nok(e* (earliest in *four nokede* four-cornered, square, *c* 1200), of obscure origin.] **1.** A corner of a square or angular thing, or of a figure bounded by straight lines. Now *rare.* **b.** A corner of land; a small triangular field 1603. **c.** A headland or promontory; also, a piece of land projecting from one division into another and terminating in a point. Now *rare.* 1487. **2.** An interior angle formed by the meeting of two walls or the like; a corner in a room or other enclosed space. late ME. **b.** A small or out-of-the-way corner ME. **c.** A secluded or sheltered spot among natural scenery 1555. **d.** A small or sheltered creek or inlet 1582. **3.** An outlying, remote, or secluded part of a country, region, etc., or of the world. late ME.

1. The lamb was slung in the n. of his plaid 1897. c. He wants my poor little Farm, because it makes a N. in his Park-wall ARBUTHNOT. 2. There were so many nooks and corners in the..room 1877. b. I write in a n. that I call my *boudoir* COWPER. c. In the deep Trosachs' wildest n. SCOTT. d. *Temp.* I. ii. 227. 3. While yet a n. is left Where English minds and manners may be found COWPER.

Comb.: **n.-rib,** *Arch.* a rib in the corner of a vault; **-shaft,** *Arch.* a shaft placed in the internal angle formed by the meeting of two contiguous faces in a compound archway; **-window,** a window in the corner of a room next the fireplace. Hence **Noo·kshotten** *a.* running out into corners or angles (now *arch.* or *dial.*) 1599.

Nook (nuk), *v. rare.* 1611. [f. prec.] **a.** *intr.* To hide in a corner. **b.** *trans.* To chip *off*, so as to form corners. **c.** To conceal.

Noology (noǫ·lŏdʒi). 1811. [f. Gr. νόος mind + -LOGY.] The science of the understanding. Hence **Noolo·gical** *a.* pertaining to n. **Noo·logist,** one who refers the origin of certain ideas to the mind itself and not to experience.

Noon (nūn), *sb.* [OE. *nón* neut., ad. L. *nona* (sc. *hora*), fem. sing. of *nonus* ninth; cf. NONE *sb.* and NONES.] †**1.** The ninth hour of the day, reckoned from sunrise according to the Roman method, or about 3 p.m. –1420. †**b.** *Eccl.* The hour or office of NONES –1561. **2.** Twelve o'clock in the day; mid-day. (The change is probably due to anticipation of the eccl. office.) ME. **b.** *transf.* The most important hour of the day 1712. **3.** The time of night corresponding to mid-day; midnight. Chiefly in phr. (*the*) *n. of night.* 1603. **b.** The place of the moon at midnight 1605. **4.** The culminating point 1600. **5.** *attrib.*, as **n.-beam,** etc., 1461.

2. The heat, bustle, and activity of n. DICKENS. *fig.* In the broad n. Of public scorn SHELLEY. b. It is 5 o'clock, the n. in Pall Mall THACKERAY. 3. Night hath climbed her peak of highest n. TENNYSON. b. To behold the wandring Moon, Riding near her highest n. MILT. 4. Thou oft Amidst thir highth of n., Changest thy countenance MILTON. *Comb.* **n.-flower,** a name given to plants of the genus *Mesembryanthemum*, and to the Goat's-beard (*Tragopogon pratensis*).

Noon (nūn), *v. U.S.* 1806. [f. prec.] *intr.* (also with *it.*) To halt or rest at noon; to stop for, or partake of, the mid-day meal.

Noonday (nū·ndēⁱ). 1535. The middle of the day; mid-day.

Nooning (nū·niŋ). Now *U.S.* 1460. [f. NOON *sb.* + -ING[1] 1.] **1.** Noontide. **2.** A noonday meal 1652. **3.** A rest at noon 1552. **b.** An interval in the middle of the day, esp. for rest or food 1865.

Noo·n-light. 1598. The light of noon; the brightest or clearest light of the day.

Noontide (nū·ntəid). [OE. *nóntīd*; see NOON *sb.* and TIDE *sb.*] **1.** The time of noon; mid-day. **2.** *transf.* The middle *of* night; the position *of* the moon at midnight 1560. **b.** *fig.*, esp. the culminating point *of* something 1578.

1. The noontide's hush and heat and shine MRS. BROWNING. *attrib.* The Noone-tide Sun SHAKS. 2. b. A Poor Relation—is..a preposterous shadow, lengthening in the n. of your prosperity LAMB.

Noose (nūs, nūz), *sb.* 1600 (? 1450.) [Origin and early history obscure; possibly a. OF. *nos* :—L. *nodus* knot.] **1.** A loop, with a running knot, which tightens as the string or rope is pulled, as in a snare, lasso, hangman's halter, etc.; a loop, a folding or doubling of a string or rope. *Running n.*: see RUNNING *ppl. a.* **2.** *fig.* **a.** The marriage tie 1600. **b.** A snare or bond 1624.

Noose (nūs, nūz), *v.* 1600. [f. prec.] **1.** *trans.* To secure as by a noose; to ensnare. **2.** To hang; to put to death by hanging 1673. **3.** To capture by means of a noose; to cast a noose round 1748. **4.** To make a noose on (a cord); to place *round* in a noose; to arrange like a noose or loop 1814.

1. He, that loves at first sight, nooses himself by vows 1710. 3. G. had..noosed the animal with his lasso 1843.

Nopal (nōᵘ·păl). 1730. [a. Sp., ad. Mexican *nopalli* cactus.] An American species of cactus (*Nopalea coccinellifera*) cultivated for the support of the cochineal-insect; a plant of this kind; a prickly pear. 1808.

Nopalry (nōᵘ·pălri). Also **-ery.** 1783. [f. prec. + -RY, after Sp. *nopalera*, F. *nopalerie*, *nopalière*.] A plantation of nopals where the cochineal-insect is bred.

Nope[1] (nōup). 1611. [app. a var. of ALP [2], OLP; see N.] The Bullfinch.

Nope[2], *U.S.* pron. of No *adv.*[3] 1.

Nor (nǭɹ), *conj.*[1] ME. [contr. of NOTHER; cf. OR *conj.*[2]] **1.** A negative particle co-ordinating two or more words, phrases, or clauses between which there is an alternative. **a.** Where a negative other than *neither* qualifies the first alternative (the normal conj. being now *or*); †formerly the second alternative might be qualified by another negative. **b.** Where the alternative is emphasized by prefixing *neither* to the first member. (The main current use.) **c.** *arch.* Introducing both alternatives (*nor* .. *nor* = *neither* .. *nor*). **d.** *arch.* Without preceding negative. **2.** and .. not.

1. a. She could not heare, nor speake, nor understand SPENSER. It requires no rhymes nor no certain number of feet or syllables CHESTERF. b. Quarter was to be neither taken nor given MACAULAY. c. Nor shapes of men nor beasts we ken COLERIDGE. d. A heart his words nor deeds can daunt BYRON. 2. Away! nor weep! BYRON.

Nor, *conj.*[2] *Sc.* and *dial.* late ME. [Origin obscure.] Than.

I know better nor you GEO. ELIOT.

Nor', abbrev. f. NORTH. late ME.

Norbertine (nǭ·ɹbəɹtin, -əin), *sb.* and *a.* 1674. [f. *Norbert* (1092–1134), founder of the order + -INE.] A member of (pertaining to) the Premonstratensian order.

No·rdenfelt. 1880. Name of a Swedish engineer, used *attrib.* and *absol.* to designate a kind of machine-gun invented by him.

Nordhausen (nǭ·ɹdhauz'n). 1849. The name of a town in Saxony, used *attrib.* as a designation of fuming sulphuric acid, orig. made there.

Nordic (nǭ·ɹdik), *a.* 1898. [ad. F. *nordique* (J. Deniker), f. F. *nord* NORTH; see -IC.] Of or pertaining to the type of northern Germanic peoples represented by the blond dolichocephalic inhabitants of Scandinavia and the north of Britain. Also *sb.*

†**Nore**, obs. var. of *nor'*, NORTH. 1612.

Norfolk (nǭ·ɹfək). [OE. *Norðfolc* 'North people'.] Name of an English county, used *attrib.* to designate things peculiar to or characteristic of the district. **b.** *spec.* **N. capon,** a red herring; **N. dumpling, turkey,** a native or inhabitant of N.; **N. jacket,** a loosely fitting jacket with a waist-belt (1866); **N. plover,** the Stone Curlew.

Norfolk Howard (nǭ·ɹfək hau·əɹd). 1865. [In the *Times* of 26 June, 1862, one Joshua Bug declared in due form that he had assumed the name of Norfolk Howard.] A bed-bug. *slang.*

‖**Noria** (nōᵊ·riă). 1792. [Sp., ad. Arab.] A device for raising water, used in Spain and in the East, consisting of a revolving chain of pots or buckets which are filled below and discharged when they come to the top.

Norimon (nǫ·rimǫn). 1616. [ad. Jap. *norimono*, f. *nori* to ride + *mono* thing; cf. KAKEMONO.] A kind of litter or palanquin used in Japan.

Norite (nōᵊ·rəit). 1878. [f. *Nor(way)* + -ITE.] *Geol.* and *Min.* A variety of gabbro or granite.

Norland (nǭ·ɹlănd). 1578. [Reduced f. NORTHLAND.] The north-country; the land in the north. **b.** *attrib.* Belonging to the north 1578. Hence **No·rlander,** a northerner 1716.

Norm (nǭɹm). 1821. [Anglicized f. next.] A rule or authoritative standard.

‖**Norma** (nǭ·ɹmă). Also *pl.* **normæ** (nǭ·ɹmī). 1676. [L. = carpenter's square.] **1.** = NORM. **2.** One of the southern constellations 1840.

Normal (nǭ·ɹmăl), *a.* and *sb.* 1530. [ad. L. *normalis*, f. *norma* (see prec.)]. **A.** *adj.* **1.** Right (angle), rectangular (*rare*) 1650. **b.** Standing at right angles; perpendicular 1696. **2.** According to or squaring with a norm; constituting, conforming to, not deviating or differing from a type or standard; regular, usual 1828. **b.** *Chem.*, in spec. uses (see quots. in N.E.D.) 1857. **3.** *N. school* [after F. *école normale*], a school for the training of teachers 1834.

B. *sb.* **1.** *Geom.* A perpendicular; a straight line at right angles to the tangent or tangent plane at any point of a curve or curved surface 1727. **2.** *Physics.* The average or mean of observed quantities 1859. **3.** The usual state or condition 1890. **b.** *ellipt.* Normal temperature 1896. Hence **No·rmalcy** (orig. *U.S.*), **Norma·lity,** n. character or state. **No·rmally** *adv.*

Normalize (nǭ·ɹmăləiz), *v.* 1865. [f. NORMAL *a.* + -IZE.] *trans.* To make normal or regular. Also *absol.* Hence **Normaliza·tion,** the action or process of making normal.

Norman (nǭ·ɹmăn), *sb.*[1] and *a.* ME. [a. OF. *Normans, -manz*, pl. of *Normant* (later *Normand*), a reduced form of Teut. or Scand. NORTHMAN.] **A.** *sb.* **1. a.** A native or inhabitant of Normandy; one belonging to the mixed Scandinavian and Frankish race there settled. **2.** = Norman-French (see B. 3 b) 1646. **B.** *adj.* **1.** Belonging or pertaining to the Normans 1589. **2.** *N. Conquest*, the conquest of England in 1066 by the Normans under William I. 1605. **3.** *Norman-English* or *-Saxon*, English as spoken by the Normans, or as influenced by them (*rare*) 1589. **b.** *Norman-French*, the form of French spoken by the Normans, or the later form of this in English legal use (Law French) 1605. **4.** The distinctive epithet of a form of architecture, or its details, developed by the Normans, and employed in England after the Conquest 1772.

1. The rage of building fortified castles..among the N. princes 1797. Hence **Normane·sque** *a.* suggestive of the N. style of architecture 1844. **No·rmanism,** prevalence of N. rule or characteristics; tendency to favour or copy the Normans 1647. **No·rmanize** *v.* **1.** *intr.* to adopt the N. tongue or manners 1623. **2.** *trans.* to make N. 1861. **Norma·nnic** *a.* of or belonging to the Normans 1710.

Norman (nǭ·ɹmăn), *sb.*[2] 1769. [= Du. *noorman*, G. *normann.*] *Naut.* A short wooden bar, thrust into one of the holes of the windlass in a merchant-ship, whereon to fasten the cable (FALCONER).

Normative (nǭ·ɹmătiv), *a.* 1880. [a. F. *normatif, -ive*; see NORMA and -ATIVE.] Establishing a norm or standard.

No·rmoblast. 1890. [f. *normo-*, as comb. form of L. NORMA + -BLAST.] *Path.* A nucleated red blood-corpuscle of a normal size.

Norn (nǭɹn). 1770. [a. ON.] One of the female Fates of Scandinavian mythology.

No·rna. 1840. Latinized form of prec.

Norroy (nǫ·roi). †Also **Norrey.** 1470. [f. AF. *nor-* north + *rey, roy* king.] Title of the third King of Arms, with jurisdiction north of the Trent.

Norse (nǭɹs), *sb.* and *a.* 1598. [prob. ad. Du. *noorsch*, var. of *noordsch*, f. *noord* NORTH + *-sch* -ISH.] **A.** *sb.* **1.** A Norwegian. Now only as collect. sing. = Norwegians. **2.** The Norwegian tongue 1688. **B.** *adj.* Norwegian; from, or belonging to, Norway 1768. Hence **No·rseland,** Norway. **No·rseman,** a Norwegian.

A. 2. *Old N.*, the language of Norway and its colonies down to the 14th c. (sometimes loosely used to include early Swedish and Danish).

Norsk, *a.* and *sb.* 1851. [a. Scand. *norsk.*] = prec.

North (nǭɹþ), *adv.*, *sb.*, and *a.* Abbrev. *nor'* in *nor'(nor')east*, etc. [Com. Teut.: OE. *norð*; not recorded in Gothic.] **A.** *adv.* **1.** Towards or in the north (see B). Also with additions, as *n. by east*, etc. **2.** quasi-*sb.* without article = B. 1. ME.; also = northerliness.

1. There is one [river] that commeth due n. CAPT. SMITH. This Bay lieth N. and South CAPT. SMITH. Phr. †*Too far n.* (slang), too clever, too knowing. 2. Most Conquests have gone from N. to South HUME. *By n.*: (see BY *prep.* 1 d).

B. *sb.* (Usu. with *the.*) **1.** That one of the four cardinal points which lies on the left-hand of a person facing due east ME. **2.** The northern part of a country or region; *spec.* **a.** of England (beyond the Humber), Great Britain, Scotland, or Ireland; the North Country ME. **b.** Of Europe: The northern lands 1579. **c.** *U.S.* The northern States bounded on the south by Maryland, the Ohio river, and Missouri, in which there was no slaveholding 1835. **3.** The north wind. Chiefly *poet.* ME. **b.** A north wind, esp. *pl.* those which blow in the West Indies 1699.

1. The Magnetic N. (=north magnetic pole), almost always, differs from the true (= north pole) 1812. 2. a. The..gray metropolis of the N. TENNYSON. b. A multitude, like which the populous N. Pour'd never from her frozen loyns MILT. 3. I will speake as liberall as the N. SHAKS.

C. *adj.* [Developed partly from OE. *norð-* in compounds.] **1.** Of, belonging to, or lying towards the north; situated on the north side OE. **b.** Facing the north 1642. **c.** Of a northern type 1820. **2.** Of the wind: Blowing from the north ME.

1. The N.-Welch MILT. N.-Britain 1708. Did ever any North-American bring his hemp to England for this bounty? FRANKLIN. Thy Master staies for thee at the N. gate SHAKS. b. A North-window is best for Butteries and Cellars FULLER. 2. When I was born, the wind was n. SHAKS. Hence **North** *v.* *rare. intr.* of the wind: to begin to blow from the north; to veer towards the north.

North abou·t. 1710. *Naut.* By a northerly route, *spec.* round the north of Scotland.

North Bri·ton. 1708. [NORTH *a.* 1.] A native of Scotland; a Scot.

North cou·ntry. ME. [NORTH *a.* 1.] The northern part of any country; *spec.* of England (beyond the Humber) or Great Britain; the country or region towards the north. Also *attrib.* Hence **North-cou·ntryman,** a native of the north of England.

North-east (nǭɹþ,ī·st, *attrib.* nǭ·ɹþ,īst), *adv.*, *sb.*, and *a.* OE. [f. NORTH and EAST.] **A.** *adv.* **1.** In the direction lying midway between north and east. **2.** quasi-*sb.* With preps., as *on, from, at* OE. **B.** *sb.* **1.** The direction, or point of the horizon, lying midway between north and east. late ME. **2.** The north-east wind. Now chiefly *poet.* late ME.

2. The wynd Tiffonyk, that is clepid north eest, or wynd of tempest WYCLIF *Acts* xxvii. 14.

C. *adj.* **1.** Of the wind: Blowing from the north-east. late ME. **2.** Situated in or towards the north-east 1440.

2. *North-east passage*, a passage for vessels along the northern coasts of Europe and Asia, formerly thought of as a possible course for voyages to the East.

North-ea·ster. 1774. [f. as prec. + -ER [1].] A wind blowing from the north-east.

North-ea·sterly, *a.* and *adv.* 1739. **A.** *adj.* Blowing from, lying towards, the north-east 1743. **B.** *adv.* From or towards the north-east 1739.

North-ea·stern, *a.* 1841. Pertaining to the north-east; lying on the north-east side.

North-ea·stward, *adv.*, *a.*, and *sb.* 1553. [f. NORTH-EAST + -WARD.] **A.** *adv.* Towards the north-east. **B.** *adj.* Situated towards the north-east 1766. **C.** *sb.* The north-east quarter 1892. Hence **North-ea·stwardly** *a.* blowing from, situated or leading towards, the north-east; *adv.* towards the north-east.

North-end. [OE. *norðende*, f. *norð* NORTH + *ende* END *sb.* In later use f. NORTH *a.*, and properly unhyphened, exc. when used *attrib.*] The northern end or extremity of anything.

Norther (nǭ·ɹþəɹ), *sb.* 1844. [f. NORTH + -ER [1].] A northerly wind; esp. a strong and cold north wind, which blows in autumn and winter, over Texas, Florida, and the Gulf of Mexico.

Norther (nǭ·ɹðəɹ), *v.* 1628. [f. NORTH *adv.* + -ER [5].] *intr.* Of the wind: To shift or veer northward.

Northerly (nǭ·ɹðəɹli), *a.* 1551. [f. NORTH; cf. *easterly*, etc.] **1.** Situated towards the north; northern. **2.** Of the wind: Blowing from the northward 1555. So **No·rtherly** *adv.* to the northward; on the north side. Hence **No·rtherliness.**

Northern (nǭ·ɹðəɹn), *a.* and *sb.* OE. [f. NORTH + *-ern* (OTeut. **rônjo-*). **A.** *adj.* **1.** Of persons or peoples: Living in, originating from, the north, esp. of England or of Europe. **b.** *U.S.* Belonging to the northern States 1836. **2.** Of the wind: Blowing from the north OE. **3.** Of things: Pertaining to, found in, characteristic of, the north. late ME. **b.** In the specific designations of animals or plants 1860. **4.** Lying or situated to the north; having a position relatively north 1590. **5.** Taking place or carried on in the north 1589.

2. That northren wynde is euer redy and destinat to all euell 1480. **3. b.** *N. diver*, the common loon (*Urinator imber* or *Colymbus torquatus*). *N. spy*, an American apple. **4.** *N. star* = NORTH STAR. *N. Lights*, the Aurora Borealis. **5.** A northerne progresse 1669.

B. *sb.* **1.** A native of the north 1774. Hence **No·rthern** *v.* to become more n. **No·rtherner,** a native or inhabitant of the n. part of any country, *esp.* (*U.S.*) of the n. States 1840. **No·rthernly** *a.* (now *rare*), northerly; †also as *adv.* **No·rthernmost** *a.* most northerly; furthest north.

Northing (nǭ·ɹþiŋ), *vbl. sb.* 1669. [f. NORTH + -ING[1].] **1.** (Chiefly *Naut.*) Progress or deviation towards the north made in sailing or travelling; difference in latitude due to moving northwards. Freq. in phr. *to make* (so much) *n.* **2.** Of heavenly bodies: Apparent movement towards the north 1808.

Northland (nǭ·ɹþlæ̆nd). [OE. *norðland* (see NORTH *a.*).] The northern part of a country, etc.; also *pl.* the lands lying in the north.

North-light. 1706. **1.** (Usu. *pl.*) = *northern lights* (NORTHERN A. 4). Now *rare.* **2.** Light coming from the north 1870.

2. The equable north-light of the artist LOWELL.

Northman (nǭ·ɹþmæ̆n). [OE. *Norðman* (see NORTH *a.*); cf. NORMAN *sb.*[1]] (Chiefly *pl.*) An inhabitant or native of Norway or of Scandinavia.

No·rthmost, *a.* Now *rare.* OE. [See -MOST.] Most northerly, northernmost.

North-north-east, *adv.* late ME. [= Du. *noordnoordoost*, etc.] In the direction lying midway between north and north-east. Also as *sb.* and *adj.*

North-north-west, *adv.* late ME. [= Du. *noordnoordwest*, etc.] In the direction lying midway between north and north-west. Also as *sb.* and *adj.*

North Sea. OE. **1.** The proper name of certain seas in northern Europe; now only, 'the German Ocean' (bounded by Great Britain, Scandinavia, and Holland) ME. †**2.** *pl.* The seas of the northern hemisphere –1726.

North star. [late ME. *north sterre.*] The pole-star.

Northu·mber. Now *rare* or *Hist.* [OE. *Norðhymbre*, f. *norð-* NORTH + *Humbre* the Humber.] *pl.* The ancient inhabitants of Northumbria, or England north of the Humber.

Northumbrian (nǭɹþɒ·mbriăn). 1612. [f. prec. + -IAN.] **A.** *adj.* Of or pertaining to Northumbria or Northumberland 1622. **B.** *sb.* **1.** An inhabitant or native of ancient Northumbria or modern Northumberland 1612. **2.** The northern dialect of ancient Northumbria or modern Northumberland 1845.

Northward (nǭ·ɹþwəɹd, *Naut.* nǭ·ɹþəɹd), *adv.*, *sb.*, and *a.* See also NORWARD. late OE. [f. NORTH + -WARD.] **A.** *adv.* **1.** Towards the north; in a northern direction. **2.** quasi-*sb.* = next 1864.

1. I am going N. for a while JOHNSON. On the Downs n. of Brighton 1885. **2.** To n. of Bautzen forty miles 1865.

B. *sb.* That direction or part which lies to the north (of a place or thing) 1624. **C.** *adj.* That moves or looks northward 1597. Hence **No·rthwardly** *adv.* in a n. direction; *adj.* having a n. situation or direction; (of the wind) blowing from the n.

No·rthwards, *adv.* and *sb.* OE. Northward.

North-west (nǭɹþwe·st, *Naut.* nǭɹwe·st; see NOR'-WEST), *adv.*, *sb.*, and *a.* OE. [f. NORTH and WEST.] **A.** *adv.* **1.** In the direction lying midway between north and west. **2.** quasi-*sb.* = next. late ME. **B.** *sb.* The direction or part lying midway between north and west; *spec.* the North-west Territories of Canada. late ME. **C.** *adj.* **1.** Of the wind: Blowing from the north-west. late ME. **2.** Pertaining to the north-west; situated in the north-west part of a country, etc. 1827.

N. Passage, a passage for vessels along the north coast of America, formerly thought of as possible for navigation between the Atlantic and the Pacific.

North-we·ster. 1737. [f. prec. + -ER[1].] **1.** A wind or gale blowing from the north-west. **2.** = NOR'-WESTER 2. 1830.

North-we·sterly, *a.* 1611. [f. NORTH-WEST, after WESTERLY.] **a.** Of the wind: Blowing from the north-west. **b.** Tending north-west.

North-we·stern, *a.* 1612. [Cf. WESTERN.] Situated or extending towards the north-west.

North-we·stward, *adv.* and *sb.* late ME. [f. NORTH-WEST + -WARD.] **a.** *adv.* In a north-westerly direction; towards the north-west. **b.** *sb.* = NORTH-WEST *sb.* 1796. Hence **North-we·stwardly** *a.* and *adv.*

Norward (nǭ·ɹwəɹd). 1618. Also *Naut.* **nor'ard** (nǭ·rəɹd). [f. *nor'* NORTH + -WARD.] **a.** *adv.* Northward. **b.** *sb.* The northern part or region 1618.

a. Nor'ard of the Dogger (*title*) 1887.

Norway (nǭ·ɹwe[i]). 1674. [ME. *Norwey*, *-wei*, OE. *Norweȝ*, ad. ON. *Norvegr*, f. *nor-*, *norðr* NORTH + *vegr* WAY.] Name of one of the Scandinavian countries, used *attrib.*, as in *N. fir, spruce*, etc.; *N. haddock, lobster, rat*, etc.; *N. deal, skiff, yawl*, etc.

Norwegian (nǭɹwī·dʒăn). 1605. [f. med.L. *Norvegia*, with *w.* from NORWAY.] **A.** *adj.* Of or pertaining to Norway; belonging to, found in, Norway 1607.

The tallest Pine Hewn on N. hills MILT.

B. *sb.* **1.** A native of Norway 1599. **2.** The language of Norway 1605. **3.** *U.S.* A kind of fishing-boat 1872.

Nor'-west. late ME. Reduced f. NORTH-WEST *a.* and *sb.*

Nor'-we·ster. 1703. [Reduced f. NORTH-WESTER.] **1.** A wind or gale from the north-west. **2.** A glass of strong liquor 1840. **3.** An oilskin hat; a sou'-wester 1851.

Norweyan (nǭɹwē[i]·ăn), *a.* 1605. [f. NORWAY + -AN.] Norwegian SHAKS.

Nose (nōuz), *sb.* [OE. *nosu*, obscurely related to OE. *nasu* and to NESE.] **I. 1.** That part of the head or face in men and animals which lies above the mouth and contains the nostrils. Also, the analogous part in lower forms of animal life. **2.** The organ of smell. late ME. **b.** The sense of smell; a (good, bad, etc.) faculty of smell or power of tracking by scent ME. **c.** Smell, odour (*dial.*) 1894. **3.** As an organ by which speech-sounds may be produced or affected. Chiefly in phr. *in* or *through the n.* 1530. **4.** *A n. of wax*, a person or thing easily moulded or influenced 1532. **5.** *slang.* A spy or informer 1812.

1. His n. on the sodaine bled LODGE. Phr. *Parson's n.*, the rump of a fowl. **2. b.** *fig.* He was a gentilman of a longe n. . . Thys Shyryffe was a coueтuouse man LATIMER. **3.** He. . pays as he speaks. . —through the n. DICKENS.

Phrases (more or less fig.). *To make a long n.* (see LONG *a.*[1]). †(*In*) *spite of one's n.*, notwithstanding one's opposition 1675. *To count*, or *tell*, *noses*, denoting the counting of supporters, deciding by mere numbers. **b.** *Under one's* (*very*) *n.*, often implying that an action is done in defiance of a person, or without his perceiving it. **c.** *To cut off one's n.*, to do something to one's own hurt or loss. *To follow one's n.*, to go straight forward, be guided by instinct. *To hold one's n.*, to compress the nostrils between the fingers and thumb in order to avoid perceiving a bad smell. *To poke, put*, or *thrust one's n.*, to poke or pry *into* something. *To turn up one's n.*, to show disdain. **d.** *To bite* or *snap one's n. off*, to answer snappishly. *To put one's n. out of joint*, etc., to displace or supplant one; to spoil one's plans; to throw one out. **e.** *To pay through the n.*, to pay excessively.

II. In transf. uses. **1. a.** The open end of a pipe or tube; the muzzle of a gun, the nozzle of a pair of bellows, etc. 1598. **b.** The beak of an alembic, retort, or still 1651. **2.** The prow, bow, or stem of a ship or boat 1538. **b.** The corresponding part of an airship, aeroplane, torpedo, etc. 1899. **3.** A prominent or projecting part; the point or extremity of anything 1592. **b.** A projecting part of a shell 1681. **c.** *Arch.* The projecting part or edge of a moulding, stair-tread, or mullion 1815.

2. One of the Gallies lost her N. with a shot 1613. **3.** The Lode-stone that alwaies holdeth his n. to the North LYLY.

attrib. and *Comb.*: **n.-ape,** the proboscis-monkey; **-cap,** a metal cap on the n. of a gun-stock; **-dive,** the forward and downward plunge of an aeroplane, etc.; also *vb.* **-leaf,** the foliaceous appendage of the nostrils in some bats; **-monkey** = *nose-ape*; **-rag,** a pocket handkerchief (*slang*); **-tube,** a tube for feeding a patient through the n.; **-worm,** the larva of the sheep-bot.

Nose (nōuz), *v.* 1577. [f. the sb.] **I.** *trans.* **1.** To perceive the smell of (something); to discover or notice by the sense of smell. **b.** To scent or smell *out* (*lit.* and *fig.*) 1630. †**2.** To confront, face, or oppose (a person, etc.) in an impudent or insolent manner. (Cf. BEARD *v.* 3.) –1824. **3.** To utter with a nasal twang; to sing through the nose 1643. **4.** To rub with the nose; to press the nose close to (something) 1777. **b.** To examine with the nose; to put the nose close to (a thing) in examining 1851.

1. *fig.* Nosing a job in every Ministerial move 1893. **2.** A sort of national convention. . nosed parliament in the very seat of its authority BURKE. **3.** It makes far better musick when you n. Sternhold's. . meeter 1643. **4.** Lambs are glad Nosing the mother's udder TENNYSON.

II. *intr.* **1.** To sniff, to smell. Also with *about* or *round* 1783. **b.** To pry or search (*after* or *for* something) 1648. **2.** To push with the nose 1891. **3.** Of strata or veins: To dip in, run *out* 1879.

1. *fig.* That fellow's still nosing round here with his gun 1895. **2.** A steamer slowly noseing round off the wharf-cranes 1891.

No·se-bag. 1796. [f. NOSE *sb.*] A bag to contain provender for a horse, suspended from the horse's head by straps fitted to the open end.

No·se-band. 1611. [f. NOSE *sb.* + BAND *sb.*[2]] The lower band of a bridle, passing over the nose, and attached to the cheek-straps.

No·se-bleed. late ME. [f. NOSE *sb.* + stem of BLEED *v.*] **1.** An old name for the plant Milfoil or Yarrow. **2.** A bleeding at the nose 1852.

Nosed (nōuzd), *a.* 1440. [f. NOSE *sb.*] **1.** Having a nose of a specified shape. **b.** (Also *well-n.*) Keen-scented 1604. **2.** Having a prominent nose, as *Nosed Monkey* 1896.

Nosegay (nōu·zge[i]). late ME. [f. NOSE *sb.* + GAY *sb.* 2.] A bunch of flowers or herbs, esp. sweet-smelling flowers; a bouquet, a posy. **b.** A perfume or scent (*spec.* one artificially prepared); an odour, smell 1855.

1. *transf.* The country is one big n. W. MORRIS.

Noseless (nōu·zlės), *a.* late ME. [-LESS.] Lacking or deprived of a nose.

No·se-piece. 1611. [f. NOSE *sb.*] **1. a.** A part of a helmet or turban serving as a guard for the nose; a nasal. **b.** A nose-band for a horse 1865. **2.** *Optics.* The part of a microscope to which the objective (or object-glass) is attached 1867.

No·se-pipe. 1784. [f. NOSE *sb.*] **1.** A pipe, or piece of piping, forming a nose or terminal to another pipe, a vessel, etc. **2.** *spec.* The blast-pipe nozzle inside the tuyère of a blast furnace 1839.

Noser (nōu·zəɹ). 1852. [f. NOSE *sb.* + -ER.] A strong head wind; *esp.* in phr. *a dead n.*

No·se-ring. 1778. [f. NOSE *sb.*] **1.** A ring fixed in an animal's nose. **2.** A ring-shaped ornament worn in the nose 1839.

†**No·se-smart.** 1589. [f. NOSE *sb.* + SMART, after L. *nasturtium.*] The plant Cress –1755.

Nose-thirl, †**-thrill, -tril,** refashioning of NOSTRIL.

†**No·se-wise,** *a.* 1566. [f. NOSE *sb.* + WISE *a.*] **1.** Conceited; clever in one's own opinion –1787. **2.** Keen-scented –1630.

Nosey, nosy (nōu·zi). 1620. [f. NOSE *sb.* + -Y[1].] **A.** *adj.* **1.** Having a large nose. **2.** Smelly 1836. **3.** *slang.* Inquisitive, prying. **B.** *sb.* One who has a large nose. (Used as a nickname.)

A. 3. *N. Parker*, an inquisitive person. B. *sb.* Had heer'd of the Duke of Wellington; he was Old N. 1851.

Nosing (nǭᵘ·ziŋ). 1771. [f. Nose *sb.* + -ING [1].] The rounded edge of a bench, or of a step projecting over the riser; also, a metal shield for the same; the prominent edge of a moulding or drip.

Noso- (nǫ·so, nǫ̆sǫ), comb. form of Gr. νόσος disease, as in †**No·socome** [a. F., ad. L. *nosocomium*, Gr. νοσοκομεῖον], a hospital (URQUHART *Rabelais*); hence **Nosoco·mial** *a.*; **Noso·graphy** [-GRAPHY], systematic description of diseases, hence **-gra·phic, -ical** *adjs.* **Nosopoe·tic** *a.*, producing or causing disease.

Nosology (nǫ̆sǫ·lŏdʒi). 1721. [ad. mod.L. *nosologia*, a. Gr. *νοσολογία; see NOSO- and -LOGY.] 1. A classification or arrangement of diseases. b. The list of known diseases 1839. 2. Systematic classification or investigation of diseases; that branch of medical science which deals with this 1727. 3. The special character of a particular disease, or the views current with regard to this 1825. Hence **Nosolo·gical** *a.* of, pertaining to, or dealing with, n. **Noso·logist**, one occupied with, or versed in, n.

Nostalgia (nǫstæ·ldʒiă). 1780. [a. mod.L. *nostalgia* (1678, rendering G. *heimweh*), f. Gr. νόστος return home + ἄλγος pain.] A form of melancholia caused by prolonged absence from one's country or home; severe home-sickness. Also **Nosta·lgy**. Hence **Nosta·lgic** *a.* of the nature of, caused by, n.; home-sick.

Nostoc (nǫ·stǫk). 1650. [Coined by Paracelsus.] *Bot.* A genus of unicellular *Algæ*, having the cells arranged in rows which intertwine with each other and form a gelatinous mass; *esp.* the ordinary species of this, *N. commune*, formerly believed to be an emanation from the stars. b. An individual plant of this genus 1851.

Nostradamus (nǫstrădē·mɒ̆s). 1668. [Latinized form of the name of Michel de *Nostredame*, a French physician (1503–1566) who published a collection of prophecies in 1555.] One who professes to foretell future events; a seer like Nostradamus.

Nostril (nǫ·stril). [OE. *nosþyrl*, f. stem of *nosu* NOSE; see THIRL.] One of the external openings in the nose of vertebrates; an analogous opening in other animals.

fig. phr. Our judgments stink in the nostrils of the people BURKE.

Nostrum (nǫ·strɒ̆m). 1602. [a. L. *nostrum*, neut. sing. of *noster* our.] 1. A medicine, or medical application, prepared by the person recommending it; *esp.* a quack remedy, a patent medicine. 2. A special device for improving or accomplishing something; *esp.* a pet scheme of political or social reform 1749.

1. The owner of a n. of some kind, called a patent food 1883. 2. Another party's n. is, more churches, more schools, more clergymen KINGSLEY. *Comb.*, as **n.-monger** (now *rare* or *Obs.*).

Nosy, var. NOSEY.

Not (nǫt), *a.* and *sb.* Now *dial.* [OE. *hnot*; etym. unkn.] †1. Close-cropped, short-haired –1633. 2. Of sheep or cattle: Hornless, polled 1587. b. *sb.* A hornless sheep 1834. †3. Of wheat or barley: Awnless, beardless –1680.

1. A not-heed hadde he, with a broun visage CHAUCER. *Comb.* as *n.-headed, -pated* adjs.

†**Not**, *v.*[1] 1530. [f. prec.] *trans.* To clip or cut short (the hair or beard) –1674.

†**Not**, *v.*[2], **note.** OE. For *ne wot* know(s) not; see NE and WIT *v.* –1614.

Not (nǫt), *adv.* and *sb.* ME. [Unstressed f. NOUGHT *adv.*] The ordinary adverb of negation. 1. Modifying an ordinary verb. a. Following the verb. Now *arch.* b. Preceding the verb. Chiefly *poet.* late ME. 2. Following an auxiliary verb. Also in the form **n't**, usu. written as one word with the verb. ME. Also *ellipt.* in replies. 3. Following the verb *to be*. Also as *n't*. late ME. b. With ellipse of vb., esp. after *if*, or in replies. late ME. 4. Preceding an infinitive or gerundial clause 1440. 5. †a. Used redundantly after vbs. of forbidding, dissuading, or preventing –1677. b. Coupled with other negatives, or repeated. Now *dial.* or *vulgar.* late ME. 6. Preceding a sentence, clause, or word. a. In introductory phrases, as *not but (that), not that*, etc. ME. b. Placed first for the sake of emphasis. late ME. c. In contrast with a following *but* 1579. d. Emphasizing a pronoun after a neg. statement, or in a reply 1625. 7. With terms of number or quantity ME. 8. After *or, if*, or *as*, with ellipse of words expressed or implied in the preceding clause. late ME. 9. Denoting contrast or opposition to what precedes, with or without *and* 1471. 10. With advs. or advb. phrases 1475. b. Modifying adjs. or pples. in agreement with a preceding sb. or pronoun 1529. c. With neg. adjs. or advs., implying the affirmative term 1657.

1. a. They wyst n. what folke they were CAXTON. 2. I'll n. offend thee with a vain tear more B. JONS. You mustn't tell me anything 1895. *ellipt.* 'You've seen this before?' 'No, n. that I can remember' (*mod.*). 3. This is n. the cause of a king, but of kings BURKE. It isn't true 1895. b. Fame if n. double-fac't is double-mouth'd MILT. 4. I knew neither what to do, or what n. to do DE FOE. 6. a. N. that I lou'd Cæsar lesse, but that I lou'd Rome more SHAKS. b. Yet n. the more Cease I to wander MILT. c. Which were borne, n. of blood,..but of God *John* i. 13. d. He is no Witch, n. he DEKKER. 7. He spoke n. a Word DE FOE. Phr. *N. a little*, a good deal. 8. Shall we give battle..or n. DE FOE. If virtue is of such a nature, it will be taught; and if n., n. JOWETT. 9. They are in heauen and n. here *Bk. Com. Prayer.* 10. N. once or twice..The path of duty was the way to glory TENNYSON. b. You have got to be regarded as n. quite right in your head 1889. c. A certain air of dignity, n. unmingled with insolence 1900.

B. *sb.* The word '*not*'; a negation or negative 1601.

They still doe returne us a n. 1608.

Comb. **n.-self** = NON-EGO.

‖ **Nota bene** (nǭᵘ·tă bī·ni). 1721. [L., 'mark well'.] Mark well, observe particularly. (Abbrev. N.B.) b. Used substantively 1731.

Notability (nǭᵘtăbi·lĭti). late ME. [a. OF., or ad. med.L. **notabilitas*; see next and -ITY.] 1. †a. A notable fact or circumstance –1470. b. A notable or prominent person 1851. 2. The quality of being notable; esp. housewifely industry or management 1786. Now *dial.*

1. b. Various other little notabilities of the neighbourhood KINGSLEY. 2. Mary has infected me with her n., and I'm going to work Mama a footstool MRS. GASKELL.

Notable (nǭᵘ·tăb'l), *a.*, *sb.*, and *adv.* ME. [a. F., ad. L. *notabilis*, f. *notare* to NOTE; see -ABLE. In sense 3 b, the pronunc. is given by some dicts. as (nǫ·tăb'l).] A. *adj.* 1. Deserving of note, esp. on account of excellence, value, or importance; remarkable, striking, eminent. 2. †a. Attracting notice; conspicuous –1621. b. Noticeable, perceptible. Now *Chem.* 1551. 3. †a. Of men: Industrious, business-like –1732. b. Of women: Capable, managing, bustling; active in household management and occupations. Now *dial.* 1718. c. Connected with household management and industry 1787.

1. Acts of n. Oppression and Injustice STEELE. You have mingled many Unworthies among them, rather Notorious than N. FULLER. 3. b. A n. Woman, who was thoroughly sensible of the intrinsick Value of Time 1718.

B. *sb.* 1. A noteworthy fact or thing (*rare*) 1483. b. A person of eminence or distinction 1815. 2. *pl. Hist.* A number of prominent men from the various estates of the realm of France, summoned by the king as a deliberative assembly in times of emergency 1568.

1. The notables of the town were fast assembling SCOTT. 2. From the very commencement of the revolution, at the first meeting of the notables 1792. Hence **No·tableness. No·tably** *adv.*

‖ **Notandum** (notæ·ndɒ̆m). Also *pl.* **notanda.** 1605. [L., neut. gerundive of *notare* to NOTE.] An entry or jotting of something to be specially noted; a memorandum, note.

Notarial (notē^ə·riăl), *a.* 1482. [ad. L. **notarialis*, f. *notarius* NOTARY *sb.*] 1. Of or belonging to a notary. b. Characteristic of notaries 1828. 2. Drawn up, framed, or executed by a notary 1622. Hence **Nota·rially** *adv.* 1847.

Notary (nǭᵘ·tări). ME. [ad. L. *notarius* shorthand-writer, clerk, secretary, f. *notare* to note, *nota* a note.] †1. A clerk or secretary to a person –1711. 2. A person publicly authorized to draw up or attest contracts, etc., to protest bills of exchange, etc., and discharge other formal duties ME. b. More fully *n. public, public* (or †*common*) *n.* 1494. †3. A noter or observer –1685.

1. *fig.* O comfort-killing Night,..Dim register and n. of shame SHAKS. 2. b. Protest is..made by a N. Publick in the presence of two credible Witnesses 1682.

Notation (notē^ı·ʃən). 1570. [ad. L. *notationem*, f. *notare* to NOTE.] †1. The explanation of a term in accordance with its etymology; the primary sense of a word. (Common in 17th c.) –1690. 2. A note or annotation. Now *rare.* 1584. 3. The action of taking or making note of something (*rare*) 1646. 4. The process or method of representing numbers, quantities, etc., by a system of signs; hence, any set of symbols or characters used to do this; *e.g.* in *Arith.* and *Algebra, Music*, etc. 1706.

1. If we may Admit that Gentleman's N. of a Libell (a Lie because False, and a Bell because Loud) 1690. 4. The ecclesiastical n. of the Greek Church.. is supposed to have originated in the Greek accents 1876.

Not-being. 1586. [NOT *adv.*] Absence of being; non-existence.

[In the philosophy of Hegel] Being and not being are thus declared to be identical 1880.

Notch (nǫtʃ), *sb.* 1577. [a. AF. *noche*, app. for **anoche*, f. *anocher* (see next).] 1. A V-shaped indentation or incision in an edge or across a surface. 2. A nick made on a stick, etc., as a means of keeping a score or record 1580. b. A run in cricket. Now *rare.* 1737. 3. *U.S.* A narrow defile through mountains; a deep narrow pass 1718. 4. An opening; a break or breach 1789.

2. Upon the Sides of this square Post, I cut every Day a N. with my Knife DE FOE. *fig.* Its prices are at the lowest notch (*U.S.*). 3. About half way between the N. of the Mountain and Hartford 1718.

Comb.: **n.-board**, a board grooved to receive the ends of the steps in a stair; **-wing**, a name of various moths.

Notch (nǫtʃ), *v.* 1597. [Aphetic a. AF. *anocher* (OF. *enochier*), f. *en-* + *oche* (mod.F. *hoche*) notch, of obsc. origin.] 1. *trans.* To cut (hair) unevenly (*rare*) –1747. 2. To make notches in; to cut or mark with notches 1600. b. To shape *into* (some form) by making notches 1768. 3. To score or record by means of notches. Also with *up* and *down*. 1623. b. To score (a run, etc.). Now *rare.* 1837. 4. To fix, secure, or insert, by means of notches 1768. b. To chop *off*, cut *out* 1820. 5. To fit the arrow to the bowstring; to nock 1635.

2. He scotcht him, and notcht him like a Carbinado SHAKS. 3. We notched the votes down on three sticks LOWELL. 4. *fig.* The houses were notched, as it were, into the side of the steep bank SCOTT. 5. His bow is bent, and he has notch'd his dart QUARLES. Hence **Notched** *ppl. a.*; *spec.* in *Bot.*, coarsely dentate or serrate; in *Zool.*, having notches or incisions.

Notching (nǫ·tʃiŋ), *vbl. sb.* 1611. [f. prec.] 1. The action of making notches, esp. in carpentry as a method of joining timbers. 2. A notch or notch-like incision 1842.

Note, *sb.*[1] *Obs.* exc. *n. dial.* [OE. *notu*, related to NEAT *sb.* and NOWT.] 1. Use, usefulness, profit, advantage. b. *dial.* The milk given by a cow; the period of giving milk; the condition of a cow when giving, or beginning to give, milk after calving 1728. 2. Office; employment, work OE.

Note (nǭᵘt), *sb.*[2] ME. [a. OF., ad. L. *nota*, a mark.] I. 1. a. A written character or sign, expressing the pitch and duration of a musical sound. b. A key of a pianoforte, etc. 1848. 2. A single tone of definite pitch, as produced by a musical instrument or by the human voice in singing ME. b. With ref. to the song, etc., of birds. late ME. 3. A strain of music, a melody. In later use only *poet.* ME. b. The musical call or song of a bird ME. 4. A cry, call, or sound of a bird or fowl ME. 5. *transf.* 1483.

2. First rehearse this song by rote, To each word a warbling n. SHAKS. b. Where birds..Sit sweetly tuning of their noates together 1613. 3. The pealing anthem swells the n. of praise GRAY. b. The deep mellow crush of the wood-pigeon's n. CAMPBELL. 4. The n. of the carrion crow.., a note-call of danger 1866. 5. We can catch clearly enough the n. of extreme..self-dependence 1877. Phr. *To change (one's) n.*: To alter (one's) way of speaking or thinking.

II. 1. A mark, sign, token, or indication *of* some quality, condition, or fact; a characteristic or distinguishing feature. late ME. b. *Theol.* One of certain characteristics by which the true Church may be known; a sign or proof of genuine origin, authority, and practice 1555.

2. A stigma or reproach. Const. *of.* Now *rare.* 1531. **3.** An objective sign, or visible token or mark, which serves to identify or distinguish a person, thing, or condition. Now *rare.* 1577. **4.** A sign or character (other than a letter) used in writing or printing; a mark *of* interrogation, etc. 1529.

1. These are the notes of the 'Neo-paganism', which began a good hundred years ago 1891. **b.** How comes subjection to the Pope to be..an essential n. of the Church? WESLEY.

III. 1. *Law.* An abstract of essential particulars relating to transfer of land by process of FINE, which was engrossed and placed on record 1483. **2.** A brief record or abstract of facts written down to assist the memory, or to serve as a basis for a fuller statement; also *transf.* a mental impression of something. (Usu. *pl.*) 1548. **b.** A brief memorandum of topics for a discourse on any subject. (Usu. *pl.*) 1693. **3.** An annotation appended to a passage in a writing or book 1560. **4.** A brief statement of particulars or of some fact; †a bill 1587. **5.** A short or informal letter 1594. **b.** A formal diplomatic communication 1796. **c.** Short for NOTE-PAPER 1883. **6.** A written promise to pay a certain sum at a specified time. Also *n. of hand.* 1683. **7.** A bank-note, or similar promissory note passing current as money 1696.

2. And 'tis out of these Notes that my Observations are compiled 1695. Phr. *To make,* or *take, a n.* or *notes. To compare notes*: see COMPARE *v.*[1] 2. **b.** He spoke for more than an hour without a n. FROUDE. 3. I found two other volumes.., enriched with manuscript notes LAMB. 4. Heere is now the Smithes n., for Shooing, And Plough-Irons SHAKS. 5. Not a n., not a line did I receive in the mean time JANE AUSTEN.

IV. 1. Distinction, mark, importance; reputation. Now *Obs.* or *arch.* 1538. **2.** Notice, regard, or attention 1598. **b.** Information; intimation (*rare*) 1598.

1. A young writer struggling into n. MACAULAY. Phr. *Of n.,* of distinction; notable. 2. Phr. *To take n. of;* No one took n. of me THACKERAY. *attrib.,* as *n.-case,* etc.

†Note, *v.*[1] [OE. *notian,* f. *notu* NOTE *sb.*[1]] *trans.* To use, make use of (something) -1560.

Note (nōut), *v.*[2] ME. [ad. OF. *noter,* ad. L. *notare,* f. *nota* NOTE *sb.*[2]] **I. 1.** *trans.* To mark carefully; to give heed or attention to; to notice, perceive. **2.** To mention separately or specially among other items committed to writing. late ME. **3.** To set down in writing; to put down as a memorandum. late ME. So with *down* 1669.

1. I received your lordship's letter, and as the merchants say, n. the contents BURKE. 2. Which thing the Evangelist notes as one of the criticall passages of his Passion 1646. 3. Ile n. you in my Booke of Memorie SHAKS.

II. †1. To denote, or signify (something) -1573. **†b.** To indicate; to point *out,* set or show *forth* -1813. **2. a.** To mark (a book, words, etc.) with a musical score (*rare*) 1440. **†b.** To distinguish by a mark -1725. **c.** To annotate 1809. **†3. a.** To affix to (one) the stigma or accusation *of* some fault, etc. -1680. **†b.** To mark or brand *with* some disgrace or defect -1652. **†c.** To stigmatize for some reason -1601.

1. b. Distinguish all betimes, with branding Fire; To n. the Tribe, the Lineage, and the Sire DRYDEN. 2. b. *To n. a bill,* is when a public notary goes as a witness, or takes notice, that a merchant will not accept or pay it CHAMBERS. 3. c. *Jul. C.* IV. iii. 2.

No·te-book. 1579. [f. NOTE *sb.*[2] + BOOK.] A book reserved for or containing notes or memoranda.

Noted (nōu·tĕd), *ppl. a.* ME. [f. NOTE *v.*[2] + -ED[1].] **1.** That is specially noticed; hence, distinguished, famous. **2.** Provided with a musical score; having musical notation 1700. Hence **No·tedly** *adv.* markedly; particularly 1603.

Noteless (nōu·tlĕs), *a.* 1616. [f. NOTE *sb.*[2] + -LESS.] **1.** Devoid of note; undistinguished, unnoticed. **2.** Unmusical; unharmonious; voiceless 1721.

1. Let her walke Saint-like, notelesse, and vnknowne DEKKER.

Notelet (nōu·tlĕt). 1824. [f. NOTE *sb.*[2] + -LET.] A short note or communication.

No·te-pa·per. 1849. [f. NOTE *sb.*[2] III. 5 + PAPER *sb.*] Paper of the various sizes now generally used for correspondence. (Also *ellipt.* note.)

Noter (nōu·tə̆ɹ). 1491. [f. NOTE *v.*[2] + -ER[1].] **†1.** A writer of the musical score in MSS. **2.** One who takes or writes notes 1589.

Noteworthy (nōu·twɒ̆ɹði), *a.* 1552. [f. NOTE *sb.*[2] + WORTHY *a.*] Worthy of notice; remarkable. Hence **No·teworthily** *adv.* **No·teworthiness.**

No·ther, *adv.* and *conj. Obs.* exc. *dial.* ME. [advb. use of *nother* pron. (OE. *nōðer,* f. NE + *ōðer, ōhwæðer* either).] = NEITHER, NOR.

Nothing (nɒ·þiŋ), *sb.* and *adv.* OE. [f. NO *adj.* + THING.] **A.** *sb.* **1.** Not any (material or immaterial) thing; nought. **2.** With dependent genitive: No part, share, etc., *of* some thing (or person) OE. **3.** A thing (or person) not worth reckoning, considering, or mentioning. late ME. **4.** *Arith.* That which is not any number, and possesses neither quantity nor value; the character representing this; NOUGHT. late ME. **5.** That which is non-existent. Also personified 1535. **b.** Denoting extinction or destruction 1590. **6.** With *a* and *pl.* **a.** A non-existent, a comparatively insignificant or worthless, thing; a trifling event 1607. **b.** A trivial or trifling remark 1601. **c.** A person of no note; a nobody 1611. **†7.** = NOTHINGNESS 1, 2, 3 (*rare*) -1682.

1. Without whom nothyng is strong, n. is holy *Bk. Com. Prayer.* Ther 's n. ill can dwell in such a Temple SHAKS. A fellow whom all the world knew to have N. in him FIELDING. Many..were heretics, or n. at all J. H. NEWMAN. Provbs. *N. venture, n. win. N. great is easy.* 2. N. of him that doth fade SHAKS. Yet had his aspect n. of severe DRYDEN. 3. Knowledge is n. compared with doing J. H. NEWMAN. 4. *fig.* Now thou art an O without a figure, I am better then thou art now, I am a Foole, thou art n. SHAKS. 5. Phr. *To dance on n.*: see DANCE *v.* 3. *To n.,* denoting the final point, stage, or state of the process of destruction, dissolution, etc. 6. The little nothings of occupied life leave a man no time for his duty 1850. **b.** To his gay nothings, n. was replied BYRON. Phr. *A new n.,* a worthless novelty. Now *dial. No n.,* n. at all. *colloq.*

Phrases, etc. *Neck or n.,* see NECK *sb.*[1] *N. else* (*but* or *than*): see ELSE *adv. N. but* (or *except*): see BUT *conj. N. doing* (slang), ellipt. formula expressing refusal or failure to do something. *One has,* or *there is, n. for it but,* denoting absence of any alternative course. *N., if not..,* above everything. *For n.*: †**a.** by no means; on no consideration; **b.** in vain, to no purpose; **c.** causelessly; **d.** gratuitously. *N. to*: **a.** of no consequence *to* one; **b.** not to be compared *to* some other person or thing. *To make n. of*: **a.** to make light of; **b.** (with *can*) to be unable to do anything; to fail to comprehend or solve. *To come to n.,* to have no result; to break down, fail. *To have n. to do with* (a thing or person): see DO *v.* IV. Also *ellipt. All to n.,* to the fullest extent (*arch.*). *N. off* (*Naut.*): an order not to let the ship fall off from the wind.

B. *adv.* Not at all, in no way OE.

I praise nothyng the knowlege of myne auncesters LD. BERNERS. †Phr. *to make n.,* not to be *of* consequence *to,* not to tell *for* or *against* -1727. To a shadie bank..He led her n. loath MILTON. The bird was n. the worse for what it had undergone SOUTHEY. *N. like* (see LIKE *a.* 2): in no way approaching (another thing) in size or quality; also advb. = not nearly, and *absol.* far from it. *N. near*: cf. NEAR *adv.*[2] 5. *N. worth,* of no value (now *rare*).

Nothingarian (nɒþiŋē·ə·riăn). 1789. [f. NOTHING *sb.* + *-arian* as in *trinitarian.*] One who holds no religious belief. Hence **Nothinga·rianism.**

Nothingism (nɒ·þiŋiz'm). 1742. [f. as prec. + -ISM.] **1.** A triviality, a trifle. **2.** = NIHILISM 1. 1890. **3.** = NIHILISM 2. 1890.

No·thingness. 1631. [f. as prec. + -NESS.] **1.** The condition or state of being nothing; non-existence; also, that which is non-existent. **b.** The cessation of consciousness or of life 1813. **2.** The worthlessness or vanity *of* something 1646. **b.** That which has no value; the condition of being worthless 1654. **3.** Utter insignificance 1652. **4.** A non-existent thing; a state of non-existence or worthlessness; a thing of no value, etc. 1652.

1. A thing of beauty is a joy for ever:..it will never Pass into n. KEATS. **b.** The first dark day of n. BYRON. 2. A sarment upon the n. of good works.. was preached SMOLLETT.

No-tho·roughfare. 1809. A way, lane, etc., from which there is no exit at one end; a cul-de-sac.

Notice (nōu·tis), *sb.* 1483. [a. F., ad. L. *notitia,* f. *notus* known.] **1.** Intimation, information, intelligence, warning. Also with *pl.* **b.** A sign, placard, etc., conveying some intimation or intelligence 1805. **2.** Formal intimation or warning of something 1594. **b.** An intimation by one of the parties to an agreement that it is to terminate at a specified time, *esp.* with ref. to quitting a house, lodgings, or employment 1837. **3.** Heed, cognizance, note, attention 1597. **4.** A brief mention in writing; *spec.* in mod. use, a paragraph or article on a newly published book, a review 1840.

1. Of these..I thought fit to give thee this n. WALTON. Phr. *To give* (and *to have*) *n. At short n.,* with little time for preparation. So *at ten minutes' n.,* etc. 2. I had the lease of the house, and the n. to quit lying at my disposal MRS. CARLYLE. **b.** The girl was under n. 1887. 3. The author speaks..of her debt, as a thing scarcely worthy of n. BURKE. 4. That brilliant n. of some..book of verses 1872. Phr. *To take n.* (const. *of*), to give heed, bestow attention; *spec.* of babies, to show signs of intelligent observation.

Notice (nōu·tis), *v.* 1450. [f. prec. Little used bef. *c* 1750.] **†1.** *trans.* To notify, intimate -1627. **2.** To make mention of; to remark upon; to speak of (something observed) 1611. **b.** To point out, make mention of, *to* one 1627. **3.** To take notice of; to perceive, observe 1757. **4.** To treat (a person) with attention and civility; to recognize or acknowledge. Now *rare.* 1746. **5.** To serve with a notice; to give notice to 1850.

2. b. She looked so much better that Sir Charles noticed it to Lady Harriet MRS. GASKELL. 3. I could n. a turbidity gathering in the air TYNDALL. 5. The men, about forty in number, were 'noticed' on Friday 1880. Hence **No·ticeable** *a.* worthy of notice; capable of being noticed 1796. **No·ticeably** *adv.* remarkably 1855.

Notifiable (nōu·tifəiăb'l), *a.* 1889. [f. NOTIFY *v.* + -ABLE.] That should be notified to some authority, *esp.* of diseases.

Notify (nōu·tifəi), *v.* late ME. [ad. F. *notifier,* ad. L. *notificare,* f. *notus* known.] **†1.** *trans.* To take note of, observe -1678. **2.** To make known, publish, proclaim; to announce. late ME. **†3.** To indicate, denote -1727. **4.** To give notice to; to inform. (Common in U.S. since 1700.) 1440.

2. The king therefore notified to the country his intention of holding a parliament MACAULAY. 4. Peter notified him, through his first minister, that he was to attend the ceremony 1843. So **Notifica·tion,** the action of notifying; an intimation, a notice. **No·tified** *ppl. a.* (now *dial.*) celebrated, notorious. **No·tifier.**

Notion (nōu·ʃən). 1567. [ad. L. *notionem,* f. *not-, noscere* to know; see -TION.] **I. 1.** A general concept under which a particular thing or person may be classed; a term expressive of such a concept. Chiefly with *under.* **†b.** A character, relation, form, etc., in which anything is conceived, mentioned, or exists -1651. **†2.** The connotation *of* a term -1713.

1. *Under the n. of,* under the concept, category, or designation of; I travelled..under the n. of a Japanese converted to Christianity 1764.

II. 1. An idea or concept 1605. **†2.** Understanding, mind, intellect -1667. **3.** An idea, view, opinion, theory, or belief 1603. **4.** An inclination, disposition, or desire to do something specified; a fancy for something 1746. Now *rare.* **5.** A product of invention 1700. **6.** *U.S.* **a.** *pl.* Wares of various kinds forming a miscellaneous cargo 1805. **b.** *pl.* Small wares, *esp.* cheap useful ingenious articles 1830.

1. Her n. of a joke is not very delicate JOHNSON. How he first Learned of the complication, I've no n. 1878. *First* and *second notions* = *First* and *second intentions* (see INTENTION II. 2). *General n.* (see GENERAL *a.* 5 c). 2. *Lear* I. iv. 245. 3. The Quaker N. of the Light within 1697. At Winchester College, a characteristic expression, tradition, custom, etc. current in the school. 4. Gloucestershire people have no n. of dying with hunger COBBETT. 5. Machines for flying in the air, and other wonderful notions EVELYN.

Notional (nōu·ʃənăl), *a.* 1597. [ad. med.L. *notionalis*; see prec. and -AL.] **1.** Of knowledge, etc.: Purely speculative; not based upon fact or demonstration. **†b.** Of persons: Given to abstract speculation; holding merely speculative views -1772. **2.** Of things, relations, etc.: Existing only in thought; imaginary 1629. **3.** Of the nature of, pertaining or relating to, a notion or idea 1861.

æ (man). ɑ (pass). au (loud). ɒ (cut). ɛ (Fr. chef). ə (ever). əi (*I, eye*). ə (Fr. eau de vie). i (sit). *i* (Psyche). ǫ (what). ǫ (got).

1. A n. work as distinguished from an experimental work M. ARNOLD. 2. Meere notionall is their [gems] value; which is in the Opinion, not in the Thing 1629. Hence **No·tionalist,** a speculative thinker; a theorist. **No·tionally** *adv.* speculatively, theoretically. **No·tionist** (now *rare*), one who holds extravagant or whimsical opinions.

No·tionate, *a.* *Sc.* and *U.S.* 1859. [f. NOTION *sb.* + -ATE [2]; cf. *opinionate.*] Full of notions, fanciful; also, headstrong.

Notitia (nō^u^ti·ʃiă). 1700. [L., f. *notus* known.] †1. Literary particulars. HEARNE. 2. An account or list; now *spec.* a register of ecclesiastical sees or districts 1797.

Noto- (nō^u^·to), comb. form of Gr. νῶτον back, as in **Notobra·nchiate** *a.* having dorsal branchiæ or gills 1870; **Notone·cta** [Gr. νήκτης swimmer] *Entom.* a species of water-beetle which swims on its back; the boat-fly 1638.

Notochord (nō^u^·tŏkǭɹd). 1848. [f. prec. + CHORD.] *Biol.* A cartilaginous band or rod forming the primitive basis of the spinal column in vertebrates. Hence **Notocho·rdal** *a.*

Notogæa (nō^u^tŏdʒī·ă). 1868. [f. Gr. νότος south wind + γαῖα earth, land.] A large zoological region, comprising the Australian, New Zealand, and Neotropical regions. Hence **No·togæ·al, -gæ·an, -gæ·ic** *adjs.*

Notopodium (nō^u^topō^u^·diŏm). 1870. [mod. L., f. NOTO- + Gr. πόδιον, dim. of πούς foot.] *Biol.* The upper or dorsal branch of a parapodium. Hence **Notopo·dial** *a.*

Notoriety (nō^u^tŏrəi·ĕti). 1592. [a. F. *notoriété*, or ad. med.L. *notorietas*, f. *notorius* NOTORIOUS *a.*; cf. *dubiety*, etc.] 1. The state or character of being notorious; the fact of being publicly or commonly known. 2. A well-known or celebrated person 1837.

1. He had been raised..to n. such as has for low and bad minds all the attractions of glory MACAULAY.

Notorious (nŏtō^ə^·riəs), *a.* 1548. [ad. med.L. *notorius*, f. *notus* known; see -ORY.] 1. Of facts: Well known; forming a matter of common knowledge 1555. 2. Of places, persons, etc.: Well or widely known (now *rare*); †famous 1555. b. Such as is generally, openly, or publicly known. Now *rare.* 1584. †3. Conspicuous; obvious, evident -1770. 4. Used attrib. with designations of persons, deeds, etc., which imply condemnation: Well known, noted (as being of this kind) 1548. 5. Noted *for* some bad practice, quality, etc.; unfavourably known or spoken on 1579.

1. Men..who deny the most n. facts JOHNSON. Phr. *It is n. that* [etc.]. 2. b. The Privy Council, whom the law recognised as the sworn and n. Councillors of the Crown 1863. 4. Declarit tratouris and notorius rebellis 1574. His mean subterfuge renders him more contemptible than his n. untruth 1807. 5. You n. stinkardly beareward B. JONS. These books were perfectly n. PALEY. Hence **Noto·rious-ly** *adv.*, **-ness.**

Notornis (nŏtǭ·ɹnis). 1848. [f. Gr. νότος south + ὄρνις bird.] *Ornith.* A New Zealand bird, now rare or extinct, related to the coots and rails.

Notothere (nō^u^·toþiəɹ). 1881. [Anglicized f. mod.L. *nototherium*, f. Gr. νότος south + θηρίον beast.] *Palæont.* An extinct marsupial of great size found in post-tertiary formations.

Not-out, *a.* 1891. *Cricket.* The phrase 'not out' (see OUT *adv.*) used attrib. to designate a batsman (his score, etc.) whose innings either is unfinished or is ended only by his side going out.

‖ **Notum** (nō^u^·tŏm). 1877. [mod.L., ad. Gr. νῶτον back.] The dorsal part of the thorax in insects.

‖ **Notus** (nō^u^·tŏs). *poet.* late ME. [L., a. Gr. Νότος.] The south wind.

Notwithstanding (nǫtwiðstæ·ndiŋ, -wiþ-), *prep.*, *adv.*, and *conj.* ME. [f. NOT *adv.* + *withstanding*, pres. pple. of WITHSTAND *v.*, after OF. *non obstant*, L. NON OBSTANTE.] A. *prep.* 1. Despite, in spite of. 2. Following *this, that*, or a sb., after OF. absolute participial construction *ce non obstant*, etc. 1490.

1. N. all her sodaine quips SHAKS. 2. These n., His hair and wrinkles will betray his age MASSINGER.

B. *adv.* Nevertheless, still, yet 1440.

He saw that it would come to pass n. SOUTHEY.

C. *conj.* Although 1449. b. Followed by *that* with dependent clause 1584.

N. objections may lie against some parts of her Liturgy,..her doctrines are exclusively scriptural WORDSW. b. N. that it were once burned by the D. of Burgundie 1596.

‖ **Nougat** (nū·ga). 1827. [F., a. Prov. *nougat* :—Rom. **nucatum*, f. L. *nuc-*, *nux* nut.] A sweetmeat composed chiefly of sugar and almonds (or other nuts).

Nought (nǫt), *sb.*, *a.*, and *adv.* [OE. *nówiht, -wuht*, f. *ne* NE + *ówiht*, var. of *āwiht*; see AUGHT *sb.*[2] and NAUGHT.] A. *sb.* 1. = NOTHING A. 1. (Now only literary.) †2. Nothingness -1711. b. *Arith.* = NOTHING A. 4. late ME. 3. With *a* and *pl.* a. A thing or person of no worth or value; a mere nothing ME. b. *Arith.* A cipher 1660.

1. I am n., I have n., I desire n. 1665. 2. He comaundide, and thingis weren maad of nouȝt WYCLIF *Ps.* xxxii[i]. Phr. *To bring, come, go*, etc., *to n.* †*N. worth*, worth nothing, of no value. †*A thing of n.*, a mere nothing. *For n.*: †in vain, to no purpose; without payment; gratis. *To set at n.*: to despise, defy, scorn, disregard. 3. b. *Noughts and crosses*: a game played with a figure containing (usu.) nine spaces which are filled alternately by the two players with noughts and crosses, the object being to get a row of one or the other.

B. *adj.* [Cf. NAUGHT *a.*, the more usual form.] †1. Of material things: Bad in condition or of their kind -1728. †b. Of actions, etc.: Bad, wicked -1607; immoral, vicious -1550. 2. Good for nothing. late ME. †3. Injurious *to*, bad *for*, a thing or person. Also without const. -1690.

1. 'Tis too plain, the Materials are n. SWIFT.

C. *adv.* [orig. the accus. of the sb.] 1. To no extent; in no way; not at all OE. †2. = NOT *adv.* -1724.

1. Vertues are laide aside, and n. accounted off 1568.

Nou·ghty, *a.* ME. *Obs.* exc. *Sc.* [f. prec. sb. + -Y [1].] = NAUGHTY.

†**Nould,** would not: see NILL *v.* 1579-1742.

Noumenon (nau·mĕnǫn). Pl. **noumena.** 1798. [ad. Gr. νοούμενον, neut. pres. pple. pass. of νοεῖν to apprehend, conceive; introduced by Kant in contrast to *phenomenon.*] *Metaph.* In Kantian philosophy: An object of purely intellectual intuition, devoid of all phenomenal attributes. Hence **Nou·menal** *a.* relating to, consisting of, noumena; given only by intuition; not phenomenal. **Nou·menally** *adv.* in a noumenal aspect.

Noun (naun). late ME. [a. AF. *noun*, OF. *non, nom* :—L. *nomen* name.] *Gram.* 1. A word used as the name of a person or thing. In older grammars including *nomen substantivum* and *nomen adjectivum* (see 2 and 3). 2. *N. substantive* = sense 1. late ME. 3. *N. adjective* = ADJECTIVE B. 1530. Hence **Nou·nal** *a.*

†**Nourice.** ME. [a. OF. *n(o)urice* :—late L. *nutricia*, fem. of *nutricius*, f. *nutric-*, *nutrix*, f. *nutrire* to nourish.] A nurse -1768.

Nourish (nʊ·riʃ), *v.* ME. [ad. OF. *noris(s)*-, lengthened stem of *norir* (mod.F. *nourrir*) :—L. *nutrire* to feed, foster, cherish, etc.] I. †1. *trans.* To bring up, rear, nurture (a child, an animal) -1618. †2. To allow (one's hair) to grow -1807. †3. To promote the growth of, tend or cultivate (plants, etc.) -1792.

1. He..left the yonger [daughter] styll in Englande, wheras she had been brought vp and norisshed 1523.

II. †1. = NURSE *v.* 1 -1551. b. To sustain (a person or living thing) with food or proper nutriment ME. c. To supply (a thing) with whatever is necessary for growth, formation, or proper condition. late ME. 2. To provide with food and sustenance. Now *rare.* late ME. 3. *absol.* To afford nutriment -1667.

1. b. The human body can be nourished on any food EMERSON. c. The mountain slopes which n. the glacier TYNDALL. 2. And thou shalt dwell in the land of Goshen.., And there wil I n. thee *Gen.* xlv. 11. 3. Sheepes Milke is sweeter, and nourisheth more 1577.

III. 1. To promote or foster (a feeling, habit, etc.) in or among persons ME. b. To cherish or nurse (a feeling) in one's own heart or mind 1560. 2. To maintain, encourage, strengthen (one's heart, mind, etc.) in or with something. late ME.

1. Freedom nourishes self-respect 1837. b. Clodius ..nourishing an implacable hate against Cicero FROUDE. 2. A man, who nourished his spirit with the contemplation of ancient heroes JAS. MILL. Hence **Nou·rishable** *a.* capable of affording, susceptive of, nourishment. **Nou·risher,** one who, or that which, nourishes; a nourishing agent. **Nou·rishing** *ppl. a.*, nutritious.

Nourishment (nʊ·riʃmĕnt). late ME. [ad. OF. *nour(r)issement*: see NOURISH *v.* and -MENT.] 1. That which nourishes or sustains; aliment, food. 2. The action, process, or fact of nourishing 1485.

1. No Dressing they require..; The Soil it self due N. supplies DRYDEN. *transf.* More substantial literary n. than could be..packed into so portable compass RUSKIN.

Nou·riture. Now *rare* or *Obs.* late ME. [a. OF. (mod.F. *nourriture*).] 1. Nourishment, sustenance, food. 2. Nurture, upbringing -1647.

‖ **Nous** (naus). 1678. [a. Gr. νοῦς.] 1. *Gr. Philos.* Mind, intellect. 2. *colloq.* or *slang.* Intelligence, common sense, gumption. (Occas. written in Greek letters.) 1706.

2. I think his doing so exhibits considerable n. in a brute 1847.

Nousel, Nousle, var. ff. NUZZLE *v.*[1] and *v.*[2]

Nouther, nowther, *pron.*, *a.*, *adv.*, *conj.* Now *dial.* [OE. *nowðer*, contr. f. *nóhwæðer*, f. *ne* NE + *ó* O *adv.* + *hwæðer* WHETHER.] A. †1. *pron.* Neither (of two) -1596. †2. *adj.* Neither. ME. only. B. *adv.* and *conj.* 1. = NEITHER A. 1. ME. †b. = NOR -1596. 2. = NEITHER A. 3. ME.

Nov., abbrev. of NOVEMBER.

‖ **Nova** (nō^u^·vă). *Pl.* **novæ** (nō^u^·vī). 1877. [L., adj. fem. sing.] *Astr.* A new star or nebula.

Novaculite (novæ·kiŭləit). 1796. [f. L. *novacula* a razor + -ITE [1] 2 b.] *Min.* A hard argillaceous slate used for hones.

Novate (novē^i^·t), *v. rare.* 1611. [f. ppl. stem of L. *novare* to make new, etc., f. *novus* new.] *trans.* To replace by something new; *spec.* in (Roman) law, to replace by a new obligation, debt, etc.

Novatian (novē^i^·ʃiăn), *sb.* and *a.* 1449. [ad. late L. *Novatiani* (pl.), f. *Novatianus* (see def.).] A. *sb.* A member of the sect founded by Novatianus, a Roman presbyter in the middle of the 3rd c. (see quots.) Chiefly *pl.* B. *adj.* Of or pertaining to Novatianus or the sect of Novatians 1630.

1. The Novatians, excepting their peculiar error, of denying reconciliation to those that fell in persecution, held other things in common with Catholiques CHILLINGW. Hence **Nova·tianism. Nova·tianist.**

Novation (novē^i^·ʃən). 1533. [ad. L. *novationem*; see NOVATE *v.*] 1. The introduction of something new; an innovation. Now *rare.* 2. *Law.* The substitution of a new debtor, creditor, contract, etc., in place of an old one 1682.

Novator (novē^i^·təɹ). 1644. [ad. L.] An innovator.

Novel (nǫ·vĕl), *sb.* 1460. [a. OF. *novelle* = It. *novella*, fem. :—L. *novella*, neut. pl. of *novellus*, f. *novus* new; see next. In sense 4, ad. late L. *novella* (sc. *constitutio*), usu. in pl. *novellæ.*] †1. Something new; a novelty -1719. †2. *pl.* News, tidings -1724. †b. *sing.* A piece of news -1736. 3. (Chiefly in *pl.*) One of the short stories contained in such works as the *Decameron* of Boccaccio, the *Heptameron* of Marguerite of Valois, etc.; a short story of this type 1566. 4. A fictitious prose narrative of considerable length, in which characters and actions representative of real life are portrayed in a plot of more or less complexity 1643. b. This type of literature. (Formerly without article; now with *the.*) 1757. 5. *Roman Law.* A new decree or constitution, supplementary to the Codex, *esp.* one of those made by the Emperor Justinian 1612.

2. Ready to bring his Maister Nouels and tidinges, whether they be true or false 1561. 4. This is no mere amatorious n. MILT. b. England has hardly received the honour she deserves as the birthplace of the modern n. 1871.

Novel (nǫ·vĕl), *a.* late ME. [a. OF. *novel* (mod.F. *nouvel, nouveau*) :—L. *novellum*, f. *novum* new. Little used bef. 1600.] 1. †a. New, young, fresh (*rare*) -1616. b. Recent; of recent origin -1727. 2. New; of a new kind or nature; strange; hitherto unknown 1475.

1. b. *N. disseisin*: disseisin of a fresh or recent date. 2. A style of decoration more n. than elegant 1870. *N. constitution* = NOVEL *sb.* 5.

Novelese (nǫvĕlī·z). 1900. [f. NOVEL *sb.* 4 + -ESE; cf. *journalese.*] The style of language characteristic of inferior novels.

Novelette (nǫvĕle·t). 1780. [f. as prec. + -ETTE.] 1. A short novel. 2. *Mus.* A pianoforte piece of free form containing a variety of themes, e.g. the *Novelletten* of Schumann 1893.

Novelism (nǫ·vĕliz'm). 1626. [f. NOVEL *sb.* + -ISM.] †1. Innovation, novelty –1703. 2. Novel-writing 1828.

Novelist (nǫ·vĕlist). 1583. [f. NOVEL *sb.* + -IST.] †1. An innovator; one who favours novelty –1727. (Common in 17th c.) †2. A newsmonger, news-carrier –1764. 3. A writer of novels 1728.

Novelize (nǫ·vĕlaiz), *v.* 1625. [f. NOVEL *sb.* + -IZE.] 1. †a. *trans.* To make new or novel –1660. b. *intr.* To introduce novelty 1823. 2. To convert into the form or style of a novel 1828.

2. Attempts to n. history 1833.

Novelty (nǫ·vĕlti). late ME. [a. OF. *novelté* (mod.F. *nouveauté*); see NOVEL *a.* and -TY.] 1. A new or unusual thing or occurrence. Also *the n.*, the newest thing. †b. A new matter of report or talk. (Usu. in *pl.*) –1595. c. An innovation 1576. 2. Novel or unusual character *of* something. late ME. 3. The quality or state of being novel; that which is novel, new, or hitherto unknown 1484.

1. They are curious, and great louers of nouelties 1632. 2. The n. of these amusements interested me 1841. 3. Any thing which has the least appearance of N. 1728.

November (nove·mbəɹ). Abbrev. **Nov.** ME. [a. L. *November* (also *Novembris*, sc. *mensis*), f. *novem* nine.] The eleventh month of the year, containing 30 days.

‖**Novena** (novī·nă). 1745. [med.L. *novena*, f. *novem* nine.] *R.C.Ch.* A devotion consisting of special prayers or services on nine successive days.

Novenary (nǫ·vĕnări). 1577. [ad. L. *novenarius*, f. *novem* nine.] A. *adj.* Pertaining to, or consisting of, the number nine (*rare*) 1603. B. *sb.* 1. An aggregate or set of nine 1577. 2. = prec. 1818.

Novennial (nove·niăl), *a.* 1656. [f. L. *novennis*, f. *novem* and *annus.*] Happening or recurring every ninth year.

Novercal (novə̄·ɹkăl), *a.* 1623. [ad. L. *novercalis*, f. *noverca* stepmother.] Characteristic of, or resembling, a stepmother.

Novice (nǫ·vis). ME. [a. OF., ad. L. *novicius, -icia*, f. *novus* new; see -ITIOUS[1].] 1. *Eccl.* One who has entered a religious house and is under probation. b. A new convert 1526. 2. One who is new to the circumstances in which he is placed; a beginner, tyro ME. 3. *attrib.* 1530. b. Appositive, as *n. hand*, etc. 1605.

1. He then assumes the dress of the Order, a cassock and bands, and becomes a n. 1859. 2. Though they came to us under the name of Veterans [they] proved to be ignorant Novices 1726.

No·viceship. 1620. [-SHIP.] = NOVITIATE 1. 1639. b. = NOVITIATE 3. 1620.

Novilu·nar, *a. rare.* 1686. [f. late L. *novilunium* (f. *novus* + *luna*), after LUNAR *a.*] Of or pertaining to the new moon.

Novitiate, noviciate (novi·ʃiĕt). 1600. [ad. F. *noviciat*; see NOVICE and -ATE[1].] 1. The probationary period of a novice. b. *transf.* and *fig.* The state or time of being a novice or beginner; time of initiation, apprenticeship, or probation 1610. 2. A novice in a religious order 1655. b. A beginner, tyro 1734. Now *rare* or *Obs.* 3. The quarters occupied by novices; a place where novices are trained 1626. 4. *attrib.* as *n. chapel*, etc. 1704. b. Appositive, as *n. candidate*, etc. 1775.

†**Novi·tious**, *a.* 1619. [ad. L. *novitius*, f. *novus*; see -ITIOUS[1].] 1. Having the character of novices. SCLATER. 2. Of recent origin –1669. So **Novi·tial** *a.*, characteristic of a novice (*rare*) 1700.

No·vity. Now *rare* or *Obs.* 1460. [a. OF. *novité*, ad. L. *novitatem*, f. *novus*; see -ITY.] †1. An innovation; a novelty –1692. 2. Novelty, newness 1569.

‖**Novodamus** (nōᵘvodē·mŏs). 1768. *Sc. Law.* [L. *de novo damus* 'we grant anew'.] A charter containing a clause (also called 'of n.') by which the superior grants afresh the matters described in the dispositive clause.

†**No·vum.** 1588. [L. *novem* nine. Cf. F., Pg. *quinquenove* (= L. *quinque* + *novem*).] An old game at dice played by five persons, the two principal throws being nine and five –1621.

Now (nau), *adv.*, *conj.*, *sb.*, and *a.* [OE. *nū*, corresp. to Skr. *nu*, *nū*, Gr. νῦ, νῦν, L. *nunc.*] I. 1. At the present time or moment. b. Under the present circumstances; in view of these facts 1508. 2. In the time directly following on the present moment; immediately OE. 3. In the time directly preceding the present moment. Now only in *just now* or (poet.) *even now*. OE. 4. At the time spoken of or referred to; by this time 1548. 5. *Now* . . . *now*, used to introduce antithetical clauses, phrases, or words. late ME. b. So *now* . . . *then*, *now* . . . *and again* (arch.), etc. 1593.

1. They will be our lords, as they are n. M. ARNOLD. Phr. (*It's*) *n. or never*, this is the moment to act, or not at all. b. I can believe anything n. MRS. STOWE. 2. I am in a hurry, and must go n. JOWETT. 3. The good Man whom I have just n. mentioned ADDISON. 4. The war was n. practically concluded 1874. 5. N. vsed in this sence, n. in that 1620. b. His walk was n. quick, and again slow JOHNSON.

Phrases. †*As n.*, at this time. *N. and again*, *anon*, †*eft*, †*n.*, at one time and another, from time to time. *N. and* (also †*or*) *then*, occasionally, fitfully, at intervals. So *Every n. and then* (or *again*).

II. 1. In sentences expressing a command or request, with the purely temporal sense weakened or effaced. Later also with ellipse of verb. OE. b. So *Now then.* (Freq. in mod. use.) OE. 2. Used to introduce a noteworthy point in an argument or proof, etc. OE. b. Inserted parenthetically, or at the end of a clause, with similar force OE. 3. Used ellipt., esp. at the beginning of a clause 1450. 4. as *conj.* Since, seeing that; as . . . now OE. b. So *now that* 1530.

1. N. your Counsels, For I am at my wits end FLETCHER. b. 'N. then,' said Amyas, 'to breakfast' KINGSLEY. 2. N. this was bad enough, . . but this was not all DICKENS. b. There's a wise young woman, n. 1760. 3. N., n., Ringwood has him WALTON. N. for it, Sneak; the enemy's at hand 1764. 4. N. they are oppress'd with trauaile, they . . cannot vse such vigilance As when they are fresh SHAKS.

III. 1. With preps., as *by*, *ere*, *for*, *or*, *till*, *unto*, *now* OE. b. *From now* (*forth*, *forward*, etc.) ME. 2. as *sb.* The present time. late ME. 3. A present point or moment of time 1630.

1. And for n. Ile leave ye FLETCHER. b. From n. till Doomsday KINGSLEY. 2. N. is an atome, it will puzzle the skill of an angell to divide FULLER. Plant the great hereafter in the n. 1851. 3. An everlasting N. reigns in nature EMERSON. Man ever with his N. at strife LOWELL.

IV. *attrib.* or *adj.* Present, of the present time 1444. (Common in 17th c.)

The dreadful treatment of the n. king BURKE.

Now-a-day, *adv.* late ME. [Cf. next and ADAY.] = next.

Now-a-days (nau·ădēᵢz), *adv.* late ME. [f. NOW *adv.* + ADAYS 2. Now freq. written as one word.] At the present day, in these times. Also *attrib.* and as *sb.*

Guineas are scarce now-a-days 1833. *sb.* The Phisitians of now a dayes 1647.

Noway (nōᵘ·weᵢ), *adv.* ME. [f. NO *a.* + WAY *sb.*] In no way or manner; not at all; by no means.

Noways (nōᵘ·weᵢz), *adv.* ME. [orig. f. gen. sing. of NONE *a.* and WAY *sb.*] = prec.

Nowch(e, obs. ff. OUCH, clasp.

Nowed (nū·ĕd, naud), *a.* 1572. [a. F. *noué* + -ED[1].] *Her.* Knotted; tied in a knot.

Nowel[1] (nōᵘe·l). late ME. [a. OF. *nouel* (mod.F. *noël* NOEL) :—L. *natalem*, acc. sing. of (*dies*) *natalis* NATAL (day).] 1. A word shouted or sung as an expression of joy at Christmas. (Retained in Christmas carols.) †2. The feast of Christmas; Christmastide –1599.

Now·el.[2] late ME. [var. of NEWEL.] †1. = NEWEL 1 –1688. 2. *Founding.* The core or inner part of a mould for casting large hollow objects 1864.

Nowhere (nōᵘ·hwēəɹ), *adv.* OE. [f. NO *adv.* + WHERE *adv.*] 1. In or at no place; not anywhere. b. To no place ME. 2. In no work or author ME. 3. as *sb.* A non-existent place; absence of all place 1831.

1. He was n. to be seen 1797. b. Mr. C. was minded to go n. this summer MRS. CARLYLE. Phrases. *N. near* or †*nigh*, not nearly, not by a long way. *To be n.* (colloq.): a. To be badly beaten (in a race, contest, etc.); to be out of the running. Also *transf.* b. *U.S.* To be utterly at a loss; to be ignorant.

No whit, *adv. arch.* 1530. [See WHIT *sb.*] Not at all, not the least.

Nowhither (nōᵘ·hwiðəɹ), *adv.* OE. [f. NO *adv.* + WHITHER *adv.*] To no place; nowhere.

Nowise (nōᵘ·waiz), *adv.* late ME. [f. NO *a.* + WISE *sb.*] In no way or manner; not at all.

Nowt (naut). *Sc.* and *n. dial.* ME. [a. ON. *naut* = OE. *nēat* NEAT *sb.*] 1. *pl.* Cattle, oxen. 2. *sing.* An ox, a bullock. late ME. b. *transf.* A stupid, coarse, or clumsy person 1806. 3. *attrib.* late ME.

Nowt(h), dial. and obs. forms of NOUGHT.

Nowy (nau·i), *a.* 1562. [ad. OF. *noé* (mod. F. *noué*), pa. pple. of *nouer* :—L. *nodare*, f. *nodus* knot.] *Her.* †1. = NOWED *a.* 2. Having a projection or curvature in or near the middle.

‖**Nox** (nǫks). 1567. [L.] Night. (Chiefly *poet.*)

No·xal, *a.* 1605. [ad. L. *noxalis*, f. *noxa* hurt, damage.] *Civil Law.* Relating to damage or injury done by a person or animal belonging to another, or to an action in respect of this.

Noxious (nǫ·kʃəs), *a.* 1612. [ad. L. *noxius*, f. *noxa.*] Injurious, hurtful, harmful; unwholesome. Hence **No·xious·ly** *adv.*, **-ness.**

†**Noy**, *sb.* ME. [Aphetic f. ANNOY *sb.*] Annoyance, trouble –1611.

†**Noy**, *v.* ME. [Aphetic f. ANNOY *v.*] 1. *trans.* To annoy, trouble, vex, harass; to harm or injure –1609. 2. *refl.* and *intr.* To vex oneself, to grieve –1587. 3. *absol.* To cause annoyance or harm –1573.

1. I ymagyn with myself whiche wayes they myght take to n. our enemyes most T. CROMWELL.

‖**Noyade** (nwaya·d), *sb.* 1819. [F., f. *noyer* :—L. *necare* to put to death (in late L. to drown).] The execution of persons by drowning, as practised by Carrier at Nantes in 1794. Hence **Noyade** *v.* and **Noyading** *vbl. sb.* 1837.

†**Noy·ance.** ME. Aphetic f. ANNOYANCE –1670.

‖**Noyau** (nwa·yo). 1797. [F. :—pop.L. **nucale*, f. L. *nuc-*, *nux* nut.] A liqueur made of brandy flavoured with the kernels of certain fruits.

†**Noy·ful**, *a.* late ME. [f. NOY *sb.* + -FUL.] Annoying; also noxious –1618.

†**Noy·ous**, *a.* ME. [Aphetic f. ANNOYOUS *a.*] Vexatious, troublesome –1675.

Nozzle (nǫ·z'l). 1608. [f. NOSE *sb.* + -LE.] 1. A socket on a candlestick or sconce, for receiving the lower end of the candle. Now *rare.* 2. A small spout, mouthpiece, or projecting aperture; a short terminal pipe or part of a pipe, as the nose of a pair of bellows, etc. 1683. b. Applied to parts of a steam-engine, *esp.* the steam-port, or the part of the cylinder enclosing this, and the exhaust-pipe or the adjustable end of this 1839. 3. *slang.* The nose 1771. 4. A small nose or beak; a projecting part or end 1850.

‖**Nuance** (niū·ăns). 1781. [F., f. *nuer* to shade, f. *nue* cloud :—pop.L. **nuba* for L. *nubes* cloud.] 1. A slight or delicate variation in expression, feeling, opinion, meaning, etc. 2. A shade of colour; a slight difference in shade or tone 1856. 3. A delicate gradation in musical expression 1879.

1. The more expert one were at *nuances*, the more poetic one should be H. WALPOLE.

Nub (nɒb). 1594. [app. a var. of KNUB.] †1. = KNUB 2. (*rare*) –1759. 2. A knob or protuberance; a lump 1727. 3. *U.S.* The point of a story or matter 1859.

Nubble (nɒ·b'l). 1818. [dim. prec.] A small knob or lump.

‖**Nubecula** (niubī·kiŭlă). *Pl.* **-læ.** 1699. [L., dim. of *nubes* cloud.] 1. *Path.* a. A cloudy formation in urine. b. A speck or small cloud in the eye 1727. 2. *Astron.* One or other of the Magellanic Clouds 1842.

Nubian (niū·biăn). 1727. [ad. med.L. *Nubianus*, or f. med.L. *Nubia*, f. L. *Nubæ*, Gr. Νοῦβαι, name of the people.] **A.** *adj.* **1.** Pertaining or belonging to the country of Nubia. **2.** In specific names of animals 1879. **B.** *sb.* **1.** A native of Nubia; a Nubian slave 1788. **2.** A Nubian horse 1790. **3.** The Nubian language 1855.

Nubiferous (niubi·fĕrəs), *a.* 1656. [f. L. *nubifer*, f. *nubes* cloud; see -FEROUS.] Cloud-bringing.

Nubilate (niū·bileit), *v.* 1691. [f. L. *nubilat-*, *nubilare*, f. *nubila* (neut. pl.), f. *nubes* cloud.] *trans.* To cloud; to obscure; to render less clear or transparent.

Nubile (niū·bil), *a.* 1642. [ad. L. *nubilis*, f. *nubere* to marry, or a. F. *nubile.*] **1.** Of females: Marriageable. **2.** Of age: Admitting of, suitable for, marriage 1831. Hence **Nubi·lity** 1813.

Nubilous (niū·biləs), *a.* Now *rare.* 1533. [ad. late L. *nubilosus*, f. L. *nubes* a cloud.] **1.** Cloudy, foggy, misty. **2.** *fig.* Obscure, indefinite.

‖ **Nucellus** (niuse·lǒs). 1882. [mod.L., app. meant as a dim. of *nucleus.*] *Bot.* The essential part of an ovule, containing the embryo-sac.

‖ **Nucha** (niū·kă). late ME. [a. med.L., a. Arab.] *Anat.* †**a.** The spinal chord. **b.** The nape of the neck. Hence **Nu·chal** *a.* of, belonging or pertaining to, the nape of the neck 1833. var. †**Nuche** (*rare*) -1601.

Nuci- (niū·si), comb. form of L. *nux*, *nucis* nut, as in **Nuci·ferous** *a.* bearing nuts. **Nu·ciform** *a.* nut-shaped. **Nuci·vorous** *a.* nut-eating.

Nuclear (niū·klĭăı), *a.* 1846. [f. NUCLEUS + -AR.] **1.** Having the character or position of a nucleus; like a nucleus; constituting a nucleus. Chiefly in *Biol.* or *Astron.* **2.** Of or belonging to a nucleus 1880.

1. A nucleolated n. cell 1846. The n. parts of the sun 1881. So **Nu·cleary** *a.* of the nature of a nucleus. **Nu·cleate** *a.* nucleated.

Nucleate (niū·klĭeit), *v.* 1864. [f. L. *nucleat-*, *nucleare* to become kernelly or hard, f. *nucleus* kernel, NUCLEUS.] **1.** *trans.* To form (anything) into, bring together as, a nucleus. **2.** *intr.* To form a nucleus; to collect about a nucleus 1883. So **Nu·cleated** *ppl. a.* having a nucleus; as a *n. cell*; clustered together 1843.

Nu·cleifo·rm, *a.* 1840. [See -FORM.] Having the form of a nucleus; tuberculated.

Nuclein (niū·klĭin). Also **-ine.** 1878. [f. NUCLEUS + -IN[1], after G. *nuklein.*] *Chem.* The principal constituent of cell-nuclei.

Nucleo- (niū·klĭo), comb. form of L. *nucleus*, used in a number of compounds, chiefly biological, as *n.-albumin*, *-proteid*, etc. **Nu·cleobranch**, *Zool.* a mollusc of the order *Nucleobranchiata*; a Heteropod 1851. **Nu·cleoplasm**, *Biol.* nuclear protoplasm 1882.

‖ **Nucleolus** (niuklī·ŏlǒs). Pl. **-li.** 1845. [L., dim. of *nucleus.*] *Biol.* A small nucleus; *esp.* a minute rounded body within the nucleus of a cell in animal and vegetable substance; also, a paranucleus. Also **Nu·cleole** 1864. Hence **Nucle·olar** *a.* of the nature of, pertaining to, a n. **Nu·cleolated** *a.*, furnished with a n.

Nucleus (niū·klĭǒs), *sb.* *Pl.* **nuclei** (niū·klĭəi) and nucleuses. 1704. [a. L. *nucleus* (*nuculeus*) kernel, inner part, f. *nucula* or *nuc-*, *nux* nut.] **I. 1.** *Astr.* The more condensed portion of the head of a comet. Also *fig.* †**2.** A supposed interior crust of the earth -1727. **3.** A central part or thing around which other parts or things are grouped, collected, or compacted; that which forms the centre of some aggregate or mass 1762. **b.** esp. *Bot.* and *Zool.* 1829. **c.** *Archæol.* A block of flint or other stone from which early implements have been made 1869.

3. Some extraneous body, which becomes the n. of the calculus 1797. About 700 individuals..were the n. of his colony of Georgia 1798. A very fair collection of modern books.., the n. of a library 1875. Hence **Nu·cleal** *a.* pertaining to, having the form or position of, a n. 1840.

‖ **Nuculanium** (niūkiulē·niǒm). 1819. [mod. L., irreg. f. L. *nucula* NUCULE.] **1.** An indehiscent fleshy fruit. **2.** A hard nut-like case in the interior of a fleshy fruit, enclosing several seeds 1849.

Nucule (niū·kiul). 1819. [a. F., ad. L. *nucula*, dim. of *nuc-*, *nux* nut.] **1.** One of the seeds of a nuculanium; a nutlet; a small stone or seed. **2.** The female organ of reproduction in the cryptogamic tribe *Chara* 1830.

Nuddle (nv·d'l), *v.* Now *dial.* 1640. [Origin obscure.] **1.** *intr.* †**a.** To push with the nose; to press close to the ground in this way; to grovel -1661. **2.** *trans.* To squeeze, press 1875.

Nude (niūd). 1531. [ad. L. *nudus.*] **A.** *adj.* **1.** *Law.* **a.** Of statements, promises, etc.: Not formally attested or recorded. **b.** Of persons, esp. *n. executor*: An executor, etc., in trust 1590. **2.** Naked, bare; without covering; devoid of furniture or decorations 1866. **b.** Of the human figure, etc.: Naked, undraped 1873.

1. a. *N. contract* or *pact*: a bare contract or promise, without any consideration. 2. b. The medals ..bear..on their obverse the n. bust of that Empress 1879.

B. *sb.* **1.** A nude figure in painting or sculpture 1708. **2.** With *the.* The undraped human figure; the representation of this in the arts 1760. **b.** The condition of being undraped 1856.

2. Modern chalk drawings, studies from the n. BROWNING.

Nudge (nvdʒ), *v.* 1675. [Origin obscure.] **1.** *trans.* To touch or push (one) slightly with the elbow to attract attention. **2.** *intr.* To give a push or thrust 1825. Hence **Nudge** *sb.* 1826.

Nudi- (niū·di), comb. form of L. *nudus* NUDE *a.*, as **Nudibra·chiate** *a. Zool.* of polyps, having arms or tentacles covered with cilia.

Nudibranch (niū·dibræŋk). 1844. [ad. F. *nudibranche*; see NUDI- and BRANCHIÆ.] *Zool.* A mollusc of the order *Nudibranchiata*, having naked gills and no shell. Also *attrib.* or as *adj.* So **Nudibra·nchial** *a.* **Nudibra·nchian** = next 1839.

Nudibra·nchiate. 1836. [See NUDI- and BRANCHIATE.] *Zool.* **A.** *adj.* Of molluscs: Having naked branchiæ; belonging to the *Nudibranchiata.* **B.** *sb.* A mollusc of this order.

Nudist (niū·dist). 1931. [f. NUDE + -IST.] An adherent of the cult of the nude.

Nudity (niū·dĭti). 1611. [a. F. *nudité*, or ad. L. *nuditatem*, f. *nudus* NUDE; see -ITY.] **1.** The condition or fact of being naked or nude; a nude or naked state. **2.** A nude figure, *esp.* as represented in the arts 1662. †**3.** *pl.* The private parts when exposed -1769.

1. In another [plate] the august n. of Downing-Street is made interesting 1900. 2. Fat Graces and other plump nudities by Rubens HAWTHORNE.

Nugacious (niugē¹·ʃəs), *a.* Now *rare.* 1652. [f. L. *nugacis*, *nugax* trifling + -OUS.] Trivial, trifling, of no moment.

Nugacity (niugæ·sĭti). Now *rare.* 1593. [ad. late L. *nugacitas*, f. *nugacis*, *nugax*; see prec. and -ITY.] **1.** Trifling, triviality, futility. **2.** A trifling or frivolous idea 1653.

Nugatory (niū·gătəri), *a.* 1603. [ad. L. *nugatorius*, f. ppl. stem of *nugari.*] **1.** Trifling, worthless. **2.** Of no force, invalid; useless, futile, inoperative 1605.

2. Those provisions of the edict..were contrived so artfully as to be nearly n. PRESCOTT. *N. payment*, one involving an immediate and formal loss, i.e. the payment of money, in return for which no service is rendered. Hence **Nu·gatoriness.**

Nugget (nv·gĕt). 1852. [app. a deriv. of s.-w. dial. *nug*, a lump, a block, etc.] **1.** A rough lump of native gold. **2.** A lump of anything 1860. **3.** *Austral.* A small compact beast or runt 1852. Hence **Nu·gget(t)y** *a.*

Nugi- (niū·dʒi), comb. form of L. *nugæ*, as in **Nu·gifying** *ppl. a.* productive of mere trifling; etc.

Nuisance (niū·săns). late ME. [a. OF., f. *nuis-*, *nuire* to hurt, harm; see -ANCE.] **1.** Injury, hurt, harm, annoyance. (In later use only as implying sense 2 or 2 b.) **2.** Anything injurious or obnoxious to the community, or to the individual as a member of it, for which some legal remedy may be found 1464. **b.** More widely: Anything obnoxious to the community or individual by offensiveness of smell or appearance, by causing obstruction or damage, etc. 1661. **c.** Applied to persons 1695. **d.** An obnoxious practice, institution, state of things, etc. 1820. **e.** A source of annoyance 1831.

2. All such Lotteries are..declared to be Common Nusances 1710. *Commit no n.*: an injunction to the public not to defile a place. **b.** The n. of the smoke of London EVELYN. **c.** He is a sort of privileged n. SCOTT. **e.** The other set,..who go little into parties, and vote balls a n. LYTTON. Hence **Nui·sancer**, one who causes a n. BLACKSTONE.

Null (nvl), *a.* 1563. [a. OF. *nul* or ad. L. *nullus*, f. *ne* not + *ullus* any.] **1.** Void, of no legal or binding force; of no efficacy, invalid. **2.** Of no value or importance; insignificant 1790. **b.** Devoid of character or expression 1850. **3.** Amounting to nothing, non-existent 1761.

1. If such consent from the father was wanting, the marriage was n. BLACKSTONE. Phr. *N. and void* 1669. 2. b. Faultily faultless, icily regular, splendidly n. TENNYSON. 3. The combined effect..is thus n. 1866. *N. method* (Electr.), a method in which the thing to be observed is the non-existence of some phenomenon; called also *zero method.*

Null (nvl), *v.* 1643. [f. prec., after *annul.*] †**1.** To reduce to nothing -1722. **2.** To annul, cancel, make void 1643.

2. The first election he nulled, because its irregularity was glaring BURKE.

‖ **Nulla bona** (nv·lă bō^u·nă). 1807. [L., 'no goods'.] The return made by a sheriff upon an execution when the party has no goods to be distrained.

‖ **Nullah** (nv·lă). *Anglo-Ind.* Also **nulla.** 1776. [Hindī *nālā* brook, ravine.] A river or stream; a watercourse, river-bed, ravine.

Nullification (nvlifikē¹·ʃən). 1630. [ad. late L. *nullificatio*; see NULLIFY and -ATION.] †**1.** Reduction to nothing DONNE. **2.** The action of rendering null or of no effect 1808. **b.** *U.S.* The action, on the part of a State legislature, of refusing to allow a general law to be enforced within the State 1799.

2. His accession..was ushered in by the n. of his father's will 1839.

Nullifidian (nvlifi·diăn). 1564. [f. L. *nulli-* comb. form of *nullus* no + *fides* faith.] **A.** *sb.* **1.** One of no faith or religion; a sceptic in religious matters. **2.** *transf.* A disbeliever 1668. **B.** *adj.* Having no faith or belief 1627.

Nullifier (nv·lifəi,əɪ). 1832. [f. next + -ER [1].] One who nullifies; *spec.* in *U.S. Hist.*, one who maintained the right of nullification on the part of any State.

Nullify (nv·lifəi), *v.* 1595. [ad. late L. *nullificare*, f. *nulli-*, *nullus* no; see -FY.] **1.** *trans.* To render legally null and void; to annul, cancel. **2.** To make of no value, use, or efficacy; to efface completely 1609.

2. They had long learnt to n. what they professed to defend 1876.

‖ **Nullipara** (nv·lipără). 1872. [mod.L., f. *nulli-* (cf. prec.) + *-para*, fem. of *-parus*; see -PAROUS.] A female who has never given birth to a child. Hence **Nullipa·rity; Nulli·parous** *a.*

Nullipore (nv·lipōəɪ). 1840. [f. L. *nulli-*, *nullus* no + PORE *sb.*[1]] A form of marine vegetation having the power of secreting lime like the coral polyp.

Nullity (nv·lĭti). 1570. [a. F. *nullité*, or med.L. *nullitas*: see NULL *a.* and -ITY.] **1.** The fact of being legally null and void; invalidity. Also (with *a* and *pl.*), an instance of this; a fact or circumstance causing invalidity. **2.** An act or thing which is null or invalid 1624. **3.** The condition of being null or nought; a state of nothingness 1589. **4. a.** A mere nothing 1591. **b.** Of persons: A nonentity 1657.

1. A petition for n. of marriage on the ground of imperfect publication of the banns 1865. The n. of all proceedings taken in contravention of them STUBBS. 2. The Court declared the deed a n. 1891. 4. a. Such a mere n. is time, to a creature to whom God gives a feeling heart COWPER. **b.** Such a miserable n., and husk of a man BROWNING.

Numb (nvm), *a.* (and *sb.*). [late ME. *nomyn*, for older *numen*, pa. pple. of NIM *v.*, to take, seize.] **1.** Deprived of feeling, or of the power of movement, *esp.* through cold 1440. **b.** Helpless, incapable 1802. **2.** Of the nature of numbness 1641. **3.** *sb.* A cold which numbs fish 1888.

1. Leaning long upon any Part maketh it Numme, and as we call it, Asleep BACON. 2. †*N. palsy*, paralysis 1772. Hence **Nu·mb-ly** *adv.* 1895, **-ness** 1571.

Numb (nɒm), *v.* 1602. [f. prec.] *trans.* To make numb.

For lazy Winter nums the lab'ring Hand DRYDEN.

Number (nɒ·mbəɹ), *sb.* ME. [a. OF. *nombre, numbre, numere* :—L. *numerum*, acc. sing. of *numerus.*] **I. 1.** The sum or aggregate *of* any collection of individual things or persons. **b.** *pl.* The title of the fourth book in the Bible, containing a census of the Israelites. late ME. **2.** A sum or total of abstract units ME. **b.** In *pl.* as a subject of study or science. late ME. **c.** A symbol or figure, or collection of these, which represents graphically an arithmetical total; a ticket or label bearing such signs 1837. **3.** The particular mark or symbol, having an arithmetical value, by which a person or thing has a place assigned to it in a series. late ME. **4.** Prefixed to a numeral, as *number two* or No. 2 (see No.), to designate things or persons by the place assigned to them in an arithmetical series. late ME. **5.** A single numbered part or issue of a book or periodical publication 1757. **b.** One of a collection of songs or poems 1878. **c.** A part or division of an opera, oratorio, etc. 1881.

1. The n. of fools is infinite SOUTHEY. 2. I hope good lucke lies in odde numbers SHAKS. Phr. *Golden n.*: see GOLDEN *a.* b. The science of numbers JOHNSON. c. A strange specimen of the human race..with a brass label and n. round his neck DICKENS. 3. To 'take' a Policeman's 'n.' 1880. Phr. *To lose the n. of one's mess*, to die, to perish. *One's n. is up* (colloq.): one is doomed to die or to come to disaster. 4. N. twenty-two wants his boots DICKENS. *N. one*, one's self, one's own person and interests; *esp.* in *to look after*, or *take care of, n. one.* 5. The old back numbers of periodicals 1851. Phr. *Back n.* (fig.), an antiquated, out-of-date person or thing. *In numbers*, in a series of separate parts published at intervals.

II. 1. The full tale or count of a collection, company, or class of persons. Also *pl.* ME. **b.** The body or aggregate of persons specified 1529. **2.** A (large, small, etc.) collection or company *of* persons or things ME. **3.** A certain (usu. a considerable) company, collection, or aggregate *of* persons or things ME. **4.** *pl.* A (great, infinite, etc.) multitude or aggregate of persons or things. late ME. **b.** Many persons, etc. 1597. **c.** In contexts denoting superiority derived from numerical preponderance 1638.

1. Hell, her numbers full, Thenceforth shall be for ever shut MILT. Is gratitude in the n. of a man's virtues? CHATHAM. 2. An infinite nombre of grassehoppers came flieng into Germany 1560. A considerable n. are employed in..workshops 1895. 3. He.. kept himself by keeping a n. of bees 1860. The testimony of a n. is more cogent than the testimony of two or three 1833. 4. The French have lost immense numbers of men WELLINGTON. b. There are numbers in this city who live by writing new books 1760. c. They overpowered the foreigners by force of numbers 1861.

III. 1. That property of things according to which they can be counted or enumerated ME. **b.** *Phren.* The faculty of numbering or calculating 1835. **2.** In phrases denoting that persons, things, etc., have not been, or cannot be, counted ME. **3.** *In n.*: in sum total; altogether ME.

1. A child..perceives a difference between many and few; and that difference it is taught to call n. 1762. 2. A shout Loud as from numbers without n. MILT.

IV. †1. Quantity, amount (*rare*) –1720. **2.** *Gram.* The property in words of denoting that one, two, or more persons or things are spoken of; the special form of a word by which this is expressed. late ME. **†3.** Conformity, in verse or music, to a certain regular beat or measure; rhythm –1667. **4.** *pl.* **a.** Musical periods or groups of notes 1579. **b.** Metrical periods or feet; hence, lines, verses 1588.

2. There are two numbers, the singular speaking of one, the plurall of moe 1591. 3. MILT. *P.L.* IV. 687. 4. In Musickes Numbers my Voyce rose and fell DRAYTON. b. I lisped in numbers, for the numbers came POPE. Hence **Nu·mberless** *a.* innumerable 1573.

Number (nɒ·mbəɹ), *v.* ME. [a. OF. *nombrer* :—L. *numerare*, f. *numerus* number.] **1.** *trans.* To count, to ascertain the number of (individual things or persons). **†b.** To compute, calculate, reckon, measure –1794. **2.** To enumerate, reckon *up.* Also *absol.* late ME. **b.** To fix the number of; to reduce to a definite number; to make few in number; to bring to a close. (Chiefly in passive.) late ME. **†c.** To collect, up to a certain number –1611. **3.** Tot check, control, or verify the number of; to count or tell *over.* Also *absol. poet.* **†b.** To count out or pay *down* (money) –1725. **c.** To apportion (one's days) with care 1535. **4.** To count, reckon, or class among certain persons or things. Chiefly const. *among, in, with.* late ME. **5.** To assign or attach a number to (a thing); *spec.* to distinguish by a number. late ME. **6.** To have lived, or to live (so many years) 1590. **7.** To comprise in a number; to have or comprise (so many things or persons) 1645. **b.** To equal, amount to 1842.

1. To n. the Votes HOBBES. b. Have you nombred the distaunce bytwene the sonne and the moone? 1530. 2. b. The Sands are numbred, that makes vp my Life SHAKS. c. N. thee an armie, like the armie that thou hast lost 1 *Kings* xx. 25. 3. c. O teach vs to nombre oure dayes, that we maye applie our hertes vnto wyszdome COVERDALE *Ps.* lxxxix. 5. 4. Make them to be noumbred with thy saynctes *Bk. Com. Prayer.* 5. The houses were not numbered MACAULAY. 6. Of as able bodie as when he number'd thirty SHAKS. 7. Otranto numbered twenty-two thousand inhabitants FREEMAN. b. The crew and passengers numbered 33. 1883. Hence **Nu·mberer** 1594.

Numb-fish. 1711. [f. NUMB *a.*] The Electric Ray or Torpedo, which numbs by the electric shocks emitted by it.

Numbles (nɒ·mb'lz). Now only *arch.* ME. [a. OF. *numbles, nombles* pl., loin of veal, fillet of beef or venison, etc., app. for **lomble(s)*, and repr. L. *lumbulus*, dim. of *lumbus* loin. Cf. UMBLES and HUMBLES.] Certain of the inward parts of a deer, etc., as used for food. Also, in early use, part of the back and loins of a hart.

‖**Numdah** (nɒ·mdā). *Anglo-Ind.* 1876. [a. Urdū *namdā*, f. Pers. *namad* carpet, rug.] A kind of felt or coarse woollen cloth; a saddle-cloth or pad made of this. Var. **Nu·mnah** 1859.

Numen (niū·mĕn). 1628. [a. L., related to *nuere* to nod (assent).] Deity, divinity; divine or presiding power or spirit.

Numerable (niū·mĕrăb'l), *a.* 1570. [ad. L. *numerabilis*, f. *numerare.*] Capable of being numbered.

Numeral (niū·mĕrăl). 1530. [ad. late L. *numeralis*, f. *numerus* number.] **A.** *adj.* **1.** Expressing or denoting number. **2.** Belonging or appertaining to number 1607.

1. *One* is a n. adjective 1824. N. characters are either letters; or figures, otherwise called digits 1727.

B. *sb.* **1.** A word expressing a number 1530. **2.** A figure or character (or a group of these) denoting a number 1686.

1. Cardinal, Ordinal, and Indefinite Numerals 1872. 2. The letters of the alphabet themselves came to be used as numerals.

Numerary (niū·mĕrări), *a.* 1726. [ad. med.L. *numerarius* (in class. L. as sb.), f. *numerus*; see -ARY.] **1.** *Eccl.* Of a canon: Forming one of the regular number. **2.** Of or pertaining to a number or numbers 1742.

Nu·merate, *v. rare.* 1721. [f. L. *numerat-*, *numerare.*] *trans.* To number, reckon. Also *absol.* Hence **Nu·merative** *a.* pertaining to numeration or numbering.

Numeration (niūmĕrē·ʃən). late ME. [ad. L. *numerationem*, f. *numerare* to number.] **1. a.** A method or process of numbering, or computing. **b.** Without article: Calculation; the assigning of number to things 1596. **2.** The action, process, or result of ascertaining the number *of* people, etc. 1533. **3.** *Arith.* The art of expressing any number in words that is already given in figures 1542.

1. a. If..time is a n. of motion 1837. b. That progress of Science, which is to destroy Wonder, and in its stead substitute Mensuration and N. CARLYLE. 2. To make an exact n. of the inhabitants of Ireland, distinguishing their religion BURKE. 3. *N. table*, a table showing the value of figures according to their place in a system of notation.

Numerator (niū·mĕrēˈtəɹ). 1542. [ad. late L., f. *numerare.*] **1.** *Arith.* **†a.** The word(s) or figure(s) by which the number of things or persons in question is denoted. **b.** The number written above the line in a vulgar fraction, which shows how many of the specified parts of a unit are taken 1575. **2.** One who or that which numbers 1675.

Numeric (niume·rik), *a.* and *sb.* 1663. [ad. mod.L. *numericus*, f. *numerus.*] **†1.** *adj.* Identical –1727. **2.** *sb.* Any number, proper or improper fraction, or incommensurable ratio 1879.

Numerical (niume·rikăl), *a.* 1624. [f. as prec. + -AL.] **1.** Pertaining to number; of the nature of, according to, number; etc. 1628. **b.** Of figures: Denoting a number 1706. **c.** In respect of numbers 1812. **d.** Characterized by the use of ordinary figures expressive of number 1840. **†2.** Particular, individual (*rare*) –1699. **†3.** With *same*: Individual, identical. So with *very.* –1716.

1. Tickets in a N. Order 1712. b. The Brahmans were the original inventors of those n. symbols MAX MÜLLER. c. Nikostratus..was not afraid of this n. superiority 1849. d. An equation is n. or algebraical according as its coefficients are numbers or algebraical symbols 1881. 3. This is that very n. Lady, with whom I am in love DRYDEN. Hence **Nume·rically** *adv.* with respect to number; by means of numbers.

Nu·merist. *rare.* 1646. [f. L. *numerus* + -IST.] One who concerns himself with numbers.

Numerosity (niūmĕrǫ·sĭti). 1589. [ad. late L. *numerositas*; see next and -ITY.] **1.** The state of being numerous; condition in respect of number 1611. **2.** Rhythmic quality.

Numerous (niū·mĕrəs), *a.* 1586. [ad. L. *numerosus*, f. *numerus* number; see -OUS.] **1.** Qualifying a sing.: abundant, copious; comprising many units. Now *rare.* **b.** Consisting of many individuals 1647. **c.** Coming from or pertaining to large numbers 1832. Now *rare.* **2.** Qualifying a pl.: Many 1622. **†3.** Containing many individuals; thronged, crowded –1831. **4.** Consisting of 'numbers' or rhythmical periods; measured, rhythmical 1589.

1. A n. Acquaintance STEELE. b. He exalted allmost all of his own n. Family CLARENDON. c. That n. voice which we designate as 'Public Opinion' 1841. 2. Contriving presses to put my books up in; they now growing n. PEPYS. 4. Eloquence..in Prose or n. Verse MILT. Hence **Nu·merous·ly** *adv.*, **-ness.**

Numismatic (niūmizmæ·tik), *a.* and *sb.* 1792. [ad. F. *numismatique*, f. L. *numismat-*, *numisma, nomisma*, a. Gr. *νόμισμα* current coin, f. *νομίζειν* to have in use.] **1.** Of, pertaining or relating to, coins or coinage. **2.** Consisting of coins 1851. **3.** *sb. pl.* The study of coins and medals 1829. Hence **Numisma·tically** *adv.* **Numismati·cian, Numi·smatist,** a student of coins. **Numismato·logy,** the science of numismatics; whence **Numismato·logist.**

Nummary (nɒ·măɹi), *a.* 1603. [ad. L. *nummarius*, f. *nummus* a coin.] **1.** Pertaining or relating to money or coinage. **2.** Dealing with coins or money 1695.

Nummular (nɒ·miūlăɹ), *a.* 1846. [f. L. *nummulus*, dim. of *nummus* coin + -AR[2].] *Path.* Coin-shaped, *esp.* of sputa 1846.

Nummulary (nɒ·miūlări), *a.* 1767. [See prec. and -ARY[1].] Nummary.

Nu·mmulated, *ppl. a.* 1873. *Path.* [f. L. *nummulus.*] = NUMMULAR.

Nummulite (nɒ·miūləit). 1811. [f. as NUMMULAR + -ITE[1] 2.] *Zool.* A genus of fossil foraminiferous cephalopods belonging to the order *Polythalamia*, found in the Tertiary strata; an individual of this genus. Hence **Nummuli·tic** *a.* (*Geol.*), containing, or formed of, nummulites.

†**Nump(s.** 1611. [Origin obscure.] A silly or stupid person –1730.

Numskull (nɒ·mskɒl). 1717. [f. NUMB *a.* + SKULL *sb.*] **1.** A blockhead, thick-head, dolt 1724. **2.** The head, pate, noddle, *esp.* that of a dull person 1717.

1. He considered them to be numskulls, and little better than idiots TROLLOPE. So **Nu·mskulled** *a.* slow-witted; stupid 1706.

Nun (nɒn). [OE. *nunne*; also ME. *nonne*; f. (ult.) eccl. L. *nonna*, fem. of *nonnus* monk (in late Gr. *νόννος, νόννα*), orig. a title given to elderly persons.] **1.** A woman devoted to a religious life under certain vows; usu., one who has vowed poverty, chastity, and obedience, and who lives in a convent under a certain rule. **†b.** A priestess or votaress of some pagan deity –1698. **2.** The name of various birds: **a.** The Blue Titmouse, *Parus cæruleus* 1589. **b.** The Smew, *Mergus albellus* 1666. **c.** A variety of domestic pigeon having a veil of white feathers covering its head 1725. **3.** A species of moth 1832.

1. For my Daughters.. They shall be praying Nunnes, not weeping Queenes SHAKS. *attrib.* and *Comb.*, as †**nun's flesh**, a cold or ascetic temperament; **nun's thread**, a fine white sewing-cotton, such as is used by nuns; **nun's veiling**, a soft thin woollen material.

Nun-bird. 1881. [f. prec.] A South American puff-bird of the genus *Monacha*.

Nun-buoy. 1703. [f. obs. *nun* child's top.] *Naut.* A buoy of circular shape in the middle and tapering towards each end.

‖**Nunc dimi·ttis.** 1552. [L., first words of the Song of Simeon in Luke ii. 29.] **1.** The canticle beginning with these words. **2.** Permission to depart; departure, dismissal 1621.

1. The sweetest Canticle is, *Nunc dimittis*; when a Man hath obtained worthy Ends, and Expectations BACON. Phr. *To sing* (one's) *nunc dimittis*, to declare oneself contented to depart from life or from some occupation.

†**Nunce.** 1566. [? a. F. *nonce*.] = NUNCIO. -1712.

Nuncheon (nʊ·nʃən). Now *dial.* [ME. *nōn(e)shench*, f. *nōn(e* NOON = *shench* [OE. *scenc*), draught, cup.] A slight refreshment of liquor, etc., orig. taken in the afternoon; a light refreshment taken between meals; a lunch.

Nunciate (nʊ·nʃieⁱt). 1596. [irreg. f. L. *nuncius* or *nunciare*, perh. after *legate*.] One who or that which announces; a messenger, nuntius.

Nunciature (nʊ·nʃiătiŭəɹ). 1652. [ad. It. *nunziatura*, f. *nunzio* NUNCIO.] The office or the period of office of a papal nuncio.

Nuncio (nʊ·nʃio). 1528. [a. earlier It. *nuncio* (now *nunzio*):—L. *nuncius* messenger.] **1.** A permanent official representative of the Roman See at a foreign court. **2.** A messenger 1601. **3.** A member of the Polish diet 1684.

Nuncius (nʊ·nʃiŏs). *rare.* 1613. [a. L.; cf. NUNTIUS.] A messenger.

Nuncle. 1589. Now *dial.* Var. of UNCLE with *n* transferred from *myn*; see N.

Nuncupate (nʊ·nkiupeⁱt), *v.* 1550. [f. L. *nuncupat-*, *nuncupare* to name, declare.] †**1.** To express (a vow) in words -1788. **2.** To declare (a will) orally 1677. †**3.** To dedicate (a work) *to* some one -1656. So **Nuncupa·tion** (in senses 1-2).

Nuncupative (nʊ·nkiupēⁱtiv, nʊnkiū·pătiv), *a.* (and *sb.*). 1546. [ad. late and med.L. *nuncupativus*; see prec. and -IVE.] **1.** Of wills: Oral, not written. **2.** Denoting nuncupation; designative (*rare*) 1619.

1. Soldiers and sailors.. when on service, may make n. wills 1883. Hence **Nuncupatively** *adv.*

†**Nuncupatory,** *a.* 1603. [Cf. prec. and -ORY.] **1.** Nuncupative, oral -1704. **2.** Dedicatory -1679.

Nundinal (nʊ·ndinăl), *a.* (and *sb.*). 1656. [ad. L. *nundinalis*, f. *nundinæ* NUNDINE.] Pertaining to a fair or market; connected with the Roman nundines.

N. letter, a letter of the alphabet (A to H) attached to each day of the Roman n. period.

Nundina·tion. 1623. [ad. L. *nundinationem*, f. *nundinari*, f. *nundinæ* NUNDINE.] Traffic, trade, buying and selling; sale.

Nundine (nʊ·ndəin). Also *pl.* 1533. [ad. L. *nundinæ* fem. pl., f. *novem* nine + *dies* day.] Among the ancient Romans, a market-day held every eighth (by Roman reckoning, ninth) day.

Nunky (nʊ·ŋki), pet form of **Nuncle** 1798.

Nunnation (nʊnēⁱ·ʃən). 1776. [ad. mod.L. *nunnatio*, f. *nūn* Arabic name of letter *n*.] **1.** The addition of a final *n* in the declension of Arabic nouns, denoted by doubling the vowel sign. **2.** The addition of inorganic *n* in Middle English forms 1838.

Nunnery (nʊ·nəri). ME. [prob. ad. AF. **nonnerie*, f. *nonne* NUN; see -ERY.] **1.** A place of residence for nuns; a building in which nuns live under religious rule and discipline; a convent. **b.** *transf.* A house of ill fame 1593. **2.** A company of nuns 1651.

1. Get thee to a Nunnerie SHAKS.

Nunnish (nʊ·niʃ), *a.* 1570. [f. NUN + -ISH.] Pertaining to a nun; nun-like.

‖**Nuntius** (nʊ·nʃiŏs). *Pl.* **nuntii** (-ʃi,əi). 1605. [L.; cf. NUNCIUS.] = NUNCIO.

Nuphar (niū·făɪ). 1845. [a. med. or mod.L., ad. Arab.-Pers. *nūfar*, reduced f. *nīnūfar* NENUPHAR.] The yellow water-lily.

Nuptial (nʊ·pʃăl), *a.* and *sb.* 1490. [a. F., or ad. L. *nuptialis*, f. *nuptiæ* wedding, f. *nupt-*, *nubere* to marry.] **A.** *adj.* Of or pertaining to marriage or the marriage ceremony.

She..at last fixed the n. day JOHNSON.

B. *sb.* Marriage, wedding. (Usu. in *pl.*) 1555.

1. The nuptials were solemnised according to Persian usage 1840. *sing.* The N. was no sooner celebrated, than he repented it 1654.

Nuptiality (nʊpʃi,æ·lĭti). 1789. [f. prec.] **1.** *pl.* Nuptial ceremonies 1863. **2.** Conjugal character.

Nuragh (nūə·ræg). 1828. [Sardinian.] A massive stone tower of ancient date, of a type peculiar to Sardinia.

Nurse (nɔ̈ɹs), *sb.*[1] late ME. [Reduced f. ME. *norice*, *nurice* NOURICE.] **1.** A woman employed to suckle, and take charge of, an infant, a WET NURSE; also, one who has general charge of a young child or children, a DRY NURSE. **b.** *transf.* One who takes care of, looks after, or advises another. late ME. **c.** *fig.* That which nourishes or fosters some quality, condition, etc. 1526. **2.** A person, usu. a woman, who attends or waits upon the sick; now *esp.* one trained for this purpose 1590. **3.** *Forestry.* A tree set in a plantation to protect smaller or newly planted ones from wind or cold 1788. **4.** *Entom.* A sexually imperfect member of a community of bees, ants, etc., upon whom devolves the care of the young brood 1818. **5.** *Zool.* An individual in the asexual stage of metagenesis 1845.

1. Shal I go, and call the a n. of the Hebrues women, to nurse ye the childe? COVERDALE *Exod.* ii. 7. The nurse's legends are for truths receiv'd DRYDEN. **c.** Time is the N., and breeder of all good SHAKS. Phr. *At n.*, in the care of a n. *To put to n.*, to commit to the care of a n. Also *fig.*, e. g. of estates in the hands of trustees. **2.** The n. sleeps sweetly, hired to watch the sick COWPER. *N.-housemaid*, a maid who combines the duties of a nursemaid and a housemaid.

Nurse (nɔ̈ɹs), *sb.*[2] 1499. [Perh. a var. of HUSS, with added (*a*)*n* (see N 2); assim. to prec.] A dog-fish or shark (of various species). So *n.-fish*, *-hound*, *-shark*.

Nurse (nɔ̈ɹs), *v.* 1526. [Ult. reduced form of *nurish* NOURISH *v.*, assim. to NURSE *sb.*[1]] **1.** Of a woman: To suckle, and otherwise attend to, or simply to take charge of (an infant) 1535. **b.** *intr.* To act as wet-nurse 1789. **2.** In *pass.* **a.** To be reared or brought up in a certain place 1526. **b.** To be brought up under certain conditions, *in* a certain environment, etc. 1601. **3.** To foster, tend, cherish (a thing); to promote the growth or development of 1542. **b.** To supply (plants) with warmth and moisture; to tend or cultivate carefully 1594. **c.** To manage (land) economically 1745. **d.** To cherish (a feeling, etc.) in one's own heart 1763. **e.** To assist or cause (a thing) to develop *into* a certain form, or *to* a certain size 1775. **4.** To bring or rear *up* with care 1603. **5.** To wait upon, attend to (a person who is ill) 1736. **b.** To try to cure (an illness) by taking care of oneself. Also with *away*. 1785. **c.** *intr.* To perform the duties of a sick-nurse 1861. **6.** To clasp (the knee, etc.) in one's hands 1849. **b.** To hold caressingly or carefully, *esp.* in the arms or on the lap 1850. **c.** To sit close to, as if taking care of (a fire) 1857. **7.** *slang.* **a.** To keep close to (a rival omnibus) so as to interfere with its custom 1858. **b.** To impede (a horse) in a race, by surrounding it with other and slower ones 1893. **8. a.** To keep in touch with (a constituency) in order to obtain votes 1869. **b.** To assist (a business house) so as to prevent its bankruptcy 1890. **9.** *Billiards.* To keep (the balls) together in order to make a series of cannons 1869.

1. So is it..comly for the own mother to nource her own childe 1546. **2.** For we were nurst upon the self-same hill MILT. **b.** O Lady, nursed in pomp and pleasure! COLERIDGE. **3.** To n. with tender care the thriving arts COWPER. **b.** I..live in Oak'n bowr, To n. the Saplings tall MILT. **c.** He nursed what property was yet left to him SCOTT. **d.** He could n. his injuries for many years 1879. **5.** The arrangements for nursing the sick have greatly improved in recent times 1881. **b.** My cold..has returned, and I am nursing it before I sail 1813. **6. b.** They..drove home again, Francesca nursing a Dying Gladiator in terra-cotta 1887. **8. a.** To n. the borough cost him £500 a year at least 1869.

Nu·rse-child. 1560. [NURSE *sb.*[1]] A foster-child.

†**Nu·rse-father.** 1564. [f. NURSE *sb.*[1] or *v.*] A foster-father. Chiefly *fig.* -1714.

Nu·rsemaid. 1657. [NURSE *sb.*[1]] A young woman employed as maid to attend to little children.

Nu·rse-mother. Now *rare.* 1579. [f. NURSE *sb.*[1] or *v.*] A foster-mother.

Nu·rser. late ME. [f. NURSE *v.* + -ER.[1]] One who, or that which, nurses, fosters, or encourages.

Nursery (nɔ̈·ɹsəri). ME. [prob. ad. AF. **noricerie*, f. *norice* NOURICE; see -ERY.] †**1.** Fosterage, upbringing, breeding; nursing -1671. **2.** The apartment which is given up to infants and young children with their nurse 1499. **3.** A practice, institution, etc., in or by which something is fostered or developed 1509. **b.** A place, sphere, etc., in which people are trained or educated; a school *of*, or *for*, certain professions, etc. 1581. †**c.** A theatre established in London for the training of young players -1683. **4.** A piece of ground in which young plants or trees are reared until fit for transplantation; †a collection of such plants. Now usu., a nursery-garden. Also *transf.* and *fig.* 1565. **5.** A place which breeds or supports animals 1661; a pond for rearing fish 1771. **b.** Of ants, etc.: The cells in which the larval and nymphal insects attain maturity 1797. **c.** A place or part in which any form of animal life is developed 1871. **6.** A race for two-year-old horses 1883. **7.** *Billiards.* A series (of cannons) made by keeping the balls close together 1869.

1. *Lear* I. i. 126. **2.** He is taught from the N., that he must inherit a great Estate SWIFT. **3.** That all subordinate treasuries, as the nurseries of mismanagement..ought to be dissolved BURKE. **4.** *fig.* Ye sacred Nurseries of blooming Youth! WORDSW. *attrib.* and *Comb.*, as (in sense 2), *n.-governess*, *school*, etc.; (in sense 4), *n.-garden*, *-gardener*, etc.

Nu·rseryman. 1672. [f. prec.] One who owns, or works in, a nursery for plants.

Nu·rse-tree. 1805. [NURSE *sb.*[1]] **1.** A tree planted to protect others. **2.** A tree supporting a parasitic plant 1857.

Nu·rsing, *vbl. sb.* 1532. [f. NURSE *v.* + -ING [1].] **1.** The action of NURSE *v.* **2.** *attrib.*, as *n.-chair*; *n. home*, a small private hospital.

Nu·rsing, *ppl. a.* 1535. [-ING [2].] **1.** That nurses, or tends like a nurse, as *n.-father*, *n.-mother*, a foster-father, -mother. **2.** That is being nursed, as, *a n. baby* (*rare*) 1860.

Nursle (nɔ̈·ɹs'l), *v.* 1596. *rare.* [var. of *nousle* NUZZLE *v.*[2], assim. to NURSE *v.*] **1.** *trans.* = NUZZLE *v.*[2] 2. **2.** To nurse, foster, cherish 1652.

Nursling, nurseling (nɔ̈·ɹsliŋ). 1557. [f. NURSE *v.* + -LING, after *suckling*.] **1.** An infant or child in relation to its nurse 1607. Also *transf.* **2.** *attrib.*, as *n. babe*, etc. 1793.

1. I was his nursling once and choice delight MILT. *transf.* Forms more real than living man, Nurslings of immortality SHELLEY.

Nurture (nɔ̈·ɹtiŭɹ, -tʃəɹ), *sb.* ME. [a. OF. *nourture*, *nurture*, var. of *noure-*, *nourriture*; see NOURITURE.] **1.** Breeding, upbringing, training, education (received or possessed by one). Now *rare.* †**b.** Moral training or discipline -1637. **2.** That which nourishes; nourishment, food. late ME. **3.** The bringing-up *of* some one; tutelage; fostering care 1676.

1. His father in his youthe had taught him good n. LD. BERNERS. **b.** Who so despiseth wisedome, and n., he is miserable *Wisdom* iii. 11. **2.** Your lovers feeble eyes you feed, But sterve their harts that needeth nourture most SPENSER. Hence **Nu·rtural** *a.* 1922.

Nurture (nɔ̈·ɹtiŭɹ, -tʃəɹ), *v.* ME. [f. prec.] **1.** *trans.* To feed or nourish; to rear. **b.** *transf.* To foster, cherish 1828. **2.** To bring up, train, educate 1526. †**b.** To discipline, chasten -1636.

1. By his Grandsyre nourisht up And nurtred from a boye 1575. **b.** To n. a secret affection 1872. **2.** They nurter the yonge wemen for to love their husbandes TINDALE *Titus* ii. 4. **b.** He that spareth the rod, hateth his childe; but he that loveth him doth instantly n. him BIBLE (Douay) *Prov.* xiii. 24. Hence **Nu·rturer.**

Nut (nʊt), *sb.* [Com. Teut.: OE. *hnutu*. OTeut. **hnut-* :—pre-Teut. **knud-*, repr. by

OIr. *cnū*, W. *cneuen*.] **I. 1.** A fruit which consists of a hard or leathery (indehiscent) shell enclosing an edible kernel; the kernel itself. †**2.** A cup formed from the shell of a coco-nut mounted in metal; also, one made of other materials to resemble this -1580. **3.** In allusive contexts 1562. **4.** In allusions to the difficulty of cracking hard-shelled nuts: **a.** A difficult question or problem 1545. **b.** A difficult undertaking; a person hard to deal with or conciliate 1662. **5.** *slang.* The head (of a person) 1858. **6.** A 'swell', dandy. *slang.* 1904. (Jocularly spelt and pronounced *knut*.)

3. More noise than nuts LONGF. They can't shoot for nuts 1899. **4. a.** He especially liked his mental nuts 1858. **b.** Fortified towns are hard nuts to crack FRANKLIN. **5.** Phr. *Off one's n.*, out of one's mind, insane. Phrases. †*Nuts to* (a person), a source of pleasure to one. *To be* (*dead*) *nuts on* or *upon*, to set great store upon, to be devoted to, or delighted with (a person or thing). *slang.*

II. 1. A small metal projection upon a spindle (of a clock, etc.) furnished with teeth, and engaging in a cog-wheel; a small spur-wheel. late ME. †**2.** A projection from the lock of a cross-bow, serving to detain the string until released by the trigger -1674. **3.** A small block of wood, iron, etc., pierced, and wormed with a female screw; used to make a bolt fast or adjust it 1611. **b.** The portion of a wooden printing-press in which the screw plays 1642. **c.** The contrivance at the lower end of a violin-bow, or the like, by which the horse-hair may be relaxed or tightened 1662. **4.** *Naut.* Either of two projections on the square part of the shank of an anchor, to secure the stock in its place 1627. **5.** *Mus.* The fixed bridge formed by a slight projection or ridge at the upper end of the strings of the violin, guitar, etc. 1698.

III. †**1.** The glans penis -1758. †**2.** = POPE'S EYE -1682. **b.** *dial.* The pancreas; also, part of the caul 1816. **3.** *pl.* Coal in small lumps 1859. **4.** A small rounded biscuit or cake. Only in *doughnut, gingerbread* or *spice nut*, q.v.

attrib. and *Comb.*, as **N.-Monday**, the first Monday in August, locally observed as a holiday; **n.-palm**, an Australian palm (*Cycus media*) which bears edible nuts; **n.-pine**, a species of pine (*Pinus sabiniana*) indigenous to N. America.

Nut, *v.* 1604. [f. prec.] To seek for, or gather nuts; *esp.* in phr. *to go* (*a*) *nutting*.

Nutant (niū·tănt), *a.* 1751. [ad. L. *nutantem, nutare* to nod.] Drooping, pendent.

Nuta·te, *v. rare.* 1880. [f. L. *nutat-, nutare*.] *intr.* To droop or bend downwards; chiefly in **Nuta·ting** *ppl. a.*

Nutation (niutē¹·ʃən). 1612. [ad. L. *nutationem*.] **1.** The action of nodding the head; an instance of this. **2.** *Astr.* A slight oscillation of the earth's axis; now *spec.* that by which the pole of the equator would describe a small ellipse in 19 years and which actually renders its motion round the pole of the ecliptic (see PRECESSION) wavy instead of circular 1715. **b.** The oscillation of a top in spinning 1879. **3.** Curvature in the stem of a growing plant 1789.

Nu·t-brown, *a.* (and *sb.*). ME. [f. NUT *sb.*] **1.** Of the colour of a ripe hazel-nut; brown as a nut; of a warm reddish-brown colour. **2.** *absol.* as *sb.* **a.** Ale 1828. **b.** A brown colour like that of nuts 1883.

1. The Nutbrowne mayd 1500. Good Nutbrowne-Ale and Tost DAVENANT. **2. b.** Her hair was of a soft nut-brown 1883.

Nu·t-crack. 1570. Now *vulgar.* [f. NUT *sb.*] = NUT-CRACKER 1.

Nu·t-cracker. 1548. [f. NUT *sb.*] **1.** An instrument for breaking the shells of nuts. Now usu., (*a pair of*) *nut-crackers*. **b.** Used *attrib.* and *Comb.* to describe the appearance of nose and chin produced by the want of teeth 1700. **2.** A brown corvine bird (*Nucifraga caryocatactes*), common in various parts of Europe, but rare in Britain 1758.

1. b. She is a toothless, nutcracker jawed old woman 1818.

Nu·t-gall. 1595. [f. NUT *sb.* + GALL *sb.*³] A gall produced upon the Dyer's Oak (*Quercus infectoria*), used esp. as a dye-stuff.

Nu·t-grass. 1830. A variety of sedge (*Cyperus Hydra*, also *C. phymatodes*), so called from its tuberous roots.

Nuthatch (nɒ·tˌhætʃ). ME. [f. NUT *sb.* The second element is conn. w. HACK *v.*¹, HAG *v.*¹, and HATCH *v.*²] A small creeping bird belonging to the genus *Sitta*, so named from the way in which it breaks nuts to feed on the kernel. The common British species is *S. cæsia.*

Nu·t-hook. 1500. A hooked stick used when nutting, to pull down the branches of the trees. †**b.** Applied to a beadle, constable, etc. -1658.

Nu·tjobber. Now *dial.* 1544. [JOBBER ¹.] = NUTHATCH.

Nu·tlet. 1856. A small nut.

Nutmeg (nɒ·tmeg). ME. [Partial tr. of AF. **nois mugue* or *muge* = med.L. *nux muscata*, f. late L. *muscus* MUSK.] **1.** A hard aromatic seed, of spheroidal form, obtained from the fruit of an evergreen tree (*Myristica fragrans* or *officinalis*), indigenous to the East Indian islands, used as spice and in medicine. **2.** Used to denote colour or appearance 1610.

1. *N.-tree*, the tree which produces the n. **2.** A Roan or N. colour'd Mare 1745. *N. liver*, a diseased condition of the liver, also called *red atrophy*.

Comb., as *n.-grater*; **n.-apple**, the fruit of the nutmeg-tree, containing the mace and n.; **-bird**, *Munia punctulata*, also called *Cowry-bird*; **n. butter**, a solid fatty reddish-brown substance, obtained by grinding the refuse nutmegs to a fine powder; **-flower**, *Nigella Sativa*, of Egyptian origin; **-pigeon**, a white pigeon (*Carpophaga ænea*), common in the Indo-Burmese countries, Ceylon, and the Andamans; **-wood**, the wood of the Palmyra palm, *Borassus flabelliformis*. Hence **Nu·tmegged** *a.* flavoured with n.; *Path.* affected with red atrophy.

Nu·t-oil. 1664. Oil obtained from nut-kernels, esp. those of the hazel and walnut, used in the manufacture of paints, varnishes, etc.

Nutria (niū·triă). 1836. [a. Sp., otter, also *lutria*, L. *lutra*.] The skin or fur of the coypu of S. America.

Nutrient (niū·triĕnt), *a.* and *sb.* 1650. [ad. L. *nutrientem* pres. pple. of *nutrire*.] **1.** Serving as nourishment; nutritious 1661. **2.** Conveying or providing nourishment 1650. **3.** *sb.* A nutritious substance 1828.

Nutrify (niū·trifəi), *v.* 1509. [f. L. *nutrire* + -(I)FY.] **a.** *trans.* To nourish. **b.** *intr.* To supply nutriment.

Nutriment (niū·trimĕnt). 1541. [ad. L. *nutrimentum*, f. *nutrire*; see -MENT.] That which nourishes; nourishing food.

Our dayly and special nutrimentes of breade and wyne 1558. *fig.* Is not Virtue in Mankind The N., that feeds the Mind? SWIFT. Hence **Nutrime·ntal** *a.* having the qualities of nutriment; nutritious; also, conveying nourishment.

Nutrition (niutri·ʃən). 1551. [ad. L. **nutritionem*, f. *nutrire*.] **1.** The action or process of supplying, or of receiving, nourishment. **2.** Food, nutriment 1603.

1. *fig.* The N. of a Common-wealth consisteth, in the Plenty and Distribution of Materials conducing to Life HOBBES. Hence **Nutri·tional, Nutri·tionary** *adjs.*

Nutritious (niutri·ʃəs), *a.* 1665. [ad. L. *nutritius, nutricius*, f. *nutric-, nutrix* nurse; see -ITIOUS¹.] Serving as or supplying nourishment. Hence **Nutri·tious-ly** *adv.*, **-ness.**

Nutritive (niū·tritiv), *a.* and *sb.* late ME. [a. F. *nutritif, -ive*, ad. med.L. *nutritivus*, f. ppl. stem of *nutrire* to nourish; see -IVE.] **1.** Having the property of nourishing; nutritious. **2.** Of, pertaining to, or concerned in, nutrition. late ME. **3.** Giving or providing nourishment 1548. **4.** *sb.* A nourishing article of food 1440. Hence **Nu·tritive-ly** *adv.*, **-ness.**

†**Nu·triture.** 1557. [ad. late L. *nutritura*, f. *nutrit-, nutrire*; see -URE.] **1.** Nourishment, nutrition -1740. **2.** Fostering; careful bringing up -1684.

Nu·tshell. ME. [f. NUT *sb.* + SHALE *sb.*, SHELL *sb.*] **1.** The hard exterior covering within which the kernel of a nut is enclosed. **2.** As an example of something without value, or of something extremely small ME. **3.** In phrases denoting great condensation, brevity, or limitation 1693. **b.** With *in*. In a few words 1831.

2. O God, I could be bounded in a n., and count my selfe a King of infinite space SHAKS. I have sometimes heard of an Iliad in a Nut-shell SWIFT. **3. b.** There, sir, is political economy in a n. T. L. PEACOCK.

Nutter (nɒ·təɹ). 1483. [f. NUT *sb.* or *v.* + -ER¹.] One who gathers nuts.

Nu·tting, *vbl. sb.* 1824. [-ING¹.] The action of gathering nuts.

Nu·t-tree. late ME. A tree that bears nuts; *esp.* the hazel (*Corylus Avellana*).

Nutty (nɒ·ti), *a.* 1662. [f. NUT *sb.* + -Y¹.] **1.** Abounding in, or productive of, nuts. **2.** Nut-like; having a taste like nuts 1836. **b.** Pleasant, full of flavour 1823. **3.** *slang.* Amorous, fond; enthusiastic. Usu. const. *upon* (a person). 1821. **4.** *slang.* Smart, spruce 1823; 'swell', dandyish 1913.

2. b. Mr. Blackmore's characteristic, leisurely, n. humor 1894. **4.** The beak wore his nuttiest wig 1839.

Nu·t-weevil. 1802. *Entom.* A small beetle (*Balaninus nucum*), which deposits its eggs in green hazel- and filbert-nuts.

‖**Nux vomica** (nɒks vǫ·mikă). 1578. [med. L., f. *nux* nut + fem. of **vomicus*, f. *vomere* to vomit.] **1.** The seed contained in the pulpy fruit of an E. Indian tree (*Strychnos Nux-vomica*), which yields the poison strychnia. **2.** The tree itself 1876.

‖**Nuzzer** (nɒ·zəɹ). 1776. [Urdū (Pers., Arab.) *nazr* gift, f. Arab. *nazara* he vowed.] In India, a present made by an inferior to a superior. So **Nuzzera·na.**

Nuzzle (nɒ·z'l), *v.*¹ late ME. [ME. *nosel*, f. NOSE *sb.* + -LE 3.] **I.** *intr.* †**1.** To bring the nose towards the ground; to grovel. ME. only. **2.** To burrow or dig with the nose; to thrust the nose into the ground or anything lying on it 1530. **3.** To poke or push with the nose *in* or *into* something 1592. **b.** With *at, about, against* 1603. **c.** Of dogs: To snuff or poke with the nose 1806. **d.** To poke with the fingers (*rare*) 1806. **4.** To nestle, lie snug in bed 1601. **b.** To nestle on or close to some part of a person 1611. **c.** To lie close *together* or *with* another 1708.

2. Like sows nuzzling for acorns T. HARDY. **3. b.** The Lambs riggle and nussle at their dugs 1657. **4.** 'Twixt the sheete and pillow I nuzled in 1601.

II. *trans.* **1. a.** To root *up* with the nose or snout 1613. **b.** To touch or rub with the nose 1812. **2.** To thrust in (the nose or head) 1594.

1. b. Twenty whale-boats were nuzzling a sand-bank KIPLING.

Nuzzle (nɒ·z'l), *v.*² Now *rare.* 1519. [Perh. f. as prec., but connexion of sense is obscure.] †**1.** *trans.* To accustom (a dog or hawk) to attack other animals or birds -1688. †**2.** To train, educate, nurture (a person) *in* some opinion, habit, etc. Freq. with *up*. -1686. †**3.** To bring up, rear, educate -1645. **4.** To nurse, to cherish fondly; to provide with a snug place of rest (cf. prec. I. 4) 1581.

†**Nyas**, *sb.* (and *a.*) 1495. [See EYAS.] **1.** An EYAS -1575. **2.** Applied allusively to persons -1616.

‖**Nychthemeron** (nikþī·mĕrǫn). 1682. [a. Gr. νυχθήμερον, neut. of νυχθήμερος lasting for a day and a night, f. νύξ, νυκτ- + ἡμέρα.] A period of twenty-four hours, consisting of a day and a night.

Nyctalope (ni·ktălōup), *sb.* and *a.* 1601. [ad. Gr. νυκτάλωψ, -άλωπος NYCTALOPS.] (One) affected with nyctalopia.

‖**Nyctalopia** (niktălōu·piă). 1684. [late L., a. Gr. *νυκταλωπία, f. νύξ, νυκτ- night + ἀλαός blind + ὤψ eye. Used by Galen in the proper sense of 'blind by night', but subseq. in that of 'seeing by night' (as if simply from νύξ and ὤψ).] **a.** Night-blindness; recurrent loss of vision after sunset. **b.** Inability to see clearly except by night; day-blindness. So **Ny·ctalopy.**

‖**Nyctalops** (ni·ktălǫps). *rare.* 1661. [L., a. Gr. νυκτάλωψ: see prec.] †**1.** Nyctalopia -1738. **2.** One affected with nyctalopia 1818.

Nycti- (ni·kti), repr. Gr. νυκτι-, a comb. form (properly locative) of νυκτ-, νύξ night, used in a few scientific terms, chiefly zoological as *Nycticardea*, the nycticorax.

‖**Nycticorax** (nikti·kŏræks). 1688. [L., a. Gr. νυκτικόραξ, f. νύξ, νυκτι- night + κόραξ raven.] The night-heron. (Cf. *night-raven.*)

Nyctitropic (niktitrǫ·pik), *a.* 1880. [f. NYCTI- + Gr. τρόπος turn; cf. *heliotropic.*] *Bot.* Turning in a certain direction at night.

Nycto- (ni·kto), repr. Gr. νυκτο-, comb. form of νυκτ-, νύξ night, as in *Nyctophilus*, a genus of bats; *nyctophobia*, dread of the night or of darkness; etc.

Nye (nəi). Now *dial.* 1470. [ad. OF. *ni*, *ny* (mod.F. *nid*):—L. *nidus* nest.] A brood (of pheasants). Cf. EYE *sb.*[2]

Nylghau (ni·lgǭ). 1770. [a. Pers. *nīlgāw*, f. *nīl* blue + *gāw* ox, cow. See also NILGAI.] A large short-horned Indian antelope, the adult male of which is of a bluish- or iron-grey colour, and has a tuft of hair on the throat.

Nymph (nimf). late ME. [a. F. *nymphe*, ad. L. *nympha*; see next.] **1.** *Myth.* One of a class of semi-divine beings, imagined as beautiful maidens inhabiting the sea, rivers, fountains, hills, woods, or trees, or attending on superior deities. **b.** *transf.* A stream, river 1591. **2.** *poet.* A young and beautiful woman; hence, a maiden, damsel 1584. **3.** A pupa 1577.

1. There is a gentle N. not farr from hence, That with moist curb sways the smooth Severn stream MILT. 2. But soft, what nimphs are these? SHAKS. **Nymph-like** *a.* and *adv.*

‖**Nympha** (ni·mfă). *Pl.* **nymphæ** (ni·mfī). 1601. [L., a. Gr. νύμφη bride, nymph.] **1.** = NYMPH 3. **2.** *pl. Anat.* The labia minora of the vulva, situated within the labia majora 1693.

‖**Nymphæa** (nimfī·ă). Also **nymphea.** 1562. [L., ad. Gr. νυμφαία, fem. of νυμφαῖος sacred to the nymphs.] The common white or yellow water-lily; a genus of aquatic plants including these and other species.

†**Ny·mphal,** *sb.*[1] [ad. L. *nymphalis*; see NYMPH and -AL.] Used by Drayton as the name of each division of his *Muses' Elysium.*

Nymphal (ni·mfăl), *a.* (and *sb.*[2]). 1656. [f. as prec.] **A.** *adj.* **1.** Belonging to a nymph; consisting of nymphs. **2.** Of the nature of, pertaining to, a pupa 1864. **3.** Including or belonging to the water-plants related to *Nymphæa* 1846. **B.** *sb.*[2] **1.** [ad. F. *nymphale.*] A name for a class of butterflies 1797. **2.** A plant belonging to the nymphal alliance 1846.

Nymphean (nimfī·ăn), *a.* 1758. [f. Gr. νυμφαῖος + -AN.] Of or belonging to a nymph or nymphs; nymph-like.

Nymphiparous (nimfi·părəs), *a.* 1835. [f. NYMPH + -(I)PAROUS.] *Entom.* Of insects: Producing nymphæ or pupæ.

Nympholepsy (ni·mfǒlepsi). 1775. [f. next, after *epilepsy.*] A state of rapture supposed to be inspired in men by nymphs; hence, an ecstasy or frenzy, esp. that caused by desire of the unattainable. So ‖**Nymphole·psia.**

Nympholept (ni·mfǒlept), *sb.* and *a.* 1813. [ad. Gr. νυμφόληπτος caught by nymphs, f. νύμφη nymph + λαμβάνειν to take.] **1.** *sb.* One who is inspired by a violent enthusiasm, esp. for an unattainable ideal. Also const. *of.* **2.** *adj.* Inspired by such enthusiasm 1902. Hence **Nymphole·ptic** *a.*

‖**Nymphomania** (nimfǒmē·niă). 1775. [f. Gr. νύμφη bride, NYMPH + μανία madness.] *Path.* A feminine disease characterized by morbid and uncontrollable sexual desire. Hence **Nymphoma·niac** *a.* and *sb.*

‖**Nymphon** (ni·mfǫn). 1855. [a. Gr. νυμφών bride-chamber, f. νύμφη.] *Zool.* A species of sea-spider.

Nymphotomy (nimfǫ·tŏmi). 1704. [a. mod. L. *nymphotomia*, f. Gr. νύμφη (see NYMPHA 2) + -τομία -TOMY.] *Surg.* Excision of the nymphæ.

‖**Nystagmus** (nistæ·gmǒs). 1822. [mod.L., ad. Gr. νυσταγμός nodding, drowsiness, f. νυστάζειν.] An involuntary oscillation of the eye-ball, usually lateral, especially common among miners. Hence **Nysta·gmic** *a.*

O

O (ōu), the fifteenth letter in the English alphabet, and the fourth vowel letter. O was the fourteenth letter in the ancient Roman alphabet, corresponding in form and value to the ancient Greek O, derived from the sixteenth letter of the Phœnician and ancient Semitic alphabet.

The normal sound of short *o* in modern English is (ǫ), low- (or mid-) back-round-wide; but it frequently stands for (*v*), as in s*o*n, d*o*th, or (*ɒ*), as in w*o*rd; and in unaccented syllables sinks to (ə), as in nati*o*n. When original short *o* comes before *r* final, or *r* + cons., as in *or, for, corn, sort*, it is now lengthened into the corresponding long sound *ǭ*; a later lengthening has taken place, chiefly in the South, before certain cons. groups, as in *cloth, cross, off, soft*, here represented by *ǭ*.

The normal sound of long *o*, as in n*o*, t*o*e, b*o*ne, is the quasi- or imperfect diphthong (ōu); but before *r*, as in bore, choral, story, the sound is that of the open quasi-diphthong (ōə).

I. 1. The letter. Pl. *Os*, O's, *os*, o's (oes). *O per se*, the letter O forming by itself a word. **b.** The sound of the letter, the vowel-sound *o*. **2.** Used to indicate serial order and distinguish things in a series, as the 'quires' or sheets of a book, etc. **3.** In *Logic*, = a particular negative. **4.** In *Chem.*, the symbol for Oxygen.

II. *Abbreviations.* **a.** O. = various proper names, as *Oliver, Olivia*, etc. **b.** = 'old', as in OE., Old English; OF., Old French; OHG., Old High German; ON., Old Norse; O.S., old style; O.T., Old Testament. **c.** = 'Order', as in D.S.O., Distinguished Service Order; O.M., Order of Merit; O.S.B., Order of Saint Benedict, etc. **d.** = 'Officer', as in O.B.E., Officer of the British Empire; O.C., Officer Commanding; O.T.C., Officers' Training Corps. **e.** O.K. (orig. *U.S. slang*) abbrev. for *oll korrect* = 'all correct', everything in order, all right: hence as vb.; O.P. (*a*) (also o.p.) 'opposite the prompter side' in a theatre, also *attrib.*; (*b*) 'over-proof': (*c*) (also o.p., *o.p.*) in booksellers' catalogues, 'out of print'.

O (ōu), *sb.*[1] ME. [From resemblance in shape to the letter O.] **1.** The Arabic zero or cipher; hence, a cipher, a mere nothing 1605. **2.** (*Pl.* **oes.**) Anything round, as a circle, round spot, orb ME.

1. Now thou art an O without a figure..thou art nothing SHAKS. 2. *Mids. N.* III. ii. 188. *Giotto's O*, the perfect circle, said to have been thrown off free hand by Giotto, the Florentine painter (1266–1336).

O', Ó, *sb.*[2] 1730. [Ir. *ó, ua*, OIr. *au*; see OY.] A prefix of Irish patronymic surnames, as *O'Connell*, etc. Hence, a person whose surname begins with *O'*.

Ireland her O's, her Mac's let Scotland boast FIELDING.

†**O,** *adv.* [OE. *á*; cf. A *adv.*, AY *adv.*] Ever, always.

†**O, oo,** *numeral adj.* ME. reduced form of *on, oon* [:—OE. *án*], ONE, used in south. and midl. bef. a cons. Cf. A *adj.*[1] –1678.

O flessh they been, and o flessh as I gesse Hath but oon herte, in wele and in distresse CHAUCER. Then Christian stept a little a to-side [= at o side] BUNYAN.

O, o' (*o*, *ŏ*, ə), *prep.*[1] ME. [Worn down f. ON *prep.*, used bef. a cons.; cf. A *prep.*[1]] = ON *prep.*, in various senses; in early use including the sense 'in'. Now only in some *arch.* or traditional phrases.

Cupid hath clapt him oth' shoulder SHAKS.

O, o' (*o*, *ŏ*, ə), *prep.*[2] ME. [Worn down f. OF *prep.*, used bef. a cons.; cf. A *prep.*[2]] = OF. In form *o'*, still used *arch.*, *dial.*, *colloq.*; e.g. in *six o'clock*; also in *John o' Groats, Jack o' lantern*, etc.

O (ōu), *int.* (*sb.*[3], *v.*) ME. [A natural exclam., expressive of sudden feeling.] **A.** *interj.* **1.** Standing bef. the sb. in the vocative relation. **2.** In other connexions, or without construction, expressing, according to intonation, appeal, entreaty, surprise, pain, lament, etc. (In 17th and 18th c., often written OH; but see OH.) ME. **3.** In ballads (chiefly *Sc.*) added after the rime-word at the end of a line 1724.

1. O Lord, our God, arise 1742. 2. O that I had wynges like a doue COVERDALE *Ps.* liv. [lv.] 6. O mee most wretched man! 1610. O, but we all live beyond our incomes 1837. It 's O for a manly life in the camp! WHITMAN. 3. The wintry sun the day has clos'd, And I'll awa to Nanie, O. BURNS.

B. as *sb.* **1.** The interj. considered as a word. So **O me, O dear,** etc., 1609. **2.** pl. *O's of Advent*, the seven Advent Anthems, each containing a separate invocation of Christ beginning with *O*, as *O Sapientia* (O Wisdom), *O Adonai*, etc. ME.

1. O me no O's, but hear B. JONS.

-o-, terminal vowel of combining forms of words, being the usual connective orig. in ethnic names, and, later, in scientific terms generally; it is affixed, not only to terms of Greek origin, but also to those derived from Latin (Latin compounds of which would have been formed with *-i-*.). Instances are *concavo-*; *chloro-*; *cumulo-*; *politico-*; *joco-*; *serio-*.

1. Primarily *-o-* qualifies adverbially the adj. to which it is prefixed; as in Gr. λευκόχλωρος 'whitely green', pale green; mod.L. *ovato-cordatus* 'ovately heart-shaped', cordate with ovate modification; *Anglo-Norman*, Norman as modified in England. **2.** Hence, used to express, shortly, almost any manner of relation between two components. *Franco-German*, orig. 'German of a French sort', may even mean 'French in conflict with German'; *Græco-Latin*, 'common to Greek and Latin'; *pneumo-gastric*, 'communicating with both lungs and stomach', etc. **3.** Appearing frequently bef. *-cracy*, *-graphy*, *-logy*, *-meter*, *-o-* tends to be permanently associated with these elements; cf. *shop-ocracy*, 'the last new *-ology*', 'galvanometers..and other *-ometers* without number', and the like.

Oad, obs. f. WOAD.

Oaf (ōuf). *Pl.* **oafs;** also 9 **oaves.** 1625. [Phonetic var. of AUF; see also OUPH.] An elf's child; a changeling left by the elves or fairies; hence, a misbegotten, deformed, or idiot child; a half-wit, dolt, booby. So **Oa·fish** *a.* 1610.

Oak (ōuk). [Com. Teut.: OE. *ác*:—OTeut. **aiks.*] **1.** Name of a forest tree, *Quercus Robur* (now divided into two sub-species, *Q. pedunculata* and *Q. sessiliflora*, DURMAST), noted for its timber, and bearing a fruit or species of mast called the ACORN; thence extended to all species of *Quercus*, trees or shrubs; the common species in N. America being *Q. alba*, the white oak, and *Q. macrocarpa*, the bur oak. **b.** With defining adjective, applied to other species of *Quercus* 1727. **2.** In Eng. versions of the Bible, used also to render Heb. *ēlāh*, the terebinth tree. late ME. **3.** With qualification, applied to trees or plants in some way resembling the oak 1551. **b.** In Australia, applied to trees of the genus *Casuarina* ('Native Oak') 1802. **4.** The wood of the oak. Hence allusively, with ref. to its hardness and enduring qualities. late ME. **b.** As the material of a ship OE. **c.** *Univ. colloq.* An oaken door; esp. in phr. *to sport one's o.*, to shut the outer door of one's rooms as a sign that one is engaged 1785. **5.** The leaves of the oak. late ME. **6.** *The Oaks*: a race for three-year-old fillies, founded in 1779, and run at Epsom on the Friday after the Derby. (So called from an estate near Epsom.)

1. Our Dance of Custome, round about the Oke Of Herne the Hunter SHAKS. **b. Black** or **Dyer's O.,** *Q. tinctoria* = QUERCITRON. **Blue O., Mountain White O.,** *Q. Douglassii* of California. **Bur, Mossy-cup,** or **Overcup O.,** *Q. macrocarpa* of N. America. **Chestnut O.,** *Q. sessiliflora*, and in N. America, *Q. Prinus* and other species having leaves like the chestnut. **Cork O.,** *Q. Suber*, a native of southern Europe and northern Africa, the bark of which furnishes cork. **Evergreen O.** = HOLM-OAK. **Italian O.,** *Q. Æsculus* of southern Europe, having edible acorns. **Kermes-oak,** *Q. coccifera*, in which the kermes insect lives. **Live O.,** a name for *Q. virens*, and other American species. **Scarlet O.,** *Q. coccinea* of N. America, so called from the colour of its foliage in autumn. **Turkey O.,** *Q. cerris* of southern Europe; in America, *Q. Catesbæi*. **Weeping O.,** *Q. lobata* of Western U.S. **White O.,** *Q. alba*, a large American tree, occas. called in England *Quebec o.* **O. of Bashan,** *Q. ægilops*. 3. **Dwarf O., Ground O.,** various species of *Teucrium*. **O. of Cappadocia,** *Ambrosia maritima*. **O. of Jerusalem** or **Paradise,** *Chenopodium Botrys*, having leaves jagged like those of an o. **Poison O.,** species of sumach. 4. With thunders from her native o. She quells the floods below COWPER. Phr. *Heart of o.*: see HEART *sb.* IV. 3. 5. Our custom of wearing o. on the twenty-ninth of May 1772.

Combs.: **O.-bark,** the bark of the o., used in tanning and as an astringent; **-beauty,** a moth (*Biston* or *Amphidasis prodromaria*), the larva of which feeds on the o.; **-button** = next; **-gall,** a gall or excrescence produced on species of o. by the punctures of gall-flies; *spec.* a gall-nut used in making ink; **-leather,** a fungus found on old oaks, and somewhat resembling white kid-leather; **-lungs,** lung-wort; **-pest,** an insect (*Phylloxera rileyi*) which infests oaks in the U.S.; **-spangle,** a kind of flattened fungus-like gall, occurring on the lower side of oak-leaves; **-wart,** an oak-gall.

Oak-apple (ōu·kˌæ:p'l). late ME. **1.** A globular form of oak-gall; *spec.* the bright-coloured spongy gall formed on the leaf-bud of the common British oak. **2.** In Australia, the young cone of the SHE-OAK 1889.

attrib., as **Oak-apple day,** the 29th of May, the day of the Restoration of Charles II, when oak-apples or oak-leaves have been worn in memory of his hiding from his pursuers in an oak, on the 6th of Sept., 1651.

Oaken (ōu·kĕn), *a.* ME. [f. OAK + -EN⁴.] 1. Made of the wood of the oak. (Now often repl. by 'oak' used *attrib.*) 2. Of, pertaining to, or forming part of the oak. *Obs.* or *arch.* (repl. by 'oak' used *attrib.*) 1450. 3. Formed of oak leaves or twigs (*arch.*) 1605. 4. Consisting of oak-trees (*arch.* and *poet.*) 1638.

1. An o. chest 1820. 3. Hee comes the third time home with the O. Garland SHAKS. 4. With breezes from our o. glades TENNYSON.

Oakling (ōu·kliŋ). 1664. [f. OAK + -LING.] A young or small oak; an oak sapling.

Oak-tree (ōu·ktrī). OE. = OAK 1.

Oakum (ōu·kŏm). [OE. *ācumbe, ācum(b)a*, (var. of *ǣcumbe, ǣcuma*), lit. 'off-combings'.] †1. The coarse part of the flax separated in hackling; hards, tow. OE. only. 2. Loose fibre, obtained by untwisting and picking old rope; used esp. in caulking ships' seams, etc. The picking of oakum was formerly a common employment of convicts and inmates of workhouses. 1481.

Oar (ōᵊɹ), *sb.* [OE. *ār* :—OTeut. **airā*; cf. Gr. ἐρ- in ἐρέτης rower, ἐρετμός oar.] 1. A stout pole, widened and flattened at one end into a blade, used as a lever to propel a boat. (See SCULL, SWEEP.) b. In ref. to slaves or criminals compelled to row in galleys; see GALLEY *sb.* 1. 1711. 2. *fig.* Anything that serves, like an oar, as a means of propulsion in the water 1586. 3. *transf.* a. A rowing-boat 1611. b. An oarsman 1608. 4. A stick, pole, or paddle, with which anything is stirred 1743.

1. Phrases. *To put in one's o.*, to interfere in another's business. *To rest, lie, on one's oars*, to lean on the handles of one's oars; *fig.* to take things easy. b. To condemn Criminals..to the O. 1711. 2. *transf.* The Oars or finny feet of Water-Fowl SIR T. BROWNE. 3. a. *Pair of oars*, a boat rowed by two men. b. He was a capital o. at Eton 1861.

Comb. **o.-fish**, a name for fishes of the family *Regalecidæ*, esp. *Regalecus Banksii*, from their compressed oar-like bodies.

Oar, *v.* 1610. [f. prec.] 1. *trans.* To propel with or as with oars; to row. 2. *intr.* To row; to advance, as if propelled by oars. Also with *it*. 1647. 3. *trans.* To make (one's way) as with oars 1801. 4. To move (one's hands, etc.) like oars 1882.

1. He..oared Himselfe with his good armes..To th' Shore SHAKS. 3. Now oaring with slow wing her upward way SOUTHEY.

Oarage (ōᵊ·rėdʒ). 1762. [f. OAR *sb.* + -AGE.] 1. The action of oars; movement of limbs like that of oars. 2. Apparatus of the nature of oars; outfit of oars; rowing apparatus 1828.

Oared (ōᵊɹd), *a.* 1590. [f. OAR *sb.* + -ED.²] Provided with oars; also in comb., as *four-oared*, etc.

Oarlock (ōᵊ·ɹlǫk). [OE. *ārloc*, f. *ār* oar + *loc* LOCK *sb.*²] = ROWLOCK.

Oarsman (ōᵊ·ɹzmæ̆n). 1824. [f. *oar's* possess. of OAR + MAN; formerly *oarman* (1608).] A 'man of the oar'; a rower. Hence **Oa·rsmanship.** So **Oa·rswoman.**

Oary (ōᵊ·ri), *a.* 1667. [f. OAR *sb.* + -Y¹.] a. Of the nature of, or having the function of, an oar or oars; oar-like. b. Furnished with oars; oared.

a. The Swan..with Oarie feet MILT.

Oasis (o‚ē·sis, ōu·ăsis). *Pl.* **oases** (-īz). 1613. [a. L., a. Gr. ὄασις, app. of Egyptian origin. The pronunc. ō·ăsis is chiefly Sc. and U.S.] A name of the fertile spots in the Libyan desert; hence *gen.* A fertile spot in the midst of a desert.

fig. My one O. in the dust and drouth Of city life TENNYSON.

Oast (ōust). [OE. *āst* :—OTeut. **aistoz*, f. root *aidh-* (Skr. *idh*) to burn.] †a. *orig.* = KILN. b. Later, A kiln for drying malt or hops, now *spec.* for drying hops.

Comb. **o.-house**, a building containing a kiln for drying hops; the whole structure composing a kiln.

Oat (ōut); usu. in pl. **oats** (ōuts). [OE. *āte*, pl. *ātan*, of obscure origin. App. *oat* denoted primarily an individual grain; cf. *groat, groats.*] 1. *pl.* The grains of a hardy cereal (see sense 2) forming an article of food for men and also a chief food of horses; usu. collectively, as a species of grain. 2. The cereal plant *Avena sativa*, which yields this grain. a. Usu. in *pl.*, collectively, as a crop. ME. b. In *sing.* (*rare*). late ME. 3. *sing.* and *collect. pl.* Applied to wild species of *Avena* (called also *Oat-grass*); esp. the **Wild O.**, *Avena fatua*, a tall grass resembling the cultivated oat. **False O.**, the Oat-like Grass, *Arrhenatherum*. OE. 4. *transf.* (*poet.*). A pipe made of an oaten straw, as a pastoral instrument of music. [After L. *avena.*] 1637.

3. Phr. *To sow one's wild oats*: to commit youthful excesses or follies (usu. implying subsequent reform). 4. That strain I heard was of a higher mood: But now my Oate proceeds MILT.

Comb.: **o.-grass**, a grass of the genus *Avena*; sometimes also applied to those of allied genera, as *Arrhenatherum, Bromus*; **-pipe, -reed**, a musical instrument made of an oat-straw.

Oat-cake. 1588. [f. OAT + CAKE *sb.*] = CAKE *sb.* 1 b.

Oaten (ōu·t'n), *a.* late ME. [f. OAT + -EN⁴.] 1. Composed of the grain of oats, or of oatmeal. 2. Made of the straw or stem of an oat. late ME. 3. Of or belonging to the oat as a plant 1588.

1. They did eate..oten bread HOLLAND. 2. Rural ditties..Temper'd to th' O. Flute MILT. 3. When Shepheards pipe on O. strawes SHAKS.

Oath (ōuþ), *sb.* *Pl.* **oaths** (ōuðz). [Com. Teut.: OE. *āþ* :—OTeut. **aiþoz* :—pre-Teut. **oitos* (cf. OIr. *oeth*).] 1. A solemn appeal to God (or to something sacred) in witness that a statement is true, or a promise binding; an act of swearing; a statement or promise corroborated by such an appeal, or the form of words in which such a statement or promise is made. b. Loosely applied to an asseveration not involving a ref. to God or anything sacred 1600. 2. A careless use of the name of God or Christ, or of something sacred, in asseveration or imprecation, or a formula of words involving this; an act of profane swearing; a curse ME.

1. *To take (an) o.*, to utter, or bind oneself by, an o.; to swear; also *to make (an) o.* *On* or *upon o.*, under the obligation of an o.; as having made an o. BIBLE *o.*, BODILY *o.*, BOOK *o.*, CORPORAL *o.*; see those words. b. *A. Y. L.* IV. i. 192–3. Hence **Oath** *v.* to utter an oath or oaths, to swear. Also *to o. it.*

Oatmeal (ōu·tmīl). late ME. [f. OAT + MEAL *sb.*¹] Meal made from oats. Also *attrib.*

†**Ob**, *sb.* 1588. [From *ob.*, abbrev. of *objection*, used in conjunction with *sol.* = *solution*, in old books of divinity.] In phr. *Ob(s) and sol(s)* = objection(s) and solution(s); scholastic or subtle disputation –1660.

†**Ob.** ME. Abbrev. of OBOLUS, used for a halfpenny –1631.

1 *Hen. IV*, II. iv. 590.

Ob., abbrev. of L. *obiit* died; used before the date of a person's death.

Ob-, *pref.* The Lat. prep. *ob* 'towards, against, in the way of', becoming, in comb. with vbs. and their derivs., *oc-* before *c-*, *of-* before *f-*, *op-* before *p-*, and app. *o-* before *m-* (in *omittere*). In Eng. use, *ob-* (*oc-, of-, op-, o-*) occurs. 1. In combs. already formed in L.; rarely in words formed in Eng. itself on L. elements; e.g. *obduce, obdurate, obedience, object, obversion, occident, occur, opponent, opposite*, etc. 2. In mod. scientific Latin, and hence in Eng., in Botany, etc., *ob-* is prefixed to adjs. in the sense 'inversely', or 'in the opposite direction', as in *obcordatus* (Linn.) OBCORDATE, *obconical, obimbricate, oblanceolate, obovoid, obvallate, obvolute*, etc.

In this use, apparently the prefix represents the *ob-* of L. *obverse* OBVERSELY, and is short for that word.

Obambulate (ǫbæ·mbiŭlēᵗt), *v. rare.* 1614. [f. L. *obambulat-*, *obambulare*, f. *ob-* (OB- 1) + *ambulare.*] *intr.* To walk about. So **Obambula·tion.**

‖**Obbligato** (ǫbligā·to, obblīgā·to), *a.* (*sb.*). Often **Obligato.** 1794. [It., 'obliged', 'obligatory'.] *Mus.* 1. That cannot be omitted; applied to a part essential to the completeness of a composition (or to the instrument on which such a part is played); esp. to an accompaniment having an independent value. Opp. to *ad libitum*. Also *transf.* forced, compulsory. 2. *sb.* An obbligato part or accompaniment 1845.

Obcordate (ǫbkǭ·ɹdēt), *a.* 1775. [OB- 2.] *Nat. Hist.* Inversely cordate; heart-shaped, with the apex serving as the base or point of attachment.

Obdiplostemonous (ǫbdiplǫ‚stī·mŏnəs), *a.* 1880. [OB- 2.] *Bot.* Diplostemonous with the disposition of the two stamen-whorls reversed; having the stamens of the outer whorl opposite to, and those of the inner whorl alternate with, the petals. Hence **Obdiploste·mony.**

†**Obdu·ce**, *v.* 1657. [ad. L. *obducere*, f. *ob-* OB- 1 + *ducere.*] *trans.* To cover, envelop –1709.

†**Obdu·ction.** 1578. [ad. L. *obductionem*, f. *obducere*; see prec.] The action of covering or enveloping –1656.

Obduracy (ǫ·bdiurăsi). 1597. [f. next; see -ACY 3.] The state or quality of being obdurate; obstinacy; persistent hardness of heart.

Obdurate (ǫ·bdiurēt, ǫbdiūᵊ·rēt), *a.* late ME. [ad. L. *obduratus, obdurare.*] 1. a. Hardened in evil; insensible to moral influence. b. Unyielding, relentless, hard-hearted, inexorable 1586. †2. Physically hardened or hard –1784.

1. a. The o. conscience of the old sinner SCOTT. b. Women are soft, milde, pittifull, and flexible; Thou, sterne, o., flintie, rough, remorselesse SHAKS. *fig.* They have joined the most o. consonants without one intervening vowel SWIFT. Hence **Obdurate·ly** *adv.*, **-ness.**

Obdurate (ǫ·bdiurēᵗt, ǫbdiūᵊ·rēᵗt), *v.* 1540. [f. prec.] *trans.* To make morally obdurate (see prec.) So **Obdura·tion**, the action of hardening or condition of being hardened 1494.

†**Obdure** (ǫbdiūᵊ·ɹ), *a.* 1608. [f. OB- 1 + *durus*, after prec.] = OBDURATE *a.* –1860. Hence †**Obdu·re·ly** *adv.*, †**-ness.**

Obdure (ǫbdiūᵊ·ɹ), *v.* Now *rare* or *Obs.* 1598. [ad. L. *obdurare*, f. *ob-* OB- 1 + *durare*, f. *durus* hard.] *trans.* = OBDURATE *v.* So **Obdu·red** *ppl. a.* = OBDURATE *a.* 1. 1585.

Obe (ōub). 1835. [ad. Gr. ὠβά.] *Gr. Hist.* A village or district in ancient Laconia; a subdivision of an original φυλή or clan.

‖**Obeah** (ōu·biă), **obi** (ōu·bi), *sb.* 1764. [West African.] 1. An amulet, charm, or fetish used by negroes for magical purposes 1796. 2. A kind of pretended sorcery or witchcraft practised by the negroes in Africa, and formerly in the West Indies 1764. 3. *attrib.*, as *obeah* (or *obi*) *-man*, a negro sorcerer, etc. 1764. Hence **O·beah, o·bi** *v. trans.* to bewitch by o.; **O·beahism** the practice of or belief in o.

Obedience (ŏbī·diĕns). ME. [a. F. *obédience*, ad. L. *obedientia*, f. *obedientem* OBEDIENT; see -ENCE.] 1. The action or practice of obeying; the fact or character of being obedient. 2. The fact or position of being obeyed, or of having others subject to one; command, authority. (Now esp. of the authority of the Church of Rome.) ME. b. *transf.* A sphere of authority or dominion, esp. ecclesiastical 1635. 3. = OBEISANCE 3. Now *arch.* and *dial.* 1503. 4. In a monastic or conventual establishment: Any office, official position, or duty, under the abbot or superior; the particular office or duty of any inmate of a convent; also, the cell, room, or place appertaining or appropriate to such an office; = med.L. *obedientia* (see Du Cange) 1700.

1. To bee brought vppe in the o. of Lawes 1602. *fig.* A heavy body falls to the ground in o. to the law of gravitation (*mod.*). *Passive o.* (*a*) (opp. to *active o.*) an obedience in which the subject suffers without resistance or remonstrance; (*b*) unqualified obedience to commands, whether reasonable or unreasonable, lawful or unlawful. 2. The two Houses decided..to return to the o. of the Papal See GREEN. b. All the English land-owners within William's o. FREEMAN. The clergy and the laity of the Roman obedience (*mod.*).

Obedient (obī·diĕnt), *a.* (*sb.*) ME. [a. OF. *obédient*, ad. L. *obedientem*, f. *obedire* to OBEY.] 1. That obeys; submissive to the will of a superior; doing what one is bidden; subservient; dutiful. b. Conventionally used as an expression of courtesy, *esp.* in phr. *your o. servant* 1548. †2. *Astrol.* Of signs of the zodiac, etc.: Subject; see OBEY *v.* 4. –1391. 3. *fig.* (chiefly of things or involuntary agents): Moving or yielding as actuated or affected by something else. late ME. †4. *sb.* One who is subject to authority; a subordinate –1662.

1. Such delight hath God in Men O. to his Will MILT. 3. Floating..o. to the streame SHAKS. Hence **Obe·diently** *adv.*

Obediential (obīdiˌeˑnʃăl), *a.* 1619. [ad. med.L. *obedientialis*, f. *obedientia*; see -AL 1.] Of, pertaining to, of the nature of, or characterized by obedience. (Chiefly *Theol.*; now *rare* or *Obs.* in gen. sense.)

Obedientiary (obīdiˌeˑnʃări). 1536. [ad. med.L. *obedientiarius*, f. *obedientia*; see -ARY.] †1. A person practising obedience; one owning allegiance; a subject; a liegeman –1603. 2. A member of a conventual establishment charged with any duty or 'obedience'. (See OBEDIENCE 4.) 1794.

Obeisance (obēˑsăns). late ME. [a. F. *obéissance*, f. *obéissant*, *obéir*.] †1. = OBEDIENCE 1. –1660. †2. *The o.* (of any one): = OBEDIENCE 2. –1678. †b. = OBEDIENCE 2 b. –1616. 3. A respectful salutation; a bow or curtsy. Often in phr. *to do, make, pay, o.* (Chiefly literary, and often *arch.*) late ME. 4. Respectfulness of manner or bearing, deference; homage, submission. (In mod. use, regarded as *fig.* from 3.) late ME.

3. He made a low Obeysance 1640. 4. A Throne to which conquered Nations yielded Obeysance STEELE.

Obeisant (obēˑsănt), *a.* ME. [a. F. *obéissant*, *obéir*:—L. *obedire*; see -ANT.] 1. = OBEDIENT 1, *Obs.* exc. as in 2. 2. Showing respect or deference; servilely obedient, obsequious 1642.

‖ **Obelion** (obīˑliǫn). 1878. [mod.L., a. Gr. *ὀβέλιον, dim. of ὀβελός spit.] *Anat.* A point on the sagittal suture, between the parietal foramina. Hence **Obeˑliac** *a.*

Obelisk (ǫˑbĕlisk, -ĭ-). 1569. [ad. L. *obeliscus*, a. Gr. ὀβελίσκος, dim. of ὀβελός.] 1. A tapering shaft of stone, usu. monolithic, and square or rectangular in section, with a pyramidal apex; a type of monument specially characteristic of ancient Egypt. b. A natural formation resembling an obelisk, e.g. a mountain peak, a cypress tree, etc. 1845. 2. A mark (either – or ÷) used in ancient MSS. to point out a spurious, corrupt, or doubtful word or passage (= OBELUS); in mod. use applied to the mark † used in printing for marginal references, foot-notes, etc. (= DAGGER *sb.* 5). *Double o.*, the double dagger (‡). 1583. Hence **Obeliˑscal** *a.*

Obelize (ǫˑbĭləiz), *v.* Also *erron.* **obolize.** [ad. Gr. ὀβελίζειν; see OBELUS and -IZE.] *trans.* To mark (a word or passage) with an obelus or obelisk; to condemn as spurious or corrupt.

‖ **Obelus** (ǫˑbĭlǒs). *Pl.* **obeli** (-ləi). late ME. [L., a. Gr. ὀβελός spit, obelus.] = OBELISK 2.

Obese (obīˑs), *a.* 1651. [ad. L. *obesus* that has eaten itself fat, pa. pple. of *obedere* to eat away, f. *ob-* OB- 1 + *edere*.] Very fat or fleshy; corpulent. Hence **Obeˑse·ly** *adv.*, **-ness.**

Obesity (obīˑsĭti, obeˑsĭti). 1611. [ad. L. *obesitas*, f. *obesus*.] The condition of being obese; corpulence.

‖ **Obex** (ōˑbeks). 1611. [L. *obex*, *-ic-*, f. *obicere*, f. *ob-* OB- 1 + *jacere* to cast.] 1. An impediment, obstacle. Now *rare* or *Obs.* 2. *Anat.* A thickening of the ependyma of the fourth ventricle of the brain at the point of the *calamus scriptorius* 1892.

Obey (ŏbēˑ), *v.* [ME. *obeien*, a. F. *obéir*:—L. *obedire*, f. *ob-* OB- 1 + *audire* to hear.] 1. *trans.* (orig. *intr.* with *dat. obj.*). a. To be obedient to. b. To comply with, perform (a command, etc.) late ME. c. To submit to, subject oneself to (a principle, authority, etc.). Now *rare* or *arch.* late ME. d. *fig.* To act as compelled by (a thing, agency, force, impulse, etc.); to be actuated by 1598. †2. *intr.* To be obedient *to* or *unto* (= 1) –1667. 3. *intr.* or *absol.* To do what one is commanded; to submit; to be obedient. late ME. b. *fig.* of a thing 1567. 4. *intr. Astrol.* Said of certain signs of the zodiac in relation to others (called *commanding* or *sovereign* signs), or of planets when in such signs. late ME. †5. To do obeisance to, bow to –1650.

1. a. The highe powers shuld be alweys obeid 1529. b. The ladies obeying the summons, came up in a group GOLDSM. c. What obeyes Reason, is free MILT. d. He marks how well the ship her helm obeys BYRON. 2. His seruants ye are to whom ye o. *Rom.* vi. 16. To their Generals Voyce they soon Obeyd MILT. 3. Will he o. when one commands? TENNYSON. b. To speak I tri'd..My Tongue obey'd MILT. 4. *Obeying Signs*, the Southern, or last six Signs of the Zodiac are so called 1679. Hence **Obeyˑable** *a.* that can, or should, be obeyed. **Obeyˑer**, one who obeys. **Obeyˑingly** *adv.*

†**Obfirm,** *v.* 1563. [ad. L. *obfirmare* (also *offirmare*), f. *ob-* OB- 1 + *firmare*, *firmus*.] *trans.* To make firm (in bad sense); to confirm (*in* an evil course, error, etc.); to make stubborn; to harden –1686. Hence †**Obfirmaˑtion,** confirming or being confirmed in evil; obduracy.

Obfuscate (ǫˑbfǒskēˑt), *v.* 1536. [f. L. *obfuscat-*, *obfuscare*, f. *ob-* OB- 1 + *fuscare*, *fuscus* dark. Cf. OFFUSCATE.] 1. *trans.* To darken, obscure (physically); to deprive of light or brightness; to eclipse. Now *rare.* 1650. †2. *fig.* To darken or obscure to the mind; to deprive of lustre or glory, throw into the shade –1702. 3. To dim (the sight); to obscure (the understanding, judgement, etc.); to stupefy, bewilder (a person) 1577.

1. Atmospheres..so dense..as may suffice to o...the Light of the Star 1734. 3. He was obfuscated with brandy and water 1893. Hence **Obfuscaˑtion,** obfuscating; the being obfuscated; *transf.* something that obfuscates. So **Obfuˑscate** *ppl. a.* Now *rare* or *Obs.* 1531.

‖ **Obi** [1], **obi-man,** etc.: see OBEAH.

‖ **Obi** [2] (ōˑbi). 1802. [Jap.] A brightly coloured sash worn round the waist by Japanese women and children; any similar sash.

Obit (ǫˑbit, ōˑbit). *Obs.* exc. *Hist.* Also freq. *obiit.* late ME. [a. OF., ad. L. *obitus*, f. *obire*, f. *ob-* OB- 1 + *ire* to go.] 1. †a. Death, decease (of a particular person) –1694. b. An obituary notice (*arch.*) 1459. 2. †a. Funeral rites, obsequies. (Also in *pl.*) –1708. b. A yearly (or other) service in commemoration of, or on behalf of the soul of, a deceased person on the anniversary or other mind-day of his death. *Obs.* exc. *Hist.* late ME.

2. b. Obits, Dirges, Masses are not said for nothing 1670.

†**Oˑbital,** *a.* and *sb.* 1690. [f. prec. *sb.* + -AL.] 1. *adj.* Recording or commemorating a death or deaths, or the celebration of obits (see prec. 2 b) –1715. 2. *sb.* An obituary WOOD.

Obiter (ǫˑbitəɹ), *adv.* and *adj.* 1573. [L. adv., orig. two words, *ob iter*, by the way.] A. *adv.* By the way, in passing, incidentally. b. *esp.* in the phr. **Obiter dictum** [L., (a thing) said by the way]: in *Law*, An expression of opinion on a matter of law, given by a judge in court, but not essential to his decision, and therefore not of binding authority; hence *gen.* Any incidental statement or remark 1812. B. quasi-*adj.* (after *obiter dictum*). Made or uttered by the way; incidental 1767.

Obitual (obiˑtiuˌăl), *a.* and *sb. rare.* 1706. [f. L. *obitus* OBIT + -AL; cf. *habitual*.] 1. *adj.* = OBITAL 1. 2. *sb.* = OBITAL 2, OBITUARY A 1. 1812.

Obituary (obiˑtiuˌări), *sb.* and *a.* 1706. [ad. med.L. *obituarius* adj. and sb., f. *obitus*; see OBIT and -ARY.] A. *sb.* 1. A register of deaths, or of obit days. 2. A notice or announcement of a death or deaths, esp. in a newspaper; usu. comprising a brief biography of the deceased 1738. B. *adj.* Relating to or recording a death (usu. with a biographical sketch of the deceased); esp. *o. notice* 1828.

Object (ǫˑbdʒĕkt), *sb.* late ME. [Partly sb. use of OBJECT *ppl. a.*; but in philosophical senses, ad. med. Schol.L. *objectum*, lit. thing thrown before (the mind). In branch II rendering L. *objectus*, thus properly a distinct wd.] I. From L. *objectum*, pl. *objecta*. †1. A statement introduced in opposition; an objection –1617. †2. Something 'thrown' or put in the way as an obstacle; a hindrance –1564. 3. Something presented to the sight or other sense; a material thing; *spec.* the thing or body observed by means of an optical instrument, or represented in drawing or perspective. late ME. b. Something which on being seen excites admiration, horror, amusement, commiseration, etc.; in colloq. use a person or thing of pitiable or ridiculous aspect 1588. 4. That to which action, thought, or feeling is directed; the thing (or person) to which something is done or about which something acts or operates (= Schol. *materia circa quam*). Const. *of* (the action, etc. or agent). 1586. 5. The thing aimed at; purpose, end 1597. 6. *Metaph.* A thing of which one thinks or has cognition, as correlative to the thinking or knowing *subject*; something regarded as external to the mind; the non-ego; also extended to include states of the ego, or of consciousness, as thought of 1651. 7. *Gram.* A substantive word, phrase, or clause, 'governed by' a verb. Also, the word 'governed by' a preposition. 1729.

3. Þe obiect of the eye is all þ[t] may be seen, & al þ[t] maye be herde is obiect to the herynge TREVISA. b. Some poor objects will be sent thither in hopes of relief BUTLER. 4. He..will be deemed a proper o. of public charity 1773. 5. How quickly Nature falls into reuolt, when Gold becomes her Obiect? SHAKS. 7. *O. clause*, a clause or subordinate sentence forming the object of a verb, as in 'we know (that) he is alive'. *Direct o.*, the word or phrase 'governed' by a transitive verb. *Indirect o.* of a (trans. or intr.) verb. ¶*No o.*: a matter of indifference (e.g. *distance no o.*).

II. [= L. *objectu-s* (*u*-stem).] †1. The fact of throwing itself or being thrown in the way (*rare*) –1555. †2. = OBJECTION 3. –1616.

2. Reason flyes the obiect of all harme SHAKS. *Comb.*: **o.-ball** (*Billiards, Croquet*, etc.), the ball at which the player aims his own ball; **-finder**, a contrivance for registering the position of an o. on a mounted microscopic slide, so as to find it again; **-lens** = OBJECT-GLASS; **-lesson**, a lesson about a material o. conveyed by actual examination of the o.; *fig.* something that exemplifies some principle in a concrete form: so *o. teaching*; **-plate** (*Microscopy*), the plate upon which the object to be examined is placed; **-staff** (*Surveying*), a levelling-staff. Hence **Oˑbjectless** *a.* devoid of an object or objects, *esp.* aimless, purposeless; so **Oˑbjectless·ly** *adv.*, **-ness.**

†**Objeˑct,** *ppl. a.* late ME. [ad. L. *objectus*, *objicere* (*obicere*), f. *ob-* OB- 1 + *jacere* to throw.] 1. Thrown or put in the way; exposed (to injury or any influence, or to sight) –1650. b. Opposite; also *fig.* opposed, contrary –1613. 2. Objected, charged (*against* a person) –1529.

Object (ǫ̆bdʒeˑkt), *v.* late ME. [f. L. *object-*, *objicere*; see prec.] 1. *trans.* To put over against or in the way of something; to expose to. *Obs.* or *arch.* 1578. b. To put in the way or interpose, as an obstacle or hindrance to progress, or a defence from attack. *Obs.* or *arch.* 1548. †c. To expose *to* danger, etc. –1677. 2. To place (something) before the eyes, etc., or the mind. *Obs.* or *arch.* 1534. 3. To bring forward as a reason, ground, or instance; to adduce. *Obs.* or *arch.* 1536. 4. To urge as an objection (*to, unto, against*). late ME. 5. To attribute to any one as a fault or crime. Const. *to, against* (†*upon*, indirect obj.). 1469. †6. *trans.* To impute, attribute (*to*) –1776. 7. *intr.* To state an adverse reason; now often merely: To express or feel disapproval. late ME. b. with *to* (occas. *against*, rarely *at*) or *inf.*: To bring forward a reason against: now usu.: To express, or merely to feel, disapproval of; to have an objection *to*, dislike. (The chief current sense.) 1513. †c. *intr.* To bring an accusation. *Acts* xxiv. 19.

1. He commanded him to be objected to a hungry and an enraged Lyon 1654. b. Pallas to their eyes The mist objected POPE. 2. Whose temperance was of proof against any meat objected to his appetite FULLER. 4. Bryant objects this very circumstance to the authenticity of the Iliad 1830. 5. When God afflicted Job, he did o. no sin to him HOBBES. 7. I think I'll have a smoke, if you don't o. (*mod.*). b. We o. to the argument on scientific grounds 1869. Hence †**Objeˑctable** *a.* that may be objected, or urged as an objection (*against* or *to*); that may be objected to –1885. **Objeˑcted** *ppl. a.* placed opposite, presented to the view or perception. *Obs.* or *arch.*

Oˑbject-glass. 1665. [OBJECT *sb.* I. 3.] The lens or combination of lenses in a telescope, microscope, etc., which is situated nearest to the object. (Cf. EYE-GLASS 3.)

Objectify (ǫ̆bdʒeˑktifəi), *v.* 1836. [f. med. L. *objectum* OBJECT *sb.* + -FY.] *trans.* To make into, or present as, an object, esp. an object of sense; to render objective. Hence **Objeˑctifiˑcaˑtion,** the action of objectifying or condition of being objectified; an instance of this.

Objection (ǫ̆bdʒeˑkʃən). late ME. [a. F., ad. L. *objectionem*, f. *objicere* to OBJECT.] 1. a. The action of stating something in opposition to a person or thing. b. That which is objected; †an accusation against a person; an adverse reason, argument, or contention. Now often merely: An expression, or feeling, of disapproval, disagreement, or dislike (esp. in phr. *to have an* or *no o.*). c. A document in which an objection is stated. †2. *transf.* and *fig.* An adverse action, an assault -1586. 3. Presentation to the view or to the mind, or that which is so presented; representation, offer -1649.

1. b. I have no o. to join with you in the enquiry 1875. Phr. *To take o.*, to bring forward a reason against something, or merely to object. Hence **Obje·ctionable** *a.* open to o.; now often, unacceptable, unpleasant. **Obje·ctionableness. Obje·ctionably** *adv.*

Obje·ctivate, *v.* 1873. [f. OBJECTIVE *a.* + -ATE.] *trans.* = OBJECTIFY. So **Obje:ctiva·tion** = OBJECTIFICATION.

Objective (ǫ̆bdʒe·ktiv), *a.* and *sb.* 1620. [ad. Schol.L. *objectivus*, f. *objectus* ppl. a., *objectum* sb.; F. *objectif, -ive.*] A. *adj.* †1. *Philos.* Pertaining or considered in relation to its object; constituting, or belonging to, an object of action, thought, or feeling; 'material', as opp. to *subjective* or 'formal' -1675. †b. Of or pertaining to the object or end as the cause of action; *o. cause* = final cause: see CAUSE *sb.* I. 4. -1678. 2. *Philos.* Used of the existence or nature of a thing as an object of consciousness (as dist. from *subjective*). †a. Opp. to *subjective* in the older sense = 'in itself': Existing as an object of consciousness; considered only as presented to the mind -1744. b. Opp. to *subjective* in the modern sense: That is the object of perception or thought, as dist. from the perceiving or thinking subject; hence, that is, or is regarded as, a 'thing' external to the mind; real 1647. 3. *transf.* (from 2 b) a. Of a person, a writing, work of art, etc.: Treating of outward things or events; regarding things from an objective standpoint. (Occas., after mod. G. *objektiv*: Treating a subject so as to exhibit the actual facts, not coloured by the feelings or opinions of the writer.) 1855. b. *Med.* Applied to symptoms 'observed by the practitioner, in distinction from those which are only felt by the patient' (*Syd. Soc. Lex.*) 1877. 4. With *to*: That is the object of sensation or thought. In *Metaph.* Related as object to subject (see OBJECT *sb.* 6). 1762. 5. *Perspective.* That is, or belongs to, the object of which the delineation is required 1706. 6. Applied to the lens or combination of lenses in an optical instrument which is nearest to the object (*o. glass*; now usu. OBJECT-GLASS, or simply *objective*) 1753. 7. *Gram.* Expressing or denoting the object of an action; *spec.* applied to that case in mod. English in which a noun or pronoun stands when it is the object of a verb, or is governed by a preposition; also to the relation of such noun or pronoun to such verb or preposition 1763. 8. *O. point*: orig. *Mil.* the point towards which the advance of troops is directed; hence *gen.* the point aimed at 1864. 9. Characterized by objecting 1814.

2. a. This confession was the o. foundation of faith; and Christ and his Apostles, the subjective JER. TAYLOR. Natural phænomena are..such as we see and perceive them: Their real and o. natures are, therefore, the same BERKELEY. b. In the philosophy of mind, subjective denotes what is referred to the thinking subject, the Ego; o. what belongs to the object of thought, the Non-Ego 1853. This [Christ's resurrection] was an historic o. fact FARRAR. 3. The book [Robinson Crusoe]..is, to use a much-abused word, eminently o.; that is, the circumstances are drawn from a real study of things as they are 1855. To complete the survey of the actualities of party politics by stating in a purely positive, or as the Germans say 'objective', way, what the Americans think about..their system BRYCE. 8. The city of Meshed being my o. point 1893.

B. *sb.* (the adj. used ellipt.) 1. Short for *o. glass* (see A. 6) 1835. 2. *Gram.* Short for *o. case* (see A. 7) 1861. 3. Short for *o. point* (see A. 8); also *fig.* something aimed at, an object or end 1881. Hence **Obje·ctively** *adv.* in an o. manner or relation (usu. opp. to *subjectively*). **Obje·ctiveness, Objecti·vity,** the quality or character of being o.

Objectivism (ǫ̆bdʒe·ktiviz'm). 1872. [f. OBJECTIVE *a.* + -ISM.] The tendency to lay stress upon what is objective or external to the mind; the philosophical doctrine that knowledge of the non-ego is prior in sequence and importance to that of the ego; the character (in a work of art, etc.) of being objective. So **Obje·ctivist,** one who holds the doctrine of o. (also *attrib.*).

Obje·ctivize, *v.* 1856. [f. OBJECTIVE *a.* + -IZE.] *trans.* To render objective.

Objectize (ǫ·bdʒĕktəiz), *v.* 1668. [f. OBJECT *sb.* + -IZE.] *trans.* To make into an object, objectify. So **Objectiza·tion.**

Object-matter. 1652. [= OBJECT *ppl. a.* + MATTER *sb.*] †1. Matter presented to view or to be employed as a means GAULE. 2. The matter that is the object of some action or study. (Usu. *subject-matter*) 1836.

Objector (ǫ̆bdʒe·ktəɹ). 1640. [f. OBJECT *v.* + -OR.] One who objects or makes an objection to something.

A conscientious o. to vaccination 1899.

Objicient (ǫ̆bdʒi·ʃiĕnt). 1864. [ad.L. *objicientem* pr. pple. of *objicere* to OBJECT.] One who objects; an opponent of a motion or proposition.

Objurgate (ǫ·bdʒɒɹgeⁱt), *v.* 1616. [f. L. *objurgat-, objurgare* to chide, rebuke, f. *ob-* OB-1 + *jurgare.*] *trans.* To chide, scold. Also *absol.* or *intr.* Hence **Objurga·tion,** chiding, scolding. **Obju·rgative, Obju·rgatory** *adjs.* **Obju·rgatorily** *adv.*

‖**Oblata** (ǫblā·tă), *sb. pl. Hist.* 1658. [L., neut. *pl.* of *oblatus*, used absol.; see next.] *Law.* Old debts, or offerings made to the king by any of his subjects, which, if not paid, were put in the sheriff's charge.

Oblate (ǫ·bleⁱt), *sb.* 1756. [ad. med.L. *oblatus*, sb. use of pa. pple. of L. *offerre* to OFFER.] A person solemnly devoted to a monastery or to a religious work; *spec.* a member of a congregation or order devoted to a specific work.

Oblate (ǫblē·t, ǫ·bleⁱt), *a.* 1696. [ad. med. or mod.L. *oblatus*, f. *ob-* OB- + *latus* in L. *prolatus* lengthened out.] *Geom.* Flattened at the poles; said of a spheroid produced by the revolution of an ellipse about its shorter axis. Opp. to *prolate.* Hence **Oblate·ly** *adv.*, **-ness.**

Oblation (ǫ̆blē·ʃən). late ME. [a. OF., ad. late L. *oblationem* offering, gift, in eccl. L. sacrifice, f. *offerre* to OFFER.] I. In religious senses. 1. The action of solemnly offering something (e.g. a sacrifice, thanksgiving, etc.) to God or to a deity. 2. The action of offering the elements of bread and wine to God in the Eucharist; also, the whole service of the Eucharist 1450. 3. That which is offered to God or to a deity; an offering, sacrifice; a victim. late ME. †Also *transf.* 4. The presentation of something to God for the services of the Church, or other pious uses; that which is so presented 1455.

1. Therfore will I offre in his dwellinge, the oblacion of thankes geuynge COVERDALE *Ps.* xxvi[i]. 6. 2. *The great o.* (Liturg.), that in which the consecrated elements are presented as sacramentally the body and blood of Christ. 3. Hee..shall bring his o. vnto the Lord *Lev.* vii. 29. 4. We humbly beseech thee most mercifully to accept our alms and oblations *Bk. Com. Prayer.*

II. In general uses. 1. The action of offering or presenting 1595. †2. A subsidy or tax; a gift to the king -1668. Hence **Obla·tional** *a.* **Obla·tionary** *sb. Eccl.* one who receives the oblations at the celebration of the Eucharist; *adj.* having the function of receiving the oblations. †**Obla·tioner,** one who makes an o.

Oblatory (ǫ·blătəri), *a.* 1611. [f. L. *oblat-, offerre*; see -ORY [2].] Pertaining to oblations.

†**Oble·ctate,** *v. rare.* 1611. [f. L. *oblectat-, oblectare* to delight, f. *ob-* (OB- 1) + *lactare*, freq. of *lacere* to entice.] *trans.* To delight, please, rejoice -1621. †So **Oblecta·tion,** delight, pleasure, enjoyment 1508.

Obley (ǫ·bli). [ME. a. OF. *oublee*, mod.F. *oublie* :—eccl. L. *oblata*, sb. from fem. pa. pple. of *offerre* to OFFER.] †1. An offering, oblation. ME. only. 2. An altar-bread or wafer. Now *Hist.* ME.

Obligant (ǫ·bligănt). 1754. [ad. L. *obligantem*, pr. pple. of *obligare* to OBLIGE.] *Sc. Law.* One who binds himself, or is legally bound, to pay or perform something.

Obligate (ǫ·bligĕt), *ppl. a.* late ME. [ad. L. *obligatus, obligare.*] †1. Bound by oath, law, or duty; obliged -1539. 2. *Biol.* That is of necessity such. *O. parasite*, an organism of necessity parasitical. 1887.

Obligate (ǫ·bligeⁱt), *v.* 1541. [f. L. *obligat-, obligare.*] 1. To bind (a person) by a moral or legal tie. Chiefly in *pass.* 1668. 2. To make (a thing) a security; to pledge, pawn, mortgage -1890. 3. = OBLIGE *v.* III. 1, 2. (In later use chiefly *dial.* and *U.S. colloq.*) 1692. b. To render (conduct, etc.) obligatory 1879.

1. Every contract..by which a debtor is obligated to pay any tax BRYCE. 3. b. An interest in him beyond what gratitude obligated 1879.

Obligation (ǫbligē·ʃən). ME. [a. OF., ad. L. *obligationem*, f. *obligare* to OBLIGE.] 1. The action of binding oneself by oath, promise, or contract to do or forbear something; a binding agreement; also, that to which one binds oneself, a formal promise. 2. *Law.* An agreement, enforceable by law, whereby a person or persons become bound to the payment of a sum of money or other performance; the document containing such an agreement; *esp.* in Eng. Law, a written contract or bond under seal containing a penalty with condition attached. Also, the right created or liability incurred by such an agreement, document, or bond. late ME. 3. Moral or legal constraint, or constraining force or influence; the condition of being morally or legally obliged or bound; a moral or legal tie binding to some performance; the binding power of a law, moral precept, duty, contract, etc. 1602. 4. Action, or an act, to which one is morally or legally obliged; one's bounden duty, or a particular duty. Occas.: An enforced or burdensome task or charge. 1605. 5. a. The fact or condition of indebtedness for a benefit or service received 1632. b. A benefit or service done or received 1618. †6. Legal liability -1758.

1. Of the obligacyon made bytwene god and us 1526. 3. Bound In filiall O., for some terme To do obsequious Sorrow SHAKS. What o. lay on me to be popular? BURKE. *Of o.*, obligatory. *Day of o.*, a day on which it is of obligation for the faithful to abstain from work and to attend divine service. 4. The o. of tribute BRYCE. 5. a. They return benefits..because o. is a pain JOHNSON. b. When a kindly face greets us, though but passing by,..we should feel it as an o. LAMB. Phr. *To be, put, under an o.*

Obligato, var. of **Obbligato.**

Obligatory (ǫ·bligătəri, ǫ̆bli·gătəri), *a.* ME. [ad. late L. *obligatorius*, f. *obligat-, obligare*; see -ORY.] 1. Imposing obligation, binding legally or morally; of the nature of an obligation; that must be done. Const. *on, upon* (†*to*, †*of*). 1502. 2. Creating or constituting an obligation ME. 3. *Biol.* = OBLIGATE *ppl. a.* 2. 1896.

1. There are situations..in which, therefore, these duties are o. BURKE. 2. *Writing (bill*, etc.) *o.* = OBLIGATION 2. Hence **O·bligato·rily** *adv.* **O·bligato·riness.**

Oblige (ǫ̆bləi·dʒ), *v.* ME. [a. OF. *obliger, -ier*, ad. L. *obligare*, f. *ob-* OB- 1 + *ligare* to bind. Formerly pronounced (ǫ̆blī·dʒ).] I. 1. *trans.* To bind (a person) by an oath, promise, contract, or any moral or legal tie (*to* a person or a course, or *to do* a thing). Now only in *Law.* Also *refl.* †2. To make (lands, property, a possession) a guarantee or security for the discharge of a promise or debt; to pledge, pawn, or mortgage -1750. 3. a. Of an oath, promise, law, command, etc.: To bind (a person) *to* some action or conduct, or *to do* something; also, *to* a person (*obs.* exc. in *Law*). late ME. b. With simple obj.: To be binding on (a person, conscience). Also *absol.* late ME.

1. It has been commonly suppos'd, That a Father could o. his Posterity to that Government of which he himself was a Subject LOCKE. The town council obliged themselves to his son to build that aisle to his memory 1890. 3. b. You say they are no Laws unless they o. the Conscience MARVELL. *To be obliged*: to be bound by a legal or moral tie.

II. †a. *trans.* To make (any one) subject or liable *to* a bond, penalty, or the like -1649. b. *refl.* To render oneself liable to punishment (L. *se obligare*). Now only *Civil Law.* late ME.

III. 1. *trans.* To bind or make indebted (†*to* oneself) by conferring a benefit or kindness; to gratify *with* or *by doing* something; to do a service to, confer a favour on. Said also of the service, kindness, etc. 1567 b. *absol.* To confer a favour; *esp.* to favour a company (with some performance). *colloq.* 1735. **2.** *pass.* To be bound *to* a person by ties of gratitude; to owe or feel gratitude. Now said freq. in ref. to small services, or formally, as in ordering goods from a tradesman, etc. 1548. **†3.** *trans.* (vaguely) To gratify, charm –1709.

1. Your early attention to this application will much o., Sir, your very faithful and obedient servant 1796. O. me with the milk DICKENS. **b.** He 'obliged' at the pianoforte 1897. **2.** I told them I was very much obliged to them for their Good-will 1726.

IV. 1. *trans.* To constrain, esp. by moral or legal force or influence 1632. **2.** To render imperative 1638.

1. Self-preservation obliged the people to these severities DE FOE. Hence **O·bligable** *a.*, **Obli·gedly** *adv.*, **-ness. Obli·ger,** one who imposes or confers an obligation.

Obligee (ǫbləidʒī·). 1559. [f. prec.; see -EE.] **1.** *Law.* One to whom another is bound by contract; the person to whom a bond is given. (Correl. to *obligor.*) **2.** One who is under obligation for benefits received 1610.

Obligement (ŏbləi·dʒmĕnt). 1584. [f. OBLIGE *v.* + -MENT.] **1.** = OBLIGATION 2. *Obs.* exc. in *Civil Law.* **2.** Obligation (moral or legal); obligation for benefits received; a kindness, favour 1611.

2. This I would endure, And more, to cancel my obligements to him DRYDEN.

Obliging (ŏbləi·dʒiŋ), *ppl. a.* 1632. [f. OBLIGE *v.* + -ING [2].] That obliges. **1.** That imposes obligation; obligatory. Now *rare.* 1638. **2.** Of persons, etc.: Ready to do services or favours 1632. **b.** Of actions, words, etc.: Courteous, civil, polite 1635.

2. Keppel had a sweet and o. temper MACAULAY. Hence **Obli·ging·ly** *adv.*, **-ness.**

Obligor (ǫbləidʒǭ·ɪ). 1541. [f. OBLIGE *v.* + -OR.] *Law.* One who binds himself to another by contract; the person who gives a bond or obligation. (Correl. to *obligee.*)

†Obliquate, *v. rare.* 1670. [f. L. *obliquat-*, *obliquare*; see OBLIQUE *v.* and -ATE [3].] *trans.* To bend aside, twist obliquely –1736. So **†Obliqua·tion,** a bending obliquely; a twisting awry.

Oblique (ŏblī·k), *a.* (*sb.*) late ME. [ad. L. *obliquus*, f. *ob-* pref. + stem *leiqw-*: *leq-* to bend. Formerly pron. (ŏbləi·k).] **1.** Having a slanting direction or position; declining from the vertical, or from the horizontal; diverging from a given straight line or course. **2.** Spec. uses. **a.** *Geom.* Of a line, a plane figure, or a surface: Inclined at an angle other than a right angle. Of an angle: Either greater or less than a right angle. Of a solid, as a cone, cylinder, or prism: Having its axis not perpendicular to the plane of its base. 1571. **b.** Astron. *O. sphere,* the celestial or terrestrial sphere when its axis is oblique to the horizon of the place; which it is at any part of the earth's surface except the poles and the equator. *O. ascension, descension*: see ASCENSION 3, DESCENSION 5. *O. horizon,* one which is oblique to the celestial equator. 1503. **c.** *Anat.* Parallel neither to the long axis of the body or limb, nor to its transverse section; esp. of certain muscles, etc. 1615. **d.** *Bot.* Of a leaf: Having unequal sides 1835. **e.** *Cryst.* = MONOCLINIC 1878. **f.** *Naut. O. sailing*: the movement of a ship when its course makes an o. angle with the meridian. 1706. **g.** *O. perspective*: see PERSPECTIVE. **3.** *fig.* Not going straight to the point; indirect. late ME. **b.** Of an end, result, etc.: Indirectly aimed at 1528. **4.** Deviating from right conduct or thought 1576. **5.** *Gram.* **a.** *O. case,* any case except the nominative and vocative (and occas., the accusative). **b.** Of speech or narration: see INDIRECT *a.* 3 (L. *oratio obliqua*) 1530. **6.** *Mus. O. motion*: when one part remains without moving while another ascends or descends. (Opp. to *similar* and *contrary.*) 1811. **B.** *sb.* An oblique muscle: see 2 c. 1800.

1. If straight thy track, or if o. [*rimes* strike], Thou know'st not TENNYSON. **2. a.** *O. hyperbola,* one the asymptotes of which are not at right angles to one another. **3.** All censure of a man's self is o. praise JOHNSON. **b.** For that the love we bear our friends.. Hath in it certain o. ends DRAYTON. **4.** There are persons to be found..who grow rich and great..by various o. and scandalous ways 1770. **5. b.** There is scarcely a single o. sentence throughout St. John's Gospel 1882. Hence **Obli·que·ly** *adv.*, **-ness.**

Oblique (ŏblī·k), *v.* 1775. [a. F. *obliquer*, f. *oblique* adj.; cf. L. *obliquare.* Formerly pron. (ŏbləi·k).] **†1.** *trans.* To turn in a sidelong direction. **2.** *intr.* To advance obliquely, esp. (*Mil.*) by making a half-face to the right or left and then marching forward 1787. **b.** Of a line, etc.: To slant at an angle SCOTT.

1. When her love-eye was fixed on me,..her eye of duty was finely obliqued SHERIDAN.

Obliquity (ŏbli·kwĭti). late ME. [a. F. *obliquité*, ad. L. *obliquitatem*; see OBLIQUE and -ITY.] **1.** The quality of being oblique; degree of this 1551. **2.** *fig.* Deviation from moral rectitude, sound thinking, or right practice; a delinquency, a fault, an error. late ME. **†3.** Deviation from directness in action, conduct, or speech; a method that is not straightforward –1818.

1. The o. of the eye, which is proper to the Chinese and Japanese DARWIN. *O. of the ecliptic,* the inclination of the plane of the ecliptic to that of the equator. **2.** The perversnesse and o. of my will DONNE. **3.** The obliquities of Eastern negotiation 1818. Hence **Obli·quitous** *a.* mentally or morally perverse.

Obliterate (ŏbli·tĕrĕt), *ppl. a.* 1598. [ad. L. *oblit(t)eratus, oblit(t)erare*; see next.] **1.** Blotted out; obliterated. Now only *poet.* **2.** *Entom.* Applied to the markings on insects, when the borders of spots fade into the ground-colour, etc. 1826.

Obliterate (ŏbli·tĕreɪt), *v.* 1548. [f. L. *oblit(t)erat-*, *oblit(t)erare* to blot out, etc., f. *ob-* OB- 1 + *lit(t)era* anything written.] **1.** *trans.* To blot out (anything written, etc.) so as to leave no distinct traces; to erase, delete, efface 1611. **b.** To cause to disappear (anything perceived by the senses) 1607. **2.** To efface, wipe out (a memory, etc.); to do away with, destroy (qualities, characteristics, etc.) 1548. **3.** *Phys.* and *Path.* To efface, close up, or otherwise destroy (esp. a duct or passage, the cavity of which disappears by contraction and adhesion of the walls). Also *intr.* for *refl.* 1813.

2. He designed to o. and extinguish the memory of heathen antiquity and authors BACON. Hence **Obliteration,** effacement, extinction. **Obli·terative** *a.* tending to o.

Oblivion (ŏbli·viən). late ME. [a. OF., ad. L. *oblivionem*, f. vb.-stem *obliv-* of *oblivisci* to forget.] **1.** The state or fact of forgetting; forgetfulness. **b.** Heedlessness, disregard 1470. **c.** Intentional overlooking, esp. of political offences 1564. **2.** The state or condition of being forgotten. late ME.

1. Make us drinke Lethe..; That for two daies o. smother griefe MARSTON. **b.** Among our crimes o. may be set DRYDEN. **c.** *Act* or *Bill of O.*, an act or bill granting a general pardon for political offences; in *Eng. Hist.* spec. applied to the Acts of 1660 and 1690, exempting those who had taken arms against Charles II and William III respectively from the consequences of their deeds. **2.** A question..which ought to have been buried in o. 1769. Hence **Obli·vionize** *v. trans.* to consign to o.

Oblivious (ŏbli·viəs), *a.* late ME. [ad. L. *obliviosus*, f. *oblivionem*; see prec. and -OUS.] **1.** That forgets; forgetful; unmindful. Const. *of.* ¶**b.** *erron.* Unconscious 1862. **2.** Of or pertaining to forgetfulness; attended by or associated with oblivion 1563.

1. The slow formality of an o. and drowsy exchequer BURKE. **b.** He was..frequently o. of what was passing around him 1862. **2.** Some sweet Obliuious Antidote SHAKS. Hence **Obli·vious·ly** *adv.*, **-ness.**

Obliviscence (ǫblivi·sĕns). 1774. [f. L. *obliviscentem, oblivisci* to forget; see -ENCE.] Forgetfulness.

†Oblocu·tion. late ME. [a. OF., ad. late L. *oblocutionem*, f. L. *obloqui*; see OBLOQUY.] Evil-speaking, obloquy, slander –1731.

Oblong (ǫ·blǫŋ), *a.* and *sb.* late ME. [ad. L. *oblongus* longish, (later) oblong; f. *ob-* + *longus* LONG.] **A.** *adj.* Elongated in one direction (usu. as a deviation from an exact square or circular form); having the chief axis longer than the transverse diameter; *spec.* in *Geom.*, rectangular with the adjacent sides unequal. **b.** Of a sheet of paper, page, book, panel, postage stamp, etc.: Rectangular with the breadth greater than the height; as an *o.* (opp. to an *upright*) *octavo* 1888. Also in *Comb.*

O. spheroid, a prolate spheroid.

B. *sb.* An oblong figure, or something oblong in form; *spec.* in *Geom.*, a rectangle of greater length than breadth 1608.

Xenophon then moved..that the march should be in a hollow o., with the baggage in the centre GROTE. Hence **Oblo·ngo-,** used in *Bot.* as comb. form of *oblong* adj. in sense 'with o. extension'.

Oblongatal (ǫblǫŋgē·tăl), *a.* 1885. [f. mod.L. *oblongatus* (as in *medulla oblongata*), pa. pple. of *oblongare*, f. *oblongus* OBLONG + -AL.] Of or pertaining to the medulla oblongata, the hindmost segment of the brain.

Oblongated (ǫ·blǫŋgeɪtĕd), *ppl. a.* 1706. [f. as prec. + -ED [1].] Prolonged; in *o. marrow,* the medulla oblongata.

Obloquy (ǫ·blŏkwi). 1450. [ad. late L. *obloquium* contradiction, f. *obloqui*, f. *ob-* OB- 1 + *loqui.*] **1.** Evil-speaking against a person or thing; abuse, detraction. †Formerly also with *an* and *pl.* **b.** The condition of being spoken against; bad repute; reproach, disgrace 1469. **†2.** *transf.* A cause of detraction or reproach; a disgrace –1621.

1. They had to..hold their convictions in the face of o. 1867. **b.** And undergo the perpetual o. of having lost a Kingdom CLARENDON. **2.** *All's Well* IV. ii. 44. So **Obloquious** (ǫblōᵘ·kwiəs), *a.* characterized by o.

Obmutescence (ǫbmiu̇te·sĕns). 1646. [f. L. *obmutescere* (f. *ob-* OB- 1 + *mutescere* to grow mute) + -ENCE.] A becoming (wilfully) mute; the action of obstinately remaining mute. So **Obmute·scent** *a.* remaining mute 1876.

Obnoxious (ŏbnǫ·kʃəs), *a.* 1581. [f. L. *obnoxiosus*, f. *obnoxius*, f. *ob-* OB- 1 + *noxa* hurt, injury; cf. NOXIOUS.] **1.** Exposed to harm; subject or liable to injury or evil of any kind. Const. *to*, †*inf.*, or †*simply.* 1597. **†2.** Liable to punishment or censure; reprehensible –1774. **†3.** Answerable, amenable (*to* some authority); dependent, subject; hence, submissive, obsequious. Const *to.* –1754. **†4.** With *to*: Exposed to the (physical) action or influence of; open *to* –1671. ¶**5.** *erron.* (by confusion with *noxious*): Hurtful, injurious –1683. **6.** That is an object of aversion or dislike; *occas.* giving offence, acting objectionably. (The chief current use, app. assoc. with *noxious.*) Const. *to.* 1675.

1. The time of Youth is most O. to forget God 1677. We are o. to so many Accidents ADDISON. **2.** A late work has appeared to us highly o. in this respect GOLDSM. **3.** An existence that is not dependent upon or o. to any other 1722. **6.** Carlyle..is becoming very o. now that he has become popular E. FITZGERALD. Hence **Obno·xious·ly** *adv.*, **-ness.**

Obnubilate (ǫbniū·bileɪt), *v.* 1583. [f. L. *obnubilat-*, *obnubilare* to cover with clouds or fog.] *trans.* To darken as with a cloud; to overcloud, obscure. Hence **Obnubila·tion,** obscuration; *spec.* clouding of the mind or faculties.

Oboe (ōᵘ·boi, ōᵘ·bōᵘ). 1700. [a. It. *oboe* (ō·*boe*), adapted spelling of F. *hautbois* HAUTBOY.] **1.** = HAUTBOY 1. 1794. **2.** Name of a reed-stop in an organ, with metal pipes, giving a penetrating tone 1700. Hence **O·boist,** a performer on the o.

Obol (ǫ·bǫl). 1670. [ad. L. *obolus.* Cf. F. *obole*: see below.] = OBOLUS 1.

O·bolary, *a. nonce-wd.* [f. L. *obolus* + -ARY.] That contributes an obolus; or, Possessing only oboli, impecunious LAMB.

Obole (ǫ·bōᵘl). 1656. [a. F., ad. L. *obolus*; see next.] A small French coin orig. of silver, later of billon, in use from 10th to 15th c. = ½ a denier; also called *maille.*

‖**Obolus** (ǫ·bŏlŏs). *Pl.* **-li** (-ləi). 1531. [L., a. Gr. ὀβολός.] **1.** A silver (later, bronze) coin of ancient Greece, = ⅙ of a drachma, or about 1½*d.* English 1579. **2.** Applied to the French OBOLE, and to other (small) coins formerly current in Europe; also, any small coin. Cf. OB. **†3.** *Apothecaries' Weight.* A weight of 10 grains, or half a scruple –1661.

Obovate (ǫbˌōᵘ·vĕt), *a.* 1785. [OB- 2.] *Nat. Hist.* Inversely ovate; egg-shaped with the broader end upmost or forward. **b.** In comb. with adj., as *o.-cuneate, -lanceolate* 1806.

Obreption (ǫbre·pʃən). 1611. [ad. L. *obreptionem*, f. *obrepere* to creep up to, steal upon, f. *ob-* OB- 1 + *repere* to creep.] The obtaining of something by craft or deceit, *spec.* in *Eccl.* and *Sc. Law,* of a dispensation, gift, etc. by false statement. (Opp. to *subreption.*)

Obreptitious (ǫbrepti·ʃəs), *a.* 1611. [f. L. *obrepticius*, f. *obreptus*, *obrepere*; see prec. and -ITIOUS[1].] Characterized by obreption; containing a false statement made for the sake of obtaining something.

Obrogate (ǫ·brŏgeⁱt), *v. rare.* 1656. [f. L. *obrogat-*, *obrogare*, f. *ob-* OB- 1 + *rogare.*] To repeal (a law) by passing a new one.

Obscene (ǫ̆bsī·n), *a.* 1593. [ad. F. *obscène* or L. *obscenus* inauspicious, filthy, indecent; etym. unkn.] 1. Offensive to modesty or decency; expressing or suggesting lewd thoughts 1598. 2. Offensive to the senses or the mind; disgusting, filthy. *arch.*

1. The rabble of Comus..reeling in o. dances MACAULAY. 2. In rags o. decreed to roam POPE. So **Obsce·ne·ly** *adv.* 1588, **-ness** 1637.

Obscenity (ǫ̆bsī·nĭti, ǫ̆bse·nĭti). 1608. [ad. L. *obscenitas*, f. *obscenus*; or ad. F. *obscénité*.] Obscene quality or character: **a.** Indecency, lewdness (esp. of language); in *pl.* obscene words or matters. †**b.** Foulness, loathsomeness; in *pl.* foul acts, dirty work -1807.

a. Worse..then the worst obscenities of heathen superstition MILT. **b.** Slovenly cooks, that after their obscenities never wash their bawdy hands BURTON.

Obscurant (ǫbskiūᵊ·rănt), *sb.* and *a.* 1799. [= G. *obscurant*, f. L. *obscurant-*, *obscurare* to darken.] **A.** *sb.* One who obscures; one who strives to prevent inquiry, enlightenment, or reform. **B.** *adj.* That obscures or darkens; of or belonging to an obscurant 1878. Hence **Obscu·rantism** [cf. G. *obscurantismus*, 18th c.], the practice or principles of those who strive to prevent enlightenment or the progress of knowledge 1834; **Obscu·rantist** *sb.* and *a.* = OBSCURANT 1838.

Obscuration (ǫbskiurēⁱ·ʃən). 1471. [ad. L. *obscurationem*, f. *obscurare.*] 1. The action of obscuring, darkening, or clouding over; obscured or dimmed state or condition; in *Astron.*, occultation, eclipse. 2. *fig.* The darkening or dimming of intellectual light, of the mental vision, of the sense of words, of truth, etc. 1611.

1. *transf.* Our old dramatists are full of such obscurations..of the *th*, making *whe'r* of *whether* LOWELL. 2. The o. of religion is superstition 1879.

Obscure (ǫ̆bskiūᵊ·ɹ), *a.* (*sb.*) late ME. [a. OF. *obscur* :—L. *obscurus*, f. *ob-* OB- 1 + *scur-*, f. root *scu-*, Skr. *sku-* to cover; cf. L. *scutum*, Gr. σκευή, etc.] 1. Devoid of light; dim; hence, gloomy, dismal. 2. Of, pertaining to, or frequenting the darkness; hence, eluding sight 1605. 3. Of colour, etc.: Dark, sombre; in later use, dingy, dull 1490. 4. Indistinct, undefined; hardly perceptible to the eye; faint, 'light' 1593. **b.** Indistinctly perceived, felt, or heard 1597. 5. Of a place: Hidden, retired; remote from observation 1484. 6. Inconspicuous, undistinguished, unnoticed 1555. **b.** Of persons, their station, etc.: Unknown to fame; humble, lowly 1548. 7. *fig.* Not manifest to the mind or understanding; hidden, doubtful, vague, uncertain 1432. **b.** Of words, statements, etc.: Not perspicuous; hard to understand. Also, of a speaker or writer. 1495.

1. His lampe shall be put out in o. darkenesse *Prov.* xx. 20. *O. rays*, the dark or invisible heat-rays of the solar spectrum. 2. The o. Bird clamor'd the liue-long Night SHAKS. 3. An o. Yellow 1662. 4. **b.** E..where it endeth, and soundeth o. and faintly JONSON. 5. They pursue, even such as me, into the obscurest retreats BURKE. 6. The small and o. beginnings of great political institutions 1854. **b.** Their homely joys, and destiny o. GRAY. 7. The Cause and seat of this Disease, which is often o. 1732. **b.** A darke, o., and crabbed style 1573. Hence **Obscu·re·ly** *adv.*, **-ness** (now *rare*).

B. *sb.* 1. Obscurity, darkness; the 'outer darkness' 1667. 2. Indistinctness of outline or colour 1792.

1. Who shall..through the palpable o. find out His uncouth way MILT.

Obscure (ǫ̆bskiūᵊ·ɹ), *v.* late ME. [f. OBSCURE *a.*, or L. *obscurare.*] †1. *trans.* To make obscure or dark, to involve in darkness; to dim 1547. 2. To dim the lustre or glory of; to outshine 1548. 3. To hide from view 1604. †**b.** *intr.* (for *refl.*) To hide oneself -1632. 4. To conceal from knowledge or observation; to keep dark; to disguise. Also *refl.* 1530. 5. To render vague or unintelligible 1584.

1. Cynthia for shame obscures her silver shine SHAKS. *transf.* In modern English speech, vowels are regularly obscured in syllables that have neither primary nor subordinate stress *N.E.D.* Introd. 2. To deface and o. Godes glory LATIMER. 5. This language..serves not to elucidate, but to disguise and o. MILL.

Obscurity (ǫ̆bskiūᵊ·rĭti). late ME. [a. F. *obscurité*, ad. L. *obscuritatem*, f. *obscurus*; see -ITY.] 1. The quality or condition of being obscure; darkness 1456. 2. The quality or condition of being unknown or inconspicuous 1619. **b.** An inconspicuous or unknown person 1822. 3. The quality or condition of not being clearly known or comprehended 1474. 4. Unintelligibleness 1538. **b.** An obscure point; an unintelligible speech or passage. late ME.

1. We waite for light, but behold obscuritie *Isa.* lix. 9. 2. Suffering Worth Lost in o. THOMSON. 3. The thought is enuoluped in obscurete CAXTON. 4. One of the most pernicious effects of haste is o. JOHNSON. **b.** The obscurities of early Greek poets 1875.

Obsecrate (ǫ·bsĭkreⁱt), *v. rare, pedantic.* 1597. [f. L. *obsecrat-*, *obsecrare*, f. *ob* on account of + *sacrare* to make sacred.] *trans.* To entreat earnestly, as in the name of something sacred; to supplicate (a person); to beg (a thing).

Obsecration (ǫbsĭkrēⁱ·ʃən). late ME. [ad. L. *obsecrationem*; see prec.] 1. Earnest entreaty; occas. in orig. L. sense, entreaty made in the name of something sacred. **b.** *Rhet.* A figure by which the orator implores the assistance of God or man 1609. 2. *spec.* One of the suffrages or prayers of the Litany beginning with the word 'by' (L. *per*) 1877.

Obsequies: see OBSEQUY[2].

Obsequious (ǫ̆bsī·kwiəs), *a.* 1450. [ad. L. *obsequiosus* compliant, f. *obsequium* OBSEQUY[1].] 1. Compliant with the will of another; prompt to serve, please, or follow directions; obedient; dutiful. Now *rare.* †**b.** Through association with OBSEQUY[2]: Dutiful in manifesting regard for the dead; proper to obsequies -1674. 2. Servilely compliant; fawning, cringing, sycophantic 1602.

1. Was no man so obsequyous and seruiceable TINDALE. **b.** Bound In filiall Obligation..To do o. Sorrow SHAKS. 2. Following him out, with most o. politeness DICKENS. So **Obse·quious·ly** *adv.*, 1599, **-ness** 1447.

†**O·bsequy**[1]. late ME. [ad. L. *obsequium*, f. *ob-* (OB- 1) + *sequi* to follow.] Ready compliance with the will of another; deferential service; obsequiousness.

Obsequy[2]; now always in pl. **obsequies** (ǫ·bsĭkwiz). late ME. [a. AF. *obsequie* (also OF.), ad. med.L. *obsequiæ*, acc. pl. *obsequias.*] Funeral rites or ceremonies; a funeral. Sometimes including or denoting commemorative rites or services.

sing. Silent obsequie and funeral train MILT. *pl.* See perform'd their Fun'ral Obsequies DRYDEN. Hence **Obse·quial** *a.*

Observable (ǫ̆bzɔ̄·ɹvăb'l), *a.* and *sb.* 1608. [ad. L. *observabilis*, f. *observare*; see -ABLE.] 1. That must or may be observed, attended to, or kept. 2. Noticeable, perceptible 1646. 3. Noteworthy; formerly, †Remarkable, notable 1609. †**B.** *sb.* A noteworthy thing, fact, or circumstance. Chiefly in *pl.* -1822.

1. Forms o. in social intercourse H. SPENCER. 2. A marked change in public sentiment became at once o. 1874. 3. We met with nothing very o. JOHNSON. **Obse·rvably** *adv.*

Observance (ǫ̆bzɔ̄·ɹvăns). ME. [a. F., ad. L. *observantia*, f. *observantem*, *observare.*] **I.** 1. The action or practice of observing (a law, duty, ceremony, custom, rule, method, etc.). Const. *of*, †*to*. late ME. **b.** The keeping of a prescribed ritual. late ME. 2. A customary rite, custom ME. **b.** An ordinance to be observed; *esp.* the rule of a religious order; *spec.* of the Observants or stricter Franciscans. late ME.

1. A Custome More honour'd in the breach, then the obseruance SHAKS. **b.** For to doon his obseruaunce to May CHAUCER. 2. Superstitious observances ..will not..mend matters with us 1729.

II. Respectful or courteous attention, dutiful service. (Rarely const. *of*.) *arch.* ME.

He compass'd her with sweet observances TENNYSON.

III. †1. Observant care, heed -1660. 2. The action of paying attention; notice; watching 1600. Now *rare.*

1. *Haml.* III. ii. 21. 2. I passed, And pried, in every place, without o. MASSINGER.

Observancy (ǫ̆bzɔ̄·ɹvănsi). 1567. [ad. L. *observantia*; see -ANCY.] 1. The quality of being observant or observing; †the action of observing. 2. Respectful or obsequious attention. *arch.* 1601. 3. A House of the Observant Order. BROWNING.

Observant (ǫ̆bzɔ̄·ɹvănt), *a.* and *sb.* 1460. [a. F., pr. pple. of *observer* to OBSERVE (formerly as *sb.*).] **A.** *adj.* 1. Attentive in observing a law, custom, principle, etc. Const. *of*. 1608. †2. Showing respect, honour, or deference; assiduous in service; obsequious. Const. *of*, *to*. -1743. 3. Heedful 1627. 4. Attentive in marking; quick to perceive. Const. *of* (†*on*). 1602.

1. O. of the little niceties of phrase and manner 1829, of contracts 1834. 3. Scrupulously o. to avoid offending the prince GOLDSM. Hence **Obse·rvantly** *adv.*

B. *sb.* †1. One who observes a law, etc. -1613. 2. *spec.* A member of that branch of the Franciscan order which observes the strict rule; the other branch being the Conventuals 1460. †3. A dutiful servant -1617.

3. *Lear* II. ii. 109.

Observantine (ǫ̆bzɔ̄·ɹvăntin, ǫbzəɹvæ·ntin). 1646. [a. F. *Observantin*, f. OBSERVANT; see -INE[1].] = OBSERVANT B. 2.

Observation (ǫbzəɹvēⁱ·ʃən). late ME. [ad. L. *observationem*, f. *observare.*] 1. = OBSERVANCE I. 1. Now *rare* or *Obs.* 1533. †2. = OBSERVANCE I. 2. -1718. †3. = OBSERVANCE II. -1721. †4. = OBSERVANCE III. 1. -1673. 5. = OBSERVANCE III. 2. 1557. **b.** The faculty or habit of taking notice 1605. **c.** Attention to presages or omens; an act of augury or divination. (Now only in general sense.) 1605. **d.** *Mil.* The watching of a fortress, of an enemy's movements, etc. 1836. 6. The action or an act of observing scientifically a phenomenon in regard to its cause or effect, or phenomena in regard to their mutual relations, these being observed as they occur in nature (and so opp. to *experiment*); also, the record of this 1559. **b.** *spec.* The taking of the altitude of the sun (or other heavenly body), in order to find the latitude or longitude; the result obtained 1559. 7. Observed truth or fact; a rule or maxim gathered from experience. Now *rare.* 1600. 8. A remark in speech or writing in ref. to something observed 1593.

1. The o. of the Sabbath MACAULAY. 4. *Temp.* III. iii. 87. 5. They were..in less danger of o. MRS. RADCLIFFE. **b.** Men of narrow o. BACON. **d.** *Army* (*corps*, etc.) *of o.*, a force employed in watching an army of the enemy. 6. O...without experiment.. can ascertain sequences and coexistences, but cannot prove causation MILL. **b.** *To work an o.*, to ascertain the latitude or longitude by means of calculations based on the sun's altitude. 7. *A. Y. L.* II. vii. 41. 8. Tut, that 's a foolish obseruation SHAKS.

attrib. and *Comb.*, as *o.-balloon*, *-post*, etc.: **o.-car**, an open railway carriage, or one with glass sides; **-mine**, a mine (originally) fired from an observing station. Hence **Observa·tional** *a.* of or pertaining to (scientific) o.

Observative (ǫ̆bzɔ̄·ɹvătiv), *a.* 1611. [f. L. *observat-*, *observare* + -IVE.] Of or pertaining to observation; observant, heedful. Now *rare.*

†**O·bservator.** 1502. [ad. F. *observateur*, ad. L. *observator.* Earlier stress *observatou·r*, *obse·rvator*, *observa·tor*.] = OBSERVER -1798.

Observatory (ǫ̆bzɔ̄·ɹvătəri), *sb.* 1676. [ad. F. *observatoire* (1670), f. L. *observat-*, *observare* OBSERVE; see -ORY.] 1. A building or place for making observations of natural phenomena; esp. for astronomical, meteorological, or magnetic observations. 2. A position or building affording an extensive view 1695. 3. (*nonce-use.*) A place of observation. STEVENSON.

1. The new Observatorie in Greenewich Park EVELYN.

Obse·rvatory, *a.* 1864. [f. L. *observat-*, *observare*; see next and -ORY.] Of or pertaining to scientific observation, as, *o. work.*

Observe (ǫ̆bzɔ̄·ɹv), *v.* late ME. [a. F. *observer*, ad. L. *observare*, f. *ob-* OB- 1 + *servare* to watch, keep.] **I.** 1. *trans.* To adhere to or abide by in practice (anything prescribed or fixed). **b.** To adhere to, follow (a method, rule, etc.) 1548. 2. To hold or keep to (a manner of life or conduct, a habit); to maintain (a quality, state, etc.). late ME. 3. To celebrate duly (a religious rite, fast, festival, etc.) 1526.

1. They..o. Circumcision PURCHAS. **b.** In ordinary writing and speaking this rule is seldom observed 1870. 2. The people o. a dead silence 1843. 3. Ye shall o. the feast of unleavened bread *Exod.* xii. 17.

II. †To treat with ceremonious respect or

reverence; to worship, honour; to court; to humour –1754. *Jul. C.* IV. iii. 45. **III.** †**1.** To give heed to (a point); to take care *that* something be done, or *to do* something –1793. **2.** To regard with attention; to watch 1567. **b.** *spec.* To inspect for purposes of divination; to watch or take note of (presages or omens). late ME. **c.** *Mil.* To watch (a fortress, the enemy's movements, etc.); also *absol.* or *intr.* 1611. **d.** *absol.* or *intr.* To make observations 1604. †**3.** *trans.* To watch for in order to avail oneself of (a proper time, an opportunity) –1642. **4.** To notice, remark, perceive, see (a thing or fact) 1560. **5.** To perceive or learn by scientific inspection (without the aid of experiment) 1559. **b.** *spec.* To make an observation (see OBSERVATION 6 b) in order to determine the altitude of (the sun, etc.), to ascertain (the latitude or longitude, etc.); also *absol.* or *intr.* 1559.

1. If we obserue to doe all these Commandements *Deut.* vi. 25. 2. d. He has not observed on the nature of vanity who does not know that it is omnivorous BURKE. 5. *absol.* When, as in astronomy, we endeavour to ascertain these causes by simply watching their effects, we *observe* 1879.

IV. To say by way of remark; to mention in speech or writing 1605. **b.** *absol.*, or *intr.* with *on* or *upon*: To make an observation, to comment (on) 1613. Hence **Obse·rve** *sb.* † = OBSERVATION 5, 6, 7. –1830; = OBSERVATION 8 *Sc.* 1711. **Obse·rvedly** *adv.* notably. **Obse·rvership,** the office of Observer. **Obse·rving** *ppl. a.* that observes; observant; engaged in scientific observation. **Obse·rvingly** *adv.*

Observer (ǫbzǝ̄·ɹvəɹ). 1555. [f. prec. + -ER [1].] **1.** One who observes or keeps a law, rule, custom, practice, method, etc. †**2.** An obsequious follower –1633. **3.** One who watches, marks, or takes notice. (A frequent title of newspapers.) 1581. **b.** One who accompanies the pilot of a flying-machine to make military or other observations 1914. **4.** One who observes phenomena scientifically; occas. the official title of the person in charge of an observatory 1795.

1. Suppos'd to be a conceal'd o. of the Jewish law 1721. 3. He is a great Obseruer, and he lookes Quite through the Deeds of men SHAKS. **b.** *Mil.* One who makes observations, esp. in connexion with the firing of artillery 1903.

Obsess (ǫbse·s), *v.* 1503. [f. L. *obsess-, obsidere*, f. *ob-* OB- 1 + *sedere* to sit.] †**1.** *trans.* To sit down before (a fortress, the enemy); to besiege, invest –1647. **2.** Of an evil spirit: To beset (a person); to haunt; to actuate from without 1540. **3.** *transf.* To beset like a besieging force or an evil spirit; in mod. use *esp.* to haunt and trouble as a 'fixed idea' 1531.

Obsession (ǫbse·ʃən). 1513. [ad. L. *obsessionem*, f. *obsidere* to OBSESS.] †**1.** The action of besieging; investment, siege –1638. **2.** Actuation by the devil or an evil spirit from without; the fact of being thus actuated 1605. **3.** *transf.* The action of any influence, notion, or 'fixed idea', which persistently assails or vexes 1680.

2. These cases belong rather to o. than possession, the spirits not actually inhabiting the bodies, but hanging or hovering about them 1871. 3. The thought of death began to haunt him till it became a constant o. 1893. Hence **Obse·ssionist. Obse·ssive** *a.*

Obsidian (ǫbsi·diăn). 1656. [ad. erron. L. *obsidianus*, in edd. of Pliny for *obsianus*; so called from its resemblance to a stone found in Ethiopia by one *Obsius* (erron. *Obsidius*).] *Min.* A dark-coloured vitreous lava or volcanic rock, of varying composition, resembling common bottle-glass; volcanic glass 1796. **b.** Also *o. stone* (*lapis Obsi*(*di*)*anus*).

Obsidional (ǫbsi·diǫnăl), *a.* 1430. [ad. L. *obsidionalis*, f. *obsidionem*, *obsidere*; see OBSESS *v.*] **1.** Of or pertaining to a siege. **2.** *fig.* Besetting, obsidious 1879.

1. *O. crown* (*coronet, garland, wreath*), tr. L. *corona obsidionalis*, a wreath of grass or weeds conferred as a mark of honour upon a Roman general who raised a siege. *O. coins*, coins struck in a besieged city to supply the want of current coins.

†**Obsi·gnate,** *v.* 1653. [f. L. *obsignat-, obsignare*, f. *ob-* OB- 1 + *signare* to seal.] *trans.* To seal; to mark as with a seal; to ratify or confirm formally –1677. So †**Obsi·gn** *v.* 1554–1670.

Obsignation (ǫbsignē̆·ʃən). Now *rare.* 1568. [ad. L. *obsignationem*; see prec.] The action of sealing; formal ratification or confirmation as by sealing.

Obsignatory (ǫbsi·gnătəri), *a.* Now *rare.* 1630. [f. L. *obsignat-, obsignare*; see -ORY.] Having the function of, or pertaining to, obsignation; ratifying or confirming as with a seal.

Obsolesce (ǫbsǫle·s), *v. rare.* 1873. [ad. L. *obsolescere* to grow old, etc., inchoative form of **obsolere*, f. *ob-* OB- 1 + *solere* to be accustomed.] *intr.* To be obsolescent; to fall into disuse.

Obsolescence (ǫbsǫle·sĕns). 1828. [f. as next; see -ENCE.] **1.** The process of becoming obsolete. **2.** *Biol.* The gradual disappearance or atrophy of an organ or part, esp. from disuse 1852.

Obsolescent (ǫbsǫle·sĕnt), *a.* 1755. [ad. L. *obsolescentem*; see OBSOLESCE *v.*] **1.** Becoming obsolete; going out of use or date. **2.** *Biol.* Gradually disappearing; imperfectly or slightly developed; said of an organ, structure, or mark, which was formerly fully developed or well-marked 1846.

1. The stronghold of o. opinions 1863.

Obsolete (ǫ·bsǫlīt), *a.* (*sb.*) 1579. [ad. L. *obsoletus*, pa. pple. of *obsolescere*; see OBSOLESCE.] **1.** That is no longer practised or used; discarded; out of date. **2.** Worn out; effaced through wearing down, atrophy, or degeneration 1832. **3.** *Biol.* Indistinct; not clearly marked; very imperfectly developed 1760. **B.** *absol.* or *sb.* One who or that which is out of date or has fallen into disuse 1748.

1. Olde and o. wordes 1579. One o. ironclad 1884. 2. Cases of o. tubercle 1897. Hence **O·bsolete** *v.* (now *rare*), *trans.* to render or account o.; to disuse. **O·bsolete-ly** *adv.*, **-ness. Obsole·tion,** the action of becoming or condition of being o. **O·bsoletism,** an o. term, phrase, custom, etc.; obsoleteness.

Obstacle (ǫ·bstăk'l). ME. [a. OF., ad. L. *obstaculum*, f. *obstare* to withstand.] **1.** A hindrance, impediment, obstruction. †**2.** Resistance, objection; in phr. *to make o.*, to offer opposition –1632.

1. He should remove the O. which prevented the Use of his Sight STEELE. *Comb.*, as **o.-race,** a race in which impediments have to be surmounted.

Obstetric, -al (ǫbste·trik, -ăl), *adjs.* 1742. [ad. mod.L. *obstetricus*, for L. *obstetricius*, f. *obstetrix*, *-tricem* midwife.] Of or pertaining to a midwife or accoucheur, or to midwifery as a branch of medical practice.

Obstetrical toad, the nurse-frog, *Alytes obstetricans.* So **Obste·trically** *adv.* 1759.

†**Obste·tricate,** *v.* 1623. [f. ppl. stem of L. *obstetricare*, f. *obstetricem.*] **1.** *intr.* To act as midwife; to aid in childbirth –1809. **2.** *trans.* To help the delivery of. Chiefly *fig.* –1741. So †**Obstetrica·tion** (*rare*) 1615–1823.

Obstetrician (ǫbstĕtri·ʃăn). 1828. [f. L. *obstetricia* midwifery + -AN.] One skilled in obstetrics; an accoucheur.

Obstetrics (ǫbste·triks). 1819. [pl. of OBSTETRIC; see -IC 2.] The branch of medical practice which deals with parturition, and its antecedents and sequels; the practice of midwifery.

Obstinacy (ǫ·bstinăsi). late ME. [ad. med. L. *obstinatia*, f. *obstinatus* OBSTINATE; see -ACY.] The quality or condition of being obstinate; stubbornness, persistency; *spec.* of a disease. Rarely in neutral or good sense. **b.** With *an* and *pl.* An act or instance of this 1628.

1. O. in a bad cause, is but constancy in a good SIR T. BROWNE. [He] adhered to his own opinion with his usual o. 1769. The o. of the disease 1808. **b.** An o. against the Laws HOBBES. So **O·bstinance, O·bstinancy** (*rare*).

Obstinate (ǫ·bstinĕt), *a.* (*sb.*) ME. [ad. L. *obstinatus*, *obstinare* (deriv. of *obstare*) to persist.] **1.** Pertinacious in adhering to one's own course; not yielding to argument, persuasion, or entreaty; inflexible, headstrong, self-willed. Rarely in neutral or good sense. **2.** Unyielding, rigid, stiff; *spec.* of a disease, etc., not yielding readily to treatment; stubborn 1638. **B.** *sb.* A stubborn or inflexible person 1502.

1. The o. Man does not hold Opinions, but they hold him 1680. 2. An o. sleeplessness JOHNSON, diarrhœa 1871. So **O·bstinate** *v.* (now *rare*), to render o.; to cause to persist stubbornly. Also *refl.* (= F. *s'obstiner*). **O·bstinate-ly** *adv.*, **-ness.** †**Obstina·tion,** obstinacy.

Obstipation (ǫbstipē̆·ʃən). 1597. [ad. L. *obstipationem*, n. of action f. **obstipare*, f. *ob-* OB- 1 + *stipare* to press together, pack.] The action of blocking or stopping up; *Med.* extreme constipation. So †**O·bstipate** *v.* (*rare*) –1702.

Obstreperous (ǫbstre·pĕrəs), *a.* 1600. [f. L. *obstreperus* (f. *obstrepere* to make a noise against) + -OUS.] **1.** Characterized by great noise or outcry, esp. in opposition; clamorous; vociferous. **2.** Turbulent or unruly, esp. in resistance 1657.

1. They [ravens] sate all night, Beating the ayre with their o. beakes B. JONS. The most careless and o. merriment JOHNSON. 2. Becoming remarkably o. when thwarted 1874. Hence **Obstre·perous-ly** *adv.*, **-ness.**

†**Obstri·nge,** *v. rare.* 1528. [ad. L. *obstringere*, f. *ob-* OB- 1 + *stringere* to tie, bind.] *trans.* To put under obligation; to bind –1660. So **Obstri·ction,** obligation.

Obstruct (ǫbstrʊ·kt), *v.* 1611. [f. L. *obstruct-, obstruere* to build against, etc., f. *ob-* OB- 1 + *struere.*] **1.** *trans.* To block, close up, or fill (a way or passage) with obstacles or impediments; to render impassable or difficult of passage. **2.** To interrupt or render difficult the passage or progress of; to impede, hinder, or retard (a person or thing in its motion) 1655. **3.** *fig.* To stand in the way of, or persistently oppose the progress or course of (proceedings, or a person or thing in a purpose or action); to impede, retard, withstand, stop 1647. **4.** To interrupt, shut out (the sight or view of) 1717.

1. The door is now so obstructed with Stones 1703. 2. The Wind..obstructs the coming of any letters from Holland 1688. 3. I don't know if it be just thus to o. the union of man and wife GOLDSM. *To o. process* (in *Law*): to commit the punishable offence of intentionally hindering the officers of the law in the execution of their duties. 4. There was nothing to o. the view GEO. ELIOT.

Obstruction (ǫbstrʊ·kʃən). 1533. [ad. L. *obstructionem*; see prec.] **1.** The action of obstructing; the condition of being obstructed; frequently in ref. to passages, organs, or functions of the body; *esp.* the ill-condition produced by constipation of the bowels. **2.** *fig.* The hindering or stopping of the course, performance, or doing of anything; *spec.* the persistent attempt to stop the progress of business, e. g. in the House of Commons 1656. **3.** Anything that stops or blocks a way or passage, or hinders or prevents progress; an obstructing obstacle 1597.

1. This does make some o. in the blood: This crosse-gartering SHAKS. He advanced without further o. to the capital 1841. O. of the Eustachian tube 1844. *Cold o.*, stoppage of the vital functions, the condition of the body in death. 2. That practice of talking against time which has more recently become famous under the name of o. 1880. 3. The great o. to generosity in our nature is jealousy 1876.

Comb., **o.-guard,** a bar, etc. fixed in front of a railway engine to remove an o. from the rails. Hence **Obstru·ctionist,** one who advocates or systematically practises o. 1846; so **Obstru·ctionism.**

Obstructive (ǫbstrʊ·ktiv), *a.* (*sb.*) 1611. [f. L. *obstruct-, obstruere* (see OBSTRUCT) + -IVE.] **A.** *adj.* **1.** Obstructing; tending to obstruct; causing impediment. Const. *of, to.* **2.** Of, pertaining to, or of the nature of obstruction of the bowels or of any bodily duct or passage 1620.

1. Academies may be said to be o. to energy and inventive genius M. ARNOLD.

B. *sb.* **1.** An obstructive agent, instrument, or force; a hindrance 1642. **2.** One who obstructs, esp. in parliamentary business 1856.

1. Episcopacy..was instituted as an o. to the diffusion of Schisme and Heresy JER. TAYLOR. Hence **Obstru·ctive-ly** *adv.*, **-ness. Obstru·ctivism.**

Obstructor (ǫbstrʊ·ktəɹ). 1649. [f. L. *obstruct-, obstruere* to OBSTRUCT.] One who or that which obstructs; a hinderer; an opponent of progress.

Obstruent (ǫ·bstruĕnt), *a.* and *sb.* 1669. [ad. L. *obstruentem*; see OBSTRUCT.] **A.** *adj.* Obstructing; *Med.* closing up the ducts or passages of the body 1755. **B.** *sb.* Something that obstructs, an obstruction; *Med.* a medicine which closes the orifices of ducts or vessels, or the natural passages of the body.

Obstupefy (ǫbstiū·pĭfəi), *v.* 1613. [f. L. *obstupefacere*, after STUPEFY.] *trans.* To stupefy, esp. mentally. So †**Obstu·pefact** *a.*, **-fa·ction, -fa·ctive** *a.*

Obtain (ǫbtēⁱ·n), *v.* [late ME. *obteine*, a. F. *obtenir*, ad. L. *obtinere*, f. *ob-* OB- 1 + *tenere* to hold, keep. Cf. CONTAIN.] **1.** *trans.* To procure or gain, as the result of purpose and effort; hence, generally, to acquire, get. Also *absol.* †**2.** To gain, win (a battle or other contest) –1649. **3.** *intr.* To gain the day, prevail; to succeed, prosper. *Obs.* or *arch.* late ME. **4.** To attain to, get as far as, reach, gain. *Obs.* or *arch.* 1477. †**b.** with *inf.* To attain or come *to be, to do*, etc.; to succeed in doing something –1703. †**5.** To hold; to possess; to occupy. (A Latin sense.) –1710. **6.** *intr.* To prevail; to be in force or in vogue; to hold good, have place, subsist, exist. 1618.

1. Blessed are the merciful: for they shall obteyne mercy TINDALE *Matt.* v. 7. Obtaining Pardon by Mony, or other rewards HOBBES. 3. This, though it failed at present, yet afterwards obtained SWIFT. 5. He who obtains the Monarchy of Heav'n MILT. 6. Laws of nature which universally o. 1764. Hence **Obtai·nable** *a.* **Obtai·nal** (*rare*) 1803, **Obtai·nment**, the action of getting. **Obtai·ner.**

Obtected (ǫbte·ktėd), *ppl. a.* 1816. [f. L. *obtectus*, *obtegere* + -ED.] *Entom.* **a.** Covered by a neighbouring part. **b.** Of pupæ: Having the limbs, etc., of the future insect indistinctly discernible through the outer covering (opp. to *coarctate*); in later use occas. including *coarctate*. Also said of the metamorphosis in which such pupæ occur.

Obtemper (ǫbte·mpəɹ), *v.* 1450. [a. F. *obtempérer*, ad. L. *obtemperare* to obey, f. *ob-* OB- 1 + *temperare* to restrain oneself.] *trans.* To comply with, submit to, obey; now only in *Sc. Law*, to obey (a judgement or order of a court). †**b.** *intr.* with *to* –1584.

Obtemperate (ǫbte·mpĕreⁱt), *v.* late ME. [f. L. *obtemperat-*, *obtemperare*; see prec.] *trans.* and *intr.* = prec.

†**Obte·nd**, *v.* 1573. [ad. L. *obtendere* to spread in front of, f. *ob-* OB- 1 + *tendere* to stretch.] **1.** *trans.* To put forward as a statement, reason, etc.; to pretend –1700. **2.** To hold out; to present in opposition; to oppose –1725.

Obtenebrate (ǫbte·nĭbreⁱt), *v.* 1611. [f. L. *obtenebrat-*, *obtenebrare*, f. *ob-* OB- 1 + *tenebrare* to make dark.] *trans.* To overshadow, darken. Hence **Obtenebra·tion**, the action of overshadowing; being overshadowed.

Obtention (ǫbte·nʃən). 1624. [a. F., f. *obtenir*, L. *obtinere*, *obtent-* to OBTAIN; cf. *detention*, etc.] The action of obtaining; obtainment.

Obtest (ǫbte·st), *v.* 1548. [ad. L. *obtestari* to protest by, f. *ob* on account of + *testari*.] **1.** *trans.* To adjure; to beg earnestly, beseech, supplicate (a person *that* . ., or *to do* something). **2.** *intr.* or with dependent clause: **a.** To make earnest supplication or entreaty. **b.** To call heaven to witness, to protest 1650.

2. Obtesting Deputies o. vainly CARLYLE.

Obtestation (ǫbtestēⁱ·ʃən). 1531. [ad. L. *obtestationem*; see prec.] **1.** A beseeching by some sacred name; supplication. **2.** The action of calling (the Deity, etc.) to witness 1555.

†**Obtre·ct**, *v.* Also **obtract.** 1596. [ad. L. *obtrectare*, f. *ob-* OB- 1 + *tractare* to drag.] *trans.* To detract from, to disparage, decry –1617. So †**Obtrecta·tion**, detraction, slander 1563. †**O·btrectator**, detractor. late ME.

Obtrude (ǫbtrū·d), *v.* 1555. [ad. L. *obtrudere*, f. *ob-* OB- 1 + *trudere* to thrust.] **1.** *trans.* To thrust forth; to eject, push out. Also *refl.* 1613. **2.** To thrust forward forcibly or unduly; to thrust (a matter, person, etc.) *upon* any one. Const. *on, upon, into* (†*to, unto*). 1555. Also *refl.* **b.** *intr.* (for *refl.*) To be or become obtrusive; to intrude, force oneself 1579.

2. A man of low birth . ., obtruded on them . . by the king for their general FULLER. Subordinate officials, who . . obtruded themselves into matters beyond their office 1847. b. Let us not o. Upon her sorrows' holy solitude 1844. Hence **Obtru·der.**

Obtruncate (ǫbtrʋ·ŋkeⁱt), *v.* 1623. [f. L. *obtruncat-*, *obtruncare* to cut off, f. *ob-* OB- 1 + *truncare*, to maim.] *trans.* To top, decapitate. So **Obtrunca·tion.**

Obtrusion (ǫbtrū·ʒən). 1579. [f. L. *obtrusionem*, f. *obtrudere* to OBTRUDE.] **1.** The action of obtruding (anything) into any space or place, or against anything else 1847. **2.** The importunate thrusting of some one or something (upon one, or upon one's attention); also *concr.* something thus thrust upon one 1641. **b.** The forcing of oneself or one's company upon any one.

2. Disturbed by the o. of new ideas JOHNSON.

Obtrusive (ǫbtrū·siv), *a.* 1667. [f. L. *obtrus-*, *obtrudere* + -IVE.] **1.** Projecting so as to be in the way 1842. **2.** Forward, unduly prominent.

2. Not obvious, not o., but retir'd, The more desirable MILT. Hence **Obtru·sive-ly** *adv.*, **-ness.**

Obtund (ǫbtʋ·nd), *v.* late ME. [ad. L. *obtundere*, f. *ob-* OB- 1 + *tundere* to beat.] *trans.* To blunt, deaden, dull, render obtuse (the faculties, physical qualities, etc.). Chiefly in medical use.

The sense of smell is obtunded 1872.

Obtundent (ǫbtʋ·ndĕnt), *a.* and *sb.* 1842. [ad. L. *obtundentem*; see prec.] **a.** *adj.* Dulling sensibility. **b.** *sb.* A substance used to do this; a demulcent.

Obturate (ǫ·btiureⁱt), *v.* 1628. [f. L. *obturat-*, *obturare* to stop up.] *trans.* To stop up, close, obstruct.

Obturation (ǫbtiurēⁱ·ʃən). 1610. [ad. L. *obturationem*; see prec.] The action of stopping up; obstruction of an opening or channel; *spec.* in *Gunnery* (see next, 2 b).

Obturator (ǫ·btiureⁱtəɹ). 1727. [a. med.L.; see OBTURATE *v.*] Something that stops up. **1.** *Anat.* (usu. *attrib.*) Name of a membrane (**o. membrane**, or **o. ligament**) which closes the thyroid foramen; applied also to structures connected with this. **2.** An artificial device for stopping an opening. *spec.* **a.** *Surg.* A plate, etc., for closing an opening of the body, esp. an abnormal opening, as in cleft palate. **b.** *Gunnery.* A gas-check. **c.** A shutter of a photographic camera. 1862.

1. **O. foramen**, a large opening in the os innominatum, representing the division between the ischium and pubis. **O. muscles**, two muscles (*o. externus* and *o. internus*) serving for rotation, etc., of the thigh. **O. nerve**, a branch of the lumbar plexus, having twigs distributed to the hip and knee joints and various muscles of the thigh.

Obtusangular (ǫbtiusˌæ·ŋgiŭlăɹ), *a.* Now *rare* or *Obs.* 1680. [See next and ANGULAR.] = *Obtuse-angled.*

Obtuse (ǫbtiū·s), *a.* 1509. [ad. L. *obtusus*, pa. pple. of *obtundere* to OBTUND.] Blunt; opp. to *acute*. **1.** *lit.* Of a blunt form; not sharp or pointed; *esp.* in *Nat. Hist.* of parts or organs of animals or plants 1589. **2.** *Geom.* Of a plane angle: Greater than a right angle; exceeding 90° 1570. **3.** *fig.* Indistinctly felt or perceived; dull 1620. **4.** Not acutely sensitive or perceptive; stupid, insensible 1509.

1. A blow with an o. weapon 1767. 2. *O. cone*, a cone of which the section by a plane through the axis has an o. angle at the vertex. *O. hyperbola*, a hyperbola lying within the o. angles between its asymptotes. 3. I . . felt an o. pain . . in my stomach 1790. 4. O. in his understanding, but kind and faithful in his disposition SCOTT. *Comb.*, as **o.-angled** *a.*, having an o. angle or angles; also in *Nat. Hist.*, with another adj., expressing a combination of forms, as **o.-ellipsoid.** Hence **Obtu·se-ly** *adv.*, **-ness.**

Obtusi- (ǫbtiū·si), comb. form of L. *obtusus* OBTUSE, as in **Obtusifo·lious** *a.*, having obtuse leaves; etc.

Obtusity (ǫbtiū·sĭti). 1805. [ad. med.L. *obtusitas*, f. *obtusus*; see -ITY.] The quality of being obtuse, obtuseness; dullness, stupidity.

His combined conceit and o. POE.

Obumbrate (ǫbʋ·mbrĕt), *a.* *rare.* 1513. [ad. L. *obumbratus*; see next.] †**a.** Overshadowed, darkened –1632. **b.** *Entom.* Concealed under some overhanging part, as the abdomen in some spiders 1826.

Obumbrate (ǫbʋ·mbreⁱt), *v.* Now *rare.* 1526. [f. L. *obumbrat-*, *obumbrare*, f. *ob-* OB- 1 + *umbrare*.] **1.** *trans.* To overshadow; to shade, darken; to obscure. ¶**2.** Misused for ADUMBRATE 3. 1632.

So **Obumbra·tion** (now *rare*) late ME.

‖ **Obus** (obüs, -z). 1871. [F., ad. G. *haubitze*; see HOWITZ.] A howitzer shell.

Obvention (ǫbve·nʃən). 1459. [a. F., or ad. L. *obventionem* revenue, f. *obvenire* to happen to.] That which comes to one incidentally; in *Eccl. Law*, an (occasional) incoming fee or revenue.

†**Obve·rsant**, *a.* 1579. [ad. L. *obversantem*, *obversari*, f. *obversus* OBVERSE.] Standing over against, opposite; also, placed in front of; hence, familiar, well-known –1754.

Obverse (ǫ·bvəɹs), *a.* and *sb.* 1656. [ad. L. *obversus*, *obvertere* to OBVERT.] **A.** *adj.* **1.** Turned towards or against; opposite. **2.** Of a figure: Narrower at the base or point of attachment than at the apex or top; *spec.* in *Nat. Hist.* Also in *comb.* = obversely, OB- 2, as *obverse-lunate*. 1826. **3.** Answering to something else as its counterpart 1875. **B.** *sb.* **1.** That side of a coin, medal, seal, etc. on which the head or principal design is struck; the opposite of *reverse* 1658. **2.** The face or side of anything intended to be presented to view; *front* as opp. to *back* 1831. **b.** *fig.* The counterpart of any fact or truth 1862. **3.** *Logic.* A proposition obtained by OBVERSION 1870.

B. 2. b. Here you have the two sides—the science of medicine, and its o., the practice of witchcraft 1862. Hence **Obve·rsely** *adv.* in an o. form or manner; with an adj. of shape = OB- 2.

Obversion (ǫbvə̄·ɹʃən). 1864. [ad. L. *obversionem*; see OBVERT.] **1.** The action of turning towards some person or thing. **2.** *Logic.* A form of immediate inference in which, by changing the quality, from one proposition another is inferred having a contradictory predicate 1870.

Obvert (ǫbvə̄·ɹt), *v.* 1623. [ad. L. *obvertere*, f. *ob-* OB- 1 + *vertere* to turn.] †**1.** *trans.* To turn (something) towards; to place fronting –1781. †**2.** To turn (a thing) in a contrary direction –1657. **3.** *Logic.* To change the quality of (a proposition) in the way of OBVERSION 1870.

Obviate (ǫ·bviˌeⁱt), *v.* 1567. [f. L. *obviat-*, *obviare*, f. *ob* against + *via* way.] †**1.** *trans.* To meet, encounter; hence, to withstand, oppose –1702. **2.** To meet and dispose of or do away with; to prevent by anticipatory measures 1598.

2. The remedies and means to o. these dangers CROMWELL. So **Obvia·tion**, prevention. late ME.

Obvious (ǫ·bviəs), *a.* 1586. [f. L. *obvius* in the way (f. *ob* against + *via* way) + -OUS.] **1.** Lying or standing in the way; placed in front of or over against; fronting. *Obs.* or *arch.* 1594. †**2.** Open *to* (action or influence); liable –1772. †**3.** Coming in one's way; frequently met or found –1772. **4.** Plain and open to the eye or mind, perfectly evident; palpable 1635. **b.** *Zool.* Plainly visible, evident, as *an o. marking* or *stripe*; opp. to *obscure*.

1. No more rejoycing in the o. Light DRAYTON. 2. The Pedant is so o. to Ridicule STEELE. 4. Things present are o. to the sense, things to come to our Reason only HOBBES. It appears o. to me, that one or the other of those two great men . . must be minister BURKE. c. quasi-*sb.*, *The obvious*: that which is obvious. Hence **O·bvious-ly** *adv.*, **-ness.**

Obvolute (ǫ·bvŏliūt), *a.* 1760. [ad. L. *obvolut-*, *obvolvere*; see next.] *Bot.* Applied to a vernation in which two leaves are so folded in the bud that half of one enrolls half of another.

Obvolve (ǫbvǫ·lv), *v.* *rare.* 1623. [f. L. *obvolvere*, f. *ob-* OB- 1 + *volvere* to roll.] *trans.* To wrap round, muffle up; to disguise. So **Obvolu·tion** (*rare*), the wrapping of a bandage round a limb; also, †a fold or twist 1578.

Obvolvent (ǫbvǫ·lvĕnt), *a.* 1857. [f. pres. pple. of *obvolvere*; see -ENT.] Wrapping round; *Entom.* curving inward or downward.

‖ **Oca** (ōu·kă). 1604. [Sp., a. Peruv. *occa.*] Either of two S. Amer. species of *Oxalis*, *O. crenata* and *O. tuberosa*, cultivated for their edible tubers.

Ocarina (ǫkărī·nă). 1877. [f. It. *oca* goose (in ref. to its shape) + -INA [1].] A musical instrument consisting of an egg-shaped terra-cotta body with a whistle-like mouthpiece and finger-holes.

Occamist (ǫ·kămist). 1550. [f. name *Occam* or *Ockham* + -IST.] A disciple or follower of William of Occam (early 14th c.), the 'Invincible Doctor', who revived the tenets of the Nominalists. Hence **O·ccamism**, the doctrine or system of the Occamists 1837.

Occamy (ǫ·kămi). 1596. [A corrupt form of *alcomye*, *alcamy*, ALCHEMY.] A metallic composition imitating silver.

Occasion (ǫkēⁱ·ʒən), *sb.* late ME. [ad. L. *occasionem* falling (of things) towards (each other), juncture, etc., in late L. also f. *occidere*, f. *ob-* OB- 1 + *cadere* to fall.] **I. 1.** A favourable juncture of circumstances; an opportunity. **b.** Personified (see FORELOCK *sb.*[2] 2). 1592. **2.** = CAUSE *sb.* I. 3. late ME. †**b.** A pretext, an excuse -1649. **3.** = CAUSE *sb.* I. 1. Const. *of*, †*that*. late ME. **b.** A subsidiary or incidental cause. Dist. from *cause* = 'efficient cause' (CAUSE *sb.* I. 4). 1605. **c.** A person who (*esp.* incidentally) brings about something 1548. †**d.** The action of causing or occasioning. Also *transf.* That which is caused or occasioned. -1600. †**4.** That which gives rise to discussion or consideration; the subject treated -1651.

1. Phr. *To take o.*, to take advantage of an opportunity (to do something); I took o. to go up and to bed in a pet PEPYS. 2. †*Evil o.*, inducement to sin, 'offence', 'stumbling-block' (= Gr. σκάνδαλον in N.T.) TINDALE. 3. *To give o. to*, to give rise to, to occasion; A mistake which had given o. to a burst of merriment JOHNSON. b. It [medicine] considereth causes of diseases, with the occasions or impulsions BACON. d. By the occasyon of duke Huon of Burdeaux, he had loste .iiii. of his nephues BERNERS.

II. 1. Necessity or need arising from a juncture of circumstances. Const. *for* (†*of*) or *inf.* 1576. †**b.** A particular, esp. a personal, need, want, or requirement. Chiefly in *pl.* = needs, requirements -1807. **2.** Necessary business; a matter, piece of business, business engagement. Chiefly *pl.*, affairs, business. Now *arch.* 1594. †**b.** *pl.* Necessities of nature -1789.

1. When he had o. to be seene, He was but as the Cuckow is in Iune, Heard, not regarded SHAKS. b. *Merch. V.* I. i. 139. 2. Such as pass on the seas vpon their lawfull occasions 1662 *Bk. Com. Prayer.*

III. †**1.** A juncture of circumstances (in itself); an event, incident, circumstance -1649. †**b.** *gen.* The course of events or circumstances SHAKS. **2.** A particular casual occurrence or juncture; the time at which something happens; a particular time marked by some occurrence or by its special character. †Formerly occas.: A case, an instance. 1568. **3. a.** A religious function; in Scotland, a Communion service. *arch.* or *Obs.* 1789. **b.** A special ceremony or celebration; a 'function', an 'event'. Chiefly *colloq.* 1860.

1. b. With-hold thy speed, dreadfull O. SHAKS. 2. Vpon the next o. that we meete SHAKS. On the o. of her marriage with Mr. — (*mod.*). 3. b. It was a great o. (*mod.*).

Phrases. *On* or *upon o.*, as o. or opportunity arises. *On* or *upon o. of*, in casual connexion with. *For (on, upon) one's o.*, on one's account, for one's sake.

Occasion (ǫkēⁱ·ʒən), *v.* 1530. [f. prec.; = F. *occasionner.*] †**1.** *trans.* To give occasion to (a person); to induce; also, to do this habitually; hence, to habituate, accustom -1684. **2.** To be the occasion or cause of (something); to cause, bring about, esp. in an incidental or subsidiary manner 1596. †**3.** *Occasioned by*, in consequence of -1725.

2. I occasioned much mirth with a ballet I brought with me PEPYS. 3. Some of which..were drowned, unable to swim to shore occasioned by age 1634. So **Occa·sioner** (now *rare*), one who or that which occasions 1452.

Occasional (ǫkēⁱ·ʒənăl), *a.* (*sb.*) 1568. [f. OCCASION *sb.* + -AL; cf. late L. *occasionaliter*, F. *occasionnel.*] †**1.** That happens casually or incidentally; casual -1654. **2.** Happening or operating on some particular occasion; limited to specific occasions; arising out of, required by, or made for, the occasion 1631. **b.** Of an article of use, building, piece of furniture, etc.: Made or constructed for the occasion; adapted for use on special occasions 1760. **c.** Of persons: Acting or employed for the occasion or on particular occasions 1759. **3.** Taking place, occurring, or met with now and then 1630. **4.** Serving as the occasion or incidental cause. Rarely const. *of*. 1646. **B.** *sb.* An occasional workman, etc. (cf. CASUAL B. 3.) 1892.

2. His o. going from the Sermon, being forced thereunto by the Extremity of the Toothach 1677. *O. Conformity*, a phr. applied after 1700 to the practice of persons who, in order to qualify themselves for office, received the Sacrament according to the rites of the Church of England, and afterwards during their office were present at any dissenting meeting for worship. *O. Conformist*, one who practised this. b. A loo, or o. table 1875. c. The o. soldier is no match for the professional soldier. MACAULAY. *O. speaker, writer*, etc., one who makes speeches for particular occasions or writes o. verses, pamphlets, etc. 3. An o. raid upon his neighbour's moveables 1881. 4. *O. cause* (*Metaph.*), (*a*) a secondary cause whereby or whereupon the primary cause comes into operation; (*b*) in the Cartesian philosophy: see next. Hence **Occasiona·lity**, the quality or fact of being o. **Occa·sionally** *adv.*, †on occasion; †incidentally; now and then.

Occasionalism (ǫkēⁱ·ʒənăliz'm). 1842. [f. prec. + -ISM, after G. *occasionalismus.*] The doctrine of the Cartesian philosopher Geulincx which accounted for the interaction of mind and matter by supposing that on occasion of every volition God produces a corresponding movement of the body and on occasion of every affection of the body a corresponding idea, mind and body thus standing to each other in the relation of occasional causes. So **Occa·sionalist** 1776.

†**Occa·sionate**, *v.* 1545. [f. med.L. *occasionat-*, *occasionare*, f. *occasionem.*] *trans.* = OCCASION *v.* 1, 2. -1647.

Occident (ǫ·ksidĕnt). Chiefly *poet.* late ME. [a. F., ad. L. *occidentem* setting, sunset, west, orig. pr. pple. of *occidere*, f. *ob-* OB- 1 + *cadere* to fall. Opp. to ORIENT.] **1.** That quarter of the sky in which the sun and other heavenly bodies set, or the corresponding region of the earth; the west. Now *rare*. **2.** Western countries, the West; i.e. orig., the countries of Western Europe, or of Europe as opp. to Asia and the Orient; also, now, America. late ME.

1. His [the sun's] bright passage to the O. SHAKS.

Occidental (ǫkside·ntăl), *a.* and *sb.* late ME. [a. F., ad. L. *occidentalis* western; see prec. and -AL. Opp. to ORIENTAL.] **A.** *adj.* **1.** Belonging to, situated in, or directed towards the Occident; of or in the west, western, westerly. **2.** Belonging to, found in, or characteristic of, western countries or regions of the earth (i.e. usu. those west of Asia); belonging to or situated in the West; Western 1553. **3.** Applied to precious stones of inferior value and brilliancy, as opp. to ORIENTAL *a.* 4. 1747.

1. *All's Well* II. i. 166. *fig.* Vpon the setting of that bright Occidentall Starre, Queene Elizabeth of most happy memory BIBLE, *Transl. Ded.* [With allusion to 2.]

B. *sb.* †**a.** A western country or region; *the o.*, the west 1829. **b.** A native or inhabitant of the West 1857. Hence **Occide·ntalism**, o. quality, style, character, or spirit; the customs, institutions, etc., of Western nations. **Occide·ntalist**, one who favours Western customs, modes of thought, etc.; one who studies the languages and institutions of Western nations. **Occidenta·lity**, **Occide·ntalize** *v.* to render o. **Occide·ntally** *adv.*

Occipital (ǫksi·pităl), *a.* (*sb.*) 1541. [ad. late or med.L. *occipitalis*, f. *occiput*, *occipit-*: see OCCIPUT and -AL.] **1.** Belonging to, or situated in or on, the occiput or back part of the head. Chiefly *Anat.*, as *o. artery, bone, condyle*, etc. **2.** Having a large occiput 1873. **B.** *sb.* **a.** The occipital bone. **b.** The occipital muscle. **c.** *pl.* A pair of occipital plates on the head of some serpents. 1758.

1. *O. bone*, the bone forming the last part of the cranium between the parietal and temporal bones. *O. muscle*, the hinder part of the occipito-frontalis muscle. Hence **Occi·pitally** *adv.*

Occipito- (ǫksi·pito), bef. a vowel occas. occipit-, used in *Anat.* as comb. form of OCCIPUT, in adjs. expressing a relation or connexion between the occiput and another part, and denominating a ligament, muscle, measurement, etc.: as, **o. -a·xial, -a·xoid**, pertaining to the occiput and the axis vertebra; **-fro·ntal**, pertaining to, or extending between, the back of the head and the forehead; also *ellipt.* as *sb.*, the *o.-frontal muscle* or *occipitofrontalis*, the large flat muscle of the scalp; **-ma·stoid**, pertaining to the occiput and the mastoid process, etc.

Occiput (ǫ·ksipʋt). late ME. [L., f. *ob-* against + *caput* head.] Chiefly *Anat.* The back or hinder part of the head. **b.** The occipital bone of the skull 1578.

†**Occi·sion.** ME. [a. F., ad. L. *occisionem.*] Killing, slaying; slaughter -1677.

Occlude (ǫklū·d), *v.* 1597. [ad. L. *occ-*, *obcludere* to shut up, f. *ob-* OB- 1 + *claudere* to close.] **1.** *trans.* To shut or stop up, obstruct (a passage), close (a vessel or opening). **2.** To prevent the passage of (a thing) by placing something in the way; to shut in, out, or off 1623. **b.** *Chem.* Of certain metals, etc.: To absorb and retain (gases) within their substance 1866. **3.** *Dentistry.* To cause the cusps of (the upper and lower teeth) to fit together; also *intr.*

So **Occlu·dent** *a.* having the property of occluding; *sb.* something having this property.

Occlusal (ǫklū·zăl), *a.* 1904. [f. L. *occlus-*, *occludere* (see prec.) + -AL.] *Dentistry.* Of or pertaining to occlusion of the teeth.

Occlusion (ǫklū·ʒən). 1645. [ad. L. **occlusionem*, f. *occludere*: see prec.] **1.** The action of occluding or fact of being occluded; stopping up, closing. (Chiefly scientific). **2.** *Chem.* The retention of gases in the pores of metals or other substances 1866. **3.** *Dentistry.* The bringing of the opposing surfaces of the teeth of the two jaws into contact 1902.

Occlusor (ǫklū·sǫɹ). 1877. [mod.L., f. L. *occludere.*] Something that occludes; chiefly *Anat.*, a structure which closes an opening. Also *attrib.*, as *o. muscle*, etc.

Occult (ǫkʋ·lt), *a.* 1533. [ad. L. *occultus*, pa. pple. of *occulere* to cover over, f. *ob-*, OB- 1 + *celere.*] Hidden (*lit.* and *fig.*). **1.** Hidden (from sight); concealed. Now *rare* or *Obs.* 1567. **b.** Applied to a line drawn in the construction of a figure, but not forming part of the finished figure; also to a dotted line 1669. **2.** Secret; communicated only to the initiated 1533. **3.** Not apprehensible by the mind; recondite, mysterious 1545. **b.** Imperceptible by the senses. Now *rare* or merged in prec. 1650. **c.** Applied to physical qualities discoverable only by experiment, or to those whose nature was unknown and unexplained; latent; also *transf.* experimental. *Obs.* exc. *Hist.* or as merged in 3. 1652. **4.** Of the nature of or pertaining to those sciences involving the knowledge or use of the supernatural (as magic, alchemy, astrology, theosophy, and the like); also *transf.* magical, mystical 1633.

1. We two will stand beside that shrine, O., withheld, untrod ROSSETTI. 3. c. The Aristotelians give the name of o. qualities..to such qualities..as they supposed to lie hid in bodies, and to be the unknown causes of manifest effects NEWTON. Hence **Occu·ltism**, the doctrine, principles, or practice of 'occult' science (see sense 4); mysticism. **Occu·ltist**, one versed in, or believing in, occultism; a mystic. **Occu·ltly** *adv.*, **-ness.**

Occult (ǫkʋ·lt), *v.* 1527. [ad. L. *occultare*, freq. of *occulere*; see prec.] *trans.* To hide, conceal; to cut off from view by interposing some other body. Now chiefly in scientific or techn. use. **b.** *spec.* in *Astron.* said of one heavenly body (as the moon, or a planet) hiding another (as a star, etc.) by passing in front of it 1764. Hence **Occu·lted** *ppl. a.*, hidden, concealed. **Occu·lting** *ppl. a.*, that occults; *spec.* in lighthouses, applied to a light cut off from view for a few seconds at regular intervals.

Occultation (ǫkʋltēⁱ·ʃən). late ME. [ad. L. *occultationem*, f. *occultare*; see prec.] **1.** Hiding, concealment; the fact of being cut off from view by something interposed. Now only scientific or techn. **2.** *Astron.* †**a.** The disappearance of a star in the sun's rays when in an apparent position near that of the sun. **b.** The concealment of one heavenly body by another passing between it and the observer. (Also, the concealment of a heavenly body behind the body of the earth; so in *circle of perpetual o.*; see CIRCLE *sb.* I. 2.) 1551. **c.** *fig.* Disappearance from view or notice 1825.

1. The Light will be under o. three times in quick succession every Minute 1882. 2. c. The prospect of the coming o. of personally disagreeable authors 1892.

Occupance (ǫ·kiŭpăns). *Sc. rare.* 1814. [f. OCCUPANT: see -ANCE.] = next, 1.

Occupancy (ǫ·kiŭpănsi). 1596. [f. as prec.: see -ANCY.] **1.** The condition of being an occupant; = OCCUPATION 1, 2. **2.** The fact of occupying or taking up (space) 1833. **3.** = OCCUPATION 4. 1826.

1. O. is the taking possession of those things, which before belonged to nobody. This..is the true ground and foundation of all property BLACKSTONE.

Occupant (ǫ·kiŭpănt). 1596. [ad. L. *occupantem*, *occupare* to OCCUPY.] A person occupying or holding in actual possession (property, esp. land, or an office or position); an occupier 1622. **b.** *Law.* One who takes possession of something having no owner, and so establishes a title to it 1596.

Occupation (ǫkiŭpē¹·ʃən). ME. [a. F., ad. L. *occupationem*, f. *occupare* to seize, OCCUPY.] **1.** The action of taking possession, esp. of a place or of land; seizure, as by military conquest, etc.; entrance upon possession ME. **2.** Actual holding or possession, esp. of a place or of land; rarely, also, of an office or position; tenure; occupancy. late ME. **3.** The taking up of space or time (*rare*) 1460. **4.** The being occupied with, or engaged in something; that in which one is engaged; employment, business ME. **b.** with *pl.* A particular action or course of action in which one is engaged; an employment, business, calling ME. †**c.** *spec.* Handicraft; trade -1607. †**5.** Use, employment (*of* a thing) -1703.

1. Its inhabitants must have possessed the art of working in metals before the Roman o. 1893. **2.** During his o. of the house and land (*mod.*). Phr. *Army of o.*, an army left to occupy a newly conquered country or region until the conclusion of hostilities or establishment of a settled government. **3.** Stooping down in complete o. of the foot-path JANE AUSTEN. **4. b.** Farewell: Othello's Occupation 's gone SHAKS. **c.** *Cor.* IV. vi. 97. *attrib.*, as **o. disease**, a disease incidental to one's occupation; **o. franchise**, the right to vote at a parliamentary election as a tenant or occupier; **o. bridge, road**, a bridge, road, for the use of occupiers of the land. **Occupa·tional** *a.*, pertaining to one's or an occupation.

Occupier (ǫ·kiŭpəiˌəɪ). late ME. [f. next + -ER[1].] **1.** One who takes, or (more usu.) holds possession; a holder, occupant. †**2.** One who uses, employs, or deals in (something); one who follows (a specified occupation) -1611. †**b.** *esp.* One who employs money or goods in trading; a trader, dealer, merchant -1611.

2. All my Auncestours were occupiers of husbandry 1577. **b.** He will..Lie faster than ten city occupiers Or cunning tradesmen 1611.

Occupy (ǫ·kiŭpəi), *v.* ME. [irreg. f. F. *occuper*, ad. L. *occupare*. The final *-y* is unexplained. Almost entirely disused in the 17th and most of the 18th c., app. because of its vulgar employment in sense 8.] †**1.** *trans.* To take possession of, seize. *Obs.* in *gen.* sense. -1614. **b.** *spec.* To take possession of (a place) by settling in it, or by conquest, etc. ME. **2.** To hold possession of; to hold (a position or office). late ME. **b.** To reside in, tenant. late ME. †**c.** *intr.* or *absol.* To hold possession or office; to dwell, reside; to stay, abide -1535. **3.** *trans.* To take up, use up, fill (space or time); also in weakened sense, To be in or at (a place or position) ME. **4.** To employ, busy, engage (a person, or the mind, attention, etc.). Often in *pass.*; also *refl.* ME. †**5.** To make use of, use (a thing) -1774. †**6.** *trans.* To employ oneself in, carry on; to follow or ply as one's business or occupation -1660. Also †*intr.* -1653. †**7.** *trans.* To employ (money or capital) in trading; to lay out, invest, trade with; to deal in. [L. *occupare pecuniam.*] -1773. †**b.** *intr.* To trade, deal -1650. †**8.** *trans.* and *intr.* To deal with sexually; to cohabit -1660.

1. b. Glencoe was to be occupied by troops MACAULAY. **2.** A married woman is now to o. the same position as her Saxon ancestress 1883. **3.** Thanne wolde it occupie a someres day CHAUCER. The voyage ..has occupied thirty days 1875. **4.** Whatever subject o. discourse COWPER. I occupied myself with my instruments 1860. **6.** They that go downe to the see in shippes, & occupie their busynesse in greate waters COVERDALE *Ps.* cvi[i] 23. **7.** *Ezek.* xxvii. 9. **b.** Occupye tyll I come TINDALE *Luke* xix. 13.

Occur (ǒkǭ·ɪ), *v.* 1513. [ad. L. *occurrere*, f. *oc-*, *ob-* OB- 1 + *currere* to run.] †**1.** *intr.* To run to meet a person, to run up (to the spot); to run against, to meet, encounter -1695. †**b.** *trans.* (by ellipsis of prep.) To meet, encounter; to oppose, resist -1767. **2.** *intr.* To present itself; to 'turn up' or appear 1516. **b.** To come into one's mind. Const. *to.* 1626. **3.** To happen, befall, take place 1549.

1. Bodies..have..a certain and determinate motion according to..the resistance of the bodies they occurr with BENTLEY. **2.** That name doth often occurre in olde evidences CAMDEN. Marble also occurs here HAWTHORNE. **b.** It could not but o. to me that you would be agreeably surprised 1809. **3.** To Mrs. Orme she told all that had occurred TROLLOPE.

Occurrence (ǒkʊ·rĕns). 1539. [f. next, after *incidence, incident.*] **1.** The fact of occurring 1725. **2.** That which occurs or is met with, or presents itself; now with *an* and *pl.*: An event, incident 1539.

1. Landslips are of frequent o. GEIKIE. **2.** The chief Occurrences of my Life STEELE.

Occurrent (ǒkʊ·rĕnt), *a.* and *sb.* Now *rare.* 1513. [prob. a. F. *occurrent*, *-ant*, ad. L. *occurrentem*; see OCCUR.] **A.** *adj.* That occurs, presents itself, or happens; occurring; current. Sometimes *spec.* Incidental. **B.** *sb.* **1.** = OCCURRENCE 2. (Now *Obs.* or a rare archaism.) 1523. †**b.** *transf.* A narration of what has happened; *pl.* news -1655. †**2.** A person or thing that meets or runs against one -1615.

1. There is neither aduersary, nor euill o. 1 *Kings* v. 4.

Ocean (ōu·ʃăn), *sb.* (*a.*) ME. [a. F. *ocëan* (*occean* 12th c.), ad. L. *oceanus*, f. Gr. ὠκεανός, orig. the great river supposed to encompass the disk of the earth; hence, the great outer sea, as opp. to the Mediterranean.] **1.** The vast body of water on the surface of the globe, which surrounds the land; the main or great sea. (Down to *c* 1650, commonly **ocean sea**, representing L. *mare oceanum*, OF. *occeanne mer*, in which *oceanum*, *occeanne* are adjs.) **2.** One of the main areas into which this body of water is divided geographically, as the *Atlantic, Pacific, Indian, Arctic*, and *Antarctic Oceans.* late ME. **3.** *transf.* and *fig.* An immense or boundless expanse of anything; *hyperbolically*, a very great or indefinite quantity 1590.

1. The deck it was their field of fame, and O. was their grave CAMPBELL. **2.** *German O.*, a former name of the North Sea; As the Atlantic and German Oceans unite at this point, a frightful tide runs here 1814. **3.** An o. of troubles 1642. Ale flowed in oceans for the populace MACAULAY.

attrib. and *Comb.*, as *o. bed, isle, monster, nymph*, etc.; *o. line, liner, power, scout, steamer*, etc.; *o.-sundered* adj.; *o.-wide* adj.; also **o. greyhound**, a swift o. steamer; **o.-lane**, a lane or track across the o.; *esp.* one prescribed for o. steamers; **o.-river, -stream**, the great stream anciently supposed to encompass the earth; **o. tramp**, a term applied to all sea-going steamships (outside the regular liners) which earn their freight solely by cargo-carrying.

Oceania (ōuʃiˌē¹·niă). 1849. [mod.L., ad. F. *Océanie*, f. L. *oceanus*, after *Asia*, etc.] A general name for the islands of the Pacific and its adjacent seas. So **Ocea·nica** 1832.

Oceanian (ōuʃiˌē¹·niăn), *a.* and *sb.* 1831. [ad. F. *océanien*, f. *océan.*] **A.** *adj.* Of or pertaining to the Pacific Ocean and its islands, or to Oceania generally. **B.** *sb.* A native of Oceania; a Polynesian 1831.

Oceanic (ōuʃiˌæ·nik), *a.* 1656. [ad. med. or mod. L. *oceanicus*, f. *oceanus*: see -IC.] **1.** Of or pertaining to, situated or living in or by, the ocean; flowing into the ocean. **2.** Ocean-like; vast COLERIDGE. **3.** = OCEANIAN A. 1842.

1. Gulls, petrels, and other o. birds 1772.

Oceanid (osī·ănid). *Pl.* **-ids, -ides** (ōusiˌæ·nidīz). 1869. [ad. Gr. ὠκεανίς, pl. -ίδες; cf. F. *Océanide.*] **1.** *Gr. Myth.* A nymph of the Ocean, one of the daughters of Oceanus and Tethys. **2.** *pl.* Marine mollusca, as dist. from *Naiades* or 'Fresh-water shells'.

Oceanography (ōu:ʃiănǫ·grăfi). 1883. [f. Gr. ὠκεανός OCEAN, after *geography.*] That branch of physical geography which treats of the ocean, its form, physical features, and phenomena; = THALASSOGRAPHY. So **Oceano·grapher. Ocea·nogra·phic, -al,** *adjs.*

Ocellar (ose·lăɪ), *a.* 1889. [f. L. *ocellus* + -AR[1].] **1.** Of or pertaining to the ocelli or small simple eyes of insects or other Arthropoda 1891. **2.** *Petrography.* Applied to that structure of rocks in which minute individual components of one mineral are arranged in radiating aggregations round another.

Ocellate (ose·lĕt, ǫ·sĕlĕt), *a.* 1857. [ad. L. *ocellatus*, f. *ocellus* eyelet; see -ATE[2].] = next.

Ocellated (ose·l-, ǫ·sĕlē¹tĕd), *a.* 1713. [f. as prec. + -ED[1].] **1.** Marked with an ocellus or ocelli; having eye-like spots. **2.** Formed like a small eye; said of a small round spot surrounded by a ring of a different colour 1828.

1. The O. Turkey of Honduras 1864.

Ocelli-, comb. form of L. *ocellus* eyelet, as in **Ocelli·ferous** *a.*, ocellated, **Oce·lliform** *a.*, having the form of an ocellus or little eye; etc.

‖ **Ocellus** (ose·lŏs). *Pl.* **ocelli** (-əi). 1819. [L., dim. of *oculus* eye.] **1.** A little eye or eyelet; *spec.* **a.** One of the simple eyes of insects and some other Arthropoda; a stemma. **b.** The simple eye or visual spot of Mollusca, Hydrozoa, etc. **c.** One of the facets or segments of a compound eye. (Usu. in *pl.*) **2.** A coloured spot surrounded by a ring or rings of different colour, as found on some feathers, etc.; an eye-like spot, an eyelet 1826.

Ocelot (ōu·silǫt). 1774. [a. F. (Buffon), shortening of Mexican *tlalocelotl*, f. *tlalli* field + *ocelotl* tiger, jaguar.] A Central and South American feline quadruped (*Felis pardalis*), about three feet in length; the prevailing colour is grey, marked with numerous elongated fawn spots edged with black; the under parts are whitish with black markings; also called *tiger-cat, leopard-cat.*

Och (oχ), *int. Irish* and *Sc.* 1528. [Ir. and Gael.] An exclamation of surprise, regret, or sorrow; oh! also *och how!* alas!

Ochlocracy (ǫklǫ·krăsi). 1584. [a. F. *ochlocratie*, a. Gr. ὀχλοκρατία, f. ὄχλος mob + -κρατία; see -CRACY.] Government by the mob; mob-rule. Hence **O·chlocrat. Ochlocra·tic, -al** *adjs.*; **-ally** *adv.*

Ochraceous (ǫkrē¹·ʃəs), *a.* 1776. [f. L. *ochra* OCHRE + -ACEOUS.] = OCHREOUS 1, 2.

Ochre, ocher (ōu·kəɪ), *sb.* late ME. [a. F. *ocre*, ad. L. *ochra* (Pliny), a. Gr. ὤχρα, f. ὠχρός pale yellow.] **1.** A native earth, or class of earths, consisting of a mixture of hydrated oxide of iron with varying proportions of clay in impalpable subdivision; varying in colour from light yellow to deep orange or brown. Much used as pigments. **b.** As a pigment; also the colour of this; esp. a pale brownish yellow. late ME. **2.** Applied to the earthy pulverulent oxides of other metals, as *antimony, bismuth, chrome, tantalic, tungstic o.* 1863. **3.** *slang.* Money, in allusion to the colour of gold coin 1854.

3. If I was flush of the o., I tell yer I'd make the thing hum 1890. Hence **O·chre, ocher** *v. trans.* to colour, mark, or rub with o.; chiefly in *pa. pple.* **O·chreish** *a.* ochreous.

Ochreous (ōu·kriˌəs), *a.* 1728. [f. mod.L. *ochreus* + -OUS.] **1.** Of the nature of, containing, or abounding in ochre. **2.** Of the colour of ochre; *spec.* of a light brownish yellow 1750.

2. A brown, bricky, o. tone, never bright RUSKIN.

Ochro- (ōu·kro), comb. form. of Gr. ὤχρα, ὠχρός (OCHRE), as in **Ochroleu·cous** *a.* [Gr. ὠχρόλευκος], yellowish-white; etc.

Ochrous (ōu·krəs), *a.* Also (*U.S.*) **ocherous.** 1757. [f. OCHRE + -OUS.] = OCHREOUS.

Ochry, ochery (ōu·kri, ōu·kəri), *a.* 1567. [f. OCHRE, *ocher* + -Y.] = OCHREOUS 1, 2.

Ochymy, var. of **Occamy.**

-ock, *suffix*, forming dims., as in *bullock, hillock*; *haddock, paddock, pollock*; also *buttock, tussock*, etc. In *bannock, hassock, mattock*, etc., *-ock* appears to be of different origin.

o'clock: see CLOCK *sb.*[1]

-ocracy, the suffix *-cracy* with connective *-o-*; also, as a nonce-word, 'the rule of any class'. So **-ocrat.** See -CRACY, -CRAT.

‖ **Ocrea** (ǫ·kriă). Also erron. **ochrea.** *Pl.* **-æ.** 1830. [L., = a greave or legging.] **a.** *Bot.* (*a*) A sheath or tube round a stem or stalk formed by the lateral cohesion of two or more stipules; (*b*) The thin sheath surrounding the seta in mosses. **b.** *Zool.* An investing part or growth similar to this; the 'boot' of a bird (see next).

Ocreate (ǫ·kriĕt), *a.* Also erron. **ochreate.** 1830. [f. prec. + -ATE[2].] **1.** Wearing or furnished with an *ocrea*, greave, or legging; booted. **2.** *Ornith.* Booted; having the tarsal envelope fused into a continuous ocrea or boot, as thrushes, nightingales, redbreasts, etc. **3.** *Bot.* Having the stipules united by cohesion into a sheath surrounding the stem 1830.

Oct-, form of OCTA-, OCTO-, bef. a vowel.

Oct., abbrev. of OCTAVO, OCTOBER.

Octa- (ǫ·ktă), a. Gr. ὀκτα-, comb. form of ὀκτώ eight. **b.** In *Chem. octa-, oct-* (occas. *octo-*) indicates the presence of eight atoms or units of an element or radical, as in *octacarbon, octachloride*, etc.

Octachord (ǫ·ktăkǭɪd), *a.* and *sb.* Also **octo-.** 1760. [ad. late L. *octachordos*, a. Gr., f. ὀκτα- OCTA- + χορδή CHORD.] **A.** *adj.* **a.**

Having eight strings. **b.** Relating to a scale of eight notes. **B.** *sb.* **a.** A series of eight notes, as the ordinary diatonic scale. **b.** A musical instrument having eight strings. 1776. Hence **Octacho·rdal** (octo-) *a.*

Octad (ǫ·ktæd). 1801. [ad. L. *octas, octad-*, a. Gr. ὀκτάς, -άδα a group of eight; see -AD 1 a.] **1.** A group or series of eight; *spec.* in ancient systems of notation: A group or series of eight characters corresponding to successive powers of ten (analogous to the groups of six figures marking millions, billions, etc. now used). **2.** *Chem.* An element or radical that has the combining power of eight units, i. e. of eight atoms of hydrogen 1877. Hence **Octa·dic** *a.*

Octagon (ǫ·ktăgǫn), *sb.* and *a.* 1656. [ad. L. *octa-, octogonos* adj., a. Gr. ὀκτάγωνος, f. ὀκτα- OCTA- + stem of γωνία corner, angle.] **A.** *sb. Geom.* A plane figure having eight angles and eight sides. Hence applied to material objects, as a fortification, of this form or section. **B.** *adj.* = OCTAGONAL 1679.

Octagonal (ǫktæ·gŏnăl), *a.* 1571. [orig. *octogonal* (so F.), ad. mod.L. *octogonalis*; see prec. and -AL.] Of the form of an octagon; eight-sided. So **Octa·gonally** *adv.* late ME.

Octahedrite (ǫktăhī·drəit, -he·drəit). Also **octo-**. 1805. [f. late L. *octa(h)edros*, a. Gr. ὀκτάεδρος + -ITE[1] 2 b.] *Min.* Native dioxide of titanium, occurring in crystals of octahedral and other related forms; also called ANATASE.

Octahedron (ǫktăhī·drǫn, -he·drǫn). Also **octo-**. *Pl.* **-ons** or **-a.** 1570. [a. Gr. ὀκτάεδρον, neut. of ὀκτάεδρος adj., eight-sided, f. ὀκτα- OCTA- + ἕδρα seat.] *Geom.* A solid figure contained by eight plane faces; usu., one contained by eight triangles; *spec.* the *regular o.*, one of the five regular solids, contained by eight equal equilateral triangles. Hence *gen.* Any material body, esp. a crystal, of this form. Hence **Octahedr·al** (ǫktăhī·drăl, -he·drăl), **-ic** *adjs.* having the form of an o.; of or belonging to an o.

Octamerous (ǫktæ·mĕrəs), *a.* Also **octo-**. 1864. [f. Gr. ὀκταμερής (μέρος part) + -OUS.] **a.** *Bot.* Having the parts of the flower in series of eight. (Often written 8-*merous*.) **b.** *Zool.* Having the radiating parts or organs eight in number, as an actinoid zoophyte.

Octameter (ǫktæ·mĭtəɹ), *a.* and *sb.* Also **octo-**. 1828. [ad. L. *octameter, -trum* adj., a. Gr. ὀκτάμετρος (μέτρον measure).] *Pros.* **A.** *adj.* Consisting of eight measures or feet. **B.** *sb.* A verse containing eight feet.

B. 'March: an Ode' [by Swinburne], is the only instance in the language of a poem written in octometers 1889.

‖**Octandria** (ǫktæ·ndriă). 1753. [mod.L., f. Gr. ὀκτώ eight + ἀνδρ- (ἀνήρ) male; see -IA[2].] *Bot.* A class in the Linnæan Sexual System, comprising plants with eight stamens. Hence **Octa·ndrous** *a.* 1830.

Octane (ǫ·ktēⁱn). 1872. [f. OCT(A-, OCT(O- + -ANE 2.] *Chem.* The paraffin of the octacarbon series (C_8H_{18}). So **O·ctene** (-īn) [-ENE], the olefine of the same series (C_8H_{16}), also called *octylene*; **O·ctine** (-əin) [-INE[5]], the hydrocarbon of the same series (C_8H_{14}) homologous with acetylene or ethine; **Octo·ic** *a.*, applied to fatty acids, etc., of the same series, as *o. acid* ($C_8H_{16}O_2$).

†**O·ctangle**, *a.* and *sb.* 1613. [ad. late L. *octangulus* adj., f. *octo* + *angulus*.] **A.** *adj.* Octagonal. **B.** *sb.* An octagon. -1726. So **Octa·ngular** *a.* octagonal.

Octant (ǫ·ktănt). 1661. [ad. late L. *octans, -tantem* a half quadrant, f. *octo* eight.] **1.** The eighth part of a circle; *i. e.* either (*a*) an arc, forming one-eighth of the circumference, or (*b*) one-eighth of the area of a circle, contained within two radii at an angle of 45°. 1750. **b.** Each of the eight parts into which a solid figure or body (*e.g.* a sphere), or the space around a central point, is divided by three planes (usu. mutually at right angles) intersecting at the central point 1790. **2.** *Astron.* That point in the apparent course of a planet at which it is 45° distant from another planet, from the sun, or from some particular point; *spec.* each of the four points at which the moon is 45° from conjunction with or opposition to the sun, or midway between the syzygies and quadratures 1661. **3.** An instrument in the form of a graduated eighth of a circle, used for making angular measurements, esp. in astronomy and navigation 1731.

‖**Octapla** (ǫ·ktăplă). Also anglicized **octaples**. 1684. [ad. Gr. ὀκταπλᾶ, neut. pl. of ὀκταπλοῦς eight-fold, after HEXAPLA.] A text consisting of eight versions, esp. of the Scriptures, in parallel arrangement.

Octarchy (ǫ·ktaɹki). 1799. [f. Gr. ὀκτώ eight + -αρχία rule.] A government by eight rulers; applied by some historians (instead of HEPTARCHY) to the kingdoms established by the Angles and Saxons in Britain.

Octastich (ǫ·ktăstik). 1577. [ad. Gr. ὀκτάστιχος: see OCTA- and STICH.] A group of eight lines of verse.

Octastichous (ǫktæ·stikəs), **octo-** *a.* 1870. [f. as prec. + -OUS.] *Bot.* Having eight leaves in the spiral row, and thus eight vertical rows in the phyllotaxis.

Octastyle (ǫ·ktăstəil), *a.* and *sb.* Also **octo-**. 1706. [ad. late L. *octastylus*, a. Gr. (στῦλος pillar).] *Arch.* **A.** *adj.* Having eight columns in front or at the end, as a building. **B.** *sb.* A building or portico having eight columns.

Octateuch (ǫ·ktătiūk). Also **octo-**. 1677. [ad. late L. *octateuchus*, a. Gr. ὀκτάτευχος (τεῦχος book).] The first eight books of the Old Testament collectively; the Pentateuch, together with Joshua, Judges, and Ruth.

Octave (ǫ·ktēv), *sb.* (*a.*) Also in sense 1 (*pl.*) †**utaves**, †**utas** (see also UTIS). ME. [a. F., ad. L. *octava*, fem. of *octavus* eighth (sc. *dies* day).] **1.** *Eccl.* (Formerly always in *pl.*) **a.** The eighth day after a festival. **b.** The period of eight days beginning with the day of a festival. **c.** *transf.* A period of festivity 1597. **2.** A group of eight lines of verse; a stanza of eight lines (*spec.* = OTTAVA RIMA); = OCTET 2. 1586. **3.** *Mus.* (Formerly EIGHTH. Occas. abbrev. 8ve.) **a.** The note eight diatonic degrees above (or below) a given note (both notes being counted), which is produced by vibrations of twice (or half) the rate. Hence, any of the notes at successive intervals of eight degrees above or below a given note (*second o.*, *third o.*, etc.). **b.** The interval between any note and its octave; an interval comprising five tones and two diatonic semitones. **c.** A series of notes, or keys of an instrument, extending through this interval. **d.** A note and its octave played or sung together. 1656. **e.** An organ-stop sounding an octave higher than the ordinary pitch; more usu. called *principal* 1716. **4.** A group or series of eight 1806. **5.** *Fencing.* (In full *o. parade.*) The position of parrying or attacking in the low outside line with the hand in supination (cf. *seconde*) 1771. **6.** A small wine-cask containing the eighth part of a pipe, or 13½ gallons 1880.

1. *In the octaves* = med.L. *in octavis* 'on the eighth day' of a festival. **c.** 2 *Hen. IV*, II. iv. 22. **2.** With monefull melodie it continued this octaue SIDNEY. **3.** *Consecutive octaves, hidden octaves*; see the adjs. **4.** *Law of octaves* (*Chem.*), the 'periodic law' as orig. stated by its discoverer Newlands 1887.

attrib. (or *adj.*) and *Comb.*: **o. flute,** (*a*) a small flute sounding an o. higher than the ordinary flute, a piccolo; (*b*) a flute-stop on an organ sounding an o. higher than the ordinary pitch; †**o. rime** = OTTAVA RIMA; **o. stanza,** a stanza of eight lines.

Octavo (ǫktēⁱ·vo). Abbrev. **8vo** or **oct.** 1582. [L., abl. of *octavus* eighth, in the phr. *in octavo* in an eighth (*sc.* of a sheet); F. *in-octavo* sb.] **1.** The size of a book, or page, when the sheets are so folded that each leaf is one-eighth of a whole sheet. Orig. in L. phr. *in octavo*, subseq. treated as Eng. prep. and sb. **2.** A book or volume *in octavo* 1712. **3.** *attrib.* or *adj.*, as in 'octavo edition' = edition *in o.* 1704.

2. Imparting his lucubrations to the world in the shape of one or two octavos 1854.

Octennial (ǫkte·niăl), *a.* 1656. [f. L. *octennium* a period of eight years (f. *octo* + *annus*) + -AL; cf. *biennial*, etc.] Of or pertaining to a period of eight years; occurring, or lasting, during eight years; recurring every eighth year. Hence **Octe·nnially** *adv.* once in eight years.

Octet, octette (ǫkte·t). 1864. [f. L. *octo*, after *duet*, etc.] **1.** *Mus.* A composition for eight singers or voices. **b.** A company of eight singers or players who perform together. **2.** A group of eight lines of verse; *spec.* the first eight lines of a sonnet 1879. **3.** *gen.* A group of eight 1894.

Octile (ǫ·ktəil), *a.* and *sb.* 1690. [ad. mod.L. *octilis*, f. *octo* eight, after *quintilis*, etc.] **A.** *adj.* Said of the 'aspect' of two planets distant 45° (= ⅛ of a circle) from each other. **B.** *sb.* = Octile aspect, OCTANT 2. 1690.

Octillion (ǫkti·lyən). 1690. [a. F., f. L. *octo* eight, after *million*; see BILLION.] The eighth power of a million, denoted by 1 followed by 48 ciphers. (In U.S., following later French usage, the ninth power of a thousand, denoted by 1 and 27 ciphers.) Hence **Octi·llionth.**

Octine (*Chem.*): see under OCTANE.

Octingentenary (ǫktindʒe·ntĭnări-, -dʒentī·nări). *rare.* 1893. [f. L. *octingenti* eight hundred, after *centenary*.] The eight-hundredth anniversary of an event.

Octo- (bef. a vowel **oct-**), comb. form of L. *octo*, and occas. of Gr. ὀκτώ eight. (The Gr. form is usu. ὀκτα-, OCTA-.) **Octoda·ctyl, -da·ctylous** *adjs. Zool.* [Gr. δάκτυλος digit], having eight digits. **O·ctofid** *a.* [L. *-fidus* = cleft], divided into eight segments, as a calyx or corolla. **O·ctofoil** *a.* [after *trefoil*, etc.: see FOIL *sb.*[1]], *sb.* an ornamental figure consisting of eight leaves or lobes; *adj.* eight-lobed (also **O·ctofoiled**). **Octo·gamy** [after *bigamy*], the marrying of eight spouses. **O·ctoglot** *a.* [Gr. γλῶττα, γλῶσσα tongue], written in eight languages. **Octola·teral** *a.* [LATERAL] eight-sided, formed of eight straight lines. **Octora·dial, -ra·diate, -ra·diated** *adjs.* [L. *radius* ray], having eight rays. **O·ctospore** *Bot.* [SPORE], each of the eight carpospores produced by certain algæ; so **Octo·sporous** *a.*, producing eight spores. **Octo·valent** *a.* [L. *valentem* having value], *Chem.* having the combining power of eight atoms of hydrogen; octadic.

October (ǫktōᵘ·bəɹ). OE. [a. L., f. *octo* eight (orig. the eighth month of the year).] **1.** The tenth month of the year (as now reckoned). **2.** Ale brewed in October 1708.

1. Bright O. was come, the misty-bright O. CLOUGH.

Octodecimo (ǫktode·simo). 1795. [For *in octodecimo*, from L. *octodecimus* eighteenth, as in *octavo*, etc.] The size of a book or page when each leaf is one-eighteenth of a whole sheet; a book of this size. Abbrev. 18mo.

‖**Octodon** (ǫ·ktŏdǫn). 1841. [mod.L., f. Gr. ὀκτώ + -όδων = -όδους -tooth.] **a.** A genus of S. Amer. rodents, resembling rats. **b.** A genus of coleopterous insects.

Octogenarian (ǫktoˌdʒĭnēᵊ·riăn), *a.* and *sb.* 1815. [f. L. *octogenarius*, f. *octogeni* eighty each, + -AN.] **A.** *adj.* Of the age of eighty; also *transf.* of or belonging to a person eighty years old 1818. **B.** *sb.* A person eighty years old 1815.

A. Blind old Dandolo! Th' o. chief BYRON. Hence **Octogena·rianism.** So **Octo·genary** *a.* and *sb.* (now *rare*) 1696.

‖**Octogynia** (ǫktoˌdʒi·niă). Also **octa-**. 1760. [mod.L., f. Gr. ὀκτώ eight + γυνή female + -IA.] *Bot.* A Linnæan order of plants comprising those with eight pistils. Hence **Octogy·nious, Octo·gynous** *adjs.*

Octoic, *a.* (*Chem.*): see under OCTANE.

Octonary (ǫ·ktonări), *a.* and *sb.* 1535. [ad. L. *octonarius* containing eight, f. *octoni* eight at a time, f. *octo*.] **A.** *adj.* Pertaining to the number eight; consisting of eight; proceeding by eights 1615. **B.** *sb.* A group of eight, an ogdoad; a group or stanza of eight lines of verse (esp. used of the 119th Psalm) 1535.

Octopartite (ǫktopā·ɹtəit), *a.* 1752. [ad. med. or mod.L. *octopartitus*, f. *octo* eight + *partitus* divided.] Divided into or consisting of eight parts; as, an †*o. indenture.*

Octoped (ǫ·ktŏped). Also **-pede.** 1822. [f. L. *octo* eight + *pes, pedem* foot.] An eight-footed animal or thing.

Octopod (ǫ·ktŏpǫd), *sb.* and *a.* 1826. [ad. Gr. ὀκτωποδ- (also ὀκταποδ-), ὀκτώπους OCTOPUS.] **A.** *sb.* An animal having eight feet; *spec.* an octopus, or other member of the suborder *Octopoda* of cephalopods 1835. **B.** *adj.* Eight-footed. So **Octo·podan** *a.* and *sb.*, **Octo·podous** *a.*

Octopus (*ǫ*ktŏ̆pŏs, *ǫ*ktō̆·pŏs). *Pl.* **octopodes** (*ǫ*ktō̆·pŏdīz), **octopuses.** 1758. [mod.L., a. Gr. ὀκτώπους, acc. ὀκτώποδα eight-footed, f. ὀκτώ eight + πούς, ποδ- foot.] A genus of cephalopod molluscs, characterized by eight 'arms' surrounding the mouth and provided with suckers; a (large and formidable) individual of this genus.

fig. We are the very o. of nations 1882.

Octoroon (*ǫ*ktŏrū·n). 1861. [irreg. f. L. *octo* eight + *-oon*, after *quadroon.*] A person having one-eighth negro blood; the offspring of a quadroon and a white; sometimes used of other mixed races.

Octosyllabic (*ǫ*:ktosilæ·bik), *a.* and *sb.* 1771. [f. late L. *octosyllabus*, in late Gr. ὀκτασύλλαβος, f. Gr. ὀκτώ, ὀκτα- eight + συλλαβή, L. *syllaba* syllable; cf. SYLLABIC.] **A.** *adj.* Consisting of eight syllables (chiefly in *Pros.* of a verse or line of poetry); composed of lines of eight syllables each. **B.** *sb.* A verse or line of eight syllables 1842.

A. The o. measure of the Lady of the Lake LOCKHART.

Octosyllable (*ǫ*ktosi·lăb'l), *sb.* and *a.* 1775. [f. L. *octosyllabus*, after *syllable.*] **A.** *sb.* = prec. B; also, a word of eight syllables. **B.** *adj.* = prec. A.

‖**Octroi** (oktrwa, *ǫ*·ktroi). Also †**octroy.** 1614. [F., f. *octroyer* (see next).] †**1.** A privilege granted by government, esp. an exclusive right of trade, etc. –1721. **2.** A tax levied on certain articles on their admission into a town (esp. in France) 1714. **b.** The barrier at which the tax is paid; also, the service, or body of officers, collecting it 1861.

Octroy (*ǫ*·ktroi), *v.* 1480. [ad. F. *octroyer*, for earlier *ot(t)royer, otreier* :—L. **auctoricare* or *auctorizare* to authorize.] *trans.* To concede, grant, accord; said of a government or appointed authority.

Octuor (*ǫ*·ktiu,*ǫ*ɪ). 1864. [F., irreg. f. L. *octo* eight, after *quatuor* four (in *Mus.* = *quartet*).] = OCTET 1.

Octuple (*ǫ*·ktiŭp'l), *a.* (*sb.*) 1603. [ad. L. *octuplus* eightfold, f. *octo* eight + *-plus*, as in *duplus* DOUBLE.] **A.** *adj.* Eightfold; eight times as much as . . ; composed of eight. **B.** *sb.* That which is eight times something else, or consists of eight parts 1692. Hence **O·ctuple** *v. trans.* to increase eightfold.

Octyl (*ǫ*·ktil). 1866. [f. OCT(A-, OCT(O- + -YL.] *Chem.* The hydrocarbon radical of the octacarbon series (C_8H_{17}); sometimes called *capryl.* Also *attrib.*, as *o. alcohol*, etc. (Earlier named *octylia.*) So **O·ctylene** = *Octene* (see under OCTANE); **Octy·lic** *a.* of or pertaining to o., as *octylic acid, alcohol*, etc. 1857.

Ocular (*ǫ*·kiŭlăɪ), *a.* and *sb.* 1503. [ad. L. *ocularis*, f. *oculus* eye.] **A.** *adj.* **1.** Of, belonging to, or connected with the eye as a bodily organ; seated in, or in the region of, the eye. *spec.* in *Entom.* Pertaining to the compound eye of an insect (dist. from *ocellar*). **b.** Used for, applied to, or relating to the eye 1599. **c.** Of the nature, form, or function of an eye 1640. **d.** Expressed by the eye 1627. **2.** Belonging to the action of the eye, and hence to the sense of sight; visual 1575.

1. b. O. remedies 1661. **d.** The o. dialect needs no dictionary EMERSON. **2.** Phr. *O. inspection, testimony, demonstration.*

B. *sb.* **1.** The eye-piece of a telescope, microscope, etc. 1835. **2.** *Joc.* for 'ocular organ', 'eye' 1825. Hence **O·cularly** *adv.* 1646.

Ocularist (*ǫ*·kiŭlărist). 1866. [a. mod. F. *oculariste*, f. *oculaire* OCULAR; see -IST.] A maker of artificial eyes.

Oculate (*ǫ*·kiŭlĕt), *a.* 1549. [ad. L. *oculatus*, f. *oculus*; see -ATE [2].] †**1.** Possessed of eyes or sight; sharp-sighted; observant –1660. **2.** *Nat. Hist.* Having eye-like spots or holes resembling eyes 1656. So **O·culated** *a.*, in sense 2.

O·culiform, *a.* 1828. [f. L. *oculus, oculi-* eye + L. *-formis* -FORM.] Having the form of an eye; eye-like.

Oculist (*ǫ*·kiŭlist). 1615. [a. F. *oculiste*, f. L. *oculus*; see -IST.] One versed in the knowledge or treatment of the eyes; a physician or surgeon who treats diseases and affections of the eye. Hence **Oculi·stic** *a.*

Oculo- (*ǫ*:kiŭlo), bef. a vowel **ocul-**, comb. form of L. *oculus* eye (see -O-); as in **Oculomotor** (-mō̆·tǫɪ) *a.*, serving to move the eye; epithet of the third pair of cranial nerves, which supply most of the muscles of the eyeballs; *sb.* the oculomotor nerve; **Oculonasal** (-nē̆ⁱ·zăl) *a.*, belonging or relating to the eye and the nose; etc.

‖**Oculus** (*ǫ*·kiŭlŏs). Pl. **oculi** (-əi). [L., eye.] †**1.** *O. Christi*: (*a*) wild sage; (*b*) *Inula O.-C.* –1658. †**2.** *O. mundi*, hydrophane –1796. **3.** *Nat. Hist.* **a.** An eye; *spec.* a compound eye, as in insects (dist. from *ocellus*). **b.** A spot resembling an eye; an ocellus. 1857. **4.** *Bot.* A leaf-bud; cf. EYE *sb.*[1] III. 1 a. 1727. **5.** *Arch.* **a.** A large circular window at the west end of a church. **b.** A round hollowed stone. 1848.

Ocydrome (*ǫ*·sidrōᵘm). 1895. [ad. mod.L. *Ocydromus*, ad. Gr. ὠκύδρομος swift-running.] *Ornith.* A bird of the genus *Ocydromus*, native of New Zealand, incapable of flight.

Ocypode (*ǫ*·sipōᵘd), *a.* and *sb.* 1864. [ad. mod.L. *Ocypoda*, f. Gr. ὠκύπους, ὠκυποδ- swift-footed.] *Zool.* **A.** *adj.* Belonging to the genus *Ocypoda* or family *Ocypodidæ* of crabs. **B.** *sb.* A crab of this genus or family; a sand-crab or racing-crab. Also **Ocypodan** (*ǫ*si·pŏdăn) *a.* and *sb.*

Od [1], **'od** (*ǫ*d). Also **odd.** 1598. A minced form of *God* (GOD *sb.*), very frequent in 17th and early 18th c. Now *arch.* and *dial.* **1.** Used interjectionally, by way of asseveration. Still *dial.* 1695. **b.** In imprecations and exclamatory phrases, as *od rat it* (*'drat it*), *od save's*, etc. Still *dial.* 1749. **2.** The possessive *'od's* (*od's, odds*, etc.) occurs like *God's* in many exclams. 1598. **b.** In *od's me, od's my life, od's my will*, and the simple *'od's, odds* it has been suggested that *'s* is for *save* 1598.

1. Od, ye are a clever birkie! SCOTT. **b.** Fools! 'od rot 'em! 1812. **2.** 'Ods pittikins: can it be sixe mile yet? SHAKS. Odzooks, I'm a young Man CONGREVE.

Od [2] (*ǫ*d, ō̆d). 1850. [Arbitrary term.] A hypothetical force held by Baron von Reichenbach (1788–1869) to pervade all nature, manifesting itself in certain persons of sensitive temperament, and exhibited esp. by magnets, crystals, heat, light, and chemical action, and held to explain the phenomena of mesmerism and animal magnetism. Also *attrib.* as *od force*, etc. (Cf. ODYL.) Hence **O·dic** *a.* **Odize** (*ǫ*·dəiz, ō̆·dəiz) *v. trans.* to charge with odic force. **b.** Forming the second element in various derivatives, as *biod* the 'od' of animal life, *thermod* heat 'od', etc.

‖**Oda** (ō̆·dă). 1625. [a. Turk. *ōṭah, ōdah* chamber, hall.] A room in a harem; *transf.* the inmates of such a room.

Odal (ō̆·dăl), *sb.* (*a.*) 1839. [a. ON. *óðal* property held by inheritance = OE. *æðel, eðel.*] Land held in absolute ownership without service or acknowledgement of any superior, as among the early Teutonic peoples. Chiefly *attrib.* See also UDAL.

‖**Odalisque** (ō̆·dălisk). 1681. [a. F., corrupt. Turk. *ōdaliq*, f. *ōdah* ODA + *-liq, -lik* expressing function.] A female slave or concubine in an Eastern harem, esp. in the seraglio of the Sultan of Turkey.

Odaller (ō̆·dăləɪ). 1860. [f. ODAL + -ER [1].] A free possessor by odal tenure; = UDALLER.

Odd (*ǫ*d), *a.* (*sb.*) and *adv.* [ME. *odde*, a. ON. *odda-* in comb. in *odda-maðr* (acc. *-mann*) third man, odd man, who gives the casting vote, in which *odda-* is genitive or comb. form of *oddi* 'point, angle, triangle', whence 'third or odd number'.] **A.** *adj.* **I.** With ref. to number. **1.** Of an individual: That is one in addition to a pair, or remaining over after division into pairs. **2.** Of a number: Having one left over as remainder when divided by two; opp. to *even.* late ME. **b.** Numbered with or known by such a number. late ME. **c.** *absol.* as *sb.* *The odd*, uneven number 1589. **3.** Added to a 'round number', and thus becoming virtually an indefinite cardinal number of lower denomination than the round number named. late ME. **b.** *ellipt.* denoting age, the word 'years' being understood (*colloq.*) 1845. **4.** Used to denote a surplus over a definite sum, or a remainder of lower denomination of money, weight, or measure. late ME.

1. *O. man*, the third (fifth, etc.) man in a body of arbitrators, a committee, etc., who, in case of an equal division of opinion, may give a casting vote. *O. trick*, in whist, the thirteenth trick, after each side has won six. **2.** This is the third time: I hope good lucke lies in odde numbers SHAKS. Phr. *O. and* (*or*) *even* (dial. *odds or evens*): a game of chance. **3.** Two hundred and o. men 1748. Fleeced of seventy o. dollars 1793. **b.** At sixty o., love, most of the ladies of thy orient race have lost the bloom of youth THACKERAY. **4.** The proceeds..amounted to 47 *l.* o. MARRYAT.

II. Transf. senses. **1.** That exists or stands alone; single, sole, solitary, singular. Now only *dial.* ME. †**2.** Singular in valour, worth, merit, or eminence. (Comp. *odder, oddest.*) –1698. †**3.** Not even, accordant, or conformable; uneven, discrepant –1596. †**b.** (*rare*) At odds (*with*) –1606. **4.** Extraneous or additional to what is reckoned or taken into account; hence, Not belonging to any particular total, set, or group; unconnected; irregular; casual. Also in weakened sense, esp. with indef. adjs., as *some o.* (= 'some or other'), *any o.* (= 'any chance', 'any stray'). *O. ends, o. things*, odds and ends (see ODDS). 1450. *O. job*, occasional employment; hence *o. job man.* **b.** Of a place: Out of the way 1576. **c.** Of an interval of time: Occurring casually 1644. **d.** Not forming part of a regular course of work, as *o. job*; whence *o. jobber*, and similarly *o. man, lad, hand*, etc, 1859. **e.** Forming part of an incomplete pair or set 1746. †**f.** Extra –1602. **5.** Extraordinary, strange. (Comp. *odder, oddest.*) 1592. **b.** Of persons, their actions, etc.: Peculiar; eccentric 1588. **c.** Of material things: Fantastic, grotesque 1613.

1. *An o. one* (n. dial.), a single one, one only. **2.** He was an Odde man indeed, for all the Popish party could not match him with his equal in Learning and Religion FULLER. **3. b.** *Tr. & Cr.* IV. v. 265. **4.** A few o. observations FIELDING. **c.** To pick up knowledge at o. moments 1893. **e.** Two o. volumes of Swift 1764. **f.** *Haml.* V. ii. 185. **5.** If she be mad.. Her madnesse hath the oddest frame of sense SHAKS. **b.** The village people thought her o., and were a little afraid of her 1882. **c.** It is the oddest carriage in the world DICKENS.

B. *sb.* (the adj. used ellipt.) **a.** An odd thing; that which is odd 1830. **b.** *Golf. The o.*: the stroke which one player has played more than his adversary.

Comb.: **o.-come-short,** a short length of cloth forming the end of a piece; an odd remainder or fragment; **o.-man-out,** a mode of singling out, by tossing, counting, or the like; **o.-pinnate** *a.*, pinnate (as a leaf) with an odd terminal leaflet. Hence **O·dd·ly** *adv.*, **-ness.**

O·ddfe·llow. 1811. [A fanciful name: cf. ODD *a.* II. 5 b.] A member of a secret society, fraternity, or order, organized under this name, for social and benevolent purposes.

Oddity (*ǫ*·dĭti). 1713. [f. ODD *a.* + -ITY.] **1.** The quality or character of being odd; strangeness, singularity 1750. **2.** An odd trait, a peculiarity 1713. **3. a.** An odd person 1748. **b.** Something odd; a fantastic object; a strange event 1834.

2. All people have their oddities DISRAELI. **3. a.** This ridiculous o. danced up to the table at which we sat SMOLLETT.

Oddments (*ǫ*·dmĕnts), *sb. pl.* 1780. [f. ODD *a.* + -MENT, after *fragment.*] Odds and ends; esp. articles belonging to broken or incomplete sets, as offered for sale.

Odds (*ǫ*dz). 1500. [app. pl. of ODD *a.* taken subst.: cf. *news.* Usu. construed as a singular bef. the 19th c.] **1.** (?) Odd or unequal things; inequalities; hence *to make odds even*, to do away with inequalities. **2.** = DIFFERENCE *sb.* 1. Now *rare.* 1542. **b.** The amount by which one quantity or thing exceeds or falls short of another; difference 1548. **c.** Difference in the way of detriment or benefit 1642. **3.** = DIFFERENCE *sb.* 3. Chiefly in *at odds* 1587. **4.** Difference in favour of one of two contending parties; balance of advantage 1574. †**b.** Superior position, advantage –1750. **c.** Equalizing allowance given to a weaker competitor or side. Also *fig.* 1591. **5.** In *Betting*, advantage conceded by one of the parties in proportion to the assumed chances in his favour 1597. **6.** 'Chances' or balance of probability in favour of something happening or being the case, esp. in *it is o.* (*that, but*), now usu. *the o. are* 1589.

7. O. and ends, odd remnants, miscellaneous articles or things (cf. *odd ends*: ODD *a.* II. 4) 1746.

1. *Meas. for M.* III. i. 41. 2. I ken nae o. o' her this many a year GALT. **b.** It [a bill] was retained by the o. of two voices 1671. **c.** Phr. *What's the o.? It is* or *makes no o.* (colloq.). 4. *At o.*, with the balance of advantage for or against one. **c.** Each side feels that it cannot allow any o. to the other 1888. 5. Phr. *To give (lay*, etc.) *o.*, to offer a wager on terms favourable to the other party; *to take o.*, to accept such a wager.

Ode (ōᵘd). 1588. [a. F., ad. late and med.L. *ōda*, earlier also *ōdē*, a. Gr. ᾠδή (contr. from ἀοιδή) song, f. ἀείδειν to sing.] **1. a.** orig., A poem intended to be sung; e.g. the Odes of Pindar, etc. *Choric Odes*, the songs of the chorus in a Greek play, etc. **b.** In mod. use: A rimed (rarely unrimed) lyric, often in the form of an address; usu. dignified or exalted in subject, feeling, and style, but sometimes simple and familiar, and rarely extending to 150 lines. **2.** *Gr. Ch.* Each of the nine Scripture canticles; also, each song or hymn of a series called the *canon of the odes* 1881.

1. O run, prevent them with thy humble o., And lay it lowly at his blessed feet MILTON.

-ode, *formative suffix*, repr. Gr. -ώδης, -ώδες, adj.-ending = 'like, of the nature of', contr. from -οειδής = -o- final of root or comb. vowel + -ειδής like; e.g. λιθώδης stony, etc. Hence Eng. sbs. in *-ode*, in the sense of 'something of the nature of' that expressed by the first element; e.g. *geode*, etc. (Not the same as *-ode* = Gr. ὁδός way, in *anode*, *cathode*, etc.)

Odelet (ōᵘ·dlėt). 1589. [f. ODE + -LET.] A short or little ode.

‖ **Odeum** (odī·ǒm). *Pl.* **odea** (odī·ă). 1682. [Late L., a. Gr. ᾠδεῖον public building for musical performances, f. ᾠδή ODE.] Among the ancient Greeks and Romans, a roofed building, akin to a theatre, for vocal and instrumental music; also, a modern hall, etc., for musical performances.

Odinism (ōᵘ·diniz'm). 1848. [f. *Odin* + -ISM.] The worship of *Odin*, called the *All-father*, the chief deity of Norse mythology, corresp. to the OE. Woden; the pre-Christian mythology and religious doctrine of the ancient Scandinavian people. So **Odi·nian, Odi·nic, Odini·tic** *adjs.* of or pertaining to Odin or Odinism; **O·dinist,** a votary of Odin; a student of O.; also *attrib.* or *adj.*

Odious (ōᵘ·diəs), *a.* late ME. [a. AF., = OF. *odieus*, ad.L. *odiosus*, f. *odium* ODIUM; see -OUS.] Deserving of hatred, hateful; causing or exciting repugnance, disagreeable, offensive, repulsive.

You told a Lye, an o. damned Lye SHAKS. The unhappy woman..whose image became more o. to him every day GEO. ELIOT. Hence **O·dious-ly** *adv.*, **-ness.**

Odium (ōᵘ·diǒm). 1602. [a. L., f. vb.-stem *od-*, *odi-* to hate.] **1.** Hatred, dislike, aversion, detestation: **a.** as a quality of the subject 1654. **b.** as a condition affecting the object 1602. **2.** Odiousness; opprobrium 1678.

a. The universal o. against him 1654. **b.** To avoid yᵗ o. vnder wᶜʰ I lye 1691. **2.** When the o. of the transaction shall be forgotten SCOTT. Phr. *Odium theologicum* (mod.L.), the hatred which proverbially characterizes theological dissensions. Hence, by imitation, *odium æstheticum, medicum, musicum*, etc.

Odometer, etc.: see HODOMETER, etc.

‖ **Odontalgia** (ǫdǫntæ·ldʒiă). Also **-algy.** 1651. [a. Gr. ὀδονταλγία toothache.] Toothache. So **Odonta·lgic** *a.* of or pertaining to toothache; *sb.* a medicine for toothache.

Odonto-, bef. a vowel **odont-,** comb. form of Gr. ὀδούς, ὀδοντ- tooth, as in **Odo·ntocete** (-sīt) [Gr. κῆτος whale] *a. Zool.* (of a cetacean) having teeth instead of whalebone, opp. to *mysticete*; *sb.* a toothed cetacean; hence **Odontoce·tous** *a.* **Odonto·geny** [-GENY], the generation or origin and development of the teeth; hence **Odontoge·nic** *a.* **Odo·ntolite** [Gr. λίθος stone], a fossil tooth; with lapidaries, a fossil tooth or other bone coloured blue by mineral impregnation, occurring in tertiary strata. **Odontosto·matous, Odonto·stomous** [Gr. στομα(τ-) mouth] *adjs.*, having jaws which bite like teeth; mandibulate (as an insect).

Odontoblast (odǫ·ntǒblast). 1878. [f. prec. + -BLAST.] A tooth-cell that produces dentine; any tooth-secreting cell. Hence **-bla·stic** *a.*

‖ **Odontoglossum** (odǫntoglǫ·sǒm). 1880. [mod.L., f. Gr. ὀδούς (see ODONTO-) + γλῶσσα tongue.] *Bot.* A genus of orchids having flowers of great size and beautiful colours; also, a plant or flower of this genus.

Odontograph (odǫ·ntǒgrɑf). 1838. [f. ODONTO- + -GRAPH.] An instrument for marking or setting out the teeth of gear-wheels.

Odontography (ǫdǫntǫ·grăfi). 1840. [f. ODONTO- + -GRAPHY.] A description, or history, of the teeth. Hence **Odontogra·phic** *a.*

Odontoid (odǫ·ntoid), *a.* and *sb.* 1797. [ad. Gr. ὀδοντοειδής tooth-like; see ODONTO- and -OID.] **A.** *adj.* **1.** Resembling or formed like a tooth; tooth-like. **2.** (*attrib.* use of B.) Of or belonging to the odontoid process, as *o. ligament, tubercle* 1840.

1. *O. process* (*o. peg*), a tooth-like projection from the body of the axis or second cervical vertebra of certain mammals and birds; when this process does not coalesce with the body of the axis, as in *Ornithorhynchus* and many reptiles, it is sometimes called the *o. bone*.

B. *sb.* The odontoid process 1854.

Odontology (ǫdǫntǫ·lŏdʒi). 1819. [f. ODONTO- + Gr. -λογία; see -(O)LOGY.] The science which treats of the structure or development of the teeth. So **Odontolo·gic, -al** *adjs.*, **-ally** *adv.* **Odonto·logist** 1788.

Odontophoran (ǫdǫntǫ·fŏrăn), *a.* and *sb.* 1877. [f. mod.L. *Odontophora* (see next).] *Zool.* **A.** *adj.* Of or belonging to the *Odontophora*, or division of molluscs having an odontophore. **B.** *sb.* A mollusc of this group.

Odontophore (odǫ·ntǒfoᵊɹ). 1870. [ad. Gr. ὀδοντοφόρος bearing teeth, f. ὀδούς, ὀδοντ- + -φόρος.] *Zool.* A ribbon-like or strap-like structure covered with teeth, forming the masticatory organ of certain molluscs; the lingual ribbon or 'tongue'. So **Odonto·phoral** *a.* of or pertaining to an o.; also, ODONTOPHORAN *a.* **Odonto·phorous** *a.* possessing an o.

‖ **Odoom** (odū·m). 1887. [Ashanti *odūm*.] A W. African timber tree (*Chlorophora excelsa*).

Odorant (ōᵘ·dŏrănt), *a.* Now *rare.* 1465. [a. F., ad. L. *odorantem*, *odorare* to scent.] = ODOROUS, ODORIFEROUS.

Odorate (ōᵘ·dŏrĕt), *a.* Now *rare.* 1626. [ad. L. *odoratus*, *odorare* to scent.] Scented fragrant.

Odoriferous (ōᵘdŏri·fĕrəs), *a.* late ME. [f. L. *odorifer* (f. *odor*, *odori-* ODOUR + *-fer*) + -OUS.] **1.** That bears or diffuses scent or smell; odorous; *rarely*, ill-smelling. **2.** *fig.* Sweet; 'fragrant' 1577.

1. The o. & swete vyolettes of all obedyence 1497. Hence **Odori·ferously** *adv.*, **-ness.**

Odorous (ōᵘ·dŏrəs), *a.* 1550. [f. L. *odor*, *odorem* ODOUR (or *odorus* fragrant) + -OUS. Formerly occas. pronounced (odoᵊ·rəs).] Emitting a smell or scent; odoriferous; more usu., sweet-smelling; fragrant.

An o. Chaplet of sweet Sommer buds SHAKS. With scents o., spirit-soothing sweets COWPER. Hence **O·dorous-ly** *adv.*, **-ness.**

Odour, odor (ōᵘ·dəɹ). ME. [a. AF. *odour*, OF. *odor*, ad. L. *odorem* smell, scent. The spelling *odor*, frequent in 17th c., is now usual in U.S.] **1.** That property of a substance that is perceptible by the sense of smell; scent, smell; occas. *spec.* sweet scent; fragrance. **2.** *transf.* A substance that emits a sweet smell or scent; a perfume; *esp.* incense, spice, ointment, etc. *arch.* or *Obs.* late ME. **3.** *fig.* **a.** 'Fragrance'; 'savour' ME. **b.** (*Good* or *bad*) Repute, favour, estimation 1847.

1. The effluvium or odor of Steel SIR T. BROWNE. The lime at dewy eve Diffusing odours COWPER. **2.** Thy Myrtles strow, thy Odours burn PRIOR. **3. a.** No o. of religious intolerance attaches to it 1873. **b.** Hartlib was in good odor during the days of the commonwealth 1864. Phr. **Odour of sanctity** (F. *odeur de sainteté*): a sweet or balsamic odour stated to have been exhaled by the bodies of eminent saints at their death, or when exhumed, and held to attest their saintship; hence, *fig.*, reputation for holiness; occas. used ironically. Hence **O·dourless** *a.* without o. or scent.

Odyl (ōᵘ·dil, ǫ·dil). Also **-yle.** 1850. [f. OD² + Gr. ὕλη material; see -YL.] = OD². Hence **Ody·lic** *a.* **O·dylism,** the doctrine of o. or od. **O·dylize** *v. trans.* to subject to or affect with o.

Odyssey (ǫ·disi). 1601. [ad.L. *Odyssea*, a. Gr. Ὀδύσσεια, f. Ὀδυσσεύς Ulysses, a king of Ithaca.] **1.** One of the two great epic poems of ancient Greece, attributed to Homer, which describes the ten years' wanderings of Odysseus on his way home to Ithaca after the fall of Troy. **2.** *fig.* A long wandering or series of travels 1889. Hence **Odyssean** (ǫdisī·ăn) *a.*

œ (at first, and now often, written separately *oe*) reproduces in modern Eng. the usual L. spelling of Gr. οι, which often in med.L., and in Romanic, was treated like simple *ē*. In words that have come into Eng. through med. L. or Fr., or other Romanic langs., Eng. has usu. a simple *e*, as in *economy*, F. *économie*, L. *œconomia*, Gr. οἰκονομία; but in recent words derived immed. from L. or Gr., *æ*, *oe* is usu. retained. This *æ*, being orig. a diphthong and subsequently a long vowel, is usu. pronounced as 'long *e*' (ī), rarely as 'short *e*' (e); when changed to *e*, it submits to the same usages as ordinary *e* from Gr. and L.

Œcist (ī·sist), **œkist** (ī·kist). Also **oikist.** 1846. [ad. Gr. οἰκιστής, f. οἰκίζειν to settle (a colony), f. οἶκος house, dwelling.] The founder of an ancient Greek (rarely a modern) colony.

Œcoid (ī·koid). Also **oikoid.** 1892. [f. Gr. οἶκος house; see -OID.] *Biol.* The colourless stroma of a red blood-corpuscle.

‖ **Œcology, eco-** (īkǫ·lŏdʒi). 1873. [mod. f. Gr. οἶκος + -(O)LOGY; after *œconomy*.] **1.** *Biol.* The branch of biology which deals with the mutual relations between organisms and their environment. **2.** The mutual relations collectively; e.g. the œ. of a plant, etc. **3.** *Sociol.* Study of the spatial distribution of a population in reference to material and social causes and effects. Hence **Œcolo·gical** *a.* **Œco·logist.**

Œconomic, -nomy: see ECONOMIC, etc.

Œcumenic (īkiumeˑnik), *a.* 1588. [ad. L. *œcumenicus*, a. Gr. οἰκουμενικός of or belonging to ἡ οἰκουμένη 'the inhabited (earth)', the whole world.] = next.

Œcumenical (īkiume·nikăl), *a.* 1563. [f. as prec. + -AL.] **1.** *Eccl.* Belonging to or representing the whole (Christian) world, or the universal church; general, universal, catholic; *spec.* applied to the general councils of the early church, and (in mod. use) of the R. C. Church; also assumed as a title by the Patriarch of Constantinople; formerly sometimes applied to the Pope of Rome. **2.** *gen.* Universal, general, world-wide 1607. Hence **Œcume·nicalism,** the theological system or doctrine of the œcumenical councils. **Œcume·nically** *adv.*

Œcumenicity (īkiūmėni·sĭti). Also **ec-.** 1840. [ad. eccl. med.L. *œcumenicitas*; see above and -ITY.] Œcumenical character.

‖ **Œdema** (idī·mă). Also **edema.** late ME. [mod.L., a. Gr. οἴδημα (-ματ-), f. οἰδέειν to swell.] *Path.* A swelling due to effusion of watery fluid into the intercellular spaces of connective tissue. **Œde·matose** *a.* = next.

Œdematous (idī·m-, ide·mătəs), *a.* Also **oid-, ed-.** 1646. [f. Gr. οἰδηματ- (see prec.) + -OUS.] Pertaining to, of the nature of, or having œdema. Hence **Œde·matously** *adv.*

Œdipean (īdipī·ăn, *U.S.* ed-), *a.* 1621. irreg. f. ŒDIPUS; see -EAN.] Pertaining to, or like that of, Œdipus; clever at guessing a riddle.

Œdipus (ī·dipǒs, *U.S.* ed-). 1557. [a. Gr. Οἰδίπους, Οἰδιποδ-, lit. 'swollen-footed', proper name.] Name of the Theban hero who solved the riddle propounded by the Sphinx; hence, one who is clever at guessing riddles.

I am not Oedipus inough, To vnderstand this Sphynx B. JONS. *Œ. complex*: a psychoanalyst's term for an infantile fixation on the mother.

‖ **Œil-de-bœuf** (öydəböf). 1826. [F., lit. 'ox-eye'.] **1.** = BULL'S EYE 6. 1849. **2.** Name of a small octagonal vestibule lighted by a small round window in the palace at Versailles; hence *transf.* and *fig.*

‖ **Œillade.** 1592. Now *arch.* [a. F., f. *œil* eye + -ADE 1 a, as in *cannonade*, etc. Formerly (ǝ̄·liad, i·liăd); now as French (öyad).] A glance of the eye, *esp.* an amorous glance, ogle. *Lear* IV. v. 25.

Œillet, œlet: see **Oillet**.

Œnanthic (*īnæ·nþik*), *a.* 1838. [f. L. *œnanthē*, a. Gr. οἰνάνθη (f. οἴνη vine + ἄνθη blossom, etc.) a vine-shoot or bud, vine-blossom, vine.] *Chem.* Having the characteristic odour of wine.

Œ. acid, an acid (or mixture of acids) $C_{14}H_{26}O_2$+ H_2O, obtained from œnanthic ether. *Œ. ether*, a mobile oily liquid, the source of the peculiar odour of wines, obtained by distillation of wine-lees. So **Œna·nthol**, œnanthylic aldehyde, furnished by the destructive distillation of castor oil. **Œna·nthyl**, $C_7H_{15}O$, the hypothetical radical of œnanthylic acid and its derivatives. **Œnanthy·lic** *a.*, in *œ. acid*, $C_7H_{14}O_2$, a transparent colourless oil, having an unpleasant odour like that of cod-fish. **Œna·nthylate**, a salt of œnanthylic acid.

Œno- (*īnǫ*), occas. **oino-** (oinǫ), comb. form of Gr. οἶνος wine, as in **Œnology** (*inǫ·lŏdʒi*), the knowledge or study of wines; so **Œnolo·gical** *a.*, **Œno·logist**. **Œnomania** (*īnomēⁱ·niă*), oino- [MANIA], (*a*) dipsomania; (*b*) delirium tremens; hence **Œnoma·niac**. **Œnometer** (*inǫ·mĭtəɹ*) [-METER], an alcoholometer. **Œnophilist** (*inǫ·filist*) [Gr. -φιλος], a lover of wine. **Œnothionic** (-þəiǫ·nik) *a.* [Gr. θεῖον sulphur], *Chem.* in *Œnothionic acid*, an acid ($C_2H_6SO_4$) obtained by treating alcohol with sulphuric acid; *ethylsulphuric* or *sulphovinic acid*.

Œnolic (*īnǫ·lik*), *a.* 1860. [a. Gr. οἶνος wine: see -OL and -IC.] *Chem.* in *Œ. acid*, any of a series of weak tannin-like acids forming the colouring matter of wine.

Œnomel (*ī·nomel*). Also †**oino-**. 1574. [ad. L. *œnomeli* (late L. *-melum*), a. Gr. οἰνόμελι, f. οἶνος + μέλι honey.] A mixture of wine and honey, used by the ancient Greeks.

fig. Those memories..Make a better œ. MRS. BROWNING.

O'er (ōəɹ), formerly **ore**, poet. and dial. contr. of OVER. dating from the 16th c.

Œsophageal (*īsofæ·dʒiăl*), *a.* Also **eso-**. 1807. [f. mod.L. *œsophageus* (f. *œsophagus*) + -AL.] Of, belonging to, or connected with the œsophagus. So **Œso·phagal**, **Œsopha·gean**, **Œsopha·giac** *adjs.* in same sense.

Œsophagitis (*īsofădʒəi·tis*). 1857. [f. ŒSOPHAGUS + -ITIS.] *Path.* Inflammation of the œsophagus.

Œsophago- (*īsǫ·făgo*), bef. a vowel **œsophag-**, comb. form. of Gr. οἰσοφάγος, ŒSOPHAGUS, as in **Œsophagectomy** (-e·ktŏmi) [Gr. ἐκτομή excision], excision of a portion of the œsophagus. **Œsophago·tomy** [Gr. -τομία], incision into the œsophagus; etc.

Œsophagus (*īsǫ·făgŏs*). Also **eso-**. late ME. [mod.L., a. Gr. οἰσοφάγος the gullet; etym. unkn.] The tube or canal extending from the mouth to the stomach, and serving for the passage of food and drink; the gullet.

‖**Œstrum** (*ī·strŏm*, *U.S.* e·s-). 1656. [med. L., var. of next.] = next.

‖**Œstrus** (*ī·strŏs*, *U.S.* e·s-). 1697. [L., a. Gr. οἶστρος gad-fly, breeze, also sting, hence frenzy.] **1.** *Entom.* A genus of dipterous insects of which the larvæ are parasitic in the bodies of various animals; an insect of this genus or of the family *Œstridæ*; a gad-fly or bot-fly. **2.** *fig.* Something that stings or goads one on, a stimulus; vehement impulse; frenzy 1850. **b.** *Physiol.* A vehement bodily appetite; *spec.* sexual orgasm; the rut of animals 1890.

2. The Impetus, the Lyrical œstrus, is gone E. FITZGERALD.

Of (*ǫv*, ŏv, əv), *prep.* See also O *prep.*[2] [OE. *of*, unaccented form of the word of which the corresp. str. form was *æf*, *af:—OTeut. *aƀa; corresp. to Skr. *apa* away from, down from, Gr. ἀπό, L. *ab*. A differentiated form of *of* is OFF.]

General Signification. The primary sense was *away, away from*, a sense now obsolete. Hence *of* was naturally used in the expression of the notions of removal, separation, privation, derivation, origin or source, starting-point, spring of action, cause, agent, instrument, material, etc. Its scope was enlarged, even in OE., by its employment to render L. *ab, de*, or *ex*, in constructions where the native idiom would not have used it; and by its employment from the 11th c. as the equivalent of F. *de*, which not merely represented L. *de* in its prepositional uses, but had come to be the Common Romanic, and so the French, substitute for the genitive case.

I. Of *motion, direction, distance*. **1.** Indicating a point of time, etc. from which something begins or proceeds. *Obs.* exc. in archaic expressions, and in such phrases as *of late, of recent years, of old, of yore*, which have come to have the sense of 'during', 'in the course of' the time indicated. OE. **2.** Away from, out of (see quots.). OE. **b.** *U.S.* In expressing the time: = To *prep.* II. 1 b. 1879.

1. One that I brought vp of a puppy SHAKS. 2. *North of, south of*, etc., *within* (a mile, an hour, an ace, etc.) *of, wide of, back of* (U.S.), *backwards of* (arch.), *upwards of* (an amount); see these words.

II. Of *liberation* and *privation*. Expressing separation from or of a property, possession, or appurtenance. **1.** In the construction of trans. etc. vbs.; as, *to cure, heal*, etc.; *to cleanse, purge*, etc.; *to free, rid of*, etc.; *to deprive, strip of*, etc. OE. **2.** In the construction of intrans. vbs.; as, *to recover*, †*lack*, etc. *of* ME. **3.** In the constr. of adjs.; as, *whole* (*of a wound*); *clean, quit, rid*, etc.; *bare, barren, void*, etc. *of* OE.

1. What little town..Is emptied of its folk this quiet morn KEATS. 2. I thinke it lacks of twelue SHAKS. 3. I am poor of thanks SHAKS.

III. Of *origin* or *source*. Indicating the person or thing whence anything originates, comes, is acquired or sought OE.

I hope you will not take it ill of me, that I offer my advice 1755. Of English parents, and of a good English family of clergymen, Swift was born in Dublin THACKERAY. You expect too much of your sister DICKENS. There was one child of the marriage 1885.

IV. Of the *source* or *starting-point of action, emotion*, etc.; *motive, cause, ground, reason*. **1.** Out of, from, as an outcome, expression, or consequence of OE. **b.** *Of oneself*, by one's own motion, spontaneously, unaided OE. **2.** Indicating the cause, reason, or ground of an action, occurrence, fact, feeling, etc. OE. **3.** After an adj. or sb., indicating that which causes or gives rise to the quality, feeling, or action: Because of, on account of. ME.

1. Phr. *Of one's own accord, of choice, course, one's own knowledge, necessity, one's own good pleasure, purpose, right*, etc. **b.** The Goats..would many of them come of themselves to be milked 1707. 2. All women labouryng of chylde *Bk. Com. Prayer*. How can wee excuse ourselues of negligence? BIBLE *Transl. Pref.* 1611. I am dying of fatigue 1843. 3. We were dead of sleepe SHAKS. I wish him ioy of her SHAKS. Sick of inaction MACAULAY.

V. Indicating the *agent* or *doer*. **1.** Introducing the agent after a passive vb. (Now usu. repl. by BY, but still in literary use.) OE. **2.** Indicating the doer of something characterized by an adj., as *it was kind of you* (= a kind thing done by you) *to help him*. Used with an adj. and sb., as *a cruel act, an odd thing*, etc.; a qualified pa. pple., as *ill done*, etc.; now only with an adj. alone, as *good, bad, rude, silly*, etc. (Usu. followed by *to do* something.) 1532. **3.** After a sb., expressing the relation of doer, or that of maker or author (= *subjective genitive*) ME.

1. Being warned of God in a dreame *Matt.* ii. 12. A wretch forsaken of God and man 1869. 2. It was most absurd of you to offer it 1887. 3. He had the secret approbation of his prince FROUDE. The Iliad of Homer. The phonograph of Edison (*mod.*).

VI. Indicating *means* or *instrument* OE.

They live of bread made of pith of trees PURCHAS. It was pouring of rain 1824.

VII. Indicating the *material* or *substance* of which anything is made or consists, or the class of which anything is an example OE.

Will you make an Asse o' me? SHAKS. On Beds of Violets blew MILT. That scamp of a [= scampish] husband of hers THACKERAY. Living quite as hard a life of it RUSKIN. A distance of over 700 yards 1896. A house of cards. The name of John. The hour of eleven. A state of rest (*mod.*). Phr. *To make much of, the best of.*

VIII. Indicating the *subject-matter of thought, feeling*, or *action*, i.e. that about which it is exercised: Concerning, about, with regard to, in reference to OE. **1.** After vbs. OE. **2.** After sbs. *Obs.* or *arch.* ME. **3.** After adjs. 1489.

1. Thus it fortuned of this adventure LD. BERNERS. Of Mans First Disobedience..Sing Heav'nly Muse MILT. To observe the young prince, and to inform himself of his character 1861. 2. Mr. Hobbs, in his Discourse of Human Nature ADDISON. 3. The same observations are true of all other contracts 1886.

IX. Representing an original *genitive dependent on a vb. or adj.* **1.** In the construction of vbs. ME. **2.** In the construction of adjs.

Many of these involve a sb., which may be taken as the subject of the genitive relation; e.g. *hopeful of*, having hope of, *envious of*, having envy of, etc.; others are verbal derivs., e.g. *expressive of* = that expresses ME.

1. Haue merci of me ME. As for the earthquake, I heard not of it 1575. Shakespear..availed himself of the old Chronicles HAZLITT. Resolutions which perhaps no single member in his heart approves of 1888. 2. The Generous Youth..studious of the Prize DRYDEN. Symbolic of the place and people too BROWNING.

X. Expressing the relation of the *objective genitive*. **1.** After a vbl. sb. in *-ing* ME. **2.** After what was formerly a vbl. sb. governed by *in* or *a*, but is now identified with a present pple. Now *dial.* or *vulgar*. 1563. **3.** After a noun of action OE. **4.** After an agent-n. ME.

1. For the auoydinge of strife 1551. We must cease throwing of stones either at saints or squirrels RUSKIN. 2. They being altering of the stage PEPYS. 3. The betrayal of a secret 1873. 4. I am a great eater of beefe SHAKS.

XI. Indicating that *in respect of* which a quality is attributed, or a fact is predicated.

Infirme of purpose SHAKS. Of able Body, sound of Limb and Wind DRYDEN. He is..fifty-three years of age 1843. He is rather hard of hearing (*mod.*).

XII. Indicating a *quality* or other mark, *time, place*, etc., by which a person or thing is characterized. (For OE. genitive; F. *de*; = *genitive of quality or description*.)

Sonne be off good chere TINDALE *Matt.* ix. 2. Are you of fourescore pounds a yeere SHAKS. One Vice, but of a minute old SHAKS. Four Misses all pretty much of a size RICHARDSON. She was all of a muck of sweat GOLDSM. Is it the hour of prayer? 1816. A boy of fourteen DICKENS. The haven of their desire R. V. *Ps.* cvii. 30 *margin*.

XIII. In *partitive* expressions; indicating things or a thing of which a part is expressed by the preceding words.

More than any of his predecessours 1523. The fairest of her Daughters Eve MILT. That sacred head of thine MILT. This was..a false step of the..general's DE FOE. It is what I desire of all things BERKELEY. As though of hemlock I had drunk KEATS. Shakespeare was of [= one of] us BROWNING. He had not been sworn of the Council MACAULAY. Whatever of best he can conceive RUSKIN. My person was indeed of [= one of, something of] the shortest 1878. Had three sons, of whom Thomas married twice 1888. The most dogged of fighters, the most dangerous of enemies 1892. There were only five of us (*mod.*).

XIV. In the sense *Belonging* or *pertaining to*: expressing possession and its converse: 'the owner of the house', 'the house of the owner'. **1.** Belonging to a place, time, or thing OE. **2.** Belonging to a person, etc. ME. **3.** Belonging to an action or the like, as that to which it relates 1534.

1. Men of Nynyue WYCLIF *Matt.* xii. 41. Justice of the Kinges Bench. late ME. Don Quixote of the Mancha 1612. He was not of an age, but for all time! B. JONS. Gideon the Judge of Israel 1662. One side of the barricadoes 1756. Companions of his exile 1844. A man of that time THACKERAY. A thing of the near future 1885. 2. I am glad you understand the reason of it 1559. But yet the pitty of it, Iago SHAKS. The tomb of England's first martyr 1886. 3. The weather is the solitary topic of conversation 1886.

XV. Indicating a *point or space of time*. **1.** At some time during, in the course of, on. Now only *colloq.*, in *of an evening, of a morning*, and the like. OE. **b.** Occas. the genitival *-s* is retained; perh. often understood as pl. 1740. **2.** During, for (a space of time). (In later use only with a neg.) *Obs.* or *arch.* late ME. **3.** *Of old, of yore, of late, of late years*: In or during the time specified (but prob. orig. in sense I. 1.) late ME.

1. Of a Thursday my dear Father and Mother were marry'd RICHARDSON. **b.** Shut up by himself of nights LAMB. 2. Not seeing or hearing from him of a long time 1760. 3. The duties have been very much lightened of late years 1885.

XVI. In *locative* and other obsolete uses. *esp.* **1.** In sense *on*. *Obs.*, *colloq.*, or *vulgar*. late ME. †**b.** esp. with *side, hand, part*, etc. –1779. **2.** In sense *in*. Mostly *Obs.* late ME. **3.** In sense *with*. Mostly *Obs.* 1523.

1. She might send him of an errand WESLEY. **b.** Six banks of paddles, three banks of a side 1779. 2. I have just been mortified enough of all conscience GOLDSM. 3. What do you want of Padre Francisco! LONGF.

XVII. Phr. **1. a.** *Of* followed by a sb. forms attrib. or advb. phrases; as, *of age, of a cer-*

tainty, of choice, of course, of necessity, of right, of a truth, etc.: see the sbs. **b.** *Of* followed by an adj. (or advb.) formerly formed advb. phrases [cf. F. *de loin, de nouveau*, etc.] *Obs.* exc. in *of a sudden*, or as repr. by worn-down forms in *a-* (*afar, afresh, alight, anew*). ME. **2.** *Of* forms the last element of many prepositional phrases: e.g. *because of; by means of, by reason of; for fear of; in behalf of, in case of, in consequence of, in face of, in lieu of, in respect of, in spite of, instead of; on account of, on behalf of, on condition of, on the point of*; etc. See the sbs.

Of-, *prefix*, the prepositional adv. OF, OFF, in comb. corresp. to L. *ab-*, Gr. ἀπο-, Skr. *apa-*, forming compounds of different ages.

1. In vbs. and their derivs. of Germanic or OE. age, retained in ME., but now obs.

2. In later combs. of OE. and ME. age, the sense of the particle is usu. 'off'. In the 16th c., *of-* in this connexion passed imperceptibly into *off-*, the form in later combinations.

Off (ǫf), *adv., prep., adj.*, and *sb.* OE. [orig. the same word as OF, *off* being at first a variant spelling, which was gradually appropriated to the emphatic form, i.e. to the adv. and the prepositional senses closely related to it. *Of* and *off* were not completely differentiated till after 1600.] **A.** *adv.* **I. 1.** To a distance, away, quite away. Also expressing resistance to motion towards; as in *ward off*, etc. **b.** *Naut.* Away from land, or from the ship; also, away from the wind 1610. **c.** *ellipt.* Gone off, just going off. Also *fig.* fallen or falling asleep. 1791. **2.** At a distance, distant. Also in AFAR *off*, FAR *off*. 1500. **b.** *fig.* Distant or remote in fact, nature, character, feeling, thought, etc. *Obs.* or *arch.* (except U.S.). 1555. **3.** Expressing separation from attachment, contact, or position on; as in *to break, cast, cut, put, shake, take off*, etc. OE. **b.** with ellipsis of pa. pple. = *come, cut, fallen off*; esp. *put* or *taken off* as clothes ME. **4.** So as to interrupt continuity or cause discontinuance; as in *break off, leave off, declare off*, etc. ME. **b.** Discontinued; no longer in operation or going on 1752. **c.** *transf.* Of a person: Disengaged, done *with* 1710. **5.** To the end; entirely, completely; as *to clear off, drink off, pay off, polish off, work off* 1440. **6.** In the way of abatement, diminution, or decay; as in *to fall off, cool off, go off*; also, *to be off* 1632. **7.** In all senses, *off* may be followed by *from*; formerly, and still *dial.*, by *of* 1526.

1. Quilp..took himself off DICKENS. **b.** Phr. *Nothing off*, to bring the ship's head nearer to the wind. **c.** I'm off for the Red Sea 1822. **2.** A street or two off FIELDING. **3.** Let it stew..then strain it off 1756. *fig.* Will. laught this off at first ADDISON. **b.** With some of his clothes on, and some off DE FOE. **4.** Upon Saturday..they break off work sooner by an hour 1657. To turn the gas off (*mod.*). **b.** When football is 'off' and cricket not yet 'on' 1901. **c.** It is best to be off wi' the old love, Before you be on wi' the new SCOTT *'Old Song'*. **d.** Away from work or duty, as *a day off* 1893. **5.** To pay off the mortgage 1818. **7.** Stand or syt a good wayе of from the fyre 1542. A fall off of a Tree SHAKS.

II. Phr. etc. **1.** BUY, COME, DASH, GET, GO, LOOK, MARK, PALM, PASS, RATTLE, TAKE OFF, etc.: see those verbs. **2.** Used with ellipsis of *come, go, take*, etc. *Off with* = take or put off. ME. **b.** *Off!* = stand off! be off! *Off with you!* = be off! 1594. **3.** *Right off, straight off*: straightway, forthwith. **4.** In *well, ill, better, worse, badly, comfortably off*, etc., *off* = '-circumstanced', '-conditioned', esp. as regards the means of life. Rarely *attrib.* or *adj.* 1733. **5.** *Either off or on*, either one way or another. See also OFF AND ON. 1549.

B. *prep.* **I.** Of motion or direction. **1.** Away from, down from, up from, so as no longer to lie, rest, or lean on OE. **2.** Of source: From the hands, charge, or possession of; esp. with *take, buy, borrow, hire*, and the like. Also expressed by FROM. 1535. **3.** Of material or substance: with *dine, eat*, etc. Now *rare.* 1815. **4.** Of deduction, etc.: From 1833.

1. A man falling off a ladder H. WALPOLE. **2.** She admitted borrowing the 1 *l.* off the plaintiff 1897. **3.** He always..eats a supper off pork steaks, nearly raw 1815. **4.** To get something taken off the price (*mod.*).

II. Of position. **1.** Away from being on; not on; no longer on 1688; *fig.* of a condition; not engaged in or upon, disinclined for 1681. **2.** Distant from (*lit.* and *fig.*) 1627. **b.** *Naut.* To seaward of; opposite or abreast of to seaward; also, away from (the wind). See also OFF-SHORE. 1669. **3.** *ellipt.* Opening or turning out of 1845. **4.** **From off**: = sense I. 1. late ME.

1. As soon as the dew is off the ground 1759. *fig.* To be off one's feed 1816. I have been off my head ever since the blow fell 1894. Phr. *To be off duty.* **2.** Two Miles off this Town ADDISON. **b.** The Stagg Rocks off the Lizard 1726. **3.** Thoroughfares off Cheapside and Cornhill 1851. **4.** Would I might neuer stirre from off this place SHAKS.

C. *adj.* [The adv. used attrib.] **1.** More distant, farther, far 1856. **b.** *Naut.* Farther from the shore; seaward 1666. **2.** *spec.* **a.** Of horses and vehicles: Right, as opp. to the *near* or left side, on which the driver walks, the rider mounts, etc. Hence *off horse* (of a pair), *off foot, leg, wheel*, etc. (Often hyphened.) 1675. **b.** *Cricket.* Applied to that side of the wicket, or of the field, opposite to that on which the batsman stands 1850. **3.** Lying off from, leading out of the main part 1851. **b.** *Off chance, off-chance*, a remote chance 1861. **4.** Said of a day, evening, season, etc., when one is 'off work'. The precise meaning depends on the context. (Occas. hyphened.) 1848. **5.** In ref. to the sale of beer, etc.: Short for 'off the premises', as in *off licence, sale, consumption*, etc. 1891.

1. It is on the 'off' side of the spectator (*mod.*). **b.** Our masts fell all over the off side 1726. **2.** Silver Blaze with his..mottled off fore leg 1894. **3. b.** There was an off-chance he might go back on the whole idea STEVENSON. **4.** That in future all such meetings be held on 'off days' in preference to 'market days' 1897.

D. *sb.* [the adj. used absol. or ellipt.] **1.** The condition or fact of being off 1669. **2.** *Cricket.* = Off side: see C. 2 b. *Comb.* **Off-drive**, a drive to the off. 1857.

Off, *v.* 1882. [From (chiefly colloq. or illiterate) uses of OFF *adv.*; cf. *to* IN, *to* BACK.] **1.** *intr.* To make off. (*illiterate.*) 1895. **2.** *Naut.* Of a ship: To move off from shore. In pr. pple. *offing.* **3.** *To off with*, to take off instantly. *illiterate* or *joc.* 1892.

Off-, *prefix.* In earlier times written *of-* (see OF-*pref.* 2). In verbs, the stress is now usu. upon the root; in the other classes (2–4) on *off-*.

1. with vbs., *off-* (ME. *of-*) enters into quasi-combination, chiefly as a separable particle, like G. *ab-* in *ab-reisen, ab-schreiben*, etc. In the pples. the adv. is still sometimes put first, and is then sometimes hyphened to the vb. Late examples are *off-drive, off-load*, etc.

2. with pres. and pa. pples., forming adjs. (stress on *off*) as *o·ff-bitten, off-standing*, etc.

3. with vbl. sbs. and nouns of action, forming sbs., sometimes concrete (stress on *off*): *o·ff-setting, off-break* (a break off), *off-look*, etc. See also Main words.

4. with other sbs., usu. with the sense 'lying or leading off from the main trunk', etc.: as in *o·ff-branch, off-spur, off-stream.*

Offal (ǫ·fǎl). late ME. [f. OFF *adv.* + FALL *sb.*[1]] **1.** That which falls, or is thrown off, as chips, dross, etc.; refuse, waste; also *pl.*, scraps of waste stuff or refuse. Now only *techn.* or *dial.* = *o. corn* or *wheat, o. leather, o. wood.* †**b.** In collect. sing. and pl.: Crumbs, leavings; relics, remnants –1786. **2. a.** The parts cut off in dressing the carcase of an animal killed for food; orig., the entrails; now, as a trade term, including the head and tail, the kidneys, heart, tongue, liver, and other parts. †Formerly also in *pl.* late ME. **b.** Contemptuously: Putrid flesh; carrion; also, opprobriously, the bodies or limbs of the slain 1581. **3.** In the fish trade: Low-priced or inferior fish as opp. to those called *prime* 1859. **4.** Refuse in general; rubbish, garbage. Now chiefly *sing.* 1598. **5.** *fig.* Refuse, offscourings, dregs, scum. Chiefly in *collect. sing.* 1581. **6.** *attrib.* or *adj.* **a.** *lit.* (See preceding senses.) 1596. **b.** *fig.* Outcast; worthless; vile. Now esp. *dial.* 1605.

2. b. Nigh burst With suckt and glutted o. MILT. **3.** Plaice, haddock, cod, ling, etc. come under the technical name of o. 1887. **5.** What trash is Rome? What Rubbish, and what Offall? SHAKS. **6. b.** He's an o. creatur as iver come about the primises GEO. ELIOT.

Off and on, *adv. phr.* (*adj.*) 1535. [OFF *adv.* I. 4, I. 1 c, II. 5.] **1.** With interruption and resumption of action; intermittently, now and again. **2.** *Naut.* On alternate tacks 1608. **b.** Used prepositionally 1708.

1. I..slept off and on..all the way to Crewe 1860. **2. b.** To stand off and on shore 1769.

B. *predicatively* or as *adj.* Sometimes off and sometimes on; intermittent; vacillating 1583.

Off-cast, offcast (ǫ·fkɑst), *ppl. a.* and *sb.* 1571. [f. OFF *adv.* + *cast*, pa. pple. of CAST *v.*] **A.** *ppl. a.* Cast off, rejected. **B.** *sb.* A thing or person that is cast off or rejected (*lit.* or *fig.*). 1587.

Off-chance: see OFF *a.* 3 b.

O·ff co·lour, o·ff-co·lour, *phr.* and *a.* orig. *U.S.* 1860. [OFF *prep.* II. 1.] Of precious stones: Not of the right colour. Hence *fig.* (*a*) Improper, 'doubtful' (*U.S.*); (*b*) out of order, in poor health, 'not up to the mark'.

Off-corn (ǫ·fkǭɹn). 1573. [OFF *adv.* I. 1.] Waste or 'offal' corn.

Offcut (ǫ·fkʊt). 1663. [f. OFF-*prefix* 3 + CUT *v.*] Something that is cut off. In *Printing*, a piece cut off a sheet to reduce it to the proper size; also, a part cut off the main sheet and folded separately, as in a sheet of duodecimo.

Offence (ǫfe·ns). late ME. Also U.S. **offense.** [Two forms: ME. *offens*, a. OF. *offens* injury, etc, ad. L. *offensus*, f. *offens-*, ppl. stem of *offendere* (see OFFEND); and ME. *offense, offence*, a. F. *offense*, ad. L. *offensa* a striking against, f. *offensus, offendere*. In U.S. *offense* is now usual.] †**1.** In Biblical use: Striking the foot against, stumbling. *lit.* and *fig.* (*rare*) –1611. **2.** A stumbling-block; an occasion of unbelief, doubt, or apostasy. late ME. **3.** Attack, assault. late ME. †**4.** Hurt, harm, injury, damage –1705. †**b.** Feeling of being hurt, pain –1674. **5.** The act or fact of offending, wounding the feelings of, or displeasing, another; usu. viewed as it affects the person offended; hence, **b.** Offended or wounded feeling. late ME. †**c.** Disfavour –1601. †**6. a.** Offensiveness. **b.** An offensive object, quality, feature, or state of things; a nuisance. –1660. **7.** A breach of law, duty, propriety, or etiquette; a transgression, sin, wrong, misdemeanour, or misdeed. Const. *against*. late ME. **b.** *spec.* in *Law.* 1780.

1. *Isa.* viii. 14. **2.** The o. of the Cross shall be my proudest boast 1865. **3.** Phr. *Arms of o.*, offensive weapons. **4.** *Jul. C.* IV. iii. 201. **b.** They leave an o. in the ear 1674. **5.** As full of Quarrell, and o. As my yong Mistris dogge SHAKS. Unfortunately, o. is usually taken where o. is meant 1882. Phr. *To give o. to*, to offend; *to take o.*, to be offended, to take umbrage; *without o.*, without giving or taking o. **6. b.** *All's Well* II. iii. 270. **7.** Phr. *To commit* (†*do, make*) *an o.*; What o. hath this man made you, Sir? SHAKS. **b.** *Offence, crime*; act of wickedness. It is used as a *genus*, comprehending every crime and misdemeanor; or as a *species* signifying a crime not indictable, but punishable summarily, or by the forfeiture of a penalty WHARTON. Hence **Offe·nceless** *a.* (chiefly *poet.*), without o.; unoffending, inoffensive; **-ly** *adv.*

Offend (ǫfe·nd), *v.* ME. [a. OF. *offendre* to strike against, etc., ad. L. *offendere*, f. *ob-* OB- 1 + *-fendere* (found only in compounds).] **I. 1.** To stumble morally; to commit a sin, crime, or fault; to transgress. Const. *against*, †*to*, †*unto*. late ME. †**2.** *trans.* To sin against; to wrong (a person); to violate (a law, etc.) –1651. †**3.** In Biblical use: To be a stumbling-block to (a person); to cause to stumble or sin –1658. †**b.** *intr.* To be caused to stumble –1611.

1. We haue offended agaynst thy holy lawes *Bk. Com. Prayer.* Great wits sometimes may gloriously o. POPE. **2.** *Meas. for M.* III. ii. 16. **3.** Yf thy hande offende the cut hym of TINDALE *Mark* ix. 43. **b.** If meate make my brother to o. 1 *Cor.* viii. 13.

II. †**1.** *trans.* To attack, assail; also *absol.* to act on the offensive –1744. †**2.** To strike so as to hurt; to give (physical) pain to; to harm –1758. **3.** To vex, annoy, displease, anger; now *esp.* To excite personal annoyance, resentment, or disgust in (any one). (Now the chief sense.) late ME.

3. The rankest compound of villanous smell, that euer offended nostrill SHAKS. *To be offended*: to be displeased, vexed, or annoyed. Now, usu., To feel hurt, take offence; He was highly offended at being passed over (*mod.*). Hence **Offe·ndedly** *adv.* in an offended manner. **Offe·nder**, one who offends; in *Law*, one who commits an OFFENCE (sense 7 b).

†**Offe·nsion.** late ME. [a. OF., ad. L. *offensionem*, f. *offendere* to OFFEND.] **1.** = OFFENCE 4–7. –1582. **2.** Stumbling; strik-

ing against some obstacle -1656. b. Spiritual stumbling, or the occasion of it WYCLIF.

Offensive (ǫfe·nsiv), *a.* (*sb.*) 1547. [ad. med.L. *offensivus*, f. *offens-*, *offendere* (see -IVE).] 1. Pertaining or tending to attack; aggressive; adapted or used for purposes of attack; characterized by attacking. Opp. to *defensive*. †2. Hurtful, injurious -1813. 3. Giving, or of a nature to give, offence; displeasing; annoying; insulting 1576. 4. Causing unpleasant sensations; now, nauseous, repulsive 1594. †5. Of the nature of a transgression -1649. B. *sb.* [absol. use of 1.] *The offensive*: the position or attitude of attack; aggressive action 1720.

1. O. and defensive arms GIBBON. 2. Water Fowl are o. to the Stomach sometimes 1732. 3. Like an offensiue wife, That hath enrag'd him on, to offer strokes SHAKS. The Prussians are very insolent, and hardly less o. to the English than to the French 1815. 4. Permitting o. smells to emanate from certain drains 1886. B. Haphazard o. is one thing; judicious o. quite another 1879. **Offe·nsive·ly** *adv.*, **-ness.**

Offer (ǫ·fəɹ), *sb.* late ME. [a. F. *offre*, vbl. sb. f. *offrir* to OFFER.] 1. An act of offering (see OFFER *v.* 3, 4); a presenting for acceptance; a proposal to give or do something. b. *ellipt.* A proposal of marriage. *arch.* 1548. c. The act of making a bid for something 1550. d. The condition of being offered; in *Comm.* the fact of being offered for sale 1794. 2. *concr.* That which is offered. Now *rare* or *Obs.* 1548. 3. An essay at doing something, or a show of this; the act of aiming at something, an aim. Now *rare* or *Obs.* 1581. b. A knob or bud showing on a stag's antler 1884.

1. A virtuous Woman should reject the first O. of Marriage ADDISON. b. It was owing to her never having had an o. W. IRVING. c. The proprietor does not bind himself to accept the highest or any o. 1890. d. Very little barley on o. 1881. 3. One sees in it a kind of O. at Modern Architecture ADDISON.

Offer (ǫ·fəɹ), *v.* [OE. *offrian*, ad. L. *offerre* to bring before, present, etc., in Vulg. and Christian L. to offer in sacrifice. The more primary senses passed into Eng. through F. *offrir* after the Norman conquest.] 1. *trans.* To present (something) to God (or to a deity, saint, etc.) as an act of worship or devotion; to sacrifice. Also with *up*. Const. *to* or †simple dative. b. *absol.* To present a sacrifice or offering; to make a donation as an act of worship OE. †2. *gen.* To give, make presentation of (*spec.* to a superior as an act of homage). Const. as in 1. -1568. 3. To tender for acceptance or refusal; to hold out (a thing) to a person to take if he will. (The prevailing sense.) late ME. †b. with *obj. cl.* To make the proposal, suggest (*that* something be done) -1727. c. *absol.* To make a proposal; to make an offer of marriage, to 'propose'. *arch.* 1596. d. *Comm.* To present for sale 1632. 4. with *inf.* To propose, or express one's willingness (to do something), conditionally on the assent of the person addressed. late ME. 5. To make an attempt to inflict or deal (violence, or injury of any kind) 1530. b. with *inf.* To essay, try, endeavour. Now *arch.* or *lit.* 1540. c. *intr.* with *at*: To make an attempt at or upon. Now *rare* or *Obs.* 1611. 6. *trans.* To bring forward or propound 1583. 7. Of a thing: To present (to sight, notice, etc.); to furnish 1576. b. *intr.* for *refl.* To present itself; to occur 1601.

1. After having washed myself, and offered up my Morning Devotions ADDISON. b. So many as are disposed, shall o. unto the poore mennes boxe *Bk. Com. Prayer*. 3. I o. thee three things; chuse thee one of them 2 *Sam.* xxiv. 12. I o. no apology 1875. Phr. *To o. battle*, etc. (cf. sense 5). 4. I offered to go to the king DE FOE. 5. Every man offerith hym wronge 1530. b. I knocke your costarde if ye o. to strike me 1553. c. He did not o. at coming in MRS. CARLYLE. 6. On this I wish to o. a few remarks (*mod.*). 7. Each age offers its characteristic riddles 1892. b. Taking the first path that offered, we soon galloped out of the forest 1809. Hence **O·fferer.**

Offering (ǫ·fəriŋ), *vbl. sb.* [OE. *offrung* vbl. sb. f. *offrian* to offer.] 1. The action of OFFER *v.*; *esp.* sacrifice; oblation. 2. *concr.* a. A sacrifice; an oblation OE. b. Something offered to a person; a present, a gift 1440.

1. The kynges that made offryng to oure lord whan he was born. late ME. 2. Plucking the intrailes of an O. forth SHAKS. *Burnt-*, *drink-*, *free-will-*, *thank-o.*, etc.; see under their first elements. b. Crowns of gold, the offerings of grateful cities GIBBON.

Offertory (ǫ·fəɹtəri). late ME. [ad. eccl.L. *offertorium* offering-place, offering, etc., f. late L. and Rom. *offeri-* ppl. stem, substituted for *oblat-*, of *offerre* to OFFER; see -ORY.] 1. An anthem sung or said in the Latin Mass immediately after the Creed, while the offerings of the people are made, and the unconsecrated elements are placed on the altar; the Scriptural sentences read or sung in the corresponding part of the English Communion Service (the *o. sentences*). 2. That part of the Mass or Communion Service at which offerings are made; the offering of these, or the gifts offered; also *spec.* the anticipatory oblation. 1539. 3. *transf.* †a. The offering *of* anything, esp. to God -1684. b. Short for *o. money*, properly, money collected at the o.; hence, a collection of money made at any religious service 1862. 4. *attrib.* 1563.

Off-hand, offhand (see below), *adv.* and *adj. phr.* 1694. [f. OFF *prep.* + HAND *sb.*] A. *adv.* (ǫ·fhæ·nd). At once, straightway, forthwith; extempore.

He..would..speak very neatly o. in Latin 1711.

B. *adj.* (*attrib.* ǫ·fhæ:nd; *pred.* ǫ·fhæ·nd). 1. Of action, speech, etc.: Done or made off-hand (see A); unpremeditated, extemporaneous, impromptu; free and easy, unstudied, unceremonious 1719. 2. *transf.* Of persons: Doing or saying things off-hand, unceremonious, curt, brusque 1708.

1. Speaking in his rapid, off-hand way DICKENS. 2. They are painfully off-hand with me T. HARDY. So **O·ff-ha·nded** *a.* = B.; whence **O·ff-ha·nded-ly** *adv.*, **-ness.**

Office (ǫ·fis), *sb.* ME. [a. AF. and OF., ad. L. *officium* service, med.L., church service; f. *ob-* OB- 1 + *-ficium* doing.] 1. Something done toward any one; a service, kindness, attention. (Chiefly with qualification.) late ME. 2. †a. *gen.* Duty towards others; a moral obligation. b. Duty attaching to one's station, position, or employment; business; function, one's part. ME. †c. Performance of a duty or function, service, etc. -1621. 3. = FUNCTION *sb.* 3. ME. †b. The proper action of an organ or faculty -1656. 4. A position to which certain duties are attached, esp. a place of trust, authority, or service under constituted authority ME. b. In absolute sense: Official position or employment; *spec.* that of a minister of state ME. c. Personified, or denoting an office-holder, or office-holders as a body 1602. 5. A ceremonial duty or service; a religious or social observance; *esp.* obsequies; now chiefly in *last office(s)*. late ME. 6. *Eccl.* a. The daily service of the Roman breviary (more fully *Divine O.*); in the Ch. of England, Morning and Evening Prayer. *To say o.*, to recite the Divine O. b. The introit, sung at the beginning of the Mass or Holy Communion; also, the service of the Mass or Holy Communion. c. Any occasional service, as the *O. for the Dead*, *of Baptism*, etc. ME. 7. An official inquest concerning any matter that entitles the king to the possession of land or chattels: = *Inquest of O.*, INQUEST 1. 8. A place for the transaction of business; often including the staff, or denominating their department. Applied to the room or department in which the clerical work of an establishment is done; also to that in which the business of any department of a large concern is conducted, as the *booking-o.*, *goods o.*, *inquiry o.*, etc. at a railway station. Formerly used of the court of an eccl. official, as still of a police court (*police o.*). late ME. b. Sometimes transferred from the place of business to the company, etc., there established, as in *Assurance* or *Insurance O.* (cf. *the Post O.*) 1646. c. (With capital O.) With defining adj., etc.: The quarters of a government department, as the *Colonial*, *Home O.*, etc.; the staff engaged in carrying on the business of the department. See FOREIGN, HOME, WAR, etc.; also POST OFFICE. 1707. d. **Holy Office** (*R. C. Ch.*): = INQUISITION 3. 1727. 9. *pl.* The parts of a house specially devoted to household work or service; the kitchen and its appurtenances: often including outhouses, the barns and cowhouses of a farm, etc. 1548. b. *sing.* A privy 1727. 10. *slang.* A hint, signal, or private intimation 1803.

1. I would I could doe a good o. betweene you SHAKS. *Ill o.*, a disservice. 2. Doe you your o., or giue vp your Place SHAKS. 3. The o. of the arteries is to lead the blood from the heart into all the parts of the body 1830. b. *Oth.* III. iv. 113. 4. The O. of Corouner. late ME. b. Phr. *To take o.*, *leave o.*, etc. *Jack in (out of) o.*: see JACK *sb.*[1] IV. 3. c. The insolence of O. SHAKS. 5. I..will be first to render thee the decent offices due to the dead SCOTT. 6. c. The O. ensuing is not to be used for any that die unbaptized *Bk. Com. Prayer*. 7. *To find an o.*, to return a verdict showing that the king is entitled to the possession of lands or chattels. *O. found*, a verdict having this effect. 8. His O. keeps your Parchment fates entire POPE. The 'Pall Mall Gazette' had its offices..in Catherine street THACKERAY. 10. Phr. *To give* (or *take*) *the o.* 11. attrib. *o.-holder*, *-seeker*.

†O·ffice, *v.* 1449. [f. prec. sb.] 1. *intr.* = OFFICIATE *v.* 1. -1502. 2. To appoint to, or place in, office -1763. 3. *slang.* To 'give the office' to (a person); see prec. sb. 10. -1819.

Office-bearer (ǫ·fisbē·ːrəɹ). 1645. One who bears or holds office; an officer.

Officer (ǫ·fisəɹ), *sb.* ME. [a. AF., OF. *officier*, ad. med.L. *officiarius*, f. *officium* OFFICE *sb.*; see -ER [2].] †1. One to whom a charge is committed, or who performs a function; a minister; an agent -1669. 2. One who holds an office, post, or place. a. One who holds a public, civil, or ecclesiastical office; a servant or minister of the king; a functionary authoritatively appointed or elected to exercise some public, municipal or corporate function. In early use, applied esp. to persons administering law or justice. ME. †b. A person engaged in the management of the domestic affairs of a great household or collegiate body, of a private estate -1611. c. A person holding the office of president, treasurer, secretary, etc. of a society or institution; an office-bearer 1711. 3. *spec.* A petty officer of justice or of the peace; a bailiff, catchpole; a constable; †a jailer; †an executioner *c* 1500. 4. A person occupying a position of authority in the army, navy, air force, or mercantile marine; *spec.* one holding a commission in the army, navy, or air force 1565. 5. A member of a grade in some honorary orders 1846.

1. MILT. *Comus* 218. 2. a. Medical O. for the Workhouse 1860. The great officers of the household ..furnish the king with the first elements of a ministry of state STUBBS. Phr. *O. of (at) arms*, a herald, pursuivant. b. *Twel. N.* II. v. 53. 3. The Theefe doth feare each bush an O. SHAKS. 4. *General*, *non-commissioned*, *staff o.*, etc.: see these words. *O. of the day*, *Orderly o.*, an officer who is in charge of the arrangements of a military force or post on a given day. *O. of the deck*, the o. temporarily in charge of the deck of a vessel, and responsible for the ship's management. See also FLAG OFFICER, PETTY OFFICER, WARRANT OFFICER. Hence **O·fficership**, the position or rank of an officer; a staff of officers 1775.

Officer (ǫ·fisəɹ), *v.* 1670. [f. prec. sb.] 1. *trans.* a. To furnish with officers. b. To command, or direct as an officer: esp. in *pass.* 2. *transf.* To command; to lead, conduct, manage; to escort 1838.

1. The French must have been very badly officered 1852.

Official (ǫfi·ʃăl), *sb.* ME. [a. F., ad. L. *officialis* sb., absol. use of *officialis* adj.] 1. *Eccl.* In the Ch. of Eng., the presiding officer or judge of an archbishop's, bishop's, or archdeacon's court; now usu. styled *O. Principal* ME. 2. One who holds a public office; as, a *government*, *municipal*, or *railway o.* 1555.

Official (ǫfi·ʃăl), *a.* 1533. [ad. L. *officialis*, f. *officium* OFFICE; see -AL.] †1. Performing some office or service; subservient *to* -1667. 2. Of or pertaining to an office, post, or place 1607. 3. Of persons: Holding office; employed in some public capacity 1833. 4. Derived from, or having the sanction of, persons in office; hence, authorized, authoritative 1854. b. *Med.* Authorized by the pharmacopœia; officinal 1884. 5. Having the manner or air usual with persons in office; formal, ceremonious 1882.

1. The Oesophagus,..a part officiall unto Nutrition SIR T. BROWNE. Phr. *O. member*, a bodily organ which serves the needs of a higher organ. 2. O. documents 1842. *O. arms* (*Her.*), arms representing those of an office or dignity, as those of a city, as used by the Mayor, etc. 3. The heavy footfall of the o. watcher of the night DICKENS. 4. The o. definition of a charity 1898. 5. Handing it with o. solemnity MISS BRADDON. Hence **Offi·cialdom**, o. routine; the domain of officials; officials collectively. (Often

in hostile sense.) **Offi·cialism**, official system or routine; officials collectively or in the abstract. (Often = *red tape, red tapeism*). **Offi·cially** *adv.* in an o. manner or capacity. **Offi·cialize** *v.* to render o., give an o. character to; to bring under o. control 1887. **Offi·cializa·tion.**

Officiality (ǒfiʃiˌæ·lĭti). 1662. [ad. late L. *officialitas*, f. *officialis* OFFICIAL; see -ITY.] 1. The office or dignity of an eccl. official (OFFICIAL *sb.* 1); the court of such, or its quarters. *Obs.* exc. *Hist.* 2. = OFFICIALISM (*rare*) 1841. b. An official post, notice, duty, etc. 1843.

Officiant (ǒfi·ʃiănt). 1740. [ad. med.L. *officiantem, officiare* to OFFICIATE; cf. F. *officiant.*] An officiating priest or minister.

Officiary (ǒfi·ʃiări), *sb.* 1545. [In I, f. as next; in II, ad. med.L. **officiaria*, f. *officiarius* OFFICER.] I. 1. An officer or official (*rare*). 2. A body of officers; an official body *U.S.* 1888. II. A division of a Highland estate, in charge of a ground officer 1799.

Officiary (ǒfi·ʃiări), *a.* 1612. [ad. med.L. *officiarius*, f. *officium* OFFICE; see -ARY[1].] Of a title, etc.: Attached to or derived from an office held. Of a dignitary: Having a title or rank derived from office.

Officiate (ǒfi·ʃieˈt), *v.* 1631. [f. med.L. *officiat-, officiare* to perform divine service, f. *officium* OFFICE.] To discharge an office. 1. *intr.* To discharge the office of a priest 1641. †b. *trans.* To perform, celebrate (a religious service or rite); to exercise (a spiritual charge or function) –1718. 2. *intr.* To perform the duties attaching to an office or place, or any particular duty or service 1683. †3. *trans.* To perform the duties of (an office or place); to execute, do (a duty or charge, business) –1727. †4. a. *trans.* To minister, supply. b. *intr.* To minister, be subservient. –1667.

2. His unmarried daughter, who officiated as his private secretary 1841. 4. a. MILT. *P. L.* VIII. 22. Hence **Officia·tion**, performance of a religious, ceremonial, or public duty. **Offi·ciator.**

‖ **Officina** (ǫfisəi·nă). 1835. [L., = workshop, etc.; contr. of *opificina*, f. *opifex* workmen.] Workshop; place of production.

Officinal (ǒfi·sinăl), *a.* (*sb.*) 1693. [ad. med.L. *officinalis*, f. *officina*; see prec. In med. L. *officina* was applied to a store-room of a monastery, in which medicines, etc. were kept.] 1. Of a herb, plant, drug, etc.: Used in medicine or the arts. Of a medical preparation: Kept in stock in apothecaries' shops; made according to the pharmacopœia. Of a scientific name: Adopted by the Pharmacopœia. (Recently repl. by OFFICIAL *a.* 4 b.) 1720. 2. Of or pertaining to a shop; 'shoppy' (*rare*) 1751. B. *sb.* An officinal drug or medicine 1693. Hence **Offi·cinally** *adv.* in o. use; according to the pharmacopœia.

Officious (ǒfi·ʃəs), *a.* 1565. [ad. L. *officiosus* obliging, dutiful, f. *officium* OFFICE.] †1. Doing or ready to do kind offices; obliging, kind –1827. †2. Dutiful; zealous in doing one's duty –1770. b. Of a thing: Serving its purpose, efficacious (*rare*) 1618. 3. Unduly forward in proffering services; doing, or prone to do, more than is asked or required; pragmatical, meddlesome 1602. †4. Pertaining to an office or business, official; hence, formal –1852. 5. *Diplomacy.* As opp. to *official*: Having an extraneous relation to official matters or duties; having the character of a friendly communication, or informal action, on the part of a government or its representatives 1852.

1. They were tolerably well-bred; very o., humane, and hospitable BURKE. †*O. lie* (L. *mendacium officiosum*): a lie told as an act of kindness to further another's interests. 2. The o. daughters pleas'd attend AKENSIDE. 3. Wolsey, that slye, o., and too Lordly Cardnall 1602. One of those o., noisy little men who are always ready to give you unasked information DISRAELI. 5. Feelers put out in the o. press 1866. Hence **Offi·cious-ly** *adv.*, **-ness.**

Offing (ǫ·fiŋ). 1627. [f. OFF *adv.* + -ING[1].] 1. The part of the visible sea distant from the shore or beyond the anchoring ground. 2. Position at a distance off the shore 1688. Also *transf.*

1. At Two this day..the Generals discovered Trump ..in the Offen 1666. 2. Phr. *To gain, get, keep, make, take an o.*

Offish (ǫ·fiʃ), *a. colloq.* 1842. [f. OFF *adv.* + -ISH[1].] Inclined to keep aloof; distant in manner. Hence **O·ffishness.**

Offlet (ǫ·fˌlėt). 1838. [f. OFF- 3 + LET *v.*[1]; cf. *inlet, outlet.*] A channel or pipe for letting water off.

Off licence: see OFF C. 5.

Off-load (ǫ·fˌlōᵘd), *v. S. Afr.* 1850. [f. OFF- 1 + LOAD *v.*, after Du. *afladen.*] *trans.* To unload.

Offprint, off-print (ǫ·fˌprint). 1885. [f. OFF- 3 + PRINT; cf. Du. *afdruk.*] A separately printed copy of an article, etc., which orig. appeared as part of a larger publication.

O·ff-re:ckoning. Usu. in *pl.* 1687. [OFF 3.- Cf. G. *abrechnung.*] A deduction; formerly, in the British army, the name of a special account between the government and the commanding officers of regiments in ref. to the clothing, etc. of the men.

O·ffsa:ddle, off-saddle, *v. S. Afr.* 1863. [f. OFF- 1 + SADDLE *v.*, after Du. *afzadelen.*] *trans.* To take the saddle off (a horse) for a rest, feeding, etc.; also *absol.*; *transf.* to make a break in a journey.

Offscouring (ǫ·fskauᵊ:riŋ). 1526. [OFF- 3.] 1. The action of scouring off 1896. 2. That which is scoured off; filth or defilement cleaned off and cast aside; refuse, rubbish (*lit.*, in *pl.* of things, and *fig.* in *collect. sing.* (after 1 Cor. iv. 13) or *pl.* of persons) 1526.

2. *fig.* White people, who are generally the dregs and offscourings of our colonies 1775.

Offscum (ǫ·fskɒm). 1579. [OFF- 3.] That which is skimmed off; scum, dross, refuse. Also *fig.* that which is rejected as vile or worthless (usu. of persons, in *collect. sing.* or *pl.*).

Offset (ǫ·fset), *sb.* 1555. [f. OFF- 3 + SET. Cf. SET-OFF.] 1. The act of setting off; outset, start. 2. A short lateral offshoot from the stem or root of a plant, serving for propagation. Also *transf.* and *fig.* 1664. b. *spec.* A person or tribe, springing collaterally from a specified family or race; a 'scion' 1711. c. A 'spur' of a mountain range 1833. 3. Something that 'sets off' something else 1675. 4. Something 'set off' against something else; anything that counterbalances, compensates, or makes up for something else; a set-off 1769. 5. *Surveying.* A short distance measured perpendicularly from a main line of measurement, as from the straight line joining the two ends of an irregular boundary, to a point (*e.g.* an angle) in the boundary, in order to calculate the area of the irregularly bounded part 1725. 6. *Arch.* A horizontal or sloping break or ledge on the face of a wall, pier, etc., formed where the portion above is reduced in thickness 1721. 7. A bend made in a pipe to carry it past an obstruction. 8. *Printing*, etc. The accidental transfer of undried ink from one surface to another, esp. to an opposite page. 1888. b. (Also *o. process*, etc.), a method of printing from a rubber surface to which a drawing or design has been transferred 1918.

Comb. **O.-pipe**: cf. 7 above; **-sheet** (*Printing*), = *set-off sheet*; see SET-OFF; **-staff** (*Surveying*), a rod used in measuring offsets.

Offset (ǫ:fse·t), *v.* Chiefly *U.S.* 1792. [f. OFF- 1 + SET *v.*] 1. *trans.* To set off as an equivalent *against* something else. Also said of the equivalent: To counterbalance, compensate. 2. *intr.* To spring, branch off, or project as an offset *from* something else 1853. b. *trans.* To furnish with an offset (see prec. 7) 1889. 3. *Printing.* = *set off* j (SET *v.*) 1888.

Offshoot (ǫ·fʃūt). 1674. [OFF- 3.] A lateral shoot or branch from the stem or main part of a plant, or anything material, as a mountain-range, a street 1814. b. *fig.* A collateral branch or descendant from a (specified) family or race 1710. c. A derivative 1801.

1. Stunted offshoots of felled trees 1814. b. An o. of the great house which had already given Dukes to Florence 1874.

Off shore, o·ff-sho·re, *adv. phr.* (*adj.*) 1720. [f. OFF *prep.* + SHORE *sb.* Opp. to IN SHORE.] 1. a. In a direction away from the shore. b. At some distance from the shore 1745. 2. *adj.* (*attrib.* ǫ·fˌʃōᵊɹ). a. Moving or directed away from the shore 1839. b. Situated, existing, or operating at a distance from the shore 1883.

1. a. The wind blowing off shore DE FOE. 2. a. The off-shore tack 1860. b. The off-shore fisheries 1883.

Off side, o·ff-si·de. *phr.* 1845. [f. OFF *prep.* + SIDE.] Away from one's own side; on the wrong side, *i.e.* in Football, Hockey, etc., between the ball and the opponent's goal (the specific meaning varying in the different games). Also *attrib.* or as *adj.* (ǫ·fˌsəid).

Offspring (ǫ·fˌspriŋ). [OE. *ofspring*, f. *of* OF, OFF + *springan* to SPRING.] 1. Children or young (more widely, descendants); progeny, issue. Applied without indef. art. to a number, or to one; with indef. art. always collective, as *a numerous o.* (Rarely of plants.) b. Rarely in *pl.*: †(*a*) = children or descendants; (*b*) in collective sense = progenies, broods, families 1548. c. *fig.* In relation to place of birth or origin 1695. 2. *fig.* Produce, product; issue, outcome, result; 'fruit' 1609. †3. Descent, derivation, origin –1715. †b. *transf.* Family, race, stock; ancestry –1612. †4. Source, original –1604.

1. c. And there Euphrates her soft Off-spring arms DRYDEN. 2. The law of nations..is the o. of modern times 1826.

Offtake (ǫ·fˌtēᵊk). 1793. [f. OFF- 3 + TAKE *sb.*] 1. The action of taking off; *spec.* the taking of commodities off the market 1885. 2. A deduction 1793. 3. A channel by which, or place where, something is taken off 1839.

Offu·scate, *ppl. a.* Now *rare.* 1603. [ad. L. *offuscatus*; see next.] = OBFUSCATE *ppl. a.*

Offu·scate, *v.* Now *rare.* 1586. [f. L. *offuscat-, offuscare* to darken, f. *of-, ob-* OB- 1 + *fuscare*, f. *fuscus* dark.] = OBFUSCATE *v.* So **Offusca·tion** = OBFUSCATION 1502.

Offward (ǫ·fwǒɹd), *adv.* 1563. [f. OFF *adv.* + -WARD.] In a direction or position off or away from something; *spec.* (*Naut.*) away from the shore. Also quasi-*sb.* in phr. *to the o.* 1600.

Oft (ǫft), *adv.* and *a.* Now *arch.*, *poet.*, or *dial.*; repr. in ordinary use by OFTEN. [Com. Teut.: OE. *oft.* See also OFTEN.] A. *adv.* = OFTEN A. Compared *ofter* (*arch.* and *dial.*), †*oftest.* b. Usu. hyphened to a ppl. adj. used *attrib.*, as *oft-told.* (In this construction still frequent.) 1586.

Many's the time and o. GOLDSM. Much in sorrow o. in woe, Onward, Christians, onward go! 1806.

†B. *adj.* = OFTEN B. (Chiefly with *vbl. sbs.*) –1671.

Warn'd by o. experience MILT.

Often (ǫ·f'n), *adv.* and *a.* ME. (first in northern texts *c* 1300). [Extended form of ME. *ofte* OFT. The pronunc. (ǫ·ftən) is now frequent in the south of England.] A. *adv.* 1. Many times; frequently. Opp. to *seldom.* Compared *oftener, oftenest.* 2. In many instances; in cases frequently occurring. late ME. 3. Usu. hyphened to a ppl. adj. used *attrib.* 1601.

1. Seldom contented, o. in the wrong DE FOE. 2. A good character is o. worth [= it often happens that a good character is worth] a great deal of money JEVONS. 3. At often-recurring intervals 1877.

B. *adj.* (The adv. used with sbs.) Done, made, happening, or occurring many times; frequent. Now *arch.* 1450.

Vse a lytell wyne for thy stommakes sake, and thyne o. diseases TINDALE 1 *Tim.* v. 23. *Comb.* With nouns denoting time, as **-while, -s** = OFTENTIME, -S. Hence **O·ftenness**, frequency (now *rare*).

O·ftentime, *adv. rare.* late ME. Variant of next. Also *adj.*

Oftentimes (ǫ·f'nˌtəimz), *adv.* Now only *arch.* or *literary.* late ME. [f. OFTEN after *oft-times.*] Many times; frequently, often.

O·ft-ti·me, *adv. Obs.* or *arch.* late ME. [f. OFT *adv.* + TIME, replacing obs. *oftsithe.*] = next. Also *adj.*

Oft-times, ofttimes (ǫ·ftˌtəimz), *adv.* Now *arch.* and *poet.* late ME. [f. OFTEN + pl. of TIME *sb.*, after †*oftsithes.*] = OFTENTIMES.

Ogdoad (ǫ·gdoˌæ̆d). 1621. [ad. late L. *ogdoas, ogdoadem*, a. Gr. ὀγδοάς, ὀγδοάδα, f. stem of ὀκτώ eight, ὄγδοος eighth.] a. The number eight. b. A group, set, or series of eight; *spec.* in *Gnosticism*, a group of eight divine beings or æons; also, the heavenly region.

Ogee (ōᵘdʒīˑ, ōᵘˑdʒī). Occas. written **OG** or **O.G.** late ME. [app. worn down from F. *ogive*, OGIVE. Prob. so called by workmen as the usual moulding employed in ogives or groin-ribs.] *Arch.* and *Joinery.* †**1.** = OGIVE **1.** -1611. **2.** A moulding consisting of a continuous double curve, convex above and concave below; a cyma reversa. In cross-section, its outline is a sort of *S* shape. 1677. **b.** Any curve or line having this form 1851. **c.** Short for *o. arch, plane* 1667.

attrib., etc., as **o. arch,** an arch formed by the union of two contrasted ogees meeting at its apex; so **o. doorway, o. window,** etc., a doorway, etc. having the form of an o. arch; **o. moulding** = OGEE **2**; **o. plane,** a joiner's moulding-plane with an o. sole. Hence **Ogee'd, ogee·d** *a.* furnished with an o. or ogees; having the form of an o.

Ogham, ogam (ǫˑgăm). 1627. [a.OIr. *ogam, ogum* (gen. *oguim*), mod.Ir. *ogham*, pl. *-uim*, Gael. *oghum*, a name conn. with its mythical inventor *Ogma.*] **1.** An alphabet of twenty characters used by the ancient British and Irish; the system of writing, or an inscription written, in such characters; also, one of the characters themselves 1677. **2.** An obscure mode of speaking used by the ancient Irish. **3.** *attrib.*, as *o. alphabet, inscription*, etc. 1784. Hence **Oghamic, ogamic** (ǫˑgămik, ogæˑmik) *a.* of or pertaining to o.; consisting of oghams 1876. var. **Ogmic.**

Ogival (oᵘdʒəiˑvăl, ōᵘdʒivăl), *a.* (*sb.*) 1841. [f. next + -AL, or a. F.] **1. a.** Having the form or outline of an ogive or pointed ('Gothic') arch. **b.** Characterized by ogives 1855. **B.** *sb.* An ogival head of a shot 1868.

Ogive (ōᵘˑdʒəiv, oᵘdʒəiˑv). ME. [a. F., of unkn. origin; see N.E.D.] *Arch.* **1.** The diagonal groin or rib of a vault, two of which cross each other at the centre. **2.** A pointed (= 'Gothic') arch 1841. **3.** *attrib.*, as *o. window*, etc. 1842. Hence **Ogived** *a.* consisting of an o. or ogives; having the form of an o. or ogee.

Ogle (ōᵘˑg'l), *sb.* 1700. [f. or cogn. w. the vb.] **1.** An eye; usu. *pl.* the eyes. Orig. *Vagabonds' cant*, in early 19th c. in *Pugilistic slang*, etc. **2.** An amorous glance; an ocular invitation to advances 1711.

Ogle (ōᵘˑg'l), *v.* 1682. [Cant word from Du. or LG.; cf. LG. *oegeln*, G. *äugeln* f. *oog* = *auge* EYE.] **1.** *intr.* To cast amorous or coquettish glances. **b.** *trans.* To turn or bring by ogling 1712. **2.** *trans.* To eye amorously; to 'make eyes' at 1698. **3.** To keep one's eyes upon; to eye 1820.

1. He sighs and ogles so, that it would do your heart good to see him 1713. **2.** As soon as the Minuet was over, we ogled one another through our Masques ADDISON. **3.** He stood ogling the wreck through his binocular 1891. Hence **O·gler. O·gling** *vbl. sb.* the throwing of amorous or languishing glances; also the glance itself.

Ogpu (ǫˑgpu). 1927. [Made up of the initials of *Otdelénie Gosudárstvenny Politicheskoy Upravy* Department of State Political Directorate.] A state department in the Russian Republic, taking the place of the cheka.

-ography: the element -GRAPHY preceded by the connective -o-; used also as *sb.* like -OLOGY.

Ogre (ōᵘˑgəɹ). 1713. [a. F., (first used by Perrault in his *Contes*, 1697).] In folk-lore and fairy tales, a man-eating monster, usu. represented as a hideous giant; hence, a man likened to such a monster.

He s the most hideous, goggle-eyed creature,.. quite an o. DICKENS. Hence **O·greish, o·grish** *a.* resembling, or characteristic of, an o. **O·greism,** the character or practices of ogres. **O·gress¹,** a female o.

Ogress². 1572. [Origin unkn.] *Her.* A representation of a cannon-ball as a bearing; = PELLET *sb.* 3.

Ogygian (odʒiˑdʒiăn), *a.* 1834. [f. L. *Ogygius*, Gr. Ὠγύγιος (f. personal name Ὠγύγης) + -AN.] Of or pertaining to the mythical Attic or Bœotian king Ogyges; of obscure antiquity; of great age.

O. deluge, a famous flood said to have taken place in the reign of Ogyges.

Oh (ōᵘ), *int.* (*sb.*) 1534. [var. spelling of O *int.*] An exclam. expressing emotion of various kinds; now chiefly used when the exclam. is detached from what follows, and esp. as a cry of pain or terror, or in expression of shame, derisive astonishment or disapprobation, in which case it is often repeated as *Oh! oh!* 1548. **B.** *sb.* The exclam. *Oh*, as a name for itself. So *Oh dear, Oh fie*, etc.

Oh sleep! it is a gentle thing COLERIDGE. **B.** Never-ending ohs and ahs 1820. Hence **Oh** *v. intr.* to exclaim 'Oh!'; *trans.* to greet with 'Oh!' Also **Oh-oh** *v.*

Ohm (ōᵘm). 1870. [f. Georg Simon *Ohm*, German physicist (1787–1854), who determined mathematically the law of the flow of electricity (*Ohm's law*).] *Electr.* The unit of electrical resistance; the resistance of a column of mercury of a constant section of one square millimetre and of a length of 106·3 centimetres, at the temperature of melting ice. Hence **Oh·mad** = OHM 1866; **Ohm·a·mmeter,** an instrument for measuring electrical current and resistance; **Oh·mic** *a.*, pertaining to or measured by the o.; **Oh·mmeter,** an instrument for measuring electrical resistance in ohms.

Oho (ohōᵘˑ), *int.* ME. [See Ho *int.*¹] An exclam. expressing surprise, taunting, exultation, etc.

Ohone (ohōᵘˑn), *int.* (*sb.*) 1480. [a. Gael. and Ir. *ochóin.*] Oh! alas! A Sc. and Ir. exclam. of lamentation.

Oh yes: see OYEZ.

-oid (oid, o₁id), *suffix*, ad. mod.L. *-oides*, Gr. -οειδής, i.e. *-o-* of prec. element or connective + -ειδής 'having the form of', 'like', f. εἶδος form; cf. L. *-i-formis* (see -FORM). In Eng. the prevalent pronunc. is with the diphthong (oi) as in *void*. Largely used in scientific terms, formed on Gr. (rarely L.) words. These are primarily adjs.; but also (as occas. in Gr.) sbs.

Examples:—(adjs.) Anat. *adenoid, thyroid*, etc.; Zool. *anthropoid, simioid*, etc.; Bot. *ovoid, scorpioid*. (sbs.) Math. *cycloid, rhomboid, spheroid*, etc.; Astron. *asteroid*; Chem. *albuminoid, alkaloid*, etc.; Bot. *fucoid*; Zool. *zooid*.

-oidal. When the form in *-oid* is a sb., an adj. is formed in *-oidal* (see -AL), as *conchoidal, rhomboidal*; so *alkaloidal, asteroidal, fucoidal*, etc.

‖ **Oidium** (o₁iˑdiɒ̆m). 1836. [mod.L., f. Gr. ᾠόν egg + -ιδιον dim. suffix.] *Bot.* Link's name for a genus of parasitic fungi, comprising species now viewed as the conidial stage of various fungi of the family *Erysipheæ*; they cause various diseases. *spec.* The species *O. Tuckeri* (*Erysiphe Tuckeri*), or the disease of the vine produced by this; grape-mildew.

Oil (oil), *sb.* [Early ME. *oli(e, oile*, a. ONF. *olie*, OF. *oil(l)e*, 16th c. *huile*:—L. *oleum.*] **1.** A substance having the following characters (or most of them): viz. those of being liquid at ordinary temperatures, of a viscid consistence and characteristic unctuous feel, lighter than water and insoluble in it, soluble in alcohol and ether, inflammable, chemically neutral. **a.** without *an* or *pl.*; orig. usu. = OLIVE-OIL ME. **b.** with *an* and *pl.*, indicating a kind or different kinds. late ME.

The oils are divided into three classes: (1) *Fatty* or *fixed oils* (see FATTY, FIXED), of animal or vegetable origin, which are chemically triglycerides of fatty acids, and produce a permanent greasy stain on paper, etc.; these are either *drying oils*, which by exposure absorb oxygen and thicken into varnishes, or *non-drying oils*, which by exposure ferment; they are used as lubricants, as illuminants, in making soap, etc. (2) *Essential* or *volatile oils* (see ESSENTIAL *a.*), chiefly of vegetable origin, which are acrid and limpid, and form the odoriferous principles of plants, etc.; they are hydrocarbons, or mixtures of hydrocarbons with resins, etc., and are used in medicine, perfumery, and (occas.) in the arts. (3) *Mineral oils*, which are mixtures of hydrocarbons, and are used chiefly as illuminants.

†**c.** *Old Chem.* One of the supposed five 'principles' of bodies -1741. **2.** In the names of the various kinds, unlimited in number. See below. late ME. **3.** In fig. and allusive uses. ME. **4.** = OIL-COLOUR. Often in pl. *oils*. 1663. **b.** *colloq.* An oil-painting. Chiefly in *pl.* 1890. **5.** *colloq.* abbrev. of OILSKIN. Chiefly in *pl.* 1891.

1. (*a*) The five foolish virgins..begd oyle JER. TAYLOR. *Holy o.*: o. used in religious or sacred rites, as the anointing of priests or kings, extreme unction, etc. **2.** (*a*) With the name of the source following *oil of*, as *o. of almonds, amber, eucalyptus, lavender*, etc. (*b*) With name of source, etc., preceding *oil*, as *cod-liver o., cottonseed o., linseed o., olive o.*, etc.; *hair o., salad o.* (see these words); **animal o.,** any o. obtained from an animal body; spec. *Dippel's animal o.*, an oil prepared by distillation from stag's horns, etc. and used in medicine; **dead o.** (see DEAD); **sweet-o.** = OLIVE-OIL. **3.** Oile of gladnesse. late ME. Phr. *To add* (*put*) *o. to the fire, flames*, etc., to aggravate fury, passion, etc.; to 'add fuel to the flame'. *To smell of o.*, to bear marks of laborious study; *to burn the midnight o.*, to study late into the night. *To pour o. upon the waters*, etc., to appease disturbance; in allusion to the effect of o. on water in agitation. *To strike o.* (U.S.), *lit.* to reach the o. (petroleum) in sinking a shaft for it; hence *fig.* to hit upon a means of growing rich quickly. †*O. of angels* (ANGEL 4), gold employed in gifts or bribes; *o. of birch, hazel, holly, hickory o., strap o.*, a flogging (with a birch-rod, hazel-stick, etc.).

attrib. and *Comb.* **1.** General: as *o.-bath, -box, -brush*, etc.; *o.-tank, -vat, -vessel*, etc.; *o.-factory, -well*, etc.; *o. gas, spirit*; *o.-engine, -lamp, -motor, -stove*; *o.-bearing, -refining* adjs.; *o.-atomizer, -refiner*, etc.; *o.-dried* (dried of o., having the o. dried up), *-driven, -fed*, adjs.; *o.-yellow* adj.

2. Special: **o.-beetle,** a beetle of the genus *Meloe*, which exudes an oily liquid when alarmed; **-bird,** name for various birds yielding o., esp. the GUACHARO, *Steatornis caripensis*: **-bush** [BUSH *sb.*²], a socket socket containing o. in which an upright spindle runs; **-can; -cellar,** (*a*) a cellar for storage of o.; (*b*) a small reservoir for o. in a piece of machinery; **-cup,** a small vessel to hold o. for lubricating, either portable, or attached to the machinery and acting automatically; **-derrick,** a derrick or frame used in boring for o.; **-field,** an area occupied by oil-bearing strata; **-garden,** a garden of olives grown for o.; **-gauge** (*-gage*), an oleometer; **-gland,** a gland which secretes o.; *spec.* the uropygial or coccygeal gland in birds, which secretes the o. with which they preen their feathers; **-meal,** ground linseed cake; **-paint** = OIL-COLOUR; **-painting,** (*a*) the action, or art, of painting in oils; (*b*) a picture painted in oils; **-palm,** a species of palm yielding o.; esp. *Elæis guineensis*, which yields palm-oil; **-paper,** paper made transparent or waterproof by soaking in o.; **-press,** an apparatus for expressing o. from fruits, seeds, etc.; so **-presser; -sand,** a stratum of sandstone yielding o.; **-shark,** any species yielding o., esp. *Galeorhinus zyopterus* of California; **-sheet,** a sheet made of oilskin or oil-paper; **-spring,** a spring of mineral o. (with or without admixture of water); **-stock,** *Eccl.* a vessel for containing holy o.; **-test, -tester,** a contrivance for ascertaining the flash-point, burning-point, lubricating quality, etc., of oils. See also OIL-BAG, etc. Hence **Oilless** (oiˑl,lės) *a.* containing no o.; not lubricated, or not requiring to be lubricated, with o. 1787.

Oil, *v.* late ME. [f. prec.] **1.** *trans.* †**a.** = ANOINT *v.* **2.** -1764. **b.** To smear or lubricate with oil 1440. **2.** *fig.* 1602. **3.** To convert (butter or grease) into oil by melting 1759. **b.** *intr.* To become of the consistency of oil 1741. **4.** *intr.* Of a ship: To take in a supply of oil 1906.

1. b. Phr. *To o. the wheels* (also *fig.*). *To o. out* (in *Painting*), to moisten (for retouching) with a thin coating of oil. **2.** Error, oiled with Obsequiousness,..has often the Advantage of Truth 1716. *To o. the hand* (*fist*), to bribe. Also with the person as obj. *To o. one's tongue*, to adopt or use flattering speech. **3. b.** Take Care the Butter do not o. 1741.

Oi·l-bag. 1713. **a.** A sac or gland in an animal which secretes or contains oil. **b.** A bag for expressing oil. **c.** A bag to contain oil for any purpose.

Oilcake (oiˑl,kēᵢk). 1757. The cake or mass of rapeseed, cottonseed, linseed, etc., which is left after the oil has been expressed; used as a fattening food for cattle or sheep, or as manure.

Oilcloth (oiˑl,klǫþ). 1697. A general name for any fabric prepared with oil, so as to be rendered waterproof. **a.** = OILSKIN. **b.** A canvas painted or coated with a preparation containing a drying oil, used for table-cloths, floor-cloths, etc. 1803.

Oi·l-co·lour. 1539. 'Colour' or paint made by grinding a pigment in oil. (Chiefly in *pl.*)

Oiled (oild), *ppl. a.* 1535. [f. OIL *v.* + -ED¹.] **1.** Smeared, or lubricated with oil 1550. **b.** Soaked, ground, or preserved in oil 1535. **c.** Impregnated with oil, as *o. cloth* = OILCLOTH, *o. silk*, etc. 1624. **2.** Melted into oil 1769. **3.** Having taken alcohol; drunk (*slang*) 1916.

Oiler (oiˑləɹ). 1846. [f. OIL *sb.* or *v.* + -ER¹.] **1.** One who, or that which, oils. Also *fig.* **2.** An oil-driven vessel 1915.

Oilery (oi·ləri). 1864. [f. OIL *sb.* + -ERY; cf. F. *huilerie.*] The business, establishment, or stock of an oilman.

Oillet (oi·lėt). late ME. [a. OF., mod.F. *œillet*, dim. of *oil, oeil* eye. Repl. by EYELET.] †1. = EYELET *sb.* 1. -1627. 2. = EYELET *sb.* 2. Now only *Hist.* late ME. 3. *attrib.*, as *o.-hole* = EYELET-HOLE. 1530.

Oilman (oi·lmæ̆n). 1440. 1. A manufacturer of or dealer in oil. 2. One who oils machinery.

Oi·l-mill. late ME. A machine in which seeds, fruits, etc., are crushed or pressed to extract oil; a factory where oil is expressed by such machines.

Oi·l-nut. 1707. A name for various nuts and large seeds which yield oil; also for the plants producing them.

spec. a. the Castor-oil Plant, *Ricinus communis*; b. the N. American Butternut, *Juglans cinerea*; c. the N. American Buffalo-nut or Elk-nut; d. the Oil Palm, *Elæis guineensis.*

Oi·l-seed. 1562. Any seed yielding oil, e.g. linseed, rapeseed, mustard-seed.

spec. a. that of the Castor-oil Plant, *Ricinis communis*; b. that of *Guizotia oleifera*, an E. Indian Composite plant, the oil of which is used for lamps and as a condiment; c. that of the False Flax, *Camelina sativa* (*Siberian oil-seed*); d. cottonseed (also attrib. *oil-seed cake*).

Oi·lskin. 1812. Cloth made waterproof by being treated with oil; a piece, or garment, of such cloth 1816. b. Often *attrib.* (made of oilskin) 1812.

Oilstone (oi·lˌstōᵘn), *sb.* 1585. A smooth and fine-grained whetstone, the rubbing-surface of which is lubricated with oil; the stone of which such whetstones are made. Hence **Oi·lstone** *v. trans.* to sharpen on an o.

O·il-tree. 1611. Name for trees, etc., yielding oil; as the Castor-oil plant, the Illupi, and the Oil Palm.

Oily (oi·li), *a.* (*adv.*) 1528. [f. OIL *sb.* + -Y.[1]] 1. Of or of the nature of oil; having the consistence or appearance of oil. *O. acid* = FATTY acid. 2. Containing oil; smeared or covered with oil; greasy, fat 1597. 3. *fig.* 'Smooth' in manner or (esp.) speech; subservient; bland, unctuous; 'slippery' 1598.

2. This oyly Rascall is knowne as well as Poules SHAKS. He mopped his o. pate BROWNING. **O. grain, †corn,** the seed of *Sesamum orientale.* 3. What had this o. scoundrel..to do with it? 1894. Hence **Oi·lily** *adv.* **Oi·liness.**

Oino-: see ŒNO-.

†Oint, *v.* ME. [f. F. *oint*, pa. pple. of *oindre* :—L. *unguere.*] *trans.* = ANOINT *v.*

Ointment (oi·ntmĕnt). [ME. *oignement*, a. OF. *oignement* :—L. **unguimentum* for *unguentum* UNGUENT. In 14th c. conformed to OINT *v.*] An unctuous preparation, used chiefly for application to the skin; an unguent.

O.K.: see O II. e.

‖**Oka, oke** (ōᵘ·kă, ōᵘk). 1625. [a. It. *oca, occa*, F. *oque, ocque*, ad. Turk. *ōqah*, Arab. *ūqiyah*; app. ad. (through Syriac) Gr. οὐγκία, L. *uncia.*] A Turkish and Egyptian measure of weight, = about 2¾ lb. English; also, a measure of capacity, = about ⅔ of a quart.

Okapi (ǫkā·pi). 1900. [Mbuba (Congo).] A bright-coloured, partially-striped ruminant of Central Africa, having points of likeness to the giraffe, the deer, and the zebra, discovered by Sir Harry Johnston in 1900.

Okenite (ōᵘ·kĕnəit). 1828. [G. *okenit*, f. Lorenz *Oken*, a German naturalist; see -ITE[1].] *Min.* A hydrous silicate of calcium, usu. forming a tough fibrous mass, of a whitish colour, and subtransparent. Also called *dysclasite.*

‖**Okimo·no.** 1888. [Japanese.] A small carved ornament worn by the Japanese.

Ok(k)er, obs. f. OCHRE.

‖**Okro, okra** (ǫ·kro, ǫ·kră). 1707. [app. W. African; see N.E.D.] A tall malvaceous plant, *Hibiscus* or *Abelmoschus esculentus*, the young mucilaginous capsules or 'pods' of which are used as an esculent vegetable and for thickening soup; the stem furnishes a fibre suitable for ropes; also the pods = GUMBO 1. a.

-ol, *suffix*, in chemical terms. 1. The termination of *alcohol*, used to form the names of substances which are alcohols in the wider sense (ALCOHOL 5), or compounds analogous to alcohol; e.g. *methol, naphthol, phenol*, etc. 2. From *phenol* the ending has been transferred to bodies belonging to the group of phenols, (which are alcohols), as *cresol, thymol*, etc., and to some phenol derivs., as *creosol, veratrol*, etc. 3. Occas. *-ol* is a deriv. of L. *oleum* oil; in which case it is more systematically written *-ole*; e.g. *furfurol*, etc.

Ola, var. of OLLA [2], palm-leaf.

Olacaceous (ōᵘlăkēⁱ·ʃəs), *a.* 1895. [f. mod. L. *Olacaceæ*, f. L. *olax* odorous; see -ACEOUS.] *Bot.* Pertaining to the order *Olacaceæ* of tropical trees or shrubs.

‖**Olam** (ōᵘlā·m). 1872. [Heb., perh. properly 'that which is hidden'.] A vast period of time, an age.

-olater, -olatry (see -O-), the forms in which -LATER, -LATRY usu. occur.

Old (ōᵘld), *a.* (*adv., sb.*) [Com. Teut.: Early ME. *old* :—OE. *ald* :—OTeut. **alđoz*, orig. a ppl. formation (= Gr. -τός, L. -*tus*) on OTeut. vb.-stem *al-*, cogn. w. L. *alere* to nourish. OTeut. **alđoz* was thus app. = 'grown up, adult', corresp. to L. *altus.* The original compar. and superl., still retained in particular uses, are ELDER (:—**alþizon*), ELDEST, q.v.; in gen. use these have been superseded by *older, oldest.*] I. 1. That has lived long; far advanced in years or life. (Opp. to *young*; less emphatic than *aged.*) b. Having the characteristics of age 1832. c. Used disparagingly; esp. *colloq.* and *slang.* 1508. 2. *transf.* Characteristic of old persons; of or pertaining to advanced life. Also *absol.* and *attrib.* ME. 3. Of a thing: Having existed long, long-made, that has been long in use. (Opp. to *new.*) Hence, Worn out, decayed, dilapidated, shabby, stale, etc.; also, Discarded after long use, disused. OE. 4. Of (any specified) age or length of existence; e.g. *How o.? Ten days o.* When used *attrib.*, usu. hyphened to *old* (*year* being used instead of *years*), as in a *two-year-old sheep*, etc. These attrib. forms are also used *absol.* as sbs.; e.g. *a flock of two-year-olds.* OE. b. The expression '*x* years old' may be preceded by a prep., as if it were a sb. phrase = 'the age of *x* years'; e.g. *a child of ten years old* ME. 5. *fig.* Of long practice and experience *in* something; experienced, skilled OE. 6. In colloq. use: = Great, plentiful, excessive, 'grand'. Now only after *good, grand, high*, and the like. 1440. b. Technically applied to a lens of high magnifying power 1667.

1. An olde Gentleman called M. Erasmus 1568. My o. bones akes SHAKS. An o. oak COWPER. *The o.* (pl.), o. people; so *o. and young, young and o.* (sc. *people*). b. An o. head upon very young shoulders 1837. c. *O. bloke, buffer, cat, codger, fogy* (see these wds.). 2. *O. age*, the latter period of life; also *absol.* and *attrib.*, as in *o.-age pension*, etc. Abraham died in a good o. age *Gen.* xxv. 8. 3. Neither do men put new wine into o. bottles *Matt.* ix. 17. Pale sherry, o. port, and cut and come again THACKERAY. Phr. *Any o...*, any..whatever (*slang*). 4. b. I was made a King, at nine months olde SHAKS. 5. Vane, young in yeares, but in sage counsell o. MILT. O. in vices 1853. O. sailors JOWETT. *O. bird*, a person who has become knowing through experience, *spec.* an experienced thief; *o.* FILE, SOLDIER, STAGER. 6. Yonders o. coile at home SHAKS. A high o. time 1898.

II. 1. a. Dating far back into the past; made or formed long ago. Also *poet.* of elemental forces, etc.: Primeval. OE. b. In personal or other particular ref.: That has been long such; not new or recent OE. c. Known or familiar from of old OE. 2. Used as an expression of familiarity, as in the colloq. *o. boy, chap, fellow, man*; also, with names of places which one has long known. Often in *good o.*, a familiar expression of appreciation. 1588. 3. Applied to the devil, a. orig. in ref. to his primeval character; in OE. *se ealda feond* and *se ealda* (= 'the old one') OE. b. also in jocular names of the devil, as in *the o. one, the o.* GENTLEMAN (*in black*); *o.* HARRY, NICK, SCRATCH, etc. 1668.

1. O. fashions please me best SHAKS. An o. and haughty Nation proud in Arms MILT. b. To pay up o. scores 1840. An o. friend of your father JOWETT. c. One of his o. tricks SHELLEY. Travelling over o. ground 1865. 2. From scenes like these o. Scotia's grandeur springs BURNS. Take another tumbler, o. man 1890. Good o. Camel Corps 1898. 3. a. *O. dragon, serpent, enemy, adversary*, etc.

III. 1. Of or pertaining to the distant past; ancient, bygone, olden. (Opp. to *modern.*) OE. b. Relating to or dealing with past times OE. c. Proper to antiquity or a bygone age; antique ME. d. Renowned in (classical) history; esp. in poetry, as an epithet with proper names 1631. 2. Belonging to an earlier period (of time, one's life, etc.) or to the earlier or earliest of two or more; possessed, occupied, practised, etc., at a former time. (Opp. to *new.*) OE. b. That was or has been (the thing designated) at a former time 1571. 3. Of earlier date, prior in time or occurrence, former, previous OE. b. With names of countries: Known or inhabited at an earlier period. 1647.

1. The Prophets o., who sung thy endless raign MILT. The 'good old times' W. IRVING. b. O. annals SHELLEY. c. What they call the o. blue, the shade seen in enamelling 1899. d. To glide adown o. Nilus SHELLEY. 2. New Presbyter is but O. Priest writ Large MILT. The o. order changeth, yielding place to new TENNYSON. b. An o. pupil of mine 1847. 3. How slow this o. Moon wanes SHAKS. *O. Year's Day*, the last day of the o. year. *O. style*: see STYLE. *O. Christmas Day, O. May-day, O. Michaelmas-day*, etc., these days according to the computation of o. style. b. *O. England, O. France, O. Spain* (opp. to the American colonies of *New England, France, Spain*; now only *Hist.*), and similarly in mod. colonial use, *the o. country, o. home* = Great Britain. *The O. Dominion*: see DOMINION. *O. World*, the Eastern Hemisphere, as opp. to the New World of America.

B. *sb.* (the adj. used ellipt.) †1. = Old man, old woman -1532. 2. *pl.* (*olds*). Old ones; old persons, etc. 1883. 3. *pl.* (*olds*). Hops more than two and less than four years old 1892. 4. = ELD 4. Chiefly in *men, times, days*, etc. *of o.* late ME. b. advb. phr. *Of o.*: of old time, long since, formerly; also, From old days, for a long time (before now). late ME.

4. Then remembred I the tymes of olde, & the yeares that were past COVERDALE *Ps.* lxxvi[i]. 5. b. You alwaies end with a Iades tricke, I know you of o. SHAKS.

C. *Old-* in Comb. 1. a. With another adj., in antithetic relation, as *o.-new, o.-young.* b. With a pr. pple., as *o.-looking.* c. With a pa. pple., in advb. sense 'of old, long, anciently', as *o.-acquainted, -established*, adjs. 2. Parasynthetic combinations: a. general, as *o.-blooded* (having o. blood), *o.-faced, -sighted*, etc., adjs.; hence *o.-sightedness* (= presbyopia). b. based on a phrase, as *o.-bachelorish, o.-boyish, o.-fogyish, o.-fogyism*, etc. 3. With a sb. (or its equivalent) forming an attrib. phrase, as *o.-book, o.-life, o.-Roman, o.-school*, etc. See also OLD-TIME, OLD-WORLD.

Special combs., etc.: **o.-clo·thes-man,** a dealer in o. or second-hand clothes; **-clo·thes-shop,** a shop for the sale of o. clothes; **o. gentleman**: see II. 3 b; **o. hand,** (*a*) one who has experience in any business, one skilful in doing something (see HAND *sb.*); (*b*) one who has been a convict; also *attrib.*; **O. Squaw** = OLD-WIFE 2; **o.-style** *a.*, belonging to the o. style, old-fashioned; **O. Tom,** a kind of strong gin. Hence **O·ldish** *a.* somewhat o. **O·ldness.**

Olden (ōᵘ·ldĕn, -d'n), *a.* late ME. [f. OLD *sb.* + -EN[4].] Belonging to a bygone time; ancient, old; esp. in phr. 'the o. time' (Shaks. *Macb.* III. iv. 75). *literary* and *arch.*

Olden (ōᵘ·ld'n), *v. rare.* 1827. [f. OLD *a.* + -EN[5].] 1. *intr.* To grow old, to age 2. *trans.* To cause to grow old, to age 1850.

1. She had oldened..as people do who suffer silently great mental pain THACKERAY.

Older (ōᵘ·ldəɹ), *a.* ME. [f. OLD *a.* + -ER[3].] The later 'levelled' comparative of OLD, which has superseded the earlier ELDER, q.v., except in special uses. So **O·ldest** *a. superl.* (cf. ELDEST).

Deposits of older date 1863. Our oldest reformation is that of Magna Charta BURKE. He is the older of the two sons, but not the eldest child (*mod.*).

Old-fangled, *a.* 1842. [f. after *new-fangled*; cf. FANGLE.] Old-fashioned. Hence **Old-fa·ngledness.**

Old-fashioned, *a.* 1604. [See FASHIONED *ppl. a.*] 1. Antiquated in form or character. 2. Attached to old fashions or ways 1687. 3. Having the ways of a grown-up person; hence, precocious, knowing. Chiefly *dial.* 1844.

1. Good, old-fashioned, long skirts 1897. 2. Old-fashioned men of wit and pleasure ADDISON. 3. The little fellow..was an old-fashioned boy DICKENS.

Old maid, 1530. 1. An elderly spinster; usu. connoting habits characteristic of such a condition. 2. A bivalve mollusc of the family *Myidæ*, also called Gaper 1865. 3. A simple round game at cards 1844. Hence **Old-mai·d·ish, -mai·denish, -mai·denly** *adjs.* **Old-mai·dery, Old-mai·dism,** the habits or characteristics of an old maid.

Old man. ME. **1.** *lit.* A man advanced in years. **b.** As a term of affectionate familiarity; see OLD *a.* II. 2. **c.** = Husband; father; 'boss' (*vulgar*). 1854. **2.** *Theol.* Unregenerate human nature (cf. *Old* ADAM). late ME. **3.** The Rainbird of Jamaica (*Hyetornis pluvialis*) 1694. **4.** In Australia: A full-grown male kangaroo 1828. **5.** A name of the Southernwood (*Artemisia Abrotanum*); perh. from its hoary foliage 1824. **6.** *Mining.* An old vein or working which has been long abandoned; also, oreless stuff 1653. **7.** *Old Man of the Sea,* a person or thing that cannot be shaken off, in allusion to the story of Sinbad the Sailor.

Comb. in plant names, as *old man's beard,* (*a*) a name of the epiphytic plant *Tillandsia usneoides*; (*b*) the Traveller's Joy, *Clematis Vitalba*; (*c*) the Strawberry Saxifrage, *Saxifraga sarmentosa*; (*d*) the South European Composite *Geropogon.*

Oldster (ōu·ldstəɹ). 1829. [f. OLD *a.* + -STER, after *youngster.*] One who is no longer a youngster (*colloq.*); *spec.* (*Naut.*) a midshipman of four years' standing.

O·ld-time, *a.* Also **-times.** 1824. Of, belonging to, or characteristic of the olden time. So **Old-ti·mer** (chiefly *U.S.*) 1882.

Old wife, old-wife. ME. **1.** An old woman. Now usu. disparaging. **2.** The Long-tailed Duck (*Harelda glacialis*) 1634. **3.** A name of various fishes, esp. of the family *Labridæ* (wrasse), *Sparidæ* (sea-bream), and *Clupeidæ* (alewife and menhaden) 1588.

1. *Old wives' fable, story, tale,* a trivial story such as is told by garrulous old women.

Old woman. late ME. **1.** *lit.* A woman advanced in years; hence, A person compared to an old woman; a man of timid and fussy character. **b.** = Wife ('my old woman'); mother (*vulgar*). 1825. **2.** A cap or cowl to prevent a chimney from smoking 1861.

1. *Old woman's fable, tale, story*: see prec. Hence **Old-wo·man-ish, -ly** *adjs.*

Old-world (ōu·ld₁wɒ̄ɹld), *a.* 1712. [The phr. *old world* used attrib.; see WORLD.] **1.** Of or pertaining to the old world or ancient order of things; characteristic of bygone times. **2.** Of or pertaining to the Old World, as opposed to the New World or America.

1. She watched the simple pastoral old-world life around her 1876.

Oleaceous (ōuli₁ēⁱ·ʃəs), *a.* 1857. [f. mod.L. *Oleaceæ,* f. *olea* olive-tree; see -ACEOUS.] *Bot.* Belonging to the N.O. *Oleaceæ,* comprising trees and shrubs chiefly of temperate regions; the typical genus is *Olea,* the Olive.

Oleaginous (ōuli₁æ·dʒinəs), *a.* 1634. [ad. F. *oléagineux,* f. L. *oleaginus, -eus, -ius,* of or pertaining to *olea* the olive-tree.] Having the properties of, or containing oil; oily, fatty, greasy. **b.** Producing oil 1696. Hence **Olea·ginousness.**

Oleander (ōuli₁æ·ndəɹ). 1548. [a. med.L.; etym. uncertain. See N.E.D.] An evergreen poisonous herb, *Nerium Oleander* (N.O. *Apocynaceæ*), a native of the Levant, with leathery lanceolate leaves, and handsome red or white flowers; rose bay. Hence, any shrub of the genus *Nerium,* as *N. odorum,* the sweet o.

Oleandrine (ōuli₁æ·ndrəin). 1885. [f. prec. + -INE⁵.] *Chem.* A yellow, poisonous, bitter alkaloid, the active principle of the leaves, etc. of the oleander.

Oleaster (ōuli₁æ·stəɹ). late ME. [a. L., f. *olea* olive-tree; see -ASTER.] **a.** The true Wild Olive (*Olea Oleaster*). **b.** A small tree of the genus *Elæagnus,* with fragrant yellow flowers, and reddish-brown inedible fruit; wild olive.

Oleate (ōu·li₁ĕt). 1831. [f. OLE-IC + -ATE⁴.] *Chem.* and *Pharm.* A salt of oleic acid; also applied to pharmaceutical preparations composed of alkaloids or metallic oxides or salts, dissolved in this.

‖**Olecranon** (ōulĕ₁krēⁱ·nǫn). 1727. [a. Gr. ὠλέκρανον, shortened from ὠλενόκρανον head or point of the elbow, f. ὠλένη + κρανίον.] *Anat.* The apophysis at the upper end of the ulna, forming the bony prominence at the elbow. Hence **Olecra·nal, Olecra·nial, Olecra·nian** *adjs.*

Olefiant (ōu·lĭfəi₁ănt, olĭ·fiănt), *a.* 1797. [a. F. *oléfiant,* in *gaz oléfiant* (1795), f. L. *oleum* OIL *sb.* + *-ficent-,* pr. ppl. stem of *-ficere* -FY.] *Chem.* Making or forming oil; only in *O. gas*: the name orig. given to what is now called ETHYLENE (C_2H_4), from its forming with chlorine an oily liquid ('Dutch oil', 'D. liquid').

Olefine (ōu·lĭfin). Also **-in.** 1860. [f. prec. with ending -INE⁵.] *Chem.* Name for the series of hydrocarbons homologous with olefiant gas or ethylene, having the general formula C_nH_{2n}; forming with chlorine and bromine oily dichlorides and dibromides analogous to Dutch liquid (see prec.). Also *attrib.,* as *o. series.*

Oleic (olī·ik, ōu·li₁ik), *a.* 1819. [f. L. *ole-um* oil + -IC.] *Chem.* Pertaining to or derived from oil; *spec.* in *O. acid*: one of the fatty acids ($C_{18}H_{34}O_2$) occurring in most fats, and a constituent of most soaps; also called *elaic acid*; in *pl.* extended to the series of acids to which this belongs. *O. ether*: a general name for the oleates of hydrocarbon radicals, esp. oleate of ethyl, $C_{18}H_{33}(C_2H_5)O_2$.

Oleiferous (ōuli₁i·fĕrəs), *a.* Also *erron.* **oliferous.** 1804. [f. L. *ole-um* OIL *sb.* + -IFEROUS.] Producing oil.

Olein (ōu·li₁in). 1838. [Fr. *oléine*; f. L. *ole-um* oil + -IN¹, after *glycerin.*] **1.** *Chem.* The trioleate of glyceryl, $C_3H_5(C_{18}H_{33}O_2)_3$, a widely diffused natural fat, obtained as a colourless oily liquid, solidifying at −6° C.; also called *elain.* In *pl.* applied to the oleates of glyceryl or glycerides of oleic acid in general; the above being distinguished as *triolein.* **2.** *Comm.* Any liquid oil obtained by pressure from partly solid oils 1893.

Oleo (ōu·lio). 1884. **1.** Commercial contr. for OLEOMARGARINE, esp. in U.S. sense of artificial butter or MARGARINE. **2.** *O. oil* (esp. U.S.) = OLEOMARGARINE 1893. **3.** Short for OLEOGRAPH.

Oleo- (ōu·lio), used **a.** as comb. form of L. *oleum* oil; as in **O·leodu:ct** [after *aqueduct*], a duct for conveying oil from an oil-well or oil-field. **O·leopte:ne** [Gr. πτηνός winged, volatile] = ELÆOPTENE. **b.** as comb. form of *oleic, olein,* as in OLEOMARGARINE.

Oleograph (ōu·liǒgrɑf). 1880. [f. OLEO- + -GRAPH.] A picture printed in oil-colours in imitation of an oil-painting. Hence **O:leogra·phic** *a.* So **Oleo·graphy** 1873.

Oleomargarine (ōu:lio₁mā·ɹgărīn, -dʒ-, -in). 1873. [f. OLEO- b + MARGARINE. Often mispronounced (-mā·ɹdʒərīn).] A fatty substance obtained by extracting the liquid portion from clarified beef fat by pressure, and allowing it to solidify; with the addition of butyrin, etc., it forms a substitute for natural butter, formerly sold as *butterine,* but now legally called *margarine.*

Oleoresin (ōu:lio₁re·zin). 1853. [f. OLEO- + RESIN.] **a.** A natural mixture of a volatile oil and a resin; a balsam. **b.** A mixture of an oil (fixed or volatile) and a resin or other active substance, artificially obtained by evaporation from an ether tincture. Hence **O:leore·sinous** *a.*

Oleraceous (ǫlĕrēⁱ·ʃəs), *a.* 1682. [f. L. (*h*)*oleraceus* (f. (*h*)*olus,* (*h*)*oler-* pot-herb) + -OUS.] Of the nature of or obtained from a pot-herb.

Olfaction (ǫlfæ·kʃən). 1846. [f. L. *olfacere,* f. *olere* to smell + *facere* to make.] The action of smelling or the sense of smell.

Olfactory (ǫlfæ·ktəri), *a.* and *sb.* 1658. [ad.L. **olfactorius,* f. *olfactor,* agent-n. from *olfacere* to smell; see -ORY.] **A.** *adj.* Of or pertaining to the sense of smell; concerned with smelling. **B.** *sb.* An organ of smelling 1823. Hence **Olfa·ctorily** *adv.*

‖**Olibanum** (oli·bănɒ̆m). late ME. [a. med.L., f. (immed. or ult.) Gr. λίβανος, late L. *libanus* (Vulg.) frankincense.] An aromatic gum resin obtained from trees of the genus *Boswellia*; formerly used as a medicine, but now chiefly as incense.

Olibene (ǫ·libīn). 1881. [f. prec. + -ENE.] *Chem.* A volatile oil, $C_{10}H_{16}$, obtained from olibanum.

Olid (ǫ·lid), *a.* 1680. [ad. L. *olidus* smelling, f. *olere* to smell; see -ID¹.] Having a strong disagreeable smell; fetid.

Oligandrous, etc.: see OLIGO-.

Oligarch (ǫ·ligāɹk), *sb.* 1610. [ad. Gr. ὀλιγάρχης, f. ὀλίγος few + ἄρχειν to rule.] A member of an oligarchy; one of a few holding power in a state. Hence **O·ligarchal, Oliga·rchic, -al** *adjs.* of, pertaining to, or of the nature of an oligarchy; carried on, administered or governed by an oligarchy; supporting or advocating oligarchy. **Oliga·rchically** *adv.* **O·ligarchize** *v. trans.* to convert into an oligarchy; to subject to an oligarchy.

Oligarch (ǫ·ligāɹk), *a.* 1884. [f. Gr. ὀλίγος few + ἀρχή origin.] *Bot.* Proceeding from few points of origin, said of the primary xylem (or wood) of the root.

Oligarchy (ǫ·ligāɹki). 1577. [ad. Gr. ὀλιγαρχία, f. as ὀλιγάρχης OLIGARCH + abstract ending -ία.] Government by the few; a form of government in which the power is confined to a few persons or families; the body of persons composing such a government.

An ignoble o. founded on the destruction of the crown, the church, the nobility, and the people BURKE.

Oligist (ǫ·lidʒist). 1828. [Named 1801 (*oligiste*) by Haüy, ad. Gr. ὀλίγιστος least.] *Min.* More fully *o. iron*: A variety of native iron sesquioxid or hæmatite so called as containing less iron than the magnetic oxide. So **Oligi·stic, -al** *adjs.*

Oligo- (ǫ·ligo), bef. a vowel **olig-,** comb. form of Gr. ὀλίγος small, little, pl. few, in forming nouns and adjs., e.g. ὀλιγόκαρπος with little fruit, oligocarpous; etc. Hence **Oliga·ndrous,** *a. Bot.,* having fewer than twenty stamens. ‖**Oligochromæ·mia** [Gr. χρῶμα colour, αἷμα blood], deficiency of hæmoglobin in the red blood-corpuscles. ‖**Oligocythæ·mia** [Gr. κύτος a hollow, αἷμα blood], deficiency of the red corpuscles of the blood; so **Oligocythæ·mic** *a.* **Oligo·merous** [Gr. μέρος part], *a. Bot.,* having fewer divisions than is normal; so **Oligo·mery. Oligoside·ric** [Gr. σίδηρος iron], *a.* containing only a small proportion of iron. **Oligosi·derite,** a stony meteorite containing a small proportion of iron. **Oligosylla·bic** [Gr. ὀλιγοσύλλαβος] *a.,* having less than four syllables. **Oligosy·llable,** a word of less than four syllables.

Oligocene (ǫ·ligosīn), *a.* 1859. [mod. f. prec. + Gr. καινός recent.] *Geol.* Of certain Tertiary strata: Of an intermediate age between the Eocene and Miocene formations.

Oligochæte, -chete (ǫ·ligokīt), *a., sb.* 1876. [f. mod.L. *Oligochæta,* f. OLIGO- + Gr. χαίτη mane, taken as 'bristle'.] **A.** *adj.* Belonging to the *Oligochæta,* one of the divisions of the *Chætopoda* (see CHÆTOPOD), including the earthworms and lugworms; so called from the small number of their bristly foot-stumps or parapodia. **B.** *sb.* A worm of this division.

Oligoclase (ǫ·ligoklēⁱs). 1832. [f. OLIGO- + Gr. κλάσις fracture; because thought to have a less perfect cleavage than albite.] *Min.* A lime- and soda-felspar resembling albite, occurring either in crystals or massive.

Olio (ōu·lio). 1643 [a. Sp. *olla,* Pg. *olha* both pron (olʸa) pot, stew, hotchpotch :—L. *olla* pot, jar; with *o* repr. final *a,* as in *armado,* etc.; cf. OLLA¹.] **1.** A dish of various meats and vegetables, stewed or boiled together, and highly spiced; hence, Any dish containing a variety of ingredients, a hotchpotch. Now *Obs.* or *arch.* **2.** *fig.* A hotchpotch, farrago, medley 1648. **b.** A collection of various pieces, as engravings, verses, etc.; a miscellany; a musical medley 1655.

1. Such a soup, or ollio..is much in vogue 1763. 2. An o. of all ages and all countries DISRAELI.

O·liphant. *arch.* ME. [a. OF. *olifant.*] Obs. f. ELEPHANT, occas. retained by mod. writers in sense 'horn of ivory': see ELEPHANT 2 b.

Olitory (ǫ·litŏri), *a.* and *sb.* Now *rare.* 1658. [ad. L. (*h*)*olitorius,* f. (*h*)*olitor* kitchen gardener, f. *holus* pot-herbs; see -ORY.] A. *adj.* Of or pertaining to pot-herbs, or to the kitchen garden. †B. *sb.* 1. A pot-herb, a culinary vegetable EVELYN. 2. A kitchen garden -1793.

‖**Oliva** (olai·vă). 1839. [L.] 1. *Zool.* A genus of gasteropod molluscs; a member of this genus; an olive-shell (see OLIVE *sb.*¹ 5). 2. *Anat.* The olivary body 1892.

Olivaceo- (olivēⁱ·ʃio), comb. form of next.

Olivaceous (olivēⁱ·ʃəs), *a.* 1776. [f. mod. L. *olivaceus*, F. *olivacé*, f. *oliva* OLIVE; see -ACEOUS.] Of a dusky green colour with a tinge of yellow; olive-green.

Olivary (ǫ·livări), *a.* 1541. [ad. L. *olivarius*, f. *oliva* OLIVE; see -ARY.] Shaped like an olive. Chiefly *Anat.*

O. body, each of two oval prominences of nerve-matter, one on each side of the medulla oblongata. Also applied to parts of or connected with the o. body.

Olive (ǫ·liv), *sb.*¹ ME. [a. F. :—L. *oliva* olive and olive-tree.] 1. An evergreen tree, *Olea europæa*, esp. *O. sativa*, with narrow entire leaves, green above and hoary beneath, and axillary clusters of small whitish four-cleft flowers; cultivated in the Mediterranean countries chiefly for its fruit and the oil thence obtained. b. Extended to the whole genus *Olea*, and to various trees and shrubs allied to or resembling the olive 1577. 2. The fruit or 'berry' of *Olea sativa*, a small oval drupe, bluish-black when ripe, with bitter pulp abounding in oil, and hard stone; valuable for its oil, and also eaten pickled in an unripe state. late ME. 3. A leaf, branch, or wreath of the common olive, an ancient emblem of peace; hence allusively. late ME. b. A child (= OLIVE-BRANCH 2); also *attrib.* 1803. 4. Olive-wood. late ME. 5. A gasteropod mollusc of the genus *Oliva* or family *Olividæ*; or its shell, of an elongated oval form and fine polish; an olive-shell 1776. 6. *Cookery.* (*pl.*) A dish composed of thickish slices of beef or veal, rolled up with onions and herbs, and stewed in brown sauce 1598. 7. A button, etc., of the shape of an olive, for fastening a garment by means of a loop of braid. 8. *Anat.* The olivary body 1899. 9. = Olive colour 1662.

1. b. **Wild O.**, the wild variety of the common o. (= OLEASTER a), or any wild species of *Olea*; also applied to various trees and shrubs resembling this. 2. The ripe Oliues overturne the stomach, and cause wambling therein 1579. 3. The three nook'd world Shall beare the Oliue freely SHAKS.

B. *adj.* a. Of the colour of the unripe fruit of the olive, a dull somewhat yellowish green. late ME. b. Also, applied to a yellowish brown or brownish yellow, in complexions 1634. c. Also, of the colour of the foliage of the olive, a dull ashy green with silvery sheen.

attrib. and *Comb.*: **o.-acanthus**, in decorative art, an ornamental form of acanthus leaf with lobes each resembling an olive leaf; **-berry** = sense 2; **o.-cautery**, a cautery with an oval head; **-crown**, a wreath of o. (as a token of victory) **o. pie**, a pie made with veal olives (see 6); **-shell** = sense 5.

Olive (ǫ·liv), *sb.*² 1541. [?] Local name of the Oyster-catcher (*Hæmatopus ostrilegus*).

O·live-branch. ME. 1. *lit.* A branch of an olive-tree. b. As an emblem of peace; hence *fig.* anything offered in token of peace and goodwill. Also in allusion to Gen. viii. 11. ME. 2. usu. *pl.* (in allusion to Ps. cxxviii. 3 (4). Children. (Now *joc.*) 1605.

Olivenite (oli·vĕnəit, ǫ·livenəit). 1820. [f. G. *oliven-* in *oliven-erz* olive-ore + -ITE ¹.] *Min.* A native arsenate of copper, occurring in crystals or masses, usu. of olive-green colour.

Oliver (ǫ·livəɹ). 1846. [Origin obsc.] A small tilt-hammer worked with the foot; used esp. in the shaping of nails, bolts, etc.

Oliver, in *a Roland for an O.*: see ROLAND.

Oliverian (ǫliviə·riăn), *sb.* and *a.* 1658. [f. *Oliver*, proper name + -IAN.] A. *sb.* A partisan of Oliver Cromwell; a Cromwellian; puritan. B. *adj.* Cromwellian; puritanical 1704.

Olivet (ǫ·livet). *Obs.* exc. as in b. ME. [ad. L. *olivetum* olive-grove.] †An olive-grove -1610. b. The Mount of Olives, the scene of the Ascension; hence allusively.

Olivetan (ǫlivī·tăn). 1691. [f. Monte Oliveto near Siena, the site of the mother convent; see -AN.] One of an order of monks founded in 1313 by John Tolomei of Siena, and subjected to the Benedictine rule.

O·live-wood. 1681. 1. The wood of the common olive, *Olea europæa*. 2. Any tree of the genus *Elæodendron* (N.O. *Celastraceæ*), furnishing an ornamental wood 1866.

Olivil (ǫ·livil). 1810. [a. F. *olivile*, f. *olive*.] *Chem.* A crystalline substance obtained from the gum of the olive tree.

Olivine (ǫ·livəin, -in). Also **-in.** 1794. [f. L. *oliva* OLIVE; see -INE ⁵.] *Min.* A variety of CHRYSOLITE, chiefly of olive-green colour, occurring in eruptive rocks and in meteorites. Also *attrib.* = **Olivi·nic** *a.*

Olla¹ (ǫ·lă). 1622. [a. Sp. *olla* (pron. o·lʸa), in Pg. *olha* pot, stew, hotchpot :—L. *olla* pot, jar.] 1. In Spain, etc., an earthen jar or pot used for cooking, etc.; also, a dish of meat and vegetables cooked in this; hence = OLIO 1. OLLA PODRIDA. 2. In parts of the U.S. formerly Spanish: A large porous earthen jar for keeping drinking-water cool 1851.

‖**Olla**². 1622. [a. Pg. *olla*, var. of *ola*, a. Malayālim *ōla* (Tamil *ōlai*).] = CADJAN 2.

‖**Ollamh, ollav** (ǫ·lăv). Also **ollave, ollam.** 1723. [a. Ir. *ollamh* (o·lav, with *nasal v*), OIr. *ollam*, learned man, doctor.] *Ir. Antiq.* A learned man; a rank equal to that of a doctor or professor in a university.

Olla podrida (ǫ·lă podrī·dă). 1599. [a. Sp., = 'rotten pot', f. *olla* (see OLLA ¹) and *podrida* = L. *putrida* putrid.] 1. = OLIO 1. 2. = OLIO 2. 1634.

-ology, Ology (ǫ·lŏdʒi), *suffix* and quasi-*sb.* 1786. 1. *suffix.* The form in which the suffix -LOGY (Gr. -λογία) usu. occurs, the *o* belonging to the prec. element (see -O-); hence regularly used in mod. formations. 2. quasi-*sb.* Any science or department of science 1811.

2. Maid-servants, I hear people complaining, are getting instructed in the 'ologies' CARLYLE.

Olp, dial. var. of ALP ²; cf. NOPE.

Olympiad (oli·mpiæd). late ME. [a. F. *olympiade*, ad. L. *Olympias*, acc. *-adem*, a. Gr. Ὀλυμπιάς, -άδ-, f. Ὀλύμπιος OLYMPIAN; see -AD.] A period of four years reckoned from one celebration of the Olympic games to the next, by which the ancient Greeks computed time, the year 776 B.C. being taken as the first year of the first Olympiad.

Olympian (oli·mpiăn), *a.* and *sb.* 1593. [ad. late L. *Olympianus*, f. earlier *Olympius*, a. Gr. Ὀλύμπιος of Olympus. Ὀλυμπία (sc. χώρα) was a district in Elis, where the Ὀλύμπια (sc. ἱερά), or Olympic games, were held.] A. *adj.* 1. Of or belonging to Olympus; heavenly, celestial 1603. 2. = OLYMPIC A. 1593.

1. Above th' O. Hill I soare MILT.

B. *sb.* 1. A native or inhabitant of Olympia; an athlete who took part in the Olympic games 1606. 2. An inhabitant of Olympus; one of the greater gods of ancient Greek mythology; *spec.* (*the O.*) Zeus or Jupiter 1843.

Olympic (ŏli·mpik), *a.* and *sb.* 1610. [ad. L. *Olympicus*, a. Gr. Ὀλυμπικός, orig. 'of Olympus', later 'of Olympia'.] A. *adj.* Of or belonging to Olympia in Elis (see prec.), in which the most famous games of ancient Greece (the *Olympic games*) were celebrated in honour of the Olympian Zeus. †B. *sb.* An Olympic game; usu. in *pl.* Also *transf.* and *fig.* -1711.

A. *O. games*, also, a quadrennial international contest at various places, the first at Athens in 1896.

Olympus (ŏli·mpŏs). 1580. [L., a. Gr. Ὄλυμπος name of several lofty mountains.] A mountain in the north of Thessaly, the fabled abode of the greater Greek gods; hence, heaven as the divine abode.

-oma, *suffix*, mod.L., a. Gr. -ωμα as in ῥίζωμα RHIZOMA, σάρκωμα SARCOMA, τρίχωμα TRICHOME, φύλλωμα PHYLLOME, f. vbs. in -οῦσθαι, as ῥιζοῦσθαι to take root. 1. Used in sbs. denoting some formation or member of the nature of that denoted by the radical part: now superseded by -OME as RHIZOME. 2. Used in names of tumours or other abnormal growths.

Omander (omæ·ndəɹ). 1843. [unkn.] Name of an E. Indian ebony obtained from the tree *Diospyros Ebenaster*; akin to calamander.

‖**Omasum** (omēⁱ·sŏm). 1706. [L., 'bullock's tripe'.] The third stomach of a ruminant; the *psalterium* or manyplies.

Ombre (ǫ·mbəɹ, Sp. o·mbre). 1660. [a. Sp. *hombre* (:—L. *hominem*) man, perh. through F. *hombre, ombre.*] 1. A card-game played by three persons with forty cards; very popular in 17th–18th c. 2. The player at this game who undertakes to win the pool 1724.

Ombro-, comb. form of Gr. ὄμβρος shower of rain: as in **Ombro·logy** [see -LOGY], the branch of meteorology that deals with rain. **Ombro·meter** [see -METER], a rain-gauge.

-ome, *suffix* = -OMA 1 and 2, but now general only in *Bot.* e.g. CAULOME, PHYLLOME, RHIZOME.

Omega (ōᵘ·mĭgă, ōᵘme·gă). 1526. [Gr. ὦ μέγα, i.e. 'great O'.] 1. The last letter of the Greek alphabet 1656. 2. *transf.* The last of a series; the last word; the end or final development 1526. 3. *attrib.* 1880.

2. *Alpha and O.*: see ALPHA 1.

Omelet, omelette (ǫ·mlėt). 1611. [a. F. *omelette*, for earlier *amelette*, app. by metathesis from *alemette* = *alemelle*, lit. thin plate.] A dish consisting of eggs whipped up, seasoned, and fried; often varied by the addition of other ingredients.

Prov. You can't make an o. without breaking eggs.

Omen (ōᵘ·mĕn), *sb.* 1582. [a. L., OL. *osmen*, perh. for **ausmen*, f. root of *audire* to hear + *-men* (as in *carmen*, etc.).] Any phenomenon or circumstance supposed to portend good or evil; a prophetic sign, prognostic, augury. b. Without *an* and *pl.*: Foreboding; prognostication 1742.

1. Far be that O. from vs [= L. *absit omen*!] HEYWOOD. b. Birds of evil o. 1876. Hence **O·men** *v. trans.* to presage, prognosticate, forebode. **O·mened** *a.* having an o., as *happy-omened*, etc.

‖**Omentum** (ome·ntŏm). *Pl.* **-a.** 1547. [L.] *Anat.* A fold or duplication of the peritoneum connecting the stomach with the liver, spleen, colon, etc.; the caul.

Three divisions of the omentum are commonly recognized: the *gastro-colic* or *greater o.* descending over a part of the intestines from the lower border of the stomach to the transverse colon; the *gastro-hepatic, hepato-gastric*, or *lesser o.* extending from the liver to the smaller curvature of the stomach; the *gastro-splenic o.* connecting the cardiac end of the stomach with the spleen. Hence **Ome·ntal** *a.* of, pertaining to, or situated in the o. 1758.

‖**Omer** (ōᵘ·məɹ). 1611. [a. Heb.] 1. A Hebrew measure of capacity equal to the tenth part of an ephah, or $5\frac{1}{10}$ pints Imperial measure. (Cf. GOMER ¹, HOMER ².) 2. A sheaf; *spec.* the sheaf of the wave-offering 1860.

2. *Counting of the O.*, the formal enumeration by Jews of the days from the eve of the 2nd day of the Passover till Pentecost. (see Leviticus xxiii. 15, 16.)

-ometer (ǫ·mĭtəɹ), the element -METER preceded by *-o-*, belonging to the prec. element, or merely connective (see -O-). Also as quasi-*sb.*

†**O·minate**, *v.* 1582. [f. L. *ominat-*, *ominari*, *-are* to prognosticate, f. *omen*, *omin-* OMEN.] 1. *trans.* To prognosticate from omens, to augur, forebode -1742. b. *intr.* To have or utter forebodings -1667. 2. *trans.* To be a prognostic of, to portend -1827. b. *intr.* To be or serve as an omen -1702. Hence †**Omina·tion**, prognostication, foreboding.

Ominous (ǫ·minəs, ōᵘ·m-), *a.* 1589. [ad. L. *ominosus*, f. *omin-* OMEN; see -OUS.] 1. Of the nature of an omen, presaging events to come, portentous 1592. †2. Of good omen; fortunate -1662. 3. Of ill omen, inauspicious 1589. b. Marked by evil omens, disastrous 1634. c. Of doubtful or menacing aspect 1877.

3. An o. shake of the head supplied the remainder of the sentence 1871. c. In the dimness or coruscation of o. light RUSKIN. Hence **O·minous-ly** *adv.*, **-ness.**

Omissible (omi·sĭb'l), *a.* 1816. [f. L. *omiss-*, *omittere* + -IBLE.] Capable of being omitted.

Omission (omi·ʃən). late ME. [ad. L. *omissionem*, n. of action from *omittere* to OMIT.] 1. The action of omitting, or fact of being omitted; also, an instance of this 1555. 2. The non-performance or neglect of action or duty; an instance of this.

1. To supply the o. in the preceding narrative

Paley. **2.** His faults to me seem only great omissions Pepys.

Omissive (omi·siv), *a.* 1629. [f. L. *omiss-*, *omittere* to Omit + -ive.] Characterized by neglecting to perform, or leaving out.

Omit (ǫmi·t), *v.* late ME. [ad. L. *omittere*, f. *o-* = *ob-* (Ob- 1) + *mittere* to send, let go.] **1.** *trans.* To leave out, not to insert or include. **2.** *trans.* To fail or forbear to use or perform; to let alone, pass over, neglect, leave undone 1533. †**b.** To leave disregarded, take no notice of Shaks. †**3.** To let go -1646.

1. So moche as they omitted or lefte vnsayd 1526. **2.** He will o. nothynge, that conserueth hys dewtie 1560. Some people..did not o. publicly to attend the worship of God De Foe. **b.** 2 *Hen. IV*, IV. iv. 27. Hence **Omi·tter.**

‖ **Omlah** (ǫ·mlā). *E. Ind.* 1778. [ad. Arab.; prop. used as a collective pl.; but occas. erron. with Eng. pl. *-s* added.] In northern India, A body or staff of native officials in a civil court.

‖ **Ommatidium** (ǫmăti·diǒm). *Pl.* **-ia.** 1888. [mod. L., f. Gr. *ὀμματίδιον, dim. of ὄμμα, ὀμματ- eye.] *Zool.* A structural element of the eyes of Invertebrates; *e.g.* one of the simple eyes which make up the compound eye of an insect. Hence **Ommati·dial** *a.*

Omneity (ǫmnī·iti). *rare.* 1638. [f. L. *omnis, omne* all + -ity.] The condition of being all; 'allness'.

So nothing became something and O. informed Nullity into an Essence Sir T. Browne.

Omni- (ǫmni), comb. form of L. *omnis* all, used in L. in forming compound adjs., and in Eng. in a multitude of words formed on L. models, or to supply a latinized equivalent to an Eng. compound in All-, as in: **Omnibene·volent** *a.* benevolent towards all; so **Omnibene·volence**, universal benevolence. **Omni·parent** [see Parent] *a.*, producing or bringing forth all things. **Omnipa·rient** *a.* = prec. **Omni·parous** [L. *-parus* producing] = *omniparent.* **Omnipa·tient** *a.*, patient of everything; having unlimited endurance. **Omniperci·pient** *a.*, perceiving all things; so **Omniperci·pience.** **Omnipre·valent** *a.*, prevailing everywhere.

Omniana (ǫmni,ēi·nă). 1807. [f. L. *omnis* all, *omnia* all things + -ana.] Notes or scraps of information about everything; '*ana*' of all kinds.

Omnibus (ǫ·mnibǒs), *sb.* and *a.* 1829. *Pl.* **-buses.** See also Bus. [a. F. (1828), a. L., 'for all', dat. pl. of *omnis*, in Fr. phr. *voiture omnibus* = *voiture pour tous* vehicle for all. **A.** *sb.* **1.** A four-wheeled public vehicle for carrying passengers, usually covered and freq. with seats on the roof as well as inside, plying on a fixed route; (also *hotel o.*), a vehicle conveying guests between a hotel and the railway station; (also *private* or *family o.*), a vehicle provided by a railway company, etc., for conveying a party and its luggage to or from a station. **2.** = *Omnibus-box*: see B. 1848. **3.** A man or boy who assists a waiter at an hotel. etc. 1888.

1. The new vehicle, called the o., commenced running this morning [4 July] from Paddington to the City 1829. **2.** Having just arrived from the o. at the Opera Thackeray.

B. *adj.* Serving for several distinct objects at once; comprising a large number of items 1854.

Phr. *O. bill, clause, order, faculty. O. box*, name of a large box on the pit tier in some theatres and opera-houses, appropriated to a number of subscribers. *O. train* [after F. *train omnibus*], a railway train stopping at all stations on the route. *O. bar, wire*, etc. (*Electr.*), one through which the whole current passes. *O.* (*book*), a volume containing several stories, etc. (usu. by a single author) published at a low price to be within the reach of all.

Omnifarious (ǫmnifē°·riəs), *a.* 1653. [f. L. *omnifarius* (Omni-; cf. *multifarius*) + -ous.] Of all kinds and forms; exceedingly various.

Omnific (ǫmni·fik), *a.* 1667. [f. med. or mod.L. *omnificus*, f. Omni- + *-ficus* making.] All-creating. *P.L.* VII. 217.

Omniform (ǫ·mnifǭım), *a.* 1647. [ad. late L. *omniformis*, f. Omni- + *forma*; see -form.] Of all forms or shapes; taking any or every form. So **Omnifo·rmity**, the quality of being omniform; the being of all forms 1644.

Omnify (ǫ·mnifəi), *v.* 1622. [f. Omni- + -fy.] †**1.** *trans.* To make everything of; to account as all in all -1668. **2.** To render universal 1810.

Omnigenous (ǫmni·dʒĭnəs), *a.* 1650. [f. L. *omnigenus* (f. Omni- + *genus* kind) + -ous.] Of all kinds.

Omnipotence (ǫmni·pǒtĕns). 1566. [ad. late L. *omnipotentia*, f. *omnipotentem*; see -ence.] The quality of being omnipotent; almightiness. **a.** *strictly*, as an attribute of deity; hence God himself = 'the Omnipotent'. **b.** *gen.* as an attribute of persons or things; hence *transf.* an omnipotent force or agency 1590.

a. The Right of Gods Soveraignty is derived from his O. Hobbes. **b.** The O. of an Ordinance of Parliament, confirmed all that was this way done Clarendon. So †**Omni·potency** 1470.

Omnipotent (ǫmni·pǒtĕnt), *a.* ME. [a. F., ad. L. *omnipotentem*, f. Omni- + *potens, -entem* able.] **1.** Almighty, infinite in power, as a deity. **2.** *gen.* All-powerful; having unlimited or very great power, force, or influence 1598. **b.** *joc.* Capable of anything; unparalleled 1596. **3.** *absol.* or as *sb.* An omnipotent being; *spec.* (with *the*) the Almighty, God 1601.

1. As helpe me verray god o. Chaucer. **2.** O o. Loue Shaks. **b.** 1 *Hen. IV*, I. ii. 121. **3.** Who durst defie th' O. to Arms Milt. Hence **Omni·potently** *adv.*

Omnipresence (ǫmni,pre·zĕns). 1601. [f. med. Schol.L. *omnipræsentia*, f. *omnipræsentem*; see -ence.] The fact or quality of being omnipresent.

Next to God's Eternitie follows his Immensitie or O., which denotes his presence in althings and al spaces 1677. The o. of casualties..threatened all projects with futility Geo. Eliot.

Omnipresent (ǫmni,pre·zĕnt), *a.* 1610. [f. med.L. *omnipræsentem*; see Omni- and Present.] Present at the same time in all places; everywhere present. Often *hyperbolical.*

The bird is o. 1867. God is not ubiquitous, but o. 1885. Hence **Omnipre·sently** *adv.*

Omniscience (ǫmni·ʃĕns, -iĕns). 1612. [ad. med. Schol.L. *omniscientia*, f. Omni- + *scientia*; see -ence.] **a.** Strictly: Infinite knowledge; hence *transf.* the omniscient Being, the Deity. **b.** *hyperbolically.* Universal knowledge 1845.

b. [Said of Whewell] 'Science is his forte, o. is his foible' Syd. Smith.

Omniscient (ǫmni·ʃĕnt, -iĕnt), *a.* 1604. [ad. mod.L. *omnisciens, -entem*, f. med.L. *omniscius*, the substituted element being L. *sciens, scientem* pr. pple. 'knowing'.] **1.** Knowing all things. Often *hyperbolical* (cf. prec.). **2.** *absol.* or as *sb.* An omniscient being or person; *spec.* (with *the*) the Deity, God 1794.

1. By no means trust to your own judgement alone; for no man is o. Bacon. So †**Omni·scious** *a.* 1588-1728.

O:mnisuffi·cient, *a. Obs.* or *rare.* 1543. [f. Omni- + *sufficientem, sufficere.*] All-sufficient, all-sufficing. So **O:mnisuffi·ciency.**

Omnium (ǫ·mniǒm). 1760. [a. L., 'of all (things, sorts)', gen. pl. of *omnis* all. In sense 1, also, *omnium gatherum.*] **1.** *Stock Exch.* The aggregate amount of the parcels of different stocks and other considerations, formerly offered by Government in raising a loan, for each unit of capital (= £100) subscribed. **b.** Colloq. applied to other combined stocks the constituents of which can be dealt with separately. **2.** (with allusion to prec.) One's 'all'. 1766.

1. In the loan of 36,000,000 *l.* contracted for in June, 1815, the o. consisted of 130 *l.* 3 per cent. reduced annuities, 44 *l.* 3 per cent. consols, and 10 *l.* 4 per cent. annuities for each 100 *l.* subscribed McCulloch.

Omnium gatherum (ǫ·mniǒm gæ·ðərǒm). *colloq.* Also hyphened. 1530. [f. L. Omnium + *gatherum*, quasi-Latin for 'a gathering'.] A gathering of all sorts; a miscellaneous collection (of persons or things); a medley.

Such an omnium gatherum as the inhabitants of a new settlement 1830.

Omnivorous (ǫmni·vǒrəs), *a.* 1656. [f. L. *omnivorus* (f. Omni- + *-vorus* devouring) + -ous.] All-devouring; that feeds on all kinds of food.

fig. He has not observed on the nature of vanity, who does not know that it is o. Burke. Hence **Omni·vorous-ly** *adv.*, **-ness.**

Omo-hyoid (ōumo,həi·oid), *a.* (*sb.*) 1840. [f. Gr. ὦμος shoulder + Hyoid.] *Anat.* Relating to, or connecting, the shoulder and the hyoid bone. Also as *sb.* the omohyoid muscle.

‖ **Omophagia** (ōumofē·dʒiă). 1706. [mod. L., a. Gr. ὠμοφαγία, f. ὠμός raw + -φαγία -phagy.] The eating of raw food, esp. raw flesh. So **Omophagic** (ōumofæ·dʒik), **Omophagous** (omǫ·făgəs) *adjs.* eating, or characterized by the eating of, raw flesh. **Omophagist** (omǫ·fădʒist), an eater of raw flesh.

Omoplate (ōu·mǒpleˈit). Also **-plat** (-plæt). 1597. [ad. Gr. ὠμοπλάτη, f. ὦμος shoulder + πλάτη broad surface, blade.] The shoulder-blade, scapula.

Omostegite (omǫ·stĭdʒəit). 1870. [f. Gr. ὦμος shoulder + στέγη covering, roof + -ite [1] 3.] *Anat.* The posterior part of the carapace, covering the thorax, in certain crustaceans.

‖ **Omosternum** (ōumostə·ɹnǒm). 1868. [f. Gr. ὦμος shoulder + mod.L. *sternum*, Gr. στέρνον breast.] *Comp. Anat.* A cartilage, or an ossification of such cartilage at the anterior extremity of the sternum. Often applied to the membrane bone overlying the front end of the sternum, and more properly called *episternum* or *interclavicle.*

†**O·mphacine,** *a.* (*sb.*) 1548. [f. Gr. ὀμφάκινος made of unripe grapes, olives, etc., f. ὄμφαξ unripe (grape, berry): see -ine [2].] In *oil o.*, an oily liquid expressed from unripe olives. Also as *sb.* = oil o. -1712.

Omphacite (ǫ·mfăsəit). 1828. [ad. mod. G. *omphazit*, f. Gr. ὄμφαξ (see prec.) + -ite [1].] *Min.* A leek-green mineral, allied to pyroxene.

Omphalitis (ǫmfăləi·tis). 1857. [f. Gr. ὀμφαλός navel + -itis.] *Med.* Inflammation of the navel.

Omphalo- (ǫmfălo), bef. a vowel **omphal-,** comb. form of Gr. ὀμφαλός navel, boss, hub. **O·mphaloce:le** (-sīl) [Gr. κήλη tumour, etc.], umbilical hernia. **O·mphaloma:ncy** [Gr. μαντεία], divination, by the number of knots on the umbilical cord at birth, of the number of future children of the mother. **O:mphalo-mesente·ric** *a.*, *Anat.* Pertaining to, or connecting, the navel and the mesentery. **O:mphalopsy·chic** (-səi·kik) *a.*, **O:mphalo·psychite** [Gr. ψυχή], one of a sect of quietists who practised gazing at the navel as a means of inducing hypnotic reverie.

‖ **Omphalodium** (ǫmfălōu·diǒm). 1839. [mod.L., f. Gr. ὀμφαλώδης navel-like, f. ὀμφαλός; see -ode.] *Bot.* The centre of the hilum of a seed, through which the nourishing vessels pass. So **O·mphalode.**

‖ **Omphalos** (ǫ·mfălǫs). 1850. [a. Gr. ὀμφαλός navel, etc.] **1.** *Gr. Antiq.* **a.** A boss on a shield, etc. 1857. **b.** A sacred stone, of a rounded conical shape, in the temple of Apollo at Delphi, fabled to mark the central point of the earth 1850. **2.** *gen.* and *fig.* A central point or portion, centre, hub 1855.

‖ **Omrah** (ǫ·mrā). 1621. [Urdū *umarā*, orig. Arab. pl. of *amīr* 'commander, lord'.] A lord or grandee of a Mohammedan court, esp. that of the great Mogul.

On (ǫn), *prep.* [OE. *an, on* adv., prep.:—O Teut. **ana* adv., prep. = Gr. ἀνά on, upon, up, Zend *ana* upon, etc. See also A *prep.*[1], An *prep.*, O *prep.*[1] In 16-18th c. the prep. was often reduced to *o'*, as in *o' my life* (Shaks.), *o' my conscience* (Sheridan), as still in north. Eng. dialects.] **I.** Of position. [OE. *on* with dative.] Of local position outside of, but close to or near, any surface. **1.** Above and in contact with, above and supported by; upon. **2.** Expressing contact with any surface, whatever its position OE. **3.** In proximity to; close to, beside, near, at OE. **4.** Expressing position with ref. to a place or thing; esp. with *side, hand, bow* (of a ship), and words of direction implying 'side', as *front, back, rear; north, south, east, west*, etc. Hence in many fig. and transf. uses of *hand, part, side, behalf*, etc. OE.

1. A citee putt on a hill may nat be hid Wyclif *Matt.* v. 14. All these hostages took a solemn oath on the gospels 1785. On life's tempestuous sea Crabbe. A colonel on half-pay 1843. During his residence on the Continent Macaulay. On the horns of a dilemma 1894. Phr. *On one's feet, knees, legs, back, face, on tiptoe, on all fours. On foot, on horse-back, on an ass, on the wing,* etc. Phr., more or less fig., *On the bench, on the cards, on the carpet, on 'Change, on the fence, on the market, on the nail, on the parish, on the rack, on the shelf, on the spot, on the streets, on the stump, on tenterhooks, on the throne, on the way*; also, *on a level, on an equality, on a par*; see the respective sbs. **2.** On Shrubs they browze DRYDEN. Isabella on its music hung KEATS. Phr. *To hang, stick on a wall*; *a fly walking on the ceiling*; *blisters on the soles of his feet*; also, *a coat on his back, shoes on his feet*. **3.** Detained long at the Douane on the Italian frontier 1832. Burton-on-Trent, Clacton-on-Sea (*mod.*). **4.** It was agreed on all hands 1747. The numbers on either side 1838.

†II. Of position *within*. Within the limits or bounds of; = IN *prep.* –1485.

III. Of time, or action implying time. **1.** Indicating the day of an occurrence, treated as a unit of time; so with *night, morning,* etc. *On the instant*, instantly. OE. **b.** = Close upon, touching upon. Also in *on time* (U.S.) = exactly at the (right, etc.) time, punctual(ly) 1843. **2.** Followed by a noun of action, etc., expressing the occasion of what is stated 1593.

1. Presented to A. B. on the occasion of his wedding (*mod.*). **b.** It is now just on post-time CARLYLE. **2.** On hearing this = when (and because) I heard this, I changed my plans (*mod.*).

IV. Of order, arrangement, manner, state. **1.** Indicating physical arrangement or grouping; = *in* (a row, a heap, pieces). *Obs.* or *arch.* OE. **2.** Indicating manner; = *in*. *Obs.* exc. in archaic phrases, as *on this wise*. OE. **3.** Of state, condition, action (see quots.) OE.

1. There lyeth nine little Ilands on a row PURCHAS. **2.** The byrthe off Christe was on thys wyse TINDALE *Matt.* i. 18. Phr. *On the cheap, on the sly, on the square*: see CHEAP C., etc. **3. a.** with a sb., as *on fire, on live, on sleep, on the tap* (now usu. *in*, occas. *on*, often *a-*, now written in comb. (*afire, alive, asleep*); **b.** with noun of action, as *on loan, on sale, on the look-out, on the move, run, wane, on the watch, on the make, on the drink, on the spree*, etc. (in these *on* is still normal); **c.** formerly with vbl. sb. as *on singing, on building* (*Obs.* or *arch.*, the vbl. sb. now functioning as a pres. pple., with *on* omitted, as 'the ark was building'). Workmen on strike 1876. On our best behaviour 1886.

V. Indicating non-material basis, ground, or footing. (fig. extension of I.) **1.** Indicating the ground, basis, or reason of action, opinion, etc. OE. **2.** Indicating that which forms the basis of income, taxation, borrowing, betting, profit, or loss 1697.

1. He..was convicted on evidence which would not have satisfied any impartial tribunal MACAULAY. Phr. *On account (of), on pretence, on purpose*; *on terms*; *on an* (or *the*) *average, on the whole*; see the sbs. **2.** The king borrowed considerable sums on his jewels 1753. Six to four on Leader 1764. The interest on the debentures 1885. The margin of profit on the sales (*mod.*).

VI. Of motion or direction towards a position. **1.** On to OE. **b.** Indicating accumulative addition, or repetition 1611. **c.** Of continued motion: *On one's way, on a journey,* etc.; also *on an errand, a message*. See these sbs. **2.** Against, towards OE. **3.** Of aspect or direction towards OE. **4.** Into, unto, to (some action, etc. Now *rare.*) OE. **5.** Indicating the person or thing to which action, feeling, etc. is directed, or that is affected by it ME. **b.** Indicating the object of desire and the like. Also *ellipt.* = bent on, set on. ME. **c.** Indicating the bank, banker, or person to whom a cheque is directed, and by whom it is payable; in *to draw on, a cheque*, etc. (*drawn*) *on* 1671. **6.** Indicating a person or thing to which hostile action is directed; against. late ME. **7.** In regard to, in reference to, with respect to, as to OE. **b.** Expressing the object to which mental activity is directed; after such verbs as *think, consider, reflect,* etc. Also after derived sbs., as *thought*, etc. OE. **c.** After *speak, write,* etc. q.v.; after *book, article, lecture,* etc., or an author's name; also ellipt. in titles and the like. late ME.

1. He threw the coins on the table. They fixed placards on the walls. A blow on the head (*mod.*). Phr. *To lay hold on, seize on*: see these vbs. **b.** With ruin upon ruin, rout on rout MILT. **2.** He bears his Rider headlong on the Foe DRYDEN. He drew his knife on her and attacked her 1894. **3.** *ellipt.* Feeling that I was on him, I pulled 1888. Phr. *To smile on, turn one's back on*. **4.** Dauid..fell on slepe BIBLE (Great) *Acts* xiii. 36. Facts which ought to have put him on enquiry 1885. **5.** On them she workes her will to uses bad SPENSER. The decision..which is binding on us 1883. Phr. *Eager, keen, mad, bent, determined, set, gone,* etc. *on*. *ellipt.* Their mind was so on their worke 1623. There was no doubt that the trout were 'on' worms 1904. **6.** Phr. *To complain, inform, tell, 'peach' on*; also *an attack, assault,* etc., *on*. Ay, 'twas he that told me on her first SHAKS. **7.** The appellants had failed on the main question 1885. **b.** The sleepless nights in which he meditated on the trophies of Miltiades 1838. **c.** Laplace's Book on the Stars CARLYLE. Coke on Littleton (*mod.*).

VII. Other senses, obs., arch., or dial. (All these orig. belonged to branches I–V.) **†1.** After verbs of *winning, gaining, taking* (by force): = from. Here orig. belonged vbs. of *wreaking* or *taking vengeance, avenging,* etc., still construed with *on* –1671. **†2.** Indicating that to which a quality has relation; In respect of –1703. **†3.** In uses now expressed by AT (esp. *on a price* or *rate*) –1794. **4.** In uses now expressed by OF. Now *dial.* and *vulgar*. ME.

VIII. 1. *On* is used in the construction of verbs like *depend*; *attend, wait*; *follow*; *believe, rely*; *feed, live*; also after the direct object, with *beget, bestow*; *spend, waste*; *congratulate*; *pride, value* oneself; or as a second construction, e.g. to *condole, consult with* a person *on* something. See these vbs. **2.** *On* was formerly frequent in connexions in which *a-* is now usual; e.g. *on back* (= aback), *on broche, on wry*, etc.

¶ *On* is used in U.S. in senses where English usage would have another preposition or expression, such as 'at, of, about, regarding, dealing with'.

On (ǫn), *adv.* (*a., sb.*). [OE. *an, on*: see prec. In mod. Eng. often an elliptic use of the prep. = on something understood.] **A.** *adv.* **1.** In the position of being in contact with, or supported by, the upper surface of something. **2.** Into the position defined in 1. OE. **3.** In the position of being attached to or covering any surface, esp. the body; on the body, as clothing or a limb ME. **4.** Into the position defined in 3. OE. **b.** *ellipt.* in *on with* = put on 1485. **5.** In a direction towards something, at; as *to* LOOK *on*. **6.** Towards something in the way of approach. late ME. **7.** Directed towards, or in a line *with*, something 1804. **8.** *Cricket.* To the on side 1882. **9.** Onward, forward in space or time OE. **b.** *ellipt.* = Go on, advance. late ME. **10.** Gone onward or ahead; in advance in space or time 1872. **b.** *Cricket,* etc.: Ahead of the opposite side 1884. **c.** *slang.* The worse for drink 1802. **11.** With onward movement or action; continuously; as *to speak on*, etc. OE. **12.** Into action or operation; as *thrash on*, proceed to thrash. late ME. **13. a.** Of persons: Engaged in some function or action; on the stage, the field, etc. 1541. **b.** Of things: In progress; in a state of activity 1605. **c.** Having a wager on (something) 1812. **d.** Ready or eager for or to do what is proposed (*colloq.*). **14.** Used idiomatically with many verbs; e.g. *to carry, catch, come on*, etc.: see the vbs.

1. Then to the well-trod stage anon, If Jonsons learned Sock be on MILT. **2.** They also set a..ham on BYRON. **3.** He had a clean Shirt on ADDISON. *Mod. slang*, Keep your hair on! **4.** He immediately drew on his Boots ADDISON. **b.** I will..on with the monk's cowl DISRAELI. **6.** It was getting on for two 1885. **7.** *Broadside on, face on, stem on,* etc., with the face, stem, etc. directed to the point of contact. **9.** They passe on through the cittie HOLLAND. From that day on, centaurs and men are foes HOBBES. **b.** On, Stanley, on SCOTT. **10.** It was now well on in the afternoon 1872. **11.** Now say on Diggon SPENSER. **12.** It came on to rain 1832. **13. a.** Supposing a slow bowler has been 'on' for some time 1888. **b.** There was a considerable sea on 1873. The water was not on (*mod.*). **d.** If there 's going to be a fight, I'm on (*mod.*).

B. *adj.* (Cf. OFF C.). **1.** *Cricket.* Applied to that side of the wicket on which the batsman stands, or to the corresponding part of the field 1851. **2.** In ref. to the licensed sale of liquors: Short for 'on the premises'; opp. to OFF C. 5. Often hyphened, as *on-licence* 1891. **C.** *sb.* *Cricket.* = On side; see B. 1. *attrib.* in *on drive, on-drive*, a drive to the on side 1881.

On-, *prefix*, unstressed form of OE. *an, on* ON, *adv., prep.*, in comb. with verbs and their derivs., and sometimes with other sbs.

1. Old verbal compounds, as *oncnáwan* to recognize, ACKNOW.

2. Later verbal compounds or collocations of adv. and verb; as **†on-become,** to befall, happen; **on-draw,** to draw on; **†on-take,** to take on, assume, behave; etc. In these the union of elements is incomplete, though less so in the inf. and pples.

3. With pr. and pa. pples. forming adjs., as *o·n-carrying* (= carrying on), etc.

4. With vbl. sbs. and nouns of action, forming sbs. (sometimes concrete), as *on-bringing* (= bringing on), etc., (which can be formed at pleasure); **on-go,** going on, progress, advance; **on-roll,** etc.; also *on-goer*, etc. See also ONLOOKER, etc.

‖ **Onager** (ǫ·nădʒəɹ). *Pl.* **-gers, -gri.** ME. [L., ad. Gr. ὄναγρος = ὄνος ἄγριος the wild ass; also both in Gr. and L. in sense 2.] **1.** A wild ass; *spec.* the species *Equus onager* (*E. hemippus*) of Central Asia. **2.** An ancient and mediæval engine of war for throwing stones 1609.

Onagraceous (ǫnăgrēi·ʃəs), *a.* 1845. [f. mod.L. *Onagraceæ*, f. L. *onagra*, fem. of ONAGER; see -ACEOUS.] *Bot.* Belonging to the N.O. *Onagraceæ*, of which *Œnothera* is the typical genus. So **Onagrad** (ǫ·năgræd), a plant of this order.

On and off, *adv. phr.* (*sb.*) 1823. = OFF AND ON, q.v.; also in more general sense (see ON *adv.* OFF *adv.*). **b.** *attrib.* **c.** *sb.* A putting on and taking off; intermittent action.

A siege which lasted on and off for twenty years 1889. Hence **On-and-off** *v.*, (*a*) *intr.* to sail on alternate tacks on and off the shore; (*b*) *trans.* to leap on and then off.

Onanism (ōu·năniz'm). 1727. [f. proper name *Onan* (Gen. xxxviii. 9) + -ISM.] Self-abuse, masturbation.

Once (wɒns), *adv.* (*conj., a., sb.*) [ME. *ānes, ōnes*, gen. case of *ān, ōn*, ONE. The final *s* retained its breath sound, and so began *c* 1500 to be spelt *-ce*, as in *hence, ice, twice*, etc.] **A.** *adv.* **1.** In strict sense: One time only. (Without any ref. to *when*.) **†b.** Firstly –1596. **2.** At any one time; ever, at all, only, merely. (Chiefly in conditional and neg. statements). ME. **†3.** *emphatically.* Once for all. Hence, To sum up; in short –1667. **4.** At one time in the past; formerly. Also *once upon a time*. late ME. **5.** At some future time; one day. Now *rare*. late ME. **6.** *Once removed*, removed by one degree of relationship 1601. **7.** Usu. hyphened to a ppl. or other adj. standing before its sb. 1668.

1. I..have read it more than o. GARRICK. *Prov.* O. bit, twice shy. **2.** *If o., when o.*, if ever, when ever; *not o.*, never. If we o. lose sight of him we shall never set eyes on him again (*mod.*). **4.** The o. famous doctrine of divine right BRYCE. O. upon a time there were gods only, and no mortal creatures JOWETT. **6.** The relationship of second cousin o. removed 1882. **7.** Seek we thy once-loved home? CAMPBELL.

Phr. **a.** *O. or twice*, a few times; *o. and again*, twice (or oftener). *O. again, o. more*. *O. for all* (*for always*, etc.), once as a final act; once and done with. So *o. and away*. *O. in a way*, as an exceptional instance; rarely. *O. in a while*, at long intervals; very occasionally. *Once-over* (U.S.), a single rapid inspection. **b.** (arising from the sense *one time*). AT ONCE. *For o.*, for one occasion. *For o. and all, for o. and away, for o. in a way*; cf. **a.** *This, that o.*: this or that time only. Hence **Oncer** (wɒ·nsəɹ), one who attends church only once on Sundays.

B. as *conjunctive adv.* = When once, if once; as soon as. (So *o. that.*) 1761.

O. I have stamped it there, I lay aside my doubts for ever SHERIDAN.

C. *ellipt.* (quasi-*adj.* and *sb.*). **1.** quasi-*adj.* **a.** = Done or performed once 1548. **b.** That once was; former. Now *rare*. 1691. **2.** quasi-*sb.* Doing a thing once, going once, etc. 1623.

1. a. O. Harrowing is generally enough 1739. **b.** The o. enemies 1880. **2.** O. a week is enough (*mod.*).

‖ **Oncidium** (ǫnsi·diɒ̆m). 1882. [mod.L., f. Gr. ὄγκος barb of an arrow, angle; so called from the form of the lower petal.] *Bot.* A large genus of American orchids, one of the best known being the Butterfly-plant (*O. Papilio*).

Onco-, comb. form of Gr. ὄγκος mass, bulk, in mod.Gr. also tumour; used in a few technical terms of medical science. **Oncograph** (ǫ·ŋkograf) [-GRAPH], an instrument, used in connexion with the *oncometer*, for recording variations in the size of an organ. **Onco·logy** [-LOGY], that part of medical science which relates to tumours; hence **Oncolo·gical** *a.* **Onco·meter** [-METER], an instrument for measuring variations in the size of an organ; hence **Oncome·tric** *a.* **Onco·tomy** [Gr. -τομία cutting], incision into, or excision of, a tumour.

Oncome (ǫ·nkvm). 1898. [f. ON- + COME *v.*; cf. *to come on.*] = next.

O·n-coming, *sb.* 1844. [See ON-.] Coming on; advance. So **O·n-coming** *ppl. a.*

Oncost (ǫ·nkǭst). 1480. [ad. (M)Du. *onkosten* pl., f. *on-* + *kost* COST *sb.*[2]] †1. (in form *uncost.*) Additional or incidental expenses -1795. *Sc.* **b.** In general use: Overhead expenses or costs 1912. **2.** *attrib.* or *adj.* Applied (esp. among miners) to work done on time wages. *O. men,* (also *oncosts*), men who work on such terms 1886.

‖**On dit** (oṅ dī). 1826. [The Fr. phr. *on dit* = 'it is said', used as a sb.] An item of gossip; something reported on hearsay.

I thought it was a mere *on dit* DISRAELI.

One (wvn, wv̆n, wən, *dial.* and *vulgar* ən), *numeral a., pron., sb.* [Com.Teut.: OE. *án* :—OTeut. **ainoz* :—pre-Teut. **oinos* = L. *unus*, older *oinos*; cf. Gr. οἴνη ace. OE. *án* became in south. and midl. dial. *on*. By 15th c., *on, oon,* had developed locally an initial *w*, which survives in the standard pronunciation.] **I.** As simple numeral. **1.** The lowest of the cardinal numbers; the number of a single thing without any more, the addition of another to which makes *two*. **2.** Joined to the tens (*twenty, thirty,* etc.), *one* orig. always preceded (*one-and-twenty,* etc.), but now often follows (*twenty-one,* etc.). So with the ordinals: *one-and-twentieth*, now usu. *twenty-first*. OE. **3.** Used before collective numerals (*dozen, score, hundred,* etc.), and fractions (*half, third,* etc.), with more precise or definite force than *a, an*; and so also in legal phraseology, etc. ME. **4.** Occas. put for *first*. late ME. **5.** *absol.* (with abstract conception of number) late ME. **6.** Hence, as *sb.* with pl., Unity; a unit; a single thing, or the abstract number denoting a single thing 1542. **b.** A single person, thing, example, etc. 1840. **c.** The symbol or figure (1. I. i) denoting unity (*mod.*). **d.** *colloq.* (now *number one*) = Oneself, one's own interest 1567.

1. We say o. book, o. page, o. line, etc.; all these are equally units BERKELEY. The principle of 'o. man, o. vote' 1891. *ellipt.* The one-and-sixpenny packet contains 100 varieties 1871. Phr. *Like o. o'clock*, vigorously, quickly. *Train due at o. twenty-five* (1 hr. 25 m.). *To go o. better* (orig. = to play a better card). 2. Phr. *O. or two* = a very few, a small number of. 3. The price of labour..is fully one-third less COLERIDGE. Three one-hundred guinea cups 1896. In the year of our Lord, One thousand, eight hundred, and ninety-nine (*mod.*). 4. Isaiah, chapter fifty-one. *In the year o.* (joc.), a long while ago, time out of mind. 5. Twenty to o. then, he is ship'd already SHAKS. O. from twenty leaves nineteen (*mod.*). 6. b. Afterwards, sauntering by ones and twos, came the village maidens THACKERAY. c. A row of ones (*mod.*). d. Humbly endeavouring to reform Number o. DARWIN.

II. Emphatic numeral. **1.** One in contrast to two or more; one only; a single OE. **2. a.** *pred.* Single, individual ME. **b.** *absol.* or as *sb.* ME. **3.** One at least, one at any rate (as dist. from 'none at all') 1481.

1. The o. and onlye way to the wealthe of a communaltye 1551. 2. a. The action is neither o., entire, nor great 1789. b. The Good or O. BERKELEY. 3. That 's o. comfort, however 1765.

III. In pregnant senses. **1.** One made up of many components, a united OE. **2. b.** *pred.* (esp. = united in marriage) 1590. **2.** One in continuity; uniformly the same; one and the same ME. **3.** One in substance; identical; the same OE. **4.** One in kind; the same in quality or nature ME. **b.** *pred.* The same; the same thing. Often *all o.* late ME. **5.** One in mind, feeling, intention, or bearing; at one ME.

1. All of them with o. voice vehemently assented JOWETT. b. We have been both o. these two Months STEELE. 2. God remains for ever o. and the same BERKELEY. 3. He is made o. with Nature SHELLEY. 4. Be of o. mynde TINDALE 2 *Cor.* xiii. 11. b. All is O. to Him, to make an Angell, or an Ant 1631. 5. Addington and I are o. again PITT.

IV. In a particularizing or partitive sense. **1.** One from amongst others; a particular, an individual. **a.** *attrib.* OE. **b.** absol. with *of*; formerly with gen. pl.; rarely without either, as in *to make o.*, to form one of a company OE. **2.** In antithesis to *one* in the sense of 'another' OE. **3.** In antithesis to ANOTHER, OTHER, *others*; with or without sb. following. *O. and another*, more than one, two or more in succession. OE. **4.** Of two things, now usu. *the one ... the other* (rarely in poetry without *the*) OE. **b.** When *the one* and *the other* refer severally to two things previously named, they are by some taken as = *the former* and *the latter*, by others as = *the latter* and *the former*. **5.** *reciprocally*, of two or more: **one another** (formerly, of two, *one ... other*, and *the o. ... the other*), *one* being grammatical subject, and *another* object, as they met *one another*, they spoke *one to another*, now usu. *to one another*, in which the grammatical relation is lost sight of, and *one another* becomes a kind of reflexive pron., with objective and possessive but no nominative case. ME.

1. a. Ae dreary, windy, winter night BURNS. *O. day*, on a particular day in the past; on some undefined day in the future; I hope to see them o. day all put downe 1588. b. O. of his Friends came and proposed to him, to make o. at a Feast 1686. 2. O. foote in sea, and o. on shore SHAKS. Phr. **One by one** (also *o. after o.*), formerly *o. and o., by o. and o.,* = o. after another, o. at a time, singly. 3. What 's o. man's meat is another man's poison FIELDING. Phr. *O. with another*, (*a*) together (*obs.* or *arch.*); (*b*) on the average. 4. The o. shall be taken and the other left *Luke* xvii. 35. Phr. *The o. and the other* = both (= F. *l'un et l'autre*). b. A Side for the Banquet..and a Side for the Houshold; The O. for Feasts and Triumphs, the Other for Dwelling BACON. The nobility and the clergy, the o. by profession, the other by patronage, kept learning in existence BURKE. 5. Yf ye shall haue loue won to another TINDALE *John* xiii. 35. Cudgel-Players, who were breaking o. another's Heads 1711.

V. Indef. pron. (with genitive *one's*). **1.** Some one, a certain one, an individual, a person (L. *quidam*). A following pronoun referring to *one* is in the 3rd pers. sing. ME. **2.** Any one of everybody; any one whatever; including (or specially meaning) the speaker himself; 'you, or I, or any o.'; a person, a man; we, you, people, they (= OE. *man*, ME. *me*, G. *man*, F. *on*). Poss. *one's*, obj. *one*; reflexive ONESELF (formerly *one's self*); also formerly and still occas. *his, him, himself*. (The pl. prons. *their, them, themselves*, formerly in general use, are now considered ungrammatical.) In this sense *one* is quite toneless (wən), proclitic or enclitic. 1477.

1. Oon Martyn luther a frere 1521. O. that lou'd not wisely, but too well SHAKS. O. with a beard 1825. He is not o. to take this lying down (*mod.*). 2. Why, may o. aske? SHAKS. If o. propose any other end unto himself 1650. One's brothers and sisters are a part of one's self 1834.

VI. Pronominal or substantival form of *a, an*. (With pl. *ones*.) **1.** An absol. form of *a*, to avoid repeating a sb.; A person or thing of the kind already mentioned ME. **2.** Added after *the, this*; *any, every, many* (*a*), etc., and (in certain phrases) after *a*; also after ordinary adjs. preceded by any of these or (in pl.) alone; in the sense of: A thing or person, pl. things or persons, of the kind in question OE. **3.** After pronominal and other adjs., without contextual ref. = Person, body, persons ME.

1. He rents a house, but I own o. I have forgotten an umbrella; I think I must buy o. (*mod.*). Phr. *O. of these days*, some time or other. 2. Ne'er a o. to be found B. JONS. The ones you mention. That o. on the table. This o. will do. (*mod.*). 3. The Consultations of the great Ones and Governours 1665. Come along, young 'un 1857. *Any o., every o., many a o., some o., such a o.*; *little ones, the Holy O., the Evil O.*, etc.: see under these words.

VII. Obs. uses. †**1.** = indef. article A. AN -1552. †**2.** *One* was formerly used with superlatives, as 'one the fairest toun' = 'a town, the fairest one', 'the one fairest town' -1613.

1. My sayde lorde was oon faythefuI man 1514. 2. He is o. The truest manner'd SHAKS.

Phr. **One and all**, every one individually and jointly. **In o.**: (*a*) in or into one place, company, or mass; together; (*b*) in unison, agreement, or harmony. Now *arch.* (*c*) in one shot or stroke; at one go. **Into o.** = *In one* (*a*). **Ones**: see ONCE.

Combs. **1.** General. **a.** attrib. phrases (unlimited in number), as *o·ne-act, -book, -clause, -year*, etc. Also *o·ne-by-o·ne, o·ne-o'clock*. **b.** Compound adjs., as *o·ne-year-o·ld*. **c.** Parasynthetic formations on such phrases as those in **a.** by adding *-ed* (also unlimited in number) as *one-a·rmed, -roomed, -storied*, etc. **d.** Parasynthetic formations in *-er* (see -ER[1] 1), as *one-decker, one-pounder*.

2. Special: **o·ne-co·loured** *a.*, of uniform colour throughout; **one·man** *a.*, consisting of, exercised, managed, or done by, one man only; **one-manual, one-pair** *a.* (in full, *one pair of stairs*), situated above one 'pair' or flight of stairs, i.e. on the first floor; **one-time** *a.*, that was so at one time or formerly, 'sometime'; **one-way** *a.*, applied to a plough which turns the furrows in one direction; also to a street in which traffic is allowed to go in one direction only, and to the traffic in such a street; **one-while** *a.* or *adv.* = *one-time.*

One (wvn), *v.* Now *rare.* [ME. *onen, anen*, f. *án*, ONE. Cf. L. *unire*, F. *unir*, f. *unus, un.*] *trans.* To make into one; to unite.

-one, *Chem.* formative suffix. [Gr. -ωνη feminine patronymic.] **a.** An ending used unsystematically in forming the names of chemical derivatives, as in *acetone, mellone, quinone*. 1848. **b.** In Hofmann's systematic nomenclature, the formative of the names of hydrocarbons of composition C_nH_{2n-4}, as in *propone* C_3H_2, *quartone* C_4H_4, etc. 1866.

O·ne-berry. 1548. †**a.** Herb Paris, *Paris quadrifolia* -1789. **b.** = HACKBERRY 2. *U.S.*

One-eyed, *a.* OE. **1.** Having only one eye; blind in one eye. **2.** *fig.* (*derogatory*) Wanting in an essential quality; *U.S.* unfair 1833.

Onefold (wv·nfōuld), *a.* 1844. [f. ONE + -FOLD.] **1.** Consisting of one member or constituent; single; simple. **2.** Simple in character; single-minded 1882.

O·ne-ha·nded, *a.* 1440. **1.** Having only one hand, or only one capable of use. **2.** Used, worked, or performed with one hand 1611.

2. The one-handed alphabet 1837. A one-handed catch 1894.

O·ne-horse, *a.* 1750. **1.** Drawn, or worked, by a single horse (as a vehicle, etc.); having or using only one horse. **2.** *fig.* (*U.S. colloq.*) On a small scale; petty; of limited resources or capacity 1854.

2. A country-clergyman, with a one-story intellect and a one-horse vocabulary O. W. HOLMES.

One-ideaed, -idea'd (wv·n₁əidī·ăd), *a.* 1849. Having, or possessed by, a single idea.

Oneiro- (onəiᵊro), also **oniro-**, bef. a vowel **oneir-**, comb. form of Gr. ὄνειρος a dream. **Oneirology** (ǫnirǫ·lŏdʒi) [Gr. ὀνειρολογία; see -LOGY], the science or subject of dreams, or of their interpretation; so **Oneiro·logist**, one versed in this. **Onei·romancy** [see -MANCY], divination by dreams. **Oneiroscopy** (-ǫ·skŏpi) [Gr. ὀνειροσκόπος an interpreter of dreams], examination or interpretation of dreams; so **Oneiro·scopist**, one versed in this.

Oneirocritic, oniro- (onəiᵊrokri·tik), *sb.* 1614. [ad. Gr. ὀνειροκριτικός pertaining to the interpretation of dreams; see -IC.] **1.** A judge or interpreter of dreams 1652. **2.** (Usu. in *pl.*) The art of interpreting dreams. So **Oneirocri·tical, oniro·** *a.*; **-ly** *adv.* Hence **Oneirocri·ticism, oniro-**, the art of interpreting dreams.

One-legged (wv·n₁legd, -le·gėd), *a.* 1842. **1.** Having only one leg 1883. **2.** *fig.* That is only a half-measure; one-sided 1842.

†**O·nement.** ME. [f. ONE *v.* + -MENT. Cf. ATONEMENT.] **1.** Physical union, conjunction. WYCLIF. **2.** = ATONEMENT 1, 2. -1598.

Oneness (wv·n₁nės). [f. ONE + -NESS. OE. had *ánnes*, whence *onnesse* in south, *annesse* in north. Recoined in 16th c.] **1.** The quality of being one in number, singleness. **b.** Uniqueness 1715. **2.** The quality of being one body or whole; integrity, unity OE. **3.** The fact of forming one whole; combination, unity, union 1657. **4.** Sameness, identity; unchangingness 1611. **5.** Unity of mind, feeling, or purpose; agreement, harmony, concord ME.

1. Our God is one, or rather very onenesse, and meere unitie HOOKER. 2. The solidarity and o. of humanity WHITTIER. 3. The closest human o., of husband and wife PUSEY.

Oner (wv·nəɹ). *slang* or *colloq.* Also **one-er.** 1840. [f. ONE + -ER[1].] **1.** *slang.* A person or thing of a unique kind; a prime one. **b.** *spec.* A heavy blow 1861. **2.** *colloq.* A person or thing in some way denoted or characterized by the number one 1889.

1. She is such a o. at eating THACKERAY. b. A o. on his ears 1885.

Onerary (ǫ·nĕrări), *a.* (*sb.*) *rare.* 1658. [ad. L. *onerarius*, f. *onus* burden; see -ARY.] **A.** *adj.* Fitted for the carriage of burdens. **B.** *sb.* A ship of burden, transport.

†**O·nerate,** *v.* 1453. [f. L. *onerat-, onerare*, f. *onus, oner-* a load.] *trans.* To load, burden, charge, oppress (*lit.* and *fig.*) -1726.

Onerous (*ǫ·nĕrəs*), *a.* late ME. [a. OF. *onereus*, F. *onéreux*, ad. L. *onerosus*, f. *onus*, *oner-* burden; see -OUS.] Of the nature of a burden; burdensome, oppressive; of the nature of a legal obligation.

Worldly cares and o. business BURTON. In *o. consideration, grant*, etc. (Sc. Law.), done or given for value received; opp. to *gratuitous*. Hence **O·nerous·ly** *adv.*, **-ness.**

Oneself (wʊnse·lf), *pron.* Also **one's self.** 1548. [orig. **one's self,** after *my self*, etc.; assim. later to *himself*, *itself*. The corresponding possess. is *one's own*.] **1.** Emphatic use: A person's self; himself or herself (including or meaning the speaker or writer) 1621. **2.** Reflexive use: objective case of ONE V. 2. (In this sense often stressless.) 1548.

1. One might wear the articles one's-self DICKENS. 2. To be pleased with o. is the surest way of offending every-body else LYTTON.

One-sided (wʊ·n₁səi·dėd; stress var.), *a.* 1793. [Parasynthetic f. *one side*; see ONE *Combs.* 1 c; partly after G. *einseitig*.] **1.** Relating to, considering, or dealing with only one side; partial 1833. **2. a.** Leaning to one side; larger or more developed on one side than on the other 1845. **b.** Unilateral 1793. **c.** Existing or occurring on one side only 1864.

1. A one-sided report of a trial 1885. 2. a. Tom's face begins to look very one-sided—there are little queer bumps on his forehead HUGHES. So **One-si·ded·ly** *adv.*, **-ness** 1831.

One-step (wʊ·nstep), *sb.* 1911. [f. ONE *a.* + STEP *sb.*] A dance in two-four time, danced by couples and characterized by various walking steps; also the music for this. Hence **O·nestep** *v.*

On-going (ǫ·ngōu:iŋ). 1825. [ON- 4.] **1.** *pl.* = Goings-on (see GOING *vbl. sb.*) **2.** *sing.* The action of going on; proceeding, continued movement (*rare*) 1890.

1. Milton had to describe the ongoings of angels 1856.

Onhanger (ǫ·nhæ:ŋəɹ). 1848. [ON- 4.] A hanger-on: see HANGER [2] 5 a.

Onion (ʊ·nyən), *sb.* ME. [a. F. *oignon* :—L. *unio, unionem* unity, union, a kind of large pearl, a single onion.] **1. a.** The edible rounded bulb of *Allium Cepa*, consisting of close concentric coats, and having a pungent flavour and smell; used as a culinary vegetable from the earliest times. **b.** The plant *Allium Cepa* itself (N.O. *Liliaceæ*). **2.** Applied to varieties of the above or other species of *Allium*, as **Rock** or **Welsh O.**, a bulbless species (*A. fistulosum*) cultivated for its leafy tops; the chibol; **Wild O.** (U.S.), *A. cernuum*, etc.; also to plants of other genera, mostly bulbous 1548. †**3.** A bunion -1846. **4.** The head (*slang*) 1922.

1. Who would ask for her opinion Between an oyster and an o.? PRIOR. He'll be rampant..at his child being lost; and the beef and the inguns not done! HOOD. 4. Phr. *Off one's onion.*

attrib. and *Comb.*, as **o.-couch, -grass, -twitch,** a species of wild oat (*Avena elatior*), so called from the rounded nodes of the root-stock; **-eyed** *a.*, having the eyes full of tears; **-shell,** name for various molluscan shells of rounded form, as those of species of *Ostrea, Lutraria*, and *Mya*. Hence **O·niony** *a.* 1838.

O·nion, *v.* 1755. [f. prec. sb.] **1.** *trans.* To flavour with onions. **2.** To apply an onion to; to produce (tears) by the application of an onion 1763.

Oniro-: see ONEIRO-.

Onliness (ōu·nlinės). Now *rare.* ME. [f. ONLY *a.* + -NESS.] **1.** The fact or condition of being alone. **2.** The fact or character of being the only one of its kind; uniqueness 1633.

On live, *phr.*, earlier form of ALIVE.

Onlooker (ǫ·nlu:kəɹ). 1606. [f. ON- 4 + LOOKER.] One who looks on; a spectator.

O·nlooking, *ppl. a.* 1663. [ON- 3.] That looks on; looking at something.

Only (ōu·nli), *a.* [OE. *ánlic*, a later form of *ǽnlic* unique, singular, excellent, f. AN, ONE + *-lic*, -LY [1].] **1.** One; solitary, lonely. Now only *dial.* **2.** One (or, by extension, two or more) of which there exist no more, or no others, of the kind OE. **b.** In later use, in ref. to relationship, also preceded by *an*, and used with a pl.; as *an o. child, o. children* 1670. †**c.** *absol.* = only one, only ones -1693. **3.** Single, one. Now *rare.* 1485. †**4.** (The thing in question) acting alone; mere, sole -1856. †**b.** Placed between a demonstrative or possessive adj. or poss. case and its sb., or bef. a sb. followed by an *of*-phrase; referring to the sb. as thus qualified -1741. **5.** Unique in quality, rank, etc.; peerless, pre-eminent. Now only as hyperbolic use of 2, = 'the only one to be counted, reckoned, or considered' OE.

2. The onely ruler of princes *Bk. Com. Prayer.* These two passages are the o. ones in which Plato makes mention of himself JOWETT. b. An o. son, sir, might expect more indulgence GOLDSM. 3. Phr. *One o.*, o. one, one and no other; This country hath one o. deanery 1630. 4. The onely odour of quick-silver killeth lice 1544. b. At the charges & only expenses of these .vi. abbeyes HOLINSHED. 5. Your onely Iigge-maker SHAKS.

Only (ōu·nli), *adv.*, *conj.* (*prep.*) [ME. (south. and south. midl.) *onliche*, f. *onlich*, ONLY *a.*, with advb. *-e* (see -LY [2]).] **A.** *adv.* **1.** As a single or solitary thing or fact. *Only* may be (*a*) dist. from *more*, or (*b*) opp. to any *other*. **b.** *Only* was formerly, and in speech is still, often placed away from the word or words limited by it; this is now avoided in careful writing 1483. †**2.** By or of itself alone, without anything else -1801. †**3.** Singularly, uniquely, specially, pre-eminently -1611. **4.** Idiomatic uses. **a.** The sense 'no more than' often passes into 'as much as'; = JUST *adv.* 5. (Cf. G. *nur*.) 1838. **b.** *O. not* = all but, little else than 1779. **c.** Not before, not till. (*Only* may precede or follow the word or phrase expressing time.) 1676. †**d.** *O. but, but o.*: (*a*) = only, merely; (*b*) except only -1711. **e.** *O. too* (*true*, etc.): see TOO.

1. I wil haue nothing else but onely this SHAKS. I have been o. twice 1805. In one o. of the casements 1838. b. Luke is o. with me CAXTON. I o. asked the question from habit JOWETT. 4. a. He is coming..if you will o. wait JOWETT. b. I was o. not a boy JOHNSON. c. *O. just*, no longer ago than the immediate past: I have o. just received it (*mod.*).

B. *conjunctive adv.*, *conj.* (*prep.*) **1.** The only thing to be added being; with this restriction, drawback, or exception only; but (*adversative*); on the other hand. late ME. **2.** Except. Now only *dial.* †**b.** Introducing a clause: Except that, were it not that -1802.

1. The flowers are lovely; o., they have no scent (*mod.*). *O. that*, except that, were it not that; O. that I know you don't love bustle, I should wish you were here 1771. 2. *O. for*, except for, but for; O. for my tea, I should have had the head-ache 1811.

O·nly-bego·tten, *a.* 1450. Begotten as an only child; tr. L. *unigenitus*, Gr. μονογενής.

Onocentaur (ǫno₁se·ntǭɹ). 1567. [ad. late L. *onocentaurus*, a. Gr. ὀνοκένταυρος, f. ὄνος ass + κένταυρος CENTAUR.] *Myth.* A fabulous creature, a centaur with the body of an ass.

Onomancy (ǫ·nŏmænsi). 1602. [Abbrev. f. obs. ONOMATOMANCY, = med.L. *onomantia*.] Divination from names or the letters of a name. Hence **Onoma·ntic, -al** *adjs.* of or pertaining to o.; practising o.

Onomastic (ǫnomæ·stik), *a.* and *sb.* 1609. [ad. Gr. ὀνομαστικός of or belonging to naming, f. ὀνομαστός named, f. ὀνομάζειν.] **A.** *adj.* Of, relating to, or connected with a name or names, or with naming; consisting of or dealing with names 1716. **b.** Used in ref. to the autograph subscription of a legal document (of which the body is in the handwriting of another person) 1802. †**B.** *sb.* A writer of an onomasticon; a vocabularist, a lexicographer -1716. So †**Onoma·stical** *a.* = A.

‖ **Onoma·sticon.** 1710. [a. Gr. ὀνομαστικόν (sc. βιβλίον) book of names, vocabulary; see prec.] A vocabulary or alphabetic list of proper names, esp. of persons. Formerly used of a vocabulary of names or nouns, or even of a general lexicon.

Ono·mato-, = Gr. ὀνοματο-, comb. form of ὄνομα, gen. ὀνόματος name.

Onomatology (ǫnǫmătǫ·lŏdʒi). *rare.* 1847. [mod. f. Gr. *ὀνοματολογία, f. ὀνοματολόγος word-gathering.] The science of the formation of names or terms; terminology. So **Onomato·logist,** one versed in o. 1695.

†**Ono·matoma:ncy.** 1652. [ad. med.L. *onomatomantia*; see ONOMATO- and -MANCY.] = ONOMANCY -1727.

Onomatop, -ope (ǫnǫ·mătǫp, -tōup). 1828. [Abbrev. f. next.] A word formed by onomatopœia.

‖ **Onomatopœia** (ǫnǫ:mătopī·a, ǫ·nŏmæ-). 1577. [a. L., a. Gr. ὀνοματοποιία the making of words, f. ὀνοματοποιός, f. ONOMATO- + -ποιος making.] **1.** The formation of a name or word by an imitation of the sound associated with the thing or action designated; this principle as a force in the formation of words; echoism. **b.** A word so formed 1842. **2.** *Rhet.* The use of naturally suggestive words, sentences, and forms for rhetorical effect 1860.

2. A good instance of o. in 'Paradise Lost' (Bk. II. 879) TENNYSON. Hence **Ono·matopœ·ic, -al** *adjs.* of, pertaining to, or characterized by o., esp. as applied to the origin of names or words; imitative; echoic; **-ally** *adv.* 1860.

‖ **Ono:matopoë·sis** (-po₁ī·sis). Also **-poiesis.** 1864. [mod. a. Gr. ὀνοματοποίησις the making of a name, f. ὀνοματοποιεῖν.] The naming of a thing, etc., from the sound associated with it; onomatopœia. So **Ono:matopoe·tic** *a.* onomatopœic 1847. **Ono:matopoe·tically** *adv.* 1866.

Onrush (ǫ·nrʊʃ). 1844. [f. ON- 4 + RUSH *sb.*] The act of rushing on; impetuous forward movement.

Onset (ǫ·nset), *sb.* 1513. [f. ON- 4 + SET *sb.*[1]] **1.** An act of setting on (an enemy); an attack, assault. **b.** (Without article.) Attack, assault 1667. **2.** The action, or an act, of beginning some operation; commencement, start 1561.

1. These troops had to bear the first brunt of the o. MACAULAY. *fig.* The o. of a fever 1789. b. Achiev'd By sudden o. MILT. 2. There is surely no greater Wisedome, then well to time the Beginnings, and Onsets of Things BACON.

†**Onse·t,** *v.* 1602. [f. ON- 2 + SET *v.*] *trans.* To make an onset upon; to set upon, attack -1648. Hence **O·nse:tter,** one who incites; one who makes an onset; *spec.* in *Coal-mining*, a workman who puts the corves or tubs into the cage at the bottom of the shaft.

On side, *phr.* 1887. In Football, Hockey, etc.: One's proper side; the opposite of OFF SIDE, q. v. Also *attrib.*

Onslaught (ǫ·nslǭt). 1625. [ad. early Du. *aenslag* (mod. *aan-*) = G. *anschlag* attempt, enterprise, modified after *slaught* (-1610). Not evidenced in the 18th c., and app. revived by Scott.] Onset, attack; *esp.* a vigorous or destructive assault or attack.

By Siege or O., to invest The Enemy 1663. The fierce o. upon that Government 1859.

Onstead (ǫ·nstėd). *Sc.* and *n. dial.* 1666. [f. ON- + STEAD, place, station, etc.] A farmhouse, with its outhouses, a farmstead; now sometimes *spec.* the offices, as dist. from the farmer's house.

On to, onto (ǫ·ntu), *prep.* 1581. [ON *adv.* + TO *prep.*, having the same relation to *on* as *into* has to *in*.] To a position on or upon (or one that is expressed by these preps.).

Please you walk forth O. the Terrace KEATS. Assisting Mr. Pickwick on to the roof DICKENS.

Onto, on to, obs. (14-16th c.) form of UNTO.

Onto-, comb. form of Gr. ὤν, ὀντ- being, neut. pr. pple. of εἶναι to be. See below.

Ontogenesis (ǫntodʒe·nĭsis). 1875. [mod. f. ONTO- + Gr. γένεσις birth.] *Biol.* The origin and development of the individual living being (as dist. from *phylogenesis*). Hence **O:ntogene·tic** *a.* of, pertaining to, or characteristic of o.; relating to the development of the individual being. **O:ntogene·tically** *adv.* with ref. to o.

Ontogeny (ǫntǫ·dʒĭni). 1872. [f. ONTO- + Gr. -γενεια birth, production, f. -γενής born, produced.] **1.** = prec. **2.** The history or science of the development of the individual being; embryology 1874. Hence **Onto·genist,** one versed in o.

Ontology (ǫntǫ·lŏdʒi). 1721. [ad. mod.L. *ontologia*, f. Gr. ὀντο- ONTO- + -λογία; see -LOGY. Cf. F. *ontologie*.] The science or study of being; that department of metaphysics which relates to the being or essence of things, or to being in the abstract. So **Onto-**

logic, -al (ǫntolǫ·dʒik, -ăl), *adjs.*, of or pertaining to, or of the nature of, o.; metaphysical. *Ontological argument, proof* (for the existence of God), the *a priori* argument that the existence of the idea of God of necessity involves the objective existence of God.

‖ **Onus** (ōu·nɒ̆s). 1640. [L.] A burden, charge, responsibility.

Onus probandi (L. phrase), the burden of proving; the obligation of proving an assertion, allegation, or charge which rests on one who makes it.

Onward (ǫ·nwǭɹd), *adv.*, *a.* late ME. [f. On *adv.* + -ward; after *inward, forward*, etc.] A. *adv.* (Formerly occ. with *of*; e.g. *o. of one's journey.*) 1. = On *adv.* 9. 1532. †2. Provisionally; *spec.* on account, 'in advance'; as an 'earnest' –1555. 3. = On *adv.* 10. late ME. Now *rare* or *arch.*

1. O. still his way he takes Gray. From..the times of Philo and four centuries o. 1839. 3. My greefe lies o. and my ioy behind Shaks.

B. *adj.* 1. Of motion, etc.: Directed onward or forward. Rarely of a thing: Moving onward, advancing. 1674. †2. Situated in front or in advance; advanced –1644.

1. Resuming his o. course W. Irving. 2. To discover o. things more remote from our knowledge Milt. Hence **O·nwardness,** advance, progression, progress 1548.

Onwards (ǫ·nwǭɹdz), *adv.* 1600. [f. prec. with advb. *-s*; see -wards.] = Onward A.

Ony, Sc. etc. f. Any.

‖**Onycha** (ǫ·nikă). late ME. [L. = Gr. ὄνυχα, accus. of ὄνυξ Onyx; in med.L. *onic(h)a*, treated as indecl., or as fem. of 1st decl. The form *onycha*, being app. not recognized as the accus. of *onyx*, was treated by mediæval writers as a distinct word; hence in Eng. versions of the Bible (Exod. xxx. 34).] One of the ingredients in the incense used in the Mosaic ritual; the operculum of a species of *Strombus*, or other marine mollusc, which emits a penetrating aroma when burnt.

‖ **Onychia** (ǫni·kiă). 1857. [mod.L., f. Gr. ὄνυξ, ὀνυχ- nail.] *Path.* Inflammation of the matrix of the nail, or of the adjacent part of finger or toe.

Onychomancy (ǫ·nikomæ:nsi). 1652. [f. Gr. ὀνυχο-, comb. form of ὄνυξ Onyx + -mancy.] Divination from the finger-nails.

Onychophorous (ǫnikǫ·fŏrəs), *a.* 1857. [f. as prec.; see -phorous.] *Zool.* Bearing nails or claws; applied to a group (*Onychophori*) of ophidian reptiles having rudimentary hind limbs, and to an order (*Onychophora*) of myriapods comprising the single genus *Peripatus*, having two chitinoid claws on each limb. So **Onycho·phoran** *a.* and *sb.*

Onymous (ǫ·niməs), *a.* *rare.* 1775. [f. Gr. ὄνυμα + -ous; after *anonymous*, etc.] Having or bearing a name.

Onyx (ōu·niks, ǫ·niks). ME. [a. L., a. Gr. ὄνυξ nail, claw, onyx-stone.] 1. A variety of quartz allied to agate, consisting of plane layers of different colours; much used for cameos. †2. = Onycha. *Ecclus.* xxiv. 15. 3. *Path.* An opacity of the lower part of the cornea of the eye, caused by an infiltration of pus behind it or between its layers, and resembling a finger-nail 1706.

attrib. and *Comb.*, as **o.-marble,** a stalagmitic limestone or marble, having a banded structure like o.; also called †*onychite* or *oriental alabaster.*

Oo- (ōu,o), bef. a vowel **o-**, comb. form of Gr. ᾠόν egg, ovum, used in scientific, chiefly biological, terms. **Oœcium** (o,ī·ʃiɒ̆m) [Gr. οἰκίον a little house], a bud-like sac in which the ova are received and fertilized in certain Polyzoa; hence **Oœ·cial** *a.* **Oo·gamous** *a.* [Gr. γάμος + -ous], *Biol.* applied to organs which reproduce (or to reproduction) by union of dissimilar (male and female) cells. **Oogenesis** (ōu,o,dʒe·nĭsis) [Genesis], the production or development of an ovum; so **Oogenetic** (ōu:o,dʒĭne·tik) *a.*, **Oogeny** (o,ǫ·dʒĭni) = *oogenesis.* **Oophyte** (ōu·ŏfəit) [Gr. φυτόν plant] = Oophore. **O·osperm** [Sperm], a. *Zool.* a fertilized ovum; b. *Bot.* = Oospore. **O·osphere** [Gr. σφαῖρα sphere], *Bot.* the female reproductive cell, esp. in the Thallophytes or lower Cryptogams, which when fertilized becomes an *oospore.* **Oostegite** (o,ǫ·stĭdʒəit) [Gr. στέγειν to cover; see -ite[1] 3], an egg-case in some Crustacea, formed by an expansion of the limbs of certain somites; hence **Oostegitic** (o,ǫ·stĭdʒi·tik) *a.* ‖ **Ootheca** (ōu,oþī·kă) [Gr. θήκη case], an egg-case in certain invertebrate animals; also, a sporangium; **Oothe·cal** *a.*

Oobit: see Woubit.

Oodles (ū·d'lz). *U.S.* 1869. [?] 'Heaps.'

Oof (ūf). *slang.* 1885. [prob. short for *ooftish*, Yiddish for G. *auf tische*, i.e. *auf dem tische* 'on the table', i.e. (money) down.] Money. Also in the fuller form **Oo·ftish.** Hence **Oof-bird,** a supplier of money. **Oo·fless** *a.* **Oo·fy** *a.*

‖**Oogonium** (ōu,ogōu·niɒ̆m). 1867. [mod. L., dim. of Gr. *ᾠογόνος egg-layer.] *Bot.* The female reproductive organ in the Thallophytes or lower Cryptogams, usu. a rounded cell or sac containing one or more *oospheres.*

Ooidal (o,oi·dăl), *a.* 1836. [f. Gr. ᾠοειδής egg-shaped + -al.] Resembling an egg; oval.

‖ **Oolakan, -chan** (ū·lăkăn). Also **ou-, eu-.** 1836. [Native name.] The candle-fish (*Thaleichthys pacificus*) of north-western America. Also *attrib.*, as *o. oil.*

Oolite (ōu·ŏləit). 1802. [a. F. *oölithe*, mod.L. *oölites*, f. Gr. ᾠόν egg + λίθος stone; see -lite.] 1. *Min.* A concretionary limestone composed of small rounded granules, like the roe of a fish, each consisting of carbonate of lime around a grain of sand as a nucleus; roe-stone. 2. *Geol.* The name of an important series of fossiliferous rocks of this character, lying between the Chalk, or the Wealden, and the Lias; sometimes applied to the whole series of limestones, sandstones, and clays, to which these belong; now usu. included, with the Lias, in the Jurassic system 1816. 3. *attrib.*, as *o. formation*, etc. 1813. Hence **Ooli·tic** *a.* of the structure of o.; pertaining to the O. formation.

Oology (o,ǫ·lŏdʒi). 1831. [mod. f. Gr. ᾠόν egg + -logy.] a. The study of, or a description of, birds' eggs, esp. in regard to their external appearance. b. The practice of collecting birds' eggs. Hence **Oolo·gic, -al** *adjs.*; **-ly** *adv.* **Oo·logist,** one versed in o.; a collector of birds' eggs.

‖ **Oolong** (ū·lǫŋ). Also **ou-.** 1852. [Chinese *wulung*, f. *wu* black + *lung* dragon.] A dark variety of cured tea.

‖ **Oomiak** (ū·miæk). 1769. Also **umiak, ooniak.** 1769. [Eskimo.] A large Eskimo boat for women and children, propelled by paddles.

-oon, the form usu. taken in Eng. by Fr. final *-on* in words stressed on the final syllable, adopted during 16–18th c., as F. *dragon*, Eng. *dragoon* (corresp. to *-on* in old adoptions, as *baron, felon*, and mod. borrowings, as *chignon*); and hence by the Fr. suffix *-on*, = It. *-one*, Sp. *-on*, L. *-o, -onem*, forming in L. masculine appellatives as *naso* big-nosed man. Examples of adopted words are *balloon, buffoon, cartoon, quadroon*; *-oon* is rare as an Eng. formative, as in *spittoon.*

Oons (ūnz), *int.* Now *rare.* 1593. [Worn-down f. *wounds* (= *God's wounds*).] = Zounds.

‖ **Oopak, oopack** (ū·pæk). 1858. [Chinese *u-pak*, Cantonese dial. form of *Hu-peh*, a central province of China.] A variety of black tea.

Oophore (ōu·ŏfoəɹ). 1875. [f. Gr. ᾠόν egg + -φόρος bearing, bearer.] *Bot.* That stage, or form of a plant, in the higher Cryptogams (ferns, mosses, etc.) which, in the alternation of generations, bears male and female organs; the 'sexual generation'; also called *oophyte.* Opp. to *sporophore* or *sporophyte.*

Oophorectomy (ōu:ofore·ktŏmi). 1872. [f. mod.L. *oophoron* ovary (see prec.) + Gr. ἐκτομή.] *Surg.* Excision of the ovary.

Oophoridium (ōu:ofori·diɒ̆m). Also **oophorid.** 1835. [f. as prec. + *-idium*, Gr. -ίδιον, dim. ending.] *Bot.* A name for the macrosporangia (or loosely, the macrospores) of certain *Lycopodiaceæ.*

Oophoritis (ōu:oforəi·tis). 1872. [f. as prec. + -itis.] *Path.* Inflammation of the ovary.

‖ **Oorali** (urā·li). 1880. Var. of Woorali.

‖ **Oosporangium** (ōu:osporæ·ndʒiɒ̆m). Also **o·ospora·nge.** 1857. [f. Oo- + Sporangium.] *Bot.* a. Thuret's term for the unilocular zoosporangium of certain fucoid Algæ (Phæosporeæ). b. A case or sac containing an oospore.

Oospore (ōu·ŏspǭəɹ). [f. Gr. ᾠόν egg + σπόρος Spore.] *Bot.* The fertilized female cell or oosphere, esp. in the lower Cryptogams, which forms the germ of a future plant.

Ootocoid (o,ǫ·tŏkoid), *a.* and *sb.* 1863. [ad. mod.L. *Ootocoidea* (neut. pl.), f. Gr. ᾠοτόκος oviparous; see -oid.] *Zool.* a. *adj.* Belonging to the *Ootocoidea*, a division of mammals comprising the marsupials and monotremes. b. *sb.* One of the *Ootocoidea.* Also **Ootocoi·dean** *a.* and *sb.*

Ooze (ūz), *sb.*[1] [In senses 1, 2, OE. *wōs* juice, sap. Sense 3 is from Ooze *v.* (itself a deriv. of sense 1).] †1. Juice, sap –1450. 2. *techn.* The liquor of a tan-vat; an infusion of oak-bark, sumach, or the like 1575. 3. The act or fact of oozing; exudation; gentle flow; also, that which oozes; a sluggish stream 1718.

Comb. (from 2) **o.-calf,** calf-skin through which the dye has been forced by mechanical means, used for the uppers of boots and shoes, and by bookbinders.

Ooze (ūz), *sb.*[2] [OE. *wáse* wk. fem.] 1. Wet mud or slime; esp. that in the bed of a river or estuary. b. A stretch of mud; a mud-bank; a marsh or fen, etc. 1500. 2. *Ocean-sounding.* White or grey calcareous matter, covering vast tracts of the ocean-floor 1860.

1. The ose or salt water mudde 1602. *fig.* Fishing a manuscript out of the o. of oblivion Lowell.

Ooze (ūz), *sb.*[3] *Obs.* or *rare.* 1555. [Etym. doubtful.] Seaweed.

Ooze (ūz), *v.* [ME. *wosen*, f. *wose*, Ooze *sb.*[1] 1, 2.] 1. *intr.* Of moisture: To pass slowly or in small quantities through the pores of a body; to exude, to percolate. b. Of a substance: To exude moisture. late ME. 2. *transf.* and *fig.* To pass as through pores, and so slowly, gradually, or imperceptibly. Often with *out, away.* 1775. 3. *trans.* To emit (moisture, etc.) slowly and gradually. Often with *out.* late ME.

1. I saw the water o. in at several crannies Swift. 2. Your valour has oozed away Sheridan. Rumours began to o. out 1867. 3. His doe-skin boots were oozing out water Mrs. Carlyle.

‖ **Oozoa** (ōu,ozōu·ă), *sb. pl.* 1881. [mod.L., f. Gr. ᾠόν egg + ζῷα, pl. of ζῷον animal.] *Zool.* A synonym of Protozoa. Hence **Oozo·an** *a.* and *sb.*

Oozy (ū·zi), *a.* [In 1 and 2, late ME. *wosie*, f. *wose* mud, Ooze *sb.*[2]; in 3, a later formation related to Ooze *v.*] 1. Of water: Charged with ooze or mud; muddy. 2. Composed of or resembling ooze, having the consistency of wet mud or slime. Of a sea-bottom: Consisting of ooze. 1563. 3. Exuding moisture; damp with exuded or deposited moisture 1714. b. Slimy or damp; said of seaweed 1742.

2. And bid the weltring waves their o. channel keep Milt. 3. The floor of the dungeon o. with wet Hawthorne. Hence **Oo·zily** *adv.* **Oo·ziness.**

Op-, the form of the L. prefix Ob- bef. *p*, as in *oppose*, etc.

Opacity (opæ·sĭti). 1560. [a. F. *opacité*, ad. L. *opacitas*, f. *opacus* Opaque.] 1. The state of being in shadow; darkness, obscurity; an instance of this 1611. b. The condition of not reflecting light 1794. 2. The quality or condition of being impervious to light; non-translucency 1634. b. *transf. Acoustic o.*, imperviousness to waves of sound 1871. 3. *fig.* a. Darkness of meaning. b. Denseness or obtuseness of intellect; *concr.* one in whom this is embodied. 1560.

Opacous (opē·kəs), *a.* Now *rare.* 1621. [f. L. *opacus* Opaque + -ous.] = Opaque *a.* Hence **Opa·cous-ly** *adv.*, **-ness.**

Opah (ōu·pă). 1750. [West African.] A rare fish of the North Atlantic (*Lampris guttatus*), of the mackerel family, conspicuous for its brilliant colour. Also called King-fish, Moon-fish.

Opal (ōu·păl). 1591. [ad. L. *opalus* (Pliny), ad. (through Gr. ὀπάλλιος) Skr. *upala* 'precious stone, gem'.] 1. An amorphous form of hydrous silica, somewhat resembling quartz, but in some species exhibiting a delicate play of colour; these when cut are valuable as gems. **2.** = OPALINE *sb.* 2. 1889. **3.** *attrib.* or *adj.* Of or resembling the opal or that of the opal, opalescent 1649.

1. *fig.* Thy minde is a very Opall SHAKS. *Common o.*, a milk-white or bluish variety, with reflexion of green, yellow, and red; *fire* or *sun o.*, a rich hyacinth-red variety from Mexico; *harlequin, precious*, or *noble o.*, a variety exhibiting a rich play of prismatic colours, which flash from minute fissures apparently striated with microscopic lines. See also CACHOLONG, GIRASOL, HYALITE.

Opalesce (ōupăle·s), *v.* 1819. [f. prec. + *-esce*, repr. L. *-escere* in *albescere*, etc., after next.] *intr.* To exhibit a play of colours or iridescence like that of the opal.

Opalescent (ōupăle·sĕnt), *a.* 1813. [f. OPAL + -ESCENT.] Exhibiting a play of colours or iridescence like that of the opal. So **Opale·sque** *a.* 1863. **Opale·scence**, the quality of being o. 1805.

Opaline (ōu·pălin, -əin), *a.* and *sb.* 1784. [f. OPAL + -INE[1].] **A.** *adj.* Opalescent; of the nature of opal. **B.** *sb.* **1.** Occas. applied to a variety of yellow chalcedony which presents an opaline semi-opacity 1861. **2.** A semi-translucent glass; also called *milk-glass* 1875. **3.** An opaline colour, surface, or expanse 1871.

Opalize (ōu·păləiz), *v.* 1811. [f. OPAL + -IZE.] **1.** *intr.* To opalesce. **2.** *trans.* To make iridescent like an opal. Chiefly in **O·palized** *ppl. a.*

O·palotype. 1873. [f. L. *opalus* OPAL + TYPE.] A positive photograph on opal glass.

Opaque (opē¹·k), *a.* (*sb.*) late ME. [ad. L. *opacus*, whence also F. *opaque*; hence the current Eng. spelling.] **1.** †Lying in shadow; darkened, obscure -1775. **b.** Of a body or surface: Not reflecting or emitting light; not lustrous, dull 1794. **2.** Impermeable to light; hence, impenetrable to sight 1641. **3.** *fig.* **a.** Hard to make out; obscure 1761. **b.** Impervious to reason, dense, obtuse 1850. **B.** *sb.* **a.** Something opaque; a medium or space through which light cannot pass 1742. **b.** A shade for the eyes 1900.

1. b. The planets are all opake, or dark bodies 1794. **3. a.** The o. but authentic Commons Journals CARLYLE. **b.** Too o. to understand her husband's jeers 1882. **B. a.** The light began to penetrate the dim o. of his understanding 1824. Hence **Opa·que·ly** *adv.*, **-ness.**

-opathy: see -PATHY.

Ope (ōup), *a.* and *sb.* ME. [Reduced from OPEN; cf. *awake(n*, etc.] = OPEN *a.* and *sb.*

Ope (ōup), *v.* late ME. [Reduced from OPEN *v.* after prec.] To open. Chiefly *poet.*

Oped his young eye to bear the blaze of greatness GRAY.

Opeidoscope (opəi·dŏskōup). 1873. [f. Gr. ὤψ, ὀπ- voice + εἶδος form + -SCOPE.] An instrument consisting of a tube closed at one end by a tense membrane, having attached to its centre a small mirror, to show the musical vibration caused by speaking or singing at the open end.

Opelet (ōu·plėt). 1860. [irreg. f. OPE *a.* + -LET.] A name of a sea-anemone, *Anemonia sulcata*, so called because the tentacles cannot be retracted.

Open (ōu·p'n), *sb.* late ME. [Partly vbl. sb. f. OPEN *v.*; partly ellipt. use of OPEN *a.*] **I. 1.** = OPENING *vbl. sb.* 2; an aperture 1470. **2.** = OPENING *vbl. sb.* 5. Now *arch.* 1711.

2. Perhaps this may leave an o. to sarcasm 1757.

II. sb. use of OPEN *a.* †**1.** Open, unconcealed, or plainly seen condition -1646. **2. a.** *The o.*: the open space. (*a*) The part of the country not enclosed; (*b*) Ground without buildings, trees, etc.; (*c*) The open water, in sea or river; (*d*) The open air 1624. **b.** An open or clear space 1796. **3.** *Stock Exchange.* The open market 1898.

1. *Hen. VIII*, III. ii. 405. **2. a.** The soldier is taught how to attack in the o. 1880. Raspberries..grown in the o. 1893.

Open (ōu·p'n), *a.* (*adv.*) [Com. Teut.: OE. *open*; OTeut. *upano-, app. from the root of UP *adv.*] **I.** Physical senses. **1.** Of a door, gate, etc.: Not 'put to', not closed or shut; 'up', set up, so as to allow free passage through. Also said of a doorway or other passage. **2.** Of a containing space, a house, box, etc.: Having its gate, door, lid, or some part of its enclosing boundary drawn aside or removed; not shut up OE. **b.** Hence, Free of entrance to all (or *to* persons specified) OE. **3.** Of a space: Not shut in; unenclosed, unwalled, unconfined. See also OPEN AIR. OE. **b.** Hence, of a battle: Fought in the open (not in a fortress, etc.), and so with full forces 1548. **4.** Not covered over or covered in; esp. in *o. boat, carriage* OE. **5.** Uncovered; bare, exposed OE. **6.** Unclosed, expanded, spread out ME. **7.** Of a line, texture, etc.: Having spaces between its parts; containing interstices, gaps, holes, or unoccupied spaces; perforated, porous 1625. **8.** Of a passage or space: Unobstructed, clear. Of a country: Free from wood, buildings, etc. Of a river, port, etc.: Free from ice. ME. **b.** Of the bodily passages: Not obstructed; *esp.* of the bowels 1562. **9. a.** Of the soil: Unbound; loose, permeable. **b.** Of weather, etc.: Free from frost, as an *o. winter.* 1615. **10.** *Naut.* †**a.** Looking unobstructedly *upon* or *to.* **b.** Seen with an opening between; clear, detached. 1478. **11.** *techn.* **a.** *Mus.* Of an organ-pipe: Not closed or shut at the top. Of a string: Not stopped by a finger. Hence, of a note, Produced by such a pipe or string, or on a wind-instrument without the aid of a slide, key, or piston. 1674. **b.** Of sounds: Uttered with the mouth open. *spec.* Of vowels: Produced with a wider opening of the oral cavity than those called *close*; e.g. *open o* and *e* (= ǭ, ę), *close o* and *e* (= ō, ē). 1485. **c.** Of a syllable: Ending in a vowel 1871.

1. The windows..were left o. SWIFT. The door burst o. FIELDING. **2.** His head was split o. with a blow 1887. Standing beside the o. grave (*mod.*). **b.** The old universities are o. to all 1891. **3.** The fields then being o. and champain BACON. The Enemy..sent a strong Party into an o. Village 1704. *O. grate, o. fireplace*, one in which the whole of the fire is visible. **b.** We our forts and lines forsake, To dare our British foes to o. fight 1706. **4.** A drive in an o. carriage and four 1854. **5.** Sow Alaternus Seeds in..o. Beds EVELYN. **6.** An o. letter in his hand TROLLOPE. **7.** Phr. *O. order* (*Mil.*), a formation in which the individual men are three or more yards apart; (*Naval*), a formation in which the individual ships are more than a cable's length apart. *O. harmony* (*Mus.*), a harmony in which the chords are separated by wide intervals. **8.** The Ice being broke, the Sound is again o. for the Ships STEELE. The Preservation of O. Spaces 1896. **10.** I found myself o. to the northern shore DE FOE.

II. Non-physical senses. **1.** Exposed to the mental view; patent, plain, easy to understand. Now only in *to lay o.*, to lay bare, 'expose'. OE. **2.** Exposed to general view or knowledge; public. Of persons: Acting in public or without concealment. OE. **3.** Not confined or limited to a few; that may be used, shared, or competed for without restriction 1460. **4.** Exposed, liable, or subject *to* 1450. **5.** Unreserved, frank, candid 1513. **6.** Free in giving. Now chiefly in *o. hand, o.-handed.* 1597. **7.** Of a question, etc.: Not finally settled; undecided; hence, uncertain 1562. **8.** Of a thing, course of action, etc.: Not closed against access; accessible, available. Const. *to* (a person). 1526. **9.** Of a person: Accessible to appeals, offers, emotions, or ideas; impressionable; amenable *to* (pity or reason) 1672.

1. A foole layeth o. his folly *Prov.* xiii. 16. **2.** Cleombrotus he treated with o. contempt 1844. **3.** *O. champion*, one who has been successful in an unrestricted championship. **4.** It seem o. to doubt 1891. **5.** One Monarch wears an honest o. Face DRYDEN. **6.** A Hand O. (as Day) for melting Charitie SHAKS. **7.** *O.* POLICY, VERDICT: see these words; certain questions brought before Parliament are treated as 'open' questions; that is, questions on which Ministers in Parliament are allowed to take opposite sides without resigning 1863. **8.** There are three..courses o. to us 1883. **9.** Those whose intelligence is quickest, openest, most sensitive M. ARNOLD. I am o. to offers (*mod.*).

Phrases, etc. *With o. arms* (sense I. 6), with arms outspread to receive; hence, with great willingness of reception. *In o. court*, in the public court of justice, before the judge and the public. *O. ear*, an attentive ear. *O. eye*, an unclosed, hence an observant or watchful eye. *O. letter*, a letter addressed to an individual but published as a matter of general interest. *With o. mouth*, with mouth open to speak; also, gaping with wonder, etc.; open-mouthed. *To keep o. doors, house*, or *table*, to provide hospitality for all comers. See also sbs. and Main words.

Comb. **a.** With a sb., forming an *attrib.* phr., as *o.-fire, -house, -view*, etc. See also Main words. **b.** Parasynthetic combs. in *-ed* (unlimited in number), as *o.-armed, -fronted, -sleeved, -windowed* (hence *o.-windowedness*). **c.** Special combs.: **o.-cast, -cut,** in *Mining*, an o. working; **-faced** *a.*, having a frank or ingenuous face; hence *openfacedness*; **-hearth,** a hearth of the reverberatory type; see HEARTH 3 b; also *attrib.*; **-minded** *a.*, accessible to new arguments or ideas, hence *open-mindedness*; **o. note,** a musical note having an open loop.

†**B.** *adv.* = Openly ME. *Twel. N.* III. iii. 37.

Open (ōu·p'n), *v.* [OE. *openian* :—OTeut. *upanōjan, f. *upano- OPEN *a.*] **I.** *trans.* **1.** To move or turn (a door, gate, etc.) away from its closed position, so as to admit of passage. Also *absol.* **2.** To make (a building, box, or enclosed space) open (OPEN *a.* I. 2); to break open, unclose, undo; to provide free access to or egress from ME. **b.** With the purpose as the main notion: To render accessible *to* (persons or the public) or *for* (some purpose) 1560. **c.** To declare open to public use by a formal ceremony 1889. **3.** To spread apart, widen, expand, unroll, extend. Also *absol.* with ellipsis of object, as 'to o. (a book) at a page', etc. OE. **4.** To make an opening in; to cut or break into ME. **b.** To make, produce, or cause (an opening or open space of some kind) ME. **5.** To loosen. (In various shades of meaning.) 1683. **6.** To clear of obstruction or hindrance; to make (a road) free for passage. Chiefly *fig.* ME. **7.** To uncover, lay bare, expose to view, display OE. **8.** *Naut.* To come in sight of, get an open view of, by rounding or passing an intervening object 1628. †**9.** To reveal, disclose, declare, make known. *Obs.* exc. as in **b.** -1804. **b.** *esp.* To disclose or divulge (one's mind, feelings, designs, etc.); *refl.* to unbosom oneself ME. †**10.** To unfold the sense of; to expound -1720. **11.** To expand, enlarge, enlighten (the mind or heart) ME. **12.** To render available for settlement, use, intercourse, etc. Usu. *o. up.* 1617. **13.** To begin, start, commence 1693. **14.** *legal.* To state (a case) to the court, as a preliminary to adducing evidence; esp. to speak first in a case, a privilege of the affirmative side. 1621. **15.** To undo, recall, or set aside (a judgement, settlement, sale, etc.) so as to leave the matter open to further action, discussion, or negotiation 1792.

1. Huy had opened its gates to the French MACAULAY. O., in the King's name LYTTON. **2.** Why, then the world 's mine Oyster, which I, with sword will o. SHAKS. Shall we o. another bottle? (*mod.*). **b.** *Mod.* To o. a shop, store, branch of a bank, registry office, etc. **3.** He too had a library, although he never opened a book 1783. *absol.* I will take the first stanza, on which I have chanced to o., in the Lyrical Ballads COLERIDGE. **4.** Who stooping op'nd my left side, and took From thence a Rib MILTON. Phr. *To o. ground*, to break up the surface of ground, as by ploughing, etc. **b.** Alpheus bold..With his trident ..opened a chasm In the rocks SHELLEY. Phr. *To o. trenches*, to dig trenches in besieging: see TRENCH. **5.** All kinds of manures o. the soil 1765. The leading troop..opens its ranks 1796. **6.** Thou op'nst Wisdoms way, And giv'st access MILT. The bowels should be well opened at the onset by a brisk purgative 1897. **7.** Herbs of every leaf..Op'ning their various colours MILT. **8.** Taking care not to o. the Obelisk on the slope of the North Head 1858. **9.** Nor o. it to others that he was Messias 1548. **b.** I have opened my mind unto you BUNYAN. **11.** My eyes had been opened, and my heart with them RUSKIN. **12.** Phr. *To o. land, to o. a country to trade.* **13.** Phr. *To o. an account, o. the ball, o. fire*, etc.: see the sbs. **14.** Phr. *To o. pleadings*, in a trial before jury, to state briefly the substance of the pleadings. **15.** The mortgagor is entitled to open the foreclosure on the usual terms 1877.

II. *intr.* (Sometimes for *refl.*, sometimes *ellipt.* or *absol.* use of the trans.) **1.** To become open, unshut, or unclosed. Hence, generally, to come apart or asunder, so as to admit of passage, disclose a vacant space, display the interior or contents; (of an abscess) to burst and discharge. OE. **2. a.** Of a door, etc.: To serve as a passage *to* or *into* 1760. **b.** Of a room or space: To have an opening or passage *to, into, out of*, etc. 1615. Also **c.** To have its opening, or outlet *towards*, to lie open *to* 1697. **3.** To expand, extend, spread apart. Also *o. out.* late ME. **b.** *fig.* To expand in intellect or sympathy 1709. **4.** To become disclosed or revealed, to begin to appear; to expand to the view, to become more and more visible 1708. **b.** *Naut.* To appear distinct or separate 1745. **5.** To speak out; to speak explicitly, explain. Now *rare.* 1641. **6.** Of hounds: To give tongue, begin to cry when in pursuit on a scent; hence, contemptuously, of men. late ME. **7.** To begin; to start operations. In theatrical parlance, To make a début, to begin a season or tour. Often *ellipt.*, for *o. fire.* 1716.

1. My wound opened again with riding DE FOE. Law offices opened at eight o'clock in those days 1870. **2. b.** A library, opening through a greenhouse on to a lawn 1801. **c.** A valley opening to the sea shore 1839. **3.** MILTON *P. L.* VI. 481. **b.** All Hearts begin to o. STEELE. **4.** The stainless sky Opens beyond them like eternity SHELLEY. **5.** When I opened, I found that this man was willing to o. too COBBETT. **6.** *Merry W.* IV. ii. 209. **7.** A battery of eight guns opened on the fleet 1894. School opens next Monday (*mod.*).

With advs. in specialized senses. **Open out.** *trans.* **a.** To unfold, unpack. **b.** To develop. **c.** To disclose, reveal, display or offer to mental view. *intr.* **d.** = sense II. 3. **e.** = sense II. 5. **O. up.** (*Up* thus added to *Open* often merely strengthens or gives emphasis, esp. in the senses following.) **a.** *trans.* To open to view, access, use, passage, or traffic; to lay open (a question previously untouched); to bring to light, disclose, raise and leave open. **b.** *intr.* To become open to passage, view, enterprise, etc. (by the removal of obstructions).

Phr. *To o. a* (or *the*) *door to*: to give access or free course to. *To o. one's eyes*, to take notice, regard; to stare with astonishment. *To o. a person's eyes*, to cause him to see, to make him aware of facts. *To o. one's mouth*, i.e. in order to swallow or eat, or (also *one's lips*) to speak; *not to o. one's lips*, to be absolutely silent.

Open air, open-air. 1526. **1.** *O·pen a·ir.* The unconfined atmosphere; hence, the unconfined space outside buildings, etc., usu. exposed to the weather. **2.** *attrib.* (usu. *o·pen-ai:r*). Existing, carried on, performed in, or characteristic of the open air 1860.

1. A Jesuit preaching in the o. BERKELEY. **2.** The hygienic and dietetic arrangements and especially the o. treatment 1896.

O·pen-bill. 1837. A bird of the genus *Anastomus*, allied to the stork, found in Africa and Asia; so called because the mandibles of its bill when shut are in contact only at the ends, leaving an open space in the middle.

O·pen-brea·sted (stress var.), *a.* 1594. Now *Obs.* or *arch.* **a.** Having the breast exposed. **b.** Of a garment: Not covering the breast 1599.

Open door. 1526. A door standing open; hence used *fig.* to typify free admission or access, freedom of admission. **b.** *International Politics.* Admission to a country, esp. for commercial intercourse, open to all upon equal terms. Used esp. with ref. to Chinese ports. 1856.

1. b. *attrib.* Coöperation between this republic and Great Britain as to the furtherance of the open door policy 1898.

Opener (ōu·p'nəɹ). 1548. [f. OPEN *v.* + -ER [1].] One who or that which opens; †an aperient.

Open-eyed (ōu·p'n,əi·d; stress var.), *a.* 1601. **1.** Having the eyes open; awake, vigilant. **b.** Done with the eyes open 1876. **2.** Having the mental 'eyes' or perceptive powers alert 1648.

1. Open-ey'd Conspiracie His time doth take SHAKS.

Open field. 1780. An unenclosed field; undivided arable land. Chiefly *attrib.* in *open-field system* by which the arable land of a village was planned out into a number of unenclosed portions or strips and distributed among the villagers.

O·pen-ha·nded (stress var.), *a.* 1601. [Parasynthetic f. *open hand.*] *lit.* Having an open hand. **a.** Free in giving, liberal, generous. †**b.** Ready to receive gifts –1785. Hence **O:penha·nded-ly** *adv.*, **-ness.**

O·pen-hea·rted (stress var.), *a.* 1611. [Parasynthetic f. *open heart.*] **1.** Disposed to communicate thoughts or feelings; not reserved, frank. **2.** Accessible to noble emotions; full of kindly feeling 1617. So **O:penhea·rted-ly** *adv.*, **-ness.**

Opening (ōu·p'niŋ, ōu·pniŋ), *vbl. sb.* ME. [-ING [1].] **1.** The action of OPEN *v.* Also with adv. as *o. out, o. up.* **2.** A gap, hole, or passage; an aperture ME. **b.** A bay, gulf, or other more or less wide indentation of the land 1719. **c.** The width of an arch between its pillars 1739. **3.** *U.S.* A tract of ground over which trees are wanting or thinly scattered, in the midst of forest tracts 1704. **4.** The action of beginning; commencement 1712. **b.** *spec.* The statement of a case made by counsel preliminary to adducing evidence 1660. **c.** *Chess.* A mode of beginning a game; *spec.* a definite sequence of moves for the purpose of establishing a line of defence or attack 1735. **5.** An opportunity; a vacancy in connexion with any business or profession 1793.

1. A confused noise of the o. of hounds BERKELEY. The opening-up of a market 1887. **4.** The days which ..preceded the o. of the session MACAULAY. **5.** She might have made him miss one or two openings in life 1855.

O·pening, *ppl. a.* late ME. [-ING [2].] That opens, in various senses. **1.** That renders open; *spec.* aperient. **b.** That opens or commences, initial; introductory. **2.** That becomes open; unclosing, unfolding, etc.

1. b. It was the o. day of the exhibition 1882. **2.** The o. eyelids of the morn MILTON.

Openly (ōu·p'nli), *adv.* OE. [-LY [2].] **1.** Without concealment; in public; publicly. **2.** Frankly, unreservedly ME. †**3.** Manifestly; clearly, plainly –1682.

1. My loue to ye, Shall shew it selfe more o. hereafter SHAKS.

Open-mouthed (ōu·p'nmau·ðd; stress var.), *a.* 1470. [Parasynthetic f. *open mouth.*] **1.** Having the mouth open; having an open mouth; hence, rapacious, in full cry, etc. 1532. **b.** Of a vessel or the like: Having a wide mouth 1660. **2.** Gaping, as with astonishment or surprise 1593. **3.** Clamorous, vociferous. Now *rare* or *arch.* 1470.

Openness (ōu·p'n,nės). 1530. [f. OPEN *a.* + -NESS.] **1.** The quality or condition of being OPEN. **2.** Absence of dissimulation, secrecy, or reserve; candour, sincerity 1611.

Open sesame (ōu·p'n se·sămi). 1826. [See SESAME.] The magic words by which, in the tale of Ali Baba and the Forty Thieves, the door of the robbers' cave was made to fly open; hence, any irresistible means of securing immediate admission.

That universal key, that *open sesame*, a bribe 1837.

†**O·pen-ti·de.** ME. = next –1744.

O·pen ti·me. 1483. The time during which anything is open: *spec.* †**a.** The time after harvest when cattle might be turned into the open fields. †**b.** The time out of Lent when no fast is imposed. **c.** That which is not close time for fish, etc.

O·pen-w·ork. 1812. [See OPEN *a.* I. 7.] **1.** Any kind of work with interstices in its substance, as in open-work of iron, etc.; *esp.* such work in knitting, netting, embroidery. **2.** *Mining.* Excavation open to the surface 1881.

Opera (ǫ·pĕră). 1644. [a. It., a. L., = labour, pains, a work produced, f. *opus, oper-* work.] **1.** A dramatic performance in which music forms an essential part, consisting of recitatives, arias, and choruses, with orchestral accompaniment and scenery; also, a dramatic or musical composition intended for this, a libretto or score. **2.** (Usu. *the o.*) As a branch of dramatic art 1759. **b.** With qualification denoting a particular branch or kind 1711.

1. Phr. *At* or *to the o.*, including the notion of the place (cf. *at the play*). **2. b.** *Comic o.* (see COMIC A. 1); *grand o.* (see GRAND A. 8); *o. bouffe* (= F. *opéra bouffe*, also ellipt. *bouffe*, and in It. form *opera buffa*), comic o., esp. an operatic extravaganza.

Comb.: **o.-cloak,** a cloak of rich material worn by ladies at the opera or in going to evening parties, dances, etc.; **-girl,** (*a*) a girl or woman who dances in the ballet of an o.; (*b*) *pl.* a greenhouse plant, *Mantisia saltatoria*, called also DANCING-GIRLS; **-glass, -glasses,** a small binocular for use at theatres, etc.; **-hat,** a hat suitable for use at the o.; *spec.* a crush-hat; **-house,** a theatre for the performance of operas.

Operable (ǫ·pĕrăb'l), *a.* 1646. [f. L. *operari* to OPERATE + -ABLE. In mod. use after the Engl. vb.] †**1.** Practicable –1677. **2.** *Med.* That admits of being operated upon 1904. Hence **O:perabi·lity.**

Operameter (ǫpĕræ·mĭtəɹ). 1829. [irreg. f. L. *opera* works + Gr. μέτρον measure.] *Mech.* A device for registering the number of revolutions made by a shaft, axle, or wheel, the strokes of a piston, the copies delivered from a printing-press, etc.

Operancy (ǫ·pĕrănsi)). *rare.* 1810. [f. OPERANT; -ANCY.] The quality or condition of being operant; operation.

Operand (ǫ·pĕrænd). 1886. [ad. L. *operandum, operari* to OPERATE.] *Math.* A quantity or symbol to be operated on.

Operant (ǫ·pĕrănt). 1602. [ad. L. *operantem, operari* to OPERATE.] **A.** *adj.* That operates; operative. **B.** *sb.* One who, or that which, operates 1700; an operative (LAMB).

Operate (ǫ·pĕreɪt), *v.* 1606. [f. L. *operat-, operari* to work, etc.; in late L., also, to have effect, produce by working, f. *opus, oper-* work.] **I.** *intr.* **1.** To be in working, exercise influence, produce an effect, act. **2.** Of persons: To bring force or influence to bear *on* or *upon.* Now *rare* or *arch.* 1650. **3.** Of drugs, medicines, etc.: To produce the desired effect; to act 1706. **4.** To perform a practical operation or series of operations; see OPERATION 5. Const. *on, upon.* 1674. **b.** *Surg.*: see OPERATION 6. 1799. **c.** *Mil.* and *Naval*: see OPERATION 7. 1808. **d.** To deal or speculate in stocks or shares; to buy and sell commodities as a broker 1859.

1. The revolutionary spirit, ceasing to o. in politics MACAULAY. **2.** He knew the Highland chieftans well, and how to o. on them 1790. **4. d.** A bull in the same jargon, is one who operates for a rise 1859.

II. *trans.* **1.** To effect by the exertion of force or influence; to bring about, accomplish 1637. **2.** To cause or actuate the working of; to work (a machine, etc.). Chiefly *U.S.* 1864. **3.** To direct the working of; to manage, conduct, work (a railway, business, etc.); to carry out, direct to an end (an undertaking, etc.) Chiefly *U.S.* 1880.

1. Now plotting to o. the ruine of the Protestant Religion MILT. **2.** The cost of operating the cars 1886. **3.** The..Company o. a large foundry 1891.

Operatic, †-ical (ǫpĕræ·tik, -ăl), *adjs.* 1730. [irreg. f. OPERA, app. after *dramatic*; see -IC, -AL.] Pertaining to, or of the nature of, opera. Hence **Opera·tically** *adv.*

Operating (ǫ·pĕreɪtiŋ), *vbl. sb.* 1674. [f. OPERATE + -ING [1].] The action of OPERATE *v.*; an instance of this, an operation.

attrib. and *Comb.*, as *o. room*; **o.-table,** one on which a patient is operated upon; **-theatre,** a room constructed for surgical operations before a class.

Operation (ǫpĕrē·ʃən). late ME. [a. OF. *operation, -cion* action, deed, ad. L. *operationem*, f. *operari.*] †**1.** Action, performance, work –1567. **2.** Working; exertion of force, energy, or influence; the way in which anything works. late ME. **b.** The condition of being in working 1818. **3.** Power to operate or work; efficacy, influence, virtue, force. Now chiefly of legal instruments. 1509. **b.** The effect produced; influence *on* something. Now *rare* or *Obs.* 1605. **4.** A particular form or kind of activity; an active process 1594. **5.** The performance of something of practical or mechanical nature, e.g. as a scientific experiment or demonstration. late ME. **b.** A (speculative) business transaction. orig. *U.S.* 1863. **6.** *Surg.* An act or series of acts performed upon an organic body with the hand alone or by means of an instrument, to remedy deformity or injury, cure or prevent disease, or relieve pain 1597. **7.** *Mil.* and *Naval.* A series of warlike or strategic acts; a movement 1749. **8.** *Math.* The action of subjecting a number or quantity to any process whereby its value or form is affected 1713. **9.** The action of operating a machine, engine, railway, business, etc. 1872.

2. There are divers manners off operacions and yet but one God which worketh all thynges TINDALE 1 *Cor.* xii. 6. The o. of the condenser pump is very simple 1824. **b.** Phr. *In o., to come into o.* **3.** He cannot..enlarge, in his own favour, the legal or equitable o. of the instrument 1884. **4.** By the operations of the mind we understand every mode of thinking of which we are conscious 1785. **7.** Phr. *Line of operations*, the line an army follows to attain its objective point 1867. Hence **Opera·tional** *a.* (esp. with reference to sense 7).

Operative (ǫ·pĕrătiv), *a.* and *sb.* 1598. [a. F. *opératif, -ive*, or ad. late L. *operativus* creative, formative, f. *operat-, operari* to OPERATE; see -IVE.] **A.** *adj.* **1.** Characterized by operating; exerting force, energy, or influence; productive *of* something; in operation 1603. **2.** Productive of the intended or proper effect; effectual, efficacious 1598. **3.** Concerned with manual or mechanical work; practical 1624. **4.** Pertaining to surgical operations 1783. **5.** Of a person: Engaged in work or production, active 1824. **6.** Engaged in production as a workman or artisan, working. (Now perh. the sb. used *attrib.*) 1831.

1. The strongest and most o. sense of duty would not satisfy you 1879. 2. Fraud was an o. instrument in the hands of this aspiring general 1818. 3. In Architecture, as in all other O. Arts, the End must direct the Operation 1624. 6. Members of the o. class C. BRONTE.

B. *sb.* **1.** One who operates or works in any branch of industry, trade, or profession; a worker 1809. **2.** A workman in any industrial art; an artisan, mechanic. Also *attrib.* 1827. Hence **O·perative·ly** *adv.*, **-ness.**

Operator (ǫ·pĕreˈtəɹ). 1597. [a. late L., f. *operari.*] One who operates. **1.** One who does or effects something; a worker, an agent 1611. **2.** One who performs the practical or mechanical operations belonging to any process, business, or investigation; a person professionally or officially so engaged 1597. **3.** One who performs surgical operations; an operating surgeon or dentist 1597. †**b.** A quack manufacturer of drugs, etc. –1710. **4.** One who carries on financial operations in stocks, shares, or commodities 1828. **5.** One who works a machine, telegraph, etc. 1870. **6.** One who works a business, undertaking, etc. *U.S.* 1877. **7.** *Math.* A symbol indicating an operation or series of operations, and itself subject to algebraical operation 1855.

Opercle (opə̄·ɹk'l). 1597. [ad. L. *operculum* cover, etc.; see -CULE.] †**1.** A cover, covering –1597. **2.** *Nat. Hist.* = OPERCULUM 1840.

Opercular (opə̄·ɹkiŭlăɹ), *a.* 1830. [f. L. *operculum* (see below) + -AR [1].] *Nat. Hist.* Of, pertaining to, or of the nature of an operculum; characterized by the presence of an operculum.

Operculate (opə̄·ɹkiŭleˈt), *a.* (*sb.*). 1775. [ad. L. *operculatus*, *operculare* to furnish or cover with a lid, etc., f. *operculum* cover, lid.] *Nat. Hist.* **A.** *adj.* Furnished with or having an operculum; effected by means of an operculum. **B.** *sb.* An operculate mollusc. In the pl. the L. form **Operculata** is usual. 1856.

Operculi-, comb. form of L. *operculum*, as in **Operculi·ferous** *a.*, having an operculum, operculate; **Ope·rculiform** *a.*, having the form of an operculum; **Operculi·genous** *a.*, producing an operculum; said of the metapodium of gastropods.

Operculum (opə̄·ɹkiŭlŏm). *Pl.* **-la.** 1713. [a. L., f. *operire* to cover; see -CULUM.] An organ or structure forming or resembling a lid or cover; *spec.* **1.** *Zool.* **a.** The gill-cover of a fish 1752. **b.** The plate which serves to close the aperture of the shell of some molluscs when the animal is retracted; also, the flap or lid in sessile cirripeds 1777. **c.** Applied to various other lid-like parts and organs 1713. **2.** *Bot.* The lid of the capsule in mosses; also, the lid of the pitcher in *Nepenthes*, and the conical limb of the calyx of *Eucalyptus* 1788. **3.** *Anat.* In the brain, the principal covering of the insula or island of Reil, which overlaps the gyri operti from above 1889.

Operetta (ǫpĕre·tă). 1770. [a. It., dim. of *opera.*] A short (orig. one-act) light opera.

Operose (ǫ·pĕrōus), *a.* 1670. [ad. L. *operosus*, f. *opus*, *oper-* work.] **1.** Made or done with, attended by, or involving much labour; laborious; elaborate 1683. **2.** Of a person: Laborious; industrious, busy.

1. Browne might himself have obtained the same conviction by a method less o. JOHNSON. 2. An o. Compiler of History 1734. So **Opero·se·ly** *adv.* 1668, **-ness** 1664. **Opero·sity**, laboriousness 1623.

Ophicalcite (ǫfikæ·lsəit). 1846. [f. Gr. ὄφις serpent + CALCITE.] *Min.* A species of rock composed of a mixture of serpentine and crystalline limestone (calcite).

Ophicleide (ǫ·fikləid). Also **-cleid.** 1834. [a. F. *ophicléide*, f. Gr. ὄφις serpent + κλείς, κλειδ- key.] A musical wind-instrument of powerful tone, a development of the ancient 'serpent', consisting of a conical brass tube bent double, with keys, forming the bass or alto to the key-bugle; also, a performer on this. **b.** A powerful reed-stop on the organ, now usu. called *tuba* 1842.

‖**Ophidia** (ofi·diă), *sb. pl.* 1802. [mod.L. neut. pl., f. assumed Gr. *ὀφιδ- or f. ὀφίδιον, f. ὄφις serpent.] *Zool.* An order of Reptiles containing the snakes or serpents.

Ophidian (ofi·diăn), *a.* and *sb.* 1813. [f. prec. + -AN.] **A.** *adj.* **1.** *Zool.* Belonging to the order *Ophidia.* **2.** Pertaining or relating to, or resembling that of, a snake or serpent; snake-like 1883. **B.** *sb. Zool.* A reptile of the order *Ophidia*; a snake or serpent 1832.

‖**Ophidium** (ofi·diŏm). 1706. [med.L., ad. L. *ophidion* (Pliny), a. Gr. ὀφίδιον 'a fish resembling the conger', dim. of ὄφις serpent.] *Zool.* A genus of acanthopterygian fishes with elongated bodies; a fish of this genus. So **Ophi·dioid** *a.* (*sb.*) belonging to (a fish of) the group *Ophidioidea*, of which O. is the typical genus.

Ophio-, comb. form of Gr. ὄφις serpent, as in ‖**Ophioglo·ssum** [Gr. γλῶσσα] *Bot.* the genus of ferns containing the adder's tongue, the type of the sub-order *Ophioglossaceæ*. **Ophio·later** [Gr. -λατρης], a serpent-worshipper. So **Ophio·latrous** *a.* given to serpent-worship. **Ophio·latry.** **Ophio·logy** [-LOGY], that branch of zoology which treats of serpents. Hence **Ophiolo·gic, -al** *adjs.*, **Ophio·logist.** **O·phioma·ncy** *rare* [Gr. μαντεία -MANCY], divination by means of serpents 1753.

Ophiomorph (ǫ·fiŏmǭɹf). [f. OPHIO- + Gr. μορφή form.] *Zool.* An amphibian of the order *Ophiomorpha* or *Ophiomorphæ* (also called *Apoda*, *Gymnophiona*, and *Ophiobatrachia*); a limbless serpentiform amphibian; a cæcilian. So **Ophiomo·rphic, Ophiomo·rphous** *adjs.* having the form of a serpent or snake; *spec.* of or pertaining to the *Ophiomorpha*; **Ophiomo·rphite**, an old name for fossil ammonite shells, from their snake-like appearance; a snake-stone.

‖**Ophiophagus** (ǫfiǫ·făgəs). *Pl.* **-gi** (dʒəi). 1555. [L., a. Gr. ὀφιοφάγος serpent-eating.] **1.** A serpent-eater. **2.** *Zool.* A genus of very venomous serpents allied to the cobra, inhabiting the East Indies, and feeding upon other snakes. One species is *O. elaps*, the HAMADRYAD 1883. So **Ophio·phagous** *a.* eating or feeding upon serpents 1650.

Ophir (ōu·fəɹ). 1595. [Heb.] The name of a place or region mentioned in the O.T., whence fine gold was obtained; its locality is uncertain.

Ophite [1] (ǫ·fəit). 1617. [ad. L. *ophites* (Pliny), a. Gr. ὀφίτης (sc. λίθος) serpentine stone, f. ὄφις serpent; see -ITE [1] 2 b.] *Min.* Name for various eruptive or metamorphic rocks, usu. green, and having spots or markings like a serpent; serpentine; serpentine marble. Also *attrib.* Hence **Ophi·tic** *a.* [1] 1883.

Ophite [2] (ǫ·fəit). 1692. [a. late L. *Ophitæ*, a. Gr. Ὀφῖται, pl. of Ὀφίτης, f. ὄφις serpent; see -ITE [1] 1.] A member of a 2nd century sect, who worshipped the serpent as an embodiment of divine wisdom. Hence **Ophi·tic** *a.* [2] 1865.

‖**Ophiuchus** (ǫfi,iū·kŏs). 1658. [L., a. Gr. ὀφιοῦχος, f. ὀφιο- OPHIO- + -εχος -holding, -holder.] One of the ancient constellations, figured as a man holding a serpent; also called *Serpentarius.*

Ophiuran (ǫ·fi,iū·răn), *a.* and *sb.* 1836. [f. mod.L. *Ophiura*, f. Gr. ὄφις serpent + οὐρά tail, in ref. to the long snake-like arms.] *Zool.* **A.** *adj.* Belonging to the genus *Ophiura*, family *Ophiuridæ*, or class *Ophiuroidea* of echinoderms. **B.** *sb.* A starfish of this genus, family, or class; a brittle-star or sand-star. So **O·phiure** (= B); **Ophiu·rid** *a.* and *sb.*; **Ophiu·roid** *a.* and *sb.*

‖**Ophryon** (ǫ·friǫn). 1878. [mod.L., f. Gr. ὀφρύς eyebrow.] *Anat.* That point in the forehead at the middle of the line joining the upper margins of the orbits of the eyes.

Ophthalmia (ǫfþæ·lmiă). late ME. Also †**Ophthalmy** (1543–1865). [late L. (Boethius), a. Gr. ὀφθαλμία, f. ὀφθαλμός eye.] *Path.* Inflammation of the eye, esp. of the conjunctiva of the eye; ophthalmitis.

Ophthalmic (ǫfþæ·lmik), *a.* and *sb.* 1605. [ad. L. *ophthalmicus*, a. Gr. ὀφθαλμικός of or pertaining to the eye, f. ὀφθαλμός eye; see -IC.] **A.** *adj.* **1.** Pertaining or relating to the eye, ocular; connected with the eye, as a nerve, etc.; affecting the eye, as a disease 1727. **2.** Good for diseases of the eye; that treats such maladies; that performs, or is used for, operations on the eye 1605. **3.** Affected with ophthalmia 1845.

1. The o. artery 1831. 2. A competent o. surgeon 1871.

B. *sb.* (the adj. used absol.) **1.** A medicine or remedy for diseases of the eye 1653. **2.** The ophthalmic or orbital nerve 1727.

Ophthalmite (ǫfþæ·lməit). 1877. [f. Gr. ὀφθαλμός + -ITE [1] 3.] *Zool.* The stalk on which the eye is borne in podophthalmous Crustacea; the ophthalmic peduncle, eye-stalk.

Ophthalmitis (ǫfþælməi·tis). 1822. [mod. L., f. Gr. ὀφθαλμός + -ITIS.] Inflammation of the eye, ophthalmia; *spec.* inflammation involving all the structures of the eye.

Ophthalmo- (ǫfþæ·lmo), comb. form of Gr. ὀφθαλμός eye. See Main words.

Ophthalmology (ǫfþælmǫ·lŏdʒi). 1842. [See above and -LOGY.] The scientific study of the structure, functions, and affections of the eye. So **Ophthalmolo·gical** *a.*, **-ly** *adv.* 1839. **Ophthalmo·logist** 1834.

Ophthalmometer (ǫfþælmǫ·mĭtəɹ). 1864. [See above and -METER.] An instrument devised by Helmholtz for measuring the curvatures of the (living) eye by means of images reflected in it. So **Ophthalmome·tric** *a.* relating to ophthalmometry. **Ophthalmo·metry**, measurement of the eye.

Ophthalmoscope (ǫfþæ·lmoskoup). 1857. [See above and -SCOPE.] An instrument for inspecting the interior of the eye, esp. the retina. So **Ophthalmosco·pic, -al** *adjs.* of or pertaining to the o. or its use; **-ly** *adv.*

Ophthalmoscopy (ǫfþælmǫ·skŏpi). 1730. [See above and -SCOPY.] †**1.** A branch of physiognomy, by which character is inferred from the appearance of the eyes –1828. **2.** Inspection of the interior of the eye; the use of the ophthalmoscope 1864.

Opiane. [f. OPIUM + *-ane* as var. of *-ine.*] Obs. synonym of narcotine. Hence chemical terms in *opian-*: **Opia·nic** *a.*, formed from narcotine; as in *o. acid* ($C_{10}H_{10}O_5$), *o. ether* ($C_{10}H_9 . C_2H_5 . O_5$). **O·pianyl** $C_{10}H_9O_4$, the radical of opianic acid and its derivs.

Opiate (ōu·piĕt), *a.* and *sb.* 1543. [ad. med. L. *opiatus*, *-um*; see next.] **A.** *adj.* Made with or containing opium; hence, inducing sleep; narcotic, soporiferous. **b.** *fig.* Inducing drowsiness or inaction 1626.

The Pastoral Reed Of Hermes, or his o. Rod MILT.

B. *sb.* Any medicine containing opium and having the quality of inducing sleep; a narcotic. *fig.* [He] began to lull my conscience with the opiates of irreligion JOHNSON.

Opiate (ōu·pieˈt), *v.* 1611. [f. prec.; see -ATE [3].] **1.** *trans.* To stupefy or put to sleep by means of opium; to narcotize. **b.** *fig.* To dull the sense or sensibility of 1762. **2.** To mix or impregnate with opium. Chiefly in **Opiated** *ppl. a.* 1611.

Opinable (opəi·năb'l, †ǫ·pinăb'l), *a.* Now *rare* or *Obs.* 1456. [ad. L. *opinabilis*, f. *opinari* to OPINE; see -BLE.] †**1.** That is a matter of opinion; disputable –1546. **2.** Capable of being opined or held as an opinion 1603.

†**Opi·native**, *a.* 1530. [ad. late and med.L. *opinativus*, f. L. *opinat-* ppl. stem; see -IVE.] **1.** Opinionative –1660. **2.** Conjectural –1829.

Opine (opəi·n), *v.* 1557. [ad. L. *opinari* (also *-are*).] **1.** *intr.* or with *obj. cl.*: To express an opinion; to say that one thinks (so and so) 1598. **b.** *esp.* To express a formal opinion, *e.g.* in council, etc. Now *rare.* 1557. **2.** To hold an opinion, or to hold as one's opinion; to think, suppose. **a.** *trans.* (usu. with *obj. cl.*) 1611. **b.** *intr.* 1656.

1. Mr. Squeers yawned fearfully, and opined that it was high time to go to bed DICKENS. 2. b. You may o. upon everything under the sun M. PATTISON. Hence

O·pinant, Opi·ner, one who opines 1611. †**Opina·tion,** an opinion 1611–1687.

†**Opinia·strous,** *a.* [f. F. *opiniastre* (see OPINIATRE) + -OUS.] Opinionated. MILTON.

Opiniated (ŏpi·ni,eitĕd), *ppl. a.* 1589. [f. stem *opini-* perh. shortened from L. *opinio* OPINION + -ATE² + -ED.] †1. Having a conceited opinion *of* –1719. 2. Opinionated 1597.

Opiniative (ŏpi·niĕtiv), *a.* Now *rare.* 1574. [See OPINIATED and -IVE.] = OPINATIVE 1. Hence **Opi·niative·ly** *adv.*, **-ness.**

†**Opinia·tre, opinia·stre,** *a.* and *sb.* 1591. [a. F. *opiniastre*, later *opiniâtre*, a Rom. formation on L. *opinio*; see -ASTER.] A. *adj.* Opinionated. B. *sb.* An opinionated person 1603. So †**Opinia·tre** *v.* 1652–1777. †**Opinia·trety, -a·strety,** the character of being o. 1619.

Opi·ning, *vbl. sb.* 1656. [f. OPINE *v.* + -ING¹.] The formation or expression of opinion; an opinion, a notion.

Opinion (ŏpi·nyən), *sb.* ME. [a. F., ad. L. *opinionem*, *-io*, f. stem of *opinari*; cf. *oblivion* and see -ION.] 1. What one opines; judgement resting on grounds insufficient for complete demonstration; belief of something as probable or as seeming to one's own mind to be true. (Dist. from *knowledge, conviction*, or *certainty*; occas. = belief.) b. What is generally thought about something. Often qualified by *common, general, public, vulgar.* late ME. 2. (With *an* and *pl.*) What one thinks about a particular thing, subject, or point; a judgement formed; a belief, view, notion. (Sometimes denoting a systematic belief, and then = *conviction.*) ME. 3. The formal statement by an expert or professional man of what he thinks, judges, or advises upon a matter submitted to him; considered advice 1470. 4. Estimation, or an estimate, *of* a person or thing. late ME. b. *spec.* Favourable estimate, esteem. (Now only with neg., or such adjs. as *great.*) 1597. †c. Self-conceit, arrogance, dogmatism; or, in good sense, self-confidence. SHAKS. †5. What is thought of one by others; standing; reputation, repute, character, credit (*of* being so and so, or *of* possessing some quality) –1705. †6. Expectation; apprehension –1658.

1. O. in good men is but knowledge in the making MILT. Phr. *In my o.*, as I think, as it seems to me. *A matter of o.*, a disputable point. b. Nothing is so easily cheated, nor so commonly mistaken, as vulgar O. 1689. This..stupid idol, o. 1753. 2. How long halt ye between two opinions? 1 *Kings* xviii. 21. Dr. Macleod had always the courage of his opinions 1876. Phr. *Pious o.*, a belief commonly accepted, but not enjoined as matter of faith. Hence *transf.*, A belief cherished in the mind, but not insisted on in practice. *To be of o.*, to hold the belief or view; to opine: often with *that*... 3. Barristers in England advise on the law by giving an o. on a case stated 1888. 4. I haue bought Golden Opinions from all sorts of people SHAKS. b. She is a selfish, hypocritical woman, and I have no o. of her JANE AUSTEN. 5. 1 *Hen. IV*, v. iv. 48. Hence †**Opi·nion** *v. trans.*, to hold the opinion, or hold as an opinion; to think, suppose 1555–1839.

†**Opi·nionate,** *a.* 1553. [f. OPINION + -ATE; see -ATE².] 1. Based on opinion, or held in the way of opinion; supposed, fancied –1661. 2. = OPINIONATED 3. –1658.

Opinionate (ŏpi·nyŏneit), *v.* Now *rare.* 1603. [f. L. *opinionem* OPINION + -ATE³.] 1. *trans.* and *intr.* = OPINE *v.* 2. 1621. †2. a. *trans.* To express as a formal opinion. b. *intr.* = OPINE *v.* 1. –1677. 3. *refl.* To become or be opinionated or obstinate. *Obs.* exc. in pa. pple.; see next. 1603.

Opinionated (ŏpi·nyŏneitĕd), *ppl. a.* 1601. [Extended f. OPINIATED; cf. next.] †1. = OPINIONED 1. –1645 †2. Possessed of a particular (*esp.* a favourable) opinion *of* –1739. 3. Thinking too highly of one's opinion; conceited or obstinate in opinion 1601. b. Obstinate, self-willed (in general sense) 1649.

Opinionative (ŏpi·nyŏneitiv), *a.* 1547. [Extended f. OPINIATIVE, after *opinion.* †1. = OPINIONATE *a.* 1. –1702. b. Relating to, or consisting in, opinion; doctrinal (as dist. from *practical*) 1638. 2. = OPINIONATE *a.* 2. 1547. So **Opi·niona·tive·ly** *adv.*, **-ness.**

Opinioned (ŏpi·nyənd), *a.* Now *rare.* 1584. [f. OPINION *sb.* + -ED.] 1. Having a (specified) opinion; holding the opinion, or of opinion (*that*..). Also in comb., as *ill-o.* 2. Thinking highly *of* oneself or one's own qualities, conceited *of* 1612. 3. Opinionated 1649.

2. He 's so opinion'd of his own Abilities, that he is ever designing somewhat DRYDEN.

Opinionist (ŏpi·nyənist). 1623. [f. as prec. + -IST.] †1. A holder of some peculiar opinion; a sectary, a faddist –1760. b. *Ch. Hist.* One of a 15th c. sect who held that only those Popes who practised voluntary poverty were true vicars of Christ 1693. 2. The holder of any specified opinion 1630.

Opisometer (ǫpisǫ·mĭtəɪ). 1872. [f. Gr. ὀπίσω backwards + μέτρον measure.] An instrument for measuring curved lines, as on a map, consisting of a small wheel turning on a screw fixed in a rod or frame.

Opistho- (opi·sþo), bef. a vowel **opisth-**, comb. form of Gr. ὄπισθεν behind, as in **Opisthoglyphic** (-gli·fik), **Opisthoglyphous** (-ǫ·glifəs) [f. mod.L. *Opisthoglyphia* neut. pl., f. Gr. γλυφή carving], *adjs. Zool.* belonging to the division *Opisthoglyphia* of snakes, having grooves on the posterior teeth. **Opisthomous** (-ōᵘ·məs) [f. mod.L. *Opisthomi* (pl.), f. Gr. ὦμος shoulder], *a. Ichthyol.* belonging to the division *Opisthomi* of teleostean fishes, having the scapular arch separate from the skull. **Opisthopulmonate** (-pɒ·lmŏnĕt) [L. *pulmo, pulmon-* lung], *a. Zool.* applied to those pulmonate or air-breathing gastropod molluscs which have the pulmonary sac behind the heart.

Opisthobranchiate (-bræ·ŋki,ĕt), *a.* (*sb.*) 1854. [ad. mod.L. *Opisthobranchiata* = *Opisthobranchia*; see prec.] *Zool.* Belonging to the order *Opisthobranchiata* or *Opisthobranchia* of gastropod molluscs, comprising aquatic forms having the gills behind the heart. b. *sb.* An opisthobranchiate gastropod. So **Opi·sthobranch** (-bræŋk), in same senses 1851.

Opisthocœlous (-sī·ləs), *a.* 1872. [f. OPISTHO- + Gr. κοῖλος hollow + -OUS.] *Comp. Anat.* Applied to vertebræ the bodies of which are concave posteriorly; dist. from *procœlous* and *amphicœlous.* Also **Opisthocœlian** (-sī·liăn), *a.*; and as *sb.* 1854.

‖**Opistho·domos.** 1706. [Gr., f. ὀπισθο- behind + δόμος house.] *Gr. Antiq.* An apartment at the back of an ancient Greek temple, corresponding to the vestibule in front.

Opisthograph (ǫpi·sþograf), *sb.* (*a.*) 1623. [ad. Gr. ὀπισθόγραφος; see OPISTHO- and -GRAPH.] *Gr.* and *Rom. Antiq.* A manuscript written on the back as well as the front of the papyrus or parchment; also, a slab inscribed on both sides. b. *adj.* = *Opisthographic.* So **Opisthogra·phic, -al** *adjs.* written or inscribed upon the back as well as the front. **Opistho·graphy,** the practice of writing on both sides; *concr.* writing of this kind.

Opisthotic (ǫpisþǫ·tik, -ōᵘtik), *a.* (*sb.*) 1870. [f. OPISTH(O- + Gr. οὖς, ὠτ- ear.] *Comp. Anat.* Epithet of one of the otic or periotic bones, situated at the back of the ear; in mammals, fused with the other otic bones, and forming that part of the petrosal bone which contains the auditory chamber. b. *sb.* The opisthotic bone.

‖**Opisthotonos** (ǫpisþǫ·tŏnǫs). Also **-us.** 1657. [Gr., f. OPISTHO- + -τονος stretched, τείνειν to stretch.] *Path.* Spasm of the muscles of the neck, back, and legs, in which the body is bent backwards; a form of tetanus. So **Opisthoto·nic** *a.* 1623.

Opium (ōᵘ·piŏm), *sb.* late ME. [a. L., a. Gr. ὄπιον 'poppy juice, opium', dim. of ὀπός vegetable juice.] The inspissated juice of a species of poppy (*Papaver somniferum*), obtained from the unripe capsules by incision and spontaneous evaporation, of a reddish-brown colour, heavy smell, and bitter taste; valuable as a sedative and narcotic drug, and much used as a stimulant and intoxicant, esp. in the East.

fig. There is no antidote against the O. of time SIR T. BROWNE.

Comb.: **o. den,** a public room, of low or mean character, kept as a resort of opium-smokers; **o. habit,** the habit of eating or smoking o. as a stimulant or intoxicant; **o. plant, o. poppy,** the white poppy. Hence **O·pium** *v. trans.* to treat with o.

‖**Opobalsamum** (ǫpobæ·lsămŏm). late ME. Also anglicized **Opoba·lsam.** [L., a. Gr. ὀποβάλσαμον, f. ὀπός juice + βάλσαμον the balsam-tree.] The balsam or oleoresin called Balm of Gilead or Balm of Mecca; see BALM *sb.* b. The tree producing this, a species of *Balsamodendron* 1737.

Opodeldoc (ǫpŏde·ldǫk). 1656. [Believed to have been coined by Paracelsus (*a* 1541); perh. containing Gr. ὀπός- vegetable juice.] †1. *orig.* The name used by Paracelsus for medical plasters of various kinds –1733. 2. Now applied to various kinds of soap liniment; *esp.* to that (*Linimentum saponis*) of the British Pharmacopœia, a solution of soap in alcohol, with camphor, oils of origanum, and rosemary added 1733.

-opolis, comb. form of -POLIS, Gr. πόλις city.

Opopanax (ǫpǫ·pănæks). late ME. [a. L., a. Gr. ὀπόπαναξ, f. ὀπός juice + πάναξ (also πανακές, neut. of πανακής adj. all-healing), name of a plant.] 1. A fetid gum-resin obtained from the root of *Opopanax Chironium*; formerly of repute in medicine. 2. In *Perfumery*, applied to a gum-resin obtained from *Balsamodendron Kataf* 1895. 3. Short for *Opopanax-tree.*

attrib. and *Comb.*, as **o. soap,** soap perfumed with o. (sense 2); **o.-tree** (*Acacia Farnesiana*), the Sponge-tree of the Southern U.S., West Indies, etc.

Oporto (wine): see PORT *sb.*⁶

Opossum (ŏpǫ·sŏm). 1610. [Amer. Indian name in Virginia.] 1. General name of the small marsupial mammals of the American family *Didelphyidæ*, mostly arboreal, some (genus *Chironectes*) aquatic, of nocturnal habits, with an opposable thumb on the hind foot, and tail usu. prehensile; esp. *Didelphys virginiana*, the common opossum of the U.S. (Colloq. shortened to POSSUM, q.v.) 2. Extended to various small or moderate-sized marsupials; *esp.* the common name in Australia and Tasmania of those of the sub-family *Phalangistinæ*, more properly called Phalangers 1777.

attrib. and *Comb.*, as **o.-mouse,** the Pygmy Flying Phalanger of Australia; **-shrimp,** a shrimp of the genus *Mysis* or family *Mysidæ*, so called from the brood-pouch in which the female carries her eggs.

Oppidan (ǫ·pidăn), *a.* and *sb.* 1540. [ad. L. *oppidanus* belonging to a town (other than Rome); as sb., a townsman, f. *oppidum* town.] A. *adj.* Of or belonging to a town, or to the town (as opp. to the country); civic; urban 1643. †b. Pertaining to a university town, as opp. to the university itself –1831. B. *sb.* 1. An inhabitant of a town 1540. †2. A 'townsman', as opp. to a 'gownsman'; also, a student not resident in a college –1696. 3. At Eton College: A student not on the foundation (who boards in the town); dist. from *colleger* 1557.

†**Oppi·gnorate, oppi·gnerate,** *v.* 1622. [f. ppl. stem of L. *oppignorare, -erare* to pledge.] *trans.* To pawn, pledge –1857.

Oppilate (ǫ·pileit), *v.* 1547. [f. ppl. stem of L. *oppilare* to stop up, f. *ob-* OB- 1 + *pilare* to ram down.] *trans.* To stop or block up, obstruct. So **Oppila·tion,** the action of stopping up or obstructing, or condition of being obstructed; an obstruction. **O·ppilative** *a.* obstructive, constipating.

†**Oppo·ne,** *v.* 1513. [ad. L. *opponere* to set against, f. *ob-* OB- 2 + *ponere* to place.] = OPPOSE –1671.

Opponency (ŏpōᵘ·nĕnsi). 1727. [f. next; see -ENCY.] 1. Antagonism, opposition. 2. The action or position of the opponent in an academical disputation as an exercise for a degree. *Obs.* exc. *Hist.* 1730.

Opponent (ŏpōᵘ·nĕnt), *a.* and *sb.* 1536. [ad. L. *opponentem, opponere*; see OPPONE, OPPOSE *v.*] A. *adj.* 1. Standing over against; opposing 1728. 2. Antagonistic, adverse, contrary, opposed. Const. *to*, †*against.* 1647. 3. *Anat.* Said of a muscle (*opponens*) of the hand in man and some quadrumana, which opposes a lateral digit to one of the other digits. Also of the digit itself. 1842. B. *sb.* 1. One who maintains a contrary argument in a disputation; correl. to *respondent. Obs.* exc. *Hist.* 1536. 2. An antagonist, adversary 1615.

2. I had already run my o. through the sword arm LYTTON.

Opportune (ǫ·pǫ̆ɹtiūn, ǫpǫ̆ɹtiū·n), *a.* late ME. [a. F. *opportun, -une* seasonable, timely; ad. L. *opportunus*, f. *ob-* OB-: cf. *Portunus* the protecting god of harbours, f. *portus* harbour, PORT, and *importunus* IMPORTUNE.] 1. Adapted to an end or purpose or the circumstances of the case; fit, suitable, appropriate; convenient. 2. Of an event, action, or thing: Fitting in regard to time or circumstances, seasonable; now chiefly, Timely, well-timed. late ME. †3. Advantageous, useful –1658.

1. *Temp.* IV. i. 26. 2. Most o. to her neede, I haue A Vessell rides fast by SHAKS. 3. It is o. to look back upon old Times, and contemplate our Forefathers SIR T. BROWNE. Hence **Opportune-ly** *adv.* late ME., **-ness** 1727.

Opportunism (ǫ·pǫ̆ɹtiuniz'm, ǫpǫ̆ɹtiū·niz'm). 1870. [f. prec., after It. *opportunismo*, F. *opportunisme*; see -ISM.] In politics, the policy of doing what is presently expedient, as opp. to rigid adherence to party principles; often used to imply sacrifice of principles or an undue spirit of accommodation to present circumstances. So **O·pportunist**, one who professes or practises o.; also *attrib.*

Opportunity (ǫpǫ̆ɹtiū·nĭti). late ME. [a. F. *opportunité*, ad. L. *opportunitas*, f. *opportunus* OPPORTUNE; see -ITY.] 1. The quality or fact of being opportune; timeliness, opportuneness. Now chiefly with ref. to the L. phrase 'felix opportunitate mortis'. 1531. 2. A time, juncture, or condition of things favourable to an end or purpose; occasion, chance. late ME. †3. Convenience or advantageousness of site or position –1781.

1. A death which, for its swiftness and its o., he might well have desired PATER. 2. I am not a little pleased with the O. of running over all the Papers STEELE. In national history o. is as powerful as purpose STUBBS. 3. Hull, a town of great strength and opportunitie both to sea and land affaires MILT.

Opposable (ǫ̆pōᵘ·zăb'l), *a.* 1667. [f. OPPOSE *v.* + -ABLE.] 1. Capable of being opposed, withstood, or placed in opposition *to* (*rare*). 2. Of a digit, esp. the thumb: Capable of being opposed to, or applied so as to meet, another 1833. Hence **Opposabi·lity**, o. quality. 1863.

Oppose (ǫ̆pōᵘ·z), *v.* late ME. [a. F. *opposer*, f. L. *ob-* OB- 2 + *poser* to place, taken as representing L. *ponere* (see POSE *v.*[1]). Repl. OPPONE *c* 1600.] I. ME. uses. †1. *trans.* = APPOSE *v.*[1] 1. –1607. 2. *absol.* and *intr.* To put objections or hard questions. *Obs.* exc. *Hist.* late ME.

II. Modern uses. 1. *trans.* To set (a thing) over against, place directly before or in front. Const. *to*, †*against.* 1593. †b. To expose, subject –1605. 2. To contrast; to put in rhetorical or ideal opposition (*to*) 1579. 3. To set (something) against by way of hindrance, check, or resistance; to place as an obstacle; also, to set or place (a person) as an antagonist 1596. †4. *refl.* and *intr.* To set oneself in opposition, contend *against*, act in opposition *to* –1717. 5. *trans.* To stand or lie over against (something); to look towards, face, front. Now *rare.* 1608. 6. To set oneself against (a person or thing); to withstand, resist, combat; to stand in the way of, obstruct 1596. Also *absol.* b. To contest. SHELLEY.

1. Her Grace sate downe..opposing freely The Beauty of her Person to the People SHAKS. b. *Lear* IV. vii. 32. 2. Memory and imagination, though we sometimes o. them, are nearly allied JOWETT. 3. I do o. My patience to his fury SHAKS. 6. The world does not o. religion as such J. H. NEWMAN. *absol.* Or to take Armes against a Sea of troubles, And by opposing end them SHAKS. Hence **Oppo·seless** *a. poet.* and *rhet.*, not to be opposed, irresistible 1605.

Opposer (ǫ̆pōᵘ·zəɹ). 1483. [f. OPPOSE *v.* + -ER[1].] 1. One who 'opposes' the defender of a thesis in an academical disputation. *Obs.* exc. *Hist.* 2. = OPPONENT B. 2. 1601.

Opposing (ǫ̆pōᵘ·ziŋ), *ppl. a.* 1608. [f. OPPOSE *v.* + -ING[2].] That opposes.

As up the o. hills they slowly creep WORDSW. All these parts of our constitution..are balanced as o. interests BURKE.

Opposite (ǫ·pŏzit), *a.*, *sb.* (*adv.*, *prep.*) late ME. [a. F., ad. L. *oppositus*, pa. pple. of *opponere*.] A. *adj.* 1. Placed or lying over against something on the other or farther side of an intervening line, space, or thing; contrary in position. Const. *to*, *from*, †*against.* b. *Bot.* (*a*) Situated in pairs on opposite sides of an axis or intervening body, as leaves on a stem; (*b*) Situated in front of an organ so as to come between it and its axis, as a stamen in front of a sepal or petal. Opp. to *alternate.* 1707. 2. Turned or moving the other way; contrary, reverse 1594. 3. Contrary in nature, character, or tendency. Const. *to*, *from.* 1580. b. With *the*: that is opposed to something else; the contrary, the other (of two related things of different character.) 1638. †4. Antagonistic, adverse, hostile. Const. *to*, *against.* –1737.

1. At the o. side of the glacier was the Aiguille Verte TYNDALL. *O. number*, either of two persons or things who occupy corresponding positions in parallel bodies, enterprises, etc. 2. We started in o. directions (*mod.*). 3. Self love takes a clean o. way, from that of charity 1650. b. The o. Sex ADDISON. 4. Be o. with a kinsman, surly with seruants SHAKS.

B. *sb.* [The adj. used *absol.*] †1. = Opposite point, esp. of the heavens –1604. †b. Opposite aspect. MILT. 2. That which is opposite; an object, fact, or quality, that is the reverse of something else; often in *pl.*, things the most different of their kind 1549. b. *Logic.* An opposite term or proposition; †a contrary argument 1588. 3. An antagonist, adversary, opponent. Now *rare* or *Obs.* late ME.

2. The most extreme opposites have some qualities in common JOWETT. 3. The opposites of this day's strife SHAKS.

C. *adv.* In an opposite position or direction 1817.

Several hon. gentlemen sat o. (*mod.*).

D. *prep.* [*ellipt.* for *o. to.*] Over against; facing or fronting on the other side 1758.

We knelt down o. each other LANDOR. Hence **O·pposite-ly** *adv.*, **-ness.**

Oppo·siti-, comb. form of L. *oppositus* opposite, used chiefly in botanical adjs., as **Opposítifo·lious**, (*a*) having opposite leaves, (*b*) situated opposite a leaf (as a peduncle or tendril). **Oppositipe·talous**, **Oppositise·palous.**

Opposition (ǫpŏzi·ʃən). late ME. [ad. L. *oppositionem*, f. *opponere*; see OPPONE, OPPOSE *v.*] 1. The action of setting opposite or against 1602. b. *spec.* Cf. OPPOSABLE *a.* 2. 1899. 2. Position over against something; opposite situation or direction 1667. 3. *Astrol.* and *Astron.* The relative position of two heavenly bodies when exactly opposite to each other as seen from the earth's surface, their longitude then differing by 180°; *esp.* the position of a heavenly body when opposite to the sun. late ME. 4. The action of placing one thing in contrast with another; the condition of being opposed or contrasted; contrast, contradistinction, antithesis 1581. †b. *Rhet.* A contrast of positions or arguments; a contrary position or argument; a counter-proposition, objection –1678. c. *Logic.* The relation between two propositions which have the same subject and predicate but differ in quantity or quality or both 1697. 5. Contrary or hostile action, antagonism, resistance; the fact or condition of being opposed, hostile, or adverse 1588. †b. Encounter, combat –1655. 6. *concr.* A political party opposed to that in office; *esp.* the party opposed to the administration in the British Parliament or other legislative body 1704. b. *transf.* Any party or body of opponents 1781. 7. *attrib.*, as *o. benches*, *cheer*, *newspaper*, etc. 1801.

1. *Haml.* v. ii. 178. 2. Phr. *In o.* (*to*), facing, fronting. 4. In the English Chronicles..the o. is made between 'French' and 'English' FREEMAN. c. *Contradictory, Contrary, Subcontrary, Subaltern O.*; see these words. 5. A disagreeable man will often dissent from you from the mere love of o. 1868. Phr. *In o.*, in the position of being opposed to the administration; They are in O. and not in office 1895. 6. Hear, hear, from the O., and laughter from the Ministerial benches 1817. Hence **Opposi·tional** *a.* **Opposi·tionist**, one who professes or practises o.; *esp.* a member of the parliamentary o.; also *attrib.* or as *adj.*

Oppositive (ǫ̆pǫ·zĭtiv), *a.* 1622. [f. L. *opposit-*, *opponere* + -IVE.] †1. = OPPOSITE A. 1, 1 b. –1857. 2. Characterized by opposing or contrasting; adversative. So **Oppo·sitive-ly** *adv.*, **-ness.**

Oppress (ǫ̆pre·s), *v.* ME. [a. OF. *oppresser*, ad. med.L. *oppressare*, f. L. *oppress-*, *opprimere*, f. *ob-* OB- 1 + *premere* to press.] 1. *trans.* †To press injuriously upon or against; to press down by force; to crush, trample down, smother, crowd –1781. b. *esp.* To bear down in battle; to overwhelm with numbers. Now *rare.* late ME. c. *fig.* Of sleep, etc.: To overpower, weigh down. (Chiefly *poet.*) 1582. 2. To lie heavy on, weigh down, crush (the feelings, mind, spirits, etc.) late ME. †3. To put down, suppress; to crush, overwhelm (a person); to put an end to (a thing or state of things, feeling, etc.) –1829. †b. To suppress, keep out of sight –1560. 4. To keep under by tyrannical exercise of power; to load or burden with cruel or unjust impositions or restraints; to tyrannize over. late ME. †5. Of an enemy, circumstances, etc.: To bear heavily upon; to reduce to straits; to harass, distress –1611. †6. *trans.* To come upon unexpectedly, take by surprise. (So L. *opprimere.*) –1603. †7. To force, ravish. (So L. *opprimere.*) –1613. 8. *Her.* = DEBRUISE *v.* 2. Chiefly in *pa. pple.* 1572.

1. Fear to put on his hat, lest he should o. his foretop RICHARDSON. b. Opprest with multitudes, he greatly fell ADDISON. c. Until the poppied warmth of sleep oppress'd Her soothed limbs KEATS. 2. The Weary World of Waters between us oppresses the imagination LAMB. 4. The powerful citizens oppressed the weak THIRLWALL. *absol.* That the man of the earth may no more o. *Ps.* x. 18.

Oppression (ǫ̆pre·ʃən). ME. [a. F., ad. L. *oppressionem*, f. *opprimere* to OPPRESS.] 1. The action of oppressing or condition of being oppressed. late ME. 2. The feeling of being oppressed or weighed down; bodily or mental uneasiness or distress. late ME. 3. Exercise of power in a tyrannical manner; cruel treatment of subjects, inferiors, etc.; the imposition of unjust burdens.

1. There gentle sleep..with soft o. seis'd My droused sense MILT. 2. Dreams, Agitations, and Oppressions, that Excess in Diet occasions in the Night 1748. 3. There is not a word in our language which expresses more detestable wickedness than *oppression* 1729.

Oppressive (ǫ̆pre·siv), *a.* 1627. [ad. med. L. *oppressivus*, f. *oppress-*, *opprimere*; see -IVE.] 1. Of the nature of oppression; unjustly burdensome, harsh, or merciless. 2. Characterized by oppressing, disposed to oppress 1712. 3. Having the quality of oppressing or weighing heavily on the mind, spirits, or senses; depressing; overpowering 1712.

1. The o. taxation of the provinces 1861. 2. The yoke of an o. aristocracy 1845. 3. A bright, o., sultry morning LYTTON. Hence **Oppre·ssive-ly** *adv.*, **-ness.**

Oppressor (ǫ̆pre·səɹ). late ME. [a. AF. *oppressour*, F. *oppresseur*, ad. L. *oppressor*, f. *opprimere* to OPPRESS.] 1. One who oppresses; *esp.* one who harasses with unjust or cruel treatment. 2. Anything that oppresses 1723.

1. I have been no avaricious o. of the people BACON.

Opprobrious (ǫ̆prōᵘ·briəs), *a.* late ME. [ad. OF. *ob-*, *opprobrieux*, or late L. *opprobriosus*, f. L. *opprobrium*; see next.] 1. Of words, language: Conveying injurious reproach; contumelious, abusive. Of persons: Using contumelious or abusive language. 2. Associated with disgrace; infamous, shameful. Now *rare.* 1510.

1. The multitude pressed round the King's coach, and insulted him with o. cries MACAULAY. 2. Neither did any thing seeme o. out of which there might arise commoditie and profit HOOKER. Hence **Oppro·brious-ly** *adv.*, **-ness.**

Opprobrium (ǫ̆prōᵘ·briə̆m). 1656. [a. L. *ob-*, *opprobrium*, f. *ob-*, *opprobrare* to reproach, taunt, f. *ob-* OB- 1 + *probrum* infamous act, infamy.] 1. The disgrace attached to conduct considered shameful; the imputation of this disgrace; infamy, reproach 1683. 2. Something that brings disgrace.

1. Great o. has been thrown on her name 1862. 2. That o. of Mankind..who now calls himself our Protector CLARENDON. So †**Oppro·bry** –1795.

Oppugn (ǫ̆piū·n), *v.* late ME. [ad. L. *oppugnare*, f. *ob-* OB- 1 + *pugnare* to fight.] †1. *trans.* To fight against, attack, besiege –1860. 2. *fig.* To call in question (a state of things), controvert (a statement, belief, etc.) 1529. b. Of things: To run counter to. Now *rare.* 1584. c. *intr.* To fight, contend, oppose 1591.

2. Then and afterwards he openly oppugned Popery 1734. b. When Law and Conscience..seem to oppugne one another, the written Law should be preferr'd HOBBES. So **Oppugnance**, **-nancy** (ǫ̆pɒ·g-

nāns, *ǫpv*·gnānsi), opposition, antagonism, conflict. **Oppugnant** (*ǫpv*·gnănt), *a.* opposing, antagonistic, contrary, repugnant. **Oppugna·tion**, attack, assault; opposition; also *fig.* **Oppu·gner** (*ǫpiū*·nəɹ), one who oppugns.

Opsimathy (*ǫ*psi·măþi). *rare.* 1656. [ad. Gr. ὀψιμαθία, f. ὀψιμαθής, f. ὀψι- late + μαθ- to learn.] Learning acquired late. So **O·psimath**, one who begins to learn late in life 1883.

Opsiometer (*ǫ*psi*ǫ*·mītəɹ). 1842. [f. Gr. ὄψις sight + -(O)METER.] = OPTOMETER.

Opsonin (*ǫ*·ps*ŏ*nin). 1903. [Discovered by A. E. Wright and S. R. Douglas (*Proc. Royal Soc.* LXXII. 366); f. Gr. ὀψώνιον victuals, provisions + -IN[1].] A substance present in blood serum which acts upon bacteria so as to render them subject to phagocytosis. Hence **Opso·nic** *a.*, **O·psonize** *v.* to affect by means of opsonins, **-iza·tion.**

Opt (*ǫ*pt), *v.* 1877. [ad. F. *opter*, ad. L. *optare* to choose; cf. *adopt.*] *intr.* To make choice (*between* alternatives); to decide (*for* one of two alternatives).

Optation (*ǫ*ptē·ʃən). 1577. [ad. L. *optationem*, f. *optare* to wish.] The action of wishing; a wish or desire. **b.** *Rhet.* The expression of a wish under the form of an exclam.

Optative (*ǫ*·ptătiv, *ǫ*ptē·tiv). 1530. [a. F. *optatif, -ive*, ad. late L. *optativus*, f. *optare* to wish; see -ATIVE. The first pronunc. is normal, but the second prevails in Eng. schools and colleges.] **A.** *adj.* **1.** *Gram.* Having the function of expressing wish or desire. **2.** Characterized by desire or choice; expressing desire. **B.** *sb. Gram.* The optative mood; an optative form of a verb 1530.

A. 1. *O. mood*: that mood or form of the verb, of which a prominent function is the expression of wish or desire, as in Gr. μὴ γένοιτο, 'may it not happen!' Hence **Optatively** *adv.* in an o. manner or sense, in expression of a wish; in the o. mood.

Optic (*ǫ*·ptik). 1541. [a. F. *optique*, ad. med.L. *opticus*, a. Gr. ὀπτικός of or pertaining to sight, f. ὀπτός seen, visible, f. stem ὀπ- (cf. ὄψομαι I shall see, etc.).] **A.** *adj.* **1.** Of or pertaining to sight; visual. (Now *rare* or *Obs.* in general sense.) 1599. **2.** *Anat.* Pertaining to or connected with the eye as the organ of sight, or with the sense of sight as a function of the brain; esp. in the names of bodily parts or structures. (Also in *Path.* and *Surg.*) 1541. **3.** = OPTICAL 2, 3. *Obs.* or *arch.* 1569. **4.** = OPTICAL 4. Chiefly in the phr. (now *arch.*) *o. glass*, a lens, or an instrument having a lens, esp. a telescope. 1607. **5.** = OPTICAL 2. 1664.

2. O. nerve, the second cranial nerve on each side, which enters the eyeball and terminates in the retina; they are the nerves of the special sense of sight. **O. thalamus,** each of two large masses of nerve-matter in the brain, one on each side of the third ventricle. **4.** The moon, whose orb Through o. glass the Tuscan artist views MILT. **5. O. angle,** (*a*) the angle between the two lines from the extremities of an object to the eye, being the angle under which it is seen, or the visual angle; (*b*) the angle between the optic axes of the eyes when directed to the same object; (*c*) the angle between the optic axes of a biaxial doubly-refracting crystal. **O. axis,** (*a*) the straight line through the centres of the pupil and crystalline lens, the axis of the eye; (*b*) a line in a doubly-refracting crystal such that a ray of light passing in the direction of it suffers no double refraction.

B. *sb.* **1.** The organ of sight, the eye; chiefly in *pl.* (Formerly learned and elegant, afterwards pedantic, now joc.) 1620. †**b.** Short for *optic nerve*; *fig.* visual power -1718. †**2.** An 'optic glass'; an eye-glass, lens, magnifying glass; a microscope or telescope -1800. †**3.** = OPTICIAN 1. -1675. †**4.** The science of sight and light, OPTICS -1869.

Optical (*ǫ*·ptikăl), *a.* 1570. [f. prec. + -AL.] **1.** Of, pertaining or relating to, the sense of sight; visual; ocular. (Now chiefly in special connexions, e.g. *an o. illusion.*) **2.** Of or pertaining to sight in relation to the physical action of light upon the eye; hence, Pertaining or relating to light, esp. as the medium of sight; belonging to optics 1570. **3.** Treating of, or skilled in, optics 1570. **4.** Constructed to assist the sight; acting by means of sight or light; devised according to the principles of optics 1748.

2. O. axis = *optic axis* (see OPTIC A. 5). **4.** *O. square*, reflecting instrument used by surveyors and others for laying off lines at right angles to each other. Hence **O·ptically** *adv.*

Optician (*ǫ*pti·ʃăn). 1687. [ad. F. *opticien*, f. med.L. *optica* OPTICS; see -ICIAN.] **1.** One versed in optics. Now *rare* or *Obs.* **2.** A maker of or dealer in optical instruments 1737.

O·ptico-, comb. f. Gr. ὀπτικός OPTIC, as in **O.-che·mical** *a.*, relating to optics and chemistry conjointly; **O.-pa·pillary** *a.*, belonging to the optic papilla.

Optics (*ǫ*·ptiks). 1579. [pl. of OPTIC *a.*, used subst. to render med.L. *optica* pl. neut., a. Gr. τὰ ὀπτικά optics; see -ICS.] The science of sight or of the medium of sight, i.e. light; that branch of physics which deals with the properties and phenomena of light. Now always construed as singular.

Optimacy (*ǫ*·ptimăsi). Now *rare.* 1579. [ad. 16th c. L. *optimatia*, f. L. *optimas*, pl. *optimates*; see next and -ACY. Repl. later by *aristocracy*.] **1.** Government, or a government, by the upper classes in a state; aristocracy; also, a state so governed 1594. **2.** The upper classes in a state; the aristocracy.

Optimate (*ǫ*·ptimĕt). 1611. [ad. L. *optimas*, as adj. aristocratic, as sb. pl. *optimates* aristocrats; f. *optimus* best. Chiefly in pl., **optimates** (*ǫ*ptimē·tīz).] A member of the patrician order in Rome; *gen.* a noble or aristocrat.

‖**Optime** (*ǫ*·ptimĭ). 1755. [a. L. adv. = 'best', 'very well', from the phr. *optime disputasti* 'you have disputed very well'.] One who has been placed in the second or third division, called respectively senior and junior optimes, in the Mathematical Tripos at Cambridge.

Optimism (*ǫ*·ptimiz'm). 1759. [a. F. *optimisme* (in mod.L. *optimismus*), f. L. *optimus* best; see -ISM.] **1.** The doctrine propounded by Leibnitz, that the actual world is the 'best of all possible worlds', being chosen by the Creator as that in which most good could be obtained at the cost of the least evil. Also applied to other doctrines of like effect. **b.** Applied to any view which supposes that good must ultimately prevail over evil in the universe 1841. **2.** The character or quality of being for the best 1795. *rare.* **3.** Disposition to hope for the best or to look on the bright side of things under all circumstances 1819.

1. Voltaire's Candide, written to refute the system of o. BOSWELL. **b.** The young reformer's social simplicity, his dreams, his optimisms 1888. **3.** 'Let it be cheerful' said he, with his gay o. 1881.

Optimist (*ǫ*·ptimist), *sb.* (*a.*) 1766. [f. as prec. + -IST.] **1.** One who holds or believes in the metaphysical principle of optimism 1783. **2.** One disposed, under all circumstances, to hope for the best 1766. **B.** *adj.* Optimistic. 1863.

2. I have always observed that good physicians are optimists 1895. **B.** The o. governess..who, when the weather was very bad, was still thankful because it was better than none at all 1865. Hence **Optimi·stic**, **-al** *adjs.* **Optimi·stically** *adv.* So **O·ptimize** *v.*

‖**Optimum** (*ǫ*·ptim*ŏ*m). 1879. [L., neut. of *optimus* best.] *Biol.* That degree or amount of heat, light, food, moisture, etc. most favourable for growth, reproduction, or other vital process. Also *attrib.* Best or most favourable.

Option (*ǫ*·pʃən). 1604. [a. F., ad. L. *optionem*, f. root *op-* of *optare* to choose.] **1.** The action of choosing; choice. Also *transf.* A thing that is or may be chosen. **2.** Power or liberty of choosing; freedom of choice 1633. **3.** The right which an archbishop formerly had on the consecration of a bishop, of choosing one benefice within the see of the latter, to be in his own patronage for the next presentation. (Abolished in 1845.) 1701. **4.** The privilege (acquired on some consideration) of executing or relinquishing, as one may choose, within a specified period a commercial transaction on terms now fixed; esp. that of calling for the delivery (a *call*), or making delivery (a *put*), or both (a *double option*), within a specified time, of some particular stock or produce at a specified price and to a specified amount 1755.

1. Plantation..must proceed from the o. of the people, else it sounds like an exile BACON. **2.** He [Peel] had no o. about accepting [office]—his sovereign sent for him, and he must come 1850. A sentence of imprisonment without the o. of a fine (*mod.*).

Optional (*ǫ*·pʃənăl), *a.* 1765. [f. prec. + -AL.] **1.** That is a matter of choice; depending on choice or preference; not obligatory 1792. **2.** Leaving something to choice.

1. Even this burthen was o., not compulsory 1818. **2.** Original writs are either o. or peremptory BLACKSTONE. **B.** *sb. U.S.* An o. subject of study 1857.

Opto-, from Gr. ὀπτός 'seen, visible', used as comb. form with the notion of 'sight, vision', or 'optic'. See Main words.

Optogram (*ǫ*·pt*ŏ*græm). 1878. [f. OPTO- + -GRAM.] Kühne's term for the image formed on the retina by the action of light, which may be rendered permanent by chemical means.

Optologist (*ǫ*pt*ǫ*·lŏdʒist). 1903. [f. OPTO- + -LOGIST.] A sight-testing optician. So **Opto·logy**, **Optolo·gical** *a.*

Optometer (*ǫ*pt*ǫ*·mītəɹ). 1738. [f. OPTO- + -METER.] A name of various instruments for testing vision; *esp.* one for measuring the refractive power of the eye and thus testing long- or short-sightedness. Hence **Opto·metrist**, **Opto·metry.**

Optophone (*ǫ*·ptofoᵘn). 1923. [f. OPTO- + Gr. φωνή sound.] An instrument to enable the blind to read printed type by the medium of sound.

Opulence (*ǫ*·piŭlĕns). 1510. [ad. L. *opulentia*; see OPULENT and -ENCE.] Wealth, riches, affluence. Also *transf.* and *fig.*

Opulent (*ǫ*·piŭlĕnt), *a.* 1601. [ad. L. *opulens, -entem* or *opulentus*, f. *ops, opem* power, might, resources, wealth; see -ULENT.] **1.** Rich, wealthy, affluent. **b.** Yielding great wealth 1664. **2.** *transf.* and *fig.* Rich in some respect: **a.** in mental wealth; **b.** in material possessions; **c.** in physical development; plump [from Fr.]. 1791. **3.** Of flowers, etc.: Rich in blossom, tint, or fragrance; splendid 1863.

1. I shall be strangely unfortunate if I meet not with some o. widow 1704. **2.** Her braided o. hair 1863. **3.** Or beast or bird or fish, or o. flower TENNYSON. Hence **O·pulent-ly** *adv.*

‖**Opuntia** (opv·nʃiă). 1601. [L. *Opuntia* (sc. *herba*), a plant growing about the Locrian city Opus (acc. *Opuntem*) in Greece; taken as a generic name.] A large genus of cactaceous plants; also, the fruit of a plant of this genus; the Prickly Pear or Indian Fig.

‖**Opus** (*ǫ*·p*ŏ*s, ōᵘ·p*ŏ*s). 1809. [L. *opus* work, pl. *opera.*] A work, a composition; *esp.* a musical composition or set of compositions as numbered among the works of a composer in order of publication. Abbrev. *Op.*

O. magnum or *magnum o.*: a L. expression signifying 'great work', frequent in Eng. use, esp. in ref. to a large or important literary work.

Opuscule (opv·skiul). 1656. [a. F., ad. L. *opusculum*, dim. of *opus* work; see -CULE.] A small work; esp. a literary or musical work of small size. var. ‖ **Opu·sculum** (pl. **-ula**).

Or (*ǭ*ɹ), *sb.* 1562. [a. F.:— L. *aurum.*] *Her.* The tincture gold or yellow in armorial bearings. **b.** *Or moulu, or molu*; see ORMOLU.

Or (*ǭ*ɹ, *ǫ*ɹ). *adv.*[1] (*prep.*, *conj.*[1]) *arch.* and *dial.* [OE. *ār* adv. 'early'; see ERE. But in all the uses exc. A. 1 the sense is that of the comparative, OE. *ǣr* earlier, sooner, before.] †**A.** *adv.* **I.** As a positive. Early; = AIR *adv.* 2, ERE A. 1. -ME. **II.** As comparative. **1.** Earlier, sooner; = ERE A. 2. ME. only. **2.** Formerly, before; = AIR *adv.* 1, ERE A. 4. -1500.

B. *prep.* **1.** Before (in time); = ERE B. 1. ME. **b.** Confused with the conjunctive *or ere* (C. 1 d) for *or e'er, or ever*, but used simply as = ere, before 1629. **2.** Bef. an adv. of time taken subst., as *long, now*, etc., forming an advb. phrase; = ERE B. 2. 1450.

1. To dye or their day 1509. **b.** The Shepherds on the Lawn, Or ere the point of dawn, Sate simply chatting in a rustick row MILTON.

C. *conj.* (or *conjunctive adv.*). **1.** Of time: Before. †**a.** in conjunctional phrases *or than, or that*; see ERE C. 1 -1721. **b.** *Or* alone, in same sense ME. **c.** with the addition of *ever, e'er* (adding emphasis). late ME. **d.** *Or ere*, for *or e'er*, or ever; see B. 1 b. 1568. **2.** Of preference: Sooner than; = ERE C. 2. ME.

1. b. Wil you drink or you go, or wil you go or you drinke? 1553. **c.** Thou accursed Spirit! damned or ever thou wert born! WESLEY. **d.** *Lear* II. iv. 288.

Or (*ǭ*ɹ, *ǫ*ɹ) *conj.*[2] (*adv.*[2]) ME. [Reduced form of the obs. OTHER *conj.* *Or* is properly the conjunction, not the associated adv. (see sense 2), which continued to be *other*, or *outher*, = mod. Eng. *either* (in *either . . or*), though *or . . or* also occurs.] **1.** *gen.* A particle co-ordinating two (or more) words, phrases, or clauses, between which there is an alternative. **b.** When singular subjects (sb. or pron.) are co-ordinated by *or*, the tendency is for the vb. and following pronouns to be plural, when the mutual exclusion of the singular subjects is not emphasized 1601. **2.** The alternative expressed by *or* is emphasized by prefixing to the first member, or adding after the last, the associated adv. EITHER, formerly OTHER or OUTHER ME. ¶**b.** For *or* occurring after *neither*, see these words and *nor* 1523. **c.** *Or* is used after *whether*; see WHETHER ME. **3.** *Or . . or* in the sense of *either . . or* is now poetic ME. †**b.** *Or . . or* occurs with alternative questions; = *whether . . or.* (*Or* alone = 'whether' is rare, prob. repr. L. *an.*) -1734. **4.** After a primary statement or an exhortation, *or* appends a secondary alternative; = otherwise, else; in any other case; if not ME. **5.** *Or else* (also formerly *orels*): = or if not, or otherwise; = sense 4; see ELSE 4. ME. **6.** *Or* connects two words denoting the same thing: = otherwise called, that is (= L. *vel, sive*) ME.

1. Did you send a verbal or a written message? 1776. A vine or two 1861. You may walk ten or even twelve miles without finding one (*mod.*). **b.** If Tintoret or Giorgione are at hand RUSKIN. Mr. Darwin or Barnum would claim him as their own 1874. **2.** You may take either the medal or its value (*mod.*). **b.** An horse that had neither good eyes or feet 1691. **3.** Or let us glory gain, or glory give POPE. **b.** Tell me where is fancie bred, Or in the heart, or in the head SHAKS. **4.** Awake, arise, or be for ever fall'n MILT. **6.** The Tame or House Spider 1608.

Or-, *pref.*, freq. in OE., and occas. in ME., now surviving in ORDEAL, and perh. in ORT. OE. *or-* was the stressed form, corresp. to Goth. *us-, ur-*, ON. *ór-, ör-*, G. *ur-*, etc., orig. an adv. and prep., meaning 'out'.

-or, a termination of words, and form of various suffixes, of L. origin.

In AF. the sound arising from Latin *ō* became (*ū*) and came *c* 1300 to be written *ou* (*onour*). The earliest adopted words in ME. had *o* or *u* (*onor, onur*), but the regular representation after 1300 was with *ou* (*onour, honour*). At the Renaissance, many of the *-our* words were conformed to the L. in *-or*; and nearly all words taken then or later from L. were spelt *-or*. In Great Britain *-our* is still written in many of the words left unchanged in the 16th c., but American usage favours *-or* in all.

1. -or (formerly often *-our*), repr. ultimately L. *-or, -orem*, in nouns of condition derived from verbal stems, as *error, horror, liquor, tenor, torpor, tremor*, etc.

2. -or (formerly often *-our*), repr. L. *-or, -orem* of agent-nouns, formed on stems identical with the supine stems of vbs. Of these there are: **a.** Those repr. L. agent-nouns other than those in *-ātor, -ētor, -itor, -ītor*; as *actor, author, confessor, doctor, inventor, tutor*, etc. **b.** Agent-nouns in L. *-ātor, -ētor, -itor, -ītor* were regularly reduced from *-ātōrem*, etc., through *-edor* to OF. *-eör, -eür*, AF. *-eour*, which became in ME. *-our*, and in F. *-eur*, and thus fell together with those from simple *-orem* in **a.** Such are *conqueror, donor, emperor* (*imperatorem*), *juror, solicitor, vendor*, etc. Also, *saviour* (AF. *sauveöur* :—OF. *salveör, salvedor*, L. *salvatorem*), which has preserved the vowel bef. *-our*. Similar are agent-nouns formed in Fr. or AF. on the vb. stem, as *purveyor, surveyor, tailor, warrior* (AF. *werreyour*, f. *werreier* to war). **c.** Agent-nouns in *-ātor, -ētor, -itor, -ītor, -ūtor*, adopted in later times in Fr., or in Eng., retain *t*, appearing in Fr. as *-ateur, -iteur*, etc., and have now in Eng. the same written form as in L., e. g. *administrator, creator, creditor*, etc. Some of these, from OF. or AF., had formerly *-our*, as *creatour, creditour*, etc.; others of later formation, immed. from L., have had the *-or* form from the first. **d. -or** is sometimes an alteration of another suffix, as of L. *-arius*, F. *-ier*, AF. *-er*, in *bachelor, chancellor*, or of Eng. *-er* :—OE. *-ere*, in *sailor*. The frequent occurrence of ME. *-our*, mod. *-or*, in legal terms denoting the person acting, as opp. to the person acted upon in *-é, -ee*, e. g. *lessor, lessee*, has given it a kind of professional character; cf. *sailor, sailer*.

3. -or (-our) sometimes represents F. *-oir*, as *manor*, OF. *manoir, maneir*, L. *manere*; *mirror*, F. *miroir*, L. **miratorium*; *parlour*, F. *parloir*, L. **parabolatorium*.

4. -or, repr. ME. = AF. *-our*, F. *-eur*, L. *-or, -orem*, a var. of *-ior*, suffix of the comparative degree of adjs., in *major, minor*. See -IOR.

Ora[1] (ōᵊ·ră). [OE., app. ad. ON. *aurar* pl.; commonly taken as ad. L. *aureus*.] **1.** A Danish money of account, reckoned in Domesday Book as = 20 pence. **2.** A measure of weight, used in Domesday Book for the ounce 1610.

‖**Ora**[2] (ōᵊ·ră). 1826. [L., = border, brim, coast, etc.] *Entom.* The inflexed or inferior lateral margin of the prothorax.

Orach, orache (ǫ·rătʃ). late ME. [Earlier *arache*, a. AF. *arasche*, F. *arroche* = It. *atrepice* :—L. *atriplicem*, nom. *atriplex*, ad. Gr. ἀτράφαξυς, -υς (ἀδρα-, ἀνδράφαξις).] A plant of the genus *Atriplex*, N.O. *Chenopodiaceæ*; esp. the Garden Orach or Mountain Spinach (*A. hortensis*).

Oracle (ǫ·răk'l), *sb.* [ME. *ora·cle*, a. F., ad. L. *oraculum* (*oraclum*), f. *orare*, with suffix *-culo-* of material instrument.] **I. 1.** *Gr.* and *Rom. Antiq.* The agency or medium by which a god was supposed to speak; the mouthpiece of the deity; the place or seat of such agency, at which divine utterances were believed to be given. **2.** A response, often ambiguous or obscure, given usu. by a priest or priestess of a god, at the shrine or seat of the deity 1598.

1. The Oracles are dumm MILT. Phr. *To work the o.*, to influence the agency or medium; to obtain the response desired by influence or manœuvring behind the scenes; also (*slang*), to raise money 1863. **2.** An o. was procured exactly suited to the purpose of the leaders of the expedition THIRLWALL.

II. *transf.* **1.** A vehicle or medium of divine communication. **a.** The holy of holies in the Jewish Temple; also, the mercy-seat within it 1440. **b.** One who or that which expounds or interprets the will of God 1548. **2.** Divine revelation; a message divinely inspired; also, *pl.* the sacred scriptures (from Rom. iii. 2). late ME.

1. a. Sion Hill..and Siloa's Brook that flowd Fast by the O. of God MILT. **b.** In his company Ione the Puzel, whom he used as an o. and a southsaier 1548. **2.** The oracles or sayinges of God 1548.

III. *fig.* **1.** Something reputed to give oracular replies or advice 1625. **b.** Something regarded as an infallible guide or indicator, esp. when its action is mysterious, as a chronometer, a compass 1726. **2.** A person reputed or affecting to be infallible 1596. **3.** A wise utterance; an authoritative and infallible declaration; undeniable truth 1569. **4.** A prognostication 1596.

1. b. He called it [a watch] his o., and said it pointed out the time for every action of his life SWIFT. **2.** I am sir O., And when I ope my lips, let no dog barke SHAKS. **3.** His Words were received as Oracles 1701. Hence **O·racle** *v. trans.* to utter as an o., *intr.* to speak as an o.

Oracular (ŏræ·kiŭlăɹ), *a.* 1631. [f. L. *oraculum* + -AR.] **1.** Of or pertaining to an oracle; that is the seat or medium of an oracle, or of direct divine communications 1678. **2.** Of the nature of an oracle 1631. **b.** Mysterious, ambiguous, or sententious, like the ancient oracles 1736. **c.** Ominous, portentous 1820. **3.** Of a person: That delivers oracular responses; also *transf.* 1821. **4.** Delivered, uttered, or decreed by an oracle 1820.

2. Whatever he said or wrote was considered as o. by his disciples MACAULAY. **b.** He opened his lips, with an o. shake of the head 1845. **3.** The o. press lays down the law 1863. Hence **Ora·cular·ly** *adv.*, **-ness.**

Oraculous (ŏræ·kiŭləs), *a.* Now *rare* or *Obs.* 1610. [f. as prec. + -OUS.] = ORACULAR.

Urim and Thummim, those o. gems On Aaron's breast MILT. He grows on a sudden o. and infallible JOHNSON. Hence **Ora·culous·ly** *adv.*, **-ness.**

Oraison, obs. f. ORISON.

Oral (ōᵊ·răl), *a.* (*sb.*) 1625. [f. L. *os, or-* mouth + -AL.] **1.** Uttered in spoken words; transacted by word of mouth: spoken, verbal 1628. **2.** Using speech only, *esp.* for the instruction of the deaf and dumb 1870. **3.** Of or pertaining to the mouth 1656. **4.** Done or performed with the mouth, as the organ of eating and drinking 1625. **B.** *sb.* Short for *oral examination, sound*, etc. 1876.

1. As for orall Traditions, what certaintie can there be in them? BP. HALL. **2.** An o. school 1880. **3.** *O. cavity*, (*a*) the cavity of the mouth; (*b*) in haustellate insects, the hollow on the lower surface of the head, from which the haustellum or sucking-mouth protrudes. **b.** *Phonetics.* Uttered through the mouth, with the nasal passage closed. **4.** The orall eating and drinking of Christ in the Sacrament 1625. **B.** The Orals, short or long, in Feel, Fill, Tulle, Full, Fool 1887. So **O·ralism**, the instruction of deaf-mutes by 'lip-language' 1883. **O·ralist** 1867. **O·rally** *adv.*, by, through, or with the mouth 1608.

Orang (ŏræ·ŋ). 1778. = ORANG-OUTANG.

Orange (ǫ·rĕndʒ), *sb.*[1], *a.* [ME. *orenge, orange*, a. OF., f. (ult.) Arab. *nāranj*, in Pers. *nārang*; cf. Pers. *nār* pomegranate. The initial *n* in Fr. and Eng. was app. absorbed in the indef. article in *une narange*.] **A.** *sb.* **1.** The fruit of a tree (see sense 2), a large globose, many-celled berry (HESPERIDIUM) with subacid juicy pulp, enclosed in a tough rind externally of a bright reddish yellow (= orange) colour. **2.** (In full *orange-tree*: An evergreen tree (*Citrus Aurantium*), a native of the East; it produces fragrant white flowers, and the fruit mentioned in sense 1. (Also applied to allied species, or subspecies, as *C. Bigaradia, C. Bergamia*; see quots.) 1615. **3.** Applied to various plants, or their fruit, mostly from some apparent resemblance in flower or fruit to the orange-tree 1817. **4.** = SEA ORANGE, a large orange-coloured holothurian (*Lophothuria fabricii*) of globose shape 1753. **5.** In full *orange-colour*: The reddish-yellow colour of the orange. Also, a pigment of this colour. 1587. **6.** *Her.* A roundel tenné (tawny-coloured) 1562.

1. *Blood* (*-red*), *Malta* or *Maltese O.*, a red-pulped variety. *Jaffa* or *Joppa O.*, a lemon-shaped and very sweet kind. *Navel O.*, a nearly seedless variety from Brazil, etc., having the rudiment of a second fruit imbedded in its apex. *Clove, Noble*, or *Mandarin O.* = MANDARIN. *Tangerine O.*: see TANGERINE. The fruit of the *Citrus Bigaradia* is called the *Bitter, Horned*, or *Seville O.*; and that of the *C. Bergamia, Bergamot O.* or BERGAMOT[1]. Phr. *To squeeze* or *suck an o.*, to extract all the juice from it; *fig.* to take all that is profitable out of anything. *Oranges and lemons*, a nursery game, in which a ditty beginning with these words is sung. **3.** **Native o.** (*Australia*), (*a*) the orange-thorn, an orange berry with a leathery skin, about one inch and a half in diameter; (*b*) the small native pomegranate, *Capparis mitchelli*. **Quito O.**, *Maclura aurantiaca*, a species of nightshade in colour, fragrance, and taste resembling an o. See also MOCK-ORANGE.

attrib. and *Comb.* **1.** General: as *o.-bloom, -grove*, etc.; *o.-girl, -merchant*, etc.; *o.-wine*; *o.-grower*; *o.-shaped* adj.

2. Special: **o.-aphis**, a black aphis (*Siphonophora citrifolii*) that infests the orange-tree; **-jelly**, (*a*) a jelly flavoured with orange-juice and orange-peel; (*b*) a variety of swede turnip; **-marmalade**, see MARMALADE; **-oil**, the essential oil obtained from the rind of the o.; **-scale**, any scale-insect which infests the orange-tree; esp. *Aspidiotus aurantii*.

B. *adj.* Of the colour of an orange (see A. 5) 1542.

Comb. In names of orange-coloured varieties of apples or pears, as *o.-bergamot, -musk, -pear, -pippin*; also in names of plants, animals, etc. of this colour (more or less), as **o. bat**, the *Phinonycteris aurantia*, inhabiting northern Australia, the male of which has fur of a bright orange; **o.-cowry**, a large handsome cowry (*Cypræa aurantia*) of a deep yellow colour; **-grass**, *Hypericum Sarothra*, having minute deep-yellow flowers; **o. lily**, *Lilium croceum*; **o. thorn**: see A. 3, quots.

Orange (ǫ·rĕndʒ), *sb.*[2] 1558. **1.** Name of a town on the river Rhone in France, formerly the capital of a small principality of the same name, from which the princes of Orange-Nassau, the ancestors of William III of England, took their title. In Eng. Hist., 'William of Orange' is an appellation of William III. **b.** *attrib.* Of or belonging to the Orange family or dynasty in Holland 1647. **2.** *Eng. Hist.* (*attrib.*) Applied to the ultra-Protestant party in Ireland, in ref. to the secret society of Orangemen formed in 1795; cf. ORANGEMAN 1795.

The members of 'The Orange Lodge' of Freemasons in Belfast and their adherents were known as 'Orange boys' and 'Orangemen'. The name of the lodge probably had ref. to William of Orange, or to the use of orange badges at the anniversary celebrations of his memory. Hence, no doubt, the use of 'Orange' as a party name.

Orangeade (ǫrĕndʒēᵊ·d). 1706. [f. ORANGE *sb.*[1] + -ADE, after *lemonade*.] A drink composed of orange and lemon juice diluted with water and sweetened. Also, now, an aerated water of an orange tint.

†Orangea·do. 1599. [Cf. Sp. *naranjada* conserve of oranges, F. *orangeat.*] Candied orange-peel -1796.

O·range-blo:ssom. 1786. The white fragrant blossom of the orange-tree. Worn by brides in wreaths, trimmings, etc., or carried in bouquets at the marriage ceremony.

O·range-flow:er. 1626. = prec.

Comb. **orange-flower water,** the aqueous solution of orange-flowers; the fragrant watery distillate left over in the preparation of neroli oil.

Orang(e)ism (ǫ·rĕndʒiz'm). 1823. [f. ORANGE *sb.*² + -ISM.] The system and principles upheld by the Orange Association; the principle of Protestant political ascendancy in Ireland.

Orangeman (ǫ·rĕndʒ,mæ̆n). 1796. [f. ORANGE *sb.*² + MAN.] A member of a political society formed, in 1795, for the defence of Protestantism and maintenance of Protestant ascendancy in Ireland; see ORANGE *sb.*²

Orangery (ǫ·rĕndʒ,ri, ǫ·rĕndʒĕri). 1664. [In sense 1, a. F. *orangerie*, f. *oranger* orange-tree; see -ERY 2.] 1. A place appropriated to the cultivation of orange-trees. †2. A scent extracted from the orange-flower; also, snuff scented with this -1744.

O·range-taw:ny, *a.* and *sb.* 1575. **A.** *adj.* Of a dull yellowish brown colour; tan-coloured with a tinge of orange. **B.** *sb.* As the name of a colour or a fabric.

Orangite (ǫ·rĕndʒəit). 1851. [From its colour.] *Min.* An orange variety of thorite.

Orang-outang (ŏræ·ŋ,ū̆tæ:ŋ). Also **orang-utan** (ōᵊ·răŋ,ū̆·tăn). 1699. [ult. ad. Malay *ōrang ū·tan* 'man of the woods'.] *Zool.* An anthropoid ape, *Simia satyrus*, of arboreal habits, inhabiting Borneo, Sumatra, and formerly Java; the male exceeds 4 feet in height and has very long arms. The *Lesser Orang-utan* is *S. morio* of Borneo.

‖**Orarion** (orēᵊ·riǫn). 1772. [Græcized f. next.] In the Greek Church, the deacon's stole.

‖**Orarium** (orēᵊ·riɒ̆m). 1706. [L., a napkin, f. *os, or-* mouth, face; see -ARIUM.] **a.** The earlier name of the stole; *spec.* in the Greek Church = ORARION. **b.** The scarf attached to a pastoral staff 1814.

Orate (ŏrē¹·t, ōᵊrē¹·t), *v.* 1600. [f. L. *orat-, orare.* Re-coined in U.S. *c* 1860, as a back-formation from *oration.*] *intr.* †1. To pray; to plead. 2. To act the orator; to hold forth, 'speechify'. Now usu. joc. or sarcastic.

1. A Rhetorician, whose businesse is to o. and persuade 1669.

Oration (ŏrē¹·ʃən), *sb.* late ME. [ad. L. *orationem*, f. *orare*; cf. prec.] 1. A prayer or petition to God; orison. Now only *Hist.* 2. A formal speech or discourse; *esp.* one delivered in connexion with some particular occasion 1502. 3. Speech, language; now only in *Gram.*, in 'direct' and 'oblique o.'

2. The greatest orations of the two first orators of any age, Demosthenes and Æschines 1844.

Ora·tion, *v. colloq.* 1633. [f. prec. sb.] *intr.* To orate; to 'speechify'.

Orator (ǫ·rătəɹ). late ME. [a. AF. *oratour* = OF. *orateur*, ad. L. *oratorem*, f. *orat-, orare*; see ORATE.] †1. An advocate, a spokesman; *spec.* a professional advocate -1650. †2. A petitioner or suppliant. (Commonly used in subscribing a letter or petition to a superior.) -1727. **b.** *Law.* The plaintiff or petitioner in a bill or information in chancery or equity (now *U.S.*). †3. One who delivers a speech or oration in public; esp. an eloquent public speaker. late ME. †4. One sent to plead or speak for another; an ambassador, envoy, or messenger -1673. 5. *Public O.*: an officer of the Universities of Oxford and Cambridge, whose functions are to speak in the name of the University on State occasions; to go in person, when required, to plead the cause of the University; to write suitable addresses, letters of congratulation or condolence; to introduce candidates for honorary degrees, and to perform other like duties 1614.

3. I come not (Friends) to steale away your hearts, I am no o., as Brutus is SHAKS. Som O. renound In Athens or free Rome MILTON.

Oratorial (ǫrătōᵊ·riăl), *a.* Now *rare.* 1546. [In sense 1, f. L. *oratorius* + -AL. In 2, referred to ORATORIO.] 1. Of, pertaining to, or proper to an orator. 2. Of or pertaining to an oratorio 1811. Hence **Orato·rially** *adv.*

Oratorian (ǫrătōᵊ·riăn). 1644. [f. L. *oratorius* of or pertaining to an orator, *oratorium* place of prayer, ORATORY *sb.*¹] **A.** *adj.* †1. = ORATORIAL 1. -1734. 2. Of or pertaining to the ORATORY (*sb.*¹ 3) 1862. **B.** *sb.* A father or priest of an oratory; *spec.* a member of the Oratory of St. Philip Neri, or other similar society (see ORATORY *sb.*¹ 3) 1656.

Orato·ric, *a.* 1656. [f. L. *oratorem* ORATOR + -IC, after *historic*, etc.] = next.

Oratorical (ǫrătǫ·rikăl), *a.* 1619. [f. as prec. + -AL.] †1. = ORATORIAN *a.* 2. 2. Of, pertaining to, or characteristic of an orator or oratory; rhetorical; also, according to the rules of oratory; characteristic of a professional advocate 1634. 3. Given to the use of oratory 1801.

2. O. Discourses 1702. 3. Americans are an o. race 1898. Hence **Orato·rically** *adv.*

Oratorio (ǫrătōᵊ·riǫ). 1727. [a. It., ad. eccl. L. *oratorium* ORATORY *sb.*¹ Named in the 16th c. from the musical services in the church of the Oratory of St. Philip Neri in Rome, these being virtually examples of the older mystery play adapted to a religious service.] A form of extended musical composition, of a semi-dramatic character, usu. founded on a scriptural theme, sung by solo voices and a chorus, to the accompaniment of a full orchestra, without the assistance of action, scenery, or dress.

O·ratorize, *v.* 1620. [f. ORATOR *sb.* + -IZE.] *intr.* To play the orator; to deliver an oration. Now usu. joc. or contemptuous: to 'speechify'.

O·ratorship. [See -SHIP.] The position or office of orator; esp. in *Public O.*, the office of Public Orator in a University.

Oratory (ǫ·rătəri), *sb.*¹ ME. [ad. L. *oratorium* place of prayer (prop. adj. 'for prayer', sc. *templum*); f. *orat-, orare*; see -ORY.] 1. A place of prayer; a small chapel; a room or building for private worship. Also in ref. to Jewish or pagan worship. †2. A faldstool at which a worshipper kneels -1771. 3. The name of certain religious societies in the R.C. Church; orig. and esp. the *O. of St. Philip Neri* or *Congregation of the Fathers of the O.*, a society of priests living in community without vows, constituted at Rome in 1564.

1. In Temples hallowed for publique vse and not in priuate Oratories HOOKER.

Oratory (ǫ·rătəri), *sb.*² 1586. [ad. L. *oratoria* (sc. *ars*).] 1. The art of the orator or of public speaking; the art of speaking eloquently; rhetoric 1593. 2. The delivery of orations or speeches; rhetorical or eloquent language.

1. That part of o., which relates to the moving of passions SWIFT. 2. It is seldom that o. changes votes 1849.

Oratress (ǫ·rătrĕs). 1586. [f. ORATOR + -ESS¹.] A female orator, †petitioner, or †plaintiff.

Orb (ǭɹb), *sb.*¹ 1526. [ad. L. *orbis* ring, circle, round disk; cf. F. *orbe.*] **I.** A circle and deriv. senses. 1. A circle, or anything of circular form, as a circular disk, etc. Now *rare.* 1590. 2. *Astrol.* The space on the celestial sphere within which the influence of a planet, star, or 'house' is supposed to act 1727. †3. *Astron.* The plane of the orbit of a planet, etc.; also, the orbit or path -1674. †4. A cyclical period, a cycle -1742.

1. And I serue the Fairy Queene, To dew her orbs vpon the green SHAKS. 3. Instruct the planets in what orbs to run POPE.

II. A sphere and deriv. senses. 1. *Old Astron.* Each of the concentric hollow spheres supposed to surround the earth and to carry the planets or stars with them in their revolution; see SPHERE. *Obs.* exc. *Hist.* 1526. 2. Anything of spherical or globular shape 1597. 3. A general name for the heavenly bodies (sun, moon, planets, or stars), in sense either of 'globe', or of 'disk'. Chiefly *poet.* or *rhet.* 1596. †**b.** *spec.* The earth; cf. L. *orbis terrarum* -1667. 4. The eye-ball; the eye. *poet.* and *rhet.* 16 . . 5. The globe surmounted by a cross forming part of the regalia; also called *mound*, formerly *globe, ball* 1702. 6. *fig.* †**a.** A 'sphere' of action or activity; rank, station. (Often with ref. to sense II. 1.) -1757. **b.** (from II. 2 or 3.) An organized or collective whole; a rounded mass; a 'world' 1603.

2. What a hell of witchcraft lies In the small o. of one particular tear! SHAKS. 3. The O. of Day GRAY. **b.** *Twel. N.* III. i. 43. 4. These eys..thir seeing have forgot, Nor to thir idle orbs doth sight appear MILT. 6. **a.** Evangelists of an higher Orbe then..Bishops 1644. *Comb.* **o.-fish,** an East Indian fish (*Chætodon* or *Ephippius orbis*).

Orb, *sb.*² 1500. [In med.L. *orba*, in Anglo-Fr. *orbe*, as if for med.L. **orba fenestra* blind window; cf. L. *orbus luminis* bereft of light, blind.] *Arch.* Blank or blind window; hence plain stone panel, blank panel.

Orb (ǭɹb), *v.* 1600. [f. ORB *sb.*¹] 1. *trans.* To enclose in, or as in, an orb or circle 1645. 2. To form or gather into an orb, disk, or globe; to round out 1600.

1. Yea Truth and Justice then Will down return to men, Orb'd in a Rain-bow MILTON.

Orbed (ǭɹbd, *poet.* ǭ·ɹbĕd), *a.* 1597. [f. ORB *sb.*¹ and *v.* + -ED.] 1. Formed into, or having the form of, an orb; rounded; arched. Also *fig.* 2. In comb., as *full-o.* (having a full orb), etc. 1667.

Orbicular (ǫɹbi·kiŭlăɹ), *a.* (*sb.*) late ME. [ad. F. *orbiculaire* or L. *orbicularis*, f. *orbiculus*; see prec. and -AR.] **A.** *adj.* 1. Round as a circle or disk; circular, of circular plan or section. **b.** *Anat.* and *Zool.* Applied to structures of circular or discoidal form; *spec.* to those muscles (*sphincters*) surrounding, and having the function of closing, natural apertures of the body, as the sphincters of the mouth, eyelids, etc. (Also in L. form *orbicularis.*) 1615. **c.** *Bot.* Of circular outline, as leaves, etc. 1731. 2. Spherical, globular. Sometimes *loosely*, Having a rounded or convex (as opp. to a flat) surface. late ME. 3. *fig.* Full-orbed, rounded, complete 1673. 4. *Nat. Hist.* Combined with other adjs. of form; (*esp.* in *Bot.* of leaves), as *o.-cordate, -ovate*, etc. 1847. 5. *O. bone* (*os orbiculare*), a very small bone of the middle ear, at the end of the incus, and articulating with the stapes 1706.

1. Quite through his bright o. targe CHAPMAN. 3. The household ruin was thus full and o. DE QUINCEY.

B. *sb. Anat.* An orbicular muscle. See A. 1. b. Also in L. form *orbicularis.* 1872. Hence **Orbicula·rity,** o. form or character. **Orbi·cular-ly** *adv.*, **-ness** (*rare*).

Orbiculate (ǫɹbi·kiŭlĕt), *a.* 1760. [ad. L. *orbiculatus*, f. *orbiculus*, f. *orbis* ORB *sb.*¹; see -CULE and -ATE² 2.] = ORBICULAR. Chiefly in *Nat. Hist.* So **Orbi·culated** *a.*

Orbiculato-, comb. f. L. *orbiculatus*, ORBICULATE, in sense 'orbiculately—', as *o.-cordate*, etc.

Orbit (ǭ·ɹbit). 1548. [ad. F. *orbite* or L. *orbita* wheel-track, orbit, f. *orbis* wheel, circle.] 1. *Anat.* The bony cavity containing the eye and its muscles, glands, etc.; the eye-socket. **b.** *Zool.* The border of, or part surrounding, the eye in a bird, insect, etc. 1774. ¶ **c.** (By confusion with ORB *sb.*¹ II. 4.) The eye-ball; the eye 1728. 2. *Astron.* The path of a heavenly body; the curved path described by a planet or comet round the sun, by a satellite about its primary, etc. (Rarely = *the ecliptic.*) 1696. ¶ **b.** Confused with *orb*; see ORB *sb.*¹ II. 1, 3, 6. 1727.

1. **c.** Or roll the lucid o. of an eye YOUNG. 2. *fig.* The backslidings of my aunt Dinah in her o. did the same service in establishing my father's system 1759. Hence **O·rbital** *a.* of, belonging to, or connected with an o.; taking place in an o., as *o. revolution.*

Orbitar (ǭ·ɹbităɹ), *a.* (*sb.*) 1741. [ad. F. *orbitaire*; see -AR.] *Anat.* 1. = ORBITAL; var. **O·rbitary.** **B.** *sb.* The zygomatic suture 1782.

Orbitelous (ǭɹbitī·ləs), *a.* 1857. [f. mod.L. *orbitelus*, F. *orbitèle*, f. L. *orbis* + *tela* web.] *Zool.* Applied to those spiders which spin circular webs, as the garden-spider. So **O·rbitele,** an o. spider.

O·rbito-, comb. form of L. *orbita* ORBIT, usu. in sense 'relating to the orbit along with (some other part)', as *o.-nasal, -temporal* adjs., etc.

Orbitolite (ǫɹbi·tŏləit). 1859. [In mod.L. *orbitolites*, f. *orbita* ORBIT + Gr. λίθος stone; see -LITE.] The fossil shell of a foraminifer of the genus *Orbitolites.*

Orbitosphenoid (ǭ·ɹbito,sfī·noid). 1854. [f. ORBITO- + SPHENOID.] **A.** *adj.* Belonging to the orbit and the sphenoid bone; applied to a small bone or bony process forming part of the eye-socket, and (in man) constituting the lesser wing of the sphenoid bone. **B.** *sb.* The o. bone or process. So **O:rbitosphenoi·dal** *a.* = prec. A.

Orby (ǭ·ɹbi), *a. rare* and *poet.* 1611. [-Y.] Of the form of an orb; moving as in a circle, 'coming round'; of the nature of, or pertaining to, a heavenly body.

Orc, ork (ǭɹk). 1590. [In sense 1, a. F. *orque*, ad. L. *orca*, a kind of whale.] **1.** A cetacean of the genus *Orca*, family *Delphinidæ*; esp. the killer (*O. gladiator* Gray). Formerly applied to more than one vaguely identified sea-monster. 1611. **2.** Occas. more vaguely (cf. L. *Orcus*, Rom. *orco*, and see OGRE): A devouring monster, an ogre 1590. Also (in sense 1) **O·rca.**

Orcadian (ǫɹkē¹·diăn), *a.* and *sb.* 1661. [f. L. *Orcades* the Orkney Islands + -IAN.] **A.** *adj.* Of or pertaining to Orkney. **B.** *sb.* A native or inhabitant of Orkney.

Orcanet (ǭ·ɹkănĕt). 1548. [a. OF. *orcanette*, altered from *arcanette*, dim. of *arcanne*, for OF. *alcanne*, ad. med.L. *alkanna*, whence ALKANET.] = ALKANET.

Orcein (ǭ·ɹsi,in). 1838. [Altered from ORCIN.] *Chem.* A red colouring-matter ($C_7H_7NO_3$) obtained from orcin by the action of ammonia and oxygen, and existing in the dye called orchil.

Orchard (ǭ·ɹtʃəɹd). [OE. *ortgeard*, the first element of which is prob. ad. L. *hortus* (late and med.L. *ortus*) garden. In 9th c. *orcgeard, orceard*, whence ME. *orchard.*] †**a.** Formerly, in general sense, A garden, for herbs and fruit-trees. **b.** Now, an enclosure for the cultivation of fruit-trees.

attrib. and *Comb.*, as **o. grass**, any grass grown in an o., *esp.* in U.S., the Cock's-foot Grass, *Dactylis glomerata*; **-house**, a glass house for the protection of fruit that is delicate, or is wanted early; **o. oriole**, a N. Amer. oriole (*Icterus spurius*) which hangs its nest from the boughs of fruit and other trees.

O·rcharding. 1664. [f. prec. + -ING¹.] **1.** The cultivation of fruit-trees in orchards. **2.** *concr.* Land laid out and planted with fruit-trees. (Chiefly Amer.) 1721.

O·rchardist. 1794. [f. as prec. + -IST.] One who cultivates an orchard.

Orchestic (ǫɹke·stik), *a.* and *sb.* 1842. [ad. Gr. ὀρχηστικός, f. ὀρχηστής dancer; see -IC.] **A.** *adj.* Of or pertaining to dancing. **B.** *sb.* (more freq. in pl.) The art of dancing 1850.

Orchestra (ǭ·ɹkĕstră). 1606. [a. L., a. Gr. ὀρχήστρα the space on which the chorus danced, f. ὀρχέεσθαι to dance. Formerly stressed *orche·stra.*] **1.** *Gk. Theatre.* A large semicircular space in front of the stage, where the chorus danced and sang. **2.** That part of a theatre or other building assigned to the band or chorus of singers 1724. **3.** The company of musicians themselves; a company of performers of concerted instrumental music in a theatre, concert-room, etc. 1720. **b.** *transf.* The set of instruments played by such a company of musicians 1834.

3. c. Also *o. chairs, stalls* (U.S.), that part of a theatre known in England as the 'stalls' (STALL *sb.*¹ 4 c). Hence **Orchestral** (ǫɹke·străl, ǭ·ɹkĕstrăl) *a.*

Orchestrate (ǭ·ɹkĕstrē¹t), *v.* 1880. [f. prec. + -ATE³.] *trans.* To compose or arrange for an orchestra; to score for orchestral performance. Hence **Orchestra·tion**, the action or art of orchestrating; the style in which a piece of music is orchestrated; instrumentation of orchestral music. **O·rchestrator.**

Orchestre, -ter (ǭ·ɹkĕstəɹ, *formerly* ǫɹke·stəɹ). 1623. [a. F., f. L. *orchestra.*] = ORCHESTRA.

Orchestric (ǫɹke·strik), *a.* 1786. [f. as prec. + -IC.] **1.** Better ORCHESTIC, q. v. **2.** Orchestral 1839.

Orchestrina (ǭɹkĕstrī·nă). Also **-ino.** 1838. [f. ORCHESTRA + -INA¹, after *concertina*, etc.] †**a.** An instrument of the keyboard kind, imitating various other musical instruments. **b.** A mechanical instrument resembling a barrel-organ, intended to imitate the effect of an orchestra. So **Orche·strion** [cf. *accordion*].

Orchid (ǭ·ɹkid). 1845. [Introduced by Lindley; f. mod.L. *Orchideæ* or *Orchidaceæ*; see ORCHIDEOUS and -ID².] Any plant of the orchis family (*Orchidaceæ* or *Orchideæ*), a large Natural Order of monocotyledons, distinguished by having one, or rarely two, sessile anthers, united with the pistil (*gynandrous*) into a central body called the *column*, and containing pollen coherent in masses (*pollinia*); the flowers have three sepals and three petals, and are often remarkable for brilliancy of colour or grotesqueness of form.

Orchidaceous (ǫɹkidē¹·ʃəs), *a.* 1838. [f. mod.L. *Orchidaceæ*; see ORCHIDEOUS and -ACEOUS.] **1.** Belonging to the N.O. *Orchidaceæ*, ORCHID. **2.** Resembling an orchid, esp. in being showy 1864.

Orchidean (ǫɹki·diăn), *a. rare.* 1821. [f. mod.L. *Orchideæ* (see ORCHIDEOUS) + -AN.] Belonging to the *Orchideæ*, orchidaceous; pertaining to or characteristic of an orchid.

Orchideous (ǫɹki·diəs), *a.* 1818. [f. mod. L. *Orchideæ* (Linn.), irreg. f. Gr. ὄρχις, L. *orchis* (with assumed stem *orchid-*).] Belonging to the *Orchideæ* or natural order of plants akin to the genus *Orchis*; orchidaceous.

Orchido-, assumed comb. form of Gr. ὄρχις (the etym. form being *orchio-*); usu. taken as if repr. ORCHID; as in **Orchido·logist**, one versed in orchidology; **Orchido·logy**, that branch of botany which deals with orchids; etc.

Orchil (ǭ·ɹtʃil). 1483. [a. OF. *orchel, orcheil*, mod.F. *orseille*. Origin uncertain; see ARCHIL.] **1.** A red or violet dye prepared from certain lichens, esp. *Roccella tinctoria*. **2.** The lichen *Roccella tinctoria*, or other species from which the dye is obtained 1758.

Orchilla (ǫɹtʃi·lă), **orchella** (ǫɹtʃe·lă). 1703. [ad. It. *orcello*, OSp. *orchillo.*] **1.** = prec. 1. **2.** (usu. *o.-weed.*) = prec. 2. 1772.

Orchis (ǭ·ɹkis). 1562. [a. L. (Pliny), the plant, a. Gr. ὄρχις testicle, also the plant orchis (so called from the usual shape of the tubers). Pl. *orchises*, for which *orchids* is often substituted.] The typical genus of *Orchidaceæ* or Orchids, comprising terrestrial herbs of temperate regions, with tuberous root (usu. having two tubers), and erect fleshy stem bearing a spike of flowers, usu. purple or red, with spurred lip; any plant of this genus, or (pop.) of other genera resembling this. **b.** With defining word (sometimes denoting an insect, etc., which the flower resembles): as BEE O., BUTTERFLY O., FINGER O., FLY O., etc. 1785.

Where..far descried High tower'd the spikes of purple orchises M. ARNOLD.

‖ **Orchitis** (ǫɹkəi·tis). 1799. [mod.L., f. Gr. ὄρχις testicle.] *Path.* Inflammation of the testicle. Hence **Orchi·tic** *a.*

Orchotomy (ǫɹkǫ·tŏmi). Also **orchio-.** 1753. [ad. Gr. ὀρχοτομία, f. ὄρχις testicle + -τομία cutting.] *Surg.* Excision of the testicles; castration.

Orcin (ǭ·ɹsin). Also **-ine.** 1840. [ad. mod. L. *orcina*, f. stem of It. *orcello* ORCHIL; see -IN.] *Chem.* A colourless crystalline substance ($C_7H_8O_2 + H_2O$) obtained from the various kinds of orchilla-weed, turning red, brown, or yellow, in contact with air, or when treated with various compounds. Cf. ORCEIN.

Ordain (ǫɹdē¹·n), *v.* ME. [a. AF. *ordeiner, -deigner*, OF. *ordener*, later *ordoner*, mod.F. *ordonner*, ad. L. *ordinare*, f. *ordo, ordinem* ORDER.] **I.** To put in order, arrange, make ready, prepare. †**1.** *trans.* To arrange in regular order; to array, marshal, order -1581. †**2.** To set or keep in proper order; to regulate, direct, conduct -1489. †**3.** To arrange the order or course of -1681. **4.** To set up (something) to continue in a certain order; to institute. Now *arch.* ME. †**5.** To plan, devise, contrive -1526. †**6.** To put in order (for a purpose); to prepare, equip; to furnish -1548. †**7.** To dispose (aright) -1502. †**8.** *intr.* To make preparation -1533.

6. He hath..ordened his arowes to destroye COVERDALE *Ps.* vii. 13.

II. To appoint, decree, destine, order. †**1.** *trans.* To appoint to a charge, duty, or office -1809. †**b.** Const. *to do* something; *to* (*on, upon*) some office, etc. -1676. **2.** *Eccl.* To appoint or admit ceremonially to the ministry of the Christian Church; to confer holy orders upon ME. †**3.** To appoint or assign (*to* or *for* a special purpose, etc.) -1618. **4.** Of the Deity, fate, etc.: To decree, predestine, destine. Also *absol.* or *intr.* ME. **5.** To decree as a thing to be observed; to enact ME. **b.** *absol.* or *intr.* To appoint, command ME. **6.** = ORDER *v.* II. 2. *Obs.* or *arch.* late ME. †**7.** = ORDER *v.* II. 3. -1621.

1. Wherefore are magistrates ordayned, but that the tranquillitie of the commune weale maye be confirmed? LATIMER. **2.** I am a young Clergyman, Ordained the very Last Ember-Week 1718. **4.** The moment..which God had ordained from the beginning 1865. The path we are ordained to tread LYTTON. **5.** That which is ordained by law they term lawful and just JOWETT. **7.** Afterward he ordeined a boat made of one tree..and went to sea in it HAKLUYT. Hence **Ordai·nable** *a.* **Ordai·ner.** **Ordai·nment**, the action or fact of ordaining.

‖ **Ordalium** (ǫɹdē¹·liŏm). 1599. Med.L. adaptation of the word *ordál*, ORDEAL; in Eng. use in the 17th c.

Ordeal (ǭ·ɹdiăl, ǭ·ɹdīl). [Com. Teut.: OE. *ordál, -dǽl*; in MHG. *urteile*, mod.G. *urteil*; thence med.L. *ordalium, ordela*, F. *ordalie*. The sb. belongs to a compound vb. of Goth. type **uzdailjan*, in MHG. and G. *erteilen*, OE. *adǽlan*, lit. 'to deal out'; hence 'to decide, give judgement'.] **1.** An ancient Teutonic mode of trial, in which a suspected person was subjected to some physical test fraught with danger, e.g. the plunging of the hand in boiling water, the carrying of hot iron, walking barefoot and blindfold between red-hot ploughshares, etc., the result being regarded as the immediate judgement of the Deity. **2.** *fig.* Anything which severely tests character or endurance; a trying experience, a trial 1658.

attrib. and *Comb.*, as *o. fire*, etc.; **o.-bean**, the poisonous CALABAR-BEAN.

Order (ǭ·ɹdəɹ), *sb.* ME. [a. OF. *ordre* :—**ordne*, ad. L. *ordinem* (nom. *ordo*).] **I.** Rank generally; a rank, grade, class. **1.** A rank, row, series. *Obs.* or *arch.* 1563. **b.** *Arch.* A series of mouldings 1845. **2.** A rank of the community; a social division, grade, or stratum; *esp.* in *higher, lower orders* ME. **b.** A definite rank in the state. late ME. **c.** Rank in the abstract. *poet.* 1667. **3.** A body of persons of the same profession, occupation, or pursuits, regarded as a separate class in the community. late ME. **4.** A class, group, kind, or sort, of persons, beings, or things, having its rank in a scale of being, or importance, or distinguished from others by nature or character 1736.

2. That part of the Catechism is written for the lower orders 1893. **b.** The most High and Sacred O. of Kings 1683. **3.** The spirit of the whole clerical o. rose against this injustice MACAULAY. **4.** He possessed talents of a high o. DISRAELI.

II. Rank in specific departments. **1.** Each of the nine ranks or grades of angels, viz. seraphim, cherubim, thrones, dominations, principalities, powers, virtues, archangels, angels ME. **2.** *Eccl.* **a.** A grade or rank in the Christian ministry, or in an eccl. hierarchy ME. **b.** The rank, status, or position of a clergyman or ordained minister of the Church. Now always *pl.*, more fully *holy orders*. ME. **c.** The conferment of holy orders, the rite of ordination ME. **3. a.** A religious society or fraternity (as of monks, nuns, friars) living under a rule; as *the Benedictine* or *Franciscan o.* ME. **b.** A fraternity of knights bound by a common rule of life, and having a combined military and monastic character; as *the Teutonic O., the O. of Knights Templars*, etc. late ME. **4.** An institution, generally founded by a sovereign, or prince of high rank, for the purpose of rewarding meritorious service by the conferring of a dignity. late ME. **b.** The badge or insignia of such a dignity 1533. **5.** *Arch.* A system of parts subject to certain uniform established proportions; esp. in *Class. Arch.*, applied to modes of architectural treatment founded upon the proportions of columns and the kind of their capitals, with the relative proportions and amount of decoration used in their entablatures, etc. 1563. **6.** *Math.* The degree of complexity of any analytical or geometrical form, equation, expression, operator, or the like, as denoted by an ordinal number (first, second, third, . . , *n*th) 1706. 7. *Nat. Hist.* One of the higher groups in the classification of animals, vegetables, or minerals, forming a subdivision of a *class*, and itself subdivided into families, or into genera and species 1760.

2. a. *Holy orders*: in the R.C.Ch., those of bishop, priest, deacon, and (since 12th c.) subdeacon; in the Anglican and Eastern Ch., only those of bishop, priest, and deacon. *Minor orders*: in the R.C.Ch., those of acolyte, exorcist, reader, and door-keeper, in the Eastern Ch., subdeacon, reader, and sometimes singer. b. The Pope has pronounced against the validity of Anglican orders (*mod.*). Phr. *To take orders*, to be ordained. *In orders*, in the position of an ordained clergyman. *In deacon's orders, in priest's* or *full orders.* c. Those five commonly called Sacraments, that is to say, Confirmation, Penance, Orders, Matrimony, and Extreme Unction *Art. Religion* xxv. 3. a. It was the Friar of Orders gray 1596. b. The hospytelers and Templars were two fygtinge orders 1550. That fair O. of my Table Round TENNYSON. 4. The honourable Ordre of the Gartier. late ME. b. To whom he will carry the O. of the Black Eagle 1710. 5. *The five Orders of Classical Architecture*, the Tuscan, Doric, Ionic, Corinthian, and Composite, rising above each other in relative height, lightness, and decoration. Of these the Doric, Ionic, and Corinthian are the original Greek orders, the Tuscan and Composite, Roman modifications or varieties. 6. *A fluxion of the second order* is a fluxion of a fluxion; *an infinitesimal of the second order* is one infinitely smaller than one of the first order. The degree of a quantic in the variables *x, y, z* . . is generally spoken of as its o. 1895. 7. *Natural O.* (of plants), a group consisting of genera or families naturally allied in general structure, as opp. to an O. in an artificial system (e.g. the Sexual System of Linnæus), the members of which agree only in some single characteristic which may be unimportant.

III. Sequence, disposition. 1. Sequence or succession in space or time; succession of acts or events; the course or method of occurrence or action ME. 2. Formal disposition or array, late ME. b. The condition in which everything is in its proper place, and performs its proper functions. late ME. c. *Mil.* Equipment for a particular purpose, as *marching o.* 1837. †3. Disposition of measures for some purpose; suitable action –1827. †4. Regular or customary mode of procedure –1715. 5. The fixed arrangement found in the existing constitution of things; a natural, moral, or spiritual system in which things proceed according to definite laws ME. 6. *Liturgiology.* A stated form of divine service, etc., prescribed by eccl. authority or custom; the service so prescribed. late ME. 7. *spec.* (from III. 4.) The prescribed or customary mode of proceeding in debates or discussions, or in the conduct of public meetings, etc., or conformity with the same 1782. 8. (= *civil* or *public o.*) The maintenance and observance of law or constituted authority; law-abiding, state; absence of insurrection, riot, turbulence, or crimes of violence 1483. 9. State or condition generally (qualified as *good, bad*, etc.); normal, healthy, or efficient condition 1568. 10. *Mil.* The position in which a rifle is held as a result of the command to 'order arms'; see ORDER *v.* 1. 1847.

1. Stand not vpon the o. of your going, But go at once SHAKS. He has inverted the natural o. 1799. 2. The crevasses are . . apparently without law or o. in their distribution TYNDALL. b. O. is Heav'n's first Law POPE. His love of o. made him always the most regular of men 1882. 3. *Meas. for M.* II. ii. 25. Phr. *To take o.*, to take measures, make arrangements. 5. The old o. changeth, yielding place to new TENNYSON. The existence of an invisible o. of things 1878. Phr. *O. of nature, of things, of the world, moral o., spiritual o.*, etc. 6. The O. of Confirmation *Bk. Com. Prayer.* 7. Here Gen. Manners called Sir Francis to o. 1812. Phr. *O. of business, to rise to a point of o., the speaker* or *motion is not in o.*, or *is out of o.* See also *O. of the day*, in V. 8. Peace and o. were maintained by police regulations of German minuteness and strictness M. PATTISON. 9. The Ships were all in prime O., all lately rebuilt 1743.

IV. The action or an act of ordering. †1. The action of putting or keeping in order; regulation, control –1690. 2. An authoritative direction, injunction, mandate; an instruction 1548. 3. *spec.* a. *Law.* A decision of a court or judge, made or entered in writing; in the Supreme Court, a direction other than a final judgement 1726. b. *Banking*, etc. A written direction to pay money or deliver property, given by a person legally entitled to dispose thereof 1673. c. *Business.* A direction to make, provide, or furnish anything, at the responsibility of the person ordering; a commission to make purchases, supply goods, etc. *A large o.* (slang), a large demand, proposal, etc. d. A pass for admission, without payment or at a reduced price, to a theatre, etc., or to a museum, park, private establishment, or the like 1763.

2. Grumio gaue o. how it should be done SHAKS. The Agamemnon was under orders to strengthen the China fleet 1884. 3. a. An o. to pay 2*s.* a month was made (*mod.*). b. I will send a Post-Office o., in repayment 1846. c. Poets indeed are not made 'to o.' BAGEHOT. Boots and shoes ready made, or to o. (*mod.*).

V. Phrases and Combinations.

O. of the day. a. In a legislative body, the business set down for debate on a particular day (= F. *l'ordre du jour*). b. Specific commands or notices issued by the commanding officer to his troops. c. *colloq.* The prevailing rule or custom of the time. **In order**: a. In proper sequence or succession. b. In proper condition; in obedience to constituted authority or usage. c. Appropriate to or befitting the occasion; suitable. d. *In* (or *on*) *short o.* (also *quick o.*): without delay, immediately *U.S.* **In o. to**: †a. In reference to; for the sake of. b. With a view to the bringing about of (something), for the purpose of (some prospective end). Now only const. inf. *In o. that*: to the end that. **Out of o.**: Not in proper sequence, orderly arrangement, or settled condition; not in proper or normal condition of action, mind, bodily health, etc.

Comb.: o. **clerk**, a clerk who enters business orders; o. **form**, a partially blank form to be filled up in giving a business order; o.-**paper**, a paper on which questions, etc., coming in the o. of the day, in a legislative assembly, are entered; -**word** (F. *mot d'ordre*), the military pass-word, a watchword. Hence **O·rderless** *a.* devoid of o. or method; disorderly 1596.

Order (ǭ·ɹdəɹ), *v.* [ME. *ordren*, f. *ordre* ORDER *sb.*] I. 1. *trans.* To give order or arrangement to; to put in order; *spec.* to draw up in order of battle, to array. *arch.* 2. To set or keep in order or proper condition; to dispose according to rule; to regulate, govern, manage; to settle 1509. b. *refl.* To conduct oneself, behave. Now *arch.* 1535. c. Of the Deity, etc.: To ordain 1642. †3. To make ready, prepare (for a purpose) –1722. †4. To bring into order or submission to lawful authority; hence, to correct, chastise –1667. †5. To treat, deal with, manage (in a specified manner) –1799.

1. He ordred his battail, like a man expert in marciall science 1548. Phr. *To o. arms* (*Mil.*): to bring a firearm into a position in which it is held vertically against the right side, the butt on the ground. 2. They o., said I, this matter better in France STERNE. b. To ordre myselfe lowlye and reuerentlye to al my betters *Bk. Com. Prayer.* c. It was ordered otherwise, and doubtless wisely FROUDE.

II. 1. To give orders for (something to be done); to bid, command, direct; to prescribe medically 1550. 2. To give orders to, command, direct (a person, *to do* something, etc.) 1628. b. *ellipt.* To command or direct (a person) to go or come *to, into, upon* (a place, etc.), *away, here, home, out*, etc. 1667. 3. To give an order for; to direct (a thing) to be furnished or supplied 1836.

1. The doctor had ordered as much fresh air as possible 1891. In U.S., also with ellipse of *to be*. These things were ordered delivered to the army 1781. 2. b. He . . was ordered to a warmer climate 1898. 3. What have you ordered for dinner? (*mod.*).

III. *Eccl.* To admit to holy orders; to ordain; formerly also, to admit or institute to a benefice. *arch.* ME. Hence **O·rderer, O·rdering** *vbl. sb.* the action of the vb.

O·rder-book. 1833. [f. ORDER *sb.* + BOOK.] A book in which orders are entered. *spec.* a. In the army, a book in which the orderly sergeants enter general and regimental orders. b. In the navy, a book kept on a man-of-war for recording occasional orders of the commander. c. In the House of Commons, a book in which motions to be submitted to the House must be entered. d. In business, a book in which the orders of customers are entered.

Orderly (ǭ·ɹdəɹli), *a.* and *sb.* 1577. [f. ORDER *sb.* + -LY[1].] A. *adj.* 1. Arranged or disposed in order; exhibiting system or method; regular. b. Of persons: Regular, methodical 1830. †2. Conformable to established order or rule; regular –1637. 3. Observant of order, rule, or discipline; well-conducted, well-behaved 1598. 4. *Mil.* Pertaining to orders or their issue; charged with the conveyance or execution of orders 1723. 5. Pertaining to the system of keeping the streets clean 1851.

1. We were . . tied together, and thus advanced in an o. line TYNDALL. 3. Elections are now conducted in an o. manner 1884. 4. *O. book*, a book kept in a regiment or company, for the entry of general or regimental orders. *O. man* = B. 1, 2. *O. officer*, the officer of the day; rarely = B. 1. *O. room*, the office and court of the commanding officer. 5. *O. bin*, a street box for the reception of refuse. So **O·rderliness** 1571.

B. *sb.* 1. A non-commissioned officer or private soldier attending upon a superior officer to carry orders or messages 1800. 2. An attendant in a military or other hospital, charged esp. with the maintenance of order and cleanliness 1809.

Orderly (ǭ·ɹdəɹli), *adv.* 1477. [f. ORDER *sb.* + -LY[2].] 1. In order; in due order or course. Now *rare.* 2. According to established order or rule; duly; in a well-conducted manner 1509.

1. I thought it good . . to wryte the same orderly vnto the (good Theophilus) COVERDALE *Luke* i. 3.

Ordinal (ǭ·ɹdinăl), *a.* (*sb.*[1]) late ME. [ad. late L. *ordinalis* denoting order in a series, f. *ordo, ordin-* ORDER; see -AL.] †1. Conformable to order, rule, or custom; orderly –1496. 2. Marking position in an order or series, as *first, second, third*, etc.; opp. to CARDINAL 1599. 3. *Nat. Hist.* Of or pertaining to an order of animals or plants, or to natural order in general 1822. 4. Relating to, or consisting of, a row or rows 1892. B. *sb.* An ordinal number (see 2) 1591.

Ordinal (ǭ·ɹdinăl), *sb.*[2] late ME. [ad. med.L. *ordinale*, adj. neut. used subst.; see prec.] †1. A book containing rules, or a body of rules or regulations –1674. 2. A book setting forth the order of the services of the Church, or of any one of them, as they existed before the Reformation; a service-book. late ME. 3. A book prescribing the rules to be observed, and containing the form of service to be used, in the ordination of deacons and priests, and the consecration of bishops 1658.

Ordinance (ǭ·ɹdinăns). ME. [a. OF. *ordenance, ordon-*, mod.F. *ordonnance*, ad. med. L. *ordinantia*, f. *ordinantem, ordinare* to ORDAIN; cf. ORDNANCE, ORDONNANCE.] †1. Arrangement in ranks or rows; esp. battle-array; also, a host in array –1601. 2. Disposition (of things or matters) according to rule; arranged condition; order. *Obs.* exc. as in b. late ME. b. = ORDONNANCE 1. 1460. †3. Provision; a preparatory step or measure; hence, provision *of* (something) –1612. †b. Apparatus, furniture –1611. 4. The action of ordering or regulating; control, disposal. *arch.* ME. b. A dispensation, decree, or appointment of Providence or of Destiny *arch.* ME. †c. Ordained place, condition, course, etc. –1601. 5. Authoritative direction how to act; system of government, polity, or discipline. *Obs.* or *arch.* ME. 6. An authoritative direction, decree, or command; e.g. of a sovereign, a local body, etc. 7. A practice or usage authoritatively enjoined or prescribed, *esp.* a religious or ceremonial observance. late ME. b. Applied esp. to the sacrament of the Lord's Supper 1830.

2. b. Verrio's invention is admirable, his ordnance full and flowing EVELYN. 3. Great ordynance of gunnes the kynge let make 1500. 4. I putte me hoolly in youre disposicion and ordinaunce CHAUCER. b. Let Ord'nance Come as the Gods fore-say it SHAKS. c. *Jul. C.* I. iii. 66. 6. According to Thy blessed Word and o. *Bk. Com. Prayer.* The Acts of the Long Parliament after 1641 were at first called *Ordinances*; one of these was the *Self-denying O.* of 1645, ordaining that no member of parliament should thenceforth hold any civil or military office. N.E.D. 7. Candidates of this sacred O. [Confirmation] 1704.

Ordinand (ǭ·ɹdinænd). 1842. [ad. L. *ordinandus, ordinare* to ORDAIN.] A candidate for ordination.

Ordinant (ǭ·ɹdinănt), *a.* and *sb. rare.* late ME. [a. OF. *ordinant*; in mod. use ad. L. *ordinantem*; see ORDAIN *v.*] A. *adj.* That arranges, regulates, or directs. B. *sb.* One who confers holy orders 1842.

Ordinarily (ǭ·ɹdinărili), *adv.* 1532. [f. ORDINARY *a.* + -LY[2].] †1. In conformity with rule; as a matter of regular occurrence

-1695. 2. In most cases; usually, commonly 1555. 3. To the usual extent 1697. 4. As is normal or usual 1831.

2. Of a more blew colour than Lead o. is 1691. 3. Phr. *More than o.*, exceptionally; I am more than o. anxious to do Justice to the Persons 1709.

Ordinary (ǭ·ɹdinări), *sb.* ME. [orig., a. early OF. and Anglo-F. *ordinarie*, ad. med.L. *ordinarius* (sc. *judex, liber*, etc.) and as neut. sb. *ordinarium*; later senses are largely ellipt. uses of ORDINARY *a.*] **I.** Applied to a person or staff of persons. 1. *Eccl.* and *Common Law.* One who has, of his own right and not by deputation, immediate jurisdiction in eccl. cases, as the archbishop in a province, or the bishop or bishop's deputy in a diocese. 2. *Civil Law.* A judge having authority to take cognizance of cases in his own right and not by delegation; *spec.* in Scotland, one of the five judges of the Court of Session who constitute the Outer House (= *Lord Ordinary*, ORDINARY *a.* 2); in *U S.*, a judge of a court of probate 1607. 3. The chaplain of Newgate prison, whose duty it was to prepare condemned prisoners for death. *Obs.* exc. *Hist.* 1700. †4. A courier conveying dispatches or letters at regular intervals; hence, post, mail. (= F. *ordinaire*) -1730. 5. Chiefly in phr. *in ordinary* (of a ship), laid up or out of commission 1754.

II. Rule, ordinance, ordinal. (= med.L. *ordinarius, ordinarium.*) †1. A formula or rule of action; an ordinance, regulation, prescript -1594. 2. A rule prescribing, or book containing, the order of divine service; the form for saying mass; the service of the mass, or that part preceding and following the canon 1494.

III. Something ordinary, regular, or usual. (From the adj. in Fr. or Eng.) †1. Customary fare; a regular daily allowance of food; hence, an allowance of anything (= F. *ordinaire*) -1668. 2. A public meal regularly provided at a fixed price in an eating-house or tavern; also, formerly, the company frequenting this 1589. b. An eating-house where such meals are provided; a dining-room in such a building 1590. c. In parts of U.S.: A tavern or inn of any kind 1774. 3. *Her.* A charge of the earliest, simplest, and commonest kind, e.g. Chief, Pale, Bend, Bend-Sinister, Fess, Bar, Chevron, Cross, Saltire 1610. 4. a. Ordinary condition, course, run, degree; ordinary state of health, etc. 1581. b. An ordinary thing or person (*rare*) 1624. 5. Applied to various things of the most usual type; e.g. an ordinary share, as dist. from preference shares, etc. 1552.

1. Giue him his ordinarie of Oats 1616. 2. He kept a daily O. (thanks being the only shot his guests were to pay) FULLER. b. The unwholsome ayre of an Eightpenny Ordinarie 1631. 4. a. *The o.*, what is customary or usual. Now *colloq.*, as in adj. phr. *out of the o.*, unusual. I see no more in you then in the o. Of Natures sale-worke SHAKS. Phr. *In o.* added to official designations: app. a modification of the simple *ordinary* (see ORDINARY *a.* 3 b), and opp. to *extraordinary*, as *chaplain-in-o.* to his Majesty, *physician-in-o.* to the Prince of Wales.

Comb. **o. table,** the table at which an o. was served and which was afterwards cleared for gambling; hence, a gambling-table or gambling-house.

Ordinary (ǭ·ɹdinări), *a.* (*adv.*) 1460. [ad. L. *ordinarius*, f. *ordo, ordin-* ORDER; see -ARY[1]. Cf. F. *ordinaire.*] †1. Conformable to order or rule; regular; orderly, methodical -1639. 2. Of a judge: Having regular jurisdiction, not deputed, *esp.* empowered *ex officio* to take cognizance of eccl. or spiritual cases. Of jurisdiction, etc.: Exercised *ex officio*. 1483. 3. Regular, normal, customary, usual 1460. b. Of officials, persons employed, etc.: Belonging to the regular staff or class of such. Now mostly *-in-ordinary*: see ORDINARY *sb.* 1555. †4. Of common occurrence; frequent; abundant -1725. †b. Customary, usual. Chiefly predicative. -1794. 5. Of the usual kind, not singular or exceptional. Often *depreciatory*: Commonplace, somewhat inferior; also (now *dial.* or *colloq.*) ordinary-looking, 'plain' 1590. †6. Not distinguished by rank or position; of low degree; common, vulgar, unrefined -1741. †B. *adv.* In an ordinary manner; ordinarily -1798.

2. *Judge o.*: (*a*) the judge of the Court for Divorce; (*b*) in Scotland, the sheriff of a county. 3. In o. life we use a great many words with a total disregard of logical precision JEVONS. Phr. *More than o.*: (*a*) more in number or amount than is usual; (*b*) with adj. or sb., To a greater degree than is usual, exceptional; also *advb.* unusually, exceptionally. *Obs., arch.*, of *dial.* So *greater, better*, (etc.) *than o.* 5. *O. seaman*, one not expert; dist. from *able seaman.* His Books are very mean and o. HEARNE. Hence **O·rdinariness.**

Ordinate (ǭ·ɹdinět), *a.* and *sb.* late ME. [ad. L. *ordinatus*, pa. pple. of *ordinare* to ORDAIN.] **A.** *ppl. a.* and *adj.* Now *Obs.* or *rare.* †**I.** Construed as *pa. pple.* Ordered, disposed; ordained, destined, appointed -1649. **II.** Construed as *adj.* †1. Conformed to order or rule; observant of order; orderly, regular -1678. 2. *Entom.* Arranged in a row or rows 1826.

Phr. *O. proportion* (*Math.*), a proportion in which the terms are in regular order. *O. line* = B. Hence †**O·rdinately** *adv.* -1763.

B. *sb. Geom.* (Formerly more fully *o. applicate.*) **a.** Any one of a series of parallel chords of a conic section, in relation to the diameter which bisects each of them; now usu. applied to half the chord (i.e. the line from the curve to the bisecting diameter), orig. called the *semi-o.* Hence, **b.** A straight line drawn from any point parallel to one of the co-ordinate axes, and meeting the other. (Correl. to ABSCISSA.) 1537.

Ordinate (ǭ·ɹdineᵗt), *v.* 1562. [f. L. *ordinat-, ordinare*; cf. prec.] †1. *trans.* = ORDAIN *v.* II. 2. -1597. 2. To order, regulate, control, govern, direct. Now *rare* or *Obs.* 1595. 3. To institute, establish, ordain, predestine. Now *rare* or *Obs.* 1610. 4. To co-ordinate 1882.

Ordination (ǭɹdinēⁱ·ʃən). late ME. [ad. L. *ordinationem.*] The action of ordaining. **I.** The action of ordering, arranging, or disposing in ranks or order; ordered condition; an arrangement or disposition 1658. b. Classification in orders 1656. **II.** The action of ordaining, or conferring holy orders; admission to the ministry of the Church; the fact of being ordained. late ME. **III.** 1. The action or fact of ordaining or decreeing, esp. as a divine action 1460. †b. Destination (*to* an end or purpose); destined function or disposition -1829. †2. That which is ordained; an ordinance, decree -1656.

1. The quality of transparency is given, by a wise o. of Providence, to the fluid substance of water 1794.

Ordinative (ǭ·ɹdineᵗiv), *a.* 1605. [ad. late L. *ordinativus*, f. *ordinat-, ordinare*; see -ATIVE.] Having the character or function of ordaining, ordering, determining, or regulating; of the nature of ordination or ordering. Now *rare.*

Ordinee (ǭɹdinī·), *a.* and *sb.* [In ME. a. OF. *ordiné*; in mod. use a new formation; see -EE.] †A. *adj.* Admitted to holy orders, or into a religious order; ordained. ME. only. **B.** *sb.* An ordained clergyman; now, usu., a newly-ordained deacon ME.

Ordnance (ǭ·ɹdnăns). late ME. [var. of *ordenance*, ORDINANCE.] †1. = ARTILLERY 1. -1644. 2. Engines for discharging missiles. **a.** = ARTILLERY 2. ME. †b. With *pl.* A large gun, piece of ordnance -1629. †c. The artillery as a branch of the army -1786. 3. The branch of the public service concerned with the supply of military stores and materials, the management of the artillery, etc. 1485. †4. Occas. var. of ORDINANCE in other senses. 5. *attrib.*, as *o. officer, stores*, etc. 1800.

2. *Piece of o.*: see PIECE. b. Gunners spunge your Ordinances CAPT. SMITH. 3. *Board of O.*, a board, partly military and partly civil, which had the management of all affairs relating to the artillery, engineers, and the matériel of the Army. It was dissolved in 1855, most of its functions as regards matériel being now discharged by the *Army Ordnance Department.*

Ordnance Survey: The official survey of Great Britain and Ireland, undertaken by the Government, and originally carried out under the direction of the Master-General of the O. Hence **o.-datum,** the datum-line or level to which all heights are referred in the O. Survey, being 12½ feet below Trinity Highwater mark, and 4½ feet above Trinity Low-water mark; **o. map,** a map prepared by the Survey.

‖**Ordo** (ǭ·ɹdo). 1849. [L., = row, series, order.] *Eccl.* An ordinal, directory, or book of rubrics; an office or service with its rubrics.

Ordonnance (ǭ·ɹdŏnăns, ‖ordǫnā·ns). 1644. [a. mod.F. *ordonnance*, for OF. *ordenance*; see ORDINANCE.] 1. Systematic arrangement, esp. of literary material, architectural parts or features, or the details of a work of art; a plan or method of composition; an order of architecture. 2. In ref. to France, etc.: An ordinance, decree, law, or by-law 1756.

Ordovician (ǭɹdovi·ʃiăn), *a.* 1887. [f. L. *Ordovices*, name of an ancient British tribe in North Wales + -IAN.] *Geol.* The name of a series of rocks, including part of the Lower Silurian of Murchison; applied also to the age in which these strata were deposited.

Ordure (ǭ·ɹdiŭɹ). late ME. [a. F., f. *ord* filthy, foul :—L. *horridus* HORRID.] 1. Filth, dirt. Formerly also in *pl. arch.* Also *fig.* of foul language, etc. 2. Excrement, dung. Formerly also in *pl.* late ME.

Ore (ōᵊɹ). OE. [Two types: (1) ME. *oor* (*e*, *oure, ur*(*e* corresp. to OE. *óra*, 'unwrought metal', 'ore'; (2) ME. *ór*, mod. *ore*, corresp. to OE. *ár* (also *ǽr*) 'brass'. Thus the mod. Eng. word app. derives its sense from OE. *óra*, but its form from OE. *ár.*] 1. A native mineral containing a precious or useful metal in such quantity, etc., as to make its extraction profitable. b. With *an* and *pl.* A quality or kind of ore OE. 2. Metal, esp. precious metal. Chiefly *poet.* 1639.

1. *fig.* The good Yeoman is a Gentleman in O. FULLER. 2. Let others toil to gain the sordid o. 1763.

attrib. and *Comb.*, as **o. body,** a body or connected mass of ore in a mine, as a vein, bed, pocket, etc.; **-hearth,** a form of small reducing furnace made of cast iron, used in lead-smelting; a Scotch or blast hearth.

Ore, O're, Ore-, obs. ff. *o'er*, OVER, OVER-.

Oread (ōᵊ·rĭæd). late ME. [ad. L. *Oreas, Oread-*, a. Gr. Ὀρειάς, Ὀρειαδ- mountain-nymph, f. ὄρος mountain; see -AD.] *Gr.* and *Lat. Myth.* A mountain-nymph.

Like a Wood-Nymph light O. or Dryad MILT.

Orectic (ore·ktik), *a. rare.* 1779. [ad. Gr. ὀρεκτικός appetitive, f. ὀρεκτός, f. ὀρέγειν to stretch out, grasp after, desire.] **a.** *Philos.* Of, pertaining to, or characterized by appetite or desire; appetitive. **b.** *Med.* Having the quality of stimulating appetite or desire.

Oreide (ōᵊ·rĭˌid). 1875. [a. F. *oréide*, f. *or* gold; see -IDE.] A kind of brass resembling gold in colour, etc., used for imitation jewellery.

‖**Oreodon** (orī·ŏdǫn). 1877. [mod.L. f. Gr. ὄρος, ὀρε-ος mountain + ὀδούς, ὀδοντ- tooth: named by Leidy in 1851.] *Palæont.* A genus of extinct ruminant mammals, typical of the family *Oreodontidæ*, the remains of which are found in the miocene tertiary formations of the western U.S. Hence **Ore·odont, -do·ntine** *adjs.*

Oreography, -ology, etc., var. OROGRAPHY, etc.

Ore-weed (ōᵊ·ɹwīd). *local.* 1586. [f. *ore*, earlier *wore, woore*, seaweed + WEED.] Seaweed.

Orexin (ore·ksin). 1891. [f. Gr. ὄρεξις desire, appetite + -IN[1].] *Chem.* The hydrochlorate of phenyl-dihydro-quinazolin, a colourless, odourless crystalline substance, used as a stomachic.

Orfe (ǭɹf). 1688. [a. G., F. *orfe, orphe*; cf. L. *orphus* (Pliny), a. Gr. ὀρφώς sea perch.] A golden-yellow variety of the ide (*Leuciscus idus*), acclimatized in England in the 19th c.

Orgal(l, obs. var. of ARGOL[1].

Organ (ǭ·ɹgăn), *sb.* OE. [ad. L. *organum*, pl. *organa*, a. Gr. ὄργανον, pl. -να, instrument, organ, musical instrument. Used in OE. in Gr. form.] **I.** A musical instrument. †1. Applied vaguely in a general sense to various musical (esp. wind) instruments -1667. 2. *spec.* A musical instrument, consisting of a number of pipes, supplied with *wind* or compressed air by means of bellows, and sounded by means of keys, which on being pressed down admit the wind to the pipes by opening valves or *pallets.* late ME. †b. Formerly in *pl.* denoting a single instrument. (The L. sing. had also the sense 'pipe'. With *the organs* cf. *the bagpipes, the pipes.*) -1825. †c. Also called *a pair*, or *set, of organs* -1714. d. Applied, with distinctive epithets, to the separate groups of stops (*partial organs*), each with its own keyboard, which make up an organ 1606. 3. Applied to other musical instruments, as in *Dutch o.* 1825. b. = BARREL-*organ* 1840. c. A keyboard wind-instrument with metal reeds; a reed-organ. *American o.*: a reed-organ in which the air is drawn inwards to the reeds. 1880.

2. d. A complete o. may be said to consist of five parts: choir o., great o., swell o., solo o., and pedal o.

..A large o. therefore consists of a number of small organs differing in quality of tone, and so arranged as to be under the control of one performer. STAINER & BARRETT.

II. A part or member of an animal or plant body adapted by its structure for a particular vital function, as seeing, hearing, speaking, digestion, respiration, etc. late ME. b. The human organs of speech or voice collectively; the larynx and its accessories as used in singing. (Somewhat *rare.*) 1601. c. *Phrenology.* One of the regions of the brain held to be the seat of particular mental faculties or tendencies 1806. d. Used in the names of special structures in the animal body, denominated after their discoverers 1877.

1. The parts of our body, by which we perceive any thing, are those we commonly call the organs of sense 1656. b. Thy small pipe Is as the maidens o., shrill, and sound SHAKS. d. *O. of Corti*, a complicated structure in the cochlea of the ear, supposed to be the essential auditory apparatus.

III. A means of action or operation, an instrument, a 'tool'; a person, body of persons, or thing by which some purpose is carried out or some function performed (*arch.*) 1548. b. A mental or spiritual faculty regarded as an instrument of the mind or soul 1656. c. An instrument, means, or medium of communication, or of expression of opinion; *spec.* applied to a newspaper or journal which is the mouthpiece of a particular party, cause, movement, or pursuit 1788.

1. An enchanteresse, an orgayne of the deuill, sent from Sathane 1548. b. Faith,—Belief,—is the o. by which we apprehend what is beyond our knowledge 1836. c. A newspaper which was generally considered throughout India to be the o. of the Government 1853.

attrib. and *Comb.*, as **o.-bird**, a name for the S. Amer. *Cyphorhinus cantans* and a Tasmanian species of *Gymnorhina*, from their notes; **-blower**, a person who works the bellows of an o.; also a mechanical contrivance for the same purpose; **-cactus**, the giant cactus, *Cereus giganteus*, from the shape of its stem resembling an organ-pipe; **-grinder**, an itinerant street musician who turns the handle of a barrel-organ (see GRIND *v.*); so *organ-grinding* adj. and sb.; **-harmonium**, a large harmonium of elaborate construction or powerful tone, adapted to take the place of an o.; **-loft**, a loft or gallery in which an o. is placed; **-point** (*Mus.*) = PEDAL-POINT; **-stop**, a stop or set of pipes of the same quality of tone, in an o.

O·rgan, *v. rare.* 1652. [f. ORGAN *sb.*] †1. *trans.* To furnish with an organ or organs –1681. 2. To play on an organ 1827.

Organdie (ǭ·ɪgăndi). 1835. [a. F. *organdi*, of unkn. origin.] A very fine and translucent kind of muslin.

Organic (ǫɪgæ·nik), *a.* 1517. [ad. L. *organicus*, a. Gr., f. ὄργανον ORGAN *sb.* Cf. F. *organique* 14th–15th c. in Anatomy.] 1. Serving as an organ; instrumental. Now *rare.* 2. Done by means of instruments; mechanical 1885. 3. *Phys.* Of or pertaining to the bodily organs; vital; *spec.* in *Path.* of a disease, Producing or attended with alteration in the structure of an organ; structural (opp. to *functional*) 1706. 4. Having organs, or an organized physical structure (of animals or plants). Opp. to *inorganic.* 1778. b. *Chem.* Applied to a class of compound substances which naturally exist as constituents of organized bodies (animals or plants), or are formed from compounds which so exist, as in *o. acid, base, compound, molecule, radical*; all these contain or are derived from hydrocarbon radicals, hence *O. Chemistry* is the chemistry of the hydrocarbons and their derivs. 1827. 5. Belonging to the organization or constitution (bodily or mental) of a living being; constitutional; fundamental. b. Structural. 1796. c. *Philol.* Belonging to the etymological structure of a word; not secondary or fortuitous (often opp. to *analogical*) 1845. 6. Of, pertaining to, or characterized by connexion or coordination of parts in one whole; organized; systematic 1850. b. *U.S.* Organizing, constitutive, as *o. act, law* 1849. 7. Organ-like 1609.

1. Those o. arts which enable men to discourse and write MILT. 4. These rocks contain no o. remains 1813. I have used it [organic nature] almost as an equivalent of the word 'living' HUXLEY. 5. My o. indolence BURNEY. 6. Consciousness is..a membered or o. whole, every part of which exists only in and through its relation to the rest 1880. So †**Orga·nical** *a.*, in all senses 1521–1837. Hence **Orga·nically** *adv.* 1662.

Organicism (ǫɪgæ·nisiz'm). 1853. [See -ISM.] 1. The doctrine that organic structure is merely the result of an inherent property in matter to adapt itself to circumstances 1883. 2. *Path.* The doctrine of the localization of disease which refers it to a material lesion of an organ.

Organific (ǭɪgăni·fik), *a.* 1840. [f. L. *organum* ORGAN *sb.* + -FIC.] Having the property or power of forming organs or organized structures; formative, organizing.

Organism (ǭ·ɪgăniz'm). 1664. [f. ORGANIZE *v.*; see -ISM.] 1. Organic structure; organization. Now *rare.* 2. An organized or organic system; a whole consisting of dependent and interdependent parts, compared to a living being 1768. 3. An organized body, consisting of mutually connected and dependent parts constituted to share a common life; the material structure of an individual animal or plant 1842.

1. The advantagious O. of the Eye 1701. 2. Paul first taught us to speak of society as an o. 1900. Hence **Organi·smal** *a.*

Organist (ǭ·ɪgănist). 1591. [f. ORGAN *sb.* + -IST, after F. *organiste.*] 1. One who plays an organ, e.g. at the services in a church. †2. A maker of organs –1653. 3. A W. Indian song-bird, a species of *Euphonia*, esp. *E. musica.* Also *o. tanager.* 1882.

Organizable (ǭ·ɪgănəizăb'l), *a.* 1679. [f. ORGANIZE *v.* + -ABLE.] Capable of being organized; *spec.* in *Biol.* Capable of being converted into organized or living tissue. Hence **O:rganizabi·lity.**

Organization (ǭ:ɪgănəizē¹·ʃən, -izē¹·ʃən). late ME. [ad. med.L. *organizatio*, f. *organizare.*] 1. The action of organizing, or condition of being organized, as a living being; also, the way in which a living being is organized; the structure of an organized body (animal or plant), or of any part of one; bodily (*rarely* mental) constitution. b. The fact or process of becoming organized or organic; in *Path.* conversion into living tissue 1804. c. *concr.* An organized structure, body, or being; an organism 1707. 2. *gen.* The action of organizing 1816. b. The condition of being organized; the mode in which something is organized; systematic arrangement for a definite purpose 1790. c. *concr.* An organized body, system, or society 1873. 3. *Mediæval Mus.* The singing of the ORGANUM 1782.

1. That being then one Plant, which has such an O. of Parts in one coherent Body LOCKE. c. Choice organisations—natures framed to love perfection GEO. ELIOT. 2. The o. of a service of transport was then proceeded with 1897. b. The Turks arrived in Europe with an o. wholly military 1832.

Organize (ǭ·ɪgănəiz), *v.* late ME. [ad. med.L. *organizare*, f. *organum* ORGAN *sb.*; see -IZE. Cf. F. *organiser, -izer.*] 1. *trans.* To furnish with organs; to give an organic structure to; to form into a living being or living tissue. Usu. in *pa. pple.* b. *intr.* for *refl.* To become organic 1880. 2. *gen.* To form into a whole with interdependent parts; to give a definite and orderly structure to; to systematize; to arrange or 'get up' something involving united action 1632. 3. *Mus.* To sing the ORGANUM to a plain-song 1782.

1. Some Cheese Mites we could see (as little..as a Mustard-seed) yet perfectly shap'd and organiz'd 1664. 2. The several orders..so organized and so acting..they were the people of France BURKE. To o. a procession, a demonstration (*mod.*). Hence **O·rganizer**, one who organizes 1849.

Organo-, comb. form of Gr. ὄργανον ORGAN; as in: **O:rganometa·llic** *a.*, *Chem.* applied to compounds in which an organic radical is directly combined with a metal. **O:rganopla·stic**, having the property of forming or producing the bodily organs. **O:rganotherapeu·tics, -the·rapy**, the treatment of disease by the administration of portions of certain animal organs or of extracts of them.

O:rganoge·nesis. 1859. [f. ORGANO- + -GENESIS.] *Biol.* = next, a. So **O:rganogene·tic** *a.* organogenic.

Organogeny (ǭɪgănǫ·dʒĕni). 1844. [f. ORGANO- + -GENY.] *Biol.* a. The production or development of the organs of a plant. b. The department of biology dealing with this. So **O:rganoge·nic** *a.* **Organo·genist.**

Organography (ǭɪgănǫ·grăfi). 1559. [f. ORGANO- + -GRAPHY.] 1. A description of instruments –1674. 2. The description of the organs of living beings; structural anatomy, esp. of plants 1806. So **O:rganogra·phic, -al** *adjs.* **Organo·graphist.**

Organology (ǭɪgănǫ·lŏdʒi). 1814. [f. ORGANO- + -LOGY.] 1. The department of biology which treats of the organs of living beings, in ref. to their structure and functions 1842. 2. Phrenology 1814. So **O:rganolo·gical** *a.* **-o·logist.**

‖ **Organon** (ǭ·ɪgănǫn). 1590. [a. Gr. ὄργανον instrument, organ, etc.; the title of Aristotle's logical treatises = 'instrument' of all reasoning; cf. ORGANUM.] †1. A bodily organ, esp. as an instrument of the soul or mind –1629. 2. An instrument of thought or knowledge; *esp.* a system of rules or principles of demonstration or investigation; spec. title of the logical writings of Aristotle 1643.

O·rgan-pi:pe. late ME. [f. ORGAN *sb.* + PIPE *sb.*] 1. One of the pipes of an organ 1440. 2. *transf.* Applied to things resembling the pipes of an organ; e.g. *pl.* to basaltic columns closely placed 1861. 3. **Organ-pipe coral**: see CORAL *sb.* 1 b. 1833.

1. *fig.* The Thunder (That deepe and dreadfull Organ-Pipe) pronounc'd The name of Prosper SHAKS.

‖ **Organum** (ǭ·ɪgănŏm). 1614. [L., a. Gr.; see ORGANON.] 1. = ORGANON 1. b. = ORGANON 2; esp. in the title of Bacon's *Novum Organum*, i.e. New Instrument for scientific investigation 1856. 2. *Mediæval Mus.* A part sung as an accompaniment below or above the melody or plain-song, usu. at the interval of a fourth or fifth; also, *loosely*, this method of singing in parts. (Also called DIAPHONY.) 1782.

Organzine (ǭ·ɪgănzīn), *sb.* 1699. [a. F. *organsin*, ad. It. *organzino*, of unkn. origin.] Silk thread, formed of several strands twisted together in the contrary direction to that in which their component filaments are twisted. Also *o. silk.* Hence **O·rganzine** *v.* to make into o.; *intr.* to twist threads of silk so as to form o.

Orgasm (ǭ·ɪgæz'm). 1684. [ad. mod.L. *orgasmus*, a. Gr. *ὀργασμός, f. ὀργάειν to swell as with moisture, to be excited.] 1. Violent excitement of feeling; rage, fury; a paroxysm of excitement or rage 1763. 2. *Physiol.* Excitement in an organ or part, accompanied with turgescence; *spec.* the height of venereal excitement in coition 1684. Hence **Orga·stic** *a.*

Orgeat (ǭ·ɪdʒăt, ‖ orʒa). 1754. [a. F. *orgeat*, f. *orge* :—L. *hordeum* barley.] A syrup or cooling drink made orig. from barley, later from almonds, and orange-flower water.

‖ **Orgia**: see ORGY.

Orgiastic (ǭɪdʒiæ·stik), *a.* 1698. [ad. Gr. ὀργιαστικός, f. ὀργιαστής, f. ὀργιάζειν to celebrate orgies; see -IC.] Belonging to, or characterized by orgies; marked by licentiousness or dissolute revelry. So **Orgia·stical** *a. rare.*

‖ **Orgueil.** ME. [a. AF. *orguil*, OF. *orgoill*, etc. = It. *orgoglio* :—Com. Rom. sb., supposed ad. OHG. **urguolî*, f. *urguol* renowned.] Pride, haughtiness. *Obs.* exc. as alien.

Orgulous (ǭ·ɪgiŭləs), **orgillous** (ǭ·ɪgiləs), *a. arch.* ME. [a. OF. *orguillus*, mod.F. *orgueilleux*, f. *orgueil*; see prec. and -OUS.] Proud, haughty. b. Splendid. c. Swelling, violent.

Orgy, orgie (ǭ·ɪdʒi); chiefly in pl. **orgies** (ǭ·ɪdʒiz), †**orgia.** 1589. [In pl. *orgies*, a. F. *orgies*, ad. L. *orgia*, a. Gr. ὄργια pl., 'secret rites', also, in L. 'secret frantic revels'. The sing. is used mainly in sense 3.] 1. *Gr.* and *Rom. Antiq.* Secret rites practised in the worship of various deities; *esp.* those connected with the festivals in honour of Dionysus or Bacchus, celebrated with extravagant dancing, singing, drinking, etc. 2. *transf.* Applied to any rites, ceremonies, or secret observances 1598. 3. Feasting or revelry; wild or dissolute revels; debauchery; often in *sing.* A drunken or licentious revel 1703.

1. The Thracian Matrons,..With Furies, and Nocturnal Orgies fir'd DRYDEN. 2. *P.L.* I. 415. 3. The worship of the beautiful always ends in an o. DIS-

RAELI. *fig.* That o. of blood and arrogance—the European tyranny of Bonaparte 1883.

-o·rial, a compound suffix, consisting of -AL, L. *-alis*, added to L. *-ori-* in *-orius, -a, -um* (see -ORY). The termination is orig. adjectival (substantival only by ellipsis). In sense, adjs. in *-orial* are usu. identical with those in *-ory*, but the former are preferred where there is a sb. in *-ory* (e.g. *purgatory, purgatorial*).

‖ **Oribi, orebi** (ǫ·rĭbi). 1795. [Cape Du. app. from Hottentot.] A small species of S. African antelope (*Antilope* or *Ourebia scoparia* or *Scopophorus ourebi*).

Orichalc (ǫ·rikælk). Also in L. form **orichalcum.** 1590. [ad. L. *orichalcum*, a. Gr. ὀρείχαλκον, lit. 'mountain-copper'. In later L. made into *aurichalcum*, as if 'golden copper'.] Some yellow ore or alloy of copper, highly prized by the ancients; perh. brass.

Oriel (ōᵊ·riĕl). ME. [a. OF. *oriol* porch, passage, corridor, gallery; cf. med.L. *oriolum* porch, entrance-hall, antechamber. Origin unkn.] †1. A portico, corridor, balcony, etc. -1500. b. In Cornwall (*orrel*), a porch or balcony at the head of an outside stair 1880. 2. A large recess with a window, of polygonal plan, projecting from the outer face of a building, usu. in an upper storey, and either supported from the ground or on corbels ME. b. for *o. window.* (Occas. used vaguely for *stained-glass window.*) 1805.

2. That small excursion out of gentlemen's halls in Dorsetshire..is commonly called an orial FULLER. b. The moon on the east o. shone SCOTT.

attrib. and *Comb.* (from 2), as *o. casement*, etc.; **o. window**, the window of an 'oriel'; a projecting window in an upper storey. b. *Oriel College* (Oxford) derives its name from a messuage called, in the reign of Henry III, *La* (or *Le*) *Oriole*, the origin of which name is unknown.

Oriency (ōᵊ·riĕnsi). Now *rare.* 1652. [f. ORIENT *a.*; see -ENCY.] 'Orient' quality; brilliancy, lustre.

Orient (ōᵊ·riĕnt). late ME. [a. F., ad. L. *oriens, orientem* rising sun, east, orig. pr. pple. of *oriri* to rise. Cf. OCCIDENT.] A. *sb.* (In sense 1 and 2 usu. with cap.) 1. That region of the heavens in which the sun rises, or the corresponding region of the world, or quarter of the compass; the east. Now *poet.* or *rhet.* 2. Eastern countries, or the eastern part of a country; the East; usu., those countries east of the Mediterranean or of Southern Europe, the countries of South-western Asia or of Asia generally (cf. ORIENTAL A. 3); occas., in mod. Amer. use, Europe or the Eastern Hemisphere. Now *poet.* or *literary.* late ME. 3. Rising (of the sun, or the daylight); sunrise, dayspring, dawn. Now *rare* or *Obs.* 1582. 4. Short for 'pearl of orient' or 'orient pearl' 1831. 5. The peculiar lustre of a pearl of the best quality 1755.

1. Lo! in the o. when the gracious light Lifts up his burning head SHAKS. 2. Sicily, Greece, will invite, and the O. 1849. Phr. *Pearl of O.*: = o. pearl, oriental pearl; a pearl from the Indian seas; hence, a brilliant or precious pearl. 3. *fig.* His life having set in the o. of his age and hopes DRUMM. OF HAWTH.

B. *adj.* 1. Situated in or belonging to the east; eastern, oriental. Now *poet.* 1450. 2. Applied to pearls, etc., of superior value and brilliancy, as coming anciently from the East; often a vague epithet: Precious; brilliant, lustrous, sparkling. late ME. b. Hence, of other things: Brilliant, lustrous, radiant, resplendent; occas. (after A. 3), Shining like the dawn, bright red (*arch.*) late ME. 3. Rising, as the sun or daylight 1598.

1. When the Sun..Pillows his chin upon an O. wave MILT. 2. He nowe shyneth as doth an o. stoone 1494. b. Banners..With O. Colours waving MILT. 3. *fig.* The o. moon of Islam SHELLEY.

Orient (ōᵊ·rient), *v.* 1727. [a. F. *orienter* to place facing the east, f. *orient* east; see prec.] 1. *trans.* To place or arrange (anything) so as to face the east; *spec.* to build (a church) with the longer axis due east and west, and the chancel or chief altar at the east end; also, to bury with the feet to the east. b. By extension: To place with the four faces towards the four points of the compass; to place in any particular way with respect to the cardinal points; also, to determine the bearings of (anything) relatively to the points of the compass 1842. 2. *fig.* To adjust, correct, or bring into defined relations, to known facts or principles; *refl.* to put oneself in the right position or relation; also, to ascertain one's bearings. Now more usu. ORIENTATE. 1850. 3. *intr.* To turn to the east, or (by extension) towards any specified direction 1896.

2. Mistress Kitty..presently began orienting herself, and getting ready to make herself agreeable O. W. HOLMES.

Oriental (ōᵊri,e·ntăl). late ME. [a. F., ad. L. *orientalis*, f. *orientem*; see -AL. Opp. to OCCIDENTAL.] A. *adj.* 1. Belonging to, or situated in, the east, eastern, easterly; *spec.* in *Astrol.* said of a heavenly body when in the eastern part of the sky, *esp.* of a planet when seen in the east before sunrise. †2. Belonging to or situated in the east of a country or place, or of the earth -1669. 3. *spec.* Belonging to, found in, or characteristic of, the countries east of the Mediterranean; belonging to Asiatic countries; also, belonging to the east of Europe, or of Christendom (as the *O. Church*); Eastern. (Usu. with capital O.) 1425. 4. Of pearls and precious stones, and hence (formerly) of other things: = ORIENT B. 2, 2b. late ME.

3. **O. sore**, an ulcerous skin-disease occurring in the East, also called *Aleppo boil, Aleppo ulcer*, etc. 4. *O. amethyst, O. emerald, O. topaz* (respectively purple, green, and yellow varieties of sapphire).

B. *sb.* †1. An oriental pearl or other gem; see A. 4. -1750. †2. *pl.* Oriental languages; see A. 3. 1734. 3. A native or inhabitant of the East; i.e. usu., an Asiatic 1701.

3. A solemn, bearded, turbanded, and robed O. BURTON. Hence **Orie·ntalism**, o. character, style, or quality; with *pl.* an o. trait or idiom; o. scholarship. **Orie·ntalist**, = B. 3; one versed in o. languages and literature. **Orienta·lity**, the quality or condition of being o. **Orie·ntally** *adv.* in an o. manner or position 1649.

Orie·ntalize, *v.* 1823. [f. ORIENTAL *a.* + -IZE.] 1. *trans.* To make oriental. 2. *intr.* a. To become oriental in character. b. To play the oriental 1829. Hence **Orientaliza·tion.**

Orientate (ōᵊ·riĕntēⁱt), *v.* 1849. [f. F. *orienter*; see -ATE [3].] = ORIENT *v.*

To o. exactly his present mode of thought 1884.

Orientation (ōᵊriĕntēⁱ·ʃən). 1839. [f. prec. or ORIENT *v.*; see -ATION. So in mod. F.] 1. The action of orienting (see ORIENT *v.* 1). b. Position or arrangement (of a natural object or formation) relatively to the points of the compass or to other parts of the same structure; the 'lie' of a thing. In *Chem.*, the relative positions of the atoms or radicals in complex molecules. 1875. c. Transference eastwards. 2. The action of turning to or facing the east, the eastward position 1875. 3. The action of ascertaining, or fact of knowing, the relative position of anything or of oneself; *spec.* in *Zool.* the faculty by which birds and other animals find their way back to a place after going or being taken to a place distant from it (as in homing pigeons and migratory birds) 1868. 4. *fig.* (from various senses): Adjustment, position, or aspect with regard to anything; determination of one's bearings in relation to circumstances, ideas, etc. 1870.

1. The o. of churches is from the rites of Etruscan augury 1881. 3. Psychical disturbance, marked by apathy,..variable temper, delusions, imperfect o. 1899. 4. The double o., one towards God, the other towards the world BARING-GOULD.

†**O·riently**, *adv.* 1515. [f. ORIENT *a.* + -LY [2].] In an 'orient' manner; brilliantly; clearly -1664. So †**O·rientness** -1661.

Orifice (ǫ·rifis). 1541. [a. F., ad. late L. *orificium*, f. *os, or-* mouth + *facere*, in comp. *-ficere* to make.] An opening or aperture, which serves as, or has the form of, a mouth, as of a tube, of the stomach, bladder, etc., of a wound; the mouth of any cavity, a perforation or vent.

The mountain resembled Ætna, being bored through the top with a monstrous o. ADDISON.

Oriflamme (ǫ·riflæm). 1475. [a. F., OF. *oriflambe*; f. L. *aurum* (F. *or*) gold + *flamma* flame.] 1. The sacred banner of St. Denis, a banderole of two (or three) points, of red or orange-red silk, attached to a lance, which the early kings of France used to receive from the hands of the abbot of St. Denis, on setting out for war. 2. *transf.* and *fig.* a. Any banner or ensign, material or ideal, that serves as a rallying point for a struggle, etc. 1600. b. Something which suggests the Oriflamme of St. Denis by its colouring, conspicuous position, etc. 1862.

2. a. And be your o. to-day the helmet of Navarre: MACAULAY. b. The new-bathed Day With o. uplifted o'er the peaks GEO. ELIOT.

Origan (ǫ·rigăn). Now *rare.* late ME. [a. F., ad. L. *origanum*; see next.] A plant of the genus *Origanum*, esp. Wild Marjoram (*O. vulgare*); formerly also applied to other aromatic labiates, as Pennyroyal (*Mentha Pulegium*).

‖ **Origanum** (ŏri·gănǝm). ME. [L., = 'wild marjoram', a. Gr. ὀρίγανον, -ος, 'an acrid herb like marjoram'.] A genus of labiates, with aromatic leaves; comprising Wild Marjoram (*O. vulgare*), Sweet Marjoram (*O. Marjorana*), Pot Marjoram (*O. Onites*), Dittany of Crete (*O. Dictamnus*), etc.

Origenist (ǫ·ridʒĕnist). 1546. [-IST.] A follower of Origen of Alexandria (*c* 185–253), or a holder of some one of the special doctrines attributed to him, among which were a threefold sense (literal, moral, and mystical) in Scripture, the pre-existence of souls, and the probable ultimate salvation of all men and of the fallen angels. So **O·rigenism.**

Origin (ǫ·ridʒin). 1563. [a. F. *origine*, ad. L. *originem, origo* beginning, source, f. *oriri* to rise.] 1. The act or fact of arising from something; derivation, rise; beginning of existence in ref. to its source or cause. b. Of a person: Descent, parentage 1605. 2. That from which anything arises, springs, or is derived 1604. b. *Anat.* The place at which a muscle, nerve, etc. arises; the root of a nerve in the brain or spinal cord 1691. c. *Math.* A fixed point from which measurement or motion commences; *spec.* the point of intersection of the axes in Cartesian co-ordinates, or the pole in polar co-ordinates. [= F. *origine.*] 1723.

1. Phr. *Certificate of o.*, a custom-house document certifying the place of o. of a commodity imported. The O. and Commencement of this greefe SHAKS. b. A distinguished man of humble o. (*mod.*). 2. We hoped..to be able to examine the glacier to its o. TYNDALL.

Original (ŏri·dʒinăl), *a.* and *sb.* ME. [a. F., ad. L. *originalis*, f. *originem* ORIGIN. Cf. F. *originel* in some of the senses.] A. *adj.* 1. Of or pertaining to the origin of something; that existed at first, or has existed from the first; primary; initial, first. b. *transf.* That is such from the beginning, or by birth; 'a born..' *rare* 1720. 2. That is the origin or source of something; primary; originative. (Now usu. merged in 1.) late ME. b. *spec.* Applied to anything in relation to that which is a representation or reproduction of it 1631. 3. Produced by or proceeding from some thing or person directly; underived, independent 1792; first-hand 1700. 4. Such as has not been done or produced before; novel or fresh in character or style 1756. b. *transf.* Of a person: Capable of original ideas or actions; inventive, creative 1803.

1. I am as sory, as if the originall fault had beene my fault 1592. Phr. *O. sin* (Theol.): the innate depravity of man's nature, held to be inherited from Adam in consequence of the Fall. (Opp. to *actual sin.*) 2. The rote and orygynall fountaine of all synne BIBLE 1551 *Rom.* Prol. O. and documentary authorities 1861. Phr. †*O. writ* (in *Law*): a writ issuing from the Court of Chancery, which formed the beginning or foundation of a real action at common law. b. The O. Texts are not corrupted 1659. It may be a misprint; you had better examine the o. document (*mod.*). 3. There is a certain quality about an o. drawing which you cannot get in a woodcut RUSKIN. 4. Even on..Aristotle's Ethics he could throw an o. light 1882. b. A great o. genius struggling with unequal conditions of knowledge JOWETT.

B. *sb.* 1. = ORIGIN 1. Now *rare* or *arch.* late ME. b. Of persons: = ORIGIN 1 b. Now *rare* or *arch.* 1555. †c. Beginning, earliest stage -1753. 2. = ORIGIN 2; an originator, an author. Now *rare* or *arch.* in gen. sense. late ME. b. *Law.* = *O. writ*: see A. 2. 1450. 3. A thing (or person) in relation to something else which is a copy, imitation, or representation of it; the pattern, archetype. late ME. 4. A work of literature or art that is not a copy or imitation; an original portrait 1683. 5. A person who acts in an original way; a singular, odd, or eccentric person 1676. 6. †a. *pl.* Original elements -1667. b. *pl.* Original inhabitants, members, etc. *rare.* 1703.

1. The Circus and Amphitheatre..all owe their o. to the Theatre 1726. 2. Spangled Heav'ns, a Shining Frame, Their great O. proclaim ADDISON. 3. The resemblance is more visible in the o. than in our translation PALEY. Cunobelin, the o. of Shakspere's Cymbeline 1892. 4. There are no absolutely undoubted originals of Queen Mary SCOTT. 5. This boy is a real o. M. ARNOLD. Hence **Ori·ginally** *adv.*

Originality (ŏridʒinæ·lĭti). 1742. [ad. F. *originalité*, f. prec.; see -ITY.] The quality or fact of being original. b. with *pl.* An original trait, act, remark, etc. 1854.

Originant (ŏri·dʒinănt), *a.* (*sb.*) 1647. [f. ORIGIN-ATE *v.* + -ANT.] A. *adj.* Originating. B. *sb.* Originating agent or influence 1892.

Originary (ŏri·dʒinări). *a.* (*sb.*) Now *rare.* 1594. [ad. late L. *originarius*, f. *originem* ORIGIN; see -ARY.] A. *adj.* †1. That originates *from* (*of*) the thing or place in question; derived *from*; aboriginal, native. 2. = ORIGINAL A. 2. 1638.

1. A Natif of Coventry, tho' o. of Cheshire 1716.

†B. *sb.* An aboriginal, a native -1716.

Originate (ŏri·dʒineᵉit), *v.* 1653. [As if f. **originat-*, **originare* (f. *originem* ORIGIN), perh. used in med. or mod.L.] 1. *trans.* To give origin to, cause to arise or begin, initiate 1657. 2. *intr.* To take its origin or rise, have its beginning; to spring, be derived. Const. *from, in, with.* 1775. b. *Anat.*, etc. To have its origin (locally); to arise (*in* or *from*) 1799.

1. Men..who have originated remarkable religious movements 1878. 2. The fire originated in the chemical room 1885. So **Origina·tion**, the action or fact of originating 1647; *spec.* †derivation (of a word) 1641-1741. **Ori·ginative** *a.* having the quality or power of originating; productive, creative. **Ori·ginator.**

‖ **Ori·llion, oreillon.** 1647. [a. F. *orillon* (oriˡyoṅ), *oreillon*, deriv. of *oreille* ear.] *Fortif.* A part of the defence of a bastion; a projecting tower at the shoulder of a bastion.

Orinasal (ōᵊrinē·zăl), *a.* (*sb.*) 1862. [f. L. *ori-*, comb. form of *os, or-* mouth + NASAL.] Pertaining to the mouth and nose; *spec.* of a vowel: Pronounced with the oral and nasal passages both open, as the 'nasal' vowels in French. B. *sb.* An orinasal vowel.

Oriole (ōᵊ·riōl). 1776. [ad. med. and mod. L. *oriolus*, in OF. *oriol* :—L. *aureolus* golden.] 1. A bird of the genus *Oriolus*, esp. *O. galbula* (the Golden Oriole), a summer visitor to Europe, with plumage of a rich yellow and black; also, any bird of the family *Oriolidæ*. 2. A bird of the genus *Icterus*, as the Baltimore Oriole (*I. baltimore*), the Orchard Oriole (*I. spurius*); or any bird of the family *Icteridæ* or subfamily *Icterinæ*, peculiar to America, mostly with similar coloration; also called *hangnests* or *hangbirds* 1792.

Orion (ŏrəi·ŏn). late ME. [L., = Gr. Ὠρίων (ī or ĭ) one of the Giants of Greek mythology, a mighty hunter.] *Astron.* A large and brilliant constellation south of the zodiac, figured as a hunter with belt and sword. *Orion's hound*, the dog-star, Sirius (S.E. of Orion).

Great O. sloping slowly to the West TENNYSON. Hence **Ori·onid**, one of a system of meteors whose radiant point is in O. 1876.

-o·rious, a compound suffix forming adjs., consisting of -OUS (L. *-osus*), added to L. *-ori-* in *ori-us, -a, -um* (see -ORY). The sense is either the same as, or closely akin to, that of adjs. in -ORY.

Orismology (ǫrizmǫ·lŏdʒi). *rare.* 1816. [For **horismology*, f. Gr. ὁρισμός definition + -LOGY.] A name for the explanation of technical terms, or for such terms collectively; terminology. Hence **Orismolo·gic, -al** *adjs.*

Orison (ǫ·rizən, -sən). *arch.* ME. [a. OF *oreisun, orison*, now *oraison* :—L. *orationem* speech, in Christian L. an address to God, a prayer; f. *orare*, f. *os, or-* mouth. Etymologically a doublet of *oration.*] A prayer. (In later use chiefly in *pl.*) b. Without *an* or *pl.* The action of praying, prayer. Now *rare.* ME.

Nimph, in thy Orizons Be all my sinnes remembred SHAKS.

Orison, -soun, -sont(e, obs. ff. HORIZON.

-o·rium, *suffix*, neut. sing. ending of L. adjs. in *-orius* (see -ORIOUS, -ORY), used subst. in sense 'place for or belonging to, thing used for', as in *auditorium* place for hearing, *prætorium* general's tent, etc. The Eng. form of these words is -ORY; but some of the L. words have been taken into historical or learned use, as *sanatorium, scriptorium*, and after these others have been formed as scientific terms.

Orle (ǭl). 1572. [a. F., OF. *urle, ourle* = It. *orlo* border, hem :—late L. **orulum*, dim. of *ora* border.] *Her.* A narrow band of half the width of the bordure, following the outline of the shield, but not extending to the edge of it 1610. b. A band of small charges arranged round the shield orlewise. Hence *in o.*, said of subordinate charges thus borne. 1572. c. The chaplet or wreath round the helmet of a knight, bearing the crest 1834.

Orleanist (ǭ·ɹlĭănist). 1848. [a. F. *Orléaniste*, f. local name *Orléans*; see next and -IST.] In French politics: An adherent of the princes of the house of Orleans, descended from the Duke of Orleans, younger brother of Louis XIV, whose descendant Louis Philippe reigned as King of the French. Also *attrib.* or as *adj.* So **O·rleanism**, the political principles of the Orleanists.

Orleans (ǭ·ɹlĭănz). 1664. [Name of a city in France.] 1. A variety of plum. 2. A fabric of cotton warp and worsted weft, brought alternately to the surface in weaving 1844.

Orlop (ǭ·ɹlǫp). 1467. [a. Du. *overloop* a covering, f. *overloopen* to run over; see OVER and LEAP *v.*] orig. The single floor or deck with which the hold of a ship was covered in, which, by the successive addition of one, two, or three complete decks above, became the lowest deck of a ship of the line; occas. applied to the lowest deck of a steamer, etc.

Ormer (ǭ·ɹməɹ). 1672. [Channel Islands Fr., = F. *ormier*, contr. f. *oreille-de-mer*, or ad. L. *auris maris* sea-ear, from its shape.] The Sea-ear, a species of univalve mollusc, *Haliotis tuberculata*, specially abundant in Guernsey, where it is used as food. Hence any species of *Haliotis*.

Ormolu (ǭ·ɹmŏlū). 1765. [a. F. *or moulu*, lit. 'ground gold'.] orig., Gold or gold-leaf ground and prepared for gilding brass, bronze, or other metal; hence, gilded bronze used in the decoration of furniture, etc. Now, An alloy of copper, zinc, and tin, having the colour of gold. b. *attrib.* and *Comb.*, as *o. clock*; **o.-varnish**, a copper, bronze, or imitation-gold varnish, also called 'Mosaic gold'.

Ornament (ǭ·ɹnăměnt), *sb.* ME. [a. OF. *ournement, ornement*, ad. L. *ornamentum* equipment, ornament, f. *ornare.*] †1. Any adjunct or accessory; equipment, furniture, attire, trappings -1747. b. *Eccl.* The accessories or furnishings of the Church and its worship, e.g. vestments, plate, organs, bells, etc. late ME. 2. Anything used, or serving to adorn; a decoration, embellishment. late ME. b. A person who adorns his sphere, time, etc. 1573. 3. The action of adorning or fact of being adorned; adornment, decoration (*lit.* or *fig.*): that in which this consists 1596. b. Mere adornment; outward show. SHAKS.

1. b. *Ornaments rubric*, the rubric immediately before the Order for Morning and Evening Prayer in the Book of Common Prayer, which refers to the 'ornaments' to be used in the Church. 2. This O. of Knighthood [the garter] SHAKS. *fig.* The o. of a meek and quiet spirit *1 Pet.* iii. 4. b. Thos singular men, the late ornaments of Cambridg and the glori of Pembrook Hal 1573. 3. There was no beauty..either of artful o., or of natural wildness 1817. b. *Merch. V.* III. ii. 97. Hence **Orname·ntal** *a.* of the nature of, or serving as, an o.; decorative; *sb. pl.* things that are ornamental (as opp. to *essentials*). **Orname·ntalism**, the principle or practice of being o. **Orname·ntalist. Orname·ntally** *adv.*

Ornament (ǭ·ɹnăment), *v.* 1720. [f. prec.] *trans.* To furnish with ornament; to adorn, embellish. Hence **O:rnamenta·tion**, the action or process of ornamenting; the state of being adorned; ornament in general. **O·rnamenter. O·rnamentist**, a professional decorator.

Ornate (ǭɹnē·t), *ppl. a.* late ME. [ad. L. *ornatus, ornare.*] †1. as *pa. pple.* Adorned, ornamented (*with*) -1771. 2. as *adj.* Ornamented; elaborately adorned or embellished 1503. b. Of literary or oratorical style: Embellished with choice language or flowers of rhetoric. late ME.

2. Femal of sex it seems, That so bedeckt, o., and gay, Comes this way sailing Like a stately Ship MILT. b. In diction Virgil is o. and Homer simple GLADSTONE. Hence **Ornate·ly** *adv.*, **-ness.**

†**Orna·te**, *v.* 1495. [f. L. *ornat-, ornare*; see -ATE [3].] *trans.* To adorn, embellish -1651.

Ornature (ǭ·ɹnătiŭɹ). *rare.* 1538. [a. F. ad. late L. *ornatura*, f. *ornat-, ornare*; see -URE.] Ornamentation, embellishment.

‖ **Ornis** (ǭ·ɹnis). 1861. [a. Gr. ὄρνις bird after use.] = AVIFAUNA.

Ornithic (ǭɹni·þik), *a.* 1854. [ad. Gr. ὀρνιθικός bird-like, f. ὄρνις bird.] Of, or pertaining to, birds; characteristic of birds; avian. b. Dealing with or skilled in birds 1876.

Ornithichnite (ǭɹniþi·knəit). 1836. [ad. mod.L. *ornithichnites* (also much used), f. Gr. ὄρνις, ὀρνιθ- bird + ἴχνος track.] A fossil footprint of a bird or bird-like reptile.

Ornitho-, bef. a vowel **ornith-**, repr. Gr. ὀρνιθο-, ὀρνιθ-, comb. form of ὄρνις bird, as in ὀρνιθο-φάγος bird-eating, etc. Used in Eng. to form many scientific terms; as ‖ **Ornithode·lphia** [Gr. δελφύς womb], *Zool.* = MONOTREMATA. **Orni·tholite** [-LITE], a fossil of a bird or part of a bird. **Ornitho·pterous** [Gr. πτερόν feather, wing], *a.* having wings like a bird. **Ornitho·tomy** [Gr. -τομια cutting; see -TOMY], dissection of birds; the anatomy of birds. See also Main words.

Ornithology (ǭɹniþǫ·lŏdʒi). 1706. [ad. mod.L. *ornithologia*, f. Gr. ὀρνιθολόγος treating of birds; see prec. and -LOGY. Cf. F. *ornithologie.*] The branch of zoology which deals with birds, their nature and habits. (By Fuller used for 'the Speech of Birds'.) So **Ornitholo·gic, -al** *adjs.* of or pertaining to o. 1802. **Ornitho·logist**, one versed in o.; a student of birds 1677.

Ornithomancy (ǭ·ɹniþomænsi). 1652. [ad. med. or mod.L. *ornithomantia*, a. Gr. ὀρνιθομαντεία; see ORNITHO- and -MANCY.] Divination by means of the flight and cries of birds; augury.

Ornithopod (ǭ·ɹniþopǫd). 1888. [ad. mod. L. *Ornithopoda*, neut. pl., f. ORNITHO- + Gr. πούς, ποδ- foot.] A. *adj.* Having feet like those of a bird; belonging to the *Ornithopoda*, a group or order of extinct saurians, containing herbivorous *Dinosauria*. B. *sb.* A member of this group. So **Ornitho·podous** *a.*

‖**Ornithorhynchus** (ǭ:ɹniþori·ŋkŏs, ǭɹnəiþo-). 1800. [f. ORNITHO- + Gr. ῥύγχος bill.] An aquatic mammal of Australia, the duck-billed platypus or duck-mole (*O. paradoxus* or *anatinus*), the only species of its genus or family in the order *Monotremata*; it has glossy dark-brown fur, webbed feet and bill like a duck's; it lays eggs with a flexible shell.

Ornithosaurian (-sǭ·riăn), *a.* and *sb.* [f. mod.L. *Ornithosauria*, neut. pl., f. ORNITHO- + Gr. σαῦρος lizard; see SAURIAN.] *Palæont.* = PTEROSAURIAN.

Ornithoscelidan (-se·lidăn), *a.* (*sb.*) 1876. [f. mod.L. *Ornithoscelida* pl. (f. ORNITHO- + Gr. σκέλος leg + *-ida*) + -AN.] *Palæont.* Of or belonging to the *Ornithoscelida*, a sub-class or order of extinct reptiles of Mesozoic and Tertiary age, which approached birds in the form of the hinder legs and the pelvic arch. B. *sb.* A member of this order.

Ornithoscopy (ǭɹniþǫ·skŏpi). 1840. [ad. Gr. ὀρνιθοσκοπία, f. ὀρνιθοσκόπος, f. ὀρνιθο- bird + -σκοπος viewing.] Observation of birds for the purpose of divination; augury.

Orocentral (ōᵊrose·ntrăl), *a.* 1884. [irreg. for **oricentral*, f. L. *os, or-* mouth + CENTRAL.] Occupying the centre of the oral side (of an echinoderm).

Orography (orǫ·grăfi), **oreography** (ǫriǫ·g-). 1846. [f. Gr. ὄρος, ὀρε- mountain + -GRAPHY. *Orography* is now usual.] That branch of physical geography which deals with the formation and features of mountains; the description of mountains. So Orogra·phic, -al *adjs.* 1802.

‖ **Orohippus** (ǫrohi·pǫs). 1877. [mod.L., f. Gr. ὄρος mountain + ἵππος horse.] A genus of fossil quadrupeds found in the Eocene beds of North America, held to be an ancestral form of the horse.

Oroide (ōᵊrǫ,id). 1875. [f. F. *or* (L. *aurum*) gold + Gr. εἶδος form; cf. -OID.] An alloy of copper and zinc, having the colour of gold.

Orology (orǫ·lŏdʒi), **oreology** (ǫri,ǫ·l-). 1781. [f. Gr. ὄρος, ὀρε- mountain + -LOGY.] The scientific study of mountains.

Oronoco, -ooko (ōᵊrǫnōᵘ·ko, -ū·ko). 1706. [Origin unkn.: app. unconnected with the river Orinoco.] A variety of tobacco from Virginia.

Orotund (ōᵊrotɒnd), *a.* (*sb.*) 1792. [f. L. phr. *ore rotundo*, lit. 'with round mouth' (Hor. *A. P.* 323).] Of the voice or utterance: Full, clear, and stronger than ordinary speech; also, contemptuously, magniloquent, inflated, pompous. **b.** *ellipt.* as *sb.* (*sc.* voice, utterance).

Orphan (ǭ·ɹfăn), *sb.* and *a.* 1483. [ad. late L. *orphanus*, a. Gr. ὀρφανός without parents, bereaved.] **A.** *sb.* One deprived by death of father or mother, or (usu.) of both; a fatherless or motherless child 1484.

fig. They..Are orphans of the earthly love and heavenly MRS. BROWNING. *Orphan's Court*, a probate court in some states of the U.S., having jurisdiction over the estates and persons of orphans. **O.-asylum, -hospital, -house**, an orphanage.

B. *adj.* Bereaved of parents; fatherless or motherless, or both 1483. Hence **O·rphan, O·rphanize,** *vbs.* to make an o. of. **O·rphancy, O·rphanhood, †O·rphanism,** the condition or position of an o.

Orphanage (ǭ·ɹfănėdʒ). 1579. [f. prec. sb. + -AGE.] **1.** The state of being an orphan. **2.** An institution or home for orphans 1865.

Orpharion (ǭɹfărəi·ǭn). 1593. [Fusion of the names Orpheus and Arion.] A large instrument of the lute kind with from six to nine pairs of metal strings played with a plectrum; much used in the 17th c.

Orphean (ǫɹfī·ăn), *a.* and *sb.* 1593. [f. L. *Orphēus* (a. Gr. Ὀρφεῖος, f. Ὀρφεύς) + -AN.] **A.** *adj.* Of or relating to Orpheus, as musician and singer, who was said to move rocks and trees by the music of his lyre; hence, melodious, entrancing, like his music. **B.** *sb.* An adherent of the Orphic philosophy 1818.

A. With other notes then to th' O. Lyre I sung of Chaos and Eternal Night MILT.

Orpheonist (ǭ·ɹfiǫnist). 1860. [a. F. *orphéoniste*, f. *Orphéon*, name of a school of vocal music established at Paris in 1833, and called after Orpheus.] A member of an *Orphéon*; a choral singer.

Orphic (ǭ·ɹfik), *a.* (*sb.*) 1678. [ad. Gr. Ὀρφικός (in L. *Orphicus*), f. Ὀρφεύς; see -IC.] **A.** *adj.* **1.** Of or connected with Orpheus, or the mysteries, writings, or doctrines associated with his name; hence, oracular. **2.** Of the nature of the music of Orpheus; melodious, ravishing 1817. **B.** *sb.* An Orphic song or hymn; chiefly in *pl.* 1855.

A. 2. An o. song indeed, A song divine of high and passionate thoughts COLERIDGE.

Orphism (ǭ·ɹfiz'm). 1880. [f. prec. + -ISM.] The system of mystic philosophy embodied in the Orphic poems, and taught to the initiated in the Orphic mysteries. So **O·rphist.**

Orphrey, orfray. (ǭ·ɹfreᵢ, -fri). [ME. *orfreis*, a. OF. *orfreis* :—**aurifrisium* for L. *auriphrygium* gold embroidery, f. *aurum* gold + *Phrygius* Phrygian; cf. *Phrygiæ vestes* Phrygian (gold-embroidered) garments. The final -*s* of *orfreis* is now treated as the pl. suffix.] **1.** Gold embroidery, or any rich embroidery; with *an* and *pl.*, a piece of richly embroidered stuff. Now only *Hist.* or *arch.* **2.** An ornamental strip or band, esp. on an eccl. vestment, often richly embroidered. late ME.

Orpiment (ǭ·ɹpimĕnt). ME. [a. OF., ad. L. *auripigmentum* (Vitruv.) gold pigment.] A bright yellow mineral substance, the trisulphide of arsenic, also called Yellow Arsenic, found native in soft masses resembling gold in colour; also manufactured by the combination of sulphur and arsenious oxide; used as a pigment under the name of King's Yellow.

O. is the original ARSENIC (sense 1 a) of the ancients. Also called *Yellow O.* to distinguish it from the so-called *Red O.* = REALGAR, disulphide of arsenic.

Orpine, orpin (ǭ·ɹpin). late ME. [a. F. *orpin*, app. altered in some way from *orpiment*.] †**1.** = ORPIMENT 1548–1725. **2.** A succulent herbaceous plant, *Sedum Telephium*, well-known in the cottage garden; from its tenacity of life, pop. called *Live-long.*

O·rpington. 1887. [f. *Orpington* in Kent.] Name of a breed of poultry.

Orrery (ǫ·rəri). 1713. [Named after Chas. Boyle, Earl of O., for whom one was made.] A piece of mechanism devised to represent the motions of the planets about the sun by means of clockwork.

Orris[1] (ǫ·ris). 1545. [app. unexplained alteration of IRIS.] **1.** A plant of the genus *Iris*, esp. *I. germanica* and *I. florentina*; the flower-de-luce 1626. **2.** Short for *orris-root*, *-powder.*

Comb.: **o.-powder**, powdered orris-root; **-root**, the rhizome of three species of Iris (*I. florentina*, *I. germanica*, *I. pallida*), which has an odour like that of violets; used as a perfume and in medicine.

Orris[2] (ǫ·ris). 1701. [Origin obsc.] A name given to lace of various patterns in gold and silver; embroidery made of gold lace.

Orse·llic, *a.* 1848. [f. med.L. *orsella* ORCHIL + -IC.] *Chem.* In *o. acid*, a crystalline solid, $C_{16}H_{14}O_7 + 2H_2O$, obtained from S. African and S. American lichens. So **O·rsellate**, a salt of o. acid. **Orselli·nic acid**, a crystalline substance, $C_8H_8O_4 + H_2O$, obtained by the action of baryta water on erythrin.

Ort (ǭɹt). Usu. in pl. **orts.** late ME. [app. cogn. w. early mod.Du. *ooraete*, *oorete* remains of food, LG. *ort*; f. *or-*, *oor-* privative + *etan* to eat.] Fragments of food left over from a meal; refuse fodder; scraps, leavings; also *fig.* *To make orts of*, to undervalue.

Let him haue time a beggers orts to craue SHAKS.

Orthian (ǭ·ɹþiăn), *a.* 1751. [f. Gr. ὄρθιος upright, high-pitched + -AN.] Applied to a style of singing, or tune, of very high pitch.

Orthid (ǭ·ɹþid). 1861. [f. mod.L. *Orthidæ*, f. *Orthis*, f. Gr. ὀρθός straight; see -ID [2].] A member of the *Orthidæ*, or genus *Orthis*, of fossil bivalves.

Orthite (ǭ·ɹþəit). 1817. [= G. *orthit*, f. Gr. ὀρθός straight; see -ITE [1].] *Min.* A variety of ALLANITE, found in long slender crystals, or straight masses. Hence **Orthi·tic** *a.*

Ortho- (bef. a vowel occas. **orth-**, comb. form of Gr. ὀρθός, used sometimes in the physical sense 'straight', sometimes in the ethical sense 'right, correct'.

1. In technical words generally: **O·rthocentre,** *Geom.* the point at which the perpendiculars from the angles of a triangle on the opposite side intersect. **Orthodia·gonal,** *Cryst.* (*a*) *sb.*, that lateral axis in the monoclinic system which is at right angles to the vertical axis; (*b*) *adj.*, belonging to or in the line of this axis (opp. to *clinodiagonal*). **O·rthodome** [DOME *sb.* 5 b], *Cryst.* a dome parallel to the orthodiagonal in the monoclinic system. **Orthopi·nacoid,** *Cryst.* one of the principal planes in the monoclinic system, parallel to the vertical axis and the orthodiagonal; hence **Orthopinacoi·dal** *a.* **Orthopy·ramid,** *Cryst.* in the monoclinic system a pyramid lying between the orthodomes and the zone of unit pyramids. **Orthosymme·tric** *a.*, *Cryst.* symmetric about two, or three, axes at right angles to each other; *spec.* = ORTHORHOMBIC. **Orthoto·mic** [Gr. -τόμος cutting], *a.* *Math.* intersecting at right angles.

2. In *Chemistry*, **a.** *Ortho-* is used to distinguish one class of acids and their salts from another denoted by the prefix *meta-*, which contain the same elements in different proportions, the *meta-* acid containing a molecule of H_2O less than the *ortho-* acid, the *ortho-* salt being also the more basic and the *meta-* salt the less basic. Thus *orthophosphoric acid* H_3PO_4, *metaphosphoric acid* HPO_3; *sodium orthophosphate* Na_3PO_4, *sodium metaphosphate* $NaPO_3$. **b.** With the names of isomeric benzene di-derivatives, *ortho-* is applied to those in which two consecutive hydrogen atoms are replaced by another element or radical, as dist. from *meta-* and *para-* derivatives, in which the two atoms are not consecutive, but unsymmetrically or symmetrically dispersed respectively. Examples: *orthodibromobenzene*, *orthopropylphenol.*

Orthocephalic (ǭ·ɹþosĭfæ·lik), *a.* 1865. [f. ORTHO- 'right, correct' + Gr. κεφαλή head + -IC.] *Ethnol.* Applied to skulls of which the breadth is from about $\frac{3}{4}$ to $\frac{4}{5}$ of the length (intermediate between *brachycephalic* and *dolichocephalic*); or, according to some, of which the height is from $\frac{7}{10}$ to $\frac{3}{4}$ of the length, or of which the height is $\frac{4}{5}$ of the breadth. So **Orthoce·phalous** *a.* **Orthoce·phaly,** the condition of being o.

‖ **Orthoceras** (ǫɹþǫ·sĕræ̆s). *Pl.* **orthocerata** (ǭ·ɹþosĕrē·tă). 1830. [f. ORTHO- 'straight' + Gr. κέρας, pl. κέρατα horn.] *Palæont.* An extinct genus of cephalopods, having long straight chambered shells; a fossil shell of this genus. Hence **Ortho·ceran** *a.*

Orthoceratite (ǭɹþose·rătəit). Also in L. form **orthoceratites** (ǭ·ɹþosĕrătəi·tīz). 1754. [f. as prec. + -ITE [1] 2.] A shell of the genus *Orthoceras* or family *Orthoceratidæ*; also, an animal of this genus or family.

Orthochromatic (ǭ·ɹþo,krǫmæ·tik), *a.* 1887. [f. ORTHO- 'correct, proper' + Gr. χρωματικός CHROMATIC.] *Photogr.* Representing colours in their correct relations, i.e. without exaggerating the deepness of some and the brightness of others (as in ordinary photography). So **Orthochromatism** (-krōᵘ·mătiz'm), the condition of being o. **Orthochro·matize** *v.*

Orthoclase (ǭ·ɹþǒklēs). 1849. [f. ORTHO- 'straight, right' + Gr. κλάσις breaking, cleavage.] *Min.* Common or potash feldspar, a silicate of aluminium and potassium, occurring in crystals or masses of various colours, characterized by two cleavages at right angles to each other. So **Orthocla·stic** *a.* having cleavages at right angles to each other.

Orthodox (ǭ·ɹþǒdǫks). 1581. [ult. ad. Gr. ὀρθόδοξος right in opinion, f. ὀρθός + δόξα. Cf. F. *orthodoxe.*] **A.** *adj.* **1.** Holding correct, i.e. currently accepted, opinions, *esp.* in theology 1611. **2.** Of opinions or doctrines: Right, correct, true; in accordance with what is authoritatively established as the true view or right practice; *orig.* in theological and eccl. doctrine 1581. **3.** Conventional; approved 1838. **4.** (*With capital.*) Specific epithet of the Eastern Church, which recognizes the headship of the Patriarch of Constantinople, and of the historical churches of Russia, Serbia, Rumania, etc., which recognize each other as of the same communion; the historical representative of the churches of the ancient East, commonly called the *Greek Church* 1772.

1. Men falsely called o. and divines 1722. **2.** To maintaine the precepts of the o. faith JAS. I. I am well aware, how much my sentiments differ from the o. opinions of one or two principal patriots SWIFT. **3.** The o. half-hour had expired LYTTON. **4.** The epithet 'Orthodox' was orig. assumed to distinguish it [the Eastern Church] from the various divisions of the Eastern Church, e.g. the Jacobite or Monophysite, Nestorian, etc.,..; but it is sometimes used by historical writers as opposed to 'Catholic'. N.E.D.

B. *sb.* An orthodox person. **b.** A member of the orthodox Eastern Church. 1587.

Was he an Heretick, or an Orthodoxe? 1641. Hence **†O·rthodoxal** *a.* **†Orthodoxa·stical** *a.*, in senses A. 1, 2. **Orthodo·xical** *a.* (now *rare*), **-ly** *adv.* **O·rthodoxism,** †orthodoxy; in derogatory sense, the treating orthodoxy as the important feature of religion. **O·rthodox-ly** *adv.*, **-ness.**

Orthodoxy (ǭ·ɹþǒdǫksi). 1630. [ad. Gr. ὀρθοδοξία, f. ὀρθόδοξος ORTHODOX.] The quality or character of being orthodox; belief in or agreement with what is, or is currently held to be, right, esp. in religious matters. **b.** with *pl.* An orthodox belief or opinion 1871.

Lanfranc was again present as the champion of o. FREEMAN. *Feast of O.*, in the Greek Church, a festival celebrated on the first Sunday in Lent, called *O. Sunday.*

Orthoepy (ǫɹþǒᵘ·ĭpi). 1668. [ad. Gr. ὀρθοέπεια correctness of diction, f. (ult.) ὀρθός ORTHO- + ἔπος, ἐπε- word.] **1.** That part of grammar which deals with pronunciation. **2.** Correct or customary pronunciation 1801.

2. Formerly they regulated their orthography by their o. 1830. So **Orthoepic** (e·pik), **-al** *adjs.*, **-ly** *adv.* **Ortho·epist.**

Orthognathic (ǭɹþǫgnæ·þik), *a.* 1849. [f. as ORTHOGNATHOUS + -IC.] = ORTHOGNATHOUS.

Orthognathous (ǫɹþǫ·gnăþəs), *a.* 1853. [f. ORTHO- 'straight' + Gr. γνάθος jaw + -OUS.] *Ethnol.* Straight-jawed; having the jaws not projecting beyond the vertical line drawn from the forehead; having a facial angle of about 90°. Said of the skull; also of persons. So **Ortho·gnathism**, the condition of being o.

Orthogonal (ǫɹþǫ·gŏnăl), *a.* 1571. [a. F., f. *orthogone*, ad. late L. *orthogonium*, neut. of *orthogonius*, a. Gr. ὀρθογώνιος right-angled; see -AL.] *Geom.* Right-angled, rectangular.

O. projection, projection in which the rays are at right angles to the plane of projection. Hence **Ortho·gonally** *adv.* at right angles.

Orthographic (ǭɹþogræ·fik), *a.* 1668. [In sense 1, f. ORTHO- 'straight, right' + -γραφος written, γραφικός of or pertaining to writing, + -AL. In sense 2, f. ORTHOGRAPHY + -IC.] 1. Epithet of a kind of perspective projection, used in maps, etc., in which the point of sight is supposed to be at an infinite distance, so that the rays are parallel. 2. Pertaining to orthography; belonging to correct spelling in general; correct in spelling 1868.

Orthogra·phical, *a.* 1589. [f. as prec.: see -ICAL.] 1. = prec. 2. 2. = prec. 1. 1706.

Orthogra·phically, *adv.* 1617. [f. prec. + -LY².] 1. In relation to spelling or orthography. 2. On the principle of orthographical projection 1669.

Orthography (ǫɹþǫ·grăfi). 1450. [a. OF. *ortografie*, later *ortographie*, ad. L. *orthographia*, a. Gr., f. ὀρθόγραφος, f. ὀρθός + -γράφος that writes, writer; see -GRAPHY.] 1. Correct spelling; spelling according to accepted usage; the way in which words are conventionally written. (By extension) Any mode or system of spelling. b. That part of grammar which treats of the nature and values of letters and of their combination; the subject of spelling 1616. 2. Orthographic projection. b. A representation in orthographic projection or section; a vertical elevation. 1645.

1. When we use the word 'orthography', we do not mean a mode of spelling which is true to the pronunciation, but one which is conventionally correct 1873. Hence **Ortho·grapher**, **Ortho·graphist**, one skilled in o. **Ortho·graphize** *v. intr.* to follow or apply o.; *trans.* to spell (a word) correctly.

Orthology (ǫɹþǫ·lŏdʒi). *rare.* 1619. [ad. Gr. ὀρθολογία, f. (ult.) ὀρθός correct + -λόγος speaking. So F. *orthologie*.] Correct speaking; that part of grammar which deals with the correct use of words. So **Ortho·loger**. **Ortholo·gical** *a.*

Orthometry (ǫɹþǫ·mĕtri). *rare.* 1775. [f. ORTHO- + Gr. -μετρία (in comb.) measurement.] The art of correct versification.

Orthomorphic (ǭɹþomǭ·ɹfik), *a. rare.* 1882. [f. ORTHO- + Gr. μορφή form + -IC.] Preserving the original shape of infinitesimal parts; applied to a class of map-projections in which small areas retain their correct shapes 1882.

Orthopædy, -pedy (ǭ·ɹþŏpīdi). 1840. [ad. F. *orthopédie*, mod.L. *orthopædia*, f. Gr. ὀρθός ORTHO- + παιδίον child, παιδεία rearing of children.] The curing or correcting of deformities in children, or in persons generally; orthopædic surgery. Hence **Orthopæ·dic, -pedic, -al** *adjs.* **Orthopæ·dics, -ped-**, orthopædy. **O:rthopæ·dist, -pedist**, an orthopædic surgeon.

‖**Orthopnœa** (ǭɹþǫpnī·ă). 1657. [L. (Pliny), a. Gr. ὀρθόπνοια, f. (ult.) ὀρθός upright + πνοή breathing, breath, πνέειν to breathe.] *Path.* A form of asthma or dyspnœa in which breathing is possible only in an upright position. So **Orthopno·ic, -pnœic**, *adjs.* affected with o. 1601.

Orthopraxy (ǭ·ɹþopræksi). *rare.* 1852. [f. ORTHO- + Gr. πρᾶξις action.] 1. Rightness of action; practical righteousness; correct practice. 2. Orthopædic surgery 1865.

‖**Orthoptera** (ǫɹþǫ·ptĕră), *sb. pl.* 1826. [mod.L., neut. pl. of *orthopterus*, f. Gr. ὀρθός straight + πτερόν wing.] *Entom.* An order of Insects, distinguished by more or less coriaceous and usu. straight and narrow fore wings, broad longitudinally-folded hind wings, and incomplete metamorphosis; comprising the cockroaches, walking-stick insects, crickets, grasshoppers, etc. Hence **Ortho·pteral, Ortho·pterous** *adjs.* belonging to the order *O.* **Ortho·pterist**, a student of *O.*

Orthoptic (ǫɹþǫ·ptik), *a.* (*sb.*) 1881. [f. ORTH(O- 'straight' + Gr. ὀπτικός of or pertaining to sight.] 1. *Fire-arms.* (*adj.* and *sb.*) Name for an opaque disk perforated with three small holes, through one of which the rifleman looks in taking aim. 2. *Math. O. locus*: the locus of intersection of tangents to any curve at right angles to each other 1882.

Orthorhombic (ǭɹþorǫ·mbik), *a.* 1868. [f. ORTHO- + RHOMBIC.] *Cryst.* Applied to that system of crystalline forms in which the three axes are mutually at right angles and unequal; also called *rectangular*, *prismatic*, *trimetric*, or *orthosymmetric*.

Orthoscopic (ǭɹþoskǫ·pik), *a.* 1875. [f. ORTHO- + Gr. -σκοπος viewing; see -IC.] Having or producing correct vision; free from, or constructed to correct, optical distortion.

Orthospermous (ǭɹþospə̄·ɹməs), *a.* 1859. [f. ORTHO- 'straight' + Gr. -σπερμος having seeds, f. σπέρμα seed.] *Bot.* Having straight seeds or fruits, as certain Umbelliferæ; also said of the seeds.

Orthostichy (ǫɹþǫ·stiki). 1875. [f. ORTHO- + Gr. στίχος row, rank, line + -Y³.] *Bot.* A vertical row or rank; an arrangement of lateral members (e.g. of leaves) inserted on an axis or stem one directly above another. Hence **Ortho·stichous** *a.*

Orthotone (ǭ·ɹþotoun), *a.* (*sb.*) 1882. [ad. Gr. ὀρθότονος, f. ὀρθός (ORTHO-) + τόνος tone, accent.] *Pros.* Having its own accent as an independent word; accented; *spec.* said of a word ordinarily unaccented when it retains or takes an independent accent. B. *sb.* An orthotone word.

Orthotropal (ǫɹþǫ·trŏpăl), *a.* 1832. [f. as ORTHOTROPOUS + -AL.] *Bot.* = ORTHOTROPOUS.

Orthotropic (ǭɹþotrǫ·pik), *a.* 1886. [f. as prec. + -IC.] *Bot.* Growing vertically upwards or downwards, as a root or stem. So **Ortho·tropism**, o. condition.

Orthotropous (ǫɹþǫ·trŏpəs), *a.* 1819. [f. mod.L. *orthotropus*, a. Gr. *ὀρθότροπος, f. ὀρθο- straight + -τροπος turning, turned + -OUS.] *Bot.* a. = ATROPOUS. b. = HOMOTROPOUS. So **Ortho·tropy**, o. condition.

Ortolan (ǭ·ɹtŏlăn). 1656. [a. F., a. Prov. *ortolan* or It. *ortolano* gardener, ad. L. *hortulanus*, f. *hortulus*, dim. of *hortus* garden; so named because it frequents gardens.] A small bird, a species of bunting (*Emberiza hortulana*), highly esteemed for its delicate flavour; the garden-bunting. Also called *o. bunting*.

Applied in America and the West Indies to two other birds, also esteemed as table delicacies, viz. the bobolink (*Dolichonyx oryzivorus*), and the soree or sora rail (*Porzana carolina*) 1666.

Orvietan (ǫɹvi,ī·tăn). *Obs.* exc. *Hist.* 1676. [ad. F. *orviétan*, or It. *orvietano*, f. *Orvieto* in Italy, where the inventor was born.] A composition, formerly held to be an antidote against poisons; 'Venice Treacle'. Hence *gen.* and *fig.* An antidote.

Orvieto (orvie·to). 1860. [From *Orvieto*; see prec.] A white wine made near the city of Orvieto.

Ory (ǭə·ri), *a.* 1549. [f. ORE + -Y¹.] Of the nature of, containing, or resembling ore; metallic.

-ory ¹, formerly **-orie**, a suffix forming sbs., originating in ONF. and AF. *-orie* = Central F. *-oire*, as in *glorie, gloire*, repr. L. *-oria*, and subseq. *-orium*, as in *oratoire*, ORATORY¹; these also took in Eng. the form *-orie*, later *-ory*, which thus came to be the normal Eng. repr. of L. *-oria, -orium*, F. *-oire*. The most numerous of these are adaptations of L. neuter sbs. in *-orium*, from adjs. in *-orius* (see -ORY²). These usu. denote a place or instrument used in some process, as *directory, dormitory, refectory*, etc.; but occas. they have other senses, as *promontory, territory*. In a few words *-ory* is the suffix *-y* added to an agent-noun in *-or*, e.g. *rectory* (the seat of a rector).

-ory ², formerly **-orie**, a suffix forming adjs. (whence also sbs.), originating in AF. *-ori*, *-orie*, OF. *-oir, -oire*, and repr. L. *-orius, -a, -um*, = the adj. formative *-i-us* added to derivative sbs. in *-or*, chiefly agent-nouns in *-tor, -sor* (see -OR), but sometimes app. from the cognate ppl. stem in *-t-, -s-*; e.g. *accusator-i-us, suasor-i-us*. Instead of *-ory*, the Eng. adj. has often -ORIAL, less frequently -ORIOUS.

Orycterope (ori·ktĕroup). 1836. [a. F. *oryctérope*, ad. mod.L. *Orycteropus* (*-pod-*), f. Gr. ὀρυκτήρ digger + πούς, ποδ- foot. Now usu. in L. form.] *Zool.* A mammal of genus *Orycteropus*; = AARD-VARK.

Orycto-, comb. form of Gr. ὀρυκτός dug up, used in mod. compounds, with the sense of 'fossil' or 'mineral'; as †**Orycto·gnosy** [Gr. γνῶσις knowledge], mineralogy; so †**Oryctogno·stic** *a.* †**Orycto·graphy** [-GRAPHY], descriptive mineralogy.

Orycto·logy. Now *rare.* 1753. [See prec. and -LOGY.] The science of 'fossils'; a. mineralogy; b. palæontology. So **Oryctolo·gical** *a.* **Orycto·logist.**

Oryx (ǫ·riks). late ME. [a. L., a. Gr. ὄρυξ (1) a pickaxe, (2) an antelope, so called from its pointed horns.] a. The ancient name of an antelope of northern Africa, perh. *O. leucoryx* or *O. beisa*. b. In mod. *Zool.*, a genus of African antelopes, of large size, with long pointed horns; one of these. The S. African species is *O. capensis*, the gemsbok.

‖**Os** ¹ (ǫs). 1548. [L., pl. *ossa*.] The Latin word for bone, commonly used in *Anat.* in the mod.L. names of particular bones.

‖**Os** ² (ǫs). 1737. [L., pl. *ora*.] The Latin word for mouth, used in *Anat.* in naming the mouths or entrances of certain passages; esp. *os uteri*, the mouth or orifice of the uterus.

Os: see OSAR.

Osage (ōu·sėdʒ). [Name of a group of Sioux Indians.] In *O. orange*, an ornamental American plant, *Toxylon pomiferum*, orig. found in the country of the O. Indians; also short for this, and in other attrib. uses (*o. plant*).

Osar (ōu·saɹ). 1854. [ad. Sw. *åsar*, pl. of *ås* ridge (of a roof or hill), a 'rigg'. In Eng. use sometimes *os*, pl. *osar*, but usu. *osar* as sing., with pl. *osars*.] *Geol.* A term for certain narrow ridges or mounds of gravel which occur in glaciated regions, essentially the same as the *kames* of Scotland and the *eskars* of Ireland, but much more elongated.

Oscheo- (ǫskio), bef. a vowel **osche-**, comb. form of Gr. ὄσχεον scrotum; in med. and surg. terms, as **O·scheocele** [Gr. κήλη tumour], scrotal hernia.

Oscillate (ǫ·sileʲt), *v.* 1726. [f. L. *oscillat-*, *oscillare* to swing; see -ATE³.] 1. *intr.* To swing backwards and forwards, like a pendulum; to vibrate; to move to and fro between two points. b. *loosely.* To move or travel to and fro 1865. c. To set up electrical oscillations 1913; esp. in wireless telephony; of a receiving apparatus, to 'howl' 1926. 2. *fig.* To fluctuate between two opinions, principles, purposes, etc.; to vary between two limits 1797. 3. *trans.* To cause to swing or vibrate to and fro 1766.

1. b. Miss Lavinia, oscillating between the kitchen and the opposite room, prepared the dining-table in the latter chamber DICKENS. 2. Human nature oscillates between good and evil JOWETT. Hence **O·scillative, O·scillatory** *adjs.*

O·scillating, *ppl. a.* 1743. [-ING².] Swinging or moving to and fro, vibrating. b. *spec.* Applied to machines or parts of them characterized by the oscillatory motion of some part or parts, which in other cases are fixed.

b. *O. cylinder*, a cylinder in a steam-engine mounted on trunnions and oscillating through a small arc, so that the piston-rod can follow the movements of the crank. *O. engine*, one having an o. cylinder.

Oscillation (ǫsilēʲ·ʃən). 1658. [ad. L. *oscillationem*, f. *oscillare*.] 1. The action of oscillating; swinging to and fro like that of a pendulum; a periodic movement to and fro, or up and down. b. In *Acoustics*, occas. = vibration; occas. = BEAT *sb.*¹ 6. *rare.* c. (Usu. *pl.*) Esp. in wireless telephony, applied to (high-frequency) alternations of electric currents. 2. *fig.* Alternating variation, fluctuation, wavering;

Math. the variation of a function between limits 1798. So **O·scillator** *spec.* a machine to produce oscillations; also, a form of wireless transmitter 1898.

‖**Oscillatoria** (ǫsilătō̆·riă). 1861. [mod.L.; see -ORY.] *Bot.* A genus of confervoid Algæ, typifying the N.O. *Oscillatoriaceæ*, growing in dense slimy tufts, in running or stagnant water, and exhibiting an oscillatory or wavy motion.

Oscillograph (ǫ·silǫgraf). 1904. [f. *oscillo-*, used as comb. f. of OSCILLATE + -GRAPH.] An instrument for recording or indicating electrical oscillations. Hence **O·scillogram.** Similarly **O·scilloscope** [see -SCOPE].

‖**Oscines** (ǫ·sinīz), *sb. pl.* 1621. [a. L., pl. of *oscen, oscin-*, f. *ob* (OB-) + *canere* to sing.] 1. *Rom. Antiq.* The birds from whose notes or voices auguries were taken, e.g. the raven, owl, etc. 2. *Ornith.* The 'Song-birds', containing those families of the *Insessores* or Passerine birds which possess true song-muscles, forming a complicated and effective musical apparatus. **O·scine, O·scinine** (-əin) *adjs.* belonging to the *O.*

Oscitancy (ǫ·sitănsi). 1619. [f. as OSCITANT; see -ANCY.] 1. Drowsiness; dullness; negligence, inattention. b. (with *pl.*) An instance of this 1677. 2. Yawning; gaping with sleepiness 1717.

1. I judge it rather the Historians oscitancie, and supine negligence 1658.

Oscitant (ǫ·sitănt), *a.* Now *rare* or *Obs.* 1625. [ad. L. *oscitantem, oscitare* to yawn; see -ANT.] Gaping from drowsiness, yawning; hence, drowsy, dull, negligent.

Southey..has been strangely o., or..has not understood the sentences COLERIDGE.

Oscitation (ǫsitē̆·ʃən). 1547. [ad. L. *oscitationem*, f. *oscitare* to open (as a mouth), also *-ari* to gape, yawn.] 1. The action of yawning or gaping from drowsiness. 2. The condition or fact of being drowsy, listless, inattentive, or negligent; an instance of this 1656.

Osculant (ǫ·skiŭlănt), *a.* 1826. [ad. L. *osculantem, osculari* to kiss.] Situated between and connecting two things; intermediate; *spec.* in *Nat. Hist.* applied to two species, genera, or families, that are united by some common characters, and to an intermediate species, genus, or group, which unites in itself the characters of two groups 1826.

Oscular (ǫ·skiŭlăı), *a.* 1828. [f. L. *osculum* little mouth, kiss; see -AR.] 1. Of or belonging to the mouth or to kissing. 2. *Zool.* Of or pertaining to the osculum of a tapeworm, or of a sponge 1881. 3. *Math.* Pertaining to a higher order of contact than the first (cf. next 4) 1869.

1. *O. muscle* (*musculus oscularis*), the *orbicularis oris* or sphincter muscle of the lips, the kissing muscle.

Osculate (ǫ·skiŭlēⁱt), *v.* 1656. [f. L. *osculat-, osculari*, f. *osculum* little mouth, kiss.] 1. *trans.* To kiss (*rare*). 2. *trans.* To bring into close contact 1671. 3. *intr.* To come into close contact or union; to have close contact with each other. In *Nat. Hist.* To have contact through an intermediate species or genus (cf. OSCULANT) 1737. 4. *Math. trans.* To have contact of a higher order with, esp. the highest contact possible for two loci; to have three or more coincident points in common with; *intr.* (for *refl.*) to osculate each other; as two curves, two surfaces, or a surface and a curve 1727. So **O·sculatory** *sb.* a representation of Christ or the Virgin, formerly kissed by the priest and people during Mass. **O·sculatory** *a.* characterized by kissing; *Math.* osculating; of or belonging to osculation.

Osculation (ǫskiŭlē̆·ʃən). 1658. [ad. L. *osculationem*, n. of action from *osculari* to kiss.] 1. The action of kissing, a kiss. 2. Close contact. a. *gen.* b. *Anat.* The mutual contact of blood-vessels. c. *Geom.* Contact of a higher order; the fact of touching at three or more coincident points (see prec. 4). 1669.

Oscule (ǫ·skiul). 1835. [ad. L. *osculum*, dim. of *os* mouth.] A little mouth or mouth-like aperture; *spec.* = next 2.

‖**Osculum** (ǫ·skiŭlǒm). *Pl.* -a. 1612. [L., see prec.] 1. A kiss. 2. *Zool.* a. A mouth or 'flue' of a sponge. b. Occas. applied to the pit-like suckers on the head of a tapeworm by which it attaches itself. 1727.

-ose [1], a suffix repr. L. *-osus*, forming adjs. from sbs., with the meaning 'full of', 'abounding in'; e.g. *annosus* full of years, *religiosus* scrupulous. As a living suffix *-osus* came down to Eng. as -OUS (ME. also *-ows*), which survives with pron. (-əs). A few words in *-ose* after L. have taken their place in the language, as *bellicose, jocose, morose*, etc. Where *-ous* and *-ose* forms are both in use, e.g. in *acinous, acinose*, those in *-ose* are more or less technical. Nouns of state from these adjs., as from those in *-ous*, end in *-osity*, as *verbosity*.

-ose [2], *Chem.*, a suffix originating in the ending of the word *glucose*, and employed in forming the names of the related carbohydrates, *saccharose* and *cellulose*, with the isomers of these three, as *dextrose, lævulose*, etc.

Osiandrian (ōusiæ·ndriăn). 1565. [f. personal name *Osiander* (see def.) + -IAN.] One of the German Protestant followers of Andreas Hosemann (latinized *Osiander*, 1498–1552), who held that the Atonement of Christ was wrought by the power of His divine and not of His human nature. Also **Osia·ndrist.**

Osier (ōu·ʒiəɹ), *sb.* (*a.*) ME. [a. F. *osier*; app. related to 9th c. L. *ausaria, osaria* 'willow-bed', which would give in F. *osière*.] 1. A species of Willow (*Salix viminalis*); much used in basket-work; also other species used for the same purpose; one of the shoots of a willow. 2. *attrib.* or *adj.* Of, belonging to, or made of osiers; covered with osiers 1578.

1. Who will make a staff of an o.? FULLER. 2. On list'ning Cherwell's o. banks reclin'd 1750.

Comb.: **o.-ait, -isle**, a small islet in a river overgrown with osiers; **-bed, -holt**, a place where osiers are grown for basket-making. **O·siered** *a.* Hence covered or adorned with osiers; twisted like osiers. **O·siery**, osiers in the mass; articles made of osiers; an osier-bed.

Osirian (osəiə·riăn), *a.* 1849. [f. proper name *Osiris* (see def.) + -IAN.] Of or pertaining to Osiris, the Egyptian deity personifying the power of good and the sunlight. So **Osi·ride, Osiri·dean** *adjs.*

-osis, *suffix*, repr. Gr. -ωσις, originating in the addition of the general suffix -σις, forming verbal nouns of action or condition, to derivative vbs. in -όω from adj. or sb. stems or combining forms in ο-; e.g. μεταμόρφωσις, f. μεταμορφόω, f. μετά + μορφή form. Many such words were also formed directly from the sbs. or adjs. themselves, e.g. ἐξόστωσις exostosis, f. ἐξ out + ὀστέον bone. Many of these Greek terms have passed through Latin into English, e.g. *apotheosis, metamorphosis*, rhetorical terms, as *miosis*, etc., and esp. medical terms, as *sclerosis, thrombosis*, etc. On the analogy of these last, others have been freely formed from Gr. elements, as *chlorosis, trichinosis*; less frequently from Latin, as *tuberculosis*.

-osity, *compound suffix* of sbs. = F. *-osité*, L. *-ositatem*; see -OSE [1], -OUS, and -ITY.

Osmanli (ǫsmæ·nli), *a.* and *sb.* 1813. [a. Turk. *osmānli* adj. 'of or belonging to Osmān'; the native word for which *Ottoman* is the usual Eng. expression.] A. *adj.* = OTTOMAN 1843. B. *sb.* An OTTOMAN.

Osmazome (ǫ·smăzōum, ǫ·z-). 1819. [a. F. *osmazôme*, irreg. f. Gr. ὀσμή scent + ζωμός soup, sauce.] *Chem.* That part of the aqueous extract of meat which is soluble in alcohol and contains those constituents of the flesh which determine its taste and smell. Hence **O:smazoma·tic, -o·matous** *adjs.*, of the nature of o.

‖**Osmeterium** (ǫsmǐtī̆ə·riǒm, ǫz-). *Pl.* -ia. Also osma-. 1816. [mod.L., f. Gr. ὀσμά-εσθαι to smell + -τήριον formative suffix, = 'instrument', 'organ', 'thing used'.] *Entom.* An organ or apparatus adapted to emit a smell or odour; *spec.* a forked process borne by some caterpillars on the segment immediately behind the head, from which they can emit a disgusting odour.

Osmiamic (ǫsmi,æ·mik, ǫz-), *a.* 1873. [f. OSMIUM + AMIC.] *Chem.* In *O. acid*: A dibasic acid, $H_2Os_2N_2O_5$, an acid amide of osmium. Its salts are **O·smiamates.**

Osmic (ǫ·smik, ǫ·z-), *a.* 1842. [f. OSMIUM + -IC.] *Chem.* Containing osmium; applied to compounds in which osmium is quadrivalent, as *o. chloride* $OsCl_4$, *o. oxide*, OsO_2.

O. acid, a name given to *osmium tetroxide* OsO_4. Its salts are **O·smiates.**

Osmio-, comb. form of OSMIUM, in names of chemical compounds in which osmium and another element enter into combination with a third, as *osmio-cyanide*.

Osmious (ǫ·smiəs, ǫ·z-), *a.* 1849. [f. OSMIUM + -OUS.] *Chem.* Containing osmium; applied to compounds in which osmium is divalent, as *o. chloride* $OsCl_2$. (Formerly to the *trichloride*, etc.)

Osmite (ǫ·smait, ǫ·z-). 1849. [f. OSMIUM + -ITE [1].] *Chem.* A salt of osmious acid.

Osmium (ǫ·smiǒm, ǫ·z-). 1804. [f. Gr. ὀσμή odour + -IUM; so called from the pungent and peculiar smell of the metal.] One of the metals of the platinum group, generally found, associated with platinum, in the alloy iridosmine. Chem. symbol Os; atomic wt. 190·8.

Osmo- [1], repr. Gr. ὀσμο-, comb. form of ὀσμή smell, odour; as in **Osmo·logy**, the study of smells, a treatise on odours; etc.

Osmo- [2], repr. Gr. ὠσμός push, thrust, impulse, used as comb. form of OSMOSE. **Osmo·meter**, an instrument for exhibiting the force of osmotic action. **Osmo·metry**, measurement of osmotic force.

Osmose (ǫ·smōus, ǫ·z-). 1854. [The common element of the words *endosmose* and *exosmose*, taken as a generalized term; cf. Gr. ὠσμός push.] The tendency of fluids separated by porous septa to pass through these and mix with each other; the action of this passage and intermixture; diffusion through a porous septum or membrane.

Osmosis (ǫsmōu·sis, ǫz-). 1867. [Latinized form of prec.] = prec. Hence **Osmo·tic** *a.* of, pertaining to, or caused by o. **Osmo·tically** *adv.* by osmotic action.

Osmund [1] (ǫ·zmǒnd). ME. [From Sw. or LG.; etym. unkn.] A superior quality of iron formerly imported from the Baltic regions, for the manufacture of arrow-heads, fish-hooks, etc. With pl., a bar of this. Also, *o. iron, o. bar.*

Osmund [2] (ǫ·smǒnd, ǫ·z-). ME. [In med.L. *osmunda*, F. *osmonde*; origin unkn.] †1. A name formerly given to various ferns –1611. 2. Now, the 'Flowering Fern', *Osmunda regalis* Linn., having large bipinnate fronds with terminal panicles of sporangia; also called *Osmund Royal, Royal Fern, King Fern.* b. Also as the Eng. name of the genus (of which six species are known). 1578.

Osmundaceous (ǫsmǒndē̆·ʃəs, ǫz-). 1857. [f. mod.L. *Osmundaceæ*; see prec. and -ACEOUS.] *Bot.* Of or belonging to the *Osmundaceæ*, one of the principal subdivisions of the N. O. *Polypodiaceæ*, the type of which is the genus *Osmunda*.

†**Osnaburg.** 1545. [f. *Osnabrück* (in later Eng. corruptly *Osnaburg*) in North Germany.] A kind of coarse linen originally made in Osnabrück –1862.

Oso-berry (ōu·so,be:ri). 1884. [? Amer. Ind.] The blue-black drupe of *Nuttallia cerasiformis*, a shrub or small tree of western North America. Also, the shrub.

‖**Osphradium** (ǫsfrē̆·diǒm). 1883. [mod.L., a. Gr. ὀσφράδιον strong scent, dim. of ὄσφρα smell.] *Zool.* The olfactory organs of some molluscs, consisting of a collection of elongated sense-cells over each gill. Hence **Osphra·dial** *a.*

Osprey (ǫ·sprēⁱ). late ME. [app. repr. L. *ossifraga*, lit. 'bone-breaker', in Pliny the name of a bird of prey, now identified with the Lammergeyer.] 1. A large diurnal bird of prey, *Pandion* (*Falco*) *Haliaëtus*; also called sea-eagle, fishing-eagle, fish-hawk. 2. A milliner's name for an egret plume worn as an ornament on a lady's hat or bonnet. (App. erron. assoc. w. *spray*.) 1885.

Ossature (ǫ·sătiŭı). 1879. [a. F., L. *os, oss-* + *-ature*, from stems in *-at-*, as *curvature*, etc.] 1. The arrangement of the bones of the skeleton. *rare.* 1885. 2. *Arch.* The skeleton or framework that supports any structure, as the beams of a roof, or the metal frame of a glass window.

Osse, oss (ǫs), *v.* Now *dial.* late ME. [Origin obscure.] †**1.** *trans.* To signify as an omen; to prophesy; to wish good luck. Also *absol.* or *intr.* –1606. **2.** *dial.* To give augury of what one is going to be or do, to shape well or ill for something; hence, to show signs of being about (to do something).

†**Osse, oss,** *sb.* 1600. [prob. f. prec.] A word of omen, a presage; a wishing of good luck. (Almost peculiar to Ph. Holland, as tr. L. *omen.*) –1611.

Ossein (ǫ·sɪ,in). Also **-ine.** 1857. [f. L. *osseus* bony + -IN [1].] *Chem.* Bone-cartilage; the organic gelatinous principle in true bony tissue; the embryonic tissue which develops into bone by the deposit of mineral salts.

Osselet (ǫ·sĕlĕt, ǫ·slĕt). 1686. [a. F., f. L. *os, oss-* bone; see -LET.] **1.** A little bone, an ossicle; one of the small bones of the carpus or tarsus. **2.** The cuttle-bone, pen, or calamary of some cephalopods 1849.

Osseo- (ǫ·sio), comb. form of L. *osseus* OSSEOUS, as in **Osseo-fi·brous** *a.* consisting of osseous combined with fibrous tissue.

Osseous (ǫ·siəs), *a.* 1682. [f. L. *osseus* bony + -OUS. Cf. F. *osseux.*] **1.** Of, consisting of, or of the nature of bone; bony; ossified 1707. **2.** Having a bony skeleton, teleostean 1828. **3.** Abounding in fossil bones 1823. **4.** *fig.* Hard or firm as bone 1682.

‖ **Osseter** (ose·tǝɹ). 1887. [a. Russ. *osëtr* sturgeon.] *Zool.* A species of sturgeon, *Acipenser Güldenstädtii.*

Ossianic (ǫsi-, ǫʃiæ·nik), *a.* 1808. [f. *Ossian*, anglicized form of *Oisin* (oʃin), name of a legendary Gaelic bard whose poems Macpherson claimed to have collected and translated.] Of or pertaining to Ossian or to the poems ascribed to him; of the style or character of Macpherson's rhythmic prose rendering of these poems; hence, magniloquent, bombastic.

Ossicle (ǫ·sik'l). 1578. [ad. L. *ossiculum*, dim. of *os, ossi-* bone.] **1.** A small bone; a small piece of bony substance; as, the *auditory ossicles* in the tympanic cavity of the ear. **2.** A small plate, joint, etc. of chitinous or calcareous substance in the animal framework; e.g. one of the plates or skeletal elements of a starfish or other echinoderm 1852.

‖ **Ossiculum** (ǫsi·kiŭlǒm). *Pl.* **-a.** 1706. [L., dim. of *os* bone.] A little bone; an ossicle; the †stone of a fruit.

Ossiferous (ǫsi·fĕrəs), *a.* 1823. [f. L. *os, ossi-* bone + -FEROUS.] Containing or yielding bones.

Ossific (ǫsi·fik), *a.* 1676. [f. L. *os, ossi-* bone + -FIC.] Bone-forming; becoming or making bone; ossifying. *O. centre*, a centre of ossification.

Ossification (ǫ:sifikē¹·ʃən). 1697. [f. OSSIFY *v.*] **1.** The formation of bone; the process of becoming bone; the condition of being ossified. **2.** *concr.* A bony formation or concretion; bone as a formation 1705.

1. O. of the arteries is most commonly the lot of old age 1830. *Centre of o.*, the point at which cartilage or connective tissue begins to ossify. Hence **O·ssified** *ppl. a.* made into bone; hardened like bone.

Ossifrage (ǫ·sifrēdʒ). 1601. [ad. L. *ossifragus, -a*, f. (ult.) *os, ossi-* bone + *frag-, frangere* to break. Cf. OSPREY.] **1.** The Lammergeyer or Geir Eagle. **2.** The Osprey or fish-hawk 1658.

1. The Eagle, and the O. [*R.V.* gier eagle], and the Ospray *Lev.* xi. 13.

Ossify (ǫ·sifəi), *v.* 1713. [f. L. *os, ossi-* bone + -FY; cf. F. *ossifier.*] **1.** *intr.* To become bone; to change from soft tissue into bone. **2.** *trans.* To convert into bone; to harden. (Chiefly in *passive.*) 1721.

1. *fig.* The natural instinct of veneration had ossified into idolatry FROUDE. 2. *fig.* Our phrases, often repeated, o. the very organs of intelligence 1860.

Ossivorous (ǫsi·vŏrəs), *a.* 1676. [f. L. *os, ossi-* bone + *-vorus* devouring + -OUS.] Bone-devouring; feeding upon bones; in *Path.* bone-destroying.

Ossuary (ǫ·siu,ări). 1658. [ad. late L. *ossuarium*, irreg. f. *os, ossi-* bone; after *mortuarium* mortuary.] A receptacle for the bones of the dead; a charnel-house; a bone-urn. **b.** *transf.* A bone-cave, or deposit formed largely of bones 1861. **c.** *fig.* That in which relics of the dead past are preserved 1872. **d.** *attrib.* or as *adj.* 1857.

The earth had confounded the ashes of these Ossuaries SIR T. BROWNE.

Osteal (ǫ·stiăl), *a.* 1877. [f. Gr. ὀστέον bone + -AL.] Of or pertaining to bone; *spec.* of the quality of sound produced by the percussion of bone.

Ostein, -ine (ǫ·sti,in). 1854. [ad. Gr. ὀστέϊνος; see prec. and -INE [1].] *Anat.* The substance of bone, bony tissue, bone as a tissue.

Osteitis (ǫsti,əi·tis). Also **ostitis.** 1839. [f. Gr. ὀστέον bone + -ITIS.] *Path.* Inflammation in the substance of a bone.

Ostend (ǫste·nd), *v.* Now *rare.* 1450. [ad. L. *ostendere* to stretch out to view, f. *obs-, ob-* (OB- 1) + *tendere* to stretch.] *trans.* To show, reveal; to manifest, exhibit.

Ostensible (ǫste·nsĭb'l), *a.* 1762. [a. F., ad. L.**ostensibilis*, f. *ostens-, ostendere*; see prec.] †**1.** That may be shown; hence, presentable; also, made to be shown –1828. †**2.** Open to public view; conspicuous, ostentatious –1828. **3.** Declared, avowed, professed; put forth as actual or genuine; often opp. to 'actual', 'real', and so = merely professed, pretended 1771.

3. The outward and o. workings of this complicated mechanism 1828. 3. My o. errand on this occasion was to get measured for a pair of shoes C. BRONTË. Hence **Ostensibi·lity. Oste·nsibly** *adv.*

Ostension (ǫste·nʃən). 1474. [a. F., ad. L. *ostens-, ostentionem*, f. *ostendere*; see OSTEND.] †**1.** The action of showing; exhibition; manifestation –1789. **2.** *Eccl.* The action of holding forth the Eucharistic elements to the sight of the people 1607.

Ostensive (ǫste·nsiv), *a.* 1605. [ad. late L. *ostensivus*, f. *ostens-, ostendere*; see -IVE.] **1.** Manifestly or directly demonstrative; *spec.* in *Logic*, Setting forth a general principle manifestly including the proposition to be proved. **2.** = OSTENSIBLE *a.* 3. 1782.

1. *O. reduction*, reduction by the direct processes of conversion, permutation, and transposition, as opp. to indirect reduction. Hence **Oste·nsively** *adv.*

Ostensory (ǫste·nsəri). Also (in F., It., or L. forms) **-oir, -orio, -orium.** 1722. [ad. med.L. *ostensorium*, f. *ostens-, ostendere*; see OSTEND and -ORY [1].] A monstrance.

Ostent [1] (ǫste·nt). Now *rare.* 1563. [ad. L. *ostentum* (pl. *-a*), something shown, a prodigy, sb. use of pa. pple. neut. of *ostendere*; see OSTEND.] A sign, portent, wonder, prodigy.

The Night waxed wan, As though with an awed sense of such o. T. HARDY.

Ostent [2] (ǫste·nt). Now *rare.* 1596. [ad. L. *ostentus* a showing, f. ppl. stem of *ostendere*: see OSTEND.] **1.** The act of showing; manifestation; display, appearance. **2.** Vainglorious display, ostentation 1598.

1. *Merch. V.* II. viii. 44. 2. Thou proud Achilles with thy great o. 1609.

Ostentate (ǫ·stĕnteɪt), *v.* Now only *U.S.* 1540. [f. L. *ostentat-, ostentare*, freq. of *ostendere*: see OSTEND.] *trans.* To make a show of, show off, display boastfully.

Ostentation (ǫstĕntē¹·ʃən). late ME. [a. F., ad. L. *ostentationem*, n. of action from *ostentare*: see prec.] †**1.** The presaging of future events; a presage; a portent, prodigy (*rare*) –1607. **2.** The action of showing; an exhibition, display (*of* something). *Obs.* or *arch.* 1534. †**b.** Mere show, appearance; false show, pretence –1649. **3.** Pretentious parade, vainglorious 'showing off' 1450.

2. Finck to ride-out reconnoitering..and to make motions and ostentations (= DEMONSTRATION 6) CARLYLE. 3. Hence o. here, with tawdry art, Pants for the vulgar praise which fools impart GOLDSM.

Ostentatious (ǫstĕntē¹·ʃəs), *a.* 1658. [f. prec.; see -IOUS.] **1.** Characterized or marked by ostentation; unduly conspicuous; boastful; pretentious. **2.** Conspicuous, showy. *Obs.* (or blending with 1). 1713.

1. His Religion was sincere, not o. ADDISON. They are not, like the Mohammedans, o. in their prayers LIVINGSTONE. So **Ostenta·tious-ly,** *adv.*, **-ness.**

Osteo- (ǫ·stio), bef. a vowel also **oste-,** comb. form of Gr. ὀστέον bone, in many derivatives, chiefly anatomical.

‖**Osteoarthri·tis,** now usually **Ostearthri·tis** [Gr. ἀρθρῖτις gout], inflammation of the bones of a joint. **O·steoblast** [Gr. βλαστός bud, germ], Gegenbaur's term for granular corpuscles found in all developing bone as the active agents of osseous growth; hence **Osteobla·stic** *a.* ‖**Osteo·clasis** [Gr. κλάσις fracture], fracture of a bone to correct a deformity; dissolution or destruction of bone tissue. **O·steoclast** [G. *osteoklast*, f. Gr. κλαστός broken], (*a*) Kölliker's term for the many-nucleated cells, found in growing bone, and concerned with the absorption of osseous tissue in the formation of the medullary spaces in cartilage; (*b*) a surgical instrument for effecting osteoclasis. ‖**Osteoco·lla** [Gr. κόλλα glue] a deposit of carbonate of lime forming an incrustation on the roots and stems of plants. **O·steocope,** also ‖**Osteo·copus** [Gr. ὀστεοκόπος, f. κόπος fatigue], violent wearing pain in the bones, esp. of syphilitic origin; syphilitic rheumatism; hence **Osteoco·pic** *a.* **Osteoge·nesis** [Gr. γένεσις GENESIS], the origination or formation of bone. **Osteo·graphy** [-GRAPHY], description of the bones; descriptive osteology. **O·steolite** [Gr. λίθος stone], compact earthy calcium phosphate, resembling lithographic stone. ‖**Osteo·ma,** *pl.* **-ata** [Gr. -ωμα, as in *carcinoma*, etc.], *Path.* a tumour composed of osseous tissue. ‖**Osteomala·cia, -mala·kia** [Gr. μαλακία softness] softening of bones due to the disappearance of earthy salts; also called *malacosteon.* **O·steomancy** [-MANCY], divination from bones. ‖**O:steomyeli·tis** [Gr. μυελός marrow], inflammation of the marrow of a bone. **O·steophyte** [Gr. φυτόν a growth], an osseous outgrowth, a bony excrescence; hence **Osteophy·tic** *a.* **O·steoplasty** [Gr. πλαστός moulded; see -PLASTY], the transplanting of a piece of bone with its periosteum to fill up a gap; hence **Osteopla·stic** *a.* ‖**O:steosclero·sis** [Gr. σκλήρωσις induration], hardening of a bone. **O·steotome** [Gr. -τομος that cuts], *Surg.* any instrument for cutting or dividing bone.

Osteoid (ǫ·sti,oid), *a.* 1847. [f. OSTE(O- + -OID.] Resembling bone; bony, osseous.

Osteologic, -al (ǫ:stiolǫ·dʒik, -ăl), *adjs.* 1777. [f. as next + -IC + -AL.] **1.** Pertaining to, dealing with, or relating to osteology. **2.** Of or pertaining to the objects of osteology, i.e. to bones, their structure, etc.; coming within the sphere of osteology 1794.

Osteology (ǫstiǫ·lŏdʒi). 1670. [ad. mod.L. *osteologia*, f. Gr. ὀστέον bone, OSTEO- + -λογία, -LOGY. Cf. F. *ostéologie.*] **1.** The science which treats of bones; that branch of anatomy which deals with the structure, genesis, and disposition of bones. **b.** A treatise on the bones 1713. **2.** *transf.* The objects of this science; the bony structure of an animal 1833. So **Osteo·logist,** one versed in o.

Osteometry (ǫsti,ǫ·mĕtri). 1878. [f. OSTEO- + -METRY.] The measurement of bones; that part of zoömetry (or *esp.* anthropometry) which has to do with the proportions of the different bones.

Osteopathy (ǫstiǫ·păþi). 1857. [f. OSTEO- + Gr. πάθος feeling; in sense 2, after *allopathy*, etc.; see -PATHY.] **1.** Disease or affection of the bones. **2.** A theory of disease and method of cure which assumes that deformation of the skeleton and consequent interference with the adjacent nerves and blood-vessels are the cause of most diseases 1897. Hence **Osteopath** (ǫ·stiopæþ), one who practises o.; **Osteopa·thic** *a.*; **Osteopa·thically** *adv.*; **Osteo·pathist,** a believer in or practiser of o.

‖ **O:steosarco·ma.** 1807. [f. OSTEO- + SARCOMA.] *Path.* **1.** Sarcoma in the bone; a disease of the bone in which a fleshy, medullary, or cartilaginous mass grows within it. **2.** A sarcoma which undergoes osseous transformation 1878.

Osteotomy (ǫsti,ǫ·tŏmi). 1844. [f. OSTEO- + Gr. -τομία cutting.] **a.** *Anat.* Dissection of the bones. **b.** *Surg.* The cutting of a bone in order to correct a deformity, etc.

‖ **Osteria** (ostĕrī·a). 1605. [It., f. *oste* :—L. *hospitem* HOST *sb.*[2]] An inn or hostelry in Italy or an Italian-speaking country.

Ostiary (ǫ·stiări). late ME. [ad. L. *ostiarius* adj., f. *ostium* door, entrance.] *Eccl.* A doorkeeper, esp. of a church; the lowest of the minor orders of the R.C. Ch. Also in L. form *ostiarius.*

Ostiole (ǫ·stiōul). Also irreg. **osteole**; and in L. form. 1835. [ad. L. *ostiolum*, dim. of *ostium* door.] A small orifice or opening; esp. *Bot.* the orifice or opening in the conceptacles and perithecia of certain algæ and fungi, through which the spores are discharged; also, openings of the stomata or breathing pores.

Osti·tis, var. of OSTEITIS.

‖ **Ostium** (ǫ·stiǒm). *Pl.* **ostia.** 1665. [L. = door, entrance, etc.] †1. The mouth of a river –1695. 2. *Anat.* Applied to the openings of the ventricles and pulmonary arteries, the Fallopian and Eustachian tubes, the urethra, etc., in the animal body 1877.

Ostler (ǫ·slər). late ME. [= HOSTELER, HOSTLER, with *h* mute.] A man who attends horses at an inn; a stableman, a groom. Also *attrib.*, as *o.-boy*. Hence **O·stleress**, a female o.

Ostlerie, -rye, obs. ff. HOSTELRY.

Ostmen (ō̆u·stmĕn), *sb. pl. Hist.* late ME. [a. ON. *Austmenn*, pl. of *Austmaðr*, men of the East; latinized *Ostmanni.*] Name given in Ireland and Iceland to invaders or settlers from Denmark and Norway.

Ostracean (ǫstrē̆ⁱ·ʃiăn), *a.* and *sb.* 1835. [f. mod.L. *Ostracea* or *-eæ*, pl., the family of bivalve molluscs containing the oyster (f. Gr. ὀστράκεος, f. ὄστρακον earthen vessel, tile, shell of oyster, etc.) + -AN.] **a.** *adj.* Belonging to the *Ostracea* or oyster family, ostraceous. **b.** *sb.* A member of the *Ostracea*, an oyster. So **Ostra·ceous** *a.* of or pertaining to the *Ostracea*; of the nature of an oyster.

‖ **Ostracion** (ǫstrē̆ⁱ·siǫn). 1658. [a. mod.L., a.Gr., dim. of ὄστρακον hard shell.] *Ichth.* A genus of fishes having their bodies covered with juxtaposed hexagonal plates; a trunk-fish or coffer-fish.

Ostracism (ǫ·străsiz'm). 1588. [ad. mod.L. *ostracismus*, a. Gr., f. ὀστρακίζειν to OSTRACIZE; see -ISM.] 1. A method of temporary banishment practised in Athens, etc., by which a too popular or powerful citizen was sent into exile for ten (later for five) years; so called because it was effected by voting with potsherds or tiles, on which was written the name of the person proposed to be exiled; hence, Temporary banishment or expatriation in general. 2. *fig.* Banishment by general consent; exclusion from society, favour, or common privileges 16..

1. By the o. a citizen was banished without special accusation, trial or defence GROTE. 2. The social o. of a heretic 1870.

Ostracite (ǫ·străsəit). 1653. [ad. L. *ostracites*, a stone mentioned by Pliny, a. Gr. ὀστρακίτης earthen, testaceous, f. ὄστρακον shell.] A fossil shell of a species or genus allied to the oyster.

Ostracize (ǫ·străsəiz), *v.* 1649. [ad. Gr. ὀστρακίζειν, f. ὄστρακον OSTRACON; see -IZE.] 1. *trans.* (*Gr. Hist.*) To banish by voting with potsherds; see OSTRACISM 1. 1850. 2. *fig.* To banish or expel as by ostracism; to exclude from society, favour, or common privileges.

2. Ostracised from society because of the drunken and violent habits of his wife 1890.

Ostraco-, bef. a vowel **ostrac-**, comb. form of Gr. ὄστρακον hard shell; as in **O·stracode·rm** [Gr. ὀστρακόδερμος] *a.*, having a bony integument or external skeleton; *sb.* an ostracoderm fish; so **O·stracode·rmal, -mous** *adjs.*

Ostracode (ǫ·străkō̆ud), *a.* and *sb.* 1865. [ad. Gr. ὀστρακώδης; see -ODE.] **a.** *adj.* Belonging to the *Ostracoda* or *Ostracopoda*, an order of entomostracous crustaceans. **b.** *sb.* A member of the *Ostracoda*. So **Ostraco·dal, Ostraco·dous** *adjs.*

Ostracon, -kon (ǫ·străkǫn). *Pl.* **-ca, -ka** (-kă). 1885. [a. Gr. ὄστρακον potsherd.] Any inscribed fragment of pottery or limestone such as those found in Upper Egypt.

Ostreaceous (ǫstri͵ē̆ⁱ·ʃəs), *a.* 1678. [f. L. *ostreaceus, f. *ostrea* oyster; see -ACEOUS.] Of the nature of the oyster or its shell; proper to an oyster; oyster-like; ostraceous.

Ostreger, ostringer (ǫ·strĕdʒəɹ, ǫ·strindʒəɹ). [ME. *ostregier, ostreger*, corruption of OF. *ostruchier, austruchier* :—late L. *austurcarius*, f. *austurcus* (:—L. *Asturicus* Austurian, from Asturia in Spain). For *ostringer*, cf. *messenger*, etc.] A keeper of goshawks.

Ostrei-, ostreo-, comb. forms of L. *ostrea*, *ostreum*, and Gr. ὄστρεον oyster. Hence: **O·streiform** *a.*, having the form of an oyster or of oysters. **O·streophage** (-fēidʒ), **Ostreophagist** (-ǫ·fădʒist) [Gr. -φάγος eating], one who or that which eats or feeds upon oysters; so **Ostreo·phagous** *a.*

Ostreiculture (ǫ·stri͵ikʊltiŭɹ). Also erron. ostr(e)a-, ostreo-, ostri-. 1861. [f. L. *ostrei-*, comb. form of *ostrea* oyster + CULTURE.] The artificial breeding of oysters for the market. Hence **O:streicu·ltural** *a.* **O:streicu·lturist.**

Ostrich (ǫ·stritʃ). [ME. *ostrice, -iche*, a. OF. *ostruce, -uche*, mod.F. *autruche* :—pop.L. *avistruthio*, from *avis* bird + late L. *struthio*, ad. Gr. στρουθίων ostrich, f. στρουθός sparrow, ostrich.] 1. A very large ratite bird, *Struthio camelus*, the only species of the genus *S.* and the family *Struthionidæ*, inhabiting the sandy plains of Africa and Arabia; it is the largest of existing birds.

There is much ref. in proverb and allusion to its indiscriminate voracity and its liking for hard substances, which it swallows to assist the gizzard in its functions; its supposed want of regard for its young; and the practice attributed to it of burying its head in the sand when pursued, through incapacity to distinguish between seeing and being seen.

b. Applied to the rhea of South America, a ratite bird resembling the ostrich; more fully *American o.* 1813. 2. *attrib.* Of or pertaining to an ostrich or ostriches; ostrich-like 1494.

1. Cruel, as an o. in desert WYCLIF *Lam.* iv. 3. Twil digest a Cathedral Church as easilie, as an Estritch a two penie nail 1589. 2. Whole nations, fooled by falsehood, fear, or pride, Their ostrich-heads in self-illusion hide MOORE.

Comb.: **o.-farm**, a farm on which ostriches are reared for the sake of their plumes; **-farming**; **-fern**, the fern *Onoclea struthiopteris* (*S. germanica*); **-tip**, the tip of an ostrich-feather.

O·strich-fea:ther. 1460. A feather of an ostrich, *esp.* one of the long curly quill-feathers of the wings or tail used as a personal ornament or for decorative purposes.

Ostrich-plume. 1637. 1. An ostrich-feather, or a bunch of two or three feathers. 2. *attrib.* Applied to a variety of Chrysanthemum 1891.

Ostringer: see OSTREGER.

Ostrogoth (ǫ·strogǫþ). 1647. [f. late L. *Ostrogothi* pl., f. OHG., OS. *ôstar* eastward, in the east :—OTeut. **aust(a)r*; see GOTH.] An East Goth; a name given to the division of the Teutonic race of Goths which conquered Italy, and in 493, under Theodoric, established a kingdom which continued till 555. Hence **Ostrogo·thian, Ostrogo·thic** *adjs.*

-ot, *suffix* [1], repr. F. *-ot*, orig. dim., but the dim. force is often lost, as in *ballot*, *chariot*, *parrot*, etc. It is not a living suffix in Eng.

-ot, *suffix* [2], repr. F. *-ote*, L. *-ota*, Gr. -ώτης, expressing nativity, as Ἠπειρώτης Epirot, native of Epirus, in which use it is often represented by -OTE. It occurs also in *helot*, *idiot*, *patriot*, *zealot*, and a few other sbs. of Greek origin.

Otacoustic (ō̆utăkū̆·stik, -ăkau·stik), *rare.* 1643. [f. Gr. οὖς, ὠτ- ear + ἀκουστικός ACOUSTIC.] An instrument to assist hearing, as an ear-trumpet. So ‖ **Otacou·sticon.**

Otaheite apple (ō̆utăhī·ti æ·p'l). 1814. [Named after *Otaheite*, or *Tahiti*, one of the Society Islands.] The fruit of *Spondias dulcis*, a native of Java, the Moluccas, and the Society Islands; it is of a golden yellow colour, the rind tasting like turpentine, and the pulp having the flavour of pine-apple.

Otalgia (ǫutæ·ldʒiă). 1657. [a. Gr. ὠταλγία ear-ache, f. οὖς, ὠτ- ear + ἄλγος pain.] Neuralgic pain in the ear. Hence **Ota·lgic** *a.*

Otary (ō̆u·tări). 1847. [ad. mod.L. *otaria*, f. Gr. οὖς, ὠτ- ear.] An eared seal; a member of the *Otariidæ*, a family of pinnipeds having very small external ears, which includes the fur seals and sea lions.

O.T.C. = Officers' Training Corps.

-ote, *suffix*, another form of -OT [2], as in *Candiote*, a native of Candia.

Otheoscope (ō̆u·þioskǫup). 1877. [f. Gr. ὠθεῖν to push + -σκοπος, -SCOPE.] A modification of the radiometer, devised by Sir W. Crookes, in which the black or driving surface is stationary, while the cooling surface is movable.

Other (ʊ·ðəɹ), *adj. pron.* (*sb.*). [Com. Teut.: OE. *ôþer*, *ôðer* = Du. and G. *ander*, etc. = Skr. *ántara-s*, and prob. L. *alter* :—Indo-Eur. **anteros*, a word formed with the usual comparative suffix of adjs., in Skr. *-taras*, Gr. -τερος, L. *-ter*, Eng. *-ther*, in *whether*, etc.] **A.** *adj.* †1. One of the two, the one (of two); L. *alter* –1596. 2. The remaining (person, thing, or group) of two; later, also, of three or more. Usu. preceded by *the* or an equivalent word (e.g. *his other foot*). OE. **b.** *Every o.*, every second, every alternate 1480. †3. That follows the first; second (of two or more). *Obs.* (exc. as in quots.) OE. 4. With plural sb. = the remaining, the rest of the; L. *ceteri* OE. 5. Existing besides, or distinct from, that already mentioned or implied; not this, not the same, different in identity; further, additional OE. **b.** In this sense, *other* may be construed with *than* ME. 6. Different (in kind or quality). Const. *than* (*from*, †*but*). ME. †7. Used to characterize things as of a different kind from those previously mentioned; e.g. *other sinful men* = other men, who are sinful –1699.

1. Her o. leg was lame SPENSER. 2. Phr. *On the o. hand*: see HAND *sb.* But (O poore Glouster) Lost he his o. eye? SHAKS. **b.** A committee every o. week SWIFT. 3. Phr. *The o. day*: †(*a*) orig. the second day, the next day; †(*b*) the preceding day, yesterday. (*c*) a day or two ago, recently. So *the o. night*, *week*, etc. They played a match the o. day against a local club 1885. 4. Satan..With Head up lift above the wave, ..his other Parts besides Prone on the Flood MILT. 5. It may chance of wheat, or of some o. graine 1 *Cor.* xv. 37. We have o. evidence..how deeply he had drunk..at classic fountains GLADSTONE. Phr. *O. such* (arch.): now usu. *such other(s)*. *O. six*, etc. (arch. or dial.), ambiguous: = the (or an) other six, or six other(s), etc. *O. the king's enemies* (arch.), ambiguous: = others, (who are) the king's enemies, or other enemies of the king. **b.** Gratuities o. than money 1866. 6. It could not be o. than pleasant to me COLERIDGE. 7. *Other sinful men* now means only 'others of such men as are sinful'.

B. *absol.*, *pron.*, or *sb.*

I. *absol.* †1. One of the two, the one; L. *alter* –ME. 2. *The o.*: The remaining one of two; later, of three or more. (Esp. contrasted with (*the*) *one*.) OE. †**b.** Instead of 'the other', the simple *other* was formerly used after *each*, *either*, *neither*, *whether* (occas. after *one*, *none*) –1657. †**c.** The simple *other* was formerly used in the sense 'each preceding one (in turn)' –1694. 3. *pl.* The remaining ones, the rest; L. *ceteri* OE. 4. absol. use of A. 5, the sb. being expressed in the context: **a.** *sing.* One besides ME. **b.** *pl.* (formerly *other* :—OE. *ôþre*, *-u*) Other things or persons of the kind mentioned OE.

2. One Monarch wears an honest open Face,..That o. looks like Nature in Disgrace DRYDEN. **b.** Priest and people interchangeably pray each for o. 1657. Phr. *Each other*, as in *they help each other*, i.e. each [helps] the other. **c.** Euery Letter he hath writ, hath disuouch'd o. SHAKS. 3. Awaking when the o. doe SHAKS. The cave where the others lay DE FOE. 4. **a.** Some time or o. we may be at leisure ADDISON. Ten years ago I used your soap; since when I have used no o. (*mod.*). **b.** I know two o. of his works J. H. NEWMAN. The very place, of all others, where it is most likely to be of real service 1877.

II. *pron.* 1. **a.** *sing.* = Another person; some one else; any one else OE. **b.** *pl.* (formerly *other*; cf. B. I. 4 b.) Other persons OE. 2. = Another thing; something else, anything else; *no* or *none o.*, nothing else. *Obs.* or *arch.* OE. 3. In reciprocal sense: = Each other, one another. In later use only *Sc.* late ME.

1. **a.** Euery one taketh before o., his owne supper 1 *Cor.* xi. 21. It is plain..she likes some o. 1811. **b.** I have pleased some and displeased o. 1607. Others indeed may talk BERKELEY. 2. This is none o., but the house of God *Gen.* xxviii. 17. He thought he could not do o. than send the two prisoners for trial 1895. 3. Nae doubt but they were fain o' ither BURNS.

III. *sb. Philos.* That which (in relation to something already mentioned) constitutes the other part of the universe of being, and is thus the counterpart or double of the former; e.g. the *non-ego* is the 'other' of the *ego*, Creation of the Creator, etc. 1863.

Other (ʊ·ðəɹ), *adv.* [1] ME. [advb. use of prec., sometimes due to ellipsis.] = OTHERWISE B. 1.

It is impossible to refer to them..o. than very cursorily 1883.

†**Other**, *conj.* and *adv.* [2] [The OE. word for 'or', *oððe*, earlier *oððа*, was superseded *c* 1130 by *oðer*, the source of which is conjectural.] **A.** *conj.* The earlier form of OR *conj.*[2] Const. *simply*, or preceded by *other*, *whether* –1574. **B.** *adv.* 1. Placed before two (or more) words, phrases, or clauses connected by *other* or *or*, so that *other*.. *other*.., and (later) *other*.. *or*..

was equivalent to mod. Eng. *either .. or ..*: see EITHER B. 3. –1588. **2.** Following an alternative clause with *or* (*rare*). ME. only. **3.** = Whether (*rare*) 1523.

Othergates (*v·ðəɹgeits*), *adv.* and *adj. Obs.* exc. *dial.* ME. [f. OTHER *a.* + GATE *sb.*² 5, with advb. genitive *-es.*] **A.** *adv.* In another way, otherwise, differently. †**B.** *adj.* Of another fashion or kind, different –1669.

A. If he had not beene in drinke, hee would haue tickel'd you other gates then he did SHAKS.

Otherguess (*v·ðəɹges*), *a.* Now only *colloq.* 1632. [Reduction of *othergets* from prec., spelt after *guess.*] = prec. B.

†**Otherguise,** *a.* 1653. [Corruption of prec. by folk-etymology, after *guise.*] = prec. –1755.

Otherness (*v·ðəɹnės*). 1587. [f. OTHER *a.* + -NESS.] The quality of being other; difference, diversity. **b.** *transf.* The fact of being other; something that is other 1821.

Other some, †**othersome,** *a.* and *pron.* Now *arch.* or *dial.* ME. [OTHER *a.*, SOME *pron.* or *a.*] *adj.* Some other; *pron.* Some others.

Otherways (*v·ðəɹwēɪz*), *adv. Obs.* exc. *dial.* ME. [f. OTHER *a.* + *ways*, advb. genitive of WAY *sb.*] = OTHERWISE.

Otherwhere (*v·ðəɹhwēəɹ*), *adv.* Also hyphened or as two words. ME. [f. OTHER *a.* + WHERE; cf. *somewhere.*] In another place; elsewhere 1541. **b.** To another place. late ME. **c.** quasi-*sb.*, esp. with *some, any*, etc. (better written separately, *some other where* = some other place) ME.

Otherwhile (*v·ðəɹhwəil*), *adv.* Now *rare* or *dial.* Also hyphened, or as two words. ME. [f. OTHER *a.* + WHILE *sb.*] **1.** At one time or other; at times; sometimes, now and then, occasionally. †**b.** quasi-*sb.* in *every otherwhile* (prop. three words), every now and then –1736. **2.** At another time, or at other times. Chiefly as *correl.* to *sometime* or an equiv. Now *arch.* late ME.

Otherwhiles (*v·ðəɹhwəilz*), *adv.* Now *rare* or *dial.* ME. [f. as prec. with advb. genitive *-s*, in later times often felt as pl.] †**1.** = prec. **1.** –1787. **2.** = prec. **2.** 1460.

Otherwise (*v·ðəɹwəiz*), *sb. phr., adv., adj.* OE. [orig. OE. *on ōðre wīsan*, in other manner, ME. *oþre wise*, at length written *otherwise*; cf. *in any wise, anywise*, etc.; see WISE *sb.*¹] **A.** Phr. with *wise*, manner, way, as distinct sb., e.g. *in other wise* (arch.).

To be led any o. than blindly BURKE.

B. *adv.* **1.** In another way, or in other ways: differently. Const. *than.* ME. **2.** In another case; in other circumstances; if not; else. late ME. **3.** In other respects 1594. †**4.** On the other hand (*rare*) –1673. **5.** *And, or o.*, and, or the opposite or the reverse 1895.

1. God saw o. PUSEY. **2.** I went at once; o. I should have missed him (*mod.*). **3.** The best men o. are not alwayes the best in regard of societie HOOKER.

C. Adjectival uses. **1.** In another state or condition; not so; different; other. late ME. **2.** as *adj.* That would otherwise be ...; that would otherwise exist 1600.

1. Some [scholars] are wise, and some are o. 1680. **2.** At the table aboue all others their o. equals 1600.

Other world, o·ther-world, *sb.* and *a.* 1884. [OTHER *a.* 2.] **1.** A world other than this: **a.** The world to come. **b.** The spirit-land of many non-Christian peoples. **c.** The world of idealism, poetry, or romance. 1888. **2.** *attrib.* Unearthly; heavenly.

2. That sweet other-world smile TENNYSON. Hence **O·therwo·rldliness,** devotion to the other world, or to the interests of a future life, *esp.* morbid, ascetic, or selfish spirituality; the quality attributed to an ideal world. **O·therwo·rldly** *a.* devoted to the concerns of the world to come, or the world of mind.

Othman. 1813. = OTTOMAN *a.* and *sb.*¹

Otic (*ōu·tik, ǫ·tik*), *a.* 1657. [ad. Gr. ὠτικός, f. οὖς, ὠτ- ear.] *Anat., Path.* Of, belonging to, or relating to the ear; auricular.

-otic (*ǫ·tik*), compound suffix, repr. Gr. -ωτικός, f. sbs. in -ωτ-ης or adjs. in -ωτ-ος (from vbs. in -όω) + -ικός -IC. Adjs. in -OTIC go in sense with sbs. in -OSIS, as *amaurotic*, of, pertaining to, or affected with *amaurosis*; so *hypnotic, narcotic*, etc. Exceptions are *erotic, exotic*, etc., which are otherwise derived, and *chaotic*, formed by analogy.

Otiose (*ōu·ʃiōus*), *a.* 1794. [ad. L. *otiosus* at leisure, f. *otium.*] **1.** At leisure or at rest; unemployed, idle; indolent 1850. **2.** Having no practical result; sterile; nugatory 1794. **b.** Superfluous, useless 1837.

1. An o. support of the Government 1850. Reposing with a vague and o. belief on the traditionary doctrines 1853. **2.** Such stories..as require..nothing more than an o. assent PALEY. **b.** The number of o. lines..which swell the piece out 1866. Hence **O·tio·se·ly** *adv.*, **-ness.**

Otiosity (*ōuʃiǫ·sĭti*). 1483. [a. OF. *occiosité*, f. *occiose*, ad. L. *otiosus* (see prec.)] The condition or state of being otiose.

‖**Otitis** (*outəi·tis*). 1799. [mod.L., f. Gr. οὖς, ὠτ- ear + -ITIS.] *Path.* Inflammation of the ear. Hence **Oti·tic** *a.*

‖**Otium** (*ōu·ʃiŏm*). 1729. The Latin word for 'leisure, ease'; used esp. in the phrase *otium cum dignitate*, dignified leisure or ease.

Oto- (*ōu·to*), bef. a vowel **ot-**, repr. Gr. ὠτο-, comb. form of οὖς, ὠτ- ear, an element of medical and other scientific words.

Otoco·nia [Gr. κονία or κόνις dust], term for the white pulverulent dust in the inner ear, the aggregation of which forms an otolith. **Oto·conite** = OTOLITH. **O·tocrane** [Gr. κρανίον the skull], the auditory capsule, the portion of the petrous bone which encloses the organ of hearing; hence **Otocra·nial, Otocra·nic** *adjs.* **O·tocyst** [Gr. κύστις bladder], term for the auditory vesicle or organ of hearing in some of the Invertebrata; hence **Otocy·stic** *a.* **O·tolite** [-LITE] = OTOLITH. ‖**Otorrhœ·a** [Gr. ῥοία a flow], purulent discharge from the ear. **Oto·steal** [Gr. ὀστέον bone], *a.* relating to the auditory ossicle.

Otolith (*ōu·tŏliþ*). 1835. [f. OTO- + Gr. λίθος stone.] *Anat.* and *Physiol.* An ear-stone; one of the calcareous bodies found in the inner ear of vertebrates and some invertebrates; in fishes often of great size. Hence **Otoli·thic, -li·tic** *adjs.*

Otology (*outǫ·lŏdʒi*). 1842. [f. Gr. οὖς, ὠτ- ear + -LOGY.] That branch of science which treats of the ear, its anatomy, functions, and diseases; a treatise on the ear. Hence **Oto·logist,** an ear-specialist. **Otolo·gical** *a.*

Otoscope (*ōu·tŏskoup*). 1849. [f. OTO- + Gr. -σκόπος observing, observer.] **1.** A modification of the stethoscope for auscultation of sounds in the ear. **2.** An optical instrument for inspection of the cavity of the ear 1853. Hence **Otosco·pic** *a.* **Oto·scopy,** the use of the o.

Ottar, var. of ATTAR, OTTO.

‖**Ottava** (*ottā·vă*). 1820. [It. = eighth, octave.] **1.** *Mus.* An octave. (Usu. abbrev. 8*va.*) 1848. **2.** *O. rima* (*rī·ma*). An Italian stanza of eight 11-syllabled lines, riming as *a b a b a b c c*; the Byronic adaptation has English heroic lines of ten syllables.

Otter (*ǫ·təɹ*), *sb.* [Com. Teut.: OE. *otr, ot(t)or, oter*:—OTeut. **otrō-z*, pre-Teut. **udrō-s*; radically akin to Gr. ὕδωρ, Skr. *udan*, Eng. *water*; cf. Gr. ὕδρος, ὕδρα water-snake.] **1.** An aquatic fur-bearing carnivorous mammal (*Lutra vulgaris*) feeding chiefly on fish, having fin-like legs, webbed feet, and long horizontally flattened tail, which enable it to swim and turn in the water with remarkable rapidity. **b.** Applied to other species of *Lutra*, and allied genera 1781. **2.** The fur or skin of any species of otter. late ME. **3.** A tackle consisting of a float with line and a number of hooks 1851.

1. An O., sir Iohn? Why an O.? *Fal.* Why? She's neither fish nor flesh SHAKS. **b. American O.,** *L. canadensis.* **Sea O.,** *L.* (*Enhydris*) *marina*, which inhabits the American shores of the North Pacific.

attrib. and *Comb.*, as **o.-dog, -hound,** a dog of a breed used for hunting the o.; **-shell,** any bivalve shell of the genus *Lutraria*; **-spear,** a spear used in hunting otters. Hence **O·tter** *v. intr.* to hunt the o., to fish with the 'o.' tackle (see sense 3).

Otter, var. of OTTO, ATTAR.

Otto (*ǫ·to*). Also formerly **otter, ottar.** 1639. An altered form of ATTAR, in *attar* or *otto of roses*, the fragrant essence of roses. **b.** Hence, *joc.*, in *o. of whisky.* THACKERAY.

Ottoman (*ǫ·tŏmăn*), *a.* and *sb.*¹ 1600. [(ult.) ad. Arab. adj., from the name *Othmān* (see below). The forms *Othoman* and *Othman* more closely represent the Arabic. The Turkish pron. is *Osmān*, whence OSMANLI.] **A.** *adj.* Of or belonging to the Turkish dynasty founded *c* 1300 by Othman or Osman I, the branch of the Turks to which he belonged, or the Turkish empire ruled by his descendants; Turkish (of the dominions of the Sultan).

O. Porte, the court or palace of the Sultan; the Turkish government; also called the Porte or Sublime Porte.

B. *sb.* A Turk of the family or tribe of Othman or Osman; a Turkish subject (of the Sultan); an OSMANLI; a Turk in the usual political sense 1605.

It is too late to change, in general use, the familiar Ottomans for the more accurate Osmans or Osmanli 1854. Hence **Ottoma·nic** *a.* and *sb.*

Ottoman (*ǫ·tŏmăn*), *sb.*² 1806. [f. prec.; prob. through F. *ottomane.*] **1.** A cushioned seat like a sofa, but without back or arms; or a small article of the same kind used as a low seat or footstool. **2.** A kind of fabric of silk, or silk and wool 1883.

†**O·ttomite.** Also **Otta-.** 1604. [f. OTTOM(AN + -ITE¹.] = OTTOMAN *sb.*¹ –1818.

Ottrelite (*ǫ·trĕləit*). 1812. [f. *Ottrez*, in Belgium, where found; see -LITE.] *Min.* A hydrous silicate of aluminium, iron, and manganese, found in greyish to black crystalline scales 1844.

‖**Ouabaïo, wabaio** (*wabai·o*). 1890. The Somāli name of the plant *Acocanthera Schimperi*, the juice of which is used to poison arrows. Hence **Ouabaïn, wabaïn** (*wabā·in*), the glucoside $C_{31}H_{48}O_{12}$, obtained from this plant, in action and composition closely resembling strophanthin.

Ouakari, var. of WAKARI, S. Amer. monkey.

‖**Oubliette** (*ublĭe·t*). 1819. [Fr., f. *oublier* to forget.] A secret dungeon, access to which was gained only through a trapdoor above; often having a secret pit below, into which the prisoner might be precipitated.

Forgotten like one in the oubliettes of the Bastille 1872.

Ouch (*autʃ*), *sb.* Now only *arch.* or *Hist.* [ME. and AF. *nouche*:—L. *nusca, nosche*:—late L. *nusca*, a. OHG. *nuscka, nuscka* buckle, clasp, app. of Celtic origin. In ME. *a nouche* was divided *an ouche*; cf. *adder.*] **1.** A clasp, buckle, or brooch (often set with precious stones); hence, a clasped necklace, bracelet, or the like; also, a buckle or brooch worn as an ornament. **2.** The gold or silver setting of a precious stone 1481.

1. Most rich and precious Ouches and Brouches 1563. **2.** Make them [ii stones] to be set in ouches of gold 1551 *Exod.* xxviii. 11. Hence **Ouch** *v. trans.* to set or adorn with, or as with, ouches.

Ought (*ǭt*), *sb.*¹ (*pron.*), *adv.*, var. of AUGHT *sb.*²

Ought, *sb.*² 1678. [OUGHT *v.* III. used as a noun.] That which is denoted by the verb *ought*; duty, obligation.

Ought, *sb.*³ *illiterate.* 1844. ['A nought' divided as 'an ought'.] = NOUGHT in sense 'cipher'.

Ought (*ǭt*), *v.* [OE. *āhte*, ME. *ohte, oȝte, oughte*, pa. t. of *āgan*, ME. *oȝen, owen*, mod. OWE *v.* q.v.] **A.** as finite verb; properly pa. t. of OWE. **I.** Pa. t. of OWE *v.* in sense 'to have or possess'; possessed, owned. *Obs.* –1670. **II.** Pa. t. of OWE *v.* in its existing sense. **1.** Had to pay; owed. *Obs.* or *dial.* ME. †**b.** *absol.* Was in debt (*to*) –1610. †**2.** *fig.* Owed, had to repay (an ill turn, shame, etc.) –1694. †**b.** Bore (ill or good will, a grudge, a spite, regarded as something yet to be paid or rendered); occas. nearly = showed, rendered (favour, allegiance, etc.) –1678. †**3.** Was indebted or beholden for; owed –1568.

1. He..sayde this other day, You o. him a thousand pound SHAKS. **2. b.** He highly inveighed against many gentlemen..that o. him no homage, as persons disaffected 1678.

III. As auxiliary of predication. The general verb to express duty or obligation of any kind, strictly used of moral obligation, but also expressing what is befitting, proper, correct, or naturally expected. Only in pa. t. (indic. or subj.), which may be either past or present in meaning. (The only current use in standard Eng.) **a.** In past sense: = Owed it to duty; was (were) under obligation (*to do* something). Now only in dependent clause, corresp. to a pa. t. in principal clause; *he said you ought* = he said it was your duty. ME. **b.** In present sense: = Am (is, are) bound or under obligation. (The most frequent sense. Formerly expressed by the pres. t., OWE *v.* III. 1.) ME. **c.** With past sense indicated by a following perf. infin. with *have*; *you o. to have known* = it was your duty to know, you should have known. (The usual modern idiom.) 1551.

a. He did not think that the defendant o. to be kept in prison any longer 1892. **b.** The precedent o. to be followed JUNIUS. **c.** We haue left vndone those things whiche we oughte to haue done *Bk. Com. Prayer.*

IV. The pa. pple. *ought* (*aught*) was formerly in literary, and is still in dial. and vulgar use, to form the perfect tense or passive voice of OWE *v.*: **a.** Owed; **b.** Possessed (*mod. Sc.*); **c.** Been obliged (*illiterate*) ME.

b. I would give half of what I am aught, to know if it is still in existence SCOTT. **c.** He hadn't o. to have done it (*mod.*).

B. as present stem, with inflexions (*oughted, oughting*, etc.). *Obs.* or *dial.* †**1.** = A. III, OWE *v.* III. 1. -1654. **2.** *Sc.* To have to pay; = OWE *v.* II. 1. 1552. **3.** *Sc.* To possess; = OWN *v.* 1. 1800.

2. We aught him the siller SCOTT. **3.** There's naebody but you and me that o. the name STEVENSON. Hence **Ou·ghtness** [f. sense III], that quality of an action that is expressed by 'ought'; moral obligatoriness (*rare*).

Ouija (wī·ya, -dʒa). 1904. [F. *oui* yes + G. *ja* yes.] A board used with a planchette for obtaining messages in spiritualistic séances.

Ouistiti, var. of WISTITI, S. Amer. monkey.

Ounce (auns), *sb.*[1] ME. [a. OF. *unce*, F. *once* :—L. *uncia* twelfth part (of a pound or a foot). Cf. INCH.] **1.** A unit of weight; orig., as still in Troy weight, the twelfth of a pound, but in avoirdupois the sixteenth of the pound. **b.** *loosely.* usu. A small quantity. late ME. **c.** *fig.* of imponderable things 1526. **2.** Used to render *onza*, a coin of Spain (= £3 12*s.*) and Sicily (= 10*s.* 3½*d.*) 1799. **3.** *attrib.* Of the weight of one ounce or (in comb.) so many ounces 1846.

1. The Troy o. consists of 480 grains, and is divided into 20 pennyweights; the avoirdupois o. contains 437·5 grains, and is divided into 16 drams; *Fluid o.*, a measure of capacity, containing an avoird. o. of distilled water at 62° Fahr. N.E.D. **b.** My sweete o. of mans flesh, my in-conie Iew SHAKS. **c.** An o. of mothers wit is worth a pound of Clergy RAY.

Ounce (auns), *sb.*[2] ME. [ad. OF. *once*, *lonce*, OF. *l'once* represents an earlier *lonce* = It. *lonza* :—pop. L. **luncia*, for L. *lyncea*, deriv. of *lyncem* LYNX.] **1.** A name orig. given to the common lynx, subseq. to various other moderate-sized feline beasts, vaguely identified. **2.** *Zool.* A feline beast (*Felis uncia*), also called *mountain-panther*, and *snow-leopard*; it resembles the leopard in marking 1774. †**b.** Applied to the Cheetah or Hunting Leopard -1821.

Ouph(e (auf). 1623. [var. of AUF(E, OAF; perh. a typographical or scribal error for *auph* or *oaph.*]

Strew good lucke (Ouphes) on euery sacred roome SHAKS.

Our (auᵊɹ), *pron.* [Com. Teut.: see below.] **A.** *personal pron.* [OE. *ūre.*] The genitive pl. of the first personal pronoun: = Of us. *Obs.* (exc. in some phrases, as *in our midst, on our behalf*, and with sense of the objective genitive, as *in our despite, our dismissal, our accusers*, and the like). late ME.

B. *possess. pron.* [OE. *ūre*, arising from inflecting the genitive pl. in A. as an adj.] **1.** Of or belonging to us, i. e. to the speakers, or the speaker and those whom he speaks for or includes. The possess. adj. corresponding to WE, US; expressing the genitive of possession; also the objective genitive, as *in our defence, our Maker*, etc.; see A. OE. **b.** Of the body of Christians, as *Our Lord*, etc., or of humanity, as *Our Father* OE. **c.** In imperial or royal use, instead of *my* ME. **d.** In vaguer sense: With whom or which we have to do; whom we have in mind; of whom (or which) we are speaking; of the writer and his readers, or merely of the writer. Cf. WE. 1612. †**2.** *absol.*: = OURS -1641. **3.** Our Father. The 'Lord's Prayer': = PATERNOSTER 1882.

1. 'Gainst us, our lives, our children, and our heirs SHAKS. **c.** Geven at Laterane the tenth yere of our popedome 1568. **d.** If we should each kill our man 1612. We must now introduce our reader to the.. fisher's cottage SCOTT.

-our, *suffix* (repr. AF. *-our*, OF. *-or*, *-ur*, *-eör*, *-eür*, mod.F. *-eur*), the earliest spelling of the suffix -OR.

Ourali, var. of WOURALI.

Ourang-outang, -utang, ff. ORANG-OUTANG.

Ourano-: see URANO-.

Ourn (auᵊɹn), *poss. pron. dial.* late ME. [f. OUR *poss. pron.*, as HERN.] = OURS.

Ours (auᵊɹz), *poss. pron.* ME. [In form a double possessive, f. poss. pron. *ur, ure*, OUR + *-es*; of north. origin.] The absol. form of the possessive pronoun OUR, used when no sb. follows: Our one, our ones; that or those belonging to us. **b.** *Of ours*: see OF XIII. ME.

He and al his is owris 1533. Ours..is 'a time of loud disputes and weak convictions' MORLEY. **b.** Let us close those wide mouths of ours CARLYLE.

Ourself (auᵊɹse·lf), *pron.* ME. [A parallel formation to next, with *self* instead of *selves.*] Emphatic and reflexive pronoun, corresponding to *we, us*; orig. = OURSELVES, but later differentiated, so as to be used mostly where *we* refers to a single person or is not definitely plural; e. g. in royal, divine, or editorial utterance, or when used indef. in the sense of *one, oneself.* **1.** *emphatic.* **a.** Standing alone as subject, as object, or predic. *poet.* or *arch.* late ME. **b.** In apposition with *we* or *us.* late ME. **2.** *reflexive*, as direct or indirect obj. ME.

1. a. Which our selfe haue granted SHAKS. Were you sick, o. Would tend upon you TENNYSON. **b.** What touches vs our selfe shall be last seru'd SHAKS. **2.** We..found ourself running among the first DICKENS.

Ourselves (auᵊɹse·lvz), *pron. pl.* 1495. [The orig. construction was nom. *wē selfe*, acc. *ūs selfe*, dat. *ūs selfum*; whence ME. *us selven.* Bef. 1500, *our(e selfs, our selves* became the standard form; cf. *yourselves*, etc., and see SELF.] **1.** *emphatic.* **a.** Standing alone as subject, as object, or after *be, become*, or the like 1591. **b.** In apposition with *we* or (rarely) *us* 1526. **2.** *reflexive*, as direct or indirect object 1495.

1. a. Our selues will heare Th' accuser SHAKS. **b.** The light..that we have attained vnto our selues BIBLE *Transl. Pref.* **2.** To see oursels as others see us BURNS.

-ous, *suffix*, repr. L. *-osus* (*-a, -um*), forming adjs., with the sense 'abounding in, full of, characterized by, of the nature of'. In Anglo-Fr. and early ME. the forms were the same as in early OF., e. g. *coveitos, -us, envios, -us*, but the vowel was soon identified with OE. long *ū*, and like it written after 1300 *ou* (*covetous, envious*), the spelling ever since retained, though the sound has passed through (*-ūs, -us*, -us) to (-*vs*, əs). Thus *-ous* became the established type of the suffix, and its addition has become the ordinary mode of anglicizing L. adjs. of many kinds, esp. those in *-eus, -ius, -uus, -er, -ris, -ax, -ox, -oci-, -endus, -ulus, -vorus, -orus*, e. g. *aqueous, conscious, arduous, alacritous, hilarious, capacious, ferocious, stupendous, garrulous, omnivorous, sonorous.*

b. The compound form *-eous* is sometimes a corruption of another suffix, e. g. in *righteous, courteous, gorgeous*; sometimes, e. g. in *bounteous, duteous*, etc., results from the addition of *-ous* to another suffix.

c. In *Chem.*, adjs. in *-ous* indicate acids and other compounds containing a larger proportion of the element indicated by the stem than those expressed by an adj. in *-ic*; e. g. *cuprous* oxide, *ferrous* salts, *sulphurous* acid, etc.; see -IC 1 b.

d. Nouns of quality from adjs. in *-ous* are usu. formed in *-ousness*, as *covetousness*; those from L. *-osus* have often also forms in *-osity*, as *curiosity*, etc.; but this termination more often accompanies adjs. in -OSE[1].

Ousel, var. OUZEL.

Oust (aust), *v.* 1588. [a. AF. *ouster* = OF. *oster*, mod.F. *ôter* to take away, etc.; deriv. unkn.] **1.** *trans. Law.* To eject, dispossess, disseise; to deprive *of* a corporeal or incorporeal hereditament. **b.** To exclude, bar, take away (a right, privilege, etc.) 1656. **2.** *transf.* To eject from any place or position. Const. *of, from*, or with double obj. 1668. **b.** To drive (a thing) out of use or fashion 1865.

1. Farmers were ousted of their leases made by tenants in tail BLACKSTONE. **2.** It was altogether impossible to o. him from command 1868. **b.** The.. waggons were built on those ancient lines whose proportions have been ousted by modern patterns T. HARDY.

Ouster (au·stəɹ). 1531. [AF. vb. infin. (see prec.) used subst.; see -ER[4].] *Law.* Ejection from a freehold, etc., deprivation of a corporeal or incorporeal hereditament; now implying a wrongful dispossession.

‖ **Ouster-le-main.** 1485. [a. AF., in L. *amovere manum* to remove the hand.] *Feudal Law.* A livery of land out of the sovereign's hands, on a judgement given for one who has pleaded that the sovereign has no title to hold it; also, a judgement or writ granting such livery. **b.** The delivery of lands out of a guardian's hands on a ward's coming of age.

Out, *sb.* 1717. [OUT *adv.*, used absol. or ellipt.] **1.** Short for *outside.* **2. a.** *pl.* The party which is out of office; usu. opp. to the *ins* 1764. **b.** = OUTSIDE A. 6. 1844. **c.** *pl.* In games: The side that is not playing; in *Cricket*, that is not in; also, the players, on either side, who are not taking part in the scrimmage at Rugby football 1895. **3.** An excursion, outing (*dial.*) 1762. **b.** *Outs and ins*, more usu. *ins and outs*; see IN *sb.* 2. 1773. **4.** *Printing.* An omission 1784. **5.** *pl.* Amounts paid out; rates and taxes (*local*) 1884. **6.** *U.S.* A blemish, flaw 1885.

2. d. *At outs* (U.S.): at odds, at variance 1901.

Out (aut), *a.* ME. [OUT *adv.* used attrib. by ellipsis of a pple. (as *lying*, etc.), or by taking the predic. use of the adv. as adj., or by resolution of compounds with *out-* (e. g. out-worker, out worker).] **1.** External, exterior. Now usu. *outer, outside, external*, or written in comb., as *out-edge*, OUTSIDE. †**2.** Outlying, or at a distance outside some place in question -1726. **3.** In cricket, football, etc.: Played *out*, or away from the home ground; played in the outer parts of the field. (Often hyphened.) 1884. **4.** Beyond the usual or normal (size) 1883.

2. In the o. Parts of his Diocess 1726. Phr. *O. isle* (*o. island*), an isle or island lying away from the mainland. (Often hyphened.) **4.** She was 'rather an o. size', as they say in the Duchy 1894.

Out, *v.* [OE. *ūtian*, f. *ūt*, OUT *adv.* Perh. formed anew in ME.] **1.** *trans.* To put out, drive out, eject, reject, get rid of, dismiss, oust (*from* a place, office, possession, etc.); to do out or deprive (*of* a possession). Now *Obs.* exc. *dial.* **b.** To put out, extinguish, blot out, abolish. *Obs.* exc. *dial.* 1502. **c.** *slang.* (orig. pugilistic): To 'knock out' or disable (an opponent); hence, To render insensible, or kill, by a blow 1896. †**2.** To set out, expose (for sale, etc.) -1670. **3.** To disclose, exhibit; to speak out, vent. *Obs.* exc. *dial.* ME. **4.** *intr.* [From the ellipt. use in OUT *adv.* I. 13.] **a.** To go out, esp. on a pleasure excursion. Also *to o. it* (colloq.) 1846. **b.** *To o. with*: To come out with; to utter (*colloq.*) 1802.

1. Outed of iurisdiction 1602. **4. a.** With that he ups and he outs 1894. **b.** He outs with his lie SPURGEON.

Out (aut), *adv.* [Com. Teut.: OE. *ūt* = Skr. *ud-* verbal prefix 'out'. Orig. only an adv., but in some Teut. langs. a prep. also. In Eng., OUT *prep.* (q.v.) is exceptional; the prepositional sense = L. *ex*, Gr. ἐξ, ἐκ, is regularly expressed by adding *of.*] **I.** Of motion or direction. **simply.* **1.** Expressing motion or direction from within a space, or from a point considered as a centre. **b.** Implying distribution and division; esp. with *deal, portion, serve, share*, and the like 1535. **2.** Away from some recognized place; e.g. the land, the shore, one's own country; away, to a distance OE. **3.** So as to project or extend beyond the general surface or limits; as in *to hang, jut, shoot*, or *stick out. To hold out*: see HOLD *v.* 1535. **b.** Expressing extension or prolongation (in space or time). late ME.

1. The children of the kyngedome shalbe caste oute into vtter darcknes 1551 BIBLE *Matt.* viii. 12. General Adams' horse struck o. and kicked me on the shin 1854. I will look o. a book for her (*mod.*). *To call one o.* (see CALL *v.*), *come o., have one o.*, i.e. to a duel. **b.** The great Empire of his Father was parcelled o. into members 1652. **2.** The Freight and Assurance o. and home STEELE. **3.** The room..built o. to serve as a library 1896. **b.** To lengthen o. the period of life GOLDSM.

***in pregnant and transf. uses.* **4.** Expressing removal from its position when *in* OE. **5.**

From one's normal or equable state of mind, or ordinary course of action. See PUT *out*. 1588. **b.** From one's harmonious relations. See also FALL *out*. 1530. **6.** So as to be no longer alight or burning; as *to do, go, put out*. late ME. **b.** From being in existence or activity; as *to die, give, go, kill o.* 1523. **7.** To an end ME. **b.** Completely, quite, outright ME. **8.** To an issue, explicit result, or solution; as *to make, find, puzzle, work out; to help out; to come, fall, turn out* 1534. **9.** To the full, complete, or utmost degree; as in *to deck, fit, rig out* 1555. **10.** From a contained or quiescent state into one of activity, accessibility, or manifestation; as *to break* or *burst out, to open out* OE. **11.** Into utterance of sound; aloud; as *to call, cry, shout, speak out*. late ME. **b.** In the way of disclosure; openly ME. **12.** Into public notice, publicity, or publication; from the printing-press 1542. **b.** Of a person: Into society; into work or service 1782. **13.** With ellipsis of intr. vb. (*go, come*, etc.); hence functioning as a verb without inflexion. late ME. **b.** So *Out with* = have out, bring out ME. **14.** With ellipsis of trans. vb. (*put, bring*, etc.) 1819.

4. Mr. Wood sat..laughing his sides o. THACKERAY. Hanmer got..run o. after a splendid hit 1843. The former member was turned o. (*mod.*). 5. Neither he nor any other sensible man puts himself o. about new books 1887. b. Wine made them fall o. 1637. 6. A Candle goes half o. in the Light of the Sun ADDISON. 7. The match to be played o. 1746. Phr. *To fight it o., talk it o. To have it o.*, to bring it to a finish. 8. Worke o. youre awne saluacion with feare and tremblynge TINDALE *Phil.* ii. 12. 10. The stars come o. M. ARNOLD. 11. Come hither Herald..And read o. this SHAKS. b. If things come o., we should keep counsel 1637. 12. Not yet set o. in Print ASCHAM. b. My sister in town bringing o. a young sister-in-law 1849. 13. O., damned spot: o., I say SHAKS. Murder will o. 1887. b. O. with your cambric, dear ladies, and let us all whimper together THACKERAY.

II. Of position. (Senses corresponding to those in I, as indicating the position resulting from the motion there expressed.)

simply*. **1. Expressing position or situation beyond the bounds of, or not within, a space, etc. late ME. **b.** Not 'in'; in the open air 1440. **c.** Away from home; on an expedition, esp. in arms 1605; *mod.* on strike. **2.** Away or at a distance from some recognized place; abroad in a distant country OE. **b.** Away from the land or shore. late ME. **3.** Projecting; protruding; *spec.* through a rent in the clothing, as *out at elbows, heels*, etc. 1553. **b.** Unfurled, displayed, as a flag, etc. 1720. **4.** Without; on the outside; externally ME.

1. If the River had been o., and the Fields under Water SIR T. BROWNE. My sword was already o. 1843. Obliged to call in money that he had lying o. (*mod.*). c. Most of the miners are 'out' 1890. d. Phr. *To be out for* (something) (orig. *U.S.*): to have all one's attention, energies, etc., directed towards securing or doing (something); so *to be out to* (do something) 1889. 4. *Merry W.* v. v. 60.

***in pregnant and transf. uses*. **5.** Removed from its own place or position. *O. of joint*: see JOINT *sb.* I. 1. ME. **b.** Not in office 1605. **c.** No longer in the game, or *in* (IN *adv.* II. 2 c); in Cricket, dismissed from the wickets 1746. **d.** No longer in prison 1885. **6.** †**a.** At fault; nonplussed, puzzled –1681. **b.** Mistaken, in error 1641. **c.** Short for *out of practice, time, tune*, etc. 1588. **d.** At variance, no longer friendly 1565. **7.** Out of pocket; in default; minus (a sum) 1632. **8. a.** No longer burning or alight; extinguished ME. **b.** No longer in vogue; not in season, as game, etc. 1660. **9.** No longer current or lasting; at an end ME. **10.** Become visible; manifest, apparent; (of a plant) in leaf, in flower 1573. **11.** Made known, no longer a secret 1713. **12.** Made public; in circulation; published (as a book, etc.) 1625. **b.** Of a girl or young woman: **a.** Introduced into society; **b.** At work, in domestic service 1814. **c.** In existence 1857.

5. I feare (sir) my shoulder-blade is o. SHAKS. b. Court newes..who's in, who's o. SHAKS. d. He's o. now on ticket-of-leave 1885. 6. a. I haue forgot my part, And I am o. SHAKS. b. If the captain is not o. in his reckoning 1887. c. One string.., which was a little o. 1837. d. Launcelet and I are o. SHAKS. 8. When the Funeral Pyre was o. and the last Valediction over SIR T. BROWNE. b. Jewels are quite o. at present GOLDSM. 9. Before the week was o., he had been duly installed 1885. 10. The trees are all o. MACAULAY. 12. b. They are not o., you know, till after the Easter ball MRS. GASKELL. c. Fanny was the worst casuist o. 1859.

III. Besides the preceding senses, *out* is used idiomatically with many verbs; e.g. to BEAR *out*, CLEAN *out*, EKE *out*, FACE *out*, etc., which see under the vbs. themselves.

Phr. **Out and about.** Going out and going about, as after an illness, etc. **O. and away.** By far; beyond all others. **O. and home. a.** To a place at a distance, and home again. **b.** *attrib.* Played alternately on their own ground and that of their opponents. **O. and in. a.** Out of a place and in again; in and out. **b.** Outside and inside.

Out, *prep.* ME. [Prep. use of the adv. for the usual OUT OF.] **1.** = OUT OF 1. *Obs.* or *arch.* exc. in *from out*. **2.** Outside beyond the limits of, beyond (*lit.* and *fig.*). *Obs.* or *dial.* ME.

1. Whan that the sunne o. the south gan weste CHAUCER. 2. Both within and o. that Wall SHAKS.

Out, *int.* late ME. [f. OUT *adv.* (see sense I. 13).] **1.** As an imperative exclam., with ellipsis of the vb.; see OUT *adv.* I. 13. **2.** An exclam. of lamentation, abhorrence, or indignant reproach (*arch.* or *dial.*) late ME.

2. O., o., (Lucetta) that wilbe illfauord SHAKS. *O. upon (on)*, arch. or dial. phr. expressing abhorrence or reproach (cf. *fie upon*.); They crie, O upon him Heretike, to the fyre with hym 1560.

Out- in *comb.* is used with sbs., with vbs. and their derivatives, and with other adverbs.

A. Forming sbs. **I.** In comb. with ordinary sbs. (Stress on *out*. The separation or hyphening of the two elements is in many cases optional.) **1.** In the sense 'Outlying, situated outside the bounds, or remote from the centre'; also, 'outside the house, out of doors'; as *out-district*, OUTFIELD, OUTHOUSE, OUTLAND, OUTPORT, *-village, -yard*, etc. **2.** In the sense 'Living, residing, or engaged outside (a house, hospital, borough, city, country, etc.)'; as *out-dweller*, OUT-PATIENT, -PENSIONER, *-pupil, -student*, etc.; also in sense 'external, foreign', as †*out-folk, -merchant, -people*. **3.** In the sense 'Exterior, external, outward' (one or other of which words would now in most cases be substituted); as in OUTLINE, OUTSIDE; also *out-bough, -branch, -edge, -end, -layer, -limit, -list, -porch*, etc. **4.** In the sense 'Out of office', as *out-party* 1817. **5.** In the sense 'Leading out', as *out-path, -trail, -way*.

II. In comb. with nouns of action, agent-nouns, and verbal sbs., cogn. w. or derived from the simple vb. followed by *out*. **1.** With nouns of action; as OUTBREAK [cf. *break out*], OUTBURST, OUTCOME, *outgush, outjet*, etc.; also *outvoyage*, etc. **2.** With agent-nouns; as OUTFITTER, OUTPUTTER, etc. **3.** With vbl. sbs. in *-ing*; as OUTGOING, etc.

B. Forming *adjs.* (Stress on *out*.) **1.** With ppl. adjs. in *-ing* (OE. *-ende*), from pres. pples.; as *outbreaking* [cf. *break out*], *outlying, outstanding*, etc. **2.** With ppl. adjs. in *-ed, -en*, etc. (from pa. pples.); as OUTBOUND, OUTCAST; also *out-flung, -pointed, -pushed*, etc. **3.** With a sb. (as obj. of *out* prep.), forming adjs., meaning 'Out of or outside the thing named'; as OUT-COLLEGE, OUTDOOR, etc. **4.** Parasynthetic derivatives from phrases in which *out* mostly means 'projecting, protruding', forming adjs.; as *out-kneed, -lipped, -shouldered*, etc.

C. *Out-* in comb. forming verbs. (Stress on the second element.) **I.** Separable or syntactic combinations. (In ME. prop. two words; in mod. use, more or less, *habitual nonce-wds.*, made up each time.) **1.** With intrans. vbs., in the same sense as the simple vb. followed by *out*; as OUTBREAK, *outflash, outflow, outgive*, etc. late ME. **2.** With trans. vbs., in the same sense as the simple vb. followed by *out*. **a.** With the force of: Out, away; out of existence; out of a socket or place, loose; outward, so as to project; forth; into the open, into manifestation; as OUTBEAR, *out-cast*, OUTPOUR, etc. **b.** With the force of 'completely, thoroughly', 'to a finish'; as OUTPLAY; also *out-tire*, etc. late ME. **3.** Forming trans. vbs. with the sense 'to put or drive out by means of' the action expressed in the simple vb. (cf. *bow out, crowd out*, etc.); as *outhiss, outjeer, outjest*.

II. Compound vbs. in *out-*, with the trans. force of exceeding or going beyond some thing or person in some action. **Formed on verbs*. **1.** To pass beyond, exceed (a defined point, a limit in time, space, degree, etc.), by or in the action expressed by the simple vb.; as OUTGROW (2), OUTLAST, OUTPASS, *out-reign*, OUTRUN, etc. 1603. **2.** To surpass, excel or outdo (a person, etc.) in the action of the simple vb. The number of these compounds is unlimited, Examples are: *out-bellow*, OUTBID, *out-bloom, outclimb, outdance*, OUTDO, *outflash, outgive, outglare, outjuggle, outlabour, outlie*, OUTLIVE, *outlove, outpace, outplan, outplay, outpray, outpreach, outreign, outroar*, OUTRUN, *outsoar, outsparkle, outspeed, outstrike, outswear, outsweeten, out-trot*, etc. **b.** To get the better of, defeat, beat, in some reciprocal action or contest; as OUTBALANCE, OUTBRAVE, *outmate, outpeer, outpoise*, OUTRIVAL, *outscold*, 1600. **c.** To overcome or defeat by the action expressed by the simple verb; as *out-baffle, outfrown, outhector, outreason, outroar*, etc. **3.** To exceed or do more than is expressed by the simple vb.; as *out-Atlas* to load more than Atlas, *outbeggar* to more than beggar, etc. late ME.

***Formed on adjectives*. **4.** To exceed or surpass in the quality expressed by the adj.; as *out-active, -black, -swift*, etc. 1605.

****Formed on sbs*. **5.** On names of qualities, actions, or objects: To exceed in the quality or action, or in ref. to the thing, expressed by the sb.; as *outlove, outlustre, outmeasure*, OUTNUMBER, OUTRANGE, *out-value, outvoice*, etc. **6.** On names of persons, actors, agents: To excel, surpass, or outdo in executing the office, or acting the part characteristic of the person or agent in question; as OUTFOOL, OUTGENERAL, etc. **7.** Hence (cf. prec. senses 2–6), esp. with proper names of persons, nations, sects, etc., in the sense of 'to outdo the person, etc., in question in his special attribute'. The classical example is Shakspere's OUT-HEROD *Herod*. Other examples are *out-Darwin, -Quixote, -Zola*, etc. See also Main words.

Out-a·ct, *v.* 1644. [OUT- C. II. 2.] *trans.* To surpass in acting or performing; to excel, outdo.

Garrick says 'She so much outacted him it is time for him to leave the stage' 1776.

Out and out, ou·t-and-ou·t. *adv. phr.* (*a.*) ME. [Cf. OUT *adv.* I. 7.] Thoroughly, completely, entirely; downright. **b.** *adj.* Complete, unqualified 1813.

She was wyckyd oute and oute. late ME. b. They're the out-and-outest young scamps 1868. Hence **Ou·t-and-ou·ter**, a thorough or perfect type of his or its kind (*colloq.* or *slang*) 1812.

Out-a·rgue, *v.* 1748. [OUT- C. II. 2.] *trans.* To get the better of in argument.

†**Outas, outes.** *Obs.* exc. *dial.* [Early ME. *uthēs*, app. repr. an OE. **ūthǣs*, f. *ūt* out + *hǣs* command; see HEST *sb.*] = OUTCRY *sb.* 1.

Out-a·sk, *v. dial.* 1642. [OUT- C. I. 2 b.] *trans.* To 'ask' the banns of marriage of (a couple) in church for the last time 1719.

Out-ba·bble, *v.* 1649. [OUT- C. I. 2, II. 2.] *trans.* **a.** To babble out. **b.** To exceed in babble or noisy talk.

Ou·tback, *adv. Austral.* 1890. Out in or to the back settlements or back-country. Also as *adj.* (1900) and *sb.* (1907).

Outbalance (autbæ·lăns), *v.* 1644. [OUT- C. II. 2 b.] = OUTWEIGH *v.*

Outbear (autbē·ɹ), *v.* ME. [OUT- C. I. 2, II. 2.] **1.** *trans.* To carry forth. **2.** *Naut.* To carry more sail than; hence, to outsail 1691.

Outbi·d, *v.* 1587. [OUT- C. II. 2, 1.] **1.** *trans.* To outdo in bidding; to offer a higher price than. **2.** *fig.* To outdo in any quality, statement, etc. 1597.

Outblaze (autblē·z), *v.* 1711. [OUT- C. I. 1, II. 2.] **1.** *intr.* To blaze forth, burst out with ardour. **2.** *trans.* To surpass in blazing; *fig.* to outshine in brilliancy 1742.

Outblu·sh, *v.* 1634. [OUT- C. II. 2.] *trans.* To outdo in blushing, to surpass in rosy colour.

Outblu·ster, *v.* 1748. [OUT- C. I. 3, II. 2 b, c.] **1.** *trans.* To drive or do out of by blustering. **2.** To outdo in blustering, to get the better of by bluster 1863.

Outboard (au·tbōᵊɹd), *a.*, *adv.* 1823. [f. OUT- B. 3 + BOARD *sb.* Cf. INBOARD.] **A.** *adj.* **a.** Situated on the outside of a ship. **b.** Outward from the median line of a ship 1893. **B.** *adv.* **a.** In a direction outward from a ship's side, or laterally away from the centre of a ship 1836. **b.** Of position: Outside a ship or boat; nearer to the outside than something else 1869.

†Ou·tborn, *a.* (*sb.*) 1450. [OUT- B. 2.] Born out of the country; of foreign birth. **B.** *sb.* A foreigner. –1550.

Ou·t-bound, *a.* 1598. [OUT- B. 2.] Outward bound.

Out-bra·g, *v.* 1565. [OUT- C. II. 2.] *trans.* To outdo in bragging; to go beyond in boastful talk.

Outbrave (autbrē·v), *v.* 1589. [OUT- C. II. 2 b.] **1.** *trans.* To face defiantly. **2.** To surpass in daring 1596. **b.** To outdo in beauty, finery or splendour of array; cf. BRAVERY 3. 1589. **c.** To outrival (in any quality) 1589.

2. b. The Lillies of the field outbraued him 1597.

Outbra·zen, *v.* 1681. [OUT- C. I. 2 b, II. 2 + BRAZEN *v.*] **1.** *trans.* To face out defiantly or impudently. **2.** To outdo in unabashedness 1702.

Outbreak (au·tbrēk), *sb.* 1602. [OUT- A. II. 1.] **1.** A breaking out; an eruption; an outburst of hostilities, of disease, etc. **2.** *Geol.* An outcrop; the emergence of a rock or stratum 1797. **3.** An insurrection 1849.

1. The flash and out-breake of a fiery minde SHAKS.

Outbreak (autbrē·k), *v.* OE. [OUT- C. I. 1.] *intr.* To break out. Now only *poet.*

Outbreathe (autbrī·ð). *v.* 1559. [OUT- C. I. 1, 2.] *trans.* To breathe out; to emit as breath. Now *poet.* Also *intr.* or *absol.*

Outbreathed (autbre·þt), *ppl. a.* 1597. [f. OUT- + BREATH + -ED.] Put out of breath. Now *poet.*

Outbuild (-bi·ld), *v.* 1742. [OUT- C. II. 2, 1, I. 2.] **1.** *trans.* To surpass in building or durability of building; also, *catachr.* to overbuild. **2.** To build out (*poet.* and *rhet.*) 1847.

Ou·t-bui:lding. 1626. [OUT- A. I. 1.] A detached building, subordinate and accessory to a main building; an out-house.

Out-bu·rn, *v.* late ME. [OUT- C. I. 2, II. 2, 1.] **1.** *intr.* To burn out or away. **2.** *trans.* To burn longer than 1742.

2. Lamps which outburn'd Canopus TENNYSON.

Outburst (au·tbɔ̄ɹst), *sb.* 1657. [OUT- A. II. 1.] **1.** An act of bursting out; an outbreak, explosion (of feeling, indignation, etc.). **2.** = OUTBREAK *sb.* 2. 1708.

1. Tom was a little shocked at Maggie's o. GEO. ELIOT.

Ou·t-by, -bye, *adv.* (*adj.*) *Sc.* and *north.* late ME. [f. OUT *adv.* + BY *adv.*] Out a little way; outside the house, abroad, in the open air; to the outside (of a house, farm, etc.).

Outcast (au·tkast), *sb.* ME. [sb. use of next.] **1.** A person 'cast out' or rejected; a pariah; an exile; a homeless vagabond. **2.** Refuse, offal; a plant thrown out from a garden. late ME.

1. I am a worme and no man: a very scorne of men and the o. of the people COVERDALE *Ps.* xxi[i]. 6.

Outcast (au·tkast), *ppl. a.* late ME. [OUT- B. 2.] **1.** Of persons: Abject, socially despised; later, Cast out from home and friends; hence, forsaken, homeless, and neglected. **2.** Of things: Rejected, discarded 1560.

1. I all alone beweep my o. state SHAKS.

Ou·tca·ste, *v.* 1867. [f. OUT- + CASTE *sb.* 2, 4, after prec.] *trans.* To put (a person) out of his caste; to cause to lose caste. So **Ou·tcaste** *sb.* one who has lost his caste; one of no caste; *adj.* of no caste.

Outcasting (au·tkastiŋ), *vbl. sb.* late ME. [OUT- A. II. 3.] The action of casting out; ejection; rendering outcast.

Outclass (autklā·s), *v.* 1870. [OUT- C.] *Sporting.* To beat (a rival) so completely as to put him virtually out of the same class; to leave 'nowhere' in a race or contest.

transf. As a liar, I out-classed every man on board 1893.

Ou·t-clea:ring, *vbl. sb.* 1875. [OUT- A. II. 1.] *Banking.* The sending out of bills of exchange and cheques to the clearing-house for settlement; hence, the bills and cheques collectively thus sent out to be cleared; the converse of IN-CLEARING.

Ou·t-co·llege, *a.* 1861. [OUT- B. 2.] Not residing within the walls of a college; applied chiefly to members of a college who reside or lodge outside.

Outcome (au·tkɒm), *sb.* ME. [OUT- A. II. 1.] **†1.** The act or fact of coming out; *Sc.* the time of year when days begin to lengthen –1715. **2.** That which comes out of something; visible or practical result, effect, or product. (orig. *Sc.* app. made Eng. by Carlyle.) 1788. **3.** An outlet 1885.

2. We do the man's intellectual endowment great wrong, if we measure it by its mere intellectual o. CARLYLE.

Outcrop (au·tkrɒp), *sb.* 1805. [OUT- A. II. 1.] *Mining* and *Geol.* The cropping out of a stratum or vein at the surface; the edge of the stratum or vein thus cropping out. **b.** *fig.* A coming into outward manifestation 1864.

Ou·tcrop, *v.* 1845. [f. prec. sb.] *intr.* **a.** *Mining* and *Geol.* To crop out (see CROP *v.*), as a stratum or vein. **b.** *fig.* To come out casually 1856. Hence **Ou·tcropper,** a miner who works an outcrop.

Outcry (au·tkrəi), *sb.* late ME. [OUT- A. II. 1.] **1.** The act of crying out; loud clamour; noise, uproar; hence, an emphatic protest. **2.** A public sale to the highest bidder; an auction. *Obs.* or *local.* 1600.

Outcry·, *v.* late ME. [OUT- C. I. 1, 2, II. 2.] **†1. a.** *intr.* To cry out. **b.** *trans.* To cry aloud, make an outcry; to proclaim. –1654. **2.** To cry louder than; to shout down 1530.

Outda·re, *v.* 1593. [OUT- C. II, 2, 2 c.] **1.** *trans.* To overcome by daring; to outbrave, defy. **2.** To dare more than 1607.

Outda·zzle, *v.* 1705. [OUT- C. II. 2.] *trans.* To outdo in brilliancy; to outshine.

Outdi·stance, *v.* 1857. [OUT- C. II. 2 b.] *trans.* To outstrip (in a race; hence, in any competition or career.)

Outdo (autdū·), *v.* ME. [OUT- C. I. 2, II. 2, 2 c.] **†1.** *trans.* To put out. (In ME. two wds.) –1603. **2.** To exceed in doing; to excel, surpass, beat; to be superior to 1607. **b.** To defeat, overcome; to exhaust 1677.

2. Wherein the Grauer had a strife With Nature, to out-doo the life B. JONS.

Ou·t-door, ou·tdoor, *a.* 1765. [OUT- B. 3.] **1.** That is done, exists, lives, or is used, out of doors, or in the open air. **2.** Relieved or administered outside or apart from residence in a workhouse, etc.; as *o. pension, relief* 1833. **3.** Applied to the outward or down stroke of a Cornish pumping engine 1875.

Ou·tdoo·rs, *adv.* 1844. [OUT *prep.*] Out of doors; in the open air; also as *sb.* = OUT-OF-DOOR B.

Ou·tdraught. 1857. [OUT- A. II. 1.] An outward draught of air; the 'back-wash' of a wave.

Outdri·nk, *v.* 1593. [OUT- C. I. 2 b, II. 2.] *trans.* **a.** To drink (anything) out or up, drink dry. **b.** To drink more than.

Outdri·ve, *v.* ME. [OUT- C. I. 2, II. 2.] **†1.** *trans.* To drive out, expel. (Prop. two wds.) ME. only. **2.** To drive faster than 1611. **3.** *Golf.* To drive farther than (*mod.*).

Outer (au·təɹ), *a.* (*sb.*[1]) late ME. [A new comparative formed on OUT, instead of UTTER from OE. *ūterra, uttra.* *Outer* is not followed by *than.*] **1.** That is farther out than another (distinguished as *inner*), exterior; farther from the centre or inside; hence, relatively far out; external; of or pertaining to the outside. **2.** Said of the objective or physical as opp. to the subjective or psychical world. late ME.

1. But the children of the kingdom shall be cast out into o. darkness *Matt.* viii. 12. **2.** Phr. *O. man,* the body (after *inner man*); hence joc., personal appearance, dress (so *o. woman*). *O. world,* the material world outside that familiar or known; also, people generally, outside one's immediate circle.

B. *ellipt.* as *sb.* In rifle-shooting, that part of the target outside the circles surrounding the bull's eye; hence, a shot that hits this part 1862.

Outer (au·təɹ), *sb.*[2] 1898. [f. OUT *v.* + -ER [1].] *Pugilism.* A knock-out blow.

Outermost (au·təɹmōst), *a.* (*adv.*) 1857. [f. OUTER *a.* + -MOST, after *out, outer.*] Farthest out from the inside or centre; most outward; most external; extremest. **b.** as *adv.* In the most outward position 1858.

Beyond the o. part of the o. Heaven 1665.

Outfa·ce, *v.* 1529. [OUT- C. II. 2 b, c.] **1.** *trans.* To outdo in facing or confronting; to look (a person) out of countenance; to stare down; hence, to put out of countenance generally. **2.** To brave, defy 1574. **†3.** To give the lie to boldly or defiantly –1686. **†b.** To maintain boldly or impudently to the face of (a person), *that,* etc. –1678. **†4.** To brazen out –1692.

1. See if thou canst out-face me with thy lookes SHAKS. **2.** They..o. you with an eye that challenges inquiry 1870.

Ou·tfall. 1629. [OUT- A. II. 1.] The outlet or mouth of a river, drain, sewer, etc., where it falls into the sea, lake, etc.

†Ou·tfangthie:f. [repr. **ūtfangenne þēof* 'out-caught thief', corresp. to *infangenne þēof* INFANGTHIEF, q. v.] *OE. Law.* Orig., the lord's right to pursue a thief (at least when the latter was 'his own man') outside his own jurisdiction, bring him back to his own court for trial, and keep his forfeited chattels on conviction. By the 13th c. its meaning had become conjectural.

Out-field, outfield (au·tfīld). 1637. [OUT- A. I. 1.] **1.** The outlying land of a farm; esp. in Scotland, the outlying land which is either unenclosed and untilled moorland or pasture, or was formerly cropped from time to time without being manured. **b.** An outlying field 1676. **2.** In *Cricket* and *Baseball*: The part of the field most remote from the batsman 1895. **b.** = OUT-FIELDER 1884.

1. *fig.* Words are enclosures from the great o. of meaning TRENCH. *O. and infield system*: see INFIELD.

Ou·t-fie:lder. 1893. [OUT- A. I. 1.] The player or fielder who stands in the out-field; see prec. 2. So **Ou·t-fie:lding** *vbl. sb.*

Outfi·ght, *v.* 1643. [OUT- C. II. 2 b.] To fight better than.

Outfit (au·tfit), *sb.* 1769. [OUT- A. II. 1.] **1.** The act of fitting out or furnishing with requisites; *ellipt.* = expenses of fitting out. **2.** The articles and equipment required for an expedition, journey, etc.; a set of things for any purpose. orig. *U.S.* 1787. **3.** A travelling party or a party in charge of cattle, etc.; a person along with his conveyance, his tools, or the like *U.S.* 1872.

2. *fig.* Man's mental and moral o. 1872.

Ou·tfit, *v.* 1840. [f. prec. sb.] *trans.* To provide with an outfit, to fit out. Also *intr.* for *refl.* or *pass.* So **Ou·tfitter,** *spec.* a dealer in outfits for travelling, athletic sports, etc.

Outfla·me, *v.* 1839. [OUT- C. II. 2, I. 1.] **a.** *trans.* To surpass in blaze or brilliancy. **b.** *intr.* To flame out, burst into blaze. *poet.*

Outflank (autflæ·ŋk), *v.* 1765. [OUT- C. II. 2 c, 1.] **1.** *trans.* To extend or get beyond the flank of the opposing army. **b.** *fig.* To 'get round', get the better of 1773. **2.** To lie or extend beyond (the flank). Also *intr.* 1796.

1. b. We were outflanked by the law 1773.

Ou·tflow, *sb.* 1800. [OUT- A. II. 1.] **1.** The act or fact of flowing out, efflux 1839. **b.** The amount that flows out 1875. **2.** *fig.* Any outward movement analogous to the outflowing of water 1800.

Outfly·, *v.* 1591. [OUT- C. I. 1, II. 1, 2.] **1.** *intr.* To fly out (*poet.*) 1599. **2.** *trans.* To outstrip or surpass in flight; to fly beyond or past 1591.

1. Out-flew Millions of flaming swords MILT.

Outfoo·l, *v.* 1638. [OUT- C. II. 2, 2 c.] *trans.* To outdo in folly or fooling; to overcome by fooling.

Outfoo·t, *v.* 1737. [OUT- C. II. 2, 5.] *trans.* To surpass in footing it; to outpace; to outstrip in dancing, running, or sailing; to outrun.

Ou·tgate, *sb.* (*adv.*) Now *Sc.* and *n. dial.* ME. [OUT- A. II. 1.] **1.** The action of going out; exit, egress; debouching. **2.** An outlet; *fig.* a way of escape or deliverance 1456.

Outge·neral, *v.* 1767. [OUT- C. II. 6.] *trans.* To outdo or defeat in generalship; to get the better of as by superior military skill.

Ou·tgo, *sb.* 1640. [OUT- A. II. 1.] **1.** The fact of going out, or that which goes out; *spec.* outlay; opp. to *income.* **2.** The action of going out; outflow 1858.

Outgo (autgōᵘ·), *v.* OE. [OUT- C. II. 1, II. 2, 1.] **1.** *intr.* To go out, go forth. (In OE. and ME. usu. two wds.) *Obs.* or *rare.* **2.** *trans.* To go faster than; to outdistance (*arch.*) 1530. **3.** To go beyond (a point, bounds, etc.); to exceed, surpass; to outdo 1553.

Ou·tgo:er. late ME. [OUT- A. II. 2.] One who goes out (see GO *v.*); esp. one who goes out of a place, office, or tenancy.

Ou·tgo:ing, *vbl. sb.* ME. [OUT- A. II. 3.] **1.** The action or fact of going out or forth. †**2.** A passage or way of exit or egress –1609. **b.** †The outer limit; the upper termination of an inclined stratum. late ME. **3.** (Usu. *pl.*) Outlay, expenses, charges 1622.

1. Men that go out of the bath and drynke muche wyne after theyr outgoyng 1562. 2. b. The coast of Manasseh also was on the north side of the river, and the outgoings of it were at the sea *Josh.* xxii. 9.

Ou·tgo:ing, *ppl. a.* 1633. [OUT- B. 1.] That goes out; issuing, outflowing. **b.** Going out from office, position, or possession.

Outgrow (autgrōᵘ·), *v.* 1594. [OUT- C. II. 2, 1, I. 1.] **1.** *trans.* To grow faster than; to grow taller or bigger than. **2.** To grow out of, to become too large for (clothes, etc.) 1691. **3.** *fig.* To leave behind in the process of growth or development 1665.

2. 'I doubt they'll o. their strength', she added GEO. ELIOT. 3. Even our gray heads o. not those errors which we have learn't before the Alphabet 1665.

Outgrowth (au·tgrōᵘþ). 1837. [OUT- A. II. 1.] The process of growing out; that which grows out of or from anything; an offshoot; an excrescence. **b.** *fig.* Of things immaterial: A natural product 1850.

b. Primogeniture is not a natural o. of the family 185.

Ou·t-guard. 1623. [OUT- A. I. 1, 3.] A guard placed at a distance outside the main body of an army, an advanced guard, an outpost.

Outhaul (au·tˌhǭl). 1840. [OUT- A. II. 1.] *Naut.* A rope used for hauling out a sail upon a spar; opp. to *inhaul.* So **Ou·thau:ler** 1793.

Outher (au·ðəɹ, ǭ·ðəɹ), *adv.* (*conj.*) Now *dial.* ME. [The neuter or uninflected form of *outher* pron. = EITHER.] An early equivalent of EITHER B. 2.

Out-Herod (autˌhe·rǫd). *v.* 1602. [OUT- C. II. 7.] *To out-Herod Herod*: to outdo Herod in violence; hence, to outdo in any excess of evil or extravagance.

Haml. III. ii. 16.

Outhouse (au·tˌhaus). ME. [OUT- A. I. 1.] A house or building, belonging to and adjoining, and subsidiary to, a dwelling-house; e.g. a stable, barn, wash-house, etc.

Outing (au·tiŋ), *vbl. sb.* 1440. [f. OUT *v.* + -ING[1].] **1.** The acting of putting or driving out. Now *rare* or *Obs.* **2.** An airing, excursion, pleasure-trip. Orig. *dial.* 1786.

Outjo·ckey, *v.* 1714. [OUT- C. II. 2 b, c.] *trans.* To get the better of by adroitness or trickery.

Ou·tkeeper. 1875. [OUT- A. II. 2.] An instrument used with the surveyor's compass, to keep tally in chaining.

Outland (au·tlǣnd), *sb.* and *a.* OE. [OUT- A. I. 1.] **A.** *sb.* **1.** A land that is outside, a foreign land. (Now only a poetic archaism.) †**2.** The outlying land of an estate or manor. In OE. and feudal tenure, that part which the lord granted to tenants. (Opp. to INLAND 1.) –1848. †**3.** *Out-lands*: the outlying lands of a province, district, or town. *Amer. Colonies.* –1731. **B.** *adj.* [In origin an attrib. use of the sb.] **1.** Of or belonging to another country; foreign, alien. Now *poet.* or *arch.* late ME. **2.** *Sc.* Outlying 1791.

Outlander (au·tlǣndəɹ). 1605. [f. prec. + -ER[1], after Du. *uitlander*, G. *ausländer.*] A man of foreign nationality; a foreigner, alien, stranger. (Now *poet.*, or a literary revival.) **b.** In ref. to S. African politics, a rendering of Du. *uitlander*, as applied, before the war of 1899–1902, to aliens settled or sojourning in the South African Republic 1892.

Outlandish (autlæ·ndiʃ), *a.* [In OE. *útlendisc*, f. *útland* OUTLAND A. 1; see -ISH.] **1.** Foreign, alien; not native or indigenous. *arch.* **2.** Foreign-looking, of foreign fashion; unfamiliar, strange; odd, bizarre, uncouth 1596. **3.** Out-of-the way, remote; far removed from civilization (now usu. derogatory) 1869.

1. But kynge Salomon loued many o. women COVERDALE 1 *Kings* xi. 1. 2. They were dressed in a quaint o. fashion W. IRVING. 3. Living in such an o. place T. HARDY. Hence **Outla·ndish-ly** *adv.*, **-ness.**

Outlast (autlɑ·st), *v.* 1573. [OUT- C. II. 1, 2.] *trans.* To last longer than or beyond; to exceed in duration; to survive.

Outlaugh (autlɑ·f), *v.* 1477. [OUT- C. II. 2, 2 c.] †**1.** *trans.* To laugh down, deride –1790. **2.** To outdo in laughing 1672.

Outlaw (au·tlǭ), *sb.* [Late OE. *útlaga*, definite form of *útlag*, *útlah* adj. 'outlawed', used absol. as sb.; a. ON. *útlagi* sb. from *útlagr* outlawed; f. *út* out, out of + OE *lagu*, LAW.] One put outside the law and deprived of its benefits and protection; one under sentence of OUTLAWRY. **b.** More vaguely: An exile, a fugitive ME.

Outlaw (au·tlǭ:), *v.* [Late OE. (*ge*)*útlagian*, f. *útlag*, *útlaga*, OUTLAW *sb.*] **1.** *trans.* To put outside the law; to proscribe; †to exile, banish; to declare an outlaw. **2.** To deprive of legal force. Now only in U.S. 1647.

1. *fig.* Charite is outelawed amonge hom WYCLIF.

Outlawry (au·tlǭri). late ME. [Anglicized repr. of AFr. *utlagerie, utlarie*, f. OE. *útlaga*, *útlah* + Rom. suffix *-aria*, F. -erie.] **1.** The action of putting a person out of the protection of the law, or the legal process by which a person is or was proclaimed or made an outlaw; the condition of one so outlawed. †In early use, often = exile, banishment. **2.** Disregard or defiance of the law 1869.

Outlay (au·tlēⁱ), *sb.* 1798. [OUT- A. II. 1.] The act or fact of laying out or expending; expenditure (of money upon something). Orig. *Sc.* and *dial.*

Outlay (autlēⁱ·), *v.* 1555. [OUT- C. I. 2.] **1.** *trans.* To lay out; to spread out, display. Now *rare* or *poet.* **2.** To lay out (money), expend 1802.

Ou·tleap, *sb.* ME. [OUT- A. II. 1.] An act of leaping out; an escape, sally, or excursion; an outburst (*lit.* and *fig.*).

Outlea·p, *v.* 1600. [OUT- C. II. 1, 2, I. 1.] **1.** *trans.* To leap over or beyond. **2.** To surpass in leaping 1629. **3.** *intr.* To leap out or forth (*poet.*) 1850.

Outlet (au·tlėt). ME. [OUT- A. II. 1.] **1.** A place or means of issue; a vent; a passage out, an exit. Also *transf.* and *fig.* **2. a.** A place into which anything is let out; *spec.* a pasture into which cattle are let out. **b.** A field, yard, or other enclosure attached to a house. 1752. †**3. a.** The outlying parts; the environs of a town. **b.** The suburban streets or roads passing into the country.–1771. **4.** Discharge, escape by outflow (*lit.* and *fig.*) 1640. **5.** *attrib.* as *o.-pipe*, etc. 1762.

1. Like the Caspian Sea, receiving all, and having no Out-let FULLER.

Outle·t, *v.* *Obs.* or *rare.* 1592. [OUT- C. I. 2.] *trans.* To let out, give egress to, pass forth.

Outlie·, *v.* 1873. [f. OUT- C. II. 1 + LIE *v.*[1]] *trans.* To lie beyond or on the outside of.

Ou·tli:er. 1610. [OUT- A. II. 2.] **1.** One who lies (i.e. sleeps or lodges) out, i.e. in the open air, or away from his place of business, etc. 1676. **b.** An outsider 1690. **c.** An outlying deer, etc. 1658. **2. a.** A boulder 1610. **b.** *Geol.* A portion of a geological formation lying *in situ* at a distance from the main body, the intervening part having been removed by denudation 1833. **c.** *gen.* An outlying portion or member of anything 1849.

2. c. Great mountain chain outliers, isolated or branching from the central chain RUSKIN.

†**Outligger, outlicker.** 1481. [prob. a dial. form of *outlier*, subseq. corrupted.] *Naut.* **1.** A spar projecting from a vessel to extend some sail, or to make a greater angle for some rope, etc. 1626. **2.** = OUTRIGGER 2. –1755.

Outline (au·tləin), *sb.* 1662. [f. OUT- A. I. 3.] **1.** *pl.* The lines, real or apparent, by which a figure is defined or bounded in the plane of vision; the sum of these lines forming the contour of a figure. **b.** *sing.* The contour thus defined 1828. **2.** A sketch or drawing in which an object is represented by lines of contour without shading 1735. **3.** A rough draught or sketch in words; a description omitting details 1759. **b.** in *pl.* The main features of any subject; the general principles 1710. **4.** *attrib.*, as *o.-map*, *-stitch*, etc. 1859.

1. b. He..beheld in the distance the black o. of a gallows SCOTT. 2. *In o.*, with only the o. drawn, represented, or visible. 3. b. His Drama at present has only the Out-lines drawn STEELE. Hence **Outli·near** *a.* of the nature of an o.

Outline (au·tləin), *v.* 1790. [f. prec. sb.] **1.** *trans.* To draw or trace the exterior line of; to draw in outline. **b.** To indicate or define the outline of 1817. **2.** To sketch in general terms 1855.

2. The scheme outlined in Mr. Bright's speech 1880.

Outlive (autli·v), *v.* 1472. [OUT- C. II. 2, 1.] **1.** *trans.* To live longer than; to survive; also, to live longer than (a thing) lasts. **b.** To outlast 1597. **2.** To live through or beyond (a specified time) 1657. **b.** To pass through (a certain state or experience); to outgrow 1641. †**3.** *intr.* To survive SHAKS. **4.** *trans.* To excel in (virtuous) living 1883.

1. Asham'd his Country's freedom to out-live 1695. 2. b. They have outlived the age of weakness JOHNSON.

Outlook (au·tluk). *sb.* 1667. [OUT- A. II. 1.] **1.** The act or practice of looking out; vigilant watch (*lit.* and *fig.*) 1815. **2.** A place from or by which a view is obtained; a look-out 1667. **3.** The view or prospect from a place or point 1828. **b.** A mental view or survey 1742. **c.** The prospect for the future 1832. **4.** *attrib.*, as *o. post*, etc. 1851.

1. Jackdaws..on the out-look for plunder 1862. 3. c. My political o. is very gloomy MACAULAY.

Outloo·k, *v.* 1595. [OUT- C. II. 2 c.] *trans.* To look or stare down; to outstare. *John* v. ii. 115.

Outlying (au·tləi:iŋ), *ppl. a.* 1663. [OUT- B. 1.] **1.** Lying or situated outside certain limits; hence *fig.* extrinsic, extraneous. Of a beast: That makes its lair outside a park or enclosure. **2.** Lying at a distance from the centre of an area; remote, out-of-the-way; living at a distance from centres of population 1689.

2. Some of these out-lying Parts of the World 1689.

Outmanœu·vre, -ver, *v.* 1799. [OUT- C. II. 2.] *trans.* To outdo in manœuvring; to get the better of by superior strategy.

Outma·rch, *v.* 1647. [OUT- C. II. 2.] *trans.* To outdo in marching, to march faster or farther than; to march so as to leave behind.

Outma·tch, *v.* 1603. [OUT- C. II. 2 b.] *trans.* To be more than a match for; to outdo.

Outmoded (autmōᵘ·dėd), *ppl. a.* 1903. [transl. F. *démodé*, f. *dé-* = OUT- B. 2 + *mode* MODE *sb.*] Out of fashion, obsolete.

Outmost (au·tmōᵘst, -məst), *a.* ME. [var. of *utmest*, UTMOST, which it gradually supplanted as superlative of *out.*] **1.** Most outward, farthest out; outermost. **b.** Hence, Most remote, farthest off, utmost 1561. †**2.** *ellipt.* The utmost point, degree, or limit; esp. in phr. *to the outmost* –1692.

Outmo·ve, *v.* 1635. [OUT- C. II. 2, 2 b.] †**1.** *trans.* To surpass or exceed in moving –1761. **2.** To defeat by a move, as in chess 1860.

Outness (au·tnės). 1709. [f. OUT *adv.* or *adj.* + -NESS.] The quality, fact, or condition of being external, esp. to the percipient or to the mind; externality.

Outnu·mber, *v.* 1670. [OUT- C. II. 5.] *trans.* To number more than.

Out of (au·tǫv, -əv), *prep. phr.* OE. [orig., and still in writing, two words, viz. OUT *adv.* followed by OF *prep.* (in its primary sense = from).] **1.** Of motion or direction: From within, from. **2.** Of position: Not in or within, outside ME. **b.** Deprived or destitute of, without 1599. **c.** Taken or derived from (*spec.* of a foal in ref. to its dam). late ME. **3.** With *sb.*, used attrib. as adj. phr., as *out-of-bounds*, *out-of-joint*, *out-of-pocket*, *out-of-the-world*, *out-*

of-work (also *sb.*); also derivatives of these, as *out-of-jointness, out-of-the-worldish.*

1. This house..wil I cast awaye out of my presence COVERDALE 2 *Chron.* vii. 20. Nothing can be made out of nothing SHAKS. Out of my doore, you Witch, you Ragge..out, out SHAKS. He quotes it out of Pliny 1662. Every body is going out of town H. WALPOLE. As you come only out of compliment to me WELLINGTON. His majesty..was thought by the physicians to be out of danger MACAULAY. He fairly laughed the Bill out of the House 1872. 2. So I were out of prison, and kept Sheepe I should be merry as the day is long SHAKS. He is but Four Miles dwelling out of Cambridg 1625. He is placed quite out of their hearing ADDISON. The Church of England is intirely out of the Dispute STEELE. To shut up the shops one day out of the seven 1866. It was expected that the meeting..would be a little out of the ordinary 1893. Our horses being out of condition 1893. b. These English are shrowdly out of Beefe SHAKS. c. Both grandsons of Eclipse and both out of Herod mares 1881. 3. Every raw, peevish, out-of-humoured, affected fop 1675. Out-of-work and sick allowances 1887.

Ou·t-of-da·te, *adj. phr.* 1628. [f. prec. 3 + DATE *sb.*] That continues to exist beyond its proper date or time; obsolete.

Ou·t-of-doo·r, -doo·rs, *adj.* and *sb. phr.* 1800. [The advb. phr. *out-of-door(s* (see DOOR) used attrib. or subst.; in the attrib. use *out-of-door* is usual.] **A.** *adj.* 1. That is outside the house, in the open air; done or grown in the open air; for use outside the house. 2. *spec.* a. Outside the Houses of Parliament; b. Carried on or given outside a workhouse, as *out-of-door relief* 1802. **B.** *sb.* (the adj. used ellipt.) The world outside the house; the open air 1856.

Ou·t-of-fa·shion, *adj. phr.* 1623. That is no longer in fashion or fashionable.

Out-office (au·t,ǫ:fis). 1624. [f. OUT- A. I. 1. + OFFICE *sb.* 9.] An outside building forming one of the offices of a mansion, farm-house, etc.; an outhouse.

Ou·t-of-the-way·, *adj. phr.* 1704. [The advb. phr. *out of the way* (see WAY *sb.*), used attrib.] 1. Remote from any frequented route; remote from any centre of population, secluded 1797. 2. Seldom met with, far-fetched; hence, extraordinary, odd 1704.

2. Out-of-the-way humours and opinions—heads with some diverting twist in them—please me most LAMB.

Ou·t-pa:rish. 1577. [OUT- A. I. 1.] **a.** A parish lying outside the walls of a city or town, though belonging to it. **b.** An outlying parish.

Outpass (autpa·s). *v.* late ME. [OUT- C. II. 1, 2.] 1. *trans.* To pass out of (bounds), beyond (a limit). 2. *fig.* To go beyond (in any quality) 1594.

Ou·t-pa:tient. 1715. [OUT- A. I. 2.] A patient who receives treatment at a hospital without being an inmate; opp. to *in-patient.* Also *attrib.*, as *o. department, treatment.*

Ou·t-pe:nsion, *sb.* 1711. [OUT- A. I. 2.] A pension given without the condition of residence in a charitable institution. So **Ou·t-pe:nsion** *v. trans.* to pension out. **Ou·t-pe:nsioner,** a non-resident pensioner; opp. to *in-pensioner* 1706.

Outpoi·nt, *v.* 1883. [OUT- C. I. 2, II. 2.] 1. *Yachting.* To outdo in pointing; to sail closer to the wind than. 2. *Boxing, etc.* To beat on points.

Ou·tpo:rt. 1642. [OUT- A. I. 1, 5.] 1. A port outside a city or town; in England, a term including all ports other than that of London. 2. A port of embarkation or exportation 1790.

Outpost (au·tpōust). 1757. [OUT- A. I. 1.] A post at a distance from the body of an army; a detachment placed at a distance from a force, when halted, to guard against surprise. Also *transf.* and *fig.* Also *attrib.*

Outpour (au·tpōᵊɹ), *sb.* 1864. [OUT A. II. 1.] The act of pouring out; that which pours out, an overflow.

Outpour (autpōᵊ·ɹ), *v.* 1671. [OUT- C. I. 2, 1.] 1. *trans.* To pour out, send forth in or as in a stream. (Chiefly *poet.*) 2. *intr.* To flow out as in a stream 1861. Hence **Ou·t-pou:ring** *vbl. sb.* the action of pouring out; an effusive or impetuous utterance. (Chiefly *pl.*)

Output (au·tput). 1839. [OUT- A. II. 1.] The act or fact of putting or turning out; production; the quantity or amount produced; the product of any industry or exertion, viewed quantitatively; the result given to the world. (Orig. a techn. or local term of iron-works, coal-mines, etc.) b. *Physiol.* Applied to the waste material expelled from the body by the lungs, skin, and kidneys; as opp. to the *income* or material taken into the system. (The undigested matter or fæces are not included.)

b. The o. may be regarded as consisting of (1) the respiratory products of the lungs, skin, and alimentary canal,..(2) of perspiration, consisting chiefly of water and salts..and (3) of the urine 1883. Hence **Ou·t-putter,** one who turns out some industrial product; a producer 1902.

Ou·t-qua:rter. 1651. [OUT- A. I. 1, 3.] *Mil.* usu. in *pl.* A station or quarter (cf. QUARTER *sb.*) away from the head-quarters of a regiment.

Outrage (au·treⁱdʒ), *sb.* ME. [a. OF. *ultrage, oultrage, outrage*:—Com.Rom. *ult-*ragium*, f. L. *ultra* beyond + suff. *-agium, -age*, see -AGE. In Eng. often taken as from OUT and RAGE.] †1. The passing beyond bounds, want of moderation, intemperance; excess. Rarely with *an* and *pl.* –1590. †b. Excess of boldness; foolhardiness; presumption –1553. 2. Extravagant, violent, or disorderly action; passionate behaviour; fury; disorder; insolence. Also rarely with *an* and *pl.* *Obs.* or *arch.* ME. 3. Violence affecting others; violent injury or harm ME. b. with *an* and *pl.* A violent injury or wrong; a gross or wanton offence or indignity. late ME. c. *transf.* Said of gross or wanton wrong or injury done to feelings, principles, or the like 1769.

2. I feare some out-rage, and Ile follow her SHAKS. I bore the diminution of my riches without any outrages of sorrow JOHNSON. 3. Wherever there is war there is misery and o. COWPER. b. Phr. *Agrarian o.*: see AGRARIAN *a.* 2. c. This unpardonable o. upon private feelings 1808. *Comb.* **o.-monger,** one who trades in outrages for political ends.

Outrage (au·treⁱdʒ), *v.* ME. [f. prec. In the obs. senses, and formerly in 2, stressed on *-ra·ge.*] †1. *intr.* To go beyond bounds; to act extravagantly or without self-restraint; to commit excesses, run riot –1718. 2. *trans.* To do violence to; to wrong grossly, treat with gross indignity or insult 1590. b. To infringe flagrantly (law, right, authority, morality, or any principle) 1725. †3. (Infl. by RAGE *v.*) To burst out into rage, to be furious, to rage; to rush out in rage –1606.

2. The king stopped, robbed, and outraged by ruffians MACAULAY. b. To o. contemporary sentiment 1871.

Outrageous (autrēⁱ·dʒəs), *a.* ME. [a. OF. *ou(l)trageus*, f. *outrage* OUTRAGE *sb.*; see -OUS.] 1. Exceeding proper limits; excessive, immoderate, extravagant; enormous, extraordinary. 2. Excessive in action; violent, furious; †excessively bold or fierce. late ME. 3. Excessive in injuriousness, cruelty, or offensiveness; of the nature of violent or gross injury, wrong, or offence, or of a gross violation of law, humanity, or morality 1456.

1. Violent and outragious Rains 1696. 2. From an o. lunatic, he sunk afterwards into a quiet, speechless idiot 1751. 3. Pelted with o. epithets TENNYSON. An o. scandal 1888. Hence **Outra·geous-ly** *adv.*, **-ness.**

Ou·trance. *Obs.* exc. as Fr. (utrāns). late ME. [a. OF. *oultrance, outrance* going beyond bounds, f. *oultrer, outrer* to pass beyond, f. L. *ultra*, F. *oltre, outre* beyond. Still occas. in literary use in the form UTTERANCE².] A degree which goes beyond bounds or beyond measure; excess.

Phr. *To* (*unto*) *o.*, beyond all limits, to extremity. *At o.*, at the last extremity. *To fight to* (*the*) or *at o.*, to fight to the death (rendering F. *combattre à outrance, à toute outrance*).

Outrange (aut,rēⁱ·ndʒ), *v.* 1858. [OUT- C. II. 5, 2, 1.] 1. *trans. Gunnery.* To have a longer range than. 2. To surpass in extent of time 1887.

Outray·, *v. Obs.* exc. *dial.* ME. [a. AFr. *ultreier, outreier*:—late L. **ultricare*, f. *ultra* beyond; cf. OUTRAGE *sb.* and *v.*] †1. *intr.* To go beyond or exceed bounds; to stray; to be or get out of array –1611. 2. To go beyond bounds; to be extravagant; to go to excess. 1440. 3. *trans.* To go beyond, overcome; to vanquish, crush; to excel. Now *dial.* late ME.

‖ **Outré** (utre), *a.* 1722. [F., pa. pple. of *outrer.*] Beyond the bounds of what is usual, correct, or proper; eccentric, out-of-the-way; exaggerated. Hence **Ou·tréness.**

Outreach (aut,rī·tʃ), *v.* 1568. [OUT- C. II. 1, 2 c, I. 1, 2.] 1. *trans.* To exceed in reach; to exceed, surpass. †2. To overreach; to outwit –1643. 3. *trans.* and *intr.* To reach out, extend (*poet.*) 1594.

Outrecuidance (utrəkwīdāns, ūtəɹkwī·dăns). *arch.* late ME. [a. F., f. *outrecuider*, f. *outre* beyond + *cuider*:—L. *cogitare* to think.] Excessive self-esteem; over-weening self-confidence or self-conceit; arrogance; presumption.

Ou·t-relie:f. 1892. = *Outdoor relief*; see OUTDOOR *a.* 2.

Outri·de, *v.* 1460. [OUT- C. I. 1, 2. II. 2, 1.] 1. *intr.* and *trans.* To ride out. *Obs.* or *poet.* 2. To ride better, faster, or farther than; to outstrip by riding 1530. 3. Of a ship: To ride out (a storm) 1647.

2. *transf.* Like a Tempest that out-rides the Wind DRYDEN.

Outrider (au·t,rəi:dəɹ). ME. [OUT- A. II. 2.] One who rides out or forth. †1. An officer of the sheriff's court who collected dues, delivered summonses, etc. –1607. †2. An officer of an abbey or convent, who attended to the external domestic requirements of the community, and looked after the manors belonging to it –1532. †3. a. A forager of an army. b. A highwayman –1625. 4. A merchant's travelling agent (*dial.*) 1762. 5. A mounted attendant who rides in advance of or beside a carriage 1530.

Outrigger (au·t,ri:gəɹ). 1748. [f. OUT *adv.* + RIG *v.*¹ + -ER ¹.] Something rigged out or projecting. 1. *Naut.* a. A strong beam passed through the port-holes of a ship, used to secure the masts and counteract the strain in the act of careening; b. A spar to haul out a sheet; c. A small spar to thrust out and spread the breast-backstays; d. A boom swung out to hang boats clear of a ship; e. Any framework rigged up outside the gunwales of a ship 1769. 2. A contrivance used with canoes in the Indian and Pacific Oceans to prevent capsizing under a press of sail 1748. 3. An iron bracket, fixed to the side of a rowing-boat, bearing a rowlock at its outer edge, so as to increase the leverage of the oar. b. An outrigged boat 1845. 4. *Building* and *Mech.* Applied to various structures placed so as to project from the face of a wall, a frame, etc. 1835. 5. An extension of the splinter-bar of a carriage, enabling a second horse to be harnessed outside the shafts; the horse so harnessed 1811. So **Ou·trigged** *ppl. a.* fitted with outriggers.

Outright (aut,rəi·t), *adv.* (*adj.*) ME. [f. OUT *adv.* + RIGHT.] 1. Straight out; straight ahead. Now *rare.* †2. Of time: Straight, straightway; forthwith, immediately –1714. 3. So that the act is finished at once; altogether, entirely 1603. 4. Fully out, entirely, quite; without reservation; openly ME.

3. Phr. *To kill o.*, i. e. so that the victim dies on the spot. *To sell or purchase o.*, i. e. so that the thing disposed of becomes at once the full property of the buyer. 4. I simper'd sometime,..But never laugh'd o. BEAUM. & FL.

B. *adj.* 1. Directed or going straight on (*rare*) 1611. 2. Direct; downright; thorough, out-and-out 1532. 3. Complete, entire (*mod.*).

2. The young are seldom tempted to o. wickedness 1851. Hence **Outri·ghtness.**

Outri·ng, *v.* late ME. [OUT- C. I. 1, 2, II. 2.] 1. *intr.* To ring out. (Prop. two wds.) 2. *trans.* To outdo in ringing, ring louder than 1635.

Outri·val, *v.* 1622. [OUT- C. II. 2 b.] *trans.* To outdo as a rival; to surpass in any competition.

†**Ou·troad.** 1560. [OUT- A. II. 1.] A riding out; *esp.* a warlike excursion; sally –1865.

That they might make outrodes by the waies of Iudea BIBLE (Genev.) 1 *Macc.* xv. 41.

Outroll (aut,rōu·l), *v.* 1585. [OUT- C. I. 2.] *trans.* To roll out or forth; to unroll, unfurl, uncoil.

†**Ou·t-room.** 1602. [OUT- A. I. 1.] An outlying room; an out-building –1668.

Outroot (autˌrū·t), *v.* 1558. [f. OUT *adv.* + ROOT; cf. F. *déraciner.*] *trans.* To root out, eradicate, exterminate.

Outrun (autˌrʊ·n), *v.* ME. [OUT- C. I. 1, II. 2. 1.] **1.** *intr.* To run out. **2.** *trans.* To outdo in running; to run faster or farther than; hence, to escape or elude. Also *fig.* 1526. **3.** *fig.* To run beyond a fixed point or limit; to go beyond in action 1655.

2. The other disciple did o. Peter, and came first to the Sepulchre *John* xx. 4. *fig.* The zeal of the flocks outran that of the pastors MACAULAY. Phr. *To o. the constable*: see CONSTABLE. 3. Thy tongue outruns thy discretion SCOTT.

Ou·trunner. 1598. [OUT- A. II. 2.] One who or that which runs out; *spec.* a horse which runs in traces outside the shaft; *fig.* a forerunner, an avant-courier.

Ou·trush. 1872. [OUT- A. II. 1.] A rushing out; a violent outflow.

Outsai·l, *v.* 1616. [OUT- C. II. 2, 1.] *trans.* To outdo in sailing; to sail faster or farther than; *transf.* and *fig.* to outstrip.

Ou·tscour. 1883. [OUT- A. II. 1.] The act of scouring out; the action of water in scouring out a channel.

Outsee·, *v.* 1605. [OUT- C. II. 2, 1.] **1.** *trans.* To surpass in length of sight or in mental insight. **2.** To see beyond (a point or limit) 1645.

Outse·ll, *v.* 1611. [OUT- C. II. 2, 2 b.] **1.** *trans.* To sell for more than; *fig.* to exceed in value. **2.** To have or secure a larger sale than 1687.

1. *Cymb.* II. iv. 102.

Ou·t-se·ntry. 1691. [OUT- A. I. 2.] A sentry placed at a distance in advance; an outpost.

Outset (au·tset). 1540. [OUT- A. II. 1.] **1.** An enclosure from the outlying moorland or common. *Sc.* **2.** Ornament or embellishment *Sc.* 1596. **3.** The act or fact of setting out upon a journey, course of action, business, etc.; start, beginning 1759. **4.** *Mining.* An elevation of the ground, or the like, round the mouth of a sinking pit, to facilitate the disposal of the debris produced in sinking 1881.

3. This is no pleasant prospect at the o. of a political journey BURKE.

Ou·t-se·ttlement. 1747. [OUT- A. I. 1.] An outlying or remote settlement.

Ou·tse·ttler. 1756. [OUT- A. I. 2, II. 2.] **a.** A settler outside of or in the outlying parts of a district. **b.** An emigrant.

Outshi·ne, *v.* 1596. [OUT- C. II. 2, I. 1.] **1.** *trans.* To shine brighter than. Also *fig.* **2.** *intr.* To shine forth (*poet.*) 1865.

1. How changed From him, who in the happy Realms of Light..didst o. Myriads MILT.

Outshoot (autˌʃū·t), *v.* 1530. [OUT- C. II. 2, 1, I. 2.] **1.** *trans.* To shoot farther or better than. **b.** To shoot beyond as a young branch; also *fig.* 1772. **2.** To shoot beyond (a mark or limit) 1545. **3.** To shoot out or forth 1658.

1. As if they out shot Robin Hood SIDNEY.

Outshow (autˌʃōᵘ·), *v.* 1558. [OUT- C. I. 2.] *trans.* To show forth, exhibit (*poet.*).

..hen high handiwork will I make my life-deed, Truth and light o. T. HARDY.

Outshri·ll, *v.* 1605. [OUT- C. II. 2.] *trans.* To outdo in shrilling; to exceed in shrillness.

Outside (au·tsəi·d, au·tsəid), *sb., adv., prep.* 1503. [f. OUT *a.*, OUT- A. I. 3 + SIDE *sb.*; cf. INSIDE.] **A.** *sb.* **1.** That part of anything which is without, or farther from the interior; the external surface 1505. **b.** The outer part or parts of anything 1598. **2.** The outer surface considered as that which is seen; the external person as dist. from the mind or spirit; outward aspect or appearance 1592. **b.** That which is merely external; outward form as opp. to substance 1660. **3.** The position or locality close to the outer side or surface of anything 1503. **4.** The outmost limit; the fullest or highest degree or quantity (*colloq.*). Chiefly in phr. *at the o.* 1707. **5.** Anything situated on or forming the outer side, edge, or border; *spec.* (*pl.*) the outermost sheets, more or less damaged, of a ream of paper 1615. **6.** Short for *o. passenger* on a coach, etc. 1804. **7.** In phr. *o. in* (usu. with *turn*): So that the outer side becomes the inner; = inside out 1771.

1. The Duke of Doria's Palace has the best O. of any in Genoa ADDISON. 2. O what a goodlie o. falsehood hath SHAKS. 3. Can I open the door from the o., I wonder? DICKENS. 4. A red light distant a quarter of a mile at the o. 1885. 7. A keeper is only a poacher turned o. in KINGSLEY.

B. *adj.* **1.** That is on, or belongs to, the outer side, surface, edge, or boundary 1634. **2.** Situated, or having its origin or operation, without; that resides without some place or area; that works out of the house, or out of a workshop or factory 1841. **3.** Not included in or belonging to the place, establishment, institution, or society in question 1881. †**4.** That has only an outside; having empty show; superficial –1728. **5.** Reaching the utmost limit; greatest, extreme 1857.

1. A Sailor, who was an o. passenger 1815. The o. walls are built hollow 1854. *O. edge* (Skating): (*To cut, do*) *the o. edge*, a particular form of fancy skating on the outer edge of the skate-iron. *O.* (*jaunting*) *car*: see JAUNTING-CAR. 2. 'Outside' work means work done entirely in the home by an 'outside' worker 1900. An o. porter (*mod.*). 3. O. opinion has evidently had its influence on the City Fathers 1881. *O. broker*, one not a member of the Stock Exchange. 5. The very o. prices that are being paid 1893.

C. *adv.* (Short for *on* or *to the o.*) **1.** Of position: On the outside of certain limits; out in the open air; in the open sea beyond a harbour; not within the body or community in question 1813. **2.** To the exterior 1889. **3.** **Outside of,** *prep. phr.* **a.** Not within the walls, limits, or bounds of; exterior to; also, To the exterior of, outward from 1839. **b.** *U.S. colloq.* Beyond the number or body of, with the exception of 1889.

1. They could..see every thing that took place o. 1813. 2. The men and women were ordered to come o. 1889. *Come o.!* (slang), a challenge to fight or to have it out. 3. a. *O. of a horse* (*colloq.*), on horseback. *To get o. of* (*slang*), (*a*) to swallow; (*b*) *U.S.* to master or understand. b. I do not often see anybody o. of my servants 1890.

D. *prep.* (Shortened from *outside of.*) **1.** Outside of; on the outer side of; external to 1817. **b.** Beyond the limits of (any domain of action or thought, any subject or matter) 1852. **2.** To the outer side of, to the exterior of, to what lies without or beyond 1856.

1. The cause of the tides is to be found o. our earth HUXLEY. b. Services, which lie o. the common routine GLADSTONE. 2. The Court cannot go o. the pleadings 1885.

Outsider (autsəi·dəɹ). 1800. [f. OUTSIDE *sb.* + -ER¹.] **1.** One who is outside any enclosure, barrier, or boundary, material or figurative; *esp.* a person without special knowledge, breeding, etc., or not fit to mix with good society (*colloq.*). **b.** *Horse-racing.* A horse not 'in the running' 1857. **2.** *lit.* One whose position is on the outside of some group or series; an outside man 1857. **3.** An outside jaunting-car 1900. **4.** *pl.* A pair of nippers which can be inserted into a keyhole from the outside so as to grasp and turn the key 1875.

1. He is only an o., and is not in the mysteries DICKENS.

Outsight (au·tsəit). 1605. [OUT- A. II. 1. Cf. G. *aussicht.*] Sight of that which is without; faculty of observation or outlook.

Outsi·ng. *v.* 1603. [OUT- C. II. 2, I. 1, 2.] **1.** *trans.* To excel in singing. Also *refl.* **b.** To get the better of by singing 1830. **2.** *intr.* To sing out 1877.

Outsi·t, *v.* 1658. [OUT- C. II. 1, 2.] **1.** *trans.* To sit beyond the time of duration of. **2.** To sit longer than 1885.

Outskirt (au·tskɔ̄ɹt). 1596. [OUT- A. I. 3.] **1.** The outer border. Now only *pl.* **2.** *attrib.* or quasi-*adj.* Situated on the outskirts 1835.

1. One of those barren parishes lying on the outskirts of civilisation GEO. ELIOT. Hence **Outski·rt** *v. rare* and *poet.*, to skirt; to border; to pass along the outskirts of.

Outslee·p, *v.* 1590. [OUT- C. II. 1, 2, I. 3.] **1.** *trans.* To sleep beyond (a specified time, etc.). **2.** To sleep longer than 1690. **3.** To sleep (a period of time) out 1784.

1. I feare we shall out-sleepe the comming morne SHAKS. 3. He has outslept the winter COWPER.

Ou·tsole. 1884. [OUT- A. I. 3.] The outer sole of a shoe, which comes in contact with the ground.

Ou·tspan, *sb. S. Afr.* 1852. [f. next.] The The action of outspanning or unyoking; the time or place of outspanning or encampment.

Outspan (au·tspæn), *v. S. Afr.* 1824. [ad. Du. *uitspannen*, f. *uit* adv. out + *spannen* to span, stretch, put horses to.] To unyoke or unhitch oxen from a wagon; to unharness horses; hence, to encamp. *trans.* and *intr.*

Outspeak (autspī·k), *v.* 1603. [OUT- C. II. 1, 2, I. 2, 1.] †**1.** *trans.* To express more than –1618. **2.** To outdo in speaking 1603. **3.** To speak (something) out; to declare 1635. **4.** *intr.* To speak out 1819.

1. *Hen. VIII*, III. ii. 127. 4. And now outspake the Corporal LYTTON.

Outspe·nd, *v.* 1586. [OUT- C. II. 1, 2.] **1.** *trans.* To exceed (resources, etc.) in spending. **2.** To spend more than (another) 1840. **3.** In *pa. pple.* **Outspe·nt,** exhausted 1818.

1. We out-spend our means 1811. 2. He outspent princes 1866. 3. Outspent with this long course, The Cossack prince rubb'd down his horse BYRON.

Outspi·n, *v.* 1616. [OUT- C. I. 1, 2 b, II. 2.] **1.** *trans.* To spin (a thread) to its full length; said *fig.* of the thread of life, etc. **2.** To outdo in spinning 1742.

Ou·tspo·ken (stress variable), *ppl. a.* orig. *Sc.* 1808. [OUT- B. 2.] **1.** Given to speaking out; candid, frank; direct in speech. **b.** Of things said: Free from reserve, distinct 1869. **2.** Spoken out, uttered 1882.

1. He is not, you know, very o. SCOTT. b. Mr. Gladstone's o. observations 1880. Hence **Outspo·ken-ly** *adv.*, **-ness.**

Outspread (au·tspred), *sb.* 1841. [OUT- A. II. 1.] **1.** The action of spreading out; expansion. **2.** *concr.* An expanse or expansion 1856.

Outspread (autspre·d), *v.* ME. [OUT- C. I. 2.] *trans.* To spread out; to expand. Hence **Ou·tspread** *ppl. a.*

Outspri·ng, *v.* ME. [OUT- C. I. 1, II. 2.] **1.** *intr.* To spring out, issue forth. (Now only *poet.*) †**b.** To spring by birth –1596. **2.** *trans.* To spring beyond or farther than 1600.

Outstand (autstæ·nd), *v.* 1571. [OUT- C. I. 2 b, 1, II. 1.] **I.** *trans.* **1.** To stand or hold out against; to resist successfully. Now *dial.* **2.** To stay out or stay beyond (in time). *arch.* 1611.

2. I haue out-stood my time SHAKS.

II. *intr.* **1.** To stand out distinctly or prominently 1755. **2.** Of a ship: To stand out from the land; to sail outwards 1866.

1. Cottages here and there outstanding bare on the mountain CLOUGH.

Ou·tsta·nding (stress variable), *ppl. a.* 1570. [OUT- B. 1.] **1.** That stands out or projects; projecting, prominent, detached. **2.** *fig.* Standing out from the rest; conspicuous, eminent; striking 1830. **3.** That stands over; that remains undetermined, unsettled, or unpaid 1797.

1. O. veins 1870. 2. The great o. facts, which our Lord has pointed out PUSEY. 3. An o. debt 1858. Phr. *O. term*: see TERM. Hence **Outsta·ndingly** *adv.* pre-eminently.

Outsta·re, *v.* 1596. [OUT- C. II. 2 b.] *trans.* To outdo in staring; to put out of countenance by staring; to look on (the sun, etc.) without blinking.

I would o. the sternest eyes that look SHAKS.

Outsta·rt, *v.* late ME. [OUT- C. I. 1, II. 1, 2.] **1.** *intr.* To start, spring forth suddenly. (Prop. two wds.) **2.** *trans.* To spring or go beyond; to take or have the start of 1593.

Ou·t-sta·tion. 1844. [OUT- A. I. 1, 3.] A station at a distance from head-quarters or from the centre of population or business.

Outstay (autstē·ⁱ), *v.* 1600. [OUT- C. II. 1, 2.] **1.** *trans.* To stay beyond the limit of; to overstay. **2.** To stay longer than 1689.

1. You are afraid of outstaying your welcome 1893. 2. Mr. Pepys, and I, outstayed the rest near an hour 1783.

Outste·p, *v.* 1759. [OUT- C. II. 1.] *trans.* To step outside of or beyond; to overstep.

Outstrea·m, *v.* late ME. [OUT- C. I. 1.] *intr.* To stream out or forth.

†**Ou·t-street.** 1585. [OUT- A. I. 1, 3.] A street outside the walls or in the outskirts of a town –1722.

Ou·tstretch, *sb.* 1863. [OUT- A. II. 1.] **1.** The act or fact of stretching out. **2.** An outstretched tract 1864. 3. The distance to which anything stretches out 1888.

Outstre·tch, *v.* late ME. [OUT- C. I. 2, 2 b, II. 1, 2.] 1. *trans.* To stretch out or forth. Chiefly *poet.* 2. To extend in area or content; to expand 1600. 3. To stretch to its limit, to strain. Now *rare.* 1607. 4. To stretch beyond (a limit, etc.) 1597.

2. The great city, which lay outstretched before him DICKENS. 3. Tymon is dead, who hath outstretcht his span SHAKS. Hence **Ou·tstretched** *ppl. a.* (esp. of the arms).

Outstri·de, *v.* 1610. [OUT- C. II. 2.] *trans.* To excel in length of stride; also *fig.*

Outstrip (autstri·p), *v.* 1580. [f. OUT- C. II. 2, 2 c, 1 + STRIP *v.*[2] 2.] *trans.* To pass in running or swift motion; to outrun, leave behind.

The deer Outstrips the active hound DEKKER. *fig.* They striue one to o. another in giuing most 1607.

Ou·tstroke. 1851. [OUT- A. II. 1.] 1. A stroke directed outwards 1874. 2. *Mining.* The act of striking out, i. e. of passing out of a working royalty into another royalty. Also *attrib.*, as *o. rent.*

Outswe·ll, *v.* 1606. [OUT- C. II. 2, 1.] 1. *trans.* To swell out more than. 2. To swell beyond (a point or limit) 1658.

†**Out-take, -taken,** *pa. pple., prep., conj.* ME. [pa. pple. of *outtake* vb. = L. *excipere.*] = EXCEPT.

Ou·t-throw, ou·tthrow, *sb.* 1855. [OUT- A. II. 1.] The act of throwing out; ejection, emission; output; matter ejected.

Out-throw, outthrow (autþrōu·), *v.* ME. [OUT- C. I. 2, II. 1, 2.] †1. *trans.* To throw out, cast out. (Prop. two wds.) –1711. 2. To throw beyond (a point), or farther than (a person) 1613.

Ou·t-thrust, *sb.* 1842. [OUT- A. II. 1.] The act or fact of thrusting or pushing forcibly outward; an outward thrusting pressure in any structure.

Out-top, outtop (aut₁tǫ·p), *v.* 1624. [OUT- C. II. 2 b.] *trans.* = OVERTOP.

Out-tra·vel, *v.* 1619. [OUT- C. II. 1, 2.] *trans.* To exceed in extent or swiftness of travelling.

Outvie (autvəi·), *v.* 1594. [OUT- C. II. 2 b.] *trans.* To vie with and excel.

Outvo·te, *v.* 1647. [OUT- C. II. 2.] *trans.* To outnumber in voting; to defeat by a majority of votes.

Ou·t-vo·ter. 1855. [OUT- A. I. 2.] One who has a parliamentary vote in a constituency in which he does not reside; a non-resident voter qualified by holding property.

Outwalk (aut₁wǭ·k), *v.* 1626. [OUT- C. II. 2, 1.] *trans.* To walk faster, farther, or better than; to walk beyond.

Ou·t-wall (-wǭl). 1535. [OUT- A. I. 3.] The outer wall of any building or enclosure. **b.** *fig.* The clothing; the body as enclosing the soul 1605.

Outward (au·t₁wǫ̆ɹd), *a.* (*sb.*[1]) [OE. *útweard*, f. *út* (see OUT *adv.*) + *-weard* -WARD.] 1. That is without or on the outer side; out, outer, external, exterior. *Obs.* or *arch.* **b.** Directed or proceeding towards the outside; pertaining to what is so directed 1700. 2. External; bodily ME. †3. External to the country; foreign –1675. 4. Of or pertaining to outer form as opposed to saner substance or reality 1526. 5. Applied to things in the external or material world, as opp. to those in the mind or thought 1573. **b.** Applied to things that are external to one's own personality, etc., or that concern one's relations with other persons and external circumstances; extrinsic 1607. 6. Dissipated, wild or irregular in conduct (*dial.*) 1875.

1. **b.** The first or O. halves of Return Tickets 1884. 2. Inward Medicines or o. Applications ADDISON. The vision was not to the o. eye 1867. *O. man* (*Theol.*), the body as opp. to the soul or spirit; *joc.* outward guise, clothing. 4. An o. and visible sign of an inward and spiritual grace *Bk. Com. Prayer.* 5. Obstinate questionings Of sense and o. things WORDSW. **b.** The law must define men's o. rights and relations 1869.

B. *sb.* (the adj. used ellipt. or absol.) †1. An outer part (of anything) –1545. 2. Outward appearance; the outside 1606. 3. in *pl.* Externals. Now *rare* or *arch.* 1627. 4. That which is outside the mind; the external world 1832.

2. So fair an O., and such stuffe Within SHAKS. Hence **Ou·tward-ly** *adv.*, 1480, †**-most** *a.*

Out-ward (au·t₁wǭɹd), *sb.*[2] 1871. [OUT- A. I. 1.] An outlying ward; a ward outside the original bounds of a borough.

Outward (au·t₁wǫ̆rd), *adv.* [OE. *útweard.*] 1. On the outside; without. **b.** From the inside to or towards the outside ME. †2. Outside of a specified or understood place; abroad –1673. †3. On, or with ref. to, the outside of the body; externally –1543. †**b.** In the body as opp. to the mind or spirit; in outward appearance as opp. to inner reality; outwardly; publicly –1673.

1. Whited tombes which appere beautyfull outwarde TINDALE *Matt.* xxiii. 28. **b.** They myght have their costes owteward & homeward 1497. 3. **b.** This o. sainted Deputie..is yet a diuell SHAKS.

Ou·tward-bou·nd, *a.* (*sb.*) 1602. [f. OUTWARD *adv.* + BOUND *ppl. a.*[1]] Directing the course outward, esp. going from a home port to a foreign one: of a ship or a person; *transf.* of a voyage. Also *absol.* as *sb.* **b.** *fig.* Dying 1809. **c.** *fig.* Bent on wandering or straying 1742.

Ou·twardness. 1580. [f. OUTWARD *a.* + -NESS.] 1. The quality or condition of being outward; outward existence; objectivity. 2. Occupation with or belief in outward things 1835.

Outwards (au·t₁wǫ̆rdz), *adv.* (*a.*) [OE. *útweardes*, f. *útweard* OUTWARD *adj.* + *-es* advb. genitive.] 1. In an outward direction; towards that which is outside. †2. In an outward position; outside; externally –1602. 3. *attrib.* (as *adj.*). For outward goods 1878.

3. The 'Outwards' department of the great goods shed 1878.

Outwatch (aut₁wǫ·tʃ), *v.* 1626. [OUT- C. II. 2, 1.] *trans.* To watch longer than; to watch (an object) till it disappears.

Outwear (aut₁wēə·ɹ), *v.* 1541. [OUT- C. I. 2, 2 b, II. 2.] 1. *trans.* To wear out, wear away; to consume by wearing. **b.** To exhaust in strength or endurance; chiefly in pa. pple. *outworn* 1610. 2. *trans.* To wear out, spend, pass (time) 1590. **b.** To outlive, outgrow 1592. 3. To wear longer than 1579.

1. **b.** By ceaseless pains outworn WORDSW. 2. If I the night out-wear POPE. 3. Teaspoons that have outworn their set 1893.

Outweary (aut₁wīə·ri), *v.* Chiefly *poet.* 1609. [OUT- C. I. 2 b.] *trans.* To weary out; to exhaust in endurance.

Some youthful Troubadour,..Who here outwearied sank M. ARNOLD.

Outweep (aut₁wī·p), *v.* 1597. [OUT- C. I. 3, II. 2.] 1. *trans.* To weep out, to expel by weeping (*poet.*). 2. To outdo in weeping 1631.

Outweigh (aut₁wē·), *v.* 1530. [OUT- C. II. 2, 2 b.] 1. *trans.* To exceed in weight; *fig.* to be too heavy for. 2. To exceed in value, importance, or influence 1632.

Outwell (aut₁we·l), *v.* 1590. [OUT- C. I. 2, 1.] †1. *trans.* To pour forth SPENSER. 2. *intr.* To well out, to gush forth 1600. Hence **Outwe·lling** *vbl. sb.* and *ppl. a.* 1821.

Outwing (aut₁wi·ŋ), *v.* 1648. [OUT- C. II. 5.] 1. *trans.* To exceed or surpass in flight; to fly beyond 1717. 2. *Mil.* Of an army: To outflank (the enemy).

Outwit (aut₁wi·t), *v.* 1652. [OUT- C. II. 5.] 1. *trans.* To surpass in wit, wisdom, or knowledge (*arch.*) 1659. 2. To get the better of by superior craft; to prove too clever for 1652.

1. Thou..Shalt outsee seers, and o. Sages EMERSON. 2. To cheat or, rather (as the Quakers word it) to O. his own Father and Brother 1705.

Ou·t₁with, *prep.* and *adv.* Chiefly *north.*; now *Sc.* ME. [f. OUT *adv.* + WITH *prep.*; cf. INWITH and WITHOUT.] Without, outside.

Outwork (au·t₁wɒɹk), *sb.* 1615. [OUT- A. I. 1, 3.] 1. Any detached or advanced work forming part of the defence of a place. Also *transf.* and *fig.* 2. (*out-work.*) Work done outside, i. e. out of doors, out of the house, out of the shop or factory, etc.; in *Cricket* = OUTFIELDING 1793.

Outwork (aut₁wɒ̄·ɹk), *v.* 1590. [OUT- C. I. 2, 2 b, II. 5, 2.] 1. *trans.* To work out to a conclusion; to complete (*poet.*). †2. To excel in work or workmanship –1782. 3. To outdo in working; to work more or faster than 1611.

Ou·t-wo·rker. 1813. [OUT- A. I. 2.] One who does outwork (see OUTWORK *sb.* 2).

Ou·t₁wo·rld, out-world, *sb.* 1647. [OUT- A. I. 3.] The outside world; an outlying or outer world.

Outworn, out-worn (aut₁wǭ·ɹn, *attrib.* au·t₁wǭɹn), *ppl. a.* 1548. [OUT- B. 2, from *wear out.*] 1. Worn out, as clothes; wasted, consumed, or obliterated by wear or by the action of time; hence *fig.* of beliefs, customs, institutions, etc. 2. Of living beings, etc.: Exhausted as to physical vigour and vitality, spent 1597.

1. A Pagan suckled in a creed o. WORDSW. 2. Inglorious, unemployed, with age o. MILT.

Outwrite (aut₁rəi·t), *v.* 1643. [OUT- C. II. 2, 1, I. 2 b.] 1. *trans.* To surpass or excel in writing. 2. To get over by writing 1837. 3. *refl.* To write oneself out 1883.

Outwrought, pa. t. and pple. of OUTWORK *v.*

Ouze, obs. f. OOZE.

Ouzel, ousel (ū·z'l) [OE. *ósle* wk. fem. :—*ǫmsla = OHG. *amsala*; ult. etym. unkn.] 1. A name of certain birds of the genus *Turdus.* **a.** The blackbird or merle (*T. merula*). Also attrib. in *o.-cock.* Now *lit.* or *arch.* **b.** Applied to *T. torquatus*, the **Ring-ouzel** 1450. †**c.** *transf.* Used of a person (prob. of dark hair or complexion) –1628. 2. Applied to other birds, pop. assoc. with the prec. 1622.

1. The Woosell cocke, so blacke of hew, With Orenge-tawny bill SHAKS. **c.** 2 *Hen. IV*, III. ii. 9. 2. **Brook O.**, the Water Rail (*Rallus aquaticus*). **Water O.**, the DIPPER (*Cinclus aquaticus*); also the American Dipper (*C. mexicanus*).

Ova, pl. of OVUM.

Oval (ōu·văl), *a.* and *sb.* 1570. [prob. ad. mod.L. *ovalis*, f. *ovum* egg.] **A.** *adj.* 1. Having the form of an egg; approximately egg-shaped, ellipsoidal 1577. 2. Having the outline of an egg as projected on a surface; having more or less the form or outline of an elongated circle or ellipse; elliptical 1610. 3. Of or pertaining to an egg (*rare*) 1646.

1. **O. chuck** = elliptic chuck; an appendage to a lathe, of such a nature that the work attached to it and cut by the tool in the usual manner becomes of an oval form. 2. *O. window*, the *fenestra ovalis* of the ear; see WINDOW. 3. Their ovall conceptions, or egges within their bodies SIR T. BROWNE. Hence **O·val-ly** *adv.*, **-ness.**

B. *sb.* 1. A plane figure resembling the longitudinal section of an egg: in *mod. Geom.* any closed curve (other than a circle or ellipse) 1570. 2. Anything having an oval or (usu.) elliptical outline 1650.

1. *Cassinian o.*: see CASSINIAN. 2. *Kennington O.*, in athletics 'the Oval', an open space at Kennington in South London, where cricket matches, etc., are played.

Ovalbumen, -in (ōuvælbiū·mĕn, -in). 1835. [f. L. *ovi albumen* (Pliny).] *Chem.* The albumen or white of egg; egg albumen.

Ovarian (ovēə·riăn), *a.* 1840. [f. OVARIUM + -AN.] Of, pertaining to, or of the nature of an ovary or ovaries.

Ovario- (ovēə·rio), comb. form of OVARIUM, expressing the participation of the ovary with some other part, as *o.-abdominal*; also with sbs. in sense 'ovarian', as *o.-insanity.*

Ovariole (ovēə·riōul). 1877. [ad. L. **ovariolum*, dim. of *ovarium*; see below.] A small ovary; one of the tubular glands of the compound ovary of some insects.

Ovariotomy (ovēəriǫ·tŏmi). 1852. [f. OVARIUM + Gr. -τομία, f. -τομος cutting, cut.] *Surg.* The operation of cutting into an ovary to remove an ovarian tumour; also oophorectomy.

Ovarious (ovēə·riəs), *a. rare.* 1730. [f. OVUM; see -ARIOUS.] Of, pertaining to, or of the nature of eggs.

‖**Ovaritis** (ōuvărəi·tis). 1857. [f. OVARIUM + -ITIS.] *Path.* Inflammation of the ovaries.

‖**Ovarium** (ovēə·riɒ̆m). *Pl.* **-ia.** 1692. [mod. L., f. *ovum* egg; see -ARIUM.] = OVARY 1 and 2.

Ovary (ōu·vări), *sb.* 1658. [ad. mod.L. *ovarium*; see prec.] 1. *Anat.* and *Zool.* The female organ of reproduction in animals, in which ova or eggs are produced. 2. *Bot.* The lowest part of the pistil in a flower, consisting of one or more carpels, which ultimately becomes the fruit or seed-vessel; the germen 1751.

Ovate (ǫ·vĕt), *sb.* 1723. [f. an assumed L. pl. *Ovates*, repr. Οὐάτεις = *vates* soothsayers, prophets, mentioned by Strabo as a third order in the Gaulish hierarchy.] An English equivalent of Welsh *ofydd*, now applied to an Eisteddfodic graduate of a third order, beside 'bard' and 'druid'.

Ovate (ōu·veit), *a.* 1760. [ad. L. *ovatus* egg-shaped, f. *ovum*; see -ATE² 2.] 1. Egg-shaped. 2. In comb. with another adj. with sense 'inclining to ovate', as *o.-lanceolate, -oblong, -rotundate*, etc. 1819. Hence **O·vately** *adv.* = ovate-, ovato- 1822.

Ovation (ovē·ʃən). 1533. [ad. L. *ovationem*, f. *ovare* to rejoice.] 1. *Rom. Hist.* A lesser triumph, granted to a commander for achievements insufficient to entitle him to the triumph proper. Also, allusively. †2. Exultation -1818. 3. *transf.* An enthusiastic reception by a concourse of people; a burst of enthusiastic applause 1831.

3. Dr. Stainer received the o. that was his due 1885.

Ovato- (ovē·to), comb. advb. form of L. *ovatus* OVATE, = 'ovately', 'ovate-', as *o.-acuminate, -oblong, -rotundate*, etc.

Oven (v·v'n), *sb.* [Com. Teut.: OE. *ofn, ofen*:—OTeut. **ohno-*:—pre-Teut. **uqno-*; cf. Gr. ἰπνός oven, furnace.] †1. A furnace -1722. 2. A chamber or receptacle of brick, stonework, or iron, for baking bread and cooking food, by continuous heat radiated from the walls, roof, or floor OE. 3. A small furnace, kiln, etc., for the heating or drying of substances in chemical, metallurgical, or manufacturing processes 1753.

1. The three Children of Israel cast into the hot fierie O. 1642. 2. I preached..in a house as warm as an o. WESLEY. *Dutch o.*, (*a*) a large pot heated by surrounding it with fuel, and placing hot coals on the lid; (*b*) a cooking utensil made of sheet-metal, placed in front of a grate and heated by radiation and reflection from the back of the chamber.

attrib. and *Comb.*, as *o. cake, man, mouth, stone, wood*; **o.-coke**, coke obtained by heating coal in a closed retort.

O·ven-bird. 1825. A name for birds which build a domed or oven-shaped nest: applied to the genus *Furnarius* of the neotropical family *Dendrocolaptidæ*, esp. *F. rufus*; also, locally, to the Willow Wren, the Long-tailed or Bottle Titmouse, and the American Golden-crowned Thrush (*Seiurus auricapillus*).

O·ver, *sb.* 1584. [OVER *adv.* used absol.] 1. That which is excessive; an excess, extreme. *Sc.* 2. An amount in excess, or remaining over; an extra 1882. 3. *Cricket.* The fixed number of balls bowled from either end of the wicket before a change is made to the other end; the portion of the game comprising a single turn of bowling from one end 1850.

Over (ōu·vəɹ), *a.* [OE. *ufer(r)a, -e, yfer(r)a, -e*, adj., early ME. *ufere, uvere*, written *over(e* bef. 1300.] 1. The upper, the higher in position. (Only *attrib.*, prec. by *the* or an equiv., and used of one of two things.) Now *Obs.* or *dial.* b. Upper, outer OE. 2. Higher in power, authority, or station; upper, superior ME. 3. That is in excess or in addition; surplus, extra 1494. 4. Too great, excessive. (Now mostly written in comb.; see OVER- 8.) 1561.

1. b. One paire of o. britches 1598. 3. O. or spoiled copies 1896. 4. Without o. care as to which is largest RUSKIN.

Over (ōu·vəɹ), *adv.* [Com. Teut.: OE. *ofer* adv. and prep. = Gr. ὑπέρ, Skr. *upari* adv. and prep., locative form of *upara* adj. 'over, higher, more advanced, later', comparative formation from *upa*, in Teut. **ufa-, uf-*, whence ABOVE.] I. In a higher position. 1. Above, on high. b. After *hang, project, jut, lean*, etc.; hence *ellipt.* projecting, leaning, or bent forward and downward 1546. 2. Above so as to cover the surface, or so as to affect the whole surface. late ME.

1. b. Don't lean o. too far, or you'll fall o. (*mod.*). 2. *To brush, cover, clothe, daub*, etc., *o.*

II. To or on the other or further side. 1. Indicating a motion or course that passes or crosses over something, usu. rising on one side and descending on the other OE.; occas. (*b*) esp. with the sense of passing above and beyond, and so *fig.* of going beyond, exaggeration 1599. 2. Hence = over the edge or brink and down, forward and down. late ME. Also, b. of a movement from the erect position, without ref. to any brink 1649; and c. in *to bend, double, fold, roll* a thing *o.*, in which the upper surface is turned upside down 1548. 3. From side to side of an interjacent surface or space OE. b. Of measurement: Across; in outside measurement 1585. c. *Cricket.* The umpire's call for the players to change ends, on a change of the bowling to the other end, after a fixed number of balls have been bowled from the one end 17... 4. Expressing transference or transition from one person, side, opinion, etc., to another 1585. 5. On the other side of something intervening, e.g. a sea, river, street; hence, merely, at some distance ME.

1. *To climb, jump, run, flow, boil o., to look o.* Toss him o. the bridge MARRYAT. b. *fig.* You haue shot ouer SHAKS. Many shot went o., but none struck us 1796. 2. *To jump, throw* oneself, *push* any one *o.* b. *To fall, tumble, topple, knock* a person, a vase, etc. *o.* c. He tourned o. the leffe, and began an order of a new life 1548. *To turn* or *roll o. and o.*, i.e. so that each part of the surface in succession rolls forward and downward, and is alternately up and down. 3. My mother will send o. every day to inquire how Miss McLean is 1894. 4. And dost thou now fall ouer to my foes? SHAKS. The balance..is brought o. into this [account] 1776. 5. Over by Dalhem a dome-spire sprang white BROWNING. *O. against* (prep. phr.), opposite to.

III. With the notion of exceeding in quantity, etc. 1. Above and beyond the quantity named or in question. a. Remaining beyond what is taken. b. In excess, in addition, more. OE. 2. Left unpaid, unsettled, or uncompleted; left till a later time or occasion 1647. †3. Beyond what has been said; moreover, besides; further -1509. 4. Too much; excessively; too ME.

1. Their wages..and something ouer SHAKS. Two and two are four, and nothing o. DICKENS. *O. or under*, more or less. 2. *To remain, lie, stand, hold, leave o.* 4. O. happy to be proud, O. wealthy in the treasure Of her own exceeding pleasure! WORDSW.

IV. Of duration, repetition, completion, ending. 1. To the end; from beginning to end. late ME. 2. Expressing repetition 1550. 3. Past, gone by, finished, at an end 1611.

1. *To read, repeat, say, tell, count o. To talk, think o.*, i.e. with detailed consideration. 2. He read it twice o. GOLDSM. *O. and o.*, many times over. 3. Now the day is o., Night is drawing nigh 1865.

Over (ōu·vəɹ), *prep.* [The same as prec. with object.] I. In sense *above*. 1. Above, higher up than OE. 2. In (or into) a position in which water, or the like, rises above one's shoes, boots, ears, head, etc. Also *fig.* 1503. 3. The spatial sense 'above' is a. combined with that of purpose or occupation, as in *o. the fire, o. a glass*; b. merged in that of having something under treatment, observation, or consideration, as in *to watch* or *talk o., make merry o.* OE.

1. Having his house burnt o. his head BERKELEY. *fig.* A grave doubt hung o. the legitimacy both of Mary and of Elizabeth MACAULAY. Phr. *O.* (one's) *signature, name*, etc., with one's signature, etc., subscribed to what is written. 2. *O. head and ears*: see HEAD *sb.* 3. Those hours..which others consume.. o. the bottle 1791. We sit down to breakfast, and talk o. it till eleven MRS. CARLYLE.

II. In sense *on, upon*. 1. On the upper or outer surface of; upon OE. 2. Upon (with vbs. of motion) OE. b. *fig.* Upon, down upon, as an influence OE. 3. a. (Position) everywhere on; here and there upon. Now esp. *all o.* OE. b. (Motion) to and fro upon; all about; throughout. Often *all o.* OE. c. Through every part of, all through 1647. d. In the above senses often placed after its object. late ME.

1. With his hat low down o. his eyes TROLLOPE. 2. Let us draw a veil o. this dismal spectacle 1861. b. A sudden change came o'er his heart 1834. 3. a. The People..began to be allarm'd all o. the Town DE FOE. b. We may range o. Europe, from shore to shore RUSKIN. c. She would have liked to go o. all his notes about his case 1892. d. A test which holds good all the world o. 1832.

III. 1. Above in authority, rule, or power OE. 2. Above or beyond in degree, quality, or action; in preference to; more than OE. †3. In addition to, further than; besides, beyond -1772. 4. In excess of, above, more than (a stated amount or number). late ME.

1. With sbs., as *king, lord o.*; *jurisdiction, rule, triumph o.*; adjs. *victorious o.*; vbs. *to reign, rule, appoint* or *set* any one *o.* Who is Lord ouer vs? *Ps.* xii. 4. 2. The preference given to him o. English captains MACAULAY. 4. A distance of o. 700 yards 1896.

IV. Across (above, or on a surface). 1. Indicating motion that passes above (something) on the way to the other side. Occas. expressing only the latter part of this, as in *falling* or *jumping over a precipice*, i.e. over the edge and down. OE. 2. From side to side of a surface or space; across, to the other side of (a sea, river, boundary, etc.); from end to end of (a line), along OE. †3. *fig.* In contravention of, contrary to -1502. 4. On the other side of; across (of position) OE.

1. O. hedge and ditch 1621. O. the ship's side 1794. The sun is peering o. the roofs 1843. 2. A free pass o. this company's line of railways 1894. 4. I have a bed o. the way offered me at three half-crowns a night 1769. *The King o. the water*, Jacobite phr. for the exiled king.

V. Of time. 1. Beyond in time; after. *Obs.* exc. *dial.* OE. 2. During, all through OE. †3. During the (eve or night) preceding; on the preceding (evening or night). *Obs.* exc. in OVERNIGHT. -1528. 4. Till the end of; for a period that includes 1806.

2. The repayment..should be spread o. a series of years 1886. 4. In case you should stay o. Wednesday MRS. CARLYLE.

Over- is used with adverbial, prepositional, and adjectival force, in comb. with sbs.; with adverbial and prepositional force in comb. with vbs.; with adverbial force in comb. with adjs., advbs., and preps. Its combs. are therefore exceedingly numerous. The following are the chief classes. (Cf. SUR-, SUPER-.)

I. In spatial and temporal senses, and in uses directly related to these. 1. With vbs., or with sbs. forming vbs., etc., in the sense 'over in space, on high, above the top or surface of', as *overcanopy*, -HANG, *-mount, -soar, -spring, -vault*, etc. Also (*b*) in sense of 'rising above', 'overtopping', as OVER-TOP, -TOWER; and (*c*) with the sense of position implying other notions of which it is a condition or element, as OVERJOY, OVERLOOK, etc. 2. With the sense 'above in power, authority, rank, station'. In vbs., as OVERMASTER, -RULE, etc. b. So in sbs. and adjs. derived from or related to vbs., as OVERRULE, -RULER, -SEER, etc.; also in other sbs., in sense of 'higher, superior', as OVER-KING, OVERLORD, etc. 3. With the sense of inclination to one side so as to lean over the space beneath. In vbs., as *overbias, -lean*, etc.; also in derived sbs. and adjs., as *overbias, overleaning*, etc. 4. With the sense of passing across overhead, and so 'away, off'. In vbs., as OVERCARRY, *-drive*, etc.; also in derived sbs. and adjs. 5. With the sense of surmounting, passing over the top, or over the brim or edge. In vbs., as OVERBOIL, -BRIM, *-climb*, -FLOW; occas. (*b*) implying 'passing over without hitting, missing', as OVERLEAP, -LOOK, -SHOOT, *-soar, -spring, -step*; also (*c*) *fig.* of surmounting or getting over an obstacle, an illness, etc., as OVERCOME. b. Also in derived or related sbs. or adjs. 6. With the sense of motion forward and down, and hence of overturning, inversion. In vbs., as OVERBALANCE, -BEAR, -THROW, -TURN, etc.; so in derived sbs. and adjs. 7. With the sense 'down upon from above'. In vbs., as OVERLEAP, -LOOK, -SEE, etc. 8. With sense 'upon the surface generally, all over, so as to prevail, or abound over, cover, hide'. In vbs., as OVERCLOUD, *-cover, -crust, -glaze, -gloom*, -GROW, *-heap, -lard, -net, -veil*, etc. b. So with ppl. adjs. and vbl. sbs. c. With sbs. in the sense of 'overlying, covering, worn over or above', 'upper or outer'; as in OVERCOAT, *-garment*, -SHOE, etc. 9. With the sense of motion over a surface generally, so as to cover in whole or part; also of motion to and fro upon or all over; as in *overflood, -glide*, -RIDE, -RUN, *-sweep*, etc.; also with derived sbs. and adjs. 10. With the sense 'across, from side to side, to the other side'; as *overcarve*, etc.; so in derived sbs. and adjs. 11. With the sense of bringing or gaining over to a party, opinion, etc. In vbs., as *Over-force, -influence*, OVERPERSUADE, *-talk*. b. So also with derived sbs. and adjs. 12. With (the sense of 'across a boundary'; hence, of transgression; as in OVERGANG, *-lash, -step*, etc. 13. With the sense 'beyond a point or limit, farther than'; in vbs., as OVERGROW, -REACH, etc.; also in derivs. **14.** As in OVERTAKE. **15.** As in OVERHEAR. **16.** With the sense 'all through' (something extended), 'through the extent of', 'from beginning to end'; in vbs., as OVERLOOK, *-name*, etc. **17.** With the sense 'through', 'to the end of' in time; 'to an end or issue', 'to extinction'; in vbs. as OVERPASS, -RUN 1603. **18.** With the sense 'beyond' in time, 'too long', 'too late'; in vbs., as *overbide*, -LIVE, -STAY. **19.** With the sense 'remaining over', or 'in addition or excess', 'surplus', 'extra'; as in vb. *overleave*; in sbs. as *overdeal*, OVERTIME. **20.** With the notion of repetition, 'over again'; in vbs. as *overact*, *-hear*, etc.; in sbs., as *overcome*, -WORD. **21.** With the sense of overcoming, putting down, or getting the better of, by the action or thing expressed; in vbs., as OVERAWE, *-brave*, -DARE; so in vbl. derivs.

II. In the sense of 'over or beyond' in degree or quality; hence, of surpassing, excelling, exceeding, excess. **1.** With the notion of doing some action over or beyond another agent, of going beyond, surpassing, or excelling in the action denoted by the simple vb. In vbs., as OVERBID 2, OVERGO 10, OVERRUN II. 1. **b.** In vbs. formed on sbs., with the sense of 'surpassing in, or in the role of', as *over-bulk*; esp. in nonce-phrases, as *over-Macpherson Macpherson*, etc. **2.** In refl. vbs., with the sense of surpassing oneself; often with the sense of exhausting oneself by the action; sometimes merely with the sense of doing too much; as *overbloom itself*, *Overdrink*, -EAT, -SLEEP *oneself*. **3.** In sense 'more than'; with vbs., as OVERBALANCE, -FILL, -MATCH, etc. **b.** So in derivs.; also in other adjs., as OVERDUE, OVERFULL. **4.** With the sense 'exceedingly, beyond measure, lavishly'. In vbs., often rendering L. *super-*, as OVERABOUND, *-glad*, *-high*, etc.; in adjs., as OVERDEAR, *-excelling*, *glorious*. Now *obs.* or *arch.* **5.** With the sense 'to a greater extent, or at a greater rate, than is usual, natural, or intended; too far'. In vbs., as OVERACT, -BID, *-drive*, *-esteem*, -ESTIMATE, *-march*, *-mount*, -RATE, etc.; in adjs., as *overawful*, etc. **6–9.** With the sense 'in or to excess, too much, too'. Now a leading use of *over-* in comb. with vbs., adjs., sbs., and advs. **6.** With vbs. (or with sbs. or adjs. forming vbs.); as *over-affect*, *-ballast*, *-burn*, *-busy*, *-cloy*, *-drink*, *-drive* -EAT, *-enter*, *-fatigue*, *-fire*, *-fish*, *-gorge*, *-leaven*, -LOAD, *-play*, *-ply*, *-pot*, -REACH, *-roast*, *-talk*, *-use*, *-water*, etc. **b.** This use is often found with pa. pples., when the other parts of the vb. occur with *over-* rarely, or not at all; as in *over-agitated*, *-assessed*, *-coached*, *-handicapped*, *-sprung*, etc. **7.** With adjs., as OVERACTIVE, *-bitter*, -BOLD, *-burdensome*, *-busy*, *-cold*, *-costly*, *-great*, *-happy*, *-hardy*, *-heavy*, *-high*, *-kind*, *-large*, *-late*, *-lavish*, *-loud*, *-officious*, *-proud*, *-rigid*, *-rigorous*, *-ripe*, *-slow*, *-strict*, *-subtle*, *-tedious*, *-weak*, etc. **b.** With pres. pples., forming ppl. adjs.; as *Overabounding*, etc. (Unlimited.) **c.** With pa. pples. in *-ed*, *-en*, etc., forming ppl. adjs., as *overacted*, *-civilized*, *-crowded*, OVERDONE, *-fraught*, etc. (Unlimited.) **d.** With adjs. in *-ed* from sbs.; as *over-brained*, *-garrisoned*, *-leisured*, etc. (Unlimited.) **8.** With sbs. **a.** Verbal sbs. in *-ing*; as *overabounding*, *-crowding*, *-doing*, *-feeding*. (Unlimited.) **b.** Nouns of action or condition allied to vbs.; as OVERCHARGE, -ISSUE; OVERACTION, -EXCITEMENT, *-haste*, *-love*, -PAYMENT, *-praise*, *-thought*, *-trust*, etc. (Unlimited.) **c.** Nouns of quality or state allied to adjs.; as OVERANXIETY, *-bitterness*, -CREDULITY, *-heat*, *-height*, *-length*, etc. (Unlimited.) **d.** Various sbs. denoting action, state, quality, etc.; as *over-care*, -CAUTION, *-cunning*, *-desire*, etc. **9.** With advs., simple or derived from adjs.; as OVERBOLDLY, *late*, -MUCH, *-soon*.

III. Combs. consisting of OVER *prep.* with object. These normally form advs. and adjs.; exceptionally they give rise to sbs. and vbs. The advs. are often written as two words, as *over all* or *overall*, *over board* or *overboard*.

O:ver-abou·nd, *v.* late ME. [OVER- II. 4, 6.] **1.** *intr.* To abound more, be more plentiful. *arch.* or *Obs.* **2.** To abound too much *with* or *in* something; of things, to be too plentiful 1597. So **O:ver-abu·ndance**, **-abu·ndant** *a.*, **-ly** *adv.*

Overact (ōᵘvəræ·kt), *v.* 1611. [OVER- II. 5, 6, 1, I. 13.] **1.** *intr.* To act in excess; to go too far in action. **2.** *trans.* To act (a part) with exaggeration; to overdo in acting 1631. †**3.** To go beyond in acting; to outdo –1661. †**4.** To actuate too powerfully; to overcome –1677.

1. You over-act, when you should under-do B. JONS. So **O:ver-a·ction**. **O:ver-a·ctive** *a.*, **-acti·vity**.

O·ver-a·ge (stress var.), *adj. phr.* 1886. [OVER *prep.* III. 4 and AGE *sb.* 3.] That is over a certain age or limit of age.

Overall (ōᵘ·vərǭl), *sb.* 1782. (OVER- III; lit. 'over everything'.) **1.** (Also *pl.*) A garment worn over the ordinary clothing as a protection against wet, dirt, etc. 1815. **2.** *pl.* Loose-fitting trousers of strong material, canvas, etc., worn as a protective outer garment; also formerly long leather or waterproof leggings 1782. Hence **O·veralled** *ppl. a.* wearing overalls.

†**Overa·ll**, *adv.* OE. [OVER- III.] **1.** Everywhere; in every direction –1596. **b.** In every-part; all over, all through –1590. **2.** Beyond everything; pre-eminently; especially –1687.

O·ver-all, *adj. phr.* 1894. [The phr. *over all* used attrib.] Including everything between the extreme points.

A..cruiser, with an 'o.' length of 335 ft. 1894.

Over and above, *phr.* late ME. [Pleonastic, for emphasis.] **A.** as *prep.* **1.** = OVER *prep.* III. 1. *rare.* 1449. **2.** = OVER *prep.* III. 3. 1521.

2. Ouer and aboue all that it had cost him 1585.

B. as *adv.* **1.** In addition, besides 1588. **2.** (Qualifying an adj.) Overmuch, too much, too. *Obs.* exc. *dial.* 1749. **b.** *attrib.* or as *adj.* Overmuch, too great, excessive (*rare*) 1865.

O:ver-a·nxious, *a.* 1741. [OVER- II. 7.] Excessively or unduly anxious, too anxious. So **O:ver-anxi·ety**, **-a·nxiously** *adv.*

Overarch (ōᵘvərā·ɹtʃ), *v.* 1667. [OVER- I. 1.] **1.** *trans.* To arch over, to bend over in or like an arch. **2.** *intr.* To form an arch overhead; to bend over as an arch 1720.

1. As the heavens over-arch the whole earth SPURGEON. Hence **Overa·rch** *sb.* an arch overhead.

O·ver-arm, *a.* 1864. *Cricket*, *Tennis.* = OVERHAND *a.* B. 2; also in *Swimming*.

Overawe (ōᵘvərǭ·), *v.* 1579. [OVER- I. 21.] *trans.* To restrain, control, or repress by awe; to keep in awe by superior influence.

Neither over-awed by Force, nor seduced by Faction 1683.

Overbalance (ōᵘvəɹbæ·lǎns), *sb.* 1641. [f. next.] **1.** Excess of weight, value, or amount; preponderance 1659. †**b.** *Commerce. spec.* Excess in the value of the exports over the imports of a country –1721. **2.** Something that outweighs or overbalances 1658.

Overbalance (ōᵘvəɹbæ·lǎns), *v.* 1586. [OVER- II. 3, I. 6.] **1.** *trans.* To do more than balance; to outweigh. Also *absol.* To preponderate. **2.** To destroy the equilibrium of; to capsize; *refl.* and *intr.* To lose one's balance 1834.

1. The expenses overbalanced the profit 1855. 2. You may o. and bring down the whole concern 1881.

O·verbank, *a.* 1879. [f. OVER *prep.* + BANK *sb.*[1]] *Artillery.* Applied to a kind of gun-carriage for muzzle-loading guns, so constructed as to allow of the gun's being fired over the parapet.

Overbear (ōᵘvəɹbēᵊ·ɹ), *v.* late ME. [OVER- I. 4, 6, II. 1.] †**1.** *trans.* To transfer, remove; to put away WYCLIF. **2.** To bear over or down by weight or physical force; to overthrow; to break or crush down 1535. **b.** *fig.* To overcome, put down, or repress, as by power, authority, or influence; to overpower, oppress 1565. **3.** To surpass in weight, importance, etc. 1712.

2. See how force oft ouerbereth ryght 1559. **b.** The barons ouerbear me with their pride MARLOWE. So **Overbea·rance**, overbearing behaviour. **Overbea·ring** *ppl. a.*, **-ly** *adv.*, **-ness**.

Overbe·nd, *v.* 1617. [OVER- I. 3, 1, II. 6.] **1.** (Only in *pple.*) **a.** *trans.* To bend (something) over or to one side. **b.** To bend over (something). **c.** *intr.* To bend or stoop over. **2.** *trans.* To bend too much or to excess 1624.

Overbid (ōᵘvəɹbi·d), *v.* 1616. [OVER- II. 5, 1.] †**1.** *intr.* To bid more than the value BEAUM. & FL. **2.** *trans.* To outbid 1645. **b.** To bid or offer more than the value of (a thing) 1646. **c.** *Bridge.* = OVERCALL *v.* 1909.

Overblow (ōᵘvəɹblōᵘ·), *v.* late ME. [f. OVER- I. 4, 6, 9, II. 6, 5 + BLOW *v.*[1]] **1.** *trans.* To blow (a thing) over the top of anything; to blow off or away. **2.** *intr.* Of a storm: To blow over, to pass away overhead; to abate in violence; hence *fig.* of danger, anger, etc. (Perf. tenses often with *be.*) late ME. **3.** *trans.* To blow (a thing) over; to blow down 1562. **4.** To blow over the surface of; to cover by blowing over (as sand or snow does). late ME. †**5.** *intr. Naut.* Of the wind: To blow too hard for topsails to be carried –1823. **6.** *trans. Mus.* To blow or play (a pipe or wind-instrument) with such force as to produce a harmonic or overtone instead of the fundamental note. Also *refl.* (of the pipe, etc.) 1852.

2. The tempest is o'erblown, the skies are clear DRYDEN.

Overboard (ōᵘ·vəɹbōᵊɹd), *adv.* OE. [f. OVER *prep.* IV. 1 + BOARD *sb.* Treated as one word from late in 18th c.] **1.** Over the side of a ship or boat, out of or from the ship into the water. **2.** *fig.* esp. in phr. *To throw o.*, to cast aside, discard, renounce 1641.

Overboil (ōᵘvəɹboi·l), *v.* 1584. [OVER- I. 5, II. 6.] **1.** *intr.* To boil over. Chiefly *fig.* 1611. **2.** *trans.* To boil too much 1584.

1. To keep the mind Deep in its fountain, lest it o. BYRON.

O·ver-bo·ld, *a.* 1530. [OVER- II. 7.] Too bold; presumptuous. Hence **O·ver-bo·ld·ly** *adv.*, **-ness**.

Overbri·m, *v.* 1607. [OVER- I. 5.] **1.** *intr.* To overflow at the brim; to brim over. (Said of the liquid or the vessel.) Mostly *fig.* **2.** *trans.* To flow over the brim of 1818.

1. If the pitcher shall o. with water SCOTT. 2. The liquor that o'erbrims the cup BROWNING. Hence **Overbri·mmed** *ppl. a.*, **Overbri·mming** *vbl. sb.* and *ppl. a.*

Overbuild (ōᵘvəɹbi·ld), *v.* Pa. t. and pple. overbuilt. 1601. [OVER- I. 1, 8, II. 6.] **1.** *trans.* To build over or upon. Chiefly *fig.* 1649. **2.** To build to excess 1642. **3.** To erect more buildings than are required upon (an area) 1601.

Overbu·rden, -bu·rthen, *sb.* 1579. [OVER- II. 8 d, I. 1.] **1.** Excessive burden; excess of burden. **2.** *Mining*, etc. The overlying waste which has to be removed in quarrying or mining, in order to get at the deposit worked 1839.

Overbu·rden, -bu·rthen, *v.* 1532. [OVER- II. 6.] *trans.* To overload, overcharge. Hence **Overbu·rdened, -bu·rthened** *ppl. a.*

Overbuy·, *v.* late ME. [OVER- II. 5, 2.] †**1.** *trans.* To buy at too high a price –1700. **2.** *refl.* and *intr.* To buy beyond one's means 1745.

Overca·ll, *v.* 1909. [OVER- II. 6.] *Bridge.* To bid more on one's hand than it is worth; to bid higher than a previous bid.

Over-ca·pitalize, *v.* 1890. [OVER- II. 6.] *trans.* To fix or estimate the capital of (a joint-stock company, etc.) at too high an amount. So **O:vercapitaliza·tion** 1882.

Overcarry (-kæ·ri), *v.* Now *rare.* late ME. [OVER- I. 10, 13, II. 5.] †**1.** *trans.* To carry over or across; to transport –1513. **b.** To carry beyond the proper point 1897. **2.** To carry too far, overdo; to do more than carry 1606. †**3.** *fig.* To carry (a person) beyond the bounds of moderation, or into error, etc.; to carry away. Also *absol.* –1648.

Overcast (ōᵘ·vəɹkast), *sb.* 1569. [f. OVERCAST *v.* or *ppl. a.*] **1.** A person or thing that is cast away; an outcast. *Obs.* exc. *dial.* **2.** Something cast or spread over; a coating; a cloud covering the sky or part of it 1686. **3.** *Mining.* A bridge which carries one subterranean air-passage over another 1867. **4.** *Needlework.* Overcast work 1891.

Overcast (ōᵘvəɹkɑ·st), *v.* ME. [OVER- I. 6, etc.] **1.** *trans.* To overthrow, overturn, cast down, upset (*lit.* and *fig.*). *Obs.* exc. *dial.* [OVER- I. 6.] **2.** To cast or throw (something) over or above something else. Now *rare.* [OVER- I. 1, 8.] ME. **3.** To cover or overspread (*with* something). Now *rare* in general sense. [OVER- I. 8.] late ME. **4.** *spec.* To cover or overspread with clouds, or with something that darkens or dulls the surface. Usu. in *pa. pple.* and of the weather. ME. **b.** *fig.* To overshadow, darken. late ME. **5.** *intr.* To become overspread with clouds; to become dark and gloomy. *Obs.* exc. *dial.* late ME. **6.** *Needlework.* To throw rough stitches over a raw edge or edges of cloth to prevent unravelling; to sew over and over; also, to strengthen or adorn such an edge by buttonhole- or blanket-stitch. [OVER- I. 5.] 1706. †**7.** To overestimate. [OVER- II. 5] –1765. †**8.** *Bowls.* (? *intr.*) To cast beyond the jack. (Also *pass.* in same sense.) [OVER- I. 13.] –1706. Hence **O·vercast** *ppl. a.* 1569.

4. A dark Cloud..overcasts the Air DE FOE. **b.** Stung to the soul, o'ercast with holy dread POPE.

O:ver-cau·tion. 1714. [OVER- II. 8 d.] Excessive caution.

O·ver-cau·tious, *a.* 1706. [OVER- II. 7.] More cautious than is needful, too cautious. Hence **Over-cau·tious-ly** *adv.*, **-ness.**

Overcharge (ōᵘvəɹ,tʃāɹdʒ), *sb.* 1611. [OVER- II. 8 b.] **1.** An excessive charge or load; an excess. **2.** The act of overcharging; an exorbitant charge 1662.

Overcharge (ōᵘvəɹ,tʃā·ɹdʒ), *v.* late ME. [OVER- II. 6; cf. F. *surcharger.*] **1.** *trans.* To load, fill, furnish, or supply to excess (*with* something). **b.** *fig.* To exaggerate, overdo. Now *rare* or *arch.* 1711. †**2.** To lay an excessive burden upon; to oppress; to overbear by superior force –1771. †**b.** To accuse too much or extravagantly –1636. **3** *spec.* To put to too great expense; now, to charge (any one) too much ME. **b.** To charge (so much) more than is justly due 1667.

1. The said Cormucke having..over-charged one of his Pistols 1681. **b.** A little overcharging the likeness ADDISON. **3.** No one likes to be overcharged for what he buys (*mod.*). **b.** The 20 pounds overcharged for the widows 1733.

O·vercheck, *a.* (*sb.*[1]) 1875. [f. OVER- I. 5 + CHECK *sb.*[1]] In *o. rein*, a rein passing over a horse's head between the ears, so as to pull upward upon the bit; *o. bridle*, a bridle having an overcheck rein.

O·vercheck, *sb.*[2] 1923. [f. OVER- I. 8 + CHECK *sb.*[2]] A pattern in which a check is superimposed upon another design.

Overcloud (-klau·d), *v.* 1592. [OVER- I. 8.] **1.** *trans.* To cloud over; to overspread or cover with or as with a cloud or clouds. **2.** *fig.* To cast a shadow over, render gloomy; to obscure 1593. **3.** *intr.* To become overclouded; to cloud over 1862.

Overcoat (ōᵘ·vəɹkōᵘt). 1848. [OVER- I. 8 c.] A large coat worn over the ordinary clothing; a great-coat, top-coat.

Overcolour (-kʋ·ləɹ), *v.* 1823. [OVER- II. 6.] *trans.* To colour too highly (usu. *fig.*); to represent too strongly. So **O:verco·louring** *vbl. sb.*

Overcome (ōᵘvəɹkʋ·m), *v.* [OE. *ofercuman*, f. *ofer-*, OVER- and *cuman*, to COME.] †**1.** *trans.* To come upon, reach, overtake. Only OE. [OVER- I. 7.] **2.** *trans.* To overpower, defeat, get the better of in any contest or struggle. Since 17th c. chiefly with non-material object. [OVER- I. 2, 21.] OE. †**b.** To win (a battle) –1585. **c.** *absol.* or *intr.* To gain the victory ME. **3.** Of some physical or mental force or influence: To overpower; to exhaust, render helpless; to affect excessively with emotion. Chiefly in *pass.*; const. *with*, rarely *by*. In *pa. pple.* occas. (euphem.) = overcome by liquor, intoxicated. [OVER- I. 2, 21.] OE. †**b.** To dominate, possess (the mind, etc.) (*rare*) –1607. †**c.** *fig.* To surpass the capacity of, overflow –1708. **4.** To get over, surmount (a difficulty); to recover from (a blow, etc.) [OVER- I. 5] ME. **5.** To go beyond, exceed, surpass (in quality, measure, etc.). Now *arch.* [OVER- I. 13.] ME. †**6.** To get through; to master, accomplish. [OVER- I. 17.] –1697. **7.** To traverse (a road, etc.) *arch.* ME. **8.** To overrun; to cover. Now *rare.* [OVER- I. 9.] late ME. †**b.** To come over suddenly SHAKS. **9.** *intr.* To 'come to', 'come round' from a swoon. Now *dial.* [OVER- I. 17.] late ME.

2. He..that is slain, is Overcome, but not Conquered HOBBES. **3.** The architect was too much overcome to speak DICKENS. Overcome by sickness 1849. **5.** The idols they had..did even o. the Egyptian idols in number 1643. **6.** I am extremely glad.. to find that you have o. your long journey 1652.

O·ver-co·nfident, *a.* 1617. [OVER- II. 7.] Too confident. So **O·ver-con·fidence,** excess of confidence. **O·ver-con·fidently** *adv.*

O:ver-corre·ct, *v.* 1867. [OVER- II. 3.] *Optics. trans.* To correct (a lens) for chromatic aberration to such an extent that the focus of the red rays lies beyond that of the violet. Opp. to *under-correct.*

Overcount (-kau·nt), *v.* 1593. [OVER- II. 1, 5.] **1.** *trans.* To outnumber 1606. **2.** To overestimate 1593.

O·ver-cre·dulous, *a.* 1605. [OVER- II. 7.] Too credulous, too ready to believe. So **O·ver-credu·lity,** too great credulity.

Overcrow (ōᵘvəɹkrōᵘ·), *v.* 1562. [OVER- I. 2, 21.] *trans.* To crow over; to exult or triumph over.

Overcrowd (ōᵘvəɹkrau·d), *v.* 1766. [OVER- II. 6.] **1.** *trans.* To crowd to excess. **2.** *intr.* To crowd together in too great a number 1899.

O·ver-cu·rious, *a.* 1561. [OVER- II. 7.] †**a.** Too careful, fastidious, or particular; **b.** Too inquisitive. Hence **O·ver-cu·rious-ly** *adv.*, **-ness.**

Overda·re, *v.* 1586. [OVER- II. 6, 1, I. 21.] **1.** *intr.* To be too daring; to dare too much. †**2.** *trans.* To surpass in or overcome by daring –1611. So **O·verda·ring** *vbl. sb.*

O·ver-dea·r, *a.* 1483. [OVER- II 4, 6] Excessively or exceedingly dear (in various senses); too costly.

Overde·ck, *v.* 1509. [OVER- I. 8, II. 6.] †**1.** *trans.* To 'deck' or cover over –1599. **2.** To deck or adorn to excess 1712.

O·ver-de·licate, *a.* 1630. [OVER- II. 7.] Too delicate. So **O·ver-de·licacy,** too great delicacy.

O:ver-deve·lop, *v.* 1869. [OVER- II. 6.] *trans.* To develop too greatly or to excess; *spec.* in *Photogr.*: see DEVELOP *v.* 5. So **O:ver-deve·lopment** 1842.

O:ver-discha·rge, *v.* 1893. [OVER- II. 6.] *trans.* To discharge too greatly; *spec.* in *Electr.*, to discharge an accumulator or storage battery beyond a certain limit, an operation injurious to the battery. So **Over-discha·rge** *sb.* the act of over-discharging or fact of being over-discharged.

Overdo (ōᵘvəɹdū·), *v.* [OE. *oferdōn*, f. *ofer-*, OVER- + DO *v.*] **1.** *trans.* To do to excess or too much; to exaggerate. **2.** *intr.* or *absol.* To do too much; to exceed the proper limit. late ME. **3.** *trans.* To carry too far 1623. **4.** To cook (food) too much. (Usu. in pa. pple. *overdone.*) 1683. **5.** To overtax the strength of; to exhaust, overcome 1822. **6.** To outdo, excel. Now *arch.* 1625.

1. Any thing so ouer-done, is from the purpose of Playing SHAKS. **2.** Some can do but they o. 1539. **5.** At night ran down too fast, and overdid myself 1858.

Overdone (ōᵘ:vəɹdʋ·n: stress var.), *ppl. a.* OE. [pa. pple. of prec.] Done too much (in various senses of OVERDO *v.*); exaggerated; overcooked; exhausted; overcome.

Overdose (ōᵘ·vəɹdōᵘs), *sb.* 1690. [OVER- II. 8.] An excessive dose, too large a dose.

Overdo·se, *v.* 1727. [OVER- II. 6.] †**1.** *trans.* To administer (medicine) in too large a dose –1777. **2.** To dose (a person) to excess; to give too large a dose to; also *transf.* 1758.

O·verdraft (-draft). 1878. [OVER- II. 6.] *Banking.* The action of overdrawing an account; the amount by which a draft exceeds the balance against which it is drawn.

O·verdraught, -draft (-draft). 1884. [OVER- I. 1.] A draught passing over or admitted from above a fire, furnace, kiln, etc.

Overdraw (ōᵘvəɹdrǭ·), *v.* late ME. [OVER- I. 10, 4, II. 6.] **I.** †**1.** *trans.* To draw over or across; (Separable comb.) late ME. only. †**b.** To draw off into another vessel –1703. †**2.** *intr.* To draw or move over or across; to pass away. late ME. only.

II. 1. *Banking.* To draw money in excess of the amount which stands to one's credit, or is at one's disposal. Also *absol.*, to make an overdraft. 1734. **2.** To exaggerate or overdo in drawing, depicting, or describing 1844.

1. My finances are not only exhausted, but overdrawn COWPER. Don't o...more than you can help 1890.

Overdre·ss, *v.* 1706. [OVER- II. 6.] **1.** *trans.* To dress to excess. Also *intr.* for *refl.* **2.** To dress or cook too much 1775.

Overdue (ōᵘ·vəɹdiū·; stress var.), *a.* 1845. [OVER- II. 3 b.] More than due; past the time when due.

O. bonds for the payment of money 1845. The train is half an hour o. (*mod.*).

O·ver-ea·ger, *a.* 1575. [OVER- II. 7.] Too eager; excessively eager or keen. Hence **O·ver-ea·ger-ly** *adv.*, **-ness.**

O·ver-ea·rnest, *a.* 1586. [OVER- II. 7.] Too earnest. Hence **O·ver-ea·rnest-ly** *adv.*, **-ness.**

Overeat (ōᵘvərī·t), *v.* 1599. [OVER- II. 6.] To eat too much, eat to excess. *intr.* or (usu.) *refl.*

Over-e·stimate, *v.* 1840. [OVER- II. 6.] To estimate too highly; to value at too high a rate. So **O·ver-e·stimate** *sb.* too high an estimate. **O·ver-estima·tion,** the action of over-estimating.

O:ver-exci·te, *v.* 1825. [OVER- II. 6.] *trans.* To excite too much. So **O·ver-excitabi·lity; -exci·table** *a.*; **-exci·tement.**

O:ver-exe·rt, *v.* 1817. [OVER- II. 6.] *trans.* To exert too much; usu. *refl.* So **O·ver-exe·rtion.**

O:ver-expo·se, *v.* 1869. [OVER- II. 6.] *trans.* Too expose too much; *spec.* in *Photogr.* to expose (a sensitized plate or film) to the light too long. So **O·ver-expo·sure.**

Overfall (ōᵘ·vəɹfǭl), *sb.* 1542. [OVER- I. 5, 6.] **1.** *Naut.* A turbulent surface of water with short breaking waves, caused by a strong current or tide setting over a submarine ridge or shoal, or by the meeting of contrary currents. **2.** A sudden drop in the sea-bottom 1798. †**3.** A waterfall in a river, a cataract or rapid –1613. **4.** A structure to allow the overflow of water from a canal or a lock on a river, when the water reaches a certain level 1791.

Overfall (ōᵘvəɹfǭ·l), *v. arch. rare.* [OE. *oferfeallan*; see OVER- I. 7, 6.] **1.** *trans.* To fall upon or over ME. **b.** To fall upon, attack OE. **2.** *intr.* To fall over 1530.

Overfault (ōᵘ·vəɹfǭlt). 1883. [OVER- I. 3 + FAULT *sb.* 9.] *Geol.* A fault of which the inclination is towards the upthrow side (hence also called *inverted* or *reverse* fault).

Over-fee·d, *v.* 1609. [OVER- II. 6.] **1.** *trans.* To feed to excess. **2.** *intr.* (for *refl.*) To take too much food 1774. So **O·ver-fe·d** (stress var.) *ppl. a.* fed to excess 1579.

Overfi·ll, *v.* [OE. *oferfyllan*, f. *ofer-* OVER- II. 3 + *fyllan* to FILL.] **1.** *trans.* To fill to overflowing. **2.** *intr.* To become full to overflowing 1615.

Over-floa·t, *v.* 1601. [OVER- I. 9, 1.] †**1.** *trans.* To overflow –1697. **2.** To float over (*lit.* and *fig.*) 1658.

Overflou·rish, *v.* 1601. [OVER- II. 6, I. 8.] **1.** *trans.* To cover with blossom or verdure 1601. †**2.** To embellish too greatly –1716.

1. *Twel. N.* III. iv. 404.

Overflow (ōᵘ·vəɹflōᵘ), *sb.* 1589. [OVER- I. 9, 5.] **1.** The act or fact of overflowing; an inundation, a flood. **2.** A flowing over from a vessel that is too full; that which flows over (*lit.* and *fig.*) 1640. **3.** Such a quantity as runs over; excess, superfluity 1589. **4.** Short for *o.-pipe* or *-drain*, a pipe or drain for carrying off excess of water 1895. **5.** *attrib.*, as *o. meeting* (of people that cannot be accommodated at the main place of meeting), *population*; *basin*, *pipe* 1837.

2. The o. of Teutons came very early thither 1852. **3.** Thy ouerflow of good, conuerts to bad SHAKS.

Overflow (ōuvəɪflōu·), *v.* *Pa. pple.* **-flowed,** †**-flown.** [OE. *oferflōwan*; see OVER- I. 9, 5.] **I.** *trans.* **1.** To flow over; to flood, inundate. **2.** *transf.* and *fig.* To pass or spread over like a flood 1533. **3.** To flow over (the brim, banks, or sides) 1548. **b.** To cause to overflow. Chiefly *fig.* 1667. †**4.** To overflow with, pour out (*rare*) -1598.

1. Trinitie Colledge greene..is in the winter time overflowne with water 1585. 2. So they overflowed his house, smoked his cigars, and drank his health R. KIPLING. 4. *Merry W.* II. ii. 157.

II. *intr.* **1.** To flow over the sides or brim by reason of fullness. †Also *transf.* and *fig.* OE. **b.** To remove from one part to another owing to want of room, etc. 1858. **2.** To be so full that the contents run over the brim. late ME.

1. This tyme at Rome the Ryver of Tiber overflowed exceedingly 1560. b. The crowd overflowed into the adjoining gardens (*mod.*). 2. *fig.* To make the comming houre oreflow with ioy SHAKS.

O·verflowing, *ppl. a.* OE. [-ING [2].] That overflows: in the senses of the vb. Hence **Overflow·ing·ly** *adv.*, **-ness.**

Overflu·sh, *v.* 1581. [OVER- II. 6, I. 8.] *trans.* **a.** To flush too much. **b.** To flush over, cover with a flush (*rare*). So **O·verflu·sh** *a.* too flush.

Overfly (ōuvəɪflai·), *v.* 1558. [f. OVER- I. 4, etc. + FLY *v.*[1]] **1.** *trans.* To cross or pass over by flying. [OVER- I. 4.] **b.** To fly beyond. Also *refl.* 1854. **2.** To surpass in flight; to fly higher, faster, or farther than. [OVER- II. 1.] 1592. †**3.** To fly (a hawk) too much. [OVER- II. 6.] -1616.

2. Out-stripping crows that strive to over-fly them SHAKS.

Overfold (ōu·vəɪfōuld), *sb.* 1883. [f. OVER- I. 3, 6 + FOLD *sb.*[2], after G. *überfaltung*.] *Geol.* A fold of strata in which the axes of the component anticline and syncline have both been tilted or pushed over beyond the vertical, so that the strata involved in the middle third of the fold are turned upside down. (Also *inclined, overturned, inverted*, or *reflexed fold*.)

Overfold (ōuvəɪfōu·ld), *v.* late ME. [OVER- I. 8, 3, 6.] **1.** *trans.* To fold over, or so as to cover. **2.** *Geol.* Of folded strata: In *pass.* To be pushed over beyond the vertical, so as to overhang or overlie the strata on the other side of the axis: see prec. 1883.

O·ver-fo·nd, *a.* 1585. [OVER- II. 7.] Too fond. **1.** Too silly. *Obs.* exc. *dial.* **2.** Too affectionate. Const. *of.* 1611. Hence **O·ver-fo·nd·ly** *adv.*, **-ness.**

O·verfo·rward, *a.* 1631. [OVER- II. 7.] Too forward. So **O·verfo·rward·ly** *adv.*, **-ness** 1593.

O·verfree·, *a.* 1639. [OVER- II. 7.] Too free. So **O·verfree·dom,** too great freedom. **O·verfree·ly** *adv.*

Overfreight (-frē·t), *v.* 1530. [OVER- II. 6.] *trans.* To overload. So **O·verfreight** *sb.* an overload.

O·verfu·ll, *a.* [OE. *oferfull*; see OVER- II. 3, 7.] Excessively full, too full. Hence **O·verfu·llness.**

Overga·ng, *v.* Now *Sc.* and *n. dial.* [OE. *ofergangan*; see OVER- I. 1, 21, 9, 13.] **1.** *trans.* To overpower. **2.** To go over, overrun ME. **3.** To go beyond, exceed 1737.

Overget (ōuvəɪge·t), *v.* ME. [OVER- I. 14, 5.] **1.** *trans.* To overtake. Now only *dial.* **2.** To get over, recover from the effects of (an illness, etc.). 1803.

Overgild (ōuvəɪgi·ld), *v.* [OE. *ofergyldan*: see OVER- I. 8 and GILD *v.*] *trans.* To gild over, cover with gilding; *fig.* to tinge with a golden colour. Chiefly in *pa. pple.* **overgi·lt.**

†**Overgi·ve,** *v.* 1444. [f. OVER- + GIVE *v.*] †**1.** *trans.* To give over or up, hand over -1711. †**2.** *intr.* To give over, desist -1592.

†**Overgla·nce,** *v.* 1588. [OVER- I. 16.] *trans.* To glance over.

I will ouerglance the superscript SHAKS.

Overgo (ōuvəɪgōu·), *v.* [OE. *ofergān*; see OVER-.] **I.** *trans.* †**1.** To come upon suddenly; to overtake, catch [OVER- I. 7, 14.] -1581. **2.** To pass over (a wall, river, boundary, etc.); to cross. *Obs.* exc. *dial.* †Also *fig.* [OVER- I. 5, 12.] OE. †**3.** To surmount. [OVER- I. 1.] -1619. **4.** *fig.* To go beyond, exceed, excel. [OVER- I. 13.] ME. **5.** To overpower, oppress, overwhelm. Now *dial.* [OVER- I. 21.] ME. †**6.** To go or spread over so as to cover. [OVER- I. 8, 9.] -1634. **7.** To overrun, overflow. Now *dial.* [OVER- I. 9.] OE. **8.** To travel through, traverse. [OVER- I. 9, 16.] ME. †**9.** To pass, live through (time); also, of time, to pass over (a person). [OVER- I. 17, 4.] -1600. †**10.** To outstrip, overtake. [OVER- II. 1.] -1635. †**11.** To pass over omit. [OVER- I. 5.] -1622.

4. Abhorring to make the punishment o. the offence SIDNEY. 8. *L. L. L.* v. ii. 196.

II. *intr.* To go or pass by; to pass over or away; to pass (in time). Now *dial.* [OVER- I. 4.] OE.

Overgo·vern, *v.* 1850. [OVER- II. 6.] *trans.* To govern too much. So **Overgo·vernment** 1861.

O·ver-gree·dy, *a.* [OE. *ofergrǣdig*; see OVER- II. 7.] Too greedy, excessively greedy. So **O·ver-gree·dily** *adv.*

O·verground, *a.* 1879. [OVER- III.] Situated over or aboveground; opp. to *underground.*

Overgrow (ōuvəɪgrōu·), *v.* late ME. [OVER- I. 8, etc.] **1.** *trans.* To grow over, to cover with growth; to overrun, overspread. (Now chiefly in *pa. pple.*) Also *transf.* and *fig.* **2.** To grow over so as to choke; to grow more vigorously than. [OVER- I. 21, II. 1.] 1523. **3.** *intr.* To grow too large; to increase unduly. (Perfect tenses often with *be.*) [OVER- II. 5.] 1490. **4.** *trans.* To grow over, above, or beyond; to outgrow (clothes, etc.). [OVER- I. 13.] 1536.

2. The tares ouergrow the wheat 1623. 4. Phr. *To o. oneself*, to grow beyond one's strength, proper size, etc.

O·vergrowth. 1602. [OVER- II. 8, I. 8.] **1.** Excessive or too rapid growth; the result of this, over-luxuriance or abundance. **2.** A growth over or upon something; an accretion 1883.

Overhair (ōu·vəɪhēəɪ). 1879. [OVER- I. 8.] In fur-bearing quadrupeds, the long straight hair that grows over or beyond the fur.

Overhand, *adv.* and *a.* 1579. [f. OVER *prep.* and *adv.* + HAND *sb.*] **A.** *adv.* (*o·verha·nd*). †**1.** Over, upside down. †**2.** Out of hand, aside -1816. **3.** With the hand over or above the object which it grasps; in *Cricket, Tennis*, etc. (with ref. to bowling, etc.), with the hand raised above the shoulder 1861. **4.** *Mining.* From below upwards (in ref. to the working or 'stoping' of a vein). **5.** *Needlework.* In *to sew o.* = OVERSEW.

B. *adj.* (*o·verhand*). †**1.** Characterized by bringing the hand from above downwards -1656. **2.** *Cricket, Tennis*, etc. Of bowling, etc.: Done with the hand raised above the shoulder 1870. **3.** *Mining.* Of the working of a vein: Performed from below upwards. **4.** *O. knot*: a simple knot made by passing the end of a rope, string, etc., over the standing part and through the loop or bight so formed 1840.

O·verhang, *sb.* 1864. [f. next.] The fact or extent of overhanging; a jutting out; also *concr.* an overhanging or projecting part. Chiefly *Naut.* the projection of the upper parts of a ship, fore and aft, beyond the water line.

Overhang (ōuvəɪhæ·ŋ), *v.* Pa. t. and pple. **overhung.** 1599. [OVER- I. 1, 3, 8.] **1.** *trans.* To hang over (something); to be suspended above; to project or jut out above. **b.** *fig.* To impend over; to threaten 1653. **2.** *intr.* To hang over; to project beyond the base; to jut out above 1667. **3.** To support from above 1887.

1. Ascend the hill which overhangs the city JOWETT. Craggie cliff, that overhung Still as it rose MILT.

O·ver-ha·rd, *a.* and *adv.* 1530. [OVER- II. 7, 9.] Too hard; excessively hard. So **Over-ha·rden** *v.* **O·ver-ha·rd·ly** *adv.*, **-ness.**

O·ver-ha·sty, *a.* 1571. [OVER- II. 7.] Too hasty; rash. So **O·ver-ha·sti·ly** *adv.*, **-ness.**

Overhaul (ōuvəɪhǭ·l), *v.* 1626. [OVER- I. 5, 14.] **1.** *Naut. trans.* To slacken (a rope) by pulling in the opposite direction to that in which it is drawn in hoisting; to release and separate the blocks of (a tackle) in this way. **2.** *Naut.* and *gen.* To pull asunder in order to examine in detail; to examine thoroughly (e.g. with a view to repairs, etc.) 1705. **3.** *Naut.* and *gen.* To overtake, come up with, gain upon 1793.

2. His own expressions of 'overhaul', for *investigate*, and 'attackable', are in the lowest style of colloquial slang DE QUINCEY. The drains..are being overhauled 1884. Hence **O·verhaul** *sb.* a thorough examination or scrutiny, esp. with a view to repairs. **Overha·uling** *vbl. sb.*

Overhead, *adv.*, *a.* OE. [*Over head* written as one wd.; see OVER- III.] **A.** *adv.* (*overhea·d*). Above one's head; aloft; up in the air or sky, *esp.* in or near the zenith; on the floor or story above 1532. **b.** So as to be completely submerged or immersed; also *fig.* (See OVER *prep.* 3.) 1653.

b. Her Husband was over-head in Debt 1706.

B. *adj.* (*o·verhead*). **1.** Placed or situated overhead, or at some distance above the ground. (Also applied to driving mechanism placed above the object driven, or to a machine having such mechanism.) 1874. **2.** Applicable to one with another; 'all-round'; general, average 1891.

1. *O. gear*, driving-gear above the object driven. *O. steam-engine*, an engine in which the cylinder is above the crank, the thrust motion being downward. 2. **O. charges, costs,** etc. (also **O·verheads** *sb. pl.*), such general expenses of a works, institution, or the like, as rent, lighting, heating, clerical establishment, etc., which cannot be charged up to any particular branch of the work.

Overhear (ōuvəɪhī·əɪ), *v.* [OE. *oferhīeran*; see OVER- I. 15. In sense 2 a new comb. in 16th c.] †**1.** *trans.* Not to hearken to; to disregard. OE. only. **2.** To hear (speech, etc.) that is not intended to reach one's ears; to hear (a speaker) without his intention or knowledge 1549.

Overheat (ōuvəɪhī·t), *v.* late ME. [OVER- II. 6.] *trans.* To heat too much, heat to excess, make too hot. Also *intr.* for *pass.* (*mod.*)

Overhouse (ōu·vəɪhaus), *a.* 1859. [f. OVER *prep.*, OVER- III. + HOUSE *sb.*] Passing over and supported by the roofs of houses (instead of posts); said of telegraph or telephone wires.

Overhung (stress var.), *ppl. a.* 1708. [f. OVERHANG *v.*] **1.** Placed so as to jut out above. **2.** Having something hanging over it 1845. **3.** Suspended or supported from above 1887. **4.** [OVER- I. 18] That has been hung too long, as meat, etc. 1895.

O·ver-indu·lge, *v.* 1741. [OVER- II. 6.] *trans.* To indulge to excess. Also *intr.* for *refl.* So **O·ver-indu·lgence,** †**-ency** 1631; also **O·ver-indu·lgent** *a.* 1728.

O·ver-info·rm, *v.* 1681. [OVER- II. 6.] *trans.* To inform, animate, or actuate to excess.

Over-i·ssue, *v.* 1837. [OVER- II. 6.] *trans.* To issue in excess; e.g. to issue notes, stocks, shares, etc., beyond the authorized amount or the issuer's ability to pay. So **O·ver-i·ssue** *sb.* an issue in excess.

Overjoy (ōuvəɪdʒoi·), *v.* late ME. [OVER- I. 1 (*c*), II. 4, 6.] †**1.** To rejoice over (tr. L. *supergaudere*) WYCLIF. **2.** *trans.* To transport with joy or gladness. (Now usu. in *pa. pple.*) 1571. **b.** *intr.* To rejoice too much 1720. Hence **Overjoy·ed** *ppl. a.*

Overju·mp, *v.* 1608. [OVER- I. 5, II. 5, 2.] **1.** *trans.* and *intr.* To jump over; *fig.* to pass over; to transcend. **2.** *trans.* To jump too far over. **b.** *refl.* To jump too far for one's strength. 1856.

O·ver-king, o·verking. ME. [OVER- I. 2 b.] *Hist.* A superior king; a king who is the superior of other rulers called kings.

Over-labour (-lē·bəɪ), *v.* 1530. **1.** *trans.* To overwork. [OVER- II. 2, 6.] **2.** To labour excessively at; to elaborate to excess. [OVER- II. 6.] 1588.

Overla·de, *v.* late ME. [f. OVER- I. 21, II. 6 + LADE *v.*] *trans.* To load with too heavy a burden, to overload. Hence **Overla·den** *ppl. a.*

O·verland, *sb. local.* 1769. Land held by a particular tenure in the west of England (see N.E.D.).

Overla·nd, over land, *adv.* 1589. [prop. two wds.; often hyphened or written as one.] Over or across land; by land (as opp. to 'by sea').

Overland (ōu·vəɪlænd), *a.* 1800. [attrib. use of prec.; see OVER- III.] Proceeding or lying over or across land; performed by land; for or connected with a journey over land.

O. route, a route entirely or partly by land; *spec.*

(1) the route to India by the Mediterranean; (2) in America, any route westward from the Atlantic to the Pacific across the continent.

O·verlander. *Australia.* 1843. One who journeyed overland from one Australian colony or capital to another (*obs.* exc. *Hist.*); *spec.* one taking cattle from one colony to another or over a long distance.

Overlap (ōu·vəılæp), *sb.* 1813. [f. next.] A partial superposition or coincidence; the part or place at which one edge or thing overlaps another; *spec.* in *Geol.* (see next, 3). **b.** *attrib.* *O. joint*, a joint in which one edge overlaps the other.

Overlap (ōuvəılæ·p), *v.* 1726. [f. OVER- I. 8 + LAP *v.*[2]] **1.** *trans.* To lap over; to overlie partially. Also *fig.* Also *absol.* or *intr.* **2.** To cover and extend beyond (*lit.* and *fig.*) 1802. **3.** *Geol.* Said of a newer formation which extends beyond the area or edge of the older one on which it mainly rests, and thus partly overlies a still older one below that: *trans.* with either of the lower formations as obj., or *absol.* 1832. **4.** To lap or ripple over (see LAP *v.*[1] 3, 4) 1863.

Overlay (ōu·vəılē), *sb.* 1725. [f. next; see OVER- I. 8.] **1.** A cravat, necktie. *Sc.* **2.** *Printing.* A piece of paper cut to the required shape and pasted over the impression-surface of a printing-press in order to make the impression darker in particular places, as in a woodcut 1824. **3.** Something laid as a covering over something else; esp. a coverlet, a small cloth laid upon a table-cloth, etc.; also *fig.* 1794.

Overlay (ōuvəılē·), *v.* *Pa. t.* and *pple.* **overlai·d.** ME. [f. OVER- + LAY *v.*] **I.** To lay over. **1.** *trans.* To lay or place over, above, or upon something else (*rare*). [OVER- I. 1, 8.] 1570. **b.** To surmount or span with something extending over (*rare*). [OVER- I. 1.] 1611. **2.** To cover the surface of (a thing) *with* something spread over it. [OVER- I. 8.] **b.** *Printing.* To put an overlay upon (see prec. 2); also *absol.* †**3.** To cover superfluously or excessively; *spec.* to overstock (a pasture *with* cattle, etc.). [OVER- I. 8, II. 6.] –1733.

1. b. To..o. With bridges rivers proud MILT. 2. The defect..of being overlaid with drapery SIR J. REYNOLDS. 3. A tree overlaid with blossoms 1633.

II. To lie over. **1.** To lie over (something else); more prop. OVERLIE. [OVER- I. 8.] late ME. **2.** *spec.* = OVERLIE 2 a. 1557. **3.** To affect like or as with a superincumbent weight. [OVER- I. 8, 21.] †**a.** To press severely upon; to distress; to overwhelm, overpower –1769. **b.** To press upon so as to impede the working or activity of; to weigh down; to smother, stifle 1609. **4.** To conceal or obscure as if by covering up 1719. **5.** *Naut.* To cross the cable or anchor of another vessel so as to cause chafing or obstruction. [OVER- I. 10.] 1796.

1. Loose shingle and boulders overlaid the mountain TYNDALL. 2. Sowes Ouerlaie and squise to death their pigges 1573. 3. a. We are on euery syde ouerlayed with aduersitee COVERDALE. b. I have been overlayd with businesse 1663. 4. Nor wou'd these scenes in empty words abound Or o. the sentiment with sound 1719. Hence **O·verlayer**, one who or that which overlays or overlies something.

Overlay·ing, *vbl. sb.* late ME. [f. OVERLAY *v.* + -ING[1].] The action of OVERLAY *v.*; *concr.* a covering.

Overleaf (ōu·vəılī·f), *adv.* 1843. [prop. two wds., OVER *prep.* and LEAF *sb.*] On the other side of the leaf (of paper).

Overleap (ōuvəılī·p), *v.* [OE. *oferhlēapan.*] **1.** *trans.* To leap over, across, or to the other side of. [OVER- I. 5.] **2.** *trans.* To pass over, omit, skip. (Now only as consciously *fig.* from 1.) OE. †**3.** To surpass in leaping; also *fig.* [OVER- II. 1.] –1603. **b.** *refl.* To leap too far. *Macb.* I. vii. 27.

1. *Macb.* I. iv. 49. 2. Whatever objection..he finds too heavy to remove, he over-leaps it 1641.

Overleather (ōu·vəıleðəı). late ME. [f. OVER *adj.* + LEATHER.] The upper leather of a shoe.

O·ver-li·beral, *a.* 1601. [OVER- II. 7.] Too liberal. So **O·ver-libera·lity.** **O·ver-li·berally** *adv.*

Overlie (ōuvəıləi·), *v.* *Pa. t.* **overlay;** *pa. pple.* **overlain.** [Early ME. *oferliggen*; see OVER- I. 8. In 17th–18th c. displaced by OVERLAY; reintroduced in 19th c.] **1.** *trans.* To lie over or upon; in *Geol.* said of a stratum resting directly on another. **2.** *spec.* **a.** To smother by lying upon ME. †**b.** To lie with (a woman) –1480. †**3.** *fig.* To oppress –1530.

2. The old idiot wretch Screamed feebly, like a baby overlain MRS. BROWNING.

O·ver-lip. Now *dial.* ME. [orig. two wds., ME. *overe lippe.*] The upper lip.

Overlive (ōuvəıli·v), *v.* Now *rare.* [OE. *oferlibban*, f. *ofer-* OVER- I. 18 + LIVE *v.*] *trans.* = OUTLIVE 1. Also *fig.* of things. **b.** *intr.* To survive OE. **c.** *refl.* To live too long 1861.

All the daies of yᵉ elders that ouerliued Ioshua 1551 *Josh.* xxiv. 31. **b.** MILT. *P. L.* x. 773.

Overload (ōu·vəılōud), *sb.* 1645. [OVER- II. 8.] An excessive load or burden; too great a load.

Overload (ōuvəılōu·d), *v.* 1553. [OVER- II. 6.] *trans.* To put an excessive load on, to overburden; to overcharge (a gun).

O·ver-lo·ng, *adv.* and *adj.* late ME. [f. OVER- II. 9, 7 + LONG *a.*[1], LONG *adv.*] **A.** *adv.* For too long a time. **B.** *adj.* Too long. late ME.

Overlook (ōu·vəıluk), *sb.* 1584. [OVER- I. 16, 7, 5.] **1.** A glance or survey; inspection or superintendence. **b.** A look down from a height; a place that affords such a view 1861. **c.** The tropical leguminous twining plant, *Canavalia ensiformis* 1837. **2.** An oversight 1887.

Overlook (ōuvəılu·k), *v.* late ME. [f. OVER- + LOOK *v.*] **1.** *trans.* To look over the top of, so as to see beyond. [OVER- I. 5.] 1559. **b.** *fig.* To overtop. *Obs.* or *rare.* 1567. **2.** To look over and beyond and thus not see; to fail to see or observe; to pass over without notice; to ignore. (The chief current sense.) [OVER- I. 5.] **3.** To look (a thing) over or through; to examine, inspect, survey; to peruse. Now *rare* or *arch.* [OVER- I. 16.] late ME. **4.** To look down upon; to survey from a higher position. [OVER- I. 7.] late ME. **b.** Of a place: To afford or command a view of 1632. †**5.** *fig.* To 'look down upon'; to despise; to slight –1794. **6.** To superintend, oversee. [OVER- I. 7.] late ME. **7.** To look upon with the 'evil eye'; to bewitch. (The popular word for this.) 1596.

1. The wall was just too high to be overlooked HAWTHORNE. **b.** The laughing Nectar overlook'd the Lid DRYDEN. 2. The French..found it prudent to o. this insult HUME. 3. *Two Gent.* I. ii. 50. 4. Have you no more manners than to o. a man when he's a writing? DRYDEN. **b.** The brow of the hill overlooking the Nairn valley 1895. 6. To..o. the other servants 1830. 7. Vilde worme, thou wast ore-look'd euen in thy birth SHAKS. Hence **O·verlooker,** one who overlooks; a spy; an overseer.

Overlord (ōu·vəılǭıd), *sb.* ME. [OVER- I. 2 b.] A lord superior; one who is the lord of other lords or rulers. Hence **Overlo·rd** *v. rare*, to lord it over; to rule as an o. **O·verlo:rdship,** the position or authority of an o.

Overly (ōu·vəıli), *a.* *Obs.* exc. *dial.* ME. [f. OVER *adv.* + -LY[1].] †**1.** Supreme. ME. only. †**2.** Superficial; cursory –1769. **3.** Supercilious, overbearing, haughty. Now only *dial.* 1627.

Overly (ōu·vəıli), *adv.* OE. [f. OVER *adv.* + -LY[2].] **1.** = OVER *adv.* III. 4. In OE., *Sc.*, and *U.S.* †**2.** Superficially, carelessly –1853. †**3.** On the surface –1573. †**4.** Haughtily, superciliously, slightingly –1650.

Overman (ōu·vəımæn), *sb.* ME. [OVER- I. 2 b.] †**1.** A superior, leader, ruler, chief –1625. **2.** An arbiter, arbitrator, umpire 1470. **3.** A foreman, overseer, esp. in a colliery 1708. **4.** [tr. G. *Uebermensch*] = SUPERMAN 1896.

Overman (ōuvəımæ·n), *v.* 1636. [OVER- II. 6.] *trans.* To furnish with too many men.

Overmantel (ōu·vəımænt'l). 1882. [OVER- III.] A piece of ornamental cabinet work, often including a mirror, placed over a mantelpiece.

Overma·ntle, *v.* 1827. [OVER- I. 8.] *trans.* To cover over like a mantle.

Overmaster (ōuvəımɑ·stəı), *v.* ME. [OVER- I. 21.] **1.** *trans.* To master completely; to get the better of, overcome, conquer. (Chiefly *fig.*) †**2.** To be master over; to hold in one's power or possession –1648. Hence **Overma·steringly** *adv.*

Overmatch (ōu·vəımætʃ), *sb.* 1542. [OVER- II. 3.] †**1.** The condition of being overmatched –1590. **2.** A person or thing that is more than a match for some other. Const. genitive or *for*. Now *rare.* 1589.

Overma·tch, *v.* ME. [OVER- II. 3.] *trans.* To be more than a match for; to defeat by superior strength or skill; to surpass, excel.

Over-measure (ōu·vəıme·ʒ'ŭı), *sb.* 1641. [OVER- I. 19, II. 8 d.] Measure above what is ordinary or sufficient: excess, surplus.

O·ver-mea·sure, *advb. phr.* late ME. [prop. two wds., OVER *prep.* and MEASURE *sb.*] Above the proper measure or amount; in excess.

O·ver-mo·dest, *a.* 1614. [OVER- II. 7.] Too modest. So **O·ver-mo·destly** *adv.* **O·ver-mo·desty.**

Overmuch (ōu·vəımʊ·tʃ; stress var.), *a.* and *adv.* ME. [OVER- II. 7, 9.] **A.** *adj.* Too much. Also *absol.* (rarely as *sb.*) **B.** *adv.* To too great an extent or degree; excessively. late ME. Hence **Overmu·chness,** excess, superabundance.

O·ver-ni·ce, *a.* ME. [OVER- II. 7.] Too nice; too fastidious, scrupulous, or particular. So **O·ver-ni·ce-ly** *adv.*, **-ness.**

Overnight, over night (ōuvəınəi·t), *advb. phr.* (*sb.*, *a.*) late ME. [f. OVER *prep.* V. 3 + NIGHT *sb.*] **1.** Before the night (as considered in relation to the following day); on the preceding evening; the night before (with implication that the result of the action continues till the following morning). **2.** During the night (till the following morning) 1535.

1. His Head ached every Morning with reading of Men o. ADDISON. 2. He preferred to stay o. with the family 1894.

B. *sb.* The preceding evening. (Now chiefly *U.S.*) 1581.

C. *attrib.* or *adj.* (*o·vernight*) Of or belonging to the previous evening; done, happening, etc., overnight 1824.

The limit of my o. journey 1870.

Overpaint (-pē·nt), *v.* 1611. [OVER- I. 8, II. 6.] †**1.** *trans.* To paint over with another colour –1614. **2.** To colour too highly 1750.

Overparted (ōuvəıpā·ıtèd), *a.* 1588. [f. OVER- II. 5 + PART *sb.* + -ED[2].] Having too difficult a part, or too many parts, to play.

Overpass (ōuvəıpɑ·s). *v.* Now somewhat *rare.* ME. [f. OVER- + PASS *v.*] **I.** Transitive senses, in which *over-* is prepositional. **1.** To pass over, travel over, move across or along. **2.** To cross ME. **3.** *fig.* To pass through (a period, an experience, etc.); often including the notion 'to get over, surmount'; more rarely, to pass, spend (time). [OVER- I. 16, 17.] ME. **4.** *fig.* To go (or be) beyond in amount, rate, value, excellence, etc.; to lie beyond the range or scope of; to exceed, excel, surpass ME. †**b.** To transgress –1597. **5.** *fig.* To pass over, leave out, omit. Now *rare.* late ME.

3. Having overpassed many rubs and difficulties 1645. 5. Some lesser errors..we o. 1831.

II. Intransitive senses, in which *over-* is adverbial. **1.** To pass over, across, or overhead ME. **2.** Of time, actions, experiences, etc.: To pass away, come to an end; to pass. Freq. in *pa. pple.* = At an end, past, over. ME. †**3.** To pass or remain unnoticed, to be let alone or omitted –1575.

2. Now that this storm is overpast MARLOWE.

Overpay (ōuvəıpē·). *v.* 1601. [OVER- II. 5.] *trans.* To pay too highly, pay more than is due. So **O·verpay** *sb.* **Over-pay·ment.**

Overpeer (ōuvəıpīə·ı), *v.* 1565. [OVER- I. 7, 1 (*b*).] **1.** *trans.* To peer over, look across from above, look down on 1589. †**b.** To 'look down upon', domineer over –1590. **2.** To rise or appear above; to tower over; to excel, outpeer 1565.

Over-peo·ple, *v.* 1683. [OVER- II. 6.] *trans.* To people too much, overstock with people. (Chiefly in *pa. pple.*)

O:ver-persua·de, *v.* 1624. [OVER- I. 11.] *trans.* To bring over by persuasion; *esp.* to persuade against one's own judgement or inclination. So **Over-persua·sion.**

Overpitch (ōuvəıpi·tʃ), *v.* 1859. [OVER- II. 5.] **1.** *Cricket.* *trans.* To pitch (a ball) too far in bowling. **2.** *fig.* To pitch too high; to exaggerate 1886.

Over-plea·se, *v.* 1611. [OVER- II. 6.] *trans.* To please too much. So **O·ver-plea·sed, O·verplea·sing** *ppl. adjs.*

Overplus (ōᵘ·vəɹplɒs), *sb.* (*adv.*, *a.*) late ME. [Partial transl. of med.L. *superplus*, F. *surplus*, f. *super*, *sur* over + *plus* more.] That which is over in addition to the main amount; an extra quantity; an amount left over, a surplus. **b.** *loosely.* Excess 1850. †**B.** *adv.* or predicatively: In addition, in excess, besides, over –1655. **C.** *adj.* Remaining over, extra, surplus 1640.

A. The landlord is paid out of the proceeds. The o. is returned to the tenant 1875. B. *Ant. & Cl.* IV. vi. 22.

Overpoise (ōᵘvəɹpoi·z), *v.* 1555. [f. OVER- I. 3 + POISE *v.*] *trans.* To weigh more than; mostly *fig.* Also *intr.* or *absol.* Hence **O·verpoise** *sb.* the act or fact of outweighing, that which outweighs.

Over-po·pulate, *v.* 1870. [OVER- II. 1.] *trans.* To over-people. (Chiefly in *pa. pple.*) So **O·ver-popula·tion. O·ver-po·pulous** *a.*, **-ness.**

Overpower (ōᵘvəɹpauᵊ·ɹ), *v.* 1593. [OVER- II. 1 b.] **1.** *trans.* To overcome with superior power; to vanquish, master. **2.** To render (a thing) ineffective or imperceptible, by excess of force or intensity 1646. **3.** To overcome by intensity; to be too much for; to crush, overwhelm 1667.

1. Those officers..were overpowered and disarmed MACAULAY. 2. Strong sauces that o. the natural flavour of the fish 1806. 3. We might be overpowered with the grandeur of the house 1881. Hence **Overpow·ering** *ppl. a.*, **-ly** *adv.*

Overpraise (ōᵘvəɹprē·z), *v.* late ME. [OVER- II. 6.] *trans.* To praise excessively; to praise more than one deserves.

Overpress (ōᵘvəɹpre·s), *v.* Now somewhat *rare.* late ME. [app. orig. a var. of OPPRESS, repr. L. *opprimere*; later assoc. w. literal senses of PRESS *v.*; see OVER-.] **I. 1.** *trans.* To oppress; to oppress beyond endurance. †**2.** To press upon with physical force, so as to overwhelm –1666. †**3.** To overburden, overload –1713.

1. My mind is overpressed with grief MILT.

II. 1. To overcome by entreaty. *rare.* 1818. **2.** To press or insist upon (a matter) unduly 1865. **3.** To put too much pressure on (a person) 1886.

2. He sometimes overpresses his point (*mod.*). So **O·ver-pre·ssure,** excessive pressure; pressing or being pressed too hard (esp. with study, etc.).

O·verprint, *sb.* 1907. [f. next.] **1.** An offprint or reprint 1911. **2.** An addition to the design or inscription of a postage stamp printed over it 1907.

Over-pri·nt, *v.* 1853. [OVER- II. 5.] **1.** *Photogr. trans.* To print (a positive) darker than it is meant to be. **2.** To impress (a printed surface) with additional print 1911. **3.** To put through the press again with added matter; also, to print too many copies of 1911.

Overprize (-prəi·z), *v.* 1589. [OVER- II. 5, 1.] **1.** *trans.* To prize too highly; to overestimate, overrate. **2.** To exceed or surpass in value. *Obs.* or *arch.* 1593.

1. Overprizing what they have already acquired, they make no further search 1663.

Over-produ·ce, *v.* 1894. [OVER- II. 6.] *trans.* To produce (a commodity) in excess of the demand or of a defined amount. So **O·ver-produ·ction,** production in excess of the demand 1822.

O·ver-proof, *a.* (*sb.*) 1807. [OVER- III.] That is 'above proof'; containing a larger proportion of alcohol than is contained in proof-spirit; see PROOF *sb.* Also *ellipt.* as *sb.* = over-proof spirit.

O·ver-propo·rtion, *sb.* 1666. [OVER- II. 8 c.] Excessive proportion; excess *of* one thing in proportion to another. So **O·ver-propo·rtion** *v. trans.* to make or estimate in excess of the true proportion.

Overrate (ōᵘvəɹrē·t), *v.* 1611. [OVER- II. 5, 6.] *trans.* To rate too highly or above the real value or amount. **b.** To assess too highly for rating purposes 1884.

Overreach (ōᵘ·vəɹrītʃ), *sb.* 1556. [f. next.] **1.** A reaching over some thing or person. **b.** Too great a reach, stretch, or strain. **2.** In ref. to a horse: The act of striking one of the fore feet with the corresponding hind foot; the injury so caused 1607. **3.** An act of overreaching in dealing 1615.

Overreach (ōᵘvəɹrī·tʃ), *v.* ME. [OVER- I. 5, 14, 9, 13, 21, II. 2, 5.] **1.** *trans.* To reach or extend over or beyond; to rise above; to stretch beyond in space or time. **2.** To overtake, come up with, attain to. Now *Sc.* ME. †**b.** To overpower –1638. **3.** *trans.* To extend or spread over (something) so as to cover it. Also *absol.* or *intr.* late ME. **4.** *intr.* Of a horse, etc.: To bring a hind foot against the corresponding fore foot in walking or running; *esp.* to strike and injure the heel of the fore foot with the hind foot. **b.** Also, generally, to bring a hind foot in front of or alongside a fore foot. 1523. **5.** *trans.* To gain an advantage over, get the better of, outdo; now always in a bad sense 1577. **6.** *refl.* To reach, stretch, strain oneself beyond one's strength, beyond one's aim, etc. 1568. Also *refl.* and *intr.* with admixture of sense 5. **7.** *intr.* To reach too far (*lit.* and *fig.*).

2. Certaine Players We ore-wrought on the way SHAKS. 5. He never made any bargain without overreaching (or, in the vulgar phrase, cheating) the person with whom he dealt FIELDING. Hence **Overrea·cher,** one who or that which overreaches.

Over-read (-rī·d), *v.* [OE. *oferrǣdan*; see OVER- I. 16, 20, II. 2.] †**1.** *trans.* To read over, read through –1648. †**2.** To re-read –1636. **3.** *refl.* and *intr.* To read too much 1805.

Over-re·ckon, *v.* 1615. [OVER- II. 6, 1.] **1.** *trans.* To overestimate. Also *absol.* 1646. †**2.** To overcharge in a reckoning –1680.

O·ver-refine (-rĭfəi·n), *v.* 1832. [OVER- II. 6.] *trans.* To refine too much; *absol.* to make over-fine distinctions. So **O·ver-refi·ned** *ppl. a.* **O·ver-refi·nement,** too subtle refinement.

Over-re·nt. *v.* 1589. [OVER- II. 6.] *trans.* To rent (land, etc.) too highly; to charge (a tenant) too high a rent.

Override (ōᵘvəɹrəi·d), *v.* [OE. *oferrīdan* to ride across; see OVER- I. 5, 9, 14, II. 1, 6.] **1.** *trans.* To ride over or across; to cross by riding (*lit.* and *fig.*). **b.** To ride all over (a country), esp. with an armed force, so as to harry, etc. ME. **2.** To ride over or upon (the fallen); to trample down by riding ME. **3.** *fig.* To trample under foot (an ordinance, right, etc.); to set at nought; to assume or have authority superior to 1827. †**4.** To overtake by or in riding; to outride –1642. **5.** To ride (a horse) too much 1596. **6.** To extend or pass over; to slip or lie over; *Surg.* to overlap, as when a bone is fractured and one piece slips over the other 1852.

2. Syr Palomydes cam vpon sir Tristram as he was vpon foot to haue ouer ryden hym MALORY. 3. Phr. *To o. one's commission,* to go beyond one's commission, discharge one's office in a high-handed and arbitrary manner. 6. A northern ice-sheet which overrode Canada GEIKIE.

O·ver-rule, *sb.* 1893. [OVER- I. 2 b.] The rule of a higher or supreme power.

Overrule (ōᵘvəɹrū·l), *v.* 1576. [OVER- I. 2.] †**1.** *trans.* To rule over, have authority over –1640. **2.** To govern or control the rule of (a person, a law, etc.) by superior power or authority 1576. **3.** To prevail over (a person) so as to change or set aside his opinion. Also *absol.* 1591. **4.** Of a thing: To prevail over, overcome 1586. **5.** To rule against, set aside, as by higher authority; *spec.* in *Law*: **a.** To set aside (a previous action or decision) as a precedent; to annul. **b.** To rule against (an argument, plea, etc.); to disallow (an action). 1593. **c.** To rule against (a person), to disallow the arguments or pleas of 1660.

2. To o. them in their prices, so as the same be not sold at any dearer rates 1596. 3. I found myself led and influenced by another's will, unpersuaded, quietly overruled C. BRONTË. 4. The general causes that o. personal aims 1877. 5. b. The chancellor overruled the objections 1875. c. Sir John Ernley..insisted.. but he was overruled MACAULAY. Hence **Overru·ler,** one who overrules, controls, or directs.

Overrun (ōᵘvəɹrʊ·n), *v.* OE. [OVER- I. 4, 5, 9, 10, 13, 16, II. 1, 2.] **I.** To run over (something). †**1.** *trans.* To run over or across (a line or surface); to pass over quickly –1649. **b.** To overflow ME. †**2.** To run through (a book, etc.); to glance through rapidly (sometimes implying omission) –1656. †**3.** To overwhelm (as waves); to run over (as a horse or vehicle), run down, trample down, crush. Also *fig.* –1667. **4.** To ride or rove over (a country) as a hostile force and so to harry and destroy; †to harass (a people) thus, to spoil (a city, etc.) late ME. **5.** Of vermin, weeds, etc.: To spread injuriously over; also of ivy, etc.: To grow over rapidly. Chiefly in *pa. pple.*, const. *with.* 1669. **6.** In various *fig.* and *transf.* senses (from 4 and 5). Now chiefly in *pa. pple.*, const. *with.* 1538. **7.** *intr.* To run over (said of a liquid or the containing vessel); to be superabundant or excessive ME.

4. The Northerne parts were overrun and harried by the Scots 1631. 5. The mouldering ruin of an abbey overrun with ivy W. IRVING. A small cell overrun with mice 1887. 6. The Wife is over-run with Affectation ADDISON.

II. To surpass in running, etc. **1.** *trans.* = OUTRUN 2; hence, to overtake or leave behind by or in running; also *fig.* to surpass. Now *rare.* late ME. **b.** To escape from by running faster than, to run away from; also *fig.* to run away from (duty, etc.); to desert, leave undone. Now only *dial.* 1583. **2.** To run farther than or beyond (a certain point, etc.); *fig.* to exceed 1633. **b.** To extend or project so as to overlie 1850. **c.** *intr.* To extend beyond the due length, or beyond any prescribed or desired limit 1864. **3.** *Printing.* (*trans.* or *absol.*) To carry over words or lines of type into another line or page to provide for the addition of new matter or the removal of matter already composed; to cause to run over 1683.

1. To o. one's age in growth, strength [etc.] SIDNEY. b. Phr. *To o. one's creditors, the* CONSTABLE. 2. Phr. *To o. the scent,* (of hounds) to continue running past a point where the hare or fox turned off, and thus to lose the scent. *To o. oneself,* to run too far; to exhaust or injure oneself with running; also *fig.* Hence **Overru·nner,** one who or that which overruns.

O·versale. 1889. [OVER- II. 8 d.] Speculative sale for future delivery to a greater amount than can be supplied; *pl.* sales beyond the available supply.

Oversco·re, *v.* 1849. [OVER- I. 8.] *trans.* **a.** To score over; to cover with scores, cuts, or deleting lines. **b.** To obliterate by scoring across.

O·ver-scru·pulous, *a.* 1597. [OVER- II. 7.] Too scrupulous. So **O·ver-scrupulo·sity, -scru·pulousness.**

Oversea (ōᵘvəɹsī), *a.* and *adv.* late ME. [f. OVER *prep.* + SEA.] **A.** *adv.* (o·ver sea·). Across or beyond the sea; abroad. **B.** *adj.* (o·versea). **1.** Of or pertaining to movement or transport over the sea; transmarine 1552. †**2.** Of foreign make –1651. **3.** Foreign 1553.

Overseas (ōᵘ·vəɹsī·z), *adv.* 1583. [f. OVER *prep.* + *seas* (app.) sb. pl.] = OVERSEA. **b.** quasi-*sb.* (with prep.). Foreign parts 1919.

Oversee (ōᵘvəɹsī·), *v.* [OE. *oferséon*, f. *ofer-* OVER- + SEE *v.*] **I. 1.** *trans.* To look down upon, overlook; to survey; to keep watch over. [OVER- I. 7.] **2.** To look over, look through; to inspect, examine; to peruse, esp. by way of revision for the printing-press. *Obs.* or *arch.* [OVER- I. 16.] late ME. **3.** To superintend, supervise; to see after the doing or working of 1449. **b.** *absol.* To act as overseer 1548. **4.** To catch sight of without the knowledge of the person seen 1742. **II. 1.** = OVERLOOK *v.* 2. *Obs.* exc. *dial.* OE. **2.** *refl.* To forget oneself, act unbecomingly; to err, blunder, act imprudently. Also *intr. Obs.* exc. *dial.* late ME.

Overseen (ōᵘvəɹsī·n), *ppl. a.* late ME. [pa. pple. of prec.] **1.** That has 'overseen himself' (see OVERSEE II. 2); deceived, deluded, in error; acting imprudently, rash in action. Now *arch.* or *dial.* †**2.** Versed, skilled, 'well seen' *in* some subject (cf. OVERSEE I. 2) –1610.

1. However Mr. Adye might have been o. in his Opinion as to the right of Seizure NELSON. Phr. *O. with* (or *in*) *drink*, also simply *o.*, intoxicated. *Obs.* exc. *dial.*

Overseer (ōᵘ·vəɹsīᵊɹ), *sb.* late ME. [f. OVERSEE + -ER[1].] **1.** One who oversees or superintends, a supervisor 1523. †**b.** A person (formerly) appointed by a testator to supervise the executor of the will -1667. c. (In full, *O. of the poor.*) An officer (appointed annually) to perform various administrative duties mainly connected with the relief of the poor 1601. †2. One who 'oversees' a book, e.g. as critic, censor, reviser, or editor -1685. Hence **O·verseership.**

Over-se·ll, *v.* 1580. [OVER- II. 5, 6.] †1. *trans.* To sell at more than the value -1768. 2. To sell more of (a stock, etc.) than one can deliver, or than exists. Also *refl.* 1879.

Overset (ōuvəɹse·t), *v.* ME. [OVER- I. 7, etc.] †1. To oppress; to press hard -1572. †2. To overcome, discomfit -1698. 3. To upset, overturn, capsize; to turn upside down. Now *rare.* [OVER- I. 6.] 1592. b. *intr.* To capsize; to be upset. Now *rare.* 1641. 4. *trans. fig.* To upset (an institution, state, or the like); to cause to fall into confusion. Now *rare.* 1679. b. To discompose (a person); to disorder, upset (the stomach, etc.) 1533. c. *intr.* To be upset, fall into disorder 1749. 5. To set up (type) in excess 1897.

3. The postilion..overset the carriage MISS BURNEY. 4. b. The news is sure to o. him DICKENS. c. While kingdoms o., Or lapse from hand to hand TENNYSON. Hence **O·verset** *sb.* the act or fact of oversetting.

Oversew (ōu·vəɹsōu), *v.* 1864. [OVER- I. 5.] *trans.* To sew overhand; to sew together two pieces of stuff, so that the thread between the stitches lies over the edges.

Overshade (ōuvəɹʃē¹·d), *v.* OE. [OVER- I. 8.] 1. *trans.* = OVERSHADOW *v.* 2. 2. To cast a shade over; to render gloomy or dark; to overshadow. Also *absol.* 1588.

Overshadow (ōuvəɹʃæ·dōu), *v.* [OE. *ofersceadwian*; see OVER- I. 8.] 1. *trans.* To cast a shadow over; to cover or obscure with darkness, overcloud; to overshade. 2. To cover or overspread with some influence, as with a shadow; to shelter, protect OE. 3. To tower above so as to cast its shadow over; hence, to rise above, 'cast into the shade' 1581.

1. *fig.* Those misfortunes which were soon to o. her FROUDE. 2. O. me in the day of battle 1578. 3. It was natural that the Crown, completely overshadowed by the great barons, should turn..to the Church 1862. Hence **Oversha·dower. Oversha·dowing** *vbl. sb.* and *ppl. a.*

Overshine (-ʃəi·n), *v.* [OE. *oferscinan*; see OVER- I. 7, 8.] 1. *trans.* To shine over or upon, to illumine. 2. To outshine; chiefly *fig.* 1588.

O·vershoe (-ʃū), *sb.* 1851. [OVER- I. 8 c.] A shoe of india-rubber, felt, etc., worn over the ordinary shoe as a protection from wet, dirt, or cold.

Over-shoe, over-shoes (ōuvəɹʃū·z), *advb. phr.* 1579. [orig. two wds.; see OVER *prep.* I. 2.] Of water, mud, etc.: So deep as to cover the shoes, shoe-deep.

A man may go ouer-shoes in the grime of it SHAKS.

Overshoot (ōuvəɹʃū·t). *v.* late ME. [OVER- I. 13, 4, 5, II. 2, 6.] 1. *trans.* To shoot, dart, run, or pass beyond (a point, limit, etc.). †b. *Naut.* To sail past (a port, etc.) -1803. 2. To shoot a missile, etc., over or above (the mark) and so to miss; to shoot beyond; also, of the missile: To pass over or beyond (the mark). Also *absol.* (*lit.* and *fig.*) 1548. †3. *fig.* To shoot too hard, utter (a word) too violently or unguardedly -1621. 4. To push or drive beyond the proper limit 1668. 5. To shoot or dart over or above 1774. b. To shoot too much over (a moor, etc.) so as to deplete it of game 1884.

1. Dogs, who running fleeter, over-shoot their game 1755. 2. *fig. To o. the mark*, to go too far, or farther than is intended or proper. *To o. oneself*, to shoot beyond or over one's mark; to miss one's mark by going too far; to exaggerate; to fall into error. †*To be overshot*, to be wide of the mark; to be mistaken or deceived.

Overshot (ōu·vəɹʃǫt), *a.* (*sb.*) 1535. [= next, with change of stress.] A. *adj.* Driven by water shot over from above. B. *sb.* The stream of water which drives an overshot wheel 1759.

A. *O. wheel*, a water-wheel turned by the force of water falling upon or near the top of the wheel into buckets placed round the circumference. *O. mill*, a mill supplied with power by an o. wheel.

Oversho·t, *ppl. a.* 1605. [pa. pple. of OVERSHOOT *v.*] 1. In the senses of the vb. 1774. 2. Said of a partially dislocated fetlock joint, in which the upper bone is driven over or in front of the lower bones 1881. 3. Having the upper jaw projecting beyond the lower 1885.

Overside, *adv.* and *a.* 1884. [Short for *over the side.*] A. *adv.* (ōuvəɹsəi·d). Over the side of a ship (into the sea, a lighter, etc.) 1889. B. *adj.* (ōu·vəɹsəid). Effected over the side of a ship; discharging over the side 1884.

Oversight (ōu·vəɹsəit). ME. [OVER- I. 7, 5.] 1. Supervision, superintendence; charge, care, management. 2. Omission or failure to see or notice, inadvertence; also, an instance of this 1477.

2. It is all rather owing to O., than to any ill Intention 1676. It [the omission] may have been an o. 1865.

O·versize, *sb.* 1849. [OVER- II. 8 d.] A size in excess of the proper or ordinary size.

Oversi·ze, *v.* 1602. [f. OVER- I. 8, II. 6 + SIZE *v.*[2]] †1. *trans.* To cover over with size. *Haml.* II. ii. 484. 2. To size too much 1878.

O·ver-si·zed (stress var.), *ppl. a.* 1801. [f. OVERSIZE *sb.* + -ED[2].] Over or above the normal size, abnormally large.

O·verskirt. *U.S.* 1883. [OVER- I. 8 c.] An outer skirt; drapery arranged over the skirt of a dress.

Overslaugh (ōu·vəɹslǭ), *sb.* 1772. [ad. Du. *overslag*, f. *overslaan* (see next); or (in sense 1) from next.] 1. *Mil.* The passing over of one's ordinary turn of duty in consideration of being required for a superior duty. 2. *U.S.* A bar or sand-bank which impedes the navigation of a river; *spec.* that on the Hudson River below Albany 1776.

Overslaugh (ōu·vəɹslǭ), *v.* 1768. [ad. Du. *overslaan* to pass over, f. *over-* OVER- I. 5 + *slaan* to strike.] 1. *trans.* To pass over, skip, omit. a. *Mil.* To pass over, skip, or remit the ordinary turn of duty of an officer, a company, etc., in consideration of his (or its) being detailed on that day for a higher duty. b. *U.S.* To pass over in favour of another, as in nomination to an office; also, generally, to pass over, ignore 1846. 2. To bar, obstruct, hinder 1864.

Oversleep (ōuvəɹslī·p), *v.* late ME. [OVER- I. 18, II. 2] 1. *intr.* and *refl.* To sleep beyond the time at which one ought to awake. 2. *trans.* To sleep beyond (a particular time) 1526.

1. They were weary, and overslept themselves DE FOE. I will not let you over-sleep, be sure 1881.

Oversleeve (ōu·vəɹslīv), *v.* 1857. [OVER- I. 8 c.] An outer sleeve covering the ordinary sleeve.

Overslide (ōuvəɹsləi·d), *v.* ME. [OVER- I. 4, 5.] †1. *intr.* To slide or slip away; to pass unnoticed. Usu. with *let.* -1560. †2. *trans.* = *to let o.* in 1. -1570. 3. To slide, slip, or glide over (a place or thing). Also *intr.* or *absol.* 1513.

Overslip (ōuvəɹsli·p), *v.* Now *rare.* late ME. 1. *trans.* To slip or pass by (*fig.*), pass over without notice; to omit, miss. [OVER- I. 4, 5.] †b. *intr.* or *absol.* To make a slip. Also *refl.* -1641. †2. *intr.* To slip or pass by; of time, to elapse (usu. implying the missing of an opportunity). [OVER- I. 4.] -1607. †3. *trans.* To slip away from, escape (a person); usu. *fig.* -1688. 4. To slip past or beyond (*lit.*). [OVER- I. 13.] 1595. †5. To slip beyond or outside of (*fig.*); to transgress through inadvertence -1592.

3. Which all this time hath overslipp'd her thought SHAKS.

O·ver-soul. 1841. [OVER- I. 2.] Emerson's name for the Deity regarded as the supreme spirit which animates the universe.

Oversow (ōuvəɹsōu·), *v.* [OE. *ofersāwan*, f. *ofer-* OVER- + SOW *v.*; repr. late L. *superseminare* (Vulg.).] 1. *trans.* To sow (seed) over other seed, or a crop, previously sown. [OVER- I. 1, 8.] 2. To sow (ground) *with* additional seed. [OVER- I. 8, 20.] OE. 3. To scatter seed over, sow *with* seed. Also *fig.* in *pa. pple.* (F. *parsemé.*) [OVER- I. 8.] 1618. 4. To sow too much of (seed). [OVER- II. 6.] 1890.

1. His enemy came and oversowed cockle among the wheate N. T. (Rhem.) *Matt.* xiii. 25.

Overspan (ōuvəɹspæ·n), *v.* 1513. [OVER- I. 10, II. 1.] 1. *trans.* To extend above and across (something else) from side to side. †2. To span (a space) with an arch, etc., to 'throw' (an arch, bridge, etc.) over a space -1817.

Overspend (ōuvəɹspe·nd), *v.* 1586. [OVER- I. 17, 13, II. 5, 2.] 1. *trans.* To spend or use till exhausted; to wear out. Usu. in *pa. pple.* **overspent**: worn out, exhausted with fatigue. 2. To spend more than (a specified amount) 1667; to spend beyond what is necessary 1857. b. *refl.* and *intr.* To spend beyond one's means 1890.

1. Harvest Hinds o'erspent with Toil and Heat DRYDEN.

Overspread (ōuvəɹspre·d), *v.* [OE. *ofersprǣdan*, f. *ofer-*, OVER- I. 8, 9.] 1. *trans.* To spread (something) over or upon something else. 2. To spread something over (something else); to cover *with* something spread upon the surface. late ME. b. in *passive* with *with* ME. 3. Of a thing: To spread or extend over (something else); to cover completely (*lit.* and *fig.*) ME.

2. With hostile forces he'll o'erspread the land SHAKS. 3. A pink flush overspread her face GEO. ELIOT.

†**Oversta·nd,** *v.* 1600. [OVER- I. 17.] *trans.* To outstay, overstay -1784.

Overstate (ōuvəɹstē¹·t), *v.* 1803. [f. OVER- II. 6, 5 + STATE *v.*] *trans.* To state too strongly; to exaggerate. So **O·versta·tement.**

Overstay (ōuvəɹstē¹·), *v.* 1646. [OVER- I. 18.] *trans.* To stay over or beyond (in time).

Overstock (ōu·vəɹstǫk), *sb.* 1565. [OVER- I. 8 c, II. 8 d.] †1. *pl.* Knee-breeches; cf. *nether-stocks* -1580. 2. A stock or store in excess of demand or requirement 1710.

Overstock (ōuvəɹstǫ·k), *v.* 1649. [OVER- II. 6.] *trans.* To stock to excess; to glut.

Overstrain (ōu·vəɹstrē¹n), *sb.* 1754. [OVER- II. 8 b.] Excessive strain.

Overstrain (ōuvərstrē¹·n), *v.* 1589. [OVER- II. 6.] To subject to excessive strain (*lit.* and *fig.*). Also *absol.* or *intr.*

Neuer will I ouerstraine my strength 1589. *fig* This argument is greatly overstrained 1863.

Overstream (ōuvəɹstrī·m), *v.* 1616. [OVER- I. 9.] *trans.* To stream over or across; to flow over in a stream.

Overstre·tch. *v.* ME. [OVER- II. 6, I. 10.] 1. *trans.* To stretch too much (*lit.* and *fig.*). 2. To stretch or extend across. late ME. So **O·ver-stretch** *sb.*

Overstrew (-strū·, -strōu·), *v.* 1570. [OVER- I. 8.] 1. *trans.* To strew or sprinkle (something) over something else. 2. To oversprinkle *with.* (Chiefly in *pa. pple.*) 1578.

Overstride (-strəi·d), *v.* ME. [OVER- I. 5, 10, 13, II. 1, 5.] 1. To stride over or across. 2. To stride or extend beyond; *fig.* to surpass 1637. 3. *intr.* To take longer strides than is natural 1899.

Overstri·ng, *v.* 1880. [OVER- I. 1, 10.] *Pianoforte-making. trans.* To arrange the strings of (a piano) in two (or three) sets crossing over one another obliquely.

Overstrung (stress var.), *ppl. a.* 1810. [OVER- II. 7 c, I. 1, 10.] 1. Too highly strung; excessively strained. 2. Of a piano: Having the strings arranged in two (or three) sets crossing one another obliquely 1880.

Overstudy (-stʊ·di), *v.* 1641. [OVER- II. 6, 2.] *trans., refl.*, and *intr.* To study too much. So **O·verstu·dy** *sb.*

O:ver-subscri·be, *v.* 1891. [OVER- II. 6.] *trans.* To subscribe for (a loan, shares, etc.) in excess of the amount required. So **O·ver-subscri·ption.**

O:ver-supply·, *sb.* 1833. [OVER- II. 8 b.] A supply in excess of the demand or requirement. So **O:ver-supply·** *v. trans.* to supply in excess.

Overswarm (-swǭ·ɹm), *v.* 1587. 1. *intr.* and *refl.* To swarm in excess. [OVER- II. 6, 2.] 2. *trans.* To swarm over (a place or region); to cover with a swarm. Also *absol.* or *intr.* [OVER- I. 9.] 1632.

Oversway (ōuvəɹswē¹·), *v.* Now *rare.* 1577. [OVER- I. 2, 21, 11, 3, 6.] †1. *trans.* To exercise sway over, govern; to domineer over, overrule, overpower -1680. †b. To prevail over by superior authority. Also *absol.* -1878. †2. To lead into some course of action; to prevail upon -1710. 3. *trans.* and *intr.* To sway over; to cause to incline to one side, or so as to be overturned; to swing or incline thus 1622.

Overswe·ll, *v.* 1586. [OVER- II. 4, 6, I. 5, 13.] 1. *trans.* or *intr.* To swell to excess.

(Chiefly in *pa. pple.* overswollen.) **2.** *trans.* To swell so as to overflow or cover. Also *absol.* or *intr.* 1595.

Overswi·m, *v.* [OE. *oferswimman*; see OVER- I. 1, 8, 9.] *trans.* To swim or float over, across, or upon.

Overt (ōu·vəɹt), *a.* ME. [a. OF. *overt* (F. *ouvert*), pa. pple. of *ovrir*, F. *ouvrir* to open.] †**1.** Open, not closed; uncovered –1552. **2.** Open to view or knowledge; evident, plain; unconcealed, not secret ME.

2. The General Judgment shall extend, not only to Mens O., but even their most secret Acts 1705. Phr. *O. act* (*Law*), an outward act, such as can be clearly proved to have been done, from which criminal intent is inferred. *Letters o.* = letters PATENT. *Market o.*, see MARKET *sb.* 1. *Pound o.*, open or public POUND. Hence **O·vertly** *adv.* openly.

Overtake (ōuvəɹtē¹·k), *v.* [Early ME. f. OVER- I. 14 + TAKE *v.*] **1.** *trans.* To come up with; to come up to in pursuit; to catch up. **b.** *fig.* To come up with in any course of action; *esp.* to get through (a task) when hindered by other business, etc.; to work off within the time ME. †**2.** To get at, reach; to reach with a blow –1680. **3.** Of some adverse agency or influence, as a storm, night, misfortune, etc.: To come upon unexpectedly, suddenly or violently; to surprise, involve. late ME. **4.** To overcome the will, senses, or feelings of; to 'take'; to overpower with excess of emotion. *Obs.* or *dial.* late ME. †**5.** To overcome the judgement of; to 'take in', deceive; in *pa. pple.* deceived, mistaken –1702. **6.** To overcome or overpower with drink, intoxicate. (Chiefly in *passive.*) Now *dial.* 1587.

1. Phrase: *Well overtaken*; Faire sir, you are well ore-tane SHAKS. **b.** It's a job you could o. with the other STEVENSON. **3.** Overtaken by a thunder storm 1794. **4.** We were all so overtaken with this good news, that the Duke ran with it to the King PEPYS. **6.** To be sure the knight is overtaken a little; very near drunk 1770.

Overta·sk, *v.* 1628. [OVER- II. 6.] *trans.* To task too heavily.

Overta·x, *v.* 1650. [OVER- II. 6.] *trans.* To tax too greatly or heavily; to exact or demand too much of. Hence **Overta·xed** *ppl. a.*; so **O·vertaxa·tion.**

Overtee·m, *v.* 1602. [OVER- II. 5, I. 21.] **a.** *intr.* To teem or breed excessively; also *fig.* **b.** *trans.* To exhaust by excessive breeding or production.

Overthrow (ōu·vəɹþrōu), *sb.* 1513.

I. [f. next.] **1.** An act of overthrowing; the fact of being overthrown; discomfiture; ruin. **2.** *Geol.* An overturning or inversion of strata 1891.

1. The dangerous consorted Traitors, That sought at Oxford, thy dire ouerthrow SHAKS.

II. [f. OVER- I. 13.] In cricket, a return of the ball by a fielder, in which it is not caught or stopped near the wicket, allowing the batsman to make more runs 1749; in baseball, a throwing of the ball over or beyond the player to whom it is thrown.

Overthrow (ōuvəɹþrōu·), *v.* ME. [f. OVER- I. 6 + THROW *v.*] **1.** *trans.* To throw (anything) over upon its side or upper surface; to upset; to knock (a structure) down, and so demolish it. **2.** *fig.* To cast down from a position of prosperity or power; to bring to ruin, reduce to impotence. late ME. **3.** To subvert, ruin, bring to nought, demolish (an order of things, a theory, plan, institution, government, etc.). late ME. **4.** †To upset in mental state; to overturn the normal sound condition of (the mind). late ME. †**5.** *intr.* To fall over or down, tumble –1587.

1. Then shal Niniue be ouerthrowen COVERDALE *Jonah* iii. 4. **2.** He..was overthrown with Thiers seven days afterwards 1894. **3.** Here's Gloster,.. That seekes to ouerthrow Religion SHAKS. **4.** O what a Noble minde is heere o're-throwne! SHAKS. Hence **O·verthrow·n** (stress var.) *ppl. a.* (*sb.*).

Overthrust (ōu·vəɹþrʊst). 1883. [OVER- I. 1, 9.] *Geol.* The thrust of the strata or series of rocks on one side of a fault over those on the other side, esp. of lower over higher strata, as in an OVERFAULT or faulted OVERFOLD.

Overthwart (ōuvəɹþwǭ·ɹt), *adv.* and *prep.* Now *Obs.* or *rare* exc. *dial.* [ME. f. OVER *adv.* + *þwert* adv.: see THWART *adv.*] **A.** *adv.* **1.** Over from side to side, or so as to cross something; across; crosswise, transversely. †**2.** *fig.* Adversely; wrongly, amiss; angrily, 'crossly' –1556. **B.** *prep.* **1.** From side to side of; so as to cross; across. late ME. †**2.** Over against, opposite –1630. **3.** On the opposite side of; across, beyond. Now *dial.* 1784.

3. Far beyond, and o. the stream COWPER.

Overthwart (ōu·vəɹþwǭɹt), *a.* and *sb.* *Obs.* exc. *dial.* ME. [f. prec.] **A.** *adj.* **1.** Placed or lying crosswise, or across something else; transverse, cross-. †**b.** *fig.* Indirect –1656. †**2.** Opposite –1692. **3.** *fig.* Inclined to cross or oppose; perverse, froward; captious, testy, 'cross', unfriendly, unfavourable ME.

1. Two crosse or ouerthwart wayes 1623. **2.** Our o'erthwart neighbours DRYDEN. **3.** Of a Spirit averse and over-thwart 1595. Hence **O·verthwart·ly** *adv.*, †**-ness.**

†**B.** *sb.* [The adj. used absol.] **1.** A transverse or cross direction –1562. **b.** A transverse passage, a by-way, a crossing; a transverse line –1631. **2.** An adverse experience; a 'cross', a rebuff –1609; contradiction; a repartee –1595.

1. Phr. *At an o., to o.*, in a transverse direction; across.

Overthwart (ōuvəɹþwǭ·ɹt), *v.* Now *rare* or *Obs.* late ME. [f. prec. adv. or adj.] **1.** *trans.* To pass or lie athwart or across; to traverse, cross. **b.** To obstruct 1654. **2.** *fig.* To act in opposition to; to thwart. Also *absol.* 1529.

Overtime (ōu·vəɹtəim), *sb.*, *adv.* 1858. [OVER- I. 19.] **A.** *sb.* Time worked over and above the regular hours; extra time. Also *attrib.* as in *o. pay.* **B.** *adv.* During extra time 1873.

Overtire (ōuvəɹtəiə·ɹ), *v.* 1557. [OVER- I. 21, II. 6.] *trans.* To tire excessively, exhaust with fatigue. Hence **Overti·red** *ppl. a.* 'tired out'.

Overtoil (ōuvəɹtoi·l), *v.* 1577. [OVER- I. 21.] *trans.* To wear out by excessive toil; to overwork, fatigue.

Overtone (ōu·vəɹtōun), *sb.* 1867. [ad. G. *oberton*, contr. of *oberpartialton* upper partial tone.] *Acoustics*, etc. An upper partial tone; a HARMONIC.

Overtone (ōuvəɹtōu·n), *v.* 1889. [OVER- II. 6.] *Photogr.* To 'tone' too much, give too deep a tone to.

Overtop (ōuvəɹtǫ·p), *v.* 1561. [OVER- I. 1.] **1.** *trans.* To rise over or above the top of; to surmount, tower above, top 1593. **2.** *fig.* To rise above in power or authority; to override 1561. **b.** To go beyond in degree or quality; to excel, surpass 1581.

1. The crabbed mountaines which overtopped it 1622. **2. b.** In them the man somehow overtops the author LOWELL.

Overto·pple, *v.* 1543. [OVER- I. 6, 3.] **1.** *trans.* To overthrow (something unstable). **2.** *intr.* To topple over 1839.

Overtow·er, *v.* 1831. [OVER- I. 1 (*b*).] *trans.* To tower over or above. So **Overtow·ering** *ppl. a.* 1639.

Overtrade (-trē¹·d), *v.* 1622. [OVER- II. 5, 2.] *Comm. intr.* and *refl.* To trade in excess of one's capital, or the needs of the market. **b.** *trans.* To do trade beyond (one's capital, stock, etc.). So **Overtra·der. Overtra·ding** *vbl. sb.* trading in excess of one's capital or the needs of the market.

Over-trai·n (-trē¹·n), *v.* 1856. [OVER- II. 6.] *trans.* To train too much, to injure by excessive training. **b.** To train (a creeping plant) too much or too high.

†**Overtrea·d,** *v.* [OE. *ofertredan*; see OVER- I. 1, 9, 13.] **a.** To trample under foot; *fig.* to oppress, subdue. **b.** To step beyond –1620.

Over-trou·ble (-trʊ·b'l), *v.* 1582. [OVER- II. 6.] *trans.* To trouble excessively. So **O·ver-trou·bled** *ppl. a.*

Overtru·mp, *v.* 1746. [OVER- II. 1.] *trans.* To play a higher trump than one already played; also *absol.* and *fig.*

Over-tru·st, *v.* ME. [OVER- II. 6.] **1.** *intr.* To trust too much; to be over-confident. **2.** *trans.* To trust (a person or thing) too much 1649.

Overtu·mble, *v.* 1600. [OVER- I. 6, 5.] *trans.* To cause to fall over; to overthrow. Now only *poet.*

Overture (ōu·vəɹtiŭɹ, -tʃŭɹ), *sb.* ME. [a. OF., mod.F. *ouverture* opening, f. *ouvert* OVERT.] †**1.** An opening, orifice, hole. Also *fig.* –1749. †**2.** A revelation, disclosure, discovery –1654. **3.** An opening of negotiations; a formal proposal, proposition, or offer. late ME. **4.** In the General Assembly of the Church of Scotland, and in the supreme court of other Presbyterian churches: A formal motion proposing or calling for legislation 1576. †**5.** An opening for proceeding to action –1768. †**6.** An opening, beginning, commencement –1741. **7.** *Mus.* An orchestral piece, of varying form and dimensions, forming the opening or introduction to an opera, oratorio, etc.; also, as an independent piece 1667. **b.** The introductory part of a poem 1870.

1. Diuers ouertures and holes were made vnder the foundacion 1548. **2.** *Lear* III. vii. 89. **3.** There have been overtures of marriage made unto him 1655.

O·verture, *v.* 1637. [f. prec. sb.] **1.** *trans.* To put forward as an overture or proposal; to offer, propose. **2.** In the supreme court of a Presbyterian church: To bring forward as an overture; to introduce as a motion 1671. **b.** To present or transmit an overture to (a church court); to approach with an overture 1864. **3.** To introduce with, or as with, a musical overture; to prelude 1870.

Overturn (ōu·vəɹtʊ̄ɹn), *sb.* 1592. [OVER- I. 6, 10.] **1.** The act of overturning or fact of being overturned; an upsetting; a revolution. **2.** *Geol.* = OVERFOLD *sb.* 1877. **3.** Turnover in the course of trade 1882.

Overturn (ōuvəɹtʊ̄·ɹn), *v.* ME. [OVER- I. 6, ? 4, 10.] †**1.** *intr.* Of a wheel, and *fig.* of time: To turn round, revolve –1649. **2.** *trans.* To turn (anything) over upon its side or face; to upset, overthrow; to cause to fall over or down ME. **b.** *intr.* To turn over, capsize, upset. late ME. **3.** *trans.* To overthrow, subvert, bring to ruin. late ME. †**4.** To upset, disorder (stomach, etc.) –1704. †**5.** To turn away; to pervert –1587.

2. They ouerturned their Canoa with a great violence 1555. **3.** We shall o're-turne it [the Kingdome] topsie-turuy downe SHAKS. Hence **Overtu·rnable** *a.* **Overtu·rner.**

Over-value (ōu·vəɹvæ:liu), *sb.* 1611. [OVER- II. 8 d.] A value or estimate greater than the worth of a thing.

Overvalue (ōuvəɹvæ·liu), *v.* 1597. [OVER- II. 5, 1 b.] **1.** *trans.* To value (a thing) above its worth; to overestimate. **b.** To put too high a money valuation upon 1641. †**2.** Of a thing: To surpass in value –1772.

1. b. If the policy be enormously overvalued, that will be evidence of fraud 1847. So **O·vervalua·tion,** the action of overvaluing.

Overwa·lk, *v.* 1533. [OVER- I. 9, 10, II. 2.] **1.** *trans.* To walk over. **2.** *refl.* To walk too much or too far 1662.

O·verwash (-wǫʃ), *sb.* 1889. [f. next.] *Geol.* The material carried by running water from a glacier and deposited over or beyond the marginal moraine.

Overwash (-wǫ·ʃ), *v.* 1577. [OVER- I. 5, 9.] *trans.* To wash or flow over (something); to bathe by flowing over.

Overwatch (ōuvəɹwǫ·tʃ), *v.* 1563. [OVER- I. 1 (c), 17, 21.] **1.** *trans.* To keep watch over 1618. †**2.** To watch all through (a night) –1590. **3.** To weary or exhaust by keeping awake or by want of sleep. Now chiefly in *pa. pple.* 1563.

Overwear (ōuvəɹwē³·ɹ), *v.* 1578. [OVER- I. 21, 17.] **1.** To wear out or exhaust with toil, etc. **2.** To wear out (clothes, etc.), wear threadbare 1630. **3.** To wear (something) away or to an end; to outwear 1581.

Overweary (ōuvəɹwī³·ri), *v.* 1576. [OVER- I. 21, II. 6.] *trans.* To overcome with weariness; to tire out.

Overween (ōuvəɹwī·n), *v.* Now chiefly in *ppl. a.* ME. [OVER- II. 5, 6.] **1.** *intr.* To have too high expectations or too high an opinion of oneself; to be arrogant or presumptuous. †**2.** To think too highly (*of*) –1621. †**3.** *trans.* (and *refl.* = 1). To over-esteem (usu. oneself, or something of one's own) –1674. †**4.** To cause to overween –1620.

1. Mowbray, you ouer-weene to take it so SHAKS. Hence **Overwee·ning** *vbl. sb.* (now *rare*), arrogance, self-conceit; over-estimation. **Overwee·ning** *ppl. a.* over-confident; conceited, arrogant, presumptuous, self-opinionated; of opinion, etc., exaggerated. **Overwee·ning·ly** *adv.*, **-ness.**

Overweigh (ōuvəɹwēⁱ·), *v.* ME. [OVER- II. 1, 5, I. 21.] **1.** *trans.* To exceed in weight (physical or moral); to overbalance, outweigh. **2.** To weigh down, overburden, oppress 1577. **3.** *intr.* To preponderate; to weigh too much 1862.

1. Say what you can; my false ore-weighs your true SHAKS.

Overweight (ōu·vəɹwēⁱt), *sb.* 1511. [OVER- I. 19, II. 8 c.] **1.** Something over the exact or proper weight; extra weight. **2.** Greater weight (than that of something else); preponderance (physical or moral) 1626. **3.** Too great weight; also *fig.* 1577.

Over-weight (ōu·vəɹwēⁱt), *a.* 1638. [OVER *prep.* + WEIGHT *sb.*] Above, or in excess of, the ordinary weight; too heavy.

I was charged a few pounds of o. luggage 1888.

Overwei·ght, *v.* 1603. [OVER- II. 6.] †**1.** *trans.* To give or attach too much weight to FLORIO. **2.** To weight too heavily; to overburden, overload (*lit.* and *fig.*). Chiefly in *pa. pple.* 1753.

†**O·ver-wet**, *sb.* 1626. [OVER- II. 7.] Too great wetness BACON. So **O·ver-we·tness.**

Overwhelm (ōuvəɹhwe·lm), *v.* ME. [f. OVER- I. 6, 8 + WHELM *v.* to roll.] **1.** *trans.* To overturn, upset; to turn upside down. *Obs.* exc. *dial.* **2.** *trans.* To cover (anything) as with something turned over and cast upon it; to bury or drown beneath this; to submerge completely (and ruin or destroy) 1450. †**b.** To overhang so as to cover more or less SHAKS. **3.** *fig.* To overcome or overpower; to bring to ruin or destruction; to crush 1529. **b.** To overpower utterly with some emotion 1535. **c.** To 'deluge' *with* 1806.

1. The earthquake..overwhelmed a chain of mountains of free stone more than 300 miles long 1796. 2. Pompeii was overwhelmed by a vast accumulation of dust and ashes HUXLEY. b. *Hen. V*, III. i. 11. 3. We Starve at home, abroad our debts orewhelm us 1692. b. I was overwhelmed with the sense of my condition DE FOE. c. The whole party ..were overwhelming him with praises 1806. Hence **Overwhe.lming** *ppl. a.*, **-ly** *adv.*, **-ness.**

Overwind (ōuvəɹwəi·nd), *v.* 1682. *Pa.t.* and *pa. pple.* overwound. [OVER- II. 5.] *trans.* To wind too tight, as in tuning a musical instrument; to wind (a watch, etc., or, in *Mining*, the hoisting rope or chain) too far.

O·ver-wi·se (-wəiz), *a.* 1588. [OVER- II. 7.] Too wise, affectedly wise. *Not over-wise*, rather deficient in wisdom. Hence **O·ver-wi·se·ly** *adv.*, **-ness. O·ver-wi·sdom.**

O·verword, *sb.* Chiefly *Sc.* 1500. [OVER- I. 20.] A word or phrase repeated again and again; *esp.* the refrain of a song.

Overwork, *sb.* [OE. *oferweorc*, f. *ofer-*, OVER- I. 1.] **I.** (ōu·vəɹwɒ̄ɹk). †**1.** A superstructure; *spec.* in OE. a sepulchral monument. OE. and ME. **2.** Extra work. [OVER- I. 19.] 1858. **II.** (ōu·vəɹwɒ̄·ɹk). Excessive work, work beyond one's capacity. [OVER- II. 8 b.] 1818.

Overwork (ōuvəɹwɒ̄·ɹk), *v.* Pa. t. and pple. **-wrought, -worked.** [OE. *oferwyrcan*, f. OVER- I. 8.] **I. 1.** *trans.* To work all over, decorate the surface of. (Only in *pa. pple.*) [OVER- I. 8.] †**2.** To work upon successfully; to gain over to a certain course. [OVER- I. 11.] –1661. **II. 1.** *trans.* To cause to work too hard; to work (a man, horse, etc.) beyond his strength; to weary or exhaust with work. [OVER- II. 6, I. 21.] 1530. **b.** To fill too full with work 1876. **c.** *intr.* To work too much 1894. **2.** To work too much upon; to elaborate to excess. (Only in *pa. pple.*) [OVER- II. 6.] 1638. **3.** *trans.* and *fig.* To stir up or excite excessively 1645.

1. Overworking my eyes by candlelight PEPYS. b. My days with toil are overwrought LONGF. 3. Till my brain became, In its own eddy boiling and o'erwrought, A whirling gulf of phantasy and flame BYRON.

Overworn (ōuvəɹwō̆ɹn; stress variable), *ppl. a.* 1565. [f. OVER- I. 21, 17 + WORN *ppl. a.*] **1.** Much worn, the worse for wear; threadbare; faded. †**2.** Obsolete –1610. **3.** Worn out, exhausted, spent, as with age or toil 1592. **4.** Spent in time; passed away 1592.

1. *fig. Twel. N.* III. i. 66. 4. Musing the morning is so much o'erworn SHAKS.

Overwrite (ōuvəɹrəi·t), *v.* 1699. [OVER- I. 8, 20, II. 6, 2.] **1. a.** *trans.* To write (something) over other writing, as a palimpsest. **b.** To write over. to cover *with* writing. **2.** To re-write 1874. **3. a.** *intr.* To write too much; **b.** *refl.* To exhaust oneself by excessive writing; **c.** To write too much about (a subject) 1837.

Overwrought (ōu·vəɹrǭ·t), *ppl. a.* 1670. [pa. pple. of OVERWORK *v.*] **1. a.** Exhausted by overwork. **b.** Worked up to too high a pitch. **2.** Elaborated to excess; over-laboured 1839.

Over-zeal (ōu·vəɹzī·l). 1747. [OVER- II. 8 d.] Too great zeal; excess of zeal. So **O·ver-zealous** (-ze·ləs) *a.* 1635.

Ovi-[1], comb. form. of L. *ovum* egg, as in **Ovi·ferous** [-FEROUS], *a. Anat.* and *Zool.* egg-bearing; applied *esp.* to special receptacles in which the ova of some crustaceans are carried. **O·viform** [-FORM], *a.* having the form of an egg, egg-shaped. **Ovigerm** (ōu·vi,dʒɔ̄ɹm) [GERM], an (unfertilized) ovum. **Ovigerous** (ovi·dʒĕrəs) [-GEROUS], *a. Anat.* and *Zool.* bearing or carrying eggs. **Ovi·vorous** [L. *-vorus* devouring + -OUS], *a.* egg-eating.

Ovi-[2], comb. form of L. *ovis* sheep, as *ovibovine, oviform, ovivorous* adjs.

Ovicapsule (ōuvikæ·psiul). 1853. [f. OVI-[1] + CAPSULE.] *Anat.* and *Zool.* A capsule or sac containing an ovum or ova; an egg-case, an ovisac. Hence **Ovica·psular** *a.*

Ovicell (ōu·visel). 1870. [f. OVI-[1] + CELL.] **1.** A receptacle for the ova in certain Polyzoa; also called *oocyst* or *oœcium*. **2.** A cell which when impregnated becomes a new individual; an egg-cell; a germ-cell; an ovum or ovule 1875.

Ovicide (ōu·visəid), *joc.* 1845. [f. OVI-[2] + -CIDE [2].] Sheep-killing. So **O·vicidal** *a.*

Ovicyst (ōu·visist). 1877. [irreg. f. OVI-[1] + CYST.] *Zool.* A receptacle in which the ova are hatched in some ascidians. Hence **Ovicy·stic** *a.*

Ovidian (ovi·diăn), *a.* 1617. [-IAN.] Belonging to or characteristic of the Latin poet Ovid (Publius Ovidius Naso, B.C. 43–A.D. 17), or his poetry.

Oviduct (ōu·vidɒkt). 1757. [ad. med. or mod.L. *oviductus* = *ovi ductus*, DUCT of the egg.] *Anat.* and *Zool.* The duct or canal forming a passage for the ova or eggs from the ovary, esp. in birds; in mammals the corresponding structure is more usu. called the Fallopian tube. So **Oviducal** (ōu·vidiū̆kăl) *a.* of the nature of an o.

Ovine (ōu·vəin), *a.* 1828. [ad. L. *ovinus*, f. *ovis*; see -INE [1].] **1.** Of, pertaining to, or characteristic of, sheep or a sheep; in *Zool.* belonging to the *Ovinæ*, a subfamily of ruminants, comprising the various kinds of sheep. **2.** *fig.* Sheeplike, sheepish 1832.

Oviparous (ovi·pārəs), *a.* 1646. [f. L. *oviparus* egg-laying (f. OVI-[1] + *-parus*, f. *parere* to bring forth) + -OUS.] *Zool.* Producing ova or eggs; applied to animals that produce young by means of eggs. (Opp. to VIVIPAROUS.) So **Oviparity** (ōuvipæ·rĭti), the condition or character of being o.

Oviposit (ōuvipǫ·zit), *v.* 1816. [f. OVI-[1] + L. *posit-*, ppl. stem of *ponere* to place; cf. *deposit.*] *Zool. intr.* To deposit or lay an egg or eggs; esp. by means of an ovipositor, as an insect. **b.** *trans.* To deposit or lay (an egg) 1847. So **Oviposi·tion.**

Ovipositor (ōuvipǫ·zitǭɹ). 1816. [f. OVI-[1] + L. *positor*, agent-n. f. *ponere.*] *Entom.* A pointed tubular organ at the end of the abdomen of the female in many insects, by means of which the eggs are deposited, and (in many cases) a hole bored to receive them.

Ovisac (ōu·visæk). 1835. [f. OVI-[1] + SAC.] *Anat.* and *Zool.* A sac, cell, or pouch containing an ovum (as a Graafian follicle), or a number of ova; an egg-case.

Ovism (ōu·viz'm). 1892. [f. L. *ovum* + -ISM; in mod.F. *ovisme.*] *Biol.* The old theory that the ovum or female reproductive cell contains the whole of the future organism in an undeveloped state, the male cell or spermatozoon acting merely as a stimulant; opp. to *spermism* or *animalculism*. So **Ovist** (ōu·vist), one who holds the theory of o. 1836. **Ovi·stic** *a.* 1893.

Ovo- (ōuvo), used irreg. as comb. form of L. *ovum* egg, as in **O:vo·rhomboi·dal**, etc.

Ovogenesis (ōuvo,dʒe·nĭsis). 1886. [mod. L., f. OVO- + GENESIS; cf. OOGENESIS.] *Biol.* The production or formation of an ovum. So **Ovogene·tic, Ovo·genous** *adjs.* contributing to the formation or growth of an ovum.

Ovoid (ōu·void), *a.* and *sb.* 1828. [ad. mod. L. *ovoides*, f. L. *ovum*; see -OID.] **A.** *adj.* **1.** Resembling an egg, egg-shaped. **2.** *Comb.*: esp. with another adj., denoting modification of the form expressed by the latter, as *o.-oblong* 1870. **B.** *sb.* A body or figure of ovoid form 1831. So **Ovoi·dal** (ovoi·dăl) *a.* 1799.

Ovolo (ōu·vŏlo). *Pl.* **ovoli** (-lī). 1663. [ad. It. †*ovolo*, now *uovolo*, dim. of †*ovo*, *uovo* :—L. *ovum* egg.] *Arch.* A convex moulding of which the section is a quarter-circle or (approx.) a quarter-ellipse, receding from the vertical downwards; also called *quarter-round* or *echinus*.

Ovology (ovǫ·lŏdʒi). 1842. [f. OVO- + -LOGY. The regular form OOLOGY is app. not used in this sense.] That part of biology or embryology which treats of the formation and structure of the ova of animals. So **Ovolo·gical** *a.* **Ovo·logist.**

‖**O:vo-te·stis.** 1877. [mod L., f. OVO- + TESTIS.] *Zool.* An organ in certain invertebrates producing both ova and spermatozoa; a hermaphrodite gland.

Ovo-viviparous (ōu:vo,vivi·pārəs), *a.* 1801. [f. OVO- + VIVIPAROUS.] *Zool.* Combining oviparous and viviparous characters; producing eggs which are hatched within the body of the parent.

Ovular (ōu·viulăɹ), *a.* 1855. [ad. mod.L. *ovularis*, f. *ovulum* OVULE; see -AR.] *Biol.* Of, pertaining to, or of the nature of an ovule.

Ovulate (ōu·viulēt), *a.* 1861. [f. mod.L. *ovulum* OVULE + -ATE [2].] Having or containing an ovule or ovules. Chiefly in comb., as *biovulate*, etc.

Ovulation (ōuviulēⁱ·ʃən). 1853. [f. OVULE + -ATION.] *Physiol.* and *Zool.* The formation and development of ovules or ova, and (*esp.*) their discharge from the ovary, as occurring in female mammals.

Ovule (ōu·viul). 1830. [a. F., ad. mod.L. *ovulum*, dim. of *ovum* egg.] **1.** *Bot.* The rudimentary seed in a phanerogamous plant; the body which contains the female germ-cell, and after fertilization becomes a *seed*. **2.** *Zool.* and *Physiol.* The female germ-cell of an animal; *spec.* the unfertilized ovum 1857. So **Ovuli·ferous** *a.* bearing or producing ovules. **O·vulist** = OVIST.

‖**Ovulum** (ōu·viulɒ̆m). *Pl.* **ovula.** 1822. [mod.L. dim. of *ovum* egg.] **1.** *Zool.* and *Physiol.* = OVULE 2. 1822. **2.** *Zool.* A genus of gastropod molluscs, including the Egg-shell (*O. ovum*) with an egg-shaped shell 1837.

‖**Ovum** (ōu·vɒ̆m). *Pl.* **ova** (ōu·vă). 1706. [L. = egg.] **1.** *Zool.* The female germ in animals, capable when fertilized by the male sperm (and in some cases without such fertilization) of developing into a new individual. **2.** *Arch.* An egg-shaped ornament or carving 1727. **3.** *attrib.*, as *o.-product*, etc.; often with pl., as *ova-duct*, etc. 1753.

Owe (ōu), *v.* [Com.Teut.: OE. *āgan* = OHG. *eigan*, etc., one of the orig. Teut. preterite-present vbs. The OE. pa. t. *āhte*, ME. *āhte*, *ōhte*, survives as OUGHT *v.*] **I.** *trans.* To have; to possess; = OWN *v.* 2. *Obs.* exc. *dial.*

The Oxe..knowes who owes him, and feedes him 1628.

II. To have to pay. **1.** To be under obligation to pay or repay (money, etc.); to be indebted in, or to the amount of; to be under obligation to render (obedience, honour, etc.). Const. with simple dat. or *to*. (The chief current sense.) ME. **b.** *absol.* To be in debt 1460. **2.** *transf.* **a.** To have towards another (a feeling, regarded as something which is yet to be rendered in action); to bear (good or ill will). *Obs.* exc. in *to owe a grudge.* late ME. **b.** To bear *to* some one or something (a relation, as dependence, etc., which has to be acknowledged); to 'own' (*rare*) 1644. **3.** *fig.* To be indebted or beholden for. Const. *to* (or simple dative). 1591. †b. Without direct obj.: To be beholden (*to* a person *for* something) -1686.

1. He seide to the firste, Hou moche owist thou to my lord? WYCLIF *Luke* xvi. 5. b. I o. euen for the clothes vpon my backe 1607. 3. We o. the discovery of the prismatic spectrum to Sir Isaac Newton 1868.

III. †1. To have as a duty; to be under obligation (*to do* something). (Followed by inf. with or without *to*). -1537. †2. quasi-*impers.* (usu. with inf. clause as subject): (It) behoves, befits, is due (to); e.g. *him owe* (or *oweth*) = it behoves him, he ought; *as him owe*, as befits him, as is due to him -1500. Hence **Ow·er**, †an owner; a debtor (*rare*). **Ow·ing** *vbl. sb.* that which one owes; debt.

Owelty (ǭu·ělti). 1579. [a. AF. *owelté*, earlier *oeltet* :—L. *æqualitatem*, f. *æqualis* equal.] *Law.* Equality.

Owenian (ǭuī·niǎn), *a.* 1883. [f. surname *Owen* + -IAN.] Of or pertaining to Robert Owen (1771–1858), a social reformer who advocated the reorganization of society on a system of communistic co-operation, which he endeavoured to carry into practice in various industrial communities. So **Ow·enist, Ow·enite,** a follower of Owen.

Owing (ǭu·iŋ), *ppl. a.* late ME. [f. OWE *v.* + -ING [2].] 1. That owes; under obligation; indebted, bounden, beholden. Now *rare* or *Obs.* 2. That is yet to be paid or rendered; owed, due. Const. *to* or simple dat. (The usual current sense.) late ME. 3. *fig.* **Owing to**: a. *pred.* That owes its existence to; attributable to; caused by, 'due to' 1655. b. Hence, as prep. phr.: In consequence of, on account of, because of 1814.

1. I am greatly o. to your Lordship for your last favour PEPYS. 2. All that was o. for the children 1782. 3. b. O. to his natural disposition to study..he had been bred with a view to the bar SCOTT.

Owl (aul), *sb.* [Com. Teut.: OE. *ūle* :—*ūlôn*, *ūwlôn*; prob. ult. echoic. Cf. L. *ulula, ululare*, and HOWL, HOWLET.] 1. A nocturnal bird of prey, well known by its doleful 'hoot', having a large head, small face, raptorial beak, and large eyes directed forwards, beset by a disk of radiating feathers; feeding on small birds, mice, and the like. b. The common British species are the *Barn O.* (White, Silver, Yellow, Church, Hissing, Hobby, Screech O.); the *Tawny O.* (Brown, Grey, Beech, Ferry, Hoot, Hooting, Ivy, Wood O.); the *Long-eared* or *Horned O.*, etc. late ME. c. *Ornith.* Any bird of the sub-order *Striges.* (The known species are about 200.) 1706. d. In provb. sayings. late ME. 2. *transf.* and *fig.* Applied to a person in allusion to nocturnal habits, to appearance of gravity and wisdom, etc. Hence = wiseacre, solemn dullard. late ME. 3. a. A name for the Lump Fish, more fully *Sea O.* 1601. b. The owl-ray 1862. 4. A variety of the domestic pigeon; also called *O.-pigeon* 1725.

1. The clamorous Owle that nightly hoots SHAKS. d. *To carry* or *send owls to Athens*, after Gr. γλαῦκ' Ἀθήναζε ἄγειν = to take a commodity where it already abounds. As drunk as owls MARRYAT.

attrib. and *Comb.*, as *o.-flight, -eyed* adj., etc.; **o.-train** *U.S. slang*, a train running during the night. b. esp. in names of animals, as **o.-monkey**, a S. Amer. monkey of the genus *Nyctipithecus*; **-moth**, a very large Brazilian moth (*Erebus strix*) resembling an owl in its colouring and in the appearance of its hind wings; **-parrot** = KAKAPO; **-pigeon**: see 4; **-ray**: see 3. Hence **Owl** *v. intr.* to behave like an owl; to pry about, prowl, esp. in the dark. Now chiefly *dial.*

Ow·ler. *Obs.* exc. *Hist.* 1690. [app. f. prec. see -ER [1] 1.] One engaged in the illegal exportation or 'owling' of wool or sheep from England; also, a vessel so employed, an owling boat. So **Ow·ling** *vbl. sb.* the trade of an o.

Owlery (au·ləri). 1817. [f. OWL *sb.* + -ERY.] 1. A place where owls are kept; a haunt of owls. 2. Owlishness 1831.

Owlet (au·lėt). 1542. [dim. of OWL; see -ET; perh. altered from HOWLET.] An owl; a young owl or little owl.

Comb. **o.-moth**, an American name for any moth of the genus *Noctua* or family *Noctuidæ.*

Ow·l-glass. 1560. [f. OWL *sb.* + GLASS *sb.* 8.] = *Eulenspiegel*, name of a German jester of mediæval times; a prototype of roguish fools; hence, A jester, buffoon.

Owlish (au·liʃ), *a.* 1611. [f. OWL *sb.* + -ISH [1].] Owl-like; resembling an owl, or that of an owl. Hence **Ow·lish·ly** *adv.*, **-ness.**

Owl-light. 1599. [f. OWL *sb.* + LIGHT *sb.*] The dim light in which owls go abroad; twilight, dusk; also (in early use) the dark.

Own (ǭun), *a.* [OE. *āgen* :—OTeut. **aiganó-*, pa. pple. of **aigan* to possess, OE. *āgan* OWE *v.* The primary sense is 'possessed, owned'.] That is possessed or owned by the person or thing indicated by the preceding sb. or pron.; of or belonging to oneself or itself; proper, peculiar, particular, individual. 1. Used after a possessive case or adj., to emphasize the possessive meaning. b. Expressing tenderness or affection; also (usu. *joc.*) in *superl.* = very own. late ME. c. *Own* in the predicate sometimes has the force of *self* in the subject, as in 'I am my own master' = 'I myself (and not some one else) am my master' 1551. 2. Without possessive preceding. Now *rare*, and usu. with *an* or in *pl.* OE. 3. *absol.* (mostly with preceding possessive): That which is (one's) own; property, possessions; (one's) own goods, kinsfolk, friends, etc. Somewhat *arch.* OE.

1. And find no spot of all the world my o. GOLDSM. The reader who loves history for its o. sake 1895. Phr. *To be one's o. man* (*woman*), to be independent; to have the full control or use of one's faculties. b. By me, thine owne true Knight SHAKS. 2. *An o. brother*, as dist. from a half-brother or brother-in-law, etc.; *o. cousins*, first cousins. 3. *Wint. T.* v. iii. 123. He gave freely of his o. 1839. Phr. *Of* (*one's*) *o.*, that is one's own; belonging to oneself.

Spec. phrases. *To hold one's o.*, to maintain one's position; not to suffer defeat or derogation. †*To tell one his o.*, to tell him the plain truth about himself. *On one's o.* (colloq.), on one's own account, responsibility, resources, etc. *To get one's o. back* (colloq.), to get even with, to revenge oneself *on* someone. Hence **Ownness** (ǭu·nnės), the fact or quality of being one's own or peculiar to oneself 1642.

Own (ǭun), *v.* [OE. *āgnian*, f. *āgen* OWN *a.* After OE. and early ME. scarcely found till 17th c., the usual word in sense 2 in the 14–17th c. being OWE.] †1. *trans.* To make (a thing) one's own; to seize, win, gain; to adopt as one's own -ME. 2. To have or hold as one's own, possess OE. †b. To have as one's function or business -1714. 3. a. To acknowledge as one's own 1610. b. To recognize as an acquaintance. *Obs.* exc. *dial.* 1650. †c. To claim for one's own -1815. 4. To acknowledge as approved or accepted; to countenance, vindicate. Somewhat *arch.* 1610. 5. To acknowledge (something) in its relation to oneself; also, to confess to be valid, true, or actual; to admit 1655. b. *intr.* To confess (*to* something) 1776. c. *To o. up* (colloq.): to confess fully or frankly. (*intr.* with or without *to*, or with *obj. clause*) 1880. 6. *spec.* To acknowledge as having supremacy, authority, or power over one; to yield obedience or submission to 1695.

2. Gardens owned by the wealthier residents 1858. b. *Wint. T.* IV. iv. 143. 3. a. Thy Brat hath been cast out..No Father owning it SHAKS. b. My Lord Chaimberlaine..who owned and spoke to me PEPYS. 5. Her age was about thirty, for she owned six and twenty FIELDING. I readily o. myself at a loss 1758. I o. to you that I have a great fear of the damage that ridicule might do 1873. b. He owns to disliking the Doctor 1853. 6. Till all Thy creatures o. Thy sway 1870.

Owner (ǭu·nəɹ). ME. [f. prec. + -ER [1].] One who owns or holds something; one who has the rightful claim or title to a thing. Also *attrib.*, as *owner-driver.*

She now lived upon an estate of which she no longer was the o. MISS BURNEY. Hence **Ow·nerless** *a.* **Ow·nership,** the fact or state of being an o.; property, proprietorship 1583.

Ox (ǫks). [Com. Teut.: OE. *oxa* wk. masc. :—OTeut. **ohs-n-* :—pre-Teut. **uksén-*. The only word in general Eng. use which retains the orig. pl. *-en*, OE. *-an*, of the weak declension.] 1. The domestic bovine quadruped (sexually dist. as *bull* and *cow*); in common use, applied to the male castrated and used for draught purposes, or reared to serve as food. 2. *Zool.* Any beast of the bovine family of ruminants, including the domestic European species, the 'wild oxen' preserved in certain parks in Britain, the buffalo, bison, gaur, yak, musk-ox, etc. OE. 3. *transf.* An ancient coin bearing a representation of an ox; also *attrib.* as *ox-coin*, etc. 1607. 4. *fig.* †a. A fool -1640. b. The *black ox*, misfortune, adversity; old age 1546.

1. A herd of Beeves, faire Oxen and faire Kine MILT. 2. *American ox*, the bison or buffalo; *Cape ox, Bos caffer*; *Indian, Brahmin*, or *Dwarf ox*, the zebu (*B. indicus*); *Musk ox*, a ruminant of arctic America, *Ovibos moschatus.* 4. a. *Merry W.* v. v. 126. b. Provb. *The black o. has trod on* (*his*, etc.) *foot.*

attrib. and *Comb.*: **o.-antelope**, a bovine antelope; in R. V. (*Num.* xxiii. 22) a marginal reading for 'wild ox', identified as *Bos primigenius*; **-bile** = *ox-gall*; **-biter**, a bird: (*a*) = *ox-pecker*; (*b*) *U.S.* the cow-bird, *Molobrus ater* or *M. pecoris*; **-fly, -gad-fly**, the gad-fly or bot-fly, *Œstrus bovis*; **-gall,** the gall of the ox, used for cleansing purposes, also in painting and pharmacy; **-god,** Apis, the sacred bull of the Egyptians; **-heart** *a.*, heart-shaped and large; applied esp. to a variety of cherry; also as *sb.*; **oxland** = OXGANG; also, plough-land; **-pecker,** the genus *Buphaga* of African birds, feeding on the parasitic larvæ that infest the hide of cattle; also called *beef-eater*; **-ray,** a fish, the large horned ray, *Cephaloptera giorna.* See also Main words.

b. In names of plants (in some of which *ox-*, like *horse-*, denotes a coarse or large species, or means 'eaten by' or 'fit for oxen'): **ox-bane,** a plant injurious to cattle; the Poison-bulb of S. Africa, *Buphane toxicaria*; **-daisy** = *Ox-eye daisy*; **-heal** or **-heel,** Bear's-foot or Fetid Hellebore, *Helleborus fœtidus*; **-mushroom,** a name for very large specimens of the common mushroom. Hence **O·x-like** *a.* and *adv.* like, or resembling that of an ox; after the manner of an ox.

Ox-, a formative of chemical terms. 1. = OXY- from *oxygen*, as in *ox-* or *oxy-acetic, oxiodic*, etc. 2. A shortening of OXAL-, as in OXAMIC, etc.

Oxal-, comb. element in chemical terms, used in the sense 'derived from or related to oxalic acid', or 'containing the radical oxalyl'. **O·xalan** [-AN 2; cf. *alloxan*] = OXALURAMIDE. **Oxale·thyline,** a poisonous oily liquid of composition $C_6H_{10}N_2$; also a general name for the series to which this belongs, as *chloroxalethyline* $C_6H_9ClN_2$. **O·xalite** *Min.*, native ferrous oxalate.

Oxalate (ǫ·ksălět). 1791. [a. F., f. OXAL- in *oxalique* OXALIC + -ATE [4].] *Chem.* A salt of oxalic acid.

Oxa·ldehyde. [f. OX- 2 + ALDEHYDE: = *oxalic aldehyde.*] *Chem.* = GLYOXAL.

Oxalic (ǫksæ·lik), *a.* 1791. [ad. F. *oxalique*, f. L. OXALIS; see -IC.] *Chem.* Of, derived from, or characteristic of the *Oxalis* or Wood Sorrel: *spec.* a. *Oxalic acid*: a highly poisonous and intensely sour acid ($C_2H_2O_4 = C_2O_2{\cdot}2HO$), the first member of the dibasic series having the general formula $C_nH_{2n-2}O_4$. b. *O. ether*, a name for neutral ethyl oxalate ($C_6H_{10}O_4 = C_2O_2{\cdot}2C_2H_5{\cdot}O_2$); also extended to the oxalates of the alcohol radicals in general.

‖ **Oxalis** (ǫ·ksălis). 1706. [L. *oxalis, -alid-*, a. Gr. ὀξαλίς, f. ὀξύς sour, acid.] *Bot.* A genus of plants, mostly herbs, with delicate five-parted flowers, and leaves usu. of three leaflets; the common British species is *O. Acetosella*, Wood Sorrel.

Oxalo-, comb. element = OXAL-, used bef. consonants; as **O·xalo·ni·trate,** a salt of oxalic and nitrate acid.

Oxaluramide (ǫksălyūə·rămaid). 1866. [See next and AMIDE.] *Chem.* The amide of oxaluric acid ($C_3H_5N_3O_3$), obtained as a white crystalline powder by the action of ammonia and hydrocyanic acid on alloxan; also called *oxalan.*

Oxaluric (ǫksălyūə·rik), *a.* 1836. [f. OXAL- + URIC.] *Chem.* In *O. acid*: a monobasic acid ($C_3H_4N_2O_4$), which may be regarded as oxalic acid and urea *minus* water, obtained as a white crystalline powder, of a very acid taste. Hence **Oxalu·rate,** a salt of o. acid.

Oxalyl (ǫ·ksălil). 1859. [f. OXAL- + -YL.] *Chem.* The hypothetical radical (C_2O_2) of oxalic acid.

Oxamic (ǫksæ·mik), *a.* 1838. [f. OX- 2 = OXAL- + AMIC.] *Chem.* In *O. acid*: a monobasic acid, $C_2H_3NO_3$ (= $NH_2{\cdot}C_2O_2{\cdot}OH$), produced by the dehydration of acid oxalate of ammonium, and in other ways; its salts are **O·xamates.** *O. ether*: an ether in which one or other of the hydrogen-atoms of oxamic acid is replaced by an alcohol-radical; e.g. *ethylic oxamate* or **Oxame·thane,** $C_4H_7NO_3$.

Oxamide (ǫ·ksămɔid). 1838. [f. OX- **2** + AMIDE.] *Chem.* The diamide $C_2O_2.N_2H_4$, representing two molecules of ammonia in which two atoms of hydrogen are replaced by oxalyl, C_2O_2; also called *oxalamide.*

Oxanilic (ǫksăni·lik), *a.* 1866. [f. OX- **2** = OXAL- + ANILIC.] *Chem.* In *O. acid* (= phenyloxamic acid): a crystalline substance ($C_8H_7NO_3$) obtained by heating aniline with an excess of oxalic acid; its salts are **Oxa·nilates.** So **Oxani·lamide** (= monophenyloxamide), a snow-white flaky substance ($C_8H_8N_2O_2$) obtained in the decomposition of cyaniline by hydrochloric acid; **Oxa·nilide** (= diphenyloxamide), a substance ($C_{14}H_{12}N_2O_2$) crystallizing in white scales, obtained by heating aniline oxalate, or in other ways; **Oxa·niline,** a base (C_6H_7NO) obtained by heating amido-salicylic acid.

O·x-bird, o·xbird. 1547. [f. OX + BIRD **2.**] A name applied to various British small wild-fowl; esp. the Dunlin (*Tringa variabilis*).

Ox-bow, oxbow (ǫ·ksbōu). late ME. [f. OX + BOW *sb.*[1]] **1.** = BOW *sb.*[1] 5. **2.** *U.S.* A semicircular bend in a river; hence, the land included in this. Also *attrib.*, as *ox-bow bend.* 1797.

Ox-eye, oxeye (ǫ·ks,ɔi). late ME. **1.** The eye of an ox; an eye like that of an ox, a large (human) eye 1688. **2.** A popular name of various birds. **a.** *esp.* the Great Titmouse (*Parus major*) 1544. **b.** Also, locally, the Dunlin, *Tringa variabilis*; etc. 1589. **3.** Applied to various plants: **a.** A species of the genus *Buphthalmum* (N.O. *Compositæ*). late ME. **b.** The British wild plants *Chrysanthemum segetum*, the Corn-marigold or Yellow Ox-eye, and *C. Leucanthemum*, the White Ox-eye, Ox-eye daisy, Dog-daisy, or Moon-daisy 1625. **c.** The American composite plant, *Heliopsis lævis*, with large yellow flowers. **4.** Applied to a drinking-cup in use at certain Oxford colleges 1703. **5.** *Naut.* = BULL'S EYE 10. 1598. Hence **O·x-ey·ed** *a.* having large full eyes like those of an ox.

Oxford (ǫ·ksfǫ̈ɹd), name of a university town in England [in OE. *Oxena-, Oxnaford* 'ford of oxen', ME. *Oxneford, Oxenford*], used attrib. in various expressions.

O. clay (*Geol.*), a deposit of stiff blue clay underlying the 'coral rag' of the Middle Oolite in the midland counties of England, and esp. in Oxfordshire; **O. corners,** in *Printing*, ruled border lines enclosing the print *of* a book, etc., crossing and extending beyond each other at the corners; **O. frame,** a picture-frame the sides of which cross each other and project at the corners; **O. man,** a man who has been educated at the University of Oxford; **O. mixture,** a very dark grey woollen cloth; **O. Movement** (*Ch. Hist.*), the movement for the revival of Catholic doctrine and observance in the Church of England, which began at Oxford about 1833; **O. oolite** (*Geol.*): the middle division of the Oolitic system; **O. School** (*Ch. Hist.*), the school of thought represented by the Oxford Movement; the body of persons belonging to this; **O. shirting,** a kind of striped material for shirts and dresses; **O. shoe,** a style of shoe laced over the instep; **O. Tracts,** the 'Tracts for the Times' issued 1833–41 in advocacy of the Oxford Movement, whence the movement is also known as TRACTARIAN. Hence **Oxfordian** (ǫksfǭ·ɹdiăn) *a.* pertaining to Oxford; in *Geol.* applied to the lower division of the Middle or Oxford Oolite.

Oxgang (ǫ·ksgæŋ). *Obs.* exc. *Hist.* Chiefly *north.* [f. OX + GANG *sb.* I. 3.] The eighth part of the CARUCATE or ploughland, varying from 10 to 18 acres, or more; a bovate.

O·x-ha·rrow. 1523. A large and powerful harrow used on clay lands; orig. drawn by oxen.

Ox-head (ǫ·kshed). 1595. [f. OX + HEAD.] **1.** The head of an ox, or a representation of one. (Used in SHAKS. *John* II. i. 292 with ref. to cuckoldry.) **2.** *transf.* A stupid person; a dolt; also *attrib.* or quasi-*adj.* stupid 1634.

O·xherd. [f. OX + HERD *sb.*[2]] A keeper of oxen; a cowherd.

Ox-horn (ǫ·kshǭɹn). 1601. [f. OX + HORN.] A horn of an ox. (Sometimes used as a drinking-vessel.)

Oxi-, earlier spelling of many words now spelt OXY-.

Oxidable (ǫ·ksidăb'l), *a.* Now *rare.* Also **oxy-.** 1790. [a. F., now *oxydable*, f. *oxider* to OXIDATE; see -ABLE.] *Chem.* Capable of being oxidated; oxidizable. Hence **O:xida·bi·lity.**

Oxidate (ǫ·ksideⁱt), *v.* Now *rare.* Also **oxy-.** 1790. [f. F. *oxider* + -ATE [3].] *Chem.* **1.** *trans.* = OXIDIZE 1. **2.** = OXIDIZE 2. 1807. Hence **Oxida·tion,** combination with oxygen; conversion into an oxide or oxygen-compound. **O·xidative** *a.* having the property of oxidizing. **O·xidator,** an oxidizing agent; an apparatus for directing a stream of oxygen into the flame of a lamp.

Oxide (ǫ·ksɔid, ǫ·ksid), *sb.* Also **oxid** (now chiefly *U.S.*), **oxyde, oxyd.** 1790. [a. F., now *oxyde*, f. *oxy*(*gène* + *-ide*, after *acide.*] *Chem.* A compound of oxygen with another element, or with an organic radical.

Oxidize (ǫ·ksidɔiz), *v.* Also **oxy-.** 1802. [f. prec. + -IZE.] *Chem.* **1.** *trans.* To cause to combine with oxygen; to convert into an oxide or oxygen-compound. (In the case of a metal, often = to rust, make rusty.) **2.** *intr.* To take up or enter into combination with oxygen; to become converted into an oxide. (Of a metal, often = to rust, become rusty.) 1826.

Oxidized silver, a name erron. given to silver with a dark coating of silver sulphide. Hence **O·xidizable,** also **oxy-,** *a.* **O:xidiza·tion,** also **oxy-,** oxidation. **O·xidizer,** also **oxy-,** an oxidizing agent.

†Oxi·dulated, *ppl. a.* Also **oxy-.** 1806. [f. obs. F. *oxidulé*, f. *oxydule*, 'lowest degree of oxidation, protoxide', dim. of *oxyde*; after L. *acidus, acidulus.*] *Chem.* Combined with a smaller proportion of oxygen than in another compound; as in *o. iron*, a former name for the magnetic oxide of iron (Fe_3O_4) as dist. from the peroxide (Fe_2O_3) –1882.

Oxime (ǫ·ksɔim), **oxim** (ǫ·ksim). 1891. [f. OX- **1** + *-ime*, shortened from IMIDE.] *Chem.* A chemical compound containing the divalent group: N(OH) joined to a carbon atom, esp. in the combination C_nH_{2n}: as *acetoxime* C_2H_4: N(OH), etc. Also called **O·ximide.**

Oxindole (ǫksi·ndoᵘl). Also **-ol.** 1872. [f. OX- **1** + INDOLE.] *Chem.* A colourless crystalline substance (C_8H_7NO), becoming an oil when heated, consisting of indole combined with one equivalent of oxygen. Hence *dioxindole*, containing two equivalents of oxygen ($C_8H_7NO_2$): see DI-[2] 2.

Oxlip (ǫ·kslip). [OE. *oxanslyppe*, f. *oxan* gen. sing. of *oxa* OX + *slyppe* slimy or viscous dropping; see COWSLIP.] The name of a flowering herb: applied to a plant intermediate between the Cowslip (*Primula veris*) and Primrose (*P. vulgaris*); now ascertained to be a natural hybrid between these. **b.** By recent botanists appropriated to *Primula elatior* (Jacq.), found in Britain only in Essex and its neighbourhood.

Oxonian (ǫksōᵘ·niăn), *a.* and *sb.* 1540. [f. *Oxonia*, latinized form of *Oxenford*, OXFORD + -AN.] **A.** *adj.* Of or belonging to Oxford 1644. **B.** *sb.* A native or inhabitant of Oxford; usu., a member of the University of Oxford 1540. **b.** A kind of shoe, which covers the instep and is buttoned 1848.

Oxo·nic (ǫksǫ·nik), *a.* 1881. [f. OX- **2** + *carb*)*onic.*] *Chem.* In *O. acid*, $C_4H_5N_3O_4$, a substance formed by the gradual oxidation of uric acid in an alkaline solution, and yielding on decomposition glyoxyl-urea and carbon dioxide. Its salts are **O·xonates.**

Ox-stall (ǫ·ksstǭl). late ME. A stall or stable for oxen.

O·x-tail. 1460. The tail of an ox; esp. as an article of food. Also *attrib.* in *ox-tail soup*, etc.

Oxter (ǫ·kstəɹ). *Sc.* and *n. dial.* 1532. [f. OE. *óxta, óhsta*, from same stem as OE. *óxn* :—**óhsna* = armpit.] The armpit; also, the under side of the upper arm.

Ox-tongue, oxtongue (ǫ·ks,tɒŋ). ME. **1.** The tongue of an ox. **2.** Pop. name of several plants: = LANGUE DE BŒUF 1. **†a.** *orig.* applied to various plants having rough leaves, more or less tongue-shaped; chiefly species of bugloss, borage, or alkanet –1611. **b.** A composite plant, *Helminthia echioides*, also called *Prickly Ox-tongue* 1760.

Oxy- (ǫksi), repr. Gr. ὀξυ-, comb. form of ὀξύς sharp, keen, acute, pungent, acid. **1.** Words of various kinds, in which *oxy-* stands for 'sharp', 'acute' (in *lit.* or *fig.* sense): as **Oxycephalic** (-sĭfæ·lik) *a.*, *Anthropol.* having a skull of pointed or conical shape; so **Oxyce·phaly.** ‖**Oxyo·pia** [mod.L., f. Gr. ὤπ- to see], *Phys.* abnormal acuteness of sight. **2.** Chemical words, in which *oxy-* is taken as the comb. form of OXYGEN (cf. HYDRO- d); denoting either simply the presence of oxygen, as in OXYACID, etc., or the addition of oxygen to the substance denoted by the simple word, and thus in effect = *oxygenated* or *oxidized.* See also OXYCHLORIDE, OXYSULPHATE, etc. A looser use is seen in **oxy-alcohol** (or **oxy-spirit**), **oxy-coal gas, oxy-house-gas,** etc., terms applied to the flame produced by mixing the vapour of a spirit lamp, ordinary house-gas, etc., with oxygen; so *oxy-alcohol blow-pipe, lamp*, etc.; **oxy-paraffin** *a.*, applied to a paraffin lamp with arrangement for the complete oxygenation of the flame. But the most frequent use of *oxy-* is as a prefix to names of organic substances, to denote a derivative or related compound in which an atom of hydrogen is displaced by one of hydroxyl (HO); in which sense *hydroxy-* is now often preferred; see OXYACID 2.

O:xy-ace·tylene, *a.* 1909. Consisting of, or involving the use of, a mixture of oxygen and acetylene.

Oxyacid, oxy-acid (ǫksi,æ·sid). Also **oxi-, ox-acid.** 1836. [f. OXY- 2 + ACID.] *Chem.* **1.** An acid containing oxygen (e.g. carbonic acid, CH_2O_3) as dist. from a *hydracid* (e.g. hydrochloric acid, HCl). **2.** *Organic Chem.* In pl., a name given to several series of acids derived from those of the fatty or the aromatic series, by the substitution of one or more hydroxyl for one or more hydrogen atoms; hence called more exactly *hydroxy-acids.*

Oxy-calcium (ǫksikæ·lsiŏm). 1865. [f. OXY- 2 + CALCIUM.] *Chem.* In *oxy-calcium light* = LIMELIGHT.

O·xychlor-, o·xychloro-. 1818. *Chem.* Containing oxygen and chlorine, as *oxychlorether*, a liquid, $CH_2Cl.CH(OH)(OC_2H_5)$, obtained by the action of water at high temperature on bichlor ether. So **Oxychlo·ride,** a combination of oxygen and chlorine with another element, as *Phosphorus oxychloride* $POCl_3$; also, a compound of a metallic chloride with the oxide of the same metal. Also called **Oxychlo·ruret.**

Oxygen (ǫ·ksidʒĕn). Also **†oxi-, †-gene.** 1790. [a. F. *oxygène* (for *principe oxygène*, earlier *oxygine*), intended for 'acidifying (principle)', *principe acidifiant* (Lavoisier); see OXY- and -GEN **1**; oxygen being at first held to be the essential principle in the formation of acids.] One of the non-metallic elements, a colourless invisible gas, without taste or smell. Symbol O: atomic weight 16.

It is the most abundant of all the elements, existing, in the free state (mixed with nitrogen), in atmospheric air, and, in combination, in water and most minerals and organic substances. It combines with nearly all other elements (forming *oxides*), the process of combination being in some cases so energetic as to produce sensible light and heat (*combustion*), in others very gradual, as in the rusting or *oxidation* of metals. It is essential, in the free state, to the life of all animals and plants, and is absorbed into the organism in *respiration*; hence it was formerly called *vital air.* Priestley, who isolated it in 1774, holding it to be common air deprived of PHLOGISTON (q. v.), called it *dephlogisticated air.*

attrib. and *Comb.* **a.** *attrib.* or *adj.* in *o. gas*, a name for oxygen in the free or gaseous state. **b.** The sb. in attrib. use or in comb.; as in *o. acid* (= OXYACID 1), *-carrier, treatment*, etc. Hence **Oxyge·nic** *a.* (*rare*) of the nature of, consisting of, o.

Oxygenate (ǫ·ksidʒĕneⁱt, ǫksi·dʒĕneⁱt), *v.* Also **†oxi-.** 1790. [a. F. *oxygéner*, f. *oxygène*; see -ATE [3].] *trans.* To supply, treat, or mix with oxygen; to cause oxygen to combine with (a substance); to oxidate, oxidize; *esp.* to charge (the blood) with oxygen by respiration. So **Oxygena·tion,** the action of oxygenating or condition of being oxygenated; oxidation. **O·xygenator,** an oxidator.

Oxygenize (ǫ·ksidʒĕnɔiz, ǫksi·dʒĕnɔiz), *v.* 1802. [f. OXYGEN + -IZE; cf. *carbonize.*] *trans.* = OXYGENATE *v.* Chiefly in *pa. pple.* (or *ppl. a.*) Hence **O·xygeni:zable** *a.* that can be oxygenized.

Oxygenous (ǫksi·dʒĕnəs), *a.* 1787. [f. OXYGEN + -OUS.] **†a.** Acidifying; *o. gas*, oxygen; *o. principle*, tr. Lavoisier's *principe oxygine* –1794. b. Of the nature of, consisting of, or containing oxygen 1822.

Oxyhæmoglobin, -hemoglobin (ǫ:ksihīmǫglōᵘ·bin). 1873. [OXY- 2.] *Chem.* The form in which hæmoglobin exists in arterial and capillary blood where it is loosely combined with oxygen.

Oxyhy·drate. 1876. *Chem.* A hydrated oxide or hydrate of a metal, as *o. of iron*.

Oxyhydrogen (ǫksihəi·drŏdʒĕn), *a.* 1827. [f. OXY- 2 + HYDROGEN.] Consisting of, or involving the use of, a mixture of oxygen and hydrogen.

O. blowpipe, a compound blowpipe in which two streams, of oxygen and hydrogen, meet as they issue; used to produce an extremely hot flame by the burning of the hydrogen in the oxygen. *O. light*, the light obtained by directing such a flame upon lime; lime-light. So *o. flame, jet, lamp*, etc. *O. microscope*, etc., one in which the object is illuminated by an o. light.

Oxymel (ǫ·ksimel). *Obs.* or *arch.* Also †oxi-, †-mell. late ME. [a. L., a. Gr. ὀξύμελι, f. ὀξύς sour + μέλι honey.] A drink or syrup compounded of vinegar and honey, sometimes with other ingredients.

‖ **Oxymoron** (ǫksimōᵊ·rǫn). 1657. [a. Gr. ὀξύμωρον adj. neut. used subst., f. ὀξύς sharp + μωρός dull, foolish.] A rhetorical figure by which contradictory terms are conjoined so as to give point to the statement or expression. (Now often *loosely* = a contradiction in terms.)

Voltaire.. we might call, by an o..., an 'Epicurean pessimist' 1890.

†**Oxymuria·tic,** *a.* 1796. [f. OXY- 2 + MURIATIC.] *Chem.* In *o. acid* (also *o. gas*): a former name of chlorine, as a supposed compound of oxygen and 'muriatic' (hydrochloric) acid –1835. Hence **Oxymu·riate**, a salt of 'o. acid'; a chlorate or chloride, as *oxymuriate of tin* = stannic chloride, *oxymuriate of potash* = potassium chlorate –1830.

Oxyni·trate. 1809. [f. OXY- 2 + NITRATE.] *Chem.* A compound of the oxide and nitrate of a metal.

Oxyntic (ǫksi·ntik), *a.* 1884. [f. Gr. *ὀξυντός, vbl. adj. from ὀξύνειν to sharpen, f. ὀξύς; see -IC.] *Physiol.* Rendering acid, acidifying; applied to certain glands of the stomach, or to cells in them, supposed to produce the hydrochloric acid of the gastric juice.

Oxyphil(e (ǫ·ksifil), *a.* 1896. [f. Gr. ὀξυ- OXY- + -φιλος -PHIL(E.] *Biol.* 'Acid-loving': applied to certain white blood-corpuscles or other cells having an affinity for acids.

Oxyrhynch (ǫ·ksiriŋk). 1839. [f. OXY- 1 + Gr. ῥύγχος snout.] 1. Any crab of the group *Oxyrhyncha*, characterized by a triangular cephalothorax with projecting rostrum. 2. A fish; = next.

‖ **Oxyrhynchus** (ǫksiri·ŋkǫs). 1661. [ad. Gr. ὀξύρρυγχος sharp-snouted, epithet of a fish.] A fish (*Mormyrus oxyrhynchus*) found in the Nile, esteemed sacred by the Egyptians.

Oxy-salt (ǫ·ksi,sǫlt). Also †oxi-. 1833. [f. OXY- 2 + SALT.] *Chem.* A salt containing oxygen; a salt of an oxyacid.

†**Oxysu·lphate.** 1802. Obs. name for a metallic sulphate containing a larger proportion of oxygen, as *o. of iron* = ferric sulphate –1815. So **Oxysu·lphide**, a compound of an element or positive compound radical with oxygen and sulphur.

Oxytocic (ǫksitǫ·sik), *a.* and *sb.* 1853. [f. Gr. ὀξυτόκιον = B., f. ὀξυ- OXY- 1 + τόκος childbirth.] *Med.* A. *adj.* Accelerating parturition. B. *sb.* A medicine having this property.

Oxytone (ǫ·ksitoᵘn), *a.* and *sb.* Also **oxyton.** 1764. [ad. Gr. ὀξύτονος having the acute accent, f. ὀξύς sharp + τόνος pitch, tone, accent.] *Gr. Gram.* A. *adj.* Having an acute accent on the last syllable. B. *sb.* A word so accented.

Oy, oe (oi, ō[i]). *Sc.* 1470. [a. Gael. *ogha.*] A grandchild.

Oyer (oi·əɹ). late ME. [a. AF. *oyer* = OF. *oir, oyr*, mod.F. *ouïr* :—L. *audire*; the inf. used subst.] *Law.* 1. Short for *oyer and terminer*; a criminal trial under the writ so called. 2. In *Common Law*, the hearing of some document read in court; esp. of an instrument in writing, pleaded by one party, when the other 'craved oyer' of it. (Abolished 1852.) 1602.

Oyer and terminer (oi·ər ənd tɔ̄·ɹminəɹ). *Law.* a. In **Commission of o. and t.**, a commission formerly directed to the King's Judges, Serjeants, etc., empowering them to hear and determine indictments on treasons, felonies, etc.; also called *Writ of o. and t.* Now, the most comprehensive of the commissions granted to judges on circuit, directing them to hold courts for the trial of offences. late ME. b. In some States of the American Union: A court of higher criminal jurisdiction 1888.

Oyez, oyes (ōᵘ:ye·s), *int.* (*sb.*). late ME. [OF. *oiez, oyez*, hear ye! imper. pl. of *oir* to hear :—L. *audiatis* pres. subj.; orig. pron. *oye·ts*, subseq. *oye·s*, and hence often written *O yes!*] A. *imper. vb.*, and *int.* 'Hear, hear ye'; a call by the public crier or by a court officer (usu. thrice uttered) to command silence and attention for the reading of a proclamation, etc.

But when the Crier cried, 'O Yes!' the people cried, 'O No! BARHAM.

B. as *sb.* A call or exclam. of 'Oyez'. Pl. †*oyesses*, also †*oyes.* 1494.

Crier Hob-goblin, make the Fairy Oyes SHAKS.

Oyster (oi·stəɹ), *sb.* ME. [a. OF. *oistre, uistre, huistre*, mod.F. *huître* = obs. It. *ostrea*, ad. L. *ostrea* fem., beside *ostreum* neut., a. Gr. ὄστρεον oyster.] 1. A well-known edible bivalve mollusc of the family *Ostreidæ*; *esp.* the common European species *Ostrea edulis*, and the N. American species, *O. virginica* of the Atlantic, and *O. lurida*, the Californian oyster, of the Pacific coast. 2. Applied also to other bivalve molluscs resembling the oyster, as the PEARL-OYSTER, *Meleagrina margaritifera*, of the family *Aviculidæ*; also with qualifications, as **Thorny o.** of the genus *Spondylus*, etc. late ME. 3. The morsel of dark meat in the front hollow of the side bone of a fowl 1883. 4. *Vegetable o.*: the salsify 1864.

attrib. and *Comb.*, as **o.-bank**, an oyster-bed; **-bed**, (*a*) a layer of oysters covering a tract of the bottom of the sea, a place where oysters breed or are bred; (*b*) a layer or stratum containing fossil oystres; †**-board**, a board or table used for displaying oysters for sale; applied contempt. to the communion-tables introduced by the early Reformers and the Puritans; **-brood**, the spat of oysters in its second year; **-farm**, a tract of sea-bottom where oysters are bred artificially; **-field** = *o.-bed*; **-fish**, †(*a*) an oyster; (*b*) the toad-fish (*Batrachus tau*); (*c*) the tautog (*Tautoga onitis*); **-green**, the seaweed *Ulva lactuca*, also *U. latissima*; **-knife**, a knife adapted for opening oysters; **-plant**, (*a*) the sea-lungwort (*Mertensia maritima*); (*b*) the salsify (*Tragopogon porrifolius*); **-plover** = OYSTER-CATCHER; **-shell**, the shell of an o.; **-tree**, the mangrove; †**-wench**, **-wife**, **-woman**, a girl or woman who sells oysters. Hence **Oy·ster** *v.* to fish for or gather oysters. **Oy·stering** *vbl. sb.* **Oy·stery** *a.* abounding in oysters; like an o.

Oy·ster-ca·tcher. 1731. A maritime wading bird of the family *Hæmatopodidæ* with black-and-white or black plumage, and bill and feet of a brilliant red.

The common European species is *Hæmatopus ostralegus* Linn.; the N. American species is *H. palliatus*.

Oz. 1548. [a. It. *ōz* or *o̅z*, 15th c. abbrev. of *onza, onze.*] An abbrev. used for 'ounce', 'ounces', as in 3 lb. 8 oz.

‖ **Ozæna, -ena** (ozī·nă). 1591. [L., a. Gr. ὄζαινα a fetid polypus in the nose, f. ὄζειν to smell.] *Path.* A fetid muco-purulent discharge from the nose, due to ulcerative disease of the mucous membrane, frequently with necrosis of the bone 1656.

Ozocerite, ozokerit(e (ozǭ·sĕrəit, ozōᵘ·kĕrit, -əit; ōᵘzosīᵊ·rəit, -kīᵊ·rəit). 1834. [a. G. *ozokerit*, arbitrarily f. Gr. ὄζειν (ὄζω I smell) + κηρός bees-wax + -ITE [1].] *Min.* A wax-like fossil resin, of brownish-yellow colour and aromatic odour; also called *native paraffin, mineral tallow*, or *mineral wax.* Used to make candles, insulate electrical conductors, etc.

Ozone (ōᵘ·zoᵘn). 1840. [a. F., f. Gr. ὄζειν to smell + -ONE.] *Chem.* An allotropic condition of oxygen, existing in a state of condensation (having three atoms to the molecule, O_3), with a peculiarly pungent and refreshing odour.

It is produced in the electrolysis of water, and by the silent discharge of electricity or the passage of electric sparks through the air (whence it is sometimes perceived after a thunderstorm). Hence **Ozonic** (ozǭ·nik) *a.* of the nature of, or containing, ozone.

Ozonify (ozōᵘ·nifəi) *v. trans.* to convert into ozone; to ozonize.

Ozonize (ōᵘ·zoᵘnəiz), *v.* 1850. [f. prec. + -IZE.] 1. *trans.* To convert (oxygen) into ozone 1858. 2. To treat or act upon with ozone 1850. Hence **O:zoniza·tion. O·zonizer**, an apparatus for producing ozone.

Ozonometer (ōᵘzoᵘnǫ·mĭtəɹ). 1862. [f. OZONE; see -METER.] An instrument or device for ascertaining the amount of ozone in the air. So **O:zonome·tric** *a.* pertaining to ozonometry. **Ozono·metry**, the measurement of the ozone in the air.

Ozonoscope (ozōᵘ·nǫskoᵘp). 1872. [f. OZONE; see -SCOPE.] An instrument for showing the presence or amount of ozone in the air. So **Ozonosco·pic** *a.*

P

P (pī), the sixteenth letter of the English alphabet, was the fifteenth in the ancient Roman alphabet, corresponding in position and value to the Greek *Pi*, Π, ח, and identical with the Phenician and general Semitic *Pe*. The letter represents the labial *tenuis*, or lip unvoiced stop, to which the corresponding sonant or voiced stop is B, and the nasal, M. In English, the simple *p* always represents this sound; but it is sometimes silent, as initially in the combinations *pn-, ps-, pt-* (repr. Gr. πν-, ψ-, πτ-), and medially between *m* and another consonant, as in *Hampstead, Hampton*, etc. See also PH.

I. 1. The letter. *Pl.* P's, p's (pīz). OE. 2. Used to indicate serial order, as in the signatures of the sheets of a book, the batteries of the Horse Artillery, etc. 3. **P and Q.** *To mind one's P's and Q's* (*peas and cues*), to be particular as to one's words or behaviour 1779.

II. Abbrevs. P. = various proper names, as Peter, Paul, etc.; P., p. = past, post; P (*Chem.*) = phosphorus; P (*chess*) = pawn; P (*Mechanics*) = pressure; p- (*Chem.*) = para-; p. = page; *p* (*Mus.*) = *piano*, softly; p. (in a ship's log) = passing showers; Π (i.e. Gr. *pi*) (*Math.*) continued product; π (*Math.*) = *pi*, the ratio of the circumference to the diameter of a circle, the incommensurable quantity 3.14159265...; Pa. (*U.S.*) = Pennsylvania; P. and O. = Peninsular and Oriental Steam Navigation Co.; P.A. = Post Adjutant; Pb (*Chem.*) = *plumbum*, lead; P.C. = Police Constable, Privy Councillor; p.c. = postcard; P.C.C. = Parochial Church Council; Pd (*Chem.*) = Palladium; pd. = paid; P.M. = Peculiar or Particular Metre or Measure, Police Magistrate; p.m. = *post meridiem*, afternoon; P.O. = post office, postal order, petty officer; P.P. = parish priest; p.p. = *per procurationem*, by proxy (see PER I); *pp* or *ppp* (*Mus.*) = *pianissimo*, very softly; P.P.C. (written on cards, etc.) = *pour prendre congé*, to take leave; p.p.i. = policy sufficient proof of interest; P.R. = proportional representation; P.R.A. = President of the Royal Academy; P.R.B. = Pre-Raphaelite Brotherhood; P.R.S. = President of the Royal Society; P.S. = *post scriptum*, postscript; P.S.A. = Pleasant Sunday Afternoon; Pt (*Chem.*) = Platinum; pt. = part, pint; P.T. = pupil teacher, physical training; P.T.O., p.t.o., = please turn over.

Pa [1] (pā). 1811. Short form of PAPA. Now *vulgar*.

‖ **Pa** [2], **pah** (pā). 1769. [Maori *pà*, f. *pà* to block up.] A native fort or fortified camp in New Zealand.

Paas, obs. f. PACE, PASCH.

‖ **Pabouch** (păbū·ʃ). 1687. [See BABOUCHE, PAPOOSH.] A heelless oriental slipper.

Pabulary (pæ·biŭlări), *a.* 1835. [ad. L. *pabularius*, f. *pabulum* fodder; see -ARY.] Of or pertaining to fodder or aliment.

†**Pa·bulous,** *a. rare.* 1646. [f. late L. *pabulosus.*] Abounding in or affording food –1755.

‖ **Pabulum** (pæ·biŭlǒm). 1678. [L., f. stem *pā-* of *pascere* to feed.] Anything taken in by an animal or plant to maintain life and growth; food, nutriment. Also *transf.* and *fig.*

Fire.. needs a *P.* to prey upon 1678. Tales of love Form the sweet p. our hearts approve CRABBE.

Paca (pæ·kă). 1657. [a. Pg. and Sp., a. Tupi *paca.*] *Zool.* A genus (*Cœlogenys*) of large dasyproctid rodents, native to Central and South America; the common species (*C. paca*) is called also *spotted cavy* and *water hare.*

Pacable (pē[i]·kăb'l), *a.* 1834. [ad. L. *pacabilis*, f. *pacare* to appease.] Placable.

Pacation (păkē·ʃən). 1658. [ad. L. *pacationem*.] The action of pacifying; pacification.

Pacchionian (pækiōu·niăn), *a.* 1811. [f. name of the Italian anatomist *Pacchioni* (1665–1726) + -AN.] *Anat.* Described by Pacchioni; as *P. corpuscle, gland, line*, etc.

Pace (pēɪs), *sb.* ME. [a. OF. *pas* :—L. *passum* (nom. *passus*), a step, lit. a stretch (of the leg), f. *pass-, pandere* to stretch.] **I.** A step, etc. **1.** A single step in walking, running, or dancing. **2.** The space traversed by one step; hence as a vague measure of distance. late ME. **3.** A definite measure of length or distance; sometimes, the distance from where one foot is set down to where the other is set down (about 2½ feet), as the *military p.*; sometimes, that between successive stationary positions of the same foot (about 5 feet), as the *geometrical p.* ME.

1. Pale cowards, marching on with trembling paces SHAKS. 2. Ten paces huge He back recoild MILT.

II. The action of stepping, etc. **1.** The action, or (usually) manner, of stepping; gait, step, walk ME. †**b.** Course, way (in walking or running) –1727. †**c.** *transf.* Movement, motion –1611. †**2.** A walking pace, walking. ME. only. **3.** Any one of the various gaits of a horse, mule, etc., esp. when trained 1589. **b.** A particular gait of the horse (or other animal); = AMBLE *sb.*, or now occas. = RACK *sb.* 5 1663.

1. The little creature accommodating her p. to mine DICKENS. 3. *fig. A. Y. L.* III. ii. 327. Phr. *To put through his paces*, to show the various accomplishments or actions of which a person is capable.

III. Rate of stepping; speed in walking or running ME. **b.** *transf.* and *fig.* Rate of movement in general; speed, velocity. late ME.

The Beggar Sings,..and never mends his p. DRYDEN. **b.** What p. is this that thy tongue keepes? SHAKS. Phr. *P. of the table* (Billiards), *of the wicket* (Cricket), the degree of elasticity of the cushions, or of the ground, as affecting the motion of the ball. *To keep p.*, to advance at an equal rate; to keep up *with*; My legs can keepe no p. with my desires SHAKS. *To go the p.*, to go at great speed; *fig.* to proceed with reckless vigour; to indulge in dissipation. *To set the p.*, to fix or regulate the speed.

IV. Special senses. **1.** A step of a stair or the like; a stage, a platform. See also FOOTPACE, HALPACE. ME. †**2.** A passage, narrow way; a pass; a strait –1617. †**3.** In a church: A passage or aisle between the seats –1828. †**4.** = PASSUS –1621.

3. *Middle p.*, the nave; *of one p.*, of a nave only. *Comb.*: **p.-maker**, a rider, runner, etc., who makes or sets the pace for another in racing or training.

Pace (pēɪs), *v.* 1513. [f. prec.] **I.** *intr.* To walk with a slow or regular pace; to step along. **b.** *trans.* with cogn. or advb. object 1598. **2.** *trans.* To walk with measured pace along (a path) or about (a place); hence, To measure by pacing 1571. **3.** *intr.* Of a horse, etc.: To move with the gait called a pace 1614. **4.** *trans.* To train (a horse) to pace; to exercise in pacing 1603. **5.** To set the pace for (a rider, boat's crew, etc.) in racing or training 1886.

1. Pacing forth With solemn steps and slow GRAY. **b.** Sentinels paced the rounds day and night MACAULAY. 2. I paced it, and found it to bee 70 of my Paces in Length 1693. 4. *fig.* The third oth' world is yours, which with a Snaffle, You may p. easie, but not such a wife SHAKS.

‖ **Pace** (pēɪ·sɪ). 1883. [abl. sing. of L. *pax* peace.] By leave of, with all deference to.

Paced (pēɪst), *a.* 1583. [f. PACE *sb.* and *v.* + -ED.] **1.** Having a (specified) pace; as *even-p.* **2.** Traversed or measured by pacing 1869. **3.** *Racing.* Having the pace set by a pace-maker 1899.

Pacer (pēɪ·səɹ). 1661. [f. PACE *v.*] **I.** *gen.* One who paces 1835. **2.** A horse whose gait is a pace 1661. **3.** *Racing.* A pace-maker 1893.

Pacha, -lik, var. ff. **Pasha, -lic.**

‖ **Pachisi** (patʃī·sɪ). 1800. [a. Hindī *pa-ch(ch)īsī*, lit. 'of *pach(ch)īs*', i. e. twenty-five.] A four-handed game, played in India, with six cowries for dice; so named from the highest throw, which is twenty-five.

Pachy- (pæ·ki, păki·), bef. a vowel also **pach-**, comb. form of Gr. παχύς 'thick, large, massive': **Pachycarpous** (-kā·ɹpəs) [Gr. καρπός], *a. Bot.* having large thick fruit. **Pachydactyl, -yle** (-dæ·ktil) [Gr. δάκτυλος], *a. Zool.* having thick fleshy digits; *sb.* an animal with thick toes. **Pachyda·ctylous**, *a.* = prec. *a.* **Pachyglo·ssal** [Gr. γλῶσσα], *a. Zool.* of or pertaining to the *Pachyglossæ*, lizards with short or thick fleshy tongues, or the *Pachyglossi*, a tribe of parrots; so **Pachyglo·ssate. Pachymeningitis** (-menindʒəi·tis) [MENINGITIS], *Path.* inflammation of the dura mater of the central nervous system, cerebral or spinal. **Pachymeter** (păki·mĭtəɹ) [-METER], an instrument for measuring the thickness of glass, metal plates, paper, etc. **Pachyote** (pæ·ki,ōut) [Gr. οὖς, ὠτ-], *a.* having thick leathery ears; *sb.* a thick-eared bat, of the genus *Pachyotus*; so **Pachyo·tous** *a.*

Pachyderm (pæ·kidɔ̄ɹm). 1838. [a. F. *pachyderme*, ad. Gr. παχύδερμος, f. παχύς thick + δέρμα skin.] *Zool.* A thick-skinned quadruped; spec. one of the *Pachydermata* of Cuvier. Also *fig.* Hence **Pachyde·rmal, -de·rmic** *adjs.*

‖ **Pachydermata** (pækidɔ̄·ɹmătă), *sb. pl.* 1823. [mod.L., f. Gr. παχύς + δέρμα, δέρματ-.] *Zool.* An order of Mammalia in Cuvier's classification (now discarded), consisting of the hoofed or ungulate quadrupeds which do not chew the cud, as the elephant, rhinoceros, hippopotamus, horse.

Pachydermatous (pækidɔ̄·ɹmătəs), *a.* 1823. [f. prec. + -OUS.] **1.** Of or belonging to the *Pachydermata*. **2.** *fig.* Thick-skinned; not sensitive to rebuff, ridicule, or abuse 1854.

Pacifiable (pæ·sifəi,ăb'l), *a.* 1618. [f. PACIFY + -ABLE.] Capable of being pacified or appeased.

Pacific (păsi·fik), *a.* and *sb.* 1548. [ad. L. *pacificus*, f. *pax, pacem* peace; see -FIC; perh. through F.] **A.** *adj.* **1.** Making, or tending to the making of, peace; conciliatory, appeasing. **2.** Of peaceful disposition, not belligerent 1641. **3.** Characterized by peace; calm, tranquil, quiet 1633. **4.** †*P. letters*, letters to the church in another city or country recommending the bearer as one in peace and communion with the Church; later, esp. letters recommending the bearer to the alms of the faithful –1725.

1. An Olive leafe he brings, p. signe MILT. 2. The old grave p. Quakers 1774. 3. *P. Ocean, Sea*, the 'Great Ocean' stretching between America and Asia; so called by Magellan, because found to be relatively free from violent storms.

B. *sb.* †**1. a.** *pl.* Peace-offerings [tr. L. *pacifica*]. **b.** An overture of peace, an Eirenicon. –1687. **2.** The Pacific Ocean. Also *attrib.* 1821.

2. Like stout Cortez, when with eagle eyes He stared at the P. KEATS. So **Paci·fical** *a.* 1485, **-ly** *adv.*

Pacificate (păsi·fikeɪt), *v.* 15... [f. L. *pacificat-, pacificare*.] †**1.** *intr.* To make peace (*with*). *rare.* –1646. **2.** *trans.* To give peace to, to pacify 1827.

Pacification (pæ:sifikē·ʃən). 1472. [a. F., ad. L. *pacificationem*.] The action or fact of pacifying; the condition of being pacified; appeasement, conciliation. **b.** A treaty of peace 1560.

His p. of friends [was] better than his execution of enemies 1615. *Edict of P.*, esp. in *French hist.*, one of the royal edicts in the 16th c. granting concessions to the Protestants; e. g. the Edict of Nantes.

Pacificator (păsi·fikeɪtəɹ). 1539. [a. L.] One who pacifies; a peacemaker. So **Paci·ficatory** *a.* tending to make peace.

Pacificism (păsi·fisiz'm), **Paci·ficist** (-ist) 1909, more regularly formed variants of next.

Pacifism (pæ·sifiz'm). 1905. [For *pacificism* (see prec.), f. PACIFIC + -ISM.] The doctrine or belief that it is desirable and possible to settle international disputes by peaceful means. So **Pa·cifist** (also *attrib.*).

Pacify (pæ·sifəi), *v.* 1460. [a. F. *pacifier*, ad. L. *pacificare*, f. *pacificus*; see -FY.] **1.** *trans.* To calm or appease (a person, passion, etc.). **2.** To bring or reduce to a state of peace; to calm, quiet 1494. **3.** *intr.* To become peaceful, calm down 1509.

1. Pray say something to p. her 1717. How..I can p. resentment JOHNSON. 2. It would take 100,000 men to p. the islands 1899. Hence **Pa·cifier.**

Pacinian (păsi·niăn), *a.* 1876. [f. name of *Pacini*, an Italian anatomist (1812–1883) + -AN.] Of or described by Pacini.

P. body, corpuscle, one of numerous oval seed-like bodies attached to nerve-endings, esp. of the cutaneous nerves of the hand and foot.

Pack (pæk), *sb.*[1] [ME. *packe, pakke*; app. a. MFlem. *pac*, or Du. or LG. *pak.*] **1.** A bundle of things enclosed in a wrapping or tied together compactly; *spec.* a bundle of goods carried by a pedlar; a soldier's valise containing his kit and carried on the back. **2.** As a measure of various commodities 1488. **3. a.** A company or set of persons; often merely contemptuous; a 'gang', 'lot' ME. **b.** A large collection, or set (of things, esp. abstract); a 'heap', 'lot'. (Usu. depreciative.) 1591. †**4.** Applied to a person of worthless character; almost always with *naughty* –1738. **5.** A number of animals kept or naturally congregating together; *spec.* of hounds for hunting, or of wild beasts (esp. wolves), and of birds (e.g. grouse) 1648. **b.** *Rugby Football.* The forwards of a side, esp. in relation to the scrum 1887. **6.** A complete set of playing-cards 1597. **7.** A large area of floating ice in pieces of considerable size 'packed' together 1791. **8.** *Hydropathy.* The swathing of the body in a wet sheet, blanket, etc.; the state of being so packed; the sheet, etc., used for this. Also *dry-pack.* 1849. **9.** The quantity (of fish, fruit, etc.) packed in a season or year 1889.

1. A pedlar's p., that bows the bearer down COWPER. 2. A p. of flour or Indian-corn meal, flax, etc. weighs 280 lbs.; of wool 240 lbs. net 1858. 3. **a.** A p. of drunken servants GOLDSM. **b.** A p. of lies 1763, of nonsense 1880. 5. He cast off his friends, as a huntsman his p. GOLDSM.

attrib. and *Comb.*, as **p.-drill**, a military punishment, in which the offender is forced to parade or march up and down in full marching order; **-house**, a warehouse; **-ice**, ice forming a p. (sense 7); **-moth**, a species of clothes-moth (*Anacampsis sarcitella*); **-sheet**, (*a*) a sheet for packing goods in; (*b*) *Med.* a wet sheet for packing a patient in; **-train**, a train of pack-beasts with their packs; **-wool**, wool done up in packs.

†**Pack**, *sb.*[2] 1571. [Goes with PACK *v.*[2]] A clandestine pact or compact; a plot, conspiracy, intrigue –1649.

Pack (pæk), *v.*[1] Pa. t. and pple. **packed** (pækt). ME. [f. PACK *sb.*[1]] **I. 1.** *trans.* To make into a pack or package; to put together as a bundle, or in a box, bag, etc., esp. for transport or for storing. Also with *up.* **b.** In *Commerce*: To prepare and put up (meat, fish, eggs, fruit, etc.) in tins, glasses, etc., so as to preserve them 1494. **c.** *absol.* To pack clothes, etc., for a journey. Often with *up.* 1684. **2.** To put together closely or compactly; to crowd together 1563. **3.** To form into a 'pack'. **a.** To form (hounds) into a pack; **b.** To place (cards) together into a pack; **c.** To drive (ice) into a pack; usu. *pass.* 1649. **4.** *intr.* for *refl.* **a.** To collect into a body; esp. to form a pack: said of wolves, grouse, etc., also of ice in the polar seas 1828. **b.** In passive sense: To admit of being packed 1846. **5.** *trans.* To cover with something pressed tightly around 1796. **b.** *Med.* To envelop (the body or a part of it) in a wet sheet or cloth 1849. **6.** To fill (a bag, box, etc.) *with* clothes or goods compactly arranged, (a crevice or interstice) *with* something fitting tightly; to cram, stuff. Also with *up.* 1581. **b.** *transf.* and *fig.* To cram, crowd (any space) *with.* Usu. *pass.*; also predicated of that which occupies the space. 1857. **7.** To load (a beast) with a pack 1596. **8.** To carry or convey in a pack or packs 1850.

1. So p. up a few things, and we'll off FOOTE. The contents of the library were all packed and carried away GEO. ELIOT. 2. Audiences so packed as to be dangerous 1887. Phr. *To p. on all sail*, to put on all possible sail; to crowd sail. Also *absol.* in same sense. 4. **b.** It..packs up easily 1867. 6. **b.** [A passage] crowded and packed with meaning 1857. 8. The ore..having been packed a distance of ten miles on mules 1877.

II. 1. *refl.* and *intr.* To take oneself off with one's belongings, be off. †**a.** *refl.* –1865. **b.** *intr.* 1440. **2.** *trans.* To send away, dismiss summarily, get rid of. Now usu. with *off.* 1589.

1. Voltaire..lost no time in packing himself CARLYLE. **b.** Sure as fate, we'll send you packing BROWNING. 2. He packed her off to bed at once 1894.

Pack, *v.*[2] 1529. [Of obsc. origin; cf. PACK *sb.*[2]] **I.** †**1.** *intr.* To agree in a secret or underhand design; to plot, conspire, scheme, intrigue –1602. †**2.** To bring or let (a person) into a plot; in *pass.* to be an accomplice or confederate in a plot -1600. †3. *trans.* To plot (something) -1694.

1. *Tit. A.* IV. ii. 155. 2. *Com. Err.* v. i. 219.

II. 1. To select or make up (a jury, etc.) in such a way as to secure a partial decision 1587. 2. To arrange or shuffle (playing-cards), so as to secure a fraudulent advantage. *Obs.* or *arch.* 1599.

2. I learned to p. cards and to cog a dye 1753. Phr. *To p. cards with*, to make a cheating arrangement with; *Ant. & Cl.* IV. xiv. 19. Hence **Pa·cking** *vbl. sb.*[2]

Package (pæ·kėdʒ). 1540. [f. PACK *v.*[1] + -AGE.] 1. The packing of goods, etc.; the mode in which goods are packed. †2. A cargo -1802. 3. A bundle of things packed up; esp. a packet, parcel. (The chief current sense.) 1722. 4. A case, box, etc., in which goods are packed 1801. Hence **Pa·ckage** *v.* (*U. S.*).

4. *Original p.*, the package or case in which goods are sent out from the place of manufacture.

Packer[1] (pæ·kəɪ). ME. [f. PACK *v.*[1] + -ER[1].] One who packs; *esp.* one who packs meat, fish, fruit, etc., for future or distant markets.

Packer[2]. 1586. [f. PACK *v.*[2] + -ER[1].] One who 'packs' cards, juries, etc.; a plotter.

Packet (pæ·kėt), *sb.* 1530. [dim. of PACK *sb.*[1]] 1. A small pack, package, or parcel; in early use, esp. the State parcel or 'mail' of dispatches to and from foreign countries. b. *fig.* A small collection (of things or persons) 1589. 2. Short for PACKET-BOAT 1709.

1. b. *To sell* (one) *a p.* (colloq.), to take him in, 'sell' him.

attrib. and *Comb.*, as *p.-ship*, *-vessel* = PACKET-BOAT; **-note**, a size of note-paper, 9 by 11 inches the sheet.

Pa·cket, *v.* 1596. [f. PACKET *sb.*; cf. F. *paqueter.*] 1. *trans.* To make up into, or wrap up in, a packet. †2. *trans.* To send by packet-boat -1747. †b. *intr.* To ply with a packet-boat -1813.

Pa·cket-boat. 1641. [f. PACKET *sb.* + BOAT.] A boat or vessel plying at regular intervals between two ports for the conveyance of mails, also of goods and passengers; a mail-boat. (Often shortened to *packet.*)

Pa·ck-horse. 1475. [f. PACK *sb.*[1] + HORSE *sb.*] A horse used for carrying packs or bundles of goods. b. *fig.* A drudge. Also *attrib.*

Packing (pæ·kiŋ), *vbl. sb.*[1] ME. [f. PACK *v.*[1] + -ING[1].] 1. The action of PACK *v.*[1] 2. *concr.* Any material used to fill up a space or interstice closely or tightly; filling, stuffing 1824.

attrib. and *Comb.*, as **p.-box**, a stuffing-box around the piston-rod of a steam-engine; **-case**; **-needle** = PACK-NEEDLE; **-sheet** (*a*) a sheet for packing goods in; (*b*) *Med.* a wet sheet in which a patient is packed in hydropathic treatment.

Packman (pæ·kmæ̆n). 1582. [f. PACK *sb.*[1] + MAN *sb.*] A man who travels about carrying goods in a pack for sale; a pedlar.

Pa·ck-nee:dle. ME. [f. PACK *sb.*[1] + NEEDLE.] A large strong needle used for sewing up packages in stout cloth.

Pa·ck-sa:ddle. ME. [f. PACK *sb.*[1] + SADDLE *sb.*] A saddle adapted for supporting a pack or packs to be carried by a pack-beast.

P. roof, a SADDLEBACK roof.

Packstaff (pæ·kstɑf). 1542. [f. as prec. + STAFF.] A staff on which a pedlar supports his pack when standing to rest himself. In phr. †*as plain as a p.* (now *pikestaff*).

Packthread (pæ·kþred). ME. [f. as prec. + THREAD *sb.*] Stout thread or twine for sewing or tying up packs or bundles.

Packwax: see PAXWAX.

‖**Paco** (pā·ko). Also **pacos.** 1604. [Sp. *paco*, a. Quichua *paco*, native name in Peru.] 1. = ALPACA. 2. *Min.* An earthy brown oxide of iron, containing minute particles of silver. (From its colour.) 1839.

Pacquet, obs. f. PACKET.

Pact (pækt). ME. [a. OF. *pact*, *pacte*, ad. L. *pactum*, neut. sb. f. *pactus*, *paciscere* to agree, covenant, f. *pac-*, *pax* PEACE.] An agreement between persons or parties, a compact.

The engagement and p. of society, which generally goes by the name of the constitution BURKE. *Nude*, *bare*, or *naked p.*, an agreement without consideration, which cannot therefore be legally enforced.

Paction (pæ·kʃən). Now chiefly *Sc.* 1471. [a. OF., ad. L. *pactionem*, f. *paciscere.*] The action of making a bargain or pact; a bargain, agreement, compact, contract. Hence **Pa·ctional** *a.* of, pertaining to, or of the nature of a pact.

Pactolian (pæktōᵘ·liăn), *a.* 1606. [f. L. *Pactolus*, Gr. Πακτωλός + -IAN.] Of, belonging or relating to, the river Pactolus in Lydia, famed for its golden sands; golden.

Pacu (pakū·, pa·kū). 1825. [a. Tupi *pacú.*] *Zool.* A freshwater fish, *Myletes pacu*, of Brazil and Guiana.

Pad (pæd), *sb.*[1] *Obs.* exc. *dial.* ME. [prob. a. ON. *padda.*] 1. †A toad; *mod. dial.* = PADDOCK *sb.*[1] 2. A star-fish 1613.

Pad (pæd), *sb.*[2] 1567. [a. Du. or LG. *pad* = OHG. *pfad*, cogn. w. English PATH; orig. vagabonds' cant.] 1. A path, track; the road, the way. *slang* or *dial.* 2. Robbery on the highway. *slang.* 1664. †3. A highway robber. Cf. FOOTPAD. -1834. 4. An easy-paced horse; also *p.-nag* 1617.

4. An abbot on an ambling p. TENNYSON.

Pad (pæd), *sb.*[3] 1554. [Of obsc. origin.] I. †1. A bundle of straw, etc. to lie on -1719. 2. A soft stuffed saddle without a tree; *esp.* that placed on an elephant 1570. b. That part of double harness to which the girths are attached 1811. 3. Something soft, as a cushion, serving esp. to diminish jarring, to fill up hollows, etc. 1700. b. A cushion or stuffing placed under a horse's foot to keep the sole moist, or under the harness to prevent galling 1843. c. In *Cricket*, etc.: A guard for the leg or shins 1851. 4. A number of sheets of blotting-, writing-, or drawing-paper fastened together at the edge to make a block; called also *blotting-*, *drawing-*, or *writing-pad* 1865.

II. 1. Any cushion-like part of the animal body 1878. 2. The fleshy elastic cushion forming the sole of the foot, or part of it, in feline or canine beasts, the camel, etc. Also, analogous parts in a bird's foot, in insects, etc. 1836. 3. The foot or paw of a fox, hare, otter, wolf, etc.; also the footprint of such 1790.

3. A silver-mounted otter-pad 1891.

III. 1. *Mech.* The socket of a brace; a tool-handle into which tools of various gauges, etc., can be fitted, as in a pad-saw 1688. 2. *Watch-* and *Clock-making.* A pallet 1696. 3. *Ship-building.* A piece of timber placed on a beam, to fill up the round of the deck 1867. 4. (Also *lily-pad.*) A broad floating leaf (of the water-lily). *U.S.* 1858.

attrib. and *Comb.*, as **p.-elephant**, an elephant having on its back a p. only (not a howdah), on which to carry burdens, baggage, game, etc.; **-saddle**, a treeless padded saddle; **-saw**: see sense III. 1.

Pad, *sb.*[4] 1579. [var. of PED.] An open pannier, usually of osiers; a measure of fish, fruit, etc., a 'basket'. 1858.

Pad, *sb.*[5] 1594. [Partly echoic, partly assoc. w. PAD *v.*[1]] The dull firm non-resonant sound of steps, or of a staff, upon the ground; also, the repeated step or footfall producing this sound.

Pad (pæd), *v.*[1] 1553. [Related to PAD *sb.*[2] But in some senses echoic.] 1. *trans.* To tramp along (a road, etc.) on foot. b. *intr.* To travel on foot; to trudge along. Also *to p. it* 1610. 2. *intr.* †a. Of a horse: To pace 1724. b. Of other quadrupeds: To walk or run with steady dull-sounding steps 1871. 3. *trans.* To tread or beat down by frequent walking (*dial.*) 1764. †4. *intr.* To rob on the highway -1736.

1. Phr. *To p. the hoof*, to go on foot, tramp (*slang*). Hence **Pa·dded** *ppl. a.*[1], trodden, beaten hard by treading. **Pa·dding** *ppl. a.*, that pads or paces on.

Pad, *v.*[2] 1821. [f. PAD *sb.*[3]] 1. *trans.* To stuff, fill out (anything) with a pad or padding; to stuff (something) in or about, so as to serve as a pad. Also *absol.* 2. *trans.* To fill *out* or expand (a sentence, story, etc.) with unnecessary or useless words or matter 1831. 3. To impregnate (the cloth) with a mordant in calico-printing 1839. 4. *East Indies.* To place or pack (big game, etc.) on the pad of an elephant 1878. 5. To track by the pad or footmarks 1861.

Pa·dded, *ppl. a.*[2] 1799. Furnished or filled out with pads or padding.

P. cell or *room*, a room in a lunatic asylum or prison, having the walls padded, to prevent the person confined from injuring himself against them.

Padder (pæ·dəɪ). 1610. [f. PAD *sb.*[2] or *v.*[1] + -ER[1].] A footpad, highwayman.

Pa·dding, *vbl. sb.* 1828. [f. PAD *v.*[2] + -ING[1].] 1. The action of PAD *v.*[2] Also *attrib.* 1839. 2. *concr.* a. That of which a pad is made; e. g. cotton, felt, hair, used in stuffing or padding anything 1828. b. Extraneous or unnecessary matter introduced into a book, speech, etc., to fill up space and make up size; in magazines, the articles of secondary interest 1869.

Paddle (pæ·d'l), *sb.*[1] 1560. [Of unkn. origin; cf. PADLE, PATTLE.] 1. A small spade-like implement with a long handle, for clearing a ploughshare, etc. 2. A short oar used without a rowlock, having a broad blade which is dipped more or less vertically into the water 1624. 3. One of the boards or floats fitted on the circumference of the 'paddle-wheel' of a steamer; a paddle-board; also, b. A float of an undershot mill-wheel. c. Short for PADDLE-WHEEL. d. Short for *paddle-boat* or *-steamer*. 4. *Zool.* A limb serving the purpose of a fin or flipper; as the foot of a duck; the wing of a penguin, etc. 1835. 5. A sliding panel or sluice in a weir or lock-gate to regulate the quantity of water allowed to flow through 1795. 6. A paddle-shaped instrument or tool, used for stirring or mixing 1662.

attrib. and *Comb.*, as *p.-blade*, etc.; 'having, or propelled by, paddles', as *p.-boat*, *-steamer*, etc.; also, **p.-beam** (*Shipbuilding*), one of two large beams lying athwart a ship, between which the paddle-wheels revolve; **-board** = sense 3; **-box**, the casing which encloses the upper part of a steamer's paddle-wheel; **-fish**, a ganoid fish, *Polyodon* or *Spatularia spatula*, having a long flat paddle-shaped snout, found in the Mississippi; **-shaft**, the revolving shaft which carries the paddle-wheels of a steamer; **staff**, (*a*) = sense 1; (*b*) *Brewing*, a wooden spade-shaped implement used in mashing; **-wood**, the light elastic wood of a S. Amer. tree, *Aspidosperma excelsum*, from which the Indians make canoe-paddles.

Pa·ddle, *sb.*[2] *Sc.* 1591. [Of unkn. origin.] The lump-fish, *Cyclopterus lumpus* = COCK-PADDLE.

Paddle (pæ·d'l), *v.*[1] 1530. [Of unkn. origin.] I. 1. *intr.* To walk or move the feet about in mud or shallow water; to wade about; to dabble in shallow water. 2. *intr.* To toy with the fingers (*in*, *on*, *with*, or *about* something) 1602. †b. *trans.* To finger idly, playfully, or fondly -1622. †3. a. *trans.* To trifle away, squander. b. *intr.* To trifle. -1840.

1. Ducks p. in the pond before the door COWPER. *fig.* Boys and girls who paddled in rhyme SWINBURNE. 2. *Oth.* II. i. 259. b. *Wint. T.* I. ii. 115.

II. *intr.* To walk with steps like those of a child; to toddle 1792. b. *trans.* To trample down by treading over (*dial.*) 1805. Hence **Pa·ddler** 1611.

Paddle, *v.*[2] 1677. [f. PADDLE *sb.*[1]] 1. *intr.* To move on the water by means of paddles, as in a canoe. Also said of the canoe. b. *transf.* To row with oars lightly 1697. c. Of a paddle-steamer, etc.: To move by means of paddle-wheels 1844. d. Of birds, etc.: To move in the water with paddle-like limbs. 2. *trans.* To propel by means of a paddle or paddles; also, to transport (a person) in a canoe 1784. 3. *trans.* To beat with a paddle or the like; to 'spank'. *U.S.* 1856.

1. b. Paddled to Barnes Railway Bridge, and rowed hard..back to Hammersmith 1866. 2. Phr. *To p. one's own canoe*, to make one's way by one's own exertions. Hence **Pa·ddle** *sb.*[3], the act of paddling or rowing lightly.

Pa·ddle-whee:l. 1685. [See PADDLE *sb.*[1] 3.] 1. A wheel used for propelling a boat or ship, having floats or paddle-boards fitted more or less radially round the circumference, so as to press backward like a succession of paddles against the water. 2. In leather manufacture, a wheel fitted with paddles (PADDLE *sb.*[1] 6) used to keep skins in constant motion in water.

Paddock (pæ·dək), *sb.*[1] ME. [f. PAD *sb.*[1] + -OCK.] 1. A frog. Now *Sc.* and *n. dial.* b. A toad. *Obs.* exc. *arch.* ME.

attrib. and *Comb.* (chiefly *dial.*), as **p.-pipe**, a species of *Equisetum* (Horse-tail), esp. *E. limosum*; also Mare's Tail, *Hippuris vulgaris*; **-stone** = TOADSTONE; **-stool** = TOADSTOOL.

Paddock (pæ·dək), *sb.*[2] 1622. [var. of PARROCK; cf. *poddish* for *porridge.*] 1. A small field or enclosure; usu. a plot of pasture-land adjoining a stable. 2. *spec.* a. A course in a park, for hounds to run matches 1678. b. *Horse-racing.* A turf enclosure near the race-course, where the horses are assembled before the race 1862. 3. *Mining.* A store-place for ore, etc. (*Colonial*) 1869. Hence **Pa·ddock** *v.* to shut up or enclose in or as in a p.; *Mining,* to store (ore, etc.) in a p.

Paddy[1] (pæ·di). 1623. [a. Malay *pādī.*] 1. Rice in the straw, or (in commerce) in the husk. 2. = PADDY-BIRD; *ellipt.* its feathers 1777. 3. *attrib.* 1698.

Paddy[2] (pæ·di). 1780. [Ir. pet-form of *Padraig* = *Patrick.*] 1. Nickname for an Irishman. 2. A bricklayer's labourer 1856. 3. A passion, temper; also PADDYWHACK. *colloq.* 1894. Hence **Pa·ddyism,** Irishism.

Pa·ddy-bird. 1727. [PADDY [1].] 1. The Java Sparrow, *Padda* (or *Munia*) *oryzivora.* 2. Anglo-Ind. name for species of white egret, which frequent the paddy-fields 1858. 3. A species of Sheathbill, *Chionis minor* 1894.

Paddymelon (pæ·dime:lən). 1827. [Corruption of an aboriginal name.] A small brush kangaroo. Also *attrib.*

Pa·ddywhack. *colloq.* 1881. [f. PADDY [2].] 1. An Irishman. 2. A rage, passion 1899.

Padesoy, obs. f. PADUASOY.

‖**Padishah, padshah** (pā·diʃā, pā·dʃā). 1612. [a. Pers. *pādshāh,* in poetry *pādĕ-, pādishah,* f. (ult.) *pati* master, lord + *šāh* SHAH.] A Persian title, taken as = 'Great King' or 'Emperor'; applied to the Shah of Persia, the Sultan of Turkey, and by natives, to the British sovereign as Emperor of India.

Padle, paidle (pē·d'l). *Sc.* 1568. [Cf. PADDLE *sb.*[1]] A field or garden hoe.

Padlock (pæ·dlǫk), *sb.* 1478. [f. *pad,* of unkn. meaning + LOCK *sb.*[2]] A detachable lock, designed to hang on the object fastened by a pivoted or sliding bow or shackle, which can be opened to pass through a staple or ring, and then locked.

fig. Put golden padlocks on Truth's lips LOWELL. Hence **Pa·dlock** *v.* to fasten with or secure by means of a p.

‖ **Padouk** (padau·k). 1858. [Burmese native name.] A Burmese leguminous tree, *Pterocarpus macrocarpus,* yielding a kind of rosewood; the wood itself.

Padre (pā·dre). 1584. [It., Sp., Pg. *padre* :—L. *patrem,* acc. of *pater.*] 'Father'; in Italy, Spain, Portugal, and Spanish America, a title of the regular clergy; in India (since *c* 1800), a minister or priest of any Christian Church; hence, applied by English soldiers and sailors to a chaplain.

‖ **Padrone** (padrō·ne). 1660. [It.] = Patron, master; applied to a. the master of a trading-vessel in the Mediterranean; b. an Italian employer of street musicians, begging children, etc.; c. the proprietor of an inn in Italy.

Paduasoy (pæ·diu,ăsoi). 1663. [prob. corruption of *pou-de-soie* or *poudesoy,* of unkn. origin, app. by association with *Padua say,* a kind of SAY or serge from Padua.] A strong corded or gros-grain silk fabric, of which POULT-DE-SOIE is the mod. representative. Also *attrib.*, and *ellipt.* a garment of this.

Pæan (pī·ăn). 1592. [a. L., a. Gr. παιάν a hymn to Apollo under the name Παιάν, Attic Παιών, the physician of the gods.] 1. A hymn or chant of thanksgiving for deliverance orig. addressed to Apollo or Artemis; esp. a song of triumph after victory addressed to Apollo; hence, any solemn song or chant. 2. *transf.* A song of praise or thanksgiving; a song of triumph 1599.

2. I sung the joyful P. clear..Waiting to strive a happy strife TENNYSON.

Pæderasty, ped- (pī·d-, pe·dĕræsti). 1609. [ad. mod. L. *pæderastia,* a. Gr., f. παιδεραστής, f. παῖς, παιδ- boy + ἐραστής lover.] Sodomy. Hence **Pæ·derast,** a sodomite. **Pædera·stic** *a.* pertaining to or practising sodomy.

Pædeutics (pīdiū·tiks); rarely sing. **-ic.** Also paid-. 1864. [ad. Gr. παιδευτικός; see -ICS.] The science or art of education.

Pædo-, pedo- (pī·do), occas. **paido-** (pai·do), bef. a vowel **pæd-, ped-,** comb. form of Gr. παῖς, παιδ- boy, child; as in **Pædogenesis** (-dʒe·nĭsis), *Zool.* production of off-spring by immature or larval animals; so **Pæ:dogene·tic** *a.* **Pædo·logy,** child study.

Pædobaptism (pīdobæ·ptiz'm). Also pedo-. 1640. [f. PÆDO- + BAPTISM.] The baptism of children; infant baptism. So **Pædoba·ptist,** one who practises or advocates infant baptism.

Pæon (pī·ǫn). 1603. [a. L. *pæon,* ad. Gr. παιών; see PÆAN.] *Prosody.* A metrical foot of four syllables, one long and three short, named, according to the position of the long syllable, a first, second, third, or fourth pæon. Hence **Pæo·nic** *a.* of or pertaining to a p. or pæons; composed of pæons; *sb.* a pæonic verse or foot.

Pæonin (pī·ŏnin). 1866. [f. L. *pæonia* PEONY (in reference to colour) + -IN.] *Chem.* = CORALLIN.

Pæony, var. of PEONY.

Pagan (pē·găn), *sb.* and *a.* late ME. [ad. L. *paganus,* orig. 'civilian', opp. to *miles* 'soldier'; in Christian L. 'heathen' as opp. to Christian or Jewish; the Christians called themselves *milites* 'enrolled soldiers' of Christ.] A. *sb.* 1. One of a nation or community which does not worship the true God; a heathen. (†In earlier use practically = non-Christian.) 2. *transf.* and *fig.* A person of heathenish character or habits, or one who holds a position analogous to that of a heathen 1841. †b. *spec.* A paramour, prostitute –1632.

1. Adue,..most beautifull P., most sweete Iew SHAKS. 2. b. 2 *Hen. IV,* II. ii. 168.

B. *adj.* 1. Not belonging to a nation or community that acknowledges the true God; heathen 1586. 2. *fig.* Heathenish 1550.

1. The ideal, cheerful, sensuous, p. life M. ARNOLD. Hence **Pa·gandom,** the pagan world; heathendom. †**Paga·nic, †-al** *adjs.* pagan. **Paga·nity,** paganism. **Pa·ganly** *adv.* †**Pa·gany,** pagandom.

Paganish (pē·găniʃ), *a.* 1583. [f. prec. + -ISH [1].] †1. Pagan –1759. 2. Resembling or befitting a pagan; of pagan character or quality; heathenish 1613. Hence **Pa·ganishly** *adv.*

Paganism (pē·găniz'm). late ME. [ad. eccl.L. *paganismus*; see -ISM.] 1. Pagan belief and practices; the condition of being a pagan; heathenism. 2. Pagan character or quality; the moral condition of pagans 1874.

1. The divisions of Christianity suspended the ruin of P. GIBBON.

Paganize (pē·gănəiz), *v.* 1615. [a. F. *paganiser*; see PAGAN and -IZE.] 1. *trans.* To make pagan. 2. *intr.* To become pagan; to act as a pagan; to assume a pagan character 1640. Hence **Pa:ganiza·tion.**

Page (pēdʒ), *sb.*[1] ME. [a. OF. *page* = It. *paggio,* med.L. *pagius,* of obsc. origin.] I. †1. A boy, youth, lad –1582. †2. A male person of the 'lower orders', or of low condition or manners; a term of contempt; cf. KNAVE 2, 3. –1529. 3. A boy or lad employed as a servant or attendant; hence, a male servant of the lowest grade in his line of service ME. 4. *Chivalry.* A boy or lad in training for knighthood, and attached to the personal service of a knight, whom he followed on foot. Now only *Hist.* ME. 5. A youth employed as the personal attendant of a person of rank 1460. b. Hence, a title of various officers of a royal or princely household, as *p. of honour, of the chamber,* etc. late ME. c. Hence, now, a boy or lad (usu. in 'buttons' or livery), employed to attend to the door, go on errands, and the like; in U.S., an attendant on a legislative body. Also *p.-boy.* d. Also applied to little boys fancifully dressed at a wedding ceremony to bear the bride's train. 1781.

1. A child þat was of half yeer age In Cradel it lay and was a propre p. CHAUCER.

II. Transf. use. *Entom.* Collector's name for a black and green S. Amer. hawk-moth of the family *Uraniidæ* 1886. Hence **Page** *v.*[1], to wait on or follow like a p.; *U.S.* to send a page-boy after (a visitor in a hotel); said also of the page. **Pa·gehood,** the state of being a p. †**Pa·gery,** the office or position of a p., service as a p. **Pa·geship.**

Page (pēdʒ), *sb.*[2] 1589. [a. F. *page* :—L. *pagina,* f. stem *pag-* of *pangere* to fasten.] 1. One side of a leaf of a book, manuscript, letter, etc. b. *Printing.* The type set up, or made up from slips or galleys, for printing a page 1727. c. *Type-founding.* One of the parcels into which new type is made up by the founders, to be sent out; usu. 8 inches by 4. 1882. 2. *fig.* a. Any page, or the pages collectively, of a writing; hence, rhetorically, writing, book, record. b. An episode, such as would fill a page in a written history. 1619.

2. Her ample p. Rich with the spoils of time GRAY. A bright p. in her military history 1885.

Comb.: *p.-proof,* a pull taken from type made up into paged form.

Page (pēdʒ), *v.*[2] 1628. [f. PAGE *sb.*[2]] 1. *trans.* To paginate. 2. To make up (composed type) into pages 1890. b. *Type-founding.* To pack up (new type) in pages for sending out 1903. Hence **Paged** (pēdʒd) *a.*, having the pages numbered; having pages of a specified kind or number.

Pageant (pæ·dʒănt, pē·dʒănt), *sb.* [Late ME. *pagyn, padgin,* etc. = Anglo-L. *pagina*; subseq. with accrescent *-t* or *-d,* as in *ancient,* etc.; see -ANT.[2] Ultimate origin obsc.: see N.E.D.] 1. A scene acted on the stage; *spec.* one scene or act of a mediæval mystery play. *Obs.* exc. *Hist.* †b. *fig.* The part played by any one in an affair, or in life; performance; esp. in *to play one's p.,* to act one's part –1878. †2. A stage or platform on which scenes were acted or tableaux represented; *esp.* in early use, the movable structure used in the open-air performances of mystery plays –1739. †b. A piece of stage machinery; also, a mechanical contrivance generally –1719. 3. Any kind of show, device, or temporary structure, exhibited as a feature of a public triumph or celebration. *Obs.* exc. *Hist.* 1511. 4. *fig.* An empty show without substance or reality 1608. 5. A spectacle arranged for effect; *esp.* a procession or parade with elaborate spectacular display 1805. Since 1907 applied to celebrations of local history consisting of a series of representations of events and personages connected with the particular place. 6. *attrib.* or *adj.* Of or acting in a pageant; stage-, puppet-; specious 1659.

1. Of paiauntis that were played in Ioyous Garde SKELTON. 3. A raree-shew (or p.) as of old, on the lord mayor's day SWIFT. *Dumb p.,* a dumb show. 4. It was a name, a shadow, an empty p. GIBBON. 5. The consecration of a King was then not a mere p. FREEMAN. Hence **Pa·geant** *v. trans.*, to carry *about* as a show or in a procession 1641; †to imitate as in a pageant or play SHAKS.

Pageantry (pæ·dʒăntri, pē·-). 1608. [See -RY.] †1. Pageants collectively –1714. 2. Splendid display; pomp. Also in *pl.* 1651. 3. Empty display, show without substance 1687.

1. *Per.* V. ii. 6. 2. The p. of war SOUTHEY. 3. Chivalry had not yet declined to mere formal pomp and p. 1854.

Paginal (pæ·dʒinăl), *a.* 1646. [ad. late L. *paginalis,* f. *pagina* leaf, page; see -AL.] Consisting of or referring to pages; page for page.

A verbal and p. reprint 1811. So **Pa·ginary** *a.*

Paginate (pæ·dʒineᴵt), *v.* 1884. [f. L. *pagina* + -ATE [3].] *trans.* To mark or number the pages of a book; to page. Hence **Pagina·tion,** the action of marking the numbers of the pages; an instance of this; the sequence of figures with which the pages are numbered.

Paging (pē·dʒiŋ), *vbl. sb.* 1775. [f. PAGE *v.*[2] + -ING [1].] The action of PAGE *v.*[2]; pagination.

‖ **Pagne** (panʸ). 1698. [F., ad. Sp. *paño* :—L. *pannum* cloth.] A cloth; the single piece of cloth variously worn by natives of hot countries; *spec.* a loin-cloth, or a short petticoat.

Pagod (pæ·gǫd). *arch.* 1582. [ad. Pg. *pagode*; see next. Pope has *pago·d* as well as *pa·god.*] 1. = next, 1. 2. An idol or image of a deity (in India, China, etc.). (Often assoc. w. *god.*) 1582. 3. = next, 3. 1598.

1. Her pagods hung with music of sweet bells TENNYSON. 2. *fig.* My poor little p., Napoleon BYRON.

Pagoda (păgōu·dă). 1618. [ad. Pg. *pagode,* pl. *pagodes,* It. *pagode,* pl. *-i*; app. a corruption of a name found by the Portuguese in India.] 1. A temple or sacred building (in India, China, etc.); *esp.* a sacred tower, usu. of pyramidal form, built over the relics of Buddha or a saint, or in any place as a work of devotion

1634. b. A small structure in imitation of an oriental pagoda 1796. †2. = prec. 2 (*rare*) –1665. 3. A gold (or silver) coin formerly current in southern India, = about 7*s.* 1618.

attrib. and *Comb.*, as **p.-flower,** the flower of the PAGODA-TREE, q.v.; **-stone,** = PAGODITE.

Pago·da-tree. 1836. 1. Name given to: a. *Sophora japonica*, cultivated in China and Japan; b. *Plumeria acutifolia*, a native of the W. Indies, cultivated in India; c. *Ficus indica*, the Banyan-tree of India. 1876. 2. *fig.* A mythical tree joc. feigned to produce pagodas (sense 3).

2. Phr. *To shake the pagoda-tree*, to make a fortune rapidly in India.

Pagodite (pæ·gŏdəit). 1837. [a. F., f. *pagode* PAGODA + -ITE¹.] *Min.* A soft mineral carved by the Chinese into figures of pagodas, images, etc.; also called *agalmatolite*.

Pagurian (păgiūᵊ·riăn), *a.* and *sb.* 1840. [f. L. *pagurus*, a. Gr. πάγουρος a kind of crab; see -IAN.] *Zool.* a. *adj.* Belonging to the genus *Pagurus* or family *Paguridæ* of decapod crustaceans. b. *sb.* One of this genus or family, a hermit-crab.

Pah (păh, pā), *int.* 1592. A natural exclam. of disgust.

Fye, fie, fie; pah, pah: Giue me an Ounce of Ciuet; good Apothecary sweeten my immagination SHAKS.

Pah, variant of PA.²

‖ **Pahlavi** (pā·lăvī), *a.* and *sb.* Also **Pehleví** (pē·lĕvī), **Pehlví.** 1777. [Pers. *Pahlavī* Parthian, f. *Pahlav*:–*Parthava* Parthia.] The name given by the followers of Zoroaster to the character in which are written the ancient translations of their sacred books, etc.; now used gen. to designate a mode of writing the language, used in Persia under the Sásánian kings; loosely, Old Persian.

In divine High piping Pehlevi..the Nightingale cries to the Rose FITZGERALD.

Paid (pēᵉid), *ppl. a.* ME. [pa. pple. of PAY *v.*¹] †1. *predicatively.* Pleased, satisfied, content –1880. 2. Remunerated with money; in receipt of pay 1862. 3. Given, as money, in discharge of an obligation; discharged, as a debt; for which the money has been given, as a bill, a cheque 1866.

2. The machinery of paid officials 1862. 3. *Paid-up capital*, that part of the subscribed capital of an undertaking which has been actually paid.

Paid-: see PÆD-.

Paigle, pagle (pēᵉi·g'l). *dial.* 1530. [Of unkn. orig.] The cowslip, *Primula veris*; also, the oxlip, the buttercup, etc.

Paijama: see PYJAMA.

Paik (pēk), *sb.* *Sc.* and *n. dial.* 1508. [Origin unkn.] A firm blow. So **Paik** *v.*

Pail (pēᵉil). ME. [Of obscure origin: cf. OE. *pægel* gill, wine-measure, and OF. *paelle, payelle* frying-pan, brazier, etc. :—L. *patella*, dim. of *patina* broad shallow dish, pan.] A vessel of wood, or of sheet-metal, usually cylindrical, and provided with a bail or hooped handle; used for carrying milk, water, etc. b. A pailful 1600.

Pailful (pēᵉi·lful). 1591. [-FUL.] As much as fills a pail.

Paillasse: see PALLIASSE.

Paillette (pælye·t). Also **-et.** 1843. [a. F. *paillette* (paˡyē·t), dim. of *paille* straw, chaff.] 1. A piece of coloured foil or bright metal, used in enamel painting 1878. 2. A spangle, used to ornament a woman's dress 1843.

Pain (pēᵉin), *sb.* [ME. a. OF. *peine* :—L. *pœna* penalty, punishment.] 1. Punishment, penalty; a fine. *Obs.* exc. in phrases (see quots.). 2. The opposite of *pleasure*; the sensation which one feels when hurt (in body or mind); suffering, distress. Also with *a* and *pl.* ME. †b. *spec.* The punishment or sufferings of hell (or of purgatory) –1598. 3. Bodily suffering; a distressing sensation as of soreness (usu. in a particular part of the body). late ME. b. *spec.* (now always *pl.*) The throes of childbirth; labour ME. 4. Mental suffering, trouble, grief, sorrow. late ME. †b. *spec.* Anxiety –1789. 5. *pl.* Trouble taken in accomplishing or attempting something. Most freq. in phr. *to take pains, to be at (the) pains.* 1528. b. In this sense *pains* pl. has been freq. construed as a *sing.* (Cf. *means, news.*) 1533.

1. Phr. *Pains and penalties. On, upon, under p. of*, followed by the penalty or punishment in case of not fulfilling the command or condition stated, as *on p. of death*; †also, the crime with which one is liable to be charged, as *on p. of felony.* †*Pain forte et dure*: see PEINE. 2. P. and pleasure are simple ideas incapable of definition BURKE. Phr. *To put out of* (one's) *p.*, etc., to dispatch (a wounded or suffering person or animal). 3. Loud he yelled for exceeding paine SPENSER. b. She bowed her selfe, and traueled, for her paynes cam vpon her BIBLE (Great) 1 *Sam.* iv. 19. 4. A Mighty p. to Love it is, And 'tis a p. that p. to miss COWLEY. 5. Yet much he praised the pains he took SCOTT. Phr. *For* (one's) *pains*: in return or recompense for one's labour or trouble; now usu. sarcastic or ironical; I had my journey for my pains 1801.

Pain (pēᵉin), *v.* ME. [a. OF. *pener*, 3rd sing. pres. *peine* :—med.L. *pœnare*, f. L. *pœna* PAIN *sb.*] †1. *trans.* To punish; to torture by way of punishment; to fine –1601. 2. To inflict pain upon; to hurt, distress. late ME. †3. *intr.* To suffer pain or distress; to suffer –1591. 4. *refl.* To take pains or trouble; to endeavour, strive. *Obs.* or *arch.* ME.

2. Transports that pain'd and joys that agonized CRABBE. Pained with the toothache HAWTHORNE. 3. So shalt thou cease to plague, and I to p. DANIEL. 4. She her paynd with womanish art To hide her wound SPENSER. Hence **Pained** *ppl. a.* ME.

Painful (pēᵉi·nfŭl), *a.* ME. [f. PAIN *sb.* + -FUL.] 1. Full of or causing pain or suffering; hurting, afflictive, grievous; annoying, vexatious. 2. Suffering or affected with (physical) pain. (Usu. of a part of the body which has been wounded or hurt.) 1590. 3. Causing or involving trouble or labour; difficult, irksome, toilsome, laborious. Now *rare* or merged in 1. late ME. 4. Characterized by painstaking. *Obs.* or *arch.* late ME. 5. Of persons: Painstaking, laborious, assiduous, careful, diligent. *Obs.* or *arch.* 1549.

1. Salutary pangs may be painfuller than mortal ones LANDOR. 2. His wound was p. 1794. 3. Quick and p. Marches DRYDEN. 5. The women be verie painefull and the men often idle 1612. Hence **Pai·nful-ly** *adv.*, **-ness.**

Painless (pēᵉi·nlės), *a.* 1591. [f. PAIN *sb.* + -LESS.] Causing no pain. Hence **Pai·nless-ly** *adv.*, **-ness.**

Painstaking (pēᵉi·nztēᵉi:kiŋ), *sb.* 1556. [f. *pains*, pl. of PAIN *sb.* + *taking*, gerund of TAKE *v.*] The taking of pains; the bestowal of careful and attentive labour in doing something. So **Pai·nstaker,** now *rare* or *Obs.*

Pai·nsta:king, *a.* 1696. [f. as prec. + *taking*, pr. pple. of TAKE *v.*] That takes pains; careful and industrious. b. Of actions, productions, etc.: Marked by attentive care 1866.

A most p. judge 1882. Hence **Pai·nsta:kingly** *adv.*

Paint (pēᵉint), *sb.* 1602. [f. next.] 1. The act of painting or colouring. 2. That with which anything is painted: a. A solid colouring matter dissolved in a liquid vehicle, used to impart colour by being spread over a surface; also, the solid colouring matter alone; a pigment 1712. b. Colouring matter laid on the face or body for adornment; rouge, etc. 1659. c. *Med.* An external medicament which is put on like paint with a brush 1899. 3. *fig.* Colour, colouring; adornment; outward show, fair pretence 1647.

attrib. and *Comb.*, as *p.-box, -brush, -pot*, etc. Hence **Pai·ntless** *a.*, destitute or devoid of paint. **Pai·nty** *a.*, of, belonging to, or abounding in paint; of a picture: overcharged with paint; hence **Pai·ntiness.**

Paint (pēᵉint), *v.* [ME. ad. OF. *peindre* (3rd sing. pres. *peint*, pa. pple. *peint*) :—L. *pingere* (pa. pple. *pinctus*) to paint.] 1. *trans.* To make (a picture, etc.) on a surface in colours; to depict, portray, delineate, by using colours. b. To adorn (a wall, window, etc.) *with* a painting or paintings. (Mostly in *pass.*) ME. c. *transf.* Said of the effect of coloured light 1831. d. *intr.* or *absol.* To practise the art of painting. late ME. 2. *fig.* a. To display vividly as by painting 1561. b. To depict in words; to call up a picture of ME. 3. To colour with a wash or coating of paint; to colour, stain; hence, to adorn with colours ME. b. *transf.* To colour by any means ME. c. *fig.* To adorn or variegate with or as with colours; to deck, beautify, ornament. late ME. 4. To put colour on (the face); to rouge; also *refl.*, and *intr.* for *refl.* late ME. †b. *intr.* (*fig.*) To change colour; to blush. *To p. white*, etc.: to turn pale. –1623. 5. *fig.* (*trans.*) To give a false colouring to; to colour highly, esp. with a view to deception. Now *rare* or *Obs.* late ME. †6. *intr.* To talk speciously. b. *trans.* To flatter or deceive with specious words. –1632. 7. *trans.* To apply with a brush, as an external medicament; to treat (any part) in this way 1861.

1. Phr. *To p.* (an object) *black, white, red, etc.*, to portray as of that colour. c. Like the Iris painted upon the cloud RUSKIN. 2. a. Desire Was painted in my looks CARY. b. What words can p. the guilt of such a conduct? 1766. *To p. black*, to represent as evil or wicked; so *not so black as he is painted.* 3. b. If God..so paints the Flowers SOUTH. c. *To p. the town red* (slang, orig. U.S.), to go on a riotous spree. 4. *intr.* Let her p. an inch thicke, to this fauour she must come SHAKS. 6. *L.L.L.* IV. i. 16. 7. The part affected should be painted with iodine (*mod.*). Hence **Pai·ntable** *a.*, suitable for a painting.

Painted (pēᵉi·ntėd), *ppl. a.* ME. [f. prec. + -ED¹.] 1. Represented in a picture; executed in colours as a picture, likeness, etc. 2. Coated or brushed over with colour or paint; ornamented with designs, etc., executed in colour; having the face artificially coloured. late ME. b. *fig.* Artificial; feigned, disguised, pretended. late ME. 3. *fig.* Highly coloured, variegated 1470.

1. As idle as a p. Ship Upon a p. Ocean COLERIDGE. 3. The pecockes paynted fethers 1526.

Comb.: **p. beauty,** a brilliant American butterfly (*Vanessa huntera*); **P. Chamber,** a chamber in the old Palace of Westminster, the walls of which were painted with a series of battle scenes; **p. cup,** †a name for (*a*) the plant *Bartsia viscosa*; (*b*) any species of the American genus *Castilleia*, having bracts more brilliant and showy than the flowers; **p. finch,** one of several species of *Passerina* or *Cyanospiza*, the nonpareil, the indigo-bird, or the lazuli-finch; **p. lady,** (*a*) a species of butterfly (*Vanessa* or *Pyrameis cardui*) of orange-red colour, spotted with black and white; (*b*) a party-coloured variety of Pink or *Dianthus*; **p. tortoise, turtle,** an American mud-turtle (*Chrysemys picta*) marked on the under surface with red and yellow.

Painter¹ (pēᵉi·ntəɹ). [ME. a. AF. *peintour* (OF. *peintour, -tor*) :—Com. Rom. **pinctorem*, for L. *pictorem*, f. *pingere.*] 1. One who paints pictures; *fig.* a pictorial describer. 2. A workman who coats or colours woodwork, ironwork, etc. with paint. late ME.

Comb., **painter's colic,** a form of colic to which painters who work with preparations of lead are liable, lead-colic. So **Pai·ntress,** a female p.

Painter² (pēᵉi·ntəɹ). ME. [Of unkn. orig.] 1. = SHANK-PAINTER. 2. A rope attached to the bow of a boat, for making it fast to a ship, a stake, etc. 1711.

2. Phr. *To cut* (or *slip*) *the p.* (*fig.*), to send a person or thing 'adrift' or away; to clear off; to sever a connexion.

Painter³. 1823. [var. of PANTHER, prob. from F. *panthère* (pronounced pantɛ̄r).] The American panther or cougar (*Felis concolor*).

Painter-Stainer. 1504. = PAINTER¹ 1 and 2. The name by which the members of the City of London Livery Company of Painters are designated in their charter.

Painting (pēᵉi·ntiŋ), *vbl. sb.* ME. [f. PAINT *v.* + -ING¹.] 1. The result or product of applying paint; colouring; pictorial decoration. 2. *concr.* A representation of an object or scene on a surface by means of colours; a picture. late ME. 3. The representing of objects or figures by means of colours laid on a surface; the art of so depicting objects 1440. b. *fig.* Representation in vivid language 1615. 4. The action of colouring or adorning with paint; the colouring of the face with paint. Also *fig.* 1497. †5. *concr.* Pigment, paint –1650.

†**Painture.** [ME. a. OF. *peinture, painture* :—late L. **pinctura* for *pictura*, f. *pingere, pict-, pinct-* to paint; see -URE.] 1. The action or art of painting. Also *fig.* –1718. 2. That which is painted; pictorial work; a painting –1668.

†**Paiocke.** Commonly taken to be a var. of PEACOCK. *Haml.* III. ii. 295.

Pair (pēᵊɹ), *sb.* [ME. a. F. *paire* :—L. *paria*, pl. neut. of *par, pari-* equal, taken as sing. fem.]

Pair is now followed by *of*; but *of* was formerly omitted, as 'a pair gloves'; cf. Ger. *ein paar handschuhe*. After a numeral *pair* was formerly used in

the sing.; 'three pair (of) shoes' = Ger. *drei paar schuhe*; but the tendency now is to say 'three pairs'.]
I. A set of two. **1.** Two separate things of a kind that are coupled in use; as 'a pair of gloves, shoes, spurs, stirrups, sculls', etc.; also (*colloq.* and somewhat *joc.*) 'a pair of eyes, ears, arms, hands, wings', etc.; also, 'a pair of folding doors, curtains', etc. **2.** In the names of single articles composed of two corresponding parts, which are not used separately; e.g. 'a pair of breeches, trousers, or stays; a pair of scissors, tongs, bellows, spectacles', etc. ME. **3.** Two persons or animals of opposite sexes. **a.** An engaged or married couple. late ME. **b.** Two partners in a dance 1770. **c.** A mated couple of animals ME. **4.** A set of two (persons, animals, or things); a couple, brace, span ME. **b.** Short for *pair of horses*, two horses harnessed together 1727. **c.** Two voters on opposite sides who mutually agree to abstain from voting in order to be absent from a division without affecting the relative position of parties 1845. **d.** Short for 'pair of oars'; see OAR *sb.* 3 a. 1885. **5.** occas. = *two*, or formerly used loosely for a few, two or three. Now usu. superseded by *a couple*. 1599.

1. Phr. *To take* or *show a clean p. of heels*, to escape by superior speed. *P. of lawn sleeves*, a bishop. *P. of oars*: see OAR *sb.* 3 a. *Another* or *a different p. of shoes* or *boots*, a different matter. 3. c. All pair'd, and each p. built a nest COWPER. 4. Phr. *P. of cards*, two of the same value (see also II. 1); *p. of colours*, two flags belonging to a regiment, one the royal, the other the regimental flag; hence, the position or commission of an ensign; *p. of dice*, a set of two.

II. A set, not limited to two. †**1.** A set (of gallows, harness, etc.); a suit (of armour); a string (of beads); a pack (of cards); a chest (of drawers), etc. All *Obs.* or only *dial.* late ME. **b.** *P. of stairs*: a flight of stairs. Often used as = *floor* or *storey*. Also *attrib.*, as in *a two p. lodging*, etc. 1530. **c.** *P. of steps*: a flight of steps; also a portable set of steps 1755. **2.** (Also written *pare*.) A company of miners working together (Cornwall, America); a team of mules carrying tin 1839.

Comb. **p.-toed** *a. Ornith.*, having the toes in pairs, two before and two behind.

Pair (pēᵊɹ), *v.*[1] 1603. [f. prec.] **1.** *trans.* To make a pair by matching (two persons or things one with another); to provide with a 'fellow' so as to make a pair 1613. †**b.** To match, equal. DRAYTON. **2.** *intr.* To go *with*, so as to match 1611. **3.** *trans.* To arrange (two persons or things) in a pair or couple 1607. **b.** To unite in love or marriage; to mate (animals) 1673. **4.** *intr.* To form a couple; esp. to make an agreement with an opponent that both shall abstain from voting on a given question or for a certain time; also *to p. off* 1711. **b.** To unite *with* one of the opposite sex; to couple or mate 1611.

2. He might have..pair'd with him in features and in shape 1756. 3. *To p. off* (a number of persons or things), to put two by two or in pairs. b. Turtles and doves of diff'ring hues unite, And glossy jett is pair'd with shining white POPE. 4. Several members had paired 1810. b. So Turtles paire That neuer meane to part SHAKS.

Phr. *To p. off*, to go off or apart in pairs; also *to p. off with* (colloq.), to marry. Hence **Paired** *ppl. a.*

Pair, *v.*[2] *Obs.* or *dial.* ME. [Aphetic f. *apeyre, apayre*, APPAIR.] †**1.** *trans.* = APPAIR 1. -1625. **2.** *intr.* = APPAIR 2. Now *dial.* ME.

1. Euer it mends Some, and paires Other BACON. Hence †**Pai·rer**, one who impairs WYCLIF. †**Pai·ring** *vbl. sb.*[2] -1617. So **Pai·rment**, IMPAIRMENT (now only *dial.*).

Pair-horse (pēᵊ·ɹhǭɹs), *a.* 1854. [From *pair of horse(s* used attrib.] For a pair of horses.

Pai·ring, *vbl. sb.*[1] 1611. [f. PAIR *v.*[1] + -ING[1].] The action of PAIR *v.*[1]

Comb. **p.-season, -time**, the season at which birds pair; the age at which the sexes begin to pair off.

Pair-oar (pēᵊ·r₁ōᵊɹ). 1854. [Condensed from *pair of oars*.] A boat rowed by a pair of oars. Also *attrib.*

Pair-royal (pēᵊɹ₁roi·ăl). Also **prial** (prəi·ăl). 1592. A set of three of the same kind. **a.** In cribbage, etc.: Three cards of the same denomination; *double pair-royal*, four such cards 1608. **b.** A throw of three dice all turning up the same number of points 1656. **c.** *transf.* A set of three persons or things; three of a kind 1592.

c. That great pair-royal Of adamantine sisters QUARLES.

Paisley (pē·zli). 1884. Name of a town in Scotland, used *attrib.* in *P. shawl*, a shawl in soft bright colours resembling a Cashmere shawl, orig. made at P.; *P. pattern*, the characteristic pattern of such a shawl; so *P. cotton, velvet*, etc., cotton, velvet, etc. having this pattern.

Pajamahs, -mas: see PYJAMAS.

Pajock, a mod. sp. of PAIOCKE, q.v.

‖**Paktong** (pæ·k₁tǫŋ). Also **paak-, packtong.** 1775. [Cantonese dial. f. Chinese *peh t'ung*, f. *peh* white + *t'ung* copper.] Chinese nickel-silver; an alloy of copper, zinc, and nickel, resembling silver.

Pal (pæl), *sb. slang* or *low colloq.* 1681. [a. Eng. Gipsy *pal* brother, mate.] A comrade, mate, partner, 'chum'; an accomplice in crime, etc. Hence **Pal** *v. intr.* to become or be a p. of another; to associate *with*. **Pa·llish, Pa·lly** *adjs.*, on terms of fellowship. **Pa·lliness.**

‖**Palabra** (pălā·bră). 1594. [Sp., = word; cf. PALAVER.] A word; speech, talk, palaver. Often in phr. *Pocas palabras* few words.

Palace (pæ·lės, -ěs), *sb.* [ME. a. OF. *palais, paleis*, F. *palais*:—L. *palatium*, orig. proper name of one of the seven hills of Rome; hence, the house of Augustus, and later the palace of the Cæsars there situated.] **1.** The official residence of an emperor, king, pope, or other sovereign ruler. **b.** The official residence of an archbishop or bishop ME. **c.** In extended applications 1526. **2.** A palatial dwelling-place. late ME. **3.** *transf.* A spacious and highly decorated building, intended as a place of amusement, entertainment, or refreshment; cf. GIN-PALACE 1834. †**4.** The 'house' of a planet. CHAUCER.

1. c. In some inchanted castle or fairy p. MISS BURNEY. Occas. applied to a ducal mansion, e.g. *Blenheim P.*; in *p. of justice*, like F. *palais de justice*, to the supreme law-court; etc. 3. *Crystal P.*, the name of the building of the Great Exhibition of 1851, when removed and erected on Sydenham Hill, near London, as a place of entertainment.

Comb. **p. car** *U.S.*, a railway-carriage fitted up in luxurious style; **-hotel**, a hotel of palatial splendour. Hence **Pa·lace** *v. trans.*, to place or lodge in a p. **Pa·laced** *a.*, having a p. or palaces; living in a p. **Pa·laceward, -wards** *adv.*

Palace Court, pa·lace-cou·rt. 1685. [= Court of the or a palace.] **1.** Name of a court formerly held at the Marshalsea and having jurisdiction in personal actions arising within twelve miles of the palace of Whitehall, the city of London excepted. **2.** The courtyard of a palace 1801.

Paladin (pæ·lădin). 1592. [a. F., ad. It. *paladino*:—L. *palatinus* of or belonging to the palace. See also PALATINE.] One of the Twelve Peers or famous warriors of Charlemagne's court, of whom the Count Palatine was the foremost; also *transf.* a knightly hero, renowned champion, knight errant. Also *attrib.*

Palæo-, *U.S.* **paleo-** (pæ:li₁o, pī:li₁o), bef. a vowel usu. **palæ-, pale-**, comb. form of Gr. παλαιός ancient (often opp. to NEO-). The spelling *pale-* is common in America. **Palæ(o)-ichthyo·logy** [Gr. ἰχθύς fish], that branch of ichthyology which treats of extinct fossil fishes. **Palæobo·tany**, the botany of extinct or fossil plants; hence **Palæobo·tanist. Palæocri·noid** *Zool.*, *sb.* a crinoid of the division *Palæocrinoidea*, comprising the earlier extinct crinoids; *a.* belonging to or characteristic of this division. **Palæocry·stic, -crysta·llic** [Gr. κρύσταλλος ice] *adjs.*, consisting of ancient ice, applied to parts of the polar seas. **Palæo·logy**, the science or study of antiquities (*rare*); **Palæo·logist. Palæonto·graphy**, the description of fossil remains; so **Palæontogra·phical** *a.* **Palæophyto·logy** [Gr. φυτόν plant] = PALÆOBOTANY. **Palæornitho·logy**, that branch of ornithology or palæontology which treats of extinct or fossil birds; so **Palæornitholo·gical** *a.* **Pa·læosaur**, a fossil saurian of the genus *Palæosaurus*. **Palæotechnic** (-te·knik) [Gr. τέχνη art] *a.*, pertaining to primitive art.

Palæography, paleo- (pæli₁ǫ·grăfi, pī·li-). 1818. [ad. mod.L. *palæographia*, f. PALÆO- + Gr. -γραφία -GRAPHY.] **1.** Ancient writing, or an ancient style or method of writing 1822. **2.** The study of ancient writing and inscriptions; the science or art of deciphering these and determining their date 1818. So **Pa·læograph**, an ancient writing. **Palæo·grapher**, occas. **-ist**, one skilled in p. **Palæogra·phic, -al** *adjs.* of or pertaining to p.; **-ly** *adv.*

Palæolithic, paleo- (pæ:liolĭ·þik, pī:li-), *a.* 1865. [f. PALÆO- + Gr. λίθος stone + -IC.] Characterized by the use of primitive stone implements; applied to the earlier part of the prehistoric 'stone age'; also to things belonging to this period: opp. to *neolithic*. So **Pa·læolith**, a primitive stone implement. **Palæoli·thoid** *a.* resembling, or of the nature of, what is p.

Palæontology, pale- (pæ:li₁ǫntǫ·lŏdʒi, pī:li-). 1838. [f. PALÆO- + Gr. ὄντα, pl. of ὄν being + -λογία -LOGY.] The study of extinct organized beings, i.e. of fossil animals and plants; often confined to that of extinct animals (palæozoology). So **Palæontolo·gic, -al** *adjs.*, **-ly** *adv.* **Palæonto·logist.**

Palæothere, paleo- (pæ·li₁oþīᵊɹ, pī·li-). Also in L. form **palæothe·rium.** 1815. [f. PALÆO- + Gr. θηρίον beast.] A perissodactyl mammal of the extinct genus *Palæotherium*, comprising several species of tapir-like form; their fossil remains are found in Eocene and Miocene strata. Hence **Palæothe·rian** *a.* of or pertaining to the p.; characterized by the palæotheres. **Palæothe·rioid, -the·roid** *adjs.* akin to the p.

Palæotype, paleo- (pæ·li₁otəip). 1867. [f. PALÆO- + TYPE *sb.*] A system of writing, devised by A. J. Ellis, in which the 'old types' (i.e. existing Roman letters, etc.) are used to form a universal phonetic alphabet. Also *attrib.* or as *adj.* Hence **Palæoty·pic** *a.*

Palæotypography, paleo- (-təipǫ·grăfi). 1872. [f. PALÆO- + TYPOGRAPHY.] Ancient typography, early printing.

Palæozoic, paleo- (pæ:li₁ozōᵘ·ik, pī:li-), *a.* 1838. [f. PALÆO- + Gr. ζωή life, ζωός living + -IC.] *Geol.* **1.** Characterized by, containing, or pertaining to ancient forms of life. Orig. applied to the Cambrian and Silurian strata; extended to all the fossiliferous strata up to the Permian, the higher strata being MESOZOIC and CAINOZOIC. **2.** *fig.* and *transf.* Belonging to the most ancient, or to the lowest, stage 1851. **B.** *sb. ellipt.* (*pl.*) Palæozoic rocks or strata 1855.

Palæozoology, paleo- (-zo₁ǫ·lŏdʒi). 1857. [f. PALÆO- + ZOOLOGY.] That department of zoology, or of palæontology, which treats of extinct or fossil animals. Hence **Pa:læozoolo·gical** *a.*

‖**Palæstra, palestra** (pălī·stră, păle·stră). late ME. [a. L. *palæstra*, a. Gr. παλαίστρα, f. παλαίειν to wrestle.] *Gr. Antiq.* A place devoted to the public teaching and practice of wrestling and athletics; a wrestling-school, gymnasium; *transf.* the practice of wrestling or athletics; also *fig.* **Palæ·stral, pale·stral** *a.* of or pertaining to the p., or to wrestling or athletics; athletic. So **Palæ·stric, -e·stric** *a.* 1774.

Palætiology (pălī:ti₁ǫ·lŏdʒi). *rare.* 1837. [(for **palæ-ætiology*), f. Gr. παλαιός ancient + ÆTIOLOGY; after *palæontology*.] Used by Whewell for the application of existing principles of cause and effect to the explanation of past phenomena. So **Palæ:tiolo·gical** *a.* **Palæ:tio·logist**, one versed in p.

Palagonite (pălæ·gŏnəit). 1863. [ad. G. *palagonit*, f. *Palagonia* in Sicily.] *Min.* A volcanic rock of vitreous structure allied to basalt.

‖**Palais de danse** (pale də dāñs). 1926. [Fr.] An elaborate public dance hall.

‖**Palampore** (pæ·lămpōᵊɹ). 1698. [Origin unkn.] A kind of chintz bed-cover formerly made in India.

Palander (pæ·lăndəɹ). *Obs.* exc. *Hist.* 1562. [app. ad. It. *palandra, palandaria*, of unkn. origin.] **1.** A flat-bottomed transport vessel used esp. (by the Turks) for transporting horses 1572. †**2.** A fire-ship; a bomb-ketch -1693.

‖**Pala·nk, -ka.** 1685. [a. F. *palanque*, It. *palanca*; so Turk. *palanqah*.] A kind of permanent entrenched camp, attached to Turkish frontier fortresses.

‖ **Palanquin, palankeen** (pælănkī·n). 1588. [orig. a. Pg. *palanquim*, repr. an E. Ind. vernacular word **pālanki*. The final nasal is app. a Pg. addition, as in *mandarin*.] A covered litter, usu. for one person, used in India and the East, carried by four or six (rarely two) men by means of poles projecting before and behind. Also *attrib.*

‖ **Palas, pulas** (pălā·s). 1799. [Hindī *palāç*, *palās*, Skr. *palāça*.] The DHĀK-tree of India, *Butea frondosa* and *B. superba*.

Palatable (pæ·lătăb'l), *a.* 1669. [f. PALATE *sb.* and *v.* + -ABLE.] Agreeable to the palate; pleasant to the taste; savoury.

fig. Truth..is seldom p. to the ears of kings 1683. Hence **Palatabi·lity, Pa·latableness. Pa·latably** *adv.*

Palatal (pæ·lătăl), *a.* and *sb.* 1828. [a. F. *palatal*, f. L. *palatum* palate + -AL.] A. *adj.* 1. *Anat., Zool.*, etc. Pertaining to the palate; palatine. 2. *Phonetics.* Of a consonant or vowel sound: Produced by placing the tongue against the palate, esp. the hard palate; now more commonly called *front*. 1828. B. *sb.* 1. *Anat.* Short for *p. bone*: = PALATINE *sb.*² 1. 1886. 2. *Phonetics.* A palatal sound; usually, a palatal or front consonant 1828. Hence **Pa·latalize** *v. trans.* to render palatal; esp. to change (a sound) by advancing the point of contact between tongue and palate. **Palataliza·tion.**

Palate (pæ·lĕt), *sb.* late ME. [ad. L. *palatum*.] 1. The roof of the mouth; the structures, partly bony and partly fleshy, which separate the cavity of the mouth from that of the nose. 2. Pop. considered as the seat of taste; hence *transf.* the sense of taste 1526. b. *fig.* Mental taste or liking. late ME. 3. *Bot.* A convex projection of the lower lip closing the throat of the corolla of a personate flower, as the snapdragon 1760. 4. *attrib.* 1611.

1. *Bony* or *hard p.*, the anterior and chief part of the palate, consisting of bone covered with thick mucous membrane. *Soft p.*, the posterior part of the palate, a pendulous fold of musculo-membranous tissue separating the mouth-cavity from the pharynx, and terminating below in the uvula; also called *veil of the p.* = VELUM 2 a. †*Falling down of the p.*, etc., relaxation of the uvula. 2. b. I heard a little too much preaching,..and lost my p. for it GEO. ELIOT.

Palate (pæ·lĕt), *v. rare.* 1606. [f. prec.] *trans.* To perceive or try with the palate, to taste; to relish. Also *fig.*

Palatial (pălē¹·ʃăl), *a.*¹ 1754. [f. L. *palatium* PALACE + -AL.] Of the nature of a palace; pertaining to or befitting a palace; splendid, magnificent (as a building). Hence **Pala·tially** *adv.*

†**Palatial,** *a.*², *sb.* 1775. Obs. irreg. form for PALATAL –1832.

Palatinate (pălæ·tinĕt, pæ·lătinē¹t). 1580. [f. PALATINE *sb.*¹ + -ATE ¹; in F. *palatinat*.] 1. The territory under the rule of a palatine or count-palatine 1658. b. In England and Ireland: A county palatine or palatine earldom: see COUNTY¹ 1 and PALATINE *a.*¹ 2b. 1614. c. *The P., Rhine P.*, a state of the old German empire, under the rule of the Pfalzgraf or Count Palatine of the Rhine 1580. 2. *attrib.* or *adj.* Of or belonging to a palatinate 1672.

2. *P. purple*, in Durham University, a light purple used in some academical robes, etc.; hence as *sb.*, a blazer of this colour awarded as a distinction in sports; the distinction itself (cf. BLUE *sb.* 8).

Palatine (pæ·lătəin, -in), *a.*¹ and *sb.*¹ late ME. [a. F. *palatin, -ine*, ad. L. *palatinus* of or belonging to the *palatium* or PALACE, as sb. 'officer of the palace, chamberlain'.] A. *adj.* 1. Of or belonging to a palace or court; palatial 1598. 2. Possessing royal privileges; having a jurisdiction (within the territory) such as elsewhere belongs to the sovereign alone. late ME. b. Of or belonging to a count or earl palatine, or to a county palatine, or palatinate 1638. 3. Of or belonging to the German Palatinate 1644.

2. *Count, Earl (Lord) P.*: see COUNT *sb.*² *County P., P. County*: see COUNTY¹ 1. *P. earldom* = County P. b. The rich p. city of Durham 1824.

B. *sb.* [the adj. used ellipt.] I. Short for Palatine Hill, *Mons Palatinus*, at Rome 1656. II. 1. An officer of the imperial palace; orig. the chamberlain, the mayor or major of the palace; a chief minister of the empire 1598. b. Hence: A lord having sovereign power over a province or dependency of an empire or realm; a great feudatory 1591. c. In England and Ireland: An earl palatine 1612. 2. *pl.* In ref. to the later Roman Empire: The troops of the palace; the prætorians 1630. †3. A county palatine or palatinate –1600. 4. An inhabitant or native of a palatinate 1610.

4. Emigrant Palatines and Saltzburghers from Germany 1773.

†III. [a. F. *palatine*: so called from the Princess Palatine, wife of the Duke of Orleans: see Littré.] A fur tippet worn by women. Also *p. tippet*. –1880.

Palatine (pæ·lătəin, -in), *a.*² and *sb.*² 1656. [a. F. *palatin, -ine*, f. L. *palatum* PALATE.] A. *adj.* 1. *Anat.*, etc. Of or belonging to the palate; situated in or upon the palate. †2. *Phonetics.* = PALATAL A. 2. –1773. B. *sb.* 1. *Anat.* (*pl.*) Short for *p. bones*: The two bones, right and left, which form the hard palate 1854. †2. *Phonetics.* = PALATAL B. 2. –1834.

Palative (pæ·lătiv), *a. rare.* 1682. [f. PALATE *sb.* + -IVE.] Appealing to the palate or taste.

Palato- (pălē¹·to, pæ·lăto), comb. form of L. *palatum* PALATE; as in **Palato-de·ntal** (*Phonetics*) *a.*, pertaining to palate and teeth; applied to consonants produced by placing the tongue against the palate immediately behind the teeth; *sb.*, a consonant so produced. **Palato-pte·rygoid** *a.*, belonging to the palatine and pterygoid bones; *sb.*, a bone composed of these united.

Palaver (pălā·vəɹ), *sb.* 1735. [ad. Pg. *palavra* word, speech, talk (= It. *parola*, F. *parole*):—L. *parabola* parable, in early med.L. 'story, tale, word'. Orig. nautical slang.] 1. A talk, parley, conference, discussion; esp. with African or other uncivilized natives. 2. Profuse or idle talk; 'jaw' 1748. b. Talk intended to wheedle 1809.

Palaver (pălā·vəɹ), *v.* 1733. [f. prec.] 1. *intr.* To talk profusely or unnecessarily; to 'jaw', 'jabber'; to talk wheedlingly. 2. *trans.* To treat with palaver; to flatter, wheedle 1785.

2. To write silly odes, and p. the great 1815. Hence **Pala·verer.**

Pale (pē¹l), *sb.*¹ ME. [a. F. *pal*, ad. L. *palus* stake.] 1. *orig.* A stake, either driven into the ground with others, to form a fence; now usu., One of the upright bars nailed vertically to a horizontal rail or rails, to form a paling. late ME. 2. A fence; a paling, palisade. *Obs.* or *arch.* ME. b. *transf.* and *fig.* Any enclosing barrier or line. *Obs.* or *arch.* 1564. c. *fig.* A limit, boundary; a restriction; a defence, safeguard. *Obs.* exc. in phr. *within* (or *outside*) *the p. of.* late ME. †3. An area enclosed by a fence; an enclosure. *Obs.* or *arch.* late ME. 4. A district within determined bounds, or subject to a particular jurisdiction; *spec.* (now only *Hist.*) b. the *English P.* in France, the territory of Calais 1494; c. the *English P.* (also simply *the P.*) in Ireland, that part of Ireland over which English jurisdiction was established 1547. 5. *Her.* An ordinary consisting of a vertical stripe or band in the middle of the shield, usu. occupying one-third of its breadth 1478. †b. A vertical stripe on cloth, etc. CHAUCER. †6. *Bot.* The 'ray' of florets in composite flowers –1683. b. = IMPALER 1676.

1. Inclosynge it with stakes or pales as his owne 1555. 2. Herds of deer not confined by any wall or p. 1792. c. Nothing within the p. or verge of Reason 1671. 5. *In p.*: said of a charge or row of charges in the position of a p.; formerly also = palewise, vertically. (*Party*) *per p.*: said of the shield when divided by a vertical line through the middle.

†**Pale,** *sb.*² 1547. [f. PALE *a.*] Paleness, pallor –1832.

Pale, *sb.*³ 1866. [ad. L. *palea.*] = PALEA.

Pale (pē¹l), *a.* [ME. a. OF. *palle, pale* (F. *pâle*), ad. L. *pallidum*, f. *pallere* to be pale.] 1. Of persons, their complexion, etc.: Of a whitish or ashen appearance; pallid; wan. b. *gen.* Of a shade of colour approaching white; faintly coloured. late ME. c. Qualifying adjs. (or sbs.) of colour 1588. d. Relatively lighter in colour 1708. 2. Wanting in brightness or brilliancy; dim. late ME. 3. *fig.* Dim, faint, feeble; lacking intensity, vigour, or robustness; timorous, etc. 1530.

1. He starte abak and waxed paale MALORY. The p. cast of Thought SHAKS. b. The p. Primrose MILT. 2. The day sterre wexeth paale and leseth hir lyht CHAUCER. 3. The p. kyngdome of Pluto 1530. Hence **Pa·le·ly** *adv.*, **-ness.**

Pale (pē¹l), *v.*¹ Now *rare.* ME. [a. OF. *paler*, f. *pal* PALE *sb.*¹: cf. L. *palare.*] 1. *trans.* To enclose with pales or a fence; to surround, fence *in*. b. *transf.* and *fig.* To encircle, hem in. Const. *in, up.* 1563. †2. To stripe, to mark with vertical stripes. (Almost always in pa. pple.) late ME.

1. b. *Hen. V*, v. Prol. 10. Hence **Paled** (pē¹ld) *ppl. a.*¹, †(*a*) = PALY; (*b*) enclosed with pales, fenced. †**Pa·ler**, an officer of a park charged with keeping the fences in repair –1800.

Pale (pē¹l), *v.*² ME. [ad. OF. *palir*, F. *pâlir*, f. *pâle* adj.] 1. *intr.* To grow pale or dim; to lose colour or brilliancy. 2. *trans.* To make, cause to become, pale; to dim. late ME.

1. The Red Rose pal'd, the White was soil'd in red 1637. 2. The Glow-worme..gins to p. his vneffectuall Fire SHAKS. Hence **Paled** *ppl. a.*², rendered pale. **Pa·ling** *ppl. a.*, growing pale.

‖ **Palea** (pē¹·li,ă). Pl. **-eæ** (-i,ī). 1753. [L., = chaff.] 1. *Bot.* A chaff-like bract or scale; *esp.* the inner bracts enclosing the stamens and pistil in the flower of grasses (opp. to the *glumes*); also, those at the bases of the individual florets in many *Compositæ*; the scales on the stems of certain ferns. 2. *Ornith.* A wattle or dewlap 1890. Hence **Palea·ceous** *a.* furnished or covered with paleæ; of the nature or consistence of chaff. So †**Pa·leous** *a.* of the nature of chaff; chaffy. Sir T. BROWNE.

Pale-face (pē¹·lfē¹s). 1822. A person who has a pale face; a name for a white man attributed to the N. Amer. Indians or 'red men'.

Pale-faced (pē¹·lfē¹st), *a.* 1592. Having a pale face.

Paleo-: see PALÆO-.

Palestra, etc.: see PALÆSTRA, etc.

Palet (pē¹·lĕt). 1880. [f. PALE *sb.*³ + -ET.] *Bot.* = PALEA 1.

‖ **Paletot** (pæ·lĕtōᵘ, pæ·ltōᵘ). 1840. [F., of unkn. origin; see PALTOCK.] A loose outer garment for men or women.

Palette (pæ·lĕt). 1622. [a. F. *palette*, dim. of *pale* shovel, blade of oar:—L. *pala* spade, etc.] 1. A flat thin tablet of wood or porcelain, used by an artist to lay and mix his colours on. b. *transf.* The set of colours used by a particular artist or for a particular picture 1882. 2. A small rounded plate formerly used in armour to protect the armpit 1834. 3. a. *Conch.* = PALLET ² 7. b. *Entom.* a flat expansion upon the legs of some insects. 1834.

Comb. **p.-knife**, a thin flexible blade of steel fitted with a handle, used for mixing colours on a palette, for distributing printing-ink on a surface, etc.

Palewise (pē¹·lwəiz), *adv.* 1721. [f. PALE *sb.*¹ + -WISE.] *Her.* In the direction of a pale; vertically. Also †**Pa·leways** 1610.

Palfrenier (pælfrĕnī³·ɹ). *arch.* 1489. [a. F. *palefrenier*; see next and -IER 2.] A man having charge of horses; a groom.

Palfrey (pǭ·lfri, pæ·l-). [ME. a. OF. *palefrei*:—late L. *palafredus*, by dissimilation from *parafredus*:—late L. *paraveredus*, f. Gr. παρά beside + *veredus* light horse, post-horse.] A saddle-horse for ordinary riding as dist. from a war-horse; *esp.* a small saddle-horse for ladies. (Now mainly *Hist.*) Also *attrib.*

A damoysel..on a fayr palfroy MALORY. [He] cried, 'My charger and her p.' TENNYSON.

Pali (pā·li), *sb.* and *a.* 1800. [Short for *pāli-bhāsā*, i.e. language of the canonical texts (as opp. to 'commentary'), f. *pāli* line, canon + *bhāsā* language.] The language used in the canonical books of the Buddhists.

Paliform (pē¹·lifǭm), *a.* 1890. [f. PALUS + -(I)FORM.] *Zool.* Resembling, or having the form of, a palus.

‖ **Palikar** (pæ·likāɹ). 1812. [ad. mod.Gr. παλικάρι lad, f. Gr. πάλλαξ, -ηξ youth.] A member of the band of a Greek or Albanian military chief.

Palil(l)ogy (păli·lŏdʒi). Also in Gr.-L. forms. 1657. [ad. L. *palil(l)ogia*, Gr. παλιλλογία, f. πάλιν again + -λογία speaking.]

Rhet. The repetition of a word or phrase for the sake of emphasis.

‖ **Palimbacchius** (pæ:limbækəi·ʊs). 1586. [L., a. Gr. παλιμβάκχειος, f. πάλιν back + βακχεῖος BACCHIUS.] = ANTIBACCHIUS. Also **Palimba·cchic.**

Palimpsest (pæ·limpsest), *sb.* and *a.* 1661. [ad. L. *palimpsestus* sb., a. Gr. παλίμψηστος scraped again, f. πάλιν again + ψηστός, f. ψῆν to rub smooth.] **A.** *sb.* †**1.** Paper, parchment, etc., prepared for writing on and wiping out again, like a slate –1706. **2.** A parchment, etc., which has been written upon twice, the original writing having been rubbed out 1825. Also *fig.* **3.** A monumental brass turned and re-engraved on the reverse side 1876. **B.** *adj.* **1.** Of a manuscript: see A. 2. 1852. **2.** Of a monumental brass: see A. 3. 1843.

Palindrome (pæ·lindrōᵘm), *sb.* and *a.* 1629. [ad. Gr. παλίνδρομος running back again.] A word, verse, or sentence that reads the same backwards as forwards. Also *adj.* Palindromic.

Subi dura a rudibus: It is P. 1638. Hence **Palindro·mic, -al** *adjs.*, **-ly** *adv.* **Pa·lindromist,** an inventor of palindromes.

Paling (pē·liŋ), *vbl. sb.* late ME. [f. PALE *v.*[1] + -ING [1].] †**1.** Decoration with 'pales' or vertical stripes CHAUCER. **2.** The action of constructing a fence with pales; fencing 1469. **3.** *concr.* **a.** Pales collectively; fencing 1788. **b.** A fence made of pales. (With *a* and *pl.*) 1558. **c.** Each of the pales of a fence; usu. in *pl.* = a set of pales, a fence 1834.

3. a. The firs answer for..p. for fences 1788.

‖ **Palingenesia** (pæ:lindʒēnī·siă). 1621. [med. L., a. Gr. παλιγγενεσία birth over again, f. πάλιν + γένεσις.] = PALINGENESY.

Palingenesis (pælindʒe·nėsis). 1818. [f. Gr. πάλιν again + γένεσις birth: cf. prec.] **1.** = PALINGENESY. **2.** *Biol.* Haeckel's term for the form of ontogenesis in which ancestral characters are exactly reproduced, without modification 1879. **3.** *Entom.* = METAMORPHOSIS 3 a. 1886. Hence **Palingene·tic** *a.* of, belonging to, or of the nature of p. (sense 2).

Palingenesy (pælindʒe·nėsi). 1643. [a. F. *palingénésie*, ad. med.L. PALINGENESIA.] Regeneration, birth over again; revival, reanimation, resuscitation.

Palinode (pæ·linōᵘd). 1599. [ad. L. *palinodia* PALINODY.] *orig.* An ode or song in which the author retracts something said in a former poem; hence *gen.* a recantation. So **Palino·dial** *a.*, of the nature of a recantation.

Palinodic (pælinǫ·dik), *a.* 1883. [ad. Gr. παλινῳδικός; see next and -IC.] *Gr. Pros.* Applied to verse in which two 'systems' of corresponding form, as a strophe and antistrophe, are separated by two others also of corresponding form but different from the former.

Palinody (pæ·linoᵘdi). Now *rare* or *Obs.* 1589. [a. F. *palinodie*, ad. L. *palinodia*, a. Gr. παλινῳδία recantation, f. πάλιν again + ᾠδή song.] = PALINODE.

Palisade (pælisē·d), *sb.* 1600. [a. F. *palissade*, f. *palisser* to enclose with pales; see -ADE.] **1.** A fence of pales or stakes. †**b.** *Gardening.* An espalier; hence *transf.* a row of trees or shrubs forming a close hedge –1712. **2.** *Mil.* A strong pointed wooden stake, of which a number are fixed deeply in the ground in a close row, as a defence 1697. **3.** *fig.* Anything likened to a fence of stakes (or one of such stakes) 1601. **b.** *pl.* Name for the lofty cliffs along the western bank of the Hudson above New York 1838.

3. A vast p. of blue ice-pinnacles 1871. *Comb.*: **p.-cell,** a cell of the **p.-tissue,** tissue consisting of elongated cells set closely side by side, as the parenchyma immediately below the epidermis of the upper surface in most leaves; **-worm,** name for various parasitic nematode worms, esp. *Strongylus armatus*, infesting the horse, etc.

Hence **Palisa·de** *v. trans.* to furnish with a p. or palisades. **Palisa·ding** *vbl. sb.* a palisade, paling.

Palisa·do, *sb. Obs.* or *arch.* 1589. [ad. Sp. *palizada*; see -ADO.] = PALISADE. Hence **Palisa·do** *v.*

Palish (pē·liʃ), *a.* late ME. [f. PALE *a.* + -ISH [1].] Somewhat pale, rather pale.

‖ **Palissé** (pa·lise), *a.* 1780. [F., pa. pple. of *palisser* to PALISADE.] *Her.* Said of a dividing line when broken into parallel vertical pointed projections, like a palisade; **b.** said of the field when divided into vertical piles of alternate tinctures.

‖ **Palkee, palki** (pā·lkī). *East Ind.* 1678. [Hindī *pālkī*.] = PALANQUIN.

Pall (pǭl), *sb.*[1] [OE. *pæll*, ad. L. *pallium*.] **I.** Cloth, a cloth. **1.** Fine or rich cloth; in OE. 'purple'. *Obs.* exc. as poet. *arch.* **2.** A rich cloth spread over or upon something; a coverlet, canopy, etc. *Obs.* or *arch.* ME. **3.** *Eccl.* **a.** An altar-cloth or frontal. *arch.* **b.** The linen cloth or linen-covered square of cardboard with which the chalice is covered. OE. **4.** A cloth, usu. of black, purple, or white velvet, spread over a coffin, hearse, or tomb 1440.

1. If p. and vair no more I wear SCOTT. 4. Mourning when their leaders fall, Warriors carry the warrior's p. TENNYSON.

II. A garment, a vestment. **1.** A robe, cloak, mantle. *Obs.* or *arch.* OE. **2.** *spec.* **a.** *Eccl.* = PALLIUM 2. Hence *transf.* The office or dignity of metropolitan or archbishop. 1480. **b.** A robe or mantle put upon the sovereign at coronation; now called the 'royal robe' 1643. **3.** *Her.* A bearing repr. the front half of an archbishop's pallium, consisting of three bands in the form of a capital Y, charged with crosses. (Also called *cross-pall.*) 1562.

1. In a long purple p.,..she was arayd SPENSER. 2. a. Besides his P., the Pope's Chamberlain, brought him from Rome, a Cardinalls hat 1650.

III. *fig.* Something that covers or conceals, a 'mantle', 'cloak'; in mod. use *esp.* something, such as a cloud, that extends over a thing or region and produces an effect of gloom 1450.

Overhead..a murky p. of smoke 1882.

attrib. and *Comb.*, as *p.-like* adj.; **p.-bearer, -holder, -supporter,** one of those attending the coffin at a funeral, to hold up the corners and edges of the p. Hence **Pall** *v.*[2], to cover with or as with a cloth or p. late ME.

Pall (pǭl), *v.*[1] late ME. [app. aphetic f. APPAL *v.*] **I.** *intr.* †**1.** To become faint; to faint, fail (in strength, virtue, etc.) –1602. †**2.** Of fermented or aerated liquors: To become flat, stale, or insipid –1703. **3.** *transf.* and *fig.* To become tasteless, vapid, or insipid to the appetite or interest 1704. **4.** To lose relish or interest; to become cloyed *with* 1765.

3. Beauty is a Thing which palls with Possession STEELE. They would satiate us and p. upon our senses RUSKIN.

II. *trans.* †**1.** To make pale, to dim –1612. †**2.** To make faint or feeble; to weaken; to appal –1686. †**3.** To render flat, stale, or insipid –1807. **4.** To satiate, cloy (the appetite, senses, etc.) 1700.

4. And p. the sense with one continu'd show ADDISON. Hence **Pall** *sb.*[2], a feeling of disgust arising from satiety or insipidity (*rare*).

Pall, var. of PAWL.

‖ **Palla** (pæ·lă). 1706. [L., obscurely related to *pallium*.] **1.** *Rom. Antiq.* A loose outer garment or wrap worn out of doors by women. **2.** *Eccl.* = PALL *sb.*[1] I. 3. 1706.

Palladian (pælē·diăn), *a.*[1] 1562. [f. L. *palladius* + -AN.] Of or pertaining to Pallas, the goddess of wisdom; hence, pertaining to wisdom, knowledge, or study.

Palla·dian, *a.*[2] 1731. [f. *Palladio* + -AN.] *Arch.* Of, belonging to, or according to the school of the Italian architect Andrea Palladio (1518–80), who imitated ancient Roman architecture without regard to classical principles.

Palladic (pælæ·dik), *a.*[1] 1857. [f. PALLADIUM [2] + -IC 1 b.] *Chem.* Applied to compounds of palladium containing a smaller proportion of the metal than those called *palladious*.

Palla·dic, *a.*[2] 1896. [Cf. PALLADIUM [1] (in sense 2) + -IC.] Name of a supposed branch of continental Freemasonry. So **Pa·lladism** 1895. **Pa·lladist.**

Palladious (pælē·diəs), *a.* 1842. [f. PALLADIUM [2] + -OUS.] *Chem.* Applied to compounds of palladium containing a larger proportion of the metal than those called *palladic*.

Palladium [1] (pælē·diʊ̆m). late ME. [a. L., a. Gr. παλλάδιον neut. of παλλάδιος of Pallas.] **1.** *Gr. and L. Myth.* The image of the goddess Pallas, in the citadel of Troy, on which the safety of the city was supposed to depend, reputed to have been brought thence to Rome. **2.** *transf.* and *fig.* Anything on which the safety of a nation, institution, etc., is believed to depend 1600.

2. The *Habeas Corpus* Act..the p. of an Englishman's liberty 1845.

Palladium [2] (pălē·diʊ̆m). 1803. [a. mod. L., f. *Pallas*. Named 1803 by Wollaston, from the newly discovered asteroid *Pallas*.] *Chem.* A hard white metal of the platinum group resembling silver, occurring in small quantities chiefly with platinum. Symbol Pd; atomic weight 126.

Pallah (pæ·lă). 1806. [ad. Sechwana *p'hala*, Zulu *im-pala*.] An antelope (*Æpyceros melampus*) inhabiting parts of S. Africa.

Palled (pǭld), *ppl. a.* late ME. [f. PALL *v.*[1] + -ED [1].] †**1.** Enfeebled, impaired –1668. **2.** Of fermented liquor, etc.: Flat, stale, vapid. late ME. **3.** Satiated, cloyed, disgusted 1691.

Pallescent (păle·sĕnt), *a. rare.* 1657. [ad. L. *pallescentem*.] Growing or becoming pale. So **Palle·scence.**

Pallet [1] (pæ·lėt). [late ME. *pailet*: cf. dial. F. *paillet* heap of straw, f. *paille* straw :—L. *palea*.] **1.** A straw bed; a mattress; a small, poor, or mean bed or couch. Also *p.-bed*, etc. †**2.** *Naut.* A small room for ballast in the hold of a ship –1867.

Pallet [2] (pæ·lėt). 1558. [a. F. *palette*, dim. of *pale* spade, blade, etc.: cf. PALETTE.] **1.** A wooden instrument consisting of a flat blade or plate, with a handle attached; *spec.* that used by potters for shaping their work. **2.** = PALETTE 1. †**3.** A flat board, plate, or disk; e.g. the blade of an oar, the float of a paddle-wheel –1808. *spec.* **b.** *Brickmaking.* A board for carrying away a newly moulded brick 1839. **c.** Each of the series of disks in a chain-pump 1875. **4.** A projection on some part of a machine, which engages with the teeth of a wheel, and thus converts a reciprocating into a rotary motion, or *vice versa*; *esp.* a projection upon the pendulum or the arbor of the balance-wheel of a clock or watch, engaging with the escapement-wheel. [So in Fr.] 1704. **5.** In an organ: Any one of the valves in the upper part of the wind-chest 1840. **6.** *Bookbinding.* A tool for impressing letters, etc. on the back of a book, consisting of a metal block mounted on a handle 1875. **7.** *Conch.* An accessory valve in some molluscs.

Pallet [3] (pæ·lėt). 1562. [dim. of PALE *sb.*[1] 5.] *Her.* An ordinary resembling the pale, but of half its breadth.

Pallial (pæ·liăl), *a.* 1836. [ad. mod.L. *pallialis*, f. PALLIUM: see -AL.] *Zool.* Of or pertaining to the pallium or mantle of a mollusc (or of a brachiopod).

†**Pa·lliament.** *rare.* 1588. [ad. med.L. *palliamentum*, f. *palliare* to cloak.] The white gown of a candidate for the Roman consulship *Tit. A.* I. i. 182.

†**Pa·lliard.** 1484. [a. F. *paillard*, f. *paille* straw; see -ARD.] A professional beggar or vagabond (who sleeps on straw in barns, etc.); *transf.* a low knave; a debauchee –1851.

Palliasse (pæ·liæs). Formerly **paillasse.** 1506. [a. F. *paillasse*, f. *paille* :—L. *palea* chaff, straw.] A straw mattress; now, usu., an under-mattress stuffed with straw, or the like.

Palliate (pæ·li,ĕt), *ppl. a.* 1548. [ad. L. *palliatus* cloaked, f. *pallium*; see -ATE [2] 2.] †**A.** as *pa. pple.* Cloaked, covered, concealed; mitigated –1650. **B.** as *adj.* †**1.** Cloaked; disguised –1648. †**2.** Of a cure: Superficial or temporary –1679. **3.** *Zool.* Having a PALLIUM (sense 3); tectibranchiate 1890.

Palliate (pæ·li,eᶦt), *v.* 1548. [f. prec.: cf. late L. *palliare* to cloak.] †**1.** *trans.* To cover with or as with a cloak. –1656. †**2.** *fig.* To hide, conceal, disguise –1812. **3.** To alleviate the symptoms of a disease; to mitigate the sufferings of; to ease 1588. **4.** To represent (an evil) as less than it really is; to extenuate, excuse 1634. †**5.** To moderate, qualify or tone down. Also *absol.* or *intr.* To take up a more moderate position, to compromise. –1796.

2. There was no palliating the fact MAR. EDGEWORTH. 3. That which cannot be cured must be pal-

liated 1876. 4. They endeavoured to p. what they could not justify 1777. Hence **Pa·lliator.** **Pa·lliatory** *a.* palliating.

Palliation (pæli,ēⁱ·ʃən). 1577. [a. F., ad. med.L. *palliationem*, f. *palliare*.] †1. The action of palliating; that which serves to conceal or hide –1794. 2. Extenuation, excuse; often in phr. *in p. of* 1605. 3. Alleviation, mitigation, relief 1626.

2. The tyrant's plea of necessity in p. of his evil deeds 1867.

Palliative (pæ·li,ātiv), *a.* and *sb.* 1543. [a. F. *palliatif, -ive*; see -IVE.] A. *adj.* †1. Serving to cloak or conceal –1656. 2. Serving to relieve (disease) superficially or temporarily, or to mitigate (pain, etc.) 1543. 3. Tending to extenuate or excuse 1779. B. *sb.* That which palliates; a palliative agent 1748; an extenuating representation 1724. Hence **Pa·lliatively** *adv.*

Pallid (pæ·lid), *a.* 1590. [ad. L. *pallidus*, f. root *pall-* in *pallere* to be pale.] Lacking depth or intensity of colour, wan, pale. Chiefly *poet.* bef. 1800, exc. in *Bot.*

P. death SPENSER. A blush suffused Her p. cheek SOUTHEY. Hence **Pa·llid·ly** *adv.*, **-ness.** **Palli·dity**, pallor.

Pallio- (pæ·lio), comb. form of PALLIUM, used in zool. terms relating to the pallium or mantle of a mollusc, etc.; as **Palliobranchiate** (-bræ·ŋkiĕt) *a.*, belonging to the *Palliobranchiata* or *Brachiopoda*, the tubes of the mantle being supposed to be branchia or gills; etc.

‖ **Pallium** (pæ·liŏm). *Pl.* **pallia.** 1564. [L.; see PALL *sb.*[1]] 1. *Antiq.* A large rectangular cloak or mantle worn by men, chiefly among the Greeks; esp. by philosophers, and by early Christian ascetics (= Gr. ἱμάτιον, HIMATION.) 2. *Eccl.* A vestment of wool worn by patriarchs and metropolitans (in R.C.Ch. conferred by the Pope) now consisting of a narrow ring-like band lying over the shoulders with a piece pendent therefrom at the front and the back. Also, a figure of this, as on the arms of the archbishopric of Canterbury. 1670. 3. a. *Zool.* The MANTLE of a mollusc (or of a brachiopod) 1872. b. *Ornith.* The MANTLE of a bird (*rare*). 4. *Meteorol.* A sheet of cirro-stratus cloud uniformly covering the whole sky 1883.

Pall-mall (pel,mel, pæl,mæl). Also formerly **pell-mell**, etc. 1568. [a. F. †*pallemaille*, a. It. *pallamaglio*, f. *palla*, var. of *balla* ball + *maglio* mallet :—L. *malleus* hammer.] †1. A mallet for striking a ball; *spec.* that used in the game described in 2. –1611. 2. A game in which a boxwood ball was driven through an iron ring suspended at a height in a long alley 1598. †3. The alley in which the game was played –1688. b. The name of a street developed from one of these alleys in London, now the centre of London club life 1656.

‖ **Pallone** (pallō·ne). 1865. [It., augm. of *palla* ball.] An Italian game, played with a large ball struck with a wooden guard, worn over the hand and wrist.

Pallor (pæ·lǒɹ). 1656. [a. L., f. root of *pallere* to be pale.] Paleness.

Pally *a.* (1895), see s.v. PAL.

Palm (pām), *sb.*[1] [OE. *palm, palma, palme*, a. L. *palma*. L. *palma* was a transf. sense of *palma* palm of the hand; see next.] 1. Any tree or shrub of the N.O. *Palmæ* or *Palmaceæ*, a large family of monocotyledons, chiefly tropical, and variously useful to man. Also applied *fig.* to a person 1800.

Palms have the stem usually upright and unbranched, a head of very large pinnate or fan-shaped leaves, and fruit of various forms (nut, drupe, or berry). The palm of Scripture is the date-palm.

b. With defining words, denoting various species of the order *Palmæ*, as **Bamboo P.**, DATE-*p.*, etc. 2. A 'branch' or leaf of the palm-tree, esp. as anciently carried or worn as a symbol of victory or triumph, and still on festal occasions ME. 3. *fig.* Victory, triumph; supreme excellence, prize. late ME. 4. A branch or sprig of any of several trees and shrubs substituted in northern countries, esp. in celebrating Palm Sunday, for the true palm; also applied to the plants themselves (e.g. the willow). late ME.

1. She dwelt vnder yᵉ palme of Debbora betwene Rama & Bethel COVERDALE *Judg.* iv. 5. *fig.* You shall see him a Palme in Athens againe SHAKS. 2. Hauyng in her hande the palme of vyctory LYDG. 3. He disputed the p. of eloquence with Cicero himself GIBBON. Phr. *To bear the p.*, *yield the p.*, etc.

attrib. and *Comb.*: **p.-branch**, a leaf of the palm-tree with its stalk, used as a symbol of victory, as a decoration, etc.; **-butter**, palm-oil in the solid state; **-cat, -civet**, (*a*) a viverrine animal of the genus *Paradoxurus* or sub-family *Paradoxurinæ*, which frequents palm-trees; (*b*) the ocelot; **-crab**, the tree-crab (*Birgus latro*), which climbs palm-trees for the fruit; **-kernel**, the kernel of the drupaceous fruit of the Oil P.; **-sugar**, see JAGGERY; **-swift**, a small Jamaican swift (*Micropus phœnicobia*) which nests in palm-leaves; **-toddy**, the juice of the Oil P., allowed to ferment, and used as a drink; **-weevil**, any one of various weevils whose larvæ bore into palm-trees; **-willow**, any species of willow the sprigs of which are used instead of palm-branches (see 4), esp. *Salix Caprea*; **-wine**, wine made from the sap of the palm-tree; **-worm**, (*a*) some large American centipede; (*b*) the larva of a palm-weevil.

Palm (pām), *sb.*[2] [ME. *paume*, a. F. *paume* :—L. *palma*; subseq. assim. to the L.] I. 1. The part of the hand between the wrist and the fingers, esp. its inner surface. b. The part of a glove that covers the palm 1852. 2. The flat expanded part of the horn in some deer, from which finger-like points project. late ME. 3. A flat widened part at the end of an arm or arm-like projection 1526; *spec.* the blade of an oar 1513; the broad triangular part of an anchor, the inner surface of the fluke 1706. 4. An instrument used by sailmakers instead of a thimble 1769.

1. *fig.* Let me tell you Cassius, you your selfe Are much condemn'd to haue an itching Palme SHAKS. *To grease* or *oil* (one's) *p.*, to bribe.

II. †1. A game resembling tennis, in which a ball was struck with the palm of the hand (= F. *la paume, jeu de la paume.*) b. The ball used in this game. –1530. 2. A measure of length, equivalent either to the breadth of the palm, i.e. about three to four inches, or to the length of the hand, i.e. about seven to nine inches 1485.

attrib. and *Comb.*, as **p.-grease** (*joc.*), money given as a douceur or bribe; so **-greasing**, petty bribery; **-play** = Sense II. 1; **-veined** *a. Bot.*, palmately veined. Hence **Pa·lmful**, as much as the p. will hold.

Palm (pām), *v.* 1673. [f. PALM *sb.*[2]: in most senses, orig. slang or low colloq.] 1. *trans.* To touch with the palm, or pass the palm across; to handle; to stroke with the hand; to shake hands with. Also *intr.* 1678. 2. *trans.* To conceal in the palm of the hand, as in cheating at cards or dice, or in juggling 1673. 3. To impose (a thing) fraudulently (*on* or *upon* a person); to pass *off* by trickery or fraud 1679. 4. To 'grease the palm' of, bribe, 'tip' 1747.

2. Is't I who cog or p. the dice GAY. 3. Thinking you cou'd pawme such stuffe on me 1679. 4. The heads of this particular firm..admit that they 'palmed' right and left 1890. Hence **Palmed** (pāmd) *ppl. a.*, concealed in the palm. **Pa·lmer** *sb.*[2] one who palms or conceals in the hand.

Palmaceous (pælmē·ʃəs), *a.* 1730. [f. mod.L. *Palmaceæ* fem. pl. (f. L. *palma* PALM *sb.*[1]) + -OUS.] *Bot.* Of or belonging to the N.O. *Palmaceæ*, *Palmæ*, or Palms.

Palma Christi (pæ·lmă kri·sti). 1548. [med.L. (= palm or hand of Christ).] 1. The Castor-oil plant, *Ricinus communis*, having leaves of a hand-like shape. †2. A name for species of *Orchis* having palmate tubers, as *O. maculata* and *O. latifolia* –1597.

Palmar (pæ·lmăɹ). 1831. [ad. L. *palmaris*, f. *palma* PALM *sb.*[2] and -AR.] A. *adj. Anat.* Pertaining to, situated in, or connected with the palm of the hand (or the analogous part of the fore-foot of a quadruped).

P. arch, the continuation of the radial artery (*deep p. arch*) and that of the ulnar artery (*superficial p. arch*) in the palm.

B. *sb.* 1. *Anat.* A palmar muscle, nerve, etc. 1890. 2. *Zool.* Name for certain joints in the 'arms' of a crinoid. (Also in L. form *palmare*, pl. *-ia.*) 1877.

Palmary (pæ·lmări), *a.*[1] 1657. [ad. L. *palmarius*, f. *palma* PALM *sb.*[1]; see -ARY.] That bears, or is worthy to bear, the palm; holding the first place, pre-eminent. So **Palma·rian** *a.* (*rare*).

Emendations of the kind which in old days would have been called 'palmary' 1888.

Pa·lmary, *a.*[2] 1696. [ad. L. *palmaris*, f. *palma* PALM *sb.*[2]; see -ARY[2].] Pertaining to the palm of the hand; palmar.

Palmate (pæ·lmeⁱt), *sb.* 1838. [f. PALM-IC + -ATE[4].] *Chem.* A salt of palmic acid.

Palmate (pæ·lmĕt), *a.* 1760. [ad. L. *palmatus*, f. *palma* PALM *sb.*[2] + -ATE[2] 2.] *Nat. Hist.* 1. Of a form like that of an open palm or hand; applied to parts of a plant or animal which have narrow or spreading divisions like fingers projecting or radiating as from a palm. 2. Of the foot of a bird: Having the toes connected by an expanded membrane; webbed 1826. So **Pa·lmated** *a.* **Palma·tion**, formation; *concr.* each of the divisions of a p. structure. Hence **Pa·lmate·ly** *adv.*

Palmati- (pælmē·ti, pælmæ·ti), comb. form of L. *palmatus* PALMATE, in botanical adjs. relating to leaves. **Palma·tifid** [L. *-fidus* split] palmately cleft at least half-way to the base. **Palma:tilo·bate**, **Palma·tilobed**, palmately divided with rounded divisions or lobes. **Palma:tipa·rted, -pa·rtite** [L. *partitus* divided] palmately divided nearly to the base; so **Palma·tisect, Palma:tise·cted** [L. *sectus* cut].

Palmchrist (pā·mkrist). 1611. Anglicized f. PALMA CHRISTI (sense 1).

†**Palmed** (pāmd), *a.* 1486. [f. PALM *sb.*[2] + -ED[2]; repr. L. *palmatus.*] Having a 'palm', as a deer's horn; palmate; carrying palmate horns –1766.

Palmer (pā·məɹ), *sb.*[1] ME. [a. AF. *palmer*, *paumer* (OF. *palmier, paumier*) :—med.L. *palmarius*, f. *palma* PALM *sb.*[1]] 1. A pilgrim who had returned from the Holy Land, in token of which he carried a palm-branch or palm-leaf; also, an itinerant monk under a perpetual vow of poverty; often simply = *pilgrim*. 2. A palmer-worm 1538. b. *Angling.* An artificial fly resembling this; a hackle 1651.

1. The Pilgrim had some home, or dwelling place, but the P. had none. The Pilgrim travelled to some certain designed place, or places, but the P. to all. The Pilgrim went at his own charges, but the P. profest wilful poverty, and went upon Alms 1674. Hence **Pa·lmer** *v.* (*Sc.* and *north.*), to wander about like a p. or vagrant.

Palmerin (pæ·lmĕrin). 1611. [f. name of a hero of romances, *Palmerin de Oliva.*] Any of the heroes of the Palmerin romances; hence, any hero of the age of chivalry.

Pa·lmer-wo:rm. 1560. [f. PALMER *sb.*[1] + WORM *sb.*] Name for various hairy caterpillars of migratory or wandering habits destructive to vegetation; in N. America, the larva of a tineid moth, *Ypsilophus pometellus*, destructive to apple-leaves.

Palmette (pælme·t). 1850. [a. F. *palmette*, dim. of *palme.*] *Archæol.* An ornament with narrow divisions or digitations, somewhat resembling a palm-leaf.

Palmetto (pælme·to). 1583. [orig. a. Sp. *palmito*, dim. of *palma* PALM *sb.*[1]; subseq. conformed to dims. in *-etto* from Italian.] Name for several smaller species of palms, esp. the dwarf fan-palm, *Chamærops humilis*, of S. Europe and N. Africa, and the cabbage palmetto, *Sabal Palmetto*, of the South-eastern U.S.

Royal P., *Sabal umbraculifera* and *Thrinax parviflora*, of the W. Indies; **Saw P.**, *Chamærops serrulata*; etc.

attrib. and *Comb.*, as *p. hat, leaf, thatch*, etc.; **p. flag**, the flag of the State of South Carolina, which bears a figure of a cabbage p. tree; so **P. State, a** name for South Carolina.

Palmi- (pælmi), comb. form of L. *palma* PALM *sb.*[1] and [2], as in **Pa·lmigrade** *a. Zool.* = PLANTIGRADE; **Pa·lmilobed** *a.*, palmately lobed; etc.

Palmic (pæ·lmik), *a.* 1838. [ad. F. *palmique*, f. L. *palma* (in PALMA CHRISTI) + -IC.] *Chem.* Of or pertaining to castor-oil; in *p. acid*, obtained by saponifying palmin and decomposing with hydrochloric acid; now called *ricinelaïdic acid.*

Palmiferous (pælmi·fĕrəs), *a.* 1664. [f. L. *palmifer* + -OUS.] Carrying 'palms' or palm-branches.

Palmin (pæ·lmin). 1838. [ad. F. *palmine*, f. L. *palma* (in PALMA CHRISTI) + -IN.] *Chem.* A fatty substance obtained by treating castor-oil with nitric peroxide. Now called *ricinelaïdin.*

Palmiped, -pede (pæ·lmiped, -pīd), *a.* and *sb.* 1610. [ad. L. *palmipes, -pedem*, f. *palma* PALM *sb.*[2] + *pes* foot.] **A.** *adj.* Of a bird: Having palmate feet 1661. **B.** *sb.* A web-footed bird 1610.

Palmist (pā·mist). 1886. [Back-formation f. PALMISTRY.] One who practises palmistry.

Palmister (pā·mistəɹ). Now *rare*. 1500. [Back-formation f. PALMISTRY.] = prec.

Palmistry (pā·mistri). late ME. [f. *paume, palme* PALM *sb.*[2] + *-estrie, -estry*, later *-istry*, of obsc. origin.] **1.** The art or practice of telling persons' characters or fortunes by inspection of the palm of the hand; chiromancy. **2.** Applied allusively to pocket-picking, bribery, etc.; also used erron. as = sleight of hand 1698.

Palmite (pæ·lməit). 1834. [ad. Sp. and Pg. *palmito* PALMETTO, S. Afr. Du. *palmiet*.] A S. Afr. aquatic plant, *Prionium Palmita* (N.O. *Juncaceæ*), growing in the beds of rivers, and bearing a tuft of large serrated sword-shaped leaves, affording a strong fibre.

Palmitic (pælmi·tik), *a.* 1857. [ad. F. *palmitique*, arbitrarily f. L. *palma* PALM *sb.*[1] + -IC.] *Chem.* Of or obtained from palm-oil; in *p. acid*: a fatty acid ($C_{16}H_{32}O_2$) contained in palm-oil and in vegetable and animal fats generally. Hence **Palmitate** (pæ·lmitĕt), a salt of this.

Palmitin (pæ·lmitin). 1857. [a. F. *palmitine*, f. as prec. + *-ine*, -IN [1].] *Chem.* A natural fat contained in palm-oil and many other fats, obtained as a white solid, the tripalmitate of glyceryl; *pl.* applied to the palmitates of glyceryl or glycerides of palmitic acid in general (cf. *tripalmitin*).

Pa·lm-oil. 1627. [In sense 1, f. PALM *sb.*[1] + OIL; in 2, f. PALM *sb.*[2], with joc. allusion to sense 1.] **1.** Oil produced by various species of palm-tree; *esp.* that obtained from the fruit-pulp of the Oil Palm (*Elæis guineensis*) of West Africa; it is used as food by the natives, and elsewhere for making soap and candles, etc. Also *attrib.* 1705. **2.** *joc.* That with which the palm is 'greased'; money given as a bribe; a 'tip' 1627.

2. Palm-oil will always produce temporary blindness in the officials 1896.

Pa·lm Su·nday. OE. The Sunday next before Easter, observed in commemoration of Christ's triumphal entry into Jerusalem by processions in which palms (see PALM *sb.*[1] 4) are carried. Also *attrib.*

Palm-tree (pā·m,trī). OE. = PALM *sb.*[1] **1.** **b.** Applied pop. to other trees, e.g. a willow, a yew-tree 1653.

Palmy (pā·mi), *a.* 1602. [f. PALM *sb.*[1] + -Y.] **1.** Containing or abounding in palms; of or pertaining to a palm or palms; palm-like. Chiefly *poet.* 1667. **2.** *fig.* Bearing or worthy to 'bear the palm'; triumphant, flourishing; esp. in *p. days*.

2. In the most high and p. state of Rome SHAKS.

Palmyra (pælməi·ᵊră). 1698. [Formerly *palmeira*, a. Pg. *palmeira* palm-tree. Erron. conformed in spelling to that of *Palmyra*, Gr. Παλμύρα, in Syria.] A species of palm (*Borassus flabelliformis*), with rounded fan-shaped leaves; commonly cultivated in India and Ceylon, and used as timber, for thatch, matting, umbrellas, hats, etc. Also *attrib.*

‖**Palolo** (pălōᵘ·lo). 1895. [Native name in Samoa and Tonga.] A nereid worm (*Palolo viridis*), abundant in parts of the Pacific, and esteemed as food by the natives.

Palp (pælp), *sb.* 1835. [a. F. *palpe*, ad. L. *palpus*.] *Zool.* = PALPUS. Hence **Pa·lpless** *a.*, having no palpi.

Palp (pælp), *v. rare.* 1534. [ad. L. *palpare* to touch softly.] *trans.* To touch, feel; to handle gently, pat. Also *fig.* To speak fair, flatter, cajole.

Palpable (pæ·lpăb'l), *a.* late ME. [ad. late L. *palpabilis*; see prec. and -ABLE.] **1.** That can be touched, felt, or handled; tangible, sensible. **b.** *Med.* Perceptible by palpation 1897. **2.** *transf.* Readily perceived by any of the other senses; perceptible; noticeable, patent. late ME. **3.** *fig.* Easily perceived; plain, evident, apparent, obvious 1545.

1. A hit, a very p. hit SHAKS. *P. darkness*, thick, gross, utter darkness. 2. The venison pasty was p. beef PEPYS. 3. Opinions of p. idolatrie HOOKER. P. falsehoods COWPER, fables 1867. Hence **Palpabi·lity, Pa·lpableness. Pa·lpably** *adv.*

Palpate (pæ·lpeᵗt), *v.* 1849. [f. L. *palpat-*, *palpare* to PALP.] *trans.* To examine by the sense of touch; to feel; *spec.* as a method of medical examination. So **Palpa·tion**, touching; gentle handling; *spec.* medical examination by feeling 1483.

‖**Palpebra** (pæ·lpĭbră). *Pl.* **-æ.** 1706. [L.] *Anat.* An eyelid. Hence **Pa·lpebral** *a.* of or pertaining to the eyelids. **Pa·lpebrate** *a.* having eyelids.

Palpi, pl. of PALPUS.

Palpicorn (pæ·lpĭkǭɹn), *a.* and *sb.* 1882. [f. mod.L. *palpicornes*, pl. of *palpicornis*, f. PALPUS + *cornu* horn.] **a.** *adj.* Having palpi like horns or antennæ; *spec.* of or pertaining to the *Palpicornes*, a tribe of pentamerous beetles having slender palpi usually longer than the antennæ. **b.** *sb.* A beetle of the tribe *Palpicornes* 1882.

Palpifer (pæ·lpifəɹ). 1841. [f. L. *palpus* PALP *sb.* + *-fer* bearing, bearer.] *Entom.* An outer lobe of the maxilla, bearing the maxillary palp. Hence **Palpi·ferous** *a.* bearing palps, esp. maxillary palps.

Palpiform (pæ·lpifǭɹm), *a.* 1819. [f. as prec. + -FORM.] Having the form of or resembling a palp.

Palpiger (pæ·lpidʒəɹ). 1841. [f. as prec. + *-ger* carrying, carrier.] *Entom.* That part of the labium of an insect which bears the labial palpi. So **Palpi·gerous** *a.* bearing palpi.

Palpitant (pæ·lpitănt), *a.* 1837. [a. F., ad. L. *palpitantem*: see next.] Palpitating.

Palpitate (pæ·lpiteᵗt), *v.* 1623. [f. L. *palpitat-*, *palpitare* to move frequently and quickly, throb, freq. of *palpare* PALP *v.*] **1.** *intr.* To pulsate rapidly and strongly, as the result of exercise, strong emotion, or as a symptom of disease; to throb. **b.** *gen.* To move with a vibrating motion 1849. **2.** *trans.* To cause to pulsate rapidly or throb 1790.

1. b. Fountains palpitating in the heat LONGF. Hence **Pa·lpitating** *ppl. a.*, **-ly** *adv.*

Palpitation (pælpitē[i]·ʃən). 1604. [ad. L. *palpitationem*, f. *palpitare* to PALPITATE.] **1.** The action of palpitating; *spec.* increased activity of the heart arising from disease of the organ itself or other parts of the body. **2.** *gen.* A trembling or quivering motion; a tremble 1677.

Palpocil (pæ·lpŏsil). Also **palpicil.** 1871. [f. *palpo-*, taken as comb. form of L. *palpus*, PALP + *cilium* eyelash.] *Zool.* A fine hairlike palp or palpus; a tactile hair.

Palpon (pæ·lpǫ̆n). 1888. [f. L. *palpus*, after *siphon*.] *Zool.* An individual member of a siphonophoran colony developed as a feeler; a dactylozooid.

‖**Palpus** (pæ·lpŭs). *Pl.* **-pi** (pəi). 1813. [L. *palpus* a feeler.] *Zool.* A jointed organ attached to the labia, maxillæ, and mandibles of insects, arachnids, etc., and serving as an organ of sense, a feeler. Also, each of the two fleshy lobes at the sides of the mouth of bivalve molluscs. Hence **Pa·lpal** *a.* of the nature of, pertaining to, or serving as a palp or feeler.

Palsgrave (pǭ·lzgrēᵗv). *Hist.* 1548. [a. 16th c. Du. *paltsgrave* = OHG. *pfalenzgrâvo*, f. *pfalenza* palace + *grâvo* count.] A count palatine. So **Pa·lsgravine**, a countess palatine.

Palsied (pǭ·lzid), *ppl. a.* 1550. [f. PALSY *sb.* or *v.* + -ED.] Affected with palsy, paralysed; *fig.* tottering, trembling.

Palstave (pǭ·lstēᵗv). Also **-staff**, ‖**paalstave, -stab.** 1851. [ad. Da. *paalstav*:—Icel. *pálstafr*, f. *páll* hoe or spade + *stafr* stave, staff.] *Archæol.* A form of celt of bronze, or other metal, shaped so as to fit into a split handle, instead of having a socket into which the handle fits.

Palsy (pǭ·lzi), *sb.* (*a.*) [ME. *parlesie, palesie*, a. OF. *paralisie*, ad. Rom. type **paralysia*, for L. *paralysis*, Gr. παράλυσις PARALYSIS.] **1.** = PARALYSIS 1. **2.** *fig.* Any influence which destroys, or seriously impairs, activity or sensibility; a condition of utter powerlessness; an irresistible tremor ME.

1. He seith to the sike man in palasie..ryse vp, take thi bed WYCLIF *Mark* ii. 10. **Bell's p.**, paralysis of the facial nerve. **Creeping p.**, gradually growing paralysis. **Scrivener's p.** = *writer's cramp*, see WRITER. **Shaking p.**, tremulous paralysis in the aged. 2. So thoroughly does the region now lie under the p. of Mohammedanism 1848.

†**B.** *adj.* (always *attrib.*, and app. attrib. use of sb.) Affected with palsy, palsied –1703.

Pa·lsy, *v.* 1582. [f. prec.] **1.** *trans.* To affect with palsy, to paralyse. Chiefly *fig.* 1615. **2.** *intr.* To shake or tremble as if palsied (*nonce-use*); to become palsied (*rare*) 1582. Hence **Pa·lsying** *ppl. a.*

Palter (pǭ·ltəɹ), *v.* 1538. [Origin unkn.] †**1.** *intr.* and *trans.* To speak indistinctly or idly; to mumble, babble –1575. **2.** *intr.* To shift, shuffle, equivocate, prevaricate; to deal crookedly; to play fast and loose. Usu. const. *with*. 1601. **b.** To haggle in bargaining; to huckster in matters of duty or honour 1611. †**c.** *trans.* To barter; to corrupt. MILT. †**3.** *trans.* To squander –1706.

2. These Iugling Fiends..,That p. with vs in a double sence, That keepe the word of promise to our eare, And breake it to our hope SHAKS. **b.** Only fools and cowards p. about morality 1883. Hence **Pa·lterer**, one who palters, a shuffler, trifler 1589. †**Pa·ltering** *ppl. a.* trifling, worthless, paltry.

†**Pa·lterly,** *a.* 1667. [app. altered f. PALTRY *a.*] Paltry, mean, shabby –1825.

†**Pa·ltock.** ME. [a. OF. *paltoc* (now *paletot*).] A short coat, sleeved doublet, or 'jack' –1658.

Paltry (pǭ·ltri), *sb.* Now only *dial.* 1556. [app. f. *palt*, var. PELT *sb.*[3] Cf. PELTRY [2].] Refuse, rubbish, trash; anything worthless.

Paltry (pǭ·ltri), *a.* 1570. [perh. attrib. use of prec.] Rubbishy, trashy, worthless; petty; despicable.

The p. trick was successful 1867. A p. fellow 1874. Hence **Pa·ltriness.**

Paludal (păl[i]ū·dăl, pæ·l[i]udăl), *a.* 1818. [f. L. *palus, palud-* marsh + -AL.] Chiefly *Med.* and *Path.* Of or pertaining to or produced by a marsh; malarial.

Paludament (păl[i]ū·dămĕnt). 1614. [ad. L. *paludamentum*.] A military cloak worn by Roman generals and chief officers; hence, a royal cloak; a herald's coat.

Paludi- (bef. a vowel **palud-**), a formative element f. L. *palus, palud-* marsh, in **Palu·dic** *a.*, of or pertaining to marshes; **Palu·dicole** *a.*, inhabiting marshes; etc.

‖**Paludina** (pæl[i]udəi·nă). 1833. [mod.L., f. L. *palus, palud-* + *-inus, -ina*; see -INE [1].] *Zool.* A genus of freshwater gastropod molluscs, also called *pond-snails*.

Paludine (pæ·l[i]udin, -əin), *a.* 1858. [f. L. *palus, palud-* + -INE [1].] Of or pertaining to a marsh. So **Palu·dinal, Palu·dinous** *adjs.*

Paludism (pæ·l[i]udiz'm). 1890. [f. as prec. + -ISM.] *Path.* = MALARIA b.

Paludous (păl[i]ū·dəs), *a. rare.* 1803. [ad. L. *paludosus* marshy; see prec. and -OUS.] Of or belonging to marshes, marshy; inhabiting marshes. So **Paludo·se** *a.*

‖**Palus** (pē[i]·lŏs). *Pl.* **-li.** 1872. [L. *palus* stake.] *Biol.* In corals, one of the thin, upright, calcareous laminæ or plates, which extend up from the bottom of a corallite to the calix, and are connected by their outer edges with the septa. Hence the dim. ‖**Pa·lulus**, pl. **paluli.**

Palustral (păl*v*·străl), *a. rare.* 1879. [f. L. *palustris* (f. *palus* marsh) + -AL.] Pertaining to or inhabiting marshes. **So Palu·strian** *a.* 1607; **Palu·strine** *a.* 1839.

Paly (pē[i]·li), *a.*[1] Chiefly *poet.* 1560. [f. PALE *a.* + -Y.] Pale, or somewhat pale. 2 *Hen. VI*, III. ii. 141.

Paly (pē[i]·li), *a.*[2] 1486. [ad. F. *palé*, f. *pal* PALE *sb.*[1]] *Her.* Said of the shield (or of a bearing) when divided palewise.

P. bendy, divided both palewise and bendwise.

Pam (pæm). 1685. [app. abbrev. of F. *pamphile*, name of the card game and of the knave of clubs in it; according to Littré, ad. Gr. name Πάμφιλος 'beloved of all'.] **1.** The knave of clubs, esp. in five-card loo, in which this card is the highest trump. **2.** Name of a card-game, akin to nap, in which the knave of clubs was the highest trump card

1691. Hence †**Pam-child**, 'knave-child', male child. H. WALPOLE.

‖ **Pampa** (pæ·mpă), usu. *pl.* **pampas** (pæ·mpăz, -ăs). 1704. [a. Sp. *pampa* (pl. *pampas*), ad. Peruv. *bamba*, a steppe, a flat.] The name given to the vast treeless plains of S. America south of the Amazon. (The similar plains north of the Amazon are called *llanos*.)

attrib. and *Comb.*, as *P. Indian*; **p.-cat**, a wild cat of the Pampas (*Felis pajeros*); **p. deer**, a small deer of S. America, *Cariacus campestris*; **p. rice**, a variety of the common Millet (*Sorghum vulgare*), with a drooping panicle.

Pa·mpas-gra·ss. 1850. [f. prec.] A gigantic grass, *Gynerium argenteum* or *Cortaderia argentea*, having ample silky panicles of silvery hue borne on stalks rising to the height of twelve or fourteen feet; a native of S. America.

Pampean, pampæan (pæmpī·ăn, pæ·mpĭăn), *a.* 1839. [f. PAMPA, after *Hyblæan*, etc.] Of or pertaining to the Pampas.

Pamper (pæ·mpəɹ), *v.* late ME. [Cf. W. Flem. *pamperen*.] **1.** *trans.* To cram with food; to over-indulge with rich food. *Obs.* exc. as in b. **b.** To over-indulge (a person) in his tastes and likings generally; to bring up daintily 1530. †**2.** *intr.* To feed luxuriously –1635.

1. After dinner I went to Snowhill; there I was pampered, and had an uneasy night JOHNSON. *P. up*, to feed up. **b.** *fig.* To p. his own vanity at the price of another's shame FIELDING. Hence **Pa·mperer.**

Pampered (pæ·mpəɹd), *ppl. a.* 1529. [f. prec. + -ED[1].] †Over-fed; luxuriously fed; over-indulged, spoiled by luxury. Also *fig.*

Pamper'd metafors MILT. P. children 1890. Hence **Pa·mperedness.**

‖ **Pampero** (pămpē·ro). 1818. [Sp., f. Peruv. *pampa* + suffix *-ero* :—L. *-arius*.] A piercing cold wind which blows from the Andes across the S. American pampas to the Atlantic.

Pamphlet (pæ·mflĕt), *sb.* ME. [app. a generalized use of *Pamphilet* or *Panflet*, a familiar name of a 12th c. L. amatory poem or comedy called *Pamphilus, seu de Amore*.] **1.** A small treatise occupying fewer pages than would make a book, composed and issued as a separate work; always unbound, with or without paper covers. **2.** More spec., a treatise of the size and form above described on some subject of current or topical interest 1592. **3.** *attrib.*, as *p. form, war*, etc. 1646.

1. In regard of the smalnesse of it, it [this Sermon] is indeed but as a little P. 1623. 2. Grattan's incomparable speech..ought to make a little separate p. BURKE.

†**Pa·mphlet**, *v.* 1592. [f. prec.] **a.** *intr.* To write a pamphlet or pamphlets. **b.** *trans.* To report or describe in a pamphlet. Chiefly in **Pa·mphleting** *vbl. sb.* and *ppl. a.* –1716.

Pamphleteer (pæmflĕtī·ɹ), *sb.* 1642. [f. PAMPHLET *sb.* + -EER.] A writer of pamphlets. (Often contemptuous.)

Pamphletee·r, *v.* 1715. [f. prec.] *intr.* To write and issue pamphlets. Chiefly in **Pamphletee·ring** *vbl. sb.* and *ppl. a.*

†**Pampina·tion.** late ME. [ad. L. *pampinationem*, *pampinare*, f. *pampinus* vine-shoot.] The pruning or trimming of vines –1846.

Pampiniform (pæmpi·nifǭɹm), *a.* 1668. [f. L. *pampinus* + -(I)FORM.] *Anat.* Curled like a vine-tendril; applied *esp.* to a convoluted plexus of veins proceeding from the testis or ovary.

Pampootie (pæmpū·ti). *local Irish.* 1846. [Origin obsc.] A kind of sandal of undressed cowskin sewn together and tied across the instep. Used in the Isles of Aran.

Pamprodactylous (pæmprodæ·ktiləs), *a.* 1899. [f. Gr. παμ- PAN- + πρό before + δάκτυλος finger or toe + -OUS.] *Ornith.* Having all the toes pointing forwards, as the colies, and a few other birds.

Pan (pæn), *sb.*[1] [OE. *panne*, *pǫnne* wk. fem. = OHG. *phanna*, *pfanna*, etc. Evidently Com. WGer. in 4th or 5th c.; history and origin unkn.] **1.** A vessel, of metal or earthenware, for domestic purposes, usu. broad and shallow, and often open. (Often in pl. with *pots*.) **b.** Often differentiated, as *bread-p.*, *saucepan*, etc. **c.** As part of any apparatus 1611. **2.** In techn. uses, applied to pan-like vessels in which substances are exposed to heat, or to mechanical processes; e.g. an open vessel used for boiling, evaporating, etc.; also in *Chem.* a closed vessel for evaporation, a vacuum pan 1674. **3.** The contents of a pan, a panful 1762. **4.** A pan-shaped depression of any vessel, or part of any structure 1764. **b.** *spec.* In obs. types of guns and pistols: That part of the lock which holds the priming 1590. **c.** A socket for a hinge, etc. 1598. **5.** A hollow or depression in the ground; *spec.* a SALT-PAN 1493. **b.** *spec.* in *S. Africa*, A dried-up salt-marsh or pool-bed 1786. **6.** = BRAIN-PAN. *Obs.* or *dial.* ME. †**b.** The patella or KNEE-PAN –1753. **7.** A hard substratum of soil, usually more or less impervious to moisture: see HARD-PAN 1784. **8.** A small ice-floe 1863.

1. Ful many a panne of bras CHAUCER. **c.** With the weights in the opposite p. of the balance 1842. *To turn the cat in the p.*: see CAT *sb.* **4. b.** *Flash in the p.*: see FLASH *sb.*[2]

attrib. and *Comb.*, as **p.-mill**, a miner's apparatus used in separating gold from the alloy of earth; **-washing**, the separating of gold from gravel, etc., by stirring it in water in a p.; **-wood**, the small coal used in salt-works.

Pan (pæn), *sb.*[2] ME. [a. Gr. Πάν.] Name of a Greek rural deity, represented as having the head, arms, and chest of a man, and the lower parts (and sometimes the horns and ears) of a goat.

He was supposed to preside over shepherds and flocks, and to delight in rural music; he was also regarded as the author of sudden and groundless terror (PANIC *sb.*[2]); and in later times, from association of his name with τὸ πᾶν the all, everything, as an impersonation of Nature.

Pan, *sb.*[3] Also **pane.** 1719. [a. F. *pan* pane, compartment; see PANE *sb.*[1]] In a timber-framed or half-timbered house, a square or compartment of timber framework, filled in with bricks or plaster 1842.

‖ **Pan, pán** (pān), *sb.*[4] 1616. [a. Hind. *pān* betel-leaf :—Skr. *parṇa* feather, leaf.] The betel-leaf; hence, the combination of betel-leaf, areca-nut, lime, etc., used as a masticatory.

Pan (pæn), *v.*[1] 1825. [f. PAN *sb.*[1]] **1.** *trans.* To wash (gold-bearing gravel) in a pan, to separate the gold; to separate by washing in a pan. Const. *off, out*. 1872. **b.** *absol.* or *intr.* To search or try for gold with the pan 1872. **2.** *transf.* and *fig.* (*U.S.* and *Colonial*.) To bring forth, yield (with *out*) 1884. **3.** *intr.* (usu. with *out*.) To yield gold, as gravel, etc. when washed in a pan; hence *transf.* of the vein or mine, to yield precious metal 1865. Also *fig.* with ref. to the issue of a project or the like. **4.** *trans.* To cook or dress in a pan 1871. **5.** *Agric.* and *dial. intr.* Of soil: To cake on the surface 1825.

1. They 'panned' the surface dirt for gold 1880. 2. The department on being searched only panned out a few copper coins 1884. 3. *fig.* Unfortunately this business did not 'pan out', to use the American phrase 1892. Hence **Pa·nning** *vbl. sb.* the action of washing sand, etc. for gold; the gold so obtained.

Pan (pæn), *v.*[2] *Sc.* and *north.* 1556. [Origin unkn.] *intr.* To fit, tally, agree. **b.** *trans.* To fit or join together 1884.

Pan-, comb. form and formative element, repr. Gr. παν- from πᾶν, neut. of πᾶς all.

1. With national names, etc., with the sense 'Of, pertaining to, or comprising all (those indicated in the second element)'; with sbs. in -ISM and -IST, gen. expressing the notion of or aspiration for the political union of all those indicated. **Pan-A·frican** *a.* of or pertaining to all persons of African birth or descent. **Pan-Ame·rican** *a.* of or pertaining to all the states of North and South America or to all Americans; hence **Pan-Ame·ricanism. Pan-A·nglo-Sa·xon** *a.* of or including all of Anglo-Saxon race. **Pan-Brita·nnic** *a.* of or comprising all the British dominions. **Pan-denomina·tional** *a.* of or embracing all religious denominations. **Pan-Ge·rman** *a.* of or pertaining to all Germans, or to the union of all Germans in one political state; *sb.* an advocate of this union; hence **Pan-Germa·nic** *a.*; **Pan-Ge·rmanism. Pan-Io·nian, -Io·nic** *adjs.* of or comprising all Ionians. **Pani·slam**, all Islam; (the conception of) a union of the Mohammedan world; so **Panisla·mic** *a.*, **Pani·slamism. Pan-Presbyte·rian** *a.* of or pertaining to all Presbyterians. **Pan-Sla·v, Pan-Sla·vic** *adjs.* of or pertaining to all the Slavic races; of or favouring **Pansla·vism**, the movement or aspiration for the union of all Slavs or Slavonic peoples in one political organization; so **Pansla·vist, Panslavi·stic** *a.* = *Pan-Slavic*. **Panslavo·nian** *a.* Pan-Slavic, Panslavistic. **Pan-Teuto·nic** *a.* of or embracing all Teutonic peoples; hence **Pan-Teu·tonism**, the principle of a union of all Teutonic peoples.

2. Other words. **Panco·smism**, *Philos.*, the doctrine that the material universe is all that exists; hence **Panco·smic** *a.* **Pane·ntheism**, the doctrine that God includes the world as part of his being; so **Panenthei·stic** *a.* **Panidiomo·rphic** *a. Min.*, having all its components idiomorphic. **Pa·nlogism** [mod.L. *panlogismus*], *Philos.*, a term formed by J. E. Erdmann on the analogy of *pantheismus*, to describe the philosophy of Hegel, as one which holds that only the rational is truly real; so **Panlo·gical, -logi·stic** *adjs.* ‖ **Panmi·xia**, *Biol.*, Weismann's term for a supposed promiscuous reproduction of all manner of ancestral qualities or tendencies, consequent on the cessation of natural selection in relation to organs which have become useless or little used. **Panomphæ·an** [Gr. ὀμφή voice of a god, oracular response], *a.* of or pertaining to Zeus, as sender of all ominous voices. **Pancha·rmacon** [Gr. φάρμακον drug], a universal remedy, a panacea. **Panpheno·menalism**, *Philos.*, a theory that the universe is purely phenomenal. **Panthele·matism, Pa·nthelism** [Gr. θελημᾰτ- will; θέλειν to will], *Philos.*, the theory of Schopenhauer that the Ultimate and Absolute is Will. **Pantheo·logy**, a synthetic theology comprehending all deities and religions. **Panzo·ism** [Gr. ζωή life], *Biol.*, a name given to a synthesis of all the elements or factors of vitality.

†**Panabase** (pæ·năbēs). 1839. [a. F., irreg. f. Gr. πᾶν all + BASE *sb.*[1]] *Min.* = TETRAHEDRITE –1896.

Panace (pæ·năsi). 1513. [ad. L. *panac-*, *panax* or *panaces*, name of a plant.] A fabulous herb, said to heal all diseases.

Panacea (pænăsī·ă). 1548. [a. L., a. Gr. πανάκεια universal remedy, f. πανακής all-healing.] **1.** A remedy, cure, or medicine reputed to heal all diseases. †**2.** = PANACE –1741. Hence **Panace·an** *a.* of the nature of a p.; all-healing. **Panace·ist**, one who believes in or applies a p.

Panache (pănɑ·ʃ). 1553. [a. F., ad. It. *pennacchio*, deriv. of *penna* feather.] A tuft or plume of feathers, esp. when used as a head-dress or an ornament for a helmet; †thence, a tassel or the like. **b.** *Astron.* A plume-like solar protuberance 1887.

He had in his cap a pennach of heron EVELYN. Hence **Pana·ched** *a.* diversified with stripes of colour like a plume.

Panada (pănā·dă). 1598. [a. Sp. *panada* = It. *panata*, F. *panade* PANADE [2], f. It. *pane*, L. *panem* bread; see -ADA.] Bread boiled to a pulp and flavoured with sugar, nutmeg, etc.

†**Panade**[1]. *rare.* ME. only. [app. related to OF. *pan-*, *penard*, cutlass; cf. med.L. *pennatus* a kind of sword.] A kind of large knife.

Panade[2] (pănē·d). 1598. [a. F.] = PANADA.

Panama (pænămā·). 1833. [Name of a town and state in Central America, and of the isthmus uniting North and South America.] *attrib.* Of or pertaining to Panama; spec. *Panama hat*, a misnomer for a hat made from the undeveloped leaves of the stemless screw-pine (*Carludovica palmata*) of tropical S. America; also *absol.* as *sb.*

Pan-Anglican (pæn,æ·ŋglikăn), *a.* 1867. [PAN- 1.] Of, pertaining to, or embracing the whole Anglican Church and its branches.

†**Pa·nary**, *sb. rare.* 1611 only. [ad. L. *panarium* bread-basket; see -ARY[1].] A storehouse for bread, a pantry.

Panary (pæ·nări), *a.* 1818. [ad. L. *panarius*, f. *panis* bread; see -ARY[1].] Of or pertaining to bread; esp. in *p. fermentation*.

‖ **Panathenæa** (pænæþinī·ă). Also **-aia.** 1603. [a. Gr. παναθήναια adj. neut. pl. (sc. ἱερά solemnities), f. παν- PAN- + Ἀθηναῖος Athenian, f. Ἀθῆναι Athens, or Ἀθήνη Athene, patron goddess of Athens.] The national festival of Athens, held, in a lesser form every year, in a greater every fifth year, to celebrate the union of Attica under Theseus. Hence **Panathenæ·an, Panathena·ic** *adjs.* of or pertaining to this festival.

Panatrope (pæ·nătrōup). 1926. [Perh. f. PAN- + Gr. -τροπος turning, after *zoetrope*.] An electrical apparatus for the reproduction of gramophone records through a loud-speaker.

Pancake (pæ·nkēk), *sb.* late ME. [f. PAN *sb.*[1] 1 + CAKE *sb.*] **1.** A thin flat cake, made of batter fried in a pan. (Often as the type of flatness.) **2.** Applied to various objects thin and flat like a pancake 1843.

1. The country is as flat as a p. 1860.

attrib. and *Comb.*: **p. day, Tuesday,** Shrove Tuesday, from the custom of eating pancakes on that day; **p.-ice,** floating ice in thin flat pieces, forming in the polar seas at the approach of winter. Hence **Pa·ncake** *v. intr.* (of an aeroplane) to descend vertically in a level position (*slang*).

†**Pa·nchart.** 1587. [ad. med.L. *pancharta*, f. Gr. παν- PAN- + L. *charta* leaf, paper.] A charter, orig. app. one of a general character, or that confirmed all special grants, but later almost any written record –1762.

Pancheon (pæ·nʃən). 1601. [app. derived from PAN *sb.*[1]] A large shallow earthenware bowl or vessel, wider at the top than at the bottom, used for setting milk to stand in, etc.

Panchroma·tic, *a.* 1904. = ORTHOCHROMATIC.

‖**Panchway, pansway** (pæ·ntʃwē, pæ·nswē). 1757. [a. Hindī *pansoi* a boat.] A light kind of boat used on the rivers of Bengal.

Panclastite (pænklæ·stəit). 1883. [f. Gr. παν- PAN- + κλαστός broken, -κλαστης breaker + -ITE[1] 4.] An explosive formed in mixing liquid nitrogen tetroxide with carbon disulphide, nitrotoluene, or other liquid combustible.

Pancratic (pænkræ·tik), *a.* 1660. [(1) f. next + -IC; (2) f. PAN- + Gr. κράτος strength + -IC.] **1.** Of or pertaining to the pancratium; hence, fully disciplined or exercised in mind. So †**-ical** 1581. **2.** Of an eyepiece: Capable of adjustment to many degrees of power 1831.

‖**Pancratium** (pænkrē·ʃiŏm), **-ion** (-iŏn). 1603. [L., a. Gr. παγκράτιον, f. παν- PAN- + κράτος bodily strength.] **1.** *Gr. Antiq.* An athletic contest, combining both wrestling and boxing. **2.** *Bot.* A genus of bulbous plants of the N.O. *Amaryllidaceæ*, bearing an umbel of large white flowers terminating a solid scape 1664. Hence **Pancra·tian** *a.* of or belonging to the p. (sense 1). So **Pancra·tiast, Pa·ncratist,** a combatant or victor in the p. **Pancratia·stic** *a.* of or pertaining to a pancratiast.

Pancreas (pæ·ŋkriˌæs). 1578. [a. mod.L., a. Gr. πάγκρεας (stem -κρεατ-) sweetbread, f. παν- PAN- + κρέας flesh.] A lobulated racemose gland situated near the stomach, and discharging into the duodenum a digestive secretion, the *pancreatic juice*; called in animals, when used as food, the *sweetbread*. Hence **Pancrea·tic** *a.* of or belonging to the p.

Pancreatin (pæ·ŋkriˌătin). 1873. [f. Gr. stem παγκρεατ- (PANCREAS) + -IN[1].] *Chem.* A proteid compound, one of the active principles of pancreatic juice; also, a preparation extracted from the pancreas and used to aid digestion. So **Pa·ncreatize** *v.* to treat with p. so as to make digestible.

‖**Pancreatitis** (pæŋkriˌătəi·tis). 1842. [f. as prec. + -ITIS.] *Path.* Inflammation of the pancreas.

Pand (pænd). *Sc.* 1561. [a. MDu., MFlem. *pand* = F. †*pand, pan* PANE *sb.*[1]] A valance.

Panda (pæ·ndă). 1835. [Said to be a Nepāl name.] A racoon-like animal (*Ælurus fulgens*) of the south-eastern Himalayas; the red bear-cat.

‖**Pandal** (pæ·ndăl). *E. Ind.* 1717. [a. Tamil *pendal* shed.] A shed, booth, or arbour, esp. for temporary use.

‖**Pandanus** (pændē·nŏs). 1846. [mod.L., ad. Malay *pandan*.] *Bot.* A genus of plants, type of the order *Pandanaceæ*, the screw-pines, found chiefly in the E. Indian archipelago. Also *attrib.*

Pandean, -dæan (pændī·ăn), *a.* and *sb.* 1804. [irreg. f. PAN *sb.*[2]] **a.** *adj.* Of or pertaining to Pan 1807. **b.** *sb.* A member of a pandean band 1804.

a. *P. band*, a band consisting mainly of players of the pan-pipe. *P. pipe* = PAN-PIPE. *P. harmonica*, a mouth-organ resembling the pan-pipe.

Pandect (pæ·ndekt). 1531. [a. F. *pandecte*, ad. L. *pandecta* or *-tes*, a. Gr. πανδέκτης an all-receiver; esp. in pl. L. *pandectæ*, Gr. πανδέκται in sense 1.] **1.** *pl.* (rarely *sing.*) A compendium in fifty books of Roman civil law made by order of the Emperor Justinian in the 6th c., systematizing the opinions of eminent jurists, to which the Emperor gave the force of law. **b.** *transf.* and *fig.* (Also *sing.*) A complete body of the laws of any country or of any system of law 1553. **2.** (*sing.*) A treatise covering the whole of a subject 1591. **3.** A manuscript copy of the whole Bible 1893.

2. That..the commons would please to form a p. of their own power and privileges SWIFT. 3. Complete Bibles ('Pandects', they are called) are very rare 1908.

Pandemian (pændī·miăn), *a.* 1818. [f. Gr. πανδήμιος of all the people + -AN.] = PANDEMIC A. 2.

Pandemic (pænde·mik), *a.* and *sb.* 1666. [f. Gr. πάνδημος, f. παν- PAN- + δῆμος people, populace; in sense 2 repr. Gr. πάνδημος ἔρως, as opp. to οὐράνιος. Cf. Plato *Symp.* 180 E.]

A. *adj.* **1.** General, universal. *esp.* Of a disease: Prevalent over the whole of a country or continent, or over the whole world. Dist. from *epidemic*, which may connote limitation to a smaller area. **2.** Of or pertaining to vulgar or sensual love 1822. **B.** *sb.* A pandemic disease 1853.

Pandemoniac (pændimōu·niæk), *a.* 1849. [f. as next, after *demoniac*.] Of or pertaining to Pandemonium; infernal. So **Pandemonia·cal** (-əi·ăkăl) *a.* characteristic of Pandemonium; esp. of din or noise.

Pandemonium (pændimōu·niŏm). Also **-dæmon-.** 1667. [In form, mod.L. f. Gr. παν- PAN- + δαίμων DEMON; coined by Milton.] **1.** The abode of all the demons; in Milton, the capital of Hell, containing the council-chamber of the Evil Spirits; in common use, = hell or the infernal regions. **2.** *transf.* **a.** A centre or headquarters of vice or wickedness. **b.** A place or gathering of wild lawless violence, confusion, and uproar 1779. **c.** A distracting fiendish 'row' 1865.

1. Pandæmonium, the high Capital Of Satan and his Peers MILT. Hence **Pandemo·nian** *a.* pandemoniac; *sb.* an inhabitant of P.

Pander (pæ·ndəɹ), *sb.* late ME. [prop. *pandar*, orig. *Pandare*, Eng. or AF. form of L. *Pandarus*, Gr. Πάνδαρος, a character in Boccaccio, and in Chaucer's *Troilus & Criseyde*. The spelling *pander* is prob. after agent-sbs. in -ER[1].] **1.** As proper name. **2.** A go-between in clandestine amours; a male bawd or procurer 1450. **b.** Less usu., a panderess 1585. **c.** *transf.* and *fig.* Said of a thing 1582. **3.** One who ministers to the baser passions or evil designs of others 1603.

1. *Tr. & Cr.* III. ii. 210. 2. He that was the Pandor to procure her NORTH. c. Make virtue a p. to vice BURKE. 3. Pandars to folly and extravagance JOHNSON. So **Pa·nderess** (now *rare*), a female p. **Pa·nderism,** the practice of a p. **Pa·nderly** *a.* of the nature of or befitting a p. (*Obs.* or *arch.*); so †**Pa·nderous** *a.*

Pander (pæ·ndəɹ), *v.* Also **-ar.** 1602. [f. prec.] **1.** *trans.* To act as a pander to; to minister to the gratification of (another's lust). Also *fig.* **2.** *intr.* To play the pander. Const. *to.* 1603.

1. *fig.* Frost..as actiuely doth burne, As Reason panders Will SHAKS.

Pandiculation (pændikiulē·ʃən). 1649. [f. L. *pandiculatus, pandiculari*, f. *pandere* to stretch.] The extension of the legs, the raising and stretching of the arms, and the throwing back of the head and trunk, accompanied by yawning, as occurring before and after sleeping, in hysteria, etc.

Pandora[1] (pændōə·ră). Also †**Pandore.** 1579. [a. Gr. πανδώρα lit. 'all-gifted', f. παν- PAN- + δῶρον gift.] *Gr. Myth.* Name of the first mortal woman, on whom, when made by Vulcan and brought to Epimetheus, all the gods and goddesses bestowed gifts.

Pandora's box, the gift of Jupiter to Pandora, a box containing all human ills, which flew forth when the box was foolishly opened by Epimetheus; according to another version, the box contained all the blessings of the gods, which, on its opening, escaped and were lost, with the exception of hope, which was at the bottom. Hence fig. and in allusive uses.

Pandora[2] (pændōə·ră), **pandore** (pændōə·ɹ). 1597. [a. It. *pandora*, F. *pandore*, ad. L. *pandura*, a. Gr. πανδοῦρα, a word prob. of foreign origin.] = BANDORE[1].

Pandour, pandoor (pæ·ndūəɹ). 1747. [= F. *pandour*, G. *pandur*; all a. Serbo-Croatian *pàndūr* a constable, etc.] **1.** In *pl.* The name borne by a local force organized in 1741 by Baron Trenck on his own estates in Croatia to clear the country near the Turkish frontier of bands of robbers; subseq. enrolled as a regiment in the Austrian army, where, under Trenck, their rapacity and brutality made *Pandour* synonymous with 'brutal Croatian soldier'. ‖**2.** In local use in Croatia, etc.: A guard; an armed retainer; a member of the local mounted constabulary 1880.

1. His style might have better suited a colonel of pandours than a Christian bishop 1791.

Pandowdy (pændau·di). *U.S.* 1846. [Origin obsc.] A kind of apple pudding, usu. seasoned with molasses, and baked in a deep dish with or without a crust.

Pandurate (pæ·ndiurēt), *a.* 1847. [f. L. *pandura* PANDORA[2] + -ATE[2].] = next.

Panduriform (pændiūə·rifǫɹm), *a.* 1753. [f. as prec. + -FORM.] Fiddle-shaped; chiefly in *Bot.* and *Entom.*

Pane (pēn), *sb.*[1] ME. [a. F. *pan*:—L. *pannum*, acc. of *pannus* a cloth, a piece of cloth.] **I.** †**1.** A cloth; a piece of cloth; any distinct portion of a garment, a lap, a skirt –1580. †**2.** A piece, width, or strip of cloth, of which several were joined together side by side, so as to make one cloth, curtain, or garment –1694. †**b.** *pl.* Strips made by cutting or slashing a garment longitudinally for ornamental purposes –1653. **II.** A piece, portion, or side of anything. †**1.** A length of a wall or fence –1672. †**2.** A side of a quadrangle, cloister, court, or town –1560. **3.** A flat side, face, or surface of any object having several sides: e.g. a side of a stone or log, of a nut or bolt-head, of the table of a brilliant-cut diamond. late ME. **III.** A division of a window, etc. **1.** One of the lights of a mullioned window (*obs.*), or a subdivision of this; now, One compartment of a window, etc. consisting of one sheet of glass held in place by a frame; the piece of glass itself, or of horn, paper, or the like 1466. **2.** = PANEL *sb.* III. 2. 1582. **3.** A rectangular division of some surface; one of the compartments of a chequered pattern 1555. **b.** Each of the blocks of burr-stone of which a mill-stone is constructed 1839. **4.** A section or plot of ground more or less rectangular in shape; *spec.* in *Irrigation*, a division of ground bounded by a feeder and an outlet drain 1805. Hence **Pa·neless** *a.*, having no panes.

Pane (pēn), *sb.*[2] 1578. [Cf. F. *panne*.] The pointed or edged end of a hammer: = north. dial. *peen*.

Pane (pēn), *v.* 1504. [f. PANE *sb.*[1]] **1.** *trans.* To make up (a piece of cloth, a garment) of strips of different sorts or colours, joined side by side. Chiefly in *pa. pple.* **2.** To fit (a window) with panes 1726.

Paned (pēnd), *ppl. a.* 1546. [f. PANE *v.* and *sb.*[1] + -ED.] **1.** Made of strips of different coloured cloth joined together, or of cloth cut into strips, between which ribs or stripes of other material or colour are inserted. **2.** Of a window or door: Having panes of glass 1756.

Panegyric (pænidʒi·rik), *sb.* and *a.* 1603. [a. F. *panégyrique*, ad. L. *panegyricus*, a. Gr. πανηγυρικός fit for a public assembly, f. πανήγυρις PANEGYRIS.] **A.** *sb.* **1.** A public speech or writing in praise of some person, thing, or achievement; a formal or elaborate encomium. Const. *on, upon,* †*of.* **2.** Eulogy; laudation 1613.

1. I profess to write, not his panegyrick..but his Life BOSWELL.

B. *adj.* = PANEGYRICAL 2. 1605. Hence †**Panegy·ric** *v. intr.* to utter or write a p.; *trans.* to praise in a p.

Panegyrical (pænidʒi·rikăl), *a.* 1592. [f. as prec. + -AL.] †**1.** Of the nature of a general assembly –1679. **2.** Of the nature of a panegyric or eulogy; encomiastic, laudatory 1592.

‖**Panegyris** (pănī·dʒiris). 1647. [a. Gr., f. παν- PAN- + ἄγυρις = ἀγορά assembly.] *Gr. Antiq.* A general assembly; *esp.* a festal assembly in honour of a god.

Panegyrize (pæ·nidʒiraiz), *v.* 1617. [ad. Gr. πανηγυρίζειν to celebrate a public festival, to deliver a panegyric.] **1.** *trans.* To pronounce or write a panegyric upon; to eulogize. **2.** *intr.* To compose or utter panegyrics 1827.

So **Panegyrist** (pæni·dʒi·rist), an encomiast; one who writes or utters a panegyric 1605.

Panegyry (pæ·nidʒiri). 1641. [f. Gr. πανήγυρις, with change of suffix.] *Gr. Antiq.* = PANEGYRIS 1. Also, A religious festival.

Panel (pæ·nĕl), *sb.* [ME. a. OF., = piece of cloth, etc., mod.F. *panneau* :—med.L. *pannellus*, dim. of *pannus* PANE *sb.*[1]]

I. A piece of cloth, etc. **1.** A piece of cloth placed under the saddle, or, now, the pad or stuffed lining of a saddle, employed to prevent galling. **2.** A kind of saddle; generally applied to a rough treeless pad 1540. **II.** A small piece or slip of parchment, etc. **1.** A slip or roll of parchment, *esp.* the slip on which the sheriff entered the names of jurors and which he affixed to the writ 1440. **2.** A list of jurymen; the jury itself. late ME. **b.** *transf.* A list of men, or of beasts 1575. **3.** *Sc. Law.* In the phr. *on* or *upon the p.* = upon (his, one's) trial. Also, later, *in the p.* 1557. **b.** The person or persons indicted, the accused 1555. **4.** A list of doctors who are prepared to accept as patients persons registered under the National Health Insurance Acts; a doctor's list of such patients 1913. **III.** A distinct portion of some surface, etc., usu. contained in a frame or border. **1.** A section or compartment of a fence or railing; a hurdle 1489. **2.** A distinct compartment of a wainscot, door, shutter, cover of a book, etc., often sunk below or raised above the general level, set in a border or frame 1600. **b.** A piece of stuff of different kind or colour, laid or inserted lengthwise in the skirt of a woman's dress 1889. **3.** A compartment in a stained glass window, containing a separate subject 1873. **4.** *Coal-mining.* **a.** A piece of coal left uncut in a mine. **b.** A compartment of a mine separated from the rest by thick masses or ribs of coal. 1747. **IV.** A thin wooden board used as a surface for oil painting; also, the painting on such a board 1688. **b.** A large size of photograph, much greater in height than width. Chiefly *attrib.* 1888. **V. 1.** *Artillery.* The carriages which carry mortars and their beds upon a march 1853. **2.** *Mining.* A heap of dressed ore 1858.

attrib. and *Comb.*, as *p.-cupboard*, *-sleeve*, etc.; (sense II. 4) *p.-doctor*, *-patient*, etc.; **-house**, a brothel in which the walls have sliding panels for the purpose of robbery (*U.S.*); **-strip**, a strip of wood or metal to cover the joint between a post and a p., or between two panels; **-thief**, a thief in a panel-house (*U.S.*); **-work**, (*a*) work in wood, etc., consisting of or containing panels; (*b*) the working of a mine by division into panels. Hence **Pa·nel(l)ed** (pæ·nĕld) *ppl. a.* **Pa·nel(l)ing**, panels collectively; p.-work.

Panel (pæ·nĕl), *v.* 1451. [f. PANEL *sb.*] **1.** *trans.* To empanel (a jury). **2.** *Sc. Law.* To bring to trial; to indict 1576. **3.** To put a panel on (a mule, ass, etc.); to saddle with a panel 1530. **4.** To fit, furnish, or adorn (a room, wall, etc.) with panels 1633. **5.** To fit or place as a panel in its frame 1832. **6.** To ornament (a skirt, etc.) with a panel or panels 1901. **7.** *Telegr.* To arrange wires in parallels 1890.

Panful (pæ·nful). 1874. [f. PAN *sb.*[1] + -FUL.] The quantity that fills a pan.

Pang (pæŋ), *sb.* 1526. [Origin obsc.] **1.** A brief keen spasm of pain which appears to shoot through the body or any part of it; a shooting pain. **2.** *fig.* A sudden sharp mental pain 1570. †**3.** A sudden transitory fit of keen feeling or emotion –1694.

1. In the pange & distresse of deth 1526. **2.** *Twel. N.* II. iv. 94. Hence **Pa·ngful** *a.* full of pangs, sorrowful (*rare*). **Pa·ngless** *a.* without a p.

Pang (pæŋ), *v.* Now *rare.* 1502. [Origin obsc.] *trans.* To afflict with pangs; to pierce or penetrate with acute physical or mental pain. Also *absol.*

Pangenesis (pændʒe·nĕsis). 1868. [f. Gr. παν- PAN- + γένεσις -GENESIS.] *Biol.* Name given by Darwin to his hypothesis, advanced to explain the phenomena of heredity, that every separate unit or cell of an organism reproduces itself by contributing its share to the germ or bud of the future offspring. So **Pangene·tic** *a.* of or pertaining to p. **Pangene·tically** *adv.*

Pangolin (pæŋgō·lin). 1774. [a. Malay *peng-gōling* roller, f. *peng-* (denominative) + *gōling* to roll, in ref. to its power of rolling itself up.] A scaly ant-eater.

Panhandle (pæ·nhæ:nd'l). 1887. [f. PAN *sb.*[1] + HANDLE.] The handle of a pan; hence *U.S.* a narrow strip of a State or Territory extending between two others. **Pa·n-ha:ndler** *U.S. slang*, a beggar. So **Pa·n-handle** *v.*

Panharmonic (pænhaɹmǫ·nik), *a.* 1875. [f. PAN- + HARMONIC.] **a.** Adapted to all the 'harmonies' or musical modes. **b.** Universally harmonic, harmonizing with all 1886. So **Panharmo·nicon**, a mechanical musical instrument of the orchestrion type, invented by J. N. Maelzel in 1800.

Panhellenic (pænhelī·nik, -e·nik), *a.* 1847. [f. PAN- 1 + HELLENIC, after Gr. πανελλήνιος, etc.] Of, concerning, or representing all men of Greek race. So **Panhe·llenism**, the idea of a political union of all Greeks; the P. spirit and aims. **Panhe·llenist**.

Panic (pæ·nik), *sb.*[1] OE. [ad. L. *panicum.*] A grass or graminaceous plant; orig. applied to *Panicum italicum* of Linnæus, otherwise called Italian Millet; also extended to other species of the genus *Panicum* and its sub-genera. **p.-grass**, any grassy species of *Panicum*.

Panic (pæ·nik), *a.* and *sb.*[2] 1603. [a. F. *panique* adj., ad. Gr. πανικός adj. of or for Pan, groundless (fear), whence πανικόν panic terror.] **A.** *adj.* (Now often taken as attrib. use of B.) In *p. fear*, *terror*, etc.: Such as was attributed to the action of the god Pan: = B. 2. **b.** Of the nature of or resulting from a panic 1741.

B. *sb.*[2] [= mod.F. *une panique.*] †**1.** Contagious emotion such as was attributed to the influence of Pan –1708. **2.** A sudden and excessive feeling of alarm or fear, usually affecting a body of persons, and leading to extravagant or injudicious efforts to secure safety. (With and without *a* and *pl.*) 1708. **b.** *spec.* A condition of widespread apprehension in relation to financial and commercial matters, leading to hasty and violent measures, the tendency of which is to cause financial disaster 1757.

1. We may..call every Passion Pannick which is rais'd in a Multitude, and convey'd by Aspect, or as it were by Contact or Sympathy SHAFTESB. **2.** The Uncertainty of what they fear'd made their Fear get greater..And this was what in after-times men call'd a Pannick SHAFTESB.

attrib. and *Comb.*: **p.-monger**, one who endeavours to create or foster a p.; an alarmist; hence **-mongering**; **-stricken**, **-struck** *adjs.*, stricken with p. Hence **Pa·nic** *v. trans.* to affect with p.; *intr.* to be affected with p. So **Pa·nical** *a. rare*, = PANIC *a.* A; **-ly** *adv.* **Panicky** (pæ·niki) *a. colloq.* of the nature of, or having a tendency to p.

Panicle (pæ·nik'l). 1597. [ad. L. *panicula*, dim. of *panus* a swelling, an ear of millet.] *Bot.* A compound inflorescence, usu. of the racemose type, forming a loose and irregularly spreading cluster, as in oats and many grasses. Hence **Pa·nicled** *a.* paniculate; furnished with a p. or panicles.

Paniculate (păni·kiŭlĕt), *a.* 1727. [ad. mod.L. *paniculatus*, f. *panicula* PANICLE + -ATE [2].] Arranged in a panicle; panicled. So **Pani·culated** *a. rare.* 1719.

Panification (pænifikē·ʃən). 1779. [a. F., f. *panifier* to make into bread.] The making into bread; conversion into the substance of bread, esp. as a chemical process.

Panjandrum (pændʒæ·ndrǒm). 1755. A nonsense formation, occurring in the string of nonsense composed by S. Foote to test the memory of Macklin, who had asserted that he could repeat anything after once hearing it. Hence, A mock title for a mysterious or exalted personage; a local magnate of great airs; a pompous pretender 1880.

And there were present the Picninnies, and the Joblillies, and the Garyulies, and the Grand P. himself, with the little round button at top FOOTE. The P. of Biblical Science and Scotch Presbyterianism 1892.

‖ **Pa·nnag.** 1611. [Heb.] 'Perhaps a kind of confection' (R.V. margin, Ezek. xxvii. 17).

Pannage (pæ·nĕdʒ). late ME. [a. OF. *pasnage*, *panage*, F. *panage* :—late L. *pastionaticum*, f. *pastionem* feeding, from *pascere*, *pastum.*] **1.** *Law.* **a.** The feeding of swine, etc. in a forest or wood; pasturage for swine; **b.** The right or privilege of pasturing swine in a forest; **c.** The payment made to the owner of a woodland for this right; the profit thus accruing. 1450. **2.** *concr.* Acorns, beech-mast, etc., on which swine feed. late ME.

‖ **Panne** (pæn, ‖pan). 1875. [F.; origin obsc.] A soft kind of cloth with a long nap, resembling velvet. Also *attrib.* as *p. velvet*.

†**Pa·nnicle.** 1590. [a. OF. *pan(n)icle*, ad. L. *panniculus*, dim. of *pannus* cloth.] ¶ **1.** App. misused as = brain-pan. SPENSER. **2.** *Bot.* A membranous covering in plants, as the scales investing a leaf-bud 1671.

Pannier (pæ·niəɹ), *sb.*[1] [ME. *panier*, a. F. *panier* :—L. *panarium* bread-basket, f. *panis* bread; see -IER 2.] **1.** A basket; *esp.* a large basket for carrying provisions, fish, etc.; in later use, mostly one of those carried by a beast of burden (usu. in pairs), or on the shoulders of a man or woman. **b.** A covered basket for holding surgical instruments and medicines for a military ambulance 1854. †**2.** *Arch.* = CORBEIL 2. **3.** A frame of whalebone, wire, etc., used to distend the skirt of a woman's dress at the hips 1877. Hence **Pa·nniered** *a.* laden with a p. or panniers.

Pannier (pæ·niəɹ), *sb.*[2] *colloq.* 1823. [Origin unkn.] The name by which the robed waiters at table are known in the Inner Temple.

Pa·nnierman. 1482. [f. PANNIER *sb.*[1]] A paid officer in the Inns of Court, who brought provisions from market (with a horse and panniers). (Abolished 1900.)

Pannikin (pæ·nikin). 1823. [f. PAN *sb.*[1] + -KIN; cf. *mannikin.*] A small metal (usu. tinned iron) drinking vessel; also, the contents of this.

Pa·nning, *vbl. sb.*: see PAN *v.*[1]

‖**Pannus** (pæ·nǒs). 1706. [perh. L. *pannus* cloth.] *Path.* A vascular condition of the cornea of the eye, with thickening and opacity.

Panoply (pæ·nǒpli). 1576. [ad. Gr. πανοπλία the full armour of the ὁπλίτης HOPLITE, f. παν- PAN- + ὅπλα arms.] A complete suit of armour, the 'whole armour' of a soldier of ancient or mediæval times. Also *trans.* and *fig.*, often with ref. to τὴν πανοπλίαν τοῦ Θεοῦ 'the whole armour of God' (Eph. vi. 11, 13).

Hee in Celestial Panoplie all armd MILT. *fig.* Patience is the P. or whole Armour of the man of God 1650. *transf.* Both of the Bears, and Orion, in golden p. dight 1887. Hence **Panoplied** (pæ·nǒplid) *a.* clad in complete armour; also *fig.*

Panoptic (pænǫ·ptik), *a.* 1826. [f. Gr. πάνοπτος seen of all, πανόπτης all-seeing + -IC.] **1.** All-seeing. **2.** In which all is seen; cf. PANOPTICON 1845.

Panopticon (pænǫ·ptikǒn). 1768. [f. Gr. παν- PAN- + ὀπτικόν, neut. of ὀπτικός OPTIC.] **1.** Bentham's name for a proposed form of prison of circular shape having cells built round a central 'well', whence the warders could at all times see the prisoners. Also *attrib.* or as *adj.* 1791. Also *transf.* and *fig.* **2.** Name given to an optical instrument 1768.

Panorama (pænŏrā·mă, -æ·mă). 1796. [f. Gr. παν- PAN- + ὅραμα view.] **1.** A picture of a landscape, etc., either arranged on the inside of a cylindrical surface round the spectator as a centre (CYCLORAMA), or unrolled or unfolded so as to pass before him in successive portions. **2.** An unbroken view of the whole surrounding region 1828. **b.** *fig.* A comprehensive survey of a subject 1801.

1. *transf.* The endless moving p. of the London streets 1876. **2.** The P. from the top of the Brocken 1836. Hence **Panora·mist**, a painter of panoramas.

Panoramic (pænŏræ·mik), *a.* 1813. [f. prec. + -IC.] Of, pertaining to, or of the nature of a panorama.

P. camera, a photographic camera made to rotate automatically so as to take an extended landscape.

‖ **Panorpa** (pănǭ·ɹpă). *Pl.* **-æ.** 1878. [mod. L. (Linnæus), of obsc. formation.] *Entom.* A genus of neuropterous insects, the type of a family *Panorpidæ*, the scorpion-flies. Hence **Pano·rpian**, **Pano·rpine** *adjs.* of or pertaining to the genus *P.* **Pano·rpid**, an insect of the family *Panorpidæ*.

Pan-pipe (pæ·npəip). Also **Pan's pipe**, **Pan's-pipe.** 1820. [PAN *sb.*[2]] A primitive musical instrument made of a series of reeds graduated in length so as to form a scale, the upper and open ends being level; its invention was ascribed to Pan; a syrinx, mouth-organ.

Pan-se·xualism. 1915. [f. PAN- 2 + SEXUAL + -ISM.] *Psychol.* The view that the sex instinct plays a part in all human thought and activity and is the chief or only source of energy. **Pan-se·xual** *a.*, **-se·xualist, -sexua·lity.**

Pansophy (pæ·nsŏfi). 1642. [f. Gr. παν- PAN- + σοφία wisdom.] **1.** Universal or cyclopædic knowledge; a scheme or cyclopædic work embracing the whole body of human knowledge. **2.** The claim or pretension to universal knowledge 1792. So **Panso·phic** *a.* of or pertaining to p. **Pa·nsophism** = 2. **Pa·nsophist,** a pretender to universal knowledge.

Panspermy (pænspə·ɹmi). Also in mod.L. form **panspe·rmia.** 1842. [ad. Gr. πανσπερμία the doctrine of Anaxagoras and Democritus that the elements were a mixture of all the seeds of things, f. πάνσπερμος.] The biogenetic theory that the atmosphere is full of minute germs which develop on finding a favourable environment. So **Panspe·rmatism, Panspe·rmism** = PANSPERMY. **Panspe·rmatist, Panspe·rmist,** one who holds the doctrine of p. **Panspe·rmic** *a.*, of or pertaining to p.

Pansy (pæ·nzi). 1500. [Formerly *pensee, pensy*, a. F. *pensée, pencée*, a fanciful application of *pensée* thought.] The common name of *Viola tricolor*; the wild plant has small flowers compounded of purple, yellow, and white; the cultivated form has large richly and variously coloured flowers. Also called HEARTSEASE, *love-in-idleness*, etc.

The Pansie freakt with jeat MILT. Hence **Pa·nsied** *a.* adorned with or abounding in pansies.

Pant (pænt), *sb.* 1500. [f. next.] **1.** One of a series of short quick efforts of laboured breathing; a gasp, a catching of the breath. **2.** A throb or heave of the breast in laboured breathing or palpitation of the heart 1581. **3.** *transf.* The regular throb and gasping sound of a steam-engine, as the valves open and shut 1840.

Pant (pænt), *v.* late ME. [perh. shortened f. OF. *pantoisier, -iser* to pant :—pop.L. **pant-, phantasiare* to be oppressed with nightmare, f. *phantasia* phantasy, nightmare.] **1.** *intr.* To breathe hard or spasmodically; to gasp for breath. late ME. **b.** To run or go panting 1713. **c.** *transf.* To emit hot air, vapour, etc. in loud puffs, as a furnace or engine 1743. **2.** To gasp (for air, water, etc.); hence *fig.* To gasp with desire; to yearn (*for, after,* or *to* with *inf.*) 1560. **3.** To throb or heave violently or rapidly; to palpitate, pulsate, beat 1460. **4.** *transf.* Of a plated ship: To have its plating bulge in and out in the struggle with the waves 1869. **5.** *trans.* To utter gaspingly; to gasp *out*, etc. 1605.

1. They blowe, and p. like discomfited souldiers 1576. *fig.* If I were..A wave to p. beneath thy power SHELLEY. **b.** As a hare..Pants to the place from whence at first he flew GOLDSM. **2.** As the Hart panteth after the water brookes, so panteth my soule after thee, O God *Ps.* xlii. 1. **3.** A breast that panted with alarms COWPER.

Pant- = Gr. παντ-, shortened form of παντο- PANTO- bef. a vowel. **Pantamo·rphic** [Gr. ἄμορφος formless], *a.* generally deformed. **Pa·ntarchy** [Gr. ἀρχή rule], a state in which the rule is vested in the whole people.

Panta- erron. f. PANTO-.

Pantagruelian (pæntăgrue·liăn). 1694. [f. *Pantagruel*, name of a giant in Rabelais' work + -IAN; cf. GARGANTUAN.] **A.** *adj.* Of, pertaining to, characteristic of, or appropriate to, Pantagruel, represented as a coarse and extravagant humorist, dealing satirically with serious subjects. **B.** *sb.* = *Pantagruelist* 1899.

Pantagruelism (pæntăgrū·eliz'm). 1835. [a. F. *pantagruélisme*, f. *Pantagruel*; see prec. and -ISM.] The theory and practice ascribed to Pantagruel, one of the characters of Rabelais; extravagant and coarse humour with a satirical or serious purpose. So **Pantagru·elist,** an imitator, admirer, or student of Pantagruel, or of Rabelais 1611. **Pa·ntagrueli·stic, -al** *adjs.*

Pantalettes, -lets (pæntăle·ts), *sb. pl.* (*rare* in *sing.*) Chiefly *U.S.* 1847. [dim. formation from *pantaloon*; see -ETTE.] Loose drawers with a frill at the bottom of each leg, worn by young girls *c* 1825–53; *transf.* euphemistically to drawers, cycling 'knickerbockers', or the like, worn by women.

Pantaloon (pæntălū·n). 1590. [a. F. *pantalon*, ad. It. *pantalone* 'a kind of mask on the Italian stage, representing the Venetian' (Baretti), of whom *Pantalone* (from *San Pantaleone* or *Pantalone*, formerly a favourite saint of the Venetians) was a nickname.] **1. a.** The Venetian character in Italian comedy, represented as a lean and foolish old man, wearing spectacles, pantaloons (see 3), and slippers. **b.** Hence, in mod. pantomime, a foolish old man who is the butt of the clown's jokes, and his abettor in his tricks 1781. **2.** Hence, a dotard, an old fool. *Obs.* exc. as echo of Shaks. 1596. **3.** Chiefly in *pl.* Applied to garments of different styles for the legs; *esp.* A tight-fitting kind of trousers fastened with ribbons or buttons below the calf, or, later, by straps passing under the boots. **b.** Hence, trousers generally (esp. in U.S.). 1798.

2. *A.Y.L.* II. vii. 158. Hence **Pantaloo·ned** *a.* wearing pantaloons; trousered. **Pantaloo·nery,** the performance of a p. in the pantomime.

Pantechnicon (pænte·knikŏn). 1830. [f. Gr. παν- PAN- + τεχνικόν adj. neut., belonging to the arts.] Orig., the name of a bazaar of all kinds of artistic work; now, a large warehouse for storing furniture; also, *colloq.* short for *p. van*, a furniture-removing van. Also *attrib.*

†**Pa·nter**¹. *Obs.* (exc. *Hist.*) [ME. *paneter*, etc., a. AF. *paneter*, F. *panetier* :—med.L. *panetarius* baker, f. L. *panem.*] Orig., a baker, but in ME. usu. the officer of a household who had charge of the pantry –1580.

Pa·nter². *Obs.* exc. *dial.* [ME. a. OF. *panter* 'tendicula, lacum'; cf. F. *pantière*, L. *panthera* hunting-net, Gr. πανθήρα.] A fowling net, a fowler's snare; a net, trap, noose. Also *fig.*

Panter³ (pæ·ntəɹ). 1700. [f. PANT *v.* + -ER¹.] **1.** One who or that which pants 1729. **2.** *slang.* The heart. (Partly a pun upon 'hart'.) 1700.

Panterer (pæ·ntərəɹ). Now only *Hist.* late ME. [Expanded f. PANTER¹.] = PANTER¹.

Pantheism (pæ·nþiˌiz'm). 1732. [f. Gr. παν- PAN- + θεός God + -ISM; app. after PANTHEIST.] **1.** The belief or theory that God and the universe are identical (implying a denial of the personality and transcendence of God); the doctrine that God is everything and everything is God. **2.** The heathen worship of all the gods 1837.

Pantheist (pæ·nþiˌist). 1705. [f. as prec. + -IST.] One who holds the doctrine of pantheism. Hence **Panthei·stic, -al** *adjs.* of or pertaining to pantheists, or pantheism; **-ly** *adv.*

Pantheon (pæ·nþiˌŏn, pænþī·ŏn). ME. [a. L., a. Gr. πάνθειον (f. παν- PAN- + θεῖος of or sacred to a god, θεός a god). Cf. F. *panthéon.*] **1.** A temple or sacred building dedicated to all the gods; *spec.* that at Rome, orig. built by Agrippa *c* 25 B.C. and also called the *Rotunda.* **b.** *fig.* 'Temple' or 'shrine of all the gods' 1596. **c.** *transf.* A building in which the illustrious dead of a nation are buried, or have memorials erected to them 1713. **2.** A habitation of all the gods; the deities of a people collectively 1550. **b.** Name for a treatise on all the gods 1698. **3.** Name of a large building in London opened as a place of entertainment in 1772; also *gen.*

Panther (pæ·nþəɹ). [ME. *pantere*, a. OF. *pantere*, mod.F. *panthère*, ad. L. *panthera*, ad. Gr. πάνθηρ.] **1.** The leopard, *Panthera pardus*; pop. applied to large leopards. **2.** Applied in America to the puma or cougar, *Felis concolor*; and, sometimes, to the jaguar, *P. onca* 1730.

attrib. and *Comb.*, as **p.-cat,** the ocelot; **-cowry,** a spotted cowry, *Cypræa pantherina* of the East Indies; **-lily,** *U.S.*, the Californian lily, *Lilium pardalinum.* Hence **Pa·ntheress,** a female p. **Pa·ntherine** (-rəin, -rin) *a.* spotted, etc., like a p.; of, belonging to, or characteristic of, a p.

Panties (pæ·ntiz). 1846. [f. PANTS: see -Y⁶.] **a.** *U.S.* Drawers. **b.** In British use, women's and children's drawers 1905.

Pantile (pæ·nˌtəil). 1640. [f. PAN *sb.*¹ + TILE *sb.* Cf. Du. *dakpan* lit. roof-pan.] **1.** A roofing tile transversely curved to an ogee shape, one curve being much larger than the other. **b.** Erron. applied to flat Dutch or Flemish paving tiles, and so to the Parade at Tunbridge Wells which was paved with these 1774. **2.** *joc.* Hard sea biscuit, etc. 1873.

Pantisocracy (pæntisǫ·krăsi, -əis-). 1794. [f. Gr. παντ- PANTO- + ἰσοκρατία ISOCRACY.] A Utopian community in which all are equal and all rule. So **Pantisocrat** (pæntəi·sŏkræt), one who advocates p. **Pantisocra·tic, -al** *adjs.* pertaining to, involving, or upholding p. **Pantiso·cratist** = *pantisocrat.*

Pantler (pæ·ntləɹ). Now only *Hist.* ME. [app. altered f. PANTER¹, PANTERER, perh. after *butler.*] = PANTER¹.

Panto (pæ·nto), abbrev. f. PANTOMIME.

Panto- (pænto, pæntǫ), bef. a vowel PANT-, repr. Gr. παντο- (παντ-), comb. f. πᾶς, πᾶν (stem παντ-) all; as in **Pa·ntograph** [Gr. -γράφος writing, writer], an instrument for the mechanical copying of a plan, etc., on the same or an enlarged or reduced scale; hence **Panto·grapher; Pantogra·phic, -al,** *adjs.*; **-ly,** *adv.* **Panto·graphy,** complete description (*rare*). †**Pa·ntomancer,** a diviner upon all kinds of things. **Panto·meter** [Gr. μέτρον measure], an instrument for measuring angles and distances, and taking elevations. **Panto·metry,** †universal measurement; the use of a pantometer; hence **Pantome·tric, -al,** *adjs.* **Pa·ntomorph** (erron. **panta-**) [Gr. παντόμορφος], that which takes any or all shapes; so **Pantomo·rphic** *a.* (**panta-**), assuming any or all forms. **Panto·phagist** [Gr. παντοφάγος all-devouring], a man or animal that devours things of all kinds; so **Panto·phagous** *a.*; **Panto·phagy. Pa·ntopragma·tic** *a.* (*joc.*) universally meddling, occupied with everything; *sb.* a pantopragmatic person.

Pantofle (pæ·ntǫf'l, -tuf'l). 1494. [a. F. *pantoufle.* Origin unkn.] A slipper; formerly applied esp. to the high-heeled cork-soled chopines; also to out-door overshoes or goloshes, sandals, and the like.

Pantology (pæntǫ·lŏdʒi). Also *erron.* **panta-.** 1819. [f. Gr. παντο- PANTO- + -λογια -LOGY.] A systematic view of all branches of knowledge; universal knowledge; also, a compendium of universal information. So **Pantolo·gic, -al** *adjs.* of or pertaining to p. Hence **Panto·logist,** one versed in all knowledge. (All joc. or sarcastic.)

Pantomime (pæ·ntŏməim), *sb.* (*a.*) Also †**Pantomimus.** 1589. [ad. L. *pantomimus* one who plays a part by dumb show, ad. Gr. παντόμιμος, f. παντο- PANTO- + μῖμος mimic, MIME.] **1.** A Roman actor, who performed in dumb show; hence, gen., a mimic actor; one who expresses his meaning by gestures and actions without words. Now only *Hist.* **2.** 'A kind of dramatic entertainment in which the performers express themselves by gestures to the accompaniment of music' (Grove *Dict. Mus.*) 1735. **3.** An English dramatic performance, orig. consisting of action without speech, but now of a dramatized tale, the dénouement of which is often a transformation scene followed by the broad comedy of clown and pantaloon and the dancing of harlequin and columbine 1739. **4.** Dumb show 1791. **5.** *attrib.* or *adj.* Of the nature of pantomime (sense 2); of, belonging to, or characteristic of the pantomime (sense 3) 1746.

3. The p. has gradually interwoven itself into our recognized Christmas festivities, so as to become an essential part of them 1892. **4.** As..he could not speak a word of French..he was obliged to convey this sentiment into p. 1871. Hence **Pa·ntomime** *v. intr.* to express oneself by p.; *trans.* to represent by p. **Pantomi·mist** = sense 1.

Pantomimic (pæntŏmi·mik), *a.* and *sb.* 1617. [ad. L. *pantomimicus*, f. *pantomimus*; see -IC.] **A.** *adj.* **1.** Of the nature of pantomime; expressed by dumb show 1680. **2.** Of or belonging to the pantomime 1805. **b.** Like a pantomime, in its sudden transformations 1895. †**B.** *sb.* = PANTOMIME *sb.* 1. –1689. So **Pantomi·mical** *a.*, **-ly** *adv.*

Pantopod (pæ·ntŏpǫd). 1887. [f. Gr. παντο- PANTO- + ποδ-, πούς foot.] *Zool.* One of the

Pantopoda, a name for the *Pycnogonidæ* or Sea-spiders, when treated as a sub-order; a sea-spider.

Pantoscope (pæ·ntŏskoup). Also *erron.* panta-. 1875. [f. Gr. παντο- PANTO- + -SCOPE.] 1. A form of photographic lens having a very wide angle. 2. A pantoscopic camera 1890.

Pantosco·pic, *a.* 1875. [f. as prec. + -IC.] Having a wide range of vision.

P. camera, a panoramic camera. *P. spectacles*, those so constructed as to have different focallengths in the upper and lower parts, the upper being for long distance vision, and the lower for short; bi-focal spectacles.

Pantry (pæ·ntri). ME. [a. AF. *panetrie*, OF. *paneterie* bread-room, f. OF. *paneter*, F. *panetier*; see PANTER [1].] A room or apartment in a house, etc., in which bread and other provisions are kept; also (*butler's* or *housemaid's p.*), one in which the plate, linen, etc. for the table are kept.

attrib. and *Comb.*: **p.-boy**, an assistant in the commissariat department on board a passenger-ship; **-man**, a man in charge of or employed in the p. (or in the commissariat department of a passenger-ship).

Pants (pænts), *sb. pl.* 1841. [Short for *pantaloons* (PANTALOON 3).] a. *U.S.* Trousers. b. In British use, men's drawers 1874.

Panurgic (pænʊ̄·ɪdʒik), *a. rare.* 1873. [ad. late Gr. πανουργικός knavish, f. πανοῦργος ready to do anything, f. παν- PAN- + ἔργον work.] Able or ready to do anything.

‖**Paolo** (pā·olo, pau·lo). 1617. [It., :—L. *Paulus* Paul.] An obs. Italian silver coin, worth about fivepence sterling, so called from Pope Paul.

Pap (pæp), *sb.*[1] [ME. *pappe*, app. from Scandinavian. Supposed to echo the sound made by an infant in feeding.] 1. A teat or nipple; a mamilla (chiefly *north. dial.* or *arch.*). 2. *transf.* Something resembling a pap in form. a. A small round tumour or swelling; a pimple 1552. b. *pl.* Formerly, a name for two (or more) conical hill summits rising side by side; still used locally 1572.

1. The pappes which gave the sucke TINDALE *Luke* xi. 27. 2. b. The great 'Paps of Jura' were hidden in the mists 1873.

Pap (pæp), *sb.*[2] late ME. [= (M)LG., G. *pappe*, Du. *pap*. For ult. origin cf. prec.] 1. Soft or semi-liquid food for infants or invalids, made of bread, meal, etc., moistened with water or milk. Also *fig.* 2. Any soft semi-liquid substance; a mash, paste, pulp. late ME. †b. The pulp of an apple, esp. when roasted –1761.

1. †*P. with a hatchet*, an ironical phr. for doing a kind thing in an unkind manner, or giving punishment in the guise of a kindness.

Comb.: **p.-boat**, (*a*) a boat-shaped vessel for holding p. for feeding infants; (*b*) a shell of the family *Turbinellidæ* used on the Malabar coast to hold anointing oil. Hence **Pap** *v.* to feed with p.; to feed *up*.

Papa [1] (păpā·). 1670. [a. F. *papa*, †*pappa*, = It. *pappa*, L. *papa* father; cf. Gr. πάππας. At first only in courtly use; now largely abandoned even by children. In early use the form varied between *papa·* and *pa·ppa*; from the latter the U.S. *po·ppa*.] A word used as the equivalent of *father*; chiefly in the voc., or preceded by a possess. pron. (as 'my papa'); also without any article; less usu. with *a* or in *pl.*

‖**Papa** [2] (pā·pă). 1559. [a. med.L. *papa* as translating Gr. πάπας, παπᾶς father.] †1. The pope (of Rome) –1861. 2. A parish priest or any of the lower clergy in the Orthodox Eastern Church. Also in Gr. form *papas*. 1591.

Papable (pē̆·păb'l), *a. rare.* 1592. [a. F., after It. *papabile* 'able to be pope', f. *papa* POPE *sb.*[1]] Qualified for the office of pope.

Papacy (pē̆·păsi). late ME. [ad. med.L. *papatia*, f. *papa* POPE.] 1. The office or position of pope (of Rome); tenure of office of a pope. 2. The papal system, ecclesiastically or politically; esp. *Hist.* the papal government as one of the states of Europe 1550.

Papagay, obs. f. POPINJAY.

Papain (păpē̆·in). 1890. [f. *papay*(*a* PAPAW + -IN [1].] *Chem.* A proteolytic ferment obtained from the half-ripe fruit of the papaw (*Carica Papaya*).

Papal (pē̆·păl), *a.* ME. [a. F., or ad. eccl. L. *papalis*, f. *papa* POPE *sb.*[1]; see -AL.] 1. Of or pertaining to a pope, or to the pope, his dignity or office. b. That is a pope 1802. †2. Adhering to or supporting the pope; belonging to the Church of Rome; popish –1814.

1. The P. benediction 1687. *P. cross*, one with three transoms; a triple cross. *P. crown*, or *tiara*, a mitre of cloth of gold, encircled with three coronets or circles of gold. 2. P. darkness SOUTHEY. Hence **Pa·palism**, the p. system. **Pa·palist**, an adherent of the p. system. **Pa·pally** *adv.* in a p. manner.

†**Papa·lity.** 1456. [a. F. *papalité*; see PAPAL and -ITY.] The papal office, dignity, or authority; the papal see –1824.

Papalize (pē̆·pălәiz), *v.* 1624. [f. PAPAL + -IZE.] 1. *intr.* To become papal or popish. 2. *trans.* To render papal; to imbue with papist principles or doctrines 1839.

†**Pa·palty.** 1577. [a. OF. *papalté*, F. *papauté*, f. *papal*.] = PAPALITY –1859.

Paparchy (pē̆·păɹki). *rare.* 1839. [f. L. *papa* pope + Gr. -αρχία sovereignty.] Papal rule.

Papaveraceous (păpē̆vәrē̆·ʃәs), *a.* 1846. [f. mod.L. *Papaveraceæ* (f. L. *papaver* poppy) + -OUS.] *Bot.* Of or belonging to the N.O. *Papaveraceæ*, the poppy family.

Papaverine (păpē̆·vәrәin). 1848. [f. L. *papaver* poppy + -INE [5].] *Chem.* An alkaloid ($C_{20}H_{21}NO_4$) contained in opium, obtained in colourless needles.

Papaverous (păpē̆·vәrәs), *a.* 1646. [f. as prec. + -OUS.] Pertaining to, resembling, or allied to the poppy; papaveraceous; *fig.* soporific.

Papaw (păpǭ·, pǭpǭ·). 1598. [Formerly *papaya*, *papay*, a. Sp. and Pg. *papaya*, *papayo* (the tree), adopted from a Carib dialect.] 1. a. The fruit of *Carica Papaya* (see b), usu. oblong and about 10 inches long, of a dull orange colour, with a thick fleshy rind, and containing numerous black seeds embedded in pulp; used in tropical countries as food. b. The tree *Carica Papaya* (N.O. *Papayaceæ*), a native of S. America, somewhat resembling a palm. The stem, leaves, and fruit contain an acrid milky juice which has the property of rendering meat tender (see PAPAIN). 1613. 2. (Only in forms *papaw*, *pawpaw*.) U. S. name for a small N. American tree, *Asimina triloba* (N.O. *Anonaceæ*), with dull purple flowers and ovate leaves (*p.-tree*); or for its edible fruit 1760. 3. *attrib.*, as *p.-bush* (= 2), etc. 1704.

Papayaceous (pæpăyē̆·ʃәs), *a.* 1846. [f. mod.L. *Papayaceæ* (f. *Papaya*; see prec.) + -OUS.] *Bot.* Belonging to the N.O. *Papayaceæ* (sometimes reckoned as a sub-order of *Passifloraceæ*), of which the Papaw-tree, *Carica Papaya*, is the type.

Papegay, -jay, -joy, obs. ff. POPINJAY.

Paper (pē̆·pәɹ), *sb.* ME. [a. AF. **paper*, = OF. *papier*, ad. L. *papyrus*, a. Gr. πάπυρος PAPYRUS.] I. Without *a* or *pl.* (exc. as denoting a particular kind). 1. A substance composed of fibres interlaced into a compact web, made from linen and cotton rags, straw, wood, certain grasses, etc., which are macerated into a pulp, dried, and pressed; it is used for writing, printing, or drawing on, for wrapping things in, for covering the interior of walls, etc. b. Also applied to other substances used for writing upon, as the PAPYRUS of the ancients; or to substances of similar texture, as that made by wasps for their nests. late ME. c. Applied familiarly to substances made from paper-pulp, as mill-board, papier mâché, etc. 1670. 2. *Comm.* a. Negotiable documents, bills of exchange, etc. collectively. b. Paper money or currency as opp. to coin, bank-notes, etc. 1674. 3. *slang.* Free passes of admission to a theatre, etc.; *transf.* persons admitted by these 1873.

1. Phr. *To commit to p.*, to write down. *To put pen to p.*, to commence writing, to write. *On p.*, in writing, in print; said esp. of a sketch or plan, in contrast to the reality; hence = in theory, theoretically. 2. a. The bankers will not look at his p. (*mod.*).

II. Individual singular with *a* and *pl.* 1. A piece, sheet, or leaf of paper 1628. b. A piece of paper serving as a wrapper or receptacle; often including the contents; a paperful; a sheet or card of paper containing pins or needles stuck in it 1511. c. A curl-paper. (Usu. in *pl.*) 1876. 2. A sheet, leaf, or piece of paper, bearing writing; a note, bill, or other legal instrument; in *pl.* written notes, memoranda, letters, official documents, etc. late ME. †b. A note, fastened on the back of a criminal undergoing punishment, specifying his offence –1688. †c. *pl.* = STATE-PAPERS, as in *Office of His* (*Her*) *Majesty's Papers*, etc. –1799. d. *pl.* The collection of documents establishing a person's identity, standing, etc.; the certificates which accompany an officer's application for permission to resign 1685. e. A set of questions in an examination; also, the written answers to these 1838. 3. = NEWSPAPER 1642. 4. A written or printed essay, dissertation, or article on some particular topic; now *esp.* a communication read or sent to a learned society. 1669.

1. But, in truth, the mind can never resemble a blank p. J. H. NEWMAN. b. A p. of sandwiches DICKENS. 2. b. 2 *Hen. VI*, II. iv. 31. d. *To send in one's papers*, to resign. *Ship's papers*, the set of papers carried by a ship for the manifestation of her ownership, nationality, destination, etc. 3. The office of the local p. STEVENSON.

III. *attrib.*, passing into *adj.* a. Of paper; made or consisting of paper 1596. b. *fig.* Like paper; slight, thin, flimsy, frail, feeble (as if made of paper) 1615. c. *fig.* Consisting of, pertaining to, or carried on by means of letters to journals, pamphlets, or books; literary 1592. d. Written on paper, in written form; *esp.* theoretical, hypothetical 1638.

a. Money of credit, which they commonly call p. currency BURKE. A *large-paper* copy of a book; see LARGE A. II. b. *P. ship*, a ship built of inferior material and badly put together 1891. d. P. profits were divided as if they were real 1893.

attrib. and *Comb.* 1. General: as *p.-case*, *-circulation*, *-factory*, *-fibre*, *-pulp*, *trade*, etc.; *p.-saving* adj.; *p.-fastener*, *-holder*, *-maker*, etc.; *p.-bound*, *-covered*, *-panelled* adjs. 2. Special: **p.-back**, a book with a p. back or cover; **p. birch** (see BIRCH *sb.* 1 b); **p. boards** (*Bookbinding*), a style of binding with paper covering the usual board stiffening; †**-book**, (*a*) a book of blank p. to write in; (*b*) *Law*, a copy of the demurrer book which contains the pleadings in an action, when the issue is one of law; **-boy**, a boy employed to sell newspapers; **-chase**, the game of hare and hounds when paper is used for the 'scent'; **-cutter**, (*a*) a paper-knife; (*b*) a machine for cutting the edges of p.; **-faced**, (*a*) having a face like p., i.e. thin or pale; (*b*) faced with p.; **-folder**, an instrument for folding p., as the folding-stick used in bookbinding; **-knife**, a knife of ivory, wood, etc., used *esp.* to cut open the leaves of an uncut book; **-marl**, a kind of marl occurring in thin layers; **-mill**, a mill in which p. is made; **-mulberry**, a small tree (*Broussonetia papyrifera*) allied to the mulberry, from the bark of which p. is made in China and Japan; **p. nautilus** = NAUTILUS a; †**P. Office** = Office of His Majesty's Papers (II. 2 c.), the STATE PAPER Office; **-rush**, the papyrus; **p. sailor**, the p. nautilus; **-tree**, name for trees or shrubs from which paper is made; **-wasp**, a wasp that constructs its nest of a papery substance made from dry wood moistened into a paste; **-weight**, a small heavy object intended to be laid upon loose papers to prevent their being disarranged; **-work**, the written work of a student in a class or examination.

Paper (pē̆·pәɹ), *v.* 1594. [f. prec.] 1. *trans.* To set down on paper; to describe in writing. Now *rare.* 2. To enclose in, put *up* in, paper; to stick (pins, etc.) in a sheet or card of paper 1599. 3. To stick paper upon (a wall, etc.); to decorate (a room) with paper-hangings 1774. b. *Bookbinding.* To paste the end-papers and fly-leaves at the beginning and end of (a volume) before putting on the cover 1875. 4. To supply with paper 1883. b. *slang.* To fill (a theatre, etc.) by means of free passes; see PAPER *sb.* I. 3. 1866. Hence **Pa·perer**, one who papers; *spec.* a paper-hanger 1844.

Pa·per-ha:nger. 1809. A man whose business it is to cover the walls of rooms, etc., with paper-hangings.

Pa·per-ha:nging. 1693. 1. *pl.* Paper, usually printed in ornamental designs, used for covering the walls of a room, etc. (so called as taking the place of the cloth hangings formerly used); wall-paper. 2. The decorating of a room with wall-paper; the occupation of a paper-hanger (*mod.*).

Pa·per mo:ney. 1691. [PAPER *sb.* I. 1, 2.] Negotiable documents used instead of money, esp. bank-notes; more strictly, a paper currency, which by the law of the country represents money and is a legal tender. Also *attrib.*

Pa·per-stai:ner. 1596. 1. One who stains or colours paper; *joc.* an (inferior) author. 2. A maker of paper-hangings 1756.

Papery (pēⁱ·pəri), *a.* 1602. [f. PAPER *sb.* + -Y [1].] Of the consistence of paper; like paper; thin or flimsy in texture.

Papess (pēⁱ·pės). 1620. [ad. F. *papesse*, It. *papessa*, f. *papa*; see -ESS [1].] A female pope. (*Hist.* of the alleged Pope Joan, A. D. 853–5.)

‖ **Papeterie** (pæpętrī·). 1847. [F., = paper-manufacture, f. *papetier* paper-maker.] A case or box for paper and other writing materials; a stationery-case.

Paphian (pēⁱ·fiăn), *a.* and *sb.* 1614. [f. L. *Paphius* adj. (f. *Paphos*) + -AN.] **A.** *adj.* **1.** Of or belonging to Paphos, a city of Cyprus sacred to Aphrodite or Venus (*the P. Goddess*). **2.** *transf.* Pertaining to love; *esp.* to unlawful sexual indulgence; belonging to the class of prostitutes 1650. **B.** *sb.* **1.** An inhabitant or native of Paphos. **2.** A devotee of the Paphian Venus; a prostitute 1811.

‖ **Papier mâché** (pa·pye mɑ·ʃe). 1753. [a. F. *papier* paper, *mâché* chewed, pa. pple. of *mâcher* :—L. *masticare* to chew. Not of French origin.] A substance consisting of paper-pulp or paper reduced to a pulp and shaped by moulding; used for boxes, jars, trays, fancy articles, etc. Also *attrib.* (usu. = made of papier mâché).

Papilionaceous (păpi:liŏnēⁱ·ʃəs), *a.* 1668. [f. mod.L. *papilionaceus*, f. L. *papilionem* butterfly; see -ACEOUS.] **1.** Of or pertaining to a butterfly or butterflies; of the nature of a butterfly; belonging to the butterfly tribe. Now *rare* or *Obs.* Also *fig.* **2.** *Bot.* Applied, from its fancied likeness to a butterfly, to that form of flower found in most leguminous plants, having an irregular corolla consisting of a large upper petal (the *vexillum* or standard), two lateral petals (the *alæ* or wings), and two narrow lower petals between these (forming the *carina* or keel). Also said of the plant. 1668.

‖ **Papilla** (păpi·lă). *Pl.* **-æ.** 1693. [L., = nipple, dim. of PAPULA.] **1.** *Zool.* and *Anat.* **a.** The nipple of the breast; the mamilla. (*rare* in Eng. use.) **b.** Any minute nipple-like protuberance, usu. soft and fleshy, in a part or organ of the body: e. g. the papillæ on the tongue 1713. **c.** *Path.* A small papule or pimple 1797. **2.** *Bot.* A small fleshy projection upon any part of a plant 1848. So **Papillar** (pæ·pilăɹ, păpi·lăɹ), **Papillary** (pæ·pilări, păpi·lări) *adjs.* of the form or nature of a p.; containing, furnished with, or consisting of papillæ; of, pertaining to, or affecting papillæ. **Pa·pillate(d** *a.* furnished or covered with papillæ; formed into a p., papillary. **Papilli·ferous** *a.* bearing papillæ. **Papi·lliform** *a.* of the form of a p.; nipple-shaped. **Pa·pillose** *a.* full of or beset with papillæ. **Papi·llous** *a.* (now *rare* or *Obs.*), papillose.

‖ **Papillitis** (pæpiləi·tis). 1892. [mod.L.; see prec. and -ITIS.] *Path.* Inflammation of the optic papilla.

‖ **Papilloma** (pæpilōᵘ·mă). *Pl.* **-ata.** 1866. [f. PAPILLA + -OMA.] *Path.* A tumour of the skin or of a mucous membrane, consisting of an overgrown papilla or group of papillæ, usu. covered with a layer of thickened epidermis or epithelium; e. g. a wart, corn, condyloma, etc. Hence **Papillo·matous** *a.* of, pertaining to, or of the nature of a p.

†**Papillote** (pæ·pilǫᵘt, -ǫt). 1748. [a. F., app. f. **papilloter*, app. f. *papillon* butterfly.] A curl-paper –1845.

Papillule (pæ·pilɩul). 1826. Also in L. form. [ad. mod.L. *papillula*, dim. of PAPILLA.] A minute papilla; esp. a small elevation or depression with a minute papilla in the centre. Hence **Papi·llulate** *a.* beset with papillules.

Papish (pēⁱ·piʃ), *a.* and *sb.* Now *dial.* 1546. [app. f. *pape*, dial. form of POPE.] **A.** *adj.* Papistical, popish. (A hostile epithet.) **B.** *sb.* = PAPIST. Now *dial.* 1604. So †**Pa·pisher** = B.

Papism (pēⁱ·piz'm). 1550. [a. F. *papisme*, or ad. 16th c. L. *papismus*, f. as next + -ISM.] The papal system; popery; Roman Catholicism.

Papist (pēⁱ·pist). 1534. [a. F. *papiste*, or ad. 16th c. L. *papista*, f. *papa* pope; see -IST.] **1.** An adherent of the pope; esp. an advocate of papal supremacy; also, more gen., a member of the Roman Catholic Church. (Usu. hostile or opprobrious.) **2.** *attrib.* or quasi-*adj.* = PAPAL 1819.

Papistic (păpi·stik), *a.* 1545. [f. as prec. + -IC.] Of, pertaining to, or of the nature of a papist or papists; adhering to the pope; of, pertaining or adhering to, the Church of Rome and its doctrines; popish. (Usu. hostile or opprobrious). So **Papi·stical** *a.* 1537, **-ly** *adv.* 1572.

Papistry (pēⁱ·pistri). 15.. [f. PAPIST + -RY.] The doctrine or system of papists; popery; the Roman Catholic religion or faith. (A hostile term.)

†**Pa·pize,** *v.* 1612. [f. L. *papa* POPE *sb.*[1] + -IZE.] **a.** *intr.* To play the pope; to act on the side of the pope or papal system; **b.** *trans.* To render papal or popish. Hence †**Pa·pized** *ppl. a.* imbued with popery. †**Pa·pizing** *vbl. sb.* and *ppl. a.* –1843.

‖ **Papoose** (păpū·s). 1634. [Algonquin.] A North-American Indian young child.

‖ **Papoosh, papouch(e** (păpū·ʃ). 1682. [a. Pers. *pāpōsh* slipper, shoe, f. *pā* foot + *pōsh* covering.] A Turkish or Oriental slipper.

Pappescent (pæ̆pe·sĕnt), *a.* Also *erron.* papesc-. 1720. [f. L. *pappus*; see -ESCENT.] *Bot.* Producing a pappus, as composite plants.

Pappose (pæpǭᵘ·s), *a.* 1691. [See next and -OSE.] *Bot.* Furnished with or of the nature of a pappus, downy. So **Pa·ppous** *a.*

‖ **Pappus** (pæ·pŏs). 1704. [mod.L., a. Gr. πάππος.] *Bot.* The downy or feathery appendage on certain fruits, esp. on the achenes or 'seeds' of many *Compositæ*, as thistles, dandelions, etc.; hence extended to the reduced calyx of *Compositæ* generally, whether downy, bristly, scaly, toothed, or membranous.

Pa·ppy, *a.* 1670. [f. PAP *sb.*[2] + -Y [1].] Of the nature or consistence of pap; soft and wet.

‖ **Paprika** (pæ·prĭkă, pæprī·kă). 1898. [Magyar.] A condiment prepared from the fruit of the *Capsicum annuum*; Hungarian red pepper.

‖ **Papula** (pæ·piŭlă). *Pl.* **-æ.** 1706. [L., = pustule, pimple, app. from a root *pap-* to swell.] = PAPULE. Hence **Pa·pular** *a.*

Papulation (pæpiulēⁱ·ʃən). 1877. [f. L. *papulare*, f. prec.] The formation of papules.

Papule (pæ·piul). 1864. [ad. L. *papula*; cf. F. *papule*.] **1.** *Path.* A small, solid, somewhat pointed swelling of the skin, usu. inflammatory, without suppuration; a pimple. **2.** *Zool.* and *Bot.* = PAPILLA 1 b, 2. 1872.

Papulo- (pæ·piulo), used as comb. form of PAPULA, PAPULE; as in **Pa:pulo-erythe·ma,** erythema accompanied by papules; etc.

Papulose (pæ·piulōᵘs), *a.* 1776. [ad. mod. L. *papulosus*; see PAPULA and -OSE.] Covered with papules or papillæ; papillose.

Papulous (pæ·piuləs), *a.* 1818. [f. as prec. + -OUS.] Covered with papules, papulose; of the nature of a papule.

Papyraceous (pæpirēⁱ·ʃəs), *a.* 1752. [f. L. *papyrus* (see PAPER) + -ACEOUS.] *Nat. Hist.* Of the thinness or nature of paper; papery.

Papyrian (păpi·riăn), *a.* Also **-ean.** 1754. [f. L. *papyrius* of papyrus + -AN.] Pertaining to or composed of papyrus.

Papyrin (pæ·pirin). Also **-ine.** 1860. [mod. f. L. *papyrus* (see PAPER) + -IN [1].] = PARCHMENT *paper*.

Papyrine (păpəi·rin), *a.* 1816. [ad. L. *papyrinus* of papyrus; see -INE [2].] Made of papyrus.

Papyro-, comb. form of Gr. πάπυρος PAPYRUS (also in sense 'paper'); as in **Papy·rotype,** name given to a modification of photolithography, in which the picture is first printed on a sensitized gelatin film supported on paper, and afterwards transferred to a lithographic stone or to zinc.

Papyrograph (păpəi·rŏgraf), *sb.* 1877. [f. PAPYRO- + -GRAPH.] Name of an apparatus for copying documents by chemical agents acting through a porous paper-stencil. Hence **Papy·rograph** *v. trans.* to copy with a p. **Pa·pyrogra·phic** *a.* pertaining to or produced by a p. or papyrography.

Papyrography (pæpirǫ·grăfi). 1848. [f. PAPYRO- + -GRAPHY.] A process of writing or drawing on paper and transferring the design to a zinc plate whence it is printed. **b.** The process of copying with a papyrograph.

Papyrology (pæpirǫ·lŏdʒi). 1898. [f. PAPYRO- + -LOGY.] The study of papyri. Hence **Papyro·logist.**

‖ **Papyrus** (păpəi·rŏs). *Pl.* **papyri** (-əi·rəi). late ME. [L., a. Gr. πάπυρος.] **1.** An aquatic plant of the sedge family, the Paper Reed or Paper Rush (*Cyperus Papyrus* or *Papyrus antiquorum*); formerly abundant in Egypt. **2.** A substance prepared, in the form of thin sheets, from the stem of the papyrus plant, by laying thin slices or strips of it side by side, with another layer crossing them, and usually a third layer again parallel to the first, the whole being then soaked in water pressed together, and dried; used by the ancient Egyptians, Greeks, Romans, etc., as a writing material 1727. **3.** (With pl. *papyri*.) An ancient manuscript or document written on papyrus 1824. **4.** *attrib.* 1837.

2. The few rolls of p. which the ancients deemed a notable collection of books LYTTON. 3. Those Biblical codices which most resemble the Herculanean papyri 1875.

Par (pāɹ), *sb.*[1] 1622. [a. L., equal, equality.] **1.** Equality of value or standing; an equal footing, a level. Now chiefly in *on* or *upon a p.* 1662. **2.** *Comm.* **a.** The recognized value of the currency of one country in terms of that of another; in full, *p. of exchange*: see EXCHANGE *sb.* 4. 1622. **b.** Equality between the market value of stocks, shares, etc., and the nominal or face value 1726. **c.** *attrib.* *P. value* = value at par 1861. **3.** An average or normal amount, quality, degree, or condition 1778. **4.** *Golf.* The number of strokes a scratch player should require for a hole or the course, calculated according to a formula, and usu. less than BOGEY 1898.

2. b. Phr. *At p.*, at the face value; *above p.*, at a price above the face value, at a premium; *below p.*, at a discount. 3. *On a p.*, on an average. *Above* or *below* (*under*) *p.*, above or below the average, normal, or usual amount, degree, condition, or quality; I think he caught a chill, and being below p. he succumbed 1886. So *up to p.*; I am about up to p., and not without hope [etc.] 1899.

Par (pāɹ), *sb.*[2] *colloq.* 1879. Abbrev. of *paragraph.*

‖ **Par** (par, pāɹ), *prep.* ME. [F., :—L. *per* through, etc.] **1.** Occurring in ME. in certain asseverations (mostly obs.), as *par charite* (where it was sometimes confused with OF. *pur*, F. *pour* :—L. *pro* for). **b.** See PERADVENTURE (*par aunter*), PARAMOUNT, PARAVAIL, PARAVANT, PERCASE, etc., which have coalesced into single words. **2.** In mod. Eng., in advb. phrases from mod.Fr., often hardly naturalized. Such are PARBLEU; *par exemple*, for instance; *par force* = PERFORCE *adv.* 1597. ‖**b. Par excellence** [L. *per excellentiam*], by virtue of manifest superiority; pre-eminently; above all others that may be so called 1695.

Par-, *prefix*, repr. F. *par-*, L. *per-* 'through, thoroughly', occurring in words from Fr., as PARBOIL, PARDON, PARVENU; esp. common in ME. in words now obs., or in which *par-* has now become PER- after L., as *parfit* PERFECT, etc.

Par, var. PARR.

‖ **Para** [1] (pā·rā). 1687. [Turkish (Pers.) *pārah* lit. piece.] A small Turkish coin, the fortieth part of a piastre, formerly of silver, but now of copper, and of the value of about one-twentieth of a penny.

‖ **Para** [2] (pā·rā). Also **parra, parah.** 1698. [Hindī.] An East Indian measure of capacity; also a weight of North Borneo.

‖ **Pará** [3] (parā·, pā·rā). 1848. Name of a seaport on the south estuary of the Amazon, in Brazil. Used *attrib.*, esp. in **P. grass,** a Brazilian forage-grass, *Panicum barbinode*, now cultivated in the Southern U. S. **P. nut** = Brazil-nut: see BRAZIL 4. **P. rubber,** an india-rubber obtained from the coagulated milky juice of *Hevea brasiliensis* (N.O. *Euphorbiaceæ*), a tree growing on the banks of the Amazon.

Para- [1] (pæră), bef. a vowel or *h* usually **par-**, repr. Gr. παρα-, παρ-, comb. form of παρά *prep.* As a prep., Gr. παρά had the sense 'by the side of, beside', whence 'alongside of, by, past, beyond', etc. In composition it had the same senses, with such cognate advb. ones as 'to one side, amiss, faulty, irregular, disordered, improper, wrong'; also expressing subsidiary relation, alteration, perversion, simulation, etc. These senses also occur in Eng. derivs.; see below and PARABLE, PARADOX, PARASITE; PARALLEL; PARENTHESIS; PARHELION; PARISH; PAROCHIAL, PARODY, PAROXYSM, etc.

1. Terms (sbs. or adjs.) chiefly *Anat.*, *Nat. Hist.*, and *Path.*, as **Paraba·sal** *a. Zool.* in crinoids, situated next to and articulated with a basal plate; also as *sb.* **Pa·rablast** [Gr. βλαστός sprout, germ], *Embryol.* the nutritive yolk of a meroblastic ovum, as dist. from the formative yolk or archiblast; hence **Parabla·stic** *a.* ‖**Parabra·nchia,** the modified osphradium of certain gastropod molluscs, considered as a secondary branchia or gill; hence **Parabra·nchial, Parabra·nchiate** *adjs.* **Parace·ntral** *a.* situated beside a centre; in *Anat.* applied to parts of the brain lying alongside the central fissure. **Paracho·rdal** *a. Embryol.* situated beside the notochord: applied to two plates of cartilage, forming the foundation of the skull in the embryo; also as *sb.* **Pa·racyst** *Bot.* one of a pair of sexual organs in certain fungi. ‖**Paræsthe·sia** *Path.* disordered or perverted sensation; a hallucination of any of the senses. **Pa·ragaster** [Gr. γαστήρ belly, stomach] *Zool.* the central or gastric cavity of a simple sponge. **Paraga·stric** *a. Zool.* (*a*) situated alongside the stomach or gastric cavity, as certain canals in *Ctenophora*; (*b*) pertaining to the paragaster of a sponge. ‖**Paraglo·ssa** [Gr. γλῶσσα tongue] *Entom.* each of two lateral appendages of the ligula in various insects; hence **Paraglo·ssal, Paraglo·ssate** *adjs.* **Para·gnathous** [Gr. γνάθος jaw] *a. Ornith.* having the mandibles of equal length. **Pa·raheliotro·pic** [Gr. ἥλιος sun, -τροπος turning] *a. Bot.* of leaves: turning their edges in the direction of incident light. **Pa·rahelio·tropism** *Bot.* a tendency in plants when exposed to brilliant light to turn their leaves parallel to the incidence of the light-rays. **Parama·stoid** *a. Anat.* situated near the mastoid process: applied to certain processes of the occipital bone, also called *paroccipital*; also as *sb.* **Paranu·cleus** *Biol.* a small subsidiary nucleus in certain *Protozoa*; hence **Paranu·clear, Paranu·cleate** *adjs.* ‖**Paraphimo·sis** *Path.* permanent retraction of the prepuce. ‖**Paraphra·sia** *Path.* incoherent or disordered speech. ‖**Para·physis** [Gr. φύσις growth], a sterile filament accompanying the reproductive organs in certain cryptogams. **Pa·raplasm** *Biol.* (*a*) Kupffer's name for the more fluid part of a cell-substance; (*b*) a neoplasm; hence **Parapla·smic, Parapla·stic** *adjs.* ‖**Parapo·dium** [Gr. ποδ- foot] *Zool.* one of the jointless lateral processes or rudimentary limbs of annelids, which serve as organs of locomotion, and sometimes of sensation or respiration; hence **Parapo·dial** *a.* ‖**Parapo·physis** [APOPHYSIS] *Anat.* an interior or ventral transverse process of a vertebra, in some animals serving as articulation for the head of a rib. **Paraspheˑnoid** *a. Zool.* and *Comp. Anat.* lying alongside the sphenoid bone; applied to a bone extending in the median line along the base of the skull in birds, reptiles, amphibians, and fishes; also as *sb.* **Paraste·rnal** [STERNUM] *a.* lying alongside the sternum or breastbone; in *p. line*, a line drawn vertically down the surface of the chest from a point in the collarbone one-third of its length from its inner end. **Para·stichy** [Gr. στίχος row, rank] *Bot.* a secondary spiral or oblique rank of lateral members around the stem or axis, in a phyllotaxis in which the leaves, scales, etc. are close together, as in certain leaf-rosettes, pine-cones, etc. **Parathe·rmic** [Gr. θερμός warm, hot] *a.* name given by Sir J. Herschel to invisible rays accompanying the orange and red rays in the spectrum, so called in ref. to the neighbouring thermic or heat rays. **Parathy·roid,** one of several bodies adjacent to the thyroid gland. **Parato·nic** *a. Bot.* pertaining to the effect of light or other external stimuli in causing movements or influencing growth in plants. **Paratri·ptic** [Gr. τριπτ-, f. τρίβειν to rub] *a.* having the property of preventing waste of bodily tissue; also as *sb.* **Para·xial** *a. Anat.* and *Zool.* lying alongside, or on each side of, the axis of the body. ‖**Parazo·a** [Gr. ζῷον animal] *sb. pl. Zool.* in some classifications, a name for the Sponges considered as a division co-ordinate with *Protozoa* and *Metazoa*; hence **Parazo·an** *a.* and *sb.* **Parelectro·nomy** *Physiol.* a condition marked by weakening of the electrical current of muscle; hence **Parelectrono·mic** *a.* ‖**Parepidi·dymis** [EPIDIDYMIS] *Anat.* the organ of Giraldes, a mass of convoluted tubules just above the epididymis. **Parocci·pital** *a. Anat.* situated at the side of the occiput, or beside the occipital bone; applied *spec.* to certain bones, or processes of bone (also called *paramastoid*), as the jugular process of the occipital bone; also as *sb.* ‖**Paroophoron** (pærọ|ǫ·fǒrǫn) [mod. L. *oophoron* ovary] *Anat.* (*a*) = *parovarium*; (*b*) a small remnant of the Wolffian body in the female, corresp. to the parepididymis. **Paro·rchid** [Gr. ὄρχις testicle] *Anat.* the epididymis. ‖**Parova·rium** *Anat.* a remnant of the Wolffian body in the female, corresp. to the epididymis in the male. **Parumbi·lical** [L. *umbilicus* navel] *a. Anat.* situated around or near the navel.

2. *Chem.* **a.** Names of substances that are (or have been supposed to be) modifications of those to the names of which *para-* is prefixed, or that have been produced along with or instead of these, or, sometimes, that merely occur with them, as **Parabe·nzene,** a hydrocarbon isomeric with benzene, occurring along with it in light coal oil. **Parachlo·ralide,** an isomer of chloral produced by the action of chloral on wood spirit. **Paracya·nogen,** an isomer or polymer of cyanogen, formed in small quantity when cyanogen is prepared from cyanide of mercury. **Paraglo·bulin,** a name given to distinguish the particular form of GLOBULIN found in blood-serum. **Parala·ctic** *a.* in *p. acid*, an isomeric modification of lactic acid, one of the two constituents of sarcolactic acid. **Para·ldehyde,** a polymer of ALDEHYDE, used as a narcotic and as a remedy against insomnia.

b. (More systematically) Names of isomeric benzene di-derivatives in which the two hydrogen-atoms replaced by another element or radical are symmetrically disposed in the benzene ring, being separated on each side by two other atoms; as 1 and 4 in the ring $1^{23}_{65}4$; e.g. *paradichlorobenzene*, $C_6ClHHClHH$. These are unlimited in number.

3. Other terms, often a. or ad. Gr. words, as **Pa·rachrose** [as if f. Gr. χρῶσις colouring] *a. Min.* that changes colour by exposure to weather. ‖**Paradiastole** (-dəi|æ·stǒlī) [L., a. Gr. παραδιαστολή] *Rhet.* a figure in which a favourable turn is given to something unfavourable by the use of an expression that conveys only part of the truth. **Paradiploma·tic** *a.* aside or apart from what is strictly diplomatic or concerned with the evidence of the manuscript texts. **Paradro·mic** [f. Gr. παράδρομος] *a.* running side by side; *p. winding*, winding in courses that run side by side. **Pa·ramorph** [Gr. μορφή form] *Min.* a pseudomorph formed by a change of physical characters without a change in chemical composition; hence **Paramo·rphic** *a.*, **Paramo·rphism.** **Paranate·llon** [Gr. ἀνατέλλων rising] *Astrol.* a star that rises at the same time as another star or other stars. **Pa·rascene** [Gr. παρασκήνιον] *Gr.* and *Rom. Antiq.* the part of an ancient theatre on either side of the stage, comprising rooms to which the actors retired. **Paraschema·tic** *a.* (*rare*) formed by a slight change of an existing element. ‖**Parasy·nesis** [Gr. παρασύνεσις] *Philol.* misunderstanding or misconception of a word, resulting in an alteration or corruption of it; hence **Parasyne·tic** *a.* ‖**Parata·xis** [Gr. παράταξις] *Gram.* the placing of propositions or clauses one after another, without indicating by connecting words the relation between them; opp. to *hypotaxis*; hence **Parata·ctic, -al** *adjs.* ‖**Parembole** (-e·mbǒlī) [Gr. παρεμβολή] *Rhet.* a kind of parenthesis. ‖**Parempto·sis** [Gr. παρέμπτωσις] = *parembole*.

Para-[2], a. F., a. It. *para-*, imperative of vb. *parare* to defend, cover from, shield, etc., orig. 'to prepare':—L. *parare* PARE *v.*; used with a sb. object, in phrases which have themselves become sbs., as *para-sole* lit. 'defend or shelter from sun', hence 'a sun-shade', etc.; on the analogy of these were formed F. *parapluie*, *parachute*, etc. Thence English has PARAPET, PARACHUTE, PARASOL, etc., with occasional unnaturalized formations, as **parapluie** [F. *pluie* rain], umbrella; **paratonnerre** [F. *tonnerre* thunder], a lightning conductor.

Parabanic (pæræbæ·nik), *a.* 1838. [f. PARA-[1], prob. in sense 'instead of' + (*allox*)*anic*, with euphonic *b*.] *Chem.* In *p. acid*, a dibasic acid, CO.2 (NH.CO), produced by the action of nitric acid on uric acid or alloxan. Hence **Pa·rabanate,** a salt of p. acid.

‖**Parabasis** (pǎræ·bǎsis). *Pl.* **-bases** (-bǎsīz). 1820. [a. Gr. παράβασις, f. παραβαίνειν to go aside, digress.] In ancient Gr. comedy, a part sung by the chorus, addressed to the audience in the poet's name, and unconnected with the action of the drama.

Parable (pæ·răb'l), *sb.* [ME. a. F. *parabole*, ad. L. *parabola* comparison; in Christian L., allegory, proverb, talk, a. Gr. παραβολή a placing side by side, f. παρα- beside + βάλλειν to cast, put.] A comparison, a similitude; any saying or narration in which something is expressed in terms of something else; an allegory, an apologue. Also, any kind of enigmatical or dark saying. *arch.* (exc. as in b). **b.** *spec.* A fictitious narrative (usually of something that might naturally occur), by which moral or spiritual relations are typically set forth, as the parables of the New Testament. late ME. **c.** *dial.* An example or illustration (to follow or avoid) 1800.

Doubtless ye will say unto me this p., Physician, heal thyself N.T. (R.V.) *Luke* iv. 23. Phr. *To take up one's p.*, to begin to discourse (*arch.*). †*Parables of Solomon*, the book of Proverbs. **b.** Heare ye therefore the p. of the sower *Matt.* xiii. 18. Hence **Pa·rable** *v.* (*rare*) *intr.* to speak or discourse in parables; *trans.* to represent or express by means of a p.

†**Pa·rable,** *a.* 1581. [ad. L. *parabilis*, f. *parare* to procure; see -BLE.] That can be readily prepared or procured -1741.

Parabola (pǎræ·bǒlǎ). 1579. [a. 16th c. L., a. Gr. παραβολή juxtaposition, application, comparison; cf. PARABLE. See note in N.E.D.] *Geom.* One of the conic sections; the plane curve formed by the intersection of a cone with a plane parallel to a side of the cone; also definable as the locus of a point whose distance from a given point (the focus) is equal to its distance from a given straight line (the directrix). **b.** Extended to curves of higher degrees resembling a parabola in running off to infinity without approaching to an asymptote, or having the line at infinity as a tangent 1664.

Cubic or *cubical p.*, a p. of the third degree. *Double p.*, a p. having the line at infinity for a double tangent. Hence **Parabo·liform** *a.* of the form of a p.

‖**Parabole** (pǎræ·bǒlī). 1589. [a. Gr. παραβολή PARABLE.] *Rhet.* A comparison, a metaphor (in the widest sense).

Parabolic (pærǎbǫ·lik), *a.* and *sb.* 1449. [ad. late L. *parabolicus*, a. late Gr. παραβολικός figurative, f. παραβολή PARABLE, PARABOLA.] **A.** *adj.* **1.** Of, pertaining to, or of the nature of a parable. **b.** Of or pertaining to parabole; metaphorical 1696. **2.** *Geom.* Of the form of, or resembling, a parabola; of which the section is a parabola: also, having relation to the parabola 1702.

1. The P. Teaching of Christ 1882. 2. *P. reflector*, a reflector, usu. of polished metal, made in the form of a paraboloid of circular section, so as to reflect parallel rays to a focus, or reflect in parallel lines the rays of a lamp placed at the focus. *P. spindle*, a figure formed by the revolution of an arc of a parabola about its (double) ordinate. *P. spiral* = HELICOID parabola.

B. *sb. Geom.* A parabolic figure; a parabola or paraboloid (*rare*) -1807.

Parabolical (pærǎbǫ·likǎl), *a.* 1554. [See -ICAL.] **1.** Of or pertaining to parable; involving, or constituting parable; having a figurative existence or value. **2.** *Geom.* = prec. A. 2. Now *rare.* 1571. Hence **Parabo·lically** *adv.*

Parabolist (pǎræ·bǒlist). 1651. [f. Gr. παραβολή PARABLE, PARABOLA + -IST.] **1.** One who deals in any way with parables or parabole. **2.** One who deals with the parabola 1831.

Parabolize (pǎræ·bǒləiz), *v.* 1600. [-IZE.] **1.** *trans.* To express in a parable. Also *absol.* **2.** To make parabolic or paraboloidal in shape 1890. Hence **Para·bolizer.**

Paraboloid (pǎræ·bǒloid), *sb.* (*a.*) 1656. [f. PARABOLA + -OID.] **A.** †**1.** = PARABOLA b. -1710. **2.** A solid or surface of the second degree, some of whose plane sections are parabolas; formerly restricted to that of circular section, generated by the revolution of a parabola about its axis, now called *p. of revolution* 1702. **B.** *adj.* Paraboloidal (*rare*) 1857. So **Paraboloi·dal** *a.* of the form of a p. 1825.

Paracelsian (pærǎse·lsiǎn). 1574. [f. proper name *Paracelsus* + -IAN.] **A.** *sb.* A follower of the Swiss physician, chemist, and natural philosopher Philippus Aureolus Paracelsus, i.e. Theophrastus Bombast von Hohenheim (1490–1541), or of his medical or philosophical principles; in the former sense opp. to GALENIST. **B.** *adj.* Of, pertaining to, or characteristic of Paracelsus 1617. Hence **Parace·lsianism,** the medical principles of Paracelsus. So **Parace·lsist** *sb.*

‖**Paracentesis** (pærǎsentī·sis). 1597. [L., a. Gr. παρακέντησις, f. παρακεντεῖν, f. παρα- PARA-[1] 1 + κεντεῖν to prick, stab.] *Surg.* The perforation of some cavity of the body, esp. for the removal of fluid or gas; tapping.

Paracentric (pærǎse·ntrik), *a.* 1704. [See PARA-[1] and CENTRIC.] Lying unevenly about a centre. **b.** Applied to the key or keyhole of a type of lock with longitudinal ribs and grooves.

P. motion (Kinetics), rendering *motus paracentricus* of Leibnitz, used by him to express that motion which, compounded with harmonic circulation, he supposed to make up the actual motion of a planet. So **Parace·ntrical** *a.*

Parachronism (pǟræ·krǫ̆niz'm). 1641. [f. Gr. παρα- PARA-[1] + χρόνος time + -ISM. Cf. F. *parachronisme*.] An error in chronology by which an event is referred to a later date than the true one. (Cf. ANACHRONISM.)

Parachute (pæră∫ū·t, pæ·ră∫ūt), *sb.* 1785. [a. F., f. PARA-[2] + *chute* fall.] **1.** An apparatus like a large umbrella used for descending safely from a great height in the air, esp. from a balloon or aeroplane. **2.** *gen.* Any contrivance, natural or artificial, serving to check a fall through the air, or to support something in the air; e.g. the expansible fold of skin or *patagium* of the flying squirrel 1833. **3.** *Mining.* A contrivance, such as a safety-catch, to prevent a too rapid descent of a cage in a shaft, or of the boring-rod in a boring 1881. Hence **Parachu·te** *v. trans.* to convey by means of a p.; *intr.* to descend by or as if by a p. **Parachu·tist.**

Paraclete (pæ·răklīt). 1450. [a. F. *paraclet*, ad. eccl. L. *paracletus*, a. Gr. παράκλητος advocate, one called to one's aid, f. παρακαλεῖν.] **1.** A title of the Holy Spirit (repr. Gr. παράκλητος in John xiv. 16, 26, etc.); prop. 'an advocate, an intercessor', but often taken as = 'comforter'. Also (rarely) repr. Gr. παράκλητος 'advocate' as applied to Christ (1 John ii. 1). †**2.** *gen.* An advocate or intercessor –1701.

1. The P., the Holy Ghost, whom the Father will send in my name N.T. (Rhem.) *John* xiv. 26.

‖**Paracme** (păræ·kmī). 1706. [a. Gr. παρακμή, f. παρα- past + ἀκμή ACME.] A point or period at which the prime is past; the point when the crisis of a fever is past. So **Parac·ma·stic** *a.* past the culmination or crisis.

†**Para·da, -a·do.** 1621. [Altered form (see -ADO 2) of F. *parade*.] = PARADE *sb.* –1690.

Parade (părē̆·d), *sb.* 1656. [a. F., ad. It. *parata*, Sp. *parada* = L. type **parata*, from *parare* to make ready, adorn.] **1.** Show, display, ostentation. **2.** A muster of troops for inspection or display; esp. one which takes place regularly at set hours or for any special purpose 1656. **3.** A march or procession; esp. in *U.S.* one organized on a grand scale, for some political purpose 1673. **b.** A crowd of promenaders 1722. **4.** A parade-ground 1704. **5.** A public square or promenade 1697. **6.** *Fencing.* = PARRY. [F. *parade*.] 1692.

1. *To make a p. of*, to display ostentatiously; Making an empty p. of knowledge which we do not really possess 1789. 3. The Rites perform'd, the Parson paid, In State return'd the grand P. SWIFT. 6. *fig.* Marks, which serve best to shew, what they [men] are..especially when they are not in P. and upon their Guard LOCKE. *Comb.* **p.-ground**, the place where troops assemble for p.

Parade (părē̆·d), *v.* 1686. [f. prec.] **1.** *trans.* To assemble (troops, etc.) for inspection or review. **2.** *intr.* To march in procession or with great display; to promenade in a public place, esp. for the sake of 'showing off' 1748. **3.** *trans.* To march through (a place of public resort) in procession or with great display; to promenade (some place), esp. for the sake of 'showing off' 1809. **4.** To march (a person) about either for show or to expose him to contempt 1807. **5.** *intr.* To make a parade; to 'show off'. *rare* or *Obs.* 1754. **6.** *trans.* To make a parade of, to 'show off' 1818.

1. The troops were paraded WELLINGTON. 4. They set him on a camel and paraded him about the city BURTON. 6. The very last..to p. his feelings 1865. Hence **Para·der**, one who parades 1748.

Paradigm (pæ·rădəim, -dim). 1483. [a. F. *paradigme*, ad. L. *paradigma*, a. Gr. παράδειγμα pattern, f. παραδεικνύναι to show side by side.] **1.** A pattern, exemplar, example. **2.** An example or pattern of the inflexion of a noun, verb, or other part of speech 1599.

1. The Universe..was made exactly conformable to its Paradigme, or universal Exemplar 1669. Hence **Paradigmatic** (pæ·rădigmæ·tik) *a.* exemplary; †*sb.* one who writes lives of religious persons to serve as examples of Christian holiness (*rare*). †**Pa·radigma·tical** *a.*, **-ly** *adv.* So †**Paradi·gmatize** *v. trans.* to set forth as a model, to make an example of.

Paradisaic (pærădisē̆·ik), *a.* 1754. [Arbitrarily f. PARADISE or L. *paradisus*.] Paradisiacal. So **Paradisa·ical** *a.* 1623. **-ly** *adv.*

Paradisal (pærădəi·săl), *a.* 1560. [f. L. *paradisus*; see next and -AL.] Of or pertaining to Paradise.

Paradise (pæ·rădəis), *sb.* [ME. a. F. *paradis*, ad. L. *paradisus*, a. Gr. παράδεισος, a. OPers. *pairidaēza* enclosure, park, in mod.Pers. and Ar. *firdaus*, f. *pairi* around + *diz* to mould, form.] **1.** The garden of Eden. Also called *earthly p.*, to distinguish it from the *heavenly p.* **2.** Heaven, the abode of God and his angels and the final abode of the righteous. (Now chiefly *poet.*) ME. **b.** The Mohammedan heaven. late ME. **c.** An intermediate place or state where the departed souls of the righteous await resurrection and the last judgement (Luke xxiii. 43) 1690. **3.** A place like Paradise; a region of surpassing beauty, or of supreme bliss ME. **b.** *fig.* A state of supreme felicity. late ME. **4.** An oriental park or pleasure-ground, *esp.* one enclosing wild beasts for the chase. **b.** Hence, an English park in which foreign animals are kept. 1613. †**5.** A pleasure-garden; *spec.* the garden of a convent –1875. **6.** *slang.* The gallery of a theatre, where the 'gods' are 1873.

1. Bytwene the grete Inde & erthly paradyse CAXTON. *Apples of p.*, the fruit of the plantain, *Musa paradisiaca*. *Bird of p.*, see BIRD *sb.* *Grains of p.*, see GRAIN *sb.*[1] I. 4. 3. [Australia] is a rather overdone P. of the working man 1891. **b.** Comfort.. seems to many Englishmen the only real p. 1902.

attrib. and *Comb.*: **p. apple**, (*a*) a variety of apple; (*b*) the Forbidden Fruit or Pomello; †**p.-bird** = bird-of-paradise; see BIRD *sb.*; **-fish**, (*a*) a species of *Polynemus*, esteemed as food in India; (*b*) a brilliantly coloured E. Indian fish (*Macropodus viridi-auratus*) sometimes kept in aquariums; **-flycatcher**, a bird of the genus *Terpsiphone*, remarkable for the length of its middle tail-feathers; **p. stock**, a hardy slow-growing apple-tree used as a stock by nurserymen for dwarfing other varieties. Hence **Pa·radise** *v. trans.* to make into P.; to make supremely blessed or beautiful.

Paradisiac (pærădi·siæk, -di·ziæk), *a.* 1632. [ad.L. *paradisiacus*, a. Gr. παραδεισιακός, f. παράδεισος PARADISE.] Of, pertaining to, or belonging to Paradise; supremely blest; peacefully beautiful; celestial. So **Paradisiacal** (pærădisəi·ăkăl, -zəi·ăkăl) 1649, **Paradi·sial, Paradi·sian, Paradi·sic, -al** (*rare*), *adjs.* in same sense.

Parados (pæ·rădǫs, ‖paradǫ). 1834. [a. F., f. PARA-[2] + *dos* back.] *Fortif.* An elevation of earth behind fortified places, to secure them from any sudden attack from the rear.

Paradox (pæ·rădǫks), *sb.* 1540. [ad. (perh. through F. *paradoxe*) L. *paradoxum*, *-on*, sb., prop. neut. of *paradoxus*, Gr. παράδοξος adj. contrary to received opinion or expectation, f. παρα- PARA-[1] + δόξα opinion.] **1.** A statement or tenet contrary to received opinion or belief; sometimes with favourable, sometimes with unfavourable connotation. (In actual use rare since 17th c.) **2.** A statement seemingly self-contradictory or absurd, though possibly well-founded or essentially true 1569. **b.** Often applied to a proposition that is actually self-contradictory, and so essentially absurd or false 1570. **3.** (Without *a* or *pl.*) = PARADOXY 2. 1589. **4.** *transf.* A phenomenon that exhibits some conflict with preconceived notions of what is reasonable or possible; a person of perplexingly inconsistent life or behaviour 1625.

1. *Ham.* III. i. 115. That pleasant and true P. of the Annual Motion of the Earth 1653. 2. The legal p., that a libel may be the more a libel for being true COLERIDGE. **b.** It is therefore no p. to say that in some case the strength of a kingdom doth consist in the weakness of it FULLER. 3. The love of p. GIBBON. 4. *Hydrostatic p.*: see HYDROSTATIC I. Hence **Pa·radox** *v. rare*, to utter paradoxes. **Parado·xal** *a.* = PARADOXICAL *a.* **Pa·radoxer, Pa·radoxist**, a propounder of paradoxes.

Paradoxical (pærădǫ·ksikăl), *a.* 1581. [f. prec.; see -ICAL.] **1.** Of the nature of a paradox, exhibiting or involving paradox. **2.** Fond of or given to paradox 1613. **3.** Of a phenomenon, circumstance, etc.: Exhibiting some contradiction with known laws or with itself 1646.

1. Comedians, p. as it may seem, may be too natural LAMB. Hence **Pa·radoxica·lity**, p. character or quality. **Paradox·ical·ly** *adv.*, **-ness.**

Paradoxi·dian, *a.* 1882. [f. mod.L. *Paradoxides*, f. Gr. παράδοξος; see PARADOX and -IAN.] *Palæont.* Of or pertaining to the *Paradoxides*, a genus of large trilobites of the Middle Cambrian age.

Paradoxology (pærădǫksǫ·lŏdʒi). 1646. [ad. Gr. παραδοξολογία, f. παραδοξολόγος telling of paradoxes; see -LOGY.] A putting forward of paradoxical opinions, a speaking by paradox.

Paradoxure (pærădǫ·ksiuə̆ɹ). 1843. [ad. mod.L. *paradoxurus*, f. Gr. παράδοξος (see PARADOX) + οὐρά tail.] *Zool.* An animal of the genus *Paradoxurus*, family *Viverridæ*, or of an allied genus, so called because of its remarkably long curving tail; a palm-cat, -marten, or -civet.

So **Paradoxurine** (pærădǫ·ksiurəin) *a.* and *sb.* [mod.L. *Paradoxurinæ*] of or pertaining to (a member of) the sub-family *Paradoxurinæ*, of which *Paradoxurus* is the typical genus.

Paradoxy (pæ·rădǫksi). 1646. [ad. Gr. παραδοξία, f. παράδοξος; see PARADOX.] †**1.** A paradox SIR T. BROWNE. **2.** Paradoxical quality or character 1796.

‖**Parænesis, paren-** (părī·nĭsis, -e·nĭsis). 1604. [late L., a. Gr. παραίνεσις exhortation, f. παραινεῖν, f. παρα- PARA-[1] + αἰνεῖν to speak of, praise.] Exhortation, advice; a hortatory composition. Hence **Paræne·tic, -ene·tic, -al** *adjs.* hortatory, advisory.

Paraffin (pæ·răfin), *sb.* Also **-ine.** 1835. [irreg. f. L. *parum* too little, barely + *affinis* having affinity; so named by Reichenbach (1830) in ref. to its neutral quality and the small affinity it possesses for other bodies.] **1.** A colourless (or white), tasteless, inodorous, crystalline, fatty substance, solid at ordinary temperatures (chemically a mixture of hydrocarbons of the series C_nH_{2n+2}), discovered by Reichenbach in 1830; obtained by dry distillation from wood, coal, peat, petroleum, wax, etc., and also occurring native in coal and other bituminous strata; used for making candles, for electrical insulators, etc. **2.** Short for *p. oil* 1861. **3.** *Chem.* A general name for the saturated hydrocarbons of the series C_nH_{2n+2}, of which the first four members, methane, ethane, propane, quartane (see -ANE), are at ordinary temperatures gaseous, those higher in the series, oily liquids, and those higher still, solids; all are remarkable for their chemical indifference, the hydrogen being combined in the highest proportion possible with the carbon 1872.

attrib. and *Comb.*, as *p. candle, lamp.*; **p. oil**, any one of several oils obtained by distillation of coal, petroleum, etc., used as illuminants and lubricants; also called simply *paraffin*, *kerosene*, or *petroleum*; **p. wax**, solid p. (= sense 1). Hence **Pa·raffin** *v. trans.* to cover, impregnate, or treat with p.

†**Pa·rage.** ME. [a. F. *parage*, perh. f. L. *par* equal; see -AGE.] **1.** Lineage, descent, rank; *esp.* noble lineage –1652. **2.** Equality of birth or station –1670. **3.** (See quot.)

3. When a fief is divided among brothers;..the younger hold their part of the elder by P., i.e. without any homage or service...This P. being an equality of duty, or service among brothers or sisters CHAMBERS.

Paragenesis (pærădʒe·nėsis). 1855. [f. Gr. παρα- PARA-[1] + γένεσις GENESIS.] **1.** *Biol.* **a.** The production in an organism of characters belonging to two different species, as in hybridism 1890. **b.** *spec.* Hybridism in which the offspring is partially sterile 1892. **c.** A name for unusual or subsidiary modes of reproduction 1891. **2.** *Min.* The formation of minerals in close contact, whereby the development of the individual crystals is interfered with, and the whole locked together in a crystalline mass; the structure so formed as in granite or marble 1855. Hence **Paragene·sic** *a.* pertaining to or of the nature of p. (sense 1). **Paragene·tic** *a.* **a.** pertaining to or originating by p.; **b.** *Min.* originating side by side, as in *p. twin* (crystal); so **Parage·nic** *a.*

Paragoge (pærăgōu·dʒi). 1656. [a. L., a. Gr. παραγωγή a leading past, addition to the end of a syllable; f. παρα- PARA-[1] + ἀγωγή carrying, leading. In F. *paragoge*.] *Gram.* The addition of a letter or syllable to a word, either inorganically as in *peasan-t*, or, as in Hebrew, to give emphasis or modify the meaning. Hence **Parago·gic, -al** *adjs.* of, pertaining to, or of the nature of p.; (of a letter) added to a word by p.

Paragon (pæ·răgǫn), *sb.* (*a.*) 1548. [a. OF. *paragon*, now *parangon*, ad. It. *paragone* (also *parangone*); etym. obscure.] **I. 1.** A pattern of excellence; a person or thing of supreme excellence. †2. A match; a mate, companion; a consort in marriage; a competitor. (Also of a thing.) –1824. †3. Comparison; competition, emulation, rivalry –1664.

1. A p. of a wife 1833. The p. of easy-chairs 1861. 3. Of both their beauties to make paragone SPENS.

II. *spec.* and *techn.* 1. A perfect diamond; now applied to those weighing more than a hundred carats 1616. †Also *p.-stone* –1698. †2. A kind of double camlet –1739. †3. A kind of black marble –1839. 4. *Printing.* A large size of type intermediate between great primer and double pica, about 3¾ lines to the inch. Also called 'two-line long primer' 1706.

B. *adj.* (*attrib.* use of sb.) Of surpassing excellence 1601.

Those jewels were p., without flaw, hair, ice, or cloud SIR T. BROWNE.

Paragon (pæ·rǎgǫn), *v.* 1586. [f. prec.] 1. *trans.* To place side by side; to parallel, compare. (Now *arch.* or *poet.*) 2. To match, mate. (Now *poet.*, etc.) 1615. †3. To surpass SHAKS. †4. To set forth as a paragon or perfect model SHAKS. †5. *intr.* To compare, compete, vie *with* –1620.

1. Lucifer, so by allusion calld, Of that bright Starr to Satan paragond MILT. 3. A Maid That paragons description SHAKS. 5. Few or none could for Feature p. with her SHELTON.

Paragonite (pæ·rǎgǫnəit). 1849. [f. Gr. παράγων pr. pple. leading aside, misleading + -ITE[1].] *Min.* A hydrous mica containing sodium, and so dist. from common or potash mica (muscovite).

P.-schist, a mica-schist in which p. takes the place of muscovite. Hence **Paragoni·tic** *a.*

Pa·ragram. 1679. [f. Gr. phr. τὰ παρὰ γράμμα σκώμματα, lit. 'jokes by the letter'.] A kind of play upon words, consisting in the alteration of one letter or group of letters of a word. So **Paragra·mmatist**, a maker of paragrams.

Paragraph (pæ·rǎgrɑf), *sb.* 1490. [a. F. *paragraphe*, ad. late L. *paragraphus*, a. Gr. παράγραφος, orig. a short horizontal stroke drawn below the beginning of a line in which a break in the sense occurs; also = παραγραφή a passage so marked; f. παρα- PARA-[1] + -γραφος written, -GRAPH.] 1. A symbol or character (now usually ¶ or ⁋) formerly used to mark the commencement of a new section; now sometimes to introduce an editorial *obiter dictum*, or as a ref. to a marginal note or footnote 1538. 2. A distinct passage or section of a discourse, chapter, or book, dealing with a particular point, the words of a particular speaker, etc. This was at first usu. indicated by the mark described above; but subseq., as now, by beginning on a new line, which is indented, and ending without running on to the next passage. 1490. b. A distinct article or section of a law or legal document, usu. numbered 1552. 3. A short passage, notice, or article in a newspaper or journal; an item of news 1769. 4. *attrib.* 1769.

2. b. I beg your Lordship's particular attention..to the 13th p. of the instructions WELLINGTON. 3. Fresh and sparkling paragraphs of Court and fashionable gossip 1882. Hence **Paragra·phic, -al** *adjs.* of, pertaining to, or of the nature of a p. or paragraphs; **-ly** *adv.*

Paragraph (pæ·rǎgrɑf), *v.* 1601. [f. prec.] †1. *trans.* = PARAPH *v.* –1652. 2. To mention in a paragraph; to write a short notice about. Also *absol.* 1764. 3. To divide into or arrange in paragraphs. (Chiefly in *pass.*) 1799.

2. No one was more paragraphed and puffed 1880. Hence **Pa·ragrapher, Pa·ragraphist**, a professional writer of newspaper paragraphs.

Paraguay (pæ·rǎgwē̆ⁱ). 1727. [Name of a river and Republic of S. America.] The S. American shrub *Ilex paraguayensis*, commonly called MATÉ, the leaves of which are dried and roasted, and infused as a beverage in the same way as tea. Hence *P.-tea*.

Parakeet (pæ·rǎkīt, pærǎkī·t). Also **paroquet**, †**-quito**, †**-keeto**, etc. 1581. The historical forms are of three types: (*a*) a. OF. *paroquet*, F. *perroquet* parrot; (*b*) from its prob. source It. *parrochetto*, dim. of *parroco* parson (cf. F. *moineau* sparrow, fr. *moine* monk); (*c*) anglicized forms of these typified by *parakeet*.] A bird of the parrot kind; now *spec.* applied to the smaller birds included in the order, esp. those having long tails. b. Applied allusively to persons, i.e. in reference to the chattering of the birds, or to their gay plumage 1596.

‖ **Paralipomena** (pærǎləipǫ·mĕnǎ), *sb. pl.* Now rarely in sing. **paralipomenon** (-leip-). ME. [late L. *paralipomena*, genit. pl. *-ōn*, a. Gr. παραλειπόμενα (things) left out, neut. pl. pres. pass. pple. of παραλείπειν to omit.] †1. (usu. *Paralipomenon*, repr. genit. pl. Παραλειπομένων (sc. βιβλία), the title in LXX and hence in the Vulgate.) The Books of Chronicles in the O.T.; so called as containing particulars omitted in the Books of Kings –1706. 2. Things omitted in the body of a work, and appended as a supplement. (Rarely in sing. *-on*.) 1662.

‖ **Paralipsis** (pærǎli·psis). Also **-leipsis**; *erron.* **-lepsis, -lepsy.** 1586. [a. Gr. παράλειψις, f. παραλείπειν to pass over, omit.] *Rhet.* A figure in which the speaker emphasizes something by affecting to pass it by without notice, usu. by such phrases as 'not to mention', 'to say nothing of'.

Parallax (pæ·rǎlæks). 1594. [a. F. *parallaxe*, ad. Gr. παράλλαξις change, alternation, mutual inclination of two lines meeting in an angle, f. παραλλάσσειν to alter, alternate.] *Astron.* Apparent displacement, or difference in the apparent position, of an object, caused by actual change (or difference) of position of the point of observation; *spec.* the angular amount of such displacement or difference of position, being the angle contained between the two straight lines drawn to the object from the two different points of view, and constituting a measure of the distance of the object 1612. b. *fig.* 1594.

There are two kinds of p., viz. *diurnal* and *annual*, the former when a celestial object is observed from opposite points on the earth's *surface*, the latter when observed from opposite points of the earth's *orbit*. As the mean or proper position of the body is that which it would have if viewed in the one case from the earth's centre (or a point in a line with it), in the other case from the centre of its orbit, the p. is actually calculated and stated from these central points, and called *geocentric* and *heliocentric* respectively. *Horizontal p.*, the diurnal p. of a heavenly body seen on the horizon. b. The sort of p. which exhibits Whitman's fame at so different an angle in his own country and in England 1892. Hence **Paralla·ctic**, †**-al** *adjs.* pertaining, relating, or due to p.

Parallel (pæ·rălel), *a.* and *sb.* 1549. [a. F. *parallèle*, ad. L. *parallelus*, a. Gr. παράλληλος beside one another, f. παρα- PARA-[1] + ἀλλήλος one another.] A. *adj.* 1. Lying or extending alongside of one another and always at the same distance apart; also of one line, etc., Extending alongside another at a continuously equal distance (const. *to*, *with*). b. *transf.* Applied esp. to mechanical contrivances of which some essential parts are parallel, or which are used to produce parallellism of movement, etc. 1594. 2. *fig.* Having the same or a like course, tendency, or purport; precisely similar, analogous, or corresponding 1604. b. Side by side in time; contemporary in duration 1746. 3. *Mus.* a. Applied to parts which move so that the interval between them remains the same; also to the movement of such parts (*p. motion*), and to the interval between such parts (usu. called *consecutive*) 1864.

1. *P. lines* (Geom.), straight lines in the same plane, which never meet however far produced in any direction, or (in mod. geometry) which intersect at infinity. *P. bars*, a pair of bars supported on posts about 4 to 6 feet above the ground, used for gymnastic exercises. b. *P. circuit* (Electr.), a term loosely applied to a circuit connecting the same two points as are connected by another circuit; so *p. connexion*, etc. *P. motion*, (*a*) the motion of anything which always remains p. to itself, i.e. in the same direction; (*b*) a mechanical device by which alternating rectilinear is converted into circular motion, and *vice versa*. *P. perspective*, perspective in which the plane of the drawing is p. to a principal surface of the object delineated. *P. rod*, the rod which connects the cranks of the driving-wheels on the same side of a locomotive; the coupling-rod. *P. ruler* (or *rulers*), an instrument for drawing p. lines, consisting of two or more straight rulers connected by jointed cross-pieces so as to be always p., at whatever distance they are set. *P. sphere*, the celestial or terrestrial sphere in that position or aspect in which the equator is p. to the horizon, i.e. at either of the poles; dist. from *oblique* and *right sphere*. 2. Having observed it to happen before in a p. Case 1758. The p. passage in the ninth book 1875.

B. *sb.* I. 1. *pl.* Parallel lines (see A. 1); rarely in *sing.* a line parallel to another 1551. b. *pl.* Things running parallel 1589. 2. *Geog.* Each of the parallel circles imagined as traced upon the earth's surface, or actually drawn upon a map, in planes perpendicular to the axis, and marking the degrees of latitude; in full, *p. of latitude*. Also *Astron.* each of the corresponding circles on the celestial sphere (*parallels of declination*), or of smaller circles parallel to the ecliptic (*parallels of latitude*), or to the horizon (*parallels of altitude*). 1555. 3. *Mil.* In a siege: A trench (usu. one of three) parallel to the general face of the works attacked, serving as a way of communication between the different parts of the siege-works 1591. 4. *Printing.* A reference-mark consisting of two parallel vertical lines (‖) 1771. 5. *fig.* A thing or person agreeing with another in essential particulars (see A. 2); a counterpart, equal, match 1599.

1. Who made the spider parallels design, Sure as Demoivre, without rule or line? POPE. 2. *attrib. P. sailing* (Naut.), sailing along a p. of latitude, i.e. directly east or west. 5. Why, this is without p., this B. JONS.

II. 1. Parallel position; parallelism 1654. 2. *fig.* Agreement in all essential particulars; analogy, parallelism 1617. 3. Comparison, or a comparison; a statement of parallelism, a simile 1599.

1. Lines that from their P. decline 1699. 2. The two republics stand in continual p. HALLAM. *In p.* (Electr.), said of two or more circuit-wires connecting the same points. 3. You are drawing Parallels between the greatest Actors of the Age STEELE. Hence **Pa·rallelist**, one who draws a p. or comparison. So **Paralleli·stic** *a.* relating to or characterized by parallelism. **Pa·rallelly** *adv.*

Pa·rallel, *v.* 1598. [f. prec.] 1. *trans.* To place (one thing) beside another (const. *with*, *to*), or (two or more things) side by side mentally, so as to exhibit a likeness between them; to compare as being like. †2. To make parallel, equalize –1669. 3. To bring forward something parallel to; to match 1606. 4. To be parallel or equal to; to match 1601. †5. *intr.* To be parallel; to correspond; to 'compare' (*with*) –1657. 6. To run parallel with, run alongside of. (Chiefly *U.S.*) 1885.

1. [He] parallels to-day's outcry against Ritualism with yesterday's against Methodism 1881. 2. His life is paralel'd Euen with the stroke and line of his great Iustice SHAKS. 3. Well may we fight for her, whom .. The world's large spaces cannot paralell SHAKS. 6. He had then..crossed over a ridge that paralleled their rear KIPLING.

Parallelepiped (pærǎlele·piped); earlier in Gr. form **parallelepipedon** (pærǎlelǐpi·pĕdǫn), pl. **-a**. Often *erron.* **parallelo-**. 1570. [ad. Gr. παραλληλεπίπεδον, f. παράλληλος PARALLEL + ἐπίπεδον plane surface, adj. neut. used sb. (f. ἐπί upon + πέδον ground).] A solid figure contained by six parallelograms, of which every two opposite ones are parallel; a prism whose base is a parallelogram. Hence **Parallelepi·pedal** *a.* having the form of a p.

Parallelism (pæ·răleliz'm). 1610. [ad. Gr. παραλληλισμός comparison of parallels, f. παραλληλίζειν to PARALLEL.] 1. The state or position of being parallel; direction parallel *to* or *with* something. b. The state or fact of remaining parallel to itself, *i.e.* of maintaining the same direction; constancy of direction 1666. 2. *fig.* The quality of being parallel (see PARALLEL *a.* A. 2) 1638. b. An instance of this; a parallel case, passage, etc. (Usu. in *pl.*) 1664. 3. *spec.* Correspondence, in sense or construction, of successive clauses or passages, esp. in Hebrew poetry; a passage exemplifying this 1778. †4. = PARALLEL *a.* B. II. 3. –1660.

2. This p. between the ancient or genuine Platonick and the Christian Trinity CUDWORTH. 3. The very laws of Hebrew composition which make the second phrase in a p. repeat the first in other words M. ARNOLD.

Parallelize (pæ·răleləiz), *v.* 1610. [ad. Gr. παραλληλίζειν, f. παράλληλος PARALLEL; see -IZE.] 1. *trans.* = PARALLEL *v.* 1. 1610. 2. = PARALLEL *v.* 3, 4. *rare.* 1634.

Parallelogram (pærăle·lǫgræm). 1570. [a. F. *parallélogramme*, ad. L. *parallelogrammum*,

a. Gr. παραλληλόγραμμον, f. παράλληλος PARALLEL + γραμμή line.] 1. *Geom.* A four-sided rectilineal figure whose opposite sides are parallel; occas. *spec.* applied to a rectangle. 2. Anything of the form of this figure, as a block of buildings, a space of ground (cf. *square*), a brick, card, domino, etc. 1820. †b. = PANTOGRAPH –1741.

1. *P. of forces* (Dynamics), a figure illustrating the theorem that if two forces acting at one point be represented in magnitude and direction by two sides of a p., their resultant will be similarly represented by the diagonal drawn from that point; hence, the theorem itself. Hence **Paralle·logramma·tic, Pa·rallelogra·mmic, -al** *adjs.* pertaining to, or of the form of, a p.

Paralogism (păræ·lŏdʒiz'm). 1565. [a. F. *paralogisme*, ad. late L. *paralogismus*, a. Gr., f. παραλογίζεσθαι to reason falsely; see -ISM.] A piece of false reasoning; a faulty syllogism; a fallacy, *esp.* (as dist. from a *sophism*) one of which the reasoner is himself unconscious. So **Para·logist**, one who commits a p. **Paralogi·stic** *a.* fallacious.

Paralogize (păræ·lŏdʒəiz), *v.* 1599. [ult. ad. Gr. παραλογίζεσθαι, f. παραλογία, f. παράλογος, f. παρά PARA-¹ + λόγος reason; see -IZE.] *intr.* To commit a paralogism; to reason falsely or illogically. So †**Para·logy**, faulty reasoning. **Paralo·gical** *a.* fallacious, illogical.

Paralyse, -ze (pæ·răləiz), *v.* 1804. [a. F. *paralyser*, f. *paralysie* (see PALSY). Cf. ANALYSE.] 1. *trans.* To affect with paralysis; to palsy. 2. *fig.* To deprive of power of action; to render helpless or ineffective; to cripple, deaden 1805.

2. His pride paralysed his love 1866. Hence **Pa·ralysa·tion. Pa·ralysed, Pa·ralysing** *ppl. adjs.*

Paralysis (păræ·lĭsis). 1525. [a. L., a. Gr. παράλυσις, f. παραλύειν to loose from beside, disable, f. παρα- PARA-¹ + λύειν to loose. The word occurs in OE. in the Gr.-L. acc. form. *paralisin*; the ME. form was *paralysie* PALSY.] 1. *Path.* An affection of the nervous system characterized by impairment or loss of the motor or sensory function of the nerves, esp. of those belonging to a particular part or organ, thus producing functional inactivity in such part. 2. *fig.* A condition of utter powerlessness, incapacity of action, or suspension of activity; the state of being 'crippled', helpless, or impotent 1813.

1. *Bell's p.*, etc.: see PALSY *sb.* *General p.* (*of the insane*), a disease characterized by a stage of mental excitement with exalted delusions, followed by dementia.

Paralytic (pærăli·tik), *a.* and *sb.* ME. [a. F. *paralytique*, ad. L. *paralyticus*, a. Gr. παραλυτικός, f. παραλύειν; see prec.] A. *adj.* 1. Affected with or subject to paralysis; palsied. 2. *fig.* Deprived of power of action; ineffective, characterized by impotency 1642. 3. Of the nature of or pertaining to paralysis 1818.

1. His shabby clothes and p. limb DICKENS. 3. A second p. attack 1818.

B. *sb.* A sufferer from paralysis, a palsied person. late ME.

General p., a sufferer from general paralysis. So †**Paraly·tical** *a.* –1788.

Param (pæ·ræm). 1866. [f. PARA-¹ 2 + AM(IDE.] *Chem.* A synonym of dicyanodiamide, a polymer of cyanamide.

Paramagnetic (pæ:rămægne·tik), *a.* 1851. [f. Gr. παρα- PARA-¹ + MAGNETIC.] Having the property of being attracted by the pole of a magnet, and hence, when suspended or placed freely in a magnetic field, of taking a position parallel to the lines of force; opp. to DIAMAGNETIC. Hence **Pa·ramagne·tically** *adv.* So **Parama·gnetism**, the quality of being p.; the phenomena exhibited by p. bodies.

Paramatta (pærămæ·tă). 1834. [f. *Paramatta* (prop. *Parramatta*) in New South Wales.] A light dress fabric having a weft of combed merino wool and a warp formerly of silk, but now usu. of cotton.

†**Pa·rament.** late ME. [a. OF. *parament*, f. L. *parare* to make ready, adorn, etc.; see -MENT.] An ornament, a decoration –1706. b. A decorated robe, a robe of state –1656.

b. Lordes in paramentz on hir courseres CHAUCER. So ‖**Parame·nto** = b.

Paramere (pæ·rămīᵊɹ). 1883. [f. Gr. παρα- PARA-¹ + μέρος part.] *Biol.* 1. One of a series of radiating parts or organs, as a ray of a star-fish; an actinomere. 2. Each of the halves of a bilaterally symmetrical animal, or of a segment or somite of such 1884. Hence **Parameric** (-me·rik) *a.*

Parameter (păræ·mĭtəɹ). 1656. [a. mod. L., in F. *paramètre*; f. Gr. παρα- PARA-¹ + μέτρον measure.] *Math.* 1. In conic sections: The third proportional to any given diameter and its conjugate (or, in the parabola, to any abscissa on a given diameter and the corresponding ordinate); this is the *p. of the given diameter. spec.* The parameter of the transverse axis (*principal p.* or *p. of the curve*), i.e. the latus rectum, or focal chord perpendicular to the axis. 2. *gen.* A quantity which is constant (as distinct from the ordinary variables) in a particular case considered, but which varies in different cases; *esp.* a constant occurring in the equation of a curve or surface, by the variation of which the equation is made to represent a family of such curves or surfaces 1852. †b. *Astron.* pl. The data necessary to determine the orbit of a heavenly body –1841. c. *Cryst.* Each of the intercepts made upon the axes in a crystal by the plane which is chosen for a face of the unit or primary pyramid 1839. Hence **Para·metral, Parame·tric, -al** *adjs.* of or pertaining to a p.

‖ **Paramo** (pa·ramo). 1760. [Sp. *páramo*; app. from a native name.] A high plateau in the tropical parts of S. America, bare of trees, and exposed to wind and thick cold fogs.

Paramount (pæ·rămaunt), *a.* (*sb.*) 1531. [a. AF. *paramont* above, f. OF. *par* by + *amont*, *à mont* adv., up, above :—L. *ad montem* to the mount or hill.] 1. Above in a scale of rank or authority; superior 1579. b. *gen.* Above all others in rank, order or jurisdiction; supreme 1531. 2. Superior *to* all others in influence, power, etc.; pre-eminent 1625. b. With ellipsis of *to* (now *rare* or *Obs.*) 1596.

1. *Lord p.*, lord superior, overlord; *spec.* the supreme lord of a fee; hence *transf.* one who exercises supreme power. So *lady p.*, a woman in supreme authority; also *transf.* the woman who has made the highest score in an archery tournament. b. To make Britain the p. power in India MACAULAY. 2. Their first duty..is p. to all subsequent engagements 1769. Matters of p. importance 1877. b. A Generall Councell is p. the Pope 1643.

B. *sb.* A lord paramount, overlord, supreme ruler or proprietor 1645. Hence **Pa·ramountly** *adv.* pre-eminently, above all. **Pa·ramoun(t)cy**, the condition or status of being p.

Paramour (pæ·rămūᵊɹ), *adv. phr.* and *sb.* [ME. a. OF. adv. phr. *par amour*, *-s*, by or through love. Early written as one word, and treated (in Eng.) as a sb.] A. *adv. phr.* †1. Through or by way of love; out of (your) love, for love's sake; *occas.*, Of your kindness, as a favour, if you please –1611. †2. For or by way of sexual love –1848. B. *sb.* †1. Love; *esp.* sexual love; an amour –1586. 2. A 'love', lover, sweetheart; also of animals and *fig.* (*arch.* and *poet.*) ME. †b. The lady-love of a knight, for whose love he did battle; hence, the object of chivalrous attachment (*poet.*) –1630. 3. An illicit lover or mistress taking the place, but without the rights, of a husband or wife. Now, the illicit partner of a man or woman. late ME.

B. 2. To wanton with the Sun her lusty P. MILT. b. Chloris, the queen of flowers:..The top of paramours B. JONS.

‖ **Parang** (pā·ræŋ). 1852. [Malay.] A large heavy sheath-knife used by the Malays as a weapon, etc.

‖ **Paranoia** (pæră̆noi·ă), **paranœa** (-nī·ă). 1857. [mod.L. a. Gr. παράνοια, f. παράνοος distracted, f. παρα- PARA-¹ + νόος, νοῦς mind.] *Path.* Mental derangement; *spec.* chronic mental unsoundness characterized by delusions and hallucinations. Hence **Paranoi·ac** *a.* afflicted with p.; also as *sb.*

Paranymph (pæ·rănimf). 1593. [ad. L. *paranymphus*, a. Gr. παράνυμφος, masc. the best man, fem. the bridesmaid, f. παρα- PARA-¹ + νύμφη bride.] 1. *Gr. Antiq.* The 'friend of the bridegroom', who accompanied him when he went to fetch home the bride; also, the bridesmaid who escorted the bride to the bridegroom; hence, a modern 'best man', or a bridesmaid 1600. 2. *transf.* and *fig.* A person or thing that woos or solicits for another; an advocate, spokesman, or orator, who speaks in behalf of another 1593.

Parapegm (pæ·răpem). Now usu. in Gr.-L. form **parapegma** (pærăpe·gmă). 1641. [ad. L. *parapegma*, pl. *-pegmata*, a. Gr. παράπηγμα, -πήγματα a thing fixed beside or near, f. παρα- PARA-¹ + πῆγμα anything fastened.] *Gr. Antiq.* A tablet set up with some public information or announcement, as a law, a proclamation, or a calendar of annals or astronomical observations; a canon, rule, or precept; a fixed date or epoch.

Parapet (pæ·răpĕt). 1590. [a. F., or It. *parapetto*, f. PARA-² + *petto* :—L. *pectus* breast.] *lit.* A defence breast-high, a breastwork. 1. *Mil.* A defence of earth or stone to cover troops from the enemy's observation and fire. 2. A low wall or barrier, placed at the edge of a platform, balcony, roof, etc., or along the sides of a bridge, pier, quay, etc., to prevent people from falling over 1598. b. *transf.* Anything resembling a parapet 1636.

Comb.: **p. line**, the line or level of the bottom of the p., esp. on a roof; **p. wall**, a low wall serving as a p. Hence **Pa·rapet** *v.* chiefly in **Pa·rapeted** *ppl. a.* furnished with or defended by a p.

Paraph (pæ·ræf), *sb.* late ME. [a. F. *paraphe*, *parafe* = med.L. *paraphus*, shortened f. *paragraphus* PARAGRAPH.] †1. A paragraph –1483. 2. *Diplomatics.* A flourish made after a signature, orig. as a precaution against forgery 1584. Hence **Pa·raph** *v.* to affix a p. to; hence to sign, esp. with initials, to initial 1667.

‖ **Parapherna** (pærăfə̄·ɹnă), *sb. pl.* 1706. [L., a. Gr. παράφερνα pl., f. παρα- PARA-¹ + φερνή dower.] 1. *Rom. Law.* Those articles of property held by a wife over and above the dowry she brought to her husband, and which remained under her own control. 2. = PARAPHERNALIA 2. 1876. Hence **Paraphe·rnal** *a.* of, belonging to, or of the nature of p.; also as *sb.* (serving as sing. to next).

Paraphernalia (pærăfəɹnē·liă), *sb. pl.* 1651. [a. med.L., short for *paraphernalia bona*, neut. pl. of *paraphernalis*, f. PARAPHERNA.] 1. *Law.* Those articles of personal property which the law allowed a married woman to keep and, to a certain extent, to deal with as her own. 2. Personal belongings, *esp.* articles of adornment or attire, trappings; appointments or appurtenances in general. Also as collect. sing. 1736.

2. The p. of justice,—the judge, and the jury, and the lawyers TROLLOPE.

‖ **Paraphonia** (pærăfōᵘ·niă). 1776. [med.L., f. Gr. παράφωνος sounding beside (f. παρα- + φωνή).] 1. *Gr. Mus.* The harmony or concord of fourths and fifths. 2. Alteration of the voice from physiological or pathological causes 1799.

Paraphragm (pæ·răfræm). 1877. [ad. Gr. παράφραγμα parapet.] *Zool.* One of the outer divisions of an endosternite in Crustacea. Hence **Paraphragmal** (pærăfræ·gmăl) *a.*

Paraphrase (pæ·răfrēⁱz), *sb.* 1548. [a. F., ad. L. *paraphrasis*, a. Gr. παράφρασις, f. παραφράζειν to tell the same thing in other words, f. παρα- PARA-¹ + φράζειν to declare, tell.] 1. An expression in other words of the sense of any passage or text; a free rendering or amplification of a passage. (Sometimes, by extension, of a musical passage.) b. Without *a* and *pl.*, as a process or mode of literary treatment 1656. †c. *fig.* A practical exemplification of or commentary upon some principle, maxim, etc. –1670. 2. In the Ch. of Scotland, etc.: Each of the hymns contained in the 'Translations and Paraphrases, in verse, of several passages of Sacred Scripture' usu. appended to the Metrical Psalter in Scottish editions of the Bible or New Testament 1745.

1. Not a literal Translation, but a kind of P. DRYDEN. *Chaldee Paraphrases*, the TARGUM. b. P., or translation with latitude, where the author is kept in view.., but his words are not so strictly followed as his sense DRYDEN. c. A glittering prelate without

inward ornaments was but the p. of a painted wall 1670.

Paraphrase (pæ·răfrēⁱz), *v.* 1606. [ad. F. *paraphraser*, f. *paraphrase*; see prec.] 1. *trans.* To express the meaning of (a word, phrase, etc.) in other words; to render or translate with latitude. Also *fig.* 2. *intr.* To make a paraphrase 1633. †3. To comment *on*, to enlarge *upon*, a subject -1683.

1. Dr. Whately..paraphrases Hume, though he forgets to cite him HUXLEY. So **Pa·raphraser** 1548.

‖**Paraphrasis** (păræ·frăsis). 1538. [L.] = PARAPHRASE *sb.* 1, 1 b.

Paraphrast (pæ·răfræst). 1549. [ad. L. *paraphrastes*, a. Gr. παραφραστής, f. παραφράζειν; see PARAPHRASE *sb.*] One who paraphrases; a paraphraser.

Paraphrastic (pærăfræ·stik), *a.* 1623. [ad. med.L. *paraphrasticus*, a. Gr. παραφραστικός, f. παραφραστής PARAPHRAST; see -IC.] Of, pertaining to, or of the nature of paraphrase; addicted to the use of paraphrase. So **Paraphra·stical** *a.* (now *rare* or *Obs.*) 1549, **-ly** *adv.* 1557.

‖**Paraphronesis** (pærăfronī·sis). 1857. [mod. L., a. Gr. παραφρόνησις wandering of mind.] = next.

‖**Paraphrosyne** (pærăfrǫ·zinī). 1693. [mod. L., a. Gr. παραφροσύνη, f. παράφρων out of one's wits, f. παρα- PARA-¹ + φρήν mind.] A mild form of delirium or temporary mental derangement.

‖**Paraplegia** (pærăplī·dʒiă). 1657. [mod.L., a. Gr. παραπληγία = παραπληξία a stroke on one side, hemiplegia, f. παραπλήσσειν to strike at the side, f. παρα- + πλήσσειν.] *Path.* Paralysis of the lower limbs and a part or the whole of the trunk, resulting from an affection of some part of the spinal cord. So **Paraple·gic** *a.* marked by or characteristic of p.; affected with p.

Paraquet, var. f. PARAKEET.

Parasang (pæ·răsæŋ). 1594. [ad. L. *parasanga*, ad. Gr. παρασάγγης, of Persian origin (cf. FARSANG).] A Persian measure of length, usu. reckoned as between 3 and 3½ English miles. Also *fig.*

Parasceve (pæ·răsīv, ‖ pærăsī·vī). 1548. [ad. late L. *parasceve* day of preparation, day before the Sabbath, a. Gr. παρασκευή preparation; f. παρα- against + σκευή equipment, etc.] 1. The day of preparation for the Jewish sabbath, the eve of the sabbath, Friday; *spec.* Good Friday (from Mark xv. 42, etc.). *Obs.* in vernacular use. †2. *gen.* Preparation -1654.

‖**Paraselene** (pæ·răsĕlī·nī). *Pl.* **-næ** (-nī). 1653. [mod.L., f. Gr. παρα- PARA-¹ + σελήνη moon (after PARHELION).] A bright spot on a lunar halo, somewhat resembling the moon itself; a mock moon. Hence **Pa:rasele·nic** *a.*

Parasite (pæ·răsəit), *sb.* 1539. [ad. L. *parasitus*, *-a*, a. Gr. παράσιτος lit. one who eats at the table of another; orig. an adj. = feeding beside; f. παρα- PARA-¹ + σῖτος food.] 1. One who eats at the table or at the expense of another (always opprobrious); a hanger-on from interested motives; a 'toady'. b. *Gr. Antiq.* One admitted to the table kept up for a public officer, or to the feast after a sacrifice 1697. 2. *Biol.* An animal or plant which lives in or upon another organism (its *host*) and draws its nutriment directly from it. Also extended to animals or plants that live as tenants of others, but not at their expense (strictly called *commensal* or *symbiotic*); also to those which depend on others in various ways for sustenance, as the skua-gull, cuckoo, etc.; and (inaccurately) to plants which grow upon others, deriving support but not nourishment from them (*epiphytes*), or which live on decaying organic matter (*saprophytes*) 1727. b. Applied, loosely or *poet.* to a plant that creeps or climbs about another plant, or a wall, trellis-work, etc. 1813. c. *fig.* A person whose part or action resembles that of an animal parasite 1883. d. *Philol.* A parasitic vowel or consonant; see PARASITIC 3 b. 1888. 3. *Min.* A mineral developed upon or within another; *spec.* [ad. G. *parasit*] a plumose variety of BORACITE, the result of alteration 1868.

1. You knot of Mouth-Friends:.. Most smiling, smooth, detested Parasites SHAKS. *fig.* Hath made his pen an hired p. BP. HALL. 2. b. Like tendrils of the p. Around a marble column SHELLEY.

Comb. **p.-diphthong**, a diphthong formed by the development of a p. beside the original vowel. Hence **Pa·rasite**, *v.* (*rare*) (*a*) *trans.* to infest as a p.; (*b*) *intr.* (*Philol.*) to develop a parasitic sound SWEET. **Pa·rasital** *a.* parasitic.

Parasitic (pærăsi·tik), *a.* 1627. [ad. L. *parasiticus*, a. Gr., f. παράσιτος PARASITE *sb.* and -IC.] 1. Of, pertaining to, or characteristic of a parasite, sycophantic. 2. *Biol.* Of, belonging to, or having the nature of a plant or animal parasite 1731. 3. *transf.* (from 2.) Applied to something subsidiary growing upon or attached to something else 1811. b. *Philol.* Applied to a non-original vowel, consonant, or other element, attached to an original phonetic element, out of which it has been developed, or to which it has been added; e.g. the sounds denoted by the *d* in *thunder*, the *e* in *flower*, etc. 1870.

1. Some parasitick Preachers 1648. So **Parasi·tical** *a.*, **-ly** *adv.*, **-ness**.

Parasiticide (pærăsi·tisəid). 1864. [f. L. *parasitus* + -CIDE 1.] *Med.* An agent that destroys parasites, e.g. such as infest the skin.

Parasitism (pæ·răsəiti:z'm). 1611. [f. PARASITE *sb.* + -ISM.] 1. Sycophancy, servile complaisance. 2. *Biol.* The condition of being a (plant or animal) parasite; parasitical quality or habits 1853. 3. *Path.* Parasitical infestation; disease caused by this 1884.

Parasitize (pæ·răsitəi:z), *v.* 1890. [f. PARASITE *sb.* + -IZE.] *trans.* To infest as a parasite. Chiefly in *pa. pple.*, infested with parasites.

Parasitology (pærăsəitǫ·lŏdʒi). 1882. [f. Gr. παράσιτος + -(O)LOGY.] That branch of biology, and of medical science, which treats of parasites and parasitism. Hence **Pa:rasitolo·gical** *a.* **Parasito·logist.**

Parasol (pærăsǫ·l, pæ·răsǫl), *sb.* 1616. [a. F., ad. It. *parasole*, f. PARA-² + *sole* sun.] 1. A small light umbrella carried by women as a defence against the sun; a sunshade 1660. †2. *transf.* Anything serving as a defence from the rays of the sun -1801.

attrib. and *Comb.*: **p. ant**, a leaf-carrying ant, esp. *Œcodoma cephalotes* of S. America; **p. pine**, the stone-pine (*Pinus Pinea*), from the form of its head of branches. Hence **Paraso·l** *v. trans.* to serve as a p. for, to shade from the sun. **Parasole·tte**, a small p.

‖**Parasynthesis** (pærăsi·nþĭsis). 1862. [a. Gr. παρασύνθεσις, f. παρα- PARA-¹ + σύνθεσις composition.] *Philol.* Derivation from a compound; conjoint combination and derivation, as a process of word-formation.

Parasynthetic (pæ:răsinþe·tik), *a.* (*sb.*) 1862. [f. Gr. παρασύνθετος (f. παρα- PARA-¹ + σύνθετος put together) + -IC.] *Philol.* Formed from a compound; formed by a conjoint process of combination and derivation. b. *sb.* A parasynthetic formation or derivative.

‖**Parathesis** (păræ·þĭsis). 1657. [mod.L., a. Gr. παράθεσις a putting beside, etc., f. παρατιθέναι, f. παρα- PARA-¹ + τιθέναι to place.] †1. *Gram.* = APPOSITION² 4. -1678. b. In Gr. and L. grammar: Simple composition of two words without change, as in Διόσκυροι, *res-publica*; opp. to *synthesis* and *parasynthesis* 1862. †2. *Rhet.*, etc. A parenthetical word, clause, sentence, or remark -1711. 3. *Gr. Ch.* A commendatory prayer 1864. So **Parathe·tic** *a.* pertaining to or characterized by p.

Paratyphoid (pærătəi·foid), *a.* and *sb.* 1903. [PARA-¹.] *Path.* Applied to a fever resembling typhoid but taking a milder course.

Paraunter, obs. f. PERADVENTURE.

Paravai·l, *adv.* (*a.*) *Obs.* exc. *Hist.* 1579. [a. OF. *par aval* down, f. *par* through, by + *aval*, *à val* adv. and prep., down :—L. *ad vallem* to the valley, as opp. to *amont*, *ad montem*.] Down below or beneath; below one in position; as *tenant paravail*, one who holds under another who is himself a tenant; *spec.* the lowest tenant, he who actually worked or occupied the land, etc Opp. to PARAMOUNT.

Paravane (pæ·răvēⁱn). 1919. [f. PARA-¹ + VANE.] An apparatus for cutting the moorings of submerged mines, towed by warships, etc., during the war of 1914-18, at a depth regulated by its vanes or planes.

†**Paravant, -aunt**, *adv.* 1590. [a. OF. *paravant* adv. and prep., 'before', f. *par* through, by + *avant* :—L. **abante* from before.] Before; in front; before the rest, pre-eminently SPENSER.

‖**Parbleu** (parblö), *int.* 1709. [F., perversion of *pardieu* by God.] A minced oath.

Parboil (pā·ɹboil), *v.* late ME. [a. OF. *parboillir*, *parbouillir* :—late L. *perbullire* to boil thoroughly, f. *per* PAR- + *bullire* to BOIL. *Par-* has been erron. identified with *part*, whence sense 2.] †1. *trans.* To boil thoroughly -1655. 2. To boil partially, half boil 1440. 3. *fig.* usu. in ref. to overheating 1566.

†**Parbreak** (paɹbrēⁱ·k), *v.* late ME. [A compound of BRAKE *v.*⁵, subseq. referred to BREAK *v.*] 1. *trans.* and *intr.* To vomit = BRAKE *v.*⁵ -1610. 2. *fig.* (*trans.*) To utter recklessly or offensively; to vomit forth -1629. Hence †**Pa·rbreak** *sb.* (*rare*).

Parbuckle (pā·ɹbɒk'l), *sb.* 1626. [orig. *parbunkle*, *-buncle*, of unkn. origin.] a. A sling formed by passing the two ends of a rope round a heavy object and through a bight of the rope, and tightening, the weight of the object serving to keep it tight. b. A rope having a bight looped round a post, etc., at the level to or from which an object is to be raised or lowered, and the two ends passed round the object, and hauled in or paid out to raise or lower it, the object acting as a movable pulley; used in hoisting casks or other cylindrical bodies. Hence **Pa·rbuckle** *v. trans.* to raise or lower (a cask, gun, etc.) by means of a p.

‖ **Parcae** (pā·ɹsī), *sb. pl.* late ME. [L.] The (three) Fates of Roman mythology; identified with the Gr. Μοῖραι.

Parcel (pā·ɹsĕl, pā·ɹs'l), *sb.* ME. [a. F. *parcelle* :—L. type **particella*, dim. of *particula*, dim. of *pars*, *partem* PART.] A. *sb.* 1. *gen.* A part *of* anything, considered separately, as a unit; a small portion, a particle (*arch.*). late ME. b. A component part (*of* something), something included in a whole. (Often without article.) *arch.* exc. in phr. *part and p.* (see PART *sb.* I. 1 c.). late ME. 2. *spec.* a. A piece of land; *esp.* as part of a manor or estate. (Often without article.) 1449. b. A small portion or instalment *of* a sum of money (now *rare* or *Obs.*) 1491; †a small portion of a book, e.g. the Bible or the Koran -1655. †3. Each of the units which make up a complex whole; an item, detail, particular, point; *esp.* an item of an account -1641. †4. A small piece, particle; a (small or moderate) quantity or amount; a lot -1830. †5. A fragment, piece. Also *fig.* -1783. 6. A small party, company, or collection (of persons, animals, or things); a detachment; a group, lot, set; a drove, flock, herd. *Obs.* exc. *dial.* or as in b. 1588. b. A 'lot', 'set', 'pack' (contemptuous) 1607. 7. A quantity of anything or a number of things (esp. goods) wrapped up in a single (small) package; an item of goods in carriage or postage; a package: now chiefly used of packages wrapped in brown paper. Also *transf.* and *fig.* 1692. b. *Comm.* A quantity (sometimes definite) of a commodity dealt with in one transaction; *esp.* in the wholesale market, a 'lot' 1832. 8. *Law.* (*pl.*) That part of a conveyance, etc., which follows the operative words, and describes the property dealt with 1766.

1. A certein parcelle of the body of a man CHAUCER. The p. of truth any..individual can seize M. ARNOLD. b. Being p. of the common mass COWPER. Phr. *Of a p. with*, consonant with. 2. a. Owners of certain parcels of Land 1720. 3. 1 *Hen. IV*, III. ii. 159. 5. *fig.* What p. of man hast thou lighted on for a Master? B. JONS. 6. Sheep are kept in small parcels 1780. b. I think the English a p. of brutes MISS BURNEY. 7. His brown-paper p. DICKENS. *fig.* A p. of half-forgotten observations HAZLITT. Phr. *Bill of parcels*: see BILL *sb.*³ 6. b. Cocoa.—At public sale to-day the parcels offered went off freely at dearer prices 1897.

attrib. and *Comb.*, as *p. boy*, *office*, *van*, etc.; **parcel(s) delivery**, the action of, or an agency for, delivering parcels (also *attrib.*); **p. paper**, stout paper, usually brown and unsized, made or used for wrapping parcels; **p. post**, that branch of the postal service which undertakes the carriage and distribution of parcels.

B. *adv.* or quasi-*adv.*, or *adj.* In part, partly. late ME.

Parcell for pride, p. for gladnesse 1430. P. lawyer, p. devil, all knave 1611. Hawkins, Frobisher and Drake, parcel-soldiers all of them 1867. *P. blind, deaf, drunk*, etc. (often hyphened, but improperly exc. when the adj. is used *attrib.*). *P. ass, poet, Protestant*, etc. (often hyphened, but properly so only when it has an adj. force).

Parcel (pā·ɹsĕl, pā·ɹs'l), *v.* 1584. [f. prec.] **1.** *trans.* To divide into 'parcels' or (small) portions. (Usu. with *out.*) **b.** To distribute in parcels 1699. **2.** To make into a parcel or parcels 1775. **3.** *Naut.* **a.** To cover (a caulked seam, etc.) with canvas strips and daub with pitch. **b.** To wrap (a rope) round with canvas strips or *parcelling* (to be then bound with spun yarn) 1627.

1. The empire.. was parcelled into twelve grand divisions 1796. 2. The mechanical art of weighing and parcelling up the tea 1887. Hence **Parcelled, parceled** (pā·ɹsĕld) *ppl. a.*

Pa·rcel-gilt, *a.* (*sb.*) 1465. [f. PARCEL *sb.* B. + GILT *ppl. a.*] Partly gilded; *esp.* of silver ware, as bowls, cups, etc., having the inner surface gilt. **b.** quasi-*sb.* Parcel-gilt ware. Also *fig.* 1610.

b. Or changing His parcell guilt to massie gold B. JONS.

Pa·rcelling, pa·rceling, *vbl. sb.* 1584. [f. PARCEL *v.* + -ING[1].] **1.** The action of PARCEL *v.* **2.** *concr.* (*Naut.*) A strip of canvas (usually tarred) for binding round a rope, to keep the interstices water-tight 1750.

Parcenary (pā·ɹsĕnări). 1544. [a. AF. *parcenarie* = OF. *parçonerie*, f. *parçonier*; see -ERY, -ARY.] *Law.* = COPARCENARY 1.

Parcener (pā·ɹsĕnəɹ). ME. [a. AF. = OF. *parçonier* = med.L. *partionarius*, for **partitionarius*, f. *partitio* PARTITION *sb.*; see -ER[2].] †**1.** One who shares, or has a part in, something with another or others; a partner; a sharer, partaker –1621. **2.** *Law.* = COPARCENER ME.

Parch (pāɹtʃ), *v.* late ME. [Origin unkn.] **1.** *trans.* To dry by exposure to great heat; to roast or toast slightly (corn, pease, and the like). **2.** To make hot and dry; to scorch; said of the action of the sun's heat, or of fever or thirst 1555. **b.** *transf.* To dry, shrivel, or wither with cold 1573. **3.** *intr.* To become very dry and hot; to shrivel up with heat 1530.

2. Parch'd are the Plains, and frying is the Field DRYDEN. b. The parching Air Burns frore, and cold performs th' effect of fire MILT. 3. We were better p. in Affricke Sunne SHAKS. Hence **Parch** *sb.* (*rare*), the action of parching or being parched. **Parched** (pāɹtʃt, pā·ɹtʃĕd) *ppl. a.*, **-ly** *adv.*, **-ness. Pa·rching** *vbl. sb.* **Pa·rching** *ppl. a.* that parches; drying to excess; scorching; that becomes parched.

Parchment (pā·ɹtʃmĕnt). Also †**parchemin.** [ME. a. F. *parchemin*, ad. L. *pergamena*, absol. use (sc. *charta*) of *Pergamena* adj. fem., of or belonging to *Pergamum*, a city of Mysia in Asia Minor. The later Eng. form in *-ment* corresponds to a med.L. by-form *pergamentum.*] **1.** The skin of the sheep or goat, etc., dressed and prepared for writing, painting, engraving, etc. **2.** A skin, piece, scroll, or roll of parchment; a manuscript or document on parchment ME. **3.** A skin or membrane resembling parchment; *spec.* the husk of the coffee-bean 1677.

1. *Cotton p.*, a parchment-like material made by soaking cotton fibre in a solution of sulphuric acid, glycerin, and water, and then rolling it into sheets. *Vegetable p.* = p.-paper (see *Comb.*). 2. I am a scribled forme drawne with a pen Vpon a P. SHAKS.

Comb.: **p.-coffee,** the coffee-bean while still in its husk; **-paper,** a tough, transparent, glossy kind of paper resembling p., made by soaking ordinary unsized paper in dilute sulphuric acid; **-skin,** a piece of p.; also *fig.*; also, a disease of the skin in which it resembles p. Hence **Pa·rchmenty** *a.* of the nature of p.

Parclose (pā·ɹklōᵘz), **perclose** (pə̄·ɹklōᵘz), *sb.* [ME. *parclos, parclose* a. OF. *parclos* m., *parclose* fem., pa. pple. of *parclore* (see next) used subst.] †**1.** Close, conclusion –1671. **2.** A partition, screen, or railing, serving to shut off a space in a building; now only, a screen or railing in a church enclosing an altar, a tomb, etc., or separating a chapel, etc. from the main body of the church ME.

1. Let the Perclose of her thoughts be this, To study what Man was, and what Man is QUARLES.

Parclo·se, perclose, *v.* 1577. [ad. OF. *parclore*, pa. pple. *parclos, -close*, f. *par-*, PAR- + *clore* :—L. *claudere* to CLOSE.] †**1.** To close, conclude –1667. **2.** *trans.* To enclose; to shut off with a parclose. *rare.* 1577.

Pard[1] (pāɹd). ME. (Now only *arch.* or *poet.*) [a. OF., ad. L. *pardus* (male) panther, a. Gr. πάρδος (from πάρδαλις), an Eastern word.] A panther or leopard.

A Soldier, Full of strange oaths, and bearded like the P. SHAKS.

Pard[2] (pāɹd). *slang*, chiefly *U.S.* 1872. [For *pardner*, PARTNER.] A partner, mate.

†**Pa·rdal.** 1553. [ad. L. *pardalis* a female panther, a. Gr. πάρδαλις fem.; see PARD[1].] A name for the panther or leopard –1661.

†‖**Parda·o.** *E. Ind.* 1582. [Pg., ad. 15th c. W. Indian form *partāb*, ult. :—Skr. *prātāp* splendour, majesty.] A coin of Goa, worth orig. about 4*s.* 6*d.*, but later only 10½*d.*; used also as a money of account –1858.

Parde(e, var. f. PARDIE.

Pardie (paɹdī·), **perdie** (pəɹdī·), *int.* or *adv. arch.* ME. [a. OF. *par dé* (mod. colloq. *pardi*), by God.] A form of oath; = 'By God!'; hence as an asseveration: Verily, assuredly, indeed.

The hous is myne, pardie 1475. *Ham.* III. ii. 305.

Pardon (pā·ɹdən, pā·ɹd'n), *sb.* [ME. a. OF. *perdun, pardun* = med.L. *perdonum*, f. *pardonner*, late L. *perdonare* (see next).] †**1.** Remission of something due, as of a debt, tax, etc. –1536. **2.** The passing over of an offence without punishment; forgiveness (but often coloured by sense 4) ME. **b.** *Theol.* Forgiveness of sins ME. **3.** *Eccl.* = INDULGENCE II. 1. ME. **b.** A church festival at which indulgence is granted; the festival of the patron saint 1477. **4.** *Law.* A remission, either free or conditional, of the legal consequences of crime 1447. **5.** The document conveying a pardon (senses 3, 4). late ME. **6.** (from 2.) The excusing of a fault or what the speaker politely treats as one; courteous forbearance or indulgence; excuse; acquittance of blame. Often in phrases of polite apology. 1548. †**b.** Leave, permission –1606. †**c.** Allowance for defect, toleration –1639.

2. Let me ask my sister p. SHAKS. 4. I hope it is some p., or repreeue For the most gentle Claudio SHAKS. *General p.*, a pardon for offences generally, or for those committed by a number of persons not named individually. 5. Their pardons, and other of their tromperye, hath bene bought and solde in Lombard strete 1542. *Meas. for M.* II. iv. 152. 6. Phr. *I beg your p.*, besides being used in its natural sense, is used also as a courteous expression of dissent or contradiction, = 'Excuse me'; e. g. 'I beg your p., it was not so'; and interrogatively = 'I do not catch what you say', or 'what you mean'. Often shortened to *Pardon.* b. *Haml.* IV. vii. 46.

Pardon (pā·ɹdən, pā·ɹd'n), *v.* late ME. [a. OF. *pardoner*, F. *pardonner* = late L. *perdonare*, f. L. *per-* PAR- + *donare* to present, give, perh. after OHG. *forgeben* FORGIVE.] †**1.** *trans.* To remit (something due, a duty, debt, fine, penalty, forfeit) –1643. **2.** To remit the penalty of (an offence); to pass over (an offence or offender) without punishment or blame; to forgive. (A more formal term than *forgive.*) late ME. **3.** To make courteous allowance for; to excuse 1509.

1. I p. thee thy life before thou aske it SHAKS. 2. He will not p. your transgressions *Exod.* xxiii. 21. In this thing the Lord p. thy seruant 2 *Kings* v. 18. *absol.* Hee will abundantly p. *Isa.* lv. 7. 3. P. my impatience 1648. Hence **Pa·rdoner**[2], one who pardons or forgives 1581. **Pardonee·.**

Pardonable (pā·ɹdənăb'l), *a.* 1548. [a. F. *pardonnable*, f. *pardonner* to PARDON; see -ABLE.] That can be pardoned or forgiven; excusable. **a.** Said of an offence. **b.** Of an offender (or his condition). Now *rare.* 1638.

a. A p. Inadvertency ADDISON. b. I dare say your daughter is p. 1803. Hence **Pa·rdonableness. Pa·rdonably** *adv.*

Pardoner[1] (pā·ɹdənəɹ). Now only *Hist.* late ME. [f. PARDON *sb.* + -ER[2] 2.] A person licensed to sell papal pardons or indulgences.

Pare (pēᵊɹ), *v.* ME. [a. F. *parer* to prepare, trim, dress :—L. *parare*; see PREPARE.] †**1.** *trans.* To get ready, to prepare; to deck out –1617. **2.** To trim by cutting off irregular or superficial parts; to cut away the outer edge or outside of (something), *e. g.* the skin or rind of (a fruit), in thin layers, slices, or flakes ME. **b.** †To prune by cutting off superfluous shoots; to reduce the thickness of (a hedge, etc.). late ME. **3.** To slice off the turf or other vegetation covering the surface of the ground 1530. **4.** To reduce (a thing) by cutting or shaving *away*; hence, to reduce little by little; to bring *down* in size or amount. Also *absol.* 1530. **5.** To cut, shave, or shear *off* or *away* (an outer border, surface, rind, etc.). late ME. **b.** *fig.* To cut off or remove 1549. **c.** To make or form by paring or cutting away 1708.

2. What a cursed wretch was I to p. my nails today! a Friday MIDDLETON. Take some pippins, p., core, and boil them 1769. Phr. *To p. to the quick*, to cut away the epidermis, etc., so deep as to reach the sensitive parts; to p. so as to hurt. Also *fig.* 3. Phr. *To p. and burn*, to cut the turf to the depth of two or three inches, and burn it, in order to use the ashes as manure. 4. To p. down the..redundance of rhetorical expression 1864. 5. To pass a halfcrown, after paring a pennyworth of silver from it MACAULAY. b. Nor haue ye a litle piece onlye of the carnall man pared awaye COVERDALE. Hence **Pared** (pēᵊɹd, *poet.* pēᵊ·rĕd) *ppl. a.*

†**Paregal, peregal,** *a.* and *sb.* ME. [a. OF. *parigal, paregal*, etc. :—L. type **perӕqualem*, f. *per-* PAR- + *ӕqualis* EQUAL.] **A.** *adj.* Fully equal; equal (esp. in power, rank, value, etc.) –1636. **B.** *sb.* An equal, peer, match –1602.

Paregoric (pærĭgǫ·rik). 1684. [ad. late L. *paregoricus*, a. Gr. παρηγορικός, f. (ult.) παρα- PARA-[1] + -αγορος speaking, f. ἀγορά assembly of the people. In F. *parégorique.*] **A.** *adj.* Of medicines: Assuaging pain, soothing. **B.** *sb.* A medicine to assuage pain, an anodyne 1704; *spec.*, in the British Pharmacopœia = *p. elixir.*

P. elixir, a camphorated tincture of opium, flavoured with aniseed and benzoic acid.

†**Pareil,** *a.* and *sb.* late ME. [a. F. *pareil* :—pop. L. **pariculum*, dim. of *par* equal.] **A.** *adj.* Equal –1610. **B.** *sb.* Equality; a mate, fellow; an equal, a match –1638.

Pareira (părēᵊ·ră). 1715. [ad. Pg. *parreira* vine trained against a wall.] A drug made of the root of a Brazilian plant, used in disorders of the urinary passages.

Parellic (păre·lik), *a.* 1866. [f. mod.L. *parella*, f. F. *parelle*, ad. med.L. *paratella*, name of a plant.] *Chem.* In *p. acid* ($C_9H_6O_4$), obtained from a crustaceous lichen, *Lecanora Parella*; also called **Pare·llin.** Hence **Pare·llate,** a salt of p. acid.

Parenchyma (păreŋkimă). *Pl.* **parenchy·mata.** Also **pare·nchym, -me.** 1651. [a. Gr. παρέγχυμα, -ματ-, f. παρα- PARA-[1] + ἔγχυμα infusion.] **1.** *Anat.* and *Zool.* The special or proper substance of a gland or other organ of the body, as dist. from the connective tissue or *stroma*, and from *flesh* proper 1657. **b.** The soft tissue composing the substance of the body in sponges, certain worms, etc. 1665. **2.** *Bot.* Tissue consisting of cells of about equal length and breadth placed side by side, usually soft and succulent; found esp. in the softer parts of leaves, the pulp of fruits, etc. (Dist. from PROSENCHYMA.) **Pare·nchymal, -ma·tic** *adjs.* of, pertaining to, or consisting of p.

Parenchymatous (pæreŋki·mătəs), *a.* 1667. [f. prec. + -OUS.] **1.** *Anat.* and *Zool.* **a.** Consisting of or having the nature of parenchyma (sense 1). **b.** Of or belonging to the parenchyma of an organ; occurring in or affecting the parenchyma 1822. **2.** *Bot.* Consisting of or having the nature of parenchyma (sense 2); of or belonging to the parenchyma 1791. So **Pare·nchymous** *a.* (now *rare*) 1666.

Parent (pēᵊ·rĕnt), *sb.* late ME. [a. OF. :—L. *parentem*, sb. use of old pr. pple. of *parĕre* to produce, beget; prop. a father or mother.] **1.** A person who has begotten or borne a child; a father or mother 1450. **b.** By extension: A progenitor, a forefather; esp. in *our first parents*, Adam and Eve. late ME. **c.** *transf.* A person who holds the position of a parent; a protector, guardian, etc. 1526. †**2.** A relative; a kinsman or kinswoman. [So in Fr., etc.] *Obs.* or *alien.* –1771. **3.** Any organism (animal or plant) considered in relation to its offspring 1774. **4.** *fig.* That from which another thing springs or is derived; a source, cause, origin 1590.

1. No man can select his own parents 1883. The crusty old parent-in-law 1899. c. *Spiritual p.*, a sponsor, god-parent; also, a person to whom one

owes one's conversion. 4. P. of sweet and solemn-breathing airs GRAY.

attrib. and *Comb.*: **p.-cell** (*Biol.*), a cell from which other cells are derived; a cytula; **-kernel**, the nucleus of the fertilized egg-cell; a cytococcus. Hence **Pa·rent** *v. rare. trans.* to be the p. of, beget, produce; to be or act as a p. to. **Pa·renthood**, the state or position of a p. **Pa·rentless** *a.* without parents, orphaned; having no (known) parents, author, or source.

Parentage (pē^ə·rĕntėdʒ). 1489. [a. F., f. *parent* PARENT + -AGE.] **1.** Exercise of the functions of a parent (*rare*). †**2.** Parents collectively (*rare*) –1590. **3.** Derivation from parents; 'birth', lineage 1565. **b.** *fig.* Origin 1581. **4.** *spec.* Hereditary degree or quality; 'family', 'birth'; *absol.* good birth 1490. †**5.** Relationship; *concr.* relations collectively –1768. **6.** Parenthood. Also *fig.* 1876.

3. The alleged p. of her son Harold was generally doubted 1870. 4. He askt me of what p. I was; I told him of as good as he SHAKS. Born of humble p. 1838.

Parental (părĕ·ntăl), *a.* 1623. [ad. L. *parentalis*; see PARENT and -AL.] **1.** Of, pertaining to, or characteristic of a parent or parents; fatherly or motherly. **2.** Of the nature of a parent; *fig.* that is the source or origin from which something springs 1647.

2. The principal, and (so to speak) p. agent in that scheme 1877. Hence **Parenta·lity**, parenthood. **Pare·ntally** *adv.*

†**Pare·ntate**, *v.* 1620. [f. L. *parentat-*, *parentare*, f. *parentem* PARENT; see -ATE[3].] *intr.* To offer funeral obsequies, esp. those of parents or relations. So **Parenta·tion**, the performance of the funeral rites of parents or relations; hence, any memorial service for the dead.

†**Parente·le.** ME. [a. F. *parentèle*, ad. L. *parentela* relationship.] **1.** Kinship; kindred –1541. **2.** = PARENTAGE 3, 4. –1734.

Parenthesis (părĕ·nþĭsis). *Pl.* **-theses** (-sīz). 1564. [a. med.L., a. Gr. παρένθεσις, f. παρατιθέναι, f. παρ(α- PARA-[1] + ἐν in + τιθέναι to place, θέσις placing.] **1.** An explanatory or qualifying word, clause, or sentence inserted into a passage with which it has not necessarily any grammatical connexion, and usu. marked off from it by round or square brackets, dashes, or commas. **2.** *transf.* An interval; an interlude; a hiatus 1599. **3.** The upright curves () collectively, used to include words inserted parenthetically; now usu. in pl. *parentheses*; 'round brackets'. Also *transf.* 1715.

1. You see the inconveniency of a long p.; we have forgot the sense that went before 1659. 2. I ne're knew tabacco taken as a p., before B. JONS. 3. *transf.* Those ingenious parentheses called cat-cradles LAMB.

Parenthesize (părĕ·nþĭsəiz), *v.* 1837. [f. prec. + -IZE.] **1.** *trans.* To insert as a parenthesis; to state in parenthesis (usu. with obj. cl.) **2.** To put between marks of parenthesis 1866.

Parenthetic (pærĕnþe·tik), *a.* 1776. [ad. med.L. *parentheticus*, a. Gr. *παρενθετικός, f. παρένθετος put in beside, f. παρεντιθέναι; see PARENTHESIS.] **1.** Of, pertaining to, or of the nature of a parenthesis; inserted as a parenthesis. **b.** *fig.* Interposed 1876. **2.** Addicted to parenthesis (*rare*) 1782.

1. They speak of him with many p. qualifications 1883. So **Parenthe·tical** *a.* 1624, **-ly** *adv.*

Parer (pē^ə·rəɪ). 1573. [f. PARE *v.* + -ER[1].] An instrument for paring; a person that pares 1862.

‖**Parergon** (pǣrɜ̄·ɹgǫn). *Pl.* **parerga.** 1601. [L., a. Gr. πάρεργον by-work, sb. use of neut. of πάρεργος, f. παρα- PARA-[1] + ἔργον work.] †**1.** In Painting: Something subordinate to the main subject; hence, *gen.* and *fig.*, ornamental accessory, grace, embellishment. **2.** By-work; work apart from one's main business or ordinary employment 1618. Hence **Pare·rgal** *a.* subsidiary, supplemental.

†**Pare·rgy.** 1646. [f. prec. with altered suffix.] A thing beside the main purpose –1656.

‖**Paresis** (pæ·rĭsis). 1693. [mod.L., a. Gr. πάρεσις letting go, paralysis, f. παριέναι, f. παρα- PARA-[1] + ἱέναι to let go.] *Path.* Incomplete paralysis, affecting muscular motion but not sensation. So **Pare·tic** *a.* of or pertaining to p.; affected with or characterized by p.

Par excellence: see PAR *prep.* 2 b.

Pargasite (pā·ɹgăsəit). 1818. [ad. G. *pargasit*, f. *Pargas* in Finland, where found; see -ITE[1] 2 b.] *Min.* A green or greenish variety of HORNBLENDE.

Parge (pāɹdʒ), *v.* 1701. [app. short for PARGET *v.*] = PARGET *v.* **1**; hence **p.-work** = PARGET *sb.* 2.

Parget (pā·ɹdʒėt), *sb.* late ME. [app. f. PARGET *v.*] **1.** Plaster spread upon a wall, ceiling, etc.; whitewash; roughcast. **2.** *spec.* Ornamental work in plaster; a facing of plaster with ornamental designs in relief or indented, used for decoration of walls; also called *pargeting*. *Obs.* or *Hist.* 1569. †**3.** *transf.* Paint (for the face) DRAYTON.

Parget (pā·ɹdʒėt), *v.* late ME. [app. a. OF. *pargeter*, *parjeter* to throw or cast over a surface, f. *par* through, all over + *jeter* to throw or cast.] **1.** *trans.* To cover or daub with parget or plaster, to plaster (a wall, etc.); to adorn with pargeting. †**b.** To daub or plaster over *with* (anything) –1698. †**c.** To cover or decorate (a surface) with ornamental work of any kind, as gilding, precious stones, etc. –1886. †**2.** *transf.* To daub or plaster (the face or body) with paint; to paint. Also *intr.* –1660. †**3.** *fig.* To 'whitewash', smooth or gloss over –1824.

1. The walles to be parieted without, and within, and diuersly paincted 1555. 2. She 's aboue fiftie too, and pargets! B. JONS. 3. Thus they did.. p., or rough-cast their vices 1640. So †**Pa·rgeter**, a plasterer; a whitewasher.

Pargeting (pā·ɹdʒėtiŋ), *vbl. sb.* late ME. [-ING[1].] **1.** The action of PARGET *v.* **2.** *concr.* = PARGET *sb.* 1, 2. late ME.

Parhelion (paɹhī·liǫn). *Pl.* **parhelia** (-iă). 1648. [a. L. *parelion*, a. Gr. παρήλιον, also παρήλιος, f. παρα- PARA-[1] + ἥλιος sun.] A spot on a solar halo at which the light is intensified (usu. at the intersection of two halos), often prismatically coloured; a mock sun.

fig. The sky was full of parhelions of delusive glory 1867. Hence **Parheliacal** (pāɹhīləi·ăkăl), **Parhelic** (paɹhī·lik or -he·lik) *adjs.* pertaining to or resembling a p.

Pariah (pē^ə·riă, pā·riă, pæ·riă). 1613. [ad. Tamil *paraiyar*, pl. of *paraiyan* lit. 'hereditary drummer', f. *parai* 'the large drum beaten at certain festivals' (Yule & Burnell).] **1.** *prop.* One of a low caste in Southern India, especially numerous at Madras, where its members supply most of the domestics in European service. **2.** Hence, A member of any low Hindoo caste, or of no caste 1711. **3.** *fig.* A social outcast 1819. **b.** = *Pariah dog* 1816. **4.** *attrib.* 1711.

Comb.: **p.-dog**, a vagabond dog of low breed which frequents towns and villages in India and the East; **-kite**, the Scavenger-kite of India (*Milvus govinda*). Hence **Pa·riahdom, Pa·riahship**, the condition of a p.

Parian (pē^ə·riăn), *a.* (*sb.*) 1638. [f. L. *Parius* of Paros + -AN.] **1.** Belonging to the island of Paros, one of the Cyclades, famed for a white statuary marble. **2.** Applied to a fine white kind of porcelain: usu. as *sb.* 1850.

Paridigitate (pæridi·dʒitĕt), *a.* 1864. [f. *pari-*, stem of L. *par* equal + DIGITATE.] *Zool.* Having an even number of toes on each foot; artiodactyl.

‖**Paries** (pē^ə·riˌīz). *Pl.* **parietes** (părəi·ĕtīz). 1727. [L. *paries, parietem* wall, partition-wall.] *Anat.*, etc. A part or structure enclosing a cavity in an animal or plant body or other natural formation; a wall (of a hollow bodily organ, an abscess or wound, a capsule of a plant, a cell of a honeycomb, etc.) Chiefly in *pl.*

Parietal (părəi·ĕtăl), *a.* (*sb.*) 1506. [a. F. *pariétal*, ad. L. *parietalis*, f. PARIES; see -AL.] **1. a.** *Anat.* and *Zool.* Belonging to or connected with the wall of the body or of any of its cavities. **b.** *Bot.* Belonging to, connected with, or attached to the wall of a hollow organ or structure, esp. of the ovary, or of a cell 1830. **2.** In U.S., Pertaining to residents and order within the walls of a college, as in *P. Board*, *P. Committee*, at Harvard College 1837. **3.** *gen.* Of or belonging to a wall (*rare*) 1845. **B.** *sb.* = Parietal bone 1706.

1. *P. bones*, a pair of bones, right and left, forming part of the sides and top of the skull, between the frontal and occipital bones.

†**Pa·rietary.** [ME. and AF. *paritarie* = OF. *paritaire*, ad. L. *parietaria*, i.e. *herba parietaria*, from *parietarius*, f. *pariet-*, PARIES.] The herb Pellitory (*Parietaria officinalis*)–1696.

Parieto- (părəi:ĕto), used as comb. form of PARIES or PARIETAL, denoting **a.** Belonging to or connected both with the parietal bone, and (the structure indicated by the second element); as **Pari:eto-ma·stoid** *a.*, etc. **b.** Belonging to or connected with the wall of (a cavity), or of the body and (some structure); as **Pari:eto-spla·nchnic** *a.* belonging to the walls of the viscera, viscero-pleural; etc.

Parillin (pări·lin). Also **pariglin** (pări·glin). 1831. [f. Sp. *parilla* (see SARSAPARILLA) + -IN[1].] *Chem.* A white or colourless, odorous, crystalline substance ($C_{40}H_{70}O_{18}$) obtained from sarsaparilla-root; also called **Pari·llic acid**, *salsaparin, sarsaparillin, sarsaparilla-saponin*, or *smilacin*.

‖ **Pari mutuel** (pari mütüel). 1881. [Fr., = mutual wager.] A form of betting in which those who have backed the winning horse divide among themselves the total of the stakes on the other horses (less a percentage for management).

Paring (pē^ə·riŋ), *vbl. sb.* ME. [f. PARE *v.* + -ING[1].] **1.** The action of pruning, or cutting off the edge or surface, or anything superficial (*lit.* and *fig.*) late ME. **2.** *concr.* A thin portion pared off the surface of anything; a shaving ME.

‖ **Pari passu** (pē^ə·rəi pæ·siū), *advb. phr.* 1567. [L., = 'with equal step'.] Side by side at an equal rate of progress; simultaneously and equally. In *Law*, On an equality, without preference.

Paripinnate (pæripi·nĕt), *a.* 1857. [f. L. *par, pari-* equal + PINNATE.] *Bot.* Pinnate with an even number of leaflets, i.e. without a terminal leaflet.

Paris (pæ·ris), name of the capital of France, in various collocations.

†**P. ball**, a tennis ball; **P. blue**, (*a*) a bright shade of Prussian blue; (*b*) a bright blue colouring matter obtained from aniline; **P. green**, a vivid light green pigment composed of aceto-arsenite of copper; **P. white**, a fine kind of whiting used in polishing.

Parish (pæ·riʃ). ME. [Two forms: (i) *paroche*, a. AF. *paroche*, OF. *pa(r)roche*, ad. late L. *parochia*; (ii) *parosshe, -ish*, etc. :—OF. *paroisse* :—pop.L. **parocia* for *parochia*. The latter was a form substituted for Christian L. *parœcia*, a. Gr. παροικία, f. πάροικος, in Christian use, 'a diocese, a parish'.] **1.** In the United Kingdom, the name of a subdivision of a county. **a.** *orig.* A township or cluster of townships having its own church and clergyman, to whom its tithes and eccl. dues are (or were) paid. **b.** A later division of such a parish for eccl. purposes only, having its own church and clergyman. **c.** A corresponding eccl. area in ancient times or in foreign countries 1839. †**d.** A parishful SHAKS. **2.** A district, often identical with an original parish, constituted for purposes of civil government, and thus designated a *civil p.*; primarily, such an area constituted for the administration of the Poor-Law, and sometimes distinguished as a *poor-law p.* 1634. **3.** The inhabitants of a parish collectively ME. **b.** *U.S.* The body of people associated for Christian worship and work in connexion with a particular church; a congregation; hence, a denomination 1851. **4.** *U.S.* In Louisiana, a territorial division corresponding to the county of other states 1839. **5.** A diocese, or district under the spiritual charge of a bishop (usu. *Hist.*, in sense of Gr. παροικία) 1587.

2. *On the p.*, in receipt of parochial relief.

attrib. and *Comb.*: often = 'parochial', as *p. bell, bounds, constable*, etc.; *p. doctor, magazine, nurse, school*; *p.-boy, poor, relief, workhouse*, etc.; also **p. lands**, landed property belonging to a p., and administered by the churchwardens; **p. priest**, the priest having the cure of souls in a p.; **p.-pump**, used allusively to denote politics or other matters of local interest and importance only; **p.- register** (cf. REGISTER *sb.*[1] 3 a); †**-top**, a whipping top kept for the use of the parishioners.

Pa·rish chu·rch. ME. The church of a parish.

Pa·rish cle·rk. late ME. An official appointed by the incumbent of a parish to assist in various duties connected with the church and its services; esp. formerly, to say the responses.

Pa·rish Cou·ncil. 1772. A council of a parish; *spec.* the local administrative body created in rural civil parishes of more than 300 inhabitants by the Act of 1894. Hence **Pa·rish Cou·ncillor**, a member of this body.

†Pari·shional, *a.* 1604. [f. PARISHION(ER + -AL.] Of or pertaining to a parish; parochial; of parishioners –1803. Hence **†Pari·shionally** *adv.*

Parishioner (păriˑʃənəɹ). 1471. [f. ME. *parishion* (in same sense, a. OF. *paroissien*, f. *paroisse* PARISH) + -ER [1].] One of the inhabitants or community of a parish.

Parisian (păriˑziăn, -iˑʒ̍ăn), *sb.* and *a.* 1530. [a. F. *parisien*, med.L. *parisianus*, f. *Parisii* Paris; see -AN.] **A.** *sb.* A native or inhabitant of Paris. **B.** *adj.* Of or pertaining to Paris; resembling Paris or that of Paris. Hence **Pari·sianism. Pari·sianize** *v. trans.* to make P.

‖ **Parisienne** (parizyen). 1886. [F. fem. of *Parisien.*] A female Parisian.

Parisite (pæ·risəit). 1846. [f. name of J. J. *Paris*, its discoverer + -ITE [1].] *Min.* A fluocarbonate of the metals of the cerium group, found in the emerald mines of California.

‖ **Parison** [1] (pæ·risǫn). *Pl.* **parisa.** 1586. [a. Gr. πάρισον neut. of πάρισος exactly balanced, f. παρ(α- PARA- [1] + ἴσος equal.] *Rhet.* An even balance in the members of a sentence. Hence **†Pari·sonal, Pariso·nic** *adjs.* characterized by p.

Parison [2] (pæ·risən). 1832. [a. F. *paraison*, f. *parer* to prepare.] *Glass-blowing.* The rounded mass into which the molten glass is first gathered and rolled when taken from the furnace.

Parisyllabic (pæ:risilæ·bik), *a.* and *sb.* 1656. [f. L. *par, pari-* equal + *syllaba* syllable, + -IC; cf. *syllabic.*] *Gram.* **A.** *adj.* Of Gr. and L. nouns: Having the same number of syllables in the nominative as in the oblique cases of the singular. **B.** *sb.* A p. noun 1893. So **†Parisylla·bical** *a.*

†Paritor (pæ·ritəɹ). 1530. [Aphetic f. APPARITOR.] An apparitor of an ecclesiastical court –1825.

Parity [1] (pæ·rĭti). 1572. [ad. L. *paritas*, f. *par* equal. Cf. F. *parité.*] **1.** The state or condition of being equal, or on a level; equality 1613. **2.** Equality of rank or status; *esp.* equality among the members, or among the ministers, of a church 1572. **3.** Likeness, analogy; parallelism; as in *p. of reason* or *reasoning.* (Cf. L. *pari ratione*) 1620. **†4.** Of numbers: Evenness –1646. **5.** *Comm.* A standard of price expressed in another currency 1886. **b.** = PAR *sb.* [1] 2 b. 1900. **6.** Equality, as legal tender or money, between coins of one metal and coins of another 1895.

3. There is..no p. of case between Spirit and Matter BERKELEY.

Parity [2] (pæ·rĭti). 1878. [f. PAROUS *a.* + -ITY.] *Obstet. Med.* The condition of being parous; the fact of having borne children.

Park (pāɹk), *sb.* [ME. a. OF. *parc* = (ult.) WGer. **parruk*, whence OE. *pearruc* (see PARROCK). In senses 5 and 6 from later uses of F. *parc*, and occas. so spelt.] **1.** *Law.* An enclosed tract of land held by royal grant or prescription for keeping beasts of the chase. (Dist. from a *forest* or *chase* by being enclosed, and from a *forest* also by having no special laws or officers.) **b.** Hence, a large ornamental piece of ground, usu. comprising woodland and pasture, attached to a country house or mansion, and used for recreation, and often for keeping deer, cattle, etc. 1715. **c.** *fig.* 1579. **2.** An enclosed piece of ground, within or near a city or town, ornamentally laid out and devoted to public recreation, a 'public park' 1661. **b.** An extensive area of land set apart as national property to be kept in its natural state for the public benefit, as the *Yellowstone P.* in the U.S. 1871. **3.** In Ireland, Scotland, etc.: An enclosed piece of ground for pasture or tillage; a field; a paddock 1581. **4.** In Colorado, Wyoming, etc.: A high plateau-like valley among the mountains 1808. **5.** *Mil.*, etc. The space occupied by the artillery, wagons, beasts, stores, etc., in an encampment; these objects themselves collectively; a complete set of artillery, of tools, etc. 1683; also, a place where motor (and other) vehicles may be left 1925. **6.** An enclosed area, overflowed at every high tide, in which oysters are bred 1867.

1. b. Hungerford Castle—a fine old place in a beautiful p. 1813. c. [Christ Church, Oxford], Learning's receptacle, Religion's parke 1606. 2. *The P.* (in London), in 17th c. St. James's Park, now esp. Hyde Park. 3. *Town parks* (Ireland), small plots of ground lying round a town or village, usu. let for tillage or pasture to the townsmen or villagers.

Comb.: **p.-hack**, a horse for riding in the p.; **-keeper**, the keeper of a park; **†-leaves**, the shrub Tutsan (*Hypericum Androsæmum*).

Park (pāɹk), *v.* 1526. [f. PARK *sb.*] **1.** *trans.* To enclose in, or as in, a park. **2.** *Mil.*, etc. To arrange (artillery, waggons, etc.) in a park 1812; to leave (a vehicle) in a car-park or other reserved space 1911. **b.** *transf.* To leave in a suitable place until required 1908.

1. How are we park'd and bounded in a pale! SHAKS. Hence **Pa·rking** *vbl. sb.* the action of the vb. (also *attrib.* as in *p.-place* for vehicles); *concr.* ground laid out like a park; in U.S., a strip of turf in the centre of a street.

Parker (pā·ɹkəɹ). ME. [a. AF., in med. L. *parcarius*, f. *parc* PARK *sb.*; see -ER [2] 2.] **1.** A park-keeper. *Obs.* exc. *Hist.* **2.** A rabbit that lives in a park 1846.

Parkin (pā·ɹkin). *n. dial.* 1828. [perh. f. proper name *Perkin* or *Parkin.*] A kind of gingerbread made of oatmeal and treacle.

Parky (pā·ɹki), *a. colloq.* 1898. [app. f. PARK *sb.* + -Y [1].] Nippingly cold.

Parlance (pā·ɹlăns). 1579. [a. AF., OF. *parla(u)nce*, f. *parler* to speak.] **1.** Speaking, speech, *esp.* debate, parleying, parley (*arch.*). **2.** Way of speaking, language, idiom; as *in common, legal, ordinary, vulgar p.*, etc. 1787.

1. Battel and not P. should determine his right, and title 1611.

Pa·rlatory. 1651. [ad. med.L. *parlatorium*, f. *parlare* PARLE *v.*] A convent parlour.

Parle (pāɹl), *sb. arch.* and *dial.* 1575. [app. f. PARLE *v.* Cf. also F. *parole.*] **1.** Speech; talk; conversation 1587. **2.** A conference, discussion, debate; *spec.* = PARLEY *sb.* 2. 1575.

2. When in an angry p. He smot the sledded Pollax on the Ice SHAKS.

Parle (pāɹl), *v. Obs.* or *arch.* and *dial.* late ME. [a. F. *parler* = med.L. *parlare*, late pop.L. *parabolare* to discourse, f. *parabola* PARABLE.] **1.** *intr.* To speak; to talk in conference. **2.** *intr.* To parley (*with* an opponent); to hold a parley 1558.

2. The Jacobite and the presbyterian..parled together DE FOE.

Parley (pā·ɹli), *sb.* 1581. [perh. f. PARLEY *v.* [1]] **1.** Speech, speaking, talk; conference; debate, argument. (Now usu. coloured by 2.) 1582. **2.** A conference for the debating of points in dispute; esp. *Mil.*, an informal conference with an enemy, under a truce, for the discussion of terms, etc. 1580.

2. Phr. *To beat* or *sound a p.*, to call for a p. by sounding a drum or trumpet; The Herald soundes a parlee, and none answers DEKKER.

Parley (pā·ɹli), *v.* [1] 1570. [perh. f. F. *parler*, imper. *parlez!*] **1.** *intr.* To speak, talk; to confer (*with*). Now *arch.* 1591. **b.** *trans.* To speak; *esp.* to speak a foreign language 1570. **2.** *intr.* To treat, discuss terms; *esp.* to hold a parley (*with* an enemy, etc.). Also *fig.* 1600. **b.** *trans.* To grant a parley to (a person); to hold discussion with, speak to 1611.

2. We..offered a truce to p. DE FOE.

Parley, *v.* [2] *U.S.* 1895. = PAROLI *v.*

Parleyvoo (pāɹlivū·), *sb. joc.* 1754. [f. F. *parlez-vous* (parlevu) in *parlez-vous français?* do you speak French?] **1.** The French language, French; French lessons. **2.** A Frenchman 1815. So **Parleyvoo·** *v. slang* or *joc. intr.* to speak French, or a foreign tongue; to palaver.

Parliament (pā·ɹlĭmĕnt), *sb.* [ME. a. OF. *parlement* speaking, f. *parler* + *-ment.*] **†1.** The action of speaking; a 'bout' of speaking; a speech; a colloquy; a discussion or debate –1542. **†b.** = PARLEY *sb.* 2. –1610. **2.** A formal conference or council for the discussion of some matter or matters of general importance; *spec.* applied to great councils of the early Plantagenet Kings (Now only *Hist.*) ME. **3.** The Great Council of the nation, which forms, with the Sovereign, the supreme legislature of the United Kingdom, consisting of the three estates, viz. the Lords Spiritual and Temporal (forming together the House of Lords), and the representatives of the counties, cities, etc. (forming the House of Commons) ME. **4.** Name of corresponding legislative bodies in the colonies, and in other countries. late ME. **5.** Applied to various consultative assemblies; (*a*) one formerly held by tinners in the Stannaries 1574; (*b*) one of the members of the Middle or the Inner Temple 1533. **b.** *fig.* and *transf.* late ME. **6.** In France (before the Revolution of 1789), the name given to a certain number of supreme courts of justice 1560. **7.** Short for *p.-cake* 1812.

1. Thus ended the parlement betwene the fader and the sone 1450. 2. They made request that it might be lawfull for them to sommon a Parlament of Gallia at a certain day 1563. 3. The privileges of p. BLACKSTONE. Phr. *Act of P.*, a statute passed by both Houses of P. and ratified by the royal assent. *Clerk of the Parliaments* (†*Parliament*), the chief official of the House of Lords, who reads the royal assent to bills before P. assembled as a corporate body in the House of Lords. *High Court of P.*, a name formerly applied collectively (as in Bk. of Com. Prayer) to the two houses of P. in session; now mostly said of P. in its judicial capacity. *To open P.* 5. b. The P. of Bees 1640, of man TENNYSON. The Cricket P. at Lord's 1903. 7. Gorging the boy with apples and p. THACKERAY.

Phrases. **Barebone's P.**, the *Little P.*, so called from Praise-God Barbon, one of the members for London. **Little P.**, the assembly of 120 members, nominated by Cromwell and his Council of Officers, which sat from 4 July to 12 Dec. 1653. **Long P.**, that which met on 3 Nov. 1640, and was finally dissolved in 1660. **Rump P.**, the remnant of the Long P., in its later history. **Short P.**, that which sat from 13 April to 5 May 1640, before the Long P.

attrib. and *Comb.*, as *p. army, buildings, news*, etc.; also **P. Act**, *spec.* the Act of Parliament passed in 1911 by which the powers of the House of Lords were restricted; **p.-cake, -gingerbread**, a thin crisp rectangular cake of gingerbread; **-chamber**, the room in which a p. meets, *spec.* that in the Old Palace of Westminster; **p. ordinance**: see ORDINANCE 6; **P. Roll**: see ROLL *of p.* Hence **†Parliame·ntal** *a.* parliamentary –1775. **Parliamentee·r** (*Hist.*) = PARLIAMENTARIAN A. 1.

Pa·rliament, *v. rare.* 1491. [late ME. *parlement*, a. OF. *parlementer.*] **†1.** *intr.* To talk, converse; to parley –1610. **2.** *intr.* To attend Parliament. Also with *it.* 1642.

Parliamentarian (pā:ɹlĭmentēᵊ·riăn). 1644. [f. as next + -AN.] **A.** *sb.* **1.** *Hist.* One who took the side or was in the service of the Parliament during the Civil War of the 17th c. **2.** One versed in parliamentary usages and tactics; a skilful parliamentary debater 1834. **B.** *adj.* = PARLIAMENTARY *a.* Hence **Pa·rliamenta·rianism**, the parliamentary principle or system.

Parliamentary (pāɹlĭme·ntări), *a.* (*sb.*) 1616. [f. PARLIAMENT + -ARY [1]; cf. F. *parlementaire.*] **1.** Of, belonging to or relating to a parliament, or parliament as an institution; of the nature of a parliament 1626. **b.** Of, belonging or adhering to, the Parliament in the Civil War of the 17th c. 1761. **2.** Enacted, ratified, or established by Parliament 1616. **3.** Consonant with the usages or agreeable to the practice of Parliament 1625. **b.** Of language: Such as is permitted to be used in Parliament; hence *allusively*, civil, courteous 1818.

1. An old P. hand GLADSTONE. *P. agent*, a person professionally employed to take charge of the interests of a party concerned in or affected by any private legislation of P. 2. Chearfully pay all p. taxes PRIESTLEY. Phr. *P. train*, a train carrying passengers at a rate not exceeding one penny a mile, which, by Act of Parliament, every railway company was formerly obliged to run daily each way over its system. So *p. carriage, fare, ticket*, etc. 3. b. Two gentlemen politely and in strictly P. language calling one another incompetent administrators 1885.

B. *sb.* **I. 1.** A member of Parliament 1626. **2.** Short for *parliamentary train*; see 2 above 1864. **II.** A person sent to parley with the enemy 1865. Hence **Parliame·ntarily** *adv.*

Parliament house. late ME. The building in which a parliament meets. (Still used of the building in Edinburgh in which the Scottish Parliament met.)

Parliament man. Now *Hist.* or *dial.* 1605. **1.** A member of the Parliament, orig. of England, also of Scotland and Ireland, later of the United Kingdom; usu. applied, like 'Member of Parliament' now, to a member of the House of Commons. **2.** = PARLIAMENTARIAN A. 1. (*rare*) 1853.

Parlour, parlor (pā·ɹləɹ). [ME. a. AF. *parlur*, OF. *parleor*, = med.L. *parlatorium*, f. *parlare* PARLE *v.* *Parlor* is usu. in U.S.] **1.** An apartment in a monastery or convent for conversation with persons from outside, or among the inmates. **2.** In a mansion, dwelling-house, town-hall, etc., *orig.* A smaller room apart from the great hall, for private conversation (e.g. a banker's parlour, the mayor's parlour in a town-hall). Hence, in a private house, the ordinary sitting-room of the family. †Formerly often simply = 'room' or 'chamber'. late ME. †**b.** Used as a dining or supper room. –*c* 1850. **3.** A room in an inn more private than the tap-room where people may converse apart 1870. **4.** *orig. U.S.* An elegantly or showily fitted apartment, for some special business or trade use, as *beauty p.*, *cinema p.*, *ice-cream p.* 1890.

2. b. To the Parler where they used to sup SIDNEY. *attrib.* and *Comb.*: **p.-boarder**, a boarding-school pupil who lives in the family of the principal; **-car** (*U.S.*), a luxuriously fitted railway carriage, a 'drawing-room' car; **-maid**, a female domestic servant who waits at table; **-organ**, a reed-organ suitable for a private room; **p. tricks** *slang*, society arts or accomplishments.

Parlous (pā·ɹləs), *a.* (*adv.*) *arch.* and *dial.* [Late ME. *perlous*, syncopated f. PERILOUS.] **A. 1.** Perilous, dangerous, hazardous. **b.** Risky to deal with; ticklish, awkward, precarious 1658. **2.** Dangerously cunning, clever, etc.; keen, shrewd; mischievous; very bad, 'shocking'; surprising, 'terrible', 'awful'. (In later use *colloq.* and *dial.*) late ME. **B.** *adv.* Excessively, 'terribly', 'awfully', 'desperately' 1599.

1. A perlous tyme 1535. **b.** A p. liquor 1658. **2.** A p. Boy: go too, you are too shrew'd SHAKS. Hence **Pa·rlous-ly** *adv.*, **-ness.**

†**Parmace·ty.** 1545. **1.** A pop. corruption of SPERMACETI –1828. **2.** In full *p. whale*: The Cachalot or Sperm whale –1851.

Parmesan (pāɹmĭzæ·n), *a.* and *sb.* 1519. [a. F. *parmesan*, It. *parmegiano*, f. *Parma*.] **A.** *adj.* Of or belonging to Parma in Northern Italy, *esp.* applied to a cheese made there and elsewhere in North Italy. **B.** *sb.* Parmesan cheese. (Now usu. with capital *P.*) 1556.

Parnassian (pāɹnæ·siăn), *a.* and *sb.* 1644. [f. L. *Parnas(s)ius*, *-eus* (f. *Parnasus*, PARNASSUS) + -AN.] **A.** *adj.* **1.** Of or belonging to Parnassus; of or belonging to poetry, poetic. **b.** *spec.* Epithet of a school of French poetry, from the title *Parnasse contemporain* of a collection of their poems published in 1866; also *transf.* **2.** *Entom.* Belonging to the genus *Parnassius* of butterflies, found in mountainous regions of the northern hemisphere. **B.** *sb.* **1.** A poet 1659. **b.** *spec.* A poet of the Parnassian school 1882. **2.** *Entom.* A butterfly of the genus *Parnassius* or subfamily *Parnassiinæ*. Hence **Parna·ssianism**, the principles or practice of the P. school of poets (see A. 1 b).

Parnassus (pāɹnæ·səs). late ME. [a. L. *Parnas(s)us*, a. Gr. Παρνασός, later Παρνασσός.] A mountain in central Greece, anciently sacred to Apollo and the Muses; hence used allusively in ref. to literature, esp. poetry. **b.** As the title of a collection of poems 1600.

Parnellism (pā·ɹnĕliz'm). 1885. [See -ISM.] The principles or policy of the Irish Home Rule party in the House of Commons led by Charles Stewart Parnell from 1880 to 1891. So **Pa·rnellite**, a member of this party.

Paroccipital: see PARA-¹.

Parochial (păr$\bar{o}$u·kiăl), *a.* (*sb.*) late ME. [a. OF. *parochial*, ad. late L. *parochialis*, f. late L. *parochia* PARISH.] **A.** *adj.* **1.** Of, belonging, or pertaining to a parish, or parishes in general. **2.** *fig.* Pertaining or confined to a narrow area or domain; narrow, provincial 1856. **B.** *sb.* (*rare*). **a.** A parish church 1637. **b.** A parish clergyman 1853.

P. church council, a parochial governing body in the Church of England, consisting of the incumbent, the churchwardens, and elected parishioners. Hence **Paro·chial-ly** *adv.*, **-ness.**

Parochialism (păr$\bar{o}$u·kiăliz'm). 1847. [See next and -ISM.] **1.** Parochial character or tendency; local narrowness of view; petty provincialism. **2.** Absorption in parish duties 1884.

Parochiality (păr$\bar{o}$ukiæ·lĭti). 1769. [f. late L. *parochialis* PAROCHIAL + -ITY.] The quality or state of being parochial (*lit.* and *fig.*). In *pl.* Affairs of the parish; narrow or restricted interests or affairs.

Parochialize (păr$\bar{o}$u·kiăləiz), *v.* 1846. [f. PAROCHIAL + -IZE.] **1.** *trans.* To make parochial. **2.** *intr.* To do parish work 1871. Hence **Paro:chializa·tion.**

†**Paro·chian**, *sb.* and *a.* [ME. *parochien*, a. OF., ad. med.L. *parochianus*, f. *parochia*.] **A.** *sb.* **1.** An inhabitant of a parish, a parishioner –1765. **2.** A parish clergyman (*rare*) –1715. **B.** *adj.* Parochial –1644.

A. 1. I gyue and bequeth to the poure parochians . . xll T. CROMWELL. **B.** The P. Pope, or independent Soveraigne in every Parish 1644.

†**Pa·rochin(e.** *Sc.* 1500. [f. late L. *parochia* or ME. *paroch(e* PARISH.] = PARISH –1824 (*Hist.*).

Parode (pæ·rōud). 1861. [ad. Gr. πάροδος entrance from the side, f. παρ(α- PARA-¹ + ὁδός way.] In ancient Gr. drama, the first ode sung by the chorus after its entrance.

†**Paro·dic**, *a.*¹ *rare.* 1684. [ad. Gr. παροδικός passing, f. πάροδος; see -IC.] *Math.* Applied to any one of the series of degrees or powers of the unknown or variable below the highest that occurs in an equation –1775.

Parodist (pæ·rŏdist). 1742. [a. F. *parodiste*, f. *parodie* PARODY.] The author of a parody. So **Pa·rodize** *v.* to parody 1658.

Parody (pæ·rŏdi), *sb.* 1598. [ult. (prob. through L. or F.) ad. Gr. παρῳδία burlesque poem or song, f. παρ(α- PARA-¹ + ᾠδή.] **1.** A composition in which the characteristic turns of thought and phrase of an author are mimicked and made to appear ridiculous, especially by applying them to ludicrously inappropriate subjects. Also applied to a burlesque of a musical work. **2.** *transf.* and *fig.* A poor or feeble imitation, a travesty 1830.

2. The Brussels riot . . is a wretched p. on the last French revolution COLERIDGE. A p. of justice 1900. So **Paro·dic** *a.*², **-al** *adjs.* of the nature of a p., burlesque.

Parody (pæ·rŏdi), *v.* 1745. [f. prec.] **1.** *trans.* To compose a parody on (a work or an author); to ridicule (a composition) by mimicking it. **b.** *intr.* To compose a parody 1875. **2.** *trans.* To imitate in a way that is no better than a parody 1801.

2. After his death, his [Pitt's] finance was parodied by incapable successors 1869.

‖**Parœmia** (părī·miă). 1586. [L., a. Gr. παροιμία by-word, proverb, f. πάροιμος by the way, f. παρ(α- PARA-¹ + οἶμος way.] *Rhet.* A proverb, adage. So **Parœmio·grapher**, a writer of proverbs. **Parœmio·logy**, the study of proverbs.

Parœmiac (părī·miæk), *a.* (*sb.*) 1699. [ad. Gr. παροιμιακός, f. παροιμία PARŒMIA.] **1.** *prop.* Of the nature of a proverb, proverbial 1820. **2.** *Gr. Pros.* (also *sb.*) (Applied to) the short line (anapæstic dimeter catalectic) with which an anapæstic system usually ends 1699.

Parol (pæ·rŏl), *sb.* and *a.* 1474. [orig. *parole*, a. AF., F. *parole* :—late pop.L. **paraula* :—**paravola* :—*parabola* PARABLE.] **A.** *sb.* **1.** Something said or spoken; an oral statement; an utterance; a word. Chiefly in *Law*; now only in phr. *by p.*, by word of mouth. **2.** *Law.* The pleadings filed in an action (formerly presented by word of mouth) 1625.

1. A tenancy at will may be created by p., or by deed 1844.

B. *adj.* [the sb. used attrib.] **1.** Expressed or given orally; verbal. Now only in *Law*, in *p. evidence*, etc. 1601. **2.** *Law.* Made (as a contract or lease) by word of mouth or in a writing not sealed 1590.

Parole (păr$\bar{o}$u·l), *sb.* 1616. [a. F. *parole* (see prec.), in sense 'formal promise', *parole d'honneur* word of honour.] **1.** In full, *p. of honour*: Word of honour given or pledged; esp. *Mil.* the undertaking given by a prisoner of war that he will not try to escape, or that, if liberated, he will return to custody under stated conditions, or will refrain from taking up arms against his captors for a stated period. A person so liberated is said to be *on p.* **b.** *ellipt.* The condition of being on parole 1667. †**2.** *Mil.* The password used only by the officers or inspectors of the guard; dist. from the *countersign* given to all the men on guard –1844. **3.** *attrib.* 1812.

1. They had broken their p. and fled 1880. **b.** This man had . . forfeited his military p. MACAULAY.

Parole (păr$\bar{o}$u·l), *v.* 1716. [f. prec.] †**1.** *intr.* To pledge one's word –1716. **2.** *trans.* To liberate (a prisoner) on parole 1863. **b.** *U.S.* To liberate (a prisoner) on his own recognizances 1888.

Paroli (pā·rŏlī), *sb.* 1701. [a. F., a. It. *paroli* 'a grand part, set, or cast, at dice' (Florio); perh. f. *paro* pair, couple.] In faro, etc., the leaving of the money staked and the money won as a further stake; the staking of double the sum before staked. Hence as vb.

My friendship goes to sleep like a p. at Pharoah, and does not wake again till their deal is over H. WALPOLE.

Paromology (pærŏmǫ·lŏdʒi). Chiefly in L. form. 1586. [ad. L. *paromologia*, Gr. παρομολογία partial admission, f. παρ(α- PARA-¹ + ὁμολογία.] *Rhet.* A figure in which something is conceded to an adversary in order to strengthen one's own position.

‖**Paronomasia** (părǫnomē·ziă, -siă). Also †parono·masy. 1579. [L., a. Gr. παρονομασία, f. παρ(α- PARA-¹ + ὀνομασία naming.] A playing on words which sound alike; a word-play; a pun. Hence **Paronoma·sial**, **Paronoma·sian** *adjs.* of or pertaining to p. So **Parono·ma·stic**, **-al** *adjs.*, **-ly** *adv.*

You catch the paronomasia, play 'po' words CALVERLEY.

‖**Paronychia** (pærŏni·kiă). 1597. [L., a. Gr. παρωνυχία a whitlow, f. παρ(α PARA-¹ + ὄνυξ, ὀνυχ- nail.] **1.** *Path.* An inflammation about the finger-nail; a whitlow. **2.** *Bot.* A genus of herbaceous plants (N.O. *Illecebraceæ*); whitlow-wort 1666.

Paronym (pæ·rŏnim). 1846. [ad. Gr. παρώνυμον adj. neut., f. παρ(α PARA-¹ + ὄνομα name word.] A word which is derived from another, or from the same root; a derivative or cognate.

Paronymous (părǫ·nimǝs), *a.* 1661. [f. Gr. παρώνυμος (see prec.) + -OUS.] **1.** Of words: Derived from the same root; radically connected, cognate. **2.** Having the same sound, but different orthography and meaning 1836.

Paronymy (părǫ·nimi). 1885. [f. Gr. παρώνυμος PARONYM + -Y³.] Formation from a word in another language with but slight change.

Paroophoron, Parorchid: see PARA-¹ 1.

Paroquet (pæ·rŏkĕt). var. of PARAKEET.

Comb. **p. (perroquet) auk**, a small auk, *Ombria psittacula* (*Cyclorhynchus psittaculus*), inhabiting the coasts and islands of the northern Pacific.

Parosteal (părǫ·stiăl), *a.* 1854. [f. PARA-¹ + Gr. ὀστέον bone.] *Anat.*, etc. = PAROSTOTIC.

‖**Parostosis** (pærǫstō·sis). 1893. [f. as prec. + -OSIS.] *Anat.*, etc. The formation of bone outside the periosteum, as in the sheaths of blood-vessels, etc. So **Parosto·tic** *a.* of or formed by p. 1870.

Parotic (părǫ·tik), *a.* 1857. [ad. mod.L. *paroticus*, f. PARA-¹ + Gr. οὖς, ὠτ- ear, ὠτικός of the ear.] *Anat.*, etc. Situated beside or near the ear; parotid.

Parotid (părǫ·tid), *a.* and *sb.* 1687. [a. F. *parotide*, or ad. L. *parotis*, *parotid-* PAROTIS.] *Anat.*, etc. **A.** *adj.* Situated beside or near the ear; applied esp. to a lobulated racemose gland just in front of the ear, and having a duct (*p. duct* or *Stenson's duct*) opening into the mouth opposite the second upper molar tooth. **B.** *sb.* The parotid gland 1770.

‖**Parotis** (păr$\bar{o}$u·tis); usu. in *pl.* **parotides** (-tidīz). 1615. [L., a. Gr. παρωτίς, παρωτιδ-, f. παρα- PARA-¹ + οὖς, ὠτ- ear; see -ID².] **1.** The parotid gland. †**2.** A parotid tumour –1893. Hence ‖**Parotidi·tis** [see -ITIS] = next.

Parotitis (pærǫtəi·tis). 1822. [irreg. for *parotiditis*, f. prec.; see -ITIS.] *Path.* Inflammation of the parotid gland, or of neighbouring structures; usu. constituting the disease called *mumps*. Hence **Paroti·tic** *a.* affected with p.

Parotoid (părōu·toid), *a.* (*sb.*) 1873. [irreg. f. PAROTIS + -OID.] *Zool.* Applied to certain glands of the skin forming warty excrescences near the ears in some batrachians, as toads. Also as *sb.*

Parous (pæ·rəs), *a.* 1896. [f. as next.] Having borne children.

-parous, *suffix*, f. L. *-parus* bearing (*parĕre* to bring forth) + -OUS, as in *multiparous*, *oviparous*, *viviparous*, etc. adjs.

‖**Parousia** (părau·siă). 1875. [Gr. παρουσία presence.] *Theol.* The second coming or advent of Christ (the sense in 1 Cor. xv. 23, etc.).

Parovarium: see PARA-¹ 1.

Paroxysm (pæ·rǫksiz'm). 1604. [a. F. *paroxysme*, ad. med.L. *paroxysmus* irritation, a. Gr. παροξυσμός, f. παροξύνειν to goad, f. παρα- PARA-¹ + ὀξύνειν to render acute.] **1.** *Path.* An increase of the acuteness or severity of a disease, usu. recurring periodically in its course; a fit. **2.** A violent access of action or emotion; a fit, convulsion 1641. **b.** (Without *pl.*) The acute stage (of any action, etc.). Now *rare.* 1650. †**3.** An open quarrel -1702.

2. He was cast into paroxysms of rage and despair 1839.

Paroxysmal (pærǫ̆ksi·zmăl), *a.* 1651. [f. prec. + -AL.] Pertaining to or of the nature of a paroxysm; marked by paroxysms; violent, convulsive. **b.** *spec.* in *Geol.* Of or pertaining to a violent natural convulsion; occas. = CATASTROPHIC, CATACLYSMIC 1830.

In a paroxismal frenzy of contending passions SHELLEY. Hence **Paroxy·smalist**, also **Pa·roxysmist** (*Geol.*), a catastrophist. **Paroxy·smally** *adv.* **Paroxy·smic** *a. rare.*

Paroxytone (pärǫ·ksitoun), *a.* and *sb.* 1764. [ad. mod.L. *paroxytonus*, a. Gr. παροξύτονος, f. παρα- PARA-¹ + ὀξύτονος OXYTONE.] **A.** *adj.* Having an acute accent on the last syllable but one. **B.** *sb.* A word so accented.

Parpen(t (pā·ɹpĕn(t). late ME. [a. OF. *parpain*, in med.L. *parpanus*, of obsc. etym.] **1.** A stone which passes through a wall from side to side. **2.** Short for *p.-wall*, a thin wall built of p. stones, as in interior partition walls.

Parquet (pā·ɹke, paɹke·t), *sb.* 1816. [a. F. *parquet*, OF. *parchet* a small compartment, etc., dim. of *parc* PARK; see -ET.] **1.** A flooring; *spec.* a flooring composed of pieces of wood, often of different kinds, arranged in a pattern; a flooring of parquetry. **2.** (Also erron. *parquette.*) Part of the auditorium of a theatre, the front part of the ground-floor nearest the orchestra. (Chiefly *U.S.*) 1848. ‖**3.** In France, etc.: The branch of the administration of law concerned with the prevention, investigation, and punishment of crime 1892. **4.** *attrib.*, as *p.-flooring*, etc. 1874. So **Pa·rquet** *v. trans.* to floor (a room) with parquet-work; to make of inlaid wood-work 1678. **Pa·rquetage** = next.

Parquetry (pā·ɹkėtri). Also ‖**parqueterie** (parkętri). 1842. [a. F. *parqueterie*, f. *parquet*; see -ERY¹.] Inlaid work of wood, in which a pattern is formed of different kinds of wood; esp. in flooring. Also *attrib.*

Parr, par (pāɹ). 1715. [app. Sc.; origin unkn.] **1.** A young salmon before it becomes a smolt; distinguished by the parallel transverse bands on its side. **2.** A young coal-fish or black cod, less than a year old; a sillock (*local*) 1769.

Comb. **p.-tail**, an artificial fly used in salmon fishing.

Parrel, parral (pæ·rĕl), *sb.* 1485. [app. aphetic f. ME. *aparail*, *-ayle*. Cf. OF. *parail* rigging.] *Naut.* A band of rope, a chain, or iron collar by which the middle of a yard is fastened to the mast. Hence **Pa·rrel, parral** *v.* to fasten by means of a p.

‖**Parrhesia** (părī·ziă, -rī·siă). 1577. [late L. *parrhesia*, a. Gr. παρρησία free-spokenness, f. παρα- PARA-¹ + ῥῆσις speech.] *Rhet.* Frankness or freedom of speech.

Parricidal (pæ·risəidăl), *a.* 1627. [ad. L. *parricidalis*, f. *parricida* PARRICIDE¹.] Of, pertaining to, or of the nature of a parricide; guilty of parricide. Hence **Parrici·dally** *adv.*

Parricide¹ (pæ·risəid). 1554. [a. F., ad. L. *par(r)icida*; perh. for **patricida*, f. *patrem*, *pater* father; see -CIDE 1.] One who murders his father or either parent or other near relative; also, the murderer of any one whose person is held sacred; *transf.* one who is guilty of treason against his country. **b.** *attrib.* = prec. 1686.

Pa·rricide². 1559. [a. F., ad. L. *parricidium*; see prec. and -CIDE 2.] The murder of a father, parent, near relative, ruler, etc.; the crime of a parricide; *transf.* the crime of treason against one's country. **b.** *attrib.* = PARRICIDAL 1806. Hence †**Parrici·dial**, †**Parrici·dious** *adjs.* parricidal.

Parrock (pæ·rək), *sb.* New chiefly *dial.* [OE. *pearroc*, *-ruc* :—WGer. **parruk*; origin obsc.] **1.** An enclosed space of ground; a small field, a paddock. **2.** A small apartment or narrow cell in a building; a stall, coop, or pen for animals 1440. Hence **Pa·rrock** *v. trans.* to enclose, shut up, confine within narrow limits.

Parrot (pæ·rət), *sb.* 1525. [Origin unkn.] **1.** A bird of the order *Psittaci*, or family *Psittacidæ*, and spec. of the genus *Psittacus*; these are scansorial and zygodactyl, and have a short hooked bill and naked cere; many of the species have beautiful plumage, and some are excellent mimics and learn to enunciate words and phrases; hence, much valued as cage-birds, esp. the Grey Parrot (*Psittacus erythacus*) of West Africa. **2.** Applied contemptuously to a person who mechanically repeats the words or imitates the action of others 1581. **3. Sea-parrot.** **a.** The coulterneb or puffin, so called from the shape of its bill 1668. **b.** Some kind of fish: see PARROT-FISH 1666.

1. A very little wit is valued in a woman, as we are pleased with a few words spoken plain by a p. POPE.

attrib. and *Comb.*, as *p. cage*, *species*, etc.; *p.-cry*, *-echo*, *-faculty*, *teacher*, etc.; **-green**, a yellowish green like the colouring of some parrots; **p. tongue**, a tongue like that of a p.; *spec.* a dry shrivelled condition of the human tongue in typhus, etc.; **-weed**, the Tree Celandine, *Bocconia frutescens*, a tropical American plant; **-work**, merely imitative repetition; **-wrasse** = PARROT-FISH a. Hence **Pa·rrotism**, mechanical repetition or imitation (*rare*). **Pa·rrotize** *v.* to parrot (*rare*). **Pa·rrotry**, the mechanical or servile repetition of the sayings, etc., of others.

Parrot (pæ·rət), *v.* 1596. [f. prec.] **1.** *intr.* To chatter like a parrot; to repeat words and phrases mechanically like a parrot. Now only as *absol.* use of next. **2.** *trans.* To repeat (words) mechanically like a parrot; to iterate to weariness; to repeat or imitate without understanding or sense 1649. **3.** *trans.* To teach to repeat in a parrot-like manner; to drill like a parrot 1775.

2. To p. the *ipsissima verba* of Kant DE QUINCEY. Hence **Pa·rroter**, one who repeats something learned by rote.

Pa·rrot-coal. *Sc.* and *n. dial.* 1789. [Origin of *parrot* unkn.] Cannel coal.

Pa·rrot-fish. 1712. A name given to some fishes from their brilliant colouring, or as having a strong hard mouth resembling the bill of a parrot. *spec.* **a.** A fish of the family *Scaridæ* found in tropical seas and having a very strong jaw. **b.** A fish of the Australian labroid genus *Labrichthys*, esp. *L. Psittacula.* **c.** One of the gymnodonts.

Parry (pæ·ri), *sb.* 1705. [f. PARRY *v.* Substituted for PARADE, a. F. *parade*, ad. It. *parata.*] **1.** = PARADE *sb.* 6. **2.** *gen.* The warding off of any attack 1709.

Parry (pæ·ri), *v.* 1672. [app. repr. F. *parez* from *parer*, ad. It. *parare* to ward a blow :—L. *parare* to make ready.] **1.** *intr.* To ward off or turn aside a weapon or blow by opposing to it one's own weapon, etc. Also *fig.* **2.** *trans.* To stop, ward off, or turn aside (a weapon, a blow, etc.) in this way 1692. **b.** *gen.* and *fig.* To turn aside (anything threatened, an awkward question, etc.); to avoid, evade 1718.

1. The Spaniards p. with the poniard. The ancients parried with their bucklers 1727. **2.** To p. a cudgel with a small sword 1824. **b.** I parried her questions by the best excuses I could offer 1859.

Parse (pāɹz, *Sc.* and *U.S.* pāɹs), *v.* 1553. [app. f. L. *pars* part.] *trans.* To describe (a word in a sentence) grammatically, by stating the part of speech, inflexion, and relation to the rest of the sentence; to resolve (a sentence, etc.) into its component parts of speech and describe them grammatically. Also *intr.* or *absol.* **b.** *intr.* for *pass.* To admit of being parsed 1880.

Let the childe, by and by, both construe and p. it ouer againe ASCHAM. **b.** Anxious..whether his sentences will p. 1880. Hence **Pa·rser**, one who parses; a book on parsing.

Parsec (pāɹse·k). 1913. [f. PAR(ALLAX + SEC(OND.] A unit of measure used for interstellar distances.

Parsee (pāɹsī·). 1615. [a. Pers. *Pārsī* Persian, f. *Pārs* Persia.] **1.** One of the descendants of those Persians who fled to India in the 7th and 8th centuries to escape Mohammedan persecution, and who still retain their religion (ZOROASTRIANISM); a Guebre. Also *attrib.* **2.** The language of Persia under the Sassanian kings 1840. **Parsee·ism**, Zoroastrianism.

Parseval (pā·ɹsėvăl). 1909. Also **Parsefal.** [f. the name of the inventor, August von *Parseval.*] Type of non-rigid German airship.

Parsimonious (pāɹsimōu·niəs), *a.* 1598. [f. L. *parsimonia* PARSIMONY + -OUS.] Characterized by parsimony; careful in the use or disposal of money or resources; sparing, saving, 'close'. Also *fig.* **b.** Of things: Yielding sparely; meagre, scanty; poor, mean 1713.

Hence **Parsimo·nious-ly** *adv.*, **-ness.**

Parsimony (pā·ɹsiməni). late ME. [ad. L. *parsimonia* or *parcimonia*, f. *parcere*, ppl. stem *pars-* to spare, save.] Carefulness in the employment of money or resources; saving or economic disposition. Also in bad sense 1561.

The misplaced parcimony of the Treasury 1896.

Phr. *Law of p.*, the logical principle that no more causes or forces should be assumed than are necessary to account for the facts.

Parsley (pā·ɹsli). [OE. *petersilie*, ad. late L. *petrosilium*, unexplained alteration of L. *petroselinum*, a. Gr. πετροσέλινον rock-parsley, f. πέτρα rock or πέτρος stone + σέλινον parsley; ME. *percil*, *-sil*, etc., a. OF. *peresil* :—late L. *petrosilium*; the later forms are app. a mixture of the OF. forms with the ending of the OE.] A biennial umbelliferous plant (*Petroselinum sativum*, sometimes classed as *Apium* or *Carum Petroselinum*), having white flowers and aromatic leaves, which are finely divided, and are used for seasoning and garnishing various dishes; in another variety (*Hamburg p.*) the large spindle-shaped root is dressed and eaten. Hence, the leaves of this plant, or the plants collectively. (Not with *a* or in *pl.*, exc. as = kind of parsley.)

Hamburg P. (see above); **Milk, Milky P.**, a name for species of *Peucedanum* and *Selinum* with milky juice; **Wild P.**, name for various wild umbellifers with finely-divided leaves. See also COW-*p.*, HEDGE-*p.*, STONE-PARSLEY, etc.

attrib. and *Comb.*, as *p. sauce*; **p.-bed**, a bed of p.; **-fern**, name for the Rock Brake (*Allosorus crispus* or *Cryptogramme crispa*), also applied to a variety of the Lady Fern (*Athyrium Filix-femina*).

Parsley-piert (-pīəɹt). Also **-pert.** 1597. [app. pop. corruption of F. *perce-pierre*, lit. 'pierce-stone'; cf. BREAKSTONE.] A dwarf annual herb (*Alchemilla arvensis*), allied to the Lady's Mantle, growing on dry barren ground, hedge-banks, etc.

Parsnip (pā·ɹsnip). [ME. *passenep*, *pasnep(e*, ult. repr. L. *pastinaca* parsnip, whence OF. *pasnaie*, of which *pasnep* may be an altered form by assoc. w. NEEP.] A biennial umbelliferous plant (*Pastinaca sativa*), having pinnate leaves, yellow flowers, and a pale yellow root, used in the cultivated state as a culinary vegetable. Hence, the root or edible part of this plant. Also extended to the genus *Pastinaca.* Also *attrib.*

Prov. *Fine* (*fair*, *soft*) *words butter no parsnips.*

Meadow P., (*a*) Cow-parsnip, *Heracleum Sphondylium*; (*b*) the N. American genus *Thaspium*; **Wild P.**, the wild form of *Pastinaca sativa* (see above). See also COW-*parsnip*, WATER-*parsnip.*

Parson (pā·ɹsən, pā·ɹs'n). [ME. *persone*, a. OF., AF. *persone*, later OF. *parsoune*, AF. *parson(e* :—L. *persona* PERSON, in med.L. 'rector of a parish'. For the genesis of the eccl. use see N.E.D.] **1.** *Eccl.* A holder of a parochial benefice in full possession of its rights and dues; a rector. **2.** Extended, in pop. use, so as to include a vicar, or any beneficed clergyman; a chaplain, a curate, any clergyman; a nonconformist minister or preacher. In the extended sense only *colloq.*, and often dyslogistic. 1588. **3.** *transf.* Applied to animals with black fur or markings, or to birds with black feathers. See also PARSON-BIRD. 1806. **4.** *fig.* A finger-post. Chiefly *dial.* 1785.

1. *P. imparsonee*: see IMPARSONEE. 2. 'Mr. C. ! He ain't a parson. He 's a Man' 1899. 3. *Isle of Wight p.*, the cormorant.

attrib. and *Comb.*: **p.-gull**, the great black-backed gull (*Larus marinus*); **p.-in-the-pulpit**, a pop. name of two plants, cuckoo-pint and monkshood; **parson's nose**, the rump of a fowl, etc.; **parson's week**, the time taken as a holiday by a clergyman who has a Sunday off, lasting usu. from Monday to the Saturday week following. Hence **Pa·rsondom**, the quality of a p.; parsons collectively. **Pa·rsoned** *ppl. a.* furnished with a p.; married in church or chapel (*colloq.*). **Pa·rsoness** (*joc.*), the wife of a p. **Parso·nic, -al** *adjs.* of or pertaining to a p.; characteristic of parsons; **-ly** *adv.*

Parsonage (pā·ɹsənėdʒ). late ME. [Altered form, as in prec., of *personage* PERSONAGE.] **1.** The benefice or living of a parson; a rectory. *Obs.* exc. in *Law.* **2.** (= *P.-house.*) The house attached to a parson's living, the rector's house. Sometimes applied to the residence provided for any minister of religion. late ME. †**3.** The parson's tithe. *Sc.* –1818. **4.** *attrib.*, as *p.-house*, etc. 1566.

3. What have I been paying stipend and teind, p. and vicarage for, ever sin' the [year] aughty-nine? SCOTT.

Pa·rson-bird. 1857. [See PARSON 3.] **1.** A New Zealand bird (*Prosthemadera novæ-zelandiæ*), so called from its dark plumage and white neck-feathers; also called *poe-bird* or *tui.* **2.** The Rook 1902.

Part (pāɹt), *sb.* (*adv.*) [In OE. ad. L. *pars, partem* (in sense 2 a); in 13th c. a. F. *part* :—L. *partem.*] **A.** *sb.* **I.** Portion of a whole. **1.** That which with another or others makes up a whole; a certain amount, but not all, of any thing or number of things; a portion, division, section, element, constituent, piece. (When denoting a number of persons or things, often taken as a noun of multitude with pl. verb.) ME. **b.** Often used without article. late ME. **c.** *spec.* An essential or integral portion; a constituent, element. (Also without article.) 1732. **2.** *spec.* †**a.** = *part of speech.* (The earliest use.) –1637. **b.** A division of a book, play, poem, etc.; also *spec.* Each of the portions of a work issued at intervals, a fascicule 1450. †**c.** An element or constituent *of* some quality or action (with no stress on its being merely a part); a point, particular. Hence *absol.* Point; matter; affair; respect. –1719. **3.** A portion of an animal body. Usu. *pl.*; also *absol.* (*euphem.*) = private parts. late ME. †**4.** A minute portion of matter; a particle –1800. **5.** *spec.* (with a numeral): Each of the equal portions of a whole; an aliquot part, exact divisor, submultiple ME. †**b.** Used by confusion as if = 'times' as in (*by*) *a thousand parts*, etc. –1625. **c.** In expressing the proportions of the ingredients of a mixture: One of a number of equal portions of indeterminate amount 1615.

1. The greatest p. of the Indian cavalry were cut to pieces 1774. Whatever is the p. of a p., is a p. of the whole 1836. b. He burneth p. thereof in the fire *Isa.* xliv. 16. Great p. perished before they could reach the wall SOUTHEY. c. The rider sate as if he had been a p. of the horse SCOTT. *P. and parcel* (emphatic). 5. Possession..being nine parts of the law 1813. c. Take of pure sulphate of copper, two parts; subcarbonate of ammonia, three parts 1811.

II. Portion allotted, share. **1.** A portion of something allotted to a particular person; a share. Also, Sharing, participation; interest, concern ME. **b.** Allotted portion; possession; one's lot in life. *Obs.* or *arch.* late ME. **2.** What one has to do; function, office, business, duty. late ME. **3.** *Theatr.* The character assigned to an actor in a dramatic performance; a rôle. Also, the words spoken by an actor in such a rôle; hence, a copy of these. 1495. **b.** *fig.* late ME. **4.** *Mus.* The melody assigned to a particular voice or instrument in concerted music, or a copy of this; each of the constituent melodies or successions of notes which make up a harmony. Hence *transf.* Each of the voices or instruments which join in a concerted piece. 1526. †**5.** A piece of conduct, an act –1632. **6.** A personal quality or attribute; almost always in *pl.* Abilities, capacities, talents. Also *absol.* = high intellectual ability, cleverness. Now *arch.* or *literary.* 1561.

1. Phr. *To have p.*, to share, partake (*in*, †*of*). *To have neither p. nor lot in*, to have no share or concern in. 2. Accuse not Nature, she hath don her p. MILT. 3. All the world 's a stage..And one man in his time playes many parts SHAKS. b. Phr. *To play* (*act*) *the p. of*, to act as or like. *To play* (*act*) *a p.*, to perform a function, or pursue a course of action; also, to sustain a feigned character, act deceitfully; He was unskilled to act a p. and speak half the truth 1886. 6. A gentleman..of very excellent good partes B. JONS. A man of Parts, but a most vile, stinking Whigg HEARNE.

III. Region; side. **1.** A portion of a country, etc., or of the world; a region, quarter. (Usu. in *pl.*; often with a vague collective sense.) late ME. †**2.** Side (*lit.*); hence, direction in space –1774. **b.** = HAND *sb.* (see *On hand* e.) Now *rare.* 1485. **3.** Side in a contest, dispute, contract, etc.; party; cause. late ME. **b.** *concr.* A party; a body of partisans; a faction. Now *rare* or *Obs.* ME.

1. To propagate the Gospel in foreign parts BERKELEY. 2. *Luke* xvii. 24. b. On the other p., I judged that I might lose nearly as much STEVENSON. 3. An agreement made..Between—..(the vendor) of the one p., and—..(the purchaser) of the other p. 1884.

IV. [f. PART *v.*] The parting of the hair. *U.S.* 1890.

Phrases. **P. of speech** (*Gram.*) [L. *pars orationis*], formerly also *p. of reason*, or simply *part*, each of the classes of words as determined by the kind of notion or relation which they express in the sentence. **Most p.**, the greatest p., most; as *adv.* mostly; †*the more p.*, the majority. **Take p.**: **a.** To share, partake *of* or *in* (cf. II. 1); **b.** To participate *in* (some action), to assist, co-operate (cf. II. 2). **For my p.**, as regards my share in the matter, as far as I am concerned; so *for his, our, your p.*, etc. **In p.**, partly. **In good p.**, favourably or without offence; *in ill p.*, unfavourably. Chiefly with *take* or the like. **On the p. of** (any one, *on his p.*, etc.), on the side of; as regards (his, etc.) share in the action; as far as (he, etc.) is concerned; also, proceeding from (the person or party mentioned) as agent; made or performed by; by.

Comb.: **p.-music**, music in parts (esp. vocal); **-singing**, singing in parts; **-writing**, composition of music in parts, combination of parts in musical composition (see II. 4).

B. *adv.* or quasi-*adv.* or *adj.* In part, partly, to some extent. Usu. hyphened when qualifying a sb. or an adj. used *attrib.* 1513.

This wretch hath p. confest his Villany SHAKS. A part-heard case of alleged dealing in bogus cheques 1891. *P.-payment*, payment in p., action of partly paying. *P.-time*, applied to a person employed for part of his or her time, or to such an employment.

Part (pāɹt), *v.* ME. [a. F. *partir* :—L. *partire* (in cl. L. usu. *partiri*) to part, divide, share, f. *pars, partem*, stem *parti-* PART *sb.*] **I. 1.** *trans.* To divide into parts; to divide, break, sever. Now somewhat *rare.* **b.** To separate (the hair), as with a comb, on each side of a dividing line or *parting* 1615. **c.** *Naut.* To break, or suffer the breaking of (a rope) so as to get loose from an anchor, a mooring, etc. 1793. **2.** *intr.* To suffer division, break, cleave, come in two or in pieces 1579. **3.** *trans.* To dissolve (a connexion, etc.) by separation of the persons or parties concerned. late ME. **4.** To put asunder, sunder (two or more persons or things, or one *from* another); to separate (combatants, companions, lovers, etc.). Also *fig.* to separate in thought, to distinguish ME. **b.** To keep asunder or separate; to separate as a boundary 1575. **c.** *spec.* in techn. uses; esp. (*Metall.*), to separate (gold and silver) from each other by an acid 1487. **d.** *intr.* or *absol.* To make or cause separation or division 1611.

1. Thou shalt p. it in pieces, and powr oyle thereon *Lev.* ii. 6. *To p. the hoof*, to have cloven hoofs; Every beast that parteth the hoofe *Deut.* xiv. 6. c. In the attempt, it parted the grappling rope 1793. 2. The frigate parted amidships MARRYAT. 3. Phr. *To p. company* (= sense II. 2). *To p. a fight, fray*, to put an end to a fight by separating the combatants. †*To p. beds*, to cease to live together in wedlock. 4. The Lord doe so to me, and more also, if ought but death p. thee and me *Ruth* i. 17. While he blessed them, hee was parted from them, and caried vp into heauen *Luke* xxiv. 51. b. Where seas or deserts p. them from the rest COWPER.

II. 1. *intr.* To become or be separated (*from* something); to be liberated or detached; to emanate; to come off (*rare*) ME. **2.** In reciprocal sense: To go or come apart, to separate. Of persons: To quit one another's company. ME. **b.** *absol.* To part with something, esp. money; to give or pay money. *slang* or *colloq.* 1873. **3.** *intr.* To take one's leave or departure; to go away; to set out (*arch.*) ME. **b.** *To p.* (*hence, out of this life*, etc.): to die ME. †**4.** *trans.* = DEPART *v.* II. 4. –1812.

2. But dearest friends, alas! must p. GAY. Here our roads parted (*mod.*). *P. from*, (*a*) to go away from, leave; *b.* = sense II. 3 b (now *rare*). *P. with* (*a*) = sense II. 2 (now *rare*); (*b*) to let go, give up; to send away, dismiss; of a body or substance: to lose, give off (heat, etc.); Oh, that I should p. with so much gold! MARLOWE. 3. But now he parted hence SHAKS. b. A [= he] parted eu'n iust betweene Twelue and One SHAKS. 4. *Rich. II*, III. i. 3.

III. 1. *trans.* To divide to or among a number of recipients; to distribute in shares. Somewhat *arch.* ME. **2.** To share with another or others; (of one person) to give a share of to another; (of several) to divide among themselves. Now *rare* or *Obs.* exc. *dial.* ME. †**3.** *intr.* To make division into shares; to give, take, or have a share; to 'go shares' (*with* a person; *of* or *in*, rarely *with*, a thing) –1670.

1. To p. her time 'twixt reading and bohea POPE. 3. They shall p. alike 1 *Sam.* xxx. 24. So †**Pa·rtable** *a.* = PARTIBLE –1632. **Pa·rter**, one who or that which parts (now *rare*).

‖**Partage** (partā·ʒ). 1456. [a. F., f. *partir* to PART; see -AGE. Formerly naturalized; now treated as F.] **1.** Division; esp. division into shares 1598. **2.** A part, share, lot 1456.

Partake (pāɹtē̆·k), *v.* 1561. [Back-formation from PARTAKER, PARTAKING, syncopated f. *part-taker, -taking*, repr. L. *particeps, -cipium.*] **I.** *trans.* **1.** To take a part in, to share in 1589. **b.** To share (a meal); hence, To eat or drink of, to 'take'. Now *rare* or *Obs.* 1611. †**c.** To be made acquainted with (news, etc.) –1667. †**2.** To impart, communicate (*to* or *with*); *esp.* to make known –1611. †**3.** To inform (a person) *of* (news, etc.) –1590.

1. The old man Partook that feeling SOUTHEY. c. Let her with thee p. what thou hast heard MILT. 2. *Wint. T.* v. iii. 132.

II. *intr.* **1.** To participate in some action or condition. Const. *in, of* (†*with*) the thing; *with* the person sharing. 1585. **b.** *esp.* (with *of*) To get, have a share or portion of. Often = to take some of, take of, take 1601. **c.** To have something *of* (a quality or attribute) 1615. †**2.** To take sides *with* a person –1627.

1. Bred in a luxurious court, without partaking in its effeminacy GOLDSM. b. Her solitary meals she partook of in the apartment next the eating room 1805. 2. When I against my selfe with thee pertake SHAKS. *Sonn.* cxlix. Hence **Parta·kable, -takeable** *a.* capable of †partaking, or of being partaken.

Partaker (pāɹtē̆·kəɹ). late ME. [f. PART *sb.* + TAKER; rendering L. *particeps.*] **1.** One who takes a part or share, a partner, participator. (Now viewed as = one who partakes.) †**2.** One who take's another's part; a supporter, partisan –1700.

1. All the other are part-takers therof more or lesse 1561. Alike p. of my joys or grief 1774. 2. To the..long unquieting of kyng Henry and his partakers 1548.

Partaking (pāɹtē̆·kiŋ), *vbl. sb.* late ME. [f. PART *sb.* + TAKING *vbl. sb.*] **1.** The taking of a part or share; participation. †**2.** The taking the part of some one; taking sides (in a dispute, etc.) –1657.

Partan (pā·ɹtăn). *Sc.* and *n. dial.* late ME. [app. Celtic; in Gael. *partan*; ult. history unkn.] A crab; *esp.* the common crab, *Cancer pagurus*; *fig.* an ill-natured person.

Parted (pā·ɹtėd), *ppl. a.* late ME. **I.** [*pa. pple.* of PART *v.*; see -ED [1].] **1.** Divided into parts; severed, cloven; divided, as the hair, by a parting 1590. **b.** *Bot.* Cleft nearly to the base, as a corolla or calyx, as *3-parted*, tripartite 1880. **c.** *Her.* = PARTY *a.* 3; hence of cloth, trappings, etc. 1478. **2.** Separated, sundered 1611. **3.** Departed, dead (*arch.*) 1593. **II.** [f. PART *sb.* + -ED [2].] †**1.** Furnished with or having (good, mean, etc.) parts; gifted, talented –1668. **2.** Charged with a dramatic part 1612.

1. A Man well p., a sufficient Scholler B. JONS.

Parterre (pāɹtē̆·ɹ). 1639. [a. F.; subst. use of *par terre* on or over the ground.] **1.** A level space in a garden occupied by flower-beds ornamentally arranged. Also *fig.* **2.** The part of the ground-floor of the auditorium of a theatre behind the orchestra; also, its occupants 1711.

Parthenic (paɹþe·nik), *a.*[1] *rare.* 1834. [ad. Gr. παρθενικός, f. παρθένος virgin.] Of or belonging to, or of the nature of, a virgin; *fig.* unviolated. So **Parthe·nian** *a.* 1656.

Parthenic (paɹþe·nik), *a.*[2] 1877. [f. L. *parthenium* (in the herbalists) camomile + -IC.] In *p. acid*, an acid obtained from some species of *Parthenium*; so **Pa·rthenine**, an alkaloid obtained from *P. Hysterophorus* and used as a remedy for fever and neuralgia.

Parthenogenesis(pā:ɹþĕnodʒe·nėsis).1849. [f. Gr. παρθένος virgin + γένεσις GENESIS.] *Biol.* Reproduction without concourse of opposite sexes or union of sexual elements. So **Pa:rthenogene·tic** *a.* pertaining to, of the nature of, or characterized by p.; reproducing by p. **Pa:rthenogene·tically** *adv.*

‖ **Parthenogonidium** (pā:ɹþĕnogoni·diŏm). 1895. [mod.L., f. Gr. παρθένος virgin + GONIDIUM.] *Bot.* A gonidium in certain algæ, as *Volvox*, by which they are reproduced asexually.

Parthenospore (pā·ɹþĕnospōᵊɹ). 1889. [f. Gr. παρθένος virgin + SPORE.] *Bot.* A reproductive cell in certain algæ, resembling a zygospore, but produced without conjugation.

Parthian (pā·ɹþiăn), *a.* and *sb.* 1526. [See -AN, -IAN.] **A.** *adj.* Of or pertaining to Parthia, an ancient kingdom of western Asia 1590.

The Parthian horsemen were accustomed to discharge their missiles backwards while in real or pretended flight; hence used allusively in *P. shaft, shot, glance*, etc.

B. *sb.* A native or inhabitant of Parthia.

Or like the P. I shall flying fight SHAKS.

‖ **Parti** (parti). 1814. [F., = party; side, match, resolution taken for oneself.] **1.** A marriageable person considered in reference to means, etc., or as a 'match'. **2.** *Parti pris*, side taken, mind made up, bias 1871.

Parti-[1], extended use of *parti-* in PARTI-COLOURED, as in †**pa·rtie-coated**, having a parti-coloured or motley coat (SHAKS.). So in †**pa·rti-me:mbered**, having members or limbs of two kinds (MILTON); etc.

Parti-[2], comb. form of L. *pars, partem*, PART; as in **parti-pa·rtial** *a.* (*Logic*), applied by Sir W. Hamilton to a proposition in which both terms are partial or particular; **parti-to·tal**, in which one is particular and one universal.

Partial (pā·ɹʃăl), *a.* (*sb.*) ME. [a. OF. *parcial*, F. *partial*, and in sense 2 *partiel*, ad. late L. *partialis.*] **A.** *adj.* **I.** Inclined antecedently to favour one party in a cause, or one side of the question more than the other; biased; interested; unfair. (Opp. to *impartial.*) **b.** Prejudiced or biased in some one's favour; hence: Favourably disposed, kindly, sympathetic. Const. *to.* Now *rare.* 1585. **c.** With *to*: Having a liking for, fond of (*colloq.*) 1696.

1. I perseaue, that God is not parciall TINDALE *Acts* x. 34. **b.** So obliging, so p. to our Sophist BENTLEY. **c.** I am not more p. to my arm chair.. than of yore 1827.

II. 1. Pertaining to or involving a part only; constituting a part only; incomplete 1641. **b.** *spec.* That is one of the parts that make up a whole; constituent, component 1481. **2.** In techn. senses. **a.** *Astron.* Applied to an eclipse in which part only of the disk of the luminary is covered or darkened 1704. **b.** *Math.* (*a*) Applied to differentials, differentiation, etc. relative to one only of the variables involved, the rest being for the time supposed constant. (*b*) *P. determinant* = MINOR *determinant* 1816. **c.** *Bot.* Forming one of the parts of a compound structure; secondary, subordinate; as *p. umbel*, each of the smaller umbels of a compound umbel; etc. 1760. **d.** *Acoustics* and *Mus.* Applied to any one of the simple tones which together form a complex tone. *Upper p. tones* (or *upper partials*): those higher in pitch than the fundamental tone; also called *harmonics* or *overtones.* 1879. **e.** *R. C. Ch.* Of an indulgence: Remitting part only of the temporal punishment of sin 1885.

1. Or p. Ill is universal Good POPE. P. damage to merchandise 1886.

B. *sb. Acoustics* and *Mus.* Short for *p. tone*; see 2 d above. Hence **Pa·rtialness.**

Partialism (pā·ɹʃăliz'm). 1864. [-ISM.] **1.** A partial theory or view, which does not take into account all the facts 1872. **2.** *Theol.* = PARTICULARISM 1. 1864.

Partialist (pā·ɹʃălist). 1597. [f. PARTIAL *a.* + -IST.] **1.** *gen.* A partial, prejudiced, or biased person; a partisan. **2.** One whose knowledge or outlook is limited 1841. **3.** *Theol.* = PARTICULARIST 1864.

Partiality (pāɹʃiæ·lĭti). late ME. [a. OF. *parci-, partialité*, med.L. *partialitas*, f. *partialis* PARTIAL; see -ITY.] **1.** The quality or character of being partial (see PARTIAL I); prejudice, bias, unfairness; an instance of this. **b.** Prepossession in favour of a particular person or thing; hence, Favourable disposition, predilection, fondness for some one or something. Const. *to, for, towards* 1581. †**2.** Party-spirit, rivalry; factiousness -1752.

1. Gyue trew iugement without ony fauoure or parsealyte LD. BERNERS.

Partialize (pā·ɹʃăləiz), *v.* 1592. [ad. F. *partialiser*, f. *partial* PARTIAL; see -IZE.] †**1.** *intr.* To be partial -1656. **2.** *trans.* To render partial; to bias 1593.

Partially (pā·ɹʃăli), *adv.* 1460. [f. PARTIAL + -LY[2].] **I.** (= F. *partialement.*) In a biased manner, with partiality; unfairly, unjustly. Now *rare.* 1495. **b.** With special favour or affection. Now *rare.* 1633.

Their own transgressions p. they smother SHAKS.

II. (= F. *partiellement.*) In a partial way or degree; incompletely; partly 1460.

Which was but p. true SIR T. BROWNE.

Partible (pā·ɹtĭb'l), *a.* 1540. [ad. post-cl. L. *partibilis*, f. *partiri* to part, divide; see -BLE.] Capable of being parted or separated; subject to partition; divisible; separable. **b.** That involves partition of inheritance 1653.

A father's land was p. among all his children 1863. Hence **Partibi·lity**, p. quality.

Participable (paɹti·sipăb'l), *a.* 1450. [a. OF., f. *participer* to PARTICIPATE; see -BLE.] †**1.** Liable to participate. **2.** Capable of being participated or shared 1610.

Participant (paɹti·sipănt), *a.* and *sb.* 1549. [ad. L. *participantem*, pr. pple. of *participare* to PARTICIPATE.] **A.** *adj.* Participating, partaking, sharing. **B.** *sb.* One who participates in anything; a sharer, partaker 1562.

The chief participants in the recent massacre 1891.

Participate (paɹti·sipĕt), *ppl. a.* Now *rare* or *Obs.* 1450. [ad. L. *participatus* made to share; see next.] †**1.** = prec. A. -1657. **2.** as *pa. pple.* Shared, participated 1850.

Participate (paɹti·sipeᶦt), *v.* 1531. [f. L. *participat-, participare*, f. *particeps, participem* a partaker, f. *parti-* PART + *-cip-*, weak form of *cap-*, stem of *capere* to take. See -ATE[3].] **I.** *trans.* **1.** = PARTAKE I. 1. †**2.** = PARTAKE I. 2. -1707.

1. The one [the soul] we p. with goddes, the other [the body] with bestes ELYOT.

II. *intr.* = PARTAKE II. 1 (but not now said of sharing in material things). Const. *with* a person, *in* (†*of*, †*with*) a thing. 1565. **b.** = PARTAKE II. 1 c. 1578.

Millie and I..participated very little in the general conversation 1873. **b.** Both members p. of harmony JOHNSON. Hence **Parti·cipating** *vbl. sb.* and *ppl. a.* (*spec.* profit-sharing). **Parti·cipatingly** *adv.*

Participation (paɹtisipēᶦ·ʃən). late ME. [a. F., ad. L. *participationem*; see prec.] **1.** The action or fact of partaking, having or forming part *of*; †the partaking of the substance, quality, or nature *of.* **2.** The fact or condition of sharing in common (*with* others, or with each other); partnership, fellowship; profit-sharing. late ME. **b.** A taking part (with others) in some action or matter 1667.

1. As for the other Sacrament, make conscience of a frequent p. thereof 1631. **2.** For thou hast lost thy Princely Priuiledge, With vile p. SHAKS. Sharing in whatever surplus profits are realised by the more efficient labour which p. calls forth 1881.

Participative (paɹti·sipeᶦtiv), *a.* 1651. [f. L. *participat-, -are*; see -IVE.] Having the quality of participating.

Participator (paɹti·sipeᶦtəɹ). 1796. [a. late L., f. *participare* to PARTICIPATE.] One who participates; a partaker, sharer. So **Parti·cipatory** *a.* characterized by participation or profit-sharing.

Participial (pāɹtisi·piăl), *a.* and *sb.* 1570. [ad. L. *participialis*, f. *participium* PARTICIPLE.] **A.** *adj.* Of the nature of a participle; of, pertaining to, or involving a participle 1591. **B.** *sb.* A verbal derivative of the nature of, or akin to, a participle 1570.

A. *P. adjective*, an adjective that is a participle in origin and form. Hence **Partici·pialize** *v.* to make p., turn into a participle. **Partici·pially** *adv.* as a participle.

Participle (pā·ɹtisip'l), *sb.* late ME. [a. OF. *participle*, by-form of *participe*, ad. L. *participium* a sharing, etc., after Gr. μετοχή.] †**1.** A person, animal, or thing that partakes of the nature of two or more different classes -1694. **2.** *Gram.* A word that partakes of the nature of a verb and an adjective; a deriv. of a verb which has the function and construction of an adjective (qualifying a noun), while retaining some of those of the verb (*e.g.* tense, government of an object); a verbal adjective. Formerly often reckoned a separate part of speech.

2. *To whom coming as unto a living stone*: the p. notes a continued motion 1681.

Particle (pā·ɹtik'l), *sb.* late ME. [ad. L. *particula*, dim. of *pars, partem* PART.] **1.** A small part or portion of a whole. Now *rare* or *Obs.*, or merged in 2. **b.** A very small part of any proposition, writing, etc.; a clause; an article of a formula 1526. **2.** A very minute portion of matter; formerly often = atom or molecule; in *Dynamics*, a minute mass of matter, which while still having inertia and attraction is treated as a point, i.e. as having no magnitude. late ME. **b.** The smallest conceivable portion of something immaterial 1620. **c.** *Liturg.* A fragment of the Host or consecrated bread 1727. **3.** *Gram.* A minor part of speech, esp. one that is short and indeclinable, a relation-word; also, a prefix or suffix having a distinct meaning, as *un-, -ly, -ness* 1533.

1. Ane p. of beif 1567. **2.** Every p. of matter attracts every other p. 1871. **b.** They had never entertained a p. of doubt PALEY.

Parti-coloured, particoloured (pā·ɹtikʊ·ləɹd; stress var.), *a.* Also **party-.** 1535. [f. *parti*, PARTY *a.*] Partly of one colour and partly of another; diversicoloured. **b.** *fig.* Varied, chequered 1622.

The Pope's parti-coloured body guard 1879. **b.** Life party-colour'd, half pleasure, half care PRIOR. Hence †**Parti-colour** *a.*; also as *sb.* -1662. †**Parti-colour** *v.* to make parti-coloured, colour variously (*rare*).

Particular (păɹti·kiŭlăɹ), *a.* and *sb.* late ME. [a. OF. *particuler* (mod. F.-*ier*), ad.L. *particularis* of or concerning a part, f. *particula* PARTICLE; see -AR[1].] **A.** *adj.* **I.** †**1.** Partial; not universal -1643. **2.** Relating to a single definite thing or person, a set of things or persons, as dist. from others; of one's (its, etc.) own; special; not general. late ME. †**b.** Proper, peculiar, restricted (*to*) -1725. **c.** *Logic.* Applied to a proposition in which something is predicated of some, not all, of a class; opp. to *universal* 1551. †**3.** Private, personal, not public -1768. **4.** That is a unit or definite one among a number; taken or considered by itself; individual, single, separate 1529. **5.** Distinguished among others of the kind; marked; special 1485. †**b.** Noteworthy; peculiar, singular -1791. †**c.** Singular, strange, odd- 1817. **d.** Used in the names of certain modifications of ordinary iambic metres common in hymns, as *Common P. Metre* (8.8.6.8.8.6.), *Long P. Metre* (8.8.8.8.8.8.), etc. Chiefly *U.S.* **6.** Relating to or dealing with the separate parts, elements, or details of a whole; detailed, minute, circumstantial 1450. †**7.** Specially attentive to a person; bestowing marked attentions; familiar in manner -1771. **b.** Closely acquainted, intimate. (Now assoc. w. 5) 1706. **8.** Attentive to or scrupulous concerning details of action; hence exacting as to details, nice in taste, fastidious 1814.

1. The Three yeares Drought, in the time of Elias, was but P., and left People Aliue BACON. **2.** These are not my p. Sentiments BURKE. *P. average*: see AVERAGE *sb.*[2] 4. *P. Baptists*, a body of Baptists holding the Calvinistic doctrines of *p. election* and *p. redemption*, i.e. the Divine election, etc., of some, not all, of the human race. **c.** 'Some lakes have an outlet' is a p. judgment 1860. **4.** Make..each p. haire to stand an end SHAKS. **5.** P. pains p. thanks do ask B. JONS. b. Johnson's mode of penmanship, which at all times was very p. BOSWELL. 6. The p. Description of the several Instruments 1669. I am thus p. in the relation of every incident 1803. 7. Never suffer this Fellow to be p. with you again FIELDING. b. These are p. friends of mine SHERIDAN. 8. People who have to work for their living must not be too p. 1879.

Phr. *P. estate* (Law), 'that interest which is granted ..out of a larger estate, which then becomes an expectancy either in reversion or remainder' (Wharton). So *p. tenant*, the tenant of a p. estate.

II. Absol. uses. 1. The p. That which is particular 1551. 2. In p. †a. (Each) by itself, individually, severally; in detail –1737. b. In distinction from others; particularly, especially 1502. †c. In private –1702. †3. In the p. In the particular or special case; opp. to *in the general* –1827.

1. This argument is from the p., to the vniuersall 1551.

B. *sb.* †1. A part of a whole; *spec.* a division or 'head' of a discourse or argument –1859. 2. A detail, item, point, circumstance 1533. b. *pl.* Items or details of statement or information; information as to details; a detailed account 1606. †3. A minute account, description, or enumeration; a minute –1846. †4. a. Each one of a number or group of things; an individual thing or article –1743. b. An individual person; occas. *spec.* a private person, one not holding a public position –1766. 5. More vaguely: A particular case or instance. (Usu. in *pl.*; opp. to *generals* or *universals.*) 1600. b. *Logic.* = *particular proposition* (see A. I. 2 c) 1551. †6. (One's) individual case; personal interest or concern; part. Chiefly in phr. *for, in, as to*, etc. (*one's*) *p.* –1790. †b. Personal or private interest, profit, or advantage –1653. †c. Personal relation, intimacy; personal interest, regard, or favour (*rare*) –1631. 7. *colloq.* or *slang.* a. Something specially belonging to, or characteristic of, a place or person, as *London p.*, a London fog 1807. b. A special friend 1828.

1. Let us devide the discourse..into foure particulars 1601. 2. Examine mee vpon the particulars of my Life SHAKS. b. But how, but how, giue me particulars SHAKS. 5. Deliberation for the most part is of Particulars HOBBES. 6. We have all admired it.. and for my own p., I return you my sincerest thanks COWPER. c. *Cor.* v. i. 3. Hence **Parti·cularly** *adv.* in a p. manner, or with a p. reference.

Particularism (pătiˑkiŭlăriz'm). 1824. [f. PARTICULAR + -ISM.] 1. *Theol.* The doctrine of particular election or particular redemption (see PARTICULAR A. I. 2) 1828. 2. Exclusive devotion to one's particular party, sect, nation, etc.; exclusiveness 1824. 3. *Politics.* The principle of leaving each state in an empire or federation free to retain its own government, laws, and rights; esp. in German politics after *c* 1850. 1853. So **Parti·cularist**, an advocate of p.; also as *adj.*

Particularity (pătikiŭlæ·rĭti). 1528. [a. F. *particularité*, ad. late L. *particularitatem*, f. *particularis* PARTICULAR; see -ITY.] 1. The quality of being particular as opp. to general or universal 1587. †b. A particular case or instance –1598. 2. The quality of being special or of a special kind; the fact of being noteworthy (now *rare*) 1570. †b. Singularity, oddity –1791. 3. An attribute belonging particularly to the thing in question; a peculiarity (now *rare*) 1588. †4. A particular point or circumstance, a detail –1796. 5. Minuteness or detailedness of description, statement, etc. 1638. †6. Special attentiveness *to* a person; familiarity –1815. 7. Attentiveness to details; scrupulous preciseness 1671.

1. b. 2 *Hen. VI*, v. ii. 44. 4. And so..entered into the particularities of the matter 1528. 6. Objectionable p. to another woman JANE AUSTEN. 7. A p. as to the saving of string 1882.

Particularize (pătiˑkiŭlăraiz), *v.* 1588. [a. F. *particulariser*; see -IZE.] 1. *trans.* To render particular (as opp. to general); to restrict to a particular thing or class (*rare*). 2. To name or state specially, or one by one; to speak or treat of individually, or in detail; to specify. (The usual sense.) 1593. b. *intr.* To go into particulars or detail 1601. 3. *trans.* To render distinct or separate; to individualize, distinguish, differentiate (*rare*) 1643.

2. In mentioning your friends, I must p. Mr. Pope 1741. b. In our hasty narrative..we have not paused to p. 1834. Hence **Parti·cularizaˑtion.**

Particulate (păɹtiˑkiŭlĕt), *a.* Only in scientific use. 1874. [ad. med. or mod.L. *particulatus*, *particulare* to divide into particles, f. *particula* PARTICLE.] Existing in the condition of minute separate particles. b. Of or relating to minute separate particles 1881.

Paˑrticule. *Obs.* exc. in sense 2, as Fr. (partĭkü·l). 1540. [a. F., ad. L. *particula* PARTICLE.] †1. A particle –1647. ‖2. *spec.* Applied to the French preposition *de* used as a prefix of nobility in personal names 1889.

‖**Partie** (partī·). 1678. [F.] a. A match in a game, a game. b. *P. carrée*, a party of four 1739.

Partile (pā·ɹtəil, -til), *a.* 1576. [ad. L. *partilis* divisible, partial, f. root of *partire* to divide; see -ILE.] †1. = PARTIAL *a.* II. –1697. 2. *Astrol.* Of an aspect: Exact to the same degree and minute, or, at least, within a degree. Opp. to PLATIC. 1610.

2. *P. conjunction*, exact conjunction; so *p. opposition*; *p. trine*, positions exactly 120° apart.

Parting (pā·ɹtiŋ), *vbl. sb.* ME. [f. PART *v.* + -ING[1].] The action of PART *v.*, partition; the result, or place, of this action; something that parts. 1. Division, breaking, cleaving 1530. b. The division or dividing line of the hair when combed 1698. 2. Separation; *spec.* in techn. uses (cf. PART *v.* I. 4 c) ME. b. The place at which two or more things separate; as the *p. of the ways* (often *fig.*); *water-p.*, a WATERSHED. late ME. c. *concr.* Something that parts or separates two things; *esp.* in techn. uses, as (*a*) *Mining* and *Geol.* A layer of rock, clay, etc. lying between two beds of different formations; (*b*) *Founding.* Fine sand (*p.-sand*) or other powdery substance used to prevent adhesion of the surfaces of the parts of a mould 1708. 3. Mutual separation of two or more persons; leave-taking ME. 4. Departure; also *fig.* (*euphem.*) decease, death (*arch.*) ME.

1. There being great danger of the ship's p. 1748. 3. P. is such sweete sorrow, That I shall say good night, till it be morrow SHAKS. The p. with a beloved Child 1705.

attrib. and *Comb.* a. *attrib.* Of or pertaining to parting; *esp.* (in adjectival construction) Given, taken, performed, etc. at parting; 'farewell', concluding, final. **p. cup**, (*a*) a drinking-cup with two handles, used by two persons in taking a draught of liquor at parting; (*b*) a kind of 'cup' or compound beverage made with ale and sherry. b. Of or pertaining to separation, as *parting-point*; *esp.* in names of technical appliances used for separating something, etc., as **p.-bead** = *p.-strip*; **-sand** (see 2 c); **-strip**, a strip of material used for separating two parts, e. g. the vertical strip of wood inserted at the side of the frame of a sash window to keep the sashes apart when raised or lowered; **-tool**, name of various tools used for separating pieces of material, for trimming, cutting fine outlines and markings, etc.

Paˑrting, *ppl. a.* late ME. [f. as prec. + -ING[2].] That parts. 1. Separating, dividing; forming a boundary between two things 1699. 2. Dividing, breaking, going to pieces 1719. 3. Going away, departing; *fig.* dying 1577. †4. Sharing, participating; *p. fellow*, sharer, partner –1514.

3. The curfew tolls the knell of p. day GRAY.

Partisan, partizan (pā·ɹtizæ̆n, pāɹtizæ·n), *sb.*[1] (*a.*) 1555. [a. F. *partisan* sb. and adj., ad. It. dial. form = Tuscan *partigiano*; f. *parte* part.] A. *sb.* 1. One who takes part or sides with another; *esp.* a zealous supporter of a party, person, or cause; often in bad sense: a blind, prejudiced, unreasoning or fanatical adherent. 2. *Mil.* A member of a party of light or irregular troops employed in scouring the country, making forays, etc.; a member of a volunteer force similarly employed, a guerrilla 1692. b. A leader of a body of such troops; a guerrilla chief 1706.

1. The clergyman must never be a p. 1866.

B. *attrib.* or as *adj.* 1. Of, pertaining to, or characteristic of a partisan; biased, prejudiced, one-sided 1842. 2. *Mil.* Of or pertaining to military partisans; pertaining to irregular or petty warfare 1708.

1. P. malice 1842, politics 1882. 2. The system of guerilla or partizan warfare [in Spain] SCOTT. *P. ranger* = RANGER 3. Hence **Partisanship**, the state, condition, or practice of a p.; zealous or blind support of one's party.

Partisan, partizan (pā·ɹtizæ̆n), *sb.*[2] *Obs.* from *c* 1700 until revived by Scott. 1556. [a. F. *partizane*, ad. It. *partesana*, var. of *partigiana*, of obsc. etym.] 1. A weapon used by infantry in the 16th–17th centuries, consisting of a long-handled spear, the blade having one or more lateral cutting projections. b. Used as a 'leading-staff' and borne as a halberd by civic and other guards 1611. 2. *transf.* A soldier, etc. armed with a partisan 1693.

1. I had as liue haue a Reede that will doe me no seruice, as a Partizan I could not heaue SHAKS.

Partite (pā·ɹtəit), *a.* 1570. [ad. L. *partitus* parted, divided. Cf. BIPARTITE, etc.] a. Divided into parts or portions. b. *Bot.* and *Entom.* Divided to the base, or nearly so, as a leaf, corolla, or insect's wing 1760.

The leaves are..palmate, five-p. 1880.

Partition (pătiˑʃən), *sb.* late ME. [a. F., ad. L. *partitionem*, f. *partire* to PART.] 1. The action of parting or dividing into parts; the fact of being so divided; division 1509. b. Division into shares or portions; distribution. late ME. 2. The action of parting or separating two or more persons or things; the fact or condition of being separated; separation, division 1530. 3. Something that separates; *esp.* that which separates one part of a space from another; *e.g.* a structure separating rooms or parts of a room (*esp.* when slighter than a wall proper); a septum or dissepiment in a plant or animal body; etc. 1545. 4. Each of the parts into which a whole is divided, as by boundaries or lines; a portion, part, division, section; a compartment; a pane, a panel; a pocket (of a bag); an apartment, chamber, room 1561. 5. *Law.* A division of real property, esp. of lands, between joint tenants, tenants in common, or coparceners, by which their co-tenancy or co-ownership is abolished and their individual interests are separated 1474. 6. *Logic.* Analysis by systematic separation of the integrant parts of a thing; enumeration of parts. (Dist. from *division.*) 1551. 7. *Math.* †a. = DIVISION 5. –1729. b. Any one of the ways of expressing a number as a sum of positive integers (*e.g.* the partitions of 4 are 1+1+1+1, 1+1+2, 1+3, 2+2) 1855. 8. *Mus.* A score. Now *rare* or *Obs.* 1597. 9. *Her.* a. The division of a shield into two parts of different tinctures by one of the dividing lines (see PARTED, PARTY *a.*). ? *Obs.* †b. An ordinary which lies between common charges on a shield. c. Each of the divisions of a parted or quartered shield. 1486.

1. The p. of the Empire 1741. b. The first p. of Poland in 1773 W. TOOKE. 2. Can we not P. make ..Twixt faire, and foule? SHAKS. 3. Great wits are sure to madness near allied, And thin partitions do their bounds divide DRYDEN. Did I not overhear your scheme..through the p.? 1763. 4. The Hold was divided in many small Partitions 1697.

attrib. and *Comb.*, as *p.-line*, etc.; **P. Treaty**, name of each of the two treaties (of 11 Oct. 1698 and 11 Oct. 1700) attempting to settle the question of the Spanish Succession after the death of Charles II; **-wall**, a wall forming a p.; *esp.* an internal wall.

Partition (pătiˑʃən), *v.* 1741. [f. prec.] 1. *trans.* To divide into parts or portions; to dismember and deal *out*. b. *spec.* To divide (land) into severalty 1880. 2. To separate by a partition; to divide *off* 1832. Hence **Partiˑtionment**, the action or fact of partitioning; *concr.* a partition, a compartment.

Partitioned (pătiˑʃənd), *ppl. a.* 1625. [f. PARTITION *sb.* and *v.* + -ED.] Having partitions; divided or separated by partitions. (Also with *off.*)

Partitive (pā·ɹtitiv), *a.* and *sb.* 1520. [ad. L. *partitivus*, f. *partitus* divided; see -IVE.] A. *adj.* Having the quality or function of dividing into parts; characterized by or indicating partition; *spec.* in *Gram.* Denoting or indicating that only a part of a collective whole is spoken of: esp. applied to a noun, etc. denoting such a part; also to the genitive used with such words in Greek, Latin, etc. (repr. in Eng. by *of* with the sb.). B. *sb. Gram.* A partitive word; a word denoting a part of a whole 1530. Hence **Paˑrtitively** *adv.* in a p. way; *Gram.* in a p. sense.

Partlet[1] (pā·ɹtlĕt). late ME. [a. OF. *Pertelote*, female proper name.] Used as the proper name of any hen, often *Dame P.*; also applied, like 'hen', to a woman.

Partlet[2]. *Obs.* exc. *Hist.* 1519. [app. corrupt f. *patelet*, a. OF. *patelette* band of stuff, dim. of *patte* paw, flap.] An article of apparel worn about the neck and upper part of the chest, chiefly by women: orig. a neckerchief; a collar or ruff. Also *attrib.*

Partly (pā·ɹtli), *adv.* 1523. [f. PART *sb.* + -LY [2].] With respect to a part; in part; in some measure or degree; not wholly. **b.** Usu. hyphened to a ppl. adj. which precedes its sb. 1888.

Reflexions, which were p. private, and p. political ADDISON. **b.** A partly-heard conversation 1888.

Partner (pā·ɹtnəɹ), *sb.* ME. [In 13th c. *partener*, app. a var. of PARCENER after PART *sb.*] **1.** One who has a share or part with another or others; a partaker, sharer. Const. *with*, rarely *of* (a person); *of*, *in*, †*to* (a thing). **2.** One who is associated in any function, act, or course of action; an associate, colleague (occas. merely = companion). Formerly often: An accomplice. ME. †**b.** One who takes part in some action -1565. **3.** *spec.* **a.** *Comm.* One who is associated with another or others in some business, the expenses, profits, and losses of which he proportionately shares 1523. **b.** A husband or wife 1749. **c.** One's companion in a dance 1613. **d.** A player associated on the same side with another in whist, tennis, etc. 1680. **4.** *Naut.* (in *pl.*) A framework of timber fitted round any hole or scuttle in a ship's deck, through which a mast, capstan, pump, etc. passes, and serving to strengthen the deck and to relieve strain 1608. **5.** *attrib.*: formerly quasi-*adj.* = associated 1639.

1. A wife worthy to be the p. of his Empire 1870. **2.** A p. in conspiracie 1602. **3.** Phr. *Sleeping* (or *dormant*) *p.*, a p. who has capital in a business and shares in its profits without taking any part in the management. *Predominant p.*: see PREDOMINANT. **b.** So forth I set..And took the p. of my life with me SOUTHEY. Hence **Pa·rtnerless**, without a p.

Partner (pā·ɹtnəɹ), *v.* 1611. [f. prec. sb.] **1.** *trans.* To make a partner, to join or associate. **2.** To be or act as the partner of; to associate oneself with as a partner 1882.

Partnership (pā·ɹtnəɹʃip). 1576. [-SHIP.] **1.** The fact or condition of being a partner. **2.** *Comm.* An association of two or more persons for the carrying on of a business, of which they share the expenses, profit, and loss 1700. **b.** The persons so associated collectively 1802. **3.** *Arith.* = FELLOWSHIP *sb.* 9. 1704. **4.** *attrib.* 1770.

1. A scandal which charged Emma herself with a p. in the deed 1877. **2.** His brother took him into p. MAR. EDGEWORTH.

Pa·rt-ow:ner. 1562. [f. PART *sb.* + OWNER; = owner in part.] One who owns something in common with another or others; each of two or more joint owners or tenants in common.

Partridge (pā·ɹtridʒ). [ME. *pertrich*, *partrich* modified a. OF. *perdriz*, altered f. *perdiz* :—L. *perdix*, *perdicem*, a. Gr. πέρδιξ, πέρδικα (the Greek) partridge.] **1.** The name of certain well-known game-birds; esp. *Perdix cinerea*, the *Common* or *Grey P.* More widely, used to include all species of the genus *Perdix*, and some allied genera. **b.** In British Colonies and U. S., pop. applied to several birds of the *Tetraonidæ* or Grouse Family and *Phasianidæ* or Pheasant Family, esp. in New England, the Ruffed Grouse (*Bonasa* or *Tetrao umbellus*), in Pennsylvania, etc. the Virginian Quail, Colin, or Bob-white (*Ortyx virginianus*) 1634. **c.** The bird, or its flesh, as used for food ME. **2.** *Ornith.* With defining words, applied to particular species of the genus *Perdix*, or of the sub-families *Perdicinæ*, *Odontophorinæ*, and *Caccabineæ*, of family *Phasianidæ*, also to some species of *Tetraonidæ*, all of order *Gallinæ*; in S. Africa, to some of order *Pterocletes* (Sand-grouse) 1611. †**3.** *Mil.* A charge for cannons consisting of a number of missiles fired together, similar to langrage or case-shot; also *p.-shot* -1867. **4.** Sea p. †**a.** The sole. [Cf. F. *perdrix de mer.*] **b.** A local name of the Golden Wrasse or Gilt-head, *Crenilabrus melops*. 1633.

1. A fat partrich CHAUCER. Plump as any p. was each Miss Mould DICKENS. **2. Bamboo P.**, of North China, *Bambusicola thoracica*; **Greek P.**, of Southern Europe (the original Gr.-L. πέρδιξ, *perdix*), *Caccabis saxatilis*; **Painted P.** (or Francolin), of S. Africa, *Francolinus pictus*; **Red-legged P.**, of Europe, *Caccabis rufa*; **Snow P.**, *Lerwa nivicola*; also *Tetraogallus Himalayensis*. Also **Night P.**, U.S. name for the American woodcock, *Philohela minor*. *attrib.* and *Comb.*, as *p.-drive*, *wing*, etc.; *p.-shooting*, etc.; also, **p.-cane** (see PARTRIDGE-WOOD 1); **-dove**, a ground-dove of Jamaica (*Geotrygon cristata*), also called mountain-witch (ground-dove); **p. pea**, (*a*) a speckled or mottled variety of field pea; (*b*) a yellow-flowered leguminous plant (*Cassia Chamæcrista*) of U.S.; also called *sensitive pea*; (*c*) a plant (*Heisteria coccinea*, N.O. *Olacineæ*) having red fruits enclosed in an enlarged fleshy calyx; **-shell**, a large univalve shell (*Dolium perdix*) with partridge-like mottlings; **-vine** = PARTRIDGE-BERRY a. Hence **Pa·rtridging** *vbl. sb.* shooting partridges.

Pa·rtridge-be:rry. 1714. Name of two N. American plants and their fruit: **a.** *Mitchella repens* (N.O. *Cinchonaceæ*), a trailing evergreen herb with edible but insipid scarlet berries; also called *partridge-vine*. **b.** *Gaultheria procumbens* (N.O. *Ericaceæ*), the CHECKER-BERRY or WINTER-GREEN, whose red berries furnish food for partridges.

Pa·rtridge-wood. 1830. **1.** A hard red wood, having darker parallel stripes, much prized for cabinet work, also used for walking-sticks, etc., from the W. Indies, supposed to be (at least in part) obtained from the leguminous tree *Andira inermis*; called also *pheasant-wood*. **2.** A name for the appearance of wood when attacked by the saprophytic fungus *Stereum frustulosum*, on account of its speckled colour 1894.

Pa·rt-song. 1850. [f. PART *sb.* + SONG.] A song for three or more voice-parts, usu. without accompaniment, and in simple harmony (dist. from *glee* and *madrigal*).

Parturiate (paɹtiū̆·rieᵢt), *v. rare.* 1660. [irreg. f. L. *parturire* + -ATE [3].] **a.** *intr.* To bring forth young; to bear fruit. **b.** *trans.* To bring forth.

Parturiency (paɹtiū̆·riĕnsi). 1652. [f. L. *parturientem*, PARTURIENT; see -ENCY.] Parturient condition or quality: usu. *fig.*

Parturient (paɹtiū̆·riĕnt), *a.* 1592. [ad. L. *parturiens*, *-ent-*, *parturire* to be in labour, desiderative of *parĕre*, *part-* to bring forth.] **1.** About to bring forth; travailing; *transf.* bearing fruit. **2.** *fig.* 'Big' or 'in travail' with (a discovery, idea, etc.) 1599. **3.** Of or pertaining to parturition 1748.

1. Allen's p. mountaines produced a..ridiculous Mouse 1657.

Parturifacient (paɹtiū̆rifē̆·ʃiĕnt), *a.* and *sb.* 1853. [f. L. *parturire* to travail + -FACIENT.] = OXYTOCIC *a.* and *sb.*

Parturition (pāɹtiŭri·ʃən). 1646. [ad. L. *parturitionem*.] The action of bringing forth or of being delivered of young; childbirth. (Chiefly *techn.*; also *fig.*)

Party (pā·ɹti), *sb.* [ME. *partie*, *-ye*, a. F. *partie* = It. *partita*, subst. use of fem. pa. pple. of L. *partire* (It. *partire*, F. *partir*) to PART.] **I.** Part, portion, side. [= F. *partie*.] †**1.** A division of a whole; a part or portion; an aliquot part: a part or member of the body -1654. †**2.** = PART *sb.* III. 1, 2. -1588. †**3.** = PART *sb.* III. 3. -1854.

3. I cannot tell on whose partie first to commence UDALL.

II. A company or body of persons. **1.** *concr.* A number of persons united in maintaining a cause, policy, opinion, etc., in opposition to others who maintain a different one ME. **b.** *abstr.* The system of taking sides on public questions; party feeling or spirit; partisanship 1701. **2.** *Mil.* A small body of troops selected for a particular service or duty 1645. **3.** A company of persons travelling together or engaged in any common pursuit; a number of persons met together for amusement, study, etc. 1773. **4.** A social gathering or entertainment, esp. of invited guests at a private house; also with qualification, as *garden-p.* 1696. †**5.** A game or match, esp. at piquet -1796.

1. My end is mirth, And pleasing, if I can, all parties 1625. **b.** [Burke] to p. gave up what was meant for mankind GOLDSM. **3.** A reading p., a house p. (*mod.*). **4.** I determined to give parties of my own 1809.

III. A single person considered in some relation. **1.** Each of two or more persons (or bodies of people) that constitute the two sides in an action at law, a contract, etc. ME. **2.** A participator; an accessory. Const. *to*. †*in*. late ME. **3.** The individual concerned or in question; more vaguely, the person (defined by some adj., etc.). (Formerly in serious use; now shoppy, vulgar, or joc., the proper word being *person*.) 1460. **b.** With *a.*: A person. Now *low colloq.* or *slang*. 1686.

1. It appears to be a narrative written by a third p. 1853. Phr. *Party-and-party* (attrib.), as between the two parties in an action at law. **2.** He was a p. to all their proceedings DICKENS. **3.** 'Tis the p., madame. What p.? Has he no name? B. JONS. 'Do you know, my Lord', (said the old p. solemnly) 1888. **b.** I should say he was a go-ahead p. 1855.

IV. Senses mostly repr. F. *parti*. †**1.** A decision on one side or the other, determination; *esp.* in *to take a p.* (cf. F. *prendre son parti*) -1760. †**2.** A person to marry; a (good or bad) match or offer -1855. †**3.** A proposal, an offer -1765.

2. A girl in our society accepts the best p. which offers itself THACKERAY.

Comb. **p.-verdict**, one person's share in a joint verdict (*Rich. II*, I. iii. 234). Hence †**Pa·rty** *v.* (*Sc. rare*) *trans.* to take the side of, side with; *intr.* to side (*with*). **Pa·rtyism**, the system of parties; party-spirit.

Party (pā·ɹti), *a.* late ME. [a. F. *parti* :—L. *partitus* divided, pa. pple. of *partir*, L. *partire* to PART.] †**1.** Parted, divided, separate; *fig.* different. ME. only. †**2.** Particoloured, variegated -1707. **3.** *Her.* Said of a shield divided into parts of different tinctures, usually into two such parts by a line in the direction of an ordinary (indicated by *per*) 1486.

2. She gadereth floures p. white & rede CHAUCER. **3.** Phr. *P. per pale*, divided by a vertical line through the middle; *p. per fess*, by a horizontal line through the middle; so *p. per bend*, *p. per chevron*: see PALE, FESS, etc. †*P. per pale* (fig.), having two different, esp. contrasted, qualities; of mixed character; half-and-half.

Pa·rty-man. 1693. [f. PARTY *sb.* + MAN.] †**1.** *Mil.* A soldier belonging to, or officer commanding, a party (PARTY *sb.* II. 2) -1724. **2.** = PARTISAN *sb.*[1] 1. 1701.

Pa·rty-wall. 1667. [f. PARTY *sb.* (used *attrib.*) + WALL *sb.*] A wall between two buildings or pieces of land intended for distinct occupation, in the use of which each of the occupiers has a partial right. Also *fig.*

Parumbilical: see PARA-[1] 1.

‖**Parure.** *Obs.* or *alien.* late ME. [a. OF. *par(e)ure* :—L. *paratura*, f. *parare* to prepare, F. *parer* to PARE.] †**1.** An apparel for an alb or amice -1552. ‖**2.** A set of jewels or other ornaments intended to be worn together; a set of decorative trimmings for a dress 1818.

Parvanimity (pāɹvăni·mĭti). 1691. [f. L. *parvus* small + *animus* mind; opp. to magnanimity.] Littleness of mind, meanness; also, an instance of this, or *transf.* a person characterized by it.

‖**Parvenu** (pā·ɹvĕniu, ‖parvənü), *sb.* and *a.* Also fem. **parvenue.** 1802. [F., sb. use of pa. pple. of *parvenir* to arrive (at a destination), to make a fortune :—L. *pervenire*.] **A.** *sb.* A person of obscure origin who has attained wealth or position; an upstart. **B.** *adj.* That has but recently risen to wealth or position; like or characteristic of a parvenu 1839.

A. The ladies their wives, who could not bear the parvenue [Rebecca] THACKERAY.

Parvi- (pāɹvi), comb. form of L. *parvus* small, as in **Parvi·potent** *a.*, having little power; **Parvi·scient** *a.*, knowing little; etc.

Parvis (pā·ɹvis). Also *erron.* **parvise.** late ME. [a. F. *parvis*, OF. *parevis*, earlier *pareïs* :—L. *paradisum* PARADISE (med. name for the atrium in front of St. Peter's at Rome, and for the courts before other churches).] **1.** The enclosed area or court in front of a building, esp. of a cathedral or church; sometimes applied to a single portico or colonnade in front of a church, and (in dictionaries) explained as a church-porch. ¶ **b.** Erron. applied to 'a room over a church-porch' 1836. †**2.** A public or academic conference or disputation. (So called from being originally held in the court or portico of a church.) -1706.

Parvitude (pā·ɹvitiud). *rare.* 1653. [f. L. *parvus*, after *magnitude*.] Smallness 1657. †**b.** An extremely small thing, atom -1709.

Parvoline (pā·ɪvǒlɔin). 1855. [f. L. *parvus* small + *-oline*, after *quinoline*.] *Chem.* A ptomaine dimethylethylpyridine, obtained as an oily liquid with a disagreeable odour, from decaying mackerel and horse-flesh, and also from certain shales and bituminous coals.

‖ **Pas** (pa). 1704. [F., = step, precedency, etc.] **1.** The right of going first; precedence. Also *fig.* 1707. **2.** A step in dancing; a kind of dance 1775. **3.** *Pas-de-souris* [F. lit. 'mouse-steps'], *Fortif.* a staircase from the ravelin to the ditch 1704.

1. Phr. *To dispute, give, take, yield, the p.* 2. *P. de deux*, a dance or figure for two persons. *P. seul*, a dance or figure for one.

Pasan, pasang (pā·zăn, -ăŋ). 1774. [a. Pers. *pāzan* the mountain goat.] A species of wild goat (*Capra Ægagrus*), found in western Asia and Crete; the bezoar-goat. ¶ Erron. identified by Buffon with the gemsbok.

Pasch (pɑsk). Now *arch.* or *Hist.* ME. [a. OF. *pasche* and *pasque* (mod.F. *pâque*), ad. L. *pascha*, a. Gr. πάσχα, ad. Heb. *pesakh* a passing over, the Passover, f. *pāsakh* to pass over. Formerly often *pl.* with *sing.* sense.] **1.** The Jewish feast of the Passover. **2.** The Christian festival of Easter (*arch.* or *local*) ME. **3.** *attrib.* ME.

Paschal (pɑ·skăl), *a.* and *sb.* late ME. [a. F. *pascal*, ad. late L. *paschalis*, f. *pascha* PASCH; see -AL.] **A.** *adj.* **1.** Of or pertaining to the Jewish Passover. **2.** Of or pertaining to Easter; used in Easter celebrations. late ME.

1. *P. lamb*, the lamb slain and eaten at the Passover; applied to Christ; hence, = AGNUS DEI b and c. 2. *P. candle*, a large candle blessed and lighted in the service of Holy Saturday, and remaining on the gospel side of the altar till Ascension day.

B. *sb.* **1.** A Paschal candle. **b.** A candlestick to hold this. late ME **2.** The Passover celebration, Passover supper, or Passover lamb 1579.

Pasch-egg (pɑ·sk₁eg). Also **paste-egg.** *Sc.* and *n. dial.* 1579. An Easter egg; an egg dyed of various colours and boiled hard.

Pash (pæʃ), *sb.*[1] *Obs.* exc. *dial.* 1611. A head.

Pash (pæʃ), *v.* Now chiefly *dial.* late ME. [app. echoic.] **1.** *trans.* To throw (something) violently, so as either to break it against something, or to break something with it. *Obs.* exc. *dial.* **2.** To dash (a thing) in pieces; to smash by blows. late ME. **3.** To strike violently, usu. so as to bruise or smash. Also *absol.* 1440. **4.** *intr.* Said of the dashing action of heavy rain (now *dial.*); also of that of a wave upon a rock 1589. Hence **Pash** *sb.*[2] a crash, heavy fall; also, debris, medley.

‖ **Pasha, pacha** (pɑ·ʃa, păʃā·). 1646. [Turkish *pāshā*, prob. = earlier *bāshā*, from *bāsh* head, chief.] A title in Turkey of officers of high rank, as military commanders, and governors of provinces. Formerly, esp. of military commanders, written BASHAW.

There are three grades of pashas, formerly distinguished by the number of horse-tails (three, two, or one) displayed as a symbol in war; a pasha of three tails being the highest in rank.

Pashalic, pachalic (pɑ·ʃalik, păʃā·lik), *sb.* (*a.*) 1745. [Turkish *pāshālik*, from *-lik*, suffix of quality or condition.] The jurisdiction of a pasha; the district governed by a pasha. **B.** *adj.* Of or pertaining to a pasha 1863.

‖ **Pashm** (pæ·ʃ'm). 1880. [Pers. *pashm* wool, down.] The under-fur of hairy quadrupeds inhabiting Tibet, etc., esp. that of the goat, of which Cashmere shawls are made. So ‖ **Pashmina** (pæʃmī·nă) [Pers. *pashmin* adj., woollen].

Pasigraphy (păsi·grăfi). 1796. [irreg. f. Gr. πᾶσι for all + -GRAPHY.] A system of writing proposed for universal use, with characters representing ideas instead of words, so as to be (like the numerals 1, 2, 3, etc.) intelligible to persons of all languages. Hence **Pa·sigraph** *v.* to represent in p. **Pasigra·phic, -al** *adjs.* of or pertaining to p.

Pasilaly (pæ·silăli). *rare.* 1805. [irreg. f. Gr. πᾶσι for all + -λαλια speaking.] A spoken language for universal use.

†**Pask, Pasque,** var. ff. PASCH.

Pasque-flower (pɑ·skflauəɪ). 1578. [orig. *passeflower*, a. F. *passe-fleur* 'a variety of anemone'; changed by Gerarde to *pasque-flower*, after *pasque*, PASCH.] A species of Anemone (*A. Pulsatilla*) blossoming in April, with bell-shaped purple flowers clothed with silky hairs. Called also *pasque-anemone*.

Pasquil (pæ·skwil), *sb.* 1533. [ad. med.L. *Pasquillus*, ad. It. *Pasquillo*, dim. of *Pasquino*; in F. *Pasquille*; see next.] †**1.** = PASQUIN 1. -1651. **2.** A pasquinade 1542. Hence †**Pa·squil** *v. intr.* to compose pasquils; *trans.* to lampoon. **Pa·squillant** *sb.* the writer of a p.; *adj.* lampooning. **Pa·squiller,** the composer of a p. or pasquils.

Pasquin (pæ·skwin), *sb.* 1566. [ult. ad. It. *Pasquino*, in L. *Pasquinus*, F. *Pasquin*. *Pasquino* or *Pasquillo* was the name given to a mutilated statue disinterred at Rome in 1501, and set up by Cardinal Caraffa at the corner of his palace near the Piazza Navona. On this satirical Latin verses were annually posted on St. Mark's Day, and the anonymous authors of these often sheltered themselves under the name 'Pasquin'.] **1.** The Roman Pasquino (man or statue), upon whom pasquinades were fathered; hence, the imaginary personage to whom anonymous lampoons were ascribed. †**2.** = PASQUINADE -1745.

1. The Grecian wits, who Satire first began, Were pleasant Pasquins on the life of man DRYDEN. 2. I hope you will not think this a pasquine SWIFT. Hence **Pa·squin** *v.* to lampoon.

Pasquinade (pæskwinē·d), *sb.* 1658. [ad. It. *pasquinata*; see prec. and -ADE.] A lampoon affixed to some public place; a squib, libel, or piece of satire generally. Hence **Pasquina·de** *v.* to satirize or libel in a p. **Pasquina·der.**

Pass (pɑs), *sb.*[1] [In ME. *pas, paas*, a. F. *pas* :—L. *passus* step, pace, etc. A doublet of PACE *sb.*; later, assoc. w. PASS *v.*] **I.** †**1.** Occasional spelling of *pas*, PACE *sb.* -1615. †**2.** = PASSUS -1647.

II. 1. A way or opening by which one passes through an otherwise impassable region, or through any barrier: *esp.* **a.** A passage through a mountainous region or over a mountain range, or (less usually) through a forest, marsh, bog, etc. ME. **b.** Chiefly *Mil.* Such a passage viewed as commanding the entrance into a country or place; hence, any place which holds the key to such entrance. Also *fig.* 1683. **c.** *gen.* A way through; a passage, road, route. Also *fig.* 1608. **d.** A place at which a river can be crossed by ford, ferry, or *rarely* a bridge. Now *rare.* 1649. **e.** A navigable channel, esp. at a river's mouth 1698. **f.** Applied to other narrow passages, e.g. in a road or street 1710. **g.** A passage for fish over or past a weir 1861. **2.** *Mining.* A wooden frame through which the ore slides down into the coffer of the stamping-mill 1671.

1. **a.** The height of the p. is 6890 feet 1833. **b.** When Philip reached Thermopylæ, he found the p. strongly guarded 1838. Phr. *To gain, hold, keep, the p.*; *to sell the pass*, often fig. to betray one's allies or one's cause.

Pass (pɑs), *sb.*[2] 1481. [Partly a. F. *passe*, f. *passer* to pass; partly f. PASS *v.*] **I. 1.** An act or the fact of passing; passage 1599. **b.** Departure from life, death. Also *fig.* 1645. †**2.** Demeanour, course of action -1603. †**3.** The fact of passing as approved; reputation; currency -1601. **4.** The passing of an examination; *esp.* in a university, the attainment of a standard that satisfies the examiners without entitling the candidate to honours. Often *attrib.* 1838.

1. Charming the narrow seas To giue you gentle Passe SHAKS. 2. *Meas. for M.* v. i. 375. 3. *All's Well* II. v. 58. 4. She managed to get a p. degree; to read a p. school (*mod.*).

II. The condition to or through which anything passes. †**1.** Event, issue; completion, accomplishment -1649. **2.** A position or situation; *esp.* a position qualified in some way; a critical position, a juncture, a predicament 1560.

1. To no other passe my verses tend Then of your graces and your gifts to tell SHAKS. Phr. (now somewhat arch.). *To bring to p.* (rarely †*unto p.*), to bring to accomplishment; to carry out; to bring about. *To come to p.*, to come to the event or issue; to be carried out, accomplished, or realized; to turn out in the event; to come about. Also, quasi-*impers.*, with *it*, and subord. cl. To come to be the fact, to come about (esp. in Scriptural lang.); It came to passe after these things, that God did tempt Abraham *Gen.* xxii. 1. 2. Where is the patriotism of bringing things to this p.? 1833.

III. Permission to pass. **a.** Permission to go or come anywhere; *esp.* a written permission to pass into, out of, or through a place; a passport; also, authorization to pass, *e.g.* through the lines of an army 1591. **b.** *Mil.* A certificate of leave of absence to a soldier for a short time 1617. †**c.** An order passing a pauper to his or her parish -1786. **d.** A document authorizing the holder to travel free on a railway, etc. Usu. *free p.* **e.** An order, etc., giving free admission to a theatre or the like. 1858.

a. The Dutch have ordered a passe to be sent for our Commissioners PEPYS.

IV. The causing of something to pass. **1.** *Fencing.* A lunge, a thrust; a bout of fencing 1598. †**b.** *fig.* A sally of wit; a witty thrust or stroke -1822. **2.** The manipulation of a juggler; the changing of the position of anything by sleight of hand; a trick 1599. **3.** A passing of the hands over or along anything; manipulation; esp. in mesmerism 1848. **4.** *Football, Hockey*, etc. A transference of the ball by one of the players to another on his own side 1891.

1. In a dozen passes between yourself and him, he shall not exceed you three hits SHAKS. **b.** *Temp.* IV. i. 244. 2. Phr. *To make the p.* (in card tricks), to alter the position of the cards in the pack, e.g. by dexterously shifting the top or bottom card.

V. More fully *p.-hemp*, the third quality of Russian hemp 1744.

attrib. and *Comb.*, as (sense I. 4) *p.-degree, examination, schools*, etc.; (sense III) *p.-inspector*, etc.; also, **p.-boat,** a broad flat-bottomed boat; a punt, or the like; **-box,** a box for transferring cartridges from the magazine to the guns on the field; **-check,** a ticket of admission to a place of entertainment allowing the holder to go out and re-enter; **-hemp:** see sense V.

Pass (pɑs), *v. Pa. t.* and *pple.* **passed; past** (now rare as pa. t.). ME. [a. F. *passer*, Com. Rom. (pop.L.) **passare*, f. *passus* PASS *sb.*[1] Cf. PACE *v.*] **A.** Intransitive uses. **I. 1.** To go on, move onward, proceed; to make one's way. Now usu. with some prep., adv., etc. **b.** Of something inanimate or involuntary: To move on under any force, to be moved, carried onward; to flow, as water, a stream, etc. ME. **c.** Of a line, string, path, etc.: To extend, 'run' 1703. **d.** To proceed in narration, consideration, or action. Now usu. only in *pass on.* late ME. **2.** With ref. to place or object of destination. Chiefly with *to* (*unto, into*). ME.

1. I was imploy'd in passing to and fro, About relieving of the Centinels SHAKS. She once had past that way TENNYSON. **c.** The path passes round a bay 1813. **d.** Er that I ferther in this tale pace CHAUCER. 2. Passing through Nature, to Eternity SHAKS. This riuer..passeth southward 1600.

II. †**1.** To go about, to travel; to move about, be astir -1585. **2.** To be handed about; to circulate, be current 1589.

2. Our money they thought would not p. BURNET. *To p. current* (†*for current*): see CURRENT *a.* *To p. for, as*, to be accepted as (often with the implication of being something else). *To p. by*, to be currently known by (a name, etc.). †*To p. on, upon*, to impose upon; to gain credit with.

III. 1. To go or be transported from one place or set of circumstances to another. (Usu. with prep.) ME. **2.** To be changed from one form or state to another; to undergo chemical, structural, or other gradual conversion *into.* late ME. **3.** *Law.* Of property: To go by conveyance, or come by inheritance *to, into the hands of.* late ME. **4.** To be uttered between two (or more) persons mutually; to be interchanged or transacted 1568.

1. To p., in descending a mountain, from snow to rain 1860. 2. The hatred of theologians has passed into a proverb 1855. 4. I know what has past between you GOLDSM.

IV. With reference to place left. **1.** To go away; to depart *from* (†*of, off*) a place, thing, or person. Of a thing: To be taken away (*from*). ME. **b.** *fig.* To depart, diverge *from* a course, practice, principle. late ME. **2.** To depart from this life, die. Now *arch.* or *dial.* when used *simply*. ME.

1. If it be possible, let this cup passe from me *Matt.* xxvi. 39. 2. Vex not his ghost, O let him passe *Lear* V. iii. 314.

V. 1. To go by. (Now the leading intr. sense of the simple verb.) ME. **b.** Of things: To be moved or impelled past; to flow past. Also *fig.* ME. **2. a.** Of time: To glide by, come to an end ME. **b.** Of things in time ME.

1. Allow me to p., please (*mod.*). b. My Lord stand backe, and let the Coffin passe SHAKS. It is done every day, and passes unregarded 1766. c. With compl. adjs., as *to p. unheeded, unnoticed.* late ME. 2. a. The first day passed without any thing doyng LD. BERNERS. b. Not to let th' occasion p. MILT.

VI. 1. To go or get through; to have, obtain, or force passage, to make one's way. Also of things. ME. **b.** Of things: e.g. to be admitted through a customs barrier 1637. **c.** To go through a duct; to be voided 1731. **2.** To go uncensured; to go without check or challenge; to pass muster; to 'do' ME. **3.** To be allowed and approved by a court, legislature, or deliberative body; to 'get through'; to be ratified 1568. **4.** To get through any trial successfully; *spec.* in an examination, to reach or satisfy the required standard 1600.

1. My Lord you passe not heere SHAKS. 2. Indeed and indeed, the trick will not p., Jonas WYCHERLEY. I never suffer a line to p. till I have made it as good as I can COWPER. 3. The bill passed without substantial alteration 1880. 4. If I p., which I trust I shall be able to do MARRYAT. *To p. master*, etc. to graduate as master, etc. (in some faculty); cf. PASSED-, PAST-MASTER.

†**VII.** To excel, to surpass; to go to excess -1611. †**b.** quasi-*impers. It passes*: it passes description, 'beats everything' -1689.

VIII. Of events: To go on in the course of things; to take place, occur, happen 1542.

I am attentive to all that passes BERKELEY.

IX. Used in ref. to process of law. **1.** Of a jury (assize, inquest): To sit in inquest *on* or *upon*; to decide or adjudicate *between* parties; to give a verdict *for* or *against* (*arch.*) ME. **b.** To serve *on* (*upon*, †*in*) a jury, assize, or trial 1574. **c.** Of a court, a judge, the law: To adjudicate, pass sentence *on, upon.* Also *transf.* 1532. **2.** Of a verdict, sentence, or judgement: To be given or pronounced; of justice: To be executed. late ME.

2. A similar sentence passed against some of his adherents GOLDSM.

†**X.** To care, to reck (usu. with neg.) -1671.

XI. Elliptical or absol. uses of B or C. **1.** *Fencing.* To make a pass (PASS *sb.*[2] IV. 1). Const. *on, upon.* 1595. **2.** *Cards* and *Dice.* **a.** In primero, poker, etc.: To throw up one's hand, retire from the game 1599. **b.** In euchre, napoleon, etc.: To decline one's opportunity (as of making the trump): see EUCHRE *sb.* 1. 1884. **3.** To pass the ball at Football, etc. (See C. III. 1 b.) 1888.

B. Transitive uses. (From A. V, VI, VII.)

I. 1. To go by, proceed past; to leave behind or on one side as one goes on ME. †**2.** *fig.* To go by without attending to; to neglect, disregard, omit -1719. **b.** To leave unmentioned 1585. **c.** orig. *U.S.* To omit payment of (a dividend, etc.) 1890. †**d.** *To p. one's flag* (Naval), to decline promotion to flag rank, and become a retired captain NELSON.

1. So p. I hostel, hall, and grange TENNYSON. 2. *John* II. i. 258.

II. To go through, across, or over (something). **1.** To go from side to side of, or across; to cross (a sea, barrier, frontier, etc.); also (less frequently) to go through, traverse (a forest, way, etc.) ME. **b.** Of a book, etc.: To go through (the printing-press, or successive editions) 1665. †**2.** To pierce, to penetrate: said of a spear, etc., also of the person driving it -1720. **3.** *fig.* To experience, undergo, endure, put up with, suffer. Now usu. *pass through.* ME. **4.** To go through the process of being considered, examined, and approved by; to come up to the standard required by. late ME.

1. The waies are dangerous to passe SHAKS. 3. The Battaile, Sieges, Fortune, That I haue past SHAKS. 4. My Bill hath passed the Lords House and was this day read in the House of Commons 1670. You'll p. your exams with distinction 1901. *To p. muster*: see MUSTER *sb.*[1] 3. *To p. the seals*, to receive royal (or other) ratification by sealing.

III. To go beyond, surpass, exceed. **1.** To go beyond (a point or place); to overshoot (a mark); to outrun; to surmount. late ME. **2.** To overstep (bounds or limits); to transgress. *fig.* To go beyond (one's province, warrant, knowledge, etc.). ME. **3.** To be too great for, transcend (any faculty or expression). late ME. **4.** To surpass in some quality; to exceed in degree (*arch.*) ME. **b.** To exceed in number, measurement, or amount. Now *rare.* ME. †**5.** To get beyond (a stage or condition of life or existence) -1685.

1. Mount Athos is so high, that it passeth the skies 1585. 2. Let not the cobler passe his pantofle 1604. He pass'd the flaming bounds of Place and Time GRAY. 3. That grief which passes show 1820. 4. Thy loue to me was wonderfull, passyng the loue of wemen BIBLE (Great) 2 *Sam.* i. 26.

IV. *To p. the lips*, †*the mouth of*: to come out of the mouth of, to be spoken or uttered by 1526.

C. Causative uses. **I. 1.** To cause or enable (a person or thing) to go, proceed, or make his way anywhere; to carry, convey, send; *esp.* to convey across a river, a ferry, etc., to transport. late ME. **2.** To make (a thing) go in any specific manner or direction; to move, draw, push (a thing) 1705. **3.** To cause to pass or go by 1852. **4.** To cause or allow (a person or thing) to go past or through some barrier or obstruction 1611. **5.** To cause or allow to pass or go by, to spend (time, one's life, a season, etc.) ME.

1. Every vagrant Person may..be..pass'd back to their last legal Settlement DE FOE. 2. *To p. one's hand over, to p. one's eye over* (to glance rapidly over), *to p. a wet sponge over* (often *fig.* to obliterate the memory of), *to pass the sweeper over* a floor, *to p. a rope* or *string round* anything, etc. 3. *To p. in review*, (orig.) *Mil.* To cause (troops) to march by for inspection; hence *fig.* 5. *To p. the winter at a place, p. one's time in sleep, p. a pleasant evening*, etc.

II. †**a.** To carry through its stages; to execute (a matter, a business); to complete (a voyage) -1748. **b.** To carry or get carried (a measure in Parliament, a resolution); to agree to, confirm, sanction, endorse 1529. **c.** To allow or enable (a person) to pass an examination 1833. †**d.** To overlook, excuse, pass over (something) -1802.

a. *Tam. Shr.* IV. iv. 57. b. Their majority will p. the bill 1799. c. I'll p. you..I can conscientiously report you a healthy subject DICKENS.

III. 1. To cause to go from one to another; to hand over, hand round, hand, transfer 1596. **b.** *Football.* To transfer (the ball) to another player on the same side. Also *absol.* (sense A. XI. 3.) 1865. **c.** To put into circulation (coin, esp. base coin, or the like). Also *fig.* 1589. **2.** *Law.* To convey, make over, with legal effect 1587. **3.** To give in pledge (one's word, promise, oath); †to pledge (one's faith, etc.) 1469.

1. P. the word to reduce the cartridges MARRYAT. They passed buckets of water from hand to hand 1901. c. Utterers of base coin have a trick of passing a bad shilling between two good ones 1864. 2. The delivery of the key of the trunk was held to p. the trunk and its contents 1891. 3. He wil not passe his word..that you are no Foole SHAKS.

IV. 1. To discharge from the body by excretion 1698. **2.** To utter, pronounce (speech, criticism, censure); rarely, to put (a question); occas., to exchange (words). 1615. **b.** To pronounce judicially 1590.

2. How to p. Complements upon Almighty God 1698. Phr. *To p. the time of day* (dial. or colloq.), to exchange salutations or gossip in passing. b. Sentence of death was passed upon him 1820.

V. †**1.** *Fencing.* To make or execute (a thrust) SHAKS. **2.** To perform the pass on a pack of cards; see PASS *sb.*[2] IV. 2. 1884.

With preps. and advs. **I.** With preps. **Pass beyond —.** a. See simple senses and BEYOND *prep.* b. To pass the limits of, exceed, transcend. **P. by —.** †a. To go through or by way of. b. To go past; to pass. c. To take no notice of, disregard, omit. **P. over —.** a. To cross, to traverse (a sea, river, or expanse). Also *fig.* b. To pass the hand over. †c. *trans.* To spend (time). d. To pass a thing without dwelling on it, or without notice or remark, to omit. **P. through —.** a. To go from side to side of, to cross, traverse. b. In ref. to times, stages, states, processes, actions, experiences, etc. c. To make or force a passage through; to penetrate; to pierce through; to send a shot through. Also *fig.* d. *causal.* To cause (a thing) to pass or go through; to put, thrust, or impel through.

II. With adverbs. **Pass away.** a. See simple senses and AWAY *adv.* b. *intr.* Of persons: To depart; also, to get or break away (as from restraint). c. *intr.* To die, expire. d. *intr.* Of time: To come to an end. e. *intr.* Of things: To come to an end, cease to be, be dissolved, perish. f. *trans.* To spend (time, etc.); to while away, to pass. †g. To transfer away (rights, etc.); to convey away (property). **P. by.** a. *intr.* To go past; to move on without stopping; to flow past. Also *fig.* and in ref. to time. b. *trans.* To go past (a thing or person) without stopping, or without taking notice; to overlook; to omit; to disregard, ignore; = *pass over* d, e. **P. forth.** a. *intr.* To go out or away (*arch.*). †b. To go forward, go on, continue. **P. in.** *trans.* To hand in (e.g. a cheque to a bank). **P. off.** a. *intr.* To go off or disappear gradually, as sensations, moisture, etc. b. *intr.* To go or be carried through (with more or less success). c. *trans.* To put into circulation, or dispose of (esp. deceptively); to palm off; to impose. d. To cause (a person) to be accepted in some false character; *esp. refl.* (with *for* or *as*) to give oneself out as what one is not, to pretend to be. **P. on.** a. *intr.* See simple senses and ON *adv.* b. *trans.* To send or hand (anything) on to the next member of a series. **P. out.** *intr.* See simple senses and OUT *adv.*; chiefly, to go out through a passage. *To p. out of*, to issue from, leave; *to p. out of sight*, to go beyond the reach of sight. **P. over.** a. *intr.* To go across; to cross to the other side. In *Chem.*, said of the volatilized substances which pass from the retort in distillation, and are condensed in the receiver. b. *intr.* Of a period of time: To go by, come to an end. c. *trans.* To hand over *to* another; to transfer. d. To pass (a thing) without touching it, or without remark or notice, esp. in narration; to omit, skip, disregard; to ignore the claims of (a person) for promotion, etc., to pass by in selection for a post, etc. e. To let go unpunished, to overlook (an offence). **P. through:** emphatic of sense A. VI. 1.

Pass-, vb.-stem or imper. of PASS *v.*, used in a few combs., as **pa·ss-out** *a.* (of a ticket) that enables the holder to pass out of and return to a place of entertainment.

Passable (pa·săb'l), *a.* late ME. [a. F., f. *passer* to PASS; see -ABLE.] **1.** That may be passed, crossed, or traversed. †**2.** Able to pass or have passage -1762. **3.** Of money: That has valid currency, current; of a book: fit for circulation. Also *fig.* 1590. **4.** That can pass muster; tolerable; sufficient, presentable 1489. **5.** quasi-*adv.* = Passably 1581.

1. The ford was not p. DE FOE. 3. The vertue of your name, Is not heere p. SHAKS. The coin may cease to be of value as a p. thing, as money 1888. 4. A p. knowledge of living languages SOUTHEY. 5. P. good Christians 1706. Hence **Pa·ssableness. Pa·ssably** *adv.* tolerably; fairly well, moderately.

‖**Passacaglia** (passăkā·lyă). 1659. [It., a. Sp. *pasacalle* (pasăka·lye), f. *pasar* to pass + *calle* street; because often played in the streets.] An early kind of dance tune (of Spanish origin) having a movement slower than the CHACONNE, generally constructed on a ground bass and written in triple time; also the dance to this.

Passade (păsē·d). *rare.* 1656. [a. F., ad. Pr. *passada* or It. *passata*, f. *passare* to PASS; see -ADE.] *Horsemanship.* A turn or course of a horse backwards and forwards on the same plot of ground. †**2.** = next, 1. -1741.

†‖**Passa·do.** 1588. [Altered f. F. *passade*, or Sp. *pasada*, It. *passata*; see prec. and -ADO.] **1.** *Fencing.* A forward thrust with the sword, one foot being advanced -1830. **2.** = PASSAGE *sb.* III. 1 b. -1656.

Passage (pæ·sėdʒ), *sb.* ME. [a. F.:—Rom. **passaticum*, f. **passare* to PASS; see -AGE.] **I.** The action of passing. **1.** A going or moving onward, across, or past; transition, transit. **b.** The passing of people; hence nearly = people passing (*rare*) 1590. **c.** The migratory flight of birds 1774. **2.** *fig.* Transition from one state or condition to another (*spec.* from this life to the next, by death); the passing of time; the course of events, etc.; a passing in thought or speech from one point, idea, or subject to another. late ME. †**b.** *absol.* Departure, death -1837. **3.** Possibility, power, or opportunity of passing; liberty, leave, or right to pass (*lit.* and *fig.*) ME. **4.** A journey; a voyage across the sea from one port to another, a crossing ME. **b.** Right of transit or conveyance as a passenger, esp. by sea; accommodation as a passenger 1632. †**5.** A charge or custom levied upon passengers -1883. †**6.** The fact of being generally accepted, as coins, customs, etc.; currency -1644. **7.** The passing into law of a legislative measure 1587. **8.** *Horsemanship.* A slow trot, in which the horse brings the diagonally opposite legs to the ground at the same moment 1727. **9.** *Med.* An evacuation of the bowels, a 'motion'; also *concr.* 1778. **10.** The action of causing something to pass; transmission, transference, etc. (*rare*) 1860.

1. The p. of the chyldren of Israel from Egypte 1526. b. *Oth.* v. i. 37. c. *Bird of p.*, a bird that migrates from one region to another at a particular season and returns at another, a migratory bird (also *fig.*). 2. Wyth good p. out of thys lyf 1430. b. *Haml.* III. iii. 86. 3. To..guard all p. to the Tree of Life MILT. 4. A rough p. 1877. b. Free p. home 1864.

II. a. That by which a person or thing passes or may pass; a way, road, path, route, channel, esp. when serving as an entrance or exit ME. **b.** *spec.* A crossing; a ford, ferry, or bridge. *arch.* ME. **c.** A corridor or alley leading to or giving access to an apartment, garden, etc. 1611.

a. A new attempt upon the North-West or North-East passages DE FOE. The liver and its bile passages 1897.

III. 1. Something that 'passes', goes on, takes place, occurs, or is done; an incident, event; an act, transaction, or proceeding. *Obs.* or *arch.* (exc. as in b and c.) 1568. **b.** A negotiation between two persons; an interchange of communications, confidences, or amorous relations 1612. **c.** (Now usu. *p. of* (or *at*) *arms.*) An exchange of blows between two persons, a fight; also *fig.* 1599. **2.** An indefinite portion of a discourse or writing, taken by itself 1549. †**b.** A digression -1663. †**c.** A remark, observation (in speech or writing); a phrase, expression -1660. **d.** *Mus.* In early use, a figure or phrase; now, a portion of a composition, of no great length, forming more or less of a unity 1727. **e.** *gen.* An indefinite portion of a course of action; an episode (*rare*) 1848.

1. *Twel. N.* III. ii. 77. **b.** Certain passages..between Will Stephen and this simple country maid 1901. **c.** Luther..had not forgotten his early p. at arms with the English Defender of the Faith 1856. **2.** To look for the p. in the original author 1802. **e.** Despite such passages of gloom he worked on 1897.

†**IV.** [The *passing* or exceeding of ten = It. *passa-dieci*, F. *passe-dix*, i. e. pass-ten.] An obsolete game at dice, played with three dice, in which the thrower *passes* or wins when he throws above ten -1755.

attrib. and *Comb.*: **p.-bed** (*Geol.*), a stratum showing transition from one formation to another; **-hawk**, a falcon taken when full-grown, during its 'passage' or migration, for the purpose of training (opp. to *eyas*); **-money**, money charged for p., fare; **-way**, a way affording passage; a passage esp. in a building (chiefly *U.S.*). Hence **Pa·ssage** *v.*[2] (*a*) to make a p., as in a ship or boat; to move across, pass; (*b*) to carry on a p. of arms; *fig.* to fence with words.

Passage (pæ·sėdʒ), *v.*[1] Chiefly in vbl. sb. **passaging.** 1796. [a. F. *passager*, altered by pop. etym. from *passéger*, ad. It. *passeggiare* to walk, pace, f. L. *passus* PASS *sb.*[1]] **a.** *intr.* To move sideways in riding, by pressure of the rein on the horse's neck and of the rider's leg on the opposite side; said of the horse, or of the rider. **b.** *trans.* To cause (a horse) to 'passage'.

Pa·ssage-boa:t. 1598. A boat for the conveyance of passengers, plying regularly between two places.

Passant (pæ·sănt), *a.* ME. [a. F. *passant*, *passer* to PASS.] †**1.** Surpassing; excelling -1485. †**2.** Passing, transitory, fugitive -1715. †**3.** Passing, going on; proceeding -1710. **4.** *Her.* Of a beast: Walking, and looking towards the dexter side, with the dexter fore-paw raised 1506. †**5.** Current, in general use, in vogue -1844. †**6.** Cursory, done in passing -1693.

2. Our p. words, and our secret thoughts 1677. **5.** Many opinions are p. concerning the Basilisk SIR T. BROWNE. **6.** On a P. review of what..I wrote to the Bp. 1693.

Pa·ss-book. 1828. [app. = book passing between bank, etc., and customer.] **1.** = BANK-BOOK. **2.** *U.S.* A book in which a merchant or trader makes an entry of goods sold to a customer, for the customer's information 1839.

‖**Passé** (pase), *a.* Also (fem.) **passée.** 1775. [F., pa. pple. of *passer* to PASS, used as adj.] Past, past the prime; *esp.* of a woman: past the period of greatest beauty; also, behind the times, superseded.

Pa·ssed-ma·ster. 1563. [f. phr. *pass master*: see PASS *v.* A. VI. 4.] One who has passed as a master; a qualified or accomplished master; cf. PAST-MASTER.

†**Passemea·sure.** 1568. [Alteration of It. *passe-*, *passa-mezzo.*] A slow dance of Italian origin, app. a variety of the pavan; the music for this, in common time. Also called *passe-measures paven*, etc., *passy measures* = It. *passe-mezzo pavana.* -1726.

Then he 's a Rogue, and a passy measures Pauyn: I hate a drunken rogue *Twel. N.* v. i. 205.

Passement (pæ·smėnt), *sb.* *Obs.* exc. *Hist.* 1535. [a. F., f. *passer* to pass; see -MENT.] = LACE *sb.* 4. †**b.** *attrib.*, as *p. lace, silk* -1613. Hence **Pa·ssement** *v.* to adorn with p. or lace; to edge (a garment) with decorative braiding 1539. So ‖**Passementerie** (pasmãntrī), trimming of gold or silver lace, or, later, of gimp, braid, or the like, or of jet or metal beads.

Passenger (pæ·sėndʒəɹ). [ME. *passager*, a. F. *passager*, *-ier*, sb. use of *passager*, *-ier* adj. passing, fleeting, etc., f. *passage* PASSAGE + *-ier* (= L. *-aris*). In late ME. *n* was intruded before *-ger* (dʒəɹ) as in *harbinger*, *messenger*, etc.] **1. a.** A passer by or through. **b.** A traveller (usu. on foot). Now unusual, exc. in *foot-passenger.* **2.** One who travels in some vessel or vehicle, esp. on board ship or in a ferry- or passage-boat; later applied also to travellers by any public conveyance entered by fare or contract. (The prevailing sense.) 1511. †**3.** A passenger-boat; a ferry-boat -1630. †**4.** A bird of passage. Also *attrib.* -1672. †**b.** *spec.* A passage-hawk; also, a name for the Peregrine falcon; in full, *p. falcon* -1694. **5.** *slang.* An ineffective member of the crew of a racing-boat, a football team, etc. 1885. **6.** *attrib.*, as *p. boat, depot, fare, ship, traffic*, etc. 1836.

Pa·ssenger-pi:geon. 1802. [See PASSENGER 4.] The 'Wild Pigeon' of N. America (*Ectopistes migratorius*), noted for its exceptional powers of long and sustained flight.

‖**Passe-partout, passepartout** (pas,partu·). 1675. [F.; f. *passer* to PASS + *partout* everywhere.] **1.** That which passes, or permits to pass, everywhere; *spec.* a master-key; also *fig.* and *attrib.* **2.** An ornamental mat or plate of cardboard, etc., with the centre cut out, serving as a mount or border to a photograph, drawing, etc. when framed. Hence *p. frame*, a frame ready made with such a mount 1867.

Passer (pɑ·səɹ). late ME. [f. PASS *v.* + -ER[1].] **1.** One who passes, travels, or goes by. **2.** One who causes to pass. (See PASS *v.* C.) 1832.

Pa·sser-by·. 1568. [f. *pass by*; see PASS *v.*] One who passes by, *esp.* a casual passer.

‖**Passeres** (pæ·sĕrīz), *sb. pl.* 1872. [L., pl. of *passer* sparrow.] *Ornith.* An order of birds typified by the genus *Passer*, including the perchers generally, and comprehending more than half of existing birds. So **Pa·sseriform** *a.* sparrow-like; *spec.* of or pertaining to the *Passeriformes* or oscinine group of *Passeres.*

Passerine (pæ·sĕrəin), *a.* (*sb.*) 1776. [f. as prec. + -INE[1].] **1.** Of or belonging to the PASSERES. **2.** Of about the size of a sparrow, as the Passerine Parrot (*Psittacula passerina*), etc. 1883. **B.** *sb.* A passerine bird 1842.

Pa·ss-guard. *Obs.* exc. *Hist.* 1548. [app. f. PASS *sb.*[2] IV. 1 + GUARD *sb.*] An item of ancient tilt armour; said to be a separate piece provided to accompany the grand guard, being screwed upon the left elbow; also *elbow-shield.*

Passible (pæ·sib'l), *a.* ME. [a. OF., ad. late L. *passibilis*, f. *pass-*, *pati* to suffer; see -IBLE.] **1.** Capable of suffering, liable to suffer; susceptible of sensation or emotion. †**2.** Liable to suffer change or decay -1655. †**3.** Capable of being suffered or felt -1621.

1. The Paradise Saints have bodies of flesh, p., and such as must have food 1691. So **Passibi·lity**, the quality of being p. **Pa·ssibleness.**

Passiflora (pæsiflō³·rä). 1763. [mod.L. (Linnæus), irreg. f. L. *passio* PASSION + *-florus* flowering.] *Bot.* The genus of plants containing the Passion-flower. Hence **Passiflo·rine** *Chem.*, an alkaloid substance obtained from the root of the Passion-flower.

‖**Passim** (pæ·sim), *adv.* 1803. [L., = 'scatteredly', f. *passus* scattered, pa. pple. of *pandere* to spread out.] Used chiefly after the name of a book or author cited, to indicate that something occurs here and there throughout the book or writings.

Passimeter (pæsi·mītəɹ). 1923. [app. f. PASSENGER + -METER.] An automatic railway ticket-booking machine.

Passing (pɑ·siŋ), *vbl. sb.* ME. [f. PASS *v.* + -ING[1].] **1.** The action of PASS *v.* in various senses. **b.** A passing-place; a ford; a railway siding 1825. **2.** *concr.* A gold or silver thread made by winding a thin strip or ribbon of the metal about a core of silk 1882.

attrib. and *Comb.*: **p.-bell** = DEATH-BELL; *fig.* the 'knell'; †**-penny**, the obolus placed by the ancient Greeks on the tongue of the dead to pay their fare over the Styx; hence, a passport to the future world; **-place**, (*a*) a ford; (*b*) a railway siding.

Pa·ssing, *ppl. a.* (*adv.* and *prep.*) ME. [-ING[2].] That passes, in various senses; *esp.* transient, fleeting; ephemeral; done, given, etc. in passing; cursory.

A p. remark 1862. Some p. traveller from distant lands 1874. The confounding of the P. with the Permanent 1899.

B. *adv.* In a passing or surpassing degree; exceedingly. Now somewhat *arch.* ME.

A man he was..p. rich with forty pounds a year GOLDSM.

†**C.** quasi-*prep.* Beyond, more than (usu. with neg.); more or better than; rather than -1830.

Men paste feare, and hardie p. measure 1561.

Hence **Pa·ssing·ly** *adv.*, **-ness.**

Pa·ssing-no·te. 1730. *Mus.* A note not belonging to the harmony, interposed between two notes essential to it, for the sake of smooth transition.

Passion (pæ·ʃən), *sb.* ME. [a. OF. *passiun*, *passion*, ad. L. *passionem* suffering, f. *pati*, *pass-* to suffer.] **I.** The suffering of pain. **1.** (Now usu. with capital.) The sufferings of Jesus Christ on the Cross (also often including the Agony in Gethsemane). Formerly also in *pl.* **b.** The narrative of the sufferings of Christ from the Gospels; also, a musical setting of this ME. **2.** The sufferings of a martyr, martyrdom (*arch.*) ME. †**3.** Suffering or affliction generally -1656. **4.** A painful disorder of the body or of some part of it. *Obs.* exc. in certain phrases. late ME.

1. By thy crosse and p.,..Good lorde deliuer us *Bk. Com. Prayer.* *Instruments of the P.*, the cross, the crown of thorns, the nails, scourge, etc. **b.** [Bach's] 'Passion according to S. Matthew' is..the finest work of the kind 1880. **3.** *Ant. & Cl.* v. i. 63. **4.** *Colic, iliac, sciatic p.*: see the adjs.

II. The being passive. [Late L. *passio*, as tr. Gr. πάθος.] **a.** The being affected from without. Now *rare* or *Obs.* late ME. †**b.** A passive quality, property, or attribute -1707.

a. The work of p. rather than of action 1846. **b.** What 's the proper p. of mettalls? B. JONS.

III. An affection of the mind. [L. *passio* = Gr. πάθος.] **1.** Any vehement, commanding, or overpowering emotion; in psychology or art, any mode in which the mind is affected or acted upon, as ambition, avarice, desire, hope, fear, love, hatred, joy, grief, anger, revenge. Occas. personified. late ME. **b.** Without article or *pl.*: Commanding, vehement, or overpowering feeling or emotion 1590. **c.** A fit or mood of excited feeling; an outburst of feeling 1590. **d.** A passionate speech or outburst. *Obs.* or *arch.* 1582. **2.** *spec.* An outburst of anger or bad temper 1530. **b.** Without *a*: Angry feeling 1524. **3.** Amorous feeling; love; †also in *pl.*, amorous desires 1588. **b.** *transf.* A beloved person 1783. **4.** Sexual desire or impulse 1641. **5.** An overmastering zeal or enthusiasm for some object 1638. **b.** *transf.* An aim or object pursued with zeal 1732.

1. We also are men of like passions with you *Acts* xiv. 15. The ruling P. conquers Reason still POPE. **b.** Is this the Nature Whom P. could not shake? SHAKS. **c.** She burst into an hysterical p. of weeping 1856. **d.** *Mids. N.* v. i. 321. **2.** Folks who put me in a p. BROWNING. **b.** P. made his dark face turn white SOUTHEY. **3.** P. lends them Power, time, meanes to meete SHAKS. The most wretched of all martyrs to this tender p. FIELDING. **5.** The growing p. for the possession of land 1874. **b.** Golf has become a p. with him (*mod.*).

attrib. and *Comb.*: **p.-music**, music to which the narrative of the P. is set (cf. I. 1 b); **-play**, a mystery-play representing the P. of Christ. Hence **Pa·ssional** *a.* of or pertaining to p. or the passions; characterized by p.

Passion (pæ·ʃən), *v.* 1468. [a. OF. *passioner*, f. *passion.*] **1.** *trans.* To affect or imbue with passion. †**2.** To affect with suffering, afflict -1626. **3.** *intr.* To show, express, or be affected by passion or deep feeling; formerly *esp.* to sorrow 1588.

1. For whose soul-soothing quiet, turtles P. their voices cooingly KEATS. **3.** 'Twas Ariadne, passioning For Theseus periury, and vniust flight SHAKS. Hence **Pa·ssioned** *ppl. a.* = PASSIONATE *a.* 2.

Passional (pæ·ʃənăl), *sb.* 1650. [ad. med. L. *passionale* (also used), neut. of *passionalis* adj. of or belonging to passion, used as sb. = *liber passionalis.*] A book containing accounts of the sufferings of saints and martyrs, for reading on their festival days. So Pa·ssionary 1475.

Passionate (pæ·ʃənět), *a.* (*sb.*) 1450. [ad. med.L. *passionatus*, corresp. to F. *passionné*; see PASSION *v.*] 1. Easily moved to angry passion; hot-tempered; irascible. †b. Enraged, angry –1817. c. Of language, etc.: Angry, wrathful 1590. 2. Of persons: Affected with passion or vehement emotion; enthusiastic, ardently desirous; †zealously devoted 1526. b. Of language, etc.: Expressive of strong emotion, impassioned 1581. c. Of an emotion: Vehement 1567. 3. Subject to passion; easily moved to strong feeling; impressible, susceptible; of changeful mood 1589. †4. *spec.* Affected with the passion of love –1704. †5. Moved with sorrow; sorrowful –1665. b. Compassionate. Now *dial.* 1594. †c. That moves to compassion –1595. B. *sb.* One who is influenced by passion, †*esp.* one who is in love 1651.

A. 1. Homer made Achilles p., Wrathfull, revengefull 1613. c. This p. expletive 1693. 2. He.. swept with p. hand the ringing harp SOUTHEY. b. Forgive this p. language *Junius Lett.* 5. She is sad and p. at your highness Tent SHAKS. b. *Rich. III*, I. iv. 121. Hence **Pa·ssionate·ly** *adv.*, **-ness.**

†**Pa·ssionate,** *v.* 1566. [f. F. *passionner*; see -ATE [3].] 1. *trans.* To excite or imbue with passion, or with a passion, as love, fear, etc. –1658. 2. To express or perform with passion –1615.

Pa·ssion-flower. 1633. [f. PASSION *sb.* I. 1 + FLOWER *sb.*; in 16th c. L. *flos passionis.*] The name of plants of the genus *Passiflora*; so called because of the fancied resemblance of parts of the flower to the instruments of the Passion.

Passionist (pæ·ʃənist), *sb.* (*a.*) 1833. [= F. *passioniste*, f. PASSION *sb.*; see -IST.] *R. C. Ch.* A member of 'The Congregation of the Discalced Clerks of the most Holy Cross and Passion of our Lord Jesus Christ' founded in Italy by Paolo della Croce in 1720. b. *attrib.* or as *adj.* 1844.

Passionless (pæ·ʃənlės), *a.* 1612. [-LESS.] Void of passion; unimpassioned.

Hopeless grief is p. 1844. Hence **Pa·ssionless·ly** *adv.*, **-ness.**

Passion Sunday. late ME. [tr. med.L. *Dominica in Passione.*] The fifth Sunday in Lent; reckoned as the beginning of Passiontide.

Pa·ssion(-)ti:de. 1861. The season immediately before Easter, in which Christ's Passion is commemorated; see prec.

Pa·ssion Wee:k. 1449. [f. PASSION *sb.* I. 1 + WEEK; cf. med.L. *hebdomada passionis.*] The week immediately before Easter, in which the Passion of Christ is commemorated; Holy Week. b. In recent use applied by some to the fifth week of Lent, beginning with Passion Sunday 1852.

Passive (pæ·siv), *a.* and *sb.* late ME. [ad. L. *passivus*, f. *pati, pass-* to suffer; see -IVE. Cf. F. *passif.*] A. *adj.* †1. Suffering, liable to suffer –1655. 2. Suffering action from without; that is the object, as dist. from the subject, of action; acted upon by external force; produced by external agency. late ME. 3. *Gram.* An epithet of voice in verbs used transitively; opp. to ACTIVE 3. Applied to that form of, or that mode of using, the verb, in which the action denoted by it is treated as an attribute of the thing towards which the action is directed. late ME. 4. *Sc. Law.* Involved by acceptance of the property of an ancestor 1576. 5. Suffering or receiving something without resistance or opposition; readily yielding to external force or influence, or to the will of another; submissive 1626. 6. Not active; quiescent, inactive, inert 1477. 7. a. *Path.* Of an inflammation, congestion, or the like: Characterized by sluggish or diminished flow of blood 1813. b. *Chem.* Not readily entering into chemical combination; inert, inactive 1849. c. *Law* and *Comm.* Of a bond, debt, or share: On which no interest is paid. Of a trust: On which the trustees have no duties to perform; nominal 1837.

2. The mind is to be considered as merely p., receiving like wax the impressions of external objects 1773. 5. P. she, all the while, mere clay in the hands of the potter CARLYLE. *P. obedience, prayer, resistance, righteousness*: see the sbs. 6. I am p. in their disputes 1710.

B. *sb.* [The adj. used ellipt.] 1. A passive thing, quality, or property. Now usu. in *pl.* late ME. 2. *Gram.* The passive voice; a passive verb 1530. 3. An unresisting or submissive person or creature. Now *rare.* 1626.

1. A due conjunction of actives and passives SIR T. BROWNE. Hence **Pa·ssive·ly** *adv.*, **-ness.**

Passivity (pæsi·vĭti). 1659. [f. L. *passivus* PASSIVE + -ITY.] †1. Passibility –1680. 2. The quality, condition, or state of being passive. Also, with *a* and *pl.*, an instance of this 1659. 3. Submissiveness 1681. 4. Want of activity, inertness, †inertia 1667.

2. The liability of matter to be shaped, and the liability of the mind to have perceptions and ideas, are pure passivities 1885.

Pass-key (pa·s,kī). 1817. [f. PASS *v.* or *sb.* + KEY *sb.*[1]] A key (other than the ordinary key) of a door or gate, *spec.* a. A master-key; also *fig.*; b. a private key to a gate, etc.; c. a latch-key.

Passless (pa·slės), *a.* 1656. [-LESS.] Impassable. *poet.*

Pass-man (pa·s,mæ̆n). 1860. [f. PASS *sb.*[2] I. 4 + MAN.] A student who takes a 'pass' degree at a university; opp. to *class-man, honours man.*

Passover (pa·sǭuvəɹ). 1530. [f. phr. *pass over*; see PASS *v.*] 1. The name of a Jewish feast, held on the evening of the fourteenth day of the (first) month Nisan, commemorative of the 'passing over' of the houses of the Israelites when the Egyptians were smitten with the loss of their firstborn. †2. *contextually*, The Paschal Lamb. b. *fig.* Applied to Christ (1 *Cor.* v. 7). –1680. 3. *attrib.* 1545.

1. *Passover*..also called the feast of unleavened bread 1840.

Passport (pa·s,poɹt), *sb.* 1500. [a. F. *passeport*, f. *passer* to PASS + *port* PORT *sb.*[1]] †1. Authorization to pass from a port, to leave a country, or to enter or pass through a country –1606. 2. A document issued by competent authority, granting permission to the person specified in it to travel, and authenticating his right to protection 1536. †b. A permit for discharged inmates of a hospital, soldiers, etc. to proceed to a specified destination –1608. 3. *Naval.* A document granted to a neutral merchant-vessel, esp. in time of war, by a power at peace with the state to which it belongs, authorizing it to proceed without molestation in certain waters; a sea-letter 1581. †4. A licence to import or export dutiable goods duty-free, or contraband goods on payment of the duties –1741. 5. *fig.* a. An authorization to pass or go anywhere 15.. b. A warrant of admission into some society, state, or sphere of action 1581. c. A voucher 1578.

1. *Letters of p.* = sense 2. 2. *transf.* Formal passports, signed and sealed for heaven 1717. 5. a. Goe lyttle Calender, thou hast a free passeporte SPENSER. b. His p. is his innocence and grace DRYDEN. c. Looke on his Letter Madam, here's my Pasport SHAKS. Hence **Pa·ssport** *v.* to furnish with a p. **Pa·ssportless** *a.*

‖**Passus** (pæ·sŏs). 1575. [L., = step, pace, etc.] A section, division, or canto of a story or poem.

Password (pa·s,wɒɹd). 1817. [f. PASS *sb.*[2] + WORD *sb.*] A word authorizing the utterer to pass; *esp. Mil.* a parole, a watchword. b. *fig.* = Watchword; secret of admittance 1836.

Passy-measures: see PASSEMEASURE.

Past (past), *ppl. a.* and *sb.* ME. [pa. pple. of PASS *v.*; cf. F. *passé*, L. *præteritus.*] A. *ppl. a.* I. Predicatively after *be*: Gone by in time; elapsed; over.

Surely the bitternesse of death is p. 1 *Sam.* xv. 32.

II. *attrib.* 1. That is passed away, bygone; elapsed (of time); belonging to former days ME. 2. Gone by immediately before the present time; just past. Often strengthened by *last* (see LAST *adv.* B. 2). ME. 3. Of or relating to bygone time; in *Gram.*, Expressing past action or state, preterite; as in *p. tense, p. participle* 1530. 4. In the use of various societies: Having served one's term of office. Cf. PAST-MASTER.

1. A narration of events, either p., present, or to come JOWETT. 2. About forty years p. (= ago) WALTON. For several months p., I have enjoyed such liberty BERKELEY. *ellipt.* I have yours of the 28th p. (= last month, *ultimo*) to acknowledge WARBURTON.

B. *sb.* [ellipt. uses of A.] 1. *The p.*: All time before the present; bygone days collectively, past time 1590. b. That which happened in the past 1665. 2. A past life, career, or history; a stage that one has passed through; *esp.* a past life over which a veil is drawn 1836. 3. *Gram.* (*ellipt.*) = *Past tense*: see A. 3. 1783.

1. The storied P. TENNYSON. 2. A woman..who has had a p. 1876.

Past (past), *prep.* and *adv.* ME. [Developed from pa. pple. of PASS *v.* (conjugated with the vb. *to be*) in uses such as 'Now is (= has) the king *passed* (*past*) the sea'.] A. *prep.* 1. Beyond in time (as the result of passing); after; beyond the age or time for. b. *ellipt.* Beyond the age of (so many years) 1560. 2. Beyond in place (as the result of passing); further on than ME. b. Of motion: By (in passing) 1542. 3. Beyond the reach, range, or compass of; incapable of. Occas. = No longer capable of or within the scope of. late ME. b. Beyond the ability or power of (*colloq.*) 1611. c. Beyond the limits of; without (now *dial.*) 1470. †4. More than, above –1668. b. Beyond in manner or degree. Now *rare.* 1611.

1. It was passed 8 of the clokke CHAUCER. After he was p. the Age of one hundred Years 1709. b. Augustus..injoin'd Marriage to all p. 25 Years 1718. 2. Until we be [*R.V.* have] p. thy borders *Num.* xxi. 22. b. Phr. *To go p.*, to pass; so *to flow, ride, run, hurry*, etc. *p.* (a person or place). 3. Phr. *P. belief, comprehension, cure, finding out*, etc.; also, *p. praying for* (colloq.): hopeless. c. *P. himself*, beside himself (now *dial.*).

B. *adv.* (absol. use of the prep.; = past the speaker or what is spoken of.) 1. So as to pass; by 1805. 2. On one side, aside. *Sc.* and *north Irel.* 1830.

1. The alarum of drums swept p. LONGF. 2. Phr. *To lay p.*, to put by or save up.

Paste (pēⁱst), *sb.* late ME. [a. OF. *paste*, mod.F. *pâte*:—Com. Rom. *pasta, perh. ad. Gr. παστη, also pl. παστά, πασταί barley porridge, subst. uses of παστός sprinkled.] 1. *Cookery.* Flour moistened and kneaded, dough; now only, with addition of butter, lard, suet, or the like. b. Applied to compositions of this consistence used as baits in angling 1653. c. A relish of some fish, crustacean, or meat, cooked, pounded or minced, and seasoned; as *anchovy-p., shrimp-p.* 1817. 2. A cement made of flour and water (sometimes with starch) boiled together; used for sticking paper, etc. 1530. 3. *gen.* Any soft and plastic composition or mixture 1604. 4. *fig.* The material of which a person is figuratively said to be made (in ref. to quality) 1645. 5. A hard vitreous composition (of fused silica, potash, white oxide of lead, borax, etc.), used in making imitations of precious stones; a gem made of this. Also called STRASS. Also *attrib.* 1662. 6. *Min.* A mineral substance in which other minerals are embedded 1828. †7. A head-dress (app. with a foundation of pasteboard) worn by women –1592.

4. The Inhabitants of that Town, methinks, are made of another p. 1645.

Comb.: **p.-cutter,** an instrument for cutting p. into shapes for pastry; **-eel,** a small nematoid worm (*Anguillula glutinis*) found in sour p.; **p. grain,** split sheep-skin with p. put on the back to harden it and give it a better grain.

Paste (pēⁱst), *v.* 1561. [f. prec.] 1. *trans.* To fasten with paste. Also *transf.* and *fig.* 2. To cover by (or as by) pasting over 1609. 3. *slang.* To beat, thrash; cf. BASTE *v.*[3] 1851.

1. *To p. up*, to stick up (on a wall, etc.) with paste. 2. Pasting a screen..all over with prints 1849.

Comb.: **p.-down,** an outer blank leaf of a book pasted on the cover; **-in** *a.*, pasted in, inserted by pasting.

Pasteboard (pēⁱ·stbōᵊɹd), *sb.* (*a.*) 1548. [f. PASTE *sb.* or *v.* + BOARD *sb.*] A. I. †1. A substitute for a thin wooden board made by pasting sheets of paper together; *esp.* a board of a book so made (cf. BOARD *sb.*) –1796. 2. A stiff firm substance made by pasting together, compressing, and rolling three or more sheets of paper; a piece of this 1562. b. *fig.* As the type of anything flimsy, unsubstantial, or counterfeit 1829. 3. *slang.* A card. a. A visiting-card 1837. b. A playing-card; also playing-cards collectively 1859. c. A railway-ticket 1901. II. *Cookery.* (Usu. with hyphen.) A board on which paste or dough is rolled out for making pastry, etc. 1858. B. *attrib.* (or as *adj.*) Made of pasteboard 1599. b. *fig.* Unsubstantial; unreal, counterfeit, sham 1659.

b. The p. triumph and the cavalcade GOLDSM.

Paste-egg: see PASCH-EGG.

Pastel[1] (pæ·stĕl). 1578. [a. F., ad. It. *pastello* woad, dim. *pasta* paste.] The plant Woad, *Isatis tinctoria*; also, the blue dye obtained from it.

Pastel[2] (pæ·stĕl). 1662. [a. F., ad. It. *pastello*; see prec.] 1. A kind of dry paste made by compounding ground pigments with gum-water, used as a crayon or for making crayons. 2. A drawing in pastel; also, the art of drawing with pastels 1855. 3. Applied to certain soft tints of dress-material; usu. *attrib.* 1899.

2. Two charming portraits,..two pastels 1893. Hence **Pa·stellist, pastelist**, an artist who works with pastels.

Paster (pē¹·stəɹ). 1737. [f. PASTE *v.* + -ER[1].] 1. One who pastes. 2. *U.S.* A small slip of gummed paper, which a voter pastes over any name he objects to on the ballot paper 1888.

Pastern (pæ·stəɹn). [ME. *pastron* = OF. *pasturon*, mod.F. *paturon*, f. OF. *pasture*; perh. the same word as OF. *pasture*, F. *pâture* PASTURE, transf. first to the tether of a horse at pasture, and then to the joint.] †1. A shackle fixed on the foot of a horse, or other beast; a hobble -1625. 2. That part of a horse's foot between the fetlock and the hoof 1530. b. The corresponding part in other animals; also *transf.* the human ankle 1555. 3. = Pastern-bone 1656.

attrib. and *Comb.*: **p.-joint**, the joint or articulation between the cannon-bone and the great pastern-bone; **p.-bone**, each of the two bones (*upper* or *great*, and *lower* or *small p.*) between the cannon-bone and the coffin-bone, being the first and second phalanges of the foot of a horse.

Pasteurism (pɑ·störiz'm). 1883. [f. name of Louis *Pasteur*, a Fr. scientist (1822–95) + -ISM.] Pasteur's method of treating certain diseases, esp. hydrophobia, by successive inoculations with attenuated virus gradually increasing in amount.

Pasteurize (pɑ·störaiz), *v.* 1881. [f. as prec. + -IZE.] 1. *trans.* To sterilize by Pasteur's method; to prevent or arrest fermentation in (milk, wine, etc.) by exposure to a high temperature so as to destroy microbes or germs. 2. To treat by the method of PASTEURISM 1886. Hence **Pa:steuriza·tion. Pa·steurizer**, an apparatus for pasteurizing milk.

‖ **Pasticcio** (pastī·ttʃo). 1752. [It., in med. L. *pasticium*, deriv. of Com. Rom. **pasta* paste.] A medley; a hotchpotch, farrago, jumble; *spec.* a. A musical composition made up of pieces from different sources, a pot-pourri; b. A picture or design made up of fragments pieced together, or in professed imitation of the style of another artist; also the style of such a picture, etc.

‖ **Pastiche** (pastī·ʃ). 1878. [F. ad. It. *pasticcio*; see prec.] = prec.

Pastil, pastille (pæ·stil, pæstī·l), *sb.* 1648. [a. F. *pastille*, ad. L. *pastillus*, *-um* a little loaf or roll of bread, etc.; app. in Romanic assoc. w. **pasta* PASTE.] 1. A small roll of aromatic paste for burning as a perfume, now esp. as a fumigator, deodorizer, or disinfectant 1658. 2. A sugared confection of a rounded flat shape (often medicated); a troche, lozenge 1648. 3. = PASTEL[2] 1. 1662. 4. *attrib.* 1833.

Pastime (pɑ·staim), *sb.* 1489. [f. PASS *v.* + TIME; in sense 1, tr. F. *passe-temps*.] 1. *gen.* That which serves to pass the time agreeably; diversion, entertainment, amusement, sport; occas. †occupation. (No *pl.*) 1490. b. With *a* and *pl.* A recreation; a sport, a game 1489. †2. A passing or elapsing of time; a space of time; an interval between two points of time -1529.

1. b. The Wood-Nymphs deckt with Daisies trim, Their merry wakes and pastimes keep MILT. Hence **Pa·stime** *v.* (now *rare*) *intr.* to pass one's time pleasantly, to entertain or amuse oneself; *trans.* to divert, amuse.

Past-master, past master (pɑ·st mɑ:stəɹ). 1762. [Later spelling of PASSED-MASTER.] 1. One who has filled the office of 'master' in a guild, civic company, freemasons' lodge, etc. 2. A thorough master (of a subject). Const. *in*, *of*. 1868. So **Pa·st-mi:stress** (in sense 2).

Pastor (pɑ·stəɹ), *sb.* [late ME. and AF. *pastour* = OF. *pastor*, *pastur*, ad. L. *pastorem*, f. *pascere* to feed.] 1. A herdsman or shepherd. Now *rare*. 2. A shepherd of souls; *spec.* the minister in charge of a church or congregation, with particular ref. to the spiritual care of his 'flock'. late ME. 3. One who protects or guides a number of people. late ME. 4. *Ornith.* A genus of starlings, of which the species *Pastor roseus* is an occasional visitor to the British islands 1825. 5. A small tropical fish (*Nomeus Gronovii*); called also *Portuguese man-of-war fish* 1902.

3. A Moses or a David, pastors of their people BACON. Hence **Pa·stor** *v.*, to take charge of (a spiritual flock) as a p. **Pa·storage** (*rare*), †the function of a p.; also, a parsonage.

Pastoral (pɑ·stŏrăl), *a.* and *sb.* late ME. [ad. L. *pastoralis*, f. *pastor* PASTOR; see -AL.] A. *adj.* I. 1. Of or pertaining to shepherds or their occupation; of the nature of a shepherd. 2. Of land: Used for pasture. Hence of scenery, etc.: Having the simplicity or natural charm associated with such country. 1790. 3. Of literature, music, etc.: Portraying country life; expressed in pastorals 1581.

1. Or sound of p. reed with oaten stops MILT.

II. Of or pertaining to a pastor or shepherd of souls; having relation to the spiritual care of a 'flock' of Christians 1526.

P. epistles, the epistles of Paul to Timothy and Titus, which deal largely with the work of a pastor. *P. staff* = CROSIER 3.

B. *sb.* (The adj. used ellipt.) I. †1. *pl.* Pastoral games SIDNEY. 2. A poem, play, etc., in which the life of shepherds is portrayed, often in a conventional manner; also extended to works dealing with country life generally 1584. b. A pastoral picture 1819. c. *Mus.* = PASTORALE 1851. 3. Pastoral poetry as a mode of literary composition 1598.

3. The Golden Age is not to be regilt; P. is gone out, and Pan extinct HOOD.

II. 1. a. 'A book relating to the cure of souls' (J.). late ME. b. A letter from a spiritual pastor to his flock; *esp.* a letter from a bishop to the clergy or people of his diocese 1865. c. *pl.* The pastoral epistles; see A. II. 1901. 2. A pastoral staff, a crosier 1658. Hence **Pa·storally** *adv.* **Pa·storalism**, p. quality or character; the p. style in literature. **Pa·storalist**, a writer of pastorals; also, one who lives by keeping flocks of sheep or cattle; *spec.* (*Australia*) a sheep-farmer, a squatter.

‖ **Pastorale** (pastorā·le, *-i*). *Pl.* **-ali** (-ā·lī), **-ales.** 1724. [It., sb. use of *pastorale* adj. PASTORAL.] *Mus.* a. An instrumental composition in pastoral style, or representing pastoral sounds and scenes; usu. a simple melody in 6–8 time. b. An opera, cantata, etc., the subject of which is pastoral.

Pastorality (pastŏræ·lĭti). 1506. [ad. med. L. *pastoralitas*, f. *pastoralis* PASTORAL; see -ITY.] Pastoral quality or character.

Pa·storalize, *v.* 1825. [-IZE.] 1. *trans.* To make pastoral or rural. 2. To put into or celebrate in a pastoral 1839.

Pastorate (pɑ·stŏrēt). 1795. [ad. med.L. *pastoratus*.] 1. The office or position of a pastor; the tenure of such office. 2. Pastors collectively 1846.

Pastorly (pɑ·stəɹli), *a.* 1616. [-LY[1].] Of, pertaining to, or befitting a pastor; pastor-like.

Pastorship (pɑ·stəɹʃip). 1563. [-SHIP.] = PASTORATE.

Pastry (pē¹·stri). 1539. [app. f. PASTE *sb.* + -RY (-ERY); cf. OF. *pastaierie*, F. *pâtisserie*.] 1. Articles of food made of or with paste (see PASTE *sb.* 1); now only, such articles when baked, as pies, tarts, etc. 2. A place where pastry is made. *Obs.* exc. *Hist.* 1570. †3. The art and business of a pastry-cook -1752.

Comb. **p.-cook**, one who makes p., *esp.* for public sale.

Pasturable (pɑ·stiŭrăb'l, -tʃər-). *a.* 1577. [f. PASTURE *sb.* or *v.* + -ABLE.] That may be pastured; fit for pasture.

Pasturage (pɑ·stiŭrĕdʒ, -tʃər-). 1533. [a. OF. *pasturage*, mod.F. *pâturage*, f. *pasturer* to PASTURE; see -AGE.] 1. The action or occupation of pasturing; grazing 1579. 2. = PASTURE *sb.* 3. 1540. 3. = PASTURE *sb.* 4. 1533.

Pasture (pɑ·stiŭɹ, -tʃəɹ), *sb.* ME. [a. OF. *pasture*, mod.F. *pâture*:—late L. *pastura*, f. *past-*, *pascere* to feed, graze; see -URE.] 1. The action of feeding (said of animals); *spec.* the grazing of cattle (*rare*). late ME. †2. Food, sustenance (*lit.* and *fig.*) -1786. 3. The growing herbage eaten by cattle ME. 4. A piece of land covered with this; grass-land. ME.

3. Twenty acres..For p. ten, and ten for plough PRIOR. *Common p.*, the use of p. by the cattle of a number of owners. *Common of p.*: see COMMON *sb.* 4. 4. *fig.* The Lord my P. shall prepare ADDISON. So **Pa·stural** *a.* of or pertaining to p.

Pasture (pɑ·stiŭɹ, -tʃəɹ), *v.* late ME. [a. OF. *pasturer*, mod.F. *pâturer*, f. *pasture*; see prec.] †1. *intr.* Of cattle, sheep, etc.: To graze. Also *fig.* 2. *trans.* To lead or put (cattle) to pasture. late ME. 3. (Of sheep or cattle) To graze upon (herbage, grass-land), to eat down; (of persons) to put sheep or cattle on (grass-land, etc.) to graze 1533.

2. Here Uzziah pastured his cattel FULLER. Hence **Pa·sturer** (*rare*), one who pastures cattle, a herdsman or grazier.

Pasty (pæ·sti, pē¹·sti), *sb.* [ME. *pastee*, a. OF. *pastée* (also *pasté*), adj. of ppl. form, f. late L. *pasta* PASTE; lit. (something) made of or with paste.] A pie, consisting usu. of seasoned venison or other meat, but sometimes of apples, jam, etc., enclosed in a crust of pastry, and baked without a dish.

The venison p. was palpable beef, which was not handsome PEPYS.

Pasty (pē¹·sti), *a.* 1607. [f. PASTE *sb.* + -Y[1].] Like paste in consistence, appearance, or colour; *esp.* of the complexion: pale and dull. b. Of or pertaining to paste jewellery 1865. Hence **Pa·stiness**, p. quality.

Pat (pæt), *sb.*[1] [late ME. *pat*, *patte*; prob. echoic.] I. The action. 1. A stroke or blow with a flat or blunt surface. *Obs.* exc. *dial.* 2. a. A stroke or tap with a flat surface, so as to flatten or smooth. b. *spec.* A gentle tap with the hand or fingers, esp. as a caress or in approbation. Also *fig.* 1804.

2. b. A word of approbation—a little p. on the back, as I may say 1898.

II. a. A small mass of some soft substance (*e.g.* butter) formed or shaped by patting 1754. b. Something of the shape and size, or appearance, of a pat of butter, etc. 1852. III. The sound. a. The sound made by striking lightly with something flat; *esp.* with the foot in walking or running 1697. b. Reduplicated, to express repetition 1876.

Pat (pæt), *sb.*[2] 1825. [abbrev. of *Patrick*.] A nickname for an Irishman; cf. PADDY[2].

Pat (pæt), *v.* 1567. [f. or related to PAT *sb.*[1]] †1. *trans.* To cause (something) to strike or hit *upon* any surface GOLDING. 2. To hit, to strike, prop. with a flat or blunt instrument; also, to drive by so striking, as a ball with the hand. *Obs.* exc. *dial.* 1591. 3. *intr.* To tap or beat lightly (*upon* any surface) 1601. 4. *trans.* To strike (something) gently with a flat surface, so as to flatten or smooth; to flatten down by such action 1607. 5. *esp.* To strike or clap gently with the fingers or hand, by way of approbation, encouragement, sympathy, etc.; hence *fig.* to express such feeling to (any one), esp. in *to p. on the back* 1714. 6. *intr.* To tap or strike lightly so as to produce a characteristic sound. Also reduplicated, *pat-pat*. 1760. 7. The vb.-stem as adv. or int. 1681.

5. The child patted Caroline's cheek 1813. We.. p. every man on the back who has the courage of his convictions 1884. 6. A short quick step she hears Come patting close behind 1801. 7. Still on, p., p., the Goblin went 1801.

Comb.: **p.-ball**, the game of rounders; also, poor or feeble lawn tennis.

Pat (pæt), *adv.* and *a.* 1578. [app. closely related to PAT *sb.*[1], *v.*; perh. from the vb.-stem.] 1. *adv.* In a way that hits its object or aim; appositely; opportunely; so as to be ready for any occasion, readily, promptly. 2. *predic.*

as *adv.* or *adj.* 1638. 3. *attrib.* or as *adj.* That comes or lies exactly to the purpose; apposite, apt; opportune. (Said esp. of things spoken.) 1646. b. *P. hand* (Poker), a hand so good when first dealt that it is not likely to be improved by drawing other cards 1889.

1. I came just p. to be a godfather PEPYS. 2. A passage..very p. to his purpose 1656. 3. A story so p., you may think it is coined COWPER. Hence **Pa·tly** *adv.* = 1. **Pa·tness**, the quality or condition of being p. or to the point; aptness.

Pa·t-a-cake. First words of a nursery rime, said or chanted to accompany the action of patting or clapping together a child's hands; also a game played in doing this.

‖**Pata·che.** 1589. [F. (pata·ʃ), or Sp. (pătaˈtʃe); origin unkn.] A small boat, used for communications between the vessels of a fleet. *Obs.* exc. *Hist.*

†**Patacoo·n.** 1584. [a. Sp. *patacon*, also *patacchina*, a. Pg. *patacão*, augm. of *pataca* piece of eight, dollar.] A Pg. and Sp. silver coin, worth, in the 17th c., about 4*s.* 8*d.* English –1749.

‖**Patagium** (pætădʒəi·ŏm). *Pl.* **-ia.** 1826. [med. L., from ancient L. *patagium* gold edging on a tunic = Gr. παταγεῖον.] a. A fold of skin or membrane extending along the side of the body of certain flying mammals and reptiles; the wing-membrane of a bat, etc. b. *Ornith.* The fold or integument occupying the angle between the upper arm and the forearm of birds. c. *Entom.* Name for each of a pair of processes or appendages on the pronotum or thorax of certain Lepidoptera. Hence **Patagial** (pătēⁱ·dʒiăl), **Pata·giate** *adjs.*

†**Pa·tagon.** 1579. [a. Sp. *patagon* large clumsy foot.] A member of a tribe of S. American Indians, whence Patagonia received its name –1773.

Patagonian (pætăgōᵘ·niăn), *a.* and *sb.* 1767. [f. *Patagonia*: see prec. and -AN.] A. *adj.* Of or pertaining to Patagonia or its inhabitants; hence †Gigantic, huge, immense. B. *sb.* A S. American Indian of a race inhabiting southern Patagonia, said to be the tallest known people; hence, *fig.* †a giant, a gigantic specimen 1767.

‖**Patas** (patā·). 1745. [F., from a dialect of Senegal.] The red monkey (*Cercopithecus patas*) of W. Africa.

Patavinity (pætăvi·nĭti). 1607. [ad. L. *patavinitas*, f. *Patavinus* of *Patavium*, now Padua, the birthplace of Livy.] The dialectal characteristics of Patavium or Padua, as shown in Livy's writings; hence *gen.* Provincialism in style; also, an instance of this.

Patch (pætʃ), *sb.*¹ [late ME. *pacche, patche*; origin unkn.] 1. A piece of cloth, leather, metal, etc., put on to mend a hole or rent, or to strengthen a weak place. b. A piece of court-plaster or the like put over a wound 1591. c. A pad worn to protect an injured eye 1598. 2. A small piece of black silk or court-plaster worn on the face, esp. in 17th and 18th centuries, either to hide a fault or to show off the complexion by contrast 1592. Also *attrib.*, esp. in *p.-box*. 3. A large or irregular spot on any surface 1573. b. A small piece or area of ground, or of anything lying or growing on it 1577. c. An area of floating pieces of ice, overlapping one another, of a circular or polygonal form 1817. d. *Anat.* and *Path.* A small well-defined area of the skin, etc. distinct in colour or appearance 1797. 4. A piece of cloth sewed together with others to form patchwork or to adorn a garment 1529. 5. A small scrap, piece, or remnant of anything 1529. 6. Anything suggesting a patch (sense 1) in the way it is fastened, or in shape or size, or otherwise 1835.

1. A foul coat full of patches HOBBES. *Phr. Not a p. on* (colloq.), not comparable to, nowhere near. 2. Your black patches you wear variously, Some cut like stars, some in half moons 1625. 3. b. A p. of April snow WORDSW. Here and there a p. of potatoes or beans 1894. 5. A King of shreds and patches SHAKS.

attrib. and *Comb.*: **p. head** (*U.S.* local), the surf-scoter, *Œdemia perspicillata*; **-ice**, pieces of ice overlapping so as to form a p.; **-leather**, leather used in patching; **-polled** *a.*, having a p. of colour on the head, esp. in *patch-polled coot* = *p. head.*

Patch (pætʃ), *sb.*² 1549. [perh. anglicized f. It. *pazzo* fool.] A domestic fool; a clown, dolt, booby. Now only *dial.* or *colloq.* applied to an ill-natured person, esp. a child, etc. Hence †**Pa·tchery**², the conduct of a p.; roguery, knavery –1607.

Patch (pætʃ), *v.* 1500. [f. PATCH *sb.*¹] 1. *trans.* To put a patch or patches on; of a thing, to serve as a patch to 1516. b. In pa. pple., said of a person in reference to his clothing, etc. 1500. 2. To mend, repair, or make whole, in various *fig.* applications. (Usu. with *up*, and implying a hasty, clumsy, or temporary manner.) 1573. 3. To make by joining pieces together as in patchwork; hence, to botch *up* 1529. 4. To put on or in as a patch. Also *fig.*; often depreciatory. 1549. b. To piece together 1630. 5. To diversify or variegate with patches. (Chiefly in pass.) 1595. 6. To adorn (a person, the face) with patches. Also *intr.* for *refl.* 1674.

1. Windows patched with rags and paper DICKENS. *P. up*, to mend by putting patches on. 2. Sin that amends, is but patcht with vertue SHAKS. You'll have to..p. up your quarrel 1875. 3. Out of what booke patched you out Cicero's Oration? LODGE. 4. b. It is just possible to p. the two narratives together 1867. 5. Grey rocks patched with moss 1774. 6. But alas, Madam, who patch'd you today? STEELE. Hence **Patched** *ppl. a.* **Pa·tcher**; also *patcher-up*. **Pa·tchery**¹, the action of patching; a patchwork (usu. *fig.*). **Pa·tching** *vbl. sb.*, the action of the vb.; also the condition of being patched.

Pa·tch-box. 1674. [f. PATCH *sb.*¹ 2 + BOX *sb.*²] A box for holding patches for the face.

Patchouli (pæ·tʃuli, pătʃū·li). 1845. [Vernacular name in Madras.] 1. An odoriferous plant (*Pogostemon Patchouli*, N.O. *Labiatæ*), native to Silhat, Penang, and the Malay Peninsula; it yields an essential oil, from which the scent (sense 2) is derived 1851. 2. A penetrating perfume made from this plant 1845. 3. *attrib.*, as *p. oil* 1881.

Patchwork (pæ·tʃ‚wɒːk). 1692. [f. PATCH *v.* or *sb.*¹ + WORK *sb.*] 1. Work made up of pieces or fragments put together, esp. in an incongruous manner; a thing patched up; a medley, a jumble. Now often viewed as *fig.* from 2. b. Work of patching up SWIFT. 2. Work consisting of small pieces of cloth of different kinds and colours sewn together by the edges, so as to make a counterpane, cushion, tea-cosy, etc. 1726. b. Any surface divided like such a counterpane 1865. 3. *attrib.*, as *p. quilt* 1713.

2. *Crazy p.*, that in which the pieces are quite irregular in shape and size. 3. Second-hand minds and p. intellects 1814.

Patchy (pæ·tʃi), *a.* 1798. [f. PATCH *sb.*¹ + -Y¹.] Abounding in or consisting of patches; resembling patchwork in appearance or structure. Hence **Pa·tchily** *adv.* **Pa·tchiness.**

Pate (pēⁱt). ME. [Origin unkn.] 1. The head, the skull; esp. the crown of the head. (Not now in serious or dignified use.) 2. The head as the seat of intellect; hence, skill, cleverness, 'brains', and formerly occas. for a person having these (*arch.* or *poet.*) 1610. 3. The skin of a calf's head 1687.

1. His vnhappynes shall come vpon his owne heade, and his wickednes shall fall vpon his owne p. COVERDALE *Ps.* vii. 16. 2. An excellent passe of p. SHAKS.

‖**Pâté** (pāte). 1704. [F. (OF. *pasté*; see PASTY *sb.*)] 1. A pie, pasty, or patty. 2. *Fortif.* (Erron. written *pate.*) A kind of oval platform, with a parapet, usu. erected in marshy grounds to cover a gate of a town 1704.

1. *P. de foie gras*, pasty of fatted goose liver, Strasburg pie.

Pated (pēⁱ·tĕd), *a.* 1580. [f. PATE + -ED ².] Having a pate (of a specified kind); as *empty-p.*

†**Patefa·ction.** 1553. [ad. L. *patefactionem*, f. *patefacere* to PATEFY.] The action of making open, visible, or known; a disclosing, revelation, declaration –1872.

†**Pa·tefy,** *v.* 1533. [ad. L. *patefacere*, f. *patere* to be open + *facere* to make; see -FY.] *trans.* To make open; to disclose, manifest –1788.

‖**Patella** (păte·lă). 1671. [L., = pan, knee-pan, dim. of *patina* PATEN.] 1. *Anat.* The knee-pan or knee-cap. Also *transf.* 2. *Archæol.* A small pan or shallow vessel; the vessel so called by the Romans 1851. 3. A natural formation in plants or animals in the form of a shallow pan 1671. 4. *Zool.* A genus of Mollusca, containing the common limpet 1753. Hence **Patellar** (pæ·tĕlăɹ, păte·lăɹ) *a.* of or pertaining to the p. or knee-pan. **Pa·tellate** *a.* furnished with, or formed into or like, a p. **Pate·lliform** *a.* having the form of a p., knee-pan, or limpet-shell.

‖**Patellula** (păte·liŭlă). 1890. [mod. L. dim. of *patella*.] A small patella; one of the sucking disks or cups on the tarsus of water-beetles.

Paten (pæ·tĕn). [ME. *patene, -eyn(e*, a. OF. *patène*, ad. L. *patena, patina* wide shallow vessel.] 1. The shallow dish, usu. circular and of silver, on which the bread is laid at the celebration of the Eucharist. 2. *gen.* A shallow dish or plate. *arch.* or *Hist.* late ME. 3. A thin circular plate of metal; anything resembling or suggesting this 1596.

3. Looke how the floore of heauen Is thicke inlayed with pattens of bright gold SHAKS.

Patency (pēⁱ·tĕnsi). 1656. [f. PATENT; see -ENCY.] 1. The state or condition of being open or exposed to view. 2. The condition of being open, expanded, or unobstructed, as a passage 1843.

Patent (pēⁱ·tĕnt, pæ·t-), *sb.* late ME. [orig. short for *letter(s) patent*: see prec.] 1. = *letters patent*: see prec. I. 1. †b. = INDULGENCE II. 1. ME. only. †c. An official certificate or licence; *esp.* a health certificate –1666. 2. A licence to manufacture, sell, or deal in an article, to the exclusion of other persons; now, a grant from a government to a person or persons conferring for a certain definite time the exclusive privilege of making, using, or selling some new invention 1588. 3. A process which has been patented 1862. 4. A territory, district, or piece of land conferred by letters patent. *U.S.* 1632. 5. *fig.* A sign or token that one is entitled to something; authority to do something; title to possess something 1590.

1. I..was examined..and gott my p. of Doctor ther 1695. 2. Abuses practised by Monopolies and Patents of priviledge 1597. 4. It is not my intent to wander far from our P. 1634. 5. Giue her pattent to offend, for if it touch not you, it comes neere no body SHAKS.

attrib. and *Comb.*, as *p. law*; **p. office**, an office where patents are issued and where the claims to patents are examined; **p.-right**, the exclusive right conferred by letters patent; **-roll**, a parchment roll containing the letters patent issued in Great Britain in any one year. Hence **Pa·tentor** (*a*) one who grants a p.; (*b*) a patentee.

Patent (pēⁱ·tĕnt, pæ·tĕnt), *a.* late ME. [In branch I, a. F., ad. L. *patentem* open, lying open; in II, directly from L. The pronunc. (pæ·tĕnt) prevails in U.S. In Eng. official use, I and II are sometimes differentiated as (pæ·tĕnt) and (pēⁱ·tĕnt).] I. 1. In *letters p.* (L. *litteræ patentes*, Fr. *lettres patentes*): An open letter or document, usu. from a sovereign or person in authority, issued for various purposes; now esp. to grant for a statutory term to a person or persons the sole right to make, use, or sell some invention. Also *fig.* 2. Conferred by letters patent; endowed with a patent. Of a person: Appointed by letters patent. 1597. 3. Of an invention: Protected or covered by letters patent. Also in the names of inventions of which the patent has expired, as *p. leather*: see LEATHER *sb.* 1. 1707. b. *fig.* and *transf.* To which one has a proprietary claim; also, special for its purpose; sovereign, superlative 1797.

1. Richard II was the first to confer the peerage by letters-p. 1863. The Letters P. were..written upon open sheets of parchment, with the Great Seal pendent at the bottom 1891. 3. The venders of p. or quack medicines 1799. b. That p. Christianity which has been for some time manufacturing at Clapham SYD. SMITH.

II. 1. Open as a door, gate, etc. 1513. 2. Open as to situation; unenclosed; freely accessible. Now *rare.* late ME. 3. Spreading, expanded; *spec.* in *Bot.* opening wide, as petals; diverging widely from the axis, as branches or leaves; *Zool.* patulous; having a wide aperture, or a shallow cavity 1753. 4. = OPEN *a.* I. 5, II. 1. 1508. 5. Open to general knowledge or use; public 1566.

2. A circular temple, p. to the sun 1839. 4. A p. fact, as certain as anything in mathematics 1874. Hence **Pa·tently** *adv.* in a p. manner; openly, evidently, clearly.

Patent (pēⁱ·tĕnt, pæ·t-), *v.* 1822. [f. PATENT *sb.* and *a.*] 1. *trans.* To grant a patent to; to admit to some privilege or rank by letters patent (*rare*) 1828. 2. To take out or obtain a patent for 1822. 3. To obtain a patent right to land *U.S.* 1874.

2. *fig.* A tendency..to fall into a style patented by Ouida 1900. Hence **Pa·tentable** *a.* capable of being patented.

Patentee (pǟtĕntī·, pæt-). late ME. [f. PATENT *sb.* + -EE[1].] One to whom letters patent have been granted; now *esp.* one who has patented an invention. Also *fig.*

‖ **Pater.** ME. [L. = father.] 1. (pæ·təɹ) = PATERNOSTER 1. 2. (pēⁱ·təɹ) Schoolboys' slang for *father* 1728.

‖ **Patera** (pæ·tĕră). *Pl.* **-æ.** 1658. [L., f. *patere* to be open. Cf. *patina, patella.*] 1. *Rom. Antiq.* A broad flat saucer or dish, used esp. in pouring out libations at sacrifices. 2. *Arch.* An ornament resembling a shallow dish; any flat round ornament in bas-relief 1776.

‖ **Paterfamilias** (pēⁱ:təɹ-, pæ:təɹfămi·liǣs). late ME. [L. (*familias*, archaic gen. of *familia*).] 1. *Rom. Law.* The head of a family or household; also, a person of either sex and any age who is *sui juris* and free from parental control 1850. 2. The (male) head of a family or household. late ME. Now chiefly *joc.*

Paternal (pătɔ̄·ɹnăl), *a.* 1605. [ad. late L. or Com. Rom. type *paternalis*, f. L. *paternus* fatherly + -AL.] 1. Of or belonging to a father or to fathers; fatherly. b. Of or belonging to one's father 1667. c. That is a father 1667. 2. Inherited or derived from a father; related on the father's side 1611.

1. *P. government*, government as by a father, paternalism. c. P. God in Filial shines, And in our Bliss with Filial joyns KEN. 2. My p. grandmother ..ran away with my p. grandfather RUSKIN. So **Pate·rnally** *adv.* 1603.

Paternalism (pătɔ̄·ɹnăliz'm). 1881. [-ISM.] 1. The principle and practice of paternal administration; government as by a father. 2. The principle of acting in a way like that of a father towards his children 1893. So **Paternali·stic** *a.* of, pertaining to, or of the nature of p.

Paternity (pătɔ̄·ɹnĭti). late ME. [a. F. *paternité*, ad. L. *paternitatem*, f. *paternus* paternal; see -ITY.] 1. The quality of being a father; the relation of a father; fatherhood 1582. †b. Patriarchal rule -1711. 2. The quality or personality of an eccl. father: used as a title, *Your, His P.*; †also, a monk or priest. late ME. 3. Paternal origin or descent. Also *fig.* 1868.

1. Having been spared the cares..of p. 1786. 3. The secret of the baby's p. 1882. *fig.* Many of the historical proverbs have a doubtful p. EMERSON.

Paternoster (pæ·təɹnǭ·stəɹ), *sb.* OE. [a. L. *pater noster* 'our Father', the first two words of the Lord's Prayer in Latin.] 1. The Lord's Prayer, esp. in Latin. b. A repetition of this as an act of worship ME. 2. *transf.* a. Any form of words repeated by way of a prayer, imprecation, or charm. late ME. b. A long nonsensical or tedious recital or utterance 1663. 3. A special bead in a rosary indicating that a paternoster is to be said; also, the whole rosary ME. 4. Anything resembling a rosary: in *Fishing*, = *p.-line* 1839.

2. a. *Black P., White P.*, names of specific charms. *Devil's P.*, a murmured or muttered imprecation. *Ape's P.*, a 'dithering' or chattering with the teeth. *attrib.* and *Comb.*: **p.-line**, a line used in fishing, with hooks attached at intervals, and weights to sink it; **-pump**, a chain-pump; **-wheel**, a device for raising water, having a number of buckets on a chain; **-while**, the time it takes to say a p. Hence **Paterno·ster** *v. intr.* to fish with a paternoster-line.

Path (paþ), *sb.* *Pl.* **paths** (pāðz). [Com. WGer.: OE. *pæþ*; ult. origin unkn.] 1. A way beaten or trodden by the feet of men or beasts, not expressly planned and constructed; a footway or footpath; hence also a walk made for foot-passengers. b. A track specially laid for foot or cycle racing. c. A track constructed for some part of machinery to run upon. 1883. 2. The way, course, or line along which a person or thing moves, passes, or travels OE. 3. *fig.* A course of action or procedure, line of conduct, etc.; less commonly, a line of thought, argument, etc. OE.

1. The perplex't paths of this drear Wood MILT. 2. Thy waye was in the see, and thy pathes in the greate waters COVERDALE *Ps.* lxxvi[i]. 19. 3. The paths of glory lead but to the grave GRAY.

Comb.: **p.-finder**, one who discovers a p. or way; an explorer; **-racer**, a bicycle made for racing upon a prepared p. or track; so **p.-racing.** Hence **Pa·thless** *a.*, **-ness.**

†**Path,** *v.* [OE. *pæþþan*, f. *pæþ* PATH *sb.*] 1. *trans.* To go upon or along, to 'tread' (a way, etc.). *lit.* and *fig.* -1807. 2. To tread, beat down by treading, as a path; usu. *fig.* -1765. 3. *intr.* To go in or as in a path; to pursue one's course. Also *refl.* -1601.

1. Pathing young Henries unadvised wayes 1598.

Pathan (paþā·n, -thā·n). 1665. [Hindustani *Paṭhān.*] One of a race inhabiting Afghanistan and noted for courage and fierceness in war.

Pathematic (pæþĭmæ·tik), *a.* *rare.* 1822. [ad. Gr. παθηματικός liable to passions, f. πάθημα, f. stem παθ-; see next.] Pertaining to the passions or emotions; caused or characterized by emotion. So **Pathema·tically** *adv.* **Pathe:mato·logy,** the doctrine of passions or emotions.

Pathetic (păþe·tik), *a.* (*sb.*) 1598. [ad. late L. *patheticus*, a. Gr. παθητικός, f. (ult.) παθ-, root of πάσχειν to suffer, πάθος suffering.] 1. Producing an effect upon the emotions; moving, stirring, affecting. *Obs.* in gen. sense. b. In mod. use: Exciting pity, sympathy, or sadness; full of pathos 1737. †2. Arising from strong emotion, passionate, earnest -1755. 3. Pertaining or relating to the passions or emotions of the mind 1649. 4. *Anat.* A name for the fourth pair of cranial nerves, also called *trochlear.* So *p. muscle*, the superior oblique muscle of the eyeball, connected with the trochlear nerve. 1681.

1. b. Our parting with our uncle was quite p. LYTTON. 3. All violent feelings..produce..a falseness in..impressions of external things, which I would generally characterize as the 'P. fallacy' RUSKIN.

B. *absol.* or as *sb.* 1. *absol. The p.*: that which is pathetic; pathetic quality, expression, or feeling 1712. 2. †a. *sing.* Pathos, or the expression of pathos -1849. b. *pl.* Pathetic expressions or sentiments; cf. *heroics* 1748. 3. *pl.* The study of the passions or emotions 1896. 4. *Anat.* Short for *p. nerve*: see A. 4. So **Pathe·tical** *a.* (now *rare*), pathetic 1573; **-ly** *adv.*; **-ness** (now *rare* or *Obs.*).

Pathic (pæ·þik), *sb.* and *a.* Now *rare* or *Obs.* 1603. [ad. L. *pathicus*, a. Gr. παθικός, f. stem παθ- to suffer.] A. *sb.* 1. A man or boy upon whom sodomy is practised; a catamite. 2. One who suffers or undergoes something 1636.

2. A mere p. to Thy devilish art MASSINGER.

B. *adj.* 1. Being, or pertaining to, a catamite 1657. 2. Undergoing something, passive (*rare*) 1857. 3. Pertaining to suffering or disease; morbid 1853.

Patho- (pæ·þo, păþǭ·), repr. Gr. παθο-, comb. form of πάθος suffering, feeling, disease, etc., as in **Pa·thogen** [-GEN], a micrococcus or bacterium that produces disease. ‖ **Pathopœ·ia** [Gr. -ποιία a making] (*a*) *Rhet.* a speech or figure of speech designed to arouse passion or emotion; (*b*) *Path.* production of disease.

Pathogenesis (pæþodʒe·nĕsis). 1876. [f. PATHO- + GENESIS.] *Med.* and *Path.* Production or development of a disease. Also **Pathoge·nesy, Patho·geny,** in same sense. So **Pathogene·tic, Pathoge·nic** *adjs.* producing, or relating to the production of, disease or bodily affection.

Pathognomonic (păþǫgnomǫ·nik), *a.* (*sb.*) 1625. [ad. Gr. παθογνωμονικός (Galen), skilled in judging of symptoms or diseases, f. παθο- PATHO- + γνωμονικός, f. γνώμων judge.] *Med.* and *Path.* A. *adj.* Specifically characteristic or indicative of a particular disease. B. *sb.* A pathognomonic sign or symptom 1704.

Pathognomy (păþǫ·gnŏmi). 1793. [f. as prec., after *physiognomy.*] 1. The knowledge or study of the passions or emotions, or of the signs or expressions of them. 2. The knowledge of the signs or symptoms by which diseases may be distinguished (*rare*) 1822. So **Pathogno·mic** *a.* of or pertaining to p. 1681. **Pathogno·mical** *a.* 1643.

Pathologic (pæþolǫ·dʒik), *a.* 1656. [ad. Gr. παθολογικός, f. παθο- PATHO-; see -LOGIC.] Of or belonging to pathology.

Patholo·gical, *a.* 1688. [f. as prec. + -AL.] 1. Pertaining to or dealing with pathology. b. That is or may be the subject of pathology; morbid 1845. 2. Pertaining to the passions or emotions (*rare*) 1800. Hence **Patholo·gically** *adv.* in relation to pathology.

Pathologist (păþǫ·lŏdʒist). 1650. [f. PATHOLOGY + -IST.] One versed in pathology; a student of or writer upon diseases.

Pathology (păþǫ·lŏdʒi). 1611. [ad. mod. or med.L. *pathologia*, f. Gr. παθο- PATHO- + -λογία -LOGY.] 1. The science or study of disease; that department of medical science, or of physiology, which treats of the causes and nature of diseases, or abnormal bodily affections or conditions. b. *transf.* The sum of morbid processes or conditions 1672. c. Extended to the study of morbid or abnormal mental or moral conditions 1842. 2. The study of the passions or emotions (*rare*) 1681.

Pathos (pēⁱ·þǫs). 1579. [a. Gr. πάθος suffering, feeling.] 1. That quality in speech, writing, music, or artistic representation (or *transf.* in events, persons, etc.) which excites a feeling of pity or sadness; power of stirring tender or melancholy emotion 1668. b. A pathetic expression or utterance (*rare*) 1579. 2. Suffering (bodily or mental). *rare.* 1693. 3. In reference to art, esp. ancient Greek art: The quality of the transient or emotional, as opp. to the permanent or ideal 1881.

1. The tale of Protestant sufferings was told with a wonderful p...by John Foxe 1874.

Pathway (pɑ·þwēⁱ). 1536. A way that constitutes or serves as a path; a path, track, way. (Often *fig.*)

A playne pathwaye to Christ and hys kyngedome BALE. High in his p. hung the Sun SCOTT.

-pathy, repr. Gr. -πάθεια, lit. 'suffering, feeling', the second element of HOMŒOPATHY, extended to ALLOPATHY, and applied, with the sense 'method of cure, curative treatment', to other compounds, as *hydropathy*, etc.

†**Pa·tible,** *sb.* ME. [ad. L. *patibulum* a fork-shaped yoke, gibbet, etc., f. *patere* to lie open + *-bulum*, forming names of instruments, etc.] A gibbet, a cross; the horizontal bar of a cross -1745.

†**Pa·tible,** *a.* 1600. [ad. L. *patibilis*, f. *pati* to suffer; see -IBLE.] 1. Capable of suffering or subject to something -1834. b. Capable of or liable to suffering; passible -1691. 2. Capable of being suffered, endurable (Dicts.) -1755.

Patibulary (păti·biŭlări), *a.* *rare.* 1646. [f. L. *patibulum* PATIBLE *sb.* + -ARY[1].] Of or pertaining to the gallows; resembling the gallows; suggesting the gallows or hanging. Chiefly *joc.*

I never saw a more p. phyz 1697. So **Pati·bulate** *v. trans.* to hang.

Patience (pēⁱ·ʃĕns). [ME. a. OF. *patience, pacience*, ad. L. *patientia*, f. *patientem* PATIENT; see -ENCE.] I. The practice or quality of being patient. 1. The suffering or enduring (of pain, trouble, or evil) with calmness and composure; the quality or capacity of so suffering or enduring. b. Forbearance under provocation of any kind; esp. bearing with others, their faults, limitations, etc. late ME. c. The calm abiding of the issue of time, processes, etc. late ME. d. Constancy in labour, exertion, or effort 1517. e. personified. late ME. 2. With *of*: The fact or capacity of enduring; patient endurance *of* (*rare*) 1530. †3. Sufferance; leave -1610.

1. That..We may with p. bear our moderate ills COWPER. b. I doe intreat your p. To heare me speake SHAKS. c. In your p. possess ye your souls *Luke* xxi. 19. He had not the p. to expect a present, but demanded one 1615. d. He learnt with p., and with meekness taught 1774. e. She sate, like P. on a Monument, Smiling at greefe SHAKS. Phrases. *To have p. with* (†*in, toward*), to show forbearance toward; so, *to have no p. with* (colloq.), to be unable to bear patiently. *Out of p.*, advb. phr. (sometimes adj.), provoked so as no longer to have p. with. 2. P. of hunger 1772. 3. I can goe no further, Sir,..by your p., I needes must rest me SHAKS.

II. Special senses. 1. A species of Dock (*Rumex Patientia*), formerly used instead of spinach, in salads, etc. *Wild P., Rumex obtusifolius.* 1440. 2. A game of cards, of which there are many varieties; usu. for one player 1816.

Patience-dock. 1776. [f. PATIENCE II. 1 + DOCK *sb.*[1]] 1. = prec. II. 1. 1884. 2. In the north of England, the Bistort (*Polygonum Bis-*

torta), there also called *Passions*, *Passion-dock*, of which the leaves are eaten as greens 1776.

Patient (pēⁱ·ʃĕnt), *a.* and *sb.* ME. [a. OF. *pacient*, *passient*, later *patient*, ad. L. *patientem*, pr. pple. of *pati* to suffer.] **A.** *adj.* 1. Bearing or enduring (evil of any kind) with composure; exercising or possessing patience. **b.** Long-suffering, forbearing (*to*, *towards*). late ME. **c.** Quietly awaiting the course or issue of events, etc. late ME. **d.** Persistent, constant, unwearied in the face of difficulties and hindrances 1590. **e.** *fig.* of things 1820. **2.** Const. *of*: Enduring or able to endure (evil, etc.). 1440. **b.** Of words, etc.: Capable of bearing (a particular interpretation) 1638. **3.** Passive. (Correl. to *agent*.) *rare.* 1611.

1. Job the patientest of men MILT. **b.** Be ȝe pacient to alle men WYCLIF 1 *Thess.* v. 14. **c.** I know twenty persevering girls for one p. one RUSKIN. **d.** P. continuance in well doing *Rom.* ii. 7. **e.** The same bright, p. stars KEATS. **2.** Neither are they so p. of hunger as of thirst 1600.

B. *sb.* †1. A sufferer; one who suffers patiently –1795. **2.** One who is under medical treatment. late ME. **3.** A person or thing that undergoes some action, or to whom or which something is done, as correl. to *agent*, and dist. from *instrument*; a recipient 1580.

2. He brings his Physicke After his Patients death SHAKS. **3.** He that is not free is not an Agent, but a P. WESLEY. Hence †**Pa·tient** *v. trans.* to make p.; esp. *refl.* to calm oneself; *intr.* to be p. **Pa·tient-ly** *adv.*, **-ness** (now *rare*).

Patina (pæ·tină). 1748. [a. L. *patina*, *-ena* a broad shallow dish or pan. In sense 2, prob. through F. *patine*.] †1. **a.** *Archæol.* The ancient Roman vessel so called. **b.** *Eccl.* = PATEN 1. –1868. **2.** A film or incrustation produced by oxidation on old bronze, usu. of a green colour. Hence extended to a similar alteration of the surface of other substances. 1748.

2. The vase is of bronze, covered by a *p.* of very fine green 1797. Hence **Pa·tinated, Pa·tinous** *adjs.* covered with a p. (sense 2). **Patina·tion,** formation of a p. So ‖**Patine** (patīⁿn) = 2.

‖ **Patio** (pā·tiₗo). 1828. [Sp., = court of a house.] 1. An inner court, open to the sky, in a Spanish, or Spanish-American house. **2.** *Mining.* A yard where ores are cleaned and sorted; also, the Spanish process of amalgamating silver ores on an open floor 1877.

‖ **Patisserie** (pati·səri). 1784. [F. *pâtisserie*, f. (ult.) med.L. *pasticium* pastry, f. *pasta* PASTE + *-erie*, -ERY.] Articles of food made by a pastry-cook; pastry.

‖ **Patois** (pæ·twa). 1643. [F. (13th c.); origin unkn.] A provincial form of a language spoken in a restricted area and having no literary status. Also *gen.* any dialect or sub-dialect. **b.** *transf.* 1790. **c.** *attrib.* or as *adj.* Of, pertaining to, or of the nature of a patois 1789.

The Dutch p. spoken in South Africa 1893. **b.** Their language is in the *patois* of fraud BURKE.

Patonce (pæt·ns), *a.* 1562. [perh. a mistaken use of F. *croix potencée*; see POTENCÉ.] *Her.* In *cross p.*, a cross with its arms usu. expanding in a curved form from the centre, having ends somewhat like those of the cross fleury.

Patrial (pēⁱ·triăl), *a.* (*sb.*) *rare.* 1629. [f. L. **patrialis*, f. *patria* fatherland.] 1. Of or belonging to one's native country. **2.** *Gram.* Applied to a word denoting a native or inhabitant of the country or place from the name of which it is derived; also to a suffix forming such words. Also as *sb.* A word of this class. 1854.

2. P. *isc*..connotes origin from a place or stock:.. *Engl-isc*, English 1870.

Patriarch (pēⁱ·triāɪk). [ME. **a.** OF. *patriarche*, ad. L. *patriarcha*, ad. Gr. πατριάρχης chief or head of a family, f. πατριά family, clan + -αρχης in comb. 'ruler'.] 1. The father and ruler of a family or tribe; *spec.* (*pl.*) in N.T., etc., the twelve sons of Jacob, from whom the tribes of Israel were descended; also, the fathers of the race, Abraham, Isaac, and Jacob, and their forefathers. **2.** In later Jewish history, applied (as repr. Heb. *nāsī* prince, chief) to the Chief or President of the Sanhedrim in Palestine (*c* 180 B.C.–A.D. 429) 1795. **3.** *Eccl.* **a.** In ref. to the primitive Church: in earliest use, an honorific designation of bishops generally, becoming at length the official title of the bishops of Antioch, Alexandria, and Rome, also, later, of Constantinople, and of Jerusalem. **b.** Hence, in the *Orthodox Eastern Ch.*, the title of the bishops of the four patriarchates of Constantinople, Alexandria, Antioch, and Jerusalem, the Patriarch of Constantinople being the *Œcumenical P.* Also the title of the heads of the other Eastern Churches. **c.** *R. C. Ch.* (*a*) A bishop second only to the Pope in episcopal, and to the Pope and Cardinals in hierarchical, rank. (*b*) The title of the Latin bishops of Constantinople, Alexandria, Antioch, and Jerusalem ME. **d.** *transf.* Applied unofficially to the chief dignitaries of other Churches 1477. **4.** The father or founder of an order, institution, etc., or of a science, school of thought, or the like 1566. **5.** A venerable old man; *esp.* the oldest man, the 'father' of a village, class, profession, etc. 1817. **b.** *transf.* The head of a flock or herd: the most venerable object of a group 1700.

4. The p. of political economy, Adam Smith 1866. 5. Mr. George Bancroft, now the p. of American literature 1888. **b.** The monarch oak, the p. of the trees DRYDEN. A goat, the p. of the flock SCOTT. Hence **Pa·triarchdom, Pa·triarchship** (*rare*) the state or office of a p.; the position or authority of an ancient p.

Patriarchal (pēⁱtriā·ɪkăl), *a.* 1570. [ad. late L. *patriarchalis*, f. *patriarcha* PATRIARCH; see -AL.] 1. Of or belonging to a patriarch; of or characteristic of the patriarchs or their times 1656. **2.** *Eccl.* Of or belonging to a hierarchical patriarch; ruled by a patriarch; of the nature or rank of a patriarch 1570. **3.** Of, pertaining to, or of the nature of a patriarchy 1828. **4.** Venerable, aged; like that of a patriarch 1837. **b.** *transf.* 1837.

1. Who could to P. years live on 1687. **2.** *P. church*, any one of the five great Roman basilicas, viz. St. John Lateran, St. Peter's, St. Paul's, St. Mary the greater, and St. Lawrence extra muros. *P. cross* (Her.), one with two transverse pieces, the upper being the shorter (an emblem of the patriarchs of the Gr. Church). **3.** The P. theory of society is..the theory of its origin in separate families, held together by the authority and protection of the eldest valid male ascendant 1883. **4. b.** Along the spoor of the p. old black buck 1850. Hence **Patria·rchally** *adv.* **Patria·rchalism,** a p. system of society or government.

Patriarchate (pēⁱ·triāɪkēⁱt). 1617. [ad. med.L. *patriarchatus*; see -ATE[1].] 1. The office, see, or residence of an ecclesiastical patriarch. **2.** = PATRIARCHY 2. 1651.

†**Patria·rchical,** *a.* 1606. [See PATRIARCH and -ICAL.] 1. = PATRIARCHAL 2. –1670. **2.** Of, pertaining to, or of the nature of the ancient patriarchs, or of the patriarchal system of government; like a patriarch, venerable –1698. Hence **Patria·rchically** *adv.* 1887.

Patriarchism (pēⁱ·triaɪkiz'm). 1666. [-ISM.] The patriarchal system of organization, government, etc.

Patriarchy (pēⁱ·triāɪki). 1561. [ad. Gr. πατριαρχία office of a patriarch.] †1. = PATRIARCHATE 1. **b.** The government of the Church by a patriarch or patriarchs. **2.** A patriarchal system of society or government; a family, tribe, or society so organized 1632.

Patrician (pătri·ʃən), *sb.*[1] and *a.*[1] late ME. [f. L. *patricius* belonging to the rank of the *patres*, 'fathers' or senators of Rome, + -AN.] **A.** *sb.* 1. A person belonging to one of the original citizen families or *gentes*, of which the ancient Roman *populus* consisted; a Roman noble 1533. **b.** In the later Roman Empire, A member of a new noble order nominated by the Emperor of Byzantium; also, an officer, orig. a member of this order, sent as representative of the Emperor to administer the western provinces of Italy and Africa. late ME. **c.** Applied to the hereditary noble citizens of some of the mediæval Italian republics, and to the higher order of the Free Cities of the German Empire 1611. **d.** *gen.* A nobleman, aristocrat 1631. **2.** One versed in the writings of the Fathers (*rare*) 1810.

1. **c.** The sentence pass'd on Michel Steno, born P. BYRON. **2.** Luther was no great P. COLERIDGE.

B. *adj.* Of, belonging to, or composed of the patricians of ancient Rome; see A. 1. 1620. **b.** *gen.* Of or belonging to the patricians in Italian or German cities; noble, aristocratic 1615. **c.** Applied to aristocratic or non-popular parties in later times 1812.

He had a p. disdain of mobs 1879. **b.** You have strange thoughts for a p. dame BYRON. Hence **Patri·cianism,** p. quality, style, or spirit; also, patricians collectively. **Patri·cianly** *adv.*

Patri·cian, *sb.*[2] 1659. [ad. L. (pl.) *Patriciani*, f. the name of their founder, *Patricius*.] *Ch. Hist.* A member of a 4th c. heretical sect, which held that the substance of the flesh was the work of the devil, not of God.

Patri·cian, *a.*[2] *rare.* 1882. [f. L. *Patricius* + -AN.] Pertaining to, or founded by, St. Patrick.

Patriciate (pătri·ʃiēⁱt). 1656. [ad. med.L. *patriciatus*, f. *patricius*; see PATRICIAN *sb.*[1] and -ATE[1].] 1. The position or rank of a patrician. **2.** A patrician order or class; the aristocracy 1795.

Patricidal (pætrisəi·dăl), *a.* 1821. [f. next + -AL.] Of, pertaining to, or resembling a patricide.

Patricide[1] (pæ·trisəid). *rare.* 1593. [f. L. **patricida*, f. L. *patrem* father + *-cida* -CIDE 1, var. *parricida* PARRICIDE.] = PARRICIDE[1].

Pa·tricide[2]. *rare.* 1625. [ad. L. type **patricidium*, after prec.; see -CIDE 2.] = PARRICIDE[2]. Also *attrib.*

Patrico (pæ·trikₒ). *Vagabonds' Cant.* 1550. [perh. f. PATTER *sb.*[1], *v.*[1] + *co*, a cant wd. for 'lad'.] A priest or parson; *esp.* a hedge-priest.

Patrimony (pæ·trimənị). ME. [a. F. *patrimoine*, *patremoine*, ad. L. *patrimonium* paternal estate, f. *patrem* father; see -MONY.] Property inherited from one's father or ancestors; heritage, inheritance. late ME. **b.** *transf.* The ancient estate or endowment of an institution, corporation, etc.; *esp.* that of a church or religious body ME. **c.** *fig.* 1581.

To reaue the Orphan of his Patrimonie SHAKS. **b.** *P. of St. Peter*, the Papal States or territory formerly held by the Pope in Italy. **c.** The p. of a poor man lies in the strength and dexterity of his hands ADAM SMITH. Hence **Patrimo·nial** *a.* pertaining to or constituting a p. **Patrimo·nially** *adv.*

Patriot (pēⁱ·triₒ̆t, pæ·t-), *sb.* (*a.*) 1596. [a. F. *patriote*, ad. late L. *patriota* fellow-countryman, ad. Gr. πατριώτης, f. πάτριος of one's fathers, πατρίς fatherland; see -OT[2].] †1. A compatriot (*rare*) –1629. **2.** One who exerts himself to promote the well-being of his country; one who maintains and defends his country's freedom or rights 1605. **b.** Assumed at various times by persons or parties whose claim to it has been denied or ridiculed by others. Hence, in 18th c. used for 'a factious disturber of the government' (J.). So sometimes, 'Irish Patriot'. 1644. ¶ **c.** Erron. (with *of* or possessive) as if = lover, devotee –1641. **B.** *attrib.* or *adj.* That is, or has the character of, a patriot; characteristic of a patriot; patriotic 1732.

A. 2. Such as were known patriots, Sound lovers of their country B. JONS. **b.** Gull'd with a Patriots name, whose Modern sense Is one that wou'd by Law supplant his Prince DRYDEN. So **Pa·triotess** (*rare*), a female p.

Patriotic (pēⁱtriₗǫ·tik, pæt-), *a.* 1653. [ad. late L. *patrioticus*, a. Gr. πατριωτικός, f. πατριώτης PATRIOT; see -IC.] †1. Of or belonging to one's country –1653. **2.** Having the character of a patriot; characteristic of a patriot; marked by devotion to the wellbeing or interests of one's country 1757.

2. The threatened invasion..roused the p. feeling of all classes 1867. So **Patrio·tical** *a.* (*rare*). **Patrio·tically** *adv.*

Patriotism (pēⁱ·triₒ̆tiz'm, pæ·t-). 1726. [f. PATRIOT + -ISM.] The character or passion of a patriot; love of or zealous devotion to one's country. Sometimes ironical (cf. PATRIOT 2. b).

P. must be founded in great principles, and supported by great virtues 1738. P. is the last refuge of a scoundrel JOHNSON.

Patripassian (pætripæ·siăn), *sb.* and *a.* 1574. [ad. late L. *patripassianus*, f. *pater*, *patri-* father + *passus* having suffered.] **A.** *sb.* One who held, as certain early heretics, that God the Father suffered with or in the person of the Son for the redemption of man. **B.** *adj.* Belonging to, or involving the doctrine of, the Patripassians 1727. Hence **Patripa·ssianism.**

Patristic (pătri·stik), *a.* and *sb.* 1837. [f. L. *patr-*, Gr. πατρ- father + -ISTIC, after G.

patristisch; cf. *Hellenistic.*] **A.** *adj.* **a.** Of or pertaining to the study of the writings of the Fathers of the Church, as in *p. learning*; **b.** hence, loosely, of or pertaining to the Fathers themselves, or their writings, as in *p. works, doctrines* 1874. **B.** *sb.* **1.** A student or adherent of the doctrines or opinions of the Fathers 1842. **2.** *pl.* The study of the lives, writings, or doctrines of the Fathers 1847. So **Pa·trist** (*rare*), one versed in the lives or writings of the Fathers. **Patri·stical** *a.* 1831, **-ly** *adv.* **Patri·s·ticism,** prop., a system founded upon the study of the Fathers; loosely, the doctrine or mode of thought of the Fathers themselves.

Patrix (pē̆i·triks). Also **patrice.** *Pl.* **patrices.** 1883. [f. L. *pater, patr-* father, as a correlative term to *matrix.*] A die, punch, or pattern used to form matrices in type-founding, etc.

†**Patro·cinate,** *v.* 1611. [f. L. *patrocinat-, patrocinari* to patronize, defend, f. *patronem* PATRON.] *trans.* To champion, maintain, patronize (a cause, etc.) –1822. So †**Patrocina·tion,** †**Patro·ciny,** patronage, protection 1450.

Patrol (pătrōu·l), *sb.* 1664. [a. F. *patrouille,* f. *patrouiller*; see next.] **1.** The action of going the rounds of a garrison, camp, etc. for the purpose of watching, guarding, and checking disorder; the perambulation of a town or district by a police constable or detachment of police for the protection of life and property. Also *fig.* and *transf.* **2.** A detachment of the guard, a police constable, or a detachment of police, told off for these purposes 1670. **3.** A detachment of troops sent out in advance of a column, regiment, etc., to reconnoitre 1702. **4.** One of the smaller units of a troop of Boy Scouts, consisting of six scouts, commanded by a *p. leader* 1908.

3. The French pushed their patroles of cavalry near the town SOUTHEY.

attrib. and *Comb.* as *p. duty,* etc.: **p.-wagon** (*U.S.*), a prison-van. Hence **Patro·lman** (chiefly *U.S.*), a man who is on p.; *spec.* a police constable attached to a particular beat or district.

Patrol (pătrōu·l), *v.* Infl. **patrolled, patrolling.** 1691. [a. F. *patrouiller,* orig. to paddle in mud, altered from *patouiller.* The military use was prob. at first a piece of French camp slang.] **1.** *intr.* To act as patrol; to reconnoitre as a patrol. **b.** To traverse a beat or district as constable or patrolman. **2.** *trans.* To go over or round (a camp, garrison, town, etc.) for the purpose of watching, guarding, etc.; to traverse (a beat or district) as constable, etc.; to traverse leisurely in all directions 1765.

Patron (pē̆i·trən), *sb.* [ME. *patroun,* a. OF. *patrun, patron,* ad. L. *patronus* protector, defender, deriv. of *pater, patrem* father.] **I.** Senses conn. w. ancient L. *patronus.* **1.** One who stands to another or others in relations analogous to those of a father; a lord or master; a protector; †a lord superior; †a founder of a religious order. **2.** *Rom. Antiq.* The former master of a manumitted slave, who retained certain legal claims upon him. **b.** A person of distinction who protected a client (see CLIENT 1) in return for certain services. Hence allusively. 1560. **c.** *Rom. Antiq.* An advocate, a pleader; hence *fig.* late ME. **3.** One who lends his influential support to advance the interests of a person, cause, art, etc.; *spec.* in 17th and 18th c. the person who accepted the dedication of a book. late ME. **b.** An advocate or champion of a theory or doctrine. Now *rare.* 1573. **c.** One who supports a practice, a form of sport, an institution, etc. Also (in tradesmen's language), a regular customer. 1605.

3. Books..ought to have no patrons but truth and reason BACON. A p. of some thirty charities TENNYSON. c. The patrons of the public-house (*mod.*).

II. Senses arising in med. Latin. **1.** One who holds the right of presentation to an eccl. benefice. (The earliest sense in Eng. use.) ME. **2.** The special tutelary saint of a person, place, craft, etc.; often *p. saint.* late ME. †**b.** A tutelary pagan divinity –1697.

2. Saint Nicholas is the great P. of Mariners 1718.

III. Senses repr. mod. Romanic uses. **1.** The captain or master of a galley, or of a coasting vessel in the Mediterranean (now *rare*). late ME. †**2.** A master or owner of slaves or captives (in the Levant, etc.) –1719. ‖**3.** The host or landlord of an inn (in Spain) 1878.

IV. Applied to things. **a.** A case for holding pistol-cartridges. (F. *patron, patronne.*) **b.** A cartridge (G. *patrone*). *Obs.* exc. *Hist.* 1683.

attrib. and *Comb.,* as *p. deity, god, martyr,* etc.: **p. saint** = sense II. 2. So **Pa·tron** *v.* (*rare*) to act as p. to, to champion as a p.; to patronize. **Patronal** (pătrōu·năl, pæ·t-, pē̆i·trŏnăl), *a.* of or pertaining to a p. or p. saint (e.g. the *p. festival* of a church); of the nature of a p. 1611. **Pa·tronate,** the position, right, or duty of a p.; the jurisdiction or possession of a p. **Pa·tronless** *a.* **Pa·tronship.**

Patron, obs. variant of PATTERN.

Patronage (pæ·trŏnėdʒ), *sb.* late ME. [a. F., = med.L. *patronaticum, -agium,* f. L. *patronus* PATRON; see -AGE.] The office or action of a PATRON. **1.** *Eccl.* The right of presentation to an eccl. benefice; advowson. **2.** Guardianship, tutelary care, as of a divinity or saint. *arch.* or *Obs.* 1582. **3.** The action of a patron in supporting, encouraging, or countenancing a person, institution, work, art, etc. Orig. implying the action of a superior. 1553. †**b.** *spec.* Protection, defence; protectorship –1844. **c.** The action of patronizing or condescending to a person 1829. **d.** In commercial or colloq. use: The financial support given by customers in making use of a line of steamers, a hotel, store, shop, etc. 1804. **4.** The control of appointments to offices, privileges, etc., in the public service 1769.

3. Henry's p. of letters was highly commendable 1839. c. There was a little savor of p. in the generous hospitality she exercised among her simple neighbors 1883.

attrib.: **P. Secretary** (in Great Britain), the Secretary of the Treasury through whom the p. of that department is administered and appointments to departments under its control made. Hence †**Pa·tronage** *v. trans.* to PATRONIZE.

Patroness (pē̆i·trənės, pæ·t-), *sb.* late ME. [ad. med.L. *patronissa,* fem. of *patronus* (after *basilissa*; see -ESS).] A female patron, patron saint, or tutelary deity; also *fig.*

P. of a ball BYRON. *fig.* Befriend me Night best P. of grief MILT.

Patronize (pæ·trŏnəiz), *v.* 1589. [f. PATRON *sb.* + -IZE.] **1.** *trans.* To act as a patron (or †patron saint) towards; to protect, support, countenance, encourage. Also *absol.* †**b.** To defend, support, stand by; to countenance –1785. †**c.** Said of things –1710. **2.** To treat with a manner or air of condescending notice 1797. **3.** In commercial or colloq. use: To frequent as a customer or visitor; to favour with one's presence, resort to 1801.

1. He patronizes the Orphan and Widow, assists the Friendless, and guides the Ignorant ADDISON. 2. The aristocracy..patronized him with condescending dexterity DISRAELI. Hence **Patroniza·tion,** the action or fact of patronizing. **Pa·tronizer. Pa·tronizingly** *adv.* with the manner or air of a patron.

Patronym (pæ·trŏnim). *rare.* 1834. [ad. Gr. πατρώνυμος, f. πατήρ, πατρ- father + ὄνομα, Doric ὄνυμα name.] = next, B.

Patronymic (pætrŏni·mik), *a.* and *sb.* 1612. [ad. L. *patronymicus,* a. Gr. πατρωνυμικός, f. πατρώνυμος; see prec. and -IC.] **A.** *adj.* Of a name: Derived from the name of a father or ancestor, esp. by addition of a suffix or prefix indicating descent. Also said of such a suffix or prefix. 1669. **B.** *sb.* A patronymic name; a name derived from that of a father or ancestor; a family name.

A. The English p. suffix corresponding to the Danish *-son* is *-ing* 1894. B. Their original p. is MacAlpine SCOTT. So **Patrony·mical** *a.* 1656; **-ly** *adv.* by a p.

Patroon (pătrū·n). 1662. [var. of PATRON in some Fr. applications. In sense 4, a. Du. *patroon.*] †**1.** = PATRON I. 3. –1697. †**2.** = PATRON III. 2. –1704. **3.** = PATRON III. 1. Now *rare.* 1743. **4.** In *U.S.* A possessor of a landed estate and certain manorial privileges, granted under the old Dutch governments of New York and New Jersey, to members of the (Dutch) W. India Company 1758. Hence **Patroo·nship,** the position, or estate, of a p.

‖**Pat(t)amar** (pæ·tămāɪ). *E. Ind.* 1598. [a. Pg. *patamar,* a. Konkani *pātamār,* Marāthī *patēmāri* dispatch-boat, f. *patta* tidings + *-māri* courier.] †**1.** A courier –1782. **2.** An Indian advice-boat or dispatch-boat; *spec.* a lateen-rigged sailing-vessel used on the west coast of India 1704.

Pat(t)ée (pate, pæ·ti), *a.* 1486. [a. F. *patté, pattée* pawed, in *croix pattée* 'a cross of which the extremities are widened in the form of an open paw' (Littré).] *Her.* Applied to a cross the arms of which are nearly triangular, being very narrow where they meet and widening out towards the extremities, so that the whole composes nearly a square.

Patten (pæ·t'n), *sb.* [late ME. a. F. *patin,* in med.L. *patinus*; perh. f. *patte* paw.] **1.** A name applied at different periods to various kinds of foot-gear, e.g. to wooden shoes or clogs, 'chopins', etc. Now only in sense b. **b.** *spec.* A kind of overshoe worn to raise the ordinary shoes out of the mud or wet; consisting of a wooden sole mounted on an iron oval ring, or the like, by which the wearer is raised an inch or two from the ground 1575. **2.** A skate (*local* or *alien*). [= F. *patin.*] 1617. **3.** *Arch.* A base or foot: the base of a column; the sole for the foundation of a wall, etc. 1643.

1. b. Good housewives..Safe thro' the Wet on clinking Pattens tread GAY. Phr. *To run on pattens* (said *fig.* of the tongue), to make a great clatter.

Comb., as **p.-maker** (now esp. as the name of one of the London City Companies). Hence **Pa·tten** *v. intr.* to go about on pattens; also, to skate (*local*). **Pa·ttened** *a.* wearing pattens.

Patter (pæ·təɪ), *sb.*[1] 1758. [f. PATTER *v.*[1], sense 3.] **1.** The cant or peculiar lingo of any profession or class; any language not generally understood. **b.** Name for the oratory of a Cheap Jack, a conjurer, or the like; also for 'jaw' 178.. **c.** *colloq.* Mere talk; chatter, gabble 1858. **2.** Rapid speech introduced into a song; also, *familiarly,* the words of a song, comedy, etc. 1876.

1. 'That's my name in your p.', said the gipsy 1875.

attrib. and *Comb.,* as *p.-speech*; **p.-song,** a humorous song in which many words are fitted to a few notes and sung rapidly.

Patter (pæ·təɪ), *sb.*[2] 1844. [f. PATTER *v.*[2]] The action or fact of pattering; a quick succession of pats, taps, etc.

Patter (pæ·təɪ), *v.*[1] late ME. [f. PATER 1 = Paternoster: from the rapid recitation of the *paternoster,* etc. as in saying the rosary.] †**1.** *intr.* To repeat the Paternoster, esp. in a rapid, mechanical, or indistinct way; to mumble one's prayers –1642. **2.** *trans.* To say over (prayers, charms, etc.) in a rapid mechanical manner. late ME. **3.** *intr.* To talk rapidly, without much regard to sense or matter; to jabber; to prattle. **b.** In *Pedlars' slang,* To talk, to speak; to 'speechify', like a Cheap Jack, or a conjurer. **c.** To talk the slang or 'patter' of thieves, beggars, etc. late ME. **4.** *trans.* (*slang.*) To talk (some language) 1812.

2. For mass or prayer can I rarely tarry, Save to p. an Ave Mary SCOTT. 4. You all p. French more or less 1857. *To p. flash,* to speak slang. Hence **Pa·tterer,** one who patters or speaks patter.

Patter (pæ·təɪ), *v.*[2] 1611. [Dim. and frequent. of PAT *v.*; see -ER [5].] **1.** *intr.* To make a rapid succession of pats, taps, or the like, as raindrops on a window-pane. **2.** To run with a rapid succession of short quick sounding steps 1806. **3.** *trans.* (*causal*) To cause to come or fall with a rapid succession of slight sounding strokes 1819.

1. The rain pattered dismally against the panes 1818. 2. Away she pattered full speed 1824.

Pattern (pæ·təɪn), *sb.* [ME. *patron,* a. F.; a doublet of PATRON. The pron. (pa·tr'n, pa·təɪn) began to be used in the 16th c., and by 1700 *patron* and *pattern* had been differentiated.] **1.** An example or model deserving imitation; a model of a particular excellence. late ME. **2.** A model, design, plan, etc., from which something is to be made. Also *fig.* ME. **3.** *spec.* In *Founding.* †**a.** A matrix, a mould. **b.** A figure in wood or metal from which a mould is made for a casting. 1508. †**4.** A copy; a likeness, similitude (*rare*) –1714. **5.** A sample. Also *fig.* 1644. **6.** An example, an instance; *esp.* a typical instance, a signal example 1555. †**7.** A precedent –1672. **8.** A decorative or artistic design, as for china, etc.; this design carried out in the manufactured article; style, type, or class of design. Also *transf.* 1582. 9. A specimen model of a proposed coin, not subsequently adopted. Dist. from a *proof.* 1837. 10. A dress-length. *U.S.* 1847. 11. *Gun-making.* The marks made by the shot from a gun on a target, in respect of their closeness together and even distribution within a given radius from the central point 1881. 12. In Ireland, A patron saint's day; hence *transf.* the festivities of the day 1745. 13. *attrib.* or *adj.* Serving as a model; typical, archetypal; ideal, model. Occas. hyphened to the sb. 1809.

1. For all an example, for no one a p. SWIFT. A p. of the domestic virtues 1870. 2. *fig.* By th' patterne of mine owne thoughts, I cut out The puritie of his SHAKS. 5. A tailor, with his books of patterns just imported from Paris 1829. 6. The only p. of consistent gallantry I have met with LAMB. 7. *Tit. A.* v. iii. 44. 8. *transf.* The broken frames..cast patterns on the ground DICKENS. 13. Two p. young ladies,..with p. deportment C. BRONTE.

attrib. and *Comb.*: **p.-book**, (*a*) a book of patterns or designs; (*b*) a blank book of cardboards to hold patterns; **-box** (*Weaving*), a box containing several shuttles, any one of which may be sent along the 'shed' as required by the pattern in colour-pattern weaving; **-card**, (*a*) a sample card (of cloth, etc.); also, a book of such cards; (*b*) *Weaving* = CARD *sb.*[2] 6; also *attrib.*, as *pattern-card cutter*, etc.; **-chain** (*Weaving*), a device for bringing the shuttles automatically from the p.-box to the picker in the required sequence; **-designer**, **-drawer**; **-maker**, one who makes patterns; *spec.* one who arranges textile patterns for weaving.

Pa·ttern, *v.* 1581. [f. prec.] **I.** †1. *trans.* a. To design, sketch, plan SIDNEY. †b. To be a pattern for; to prefigure -1654. 2. To make (something) after a pattern or model; to model, fashion. Const. *after, on, upon*; †also *by, from, to* 1608. 3. To match, to parallel, to equal; to compare (a person or thing *to* or *with* another). *Obs.* or *arch.* 1586. 4. To take as a pattern; to imitate, copy (*rare*) 1601.

1. b. *Meas. for M.* II. i. 30. 2. To patterne our obedience to the holy Angels 1608. †*P. out*, to work out according to some p. 3. *Wint. T.* III. ii. 37.

II. 1. *trans.* To work or decorate with a pattern; also *transf.* to adorn with light and shade, or with variegated colouring 1857. 2. *intr.* Of a gun: To distribute the shot in a pattern: see PATTERN *sb.* 11.

1. The walls..that Giotto patterned RUSKIN. Hence **Pa·tterning** *vbl. sb.* the production or arrangement of patterns; *concr.* work done according to a pattern. **Pa·tterner**, one who draws or composes patterns.

Pattinsonize (pæ·tinsənəiz), *v.* 1859. [f. name of H. L. *Pattinson*, inventor of the process.] *trans.* To extract silver from (argentiferous lead-ore) by the Pattinson process. So **Pattinsoniza·tion** 1881.

Pattle, pettle (pa·t'l, pe·t'l). *Sc.* and *n. dial.* late ME. [Origin obsc.] A tool like a small spade with a long handle, used chiefly to remove the earth adhering to a plough.

Patty (pæ·ti). 1710. [Altered f. F. *pâté*, OF. *pasté* PASTY.] A little pie or pasty. Hence **Pa·tty-cake**; ¶ also erron. for PAT-A-CAKE.

Pattypan (pæ·tipæn). 1660. [f. prec. + PAN *sb.*[1]] †1. = PATTY -1700. 2. A small tin pan or shape in which patties are baked 1694.

Patulous (pæ·tiŭləs), *a.* 1616. [f. L. *patulus*, f. root of *patere* to be open.] 1. Open; expanded; wide open. 2. Spreading; said esp. of the boughs of a tree 1682. 3. *Bot.* Spreading outwards 1756.

2. His hands and feet are large and p. 1875. Hence **Pa·tulous-ly** *adv.*, **-ness**.

Pauci- (pǭ·si), comb. form of L. *paucus* few, little, as in **Pauci·loquent**, uttering few words; whence **Pauci·loquently** *adv.* **Pauci·loquy**, sparingness of speech. **Paucispi·ral** *a.* having few whorls, as a shell; so **Paucispi·rated** *a.*

Paucity (pǭ·sĭti). late ME. [a. F. *paucité*, or ad. L. *paucitas*, f. *paucus* few, little; see -ITY.] 1. Fewness; a small number. 2. Smallness of quantity; scantiness 1650.

1. Having to capitulate owing to..the p. of its defenders JOWETT. 2. P. of evidence 1858.

Paughty (pǭ·ti, *Sc.* pāχti), *a.* *Sc.* and *n. dial.* 1572. [Origin unkn.] Haughty; insolent.

Paul (pǭl). late ME. [a. OF. *Pol*, mod.F. *Paul*:—L. *Paulum*, nom. *Paulus.*] 1. English form of L. *Paulus*, the 'Apostle of the Gentiles' (Acts xiii. 9). 2. [repr. It. *Paolo*, Paul.] = PAOLO 1767. 3. **Paul Pry**: a very inquisitive person (name of a character in a comedy by John Poole, 1825); also *attrib.* 1829. b. Hence **Paul-Pry** *v. intr.* to be impertinently prying 1839. †4. **Paul's**: pop. name of St. Paul's Cathedral in London; formerly a resort of loungers and gossips. (Now always *St. Paul's.*) Hence *attrib.* in *Paul's Alley, Cross*, etc. late ME.

1. For proverbial phr. cf. PETER. 3. *attrib.* It will cure her of her Paul-Pry tricks 1870. 4. This oyly Rascall is knowne as well as Poules SHAKS.

Comb. with *Paul's*: **Paul's betony**, a species of *Veronica*, the Wood Speedwell (*V. officinalis*).

Pauldron. 1594. Var. of POULDRON.

Paulian (pǭ·liăn). 1449. [f. L. *Paulus* Paul; cf. *Christian.*] *Ch. Hist.* One of a sect who rejected the personality of the Logos and the Holy Spirit, and denied the pre-existence of Christ as 'the eternal Son of God'; founded by Paul of Samosata in the 3rd c. So **Pau·lianist, Pau·lianite.**

Paulician (pǭli·ʃiăn), *sb.* and *a.* 1574. [ad. L. *Pauliciani*, a. Gr. Παυλικιανοί, perh. from *Paulus* Paul.] *Ch. Hist.* A. *sb.* A member of a sect which arose in Armenia in the 7th c., holding modified Manichæan opinions. B. *adj.* Of or belonging to this sect.

Pauline (pǭ·ləin), *a.* and *sb.* late ME. [ad. L. *Paulinus* adj., f. *Paulus* Paul; see -INE[1].] A. *adj.* Of, pertaining to, or characteristic of St. Paul, his writings, or his doctrines 1817.

The P. Epistles 1876.

B. *sb.* 1. A member of certain religious orders so named. late ME. 2. A scholar of St. Paul's School, London 1867.

1. Some be Paulines, some be Antonynes 1550. 2. The Paulines were especially famous for caligraphy 1867. Hence **Pau·linism**, P. theology. **Pau·linist**, an adherent of St. Paul or his doctrine. **Paulini·stic** *a.* of or pertaining to a Paulinist or Paulinism.

Paulism (pǭ·liz'm). 1823. [f. *Paul* + -ISM.] The doctrine of St. Paul; Paulinism.

Paulist (pǭ·list). 1678. [f. as prec. + -IST.] 1. In India, a name for a Jesuit, from their church of St. Paul in Goa. 2. A member of a Roman Catholic association, the Congregation of the Missionary Priests of St. Paul the Apostle, founded at New York in 1858.

Paulite (pǭ·ləit). 1839. [f. name of St. *Paul*, L. *Paulus* + -ITE[1] 1.] One of an order of monks, also called Hermits of St. Paul, founded in 1215, at Budapest. Also *attrib.*

Paulo-post-future (pǭ·lo,pōust,fiū·tiŭı, -tʃəı), *a.* and *sb.* 1824. [ad. mod.L. *paulo post futurum*, tr. Gr. ὁ μετ' ὀλίγον μέλλων the future after a little. In 19th c. grammars called also 'third future', 'futurum exactum', 'futurum perfectum', 'future perfect'.] 1. A name of a tense of the passive voice of Greek verbs, used chiefly to state that an event will take place immediately. 2. *allusively.* A future which is a little after the present; a by-and-by; (belonging to) an immediate or proximate future 1848.

2. Shelley's..anticipated profits were in the paulo-post-future 1887. So **Pau·lo-po·st** *a.* [L. *paulo post*], a little subsequent; also **Pau·lo-pa·st** *a.* relating to something lately finished. (*nonce-wds.*)

‖ **Paulownia** (pǭlō·vniă, pǭlōu·niă). 1847. [After Anna *Paulovna*, daughter of the Tsar Paul I.] *Bot.* A genus of *Scrophulariaceæ*, comprising the single species *P. imperialis*, a Japanese ornamental tree with purplish trumpet-shaped flowers blossoming in early spring.

Paunch (pǭnʃ), *sb.*[1] [late ME. a. ONF. *panche* = OF. *pance*, now *panse*:—Com. Rom. **pantica*, f. L. *pantex, panticem.*] 1. = BELLY *sb.* 5. Now usu. dyslogistic, implying prominence, gluttony, etc. 2. The first and largest stomach of a ruminant; the rumen. late ME. b. esp. as used for food; tripe. late ME.

Paunch, panch (pǭnʃ), *sb.*[2] 1626. [app. the same word as prec.] *Naut.* a. A thick strong mat, made of interlaced spun yarn or strands of rope, used on a ship to prevent chafing. b. A wooden covering or shield on the fore side of a mast (*rubbing p.*), to preserve it from chafing when the masts or spars are lowered.

Paunch (pǭnʃ), *v.* Now *rare* or *dial.* 1530. [f. PAUNCH *sb.*[1]] 1. *trans.* To stab in the paunch; also *loosely*, to stab. 2. To cut open the paunch of (an animal); to disembowel, eviscerate 1570. †3. To fill the belly, to glut. (Also *intr.* for *refl.*) -1635.

1. Batter his skull, or p. him with a stake SHAKS.

Paunchy (pǭ·nʃi), *a.* 1598. [f. PAUNCH *sb.*[1] + -Y[1].] Having a large paunch; big-bellied. Hence **Pau·nchiness.**

Pauper (pǭ·pəı). 1516. [a. L. *pauper* poor.] 1. A poor person. a. In Law: One allowed, on account of poverty, to sue or defend in a court of law, without paying costs (*in forma pauperis*) 1631. b. *gen.* A person destitute of means of livelihood; a beggar. (Now assoc. with c.) 1516. c. *spec.* A person in receipt of poor-law relief 1775. 2. a. *attrib.* (in apposition) or as *adj.* That is a pauper; destitute 1809. b. *attrib.* Of, belonging or relating to, or intended for a pauper or paupers, as *p.-asylum, -grave, -rate, -system* 1823.

1. c. The p. lives better than the free labourer; the thief better than the p. EMERSON. 2. a. Educating p. children 1846. Hence **Pau·perdom**, the condition of a p., destitution; paupers collectively. **Pau·perism**, the condition of paupers; the existence of a p. class; poverty, with dependence on public relief; *concr.* paupers collectively.

Pauperize (pǭ·pərəiz), *v.* 1834. [f. prec. + -IZE.] *trans.* To reduce to the condition of a pauper; *esp.* to make dependent on public relief. Also *absol.*

The charity that pauperizes 1902. Hence **Pau:periza·tion.**

Pausal (pǭ·zăl), *a.* (*sb.*) 1877. [f. PAUSE *sb.* + -AL.] Of or pertaining to a pause or the pause in a sentence; in *Heb. Gram.* applied to the form which a word receives in the pause.

Pause (pǭz), *sb.* 1440. [a. F., ad. L. *pausa* halt, stop, ad. Gr. παῦσις, f. παύειν to cease; in the musical sense ad. It. *pausa.*] 1. A short interval of inaction or silence; occas. *spec.* an intermission arising from uncertainty, a hesitation. b. (Without article.) Intermission, waiting, hesitation, suspense 1593. 2. *spec.* An intermission, stop, or break made, according to the sense, in speaking or reading; in *Prosody*, a cæsura; also, a break of definite length in a verse, occupying the time of a syllable or a number of syllables. Also *transf.* in a piece of music. 1440. 3. *Mus.* †a. A character denoting an interval of silence; a rest -1674. b. The character 𝄐 or 𝄑 placed over or under a note or rest to indicate that it is to be lengthened indefinitely. (Also placed over a double bar at the conclusion of a piece, and rarely over a single bar in the course of it.) 1806.

1. There was a p. before the preacher spoke again GEO. ELIOT. b. Sad p. and deep regard beseem the sage SHAKS. Phr. *To give p. to, to put to a p.*, to cause to stop or hesitate; to 'pull up'. *At p.*, pausing, not proceeding; in suspense; You stand there at p., and silent RUSKIN. Hence **Pau·seful** *a.*, **-ly** *adv.* **Pau·seless** *a.*, **-ly** *adv.*

Pause (pǭz), *v.* 1526. [f. prec., or ad. L. *pausare* or F. *pauser* to halt, cease.] 1. *intr.* To make a pause; to stop (temporarily), to wait; to stop for deliberation or on account of uncertainty; to hesitate, hold back. †b. *refl.* in same sense 2 *Hen. IV.* IV. iv. 9. 2. To dwell, linger *upon*, some particular word or thing 1530.

1. Why doth the Iew p.? take thy forfeiture SHAKS. I p. for a Reply SHAKS. 2. Other Offenders we will p. vpon SHAKS. Hence **Pau·ser** (*rare*), one who pauses. **Pau·singly** *adv.*

‖ **Pauxi** (pǭ·ksi). 1753. [a. Sp. *pauxi*, now *pauji* (pau·χi), a. Mexican *pauxi* (pau·ʃi).] The Galeated Curassow (*Pauxis galeata*).

Pavage (pē¹·vėdʒ). ME. [a. F., f. *paver* to PAVE; see -AGE.] 1. A tax or toll towards the paving of highways or streets; also, the right to levy this. 2. The action of paving, the laying of a pavement. Also *attrib.* 1553.

Pavan (pæ·văn). 1535. [a. F. *pavane*, ad. It. *pavana*, or Sp. *pavana*; perh. f. Sp. *pavo* peacock.] A grave and stately dance, in which the dancers were elaborately dressed; introduced into England in the 16th c. b. Music for this dance or in its rhythm, which is duple and very slow 1545.

Pave (pē¹v), *v.* ME. [a. OF. *paver*, either from L. *pavire* to beat, strike, ram, or a back formation from F. *pavement* PAVEMENT.] 1. *trans.* To lay or cover with a pavement (a road, street, yard, etc.; hence, a town, house, etc.); see PAVEMENT 1. b. To overlie as a pavement 1600. 2. *fig.* To cover or overlay as with a pavement. late ME.

1. The court is pavid with Mosaique stone 1585. b. They had more Rubies than wold paue Cheapside 1600. 2. Hell is paved with good intentions 1771. Phr. *To p. the way*, to prepare the way (*for* something to come); to lead on to an object in view.

|| **Pavé** (pave). 1764. [F., sb. use of pa. pple. *pavé* paved.] 1. A paved street, road, or path. 2. A setting of diamonds, etc., placed close together like the stones of a pavement, so that no metal is visible. Also *attrib.*, as *p.-effect* 1871.

1. *On the pavé*: see *on the* PAVEMENT.

Paved (pēⁱvd), *ppl. a.* late ME. [f. PAVE *v.* + -ED[1].] Laid with a pavement; having a pavement; †set or laid together as a pavement.

There was vnder his feet, as it were a paued worke of a Saphire stone *Exod.* xxiv. 10.

Pavement (pēⁱ·vmĕnt), *sb.* ME. [a. OF., ad. L. *pavimentum* a beaten or rammed floor, f. *pavire* to beat, ram, tread down.] 1. A piece of paved work, a paved surface; the superficial covering of a floor, yard, street, etc., formed of stones, bricks, tiles, or, in later times, blocks of wood, fitted closely together; also, an undivided surface of cement, concrete, asphalt, etc. b. The paved part of a public thoroughfare; now only *spec.* the paved footway by the side of a street, as dist. from the roadway ME. c. *U.S.* = ROADWAY 2. d. The floor of a mine 1839. e. A seam of fire-clay underlying a seam of coal. 2. *Anat.* and *Zool.* A level hard surface formed by close-set teeth, bony plates, or the like 1847.

1. b. *On the p.* (after F. *sur le pavé*), walking the streets, without lodging, abandoned; I was left completely on the p. 1818. *fig.* Or like a gallant Horse falne in first ranke, Lye there for pauement to the abiect reere SHAKS.

attrib. and *Comb.*, as *p.-stone*, etc.; **p.-artist**, one who draws figures or scenes on the flagged p. in coloured chalks in order to get money from passers-by; **-tooth**, a broad flat tooth forming with others a p. in sense 2, as in the Port Jackson shark. Hence **Pa·vement** *v. trans.* to lay with a pavement; to pave (chiefly in *pa. pple.*) 1634.

Paven (pēⁱ·vĕn), *ppl. a.* Chiefly *poet.* 1634. [irreg. f. PAVE *v.*, after *shaven*, etc.] = PAVED.

Paver (pēⁱ·vəɹ). ME. [f. PAVE *v.* + -ER[1].] 1. One who paves, a paviour. 2. A paving-stone or tile 1696.

|| **Pavia** (pēⁱ·viă). 1753. [mod.L.; named after Peter Paaw (Pavius), Professor of Botany at Leiden 1589–1617.] *Bot.* A genus of trees and shrubs (N.O. *Sapindaceæ*) closely allied to the Horse-chestnut, but distinguished by having a smooth, not prickly, capsule; hence called Buck-eye, or Smooth-fruited Horse-chestnut. Hence **Paviin** (pēⁱ·vi,in), *Chem.* a fluorescent substance, $C_{16}H_{18}O_{10}$, existing in the bark of *P.* and other trees; also called FRAXIN.

Pavid (pæ·vid), *a. rare.* 1656. [ad. L. *pavidus*, f. stem of *pavere* to quake with fear.] Fearful, timid.

Pavilion (păvi·lyən), *sb.* [ME. a. F. *pavillon* tent, canopy, standard :—L. *papilionem* butterfly, moth, transf. tent, pavilion.] I. 1. A tent, esp. a large one, rising to a peak above. b. *Her.* A tent as a heraldic bearing 1725. †c. A canopied litter –1703. 2. *fig.* Anything likened to a tent 1535.

1. This mountaine..resembling perfectly the fashion of a p., or of a sugar loafe 1604. 2. He made darknes his pauylion rounde aboute him COVERDALE 2 *Sam.* xxii. 12.

II. In transf. and techn. uses, chiefly from French. 1. A French gold coin struck by Philip VI of Valois in 1329, the obverse of which represented the king seated under a canopy or *pavillon*. Also applied to the *royal d'or* struck by the Black Prince for use in Guienne, etc. 1755. 2. A light ornamental building or pleasure-house; also, a building attached to a cricket or other ground, for the convenience of spectators and players 1687. 3. A projecting subdivision of a building or façade, often elaborately decorated, forming an angle, or the central feature of a large pile 1676. b. A detached or semi-detached subdivision of a hospital 1858. †4. A flag or ensign –1778. †5. *Bot.* The spreading part of the corolla of a flower; the *vexillum* or standard in a papilionaceous flower –1796. 6. The part of a brilliant-cut diamond between the girdle and the collet 1751. 7. *Anat.* a. The pinna or auricle of the ear 1842. b. The fimbriated extremity of a Fallopian tube 1857.

2. The handsome p. which was recently built [at Lord's] 1891.

attrib. and *Comb.*: **p.-facet**, any one of the four largest facets in the p. of a brilliant-cut diamond.

Pavilion (păvi·lyən), *v.* ME. [f. prec.] 1. *trans.* To set, place, or enclose in or as in a pavilion; to canopy. 2. To furnish or set (a field, etc.) with pavilions 1667.

2. The field Pavilion'd with his Guardians bright MILT.

Paving (pēⁱ·viŋ), *vbl. sb.* late ME. [-ING[1].] The action of PAVE *v.*; *concr.* a pavement; the material of which a pavement is composed. Also *attrib.*, as *p.-stone, -tile*, etc.

Paviour, -ior (pēⁱ·viəɹ). late ME. [f. PAVE *v.*; var. (perh. after *saviour*) of *pavier, -yer*, altered f. PAVER, after sbs. in -IER 1.] 1. One who paves or lays pavements. Also *fig.* b. A rammer for driving paving-stones 1875. 2. = PAVER 2. 1611.

Pavis, pavise (pæ·vis), *sb.* Now *Hist.* [ME. *paveys, -eis*, a. OF. *pavais*, F. *pavois*, ad. It. *pavese*; app. f. *Pavia* in Italy, where orig. made.] 1. A convex shield, large enough to cover the whole body, used as a defence against archery, and esp. in sieges; hence, any large shield. †b. As used on board a ship (ranged along the sides as a defence against archery) –1562. †2. A screen of pavises; a pavisade; any screen or shelter used in fighting –1582. †3. *fig.* A defence, protection –1534.

3. He was their bulwark, their paues, and their wall 1529. Hence **Pavis, pavise** (pæ·vis) *v.* to cover, shelter, or defend with a p. (*Obs.* or *Hist.*) **Pavisa·de, pavesa·de, †Pavisa·do, pavesa·do**, a defence or screen made of pavises or shields joined together in a continuous line; hence, a screen of canvas run round the sides of a ship for protection against missiles, etc. **Pa·viser, -or**, a man armed with or bearing a p.

†**Pavo·ne.** *rare.* [ad. It. *pavone* :—L. *pavo, pavonem.*] A peacock SPENSER.

Pavonian (păvōᵘ·niăn), *a.* 1793. [f. L. *pavo, pavonem* peacock + -IAN.] Of or pertaining to a peacock; pavonine.

Pavonine (pæ·vŏnəin), *a.* and *sb.* 1656. [ad. L. *pavoninus*, f. *pavonem* peacock; see -INE[1].] A. *adj.* 1. Of or pertaining to, resembling or characteristic of a peacock. b. *Zool.* Of or pertaining to the genus *Pavo* or sub-family *Pavoninæ*, including the peafowl 1895. 2. Resembling the neck or the tail of the peacock in colouring 1688. B. *sb.* 1. An iridescent lustre found on some ores or metals; peacock-tail tarnish 1805. 2. *Zool.* A bird of the sub-family *Pavoninæ* 1895.

Pavy (pēⁱ·vi). 1675. [a. F. *pavie*, f. *Pavie* Pavia.] A hard clingstone peach or nectarine.

Paw (pǭ), *sb.* [ME. a. OF. *powe, poue*, var. of *poe* (*pooe*) = Pr. *pauta*; app. of Frankish origin; cf. HG. *pfote* paw.] 1. The foot of a beast having claws or nails. (Dist. from *hoof.*) b. The foot of any animal; *esp.* the claw of a bird (*rare*). late ME. 2. *joc.* The hand, esp. when clumsy or awkwardly used (*colloq.*) 1593. b. Handwriting; 'fist'; signature 1702. 3. [f. PAW *v.*] The action, or an act, of pawing 1611.

1. Whatsoeuer goeth vpon his pawes, among all maner of beasts *Lev.* xi. 27.

†**Paw** (pǭ), *a. slang* or *colloq.* 1668. [app. a var. of *pah*, adj. use of PAH *int.*] Improper, naughty, obscene –1730.

Paw (pǭ), *v.* 1604. [f. PAW *sb.* Cf. *to claw.*] 1. *trans.* and *intr.* To touch or strike with the paw 1611. 2. To strike or scrape the ground with the hoofs; said of a horse, etc. 1611. 3. a. *trans.* To pass the hand over, handle, *esp.* awkwardly, coarsely, or rudely (*colloq.*) 1604. b. *intr.* To pass the hand clumsily, etc. 1848.

2. He paweth in the valley, and reioyceth in his strength *Job* xxxix. 21. 3. a. Our great court-Galen..paw'd his beard, and mutter'd 'catalepsy' TENNYSON.

Pawk, pauk (pǭk). *Sc.* and *n. dial.* 1513. [Origin obsc.] Trick, artifice, cunning device. Hence **Paw·ky** *a.* tricky, artful, sly, cunning, shrewd; esp. dryly humorous. **Paw·kily** *adv.* **Paw·kiness.**

Pawl (pǭl), *sb.* 1626. [perh. = F. *pal* stake, L. *palus* stake, prop, stay, or Du. *pal* (used in sense 2).] 1. *Naut.* Each of the short stout bars made to engage with the whelps, and prevent a capstan, windlass, etc. from recoiling. 2. A bar pivoted at one end to a support, and engaging at the other with the teeth of a ratchet-wheel or ratchet-bar, so as to hold it in a required position 1729.

Comb., as **p.-bitt, -post** (*Naut.*), a strong vertical post in which the pawls of a windlass are fixed; **-head** (*Naut.*), the part of the capstan to which the pawls are attached; **-rim** (*Naut.*), a notched cast-iron ring for the pawls to catch in.

Pawl, *v.* Chiefly *Naut.* 1704. [f. prec.] 1. *trans.* To stop or secure (a capstan, ratchet-wheel, etc.) by means of a pawl or pawls. 2. *fig.* (*colloq.* or *slang.*) a. *trans.* To bring to a standstill, stop, check, 'pull up'. b. *intr.* To stop, cease, *esp.* to stop talking. 1825.

Pawn (pǭn), *sb.*[1] [late ME. *poune*, a. AF. *poun*, OF. *poon, paon*, var. of *peon*, earlier *pedon* foot-soldier, pawn at chess :—L. *pedo, pedonem*, f. *pes, ped-* foot.] One of the pieces of smallest size and value in the game of chess. Also *fig.* (usu. of a person).

Councillors of State..playing their high chess-game, whereof the pawns are Men CARLYLE.

Pawn (pǭn), *sb.*[2] 1496. [a. OF. *pan* pledge, security, surety, also booty; cf. G. *pfand.* Ult. history obsc.] 1. A thing (or person) given, deposited, or left in another's keeping, as security for a debt, or for the performance of some action; a pledge, surety, gage. (Now *rare.*) b. *fig.* 1573. †c. = GAGE *sb.*[1] 2. SHAKS. d. A person held as security for a debt, and used as a slave 1837. 2. The state of being pledged, or held as a pledge (*lit.* and *fig.*). Usu. in phr. *in p.*, *at p.*, †*to p.* (The usual sense.) 1554. b. The action of pawning 1824.

1. He must leave behind, for pawns, His mother, wife, and son DRYDEN. c. *Rich. II*, I. i. 74. 2. Her plate and jewels are at pawne for money PEPYS. b. The Contract of P. as it exists at Common Law 1883.

Comb. **p.-ticket**, a ticket issued by a pawnbroker in exchange for a pledge deposited with him, and bearing particulars of the loan.

†**Pawn**, *sb.*[3] 1548. [= Du. *pand*; a Du. development of F. *pan*; see PANE *sb.*[1] II. 1, 2.] A gallery or colonnade, a covered walk or passage, esp. one in a bazaar, exchange, etc. alongside which wares are exposed for sale –1888.

Pawn (pǭn), *v.* 1567. [f. PAWN *sb.*[2]; cf. G. *pfänden.*] *trans.* To give or deposit as security for the payment of a sum of money, or for the performance of some action (something to be forfeited in case of non-payment or non-performance); to pledge; to stake, wager; to risk. a. *lit.* 1570. b. *fig.* (e.g. one's life, honour, word, etc.) 1567.

a. He is over head and ears in debt, and has pawned several things SWIFT. b. I will p. my life for her, she will never be pert RICHARDSON. Hence **Paw·nable** *a.* that can be pawned.

Pawnbroker (pǭ·nbrōᵘ:kəɹ). 1678. [f. PAWN *sb.*[2] + BROKER 2.] One engaged in the business of lending money upon interest on the security of articles of personal property pawned or pledged. Hence **Paw·nbro:king** *vbl. sb.* the action or business of a p.

Pawnee (pǭnī·) 1683. [f. PAWN *v.* + -EE.] The person with whom something is deposited as a pawn or pledge. (Correl. to next.)

Pawner (pǭ·nəɹ). Also (in legal use) **-or.** 1745. [f. PAWN *v.* + -ER[1] or -OR.] One who pawns; one who deposits something as a pledge, esp. with a pawnbroker.

Pawnshop (pǭ·nʃŏp). 1849. [f. PAWN *sb.*[2] + SHOP.] A pawnbroker's shop or place of business.

Paw-paw (pǭ·pǭ:), *a. slang* or *colloq.* ?*Obs.* 1720. [Redupl. of PAW *a.*] Nursery term for 'nasty, improper, naughty', used euphem. for 'indecent, obscene, immoral'.

Pawpaw, var. of PAPAW.

Pax[1] (pæks). late ME. [a. L. *pax* peace.] ||1. The L. word meaning 'peace' 1485. b. *Eccl.* In L. salutations, etc., as *P. vobis* peace be with you 1593. c. quasi-*int.* (in schoolboy slang). 'Keep quiet!' 'Truce!' 1852. 2. *Eccl.* The kiss of peace: see PEACE *sb.* 4; the ceremony of kissing the pax: see sense 3. *rare.* 1440. 3. *Eccl.* A tablet with a projecting handle behind, bearing a representation of the Crucifixion, etc., which was kissed by the officiating priests and congregation at Mass; an osculatory. late ME. 4. *transf.* (Public school slang.) A friend; good friends 1781.

1. *P. Dei, Ecclesiæ, Regis*, the peace of God, the Church, the king's peace. *P. Romana*, the peace within the Roman empire; so *p. Britannica*, the peace imposed by British rule. 4. *To be good p.*, to be good friends.

†**Pax**[2]. 1641. Corrupt f. Pox -1716.

‖**Paxilla** (pæksi·lă). *Pl.* **-æ.** 1870. [mod. L., f. cl.L. *paxillus* small stake, peg.] *Zool.* A pillar-like pedicel in echinoderms, surmounted by a tuft of minute calcified spinelets attached to the integument. Hence **Paxi·llar** *a.* **Paxi·llate** *a.* having paxillæ. **Paxi·lliform** *a.*

Paxillose (pæ·ksilōus), *a.* 1882. [f. L. *paxillus* (see above) + -OSE.] **a.** *Geol.* Resembling a small stake. **b.** Of or pertaining to the *Paxillosæ*, a group of echinoderms bearing paxillæ 1895.

Paxwax (pæ·ks,wæ·ks). Now *dial.* and *colloq.* late ME. [Earlier *fax-wax, fex-wex*, the second element being prob. from OE. *weaxan* to grow, WAX *v.*[1]] The stout elastic tendon extending from the dorsal vertebræ to the occiput, and serving to support the head; the nuchal ligament.

Pay (pēi), *sb.* ME. [a. OF. *paie*, f. *payer* to PAY.] †**1.** Satisfaction, liking -1602. **2.** The action of paying, payment (esp. of wages or hire) 1440. **b.** The condition of being paid, or receiving wages or hire 1596. **3.** *concr.* Money paid for labour or service; wages, hire, salary, stipend ME. **4.** *fig.* Retaliation or punishment inflicted; penalty or retribution suffered; recompense, etc. bestowed. Now *rare* or *Obs.* ME. **5.** *Mining.* A remunerative yield of metal in a bed of ore 1877.

2. Rather to score it up against the future, than require present p. 1647. 3. I take the Queen's P. in Quin's Regiment THACKERAY. Phr. †*Dead p.*: see DEAD PAY. 5. It is in this stratum..where the rich p. will be found RAYMOND.

Phr. *To be good* (etc.) *p.*, to be sure to pay one's debts (colloq.); *fig.* to afford profit.

Pay (pēi), *v.*[1] Pa. t. and pple. **paid** (pēid). [ME. a. F. *payer* = It. *pagare* :—L. *pacare* to appease, pacify, in med.L. also 'to pay', f. *pax, pacem* peace.] †**1.** *trans.* = APAY *v.* 1. Chiefly in *pa. pple.* Satisfied, content, pleased -1501. **2.** *trans.* To give to (a person) what is due in discharge of a debt, or as a return for services done, or goods received, etc.; to remunerate, recompense ME. **3.** *fig.* or *gen.* To reward, recompense, requite, give what is due or deserved to (a person). late ME. **b.** To give (one) his deserts, punish 1450. **c.** *spec.* To beat, flog. Now *dial.* or *slang.* 1581. **4.** To recompense, reward (a service, work, etc.); in good or bad sense. Also, of a thing, To yield or recompense for. late ME. **5.** To hand over (money, etc.) in return for goods or services, or in discharge of an obligation; to render (a sum or amount owed). Also *transf.*; cf. 6 b. ME. **6.** To give money in discharge of (a debt, dues, tribute, tithes, ransom, hire, etc.). late ME. **b.** *transf.* Of a thing: To furnish (money, etc.) for the discharge of (a debt, etc.) 1656. **7.** *fig.* To give or render (anything owed, due, or deserved); to discharge (an obligation). In good or bad sense. ME. **b.** *Arith.* In subtraction, to compensate for 'borrowing' (see BORROW *v.*[1] 1 c) by mentally adding a unit to the subtrahend of the next higher denomination. Usu. *to p. back.* 1897. **8.** (With the notion of debt weakened or lost.) To render, bestow (attention, respect, a compliment, a visit, etc.). 1590. **9.** *absol.* or *intr.* To give money, etc., in return for something or in discharge of an obligation; also *fig.* ME. **10.** *absol.* or *intr.* Of a thing or action: To yield an adequate return; to be profitable or advantageous 1812. **b.** *trans.* To be profitable to (a person) 1883. **11.** *P. for*: To give money or other equivalent value for. Also *transf.* of a thing, sum of money, etc.: To furnish an equivalent for; to be sufficient to defray the cost of. late ME. **b.** *fig.* To atone for; more usu., To suffer or be punished for. late ME. †**12.** *trans.* = *pay for*: see 11. -1842. †**b.** *fig.* To make up for -1790. **13.** *Naut.* To let out (a rope or chain) by slackening it. (Also in ref. to something let out by the rope.) Now always with *out* or *away.* 1627. **14.** *Naut.* (*trans.*) To cause (a ship) to fall to leeward, or fall away from the wind. Now always with *off.* 1627. **b.** *intr.* for *pass.* To fall to leeward 1625.

2. He had been..paid by the job 1813. Phr. *To p. off* (rarely *up*), to pay in full and discharge; *spec.* to pay and discharge the crew of (a ship) upon completion of a commission. Also *intr.* for *pass.* *To p. out*, to get rid of by paying; The Man in Possession had been paid out 1887. 3. b. They, in return, (as the vulgar phrase has it,) 'p. him out' 1863. c. Thence home, and find the boy out of the house and office.. I did p. his coat for him PEPYS. 4. Haste still paies haste SHAKS. It will more than p. the trouble I have taken to write it CHESTERF. 5. Have pacience with me, and I will paye the all TINDALE *Matt.* xviii. 29. Phr. *To p. away, in, over, out*, etc. *P. down*, to lay down (money) in payment; to pay on the spot (also *fig.*). 6. Phr. *P. off*, to p. in full; to clear off (a debt) by payment. *P. up*, to make up arrears of payment. b. That this estate should be liable to p. these debts 1818. 7. Ye traytours were payed ther desertes LD. BERNERS. Made mee p. the price of pillage with my bloud 1587. Praise, everlasting praise, be paid To him that earth's foundation laid WATTS. To forget the pain he paid for his discoveries 1890. Phr. *To p. one's debt to nature*, or *nature's debt*, (*spec.*) to die; see DEBT *sb.* 8. They paid little heed to the sermon 1882. 9. The vngodly borroweth and paieth not agayne COVERDALE *Ps.* xxxvi[i]. 21. 10. You won't find it p. in the long run 1885. 11. [He] shal paye for al þat by the wey is spent CHAUCER. b. Lot payes deare for his rashnesse BP. HALL.

Phr. *The* DEVIL *to p.*, *to p. through the* NOSE, *to p. the* PIPER, *to p. one's* WAY: see these sbs. Hence **Pay·ing** *vbl. sb.*; also with advs., as *paying-in*, etc. **Pay·ing** *ppl. a.* that pays, remunerative.

Pay (pēi), *v.*[2] Chiefly *Naut.* Pa. t. and pple. **payed (paid).** 1594. [a. ONF. *peier* :—L. *picare*, f. *pix, picem* pitch.] *trans.* To smear or cover with pitch, tar, resin, tallow, or the like, as a defence against wet, etc.

Pay- in comb. [PAY *sb.* or stem of PAY *v.*[1]]

1. In sbs. denoting persons or things connected with the payment of money, esp. wages; as *p.-clerk, -inspector*; PAYMASTER, PAYMISTRESS; *p.-bill, -book, -list, -roll, -sheet*; *p.-envelope*; *p.-office, -room, -train*; PAY-DAY, *p.-night, -week.*

2. *Mining.* Containing mineral in sufficient quantity to be profitably worked; as *p.-channel, -dirt* (also contemptuous for 'money'), *-gravel, -ore, -rock, -vein.*

3. The vb.-stem in comb. with object; as **p.-all**, he who or that which pays all, or bears the whole charge; **-rent** *a.*, furnishing money to p. the rent.

Payable (pēi·ăb'l), *a.* 1447. [f. PAY *v.*[1] + -ABLE. Cf. F. *payable.*] **1.** *Comm.* Of a sum of money, a bill, etc.: That is to be paid; due; falling due (usu. *at* or *on* a specified date, or *to* a specified person). **b.** Of a person: That is to be paid 1617. **2.** *Mining.* (In active sense.) Of a mine, a bed of ore, etc.: That can be made to pay; capable of being profitably worked. Hence *transf.* Commercially profitable; paying 1859.

1. A bill..p. here at the shortest sight 1725. 2. Never again did we hit upon p. gold 1879. Hence **Payabi·lity** (*rare*), capability of being profitably worked (as a mine). **Pay·ably** *adv.*

Pay·-day. 1529. [PAY- 1.] The day on which payment is, or is to be, made; *esp.* a periodically recurring day for the payment of wages; on the *Stock Exchange*, the day on which a transfer of stock has to be paid for.

Payee (pēi,ī·). 1758. [f. PAY *v.*[1] + -EE.] The person to whom a sum of money is, or is to be, paid; *esp.* the person to whom a bill or cheque is made payable.

†**Pay·en.** ME. [a. OF. :—L. *paganus.*] = PAGAN -1550.

Payer (pēi·əɹ). late ME. [f. PAY *v.*[1] + -ER [1].] One who pays; *esp.* one who pays a sum of money. (As correl. to *payee* occas. spelt *payor.*)

Paymaster (pēi·mαːstəɹ). 1550. [f. PAY- 1 + MASTER.] An official (*esp.* an officer in the army or navy) whose duty it is to pay troops, workmen, or other persons. Also *fig.*

P.-general, the officer at the head of the department of the Treasury through which payments are made. Hence **Pay·ma·stership, Pay·master-ge·neralship.**

Payment (pēi·mĕnt). ME. [a. F. *paiement*, f. *payer* PAY *v.*[1]; see -MENT.] **1.** The action, or an act, of paying. **2.** A sum of money (or other thing) paid; pay, wages; price 1449. **3.** *fig.* The action, or an act, of rendering to a person anything due, deserved, or befitting, or of discharging an obligation; the thing so rendered ME. **4.** *attrib.* 1581.

1. The great principle of p. by results 1892. When goods are offered in exchange for goods, it is popularly distinguished as 'payment in kind' 1893.

Paymistress (pēi·mi:strĕs). 1583. [f. PAY- + MISTRESS, after *paymaster.*] A woman who superintends the payment of persons or services; also *fig.*

Paynim (pēi·nim), *sb.* (*a.*) *arch.* [ME. a. OF. *paienime*, earlier *-isme* :—late L. *paganismus* PAGANISM.] **A.** *sb.* A pagan, a heathen; a non-Christian; *esp.* a Mohammedan, a Saracen. *arch.* and *poet.* late ME. **B.** *adj.* (orig. *attrib.* use of sb.) Of pagans; pagan, heathen; non-Christian; chiefly = Mohammedan or Saracen. In mod. writers *poet.* or *Hist.* ME.

Champions bold Defi'd the best of Panim chivalry To mortal combat MILT. Hence **Pay·nimry**, paynims collectively, heathenry.

Paynize (pēi·nəiz), *v.* 1844. [f. *Payne*, inventor's name.] *trans.* To impregnate (wood) with a solution of calcium (or barium) sulphide followed by one of calcium sulphate, to harden and preserve it.

‖**Paysage.** *Obs.* exc. as F. (peizā·ʒ). 1611. [F., f. *pays* country; see -AGE.] **a.** A representation of rural scenery. **b.** A rural scene, landscape. Hence **Paysagist** (pēi·zădʒist), a landscape-painter.

‖**Paysanne** (peizα·n). 1748. [F., fem. of *paysan* PEASANT.] A peasant-woman; a countrywoman.

Paytamine (pēi·tămәin). 1879. [f. *Payta* + AMINE.] *Chem.* An amorphous alkaloid, obtained from *Payta-bark*, a pale variety of cinchona bark, shipped from Payta in Peru. So **Paytine** (pēi·təin), a crystallizable alkaloid obtained with p. 1875.

Pea[1] (pī). 1666. [New sing. f. the earlier sing. and pl. PEASE, sometimes written *peas*, where *s* was regarded as a pl. inflexion.] **I.** The seed or plant. **1.** The round seed of *Pisum sativum* (see 2), used for food. **2.** The plant *Pisum sativum*, a hardy climbing leguminous annual, with large papilionaceous flowers succeeded by long pods each containing a row of round seeds. Usu. dist. as *p.-plant.* 1699. **3.** Applied with defining words to leguminous plants allied to the common pea 1783.

1. To find the p., which I put under one of my thimbles BORROW. *Green peas*, peas gathered for food while still green and unripe. Provb. *As like as two peas.* 3. **Angola P.** = *Congo Pea*; **Beach-p.** = *Sea-pea*; **Butterfly-p.**, *Clitoria Mariana* of S. America and India; **Congo P.**, a variety (*bicolor*) of *Cajanus indicus*, with yellow flowers marked with crimson; **Egyptian P.**, the CHICK-PEA; **Everlasting P.** (see EVERLASTING A. 4. b.); **Hoary P.**, the genus *Tephrosia*, which has leaves covered with a grey down; **Milk-p.**, the N. American genus *Galactia*; **Sea-p., Sea-side P.**, *Lathyrus maritimus* (*Pisum maritimum*), a sea-coast species rare in England; also SWEET PEA.

II. Something small and round like the seed; the eggs, roe, or spawn of certain fishes 1758.

attrib. and *Comb.*, as *p.-bloom, -blossom*, etc.; **p.-bean** (see BEAN 3); **-beetle, -bug**, a small coleopterous insect (*Bruchus pisi*), a native of S. America, which infests peas; **-comb**, a triple comb occurring in some varieties of domestic fowl; **-crab**, a small crab of the genus *Pinnotheres*, commensally inhabiting the shell of a bivalve mollusc, as a mussel or oyster; **-dove**, a species of pigeon, *Zenaida amabilis*, found in W. Indies and Florida; **-flour**, flour made of peas, pease-meal; **-green** *a.* and *sb.*, (of) a colour like that of fresh green peas, a nearly pure but not deep green; **-grit**, a coarse pisolitic limestone; **-maggot**, a caterpillar which infests peas, the larva of the *pea-moth*; **-moth**, a small moth (*Tortrix pisi*) which lays its eggs on pea-pods; **-rifle**, a rifle with a thick barrel and a small round bullet like a p.; **-shooter**, a toy weapon, consisting of a tube from which peas are shot by the breath; **-time** (*U.S.*), phr. *the last of p.-t.*: the last stage of anything; **-vine** (*U.S.*), the 'vine', or climbing stem of any p.-plant; *esp.* (*a*) the Hog-peanut; (*b*) an American vetch, *Vicia americana*; **-weevil** = *p.-bug.*

Pea[2] (pī). Also **pee.** 1833. [perh. shortened from *peak.*] = PEAK *sb.*[2] 3 c.

Pea.[3] *local.* 1761. [prob. f. *pease*, PEISE weight, taken as a pl.] The sliding weight used on a steelyard, safety-valve, etc.

Peaberry (pī·beri). 1879. [f. PEA[1] + BERRY *sb.*[1]] A single round seed of the coffee-plant, occurring towards the end of the branches, through abortion of one of the usual two seeds in the fruit.

Peace (pīs), *sb.* [Early ME. *pais*, a. OF. *pais*, mod.F. *paix* :—L. *pacem* (nom. *pax*) peace.] **1.** Freedom from, or cessation of, war or hostilities; that condition of a nation or community in which it is not at war with another. **b.** (With article.) A ratification or treaty of peace between two powers previously at war. (†Also, formerly, a truce.) late ME. †**c.** With *possessive* or *of*. A state of peace, concord, and amity with a person –1576. **2.** Freedom from civil commotion; public order and security ME. **3.** Freedom from disturbance or perturbation (esp. as a condition in which an individual is); quiet, tranquillity. Also emphasized as *p. and quiet(ness.* ME. **b.** In or after Biblical use, in expressions of salutation, etc. ME. **4.** Freedom from quarrels or dissension between individuals; concord, amity ME. †**b.** *transf.* An author or maintainer of concord –1560. **5.** Freedom from mental or spiritual disturbance or conflict arising from passion, sense of guilt, etc.; e.g. *p. of mind, soul,* or *conscience* ME. **6.** Absence of noise, movement, or activity; stillness, quiet ME. **b.** *ellipt.* as exclam. after L. *pax*, F. *paix*, etc. (Cf. PEACE *v.* 1.) **7.** In generalized sense. late ME.

1. In this weake piping time of P. SHAKS. P. hath her victories No less renownd then warr MILT. b. The P. of Amiens CANNING. 3. Let him sleep in p. GRAY. *Bill of p.*, a bill brought by a person to establish a right, with the object of securing freedom from perpetual litigation. b. P., p., be unto thee, and p. be to thine helpers 1 *Chron.* xii. 18. 4. *Kiss of p.*, a kiss given in sign of friendliness; *spec.* a kiss of greeting given in token of Christian love (see PAX) at religious services in early times; now, in the Western Ch., usu. only at High Mass. b. And he shalbe our p. BIBLE (Genev.) *Micah* v. 5. 6. Calm and deep p. on this high wold TENNYSON. 7. Every thing that is sincerely good..With Truth, and P., and Love shall ever shine MILT.

Phrases. **a.** Belonging to 1. *P. at any price. P. with honour.* **b.** Belonging to 2. *The king's p.*, orig. the protection secured to certain persons by the king, as those travelling on the king's highway, etc.; hence, the general peace of the kingdom under the king's authority. *The p.* = the king's peace, in its wider sense; as in *to keep the p.*, *breach of the p.*; *to swear the p. against* (any one), to swear that one is in bodily fear of another, so that he may be bound over to keep the peace; also, *commission, justice, officer, of the p.*, etc. *God's p.*, God's requirement of peace and good order. The *Roman p.* = *pax Romana*, the *British p.* = *pax Britannica*; see PAX[1] 1. *To keep the p.*, to refrain, or prevent others, from disturbing the public peace. **c.** In various senses. *At p.*, not at strife or variance; quiet, peaceful. *To hold* (occas. *keep*) *one's p.*, to keep silence (*arch.*). *To make p.*, (*a*) to effect a reconciliation between parties at variance; to conclude peace with a nation at the close of a war; (*b*) to enter into friendly relations with a person; (*c*) to enforce public order. *To make* one's, or a person's, *p.*, to come, or bring some one, into friendly relations (*with* another).

Comb.: **p.-breaker**, one who breaks or violates p.; one who commits a breach of the p.; **p. establishment**, the reduced troops under arms and military supplies maintained in a standing army in time of p.; **-monger**, hostile term for one who advocates p.; **officer**, a civil officer appointed to preserve the public p., as a constable; **-warrant**, a warrant for arrest, issued by a Justice of the Peace. Hence **Pea·celess** *a.* devoid of p., unquiet; **-ness.**

Peace (pīs), *v.* late ME. [f. prec. At first in the imper.; prob. interjectional use of prec.] **1.** *intr.* imper., as exclam.: Be silent, keep silence (*arch.*). †**2.** *intr.* To be or become still or silent; to keep silence –1633.

1. He..sayde vnto the see: p. and be still TINDALE *Mark* iv. 39. 2. When the Thunder would not p. at my bidding SHAKS.

Peaceable (pī·săb'l), *a.* [ME. *peisible*, a. OF. *pais-*, *peisible*, f. *pais* PEACE *sb.*; see -BLE.] **1.** Disposed to, or making for, peace; not quarrelsome or pugnacious. †**b.** Not talkative, taciturn, calm; quiet in behaviour –1826. **2.** = PEACEFUL 2 (now the usual word) ME. Hence **Pea·ceableness. Pea·ceably** *adv.*

Peaceful (pī·sfŭl), *a.* ME. [f. PEACE *sb.* + -FUL.] **1.** Disposed to or making for peace; friendly, pacific. (Now usu. *peaceable.*) **2.** Full of or characterized by peace; free from strife; untroubled, tranquil, quiet. (Now the usual sense.) ME. **3.** Belonging to a time or state of peace 1586.

1. And smooth the frownes of War, with peacefull lookes SHAKS. 2. The p. hermitage MILT. 3. Peacefull plenty 1586. Hence **Pea·ceful-ly** *adv.*, **-ness.**

Peacemaker (pī·s,mē̆ːkəɹ). late ME. [f. PEACE *sb.* + MAKER.] One who makes or brings about peace; one who reconciles opponents. **b.** *joc.* A revolver, warship, etc. 1841.

Blessed are the peacemakers TINDALE *Matt.* v. 9. So **Pea·cema·king** *sb.* and *a.*

Pea·ce-o·ffering. 1535. [f. PEACE *sb.* + OFFERING.] **1.** An offering or sacrifice presented as a thanksgiving to God, under the Levitical law. **2.** An offering made to make peace; a propitiatory sacrifice or gift 1661.

Peach (pītʃ), *sb.*[1] [late ME. *peche*, a. F. *pêche*, OF. *peche*, earlier *pesche* (= It. *persica*, *pesca*) :—late L. *persica*, for cl. L. *persicum*, ellipt. for *Persicum malum* lit. Persian apple; so *Persica malus* or *arbor* peach-tree.] **1.** The fruit of the tree *Amygdalus persica* (see 2), a large drupe, usually round, of a whitish or yellow colour, flushed with red, with downy skin, highly flavoured sweet pulp, and rough furrowed stone. **2.** The tree *Amygdalus* (*Prunus*) *persica*, N.O. *Rosaceæ*, a native of Asia; the peach-tree. late ME. **3.** Applied to other edible fruits resembling the peach, or to the plants producing them; esp. *Sarcocephalus esculentus*, a climbing shrub of West Africa (*Guinea*, *Negro*, or *Sierra Leone P.*), bearing a large juicy berry 1760. **4.** Short for *p.-brandy* (U.S.) 1853. **5.** = *P.-colour*; also *attrib.* or as *adj.* 1848. **6.** *slang.* (orig. *U.S.*) Applied to anything particularly good of its kind, as in *she's a p.* 187..

attrib. and *Comb.*, as *p.-stone*, etc.; also **p.-bloom**, (*a*) the delicate powdery deposit on the surface of a ripe peach; hence in ref. to complexion; (*b*) = PEACH-BLOSSOM 1; **-borer**, any insect whose larva bores through the bark of the peach-tree; *spec.* a moth, *Ægeria exitiosa*, and a beetle, *Dicerca divaricata*; **-brandy**, a spirituous liquor made from the fermented juice of peaches; **-colour**, (*a*) the colour of a ripe p., a soft pale red; (*b*) the colour of PEACH-BLOSSOM, a delicate rose or pink; also *attrib.* or as *adj.*; so **-coloured** *a.*; **p. Melba** = PÊCHE MELBA; **-tree** = 2.

Peach, *sb.*[2] 1778. [f. prec.] *Min.* Cornish miners' term for chlorite slate. Hence **Pea·chy** *a.*[2] containing a large proportion of p. 1814.

Peach (pītʃ), *v.* 1460. [Aphetic f. *apeche*, APPEACH.] †**1.** *trans.* To accuse (a person) formally; to impeach –1727. **b.** To inform against (an accomplice or associate); to 'round upon'. Now *rare.* 1570. **c.** *transf.* To blab, divulge (*colloq.*) 1852. **2.** *intr.* or *absol.* To turn informer. Const. *upon*, *against*. Now chiefly *slang* or *colloq.* 1596.

2. If I be tane, Ile p. for this SHAKS. Save my life, and I'll p. 1717. Hence **Pea·cher**, an informer.

Pea·ch-blo·ssom. 1664. **1.** The blossom of the peach-tree. **2.** *attrib.*, *esp.* Of the colour of a peach-blossom, a delicate purplish pink 1702. **3.** A species of moth (*Thyatira batis*), from the colour of the spots on its wings 1819.

Pea·ch-blow. 1861. [See BLOW *sb.*[3]] A delicate purplish-pink colour; cf. prec. 2. **b.** A glaze of this colour on some oriental porcelain. Also *attrib.* 1886. **c.** A variety of potato of this colour 1868.

Pea·-chick. 1542. The young of the peafowl. **b.** A young and vain person 1746.

Peachy (pī·tʃi), *a.*[1] 1599. [f. PEACH *sb.*[1] + -Y[1].] Of the nature or appearance of a peach; chiefly of the cheeks: Round, soft, and having a delicate pink flush. Hence **Pea·chiness.**

Pea·-coat. 1845. [f. after *pea-jacket.*] = PEA-JACKET.

Peacock (pī·kǫk), *sb.* [ME. f. *pe :—OE. *péa* + COCK *sb.*[1]; beside which ME. had *pocock*, f. *po*, *poo*, and *pacock*, f. (northern) *paa*, *pa-*, both repr. OE. *páwa*, a. L. *pavo.*] **1.** The male bird of any species of the genus *Pavo* or peafowl, esp. of the common species *P. cristatus*, a native of India, well known as the most imposing and magnificent of birds; often treated as a type of ostentatious display and vainglory. **b.** *transf.* and *fig.* late ME. **c.** The bird or its flesh as an article of food 1460. **2.** A southern constellation (*Pavo*) 1674. **3.** Short for *p.-butterfly*, *p.-moth* 1827.

1. The self-applauding bird, the p. COWPER. b. Phr. *To play the p.*, to comport oneself vain-gloriously.

attrib. and *Comb.*: **p.-blue**, the lustrous blue of a peacock's neck; **-butterfly**, a European butterfly (*Vanessa Io*) with ocellated wings; **-coal**, iridescent coal; **-eye**, the ocellus on a peacock's feather; also *attrib.*; **-moth**, *Macaria notata* and *M. alternata*, of family *Geometridæ*; **-throne**, the former throne of the kings of Delhi; adorned with the representation of a peacock's tail fully expanded, composed of precious stones. Hence **Pea·co·ckery, Pea·cockism**, foppery. **Pea·cockish** *a.* like a p. or that of a p.; **-ly** *adv.*; **-ness. Pea·cocklike** *a.* peacockish; *adv.* after the manner of a p. **Pea·cocky** *a.* suggesting a p. in walk, bearing, self-display, or showiness.

Peacock (pī·kǫk), *v.* 1586. [f. prec.] **1.** *trans.* To make like a peacock; to puff up with vanity; *esp. refl.* to strut about or pose like a peacock. **2.** *intr.* To strut about ostentatiously; to make a vainglorious display, pose 1818.

2. People of various nationalities..p. about in fine feathers 1890.

Peacock's feather, peacock-feather. late ME. A feather of the peacock; *spec.* one of the long tail-feathers, adorned with iridescent ocelli or 'eyes'. Hence taken as a symbol of vainglory, or a decoration of rank, etc.

Pea·cock-fi·sh. 1661. A European labroid fish, the blue-striped wrasse (*Crenilabrus pavo*); from its green, blue, red, and white colouring.

Peacock's tail. 1570. The tail-coverts of the peacock collectively, which the bird is able to erect in a resplendent vertical circle behind its body. **b.** Hence *transf.*; esp. in *peacock's tail* (*peacock-tail*) *tarnish* = PAVONINE B. 1.

Pea·-flower. 1825. The flower of the pea, or any flower resembling this.

Peafowl (pī·faul). 1804. A bird of the genus *Pavo*; a peacock or peahen.

†**Pe·age.** 1456. [a. F. *péage* :—late pop.L. *pedaticum*, f. *pes*, *pedem* foot; see -AGE.] Toll paid for passing through a place –1846.

Peahen (pī·hen). [late ME. *pehen(ne*, f. *pe-*, OE. *péa* + *henne* HEN. Cf. PEACOCK.] A female peafowl, the female of the peacock.

‖**Peai** (pi,ai·), *sb.* 1613. [ad. Carib *piai.*] A medicine-man or witch-doctor, among the Indians of S. America; cf. PIACHE.

Pea·-ja·cket. 1725. [app. f. PEE *sb.*[1] + JACKET.] A short stout overcoat of coarse woollen cloth, now commonly worn by sailors.

Peak (pīk), *sb.*[1] [OE. *Péac* (only in *Péaclond*) of unkn. origin.] Name of the hilly district in the north-west of Derbyshire, England; the High Peak and the Low or Lower Peak.

Peak (pīk), *sb.*[2] 1530. [A later equiv. of PIKE *sb.*[1]] **I. 1.** A projecting point; a pointed or tapering extremity; †a beak or bill. Now *rare.* 1578. **b.** *spec.* †The projecting front of a widow's hood –1719; †any pointed part of a garment, etc. –1818; the point of a beard 1592; the projecting part of the brim of a man's cap 1660; a point formed by the hair on the forehead, a 'widow's peak' 1833. **2.** A headland. Now *local.* 1548. **3.** *Naut.* **a.** The narrowed end of a ship's hold at the bow, the FOREPEAK; also the corresponding part at the stern, the *after-peak* 1693. **b.** 'The upper outer corner of those sails which are extended by a gaff' (Smyth); also, the upper end of a gaff. Hence *gaff p.*, *mizzen p.* 1711. **c.** The point at the end of the fluke of an anchor 1793.

1. The moon put forth a little diamond p. KEATS.

II. Later form of PIKE *sb.*[2] **a.** The pointed top of a mountain; a mountain or hill having a pointed summit, or of conical form 1634. **b.** *fig.* Highest point, summit 1784. **c.** *transf.* The pointed top of anything 1840. **d.** *Electr.*, etc. The highest point of a load curve, as of the load-time curve of a power station; the maximum value of an alternating quantity during a cycle; *transf.* the (time of) greatest frequency or maximum of other varying quantities, as traffic, trade, prices, etc. 1902.

a. The top of the high Peake of Damoan..like a Sugar-loafe SIR T. HERBERT. b. Also *attrib.*, as in *p. month*, *year*, in which the allusion is now often to the high points of a graph record. c. A conical roof going up into a p. DICKENS. d. P. load.

†**Peak,** *sb.*[3] 1529. [Origin unkn.] A dolt, noodle. See HODDYPEAK. –1580.

Peak (pīk), *v.*[1] 1550. [Origin unkn.] †**1.** *intr.* To shrink, to slink –1642. †**2.** To move about dejectedly or silently –1603. **3.** To droop in health and spirits, waste away; to look sickly or emaciated. Chiefly in *p. and pine.* 1605.

2. Yet I..peake Like John a-dreames..And can say nothing SHAKS. **3.** Wearie Seu'nights, nine times nine, Shall he dwindle, peake, and pine SHAKS.

Peak (pīk), *v.*² 1577. [f. PEAK *sb.*²] **1.** *intr.* To project or rise in a peak. **2.** *trans.* To bring to a head; *fig.* to accentuate 1887.

Peak, *v.*³ 1626. [f. *pike* or *peak* in the adv. *a-pike*, A-PEAK = vertically, or aphet. f. the adv. itself.] *Naut.* (*trans.*) To place, put, or raise a-peak or vertically. **a.** To tilt up a yard vertically, or nearly so, by the mast; to top a yard; esp. *to p. the mizzen.* **b.** *To p. the oars*: to raise the oar blades out of the water to an almost vertical position 1875. **c.** Of a whale: To raise (his tail or flukes) straight up in diving vertically. Also *intr.* 1839.

Peaked (pīkt, pī·kėd), *a.* 1450. [f. PEAK *sb.*² + -ED².] **1.** Having a peak; pointed; brought to a peak or point. **b.** *spec.* Of a mountain: Having, or rising into, a peak. Also in comb., as *twin-p.*, etc. So of a roof. 1670. **2.** Sharp-featured, thin, pinched, as from illness or want; sickly-looking. Chiefly *colloq.* 1835.

1. [Charles the first] his Vandyke dress,..and his p. beard MACAULAY. **2.** As pale and p. as a charity-school-girl 1883. Hence **Pea·kedness.**

Peaking (pī·kiŋ), *ppl. a.* Now *dial.* 1598. [f. PEAK *v.*¹ + -ING².] **1.** Sneaking, skulking; mean-spirited. **2.** Emaciated, sickly, pining, peaky 1700.

Peakish (pī·kiʃ), *a.*¹ 1519. [f. PEAK *sb.*³; sense 2 goes with prec.] †**1.** Slothful, spiritless; stupid; ignorant -1603. **2.** Somewhat 'peaky' (PEAKY *a.*²) 1836. Hence †**Pea·kishness.**

†**Pea·kish,** *a.*² 1567. [f. PEAK *sb.*¹ + -ISH¹.] Of, pertaining to, or resembling that of the district of the Peak in Derbyshire -1646.

That p. caue HOLLAND. His p. dialect BP. HALL.

Peaky (pī·ki), *a.*¹ 1832. [f. PEAK *sb.*² + -Y¹.] **1.** Abounding in, or characterized by having, peaks. **2.** Peaked, pointed; peak-like 1869.

1. Hills with p. tops engrail'd TENNYSON. **2.** A p. nose 1887.

Pea·ky, pee·ky, *a.*² *colloq.* and *dial.* 1853. = PEAKING *ppl. a.* 2.

Peal (pīl), *sb.*¹ [Late ME. *pele*; in sense I and perh. in other senses, aphetic f. *apele*, APPEAL.] †**I.** = APPEAL *sb.* -1471. **II.** †**1.** The ringing of a bell as a call or summons -1675. **2.** The ringing of a bell, or of a set of bells; *spec.* a series of changes rung on a set of bells. Also *transf.* and *fig.* 1511. **3.** A set of bells tuned to one another; a ring of bells 1789. **4.** A discharge of guns or cannon so as to produce a loud sound; esp. as an expression of joy, a salute, etc. *Obs.* exc. *Hist.* 1515. **5.** A loud outburst or volley of sound 1535.

2. The bells ring..a joyous p. 1812. *transf.* My pockets ring A golden p. MASSINGER. **4.** The Castle discharged a peale of ordinaunce 1577. **5.** Still gazing in a doubt Whether those peales of praise be his or no SHAKS. A rattling p. of thunder DRYDEN.

Peal, peel (pīl), *sb.*² [In 1533 *salmon pele*; origin unkn.] **a.** A grilse or young salmon; **b.** A smaller species of salmon, *Salmo cambricus* (or *S. trutta*).

Peal (pīl), *v.*¹ Now *dial.* late ME. Aphetic f. *apele*, APPEAL *v.*

Peal (pīl), *v.*² 1632. [f. PEAL *sb.*¹] **1.** *intr.* To sound forth in a peal, to resound. †**2.** *trans.* To storm, din, or assail (the ears, or a person) *with* (loud noise, etc.) -1719. **3.** To give forth in a peal or peals 1714.

1. There let the pealing Organ blow, To the full voic'd Quire below MILT. **3.** Loud thunder is pealed from the skies 1887.

Pean (pīn). 1562. [Origin obsc.] *Her.* One of the furs, represented as sable powdered with 'spots' of or.

Peanut (pī·nɒt). 1835. [f. PEA¹ + NUT *sb.* I. 1.] The fruit or seed of *Arachis hypogæa*, or the plant itself, much cultivated in warm climates; the fruit is a pod ripening underground, containing two seeds like peas, valued as food and for their oil. (Also called *ground-nut* or *ground-pea.*) **b.** *attrib.* 1875.

b. *P. politics* (U.S. slang), underhand and secret tactics; so **p. politician.**

Pear (pēᵊɹ). [OE. *pere*:—WGer. **pera*, a. late L. *pira*, *pera*, fem. sing., for L. *pira* pl. of *pirum* pear.] **1.** The fleshy fruit of the pear-tree (see 2), a pome of a characteristic shape, tapering towards the stalk. **2.** The tree *Pyrus communis* (N.O. *Rosaceæ*), or other species with similar fruit; widely grown in many varieties for the fruit (sense 1). More usually *p.-tree.* late ME. **3.** Applied, with defining words, to various other fruits or plants in some way resembling the pear; as ALLIGATOR *p.*, PRICKLY P., etc. **4.** *transf.* Applied to things resembling a pear in shape; *e.g.* the fruit or hip of the rose; a pear-shaped pearl, etc. 1576.

1. Appeles and peres that semen very gode, Ful ofte tyme are roten by the core LYDG.

attrib. and *Comb.*, as *p.-shaped*, etc.; **p.-blight,** (*a*) a destructive disease of pear-trees, caused by a bacterium (*Micrococcus amylovorus*) which turns the leaves rapidly brown; (*b*) a disease of pear-trees caused by a beetle (*Xyleborus*) which bores into the bark (*pear-blight beetle*, also called *pin-borer*); **-drop,** (*a*) a p.-shaped sweetmeat, usu. flavoured with jargonelle-p. essence; (*b*) a p.-shaped jewel used as a pendant; **-gauge,** a gauge invented by Smeaton, consisting of a pear-shaped glass vessel and a hermetically closed tube, for measuring the degree of exhaustion of air in an air-pump; **-slug,** the slug-like larva of a saw-fly, *Selandria cerasi* (*Eriocampa limacina*), which infests the leaves of the pear and other fruit-trees; also called *plum-slug*, *slug-worm*, etc.; **-tree** = 2; also the wood of this tree.

Pearl (pɔ̄ɹl), *sb.*¹ [ME. a. F. *perle*, ad. pop. L. **perla* (It. *perla*), obscurely related to L. *perna* kind of mussel (It. dial. *perna* pearl).] **I. 1.** A nacreous concretion formed within the shell of various bivalve molluscs around some foreign body (e.g. a grain of sand), composed of filmy layers of carbonate of lime interstratified with animal membrane; it is of hard smooth texture, of globular, pear-shaped, oval, or irregular form, and of various colours, usually white or bluish-grey; often having a beautiful lustre, and hence prized as a gem; formerly also used in medicine. (The chief source is the PEARL-OYSTER.) **b.** (without *a* or *pl.*) As name of the substance ME. **c.** = MOTHER-OF-PEARL. Chiefly *attrib.* **2.** *Her.* In blazoning by precious stones, the tincture argent or white 1500. **3.** *fig.* Something especially precious, noble, or choice ME.

1. b. Like the wounded oyster, he mends his shell with p. EMERSON. **3.** He is the very p. Of curtesie SHIRLEY. Provb. *To cast pearls before swine*, to offer a good thing to one who is incapable of appreciating it. (From Matt. vii. 6.)

II. In transf. senses. **1.** A thin white film or opacity growing over the eye; a kind of cataract. *Obs.* or *dial.* late ME. **2.** A small and round pearl-like drop or globule; e.g. a dewdrop, a tear 1460. **3.** Applied rhet. to teeth. Cf. 'ivory'. 1586. **4.** One of the bony tubercles encircling the bur or base of a deer's antler 1575. **5.** One of several small white or silver balls set on a coronet; a similar ball as a heraldic bearing 1688. **6.** *Printing.* Name of a size of type intermediate between agate and diamond, equal to 5-point 1656.

This line is printed in pearl type.

7. A small fragment or size of various substances, e.g. of molten metal; a small piece of clean coal; a small pill or pilule 1873. **8.** One of the stages in sugar-boiling 1883. **9.** The colour of a pearl, a clear pale bluish-grey. Also *attrib.* or as *adj.* = *p.-coloured.* 1688.

2. Now hung with pearls the dropping trees appear POPE. **3.** A girle, Rubie-lipt and tooth'd with p. HERRICK.

attrib. and *Comb.*, as *p.-fisher*, *-fishery*, etc.; **p.-button,** a button made of a p., or of mother-of-pearl or an imitation of it; **-diver,** one who dives for pearl-oysters; **-eye,** †(*a*) = II. 1; (*b*) an eye of a pigeon, etc., resembling a p.; so **-eyed** *a.*; **-fish,** †(*a*) a shell-fish producing pearls; (*b*) a fish (*e.g.* the bleak) from the scales of which artificial p. is made; **-grain,** the grain or unit of weight by which the value of pearls is estimated; a carat-grain, one fourth of a carat; **-grass,** the large quaking-grass (*Briza maxima*), from the shape of its spicules; **-hen,** the guinea-fowl; **-moss,** carrageen (*Chondrus crispus*); **-moth,** a pyralid moth of the genus *Botys* or *Margaritia*, so called from its shining appearance; **-mussel,** a species of mussel bearing pearls; **-nautilus,** the pearly nautilus; **-powder,** a cosmetic used to impart whiteness to the skin; = *p.-white*; **-sago,** sago in small hard rounded grains; **-stone** = PERLITE; **-white** *a.*, pearly-white; *sb.* white oxide of bismuth; = *p.-powder.*

Pearl (pɔ̄ɹl), *sb.*² 1824. [app. a var. of PURL *sb.*¹] One of a row of fine loops forming a decorative edging on pillow-lace, braid, ribbon, gold-lace, etc. Chiefly in Comb., as *p.-edge*, *-loop*, etc.

Pearl (pɔ̄ɹl), *v.* late ME. [a. F. *perler*, f. *perle*, or directly f. PEARL *sb.*¹] **1.** *trans.* To adorn, set, or stud with or as with pearls, or with mother-of-pearl. (Only in *pa. pple.*) **2.** To sprinkle with pearly drops 1595. **3.** To make pearly in colour or lustre 18... **4.** To reduce (barley, sago, etc.) to the shape of small round pearls 1600. **5.** To cover with a coating of 'pearl' sugar (PEARL *sb.*¹ II. 8) 1883. **6.** *intr.* To form pearl-like drops or beads 1595. **7.** To seek or fish for pearls 1639.

2. The evening dew had pearl'd their tresses KEATS. **7.** We've pearled on half-shares in the Bay KIPLING. Hence **Pea·rling** *vbl. sb.* seeking or fishing for pearls; coating of comfits with 'pearl' sugar; formation into pearl-like grains.

Pea·rl-ash. 1726. The potassium carbonate of commerce, so called from its pearly hue. Orig. only in pl.

Pea·rl-ba·rley. 1710. [Cf. PEARL *v.* 4.] Barley reduced by attrition to small rounded grains.

Pearled (pɔ̄ɹld), *ppl. a.* late ME. [f. PEARL *sb.*¹ and *v.* + -ED.] **1.** Furnished, set, or adorned with pearls or mother-of-pearl. **2.** Formed into pearly drops; dew-besprinkled 1586. **3.** Formed into small rounded grains 1600. **4.** Of sugar: Boiled to the degree called 'pearl' (PEARL *sb.*¹ II. 8) 1706.

Pearler (pɔ̄·ɹləɹ). 1887. [f. PEARL *v.* + -ER¹.] A trader engaged in pearl-fishing; also, a small vessel employed in this trade.

Pearling (pɔ̄·ɹliŋ). *Sc.* and *n. dial.* 1621. [Goes with PEARL *sb.*²; see -ING¹.] A kind of lace of thread or silk for trimming the edges of garments; also called *p.-lace.* In *pl.*, edgings of this lace; also *transf.* clothes trimmed with it.

Pearlite (pɔ̄·ɹləit). 1833. [f. PEARL *sb.*¹ + -ITE¹.] **1.** = PERLITE. **2.** *Metall.* One of the forms in which carbon and iron are combined in cast steel 1889.

Pea·rl-oy·ster. 1668. A pearl-bearing bivalve mollusc of the family *Aviculidæ*; spec. *Meleagrina margaritifera* of the Indian seas.

Pea·rl-shell. 1614. **1.** A shell having a nacreous coating; mother-of-pearl. Also *rhet.* something resembling such a shell. **2.** Any shell producing pearls; a pearl-mussel 1788. **3.** *attrib.* Of or resembling a pearly shell 1618.

Pea·rlwort. 1660. A book-name for the genus *Sagina* of caryophyllaceous plants. Also **Pea·rlweed.**

Pearly (pɔ̄·ɹli), *a.* (*adv.*, *sb.*) late ME. [f. PEARL *sb.*¹ + -Y¹.] **1.** Round and lustrous like a pearl, as a dewdrop, etc. **b.** Like pearl in appearance or lustre 1603. **2.** Abounding in, having, or bearing pearls 1619. **b.** Nacreous 1667. **3.** Made of, set with, adorned with pearls or pearl 1742. **4.** Of the colour of pearl 1790. **5.** *fig.* Exceedingly precious; of supreme (spiritual) purity or lustre 1760. **B.** *adv.* After the manner of, or in respect of, pearl or pearls 1818. **C.** *sb.* in *pl.* Pearl-buttons; clothes adorned with these, as worn by costermongers. 1886.

A. 1. b. Her teeth were of a p. whiteness GIBBON. **2.** A diver in the p. seas KEATS. **b.** Pearlie shells MILT. Hence **Pea·rliness,** p. quality or character.

Pearmain (pēᵊ·ɹmēn). [late ME. a. OF. *par-*, *permain*, app. ad. L. **parmanus* of Parma.] †**1.** A variety of pear; app. the same as the WARDEN -1611. **2.** A variety of apple 1597. **3.** *attrib.* late ME.

Peart (pīᵊɹt), *a.* Variant of PERT *a.* (q. v.) from 15th c.; still dial. or arch.; *esp.* **a.** Lively, brisk, active; **b.** Clever, intelligent, sharp.

Peasant (pe·zănt), *sb.* 1475. [a. AF. *paisant*, OF. *païsent*, *-enc*, mod.F. *paysan*, f. *païs*, *pays*:—L. *pagensis*, sc. *ager* territory of a *pagus* or canton, the country.] **1.** One who lives in the country and works on the land; a countryman, a rustic. (In early use, prop. only of foreign countries; often connoting the lowest rank, antithetical to *noble.*) †**b.** Serf, villein; also boor, clown -1613. †**c.** A low fellow -1601. **2.** *attrib.* **a.** That is a peasant, as *p.-proprietor*; †formerly, of peasant nature, base 1550. **b.** Of or pertaining to a peasant or peasants 1597.

1. Heaven lies no more open to a Noble mans performances and merits, then a pezants 1642. **2. a.** Oh what a Rogue and Pesant slaue am I SHAKS. **b.** The Tuscan peasant-plays 1878. Hence **Pea·santly** *a.* (*rare* or *Obs.*) of, pertaining to, or characteristic of a p. or peasants.

Peasantry (pe·zăntri). 1553. [f. as prec. + -RY.] **1.** Peasants collectively; a body of peasants. **2.** The condition of being a peasant; the legal position or rank of a peasant; rusticity 1596.

1. A bold p., their country's pride, When once destroy'd, can never be supplied GOLDSM. 2. Colours so borne, shew Bastardy, peasantry, or dishonor 1622.

Peascod: see PEASECOD.

Pease (pīz), *sb.* [OE. *pise* wk. fem., pl. *pisan*, a. L. *pisa* (pl. -æ), late collateral form of *pisum*, pl. *pisa*, a. Gr. πίσον, earlier πίσος, pulse, pease. In ME. *pese*, pl. *pesen*; 16th c. *pease*, pl. *peasen*, *peses*, *pease*. See also PEA [1].] **1.** The plant, PEA [1] 2. **2.** A single seed, a pea (PEA [1] 1). *Obs.* or *arch.* OE. Also *collect.* esp. in *green p.*, †*peasen = green peas*; see PEA [1] 1440.

Comb., as *p.-porridge*, *pudding*, etc.; **p.-meal**, meal made by grinding peas; also *fig.* a medley, 'mess'.

†**Pease**, *v.* [ME. *paisen*, a. OF. *pais(i)er*, f. *pais*, PEACE *sb.* Also partly aphetic f. APPEASE.] **1.** *trans.* To make peace between, reconcile (two persons, or one *with* another). Also *intr.* -1652. **2.** *trans.* To quell the hostility of, to appease (a person); to satisfy, content. Also, to quiet, pacify. -1561. **3.** To reduce to peace, still, appease (strife, wrath, etc.). Also, to quiet, pacify (sorrow, violent feeling). -1541. **4.** To pacify (a country or community) -1548. **5.** To reduce to stillness or silence -1526.

Peasecod, peascod (pī·zkǫd). Now *arch.* or *dial.* late ME. [f. PEASE *sb.* + COD *sb.*[1] 2.] The pod or legume of the pea-plant; a pea-pod.

Peason, -en (pī·zən). *arch.* and *dial.* pl. of PEASE q.v.

Pea·-sou·p. Also **pease-soup.** 1711. [f. PEASE *sb.*, PEA [1] + SOUP.] A soup made from peas. Also *attrib.* (in ref. to its colour and consistency). Hence **Pea·-sou·py** *a. colloq.*, resembling pea-soup (said esp. of a thick yellow fog).

Peastone (pī·stōun). 1821. [f. PEA [1] + STONE *sb.*] A variety of limestone consisting of large rounded grains like peas; PISOLITE.

Peat [1] (pīt). [In 14th c. *pete*, in Anglo-L. *peta*; origin unkn.] **1.** (With *a* and *pl.*) A piece of the substance described in sense 2, usually roughly brick-shaped, for use as fuel. (Chiefly *Sc.* and *n. dial.*) **2.** Vegetable matter decomposed by water and partly carbonized by chemical change, often forming bogs or mosses of large extent, whence it is dug or cut out and 'made' into peats (in sense 1). late ME.

Comb.: **p.-bog**, a bog composed of p.; **-coal**, a soft earthy lignite; **-hag**, broken ground whence peats have been dug; **-moss**, a peat-bog (the regular name in the North); the substance p.; also, the bog-moss (*Sphagnum*); *pl.* the family of mosses that grow in peat-bogs; **-reek**, the smoke of a peat-fire; also *attrib.*; hence, a cant name for whisky distilled over a peat-fire and so flavoured with peat-smoke; also, loosely, Highland whisky generally. Hence **Pea·ty** *a.*

Peat [2] (pīt). *Obs.* or *arch.* 1568. [Re-introduced by Scott. Origin unkn.] †**1.** As a term of endearment = pet of a woman; hence = girl simply, light or merry girl, spoilt girl, etc. -1632. **2.** As a term of obloquy for a woman; esp. in *proud p.* 1599. **b.** As a term of dislike for a man 1818. †**3.** 'Formerly, a lawyer, supposed to be under the peculiar patronage of any particular judge, was invidiously termed his peat or pet' (Scott *Redgauntlet* Let. xiii, note) -1824.

Pea·-tree. 1822. Name for several leguminous trees or shrubs with flowers resembling those of the pea; esp. the genus *Caragana*, of Siberia, China, etc., and the tropical *Sesbania*.

Peav(e)y (pī·vi). *U.S.* 1878. [Inventor's name.] *Lumbering.* A cant-hook having a spike at the end of the lever.

‖**Peba** (pī·ba). 1834. [Shortened from Tupi *tatu-peba = tatu* armadillo and *peba* low.] An American armadillo, *Tatusia* (*Dasypus*) *peba*; the seven- or nine-banded armadillo.

Pebble (pe·b'l), *sb.* ME. [First element of OE. *papol-*, *popelstān*; origin obsc.] **1.** A small stone (less than a *boulder* or *cobble*) worn and rounded by the action of water. Also, a stone rounded by attrition of ice or sand. **2.** Applied to: **a.** A colourless transparent kind of rock-crystal, used instead of glass in spectacles; a lens made of this. **b.** Various kinds of agates, etc., as *Scotch*, *Egyptian*, *Mocha p.* **c.** *rhet.* The loadstone. 1600. **d.** A kind of earthenware invented by Wedgwood 1768. **3. a.** Short for *p.-leather.* Also, the grain produced on leather by pebbling 1875. **b.** Short for *p. powder* 1880. **4.** *attrib.* Of or pertaining to a pebble or pebbles; made or consisting of pebbles, or of agate or 'Scotch pebble' 1725.

1. A pibble out of the brook BP. HALL. 2. **c.** More than the diamond Koh-i-noor, ..they prize that dull p...whose poles turn themselves to the poles of the world EMERSON.

Comb.: **p.-dashed** *a.*, treated with **p.-dash** or **-dashing**, i. e. mortar with pebbles in it; **-leather**, pebbled leather (see next 2); **p. powder**, a slow-burning gunpowder in the form of cubes or prisms of the size of pebbles; **-ware**, a kind of Wedgwood ware in which clays of different colours are incorporated in the paste. Hence **Pe·bbly** *a.*

Pebble (pe·b'l), *v.* 1605. [f. prec. sb.] **1.** *trans.* To pelt with (or as with) pebbles. **2.** *Leather Manuf.* To produce a rough surface, such as might be produced by the pressure of pebbles, upon (leather), by means of a roller having a pattern upon it.

Pebbled (pe·b'ld), *a.* 1600. **1.** [f. PEBBLE *sb.* + -ED [2].] Covered, strewn, or heaped with pebbles; pebbly. (Chiefly *poet.*) **2.** [f. PEBBLE *v.* + -ED [1].] Of leather: Treated by the pebbling process (see prec. 2).

1. Like as the waues make towards the pibled shore SHAKS.

Pe·bble-stone. OE. = PEBBLE *sb.* 1.

‖**Pébrine** (pebrī·n). 1870. [mod. F. ad. Pr. *pebrino*, f. *pebre* pepper, in ref. to the black spots.] A destructive epidemic disease of silkworms, marked by black spots and stunted growth.

Pecan (pĭkæ·n). 1773. [In 18th c. *paccan* = F. *pacane*, from the native name in Algonkin dialects.] The nut or fruit, olive-shaped and finely flavoured, of a species of hickory (*Carya olivæformis*) common in the Ohio and Mississippi valleys, often attaining a very great height; also, the tree itself, the pecan-tree. **b.** *Bitter p.*, bitter-seeded hickory (*Carya aquatica*); also called *water-* or *swamp-hickory*.

Peccable (pe·kăb'l), *a.* 1604. [a. F., or ad. med.L. *peccabilis*, f. *peccare* to sin, after L. *impeccabilis* IMPECCABLE.] Capable of sinning, liable to sin.

We hold all mankind to be p. and errable, even the Pope himself BERKELEY. Hence **Peccabi·lity**, liability to sin.

Peccadillo (pekădi·lo). 1591. [a. Sp. *pecadillo* (-dī·lyo), dim. of *pecado* sin.] A small or venial fault or sin; a trifling offence. So †**Peccadill.**

Peccancy (pe·kănsi). 1611. [ad. L. *peccantia*, f. *peccant-*; see next and -ANCY.] **1.** The quality or condition of being peccant; sinfulness 1656. **b.** A sin, offence 1648. †**2.** Faultiness, incorrectness CHAPMAN.

Peccant (pe·kănt), *a.* 1604. [ad. L. *peccantem*, pr. pple. of *peccare* to sin; in sense 3, a. OF. *peccant.*] **1.** Sinning, offending. Also said of things. †**2.** Faulty, incorrect -1841. **3.** Causing disorder of the system; morbid, unhealthy, corrupt; also, inducing disease 1604.

1. The p. Officials..fell on their knees CARLYLE. 3. The patient..pointing to the p. tooth as the source of his woe 1899. Hence **Pe·ccant-ly** *adv.*, **-ness.**

Peccary (pe·kări). 1613. [ad. Carib *pakira*, *paquira.*] An American gregarious quadruped, allied to the swine.

‖**Peccavi** (pekē·vəi). 1553. [L., pa.t. of *peccare* to sin.] 'I have sinned' in phr. 'to cry *p.*'; hence, an acknowledgement of guilt.

So *pecca·vimus* 'we have sinned'; *pecca·vit* 'he has sinned'.

‖**Pêche Melba** (pēiʃ me·lbă). [Fr.; *pêche* PEACH + name of Dame Nellie *Melba*, Australian prima donna.] A confection of ice-cream and peaches flavoured with liqueurs, etc.

Peck (pek), *sb.*[1] [ME. *pek* = OF. *pek*; history unkn.] **1.** A measure of capacity for dry goods; the fourth part of a bushel, or two gallons. **2.** A vessel used as a peck measure. late ME. **3.** *loosely.* A large quantity or number, a great deal, a 'heap', 'lot'. Chiefly *fig.* in phr. *a p. of troubles.* 1535.

1. O, Willie brew'd a peck o' maut BURNS. Prov. Every man must eat a p. of dirt in his life 1710.

Comb. **p. loaf**, a loaf made from a p. of flour.

Peck (pek), *sb.*[2] 1567. [f. PECK *v.*[1]] **1.** An act of pecking; a stroke with the beak or bill; *joc.* a perfunctory kiss 1611. **2.** The mark made by pecking; a prick, hole, or dint; a dot 1591. **3.** *slang*, orig. *Thieves' Cant.* Food, 'grub'; provender 1567.

3. *P.-alley*, the throat.

Peck (pek), *v.*[1] late ME. [app. var. of PICK *v.*[1]] **I. 1.** *trans.* To strike with the beak, as a bird; to indent or pierce by thus striking. **b.** To make (a hole, etc.) by pecking 1768. **2.** *intr.* To strike with or use the beak, as a bird. late ME. **3.** *trans.* Of birds: To take (food) with the beak; esp. in small bits at a time. Often with *up.* late ME. **4.** *trans.* and *intr.* Of persons: **a.** To eat, to feed. *colloq.* (orig. *Thieves' Cant*). **b.** To bite, to eat daintily or in a nibbling fashion. 1550.

1. These parrots p. the fairest fruit DRYDEN. 2. They p. and combat with their claws GOLDSM. *P. at*, to aim at with the beak, to try to p.; also *transf.*; 'Tis not long after But I will weare my heart vpon my sleeue For Dawes to pecke at SHAKS. *P. at* (fig.), to try to pick holes in; to carp or nag at; The Scripture hee pecks at 1641. 3. Little birds..Light on the floor, and p. the table-crumbs 1804.

II. *trans.* To strike (something) with a pick, etc., so as to indent, pit, pierce. †Also *intr.* 1530. Hence **Pecked** (pekt) *ppl. a.* *Pecked line*, a line formed by short strokes thus - - - - - -.

Peck, *v.*[2] Now chiefly *dial.* 1611. [var. of PICK *v.*[2] = PITCH *v.*[1]] **1.** *trans.* To pitch, cast, fling, throw; to jerk. *Obs.* exc. *dial.* **2.** *intr.* To pitch forward; *esp.* of a horse: to stumble through striking the ground with his toe (*dial.* and *colloq.*) 1770.

1. *Hen. VIII*, v. iii. 94. 2. The horse pecked and stumbled, and I fell forward on his neck 1898.

Pecker (pe·kəɹ). 1587. [f. PECK *v.*[1] + -ER [1].] **1.** One who, or that which, pecks; a bird that pecks, as FIG-*p.*, FLOWER-*p.*, etc.; also short for WOODPECKER 1697. **2.** An implement for pecking; a kind of hoe 1587. **3.** *slang.* Courage, resolution. Chiefly in phr. *to keep one's p. up.* 1848.

Peckish (pe·kiʃ), *a. colloq.* 1785. [f. PECK *v.*[1] + -ISH [1].] Disposed to 'peck' or eat; somewhat hungry.

Pecksniff (pe·ksnif). 1844. Name of a character in Dickens's 'Martin Chuzzlewit', represented as an unctuous hypocrite, always prating of benevolence, etc., used allusively. Hence **Pecksni·ffery, Pe·cksniffism. Pecksni·ffian** *a.*

Pectase (pe·kteis). 1866. [f. PECT(IN or PECT(OSE, after *diastase.*] *Chem.* A ferment having the property of converting pectin into pectic and other related acids.

Pectate (pe·ktēt). 1831. [f. PECTIC + -ATE [1].] *Chem.* A salt of pectic acid.

Pecten (pe·kten). *Pl.* **pectines** (pe·ktinīz), **pectens.** late ME. [a. L. *pecten*, *pectin-*, f. *pectere* to comb, cogn. w. Gr. πέκειν to comb.] *Anat.* and *Zool.* †**1.** The metacarpus -1541. **2.** The pubes; also, the pubic bone or share-bone. ? *Obs.* 1661. **3.** Applied to various comb-like structures in animal bodies. **a.** A pigmented vascular process which projects from the choroid coat of the eye into the vitreous humour in birds, and in certain reptiles and fishes; also called *marsupium* 1713. **b.** Each of two comb-like appendages behind the posterior legs in scorpions 1826. **c.** The pectinated structure on the claws of certain birds. **d.** = CTENOPHORE 1. **4.** A genus of bivalve molluscs, having a rounded shell with radiating ribs suggesting the teeth of a comb; an animal of this genus, a scallop 1682.

Pectic (pe·ktik), *a.* 1831. [ad. Gr. πηκτικός, f. πηκτός, congealed, curdled, f. stem πηγ- in πηγνύειν to make firm or solid.] *Chem.* In *p. acid*, a transparent gelatinous substance formed by chemical action from PECTIN, and forming an important constituent of fruit-jellies.

Pectin (pe·ktin). 1838. [f. PECT(IC + -IN [1].] *Chem.* A white neutral substance, soluble in water, formed from PECTOSE by heating with acids, or naturally in the ripening of fruits, and constituting the gelatinizing agent in vegetable juices.

†**Pectinal** (pe·ktinăl), *a.* 1541. [ad. med. L. *pectinalis*, f. L. *pecten, pectin-*; see -AL.] 1. *Anat.* Belonging to the 'pecten' or pubes; *p. bone*, the pubic bone –1541. 2. *Nat. Hist.* Of the nature of or resembling a comb –1705.

Pectinate (pe·ktinět), *a.* 1793. [ad. L. *pectinatus*, f. *pecten* comb; see -ATE [2].] = PECTINATED. Hence **Pe·ctinately** *adv.* like the teeth of a comb.

Pectinate (pe·ktineᶦt), *v.* 1646. [f. L. *pectinat-, pectinare*, f. *pecten* comb.] *trans.* and *intr.* To fit together in alternation like the teeth of two combs; to interlock.

Pectinated (pe·ktineᶦtėd), *ppl. a.* 1671. [f. as PECTINATE *a.* + -ED.] Chiefly *Nat. Hist.* Formed like a comb; having straight narrow closely-set projections or divisions like the teeth of a comb.

Pectination (pektinēᶦ·ʃən). 1646. [f. L. *pectinare* to PECTINATE; see -ATION.] 1. The action of interlocking or condition of being interlocked like the teeth of two combs. ? *Obs.* 2. The condition or character of being pectinated; *concr.* a comb-like structure 1819.

Pectineal (pekti·niˌăl), *a.* 1840. [f. mod. L. *pectineus*, f. *pecten* comb + -AL.] *Anat.* Pertaining to the pecten or pubic bone; applied to certain parts of this bone and connected structures.

‖ **Pectineus** (pekti·niˌŏs). 1704. [mod.L., f. *pectin-* PECTEN.] *Anat.* For *p. musculus*, a flat muscle arising from the pectineal eminence of the pubic bone and inserted into the thigh-bone just behind the small trochanter.

Pectini-, bef. a vowel **pectin-**, comb. form of L. *pecten* comb.

Pe·ctinibranch (-bræŋk), **-bra·nchian, -bra·nchiate** [BRANCHIA], *adjs.* belonging to the *Pectinibranchia* (or *-branchiata*), a family of gastropod molluscs having comb-like gills (also called *Ctenobranchia*); also as *sb.*, a mollusc of this family. **Pe·ctinicorn** [L. *cornu* horn] *a.* having pectinated antennæ, as the division *Pectinicornia* of lamellicorn beetles; *sb.* a beetle of this division. **Pe·ctiniform** *a.*, (*a*) comb-shaped; (*b*) of the form of a scallop (PECTEN 4).

Pectinite (pe·ktinəit). 1677. [f. L. *pectin-* PECTEN + -ITE [1].] *Palæont.* A fossil pecten or scallop.

Pectize (pe·ktəiz), *v.* 1882. [f. Gr. πηκτός fixed, congealed (cf. PECTIC) + -IZE.] *trans.* and *intr.* To change into a gelatinous mass; to congeal.

Pectolite (pe·ktŏləit). 1828. [f. as prec. + -LITE.] *Min.* A whitish or greyish hydrous silicate of calcium and sodium, found in close aggregations of acicular crystals, usually fibrous and radiated in structure.

Pectoral (pe·ktŏrăl), *sb.* and *a.* 1440. [As sb., in sense 1, a. OF. *pectoral*, ad. L. *pectorale* breast-plate, sb. use of adj., f. *pectus* breast; as adj., ad. the L. adj.] **A.** *sb.* 1. Something worn on the breast. **a.** An ornamental breast-plate; *spec.* that worn by the Jewish High Priest (= BREAST-PLATE 2) 1440. **b.** = BREAST-PLATE 1. 1590. †**c.** An ornamental cloth for the breast of a horse –1662. 2. A medicine, food, or drink, good for affections of the chest, i. e. the lungs, etc. 1601. 3. *Anat.* Short for *p. muscle, p. fin* 1758. **B.** *adj.* 1. Of, pertaining to, situated or occurring in or upon, the breast or chest; thoracic. Chiefly *Anat.* 1578. 2. *Med.* Of a medicine, food, or drink: Good for diseases or affections of the chest (or, loosely, the internal organs generally) 1576. 3. Worn, or to be worn, on the breast; as the *p. cross* of a bishop. 1616. 4. *fig.* Proceeding from the 'breast' or 'heart' 1630.

1. *P. arch* or *girdle*, the shoulder-girdle (see GIRDLE *sb.*[1] 4. a.). *P. fins*, the pair of lateral fins attached to the pectoral arch in fishes. *P. muscles*, the muscles of the chest, esp. the *pectoralis major* and the *pectoralis minor*. 2. Some p. physick to ease his cough 1637. 4. His words are then so pithy and so pectorall 1633. Hence **Pe·ctorally** *adv.* (*rare*), in a p. manner or position.

Pectoriloquy (pektŏri·lŏkwi). 1834. [ad. F. *pectoriloquie*, f. L. *pectus, pector-* breast + *-loquium* speaking.] *Path.* The transmission of the sound of the voice through the wall of the chest to the ear in auscultation; usu. a sign of a cavity or some other affection in the lung. So **Pectorilo·quial, Pectori·loquous** *adjs.* of, or of the nature of, p. 1824. **Pectori·loquism,** pectoriloquy 1820.

Pectose (pe·ktōᵘs). 1857. [f. PECT(IC + -OSE.] *Chem.* An insoluble substance related to cellulose and occurring with it in vegetable tissues, esp. in unripe fruits; by the action of acids, etc. it is converted into PECTIN. Hence **Pectosic** (pektǫ·sik) *a.*, in *pectosic acid*, an acid formed immediately from pectin by the action of alkalis, etc., and converted by further action of the same into pectic acid.

Pectous (pe·ktəs), *a.* 1861. [f. as PECTIZE + -OUS.] *Chem.* **a.** Congealed, solidified; said of substances normally fluid. **b.** Related to pectin. *P. acid*, an acid related to pectic acid.

‖ **Pectus** (pe·ktŏs). *Pl.* **pectora** (pe·ktŏră). 1693. [L.] *Anat.* and *Zool.* **a.** The breast or chest. **b.** *Entom.* The lower surface of the thorax or prothorax of an insect.

Peculate (pe·kiŭleᶦt), *v.* 1749. [f. L. *peculat-, peculari* to embezzle, f. *peculium* private property, f. *pecu* cattle, money.] †1. *trans.* To rob (the state or country) by peculation –1749. 2. To embezzle or pilfer (money) 1802. Also *intr.* So **Pe·culator,** an embezzler, esp. of public money or property 1656.

Peculation (pekiŭlēᶦ·ʃən). 1658. [f. L. *peculari* to PECULATE; see -ATION.] The appropriation of public money or property by one in an official position; the embezzlement of money or goods entrusted to his care.

Peculiar (pĭkiū·liăɹ), *a.* and *sb.* 1460. [a. obs. F. *peculier*, or ad. L. *peculiaris* of or relating to private property, f. *peculium* (see PECULATE *v.*).] **A.** *adj.* 1. That is one's own private property; that belongs exclusively to an individual person, place, thing, or group. Const. with preceding possessive, or with *to.* †2. Of separate constitution or existence; independent, particular, individual; single –1799. 3. Particular, special 1590. 4. Unlike others, singular, strange, odd, queer 1608.

1. All other goods by fortune's hand are giv'n, A Wife is the p. gift of heav'n POPE. A timidity p. to your sex 1766. †*P. institution*, a cant phrase in U.S. for negro slavery. 2. The single and p. life is bound ..To keepe it selfe from noyance SHAKS. 3. A more proper subject of p. taxation ADAM SMITH. 4. Mr. Weller's knowledge of London was extensive and p. DICKENS. A girl of p. temper 1888.

Phrases. *P. jurisdiction* (*authority*, etc.), in *Canon Law*, a jurisdiction proper to itself, exempt from the jurisdiction of the bishop of the diocese. *P. measure* (in hymns, etc.), any metre other than Common, Long, or Short. *P. People*, (*a*) the Jews, as God's own chosen people; hence *transf.*; (*b*) A religious denomination founded in 1838, holding the plenary inspiration of Scripture and practising baptism of believers and divine healing. †*In p.*, as a peculiarity.

B. *sb.* (the adj. used absol.) **I.** *gen.* 1. **a.** A property or privilege exclusively one's own 1650. †**b.** = *P. people*: said of the Jews, and of Christian believers –1659. †2. A peculiarity –1750. **II.** Spec. and techn. 1. *Eccl.* A parish or church exempt from the jurisdiction of the ordinary or bishop in whose diocese it lies 1562. **b.** *transf.* and *fig.* A place, district, office, etc. exempt from ordinary jurisdiction 1591. 2. **a.** A nickname in Oxford (*c* 1837-8) for members of the Evangelical party 1837. **b.** One of the Peculiar People 1876.

1. *Court of Peculiars*, a branch of the Court of Arches having jurisdiction over the peculiars of the archbishop of Canterbury. 2. **a.** 'Puseyites and Peculiars' stood shoulder to shoulder 1895. Hence **Pecu·liar-ly** *adv.*, **-ness** (now *rare*).

Peculiarity (pĭkiūliˌæ·rĭti). 1610. [f. prec. + -ITY.] †1. Exclusive possession; private ownership BP. HALL. 2. The quality of being peculiar to a single person or thing; also, that which is peculiar to a single person or thing 1646. †3. A particular liking; a partiality –1847. †**b.** Special attentiveness to a person RICHARDSON. 4. The quality of being *sui generis*; singularity, oddity; an odd trait or characteristic 1751. †5. The doctrine or practices of 'Peculiars' (see PECULIAR B. II. 2. a.) *rare.* –1838.

2. We shall speak first of those things wherein they agree; and of their peculiarities afterwards 1726. 4. There is another..p. about Mr. Talfourd; he can't spell 1817.

Peculiarize (pĭkiū·liărəiz), *v.* 1624. [f. as prec. + -IZE.] *trans.* To make peculiar; †to appropriate exclusively *to* –1704.

‖ **Peculium** (pĭkiū·liŏm). 1681. [L. = private property, f. *pecu* cattle.] 1. *Rom. Law.* The property which a father allowed his child, or a master his slave, to hold as his own 1706. 2. A private or exclusive possession, property, or appurtenance.

2. This is the p. of blame, which your lordship has portioned out to me, and separated from the common stock BURKE.

†**Pecu·nial,** *a.* late ME. [ad. L. *pecunialis*, f. *pecunia* money.] 1. = PECUNIARY *a.* 1. **b.** Having to do with pecuniary penalties. –1726. 2. = PECUNIARY *a.* 2. –1530.

Pecuniarily (pĭkiū·niărili), *adv.* 1614. [f. next + -LY [2].] In a pecuniary manner; in respect of money; †by exaction of money.

Pecuniary (pĭkiū·niări), *a.* (*sb.*) 1502. [ad. L. *pecuniarius*, f. *pecunia*; see -ARY [1]. In F. *pécuniaire.*] 1. Consisting of money; exacted in money. **b.** Of an offence or law: Having a money penalty 1610. 2. Of, belonging to, or having relation to money 1623. 3. Of which money is the object 1672. †**B.** *sb.* Money; *pl.* resources in money; money matters –1767.

A. 1. P. aids STUBBS. 2. Paltry p. difficulties EMERSON. 3. P. Matches SIR T. BROWNE.

Pecunious (pĭkiū·niəs), *a.* Now *rare.* late ME. [ad. L. *pecuniosus*, f. *pecunia*; see -OUS. Cf. F. †*pécunieux.*] Well provided with money. So **Pecunio·sity,** the state of being p. 1883.

Ped. late ME. [Origin unkn.] A wicker pannier; a hamper with a lid.

Pedage (pe·dėdʒ). *Obs.* exc. *Hist.* late ME. [ad. med.L. *pedagium*, for earlier L. *pedaticum*; see PEAGE.] = PEAGE.

Pedagogic (pedăgǫ·dʒik), *a.* and *sb.* 1781. [mod. f. L. *pædagogicus*, a. Gr. παιδαγωγικός, f. παιδαγωγός pedagogue; see -IC. So F. *pédagogique.*] **A.** *adj.* Of, pertaining to, or characteristic of a pedagogue or pedagogy; having the office or character of a pedagogue. **B.** *sb.* (usu. *pl.* Pedagogics.) The science, art, or principles of pedagogy 1864. So **Pedago·gical** *a.* 1619, **-ly** *adv.*

Pedagogue (pe·dăgǫg), *sb.* late ME. [a. OF. *pedagoge, pedagogue*, ad. L. *pædagogus*, a. Gr. παιδαγωγός, f. παῖς, παιδ- boy + ἀγωγός leader.] 1. A man having the oversight of a child or youth; an attendant who led a boy to school. *Obs.* exc. in ref. to ancient times. 1483. †Also *fig.* –1653. 2. A schoolmaster, teacher, preceptor. (Now usu. hostile, with implication of pedantry, dogmatism, or severity.) late ME.

1. *fig.* S. Paul teaching that the whole law was a p. guiding men to Christ 1609. 2. A Welsh schoolmaster, a good scholar but a very p. PEPYS. Hence **Pe·dagogue** *v.* to instruct as a p.

Pedagoguism, pedagogism (pe·dăgǫg-i·z'm, -gǫdʒi·z'm). 1642. [f. prec. + -ISM.] The character, spirit, or office of a pedagogue: the system of pedagogy.

This tetter of Pedagoguisme MILT.

Pedagogy (pe·dăgǫgi, -goᵘdʒi, -gǫdʒi). Also pædagogy. 1583. [a. F. *pédagogie*, ad. Gr. παιδαγωγία office of a παιδαγωγός; see PEDAGOGUE.] 1. The function, profession, or practice of a pedagogue; pedagogics 1623. 2. *fig.* Instruction, discipline, training; a means or system of introductory training. (Cf. *Gal.* iii. 24.) 1583. 3. A place of instruction; a school or college. (Also *fig.*) *Obs.* exc. *Hist.* 1625.

Pedal (pe·dăl), *sb.* 1611. [app. a. F. *pédale*, ad. It. *pedale* a foot, footstool, footstalk, stock of a tree, etc., f. L. *pedalis* adj.; see next.] 1. A lever worked by the foot, in various musical instruments, and with various functions.

a. In the organ: (*a*) Each of the (wooden) keys played upon by the feet, together constituting the *p. keyboard* or *p.-board*, and usu. operating upon a separate set of pipes of bass tone (*p.-pipes*) forming the *p. organ* (see ORGAN *sb.* 2 d). (*b*) A foot-lever for drawing a number of stops out or in at once, or for other purposes. (*c*) Short for *p. organ* or *keyboard*. **b.** In the pianoforte, etc.: (*a*) A foot-lever for raising the dampers from the strings, thus rendering the tone fuller (*damper p.*, also loosely called *loud* or *forte p.*). (*b*) One for softening the tone (*soft* or *piano p.*). (*c*) Any one of various others occasionally used for sustaining or otherwise modifying the tone, or for special effects.

2. A lever worked by the foot in various machines; a treadle; *esp.* in a bicycle or tricycle 1789. 3. *Mus.* A note sustained (or reiterated) in one part, usu. in the bass, through a succession of harmonies some of which are independent of it; in organ-music usu. sustained by holding down a pedal 1854. 4. *Geom.* A curve or surface which is the locus of the feet of the perpendiculars let fall from a fixed point (the *p. origin* or *pole*) upon the tangents to a given curve or surface 1863.

attrib. and *Comb.* Of, belonging to, connected with, worked by, having, or constituting a p. or pedals (in sense 1 or 2), as *p. action, harp, key, keyboard, mechanism*, etc.; played upon the pedals of an organ, or constituting or involving a p. (in sense 3), as *p. bass, note, passage*; in *Geom.* relating to a p. curve or surface; **p.-board** (see 1 a); **-piano**, a pianoforte fitted with a pedal-board like that of an organ; **-point** = sense 3.

Pedal (pe·dăl, pī·dăl), *a.* 1625. [ad. L. *pedalis*, f. *pes, ped-* foot; see -AL. (Pronounced pī·dăl only in senses 1, 1 b.)] 1. Of, pertaining to, or connected with the foot or feet (*rare* in *gen.* sense). b. *Anat.* and *Zool.*: usu. in reference to the foot or *podium* of a mollusc 1851. 2. *Geom.* Relating to the feet of perpendiculars; of or pertaining to the pedal of a curve or surface 1863. 3. *Mus.* That is, or relates to, a pedal or pedals; see PEDAL *sb.* 1, 3.

2. *P. curve* or *surface* = PEDAL *sb.* 4. *P. origin, pole*: see PEDAL *sb.* 4.

Pedal (pe·dăl), *a.*[2] 1887. [ad. It. *pedale* stem of a plant.] Applied to the lower and thicker part of a kind of straw grown in Italy for plaiting; *ellipt.*, a plait made with this straw.

Pedal (pe·dăl), *v.* 1866. [f. PEDAL *sb.*] *intr.* a. To play upon the pedals of an organ. b. To work the pedals of a bicycle 1888.

Pedalier (pedălīə·ɪ). 1881. [a. F. *pédalier*, f. *pédale* PEDAL *sb.*] The pedal keyboard of an organ; similar pedals attached to a pianoforte.

Pedant (pe·dănt), *sb.* (*a.*) 1588. [a. F. *pédant* or It. *pedante* teacher, etc. Origin unkn.] †1. A schoolmaster, teacher, or tutor –1704. 2. A person who overrates book-learning or technical knowledge, or parades it; one who has mere learning without practical judgement; one who lays excessive stress upon details or upon strict adherence to formal rules; occas., one who is possessed by a theory, a doctrinaire 1596. 3. *attrib.* or *adj.* That is a pedant; of or pertaining to a pedant; pedantic 1616.

1. Like a P. that keepes a Schoole i'th Church SHAKS. 2. A Man who has been brought up among Books, and is able to talk of nothing else, is..what we call a P. ADDISON.

†**Peda·nte, -a·ntie, -a·nty.** 1593. [app. a. It. *pedante* PEDANT.] 1. = PEDANT –1630. 2. A company of pedants MILT.

Pedantic (pĭdæ·ntik), *a.* 1600. [f. PEDANT or It. *pedante* + -IC.] Having the character of, or characteristic of, a pedant; characterized by or exhibiting pedantry.

He does not..sacrifice sense and spirit to p. refinements MACAULAY. So **Peda·ntical** *a.* (now *rare*) 1588, **-ly** *adv.* **Peda·nticism**, a p. expression or notion; a piece of pedantry. **Peda·nticly** *adv.* (now *rare*).

Pedantism (pe·dăntiz'm). Now *rare.* 1593. [f. PEDANT + -ISM.] †1. The office or authority of a schoolmaster; the state of being under a schoolmaster, pupillage. Also *fig.* –1658. 2. Pedantic phraseology, treatment, or method; pedantry 1593. 3. With *a* and *pl.* A piece of pedantry 1656.

3. History-Books, opulent in nugatory pedantisms CARLYLE.

Pedantize (pe·dăntəiz), *v.* 1611. [f. as prec. + -IZE.] 1. *intr.* To play the pedant; to speak or write pedantically. Also *to p. it.* 2. *trans.* To turn into a pedant; to make pedants 1734.

Pedantocracy (pedăntǫ·krăsi). 1859. [f. PEDANT + -OCRACY; app. coined (in F. form) by J. S. Mill.] A system of government by pedants; a governing body of pedants. So **Peda·ntocrat. Pedantocra·tic** *a.*

Pedantry (pe·dăntri). 1612. [ad. It. *pedanteria*, f. *pedante*; see PEDANT and -RY.] 1. The character, habit of mind, or mode of proceeding, characteristic of a pedant; mere learning without judgement; unseasonable display of learning or technical knowledge. b. with *pl.* A piece of pedantry 1656. 2. Undue insistence on forms or details; slavish adherence to rule, theory, or precedent 1845.

1. P. proceeds from much Reading and little Understanding STEELE. That men are frighted at Female p. is very certain 1766.

Pedarian (pĭdēə·riăn), *a.* and *sb.* 1753. [f. L. *pedarius* of or belonging to a foot, of a foot long, f. *pes, ped-* foot; see -ARY[1] and -AN.] *Rom. Antiq.* A. *adj.* Applied to Roman senators of an inferior grade, who had no vote of their own, but could merely signify their assent to that of another. B. *sb.* A pedarian senator.

Pedate (pe·dēˈt), *a.* 1760. [ad. L. *pedatus* having feet, f. *pedem* foot; see -ATE[2].] *Nat. Hist.* 1. Having divisions like toes, or like the claws of a bird's foot; *spec.* in *Bot.* applied to a compound or lobed leaf having a slender midrib passing through the central leaflet or lobe, and two thicker lateral ribs which branch at successive points to form the midribs of the lateral leaflets. Applied also to the venation of a simple leaf when thus arranged. So †**Pedated.** 2. *Zool.* Furnished with feet 1816. 3. *Anat.* Expanded (at the end) like a foot 1870. **Pe·dately** *adv.*

Pedati-, comb. form of L. *pedatus* PEDATE, in adjs. relating to leaves: **Pedatifid** (pĭdæ·tifid) [L. *-fidus* split], pedately cleft or divided at least half-way to the base; **Pedatipa·rtite** (pĭdēˈti-) [PARTITE], pedately divided nearly to the base; so **Peda·tisect, Pedatise·cted** (pĭdēˈti-) [L. *sectus* cut]; etc.

Peddle (pe·d'l), *v.* 1532. [In I, app. back-formation from *pedler* PEDLAR; in II perh. alteration of PIDDLE *v.*] I. 1. *intr.* To follow the occupation of a pedlar; to go about carrying small wares for sale. 2. *trans.* To trade or deal in as a pedlar; to carry about and offer for sale. Chiefly *U.S.* 1837. b. *fig.* To deal out in small quantities; to 'retail' 1837.

2. b. Going around peddling his griefs in private ears 1864.

II. *intr.* To busy oneself with trifles; to trifle, dally. (Cf. PIDDLE *v.*) 1597. b. *trans.* with *away*: To fritter away on trifles 1880. So **Pe·ddling** *vbl. sb.* the occupation of a pedlar; also, dealing in trifles or in a trifling manner.

Peddling (pe·dliŋ), *ppl. a.* 1532. [See PEDDLE *v.* and -ING[2].] 1. Plying the trade of a pedlar; going about with small goods for sale. 2. a. Of persons: Busying oneself with trifles, or in a trifling way. b. Of things: Trifling, contemptible, petty, trashy 1597.

2. Poor p. Dilettantism CARLYLE. Hence **Pe·ddlingly** *adv.*

Pederast, etc.: see PÆDERAST, etc.

‖**Pedesis** (pĭdī·sis). 1878. [a. Gr. πήδησις leaping.] A name given to the *Brownian movement* of minute particles; see BROWNIAN *a.*

Pedestal (pe·dĕstăl), *sb.* 1563. [a. F. *piédestal*, ad. It. *piedestallo*, †*piedistallo*, i. e. *pie di stallo* foot of a stall, f. *piè, piede* foot + *stallo* stall, hovel, shed, stable. In Eng. refash. after L. *pedem.*] 1. The base supporting a column or pillar in construction; the base of an obelisk, statue, vase, or the like; also, each of the two supports of a knee-hole writing-table. 2. A base, support, foundation 1591. 3. *techn.* †a. On a railway, the 'chair' used to support the rails, or a base to support the chair; b. an axle-guard or horn-plate; c. the standard or each of the standards or supports of various machines or pieces of mechanism; e.g. the standard of a pillow-block, etc. 1774.

2. Self-denial and Mortification, which are the P. of the Crosse JER. TAYLOR. Fain would he make the world his p. YOUNG.

attrib. and *Comb.*: **p.-coil, -coiler**, an upright coil of steam-pipe for use as a radiator; **-cover**, the cap of a pillow-block; **-table**, one with a massive central support or foot. Hence **Pe·destal** *v. trans.* to set or support upon a p.; to furnish with a p. (*lit.* and *fig.*). **Pe·destalled, -aled** *a.* provided with, set upon, or having a p.

Pedestrial (pĭde·striăl), *a.* 1611. [f. L. *pedester* on foot, going on foot (f. *pes, ped-* foot) + -AL.] †1. = PEDESTRIAN –1634. 2. Fitted for walking, as the *p. legs* of a crab 1890. Hence **Pede·strially** *adv.*

Pedestrian (pĭde·striăn), *a.* and *sb.* 1716. [f. L. *pedester* (see prec.) + -AN.] A. *adj.* 1. On foot, going on foot; performed on foot; of or pertaining to walking 1791. b. Of a statue: Representing a person on foot 1822. 2. [After L. *pedester*, Gr. πεζός] Applied to plain prose as opposed to verse; prosaic, commonplace 1716.

1. A p. tour WORDSW. 2. P. Muses BYRON. Verse ..of a very p. order 1888.

B. *sb.* One who goes or travels on foot; a walker 1793. Hence **Pede·strianism,** the practice of a p., walking; prosaic or commonplace quality or style. **Pede·strianize** *v. intr.* (also with *it*) to act the pedestrian; to go or travel on foot; to walk 1811.

†**Pede·strious,** *a.* 1646. [f. L. *pedester* + -OUS.] Going on foot –1822.

Pedetentous (pedĭte·ntəs), *a. rare.* 1837. [f. L. *pedetentim* step by step + -OUS.] Proceeding step by step; advancing cautiously.

Pedetic (pĭde·tik), *a.* 1878. [ad. Gr. πηδητικός, f. πηδητής leaper; cf. PEDESIS.] Of or pertaining to pedesis.

Pedi-, comb. form of L. *pes, pedem* foot, as in L. *pedisequus*, Eng. *pedicure*, etc.

Pe·diform, *a.* having the form of a foot; said chiefly of the organs of insects. **Pedigerous** (pĭdi·dʒĕrəs), *a.* bearing feet or legs.

Pediad (pe·diæd), *a.* 1899. [ad. Gr. πεδιάς, -άδα adj. flat, level, f. πεδίον PEDION.] *Cryst.* Of, pertaining to, or consisting of pedia.

Pedicel (pe·disĕl). 1676. [ad. mod.L. *pedicellus*, dim. of *pediculus* little foot, footstalk, dim. of *pes, ped-* foot. In mod.F. *pédicelle.*] 1. *Bot.* A small stalk or stalk-like structure in a plant; *esp.* each of the subordinate stalks which immediately bear the flowers in a branched inflorescence (the main stalk being the *peduncle*); also, a small peduncle. 2. *Zool.* and *Anat.* Applied to various small stalk-like structures in animals (mostly also called PEDUNCLE) 1826.

a. In insects, the third joint of an antenna; also, the basal joint of the abdomen when long and slender. b. The eye-stalk in some Crustacea, etc. c. The stalk by which a brachiopod, etc., is attached. d. Each of the ambulacral feet of an echinoderm. e. The PEDICLE of a vertebra.

3. *attrib.*, as *p.-cell*, a cell forming a p. 1882. Hence **Pedice·llar** *a.* pertaining to, or of the nature of, a p. **Pe·dicelled, -eled** *a.* pedicellate.

‖ **Pedicellaria** (pe:disĕlēə·riă). *Pl.* **-æ.** 1872. [mod.L., f. *pedicellus* PEDICEL.] *Zool.* In echinoderms, Each of a number of small pincer-like organs, with two, three, or four valves, on the outside of the body, usually among and around the spines.

Pedicellate (pe·disĕlēˈt), *a.* 1824. [f. mod.L. *pedicellus* PEDICEL + -ATE[2].] *Bot.* and *Zool.* Having a pedicel or pedicels; *spec.* in *Zool.* belonging to the division *Pedicellata* of echinoderms. So **Pe·dicellated** *a.* 1821. **Pedicella·tion**, the condition of being p.

Pedicle (pe·dik'l). 1626. [ad. L. *pediculus* footstalk, dim. of *pes, ped-* foot; see -CULE.] *Nat. Hist.*, etc. 1. *Bot.* A small stalk, footstalk, pedicel; formerly, the stalk of a leaf (= *petiole*), or of a flower or fruit (= *peduncle*); now usu., a minute stalk-like support, as those of seeds, glands, etc. 2. *Zool.*, etc. A small stalk; a pedicel or peduncle.

spec. a. *Path.* A stalk by which a tumour, etc., is attached to a part of the body. b. *Anat.* Each of the two narrow thickened parts of a vertebra connecting the centrum with the lamina. c. *Zool.* The process of bone supporting the horn of a deer, etc. 1753. Hence **Pe·dicled** *a.* having a p., pediculated.

Pedicular (pĭdi·kiŭlăɪ), *a.* 1660. [ad. L. *pedicularis*, f. *pediculus* louse. Cf. F. *pédiculaire.*] Of or pertaining to a louse or lice; lousy.

Pediculate (pĭdi·kiŭlēˈt), *a.* (*sb.*) 1857. [f. L. *pediculus* footstalk + -ATE[2].] *Nat. Hist.* 1. = next. 2. Belonging to the group *Pediculati* of teleost fishes, characterized by the elongated basis of the pectoral fins, resembling an arm. Also as *sb.* A member of this group. 1880.

Pediculated (pĭdi·kiŭlēˈtĕd), *a.* 1822. [f. as prec. + -ED[2].] Having, or borne upon, a pedicle; stalked. (Chiefly in *Path.* of morbid growths.)

Pedicula·tion. 1719. [ad. late L. *pediculationem*, f. *pediculus* louse; see -ATION.] *Path.* = PEDICULOSIS.

‖**Pediculo·sis.** 1890. [f. L. *pediculus* louse + -OSIS.] *Path.* Phthiriasis.

Pediculous (pĭdi·kiŭləs), *a.* 1550. [ad. L. *pediculosus*, f. *pediculus* louse.] Infested with lice, lousy; also, of or pertaining to a louse, or characterized by lice.

Pedicure (pe·dikiuəɹ), *sb.* 1842. [a. F. *pédicure*, f. L. *pes, pedi-* foot + *curare* to take care of.] 1. One whose business is the surgical care and treatment of the feet. 2. The surgical treatment of the feet, esp. in the removal or cure of corns, bunions, etc. 1863. So **Pe·dicure** *v.* to cure or treat (the feet) by the removal of corns, etc. **Pe·dicurism**, the art of a p. **Pe·dicurist** = sense 1.

Pedigree (pe·digrī). late ME. [In 15th c. *pedegru, pee-de-grew*, etc., app. AF. forms = F. *pié (pied) de grue* crane's foot; so called 'from a three-line mark (like the broad arrow) used in denoting succession in pedigrees' (Skeat).] 1. A genealogical stemma or table; a genealogy drawn up in tabular form. 2. One's line of ancestors; ancestry; descent 1440. b. Of animals 1608. c. *transf.* Origin, line of succession; etymological descent 1566. 3. (Without article.) Descent in the abstract; esp. ancient descent; 'birth' 1460. 4. A line of succession; *loosely*, a long series or 'string' of people 1532. 5. *attrib.* and *Comb.* Of, pertaining to, or having a recorded line of descent, as *p. cattle*, etc. 1863.

1. I wish..you would make a p. for me 1711. 2. Who had no better cover for his sordid extraction than a Welch pedegrew SIDNEY. c. The origin and p. of our moral judgments 1833. 3. Vertue lieth not in P. HOBBES. 5. Pedigree-mongers nowadays invent pedigrees 1871. Hence **Pe·digreed** *a.* having a recorded p., as cattle.

‖**Pediluvium** (pedil*i*ū·vi*ɒ*m). *Pl.* **-ia.** 1693. [med. or mod.L., f. *pes, pedi-* foot + *-luvium* washing, f. *luere* to wash.] A foot-bath; a washing of feet. Also *attrib.* Hence **Pedilu·vial** *a.*; also *sb. pl.* ceremonies connected with the washing of feet (as a religious act).

Pedimane (pe·dimēⁱn). 1835. [a. F. *pédimane*, f. L. *pes, pedi-* foot + *manus* hand.] *Zool.* A pedimanous quadruped (see next).

Pedimanous (pĭdi·mănəs), *a.* 1839. [f. as prec. + -OUS.] *Zool.* Having feet like hands; applied to the lemurs and opossums in ref. to their hind feet.

Pediment (pe·dimĕnt). 1592. [An alteration of *periment, peremint*, perh. a workman's corruption of *pyramid*.] 1. The triangular part, resembling a low gable, crowning the front of a building in the Grecian style of architecture, esp. over a portico. Also, a similarly-placed member in the Roman and Renaissance styles. Hence, in *Decorative art*, Any member of similar form and position, as one placed over the opening in an ironwork screen, etc. 2. Referred to L. *pes (ped-)* 'foot', and used for: A base, foundation; a pavement 1726. Hence **Pe·dimented** *a.* having a p.; formed with or made like a p.

Pedime·ntal, *a.* 1851. [f. prec. + -AL.] 1. Of or pertaining to a pediment, of the nature of a pediment. b. Shaped like a pediment, rising to a vertical angle 1890. 2. Of or pertaining to a pedestal (see PEDIMENT 2). G. MEREDITH.

Pedion (pe·di*ǫ*n). *Pl.* **pedia.** 1899. [a. Gr. πεδίον a plane, a flat surface.] *Cryst.* A term for any face of an anorthic crystal, each face being bounded by a set of faces of which no two are necessarily parallel, and which are connected only by a law of rational indices.

Pedipalp (pe·dipælp). Also in L. form **pedipalpus**, pl. **-i.** 1826. [ad. mod.L. *Pedipalpi* sb.pl., f. L. *pes, pedi-* foot + *palpus* PALP.] *Zool.* 1. An arachnid of the group *Pedipalpi*, distinguished by large pincer-like palps; formerly including the true scorpions, now only the *Phrynidæ* and *Thelyphonidæ*, or whip-scorpions 1835. 2. Each of a pair of palps or feelers attached to the head just in front of the ambulatory limbs in most Arachnids; in some cases large and pincer-like or chelate 1826. Hence **Pedipa·lpal** *a.* **Pedipa·lpate** *a.* provided with pedipalps. **Pedipa·lpous** *a.* belonging to the group *Pedipalpi* (see 1); having large pedipalps.

Pedlar (pe·dlaɹ), *sb.* Also *U.S.* **ped(d)ler.** late ME. [Origin obsc. Cf. earlier *pedder*.] 1. One who goes about carrying small goods for sale (usu. in a bundle or *pack*); a travelling chapman. (Cf. HAWKER.) Also *fig.* 2. One who peddles, or works in a petty, incompetent, or ineffective way 1585. 3. *attrib.* 1553.

1. All as a poore pedler he did wend, Bearing a trusse of tryfles at hys backe SPENSER.

Comb. **Pedlar's French,** rogues' and thieves' cant; hence, unintelligible jargon, gibberish.

Pedlary (pe·dləri), *sb.* (*a.*) 1530. [f. prec. + -Y³; cf. *beggary*.] **A.** *sb.* 1. The business or practice of a pedlar. Also *fig.* 1604. b. Pedlars' wares 1593. 2. Trifling practices or things; trumpery, trash, rubbish 1530. **B.** *attrib.* or as *adj.* Pedlar's 1550. *fig.* Peddling, trashy –1674.

A. 2. Ear-confession and pardons, with like p. 1530.

Pedo-: see PÆDO-.

Pedology (pĭd*ǫ*·lŏdʒi). 1925. [f. Gr. πέδον ground + -LOGY.] The science of soils.

Pedometer (pĭd*ǫ*·mĭtəɹ). 1723. [ad. F. *pédomètre*, hybrid f. *pedo-* for L. *pedi-* PEDI- + Gr. μέτρον measure, -METER.] An instrument for recording the number of steps taken, and thus approximately measuring the distance travelled on foot; usu. resembling a watch, having a dial-plate marked with numbers, round which a pointer or index-hand travels. Hence **Pedome·tric, -al** *adjs.* of, pertaining to, or of the nature of, a p.; **-ly** *adv.*

Pedomotive (pe·dŏmōᵘtiv), *a.* and *sb.* 1824. [erron. f. *pedo-* for PEDI- + MOTIVE; cf. *locomotive*.] (A vehicle) actuated by the foot or feet.

Pedrail (pe·drēⁱl). 1902. [f. L. *pes, pedem* foot + RAIL *sb.*²] A device for facilitating progress of heavy vehicles over rough ground by attachment of broad foot-like supporting surfaces to the wheel-rims.

‖**Pedregal** (pedrega·l, pe·dregăl). Also *erron.* **pedra-.** 1839. [Sp. *pedregal* a stony place, f. *piedra* stone = L. *petra*.] In Mexico and s.w. U.S., a rough and rocky tract; an old lava-field. Also *transf.* an ice-field.

Pedrero (pedrē·ro). Now *Hist.* 1440. [a. Sp. *pedrero*, repr. L. type **petrarius, -um*, in med.L. *petraria* a stone-throwing engine, f. *petrarius*, adj., f. *petra* stone.] A piece of ordnance orig. for discharging stones, formerly also broken iron, etc., and for firing salutes.

Peduncle (pĭd*ɒ*·ŋk'l). 1753. [ad. mod.L. *pedunculus* footstalk, dim. of *pedem, pes* foot.] 1. *Bot.* The stalk of a flower or fruit, or of a cluster of flowers or fruits; the primary stalk, or one of the general stalks of an inflorescence, which bears either a solitary flower, a number of sessile flowers, or a number of subordinate stalks (*pedicels*) directly bearing the flowers. (Dist. from a leaf-stalk or *petiole*.) 2. *Zool.*, etc. A stalk or stalk-like process in an animal body, either normal or morbid; = PEDICEL 2 a, b, c, PEDICLE 2 a; also, applied to several bundles of nerve-fibres in the brain, connecting one part of it with another 1797. So **Pedu·ncled** *a.* pedunculate. **Pedu·ncular** *a.* (*Nat. Hist.*) of, pertaining to, or of the nature of, a p.

Pedunculate (pĭd*ɒ*·ŋkiŭlĕt), *a.* 1760. [ad. mod.L. *pedunculatus*, f. *pedunculus*; see prec. and -ATE².] *Nat. Hist.* Having a peduncle or peduncles; supported by a peduncle; stalked. So **Pedu·nculated** *a.* 1752.

†**Pee**, *sb.*¹ 1483. [= late MDu. *pîe* (now *pij*) coat of coarse woollen stuff; found from 14th c. in *courtepy* = Du. *korte pîe* short coat of this kind; history obsc. Now only in PEA-COAT, PEA-JACKET.] A coat of coarse cloth worn by men, esp. in the 16th c. –1635.

Pee (pī), *sb.*² 1653. [History unkn.] *Mining.* The portion common to two veins which intersect.

Pee, *sb.*³ 1747. [Cf. PEA³.] *Mining.* A small piece of ore.

Pee (pī), *v.* 1788. To urinate. Also *sb.*

Peek (pīk), *v.* [ME. *pike, pyke*; origin unkn., but cf. PEEP *v.*² and KEEK (ME. *kike*).] *intr.* To look through a crevice, or out of or into a recess, etc.; to peer, peep, pry, look *in* or *out*. Hence **Peek** *sb.* a peep, a glance 1844.

Peek-bo, peek-a-boo. Now chiefly *U.S.* 1599. [f. PEEK *v.*] = BO-PEEP, PEEP-BO.

Peel (pīl), *sb.*¹ [ME. *pel, pele* = AF. *pel*, OF. *piel* (mod.F. *pieu*) stake:—L. *palus, palum*.] †1. A stake (*rare*). ME. only. †2. A palisade formed of stakes; a stockade; a stockaded or palisaded (and moated) enclosure –1596. †3. A castle; esp. a small castle or tower –1679. 4. The general name, in modern writers, for the massive square towers or fortified dwellings built in the 16th c. in the border counties of England and Scotland, for defence against forays 1726. 5. Hence, the proper name of a place in the Isle of Man 1718. 6. *attrib.*, as **p.-house, -tower** = sense 4. 1505.

Peel (pīl), *sb.*² [late ME. a. OF. *pele* (mod. F. *pelle* shovel):—L. *pala* spade, shovel, etc.] 1. A shovel or shovel-shaped instrument. 2. *spec.* A baker's shovel for thrusting loaves, pies, etc. into the oven and withdrawing them from it. late ME. 3. *Printing.* A T-shaped instrument used to hang up damp freshly printed sheets to dry 1683. 4. The blade or wash of an oar. *U.S.* 1875.

Peel (pīl), *sb.*³ 1583. [var. of PILL *sb.*¹, after PEEL *v.*] The rind or outer coating of any fruit; esp. in *orange-, lemon-, citron-p.*; **candied p.**, the candied rind of species of *Citrus*, esp. the citron.

Peel (pīl), *v.* ME. [var. of PILL *v.*¹, in later use appropriated to the sense 'decorticate'.] †I. To pillage. *trans.* = PILL *v.*¹ 1. –1732. II. To decorticate, strip. 1. To strip anything of its outer layer, as an orange, potato, etc., of its skin or rind, a tree of its bark; also usu. with *off*, to strip off (skin, bark, etc.). late ME. b. To make by peeling 1885. 2. *intr.* Of trees, animal bodies, etc.: To become bare of bark, skin, etc.; to cast the epidermis as after a fever. Of skin or bark: To become detached, scale off. Also b. To admit of being peeled or barked. 1599. 3. *absol.* or *intr.* To strip, as for exercise, etc. (Now *slang* or *colloq.*) 1785.

1. b. And Jacob took him rods of fresh poplar..and peeled [*A. V.* pilled] white strakes in them *Gen.* xxx. 37 (R. V.). 2. b. A meanes to make them peele better 1641. 3. He began to p., as the boxers call it MARRYAT.

Peeled (pīld), *ppl. a.* 1470. [f. prec. + -ED¹. See also PILLED.] 1. Stripped of possessions, plundered 1508. 2. = PILLED *ppl. a.* 2. 1470. 3. Worn threadbare, as a garment; bare of herbage, as ground. b. *transf.* Beggarly, mean, wretched. 1510. 4. Stripped of skin, bark, rind, etc. 1725. 5. Phr. *Scattered and peeled* (Isa. xviii. 2), prob. a mistranslation; but *peeled* has been vaguely associated with one or more of the senses above 1611.

1. Is thy land p., thy realm marauded? EMERSON. 4. Phr. *To keep (one's) eyes p.*, i. e. open, on the alert. *U.S. colloq.* 5. A people scattered and peeled and trodden under foot WESLEY. Hence **Pee·ling** *vbl. sb.* the action of the vb.; *concr.* that which is peeled or peels off.

Peeler¹ (pī·ləɹ). ME. [f. as prec. + -ER¹. See also PILLER.] †1. = PILLER 1. –1608. b. A plant that robs or impoverishes the soil 1573. 2. One who or that which peels 1597.

Peeler² (pī·ləɹ). 1817. [-ER¹.] A nickname for members of the Irish constabulary, founded (1812–18) by Mr. (later Sir) Robert *Peel*; hence, for a policeman in England. See BOBBY 2.

Peelite (pī·ləit). 1853. [See -ITE¹.] A name given to those Conservatives who sided with Sir Robert Peel when he introduced his measure for the repeal of the Corn Laws in 1846. So **Pee·lism.**

Peen (pīn). *dial., techn.*, and *U.S.* 1683. [17th c. *pen*; of obsc. origin.] The sharp or thin end of a hammer-head, opposite to the face; = PANE *sb.*²

Peenge (pīndʒ), *v.* *Sc.* and *n. dial.* Also **pinge.** 15... [perh. after *whinge* to whine, infl. by *peek, peevish*, etc.] *intr.* To whine, complain in a whining voice.

Peep (pīp), *sb.*¹ late ME. [f. PEEP *v.*¹] 1. An imitation of the feeble shrill sound made by young birds, mice, etc.; the sound itself; a cheep or faint squeak. Now *arch.* or *local.* 1470. 2. A pop. name of certain birds, e.g. species of sandpiper, the meadow-pipit, etc. 1794.

Peep (pīp), *sb.*² 1530. [f. PEEP *v.*²] An act of peeping; a surreptitious, furtive, or peering glance 1730. b. *fig.* Said esp. of the first appearance of daylight, as in *p. of dawn*, P. OF DAY, etc. Also, a tiny speck of light. 1530. c. = PEEP-BO. *Obs.* exc. *dial.* 1677.

Hence that wild suspicious p., Like a rogue that steals a sheep SWIFT. b. Oft have we seen him at the p. of dawn GRAY.

attrib. and *Comb.*; **p. hawk** (*dial.*), a kestrel; **-sight,** a backsight for rifles with a slit for bringing the foresight into line with the object aimed at.

Peep (pīp), *v.*[1] [late ME. *pepen*, repl. earlier *pipen*, *pypen* = OF. *piper*; echoic. See PIPE *v.*[1]] **1.** *intr.* To utter the weak shrill sound proper to young birds, mice, and some frogs; to cheep, chirp, squeak. **2.** *transf.* Of persons: To squeak; to 'sing small'. (Chiefly contemptuous.) 1550.

1. There was none that moved the wing, or opened the mouth, or peeped [R. V. chirped] *Isa.* x. 14. 2. Wizards that peepe and that mutter *Isa.* viii. 19.

Peep (pīp), *v.*[2] 1460. [app. related to PEEK *v.*] **1.** *intr.* To look through a narrow aperture as through the half-shut eyelids or through a crevice, chink, etc. into a larger space; hence, to look furtively, slyly, or pryingly. **2.** *fig.* To emerge into view; to begin to appear or show itself; said of daylight, flowers, distant eminences, etc.; freq. with the suggestion of looking out or over something. 1535. **b.** Of a plant, seed, etc.: To sprout 1593. **c.** Of a characteristic: To come slightly into view unconsciously 1579. **3.** *trans.* To cause to appear slightly; often with *out* 1573. **b.** To cause or allow (the eye) to peep. *rare.* 1818.

1. Some that will euermore peepe through their eyes, And laugh like Parrats at a bag-piper SHAKS. 2. Sweet as the primrose peeps beneath the thorn GOLDSM. c. The way the retired statesman peeps out in his essays LAMB. 3. This love..Peeps out his coward head to dare my age DRYDEN.

Peep-bo (pī·pbōu:). *colloq.* 1837. = BO-PEEP.

Peeper[1] (pī·pəɹ). 1591. [f. PEEP *v.*[1] + -ER[1].] **1.** One who or that which peeps or cheeps 1611. **2.** *spec.* **a.** A young chicken or pigeon 1591. **b.** *U.S.* One of various tree-frogs, esp. the Hylodes 1884.

Peeper[2] (pī·pəɹ). 1652. [f. PEEP *v.*[2] + -ER[1].] **1.** One who peeps or peers; *esp.* a 'Paul Pry'. **2.** *slang.* An eye. Chiefly *pl.* 1700. **3.** *Cant.* A looking-glass; also, a spy-glass; *pl.* a pair of spectacles 1694.

1. What would not I give for a peeper's place at the meeting 1663.

Peep-hole (pī·phōul). 1681. A small hole through which one can peep.

Pee·ping, *ppl. a.* 1592. [f. PEEP *v.*[2] + -ING[2].] That peeps or peers; that peeps forth. *P. Tom* (see quot.); hence allusively.

The story [of Godiva] is embellished with the incident of P. Tom, a prying inquisitive tailor, who was struck blind for popping out his head as the lady passed 1837.

Peep of day. 1577. [See PEEP *sb.*[2] b. Cf. *day-peep* (1530).] The first appearance of daylight.

Peep-of-day boys, a Protestant organization in the North of Ireland (*c* 1784–95), whose members visited the houses of their Roman Catholic opponents at daybreak in search of arms.

Peep-show (pī·pʃōu). 1861. [f. PEEP *v.*[2] or *sb.*[2] + SHOW *sb.*] A small exhibition of pictures, etc., viewed through a magnifying lens inserted in a small orifice. Also *fig.*

‖ **Peepul, pipal** (pī·pʊl). 1788. [Hindī *pīpal* :—Skr. *pippala*.] = BO-TREE. Also *p.-tree.*

Peer (pīəɹ), *sb.* (*a.*) [ME. *per*, *pe(e)re*, a. OF. *per*, *peer*, F. *pair* = L. *parem*, *par* equal.] **1.** An equal in standing or rank; one's equal before the law. **2.** An equal in any respect ME. **3.** One matched with another; a companion, mate; a rival. *Obs.* or *arch.* ME. **4.** A member of one of the degrees of nobility in the United Kingdom; a duke, marquis, earl, viscount, or baron. Also *transf.* and †*gen.* ME. **5.** *attrib.* That is a peer 1693. **6.** *adj.* or quasi-*adj.* Equal (*to*) 1567.

1. Nor must Strafford suffer by an ordinary way of judicature by his peers,..he must die by Act of Parliament 1660. 2. Ulysses..Jove's p. in wisdom COWPER. 3. To stray away into these forests drear, Alone, without a p. KEATS. 4. *Peers of the United Kingdom* or *of the realm* (up to 1707 called *peers of England*, from 1707 to 1801 *peers of Great Britain*), all of whom may sit in the House of Lords. *Peers of Scotland*, of whom sixteen are elected to each Parliament as representative members to sit in the House of Lords. *Peers of Ireland*, of whom twenty-eight representatives are elected for life to the House of Lords. *Peers of France*, (*a*) = DOUZEPERS; (*b*) those who possessed a territory which had been erected into a lordship and who had a right to sit in the Parliament of Paris; (*c*) members of the Upper Legislative Chamber, 1814–1848. **6.** More than one artist whose hand has not been p. to his feeling 1881. Hence **Pee·rship** = PEERAGE 2, PEERDOM 3.

Peer (pīəɹ), *v.*[1] late ME. [a. OF. *perer*, var. of *pairier*, *parer* :—L. *pariare* to make equal, f. *parem* PEER.] †**1.** *trans.* To make, or class, as equal; to rank *with* –1662. **2.** To equal, to rank with 1440. **3.** *intr.* To be equal, to rank on an equality. late ME. **4.** [f. prec. sb.] *trans.* To make (a man) a peer. *colloq.* 1753.

2. O, that's the queen o' womankind, And ne'er a ane to p. her BURNS.

Peer (pīəɹ), *v.*[2] 1450. [Origin obsc.; perh. connected with *pear*, *pere*, aphet. f. APPEAR.] **1.** *intr.* To look narrowly, esp. in order to make something out. **2.** *fig.* Said of inanimate things: To 'peep out' so as just to be seen; to appear slightly 1592. **3.** *transf.* To show (itself); to appear 1592. †**4.** *trans.* To make to peep out SHAKS.

1. Peering in Maps for ports, and peers, and rodes SHAKS. Deep into that darkness peering, long I stood POE. 2. Already streaks of blue p. through our clouds CARLYLE. 3. No Shepherdesse, but Flora Peering in Aprils front SHAKS. Hence **Pee·ring** *ppl. a.* that peers 1629.

Peerage (pīə·rėdʒ). 1454. [f. PEER *sb.* + -AGE.] **1.** The body of peers. **b.** *gen.* Nobility, aristocracy 1725. **2.** The rank or dignity of a peer 1671. †**b.** The territory of a peer –1759. **3.** A book containing a list of the peers, with their genealogy, connexions, etc. 1766. **4.** *attrib.* as *p.-book*, etc. 1727.

1. When Charlemain with all his P. fell By Fontarabbia MILT. 3. His name was in the P. 1856.

Peerdom (pīə·ɹdəm). 1603. [f. PEER *sb.* + -DOM.] **1.** = PEERAGE 2. †**2.** The territory of a French peer –1762. **3.** Equality 1891.

Peeress (pīə·rės). 1689. [f. PEER *sb.* + -ESS.] The wife of a peer.

P. in her own right, a woman having the rank of a peer by creation or descent.

Peerless (pīə·ɹlės), *a.* ME. [-LESS.] Without peer; unequalled, matchless.

The moon..Apparent Queen unvaild her **p.** light MILT. Hence **Pee·rless-ly** *adv.*, **-ness.**

Peery (pīə·ri), *a.* 1700. [f. PEER *v.*[2] + -Y.] Inclined to peer; hence, prying, inquisitive. **b.** *Rogues' Cant.* Knowing, sly 1757.

Two p. gray eyes, which had a droll obliquity of vision SCOTT.

Peesweep (pī·zwīp). *Sc.* and *dial.* 1796. [From the cry.] The lapwing.

Peetweet (pī·twīt). *U.S.* 1844. [Echoic; cf. *peewit*.] The spotted sand-piper or sand-lark of N. America (*Tringoides macularius*).

Peeved (pīvd), *ppl. a.* Orig. *U.S.* 1918. [f. PEEV(ISH + -ED[1].] Annoyed, vexed.

Peevish (pī·viʃ), *a.* late ME. [Origin unkn.] †**1.** Silly, senseless –1676. †**b.** Beside oneself; mad –1591. †**2.** Spiteful, malignant, mischievous, harmful –1601. †**3.** An epithet of dislike, hostility, etc., expressing rather the speaker's feeling than any quality of the object referred to –1548. †**4.** Perverse; headstrong, obstinate; skittish, capricious, coy –1671. **5.** Morose, querulous, ill-tempered, childishly fretful 1530. **b.** Of personal qualities, actions, etc.: Characterized by petty vexation 1577. **6.** in advb. constr. = *peevishly* 1529.

1. P. chattering FORD. 2. Peeuishe and mocking rymes GRAFTON. 3. Sirs, howe is it thus..that this peuysshe douehouse holdeth agaynst vs so longe? 1523. 4. *Two Gent.* v. ii. 49. 5. Some men fast to mortifie their lust: and their fasting makes them p. JER. TAYLOR. b. With a p. whine in his voice HAZLITT. Hence **Pee·vish-ly** *adv.*, **-ness.**

Peewit: see PEWIT.

Peg (peg), *sb.*[1] 1440. [app. of LG. origin; cf. dial. Du. *peg*, plug, peg, small wooden pin, LG. *pigge* peg, etc.] **1.** A pin or bolt, orig. of wood, also of metal, etc., used to hold together parts of a framework, of machinery, etc., for stopping up a hole, as the vent of a cask, for hanging up hats, clothes, etc., for holding the ropes of a tent, etc., or for marking boundaries, levels, the score in cribbage, etc. Also short for *clothes-p.* **b.** A cricket stump. *colloq.* 1909. **2.** *spec.* **a.** In stringed musical instruments, A pin of wood or metal to which the strings are fastened at one end, and which is turned to adjust the tension in tuning; a tuning-peg. Often in fig. expressions. 1589. **b.** One of a set of pins fixed in a drinking-vessel to measure the quantity each person was to drink 1617. **c.** *Shoemaking.* A pin of wood, etc., used to fasten the uppers to the sole, or the lifts to each other 1765. **d.** The metal pin on which a peg-top spins 1740. **3.** *fig.* ? The interval between two pegs; a step, degree 1589. **4.** A drink; esp. of brandy and soda-water. Chiefly in Anglo-Indian slang. (Cf. 2 b.) 1864. **5.** An implement furnished with a pin, claw, or hook, used for tearing, harpooning, etc. 1731.

1. Phr. *A round p. in a square hole* (or *vice versa*), a man placed in a position unsuited or uncongenial to him. *A p. to hang* (a discourse, opinion, etc.) *on*, an occasion, pretext, excuse for. *To move, start, stir a p.*, to move a limb, make a move. 2. a. *Oth.* II. i. 202. b. Come, old fellow, drink down to your p. LONGF. 3. Phr. *To take, bring, let* (a person) *down a p.* (*or two*), *a p. lower*, etc., to lower him a degree in his own or the general estimation. Also, *to come down a p.*

attrib. and *Comb.*, as *p.-hole*, etc.; **p.-board,** a board with holes and pegs, used in some games; **-ladder,** a ladder with a single standard having rungs fixed through it, or to one side; **p. leg,** a wooden leg; **-tankard,** one with pegs inserted at intervals to mark the quantity each person is to drink; **-tooth,** a peg-shaped tooth, a canine tooth.

Peg (peg), *sb.*[2] 1694. [Altered from *Meg* = MARGARET; cf. *Poll* = *Moll*, *Mary*.] **1.** A pet form of *Margaret*. **2.** *Old Peg* (dial.): Skim-milk cheese 1785.

Peg (peg), *v.* 1543. [f. PEG *sb.*[1]] **I. 1.** *trans.* To fix with a peg; to fasten with or as with a peg or pegs. Also with *down*, *in*, *out*, *up*. 1598. **b.** *fig.* To confine; to tie or bind *down* 1824. **c.** *fig.* To fix the market price by buying or selling freely at a given price. *Stock Exchange slang.* 1882. **2.** To insert a peg into. †**a.** To thrust a peg into the nose of (a swine, etc.) to prevent it from routing –1631. †**b.** To plug; to spike (a cannon) –1747. **3.** To strike or pierce with a peg; to strike with a turtle-peg; to harpoon. **b.** *intr.* To aim *at* with a peg or peg-top. 1740. **4.** *Cribbage.* To mark (the score) with pegs on a cribbage-board (also *absol.*); hence *transf.* to score (so many) 1821. **5.** To mark with pegs; *esp.* to mark the boundaries of (a piece of ground, a claim, etc.) with pegs placed at the corners; usu. *p. out* 1852.

3. Silas pegged at him with his wooden leg DICKENS. 5. Several other claims have been pegged out 1890.

II. †**1.** To drive *in* as a peg by repeated blows –1647. **2.** *intr.* To make one's way with vigour or haste. *dial.* and *colloq.* 1808. **3.** To work on persistently; to 'hammer' away 1805. (Senses 2 and 3 esp. with *away*, etc.)

2. Down the street I pegged like a madman 1884. 3. It is no good pegging away at one little point 1867.

Peg out. a. *Croquet.* To put (a ball) out by making it hit the winning-peg. **b.** *intr. Cribbage.* To win the game by reaching the last holes before the show of hands. **c.** *intr.* To peg or pitch one's tent. **d.** To die; to be ruined (*slang*). Hence **Pe·gger,** one who pegs; also, a pegging-machine.

Pegamoid (pe·gămoid). 1895. Trade name of a waterproof cloth or imitation leather.

Pegasus (pe·găsŏs). late ME. [L., a. Gr. Πήγασος, f. πηγή spring, fount; named from the πηγαί or springs of Ocean, near which Medusa was said to have been killed. Formerly also, **Pe·gase,** in late ME. **Pegasee.**] **1.** *Gr.* and *L. Myth.* The winged horse fabled to have sprung from the blood of Medusa, and with a stroke of his hoof to have caused the fountain HIPPOCRENE to well forth on Mount Helicon. Hence, represented as the favourite steed of the Muses, and said allusively to bear poets in their poetic 'flights'. Also *attrib.* **b.** *Her.* A winged horse as a bearing, etc. 1562. **c.** *Astron.* A northern constellation, figured as a winged horse, containing three stars of the 2nd magnitude forming with one star of Andromeda a large square (the *square of P.*) 1696. **2.** *Zool.* A genus of fishes, typical of the family *Pegasidæ*, with body somewhat like a horse's head, and one dorsal and one anal fin, suggesting wings; also called *flying sea-horses* 1835.

1. Each spurs his jaded P. apace BYRON. Hence **Pega·sean, -a·sian** *adjs.* pertaining to, connected with, or resembling P.; swift; poetic.

Pegging (pe·giŋ), *vbl. sb.* 1611. [f. PEG *v.* + -ING[1].] **1.** The action of the vb. PEG. **2.** *concr.* Pegs collectively, material for pegs.

attrib. and *Comb.*: **p.-awl,** an awl for drilling

holes for the pegs of shoes; **-machine**, a machine for driving in the pegs of shoes.

Peggy (pe·gi). [Alteration of *Meggy, Maggie* = MARGARET. Cf. *Polly.*] **1.** A local name of various warblers (*Sylvia*) and allied genera; also of the Pied Wagtail 1836. **2.** = DOLLY *sb.*[1] 4 a. Also p.-tub. 1823. **3.** *P.-with-(her-) lantern* = JACK-O'-LANTERN 1855.

†**Pe·gma, pegme.** 1603. [a. L. *pegma*, a. Gr. πῆγμα framework fixed together, etc., f. πηγνύειν to fasten.] A kind of framework or stage used in theatrical pageants, sometimes bearing an inscription; hence *transf.* the inscription itself –1647.

Pegmatite (pe·gmătəit). 1832. [f. Gr. πῆγμα, πηγματ- thing joined together + -ITE [1].] *Min.* A coarsely crystallized kind of granite, containing little mica. Hence **Pegmati·tic, Pe·gmatoid** *adjs.*

Pe·g-top, pe·gtop. 1801. [f. PEG *sb.*[1] + TOP *sb.*] **1.** A pear-shaped wooden spinning-top, with a metal peg forming the point, spun by the rapid uncoiling of a string wound about it. **b.** A game of spinning peg-tops 1828. **2.** *pl.* = *p. trousers* 1859. **3.** *attrib.* Having the shape of a peg-top, as *p. whiskers*; **p. trousers**, trousers very wide in the hips and narrow at the ankles 1858.

Pehlevi, Pehlvi: see PAHLAVI.

‖ **Peignoir** (pęnʸwar). 1835. [F., f. *peigner* to comb.] A loose dressing-gown worn by women while their hair is being combed, or on coming out of a bath; misapplied to a woman's morning gown.

‖**Peine** (pēⁱn, ‖pen). 1554. [F. = PAIN.] Pain, punishment. In phr. *p. forte et dure*: 'severe and hard punishment', formerly inflicted on persons arraigned for felony who refused to plead; pressing to death. Also used allusively.

Peirastic (pəiræ·stik), *a. rare.* Also **pir-.** 1656. [ad. Gr. πειραστικός tentative, f. πειρᾶν to try.] Involving, or performing, an attempt; experimental, tentative. So **Peira·stically** *adv.*

†**Pei·sage, pesage.** 1455. [ME. a. OF. *pesage*, f. *peser* PEISE *v.*] A duty paid for the weighing of goods –1706.

Peise (pēⁱz, pīz), *sb. Obs.* exc. *dial.* [ME. *peis, peys*, a. early OF., ONF., and AF. *peis* (OF. *pois*, F. *poids*) :—L. *pensum* something weighed, weight, f. *pendere* to weigh.] †**1.** The quality of being heavy; heaviness, weight. Also in semi-*concr.* sense; cf. *load, burden.* –1624. †**b.** Gravity, importance; burden (of blame, etc.); 'ballast' –1602. †**2.** Definite or specified weight; the amount that a thing weighs –1610. **3.** *concr.* A weight; *spec.* (*a*) a standard weight for goods; (*b*) one of the weights of a clock. Now *dial.* ME. †**4.** Forcible impact, as of a heavy body; momentum; a heavy blow or fall –1602. **5.** Balance, poise, equilibrium; suspense; the act of holding poised. Now *dial.* late ME.

Peise (pēⁱz, pīz), *v. Obs.* exc. *dial.* [ME., repr. the stem-stressed form of OF. *peser* :—L. *pensare* to weigh, freq. of *pendere.*] †**1.** *trans.* To weigh, as in a balance. Also *absol.* –1609. **b.** To estimate the weight of, as by poising in the hand. Now *dial.* late ME. †**2.** *fig.* To weigh in the mind; to ponder; to estimate –1633. †**3.** To keep or place in equilibrium; to balance, poise –1633. †**b.** To balance (two things), or (one thing) against another; to make equal in weight. Usu. *fig.* –1622. †**c.** To be of equal weight with, balance, counterbalance –1607. †**4.** To put a weight upon; to load, burden; to weigh down; to oppress (*lit.* and *fig.*) –1627. **5.** *intr.* To weigh (so much). Now *dial.* late ME.

4. Lest leaden slumber peize me down SHAKS. Hence †**Pei·ser**, one who weighs; *spec.* an officer appointed to weigh the tin from the Cornish mines.

†**Pei·trel, pey·trel, pe·trel.** [ME. a. AF. *peitrel* = OF. *peitral* (mod.F. *poitrail*) :—L. *pectorale*; see PECTORAL.] = POITREL –1687.

Pejorate (pī·dʒŏreⁱt), *v.* 1644. [f. L. *pejorat-*, *pejorare* to make worse, f. *pejorem* worse.] *trans.* To make worse, deteriorate, worsen. Hence **Pejora·tion.**

Pejorative (pī·dʒŏrĕtiv, pīdʒǫ·rătiv), *a.* and *sb.* 1882. [See prec. and -IVE. So F. *péjoratif.*] **A.** *adj.* Tending to make worse; depreciatory; applied esp. to a derivative word in which the meaning of a root word is lowered by the addition of a suffix, etc. **B.** *sb.* A word of this character, as *poetaster*, etc. Hence **Pe·joratively** *adv.* in a deteriorated sense.

Pekan (pe·kăn). 1796. [Canadian Fr. *pekan*, ad. Abnaki *pékané.*] A carnivorous beast (*Mustela pennanti*) of the weasel family, valuable for its fur; also, its fur.

Peke (pīk), **Pekie** (pī·ki). 1920. Abbrev. of PEKIN(G)ESE *dog.*

Pekin, -king (pī·ki·n, -ki·ŋ). 1783. [a. F. *pékin*, ad. Chinese *Pē-kīng* (pē·kī·ŋ), lit. 'northern capital' (opp. to *Nānking* 'southern capital'), the capital of China.] **1.** A kind of silk stuff. ‖**2.** Fr. *pékin, péquin* (pekę̃n): A name orig. given by the soldiers under Napoleon I to any civilian; occasional in Eng. use 1827.

Pekin(g)ese (pīkiŋī·z, pīkinī·z), *a.* 1907. [f. PEKIN + -ESE.] Of or belonging to Pekin: *spec.* in *P. dog* or *spaniel*, a small long-haired dog, of the pug type, orig. brought from the Imperial Palace at Pekin; also as *sb.*

Pekoe (pe·ko, pī·ko). 1712. [a. Chinese (Amoy dial.) *pek-ho*, f. *pek* white + *ho* down, hair.] A superior kind of black tea, so called from the leaves being picked young with the down still on them.

Pelage (pe·lėdʒ). 1828. [a. F. *pelage*, f. OF. *peil, pel*, F. *poil* hair, down + -AGE.] A general and collective term for the fur, hair, wool, etc., of a quadruped. (Cf. *plumage.*)

Pelagian (pǐlēⁱ·dʒiăn), *a.*[1] and *sb.*[1] 1449. [f. L. *Pelagianus*, f. *Pelagius*, latinized form of the name of a British monk of the 4th and 5th centuries.] **A.** *adj.* Of or pertaining to Pelagius or his doctrines. (He denied the Catholic doctrine of original sin.) 1565. **B.** *sb.* A follower of the doctrine of Pelagius 1449.

The sect of Pelagianys, which helden that a man bi his fre wil mai deserue heuen withoute grace 1449. Hence **Pela·gianism. Pela·gianize** *v. intr.* to hold or express P. views.

Pelagian (pǐlēⁱ·dʒiăn), *a.*[2] and *sb.*[2] 1601. [f. L. *pelagius*, a. Gr. πελάγιος of the sea + -AN.] **A.** *adj.* †**1.** Of or pertaining to the *pelagiæ conchæ* or sea shells whence purple dye was obtained HOLLAND. **2.** = PELAGIC 1746. **B.** *sb.* An inhabitant of the open sea or ocean 1854.

A. 2. Some [shell-fish] are p., or inhabit only the deeps of the sea 1776.

Pelagic (pǐlæ·dʒik), *a.* 1656. [ad. L. *pelagicus*, a. Gr. *πελαγικός, f. πέλαγος the sea.] Of or pertaining to the open or high sea, as dist. from the shallow water near the coast; oceanic; now *spec.* living on or near the surface of the open sea or ocean, as dist. from its depths. **b.** Of sealing: Carried on or performed on the high seas. So *p. sealer.* 1891. So †**Pela·gious** *a.*

Pelamyd, -mid (pe·lămid). Also in L. form. 1598. [ad. L. *pelamys, -myd-, pelamis*, a. Gr. πηλαμύς, -μυδα.] **1.** A small Mediterranean fish; a young tunny. **2.** Applied to the genus *Pelamys* of scombroid fishes 1863.

Pelargonic (pelaɹgǫ·nik), *a.* 1848. [f. PELARGONIUM; see -IC.] *Chem.* Of or derived from the genus *Pelargonium*; esp. in *P. acid*, a fatty acid, $C_9H_{18}O_2$, prepared from the volatile oil of plants of this genus; nonylic acid.

‖**Pelargonium** (pelăɹgōᵘ·niŏm). 1819. [mod. L., f. Gr. πελαργός stork; app. after *geranium.*] *Bot.* A large genus of plants of the N.O. *Geraniaceæ*, having showy flowers and fragrant leaves, commonly cultivated under the name of *geranium.*

Pelasgian (pǐlæ·zdʒiăn), *a.* and *sb.* 1585. [f. L. *Pelasgius*, a. Gr. Πελάσγιος, of or pertaining to the Πελασγοί or Pelasgi.] **A.** *adj.* = next. **B.** *sb.* One of the *Pelasgi*, an ancient race widely spread over the coasts and islands of the Eastern Mediterranean and Ægean, and believed to have occupied Greece before the Hellenes.

Pelasgic (pǐlæ·zdʒik), *a.* 1785. [ad. L. *Pelasgicus*; see prec.] Of, pertaining to, or characteristic of the Pelasgi or Pelasgians. *P. architecture, building*, the oldest form of masonry found in Greece, constructed of rough or unhewn stones piled up without cement.

Pelecoid (pe·lǐkoid), *a.* and *sb.* 1727. [ad. Gr. πελεκοειδής, f. πέλεκυς axe, hatchet + -ειδης -shaped.] **A.** *adj.* Hatchet-shaped. **B.** *sb.* A figure bounded by a semicircle and two concave quadrants meeting in a point, and so resembling the blade of a battle-axe.

Pelecypod (pǐle·sipǫd), *a.* and *sb.* 1857. [f. Gr. πέλεκυς hatchet + -ποδος -footed.] *Zool.* **A.** *adj.* Having a hatchet-shaped foot, as a bivalve mollusc; pertaining to such a mollusc. **B.** *sb.* A p. mollusc. Hence **Pelecy·podous** *a.*

Pelerine (pe·lĕrin, -īn). 1744. [a. F. *pèlerine*, transf. use of fem. of *pèlerin* PILGRIM = pilgrim's mantle or cape.] A name for various kinds of mantles or capes worn by women; in recent use, a long narrow cape or tippet, with ends coming down to a point in front.

Pelf (pelf). [ME. a. ONF. **pelfe* (mod. Norman *peufe*), var. of OF. *pelfre, peufre* spoil; perh. related to L. *pilare* to pillage, F. *piller.*] †**1.** Spoil, booty –1470. †**2.** Property, goods, gear –1847. **3.** Money, wealth, riches; now 'filthy lucre' 1500. †**4.** Trash; frippery –1632. **b.** Refuse; now *dial.*, vegetable refuse 1589.

3. Ye rich men cannot think to carry your pelfe with you into Heaven BP. HALL. So †**Pe·lfry** (*a*) = sense 1. –1565; (*b*) = sense 4. –1551.

Pelham (pe·lăm). 1849. [From the surname.] In full, *P. bit*, a form of bit combining the snaffle and the curb in one. So *P. bridle.*

Pelican (pe·likăn). OE. [ad. late L. *pelicanus, pelecanus*, ad. Gr. πελεκάν; app. related to πελεκᾶς woodpecker, perh. f. πέλεκυς axe, from the appearance or action of the bill.] **I.** The bird. **1.** One of a genus, *Pelecanus*, of large gregarious fish-eating water-fowls, having an enormously distensible membranous pouch depending from the lower mandible of the long hooked bill, which is used for the storing of fish when caught. **b.** In ref. to the fable that the pelican feeds her young with her own blood. late ME. †**c.** Hence applied symbolically to Christ –1814. **2.** A representation of the pelican. late ME.

1. b. What, would'st thou have me turn P., and feed thee out of my own Vitals? CONGREVE. **c.** [St. John] who lay Upon the bosom of our p. CARY. **2.** *P. in her piety* (*Her.*), a pelican represented as vulning (*i. e.* wounding) her breast in order to feed her young with her blood.

II. *transf.* **1.** An alembic having a tubulated head, from opposite sides of which two curved tubes pass out and re-enter at the body of the vessel; used in distilling liquors by fermentation 1559. **2.** An instrument having a strong curved beak, formerly used for extracting teeth 1597. **3.** An ancient piece of artillery; also, the shot from it 1727.

attrib. and *Comb.*, as *p.-brood*, etc.; **p.-fish**, an eel-like fish (*Eurypharynx pelecanoides*), dredged from a great depth near the Canary Islands; so called from its enormously developed jaws and gular pouch; **-flower**, a W. Indian climbing plant (*Aristolochia grandiflora*), Poisonous Hogweed; **p. ibis**, an Asiatic wood-ibis (*Tantalus leucocephalus*); **pelican's foot**, a gastropod shell (*Aporrhais pes-pelecani*), so called from its digitate outer lip. Hence **Pe·licanry**, a place where pelicans breed.

Pelisse (pĕlī·s). 1718. [a. F., = It. *pelliccia* 'any kind of furred garment' (Florio) :—med.L. *pellicia*, for L. *pellicia* (or *-icea*) *tunica* or *vestis*, a garment of fur, f. *pellis* skin.] **1.** †**a.** A garment of fur. **b.** A long mantle or cloak lined with fur. **2.** A long mantle of silk, velvet, cloth, etc., worn by women, reaching to the ankles, and having arm-holes or sleeves 1755. **b.** A garment worn out of doors by young children over their other clothes 1852.

Pell (pel). *Obs.* exc. *Hist.* [ME. a. AF. *pell*, OF. *pel*, mod.F. *peau* :—L. *pellem* skin, leather, parchment.] †**1.** A skin or hide; *esp.* a furred skin used as the lining of a cloak; a cloak so lined, a fur –1596. **2.** A skin or roll of parchment, a parchment; *spec.* each of the two pells, of receipt (*pellis receptorum*) and disbursement (*pellis exituum*), kept at the Exchequer. **b.** In *pl.* The Office of the Exchequer in which these were kept. *Obs.* exc. *Hist.* 1454.

2. *Clerk of the Pells*, an officer formerly charged with the entry of receipts and disbursements on the parchment rolls in the Exchequer. So *Master of the Pells. Obs.* exc. *Hist.*

†**Pellage.** ME. [f. AF. *pell* PELL + -AGE.] An impost formerly levied on exported skins –1691.

‖ **Pellagra** (pelǝ̄ⁱ·gră, -æ·gră). 1811. [It. and mod.L.; perh. orig. It. *pelle agra* 'rough skin'.] *Path.* An endemic disease often ending in insanity (frequent among the peasantry of Lombardy, etc.), in which the skin reddens, dries, and cracks, and the epidermis peels off. Hence **Pella·grin**, a person afflicted with p. **Pella·gric, Pella·grous** *adjs.* of the nature of or pertaining to p.; affected with p.

Pellet (pe·lėt), *sb.* late ME. [a. F. *pelote* = It. *pillotta*, med.L. *pelota, pilota*, deriv. of It. *pila*, L. *pila* ball.] **1.** Any (small) globe, ball, or spherical body; a bolus, a pill, etc. **2.** *spec.* A ball, usu. of stone, used as a missile during the 14th and 15th centuries, and shot from mortars, etc.; later, a bullet; now applied to small shot. Also *fig.* late ME. **b.** A toy bullet of clay, wood, paper, etc. 1553. **3.** *Her.* A roundel sable 1572. **4.** A circular boss, rounded or flat, in coins or decorative work 1842.

2. As swifte as pelet out of gonne CHAUCER.

Comb. **p. moulding** *Arch.*, a moulding consisting of a flat band on which are circular flat disks (Gwilt). Hence **Pe·llet** *v. trans.* †(*a*) to form or shape into pellets; to send as a pellet; (*b*) to hit with (paper) pellets, small shot, etc. **Pe·lleted** *ppl. a.* marked or charged with (heraldic) pellets.

Pelletierine (peletīǝ·rǝin). 1881. [f. name of F. chemist, Bertrand *Pelletier* (1761–97) + -INE.] *Chem.* A colourless alkaloid ($C_8H_{13}NO$) obtained from the bark of a pomegranate.

Pe·llety, *a.* 1572. [f. PELLET *sb.* 3 + -Y 5.] *Her.* Charged with pellets; pelleted.

Pellicle (pe·lik'l). 1541. [ad. L. *pellicula*, dim. of *pellis* skin.] A small or thin skin; a membrane, cuticle, film. Chiefly in scientific use, and applied to natural formations, as a thin membrane in an animal or plant body, etc. So **Pe·llicule** (*rare*). late ME. **Pelli·cular** *a.* of, pertaining to, or of the nature of a p.

Pellitory (pe·litǝri). 1533. [In sense 1 var. of earlier *peletre, peletyr*, with changed suffix; in sense 2 alteration of **peretarie, paretarie*, PARIETARY, by dissimilation of *r..r* to *l..r*.] **1.** A composite plant, *Anacyclus Pyrethrum*, called distinctively *P. of Spain*, a native of Barbary, the root of which has a pungent flavour, and is used as a local irritant and salivant and as a remedy for toothache. Also, the root (*radix pyrethri*) as thus used. †**b.** Applied to other plants resembling this; *esp.* (*a*) Masterwort, *Peucedanum Ostruthium* (also *Great* or *False P. of Spain*); (*b*) Sneezewort, *Achillea Ptarmica* (also *Wild* or *Bastard P.*) –1760. **2.** A low bushy plant (*Parietaria officinalis*, N.O. *Urticaceæ*) with small ovate leaves and greenish flowers, growing upon or at the foot of walls; commonly distinguished as *P. of the wall.* Also extended to the whole genus *Parietaria.* 1548. **3.** *attrib.*, as *p. root* 1713.

Pell-mell (pe·lme·l), *adv.* (*a.*, *sb.*) 1579. [a. F. *pêle-mêle*, in OF. *pesle mesle, pelle-melle.* The second element was app. the stem of the vb. *mesler, mêler* to mix, mingle. Prob. a riming combination, as in *tire-lire*, Eng. *helter-skelter*, etc.] **1.** With disorderly or confused mingling; promiscuously 1596. **b.** Of combatants: Without keeping ranks; hence, hand to hand; in a mêlée 1579. †**2.** Indiscriminately; in the mass –1659. **3.** In disorder and hurry; headlong, recklessly 1594.

1. [They] were so closely followed, that our Soldiers entred with them p. into the City 1677. 3. I went to work p., blotted several sheets of paper with choice floating thoughts W. IRVING.

B. *adj.* (pe·lmel) Tumultuous; confused, indiscriminate 1585. **C.** *sb.* Promiscuous mingling; a hand-to-hand fight, a mêlée 1590.

High deeds Haunt not the fringy edges of the fight But the p. of men CLOUGH.

Pell mell, obs. f. PALL-MALL.

Pellock, -ack, -och (pe·lǝk, -ǝχ). *Sc.* ME. [Of obscure origin.] The porpoise.

Pellucid (pěl*ū*·sid), *a.* 1619. [ad. L. *pellucidus*, f. *pel-*, *perlucere* to shine through. Not in colloq. use.] **1.** Translucent, transparent; clear. **2.** *fig.* †**a.** Easy to 'see through'; 'transparent' –1661. **b.** Clear in style or expression. **c.** Mentally clear. 1822.

1. I will..send the rays..through this slab of p. ice TYNDALL. *P. zone*: see ZONE. 2. a. Their craft was p. 1644. Hence **Pelluci·dity**, p. quality or condition. **Pellu·cid·ly** *adv.*, **-ness.**

Pelmanism (pe·lmăniz'm). 1918. [f. *Pelman* (coined in 1899), proprietary name of an educational institute + -ISM.] The memory-training system of the Pelman Institute.

Pelmatozoan (pe:lmătozō*u*·ăn), *a.* and *sb.* [f. mod.L. *Pelmatozoa*, neut. pl. (f. Gr. πελματο- sole of the foot + ζῷον animal) + -AN.] (An echinoderm) of the division *Pelmatozoa*, characterized by a stalk by which it is fixed. So **Pe:lmatozo·ic** *a.*

Pelmet (pe·lmėt). 1821. [?] A horizontal curtain or valance fixed over a door, window, etc. to hide the fittings of hanging curtains, etc.

Pelo-, comb. form of Gr. πηλός clay, mud; as in **Peloli·thic** [Gr. λίθος stone] *a.*, *Geol.* applied to rock-strata consisting of clay; etc.

‖ **Peloria** (pĭlō*ᵊ*·riă). 1859. [mod.L., f. Gr. πέλωρος monstrous, f. πέλωρ monster.] *Bot.* Regularity or symmetry of structure occurring abnormally in flowers normally irregular or unsymmetrical. **Pelo·rian, -o·riate, -o·ric** *adjs.*

‖ **Pelota** (pĭlō*u*·tă). 1895. [Sp. *pelota* ball, augment. of *pella* :—L. *pila* ball.] A Basque game somewhat resembling tennis or rackets, played in a large court with a ball and a racket of wicker-work fastened on the hand.

Pelt (pelt), *sb.*[1] ME. [perh. a back-formation from PELTRY 1.] **1.** The skin of a sheep or goat with short wool on; also, the undressed skin of a fur-bearing animal; a fell. **2.** *spec.* A raw skin of a sheep, goat, etc., stripped of its wool or fur 1562. **3.** The human skin (*joc.* or *dial.*) 1605. **4.** †**a.** A garment made of a skin or fell –1649. **b.** Untanned sheepskin used to form a printer's inking-pad; a pelt-ball 1683. **5.** The dead quarry of a hawk, esp. when mangled 1615.

1. Some others of them [Saints] went about in peltes and goates skinnes FOXE.

attrib. and *Comb.*, as **p.-ball** = sense 4 **b**; **-monger**, one who deals in skins; **-rot**, a skin-disease in sheep.

Pelt, *sb.*[2] 1513. [f. PELT *v.*] **1.** An act of pelting; the act of pelting with missiles or (*fig.*) with obloquy. **b.** The beating of rain or snow 1862. **2.** An outburst of temper, a rage. *Obs.* exc. *dial.* 1573. **3.** The action of pelting (PELT *v.* 6) esp. in *full p.*, (at) full speed 1819.

3. Just fancy a horse that comes full p. HOOD.

Pelt, *sb.*[3] Now only *dial.* 1567. [Of obsc. origin; cf. dial. *palt* in same sense.] †Trash or rubbish; rags; also *mod. dial.* Refuse, waste.

Pelt (pelt), *v.* 1500. [Origin unkn.] **1.** *trans.* To strike with many or repeated blows (now, with something thrown); to assail with missiles. **b.** *fig.* To assail with reproaches or obloquy 1658. **2.** *intr.* To go on striking vigorously. Also *fig.* 1535. **3.** To strike *at* vigorously with missiles; to go on firing. Also *fig.* 1565. **4.** *trans.* To go on throwing (missiles) with intent to strike. Also *fig.* 1683. †**5.** *intr.* To throw out angry words –1706. **6.** To move at a vigorous and rapid pace 1831.

1. A crowd..pelting one another with Cudgels 1687. Make snowballs and p. each other 1835. 2. The smith..pelting away at his hot iron HOOD. The rain began to p. 1879. 6. I saw the rhinoceros pelting away 1872. Hence **Pe·lter**, one who pelts; a pelting shower; (*dial.*) a rage, 'temper'. **Pe·lting** *ppl. a.* that pelts; (*dial.*) violent, passionate.

‖ **Pelta** (pe·ltă). *Pl.* **-tæ** (-tī). 1600. [L., a. Gr. πέλτη a small light shield of leather.] **1.** *Antiq.* A small light shield used by the ancient Greeks, Romans, etc. **2.** *Bot.* The apothecium of a lichen when without a rim; also, a bract or scale attached by the middle like a peltate leaf 1760.

Peltast (pe·ltæst). 1623. [ad. L. *peltasta*, ad. Gr. πελταστής, f. πέλτη PELTA.] *Gr. Hist.* A kind of foot-soldier, armed with a pelta and short spear or javelin.

Peltate (pe·lte*ⁱ*t), *a.* 1760. [ad. L. *peltatus* armed with the PELTA.] *Bot.* and *Zool.* Shield-shaped; usu. of a leaf: Having the petiole joined to the under-surface of the blade at or near the middle (instead of at the base or end); hence, said of other stalked parts similarly attached. So †**Pe·ltated** *a.* 1753. **Pe·ltately** *adv.* in the manner of a p. leaf. **Pelta·tion,** p. condition, or a p. formation.

Pelti-, comb. form of PELTA, in some rarely used scientific terms; as **Pe·ltiform** *a.*, shield-shaped; of a peltate form; etc.

Pe·lting, *a. arch.* 1540. [app. related to PELTRY 2.] Paltry, mean, insignificant, trumpery; worthless.

Like to a Tenement or pelting Farme SHAKS.

Peltry 1 (pe·ltri). late ME. [a. AF. *pelterie* = OF. *peleterie*, mod.F. *pelleterie*, f. *peletier, pelletier* furrier, f. OF. *pel* :—L. *pellem*, *-is* skin. In mod. use a new adoption.] **1.** Undressed skins; esp. fur-skins; pelts collectively. **b.** *pl.* Kinds of peltry 1809. **2.** *attrib.*, as *p.-man*; †**p.-ware** = sense 1. late ME.

†**Pe·ltry** 2. Chiefly *Sc.* 1550. [app. a var. of PALTRY *sb.*] Refuse, rubbish, trash; a piece of rubbish –1808.

‖ **Peludo** (pĭl*ū*·do). 1845. [Sp., subst. use of *peludo* hairy, f. *pelo* :—L. *pilus* hair.] The hairy armadillo (*Dasypus villosus*) of S. America.

Pelvi-, comb. form of L. *pelvis* (see below); as in **Pe·lviform** *a.* basin-shaped. **Pelvi·meter** [-METER] an instrument for measuring the diameters of the pelvis; so **Pelvi·metry**; etc.

Pelvic (pe·lvik), *a.* 1830. [irreg. f. L. *pelvis* + -IC.] **1.** Of, pertaining to, contained in, or connected with the pelvis (PELVIS 1). **2.** Of or pertaining to the pelvis of a crinoid 1849.

1. *P. arch, p. girdle*, the girdle formed by the bones of the pelvis, the hip-girdle. *P. limbs*, the limbs supported by the pelvic arch; as the legs of a man.

‖ **Pelvis** (pe·lvis). *Pl.* **pelves** (pe·lvīz). 1615. [L. *pelvis* basin, laver.] **1.** The basin-shaped cavity formed (in most vertebrates) by the haunch bones or *ossa innominata* together with the *sacrum* and other vertebræ. **2.** The basin-like cavity of the kidney, into which the uriniferous tubules open 1678. **3.** The basal part of the calyx of a crinoid 1839.

1. *True p.*, that part of the (human) pelvis below the ilio-pectineal line; *false p.*, the space above this between the iliac fossæ.

Pembroke (pe·mbrǒk). 1778. Name of a town and shire in Wales and of an earldom in the British peerage. Hence **P. table**, or *ellipt.* **Pembroke**, a table supported on four fixed legs, having two flaps, which can be spread out horizontally and supported on legs connected with the central part by joints.

Pemmican (pe·mikăn). Also **pemican.** 1801. [a. Cree *pimecan, pimekan*, f. *pime* fat.] A preparation made by certain N. American Indians, consisting of lean meat, dried, pounded, and mixed with melted fat, so as to form a paste, and pressed into cakes; hence, beef similarly treated, and usu. flavoured with currants, etc., for the use of arctic explorers, soldiers, etc., as containing much nutriment in little bulk, and keeping for a long time. **b.** Extremely condensed thought or matter 1870.

b. *attrib.* A certain tendency to..the p. style 1900.

‖ **Pemphigus** (pe·mfigǒs). 1779. [mod.L., f. Gr. πέμφιξ, πεμφιγ- bubble.] *Path.* An affection of the skin characterized by the formation of watery vesicles or eruptions (*bullæ*) on various parts of the body. Hence **Pe·mphigoid, Pe·mphigous** *adjs.*

Pen (pen), *sb.*[1] [OE. *penn*, of unkn. origin.] **1.** A small enclosure, for cows, sheep, swine, poultry, etc.; a fold, sty, coop, etc. **b.** *transf.* A number of animals in a pen, or sufficient to fill a pen 1873. **2.** Applied to various enclosures resembling these 1620. **3.** A contrivance for penning the water in a river or canal, so as to form a head of water; a weir, dam, etc. ? *Obs.* 1585.

1. Tel..how my Father stole two Geese out of a P. SHAKS. b. A p. of Plymouth Rocks 1904. 2. The place where visitors were allowed to go was a little p. at the left of the entrance 18...

Pen (pen), *sb.*[2] [ME. a. OF. *penne* = It. *penna* feather, etc. :—L. *penna* feather, wings, in late L. writing pen.] **I.** A feather, a quill, etc. **1.** A feather of a bird, a plume. *Obs.* or *dial.* late ME. **b.** In *pl.* The flight-feathers (*remiges*) of birds regarded as the organs of flight; hence put for 'wings'. Now a poetic archaism. late ME. **2.** *spec.* The quill or barrel of a feather; the quill of a porcupine. *Obs.* or *dial.* late ME. **3.** *transf.* The internal, somewhat feather-shaped shell of certain cuttle-fishes, as the squids 1872.

1. b. On mighty pens uplifted soars the eagle aloft 1800.

II. A writing tool, etc. 1. A quill feather or part of one, with the quill pointed and split into two nibs at its lower end, for writing with ink; a quill-pen. Hence, a small instrument made of steel or other metal, pointed and split like the end of a quill-pen; a pen-nib; such a nib with the pen-holder into which it is fitted. Also, any instrument adapted for writing with fluid ink. ME. b. Viewed as the instrument of authorship; hence, the practice of writing or literature; †literary ability; manner, style, or quality of writing 1447. c. Hence, a writer or author. Now *rare*. 1563. 2. Anything having the function of a writing pen. †a. A stylus; a graver -1650. b. A black-lead or other pencil. Now *dial.* 1644.

1. The penne of a ready writer *Ps.* xlv. 1. DRAWING-*p.*, MUSIC-*p.*; FOUNTAIN-*p.*, STYLOGRAPHIC *p.*, see these words. Phr. *P.-and-pencil* (attrib.), using both pen and drawing-pencil or brush; *p.-and-wash*, using both pen and brush; also PEN-AND-INK. b. Tyranny has no enemy so formidable as the p. COBBETT. c. [A book] wherein a second P. had a good share JONSON. 2. *Electric p.*, *pneumatic p.*, modern inventions which perforate the lines of writing in fine dots, whence copies are made in ink by stencilling.

Comb.: **p.-case**, a case or receptacle for a p. or pens; **craft**, the craft or art of the p.; skill in writing; **-name** tr. NOM-DE-PLUME, q.v.; **-picture**, a picture drawn with the p.; usu. *fig.* a picturesque description; **-plume** = PEN-FEATHER; **-point**, (*a*) the point of a p.; (*b*) *dial.* a steel p. or nib; **-portrait** (cf. *p.-picture*); **-tray**, a tray for pens.

Pen, *sb.*[3] 1550. [Origin unkn.] A female swan.

Pen, *sb.*[4] *local.* [a. Brythonic *pen* head.] A word orig. meaning 'head', frequent in place-names in Cornwall, Wales, etc., as Penzance, Penmaenmawr, etc.; in the south of Scotland, etc., used as a separate word in names of hills, e.g. Ettrick Pen, Lee Pen, etc.; rarely as common noun, 'the pen'.

Pen, *v.*[1] Pa. t. and pple. **penned** (pend); also †**pend**. [ME. *pennen*, repr. OE. **pennian*, app. f. *penn*, PEN *sb.*[1]] 1. *trans.* To fasten, make fast. Now *dial.* 2. To shut in, shut up, confine. Often with *up*; also *in*. ME. 3. *spec.* a. To dam up (the water) in a river or canal. Now *rare*. 1576. b. To confine or shut up (cattle, poultry, etc.) in a pen; to put or keep in a pen 1610.

2. Sonne-bright honour pend in shamefull coupe SPENSER. 3. Where Shepherds p. thir Flocks at eeve In hurdl'd Cotes MILT. Hence **Penned** (pend) *ppl. a.*[1] shut up in a pen; confined, as water, by a weir or lock; also with *in*, *up*.

Pen, *v.*[2] Pa. t. and pple. **penned** (pend). 1490. [f. PEN *sb.*[2] II. 1.] *trans.* To write *down* with a pen; to write; to draw up (a (document); to compose and write, to indite. †b. To set forth in writing -1659.

Panegyrick upon Folly, penn'd in Latin by Erasmus 1683. Penning a letter to the *Times* 1880. Hence **Penned** (pend), *ppl. a.*[2] written (with a pen); set down in writing; also with adv., as *well-penned*.

Penacute (pīnăkiū·t), *a.* 1751. [f. L. *pene* almost + ACUTE.] *Heb.* and *Gr. Gram.* Having an acute accent on the penultimate; also as *sb.*

Penal (pī·năl), *a.* late ME. [a. F. *pénal*, ad. L. *penalis* of or belonging to punishment, f. *pœna* penalty, ad. Gr. ποινή quit-money, fine.] 1. Of, pertaining to, or relating to punishment. a. Punitive; prescribing or enacting the punishment of an offence or transgression. b. Of an act or offence: Punishable, esp. by law 1472. c. Constituting punishment; inflicted as, or in the way of, punishment 1600. d. That is payable or forfeitable as a penalty 1623. e. Used or appointed as a place of punishment 1843. f. Involving, connected with, or characterized by, a penalty or legal punishment. g. Of, pertaining to, or subject to the penal law, penal servitude, etc. 1647. †2. Painful; severe, esp. in the way of punishment -1709.

1. a. *P. Laws*, laws which impose a penalty for the commission of any act; *spec.* the laws inflicting penalties upon Nonconformists and Papists. *P. Code* (in Ireland), a name applied to the successive penal statutes passed in 17th and 18th centuries against Papists. b. A second edict made it p. to pay more 1872. c. *P. servitude*, imprisonment with hard labour at any p. establishment in Great Britain or its dominions; substituted for transportation in 1853. d. Let another hand..exact Thy p. forfeit MILT. e. P. settlements 1843. Cayenne is..the p. colony of France 1876. Hence **Pe·nally** *adv.* in the way of punishment.

Penality (pīnæ·lĭti). Now *rare*. 1495. [a. F. *pénalité*, or ad. med.L. *pœnalitas* PENALTY.] †1. = PENALTY 1. -1513. †2. = PENALTY 2. -1548. 3. The character or fact of being penal 1650.

Penalize (pī·nălaiz), *v.* 1868. [f. PENAL *a.* + -IZE.] 1. *trans.* To make (an action) penal 1879. 2. *Sport.* To subject to a penalty; hence *gen.*, to handicap 1868. Hence **Penaliza·tion**.

Penalty (pe·nălti). 1512. [Ult. ad. med.L. *pœnalitas*, f. *pœnalis* PENAL; cf. PENALITY.] †1. Pain, suffering (*rare*) -1642. 2. A punishment imposed for breach of law, rule, or contract; a loss, disability, or disadvantage of some kind, either fixed by law for some offence, or agreed upon in case of violation of a contract; occas. *spec.* the payment of a sum of money imposed in such a case, or the sum of money itself; a fine, mulct. b. *fig.* Suffering, disadvantage, or loss, esp. that resulting from an error or fault, or incident to some position or state 1664. c. *Sport.* A disadvantage imposed on a competitor or side as punishment for a breach of rules; also, a handicap 1885. 3. *attrib.*, esp. in *p. goal, kick*, etc. 1889.

2. In the day thou eat'st, thou di'st; Death is the penaltie impos'd MILT. Phr. *On, upon, under p.*, with the liability of incurring p. in case of not fulfilling the command or condition stated. 3. **p. envelope** *U.S.* an envelope for the unauthorized use of which a penalty is imposed.

Penance (pe·năns), *sb.* ME. [a. OF. *pen(e)ance, pennance* :—L. *pænitentia*, f. *pænitentem* PENITENT; see -ANCE.] †1. Repentance, penitence -1699. 2. *Theol.* The sacramental ordinance in which remission of sins is received by a penitent through the absolution of a priest, the necessary parts being contrition, confession, satisfaction, and absolution ME. 3. The performance of some act of self-mortification or submission to some penalty, as an expression of penitence; penitential discipline or observance; *spec.* in *Eccl.* use, such discipline or observance officially imposed by a priest after confession ME. b. Temporal punishment for sin. late ME. 4. *transf.* ME. †5. Punishment -1769.

1. Phr. *To do p.* [L. *agere pænitentiam*], to repent. 3. Phr. *To do p.*, to perform acts of self-mortification or undergo penitential discipline. b. Trentals, seyde he, delieueren fro penaunce Hir freendes soules CHAUCER. 4. We..made our horses do p. for that little rest they had DE FOE. 5. He..shall, for his obstinacy, receive the terrible sentence of *p.*, or *peine forte et dure* BLACKSTONE. Hence **Pe·nance** *v. trans.* to subject to penance; to discipline, chastise.

Pen and ink, pen-and-ink, *phr.* 1463. A. as *sb.* 1. *lit.* The instruments of writing. 2. Short for *pen-and-ink drawing* 1890. B. as *adj.* (prop. hyphened.) 1. Using pen and ink; clerkly. Now *rare* or *Obs.* 1676. 2. Done, made, or executed with pen and ink, as a drawing; also, done or described in writing 1842.

B. 1. The Duke of Bedford..says he is tired of being a pen and ink man H. WALPOLE. So †**Pen and inkhorn**, as writing instruments, carried by clerks, etc.; usu. *attrib.* or as *adj.* (with hyphens): Engaged in writing, clerkly; learned, pedantic.

Penang lawyer: see LAWYER 4.

Penannular (pīnæ·niŭlăɹ), *a.* 1851. [f. L. *pæne*, PENE- + ANNULAR.] Nearly annular; of the form of an almost complete ring.

‖ **Penates** (pīnē·tīz), *sb. pl.* 1513. [L., perh. f. *penus* innermost part of a temple of Vesta.] *Roman Myth.* The guardian deities of the household and of the state, who were worshipped in the interior of every house; often coupled with *Lares* (see LAR); household gods. Also *transf.* and *fig.*

Pence (pens), collect. pl. of PENNY, q. v.

Pencel, pensel, -il (pe·nsĕl). Now only *Hist.* or *arch.* ME. [a. AF. *pencel*, reduced from *penoncel*, PENNONCEL, dim. of *penon*, PENNON.] A small pennon or streamer. †b. A lady's token worn or carried by a knight -1485.

‖ **Penchant** (paṅʃaṅ). 1672. [F., sb. use of pr. pple. of *pencher* to slope, incline :—L. type **pendicare* from *pendere* to hang.] A (strong or habitual) inclination; a favourable bias, bent.

She had a *p.* for brown MISS MITFORD.

Pencil (pe·nsĭl, pe·ns'l), *sb.* [late ME. a. OF. *pincel*, mod.F. *pinceau* :—pop.L. **penicellum*, for cl.L. *penicillum*, dim. of *peniculus* brush, dim. of *penis* tail.] I. 1. An artist's paint-brush of camel's hair, fitch, sable, etc., gathered into a quill; esp. a small and fine one. Now *arch.* b. Put for the painter's art, skill, or style; and transferred to word-painting. late ME. c. *fig.* 1581. 2. An instrument for marking, drawing, or writing; formed of black lead, white or coloured chalk, charcoal, soft slate, aniline, etc., and having a tapering point; *spec.* a thin strip of such substance (usu., when not otherwise described, of plumbago or graphite), enclosed in a cylinder of soft wood, or in a metal case with a tapering end. (Now the prevailing sense.) 1612.

1. b. Truth needs no colour, with his colour fix'd; Beauty no p. SHAKS. c. Tinted by the golden p. of autumn DISRAELI.

II. 1. A small tuft of hairs, bristles, feathers, or the like, springing from or close to a point on a surface. Now only in *Nat. Hist.* 1599. 2. *Optics.* A set of rays converging to or diverging from a single point, or such number of them as may fall upon any surface or be considered collectively 1673. 3. *Geom.* The figure formed by a set of straight lines meeting in a point 1840. 4. Anything pencil-shaped 1837.

2. *Optic p.*, the rays that pass from any point through the crystalline lens, and are again brought to a focus on the retina, thus forming a double cone with the crystalline as common base.

Comb.: **p. cedar**, any of several species of juniper the wood of which is used for the casing of lead-pencils; **p. diamond** (see sense II. 4); **p. flower**, a name for the genus *Stylosanthes* of leguminous plants; **p.-lead**, black-lead or graphite as used for making pencils; a slender stick of this for fitting into a pencil-case, etc.; **-sharpener**, an instrument for sharpening a black-lead or slate p. by pushing or rotating it against a cutting edge.

Pencil (pe·nsĭl, -s'l), *v.* 1532. [f. prec.] 1. *trans.* To paint with a pencil or brush (*obs.* or *arch.*); now, usu., to colour, tint, or mark with or as with a black-lead pencil. Also *fig.* b. To depict or represent with the pencil or brush; †*transf.* to depict in words; also (in later use) to outline, sketch, or delineate in pencil. Also *fig.* 1610. 2. To write or jot down with a pencil 1760. †3. *intr.* To form into pencils (of light) -1774. 4. *trans.* To treat or 'paint' (a wound, etc.) *with* something applied with a fine brush 1822.

1. Time enough to pencill it over with all the curious touches of art MILT.

Pe·ncil-ca·se. 1552. A holder for the reception of a pencil or pencil-lead, etc., usually of metal; also, a case of wood, leather, etc., for keeping pencils in.

Pencilled, -iled (pe·nsĭld, -s'ld), *ppl. a.* 1592. [f. PENCIL *sb.* and *v.* + -ED.] 1. Having a pencil 1593. 2. Painted with a 'pencil' or fine brush; depicted with or as with a 'pencil'; now, usu., drawn or sketched in pencil 1593. 3. Marked with or as with a lead pencil 1592. 4. Written with a pencil 1794. 5. Having pencils of rays; radiate 1853. 6. *Zool.* and *Bot.* Tufted; brushy; penicillate 1846.

3. Small pensild eye browes KYD.

Pencilling (pe·nsĭliŋ, -s'liŋ), *vbl. sb.* 1706. [-ING[1].] 1. The action of PENCIL *v.*; *esp.* fine colouring or drawing; also *transf.* 2. *concr.* A drawing or sketch with a pencil; a jotting or note, made in pencil; *fig.* a literary sketch or portrait 1830. 3. Drawing a line of white paint along a mortar-joint in a brick wall 1875.

1. Whether they are..made by the pencilings of art or nature HOGARTH.

†**Pe·n-clerk.** late ME. [f. PEN *sb.*[2] + CLERK.] A 'clerk' whose scholarship extended only to the use of the pen (as dist. from *clerk* = clergyman or scholar); a clerk, a secretary; also *fig.* -1634.

Pencraft (pe·nkraft). *rare.* 1600. [f. PEN *sb.*[2] + CRAFT *sb.*] The craft or art of writing; penmanship, authorship.

Pend, *v.* 1480. [app. a. F. *pendre* :—late L. *pendere* to hang. But occas. aphetic f. *apend*, APPEND *v.*[2], or of *depend*.] †1. *trans.*

To hang; to append -1660. **2.** *intr.* To hang; to depend (*lit.* and *fig.*) 1480.

Pendant (pe·ndănt), *sb.* ME. [a. F. *pendant*, sb. use of pr. pple. of *pendre* to hang.] †**I.** = F. *pendant* = *pente.* Slope, declivity, inclination (of a hill, etc.) -1641. **II.** Something that hangs or is suspended. **1.** A loose hanging ornament; now chiefly, an ornament of some precious metal or stone, attached to a bracelet, necklace, etc.; rarely, an ornamental fringe ME. †**b.** *spec.* The end of a belt or girdle which remained hanging down after passing through the buckle -1577. **c.** *spec.* The pendant part of an ear-ring 1555. **d.** *transf.* 1586. †**2.** A natural hanging part; as *Bot.* an anther -1790. **3.** Applied to mechanical constructions; as †a pendulum -1653; a hanging chandelier, etc. 1858; †a hanging shield -1727. **4.** *Arch.* **a.** In the Decorated and Perpendicular styles: A knop or other terminal together with the stem suspending it, hanging from a vault or from the framing of an open timber roof. **b.** In *Carpentry*, A similar object on the lower end of the newel at the angle of a staircase when this projects below the string. **c.** A representation of fruit, flowers, etc., in a hanging position, as a decorative feature. ME. **5.** *Arch.* In open timber roofs: **a.** A wooden post placed against the wall, usu. resting on a corbel, its upper end secured to the hammer-beam or to the lower end of the principal rafter; also called *p. post.* **b.** A spandrel formed by the side-post, the curved brace, and the tie-beam or the hammer-beam. **c.** In stone-work: A shaft worked on the masonry of the wall, supporting the ribs of a vault or an arch or the pendant-post of an open timber roof, and resting on a corbel or terminating in a decorated boss. ME. **6.** *Naut.* (*Rigging p.*) A short rope hanging from the head of a (main or fore) mast, yard-arm, or clew of a sail, and having at its lower end a block or a thimble spliced to an eye for receiving the hooks of the fore and main tackles. Also a similar device used in other parts of the ship. late ME. **7.** *Naut.* A tapering flag, very long in the fly and short in the hoist; *spec.* that flown at the masthead of a vessel in commission, unless distinguished by a flag or broad pendant. The official form is PENNANT. 1485. **b.** *Broad p.*: a short swallow-tailed pendant flown as the distinctive mark of a commodore's ship in a squadron 1716.

1. b. The buckles and pendentes were all of fyne golde 1548. d. Man, ordinarily a p. to events, only half attached EMERSON. 7. I hoisted my P. on the Irresistible NELSON.

III. 1. That by which something is hung or suspended; now *spec.* the pendant-shank or stem and the pendant-ring or bow of a watch 1580. **2.** A thing, esp. a picture, forming a parallel, match, or companion to another. Also said of a person Often pron. as F. (paṅdaṅ). 1788. **b.** A complementary statement, consideration, etc.; a counterpart 1841.

2. When St. Catharine is grouped with other saints, her usual p. is St. Barbara 1848.

Comb.: **p.-bow**, the ring or 'bow' of a watch-stem; **-fittings**, hanging fittings for electric light; **-post** *Arch.* = sense II. 5 a; **-tackle**, a tackle rigged from the masthead p.

Pendency (pe·ndĕnsi). 1637. [f. PENDENT; see -ENCY.] **1.** The state or condition of being pendent, or awaiting settlement. **2.** Pendent position; droopingness, droop (*rare*) 1770.

Pendent, -ant (pe·ndĕnt, -ănt), *a.* (*prep.*) late ME. [orig. *penda(u)nt*, a. F. *pendant*; see PENDANT *sb.* About 1600, refash. after L. *pendens, pendentem.* But *pendant* is still freq. used.] **1.** Hanging; dependent. Of a tree: having down-hanging branches. **2.** Overhanging; jutting or leaning over; also, slanting; placed or hanging on a steep slope. late ME. Also *fig.* **3.** Hanging unsupported in the air or in space; supported above the ground on arches, columns, etc. Now *rare* or *Obs.* 1600. **4.** Hanging in the balance, undecided, pending 1633. **5.** *Gram.* Of which the grammatical construction is left incomplete 1849.

1. The p. woodbine WORDSW. 2. Another pendant towre like that at Pisa EVELYN. 3. To be..blowne with restlesse violence round about The pendant world SHAKS. Hence **Pe·ndently, -antly,** *adv.*

‖ **Pendente lite** (pende·nti ləi·ti). 1736. [L., lit. 'with the lawsuit pending'.] *Law.* While a suit is pending; during litigation.

Pendentive (pende·ntiv), *sb.* (*a.*) 1727. [ad. F. *pendentif, -ive*, f. L. *pendentem* hanging; see -IVE.] **1.** *Arch.* Each of the spherical triangles formed by the intersection of a hemispherical dome by two pairs of opposite arches springing from the four supporting columns; *orig.* supporting an independent dome, cupola, or the like. Also (as in Gothic architecture) extended to each of the similar segments constituting that part of a groined vault resting on a single impost. ¶ **2.** Incorrect uses: = PENDANT II. 4, 5. 1845. **B.** *adj.* Of or belonging to pendentives; of the form of or having pendentives 1790.

Pendicle (pe·ndik'l). Chiefly *Sc.* 1488. [ad. L. **pendiculum*, f. *pendere* to hang + *-culum*, suffix forming names of instruments, also often dim.] **1.** A hanging ornament, a pendant. Now *rare.* **2.** Something dependent on something else; an appurtenance, appendage, dependency; *spec.* a small piece of property, esp. when separately sublet 1530. Hence **Pe·ndicler,** the holder of a p.; an inferior tenant.

Pending (pe·ndiŋ), *ppl. a.* and *prep.* 1642. [Formed after F. *pendant*, L. *pendens* hanging, in suspense, with Eng. ppl. ending -ING [2].] **A.** *ppl. a.* **1.** Remaining undecided, awaiting settlement; orig. of a lawsuit. 1797. **2.** Impending, imminent (*rare*) 1806.

1. The p. negotiations 1838. 2. These p. ills 1833.

B. *prep.* or quasi-*prep.* During, throughout the continuance of, in the process of. (Orig. used in a construction corresp. to the abl. absol.; thus L. *pendente lite*, F. *pendant le procès* (= *le procès pendant*). The pple. when it stood before the sb. came to be viewed as a prep.) 1642. **b.** While awaiting, until 1838.

b. P. his return, Kate and her mother were shown into a dining-room DICKENS.

Pendle (pe·nd'l). *local.* 1808. [Origin obsc.] A term for various kinds or beds of stone as occurring in quarries. Also *p.-rock, -stone.*

Pendragon (pen͵dræ·gən). 1470. [Welsh = chief leader in war, f. *pen* head + *dragon* dragon, f. L. *draco, draconem* dragon, the standard of a cohort.] A title given to an ancient British or Welsh prince holding or claiming supreme power; chief leader or ruler.

Hit befel in the dayes of Vther p. when he was kynge of all Englond MALORY. Hence **Pendra·gonship,** the rank of p.

Pendulant (pe·ndiŭlănt), *a.* Also **-ent.** 1650. [See PENDULATE.] Pendulous, pendent.

Pendular (pe·ndiŭlăı), *a.* 1878. [f. PENDULUM + -AR [1].] Of or pertaining to a pendulum; resembling that of a pendulum, as a simple vibration.

Pendulate (pe·ndiŭleit), *v.* 1698. [f. L. **pendulare* = It. *pendolare*, f. *pendulus* PENDULOUS; see -ATE [3].] *intr.* **a.** To swing like a pendulum. **b.** *fig.* To oscillate between two opposite conditions, be in suspense or undecided.

Pe·ndule. Now *rare.* 1578. [In sense 1, app. ad. L. *pendulus* PENDULOUS; in senses 2, 3, a. F. *pendule.*] **1.** Something pendulous or suspended. †**2.** A pendulum. [F. *pendule* masc.] -1798. **3.** A time-piece having a pendulum. Now only as Fr. *pendule* (paṅdül) fem. 1661. †**4.** *attrib.*, as *p. clock* -1677.

Penduline (pe·ndiŭləin), *a.* (*sb.*) 1802. [a. F. *penduline*, mod.L. *pendulinus*, f. L. *pendulus* PENDULOUS; see -INE [1].] **1.** Applied to a bird that builds a pendulous nest, esp. the *p. titmouse* of Southern and Eastern Europe (*Ægithalus pendulinus*). **2.** Pendulous, as a bird's nest 1885. **B.** *sb.* A titmouse of the genus *Pendulinus*, or allied to this 1890.

Pendulous (pe·ndiŭləs), *a.* 1605. [f. L. *pendulus* hanging down, pendent (f. *pendere* to hang) + -OUS.] **1.** Suspended; hanging down, pendent, drooping. Freq. in *Nat. Hist.* 1656. †**b.** Suspended overhead; overhanging. Also *fig.* Impending. -1800. **c.** Hanging or floating in air or space. Now *rare* or *Obs.* 1638. **2.** *spec.* Suspended so as to swing; oscillating; hence, of movement: Oscillatory, undulating; consisting of simple vibrations 1706. **3.** *fig.* Wavering between two opinions, purposes, or tendencies; vacillating, undecided, doubtful. Now *rare.* 1624.

1. Ears long, broad, and p. 1782. b. *Lear* III. iv. 69. c. The p. round Earth MILT. 3. The Kings mind was wholy p. (or doubtfull) PRYNNE. So **Pendulo·sity** (*rare*) the quality or condition of being p. **Pe·ndulous-ly** *adv.*, **-ness.**

Pendulum (pe·ndiŭlŏm). *Pl.* **-ums,** formerly (*rare*) **-a.** 1660. [a. mod.L. *pendulum*, sb. use of neut. of L. *pendulus* PENDULOUS, lit. a free-hanging body.] **1.** A body suspended so as to be free to swing or oscillate; usu., an instrument consisting of a rod, with a weight or *bob* at the end, so suspended as to swing to and fro by the action of gravity; esp. as an essential part of a clock, serving (by the isochronism of its vibrations) to regulate and control the movement of the works. **2.** *fig.* In ref. to oscillation between two opposites 1769. †**3.** A pendulum-clock, a pendulum-watch -1706. **4.** *attrib.* 1664.

1. **Compound p.,** (*a*) a p. consisting of a number of weights at fixed distances; an actual material p. regarded theoretically, as opp. to a *simple p.*; (*b*) a compensation p. whose rod consists of bars of different metals. **Conical p.,** a p. so contrived that the bob revolves in a circle, the rod thus describing a cone. **Mercurial** (or †**Quicksilver**) **p.,** a compensation p. with a cylindrical bob containing mercury, whose upward expansion by heat counteracts the lengthening of the rod. **Simple p.,** (*a*) a theoretical p. consisting of a particle having weight but no magnitude, suspended by a weightless inextensible rod, and moving without friction; (*b*) a p. consisting simply of a bob suspended by a cord or wire; (*c*) a p. unconnected with any mechanism. **Spherical p.,** = *conical p.* See also BALLISTIC *p.*, COMPENSATION *p.*, GRIDIRON *p.*, etc. 2. Man! Thou p. betwixt a smile and tear BYRON.

Comb.: **p.-ball, -bob,** the heavy ball or bob forming the lower end of a p.; **-clock,** a clock that goes by means of a p.; **-level,** a plumb-level; †**-watch,** a watch of the modern type, with a balance-wheel provided with a spring and oscillating regularly, thus having the function of the p. of a clock; **-wheel,** (*a*) the escapement wheel of a clock; †(*b*) the balance-wheel of a watch.

Pene- (pīni), *prefix*, repr. L. *pæne* nearly, almost, all but, bef. a vowel *pæn-*, *pen-*, in a few words of rare occurrence, as **Pe:necontempora·neous** *a.*; **Pe·neplai:n** (also **-plane**), a tract of land almost a plain; etc.

‖ **Penelope** (pĭne·lŏpi). 1581. [a. Gr. Πηνελόπη.] **1.** Name of the wife of Ulysses in ancient Greek legend, who, during her husband's long absence, nightly unravelled the web she had woven during the day, and thus put off the suitors whose offers were to wait till the web should be finished; hence, allusively, for 'chaste wife'. **2.** *Zool.* A genus of gallinaceous birds of Central and South America, typical of the subfamily *Penelopinæ* or guans 1605.

1. Our absent Penelopes were, doubtless, dreaming 1835. Hence **Penelope·an** *a.* of or pertaining to, or resembling the web or weaving, or time-gaining policy of P. **Pene·lopine** *a. Zool.* belonging to the subfamily *Penelopinæ* of gallinaceous birds.

Penetrability (pe:nĭtrăbi·lĭti). 1609. [f. next; see -ITY.] †**1.** Capacity of penetrating -1687. **2.** Capability of being penetrated; *spec.* in *Nat. Phil.* the capacity of simultaneously occupying the same space as something else 1648.

Penetrable (pe·nĭtrăb'l), *a.* late ME. [ad. L. *penetrabilis*, f. *penetrare* PENETRATE; see -BLE.] †**1.** Having the quality or capacity of penetrating; penetrative, penetrating -1668. **2.** Capable of being penetrated or pierced; into or through which access may be gained 1538.

2. It is not p. by the eye of man TOPSELL. *fig.* I am ..p. to your kinde entreaties SHAKS. Hence **Pe·netrableness,** penetrability. **Pe·netrably** *adv.* †**a.** penetratingly; **b.** so as to be p.

Penetral (pe·nĭtrăl). Now *rare.* 1589. [a. L. *penetral(e* (usu. in pl. *penetralia*; see next), f. *penetralis* interior, innermost, f. stem of *penetrare* PENETRATE.] The innermost part; of a temple, the sanctuary; usu. in *pl.* = next.

‖ **Penetralia** (penĭtrē·liă), *sb. pl.* 1668. [L., pl. of *penetral(e*; see prec.] The innermost parts of a building; *esp.* of a temple, the sanctuary or inmost shrine; hence *gen.* Innermost parts.

The p. of the harams of the East 1779. Hence **Penetra·lian** *a. rare.*

†**Pe·netrancy.** 1578. [f. L. *penetrantem* PENETRANT; see -ANCY.] Penetrating quality; penetrativeness (*lit.* and *fig.*) -1692.

Penetrant (pe·nĭtrănt), *a.* 1543. [ad. L. *penetrantem* pr. pple. of *penetrare* PENETRATE, or F. *pénétrant.*] **1.** *lit.* Having the property of penetrating, piercing, or making its way into anything. 2. *fig.* Of the mind, intellect, etc.: Acute, subtle 1599.

Penetrate (pe·nĭtreᶦt), *v.* 1530. [f. L. *penetrat-*, *penetrare* to place within, enter within, etc.; related to *penitus* interior, etc.; see -ATE [3].] 1. *trans.* To make or find its (or one's) way into or right through (something); usu. implying force or effort; to gain access within; to pierce. b. To permeate. Also with personal subj.: To cause to be permeated; to imbue (*with* something). 1680. 2. *intr.* To make its (or one's) way *into* or *through* something, or *to* some point or place (implying remoteness or difficulty of access); to gain entrance or access 1530. 3. *fig.* (*trans.*) To pierce the ear, heart, or feelings of; to 'touch' 1591. b. *intr.* To touch the heart SHAKS. 4. *trans.* To gain intellectual access into the inner content or meaning of; to see into or through; to find out, discover, discern 1560. b. *intr.* To see *into* or *through* 1589.

1. A cloud which it was almost impossible to p. 1860. b. The reader..should have penetrated himself..with the atmosphere of the times 1887. 2. Born where Heav'n's influence scarce can p. POPE. 3. A Man penetrated with..Grief 1720. b. *Cymb.* II. iii. 14. 4. Clive penetrated and disappointed his designs 1818. Hence **Pe·netrating** *ppl. a.*, -**ly** *adv.*, -**ness**.

Penetration (penĭtrēᶦ·ʃən). 1623. [ad. late L. *penetrationem*, f. *penetrare* PENETRATE.] 1. The action, or an act, of penetrating; also, mutual permeation as of two fluids. b. *Nat. Phil.* The occupation of the same space by two bodies at the same time; formerly *p. of dimensions* 1661. 2. Power of penetrating, as a measurable quantity or quality. a. *Gunnery.* The depth to which a bullet, etc. will penetrate any material against which it is fired 1807. b. *Optics.* The power of an optical instrument to enable an observer to see into space, or into an object 1799. 3. *fig.* Insight, acuteness, discernment 1605.

1. His Magnetic beam,..to each inward part With gentle p.,..Shoots invisible vertue even to the deep MILT. 2. a. The more p. shells have the better 1901. 3. You can pretend to be a Man of P. STEELE.

Penetrative (pe·nĭtreᶦtiv), *a.* late ME. [ad. med.L. *penetrativus*, f. *penetrat-*, *penetrare* to PENETRATE; see -ATIVE.] 1. Having the quality of penetrating; *spec.* Having the quality of entering through the senses, or of keenly affecting the sense organs; sharp, pungent. Also said of the eye or sight. 2. *fig.* That penetrates to the seat of the feelings SHAKS. 3. *fig.* Having the power of mental penetration; intellectually acute 1727.

1. The p. character of temptations TRENCH. 2. *Ant. & Cl.* IV. xiv. 75. 3. So..minutely p. was the quality of his understanding MORLEY. Hence **Pe·netrative-ly** *adv.*, -**ness**.

Pen-feather (pe·n,feːðəɹ). 1602. [f. PEN *sb.*[2] + FEATHER.] 1. A quill-feather of a bird's wing. 2. = PIN-FEATHER 1877. So **Pe·n-fea:thered** *a.* = PIN-FEATHERED. Also said of a horse or his hair when rough or bristly.

Pen-fish. 1763. [f. PEN *sb.*[2] + FISH *sb.*[1]] 1. A squid 1835. 2. The sparoid fish *Calamus penna* of the Caribbean Sea 1763.

Penfold (pe·n,fōuld), *sb.* and *v.* 1575. [f. PEN *sb.*[1] + FOLD *sb.*[1]] = PINFOLD *sb.* and *v.*

Penguin (pe·ŋgwin, pe·ngwin). 1578. [Origin obsc.] †1. The Great Auk or Gare-fowl (*Alca impennis*) –1792. 2. Any bird of the family *Spheniscidæ*, including several genera of sea-fowl inhabiting the southern hemisphere, distinguished by having the wings represented by scaly 'flippers' or paddles with which they swim under water 1588.

Comb.: **p. duck**, a variety of the common duck having the feet placed so far back as to induce a nearly erect attitude like that of a p.; **p. grass**, the tussock-grass of the Falkland Islands, *Poa flabellata*. Hence **Pe·nguinery**, a colony of penguins; a place where penguins congregate and breed.

Penholder (pe·nhōuːldəɹ). 1815. [f. PEN *sb.*[2] + HOLDER [1].] A holder for a (steel or other) pen; the pen and penholder together forming a writing instrument or 'pen' of which the penholder forms the handle.

Penial (pī·niăl), *a.* 1877. [f. PENIS + -AL.] *Anat.* Belonging to or connected with the penis.

Pe·nible, *a.* late ME. [a. F. *pénible*, f. *peine* pain; see -BLE.] †1. Painstaking; hard-working –1481. 2. Causing or involving pain or trouble; painful. *Obs.* or *rare arch.*

Penicil (pe·nisil). 1826. [ad. L. *penicillus* PENCIL.] *Nat. Hist.* A small bundle or tuft of slightly diverging hairs, resembling a paint-brush.

Penicillate (pe·nisilĕt), *a.* 1819. [f. L. *penicillus* PENCIL + -ATE [2].] *Nat. Hist.* a. Furnished with a penicil or pencils; having a small tuft or tufts of hairs, scales, etc. b. Formed into or forming a small tuft or brush. c. Streaked, pencilled.

Penicilliform (penisi·lifǭɹm), *a.* 1811. [ad. mod.L. *penicilliformis*, f. *penicillus* PENCIL; see -FORM.] Of the form of, or resembling, a hair-pencil.

Peninsula (pĭni·nsiŭlă). *Pl.* **-as** (-ăz), formerly -æ. 1538. [a. L. *pæninsula*, f. *pæne-* PENE- + *insula* island.] A piece of land that is almost an island, being nearly surrounded by water; hence, any piece of land projecting into the sea so that its boundary is mainly coastline. b. (*spec.*) *The P.*: Spain and Portugal.

Peninsular (pĭni·nsiŭlăɹ), *a.* (*sb.*) 1612. [f. prec. + -AR.] Of, belonging to, or of the nature of a peninsula. b. *spec.* (usu. with capital.) Of or pertaining to the peninsula of Spain and Portugal, or (*esp.*) the war carried on there in 1808–14. 1812. B. *sb.* a. An inhabitant of a peninsula. b. A soldier of the P. war. 1888.

Peninsulate (pĭni·nsiŭleᶦt), *v.* 1538. [f. as prec. + -ATE [3]; after *insulate.*] *trans.* To make into a peninsula; to divide into peninsulas.

A detached tract peninsulated by sea, lake, or river 1774.

‖**Penis** (pī·nis). *Pl.* **penes** (-īz). 1693. [L., orig. = *cauda* tail.] The intromittent or copulatory organ of any male animal.

Penistone (pe·nistǝn). 1551. [Name of a small town in Yorkshire, where the cloth was made.] †1. A kind of coarse woollen cloth formerly used for garments, linings, etc. Also *attrib.* –1834. 2. *P. flags*, sandstone flags from the coal measures around Penistone, used for paving-stones 1688.

Penitence (pe·nitĕns). ME. [a. OF. *pénitence*, ad. L. *pænitentia*, f. *pænitens* PENITENT; see -ENCE.] 1. = PENANCE *sb.* 3. Now *rare*, and usu. including sense 2. 2. The fact or state of being penitent; contrition, with desire and intention of amendment; repentance 1591.

2. By P. th' Eternalls wrath's appeas'd SHAKS.

†**Pe·nitencer.** ME. [a. F. *pénitencier*, ad. med.L. *pæni-*, *pœnitentiarius.*] In the mediæval Church, a priest appointed to hear confession, assign penance, and give absolution in extraordinary cases; a penitentiary.

Penitency (pe·nitĕnsi). Now *rare.* 1450. [ad. L. *pænitentia*; see PENITENCE and -ENCY.] 1. Penitence as a state; repentance. †2. A penitential practice or discipline (*rare*) –1676.

Penitent (pe·nitĕnt), *a.* and *sb.* late ME. [a. OF. *pénitent*, ad. L. *pænitentem*, pr. pple. of *pænitere* to repent.] A. *adj.* 1. That repents, with intention to amend the sin or wrongdoing; contrite. b. *transf.* of things: Expressive of repentance 1723. †2. Regretful, grieved; relenting, sorry, vexed. Const. *of*, *upon*. *rare.* –1609. 3. Undergoing penance 1590.

1. A p. prodigal 1840. b. Several p. letters DE FOE. 3. *Com. Err.* I. ii. 52.

B. *sb.* 1. One who repents; a repentant sinner. late ME. 2. A person performing (ecclesiastical) penance; one under the direction of a confessor. late ME. 3. *pl.* A name designating various R. C. congregations or orders, associated for mutual discipline and charitable works. Rarely in *sing.*, a member of one of these. 1693.

attrib. p.-form, a form or bench for penitents. Hence **Pe·nitently** *adv.*

Penitential (penite·nʃăl), *a.* and *sb.* 1508. [ad. med.L. *pœnitentialis*, f. *pæni-*, *pœnitentia* PENITENCE; see -AL.] A. *adj.* 1. Of, pertaining to, or expressive of penitence or repentance. 2. Pertaining to, expressive of, or constituting ecclesiastical penance; of the nature of a penance 1535. Also *fig.*

1. *P. Psalms*, seven psalms (vi, xxxiii, xxxvii; li, cii, cxxx, cxliii) which are used as penitential devotions. 2. *P. robe*, a robe worn by a public penitent.

B. *sb.* 1. A penitent. †Also *joc.* a prisoner. 1627. 2. A book containing in codified form the canons of the Church relating to penance, its imposition, etc. 1618. 3. *pl.* Short for *P. Psalms*: see A. 1. 1641. 4. *pl.* †a. The demeanour, appearance, or behaviour of a penitent. b. Mourning garments; black clothes (*colloq.*). 1748. Hence **Penite·ntially** *adv.*

Penitentiary (penite·nʃări), *a.* and *sb.* late ME. [ad. med.L. *pœnitentiarius* adj. and sb., f. L. *pæni-*, *pœnitentia* PENITENCE; see -ARY [1].] A. *adj.* 1. Of or pertaining to penance; administering or undergoing penance 1577. 2. Pertaining to, or expressive of, penitence; repentant (*rare*) 1634. 3. Intended for or relating to the penal and reformatory treatment of criminals 1776. 4. Of an offence: Punishable by imprisonment in a penitentiary (*U.S.*) 1856.

1. The p. books and canons 1678. 2. A p. letter 1806. 3. *P. House* = B. III. 3. *P. Act*, the Act 19 Geo. III, c. 74. 4. It had been a p. offence to teach a black to read and write 1896.

B. *sb.* I. = med.L. *pœnitentiarius.* 1. A person appointed to deal with penitents or penances; *spec.* in R. C. Ch., an officer vested with power to deal with extraordinary cases 1475. †2. = PENITENT *sb.* 1 and 2. –1654. 3. A member of a religious order so called 1631.

1. *Grand, High* (*Chief, Great*) *P.*, a cardinal who presides over the office called 'penitentiary' (see II), and has the granting of absolution in cases reserved for the papal authority.

II. = med.L. *pœnitentiaria.* *R. C. Ch.* The office or dignity of a penitentiary; an office or congregation in the Papal Court, presided over by the Grand Penitentiary, and forming a tribunal for deciding upon questions relating to penance, dispensations, etc. 1658. III. = OF. *pen(e)ancerie.* †1. A place of penitential discipline or punishment for ecclesiastical offences –1644. 2. An asylum for penitent prostitutes 1806. 3. A reformatory prison; a house of correction 1816. 4. *U.S.* A prison 1898. IV. = PENITENTIAL *sb.* 2 (*rare*) 1853. Hence †**Penite·ntiaryship**, the office of p. (see B. I. 1).

Penknife (pe·n,nəif). late ME. [f. PEN *sb.*[2] + KNIFE.] A small knife, usu. carried in the pocket, used orig. for making and mending quill pens. (Formerly provided with a sheath; now made with a jointed blade or blades which fit inside the handle when closed.)

Penman (pe·nmæ̆n). *Pl.* **penmen** (pe·nmen). 1591. [f. PEN *sb.*[2] + MAN *sb.*] 1. A man employed to write or copy documents, etc.; a clerk, secretary, notary, scrivener. Now *rare.* 1612. 2. A man skilled in penmanship; a calligrapher. (Qualified as *good*, *expert*, *swift*, etc.) 1591. 3. An author, a writer 1592. b. Const. *of* (that which is written). Now *rare.* 1610.

1. *Penmen of God* or *of the Holy Ghost*, applied to the writers of Scripture regarded as writing from divine dictation or command; St. Paul, one of the first Pen-men of the Holy Ghost 1656. Hence **Pe·nmanship,** the action or performance of a p.

Pennaceous (penēᶦ·ʃəs), *a.* *rare.* 1819. [f. mod.L. *pennaceus* (f. *penna* feather) + -OUS; see -ACEOUS.] a. *Ornith.* Having the structure of a pen-feather or quill-feather. b. *Entom.* and *Bot.* Applied to markings resembling feathers, or to surfaces or structures having such markings.

†**Pe·nnage.** *rare.* 1601. [a. F. *pennage*, f. *penne* plume; see -AGE.] = PLUMAGE –1857.

Pennant [1] (pe·nănt). 1611. [app. a compromise between PENDANT and PENNON.] 1. = PENDANT *sb.* II. 6. 2. = PENDANT *sb.* II. 7, PENNON 3. 1698. b. = PENNON 1. 1815. c. *U.S.* A flag awarded as a distinction 1888.

Pennant [2] (pe·nănt). 1756. [a. Welsh *pennant*, lit. 'dale-head', f. *pen(n* head + *nant* valley; also, a common Welsh place-name.] Now usu. *P. grit*: the name of an unproductive series of gritty strata lying between the Upper and Lower Coal-measures, in South Wales, etc. Also *P. flag, rock, stone.*

Pennate (pe·nĕt), *a.* *rare.* 1857. [ad. L. *pennatus* winged, f. *penna* feather; see -ATE [2].] 1. *Nat. Hist.* = PINNATE. 2. = PENNIFORM 1877. So **Pe·nnated** *a.* (in senses 1, 2); also, feathered 1727.

Pennati-, comb. form of L. *pennatus* PENNATE, as in **Pennatifid** *a.*, etc. = PINNATIFID, etc. (see PINNATI-).

Pennatulacean (penætiŭlēᶦ·ʃiăn), *a.* and *sb.* 1857. [f. mod.L. *Pennatulacea* neut. pl., f. *Pennatula*, the typical genus.] A. *adj.* Belonging to the order *Pennatulacea* of alcyonarian polyps. B. *sb.* A polyp of this order. So

Pennatula·ceous *a.* **Penna·tulid,** a polyp of the family *Pennatulidæ*, of which *Pennatula*, the sea-pen, is the typical genus.

Penner[1] (pe·nəɹ). *Obs.* or *dial.* late ME. [ad. med.L. *pennarium*, f. *penna* pen; see -ARIUM, -ER[2] 2.] A case or sheath for pens; a pen-case; in later use, occas., a writing-case.

Penner[2] (pe·nəɹ). 1570. [f. PEN *v.*[2] + -ER[1].] One who pens or words a writing, document, etc.; a writer *of* something.

Penni-, comb. form of L. *penna* feather, PEN *sb.*[2], as in **Penni·ferous** [L. *pennifer*] *a. Nat. Hist.* bearing or producing feathers; feathered. **Pe·nniform** [mod. L. *penniformis*] *a. Nat. Hist.* having the form or appearance of a feather; *spec.* applied to a muscle whose fibres are obliquely arranged on each side of a central tendon. **Pennigerous** (peni·dʒěrəs) [L. *penniger*] *a.* feather-bearing, feathered. **Pe·nninerved** [NERVE] *a. Bot.* (of a leaf) having nerves or veins diverging on each side of a midrib; feather-veined, pinnately veined; also **Penni·ne·rvate** *a.* **Pe·nniveined** [VEIN] *a. Bot.* = prec.

Penniless (pe·nilės), *a.* ME. [f. PENNY + -LESS.] Not having a penny; having no money; poor, destitute.

†*P. bench*, name of a covered bench which formerly stood beside Carfax Church, Oxford; and app. of similar open-air seats elsewhere; prob. as being the resort of destitute wayfarers; hence allusively. Hence **Pe·nniless-ly** *adv.*, **-ness.**

‖**Pennill** (pe·nilʰ), usu. in *pl.* **pennillion** (peni·lʰiǫn). 1784. [Welsh.] A form of improvised verse adapted to an air played on the harp, sung at the Eisteddfod, etc.; a stanza of such verse.

Pennon (pe·nən). [late ME. a. OF. *pen(n)on*, prob. a Rom. deriv. of L. *penna*, F. *penne* feather, plume, wing.] **1.** A long narrow flag or streamer, triangular and pointed, or swallow-tailed, formerly borne as a distinction by a knight under the rank of banneret; now a military ensign of the lancer regiments. **b.** Any flag or banner. late ME. **c.** *fig.* Applied to things of the shape of a pennon 1618. †**2. a.** A knight-bachelor. **b.** An ensign-bearer. -1661. **3.** The long pointed streamer of a ship; also called PENDANT and PENNANT 1627. **4.** *poet.* Used by Milton, and others after him, for: A wing, pinion 1667.

1. c. A pillar of dark smoke, which..spread its long dusky p. through the clear ether SCOTT. **3.** Yachts with pennons flying 1884. **4.** Fluttring his pennons vain plumb down he drops MILT. Hence **Pe·nnoned** (pe·nənd) *a.* having, bearing, or furnished with a p.

Pennoncel (pe·nənsel). *Obs.* exc. *Hist.* late ME. [a. OF. *penoncel*, dim. of *penon*, PENNON.] A small pennon borne upon a helmet or lance, a PENCEL; a pennon or pendant of a ship.

Penny (pe·ni). *Pl.* **pennies** (pe·niz), **pence** (pens). [OE. *pęn(n)ing, pęnding*, later *pęnig* (whence ME. *peni, peny*). Evidently of WGer. origin, but the source is unkn.] **I.** Original senses. **1.** An English coin of the value of $\frac{1}{12}$ of a shilling or $\frac{1}{240}$ of a pound; orig. of silver, later of copper, now of bronze. Denoted (after a numeral) by *d.* (for *denarius, denarii*); thus 5*d.*, fivepence. **b.** The pl. *pennies* is now used only of the individual coins (exc. in U.S.); *pence* is usu. collective, and is especially used after numerals, where from *twopence* to *elevenpence* (rarely *twelvepence*) and in *twentypence*, it is stressless (tʊ·pěns, etc.) and now written in comb. With other numbers *pence* is written separately (or hyphened) and has a separate stress, as *eighteen pence* (ē·tīn,pe·ns). OE. **2.** Rendering L. *denarius* (see DENARIUS); also occas. *argenteus* ('piece of silver'), and *nummus* (= *nummus sestertius*, SESTERCE). Now only in Biblical use. OE. **b.** In U.S. *colloq.* a cent 1889.

1. *Scots p.*, a coin equal in 17th c. to one-twelfth of the English penny. **2.** Shew me a p. Whose image and superscription hath it? And they said, Cæsar's. *Luke* xx. 24 (R.V.)

II. From the fact that the (silver) penny was for long the chief or only coin in circulation, the name came to be used in the following senses: **1.** A coin: applied to coins of distinct origin from the ordinary penny. Now *Hist.* 1483. **2.** Used vaguely for a piece of money; hence, a sum of money, money. Now chiefly in phr. *a pretty p.* ME. **b.** In *pl.* = money; orig. as consisting of (silver) pennies; in later use, often depreciative, 'small money', 'coppers', 'small earnings' ME. †**c.** (*Sing.*) With ordinal numeral, expressing an aliquot part of a sum of money, as *the fifth p.*, *i.e.* every fifth penny in any number of pennies = one-fifth of the whole amount -1844. **d.** The particular amount of some tax, impost, or customary payment. With defining word, as EARNEST-P., GOD'S P., PETER-P. (*pence*), etc. ME. **3.** As the type of a coin of small value, or of a small amount of money. Often in contrast with *pound.* ME.

1. *P. of twopence*, a silver coin of the value of twopence, a half-groat. *Gold p.*, a gold coin of the value of 20 shillings. **2.** They may..there be lodged..without paying of any pennie 1585. †*First p.*, prime cost, cost price. **b.** Dispensers of treasure..without price to them that have no pence MILT. **3.** A peny yn seson spent wille safe a pounde 1457.

III. Transf. uses; chiefly ellipt. †**1.** = PENNYWEIGHT -1590. †**2.** The amount bought for a penny -1591.

Phr. and Prov. *A p. for your thoughts*, I would give something to know what you are thinking about (addressed to one in a 'brown study'). *A p. saved is a p. gained* (*got, earned*). *A pretty* (*fine*, etc.) *p.*, a considerable sum (in the way of gain or cost). *In for a p., in for a pound*, having entered upon a matter one must carry it through at any cost. *No paternoster, no p.*, no work, no pay. *Take care of the pence and the pounds will take care of themselves. To turn* (*wind*) *the* (*a*) *p.*, to employ one's money profitably; or, to gain money. *Obs.* exc. in *to turn an honest p.* (see HONEST *a.* 4 b).

attrib. and *Comb.* **1.** *attrib.* or as *adj.* Of the price or value of a penny, costing a penny, as *p. bun, newspaper*, etc.; *p. dreadful* (see DREADFUL C); so with prefixed numeral, as *fivepenny nail*, a size of nail (orig. a nail which cost 5*d.* a hundred), *tenpenny nail*, etc.; for the use of or admission to which the charge is a penny, as *p. boat, bus, gaff* (GAFF *sb.*[3]), etc.; (of a game) at which the stake is a penny, as *p.-nap*, etc.; (of a person) selling something or doing some work for a penny or cheaply; hence, engaged in inferior work, as *p.-barber, poet, wit.* **2.** *Comb.*: **p.-bank,** a savings bank at which as little as a p. may be deposited; **-cress,** the plant *Thlaspi arvense*, or some other cruciferous plant with flat round pods; **-dog,** a kind of dogfish, also called *miller's dog* or *tope*; †**-farm** (**-ferme**), a money rent, instead of services; **-farthing** *colloq.*, an old fashioned high bicycle having a large and a small wheel; **-father,** one who is too careful of his pence; a niggard, skinflint; **-fee** *Sc.*, a payment of a p.; 'wages paid in money' (Jam.); **-fish,** the John Dory, so called as having a round spot upon either side; **-in-the-slot** *a.* [from the direction 'Put a penny in the slot'], (of mechanical devices for the automatic supply of commodities) actuated by the fall of a p. inserted through a slot; also *fig.*; **-land,** land valued at a p. a year (*Obs.* or *dial.*); **-piece,** a piece of money of the value of a p., a p.; †**-rent,** rent paid in money; periodical payment in cash; **-trumpet,** a toy trumpet costing a p.; also *fig.* in reference to petty boasting; **p. wedding,** a wedding at which each of the guests contributes money to the expenses of the entertainment and to the setting up of the newly-married couple.

Pe·nny-a-li·ne, *a.* 1833. [The phr. (*a*) *penny a line* used attrib.] Of writing or a writer: Paid at the rate of a penny a line; of cheap and superficial literary quality. So **Pe·nny-a-li·ner,** a writer who is paid at a penny a line, or at a low rate (usu. implying one who writes in an inflated style so as to fill as much space as possible); a hack-writer for the press.

Pe·nny-grass. late ME. [f. PENNY + GRASS.] Pop. name of: **a.** Navelwort or Wall Pennywort, *Cotyledon Umbilicus*; **b.** Marsh Pennywort, *Hydrocotyle vulgaris* (in both cases from the round leaves); **c.** Yellow-rattle, *Rhinanthus Crista-galli* (from the flat roundish pods).

Penny post, penny-post. 1680. [See POST *sb.*[1]] An organization for the conveyance of letters or packets at an ordinary charge of a penny each; *esp.* that established in the United Kingdom on 10 Jan. 1840 on the initiative of Rowland Hill. Also *attrib.* So **Pe·nny-po·stage,** the postage of letters, etc. at a charge of a penny each.

Pennyroyal (peniroi·ăl). 1530. [app. an alteration of earlier *pulyole ryale*, in AF. *puliol real* = OF. *poliol* thyme (:—L. type **pulegiolum*, dim. of *pulegium* thyme) + *real, royal* royal.] A species of mint (*Mentha Pulegium*), with small leaves and prostrate habit; formerly cultivated for its supposed medicinal virtues. Also applied, usu. with qualifying words, to other aromatic labiates, or other plants. Also *attrib.*

Bastard or *False P.*, names of two N. American labiates, *Trichostemma dichotomum* and *Isanthus cæruleus.*

attrib.: **p.-water,** a liquor distilled from the leaves of p., formerly used in medicine.

Pennyweight (pe·niwēᵢt). late ME. [f. PENNY + WEIGHT *sb.*] A measure of weight, = 24 grains, $\frac{1}{20}$ of an ounce Troy, or $\frac{1}{240}$ of a pound Troy. (Formerly = $\frac{1}{240}$ of a Tower pound, i. e. $22\frac{1}{2}$ grains, the actual weight of a silver penny.) Abbrev. *dwt.* **b.** A proportional measure of one-twelfth used in stating the fineness of silver (thus, pure silver is 12 pennyweights fine) 1758.

Pe·nny-wi·se, *adj. phr.*, or *a.* 1607. [cf. PENNY II. 3.] Wise or prudent in regard to pence, *i.e.* careful (*esp.* over-careful) in small expenditures; usu. in phr. *penny-wise* (*and*) *pound-foolish*, thrifty in small matters while wasteful in large ones. Hence **Penny-wisdom,** the quality of being penny-wise.

Pennywort (pe·niwɒɹt). late ME. [f. PENNY + WORT.] **1.** (In full, *Wall P.*) *Cotyledon Umbilicus* (N.O. *Crassulaceæ*), having peltate leaves of a rounded concave form, and growing in the crevices of rocks and walls; navelwort. **2.** (*Marsh P.* or *Water P.*) *Hydrocotyle vulgaris*, a small umbelliferous plant with rounded peltate leaves, growing in marshy places. Also extended to other species. 1578.

Pennyworth (pe·niwɒɹþ), contr. **penn'orth** (pe·nəþ). OE. [f. PENNY + WORTH.] **1.** The amount which may be bought for a penny; as much as is worth a penny. **b.** *fig.* Amount, sum; *esp.* a very small, or the least, amount; often with neg. = not the least bit; *ironically*, 'a deal', 'a lot'. late ME. †**2.** That which is or may be bought for a given sum, in contrast to the money itself. (Often in *pl.*) -1656. **3.** Money's worth, value for one's money; a bargain; †profit, advantage obtained. Usu. qualified as *bad, cheap, dear, good*, etc.; also *absol.* A good bargain. Also *fig.* ME. †**b.** Price in proportion to value; (cheap, etc.) rate -1729.

1. She..will never buy anything by single pennyworths JOHNSON. **3.** You take your peniworths now. Sleepe for a weeke SHAKS. You will not find it a dear p. 1868. **b.** *At a* (*good*, etc.) *p.*: This tract of land he bought at a very great penny-worth SWIFT.

Penology (pinǫ·lŏdʒi). 1838. [f. Gr. ποινή fine, penalty, L. *pœna* punishment + -OLOGY.] The scientific study of the prevention and punishment of crime; the science of prison and reformatory management. Hence **Penolo·gical** *a.* of, pertaining or relating to, p. **Peno·logist,** one versed in p.

Pens, obs. f. PENCE, pl. of PENNY.

‖**Pensée.** ME. [In sense 1, a. OF. *pensee*; in 2, only as Fr.] †**1.** Thoughtfulness, a thought -1477. ‖**2.** (paṅse) A thought or reflection put in literary form 1886.

‖**Penseroso** (pensěrōᵘ·so), *a.* and *sb.* 1765. [From the title of Milton's poem *Il Penseroso*, a. obs. It. *penseroso*, now *pensieroso*, f. *pensiere* thought.] **A.** *adj.* Meditative, brooding, melancholy. **B.** *sb.* A brooding or melancholy person or personality.

Pensile (pe·nsəil, -sil), *a.* 1603. [ad. L. *pensilis* pendent, f. *pens-, pendere* to hang; see -ILE.] **1.** Hanging down, pendulous. **b.** 'Hanging' or situated on a declivity 1750. **2.** Hanging in the air or in space; suspended on arches, with void space beneath; vaulted 1613. **3.** That constructs a pensile nest 1802.

1. The p. nests of the weaver bird 1854. **b.** His azure stream, with p. woods enclos'd SHENSTONE. **2.** Babylon..was then the wonder of the world for its walls and p. gardens 1703. **3.** The P. Warbler 1802. Hence **Pe·nsileness, Pensi·lity** (*rare*).

Pension (pe·nʃən), *sb.* late ME. [a. F. *pension, -un*, ad. L. *pensionem* payment, rent, f. *pens-, pendere* to weigh, to pay; see -ION.] †**1.** A payment; a tribute, tax, charge, imposition; a contribution; a price paid or received; an expenditure. Also *fig.* -1638. **2.** *Eccl.* A fixed payment out of the revenues of a benefice, upon which it forms a charge. late ME. †**3.** Stipend, salary, wages; fee -1776. **b.** A payment made to one who is not a professed servant or employee, to retain his good will, secret service, etc.; a subvention, a fixed allowance. **c.** A regular payment to persons of rank, royal favourites, etc., to enable them to maintain their state; also to men of learning or science, artists, etc., to enable them to carry on work of public interest or value. 1500. **4.** An annuity or other periodical payment made, esp. by a government, a company, or an employer of labour, in consideration of past services or of the relinquishment of rights, claims, or emoluments 1529. †**5.** The annual (or other periodical) payment made by each member of a gild, college, or society, towards its general expenses; *esp.* that levied upon each member of an Inn of Court to defray its standing charges –1838. †**6.** Payment for board and lodging, or for the board and education of a child, etc. –1803. **b.** A boarding-house, a lodging-house at a fixed rate; occas. a boarding-school; †also formerly a tavern. Now only as F. (paṅsyoṅ). 1644. **7.** [from 5] A consultative assembly of the members of Gray's Inn, one of the Inns of Court in London 1570.

3. He commanded to giue to all that kept the city, pensions and wages 1 *Esdras* iv. 56. **b.** *Pension*, an allowance made to any one without an equivalent. In England it is generally understood to mean pay given to a state hireling for treason to his country JOHNSON. 4. *Old age p.*, a payment of so much per week or month paid to a workman or poor person (or to every one) on reaching a specified age.

Pension (pe·nʃən), *v.* 1642. [f. prec.] **1.** *intr.* To live or stay in a pension or boarding-house; to board and lodge. **2.** *trans.* To grant a pension to; also (contextually) to buy over with a pension. *To p. off*, to dismiss with a pension. 1702. Hence **Pe·nsionable** *a.* entitled to a pension; of service, etc.: entitling to a pension.

Pensionary (pe·nʃənări), *sb.*[1] 1536. [ad. med.L. *pensionarius*; see PENSION *sb.* and -ARY[1] B. 1.] **1.** = PENSIONER 1. 1548. **2.** [= Du. *pensionaris.*] Formerly, the chief municipal magistrate of a Dutch city, with the function of a legal adviser or speaker. *Hist.* 1587. **b.** *esp.* (prop. *Grand P.* = Du. *Groot Pensionaris*): The first minister of the province of Holland and Zealand in the Seven United Provinces of the Netherlands (1619–1794) 1655. **c.** *transf.* Satirical nickname for English statesmen 1771.

1. The Nabob sank into a p. 1874. 2. c. The grand p. [Pitt], that weathercock of patriotism SMOLLETT.

Pensionary (pe·nʃənări), *sb.*[2] 1582. [f. PENSION *sb.* + -ARY[1] B. 2.] A place of residence for pensioners; formerly, at Cambridge, a residence for undergraduates not on the foundation of a college.

Pensionary (pe·nʃənări), *a.* 1548. [ad. med.L. *pensionarius*; see PENSION and -ARY[1] A.] **1.** That is in receipt of a pension; hence, mercenary, hireling, venal. **2.** Consisting, or of the nature, of a pension 1631.

1. An extensive p. clergy 1825. 2. P. favours 1771.

Pensioner (pe·nʃənəɹ). late ME. [a. AF. *pensionner* = OF. *pensionnier*, f. *pension*, PENSION; see -ER[2].] **I.** One who receives a pension. **1.** One who is in receipt of a pension or regular pay; one who is in the pay of another; in early use, a mercenary; in 17th–18th c. often, a hireling, tool, creature 1487. **b.** *spec.* One who is in receipt of a pension in consideration of past services or on account of injuries received in service; esp. one of the inmates of Chelsea and Greenwich Hospitals 1706. †**2.** *spec.* = *Gentleman p.*; see GENTLEMAN 2. –1737. †**b.** A member of a bodyguard, a retainer. Also *fig.* –1632. **3.** The officer of the Inns of Court who collected the pensions, kept the pension-book or pension-roll, etc. *Obs.* exc. *Hist.* late ME. †**4.** = PENSIONARY *sb.*[1] 2, 2 b. –1756.

1. Charles [II.] became the p. of the French king 1863. 2. b. *fig.* I serue the Fairy Queene,..The Cowslips tall, her pensioners bee SHAKS.

II. One who makes a stated periodical payment. **1.** At Cambridge University: An undergraduate who is not a scholar on the foundation of a college, or a sizar; one who pays for his own commons, etc.; = *Commoner* at Oxford 1450. †**2.** A boarder; *esp.* a girl or woman living *en pension* in a convent or school in France, Belgium, etc.; = F. *pensionnaire* –1827. **3.** *attrib.*, as *p. messenger*, etc. 1678.

Pensionnaire (paṅsyonēr). 1598. [F. = med. L. *pensionarius.*] **a.** One in receipt of a pension; a pensioner, a paid retainer (*rare*). **b.** One who boards in a French lodging-house, institution, or family. **c.** A junior member of the *Comédie Française.*

†**Pe·nsionry.** [f. PENSIONER; see -RY.] A body of pensioners or paid retainers MILTON.

Pensive (pe·nsiv), *a.* (*sb.*) late ME. [a. F. *pensif, -ive*, f. *penser* to think; see -IVE.] **1.** Plunged in thought; meditative; reflective; often with some tinge of melancholy. †**2.** Full of anxious thought or foreboding; anxious, apprehensive –1654. **3.** 'Sorrowfully thoughtful, sorrowful; mournfully serious; melancholy' (J.); gloomy, sad. late ME. **4.** *transf.* Of things: Associated with thought, anxiety, or melancholy 1548. **5.** *absol.* as *sb.* Pensive manner or mood 1775.

1. He had a greater feare of those who were p. as Brutus 1639. 3. The heavie burthen of my p. brest DRAYTON. 4. P. Twilight in her dusky car S. ROGERS. Hence †**Pe·nsived** *a.* ? rendered p. or sad. SHAKS. **Pe·nsive·ly** *adv.*, **-ness.**

Penstock (pe·nˌstǫk). 1607. [f. PEN *sb.*[1] + STOCK *sb.*[1]] **1.** A sluice for restraining or regulating the flow from a head of water formed by a pen (PEN *sb.*[1] 3), as in a water-mill. Also *attrib.* **2.** = PENTROUGH. (*U.S.*) **b.** A tube by which water is conveyed from a head of water into a turbine. **c.** Also applied to the barrel of a pump. 1828.

‖**Pensum** (pe·nsǒm). *rare.* 1705. [L., weight, charge, duty, f. *pendere* to weigh.] A school-task or lesson to be prepared; also, a school 'imposition'.

Pent (pent), *sb.* 1754. [Short for PENTHOUSE.] A sloping roof or covering, a PENTHOUSE.

Pent (pent), *pa. pple.* and *ppl. a.* 1550. [In form, pa. pple. of *pend*, obs. var. of PEN *v.*[1]] **1.** Shut up or confined within narrow limits. Often with *in, up.* **2.** Of a place, room, etc.: Shut *up*, confined 1594. †**3.** Having something pent within it; distended or strained by being overfull of something –1728.

1. Long in populous City p. MILT. In vain our p. wills fret M. ARNOLD. Pent-up emotion 1879.

Penta- (pentă), bef. a vowel **pent-**, a. Gr. πεντα-, comb. form of πέντε five. In *Chem.* it indicates the presence of five atoms of some element, as in *pentacarbon, pentachloride, pentasulphide, pentoxide*, etc.

Pentabasic (-bē¹·sik) *a. Chem.* having five atoms of a base, or of replaceable hydrogen. **Pentaca·psular** *a.* having five capsules. **Pentachromic** (-krōᵘ·mik) *a.* of five colours, capable of distinguishing (only) five colours in the spectrum. **Pentada·ctyl(e** [Gr. δάκτυλος finger] *a.* having five toes or fingers; *sb.* a person or animal with five digits on each limb. So **Pentada·ctylous** *a.* **Pentadelphous** (-ăde·lfəs) [Gr. ἀδελφός brother] *a. Bot.* (of stamens) united by the filaments in five bundles; (of a plant) having the stamens so united. **Pe·ntafid** [L. *-fidus* split] *a. Bot.* cleft into five. ‖**Pentagy·nia** [Gr. γυνή woman, in sense 'pistil'], an order of plants in the Linnæan system, comprising those having five pistils. Hence **Pentagy·nian, Penta·gynous** *adjs.* **Pentaha·loid** *a. Chem.* containing five atoms of a halogen in the molecule. **Penta·ndria** [Gr. ἀνδρ-, ἀνήρ man, in sense 'stamen'] *Bot.* the fifth class in the Linnæan system, comprising plants having five stamens not cohering. So **Penta·ndrian, Penta·ndrous** *adjs.* **Pentape·talous** *a. Bot.* having five petals. **Pentaphyllous** (-fi·ləs) [Gr. φύλλον leaf] *a.* five-leaved. **Pe·ntaptote** [ad. Gr. πεντάπτωτος adj.] *Gram.* a noun having five cases. **Pe·ntaptych** (-ptik) [Gr. πτυχή fold, after DIPTYCH, etc.], an altar-piece or the like consisting of five leaves, i. e. a central piece and two folding pieces on each side. **Penta·rsic** [ARSIS] *a. Pros.* having five stresses. **Pentase·palous** *a. Bot.* having five sepals. **Pentaspe·rmous** [Gr. σπέρμα seed] *a. Bot.* having five seeds. **Pe·ntastyle** [Gr. στῦλος pillar] *a. Arch.* having five columns in front or at the end; *sb.* a pentastyle building or portico.

Pentachord (pe·ntăkǭɹd). 1721. [f. PENTA- + Gr. χορδή string.] *Mus.* **1.** A musical instrument with five strings. **2.** A system or series of five notes 1811.

Pentacle (pe·ntăk'l). 1594. [In med.L. *pentaculum*, app. f. PENTA- + *-culum*, dim. or instrumental suffix.] A certain figure used as a symbol, esp. in magic; app. prop. the same as PENTAGRAM; but also used for the *hexagram* or six-pointed star formed by two interlaced triangles, etc. Hence **Penta·cular** *a.*

Pentacrinite (pentæ·krinəit). 1818. [f. mod.L. *Pentacrinus* sea-lily (f. Gr. πεντα- five + κρίνον lily) + -ITE[1] 2 a.] *Palæont.* An encrinite or fossil crinoid of the genus *Pentacrinus* or family *Pentacrinidæ*. So **Penta·crinoid** *a.* allied to or resembling the genus *Pentacrinus* or family *Pentacrinidæ*; *sb.* a pentacrinoid crinoid.

Pentad (pe·ntæd). 1653. [ad. Gr. πεντάς, -άδα, later form of πεμπάς, -άδα a group of five, see -AD 1 a.] **1.** The number five (in the Pythagorean system); a group of five. **2.** A period of five years 1880. **3.** *Chem.* An element or radical that has the combining power of five units, i.e. of five atoms of hydrogen. Also *attrib.* or *adj.* 1877. Hence **Penta·dic** *a.* of the nature of a p. (sense 3), pentavalent; whence **Pentadi·city,** the fact of being a p.

Pentadecane (pe·ntădi̇kēⁱn). 1872. [f. late Gr. πεντάδεκα- for πεντεκαίδεκα fifteen + -ANE 2 b.] *Chem.* The paraffin of the 15-carbon series, $C_{15}H_{32}$. So **Pe·ntadecine** (-dĭsəin), the corresponding hydrocarbon of the ethine series, $C_{15}H_{28}$; **Pentade·cyl,** the radical $C_{15}H_{31}$.

Pentagon (pe·ntăgǫn), *a.* and *sb.* 1570. [In A, ad. L. *pentagonus*, a. Gr. πεντάγωνος, f. πεντα- PENTA- + -γωνος from stem of γωνία angle. In B, ad. L. *pentagonum*, Gr. πεντάγωνον adj. neut. used as sb.] †**A.** *adj.* Having five angles; pentagonal –1669. **B.** *sb.* A figure, usu. a plane rectilineal figure, having five angles and five sides. In *Fortif.* A fort with five bastions. 1571.

Pentagonal (pentæ·gŏnăl), *a.* (*sb.*) 1570. [f. prec. + -AL.] **1.** *Geom.*, etc. Of or pertaining to a pentagon; of the form of a pentagon, five-cornered or five-sided 1571. **b.** Applied to a solid figure or body of which the base or section is a pentagon 1570. **c.** Contained by pentagons, as a solid figure 1851. **2.** *P. numbers*: the series of POLYGONAL numbers 1, 5, 12, 22, 35, 51, etc. formed by continuous summation of the arithmetical series 1, 4, 7, 10, 13, 16, etc. **b.** as *sb.* A pentagonal number 1795. Hence **Penta·gonally** *adv.* in a p. form. var. †**Penta·gonous** *a.*

Pentagram (pe·ntăgræm). 1833. [ad. Gr. πεντά-, πεντέγραμμον adj. neut. used as sb., f. πέντε five + γραμμή line, mark.] A five-pointed figure formed by producing the sides of a pentagon both ways to their points of intersection, so as to form a five-pointed star; the 'five straight lines' of which the figure consists form one continuous line or 'endless knot'. Formerly a mystical symbol credited with magical virtues. (Also called *pentacle*, †*pentagonon, pentalpha, pentangle.*)

Pentahedral (pentăhī·drăl, -he·drăl), *a.* Also **pentaedral.** 1804. [f. PENTA- + Gr. ἕδρα seat, base + -AL.] Of a solid figure or body: Having five faces; *esp.* having five lateral faces, five-sided (as a prism of pentagonal section). So †**Pentahe·drical, Pentahe·drous** *adjs.* **Pentahe·dron,** a solid having five faces.

‖**Pentalpha** (pentæ·lfă). 1818. [a. Gr. πένταλφα, a synonym of πεντάγραμμον PENTAGRAM, f. πέντε five + ἄλφα the letter A; from its presenting the form of an A in five different positions.] = PENTAGRAM.

Pentamerous (pentæ·mĕrəs), *a.* 1826. [f. PENTA- + Gr. μέρος part + -OUS.] Having, consisting of, or characterized by, five parts or divisions. **1.** *Bot.* Having the parts of the flower-whorl five in number. (Often written *5-merous.*) 1835. **2.** *Zool.* **a.** Consisting of five joints, as the tarsi of certain insects; also applied to such insects themselves, as the beetles of the group *Pentamera*. **b.** Having five radiating parts or organs, as a star-fish, etc. 1826. So **Penta·meral** *a.* **Penta·meran,** a p. beetle. **Penta·merism,** the condition of being p.

Pentameter (pentæ·mǐtəɹ), *sb.* and *a.* 1546. [a. L. *pentameter* sb., ad. Gr. πεντάμετρος adj. consisting of five measures, f. πεντα- five + μέτρον measure.] **A.** *sb.* A verse or line consisting of five feet. **1.** *Gr.* and *L. Pros.* A form of dactylic verse composed of two similar halves (penthemimers), each consisting of two feet and a long syllable; in the first penthemimer each of the two feet may be either dactyl or spondee, in the second they must both be dactyls. Most commonly used in *elegiac* verse; see ELEGIAC

A. 1. (The verse was erroneously analysed as two dactyls (or spondees), a spondee, and two anapæsts; hence the name.) 1589. **2.** Applied to lines of verse consisting of five feet in other languages; e.g. the English heroic verse of ten syllables 1706.

1. In the hexameter rises the fountain's silvery column, In the p. aye falling in melody back COLERIDGE.

B. *adj.* (Now attrib. use of sb.) Consisting of five metrical feet; having the form of a pentameter 1546.

Pentane (pe·ntēin). 1877. [f. Gr. πέντε five + -ANE 2 b.] *Chem.* The general name of the paraffins of the pentacarbon series, C_5H_{12}; also called *quintane* and *pentyl hydride.* Three such hydrocarbons are known, all colourless mobile fluids, occurring in petroleum, etc. *attrib.*, as *p. lamp, vapour*, etc. So **Pentene** (pe·ntīn), an olefine of the pentacarbon series, C_5H_{10}; comprising four known forms, one of which is AMYLENE; **Pentine** (pe·ntəin), also **Pe·ntinine, Pe·ntylene,** the hydrocarbon C_5H_8, of the same series, homologous with acetylene or ethine; **Pento·ic** *a.* applied to fatty acids, aldehydes, etc. of the same series, as *Pentoic* or Valeric acid; **Pe·ntone, Pe·ntonene,** a hydrocarbon of the formula C_5H_6; **Pe·ntyl,** the radical C_5H_{11}, of which one form is AMYL; hence **Penty·lic** *a.*

Pentangle (pe·ntæŋg'l). †Also **pentagle.** ME. [In form a hybrid, f. Gr. πεντα- + ANGLE; but, in sense 1, perh. a var. of *pentagle*, PENTACLE.] **1.** = PENTACLE, PENTAGRAM. **2.** = PENTAGON (*rare*) 1658.

Pentangular (pentæ·ŋgiŭlăɹ), *a.* 1661. [f. as prec. + *angular.*] Having five angles or angular points; pentagonal.

Pentapody (pentæ·pŏdi). 1864. [f. Gr. πεντάπους of five feet, f. πεντα- PENTA- + πούς foot; cf. DIPODY.] *Pros.* A verse or line consisting of five feet, or a sequence of five feet in a verse.

‖ **Pentapolis** (pentæ·pŏlis). 1838. [L., a. Gr. πεντάπολις, f. πεντα- PENTA- + πόλις city.] A confederacy or group of five towns; applied in ancient times to several such groups. So **Pentapo·litan** *a.* of or pertaining to a p., spec. to that of Cyrene in Lybia 1727.

Pentarch (pe·ntaɹk), *sb.* 1793. [f. Gr. πέντε five + -αρχος ruler.] **a.** The ruler of one of a group of five districts or kingdoms. **b.** One of a governing body of five persons.

Pentarch (pe·ntaɹk), *a.* 1884. [f. as prec. + ἀρχή beginning.] *Bot.* Arising from five distinct points of origin, as the woody tissue of a root.

Pentarchy (pe·ntaɹki). 1587. [ad. Gr. πενταρχία a rule of five, f. πέντε five + -αρχία rule.] **1.** A government by five rulers; a group of five districts or kingdoms each under its own ruler. **2.** Government by a body of five persons; a governing body of five. Also *fig.* 1633.

2. *fig.* The P. of sences 1651.

Pentastich (pe·ntăstik). 1658. [ad. mod. L. *pentastichus*, a. Gr. πεντάστιχος, f. PENTA- + στίχος row, line.] *Pros.* A group of five lines.

Pentastichous (pentæ·stikəs), *a.* 1857. [f. as prec. + -OUS.] *Bot.* Arranged in five rows, five-ranked; *esp.* of a stem; having five leaves in the spiral row, and thus five vertical rows in the phyllotaxis.

Pentastom(e (pe·ntăstŏm, -oᵘm). 1857. [ad. mod.L. *Pentastomum*, f. PENTA- + Gr. -στομος adj. formative f. στόμα mouth; so called from the appearance of the mouth and the two pairs of chitinoid hooks adjacent to it.] *Zool.* An animal of the genus *Pentastomum* or *Pentastoma*, comprising internal parasites infesting man and other animals; an aberrant group of *Arachnida*, formerly classed as trematode worms. So **Penta·stomous** *a.* having five mouths or openings.

Pentasyllabic (pe:ntăsilæ·bik), *a.* 1771. [f. L. *pentasyllabus*, a. Gr. πεντασύλλαβος + -IC, after SYLLABIC.] Of five syllables. So **Pentasy·llable**, a word of five syllables.

Pentateuch (pe·ntătiŭk). 1530. [ad. L. *pentateuchus, -um*, f. Gr. ἡ πεντάτευχος the pentateuch, sb. use (sc. βίβλος) of πεντάτευχος adj. 'of five books', f. πεντα- PENTA- + τεῦχος implement, vessel, in late Gr. 'book'.] **1.** Name for the first five books of the Old Testament taken as a connected group, traditionally ascribed to Moses (hence called 'the five books of Moses'). **2.** *transf.* A volume composed of five books, etc. (*rare*) 1656.

2. The Hebrew Psalter came together not as a book but as a P. 1891. Hence **Pentateu·chal** *a.*

Pentathionic (pe:ntăþəi,ǫ·nik), *a.* 1848. [irreg. f. PENTA- + Gr. θεῖον sulphur + -IC; see DITHIONIC.] *Chem.* In *p. acid*, an acid containing five atoms of sulphur in the molecule, $H_2S_5O_6$, colourless, inodorous, and of bitter taste. Hence **Pentathi·onate,** a salt of p. acid.

Pentathlete (pentæ·þlīt). 1828. [ad. Gr. πενταθλητής, f. πένταθλον; see next.] An athlete who contended in the pentathlon.

‖ **Pentathlon** (pentæ·þlǫn). Also in L. form **pentathlum.** *Pl.* **-a.** 1706. [a. Gr. πένταθλον, f. πέντε five + ἆθλον contest.] *Gr.* and *Rom. Antiq.* An athletic contest consisting of five exercises (leaping, running, throwing the discus, throwing the spear, and wrestling) performed on the same day by the same athletes.

Pentatomic (pentătǫ·mik), *a.* 1872. [f. Gr. πέντε five + ἄτομος ATOM + -IC; cf. *atomic.*] *Chem.* Containing five atoms of some substance in the molecule; *spec.* containing five replaceable hydrogen atoms; also = PENTAVALENT.

Pentatonic (pentătǫ·nik), *a.* 1864. [f. PENTA- + Gr. τόνος TONE *sb.* + -IC.] *Mus.* Consisting of five notes or sounds; *esp.* applied to a form of scale without semitones.

Pentavalent (pentæ·vălĕnt), *a.* 1871. [f. PENTA- + L. *valentem* having power or value.] *Chem.* Having the combining power of five atoms of a univalent element; quinquivalent.

Penteconta- (pentīkǫ·ntă), bef. a vowel **-cont-**, comb. form of Gr. πεντήκοντα fifty; as in †**Penteco·ntarch** [ad. Gr. πεντηκόνταρχος], a commander of fifty men; etc.

‖ **Penteco·nter**[1]. 1623. [a. Gr. πεντηκοντήρ.] *Gr. Antiq.* A commander of a troop of fifty men.

‖ **Penteco·nter**[2]. 1790. [ad. Gr. πεντηκοντήρης.] *Gr. Antiq.* A fifty-oared ship of burden.

Pentecost (pe·ntīkǫst). OE. [a. Christian L. *pentecoste*, a. Gr. πεντηκοστή (sc. ἡμέρα or ἑορτή) fiftieth (day or feast), in Tobit ii. 1, 2 Maccabees xii. 32.] **1.** A name of Hellenistic origin for the Jewish harvest festival (in O.T. the Feast of Weeks) observed on the fiftieth day of the OMER (q.v. sense 2). **2.** A Christian festival observed on the seventh Sunday after Easter, in commemoration of the descent of the Holy Ghost upon the disciples on the day of Pentecost (Acts ii); Whit Sunday OE. **3.** *fig.* in allusion to the gift of the Holy Spirit, or the circumstances recorded in Acts ii. 176..

2. Come Pentycost as quickely as it will SHAKS. 3. Ever the fiery P. Girds with one flame the countless host EMERSON. Hence **Penteco·stal** *sb.* (usu. pl.) offerings formerly made in the Church of England at Whitsuntide to the priest, or to the mother-church; *a.* of or pertaining to P.; like that of the Day of P. in Acts ii.

‖ **Pentecostys** (pentīkǫ·stis). Also irreg. anglicized **pe·ntekosty.** 1808. [a. Gr. πεντεκοστύς f. πεντηκοστός fiftieth.] *Gr. Antiq.* A body of fifty men, as a division of the Spartan army.

Pentelic (pente·lik), *a.* 1579. [ad. L. *Pentelicus*, a. Gr., f. Πεντελή name of a deme of Attica.] Of or from Mount Pentelicus, near Athens; esp. applied to the white marble there quarried. So †**Penteli·cian, Pente·lican** *adjs.*

Penthemimer (penþi̇mi·məɹ). 1586. [ad. Gr. πενθημιμερής consisting of five halves, f. πέντε five + ἡμιμερής halved (ἡμι- half + μέρος part).] *Anc. Pros.* A group or catalectic colon of five half-feet; esp. as constituting each half of a pentameter, or the first part of a hexameter when the cæsura occurs in the middle of the third foot. Hence **Penthemi·meral** *a.* applied to a cæsura in the middle of the third foot.

Penthouse (pe·nthaus), **pentice** (pe·ntis), *sb.* [ME. *pentis*, rarely *pendis*, app. aphet. f. OF. *apentis, apendis, -deis*; cf. med.L. *appenditium* 'a small sacred building dependent upon a larger church' (Du Cange), post-cl.L. *appendicium* appendage. As a 'lean-to' has usually a roof with one slope only, the word was associated early with F. *pente* slope; hence, by pop. etymology, *penthouse* for *pentis.*] **1.** A subsidiary structure attached to the wall of a main building. **a.** Such a structure having a sloping roof, formerly sometimes forming a covered walk, arcade, or colonnade, in front of a row of buildings; a sloping roof or ledge placed against the wall of a building, etc., for shelter from the weather; *occas.*, the eaves of a roof when projecting considerably. †**b.** Any small building attached to a main one, an annex -1886. **c.** A shed with a sloping roof, as a separate structure 1816. **2.** Anything of the nature of or akin to a sloping roof; an awning; a canopy, etc. 1530. **3.** *fig.* Applied to things likened to a penthouse (*e.g.* the eyebrows) 1589. attrib. *L.L.L.* III. i. 17.

Hence **Pe·nthouse** *v.* (usu. in pa. pple.) to furnish with or as with a p.; to cause to project like a p.

Pentode (pe·ntoᵘd), *a.* 1919. [f. Gr. πέντε five + ὁδός way.] Applied to a five-electrode wireless valve. Also as sb.

Pentoxide (pentǫ·ksəid). 1863. [PENTA-.] *Chem.* A binary compound containing five equivalents of oxygen.

Pent-roof (pe·nt,rūf). 1835. [f. *pent-* in PENTHOUSE + ROOF *sb.*] A shed-roof.

Pentrough (pe·n,trǫf). 1793. [f. PEN *sb.*[1] 3 + TROUGH.] A trough, channel, or conduit constructed to convey the water formed by a pen to the wheels of a water-mill, etc.

Pen(t)stemon (pen(t)stī·mən). 1760. [mod. L., irreg. f. Gr. πέντε five + στήμων, taken as = stamen.] *Bot.* A genus of herbaceous plants of the N.O. *Scrophulariaceæ*, natives of America, having showy clustered flowers, usu. tubular and two-lipped, and of various colours.

Penult (pǐnʊ·lt), *a.* and *sb.* 1539. [orig. abbrev. of PENULTIMA, PENULTIMATE.] **A.** *adj.* Last but one, penultimate. (Now chiefly scientific.) **B.** *sb.* †**1.** The last day but one of a month. *Sc.* -1678. **2.** *Gram.* The last syllable but one 1650.

A. The p. joint of the eight posterior legs DANA.

Penu·ltim(e, *a.* and *sb.* 1532. [ad. L. *pænultimus*; see next.] = PENULTIMATE.

‖ **Penultima** (pǐnʊ·ltimă). 1589. [L. *pænultima* (sc. *syllaba*) adj. fem., f. *pæne* almost + *ultimus* last.] The last syllable but one (of a word or verse).

Penultimate (pǐnʊ·ltimėt), *a.* and *sb.* 1677. [f. PENE- + ULTIMATE, after L. *pænultimus.*] **A.** *adj.* Last but one. (Chiefly scientific and techn.) Also, occurring on the last syllable but one. **B.** *sb.* The last member but one of a series; *spec.* in *Gram.* the last syllable but one of a word 1727.

‖ **Penumbra** (pǐnʊ·mbră). 1661. [mod.L. (Kepler), f. PENE- + UMBRA shadow.] **1.** The partially shaded region around the shadow of an opaque body; the partial shadow, as dist. from the total shadow or umbra; *esp.* that surrounding the total shadow of the moon, or of the earth, in an eclipse. **b.** The lighter outer part of a sun-spot, surrounding the darker central nucleus or umbra 1834. **2.** *fig.* A partial shade or shadow, esp. as bordering upon a fuller or darker one 1801.

2. It is but a p., a twilight of virtue and happiness 1836. Hence **Penu·mbral, Penu·mbrous** (*rare*), *adjs.* of, pertaining to, or characterized by a p. or partial shadow; also *fig.*

Penurious (pǐniūᵊ·riəs), *a.* 1596. [ad. med.L. *penuriosus*, f. L. *penuria*; see PENURY and -OUS.] **1.** In want; needy, poverty-stricken (also *fig.*); †with *of*, wanting in. †**b.** Of things, circumstances, etc.: Of, pertaining to, or associated with want; poor, exiguous; barren, unfertile -1789. **2.** Niggardly, parsimonious, grudging; *transf.* meagre, slight, 'shabby', mean 1634. †**3.** Fastidious, dainty (*rare*) -1730.

1. Dives, rich in this world, became exceeding p. in the other 1614. b. Seven most scant and p. yeares of great famine 1639. 2. As a p. niggard of his wealth MILT. Hence **Penu·rious-ly** *adv.*, **-ness.**

Penury (pe·niŭri). late ME. [ad. L. *penuria, pænuria* want, need.] **1.** Destitution, indigence; poverty. **2.** Lack, scarcity, want (*of* something material or immaterial) 1447. **3.** Penuriousness, miserliness. Now *rare.* 1651.

1. Chill P. repress'd their noble rage GRAY. 2. You owe..to your stars your p. of sense 1699. 3. God sometimes punishes..p. with oppression JER. TAYLOR.

Penwiper (pe·nwəi:pəɹ). 1848. [f. PEN *sb.*² II. 1 + WIPER.] A contrivance, usu. consisting of one or more pieces of cloth folded or fastened together, for cleaning a pen by wiping the ink from it.

Penwoman (pe·nwu:măn). 1748. [f. as prec. + WOMAN, after *penman.*] A woman skilled in the use of the pen. (Usu. qualified as *good, fine,* etc.)

Peon (pī·ǫ̆n). 1609. [In sense 1, ad. Pg. *peão* pedestrian, and F. *pion* foot-soldier; in sense 2, a. Sp. *peon* in same senses, f. (ult.) L. *pes, pedem* foot. A doublet of PAWN *sb.*¹] 1. In India: a. A foot-soldier. b. A native constable. c. An attendant or orderly; a footman or messenger. 2. In Spanish America: A day-labourer; in S. America, a man or boy leading a horse or mule; in Mexico *spec.* a debtor held in servitude by his creditor till his debts are worked off. Also *attrib.* 1828. Hence **Pe·onage, Pe·onism,** the work or service of a p.; the system of having or using peons; in Mexico *spec.* the condition of a p. serf.

Peony (pī·ŏni). Also **pæony.** [In OE. *peonie,* in ME. *pione* from OF., in 15th c. conformed to their ult. source, late L. *peonia,* L. *pæonia,* a. Gr. παιωνία the peony, f. Παιών Pæon, physician of the gods.] 1. A plant or flower of the genus *Pæonia* (N.O. *Ranunculaceæ*), comprising stout herbs, or rarely shrubs, with large handsome red or white globular flowers, often double under cultivation; esp. *P. officinalis.* 2. *attrib.* or as *adj.* Dark red; esp. of the cheeks, plump and rosy 1548.

People (pī·p'l), *sb.* ME. [a. AF. *poeple, people* = OF. *pople, poeple, peuple,* etc. :—L. *populum,* acc. of *populus* the people, the populace.] 1. = FOLK 1. a. In sing., as a collective of unity. b. In sing. form, construed as pl. ME. c. *pl.* Nations, races (= L. *populi, gentes*). late ME. †d. Used in sing. in the sense 'nations' –1793. e. *transf.* of animals. late ME. 2. The persons belonging to a place, constituting a particular concourse, congregation, company, or class. Construed as *pl.* ME. †b. As *collect. sing.* A company, a multitude. Also with *pl.* –1662. 3. Persons in relation to a superior, or to some one to whom they belong. Chiefly with possessive. a. The subjects of a king or other ruler; the servants of God, or of Christ; the congregation or flock of a pastor, etc. Const. as *pl.* ME. b. The body of attendants, armed followers, retinue, work-people, servants, etc. Const. as *pl.* ME. c. Those to whom any one belongs, one's tribe, clan, etc. collectively: *esp.* (colloq.) one's parents, brothers and sisters, and other relatives at home. Const. as *pl.* late ME. 4. The commonalty, as dist. from the nobility and ruling or official classes. Const. as *pl.* ME. 5. *Politics.* The whole body of enfranchised or qualified citizens, considered as the source of power; esp. in a democratic state, the electorate 1646. 6. Men or women indefinitely; persons, folk. Const. as *pl.* ME. b. *emphatically* = Human beings 1450. c. *transf.* Living creatures. *poet.* or *rhet.* 1667. 7. Unemphatically, *people* = F. *on,* G. *man*; in colloq. use repl. *men* ('men say', etc.) ME.

1. a. A people's voice! we are a p. yet TENNYSON. b. Should not a p. seeke vnto their God? *Isa.* viii. 19. c. All our English-speaking peoples MORLEY. d. Hee shall iudge among the nations, and shall rebuke many p. [WYCLIF puples, *R.V.* peoples] *Isa.* ii. 4. e. The Ants are a p. not strong *Prov.* xxx. 25. 2. The p. here want sadly to know what I am 1711. b. He ..gaderyd a grete peple of menne 1482. 3. The p. of the Prince that shall come *Dan.* ix. 26. b. The Douglas p. are in motion on both sides of the river SCOTT. c. Mrs. Sterling..had lived..with his Father's p. CARLYLE. 4. I speak to the p. as one of the p. *Junius Lett.* 5. The will of the p. MILL. 6. I have bought Golden Opinions from all sorts of p. SHAKS. *Good p.,* formerly a courteous way of addressing an assemblage; cf. GOOD *a.* 2. b. *Raskall* is properly the hunters terme giuen to young deere.., and not to p. PUTTENHAM. c. *The little p., the good p.,* the fairies. 7. P. cannot understand a man being in a state of doubt J. H. NEWMAN. Hence **Peo·ple-less,** having no p. or population 1621.

People (pī·p'l), *v.* 1489. [a. F. *peupler,* f. *peuple*; see prec.] 1. *trans.* To furnish with people or inhabitants; to populate 1500. b. *transf.* To fill or stock (with animals, inanimate objects, etc.) 1533. c. *fig.* To imagine or represent as peopled 1817. 2. To fill or occupy as inhabitants; to constitute the population of (a country, etc.) 1489. b. *transf.* and *fig.* of animals, inanimate objects, etc. 1593. †c. *absol.* To form a settlement –1604. 3. *intr.* (for *refl.*) To grow populous 1659.

1. The nearest Regions must have been first and most fully peopled 1696. c. This silent spot tradition old Had peopled with the spectral dead SHELLEY. 2. What vary'd Being peoples every star POPE. b. The gay motes that p. the Sun Beams MILT. Hence **Peopled** (pī·p'ld) *ppl. a.* occupied by people; full of inhabitants; inhabited; also *fig.* **Peo·pler,** one who peoples or causes the peopling of a country; a colonizer; an inhabitant.

†**Peoplish,** *a.* [-ISH¹.] Clownish, vulgar CHAUCER.

Pep (pep). 1915. orig. *U.S.* [abbrev. of PEPPER *sb.*] *slang.* Vigour, energy, 'go'.

‖ **Peperino** (pepĕrī·no). Also **pip-.** 1777. [It., f. *pepere* pepper; so called from its consisting of small grains.] *Geol.* A light porous volcanic rock or tuff, formed of sand, cinders, etc. cemented together; a name first given to the tufas of Monte Albano near Rome. Hence **Pe·perine** *a. rare,* consisting or composed of p.

‖ **Peplos, peplus** (pe·plǫs, -ŏs). 1776. [a. Gr. πέπλος, in pl. πέπλα, whence L. *peplus, peplum.*] An outer robe or shawl worn by women in ancient Greece; *spec.* that woven yearly for the statue of the goddess Athene at Athens, carried in procession to her temple at the greater Panathenæa.

‖ **Peplum** (pe·plŏm). 1678. [L.; see prec.] 1. = PEPLOS. 2. A kind of overskirt, supposed to resemble the ancient peplum 1893.

‖ **Pepo** (pī·po). 1861. [L. *pepo* pumpkin, a. Gr. πέπων, short for πέπων σίκυος, a gourd eaten when ripe, f. πέπων ripe.] *Bot.* Any fleshy fruit, with numerous seeds attached to parietal placentæ, and a firm rind; as the gourd, melon, cucumber, etc.

Pepper (pe·pəɹ), *sb.* [OE. *pipor*; Com. WGer. a. L. *piper* = Gr. πέπερι, of Oriental origin.] 1. A pungent aromatic condiment, derived from species of *Piper* and allied genera, used for flavouring, and acting as a digestive stimulant and carminative; *esp.* the dried berries of *Piper nigrum,* either whole (PEPPERCORNS) or ground into powder. b. Also, the pungent condiments yielded by other plants; see 3. 1838. 2. The plant *Piper nigrum,* an E. and W. Indian climbing shrub, having alternate stalked leaves, with pendulous green flower-spikes opposite the leaves, succeeded by small berries turning red when ripe. Also, any plant of the genus *Piper* (including *Chavica*), or (by extension) of the N.O. *Piperaceæ.* late ME. 3. With qualifying words, applied to other plants furnishing pungent condiments; sometimes to plants having leaves of a pungent flavour 1538. 4. In allusive or proverbial expressions. late ME.

1. P. was a favourite ingredient of the most expensive Roman cookery GIBBON. *Black p.,* that form of the condiment which is prepared from the berries dried when not quite ripe. *White p.,* a less pungent form, from the same berries when fully ripe, or from the black by removing the husk. *Long p.,* a similar condiment prepared from the immature fruit-spikes of the allied plants *Piper* (*Chavica*) *officinarum* and *P. longum,* formerly supposed to be the flowers or unripe fruit of *P. nigrum.* 3. **African p.,** (*a*) *Habzelia* (*Xylopia*) *æthiopica* or other species (N.O. *Anonaceæ*); (*b*) *Capsicum fastigiatum.* **Chili p.** (*a*) = PEPPER-TREE a; (*b*) erron. = CHILLI. **Chinese p.** = *Japanese pepper.* **Guinea p.,** (*a*) see GUINEA P.; (*b*) = *African p.* **Japanese p.,** *Xanthoxylon piperitum* of Japan and China. **Melegueta p.** = *grains of Paradise*: see GRAIN *sb.*¹ 4. See also CAYENNE *p.,* CUBEB *p.,* JAMAICA *p.,* RED *p.* etc. 4. Heere's the Challenge, reade it: I warrant there's vinegar and p. in 't SHAKS. †*To take p. in the nose,* to take offence. So †*to snuff p.*

attrib. and *Comb.,* as **P. Alley,** name of an alley in London, hence allusively in pugilistic slang; **p.-cake,** local name for gingerbread; **-elder,** name for plants of the genera *Peperomia, Enckea,* and *Artanthe,* allied to the common p.; **-grass,** (*a*) any species of *Lepidium* (as *L. sativum,* garden-cress), from the pungent taste; (*b*) = PILLWORT; **-mill,** a small hand-mill for grinding p.; **-moth** = PEPPERED *moth*; **-plant,** the plant *Piper nigrum* or any plant producing pepper; **-pod,** the pod of any species of *Capsicum*; **-root,** any species of *Dentaria,* esp. *D. diphylla,* so called from the pungent root; **-sauce,** a pungent sauce or condiment made by steeping 'red peppers' (capsicum pods) in vinegar.

Pepper (pe·pəɹ). 1581. [f. prec. (OE. had *piporian, piprian,* etc. in the same sense.)] 1. *trans.* To sprinkle with pepper; to flavour or season with pepper. Also *absol.* 2. To sprinkle (a surface) as with pepper; to besprinkle, dot, stud. Also *fig.* (Mostly in *pa. pple.*) 1612. 3. To sprinkle like pepper. Also *fig.* 1821. 4. To pelt with shot or missiles. Also *fig.* 1644. b. *intr.* To discharge shot, etc. (*at* something) 1767. 5. *trans.* To 'give it (a person) hot'; to beat severely, trounce. Hence †b. To give one his death-blow (*lit.* and *fig.*), to 'do for', ruin. 1500. 6. To give pungency, spice, or flavour to (speech or writing) 1835. †b. To dose with flattery –1784. †7. To infect with venereal disease. (F. *poivrer.*) –1723.

2. Every page was peppered with italic 1896. 4. You may p. the bishops a little GEO. ELIOT. b. Peppering away at the pheasants 1890. 5. I am pepper'd I warrant, for this world SHAKS. 6. b. Who pepper'd the highest, was surest to please GOLDSM. Hence **Pe·ppering** *vbl. sb.* the action of the vb.; pelting with shot, missiles, etc. **Pe·ppering** *ppl. a.* that peppers; pungent; falling heavily (as rain).

Pe·pper-and-sa·lt. 1774. Name for a kind of cloth made of dark- and light-coloured wools woven together, showing small dots of dark and light closely intermingled; also, a garment made of this. Usu. *attrib.* or *adj.*

Pe·pper-box. 1546. 1. A small box, usu. cylindrical, with a perforated lid, for sprinkling powdered pepper. 2. *transf.* Applied contemptuously to a small cylindrical turret or cupola 1821. 3. The irregular buttress sticking into the fives-court at Eton 1865. 4. *fig.* A hot-tempered person 1867. 5. *attrib.* 1825.

1. Hee cannot creepe into a halfe-penny purse, nor into a Pepper-Boxe SHAKS.

Pe·pper-ca·stor, -ca·ster. 1676. [See CASTOR².] 1. A small vessel with a perforated top, usu. one of the castors of a cruet-stand, for sprinkling pepper at table. 2. *transf.* a. = prec. 2. 1859. b. *slang.* A revolver 1889.

Peppercorn (pe·pəɹkǭɹn). OE. [f. PEPPER *sb.* + CORN *sb.*¹ 2.] 1. The dried berry of black pepper. b. Stipulated for as a quit-rent or nominal rent 1607. 2. *attrib.* Of or consisting in a peppercorn, as *p. rent*; also *fig.* very small, insignificant 1791.

1. b. In modern times building leases sometimes reserve a pepper-corn as rent 1898.

Peppered (pe·pəɹd), *ppl. a.* 1581. [f. PEPPER *v.* + -ED¹.] Sprinkled or seasoned with pepper; sprinkled with small dots like grains of pepper; pelted with shot, etc.

P. moth, collector's name of the Geometrid moth *Amphydasis* (*Biston*) *betularia.*

Pepperer (pe·pərəɹ). ME. [In 1, f. PEPPER *sb.* + -ER²; in 2, f. PEPPER *v.* + -ER¹.] 1. A dealer in pepper and spices; a grocer. (The original name of the Grocers' Company of London.) *Obs.* exc. *Hist.* 2. One who or that which peppers; *fig.* a hot-tempered person; something pungent 1711.

Pepperidge (pe·pəridʒ). Also **-age.** 1823. 1. Var. of PIPPERIDGE. 2. *U.S.* The Black Gum, Sour Gum, or Tupelo, a N. Amer. tree of the genus *Nyssa,* having very tough wood 1826.

Peppermint (pe·pəɹmint). 1696. [f. PEPPER *sb.* + MINT *sb.*², app. after Bot. L.] 1. A species or subspecies of mint (*Mentha piperita*), cultivated for its essential oil (*oil of p.*). 2. The essential oil of peppermint, or some preparation of it 1836. b. A lozenge flavoured with peppermint, a peppermint-drop 1884. 3. (In full *p.-tree.*) Name for several Australian species of *Eucalyptus* (*E. amygdalina, piperita,* etc.) yielding an aromatic essential oil resembling that of peppermint 1790.

Comb.: **P.-camphor** = MENTHOL; **p.-drop, -lozenge,** a lozenge made of sugar, flavoured with p.; **-tree** (see 3).

Pe·pper-pot. 1679. 1. = PEPPER-BOX 1. Also in allusive and fig. uses. 2. A W. Indian dish composed of meat (or fish, game, etc.) and vegetables stewed with cassareep and red pepper or other hot spices 1704. 3. *attrib.* 1883.

Pe·pper-tree. 1691. a. An evergreen tree or shrub of S. America, *Schinus Molle* (N.O. *Anacardiaceæ*), having a pungent red fruit; b. A tree of Australia and Tasmania, *Drimys* or

Tasmannia aromatica, or other species (N.O. *Magnoliaceæ*), having small pungent fruit used as pepper.

Pepperwort (pe·pəɹwɒ̈ɹt). 1562. **1.** A species of cress (*Lepidium latifolium*), formerly also called dittander or dittany; also the genus *Lepidium* in general. **2.** *pl.* A name for the N.O. *Marsileaceæ*, consisting of small aquatic plants allied to the ferns 1846. **b.** Lindley's name for N.O. *Piperaceæ* 1846.

Peppery (pe·pəri), *a.* 1699. [f. PEPPER *sb.* + -Y [1].] **1.** Abounding in pepper; of the nature of or resembling pepper; pungent, 'hot'. **2.** *fig.* **a.** Of speech or writing: Sharp, stinging, pungent. **b.** Of a person, etc.: Hot-tempered, irascible, testy. 1826.

2. a. Some good, strong, p. doctrine DICKENS. Hence **Pe·pperi·ly** *adv.*, **-ness.**

Pepsin (pe·psin). Also formerly **-ine.** 1844. [f. Gr. πέψις digestion (f. stem πεπ- to cook, digest) + -IN [1].] A ferment contained in the gastric juice, having the property of converting proteids into peptones in the presence of a weak acid; also used medicinally in cases of indigestion, etc. Hence **Pe·psinate** *v.* to mix or treat with p.

Peptic (pe·ptik), *a.* and *sb.* 1651. [ad. Gr. πεπτικός able to digest, f. πεπτός cooked, digested.] **A.** *adj.* **1.** = DIGESTIVE A. 1; used *spec.* in relation to the digestion in which pepsin is concerned. **2.** = DIGESTIVE A. 2. 1661. **3.** = EUPEPTIC A. 2. CARLYLE.

1. *P. digestion*, stomachic or gastric digestion. *P. glands*, the glands which secrete the gastric juice.

B. *sb.* **1.** A substance which promotes digestion 1842. **2.** *pl.* The digestive organs (*joc.*) 1842. Hence **Pe·ptical** *a.* = A. **Pepti·cian,** a person who has good digestion CARLYLE. **Pepti·city,** good p. condition.

Peptogen (pe·ptŏdʒen). 1875. [f. Gr. πεπτός (see prec.) + -GEN.] A general name for substances which stimulate the formation of pepsin in the gastric juice. So **Peptoge·nic, Pepto·genous** *adjs.* having the quality of forming, or stimulating the formation of, pepsin; also, of converting proteids into peptones.

Peptone (pe·ptoun). 1860. [ad. G. *pepton*, ad. Gr. πεπτόν, neut. of πεπτός PEPTIC.] The general name for a class of albuminoid substances into which proteids (the nitrogenous constituents of food) are converted by the action of pepsin or trypsin; differing from proteids in not being coagulable by heat, and in being easily soluble and diffusible through membranes, and thus capable of absorption into the system. Also *attrib.* Hence **Pe·ptonize** *v. trans.* to convert (a proteid) into a p.; *esp.* to subject (food) to an artificial process of predigestion by means of pepsin or pancreatic extract; also *fig.* **Pe·ptoniza·tion. Pe·ptonizer.**

‖ **Peptonuria** (peptoniū̆ə·riă). 1891. [mod. L., f. as prec. + Gr. οὖρον urine; see -URIA.] *Path.* The presence of peptones in the urine.

Peptotoxin (pepto,tǫ·ksin). 1890. [f. Gr. πεπτός (see PEPTIC) + TOXIN.] A poisonous alkaloid formed from peptones during digestion.

Per (pəɹ), *prep.* A Latin prep. (whence It., OF. *per*, F. *par*) meaning 'through, by, by means of'; in med. L. also = 'for every.., for each..': used in English in various L. and OF. phrases, and ult. becoming practically an Eng. prep. used freely with sbs.

I. In Latin (med.L. and It.) phrases. **1. per accidens** [= Gr. κατὰ συμβεβηκός] by accident, by virtue of some non-essential circumstance, contingently, indirectly. (Opp. to *per se*.) 1528. **b.** In *Logic* applied to conversion in which the quantity of the proposition is changed from universal to particular 1677. **2. per annum,** (so much) by the year, every year, yearly 1601. **3. per consequens,** by consequence, consequently. late ME. **4. per contra** [It.], on the opposite side (of an account, etc.); on the other hand; as a set-off 1554. **b.** as *sb.* The opposite side (of an account, etc.) 1894. **5. per diem,** (so much) by the day, every day, daily 1520. **b.** as *sb.* An amount of so much every day (*U.S.*) 1888. **6. per mensem,** (so much) every month 1647. **7. per procurationem** (abbrev. *per proc., per pro., p.p.*; sometimes *per procuration*), by proxy or deputy (often used in signatures to documents on behalf of a firm, etc.) 1819. **8. per saltum,** by a leap, at one bound, all at once 1600. **9. per se,** by or in itself (himself, herself, themselves); intrinsically, essentially; without reference to anything (or any one) else 1572. †**b.** Formerly used in naming a letter which by itself forms a word (*A per se*), or as a symbol which by itself stands for a word (*and per se* = &, AMPERSAND); hence allus. 1475. **10.** In various phr., as *per arsin*, etc. (see ARSIS, etc.); **per capita** (*Law*), 'by heads', applied to succession when divided among a number of individuals in equal shares (opp. to *per stirpes*); **per fas et (aut) nefas,** by right and (or) wrong, by means fair or foul; **per pares,** by (his) peers; **per stirpes** (*Law*), by 'stocks' or 'families'; applied to succession when divided in equal shares among the branches of a family, the share of each branch being then subdivided equally among the representatives of that branch (opp. to *per capita*). late ME.

II. **1.** In OF. phrases, some of which occur with PAR, q. v., as *per charite*, etc.; also †**per maistrie,** by conquest; **per my et per tout** (*Law*), 'by half and by all', by joint-tenancy; **per pais, per pays** (*Law*), 'by the country'. See also PERADVENTURE, PERCHANCE, PERFORCE, etc. ME. **2.** *Her.* In phr. denoting partition of the shield in the direction of any of the principal ordinaries (*per* BEND, *per* CHEVRON, etc.).

III. As an Eng. preposition. **1.** By, by means of, by the instrumentality of; esp. in phrases relating to conveyance, as *per bearer, per carrier, per post*, etc. Also = according to, as stated or indicated by, as (*as*) *per invoice*, (*as*) *per margin*; as laid down by (a judge) 1588. So in joc. slang use, (*as*) *per usual* = as usual. **2.** In distrib. sense, following words of number or quantity, in expressions denoting rate or proportion: For each.., for every... See also PER CENT. 1598.

Per-, *prefix* [1]. The L. prep. *per* (see prec.) used in composition with vbs., adjs., and their derivatives.

I. In senses: **1.** Through, in space or time; throughout, all over; with verbs (and derivs.), as PERAMBULATE, PERFORATE, PERVADE. **2.** Through and through, thoroughly, completely, to completion, to the end; with verbs (and their derivs.), as PERFECT, PERMUTE, PERPETRATE, PERTURB, etc. **3.** Away entirely, to destruction, 'to the bad'; with verbs (and their derivs.), as PERDITION, PERISH, PERVERT, etc. **4.** Thoroughly, perfectly, extremely, very; with adjs. and advbs., as PERFERVID, etc. Formerly also with derived sbs. (or their analogues), in sense 'very great', 'extreme', as *perdiligence*, etc.

II. *Chem.* (from I. 4). Forming sbs. and adjs. denoting the maximum (or supposed maximum) of some element in a chemical combination; esp. **a.** With names of binary compounds in -IDE (formerly *-uret*), designating that in which the element or radical combines in the largest proportion with another element, e. g. PEROXIDE, PERCHLORIDE 1804. **b.** With adjs. in -IC, naming oxides, acids, etc., designating that compound which contains the greatest proportion of oxygen (and, consequently, the least of the element named), as PERCHLORIC, -MANGANIC, etc. Also in names of salts of these acids, and analogous bodies, as PERCHLORATE, -MANGANATE, etc. Formerly *per-* was also prefixed to adjs. in *-ous*, where *hypo-* is now used, as *persulphurous* = HYPOSULPHUROUS; etc.

Per-, *prefix* [2], repr. OF. *per* or F. *par* (see PAR *prep.*, PER *prep.* II), in phr. which have coalesced into single words, as PERADVENTURE, PERCHANCE, etc.; so also PERHAPS, q. v.

Peract (pəræ·kt), *v.* Now *rare.* 1621. [f. L. *peract-*, *peragere*, f. *per* (PER- [1] 2) + *agere*.] *trans.* To practise, perform; to accomplish.

Peracute (pɔ̄răkiū̆·t), *a.* Now *rare.* late ME. [ad. L. *peracutus*; see PER- [1] 4 and ACUTE.] *Path.* Of diseases: Very acute or severe; attended with much inflammation.

Peradve·nture, *sb.* 1450. [sb. use of next.] The possibility of a thing being so or not; uncertainty, doubt; a contingency; a conjecture, chance.

Some to be saved infallibly, and others to be left to a p. COWPER. Phr. *Out of, past, beyond, without (all) p.*, beyond question, without doubt. †*By, at (a) p.*, by haphazard; at random, randomly.

Peradventure (perădve·ntiūr, -tʃəɹ), *adv. arch.* [ME. *per-*, *parauenture*, a. OF. phrase *per* or *par aventure*, by chance. Refash. after L. in 15th c.] †**1.** In a statement of fact: By chance; as it happened –1624. **2.** In a dependent clause expressing hypothesis or purpose (with *if, unless, that, lest*): By chance or accident, perchance; *if p.*, if it chance that ME. **3.** In a hypothetical or contingent statement: Perchance, haply; maybe, perhaps; not improbably, belike ME. **b.** Qualifying a word or phr., usu. by ellipsis ME.

2. Unless, p., their wives were comely and young LYTTON. 3. Peraduenture there be fifty righteous within the citie *Gen.* xviii. 24. b. Lo, where he commeth towards, peraduenture to his paine 1575.

Peragrate (pe·răgreɪt), *v.* Now *rare.* 1542. [f. L. *peragrat-*, *peragrare*, f. *per* through + *agrum* field, country.] *trans.* To travel or pass through (a country, etc.). Also *fig.* Hence **Peragra·tion** (now *rare*), a travelling through or traversing; as †*month of p.*, the period of the moon's revolution; a sidereal (or tropical) month 1561.

Perai (pirai·), **piraya** (pirā·yă). 1753. [ad. Tupi *piraya*, lit. 'scissors'.] A voracious freshwater fish, *Serrasalmo piraya*, of the Orinoco, etc.

Perambulate (pĕræ·mbiū̆leɪt), *v.* 1568. [f. L. *perambulat-*, *perambulare* (f. *per* through + *ambulare* to walk); see -ATE [3].] **1.** *trans.* To walk through, over, or about (a place); formerly to travel through. Also *fig.* **b.** *intr.* To walk about; to move about 1607. **2.** *spec.* **a.** *trans.* To travel through and inspect (a territory). **b.** To walk officially round the boundaries of (a forest, manor, parish, etc.) for the purpose of formally determining or preserving them 1612.

1. There is a great deal of Spain that has not been perambulated JOHNSON. So **Pera·mbulant** *a.* (*rare*) perambulating, itinerant.

Perambulation (pĕræmbiū̆lēɪ·ʃən). 1472. [a. AF., med.L. *perambulatio*, f. *perambulare*; see prec. and -ATION.] **1.** The action of walking through; a walk, a journey on foot; formerly, the action of travelling through or about 1485. **2.** The action of travelling through and inspecting a territory or region; a survey. **b.** *transf.* A written account of a survey. 1576. **3.** The ceremony of walking officially round (a forest, manor, parish, or holding) for the purpose of asserting and recording its boundaries; beating the bounds 1472. **b.** *transf.* A record of a perambulation 1610. **4.** The boundary traced, or the space enclosed, by a perambulation; bounds; extent (*lit.* and *fig.*) 1601. †**5.** *fig.* Comprehensive relation or description; also, circumlocution –1652. **6.** *attrib.* 1670.

1. His daily perambulations at Lasswade 1877. 2. Discrete persons..to make parambulacions & to appoint..wher the boundes..shal extend 1540.

Perambulator (pĕræ·mbiū̆leɪtəɹ). 1611. [f. L. *perambulare* to PERAMBULATE; see -OR 2.] **1.** One who perambulates (see the vb.). Now *rare* or *Obs.* †**2.** A machine for measuring distances; a hodometer, waywiser –1828. **3.** A hand-carriage for young children, pushed from behind. (Often colloq. shortened to *pram*.) 1857.

‖ **Perameles** (perămī·līz). 1886. [mod.L., f. Gr. πήρα bag, pouch + L. *meles, melis* marten or badger.] *Zool.* A genus of small marsupials of Australia and New Guinea, typical of the family *Peramelidæ*, or true bandicoots.

Percale (pəɹkē̆·l, ‖ perkā·l). 1618. [So in F. Origin unkn.] **a.** A fabric imported from the East Indies in the 17th and 18th centuries. **b.** A closely woven cotton fabric, like muslin, but without gloss 1840.

Percaline (pɔ̄ıkălī·n, pɔ̄·ıkălin). 1858. [a. F., dim. of *percale*.] A glossy kind of French cotton cloth, usually dyed of one colour.

Percarbide (pəɹkā·ɹbəid). 1826. [f. PER- [1] II. a + CARBIDE.] *Chem.* A compound containing the maximum proportion of carbon with another element. Also †**Perca·rburet.** So **Perca·rburetted** *a.* containing a maximum of carbon, as *percarburetted iron*.

Perca·se, *adv. Obs.* (exc. *dial.*) [ME. a. AF. *per cas*, *par cas*, OF. *par cas*; see PER and CASE *sb.* [1]] †**1.** = PERADVENTURE *adv.* 1, PERCHANCE 1. –1513. †**2.** *If (except, lest*, etc.) *p.*, if (lest, etc.) by chance –1575. **3.** In a hypothetical or contingent statement: It may (might) chance or be the case that..; maybe, perchance ME. †**b.** = PERADVENTURE *adv.* 3 b. –1600.

Perceant (pɔ̄·ɹsănt), *a. poet. arch.* or *Obs.* late ME. [a. F. *perçant*, pr. pple. of *percer* to pierce.] Penetrative, keen, piercing.

The sophist's eye,..Keen, cruel, p., stinging KEATS.

Perceivable (pəɹsī·văb'l), *a.* Now *rare.* 1450. [orig. a. OF. *percevable*; now referred to PERCEIVE *v.*] Perceptible; sensible; intelligible, appreciable. Hence **Percei·vably** *adv.*

Percei·vance. *Obs.* exc. *dial.* 1534. [a. OF. *percevance*; see PERCEIVE and -ANCE.] The capacity of perceiving, discernment, wisdom; perception (mental or physical).

Perceive (pəɹsī·v), *v.* ME. [a. OF. **per-*

ceivre, north. f. *perçoivre*, now *percevoir* :—L. *percipere*, f. *per* thoroughly + *capere* to lay hold of.] **I.** To take in with the mind or senses. **1.** *trans.* To apprehend with the mind; to become aware of; to observe, understand. Also *absol.* †**b.** Of an inanimate object: To be affected by –1626. **2.** To become aware of by sight, hearing, or other sense; to observe ME. †**3.** To apprehend what is not present to observation; to see through, see into –1660.

1. Do you not perceiue the iest? SHAKS. b. The Vpper Regions of the Aire perceiue the collection of the matter of Tempest and Winds, before the Aire here below BACON. 2. They went awaye by nyght so pryvely, that the enemy perceived it not 1560. 3. They think their designes are too subtile to be perceived HOBBES.

†**II.** To take into possession. **a.** *trans.* To receive (rents, profits, dues, etc.) –1625. **b.** *gen.* To receive, get, obtain –1748.

b. *Two Gent.* I. i. 144. Hence **Perceivedly** (pəɹsī·vėdli) *adv.* **Percei·ver.**

Per cent (pəɹ se·nt), *phr.* (*sb.*) 1568. [See PER III. 2 and CENT[1]. Also written with full stop (*per cent.*), as if an abbrev. of per centum.] **A.** *phr.* By the hundred; for, in, or to every hundred; expressing a proportion, *esp.* of interest to principal. **b.** Used *attrib.* ('four per cent loan') or as *sb.* in *pl.* ('three per cents') 1720. **B.** *Per cents* as *sb. pl.* Percentages; *spec.* in U.S. schools 1850.

Percentage (pəɹse·ntėdʒ). 1789. [f. prec. + -AGE.] A rate or proportion per cent; a quantity or amount reckoned as so much in the hundred; *loosely*, a proportion (*of* something).

A serious p. of books are not worth reading at all 1886.

Percentile (pəɹse·ntəil, -il), *a.* and *sb.* 1885. [f. *per cent*(*um* (see above), app. after *bissextile*, etc.] **A.** *adj.* Pertaining to percentage; reckoned as a percentage 1890. **B.** *sb.* Each of a series of values obtained by dividing a large number of quantities into a hundred equal groups in order of magnitude 1885.

Percept (pɔ̄·ɹsept). 1837. [f. L. *perceptum*, f. *percipere* to PERCEIVE, after *concept.*] *Philos.* **1.** An object of PERCEPTION. **2.** The mental product of perceiving 1876.

2. A p. is the abstract of sensations 1876. So **Perce·ptual** *a.* of or pertaining to perception; of the nature of percepts.

Perceptible (pəɹse·ptĭb'l), *a.* 1551. [ad. late L. *perceptibilis*, f. *percipere*, *percept-* to PERCEIVE; see -BLE.] †**1.** Percipient, perceptive *of* –1772. **2.** Capable of being perceived, cognizable, apprehensible; observable 1603.

2. The soule is not p. by any sense HOLLAND. Hence **Perce·ptibi·lity**, †perceptivity; capability of being perceived. **Perce·ptibly** *adv.* in or to a p. degree.

Perception (pəɹse·pʃən). 1475. [In earlier senses, a. OF. *perception*; in later, perh. ad. L. *perceptionem*, f. *percipere* to PERCEIVE.] **I.** From L. *percipere*, to take, receive. **1.** The collection or receiving of rents, etc. Now only in legal use. 1475. †**2.** The partaking of the Eucharist –1674. **II.** From L. *percipere*, to be or become cognizant of. **1.** The taking cognizance of objects in general; occas. practically = consciousness. In Locke esp. as dist. from *volition*. 1611. †**b.** The being affected by an object without contact, though consciousness is absent BACON. **2.** The taking cognizance of a sensible or quasi-sensible object 1704. **3.** The intuitive recognition of a moral or æsthetic quality, e. g. the truth of a remark, the beautiful in objects 1827. **4.** *Philos.* The action of the mind by which it refers its sensations to an external object as their cause. (Dist. from *sensation*, *conception* or imagination, and *judgement* or inference.) 1762. **5.** The (or a) faculty of perceiving (in any of these senses) 1712. **6.** = PERCEPT 2. 1690.

1. The two..principal Actions of the Mind..are these two: P., or Thinking, and Volition, or Willing LOCKE. 2. The whole apparatus of vision, or of p. by any other of our senses 1736. 4. External things and their attributes are objects of p.: relations among things are objects of conception 1762. 5. He is a new man, with new perceptions EMERSON. Hence **Perce·ptional** *a.* of, pertaining to, or of the nature of p.

Perceptive (pəɹse·ptiv), *a.* (*sb.*) 1656. [f. L. *percept-*, *percipere* to PERCEIVE + -IVE.] **1.** Characterized by or capable of perceiving; pertaining to or having perception; instrumental to perception. **b.** Of ready perception. Also with *of*. 1860. †**2.** Perceptible –1813. **B.** *sb. pl.* The perceptive faculties or organs 1858.

1. Your mother's p. faculties are extraordinary 1897. Hence **Perce·ptive·ly** *adv.*, **-ness. Percepti·vity**, p. quality.

Perch (pɔ̄ɹtʃ), *sb.*[1] ME. [a. F. *perche* :—L. *perca*, a. Gr. πέρκη.] **1.** A common spiny-finned freshwater fish (*Perca fluviatilis*) of Europe and the British Isles. Also, the common yellow perch of N. America (*P. americana* or *flavescens*), or species of the family *Percidæ* in general. (Now rare in pl., the collect. sing. being used instead.) **b.** Applied on the Pacific coast to any fish of the viviparous family *Embiotocidæ* or surf-fishes, and locally to various other fishes 1882. **2.** With qualifying word, applied to various fishes of the family *Percidæ*, and of other families, resembling the common perch or taking its place as food 1611.

2. **Black p.**, a name for dark-coloured species of *Centropristis*, also called *black bass*; also for other dark-coloured fishes allied to the common p.; **Blue p.**, the BURGALL or CUNNER; **Red p.**, the rose-fish, *Sebastes marinus*; **White p.**, (*a*) *Morone americana*, family *Labracidæ*; (*b*) various species of the *Embiotocidæ*; **Yellow p.** (see 1).

Perch (pɔ̄ɹtʃ), *sb.*[2] ME. [a. F. *perche* :—L. *pertica* pole, measuring-rod.] **I.** A pole, rod, stick, or stake, used *e.g.* for a weapon, a prop, etc. *Obs.* or *dial.* in gen. sense. **b.** A pole set up in the sea, a river, etc., to serve as a mark for navigation 1465. **c.** The centre pole connecting the hinder to the fore-carriage in some four-wheeled vehicles 1668. **II. 1.** A bar fixed horizontally to hang something upon; a peg. *Obs.* or *Hist.* †**b.** A bar to support a candle or candles –1565. **2.** A bar fixed horizontally for a hawk or tame bird to rest upon. late ME. **b.** Anything serving for a bird to alight or rest upon; also *transf.* 1470. **c.** *fig.* An elevated or secure position or station 1526. **d.** *colloq.* An elevated seat on a vehicle for the driver 1841. **3.** A wooden bar, or frame of two parallel bars, used in examining and dressing cloth, blankets, etc. *Obs.* or *dial.* 1553.

2. As Chauntecleer among hise wyues alle Sat on his perche CHAUCER. b. *To take one's p.*, to perch, to alight. Phr. *To knock off one's p.*, to upset, vanquish, 'do for', be the death of. So *hop the p.*, to die.

III. A rod of a definite length for measuring land, etc.; hence **a.** A measure of length, esp. for land, etc.; in Standard Measure = $5\frac{1}{2}$ yards, but varying locally. Also called POLE or ROD. late ME. **b.** A superficial measure of land; a square perch or pole (normally $\frac{1}{160}$ of an acre) 1442. **c.** A solid measure used for stone, containing a lineal perch (see a) in length, and usually $1\frac{1}{2}$ feet in breadth and 1 foot in thickness; but varying locally 1823.

Perch (pɔ̄ɹtʃ), *v.* ME. [a. F. *percher*, f. *perche* PERCH *sb.*[2]] **I. 1.** *intr.* To alight or rest as a bird upon a perch. Hence *transf.* of persons or things: To alight or settle, or to stand, sit, or rest, upon something. 1486. **2.** *trans.* To set or place upon a perch; to set up on a height, or as on a perch. Also *refl.* 1575. **3.** *pa. pple.* Standing, seated, or settled upon a perch; set up on an eminence. late ME.

1. Birds of dazzling plume P. on the loaded boughs 1804. 3. The heights on which the old town is perched 1884.

II. To stretch (cloth from the loom) upon a perch (PERCH *sb.*[2] II. 3), for the purpose of examining it, etc. 1552.

Percha (pɔ̄·ɹtʃă). Short for GUTTA-PERCHA.

Perchance (pəɹtʃɑ·ns), *adv. arch.* [ME. a. AF. *par chance*, f. OF. *par* by + *chance* CHANCE.] **1.** = PERADVENTURE *adv.* 1. *Obs.* exc. *arch.* **2.** = PERADVENTURE *adv.* 2. late ME. **3.** = PERADVENTURE *adv.* 3. late ME. **b.** Qualifying a word or phr., by ellipsis. late ME.

3. b. To sleepe, p. to Dreame: I, there's the rub SHAKS.

Perched (pɔ̄ɹtʃt, *poet.* pɔ̄·ɹtʃėd), *ppl. a.* late ME. [f. PERCH *v.*, *sb.*[2] + -ED[1] and [2].] **1.** Seated as a bird upon a perch; set up on a high point; *spec.* in *Geol.* applied to a block or boulder left resting upon a pinnacle or the like by the melting of the ice which carried it. **2.** Furnished with a perch or perches 1671.

Percher[1] (pɔ̄·ɹtʃəɹ). 1775. [f. PERCH *v.* + -ER[1].] **1.** A person or animal that perches. **2.** *spec.* One of the *Insessores* or perching birds 1835. **3.** A workman employed in perching cloth (see PERCH *v.* II) 1882.

†**Percher**[2]. ME. [f. PERCH *sb.*[2] II. 1 b.] A tall candle –1706.

‖**Percheron** (pęrʃəron̄). 1875. [Fr. adj. from *le Perche*, a district of France.] A horse of a noted breed raised in le Perche, combining strength with lightness and speed.

Perchlor-, perchloro-. 1857. Comb. form of *perchloric*, *perchloride*, *perchlorinated*; chiefly indicating a compound in which there is the maximum replacement of hydrogen by chlorine, as in *perchlo:race·tic*, *perchlo:roqui·none*, etc.

Perchlorate (pəɹklō·rėt). 1826. [f. PER-[1] II. b + CHLORATE.] *Chem.* A salt of perchloric acid. Hence **Perchlo·rated** *ppl. a.*

Perchloric (pəɹklō·rik), *a.* 1818. [f. PER-[1] II. b + CHLORIC.] *Chem.* In *P. acid*, hydrogen perchlorate, $HClO_4$, the oxygen acid of chlorine, containing more oxygen than CHLORIC acid ($HClO_3$).

Perchloride (pəɹklō·rəid). 1818. [PER-[1] II. a.] *Chem.* A compound of chlorine with another element or radical, containing the maximum proportion of chlorine. So **Perchlo·rinated**, combined with the maximum proportion of chlorine; hence **Perchlorina·tion.**

Perciform (pɔ̄·ɹsifǭɹm), *a.* 1880. [ad. mod. L. *perciformis*, f. L. *perca* perch; see -FORM.] *Ichthyol.* Of the form of, or resembling, a perch; *spec.* belonging to the division *Perciformes* comprising the *Percidæ* and several allied families.

Percipience (pəɹsi·piĕns). 1768. [f. L. *percipientem* PERCIPIENT; see next and -ENCE.] The action or condition of perceiving; perception. So **Perci·piency**, the quality of being percipient.

Percipient (pəɹsi·piĕnt), *a.* and *sb.* 1662. [ad. L. *percipientem*, pr. pple. of *percipere* to PERCEIVE.] **A.** *adj.* That perceives or is capable of perceiving; conscious 1692. **B.** *sb.* One who or that which perceives; *spec.* in *Telepathy*, etc., one who perceives something outside the range of the senses 1885.

Percoid (pɔ̄·ɹkoid), *a.* and *sb.* 1840. [f. L. *perca* PERCH *sb.*[1] + -OID; first in F., in pl. *Percoïdes*, the perch family of acanthopterygious fishes (*Percidæ*).] *Ichthyol.* **A.** *adj.* Resembling or akin to a perch; belonging to the family *Percidæ*. **B.** *sb.* A fish of the perch family. So **Percoi·dean** *a.* and *sb.* **Percoi·deous** *a.*

Percolate (pɔ̄·ɹkŏlėt), *sb.* 1885. [ad. L. *percolatum* strained; see next.] A product of percolation.

Percolate (pɔ̄·ɹkŏleⁱt), *v.* 1626. [f. L. *percolat-*, *percolare*, f. *per* PER-[1] 1 + *colare* to strain, f. *colum* a strainer.] **1.** *trans.* To cause (a liquid) to pass through the interstices of a medium; to strain or filter. Also *fig.* **2.** *intr.* Of a liquid: To filter, ooze, or trickle through a porous substance or medium 1684. **b.** *fig.* 1867. **3.** *trans.* Of a liquid: To permeate (a porous body or medium). Also *fig.* 1794.

2. The water which has percolated through the sandy beds HUXLEY. b. The worship of Isis had percolated..into the Greek Peninsula GLADSTONE.

Percolation (pəɹkolēⁱ·ʃən). 1613. [ad. L. *percolationem*, f. *percolare* to PERCOLATE.] The action or process of percolating; filtration; *spec.* in *Pharmacy*, the process of obtaining an extract by passing a dissolving liquid through a pulverized substance until all the soluble matters are extracted. **b.** An oozing through 1646.

Percolator (pɔ̄·ɹkŏleⁱtəɹ). 1830. [f. L. *percolare* to PERCOLATE.] One who or that which percolates. **b.** An apparatus for percolating or straining a liquid (e. g. coffee).

Percomorph (pɔ̄·ɹkŏmǭɹf), *a.* and *sb.* 1885. [f. mod. L. *Percomorphi* pl.] *Ichthyol.* **A.** *adj.* Belonging to the order *Percomorphi*, comprising most of the spiny-finned fishes. **B.** *sb.* A fish of this order.

Percur (pəɹkɒ̄·ɹ), *v. rare.* 1657. [ad. L. *percurrere* to run through, f. PER-[1] 1 + *currere* to run.] *trans.* To run through, traverse. So **Percu·rrent** *a. rare*, running through; *spec.* in *Bot.* said of a midrib, etc., extending from the base to the apex of a leaf.

Percursory (pəɹkṓ·ɹsŏri), *a. rare.* 1837. [f. L. *percursor* one who runs through; see -ORY [2].] Characterized by running through something rapidly or hastily.

Percuss (pəɹkṓ·s), *v.* 1560. [f. L. *percuss-*, *percutere*, f. PER-[1] 1 + *quatere* to shake, strike, etc.] †1. *trans.* To strike so as to shake; hence *gen.* to strike, hit, knock. Also *fig.* -1694. 2. *Med.* To tap or strike gently (some part of the body), for purposes of diagnosis, or of therapeutics. Also *absol.* or *intr.* 1834.

1. Solid Bodies, if..softly percussed, give no Sound BACON.

Percussion (pəɹkṓ·ʃən), *sb.* 1544. [ad. L. *percussionem* n. of action from *percutere*; see prec.] 1. The striking of one body with or against another with some degree of force; impact; a stroke, knock. Usu. in reference to solid bodies. b. *transf.* and *fig.* 1607. 2. *spec.* a. The striking of a fulminating powder, or *p. cap*, so as to produce a spark and explode the charge in a fire-arm 1810. b. *Med.* The action of striking or tapping with the finger, or with a small hammer, upon a part of the body, either to ascertain the condition of some organ by the sound produced, or for therapeutic purposes. 1834. c. *Instrument of p.*: a musical instrument played by percussion 1776. d. Instruments of percussion, collectively.

1. *Centre of p.* see CENTRE *sb.* b. With..The Thunder-like p. of thy sounds Thou mad'st thine enemies shake SHAKS.

attrib. and *Comb.*, as *p. bullet, fuse, gun, match,* etc. (made so as to be ignited or exploded by p.); *p. massage*, etc.; **p. cap**, a small copper cap or cylinder containing fulminating powder, exploded by the p. of a hammer so as to fire the charge of a fire-arm; **-drill**, a drill worked by p.; **-lock**, a form of lock for a fire-arm in which a charge is fired by a *p. cap*; **p. powder**, the powder used in p. caps, consisting, since *c* 1823, of mercury fulminate; **-sieve**, an apparatus for sorting ores according to size by means of two inclined sieves agitated by levers; **-table**, an apparatus for sorting ores according to weight, consisting of a slightly inclined table which is shaken by a mechanical appliance. Hence **Percu·ssion** *v.* to fit (a fire-arm) for being fired by p.; to treat with p. massage.

Percussive (pəɹkṓ·siv), *a.* 1793. [f. L. *percuss-*, *percutere* (see PERCUSS) + -IVE.] Having the property of striking; of, pertaining to, or connected with percussion.

Percutient (pəɹkiū·ʃiĕnt), *a.* and *sb.* ? *Obs.* 1626. [ad. L. *percutientem*; see PERCUSS.] A. *adj.* Striking, percussive. B. *sb.* Something that strikes; a striking agent or body.

Perdie, var. of PARDIE.

†Pe·rdifoil, pe·rdifol. *rare.* 1657. [f. mod. L. *perdifolius*, f. *perdere* to lose + *folium* leaf.] A plant which annually loses its leaves -1803.

Perdition (pəɹdi·ʃən). [ME. a. OF. *perdiciun*, F. *perdition*, ad. L. *perditionem*, f. *perdere* to destroy, lose; f. PER-[1] 3 + *dare* to give, put.] 1. Utter destruction, complete ruin. Now *rare.* †b. Loss, diminution (*rhet.*) SHAKS. c. That wherein ruin lies. *Obs.* or *arch.* 1625. 2. *Theol.* The condition of final damnation; the fate of those in hell, eternal death. late ME. b. In imprecations 1604. †c. The place of destruction -1627.

1. A Man may be cheaply vitious, to the p. of himself SIR T. BROWNE. b. *Ham.* v. ii. 117. 2. Children of p. and inheritors of hell fire 1563. b. *Oth.* III. iii. 90. c. Down To bottomless p. MILT. Hence **Perdi·tionable** *a.* deserving p.

‖ **Perdix** (pɔ̄·ɹdiks). 1609. The L. word for 'partridge', retained in the Douay Bible and used in Ornithology as a generic name.

Perdu, perdue (pɔ̄·ɹdiu, pəɹdiū·, ‖pęrdü), *a.* and *sb.* 1591. [a. F. *perdu* lost; app. orig. introduced in the F. mil. phrase *sentinelle perdue*, and so spelt *perdue*; now usu. treated as alien, and written *perdu* or *perdue* according to gender.] A. *adj.* (or *pa. pple.*) †1. In *sentinel perdue*: a. The post of a sentinel in a very dangerous position. b. A sentinel posted in such a position. -1688. 2. †a. Placed in an extremely hazardous position; hence, in a desperate case, lost -1656. b. Lying hidden; disguised. Now chiefly as Fr. 1734. 3. In phrase *to lie perdu*. a. *Mil.* Placed as an outpost, scout, etc., in a hazardous position; (lying) in ambush, in wait. Often *transf.* or *fig.* 1607. b. Hidden; out of sight 1701.

2. b. A Huguenot perdue in the Louvre 1837. 3. a. It is unfitting he should lie Perdue, who is to walk the round FULLER. b. [It] had lain perdu in my head all that time 1893.

†B. *sb.* [Partly short for *sentinel perdue* or F. *enfants perdus*, partly ellipt. uses of A. 3.] 1. A soldier placed in a position of special danger, or ordered on a forlorn hope -1706. b. *collect.* The watch, guard -1654. c. *pl.* = FORLORN HOPE [F. *enfants perdus*] -1656. d. *transf.* One who acts as a watcher, scout, or spy -1734. 2. A desperado; a roué. CHAPMAN.

1. Shepheards lying constant Perdues in defence of their flocks FULLER.

Perduellion (pɔ̄ɹdiu,e·liŏn). 1533. [ad. L. *perduellionem*, f. (ult.) PER through + *duellis* warrior.] *Rom.* and *Sc. Law.* Hostility against the state or government; treason.

Perdurable (pəɹdiū·răb'l, pɔ̄·ɹdiŭrăb'l), *a.* ME. [a. OF. *per-*, *pardurable*, ad. late L. *perdurabilis*, f. *perdurare*; see next and -BLE.] Enduring continuously, lasting, permanent. b. *esp.* (in theol. lang.) Everlasting, eternal. late ME. c. Of material things: Imperishable; lasting indefinitely. late ME.

Leaving a name p. on earth SOUTHEY. Hence **Perdurabi·lity, Perdurableness,** the quality of being p. **Perdurably** *adv.*

Perdure (pəɹdiūᵊ·ɹ), *v.* Now *rare.* 1450. [a. obs. F. *par-*, *perdurer*, ad. L. *perdurare*, f. PER-[1] 2 + *durare* to harden, endure.] *intr.* To continue, endure, last on. So **Perdu·rance**, permanence, duration. **Perdura·tion** (*arch.*), continuous duration.

Peregrinate (pe·rĕgrineɪt), *v.* 1593. [f. L. *peregrinat-*, *peregrinari* to sojourn or travel abroad, f. *peregrinus* PEREGRINE.] *intr.* To travel, journey. b. To sojourn in a foreign country 1755. c. *trans.* To travel along or across 1835. So **Pe·regrinator** (now only *affected*) one who peregrinates; a traveller; a pilgrim.

Pe·regrinate, *a. rare.* 1588. [f. L. *peregrinatus*, pa. pple. of *peregrinari*; see prec.] Foreign-fashioned; having the air of one who has travelled abroad.

Peregrination (pe:rĕgrinē·ʃən). 1523. [a. F. *pérégrination*, or ad. L. *peregrinationem*, f. *peregrinari* to PEREGRINATE.] 1. The action of travelling in foreign lands, or from land to land; hence, from place to place 1548. b. With *a* and *pl.* A course of travel; a journey, esp. on foot; in *pl.* = travels 1548. c. *fig.* A systematic going through a subject, course of study, etc. d. The 'journey' of life. 1615. †2. A sojourning in a foreign land -1697. †b. *fig.* Man's life on earth viewed as a 'sojourn in the flesh' -1733.

1. b. My peregrinations about this great metropolis 1820. 2. b. In the eighty third year of his p. 1702.

Peregrine (pe·rĕgrin), *a.* and *sb.* late ME. [ad. L. *peregrinus* coming from foreign parts, foreign, f. *pereger* that is abroad or on a journey, *peregre* adv. abroad, f. *per* through + *ager* field.] A. *adj.* 1. Foreign; outlandish, strange; imported from abroad; also, †foreign to the matter in hand 1530. 2. *Astrol.* Of a planet: Situated in a part of the zodiac where it has none of its essential dignities 1588. †3. Upon a pilgrimage; travelling abroad -1768. 4. P. falcon: a typical species of falcon (*Falco peregrinus*), formerly esteemed for hawking. (So named because caught on their passage or 'pilgrimage' from their breeding-place; cf. *passage-hawk.*) late ME.

1. *P. tone* (med.L. *tonus peregrinus*), name of one of the Gregorian 'tones' or chants. 4. A Faucon peregryn thanne semed she Of fremde Land CHAUCER.

B. *sb.* 1. A sojourner in a foreign land; now only in *Rom. Antiq.* An alien denizen in ancient Rome 1593. †2. A pilgrim; a traveller in a foreign land -1654. 3. = *P. falcon* 1555.

Peregrinity (perĕgri·nĭti). 1591. [a. F. *pérégrinité*, or ad. L. *peregrinitas*, f. *peregrinus* PEREGRINE; see -ITY.] The condition of being a foreigner or alien; †the quality of being foreign; outlandishness. b. A journeying abroad CARLYLE.

Peremptory (pe·rĕmᵖtəri), *a.* (*adv.*, *sb.*) 1513. [ad. (through F.) L. *peremptorius* destructive, decisive, f. *peremptus*, *perimere* to cut off, destroy (f. PER-[1] 3 + *emere* to buy; orig., to take); see -ORY [2].] A. *adj.* 1. In Rom. Law, used in the sense 'that puts an end to, or precludes all debate, question, or delay', hence 'decisive, final'; hence, in Eng. Law in same sense (see quots.) 1530. b. †(*a*) Of a conclusion, statement, etc.: Incontrovertible; conclusive, final (now merged in 4) -1718. (*b*) Of a command, etc.: Admitting no refusal; imperative 1576. 2. *Law.* Said of a day or time decreed for the performance of some act. ? *Obs.* 1513. b. Hence, Positively fixed; absolutely requisite, essential 1596. †c. *colloq.* 'Absolute', utter B. JONS. †3. Resolute; resolved, determined (*to do* something, or *that*, etc.); also, obstinate, self-willed -1759. 4. Of persons, their actions, etc.: Positive in opinion or action; *esp.* in bad sense, intolerant of debate or contradiction; over-confident, dogmatic 1586. 5. Intolerant of refusal or opposition; imperious, dictatorial. (Now the most usual sense.) 1591. †6. Deadly, destructive -1614.

1. *P. challenge* or *exception* (*Law*), an objection without showing any cause allowed to a prisoner, against a certain number of jurymen. *P. mandamus*, a mandamus in which the command is absolute. *P. writ*, an original writ directing the sheriff to enforce the defendant's appearance in court without option; so *p. citation*, etc. b. The orders of the Senate were p. 1878. 2. b. It is a p. point of virtue that a man's independence be secured EMERSON. 4. His humour is lofty, his discourse peremptorie SHAKS. 5. The p. tone in which he sent forth his sublime commands GOLDSM.

†B. as *adv.* a. *colloq.* Absolutely, entirely. b. By a peremptory order; without fail. -1709.

†C. *ellipt.* as *sb.* Short for *p. challenge, writ,* etc. -1753. Hence **Pe·remptori·ly** *adv.*, **-ness.**

Perennial (pĕre·niăl), *a.* and *sb.* 1672. [f. L. *perennis* lasting through the year or years (f. *per* through + *annus* year) + -AL.] A. *adj.* 1. Lasting or continuing throughout the year; said esp. of a spring or stream which flows through all seasons of the year 1703. 2. Lasting through a long, indefinite, or infinite time; enduring, never-failing; everlasting, eternal 1750. b. Of plants, their roots, etc.: Remaining alive through a number of years; opp. to *annual* and *biennial* 1672.

2. A constant and p. softness of manner JOHNSON. b. P. herbs and shrubs 1880.

B. *sb.* 1. A perennial plant; see A. 2 b. 1763. 2. Something that lasts through a succession of years. (With conscious allusion to sense 1.) 1771. Hence **Pere·nnially** *adv.*

Perennibranch (pĕre·nibræŋk), *a.* and *sb.* 1835. [f. mod.L. *Perennibranchia* neut. pl., f. *perennis* PERENNIAL + BRANCHIA.] A. *adj.* Having permanent gills; belonging to the division *Perennibranchia* (or *Perennibranchiata*) of Amphibians. B. *sb.* An amphibian of this division. Also **Perennibra·nchiate** *a.* and *sb.*

Perennity (pĕre·nĭti). 1597. [ad. L. *perennitas*, f. *perennis* PERENNIAL; see -ITY.] The quality of being perennial; perpetuity.

†Pererra·tion. 1608. [f. L. *pererrare.*] A wandering or travelling about -1658.

Perfay (pəɹfē·), *int. arch.* [ME. a. OF. *par fei*, f. *par* by (PAR *prep.* 1) + OF. *fei*, mod.F. *foi* :—L. *fidem.*] By (my) faith; verily, truly.

Perfect (pɔ̄·ɹfĕkt), *a.* (*adv.*, *sb.*) [orig. ME. *parfit(e*, a. OF. *parfit(e* :—L. *perfectum, -am*, pa. pple. of *perficere* to accomplish, f. PER-[1] 2 + *facere*; subseq. conformed to L. *perfectus.*] A. *adj.* I. *gen.* †1. Thoroughly made, formed, done, performed, carried out, accomplished; of full age -1773. 2. Fully accomplished, versed, trained, conversant. Const. *in, with,* †*of, arch.* ME. †b. Made ready -1568. c. Thoroughly learned or acquired. Also of a person: Having learnt one's lesson, etc. thoroughly. 1581. 3. Complete; not deficient in any particular ME. †b. Sound; of sound mind, sane -1619. 4. Free from any imperfection; faultless. But often used of a near approach to such a state, and hence capable of comparison. ME. b. *spec.* Of supreme moral excellence ME. 5. Completely corresponding to a definition, pattern, or description. late ME. b. Of a copy, representation, etc.: Exact, correct 1540. c. Entire, unqualified; pure, unalloyed 1590. d. Sheer; unmitigated, utter. Chiefly *colloq.* 1611. †6. Completely assured, certain; of a statement or speaker (*rare*). †7. Satisfied, contented SHAKS.

1. Sonnes at p. age SHAKS. 2. The Hawke that is

most p. for the flight GREENE. **c.** Mrs. Grimley.. undertook to prompt, as the performers were not all very p. 1844. **3.** Perfecte God, and perfecte man *Athan. Creed* 1548. A man of..p. sincerity 1841. **b.** *Lear* IV. vii. 63. **4.** Good and perfit English 1590. **b.** Marke the p. man, and behold the vpright *Ps.* xxxvii. 37. Guide me in thy p. way WESLEY. **5.** The p. octahedron 1823. **b.** A more p. copy procured at Aleppo PALEY. **c.** You talk..like a p. stranger 1699. **d.** A man whose chin terminated in a point..would be a p. horror 1804. **6.** *Cymb.* III. i. 73. **7.** *Macb.* III. iv. 21.

II. *techn.* **1.** *Arith.* Applied to a number which is equal to the sum of its aliquot parts. late ME. **2.** *Gram.* Applied to the tense which denotes a completed event or action viewed in relation to the present; hence (with qualification) to any tense expressing action completed at the time indicated 1530. **3.** *Mus.* (Opp. to IMPERFECT *a.* II. 3.) 1597. **4.** *Physiol., Anat.*, etc. Having its proper characteristics developed to the fullest degree; typical 1693. **5.** *Bot.* Having all four whorls of the flower (calyx, corolla, stamens, and pistils) 1706. **6.** *Entom.* In the most completely developed form or phase, as *p. insect, state*, etc. 1834. **7.** *Physics.* Conceived as existing in a state of ideal perfection, as *p. elasticity, gas*. 1849.

1. The partes of 6 are 1, 2, 3..wherefore 6 is a p. number 1570. **3.** *P. concords* or *consonances*, a name including the concords of a unison, fifth, and octave, and sometimes a fourth. Hence, applied to the intervals of a fourth, fifth, and octave, in their normal form (opp. to *augmented* and *diminished*). So *p. chord* or *triad*, a name for the common chord in its direct position (involving a perfect fifth). *P. cadence*: a cadence consisting of the direct chord of the tonic preceded by a dominant or subdominant chord (authentic or plagal cadence), and forming a full close.

B. as *adv.* = Perfectly. Obs. exc. *dial.* or *poet.* 1470. **C.** quasi-*sb.* **1.** That which is perfect, perfection (*rare*). *poet.* 1842. **2.** *Gram.* ellipt. for *p. tense*; see A. II. 2. 1841. Hence **Pe·rfect-ly** *adv.*, **-ness.**

Perfect (pɔ̄·ɹfėkt, pəɹfe·kt), *v.* late ME. [f. PERFECT *a.*] **1.** *trans.* To complete; to carry through, accomplish 1494. **b.** *Printing.* To complete the printing of a sheet by printing the second side 1824. †**2.** To bring to full development –1607. **3.** To make perfect or faultless; *loosely*, To bring nearer to perfection; to improve 1449. **4.** To make (a person) perfect *in* some art, etc.; †to inform completely 1603.

1. Labour perfected, with the evening ends QUARLES. Then urg'd, she perfects her illustrious toils POPE. **3.** George especially perfected his accent so as to be able to pass for a Frenchman THACKERAY. **4.** *Meas. for M.* IV. iii. 146. Hence **Perfecter,** one who perfects, completes, or finishes.

Perfectibility (pəɹfektibi·lĭti). 1794. [f. next.] **1.** Capability of being perfected or becoming perfect; *spec.* the capacity of man to progress indefinitely towards perfection; the doctrine of this capacity. **2.** *loosely.* A state of perfection (*rare*) 1809. Hence **Perfe:ctibilita·rian,** an upholder of human p.

Perfectible (pəɹfe·ktĭb'l, pɔ̄·ɹfėktĭb'l). 1635. [f. PERFECT *v.* or *a.* + -IBLE; cf. F. *perfectible.*] Capable of being perfected or brought to perfection. So **Perfectibi·lian, Perfecti·bilist,** one who holds the doctrine of **Perfecti·bilism,** the theory of the perfectibility of man.

Perfecting (pɔ̄·ɹfėktiŋ, pəɹfe·ktiŋ), *vbl. sb.* 1494. [-ING [1].] The action of PERFECT *v.*

attrib. **P. machine** or (U.S.) **press,** a printing machine on which the sheet, as it passes through, is printed first on one side and then on the other before leaving the machine.

Perfection (pəɹfe·kʃən), *sb.* ME. [a. OF., ad. L. *perfectionem*, f. *perfect-, perficere*; see PERFECT *a.*] **1.** The action, process, or fact of making perfect; completing, accomplishing. late ME. †**2.** Completed state, completeness –1679. **b.** The full growth or development of anything 1500. †**c.** *Mus.* The condition of being 'perfect' (see PERFECT *a.* II. 3) –1880. **3.** Flawlessness, faultlessness. Also often, Comparative excellence. ME. **b.** *concr.* A perfect person, place, etc. 1594. **4.** The condition of being morally perfect; holiness; †in ME. *spec.* Monastic discipline ME. **5.** The most perfect degree, the highest pitch (*of* a quality, faculty, etc.); the extreme or height (*of* anything good or evil) ME. **6.** (With *a* and *pl.*) A quality, feature, accomplishment, etc. of a high order or great excellence 1572.

1. To study your own p. LAW. **2. b.** They..bring no fruite to p. *Luke* viii. 14. **3.** In different glaciers, ..these veins display various degrees of p. TYNDALL. **b.** Is this the citie that men call the p. of beauty? *Lam.* ii. 15. **4.** A p. like Buddha's 1882. *Counsel of p.*, see COUNSEL *sb.* 2. **5.** The p. of goodness 1729. **6.** [He] hathe many perfections in him 1572.

Phr. *To p.*, completely, perfectly. Hence **Perfe·ction** *v. trans.* (*rare*) to perfect. **Perfe·ctional** *a.* of, pertaining to, or of the nature of p. So **Perfe·ctionate** *v. trans.* (now *rare*) To make perfect or complete; **Perfectiona·tion,** the action or fact of being made perfect. **Perfe·ctionize** *v. trans.* (*rare*) to bring to p. **Perfe·ctionment,** the action of perfecting.

Perfectionism (pəɹfe·kʃəniz'm). 1846. [f. after next; see -ISM.] A system or doctrine of perfection; *esp.* the theory of the moral perfectibility of man.

Perfectionist (pəɹfe·kʃənist). 1657. [f. PERFECTION *sb.* + -IST.] One who holds any theory or follows any practice for the attainment of religious, moral, social, or political perfection; *esp.* one who holds that religious or moral perfection may be attained; *spec.* (with cap.) a member of the communistic community of Oneida Creek, N.Y. Also *attrib.*

Perfectist (pɔ̄·ɹfėktist). *Obs.* exc. *Hist.* 1618. [f. PERFECT *a.* + -IST] = PERFECTIONIST.

Perfective (pəɹfe·ktiv), *a.* 1596. [See PERFECT *v.* and -IVE.] **1.** Tending to make perfect or complete; usu. with *of*. Now *rare*. **2.** In process of being perfected. *rare*. 1848. **3.** *Gram.* Expressing completion of action; opp. to IMPERFECTIVE 1844.

1. That which is..perfectiue of his kind 1620. **2.** Dugès was..able to see..the eight legs in a p. state 1848. Hence **Perfe·ctively** *adv.* in a way tending to completeness.

Perfervid (pəɹfɔ̄·ɹvid), *a.* 1856. [ad. mod. L. *perfervidus*, f. PER-[1] 4 + *fervidus* FERVID; chiefly in the phr. *perfervidum ingenium Scotorum*, founded on Buchanan's *Scotorum præfervida ingenia.*] Very fervid, glowing, or ardent.

Perficient (pəɹfi·ʃėnt), *a.* (*sb.*) *rare*. 1641. [ad. L. *perficientem*, pr. pple. of *perficere* to complete.] **A.** *adj.* That accomplishes something; effectual, actual 1659. †**B.** *sb.* One who perfects or completes –1662.

Perfidious (pəɹfi·diəs), *a.* 1598. [ad. L. *perfidiosus*, f. *perfidia* PERFIDY; see -OUS.] Characterized by perfidy; guilty of breaking faith or violating confidence; treacherous.

P. dealing 1759. The victim of a p. woman LYTTON. Hence **Perfi·dious-ly** *adv.*, **-ness.**

Perfidy (pɔ̄·ɹfidi). 1592. [a. F. *perfidie*, ad. L. *perfidia*, f. (ult.) PER-[1] 3 + *fides* faith.] The deceitful violation of faith or promise; base breach of faith or betrayal of trust; often, the profession of friendship in order to betray.

Many other things he reporteth of the p. of the French nation 1607. The name of Judas has become a byword of covetousness and p. 1885.

†**Perfla·ble,** *a.* late ME. [ad. L. *perflabilis*, f. *perflare* PERFLATE.] That may be blown through; allowing of ventilation –1620.

Perflate (pəɹflē·t), *v.* Now *rare*. 1540. [f. L. *perflat-, perflare*, f. PER-[1] 1 + *flare* to blow.] *trans.* To blow through, ventilate. So †**Perfla·tile** *a.* exposed to wind; airy. **Perfla·tion,** free passage of wind or air; ventilation.

Perfluent (pɔ̄·ɹfluĕnt), *a.* 1673. [ad. L. *perfluentem*, pr. pple. of *perfluere* to flow through; see PER-[1] 1.] Flowing through.

P. battery, a kind of galvanic battery actuated by a liquid flowing through.

Perfoliate (pəɹfōu·liĕt), *a.* 1687. [f. PER-[1] 1 + L. *folium* leaf; see -ATE [2] 2.] **1.** *Bot.* Having the stalk apparently passing through the leaf, the edges of the basal lobes uniting round the stem. Said orig. of a plant and its stalk; later *transf.* of the leaf. **2.** *Entom.* Of antennæ: Having the joints dilated or expanded laterally all round. Also **Perfo·liated.** 1752. Hence **Perfolia·tion.**

Perforate (pɔ̄·ɹfŏrĕt), *ppl. a.* 1540. [ad. L. *perforatus*, pa. pple. of *perforare*; see next.] = PERFORATED.

Perforate (pɔ̄·ɹfŏreit), *v.* 1538. [f. L. *perforat-, perforare*, f. PER-[1] 1 + *forare* to bore.] **1.** *trans.* To make a hole or holes right through; to pierce with a pointed instrument or projectile; *spec.* to make rows of small holes separating coupons, stamps, etc., in a sheet. **b.** To bore into (a thing) 1712. **c.** To 'pass through' in position; to extend or be continued through 1820. **2.** To form (a hole, etc.) by boring 1876. **3.** To make or suffer perforation 1775.

Perforated (pɔ̄·ɹfŏreitėd), *ppl. a.* 1486. [f. prec. + -ED [1].] **1.** Pierced with one or more holes. **b.** *Nat. Hist.* Cribrose 1678. **2.** Made or outlined by perforations (*rare*) 1790.

2. P. Initials on Stamps 1891.

Perforation (pɔ̄ɹfŏrē·ʃən). ME. [ad. late L. *perforationem*, f. *perforare* to PERFORATE.] **1.** The action of perforating, boring through, or piercing; the fact or condition of being perforated 1440. **b.** *Surg.* The formation, through accident or disease, of a hole through the thickness of any structure, as through the wall of the intestine, etc. 1666. **2.** A hole made by boring, punching, or piercing; an aperture passing through or into anything 1543. **3.** The natural orifice of an organ or part of the body –1797.

2. [Stamps] with pin-pricked perforations 1870.

Perforative (pɔ̄·ɹfŏrĕtiv), *a.* 1597. [a. F. *perforatif, -ive*, f. L. *perforat-, perforare* to PERFORATE + -IVE.] Having the character of perforating; tending to perforate.

Perforator (pɔ̄·ɹfŏreitəɹ). 1739. [f. L. *perforare* to PERFORATE.] One who or that which perforates; *esp.* (*Surg.*) an instrument for penetrating the fœtal skull.

Perforce (pəɹfōə·ɹs), *adv., sb.* [ME. a. OF. *par force* by force.] **A.** *adv.* †**a.** By violence; forcibly –1670. **b.** By moral constraint; compulsorily, of necessity 1542. **c.** quasi-*adj.* 1580.

Patience p., see PATIENCE *sb.* 1. *P. of*, prop. 'per force of', by force of, by dint of.

B. quasi-*sb.* In phrases *by p.*, by compulsion; *of p.*, of necessity 1525.

†**Perfo·rce,** *v.* 1509. [a. OF. *parforcier, -forcer*, f. *par* through + *forcer* to FORCE.] *trans.* To force, constrain –1610.

Perform (pəɹfǭ·ɹm), *v.* [ME. a. OF. *par-, perfourmer, -former*; f. *par-* PER-[1] 2 + *former* FORM *v.*, or *forme* FORM *sb.*, or perh. an alteration of *parfournir* to accomplish completely.] †**1.** *trans.* To carry through to completion (an action, process, work, etc.) –1620. †**b.** To complete by adding what is wanting. Also with *up*. –1537. †**2.** To make, construct (a material object); to execute (a piece of work, literary or artistic) –1774. †**3.** To bring about, produce (a result) –1715. **4.** To carry out in action, execute (a command, promise, undertaking, etc.) ME. **5.** To carry out, achieve (any undertaking); to go through and finish, do, make ME. †**b.** *loosely.* To grant, pay, etc. that which is promised –1661. **c.** *absol.* or *intr.* To discharge one's function, do one's part; to do, act (well, ill, etc.). late ME. **6.** *spec.* To do, go through, execute (a duty, public function; a piece of music, play, etc.) 1613. **b.** To play (a part or character) 1610. **c.** *absol.* or *intr.* To act in a play; to play or sing 1836.

2. A garland..of Mosaic, or inlaid work, and not ill performed 1774. **3.** *Temp.* I. ii. 194. **4.** Yt I maye daylie performe my vowes COVERDALE *Ps.* lx[i]. 8. **5.** Murthers haue bene perform'd Too terrible for the eare SHAKS. **b.** Performing Life to those to whom he promised it FULLER. **c.** *Cor.* I. i. 271. **6.** The Opera..was performed with great Applause STEELE. **b.** In Acting, barely to p. the Part is not commendable STEELE. **c.** He..performed skilfully on the flute MACAULAY. Hence **Perfo·rmable** *a.* that may be performed or done. **Perfo·rmer,** one who (or that which) performs. **Perfo·rming** *ppl. a.* that performs; applied *spec.* to animals trained to execute feats or tricks at a public entertainment.

Performance (pəɹfǭ·ɹmăns). 1494. [f. prec. + -ANCE.] **1.** The carrying out of a command, duty, etc. (Often antithetical to *promise.*) 1531. **2.** The accomplishment, carrying out, doing of any action or work; working, action 1494. **b.** An action, act, deed. Often emphatic: A notable deed. 1599. **c.** A piece of work; a composition. Now *rare*. 1665. **3.** *spec.* The action of performing a ceremony, play, part, piece of music, etc. 1611. **b.** A public exhibition or entertainment 1709.

1. Promises are not binding, where the p. is unlawful PALEY. **2.** The p. of some experiment 1879. **b.** Besides her walking, and other actuall performances, what..haue you heard her say? SHAKS. **c.** His performances in prose are bad enough 1875.

†**Pe·rfricate,** *v.* 1597. [f. L. *perfricat-*, *perfricare*; cf. FRICTION.] *trans.* To rub thoroughly or all over –1755. Hence **Perfrica·tion** 1607.

Perfume (pə·ɹfiŭm, pəɹfiū·m), *sb.* 1533. [a. F. *parfum*, sb. f. *parfumer*; see next.] **1. a.** *orig.* The odorous fumes given off by the burning of any substance, e.g. of incense. **b.** Hence, The volatile particles, scent, or odour emitted by any sweet-smelling substance; fragrance. **c.** *fig.* Fragrance, savour; repute 1586. **2.** A substance, natural or prepared, which emits an agreeable odour; scent 1542.

1. b. Three April perfumes in three hot Junes burn'd SHAKS. 2. Cinamome,..Spekenarde, Cassia, sweete perfumes EDEN.

Perfume (pəɹfiū·m), *v.* 1538. [a. F. *parfumer*, f. *par-* PER-[1] 1, 2 + *fumare* to smoke.] **1.** *trans.* To fill or impregnate with the smoke or vapour of some burning substance; esp. of incense or the like. **2.** To impart a sweet scent to. (Now the ordinary sense.) Also *fig.* 1539.

1. They p. their temples with frankensence EDEN. Hence **Perfu·mer**, one who perfumes; one engaged in making or selling perfumes 1573.

Perfumery (pəɹfiū·məri). 1788. [f. PERFUMER; see -ERY. In mod.F. *parfumerie.*] **a.** The preparation of perfumes; the business of a perfumer. **b.** Perfumes as a class of substances. **c.** A perfumer's place of business.

Perfunctory (pəɹfʊ·ŋktəri), *a.* 1581. [ad. late jurid. L. *perfunctorius* done carelessly or superficially, negligent, f. *perfunct-*, *perfungi* to get done with; see -ORY.] **1.** Of a thing: Done merely for the sake of getting rid of the duty; done as a piece of routine or for form's sake only, and so without interest; formal, mechanical; superficial, trivial. **b.** Of a person: Acting merely by way of duty; official; formal; lacking interest or zeal 1600. †**2.** Stated in formal terms CLARENDON.

1. [He] glanced at the two documents in a p. manner 1885. b. The presumptuous rashnesse of a p. licencer MILT. Hence **Perfu·nctorily** *adv.* **Perfu·nctoriness.** So †**Perfuncto·rious** *a.*, †**-ly** *adv.*

Perfuse (pəɹfiū·z), *v.* 1526. [f. L. *perfus-*, *perfundere*, f. PER-[1] 1 + *fundere* to pour out.] **1.** *trans.* To overspread with any moisture; to besprinkle (*with* water, etc.); to cover or suffuse (*with* radiance, colour, grace, etc.) **2.** To pour (something) through; to diffuse through or over. Also *fig.* 1666. So **Perfu·sive** *a.* having the character of being shed all over, or diffused all through.

Perfusion (pəɹfiū·ʒən). 1574. [ad. L. *perfusionem*, f. *perfundere*; see prec.] The action of perfusing; *spec.* the pouring over of water in baptism, as opp. to immersion.

Pergameneous (pəɹgămī·niəs), *a.* 1826. [f. L. *pergamena* PARCHMENT + -EOUS.] Of the nature or texture of parchment. So **Pergamenta·ceous** *a.*

‖ **Pergola** (pə̄·ɹgŏlă). 1654. [a. It. :—L. *pergula* projecting roof, f. *pergere* to come forward.] **1.** An arbour or covered walk formed of growing plants trained over trellis-work 1675. †**2.** An elevated balcony –1656.

‖ **Pergunnah, pergana** (pəɹgʊ·nă). 1765. [a. Pers. and Urdu *parganah* district.] A division of territory in India, comprising a group of villages.

Perhaps (pəɹhæ·ps), *adv.* (*sb.*) Also (*colloq.*) **p'raps.** 1528. [f. PER *prep.* II. 1 + *happes*, *haps*, pl. of *happe*, HAP *sb.*] **1.** A word qualifying a statement so as to express possibility with uncertainty; = PERCHANCE 3. **2.** = PERCHANCE 2. 1576. **B.** *sb.* **a.** A statement qualified by 'perhaps'. **b.** A mere possibility. 1534.

A. 1. P. I may give farther answer to this query JOHNSON. There are three, or p. four, courses open to us 1883. 2. Pray God, if p. the thought of thine heart may be forgiven thee *Acts* viii. 22.

Peri (pī·ri). 1777. [ad. Pers. *pārī* or *pĕrī*.] In Persian mythology, one of a race of superhuman beings, orig. represented as of malevolent character, but subsequently as good genii, endowed with grace and beauty. Hence *transf.* 'a fair one'.

Peri-, *prefix*, repr. Gr. περί prep. and adv., 'round, around, round about, about'.

In numerous scientific terms, chiefly anatomical and pathological, in which *peri-* has a prepositional relation to the implied sb. **a.** In adjs. = situated or occurring about or around, surrounding or enclosing (the part, organ, etc. denoted by the second element); occas. also = pertaining to the part, or thing, denoted by a corresponding sb.; as in: **Peribra·nchial**, around the branchiæ or gills. **Peribro·nchial**, around the bronchial tubes. **Perice·llular**, around a cell or cells. **Pericho·rdal** (-kǭ·ɹdăl), around the notochord or spinal chord. **Perio·tic** [Gr. ὠτικός of the ear], *Anat.* surrounding the ear; applied to those bones of the skull which constitute a protective case for the internal ear; also as *sb.* **Pe·ristoma·tic,** *Bot.* surrounding a stoma of a leaf.

b. In sbs. (mostly in L. form) denoting a part, organ, etc., surrounding or enclosing that denoted by the second element; as PERIANTH, etc.; **Pe·riblem** [Gr. περίβλημα anything thrown round], *Bot.* the embryonic cells of the growing-point of phanerogams from which the primary cortex is developed. ‖**Perica·mbium** = *pericycle.* ‖**Perichæ·tium** [Gr. χαίτη long hair], *Bot.* a whorl or cluster of modified leaves at the base of a group of reproductive organs, or of the fructification, in mosses and some liverworts. ‖**Pericho·ndrium** [Gr. χόνδρος cartilage], *Anat.* a membrane consisting of fibrous connective tissue, enveloping the cartilages except at the joints. **Pe·richord,** the sheath or investment of the notochord. ‖**Pericli·nium** [Gr. κλίνη couch], *Bot.* the involucre of *Compositæ.* **Pe·ricycle** [Gr. περίκυκλος all round], *Bot.* the outer portion of the vascular cylinder, lying between the vascular bundles internally, and the endodermis or innermost layer of the cortex externally. ‖**Perie·nteron** [Gr. ἔντερον intestine], *Embryol.* and *Zool.* a space between the outer and inner layers of a gastrula, the remnant of the blastocœle persisting after gastrulation. **Pe·rilymph,** *Anat.* the clear fluid contained within the osseous labyrinth of the internal ear, and surrounding the membranous labyrinth. **Pe·rimorph** [Gr. μορφή form], *Min.* a mineral enclosing another. ‖**Perimy·sium** [Gr. μῦς muscle], *Anat.* the sheath of connective tissue enveloping a muscle. ‖**Perine·phrium** [Gr. νεφρός kidney], the connective tissue which envelops the kidneys. ‖**Perio·stracum** [Gr. ὄστρακον shell of a mussel], *Zool.* the outer horny covering of the shell of a mollusc or brachiopod. **Pe·riproct** [Gr. πρωκτός anus], *Zool.* that part of the body-wall of an echinoderm which surrounds the anus. **Pe·risarc** [Gr. σάρξ, σαρκ- flesh], *Zool.* the horny or chitinous case investing the cœnosarc in some Hydrozoa. **Pe·risome** [Gr. σῶμα body], *Zool.* the integument or body-wall of an echinoderm, upon which the external calcareous skeleton is developed. **Pe·risperm** [Gr. σπέρμα seed], *Bot.* the mass of nutritive tissue outside the embryo-sac in some seeds; also, the tissue of the nucellus, which sometimes persists in the ripe seed. **Pe·rispore** [Gr. σπόρος seed], *Bot.* the skin or integument of a spore. **Pe·ritreme** [Gr. τρῆμα hole], *Zool.* (*a*) a small chitinous ring surrounding a breathing-hole in an insect; (*b*) = PERISTOME 2 a.

c. *Path.* In sbs. in -ITIS (-əi·tis), denoting inflammation in the parts around or about that denoted by the second element, or in the part denoted by a corresponding sb. (see b); with corresponding adjs. in -*itic* (-i·tik); as PERICARDITIS, etc. **Pe·riadeni·tis** [Gr. ἀδήν gland], inflammation of the connective tissue round a gland. **Pe·richondri·tis,** of the *perichondrium* (see b). **Pe·rinephri·tis,** of the *perinephrium* (see b). **Pe·riprocti·tis** [Gr. πρωκτός the anus], of the connective tissue about the anus. **Pe·rityphli·tis** [Gr. τυφλόν cæcum], of some part around or adjacent to the cæcum (when seated in the *appendix vermiformis*, now called *appendicitis*).

Perianth (pe·ri,ænþ). Formerly in L. form **perianthium.** 1706. [app. after F. *périanthe*, ad. mod.L. *perianthium*, f. Gr. περί about + ἄνθος flower; cf. PERICARP.] *Bot.* A floral envelope; formerly, a synonym of CALYX; now, the outer part of a flower, which encloses the essential organs (stamens and pistils); either *double*, i.e. the calyx and corolla collectively; or *single*, when there is only one 1828. **b.** In liverworts, a leafy or membranous covering surrounding the archegonium; in mosses, the cluster of leaves surrounding the sexual organs in the 'flower' 1857. Also *attrib.*

Periapt (pe·ri,æpt). Also formerly in Gr. form **periapton,** pl. **-a.** 1584. [a. F. *périapte*, ad. Gr. περίαπτον, f. περί + ἅπτος fastened, f. ἅπτειν to fasten.] Something worn about the person as a charm; an amulet.

Helpe ye charming Spelles and Periapts SHAKS.

Periaster, periastron (peri,æ·stəɹ, -æ·strŏn). Also **periastre.** 1851. [f. Gr. περί PERI- + ἄστρον star, after PERIHELION, etc.] *Astron.* That point in the orbit of a heavenly body revolving round a star at which it is nearest to the star. Also *attrib.* Hence **Peria·stral** *a.* of or pertaining to the p.

Periblast (pe·riblæst). 1857. [f. Gr. περί PERI- + -BLAST.] *Biol.* **a.** = PERIPLAST b. **b.** The outer layer of protoplasm in the egg of a teleostean fish, surrounding the central yolk. Hence **Peribla·stic** *a.* (*a*) in Haeckel's nomenclature, applied to one stage in the development of a meroblastic ovum which germinates by segmentation of the superficial part; (*b*) of or pertaining to the p. (sense b).

‖ **Peribolus** (pĕri·bŏlŏs), **-os** (-ǫs). 1706. [a. Gr. περίβολος circuit, enclosure; f. περί PERI- + βολ-, from βάλλειν to throw.] *Gr. Antiq.* An enclosure or court around a temple; the wall bounding this.

Pericardiac (perikā·ɹdiæ̆k), *a.* 1822. [f. PERICARDIUM, after *cardiac.*] = next.

Pericardial (perikā·ɹdiăl), *a.* 1654. [f. as prec. + -AL.] Of, pertaining to, occurring in, or connected with the pericardium. So **Perica·rdian, Perica·rdic** *adjs.* 1656.

‖ **Pericarditis** (pe:rikaɹdəi·tis). 1799. [f. as prec. + -ITIS.] *Path.* Inflammation of the pericardium.

‖ **Pericardium** (perikā·ɹdiŏm). 1576 (-ion), 1615 (-ium). [Latinized f. Gr. (τὸ) περικάρδιον adj. neut. used as sb., f. περί PERI- + καρδία heart.] *Anat.* The membranous sac, consisting of an outer fibrous and an inner serous layer, which encloses the heart.

Pericarp (pe·rikāɹp). 1759. [= F. *péricarpe*, ad. mod.L. *pericarpium*, a. Gr. περικάρπιον pod, husk, shell, f. περί PERI- + καρπός fruit.] *Bot.* A seed-vessel; the wall of the ripened ovary or fruit of a flowering plant. Hence †**Perica·rpial, Perica·rpic** *adjs.* of or pertaining to a p.

‖ **Pericarpium** (perikā·ɹpiŏm). Now *rare.* 1691. [mod.L.] = prec.

Pericentral (pe·risentrăl), *a.* 1889. [f. PERI- a + CENTRE + -AL.] *Bot.* Arranged round a centre or central body.

Pericentre (pe·risentəɹ). 1902. [f. PERI- + CENTRE, after *perihelion.*] That point in the (eccentric) orbit of a body revolving round a centre, at which it is nearest to that centre.

Perichætous (perikī·təs), *a.* 1870. [f. mod. L. *Perichæta* (f. PERI- + Gr. χαίτη long hair, 'bristle') + -OUS.] *Zool.* Surrounded by bristles; having segments so surrounded, as earthworms of the genus *Perichæta.*

‖ **Perichoresis** (pe:rikorī·sis). 1858. [a. Gr. περιχώρησις.] *Theol.* = CIRCUMINCESSION.

Periclase (pe·riklēs). 1844. [ad. mod.L. *periclasia*, erron. f. Gr. περι- exceedingly + κλάσις fracture; referring to its perfect cleavage.] *Min.* A mineral consisting of magnesia and a little protoxide of iron, found in greenish crystals or grains, at Vesuvius and elsewhere. Also called **Peri·clasite.**

Periclean (periklī·ăn), *a.* 1822. [f. *Pericles* + -AN.] Of or pertaining to Pericles (*c* 495–429 B.C.) and his age in Athenian history; the period of the intellectual and material preeminence of Athens. Also *transf.*

Periclinal (periklai·năl), *a.* 1876. [f. Gr. περικλινής sloping on all sides + -AL.] **1.** *Geol.* = QUAQUAVERSAL. **2.** *Bot.* [= G. *periklinc*]. Applied to those cell-walls at a growing-point which run in the same direction as the circumference of the shoot. Also as *sb.* = p. wall or plain. 1882.

†**Peri·clitate,** *v.* 1623. [f. L. *periclitat-*, *periclitari*, f. *periculum*, *periclum.*] *trans.* To expose to peril; to endanger, risk –1765.

They would p. their lives 1657. So †**Periclita·tion,** the action of exposing or condition of being exposed to peril; also, an experiment; a venture –1897.

‖ **Pericope** (pĕri·kŏpi). 1658. [Late L., a. Gr. περικοπή a section, f. περί PERI- + κοπή cutting.] A short passage, section, or paragraph in a writing; esp. (*Eccl.*) a portion of Scripture appointed for reading in public worship.

‖ **Pericranium** (perikrē·niŏm). 1541. [med. or mod.L., a. Gr. περικράνιον adj. neut. used as sb., f. περί PERI- b + κρανίον skull.] **1.** *Anat.* The membrane enveloping the skull, being the external periosteum of the cranial bones. **2.** *loosely* (usu. *affected* or *joc.*): **a.** The skull; **b.** The brain, esp. as the seat of mind. Now *rare.* 1590. So †**Pe·ricrane** (chiefly in sense 2); †Pe·ricrany. Hence **Pericra·nial** *a.* of or pertaining to the p., -ly *adv.*

†Peri·culous, *a.* 1547. [ad. L. *periculosus*, f. *periculum* danger; see -OUS.] Perilous -1835.

Periderm (pe·ridəɹm). 1849. [mod. f. Gr. περί PERI- + δέρμα skin.] **1.** *Zool.* A hard or tough covering investing the body in certain Hydrozoa 1870. **2.** *Bot.* orig., applied to the corky layers of plant-stems; later, the whole of the tissues formed from the cork-cambium. Hence **Peride·rmal** *a.*

‖ **Peridiastole** (pe:ridəi,æ·stŏlī). 1842. [mod. f. Gr. περί over, beyond + DIASTOLE.] *Physiol.* The interval between the diastole of the heart and the following systole. Hence **Peridiasto·lic** *a.*

‖ **Peridium** (pĭri·diŏm). *Pl.* **-ia.** 1823. [a. Gr. πηρίδιον, dim. of πήρα wallet.] *Bot.* The outer coat or envelope of certain fungi, which encloses the spores. Hence **Peri·dial** *a.*

Peridot (pe·ridǫt). ME. [a. F. *péridot*; prob. of Oriental origin.] **†a.** In ME. The chrysolite -1460. **b.** A jeweller's term for OLIVINE 1706. Hence **Perido·tic** *a.* **Pe·ridotite** *Min.* [-ITE [1] 2 b], a mineral consisting of p. (olivine) and various other minerals.

‖ **Periegesis** (pe:ri,ĭdʒī·sis). 1627. [a. Gr. περιήγησις, f. περί PERI- + ἥγησις leading.] A description of a place or region.

Perigee (pe·ridʒī). 1594. Also in L. forms. [a. F. *périgée*, ad. late L. *perigeum, perigæum*, ad. late Gr. περίγειον, in Ptolemy 'perigee', f. περί PERI- + γέα, γῆ earth. Used earlier in its Gr. or L. form.] **1.** That point in the orbit of a planet (now usu., the moon) at which it is nearest to the earth. (Opp. to APOGEE 1.) **†2.** The point of the heaven at which the sun has the least altitude at noon; i.e. at the winter solstice. (Opp. to APOGEE 2.) -1646. **†3.** *fig.* (cf. APOGEE 3) -1670. So **Perige·al, Perige·an** *adjs.* of or pertaining to p.

Perigone (pe·rigo͡un). Also in L. form. 1819. [a. F. *périgone*, ad. mod.L. *perigonium*, f. Gr. περί PERI- + γόνος offspring, seed.] **1.** *Bot.* **a.** = PERIANTH. **b.** The male perianth in mosses (PERIANTH b) 1863. **2.** *Zool.* A sac formed by the outer parts of the gonophore of a hydroid 1871. Hence **Peri·gonal, Perigo·nial** *adjs.* pertaining to a p.

‖ **Périgord** (perigor). 1752. A district in the south-west of France, famous for its truffles. Hence **P. pie**, a meat pie flavoured with truffles.

‖ **Perigynium** (peridʒi·niŏm). Rarely **perigyn** (pe·ridʒin). 1821. [mod.L., f. Gr. περί PERI- b + γυνή, in Bot. 'pistil'.] *Bot.* **a.** A membranous sac, investing the ovary in the Sedges (*Carex*). **b.** A part of the leafy investment of the female organs of mosses. **c.** In liverworts: = PERIANTH b.

Perigynous (pĕri·dʒinəs), *a.* 1807. [f. mod.L. *perigynus* (f. as prec.) + -OUS.] *Bot.* Situated around the pistil or ovary; said of the stamens when growing upon a part surrounding the ovary; also of a flower in which the stamens are so placed. So **Peri·gyny,** p. condition.

‖ **Perihelion** (perihī·liŏn). †Also **-ium.** *Pl.* **-ia.** 1666. [Græcized f. mod.L. *perihelium* (f. Gr. περί PERI- + ἥλιος sun).] *Astr.* That point in the orbit of a planet, comet, etc., at which it is nearest to the sun. Opp. to APHELION. **2.** *fig.* Highest point, 'zenith' 1804. Hence **Perihe·lial, Perihe·lian** *adjs.*

Perijove (pe·ridʒōuv). 1837. [= F. *périjove*, mod.L. *perijovium*, f. PERI- + L. *Jovem* Jupiter, after *perigee.*] *Astr.* That point in the orbit of any of Jupiter's satellites at which it is nearest to Jupiter.

Peril (pe·ril), *sb.* ME. [a. F. *péril*:—L. *periculum*, trial, danger, f. root of *experiri* to try + *-culum*, suffix naming instruments.] **1.** Risk, jeopardy, danger. **2.** (with *a* and *pl.*) A case or cause of peril; *pl.* dangers, risks ME. **†3.** A matter of danger. Const. *it is p.*, it is dangerous (to do something). -1540.

1. Glory Is the fair child of p. SMOLLETT. At the p. of his life PALEY. A vessel in p. of wreck GEO. ELIOT. Phr. *At* (*ton, to*) *your* (*his*, etc.) *p.*, you (etc.) taking the risk. *Yellow p.*: see YELLOW *a.* 2. *P. of the sea* (Marine Insurance), strictly, the natural accidents peculiar to the sea, but in law extended to include capture by pirates, losses by collision, etc.

Peril (pe·ril), *v.* 1567. [f. prec.] **1.** *trans.* To expose to danger; to imperil, risk. **†2.** *intr.* To be in danger (*rare*) -1647.

1. Jonathan perilled his life..for..David 1647.

‖ **Perilla** (pĕri·lă). 1788. [mod.L.] *Bot.* A small genus of Labiates; esp. *P. ocimoides*, grown on account of its deep-purple leaves.

Perilous (pe·riləs), *a.* (*adv.*) ME. [a. AF. *perillous*:—L. *periculosum*, f. *periculum* PERIL; see -OUS.] **1.** Fraught with peril; full of risk; dangerous; hazardous. **†2.** = PARLOUS A. 2. -1606. **†B.** *adv.* = PARLOUS B. -1849.

1. In a p. predicament 1836. 2. A p. clymbyng whan beggers up arise To hye estate LYDG. Hence **Pe·rilous-ly** *adv.*, **-ness.**

Perimeter (pĕri·mĭtəɹ). 1592. [ad. L. *perimetros*, a. Gr. f. περί PERI- + μέτρον measure.] **1.** The outer boundary of a closed geometrical figure (curved or rectilineal), or of any area or surface; circumference; also, the length of this. **2.** An instrument for measuring the field of vision, and determining the visual powers of different parts of the retina 1875. Hence **Perime·tric** *a.* pertaining to a p. or circumference; pertaining to or obtained by a p. (sense 2) or perimetry. **Perime·trical** *a.*, **-ly** *adv.*

Perimetry (pĕri·mètri). 1570. [f. as prec. + -Y.] **1.** Measurement round; perimeter. Now *rare.* **2.** Measurement of the field of vision by means of the perimeter (sense 2) 1893.

Perineal (perinī·ăl), *a.* 1767. [f. PERINEUM + -AL.] Of, pertaining to, or situated in the perineum.

P. body, the mass of tissue of which the surface of the perineum forms the base.

Perineo-, comb. form of PERINEUM, in a few terms of pathology, etc.; **Perine·opla:sty,** a plastic operation on the perineum; **Perineorrhaphy** (-ǫ·răfi) [Gr. ῥαφή sewing], suture of the perineum when ruptured; etc.

‖ **Perineum, -æum** (perinī·ŏm). 1632. [late L., a. Gr. περίναιον, περίνεος (or πηριν-).] *Anat.* The region of the body between the anus and the scrotum or vulva; denoting either the surface of this or the perineal body.

‖ **Perineuritis** (pe:ri,niurəi·tis). 1878. [mod. L., f. next + -ITIS.] *Path.* Inflammation of the perineurium.

‖ **Perineurium** (peri,niū·riŏm). 1842. [mod. L., f. Gr. περί PERI- + νεῦρον nerve.] *Anat.* The sheath of connective tissue enveloping a bundle of nerve-fibres. Hence **Perineu·rial** *a.* of or pertaining to the p.

Period (pīə·riŏd), *sb.* late ME. [a. F. *période*, ad. L. *periodus*, a. Gr. περίοδος going round, cycle of years, etc., f. περί PERI- + ὁδός way.] **I.** A course or extent of time. **†1.** Time of duration -1672. **2.** *Chronol.* A round of time marked by the recurrence of astronomical coincidences, used as a unit in chronology; e.g. the *Dionysian, Julian*, etc., *p.* (Cf. CYCLE *sb.* 2) 1613. **b.** *Astron.* The time in which a planet or satellite performs its revolution 1727. **c.** *Physics.* The interval between the recurrence of phases in a vibration, etc. 1865. **d.** Any round or portion of time occupied by a recurring process or action 1850. **3.** *Path.* The time during which a disease runs its course; also, each of its marked phases 1543. **b.** *pl.* (in full *monthly periods*), the menses 1822. **4.** An indefinite portion of time, of history, or of some continuous process, as life. 1712. **b.** *Geol.* One of the larger divisions of geological time 1833.

1. Many Temples early gray have out-lived the Psalmist's p. SIR T. BROWNE. **d.** The heart beats by periods TYNDALL. 4. A former p. of language 1870. *The p.*, the time in question; *esp.* the present day; The girl of the p. is a creature who dyes her hair and paints her face 1868. Also *attrib.* = belonging to a particular period, e.g. *p. costume.*

II. Completion, end of any course. **1.** The point of completion; consummation, conclusion, end. late ME. **†b.** The final stage; the concluding sentence, peroration; the finish, issue, outcome -1769. **†c.** Death -1682. **†2.** The highest point reached; the acme -1608. **†3.** A point or stage of advance; a moment, occasion -1841. **†4.** Appointed end (of a journey, etc.) -1789. **†5.** *fig.* The goal -1674.

1. The p. of thy Tyranny approacheth SHAKS. Phr. *To put a p. to*: to put an end to. 5. There's his p. To sheath his knife in vs SHAKS.

III. In Grammar, Rhetoric, etc. **1.** A complete sentence; esp. one of several clauses, grammatically connected, and rhetorically constructed 1579. **b.** In *Ancient Pros.* A group of two or more cola (COLON [2] 1) 1837. **2.** A full pause such as is properly made at the end of a sentence 1587. **b.** The point that marks the end of a complete sentence; a full stop (.) 1609. **3.** *Mus.* 'A complete musical sentence' (Stainer) 1866. **4.** *Arith.* A set of figures in a large number marked off by commas placed between or dots placed over, as in numeration, circulating decimals, and the extraction of the square or cube root 1674. **5.** *Math.* The interval between any two successive equal values of a periodic function 1879.

1. Not a p. Shall be unsaid for me MILT. 2. Make periods in the midst of sentences SHAKS. Hence **†Pe·riod** *v. trans.* to put a period to; to end; to dissolve; *intr.* to come to a conclusion.

Periodate, per-iodate (pərəi·ŏdeᵊt). 1836. [See PER-[1] II.] *Chem.* A salt of periodic acid. So **Periodic, per-iodic** (pərəi,ǫ·dik), *a.*, as in *Periodic acid*, H_5IO_6, an acid containing a larger proportion of oxygen than iodic acid. **Peri·odide** or **†Perio·duret,** a combination of iodine with another element or radical in a larger proportion than in a simple iodide.

Periodic (pīəri,ǫ·dik), *a.*[1] 1642. [a. F. *périodique*, ad. L. *periodicus*, a. Gr., f. περίοδος PERIOD; see -IC.] **1.** Of, pertaining, or proper to the revolution of a heavenly body in its orbit, as *p. motion.* **2.** = PERIODICAL *a.* 2; *spec.* in *Path.* having regularly recurring symptoms, as *p. fever* 1661. **3.** Pertaining to a rhetorical or grammatical period; expressed in periods 1701.

1. A direct method of ascertaining the p. time of each planet HERSCHEL. 2. *P. function* (*Math.*), one whose values recur in the same order while that of the variable increases or decreases continually. *P. inequality* (*Astron.*), see INEQUALITY. *P. law* (*Chem.*), the statement of the fact that the properties of the chemical elements are p. functions of their atomic weights; i.e. that when arranged in the order of these weights, the elements fall into recurring groups or series, so that those having similar chemical and physical properties recur at regular intervals. 3. Anaxagoras never attained to a connected or p. style JOWETT.

Periodic, *a.*[2]; see under PERIODATE.

Periodical (pīəri,ǫ·dikăl), *a.* (*sb.*) 1601. [f. as PERIODIC *a.*[1] + -AL.] **1.** = PERIODIC *a.*[1] 1. 1603. **2.** Recurring at regular periods or intervals; *loosely*, reappearing at intervals, intermittent 1601. **3.** *Arith.* Of, pertaining to, or expressed in, periods (sense III. 4). *rare.* 1674. **†4.** = PERIODIC *a.*[1] 3. -1780. **5.** Of magazines, etc.: Published at regular intervals longer than a day, as monthly, etc. **b.** Written in or characteristic of such publications; writing for magazines, etc. 1716. **B.** *sb.* A magazine or miscellany published at regular intervals 1798.

A. 5. b. He..knows good from bad, which is not very often the case with p. critics SOUTHEY. Hence **Perio·dical-ly** *adv.* at regularly recurring intervals; also *loosely*, every now and then; **-ness** (*rare*).

Periodicity (pīə:riŏdi·sĭti). 1833. [ad. F. *périodicité*, f. L. *periodicus* PERIODIC; see -ITY.] **1.** The quality or character of being periodic, or regularly recurrent. **2.** *Physiol.* Menstruation; cf. PERIOD *sb.* I. 3 b. 1848.

‖ **Periœci** (peri,ī·səi), *sb. pl.* 1594. [med.L., a. Gr. περίοικοι, pl. of περίοικος, lit. dwelling around, neighbouring.] **1.** Dwellers under the same parallel of latitude, but opposite meridians. (Cf. ANTŒCI.) **2.** *Gr. Hist.* The dwellers in the country round a city, or in the surrounding country towns and villages 1846.

Periosteal (peri,ǫ·stiăl), *a.* 1830. [f. PERIOSTEUM + -AL.] Surrounding or occurring round a bone; of, pertaining to, or connected with the periosteum.

‖ **Periosteum** (peri,ǫ·stiŏm). 1597. [mod. L., f. (ult.) Gr. περί PERI- + ὀστέον bone.] *Anat.* The dense fibro-vascular membrane which envelops the bones (except where they are covered by cartilage). Hence **Periosteo-,** comb. form. ‖ **Periosti·tis** *Path.* inflammation of the p.; **Periosti·tic** *a.*

†Peripate·tian. 1533. [For *peripatetician; see PERIPATETIC, -IAN.] A peripatetic -1753.

Peripatetic (peripăte·tik), *a.* and *sb.* late ME. [a. F. *péripatétique*, ad. L. *peripateticus*,

a. Gr. περιπατητικός given to walking about, f. (ult.) περί PERI- + πατεῖν to walk; in reference to the custom of Aristotle, who taught while walking in a περίπατος or walk in the Lyceum at Athens.] A. *adj.* 1. Of or belonging to the school of Aristotle; Aristotelian; held or believed by this sect of philosophers. (With capital P.) 1566. 2. Walking about in connexion with one's calling; itinerant 1642.

1. The old peripatetick principle, that Nature abhors a Vacuum 1751.

B. *sb.* 1. A disciple of Aristotle; an Aristotelian. late ME. 2. One who walks about; a traveller; an itinerant dealer. (Mostly *joc.*) 1617. So **Peripate·tical** *a.* (now *rare*), **-ly,** *adv.* **Pe·ripate·ticism,** the system of philosophy; (*joc.*) the practice of walking about.

‖ **Peripatus**[1], **-os** (pĕri·pătɒ̆s, -ɒs). 1660. [L. = Gr περίπατος, f. περί PERI- + πάτος path.] The walk in the Lyceum where Aristotle taught; hence *transf.* the school of Aristotle.

‖ **Peripatus**[2] (pĕri·pătɒ̆s). 1840. [mod.L., a. Gr. περίπατος (one) walking about; see prec.] *Zool.* A remarkable genus of Arthropods, constituting the family *Peripatidæ*. The species are worm-like creatures, inhabiting damp places among decaying wood and the like, in tropical America, S. Africa, Australasia.

‖ **Peripeteia, -tia** (pe:ripĕtəi·ă, -tī·ă). Also peripety (pĕri·pĭti). 1591. [a. Gr. περιπέτεια, f. (ult.) περί PERI- + stem πετ- of πίπτειν to fall.] A sudden change of fortune or reverse of circumstances (in a tragedy, etc., or in life).

Peripheral (pĕri·fĕrăl), *a.* 1808. [f. Gr. περιφερής (see PERIPHERY) + -AL.] Of, pertaining to, or situated in, the periphery; constituting the external surface; esp. in *Anat.*, etc., of the surface or outward part of an organic body. Hence **Peri·pherally** *adv.* in a p. way or position; at the periphery. So **Peripheric, -al** *adjs.*, **-ly** *adv.* in same senses.

Periphery (pĕri·fĕri, pe·riferi). 1571. [ad. late L. *peripheria* (also used), a. Gr. περιφέρεια circumference, f. περιφερής moving round, f. περί PERI- + φέρειν to bear, carry.] The line that forms the boundary, esp. of any round or rounded surface. **b.** *spec.* in *Geom.* The circumference of any closed curvilinear figure; also, the sum of the sides of a polygonal figure; a perimeter. Also *fig.* **c.** The external boundary or surface of any space or body 1666. **d.** *loosely*, A surrounding area 1759.

Periphractic (perifræ·ktik), *a.* 1881. [f. Gr. περίφρακτος fenced around (φράσσειν to fence) + -IC.] *Geom.* Said of a region having one or more internal bounding surfaces (or curves, when the region is plane) unconnected with the external boundary.

Periphrase (pe·rifrēⁱz), *sb.* 1589. [ad. F. *périphrase*, ad. L. *periphrasis*.] = PERIPHRASIS.

Periphrase (pe·rifrēⁱz), *v.* 1624. [a. F. *périphraser*; see prec.] 1. *trans.* To express by periphrasis. 2. *intr.* To use circumlocution 1652.

Periphrasis (pĕri·frăsis). *Pl.* **-ses** (-sīz). 1533. [a. L., a. Gr. περίφρασις, f. (ult.) περί round about + φράζειν to declare.] 1. That figure of speech which consists in expressing the meaning of a word or phrase, etc., by many or several words instead of by few or one; a wordy or roundabout way of speaking; circumlocution. 2. An instance of this 1579. †**b.** *fig.* An amplification –1658.

1. The loose clumsiness of perpetual p. 1864.

Periphrastic (perifræ·stik), *a.* 1805. [ad. Gr. περιφραστικός, f. περιφράζειν to express by periphrasis; see -IC.] Of the nature of, characterized by, or involving periphrasis; circumlocutory, roundabout.

P. conjugation (in Grammar), a conjugation formed by the combination of a simple verb and an auxiliary. *P. genitive*, a genitive formed with *of* in Eng., *de* in Fr., etc. So **Periphra·stical** *a.*, **-ly** *adv.*

Periphraxy (pe·rifræksi). 1881. [f. late Gr. περίφραξις a fencing round.] *Geom.* The condition of being PERIPHRACTIC (q.v.).

Periplast (pe·riplæst). 1853. [f. Gr. περί PERI- + πλαστός moulded.] *Biol.* †**a.** The intercellular substance in which the organized structures of a tissue are embedded. **b.** The main substance or body of a cell, as dist. from the cell-wall and the internal nucleus. **c.** A cell-wall or cell-envelope. Hence **Peripla·stic** *a.*

‖ **Periplus** (pe·riplɒs). 1776. [L., a. Gr. περίπλους, f. περί PERI- + πλοῦς voyage.] Circumnavigation; a voyage round a coast-line, etc. **b.** *transf.* A narrative of such a voyage.

Peripneumony (peripniū·mŏni), ‖ **peripneumonia** (-pniumōᵘ·niă). Now *rare* or *Obs.* 1550. [ult. a. Gr. περιπνευμονία, f. περί PERI- + πνεύμων lungs.] *Path.* = PNEUMONIA. Hence **Peripneumonic** (-mǫ·nik) *a.* pertaining to or having pneumonia; *sb.* one so affected.

Peri·pter, -ere. *rare.* 1696. [a. F. *périptère*, ult. ad. Gr. περίπτερον, f. περί PERI- + πτερόν wing.] *Arch.* A peripteral building. So **Peri·pteral** *a.* having a single peristyle or row of pillars surrounding it, as a Greek temple.

Perique (pĕrī·k). 1895. [Fr. of unkn. origin.] Dark or black tobacco from Louisiana.

Periscian (peri·siăn, -ʃiăn), *a.* and *sb.* 1594. f. L. *Periscii* + -AN.] A. *adj.* Of or pertaining to the Periscii. B. *sb.* (in *pl.*) = PERISCII.

‖ **Periscii** (pĕri·si,əi, -i·ʃi,əi), *sb. pl.* 1625. [med.L., a. Gr. περίσκιοι, pl. of περίσκιος, f. περί PERI- + σκιά shadow.] Those who dwell within the polar circles, whose shadows revolve around them on a summer day.

Periscope (pe·riskoᵘp). 1865. [f. Gr. περί PERI- + σκοπός look, σκοπεῖν to look.] 1. A variety of photographic object-glass. 2. An apparatus used in a submarine or trench, for obtaining a view of objects above the surface by a system of mirrors 1899. Hence **Perisco·pic** *a.* enabling one to see distinctly for some distance around the axis of vision. **Pe·riscopism,** the faculty of periscopic vision.

Perish (pe·riʃ), *v.* [ME. a. OF. *periss-*, *perir* :—L. *perire* to pass away entirely, etc., f. PER-[1] 3 + *ire* to go.] 1. *intr.* To come to an untimely end; to suffer destruction; to lose its life. (Chiefly of living beings.) **b.** To incur spiritual death; to suffer moral ruin ME. **c.** Of material things: *spec.* as opposed to things spiritual or eternal, or as the effect of decay or exposure to destructive conditions. late ME. **d.** Of immaterial things: To come to an end, pass away ME. **e.** In imprecations 1526. 2. In *pa. pple.* with *be*, expressing the resulting state ME. 3. *trans.* To bring to destruction; to put to death, kill (a person, etc.), wreck (a ship, etc.) *Obs.* or *arch.* late ME. †**b.** To destroy spiritually; to ruin morally –1750. **c.** Said of the effect of cold, hunger, or privation, in shrivelling up, or reducing to a moribund condition. Now chiefly *dial.* 1719.

1. The common rout, That..Grow up and p. as the summer flie MILT. **b.** Knowledge is good..yet man perished in seeking knowledge RUSKIN. **c.** The joints are apt to 'perish' by the action of the acids 1885. **d.** Bards..whose Songs have perished in the Wreck of Time 1763. **e.** P. the man, whose mind is backward now SHAKS. 2. We were all perished with cold 1845. Hence †**Pe·rishment,** destruction, damage, loss.

Perishable (pe·riʃăb'l), *a.* (*sb.*) 1611. [f. prec. + -ABLE.] 1. Liable to perish; *esp.* naturally subject to speedy decay. 2. **a.** *absol.* quasi-*sb.* *The p.*, that which is transitory 1821. **b.** *sb. pl.* Things liable to decay; said chiefly of food-stuffs in transit 1742.

1. Thou p. flesh and form of clay COWPER. **b.** Perishables like fish and flowers 1895. Hence **Perishabi·lity** (*rare*), **Pe·rishableness,** p. quality. **Pe·rishably** *adv.*

Perisher (pe·riʃəɹ). 1888. [f. as prec. + -ER[1].] *slang.* An extreme (of any course of action); also applied contemptuously to persons.

Those perishers in the gallery didn't know anything about Shakespeare 1896. So **Pe·rishing** *a. slang*, 'blighted', 'blinking'; also *adv.* (e.g. *p. cold*).

Perispome (pe·rispōᵘm), *a.* and *sb.* 1818. [abbrev. of perispo·menon (also used) = Gr. περισπώμενον, neut. of pr. pple. pass. of περισπᾶν to draw around, mark with the circumflex.] A. *adj.* Having a circumflex accent on the last syllable. B. *sb.* A word so accented.

Perissad (pĕri·sæd), *sb.* (*a.*) 1870. [f. Gr. περισσός uneven, odd (f. περί 'over, beyond') + -AD.] *Chem.* An element or radical whose quantivalency is represented by an odd number, as a monad, triad, etc.; opp. to ARTIAD. Also as *adj.*

Perissodactyl, -yle (pĕrisodæ·ktil), *a.* and *sb.* 1849. [ad. mod.L. *perissodactylus*, f. Gr. περισσός uneven + δάκτυλος digit.] *Zool.* A. *adj.* Having an odd number of toes on each foot, as an ungulate mammal; belonging to the division *Perissodactyla* of *Ungulata*. B. *sb.* A perissodactyl ungulate or hoofed animal; *pl.* in -*s* or -*a*. Opp. to ARTIODACTYL. 1854.

†**Perisso·logy.** 1583. [ad. late L. *perissologia*, a. Gr., f. περισσός redundant + λόγος speech.] *Rhet.* Redundance of speech; use of more words than are necessary; pleonasm –1776. Hence **Perissolo·gical** *a.* (*rare*), redundant in words.

‖ **Peristalsis** (peristæ·lsis). 1859. [mod.L.; see next. *Physiol.* Peristaltic movement.

Peristaltic (peristæ·ltik), *a.* 1655. [ad. Gr. περισταλτικός, f. περιστέλλειν lit. to send round.] *Physiol.* Applied to the automatic muscular (vermicular) movement, consisting of rhythmic wave-like contractions in successive circles, by which the contents of the alimentary canal or other tubular organ are propelled along it. Hence **Perista·ltically** *adv.*

Peristerite (pĕri·stĕrəit). 1843. [f. Gr. περιστερά pigeon + -ITE[1] 2 b.] *Min.* A variety of ALBITE exhibiting a slight iridescence like that on a pigeon's neck.

Peristeronic (pĕristĕrǫ·nik), *a.* 1868. [app. f. Gr. περιστερών dove-cot (cf. prec.) + -IC.] Pertaining to or concerned with pigeons.

Peristome (pe·ristoᵘm). Also **peri·stoma** (pl. **-ata**), peristo·mium (pl. **-ia**). 1796. [ad. mod.L. *peristoma*, f. Gr. περί PERI- + στόμα mouth; altered to *peristomium* after *pericarpium*, etc.] 1. *Bot.* The fringe of small teeth around the mouth of the capsule in mosses. 2. *Zool.* **a.** The margin of the aperture of the shell of a mollusc 1828. **b.** Any special structure or set of parts around the mouth of invertebrates 1875. Hence **Peristo·mal, Peristo·mial** *adjs.*

Peristrephic (peri,stre·fik), *a.* 1827. [irreg. f. Gr. περιστρέφειν to turn round + -IC.] Turning round, revolving, rotatory (as a panorama).

Peristyle (pe·ristəil). 1612. [a. F. *péristyle*, ad. L. *peristylum*, *-ium*, in Gr. περίστυλον sb., f. περί PERI- + στῦλος pillar.] *Arch.* A row of columns surrounding a temple, etc., or a court, cloister, etc.; less properly, the space so surrounded. ¶ **b.** Applied to the columned porch of a church, to a pillared verandah, etc. 1694.

‖ **Perisystole** (perisi·stŏlĭ). 1664. [mod.L., f. Gr. περί PERI- + συστολή SYSTOLE.] *Physiol.* The interval between the systole and the following diastole of the heart, inappreciable except when the heart's action is failing. Hence **Perisysto·lic** *a.*

†**Peri·te,** *a.* 1524. [ad. L. *peritus*.] Experienced, skilled –1820.

‖ **Perithecium** (peripī·siŏm, -ʃiŏm). Pl. **-ia.** Also perithece (pe·ripīs). 1832. [mod.L., f. Gr. περί PERI- + θήκη case; cf. *pericarpium*.] *Bot.* A cup-shaped or flask-shaped receptacle, inclosing the fructification in certain fungi, etc. Hence **Perithe·cial** *a.*

‖ **Peritoneum, -æum** (pe:ritŏnī·ŏm). 1541. [L., a. Gr. περιτόναιον (-ειον) adj. neut. used sb., f. (ult.) περί PERI- + -τονος, from τείνειν to stretch; cf. TONE.] *Anat.* The double serous membrane which lines the cavity of the abdomen. In vertebrates below mammals, which have no diaphragm, the membrane lining the whole body-cavity, corresponding to the mammalian p. and pleura combined. Hence **Peritone·al, -æ·al** *a.* of, pertaining to, situated in, or affecting the p. **Peritonitis** (pe:ritŏnəi·tis), inflammation of the p., or of some part of it 1776.

Peritrichan (pĕri·trikăn), *a.* and *sb.* 1875. [f. mod.L. *Peritricha*, f. Gr. περί PERI- + τριχ-, θρίξ hair.] *Zool.* A. *adj.* Belonging to the division *Peritricha* of *Infusoria*, having a band of cilia round the body. B. *sb.* An infusorian of this division. So **Peri·trichous** *a.*

‖ **Peritrochium** (peritrōᵘ·kiŏm). 1704. [mod. L., a. Gr. περιτρόχιον wheel, f. περίτροχος circular.] *Mech.* A wheel, as constituting part of the mechanical power called the wheel-and-axle.

Peritropal (pĕri·trŏpăl), *a. rare.* 1819. [f. mod.L. *peritropus* + -AL.] *Bot.* Of an embryo or ovule: = AMPHITROPAL, HEMITROPOUS 2. Also **Peri·tropous** *a.*

Periwig (pe·riwig), *sb.* Now only *Hist.* 1529. [In 16th c. *pe·rwyke*, altered f. *pe·rruck*, *pe·rug*, a. F. *perruque*; see PERUKE.] **1.** An artificial imitation of a head of hair (or part of one); a WIG. †**2.** An alleged kind of marine animal –1674. Hence **Pe·riwig** *v. arch.*, to dress or conceal with, or as with, a p. **Pe·riwigged** *ppl. a.* wearing or having a p.

Periwinkle[1] (pe·riwiŋk'l). [In OE. *peruince*, a. L. *pervinca*; etym. unkn.] The common name of plants of the genus *Vinca* (N.O. *Apocynaceæ*), esp. *V. minor* and *V. major*, the Lesser and Greater Periwinkle, evergreen trailing sub-shrubs with light blue starry flowers, varying in *V. minor* with pure white. Also *attrib.*

Periwinkle[2] (pe·riwiŋk'l). 1530. [OE. had in the same sense pl. *pinewinclan* (or ? *winewinclan*).] A gastropod mollusc of the genus *Littorina*, esp. *L. littorea* the common European coast species, much used for food.

Perjink (pəɹdʒi·ŋk), *a. Sc.* [Origin unkn.] Exact, precise; prim.

†**Pe·rjure**, *sb.* (*a.*) late ME. [a. AF. *perjur*, *parjur*, or ad. L. *perjurus.*] A perjurer –1615. **b.** as *adj.* Perjured –1600.

Perjure (pə̄·ɹdʒŭɹ), *v.* 1477. [a. OF. *parjurer* :—L. *perjurare*, f. PER-[1] 3 + *jurare* to swear.] †**1.** *intr.* To commit perjury; to be false to an oath, promise, etc. –1789. **b.** *refl.* *To p. oneself*: to forswear oneself. Now the usual const. 1755. **c.** quasi-*pass.* *To be perjured*: to be guilty of perjury 1477. †**2.** *trans.* To prove false to or break (an oath, vow, etc.) –1809. †**3.** To cause to commit perjury SHAKS. †**4.** To prove false to (a person) to whom one has sworn faith –1610.

1. b. A person who has..perjured himself [is] the bane of society 1772. 4. She..did pray For me that perjur'd her FLETCHER.

Perjured (pə̄·ɹdʒŭɹd), *ppl. a.* (*sb.*) 1453. [pa. pple. of prec. vb., after AF. *perjuré*, OF. *parjuré* pa. pple. of the intr. vb., lit. (one) that has committed perjury. (Viewed in Eng. as passive; whence prec. 1 c.)] **1.** That has committed perjury; forsworn. Also *absol.* †**2.** Characterized by perjury; perjurious –1814. †**3.** Falsely sworn –1697.

1. P. traitors 1859. 3. Their periured oth SPENSER.

Perjurer (pə̄·ɹdʒŭrəɹ). 1553. [app. a. AF. *par-*, *perjurour*, f. *parjurer* to PERJURE.] One who commits perjury, *spec.* in the legal sense; one who is forsworn.

Perjurious (pəɹdʒūə·riəs), *a.* 1540. [ad. L. *perjuriosus*, f. *perjurium* PERJURY.] †**1.** Of persons: Guilty of perjury –1829. **2.** Of actions, etc.: Characterized by perjury 1602.

2. P. suits for nullification of marriage 1872. Hence **Perju·rious-ly** *adv.*, **-ness** (*rare*). So †**Pe·rjurous** *a.*

Perjury (pə̄·ɹdʒŭri). late ME. [a. AF. *perjurie*; in mod.F. *parjure*, ad. L. *perjurium*, f. *perjurare* to PERJURE.] The action of swearing to a statement known to be false; *spec.* in *Law*, the crime of wilfully uttering false evidence while on oath. **b.** Applied also to the violation of a promise made on oath 1532. **c.** with *a* and *pl.* 1440.

c. At Louers periuries They say Ioue laught SHAKS.

Perk (pə̄ɹk), *a.* 1579. [Goes with PERK *v.*] Self-assertive, pert, 'cocky'; brisk; smart.

Perk (pə̄ɹk), *v.* late ME. [Origin obsc.] **I.** *intr.* To carry oneself smartly, briskly, or jauntily. **b.** To lift one's head, thrust oneself forward briskly, boldly, or impudently. Also with *up*. Also *fig.* 1529. **c.** With *up*: To recover liveliness, as after depression or sickness (*colloq.*) 1656.

b. The old woman perk'd up as brisk as a bee BARHAM. *fig.* He knew that Hagar would quickly p. up, and domineer over Sarah 1703. High garret gable-windows perking into the roofs DICKENS.

II. *trans.* **1.** To make spruce or smart; to prank or trim, as a bird its plumage. Also with *up*, *out.* 1485. **2.** To prick up; to hold *up* briskly or self-assertively 1591.

2. [The blackbird] perks his tail up, and challenges the world with the call already mentioned JEFFERIES.

Perkinism (pə̄·ɹkiniz'm). *Hist.* 1798. [-ISM.] *Med.* A method of treatment introduced by Elisha *Perkins*, an American physician, for the cure of rheumatic diseases; it consisted in drawing two small pointed rods, one of steel and one of brass, called 'metallic tractors', over the affected region; tractoration. So **Perkine·an, Perkini·stic** *adjs.* **Pe·rkinize** *v.* to practise P.

Perky (pə̄·ɹki), *a.* 1855. [f. PERK *v.* or *a.* + -Y[1].] Inclined to be self-assertive or to thrust oneself forward; also, smart, brisk.

transf. Amid p. larches and pine TENNYSON. Hence **Pe·rkily** *adv.* **Pe·rkiness.**

Perla·ceous, *a.* 1777. [f. med.L. and Rom. *perla* PEARL + -ACEOUS.] Nacreous.

Perlite (pə̄·ɹləit). Also **pearlite.** 1833. [= F. *perlite*, f. *perle* PEARL; see -ITE[1] 2 b.] *Min.* Obsidian or other vitreous rock in form of enamel-like globules; pearlstone. **Perli·tic** *a.*

Perlustrate (pəɹlʊ·streⁱt), *v.* *Obs.* exc. in techn. use. 1535. [f. ppl. stem of L. *perlustrare* to wander through, f. PER-[1] 1, 2 + *lustrare* to traverse, survey.] *trans.* To travel through and survey thoroughly. Also *absol.* Hence **Perlustra·tion**, the action of perlustrating 1640.

Perm (pə̄ɹm). 1928. Colloq. abbrev. of PERMANENT *wave.* So **Permed** (pə̄ɹmd) *ppl. a.*

Permalloy (pə̄·ɹmăloi). 1924. [f. PERM(EABLE) + ALLOY.] Trade name for an alloy of nickel and iron very sensitive to magnetic forces.

Permanence (pə̄·ɹmănĕns). ME. [ad. med. L. *permanentia*, f. *permanentem* PERMANENT; see -ENCE.] The fact or quality of being permanent; continuance; abidingness.

Permanency (pə̄·ɹmănĕnsi). 1555. [f. as prec. + -ENCY.] **1.** = prec. 2. **2.** A (concrete) example of something permanent; a permanent person, thing, position, etc. 1841.

2. A temporary engagement, not a p. (*mod.*).

Permanent (pə̄·ɹmănĕnt), *a.* late ME. [ad. L. *permanentem*, pr. pple. of *permanere* to stay to the end, f. PER-[1] 1, 2 + *manere* to stay; perh. through F.] **1.** Lasting or designed to last indefinitely without change; enduring; persistent: opp. to *temporary*. †**2.** Of persons: Continuing steadfast *in* a course –1548. **3.** *absol.* *The p.*, that which endures or persists 1826.

1. Human institutions perish, but nature is p. 1780. *P. gas*, a name formerly given to gases supposed to be incapable of liquefaction, as oxygen, hydrogen. *P. magnet*, a magnet whose property continues after the magnetizing current has ceased to pass through it. *P. wave*, applied to a method of waving the hair supposed to be p. *P. way* (*road*), the finished road-bed of a railway, as dist. from a contractor's temporary way. Hence **Pe·rmanently** *adv.*

Permanganate (pəɹmæ·ŋgănĕt). 1841. [f. next; see -ATE[4].] *Chem.* A salt of permanganic acid, as *potassium p.* or *p. of potash*, $KMnO_4$, which dissolves in water with a fine purple red, and is used as a disinfectant.

Permanganic (pə̄ɹmæŋgæ·nik), *a.* 1836. [f. PER-[1] II. b + MANGANIC.] *Chem.* In *p. acid*, the acid $HMnO_4$, obtained from manganese.

†**Perma·nsion.** 1646. [ad. L. *permansionem*, f. *permanere*; see PERMANENT.] = PERMANENCE 1. –1659.

Permeability (pə̄ːmiăbi·lĭti). 1759. [f. next + -ITY.] The quality or condition of being permeable; perviousness.

Magnetic p., conducting power for lines of magnetic force.

Permeable (pə̄·ɹmiăb'l), *a.* ME. [ad. L. *permeabilis* that can be passed through, f. *permeare* to PERMEATE; see -BLE.] **1.** Capable of being permeated or passed through; penetrable, pervious. Const. *by, to.* †**2.** Penetrative –1752.

1. Cast steel is..p. to ether 1893. Hence **Pe·rmeably** *adv.*

Permeant (pə̄·ɹmiănt), *a.* 1646. [ad. L. *permeantem* pr. pple. of *permeare* to PERMEATE; see -ANT[1].] Permeating. So **Pe·rmeance.**

Permeate (pə̄·ɹmieⁱt), *v.* 1656. [f. L. *permeat-*, *permeare*, f. PER-[1] 1 + *meare* to go, pass.] **1.** *trans.* To pass, spread, or diffuse itself through; to penetrate, pervade, saturate 1660. **2.** *intr.* with *through, into, among*, etc. 1656. Hence **Permea·tion**, penetration; pervasion 1623. **Pe·rmeative** *a.* penetrative; pervasive.

Permian (pə̄·ɹmiăn), *a.* (*sb.*) 1841. [f. *Perm* in Eastern Russia, where these strata are extensively developed.] *Geol.* Name of the uppermost division of the Palæozoic series of strata, lying below the Trias and above the Carboniferous formation, and consisting chiefly of red sandstone and magnesian limestone. Also *ellipt.* as *sb.* The Permian system, or a formation belonging to it; *pl.* = P. strata.

Permissible (pəɹmi·sĭb'l), *a.* late ME. [a. OF., prob. ad. med. L. *permissibilis*, f. *permiss-*, *permittere* to PERMIT.] That can be or ought to be permitted; allowable. Hence **Permissibi·lity, Permi·ssibleness**, the quality of being p. **Permi·ssibly** *adv.*

Permission (pəɹmi·ʃən). late ME. [ad. L. *permissionem*, f. *permittere* to PERMIT.] The action of permitting or giving leave; liberty or licence granted to do something; leave.

Do as thou find'st P. from above MILT.

Permissive (pəɹmi·siv), *a.* late ME. [a. OF. *permissif, -ive*, f. L. *permiss-*, *permittere* to PERMIT; see -IVE.] **1.** Having the quality of permitting or giving permission; not forbidding or hindering 1603. **2.** Permitted, allowed; done, or acting, under permission; optional.

1. Not a Positive but a P. command H. MORE. 2. *P. waste* (Law), waste that is allowed to happen by neglect of repairs. Hence **Permi·ssive-ly** *adv.*, **-ness.**

†**Permi·stion.** 1612. [ad. L. *permistionem* (var. of *permixtionem*).] = PERMIXTION –1674.

Permit (pə̄·ɹmit), *sb.* 1714. [f. PERMIT *v.*] **1.** A written order giving permission, a warrant, a licence; esp. a licence for the landing or removal of dutiable or excisable goods. **2.** Permission, leave (esp. formally given). (Formerly stressed *permi·t.*) 1730.

Permit (pəɹmi·t), *v.* 1489. [ad. L. *permittere* to let go, surrender, permit, f. PER-[1] 1, 3 + *mittere* to let go, let loose, send.] **I. 1.** *trans.* To admit or allow the doing or occurrence of; to give leave or opportunity for. **2.** To allow (a person or thing) to do (or undergo) something 1514. **b.** *refl.* with *in*: To allow oneself to indulge in or commit 1678. **3.** *absol.* or *intr.* To allow 1553. **b.** *intr.* with *of*: To allow of, admit of 1860.

1. Pitt..would by no means p. the introduction of Sunday papers into his household THACKERAY. 2. P. me to recommend him to your Grace's protection *Junius Lett.* 3. To examine over all the noted words, as time permits 1612.

II. †**1.** *trans.* To commit, submit, hand over; to give up, leave; to refer (*to* the will of). Const. *to* (*unto*). –1802. †**2.** To leave undone, unused, etc.; to pretermit, omit –1692.

1. What thou livst Live well, how long or short p. to Heav'n MILT. Hence **Permittee·, Permi·tter.**

Permittance (pəɹmi·tăns). *Obs.* or *arch.* 1580. [f. PERMIT *v.* + -ANCE.] Permission.

†**Permi·x**, *v.* 1678. [Back-formation f. next.] *trans.* To mix thoroughly, intermingle –1683.

†**Permi·xed, permi·xt**, *ppl. a.* late ME. [orig. ad. L. *permixtus*, f. *permiscere* to mix thoroughly.] Thoroughly mixed, intermixed, intermingled –1660.

†**Permi·xtion.** late ME. [ad. L. *permixtionem*, f. *permiscere* to mix thoroughly, f. PER-[1] 2 + *miscere* to mix.] A thorough mixture or mingling; intermingling –1685.

Permutable (pəɹmiū·tăb'l), *a.* 1662. [ad. late L. *permutabilis*, f. *permutare* to PERMUTE and -ABLE.] **1.** Capable of being exchanged; interchangeable 1776. **2.** Liable to change 1662. Hence **Permutabi·lity**, the quality or condition of being p. **Permu·tableness. Permu·tably** *adv.*

Permutation (pə̄ɹmiutēⁱ·ʃən). late ME. [a. OF. *permutacion*, ad. L. *permutationem*, f. *permutare* to PERMUTE.] †**1.** Exchange of one thing for another; commutation; barter –1754. **2.** Alteration; transmutation. Now *rare.* ME. **3.** *Math.* The action of changing the order of a set of things lineally arranged; each of the different arrangements of which such a set is capable. Hence *gen.*, in *pl.* (usu. in phr. *permutations and combinations*): Variations of order or arrangement. 1710. **4.** *Philol.* The interchange of consonants occurring regularly in cognate words belonging to related

languages, as in L. and Gr. *duo*, Eng. *two*, G. *zwei*; L. and Gr. *tria*, Eng. *three*, G. *drei* 1843.
2. The violent convulsions and permutations that have been made in property BURKE. *Comb.* **p.-lock,** a lock in which the parts can be transposed or shifted, so that it is necessary to arrange them in some particular way in order to shoot or withdraw the bolt.

Permute (pəɹmiū·t), *v.* late ME. [ad. L. *permutare*, f. PER-[1] 2 + *mutare* to change.] †1. *trans.* To change one for another; to exchange, interchange –1657. 2. To change thoroughly; to transmute. Now *rare* or *Obs.* 1440. 3. *Math.* To subject to permutation (see prec. 3) 1878. 4. *Philol.* (in *pass.*). To undergo permutation (see prec. 4) 1846. Hence **Permu·ter,** one who permutes.

Pern (pɔ̄ɹn). 1840. [ad. mod.L. *pernis*, erron. ad. Gr. πτέρνις a kind of hawk.] A bird of the genus *Pernis*; the HONEY-BUZZARD.

Pernancy (pɔ̄·ɹnănsi). 1642. [f. OF. *pern-* = *pren-*, stem of *prendre* to take + -ANCY.] *Law.* The taking or receiving of anything; taking into possession; receipt, as of rents, tithes, etc.

†**Pe·rnel.** late ME. [Earlier *parnel*, a. OF. *Peronele* :—L. *Petronilla*, taken as fem. of *Petrus* Peter.] A priest's concubine; a wanton young woman; an effeminate man –1581.

†**Perni·cion.** 1530. [ad. late L. *pernicionem* = cl. L. *pernicies*.] Total destruction –1736.

Pernicious (pəɹni·ʃəs), *a.*[1] 1521. [ad. F. *pernicieux*, ad. L. *perniciosus*, f. *pernicies* destruction, death, f. PER-[1] 2 + *nex*, *necem* death.] Having the quality of destroying; destructive, ruinous; fatal. b. Wicked; villainous. Now *rare* or *Obs.* 1555.
Men of p. principles 1704. P. anæmia 1898. b. Victims of a p. woman's crime COWPER. Hence **Perni·cious·ly** *adv.*, **-ness.**

Perni·cious, *a.*[2] *rare.* 1656. [f. L. *pernix*, *pernici-* fleet + -OUS.] Rapid, swift. So †**Perni·city,** swiftness, celerity 1592.

Pernickety (pəɹni·kėti), *a.* 1808. [orig. Sc.; origin unkn.] Of persons, etc.: Particular about trifles; precise; fastidious. Of things: Requiring precise handling or care; ticklish.

Pernoctate (pəɹnǫ·kteⁱt), *v.* 1623. [f. L. *pernoctat-*, *pernoctare*, f. PER-[1] 1 + *noct-*, *nox* night.] *intr.* To pass the night; see next.

Pernoctation (pɔ̄ɹnǫktēⁱ·ʃən). 1633. [ad. L. *pernoctationem*, f. *pernoctare*.] The action of spending the night; esp. in *Eccl.* use, spending the night in prayer; in University use, passing the night within the bounds of the university in order to keep residence.

†**Pernor.** ME. [a. AF. *pernour* = OF. *preneor*, *-eur*, f. *prendre* to take.] *Law.* A taker or receiver, esp. of rents or profits of land –1642.

Perofskite (pĕrǫ·fskəit). Also **perov-,** **perow-.** 1844. [f. name *Perovski*; see -ITE[1] 2 b.] *Min.* Titanate of calcium, occurring in crystals varying in colour from yellow to black.

‖**Perone** (pe·rǒnī). 1693. [mod.L., a. Gr. περόνη a pin, etc.] *Anat.* = FIBULA 2.

Peroneal (perǫnī·ăl), *a.* 1831. [f. mod.L. *peronæus* PERONEUS + -AL.] *Anat.* Pertaining to or connected with the *perone* or fibula. Hence **Perone·o-,** comb. form.

‖**Peroneus** (perǫnī·ɒ̆s). 1704. [mod.L. (sc. *musculus* muscle), f. PERONE.] *Anat.* Name for various muscles connected with the fibula.

‖**Peronospora** (perǫnǫ·spŏră). 1884. [mod. L., f. Gr. περόνη pin + σπόρος seed.] *Bot.* A genus of minute parasitic fungi (moulds or mildews) of which several species cause diseases in plants.

Perorate (pe·rŏrēⁱt), *v.* 1603. [f. L. *perorat-*, *perorare*, f. PER-[1] 1 + *orare* to speak.] 1. *intr.* To speak at length. b. *trans.* To declaim 1681. 2. *intr.* To sum up or conclude a speech 1808.
1. Now hauing perorated (as he thinkes) sufficiently, he beginnes to growe to a conclusion 1603.

Peroration (perŏrēⁱ·ʃən). 1440. [ad. L. *perorationem*, f. *perorare*; see prec.] 1. The concluding part of an oration, speech, or written discourse, in which the speaker or writer sums up; any rhetorical conclusion to a speech. 2. A discourse; a rhetorical passage 1593.

Peroxide (pərǫ·ksəid). 1804. [f. PER-[1] II. a + OXIDE.] *Chem.* That compound of oxygen with another element which contains the greatest possible proportion of oxygen.
Used colloq. for *p. of hydrogen*, which is used to bleach the hair, etc. Hence **Pero·xided,** treated or dyed with hydrogen p. †**Pero·xidate, Pero·xidize** *vbs. trans.* and *intr.*, to convert, or become converted, into a p.; whence **Peroxida·tion, Pero·xidizement,** conversion into a p.

Perpend (pəɹpe·nd), *v. arch.* 1527. [ad. L. *perpendere*, f. PER-[1] 2 + *pendere* to weigh.] *trans.* To weigh mentally, ponder, consider. Also *absol.* or *intr.*
P. my words O Signieur Dewe, and marke SHAKS.

†**Perpe·ndicle.** *rare.* late ME. [a. OF., ad. L. *perpendiculum*, f. (ult.) PER-[1] 2 + *pendere* to hang.] A plumb-line –1867.

Perpendicular (pɔ̄ɹpĕndi·kiŭlăɹ), *a.*, *adv.*, and *sb.* late ME. [a. OF. *perpendiculer*, *-ier*, ad. L. *perpendicularis*, f. *perpendiculum*; see prec.] A. *adj.* 1. Situated at right angles to the plane of the horizon, or directly up and down; vertical. b. Of an ascent, etc.: Very steep, precipitous 1596. c. Of persons: Of erect figure or attitude; also, upright; (*joc.*) in a standing position 1768. †d. *fig.* Directly leading *to* –1651. 2. *Geom.* Of a line or plane: Having a direction at right angles to a given line, plane, or surface. Const. *to* (†*with*). 1570. 3. *Arch.* Applied to the third or florid style of English pointed architecture, which prevailed from the end of the 14th to the beginning of the 16th century, characterized by the vertical lines of its tracery 1812.
1. In the Sunnes p. glances, wee found it hot 1638. d. Causes p. to their effects SIR T. BROWNE.
†B. *adv.* Perpendicularly, vertically –1792.
C. *sb.* 1. An appliance for indicating the vertical line from any point; e.g. a mason's plumb-level, etc. 1603. 2. A line at right angles to the plane of the horizon, a vertical line; also, a vertical plane or face; *loosely*, a steep. *The p.* (sc. line, direction). 1632. b. Upright position; also *fig.* 1859. c. *slang.* A meal, party, etc., at which most of the guests stand 1871. 3. *Geom.* A straight line at right angles to a given line, plane, or surface 1571. Hence **Pe:rpendicula·rity,** verticality; p. position or direction. **Perpendi·cularly** *adv.*

†**Perpe·nsion.** 1646. [f. L. *perpendere*, *perpens-* to PERPEND.] Mental weighing; thorough consideration –1674.

†**Perpe·nsity.** [f. L. *perpensus* deliberate, pa. pple. of *perpendere* to PERPEND + -ITY.] Attention. SWIFT.

†**Perpe·ssion.** 1603. [ad. L. *perpessionem*, f. PER-[1] 1, 2 + *passionem* PASSION.] Endurance of suffering –1659.

Perpetrable (pɔ̄·ɹpĕtrăb'l), *a.* [ad. late L. *perpetrabilis*, f. *perpetrare*; see next and -ABLE.] Capable of being perpetrated.

Perpetrate (pɔ̄·ɹpĕtreⁱt), *v.* 1547. [f. L. *perpetrat-*, *perpetrare*, f. PER-[1] 1 + *patrare* to effect.] *trans.* To perform, execute, or commit (a crime or evil deed; also (*colloq.*) a pun, or anything treated as shocking).
Sir Philip induced two of his sisters to p. a duet C. BRONTE. All the usual atrocities were perpetrated by the brutal soldiery 1855. Hence **Perpetra·tion,** the action of perpetrating (an evil deed); the action perpetrated; an atrocity. **Pe·rpetrator.**

Perpetuable (pəɹpe·tiu̦ăb'l), *a. rare.* 1885. [f. L. *perpetuare* to PERPETUATE; see -ABLE.] Capable of being perpetuated.

Perpetual (pəɹpe·tiu̦ăl), *a.* (*adv.*) ME. [a. F. *perpétuel*, ad. L. *perpetualis*, f. *perpetuus*, f. PER-[1] 1 + *petere* to seek.] 1. Lasting for ever; eternal; permanent (during life). b. That is applicable, or remains valid for ever, or for an unlimited time 1450. 2. Continuing or continued without intermission; continuous. late ME. B. *adv.* = Perpetually. late ME.
A. 1. [Mountains] enveloped in p. snow HUXLEY. *P. curate*, see CURATE 1; so *p. curacy*, *cure*. *P. motion*, motion that goes on for ever; *spec.* that of a hypothetical machine, which being once set in motion should go on for ever, or until stopped by external force or worn out. b. Phr. *P. injunction*, *settlement*. *P. calendar*, one that may be adjusted so as to supply information for any year or for many years. 2. [It] will keep her spirits in a p. flutter 1755. Hence **Perpe·tually** *adv.* eternally; for the rest of one's life (*arch.*); incessantly; persistently. **Perpe·tualness.** †**Perpe·tualty,** = PERPETUITY 1.

Perpetuance (pəɹpe·tiu̦ăns). 1558. [a. OF. *perpétuance*, f. *perpétuer* to perpetuate; see -ANCE.] Perpetuation.

Perpe·tuate, *ppl. a.* 1503. [ad. L. *perpetuatus*, *perpetuare* to PERPETUATE.] Made perpetual; perpetually continued.

Perpetuate (pəɹpe·tiu̦eⁱt), *v.* 1530. [f. L. *perpetuat-*, *perpetuare*, f. *perpetuus* PERPETUAL; see -ATE[3].] *trans.* To make perpetual; to continue indefinitely; to preserve from extinction or oblivion.
Each courts its Mate, And in their Young themselves p. KEN. Hence **Perpetua·tion,** the action of perpetuating; permanent continuation. **Perpe·tuator.**

Perpetuity (pɔ̄ɹpėtiū·ĭti). [late ME. *perpetuite*, a. F. *perpétuité*, ad. L. *perpetuitatem*, f. *perpetuus* perpetual; see -ITY.] 1. The quality or state of being perpetual. 2. A perpetual possession, tenure, or position. late ME. b. *Law.* Of an estate: The quality or condition of being inalienable perpetually, or for a period beyond certain limits fixed by the general law; an estate so restricted or perpetuated 1596. 3. A perpetual annuity. Hence, The amount or number of years' purchase required to buy a perpetual annuity. 1806.
1. A third attribute of the king's majesty is his p... The king never dies BLACKSTONE. Phr. *In*, *to*, *for p.*, for ever, for an unlimited period. 2. b. The Perpetual Advouson of Staplehurst,..is to be disposed of, either the P., or the next Presentation 1702.

†**Perplex,** *sb. rare.* 1652. [ad. L. **perplexus* after next.] Perplexity; entanglement –1762.

†**Perple·x,** *a.* late ME. [ad. L. *perplexus* involved, f. PER-[1] 2 + *plexus*, *plectere* to plait, interweave.] 1. Perplexed, puzzled –1546. 2. Of things: Intricate; involved, tangled –1684. Hence †**Perple·xly** *adv.* MILT.

Perplex (pəɹple·ks), *v.* 1595. [f. prec. and PERPLEXED *ppl. a.*, and at first used only in pa. pple.] 1. *trans.* To fill (a person) with uncertainty as to the nature or treatment of a thing by reason of its involved or intricate character; to bewilder, puzzle. 2. To make (a thing) uncertain through intricacy; to complicate, confuse 1619. 3. To cause to become tangled; to entangle, intertwine; to intermingle 1620.
1. We are perplexed, but not in despaire 2 *Cor.* iv. 8. Their contradictory accounts..serve only to p... the student 1855. 2. It is possible by a cloud of unmeaning words to p. the question GROTE. 3. Now to p. the ravell'd noose GOLDSM.

Perplexed (pəɹple·kst), *ppl. a.* 1477. [f. L. *perplexus* PERPLEX *a.* + -ED.] 1. Involved in doubt and anxiety about a matter on account of its intricate character; bewildered, puzzled. Formerly: Troubled. 2. Of things: Intricate, involved, complicated 1529. 3. Of material objects: Intricate, entangled 1605. Hence **Perple·xed·ly** *adv.*, **-ness.**

Perplexing (pəɹple·ksiŋ), *ppl. a.* 1631. [-ING[2].] That perplexes; causing perplexity.
With p. thoughts To interrupt the sweet of Life MILT.

Perplexity (pəɹple·ksĭti). ME. [ad. post-cl. L. *perplexitas*, f. *perplexus* PERPLEX *a.*, or a. F. *perplexité*.] 1. Puzzled condition, bewilderment, distraction. †b. Trouble, distress –1658. 2. With *a* and *pl.* a. An instance of this condition 1451. b. Something that causes perplexity 1598. 3. An entangled or confused state *of* anything 1664.
2. a. Accidents which produce perplexities, terrors, and surprises JOHNSON. b. The perplexities of Loue 1598.

Per pro.: see PER *prep.* I. 7.

Perquisite (pɔ̄·ɹkwizit). 1450. [ad. L. *perquisitum*, f. *perquirere* to make diligent search for, f. PER-[1] 2 + *quærere* to seek.] †1. *Law.* Property acquired otherwise than by inheritance –1704. 2. *Law.* Casual profits that come to the lord of a manor in addition to his regular revenue 1552. 3. *gen.* Any casual emolument in addition to salary or wages 1565. b. Any article that has served its primary purpose, which subordinates or servants claim a customary right to take for their own use 1709. c. A customary 'tip' 1721. d. The emoluments of any office 1712. †4. *concr.* An adjunct of anything –1686. 5. *fig.* A thing to which one has the sole right 1793.
3. The queen..is intitled to an antient p. called queen-gold, or *aurum reginæ* BLACKSTONE. *fig.* The

best Perquisites of a Place are the Advantages it gives a Man of doing Good ADDISON. 4. My wife very fine to-day, in her new suit of laced cuffs and perquisites PEPYS. 5. The government kept a most jealous eye upon what it regarded as its own peculiar perquisites 1838.

Perquisition (pǝːkwizi·ʃǝn). 1461. [a. F., ad. L. *perquisitionem*, f. *perquirere*; see prec.] †1. The gaining of something otherwise than by inheritance (*rare*). 2. A thorough or diligent search; *spec.* (after F. use) a domiciliary or other search ordered by law for the discovery of a person, incriminating documents, etc. 1611.

Perradial (pǝːrē¹·diăl), *a.* 1880. [f. PERRADIUS + -AL.] *Zool.* Pertaining to the *perradii* of a cœlenterate; primarily radial. Also *sb.* a p. tentacle.

‖ **Perradius** (pǝːrē¹·diǝs). *Pl.* **-ii** (-iˌǝi). 1880. [mod.L., f. PER-¹ 4 + RADIUS.] *Zool.* Each of the primary rays or radiating parts of certain cœlenterates.

†**Pe·rrie, -y.** Chiefly *poet.* ME. [a. AF. *perrie, OF. *pierrie*, for *p(i)errerie*, f. *pierre* stone; see -ERY 1.] Precious stones collectively; jewellery -1560.

†**Perrier.** late ME. [a. OF. *perrier* (now *pierrier*), f. F. *pierre* stone; cf. PEDRERO.] A ballistic engine or cannon for discharging stones; later, = PEDRERO -1696.

Perron (pe·rǝ̆n, ‖peroǹ). late ME. [a. F., f. *pierre* stone.] 1. A large block or solid erection of stone, used as a platform, the base of a market-cross, etc. 2. *Arch.* A platform, ascended by steps, in front of a church, mansion, etc., and upon which the door or doors open; sometimes applied to a double flight of steps ascending to such a front door 1723.

Perroquet, p. auk: see PARAKEET, PAROQUET.

Perruque: see PERUKE.

‖ **Perruquier** (perükye). 1753. [F., f. *perruque* PERUKE.] One who makes, dresses, or deals in perukes; a wig-maker.

†**Perry** [1], **pery, pirie.** [OE. *pir(i)ge, pirie*, :—L. *pirea, f. *pirum* PEAR *sb.* Frequent in place-names.] A pear-tree. Also *attrib.* -1603.

Perry [2] (pe·ri). [ME. *pereye*, a. OF. *peré, perey*, f. (ult.) late L. *pera* = L. *pirum* pear.] A beverage resembling cider made from the juice of pears. Also *attrib.*

Persalt, per-salt (pǝ̄·ɹsǫlt). 1820. [f. PER-¹ II. + SALT.] *Chem.* A salt formed by combination of an acid with the peroxide of a metal.

Perscrutation (pǝ̄ɹskrutē¹·ʃǝn). 1603. [a. obs. F., ad. L. *perscrutationem*, *perscrutare*, f. PER-¹ 2 + *scrutare* to search closely.] A thorough searching; careful scrutiny, examination.

Perse (pǝɹs), *a.* and *sb.* *arch.* [late ME. a. OF. *pers, -e* :—late L. (Rom.) *persus, -a.* The Rom. word was prob. a back-formation from L. *Persicus* PERSIC.] In early writers, Blue, bluish, bluish-grey; later, often taken (after Italian) as purplish black; also *sb.* the colour, or a stuff of the colour.

A long surcote of pers vp on he hade CHAUCER.

‖ **Persea** (pǝ̄·ɹsiă). 1601. [L., a. Gr. περσέα.] a. *Ancient Mythol.* A sacred fruit-bearing tree in Egypt and Persia. b. *Bot.* A genus of trees and shrubs, N.O. *Lauraceæ*, common in tropical America and the West Indies.

Persecute (pǝ̄·ɹsikiūt), *v.* 1477. [a. F. *persécuter*, f. L. *persecut-*, *persequi* to PURSUE.] †1. *trans.* To pursue, hunt, drive (with missiles, or with attempts to catch, kill, or injure) -1697. 2. To pursue with malignancy or injurious action; *esp.* to oppress for holding a heretical opinion or belief 1482. 3. To harass, worry; to importune 1585.

2. Blessed are ye when men shall revyle you, and p. you,..ffor my sake TINDALE *Matt.* v. 11. 3. He may ..p. with Rhyme POPE.

Persecution (pǝ̄ɹsikiū·ʃǝn). [ME. *persecucion*, etc., a. OF., ad. L. *persecutionem*, f. *persequi* to PERSECUTE.] 1. The action of persecuting, *esp.* the infliction of death, torture, or penalties for adherence to a particular religious belief or opinion; the fact of being persecuted; an instance of this. b. A particular course or period of systematic infliction of punishment directed against those holding a particular (religious) belief. late ME. c. *transf.* Persistent injury or annoyance from any source 1585. †2. The action of pursuing; prosecution (of an aim, etc.); quest -1647.

1. P. is a bad and indirect way to plant Religion SIR T. BROWNE. c. The..persecutions of the skie SHAKS.

Persecutive (pǝ̄·ɹsikiūtiv), *a.* *rare.* 1659. [See PERSECUTE and -IVE.] Tending or addicted to persecution.

Persecutor (pǝ̄·ɹsikiūtǝɹ). 1484. [orig. a. AF. *persecutour*, ad. L. *persecutorem*, f. *persequi* to PERSECUTE; see -OR. Also with *-er*; see -ER¹.] One who persecutes; *esp.* one who harasses others on account of opinions or beliefs. So **Pe·rsecutress, Pe·rsecutrix** (*rare*), a female p.

Perseid (pǝ̄·ɹsiˌid). 1876. [ad. mod.L. *Perseis*, pl. *-ides*, daughter of Perseus.] *Astron. pl.* A group of meteors which appear to radiate from the constellation Perseus. Also *attrib.*

Perseity (pǝɹsī·iti). 1694. [ad. med.L. *perseitas* (Duns Scotus), f. *per se* by itself = Gr. καθ' αὑτό (Aristotle).] The quality or condition of existing independently, or of being predicated essentially of a subject.

Perseverance (pǝ̄ːsīvī·răns). ME. [a. F., ad. L. *perseverantia*, f. *perseverantem*; see next and -ANCE. Formerly (pǝɹse·vĕrăns).] 1. The fact, process, condition, or quality of persevering; constant persistence in an undertaking; steadfast pursuit of an aim. 2. *Theol.* Continuance in a state of grace leading finally to a state of glory 1555.

1. Job, Whose constant p. overcame Whate're his cruel malice could invent MILT. 2. *Final p., p. of the saints*, the doctrine that those who are elected to eternal life will never permanently lapse from grace or be finally lost: one of the 'Five points of Calvinism'.

Perseverant (pǝ̄ɹsīvī·rănt), *a.* Now *rare.* ME. [a. F. *persévérant*, f. *persévérer* to PERSEVERE. Formerly (pǝɹse·vĕrănt).] Steadfast, persistent, persevering. Hence **Perseve·rantly** *adv.* (now *rare*).

Persevere (pǝ̄ɹsīvī·ɹ), *v.* Also †**persever.** late ME. [a. F. *persévérer*, ad. L. *perseverare* to abide by strictly, f. (ult.) PER-¹ 4 + *severus* strict. Formerly (pǝɹse·vǝɹ).] 1. *intr.* To continue steadfastly in a course of action (formerly, also, in a condition, state, or purpose), esp. in the face of difficulty; to continue constant. Const. *in, with.* †b. Const. *to* with *infin.* -1796. †2. a. To continue in a place, state or condition -1784. †b. Of things: To continue, last, endure -1696. †3. *trans.* To cause to continue; to keep constant, preserve -1655.

1. I will perseuer in my course of Loyalty SHAKS. Thrice happie if they know Thir happiness, and p. upright MILT. Hence **Perseve·ringly** *adv.*

Persian (pǝ·ɹʃăn). [orig. ME. *Persien*, a. F., ad. L. *Persianus, f. *Persia*, name of the country.] A. *adj.* 1. Of or pertaining to Persia, its inhabitants, or language. 2. In specific names of productions found in or imported from Persia; e.g. *P. carpet*, etc. 1632. 3. *Arch.* Applied to figures of men serving instead of columns to support entablatures 1727.

1. I do not like the fashion of your garments. You will say they are P. SHAKS. 2. **P. berries**, the unripe fruit of *Rhamnus infectorius*, coming from Persia; **P. blinds** = PERSIENNES; **P. cat**, the Angora cat, with long silky hair, and thick bushy tail; **P. drill**, a hand drill operated by the movement of a nut backward and forward on the thread of a revolving screw, which carries the drill; **P. earth** = *Indian red*; **P. fire**, *Path.* = ANTHRAX 1; **P. insect-powder**, an insecticide made of the flowers of *Pyrethrum roseum*; **P. lily**, a fritillary (*Fritillaria persica*); **P. morocco**, a kind of morocco leather made from the skin of a hairy sheep called the Persian goat.

B. *sb.* 1. A native or inhabitant of Persia. late ME. Also short for *P. cat, P. morocco.* 2. The native language of Persia 1634. 3. *Arch.* A male figure dressed in the ancient Persian manner serving instead of a column or pilaster to support an entablature 1823. †4. A thin soft silk, used for linings. Also called *Persia* or *P. silk.* -1838. 5. = PERSIENNES 1786.

Persic (pǝ̄·ɹsik), *a.* and *sb.* 1606. [ad. L. *Persicus*, f. *Persæ* Persians; see -IC.] A. *adj.* = PERSIAN *a.* B. *sb.* The Persian tongue 1753.

‖ **Persicaria** (pǝɹsikē·riă). 1597. [med. or mod.L., f. L. *persicum* (*malum*) peach.] The plant *Polygonum Persicaria*, or Peachwort.

Persico(t (pǝ̄·ɹsiko, -kōu, -kǝt). 1709. [a. F., a. It. *persico*, L. *persicum* peach.] A cordial made by macerating the kernels of peaches, apricots, etc. in spirit.

‖ **Persiennes** (pǝɹsie·nz, ‖pęrsyęn), *sb. pl.* 1842. [Fr., pl. fem. of adj. *persien* Persian.] Outside window-shutters, or blinds, made of light laths horizontally fastened to a frame, so as to be movable, like those of Venetian blinds.

‖ **Persiflage** (pǝ̄·ɹsiflāʒ, ‖pęrsiflāʒ). 1757. [Fr., f. *persifler* to banter; see -AGE.] Light banter or raillery; a frivolous manner of treating any subject. So ‖ **Persifleur** (pęrsiflör), a person addicted to p.

Persimmon (pǝɹsi·mǝn). 1612. [Corruption of native name in Powhatan dialect.] 1. The plum-like fruit of the tree *Diospyros virginiana*; the American Date-plum; it is very astringent until softened by frost, when it becomes sweet and edible. Also, The large red fruit of the Japanese species *D. Kaki.* 2. (More fully *p.-tree.*) The tree *Diospyros virginiana* (N.O. *Ebenaceæ*). Also applied to Japanese P., *D. Kaki*, and other species. 1737.

Persist (pǝɹsi·st), *v.* 1538. [ad. L. *persistere*, f. PER-¹ 2 + *sistere* to stand.] 1. *intr.* To continue firmly or obstinately *in* a state, opinion, purpose, or course of action, esp. against opposition. b. To persist in saying or asserting 1698. 2. To remain in existence; to last 1760.

1. Thus to p. In doing wrong, extenuates not wrong SHAKS. b. [Callisthenes] persisted in his innocence to the last GOLDSM. 2. The Calyx..Persisting, till the Fruit is come to Maturity 1760. Hence **Persi·ster** (*rare*) one who persists.

Persistence (pǝɹsi·stĕns). 1546. [a. F. *persistance*; subseq. refash. after L.] 1. The action or fact of persisting; obstinate continuance in a particular course. Also = PERSISTENCY 1. 2. Continued existence in time or (*rarely*) in space; endurance; continuous occurrence 1621.

2. *P. of an impression*, the continuance of a sensible (esp. of a visual) impression after the exciting cause is removed. *P. of force* or *energy*, *p. of matter*, names for the two principles of the conservation of energy and the permanence of matter.

Persistency (pǝɹsi·stĕnsi). 1597. [f. L. *persistentem*; see next and -ENCY.] 1. The quality of persisting or being persistent; also = PERSISTENCE 1. 2. = PERSISTENCE 2. 1833.

Persistent (pǝɹsi·stĕnt), *a.* 1826. [ad. L. *persistentem*, pr. pple. of *persistere* to PERSIST.] 1. Persisting in some action, course, etc., esp. against opposition, or in spite of failure 1830. 2. Existing continuously in time; enduring 1853. b. Of an action or condition: Continuous; constantly repeated 1857. 3. *spec.* a. *Zool.* and *Bot.* Of parts of animals and plants (as the horns, hair, calyces, etc.): Remaining after the period at which such parts in other cases fall off or wither; permanent; continuing; opp. to *deciduous* or *caducous* 1826. b. *Geol.* Of a stratum: Extending continuously over the whole area occupied by the formation 1833. Hence **Persi·stently** *adv.* So **Persi·sting** *ppl. a.* (in sense 3). **Persi·stingly** *adv.*

Persi·stive, *a.* 1606. [f. PERSIST *v.* + -IVE.] Persisting, tending to persist.

Person (pǝ̄·ɹsǝn, pǝ̄·ɹs'n), *sb.* ME. [a. OF. *persone*, mod.F. *personne* :—L. *persona* a mask used by a player, a character acted; in late use, a human being; connected by some with L. *personare* to sound through.] I. A part played in a drama, or in life; hence, function, office, capacity; guise, semblance; character in a play or story. (Now chiefly in the phr. *in the p. of* = as representing.)

He comes to disfigure, or to present the p. of Moone-shine SHAKS.

II. An individual human being; a man, woman, or child ME. b. (Now only with qualification) A man or woman of distinction or importance; a personage. late ME.

Ninety and nine iust persons *Luke* xv. 7. A p. in trade MISS BURNEY. *Young p.*, a young man or young woman; now esp. the latter, when the speaker does not desire to specify her position as 'woman' or 'lady'; They are not young ladies, they are young persons W. S. GILBERT. b. A man of my parts and talents..is a p. DRYDEN.

III. 1. The living body of a human being; either (*a*) the actual body, as distinct from clothing, etc., or from the mind or soul, or (*b*) the body with its clothing, etc. Usu. with *of* or possessive. ME. †b. (With qualifying adj.) A man or woman of (such and such) a figure –1805. 2. The actual self of a man or woman, individual personality. With *of* or poss. late ME.

1. For her owne P., It beggerd all description SHAKS. One of his advantages was a fine p. GEO. ELIOT. b. A fair persone he was and fortunat CHAUCER. A pale thin p. of a man STERNE. 2. Phr. *His* (*own*) *p.* = himself; *your p.* = yourself, you personally.

IV. *Law.* A human being (*natural p.*) or body corporate or corporation (*artificial p.*), having rights or duties recognized by law 1444.

V. *Theol.* a. Applied to the three modes of the divine being in the Godhead (Father, Son, and Holy Spirit) which together constitute the Trinity ME. b. The personality of Christ, esp. as uniting the two natures, divine and human 1562.

a. Þe trinite þat is o god and persones þre ME.

VI. *Gram.* Each of the three classes of pronouns, and corresponding distinctions in verbs, denoting respectively the person speaking (*first p.*), the person spoken to (*second p.*), and the person or thing spoken of (*third p.*); each of the different forms or inflexions expressing these distinctions 1520.

VII. *Zool.* Each individual of a compound or colonial organism; a zooid 1878.

Phr. *In* one's (*own*) *p.*, formerly also *in* (one's) *proper p.*: †a. = in person; b. In one's own character (not as representing another). *In p.*: personally; oneself. *In the p. of* (*in his* or *her p.*): a. as the representative of: b. embodied in; impersonated in; (as) personally represented by. *To accept, respect persons*, or *the p. of* any one, to look upon with favour (see Ps. lxxxi. 2, Luke xx. 21, Rom. ii. 11, etc.).

†Pe·rson, *v.* [f. prec.] = PERSONATE *v.* 4. MILT.

‖ **Persona** (pəɹsōᵘ·nă). [L.: see PERSON *sb.*] 1. **P. grata** (grēⁱ·tă), an acceptable person or personage: orig. applied to a diplomatic representative who is personally acceptable to the personage to whom he is accredited. 2. *In propria persona*: see IN *Lat. prep.*

Personable (pə̄·ɹsənăb'l), *a.* late ME. [f. PERSON *sb.* + -ABLE.] 1. Having a well-formed person; handsome; presentable. (Now chiefly in literary use.) †2. *Law.* Having the status of a legal person (PERSON *sb.* IV), and as such competent to maintain a plea in court, or to take anything granted or given –1660.

1. Certainly, he was a p. young man 1890. Hence **Pe·rsonableness**, personal handsomeness.

Personage (pə̄·ɹsənėdʒ). 1461. [a. OF. *personage*, mod.F. *personnage* = med.L. *personaticum, -agium*, f. *persona* PERSON; see -AGE.] †1. A representation or figure of a person –1711. †2. = PERSON *sb.* III. 1. –1785. †b. = PERSON *sb.* III. 1 b. –1807. 3. A person of high rank, distinction, or importance; a person of note. (Orig. always with *great* or the like.) 1503. b. A person; a man or woman (of unspecified status) 1555. †4. The sort of person any one is –1598. 5. One of the characters of a drama, dramatic poem, story, etc. 1573. b. Hence, the acting of such a character, the part acted 1559.

2. The Armenians are..of comely P. 1680. 3. He was fast becoming a p. DISRAELI. b. That ready-witted and helpful p. 1890. 5. Only three speaking personages should appear at once upon the stage JOHNSON. b. Phr. *To take upon oneself, put on, play, assume the p. of*; also *fig.* and *transf.* in *to represent the p. of.*

Personal (pə̄·ɹsənăl), *a.* (*sb.*) late ME. [a. OF., ad. L. *personalis*, f. *persona* PERSON; see -AL.] 1. Of, pertaining to, concerning or affecting the individual person or self; individual; private; one's own. 2. Done, made, performed, held, etc. in person. late ME. †b. Present or engaged in person –1617. 3. Of or pertaining to one's person, body, or figure; bodily. late ME. 4. Directed to, aimed at, or referring to some particular person or to oneself personally, *spec.* in a hostile sense or manner 1614. b. *transf.* Making, or addicted to, personal remarks or reflections 1607. 5. Of, pertaining to, or having the nature of a person, as opposed to a thing or abstraction 1651. 6. *Law.* Opp. to *real*: †a. orig. in *p. action* (or *plea*), an action wherein the claim was the recovery of damages from the *person*; dist. from a *real* action, for the restitution of the thing itself, and from a *mixed* action in which both restitution and damages were demanded –1888. Hence b. *p. property* (*estate*, etc.), things recoverable in the personalty or by a personal action, i. e. chattels and chattel interests in land, or generally all property except land and those interests in land which pass on the owner's death to his heir (cf. REAL) 1544. 7. *Gram.* Of or pertaining to the three persons; denoting one of these; esp. in *p. pronoun* 1481.

1. I know no personall cause, to spurne at him, But for the generall SHAKS. This is p. to himself 1874. *P.* EQUATION, *p.* IDENTITY; see these words. 2. Bound by law to p. service in the cavalry 1844. Any p. interview 1880. b. When hee was personall in the Irish Warre SHAKS. 3. He shall have no p. ill-usage SCOTT. The p. ornaments of the Bronze age 1865. 4. P. invectives 1614, abuse 1801. The strong p. vanity of the man 1830. b. Where have I been particular? where p.? B. JONS. 5. Grief is certainly a p. affection, of which a quality is not capable 1659. 6. *P. contract*, one which depends upon the existence, or the personal qualities, skill, or services of one of the parties; e. g. a contract of marriage. *P. representative*, an executor or administrator. 7. *P. verb*, a verb that has inflexions for all three persons (opp. to *impersonal*; now *rare*).

B. *sb. pl.* Personal matters or things; †*spec.* personal property, personalty. 1497. b. *pl.* Short for *p. remarks* (now rare), *p. paragraphs* (U.S.), *p. pronouns* (rare).

Personalism (pə̄·ɹsənăliz'm). 1846. [f. prec. + -ISM.] The quality or character of being personal; variously used to denote some personal theory, method, characteristic, etc.

Personality (pə̄ɹsənæ·liti). late ME. [a. OF. *personalité*, mod. *personnalité*, ad. late L. *personalitas*, f. *personalis* PERSONAL; see -ITY.] 1. The quality or fact of being a person; that quality which makes a being personal. b. The property ascribed to the Deity of consisting of distinct persons (see PERSON *sb.* V.) 1492. c. Personal existence; personal identity 1835. 2. Distinctive individual character, esp. when of a marked kind 1795. 3. A personal being, a person 1678. 4. The fact of relating to an individual person, or to particular persons; *spec.* the quality of being aimed at an individual, esp. in a hostile way 1772. b. (Usu. in *pl.*) A statement or remark aimed at or referring to an individual person 1769. 5. *Law.* = PERSONALTY (*rare*) 1658.

1. These capacities constitute p., for they imply consciousness and thought PALEY. c. The age of Homer is surrounded with darkness, his very p. with doubt RUSKIN. 4. He had attacked Wolsey himself with somewhat vulgar p. 1856. b. The Senator resorted to personalities 1850.

Personalize (pə̄·ɹsənăləiz), *v.* 1727. [f. PERSONAL *a.* + -IZE.] *trans.* To render personal; to personify; to impersonate. Hence **Pe:rsonaliza·tion.**

Personally (pə̄·ɹsənăli), *adv.* late ME. [f. PERSONAL *a.* + -LY [2].] In a personal manner, capacity, etc. 1. In person: = (by) himself, themselves, etc. b. In objective sense, expressing the relation of an action, feeling, etc. to the actual person mentioned 1483. 2. As a person 1597. 3. In one's personal capacity; as regards oneself; *esp.* 'for myself' 1849.

1. He..must answer the damage p. 1765. Phr. *P. conducted*, conducted by some one in person. b. The amended writ ought to have been served on them p. 1891. 2. God the Word, when He took human nature, came into it p. PUSEY. 3. P. I don't despair 1902.

Personalty (pə̄·ɹsŏnălti). 1481. [ad. late AF. *personaltie* = med.L. *personalitas* PERSONALITY; cf. *reality, realty.*] †a. (See quot.) b. Personal goods, personal estate; also *gen.* personal belongings.

a. Actions were said to be or to sound *in the realty* or *in the p.*, according to the nature of the relief afforded therein. Next the terms, *the realty, the p.* were applied to the things recoverable in real or personal actions 1888.

Personate (pə̄·ɹsŏnĕt), *a.* 1597. [ad. L. *personatus* masked, etc., f. *persona* PERSON; see -ATE [2].] †1. Personated, counterfeit –1822. †2. Personal; impersonated –1689. 3. *Bot.* Mask-like; applied to a two-lipped corolla having the opening between the lips closed by an upward projection of the lower lip, as in the snapdragon. (Dist. from *ringent*). 1760.

Personate (pə̄·ɹsŏneⁱt), *v.* 1591. [f. L. *personat-*, *personare*, f. *persona* mask, etc.; see PERSON *sb.*] 1. *trans.* To act or play the part of (a character in a drama, etc.); to act (a drama, etc.); to represent dramatically 1598. b. To assume the character of 1704. c. *absol.* To play or act a part 1642. 2. To pretend to be (another), usually for purposes of fraud 1613. †3. To counterfeit (a quality) –1633. †4. To represent (a person, etc.) in writing (*esp.* as saying so and so); occas., to symbolize –1693. 5. To stand for, represent, symbolize, signify; to stand in the place of; to impersonate. Now *rare* or *Obs.* 1611. †6. To represent as a person (*rare*) –1823.

1. They [i. e. Stage-players] can act to the life those whom they p. 1647. c. The actor's first duty..is to p. SIR H. IRVING. 2. A yong woman..that personated a man 1694. 3. His sorrow is not personated 1633. 5. *Cymb.* v. v. 454. Hence **Pe·rsonated** *ppl. a.* acted, feigned; also = prec. 3. **Persona·tion**, the action of personating (in various senses). **Pe·rsonator.**

Personeity (pəɹsŏnī·iti). *rare.* 1822. [irreg. f. PERSON, after *corporeity*.] a. That which constitutes a person. b. *concr.* A personal being. COLERIDGE.

Personification (pəɹsǫ:nifikēⁱ·ʃən). 1755. [f. next. 1. The act of personifying; esp. as a rhetorical figure or species of metaphor. b. An imaginary person conceived as representing a thing or abstraction 1850. 2. A person or thing viewed as embodying a quality, etc., or as exemplifying it in a striking manner; an 'incarnation' (*of* something) 1807. 3. A dramatic representation, or literary description, of a person or thing 1814.

1. The personifications of church and country as females 1875. 2. He was popularly regarded as the p. of the Latitudinarian spirit MACAULAY.

Personify (pəɹsǫ·nifəi), *v.* 1727. [a. F. *personnifier*; see PERSON and -FY.] 1. *trans.* To figure or represent (a thing or abstraction) as a person, esp. in speech or writing; in art, to symbolize by a figure in human form. 2. To embody (a quality, etc.) in one's person or self; to exemplify in a typical manner. Chiefly in *pa. pple.* 1803.

1. Greek philosophy has a tendency to p. ideas JOWETT. 2. The natives of this country are rashness personified 1803. Hence **Perso·nifier,** one who personifies.

†Personize (pə̄·ɹsənəiz), *v.* 1593. [f. PERSON + -IZE.] 1. *intr.* To act a part –1593. 2. *trans.* To personify –1762.

2. Milton has Personiz'd them 1734.

‖ **Personnel** (pəɹsŏne·l). 1857. [F., sb. use of *personnel* adj., as contrasted with *matériel*.] The body of persons engaged in any service or employment, esp. in a public institution, as an army, navy, hospital, etc.; the human equipment (*of* an institution, etc.).

†Perspe·ction. 1549. [ad. L. *perspectionem*; see PERSPECTIVE *a.*] A looking through, into, or at something; contemplation; outlook. *lit.* and *fig.* –1682.

Eye-gate was the place of p. BUNYAN.

Perspective (pəɹspe·ktiv), *sb.* late ME. [ad. med.L. *perspectiva* (sc. *ars*), the science of optics.] I. †1. The science of sight; optics –1658. †2. An optical instrument for viewing objects with –1789.

2. Phr. *To look through the wrong end of the p.*, to look upon something as of less importance than it is.

II. 1. The art of delineating solid objects upon a plane surface so as to produce the same impression of relative positions and magnitudes, or of distance, as the actual objects do when viewed from a particular point. (Formerly also *pl.* in same sense.) 1583. b. *transf.* The appearance presented by visible objects, in regard to relative position, apparent distance, etc. c. *Mod. Geom.* = HOMOLOGY 4. 1857. d. *fig.* The proportion in which the parts of a subject are viewed by the mind 1605. 2. *concr.* A drawing or picture in perspective; a 'view' 1644. †b. A picture or figure constructed so as to produce some fantastic effect –1610. 3. A visible scene, view, or prospect; *esp.* a vista 1620.

1. AERIAL *p.*, ISOMETRIC *p.*, LINEAR *p.*: see these words. *Angular* or *oblique p.*, that in which neither side of the principal object is parallel to the plane of delineation. d. Evolution..has thrown the universe into a fresh p. 1894. 2. Hogarth's lively p. of Cheapside THACKERAY. b. *Rich. II*, II. ii. 18. 3. The lofty towers and long perspectives of the church GRAY. *fig.* I saw a long p. of felicity before me GOLDSM.

Phr. *In p.*, **a.** in mental view; in prospect; **b.** drawn or viewed in accordance with the principles of p.; also *fig.*

†**III.** Close inspection; insight -1649.

Perspective (pəɹspe·ktiv), *a.* late ME. [ad. late L. *perspectivus*, f. *perspicere* to look through, view, f. PER-[1] I + *specere* to look.] **I.** †**1.** Relating to sight; optical -1592. †**2.** Useful for looking or viewing; applied to various instruments, etc. Usu. in phr. *p. glass* = prec. I. 2. Also *fig.* -1729.

II. Of or pertaining to, or drawn according to, perspective 1606. Hence **Perspe·ctively** *adv.* †optically; †clearly; in perspective.

†**Pe·rspicable,** *a.* 1660. [ad. late L. *perspicabilis*, f. **perspicari* = *perspicere*.] Capable of being beheld; visible -1665.

Perspicacious (pɔ̄ɹspikēⁱ·ʃəs), *a.* 1616. [f. L. *perspicax, -cacem*, f. *perspicere*; see PERSPECTIVE and -ACIOUS. Cf. F. *perspicace*.] **1.** Of clear and penetrating sight; clear-sighted. *arch.* **2.** Of penetrating mental vision or discernment 1640. Hence **Perspica·cious·ly** *adv.*, **-ness.**

Perspicacity (pɔ̄ɹspikæ·sĭti). 1548. [ad. L. *perspicacitas*, f. *perspicax*; see prec. and -ITY; cf. F. *perspicacité*.] **1.** Keenness of sight. *Obs.* or *arch.* 1607. **2.** Clearness of understanding; penetration, discernment. So †**Pe·rspicacy.**

†**Pe·rspicil.** 1611. [ad. med. or mod.L. *perspicillum*, f. *perspicere* + *-illum*, dim. and instrumental suffix; cf. *aspergillum*.] An optic glass; a lens; a telescope or microscope. Also *fig.* -1680.

Perspicuity (pɔ̄ɹspikiū·ĭti). 1477. [ad. L. *perspicuitas*, f. *perspicuus*, (see next and -ITY); cf. F. *perspicuité*.] †**1.** Transparency, translucency -1750. **2.** Clearness of statement or exposition; lucidity 1546. †**3.** Conspicuousness (*rare*) -1634. ¶**4.** *improp.* Perspicacity 1662.

Perspicuous (pəɹspi·kiu,əs), *a.* 1477. [f. L. *perspicuus* transparent, clear (f. *perspicere* to see through) + -OUS.] †**1.** Transparent, translucent -1750. **2.** Clear; clearly expressed, lucid; evident 1586. **b.** Of persons: Clear in statement or expression 1593. †**3.** Conspicuous -1805. ¶**4.** *improp.* Perspicacious (*rare*) 1584.

2. The most p. and energetick language BOSWELL. **b.** Prethee.., be plaine and p. with mee DEKKER. Hence **Perspi·cuous·ly** *adv.*, **-ness.**

Perspirable (pəɹspəiə·răb'l), *a.* 1604. [f. PERSPIRE *v.* + -ABLE.] **1.** Capable of perspiring; liable to perspire. **b.** Of, pertaining to, or attended with perspiration 1805. †**2.** Liable to be blown through; airy -1669. **3.** Capable of being thrown off in perspiration 1646.

1. b. *P. point*, point of perspiration. Hence **Perspirabi·lity,** liability to perspire.

Perspiration (pɔ̄ɹspirēⁱ·ʃən). 1611. [a. F., f. *perspirer*, ad. L. *perspirare* to PERSPIRE.] †**1.** Breathing out or through -1710. †**2.** Evaporation, exhalation -1707. **3.** The excretion of moisture through the pores of the skin; sweating 1626. **4.** *concr.* That which is perspired; sweat 1725.

Perspirative (pəɹspəiə·rătiv, pɔ̄ɹspirēⁱtiv), *a. rare.* 1730. [f. L. *perspirat-*, ppl. stem of *perspirare* to PERSPIRE + -IVE.] = next.

Perspiratory (pəɹspəiə·rătəri), *a.* 1725. [f. as prec. + -ORY[2].] **1.** Promoting or subservient to perspiration. **2.** Of, pertaining to, or of the nature of perspiration 1805.

Perspire (pəɹspəiə·ɹ), *v.* 1646. [ad. L. *perspirare* (f. PER-[1] I + *spirare* to breathe).] †**1.** *intr.* Of the wind: To breathe gently through HERRICK. †**2.** *intr.* Of any volatile matter: To pass out or escape through pores; to evaporate; to exhale -1799. **3.** *intr.* To give out watery fluid through the pores of the skin. (Now the ordinary sense.) 1725. **4.** *trans.* To give off (liquid) through pores, either insensibly as vapour, or sensibly as moisture; said of organic bodies. Also *fig.* 1707.

2. The cork being..porous, part of the spirits..p. 1676. **4.** After the blossom unfolds it perspires a sweet honey-like fluid 1837.

Perstringe (pəɹstri·ndʒ), *v.* 1549. [ad. L. *perstringere*, f. PER-[1] 2 + *stringere* to tie, bind.] **1.** To censure; to criticize adversely. †**2.** To touch on; to glance at -1797. †**3.** To dull (the eyes, or light); to dazzle; to dim -1664. Hence †**Perstri·ction** (*rare*), stricture.

Persuadable (pəɹswēⁱ·dăb'l), *a.* 1530. [f. PERSUADE *v.* + -ABLE.] †**1.** Persuasive -1530. **2.** = PERSUASIBLE 2. 1598. Hence **Persuadabi·lity, Persua·dableness; Persua·dably** *adv.*

Persuade (pəɹswēⁱ·d), *v.* 1513. [ad. L. *persuadere*, f. PER-[1] I + *suadere*; see SUASION.] **I.** To persuade *a person.* **1.** *trans.* To induce (a person) to believe something. Const. *that* (a thing is so); *of* (a fact, etc.), rarely *into, out of* (a belief, etc.). Somewhat *arch.* Also *refl.* Also *absol.* **b.** *pa. pple.* Led to believe; assured, sure 1553. **2.** To prevail upon (a person) to do something. Const. *to* with *inf.*; *to, unto, into* (an action); also *from, out of.* Also *absol.* 1513. †**3.** To seek to induce (a person) to (or from) a belief, a course of action, etc.; to assure (one) *that*; to counsel strongly -1801.

1. These..perswade women that they can foretell them their fortune 1600. *refl.* Yet can I not perswade me thou art dead MILT. **2.** To p. the lady into a private marriage 1771. The man was persuaded to open the door 1875.

II. To persuade *a thing.* †**1.** To induce belief of (a fact, statement, etc.); to prove -1685. **2.** To lead one to do or practise; to urge successfully upon one (*arch.*) 1538. †**3.** To urge (a statement, opinion, etc.) as credible or true; to go to prove, make probable -1687. †**4.** To commend to adoption, advise, advocate, recommend (an act, course, etc.) -1781.

2. Your King..Sends me a Paper to perswade me Patience SHAKS. **3.** Disputing and perswading the things concerning the Kingdom of God *Acts* xix. 8.

III. *intr.* To use persuasion; to succeed in bringing over or inducing 1526.

How I perswaded, how I praid, and kneel'd SHAKS. Phr. †*To p. with*, to use persuasion with, plead with; occas., to prevail with; †*fig.* to prevail or avail with. Hence **Persua·ded** *ppl. a.* prevailed upon; convinced; induced by persuasion; †proved. **Persua·ded·ly** *adv.*, **-ness.**

Persuader (pəɹswēⁱ·dəɹ). 1538. [f. prec. + -ER[1].] One who or that which persuades; esp. (*slang*) a weapon, spurs, etc.

Persuasible (pəɹswēⁱ·sĭb'l, -zĭb'l), *a.* late ME. [ad. L. *persuasibilis*, f. *persuas-, persuadere* to PERSUADE; see -BLE.] †**1.** Persuasive -1647. **2.** Capable of being persuaded; open to persuasion 1502. †**3.** Credible, plausible -1643. Hence **Persuasibi·lity, Persua·sibleness,** the quality of being p. **Persua·sibly** *adv.*

Persuasion (pəɹswēⁱ·ʒən). late ME. [ad. L. *persuasionem*, perh. through F.] **1.** The action, or an act, of persuading or seeking to persuade; the presenting of inducements or winning arguments to a person to induce him to do or believe something. †**b.** An argument or inducement -1624. **c.** Persuasiveness 1601. **2. a.** The fact or condition of being persuaded; conviction, assurance 1534. **b.** with *pl.* A belief, conviction 1510. **3.** *spec.* Religious belief or opinion; a creed 1623. Hence **b.** A sect holding a particular belief, a denomination 1727. **c.** *slang.* Nationality; sex; kind; sort; description 1864.

1. The English Lords By his perswasion, are againe falne off SHAKS. **c.** Ist possible that my deserts to you Can lacke perswasion? SHAKS. **2. a.** My doubts were..converted into a full p. 1777. **3.** All his Subjects of what perswasion soever *Bk. Com. Prayer.* Pref. The Roman Catholic p. 1813. **b.** The Essenes, a p. that reject pleasure as a positive evil 1863. **c.** A dark little man..of French p. 1903.

Persuasive (pəɹswēⁱ·siv, -ziv), *a.* and *sb.* 1589. [ad. med.L. *persuasivus*, f. *persuas-, persuadere* to PERSUADE; see -IVE.] **A.** *adj.* Having the power of persuading; winning. **B.** *sb.* Something adapted to persuade; a motive or inducement presented 1641.

A. A most p. Preacher 1639. Hence **Persua·sive·ly** *adv.*, **-ness.** So **Persua·sory** *a.* = PERSUASIVE *a.* (now *rare* or *Obs.*).

†**Pe·rsue.** Also **parcy,** etc. 1530. [app. orig. **parcee*, **percee*, a. F. *percée* act of piercing. Later confused with *pursue.*] *Venery.* The track of blood left by a stricken deer or other wounded beast of the chase -1661.

Persulphate (pəɹsʊ·lfĕt). 1813. [PER-[1] II. b.] *Chem.* That sulphate which contains the greatest proportion of oxygen, or of the sulphuric acid radical SO_4; as *p. of iron*, now named *ferric sulphate*, $Fe_2(SO_4)_3$; etc.

Persulphide (pəɹsʊ·lfəid). 1856. [PER-[1] II.] *Chem.* That sulphide of any element or basic radical which contains the greatest proportion of sulphur; orig. called *persulphuret.*

Pert (pɔ̄ɹt), *a.* (*sb.*, *adv.*) ME. [Aphetic f. APERT, partly repr. L. *apertus*, partly = OF. *aspert, espert* :—L. *expertus.* (From 15th c., evidenced with a long vowel, *peert*, later *peart, piert.*)] **I.** †**1.** Open, unconcealed; manifest -1579. †**2.** Of personal appearance. **a.** (in early use) Beautiful. **b.** (later) Smart, dapper. -1684. **II.** †**a.** Expert, skilled; ready -1500. **b.** Sharp, intelligent; adroit, clever. late ME. **III. 1.** Forward in speech and behaviour; saucy, 'cheeky', malapert. Now the ordinary sense. late ME. †**b.** As a vague expression of disfavour -1752. **2.** Bold (esp. in a bad sense); forward; audacious. *Obs.* (exc. as merged in prec.) 1535. **3.** Lively; brisk, sprightly; in good spirits, 'jolly'. Often used of the state of an invalid: 'bright', 'chirpy' (esp. in form *peart*). Now *dial.* and *U.S.* 1581.

1. The p. talk of children 1702. As p. a genius as the applause of a common-room ever..spoiled DISRAELI. **b.** A p. bad apartment H. WALPOLE. **3.** The p. Fairies and the dapper Elves MILT. Quick she had always been and 'peart', as we say on Exmoor BLACKMORE.

B. *sb.* (the adj. used *absol.*) A pert person or thing. late ME.

C. *adv.* or quasi-*adv.*: in various senses of the adj. late ME. Hence **Pe·rt-ly** *adv.*, **-ness.**

Pertain (pəɹtēⁱ·n), *v.* [ME. *par-, pertene*, a. OF. *partenir* :—L. *pertinere* to extend, tend (to), belong (to), f. PER-[1] I + *tenere* to hold.] **1.** *intr.* To belong; e. g. as a native, as part of a whole, as an accessory, as dependent, etc. Const. *to.* **b.** To belong as one's care or concern. *To p. to*: to concern. *Obs.* or *arch.* late ME. **c.** To be appropriate *to.* late ME. **2.** To have reference, relate *to.* late ME. †**3.** Phr. *As pertains to* (used impersonally), *as pertaining to* = as regards, in relation to. -1568.

1. If she pertaine to life, let her speake too SHAKS. **b.** The cares of war P. to all men born in Troy 1870. **c.** The things which perteine to peace 1577. **2.** This law pertains, first to vows made to God himself 1770.

Pertinacious (pɔ̄ɹtinēⁱ·ʃəs), *a.* 1626. [f. L. *pertinaci-, pertinax* (f. PER-[1] 4 + *tenax* tenacious) + -OUS.] Persistent or stubborn in holding to one's own opinion or design; resolute; obstinate. Chiefly as a bad quality. **b.** Obstinately or persistently continuing 1646.

P. importunity 1626. As p. as ivy climbing a wall 1805. Hence **Pertina·cious·ly** *adv.*, **-ness.**

Pertinacity (pɔ̄ɹtinæ·sĭti). 1504. [a. F. *pertinacité*, f. (ult.) L. *pertinacem, pertinax*; see prec.] The quality of being pertinacious; persistency; usu. in a bad sense: perverse obstinacy or stubbornness. So †**Pe·rtinacy.** late ME.

†**Pe·rtinate,** *a.* 1534. [irreg. formation, perh. after *intimate, intimacy*, etc.] = PERTINACIOUS -1552. So †**Pe·rtinately** *adv.* late ME.

Pertinence (pɔ̄·ɹtinĕns). late ME. [In sense 1, a. OF. *partenance*, f. *partenant, partenir* to belong; in 2, f. PERTINENT; see -ENCE.] †**1.** = PURTENANCE, APPURTENANCE 1, 2. -1552. **2.** The fact of being pertinent 1659.

Pertinency (pɔ̄·ɹtinĕnsi). 1598. [f. L. *pertinentem* PERTINENT; see -ENCY.] **1.** The quality of being pertinent; relevancy, appositeness. †**2.** = APPURTENANCE 1. 1651.

1. Loving p., and by consequence brevitie FLORIO.

Pertinent (pɔ̄·ɹtinĕnt), *a.* and *sb.* late ME. [ult. f. L. *pertinentem*, pr. pple. of *pertinere* to PERTAIN; but in early use immed. a. OF. *partenant.*] **A.** *adj.* †**1.** Pertaining or belonging (*to*) -1635. †**2.** Appropriate, suitable in nature or character -1697. **3.** Pertaining to the matter in hand; relevant; apposite. Const. *to.* late ME.

3. Judges who make p. remarks on the case JOWETT.

B. *sb.* (Chiefly *Sc.*) A minor property, appurtenance. Usu. in *pl.* late ME. Hence **Pe·rtinent·ly** *adv.*, **-ness** (*rare*).

Perturb (pəɹtɔ̄·ɹb), *v.* late ME. [a. OF. *per-, partourber, -turber*, ad. L. *perturbare*, f. PER-[1] 2 + *turbare.*] **1.** *trans.* To disturb greatly (physically); to unsettle, derange, throw into confusion. **2.** To disturb greatly (mentally); to agitate, discompose ME.

2. His childish imagination was perturbed at a phenomenon for which he could not account SCOTT.

Hence †**Pertu·rbance**, great disturbance; molestation; perturbation. **Pertu·rbed** *ppl. a.* disquieted, agitated; confused, deranged. **Pertu·rbedly** *adv.* **Pertu·rber**, a disturber, troubler.

Perturbate (pǝ·ɹtɒɹbeˈt, pǝɹtǝ̄·ɹbeˈt), *a.* 1570. [ad. L. *perturbatus*; see prec.] Disturbed, put out of order.

Perturbate (pǝ·ɹtɒɹbeˈt, pǝɹtǝ̄·ɹbeˈt), *v. rare.* 1547. [f. ppl. stem of L. *perturbare* to PERTURB.] *trans.* = PERTURB. Hence **Pe·rturbator** (now *rare*) = PERTURBER.

Perturbation (pǝ̄ɹtɒɹbēˈ·ʃǝn). late ME. [a. OF., ad. L. *perturbationem*, f. *perturbare* PERTURB.] 1. The action of perturbing; the fact or condition of being perturbed; disorder; mental agitation; trouble. Also occas. cause of disturbance. 2. Disturbance of the regular order or course 1567. b. *Astron.* The deviation of a heavenly body from its theoretically regular orbit, caused by the attraction of bodies other than its primary, or by the imperfectly spherical form of the latter 1812.

1. *Rich. III*, v. iii. 161, 2 *Hen. IV*, IV. v. 23. These various perturbations of mind, which are characteristic of a bad conscience NEWMAN. Hence **Perturba·tional** *a.* of, pertaining to, of the nature of p.

Perturbative (pǝɹtǝ̄·ɹbǎtiv, pǝ̄·ɹtɒɹbeˈtiv), *a.* 1638. [ad. late L. *perturbativus*, f. *perturbare* to PERTURB; see -IVE.] Causing or apt to cause perturbation or disturbance.

Pertuse (pǝɹtiū·s), *a. rare.* 1721. [ad. L. *pertusus*, *pertundere* to punch or bore into a hole, f. PER-¹ 1 + *tundere* to beat.] Bored through, pierced with holes; spec. in *Bot.*, applied to a leaf. So **Pertu·sed** *a.* †**Pertu·sion**, the action of punching or boring; a hole punched or bored 1626.

‖ **Pertussis** (pǝɹtɒ·sis). 1799. [mod.L., f. PER-¹ 4 + *tussis* cough.] *Path.* = HOOPING-COUGH. Hence **Pertu·ssal** *a.*

Peruke (pĕrū·k), *sb.* 1547. [a. F. *perruque*; origin unkn.] †1. A natural head of hair -1590. 2. A periwig or wig 1565. 3. *attrib.*, as *p.-block*, etc. 1547. Hence **Peru·ke** *v. trans. rare*, to furnish with a p.

Perule (pe·rūl). 1825. [a. F. *pérule*, ad. mod.L. *perula*, dim. of *pera*, a. Gr. πήρα purse, wallet.] *Bot.* †a. The covering of a seed. b. The scaly covering of a leaf-bud. c. A kind of sac formed by the adherent bases of the two lateral sepals in certain orchids.

Perusal (pĕrū·zăl). 1600. [f. next + -AL.] 1. Survey, examination, scrutiny. *Obs.* or *arch.* 1602. 2. A reading through or over.

1. He fals to such perusall of my face, As he would draw it SHAKS.

Peruse (pĕrū·z), *v.* 1479. [In sense 1, f. PER-¹ 1 or 2 + USE *v.*; in the other senses the element *-use* is not accounted for.] †1. *trans.* To use up -1570. †2. *trans.* To go through, deal with, describe, examine (a number of things) one by one -1716. b. To consider in detail (*arch.*) 1533. c. To travel through scrutinizingly. *Obs.* exc. *dial.* 1523. 3. *intr.* †To go from one to another of a series, to continue; to travel (*joc.*) 1523. †4. *trans.* To go over (a writing, etc.) again; to revise -1632. †b. To go through (a book) critically; to criticize; to set forth or expound critically -1551. 5. To read through or over; hence (loosely) to read 1532.

2. b. My self I then perus'd, and Limb by Limb Survey'd MILT. 5. I will show what to turn over unread and what to p. STEELE. Hence **Peru·se** *sb.* †perusal; *sailors' colloq.* a 'look round' ashore. **Peru·ser.**

Peruvian (pĕrū·viăn), *a.* (*sb.*) 1663. [f. mod.L. *Peruvia* + -AN.] Of, pertaining to, or native to Peru, in South America.

P. bark, the bark of the Cinchona tree; see BARK *sb.*¹ 6, CINCHONA.

B. *sb.* A native or inhabitant of Peru. b. *pl.* Peruvian stocks, bonds, etc. 1656.

Pervade (pǝɹvēˈ·d), *v.* 1653. [ad. L. *pervadere*, f. PER-¹ 1 + *vadere* to go, walk.] 1. *trans.* To pass through; to flow or extend through. Now *rare* 1656. 2. To diffuse itself throughout; to permeate, saturate 1659. b. *intr.* To diffuse itself. Now *rare* 1653.

1. I pervaded Westminster Hall and looked into most of the Courts 1892. 2. An ardent spirit of enquiry pervaded..Europe 1791. Hence **Perva·dingly** *adv.*, **-ness.** **Perva·sion**, the action of pervading; the condition of being pervaded. **Perva·sive** *a.* having the quality or power of pervading; **-ly** *adv.*; **-ness.**

Perverse (pǝɹvǝ̄·ɹs), *a.* late ME. [a. F. *pervers*, *-e*, ad. L. *perversus*, f. *pervertere* to PERVERT.] 1. Turned away from what is right; perverted; wicked. b. Incorrect; wrong 1568. c. *spec.* Of a verdict: against the weight of evidence or the direction of the judge on a point of law 1854. 2. Obstinate or persistent in what is wrong; self-willed or stubborn (in error) 1579. 3. Disposed to be obstinately contrary to what is true or good or to go counter to what is reasonable or required. late ME. †b. Of things or events: Adverse, unpropitious -1713.

1. O faithless and p. generation, how long shall I be with you *Matt.* xvii. 17. 2. P. neglect of the most salutary precepts JOHNSON. 3. I married the most p. woman in the world 1660. Hence †**Perve·rsed** *ppl. a.* (chiefly *Sc.*) = sense 1; †**-ly** *adv.*; †**-ness.** **Pe·rverse·ly** *adv.*, **-ness.**

Perversion (pǝɹvǝ̄·ɹʃǝn). late ME. [ad. L. *perversionem*, f. *pervertere* to PERVERT.] The action of perverting or condition of being perverted; turning aside from truth or right; diversion to an improper use; corruption, distortion; *spec.* change to error in religious belief (opp. to CONVERSION II. 1); *transf.* a perverted form *of* something.

Women to govern men,..slaves freemen,..being total violations and perversions of the laws of nature and nations BACON.

Perversity (pǝɹvǝ̄·ɹsĭti). 1528. [a. F. *perversité*, ad. L. *perversitas*, f. *perversus* PERVERSE.] Perverseness.

Perversive (pǝɹvǝ̄·ɹsiv), *a.* 1817. [f. L. *pervers-*, *pervertere* to PERVERT; see -IVE.] Having the character or quality of perverting in nature, character, or use.

Pervert (pǝɹvǝ̄·ɹt), *v.* late ME. [ad. F. *pervertir*, ad. L. *pervertere*, f. PER-¹ 2, 3 + *vertere* to turn.] †1. To turn upside down; to upset; to subvert -1656. 2. To turn aside from its right course, aim, meaning, etc. late ME. †b. To divert SHAKS. 3. *trans.* To turn (a person, the mind, etc.) away from right opinion or action; to lead astray; to corrupt. late ME. b. *spec.* To turn (any one) aside from a right religious belief or system. late ME. c. *intr.* To become a pervert. late ME.

2. They perverted the course of justice 1868. 3. How He [Satan] in the Serpent had perverted Eve, Her Husband shee MILT. Hence †**Perve·rt** *a.* perverted. **Pervert** (pǝ̄·ɹvǝɹt) *sb.* one who has been perverted or corrupted; an apostate. **Perve·rter**, one who perverts (a person or thing). **Perve·rtible** *a.* capable of being perverted.

†**Perve·stigate**, *v.* 1610. [f. L. *pervestigat-*, *pervestigare*, f. PER-¹ 2 + *vestigare* to track.] *trans.* To investigate diligently; to find out by research -1688. Hence †**Pervestiga·tion**, diligent investigation -1715.

†**Pe·rvial**, *a. rare.* 1595. [f. L. *pervius* PERVIOUS + -AL.] Pervious. CHAPMAN. Hence †**Pe·rvially** *adv.* clearly.

Pervicacious (pǝ̄ɹvikēˈ·ʃǝs), *a.* Now *rare.* 1633. [f. L. *pervicax*, *-cacem* stubborn (f. root *pervic-* of *pervincere*, f. PER-¹ 1 + *vincere* to conquer, prevail against) + -IOUS.] Very obstinate; headstrong, wilful; refractory. Hence **Pervica·cious·ly** *adv.*, **-ness.**

Pervicacity (pǝ̄ɹvikæ·sĭti). Now *rare.* 1604. [f. as prec. + -ITY.] The quality or state of being pervicacious. So †**Pe·rvicacy** 1537-1748.

Pervious (pǝ̄·ɹviǝs), *a.* 1614. [f. L. *pervius* (f. PER-¹ 1 + *via* way) + -OUS.] 1. Allowing of passage through; lying open *to* 1631. b. *esp.* Permeable 1627. c. *fig.* (*a*) Fully intelligible, 'transparent'; (*b*) Of a person or the mind: Accessible to influence or argument 1614. d. *Zool.* and *Bot.* Open, patent, patulous 1806. 2. Having the quality of passing through; pervasive. Now *rare* or *Obs.* 1684.

1. Every Country is p. to a wise Man 1659. b. A coarse argillaceous gravel, p. to water 1807. Hence **Pe·rviousness.**

‖ **Pes** (pīz). *Pl.* **pedes** (pe·dīz). 1842. [L., = foot.] 1. *Comp. Anat.* The terminal segment of the hind limb of a vertebrate animal. 2. *Bot.* A foot-like part or organ; a peduncle.

‖ **Peseta** (pĕsē·tă). 1811. [Sp., dim. of *pesa* weight.] A modern Spanish silver coin, equivalent to the French franc; now the unit of value in Spain.

‖ **Peshito** (pĕʃī·to), **Peshitta** (pĕʃī·tta), *a.* and *sb.* 1793. [Syriac *p'shīṭā, -ṭō, p'shīṭṭā, -ṭō*, 'the Simple' or 'Plain'.] The principal version of the Old and New Testaments in ancient Syriac, sometimes styled the Syriac Vulgate.

‖ **Peshwa** (pē·ʃwā). 1698. [Pers. = 'chief'.] The chief minister of the Maratha princes (from *c* 1660), who made himself in 1749 the hereditary sovereign of the Maratha state.

Pesky (pe·ski), *a. U.S. colloq.* 1845. [perh. alteration of *pesty* (E. A. Poe), f. PEST.] 'Plaguy', 'confounded'; annoying, disagreeable; hateful, abominable.

‖ **Peso** (pē·so). 1555. [Sp., = 'weight':—L. *pensum*; see PEISE *sb.*] A coin, either of gold or silver, formerly current in Spain and its colonies; now, a standard silver coin used in most of the S. American republics.

Pessary (pe·sări). late ME. [ad. med.L. *pessarium*, f. L. *pessum*, *-us*, a. Gr. πεσσός an oval stone used in playing a game like draughts; hence, a medicated plug.] 1. *Med.* A medicated plug of wool, lint, etc., to be inserted in the neck of the womb, etc., for the cure of various ailments; a suppository. 2. *Surg.* An instrument worn in the vagina to prevent or remedy various uterine displacements 1754.

Pessimism (pe·simiz'm). 1794. [f. L. *pessimus* worst + -ISM, after *optimism*.] †1. The worst condition possible; cf. OPTIMISM 2. -1812. 2. The tendency to look at the worst aspect of things; cf. OPTIMISM 3. 1815. 3. The doctrine that this world is the worst possible, or that everthing naturally tends to evil; opp. to OPTIMISM 1. 1878.

Pessimist (pe·simist), *sb.* (*a.*) 1836. [f. as prec. + -IST.] 1. a. One who habitually takes the worst view of things. b. One who holds the metaphysical doctrine of pessimism. B. *adj.* (the sb. used *attrib.*) Characterized by pessimism 1861.

A p. view of the situation 1868. Hence **Pessimi·stic**, **-al** *adjs.* pertaining to, of the nature of, or characterized by pessimism; disposed to take the worst view of things; **-ly** *adv.*

‖ **Pessulus** (pe·siŭlǝs). 1890. [L., a bolt.] *Anat.* In some birds, the cartilaginous or bony bar extending vertically across the lower end of the windpipe, and forming part of the syrinx.

Pest (pest). 1568. [a. F. *peste*, ad. L. *pestis* plague.] 1. Any deadly epidemic disease; pestilence; *spec.* the bubonic plague. Now *rare.* 2. Any thing or person that is noxious, destructive, or troublesome; a bane, curse, plague 1609.

1. The p. came to Edinburgh 1637. 2. Philippe IV, the p. of France 1852. *Comb.* **p.-cart** (now *Hist.*), the cart used to carry away the bodies of the dead during a plague or pestilence. Hence †**Pe·stful** *a.* pestiferous, pestilential.

Pestalozzian (pestălǫ·tsiăn), *a.* (*sb.*) 1826. [f. surname *Pestalozzi* + -AN.] A. *adj.* Of or pertaining to the system of education introduced by Jean Henri *Pestalozzi* (1746-1827), a Swiss teacher, which aimed at the development of the faculties in a natural order, beginning with the perceptive powers. B. *sb.* An adherent of the system of Pestalozzi 1868. Hence **Pestalo·zzianism**, Pestalozzi's system of education.

Pester (pe·stǝɹ), *v.* 1524. [perh. aphetic f. OF. *empestrer*, also *empasturer* (Walloon *epasturer*) to hobble a horse while feeding, f. (ult.) L. *in* + *pastorium* tether for a horse, f. *pasci* (stem *past-*) to feed. Influenced later by PEST, whence the sense 'plague'.] †1. *trans.* To clog, embarrass, obstruct the movements of; to encumber (*lit.* and *fig.*) -1676. †2. To obstruct (a place) by crowding; to overcrowd -1748. †3. To crowd (persons or things *in* or *into*) -1686. 4. To annoy, trouble persistently, plague. (The current sense.) 1562.

4. I pestered him with questions 1795. [Malabar] is..pestered with green adders 1796. Hence **Pe·ster** *sb.* †obstruction; bother; nuisance. Hence **Pe·sterer.** **Pe·sterment** (*Obs.* exc. *dial.*), pestering or being pestered; †overcrowding; annoyance, worry. **Pe·sterous** *a. rare*, having the quality of pestering; cumbersome; troublesome.

Pe·st-house. 1611. [f. PEST + HOUSE *sb.*] A hospital for persons suffering from any infectious disease, esp. the plague; a lazaretto.

†**Pe·stiduct.** 1624. [f. L. *pestis* plague + *ductus* DUCT.] A channel of the plague, or of any infectious epidemic –1672.

Pestiferous (pesti·fĕrəs), *a.* 1458. [f. L. *pestifer, -ferus*, f. *pestis* PEST + *-fer*; see -FEROUS. In F. *pestifère*.] **I. 1.** Bringing pest or plague; noxious, deadly; of the nature of a pest, pestilential 1542. **2.** *fig.* Bearing moral contagion; mischievous, pernicious 1458.

1. These women are a p. kinde of animals 1600. Regions almost desolated by p. exhalations HERSCHEL. 2. P. hordes of gamblers 1824.

II. [= F. *pestiféré*.] Plague-stricken 1665.

Multitudes of poore p. creatures begging almes EVELYN. Hence **Pesti·ferous-ly** *adv.*, **-ness.**

Pestilence (pe·stilĕns). ME. [a. F., ad. L. *pestilentia*, f. *pestilentem* PESTILENT; see -ENCE.] **1.** Any fatal epidemic disease, affecting man or beast, and destroying many victims. **b.** *spec.* The bubonic plague, the plague *par excellence*. late ME. **2.** *fig.* That which is morally pestilent; that which is fatal to the public peace or well-being. Now *rare*. ME. †**3.** That which plagues in any way –1555. †**4.** As an imprecation –1612.

1. The p. that walketh in darkness *Ps.* xci. 6. **b.** This yere was the iij. great pestelens 1556. 2. O flaterie! o lurkyng p. HOCCLEVE. 4. A verray p. vpon yow falle CHAUCER. *Comb.* **p.-weed, -wort,** the Butterbur, *Petasites vulgaris* (from its repute against the plague).

Pestilent (pe·stilĕnt), *a.* (*adv.*) late ME. [ad. L. *pestilens, -entem*, a ppl. deriv. from *pestis* plague, PEST; also *pestilentus*.] **1.** Destructive to life; deadly; poisonous. **2.** Infectious as a disease or epidemic; pestilential. Now *rare*. 1613. **3.** *fig.* Injurious to religion, morals, or public peace; noxious, pernicious 1513. **4.** That pesters or annoys; plaguy. Often *joc.* 1592. †**B.** *adv.* Confoundedly; 'plaguy' –1700.

A. 1. The influence of a p. planet 1564. P. opium 1880. **2.** Vapour, and Mist, and Exhalation hot, Corrupt and P. MILT. **3.** P. books 1758. **4.** What a p. knaue is this same SHAKS. **B.** *Oth.* II. i. 251. Hence **Pe·stilent-ly** *adv.*, **-ness.**

Pestilential (pestile·nʃăl), *a.* late ME. [ad. med.L. *pestilentialis*, f. L. *pestilentia* PESTILENCE; see -AL.] **1.** Producing or tending to produce pestilence; noxious to life or health; pestiferous. **2.** Of the nature of or pertaining to pestilence, *esp.* bubonic plague 1530. **3.** Morally baneful or pernicious 1531.

1. A p. malignancy in the air, occasioned by the comet SWIFT. 2. A p. disease GIBBON. 3. So p., so infectious a thing is sin JER. TAYLOR. Hence **Pestile·ntially** *adv.* So †**Pestilentious** *a.*

Pestle (pe·s'l, pe·st'l), *sb.* [ME. a. OF. *pestel, -eil*:—L. *pistillum, -us*, dim. of **pistrum*, f. *pistum, pinsere* to pound, etc.] **1.** An instrument, (usu. club-shaped) for bruising or pounding substances in a mortar. Also *fig.* **2.** Applied to various appliances for pounding, stamping, pressing, etc.; e.g. a stamp, etc. 1604. **3.** The leg of certain animals, used for food, *esp.* the haunch of a pig. Now *dial.* ME. †**4.** A constable's truncheon or club CHAPMAN. †**5.** *Bot.* Early form of PISTIL, q.v.

1. *P. and mortar*, esp. those used by an apothecary in compounding drugs; hence taken as the symbol of the profession. 3. Phr. †*The p. of a lark, fig.* a trifle, something very small.

Pe·stle, *v.* late ME. [a. OF. *pesteler*, f. *pestel*; see prec.] **1.** *trans.* To beat, pound, or triturate, with or as with a pestle. **2.** *intr.* To use or work with a pestle 1866.

Pestology (pestǫ·lŏdʒi). 1921. [f. PEST *sb.* + -OLOGY.] The study of pests, *esp.* of insect pests.

Pet (pet), *sb.*[1] 1508. [orig. Sc. and north. Eng.; origin unkn.] **1.** Any animal that is domesticated or tamed and kept as a favourite, or treated with fondness; esp. applied to a lamb reared by hand. **2. a.** An indulged (and, usu., spoiled) child 1508. **b.** Any person who is specially indulged; a darling, favourite. Also *transf.* of a thing. 1825. **3.** *attrib.* **a.** Of an animal: kept as a pet 1584. **b.** Specially cherished; favourite. Also (*joc.* or ironically) *p. aversion*, that which one specially dislikes. 1832. **c.** Expressing fondness, endearing; chiefly in **p. name** (often hyphened), a hypocoristic name 1829.

1. The other has transferred the amorous Passions of her first Years to the Love of Cronies, Petts and Favourites STEELE. 2. **b.** The p. of society 1902. 3. **a.** The P. Lamb WORDSW. (*title*). **b.** My own particular p. scrubbing brush has been used for black-leading 1898. Hence **Pet** *v.*[1] to make a p. of; to indulge; to fondle; often in **Pe·tting** *vbl. sb.*

Pet (pet), *sb.*[2] 1590. [Origin obsc.] Offence at being (or feeling) slighted or not made enough of; a fit of ill humour from this cause.

To take (the) p., to take offence and become sulky. Hence †**Pet** *v.*[2] *intr.* to be in a p.; to take offence at one's treatment; to sulk –1837.

Petal (pe·tăl). 1726. [ad. mod.L. *petalum* (cf. PETALON) in ancient L. in sense 'metal plate', a. Gr. πέταλον thin plate, leaf, f. root πετ- to spread.] *Bot.* Each of the divisions (modified leaves) of the corolla of a flower (see COROLLA 2), esp. when separate. Hence **Petali·ferous** *a.* bearing petals. **Pe·taliform** *a.* petaloid. **Pe·taline** *a.* pertaining to a p.; situated on a p.; consisting of petals; petaloid. **Pe·talled, petaled** *a.* having petals; also in parasynthetic compounds, as *crimson-petalled, six-petalled*.

Petalism (pe·tăliz'm). 1612. [ad. Gr. πεταλισμός, f. πέταλον leaf; see -ISM.] *Anc. Hist.* A method of temporary banishment (for five years) practised in ancient Syracuse, similar to the OSTRACISM of Athens, but effected by writing the name of the person on an olive leaf.

Petalite (pe·tăləit). 1808. [f. Gr. πέταλον leaf + -ITE.] *Min.* A silicate of aluminium and lithium, occurring in whitish or greyish masses having leaf-like cleavage.

Petalody (pe·tălōudi). 1869. [f. Gr. πεταλώδης leaf-like, f. πέταλον leaf; see -ODE.] *Bot.* The condition of having other organs or parts of the flower modified into the form of petals; e.g. the stamens in most 'double' flowers.

Petaloid (pe·tăloid), *a.* 1730. [ad. mod.L. *petaloideus*, f. L. *petalum* PETAL; see -OID.] **1.** *Bot.* Of the form of, or resembling, a petal. **b.** Belonging to the *Petaloideæ*, a division of monocotyledons having normally flowers with ordinary coloured petals or p. parts, as lilies, orchids, etc. 1836. **2.** *Zool.* Applied to the ambulacra of certain echinoids, which have a dilated portion and a tapering extremity, suggesting the petals of a flower 1862. So **Petaloi·dal** *a.*

‖**Petalon** (pe·tălǫn). 1678. [a. Gr. πέταλον.] The plate of gold worn on the linen mitre of the Jewish high priest.

Petalostichous (petălǫ·stikəs), *a.* [f. mod. L. *Petalosticha* (f. Gr. πέταλον leaf + στίχος row) + -OUS.] *Zool.* Having petaloid ambulacra; belonging to the division *Petalosticha* of Echinoids.

Petalous (pe·tăləs), *a. rare.* 1730. [f. L. *petalum* + -OUS.] Having petals: opp. to *apetalous*.

Petard (pĭtā·ɹd, pĭtā·ɹ), *sb.* 1598. [a. F. *pétard*, f. *péter* to break wind; see -ARD.] **1.** A small engine of war used to blow in a door or gate, or to make a breach in a wall, etc.; orig. of metal and bell-shaped, later a cubical wooden box, charged with powder, and fired by a fuse. Also *fig.* **2.** A kind of firework; a cracker 1634.

1. To haue the enginer Hoist with his owne petar SHAKS. Hence †**Peta·rd** *v.* to blow open, or breach, with a p. †**Petardee·r, -ier,** a soldier who manages a p.

‖**Petasus** (pe·tăsŏs). 1599. [L., a. Gr. πέτασος, f. root πετ- spread out.] A low-crowned broad-brimmed hat worn by the ancient Greeks; also, the winged hat of Hermes.

Petaurist (pĭtǭ·rist). 1656. [ad. Gr. πεταυριστής a performer on the πέταυρον or spring-board.] †**1.** An acrobat, tumbler, rope-dancer (*rare*) –1658. **2.** *Zool.* Any marsupial of the genus *Petaurista* or subfamily *Petaurinæ*, most of which have a parachute enabling them to take flying leaps; a flying phalanger, etc.

Pet-cock. 1848. [app. f. PET *sb.*[1] + COCK *sb.*[1]] A small plug-cock fastened in a pipe or cylinder, as in a pump or a steam-engine, for purposes of draining or testing.

‖**Petechia** (pĭtī·kiă); usu. in pl. **petechiæ** (-kiį). 1794. [mod.L., a. It. *petecchia* a freckle, etc. Origin unkn.] *Path.* A small red or purple spot in the skin caused by extravasation of blood, occurring in certain fevers, etc. So **Pete·chial** *a.* of the nature of, pertaining to, or characterized by petechiæ 1710.

Peter (pī·təɹ), *sb.* [In 12th c. *Peter*, ad. L. *Petrus*, a. Gr. Πέτρος, lit. 'stone', translating Syriac *kēfā* (græcized *Cephas*) 'stone', the surname conferred by Christ upon Simon Bar-jona (Matt. xvi. 17), historically known as St. Peter.] A male Christian name; hence in many transf. uses, mostly referring directly or indirectly to St. Peter.

1. Used in proverbial phrases in conjunction with *Paul*; esp. in *to rob P. to pay Paul*, to take away from one person, cause, etc. in order to pay another; to discharge one debt by incurring another. late ME. 2. *Thieves' Cant.* A portmanteau or trunk; a bundle or parcel 1668. 3. **Blue Peter,** see BLUE *a.* (also simply *Peter*).

Comb. **(St.) Peter's bark, boat,** the (Roman) Catholic Church; **(St.) Peter's fish,** the haddock, or other fish, having marks affirmed in legend to have been made by St. Peter's thumb and finger when he caught the fish for the tribute-money (Matt. xvii. 27); **Peter's penny**: see PETER-PENNY. **St. Peter's wort** (also **(St.) Peterwort**), (*a*) the Cowslip (= Herb Peter); (*b*) certain species of *Hypericum*; also *Ascyrum*; (*c*) Feverfew, *Pyrethrum Parthenium*.

Peter (pī·təɹ), *v. slang* or *colloq.* 1812. [Origin unkn.] **1.** *trans.* To stop, leave off (*slang*). **2.** *intr.* *To p. out* (orig. *U.S. Mining colloq.*): to run out and disappear (as a stream, a vein of ore); to die out, fail 1865.

Pe·ter-boat. 1540. [app. f. PETER *sb.* + BOAT.] Local name (on the Thames, etc.) for a decked fishing-boat smaller than a smack or yawl; also a dredger-man's double-ended boat.

Peterman (pī·təɹmæ̆n). late ME. [app. f. PETER *sb.* (in allusion to the occupation of Simon Peter).] A fisherman.

Pe·ter-pe·nny, Peter's penny. Usu. in pl. Peter's pence. ME. [f. PETER *sb.* (in ref. to the claim of the see of Rome to the patrimony of St. Peter) + PENNY.] **1.** *Hist.* An annual tax or tribute of a penny from each householder having land of a certain value paid before the Reformation to the papal see. **2.** Applied to voluntary contributions of Roman Catholics to the papal treasury since 1860.

Petersham (pī·təɹʃăm). 1812 [f. Viscount *Petersham*, c 1812.] (*attrib.*, or *ellipt.* as *sb.*) **a.** Name for a heavy overcoat or breeches formerly fashionable; also for the cloth of which such overcoats are made. **b.** A thick kind of ribbon of ribbed or corded silk, used for hat-bands, etc.

Petiole (pe·tioul). 1753. [ad. L. *petiolus* little foot, stem, stalk of fruit.] **1.** *Bot.* The footstalk of a leaf, by which it is attached to the stem; a leaf-stalk. **2.** *Zool.* A slender stalk-like structure supporting some part, as the eye-stalk in certain Crustacea, etc. 1782. Hence **Pe·tiolar** *a.* of, pertaining to, or of the nature of a p. **Pe·tiolate(d)** *adjs.* having a p.; stalked; borne upon a p. **Pe·tioled** *a.* petiolate.

Petiolule (pe·tiǫliul). 1832. [ad. mod.L. *petiolulus*, dim. of *petiolus*.] *Bot.* A partial or secondary petiole; the footstalk of a leaflet in a compound leaf. Hence **Petio·lulate** *a.* having, or borne upon, a p.

Petit (†pe·tit), *a.* (*sb.*) ME. [a. F. *petit*, fem. *petite*; perh. from a Celtic root *pett-*; whence also It. *pezza*, F. *pièce*, Eng. *piece*.] †**1.** Of small size, small –1675. †**2.** = PETTY *a.* 2. –1759. †**3.** = PETTY *a.* 3. –1641. **4.** In special collocations (rarely hyphened) as a var. of *petty*: **Petit Bag, Officer**: see PETTY BAG, PETTY OFFICER; also petit SESSIONS, TREASON, etc. **5. P. point** = TENT-STITCH. ‖**6.** (pəti) In mod.F. petit verre, a glass of liqueur [*lit.* small glass] 1858. †**B.** *sb.* A junior schoolboy. Also *transf.* –1691.

Petite (pətī·t, pĕtī·t), *a.* 1712. [See prec.] †**1.** A var. of PETIT (without ref. to gender or sex). **2.** Of a woman or girl: Little, of small stature or size, tiny 1784. **3.** In F. **petite morale,** minor morals; **petite pièce,** a minor performance; in *pl.* the minor writings of an author (formerly as Eng. *petite pieces*) 1712.

‖**Petitio** (pĭti·ʃiō). 1706. [L.; see next.] The L. word for 'asking, begging, petitioning, petition', in some phrases: esp. ‖**P. induciarum** (indiuʃiē·rǒm). *Law* = IMPARLANCE 2.

1706; ‖**P. principii** (pĭti·ʃio prinsi·piˌəi). *Logic* [lit. taking the beginning or a principle for granted], the fallacy of taking for granted a premiss which is either equivalent to, or itself depends on, the conclusion; an instance of this 1531.

Petition (pĭti·ʃən), *sb.* ME. [a. F. *pétition*, ad. L. *petitionem*, f. *petere*.] **1.** The action of formally asking, begging, supplicating, or humbly requesting late ME. **2.** A supplication or prayer; an entreaty; *esp.* a solemn and humble prayer to the Deity, or to a sovereign or superior; also, one of the clauses of a prayer ME. **b.** *transf.* The thing asked or entreated 1440. **3.** A formally drawn up request or supplication; *esp.* a written supplication addressed to a superior, or to a person or body in authority (as a sovereign or legislature), soliciting some favour, right, or mercy, or the redress of some wrong or grievance 1450. **4.** *Law.* A formal application in writing made to a court (*a*) for judicial action concerning the matter of a suit then pending before it; (*b*) for something which lies in the jurisdiction of the court without an action, as a writ of *habeas corpus*, etc.; (*c*) in some forms of procedure initiating a suit or its equivalent 1737. †**5.** *Math.* A postulate; an axiom –1795.

1. P., peaceable p., is the course COBBETT. **2.** Our p. in the Litany, against sudden death RUSKIN. **b.** *Jul. C.* II. i. 58. **3.** Phr. *P. and Advice* (*Eng. Hist.*), the Remonstrance presented by Parliament to Cromwell on 4 Apr. 1657. *P. of Right*, the parliamentary declaration of the rights and liberties of the people, assented to by King Charles I in 1628. **4.** *P. of right* (*Law*), an ancient Common Law remedy against the Crown for obtaining possession or restitution of real or personal property 1467.

Petition (pĭti·ʃən), *v.* 1607. [f. prec.] **1.** *trans.* To address a petition to; to make a humble request or supplication to; *spec.* to address a formal written petition to (a sovereign, legislature, court, etc.) **b.** To beg for (a thing) 1631. **2.** *absol.* or *intr.* To address or present a petition; to ask humbly (*for* something) 1634.

1. You haue, I know, petition'd All the Gods for my prosperitie SHAKS. **b.** All that I hope, p., or expect CRABBE. Hence **Peti·tioning** *vbl. sb.* the action of making or presenting a petition; *ppl. a.* that petitions; *petitioning creditor*, one who asks for a declaration of bankruptcy against his debtor.

Petitionary (pĭti·ʃənări), *a.* 1579. [ad. med.L. *petitionarius*, f. *petitionem* PETITION; see -ARY [1].] **1.** Of the nature of, containing or characteristic of a petition. **2.** Of persons: Suppliant. *Obs.* or *arch.* 1607. †**3.** Containing a *petitio principii* SIR T. BROWNE.

2. To say no to a poor p. rogue LAMB. Hence **Peti·tionarily** *adv.* in a p. manner.

Petitionee (pĭtiʃənī·). 1764. [f. PETITION *v.* + -EE.] *U.S. Law.* The person or party against whom a petition is filed.

Petitioner (pĭti·ʃənəɹ). late ME. [f. PETITION *sb.* + -ER [2].] **1.** One who presents a petition. **b.** *Hist.* One of those who signed the address to Charles II in 1680, petitioning for the summoning of Parliament 1757. **2.** *Law.* **a.** A plaintiff in an action commenced by petition. **b.** A petitioning creditor 1503.

‖**Petit-maître** (pətiˌmɛ̄tr). 1711. [F., = little master.] An effeminate man; a dandy, coxcomb. Also *attrib.*

‖**Petit mal** (pəti mal). 1891. [F., = little evil.] The milder form of epilepsy.

†**Peti·tor.** *rare.* 1613. [a. L., f. *petere* to seek.] A seeker, applicant, candidate –1655.

Petitory (pe·titəri), *a.* 1579. [ad. late L. *petitorius*; see prec. and -ORY.] **1.** Petitionary, supplicatory. Now *rare.* **2.** *Law.* Characterized by laying claim to something; in *p. action*, etc., an action claiming title or right of ownership, as distinct from mere possession, in anything 1602.

‖**Petit souper** (pəti supe). 1765. [F.] A little supper; an unceremonious supper for a few intimates.

Petralogy: see PETROLOGY.

Petrarchal (pĭtrā·ɹkăl), *a.* 1818. [f. *Petrarch*, It. *Petrarca*, surname + -AL.] Of, pertaining to, or in the style of the Italian poet Petrarch (1304–74). So **Petra·rchan** *a.* (also *sb.* = *Petrarchist*) 1827. **Petra·rchian** *a.* 1801. **Pe·trarchist**, an imitator of Petrarch 1823.

Petrary (pe·trări). Now *Hist.* 1610. [ad. med.L. *petraria* fem., f. *petra* stone.] A mediæval military engine for discharging stones.

Petre (pī·təɹ). 1594. [In sense 1, abbrev. of SALTPETRE; in 2, ad. L. *petra*, Gr. πέτρα rock.] **1.** = SALTPETRE. (Now only *technical colloq.*) †**2.** *Oil of p.*: rock-oil, petroleum –1741.

Petrean (pĭtrī·ăn), *a. rare.* 1632. [f. L. *petræus* (a. Gr. πετραῖος rocky, f. πέτρα rock) + -AN.] Rocky; of or pertaining to rocks or stones; of Arabia Petræa.

Petrel (pe·trĕl). 1676. [orig. *pitteral*; perh. repr. a. L. dim. of *Petrus*, St. Peter.] A small sea-bird, *Procellaria pelagica*, with black and white plumage and long wings; hence extended to any species of the genus *Procellaria* (Storm-Petrels or Stormy Petrels), or of the family *Procellariidæ*, or order *Tubinares*.

†**Petrescent** (pĭtre·sĕnt), *a.* 1663. [f. L. *petra* stone + -ESCENT.] prop. Becoming petrified; but usu., petrifactive. So †**Petre·scence**, †**-ency**, the process of petrifaction; formation of calculus.

Petrifaction (petrifæ·kʃən). 1646. [f. PETRIFY; see -FACTION.] **1.** The action of petrifying, or condition of being petrified; conversion into stone or stony substance; in *Path.* formation of 'stone' or calculus. **2.** *concr.* Something petrified, or formed by conversion into stone; a stony concretion, as in fossils, stalactites and stalagmites 1686.

1. *fig.* This is making a p. both of love and poetry HAZLITT. **2.** *fig.* He gives you the p. of a sigh HAZLITT. So **Petrifa·ctive** *a.* causing p.

Petrific (pĭtri·fik), *a.* Now *rare.* 1667. [ad. med.L. *petrificus*, f. *petra* rock, stone; see -FIC.] **1.** Having the quality of petrifying; petrifactive; in *Path.* causing the formation of 'stone' or calculus. **2.** *loosely.* Petrified, stony 1804.

1. Death with his Mace p. MILT. *fig.* A look meant to be nothing less than p. MISS BURNEY.

Petrification (pe:trifikēⁱ·ʃən). Now *rare.* 1611. [a. F. *pétrification*, ult. f. L. **petrificare*; see next.] = PETRIFACTION.

Petrify (pe·trifəi), *v.* 1594. [a. F. *pétrifier*, ad. L. type **petrificare*, f. *petra* rock; see -FY.] **1.** *trans.* To convert into stone or stony substance; *spec.* to turn (an organic body) into a stony concretion by replacing its original substance by a calcareous or other mineral deposit; also, *loosely*, to encrust with such a deposit. Also *absol.* **2.** *fig.* To change as if into stone. **a.** To harden, benumb, deaden, stiffen 1626. **b.** To make motionless or rigid, e.g. with fear, etc. (Chiefly *passive.*) 1771. **3.** *intr.* (for *pass.*) To become converted into stone or stony substance 1646.

1. Albertus gives an account of a tree..with a nest and birds petrified 1750. **2. a.** To p. a doctrine into an outward formula 1892. **b.** I was almost petrified with horror at the intelligence 1786. **3.** *fig.* Like Niobe we marble grow, And p. with grief DRYDEN. Hence **Pe·trified** *ppl. a.* changed into stone or stony substance; represented or embodied in stone; stupefied, 'paralysed' with surprise, etc.

Petrine (pī·trəin), *a.* 1846. [f. L. *Petrus* PETER + -INE; cf. PAULINE.] Of, pertaining to, or characteristic of the Apostle Peter.

P. claims, the claims of the popes as successors of St. Peter.

Petro- (petro), properly comb. form of Gr. πέτρος stone or πέτρα rock, as in PETROGLYPH, etc. In *Anat.* used to form adjs. descriptive of parts connected with the petrous portion of the temporal bone and some other part: as **Petrohy·oid, Petroma·stoid**, etc.

Petrobrusian (petrobrū·siăn). 1559. [ad. L. *Petrobrusiani* pl., f. name of Pierre de Bruys (*Petrus Brusianus*).] *Ch. Hist.* A member of a sect founded by Peter or Pierre de Bruys in the South of France in the 12th c., who rejected infant baptism, transubstantiation, etc.

Petroglyph (pe·trŏglif). 1870. [ad. F. *pétroglyphe*, f. Gr. πέτρα rock + -γλυφή carving.] A rock-carving (usu. prehistoric). So **Petrogly·phic** *a.* belonging to or of the nature of a p. **Petro·glyphy**, rock-carving.

Petrography (pĭtrǫ·grăfi). 1651. [f. Gr. πέτρα rock + -GRAPHY.] The scientific description of the composition and formation of rocks; descriptive petrology. So **Petrogra·phic, -al** *adjs.* of or pertaining to p.; dealing with p.

Petrol (pe·trǫl). 1585. [a. F. *pétrole, petrolle*, ad. med.L. PETROLEUM.] †**1.** = PETROLEUM –1811. **2.** *Chem.* A hydrocarbon (C_8H_{10}) occurring in petroleum 1866. **3.** [Reintroduced from Fr.] A name for refined petroleum as used in motor-cars, etc. Also *attrib.*, as *p. engine, pipe, pump.* 1895.

‖**Petrolatum** (petrǒlēⁱ·tǒm). 1887. [mod. L., f. PETROL + -*atum* in *acetatum*, etc.; see -ATE [1] c.] The official name in the U. S. Pharmacopœia for pure petroleum jelly, called in the British Pharmacopœia *paraffinum molle*.

Petroleum (pĭtrōᵘ·liǒm). 1526. [a. med. L. *petroleum*, f. L. *petra* (Gr. πέτρα) rock + *oleum* oil.] A mineral oil, varying from light yellow to dark brown or black, occurring in rocks or on the surface of water in various parts of the world, used esp. as a source of oils for illumination and mechanical power; rock-oil.

attrib. and *Comb.*, as *p.-car, -filter, -lamp*, etc.; **p.-ether**, a volatile oil obtained from p., also called *naphthalic ether*; **-oil** = petroleum; in mod. use dist. from **p.-spirit**, whose vapour flashes at lower temperatures. Hence **Petro·leous** *a.* abounding in or containing p.

‖**Pétroleur** (petrolör). 1871. [F., f. *pétrole* + -*eur*, ending of masc. agent-nouns.] A (male) incendiary who uses petroleum. Also ‖**Pétroleuse** (petrolöz) [fem. of this], a female who does the same.

Petrolic (pĭtrǫ·lik), *a.* 1899. [f. PETROL + -IC.] Of or pertaining to petrol or petroleum.

Petrolin (pe·trolin). 1831. [f. PETROLEUM or PETROL + -IN.] A substance obtained from Rangoon petroleum, identical with *paraffin*. **b.** Trade name for an oil obtained from petroleum.

Petrology (pĭtrǫ·lŏdʒi). 1811. [f. Gr. πέτρα rock + -OLOGY; orig. formed erron. as *petralogy*.] That branch of geology which deals with the origin, structure, and composition of rocks. So **Petrolo·gic, -al** *adjs.*, **-ly** *adv.* **Petro·logist**, one versed in p.

Petronel (pe·trǒnĕl). Now *Hist.* or *arch.* 1577. [a. F. *petrinal*, dial. form of *poitrinal*, f. *poitrine* breast, chest, f. (ult.) L. *pectus*, pl. *pectora*. So called because the butt end rested against the chest in firing.] A kind of large pistol or carbine, used in the 16th and early 17th c., esp. by horse-soldiers.

Petrosal (pĭtrōᵘ·săl), *a.* (*sb.*) 1741. [f. L. *petrosus* rocky + -AL.] *Anat.* Applied to the petrous portion of the temporal bone (med.L. *os petrosum*), and parts connected with it. **b.** *absol.* as *sb.* = Petrosal bone 1848.

Petrosilex (petroˌsəi·leks). 1770. [mod. L., f. *petrus* stone + *silex* flint.] *Min.* A hard rock; an early name for felsite. Hence **Pe:trosili·ceous** *a.* consisting of or containing p.

Petrous (pe·trəs), *a.* 1541. [f. L. *petrosus* stony, rocky.] Of the nature of, or as hard as, stone or rock; stony, rocky; in *Anat.* applied to the hard part of the temporal bone protecting the internal ear.

Petted (pe·tĕd), *ppl. a.* 1724. [f. PET *v.*[1] + -ED [1].] Treated as a pet or favourite; spoiled by petting or indulgence.

Pettichaps (pe·tiˌtʃæps). 1674. [f. PETTY *a.* + (app.) CHAP *sb.*[2] or [3].] The Garden Warbler (*Sylvia hortensis*). Also applied to other species of warblers; *dial.* the long-tailed titmouse.

Petticoat (pe·tikoᵘt), *sb.* (*a.*) late ME. [orig. two words, *petty coat*, lit. little or small coat.] **1.** †A small coat worn by men beneath the doublet –1542. **2.** *gen.* A garment worn by women, girls, and young children 1464. *spec.* **a.** A skirt as dist. from a bodice, worn either externally, or beneath the gown or frock 1602. **b.** An underskirt 1596. †**c.** The skirt of a woman's riding-habit –1824. **d.** The rudimentary garment worn by women among primitive or uncivilized peoples 1698. **3.** *pl.* Skirts collectively; also, skirts worn by young children; chiefly in phr. (said of a boy) *in petticoats* 1600. **4.** (Chiefly *pl.*) As the typical feminine garment; hence as the symbol of the female sex or character 1593. **b.** (*sing.*) A female; the female sex 1600. **5.** Applied joc. or contemp-

ö (Ger. Köln). ǒ (Fr. peu). ü (Ger. Müller). ŭ (Fr. dune). ǝ̆ (curl). ē (ēº) (there). ē (ēⁱ) (rein). ɛ̄ (Fr. faire). ɜ (fir, fern, earth).

tuously to the skirts of a clergyman's dress; also descriptively to the kilt of the Highlander, the fustanella of the Greek, etc. 1730. **6.** Anything resembling a petticoat; e.g. a toilet-table cover reaching down to the floor 1864; the inverted cup of a p. insulator (see below); also = *p. insulator* 1906.

2. a. A winning wave (deserving note) In the tempestuous petticote HERRICK. She was in her new suit of black sarcenet and yellow petticoate very pretty PEPYS. **b.** A good flannel p. ought to be little the worse for one year's wear 1844. **3.** I have known him ever since he was in petticoats 1877. **4.** Beatrice Cenci is really none other than Percy Bysshe Shelley himself in petticoats KINGSLEY. **b.** Can't do business with a p. in the room 1864.

II. *attrib.* (often = adj.) **a.** In petticoats; female; womanish. (Often hyphened.) Now *rare.* 1625. **b.** Executed, performed, wielded by a woman; feminine 1660.

a. To ridicule the p. pedant 1797. **b.** P. influence 1850.

Comb.: **p. government,** (undue) predominance of women in the home or in politics. **p. insulator,** an inverted cup-shaped insulator of porcelain or the like that supports a telegraph wire; **p.-pipe,** a bell-mouthed pipe in the chimney of a locomotive into which the exhaust-steam enters and which serves to equalize the draught. Hence **Pe·tticoated** *a.* having or wearing petticoats; also *transf.*

Pettifog (pe·tifǫg), *v.* 1611. [app. back-formation from PETTIFOGGER.] *intr.* To act as a pettifogger; to conduct a petty case in a minor court of law; to practise legal chicanery; also *transf.* to quibble about very small points.

Pettifogger (pe·tifǫgəɹ). 1564. [f. PETTY + FOGGER[1].] **1.** A legal practitioner of inferior status, who gets up or conducts petty cases; *esp.* one who employs mean, cavilling practices. **2.** *transf.* A petty practitioner in any department; an empiric, pretender 1602.

Hence **Pe·ttifoggery,** pettifogging practice; legal chicanery.

Pettifogging (pe·tifǫgiŋ), *vbl. sb.* 1580. [f. as PETTIFOG *v.* + -ING[1].] The action of a pettifogger; chicanery, pettifoggery; quibbling.

Pettifogging (pe·tifǫgiŋ), *ppl. a.* 1603. [f. as prec. + -ING[2].] Acting as a pettifogger; mean, shifty, quibbling; also, pertaining to or characteristic of pettifoggers.

Pettish (pe·tiʃ), *a.* 1591. [f. PET *sb.*[2] + -ISH[1].] Subject to fits of offended ill humour; in a pet; pertaining to, or of the nature of a pet; peevish, petulant; easily put out.

I checked her, which made her mighty p. PEPYS. Hence **Pe·ttish-ly** *adv.*, **-ness.**

Pettitoes (pe·titōuz), *sb. pl.* Rarely in *sing.* 1555. [Origin obsc.] **1.** Pig's trotters, esp. as used for food; in earlier use the word included the heart, liver, lungs, etc. of pigs, calves, sheep, and other animals. †Also *fig.* in expressions of contempt. **2.** The feet of a human being, esp. of a child 1589.

Pettle (pe·t'l), *v. Sc.* and *n. dial.* 1719. [freq. of PET *v.*[1]; see -LE.] *trans.* To pet, fondle, indulge.

‖ **Petto** (pe·tto). 1674. [It. :—L. *pectus.*] The breast.

In p. (It.), in one's own breast; in contemplation; undisclosed.

Petty (pe·ti), *a.* (*sb.*) [In late ME. *pety*; phonetic spelling, after F. pronunciation, of PETIT.] †**1.** Small (in size or stature) –1688. **2.** Of small importance, trivial 1581. **b.** Little-minded, mean 1713. **3.** Minor, inferior; subordinate; on a small scale 1523.

2. Those p. evils, which make prosperous men miserable 1824. **b.** Our p. animosities STEELE. **3.** I fly from p. tyrants to the throne GOLDSM. P. shopkeepers 1831.

Special collocations: **p. average:** see AVERAGE *sb.*[2] 2; **p. cash,** small cash items of receipt or expenditure; whence petty-cash-book; **p. dancers,** the Northern Lights. See also PETTY BAG, P. OFFICER, etc.; and *petty* JURY, LARCENY, SESSION, TREASON, etc. Hence **Pe·ttily** *adv.* **Pe·ttiness.**

†**B.** *sb.* **1.** A little boy at school; a boy in a lower form –1855. **2.** A privy or latrine.

Petty Bag, petty-bag. *Obs.* exc. *Hist.* 1631. [From the small leather bag in which records were put.] An office formerly belonging to the Common Law jurisdiction of the Court of Chancery, for suits for and against solicitors and officers of that court, and for process and proceedings by extents on statutes, recognizances, *scire facias*, to repeal letters patent, etc.

†**Pe·tty ca·non, pe·ttica·non.** 1530. A minor canon –1769.

†**Pe·tty ca·ptain, pe·ttica·ptain.** late ME. An officer below the rank of captain; a lieutenant; a centurion.–1633.

Petty officer. 1577. [PETTY *a.* 3.] **1.** *gen.* A minor officer. **2.** *spec.* An officer in the navy corresponding in rank to a non-commissioned officer in the army 1760.

Petulance (pe·tiŭlăns). 1610. [a. F. *pétulance*, ad. L. *petulantia.*] The fact or quality of being petulant. **1.** Wanton, pert, or insolent behaviour or speech. Now *rare* or *Obs.* **b.** A petulant or saucy expression 1741. **2.** Peevish impatience of opposition or restraint 1784.

1. With the p. of youth she pursued her triumph over her prudent elder sister SCOTT.

Petulancy (pe·tiŭlănsi). 1559. [ad. L. *petulantia*, f. *petulantem* PETULANT; see -ANCY.] †**1.** = PETULANCE 1. –1748. **2.** = PETULANCE 2 (*rare*) 1712.

Petulant (pe·tiŭlănt), *a.* (*sb.*) 1599. [a. F., ad. L. *petulantem*, pr. pple. of **petulare*, dim. of *petere* to aim at. In sense 3, app. infl. by *petted, pettish.*] **1.** Forward; wanton, lascivious (now *rare*). **2.** Pert; insolent; rude (now *rare*) 1605. **3.** Displaying peevish impatience and irritation, esp. on slight occasion 1755. **B.** *sb.* A petulant person 1682.

A. 2. The p. scribblers of this age DRYDEN. **3.** Laud was p., passionate, and impatient of contradiction 1830. Hence **Pe·tulantly** *adv.*

†**Petum, -un.** 1577. [a. F. *petun*, a. Guarani *petȳ.*] Native S. Amer. name of Tobacco –1763.

Petunia (pǐtiū·niă). 1825. [mod.L., f. F. *petun*; see prec.] *Bot.* **1.** A genus of ornamental herbaceous plants (N.O. *Solanaceæ* or *Atropaceæ*) nearly allied to tobacco, natives of S. America; they bear white, violet or purple, and variegated funnel-shaped flowers. Also, a plant or flower of this. **2.** The dark violet colour of the petunia. Also *attrib.* 1891.

‖ **Petuntse** (petu·ntsĕ, pǐtʊ·ntsĕ). 1727. [Chinese (Mandarin) *pai-tun-tzə*, f. *pai* white, *tun* mound, stone + *-tzə* formative ending.] A white earth, consisting of pulverized granite; used in combination with kaolin in the manufacture of Chinese porcelain. Also *attrib.*

Petzite (pe·tsəit). 1849. [f. name of W. *Petz*, a chemist, who analysed it; see -ITE[1] 2.] *Min.* Telluride of silver, containing a variable amount of gold.

Peucedanin (piuse·dănin). 1836. [f. L. *Peucedanum*, a. Gr. πευκέδανον the herb hog's fennel (f. πεύκη pine + ἔδανον eatable, food) + -IN[1].] *Chem.* A neutral substance ($C_{12}H_{12}O_3$) contained in the root of masterwort, *Peucedanum* (*Imperatoria*) *Ostruthium*, and other umbelliferous plants; also called *imperatorin.*

Peucyl (piū·sil). 1857. [f. Gr. πεύκη pine + -YL.] *Chem.* An oily hydrocarbon obtained from turpentine-oil; also called *terebilene.*

‖ **Peulvan, -ven** (pölvaṅ). 1841. [F., a. Breton *peŭlvan*, f. *peŭl* stake, pillar + *van*, mutate of *man* appearance.] *Archæol.* An upright long stone, an undressed stone pillar of prehistoric age; prop. applied to those in Brittany.

Pew (piū), *sb.* [late ME. *puwe, pywe, pewe*, OF. *puye, poye* parapet, balustrade, balcony :—L. *podia*, pl. of *podium*, a. Gr. πόδιον base, pedestal, dim. of πούς, ποδ- foot.] †**1.** A raised standing-place, stall, or desk in a church; often differentiated, as *minister's p.*, a pulpit, *reader's p.*, the desk at which the service is read, etc. 1479. **2.** A place (often enclosed), usu. raised on a footpace, seated for and appropriated to certain of the worshippers, e.g. for a great personage, a family, etc. late ME. **b.** Now applied to the fixed benches with backs in a church or chapel, each seating a number of worshippers 1631. **3.** A raised seat or bench, for judges, lawyers, etc.; a rostrum used by public speakers, etc.; a 'box' in a theatre, etc. Now only as transf. from 2. 1558.

Comb. †**p.-fellow,** one who sits in the same pew; one of the same communion or persuasion; an associate; **p.-rent,** the rent paid for a p., or for sittings in a church. Hence **Pew** *v. trans.* to fit up with pews; to shut up in or as in a p. **Pew·age,** the provision of pews; rent paid for pews.

Pewee (pī·wī). *U.S.* and *Canada.* 1810. [Echoic.] A name for some small olivaceous fly-catchers of the family *Tyrannidæ*, and so identified with PEWIT 3; by others restricted to the genus *Contopus*, as *C. virens*, the *Wood-p.* of the U. S. and Canada.

Pewit, peewit (pī·wit, piū·it). 1529. [Echoic, from the cry of the bird.] **1.** The Lapwing (*Vanellus vulgaris* or *cristatus*). **b.** The wailing cry of this bird 1812. **2.** (In full **p. gull.**) The black-headed Gull (*Larus ridibundus*); from its cry 1661. **3.** In *U.S.* A name of species of Tyrant Flycatchers, as the Common P., *Sayornis fusca* or *S. phœbe* 1817.

Pewter (piū·təɹ). [late ME. a. OF. *peutre, peautre, peaultre*, etc., repr. an earlier **peltre* = It. *peltro.* Origin unkn.] **1.** A grey alloy of tin and lead, or (sometimes) other metals. **b.** Pewter ware 1573. **2.** A pewter pot. Also *fig.* 1839. **3.** A polishing medium used by marble-workers, made by the calcination of tin 1875.

Comb.: **p.-solder,** soft solder, of similar composition to p., but containing a greater proportion of lead. So **Pew·terer,** a worker in p. ME. **Pew·tery** *a.* of the nature of, or characteristic of, p.

Pewterwort (piū·təɹwɒɹt). 1597. [f. prec. + WORT.] *Herb.* The plant *Equisetum hyemale*, so named on account of its use in polishing pewter utensils.

Peyerian (pəi,ī°·riăn), *a.* 1799. [f. proper name *Peyer* + -IAN.] *Anat.* Of, pertaining to, or named after the Swiss anatomist J. K. Peyer (1653–1712); as the *P.* (or *Peyer's*) *glands* or *patches*, groups of follicles in the wall of the small intestine.

‖ **Peziza** (pǐzəi·ză). 1833. [mod.L.; cf. L. *pezica* or *pezita*, f. Gr. πέζις a stalkless mushroom.] *Bot.* A large genus of discomycetous fungi, of cup-like shape, and often of brilliant colour. Hence **Pezi·ziform, Pezi·zoid** *adjs.* of the form of a P.

‖ **Pfennig, -ing** (pfe·nig, -iŋ). 1547. [G. *pfennig.* OHG. *pfenning* :—WGer. **pani(n)g*, whence PENNY.] A small copper coin of Germany, now the hundredth part of a mark.

Ph, a consonantal digraph, usu. having the phonetic value of F. It was the combination used by the Romans to represent the Gr. letter Φ, φ named Φῖ, *Phī.* In late pop. and med. Latin, and in the Romanic languages, *f* was often substituted for *ph*, as now regularly in Italian and Spanish, and in some French words, whence the spelling of English *fancy* (cf. *phantasy*), *fantastic.* In *phantom* and *pheasant* (F. *fantôme, faisan*), there has been etymological reversion to *ph.*

Phacochœre (fæ·kŏkiəɹ). Also **-chere.** 1842. [ad. mod.L. *phacochœrus*, f. Gr. φακός wart + χοῖρος pig.] *Zool.* A wart-hog.

Phacolite (fæ·kŏləit). Also **phako-.** 1843. [ad. G. *phakolit*, f. Gr. φακός lentil + λίθος stone.] *Min.* A colourless variety of CHABAZITE, occurring in crystals of lenticular form.

Phæacian (fi,ēi·ʃăn). 1788. [f. L. *Phæacia*, Gr. Φαιακία Scheria + -AN.] One of the inhabitants of Scheria (Corcyra), noted for their luxury; hence, a gourmand.

Phænogam, phe- (fī·nŏgæm). 1846. [f. mod.L. *phænogama*, sc. *vegetabilia*, f. Gr. φαινο- showing + γάμος marriage.] = PHANEROGAM. So **Phænoga·mian, Phænoga·mic, Phæno·gamous** *adjs.*

Phaeton (fē·tən). 1593. [a. Gr. φαέθων shining, also as proper name of the son of Helios, famous for his unlucky driving of the sun-chariot.] †**1.** A rash charioteer like Phaethon; any charioteer; something that, like Phaethon, sets the world on fire –1747. **2.** A species of light four-wheeled open carriage; usu. drawn by a pair of horses, and with one or two seats facing forward 1742.

‖ **Phagedæna, -ena** (fædʒǐdī·nă, fægǐ-). 1657. [L., a. Gr. φαγέδαινα, f. φαγεῖν to eat.] *Path.* An eating ulcer; spreading erosion occurring in an ulcer or sore. So **Phagedænic, -enic** (fædʒǐdī·nik, -e·nik, fægǐ-), **Phagedæ·nous,** *adjs. Path.* of the nature of, characterized by, or affected with P.

Phagocyte (fæ·gǒsəit). 1884. [mod. f. Gr. φαγο- eating + -CYTE.] *Physiol.* A leucocyte which has the power of guarding the system against infection by absorbing and destroying pathogenic microbes. Hence **Pha·gocytism, Pha·gocyto·sis**, the destruction of micro-organisms by phagocytes.

-phagous, *suffix*, f. L. *-phagus*, Gr. -φαγος eating + -OUS; as *anthropophagous* man-eating, etc. Also **-phagy**, ad. Gr. -φαγία eating (*sb.*); as *ichthyophagy*.

Phako-: see PHACO-.

Phalangal (fălæ·ŋgăl), *a. rare.* 1848. [f. L. *phalanx, phalang-* + -AL.] = PHALANGEAL. Also **Phala·ngar** *a.*

Phalange (fæ·lændʒ). 1560. [a. F. *phalange*, ad. L. *phalangem*, PHALANX.] †1. = PHALANX 1. –1689. 2. = PHALANX 3, 4. 1864.

Phalangeal (fălæ·ndʒiăl), *a.* 1831. [f. mod.L. *phalangeus*, f. *phalanx, phalang-* + -AL.] *Anat.* and *Zool.* Pertaining to, or of the nature of, a phalanx or phalanges (PHALANX 3). Also *sb.*

Phalanger (fălæ·ndʒəɹ). 1774. [a. mod.L., f. Gr. φαλάγγιον spider's web; in ref. to the webbed toes of the hind feet.] *Zool.* A quadruped of the genus *Phalangista*, or of the subfamily *Phalangistinæ*, Australian marsupials of arboreal habits; the typical genera (Australian opossums) have prehensile tails; the *flying phalangers* have non-prehensile tails and a flying membrane or parachute.

Phalangid (fălæ·ndʒid). 1835. [ad. mod. L. *Phalangidæ*, f. PHALANGIUM; see -ID³.] *Zool.* An arachnid of the family *Phalangidæ* or order *Phalangidea* (typical genus *Phalangium*), related to the mites, but more resembling spiders, without spinnerets or poison-glands, and usu. with very long and slender legs; the common species are known as *harvest-spiders* or *harvestmen*.

Phalangist (fălæ·ndʒist, fæ·lăndʒist). 1835. [ad. mod.L. *Phalangista*, Cuvier's substitute for PHALANGER.] *Zool.* = PHALANGER. So **Phala·ngistine** *a.* belonging to the subfamily *Phalangistinæ*; *sb.* a marsupial of this subfamily.

Phalangite (fæ·lændʒəit). *Hist.* 1839. [ad. L. *phalangita* or *-ites*, a. Gr., f. φάλαγξ; see -ITE.] A soldier belonging to a phalanx.

Phalanstery (fæ·lænstĕri). 1850. (Earlier in F. form.) [Anglicization of F. *phalanstère*.] In Fourier's scheme for the reorganization of society. A building or set of buildings occupied by a *phalanx* or socialistic community; hence, such a community numbering about 1800 persons. So **Phalansterian** (fælænstīə·riăn) *a.* and *sb.* of, pertaining or relating to a p.; a member of a p. 1843.

Phalanx (fæ·læŋks). *Pl.* **pha·lanxes**, ‖ **phalanges** (fălæ·ndʒīz). 1553. [a. L., Gr. φάλαγξ, -αγγες.] 1. *Gr. Antiq.* A line or array of battle; *spec.* a body of heavy-armed infantry drawn up in close order, with shields joined and spears overlapping. Hence **b.** any compact body of troops 1814. 2. *transf.* A compact body of persons or animals massed or ranged in order, as for attack, defence, etc. 1733. **b.** *fig.* A number or set of persons banded together for a common purpose; a 'united front'; the combination of such (in phr. *in p.*) 1600. **c.** A community of persons living together in a PHALANSTERY, q.v. 1843. 3. *Anat.* and *Zool.* Each bone of the digits (fingers and toes, or homologous parts). Usu. in pl. *phalanges*. 1693. 4. *Bot.* A bundle of stamens united by their filaments 1770.

1. The square (whiche the Macedons call p.) 1553. *attrib.* The p. order of battle 1838. 2. a. The sheep ..All huddling into p., stood and gaz'd COWPER. b. The crown lawyers opposed in p. 1817. Hence **Pha·lanxed** *a.* drawn up in a p.

Phalarope (fæ·lărōup). 1776. [a. F., irreg. ad. mod.L. *Phalaropus*, f. Gr. φαλαρίς a coot + πούς, ποδ- foot.] *Ornith.* A name applied to several small wading and swimming birds of the family *Phalaropodidæ*, order *Limicolæ*, related to the snipes.

Phaleucian (fălū·siăn), *a.* 1571. [f. L. *Phaleucius* (for *Phalæcius*) + -AN.] Pertaining to Phalæcus, an ancient Greek poet; applied to a metre consisting of a spondee, a dactyl, and three trochees.

Phallic (fæ·lik), *a.* 1789. [ad. Gr. φαλλικός, f. φαλλός penis.] Of or relating to the phallus or phallism; symbolical of the generative power in nature. Hence **Pha·llicism, Pha·llism**, the worship of the phallus, or of the organs of sex, as symbols of the generative power in nature.

‖ **Phallus** (fæ·lǒs). *Pl.* **-i.** 1613. [L., a. Gr. φαλλός penis.] 1. An image of the male generative organ, symbolizing the generative power in nature, venerated in various religious systems; *spec.* that carried in procession in the Dionysiac festivals in ancient Greece. 2. *Bot.* A genus of gasteromycetous fungi, so called from their shape, including the common stinkhorn, *P. impudicus* 1857.

Phane, obs. var. FANE *sb.*¹ 2 = VANE.

Phanero- (fæ·nĕro), bef. a vowel **phaner-**, comb. form of Gr. φανερός visible, evident (opp. to CRYPTO-); used in: **Pha:nerocodo·nic** [Gr. κώδων a bell] *a.*, bell-shaped: said of the gonophores of hydrozoans when possessing a developed umbrella; **Pha:nerocry·stalline** *a.*, of evident crystalline structure; **Pha:neroglo·ssal, -glo·ssate, -glo·ssous** [Gr. γλῶσσα] *adjs.* having a distinct tongue, as certain frogs.

Phanerogam (fæ·nĕrogæm). 1861. [a. F. *phanérogame*, in mod.L. *phanerogamus* adj., f. Gr. φανερός PHANERO- + γάμος sexual union.] *Bot.* A phanerogamic or flowering plant. (Opp. to CRYPTOGAM. Chiefly in pl. So **Phanerogamous** (fænĕrǫ·gămǝs) *a.* flowering 1816.

‖ **Phanerogamia** (fæ:nĕrogæ·miă). 1821. [mod.L., sing. fem. abstr. f. *phanerogamus*; see prec.] *Bot.* A primary division of the vegetable kingdom, comprising plants having obvious reproductive organs, i.e. stamens and pistils; the sub-kingdom of flowering plants. Hence **Phanerogа·mic** *a.* phanerogamous 1830.

Phantascope (fæ·ntăskōup). 1866. [irreg. f. Gr. φαντός visible + -SCOPE.] 1. A contrivance for exhibiting phenomena of binocular vision. 2. = PHENAKISTOSCOPE 1876.

Phantasia, var. form of FANTASIA.

Phantasiast (fæntē̆·ziæst). 1680. [ad. eccl. Gr. Φαντασιαστής, f. φαντασία FANTASY.] One of those Docetæ who held that the body of Jesus Christ was a mere phantasm.

Phantasm (fæ·ntæz'm). ME. [orig. a. F. *fantasme*, ad. L. *phantasma*, a. Gr. φάντασμα; see next.] I. 1. a. Illusion, deceptive appearance. *Obs.* or *arch.* b. With *a* and *pl.* An illusion; a deception; a phantom. late ME. c. An illusive likeness (*of* something), a 'ghost' or 'shadow'; a counterfeit 1638. †d. A counterfeit, an impostor –1641. 2. An apparition, a ghost. Now only *poet.* or *rhet.* late ME. b. *Psychics.* The supposed vision or perception of an absent person, living or dead, presented to the senses or mind of another 1884.

1. b. A fantasm bred by the feaver which had then seis'd him MILT. 2. That those phantasms..do frequent Cemeteries, Charnel-houses, and Churches, it is because these are the dormitories of the dead SIR T. BROWNE.

II. 1. *Philos.* A mental image, appearance, or representation, considered as the immediate object of sense-perception 1594. †2. Imagination, fancy –1689. b. An imagination, a fancy (now always with emphasis on its unreality) 1672.

1. When they are objects of memory and of imagination, they get the name of phantasms 1785. Hence **Phanta·smal, †Phantasma·tical, Phanta·smic**, *adjs.* of the nature of a p.; spectral; imaginary, unreal. **Phanta·smally** *adv.*

Phantasma (fæntæ·zmă). †Also **fantasma.** *Pl.* **-as** (ăz), **-ata** (ătă). 1598. [a. It. *fantasma* = L. *phantasma*, a. Gr. φάντασμα, f. φαντάζειν to present to (or as to) the eye, f. φαντός visible, f. stem φαν- of φαίνειν to show.] a. An illusion, vision, dream; b. An apparition, a spectre.

Phantasmagoria (fæntæzmăgō·riă). Also **Phanta·smagory.** 1802. [f. Gr. φάντασμα + (?) ἀγορά assembly.] 1. An exhibition of optical illusions produced chiefly by means of the magic lantern, first given in London in 1802. Also *transf.* 2. A shifting series of phantasms or imaginary figures as seen in a dream or fevered condition or as called up by the imagination 1828. 3. *transf.* A shifting and changing external scene consisting of many elements 1822.

2. Milton's genius has filled the atmosphere with a brilliant p. of contending angels 1875. Hence **Phantasmago·rial, Phantasmago·ric, -al** *adjs.*

Phantasmascope (fæntæ·zmăskōup). 1835. [irreg. f. PHANTASMA + -SCOPE.] = PHENAKISTOSCOPE.

Phantast, -asy: see FANTAST, -ASY.

Phantom (fæ·ntǝm). [ME. *fantosme, fantome*, a. OF. *fantosme* :—L. *phantasma*; see PHANTASMA.] †1. Illusion, unreality; vain imagination; delusion, falsity –1692. †b. With *a* and *pl.* An instance of this; a deception; a lie –1686. 2. Something that has only an apparent existence; an apparition, a spectre; a spirit, a ghost. late ME. b. A (material or optical) image *of* something 1707. c. *fig.* A 'vain show'; a person, institution, etc., having the show but not the substance of power; a cipher 1661. 3. A mental illusion; an image which appears in a dream or which is formed or cherished in the mind; also, a haunting thought 1590. b. The mental concept of an external object 1681. 4. *attrib.* or *adj.* That is a phantom; merely apparent, illusive. late ME.

2. The pale phantoms of the slain Glide nightly o'er the silent plain SMOLLETT. c. The caprice of the Barbarians..once more seated this Imperial p. [Maximus] on the throne GIBBON. 3. She was a P. of delight When first she gleamed upon my sight WORDSW. 4. The Phantome-nations of the dead POPE. *Comb.* **p.-tumour**, a temporary abdominal swelling resembling an actual tumour. Hence **Phantoma·tic** *a.* phantom-like, unreal. **Phanto·mic, Phanto·mical** *adjs.* of the nature of, resembling a p.

Phantoscope (fæ·ntǒskōup). 1894. [f. Gr. φαντός visible + -SCOPE.] A modification of the kaleidoscope.

-phany, repr. Gr. -φανία, -φάνεια appearance, manifestation, f. stem φαν- of φαίνειν to show, appear; as in EPIPHANY, etc.

Pharaoh (fēə·ro). [OE. *Pharaon*, ad. L. *Pharao, Pharaonem*, a. Gr. Φαραώ, a. Heb., ad. Egypt. The Eng. final *h* is from Heb.] 1. The generic appellation of the ancient Egyptian kings; an Egyptian king. b. *fig.* A tyrant or taskmaster 1630. †2. = FARO –1843.

1. **P.'s chicken**, the Egyptian vulture (*Neophron percnopterus*); **P.'s mouse** or **rat**, the ichneumon; **P.'s serpent**, a chemical toy composed of sulphocyanide of mercury, which fuses in a serpentine form. Hence **Pharao·nic, †-al** *adjs.* of, pertaining to, or like P.

Phare (fēəɹ). 1615. [a. F., ad. L. *pharus*, a. Gr. φάρος.] 1. A lighthouse. †2. A strait or channel lighted by a pharos; the Strait of Messina –1723.

†**Pha·rian**, *a.* 1591. [f. L. *Pharius* of PHAROS.] Of or pertaining to the island of Pharos; *poet.* Egyptian, Nilotic. b. *sb.* An Egyptian. 1729.

And past from P. fields to Canaan land MILT.

Pharisaic (færisē̆·ik), *a.* 1618. [ad. L., a. Gr. φαρισαϊκός; see PHARISEE and -IC.] 1. Of or belonging to the Pharisees. Also **Pharisæ·an, -e·an.** 1643. 2. Resembling the Pharisees in being strict in doctrine and ritual, without the spirit of piety; laying stress upon the outward show of religion and morality, and assuming superiority on that account; hypocritical; formal; self-righteous.

1. The Pharisaick Sect amongst the Jews CUDWORTH. 2. Wee are so Punctuall and Precise In Doctrine (Pharisaik-wise) 1618. So **Pharisa·ical** *a.*, **-ly** *adv.*, **-ness** 1599.

Pharisaism (fæ·risē,iz'm). 1601. [f. mod. L. *Pharisaïsmus*, f. Gr. φαρισαῖος PHARISEE + -ISM.] 1. The doctrine and practice of the Pharisees; the fact of being a Pharisee 1610. 2. The character and spirit of the Pharisees; hypocrisy; formalism; self-righteousness.

2. Of all the Pharisaisms of the day, our Churchgoing seems to me the masterpiece PUSEY.

Pharisee (fæ·risī). OE. (in L. form). [ME. *ph-, farise*, a. OF. *farise*, ad. L. *pharisæus, -eus*, a. Gr. φαρισαῖος, ad. Aramaic *p'rīshaiyā*, emphatic pl. of *p'rīsh* = Heb. *pārūsh* separated, hence separatist.] 1. One of an ancient Jewish sect distinguished by their strict observance of the traditional and written law, and by their pretensions to superior sanctity. 2. A person of this disposition; a self-righteous person; a formalist; a hypocrite 1589.

1. Oon a Pharise and the tothir a pupplican WYCLIF *Luke* xviii. 10. 2. Not the nation, but the affection makes a P. 1599. Hence **Pha·riseeism**, Pharisaism.

Pharmaceutic (fāɹmăsiū·tik, -kiū·tik), *a.* and *sb.* 1541. [ad. L., a. Gr. φαρμακευτικός, f. φαρμακευτής = φαρμακεύς poisoner, druggist, f. φάρμακον poison, medicine.] **A.** *adj.* Pertaining or relating to pharmacy; pharmaceutical. Now *rare.* 1656. **B.** *sb.* (Usu. in pl. **pharmaceutics.**) The science of pharmacy, or of the use of medicinal drugs. 1541. So **Pharmaceu·tical** *a.* pertaining to or engaged in pharmacy; relating to the preparation, use, or sale of medicinal drugs 1648; **-ly** *adv.* **Pharmaceu·tist,** a pharmacist, druggist.

Pharmacist (fā·ɹmăsist). 1834. [f. PHARMACY + -IST.] A person skilled in pharmacy; a druggist or pharmaceutical chemist.

Pharmaco-, repr. Gr. φαρμακο-, comb. form of φάρμακον drug, medicine, poison, as in:

Pha:rmacodyna·mic *a.* relating to the powers or effects of drugs; so **Pha:rmacodyna·mics** *sb. pl.* the science or subject of the powers or effects of drugs. **Pharmacognosy** (fāɹmăkǫ·gnǒsi) (also **-gno·sia,** and less correctly **-gno·sis**), the knowledge of drugs, *esp.* in their natural or unprepared state.

Pharmacolite (fā·ɹmăkǒləit). 1805. [f. Gr. φάρμακον poison + -LITE.] *Min.* Hydrous arsenate of calcium, occurring in silky fibres.

Pharmacology (fāɹmăkǫ·lŏdʒi). 1721. [ad. mod.L. *pharmacologia*; see PHARMACO- and -LOGY.] That branch of medical science which relates to drugs, their preparation, uses, and effects, the science of pharmacy. Hence **Pha:rmacolo·gical** *a.*, **-ly** *adv.* **Pharmaco·logist.**

Pharmacopœia (fā:ɹmăkǒpī·ă). 1621. [mod. L., (ult.) f. Gr. φαρμακο- PHARMACO- + -ποιος making, maker.] 1. A book containing a list of drugs and other medicinal substances or preparations, with directions for their preparation and identification; *spec.* one officially published and revised from time to time. 2. A stock of drugs 1721. Hence **Pharmacopœ·ial** *a.* pertaining to a p.; *spec.* recognized in, or prepared according to the directions of, the official Pharmacopœia.

Pharmacosiderite (fā:ɹmăkosəi·dĕrəit). 1835. [f. Gr. φάρμακον poison + σίδηρος iron + -ITE.] *Min.* Hydrous arsenate of iron, occurring in minute greenish or brownish crystals of cubic form; also called *cube-ore.*

Pharmacy (fā·ɹmăsi). late ME. [a. OF. *farmacie, pharmacie* (16th c.), a. late L. *pharmacia*, a. Gr. φαρμακεία.] 1. The use or administration of drugs or medicines. (Now chiefly *poet.* or *rhet.*) 2. The art or practice of collecting, preparing, and dispensing drugs, esp. medicinally; the compounding of medicines; the occupation of a druggist or pharmaceutical chemist. (The chief current sense.) 1651. 3. A drug-store or dispensary 1833.

Pharo: see PHARAOH 2.

Pharos (fē³·rǫs). 1552. [a. L., a. Gr. Φάρος; It. *faro* (occas. in Eng.).] 1. Name of an island off Alexandria, on which King Ptolemy Philadelphus built a famous tower lighthouse; hence the lighthouse itself 1575. 2. Any lighthouse or beacon to direct mariners 1552. 3. *transf.* Any conspicuous light; a lamp, etc. 1759.

1. A most high Tower, like to the Pharo of Alexandria 1617. 2. *fig.* Their eyes sweet splendor seems a P. bright SYLVESTER.

Pharyngal (fări·ŋgăl), *a.* (*sb.*) 1835. [f. mod.L. *pharynx* + -AL.] = next.

Pharyngeal (fări·ndʒīăl), *a.* (*sb.*) 1828. [f. mod.L. *pharyngeus* (f. *pharynx, pharyng-*) + -AL.] Of, pertaining to, or connected with the pharynx. **b.** *sb.* Short for *p. artery, bone,* etc.; esp. applied to the pharyngeal bones in fishes 1834.

‖**Pharyngitis** (færindʒəi·tis). 1844. [mod. L., f. Gr. φάρυγξ, φαρυγγ- PHARYNX + -ITIS.] *Path.* Inflammation of the pharynx. Hence **Pharyngi·tic** (-i·tik), *a.*

Pharyngo- (făriŋgo), comb. form of PHARYNX; as in:

Phary·ngobranch (-bræŋk), *a.*, belonging to the *Pharyngobranchii*, the lowest group of vertebrates, characterized by the pharynx being perforated by the branchial slits; *sb.* an animal of this group, an *Amphioxus* or lancelet; so **Pharyngobra·nchial, Pharyngobra·nchiate** *adjs.* = prec. adj. **Phary·ngognath** [Gr. γνάθος jaw] *a.* belonging to the order *Pharyngognathi* of fishes, having the inferior pharyngeal bones ankylosed; *sb.* a fish of this order. **Pharyngo-laryngeal** (-lări·ndʒīăl) *a.* pertaining to the pharynx and larynx; applied to the lower cavity of the pharynx. **Phary·ngotome** [Gr. -τομος cutting], an instrument for making an incision into the pharynx; so **Pharyngo·tomy,** incision into the pharynx.

Pharynx (fæ·riŋks). 1693. [a. mod.L. *pharynx*, a. Gr. φάρυγξ throat.] *Anat.* The cavity, with its enclosing muscles and mucous membrane, situated behind, and communicating with the nose, mouth, and larynx, and continuous below with the œsophagus. **b.** A more or less corresponding cavity in many invertebrates 1826.

Phascolome (fæ·skolǒᵘm). 1838. [ad. mod. L. *Phascolomys*, f. Gr. φάσκωλος purse + Gr. μῦς mouse.] *Zool.* An animal of the marsupial genus *Phascolomys*, containing the three species of the WOMBAT.

Phase (fēⁱz). 1812. [Partly ad. F. *phase*, partly a sing. deduced from pl. *phases* of PHASIS, q. v.] 1. Each of the aspects presented by the moon or any planetary body, according to the extent of its illumination. 2. Aspect; appearance; *esp.* any one aspect of a thing of varying appearances; a state or stage of change or development. 3. *Physics.* A particular change or point in a recurring sequence of movements or changes, e.g. a vibration or undulation 1864.

2. The most attractive p. of her character LYTTON.

‖**Phasis** (fēⁱ·zis, fēⁱ·sis). *Pl.* **phases** (fēⁱ·zīz, fēⁱ·sīz). 1660. [mod. L., a. Gr. φάσις, f. root φα-, φαν- of φαίνειν to show, appear.] 1. = PHASE 1. **b.** The first appearance of the new moon 1880. 2. = PHASE 2. 1665.

2. It is..only a new p. of an old thing 1886. Hence **Pha·sic** *a.* 1890.

†**Phasm.** 1656. [ad. L. *phasma*, a. Gr. φάσμα, f. φάω I shine, or φαίνειν to show, appear. (See next.)] †1. An extraordinary appearance; *esp.* a meteor –1686. 2. Anything visionary; a phantom, apparition. –1822.

‖**Phasma** (fæ·zmă). 1635. [See prec.] †1. Earlier form of PHASM, q. v. 2. *Zool.* A genus of cursorial orthopterous insects, typical of the family *Phasmidæ*, known as spectre-insects or walking-sticks. Hence **Pha·smid** 1872.

Pheasant (fe·zănt). [ME. a. AF. *fesant*, OF. *fesan*, F. *faisan* :—L. *phasianus*, Gr. φασιανός (sc. ὄρνις) the Phasian bird, f. Φᾶσις the Phasis, a river of Colchis.] 1. Name of a well-known game-bird, *Phasianus colchicus*, naturalized in Britain and other parts of Europe; hence, applied to all the species of *Phasianus*, and to some related genera. **b.** Locally applied to birds of other families, as the Ruffed Grouse (*Bonasa umbellata*) of the U. S., etc. 1637. **c.** The bird or its flesh as food. late ME. 2. *Ornith.* With defining words, applied to particular species of the genus *Phasianus* and allied *Phasianinæ*, and *Pavoninæ*; also to other birds in some way resembling the pheasant 1743. **b.** *Sea p.*, the Pintail Duck, *Dafila acuta* 1633.

2. **Firebacked P.**, of the Malay archipelago, etc., *Euplocamus ignitus*; **Gold** or **Golden P.**, of China and Tibet, *Thaumalea picta* or *Chrysolophus pictus*; **Lyre-** or **Lyre-tailed P.**, of Australia = LYRE-BIRD; **Ring-necked P.**, of China, *Phasianus torquatus*; **Silver P.**, of China, *Euplocamus nycthemerus*; **Water P.**, the pheasant-tailed Jacana, *Hydrophasianus chirurgus*.

attrib. and *Comb.*, as *p.-driving*, etc.; **p.-cock,** the male p.; **-coucal, cuckoo,** *Centropus phasianus*, of New South Wales; **-duck** = *Sea pheasant*; **-hen,** the female p.; **-Malay,** a variety of the domestic fowl; **-wood** = PARTRIDGE-WOOD 1. Hence **Phea·santry,** a place where pheasants are reared or kept.

Pheasant's eye. 1731. 1. Any plant of the genus *Adonis*, esp. *A. autumnalis*. 2. The common white Narcissus (*N. poeticus*) 1872. 3. (also **pheasant-eye, pheasant's eye pink**): The ring-flowered variety of the Garden Pink (*Dianthus plumarius* var. *annulatus*) 1753. So **Phea·sant-e·yed,** *a.* marked like the eye of a pheasant; applied to the flowers of these plants.

Pheasant-shell. A shell of the gastropod genus *Phasianella*, of the Australian seas; named from the brilliantly coloured and polished surface.

Phello- (felo), comb. form of Gr. φελλός cork. **Phe·lloderm** [Gr. δέρμα skin], *Bot.* a layer of parenchymatous cells containing chlorophyll, formed in the stems of some plants from the inner cells of the phellogen. **Phe·llogen** [see -GEN], *Bot.* the layer of meristematic cells from which the cork-cells are formed, the cork-cambium. **Phellopla·stic,** a cork model or figure; the art of cutting figures or models in cork (also **Phellopla·stics**).

Phen-: see PHÆN-.

Phen-, pheno-, formative element in *Chem.* (for *phæn(o-)* f. Gr. φαινο- shining, φαίνειν to show, φαίνεσθαι to appear. First used by Laurent, 1841, in 'hydrate de phényle', and 'acide phénique', names for the substance subseq. called PHENOL. These names indicated that the substance was a coal-tar product, arising from the manufacture of *illuminating* gas. Hence *phen-, pheno-* was gradually used as the basis of the names of all the bodies derived from benzene. **Phenacetin** (fĭnæ·sĭtin), the acetyl deriv. of phenetidin, the ethylic ether of paramido-phenol $C_6H_4 . OC_2H_5 . NH(CH_3CO)$, used as an antipyretic 1889. **Phena·nthrene,** a solid hydrocarbon, $(C_6H_4 . CH)_2$, prepared from crude anthracene (with which it is isomeric), crystallizing in colourless shining laminæ. **Phene·tidin,** the ethyl deriv. of amidophenol. **Phe·netol,** ethyl phenyl ether, or phenate of ethyl, $C_2H_5 . OC_6H_5$, a volatile aromatic-smelling liquid.

Phenacite (fe·năsəit), **-kite** (-kəit). 1834. [f. Gr. φέναξ, φενακ- cheat (as having been mistaken for quartz) + -ITE [1].] *Min.* A silicate of glucinum, occurring in quartz-like transparent or translucent crystals.

Phenakistoscope (fenăki·stǒskoᵘp). 1834. [f. Gr. φενακιστής cheat, f. φενακίζειν to cheat + -SCOPE.] A disk with figures upon it arranged radially, representing a moving object in successive positions; on turning it round rapidly, and viewing the figures through a fixed slit (or their reflexions in a mirror through radial slits in the disk itself), the persistence of the successive visual images produces the impression of actual motion.

†**Phene** (fīn). 1857. [a. F. *phène*; see PHEN-.] *Chem.* An early name proposed for BENZENE. Hence **Phenic** (fī·nik, fe·nik) *a.* = PHENYLIC. *P. acid,* PHENOL or carbolic acid. Its salts are **Phe·nates.**

Phenicine, -in (fe·nisəin, -in). 1826. [Etymologically *phœnicin(e*, f. Gr. φοῖνιξ a purple-red, lit. a Phœnician (in ref. to Tyrian purple) + -IN.] *Chem.* A colouring matter produced by the action of nitro-sulphuric acid on phenylic alcohol; indigo carmine.

Phenol (fī·nǫl). 1852. [f. Gr. φαινο- (see PHEN-) + -OL 1 (= alcohol).] *Chem.* A hydroxyl derivative of benzene, $C_6H_5(OH)$, commonly known as CARBOLIC *acid*, q.v. (also *phenic* or *phenylic acid, phenyl hydrate*). **b.** In pl. **phenols,** the hydroxyl derivatives of the aromatic or benzene series of hydrocarbons 1857. Hence **Pheno·lic** *a.* carbolic.

Phenology (fīnǫ·lŏdʒi). Also **phæn-.** 1884. [f. *pheno-* (in *phenomenon*) + -LOGY.] The study of the times of recurring natural phenomena. So **Phenolo·gical** *a.* 1875.

Phenomenal (fĭnǫ·menăl), *a.* (*sb.*) Also **phæn-.** 1825. [f. PHENOMENON + -AL.] 1. Of the nature of a phenomenon; consisting of phenomena; apparent, sensible, perceptible. (Opp. to *real, absolute,* etc., and in Philosophy to *noumenal.*) Also *absol.*, *the p.*, that which is cognizable by the senses. **b.** Of, relating to, or concerned with phenomena, esp. with the phenomena of any science 1840. 2. Of the nature of a remarkable phenomenon; extraordinary, exceptional; 'prodigious' 1850. Hence **Pheno·menal·ism,** a. that manner of thinking which considers things from the point of view of phenomena only; **b.** the doctrine that phenomena are the only objects of knowledge, or the only realities. So Pheno·menalist. 1856. Pheno·menalize *v. trans.* to render p.; to conceive or represent as p.

Phenomenology (fīnǫmenǫ·lŏdʒi). 1797. [f. next + -LOGY.] **a.** The science of phenomena as distinct from that of being (ontology). **b.** That division of any science which describes and classifies its phenomena.

Phenomenon (fīnǫ·menǫn). *Pl.* **-a.** 1576. [a. L. (post-cl.) *phænomenon*, pl. *-a*, a. Gr. φαινόμενον, pl. -μενα appearing, apparent, pres. pple. neut. of φαίνεσθαι to appear.] **1.** A thing that appears, or is perceived or observed; applied chiefly to a fact or occurrence, the cause of which is in question. **2.** *Philos.* That of which the senses or the mind directly takes note; an immediate object of perception. (Opp. to NOUMENON.) 1788. **3.** A highly exceptional or unaccountable fact or occurrence; *colloq.* a prodigy 1771.

1. The common p. of a piece of metal being eaten away by rust 1878. Phr. †*To save* (or *salve*) *the phenomena* (tr. Gr. σώζειν τὰ φαινόμενα): to reconcile the admitted facts with some theory with which they appear to disagree. 3. This, Sir,..this is the infant p.—Miss Ninetta Crummles DICKENS. Hence **Pheno·menism** = PHENOMENALISM b. **Pheno·menist** = PHENOMENALIST 1830.

Phenose (fī·nōus). 1878. [f. PHEN- + -OSE [2].] *Chem.* A sweetish amorphous deliquescent compound formed by the action of hypochlorous acid on benzene, and having the general formula $C_6H_{12}O_6$ of the carbohydrates.

Phenyl (fī·nil, fe·nil). 1850. [f. PHEN- + -YL, lit. 'radical of benzene (*phene*)'.] *Chem.* The monovalent organic radical C_6H_5 (also symbolized Ph), which exists in the free state as DIPHENYL, $H_5C_6-C_6H_5$, and enters as a radical into benzene (*phenyl hydride*), phenol (*phenyl hydroxyl*), aniline (*phenylamine*), and a very extensive series of organic compounds. Also *attrib.* and *Comb.*, as *p. acetate*; **p.-ace·tamide** = ACETANILIDE; **p.-hy·drazine**, $C_6H_5.NH.NH_2$; etc. Hence **Phe·nylami·ne**, the systematic name of ANILINE (*monophenylamine*), $NH_2.C_6H_5$, and of many other 'organic bases derived from ammonia by the substitution of one or more atoms of phenyl for an equivalent quantity of hydrogen' (Watts). **Phe·nylene**, the hydrocarbon C_6H_4. **Phenylic** (fīni·lik) *a.* of or derived from phenyl; *phenylic acid*, *alcohol*, other names for phenol or carbolic acid.

Pheon (fī·ǫn). 1486. [Etym. unkn.] *Her.* 'A charge representing a broad barbed arrow, or head of a javelin' (Fairholt). Either identical with the 'broad arrow', or differing only in being engrailed on the inner edge.

Phew (fiŭ, fiu), *int.* 1604. [Representing the action of puffing or blowing away with the lips.] A vocal gesture expressing impatience, disgust, or weariness.

Phi (fəi). The Greek letter (Φ, φ) = ph.

Phial (fəi·ăl), *sb.* [ME. a. OF. *fiole*, also *phiole*, ad. late L. *phiola*, L. *phiala*, ad. Gr. φιάλη a broad flat vessel.] A vessel for holding liquids, esp. drinks; now usu. a small glass bottle, esp. for liquid medicine. Hence **Phi·al** *v. trans.* to store or keep in a p.

Phil-, form of PHILO- used bef. a vowel or *h*.

-phil (fil), **-phile** (fəil), comb. element repr. Gr. φίλος loving, dear. In Gr., found only in personal names, with the sense 'dear, beloved', as Θεόφιλος Theophilus (dear to God). In med. and mod.L. often used in form *-philus*, *-phila* with sense 'lover, loving'. Hence in French words *-phile*, in Eng. *-phile* or *-phil*, as *Anglophil(e*, etc., for which forms with the prefix PHILO- are etymologically more correct.

Philabeg, erron. f. FILIBEG, a kilt.

Philadelphian (filăde·lfiăn), *a.* and *sb.* 1615. [In sense A. 1, f. Gr. φιλαδελφία brotherly love + -AN; in sense A. 2 in part, and in B., f. Gr. Φιλαδέλφεια, *Philadelphia* (i.e. the city of Ptolemy Philadelphus).] **A.** *adj.* **1.** Brotherloving; loving the brethren. **2.** Of or pertaining to the Philadelphians; see B. and cf. Rev. iii. 7–13. 1693. **3.** Of or pertaining to any city of the name of Philadelphia, esp. that in Pennsylvania, U.S.A. **4.** Of or pertaining to Ptolemy Philadelphus. **B.** *sb.* (*pl.*) A religious society (the *Philadelphian Society*) organized in England towards the end of the 17th c. 1693. **b.** A native or inhabitant of Philadelphia (cf. A. 3) 1792.

Philander (filæ·ndəɹ), *sb.* 1737. [ad. Gr. φίλανδρος adj., fond of men, (of a woman) loving her husband, f. φιλο-, PHILO- + ἀνδρ-, ἀνήρ; in later use, a proper name for a lover.] †**1.** A lover; one given to making love –1813. **2.** A name for certain marsupial animals: **a.** A small wallaby (*Macropus brunnii*) first described by Philander de Bruyn. **b.** A S. Amer. opossum (*Didelphys philander*). **c.** An Australian bandicoot (*Perameles lagotis*). 1737. Hence **Phila·nder** *v. intr.* to make love, esp. in a trifling manner; to dangle after a woman. Whence **Phila·nderer**, one who philanders; a male flirt 1841.

Philanthrope (fi·lǣnþrōup). 1734. [ad. Gr. φιλάνθρωπος adj., f. φιλο- PHILO- + ἄνθρωπος man.] = PHILANTHROPIST.

Philanthropic, -al (filǣnþrǫ·pik, -ăl), *adjs.* 1789. [ad. F. *philanthropique*, f. Gr. φιλάνθρωπος (see prec.) + -IC + -AL.] Characterized by philanthropy; benevolent, humane. So **Philanthro·pically** *adv.* 1787.

Philanthropine (filæ·nþrŏpin). 1802. [ad. G. *Philanthropin*, a. Gr. φιλανθρώπινον adj. neut. (formed after ἀνθρώπινον).] Name for the school founded in 1774 by Basedow or Bassedau at Dessau, in Germany, for the education of children by his 'natural system', in the principles of philanthropy, natural religion, etc.; also any similar institution. Hence **Philanthro·pinist**, an advocate of Basedow's system; also, a pupil at a p.

Philanthropism (filæ·nþrŏpiz'm). 1835. [f. PHILANTHROPY + -ISM.] The profession or practice of philanthropy; a philanthropic theory or system.

Philanthropist (filæ·nþrŏpist). 1730. [f. as prec. + -IST.] One who practises philanthropy; one who loves his fellow-men and exerts himself for their well-being. Formerly with the wider sense of 'friend or lover of man'.

Philanthropize (filæ·nþrŏpəiz), *v.* 1826. [f. as prec. + -IZE.] **1.** *intr.* To practise philanthropy. **2.** *trans.* To make (persons) objects of philanthropy 1830.

Philanthropy (filæ·nþrŏpi). 1608. [ad. late L. *philanthropia*, a. Gr., f. φιλάνθρωπος; see PHILANTHROPE.] Love towards mankind; practical benevolence towards men in general; the disposition to promote the well-being of one's fellow-men. †**b.** *spec.* (cf. *Titus* iii. 4). The love of God to man –1711.

Philately (filæ·tĭli). 1865. [ad. F. *philatélie*, f. Gr. φιλ(ο-, PHILO- + ἀτελής free from charge, ἀτέλεια exemption from payment (ἐξ ἀτελείας *franco*), Gr. ἀτελής = *free* or *franco*, has been taken as = 'postage-stamp', the substitute for the original impressed receipt stamp for the amount prepaid.] Stamp-collecting. Hence **Philate·lic** (-ăte·lik) *a.* relating to or engaged in p. **Phila·telist**, a stamp-collector.

-phile: see -PHIL.

Philharmonic (filhaɹmǫ·nik), *a.* and *sb.* 1762. [a. F. *philharmonique*, after It. *filarmonico*, f. Gr. φιλ(ο-, PHIL(O- + ἁρμονικός HARMONIC.] **A.** *adj.* Loving harmony; devoted to music 1813. **B.** *sb.* A lover of harmony; a person devoted to music.

A. *P. Society*, name of various musical societies, *esp.* that founded in London in 1813 for the promotion of instrumental music; hence *P. concert*, one given by the P. society.

Philhellene (fi·lhelīn), *a.* and *sb.* 1825. [ad. Gr. φιλέλλην adj., loving the Greeks, f. φιλ(ο- + Ἕλλην HELLENE.] **A.** *adj.* = next. **B.** *sb.* = PHILHELLENIST.

Philhellenic (filhelī·nik, -e·nik), *a.* 1830. [f. as prec. + HELLENIC.] Friendly to Greece or the Greeks (esp. in relation to national independence). So **Philhellenism** (filhe·lĭniz'm), the principle of supporting the Greeks. **Philhellenist** (filhelī·nist), a friend or supporter of Greece.

Philibeg, var. of FILIBEG.

Philip (fi·lip). 1482. [a. Gr. Φίλιππος, lit. lover of horses.] **1.** A man's name; e.g. that of the king of Macedon, in the expression 'to appeal from Philip drunk to Philip sober' 1568. †**2.** Name of old French, Spanish, and Burgundian coins, issued by kings or dukes of this name –1769. **3.** A former name for a sparrow; contracted to *Phip. Obs.* exc. *dial.*; also *dial.* applied to the hedge-sparrow 14...

Philippic (fili·pik), *sb.* (*a.*) 1592. [ad. L. *Philippicus*, a. Gr. φιλιππικός, f. Φίλιππος Philip (of Macedon). So mod.F. *philippique.*] **A.** *sb.* Epithet of the orations of Demosthenes against Philip king of Macedon; hence applied to Cicero's orations against Antony, and *gen.* to any discourse of the nature of a bitter invective. **B.** *adj.* **a.** Of or pertaining to any person called Philip; **b.** of Philippi; **c.** of the nature of a philippic or invective 1614.

Philippina (filipī·nă), **philippine, philopœna.** 1848. [repr. (like F. *philippine*, Du. *filippine*, etc.) G. *vielliebchen*, dim. of *viellieb* very dear (cf. *liebchen* darling), altered into *Philippchen* (= little or darling Philip).] An amusement in which, at a dinner party, a person finding an almond or other nut with two kernels eats one kernel, and gives the other to a person of the opposite sex; when the parties next meet, the one who first says 'Good morning, Philippine!' is entitled to a present from the other. Also applied to the double nut or kernel, and to the present claimed or given.

Philippize (fi·lipəiz). *v.* 1607. [ad. Gr. φιλιππίζειν, f. Φίλιππος Philip; see -IZE.] *intr.* To favour, or take the side of, Philip of Macedon; also *gen.* to speak or write as one is corruptly inspired or influenced.

The oracles will P., as long as Philip is the master 1875.

‖ **Philister** (fili·stəɹ). 1828. [G., f. L. *Philistæus*, Gr. Φιλιστιαῖος; see PHILISTINE.] = PHILISTINE *sb.* 3, 4.

Philistia (fili·stiă). 1535. [med.L. = Gr. Φιλιστία; ult. repr. Heb. *p'lesheth.*] **1.** The country of the Philistines, in south-west Palestine; also, the people. **2.** The class of 'Philistines' (sense A. 4) 1857. Hence **Phili·stian** *a.* of or pertaining to Philistia or the Philistines.

Philistine (fi·listəin, -tin), *sb.* and *a.* late ME. [a. F. *Philistin*, ad. late L. *Philistinus*, usu. in pl. *Philistini*, etc., ad. late Gr. Φιλιστῖνοι, Παλαιστῖνοι; ad. ult. Heb. *p'lishtīm* (or *-iim*).] **A.** *sb.* **1.** One of an alien warlike people who occupied the southern sea-coast of Palestine, and constantly harassed the Israelites. **2.** *fig.* Applied (humorously or otherwise) to 'the enemy', into whose hands one may fall, e.g. bailiffs, literary critics, etc.; formerly, also, to the debauched or drunken 1600. **3.** = PHILISTER, applied by German students to one not a student at a university 1824. **4.** A person deficient in liberal culture; one whose interests are material and commonplace 1827.

2. That bloodthirsty P., Sir Lucius O'Trigger SHERIDAN. 4. The people who believe most that our greatness and welfare are proved by our being very rich,..are just the very people whom we call the Philistines M. ARNOLD.

B. *adj.* **1.** Of or pertaining to the people of Philistia 1842. **2.** Like the modern 'Philistine'; uncultured; commonplace; prosaic. (Of persons and things.) 1831.

2. Byron..had in him a cross of the true P. breed SWINBURNE.

Philistinism (fi·listiniz'm, -əiniz'm). 1831. [f. prec. + -ISM.] The opinions, aims, and habits of social Philistines (see prec. A. 4); the condition of being a Philistine.

Philistinism! we have not the expression in English. Perhaps we have not the word because we have so much of the thing M. ARNOLD.

Phillipsite (fi·lipsəit). 1825. [f. J. W. *Phillips*, Eng. mineralogist; see -ITE [1].] *Min.* A hydrous silicate of aluminium, calcium, and potassium, found in cruciform twin crystals of a white colour.

Phillis (fi·lis). Also **Phyllis.** 1632. [a. L. *Phyllis*, a girl's name, a. Gr. Φυλλίς female name, lit. foliage, f. φύλλον leaf.] A generic proper name in pastoral poetry for a rustic maiden, or for a sweetheart; also applied (after Milton) to a 'neat-handed' table-maid or waitress.

‖ **Phillyrea** (fili·rīă, filirī·ă). 1664. [Bot.L. *phyllyrea*, erron. for *philyrea*, a. Gr. φιλυρέα, app. deriv. of φιλύρα lime-tree. Often spelt erron. *phyll-* and *phyl-*.] *Bot.* A genus of ornamental evergreen shrubs (N.O. *Oleaceæ*), natives of the Mediterranean region and the East; also called *jasmine-box* or *mock privet.*

Phillyrin (fi·lirin). 1838. [f. prec. + -IN [1].] *Chem.* A white crystallizable bitter substance obtained from the bark of *Phillyrea latifolia.*

Philo- (filo), bef. a vowel (or *h*) usu. **phil-** (fil), repr. Gr. φιλο-, φιλ-, comb. form from root of φιλεῖν to love, φίλος dear, friend. Employed in English to form new compounds, after the Gr. model, the second element of which is properly Greek, but often Latin, and even English; esp. frequent with national names, as *p.-German*, *p.-Turk*, and the like.

Philobi·blic [Gr. βίβλος book], *a.* fond of books; devoted to literature. **Philogynist** (filǫ·dʒinist) [Gr. γυνή woman], a lover or admirer of women. **Phi·lomath** [Gr. μαθ-, root of μανθάνειν to learn], a lover of learning; a student, esp. of mathematics; formerly applied to an astrologer; so **Philoma·thic** *a.*, **Philo·mathy.** (All now *rare.*) **Philo·te·chnic** [Gr. τέχνη art], *a.* fond of or devoted to the arts, esp. the industrial arts.

Philologer (filǫ·lŏdʒəɹ). 1588. [f. PHILOLOGY + -ER.] = PHILOLOGIST. Now *rare.*

Philologist (filǫ·lŏdʒist). 1648. [f. next + -IST.] **1.** One devoted to learning or literature; a scholar, *esp.* a classical scholar. Now *rare.* **2.** A person versed in the science of language; a student of language 1716.

Philology (filǫ·lŏdʒi). 1614. [ad. L. *philologia*, a. Gr. φιλολογία, f. φιλόλογος fond of speech or learning, literary, f. φιλο- + λόγος speech.] **1.** Love of learning and literature; the study of literature, in a wide sense; literary and classical scholarship; polite learning. Now *rare.* **2.** The science of language; linguistics. (See also COMPARATIVE.) 1716. Hence **Philolo·gic, -al** *adjs.* of, pertaining to, concerned with, or devoted to the study of p. **Philolo·gically** *adv.*

Philomel (fi·lŏmel), **Philomela** (filŏmī·lă). *poet.* late ME. Also early and erron. **philomene.** [a. F. *philomèle*, ad. L. *philomela*, a. Gr. φιλομήλα, supposed to be f. φιλο- PHILO- + μέλος song, with vowel lengthened.] A poetic name for the nightingale. (Now always with capital P, usu. with ref. to the myth of Philomela metamorphosed into a nightingale.)

And Philomele her song with teares doth steepe SPENSER.

Philonian (fəilōu·niăn), *a.* 1874. [ad. L. *Philonianus*, f. *Philo*, *-onem*, ad. Gr. Φίλων; see -AN.] Of or pertaining to the Jewish philosopher Philo, who flourished at Alexandria about the beginning of the Christian era. So **Philo·nic** *a.* **Phi·lonism,** the system of Philo.

Philoprogenitive (fi:lo,prodʒe·nitiv), *a.* 1865. [irreg. f. PHILO- + L. *progenit-*, *progignere* to beget + -IVE.] **1.** Inclined to production of offspring; prolific. **2.** *Phrenol.* Loving one's offspring; of or pertaining to love of offspring 1876. So **Phi:loproge·nitiveness** 1815.

†**Philosoph, -ophe.** OE. [ad. L. *philosophus*, a. Gr. φιλόσοφος, f. φίλος loving + σοφός wise, a sage.] = PHILOSOPHER **1**; now also PHILOSOPHIST **2**.

Philosophaster (filǫ·sŏfæstəɹ, filǫsofæ·stəɹ). 1611. [a. L., f. *philosophus*; see -ASTER.] A shallow or pseudo-philosopher.

Philosopheme (filǫ·sŏfīm). 1678. [ad. late L. *philosophema*, a. Gr. φιλοσόφημα, f. φιλοσοφεῖν to philosophize.] A philosophic conclusion or demonstration; a philosophical statement, theorem, or axiom.

Philosopher (filǫ·sŏfəɹ). [In 14th c. *philosophre*, *filo-*, *-sofre*, AF. var. of OE. *philosophe* PHILOSOPH.] **1.** A lover of wisdom; one versed in philosophy or engaged in its study; formerly embracing men learned in physical science as well as those versed in the metaphysical and moral sciences, but now, when unqualified, restricted to the latter. Also differentiated, as *moral p.*, *political p.*; *natural p.* (= physicist). †**2.** An adept in occult science, as an alchemist, diviner, weather-prophet, etc. –1485. **3.** One who regulates his life by the light of philosophy; one who speaks or behaves philosophically 1599.

1. I feare hee will proue the weeping Phylosopher [Heraclitus] when he growes old SHAKS. Pythagoras..is said to have first named himself p. or lover of wisdom COLERIDGE. **3.** For there was neuer yet P. That could endure the tooth-ake patiently SHAKS. Phr. *Oil of philosophers*, an old drug compounded of powdered brick and linseed oil.

Philosopher's stone. late ME. [tr. med. L. *lapis philosophorum* (see prec. 2).] A reputed solid substance or preparation supposed by the alchemists to possess the property of changing other metals into gold or silver, the discovery of which was the supreme object of alchemy. Also *transf.* and *fig.*

Philosophic (filŏsǫ·fik), *a.* (*sb.*) 1644. [ad. post-cl. L. *philosophicus*; see -IC.] **A.** *adj.* = next. **B.** *sb.* (*pl.*) Studies, works, or arguments pertaining to philosophy 1734.

Philosophical (filŏsǫ·fikăl), *a.* (*sb.*) late ME. [f. as prec. + -AL; see -ICAL.] **1.** Of or pertaining to a philosopher or philosophy; of the nature of, consonant with, or proceeding from philosophy or learning; in earlier use including 'scientific' 1500. **b.** Physical, scientific. Now *Obs.* or *arch.* 1471. **2.** Of persons, etc.: Skilled in or devoted to philosophy or learning (formerly including physical science); learned. late ME. **3.** Characterized by practical philosophy or wisdom; befitting a philosopher in respect of wisdom or temperance 1638. †**B.** *sb.* (*pl.*) The subjects of study in a course of philosophy –1716.

1. The cuddy is a fish of which I know not the p. name JOHNSON. My mind is in a state of p. doubt as to animal magnetism COLERIDGE. **b.** Young Watt ..exhibited a box of p. toys 1843. **2.** The P. Transactions (of the Royal Society) (*title*). A p. chemist would probably make a very unprofitable business of farming SIR H. DAVY. **3.** His patience was more Philosophicall than his Intellect 1638. Hence **Philoso·phically** *adv.*

Philoso·phico-, comb. form of PHILOSOPHIC: = philosophically-, philosophical and.. as in *p.-historic*, etc. 1743.

Philosophism (filǫ·sŏfiz'm). 1792. [a. F. *philosophisme*, f. Gr. φιλόσοφος; cf. *sophism*.] Philosophizing, or a philosophizing system; usu., in a hostile sense, affectation of philosophy.

The Dryasdust Philosophisms and enlightened Scepticisms CARLYLE.

Philosophist (filǫ·sŏfist). Now *rare.* 1589. [app. in sense **1**, from L. *philosophia* + -IST In sense **2** = F. *philosophiste*.] †**1.** = PHILOSOPHER **1.** Puttenham. **2.** One who philosophizes erroneously; applied polemically to the French Encyclopædists, and hence to rationalists generally 1798. Hence **Philosophi·stic, -al** *adjs.* rationalistic, sceptical.

Philosophize (filǫ·sŏfəiz), *v.* 1594. [f. Gr. φιλόσοφος; see PHILOSOPH and -IZE **1**.] **1.** *intr.* To play the philosopher; to think, reason, or argue philosophically; to speculate, theorize. Also *trans.* with *into*. **2.** *trans.* To render philosophic; to explain, treat, or construct philosophically 1658.

1. Man philosophises as he lives. He may philosophise well or ill, but philosophise he must 1836. Hence **Philo·sophizer.**

Philosophy (filǫ·sŏfi). [ME. a. OF. *filo-*, *philosophie*, ad. L. *philosophia*, a. Gr., f. φιλόσοφος PHILOSOPH.] **1.** (In the original and widest sense.) The love, study, or pursuit of wisdom, or of knowledge of things and their causes, whether theoretical or practical. †**b.** Occas. used esp. of practical wisdom –1750. **2.** That more advanced study, to which, in the mediæval universities, the seven liberal arts were introductory; it included the three branches of *natural*, *moral*, and *metaphysical philosophy*, commonly called *the three philosophies.* Hence the degree of *Doctor of Philosophy.* late ME. **3.** (= *natural p.*) The knowledge or study of natural objects and phenomena; now usu. called 'science'. Now *rare* or *Obs.* ME. **4.** (= *moral p.*) The knowledge or study of the principles of human action or conduct; ethics. late ME. **5.** (= *metaphysical p.*) That department of knowledge or study which deals with ultimate reality, or with the most general causes and principles of things. (Now the most usual sense.) 1794. **6.** Occas. used esp. of knowledge obtained by natural reason, in contrast with revealed knowledge. late ME. **7.** With *of*: The study of the general principles *of* some particular branch of knowledge, experience, or activity; also, less properly, *of* any subject or phenomenon 1713. **8.** A philosophical system or theory. (With *a* and *pl.*) late ME. **9. a.** The system which a person forms for the conduct of life. **b.** The mental attitude or habit of a philosopher; serenity; resignation; calmness of temper 1771.

1. Depth in Philosophie bringeth Men about to Religion BACON. **b.** The chiefe of all p. consisteth to serve God, and not to offend men 1557. **4.** History is P. teaching by example BOLINGBROKE. **5.** I regard P. then..as the study which 'takes all knowledge for its province' 1902. **6.** Let Phylosophy not be asham'd to be confuted 1640. **7.** The great professor ..of the p. of vanity [Rousseau] BURKE. **8.** *Ham.* I. v. 167. **9.** My own infirmities..and the public news coming altogether have put my utmost p. to the trial 1774.

-philous, terminal element in modern formations = 'lover', 'loving', f. med.L. *-philus*, Gr. -φιλος -PHIL (q.v.) + -OUS, as in *ammophilous*, *dendrophilous*, *hygrophilous*; hence **-philism, -phily** (Gr. -φιλία), expressing the state or quality of being what is denoted by *-philous*, and occas. *-philist* = lover (of), as *œnophilist.*

Philtre, philter (fi·ltəɹ), *sb.* 1587. [a. F. *philtre*, ad. L. *philtrum* (also formerly used), a. Gr. φίλτρον love-potion, f. φιλ-, stem of φιλεῖν to love, φίλος loving + -τρον suffix of instrument.] A love-potion or love-charm. Sometimes *loosely*, a magic potion. Hence **Phi·ltre, phi·lter** *v. trans.* to charm with a love-potion; *fig.* to bewitch.

‖ **Phimosis** (fəimōu·sis). 1674. [mod.L., a. Gr. φίμωσις muzzling.] *Path.* Contraction of the orifice of the prepuce, so that it cannot be retracted.

Phit (fit), imitation of a sound like that made by a rifle-bullet 1894.

Phiz (fiz). *joc. colloq.* 1688. [abbrev. of *phiznomy*, PHYSIOGNOMY.] Face, countenance; expression of face.

Phleb-, bef. a cons. **phlebo-,** comb. form of Gr. φλέψ, φλεβ- vein, an element in terms of physiology, pathology, etc.

‖ **Phlebitis** (flĭbəi·tis). 1822. [mod.L., f. Gr. φλέψ, φλεβ-; see -ITIS.] *Path.* Inflammation of the walls of a vein. Hence **Phlebi·tic** *a.*

Phlebo-, comb. element: see PHLEB-.

Phlebograph (fle·bŏgrɑf) [-GRAPH], an instrument (sphygmograph) for recording diagrammatically the pulsations of a vein. **Phlebolite** (fle·bŏləit), **Phle·bolith** [Gr. λίθος; see -LITE], a morbid calcareous concretion in a vein, a vein-stone. **Phlebology** (flĭbǫ·lŏdʒi) [-LOGY], that part of physiology or anatomy which treats of the veins; etc.

Phlebotomize (flĭbǫ·tŏməiz), *v.* 1596. [a. F. *phlébotomiser*, f. med.L. *phlebotomus*, Gr. φλεβότομος; see next and -IZE.] **a.** *intr.* To practise phlebotomy; to let blood by opening a vein. **b.** *trans.* To bleed (a person, etc.); also *transf.* and *fig.* **c.** *intr.* for *pass.* To be bled. Hence **Phlebo:tomiza·tion,** blood-letting.

Phlebotomy (flĭbǫ·tŏmi). ME. [a. OF. *flebothomie*, ad. L. *phlebotomia*, a. Gr. f. (ult.) φλεβο- PHLEBO- + -τομος -cutting, -cutter.] **1.** The action or practice of cutting open a vein so as to let blood flow, as a therapeutical operation; venesection, bleeding. **2.** *transf.* and *fig.* The drawing of blood in any way (*lit.* or *fig.*); *esp.* bloodshed; 'bleeding' in purse or pocket 1589.

2. Warre is the P. of the Body Politique 1646. Fiscal P. 1827. Hence **Phlebo·tomist,** one who practises p.; a blood-letter.

‖ **Phlegethon** (fle·gĭþǫn, fle·dʒ-). late ME. [a. Gr. Φλεγέθων, -οντ- = lit. 'blazing'.] *Gr.* and *Lat. Myth.* Name of a fabled river of fire, one of the five rivers of Hades.

Phlegm (flem). [ME. *fleem*, *fleume*, *fleme*, a. OF. *fleume*, *flemme*, mod.F. *flegme*:—L. (post-cl.) *phlegma*, a. Gr. φλέγμα inflammation, morbid clammy humour (as the result of heat), f. φλέγειν to burn, blaze. In 16th–17th c. conformed in spelling to Gr.-L. original.] **1.** The thick viscous semifluid substance secreted by the mucous membranes, esp. of the respiratory passages; mucus. **a.** In old physiology, regarded as one of the four bodily 'humours', described as cold and moist. late ME. **b.** In mod. use; esp. when morbid, and discharged by cough, etc. (Not now applied to the mucus of the nasal passages.) 1486. †**c.** With *a* and *pl.* A mass of phlegm or mucus –1727. †**2.** *Old Chem.* One of the five 'principles' of bodies, also called *water*; any watery inodorous tasteless substance obtained by distillation –1812. **3.** The character supposed to result from predominance of phlegm (sense 1 a) in the bodily constitution; phlegmatic temperament; coldness or dullness of character; coolness or evenness of temper 1578.

3. The patience of the people was creditable to their p. MEREDITH. Hence **Phlegma·tic** (flegmæ·tik) *a.* of the nature of or abounding in p.; cold, sluggish, apathetic; cool, self-possessed. **Phlegma·tically** *adv.*

‖ **Phlegmasia** (flegmēⁱ·siă, -ziă). *Pl.* **-æ.** 1706. [mod.L., a. Gr. φλεγμασία.] *Path.* Inflammation, *esp.* inflammation accompanied by fever.

P. dolens, or *p. alba dolens*, milk-leg or white-leg.

Phlegmon (fle·gmǫ̆n). [ME. a. L. *phlegmon* or *phlegmona*, a. Gr. φλεγμονή inflammation, etc., f. φλέγειν to burn.] *Path.* An inflammatory tumour, a boil or carbuncle; inflammation, esp. of the cellular tissue, tending to suppuration. Hence **Phlegmo·nic, Phle·gmonous** *adjs.* pertaining to or of the nature of a p. **Phle·gmonoid** *a.* resembling a p.

Phlegmy (fle·mi), *a.* 1550. [f. PHLEGM + -Y[1].] **1.** Mucous; containing or characterized by phlegm. **2.** = PHLEGMATIC 1607.

Phloem (flōᵘ·em). 1875. [mod., f. Gr. φλόος = φλοιός bark + -ημα, passive suffix.] *Bot.* The softer portion of the fibrovascular tissue, as dist. from the xylem or woody portion; the bast with its associated tissues.

Phlogistic (flǫdʒi·stik, -gi·stik), *a.* 1733. [In sense 1, f. PHLOGISTON + -IC; in 2 and 3, immed. ad. Gr. φλογιστός inflammable.] **1.** *Chem.* Of the nature of or consisting of phlogiston; connected with or related to phlogiston. **2.** *Path.* Inflammatory 1754. †**3.** Fiery, heated, inflamed (*lit.* and *fig.*) –1855.

Phlogi·sticate, *v. Obs.* exc. *Hist.* 1774. [f. prec. + -ATE[3].] *trans.* To render phlogistic; to combine with phlogiston. Chiefly in *pa. pple.*

†*Phlogisticated air* or *gas*, names for nitrogen in the phlogistic theory. (Cf. DEPHLOGISTICATED.) So †**Phlogistica·tion,** combination with phlogiston; now called *deoxidation.*

Phlogiston (flǫdʒi·stǫ̆n, -gi·stǫ̆n). 1733. [mod.L., a. Gr. φλογιστόν, f. φλογίζειν to set on fire, f. φλόξ, φλογ- flame, ablaut deriv. of φλεγ-, root of φλέγειν to burn.] *Chem.* A hypothetical substance or principle, formerly supposed to exist in combination in all other combustible bodies, and to be disengaged in the process of combustion; the 'principle of inflammability'; the matter of fire, conceived as fixed in inflammable substances. Hence **Phlogi·stian, Phlogi·stonist,** a believer in the existence or theory of p.

Phlogogenetic (flǫ·godʒĭne·tik), *a.* 1893. [f. Gr. φλογο-, comb. f. φλόξ flame + -GENETIC.] *Path.* Producing inflammation. Also **Phlogoge·nic, Phlogo·genous** *adjs.* in same sense.

Phlogopite (flǫ·gǫ̆pəit). 1850. [f. Gr. φλογωπός fiery (f. φλογ- flame + ὤψ, ὠπ- face) + -ITE[1].] *Min.* A magnesia mica, found in crystalline limestone and serpentine.

‖ **Phlogosis** (flogōᵘ·sis). *Pl.* **-es** (-īz). 1693. [mod.L., a. Gr., f. φλόξ, φλογ- flame.] *Path.* Inflammation. Hence **Phlogosed** (-ōᵘ·zd) *ppl. a.* inflamed. **Phlogosin** (-ōᵘ·sin) *Chem.* a product of cultures of certain bacteria, which produces acute local inflammation. **Phlogotic** (-ǫ·tik) *a.* inflammatory.

Phlorizin (florəi·zin, flǫ·rizin). Also formerly called †**phloridzite.** 1835. [f. Gr. φλόος, φλοιός bark + ῥίζα root + -IN.] *Chem.* A bitter substance ($C_{21}H_{24}O_{10}$), crystallizing in silky needles, obtained from the bark of the root of the apple, pear, plum, and cherry trees.

Phloro-, bef. a vowel **phlor-,** used in *Chem.*, to form names of substances connected with PHLORIZIN, as

Phloramine (flǫ·rămən) [AMINE], the amine ($C_6H_7NO_2 = C_6H_5O_2.NH_2$) obtained in thin shining films by the action of ammonia on phloroglucin. **Phloretin** (flōᵊ·rītin), a sweet crystalline substance ($C_{15}H_{14}O_5$) produced by the action of dilute acids on phlorizin; hence **Phloretic** (flore·tik) *a.*, applied to an *acid* ($C_9H_{10}O_3$) obtained from phloretin by the action of potash; also to *ethers* (*phloretic ethers*) in which an organic radical takes the place of 1 atom of hydrogen in phloretic acid (Watts). **Phloroglucin** (flǫroglū·sin) [Gr. γλυκύς sweet + -IN[1]], a colourless or yellowish crystalline, intensely sweet substance ($C_6H_6O_3$), obtained from phloretin, and occurring widely distributed in plants. **Phlorol** (flǫ·rǫl), a phenol, an oily substance ($C_8H_{10}O$) obtained from salts of phloretic acid, or from creosote. **Phlorone** (flǫ·rōᵘn), a yellow crystalline substance ($C_8H_8O_2$), homologous with quinone, obtained by distillation of beech-wood and coal-tar.

Phlox (flǫks). 1706. [a. L., a. Gr. φλόξ a plant (prob. *Silene*), lit. flame.] *Bot.* A N. American genus of herbaceous (rarely shrubby) plants (N.O. *Polemoniaceæ*), with clusters of salver-shaped flowers of various colours. **b.** *attrib.* **p.-worm,** the larva of an American moth, *Heliothis phlogophagus*, which feeds upon phloxes.

‖ **Phlyctæna, -ena** (fliktī·nă). 1693. [mod. L., a. Gr. φλύκταινα a blister, f. φλύειν, φλύζειν to swell.] *Path.* An inflammatory vesicle, pimple, or blister upon the cuticle or the eye-ball. Hence ‖**Phlycte·nula** (-æn-), pl. **-æ** [mod.L. dim. of *phlyctena*], a small p., esp. upon the conjunctiva or cornea of the eye; whence **Phlycte·nular** (-æn-) *a.*

-phobe, a. Fr. *-phobe*, ad. L. *-phobus*, a. Gr. -φόβος -fearing, adj. ending, f. φόβος fear; as in *hydrophobe, Anglophobe*, etc.

-phobia, a. L. *-phobia*, a. Gr. -φοβία, forming abstr. sbs. from the adjs. in -φόβος (see prec.) with sense 'dread, horror'; as in *hydrophobia, Russophobia*, etc. Hence **-pho·bic** forming adjs., **-pho·biac, -phobist** forming sbs.

Phobia (fōᵘ·biă). 1801. [prec. used as a separate word.] Fear, horror, or aversion, esp. of a morbid character.

‖ **Phoca** (fōᵘ·kă). *Pl.* **phocæ** (fōᵘ·sī), **phocas.** 1599. [L., a. Gr. φώκη seal.] *Zool.* A seal; in mod. zoology, restricted to the genus typified by the Common Seal, *P. vitulina.* Hence **Phoca·cean** *a.* of or pertaining to the *Phocidæ* or seal family; *sb.* a member of this family. **Pho·cal** *a.* of or pertaining to a seal. **Pho·cine** (fōᵘ·səin) *a.* pertaining to the subfamily *Phocinæ*, containing the seals proper; *sb.* a member of this family.

Phocenic (fosī·nik, -se·nik), *a.* 1836. [for **phocænic*, f. Zool. L. *Phocæna* (a. Gr. φώκαινα porpoise, f. φώκη seal) + -IC.] *Chem.* Applied to an acid obtained from porpoise- or dolphin-oil, orig. called DELPHINIC, and subseq. identified with VALERIC acid $(CH_3)_2.C_2H_3.CO_2H$. So **Pho·cenil, Pho·cenin,** glyceryl valerate, or trivalerin, = DELPHIN *sb.* 2.

Phocodont (fōᵘ·kǒdǫnt), *a.* (*sb.*) [f. Gr. φώκη seal + ὀδούς, ὀδοντ- tooth.] *Zool.* Of or pertaining to the *Phocodontia*, an extinct suborder of *Cetacea*, furnishing connecting links with the *Phocidæ* or seals. **b.** *sb.* Any member of the *Phocodontia.*

‖**Phœbe**[1] (fī·bi). *poet.* 1590. [a. L., a. Gr. Φοίβη, fem. of φοῖβος bright; cf. PHŒBUS.] Name of Artemis or Diana as goddess of the moon; the moon personified.

To morrow night, when P. doth behold Her siluer visage, in the watry glasse SHAKS.

Phœbe[2] (fī·bi). 1700. [Echoic, but spelt after prec.] = PEWIT 3, PEWEE.

‖ **Phœbus** (fī·bǒs). late ME. [a. L., a. Gr. Φοῖβος lit. bright, shining.] A name of Apollo as the Sun-god; the sun personified. Chiefly *poet.* **b.** Apollo as the god of poetry and music, presiding over the Muses; hence, the genius of poetry 1809. So **Phœbe·an** *a.*

Phœnician (fĭni·ʃăn), *sb.* and *a.* [ME. *Phenicien*, a. F. *phénicien*, f. L. *Phœnicia* (sc. *terra*) = L. *Phœnice*, a. Gr. Φοινίκη the country of the Φοίνικες (Φοῖνιξ); see -AN. The primary sense of Gr. Φοῖνιξ is uncertain.] **A.** *sb.* **1.** A native or inhabitant of Phœnicia, an ancient country on the coast of Syria, which contained the cities of Tyre and Sidon; also of any Phœnician colony. **2.** The language spoken by this people 1836.

1. Astoreth, whom the Phœnicians call'd Astarte, Queen of Heav'n MILT.

B. *adj.* Of or pertaining to ancient Phœnicia, or its inhabitants or colonists; hence, Punic, Carthaginian 1601.

Phœnicopter (fī·nikǫptəɹ). 1570. [ad. L. *phœnicopterus*, a. Gr. φοινικόπτερος flamingo, lit. red-feathered, f. φοῖνιξ, φοινικ- crimson + πτέρον feather.] *Ornith.* Adopted form of the Gr. and L. name of the flamingo of Southern Europe (*Phœnicopterus roseus* or *antiquorum*).

Phœnix[1], **phenix** (fī·niks). [OE. and OF. *fenix*, a. med.L. *phenix*, L. *phœnix*, a. Gr. φοῖνιξ the bird, identical with φοῖνιξ Phœnician, purple-red. The Eng. spelling was assimilated to L. in 16th c.] **1.** A mythical bird, of gorgeous plumage, fabled to be the only one of its kind, and to live five or six hundred years in the Arabian desert, after which it burnt itself to ashes on a funeral pile, and emerged from its ashes with renewed youth, to live through another cycle of years. **2.** *transf.* and *fig.* **a.** A paragon ME. **b.** That which rises from the ashes of its predecessor 1591. **3.** *Astr.* One of the southern constellations 1674.

1. But from himself the P. only springs: Self-born, begotten by the Parent Flame In which he burn'd, Another and the Same DRYDEN.

‖ **Phœnix**[2] (fī·niks). 1601. [mod.L. (Linn.) a. Gr. φοῖνιξ date palm, date.] A genus of palms, distinguished by their pinnate leaves. (*P. dactylifera* is the Date Palm.)

‖ **Pholas** (fōᵘ·læs). *Pl.* **pholades** (fōᵘ·lădīz). 1661. [mod.L., a. Gr. φωλάς, φωλαδ- adj. lurking in a hole (φωλεός).] *Zool.* A genus of boring bivalve molluscs (family *Pholadidæ*); an animal of this genus, a piddock. So **Pho·lad, -a·dean, Pho·ladid.**

Phonate (fōᵘ·neⁱt), *v.* 1876. [f. Gr. φωνή voice + -ATE[3].] *Physiol. intr.* To utter vocal sound; *trans.* to sound vocally. Hence **Pho·natory** *a.* pertaining or relating to phonation.

Phonation (fonēⁱ·ʃən). 1842. [f. Gr. φωνή voice + -ATION.] *Physiol.* The production or utterance of vocal sound; usu. as dist. from *articulation*; occas. *gen.* vocal utterance, voice-production.

Phonautograph (fonǭ·tǒgraf). 1859. [f. Gr. φωνή voice + αὐτο- self + -GRAPH -writer (i. e. recorder).] An apparatus for automatically recording the vibrations of sound by means of a membrane set in vibration by the sound-waves, and having a point attached which makes a tracing upon a revolving cylinder.

Phone (fōᵘn), *sb.*[1] 1890. [ad. Gr. φωνή voice.] *Phonetics.* An elementary sound of spoken language; a simple vowel or consonant sound. Also, any of the variants of a phoneme.

Phone, *sb.*[2] and *v.* 1884. Colloq. abbrev. of TELEPHONE; also of *ear-* or *head-phone.*

Phoneidoscope (fonəi·dǒskōᵘp). 1878. [f. Gr. φωνή voice + εἶδος form + -SCOPE.] An instrument for exhibiting the colour-figures produced by the action of sound-vibrations upon a thin film, e.g. of soap-solution.

Phoneme (fōᵘ·nīm). 1923. [ad. F. *phonème*, ad. Gr. φώνημα sound, speech.] *Philol.* A speech-sound considered in respect of its functional relations in a linguistic system.

Phonetic (fǒne·tik), *a.* 1826. [ad. mod.L. *phoneticus*, a. Gr. φωνητικός adj., f. (ult.) φωνεῖν to utter sound.] **1.** Representing vocal sounds; applied to signs which represent the (elementary) sounds of speech, or which express the pronunciation of words. **b.** Applied to systems of spelling in which each letter represents invariably the same spoken sound 1848. **2.** Of, pertaining or relating to the sounds of spoken language; consisting of vocal sounds 1861. **b.** Involving vibration of the vocal chords (as opp. to mere breath or whisper) 1880. Hence **Phone·tical** *a.* (*rare*), phonetic; **-ly** *adv.* **Phoneti·cian** (fōᵘnĭti·ʃăn) = PHONETIST 1. 1848. **Phone·ticism,** p. quality, or the p. system, of writing or spelling. **Phone·ticist,**

an advocate of p. spelling. **Phone·ticize** *v. trans.* to render p., to write phonetically.

Phonetics (fōne·tiks), *sb. pl.* 1841. [See prec. and -ICS.] That section of linguistic science which treats of the production of the sounds of speech and their representation; the phonetic phenomena (of a language or dialect).

Phonetism (fōu·nĭtiz'm). 1879. [f. Gr. φωνητός to be spoken (f. φωνεῖν) + -ISM.] Phonetic representation; reduction to a phonetic system of writing or spelling.

Phonetist (fōu·nĭtist). 1864. [f. as prec. + -IST.] 1. A person versed in phonetics; one who studies the sounds of speech. 2. A phoneticist 1875.

Phoney (fōu·ni), *a.* *U.S. slang.* 1902. [perh. var. of *fawney* (worthless) ring, f. Ir. *fáinne* ring.] Counterfeit, sham.

Phonic (fǭu·nik), *a.* 1823. [f. Gr. φωνή voice + -IC.] 1. Acoustic. 2. = PHONETIC 2, 2 b. 1843. Also *sb. pl.* (1683), †acoustics –1842; phonetics (*rare*) 1844.

Phono- (fōuno), bef. a vowel **phon-**, comb. form of Gr. φωνή voice, sound, used extensively in modern technical terms, as PHONOGRAPH, PHONOLOGY, etc.; and also in **Phonoca·mptic** [Gr. καμπτός, -ικός, f. κάμπτειν to bend] *a.* (*rare*) having the property of reflecting sound, or producing an echo; cataphonic; hence **Phonoca·mptics**, cataphonics, catacoustics. **Pho·nofilm**, a cinematographic film in which the characters speak 1922. **Phono·meter** [Gr. μέτρον measure], an instrument for measuring or recording the number or force of sound-waves. **Pho·noscope** [-SCOPE], (*a*) name for various instruments by means of which sound-vibrations are represented in a visible form; (*b*) = MICROPHONE.

Phonogram (fōu·nŏgræm). 1860. [f. PHONO- + -GRAM; in sense 2, after *telegram*.] 1. A character representing a spoken sound; *spec.* a letter of (Pitman's) phonography. 2. The sound-record made by a phonograph; a phonographic record or message 1884.

Phonograph (fōu·nŏgraf), *sb.* 1835. [f. Gr. φωνή voice + (in sense 1) -(ό)γραφος written, (in sense 2) -γράφος writing, writer; see -GRAPH.] †1. = prec. 1 (*rare*) –1857. †2. = PHONAUTOGRAPH 1863. 3. (spec. *talking p.*) An instrument, invented by Thomas A. Edison, by which sounds are automatically recorded and reproduced 1877. Hence **Pho·nograph** *v. trans.* a. to report in (Pitman's) phonography; b. to record or reproduce by or as by a p.

Phonography (fŏnǫ·grăfi). 1701. [f. Gr. φωνή voice (see PHONO-) + -GRAPHY.] †1. The art or practice of writing according to sound; phonetic spelling –1851. 2. *spec.* Pitman's system of phonetic shorthand 1840. 3. The automatic recording of sounds, as by the PHONAUTOGRAPH, or the recording and reproduction of them by the PHONOGRAPH; the construction and use of phonographs 1861. Hence **Phono·grapher**, a phonetist; one who uses p. (sense 2), or the phonograph. **Phonogra·phic** *a.* phonetic; of, pertaining to, or using p. (sense 2); of, pertaining to, or produced by the phonograph; **-ally** *adv.*

Phonolite (fōu·nŏləit). 1828. [f. PHONO- + -LITE.] *Min.* Name for various volcanic rocks which ring when struck; clinkstone. Hence **Phonoli·tic** *a.*

Phonology (fŏnǫ·lŏdʒi). 1799. [f. Gr. φωνή (see PHONO-) + -LOGY.] The science of vocal sounds (= PHONETICS), esp. of those of a particular language; also, the system of sounds and phonetic features or conditions of a language. Hence **Phonolo·gic, -al** *adjs.* phonetic; **-ly** *adv.* **Phono·logist**, a phonetist.

Phonopore (fōu·nŏpoəɹ). 1886. [f. PHONO- + Gr. πόρος passage.] An apparatus by means of which electrical impulses produced by induction, as in a telephone, may be used to transmit messages along a telegraph wire, without interfering with the current by which ordinary messages are simultaneously transmitted. **Phonopo·ric** *a.* Also **Pho·nophore**.

Phonotype (fōu·nŏtəip), *sb.* 1844. [f. PHONO- + TYPE.] A character of a phonetic alphabet adapted for printing; (without *a* and *pl.*) phonetic print or type. Hence **Pho·notype** *v. trans.* to print in p. **Phonoty·pic, -al**, *adjs.*, **-ly** *adv.* **Pho·notypist** (-təipist), an advocate or user of p. **Pho·notypy** (-təipi), a method or system of phonetic printing.

-phore (fōəɹ), mod.L. *-phorus, -phorum*, a. Gr. -φόρος, -ον bearing, bearer, f. φέρειν to bear, used to form various technical words, as *semaphore, gonophore, phonophore.* Hence -PHOROUS.

‖ **Phorminx** (fǭ·ɹmiŋks). 1776. [mod.L., a. Gr. φόρμιγξ.] A kind of cithara or lyre used by the ancient Greeks to accompany the voice.

‖ **Phormium** (fǭ·ɹmiŏm). 1852. [mod.L., a. Gr. φορμίον a species of plant.] *Bot.* A genus of liliaceous plants (suborder *Hemerocalleæ*), comprising a single variable species, *P. tenax*, the New Zealand flax; any of these.

Phorone (forōu·n). 1859. [Shortened from *camphorone* (f. CAMPHOR + -ONE).] †a. A substance, $C_9H_{14}O$, now called *camphor-phorone*; b. An isomer of this substance, *diisopropylidene acetone*, a colourless oil with aromatic odour.

Phoronomy (forǫ·nŏmi). 1877. [ad. mod. L. *phoronomia*, f. Gr. φορά motion (f. φέρειν to bear) + *-nomia*: cf. ASTRONOMY.] The purely geometrical theory of motion; kinematics. Hence **Phorono·mic** *a.* kinematic. **Phorono·mics** *sb.* = *phoronomy*.

-phorous (fŏrəs), comb. element, f. mod.L *-phorus*, -φόρος + -OUS, forming adjs.; synonymous with -FEROUS, but properly used only in words derived from Gr., e.g. *carpophorous, oophorous, phonophorous*, etc.

Phosgene (fǫ·sdʒīn). Also **-gen** (-dʒen). 1812. [f. Gr. φῶς light + *-gene*, -GEN.] *Chem.* A name for the gas carbon oxychloride, $COCl_2$, orig. obtained by exposing equal volumes of chlorine and carbonic oxide to the sun's rays. Also called *p. gas.*

Phosgenite (fǫ·sdʒĭnəit). 1849. [f. prec. + -ITE [1].] *Min.* A mineral consisting of nearly equal parts of carbonate and chloride of lead, occurring in tetragonal crystals.

Phosph- = PHOSPHO-, comb. form of PHOSPHORUS.

Phospham (fǫ·sfæm). 1866. [f. PHOSPH- + AM(MONIA).] *Chem.* The nitril of phosphoric acid (PHN_2), a white, reddish, or yellowish-red powder.

Phosphate (fǫ·sfĕt). 1795. [a. F., f. PHOSPH- + -ATE [4].] *Chem.* A salt of phosphoric acid. b. In *pl.*, esp. the phosphates of lime or iron and alumina, as constituents of cereals, etc. 1858. Hence **Pho·sphated** *a.* converted into a p.; combined with or containing phosphoric acid. **Phospha·tic** *a.* of the nature of, characterized by the presence of, or containing a p.

Phosphaturia (fǫsfătiūə·riă). 1876. [f. prec. + -URIA.] *Path.* A morbid state evidenced by the excess of phosphates in the urine. Hence **Phosphatu·ric** *a.*

Phosphene (fǫ·sfīn). 1872. [irreg. f. Gr. φῶς light + φαίνειν to show.] An appearance of rings of light produced by pressure on the eyeball, due to irritation of the retina.

Phosphide (fǫ·sfəid). 1849. [f. PHOSPH- + -IDE.] *Chem.* A combination of phosphorus with another element or a radical. (Earlier name *phosphuret*.)

Phosphine (fǫ·sfəin). 1871. [f. PHOSPH- + -INE [5]; cf. AMINE.] *Chem.* 1. A name for phosphuretted hydrogen gas, PH_3 (as an analogue of ammonia, NH_3) 1873. 2. A phosphorus ammonia; a compound having the structure of an *amine*, with phosphorus in place of nitrogen; e.g. *monoethyl p.*, $C_2H_5.P.H_2$. 1871. Hence **Phosphi·nic** *a.* of, pertaining to, or derived from p.; in *phosphinic acid*, any one of various acids formed from the primary and secondary phosphines by fixation of 3 and 2 atoms of oxygen respectively.

Phosphite (fǫ·sfəit). 1799. [a. F., f. PHOSPH- + -ITE [1].] *Chem.* A salt of phosphorous acid.

Phospho- (fǫ·sfo), bef. a vowel **Phosph-**, comb. form, shortened from PHOSPHORUS.

Phosphonium (fǫsfōu·niŏm). 1866. [f. PHOSPH(ORUS + ending of AMMONIUM.] *Chem.* A combination of hydrogen and phosphorus, PH_4, analogous to ammonium, entering as a monovalent radical into many compounds, as *p. iodide*, PH_4I, etc. Hence **Phospho·nic** *a.*, in *p. acid*, any one of several compounds derived from phosphoric acid by the replacement of hydroxyl (OH) by a hydrocarbon group. Occas. called *phosphinic*, or *phosphenilic acid.*

Phosphor (fǫ·sfǭɹ), *sb.* (*a.*) 1635. [ad. L. *phosphorus* PHOSPHORUS.] 1. (With capital P.) The morning star; the planet Venus when appearing before sunrise; Lucifer. Now only *poet.* †2. = PHOSPHORUS 2. –1819. 3. = PHOSPHORUS 3; esp. in *p.-bronze, -copper, -tin, -zinc*, alloys of phosphorus with these metals; see BRONZE, etc. †B. *adj.* Light-giving; phosphorescent –1820.

1. Bright P., fresher for the night TENNYSON.

Phosphorate (fǫ·sfŏreit), *v.* 1789. [f. PHOSPHORUS + -ATE [3].] Orig. and chiefly in *ppl. a.* **Pho·sphorated.** *trans.* To combine or impregnate with phosphorus.

Phosphoreal (fǫsfōə·riăl), *a.* 1745. [f. (doubtful) L. *phosphoreus* (f. *phosphorus*) + -AL.] Of or pertaining to phosphorus; resembling that of phosphorus.

Phosphoresce (fǫsfŏre·s), *v.* 1794. [f. PHOSPHORUS + L. *-escere*, formative of inceptive vbs.] *intr.* To emit luminosity without combustion (or by gentle combustion without sensible heat); to shine in the dark.

Phosphorescent (fǫsfŏre·sĕnt), *a.* (*sb.*) 1766. [f. PHOSPHORUS; see -ESCENT.] Having the property of shining in the dark; luminous without combustion or without sensible heat; self-luminous. B. *sb.* A phosphorescent substance 1863. Hence **Phosphore·scence**, the condition or quality of being p.

Phosphoric (fǫsfǫ·rik), *a.* 1784. [ad. F. *phosphorique*; see PHOSPHOR and -IC.] 1. Pertaining to or of the nature of a phosphorus (sense 2); phosphorescent. 2. *Chem.* Of or pertaining to the element phosphorus; *spec.* applied to compounds in which phosphorus has its higher valency (pentavalent) as opp. to PHOSPHOROUS; esp. in *p. acid* = trihydrogen phosphate, $H_3PO_4 = P(OH)_3O$, a colourless, inodorous, intensely bitter acid 1791.

Phosphorite (fǫ·sfŏrəit). 1796. [f. PHOSPHORUS + -ITE [1]] *Min.* A name orig. applied to APATITE, or native phosphate of lime; now only to a non-crystallized variety from Estremadura, Spain, and elsewhere.

Phosphorize (fǫ·sfŏrəiz), *v.* 1799. [a. F. *phosphoriser*, f. PHOSPHORUS; see -IZE.] = PHOSPHORATE. Orig. and chiefly in *ppl. a.* **Pho·sphorized.**

Phosphoro-, comb. form of PHOSPHORUS, used to form chemical and other terms; as **Phosphorogenic** (-dʒe·nik) *a.*, causing phosphorescence; *spec.* applied to those rays of the spectrum which excite phosphorescence in certain objects.

Phosphoroscope (fǫ·sfŏrŏskōup). 1860. [-SCOPE.] a. An apparatus for observing and measuring the duration of phosphorescence in such substances as emit light for a very short period; b. A scientific toy consisting of an arrangement of glass tubes containing various phosphorescent substances, each glowing with a different coloured light.

Phosphorous (fǫ·sfŏrəs), *a.* 1777. [f. next + -OUS; in sense 2, ad. F. *phosphoreux*; see -OUS c.] 1. = PHOSPHORESCENT *a.* 2. *Chem.* Abounding in phosphorus; *spec.* applied to compounds into which phosphorus enters in its lower valency (trivalent), as opp. to *phosphoric*; esp. in *p. acid* = $P(OH)_3$. 1794.

Phosphorus (fǫ·sfŏrŏs). 1629. [a. L., a. Gr. φωσφόρος adj. (f. φῶς light + -φόρος bringing); hence as sb. (sc. ἀστήρ) the morning star.] 1. (with capital P): The morning star: = PHOSPHOR 1. Now *rare.* 2. Any substance or organism that phosphoresces; *esp.* (in later use) a substance that absorbs sunlight, and shines in the dark. *Pl.* †phosphoruses, †'-s,

phosphori. Now *rare.* 3. *Chem.* One of the non-metallic elements, a yellowish translucent substance resembling wax, widely distributed in nature in combination with other elements; it is extremely inflammable, undergoing slow combustion at ordinary temperatures, and hence appearing luminous in the dark. (Symbol P.) 1680.

attrib. and *Comb.*, as *p. matches, poisoning*; in Chem. = of p., as *p. oxychloride*, etc.; **p. necrosis,** gangrene of some part of the jaw-bone, due to the fumes of p., a disease affecting persons engaged in the manufacture of matches; **p. paste,** a paste containing p., used to kill vermin.

†**Phosphuret** (fǫ·sfiŭret). Also **-oret.** 1799. [ad. mod.L. *phosphoretum*, after F. *phosphure* phosphide; see -URET.] *Chem.* = PHOSPHIDE –1868. Hence **Pho·sphuretted** *a.* (also **phosphor-**), combined chemically with phosphorus, as *phosphuretted hydrogen* = PHOSPHINE.

Phossy (fǫ·si), *a. colloq.* Also **fossy.** 1889. [f. *phos*, colloq. abbrev. of PHOSPHORUS + -Y [1].] In **p. jaw,** pop. name for phosphorus necrosis of the jaw.

Photic (fōu·tik), *a. rare.* 1843. [f. Gr. φῶς, φωτ- light + -IC.] Pertaining or relating to light. So **Pho·tics** *sb. pl.*, (*a*) the science of light and its intrinsic properties (occas. used instead of *optics*); (*b*) applied in U. S. to that class of mechanical inventions embracing illuminating apparatus generally.

Photo (fōu·to). 1870. Colloq. abbrev. of PHOTOGRAPH.

Photo- (fōutŏ), bef. a vowel properly **phot-** (but also in full from *photo-*), repr. Gr. φωτο-, comb. form of φῶς, φωτ- light. 1. Words in which *photo-* simply denotes 'light'.

‖**Pho·tobacte·rium,** a phosphorescent bacterium. **Photoche·mical** *a.* of or pertaining to the chemical action of light; so **Photoche·mistry. Pho·todyna·mic, -al** *adjs.* [see DYNAMIC], pertaining or relating to the energy of light; so **Pho·todyna·mics,** that part of physics which deals with the energy of light, esp. in relation to growth or movement in plants. **Pho·tomagne·tic** *a.*, applied to certain rays of the spectrum having, or supposed to have, a magnetic influence; so **Photoma·gnetism,** photomagnetic property or character; that branch of physics which deals with the relations between light and magnetism. **Photopho·bia** [-PHOBIA], dread of or shrinking from light, esp. as a symptom of disease of the eyes. **Pho·tophore** [-PHORE], an apparatus with an electric light, used for examination of internal organs of the body, etc. **Photothe·rapy,** a system of treatment of certain skin diseases by exposure to particular light-rays, introduced by N. R. Finsen of Copenhagen.

2. Words in which *photo-* indicates connexion with photography, or some photographic process; being sometimes practically equivalent to PHOTOGRAPHIC, as in *p.-process, -radiogram, -telegram, -tracing, -transfer, -zincograph*, vb., etc.

Pho·to-ele·ctrotype, a process in which a photographic picture is produced in relief, so as to afford, by electro-deposition, a matrix for a cast, from which impressions in ink may be obtained. **Photogra·mmeter** [f. PHOTOGRAM + -METER], a photographic camera combined with a theodolite, for use in surveying, or for taking pictures for use in map-making. **Pho·to-mecha·nical** *a.* combining a photographic and a mechanical process. **Pho·to-relie·f,** an image in relief produced by a photographic process. **Photo-scu·lpture,** a process in which the subject is photographed simultaneously from a number of different points of view all round, and the photographs are used to trace successive outlines on a block of modelling clay which is afterwards finished by hand. **Photo-te·lescope,** a telescope with photographic apparatus, used for photographing stars or other heavenly bodies. **Pho·totypo·graphy** [TYPOGRAPHY], printing from an engraving in relief produced by a photo-mechanical process. **Pho·to-xylography** (-zəilǫ·grăfi) [XYLOGRAPHY], a process of employing photography in the preparation of wood blocks for printing from.

3. Prefixed to the names of chemical salts, etc., and of chemical processes to express the effect of light in changing the molecular constitution of the salt, etc. (by virtue of which it can be employed in photography.) Thus **Pho·to-sa·lt,** a general term for any salt so modified by light; so **photo-bro·mide, -su·lphate,** etc.

Photochromatic (fōu:tŏkromæ·tik), *a.* 1888. [f. PHOTO- + CHROMATIC.] Of or pertaining to the chromatic or colouring action of light; pertaining to or produced by photochromy. So **Pho·tochrome,** name for a coloured photograph. **Photo·chro·motype,** a picture in colours printed from plates prepared by a photo-relief process. **Pho·tochromy,** (*a*) the art or process of colouring photographs; (*b*) colour-photography.

Pho:to-ele·ctric, *a.* Also **photelectric.** 1863. [f. PHOTO- + ELECTRIC.] **a.** Pertaining to, furnishing, or employing electric light 1863. **b.** Of or pertaining to photo-electricity; producing an electric effect by means of light 1880. **c.** Used for taking photographs by electric light. So **Pho:to-electri·city,** electricity generated or affected by light.

Photoelectrotype: see PHOTO- 2.

Pho:to-engra·ving. 1872. [f. PHOTO- 2 + ENGRAVING.] Any process in which, by the action of photography, a matrix is obtained from which prints in ink can be taken. (Usu. restricted to those cases in which the matrix is in relief, as dist. from PHOTOGRAVURE.)

Pho:to-galvano·graphy. 1855. [f. PHOTO- 2 + GALVANOGRAPHY.] A process of obtaining from a positive photograph, by means of a gutta-percha impression from a relief negative in bichromated gelatine, an electrotype plate capable of being used as in copper-plate printing. So **Pho:to-galva·nograph,** a print thus formed. **Pho:to-galvanogra·phic** *a.*

Photogen (fōu·tŏdʒen). 1864. [f. Gr. φῶς, φωτ- (PHOTO- 1) + -GEN.] A kind of paraffin oil; kerosene.

Photogene (fōu·tŏdʒīn). 1864. [See PHOTO- 1 and -GEN 2.] *Physiol.* A visual impression (usu. negative) continuing after the withdrawal of the object which produced it; an after-image.

Photogenic (-dʒe·nik), *a.* 1839. [See PHOTO-, -GEN, -IC.] 1. Produced by light; †photographic (–1867). 2. Producing or emitting light 1863. 3. That is an apt subject for artistic photography.

Photoglyph (fōu·tŏglif). 1852. [f. PHOTO- 2 + γλυφή GLYPH.] An engraved plate, such as can be printed from, produced by the action of light. So **Photogly·phic, Photogly·ptic** *adjs.* **Pho·toglyphy,** the art or process of engraving by means of the action of light and certain chemical processes; the production of photoglyphic plates and photoglyphs or photogravures.

†**Photogram** (fōu·tŏgræm). 1859. [f. PHOTO- 2 + -GRAM as in *telegram*).] = PHOTOGRAPH.

Photograph (fōu·tŏgraf), *sb.* 1839. [f. Gr. φῶς PHOTO- 1 + -γραφος written, delineated (cf. AUTOGRAPH, PARAGRAPH).] A picture, likeness, or facsimile obtained by photography.

Photograph (fōu·tŏgraf), *v.* 1839. [f. prec. sb.] 1. *trans.* To take a photograph of. **b.** *absol.* or *intr.* To take photographs 1861. **c.** *intr.* (for *pass.*) To 'take' (well or badly) 1893. 2. *trans. fig.* To portray vividly in words; to fix on the mind or memory 1862.

1. When a distant landscape is photographed, a large number of rays of light are concentrated upon the film 1883. **c.** I do not p. at all well 1893. 2. Indelibly photographed on a memory from which few things..have been effaced 1862.

Photographer (fŏtǫ·grăfəɹ). 1847. [f. prec. + -ER [1].] One who practises photography, *esp.* as a business. So †**Photo·graphist** 1843.

Photographometer (fōu:tŏgrăfǫ·mĭtəɹ). 1849. [f. as prec. + -OMETER, -METER.] An instrument for ascertaining the degree of sensitiveness of photographic films to the chemical action of light.

Photography (fŏtǫ·grăfi). 1839. [f. Gr. φῶς PHOTO- 1 + -γραφία writing, delineation; see -GRAPHY.] The process or art of producing pictures by means of the chemical action of light on a sensitive film on a basis of paper, glass, metal, etc.; the business of producing and printing such pictures. So **Photogra·phic, -al** *adjs.* of, pertaining to, used in or produced by p.; engaged or skilled in p.; **-ly** *adv.*

Photogravure (fōu:tŏ,grăviū̆ə·ɹ), *sb.* 1879. [a. F., f. PHOTO- + *gravure* engraving.] Photo-engraving; *esp.* the process of preparing a matrix by transferring a photographic negative to a metal plate, and then etching it in; a picture produced by this process. Hence **Photogravu·re** *v. trans.* to reproduce by p.

Photoheliograph (fōu:tohī·liograf). 1861. [f. PHOTO- + Gr. ἥλιος sun + -GRAPH.] = HELIOGRAPH 2.

Photolithography (fōu:to,liþǫ·grăfi). 1856. [f. PHOTO- 2 + LITHOGRAPHY.] The art or process of producing, by photography, designs upon lithographic stone, etc., from which prints may be taken as in ordinary lithography. So **Photoli·thograph,** a print produced by p. 1855. **Pho:tolitho·grapher,** one who practises p. **Pho:tolithogra·phic** *a.*

Photology (fotǫ·lŏdʒi). *rare.* 1828. [f. Gr. φῶς PHOTO- 1 + -LOGY.] The science of light; optics. Hence **Photolo·gic, -al** *adjs.* optical. **Photo·logist,** one versed in p.

Photometer (fotǫ·mĭtəɹ). 1760. [f. Gr. φῶς PHOTO- 1 + -METER.] An instrument for measuring the intensity of light or comparing the intensity of light from various sources.

Photometry (fotǫ·mĕtri). 1824. [ad. mod. L. *photometria*, f. Gr. φῶς PHOTO- 1 + -μετρία -METRY.] Measurement of light; comparison of the intensity of light from various sources; the use of a photometer. Hence **Photome·tric, -al** *adjs.*; **-ly** *adv.* **Photometrician** (-i·ʃăn).

Photomicrograph (fōuto,məi·krŏgraf). 1858. [f. PHOTO- 2 + Gr. μικρός MICRO- + -GRAPH.] A photograph of a microscopic object on a magnified scale. So **-micro·graphy.**

Photon (fōu·tǫn). 1926. [f. Gr. φωτ-, φῶς light, after *electron*.] *Physics.* A corpuscle or unit particle of light.

Photophone (fōu·tŏfōun). 1880. [f. Gr. φῶς PHOTO- 1 + -φωνος sounding, sounder, φωνή voice, sound.] An apparatus in which sounds are transmitted by light; *esp.* that invented by A. Graham Bell and Sumner Tainter in 1880. See RADIOPHONE. Hence **Photopho·nic** *a.* **Photo·phony,** the use of the p.; the conveyance of sound-vibrations by means of light.

Photoscope (fōu·tŏskōup). 1872. [f. PHOTO- 1 + -SCOPE.] **a.** A means of examining light, e.g. for purposes of analysis. **b.** [with *photo-* taken as = *photograph*.] A lens or apparatus with lenses, through which photographs are viewed. Hence **Photosco·pic** *a.* pertaining to the examination of light; belonging to a p.

Photosphere (fōu·tŏsfīəɹ). 1664. [f. PHOTO- 1 + Gr. σφαῖρα ball, SPHERE.] 1. A sphere or orb of light. 2. *Astron.* The luminous envelope of the sun (or a star), from which its light and heat radiate 1848. Hence **Photosphe·ric** *a.*

Photostat (fōu·tŏstæt). 1912. [f. PHOTO- 2 + -STAT.] A trade name for a photographic apparatus designed for taking a copy of a flat original on sensitized paper, and giving a negative image; a copy so made. Hence as vb. and **Photosta·tic** *a.*

Photosynthesis (fōuto,si·nþĭsis). 1904. [f. PHOTO- + SYNTHESIS.] Chemical combination caused by the action of light; *spec.* in plants the conversion of the carbon dioxide and water of the air into carbohydrates brought about by exposure to light. Hence **Photosy·nthesize** *v. trans.* to convert (carbon dioxide and water into carbohydrates) by p. **Pho:tosynthe·tic** *a.* of or belonging to p. **-the·tically** *adv.*

‖ **Phototonus** (fotǫ·tŏnŏs). 1875. [mod.L. f. Gr. φῶς, φωτο- PHOTO- + τόνος tension, TONE.] *Bot.* The normal condition of sensitiveness to light in leaves and other organs, maintained by continued exposure to light. Hence **Phototo·nic** *a.*

Phototropic (fōutotrǫ·pik), *a.* 1899. [f. PHOTO- + Gr. -τροπος turning + -IC.] *Bot.* Bending or turning under the influence of light; a more accurate substitute for HELIOTROPIC.

Phototype (fōu·tŏtəip), *sb.* 1859. [f. Gr. φῶς PHOTO- + -TYPE.] A plate or block for printing from, produced by a photographic process; also, the process by which such a plate is produced, or a picture, etc., printed from it. Hence **Pho·totype** *v. trans.* to reproduce by means of phototypy. **Phototy·pic** *a.* **Pho·totypy,** the art or process of making phototypes.

Photozincography (fōu:toziŋkǫ·grăfi). 1860. [f. PHOTO- + ZINC + -GRAPHY.] The art or process of producing by photographic methods a design on a zinc plate from which prints can be taken. Hence **Photozi·ncograph** *sb.* a plate, or a picture or facsimile, produced by p. **Photozi·ncograph** *v. trans.* to produce or copy by p. **Pho:tozincogra·phic, -al** *adjs.*

Phra·gmocone. Also *erron.* **phragma-.** 1847. [f. Gr. φραγμός fence + κῶνος CONE.] *Zool.* The conical chambered internal skeleton of a fossil belemnite; also, by extension, the corresponding part in other fossil cephalopods.

Phrase (frēⁱz), *sb.* 1530. [ad. late L. *phrasis* (formerly also used), a. Gr., f. φράζειν to point out, tell.] **1.** Manner or style of expression; diction, phraseology, language. **2.** A small group of words expressing a single notion, or entering with some degree of unity into the structure of a sentence; an expression; esp. a characteristic or idiomatic expression 1530. †**b.** Applied to a single word –1699. **c.** *Gram.* A group of words equivalent to a noun, adjective, or adverb, and having no finite verb of its own 1852. **3.** A short, pithy, or telling expression; sometimes, a meaningless, trite, or high-sounding form of words 1579. **4.** *Mus.* Any (comparatively) short passage, forming a more or less independent member of a longer passage, or of a whole movement 1789.

1. Conforme the stile thereof with the P. of our Englishe 1540. 2. 'If I were you' is a p. often on our lips 1875. b. 2 *Hen. IV*, III. ii. 79. 3. A man.. That hath a mint of phrases in his braine SHAKS. The p. was tossed about till it bore no certain meaning 1841.

Comb.: **p.-book,** a book containing a collection of idiomatic phrases; **-mark,** a sign in musical notation to indicate the proper phrasing; **-monger,** one who deals in fine-sounding phrases; so *p.-maker.* Hence **Phra·sal** *a.* of the nature of or consisting of a p.

Phrase, *v.* 1550. [f. prec. sb.] **1.** *intr.* To employ a phrase or phrases. **2.** *trans.* To put into words; to express in words or a phrase; to express 1570. **3.** To call, designate; †to signify. Now *rare* or *arch.* 1585. **4.** *Mus.* To divide or mark off into phrases, esp. in execution. Also *absol.* 1796.

2. *To p. it,* to express the thing, to 'put it'; He has had, as he phrased it, 'a matter of four wives' JOHNSON. 3. The papists..p. the preachers to be uncircumcised Philistines 1585.

Phraseogram (frēⁱ·ziŏgræm). 1847. [irreg. f. Gr. φράσις + -GRAM.] A written character or symbol representing a phrase, *esp.* in systems of shorthand. So **Phra·seograph** [-GRAPH] (*Shorthand*) a phrase for which there is a phraseogram 1845.

Phraseological (frēⁱzi,ŏlǫ·dʒikăl), *a.* 1664. [f. PHRASEOLOGY + -IC + -AL.] **1.** Using phrases or peculiar expressions; expressed in a special phrase or phrases. **2.** Of or pertaining to phraseology; dealing with phrases or phraseology 1664.

2. A p. peculiarity of these tracts 1899. Hence **Phraseolo·gically** *adv.*

Phraseology (frēⁱzi,ǫ·lŏdʒi). 1664. [ad. mod.L. *phraseologia,* Gr. φρασεολογία, erron. f. Gr. φράσις speech + -λογία -LOGY.] †**1.** A phrase-book –1776. **2.** Manner or style of expression; the particular form of speech or diction which characterizes a writer, language, etc. 1664.

2. Men, according to their habits and professions, have a p. of their own BURKE. Hence **Phraseo·logist,** one who treats of p.; a phrase-monger.

Phrasing (frēⁱ·ziŋ), *vbl. sb.* 1611. [f. PHRASE *v.* + -ING¹.] **1.** The action of PHRASE *v.*; manner or style of verbal expression; phraseology, wording. **2.** *Mus.* The rendering of musical phrases 1880.

Phratry (frēⁱ·tri). 1833. [ad. Gr. φρατρία, f. φράτηρ clansman; cogn. w. Skr. *bhrātā,* L. *frater,* Goth. *brōþar* BROTHER.] **1.** *Ancient Gr. Hist.* A politico-religious division of the people; in Athens, each of the three subdivisions into which the phyle was divided; a clan. **2.** *transf.* Applied to tribal or kinship divisions existing among primitive races 1876.

‖ **Phrenesis** (frĭnī·sis). 1547. [L., a. late Gr., f. φρήν, φρεν-: see next and cf. FRENZY.] *Path.* = PHRENITIS.

Phrenetic (frĭne·tik), *a.* (*sb.*) [late ME. *frenetik*(*e,* a. OF. *frenetike,* ad. L. *phreneticus,* a. late Gr. φρενητικός, f. φρήν, φρεν- heart, mind. Formerly stressed *phre·netic.*] †**1.** Of persons: = FRANTIC *a.* **1.** –1778. **2.** *transf.* Fanatic, *esp.* in religious matters 1540. **3.** = FRANTIC *a.* **2.** 1529. **B.** *sb.* A madman 1612. So †**Phrene·tical** *a.,* **-ly** *adv.*

Phrenic (fre·nik), *a.* (*sb.*) 1704. [ad. mod. L. *phrenicus,* f. Gr. φρήν, φρεν- diaphragm, mind; see -IC.] **1.** *Anat.* and *Path.* Of, pertaining to, or affecting the diaphragm. †**2.** Mental –1847. **B.** *sb.* **1.** *Anat.* Short for *p. nerve* 1776. **2.** *pl.* **Phrenics**: That branch of science which relates to the mind; psychology 1841.

‖ **Phrenitis** (frĭnəi·tis). 1621. [Late L., a. Gr. φρενῖτις delirium, f. φρήν, φρεν- + -ITIS.] *Path.* Inflammation of the brain or of its membranes, attended with delirium and fever; brain-fever. Hence **Phreni·tic** *a.* affected with p.

Phreno-, bef. a vowel **phren-,** a. Gr. φρενο- (comb. form of φρήν, stem φρεν- midriff, mind), usu. in sense of 'the mind, mental faculties'; as in

Phre·nogram, the curve or tracing made by the phrenograph. **Phre·nograph,** (*a*) an instrument for recording the movements of the diaphragm in respiration; (*b*) a phrenological 'chart' of a person's mental characteristics. **Phreno-ma·gnetism,** the excitation of the phrenological organs by magnetic influence; hence **Phreno-magne·tic** *a.*

Phrenology (frĭnǫ·lŏdʒi). 1815. [f. Gr. φρήν, φρεν- mind + -LOGY; lit. 'mental science'.] The scientific study or theory of the mental faculties; *spec.* (and in ordinary use), the theory originated by Gall and Spurzheim, that the mental powers of the individual consist of separate faculties, each having its organ and location in a definite region of the surface of the brain; hence, the study of the external conformation of the cranium as an index to the development and position of these organs, and thus of the degree of development of the various faculties. Hence **Phrenolo·gic, -al,** *adjs.* of or belonging to p.; **-ly** *adv.* **Phreno·logist,** one skilled in p. **Phreno·logize** *v. trans.* to examine or analyse phrenologically.

Phre·nosin. 1878. [f. Gr. φρήν, φρεν- mind + -OSE + -IN¹ (after *myosin*).] *Chem.* A substance ($C_{34}H_{67}NO_8$) obtained from the brain.

Phrensy, -zy, etc. var. of FRENZY.

Phrontistery (frǫ·ntistĕri). Often in Gr. or Latinized forms **phrontiste·rion, phrontiste·rium.** 1614. [ad. Gr. φροντιστήριον, f. φροντιστής a deep thinker, f. φροντίζειν, f. φροντίς thought.] A place for thinking; a 'thinking-shop': a term applied in ridicule to the school of Socrates; hence applied to modern educational institutions.

Phrygian (fri·dʒiăn), *a.* (*sb.*) 1579. [ad. L. *Phrygianus,* f. *Phrygia*; see -AN.] Of or pertaining to Phrygia, an ancient country of Asia Minor, or its inhabitants.

P. cap, a conical cap or bonnet with the peak turned over in front, now identified with the cap of liberty. *P. mode* (*mus.*): (*a*) an ancient Greek mode of a warlike character, derived from the ancient Phrygians; (*b*) the second of the 'authentic' ecclesiastical modes, having its 'final' on E and 'dominant' on C.

B. *sb.* **a.** A native or inhabitant of Phrygia. **b.** A CATAPHRYGIAN. 1585.

Phthalic (fþæ·lik), *a.* 1857. [abbrev. from NAPHTHALIC.] *Chem.* Of, pertaining to, or obtained from naphthaline, as *p. anhydride,* etc. *P. acid,* a white crystalline compound ($C_8H_6O_4$) produced by the action of nitric acid on naphthaline, alizarin, purpurin, etc. Also called ALIZARIC *acid.*

So **Phtha·late,** a salt of p. acid. **Phthalein** (fþæ·lĭ,in) [-IN¹], one of a series of organic dyes produced by combining p. anhydride with the phenols, with elimination of water. **Phthalide** (fþæ·ləid) [-IDE, here short for *anhydride*], the anhydrous form of p. acid, a white crystalline substance, $C_8H_4O_3 = C_6H_4(CO)_2O$, obtained by distilling the acid. **Phtha·limide** [see IMIDE], a derivative of ammonia in which two atoms of hydrogen are replaced by phthalyl; a colourless crystalline inodorous and tasteless body, $C_8H_4O_2.NH$. **Phthalin** (fþæ·lin) [-IN¹], a colourless crystalline substance obtained from phthalein. **Phthalyl** (fþæ·lil) [-YL], the radical of p. acid ($C_8H_4O_2$).

‖ **Phthiriasis** (þəirəi·ăsis, þəiᵊri,ēⁱ·sis, fþ-). Also **phtheir-.** 1598. [L., a. Gr., f. φθειριᾶν to be lousy.] *Path.* A morbid condition of the body in which lice multiply excessively, causing extreme irritation; pediculosis.

Phthisic (ti·zik), *sb.* and *a.* Now *rare.* [ME. *tisik*(*e* sb., a. OF. *tisike, -ique,* later *ptisique, thisique* = It., Sp. *tisica* consumption, repr. a Rom. *phthisica, thisica,* f. (ult.) Gr. φθίσις PHTHISIS.] **1.** A wasting disease of the lungs; pulmonary consumption. †**2.** *loosely.* A severe cough; asthma –1741. **B.** *adj.* = PHTHISICAL *a.* late ME. Hence **Phthi·sical** (ti·zikăl), *a.* of, pertaining to, characterized by, or affected with phthisis. **Phthi·sicky** (ti·ziki), *a.* phthisical, consumptive; asthmatic, wheezy.

‖ **Phthisis** (þəi·sis, təisis, fþi·sis). 1543. [L., a. Gr. φθίσις, f. φθίνειν (root φθι-) to decay, waste away.] A progressive wasting disease; *spec.* pulmonary consumption. Hence **Phthisiology** (fþ-, þiziǫ·lŏdʒi), the science or study of p., or a treatise on p.

Phut (fʊt). *slang.* 1892. [f. Hind. *phatna* to burst.] *To go p.*: to be a failure, fizzle out.

Phycic (fəi·sik), *a.* 1864. [f. Gr. φῦκος fucus, seaweed + -IC.] In *p. acid,* a crystalline substance extracted from *Protococcus vulgaris* by alcohol.

Phycite (fəi·səit). 1864. [f. as prec. + -ITE¹ 4.] *Chem.* A sweet-smelling crystalline substance ($C_4H_{10}O_4$) extracted from *Protococcus vulgaris*; also called *erythromannite.*

Phyco- (fəi·ko), comb. form of Gr. φῦκος (L. *fucus*) seaweed; used in the formation of mod. scientific terms relating to seaweeds or algæ, as

Phycochrome (fəi·kŏkrōᵘm), the bluish-green colouring matter of some algæ, being chlorophyll modified by an admixture of phycocyanin. **Phycocyan** (fəi·ko,səi·ăn), **Phycocy·anin, Phycocya·nogen,** the blue colouring matter which is combined with chlorophyll in certain algæ. **Phy:co-e·ry·thrin,** the red colouring matter found similarly in *Florideæ.* **Phyco·logy** [-LOGY], the branch of botany treating of seaweeds; algology. **Phycomycetous** (fəi·ko məisī·təs) *a.,* of or pertaining to the *Phycomyceteæ,* a division of Fungi, of which the genus *Phycomyces* is the type. **Phycophæ·in** [Gr. φαιός dusky], a reddish-brown pigment found in the olive-brown seaweeds, as the *Fucaceæ,* etc. **Phycoxa·nthin,** = DIATOMIN.

Phylactery (filæ·ktĕri). [Late ME. ad. L. *fyl-, phylacterium* (Vulg.), a. Gr. φυλακτήριον, f. φυλακτήρ a guard, f. stem φυλακ- of φυλάσσειν to guard.] **1.** A small leathern box containing four texts of Scripture, Deut. vi. 4–9, xi. 13–21, Ex. xiii. 1–10, 11–16, written in Hebrew letters on vellum, and worn by Jews during morning prayer on all days except the sabbath, as a reminder of the obligation to keep the law. Cf. Deut. xi. 18. **b.** *fig.* A reminder; a religious observance or profession of faith; an ostentatious display of piety or rectitude, a mark of Pharisaism 1645. **2.** An amulet worn as a preservative against disease, etc.; also *fig.* a charm, safeguard 1809. **3.** A vessel or case containing a holy relic. late ME. **4.** In mediæval art, The inscribed scroll proceeding from a person's mouth or held by him, to indicate his words; *fig.* a record, a roll. Also, the infula of a mitre. 1855.

1. b. Happy are they who..make their Phylacteries speak in their Lives SIR T. BROWNE. Phr. *To make broad the p.* (from Matt. xxiii. 5), to vaunt one's righteousness.

Phyla·ctocarp (fəil-). 1883. [f. Gr. φυλακτός, vbl. adj. f. φυλάσσειν to guard + καρπός fruit.] *Zool.* A 'fruit-case'; a receptacle in certain hydroids protecting the gonothecæ.

Phylactolæ·matous (fəil-), *a.* 1877. [f. mod.L. *Phylactolæmata,* f. Gr. φυλακτο-, f. φυλάσσειν to guard + λαιμός throat + L. *-ata* (pa. pple.); see -OUS.] *Zool.* Belonging to the *Phylactolæmata,* an order of Polyzoa, having the lophophore bilateral, and the mouth overhung by a small ciliated mobile lobe, the epistome.

Phylarch (fəi·lāɹk). 1551. [ad. L. *phylarchus,* a. Gr. φύλαρχος chief of a tribe, f. φυλή tribe + -αρχος, f. ἄρχειν to rule.] **1.** The chief of a phyle or tribe in ancient Greece; hence, any tribal chief 1656. **2.** In ancient Attica, An officer elected to command the cavalry of each of the ten phylæ 1830. **3.** The title of certain magistrates in the ideal commonwealths of Plato, More, etc. 1551. Hence **Phy·larchy,** the office of a p., tribal government.

‖ **Phyle** (fəi·lī). *Pl.*- **æ.** 1863. [a. Gr. φυλή tribe.] In ancient Greece, a clan or tribe, based on supposed kinship; in Attica, a political, administrative, and military unit; also the cavalry brigade furnished by an Attic tribe.

Phyletic (fəile·tik), *a.* 1881. [ad. Gr. φυλετικός, f. φυλέτης a tribesman, f. φυλή a tribe.] *Biol.* Of or pertaining to a phylum or race; racial.

Phyllis: see PHILLIS.

Phyllite (fi·ləit). 1828. [f. Gr. φύλλον leaf + -ITE [1].] *Min.* **a.** A species of magnesia-mica, occurring in small scales in argillaceous schist or slate. **b.** A rock consisting of an argillaceous schist or slate containing scales or flakes of mica.

Phyllo- (filo), repr. Gr. φυλλο-, comb. form of φύλλον leaf.

Phyllobranchia (-bræ·ŋkiă), pl. **-æ,** [Gr. βράγχια gills], *Zool.* each of the leaf-like foliaceous, or lamellar gills of certain crustaceans. **Phyllocyanin** (-səi·ănin) [see CYANIN], *Chem.* a blue or bluish-green substance supposed to be a constituent of chlorophyll. **Phy·llocyst** (-sist), *Zool.* a cyst or cavity in the hydrophyllium of certain Hydrozoa. **Phyllomorphic** (-mǭ·ɹfik) [Gr. μορφή form] *a.* leaf-shaped; so **Phyllomo·rphous** *a.*; **Phy·llomorphy** = PHYLLODY *a.* **Phy·llophore** (-fōᵊɹ) [Gr. φυλλοφόρος leaf-bearing], *Bot.* the growing-point or terminal bud from which the leaves arise, esp. in palms; so **Phyllo·phorous** *a.*, leaf-bearing; in *Zool.*, bearing parts resembling leaves, as the nose-leaf of certain bats. **Phy·llosome** [Gr. σῶμα body], *Zool.* the larval form of certain macrurous crustaceans; a glass crab. **Phylloxanthin** (filǫksæ·nþin) [a. F. *phylloxanthine*, f. Gr. ξανθός yellow], *Chem.* a yellow constituent of chlorophyll, also called XANTHOPHYLL.

Phylloclade (fi·lǫklēⁱd). 1858. [ad. mod. L. **phyllocladium** (filǫklēⁱ·diǒm), f. Gr. φύλλον leaf + κλάδος branch.] *Bot.* A branch of an enlarged or flattened form, resembling or performing the functions of a leaf, as in the *Cactaceæ*.

Phyllode (fi·lōᵘd). 1848. [a. F. *phyllode*, ad. mod.L. **phyllodium** (filōᵘ·diǒm), also in Eng. use, f. Gr. φυλλώδης leaf-like, f. φύλλον leaf; see -ODE.] *Bot.* A petiole or leaf-stalk of an expanded and (usu.) flattened form, resembling and having the functions of a leaf, as in many Acacias.

Phyllody (fi·lǫdi). 1888. [f. prec. + -Y [3].] *Bot.* **a.** The condition in which certain organs, esp. parts of the flower, are metamorphosed into ordinary leaves. **b.** The condition in which the leaf-stalk is metamorphosed into a phyllode.

Phylloid (fi·loid), *a.* and *sb.* 1858. [f. mod. L. *phylloides*, f. Gr. φύλλον leaf; see -OID.] **A.** *adj.* Resembling a leaf; foliaceous. **B.** *sb.* A part in lower plants analogous to a leaf.

Phyllome (fi·lōᵘm). 1875. [ad. mod.L. *phylloma*, f. Gr. φύλλωμα foliage, f. φυλλοῦν to clothe with leaves, f. φύλλον leaf.] The general name for a leaf or any organ homologous with a leaf (as a sepal, petal, stamen, carpel, etc.)

Phyllophagan (filǫ·făgăn). 1842. [f. mod. L. *phyllophaga* pl., f. φύλλον leaf + -φάγος eating.] *Zool.* A member of the *Phyllophaga*, a name applied to various groups of animals which feed on leaves. So **Phyllo·phagous** *a.* leaf-eating; belonging to the *Phyllophaga*.

Phyllopod (fi·lǒpǫd), *sb.* and *a.* 1863. [f. mod.L. *Phyllopoda* pl., f. Gr. φύλλον leaf + ποδ-, πούς foot.] *Zool.* **A.** *sb.* A member of the *Phyllopoda*, a group of entomostracous crustaceans, having lamellate or foliaceous swimming feet; a leaf-footed crustacean. **B.** *adj.* Belonging to the *Phyllopoda*; leaf-footed. So **Phyllo·podous** *a.* = prec. B. 1835.

Phyllorhine (fi·lǒrəin), *a.* and *sb.* [ad. mod.L. *Phyllorhinus*, f. Gr. φύλλον leaf + ῥιν-, ῥίς nose.] *Zool.* **A.** *adj.* Of a bat: Having a nose-leaf; leaf-nosed; *spec.* belonging to the *Phyllorhininæ*, a subfamily of the horseshoe-bats. **B.** *sb.* A leaf-nosed bat; *spec.* one of the *Phyllorhininæ*.

Phyllostome (fi·lostōᵘm). 1858. [ad. mod. L. *Phyllostoma*, f. Gr. φύλλον leaf + στόμα, στοματ- mouth.] *Zool.* A bat of the genus *Phyllostoma* or family *Phyllostomatidæ*, having a nose-leaf or other appendage of the snout. Also **Phyllo·stomid.**

‖ **Phyllotaxis** (filotæ·ksis). 1857. [mod.L., f. Gr. φύλλον leaf + τάξις arrangement.] *Bot.* The arrangement of leaves (or other lateral members) upon an axis or stem; the geometrical principles of such arrangement. Also **Phy·llotaxy.** So **Phyllota·ctic, -al** *adjs.*

‖ **Phylloxera** (filǫksīᵊ·ră). 1868. [mod.L., f. Gr. φύλλον leaf + ξηρός dry.] *Entom.* A genus of *Aphididæ* or plant-lice; esp. *P. vastatrix*, also called *vine-pest*, which is very destructive to the European grape-vine. Hence **Phylloxeral** (-īᵊ·răl), **Phylloxeric** (-e·rik) *adjs.* pertaining or relating to the p. **Phyllo·xerated, Phyllo·xerized** *ppl. adjs.* infested with the p.

Phylo-, bef. a vowel **phyl-**, comb. form of Gr. φῦλον, φυλή a tribe, used mostly in biological terms.

Phylogenesis (fəilodʒe·nĭsis). 1875. [mod. f. PHYLO- + -GENESIS.] *Biol.* The evolution of the tribe or race, or of any organ or feature in the race. So **Phy·logene·tic** *a.* of, pertaining to, or characteristic of p. or phylogeny; relating to the race history of an organism or organisms; so **Phy·logene·tical** *a.*, **-ly**, *adv.*

Phylogeny (fəilǫ·dʒĭni). 1870. [ad. mod. G. *phylogenie*, f. Gr. φῦλον race + -γενεια birth, origin.] *Biol.* **1.** = prec. 1872. **2.** The race history of an animal or vegetable type; tribal history 1875. **3.** A pedigree showing the racial evolution of a type of organisms 1870. Hence **Phyloge·nic** *a.* phylogenetic. **Phylo·genist,** one versed or skilled in p.

‖ **Phylum** (fəi·lǒm). *Pl.* **-la.** 1876. [mod. L., a. Gr. φῦλον race.] *Biol.* A tribe or race of organisms, related by descent from a common ancestral form; a primary division or subkingdom of animals or plants supposed to be so related.

‖ **Phyma** (fəi·mă). *Pl.* **-ata.** 1693. [L., a. Gr. φῦμα, φυματ- swelling, tumour.] *Path.* An inflamed swelling; an external tubercle.

‖ **Physa** (fəi·să). 1842. [mod.L., a. Gr. φῦσα bellows.] *Zool.* A small freshwater gastropod.

‖ **Physalia** (fəisēⁱ·liă). 1842. [mod.L., f. Gr. φυσαλέος inflated with wind, φυσαλλίς bladder, bubble.] *Zool.* A genus of oceanic hydrozoa; the Portuguese man-of-war; see MAN-OF-WAR. Hence **Physa·lian** *a.* belonging to this genus; *sb.* a species of P.

Physeter (fəisī·təɹ). 1591. [a. L. *physeter* a cachalot, a. Gr. φυσητήρ a blower, a whale, f. φυσᾶν to blow.] †**1.** A large blowing whale –1786. **2.** *Zool.* Generic name of the cachalots or larger sperm-whales 1753. **3.** A filter acting by air-pressure 1842.

Physic (fi·zik), *sb.* [ME. *fisike*, a. OF. *fisique*, ad. L. *physica*, a. Gr. φυσική (ἐπιστήμη) the knowledge of nature; see next.] **1.** = PHYSICS 1. Now *rare.* **2.** The theory of diseases and their treatment; medical science, medicine. *Obs.* or *arch.* late ME. **3.** The art or practice of healing; the medical profession ME. **b.** The medical faculty personified; physicians. late ME. †**c.** Medical treatment –1700. **4.** = MEDICINE *sb.*[1] 2. (Now *colloq.*) 1591. **b.** *spec.* A cathartic or purge 1617. †**5.** *fig.* Wholesome regimen or habit –1699. †**b.** Mental, moral, or spiritual remedy –1703.

1. Physike, which is the studie of naturall things: metaphysike, which is of supernaturall things 1586. 2. A..good learned company, many Doctors of Phisique PEPYS. 3. c. Farewel Phisik; go ber the man to chirche CHAUCER. 4. Throw Physicke to the Dogs, Ile none of it SHAKS. 5. b. He is a madman. It is good p. to whip him 1656.

Comb.: **p.-ball,** medicine in the form of a ball or bolus for a horse, dog, etc.; †**p. garden,** a garden for the cultivation of medicinal plants; hence, a botanic garden. Hence **Phy·sicky** *a.* having the taste, smell, or other qualities of p. or medicine.

Physic (fi·zik), *a.* Now *rare.* ME. [a. F. *physique*, ad. L. *physicus*, a. Gr. φυσικός, f. φύσις nature, f. φύειν to produce.] **1.** Physical, natural 1563. †**2.** Medical; medicinal. (= prec. *sb. attrib.*) –1736.

Physic (fi·zik), *v.* Infl. **physicked, physicking.** late ME. [f. PHYSIC *sb.* 3–5.] *trans.* To dose with physic, esp. with a purgative. Now *colloq.* **b.** *fig.* To treat with remedies, relieve 1589.

b. The labour we delight in, Physicks paine SHAKS.

Physical (fi·zikăl), *a.* late ME. [ad. med. L. *physicalis*, f. *physica* PHYSIC *sb.*; see -AL.] **I. 1.** Of or pertaining to material nature; pertaining to or connected with matter; material; opp. to *psychical, mental, spiritual* 1597. **b.** Belonging or relating to Natural Philosophy or Natural Science; relating to or in accordance with the regular processes or laws of nature 1580. **c.** Of persons: Dealing with or devoted to natural science 1678. **2.** Belonging to the science of physics; see PHYSICS 2. 1734. **3.** Of the body; bodily, corporeal 1780.

1. Phr. *P. cause, energy, power; p. possibility, impossibility*, etc. b. The law of gravitation is a p. axiom HERSCHEL. 2. The p. properties of matter may be altered without affecting its deeper chemical constitution HUXLEY. 3. The man gave me the impression of p. strength 1860. The lads..went through a course of p. drill 1899. *P. exercises, jerks, training*, muscular exercises designed to strengthen or keep the body healthy. So *p. culture*.

II. 1. Of or belonging to medicine; medical. Now *rare.* 1450. †**b.** Of persons: Practising medicine; medical –1796. †**2.** Used in medicine, medicinal –1828; curative, remedial; good (*for* one's health) –1633. **3.** In special phrases 1817.

1. The Medical and P. Journal (*title*) 1799. 3. **P. astronomy,** that branch of astronomy which treats of the motions, masses, positions, light, heat, etc. of the heavenly bodies. **P. chemistry,** that branch of chemistry which deals with the structure of molecules. **P. force,** material as opp. to moral force; in politics, the use of armed power, to effect or repress political changes. **P. geography,** that branch of geography which deals with the natural features of the earth's surface. **P. geology,** the study of the formation and history of strata and eruptive rocks apart from palæontology. **P. optics,** that branch of optics which deals with the properties of light itself (as dist. from the function of sight). **P. point,** a point conceived as infinitely small, and yet a portion of matter. **P. science** = PHYSICS. **P. sciences,** the sciences that treat of inanimate matter, and of energy apart from vitality. **P. sign,** a symptom of health or disease ascertainable by bodily examination. Hence **Phy·sically** *adv.* according to nature, or the material laws of nature; according to natural philosophy or science; corporeally; †by medical rules.

Physician (fizi·ʃăn), *sb.* [ME. *fisicien*, a. OF., f. L. *physica*; see PHYSIC and -ICIAN.] †**1.** A student of physics –1833. **2.** One who practises the healing art, including medicine and surgery ME. **b.** One legally qualified to practise the healing art as above; *esp.* as dist. from one qualified as a surgeon only. late ME. **3.** *transf.* and *fig.* A healer; one who cures moral, spiritual, or political maladies. late ME.

2. More needs she the Diuine, then the Physitian SHAKS. b. O lord, whi is it so greet difference bitwixe a cirurgian & a phisician 1400. 3. Time must be her p. 1805. Hence **Physi·cian** *v. trans.* (*a*) to make into a p.; (*b*) to put under the care of a p. **Physi·cianer** *dial.* = PHYSICIAN 2. **Physi·cianship,** the office or position of p.

Physicism (fi·zisiz'm). 1869. [f. PHYSIC *sb.* + -ISM.] A doctrine of physical phenomena; *esp.* one which refers all the phenomena of the universe, including life itself, to physical or material forces; materialism.

In the progress of the species..anthropomorphism grows into theology, and p. (if I may so call it) develops into Science HUXLEY.

Physicist (fi·zisist). 1840. [f. PHYSIC *sb.* + -IST.] **1.** A student of physics (PHYSICS 2). **b.** A student of nature or natural science in general (cf. PHYSICS 1) 1858. **2.** A believer in physicism; opp. to *vitalist* 1871.

Phy·sic-nut. 1657. [f. PHYSIC *sb.* 4 + NUT.] The fruit of the euphorbiaceous shrub *Jatropha Curcas* (*Curcas purgans*), of tropical America, used as a purgative; the Barbadoes- or purging-nut; also the plant itself.

Physico- (fi·ziko), comb. form of Gr. φυσικός natural, physical, usu. an advb. or adj. qualification of the second element, 'physically', 'physical' (see -O- 1); also, sometimes expressing any relation, as simple combination or contact (see -O- 2); as in **Phy:sico-che·mical** *a.* of or belonging to physical chemistry; of or pertaining to physics and chemistry. **Phy:-**

sico-mathema·tical *a.* of or pertaining to the application of mathematics to physics or mixed mathematics. **Phy:sico-mecha·nical** *a.* of or pertaining to the dynamics of natural forces, or the mechanical branch of natural philosophy. **Phy:sico-me·ntal** *a.* pertaining to both body and mind. So **Phy:sico-mo·ral** *a.*

Phy:sico-theo·logy. 1712. [See prec.] A theology founded upon the facts of nature, and the evidences of design there found; natural theology. So **Phy:sico-theolo·gical** *a.* **Phy:sico-theo·logist.**

Physics (fi·ziks). 1589. [pl. of PHYSIC *a.* used subst., rendering L. *physica* neut. pl., a. Gr. *τὰ φυσικά* lit. 'natural things', the collective title of Aristotle's physical treatises: in Eng., pl. in origin and form, but now constr. as a sing.: cf. *metaphysics*, etc.] **1.** Natural science in general; in the older writers *esp.* the Aristotelian system; hence, natural philosophy in the wider sense. Also, a treatise on this, as *Aristotle's Physics.* **2.** In current usage, restricted to The science, or sciences, treating of the properties of matter and energy, or of the action of the different forms of energy on matter in general (excluding Chemistry and Biology) 1715.

2. P. is divided into *general p.*, dealing with the general phenomena of inorganic nature (dynamics, molecular physics, physics of the ether, etc.), and *applied p.*, dealing with special phenomena (astronomy, meteorology, terrestrial magnetism, etc.). There is a tendency now to restrict the word to the former group. N.E.D.

Physio- (fi·ziǫ), comb. element, repr. Gr. *φυσιο-*, f. *φύσις* nature; used as a formative with the sense 'nature' or 'natural', as in PHYSIOGNOMY, PHYSIOLOGY, etc. **Phy:sio-philo·sophy,** a name for the philosophic system of nature of Oken, who 'aimed at constructing all knowledge *a priori*, and thus setting forth the system of nature in its universal relations' 1847.

Physiocrat (fi·ziǫ,kræt). Also in F. form **-crate.** 1798. [a. F. *physiocrate*, f. *physiocratie*; see PHYSIO- and -CRAT.] One of a school founded by F. Quesnay in France in the 18th c., who maintained that society should be governed according to an inherent natural order, that the soil is the only source of wealth and the only proper object of taxation, and that security of property and freedom of industry and exchange are essential. So **Physio·cracy,** government according to natural order; *spec.* the doctrine of the physiocrats. **Phy:siocra·tic, †-al** *adjs.*

Physiogeny (fiziǫ·dʒĭni). 1858. [ad. mod. L. *physiogenia*, f. Gr. *φυσιο-* PHYSIO- + *-γένεια* -GENY.] *Biol.* The genesis of vital functions; the development of the functions of living organisms, which are the province of physiology; the science or history of this.

Physiognomic (fi:ziǫnǫ·mik, fi:ziǫgnǫ·mik), *a.* 1704. [ad. late L. *physiognomicus*, corruption of Gr. *φυσιογνωμονικός*; see PHYSIOGNOMY and -IC.] **1.** Of the nature of physiognomy; characteristic. **2.** Of, pertaining to, or skilled in physiognomy 1755.

Physiogno·mical, *a.* 1588. [f. as prec. + -AL.] **1.** Pertaining to, dealing with, or skilled in physiognomy. **2.** Of or pertaining to the face or form (prop.) as an index of character, but often used simply in ref. to personal appearance 1811. Hence **Physiogno·mically** *adv.*

Physiognomist (fiziǫ·nǒmist, -ǫ·gnǒmist). 1570. [a. OF. *physionomiste*, f. *physionomie*; see -IST.] One skilled in physiognomy; formerly, one who professed to tell destiny from the face.

Physiognomonic (fiziǫgnǫmǫ·nik), *a.* (*sb.*) *rare.* 1755. [ad. med.L. *physiognomonicus*, a. Gr. *φυσιογνωμονικός* adj., f. *φυσιογνωμονία*; see next and -IC.] The etymological form for PHYSIOGNOMIC. So **†Physio:gnomo·nical** *a.* -1814.

Physiognomy (fiziǫ·nǒmi, -ǫ·gnǒmi). Vulgarly abbrev. *physiog.*, *phizog.*, and PHIZ. [ME. *fisnomye, fis-, phisonomye*, etc., a. OF. *fiz-, phis-, phizonomie*, ad. med.L. *phisonomia, physionomia*, **physiognomia*, ad. Gr. *φυσιογνωμονία*, f. *φύσις* nature (PHYSIO-) + *γνώμων, γνωμον-* judge, interpreter; wrongly written *φυσιογνωμία* in Stob. Ecl., whence the med. L. form.] **I. 1.** The art of judging character and disposition from the features of the face or the form and lineaments of the body generally. **†2.** The foretelling of destiny from the features and lines of the face, etc.; the fortune so foretold; *loosely*, fortune foretold (or character divined) by astrology -1651.

1. We know your skill in p...Read that countenance C. BRONTE. 2. According to my little skill in P., I hope he may live yet many a yeer 1651.

II. 1. The face, esp. viewed as an index to the mind and character; expression of face; also, the general cast of features, type of face (of a race); vulgarly, the face or countenance. late ME. **†b.** A portrait -1603. **2.** *transf.* The external features of anything material; e.g. the contour of a country 1567. **3.** *fig.* The ideal, mental, moral, or political aspect of anything as an indication of its character 1680.

1. She did abhorre her husbands phisnomy BURTON. 3. There is a Kind of P. in the Titles of Books, no less than in the Faces of Men 1680. Hence **Physio·gnomize** *v. trans.* to study physiognomically; to deduce the character from the face.

Physiogony (fiziǫ·gǒni). 1834. [f. Gr. *φύσις* nature + *-γονία* begetting.] The generation or production of nature.

Physiography (fiziǫ·grăfi). 1828. [f. Gr. *φύσις* nature + *-γραφία* -GRAPHY.] **1.** A description of nature, or of natural phenomena or productions generally. **2.** A description of the nature of a particular class of objects (e.g. minerals) 1888. **3.** Physical geography 1873. So **Physio·grapher,** one versed in p. **Phy:siogra·phic, -al** *adjs.* 1796, **-ly** *adv.*

Physiolater (fiziǫ·lătəɹ). 1860. [f. as prec. + Gr. *-λατρης* worshipper.] A worshipper of nature. So **Physio·latry,** nature-worship.

Physiologer (fiziǫ·lǒdʒəɹ). Now *rare* or *Obs.* 1598. [f. PHYSIOLOGY + -ER[1].] **1.** A student or teacher of natural science; *spec.* a philosopher of the Ionic sect. **2.** = PHYSIOLOGIST 2. 1680.

Physiologist (fiziǫ·lǒdʒist). 1664. [f. as prec. + -IST.] **†1.** = PHYSIOLOGER 1. 1827. **2.** One versed in animal (or vegetable) physiology; a student or teacher of the science of the functions and properties of organic bodies 1778.

Physiology (fiziǫ·lǒdʒi). 1564. [ad. L. *physiologia*, a. Gr., f. *φυσιολόγος* one who discourses on nature, f. *φύσις* nature; see -LOGY.] **†1.** The study and description of natural objects; natural science; also, a particular system or doctrine of natural science -1797. **2.** The science of the normal functions and phenomena of living things 1615.

It comprises *animal* and *vegetable p.*; that part of the former which refers specially to the vital functions in man is called *human p.* N.E.D. So **Phy:siolo·gic, -al** *adjs.* †of or belonging to natural science; pertaining or relating to p.; **-ly** *adv.* **†Phy:sio·logize** *v.* †*intr.* to speculate or reason on nature; †*trans.* to explain in accordance with natural science.

Physique (fizī·k). 1826. [a. F., absol. use of *physique* PHYSIC *a.*] The physical or bodily structure, organization, and development; the characteristic appearance or physical powers (of an individual or a race).

Physnomy, obs. f. PHYSIOGNOMY.

Physo- (fəisǫ), repr. Gr. *φυσο-*, comb. form of Gr. *φῦσα* bellows, bladder, bubble; used in

Phy·sograde [ad. mod.L. *Physograda*, f. *-gradus*], *Zool.* **a.** *adj.* moving by means of a hollow vesicular float or buoy; of or pertaining to the *Physograda*, a group of oceanic hydrozoa furnished with such floating organs; **b.** *sb.* a member of this group. ‖ **Physometra** (-mī·tră) [Gr. *μήτρα* womb], *Path.* the presence of gas in the uterus. **Physopod** (fəi·sǫpǫd) [Gr. *πούς, ποδ-* foot], a mollusc of the division *Physopoda* or *Thysanoptera*, rhipidoglossate gastropods, with a sort of sucker on the foot.

Physoclist (fəi·sǫklist), *a.* and *sb.* 1887. [f. mod.L. *Physoclisti* (pl.), f. Gr. *φῦσα* bladder + *-κλειστος* shut, closed.] *Ichthyol.* **A.** *adj.* Belonging to the *Physoclisti*, a group of teleost fishes having the duct between the air-bladder and the intestine closed. **B.** *sb.* A member of this group. So **Physocli·stic, Physocli·stous** *adjs.*

‖ **Physophora** (fəisǫ·fŏră). 1869. [mod.L., f. Gr. *φῦσα* bladder + *-φορος* bearing, borne.] *Zool.* A genus of oceanic hydrozoa, the species of which float by means of numerous vesicular organs. So ‖**Physo·phoræ** *pl.* (occas. **Physophora**), a suborder or division of *Siphonophora* (an order of *Hydrozoa Craspedota*) having the proximal end modified into a pneumatophore or float. **Physo·phoran** *a.* of or pertaining to the *Physophoræ*; *sb.* a member of this division.

‖ **Physostigma** (fəisǫsti·gmă). 1864. [mod. L., f. Gr. *φῦσα* bladder + *στίγμα* STIGMA.] *Bot.* A genus of leguminous plants, the flower of which has a spiral keel, and a bent style continued into an oblique hood above the stigma; the only species, *P. venenosum*, produces the highly poisonous Calabar bean. Hence, the Calabar bean, or its extract as a drug. Hence **Physosti·gmine** the alkaloid $C_{15}H_{21}N_3O_2$, constituting the active principle of the Calabar bean.

Physostome (fəi·sǒstoum), *a.* and *sb.* 1880. [f. mod.L. *Physostomi*, f. Gr. *φῦσα* bladder + *στόμα* mouth, *-στομος* -mouthed.] *Ichthyol.* **A.** *adj.* Belonging to the *Physostomi*, a group of teleost fishes, in which the air-bladder is connected with the alimentary canal by an air-duct. **B.** *sb.* A member of this group. So **Physosto·matous, Physo·stomous** *adjs.*

Phyt- (fəit), comb. form used bef. a vowel for PHYTO-, as in **Phyta·lbumin,** vegetable albumin. **Phyta·lbumose,** a form of albumen occurring in plants.

-phyte, a terminal element repr. Gr. *φυτόν* a plant, and denoting a vegetable organism, as *microphyte*, etc. See also ZOOPHYTE.

Phyto- (fəitǫ), comb. form of Gr. *φυτόν* a plant, lit. that which has grown, f. *φύειν* to grow; used chiefly to form botanical words.

Phytoche·mistry, the chemistry of plants; so **Phytoche·mical** *a.* **Phy:togeo·graphy,** the geographical distribution of plants; so **Phy:togeogra·phic, -al** *adjs.* **Phytoglyphy** (fəitǫ·glifi, fit-) [see GLYPH], nature-printing, as orig. used for plants; hence **Phytogly·phic** *a.* **†Phyto·gnomy,** [after *physiognomy*; see GNOMIC], vegetable physiognomy. **Phyto·nomy** [see -NOMY], the science of the laws of plant-growth. **Phy:topatho·logy,** (*a*) the study of the pathology or diseases of plants; (*b*) the pathology of diseases due to vegetable organisms, as fungi; mycology; hence **Phy:topatholo·gical** *a.*; **Phyto-patho·logist,** one versed in phytopathology (*a*). **Phy:tophysio·logy,** vegetable physiology. **Phyto-pla·nkton,** floating plant organisms collectively.

Phytogenesis (fəitǫdʒe·nĭsis). 1858. [f. prec. + -GENESIS.] The generation or evolution of plants. Also **Phyto·geny,** in same sense. So **Phytogene·tic, -al** *adjs.*

Phytography (ɪəitǫ·grăfi). 1696. [ad. mod.L. *phytographia*; see PHYTO- and -GRAPHY.] **1.** Description of plants; descriptive botany. **2.** = PHYTOGLYPHY. Hence **Phytogra·phic, -al** *adjs.*

‖ **Phytolacca** (fəitolæ·kă). 1753. [mod.L., f. Gr. *φυτόν* plant + mod.L. *lacca* crimson lake.] *Bot.* The genus of plants including the Pocan, Virginian Poke, Pokeweed, or Red-ink plant (*P. decandra*); also various preparations of the plant used medicinally.

Phytology (fəitǫ·lǒdʒi). 1658. [ad. mod. L. *phytologia*, f. Gr. *φυτόν* plant + *-λογία*; see -LOGY.] The science of plants; botany. So **Phytolo·gical** *a.* relating to the study of plants; botanical 1654; **-ly** *adv.* **Phyto·logist,** one versed in p. (All now *rare.*)

Phytomer (fəi·tǫməɹ). 1880. [ad. mod.L. *phytomeron*, pl. *-a*, f. Gr. *φυτόν* plant + *μέρος* part.] = next.

Phyton (fəi·tǫn). 1848. [a. F., a. Gr. *φυτόν* plant, f. *φύειν* to produce.] *Bot.* A plant-unit; the smallest part of root, stem, or leaf which will grow when severed from the parent.

Phytophagic (fəitǫfæ·dʒik), *a.* 1866. [f. as next + -IC.] *Zool.* Of or pertaining to, caused by, the habit of feeding on plants or vegetable matter; said of variation of the colouring of insect larvæ.

Phytophagous (fəitǫ·făgəs), *a.* 1826. [f. Gr. *φυτόν* plant + *-φάγος* eating + -OUS (see -PHAGOUS); cf. mod.L. *Phytophaga, -phagi.*] *Zool.* **a.** Feeding on plants or vegetable substances, as insects, molluscs, etc. **b.** Belonging to the *Phytophaga* = (*a*) leaf-beetles and their allies, (*b*) sawflies and horn-tails, (*c*) certain cyprinoid fishes, (*d*) the plant-eating edentates, (*e*) the plant-eating placental mammals.

Phytotomy (fəitǫ·tŏmi). 1844. [f. Gr. φυτόν plant + -τομία a cutting.] The dissection of plants; vegetable anatomy. Hence **Phyto·tomist**, one versed in p.

‖**Phytozoon** (fəitozōu·ǫn). Also **-zo·um.** *Pl.* **-zo·a.** 1842. [f. Gr. φυτόν plant + ζῷον animal; lit. 'plant-animal'; cf. *zoophyte.*] **1.** *Zool.* A plant-like animal or zoophyte; a single polyp in a zoophyte. **2.** *Bot.* A male generative cell, a spermatozoid 1861.

Pi (pəi), *sb.* Name of the Greek letter π (in Gr. πῖ, pī); used in *Math.* to express the ratio of the circumference or periphery (περιφέρεια) of a circle to its diameter; see P (the letter).

Pi (pəi), *a. School* and *university slang.* 1870. [abbrev. of PIOUS.] Pious, sanctimonious.

Pi jaw [JAW *sb.* 6], religious or moral exhortation.

Pia (pəi·ă). *Anat.* Short for PIA MATER.

Piaçaba: see PIASSABA.

‖**Piache** (pi̯a·tʃe). 1555. [Tamanac *piache* = Carib *piai* PEAI.] A medicine-man or witch-doctor among the Indians of Central and Southern America; a PEAI.

Piacle (pəi·ăk'l). Now *rare.* 1490. [a. OF. *piacle* or ad. L. *piaculum*, f. *piare* to appease; see -CULE.] †**1.** Expiation; expiatory offering -1711. **2.** A wicked action which calls for expiation 1644.

Piacular (pəi,æ·kiŭlăı), *a.* 1610. [ad. L. *piacularis* expiatory; see prec. and -AR[1].] **1.** Making expiation or atonement; expiatory 1647. **2.** Calling for expiation; sinful, wicked, culpable 1610.

2. They held it p. to eat with sinners 1657. Hence **Piacula·rity**, the quality of being p.: (*a*) expiatory character, (*b*) criminality.

Piaffe (pi,æ·f), *v.* 1761. [a. F. *piaffer*; ult. origin unkn.] *Horsemanship* (*intr.*) To move with the same step as in the trot, but more slowly. So **Pia·ffer** *sb.* the action of piaffing 1862.

‖**Pia mater** (pəi·ă mē·təı). late ME. [med. L., tr. Arabic *umm raqīqah* 'thin or tender mother'. Cf. DURA MATER.] *Anat.* A delicate fibrous and very vascular membrane which forms the innermost of the three *meninges* enveloping the brain and spinal cord. Hence **Pi·al** *a.* of or pertaining to the pia mater.

Pian (pi,æ·n, ‖pyañ). Also **epian**, and in pl. **pians.** 1803. [= Sp., Pg. *epian* and *pian*, a. Galibi (Rio de Janeiro) *pian.*] = YAWS.

‖**Pianissimo** (pi̯āni·simo), *a.* (*adv.*) *sb.* 1724. [It.:—L. *planissimus*, superl. of *planus*: see PIANO *a.*)] *Mus.* **A.** *adj.* Very soft. **B.** *adv.* Very softly. **C.** *sb.* A very soft passage. Abbrev. *pp.* or *ppp.*

Pianist (pī·ănist). 1839. [ad. F. *pianiste*: see PIANO[2] and -IST.] A player on the pianoforte. So ‖**Piani·ste** [F.] = prec.; but often used in Eng. as the feminine form.

‖**Piano** (pi,ā·no), *adv.*, *a.*, *sb.*[1] 1683. [It.:—L. *planus* flat, later of sound, soft, low.] **A.** *Mus.* (abbrev. *p*) *adv.* and *a.* Soft(ly); also *fig.* subdued(ly). **B.** *sb.* A flat or floor in an Italian dwelling-house, hotel, etc. 1860.

Piano (pi,æ·no), *sb.*[2] 1803. [a. It., shortened from next or FORTEPIANO.] **1.** = next. **2.** A keyboard machine for perforating cards for a Jacquard apparatus 1881.

Comb. **p.-player** = PIANOLA 1907.

Pianoforte (pi,æ·no,fǭ·ɹte, pi,æ·nofǭɹt). 1767. [a. It., earlier *piano e forte* (*pian e forte*) 'soft and strong', used by Cristofori, its inventor, to express the gradation of tone of which it is capable. Now usually PIANO[2].] A musical instrument producing tones by means of hammers, operated by levers from a keyboard, which strike metal strings, the vibrations being stopped by dampers; it is commonly furnished with pedals for regulating the volume of sound. It is essentially a dulcimer provided with keys and dampers, but in other respects imitates the harpsichord and clavichord.

Grand p. or *piano*, a large p., harp-shaped like the harpsichord, and having the strings horizontal and at right angles to the keyboard. *Square p.*, rectangular like the clavichord, having the strings horizontal, but parallel to the keyboard. *Upright* or *cabinet p.*, rectangular upon edge, having the strings vertical. *Oblique* or *cottage p.*, upright but lower, having the strings ascending obliquely or diagonally.

Pianola (pi̯ānōu·lă). 1901. [app. intended as a dim. of PIANO.] Trade name for a mechanical attachment for playing the piano; also, a piano equipped with this.

Pia·no-o:rgan. 1844. A mechanical piano constructed like a barrel-organ.

Piarist (pəi·ărist). 1842. [ad. F. *Piariste*, etc. f. mod. L. title *patres scholarum piarum* fathers of the religious schools, the Piarists being the regular clerks of the *Scuole Pie* or religious schools.] A member of a Roman Catholic secular order, founded at Rome shortly before 1600. They devote themselves without pay to the instruction of the young.

‖**Piassaba** (pi̯āsā·bă). Also **piassava, piaçaba.** 1857. [a. Pg., a. Tupi *piaçába.*] A stout woody fibre obtained from the leaf-stalks of two Brazilian palm-trees, *Attalea funifera* and *Leopoldinia Piassaba*, and imported for the manufacture of brooms, brushes, etc. (Also *p. fibre.*)

Piastre, piaster (pi,æ·stəɹ). 1611. [a. F. *piastre*, ad. It. *piastra* 'any kind of plate or leafe of mettall' (Florio); as applied to a coin, short for *piastra d'argento* 'plate of silver'.] **1.** A name for the Spanish *peso duro*, piece of eight, or dollar, and its representatives in Spanish America and other countries 1630. **2.** Name of a small Turkish coin called *ghūrūsh*, $\frac{1}{100}$ of a Turkish pound.

Piazza (pi,æ·ză). 1583. [a. It. *piazza* (pia·ttsa) square, market-place (= Eng. PLACE):—Com. Rom. **plattia*, for **platia*, L. *platea*, a. Gr. πλατεῖα (ὁδός) broad street.] **1.** A public square or market-place, usu. one in an Italian town; but in 16th to 18th c. often applied to any open space surrounded by buildings. **2.** Erron. applied to a colonnade or covered gallery surrounding an open square, and hence to a single colonnade in front of a building. Now *rare.* 1617. **b.** (Chiefly U.S.) The verandah of a house 1787.

2. They live in one of the Piazzas in Covent Garden 1695.

Pibroch (pī·brŏχ). 1719. [ad. Gael. *piobaireachd* the art of playing the bagpipe, f. *piobair* a piper (f. *piob* a pipe, a. Eng. *pipe*) + *-achd*, suffix of function.] In the Scottish Highlands, a series of variations for the bagpipe, chiefly martial, but including dirges. ¶ Erron. used as if = bagpipe.

Some pipe of war Sends the bold p. from afar SCOTT.

‖**Pic, pike** (pīk). 1599. [= F. *pic*, a. Turk. *pik*, ad. Gr. πῆχυς ell, cubit.] A Turkish measure of length, used for cloth, etc., and varying from 18 to 28 inches, there being a long and a short standard.

Pica[1] (pəi·kă). 1497. [med. (Anglo-) L. (cf. *pica* PIE *sb.*[1], magpie), found in sense 1, beside the Eng. *pye*, PIE *sb.*[3], from end of 15th c. Sense 2 is prob. from sense 1.] †**1.** = PIE *sb.*[3] **1.** (Only Anglo-L.) **2.** *Typogr.* A size of type, next below English, of about 6 lines to the inch, equal to 12 point. Used also as a standard of measurement for large type, leads, borders, etc. *Small p.*, a size between long primer and pica, equal to 11 point 1588.

This is Pica type.

This is Small Pica type.

Two-line p., the size of type having a body equal to two lines of p. *Double p.* (prop. *double small p.*), a size of type equal to two lines of small p.

‖**Pica**[2] (pəi·kă). 1563. [mod. or med. L., = magpie, prob. tr. Gr. κίσσα, κίττα magpie, also false appetite.] *Path.* A perverted craving for substances unfit for food, as chalk, etc.

‖**Picador** (pi·kădǭɹ). 1797. [Sp., lit. 'pricker', f. *picar* to prick.] In a bull-fight, A mounted man, who opens the game by provoking the bull with a lance.

Picamar (pi·kămāɹ). 1835. [f. L. *pix*, *picem* pitch + *amarus* bitter.] *Chem.* An intensely bitter, thick transparent oil, obtained in the distillation of wood-tar.

Picaresque (pikăre·sk), *a.* 1810. [ad. Sp. *picaresco*, f. *picaro* rogue; see -ESQUE.] Belonging or relating to rogues or knaves; applied esp. to a style of fiction dealing with the adventures of rogues, chiefly of Spanish origin.

Picaroon (pikărū·n), *sb.* 1624. [a. Sp. *picaron*, augm. of *picaro* rogue.] **1.** A rogue; a knave; a thief; a brigand 1629. **2.** A pirate, sea-robber, corsair 1624. **3.** A privateer or corsair 1625.

1. I see in thy countenance something of the pedlar—something of the p. SCOTT. Hence **Picaroo·n** *v. intr.* to play the pirate or brigand.

Picayune (pikăyū·n), *sb.* and *a.* *U.S.* 1852. [Origin unkn.] **A.** *sb.* The U. S. 5-cent piece or other coin of small value; hence *colloq.* an insignificant person or thing. **B.** *adj.* Mean, contemptible 1856. Hence **Picayu·nish** *a.*

†**Pi·ccadill, pi·ckadill.** 1607. [a. F. *pica-*, *piccadilles* 'the seuerall diuisions or peeces fastened together about the brimme of the collar of a doublet' (Cotgr.), app. repr. a Sp. **picadillo*, dim. of *picado* pricked, pierced, slashed. Hence the name of the street called Piccadilly (see N.E.D.).] **1. a.** A border of cut work or vandyking inserted on a collar or ruff, etc. **b.** *transf.* An expansive collar, usu. with a broad laced or perforated border, fashionable early in the 17th c. -1821. **2.** A stiff band of linen-covered pasteboard or wire, worn in the 17th c. to support the wide collar or ruff -1688. **3.** *transf.* A halter (*joc.*) -1678.

Piccalilli (pi·kălili). 1769. [Origin unkn.] A pickle composed of a mixture of chopped vegetables and hot spices.

Piccaninny, pickaninny (pi·kănini), *sb.* (*a.*) 1657. [A West Indian Negro deriv. of Sp. *pequeño* or Pg. *pequeno* little, small.] A little one, a child: applied esp. to the children of negroes, or of South African or Australian natives. **b.** *joc.* A child, in general 1785. **B.** *adj.* Very small; tiny, baby 1876.

Piccolo (pi·kǒlo). 1856. [a. It., = small; hence absol., a small flute.] **1.** (orig. *p. flute.*) A small flute, an octave higher in pitch than the ordinary flute; also called the *octave flute.* **2.** An organ stop having the tone of the piccolo 1875. **3.** (for *p. piano.*) A small upright pianoforte 1858.

‖**Pice** (pəis). 1615. [ad. Hindī *paisā.*] A small E. Indian copper coin equal to one fourth of an anna.

Piceous (pi·sĭ,əs), *a.* 1646. [f. L. *piceus* pitchy (f. *pix*, *picem* PITCH *sb.*[1]) + -OUS.] Of, pertaining to, or resembling pitch: **a.** Inflammable, combustible; **b.** Pitch-black, brownish or reddish-black.

‖**Pichey** (pi·tʃi). 1827. [app. Guarani.] The Little Armadillo, *Dasypus minutus*, of La Plata.

‖**Pichiciago** (pitʃi,syē·go). 1825. [ad. Sp. *pichiciego*, f. (?) Guarani *pichey* (see prec.) + Sp. *ciego* (:—L. *cæcus*) blind.] A small burrowing edentate animal of Chili, *Chlamyphorus truncatus*, allied to the Armadillos; its back and head are covered with a hard leather-like shell attached only along the spine.

‖**Pichurim** (pi·tʃŭrim). 1842. [Tupi.] A lauraceous S. Amer. tree, *Nectandra Puchury.*

P. bean, the aromatic cotyledon of the seed of this tree, used in cookery and medicinally. Hence **Pichu·ric** *a. Chem.* of, pertaining to, or derived from p. beans; *pichuric acid* = LAURIC *acid.*

Piciform (pəi·sifǭɹm), *a.* 1872. [ad. mod. L. *piciformis*, f. *picus* woodpecker; see -FORM.] Having the form of, or resembling, a woodpecker; of or pertaining to the *Piciformes*, a group of birds of the order *Picariæ.*

Pick (pik), *sb.*[1] ME. [app. a collateral form, with short vowel, of PIKE *sb.*[1]] **I.** A tool consisting of an iron bar, usu. curved, steel-tipped, tapering squarely to a point at one end, and a chisel-edge or point at the other, attached through an eye in the centre to a wooden handle placed perpendicularly to its concave side; a pickaxe, mandril, mattock, 'slitter'; used for breaking up stiff ground or gravel, etc. **b.** A pointed hammer used for dressing mill-stones, etc., 1483.

II. †**1.** = PIKE *sb.*[1] II. **1.** -1688. **2.** The name of various pointed or pronged instruments; esp. (*Fishing*) a kind of gaff; an eel-spear (*dial.*) 1875. **3.** An instrument for picking: chiefly in *Comb.*, as TOOTHPICK, etc. 1619.

1. Take down my Buckler, and sweep the Cobwebs off: and grind the p. ont BEAUM. & FL.

III. The diamond in playing-cards. Also *transf.* Now *n. dial.* 1598.

Comb.: **p.-dressing**, in masonry, a pitted facing

produced by a pointed tool, broached hewn-work; **-hammer,** a pick with one blunt end, like a hammer.

Pick, *sb.*[2] 1513. [f. PICK *v.*[1]] **1.** An act of picking; a stroke with something pointed. **2.** An act of choosing or selecting; *transf.* that which is selected; the choicest portion or example; the choicest product or contents 1760. **3.** The quantity or portion of any crop picked or gathered at one time; a gathering 1887. **4.** *Printing.* **a.** A speck of hardened ink or dirt that gets into the hollows of types in forme and causes a blot on the printed page. **b.** An intrusive bit of metal on an electrotype or stereotype plate. 1683.

2. Mamma—I wish you would not say 'the pick of them'..it is rather a vulgar expression GEO. ELIOT.

Pick, *sb.*[3] *n. dial.* 1627. [f. PICK *v.*[2]] **1.** = PITCH *sb.*[2] **2.** *Weaving.* A cast or throw of the shuttle; the stroke that drives the shuttle; taken as a unit of measurement in reckoning the speed of the loom 1851. **b.** *transf.* In textiles, A single thread of the weft (produced by one pick of the shuttle); esp. used in ref. to the number of threads in the inch, as determining the fineness of the fabric 1860.

Pick (pik), *v.*[1] [OE. has *picung* vbl. sb. (*ī* or *ĭ*), implying a vb. *pician* or *pīcan* to puncture. Otherwise no examples occur before 1300. History obscure.] **I. 1.** *trans.* To pierce, indent, dig into, or break the surface of (anything) by striking it with something sharp and pointed, as to break up (ground, etc.) with a pick. Also *absol.*, to ply the pick, mattock, etc. ME. **†b.** Of a bird: To pierce with the bill, to peck; of an insect: to puncture –1645. **c.** To make by picking; in phr. *to p. a hole* or *holes in* something 1648. **2.** To probe or penetrate with a pointed instrument or the like, so as to remove any extraneous matter; e.g. *to p. the teeth.* late ME. **b.** Applied to a similar use of the finger-nails to remove a pimple, etc. 1676.

1. b. Isopes frogges to whom..Iupiter sent a hearon to picke them in the hedes 1555. 2. He picked his Nose, which you know is neither graceful or royal 1768.

II. 1. To clear or cleanse (a thing), with the fingers or the like, of any extraneous or refuse substance, as to pick a fowl (of its feathers), fruit, as currants, etc. (of their stalks, etc.). ME. **†2.** To cleanse, trick out, prank; to adorn; of a bird: to preen (its feathers) –1681.

1. Phr. *A crow to p.* (prop. *pluck*): see CROW *sb.*[1] *To p. a bone*, to clear it of all adherent flesh; so *to p. a carcass*, etc. *To have a bone to p. with any one*; see BONE *sb.*

III. 1. To pluck, gather, cull (fruit, growing flowers, etc.); said also of a bird ME. **†b.** *fig.* To 'gather' with the mind; to infer, make out –1621. **2.** Of birds and some beasts: To take up (grains or small bits of food) with bill or teeth; also, of persons, to bite or eat in small bits; *colloq.* to eat. (Cf. PECK *v.*[1]) late ME. **b.** *intr.* To eat with pecking or small bites; of a person, to eat fastidiously; *slang* or *colloq.* to eat 1584.

1. b. Trust me sweete, Out of this silence yet, I pickt a welcome SHAKS. 2. I think..that I could p. a little bit of pickled salmon DICKENS. b. I could never do mair than pyke at food STEVENSON.

IV. 1. To choose out, select carefully, cull. Now chiefly in *to p. one's men, one's words*, etc. late ME. **2.** To seek and find an occasion of; as *to p. a quarrel with* a person 1449. **†***To p. a thank* (*thanks*) *of* (*with*): to curry favour with.

1. Phr. *To p. one's way, steps*, to choose a way carefully through dirty or dangerous ground. *To p. and choose*, to select fastidiously. 2. Phr. **†***To p. occasion to do* (something).

V. 1. To rob, plunder (a person or place); to rifle the contents of (anything); †to steal (goods, etc.). Now only in phr. *to p.* a person's *pocket* or *purse*, also *fig.* his *brains.* ME. **b.** *intr.* or *absol.* In later use as a kind of euphemism for: To practise petty theft; to pilfer, filch. Chiefly in phr. *p. and steal.* late ME. **2.** To open (a lock) with a pointed instrument, a skeleton key, or the like; to open clandestinely (esp. in order to rob) 1546.

1. He hath as fine a hand at picking a pocket as a woman GAY. b. To kepe my handes from picking and stealing *Bk. Com. Prayer.* 2. She mynded..To picke the..locke 1546.

VI. 1. To separate by picking, to pull or comb asunder 1536. **b.** *intr.* for *pass.* To admit of being picked 1794. **2.** To pluck the strings of a banjo, etc. *U.S.* 1860.

1. They'll p. you to pieces a little among themselves TROLLOPE. Picking oakum in penal servitude 1874. b. The yarn..will p. into oakum 1794.

VII. Intr. uses with preps. **1.** *To p. at* —: **a.** To make a motion to pick (in various senses) 1525. **b.** *fig.* To gird at, nag at; to carp at. Now only *dial.* and *U.S.* 1670. **2.** *To p. on, upon* —: = prec. b. Now *U.S. dial.* late ME.

Combs. with adverbs. **P. away:** see senses I. 1 and III. 1 and AWAY. **P. in.** To work in or fill in, in a painting or drawing. **P. off. a.** See sense III. 1 and OFF. **b.** To shoot with deliberate selection and aim. **P. out. a.** To extract by picking; to dig out, peck out. **b.** To choose out with deliberation; said also of natural agents, as diseases. **c.** To distinguish from surrounding objects, etc. with the senses. **d.** To make out or gather (sense or meaning); to piece out and ascertain (facts) by combining separate items of information. **e.** To identify the notes of (a tune) and so play it by ear. **f.** To deck out, to adorn; now *spec.* to lighten or relieve the ground colour (of anything) by lines or spots of a contrasted colour following the outlines, mouldings, etc. **P. up. a.** To break up (ground) with a pick; to take up. **b.** To take up with the fingers or beak; to lay hold of and take up from the ground or any low position; in *Knitting*, to take up (stitches) with a knitting-needle. *To p. oneself up*, to recover oneself smartly from a fall, etc. **c.** To acquire, gain, collect as chance offers; to make (a livelihood) by occasional opportunity. **d.** To seize, snap up, capture (a vessel); to capture in detail. Now *rare.* **e.** To take (a person or thing overtaken) along with one, or into a vessel or vehicle; also said of a vehicle, a ship, etc. **f.** To come upon, find (a path, etc., wireless station, wave-length, etc.), *esp.* to recover (a trail, etc.). *To p. up a wind*, to run from one prevalent wind into another with as little intervening calm as possible. *To p. up the range* (of a rifle or gun). **g.** Phrases. *To p. up flesh*, to put on flesh again. *To p. up* (*one's*) *spirit, courage*, etc. **h.** *intr.* To recover, improve, 'look up' after an illness, or any check or depression. **i.** To enter into conversation, make acquaintance *with* (some one casually met). **j.** *colloq.* To take (a person) up sharply.

Pick (pik), *v.*[2] Now only *dial.* or *techn.* ME. [Collateral form of PITCH *v.*[1]] **†1.** *trans.* To fix, stick, plant (something pointed) in the ground, etc.; to pitch (a tent or the like) –1602. **2.** To thrust, drive; to pitch, hurl; to throw. Now *dial.* 1525.

2. As high As I could picke my Lance SHAKS.

Pick- in *Comb.* Mostly the stem or imperative of PICK *v.*[1] with an object, forming sbs. **Pick-cheese** *dial.*, the great and blue tits; the fruit or cheese of the mallow. **†Pick-fault,** a fault-finder. See also Main words.

Pi·ck-a-back, *adv. phr.* (*a.*, *sb.*) Also a pick back, pickback, pick-pack, piggy-back, etc. 1565. [Origin unkn. See N.E.D.] On the shoulders or back like a pack or bundle; said in ref. to a person (or animal) carried in this way. **b.** quasi-*adj.* and *sb.* 1590.

b. A p. ride through the surf in a dirty fellow's grasp 1864.

Pickaninny, var. of PICCANINNY.

Pickaxe (pi·kˌæks), *sb.* Also **-ax.** [ME. *pikoys, picois*, a. OF. *picois* pickaxe, conn. w. OF. *pic*; see PIKE *sb.*[1] The later form arose through confusion of the suffix with AXE *sb.*] A miner's, quarryman's, or digger's pick; = PICK *sb.*[1] I. Hence **Pi·ckax(e** *v. trans.* to break with a p.; *intr.* to use a p.

Pickback, var. of PICK-A-BACK.

Picked (pi·kėd), *a.* late ME. [f. PICK *sb.*[1] II. 1 + -ED[2].] **1.** Acuminated, pointed, spiked. Now *arch.* or *dial.* **b.** In names of animals, etc.: Having prickles, spiny 1758. **†2.** Peaked, tapering to a thin end –1771.

1. The shield to be made p. at both ends 1660. b. The p. dog-fish (*Spinax acanthius*). 2. The head of a man, with a hat and p. beard H. WALPOLE.

Picked (pikt, *poet.* pi·kėd), *ppl. a.* late ME. [f. PICK *v.*[1] + -ED[1].] **1.** In senses of PICK *v.*[1] **†2.** Adorned, ornate; spruce, nice, finical, fastidious –1636. **3.** Chosen out, esp. for excellence or efficiency, or for a definite purpose 1548.

1. A gill of p. shrimps 1806. 2. *Ham.* v. i. 151. 3. Only a few p. craftsmen can manage it M. ARNOLD. Hence **†Pi·cked-ly** *adv.*, **†-ness.**

†Picke-devant, pique devant, 1587. [app. either for F. *pique* (or *pic*) *devant*, meant for 'peak in front', or for *piqué devant*, 'peaked in front'.] A peaked or Vandyke beard –1638.

†Picked-hatch. 1598. [f. PICKED *a.* + HATCH *sb.*[1]] A hatch or half door, surmounted by a row of pikes or spikes, to prevent climbing over; *spec.* a brothel.

Goe..to your Mannor of Pickt-hatch SHAKS.

Pickeer (pikīᵊ·ɹ), *v.* 1645. [Origin unkn.] **†1.** *intr.* To maraud, pillage, plunder; to practise piracy –1718. **2.** *trans.* To skirmish, reconnoitre, scout (in war), to bicker (*with* the enemy) 1645. **3.** *fig.* **a.** To scout 1649. **†b.** To dally, flirt –1709. **†c.** To wrangle –1717.

‖ **Pickelhaube** (pi·kəlhau:bə). 1890. [G., :—MHG. *beckelhûbe, beckenhûbe* basinet, f. *becken* basin + *hûbe* cap, bonnet. The form has app. been influenced by G. *pickel* spike.] The spiked helmet of the German army.

Picker[1] (pi·kəɹ). 1526. [f. PICK *v.*[1] + -ER[1].] **1.** *gen.* A person who picks, in any sense. Also a second element in many combinations, as *fruit-, hop-, potato-, rag-p.*, etc. **2.** A tool or instrument for picking. **a.** In agriculture: (*a*) A sort of mattock or pickaxe; (*b*) a part of a picking-machine which separates the potatoes from the soil. Often in comb. as *potato-p.* 1707. **b.** In the textile industries: (*a*) A machine for separating and cleansing the fibres of cotton, wool, and the like; (*b*) an implement for burling cloth 1795. **c.** In *Mining* and *Metallurgy*: in Cornwall, a miner's hand-chisel; a miner's needle for picking out the tamping of an unexploded charge. In *Founding*, a light pointed steel rod, used for lifting small patterns from the sand into which they have been rammed; a tool for piercing a mould. 1874.

1. They are pickers and choosers of God's word 1870. *Pickers and stealers* (see PICK *v.*[1] V. 1), *colloq.* hands. *A p. of quarrels*, one who seeks occasion for quarrels. *Comb.* with *adv.*, as **picker-up;** A mere picker-up of trifles 1874.

Picker[2] (pi·kəɹ). 1841. [f. PICK *v.*[2] + -ER[1].] *Weaving.* In a loom, the small instrument which travels backwards and forwards in the shuttle-box and drives the shuttle to and fro through the warp.

Pickerel (pi·kĕrĕl). ME. [dim. of PIKE *sb.*[4]; see -REL.] A young pike. **b.** In U. S. and Canada, any of several species of *Esox*, esp. the smaller species; about the Great Lakes, the true pike; also the pike-perch, wall-eye, or glass-eye (*Stizostedion vitreum*).

Pi·ckerel-wee:d. 1653. [f. prec. + WEED.] **1.** A name locally applied to certain weeds, found in still waters, amongst which pike breed; *esp.* species of *Potamogeton* or Pondweed. **2.** In N. America, Any species of *Pontederia*, lacustrine plants, with sagittate leaves, and spikes of blue flowers 1836.

Pickery (pi·kəri). 1508. [f. PICKER[1]; see -ERY.] Petty theft. *Sc. Law.*

Picket (pi·kėt), *sb.* 1690. [a. F. *piquet* pointed stake, etc., f. *piquer* to pierce; see -ET.] **I. 1.** A pointed stake, post, or peg, driven into the ground; used e.g. in the construction of a stockade or fence; to mark positions in surveying, etc.; to fasten a rope or string to, esp. in order to tether a horse, or to secure a tent 1702. **2.** A stake with pointed top, used in a military punishment in vogue in the 17th and 18th c. Hence, a name for this punishment. 1690.

II. 1. *Mil.* A small detached body of troops, sent out to watch for the approach of the enemy or his scouts (*outlying p.*), or held in quarters in readiness for such service (*inlying p.*); also applied to a single soldier so employed. In the Army Regulations spelt *piquet.* 1761. **b.** A camp-guard, sent out to bring in men who have exceeded their leave 1787. **c.** *transf.* and *fig.* A party of sentinels; an outlying post 1847. **2.** (usu. *pl.*) Applied to men stationed by a trade-union or the like, to watch men going to work during a strike, and to endeavour to dissuade or deter them 1867.

III. An elongated rifle bullet, with a conoidal front; a cylindro-conoidal bullet. (Said to have been made for Col. Pickett.) *Hist.* 1858.

attrib. and *Comb.*, as *p.-fence, rope*, etc.; **p.-guard,** an inlying p., also a p. protecting a position; **-line,** (*a*) a tether; (*b*) a line held by pickets.

Picket (pi·kėt), *v.* 1745. [f. prec. sb.] **1.** *trans.* To enclose or secure with stakes; to palisade. **b.** To tether (a horse, etc.) to a peg fixed in the ground 1814. **2.** To punish or torture with the picket. *Obs.* exc. *Hist.* 1746. **3.** *Mil.* To post as a picket. **b.** *intr.* (for *refl.*) To act on picket duty. 1775. **4.** In strikes, etc.: **a.** *intr.* To act as a picket; **b.** *trans.* To beset with pickets. 1838. Hence **Pi·cketing** *vbl. sb.* the action of the vb.; *spec.* in a labour dispute, the posting of men to intercept non-strikers on their way to work and prevail upon them to desist.

Picking (pi·kiŋ), *vbl. sb.* ME. [f. PICK *v.*[1] + -ING [1].] **1.** The action of PICK *v.*[1] **2.** *spec.* **a.** Stealing, theft; in later use, petty theft, pilfering; esp. in *p. and stealing*. late ME. **b.** *Weaving.* A finishing process of cloth-making 1875. **c.** *Metall.* Rough sorting of ores 1839. **3.** *concr.* That which is or may be picked or picked up; the amount picked; a scrap; *pl.* portions of anything worth picking up 1642. **b.** Chiefly *pl.* Perquisites dishonestly come by; pilfering 1765.

Picking (pi·kiŋ), *ppl. a.* 1535. [f. PICK *v.*[1] + -ING [2].] **1.** That picks (see PICK *v.*[1]); *spec.* thievish. †**2.** Dainty; fastidious –1678.

1. Little p. thievish hands KIPLING.

Pickle (pi·k'l), *sb.*[1] late ME. [app. a. MDu. *pekel(e* brine, pickle; ult. origin unkn.] **1.** Brine, vinegar, or other salt or acid liquor, in which flesh, vegetables, etc., are preserved 1440. **2.** Some article of food preserved in pickle; usu. (*pl.*) Vegetables pickled and eaten as a relish 1707. **3.** An acid solution used for cleansing metal or wood, or for other purposes 1776. **4.** *fig.* A condition or situation, usu. disagreeable; a sorry plight. Now *colloq.* 1562. **5.** A troublesome or mischievous child. *colloq.* 1779.

1. Phr. *In p.* (*fig.*), kept in preparation for use; esp. in *a rod in p.*, a punishment in reserve, ready to be inflicted on occasion. 2. Received a present of pickles from Miss Pilcocks JOHNSON. 4. I could see no way out of the p. I was in STEVENSON. 5. Young Sam Tyler,..a thorough P. 1837.

Pickle (pi·k'l), *sb.*[2] *Sc.* and *north.* 1552. [Origin unkn.] **1.** A single grain or corn of wheat, barley, or oats. **2.** A small quantity or amount; a little. (Followed by sb. without *of.*) 1724.

Pickle (pi·k'l), *v.* 1552. [f. PICKLE *sb.*[1]] **1.** *trans.* To put into pickle; to preserve in pickle. (Sometimes, to salt, as butter.) **2.** *Naut.* To rub salt, or salt and vinegar, on the back after flogging or whipping; formerly practised as a punishment. *Obs.* exc. *Hist.* 1706. **3.** To treat with some acid or the like, for cleansing or other purposes 1844.

1. *fig.* You are pickling a rod for your own back 1904. So **Pickled** (pi·k'ld) *ppl. a.* preserved in pickle; steeped in acid, etc.; *pickled herring*: see next.

Pi·ckle-he·rring. Now *rare.* 1552. [orig. *pickled herring*; later *pickle-herring*, after MDu. *peeckel-harinck.*] †**1.** *lit.* A pickled herring –1607. **2.** A clown, a buffoon, a merry-andrew. [Of German origin.] 1716.

Pi·ckler. 1683. [f. PICKLE *v.* + -ER [1].] **1.** A cucumber, onion, etc., grown for pickling. **2.** A person or thing that pickles (*lit.* and *fig.*). Also, a pickling-jar. 1862.

Picklock (pi·k,lǫk), *sb.* and *a.* 1553. [f. PICK *v.*[1] + LOCK *sb.*[2]] **1.** A person who picks a lock; *spec.* a thief who does this. **2.** An instrument for picking locks 1581. **B.** *adj.* Used for picking a lock; *esp.* in *p. key* = sense 2. 1607.

1. *fig.* Some crafty fellow, some picklocke o' the Law! B. JONS.

Pi·ck-me-up. *colloq.* 1867. [phr. used as sb.] *orig.* A stimulating alcoholic drink; extended to beverages, medicinal preparations, etc., supposed to have tonic qualities. **b.** *fig.* Anything having a bracing effect 1876.

Pickpocket (pi·kpǫ·kėt). 1591. [f. PICK *v.*[1] + POCKET; see PICK-.] One who steals from or 'picks' pockets.

†**Pi·ckpurse.** late ME. [See PICK-.] One who steals purses or from purses –1727.

fig. I am no pick-purse of anothers wit SIDNEY. Phr. *Purgatory p.*, *p. purgatory*, a term used orig. app. by Latimer in ref. to the use made of the doctrine of purgatory to obtain payments for masses for departed souls, etc.

Pickthank (pi·kþæŋk), *sb.* and *a.* *arch.* and *dial.* 1500. [See PICK *v.*[1] IV. 2 and PICK-.] **A.** *sb.* One who 'picks a thank', i. e. curries favour with another; a flatterer, sycophant; a tell-tale. **B.** *adj.* (*sb.* used attrib.) Flattering, sycophantic, tale-bearing 1561.

a. 1 *Hen. IV*, III. ii. 25.

Picktooth (pi·ktūþ), *sb.* and *a.* pl. **picktooths.** Now *rare* or *arch.* 1542. [f. PICK *v.*[1] + TOOTH; see PICK-.] **A.** *sb.* A toothpick. **B.** *adj.* Idle, easy, leisurely 1728.

Pick-up, *sb.* (*a.*) 1859. [f. phr. *to pick up*; see PICK *v.*[1]] The act of picking up; *spec.* of picking up sides in a game; in *Cricket*, the picking up of the ball. Also, one who or that which is picked up. 1860. **b.** An electrical device fitted to a gramophone in place of the sound-box, for converting the sound into electric current 1926. **c.** *Wireless.* An electrical arrangement for connecting to a studio, etc. a programme produced outside 1925. **B.** *attrib.* or as *adj.* **a.** = that picks up, as in *pick-up apparatus, water-trough*, etc. **b.** = picked up for the nonce, as in *pick-up crew, dinner*, etc. 1859.

Pickwickian (pikwi·kiăn), *a.* (*sb.*) 1837. [f. *Pickwick*, surname in Dickens's *Pickwick Papers* (1837).] Of or pertaining to Mr. Pickwick, or the Pickwick Club; chiefly *joc.*, said of words used in a technical, constructive, or esoteric sense, or of language 'unparliamentary' in its natural sense. **B.** *sb.* A member of the Pickwick Club 1837.

Picnic (pi·knik), *sb.* Also earlier **pick-nick, pic-nic.** 1748. [ad. F. *pique-nique*; origin unkn.] **1.** *orig.* A fashionable social entertainment in which each party present contributed a share of the provisions; now, A pleasure party in which all partake of a repast out of doors. Also *transf.* and *fig.* **2.** *attrib.* Pertaining to or of the nature of a picnic 1802.

1. They held impromptu pic-nics on breezy heights 1866. Phr. *No* or *not a p.*, not an easy job. Hence **Pi·cnic** *v.* (inflected **picnicked, -nicking**) *intr.* to hold or take part in a p., to eat in p. fashion. **Pi·cnicker** (pi·knikər), one who takes part in a p.

Picoid (pəi·koid), *a.* 1809. [f. L. *picus* woodpecker + -OID.] Like the woodpeckers.

Picoline (pi·kŏləin). 1853. [f. L. *pix*, *picem* pitch + *ol-eum* oil + -INE [5].] *Chem.* A colourless liquid compound (C_6H_7N) obtained from bone-oil, coal-naphtha, tar, peat, etc.

‖**Picot** (pīko). 1869. [F., dim. of *pic* peak, point, prick.] A small loop of twisted thread, one of a series forming an edging to lace, etc. Also *attrib.*, as *p.-edge*. Also as vb.

Picotee (pikŏtī·). 1727. [a. F. *picoté, -ée*, pa. pple. of *picoter* to mark with pricks or points: see PICOT.] A variety of the carnation (*Dianthus Caryophyllus*), the flowers of which have a light ground, the petals being edged with a darker colour.

Picquet: see PIQUET.

‖**Picra,** short for HIERA PICRA.

Picric (pi·krik), *a.* 1838. [f. Gr. πικρός bitter + -IC.] *Chem.* In *p. acid*, also called *trinitro-carbolic* or *carbazotic acid*, *artificial indigo-bitter*, a yellow intensely bitter substance ($C_6H_3N_3O_7$), crystallizing in yellow shining prisms or laminæ, used in dyeing, medicine, and in the manufacture of explosives. So **Pi·crate,** a salt of p. acid. **Pi·cryl,** a synonym of trinitrophenyl, the radical of p. acid.

Picrite (pi·krəit). 1814. [f. as prec. + -ITE [1].] *Min.* A dark grey-green rock consisting mainly of chrysolite.

Picro- (pi·kro), bef. a vowel sometimes **picr-**, comb. form of Gr. πικρός bitter, (*a*) in the sense 'having a bitter taste or smell', esp. in the names of magnesium minerals, because magnesium salts have a bitter taste; (*b*) in names of derivs. of PICRIC acid, as *picramic acid, picramine*, etc.

Among these are **Pi·crolite** [Gr. λίθος stone], *Min.* a fibrous dark-green variety of serpentine. **Pi·cromel** [Gr. μέλι honey], a bitter-sweet substance obtained from bile. **Picroto·xin** [cf. TOXIN], formerly **picrotoxia,** *Chem.* the bitter poisonous principle ($C_{12}H_{14}O_5$) of the seeds of the *Cocculus indicus*.

Pict (pikt). late ME. [ad. late L. *Picti*, perh. = 'painted or tattooed people'; or the L. may represent a native name. OE. *Peohtas* (mod. Sc. *Pecht*) represents an earlier **Pihtas.*] One of an ancient people of disputed origin, who formerly inhabited parts of north Britain.

Picts' houses, underground structures attributed to the Picts, found in Orkney, etc. Hence **Pi·ctish** *a.*

Pictograph (pi·ktŏgraf). 1851. [f. L. *pictus* painted + -GRAPH.] A pictorial symbol or sign; a writing or record consisting of pictorial symbols. Hence **Pictogra·phic** *a.*

Pictorial (piktōᵊ·riăl), *a.* (*sb.*) 1646. [f. late L. *pictorius* (f. *pictor* painter) + -AL.] **1.** Of, belonging to, or produced by the painter; of or pertaining to painting or drawing. Now *rare.* **2.** Consisting of, expressed in, or of the nature of, a picture or pictures 1807. **3.** Containing a picture or pictures; illustrated 1826. **4.** *fig.* Like a picture; picturesque, graphic 1829. **B.** *sb.* A journal of which pictures are the main feature 1880.

1. Far be it from me to say that the p. calling is not honourable THACKERAY. 2. The hieroglyphs or p. forms were used..above one thousand years after they ceased to represent the vernacular..language of Egypt 1876. 3. P. Dutch tiles HOOD. 4. Of all poets Spenser excelled in the p. faculty 1841. Hence **Picto·rially** *adv.*

Pi·ctural, *a.* *rare.* 1656. [f. L. *pictura* PICTURE + -AL.] Of or pertaining to pictures; pictorial.

Picture (pi·ktiŭr, pi·ktʃər), *sb.* late ME. [ad. L. *pictura*, f. *pict-*, ppl. stem of *pingere* to paint.] †**1.** The action or process of painting or drawing; the fact of being painted or pictorially represented; the art of painting; pictorial representation –1844. **2.** The concrete result of this process. †**a.** Painting –1580. **b.** An individual painting, drawing, or representation on a surface, of an object or objects; *esp.* as a work of art. (Now the prevailing sense.) 1484. **c.** *spec.* The portrait or likeness of a person. Now *colloq.* or *affected.* 1505. †**d.** A likeness in the solid, esp. a statue or monumental effigy –1771. **e.** A person so strongly resembling another as to seem a likeness of him. Const. *of* 1712. **f.** A tableau; *spec.* at the end of an act or play. Also *living p.* (F. *tableau vivant*). 1865. **g.** In full *cinematograph, cinema*, or *moving p.*, a cinematograph film; *the p-s*, the cinema (*colloq.*) 1912. **h.** *fig. colloq.* A very picturesque object. **i.** *Into the p.*, so as to be obvious. *In the p.*, in evidence 1919. **3.** *transf.* A scene; the total visual impression produced by something; hence = IDEA III. 1. 1547. **4.** *fig.* A graphic description, written or spoken, of an object, capable of suggesting a mental image 1588. **5.** A symbol, type, figure; an illustration 1656.

1. P. took her feigning from Poetry B. JONS. 2. **b.** Every noble p. is a manuscript book, of which only one copy exists RUSKIN. **c.** *Twel. N.* III. iv. 228. **e.** The sons are the very p. of their father DE FOE. **g.** I saw it done in the pictures, Sir 1916. **h.** The little girl is a p. (*mod.*). 3. *Clinical p.*, the total impression of a diseased condition, formed by the physician. 5. He looks the p. of health 1871.

attrib. and *Comb.* **a.** General: as *p.-dealer, -shop*, etc.; *p.-language, -puzzle*, etc.; *p.-cover, -paper*; *p.-cleaner, cleaning, -restorer*, etc.

2. Special: as **p.-book**; **-card,** a court-card in a pack of cards; **-frame**; **-frock,** a frock designed in imitation of the style of an earlier period, esp. such a frock copied from a portrait; **p. gallery,** a hall or building containing a collection of pictures; the collection itself; **p. hat,** orig. a lady's wide-brimmed hat, usually black and adorned with ostrich feathers, as in the paintings of Reynolds and Gainsborough; hence, any wide-brimmed hat, usu. of straw and with a curving brim; **p.-house,** a cinema; **p.-moulding,** a horizontal wooden moulding, parallel to the ceiling of a room, for hanging pictures; **p. palace,** a cinema; **p. play,** a cinematograph film; **p. postcard,** a postcard having on the back of it a p.; **-rail, -rod,** a rod occupying the place of a *picture-moulding*; **-theatre,** a cinema.

Picture (pi·ktiŭr, -tʃər), *v.* 1489. [f. prec. sb.] **1.** *trans.* To represent in a picture; to draw, paint, depict; *transf.* to reflect as in a mirror. Also with *out*. **b.** To figure, to represent symbolically 1526. **2.** To describe graphically. Also with *out, forth.* 1586. **3.** To form a mental picture of, to imagine. Often *to p. to one's self.* 1738.

1. A cunning painter thus..would p. Justice MASSINGER. **b.** The anxiety of his mind was strongly pictured upon his face 1782. 3. We must not..p. the early Puritan as a gloomy fanatic 1874. Hence **Pi·cturable** *a.* capable of being painted or pictured. **Pi·ctured** *ppl. a.* represented in or as in a picture;

illustrated with a picture or pictures, or *fig.* with word-painting.

Picturesque (piktiūre·sk, -tʃər-), *a.* 1703. [ad. F. *pittoresque*, ad. It. *pittoresco*, f. *pittore* :—L. *pictorem* painter; see -ESQUE; prop. 'in the style of a painter'; but in Eng. use 'in the style of a picture'.] **1.** Like a picture; fit to be the subject of an effective picture; possessing pleasing and interesting qualities of form and colour. **2.** Of language, etc.: Strikingly graphic or vivid; sometimes implying disregard of fact 1734. **3.** Having a perception of the picturesque. Now *rare.* 1795. **4.** *absol.* as *sb. The p.*, that which is picturesque; picturesqueness 1794.

1. Susceptible observers..say of a scene 'How picturesque'—meaning by this a quality distinct from that of beauty, or sublimity, or grandeur; meaning to speak..of its fitness for imitation by art BAGEHOT. *P. gardening*, the romantic style of gardening, aiming at irregular and rugged beauty; so *p. gardener*. 2. P. history is seldom to be trusted 1868. Hence **Picture·sque-ly** *adv.*, **-ness.**

Pi·cture-wri·ting. 1741. The method of recording events or expressing ideas by pictures which literally or figuratively represent the things and actions; *concr.* a writing or inscription consisting of pictorial symbols.

‖**Picul** (pi·kɒl). 1588. [Malay-Javanese *pikul* a man's load.] A measure of weight used in China and the East generally, equal to 100 catties, i. e. about 133⅓ lbs. avoirdupois.

Piculet (pi·kiŭlėt). 1849. [f. L. *picus* woodpecker + -ET.] *Ornith.* A bird of the subfamily *Picumninæ*; a small soft-tailed woodpecker.

Piddle (pi·d'l), *v.* 1545. [Origin obsc. Cf. *paddle, peddle.*] **1.** *intr.* = PEDDLE *v.* II. (Always depreciatory.) Now *rare.* **b.** To trifle with one's food; to pick at one's food instead of eating heartily 1620. **2.** To make water. Now *vulgar* 1796. Hence **Pi·ddler. Pi·ddling** *ppl. a.* trifling, insignificant, paltry.

Piddock (pi·dǫk). 1730. [Origin unkn.]. A bivalve mollusc of the genus *Pholas* or family *Pholadidæ.*

Pidgin, pigeon (pi·dʒin, -ən). Also **pidjin.** 1850. A Chinese corruption of Eng. *business.* Hence **Pidgin-English**, the jargon, consisting chiefly of English words, often corrupted in pronunciation, and arranged according to Chinese idiom, used for intercommunication between Chinese and Europeans at seaports, etc.

Pie (pəi), *sb.*¹ ME. [a. OF., :—L. *pica* magpie.] **1.** The bird now called the MAGPIE. **2.** *fig.* Applied to †**a.** a cunning or wily person; **b.** a chattering or saucy person 1542. **3.** Applied locally to other birds, usu. having black-and-white ('pied') plumage. (See also SEA-PIE.) 1883. **b.** *French p., rain-p., wood-p.*: applied to various species of woodpecker 1677. **4.** *attrib.* In compounds denoting 'parti-coloured', as *p.-coated* adj. See PIEBALD. 1630.

Pie (pəi), *sb.*² ME. [Not known outside Eng. (exc. in Gael. *pighe*, from Eng. or Lowland Sc.) Origin obsc.] **1.** A dish composed of meat, fowl, fish, fruit, or vegetables, enclosed in or covered with a layer of paste and baked. **b.** With defining word, as APPLE-PIE, *venison-pie*, etc.; also PÉRIGORD *p.* 1602. **2.** Any object resembling a pie 1842. **3.** *fig.* A prize, a treat; a bribe. *U.S. slang.* 1895.

1. He koude..wel bake a pye CHAUCER. Phr. *To have a finger in the p.*, to have a share (often officious) in the doing of something. See also HUMBLE PIE. The term is extended to other dishes (*potato p.*) which have a crust when baked. The use of *pie* as distinguished from *tart* varies locally. 2. *Bran p.*, a tub full of bran with toys, etc. hidden in it, to be drawn out at random, at Christmas festivities, etc. DIRT-PIE, MUD-PIE.

Comb.: **p.-dish**, the deep dish in which a p. is made (and cooked).

Pie, pye, *sb.*³ Now only *Hist.* 1477. [= med.L. *pica*; see PIE *sb.*¹ and PICA¹.] **1.** A collection of rules, adopted in the pre-Reformation Church of England, to show how to deal with the concurrence of more than one office on the same day. **b.** Hence app. COCK AND PIE, q. v. †**2.** (Usu. pye book.) An alphabetical index to rolls and records –1788.

Pie (pəi), *sb.*⁴ 1659. Also †**pye,** (*U.S.*) **pi.** 1659. [perh. transf. use of PIE *sb.*²] A mass of type mingled indiscriminately, such as results from the breaking down of a forme of type. **b.** *transf.* A jumble, medley, confusion, chaos; a 'mess' 1837.

‖**Pie** (pəi), *sb.*⁵ Also **pai, pi.** 1859. [a. Hindī, etc. *pā'ī*; cf. Skr. *pad, padī* quarter from *pice.*] The smallest current Anglo-Indian copper coin, the twelfth part of an anna; before the depreciation of the rupee, about one-eighth of a penny.

Pie. *v.* 1870. [f. PIE *sb.*⁴] *Printing. trans.* To make (type) into 'pie'; to mix up indiscriminately.

Piebald (pəi·bǫld), *a.* (*sb.*) 1589. [f. PIE *sb.*¹ + BALD *a.* 4.] Of two different colours, esp. white and black (like the plumage of a magpie), usu. arranged irregularly; pied; usu. of animals, esp. horses. Loosely, parti-coloured 1594. **b.** *fig.* Of mixed characters or qualities (always in bad sense); motley, mongrel 1589. **B.** *sb.* A piebald animal, esp. horse. *fig.* A person or thing of mixed character, a 'mongrel' 1765.

Dusky woods, p. with snow DARWIN. **b.** Shall hurl his p. Latin at thy head 1763. **B.** Three pyebalds and a roan TENNYSON. Hence **Pie·baldness, -ly** *adv.*

Piece (pīs), *sb.* [ME. *pece*, later *piece*, a. OF. *pece, piece*, mod.F. *pièce*, f. late L. **pettia*, **pettium.* Ulterior etym. unkn.] **I.** In general sense; or followed by *of.* **1.** A separate portion, part, bit, or fragment of anything; one of the distinct portions of which anything is composed. †**2.** A part *of* a whole, considered as distinct; a portion *of* an immaterial thing. (Now repl. by *part, portion.*) –1755. **b.** A limited portion *of* land, enclosed, marked off by bounds, or viewed as distinct 1450. **3.** A portion or quantity *of* any substance or kind of thing forming a single (usu. small) body or mass; a bit. late ME. **b.** Of something non-material, as *a p. of prose, of music*, etc. 1601. **4.** A length (varying according to the material) in which cloth, etc., is woven; also, a length *of* wall-paper as made (in England, usually 12 yards) 1523. **5.** A cask *of* wine or brandy, usually equivalent to the butt, or to two hogsheads. [Fr. *pièce.*] 1490. **6.** A single object or individual forming a unit of a class or collective group, as *a p. of furniture, of plate, of ordnance*, etc. late ME. **7.** *P. of work*: **a.** A product of work, a (concrete) work 1540. **b.** A task, difficult business; *fig.* a commotion (*colloq.*) 1594. **8.** An individual instance, or example, *of* any form of action or activity, function, abstract quality, etc. 1568.

1. *In pieces*, broken, in fragments; *fig.* at variance. *To pieces*, into fragments, asunder. *To go* or *come to pieces*, to break up. *To take to pieces*, to separate into its parts. 2. After waiting a day and p. in Winchester WASHINGTON. Phr. *A p. of one's mind*, something of what one thinks; one's candid opinion; a rebuke. **b.** I haue bought a p. of ground *Luke* xiv. 18. 3. A hard peece of wood 1657. *P. of water*, a small detached sheet of water, a small lake. *P. of money, of gold, of silver*, a coin. *P. of flesh*, a human being; *p. of goods*, a woman or child (*joc.*) Now *dial.* **b.** Here doth lye Ben Ionson his best p. of poetrie B. JONS. 4. A *p.* of muslin is 10 yards; of calico, 28 yards; of Irish linen, 25 yards 1858. 5. Pieces of Conyack Brandy in 32 Lotts 1687. 7. **a.** What a p. of worke is a man! how Noble in Reason! [etc.] SHAKS. 8. A..delicate P. of Architecture 1686. A rare p. of luck 1876.

II. Absolute uses, without *of* and specification of the substance, etc. **1.** A person, a personage, an individual. *arch.* and *dial.* ME. **2. a.** A piece of armour. late ME. †**b.** A fortified place, stronghold –1721. **3.** A weapon for shooting, fire-arm 1550. **4.** Each of the pieces of wood, ivory, etc., also called 'men', with which chess, draughts, backgammon, etc., are played 1562. **5.** A piece of money; a coin. Often defined as *crown p., penny p.*, etc. 1575. †**b.** *spec.* Popularly applied to the sovereign, and guinea, as either was the current coin –1741. **6.** A portion of time or space. Now *dial.* ME. **7.** A (small) portion of some specific substance. late ME. **b.** Short for 'piece of bread' (with or without butter); *spec.* such a piece eaten by itself, not as part of a meal. *Sc.* and *dial.* 1787. **c.** pl. *pieces.* An inferior quality of crystallized sugar 1867. **8.** A production, specimen of handicraft, work of art; a contrivance. *Obs.* in general sense. See also MASTERPIECE. 1604. **b.** A painting, a picture 1574. **c.** A literary composition, usu. short 1533. **d.** A drama, a play 1643. **e.** A musical composition, usu. short 1825.

1. Hee is another manner of peece then you think for B. JONS. Xanthus having a kind of a Nice froward P. to his wife 1694. 3. The stocke of his p. is ..made..somewhat like a fowling p. 1591. So from a p. two chained bullets flie 1600. 4. In order to begin the game, the pawns must be moved before the pieces 1797. 5. *P. of eight*, the Spanish dollar, or *peso*, of the value of 8 *reals*, or about 4*s.* 6*d.*, marked with the figure 8. 8. **b.** The walls were thickly covered, chiefly with family pictures:..now and then some..battle-piece LYTTON. **d.** On the first night of a new p. they always fill the house with orders to support it SHERIDAN.

Phr. *A p., the p., each* or *every p.*, each piece of a number of pieces; each unit of a number, set, or company; each of them or these; esp. in stating the share or price of each unit or individual member. Hence, *advb.*, APIECE, q. v.. *the p., per p.* *By the p.*, at a rate of so much for a definite amount or quantity. *On the p.*, at piece-work. *In* or *of one p.*, consisting of a single or undivided p. or mass. *Of a p.* (*with*), of one p., in one mass; often *fig.* of one and the same kind or quality; uniform; in agreement, in keeping. *P. by p.*, one p. or part after another in succession; a p. at a time, gradually.

Comb.: **p.-goods** *sb. pl.*, textile fabrics, woven in recognized lengths for sale; now esp. Lancashire cotton goods exported to the East; **-market**, the market for goods sold by the p.; **-rate**, rate of payment for piece-work; **-work**, work done and paid for by the p.; **-worker.**

Piece (pīs), *v.* late ME. [f. prec. sb.] **1.** *trans.* To mend, make whole, or complete by adding a piece or pieces; to patch. **2.** To put together so as to form one piece; to mend (something broken) by joining the pieces; *absol.* in spinning, to join or piece up threads 1483. **b.** *fig.* To join, unite; *refl.* to join oneself *to*, unite *with* 1579. †**3.** *intr.* To unite, come together; to agree; to join on –1692.

1. *fig. Ant. & Cl.* I. v. 45. 2. I cannot p. the leg as the doctor can MRS. GASKELL **b.** Piecing fragments of empty signification MEREDITH. 3. New Things peece not so well BACON.

Comb. with adverbs. **P. on.** *trans.* and *intr.* To fit on (as the corresponding piece). **P. out.** *trans.* To complete, eke out, or enlarge by the addition of a piece. **P. together.** *trans.* To join together (pieces or fragments) into a whole; to make up of pieces so combined. **P. up.** *trans.* To make up (esp. that which is broken); to patch up.

‖**Pièce** (pyęs). 1789. The French for 'piece'; occurring in French phrases in Eng. use. **a.** A document used as evidence; esp. in *p. justificative*, a document serving as proof of an allegation. **b.** *P. de résistance* (pyęs də rezistāṅs): the most substantial dish in a repast; also *fig.* the chief item in a collection, group, or series.

Piecemeal (pī·smīl), *adv.* (*sb., a.*) [ME. f. PIECE *sb.* + -MEAL.] **1.** One part at a time; piece by piece, by degrees; separately. Also with *by* (rarely *in*). **2.** Piece from piece; into or in pieces; with *break, tear, cut*, etc. 1570. †**B.** quasi-*sb.* (with *pl.*) A small piece, portion, or fragment; chiefly in phr. *by piecemeals* –1762. **C.** *adj.* (the adv. used *attrib.*) Consisting in pieces; done bit by bit 1600.

1. The business will be done covertly and p. BURKE. 2. Bruse Thou shalt and peecemeale breake These men like potshards weake SIDNEY. **C.** Giving no opinion on p. reform 1831. Hence **Pie·cemeal** *v.* (now *rare*) to divide p.; to dismember.

Piecen (pī·s'n). *v.* *local* or *techn.* 1835. [f. PIECE *sb.* + -EN⁵ 2.] *trans.* To join, to piece; chiefly, to join broken threads in spinning.

Piecener (pī·s'nəɹ). 1835. [f. prec. + -ER¹.] One who pieces or piecens; a piecer; *spec.* a young person employed in a spinning-mill to keep the frames filled with rovings, and to join together the ends of threads which break; formerly also, to join the cardings or slivers for the slubber, a work now done by machinery.

Piecer (pī·səɹ). 1825. [f. PIECE *v.* + -ER¹.] **1.** *gen.* One who pieces; a patcher 1836. **2.** *spec.* In a spinning-mill: see PIECENER 1825.

Piecrust (pəi·krɒst). 1582. [PIE *sb.*²] The baked paste forming the crust of a pie.

Prov. Promises are like pie-crust, made to be broken.

Pied (pəid), *ppl. a.* late ME. [As if pa. pple. of a verb *pie*, f. PIE *sb.*¹; see -ED.] Parti-coloured; orig. black and white like a magpie. Also, wearing a parti-coloured dress, e.g. *pied piper*. **b.** Construed as *pa. pple.* = variegated 1632. **c.** In the specific names of many birds and animals 1837.

To weare the p. coate off a foole 1575. **b.** Meadows trim with Daisies pide MILT. **c. P. antelope** = BONTEBOK; **p. blackbird,** any Asiatic thrush of the genus *Turdulus*; **p. finch,** the chaffinch, *Fringilla cœlebs*; **p. flycatcher** (*Muscicapa atricapilla*). Hence **Pie·dness.**

‖**Pied-à-terre** (pyetatɛ̄r). 1839. [Fr. 'foot to earth'.] A place to rest or stay at.

Piedmontite (pī·dmǫntəit). 1854. [f. *Piedmont* (It. *Piemonte*), its locality + -ITE [1] 2 b.] *Min.* A brownish-red or reddish-black silicate of aluminium, iron, manganese, and calcium, resembling epidote; manganese epidote.

Pieman (pəi·mǣn). 1820. A man who makes pies for sale; a vendor of pies. So **Pie·-wo:man** 1817.

Piepowder (pəi·paudəɹ), *a.* and *sb.* ME. [ult. = med. (Anglo-) L. *pede-pulverosus* dusty-footed, also as sb., a wayfarer, itinerant merchant, etc.] †**A.** (*piepoudrous*, etc.) *adj.* Wayfaring, itinerant; *absol.* as *sb. sing.* and *pl.* = B. -1609. **B.** (*piepowder*) *sb.* †A travelling man, a wayfarer, *esp.* an itinerant merchant or trader. Chiefly used in *Court of Piepowders*, a summary court formerly held at fairs and markets to administer justice among itinerant dealers, etc. -1735. **b.** *attrib.* and *sb. sing.*, *P. Court*, *Court of P.* = *Court of Piepowders* 1574.

Pier (piəɹ). [In 12th. c. *per*, rendering med. L. *pera*, of unkn. origin.] **1.** One of the supports of the spans of a bridge, whether arched or otherwise formed. **2.** A solid structure of stone, or of earth faced with piles, extending into the sea or a tidal river, to protect or enclose a harbour and form a landing-stage; also, one of iron or wood, open beneath, forming a pleasure promenade, and often a landing-place; also, a projecting landing-stage or jetty on the bank of a river or lake 1453. †**b.** *transf.* A haven -1721. **3.** *Arch.* and *Building.* A solid support of masonry or the like designed to sustain vertical pressure: **a.** A square pillar or pilaster; **b.** The solid masonry between doors, windows, etc.; **c.** Each of the pillars from which an arch springs 1663.

attrib. and *Comb.*, as **p.-glass,** a tall mirror; orig. one fitted to fill up the p. between two windows, or over a chimney-piece; **-table,** a low table occupying the space between two windows. Hence **Pie·rage,** the toll paid for the use of a pier or wharf.

Pierce (pīəɹs), *v.* ME. [a. OF *percer*, earlier *percier*; ult. origin unkn.] **1.** *trans.* To penetrate (a substance), as a sharp-pointed instrument does; of an agent: to stab, prick, puncture (anything) *with* such an instrument. **b.** *transf.* and *fig.*; *spec.* said of the penetrating action of cold. late ME. **2.** To make a hole, opening, or tunnel into or through (something); to bore through; to broach (a cask, etc.) ME. **b.** To make (a hole, etc.) by piercing. late ME. **3.** To force one's way through or into; to break (an enemy's line) ME. **4.** To reach or penetrate with the sight or mind; to discern. late ME. **5.** To penetrate with pain, grief, or other emotion; to wound; to move deeply. late ME. **6.** *intr.* To enter, penetrate, or pass *into* or *through*; *transf.* to project or jut sharply. late ME. **b.** *transf.* and *fig.* To see *into* (anything) 1549.

1. They shall loke on hym, whom they pearsed TINDALE *John* xix. 37. His only son..was pierced through the heart by a javelin GIBBON. **2.** Le Ceres, French ship privateer, pierced for 14 guns 1798. **4.** He pierced the mysteries of nature 1850. **5.** Can no prayers p. thee? SHAKS. **6.** Narrow promontories, piercing out into the water 1872. Hence **Pierce** *sb.* the act or process of piercing.

Pierced (pīəɹst, *poet.* pīə·ɹsėd), *ppl. a.* late ME. [f. prec. + -ED [1].] In the senses of PIERCE *v.* **b.** *spec.* in *Her.* (*a*) Said of a charge represented as perforated with a hole, so that the tincture of the field appears through. (*b*) Said of an animal used as a charge, represented as having an arrow, spear, etc., fixed in its body, but not passing through it. 1572.

Piercer (pīə·ɹsəɹ). late ME. [= F. *perceur*, f. *percer* to pierce; see -ER [1] 2.] **1.** *gen.* One who or that which pierces. **2.** An instrument or tool for piercing or boring holes, as an auger, awl, gimlet, stiletto, etc. late ME. **b.** The sting or the ovipositor of an insect 1691. **3.** A person employed in perforating metal or wood work 1736.

Piercing (pīə·ɹsiŋ), *ppl. a.* late ME. [f. PIERCE *v.* + -ING [2].] **1.** Perforating, penetrating, as a sharp-pointed instrument. **2.** Able to 'see into' a thing; having penetration ME.

1. Sorrow's p. dart GRAY. A p. shriek rang through the..air 1884. *fig.* A state of the most p. inquietude 1791. **2.** The most p. eyes I ever beheld are those of Voltaire 1779. Hence **Pie·rcing-ly** *adv.*, **-ness.**

Pier-head. 1682. [f. PIER + HEAD *sb.*] The outward or seaward end of a pier.

Pierian (pəi,ĭə·riǎn), *a.* 1591. [f. L. *Pierius* adj. + -AN.] Belonging to Pieria, a district in N. Thessaly, the reputed home of the Muses; *spec.* an epithet of the Muses; hence in ref. to poetry or learning.

A little learning is a dang'rous thing; Drink deep, or taste not the P. spring POPE.

Pieridine (pəi,e·ridəin), *a.* [ad. mod.L. *Pieridinæ*, f. *Pieris*, the typical genus.] *Entom.* Belonging to the family *Pieridæ*, or subfamily *Pieridinæ* of *Papilionidæ*, containing the cabbage butterflies.

Pierrette (pī̆ěre·t, ‖pyɛrɛt). 1888. [F., fem. dim. of *Pierre* Peter, corr. to PIERROT.] A female member of a company of pierrots.

Pierrot (pī·ěro, ‖pyɛro). 1741. [F., dim. of *Pierre*, applied to a buffoon:—L. *Petrum*, nom. *Petrus* PETER. Cf. *zany*.] A typical character in French pantomime; applied in English use to a singer or instrumentalist having usu. a whitened face and wearing loose white fancy dress.

Piet, pyet, pyot (pəi·ət). Now only *Sc.* and *n. dial.* [In ME. *piot*, f. PIE *sb.* [1] + -OT [1], written later -ET.] **1.** The magpie. **b.** The dipper or water-ouzel. Also *water-piet*. 1839. **2.** *fig.* Applied to a talkative or saucy person 1574. **3.** *attrib.* Pied, piebald 1508.

‖**Pietà** (pyeta·) 1644. [It. :—L. *pietatem* PIETY.] A representation, in painting or sculpture, of the Virgin Mary (and other holy women) mourning over the dead Christ.

Pietism (pəi·ėtiz'm). 1697. [ad. G. (mod. L.) *pietismus*, formed after PIETIST; see -ISM.] **1.** *Ch. Hist.* The movement for the revival and advancement of piety in the Lutheran church (see next, 1); the principles or practices of the German Pietists. **2.** Pious sentiment; often implying an affectation or exaggeration of piety 1829.

1. Say what you will of P., no one can deny the real worth of the characters which it formed 1877.

Pietist (pəi·ėtist). 1697. [a. G., f. L. *pietas* PIETY + -IST. Applied in derision to the followers of Spener, in ref. to the *collegia pietatis* formed by them *c* 1690.] **1.** *Ch. Hist.* One of the party of reformers in the Lutheran church who followed Philipp Jakob Spener in the movement begun by him at Frankfort about 1670 for the deepening of piety and the reform of religious education. **2.** A person characterized by or professing special piety; one who cultivates, or lays stress on, depth of religious feeling or strictness of religious practice, esp. as dist. from intellectual belief. 1767. **3.** *attrib.* That is a pietist; pietistic 1705. Hence **Pieti·stic** *a.*; **-ical** *a.*; **-ly** *adv.*

Piety (pəi·ėti). ME. [a. OF. *piete*, ad.L. *pietas*, f. *pius* PIOUS.] †**I.** An early form of PITY, in various senses -1606.

Thou art a mercifull God..and of a great pietie *Bk. Com. Prayer, Commination*, 1548-9.

II. The quality or character of being pious. **1.** Habitual reverence and obedience to God (or the gods); godliness, devoutness, religiousness 1604. **2.** Faithfulness to the duties naturally owed to parents and relatives, superiors, etc.; dutifulness, esp. to parents 1579. **3.** With *a* and *pl.* A pious act, observance, or characteristic 1652.

1. True p. is cheerful as the day COWPER. **2.** Let them learne first to shew pietie at home, and to requite their parents 1 *Tim.* v. 4. Phr. *Mount, Mountain of p.*: see MOUNT *sb.* [1] II. 1. *Pelican in her p.*: see PELICAN I. 2.

Piezometer (pəi,ezǫ·mǐtəɹ). 1820. [f. Gr. πιέζειν to press + -(O)METER.] An instrument for measuring pressure (or something connected with pressure); e.g. for measuring the compressibility of liquids, measuring the pressure of water at any point in a water-main, etc.

‖**Piffero** (pi·fero). 1724. [It. = Sp. *pifaro*, F. *fifre* a fife or pipe, ad. OHG. *pfîfari*, f. *pfîfa* PIPE, FIFE.] A small flute; also, a primitive kind of oboe, or a bagpipe with an inflated sheepskin for reservoir.

Piffle (pi·f'l), *v.* *dial.* and *slang.* 1847. [perh. onomatopœic, with dim. ending.] *intr.* To talk or act in a feeble or ineffective way. Hence **Pi·ffle** *sb.* foolish nonsense; twaddle. **Pi·ffler,** a trifler, a twaddler. **Pi·ffling** *a.* twaddling, foolish, trivial.

Pig (pig), *sb.* [1] [Early ME. *pigge*:—prob. OE. **picga*, **pigga*; etym. unkn.] **I. 1.** The young of swine; 'a young sow or boar' (J.). **2.** By extension: A swine of any age; a hog 1663. **b.** The figure of the animal used as an ornament, etc. *Sussex p.*, a drinking vessel in this form. 1884. **3.** The animal or its flesh as food (*joc.*, exc. with ref. to a young or sucking pig) late ME. **4.** Any of various species of the family *Suidæ*, as *bush-p.*, *wood-p.*; also extended to animals resembling the pig, as *sea-pig*, (*a*) the porpoise, (*b*) the tunny. See also GUINEA-PIG. 1664. **5.** Applied opprobriously to a person, etc. (Cf. F. *cochon*.) 1546.

3. A Dissertation upon Roast P. LAMB.

II. Technical uses. **1.** An oblong mass of metal, as obtained from the smelting-furnace; esp. of iron. Also, in mod. use (without *a* or *pl.*), short for *pig-iron*. *P. of ballast*, a pig of iron (rarely of lead) used as ballast. 1589. **b.** Applied to the moulds or channels in the pig-bed 1805. **2.** In various techn. and local uses: e.g. a block or cube of salt; a segment of an orange or apple; etc. 1825. **3.** *Pigs in clover*, a game which consists in rolling a number of marbles into a recess or pocket in a board by tilting the board 1900.

Phrases. *To buy a p. in a poke* (or *bag*), to buy a thing without seeing it or knowing its value. *Please the pigs*, if all 's well. *To carry pigs to market*, to try to do business or attain to results. *To drive* (or *bring*) *one's pigs to a fine, pretty*, etc. *market*, (usu. ironical) to be unsuccessful in a venture. *Prov.* Pigs might fly: an expression of incredulity.

Comb.: **p.-market,** (*a*) a market for the sale of swine; (*b*) a name for the proscholium or ante-chamber of the Divinity School at Oxford; **-mould,** one of the channels in a pig-bed; **-fish,** a pop. name in America and Australia of several fishes; **-ring,** a ring fixed in the snout of a hog to prevent it from grubbing; **-yoke,** a sextant or quadrant (*slang*).

Pig (pig), *sb.* [2] Now *Sc.* and *Northumb.* late ME. [Cf. PIGGIN.] An earthenware pot, pitcher, jar, or other vessel; a crock.

Pigs and whistles, fragments; trivialities; *to go to pigs and whistles*, to be ruined.

Pig, *v.* 1532. [f. PIG *sb.* [1]] **I.** Of a sow: To bring forth pigs; to farrow. Also *transf.* and *fig.* **2.** *intr.* To huddle or herd together like pigs; to sleep in a place like a pigsty. Also *to p. it* (mod. colloq.). 1675. **b.** *trans.* To crowd (persons) together like pigs 1745.

Pi·g-bed. 1821. [f. PIG *sb.* [1] + BED *sb.*] **1.** A pigsty, a pig's lair. **2.** The bed of sand in which pigs of iron are cast 1884.

Pigeon (pi·dʒin, -ən), *sb.* [ME. *pyjon*, *pejon*, a. OF. *pijon*, *pyjoun* young bird, young dove, dove, mod.F. *pigeon* (whence the mod. Eng. spelling), :—late L. **pibionem*, for *pipionem* (*pipio*) a young cheeping bird, f. *pipire* to cheep.] †**1.** A young dove -1601. **2.** A bird of the family *Columbidæ*, a dove, either wild or domesticated 1494. **3.** *fig.* †**a.** A young woman, a girl; a sweetheart; also, a coward -1682. **b.** One who lets himself be swindled, esp. in gaming; a dupe, gull 1593. **4.** A flying target, used as a substitute for a real pigeon.

2. At Modena..pigeons are taught to carry letters to a place appointed, and bring back answers 1756. CARRIER-PIGEON, *homing p.*, *nun p.*, *pouter p.*, *tumbler p.*, etc.; **fruit p., ground p.,** PASSENGER-P., **rock p., wild p., wood-p.:** for the more important of these see the qualifying word. **3. b.** He was a famous p. for the play-men; they lived upon him THACKERAY. Phr. *To pluck a p.*, to 'fleece' a person. **4.** *Clay p.*, a saucer of baked clay thrown into the air from a trap, as a mark at shooting-matches. Phr. *To fly the blue p.* (Naut. slang): to heave the deep-sea lead.

Combs.: **p.-express** = *pigeon-post*; **-fancier:** see FANCIER 3; **-flyer,** one who lets homing pigeons fly, or takes part in pigeon-races; **-hearted** *a.*, faint-

hearted, timid; †-livered *a.*, gentle, meek; **-match,** a match at shooting pigeons released from traps; **-post,** etc. by homing pigeons; **-poult,** the young of a p.; **-woodpecker** (*U.S.*) = FLICKER *sb.*[2]
b. Combs. with *pigeon's*: **pigeon's blood,** *attrib.* (of a ruby) dark red, rather lighter than beef's blood; **pigeon's egg,** a bead of Venetian glass, of the shape and size of the egg of a p.; **pigeon's-foot** (= F. *pied de pigeon*), dove's-foot (*Geranium columbinum*).

Pigeon, *v. arch.* 1675. [f. prec.] *trans.* To make a pigeon of; to gull, cheat, delude, swindle, esp. at cards or any kind of gaming.

Pigeon (English): see PIDGIN.

Pi·geon-be:rry. 1775. [f. PIGEON *sb.* + BERRY *sb.*[1]] In N. America, the Poke-weed, *Phytolacca decandra*; also its berry; in Bermuda *Duranta Plumieri*.

Pi·geon-breast. 1849. *Path.* A deformity of the human chest, in which it is laterally constricted so that the sternum is thrust forward, as in a pigeon. So **Pi·geon-brea:sted** *a.* 1815; also **Pi·geon-che:sted** *a.*

Pi·geongram. 1885. [f. PIGEON *sb.*, after *telegram*.] A message transmitted by a homing pigeon.

Pi·geon-hawk. 1807. A hawk that preys on pigeons; in England a name for the sparrow-hawk, and sometimes the goshawk; in U. S. the American merlin (*Falco columbarius*) and related species; also sometimes, the sharp-shinned hawk (*Accipiter velox*).

Pi·geon-hole, *sb.* 1592. [f. PIGEON *sb.* + HOLE *sb.*] 1. A hole (usu. one of several) in a wall or door for the passage of pigeons; hence *transf.* 1683. 2. A small recess or hole (usu. one of a series) for domestic pigeons to nest in; hence, any small hole, recess, or room for sitting or staying in 1622. †3. A cant name for the stocks -1694. 4. *Printing.* An excessively wide space between two words. Not now common. 1683. 5. One of a series of compartments, in a cabinet, writing-table, or range of shelves, open in front, and used for the keeping of documents, etc., also of wares in a shop 1789.

5. Abbé Sieyes has whole nests of pigeon-holes full of constitutions ready made, ticketed, sorted, and numbered BURKE. *fig.* Incapable of arranging his thoughts in orderly symmetrical pigeon-holes 1902.

Pi·geon-hole, *v.* 1848. [f. prec. sb.] 1. *trans.* To deposit in a pigeon-hole (5); hence, to put aside (a matter) for future consideration, shelve for the present 1861. 2. To place or label mentally; to classify or analyse exhaustively 1870. 3. To furnish with or divide into a set of pigeon-holes 1848.

1. Lord Lyveden, by duly pigeon-holing the complaint, added another to the long list of his public services in that line 1861.

Pi·geon-house. 1537. A columbarium, dovecot.

Pi·geon-pea. 1716. [= F. *pois-pigeon.*] The seed of a leguminous shrub, *Cajanus indicus*, native of the E. Indies; also, the plant.

Pi·geon-plum. 1747. 1. A tree of the W. Indies and Florida, *Coccoloba Floridana*, N.O. *Polygonaceæ*, the wood of which is used in cabinet-making; also, its edible grape-like fruit. 2. A W. African tree of the genus *Chrysobalanus*, N.O. *Rosaceæ*; also, its succulent edible fruit 1884.

Pi·geonry. 1840. [-RY.] A pigeon-house.

Pigeon's milk. 1777. 1. The partly digested food with which pigeons feed their young 1888. 2. An imaginary article for which children are sent on a fool's errand.

Pi·geon-toe:d, *a.* 1801. 1. *Ornith.* Having the toes arranged on a level, as in pigeons; peristeropod 1890. 2. Of persons or horses: In-toed.

Pigeon-wood (pi·dʒənwud). 1745. A name given to the wood of various tropical or subtropical trees or shrubs, mostly used in cabinet-work, so called from the marking or colouring.

Piggery (pi·gəri). 1804. [f. PIG *sb.*[1] + -ERY.] 1. A place where pigs are kept. 2. Piggish condition; piggishness 1867.

Piggin (pi·gin). Chiefly *dial.* 1554. [perh. f. PIG *sb.*[2]] A small pail, esp. a wooden one with one stave longer than the rest serving as a handle; a milking pail; a vessel to drink out of.

Piggish (pi·giʃ), *a.* 1792. [f. PIG *sb.*[1] + -ISH[1].] Pertaining to a pig, piglike; stubborn; selfish, mean; unclean, vile. Hence **Pi·ggishly** *adv.*, **-ness.**

Pigheaded (stress var.), *a.* 1620. [Parasynthetic deriv. of PIG *sb.*[1] + HEAD *sb.* + -ED[2].] Having a head like that of a pig; usu. *fig.*, having the mental qualities ascribed to a pig, obstinate, stupid, perverse. Hence **Pi·ghea·d·ed·ly** *adv.*, **-ness.**

Pight, arch. pa. t. and pa. pple. of PITCH *v.*[1]

Pightle (pəi·t'l). *local.* ME. [Origin obsc.] A small field or enclosure; a close or croft.

Pig-iron. 1665. [f. PIG *sb.*[1] II. 1.] Cast iron in pigs or ingots, as first reduced from the ore.

Pigment (pi·gmĕnt). late ME. [ad. L. *pigmentum*, f. *pig-*, *pingere* to paint.] A colouring matter or substance. a. A paint, dye, 'colour'; in techn. use, a dry substance, usu. in the form of a powder, which, when mixed with a vehicle, constitutes a 'paint'. b. *Nat. Hist.* Any organic substance occurring in and colouring any part of an animal or plant; the natural colouring-matter of a tissue 1842. Hence **Pigme·ntal** *a.* pigmentary; **-ly** *adv.* **Pi·gmented** *a.* charged or coloured with p.

Pigmentary (pi·gmĕntări), *sb.* and *a.* late ME. [ad. L. *pigmentarius* adj., of or belonging to paints or unguents; sb., a dealer in these, f. *pigmentum*; see prec. and -ARY[1].] †A. *sb.* An apothecary. late ME. only. B. *adj.* †1. Pertaining to an apothecary or maker of aromatic confections. late ME. only. 2. Of, pertaining or belonging to, or consisting of pigment; producing or containing colouring-matter; in *Path.* characterized by the formation or presence of pigment 1851.

Pigmentation (pigmĕntēi·ʃən). 1866. [f. L. *pigmentatus* painted + -ION; see -ATION.] *Biol.*, *Nat. Hist.*, etc. Coloration or discoloration by formation or deposition of pigment in the tissues.

Pi·g-me:tal. 1731. [f. PIG *sb.*[1] II. 1. + METAL; cf. SOW-METAL.] Metal, usu. iron, in the form of pigs.

Pigmy, var. of PYGMY.

Pignorate (pi·gnŏreit), *v.* Also **pignerate.** 1623. [ad. L. *pignerare* (*pignorare*) to give as a pledge, f. *pignus* (*pigner-*, *-or-*) pledge; see -ATE[3].] *trans.* To give or take as a pledge; to pledge, pawn. Hence **Pignora·tion,** the action of pledging or pawning. **Pi·gnorative** *a.* pledging, pawning.

Pi·g-nut. 1610. [f. PIG *sb.*[1] + NUT.] 1. = EARTH-NUT 1. 2. = HOG-NUT 2. 1760.

Pi·gskin. 1855. [f. PIG *sb.*[1] + SKIN.] The skin of the pig or hog; leather made of this. Hence in *Sporting slang*, a saddle.

Pi·gsney, -ny. *arch.* and *dial.* [ME. f. *pigges* pig's + *neyȝe* = *eye* with prosthetic *n*, app. derived from *an eye, min eye.*] 1. A darling, pet; an endearing form of address, chiefly to a girl or woman. †2. An eye; a 'dear little eye' -1774.

1. And the little pigsny has mamma's mouth FARQUHAR.

Pigsticking (pi·gˌsti:kiŋ). 1848. [f. PIG *sb.*[1] + *sticking* vbl. sb.] The hunting of the wild boar with a spear. **Pi·gstick** *v. intr.* to hunt the wild boar. **Pi·gsticker,** (*a*) one who follows this sport; (*b*) a horse trained to this sport; (*c*) *colloq.* a long-bladed pocket-knife.

Pigsty (pi·gstəi). 1591. A sty or pen for pigs, including a shed. b. *transf.* A miserable dirty hovel.

Pi·g's wash, pi·gwash. 1630. The swill of a brewery or kitchen given to pigs; = HOGWASH. Also *transf.*

Pi·gtail. 1688. [From resemblance to the tail of a pig.] 1. Tobacco twisted into a thin rope. 2. A plait or queue of hair hanging down from the back of the head, applied *spec.* to that worn formerly by soldiers and sailors, and still occasionally by young girls, and now *esp.* to that customary among the Chinese 1753. b. *transf.* A Chinese 1886. 3. *attrib.*, esp. in sense 'characteristic of the period when pigtails were worn', old-fashioned, pedantic, formal 1746. Hence **Pi·gtailed** *a.* having a tail like a pig's; having a p.; tied up into a p.

Pi·gweed. 1844. Various herbs devoured by swine, as the Goosefoots, Cow-parsnip, etc.

Pi-jaw: see PI *a.*

‖ **Pika** (pəi·kă). 1827. [ad. *piika*, native name among the Tungus of Siberia.] A small rodent quadruped, *Lagomys alpinus*, allied to the guinea-pig, inhabiting boreal and alpine regions of Europe and Asia.

Pike (pəik), *sb.*[1] [Found in OE. as *piic*, *pic*, in ME. *pik* (pl. *pīkes*), later *pȳke*, *pīke*; cf. PICK *sb.*[1]] I. A pickaxe; a pick used in digging, breaking up ground, etc. Now only as *dial.* form of PICK *sb.*[1] II. 1. A sharp point, a spike, as the pointed end of a staff, or of an arrow or spear, the spike in the centre of a buckler ME. b. A prickle, a thorn; a hedgehog's prickle or spine. Chiefly *Sc.* *Obs.* or *dial.* ME. 3. A staff having an iron point or spike, a pikestaff. Now *dial.* ME. b. A pitchfork, a hay-fork. Now *dial.* late ME. III. 1. = PEAK. a. The long peak of a shoe; a poulaine. *Obs.* exc. *Hist.* late ME. b. The 'beak' of an anvil. *Obs.* or *dial.* 1677. 2. *dial.* A narrow pointed piece of land at the side of a field of irregular shape 1585.

attrib. and *Comb.*, as **p.-pole** *U.S.*, a pole with a spike and a hook, used by lumbermen in driving logs, also as a boat-hook; **piketail** *U.S.*, the pintail duck.

Pike (pəik), *sb.*[2] *north. Eng.* ME. [app. a local use of prec., or of Norse origin.] 1. A name for a pointed or peaked summit, or a mountain or hill with a pointed summit; used extensively in the English Lake district. b. A cairn, also, a beacon, tower, or pile, on an eminence 1751. 2. A pointed or peaked stack of hay, made up temporarily in the hayfield; also, a stack of corn, circular in form, pointed, and of no great size 1641.

1. Then there came down from Langdale P. A cloud SHELLEY.

†**Pike** (pəik), *sb.*[3] 1555. [ad. Sp. *pico* beak, bill, peak, Pg. *pico* summit, top. Distinct from prec., as being of general use; its later form is PEAK *sb.*[2].] 1. The earlier form of PEAK *sb.*[2], the conical summit of a mountain. (Used first in the name *Pike* (*Picke*) of *Teneriffe.*) -1776. b. Hence, Any mountain peak; *esp.* a volcanic cone -1796. 2. *Naut.* Phr. *On* (*the*) *p.*, vertically, straight up and down -1628.

Pike (pəik), *sb.*[4] ME. [app. short for *pike-fish*, from PIKE *sb.*[1], in ref. to its pointed beak; cf. GED and F. *brochet*, f. *broche* spit.] 1. A large, voracious freshwater fish of the northern temperate zone, *Esox lucius*, with a long slender snout; a jack, luce. Hence, any fish of the genus *Esox* or of the family *Esocidæ*. 2. Applied in the colonies, etc., to various fishes resembling the pikes proper: e.g. two cyprinoid fishes, *Ptychochilus lucius* and *Gila grandis*, of California, and species of *Sphyræna* of Australia 1871. b. Also with distinctive epithets 1810.

1. He..Saw the p., the Maskenozha LONGF. 2. b. **Glass-eyed, Goggle-eyed, Wall-eyed P.,** the pike-perch, *Stizostedion americanum* (or *S. vitreum*); **Sand-p.,** the lizard-fish, *Synodus fœtens*; **Sea P.,** the common garfish or gar-pike, *Belone vulgaris*; see also GAR-PIKE.

attrib. and *Comb.*, as **p.-perch,** a percoid fish of the genus *Stizostedion*; esp. *S. americanum* and *S. vitreum*; **-whale** = *piked whale*: see PIKED *a.*

Pike (pəik), *sb.*[5] Also †**pique,** †**pyke.** 1511. [a. F. *pique* sb. fem., a military term; from the same root as F. *piquer* to pierce, puncture.] 1. A weapon consisting of a long wooden shaft with a pointed head of iron or steel; in the 18th c. superseded by the bayonet. †2. *transf.* = PIKEMAN[1] -1649.

1. Phr. *To trail a p.*: see TRAIL *v.* †*To run* (*push, cast oneself*, etc.) *upon the pikes*, (*fig.*) to rush to destruction.

Pike, *sb.*[6] *dial.* or *local colloq.* and *U.S.* 1837. [Short for TURNPIKE.] 1. A toll-bar or toll-gate. b. *transf.* The toll paid at a turnpike-gate 1837. 2. A turnpike road 1852.

Piked (pəikt, pəi·kĕd), *a.* ME. [f. PIKE *sb.*[1] + -ED[2].] 1. = PICKED *a.* 1, 1 b. 2. Tapering to a point or peak; pointed, peaked 1538.

2. **P. horn,** a tall conical head-dress worn by ladies in the 14th and 15th c. **P. shoe,** a shoe with a long

peak at the toes; a poulaine. **P. whale,** the lesser rorqual, or pike-headed whale, *Balænoptera rostrata.*

Pikelet (pəi·klėt). 1790. [Shortened from *barapicklet* (W. *bara pyglyd*).] A local name for a crumpet.

Pikeman[1] (pəi·kmæ̆n). *Obs.* exc. *Hist.* ME. [f. PIKE *sb.*[5] + MAN.] A soldier armed with a pike.

Pikeman[2] (pəi·kmæ̆n). 1845. [f. PIKE *sb.*[1] + MAN *sb.*] A pickman; a miner; one who hews the coal with a pickaxe.

Pi·keman[3]. 1857. [f. PIKE *sb.*[6] + MAN *sb.*] The keeper of a turnpike.

Pikestaff (pəi·kˌstɑf). ME. [f. PIKE *sb.*[1] + STAFF; in sense 2, f. PIKE *sb.*[5]] **1.** A walking stick with a metal point at the lower end like an alpenstock. **2.** The wooden shaft of a pike (the weapon) 1580.

Phr. *As plain as a p.*, earlier *as plain as a* PACK-STAFF (in ref. to its plain surface).

Pilage (pəi·lėdʒ). 1825. [f. PILE *sb.*[4] + -AGE.] = PELAGE.

Pilaster (pilæ·stəɹ). 1575. [a. F. *pilastre*, a. It. *pilastro*, in med.L. *pilastrum*, f. *pila* pillar; see -ASTER.] *Arch.* **1.** A square or rectangular column or pillar; *spec.* such a pillar engaged in a wall, from which it projects a third, fourth, or other portion of its breadth; an anta; formerly also, the square pier of an arch, abutment of a bridge, etc. Hence **Pila·stered** *a.* furnished with or supported on pilasters.

Pilate (pəi·lĕ̆t). late ME. [a. F., ad. L. *Pilatus.*] The name (Pontius Pilate) of the Roman procurator of Judæa concerned in the trial of Jesus Christ; hence allus. as a term of reproach.

|| **Pilau, pilaw** (pilau·, pilǭ·, pilǭu·), **pilaff** (pilɑ·f). 1612. [a. Pers. *pilāw* boiled rice and meat. *Pilaff* represents mod. Turk. pronunciation.] An oriental dish, rice boiled with fowl, meat, or fish, and spices, raisins, etc.

Pilch (piltʃ), *sb.* [OE. *pylece*, ad. med.L. *pellicea*, furred garment, fem. of *pelliceus* adj. f. *pellis* a skin. Cf. PELISSE.] **1.** An outer garment made of skin dressed with the hair; later, a leathern or coarse woollen outer garment. *Obs.* exc. *Hist.* **2.** A light frameless saddle for children 1552. **3.** A triangular flannel wrapper for an infant, worn over the diaper or napkin 1674.

Pilchard (pi·ltʃăɹd). 1530. [Origin unkn. The *d* is excrescent.] A small sea fish, *Clupea pilchardus*, closely allied to the herring; it is taken in large numbers on the coasts of Cornwall and Devon.

Fooles are as like husbands, as Pilchers are to Herrings SHAKS.

Pi·lcorn. ME. [For *pildcorn*, f. PILLED *ppl. a.* + CORN.] A kind of oat, in which the glumes or husks do not adhere to the grain, but leave it bare. Also called *pilled oats.*

Pilcrow (pi·lˌkrōu). *arch.* 1440. [app. for *pilled crow.* History obscure.] A paragraph mark.

Pile (pəil), *sb.*[1] [OE. *pīl* masc., a. L. *pilum*, the heavy javelin of the Roman footsoldier, orig. 'pestle'.] †**1.** A dart; a shaft. –1400. †**b.** The pointed metal head of a dart, lance, or arrow –1700. **c.** Used to render L. *pilum*, the heavy javelin of the Roman footsoldier 1620. **2.** A (pointed) blade (of grass) 1513. **3.** A pointed stake or post; *spec.* in later use, a large and heavy beam of timber, usu. sharpened at the lower end, of which a number are driven into the bed of a river, or into marshy or uncertain ground, for the support of a bridge, pier, quay, wall, etc. Also extended to cylindrical or other hollow iron pillars used for the same purposes. OE. **4.** *Her.* A charge, one of the ordinaries or subordinaries, having the form of a wedge, usu. issuing from the chief or top of the escutcheon, with the point downwards. *In p.*: arranged in the form of a pile. *Party per p.*: divided by lines in the form of a pile. 1486.

2. Every p. of the grass that springs so sweetly in the meadows 1895. **3.** The houses of Amsterdam, which are reported to stand upon piles driven deep into the quagmire 1768.

attrib. and *Comb.*, as *p.-breakwater*; *p.-village*, etc.; also **p.-building,** a building erected on piles, esp. a prehistoric dwelling; **-cap,** a cap or plate for the head of a pile; also, a beam connecting the heads of piles; **-dwelling,** a dwelling built on piles, esp. in a lake, but sometimes on dry ground; hence **-dweller**; **-house,** a pile-dwelling; **-worm,** the teredo.

Pile (pəil), *sb.*[2] late ME. [a. F., = heap, etc. :—L. *pila* pillar, pier, or mole of stone.] †**1.** A pillar; a pier, esp. of a bridge –1730. †**2.** A mole or pier in the sea –1652. **3.** A heap of things lying one upon another; also *fig.* 1440. **b.** A series of weights fitting one within or upon another, so as to form a solid cone or other figure. (So F. *pile.*) 1440. **c.** *spec.* A heap of combustibles on which a dead body is burnt (*funeral pile*) 1615. **d.** *Metall.* A rectangular mass of cut lengths of puddled iron bars, laid upon each other in rows, for the purpose of being rolled after being raised to a welding temperature 1839. **e.** *ellipt.* (for *p. of wealth, money*, etc.) A heap of money, a fortune. Chiefly in colloq. phr. *to make one's p.* 1731. **4.** A lofty mass of buildings; a large building 1607. **5.** A series of plates of two dissimilar metals, such as copper and zinc, laid one above the other alternately, with cloth or paper moistened with an acid solution placed between each pair, for producing an electric current (*galvanic* or *electric p.*). Also extended to other arrangements of such plates: cf. BATTERY. 1800.

3. A large p. of letters and packages 1891. **e.** On the old Californian principle of 'making a "pile" and vamosing the ranché' 1852. **4.** The magnificent p. of the Escorial 1855. **5.** *Dry p.*, a voltaic p. in which no liquid is used, and which generates a feeble but very permanent current.

Pile (pəil), *sb.*[3] *arch.* late ME. [a. OF., in med.L. *pila*; app. the same word as in prec. In F. opp. to *croix*, as in Eng. to 'cross'.] †**1.** The under iron of the minting apparatus with which money was struck; its surface bore the die of which the impression was made on the reverse side of the piece; opp. to *trussell* –1876. **2.** Hence, The side of a coin opposite to the 'cross' or face; the reverse (*arch.*) late ME.

2. *Cross and (or) p.*, in phrases: see CROSS *sb.* 15.

Pile (pəil), *sb.*[4] ME. [ad. L. *pilus* hair.] **1.** Hair, *esp.* fine soft hair, down; *rarely*, a single hair of this kind; the wool of sheep, etc. **2.** A nap upon cloth; now *esp.* the downy nap of velvet, plush, etc.; also, loops in a carpet forming a nap 1568. **b.** Each of the fine hair-like fibres of velvet, flannel, etc. 1787. **c.** *transf.* The burr on a plate in etching 1885.

2. *Double p., p. upon p., two-p., three-p.*, attrib. phr.: having the pile of double or treble closeness.

Comb.: **p.-beam,** a separate warp-beam, upon which the pile-warp is wound and carried; **-warp,** the secondary warp, which furnishes the substance of the p., also called *nap-warp*; it may consist of one, two, or three threads in the loop, producing *single-*, *double-*, or *three-pile velvet.* Hence **Piled** *ppl. a.*[2] covered with p.; having a p. or long nap.

Pile (pəil), *sb.*[5] Usu. *pl.* **piles.** late ME. [Origin unkn.] *Path.* A disease characterized by tumours of the veins of the lower rectum; hæmorrhoids.

Pile (pəil), *v.*[1] 1440. [f. PILE *sb.*[1] sense 3.] **1.** *trans.* To furnish or strengthen with piles (esp. of timber); to drive piles into. †**2.** To fix, drive in (as a stake or pile) –1613.

Pile, *v.*[2] 1576. [f. PILE *sb.*[2]] **1.** *trans.* To form into a pile; to heap up. Often with *up, on.* **b.** *Metall.* = FAGGOT *v.* 2. 1839. **2.** *transf.* and *fig.* To amass, accumulate 1844. **3.** *intr.* for *refl.* or *pass.* 1613. **4.** *trans.* To cover or load *with* things heaped on 1667. Hence **Piled** *ppl. a.*[1] laid or reared in a pile or piles, heaped. **Pi·ler,** one who piles.

1. *To p. arms* (*Mil.*), to place muskets or rifles (usu. three) in a position in which their butts rest on the ground and their muzzles come together, so as to form a pyramidal figure. **2.** Phr. *To p. up* (or *on*) *the agony* (*colloq.*), to add fresh elements or details to anything already painful. So *to p. it on.* **3.** Money ..continues to p. up and up at the bankers 1897. **4.** Its floor Piled with provender for cattle BROWNING.

Pileate (pəi·liˌĕt), *a.* 1828. [ad. L. *pileatus* capped, f. *pileus*; see PILEUS 2.] *Nat. Hist.* Having a pileus or cap.

Pileated (pəi·liˌeitėd), *a.* 1728. [f. as prec. + -ED.] **1.** *Nat. Hist.* = prec.; *spec.* applied to certain Echini or sea-urchins; also, to certain birds, as the *P. Woodpecker* (*Picus pileatus*) of N. America. **2.** Wearing the *pileus* (see PILEUS 1) 1856.

Pi·le-dri:ver. 1772. A machine for driving piles (PILE *sb.*[1] 3) into the ground, usu. consisting of a heavy block of iron, suspended in a frame between two vertical guide-posts, and alternately let fall upon the pile-head, and raised by steam, manual, or other power.

|| **Pileorhiza** (pəiliˌorəi·ză). Also **-rrh-, -rhize.** 1857. [mod.L., f. *pileus* cap + Gr. ῥίζα root.] *Bot.* The mass of tissue which covers and protects the growing-point of a root; the root-cap.

Pileous (pəi·liˌəs), *a.* *rare.* 1842. [f. L. **pileus* (f. *pilus* hair) + -OUS.] Pertaining to or consisting of hair, hairy.

Piles, hæmorrhoids; see PILE *sb.*[5]

|| **Pileum** (pəi·liˌŏm). 1874. [L., collateral form of *pileus*; see next.] *Ornith.* The whole of the top of the head of a bird, comprising the *frons, corona,* and *occiput.*

|| **Pileus** (pəi·liˌŏs). *Pl.* **pilei** (pəi·liˌəi). 1760. [L. *pileus* felt cap. Cf. Gr. πῖλος.] **1.** *Antiq.* A felt cap without a brim, worn by the ancient Greeks and Romans 1776. **2.** *Bot.* A cap-like formation in various Fungi, esp. in the *Hymenomycetes* (mushrooms, etc.) 1760. **3.** *Ornith.* = PILEUM.

Pilewort (pəi·lwɒɹt). 1578. [f. PILE *sb.*[5] + WORT, from its reputed efficacy against piles; cf. FIGWORT.] The Lesser Celandine or Figwort (*Ranunculus Ficaria* or *Ficaria verna*). Also used for the whole genus *Ficaria.*

†**Pilfer** (pi·lfəɹ), *sb.* late ME. [In earlier use a. OF. *pelfre* spoil; see PELF. Later, formed on the verb.] That which is pilfered; spoil, plunder, booty –1791.

Pilfer (pi·lfəɹ), *v.* 1548. [app. a. AF., OF. *pelfrer* to pillage, rob: see PELF.] **1.** *trans.* To plunder, steal; esp. in small quantities 1550. **b.** To plunder (a person or place). *rare.* 1838. **2.** *intr.* or *absol.* To pillage, plunder; *spec.* to commit petty theft 1548.

1. *fig.* And not a year but pilfers as he goes Some youthful grace that age would gladly keep COWPER. Hence **Pi·lferer.** **Pi·lfering** *vbl. sb.* petty theft. **Pi·lferingly** *adv.*

Pilgarlic (pilgā·ɹlik). 1529. [f. PILLED, PEELED *ppl. a.* + GARLIC.] A 'pilled' or bald head; a bald-headed man; from 17th c. applied in a ludicrously contemptuous way: 'poor creature'. Now *dial.* **b.** (usu. *poor P.*) = poor I, poor me. *dial.* and *U.S. colloq.* or *slang.* 1694.

Pilgrim (pi·lgrim), *sb.* [Early ME. *pele-, pilegrim*, repr. OF. **pelegrin* :—L. *peregrinum* stranger, f. *peregre* adv., from abroad, abroad, f. *per* through + *ager* country, land. In Eng. (rarely in OF.) final *n* became *m*, making *pelegrim, pilgrim.*] **1.** One who travels from place to place; a wanderer; a sojourner. (Now *poet.* or *rhet.* in gen. sense.) **2.** *spec.* One who journeys (usu. a long distance), to some sacred place, as an act of religious devotion. (The prevailing sense.) ME. **3.** *Amer. Hist.* Name given to those English Puritans who founded the colony of Plymouth, Massachusetts, in 1620. Now usu. **Pilgrim Fathers.** 1798. **4.** *U.S.* and *Colonial.* An original settler; a recent immigrant (also said of animals) 1851.

1. Any man may be called a p. who leaveth the place of his birth ROSSETTI. **2.** Pilgrimes were they alle That toward Caunterbury wolden ryde CHAUCER. *fig.* The Pilgrim's Progress from this World to That which is to come BUNYAN (*title*). **3.** The Feast of the 'Sons of the Pilgrims' 1798.

attrib. and *Comb.* **a.** *attrib.* That is a pilgrim; going on pilgrimage; consisting of pilgrims; of, pertaining or relating to, a pilgrim or pilgrims; as *p. chief, city, foot, garland, train*, etc. **b.** *spec.* (often with *pilgrim's*): **p.-bottle, pilgrim's bottle** = COSTREL; **P. Fathers** (*Amer. Hist.*): see sense 3; **pilgrim's shell,** a cockle- or scallop-shell carried by a pilgrim as a sign of having visited some sacred place; **pilgrim's sign,** a medal, etc., presented to a pilgrim at a shrine as a sign of his having visited it. Hence **Pi·lgrim** *v. intr.* to make a pilgrimage; to travel or wander like a p. **Pi·lgrimer** (*rare*), a p.

Pilgrimage (pi·lgrimėdʒ), *sb.* [ME. *pelrimage* (rarely *pelrin-*), a. OF. *pelrim-, pelryn-, pelerinage*, f. *peleriner* to go as a pilgrim; see -AGE.] **1.** A journey made by a pilgrim; the action of taking such a journey. **b.** *transf.* and *gen.* A journey; peregrination; sojourning

ME. c. *fig.* The course of mortal life figured as a journey ME. 2. *transf.* A place to which a pilgrimage is made 1517.

1. b. A p. of pleasure 1797. c. Se that ye passe the tyme off your pilgremage in feare TINDALE 1 *Pet.* i. 17. Hence **Pi·lgrimage** *v. intr.* †to live among strangers; to make a p.; to go on p.

Pilgrimize (pi·lgrimaiz), *v.* 1598. [See -IZE.] *intr.* To play the pilgrim, go on pilgrimage. Also *to p. it.*

‖ **Pilidium** (paili·diŏm). 1842. [mod.L., a. Gr. πιλίδιον, dim. of πῖλος a felt cap.] *Zool.* A name of the cap-shaped larvæ of some species of Nemertean worms, formerly considered as a distinct genus 1877.

Piliferous (paili·fĕrəs), *a.* 1846. [f. L. *pilus* hair + -FEROUS.] Bearing or having hair; *spec.* in *Bot.* bearing hairs or tipped with a hair.

Piliform (pai·lifǭɹm), *a.* 1826. [ad. mod. L. *piliformis*, f. L. *pilus* hair: see -FORM.] Having the form of a hair; hairlike.

Piligerous (paili·dʒĕrəs), *a.* 1835. [f. L. *pilus* hair + -GEROUS.] Bearing hair, clothed with hair.

Piling (pai·liŋ), *vbl. sb.*¹ 1440. [f. PILE *v.*¹ + -ING¹.] 1. The action of PILE *v.*¹ 2. A mass of piles; pilework; wood for piles 1488.

Piling (pai·liŋ), *vbl. sb.*² ME. [f. PILE *v.*² + -ING¹.] The action of heaping up. b. *Leather-making.* The putting of hides in a pile or heap in order to sweat them and cause the hair to come off. *U.S.* 1875.

Pill (pil), *sb.*¹ Now *dial.* late ME. [app. related to PILL *v.*¹] = PEEL *sb.*³

Pill (pil), *sb.*² 1484. [Prob. ad. MDu., MLG. *pille*, ad. L. *pilula*, dim. of *pila* ball.] 1. A small ball of medicinal substance, of a size convenient to be swallowed whole. b. *fig.* Something disagreeable that has to be 'swallowed' or endured 1548. 2. Any small pill-like body; a pellet 1575. b. A cannon-ball; a bullet (*joc.*) 1626. c. in *pl.* = BILLIARDS (*slang*) 1896. d. A ball (*slang*). 3. An objectionable person; a bore (*slang*) 1897. 4. (Also *Pills.*) Nickname for a physician (*slang*) 1860.

1. The cannon-shot, and doctor's p. With equal aim are sure to kill 1763. b. It was a bitter p. for the King..to swallow H. WALPOLE.

attrib. and *Comb.*: **p.-beetle**, a small beetle of the genus *Byrrhus*, which, when it feigns death, contracts itself into a ball; **-crab** = *pea-crab*.

Pill (pil), *sb.*³ Also **pyll.** [In 16th c. *pille, pill*, app. :—OE. *pyll*, var. of *pull, pul* pool, creek.] A local name on both sides of the Bristol Channel, in Cornwall, etc., for a tidal creek on the coast, or a pool in a creek, etc.

Pill (pil), *v.*¹ OE. [Found in forms which point to an OE. **pilian*; prob. influenced by F. *piller* to pillage and *peler* to peal.] I. To pillage, rob: = PEEL *v.* I. 1. *trans.* To plunder, pillage; to despoil (a person or country) *of* (anything). Now *arch.* ME. †b. To exhaust, impoverish (soil) –1610. †2. *absol.* To rob, plunder –1678. †3. *trans.* To take by violence; to make a prey of –1618. †4. To pluck, pull, tear –1605.

1. The Commons hath he pil'd with greeuous taxes SHAKS. 2. Large-handed Robbers your graue Masters are, And p. by Law SHAKS. 3. *Rich. III*, I. iii. 159.

II. To decorticate: = PEEL *v.* II. 1. *trans.* = PEEL *v.* II. 1, 1 b. Now *arch.* and *dial.* late ME. 2. *intr.* Of skin, bark, etc.: To become detached, come off, scale or peel *off.* b. Of animal bodies, trees, etc. = PEEL *v.* II. 2. Now *dial.* OE. †3. *trans.* To make bare of hair, remove the hair from; to remove (hair) –1648. †b. *intr.* To become bald –1614. 4. To bare (land) by eating or shaving off, or cutting down crops, etc., close to the ground 1555.

1. The skilfull shepheard pil'd me certaine wands SHAKS. 2. The whitenesse pilled away from..his eyes *Tobit* xi. 13. 3. Doe they first p. thee, next pluck off thy skin? HERRICK. Phr. *P. and poll*, to ruin by depredations or extortions; to rifle, pillage. Hence †**Pi·ller**, a robber, plunderer; a thief –1674.

Pill, *v.*² 1736. [f. PILL *sb.*²] 1. *trans.* To dose with pills. 2. To blackball (*slang*) 1855. b. To fail (a candidate) in an examination (*slang*) 1908.

Pillage (pi·lėdʒ), *sb.* late ME. [a. F., f. *piller* (PILL *v.*¹).] 1. The action of plundering; spoliation, plunder; chiefly that practised in war; also, wholesale robbery or extortion. †2. Goods forcibly taken, esp. from an enemy in war; booty, spoil, plunder –1750.

Pillage (pi·lėdʒ), *v.* 1592. [f. prec.] 1. *trans.* To rob, plunder, sack (a person, place, etc.), esp. as practised in war. 2. To carry off as booty; to make a spoil of; to appropriate wrongfully 1600. 3. *absol.* or *intr.* To plunder; to rob with open violence 1593.

1. He pillaged many Spanish towns, and took rich prizes FULLER. 3. They were suffered to p. wherever they went MACAULAY. Hence **Pi·llager.**

Pillar (pi·lăɹ), *sb.* ME. [a. OF. *piler* (mod. F. *pilier*) :—late pop.L. *pilare*, deriv. of L. *pila* pillar, pier, mass.] 1. *Arch.* A detached vertical structure of stone, brick, wood, metal, etc., slender in proportion to its height, and of any shape in section, used either as a support for some superstructure, or standing alone as a monument, etc. Cf. COLUMN. b. = PILLAR-BOX 1865. 2. A post, a pedestal; e.g. one of the four posts of a bedstead; the single central support of a table, a machine, etc.; also *attrib.* as *p.* (*and claw*) *table, stand*, etc. ME. 3. *fig.* a. An imaginary prop on which the heavens or the earth is represented as resting ME. b. A person who is a main supporter of an institution, principle, etc. ME. c. A fact or principle which is a main support of something 1578. 4. *transf.* An upright pillar-like mass or 'column' of air, vapour, water, sand, etc. ME. †5. A portable pillar borne as an ensign of dignity or office. *Obs.* exc. *Hist.* 1518. 6. *Mining.* A solid mass of coal or other mineral, of rectangular section, left to support the roof of the working 1708. 7. *Anat.* and *Phys.* Applied to certain bodily structures in ref. to their form and function 1807.

1. All good architecture adapted to vertical support is made up of pillars RUSKIN. 2. A round table is generally described as having 'pillars and claws' 1881. 3. The pileris of heuene togidere quaken WYCLIF *Job* xxvi. 11. b. The p. of the orthodox faith GIBBON. 4. Blood, and fire, and pillars of smoke *Joel* ii. 30. 5. *Hen. VIII*, II. iv. (*Stage direct.*). 7. *Pillars of fauces*, two arching folds of mucous membrane containing muscular fibres, which pass from the base of the uvula outwards and downwards on either side.

Phr. *From p. to post*, orig. *from post to p.*: from one party or place of appeal or resource to another; hither and thither; implying repulse and harassment. Orig. a figure drawn from the tennis-court.

attrib. and *Comb.*: **p. apostle**, a chief apostle, as Peter, James, or John (see Gal. ii. 9); **p. plate**, the plate of a watch movement next behind the dial; **-post** = *pillar-box*; **-saint** = PILLARIST.

Pillar (pi·lăɹ), *v.* 1607. [f. prec. sb.] 1. *trans.* To support or strengthen with or as with pillars. 2. To embody in the form of a pillar; to display in the figure of a pillar (*rare*) 1812.

Pi·llar-box. 1858. A hollow pillar about five feet high, erected in a public place, containing a receptacle for posting letters.

Pillared (pi·lăɹd), *ppl. a.* ME. [f. PILLAR + -ED.] 1. Having, supported on or by, or furnished with a pillar or pillars. 2. Fashioned into or like a pillar or pillars 1698.

1. *fig.* The pillar'd firmament MILT. 2. P. basalt 1887.

Pillarist (pi·lărist). 1638. [f. PILLAR *sb.* + -IST. A pillar-saint, a stylite.

Pill-box (pi·lbǫks). 1737. [f. PILL *sb.*² + Box *sb.*²] 1. A shallow cylindrical box of cardboard for holding pills. b. Jocularly applied to various boxes, closed vehicles, etc. 1835, a small round concrete emplacement 1918. c. *attrib.* and *Comb.* Like a pill-box in shape, or size, as *pill-box hat, house* 1836.

Pilled (pild), *ppl. a.* *arch.* and *dial.* late ME. [f. PILL *v.*¹ + -ED¹.] 1. Stripped of skin, bark, rind, etc. *Obs.* or *dial.* 2. Bereft of hair, feathers, etc.; bald, shaven, tonsured. *Obs.* or *dial.* late ME. †3. Bare, threadbare; bare of pasture; poor. Also *fig.* –1613. 4. Plundered, pillaged. *arch.* or *dial.* 1514.

2. As piled as an Ape was his skulle CHAUCER.

Pillion (pi·lyən). 1503. [app. of Celtic origin, a. (ult.) L. *pellis* skin, pelt, felt.] A kind of saddle, *esp.* a woman's light saddle. Also, a pad or cushion attached to the hinder part of an ordinary saddle for a second person (usu. a woman). *Obs.* exc. *Hist.* b. A pad or spring seat for a second person on the back of a motor-bicycle 1911.

The straps of my wife's p. broke down GOLDSM.

Comb. (sense b), as *p.-rider, -riding, -seat*, etc.

Pilliwinks (pi·liwiŋks). Also **pilnie-.** *Hist.* late ME. [Origin unkn.] An instrument of torture for squeezing the fingers.

Pillory (pi·lŏri), *sb.* [ME. *pillori*, a. OF. *pellori, pilori*, etc. Origin unkn.] A wooden framework erected on a post or pillar, having holes through which the head and hands of an offender were thrust, in which state he was exposed to public ridicule and molestation. In other forms, the culprit was fastened to a stake by a ring round his neck and wrists. Hence **Pi·llorize** *v. trans.* = next.

Pi·llory, *v.* 1600. [f. prec. sb.] *trans.* To set in the pillory; to punish by exposure in the pillory. b. *fig.* To expose to public ridicule or abuse 1699.

b. He has Pilloried himself for 't in Print, as long as that Book shall last 1699.

Pillow (pi·lou), *sb.* [OE. *pyle, pylu* :— **pulwi*, repr. with cognates a WGerm. **pulwi(n)*, a. L. *pulvinus* cushion.] 1. A support for the head in sleeping or reclining; *spec.* a case made of linen, etc., stuffed with feathers, down, etc.; esp. as forming part of a bed. Also applied to any object improvised for the same purpose. b. In various fig. uses. 2. A pad 1607; a padded support upon which bone lace is made 1781. 3. In techn. applications; esp. *Naut.* the block of timber on which the inner end of a bowsprit rests 1626. 4. A kind of plain fustian 1839.

1. Coleridge..slept with the *Observations on Man* under his p. J. MARTINEAU. Phr. *To take counsel of one's p.*, etc.: to 'sleep upon' a matter of importance. b. As we..smoothed down his lonely p. WOLFE. 2. Yon cottager, who weaves at her own door, P. and bobbins all her little store COWPER.

attrib. and *Comb.*: **p.-block**, a cradle or bearing to hold the boxes or brasses forming the journal-bearing of a shaft or roller; **-fight**, a fight with pillows; **-lace**, lace worked on a p. (sense 2); **-slip, -tie** = PILLOW-CASE.

Pi·llow, *v.* 1629. [f. prec. sb.] 1. *trans.* To rest or place (the head, etc.) on or as on a pillow. b. Of a thing: To serve as a pillow for 1801. c. In *pa. pple.* Laid on, or as on, a pillow 1794. 2. *trans.* To support or prop *up* with pillows 1839.

1. When the Sun in bed,..Pillows his chin upon an Orient wave MILT. Hence **Pi·llowed** (-oud) *ppl. a.*

Pi·llow-case. 1745. The washable case of a pillow, usu. of white linen or cotton cloth.

Pillowy (pi·loui), *a.* 1798. [f. PILLOW *sb.* -Y¹.] Having the quality or appearance of a pillow; soft; yielding.

Pillwort (pi·lwɒɹt). 1861. [f. PILL *sb.*² + WORT; so called from its small globular involucres.] Any plant of the cryptogamous genus *Pilularia*, esp. *P. globulifera.*

Pilo- (pai·lo), comb. form of L. *pilus* hair, as in **Pilomo·tor** *a.* applied to those nerves which produce movement of the hairs; **Pi·lo-seba·ceous** *a.* applied to sebaceous glands that open into hair-follicles.

Pilocarpine (pailokā·ɹpain). 1875. [f. mod. L. *Pilocarpus*, generic name in Bot. (f. Gr πῖλος wool, felt + καρπός fruit) + -INE⁵.] *Chem.* A white crystalline or amorphous alkaloid, $C_{11}H_{16}N_2O_2$, obtained from the leaves of jaborandi, *Pilocarpus pinnatifolius* (or other species), used in pharmacy.

Pilose (pai·lōus), *a.* 1753. [ad. L. *pilosus*, f. *pilus* hair.] Covered with hair, esp. with soft flexible hair; hairy, pilous. So **Pilo·sity**, the quality or state of being p.; hairiness 1605.

Pilot (pai·lət), *sb.* 1530 [a. early mod.F. *pillotte, pilot*, mod.F. *pilote*, ad. It. *pilota, -to*, perh. altered from It. *pedota*, in OF. *pedot.*] 1. One who directs the course of a ship; a steersman; *spec.* a person duly qualified to steer ships into and out of a harbour or wherever local knowledge is required. b. One who navigates an aeroplane, etc. 1848. c. *transf.* and *fig.* A guide through some unknown place or through difficulties and dangers; a leader in the hunting-field 1593. d. Short for *p. boat, engine* 1896. 2. = *pilot-cloth* 1844. 3. = COW-*catcher. U.S.* 1864. 4. = PILOT-FISH 1. 1835.

1. I was like a ship without a p., that could only run

before the wind DE FOE. Phr. *To drop the p.* (after his duties on board are finished); hence freq. in allusive and fig. use. c. I hope to see my P. face to face When I have crost the bar TENNYSON.

attrib. and *Comb.*, Of or pertaining to a p. or pilots, as *p.-brig*, *-coble*, etc.; that acts as a p. or in any way as a guide, as *p.-balloon*, *-engine*, *-train*, etc.; **p.-bread**, name in the W. Indies for hard or ship biscuit; **-cloth**, an indigo-blue woollen cloth, used for greatcoats, etc.; **-coat** = PEA-JACKET; **-jack**, the 'jack' surrounded by a white border, a signal for a p.; **-jacket**=PEA-JACKET; **-light**, a small permanent light used to ignite gas at a burner; **-snake**, (*a*) a large N. Amer. snake, *Coluber obsoletus*; (*b*) the pine-snake, *Pituophis melanoleucus*; (*c*) the copper-head; **-water** (also **pilot's water**), a piece of water in which a pilot must be employed; **-whale**, the round-headed porpoise or ca'ing whale. Hence **Pi·lotism**, the practice of a p.; pilotage. **Pi·lotless** *a.* (of an aeroplane), not having a p.

Pi·lot, *v.* 1649. [f. prec., or a. F. *piloter.*] 1. *trans.* To conduct as a pilot; to steer, guide 1693. 2. *transf.* and *fig.* To guide through unknown or dangerous paths or places, or through a difficult course of affairs; to conduct as a 'pilot' in the hunting-field 1649. 3. To act as pilot on, in, or over (a course, etc.) 1725.

3. Morn and eve, night and day, Have I piloted your bay BROWNING.

Pilotage (pəi·lətedʒ). 1618. [a. F., f. *piloter*; see prec. and -AGE.] 1. The action or practice of piloting; the function or office of a pilot; pilotship. Also *transf.* and *fig.* 2. The charge for piloting; pilotage dues 1622. 3. *attrib.*, as *p. certificate*, etc. 1830.

Pi·lot-bird. 1678. [f. PILOT *sb.* + BIRD.] A name for: †a. A sea-bird of the W. Indies; b. An Australian bird, *Pycnoptilus floccosus*.

a. The *P. Bird*, a certain Bird about the Caribe Islands, which gives notice to Ships that sail that way, when they come near any of those Islands 1678.

Pi·lot-boat. 1588. A boat in which pilots cruise off shore in order to meet incoming vessels.

Pi·lot-fish. 1634. [f. PILOT *sb.* + FISH *sb.*[1]] 1. A small carangoid fish of warm seas, *Naucrates ductor*, reputed to act as a guide to the shark. 2. A general term for the *Carangidæ*, as the rudder-fish (*Seriola zonata*) 1792.

Pilous (pəi·ləs), *a.* 1658. [ad. L. *pilosus* hairy; see -OUS.] Characterized by or abounding in hair; consisting of hair; hairy, pilose.

Pilular (pi·liŭlăr), *a.* 1802. [f. L. *pilula* PILL *sb.*[2]; see -AR.] Of or pertaining to pills; of the nature of a pill or pills.

Pilule (pi·liul). late ME. [a. F., ad. L. *pilula*; see PILL *sb.*[2]] A pill; a small pill.

Pilulous (pi·liŭləs), *a.* 1872. [f. L. *pilula* + -OUS.] Resembling a pill; pill-like, minute.

Pily (pəi·li), *a.*[1] 1638. [f. PILE *sb.*[1] + -Y[5].] *Her.* Divided into a number of piles, the number and direction usu. being indicated.

Pily (pəi·li), *a.*[2] 1533. [f. PILE *sb.*[4] + -Y[1].] Having a pile or nap; of the nature of a pile.

Pimaric (pimæ·rik, pəi-), *a.* 1857. [mod. f. *Pi(nus) mar(itima)* + -IC.] *Chem.* In *p. acid*, an acid resin ($C_{20}H_{30}O_2$) occurring in the turpentine of *Pinus maritima*.

Pimelic (pime·lik), *a.* 1838. [f. Gr. πιμελή fat + -IC.] *Chem.* In *P. acid*, an acid ($C_7H_{12}O_4$) obtained in small crystalline grains by the action of nitric acid on various fatty substances.

Pimelite (pi·mĕləit). 1808. [f. as prec.; see -ITE[1].] *Min.* A hydrous silicate of aluminium, iron, nickel, and magnesium, of apple-green colour, greasy in appearance and to the touch.

Pimento (pime·nto). 1690. [ad. Sp. *pimienta*, Pg. *pimenta* pepper, repr. L *pigmentum* spice, pepper.] †1. Formerly, Cayenne or Guinea pepper –1697. 2. Now, The dried aromatic berries of the tree *Eugenia Pimenta* (see 3); also called *Jamaica pepper* or *allspice* 1690. 3. The tree which yields this spice, *Eugenia Pimenta* or *Pimenta officinalis* (N.O. *Myrtaceæ*), an evergreen, much cultivated in Jamaica; also, its wood 1756.

Pimlico (pi·mliko). 1848. [Echoic, from the cry of the bird.] The Australian friar-bird.

Pimp (pimp), *sb.* 1607. [Origin obsc.] A pander, procurer. Hence **Pimp** *v. intr.* to act as p.; to pander.

Pimpernel (pi·mpəɹnĕl). late ME. [a. OF. *pimprenele*, *pimpernelle*, mod.F. *pimprenelle* = med.L. *pipinella*, a corruption of *bipinnella*, dim. of *bipinnula*, dim. deriv. of *bipennis* two-winged, pern. in ref. to the pinnate leaves.] †1. The Great Burnet, *Sanguisorba officinalis*, and Salad Burnet, *Poterium Sanguisorba* –1578. 2. The common name of *Anagallis arvensis* (N.O. *Primulaceæ*), a small annual with smooth ovate opposite leaves, and scarlet (also blue, or, occas., white) flowers, which close in rainy or cloudy weather; distinctively called *Scarlet Pimpernel*. Hence extended to the whole genus. late ME.

2. **Water P.**, (*a*) the greater and lesser Brooklime, *Veronica Beccabunga* and *V. Anagallis*; (*b*) Brookweed, *Samolus Valerandi* or other species.

Pi·mping, *a.* 1687. [Origin unkn.] Small, petty, mean; in poor health or condition, sickly.

Pimple (pi·mp'l), *sb.* late ME. [Origin unkn.] 1. A small solid rounded tumour of the skin, usu. inflammatory; a papule or pustule. 2. *fig.* A small rounded swelling, as a bud, etc. 1582. 3. *attrib.*, as *p.-faced*, etc. 1607.

1. The distilled water..is good against the freckles, spottes, and pimpels of the face 1578. 2. He pinches from the second stalk A p., that portends a future sprout COWPER. Hence **Pi·mple** *v.* (now *rare*), to make or become pimply. **Pimpled** (pi·mp'ld), *a.* having, or characterized by, pimples. **Pi·mply** *a.* full of pimples; covered or spotted with pimples.

Pin (pin), *sb.* [Com. LG.; late OE. *pinn*; held to be ad.L. *pinna* point, etc.] I. Primary sense: = *peg*. 1. A small piece of wood, metal, etc., usu. cylindrical, used to fasten or hold together parts of a structure, to hang something upon, to stop up a hole, etc.; a peg, bolt. b. An indicator of a long or pointed shape; as †the index of a balance, etc. 1440. †c. A peg fixed in the centre of a target –1642. d. = PEG *sb.*[1] 2 a. 1587. e. = PEG *sb.*[1] 2 b. 1592. f. *Naut.* (*a*) A thole-pin. (*b*) Applied to various pegs or bolts used in a ship, e. g. to make fast the rigging (BELAYING-*pins*), etc. 1832. g. *Carpentry.* The tenon of a dovetail joint 1847. h. *Quoits.* The peg at which the quoit is aimed 1857. i. *Golf.* An iron rod bearing a small flag, to mark the position of a hole 1901. †2. *fig.* That on which something hangs or depends. late ME.

1. Oak is excellent for..pinns and peggs for tyling, &c. EVELYN. e. No jovial din Of drinking Wassail to the p. LONGF.

II. = ME. and Sc. *preen*, F. *épingle*. 1. A slender piece of wire (now usu. of brass or iron, tinned), with a sharp tapered point and a flattened round head, used for fastening together parts of dress, loose papers, etc., and for various purposes. Also applied to larger articles of the same kind made of steel, gold, silver, etc. See also DRAWING-*pin*, HAIRPIN, HAT-*pin*, SAFETY PIN, etc. (The most frequent use.) late ME. b. *allusively.* Something very small, or of little value ME. 2. *transf.* The incipient bur or blossom of the hop 1900.

1. He that will not stoop for a p. will never be worth a pound PEPYS. Phr. *Pins and needles* (colloq.): the pricking or tingling sensation felt in a limb after numbness. *On pins and needles*: in a state of excessive uneasiness. b. Phr. *Not worth a p.*, *not to care a p.*, etc. So *Pin's head*, *pin's point*.

III. (Cf. med.L. *pinna*, Du. *pinne* pinnacle.) 1. A point, peak, apex. *Obs.* exc. *dial.* 1450. 2. The projecting bone of the hip, esp. in horses or cattle. Now *dial.* 1703.

IV. Transf. uses. 1. A leg; usu. in *pl. colloq.* or *dial.* 1530. 2. A skittle; in *pl.* the game of skittles 1580. †3. A knot in wood –1585. 4. A small cask or keg holding half a firkin, or $4\frac{1}{2}$ gallons 1570. †5. A piece at chess, etc. –1784. 6. Short for ROLLING-*pin*, KNITTING-*pin*, etc. 1894.

1. I never saw a fellow better set upon his pins 1781. 5. The Queene is the next p. in height to the King 1688.

V. Phraseological uses. 1. In the phrase *in a merry p.*, in a merry humour or frame of mind. *arch.* or *dial.* late ME. †2. Pitch; degree; step; esp. with *higher*, *lower*, *utmost*, *raise*, *take down*. (Orig. taken from a musical tuning-peg; see I. 1 d.) –1776. 3. Phr. *To put in the p.* (*colloq.* or *slang*): to call a halt; *esp.* to give up drinking. So *to let loose a p.* 1832.

1. Right glad to find His friend in merry p. COWPER.

attrib. and *Comb.*, as **p.-buttock**, a narrow or sharp buttock; **p. connexion**, a connexion of the parts of an iron or steel bridge by pins (instead of rivets, etc.; cf. *pin-joint*); **p.-drill**, a drill with a projecting central pin surrounded by a cutting face, used for countersinking, etc.; **-dust**, dust formed of filings of brass or other metal produced in the manufacture of pins; **-joint**, a form of joint in which two parts are connected by a pin passing through an eye in each; **-spot**, each of a number of round spots like pins' heads forming a pattern upon a textile fabric; **-stripe**, a narrow ornamental stripe of the thickness of a pin; hence **p.-striped** *a.*; **p. switch** (*Telegr.*), a switch in which electric connexion is made by pins passing through holes in metal plates; **-worm**, a small thread-worm, *Oxyuris vermicularis*, which infests the rectum, esp. in children.

Pin (pin), *v.* ME. [In branch I., f. prec. In branch II., perh. worn down from PIND *v.*] I. To transfix, etc., with a pin. 1. *trans.* To fasten (things *together*) with one or more pins, pegs, or bolts. 2. To fasten with a pin, or with a brooch, hairpin, or hat-pin; to transfix with a pin; also with a lance or the like. late ME. 3. *fig.* To attach firmly *to* a person, or ostentatiously *to* or *on* his SLEEVE; to make absolutely dependent or contingent *on* a person or thing; to append, fix, tack on. Now *rare.* 1579. 4. *transf.* To hold (a man or animal) *down* or *against* something by force; to seize and hold fast 1814. 5. *fig.* To hold or bind (a person) strictly *to* a promise, etc.; often with *down* 1710.

1. Great peeces of tymber pinned together 1579. 2. The wardrobe woman was pinning up the Queen's hair MME. D'ARBLAY. The first object is to p. the insect 1852. 3. Phr. *To p. one's faith upon, on* (a thing, or person, or his SLEEVE), to place entire or openly professed trust or belief in. 4. While I pinned his arms from behind, Mr. Taylor seized his whip 1859. 5. One of those pestilent fellows that p. a man down to facts W. IRVING.

II. Cf. PIND *v.* 1. To enclose by or as by means of bolts or bars; to hem in, shut *up*; *spec.* to put in a pinfold, impound (a beast). late ME. †2. To confine, restrict –1638.

1. Pinn'd like a flock, and fleeced too in their fold BYRON.

‖ **Piña** (pī·nʸă). 1577. [S. Amer. Sp., (formerly *pinna*), Pg. *pinha* pine-apple, orig. pine-cone (ad. L. *pinea*).] †1. (Spelt *pina*, *pinna*, *pinia*.) The pine-apple –1622. 2. Pine-apple leaf fibres; a fine fabric made of these, also called **p.-cloth**, **p.-muslin** 1858.

Pinacoid, pinakoid (pi·năkoid), *a.* and *sb.* 1876. [f. Gr. πίναξ, πινακ- slab; see -OID.] A. *adj.* Applied to any plane, in a crystallographic system, intersecting one of the axes of co-ordinates and parallel to the other two 1895. B. *sb.* A pinacoid plane, or a group of such planes constituting a 'form'.

Pinacolin (pinæ·kŏlin). 1866. [f. next + -OL + -IN[1].] *Chem.* A colourless oily liquid ($C_6H_{12}O$), having an odour of peppermint, variously produced from pinacone.

Pinacone (pi·năkoun). 1866. [f. Gr. πίναξ tablet + -ONE.] *Chem.* A white crystalline substance ($C_6H_{14}O_2$), crystallizing in large tablets, produced by the action of sodium or sodium-amalgam on aqueous acetone.

‖ **Pinacotheca** (pi:năkoþī·kă). Also **pi·nacotheːk** (-þek). 1624. [L., a. Gr. πινακοθήκη, f. πίναξ, πινακ- tablet, picture + θήκη repository.] A place for the keeping and exhibition of works of art.

Pinafore (pi·năfoəɹ), *sb.* 1782. [f. PIN *v.* + AFORE, because orig. pinned upon the dress in front.] A covering of washable material worn by children or others over the frock or gown, to protect it from being soiled. Hence **Pi·nafored** *a.* attired in a p.

Pinaster (pəinæ·stəɹ). 1562. [a. L., = wild pine, f. *pinus* pine; see -ASTER.] *Bot.* A species of pine indigenous to south-western Europe.

‖ **Pinax** (pi·næks). *Pl.* **pinaces** (pi·năsīz); also **pinakes**. 1682. [L., a. Gr. πίναξ board, etc.] †1. A tablet; hence a list, register, etc. inscribed on a tablet; a catalogue, index –1785. 2. *Antiq.* A plate, platter, or dish; *esp.* one with anything painted or engraved on it 1857.

‖ **Pince-nez** (pęns͵ne). 1880. [F., = 'pinch-nose'.] A pair of eyeglasses with a spring which clips the nose.

Pincers (pi·nsəɹz), *sb. pl.* [In ME. *pinsour(s*, etc., app. AF. agent-n. from *pincer* vb.;

see PINCH.] 1. A tool for grasping or nipping anything, consisting of two limbs pivoted together, forming a pair of jaws with a pair of handles or levers by which they can be pressed tightly together. (Usu. *a pair of pincers*; rarely *a pincers*.) 2. An organ (or pair of organs), in various animals, resembling pincers, and used for grasping or tearing; as the chelæ of crustaceans, etc. 1658. Hence Pi·ncer *v. trans.* to compress with or as with pincers; to torture with or as with pincers.

Pinch (pinʧ), *sb.* 1489. [f. next.] **I. 1.** An act of pinching; a firm compression between the finger and thumb or two surfaces; a nip, a squeeze; †a bite 1591. 2. *fig.* Pressure (usu. of want, etc.); difficulty, hardship 1605. †3. The pang of death, or of remorse, shame, etc. -1681. 4. A strait, exigency, extremity. Now usu. in phr. *at* (*on*) *a p.* 1489. b. The crucial point of a matter. Now *rare.* 1639.

1. The stroke of death is as a Louers p. SHAKS. 2. Necessities sharpe p. SHAKS. 3. *Temp.* v. i. 77. 4. But that Apprehension appeared Groundless when it came to the p. 1681. b. The very P. of the Argument 1720.

II. A place or part at which something is pinched. †1. A pleat or gather, in a skirt, etc. b. A bend or fold in the brim of a hat. -1860. 2. A steep or difficult part of a road. Now *dial.* 1754. **III.** As much of something (esp. snuff) as may be taken with the tips of the finger and thumb; hence *fig.* a very small quantity 1583. **IV.** A crow-bar 1816.

Pinch (pinʧ), *v.* ME. [a. ONF. **pinchier*, 3rd sing. pr. *pinche* = mod.F. *pincer*; ult. origin unkn.] **I. 1.** *trans.* To compress between the tips of the finger and thumb, with the teeth, an instrument, etc.; to nip, squeeze. (The principal literal sense.) Also *absol.* or *intr.* b. Said of a tight shoe, etc. which presses painfully upon the part which it covers. (Usu. *absol.* or *intr.*) late ME. c. *pass.* To be jammed between two solid objects so as to be crushed 1896. 2. With *adv.* or *compl.* To bring or get into some state or position by pinching ME. b. *Hort.* To nip off part of (a shoot). With *out, back, down.* 1693. c. To force out by compression, squeeze out; *fig.* to extort, 'squeeze' (money) *from* or *out of* a person 1770. †3. To seize, compress, or snap with the teeth. Often *absol.* -1700. †4. Said of actions causing a painful bodily sensation: To pain, torture, torment -1607. 5. Said of the action of cold, hunger, exhaustion, or wasting disease: including the painful physical sensations and often the mental affliction. In ref. to plants: To nip, to cause to shrivel up. 1548.

1. b. Phr. *To know where the shoe pinches*, i. e. to know (by direct experience) the cause of a trouble or difficulty. (Usu. *absol.* or *intr.*) c. He was pinched between the train and the platform 1899. 3. 3 *Hen. VI*, II. i. 16. 5. Pinched with pouertie & aduersitie 1581. The polyanthuses were a little pinched by the easterly winds 1772.

II. In non-physical and fig. senses. 1. To straiten; to afflict, harass. *Obs.* exc. as *fig.* from I. 1 or 5. 1548. Also *intr.* or *absol.* †2. *intr.* a. To encroach *on*; b. to put stress *upon* -1734. 3. †a. To be close-fisted, meanly parsimonious, or miserly; to drive hard bargains -1617. b. *trans.* To stint; to give barely, or with short measure or weight; to give grudgingly. Now *dial.* 1530. Also *intr.* in refl. or pass. sense. 1549. 4. *trans.* To restrict narrowly. Now *rare* or *Obs.* 1570. b. To reduce to straits (in argument, etc.); to 'put in a tight place'. Now *rare.* 1692.

3. b. I am..pinched for time COWPER. *intr.* I'm forc'd to p., for the Times are hard SWIFT. 4. That doctrine which pincheth our liberty within so narrow bounds 1677.

III. Technical and slang. 1. a. *Racing.* To press (a horse); to exhaust by urging 1737. b. *Naut.* To sail (a vessel) close-hauled 1895. 2. *intr. Mining.* Of a vein, etc.: To become narrow or thin; with *out*, to come to an end 1872. 3. *trans.* a. To purloin (a thing); to rob (a person). *slang.* 1673. b. To take into custody. *slang.* 1860.

Pinch- in Comb. [chiefly the imperative or vb.-stem; sometimes the sb.]: **P.-bar** = PINCH *sb.* IV.; **-cock** *Mech.*, a clamp used to compress a flexible or elastic tube so as to regulate the flow of liquid, etc.; **-fist,** a niggard, miser; **†-gut,** one who stints himself or others of food; also *attrib.*

Pinchbeck (pi·nʧbek), *sb.* (*a.*) 1734. [f. Christopher *Pinchbeck*, the inventor, a watchmaker (died 1732).] 1. An alloy of about five parts of copper with one of zinc, resembling gold: used in clock-making, cheap jewellery, etc. 2. *fig.* As a type of what is counterfeit or spurious 1859. 3. *attrib.* or *adj.* a. Made of pinchbeck 1746. b. Spurious; sham 1850.

2. Those golden locks were only p. THACKERAY.

Pinched (pinʧt), *ppl. a.* 1530. [f. PINCH *v.* + -ED.[1]] 1. Compressed between the finger and thumb, or two opposing bodies; nipped, squeezed; shaped as if compressed. 2. Said in ref. to the physical effects of cold, hunger, pain, or old age 1614. 3. Straitened in extent 1649; straitened in circumstances 1716.

Pincher (pi·nʧəɹ). 1440. [f. PINCH *v.* + -ER [1].] 1. One who or that which pinches; *fig.* a miser; a haggler. 2. An instrument for pinching or grasping; in pl. *pinchers* often = PINCERS 1575.

Pinching (pi·nʧiŋ), *vbl. sb.* 1440. [f. PINCH *v.* + -ING [1].] The action of PINCH *v.*, in various senses. 1. Nipping, squeezing, pressure 1693. 2. The sensation caused by pinching or gripping; the pressure of pain. Also *fig.* 1495. 3. Parsimony 1440.

Comb.: p.-bar = *pinch-bar* (PINCH-); **-nut** = *jam-nut* (JAM *sb.*[1]).

Pinc-pinc (pi·ŋkpiŋk). 1868. [Echoic.] A South-African warbler, *Drymœca* or *Cisticola textrix.*

Pincushion (pi·nkuːʃən). 1632. A small cushion used for sticking pins in, to keep them ready for use.

Pind, *v. Obs.* exc. *dial.* [OE. (*ge*)*pyndan*, f. **pund* POUND *sb.*[2]] *trans.* To shut up, enclose; to dam up (water) -1483. b. *spec.* To put (beasts) in a pound, to impound ME.

‖ **Pi·nda, pi·ndar.** 1707. [ad. Pg. *pinda*, ad. Congo *mpinda*, Mpongwe *mbenda*; carried by negroes to America.] W. Indian and Southern U. S. for the ground-nut or pea-nut (*Arachis hypogæa*).

‖ **Pindari** (pindā·rī), *sb.* (*a.*) 1788. [a. Hindustani *pinḍārī, pinḍārā*, for Marathi *penḍhārī*; perh. from a place-name *Pandhār.*] 1. One of a body of mounted marauders who arose in Central India in the 17th c. Also as *adj.* 2. The dialect of these and their descendants 1901.

Pindaric (pindæ·rik), *a.* and *sb.* 1640. [ad. L. *Pindaricus*, a. Gr., f. Πίνδαρος Pindar.] **A.** *adj.* Of or pertaining to the poet Pindar; written, writing, etc., in the style of Pindar. **B.** *sb.* An ode, poem, metre, or form of verse, in imitation of Pindar. Chiefly in *pl.* 1685.

A. Those admirable English Authors who call themselves Pindarick Writers ADDISON. B. A Pindarick on the Death of Our Late Sovereign 1685. So †**Pinda·rical** *a.* Pindaric. **Pi·ndarism,** imitation of Pindar. **Pi·ndarist,** a writer of P. verses.

Pinder (pi·ndəɹ). ME. [f. PIND *v.* + -ER [1].] An officer of a manor who impounds stray beasts.

Pine (pəin), *sb.*[1] *Obs.* or *arch.* [Early ME. *pīne*:—OE. **pīn*, a. L. *pœna* punishment, pain. †1. Punishment; torment, torture; *spec.* the penal sufferings of hell or purgatory. †2. = PAIN *sb.*[1] 3. -1600. b. = PAIN *sb.*[1] 4. *Obs.* or *arch.* ME. †3. The condition of pining for food; famine; want; starvation -1725.

1. Of Proserpyne That quene ys of the derke pyne CHAUCER.

Pine (pəin), *sb.*[2] [OE. *pīn*, ad. L. *pinus*; in ME. a. F. *pin* :—L. *pinus*.] 1. A tree of the genus *Pinus*, or of various allied coniferous genera, having evergreen needle-shaped leaves, of which many species afford valuable timber, and some have edible seeds. b. The wood of these trees. late ME. 2. With qualifying words, applied to various species of *Pinus* or other coniferous genera (or to their wood) 1731. b. Also applied to plants of other orders, resembling the true pine in some respect: e. g. certain species of *Lycopodium* or Club Moss (Festoon Pine, *L. rupestre*; Moonfruit Pine, *L. lucidulum*; etc.) 1760. 3. *transf.* Something made of pine-wood: e. g. a torch, a ship, a mast. Chiefly *poet.* 1586. 4. = PINE-APPLE 2. 1661. 5. A figure of a pine-apple or pine-cone 1790.

1. His Spear, to equal which the tallest P., Hewn on Norwegian hills,..were but a wand MILT. 2. **Norfolk Island P.,** *Araucaria excelsa*; **Norway P.,** (*a*) the Spruce Fir, *Abies* (*Picea*) *excelsa*; (*b*) (in U.S.) the N. American Red Pine, *Pinus resinosa*; (*c*) a variety of the timber of *Pinus sylvestris*; **Nut-pine** (see NUT); **Red P.,** (*a*) *Pinus resinosa* of N. America; (*b*) (of Australia) *Frenela Endlicheri*; (*c*) (of New Zealand) *Dacrydium cupressinum*; also the timber = *Riga pine*; **Riga P.,** a variety of the timber of *Pinus sylvestris*; **Scotch P.,** *Pinus sylvestris*, commonly called *Scotch* FIR; **Sugar P.,** *Pinus Lambertiana* of California, which yields a sweet resin used for sugar; **White P.,** various species with light-coloured wood, esp. the Norway pine or Spruce, *Pinus Strobus* of N. America, and species of *Frenela* and *Podocarpus* of Australia, etc.

attrib. and *Comb.*, as *p.-bark, -plantation*, etc.; **p.-beetle,** any one of various small beetles destructive to the bark or wood of pines; **-cone,** the cone or fruit of the pine-tree; **-drops,** the N. Amer. plant *Pterospora andromedea*, parasitic on the roots of pine-trees; **-finch,** (*a*) = *pine grosbeak*; (*b*) = *pine-siskin*; **p. grosbeak,** a large finch, *Pinicola enucleator*, inhabiting pine-woods in Europe and N. America; **p. gum,** a resin resembling sandarach, obtained from Australian trees of the genus *Callitris* or *Frenela*; **p. hawk-moth,** a species of hawk-moth, *Sphinx pinastri*, whose larva feeds on the pine-tree; **-lizard,** the common brown lizard of N. America, *Sceloporus undulatus*; **-marten** (see MARTEN); **-needle,** the needle-shaped leaf of the p.; **-oil,** name for various oils obtained from the leaves, twigs, wood, or resin of pine-trees; **-sap,** a reddish fleshy plant, *Monotropa Hypopitys*, formerly supposed to be parasitic on the roots of pine-trees; **-siskin,** a small N. American siskin or finch, *Chrysomitris pinus*, found in pine-woods; **-snake,** a large harmless snake of the N. Amer. genus *Pityophis*, found in pine-woods.

Pine (pəin), *v.* [OE. *pīnian*, f. **pīn* PINE *sb.*[1]] †1. *trans.* To afflict with pain or suffering; to torment, trouble, distress. Also *absol.* -1724. 2. To exhaust or consume (a person, animal, etc.) by suffering of body or mind; to cause to languish; to wear out, emaciate; to deprive or stint of food, to starve. Also with *away, to death*, etc. Now *rare* exc. *dial.* ME. 3. *intr.* To languish, waste away, esp. from intense grief, etc., wasting disease, or want of sustenance 1440. b. *transf.* Of things: To lose bulk, vigour, or intensity; to languish 1727. c. *trans.* with *away* or *out*: To spend (life, health, etc.) in pining 1725. 4. *intr.* To long eagerly; to languish with intense desire. Const. *for, after*, or *inf.* 1592. 5. To repine, fret 1687. b. *trans.* To mourn (*arch.*) 1667. 6. *Sc.* To cause (fish) to shrink in the process of curing 1560.

1. O tell him..how my soule is pin'd 1635. 3. He ten times pines, that pines beholding food SHAKS. They generally p. away..and die in a short time GOLDSM. c. Barristers pining a hungry life out in chambers THACKERAY. 4. Who did there pining for their native home 1748. 5. b. We..see, and p. our loss SWINBURNE.

Pineal (pi·nɪ̆ăl, pəi·nɪ̆ăl), *a.* 1681. [a. F. *pinéal*, f. L. *pinea* pine-cone; see -AL.] *Anat.* Resembling a pine-cone in shape: applied to a small somewhat conical body (the *p. body* or *p. gland*), situated behind the third ventricle of the brain, and containing sand-like particles. b. Pertaining to or connected with the pineal body, as *p. eye, ventricle* 1888.

Pine-apple, pineapple (pəi·nˌæːp'l). late ME. [f. PINE *sb.*[2] + APPLE.] 1. The fruit of the pine-tree; a pine-cone. *Obs.* exc. *dial.* b. A figure or image of a pine-cone 1483. 2. The large collective fruit of the ananas, *Ananassa sativa*; so called from its resemblance to a pine-cone. b. The plant which bears this, a native of tropical South America. 1664.

Pi·ne-ba:rren. *U.S.* 1737. [f. PINE *sb.*[2] + BARREN *sb.* 2 a.] A level sandy tract of land, scantily covered with pine-trees, chiefly in the Southern States.

Pinery (pəi·nəri). 1758. [f. PINE *sb.*[2] + -ERY.] 1. A place in which pine-apples are grown. 2. A plantation of pine-trees 1831.

Pine-tree. OE. = PINE *sb.*[2] 1.

attrib. **Pine-tree State,** Maine, U.S., so called from its extensive pine-forests.

‖ **Pinetum** (pəinī·tɒ̆m). *Pl.* **-a, -ums.** 1842. [L., 'pine-grove', f. *pinus* PINE *sb.*[2]] A plantation or collection of pine-trees of various species, for scientific or ornamental purposes.

Pi·ne-wood. 1813. [f. PINE *sb.*[2] + WOOD *sb.*] **1.** The wood of the pine-tree 1815. **2.** A wood or forest of pines.

Piney (pəi·ni), **pinnay** (pi·neɪ). Also **piny.** 1857. [ad. Tamil *pinnai* or *punnai*, in Skr. *punnāga.*] Name of two E. Indian resinous trees, *Calophyllum inophyllum* (N.O. *Clusiaceæ*), called also **piney-tree,** and *Vateria indica* (N.O. *Dipteraceæ*), used *attrib.*, as in **piney dammar, resin, varnish,** the resin obtained from *Vateria indica*, also called *white dammar, Indian* or *Malabar copal*, or *gum animé*; **piney oil, piney tallow,** a fatty or waxy substance from the fruit of the same tree, used in making candles.

Pin-eyed (pi·n,əi:d), *a.* 1810. [f. PIN *sb.* + EYED *ppl. a.*] Applied to the long-styled form of a flower (esp. *Primula*), which shows the stigma resembling a pin's head, at the top of the corolla-tube.

Pin-feather (pi·nfe:ðəɹ), *sb.* 1775. [f. PIN *sb.* + FEATHER *sb.*] Any young feather from the time that it first pierces the skin, much in the form of a peg, until it bursts its confining sheath and expands its vanes. Hence **Pi·n-fea:thered** *a.* having immature feathers; also *fig.*

Pi·n-fire, *a.* (*sb.*). 1870. [f. PIN *sb.* + FIRE *v.*] Applied to a form of cartridge for breech-loading guns fitted with a pin which, on being struck by the hammer of the lock, is thrust into the fulminate and explodes it. Also applied to a gun in which this is used.

Pinfold (pi·nfōuld), *sb.* [Late OE. *pundfald*, f. **pund* POUND *sb.*[2] + *fald* FOLD *sb.*[1] From *c* 1400 assoc. w. the verb *pyndan* PIND, and perh. with PIN *v.*] A place for confining stray or distrained cattle, etc.; a pound; later, occas., a fold for sheep, cattle, etc.

fig. Confin'd, and pester'd in this pin-fold here MILT. Hence **Pi·nfold** *v. trans.* to shut up in a p.; hence *fig.* to confine within narrow limits.

Ping (piŋ), *sb.* 1856. [Echoic.] An abrupt ringing sound, such as that made by a rifle bullet in flying through the air, by a mosquito, etc. So **Ping** *v. intr.* to make such a sound.

Pingle (pi·ŋg'l). *Obs.* exc. *dial.* 1523. [Origin obsc.] A small enclosed piece of land; a paddock, a close.

Ping-pong (pi·ŋpǫŋ). 1900. [Echoic.] A parlour game resembling lawn-tennis, played on a table with bats and celluloid balls; so called from the 'ping' of the bat when striking.

Pinguedinous (piŋgwe·dinəs), *a.* 1599. [f. L. *pinguedinem* (f. *pinguis*) + -OUS.] Fatty.

Pinguefy (pi·ŋgwĭfəi), *v.* Now *rare.* 1597. [ad. L. *pinguefacere* to fatten.] **1.** *trans.* To cause to become fat or greasy; also to make (soil) rich or fertile 1599. †**2.** *intr.* To become fat –1825.

Pinguescent (piŋgwe·sĕnt), *a.* 1797. [ad. L. *pinguescentem*, *pinguescere* to grow fat, f. *pinguis* fat.] Becoming or growing fat, fattening. So **Pingue·scence** (*rare*).

‖ **Pinguicula** (piŋgwi·kiŭlă). 1597. [L. fem. (sc. *planta*) of *pinguiculus*, dim. of *pinguis* fat.] **1.** *Bot.* = BUTTERWORT. **2.** *Path.* A small blotch or growth of the conjunctiva, usu. near the edge of the cornea 1858.

Pinguid (pi·ŋgwid), *a.* Now usu. *joc.* or *affected.* 1635. [f. L. *pinguis* adj. + -ID; cf. *gravid*, etc.] Of the nature of, resembling, or abounding in fat; unctuous, greasy, oily; (of soil) rich, fertile. Also *transf.* and *fig.* Hence **Pingui·dity,** fatness, fatty matter.

Pinguin (pi·ŋgwin). 1696. [Origin obsc.] A W. Indian plant (*Bromelia Pinguin*) or its fruit; used in fevers and as an anthelmintic.

Pin-head (pi·nhed). 1662. [f. PIN *sb.* + HEAD *sb.*] The head of a pin. Used as a type of something of very small size or value, etc. **b.** *attrib.* Resembling a pin's head; very small and of rounded form 1835.

b. His sharp-nose and pin-head eyes O. W. HOLMES.

Pin-hole (pi·nhōul). 1676. **1.** A hole into which a pin or peg fits 1677. **2.** A hole made by a pin; any very small aperture or perforation 1676. **3.** *attrib.* (in sense 2). Of the nature of a p. or very small aperture; of the size of a pin-prick 1853.

P. camera, one with a minute hole instead of a lens.

Pinic (pəi·nik), *a.* 1831. [ad. F. *pinique*, f. L. *pinus* PINE *sb.*[2]; see -IC.] *Chem.* Of, pertaining to, or derived from the pine-tree; spec. in *p. acid*, an acid ($C_{20}H_{30}O_2$) obtained from pine resin.

Pinion (pi·nyən), *sb.*[1] ME. [a. OF. *pignon*, collateral form of OF. *penon, pennon* = It. *pennone*, a Rom. augmentative of L. *penna* (*pinna*) PEN *sb.*[2]] **1.** The distal or terminal segment of a bird's wing; hence (chiefly *poet.* or *rhet.*) a wing (always with ref. to its use for flight) 1440. **b.** *Carving.* The part of a wing corresponding to the fore-arm; formerly applied to the whole wing 1655. **2.** *fig.* (In ref. to things poetically represented as having wings.) 1602. **3.** The outermost feather, or any flight-feather, of a bird's wing 1545. **4.** The anterior border of an insect's wing 1720.

1. First a speck, and then a vulture, Till the air is dark with pinions LONGF. **2.** Hope humbly then; with trembling pinions soar POPE. Hence **Pi·nioned** *a.* having pinions or wings; winged.

Pinion (pi·nyən), *sb.*[2] 1659. [ad. F. *pignon*, perh. a use of OF. *pignon* battlement.] *Mech.* A small cog-wheel the teeth of which engage with those of a larger one; also a spindle, arbor, or axle, having cogs or teeth which engage with the teeth of a wheel.

P. and rack, also *rack and p.*: see RACK *sb.*[2]

Pinion (pi·nyən), *v.* 1558. [f. PINION *sb.*[1]] **1.** *trans.* To cut off the pinion of one wing, or otherwise disable the wings, in order to prevent a bird from flying. (With the bird, or the wing, as obj.) 1577. **2.** To bind the arms of any one; to disable by so binding; to shackle. (With the person, or the arms, as obj.) 1558. **b.** To bind fast *to* something, or together 1652.

2. *transf.* Yon ancient prude..Her elbows pinioned close upon her hips COWPER.

Pinite[1] (pi·n-, pəi·nəit). 1805. [ad. G. *pinit*, from its locality, the Pini mine, Schneeberg, Saxony: see -ITE[1] 2 b.] *Min.* A hydrous silicate of aluminium and potassium, occurring in various crystalline forms.

Pinite[2] (pəi·nəit). 1857. [a. F., f. L. *pinus* PINE *sb.*[2]; see -ITE[1] 4.] *Chem.* A crystallizable saccharine substance ($C_6H_{12}O_{10}$) obtained from the sap of two species of pine-tree, *Pinus lambertiana* and *P. sabiniana.*

Pink (piŋk), *sb.*[1] Now chiefly *Hist.* 1471. [app. a. MDu. *pincke, pinke* small sea-going ship, fishing-boat; ult. origin unkn.] A sailing-vessel: orig. one of small size, flat-bottomed and having bulging sides; later, applied to warships, etc. *Comb.* **p.-stern,** a stern like that of a p.; hence, a small vessel having a narrow stern.

Pink (piŋk), *sb.*[2], **penk** (peŋk). 1490. [Origin obsc.] **1.** A minnow. Now *dial.* **2.** A young salmon before it becomes a smolt; a samlet, parr 1533.

Pink (piŋk), *sb.*[3] 1512. [f. PINK *v.*[1]] †**1.** A hole or eyelet punched in a garment for decorative purposes; also, scalloping done for the same purpose –1632. †**2.** A stab with a poniard, etc. –1638. **b.** A shot-wound 1885.

Pink, *sb.*[4] and *a.* 1573. [Origin obsc.] **A.** *sb.* **I. 1.** General name of various species of *Dianthus* (N.O. *Caryophyllaceæ*), esp. of *D. plumarius*, a garden plant with very numerous varieties, having pure white, pink, crimson, or variegated sweet-smelling flowers. **b.** Applied with qualifying words to other species of *Dianthus*, and to other plants allied to or resembling the pink 1573. **2.** *fig.* The 'flower' of excellence; the embodied perfection (*of* some good quality) 1592. **b.** The most perfect condition or degree *of* something; the height, extreme 1767. †**c.** A beauty; an exquisite –1827.

1. b. China or **Chinese P.,** *Dianthus chinensis*; see CHINA *sb.*; **Clove P.,** *D. Caryophyllus*; see CLOVE *sb.*[2]; **Maiden, Maidenly,** or **Meadow P.,** *Dianthus deltoides*; **Pheasant's eye P.** = PHEASANT'S EYE 3; **Sea P.,** Thrift, *Statice Armeria*; **Wild P.,** any wild species of *Dianthus*. **2.** Nay, I am the very pinck of curtesie SHAKS. **b.** In the very p. of the mode THACKERAY. Phr. *In the p.*, in perfect health (*colloq.* or *slang*).

II. sb. use of B. **1.** A light or pale red colour with a slight purple tinge 1846. **2.** Scarlet when worn by fox-hunters; a scarlet hunting-coat, or the cloth of which it is made 1834. **b.** *transf.* A fox-hunter 1828.

2. Although not in p., [I] was the best mounted man in the field DISRAELI.

B. *adj.* [orig. attrib. use of sense I. 1 of the sb.] **1.** Of the colour of the pink (sense I. 1) in its single natural state; of a pale or light red colour, slightly inclining towards purple; of a pale rose-colour 1720. **2.** Applied to the colour of a hunting-coat 1857.

Comb.: **p. salt,** the ammonium salt of tetrachloride of tin, $2NH_4Cl \cdot SnCl_4$, used in calico-printing; **p. saucer,** a saucer containing a pigment used to give a pink tint to the skin, or to garments; *transf.* the pigment itself. Hence **Pi·nkish** *a.* somewhat p. **Pi·nkness,** the quality or state of being p.

Pink, *sb.*[5] 1634. [Origin obsc.] A yellowish or greenish-yellow pigment or 'lake' obtained by the combination of a vegetable colouring matter with some white base, as a metallic oxide; as *Brown p., French p., Dutch, English, Italian p.*

Pink, *a.*: see PINK *sb.*[4] B.

Pink (piŋk), *v.*[1] ME. [Cf. LG. *pinken* to strike, peck, said to be a nasalized modification of *picken* PICK *v.*[1]] **1.** *intr.* To make holes; to prick, thrust, stab. Now *rare.* **2.** *trans.* To pierce, prick, or stab with any pointed weapon or instrument 1598. **3.** To ornament (cloth, leather, etc.) by cutting or punching eyelet-holes, figures, etc.; to perforate; also, now, to decorate the raw edge of silk, etc., by scalloping and punching out a pattern on it. Also *to p. out.* 1503. **4.** To adorn, deck 1558.

2. One of them pink'd the other in a duel ADDISON.

Pink (piŋk), *v.*[2] 1540. [= Du. *pinken* to shut the eyes, to wink, to leer. History unkn.] **1.** *intr.* **a.** Of the eyes: To be half shut, to blink; to peer, peep. Now *dial.* **b.** Of a person: To blink or wink; to look slyly. Now *dial.* 1587. **2.** *P. in* (of daylight, etc.): to diminish, 'draw in'. *dial.* 1886.

Pink (piŋk), *v.*[3] 1920. [Echoic.] *intr.* Of a motor-engine: To 'knock'.

Pinked (piŋkt), *ppl. a.* 1598. [f. PINK *v.*[1] + -ED[1].] **1.** Pierced, pricked, wounded; tattooed 1608. **2.** Of cloth, leather, etc.: Ornamented with perforations, or (later) cut edges; slashed, scalloped 1598. **b.** Of flounces, frills, ribbons, etc.: Having the raw edge stamped or cut into scallops, jags, or narrow points. Often *p. out.* 1884.

Pi·nk-eye. 1795. [f. PINK *a.* + EYE *sb.*[1]] **1.** (Also *pink-eye potato.*) A variety of potato having pink eyes or buds. **2.** A contagious form of influenza in the horse, so called from the colour of the inflamed conjunctiva. **b.** A contagious form of ophthalmia in man, marked by redness of the eyeball 1882.

Pink-eyed (pi·ŋk,əid), *a.*[1] *Obs.* exc. *dial.* 1519. [Parasynthetic f. *pink* or *pinkie eye* (cf. Du. *pinkoogen* to wink).] Having small, narrow, or half-closed eyes; also, squint-eyed.

Pink-eyed, *a.*[2] [f. PINK *a.*] Having a pink or light red eye or eyes.

Pinkie, -y (pi·ŋki). 1874. Dim. of PINK *sb.*[1]

Pinking (pi·ŋkiŋ), *vbl. sb.* 1503. [f. PINK *v.*[1] + -ING[1].] The action of PINK *v.*[1]; decorating cloth, leather, etc., with holes, or (later) scalloped edges; *concr.* work so treated.

Comb., as **p.-iron,** a sharp instrument for cutting out pinked borders; also *joc.*, a sword.

Pinkroot (pi·ŋk,rūt). 1763. [f. PINK *sb.*[4] + ROOT.] **a.** The root of *Spigelia marilandica*, or of *S. Anthelmia*, used as vermifuges and purgatives. **b.** The herb *Spigelia marilandica* (N.O. *Loganiaceæ*), a native of the Southern U. S., called *Carolina Pink, Indian Pink*, or *Worm-grass*; also, *S. Anthelmia*, of the W. Indies and S. America (*Demerara P.*).

‖ **Pinkster** (pi·ŋkstəɹ). *U.S.* (N.Y.) Also **pingster, pinxter.** 1821. [Du., prob. through Gothic *paintêkustê*, a. Gr. πεντηκοστή Pentecost.] Whitsuntide; usu. *attrib.*

Pinxter-flower, U.S. name for *Azalea nudiflora*.

Pinky (pi·ŋki), *a.* 1776. [f. PINK *sb.*[4] or *a.* + -Y[1].] Tinged with or inclining to pink.

Pin-money (pi·nmɒ:ni). 1697. [f. PIN *sb.* II. 1 + MONEY.] A sum of money allotted by a man to his wife for personal expenses, *esp.* such a sum provided by a settlement.

‖ **Pinna**[1] (pi·nă). 1520. [L., var. of *pina*, a. Gr. πίνα (also πίννα, πίννη), in same sense.]

Zool. A genus of bivalve molluscs, having a large silky byssus or 'beard'.

‖ **Pinna** [2] (pi·nă). *Pl.* **-æ** (formerly also -as). 1785. [mod.L. uses of L. *pinna* = *penna*.] 1. *Anat.* The broad upper part of the external ear; also, the whole external ear 1840. 2. *Bot.* Each primary division (leaflet, petiole with leaflets, or lobe) of a pinnate or pinnatifid leaf, esp. in ferns 1785. 3. *Zool.* a. The fin of a fish; any fin-like structure, as the flipper of a seal, etc. b. A wing-like expansion or branch in certain polyps or other invertebrates. 1846.

Pinnace (pi·něs). 1546. [a. F. *pinasse*, *pinace*, usu. referred to L. **pinacea*, f. L. *pinus* pine-tree.] 1. A small light vessel, usually two-masted and schooner-rigged; often employed as a tender, scout, etc. Since c 1700 only *Hist.* and *poet.* 2. A double-banked boat (usu. eight-oared) forming part of the equipment of a man-of-war; also applied to other small boats 1685. †3. *fig.* A woman; also *spec.* a mistress; a prostitute -1693.

1. Full of flats and shoulds that our Pinnasse could not passe CAPT. SMITH.

Pinnacle (pi·năk'l), *sb.* [ME. *pinacle*, a. OF. and F. *pinacle*, ad. late L. *pinnaculum*, dim. of *pinna* wing, pinnacle, point.] 1. A small ornamental turret, usu. terminating in a pyramid or cone, crowning a buttress or rising above the roof or coping of a building. †b. *transf.* A vertical pointed structure resembling the above; a pyramid -1703. 2. Any natural peaked formation; *esp.* a peak ME. 3. *fig.* The highest point or pitch; the culmination; the acme, climax. late ME.

1. They fancied these to be cities adorned with towers and pinnacles 1777. 2. The pure-white p. of the Weisshorn 1878. 3. The highest P. of my Ambition 1659. Hence **Pi·nnacled** *ppl. a.* having a p. or pinnacles; elevated on or as on a p.

Pi·nnacle, *v.* 1656. [f. prec. sb.] 1. *trans.* To set on or as on a pinnacle; to rear as a pinnacle. 2. To form the pinnacle of 1818.

Pinnate (pi·nět), *a.* 1727. [ad. L. *pinnatus*, f. *pinna* feather, wing; see PINNA [2] and -ATE [2].] Resembling a feather; having lateral parts or branches on each side of a common axis. a. *Bot.* Applied to a compound leaf having a series of leaflets arranged on each side of a common petiole, the leaflets being usu. opposite, sometimes alternate (*alterni-pinnate*). b. *Zool.* Having branches, tentacles, or other lateral parts arranged on each side of an axis 1846. Hence **Pi·nnately** *adv.*

Pinnated (pi·neitėd), *a.* 1753. [f. as prec. + -ED [1].] 1. = prec. Chiefly *Bot.* and *Zool.* 2. *Zool.* Having parts like wings, or like fins 1776.

P. Grouse, any bird of the genus *Cupidonia*, having wing-like tufts of feathers on the neck, as the prairie-hen of N. America, *C. cupido*.

Pinnati- (pinē·ti, pinæ·ti), comb. form of L. *pinnatus* PINNATE; chiefly in botanical terms relating to leaves: **Pinna·tifid** (-æti-) *a.*, (of a leaf) pinnately cleft or divided at least half-way to the middle; **Pinna:tilo·bate, Pinna·tilobed** (-ēti-) *adjs.*, pinnately divided with rounded divisions or lobes; **Pinna:tipa·rtite** (-ēti-) *a.*, pinnately divided nearly to the midrib.

Pinnatiped (pinæ·tiped), *a.* and *sb.* 1828. [f. mod.L. *pinnatipes*, *-pedem*, f. *pinnatus* winged + *pes* foot.] *Ornith.* A. *adj.* Having the toes furnished with lobes; lobiped, fin-footed. B. *sb.* A pinnatiped bird; a bird of the group *Pinnatipedes*, having this character.

Pinner [1]. Now *local.* 1495. [var. of PINDER, f. PIN *v.* II. 1 = PIND *v.*] An officer who impounds stray beasts.

Pinner [2]. 1652. [f. PIN *v.* + -ER [1].] One who or that which pins. 1. A coif with two long flaps, one on each side, pinned on and hanging down; worn by women, esp. of rank, in the 17th and 18th centuries. Now only *Hist.* 1652. 2. *dial.* A pinafore or apron with a bib 1846.

Pinni- (pi·ni), comb. form. of L. *pinna*, *penna* wing, as **Pi·nnigrade** [L. *-gradus* walking] *a.*, *Zool.* walking by means of fin-like organs or flippers, as the pinniped Carnivora; also as *sb.* a p. animal.

Pinniform (pi·nifǭm), *a.* 1752. [f. PINNI- + -FORM.] a. Having the form of, or resembling, a fin. b. = PENNIFORM. c. Of a pinnate form. d. Resembling the mollusc called *Pinna* (PINNA [1]).

Pinniped (pi·niped), *a.* and *sb.* 1842. [ad. mod.L. *Pinnipes* (neut. pl. *Pinnipedia*), L. *pinnapes*, *pennipes* wing-footed, used in Zool. in sense 'fin-footed'; f. L. *pinna* + *pes*, *ped-* foot.] A. *adj.* Having feet resembling fins, fin-footed; *spec.* belonging to a suborder (*Pinnipedia*) of *Carnivora*, which have fin-like limbs or flippers. B. *sb.* A pinniped mammal; a seal or walrus.

Pinnothere (pi·nopīəɹ), **pinnotere** (pi·notīəɹ). 1601. [ad. L. *pinno-*, *pinoteres* (*-theres*), a. Gr. πιννοτήρης, f. πῖνα, πίννα PINNA [1] + τηρεῖν to guard.] Any of the small crabs of the genus *Pinnotheres*, which commensally inhabit the shells of various bivalves, as oysters and mussels; a pea-crab. So **Pinnothe·rian** *a.* and *sb.*

Pinnule (pi·niul). Also (in sense 1) **pinule**, (in senses 2 and 3) **pinnula** (pl. -æ). 1594. [ad. L. *pinnula*, dim. of *pinna* plume, wing; see PINNA [2].] 1. Each of the two sights at the ends of the 'alidade' or index of an astrolabe, quadrant, etc. 2. *Bot.* Each of the secondary or ultimate divisions of a pinnate leaf; a subdivision of a pinna; esp. in ferns 1776. 3. *Zool.* A part or organ resembling a small wing or fin, or a barb of a feather; *spec.* each of the lateral branches of the arms in crinoids 1748. Hence **Pi·nnulate, Pi·nnulated** *adjs.* having pinnules.

Pinny (pi·ni). Nursery and colloq. abbrev. of PINAFORE.

Pinnywinkles, var. PILLIWINKS.

Pinocle (pi·nǫk'l) *U.S.* Also **-chle**. 1890. [Origin unkn.] A game of cards resembling bezique; also, the occurrence of the queen of spades and knave of diamonds together in this game.

‖ **Pinole** (pinō·le). *U.S.* Also **pino·la, pinol** (pinōu·l). 1853. [a. Amer. Sp., ad. Aztec *pinolli*.] A meal made from parched cornflour mixed with sweet flour of mesquit-beans, or with sugar and spice.

Pinoleum (pinōu·liŏm). 1878. [f. L. *pinus* PINE *sb.*[2] + *oleum* OIL *sb.*] A material for sun-blinds, composed of slender slips or rods of pine-wood coated with oil-paint and threaded close to each other so as to form a sheet which can be rolled up.

‖ **Piñon** (pinyǫ·n, pi·nyən). Also **pinion**. 1851. [Sp. (pinʸo·n):—late L. **pinionem*, f. L. *pinea* pine-cone.] The American nut-pine, *Pinus edulis*, also the species *P. monophylla*, *P. Parryana*; the fruit or nut of these.

Pi·n-prick. 1862. [f PIN *sb.* II. + PRICK *sb.*] 1. The prick of a pin; a minute puncture. 2. *fig.* A petty annoyance, a minute irritation 1885.

2. *Policy of pin-pricks*, a course of petty hostile acts maintained as a national or a party policy.

Pint (pəint). [ME. *pynte*, a. F. *pinte*; ult. source unkn.] A measure of capacity for liquids (also for corn and other dry substances), equal to half a quart or $\frac{1}{8}$ of a gallon. b. A vessel containing a pint; a pint-pot 1483. c. *ellip.* A pint of ale, beer, etc. 1767.

Pintado (pintā·do). 1602. [a. Pg. (and Sp.) *pintado*, lit. 'painted':—late L. **pinctare*, f. late pa. pple. **pinctus* (for *pictus*) of *pingere* to paint.] †1. A kind of Eastern chintz -1727. 2. A species of petrel, *Daption capensis*, also called Cape Pigeon. Now *p. bird*, *petrel*. 1611. 3. The Guinea-fowl 1666.

Pintail (pi·n,tēl). 1768. [f. PIN *sb.* I. + TAIL.] 1. (In full *p. duck*.) A species of duck (*Dafila acuta*), of which the male has the tail of a pointed shape, the two middle feathers being longer than the rest. 2. A species of grouse having a pointed tail, as the pintailed sand-grouse (*Pterocles setarius*) of the Old World, and the pintailed or sharp-tailed grouse (*Pediœcetes phasianellus*) of N. America (also called *p. chicken*) 1879. Hence **Pi·ntailed** *a.*

Pintle (pi·nt'l). [OE. *pintel* (-*el* perh. dim.: see -LE); of unkn. history.] 1. The penis. Now *dial.* or *vulgar*. 2. A pin or bolt; esp. one on which some other part turns, as in a hinge, etc. 1486.

Pint-pot. 1563. A (pewter) pot containing a pint 1622. †b. *joc.* A seller of beer -1596.

‖ **Pinto** (pi·nto). *U.S.* 1867. [a. Amer. Sp.:—**pinctus* (see PINTADO).] Piebald (horse).

Pi·n-wheel. 1696. [f. PIN *sb.* I. + WHEEL.] 1. a. 'A wheel in the striking train of a clock in which pins are fixed to lift the hammer' (F. J. Britten). b. 'A contrate wheel in which the cogs are pins set into the disk' (Knight). 2. A firework, a small catherine-wheel 1869.

Piny (pəi·ni), *a.* 1627. [f. PINE *sb.*[2] + -Y [1].] Abounding in, covered with, or consisting of pine-trees; of or pertaining to a pine-tree.

The long low lines of p. hills RUSKIN.

‖ **Piolet** (pyolḗ). 1868. [F., prop. Savoy dial., dim. of *piolo*, app. cogn. w. F. *pioche*, *pic*.] An ice-axe used by Alpine climbers.

Pioneer (pəi,ŏnīə·ɹ), *sb.* 1523 [a. F. *pionnier*, OF. *paonier*, orig. foot-soldier, (later) pioneer. See PEON, PAWN, and -IER.] 1. *Mil.* One of a body of foot-soldiers who march with or in advance of an army or regiment, having spades, pickaxes, etc., to dig trenches, and clear and prepare the way for the main body. †2. *gen.* A digger, excavator; a miner -1640. 3. *fig.* One who goes before to prepare the way; one who begins some enterprise, course of action, etc.; an original investigator, explorer, or worker; an initiator (*of*) 1605.

3. The great p. of Arctic travel, Sir Edward Parry 1856.

Pionee·r, *v.* 1780. [f. prec. sb.] 1. *intr.* To act as pioneer; to prepare the way as a pioneer. 2. *trans.* To prepare, clear, open (a way, road, etc.) as a pioneer (*lit.* and *fig.*) 1794. 3. To act as a pioneer to, be the pioneer of; to prepare the way for 1819.

Pious (pəi·əs), *a.* 1602. [f. L. *pius* dutiful, pious + -OUS.] 1. 'Careful of the duties owed by created beings to God' (J.); devout, godly, religious. b. Of fraud and the like: Practised for the sake of religion or for a good object, or 'under the appearance of religion' (J.); see also FRAUD *sb.* 1637. 2. Faithful to the duties naturally owed to parents, friends, superiors, etc.; dutiful, duteous. Of persons (also of birds), or actions, etc. Now *rare* or *arch.* 1626.

1. Campbell is a good man, a p. man..he never passes a church without pulling off his hat JOHNSON. Old p. tracts, and Bibles bound in wood CRABBE. *P. founder*, the founder of a college or other endowment for the glory of God and the good of men. b. He sought the presence of his deare brother Benjamin by a p. kind of fraud 1637. 2. With p. care She..the aged gossip led KEATS. Hence **Pi·ous-ly** *adv.*

Pip (pip), *sb.*[1] late ME. [app. a. MDu. *pippe*, Du. *pip* = WG. **pipit*, a. pop. L. **pipita*, app. an unexplained alteration of PITUITA.] A disease of poultry and other birds, characterized by the secretion of a thick mucus in the mouth and throat, often with a white scale on the tip of the tongue (often applied to this scale itself). b. Applied (usu. *joc.*) to various diseases in human beings; also to any depressed state of mind. late ME.

b. The children ill with the p., or some confounded thing THACKERAY. Phr. *To give* (or *have*) *the p.*

Pip, *sb.*[2] 1596. [Orig. *peep*, still used dial.; cf the dial. *ship* for *sheep*. Origin unkn.] 1. Each of the spots on playing-cards, dice, or dominoes. 2. A spot or speck; *spec.* a spot on a spotted dress fabric; *pl.* specks appearing to dance before the eye. Now *dial.* 1676. 3. *Gardening.* Each single blossom of a clustered inflorescence, esp. in the cowslip and polyanthus 1753. 4. Each of the rhomboidal segments of the surface of a pine-apple 1833. 5. *colloq.* A star on an army officer's uniform, indicating his rank 1919.

Pip, *sb.*[3] 1598. [app. short f. PIPPIN.] †1. = PIPPIN 2. -1601. 2. = PIPPIN 1. 1797.

Pip, *sb.*[4] 1920. Signallers' name for the letter P, used in abbrev., as *pip emma*, P.M.

Pip, *v.*[1] 1659. [app. var. of PEEP.] 1. *intr.* To chirp, as a young bird. 2. *trans.* To crack (the shell of the egg), as a young bird.

Pip, *v.*[2] *colloq.* or *slang.* 1880. [f. PIP *sb.*[2] (or [3]) taken *fig.*; cf. PILL *v.*[2]] *trans.* To blackball; to defeat, beat; to hit with a shot.

‖ **Pipa** (pipā, pəi·pă). Also **pipal**. 1718. [a. Surinam negro *pipál* masc., *pipá* fem.] The Surinam toad (noted for its manner of hatching its young; see quot.); hence in *Zool.* the genus of tailless batrachians of which this is the only species.

The male *Pipa*,..as soon as the eggs are laid, places them on the back of the female, and fecundates them...The skin of her back..forms cellules, in which the eggs are hatched, and where the young pass their tadpole state 1838.

Pipage (pəi·pėdʒ). Also **pipeage.** 1612. [f. PIPE *sb.*^{1} + -AGE.] The conveyance of water, gas, petroleum, etc. by means of pipes; the laying down of pipes for this purpose; such pipes collectively.

Pipe (pəip), *sb.*^{1} [OE. *pīpe*, (ult.) a. late L. **pipa*, f. *pipare* to peep, pipe, chirp.] **I.** A musical tube. **1.** A musical wind-instrument consisting of a single tube of reed, straw, or (now usu.) wood, blown by the mouth. **b.** Each of the tubes (of wood or metal) by which the sounds are produced in an organ; see ORGAN-PIPE 1440. **c.** *Naut.* The boatswain's whistle; the sounding of this as a call to the crew 1638. **d.** *pl.* = *Bagpipes.* Also *poet.* in *sing.* 1706. **2.** *transf.* The voice, esp. in singing; the song or note of a bird, etc. 1580.

1. Their scrannel Pipes of wretched straw MILT. **2.** Thy small p. Is as the maidens organ, shrill, and sound SHAKS. The earliest p. of half-awaken'd birds TENNYSON.

II. A cylindrical tube or stick for other purposes. **1.** A hollow cylinder of wood, metal, etc., for the conveyance of gas, water, vapour, etc., or for other purposes; a tube OE. **2.** †**a.** The account of a sheriff or other minister of the Crown, as sent in and enrolled at the Exchequer. [AF.] **b.** The department of the Exchequer that drew up the 'pipes', or enrolled accounts, of sheriffs and others (= *pipe-office*) 1455. **3.** A tubular organ, passage, canal, or vessel in an animal body; applied now *esp.* to the respiratory passages. Usu. in *pl.* late ME. **4.** *Mining* and *Geol.* (*a*) A vein of ore of a more or less cylindrical form; also called *pipe vein, pipe-work.* (*b*) A vertical cylindrical hollow filled with sand or gravel, occurring in a stratum of chalk; also called *sand-pipe* or *sand-gall.* (*c*) The vertical eruptive channel which opens into the crater of a volcano. (*d*) Each of the vertical cylindrical masses of blue rock in which diamonds are found embedded in S. Africa (see KIMBERLITE). 1667. **5.** Each of the channels of a decoy for wild fowl 1634.

2. b. The Office of the Clerk of the Pipe 1455. **3.** He loves to clear his Pipes in good Air (to make use of his own phrase) ADDISON.

III. A narrow tube of clay, wood, etc., with a bowl at one end, for drawing in the smoke of tobacco (or other narcotic or medicinal substance); also, a quantity of tobacco which fills the bowl; a pipeful. (See TOBACCO-PIPE.) 1594.

Happy mortal! he who knows Pleasure which a P. bestows 1736. *P. of peace*, the CALUMET of the American Indians. Also allusively *Queen's* (*King's*) *P.*, joc. name for a furnace at the London Docks, used formerly for burning contraband tobacco, now for burning tobacco-sweepings, etc. *To put* a person's *p. out*, to take the 'shine' out of, extinguish. *Put that in your p. and smoke it*, put up with that if you can. *attrib.* and *Comb.*: **p.-dream** *U.S.*, a fantastic notion likened to a dream produced by opium-smoking; **-light**, a strip of paper folded or twisted for lighting a p., a spill; **-major**, the chief player of a band of bagpipe-players; **-metal**, an alloy of tin and lead, with or without zinc, used for organ-pipes; **-office**, the office of the Clerk of the P. in the Exchequer (see II. 2); **-ore**, iron ore (limonite) in vertical pillars, imbedded in clay; **-organ**, an organ with pipes, esp. as dist. from a *reed-organ*; **-rack**, (*a*) in an organ, a wooden shelf with perforations by which the pipes are supported; (*b*) a rack for tobacco-pipes; **-stopper**, a small plug for compressing the tobacco in the bowl of a p.; **p. vein** (*Mining*): see II. 4 a; **-vine**, a name for the N. American plant *Aristolochia Sipho*, from the shape of the flowers and the twining growth (also called *Dutchman's pipe*); **-work** (*Mining*), a p. vein of ore; **-wrench**, a tool with one jaw fixed on a shank and the other movable on a pivot, for gripping a p. when turned in one direction round it.

Pipe, *sb.*^{2} late ME. [a. OF., F. In origin, the same word as prec., in sense of a cylindrical vessel.] A large cask with its contents (wine, beer, cider, beef, fish, etc.), or as a measure of capacity, equivalent to half a tun, or 2 hogsheads, or 4 barrels, i.e. usu. containing 105 imperial gallons. Sometimes identified with BUTT *sb.*^{2} 1.

Pipe (pəip), *v.*^{1} [In branch I, OE. *pīpian* to blow the pipe, ad. L. *pipare*, f. *pipa* PIPE *sb.*^{1} In branch II, ME. *pipen* :—L. *pipare* to peep, cheep, chirp.] **I. 1.** *intr.* To blow or play on a pipe. **b.** To whistle, as the wind, a man, a bird: see II. **2.** *trans.* To play (a tune, music) upon a pipe. late ME. **b.** *transf.* To lead by the sound of a pipe; to entice or decoy, as wild fowl 1546. **3.** *Naut.* To summon, as a boatswain the crew, to some duty, or to a meal, by sounding the pipe or whistle. (*trans.* and *intr.*) 1706.

1. We have pyped vnto you, and ye have nott daunsed TINDALE *Luke* vii. 32. **2.** Piping down the valleys wild, Piping songs of pleasant glee BLAKE. **3.** The hands had just been piped to breakfast 1884. *To p. away, down*, to dismiss by sounding the p.

II. †**1.** *intr.* To utter a shrill and weak sound; to cheep, squeak, peep. Repl. by PEEP *v.*^{1} -1483. **2.** Variations of sense II. 1, infl. by sense I. 1. **a.** To whistle: said of the wind, a man, a marmot; also to hum or buzz shrilly; to whistle or whizz as a bullet 1513. **b.** To whistle or sing as a bird 1591. **c.** To talk loud and shrilly 1784. **d.** To weep, to cry. *colloq.* or *slang.* 1797. **3.** *trans.* To utter **a.** in a cheeping voice, as a mouse; **b.** in a loud shrill or clear voice, as a bird, a singer, or speaker. late ME. **4.** *To p. one's eye* or *eyes* (orig. *Naut. slang*): to shed tears, weep, cry 1789.

2. a. While rocking Winds are Piping loud MILT. **b.** The thrush piped from the hawthorn 1822. **3.** The boys piped out an hurrah THACKERAY.

III. *Pugilistic slang.* (*intr.*) To pant from violent exertion or exhaustion 1814. **IV.** *P. up.* **a.** *trans.* To begin to play or sing, strike up. late ME. **b.** *intr.* To speak up in a piping voice; to rise, as the wind 1889.

Pipe (pəip), *v.*^{2} 1788. [f. PIPE *sb.*^{1}] **I.** *trans. Gardening.* To propagate (pinks, etc.) by cuttings taken off at a joint of the stem. **II.** To trim or ornament (a dress, etc.), to ornament (a cake, etc.), with piping 1841. **III. 1.** *trans.* To furnish or supply with pipes 1884. **2.** To convey (water, gas, oil, etc.) through or by means of pipes 1889. **3.** *Mining.* To direct a jet of water from a pipe upon (gravel, etc.): see HYDRAULIC *a.* 1; to supply with water for this purpose 1882.

Pi·pe-clay, *sb.* 1779. A fine white kind of clay, which forms a ductile paste with water; used for making tobacco-pipes, and (esp. by soldiers) for cleaning white trousers, etc. Hence *allus.*, excessive attention to the minutiæ of dress and appearance in the management of regiments. Hence **Pi·pe-clay** *v. trans.* to whiten with pipe-clay; *fig.* to put into spick-and-span order.

Piped (pəipt), *ppl. a.* 1520. [f. PIPE *sb.*^{1} and *v.*^{2}] **1.** Furnished with a pipe or pipes; having the form of a pipe, tubular. **2.** Formed into, or ornamented with, piping 1884. **3.** Conveyed by pipes 1883.

Pi·pe-fish. 1769. [PIPE *sb.*^{1}] A fish of the genus *Syngnathus* or family *Syngnathidæ*, having a long slender body and a long snout.

Pipeful (pəi·pful). 1605. [f. PIPE *sb.*^{1} and ^{2} + -FUL.] **1.** [f. PIPE *sb.*^{2}] A quantity (of liquor, etc.) sufficient to fill a pipe or large cask. *rare.* **2.** [f. PIPE *sb.*^{1}] A quantity (of tobacco, etc.) sufficient to fill the bowl of a pipe 1613.

Pipe-layer (pəi·p,lēⁱəɹ). 1851. [f. PIPE *sb.*^{1} + LAYER *sb.*] **a.** A workman who lays pipes for the conveyance of water, gas, etc. **b.** *U.S. political slang.* One who schemes to procure corrupt votes. So **Pi·pe-lay:ing** 1848.

Pi·pe-line. 1883. A conduit of iron pipes for conveying petroleum from the oil-wells to the market or refinery, or for supplying water to a town or district.

Pipemouth (pəi·pmauþ). A fish of the genus *Fistularia* or family *Fistulariidæ*, characterized by a long pipe-like snout.

Piper (pəi·pəɹ). [OE. *pīpere*, f. *pīpe* PIPE *sb.*^{1} + *-ere* -ER^1.] **1.** One who plays on a pipe (*esp.* a strolling musician), in Scotland *spec.* a bagpiper. **2.** Pop. name for several kinds of fish; *esp.* a species of gurnard, *Trigla lyra*, so called from the sound it makes when caught; in New Zealand, the garfish 1601. **3.** A broken-winded horse; cf. *roarer* 1831.

1. Let's haue a dance...Strike vp Pipers SHAKS. Phr. *To pay the p.*, i.e. for piping to lead the dance; hence, to defray the cost, or bear the loss, incident to some proceeding; Londoners had paid the p., and should choose the tune 1895.

Piperaceous (pipĕrēⁱ·ʃəs), *a.* 1674. [f. L. *piper* PEPPER + -ACEOUS.] †**a.** Of the nature of pepper; pungent. **b.** *Bot.* Belonging to the N.O. *Piperaceæ*, the pepper tribe (typical genus *Piper*; see PEPPER).

Piperazine (pi·pĕrăzəin). 1891. [f. L. *piper* (see next) + AZ(O- + -INE^5.] *Pharm.* A compound allied to spermin, chemically *diethylenediamine.*

Piperic (pipe·rik), *a.* 1866. [f. L. *piper* PEPPER + -IC.] *Chem.* Pertaining to or derived from pepper; in *p. acid*, an acid obtained by boiling piperine with potash.

Piperidine (pipe·ridəin). 1857. [mod. f. L. *piper* PEPPER + -IDE + -INE^5.] *Chem.* 'A volatile base ($C_5H_{11}N$) produced by the action of alkalis on piperine' (Watts).

Piperine (pi·pĕrəin). 1820. [f. as prec. + -INE^5.] *Chem.* An alkaloid obtained from species of pepper (*Piper nigrum* and *P. longum*), crystallizing in colourless prisms.

Pi·pe-roll. 1612. [f. PIPE *sb.*^{1} 2 + ROLL *sb.*] The Great Roll of the Exchequer, comprising the various 'pipes', or enrolled accounts, of sheriffs and others for a financial year.

Pi·pe-stone. 1809. [f. PIPE *sb.*^{1} + STONE.] = CATLINITE.

Pipette (pipe·t). 1839. [a. F., dim. of *pipe* PIPE *sb.*^{1}; see -ETTE.] A small pipe or tube, used (esp. in chemistry, etc.) to transfer or measure small quantities of a liquid or gas.

Pipewort (pəi·pwɒɹt). 1806. [f. PIPE *sb.*^{1} + WORT.] Any plant of the genus *Eriocaulon* of aquatic or marsh herbs allied to grasses, with a membranous tube surrounding the ovary.

Piping (pəi·piŋ), *vbl. sb.*^{1} ME. [f. PIPE *v.*^{1} + -ING^1.] The action of PIPE *v.*^{1} **1.** Playing on a pipe; the music of pipes or wind-instruments. **2.** The utterance of a shrill sound, or the sound itself (see PIPE *v.*^{1} II.) ME. **3.** Weeping, crying. *slang* or *colloq.* 1779.

Pi·ping, *vbl. sb.*^{2} 1660. [f. PIPE *v.*^{2} and *sb.*^{1} + -ING^1.] **1.** The action of PIPE *v.*^{2}, q.v. **2.** *Dressmaking.* The trimming or ornamentation of the edge of stuff or the seams of a garment, by means of a fine cord enclosed in a pipe-like fold; *concr.*, the tubular kind of trimming thus formed 1858. **3.** *Confectionery.* The action or art of ornamenting cakes, etc. with cord-like lines of sugar; *concr.* the lines so used 1883.

Pi·ping, *ppl. a.* late ME. [f. PIPE *v.*^{1} + -ING^2.] **1.** Playing on a pipe 1638. **b.** Characterized by piping, i.e. the music of the pastoral pipe (as dist. from martial music): in the Shaksperian phr. *p. time*(*s*) *of peace* 1594. **2.** Sounding shrilly; whistling 1513. **3.** quasi-*adv.* in phr. **p. hot,** so hot as to make a piping or hissing sound as a dish freshly cooked; hissing hot; hence *gen.* very hot ME. **b.** *fig.* Fresh, just come out 1607.

2. P. bullfinch, a bullfinch trained to whistle a tune; **p. crow,** the Australian genus *Gymnorhina*; **p. hare,** the pika or calling hare, *Lagomys*; **p. plover,** *Ægialites melodus*, of N. America.

Pipistrelle, -el (pipistre·l). 1771. [a. F., ad. It. *pipistrello* bat, var. *vipistrello* repr. late L. **vespertilio* for L. *vespertilio* bat, f. *vesper* evening.] A small species of bat, *Vesperugo pipistrellus*, common in Europe.

Pipit (pi·pit). 1768. [prob. imitative of the bird's note.] Any bird of the genus *Anthus* or several allied genera of the family *Motacillidæ*, having a general resemblance to larks.

Pipkin (pi·pkin). 1565. [Origin obsc.] A small earthenware pot or pan, used chiefly in cookery. (Formerly including metal pots. Now local.) Hence **Pi·pkinet,** a small p.

Pipperidge (pi·pəridʒ). 1538. [Origin obsc.] **1.** A local name of the Barberry, fruit or shrub. **2.** = PEPPERIDGE 2. 1828.

Pippin (pi·pin). [ME. a. OF. *pepin*, mod. F. *pepin, pépin* pip. Origin obsc.] **1.** The seed of certain fruits, including those now called *pips*, and others. *Obs.* exc. *n. dial.* **2.** The name of numerous varieties of apple. late

ME. 3. Applied to a person (*slang*) 1664. 4. *attrib.*, as p. face, a round red face 1598.

|| **Pipsissewa** (pipsi·sīwă). 1818. [ad. N. Amer. Indian name *sip-si-sewa*; perh. a white man's corruption.] A low creeping evergreen with whitish flowers, *Chimaphila umbellata* (N.O. *Ericaceæ* or *Pyrolaceæ*), also called Prince's pine. Also, the leaves of this used as a diuretic and tonic.

Pi·p-squeak. *slang.* 1910. 1. An insignificant or contemptible person or thing. 2. A shell distinguished by its sound in flight 1916.

Pipy (pəi·pi), *a.* 1724. [f. PIPE *sb.*[1] + -Y[1].] Containing pipes; of the form of a pipe.

Piquancy (pī·kănsi). 1664. [f. next; see -ANCY.] The quality of being piquant, in various senses; sharpness; appetizing flavour; etc.

Piquant (pī·kănt), *a.* (*sb.*) 1521. [a. F., pr. pple. of *piquer* to sting; see PICK *v.*[1] Now also **piquante** (pīkɑ·nt), usu. repr. F. fem. *piquante.*] 1. That pierces or stings; keen, trenchant; severe, bitter. Chiefly *fig. Obs.* or *arch.* 2. Agreeably pungent of taste; sharp, stinging, biting; appetizing 1645. 3. *fig.* That stimulates or excites keen interest or curiosity; pleasantly stimulating or disquieting 1695. B. *sb. rare.* That which is piquant. a. A hedgehog's prickle; b. A piquant dish; a whet. 1835.

2. As p. to the Tongue as Salt it self ADDISON. 3. She disapproved entirely of the p. neatness of Caroline's costume C. BRONTE. That picquante letter-writer, Madame de Sévigné 1873. Hence **Pi·quantly** *adv.*

Pique (pīk), *sb.*[1] 1532. [a. F., n. of action f. *piquer* to prick, etc.; see PIQUE *v.*[1]] 1. A personal quarrel between two or more persons; ill-feeling, animosity, enmity. 2. A feeling of anger, resentment, or ill-will, resulting from some slight or injury; offence taken 1592.

2. A Bishop who had turned monk in a momentary fit of p. FREEMAN.

Pique (pīk), *sb.*[2] 1668. [a. F. *pic*, in same sense; origin unkn.] In piquet, the winning of thirty points on cards and play, before one's opponent begins to count, entitling the player to begin his score at sixty.

Pique (pī·ke, pīk), *sb.*[3] 1748. [a. Sp. Amer., ad. Quichua *piqui, piki.*] = CHIGOE.

Pique, *sb.*[4] 1826. Erron. f. PEAK *sb.*[2]

Pique (pīk), *v.*[1] 1664. [a. F. *piquer* to prick, etc.; *se piquer*, to take offence.] 1. *trans.* To irritate; to offend by wounding pride or vanity 1671. 2. *trans.* To excite to action by arousing envy, rivalry, jealousy, etc.; to arouse, awake (curiosity, interest). †b. *refl.* To put oneself on one's mettle. 1698. †3. *absol.* or *intr.* To arouse a feeling of pique; to stimulate -1710. 4. *refl.* (rarely *intr.*). To take pride *in*, plume oneself *on*. Const. *on, upon*, rarely *at, in*. (= F. *se piquer de.*) 1705.

1. A little picqued by the excess of his mirth 1796. 2. You have piqued my curiosity 1870. 3. Every Verse hath something in it that piques ADDISON. 4. Men who are thought to p. themselves upon their wit POPE.

Pique, *v.*[2] 1659. [f. PIQUE *sb.*[2]] In *Piquet*: a. *trans.* To score a pique against (one's opponent). b. *intr.* To score a pique.

|| **Piqué** (pī·ke), *sb.* (*a.*) 1852. [F., pa. pple. of *piquer* (see PIQUE *v.*[1])] A rather stiff cotton fabric woven in a strongly ribbed or raised pattern; quilting. b. The raised pattern of such a fabric 1890. B. *ppl. a.* Inlaid (with little points of gold, etc.). Also as sb. = *p. work* (*a*) decorative needlework in which a pattern is formed by stitching; (*b*) ornamental work in tortoise-shell, etc., formed by means of minute inlaid designs traced in points of gold, etc.

Piquet (pike·t, pi·kĕt). Also **picket, picquet**, etc. 1646. [a. F.; origin unkn.] A card-game played by two persons with a pack of 32 cards (the low cards from the two to the six being excluded).

|| **Pir** (pī·əɪ). 1672. [Pers. = old man.] A Mohammedan saint; also, a holy place.

Piracy (pəi·răsi). 1552. [ad. med.L. *piratia*, a. Gr. πειρατεία, f. πειρατής PIRATE; see -ACY.] The action or practice of a pirate. 1. Robbery and depredation on the sea or navigable rivers, or by descent from the sea upon the coast, by persons not holding a commission from a civilized state; with *a* and *pl.*, an instance of this. 2. *fig.* Infringement of rights conferred by a patent or copyright 1771.

Piragua (piræ·gwă), **periagua** (peri,æ·gwă). 1609. [orig. a. Sp., a. Carib *piragua* a dug-out; subseq. corrupted.] 1. A long narrow canoe hollowed from the trunk of a single tree. 2. An open flat-bottomed schooner-rigged vessel; a sort of two-masted sailing-barge 1667.

Pirate (pəi·rĕt), *sb.* ME. [ad. L. *pirata*, a. Gr. πειρατής, f. πειρᾶν to attempt, attack.] 1. One who robs and plunders on the sea, etc.; a sea-robber. 2. *transf.* A vessel employed in piracy or manned by pirates; a pirate-ship 1600. 3. Any one who roves about in quest of plunder; one who robs with violence; a marauder, despoiler 1526. 4. *fig.* One who appropriates or reproduces without leave, for his own benefit, a composition, idea, or invention that he has no right to; esp. one who infringes on the copyright of another 1701. 5. An omnibus which infringes on the recognized routes; now often applied to any omnibus owned by a private firm or person. Also *transf.* The driver of such an omnibus. 1889. b. *attrib.* and *Comb.*, as *p.-ship*, etc. P. bus, omnibus (see 5).

1. Notable Pyrate, thou salt-water Theefe SHAKS. 3. Pirates of the desert 1850. 4. In 1599 two of them [Shakspere's Sonnets] were printed by the p. Jaggard 1887.

Pirate (pəi·rĕt), *v.* 1574. [f. prec. sb.] 1. *trans.* To practise piracy upon; to rob, plunder. 2. *intr.* To play the pirate, practise piracy 1685. 3. *fig. trans.* To appropriate or reproduce (the work or invention of another) without authority, for one's own profit 1706.

3. He had no right to p. a peculiar trade mark 1850.

Piratic (pəiræ·tik), *a.* 1640. [ad. L. *piraticus*, a. Gr., f. πειρατής pirate; see -IC.] Of or pertaining to a pirate or pirates; like a pirate. *P. war*, that waged by Pompey against the pirates in the Mediterranean.

Piratical (pəiræ·tikăl), *a.* 1565. [f. as prec. + -AL.] 1. Of or pertaining to a pirate or piracy; of the nature of, characterized by, given to, or engaged in piracy; pirate-like 1579. b. *fig.* Given to literary piracy, etc. 1736. 2. Obtained by piracy; pirated 1565.

1. The Moors established the p. states of Algiers and Tunis 1872. b. P. publishers 1877. 2. Two legal editions—two p. ones 1838. So **Pira·tically** *adv.* 1549.

Pirl (pəɹl, *Sc.* pi·r'l), *v. arch.*, *Sc.* and *dial.* 1500. [Perh. onomatopœic.] 1. *trans.* To twist, wind, or spin (threads, etc.) into a cord; now esp. *dial.* to twist (horsehair) into fishing-lines, etc. 2. To cause to revolve, to spin. Also *intr.* To spin. 1791.

Pirn (pəɹn, *Sc.* pirn). Now *Sc.* and *dial.* late ME. [Origin obsc.] 1. A weaver's bobbin, spool, or reel 1440. b. A reel of sewing cotton 1820. 2. Any device like a reel, or used for winding; *esp.* a fishing-reel 1782.

Pirogue (pirōᵘ·g). Also **per(i)oque, periogue, piroque.** 1666. [a. F. *pirogue*, prob. from Galibi, the Carib dialect of Cayenne.] Another form of PIRAGUA; extended to local kinds of open boats, with or without sails.

Pirouette (piruˌe·t), *sb.* 1706. [a. F., = spinning top, teetotum, etc., cf. It. *piru(o)lo*, dim. of **piro* pin, peg.] 1. The act of spinning round on one foot, or on the point of the toe, as performed by ballet-dancers. 2. In the manège: 'A turn or circumvolution which a horse makes, without changing his ground' (Chambers) 1727. So **Piroue·tte** *v. intr.* to dance a p., spin or whirl on the point of the toe; to move with a whirling motion.

Pirrie, -y (pi·ri). Now only *dial.* late ME. [app. onomatopœic.] A blast of wind; a squall; a sudden storm of wind, 'half a gale'.

|| **Pis aller** (pizale). 1676. [F., from *au pis aller* lit. at the worst going.] The worst that can be, or can happen; what one accepts when one can do no better; a last resource.

Piscary (pi·skări). 1474. [ad. med.L. *piscaria*, neut. pl. of *piscarius* adj., f. *piscis* fish.] 1. The right of fishing (as a thing owned). Now usu. in *common of p.* 2. A place where fish may be caught; a fishing-ground 1625.

1. Common of p. is a liberty of fishing in another man's water, in common with the owner of the soil, and perhaps also with others 1880.

Piscation (piskēⁱ·ʃən). *rare.* 1624. [ad. L. *piscationem.*] Fishing.

|| **Piscator** (piskēⁱ·tǫɹ, -əɹ). 1653. [L., f. *piscari* to fish.] A fisherman; an angler.

Piscatory (pi·skătəri), *a.* 1633. [ad. L. *piscatorius* adj., f. *piscator*; see -ORY[2].] 1. Of or pertaining to fishers or to fishing. So **Piscato·rial** *a.* 2. Employed in or addicted to fishing 1661.

1. *P. ring*, the signet ring worn by the pope as successor of St. Peter (cf. Matt. iv. 19, etc.).

|| **Pisces** (pi·sīz). late ME. [L., pl. of *piscis* fish.] 1. *Astron.* The twelfth zodiacal constellation, the Fishes; also the twelfth sign of the Zodiac (orig. coincident with the constellation), which the sun enters about Feb. 20. 2. *Zool.* Fishes, as a class of Vertebrata 1841.

Pisciculture (pi·sikɒltiŭɹ, -tʃəɹ). 1859. [f. L. *piscis* fish + *cultura* CULTURE.] The breeding, rearing, and preserving of (living) fish by artificial means. Hence **Piscicu·ltural** *a.*; **-ly** *adv.* **Piscicu·lturist**, a person engaged or interested in p.

Pisciform (pi·sifǭɹm), *a.* 1828. [f. L. *piscis* + -FORM.] Having the form of a fish.

Piscina (pisī·nă, pisəi·nă). *Pl.* **-æ, -as.** 1599. [a. L., = fishpond, etc., f. *piscis* fish.] 1. A fishpond; a pond, basin, or pool; among the ancient Romans, a bathing-pond. 2. *Eccl.* A perforated stone basin for carrying away the ablutions, generally placed in a niche on the south side of the altar 1793.

Piscine (pi·sin, pisī·n), *sb.* ME. [a. OF., F., ad. L. *piscina*; see prec.] = PISCINA 1, 2.

Piscine (pi·səin), *a.* 1799. [f. L. *piscis* fish; see -INE[1].] Of, pertaining to, of the nature of, or characteristic of a fish or fishes.

Piscivorous (pisi·vŏrəs), *a.* 1668. [f. L. *piscis* + *-vorus* devouring + -OUS.] Fish-eating; ichthyophagous.

|| **Pisé** (pī·ze). 1797. [a. F., subst. use of pa. pple. of *piser* to beat:—L. *pisare, pinsare* to beat, pound, stamp.] Stiff clay or earth kneaded, or mixed with gravel, used for building cottages, walls, etc., by being rammed between boards which are removed as it hardens; also, this mode of building. Also *attrib.*

Pisgah (pi·zgă). 1650. The name of a mountain east of Jordan, whence Moses was allowed to view the Promised Land (Deut. iii. 27); hence allusively, esp. *attrib.*, as *P. glance, prospect, view.*

Pish (piʃ), *int.* and *sb.* 1592. **A.** *int.* A natural exclam. expressing contempt, impatience, or disgust. **B.** *sb.* The utterance of this exclam. 1594. Hence **Pish** *v. intr.* to say 'pish' (often with *at*); *trans.* to say 'pish' to.

Pisiform (pəi·sifǭɹm, pi·zi-), *a.* (*sb.*) 1767. [ad. mod.L. *pisiformis*, f. *pisum* PEA[1]; see -FORM.] **A.** *adj.* Pea-shaped; of small globular form. **B.** *sb.* Short for *p. bone.* (Also in L. form pisiforme.) 1808.

A. *P. bone* (Anat.), a small pea-shaped bone of the upper row of the carpus. *P. iron-ore*, iron-ore occurring in small concretions like peas.

Pismire (pi·smaiəɹ). *Obs.* exc. *dial.* [ME. *pissemyre, -mire*, etc., f. PISS + *mire* ant; from the urinous smell of an anthill.] An ant. b. *fig.* Applied contempt. to a person 1569.

Pisolite (pi·zŏləit, pəi·sŏ-). 1708. [ad. mod.L. *pisolithus*, f. Gr. πίσος, -ον pea + -LITE.] = PEASTONE. Hence **Pisoli·tic** *a.* of the nature of, consisting of, or resembling p.

Piss (pis), *sb.* Not now in polite use. late ME. [f. next.] Urine, 'water'.

Piss (pis), *v.* Not now in polite use. [a. OF. *pissier*, F. *pisser*; prob. onomatopœic.] 1. *intr.* To urinate, make water. Also *transf.* 2. *trans.* To discharge as or with the urine. Also *transf.* and *fig.* ME. 3. To wet with urine; to put *out* (fire) in this way ME.

Pissabed (pi·săbed). *Obs.* exc. *dial.* 1565. [f. PISS *v.* + ABED, from its diuretic property. So F. *pissenlit.*] The dandelion.

Pissasphalt (pi·sæsfælt). Also in alien forms. 1601. [ad. L. *pissasphaltus*, a. Gr., f. πίσσα pitch + ἄσφαλτος ASPHALT.] A semi-liquid variety of bitumen, mentioned by ancient writers.

Pist, var. PST.

Pistachio (pistā·ʃio, -ā·tʃᵢo, -ē·ʃio). late ME. [ad. L. *pistacium*, a. Gr. πιστάκιον, f. πιστάκη pistacia, from OPers., with assimilation to F. *pistache*, It. *pistacchio*, or Sp. *pistacho*.] **1.** (Also *p. nut.*) The 'nut' or dry drupe of *Pistacia vera* (see b), or its edible kernel, of a greenish colour. 1533. **b.** (Also *p. tree.*) The tree *Pistacia vera* (N.O. *Anacardiaceæ*), a native of Western Asia. late ME. **2.** (Also *p. green.*) A green colour like that of the pistachio nut. Also *attrib.* or as *adj.* 1791. **3.** *attrib.*, as *p. green* (sb. and adj.), *nut*, *tree*, etc. 1598.

‖ **Pistacia** (pistē·ʃiă). late ME. [L., = pistachio tree, f. Gr. πιστάκη; see prec.] The pistachio tree = prec. 1 b; in *Bot.* the name of the genus, including also the mastic-tree and the terebinth; the species are collectively called *turpentine-trees*. †**b.** = prec. 1 a –1583.

Pistacite (pi·stăsəit). 1828. [ad. G. *pistazit*, f. prec. + -ITE; so named from its colour.] *Min.* = EPIDOTE, or a variety of it.

Pistareen (pistărī·n). 1774. [app. f. PESETA.] An Amer. or W. Ind. name for a small coin formerly current there. **b.** *attrib.* or as *adj.* Petty, paltry (cf. PICAYUNE).

Pistic (pi·stik), *a.* 1646. [ad. L. *pisticus*, a. Gr. πιστικός perh. 'genuine, pure', f. πίστις faith; perh. a local name.] In *nard p.*, *p. nard* = Gr. νάρδος πιστική in Mark xiv. 3, John xii. 3 (in Bible versions translated *spikenard*).

Pistil (pi·stil). 1578. [In sense 1, the same word as PESTLE, OF. *pestel* :—L. *pistillum*. For sense 2, the L. word itself was first used, subseq. its Fr. adaptation *pistil*.] *Bot.* †**1.** In early use (in form *pestle*, *pestill*), the thick pestle-like spadix of araceous plants –1672. **2.** The female organ of a flower, comprising (in its complete form) the ovary, style, and stigma 1718. So **Pi·stillary** *a.* of, pertaining to, or of the nature of a p. **Pi·stillate** *a.* having a p. or pistils (and no stamens); female: opp. to *staminate*. **Pistilli·ferous** *a.* pistillate: opp. to *staminiferous*. **Pi·stilline** *a.* pistillate; pistillary.

‖ **Pistillidium** (pistili·diǒm). *Pl.* **-ia.** 1854. [mod.L., f. *pistillum* PISTIL + *-idium* = Gr. -ιδιον, dim. suffix.] *Bot.* The female organ in the higher Cryptogams, the ARCHEGONIUM.

†**Pistle.** [OE. *pistol*, aphet. f. *epistol*, ad. L. *epistola* EPISTLE.] **1.** = EPISTLE *sb.* 1–3. –1787. **2.** A (spoken) story or discourse –1550.

Pistol (pi·stəl), *sb.* 1570. [a. obs. F. *pistole* pistol; app. shortened f. PISTOLET [1].] A small fire-arm with a more or less curved stock, adapted to be held in, and fired with, one hand.

Volta's p., a metallic tubular vessel, closed with a cork, in which an explosive mixture of gases may be ignited by an electric spark.

attrib. and *Comb.*: **p.-arm**, the arm with which the p. is held when fired; **-carbine**, a p. with a detachable butt-piece, which can be fired either as a p. or as a carbine; **-pipe** (*Metallurgy*), the blast-pipe of a hot-blast furnace; **-shot**, a shot from a p.; the distance to which a shot can be fired from a p. Hence **Pi·stol**, *v. trans.* to shoot with a p.

Pistole (pistōᵘ·l). 1592. [a. F., = the coin, app. shortened from *pistolet*.] A name formerly applied to certain foreign gold coins; occas. = PISTOLET [2]; *spec.* from 1600 applied to a Spanish gold coin worth 16*s.* 6*d.* to 18*s.*

Pistoleer (-īə·ɪ). 1832. [See -EER.] A soldier armed with a pistol.

†**Pi·stolet** [1]. 1550. [a. F., app. dim. from stem of It. *pistolese* 'a great dagger', sb. use of *Pistolese* adj., of or pertaining to Pistoia, a town of Tuscany.] A small fire-arm; the earlier name of the PISTOL –1650.

†**Pistolet** [2]. 1553. [a. F. History obsc.] A name given to certain foreign gold coins; in the 16th c. usu. ranging in value from 5*s.* 10*d.* to 6*s.* 8*d.*; in later times = PISTOLE –1659.

Piston (pi·stən). 1704. [a. F., ad. It. *pistone*, var. of *pestone* great pestle, augm. from stem *pest-* in *pestello* pestle :—late L. *pistare*, freq. of *pist-*, *pinsere* to pound, beat.] **1.** A disk or short cylinder of wood, iron, etc., which fits closely within a hollow cylinder or tube, and can be driven with a reciprocating motion up and down the tube, or backwards and forwards in it; on one side it is attached to a rod (*piston-rod*) by which it imparts motion to machinery (e.g. in a steam-engine), or by which motion is imparted to it (e.g. in a pump). **2.** In the cornet, etc., a sliding valve which moves in a cylinder like a piston, used for increasing the length of the air-passage and thus lowering the pitch of the note 1876.

attrib. and *Comb.*: **p.-head**, the disk of a p., which slides in the tube, as dist. from the *piston-rod*; **-rod** (see 1); **-valve**, (*a*) a valve in a p., as that in a pump; (*b*) a valve formed by a p. sliding backwards and forwards in a tube, for admitting steam into, or exhausting it from, the cylinder of a steam-engine.

Pit (pit), *sb.* [OE. *pytt*, ME. *pyt(t*, *pit*, *put(t*, *pet*; repr. WGer. **puttjoz*, a. L. *puteus* well, pit, shaft.] **1.** A hole or cavity in the ground, either natural or formed by digging. **b.** An open deep hole made in digging for some mineral deposit, as CHALK-, CLAY-, GRAVEL-*pit* OE. **c.** A hole made for a special purpose in various industries, as sawing, tanning, etc. OE. **d.** *Agric.* and *Gardening.* A hole made for storing and protecting edible roots, etc. through the winter; or one (usu. with a glazed frame) for protecting young or tender plants 1500. **e.** A dungeon. *Obs.* exc. *Hist.* 1500. **f.** A covered hole to serve as a trap for wild beasts (or enemies); a pitfall 1611. **2.** A well, a water-hole; a pond, pool. *Obs.* or merged in **1.** OE. **3.** A grave. *Obs.* or *dial.* (exc. as in *plague-pit*, etc.) ME. **4.** The abode of evil spirits and lost souls; hell, or some part of it. Often in phr. *pit of hell*. ME. **5.** An enclosure in which animals were or are set to fight for sport; *esp.* = COCKPIT 1. 1568. **b.** = COCKPIT 2. **6.** The shaft of a coal-mine; also, the mine as a whole 1447. **7.** *Pit and gallows*, in *Sc. Law*, the privilege, formerly conferred on barons, of executing thieves or other felons by hanging the men on a gallows and drowning the women in a pit (see sense 2) ME.

1. There in the ghastly p. a body was found TENNYSON. **e.** Then took they Jeremiah, and cast him into the dungeon [*marg.* or pit] of Malchiah R.V. *Jer.* xxxviii. 6. **f.** He [a young lion] was taken in their p. *Ezek.* xix. 4. *fig.* He fals himselfe that digs anothers p. DEKKER. **3.** O Lord..thou hast kept me alive, that I should not go down to the p. *Ps.* xxx. 3. **5.** Phr. *To fly* or *shoot the p.*, to turn and fly out of the p., as a craven cock; hence *fig.*

II. 1. A hollow or indentation in an animal or plant body, or in any surface: *spec.* A natural hollow or depression in the body, as the ARMPIT ME. **b.** A depressed scar, such as those left on the skin after small-pox 1677. **c.** *Bot.* A minute depression on the inner side of the wall of a cell or vessel, as in the wood-cells of conifers; also, a minute depression on the surface of a seed 1857. **2.** That part of the auditorium of a theatre which is on the floor of the house; now usu. only the part of this which is behind the stalls. Also *transf.* the people occupying this. 1649. **3.** *U.S.* A part of the floor of an Exchange appropriated to a special branch of business, e.g. *grain p.*, *wheat p.* 1886. **b.** Hence, the name of a card game, which mimics a corn exchange 1904.

1. a. *P. of the stomach*, the slight depression in the region of the stomach between the cartilages of the false ribs. **2.** Speak more to the p...—the soliloquy always to the p., that's a rule SHERIDAN. **3.** The world's food should not be at the mercy of the Chicago wheat p. 1903.

Comb.: **p.-bank**, the bank at a pit-head where the coal is sorted and screened; **-brow**, the brow or edge of a p.; **-frame**, a framework at the top of a p. or shaft, supporting the pulley; **-head**, the top of a p. or shaft, or the ground immediately around it; **-kiln**, an oven for making coke from coal; **-saw**, a large saw for cutting timber, worked in a sawpit, with handles at the top and bottom; **-sawyer**, the man who stands in a sawpit and works the lower handle of a pit-saw (opp. to *top-sawyer*); **-stall**, a seat situated between the stalls and the pit; **-viper**, a venomous serpent of the family *Crotalidæ*, characterized by a p. or depression in front of each eye; **-work**, the system of pumps and machinery connected with them in a p. or shaft.

Pit, *v.* 1456. [f. prec.] **I. 1.** *trans.* To put or cast into a pit; *esp.* to put (roots, vegetables, etc.) into a pit for storage. **2.** To set (cocks, dogs, pugilists, etc.) to fight for sport, prop. in a 'pit' or enclosure 1760. **3.** *fig.* To match, oppose (persons or things). Const. *against*. Often in passive. 1754.

1. They..liued like beasts, and were pitted like beasts, tumbled into the graue 1621. **2.** Two of the gamest little men ever pitted for twenty-five guineas 1814.

II. 1. To make pits in. **a.** To make hollows or depressions in or upon; to mark with small scars or spots, as those left on the skin after small-pox. Usu. in *pass.* Also *absol.* or *intr.* 1487. **b.** To furnish with pits or holes; to dig pits in 1764. **2.** *intr.* for *pass.* To sink in or contract so as to form a pit or hollow. Also, to become marked with pits. 1737.

1. a. A Gentlewoman, whose Nose was pitted with the Small Pox 1661. Great drops of rain began to p. the white dusty roads 1891.

‖ **Pita** (pī·ta). 1698. [Sp., a. Peruvian (Quichua) *pita* fine thread from bast.] **a.** Name for the 'American aloe' (*Agave americana*) and allied species. **b.** The tough fibre obtained from these, used for cordage, etc.; also called *p.-fibre*, *-flax*, *-hemp*, *-thread*. **c.** *P.-wood*, the pith-like wood of *Fourcroya gigantea*.

‖ **Pitahaya** (pītahā·ya). 1783. [Sp., a. Haytian.] Name (in Mexico and South-western U.S.) for the giant cactus (*Cereus giganteus*) or other tall species bearing edible fruit.

Pit-a-pat (pi·tăpæ:t), **pit-pat** (pi·tpæt), *adv.*, *adj.*, *sb.* 1522. [Echoic.] An imitation of the alternated sound made by the strong beating of the heart in excitement or emotion; also of that of light and rapid footsteps, etc. **A.** *adv.* With such a sound or sounds; palpitatingly; patteringly: usu. in phr. *to go pit-a-pat*. **B.** *adj.* Palpitating, pattering 1637. **C.** *sb.* The sound itself, or the action producing it 1582.

A. Her feet went pit-a-pat with joy 1760. **C.** 'Tis but the pit-a-pat of two young hearts DRYDEN. Hence **Pit-a-pat** *v. intr.* to go pit-a-pat, to palpitate, to patter.

Pitch (pitʃ), *sb.*[1] [OE. *pic*, ad. L. *picem*, *pix*.] **1.** A tenacious, resinous substance, of a black or dark-brown colour, hard when cold, a thick viscid semi-liquid when heated; obtained as a residuum from the boiling of tar, also from the distillation of turpentine; used to stop the seams of ships after caulking, to protect wood from moisture, etc. **2.** Applied to various bituminous substances (*mineral p.*); esp. (*Jew's p.*) = ASPHALT 1, BITUMEN 1. late ME. **3.** Improp. applied to the resin or crude turpentine which exudes from pines and firs. late ME.

2. A Vessel of huge bulk,..Smeard round with P. MILT. **3.** *Burgundy* or *white p.*: see BURGUNDY. *Greek p.* = COLOPHONY.

Phrases. *Black* or *dark as p.*; *He that toucheth p. shall be defiled therewith* (Ecclus. xiii. 1), etc.

Comb.: **p.-black** *a.*, of the brownish-black colour of p.; also, intensely black; **-dark** *a.* (two words when predicative), 'as dark as p.', intensely dark; hence **-darkness**; **-ore**, (*a*) a dark-brown ore of copper, containing bitumen; (*b*) = PITTICITE; (*c*) = PITCH-BLENDE.

Pitch (pitʃ), *sb.*[2] 1500. [f. next, but the sense-development is obsc.] **I.** Act or manner of pitching. †**1.** An act of setting, laying, or paying down; *concr.* that which is laid or thrown down (*rare*). **b.** An act of pitching upon a thing or place 1791. **2.** An act of plunging head-foremost; *spec. Naut.* The downward plunge of a ship's head in a seaway 1762. **3.** The act of pitching or throwing underhand. **a.** *Cricket.* The act or manner of delivering the ball in bowling, or the way in which it alights. **b.** *Baseball.* The act of serving the ball to the batter; the right or turn to do this. **c.** *Golf.* The action of 'lofting' the ball. 1833. **II.** Something that is pitched, or used for pitching. **a.** The quantity of hay, etc. thrown up by a pitchfork 1778. **b.** The quantity of some particular commodity pitched or placed in a market for sale 1866. **III.** Place of pitching. **1.** A place at which one stations oneself or is stationed; *esp.* a spot at which a street performer, a bookmaker, a crossing-sweeper, etc., stations himself 1765. **2.** *Agric.* and *Mining* (Cornw.). A definite portion of a field or of a mine, allotted to a particular workman 1805. **3.** *Cricket.* The piece of ground between and about the wickets 1886.

IV. Highest point, height, etc. †**1.** The highest (or extreme) point, top, apex, vertex –1667. †**2.** A projecting point of some part of the body, as the shoulder, the hip –1611. **3.** The extreme point of a cape or headland 1677. **4.** The height to which a falcon, etc., soars before swooping down on its prey. Often in phr. *to fly a p.* 1591. †**b.** Altitude, elevation –1774. **5.** *fig.* Highest or supreme point or degree; acme, climax. Now *rare* exc. in *at the p. of* *one's voice.* 1624. †6. Height, stature –1807. 7. Height of an arched roof, or of any roof or ceiling, above the floor, or of the vertex of an arch above the springing line 1615.

4. And beares his thoughts aboue his Faulcons P. SHAKS. *fig.* Rabelais flew to a higher p., too, than Sterne 1798. 5. When the general hilarity was at its p. 1873.

V. Height in a fig. sense, degree. **1.** Comparative height or intensity of any quality or attribute; degree, elevation, stage, status, level. Almost always used of a high or intense degree. 1568. **2.** *Mus.* That quality of a musical sound which depends on the comparative rapidity of the vibrations producing it; degree of acuteness or graveness of tone. (Sometimes also in ref. to the tone of the voice in speaking.) Also a particular standard of pitch for voices or instruments, as *concert p.* (also *transf.* and *fig.*) 1797. **b.** *transf.* Applied to light, etc., as being analogous to sound 1871.

1. To lowest p. of abject fortune thou art fall'n MILT. 2. Screaming out..in every conceivable key and p. of shrillness 1867. **b.** The p. of the light.. heightens 1871.

VI. Inclination, slope, declivity. Degree of inclination to the horizon, slope; a sloping part or place. *spec.* **a.** A steep place, declivity; a descent, usu. sloping, sometimes perpendicular 1542. **b.** *Mining.* The inclination of a vein of ore or seam of coal from the horizontal 1719. **c.** *Arch.* The inclination of a sloping roof, or of the rafters, to the horizontal; the proportion of the height of a roof to its span 1703. **d.** The slope of a flight of steps; *concr.* a flight of steps 1703. **e.** The setting of a ploughshare for a required depth of penetration. **f.** The rake or inclination of the teeth of a saw. **g.** The inclination of the bit of a plane to the surface that is being planed. 1707. **VII.** *Mech.* The fixed distance between successive points or lines. **a.** The distance between the centres of any two successive teeth of a cog-wheel or pinion, or links of a gear-chain, measured along the *pitch-line* or *pitch-circle* (see *Combs.*); the distance between the successive paddles of a paddle-wheel, measured on the circle passing through their centres. **b.** The distance between the successive convolutions of the thread of a screw, measured in a direction parallel to the axis. **c.** The distance between the centres of successive rivets or stays. 1815.

Comb.: **p.-chain**, a chain consisting of links riveted or bolted together so as to work in the teeth of a toothed wheel; **-circle**, a circular *pitch-line*; **-line**, the imaginary line, usu. a circle, passing through the teeth of a cog-wheel, pinion, rack, etc. so as to touch the corresponding line in another cog-wheel, etc., when the two are geared together; **-point**, the point of contact of the pitch-lines of two cog-wheels, etc. which engage with each other; **-wheel**, a toothed wheel engaging with another.

Pitch (pitʃ), *v.*[1] [ME. *piche(n, picche(n*; pa. t. *pight(e*, pa. pple. *pight*; also later *pitched*. Origin and history obsc.] **I.** To thrust in, fix in; make fast, settle; set, place. †**1.** *trans.* To plant, implant; to fix, stick, fasten. Later, approaching the sense 'to place'. –1775. **2.** To place and make fast with stakes, poles, pegs, etc., as a net or the like. Now *rare.* 1545. **3.** *spec.* To fix and erect (a tent, pavilion, etc.) as a place of lodgement ME. **b.** *absol.* or *intr.* To encamp 1440. **4.** *trans.* To set, plant, place (anything) in a fixed or definite position; to found or set up (a building, pillar, etc.) ME. **b.** *spec.* To set (a stone, etc.) upon end; to set a stone on edge for paving 1623. †**5.** *fig.* To place, implant, plant, set, fix (one's trust, hope, desire, thought, sight, etc.) *in* or *on* some object, or *in* some state –1820. **6.** To place or lay out (wares) in a fixed place for sale; hence, to expose for sale in the market, etc. 1530. **7.** *intr.* (or *refl.*) To place or locate oneself; to take up one's position, settle, alight. Now *rare* or *arch.* 1609. **8.** *trans.* To set, plant, fill, furnish (something) *with* things or persons stuck or placed in or on it; *esp.* to pave (a road, path, etc.) with stones set on end. Also, to form a foundation for a macadamized road with larger stones placed on edge. 1550.

1. Phr. *To p. the wickets* (Cricket), to stick or fix the stumps in the ground and place the bails. 2. The dext'rous Huntsman..pitches Toils to stop the Flight DRYDEN. 3. The tents were pitched where I chose to rest JOHNSON. Phr. *To p. a camp, a caravan*, etc. **b.** To choose a commodious place to p. in HOBBES. 4. Their mightier Empire, there, the middle English pight DRAYTON. 6. †*P. and pay* (absol. or intr.), ? to pay down at once; The word is, P. and pay: trust none SHAKS. 8. He wore a gown of purple velvet, pight with pieces of gold FULLER. Paved with bricks or pitched with pebble 1811

II. To set in order, arrange; to fix the order, position, rate, price, or pitch of. **1.** *trans.* To set in order for fighting, to arrange (a battle, field of battle); to set in array. *Obs.* exc. in PITCHED *ppl. a.* (q.v.). 1470. **2.** To pit (one person) *against* another (*rare*) 1801. †**3.** To determine (something that is to be); to fix, settle –1649. †**4.** To fix, settle, or place in thought; to determine (an existing fact); to ascertain; to come to a conclusion about –1687. **5.** To set at a particular pitch or degree (high, low, etc.). In mod. use mostly *fig.* To set in a particular 'key', or style of expression, feeling, etc. 1633. **b.** *Mus.* To determine the pitch of (a tune, the voice, an instrument) 1674. **6.** *intr.* with *on* or *upon*: To fix upon, decide upon; to select, choose; in mod. use, to select more or less casually; to let one's choice fall *upon* 1628.

1. Our battle, then, in martial manner pitch'd MARLOWE. 4. First they p. their conclusion, and then hunt about for premises to make it good 1640. 5. His conversation was pitched in a minor key 1874. 6. The place which he pitched upon for his trading post 1836.

III. To cast or throw in particular ways. **1.** *trans.* To cast, throw, or fling forward; to hurl; to throw (a thing) underhand so that it may fall and rest on a particular spot. Also *absol.* late ME. **b.** To throw (sheaves, hay, etc.) with a pitchfork. Often *absol.* late ME. **c.** In *Baseball*, etc.: To deliver or serve (the ball) to the batter. In various games, to throw a flat object towards a mark. Also *absol.* 1773. **d.** *slang.* To utter, tell 1867. **2.** *intr.* for *pass.* To fall headlong heavily, or strike forcibly against something, by being thrown ME. **3.** *intr.* Of a ship: To plunge with the head into the trough of the sea; hence, to rise and fall alternately at bow and stern; to plunge in a longitudinal direction (as dist. from *rolling*) 1687. **b.** *trans.* To cast (*away, overboard*, etc.) by this movement 1727. **c.** *intr.* Of a person or animal: To plunge forward like a pitching ship 1849.

1. Mrs Villiers, in galloping to cover the other day ..was pitched off 1836. **d.** If he had had the sense to..p. them a tale, he might have got off 1867. 2. On his head unhappily he pight SPENSER.

IV. *intr.* To incline forwards and downwards; to dip. Now only in *Mining*, said of a vein of ore or other stratum. 1519. **b.** *intr.* To settle down, as a swelling or loose soil; *fig.* to lose flesh (*dial.*) 1794. **V.** with *adv.* or *prep.* **a.** *P. in*: to set to work vigorously. *colloq.* (chiefly *U.S.*) 1847. **b.** *P. into*: to attack forcibly (with blows, etc., or with words); to reprimand (*colloq.*) 1843. **VI.** The verb-stem in comb. forming *sbs.*, in names of games, in which coins, etc., are thrown at a mark, or into a hole or vessel; as PITCH-AND-TOSS, PITCH-FARTHING, etc.

Pitch (pitʃ), *v.*[2] [OE. *(ge)pician*, f. *pic* PITCH *sb.*[1]] *trans.* To cover, coat, or smear with pitch; to brand (a sheep, etc.) with pitch; to stain with pitch.

Pi·tch-and-to·ss. 1810. [From name of the two actions.] A game of combined skill and chance.

Each player pitches a coin at a mark; the one whose coin lies nearest to the mark then tosses all the coins and keeps those that turn up 'head'; the one whose coin lay next in order does the same with the remaining ones, and so on, till none are left.

Pitch-blende (pi·tʃblend). 1770. [ad. G. *pechblende*, f. *pech* PITCH *sb.*[1]; see BLENDE.] *Min.* Native oxide of uranium, found in blackish pitch-like masses, more rarely crystalline; URANINITE.

Pi·tch-brand. 1631. [f. PITCH *sb.*[1] + BRAND *sb.*] A mark of ownership made upon a sheep, etc.; also *fig.* a distinctive evil mark or characteristic.

Pitched (pitʃt), †**pight** (pəit), *ppl. a.* ME. [pa. pple. of PITCH *v.*[1] The form *pight* has been obs. since *c* 1600.] †**1.** Fixed in the ground, staked; set in anything; set with jewels –1615. **2.** Set in orderly array for fighting; said of a battle of which the plans and ground have been chosen and fixed beforehand; a regular battle as dist. from a skirmish, etc.; also *pitched field* 1549. **3.** In other senses of PITCH *v.*[1] 1605. **4.** [Partly f. PITCH *sb.*[2]] Having a (high, low, etc.) pitch, as a roof, building, plough 1615. **b.** Having a specified musical pitch 1622.

Pitcher[1] (pi·tʃəɹ). [ME. *picher, pecher*, a. OF. *pichier, picier, picher* (mod.F. *pichet*):—pop. L. **piccarium*, in med.L. *picarium, bicarium*; see BEAKER.] **1.** A large vessel usu. of earthenware, with a handle (or two ears) and usu. a lip, for holding liquids. **2.** *Bot.* A leaf, or part of one, modified into the form of a pitcher (see PITCHER-PLANT): = ASCIDIUM 2. 1797.

1. Prov. *Pitchers have ears* (with pun on EAR): used as a warning that one may be overheard; in *little pitchers have long* or *wide ears* (etc.) said in ref. to children. *The p. goes often to the well, but is broken at last* (etc.): said of long-continued success (or impunity), ending at length in failure (or punishment). Hence **Pi·tcherful**, the quantity that fills a p.

Pitcher[2] (pi·tʃəɹ). 1707. [f. PITCH *v.*[1] + -ER[1].] **1.** One who pitches anything; e. g. in *Harvesting*, one who pitches the hay or sheaves to the loader on a cart or rick 1722. **b.** A street vendor who pitches a stall at a definite place or occupies a 'pitch' 1896. **2.** A player who pitches or delivers a ball, *esp.* in *Baseball* 1870. **3.** Something pitched, or used for pitching; *esp.* a stone used for paving; the brick-shaped granite 'setts' used for crossings, etc. 1707.

Pi·tcher-plant. 1835. [f. PITCHER[1] + PLANT *sb.*[1]] Name for several plants, which have the leaves, or some of them, modified into the form of a pitcher, often containing a liquid secretion by means of which insects are captured and assimilated by the plant; *esp.* the E. Indian genus *Nepenthes*, and the N. American genus *Sarracenia*.

Pi·tch-fa·rthing. 1742. [PITCH *v.*[1] III. 1.] = *chuck-farthing* (CHUCK *v.*[2]) q. v.

Pitchfork (pi·tʃfǫɹk), *sb.*[1] 1452. [Also, earlier, *pickfork*; app. orig. f. PICK *sb.*[1] and subseq. assoc. w. PITCH *v.*[1]] A long-handled fork with two sharp prongs for lifting and pitching hay, straw, or sheaves.

Pi·tchfork, *sb.*[2] 1881. [f. PITCH *sb.*[2] V. 2 + FORK *sb.*, after PITCH-PIPE.] A tuning-fork for setting the pitch of a tune or instrument.

Pi·tchfork, *v.* 1837. [f. PITCHFORK *sb.*[1]] **1.** *trans.* To cast with, or as with, a pitchfork; to pitch forcibly or roughly. **b.** *fig.*; *esp.* to thrust (a person) forcibly or unsuitably into some position or office 1844. **2.** To stab or attack with a pitchfork 1854.

1. **b.** Whether he was pitchforked into the service or rose meritoriously is now a matter of indifference 1863.

Pitching (pi·tʃiŋ), *vbl. sb.* late ME. [f. PITCH *v.*[1] + -ING[1].] **1.** The action of PITCH *v.*[1] **2.** *spec.* The action of setting stones in paving; also, the facing of a bank or slope with stones set on edge close together, as a protection against waves or currents 1703. **b.** *concr.* Pavement composed of cobbles or granite 'setts' firmly set up; also, a facing of stone on a bank or slope 1693. **c.** The foundation of a macadamized road made of stones 6 or 8 inches deep, laid on edge so as to form an arched support for the broken metalling 1830. **3.** The action of throwing, hurling, or lofting something; *esp.* a ball in baseball, golf, etc. 1652.

Comb. **p.-piece**, a piece of timber at the top of a wooden staircase, supporting the 'carriage' or framework (correlative to the *apron-piece* at the bottom).

Pitch-ore: see PITCH *sb.*[1]

Pitch-pine. 1754. [f. PITCH *sb.*[1] + PINE *sb.*[2]] Name of several species of pine with specially resinous wood, or from which pitch or turpentine is obtained; esp. *Pinus rigida* of N. America.

Pi·tch-pipe. 1711. [f. PITCH *sb.*[2] V. 2 + PIPE *sb.*[1]] A small musical pipe, blown by the mouth (either a flue-pipe or a reed-pipe), used to set the pitch for singing or tuning an instrument.

Pitchstone (pi·tʃstōᵘn). 1784. [f. PITCH *sb.*[1] + STONE *sb.*, tr. G. *pechstein.*] An old volcanic rock; obsidian or other rock looking like hardened pitch.

Pitchwork (pi·tʃwɔːk). 1858. [f. PITCH *sb.*²] Mining work in which the workmen are paid by receiving a fixed proportion of the output.

Pitchy (pi·tʃi), *a.* (*adv.*) 1513. [f. PITCH *sb.*¹ + -Y ¹.] **1.** Full of pitch; bituminous, resinous; coated, smeared, or soiled with pitch; *fig.* sticky like pitch, thievish. **2.** Like pitch; tenacious, viscid; bituminous 1552. **3.** *Nat. Hist.*, etc. Of the colour of pitch; dark-brown inclining to black. Hence *pitchy-black.* 1828. **4.** *fig.* 'As black as pitch'; pitch-dark; of darkness, Intense, thick 1586. **b.** Morally 'black'; grossly wicked 1612.

4. The pitchie night had bereft vs of the conduct of our eyes 1615. **b.** The p. taint of general vice CRABBE. Hence **Pi·tchiness,** intense darkness or blackness.

Pit-coal. Now *rare* or *arch.* 1483. [f. PIT *sb.* + COAL.] Coal obtained from pits or mines (as dist. from *charcoal*), now called simply *coal* (COAL *sb.* 4).

Piteous (pi·tiəs), *a.* [ME. *pytos, pitous,* a. OF. *pitos, piteus,* AF. *pitous* :—L. **pietosus,* f. *pietatem* PIETY.] †**1.** Full of piety; godly, devout -1570. **2.** = PITIFUL 2. ME. **3.** = PITIFUL 3. ME. **b.** as *adv.* Piteously. late ME.

1. The Lord knew for to delyuere pitouse men of temptacioun WYCLIF 2 *Pet.* ii. 9. **2.** He hath with a p. eye Beheld us in our misery MILT. **3.** A p. thinge was it to se COVERDALE 2 *Macc.* vi. 9. Hence **Pi·te·ous·ly** *adv.*, **-ness.**

Pitfall (pi·tfǭl). late ME. [app. f. PIT *sb.* + FALL *sb.*², OE. *fealle* a falling trap-door, a trap. Now usu. taken as a 'pit into which one may fall'.] †**1.** A trap for birds in which a trap-door or the like falls over a cavity or hollow -1706. **2.** A concealed pit into which animals or men may fall and be captured. late ME. **3.** *fig.* A 'trap' for the unsuspecting or unwary; any hidden danger or error into which a person may fall unawares 1586.

3. The snares and pitfalls of the law 1827.

Pith (piþ), *sb.* [OE. *piþa* pith of a tree or vegetable, etc. :—WGer. **piþon-,* **pippon-,* represented only in the LG. group.] **1.** The central column of spongy cellular tissue in the stems and branches of dicotyledonous plants; the medulla; applied also to the internal tissue of other stems, and to that lining the rind in certain fruits (e.g. the orange). **2.** The spinal cord 1594. **3.** Applied to other substances analogous to the pith of a tree; e.g. the core of various epidermal appendages, as feathers, horn, and hair. late ME. **4.** *fig.* The central or inward part; hence, the essential or vital part (*of* anything); spirit, essence. So *p. and marrow.* OE. **5.** Physical strength or force; vigour; mettle, 'backbone' ME. **b.** Force, energy (of words, speech, etc.) 1526. †**6.** Substance, substantial quality (of words, writings, etc.) -1590. **7.** Importance, gravity, weight 1602.

4. The very p. and marrow of Mr. Wesley's views 1831. **5.** A man of Sampsons p. 1601. **b.** Cool vigour and laconic p. CARLYLE. **6.** It hath in it some p. 1529. **7.** Enterprizes of great p. and moment SHAKS.

attrib. and *Comb.*, as **p. hat, helmet,** a helmet-shaped sun-hat made of the dried p. of the Indian Solah or Spongewood of Bengal (*Æschynomene aspera*); **-paper,** a paper made from the p. of various plants; **-plant,** the Chinese rice-paper tree (*Aralia* or *Fatsia papyrifera*). Hence **Pi·thless** *a.* having no p.

Pith (piþ), *v.* 1805. [f. prec. sb.] *trans.* To pierce or sever the pith or spinal cord of (an animal), so as to kill it or render it insensible; *spec.* to slaughter (cattle) in this way.

Pithecanthrope (piþĭkæ·nþrōᵘp). Also **Pithecanthropos, -us.** 1876. [f. Gr. πίθηκος ape + ἄνθρωπος man.] An ape-man or man-like ape; Haeckel's name for a hypothetical link between the Apes and Man.

Pithecian (piþī·siăn), *a.* 1890. [ad. F. *pithécien,* f. Gr. πίθηκος ape; see -IAN.] *Zool.* Of or pertaining to *Pithecia,* the typical genus of the *Pitheciinæ,* a subfamily of the *Cabidæ,* S. Amer. monkeys commonly called Sakis.

Pithecoid (piþī·koid), *a.* (*sb.*) 1861. [ad. F. *pithécoïde,* f. Gr. πίθηκος ape; see -OID.] Resembling in form or pertaining to the apes, esp. the higher or anthropoid apes; simian, ape-like. Also *sb.*

Pi·t-hole. 1601. A hole forming a pit; a pit-like hollow or cavity; *spec.* a grave.

Pithy (pi·þi), *a.* ME. [f. PITH *sb.* + -Y ¹.] **1.** Consisting or of the nature of pith; abounding in pith 1562. **2.** *fig.* Full of strength; vigorous; of liquor, containing much alcohol. Now *dial.* or *Obs.* ME. **3.** Full of substance or significance; solid; *esp.* of speech, etc.: Containing much matter in few words; condensed; sententious; terse. (Now the prevailing sense.) 1529. **b.** *transf.* of a speaker or writer 1548.

1. The p. bunch of unripe nuts 1821. **3.** Very piththie is this pronown I 1571. He preached..a plain, short, p. sermon 1893. **b.** In all these particulars [he] was very short but p. ADDISON. Hence **Pi·thily** *adv.* **Pi·thiness.**

Pitiable (pi·tiăb'l), *a.* [ME. a. OF. *piteable, pitiable, pitoiable* (mod.F. *pitoyable*) pitiable (in active and passive sense), f. OF. *piteer, pitier, pitoyer* to PITY; see -ABLE.] **1.** = PITIFUL 3. 1456. **2.** = PITIFUL 4. 1789.

1. Theese pytoyable thynges thus y-happed CAXTON. **2.** The p. display of short-sighted greed over the Factory Bill 1891. Hence **Pi·tiableness. Pi·tiably** *adv.*

Pitiful (pi·tiful), *a.* 1449. [f. PITY *sb.* + -FUL.] †**1.** Pious (*rare*) -1570. **2.** Full of or characterized by pity; compassionate, tender 1491. **3.** Exciting or apt to excite pity; deplorable, lamentable 1450. †**b.** as *adv.* Pitifully -1599. **4.** To be pitied for its littleness or meanness; despicable, contemptible 1582.

2. The lorde is very pitifull and mercifull TINDALE *Jas.* v. 11. **3.** The p. fate of his friend 1871. **4.** A p. copy of verses PEPYS. Hence **Pi·tiful-ly** *adv.*, **-ness.**

Pitiless (pi·tilės), *a.* late ME. [-LESS.] Without pity or compassion; merciless.

The pelting of this pittilesse storme SHAKS. Hence **Pi·tiless-ly** *adv.*, **-ness.**

Pitman (pi·tmæn). 1609. [f. PIT *sb.* + MAN *sb.*] †**1.** The digger of a common grave. J. DAVIES. **2.** A man who works in a pit or mine; *esp.* a collier 1761. **3.** A pit-sawyer 1703. **4.** (*transf.* from 3.) In machinery, a connecting-rod. Chiefly *U.S.* 1846.

‖**Piton** (pītǭ·n). 1920. [Fr.] *Mountaineering.* A peg or cramp stuck into a rock-face.

Pitpan (pi·tpæn). 1798. [Mosquito.] = DUG-OUT *sb.* 1, used in Central America.

Pit-pat: see PIT-A-PAT.

‖**Pitta** (pi·tă). 1840. [mod.L., a. Telugu *piṭṭa* anything small, a pet.] *Ornith.* A family of passerine birds, type of the family *Pittidæ,* the Ant-thrushes of the Old World, species of which inhabit China, India, and Australia, and one, *P. angolensis,* the W. Coast of Africa.

Pittacal (pi·tăkæl). 1835. [a. G., f. Gr. πίττα pitch + καλός beautiful.] *Chem.* A dark-blue solid substance obtained from the high-boiling portions of wood-tar.

Pittance (pi·tăns). [ME. *pita(u)nce,* a. OF. *pitance, -ence,* app. the same word as *pitance, pietance* pity, ad. L. **pietantia,* deriv. of *pietas* (see PIETY).] **1.** A pious donation or bequest to a religious house or order, to provide extra food, etc., on particular occasions; hence, the allowance or dole itself. Now only *Hist.* **b.** An alms, dole. late ME. **2.** A small allowance of food and drink; scanty rations or diet. Now *rare.* late ME. **b.** A (bare) allowance, remuneration, or stipend, by way of livelihood 1714. **3.** A (small or sparing) allowance, share, or allotment (*of* anything) 1616. **b.** A small proportion of a whole 1561.

1. **b.** Their usual requests for pittances of food and clothing 1838. **2. b.** Yon cottager,..Just earns a scanty p. COWPER. **3.** Her small p. of wages FIELDING. **b.** A small p. of Reason and Truth LOCKE.

Pitted (pi·tėd), *ppl. a.* OE. [f. PIT *v.* + -ED ¹; and partly f. PIT *sb.* + -ED ².] **1.** Marked or spotted with pits; *spec.* in *Bot.* of cells, vessels, etc. (see PIT *sb.*). Also, marked *with* small-pox. **2.** Placed or planted in a pit 1799.

Pitter (pi·təɹ), *v. dial* 1592. [Echoic.] *intr.* To make a rapid repetition of a sound in quality approaching short *i,* as in the sound made by the grasshopper, or by a thin stream of water running over stones.

Pi·tter-pa·tter, *sb.* (*adv.*) late ME. [Redupl. from PATTER *v.*¹ and ².] †**1.** Pattering repetition -1561. **2.** An imitation of a rapid alternation of light beating sounds, as those made by rain, light footfalls, etc. **a.** orig. as *adv.* 1679. **b.** as *sb.* A designation of such a sound 1863.

Pitticite (pi·tisəit). 1826. [ad. G. *pittizit,* f. Gr. πίττα pitch: see -IC and -ITE ¹.] *Min.* Hydrous sulpharsenate of iron having a vitreous or greasy lustre, occurring in yellowish or reddish-brown, red, and white reniform masses. Also called *pitchy iron ore.*

Pittite¹ (pi·təit). 1808. [See -ITE ¹ 1.] An adherent of the English statesman William Pitt (1759–1806), or of his policy. So **Pi·ttism,** Pitt's policy.

Pittite² (pi·təit). 1807. [f. PIT *sb.* + -ITE ¹.] *colloq.* One who occupies a seat in the pit of a theatre.

‖**Pituita** (pitiu,əi·tă). 1699. [L.] *Physiol.* The secretion of the mucous membrane; phlegm, mucus. Also *attrib.* = next.

Pituitary (pitiū·itări), *a.* 1615. [ad. L. *pituitarius,* f. *pituita;* see prec.] *Physiol.* etc. Of, pertaining to, or secreting pituita or phlegm; mucous. **b.** *absol.* or as *sb.* (*a*) = p. membrane; (*b*) = p. gland 1845.

P. body, gland, a small bilobed ductless gland attached to the infundibulum at the base of the brain.

Pituitous (pitiū·itəs), *a.* 1607. [ad. L. *pituitosus;* see -OUS.] Of, pertaining to, consisting of, or of the nature of pituita or mucus; of diseases, etc.: Characterized or caused by excess of mucus. **b.** = PHLEGMATIC 1658.

‖**Pituri** (pi·tiŭri). 1863. Native name of an Australian shrub, *Duboisia Hopwoodii,* the leaves, etc. of which are used as a narcotic.

Pity (pi·ti), *sb.* [ME. *pite,* a. OF. *pite, pitet,* mod.F. *pitié,* ad. L. *pietatem, pietas* PIETY. In ME. both *pite* and *piete* are found first in the sense 'compassion', later both are found also in the sense 'piety'; they were not completely differentiated before 1600.] †**1.** The quality of being pitiful; clemency, mercy, mildness, tenderness -1613. **2.** A feeling of tenderness aroused by the suffering or misfortune of another, and prompting a desire for its relief; compassion, sympathy ME. **3.** *transf.* A ground or cause for pity; a regrettable fact or circumstance; a thing to be sorry for. In early use without *a.* late ME. **b.** Idiomatically with *of* (= in respect of). *Obs.* or *arch.* 1450. †**4.** Remorse. *To have p.,* to repent. -1591.

2. Griefe, for the Calamity of another, is Pitty HOBBES. *To have* or *take p.,* prop. to conceive or feel p.; usu. to exercise p., to be compassionate. Const. *on, upon. For pity's sake,* exclam. of entreaty. **3.** Phr. *It is, was, would be* (*a*) *p., the more* (*is*) *the p., a thousand pities, a great p.,* etc. What a p. it is I was not born in the golden age of Louis the Fourteenth H. WALPOLE. It would be a p. to alter it 1880. **b.** But yet the pitty of it, Iago! SHAKS.

Pity (pi·ti), *v.* 1515. [f. prec. sb.] **1.** *trans.* To feel pity for; to be sorry for. (Sometimes implying slight contempt.) 1529. †**2.** To move to pity; to grieve. Usu. impersonal. -1835. †**3.** *intr.* (or *trans.* with *inf.* or *obj. cl.*) To be moved to pity; to grieve -1670.

1. Like as a father pitieth his children, so the Lord pitieth them that feare him *Ps.* ciii. 13. **2.** Thy seruantes haue a loue to hir stones, and it pitieth them to se her in the dust COVERDALE *Ps.* ci[i]. 14. **3.** I pitie to see you go from suche good beginnynges COVERDALE. Hence **Pi·tier,** one who pities. **Pi·tying** *ppl. a.* that pities; compassionate. (In mod. use occas., Feeling slight contempt.) **Pi·tyingly** *adv.*

‖**Pityriasis** (pitirəi·ăsis). 1693. [mod.L., a. Gr. πιτυρίασις scurf, f. πίτυρον bran.] *Path.* A condition of the skin characterized by the formation and falling off of irregular patches of small bran-like scales, without inflammation; the (diseased) formation of dandruff or scurf.

Pivot (pi·vət), *sb.* 1611. [a. F., = pivot, hinge. Origin unkn.] **1.** A short shaft or pin, forming the fulcrum and centre on which something turns or oscillates; a pintle, gudgeon. **2.** *Mil.* The officer or man on whom a body of troops wheels; also that flank by which the alignment is corrected 1796. **3.** *fig.* That on which anything turns; a cardinal or central point 1813. **4.** *attrib.* or *adj.* That is the pivot; cardinal; pivotal 1861.

3. The paper-money is the p., on which their all turns COBBETT.

Comb.: **p.-bridge,** a swing-bridge pivoted on a central pier; **-broach, -drill,** watchmakers' tools; **-gun,** a gun which may be turned freely on a p., to alter the direction.

Pi·vot, *v.* 1841. [a. F. *pivoter*, f. *pivot*; see prec.] **1.** *trans.* To furnish with, mount on, or attach by means of, a pivot or pivots. (Chiefly in *pass.*) Also *fig.* 1851. **2.** *intr.* To turn as on a pivot; to hinge; in *Mil.* to swing round a point as centre. Chiefly *fig.* 1841.

Pivotal (pi·vətăl), *a.* 1844. [f. PIVOT *sb.* + -AL.] Of, pertaining to, of the nature of, or constituting a pivot; central, cardinal, vital.

To have for p. motive nothing but the fear of death from hunger 1844. Hence **Pi·votally** *adv.* as on a pivot.

Pix: see PYX.

Pixy, pixie (pi·ksi). Also *w. dial.* **pisky.** 1630. [Origin obsc.] A supposed supernatural being akin to a fairy.

attrib. and *Comb.*: **p.-ring** = FAIRY-RING; **p. stool,** a toadstool or mushroom.

Pixy-led, *a.* 1659. Led astray by pixies; bewildered.

‖ **Pizzicato** (pittsīkā·to), *a.*, *adv.*, *sb.* 1845. [It., f. *pizzicare* to pinch, twang, etc.] *Mus.* **A.** *adj.* and *adv.* Said of a note or passage played on a violin, etc. by plucking the string with the finger instead of using the bow. (Abbrev. *pizz.*) 1880. **B.** *sb.* A note or passage so played.

Pizzle (pi·z'l). Now *dial.* or *vulgar.* 1523. [= Flem. *pezel*, LG. *pesel*, dim. of OLG. **pisa* sinew.] The penis of an animal; often that of a bull, used as a flogging instrument.

Placable (plæ·kab'l, plē¹·kăb'l), *a.* [Late ME. a. OF., ad. L. *placabilis*; see -ABLE.] †**1.** Pleasing, agreeable -1542. **2.** Capable of being, or easy to be, pacified; gentle, forgiving 1586. ¶ **3.** Peaceable, quiet. (*Catachrestic.*) 1611.

2. Methought I saw him p. and mild MILT. Hence **Pla·cableness. Pla·cably** *adv.*

Placard (plæ·kā̆ɹd), *sb.* 1481. [a. OF. *plackart*, *placard*, *-art*, etc., mod.F. *placard*, f. OF. *plaquier* (mod.F. *plaquer*) to plate, lay flat, plaster, etc.; see -ARD.] **I.** An official or public document. **1.** A formal document (orig.) authenticated by a thin seal affixed to its surface; an edict, ordinance, proclamation, official announcement. *Obs.* exc. *Hist.* 1482. **b.** esp. in 17th c., A decree or ordinance of the States General or other competent authority in the Netherlands. In this sense often spelt *placaert*, *placaet*, *placaat*, after Du. *Hist.* 1589. **2.** A notice, or other document, written or printed on one side of a single sheet, to be posted up, or otherwise publicly displayed; a bill, a poster 1560.

1. All Placarts or Edicts are publish'd in his name 1645.

II. †**a.** A piece of armour; a breast- or back-plate; esp. an additional plate of steel, iron, etc., worn over or under the cuirass -1826. †**b.** An article of dress, sometimes richly embroidered, app. worn by both sexes in the 15th and 16th c., beneath a coat or gown -1548.

Placard (plæ·kā̆ɹd), *v.* 1813. [f. prec. sb.] **1.** *trans.* To affix or set up placards on or in (a wall, window, town, etc.). **2.** To make public, advertise (something) by means of placards; to display (a poster, notice, etc.) as a placard 1818.

2. Bills..were placarded on all the walls DICKENS.

Placate (plăkē¹·t, pleikē¹·t), *v.* 1678. [f. L. *placat-*, *placare*; see -ATE [3].] *trans.* To render friendly; to pacify, conciliate; to propitiate.

A victory so complete..failed to p. the indignant young actress 1894. Hence **Placa·tion,** the action of placating; conciliation, propitiation. **Placatory** (plæ·kătəri, plē¹·k-) *a.* propitiatory.

Pla·ccate. *Obs.* exc. *Hist.* 1588. [app. a var. of PLACARD (in sense II. a.). See also PLACKET.] = PLACARD *sb.* II. a. Also, a leather doublet lined with strips of steel, worn under the outer armour 1632.

Place (plē¹s), *sb.* [ME. a. F. :—late L. **plattia*, for class. L. *platea* open space, ad. Gr. πλατεῖα (ὁδός) broad street.] **I.** An open space in a city; a square, a market-place. †**a.** Used in OE. as tr. L. *platea* (Vulg.). **b.** In mod. use, forming the second element in the name of a group of houses in a town or city, now or formerly possessing some of the characters of a square, chiefly that of not being properly a street 1585. **II.** A material space. **1.** Space; extension in two (or three) directions; 'room' (*arch.*) ME. **b.** *gen.* Space, extension. (Chiefly *rhet.*, and opp. to *time.*) 1631. **2.** A particular part of space, of definite situation. (= L. *locus.*) Sometimes applied to a part of the earth's surface. ME. **b.** The portion of space actually occupied by a person or thing; locality; situation 1570. †**c.** Short for 'place of battle', 'field' -1705. **3. a.** A general designation for a city, town, village, hamlet, etc. ME. **b.** A residence, dwelling, house; a seat, mansion; *spec.* a manor-house; a country-house with its surroundings ME. †**c.** A fortress, citadel, 'strong place' -1819. **d.** A building, apartment, or spot devoted to a specified purpose; as *a place of amusement*, etc. 1530. **4.** A particular part or spot in a body or surface. late ME. **5.** A particular part, page, etc. in a book or writing ME. †**b.** A text, extract -1743. †**c.** A subject, a topic; esp. in *Logic* and *Rhet.* = LOCUS *sb.* 2. -1697. **6.** In techn. uses: **a.** *Astron.* The apparent position of a heavenly body on the celestial sphere 1669. **b.** *Falconry.* The point or pitch attained by a falcon, etc., before swooping down on its quarry. *Obs.* (or *arch.* after Shaks.) 1605. **c.** *Mining.* A drift or level driven from side to side of a wide lode as a beginning of a slide.

II. 1. Men .. calling 'Place! Place!' to clear the way for their master 1852. Phr. *Give p.*: see Phrases. **b.** He pass'd the flaming bounds of P. and Time GRAY. **2.** I haue no p. to fle vnto COVERDALE *Ps.* cxli. 4. **b.** We say it hath kept the same P.:.. it hath changed its P. LOCKE. **3.** Schools at Tours and other places in France 1843. **b.** Mr. Rodney's p. in Hampshire 1902. **d.** The Coffee-houses have ever since been my chief Places of Resort ADDISON. *Another p.*, in House of Commons phraseology, the other house, the House of Lords. *P. of worship*: see Phrases. **4.** Who..would..Kiss the p. to make it well? 1804. **5.** They shut up her lesson-books and lost her p. 1861. **6. b.** A Faulcon towring in her pride of p. SHAKS.

III. Position in some scale, order, or series. **1.** Position or standing in the social or any scale; rank, station, whether high or low. **b.** *absol.* High rank or position; dignity ME. **c.** *Racing.* A position among the placed competitors; see PLACE *v.* 5 b. 1885. **2.** *Arith.* The position of a figure in a series, in decimal or similar notation, as indicating its value or denomination; in *pl.* with numeral, used to express the number of figures, esp. after the decimal point in a decimal fraction 1542. **3.** A step or point in the order of progression; as *in the first* (*next*, *last*) *p.*, etc. 1639.

1. As an English critic of English literature, his p. is in the front rank 1893. **2.** He also calculated the ratio to 55 decimal places 1841.

IV. Position or situation with ref. to its occupation or occupant. **1.** A proper, appropriate, or natural place (for the person or thing in question to be in or occupy). late ME. **b.** *fig.* A fitting time; occasion, opportunity. late ME. **c.** *fig.* 'Room'; reasonable ground 1638. **d.** = PLACE-KICK. **2.** The space which one person occupies by usage, allotment, or right; a seat or accommodation in a public building, conveyance, or the like, a seat at table. late ME. **b.** With *possessive* or *of*: The space previously or customarily occupied by some other person or thing; room; stead 1450. **3.** An office, employment, situation; occas. *spec.* a government appointment 1558. **b.** Without *a* or *pl.*: Official position, esp. of a minister of state 1568. **c.** The duties of any office or position; (one's) duty or business 1652.

1. Heere's no p. for you maids SHAKS. **c.** In the Sacred Writings there's no p. for Conjectures or Emendations 1721. **2.** After having fee'd very high for places at Mrs. Siddons's benefit 1806. **b.** O God, that Somerset..were in Talbots p. SHAKS. Phr. *In the p. of*, instead of, in substitution for. *To take the p. of*, to be substituted for. **3.** Couldn't let you do it, sir. Much as my place 's worth 1871. **b.** P. shows the man 1702.

Phrases. *With other sbs. **Place of arms** [ad. F. *place d'armes*]. **a.** An open space for the assembling of troops. **b.** A strongly fortified city or a fortress, used as an arsenal or magazine, or as a place of retreat. **P. of worship.** A place where religious worship is performed; *spec.* a building (or part of one) appropriated to assemblies or meetings for religious worship 1689. **With preps. **From p. to p.** From one p. to another, and so on in succession.* **In p.** †**a.** On the spot. So *upon the p.* **b.** In its original or proper position; in position; *in situ*; *spec.* in *Geol.*; in *Mining*, applied to a vein or lode situated between fixed rocks. **c.** *fig.* In his or its proper or fitting position; in one's element, at home; timely. **d.** *In* (some one's) *p.*: situated as (he) is. **Out of p.** Not situated in the natural or appropriate position; misplaced; *fig.* unsuitable, unseasonable. ***With verbs. **Find p.** To find room to dwell or exist, to have being (*in* something). **Give p.** To make room, get out of the way; to give way *to*; to be succeeded by. *arch.* exc. *fig.* **Have p.** To have room to exist; to exist; to be situated. **Take p. a.** To take effect; to be accomplished or realized. *Obs.* or *arch.* †**b.** To find acceptance. †**c.** To take precedence *of.* †**d.** To be present. **e.** To come into existence, happen; to occur (in place or time).

attrib. and *Comb.*, as *p.-name*; *p.-monger*; **p. act,** the Act of Parliament excluding persons holding office under the Crown from sitting in the House of Commons; **p. betting,** backing a horse, etc. for a p.; **p. horse,** one which comes in among those placed; see PLACE *v.* 5 b. See also Main words.

Place (plē¹s), *v.* *Pa. t.* and *pple.* **placed** (plē¹st). 1548. [f. prec.] **1.** *trans.* To put or set in a particular place, position, or situation; *fig.* to set in some condition or relation to other things. Often a mere synonym of *put*, *set*. 1551. **b.** To put or set (a number of things) in their proper places; to arrange 1548. **2.** To appoint (a person) to a place; *spec.* to induct to a pastorate 1550. **b.** To find a place or situation for; to settle 1596. **3.** *spec.* **a.** To put out (money, funds) at interest. Often with *out*. **b.** To put (an order for goods) into the hands of a (selected) person or firm. **c.** To dispose of to a customer. **d.** To arrange for the performance or publication of (a play, book, etc.). 1700. **4.** *fig.* To fix, repose (faith, confidence, etc.) *in* or *on* a particular person or thing 1621. **5.** To assign a place to; to locate; to rank, class; to date 1597. **b.** *Racing.* To state the position of (a horse, etc., usu. the first three only) among the competitors when passing the winning post; *to be placed*, to obtain a place among the first three 1831. **c.** To identify fully; to determine who (or what) a particular person (or thing) is; to assign to a class (orig. *U.S.*) 1855. **6.** To ascribe; to hold (a quality, etc.) to reside or consist *in* something; †to 'put down' *to* 1608. **7.** *Rugby Football.* To get (a goal) from a place-kick 1890.

1. He used to p. the patient under a pump 1800. **b.** (Stage direction) Places chairs SHERIDAN. **3. b.** Many large orders have already been placed for next season 1889. **4.** No confidence could be placed in any of the twelve Judges MACAULAY. **6.** They did not p. honour or honesty simply in victory 1631.

‖ **Placebo** (plăsī·bo). *Pl.* **-os, -oes.** ME. [a. L., (I shall be pleasing or acceptable) 1st sing. fut. ind. of *placere* to please.] **1.** *Eccl.* In the Latin rite: Vespers for the Dead, the first antiphon of which is *Placebo Domino* [etc.], Ps. cxiv. 9, Vulg. †**2.** A flatterer, sycophant -1651. **3.** *Med.* A medicine given more to please than to benefit the patient 1811.

1. Phr. *To sing* (*a*) *p.*, etc., to be servile or time-serving.

Pla·ce-brick. 1703. *orig.* A brick made of soft clay, and laid on a prepared 'place' to harden before being burnt; now, a brick which has been imperfectly burnt, through being on the windward side of the kiln or clamp.

Pla·ce-ho·lder. 1818. One who holds office under the government.

Pla·ce-hu·nter. 1713. One who seeks persistently for a post in the public service. (With unfavourable connotation.) So **Pla·ce-hunting** *sb.* and *a.*

Pla·ce-kick, *sb.* 1845. [f. PLACE *sb.* + KICK *sb.*[1]] *Rugby Football.* A kick made by a player when the ball is previously placed on the ground for that purpose by another player. So **Pla·ce-kick** *v.*

Placeless (plē¹·slės), *a.* 1598. [-LESS.] **1.** Not confined to place; not bounded or defined. **2.** Having no stated place or locality 1644. **3.** Out of office or employment 1831.

Placeman (plē¹·smăn). 1741. [f. PLACE *sb.* + MAN *sb.*] One who holds an appointment in the service of the sovereign or state; usu. in hostile sense: One who is appointed to (or seeks) such a position from motives of interest, without regard to fitness.

Placement (plē¹·smĕnt). 1844. [f. PLACE *v.* + -MENT.] The action of placing, or fact of being placed; placing, arrangement.

‖ **Placenta** (plăse·ntă). 1677. [L., cake, ad. Gr. πλακοῦντα, acc. of πλακοῦς flat cake, f. root πλακ- of πλάξ flat plate.] **1.** *Zool.* and *Anat.* (orig. *p. uterina* uterine cake.) The spongy vascular organ, of flattened circular form, to which the fœtus is attached by the umbilical cord, and by means of which it is nourished in the womb, in all the higher mammals, and which is expelled in parturition; the afterbirth 1691. **2.** *Bot.* That part of the carpel to which the ovules are attached. So **Placenti·ferous** *a.* bearing or having a p. 1667.

Placental (plăse·ntăl), *a.* (*sb.*) 1808. [ad. mod.L. *placentalis*, f. prec.; see -AL.] **1.** *Zool.*, etc. Of or pertaining to the placenta. **b.** Furnished with a placenta 1840. **2.** *Bot.* Pertaining to the placenta of a plant 1857. **B.** *sb.* A placental mammal 1847.

‖ **Placentalia** (plæsĕntē¹·liă), *sb. pl.* 1842. [mod.L., neut. pl. of *placentalis*, adj.; see prec.] *Zool.* Placental mammals; a primary division of Mammalia, comprising those provided with a placenta; contrasted with *Marsupialia* and *Monotremata*.

Placentary (plæ·sĕntări, plăse·ntări), *a.* (*sb.*) 1843. [ad. mod.L. *placentarius*, f. PLACENTA; see -ARY [1].] Of, pertaining or relating to the placenta; placental (*Zool.* and *Bot.*). **b.** *Zool.* Of or pertaining to the *Placentalia*. **B.** *sb. Zool.* A placental mammal 1890.

Placentation (plæsĕntē¹·ʃən). 1760. [a. F., f. PLACENTA; see -ATION.] **1.** *Zool.* The formation and disposition of the placenta in the uterus 1880. **2.** *Bot.* The disposition of the placenta or placentas in the ovary.

Place·ntiform, *a.* 1858. [f. as prec. + -FORM.] *Zool.* and *Bot.* Having the form of a placenta; discoid; cake-shaped.

Placer [1] (plē¹·səɹ). 1579. [f. PLACE *v.* + -ER [1].] One who places, puts, or sets; often *techn.*, e.g. in *Bookbinding*, a workman who arranges the sheets.

Placer [2] (plē¹·səɹ). (Chiefly *U.S.*) 1848. [a. Amer. Sp. *placer* (plase·r) deposit, shoal, f. *plaza* place.] A deposit of sand, gravel, or earth, in the bed of a stream, or any alluvial or diluvial detritus, containing valuable minerals in particles; a place where this is washed for gold, etc.

Placet (plē¹·set). 1572. [a. L., 'it pleases'.] ‖ **1.** The Latin for 'it pleases (me or us)'; part of the formula used in the old universities in voting for or against a measure 1592. **2.** as *sb.* **a.** The expression of assent or sanction (by this word) 1589. **b.** A vote of assent in a council, or in the congregation or convocation of a university 1883.

Placid (plæ·sid), *a.* 1626. [ad. L. *placidus*, f. root of *placere* to please; see -ID [1].] Of peaceful or tranquil appearance, character, or disposition.

That p. aspect and meek regard MILT. The male population is distinctly of a p. temperament 1871. Hence **Placidity** (plăsi·dĭti), the quality of being p. 1619. **Pla·cid-ly** *adv.*, **-ness.**

‖ **Placitum** (plæ·sitŏm). *Obs.* exc. *Hist. Pl.* placita. 1668. [L., neut. pa. pple. of *placere* to please; in med.L. the sentence of a court, a fine, a trial, a plea.] The decree of a judge, the decision or determination of a public assembly, a court of justice, or the like. Also, in *pl.* the proceedings at such assemblies or courts, trials at law, pleadings or pleas.

Plack (plæk). *Sc.* and *n. dial. Obs.* exc. *Hist.* 1473. [prob. a. Flem. *placke*, *plecke*, a small coin of Brabant and Flanders. Orig. 'flat disk, tablet'.] †**a.** A coin of the Netherlands of the 15th and 16th centuries –1526. **b.** A small copper coin current in Scotland in the 15th and 16th centuries, worth 4 pennies Scots 1473. **c.** The type of something of very small value; a farthing; a bit 1550. **d.** *attrib.* Worth or costing a plack 1560.

c. Phr. *Not worth a p.*, utterly worthless. *P. and bawbee, p. and boddle*, in full, every penny. *Two and a p.*, a trifle.

Placket (plæ·kĕt). 1546. [app. var. of PLACARD *sb.*] **1.** An apron or petticoat; hence *transf.* a woman. *Obs.* or *arch.* 1606. **2.** The slit at the top of a skirt or petticoat, for convenience in putting on and off 1546. **3.** A pocket, esp. that in a woman's skirt 1663. *Comb.* **p.-hole**, an opening in the outer skirt to give access to the pocket within; also = sense 2.

Placo- (plæ·ko), bef. a vowel **plac-**, comb. form of Gr. πλάξ, πλακ- a flat plate, tablet. **Pla·coderm** [Gr. δέρμα] *a.*, having the skin encased in broad flat bony plates, as certain fossil fishes; of or belonging to the *Placodermata* or *Placodermi*, an order of Palæozoic fishes having the head and pectoral region thus protected; *sb.* one of the *Placodermata*. **Placoga·noid** [GANOID] *a.*, of or pertaining to the *Placoganoidei*, a division of fossil Devonian fishes, having the head and part of the body protected by large ganoid plates; *sb.* a fish of this division; also **Placoganoi·dean** *a.* and *sb.*

Placoid (plæ·koid), *a.* and *sb.* 1842. [f. Gr. πλάξ, πλακ- flat plate, tablet; see -OID.] *Zool.* **A.** *adj.* **1.** Having the form of a plate; applied to the horny scales and tubercles of the *Placoidei*; see B. **2.** Having placoid scales; of or pertaining to the *Placoidei* 1847. **B.** *sb.* A fish of the division *Placoidei*, containing the sharks and rays, distinguished by having the skin protected by irregularly disposed bony scales, sometimes bearing spines 1852. Hence **Placoi·dean** *a.* and *sb.* 1836.

‖ **Plafond** (plafoñ). 1664. [F., f. *plat* flat + *fond* bottom.] *Arch.* A ceiling; hence, a painting executed on a ceiling.

Plagal (plē¹·găl), *a.* 1597. [ad. med.L. *plagalis*, f. med.L. *plaga* the plagal mode, app. a back-formation from med.L. *plagius*, a. med. Gr. πλάγιος plagal, in class. Gr. 'oblique', f. πλάγος side.] **a.** In *Gregorian Music*, applied to those eccl. modes which have their sounds comprised between the dominant and its octave, the final being near the middle of the compass. Cf. AUTHENTIC *a.* 8. **b.** *P. cadence*: that in which the chord of the subdominant immediately precedes that of the tonic.

Plage (plāʒ). late ME. [a. OF., f. (ult.) L. *plaga* a region.] †**1.** A region, district, clime; occas., a zone –1613. †**2.** Any one of the four principal quarters of the compass; direction, side –1652. ‖ **3.** A seashore, seaside resort 1920.

1. From the frozen p. of Heaven MARLOWE.

Plagiarism (plē¹·dʒiăriz'm). 1621. [f. as PLAGIARY + -ISM.] **1.** The action or practice of plagiarizing; the taking and using as one's own of the thoughts, writings, or inventions of another. **2.** A purloined idea, design, passage, or work 1797. Hence **Pla·giarist**, one who is guilty of plagiarism 1674. **Plagiari·stic** *a.*, **-ally** *adv.*

1. If an author is once detected in borrowing, he will be suspected of p. ever after HAZLITT. **2.** They are full of plagiarisms, inappropriately borrowed 1875.

Plagiarize (plē¹·dʒiărəiz), *v.* 1716. [f. next + -IZE.] **1.** *trans.* To practise plagiarism upon (a thing, rarely a person). **2.** *intr.* To practise or commit plagiarism 1832.

Plagiary (plē¹·dʒiări), *sb.* and *a.* 1597. [ad. L. *plagiarius* a kidnapper; a seducer; also, a literary thief.] **A.** *sb.* †**1.** A kidnapper, a man-stealer –1697. **2.** = PLAGIARIST 1601. **3.** = PLAGIARISM 1; literary theft 1646. **b.** = PLAGIARISM 2. 1677.

2. Why? the ditt' is all borrowed; 'tis Horaces: hang him p. B. JONS.

B. *adj.* †**1.** That plagiarizes; plagiarizing –1662. †**2.** Obtained by plagiarism; plagiarized –1820.

Plagihedral (plēdʒihī·drăl, -he·drăl), *a.* 1805. [f. PLAGI(O- + Gr. ἕδρα seat, base.] *Cryst.* Having certain faces obliquely situated; also said of such faces.

Plagio- (plē¹·dʒio-, plæ·gio-), bef. a vowel or *h* **plagi-**, comb. form, repr. Gr. πλάγιος oblique, slanting, f. πλάγος side.

Plagiocephalic (plē¹·dʒiosĭfæ·lik) *a.* [Gr. κεφαλή head + -IC] characterized by plagiocephaly; so **Plagioce·phalous** *a.* in same sense. **Plagioce·phaly**, oblique deformity of the skull, consisting in the greater development of the anterior part on one side and of the posterior part on the other. **Pla·gioclase** [Gr. κλάσις cleavage] *Min.* name for the group of triclinic feldspars, the two prominent cleavage directions in which are oblique to one another; so **Plagiocla·stic** *a.* having oblique cleavage; opp. to ORTHOCLASTIC. **Pla·giostome** [F.; Gr. στόμα mouth] *sb.* (*a.*) a member of the *Plagiostomi*, cartilaginous fishes, including the sharks and rays, which have the mouth placed transversely beneath the snout; so **Plagio·stomous** *a.* of or pertaining to the plagiostomes; having the mouth placed transversely beneath the snout. **Plagiotro·pic** [Gr. τροπικός inclined, f. τρόπος turning] *a. Bot.* said of members or organs of plants, the two halves of which react differently to the influences of light, gravitation, and other external forces, and which therefore take up an oblique position; opp. to ORTHOTROPIC; hence **Plagio·tropism**, p. character.

Plagionite (plē¹·dʒiŏnəit). [ad. G. *plagionit*, f. Gr. πλάγιος, -ον oblique + -ITE [1].] *Min.* A sulphide of lead and antimony occurring in monoclinic thick tubular crystals of a blackish grey colour.

‖ **Plagium** (plē¹·dʒiŏm). 1577. [L.] *Civil Law.* Kidnapping, man-stealing.

Plague (plē¹g), *sb.* [ME. *plage*, a. OF. *plage*, *plague*, ad. L. *plaga* stroke, wound, in late L. plague, pestilence (Vulg.), f. root *plag-* of *plangere* to strike.] †**1.** A blow, a stroke; a wound –1538. **2.** An affliction, calamity, evil, 'scourge'; *esp.* a visitation of divine anger or justice. late ME. **b.** In weakened sense: A nuisance; *colloq.* trouble 1604. **c.** Applied to a person or animal 1551. **3.** A general name for any malignant disease with which men or beasts are stricken. †**a.** An individual affliction, e.g. leprosy –1672. **b.** *esp.* An epidemic attended with great mortality; a pestilence 1548. **c.** *spec.* *The p.*: the oriental or bubonic plague 1601.

2. Egipte was smyten with x. plages and diseases 1432. This p. of rayne and waters *Bk. Com. Prayer*. **b.** She disliked stiles, she found it such a p. to get over them 1825. **c.** What a P. to Society is a Man who has written a Book 1707. **3. b.** The famous 'plagues', which ravaged Europe, were forms of typhus fever 1871. **c.** His servant died—a bubo on his right groine, and two spots on his right thigh, which is the p. PEPYS.

attrib. and *Comb.*, as **p.-bill**, an official return of the deaths caused by the p. in any district; **-mark** = PLAGUE-SPOT 1; **p. pit**, a deep pit for the common burial of plague victims.

Plague (plē¹g), *v.* 1481. [f. prec.] **1.** *trans.* To afflict with plague or calamity (esp. in ref. to divine punishment). Now *rare* or *arch.* **2.** In weakened sense: To torment, tease, trouble, bother, annoy 1594.

1. Christians were too intent on plaguing Jews 1787. **2.** Husbands and wives..plaguing one another GAY. Hence **Pla·guer**, one who plagues or harasses. **Pla·guesome** *a.* troublesome, vexatious, plaguy.

Pla·gue-spot. 1711. **1.** A spot on the skin characteristic of the plague, or of some disease so called. **2.** A locality infested with plague. Often *fig.* 1895.

Plaguy (plē¹·gi), *a.* (*adv.*). 1574. [f. PLAGUE *sb.* + -Y [1].] **1.** Pestiferous, pestilential, pernicious. Now *rare* or *arch.* **b.** Plague-stricken. Now *rare* or *Obs.* 1604. **2.** That is a plague; that causes severe affliction 1598. **b.** In weakened sense: Vexatious, troublesome, annoying, disagreeable; hence *colloq.* = 'pestilent', 'confounded', excessive 1615. **B.** as *adv.* = Plaguily (*colloq.*) 1584.

2. They make charming mistresses but p. wives GAY. **b.** A p. rise in the price of everything 1879. **B.** You've been a p. long time in coming 1884. Hence **Pla·guily** *adv.* in a p. manner; confoundedly.

Plaice (plē¹s). [ME. *plais*, *plaice*, a. OF. *plaïz*, early mod.F. *plaïse*, *pleïsse*, *pladisse*:—late L. *platessa*, app. f. Gr. πλατύς broad, or root πλατ- flat.] A European flat-fish, *Pleuronectes platessa*, much used as food; in America extended to various allied species of this genus or of the family *Pleuronectidæ*. (Pl. now rare; the collect. sing. *plaice* being used instead.) **2.** *dial.* = FLUKE *sb.*[1] 2. 1722.

attrib. and *Comb.*, as **p.-mouth**, a small puckered or wry mouth; also *attrib.*; so **-mouthed** *a.*

Plaid (plæd, *Sc.* plēd). 1512. [Gael. *plaide*; etym. unkn.] **1.** A long piece of twilled woollen cloth, usu. having a chequered or tartan pattern, forming the outer article of the Highland costume. The Lowland 'shepherd's plaid', of a black chequer pattern on white, is commonly called a MAUD. **2.** The cloth of which plaids are made 1634. **3.** *transf.* A man wearing a plaid; a Highlander. SCOTT.

Comb. p.-**nook** (-neuk) *Sc.*, one end of the folded p. sewn up so as to form a large pocket.

Plaided (plæ·dèd, *Sc.* plē·dèd), *a.* 1802. [f. PLAID + -ED².] 1. Dressed in or wearing a plaid. 2. Made of plaid; having a plaid pattern 1814.

Plaidie, -y (plæ·di, *Sc.* plē·di). *Sc.* 1719. [f. PLAID + -IE.] A small plaid; also, a childish, sentimental, or poetic name for a plaid.

Plaiding (plæ·diŋ, plē·diŋ). 1566. [f. PLAID + -ING¹.] 1. Material for plaids; a twilled woollen cloth; a cloth of tartan pattern. 2. A plaid or checkered pattern 1889.

Plain (plēⁱn), *sb.* ME. [a. OF. :—L. *planum* a plain, prop. neut. of *planus* PLAIN *a.*¹] 1. A flat tract of country; an extent of level ground or flat meadow land; applied *spec.* in *Salisbury Plain*, etc. **b.** Chiefly *pl.* In colonial and U.S. use, any treeless level tract of country; prairie 1779. **c.** *transf.* The level expanse of sea or sky 1567. 2. An open space as the scene of battle or contest; the field. Now *poet.* late ME. †3. A level or flat surface (ideal or material). Now spelt *plane.* = PLANE *sb.*³ 1. -1863. 4. The floor of the hall in which the French National Convention met at the time of the Revolution; hence applied to the more moderate party who had seats there. (Cf. MOUNTAIN I. 5.) 1827.

1. *Cities of the P.* (sc. *of the Jordan*), Sodom, Gomorrah, etc., before their destruction; Lot dwelled in the cities of the plaine, and pitched his tent toward Sodome *Gen.* xiii. 12. **c.** The sick'ning stars fade off th' æthereal p. POPE. 2. I will leade forth my Soldiers to the plaine SHAKS.

attrib. and *Comb.*, as *p.-station*; *plain-like* adj.; also with *plains-*, as *plains-people*, etc.

Plain (plēⁱn), *a.*¹ and *adv.* ME. [a. OF. :—L. *planus* flat.] **A.** *adj.* I. 1. Flat, level, even; free from elevations and depressions. †**b.** *gen.* Flat -1650. †**c.** *Geom.* Now PLANE *a.* 1. -1727. 2. Smooth, even. *Obs.* exc. in comb. or phrases. ME. 3. Free from obstructions or interruptions; clear, open; public. *Obs.* exc. *dial.* ME. **b.** *transf.* Unobstructed, clear (*view, sight*) 1613.

1. Follow me then to plainer ground SHAKS. 3. Able to give him battell in the plaine sea 1579.

II. 1. Open, clear; evident, obvious ME. 2. That is clearly what the name expresses; manifest; downright, mere, 'flat', absolute ME. 3. Simple, readily understood. Also *transf.* of a speaker or writer. late ME. 4. Not complicated; simple 1659.

1. Practical Christianity..is a p. and obvious thing BUTLER. 2. He reaped p. unequivocal hatred LAMB. 3. Tell her distinctly what you want..in few p. words 1861. 4. P. sewing 1895.

III. 1. Unembellished, not ornate; (of the hair) worn straight, not curled; (of drawings, etc.) not coloured. Also *fig.* ME. **b.** *Cards.* (*a*) Applied to the common as opp. to the picture cards. (*b*) Not trumps. 1844. 2. Of simple composition; not elaborate. Of food: Not rich or highly seasoned 1655.

1. A young Man..with long p. Hair 1655. Picture-postcards, p. or coloured (*mod.*). 2. [As a] school-boy counts the currants in an unusually p. cake 1879. *P. bread and butter*, i. e. without preserves, etc. *A p. tea*, tea with p. bread and butter. *P. water*, water without any addition.

IV. 1. Open in behaviour; free from duplicity or reserve; candid, frank. *Obs.* exc. in sense: Plain-spoken. late ME. 2. Free from evasion or subterfuge, straightforward, direct 1500.

1. I wil sing a Song if any body wil sing another; else, to be p. with you, I wil sing none WALTON. 2. If you do not give a p. answer to a p. question, you will be committed 1776. Phr. *P. truth* (often with the notion 'uncoloured'). *P. English*: see *Comb.*

V. 1. Ordinary, simple, unsophisticated; such as characterizes ordinary people 1586. 2. Not distinguished by rank or position; ordinary 1580. 3. Homely, unaffected 1601. 4. Simple in dress or habits; frugal 1613. 5. Of homely appearance; often euphemistically for: Ill-favoured, ugly 1749.

1. I pray thee vnderstand a plaine man in his plaine meaning SHAKS. 2. I preached to several hundred of p. people WESLEY. 3. They spoke of.. their Queen..'She is a p. woman, a very p. woman like ourselves' 1904. 4. His habits of life were remarkably p. and frugal 1871. 5. Handsome young men must have something to live on, as well as the p. JANE AUSTEN.

Phrases. *P. as a pikestaff* (earlier *packstaff*). *P. as the sun at noonday, as Salisbury* (pun on Salisbury Plain). See also DUNSTABLE.

B. *adv.* (Advb. uses of the adj.) 1. With clearness of expression; clearly, intelligibly, candidly. late ME. 2. With clearness of perception or utterance; clearly, manifestly 1590.

1. Sir to tell you plaine, I'le finde a fairer face not washt to day SHAKS. 2. Did not Torquato Tasso speak p. at six months old? 1784.

Comb.: p. **clothes**, ordinary citizen dress, mufti; opp. to UNIFORM; also *attrib.*, as *plain-clothes constable*; p. **cook** *sb.*, a person, usu. a woman, capable of preparing simple dishes; p.-**cook** *v. intr.*, to do plain cooking; p. **English**, plain straightforward language, plain terms; also, a plain or clear statement; p. **language**, *spec.* the manner of speech used by Quakers; p.-**sail** *Naut.*, sail ordinarily carried; p. **service**, divine service said without music; -**singing** = PLAINSONG. Hence **Plai·nly** *adv.*, -**ness.**

†**Plain**, *a.*² [ME *plein, playn*, a. F. *plein* (†*plain*) :—L. *plenus* full.] 1. Full, plenary, entire, perfect -1653. 2. Full or complete in number, extent, etc.; esp. of a council, assembly, or court -1677. 3. In phr. *in p. battle* (*combat, war*), in regular open battle, etc. -1718.

Plain (plēⁱn), *v. arch.* or *dial.* [ME. *plei(g)ne, playne*, etc., a. OF. *plaign-*, stem of *plaindre* to lament :—L. *plangere* to beat (the breast), lament, f. root *plag-* strike.] = COMPLAIN *v.* in various senses.

I did many times p. my ill hap 1617. Small Cause, I ween, has lusty Youth to p. 1710.

Plai·n chant. 1727. [a. F. *plain chant*, = med.L. *cantus planus.*] = PLAINSONG, CANTO FERMO.

Plain dealer, plain-dealer. Now *rare.* 1571. [f. PLAIN *a.*¹ + DEALER; cf. next.] One who is straightforward and candid in his dealings with others.

Plain dealing, plain-dealing, *sb.* 1573. [f. PLAIN *a.*¹ + DEALING *vbl. sb.*; cf. DOUBLE-DEALING.] Openness of conduct; candour, straightforwardness.

Plai·n-dea·ling, *a.* 1566. [f. PLAIN *adv.* + *dealing* pr. pple.] That deals plainly; straightforward in conduct.

Plain-hearted, *a.* Now *rare.* 1608. [f. *plain heart* (PLAIN *a.*¹) + -ED².] Having a sincere and open heart; without guile; ingenuous, innocent. Hence **Plai·n-hea·rted-ly** *adv.*, -**ness.**

Plaining (plēⁱ·niŋ), *vbl sb. arch.* ME. [-ING¹.] The action of PLAIN *v.*; lamentation; complaint.

Plai·n sai·ling, *sb.* 1827. [prob. pop. use of PLANE SAILING, formerly also spelt *plain sailing*, but used with sense of PLAIN *a.*¹ I. 3.] Sailing or going on in a plain course, in which there is no difficulty or obstruction; simple or easy course of action.

Plainsman (plēⁱ·nzmæ̆n). 1881. [f. PLAIN *sb.* + MAN *sb.*] A man of the plain or plains; an inhabitant of a flat country, or of wide open plains.

Plainsong (plēⁱ·nsǫŋ). 1447. [tr. med.L. *cantus planus*, F. *plain chant*, etc.] 1. A form of vocal music believed to have been used in the Christian Church from the earliest times, consisting of melodies composed in the mediæval modes (see MODE I. 1 b) and in free rhythm depending on the accentuation of the words, and sung in unison. See AMBROSIAN, GREGORIAN. 2. A simple melody or theme; often accompanied by a running melody or 'descant' (see DESCANT *sb.*); hence in *fig.* applications. *Obs.* or *Hist.* 1566.

2. *attrib.* The plainsong Cuckow gray SHAKS.

Plain-speaking, *sb.* and *a.* 1852. **A.** *sb.* Plainness of speech, candour, frankness. **B.** *adj.* = next 1884.

Plain-spoken, †plain-spoke, *a.* 1678. [f. PLAIN *adv.*; cf. OUTSPOKEN.] 1. Given to speaking plainly; outspoken. 2. Plainly spoken; clearly expressed; candid, frank 1703.

2. A rough, bluff, hearty, plain-spoken way of eulogising them to their faces 1836. Hence **Plain-spo·kenness.**

Plaint (plēⁱnt), *sb.* [In ME. two words (i) *plainte, pleinte*, a. OF. *plainte* :—pop.L. *plancta* sb., f. fem. pa. pple. of *plangere* to lament; (ii) *plaint*, a. OF. *plaint, pleint* :—L. *planctus.*] 1. The action or an act of plaining; lamentation, grieving. (Now chiefly *poet.*). 2. A statement or representation of wrong, injury, or injustice; a complaint. (Now *rare.*) ME. 3. *spec.* An oral or written statement of grievance made to a court of law, for the purpose of obtaining redress; an accusation, charge, complaint. late ME.

1. The hapless Paire Sate in their sad discourse, and various p. MILT. 2. Shee with teares made vnto him her p. 1605.

Plaintiff (plēⁱ·ntif). late ME. [a. OF. *plaintif*, subst. use of *plaintif* adj. PLAINTIVE.] *Law.* The party who brings a suit into a court of law; a complainant, prosecutor; opp. to *defendant.*

Plaintive (plēⁱ·ntiv), *a.* [ME. a. OF. *plaintif, -ive* = L. **planctivus*, f. *planctus* PLAINT; see -IVE.] 1. Complaining, lamenting; †suffering. Now *rare.* †2. Being or pertaining to the plaintiff in a suit -1596. 3. Expressive of sorrow; mournful, sad 1579.

3. The fiddle screams P. and piteous COWPER. Hence **Plai·ntive·ly** *adv.*, -**ness.**

Plai·n-work, plain work. 1715. 1. Work of a simple kind, as dist. from ornamental or 'fancy' work; *spec.* plain needlework or sewing. 2. *Masonry.* The even surface produced on stone by the chisel, without taking away more than the mere inequalities 1823.

Plaisance, obs. var. of PLEASANCE.

Plaister, obs. f. PLASTER.

Plait (plæt, *Sc.*, *U.S.* plēⁱt), *sb.* [ME. *pleyt, playt*, a. OF. *pleit*, later *ploit*, fold, etc. :—pop.L. **plictum* = L. *plicitum* a thing folded, pa. pple. neut. of *plicare* to fold.] 1. (Now superseded in gen. use by *pleat.*) A fold, crease, or wrinkle; esp. a flattened fold of cloth made by doubling the material upon itself. **b.** A fold, wrinkle, or crease in any natural structure, e.g. in the lip, brow, or ear 1592. **c.** *fig.* A sinuosity or twist of nature or character; a hidden recess; usu. implying artifice or deceit. *Obs.* or *arch.* 1589. 2. A contexture of three or more interlaced strands of hair, ribbon, straw, etc.; *esp.* a braided tress of hair, a queue, a pigtail 1530.

1. Then smoothed down the plaits of her apron 1850. **b.** I should fear Some p. between the brows MRS. BROWNING. 2. Wearing their hair in long plaits down their backs 1880.

Plait (plæt, *Sc.*, *U.S.* plēⁱt), *v.* ME. [f. prec.] 1. *trans.* = PLEAT *v.* 1 (by which it is superseded). 2. To braid or intertwine (hair, straw, rushes, narrow ribbons, etc.) so as to form a plait, band, or rope.

1. [He] wore his shirt frill plaited and puffed out W. IRVING. 2. Little Margery..who plaited straw DICKENS. Hence **Plai·ter,** one who or that which plaits.

Plaited (plæ·tèd, *Sc.*, *U.S.* plēⁱ·tèd), *ppl. a.* late ME. [f. prec. + -ED¹.] 1. Folded, doubled; furnished with pleats. In this sense superseded by *pleated.* 1440. **b.** Wrinkled, corrugated, fluted, striated 1519. 2. Braided, formed into a plait; interlaced, interwoven 1594.

2. P. alleys of the trailing rose TENNYSON.

Plan (plæn), *sb.* 1678 [a. F., a plane surface, etc., sb. use of *plan, plane* adj., ad. L. *planus* flat (being a learned and techn. doublet of *plain, plaine* flat, PLAIN).] I. 1. A drawing, sketch, etc. of any object, made by projection upon a flat surface (opp. to ELEVATION II. 3); *spec.* (*a*) A drawing showing the relative positions of the parts of a building, or of any one floor of a building on a horizontal plane. (*b*) A large-scale, detailed map of a town or district. See also GROUND-PLAN. **b.** A table or programme indicating the relations of some set of objects, or the times, places, etc. of some intended proceedings 1780. 2. A scheme of arrangement; *transf.* disposition of parts; a type of structure (viewed as designed); configuration (of a surface) 1732. 3. A scheme of action, project, design; the way in which it is proposed to carry out some proceeding. Also in weakened sense: Method, way of proceeding 1706.

2. A mighty maze! but not without a p. POPE. I have not yet drawn out a p. for my stories, but certain germs thereof are budding in my mind THACKERAY. 3. The good old rule..the simple p., That they should take, who have the power, And they should

keep who can WORDSW. Change your whole p. of campaign 1837.

II. After F. *plan*. **a.** *Perspective.* Any one of a number of ideal planes perpendicular to the line of vision passing through the objects represented in a picture 1678. **b.** *Sculpture.* The plane on which the figures in a bas-relief are raised above the ground, *esp.* one of several such planes giving more or less relief to different figures in the design 1780.

Plan (plæn), *v.* 1728. [f. prec. sb.] **1.** *trans.* To make a plan of (a piece of ground, a building, etc.); to plot down, lay down. Also to construct (a plan or diagram). 1748. **2.** To make a plan of (a building, etc., to be constructed); hence to devise, contrive, design (a building, etc., to be constructed) 1728. **3.** To devise, design (something to be done, or some action, etc., to be carried out); to arrange beforehand. Also with clause or *absol.* 1737.

2. The gardens were planned by the best landscape gardeners of the day 1893 **3.** We had planned an ascent of Monte Rosa together TYNDALL.

Planar (plēⁱ·năɹ), *a.* 1850. [ad. L. *planaris*, f. *planum* PLANE *sb.*³; cf. *linear.*] *Math.* Belonging to, situated in, or related in some way to, a plane.

‖ **Planaria** (plănēᵊ·riă). 1819. [mod.L. generic name, sb. use of fem. of L. *planarius* adj. (used as = 'flat').] *Zool.* A genus of the sub-order *Planarida* of turbellarian worms. Hence **Plana·rian** *a.* belonging or related to the genus *Planaria*; *sb.* a planarian worm, a flatworm. **Plana·ridan** *a.* belonging to the sub-order *Planarida*; *sb.* a planaridan worm. **Planariform** (-ēᵊ·rifǭɹm) *a.*, **Planarioid** (-ēᵊ·ri,oid) *a.*, of the form of or resembling a planarian.

Planch (plɑnʃ). late ME. [a. F. *planche* plank, slab; see PLANK.] **1.** A plank; *dial.* a floor. *Obs.* exc. *dial.* **2.** A slab of metal, stone, baked clay, etc.; *spec.* in *Enamelling*, a slab of baked fire-clay used to support the work during the process of baking 1578.

Plancher (plɑ·nʃəɹ). *Obs.* exc. *dial.* ME. [a. OF. *plancher*, *-ier* planking, f. *planche* PLANCH *sb.*] †**1.** A plank, a board; planking, boarding -1720. **2.** A floor (*dial.*) or †platform of planks or boards 1449. †**3.** = PLANCIER -1728.

Planchet (plɑ·nʃĕt). 1611. [dim. of PLANCH; see -ET.] The plain disk of metal of which a coin is made; a coin-blank.

Planchette (plānʃe·t, ‖ plānʃęt). 1860. [a. F., dim. of *planche* PLANK.] A small board, supported by two castors and a vertical pencil, which, when one or more persons rest their fingers lightly on the board, is said to trace lines or letters, and even to write sentences, without conscious direction or effort.

Plancier (plænsīᵊ·ɪ). 1664. [ad. OF., collateral form of *planchier*; see PLANCHER.] The under side of the corona of a cornice.

Plane (plēⁱn), *sb.*¹ late ME. [a. F., earlier OF. *plasne* :—L. *platanus*, a. Gr. πλάτανος the Oriental Plane, f. πλατύς broad, because of its broad leaves.] **1.** A tree of the genus *Platanus*, comprising lofty spreading trees, with broad angular palmately-lobed leaves, and bark which scales off in irregular patches; orig. and esp. *P. orientalis*, the Oriental Plane, a native of Persia and the Levant; also *P. occidentalis*, the Occidental or Virginian Plane or Buttonwood. **2.** In Scotland and the north of England applied to the species of maple commonly called 'sycamore' (*Acer pseudoplatanus*), the leaves of which resemble those of *Platanus*; also called False, Mock, or Scotch Plane 1778.

Plane (plēⁱn), *sb.*² ME. [a. F. :—late L. *plana* a plane, f. *planare* to plane.] **1.** A tool resembling a plasterer's trowel, used by plumbers, bricklayers, etc., for smoothing the surface of sand, clay in a mould, etc. **2.** A tool used by carpenters and others, for levelling down and smoothing the surface of woodwork by paring shavings from it.

It consists of a *stock* of wood or metal, with a smooth base or *sole* which slides over the surface of the wood, and a steel blade set in it at an angle so that its edge projects slightly through a slit or *mouth* in the sole. BENCH-*p.*, JACK-P., TRYING-*p.*, etc.: see these words.

Plane (plēⁱn), *sb.*³ 1570. [ad. L. *planum*, adj. neut. used sb.; introduced in 17th c. to express the geometrical and allied uses of PLAIN. Cf. next.] **1. a.** A plane superficies; in *Geom.*, a surface such that every straight line joining any two points in it lies wholly in it, or such that the intersection of two such surfaces is always a straight line; the simplest kind of geometrical surface. Hence *gen.*, An imaginary superficies of this kind in which points or lines in material bodies lie. **b.** A flat or level surface of a material body 1571. **c.** *Cryst.* and *Min.* Each of the natural faces of a crystal; also, an imaginary plane surface related to these in some way 1800. **d.** *Anat.* Any one of certain imaginary plane surfaces used as standards of ref. for the positions of bodily organs, or (in *Craniometry*) of parts of the skull 1830. **e.** (*a*) = AEROPLANE 1. 1891. (*b*) = AEROPLANE 2. 1915. **2.** *Mining.* Any main road in a mine, along which coal, etc., is conveyed in cars or trucks 1877. **3.** *fig.* in ref. to thought, knowledge, moral qualities, social rank, etc.: Higher or lower level, grade, degree 1850.

1. *P. of projection*, a plane upon which points, lines, or figures are projected. *Objective p.* (Perspective), any plane situated in the object itself. *Perspective p.*, a transparent plane, usu. perpendicular to the horizon, supposed to be interposed between the object and the eye, and intersected by straight lines passing from one to the other, which determine the points of the drawing; also called *p. of delineation* or *p. of the picture*. *P. of polarization* (Optics), in polarized light, the plane which passes through the incident ray and the polarized ray, and is perpendicular to the plane of vibration of the ether in the polarized ray. **b.** *Inclined p.*: see INCLINED *ppl. a.* 1. **3.** The superstitious man is on the same p. as the savage 1885.

Plane (plēⁱn), *a.* 1570. [ad. L. *planus* flat, level; or, prop., a refash. of PLAIN *a.*, in certain senses.] **1.** *Geom.* Of a surface: Perfectly flat or level, so that every straight line joining any two points in it lies wholly in it (see prec. 1 a). Hence applied to an angle, figure, or curve which lies wholly in such a surface. **b.** *transf.* Relating to or involving plane surfaces or magnitudes 1704. **2.** Of a material surface, etc.: Flat, level; not convex or concave 1666.

p. chart (†*plain chart*), a chart on which the meridians and parallels of latitude are represented by equidistant straight lines (cf. PLANE SAILING); **p. scale** (†*plain scale*), a scale or ruler marked with lines denoting chords, rhumbs, sines, tangents, secants, etc., formerly used, esp. in navigation.

Plane (plēⁱn), *v.*¹ ME. [a. F. *planer* :—L. *planare* to make flat, level, or smooth, f. *planus* PLANE, PLAIN.] **I.** In gen. sense. **1.** *trans.* To make (a surface) plane, even, or smooth; to level, to smooth. Also *fig.* (Now chiefly in arch. phr. *to p. the way*, or as *fig.* of sense II. 1.) †**2.** *fig.* To make plain or intelligible; to explain, display, show -1659.

1. You planed her path To Lady Psyche TENNYSON.

II. 1. *trans.* To dress with a plane or planing-machine; to smooth down (wood, metal, etc.) with or as with a plane. late ME. **2.** *intr.* To use or work with a plane 1703.

1. Phr. *To p. away*, *off*: to remove by or as by planing.

Plane (plēⁱn), *v.*² 1611. [a. F. *planer*, f. *plan* plane, because a bird when soaring extends its wings in a plane.] *intr.* Of a bird: To be poised on outspread motionless wings. **b.** [f. PLANE *sb.*³ 1 e.] To travel in an aeroplane; *esp.* to glide *down* 1909.

Planer (plēⁱ·nəɹ). 1560. [f. PLANE *v.*¹ + -ER ¹.] **1.** One who makes level or levels down. **2.** One who planes 1598. **3.** Formerly, a plane; now, a planing-machine 1596. **4.** *Printing.* A block of wood used in beating down projecting types in a form 1858.

Plane sailing. Also formerly **plain s.** 1699. [f. PLANE *sb.*³, formerly spelt *plain.*] In *Navigation*, The art of determining a ship's place on the theory that she is moving on a plane, or that the surface of the earth is plane instead of spherical; navigation by a *plane chart*: see PLANE *a.* **b.** *fig.* A course so simple as to leave no room for mistakes. Now usu. PLAIN SAILING, q. v. 1858.

Planeshear (plēⁱ·nʃīᵊɹ), **planksheer** (plæ·ŋkʃīᵊɹ). 1711. [Corruption of PLANCHER *sb.*] A continuous planking covering the timber-heads of a wooden ship, in men-of-war forming a shelf below the gunwale; also loosely applied to the gunwale.

Planet ¹ (plæ·nĕt). [ME. a. OF. *planete* (F. *planète*), ad. late L. *planeta* or *planetes*, a. Gr. πλανήτης wanderer, hence, in *pl.* (ἀστέρες) πλανῆται wandering stars, f. πλανᾶν to lead astray, pass. to wander.] †**1.** *Old Astr.* A heavenly body distinguished from the fixed stars by having an apparent motion of its own among them. (The seven planets, in the order of their accepted distance from the Earth, were the Moon, Mercury, Venus, the Sun, Mars, Jupiter, and Saturn.) **b.** *esp.* in *Astrol.*, said with ref. to the supposed 'influence' of any one of these bodies in affecting persons and events; in later use said vaguely of an occult controlling fateful power ME. **2.** *Mod. Astron.* The name given to each of the heavenly bodies that revolve in approximately circular orbits round the sun (*primary planets*), and to those that revolve round these (*secondary planets* or SATELLITES) 1640.

The primary planets comprise the *major planets*, viz., in order of distance from the sun, Mercury, Venus, the Earth, Mars, Jupiter, Saturn, Uranus, and Neptune, and the *minor planets* or ASTEROIDS, the orbits of which lie between those of Mars and Jupiter.

1. b. I was born under a Threepenny P., never to be worth a Groat SWIFT. **2.** *fig.* Two such political planets 1790.

Comb.: **p.-gear**, **-gearing**, a system of gearing in which planet-wheels are introduced; a mechanical combination for converting power into speed; **-wheel**, the exterior wheel which revolves round the central or sun-wheel, in the sun-and-planet motion.

Planet ² (plæ·nĕt), ‖**planeta** (plănī·tă). 1602. [ad. med.L. *planeta* chasuble, orig. = *pænula*, a large cloak worn by travellers; perh. f. Gr. πλανήτης a wanderer.] A chasuble.

Pla·ne-ta:ble, *sb.* Also †**plaintable.** 1607. [f. PLANE *a.* + TABLE *sb.*] A surveying instrument used for measuring angles in mapping, consisting of a circular drawing-table mounted horizontally on a tripod, and having an alidade pivoted over its centre. Hence **Pla·ne-ta:ble** *v. trans.* to survey with the plane-table.

‖**Planetarium** (plænĕtēᵊ·riǒm). 1774. [mod. L., f. *planetarius*; see -ARIUM.] An ORRERY. **b.** A model representing the planetary system 1860.

Planetary (plæ·nĕtări), *a.* and *sb.* 1593. [ad. late L. *planetarius*, prop. adj., but only occurring as sb., an astrologer.] **A.** *adj.* **1.** Belonging to or connected with a planet or planets; of the nature of or resembling a planet; having some attribute of a planet 1602. **b.** esp. in *Astrol.* with ref. to the supposed 'influence' of a planet 1607. **c.** *P. hour*, the twelfth part of the natural day or night. (In *Astrol.* supposed each to be ruled by a planet.) 1593. **2.** Belonging to this planet; terrestrial, mundane 1831. **3.** *fig.* Wandering; erratic 1607.

1. *P. nebula*, one resembling a planet from its disk being round or slightly oval. *P. system*, the system comprising the sun and planets, the solar system; also *fig.* a system of correlated parts. *P. year*: see YEAR. **c.** I was born in the P. hour of Saturn SIR T. BROWNE. **3.** His..erratical and p. life FULLER. Hence **Pla·netarily** *adv.*

B. *sb.* †**1.** An astrologer, star-gazer -1716. **2.** A planetary body 1819.

Planetesimal (plænĕte·simăl), *a.* and *sb.* 1906. [f. PLANET *sb.*¹ + *-esimal*, after *infinitesimal.*] **A.** *adj.* Pertaining to the minute bodies of space. **B.** *sb.* A minute planetary body.

Planetoid (plæ·nĕtoid), *sb.* (*a.*) 1803. [f. PLANET *sb.*¹ + -OID.] A body resembling a planet; a minor planet or asteroid. **b.** *adj.* (or *attrib.*) Of or belonging to the asteroids 1862.

Plane-tree (plēⁱ·n,trī). late ME. [f. PLANE *sb.*¹ + TREE.] = PLANE *sb.*¹

Pla·net-stri:cken, *a.* 1600. = next.

Pla·net-struck, *a.* 1600. [f. PLANET *sb.*¹ 1 b + pa. pple. of STRIKE *v.* Cf. *moon-struck.*] Stricken by the supposed malign influence of an adverse planet; blasted.

They being affrighted (as it were Planet-struck) and confounded with shame 1658.

Plangent (plæ·ndʒĕnt), *a.* 1822. [ad. L. *plangentem*, pr. pple. of *plangere* to strike noisily, beat the breast, etc.] **1.** Making the noise of waves beating on the shore, etc. **2.**

Loud-sounding; applied sometimes to a metallic, sometimes to a loud thrilling or plaintive sound 1858.

1. With pulse of p. water like a knell SWINBURNE. 2. This rugged young King, with his p. metallic voice CARLYLE. Hence **Pla·ngency,** the quality of being p. **Pla·ngently** *adv.*

Plani- (plē̆ⁱni), comb. form of L. *planus* level, flat, smooth.

Planiform (plēⁱ·nifǭɹm) *a.*, having a flattened shape; *spec.* in *Anat.* = ARTHRODIAL. **Planipennate** (plēⁱnipe·nēt) [L. *pennatus* winged] *a.*, *Zool.* having flat wings; (*b*) *spec.* in *Entom.* belonging to the suborder *Planipennia* of neuropterous insects, characterized by flat wings not folded when at rest. **Planipe·talous** *a.*, *Bot.* having flat petals.

Planimeter (plăni·mĭtəɹ). Also **-metre.** 1858. [ad. F. *planimètre*, f. PLANI-; see -METER.] An instrument for mechanically measuring the area of an irregular plane figure. So **Planime·tric, -al** *adjs.* **Plani·metry,** the measurement of plane surfaces; plane geometry.

Planing (plēⁱ·niŋ), *vbl. sb.* late ME. [-ING [1].] The action of PLANE *v.*[1] *Comb.*: **p.-machine,** a machine (of various kinds) for planing wood or metal; **-mill,** = planing-machine; also, a workshop where planing is done.

Planish (plæ·niʃ), *v.* late ME. [f. obs. F. *planiss-*, *planir* to smooth (F. *aplanir*), f. *plan* level, flat; see -ISH [2].] *trans.* To make level or smooth; to level. **b.** *spec.* To flatten (sheet-metal or metal-ware) on an anvil by blows of a smooth-faced hammer, etc.; to flatten and reduce in thickness; to reduce (coining-metal) to the required thickness by passing between rollers; to polish (paper, etc.) by means of a roller 1688. Hence **Pla·nisher,** a person who planishes; a tool or instrument used for planishing. **Pla·nishing** *vbl. sb.*, chiefly *attrib.* and *Comb.*, as **p. hammer,** a hammer with polished slightly convex faces, used for planishing sheet-metal; **-roller,** a roller used in planishing; *esp.* in *pl.*, the second pair of rollers, of hardened and polished iron, between which coining-metal is passed to reduce it to the proper thickness.

Planisphere (plæ·nisfīəɹ). [In ME. form *planisperie*, ad. med.L. *planisphærium*, f. L. *planus* PLANE *a.* + *sphæra*, Gr. σφαῖρα SPHERE; in form *planisphere*, a. OF. *planisphère.*] A map or chart formed by the projection of a sphere, or part of one, on a plane; now *esp.* a polar projection of half (or more of) the celestial sphere, as in one form of the astrolabe.

Revolving p., a device consisting of a polar projection of the whole of the heavens visible in a particular latitude, covered by a card with an elliptical opening, which can be adjusted so as to show the part of the heavens visible at a given time. Hence **Planisphe·ral, -sphe·ric, -al** *adjs.*

Plank (plæŋk), *sb.* [ME. *planke*, a. ONF. *planke*, = F. *planche*:—post-Aug. L. *planca* board, plank, slab.] **1.** A long flat piece of smoothed timber, thicker than a BOARD; *spec.* a length of timber sawn to a thickness of from two to six inches, a width of nine inches or more, and eight feet or upwards in length. **b.** Without *a* and *pl.* Timber cut into planks; planking 1559. **c.** *fig.* esp. in ref. to the use of a plank to save a shipwrecked man from drowning. **2.** Applied to various things consisting or formed of a flat slab of wood, as a narrow foot-bridge, a table or board, etc. late ME. **3.** *fig.* An item of a political or other programme. (Cf. PLATFORM III. 5 b.) Orig. and chiefly *U.S.* 1848.

1. c. This is indeed the only p. we have to trust to, that can save us from shipwreck 1690. 3. Another 'plank' is the restriction of Chinese immigration 1884.

Phrases. *P.-over-p.*, with the outside planks overlapping as in a clinker-built vessel. *To walk the p.*, to walk blindfold along a p. laid over the side of a ship until one falls into the sea (as pirates are said to have made their captives do).

attrib. and *Comb.*, as **p.-bed,** a bed of boards resting on low trestles, without a mattress, used as part of the discipline of convents, prisons, etc.; **-road,** a road made of a flooring of planks laid transversely on longitudinal bearing timbers (*U.S.*); **-way,** the narrow portion of deck between the side and the frame of the hatch in a wherry, etc.

Plank (plæŋk), *v.* late ME. [f. prec. sb.] **1.** *trans.* To furnish, lay, floor, or cover with planks. Also with *over.* **b.** To fasten *together* or *down* with planks 1864. **2. a.** To put down; to deposit, plant. *colloq.* 1859. **b.** To table or lay down money; to pay on the spot. Const. *down, out, up. U.S. colloq.* 1824. **3.** *techn.* **a.** To splice together (slivers of wool) into rovings. **b.** To harden (a hat) by felting. 1874. **4.** *U.S.* To fix on a board (a fish that has been split open, or meat) and cook at a hot fire 1855. **5.** *intr.* (also with *it*). To sleep on a plank or a hard surface 1829.

1. The Sides were planck'd with Pine DRYDEN. b. Boats planked together two and two CARLYLE.

Planked (plæŋkt), *ppl. a.* 1608. [f. prec. + -ED [1].] **1.** Furnished, laid, etc. with planks. **2.** Of fish, etc.: see sense 4 above.

Planking (plæ·ŋkiŋ). *vbl. sb.* 1495. [f. PLANK *v.* + -ING [1].] **1.** The action of PLANK *v.* **2.** *concr.* Planks in the mass; plank-work; the planks of a structure; *spec.* those forming the outer shell and inner lining of a ship 1751.

Plankton (plæ·ŋktǫn). 1892. [a. G., a. Gr. πλαγκτόν, neut. of πλαγκτός vbl. adj., drifting, f. πλάζεσθαι to drift.] *Biol.* A collective name for all the forms of floating or drifting organic life found at various depths in the ocean, or in bodies of fresh water. Hence **Plankto·nic** *a.*

Planner (plæ·nəɹ). 1716. [f. PLAN *v.* + -ER [1].] One who plans or makes a plan; *spec.* in *Sc.*, a landscape gardener.

Plano- [1] (plēⁱno), used as comb. form of L. *planus* flat, smooth, level; denoting (*a*) flatly, in a flattened manner, with modification of a specified form in the direction of a plane, as *p.-conical, -orbicular*; (*b*) a combination of a plane with another surface, esp. plane on one side, and of another surface on the other, as PLANO-CONCAVE, -CONVEX, etc. Also **p.-horizontal,** having a plane horizontal surface or position; **-subulate,** of a flat, awl-shaped form.

Plano- [2] (plæno), bef. a vowel or *h* **plan-,** comb. form of Gr. πλάνος wandering, as in **Pla·noblast** [Gr. βλαστός sprout, shoot], *Zool.* the free-swimming generative bud or gonophore of certain Hydrozoa, usu. a craspedote medusa or medusoid.

Pla:no-co·ncave, *a.* 1693. [f. PLANO-[1] + CONCAVE.] Having one surface plane and the opposite one concave, as a lens.

Pla:no-co·nvex, *a.* 1665. [f. as prec. + CONVEX.] **1.** Having one surface plane and the opposite one convex; chiefly of lenses. **b.** Of a crystal: Having some faces plain and others convex 1805. **2.** Having a flattened convex form 1843.

‖**Planorbis** (plănǭ·ɹbis). 1833. [mod.L., f. *planus* PLANE *a.* + *orbis* ORB.] *Zool.* A genus of fresh-water snails (pond-snails), characterized by a flat rounded spiral shell.

Plant (plɑnt), *sb.* [In sense 1, OE. *plante* fem., ad. L. *planta* sprout, slip, cutting. Later senses are affected by med. or mod. uses of L. *planta*, and by F. *plante*, or are derivs. of PLANT *v.*] **I. 1.** A young tree, shrub, or herb for planting; a set, cutting, slip; a sapling. *Obs.* or *dial.* (In local use the name for seedling vegetables at this stage, as 'healthy cabbage plants', etc.) **b.** A young sapling used as a pole, staff, or cudgel. Now chiefly *dial.* late ME. **c.** *fig.* Anything planted; a scion, offshoot, nurseling; a young person; a novice. Now *rare.* late ME. **2.** A member of the vegetable kingdom; a vegetable; generally distinguished from an animal by the absence of locomotion and of special organs of sensation and digestion, and by the power of feeding wholly on inorganic substances. Often restricted to the smaller, esp. herbaceous plants, to the exclusion of trees and shrubs 1551.

1. b. Take a p. of stubborn oak And labour him with many a sturdy stroke DRYDEN. 2. *fig.* Government has been a fossil; it should be a p. EMERSON.

II. Chiefly from PLANT *v.* **1.** *collect.* A crop 1832. **b.** *abstr.* Growth 1844. **2.** The way in which one plants himself; footing, pose 1817. **3.** A deposit of fish-spawn, fry, or oysters; *ellipt.* an oyster which has been bedded or is intended for bedding, as dist. from a native. *U.S.* 1868. **4.** The fixtures, implements, machinery, and apparatus used in carrying on any industrial process. (In Great Britain rarely with *a* or *pl.*) 1789. **b.** *fig.* with ref. to spiritual or intellectual work 1861. **5.** [f. PLANT *v.* III. 2.] A hoard of stolen goods; also the place where they are hidden. *Thieves' slang.* 1796. **6.** A swindle; an elaborately planned burglary or other form of theft or robbery (*slang* or *colloq.*) 1825. **7.** [f. PLANT *v.* I. 2 c.] A spy, a detective; a picket of detectives (*slang*) 1812.

1. b. *In p.*, growing, in leaf; *to lose p.*, to die off; *to fail in* or *miss p.*, to fail to spring from seed. 6. 'It's a conspiracy', said Ben Allen. 'A regular p.', added Mr. Bob Sawyer DICKENS.

Comb.: **p.-beetle,** a beetle of the family *Chrysomelidæ*, feeding on plants, a leaf-beetle; **-bug,** any one of various hemipterous insects (esp. of the family *Capsidæ*) that infest, and feed upon the juices of, plants; **-cane,** a sugar-cane of one year's growth; **-cutter,** a passerine bird of the S. American genus *Phytotoma*, having the habit of biting off the shoots of plants; **-louse,** any small hemipterous insect that infests plants; *esp.* an aphis.

Plant (plɑnt), *v.* [OE. *plantian*, and OF. *planter*, ad. L. *plantare* to plant, fix in place, f. *planta* PLANT *sb.*] **I.** To plant a thing in or on a place. **1.** *trans.* To set in the ground so that it may take root and grow (a tree or herb, a shoot, cutting, root, bulb, or tuber; occas., a seed; hence, a crop, a garden, forest, etc.). **b.** To introduce (a breed of animals) into a country; to deposit (young fish, spawn, oysters) in a river, tidal water, etc.; to naturalize 1899. **2.** To place firmly, to fix *in* or *on* the ground, etc.; to set *down* or *up* in a firm position; to fix in position; to post, station. late ME. **b.** To place (artillery) in position for firing 1560. **c.** To station (a person); *esp.* (in slang or vulgar use) to post as a spy or detective 1693. **d.** *refl.* To place, station, post oneself; to take up one's position 1703. **3.** To found, establish, institute (a community, etc., esp. a colony, city, or church). Now *rare.* OE. **b.** To settle (a person) in a place as a colonist, etc. ME. **c.** *refl.* To establish oneself, settle 1560. **4.** To place *in* some local position; to locate, situate; in *pa. pple.* situated 1558. **5.** *fig.* from prec. senses. **a.** To implant, cause (an idea, etc.) to take root in the mind. late ME. **b.** To settle, establish firmly, as a principle, religion, practice, etc. 1529. **c.** To set up (a person or thing) in some position or state 1562.

1. Plaunt þou a vine WYCLIF. Phr. *P. out*, to transfer from a pot or frame to the open ground; to set out (seedlings) at intervals, so as to give room for growth. 2. He planted the British Colours on the Castle 1714. b. Four swivel guns..were planted at the mouth of each funnel 1748. c. He was planted (to use a vulgar phrase) upon me by his party COBDEN. d. One grisly old wolf-dog..had planted himself close by the chair SCOTT. 3. Planting..schools for the education of youth 1656. b. My being planted so well in Brazil DE FOE. 4. A Town.. finely built, but foolishly planted 1624. 5. a. That noble Thirst of Fame and Reputation which is planted in the Hearts of all Men STEELE. c. A man in all the worlds new fashion planted SHAKS.

II. With the place as object. **a.** To furnish (a piece of land) with growing plants 1585. **b.** To furnish *with* a number of things disposed over the surface. late ME. **c.** To furnish a district *with* settlers or colonists; to stock *with* inhabitants, cattle, etc. 1608.

a. With wild Thyme and Sav'ry, p. the Plain DRYDEN. b. A vast Ocean planted with innumerable Islands ADDISON.

III. Colloquial uses, orig. slang or vulgar. **1.** To deliver (a blow, etc.) with definite aim. *Pugilistic slang.* 1808. **2.** To hide, conceal; esp. stolen goods. Orig. *Thieves' slang.* 1610. **3.** To 'salt' a mining claim. *Gold-digging slang.* 1850. **b.** To devise as a 'plant' or fraudulent scheme 1892. **4.** To abandon. [Cf. F. *planter là.*] *rare.* 1821.

1. I planted a stomacher in his fifth button MARRYAT. 4. He makes her a most exemplary husband; and then, all at once, he plants her; plants her at once and for ever 1858. Hence **Pla·ntable** *a.* capable of being planted; fit for planting or cultivation.

†**Pla·ntage.** 1606. [a. F., f. *planter*; see prec. and -AGE.] **1.** The cultivation of plants; planting –1688. **2.** Plants in the mass; vegetation, herbage –1825.

2. As true as steele, as p. to the Moone SHAKS.

Plantain [1] (plæ·nteⁱn, -tĕn). [ME. a. OF. *plantain*, *-ein*:—L. *plantaginem* (nom. *plantago*) plantain, app. from the root of *planta* sole of the foot, in ref. to its broad prostrate leaves.]

1. A plant of the genus *Plantago*, esp. the Greater Plantain, *P. major*, a low herb with broad flat leaves spread close to the ground, and close spikes of inconspicuous flowers, followed by dense cylindrical spikes of seeds. 2. Applied with defining words to other plants resembling the plantain 1538.

1. Plantayne or weybrede..is called also..grete plantayne, and groweth in moyst places & playne feldes 1516. Long, Narrow-leaved, or Ribwort P., *Plantago lanceolata*. 2. **Bastard P.**, *Limosella aquatica*. **Water P.**, *Alisma Plantago*.

Plantain [2] (plæ·ntéin, -tėn). Now *Obs.* or *rare*. 1535. [a. obs. F., used beside *platane*, ad. L. *platanus*; cf. next.] The Plane (*Platanus orientalis*).

Plantain [3] (plæ·ntéin, -tėn). 1555. [In 16th c. *platan*, *plantan(e*, ad. Sp. *plátano*, *plántano*, in same sense, identical in form with *plátano*, *plántano* plane-tree.] 1. A tree-like tropical herbaceous plant (*Musa paradisiaca*) closely allied to the Banana (*M. sapientum*), having immense undivided oblong leaves, and bearing its fruit in long densely-clustered spikes 1604. 2. The fruit of this plant, a long, somewhat pod-shaped, or cucumber-like, fleshy fruit (botanically a berry); it forms a staple food in most countries within the tropics.

attrib. and *Comb.*, as **p.-cutter**, **-eater**, a bird of the genus *Musophaga* or of the family *Musophagidæ*, a TOURACO; **-meal**, the powdered substance of the dried fruit of the p.

Plantal (plæ·ntăl), *a.* Now *rare*. 1642. [f. PLANT + -AL, after *animal*.] Pertaining or relating to a plant; vegetable; used by Henry More as tr. Gr. φυτικός.

Pla·nt-a·nimal. Now *rare*. 1621. [a. early mod. L. *plantanimal*, tr. Gr. ζωόφυτον.] A zoophyte or 'animal plant'.

Plantar (plæ·ntăɹ), *a.* 1706. [ad. L. *plantaris* adj., f. *planta* sole.] *Anat.* Pertaining or relating to the sole of the foot.

Plantation (plɑntēⁱ·ʃən). 1450. [ad. L. *plantationem*, n. of action f. *plantare* to plant; see -ATION.] 1. The action of planting, the placing of plants in the soil so that they may grow. Now *rare*. b. The settlement of persons in some locality; *esp.* colonization 1586. 2. An assemblage of growing plants of any kind which have been planted 1569. b. Now *esp.*, a wood of planted trees 1669. †3. *fig.* That which has been planted, founded, or settled, as an institution, a mission station -1704. 4. A settlement in a new or conquered country; a colony. Also *transf. Obs.* exc. *Hist.* 1614. †b. A company of settlers or colonists -1715. 5. An estate or farm, esp. in a tropical country, on which cotton, tobacco, sugar-cane, coffee, or other crops are cultivated, formerly chiefly by servile labour 1706.

1. *fig.* The p. of churches and the propagation of the gospel 1795. b. The first p. of Inhabitants, immediately after the Deluge 1625. 2. b. A plain.. covered with corn, grass, or plantations 1806. 4. Ireland and the Plantations in America..are a Burthen to England PETTY. Phr. *To send* (prisoners, etc.) *to the plantations*, i.e. to penal servitude or indentured labour in the colonies, a method of punishment in the 17th and 18th c. *Comb.* †**P. Office**, early name of the Colonial Office.

Planted (plɑ·ntėd), *ppl. a.* ME. [f. PLANT *v.* + -ED [1].] 1. Set in the ground, as a plant; fixed in the ground, set up, established, etc. (see PLANT *v.*). 2. Furnished with plants, trees, etc. late ME.

Planter (plɑ·ntəɹ). ME. [f. PLANT *v.* + -ER [1].] I. Of persons. 1. One who plants or sows; hence, a cultivator of the soil, a farmer, an agriculturist. Also *fig.* 2. An early settler; a pioneer; a colonist; in Ireland, one of the English or Scotch settlers planted on forfeited lands in the 17th c. *Hist.* 1620. b. In Ireland, A person settled in the holding of an evicted tenant 1890. 3. The proprietor or occupier of a plantation or cultivated estate, *esp.*, now, in tropical and sub-tropical countries. Often in comb., as *cotton-*, *sugar-*, *tobacco-p.* 1647.

II. Of things and beasts. 1. A machine for planting or sowing seeds, as *potato p.*, etc. 1856. 2. *U.S.* A snag formed by a tree-trunk embedded in a more or less erect position in a river 1802. 3. *colloq.* A horse that has the habit of refusing to move 1864. Hence **Pla·ntership**, the office or condition of a p.

Plantigrade (plæ·ntigrēⁱd), *a.* (*sb.*) 1831. [a. F., f. L. *planta* sole + *-gradus* going, walking.] Walking upon the soles of the feet (opp. to DIGITIGRADE); also said of the feet, or of the walk, of an animal. Commonly restricted to the former tribe *Plantigrada* of carnivorous mammals; comprising the bear, wolverene, badger, racoon, etc. b. In ref. to human beings: Placing the whole sole of the foot upon the ground at once in walking 1837. c. *transf.* Of or belonging to a plantigrade animal, as a bear 1853. B. *sb.* A plantigrade animal; *esp.* one of the order *Plantigrada* 1835.

Pla·nting, *vbl. sb.* OE. [f. PLANT *v.* + -ING [1].] 1. The action of PLANT *v.*, q.v. 2. A clump or bed of things planted; *esp.* a clump or wood of planted trees; a plantation. Chiefly *Sc.* and *n. dial.* 1632.

Pla·ntlet. 1816. [f. PLANT *sb.* + -LET.] An embryo plant; a diminutive plant.

Planto·cracy. 1846. [irreg. f. PLANT(ER + -OCRACY, after *aristocracy*, etc.] A dominant class or caste consisting of planters (in the W. Indies, etc.).

Plantule (plæ·ntiul). 1733. [ad. mod.L. *plantula*, dim. of *planta* a shoot.] *Bot.* An embryonic or rudimentary plant.

‖**Planula** (plæ·niŭlă). *Pl.* -æ. 1870. [mod. L., a little plane, dim. of *planus* PLANE *a.*] *Zool.* The flat-shaped ciliated free-swimming embryo of certain Hydrozoa; hence extended to a similar embryo in Cœlenterates generally.

Planxty (plæ·ŋksti). 1790. [Origin unkn.] *Irish Music.* 'A harp tune of a sportive and animated character, moving in triplets' (Stainer and Barrett).

Plap (plæp), *v.* 1846. [Onomatopœic. See also PLOP.] *intr.* To come down or fall with a flat impact, and with the sound that this makes. Also as *sb.* or *adv.*

‖**Plaque** (plɑk). 1848. [F., ad. Du. *plakke* PLACK.] 1. An ornamental tablet of metal or porcelain, either plain or decorated, intended to be hung up on a wall, inserted in a piece of furniture, etc. 1875. b. A small tablet worn as a badge of high rank in an honorary order 1848. 2. *Path.* A patch of eruption or the like 1876. So ‖**Plaque·tte**, a small p.

Plash (plæʃ), *sb.*[1] [OE. *plæsc*, ME. *plasch*; prob. onomatopœic.] A shallow piece of standing water; a marshy pool; a puddle.

Two frogs..consulted when their p. was drie whither they should go BACON.

Plash, *sb.*[2] (*adv.* or *int.*) 1513. [Goes with PLASH *v.*[2]] 1. The noise made when a body strikes the surface of water so as to break it up, or plunges into or through it; an act accompanied by this noise; a plunge, a splash. b. The like noise produced when water, etc., falls upon a body, or when masses of water dash against each other; an act producing this noise 1808. 2. *advb.* or *int.* With a plash 1842.

2. We go p., p., p., in the lawn-like glade LIVINGSTONE.

Plash, *sb.*[3] *Obs.* or *dial.* 1638. [f. next.] A plashed bough or bush; a plashed thicket.

Plash (plæʃ), *v.*[1] late ME. [a. OF. *plais-s(i)er*, *plai(s)cier*, etc. :—late L. **plectiare*, f. **plectia* twined or plaited hedge, f. L. *plectere* to plait. Cf. PLEACH.] 1. *trans.* To bend down and interweave (stems half cut through, branches, and twigs) so as to form them into a hedge or fence 1495. †b. To bend down, break down (trees, bushes, etc.) for other purposes -1727. †c. To interlace (a fruit-tree in trellis-work); to train against a trellis or a wall -1676. †d. To intertwine, like plants in a thicket -1735. 2. a. To make, dress, or renew (a hedge) by cutting the stems half through, and interlacing stems, branches, and twigs, so as to form a close low fence; to 'lay' (a hedge) 1523. †b. To treat (a wood, etc.) in the same way, in order to obstruct a pass or entrance, or defend a fastness; to form hurdles, weirs, etc. by such interweaving -1796.

Plash (plæʃ), *v.*[2] 1582. [Cf. PLASH *sb.*[2]] 1. *trans.* To strike the surface of (water) so as to break it up; to plunge into (water, etc.) or drive it against a body or against itself with commotion and noise; to splash. b. To dash with breaking water, etc., so as to wet; to splash. Also *absol.* 1602. c. To splash (a wall) with wet colouring matter 1864. 2. *intr.* a. To splash through, or dash about in water with commotion and noise 1650. b. Of water, etc.: To dash against or upon a body; to tumble about in agitation, with the noise of breaking water 1665.

1. b. The floor all plashed with blood 1856. 2. a. The fish were jumping and plashing THACKERAY. b. Far below him plashed the waters LONGF.

Pla·shing, *vbl. sb.* 1495. [f. PLASH *v.*[1] + -ING [1].] The action of PLASH *v.*[1] Also *concr.* A piece of plashed hedge or thicket.

Plashy (plæ·ʃi), *a.*[1] 1552. [f. PLASH *sb.*[1] + -Y [1].] Abounding in puddles; marshy, swampy, boggy; wet and sloppy; full of plashes of rain.

Those slymie plashie fieldes 1599.

Pla·shy, *a.*[2] 1582. [f. PLASH *sb.*[2] + -Y [1].] That plashes; that dashes or falls with a plash, as water; that splashes the water.

Plasm (plæ·z'm). 1620. [ad. late L. *plasma*; see next.] †1. A mould or matrix in which something is cast or formed; the cast of a fossil. Also *fig.* -1764. 2. *Phys.* = PLASMA 3. 1876. 3. *Biol.* The living matter of a cell, protoplasm; occas. *spec.* the general body of protoplasm as dist. from the nucleus 1864.

‖**Plasma** (plæ·zmă). 1712. [Late and eccl. L., a thing formed or moulded, a. Gr. πλάσμα, f. πλάσσειν to mould.] †1. Form, mould, shape (*rare*) -1829. 2. A subtranslucent green variety of quartz, allied to chalcedony and heliotrope, anciently used for ornaments 1772. 3. *Phys.* The colourless coagulable liquid part of blood, lymph, or milk, in which the corpuscles (or, in milk, oil-globules) float; also, the similar liquid obtained from fresh muscle 1845. 4. *Biol.* = PLASM 3. 1864. So **Plasma·tic** *a.*, relating to the p., esp. of the blood.

Plasmic (plæ·zmik), *a.* 1875. [f. PLASM or PLASMA + -IC.] Pertaining to or consisting of plasm; protoplasmic.

Plasmin (plæ·zmin). 1866. [ad. F. *plasmine* f. PLASMA + *-ine*, -IN [1].] *Chem.* A proteid substance obtained from the plasma of the blood, soluble in water, the solution coagulating into fibrin.

Plasmo-, bef. a vowel **plasm-**, shortened comb. form of Gr. πλάσμα, πλασματ- plasm. (The fuller form is *plasmato-*.)

‖**Plasmodium** (plæzmōᵘ·diŏm). *Pl.* -ia. 1875. [mod.L., f. PLASMA + *-odium*; see -ODE.] *Biol.* 1. A mass or sheet of naked protoplasm, formed by the fusion, or by the aggregation, of a number of amœboid bodies, and having an amœboid creeping movement. 2. Name given to certain parasitic organisms found in the blood of patients with recent malaria, and quartan and tertian ague 1895. Hence **Plasmo·dial**, **Plasmodic** (-ǫ·dik) *adjs.* pertaining to, of the nature of, or arising from a p.

Plasmogen (plæ·zmŏdʒėn). 1888. [f. PLASMO- + -GEN.] *Biol.* The chemically highest or most elaborate form, stage, or part of protoplasm, which by its vital activity forms the tissues or other organic products; true or formative protoplasm; bioplasm.

Plasmogeny (plæzmǫ·dʒėni), **-gony** (-gŏni). 1876. [f. PLASMO- + -GENY; in form *plasmogony*, with suffix repr. Gr. -γονία generation.] *Biol.* A mode of spontaneous generation.

Plasmology (plæzmǫ·lŏdʒi). 1888. [f. as prec. + -LOGY.] The study of the ultimate corpuscles of living matter.

‖**Plasmolysis** (plæzmǫ·lisis). 1885. [f. PLASMO- + Gr. λύσις loosing, setting free.] *Biol.* Contraction of the protoplasm of a vegetable cell with separation or freeing of the lining layer from the cell-wall, due to the withdrawal of liquid by exosmosis when the cell is placed in a liquid of greater density than the cell-sap. Hence **Pla·smolyse** *v.* to subject to p. **Plasmoly·tic** *a.* pertaining to, showing, or causing p.

Plasson (plæ·sǫn). 1879. [a. G. *plasson*, a. Gr. πλάσσων, -ον, pres. pple. of πλάσσειν to mould.] *Biol.* The homogeneous protoplasm of hypothetical primitive organisms, not yet differentiated into nucleus and general cell-substance, or that of non-nucleated cells or cytodes.

-plast, comb. element repr. Gr. πλαστός formed, moulded, in *bioplast, endoplast*, etc.

Plaster (plɑ·stəɹ), *sb.* Also *Sc.* and *north. dial.* plaister (plē·stəɹ). [OE. *plaster*, ad. pop. L. *plastrum*, shortened from *emplastrum*, a. Gr. ἔμπλαστρον, var. of ἔμπλαστον plaster, salve, f. ἐμπλαστός vbl. adj. 'daubed on or over'. In ME. reinforced by OF. *plastre*, mod.F. *plâtre*, only in branch II. The history of the form *plaister* is obscure.] **I.** An external curative application, consisting of a more or less solid substance spread upon a piece of muslin, skin, etc., and of such nature as to be adhesive at the temperature of the body; used for the local application of a medicament, or for closing a wound, etc. See also COURT-P., STICKING-P. **b.** *fig.* A healing or soothing means or measure ME.

b. The breath of the people being but a sorry plaister for a wounded conscience 1625.

II. 1. A composition which may be spread or daubed upon a surface, as of a wall, in a plastic state, to harden; *spec.* a mixture of lime, sand, and (usu.) hair, used for covering walls, ceilings, etc. ME. **2.** Sulphate of lime, gypsum: †(*a*) in its natural state; (*b*) powdered, but not calcined; used as a ground for painting and gilding, or for work in relief; (*c*) calcined; = PLASTER OF PARIS. late ME.

attrib. and *Comb.*, as **p.-bronze**, a plaster cast covered with bronze dust, to resemble a bronze; **-jacket**, in orthopædic surgery, a body casing or bandage stiffened with p. of Paris, for correcting curvature of the spine, etc.; **-rock, -stone**, raw gypsum.

Pla·ster, *v.* ME. Also **plaister** (see prec.). [f. prec. sb., or a. F. *plastrer*, mod.F. *plâtrer*, to plaster (a wall).] **1.** *trans.* To overlay, or cover with builder's plaster or the like. **b.** *transf.* To bedaub, cover with any adhesive substance; to overlay with excess of (vulgar) ornament. late ME. **c.** *fig.* To cover, load to excess, e.g. with praise; also, to gloze over; to botch, mend, or restore superficially. Also with *over, up.* 1546. **2.** To treat medically with a plaster. Also *absol.* late ME. **b.** *fig.* To soothe, alleviate; hence, *joc.* to give compensation for. late ME. **3.** To apply (something) like plaster (or a plaster) upon a surface 1864. **4. a.** To treat (wine) with gypsum or sulphate of potash to neutralize acidity. **b.** To dust (vines) with gypsum to prevent rot or mildew of the berries. **c.** To treat (land) with plaster of Paris. 1819.

1. Why could he not plaster the chinks? RUSKIN. **b.** The Great Duke (the breast of whose..coat was plastered with some half-hundred decorations) THACKERAY. **c.** To p. his friends with praise 1865. **2. b.** Clare..gave the man five shillings to p. the blow T. HARDY. Hence **Pla·sterer, †plai·sterer,** one who plasters buildings; one who moulds or casts figures in plaster. **Pla·stery** *a.* of the nature of or like plaster; viscid, tenacious.

Pla·stering, *vbl. sb.* 1440. Also **plaistering.** [-ING[1].] **1.** The action of PLASTER *v.* **2.** *concr.* Plastered work; a coating of plaster, or of anything plastered or daubed on 1538.

Plaster of Paris (plɑ·stərəvpæ·ris). ME. [PLASTER *sb.* II. 2.] A fine white plaster, consisting of gypsum rendered anhydrous by calcination, which swells and rapidly sets when mixed with water; used for making moulds and casts, as a cement, etc.; so called because prepared from the gypsums of Montmartre, Paris.

Plastic (plæ·stik), *a.* 1632. [ad. L. *plasticus*, a. Gr. πλαστικός that may be moulded, f. πλαστός moulded, f. πλάσσειν to mould, form.] **I.** In active sense. **1.** Characterized by moulding, or giving form to clay, wax, etc.; capable of shaping or moulding formless matter. **b.** In surgery: Concerned with remedying a deficiency of structure; reparative of tissue; as *p. surgery, a p. operation* 1879. **2.** Causing the growth or production of natural forms, esp. of living organisms; formerly as an attribute of an alleged principle, virtue, or force in nature; formative, procreative; creative 1646. **3.** *fig.* in ref. to immaterial things, conditions, or forms, literary productions, etc. 1662.

1. *P. art*, the art of shaping or modelling; any art in which this is done, as sculpture or ceramics. So *p. artist*; God, the great p. Artist 1741. **2.** In what diminutives the plastick principle lodgeth is exemplified in seeds SIR T. BROWNE. **3.** The p. energy of the imagination 1877.

II. In neuter and passive sense. **1.** Pertaining to moulding or modelling; produced by moulding, modelling, or sculpture, as dist. from that which is drawn on a surface 1726. **2.** Susceptible of being moulded; readily assuming a new shape 1791. **3.** Of immaterial things and conditions: Impressionable, pliable; susceptible to influence; pliant, supple, flexible 1711. **4.** *Biol.* and *Path.* Capable of forming, or being organized into, living tissue, as *p. lymph*, etc.; pertaining to or accompanied by such a process, as *p. bronchitis* 1834.

2. *P. sulphur*, an allotropic form of sulphur; see N.E.D. *P. clay* (*Geol.*), a name given (after F. *argile plastique*) to the middle group of the Eocene beds, immediately underlying the London clay, now called the Woolwich and Reading series. **3.** While his mind 's ductile and p., I'll place him at Dotheboys Hall 1842.

III. absol. *The p.*: †**a.** The plastic principle or virtue; **b.** plastic art, plastic beauty 1661. Hence **Pla·stically** *adv.* **Plasti·city,** the quality of being p.

Plasticine (plæ·stisīn). 1897. [f. prec. + -INE[4].] Proprietary name of a plastic composition, used in schools, etc. as a substitute for modelling clay.

Plastid (plæ·stid). 1876. [a. G. (Haeckel), f. Gr. πλαστός (see -PLAST) + *-id*, after Gr. -ίδιον, dim. suffix.] **1.** *Biol.* An individual mass or unit of protoplasm, as a cell or unicellular organism. **2.** *Bot.* A differentiated corpuscle or granule occurring in the protoplasm of a vegetable cell; e.g. a chlorophyll-granule, a chromoplastid, or a leucoplastid 1885.

Plastidule (plæ·stidiul). 1877. [a. G. *plastidul* (Haeckel), dim. of *plastid*; see -ULE.] *Biol.* A hypothetical molecule or ultimate particle of protoplasm, constituting a vital unit, and forming an element or constituent of a plastid or cell.

Plastin (plæ·stin). 1889. [f. Gr. πλαστός (see -PLAST) + -IN[1], after *chromatin*.] *Biol.* A viscous substance found in the nucleus of a cell.

Plastogamy (plæstǫ·gămi). 1891. [f. Gr. πλαστός moulded + -γαμία marriage.] *Biol.* The fusion of the protoplasm of two or more cells or unicellular organisms, as in the formation of a plasmodium. Hence **Plastoga·mic** *a.*

Plastron (plæ·strǫn). 1506. [a. F., breast-plate, etc., ad. It. *piastrone*, augm. of *piastra* breast-plate, prop. plate of metal; see PIASTRE, PLASTER.] **1.** A steel breast-plate formerly worn beneath the hauberk. *Obs.* exc. *Hist.* **b.** A leather-covered wadded shield or pad, worn by fencers over the breast 1693. **2.** In women's dress, A kind of ornamental front to a bodice; also, a loose front of lace, etc. 1876. **b.** In men's dress, a starched shirt-front 1890. **3.** *Zool.* (After Cuvier.) The ventral part of the shell of a tortoise or turtle 1831. **b.** Applied to the corresponding part in various other animals, as in certain echinoderms, etc. 1854.

-plasty, comb. element, repr. Gr. -πλαστία, f. πλαστός formed, used in sense 'moulding, formation', as in *dermatoplasty, osteoplasty*, etc.

Plat (plæt), *sb.*[1] *arch.* or *dial.* ME. [app. a. OF., flat surface or thing, dish, etc., sb. use of adj. *plat, plate* flat; see PLAT *a.*] **I.** A flat thing, part, or surface. †**1.** A flat piece, a plate (of metal); a sheet, slice –1503. **2.** The flat part or side of anything; †**a.** The flat of a sword; **b.** The mould-board of a plough (*dial.*) late ME. **3.** A flat country, a plateau or tableland. *U.S.* 1812. **4.** *Mining.* A widened space in a level, near the shaft, where trucks may cross, or ore is collected for hoisting, etc. 1874. **II.** A surface or place generally. †**1.** A surface in general (whether plane or not) –1593. **2.** A place, spot, point of space; a locality or situation. *Obs.* exc. *dial.* 1558.

Plat (plæt), *sb.*[2] 1511. [Collateral f. PLOT *sb.*, infl. by prec.] **I.** = PLOT *sb.* I. 2 (which is found earlier). A piece of ground (usually) of small extent; a patch; as *grass-p.*, etc. 1517.

On a P. of rising ground, I hear the far-off Curfeu sound MILT.

II. = PLOT *sb.* II. 1. Now only *U.S.*

Plat (plæt), *sb.*[3] *Obs.* or *dial.* 1503. [Collateral f. PLAIT *sb.*, going with PLAT *v.*[1]] **1.** = PLAIT *sb.* 2. 1535. **2.** *Naut. pl.* Flat ropes made of rope-yarn, and plaited one over another.

1. Her haire nor loose nor ti'd in formall p. SHAKS.

‖ **Plat** (pla), *sb.*[4] 1763. [F., dish; see PLATE *sb.*] A dish.

Olives..a favourite 'plat' of mine BYRON.

Plat (plæt), *a.* and *adv.* *Obs.* exc. *dial.* ME. [a. F.:—late pop. L. **plattus* adj., flat, smooth; perh. f. Gr. πλατύς broad, flat. Cf. PLACE, PLATE.] **A.** *adj.* †**1.** Flat, level; plane; plain –1584. †**2.** *fig.* 'Flat', plain, blunt, straightforward, downright, unqualified; esp. in phr. *p. and plain* –1560. **B.** *adv.* †**1.** Of position: In or into a flat position, flatly, flat; level with the ground or any surface –1598. **2.** Of manner: Flatly, bluntly, straightforwardly. Often *p. and plain.* Now *Sc.* and *n. dial.* late ME.

Plat (plæt), *v.*[1] *Pa. t.* and *pple.* **platted.** late ME. [Parallel form of PLAIT *v.*, going with PLAT *sb.*[3]] *trans.* To intertwine, intertwist; to plait (hair, straw, etc.); to form (hats, etc.) by plaiting; = PLAIT *v.* 2. Now a less usual spelling than PLAIT (which, however, in this sense, is usu. pronounced *plat*).

Plat, *v.*[2] 1556. [In origin, collateral form of PLOT *v.*] †**1.** *trans.* To plan; to sketch –1609. **2.** = PLOT *v.* 3. Now only *U.S.* 1751.

Platan (plæ·tăn). Also **-ane.** late ME. [ad. L. *platanus* PLANE *sb.*[1]] The Oriental Plane-tree (*Platanus orientalis*): = PLANE *sb.*[1] 1.

‖ **Platanus** (plæ·tănǫs). late ME. [L., a. Gr. πλάτανος PLANE *sb.*[1]] **1.** = prec. Also *p.-tree.* Now *rare.* **2.** *Bot.* The name of a genus of trees constituting the N.O. *Platanaceæ.*

Platband (plæ·tbænd). 1696. [a. F. *plate-bande*, f. *plate* fem., flat + *bande*.] **1.** *Arch.* **a.** A flat rectangular moulding or fascia, the projection of which is less than its breadth. **b.** The list or fillet between the flutings of a column. **2.** *Hort.* A narrow bed of flowers or strip of turf forming a border 1727.

Plate (plēit), *sb.* [ME. a. OF. *plate* thin plate, lamina of metal, etc., orig. fem. form of F. *plat, plate*:—late and med.L. *plattus, -a, -um* adj. 'flat'; see PLAT *a.*] **I.** A flat sheet of metal, etc. **1.** A flat, thin, usu. rigid sheet, slice, leaf, or lamina of metal or other substance, of more or less uniform thickness and even surface. **b.** *Anat., Zool.*, and *Bot.* A thin flat organic structure or formation 1658. **2.** As a material: Metal beaten, rolled, or cast into sheets. late ME. **3. a.** One of the thin pieces of iron or steel composing plate-armour. **b.** (without *a* and *pl.*) Plate-armour; often *attrib.* Cf. BREAST-PLATE, etc. Now *Hist.* or *arch.* ME. **4.** A flat piece or slab of metal, wood, etc., forming or adapted to form part of a piece of mechanism, etc.; e.g. **a.** each of the parallel sheets of metal forming the back and front walls of a lock, or of a watch or clock; **b.** one of the sheets of which ship's armour, steam-boilers, etc. are composed; **c.** (*Dentistry*) the portion of a denture which fits to the mouth and holds the teeth; **d.** a CENTRE-BOARD. late ME.; **e.** (*Wireless*) the anode of a thermionic tube, orig. a flat plate, now a cylinder surrounding the cathode or filament 1918. **5.** A smooth or polished plate of metal, etc. for writing or engraving on. late ME. **b.** Such a plate of metal, etc., bearing a name or inscription, for affixing to anything, as BRASS *p.*, DOOR-*p.*, NAME-*p.* 1668. **c.** *Photogr.* A thin sheet of metal, porcelain, or (now usu.) glass, coated with a film sensitive to light, on which photographs are taken 1840. **6.** A polished sheet of copper or steel engraved to print from; hence **b.** an impression from this, an engraving. Also short for BOOK-PLATE. **c.** A stereotype or electrotype cast of a page of composed movable types, from which the sheets are printed 1824. **7.** *Arch.* A horizontal timber at the top or bottom of a framing, as *ground, roof, wall, window p.* 1449. **8.** A wheel-track consisting of a flat strip of iron or steel with a projecting flange to retain the wheels, on which colliery trams are run; an early form of railroad; also *p.-rail.* Locally retained for a railway rail; cf. PLATE-LAYER. 1825. **9.** *Mining* Shale, thin slaty rock 1794.

1. Plates of glass 1665. **b.** *Blood-p.* = HÆMATO-

BLAST a. 3. In mail and p. of Milan steel SCOTT. 5. c. A *whole-plate* measures $8\frac{1}{2}\times6\frac{1}{2}$ inches; *half-plate* (English) $6\frac{1}{2}\times4\frac{1}{4}$ inches; (*U.S.*) $5\frac{1}{2}\times4\frac{1}{4}$ inches; *quarter-plate*, $4\frac{1}{4}\times3\frac{1}{4}$ inches. *Dry p.*: see DRY *a.*

II. A thin piece of silver or gold; silver or gold utensils. †**1.** A silver coin; usu. in full *p. of silver, silvern p.*; *spec.* from 16th c. the Spanish coin *real de plata*, the eighth part of a piastre –1606. **2.** Precious metal; bullion; from 16th c. usu. silver, after Sp. *plata*. Now only *Hist.* late ME. **3.** *collect. sing.* Utensils for table and domestic use, ornaments, etc., **a.** orig. of silver or gold. late ME. **b.** Extended to plated ware, and to other kinds of metal, as *pewter p., electro-p.*, etc. 1545. **4.** *Her.* A roundel argent 1562. **5.** Orig., in *Horse-racing*, a prize consisting of a gold or silver cup or the like given to the winner of a race; now, also, a prize in other contests; loosely, a contest in which the prize is a plate 1675.

1. Realms & Islands were As plates dropt from his pocket SHAKS. **3.** A salt-cellar of silver,..one of the neatest pieces of p. that ever I saw PEPYS. **b.** Spoons and forks of real silver, not trumpery p. 1889. **5.** *Selling-p.*, a horse-race the condition of entry to which is that the winner must be sold at a price previously fixed.

III. A shallow, usu. circular vessel, orig. of metal or wood, now commonly of earthenware or china, from which food is eaten; as *dessert, dinner, fruit, soup p.* 1450. **b.** *transf.* That which is placed on a plate; *spec.* †(*a*) a supply of food; eating and drinking; †(*b*) a dish or course 1577. **c.** A similar vessel of metal or wood used for taking the collection at places of worship, etc.; hence *colloq.*, the amount taken up. 1779.

attrib. and *Comb.*: **p.-basket,** (*a*) a baize-lined basket in which silver spoons, forks, etc. are kept; (*b*) a metal-lined basket for removing plates, etc. which have been used at table; **-bolt,** (*a*) a bolt which slides on a flat plate; (*b*) a bolt having a wide flat head; **-bone,** the shoulder-blade; **-cultivation, -culture,** the culture of micro-organisms on glass plates; **-day,** the day of the race for a p.; **-horse** = PLATER 3; **-lock,** a lock having the outer case of wood; also, a lock in which the works are pivoted on an iron plate; **-man,** a man who has charge of plate (sense 3); **-matter,** stereotype matter for newspapers such as is sometimes supplied from a central establishment to local journals; **-paper,** paper of fine quality on which engravings are printed; **-powder,** a polishing powder for silver ware; **-rack,** a frame in which plates are placed to drain, or in which they are usu. kept; also, a grooved frame for draining photographic plates; **p. tracery,** *Arch.* that kind of solid tracery which appears as if formed by piercing a flat surface with ornamental patterns; **-wheel,** a wheel in which the hub is connected with the rim by a p., instead of by spokes.

Plate (plēit), *v.* late ME. [f. prec.] **1.** *trans.* To cover or overlay with plates of metal, for ornament, protection, or strength; to cover (ships, locomotives, etc.) with armour-plates. **2.** To cover articles made of the baser metals with a coating of gold or silver; also iron with tin 1704. **b.** with *on, upon*, and construction reversed 1790. **3.** To make a stereotype or electrotype plate of for printing 1907. **4.** *Philately.* To assign (a stamp, etc.) to its place as originally printed on a sheet; to reconstruct (a sheet of stamps) thus 1896.

Plateau (plæ·tou, plătōu·). *Pl.* **plateaux, -eaus** (-ōuz). 1791. [a. F.:—OF. *platel* flat piece of metal, etc., dim. of *plat*; see PLAT *a.*] **1.** *Geog.* An elevated tract of comparatively flat or level land; a table-land 1796. **2.** *Hist.* **a.** An ornamented tray or dish for table-service. **b.** A decorative plaque 1791.

Plateful (plēi·tful). 1766. [-FUL.] The quantity with which a plate is filled.

Pla·te-gla·ss. 1727. [f. PLATE *sb.* + GLASS *sb.*] A fine quality of thick glass, cast in plates, used for mirrors, shop-windows, etc.

Plate-layer (plēi·t,lēiːəɹ). 1836. *orig.* One who lays, keeps in order, and renews the plates (see PLATE *sb.* I. 8) on a tramway or railway; hence, a man employed in fixing and keeping in order the permanent way of a railway. So **Pla·te-lay·ing.**

Pla·te-mark. 1858. [f. PLATE *sb.* + MARK *sb.*[1]] **1.** A name for the various marks legally impressed on gold and silver plate for the purpose of indicating maker, degree of purity, hall or place of assay, date, etc.; = HALL-MARK. **2.** The impression left on the margin of an engraving by the pressure of the plate 1889. Hence **Pla·te-marked** *a.* having a plate-mark.

Platen, platten (plæ·tĕn, -'n). [ME. *plateyne*, a. OF. *platine*, flat piece, metal plate, f. *plat* adj.; see PLAT *a.* and -INE [4].] †**1.** A flat plate of metal for various purposes –1813. †**2.** = PATEN 1. **3.** *Printing.* An iron (formerly wooden) plate in a printing-press, which presses the paper against the inked type so as to secure an impression. Also applied to similar parts in other machines. 1594.

Comb. **p.-machine, p. printing machine,** a press having a p., as opp. to a rotary or cylinder-press.

Plater (plēi·təɹ). 1771. [f. PLATE *v.* and *sb.* + -ER [1].] **1.** One who plates articles with a film of gold, silver, etc., as *electro-p.*, etc. **2.** A man who manufactures or applies metal plates, esp. in shipbuilding 1864. **3.** *Horse-racing.* A horse that competes chiefly in plate or prize races; an inferior race-horse 1859.

Plateresque (plætəre·sk), *a.* 1842. [ad. Sp. *plateresco*, f. *platero* a silversmith, etc. (f. *plata* silver) + *-esco*; see -ESQUE.] Resembling silver work; applied to a rich grotesque style of decoration, etc.

Platform (plæ·tfǫɹm), *sb.* 1550. [a. F. *plateforme*, lit. 'flat form', 'plane figure', etc.; see PLAT *a.* and FORM *sb.*] **I.** A plane surface; a plane on the flat. †**1.** *Geom.* A plane figure (as a triangle, etc.); also, a plane surface, a plane; any surface –1674. †**2.** A plan or representation on the flat (*of* any structure existing or projected); a ground-plan; a chart, map; a draught to build by 1551. **II.** Fig. uses derived from sense I. 2. †**1.** A plan, design; a model –1827. †**b.** A written outline or sketch; a scheme; a description –1727. †**2. a.** A plan of action; a scheme, design –1815. **b.** *spec.* A plan or draught of church government and discipline. Now *Hist.* 1573. †**c.** A plan of government or administration; a plan of political action –1757.

II. 1. You will..follow the p. of the London petition BURKE **2. b.** No existing Church can find any pattern or p. of its government in those early days 1881.

III. The surface or area on which anything stands. †**1.** The site of a group of buildings, a fort, a camp, or any structure –1796. †**b.** *fig.* The ground, or basis *of* an action, event, calculation, condition, etc. –1832. **c.** *fig.* A plane or level *of* action, thought, etc. *rare.* 1870. **2.** A raised level surface or area: **a.** A level place for mounting guns in a battery 1560. **b.** A natural or artificial terrace; a table-land, a plateau 1580. †**3.** A division of the orlop of a man-of-war, between the cock-pit and the main-mast –1741. **4.** A raised level surface formed with planks, boards, or the like 1727. **b.** A horizontal piece of flooring resting on wheels, as in a railway carriage, truck, or tram-car 1832. **c.** A raised floor along the side of the line at a railway station, for convenience in entering and alighting from the trains 1838. **5.** *spec.* A piece of raised flooring in a hall, or in the open air, from which a speaker addresses his audience, and on which the promoters of a meeting sit; hence *transf.* or allusively in ref. to discussion on a platform, platform oratory, etc 1820. **b.** *fig.* A basis on which persons unitedly take their stand and make their public appeal; *spec.* in U. S. politics, a public declaration of principles and policy issued by the representatives of the party assembled to nominate candidates for an election 1844.

1. c. Conversation in society is found to be on a p. so low as to exclude science, the saint, and the poet EMERSON. **2. b.** The station chosen..was on a grassy p. 1860. **4. c.** Subway to platforms 1, 2, 3, and 4 (*mod.*). **5.** He lamented the growth of the p. He ignored the Press. 1901. **b.** I care nothing for names. All I ask for is a p. and an issue 1847.

attrib. and *Comb.*, as **p.-car** (*U.S.*), **-carriage,** a low four-wheeled wagon or truck without sides, for transporting mortars and other heavy articles; **-crane,** a crane mounted on a railway-truck; **-scale,** a weighing-machine with a p. on which the object to be weighed is placed.

Pla·tform, *v.* 1592. [f. prec.] †**1.** *trans.* To plan, outline, sketch, draw up a scheme of (*lit.* and *fig.*) –1641. †**2.** To furnish (a building) with a platform –1796. **3.** To place on or as on a platform 1793. **4.** *intr.* To speak on a platform 1859.

1. To grant that church discipline is platformed in the Bible MILT. Hence **Pla·tformer.**

Plathelminth: see PLATYHELMINTH.

Platic (plæ·tik), *a.* 1625. [ad. late and med.L. *platicus*, ad. late Gr. πλατικός, -ικός broad, diffuse, f. πλατύς broad; see -IC.] *Astrol.* Of an aspect: Not exact or within a degree, but within half the sum of the 'orbs' of two other planets.

Platin- (plæ·tin), comb. f. PLATINUM bef. a vowel, as in *platinamine*, an amine of platinum.

Platina (plæ·tină, plătī·nă). Now *rare* or *Obs.* 1750. [a. Sp., (platī·na) platinum, dim. of *plata* silver; see -INE [4].] The earlier name of PLATINUM.

Plating (plēi·tiŋ), *vbl. sb.* 1543. [f. PLATE *v.* + -ING [1].] **1.** The action of PLATE *v.*; *esp.* **a.** The process of coating with a thin layer of precious metal 1825. **b.** Plate-racing 1865. **2.** *concr.* The result or product of this action; *esp.* an external layer or sheath of plates 1843; the surface of precious metal with which copper, etc. is plated 1833. **3.** *attrib.* = 'occupied or used in plating', as **p. hammer,** (*a*) a heavy hammer for clinching; (*b*) a steam-hammer for working on armour-plate, etc. 1543.

Platinic (plăti·nik), *a.* 1842. [f. PLATINUM + -IC.] *Chem.* Applied to those compounds of platinum in which it exists in its higher degree of valency, i.e. as a tetrad; as *p. chloride* $PtCl_4$; opp. to PLATINOUS.

Platiniferous (plætini·fĕrəs), *a.* 1828. [f. PLATINUM + -FEROUS.] Bearing or yielding platinum.

Platinize (plæ·tinəiz), *v.* 1825. [f. PLATINUM + -IZE.] *trans.* To coat with platinum. Hence **Platiniza·tion.**

Platino- (plæ·tino), comb. form of PLATINUM; *spec.* in *Chem.* denoting compounds in which it is divalent.

Platinode (plæ·tinōud). 1839. [f. PLATINUM + Gr. ὁδός path, as in *anode*, etc.] *Electr.* The negative plate or pole (cathode) of a voltaic cell (often of platinum); opp. to ZINCODE.

Platinoid (plæ·tinoid), *a.* and *sb.* 1864. [f. PLATINUM + -OID.] **A.** *adj.* Resembling platinum. **B.** *sb.* Name for an alloy of nickel, zinc, copper, and tungsten, of a silvery white colour, and resembling platinum in non-liability to tarnish, etc. 1885.

Platino·so-, comb. form of mod.L. *platinosus* PLATINOUS.

Platinotype (plæ·tinŏtəip). 1880. [f. PLATINO- + TYPE.] *Photogr.* A process of photographic printing by which prints in platinum-black are produced; a print produced by this process 1884.

Platinous (plæ·tinəs), *a.* 1842. [f. next + -OUS c.] *Chem.* Applied to those compounds of platinum in which it exists in its lower degree of valency, i.e. as a dyad. Cf. PLATINIC.

Platinum (plæ·tinŏm). 1812. [mod.L., altered from PLATINA, after the names of other metals in *-um*.] **1.** A somewhat rare metal (orig. named PLATINA), of a white colour like silver, but less bright, very heavy, ductile, and malleable, unaffected by all simple acids, and fusible only at an extremely high temperature; used chiefly in chemical and other scientific processes, and in setting precious stones. Symbol Pt. **2.** *attrib.* **a.** Made or consisting of platinum 1840. **b.** Of, related to, containing, or combined with platinum; as *p. ore, p. salts*; with names of other metals denoting alloys, as *p.-iridium, -steel* 1849.

Comb.: **p.-black,** a black powder resembling lamp-black, consisting of p. in a finely-divided state; **-lamp,** an incandescent lamp having the filament made of p.; **-metals,** name for the class of metals comprising p. and certain others, viz. iridium, osmium, palladium, rhodium, and ruthenium, associated with it; **-zinc** *a.* formed of plates alternately of p. and zinc, as a voltaic cell.

Platitude (plæ·titiūd). 1812. [a. F., f. *plat* PLAT *a.*, after *altitude*, etc.; see -TUDE.] **1.** Flatness, dullness, insipidity, commonplaceness (in speech or writing). **2.** A flat, dull, or commonplace remark or statement; esp. one uttered with an air of importance 1815.

1. A repartee which has all the profound p. of mediæval wit ROSSETTI. Hence **Platitu·dinize** *v.* to utter platitudes.

Platitudinarian (plætitiūdinē·riăn), *sb.* and *a.* 1854. [f. PLATITUDE, after *latitudinarian.*] **A.** *sb.* One who utters or deals in platitudes. **B.** *adj.* Characterized by platitude; addicted to the use of platitudes 1866.

A. A political p. as insensible as an ox to everything he can't turn into political capital GEO. ELIOT. Hence **Platitudina·rianism.**

Platitudinous (plætitiū·dinəs), *a.* 1862. [f. as prec. + -OUS; cf. *multitudinous.*] Characterized by or of the nature of a platitude; full of platitudes; uttering or writing platitudes. Hence **Platitu·dinous·ly** *adv.*, **-ness.**

Platonic (plătǫ·nik), *a.* and *sb.* 1533. [ad. L. *Platonicus*, a. Gr., f. Πλάτων Plato; see -IC.] **A.** *adj.* **1.** Of or pertaining to Plato (B.C. 429–*c* 347), or his doctrines; conceived or composed after the manner of Plato. **b.** Of a person: That is a follower of Plato 1654. **2.** Applied to love that is purely spiritual for one of the opposite sex. (As orig. used, *amor platonicus* was a synonym of *amor socraticus*, which denoted the kind of interest in young men with which Socrates was credited, and had no ref. to women.) 1636. **b.** Feeling or professing Platonic love 1650.

†*P. bodies* (Geom.), a former name for the five regular solids (tetrahedron, cube, octahedron, dodecahedron, icosahedron). *P. year*, a cycle in which the heavenly bodies were supposed to go through all their possible movements and return to their original relative positions; sometimes identified with the period of revolution of the equinoxes (about 25800 years; see PRECESSION).

B. *sb.* †**1.** A follower of Plato; a Platonist –1840. †**2.** A Platonic lover –1757 **3.** (Usu. *pl.*) Platonic love; the acts or doings of a Platonic lover 1796. So **Plato·nical** *a.* = above adj. in all senses; **-ly** *adv.*, **-ness.**

Platonism (plē¹·tŏniz'm). 1570. [ad. mod. L. *platonismus*, f. Gr. Πλάτων Plato; see -ISM.] **1.** The philosophy of Plato, or of his followers. **2.** (with *pl.*) A doctrine or tenet of Platonic philosophy; a saying of, or like those of, Plato 1610. **3.** The doctrine or practice of Platonic love 1782.

Platonist (plē¹·tŏnist). 1549. [ad. med.L. *platonista*, f. Gr. Πλάτων; see -IST.] A follower of Plato; one who holds the doctrines or philosophy of Plato. **b.** A Platonic lover 1756.

Platonize (plē¹·tŏnəiz), *v.* 1608. [ad. Gr. πλατωνίζειν, f. Πλάτων Plato; see -IZE.] **1.** *intr.* To follow the doctrine of Plato; to philosophize after the manner of Plato; to be a Platonist. **2.** *trans.* To give a Platonic character to; to render Platonic 1850.

Platoon (plătū·n), *sb.* 1637. [ad. F. *peloton* little ball, platoon, dim. of *pelote*; see PELLET *sb.* and -OON.] **1.** *Mil.* A small body of foot-soldiers, operating as an organized unit; a squad detached for purposes of drill or firing a volley, etc.; disused from *c* 1850 to 1913, since when it has denoted: A quarter of a company. †**b.** *transf.* A volley fired by a platoon –1889. **2.** *fig.* A squad; a company or set of people 1711.

2. If you speak of the age, you mean your own p. of people EMERSON.

Platter (plæ·təɹ). Now chiefly *arch.* or *U.S.* [ME. *plater*, a. AF., f. *plat* dish.] A flat dish or plate for food; later, often a wooden plate.

Comb. †**p.-faced** *a.* having a broad, round, flat face.

Pla·tting, *vbl. sb.* 1483. [f. PLAT *v.*¹ + -ING¹.] **1.** Plaiting. **2.** Plaited straw, grass, palmetto, or the like, in ribbon-like strips, for making hats, etc. 1725.

Platy (plē¹·ti), *a.* 1533. [f. PLATE *sb.* + -Y¹.] †**1.** Consisting or formed of plates; plate-like –1612. **2.** *Geol.* Consisting of or easily separating into plates; flaky 1806.

Platy- (plæti), = Gr. πλατυ-, comb. form of πλατύς broad, flat.

Platycephalic (-sĭfæ·lik), **-cephalous** (-se·făləs) [Gr. κεφαλή head] *adjs.*, having a flat or broad head; *spec.* in *Craniom.* applied to a skull of flattened form, having a vertical index of less than 70. **Platycnemic** (-knī·mik) [Gr. κνήμη tibia] *a.*, *Anat.* of the tibia, broad and flat; also, of a person, having such tibiæ; so ‖**Platycne·mia** [mod.L.], **-cne·mism, -cne·my,** platycnemic condition. **Platymeter** (plăti·mĭtəɹ) [-METER], *Electr.* an apparatus for measuring the inductive capacity of different dielectrics in the form of plates or disks.

Platyhelminth (plætihe·lminþ). Also **plathelminth.** 1890. [f. mod.L. pl. *Platyhelmintha*, *-thes*, f. PLATY- + Gr. ἕλμινς (ἑλμινθ-) worm: see HELMINTH.] *Zool.* An animal of the group *Platyhelmintha* or *Platyhelminthes*, comprising the nemertean, trematode, cestode, and turbellarian worms; a flat-worm.

Platypod (plæ·tipǫd), *a.* and *sb.* 1846. [f. Gr. πλατύπους, πλατυποδ- flat-footed; cf. next.] *Zool.* Having broad or flat feet; *spec.* belonging to the group *Platypoda* of monotrematous mammals (typical genus *Platypus*), or to the group *Platypoda* of gastropod molluscs, having a broad flat foot adapted for crawling; also in *Ornith.* syndactyl. Also *sb.*, an animal of this group.

‖**Platypus** (plæ·tipŏs). 1799. [mod.L., a. Gr. πλατύπους, f. πλατύς flat + πούς foot.] *Zool.* A name of the ORNITHORHYNCHUS or duck-mole of Australia.

Platyrrhine, platyrhine (plæ·tirəin), *a.* (*sb.*) 1842. [ad. mod.L. *platyrrhinus*, f. Gr. πλατύς PLATY- + ῥίς, ῥιν- nose.] **1.** *Zool.* Belonging to the division *Platyrrhini* of the order *Quadrumana*, including all the apes of the New World and comprising those apes or monkeys which have the nostrils considerably apart and directed forwards or sideways, and the thumbs nearly or quite non-opposable. **b.** *sb.* A platyrrhine monkey. **2.** *Anthropol.* Having the nose, or the nasal bones, flat or broad; having a nasal index of from 51 to 58. **b.** *sb.* A platyrrhine person or skull 1886.

Plaud, *v.* Now *rare* or *Obs.* 1598. [ad. L. *plaudere* to applaud, clap the hands.] *trans.* To applaud; to praise. Hence **Plaud** *sb.* applause, praise.

Plaudit (plǭ·dit). 1624. [Shortened from next.] An act of applauding; a round of applause; any emphatic expression of approval.

The noisy plaudits of the pit and gallery 1883.

‖**Plaudite** (plǭ·ditĭ). 1567. [a. L., 2 pl. imper. of *plaudere* to applaud; the customary appeal for applause made by Roman actors at the end of a play. The final *-e* ult. became mute, whence PLAUDIT.] An appeal for applause at the end of a performance.

Plau·ditor. [irreg. f. PLAUDIT + -OR; cf. *auditor.*] One who applauds. COLERIDGE. So **Plau·ditory** *a.* applauding, applausive.

Plausibility (plǭzĭbi·lĭti). 1596. [f. L. *plausibilis* (see PLAUSIBLE) + -ITY.] The quality of being plausible. †**1.** Readiness to applaud –1644. †**2.** The quality of deserving applause or approval; agreeableness of manner or behaviour, affability; with *pl.* an instance of this –1681. **3.** Of an argument, statement, etc.: Appearance of reasonableness; speciousness 1649. **b.** (with *pl.*) A plausible argument, statement, or the like 1660. **c.** Of a person: Fair-spokenness 1754.

3. The last excuse..was allowed..to have more p., but less truth SWIFT. **b.** Political plausibilities will reconcile men to everything, save the deprivation of their property 1881.

Plausible (plǭ·zĭb'l), *a.* (*sb.*) 1541. [ad. L. *plausibilis*, f. *plaus-*, ppl. stem of *plaudere* to applaud; see -IBLE.] †**1.** Deserving of applause; praiseworthy, commendable –1711. †**2.** Acceptable, agreeable, pleasing; generally acceptable, popular –1828. †**b.** Of persons, etc.: Agreeable, ingratiating, winning –1841. **3.** Having a show of truth, reasonableness, or worth; apparently acceptable; fair-seeming, specious. (Chiefly of arguments or statements.) 1565. **b.** Of persons: Fair-spoken (with implication of deceit) 1846. **B.** *absol.* or as *sb.* That which is plausible; a plausible statement, etc. 1654.

3. Little aided by conjecture, however p. 1876. **b.** A p., cunning kind of fellow 1875. Hence **Plau·sibleness** (now *rare*), plausibility. **Plau·sibly** *adv.*

Plausive (plǭ·siv), *a.* Now *rare.* 1598. [f. L. *plaus-*, *plaudere* + -IVE.] **1.** Having the quality of applauding; applausive. †**2.** = PLAUSIBLE 1, 2, 3. SHAKS.

2. *Ham.* I. iv. 30; *All's Well* IV. i. 29.

Plautine (plǭ·təin), *a.* 1881. [ad. L. *Plautinus.*] Pertaining to, characteristic of, or in the style of the Roman comic poet Plautus (died B.C. 184).

Play (plē¹), *sb.* [OE. *plega* (*plæga*, *plaga*), wk. sb. from root of *pleg(e)an*, *-ian*, etc. to PLAY, q.v.] **I.** Exercise, free movement or action. †**1.** Of living beings: Active bodily exercise; brisk and vigorous action of the body or limbs, as in dancing, leaping, etc. –ME. **b.** The action of lightly and briskly wielding and plying (a weapon, etc.). Also in comb., as *sword-p.* OE. **2.** Of physical things: Rapid, brisk, or light movement; elusive change or transition (of light or colour); light motion about or impact upon something 1628. **3.** *fig.* and *gen.* Action, activity, operation, working; often implying the ideas of rapid change, variety, etc. (Now usu. of feeling, fancy, thought, etc.; formerly of persons.) 1599. **4.** Free or unimpeded movement (usu. from or about a fixed point); the proper motion of a piece of mechanism, or a part of the living body 1653. **b.** Freedom or room for movement; the space in or through which anything can or does move 1659. **c.** *fig.* and *gen.* Free action; scope for activity 1641.

2. Iridescent p. of colours 1875. 3. Euen p. of Battaile SHAKS. The lively p. of fancy 1875. Phr. *In full p.*: acting with its full force. *To hold* or *keep* (a person, etc.) *in p.*: to keep exercised, occupied, or engaged; to give (a person) something to do (usu. in the way of self-defence or delay). *To come into p.*: to come into action or operation. *To bring* or *call into p.*: to bring into action, make active. *To make p.*: in *Racing* and *Hunting*, to exercise pursuers or followers; in *Pugilism*, to deliver blows actively; hence *gen.* to act effectively; to hasten or hurry on. *To make p. with*: to exercise or display freely. 4. Give him [the chub] p. enough before you offer to take him out of the water WALTON. The girl was an arch, ogling person, with..a great p. of shoulders 1897.

II. Exercise or action for amusement, etc. **1.** Exercise or action by way of recreation; amusement, sport. *At p.*, engaged in playing. ME. †**b.** Amorous disport; dalliance. –1667. **2.** Jest, fun, sport (as opp. to *earnest*); trifling. Often in phr. *in p.* ME. **3.** (with *pl.*) A particular diversion; a game, a sport. Now *rare* or *Obs.* OE. †**4.** A trick, dodge, 'game' (*Obs.* exc. as in 7) –1746. **5.** The playing of a game 1450. **b.** Manner or style of playing; skill in playing 1531. **c.** A point in playing, a special device in a game 1778. **6.** *spec.* Gaming, gambling ME. **7.** In phrases *fair p.*, *foul p.*: rarely *lit.*; usu. *fig.* action, conduct, dealing; see FAIR *a.*, FOUL *a.* 1440. **8.** [from the notion of recreation, sense II. 1] Cessation or abstinence from work; the condition of being idle, or not at work 1601.

1. All work and no p. makes Jack a dull boy *Prov.* 2. The king..made her answer part in ernest, part in p. merely 1513. Phr. †*P. of words*: a playing or trifling with words so as to produce a rhetorical or fantastic effect. *P. on* or *upon words*: a pun. 3. She was fond of all boy's plays JANE AUSTEN. 5. P. was very slow,..twenty minutes being consumed in getting ten runs 1882. Phr. *In p.*: said of a ball, etc. = being played with. So *out of p.* Hence *p.*, transf. (in *Cricket* and *Football*), that part of the ground within definite boundaries, in which the game is carried on. *Child's p.*, a very easy or trifling matter. 6. A young nobleman,..ruined by p. 1769. 7. It was hardly fair p.—it was almost swindling LYTTON. 8. When miners and colliers strike they term it going to p. DISRAELI.

III. Mimic action. **1.** A dramatic or theatrical performance OE. **b.** *transf.* A performance, proceeding, piece of action (in real life) 1581. **2.** A dramatic piece, a drama 1440.

1. Wee had a p. called Twelve Night 1601. Phr. *at* or *to the p.* **b.** This little p. being achieved, the Marquis of Steyne made..two profound bows..and passed on THACKERAY.

†**IV.** Performance on a musical instrument. *rare.* –1755.

attrib. and *Comb.*, as **p.-acting,** the performance of a play or plays; now usu. *joc.* playing a part, posing; **-actor,** an actor of plays, a dramatic performer; **-actress,** a female actor of plays; †**-club** (*Golf*), a driver; **-right,** the author's proprietary right of performance of a musical or dramatic composition; **-room,** a room in which children may play; **-table,** a gaming table.

Play (plē¹), *v.* [OE. *plegan* (cf. prec.), corresp. to MDu. *pleyen*, *pleien*, *playen* to dance for joy, rejoice, be glad. Primary notion: 'to bestir or busily occupy oneself'.] **I.** To exercise oneself, act or move energetically; to actuate, exercise (a craft, etc.). †**1.** *intr.* To exercise or occupy oneself; to act, operate, work –1677. **b.** To strut, dance, or otherwise display itself, as a cock bird before the hens. Also *p. up.* 1765. **2.** Of living beings: To move about swiftly, with a lively or capricious motion; to fly, dart to and fro; to frisk; to flit, flutter OE. **3.** Of things; To move briskly or lightly, esp. with irregular motion, as lightning, flame, etc.; to change rapidly, as colours in iridescence; to strike lightly upon something, as waves, wind, light, etc. 1590. 4. To bubble and roll about as a boiling liquid; to boil. *Obs.* exc. *dial.* late ME. 5. To move, revolve, or oscillate freely (usu. within a definite space); to have its proper unimpeded movement, as a piece of mechanism, a limb, etc.; to have free play 1595. 6. *trans.* To cause to play, to ply. a. To wield (something) lightly and freely; to keep in motion or exercise 1589. b. To discharge, fire, let *off* (artillery, etc.) *on* or *upon* persons or things; to cause (a fountain, etc.) to play 1595. c. *Angling.* To give play to (a fish); to allow (it) to exhaust itself by pulling against the line 1741. d. To cause to move or pass lightly, flutter, glitter, etc.; to exhibit with brilliant effect; to draw lightly upon a surface 1716. 7. *intr.* To operate artillery, to fire (*on* or *upon* persons or things); also said of the artillery, or of a mine, etc.: To be discharged or fired 1601. 8. Of a fire-engine, fountain, etc.: To emit a jet of water, to spout. Also said of the water, or of a fireman, etc. 1666. 9. *trans.* To practise, perform, do (some action); to execute (a movement); usu. to practise in the way of sport, deceit, etc. (a trick, joke, etc.: const. *on* or *upon*, or with simple dative). In mod. use also with *off* (implying successful action; see OFF A). late ME.

1. There is an invisible Agent,..who plays in the dark upon us SIR T. BROWNE. 2. Bats..as they p. over pools and streams 1767. 3. A splendid silk.. Where like a shoaling sea the lovely blue Play'd into green TENNYSON. *fig.* Alfred allows his fancy to p. round the idea 1869. 5. Warme life playes in that infants veines SHAKS. The Tiller playeth in the Gunroome 1627. 6. a. †*To p.* (*a good*) *knife and fork*, to eat (well or heartily); so *to p. a good stick*, to fence well. 7. The Cannon on each Side began to p. STEELE. 8. The fountains played in his honour MACAULAY. 9. Man..Plaies such phantastique tricks before high heauen, As makes the Angels weepe SHAKS.

II. To exercise oneself in the way of diversion or amusement. 1. *intr.* To amuse or divert oneself in any way; to sport, frolic OE. b. To sport amorously; *euphem.* to have sexual intercourse. Now *rare* or *Obs.* OE. 2. *P. with*: to amuse oneself with; to treat (anything) lightly or frivolously; to dally, trifle, or toy with ME. 3. To trifle *with.* late ME. 4. To make sport or jest at another's expense; to mock. Now *rare.* OE. 5. To abstain from work; to take a holiday. [From sense II. 1.] Now *dial.* (esp. of men on strike or out of work). late ME.

1. To playe with fooles, oh, what a foole was I 1576. 2. As children, we p. with our meat when we should eat it BAXTER. 3. I'd recommend you not to p. with 'post captains' MARRYAT. *P. on* or *upon a word* or *words*, to pun. 4. *P. with*, to make sport of, ridicule, mock at; to befool. 5. Master Slender is let the Boyes leaue to play SHAKS. Of the 70,000 men 'playing', 40,000 are non-unionists 1894.

III. To engage in a game, etc. 1. *trans.* To exercise oneself in, engage in, practise (a definite game) OE. b. To represent or imitate in sport; to practise or deal with in a trifling way. Also with *obj. cl.* to pretend (*that* ...) for sport. late ME. 2. *intr.* To take part in a game. In *Cricket* said esp. of the batsman. ME. b. *spec.* To play for stakes; to game, gamble 1511. c. imper. *Play!* In *Cricket*, said by the bowler immediately before the delivery of the ball, or by the umpire at the beginning of a match or innings; also in *Lawn Tennis* by the server at the beginning of each service 1787. d. *transf.* In *Cricket*, said of the 'wicket' in ref. to the effect of its condition upon the play 1866. 3. *fig.* or *gen.* To act, behave, conduct oneself (in some specified way) 1440. 4. *P. at*: a. To take part in (a specified game); also *fig.* ME. b. To represent in sport 1840. 5. *trans.* with personal object. a. To play against. late ME. b. *Cricket*, etc. To employ in a match; to include in a team 1887. 6. To stake in a game; to hazard at play 1483. b. To play for, or in order to gain (something); to gain by playing; in phr. *to p.* BOOTY, *to p. a* PRIZE. 7. a. *Chess*, etc. To move (a man) to another square on the board 1562. b. *Cards.* To take (a card) from one's 'hand' and lay it face upwards on the table, in one's turn 1680. c. In cricket, and other ball-games: To strike (the ball) with the bat, racket, stick, cue, etc., or to deliver it with the hand, so as to send or place it in a particular direction or position 1850. d. *P. on* (*Cricket*): of a batsman, to play the ball on to his own wicket, putting himself 'out' 1882. 8. To bring into some condition by playing, e.g. *to p. oneself in*, to get into form for play 1869. 9. *fig.* a. To use or treat as a counter or plaything. COWLEY. b. To pit (one person, thing, or party *against* another), esp. for one's own advantage. Now usu. *p. off.* 1643. c. *P. off*: to cause (a person) to exhibit himself disadvantageously 1712. d. To palm off 1768.

1. To p. BO-PEEP, DUCK AND DRAKE, FAST AND LOOSE (see these words). *To p. the game*: i.e. according to the rules, fairly; hence to 'play fair', act honourably (*colloq.*). b. We played that we were gypsies 1890. 2. Well played, sir! 1884. b. Playing for his last stake 1809. 3. *To p. fair*: to play according to the rules, without cheating; hence, to act justly or honourably. *To p. false, foul, foully*; also *to p.* a person *false*: to cheat in a game or contest; to deceive, betray. *To p. into the hands of*: to act so as to give an advantage to (another, either partner or opponent). *To p. it on*: to p. a trick upon, take in, cheat; so *to p.* (*low*) *down on*, to take a mean or unfair advantage of (slang or colloq.). *To p. on* or *upon the square* (see SQUARE). 4. a. The kyng & the Emperor playd at tennice 1548. There, two can p. at that game LYTTON. b. To p. at holding courts and receiving petitions MACAULAY. 5. a. 'I'll p. you for a hundred pounds, Doctor!' 1832. b. Bowlers who are played for their bowling only 1892. 6. *Twel. N.* II. v. 207. *P. away*: to lose in gambling; *fig.* to waste, squander. 7. b. *fig. To p. one's cards well* (fig.), to make good use of one's resources or chances. 8. *To p. time out*, to extend the play until the appointed time. 9. b. The Sultan likes to p. off one Power against another 1885.

IV. To perform instrumental music. 1. *intr.* To perform upon a musical instrument. Const. *on, upon.* OE. b. Said of the instrument or the music itself 1588. 2. *trans.* To perform (music, a piece of music) on an instrument 1509. 3. To perform on (a musical instrument); to cause (it) to sound 1727. 4. With *in, out, off, down, up*, etc.: To lead, dismiss, or accompany (persons) with instrumental music 1844. 5. *fig.* a. *P. on* or *upon*: to practise upon 1602. b. *To p. first*, etc., *fiddle*: see FIDDLE *sb.* So *to p. second*, to take a subordinate part. 1809.

1. Ther herd I pleyen vpon an harpe..Orpheus ful craftely CHAUCER. 2. When thou, my music, music play'st, Upon that blessed wood SHAKS. 5. You would p. vpon mee; you would seem to know my stops SHAKS.

VI. To perform dramatically, etc. 1. *trans.* To perform as a spectacle upon the stage, etc.; to act (a drama, etc.). late ME. 2. *P. out*: to perform to the end; *fig.* to bring to an end; *refl.* to become obsolete or effete 1596. b. *intr.* for *refl.* or *pass.* 1835. c. pa. pple. *Played out*: performed to the end, over and done with; also, exhausted, effete, worn out 1863. 3. *trans.* To act the part of. late ME. 4. Hence *fig.* in real life: To sustain the character of. (Almost always with *the* before the object.) late ME. 5. To act (*a part, the part of*). *lit.* or *fig.* 1470. 6. *intr.* To act a drama, or a part in a drama; to perform 1580. 7. *P. up to* (*Theatr. slang*): to act in a drama so as to assist another actor; hence, to back up; to flatter, toady 1809.

1. The whil'st this Play is Playing SHAKS. 2. He was decidedly of opinion that Mr. Gladstone was played out 1887. 3. I could p. Ercles rarely SHAKS. 4. Phr. *To p. the* DEVIL, *the* FOOL, *the* MAN, *the* MISCHIEF, POSSUM, TRUANT, etc.: see the sbs. 5. In the final struggle..England played her part well 1881. Hence **Play·able** *a.* capable of being played; (of a cricket or football ground) fit for playing on.

Play-bill (plēⁱ·bil). 1673. A bill or placard announcing a play and giving the names of the performers.

Play-book (plēⁱ·buk). (Also as one word or two.) 1535. A book of plays.

Play-day (plēⁱ·dēⁱ). 1601. A day given up to play; *esp.* a school holiday. *Obs.* or *arch.* b. A week-day on which miners, etc. do not work 1892.

Player (plēⁱ·əɹ). [OE. *plegere*, f. *plegan*, PLAY *v.* + -ER[1].] 1. One who plays; one who is practised or skilful at some game, usu. specified in the context. late ME. b. A gambler 1483. c. A professional player (at a game or sport) 1861. 2. A dramatic performer; an actor 1453. 3. One who plays on a musical instrument 1463. 4. *Billiards* (*Pool*), *Croquet.* The ball which, after the person playing has finished his break, will play on his ball 1866.

1. The by standers (whiche commonlye see more then the plaiers) 1562. 2. *A. Y. L.* II. vii. 140. 3. *Comb.* **P.-piano**, a piano fitted with an apparatus enabling it to be played automatically.

Pla·yfe:llow. 1513. A companion in play; usu. said of children or young people.

Playful (plēⁱ·fŭl), *a.* ME. [f. PLAY *sb.* + -FUL.] Full of play, frolicsome, sportive; also, pleasantly humorous or jocular, merry. Hence **Play·ful·ly** *adv.*, **-ness.**

Playgoer (plēⁱ·gōᵘəɹ). 1822. [f. PLAY *sb.* + GOER; cf. *church-goer.*] One who (habitually) goes to the theatre. So **Play·-go:ing** *sb.* and *a.*

Play·ground. 1794. A piece of ground used for playing on, esp. one attached to a school; hence, any place of recreation.

fig. Switzerland, the p. of Europe (*mod.*).

Play·house. 1599. A building in which plays are acted; a theatre.

Playing (plēⁱ·iŋ), *vbl. sb.* ME. [f. PLAY *v.* + -ING[1].] The action of PLAY *v.*

attrib. and *Comb.*, as **p.-card** = CARD *sb.*[2] 1; **-field**, a field or piece of ground for playing in; orig. applied esp. to the playgrounds at Eton, now to any school fields used for games.

Play·let. 1911. [See -LET.] A short play.

Playmate (plēⁱ·mēⁱt). 1642. [f. PLAY *sb.* + MATE *sb.*[2]] A companion in play, a playfellow.

Play·-off. 1906. [f. PLAY *v.* + OFF *adv.*] An additional match to decide a draw or tie; a replay.

Playsome (plēⁱ·sŏm), *a.* Now chiefly *dial.* 1612. [f. PLAY *sb.* + -SOME.] Inclined to play; playful. Hence **Play·some·ly** *adv.*, **-ness.**

Plaything (plēⁱ·þiŋ). 1675. [f. PLAY *sb.* + THING.] A toy to play with. b. *fig.* A man, animal, or thing, treated as a toy 1680.

Playtime (plēⁱ·təim). 1661. [f. PLAY *sb.* + TIME *sb.*] A time for play or recreation.

Play·wright. 1687. [f. PLAY *sb.* + WRIGHT.] A maker or author of plays; a dramatist.

‖ **Plaza** (plā·þa, plā·sa). 1683. [Sp. :—pop. L. **plattia* :—L. *platea*; see PLACE *sb.*] In Spain, etc., A market-place, square.

Plea (plī). [ME. *plaid, plai*, a. OF. *plaid* :—L. *placitum*; sb. use of pa. pple. neut. of L. *placere* to please; see PLACITUM.] I. In Law. 1. A suit or action at law; the presentation of an action in court. Now *Hist.* and *Sc.* 2. a. A pleading; an allegation formally made by a party to the court, in support of his case. late ME. b. A formal statement, written or oral, made by or on behalf of a prisoner or defendant, alleging facts either in answer to the indictment, or to the plaintiff's declaration, bill, or statement of claim, or showing cause why the prisoner or defendant should not be compelled to answer 1449. c. *Special plea*: in civil or criminal law, a plea either in abatement or in bar of an action or prosecution, alleging some new fact; opp. to *the general issue* 1699.

1. A p. between two country squires about a barren acre upon a common 1735. Phr. *To hold pleas*, to try actions at law, to have jurisdiction; *to hold a p.*, to try an action. *Common pleas*: orig., legal proceedings on matters over which the Crown did not claim exclusive jurisdiction; later, actions at law brought by one subject against another, identified with *civil actions. Pleas of the Crown* (*placita Coronæ*): orig., legal proceedings on matters over which the Crown claimed an exclusive jurisdiction, as being breaches of the king's peace; later, in England, including all criminal proceedings, as opp. to common pleas or civil proceedings. 2. b. *Declinatory, dilatory*, etc. *p.*: see the adjs.

II. 1. Controversy, quarrel, strife. Now only *Sc.* ME. 2. That which is pleaded in justification or excuse; a pleading; an apology, pretext, excuse 1550. †3. That which is demanded by pleading; a claim. SHAKS.

2. So spoke the Fiend, and with necessity, The tyrant's p., excused his devilish deeds MILT. 3. *Merch. V.* IV. i. 198, 203.

Pleach (plītʃ), *v.* [ME. *pleche*, a. OF. **plechier*, dial. form of OF. *plessier, plaissier* PLASH *v.*[1]] 1. *trans.* = PLASH *v.*[1] 1. 2. = PLASH *v.*[1] 2. 1523. 3. *gen.* To entwine, interlace, tangle, plait 1830.

3. Poppied hair of gold Persephone Sad-tressed and pleached low down about her brows SWINBURNE.

Pleached (plīʃt, *poet.* plī·tʃéd), *ppl.a.* 1599. [f. prec. + -ED [1].] 1. Of boughs: Interlaced, tangled; *transf.* of the arms, folded together 1606. 2. Fenced or overarched with pleached boughs, as an arbour. Now as a Shaksperian expression revived by Scott.

2. Walking in a thick p. alley in my orchard SHAKS.

Plead (plīd), *v.* *Pa. t.* and *pple.* **pleaded**: also pled (now *Sc.*, *dial.*, and *U.S.*), †plead. [ME. *plaiden, plaidi*, a. OF. *plaidier*, f. *plaid*; see PLEA *sb.*] I. Intransitive uses. †1. To litigate -1550. b. *fig.* To wrangle, argue *with*, *against* -1593. 2. To address the court as an advocate on behalf of either party ME. b. Hence *fig.* To urge a suit or prayer; to make an earnest supplication; to beg, implore. Const. *with* the person appealed to; *for* the thing desired, or the person for whom one speaks; also *against*. late ME. 3. To put forward a plea. Cf. PLEADING *vbl. sb.* 3. 1444. b. *esp.* To put forward an answer or objection to the plaintiff's bill. late ME.

2. b. All Roger's services could not p. against this ill-timed tenderness to a foe 1869. 3. a. *P. over*, to follow up an opponent's pleading by replying, etc., so overlooking some defect to which exception might have been taken WHARTON.

II. Transitive uses. †1. To go to law with, sue (a person) -1500. 2. To maintain (a plea or cause) by argument in a court of law. Also *transf.* 1482. 3. To sue for in a court of law. Also *transf.* To beg, entreat for. ME. 4. a. To allege formally in the course of the pleadings. (Cf. PLEA *sb.* I. 2 a.) 1460. b. To allege formally as a plea (PLEA *sb.* I. 2 b). *P. specially*, to allege as a special plea (PLEA *sb.* I. 2 c) 1531. c. Hence *fig.* To allege as a plea, esp. in defence, apology, or excuse, or as extenuating an offence 1454.

2. P. the widow's cause 1777. 4. b. It would be vain to p...the king's command to do an unlawful act 1863. c. I can only p. my inexperience in this branch of literature W. IRVING. Phr. *To p. not guilty* (in civil and criminal law), to deny liability or guilt; in Law-French, *plaider de rien coupable*. So *to p. guilty*; also *fig.* to confess to an accusation or imputation. *Guilty* is technically not a *plea*, but a confession.

Pleadable (plī·dăb'l), *a.* [ME. a. AF. *pledable* = OF. *plaidable*, f. *plaidier* to PLEAD; see -ABLE.] That may be pleaded. b. *gen.* That may be claimed, urged or alleged in behalf of a cause 1565.

Pleader (plī·dəɹ). [ME. *playdur, -our*, a. OF. *plaideor*, F. *plaideur*, f. OF. *plaidier, plaider* to PLEAD; see -OUR, -ER [1].] 1. One who pleads in a law-court; an advocate. 2. *gen.* One who pleads, entreats, or intercedes 1607. 3. See SPECIAL PLEADER.

2. But sure if you Would be your Countries P., your good tongue..Might stop our Countryman SHAKS.

Pleading (plī·diŋ), *vbl. sb.* ME. [f. PLEAD *v.* + -ING [1].] The action of PLEAD *v.* †1. Litigation; hence, a lawsuit, action; a controversy -1556. 2. The advocating of a cause in a court of law; the art of drawing pleadings; the body of rules, etc. constituting this art. late ME. 3. A formal allegation now usually in writing, setting forth the cause of action or the defence; in pl. *pleadings*, the formal statements on both sides; in strict use, excluding the count or declaration 1531. 4. *gen.* Intercession, advocacy, earnest entreaty. late ME. 5. See SPECIAL PLEADING.

Plea·ding, *ppl. a.* 1818. [-ING [2].] That pleads. Hence **Plea·ding·ly** *adv.*, -ness.

Pleasance (ple·zăns). [Late ME. a. OF. *plaisance*, f. *plaisant*, *plaisir* to please; see -ANCE.] 1. The condition or feeling of being pleased; delight, pleasure, joy. *arch.* and *poet.* †2. The disposition to please; complaisance; courtesy -1599. b. A pleasantry. *Obs.* exc. *poet.* 1681. 3. Pleasure-giving quality; pleasantness. *Obs.* exc. *poet.* late ME. b. That in which one delights. *Obs.* exc. *poet.* 1485. 4. A pleasure-ground, usu. attached to a mansion. (Now sometimes surviving as the name of a street or 'place'.) 1585.

1. Thus is this quyen in plesaunce & in Ioye CHAUCER. 3. With pleasaunce of the breathing fields yfed SPENSER. 4. A charming old pleasaunce with bowling-green and long grass walks 1888.

Pleasant (ple·zănt), *a.* (*adv.*) [Late ME. a. OF. *plais-, pleisant*, prop. pr. pple. of *plaisir* = mod.F. *plaire* to please; see PLEASE *v.*] 1. *orig.*, = PLEASING; now, more vaguely: Agreeable to the mind, feelings, or senses; such as one likes. 2. Having pleasing manners, demeanour, or aspect; agreeable, good-humoured 1560. †3. Humorous, facetious; merry, gay -1782. b. Hilarious from drink (*rare* or *arch.*) 1596. †4. Amusing, ridiculous, funny -1760.

1. The pleasantest time of all the twenty-four hours KINGSLEY. *Pleasant Sunday Afternoon* (abbrev. *P.S.A.*): a kind of service usu. held in a place of worship on a Sunday afternoon, diversified with music and addresses. 2. Content and even p. under Hardships 1705. A clever woman is always a pleasanter companion than a clever man 1873. 4. With such other like p. iestes 1583. Hence **Plea·santl·y** *adv.* -ness.

Pleasantry (ple·zăntri). 1655. [a. F. *plaisanterie*, f. *plaisant* PLEASANT, jocose; see -RY.] 1. A pleasant and sprightly humour in conversation; jocularity; raillery. b. With *a* and *pl.* A humorous passage, action, or (now esp.) speech; a joke 1701. †2. Pleasure, pleasantness, enjoyment -1790.

1. Pumping his brain for p., and labouring for wit to entertain the sneering crowd around him 1763. b. With their Censorious Plaisanteries upon the greatest of Authors and Worthies 1716.

Please (plīz), *v.* [ME. *plaise, pleise, plese*, a. OF. *plaisir* :—L. *placere*, f. root *plac-* in *placidus* gentle, mild, *placare* to calm, soothe.] I. †1. *intr.* To be agreeable; to give pleasure. Const. *to*, *with*. ME. only. 2. *trans.* To be agreeable to; to gratify, satisfy, delight. Also *absol.* ME. b. *refl.* To gratify oneself. Also *colloq.* to do as one likes. 1586. 3. *Impersonally*, with formal subject *it*: To seem good to one; to be one's will or pleasure. (Equiv. to 'will', 'choose', 'think proper', etc., with the person as subject.) ME. b. With omission of *it*: in *p. your honour*, *p. God*, etc. 1440. 4. *Passive. To be pleased*: to be gratified or delighted. Const. *with*. late ME. b. with *inf.* (or *clause*) expressing the subject of satisfaction. Also (*b*) To have the will or desire, to be moved; (*c*) To think proper, vouchsafe, choose; to be so obliging as; (*sarcastically*) to have the humour. late ME. 5. *trans.* To appease, pacify, satisfy. *Obs.* or *dial.* late ME.

2. The thing pleased the king, and he did so *Esther* ii. 4. *absol.* For we that live to p., must p. to live JOHNSON. b. *A.Y.L.* v. iv. 78. 3. It pleased Silas to abide there still *Acts* xv. 34. 4. Nor can God be pleased with the perverted adoration 1850. b. Be pleased then To pay that dutie which you truly owe SHAKS. My dear Sir! you are pleased to be amusing this morning DISRAELI.

II. *intr.* To be pleased, to like; to have the will or desire; to have the humour; to think proper. (Partly from the impersonal use (sense I. 3); cf. LIKE *v.*) 1500.

You may make what use of it you p. ADDISON. Phrases. *If* (†*and, an*) *you p.*: if it please you, if you like, if it is your will or pleasure; a courteous qualification to a request, etc.; also (parenthetically) a sarcastic way of emphasizing any surprising statement, as if asking leave to make it. *Please!* (imper. or optative) was app. short for *p. you* (I. 3 b) = 'may it (or let it) please you'; but is now taken as = 'Be pleased' (imper. of II), or as short for 'if you please'. *Come here, p.* (= if you p.); *P.* (= be pleased) *not to lose the book*. Hence **Plea·ser**, one who or that which pleases or aims at pleasing.

Pleased (plīzd), *ppl. a.* late ME. [f. prec. + -ED [1].] Affected by feelings of satisfaction or pleasure; contented, gratified. Hence **Plea·sed·ly** *adv.*, -ness.

Pleasing (plī·ziŋ), *vbl. sb.* late ME. [-ING [1].] 1. The action of PLEASE *v.* †2. = PLEASINGNESS -1594.

Plea·sing, *ppl. a.* late ME. [-ING [2].] That pleases. Hence **Plea·sing·ly** *adv.*, -ness.

Pleasurable (ple·ʒ'ŭrăb'l), *a.* 1579. [f. next + -ABLE, after *comfortable*.] 1. Affording, or capable of affording, pleasure; agreeable. †2. Pleasure-seeking, pleasure-loving -1709. Hence **Plea·surableness**, **Plea·surably** *adv.*

Pleasure (ple·ʒ'ŭɹ), *sb.* [ME. *plesir, plaisir*, a. OF. :—L. *placere* to please. Late ME. *plēser* (cf. mod. dial. *pleezer*), by assimilation to *measure*, became *pleasure*.] 1. The condition of consciousness induced by the enjoyment or anticipation of what is felt or viewed as good or desirable; enjoyment, delight, gratification. The opposite of *pain*. b. In bad sense: Sensuous enjoyment as a chief object of life or end in itself 1526. c. In strictly physical sense: Sensual gratification 1450. 2. One's will, desire, choice. late ME. 3. A source or object of pleasure or delight 1495. 4. The quality which gives pleasure; pleasureableness 1530. 5. *attrib.* as *p.-boat*, *-ground*, *-house*, *-resort*, etc. 1712.

1. Pain and p. are simple ideas, incapable of definition BURKE. P. is what all creatures desire 1894. b. Men, some to Bus'ness, some to P. take; But every Woman is at heart a Rake POPE. But pleasures are like poppies spread, You seize the flower, the bloom is shed BURNS. 2. I will wait vpon his p. SHAKS. They were determined not to submit..to her will and p. HUME. 3. Your..love of truth renders this a duty as well as a p. 1858. 4. The p. of pale colours 1869.

Phrases. *At* (*one's*) *p.*, *at p.*: as or when one pleases; at will, at discretion. *During* (*one's*) *p.*: while one pleases. *To do* (*one*) *a p.*: to do a favour; to please, gratify. *Man* (*woman*) *of p.*: one who is devoted to the pursuit of sensual pleasure. *To take* (*a*) *p.*: to be pleased, to delight (*in*, *to do* something, etc.). Hence **Plea·sureful** *a.* full of or fraught with p. **Plea·sureless**, devoid of p., joyless.

Pleasure (ple·ʒ'ŭɹ), *v.* 1538. [f. prec. sb.] 1. *trans.* To give pleasure to; to gratify (now *rare*) 1559. 2. *intr.* To take pleasure, to delight. Const. *in* or *to* with *inf.* 1538.

Plea·surer. 1833. [f. PLEASURE *sb.* or *v.* + -ER [1].] A pleasure-seeker: a holiday-maker.

Plea·sure-see·ker. 1852. One who seeks pleasure; *spec.* a holiday-maker.

Plea·surist. 1682. [f. PLEASURE *sb.* + -IST.] a. A devotee of pleasure, a voluptuary. b. A pleasure-seeker.

Pleat (plīt), *sb.* 1495. [By-form of PLAIT *sb.*] = PLAIT *sb.* 1. 1581. *Box-p.*: see BOX *sb.*[2]

Pleat (plīt), *v.* late ME. [By-form of PLAIT *v.*, going with prec. sb.] 1. *trans.* To fold (cloth, etc.); now *esp.* to gather (loose or flowing drapery) into pleats or regular folds fixed in position at the edge. 2. = PLAT *v.*[1] *dial.* 1483.

Accordion-pleated, pleated (by machinery) with very fine equal single pleats; *knife-pleated*, pleated by hand with the blade of a knife (or by a machine producing the same result).

Plebe (plīb). 1612. [In sense 1, app. a. F. *plèbe*, ad. L. *plebs*, *plebem*: see PLEBS. In sense 2, shortened from PLEBEIAN.] †1. The Roman plebs; hence, the commonalty of any nation -1635. 2. *U.S. colloq.* A member of the lowest class at a military or naval academy; a freshman. Also *pleb.* 1884.

Plebeian (plĭbī·ăn). 1533. [f. L. *plebeius* + -AN. In Shaks. occas. stressed *ple·bean*.] A. *sb.* a. A member of the Roman plebs; a Roman commoner, as opp. to the patricians, etc. b. *gen.* One of the common people, a commoner 1586.

a. The dull Tribunes, That with the fustie Plebeans, hate thine Honors SHAKS. b. A Yeoman, or Plebeyan;..any lay man that is no Gentleman 1611. *fig.* To the brave, there is but one sort of p., and that is the coward LYTTON.

B. *adj.* a. Of or belonging to the Roman plebs; that was a plebeian 1566. b. Of low birth or rank; pertaining to or connected with the common people; popular 1600. c. Having qualities attributed to the lower classes; commonplace, undistinguished; vulgar or vulgar-looking 1615.

c. An important gentleman..of rather p. countenance DICKENS. Hence **Plebei·anism**, p. character or style. **Plebei·anize** *v. trans.* to reduce to p. rank; to make common. **Plebei·an·ly** *adv.*, -ness.

Plebiscite, -it (ple·bisəit, -it). Also **plé-biscite**. 1533. [a. F. *plébiscite*, ad. L. *plebiscitum*.] 1. *Rom. Hist.* = PLEBISCITUM 1. 2. In mod. politics, A direct vote of the whole of the electors of a state to decide a question of public importance; also by extension, a public expression, with or without binding force, of the wishes or opinion of a community 1860.

2. He [Louis Napoleon] knew how to strangle a nation in the night-time with a thing he called a 'P.' KINGLAKE. Hence **Plebi·scitary** *a.* relating to, based on, favouring, or of the nature of a p.

‖ **Plebiscitum** (plĭbisəi·tǒm). *Pl.* -a. 1577. [L. (also *plebis scitum*, *plebi scitum*, lit. an ordinance of the plebs), f. *plebis*, genitive of *plebs* + *scitum* ordinance, decree.] 1. *Rom. Hist.* A law enacted by the plebs assembled in the *comitia tributa*. 2. = PLEBISCITE 2. 1859.

Plebs (plebz). 1647. [L., (earlier *plebes*).] *Rom. Hist.* The commonalty, orig. comprising all citizens that did not belong to one of the patrician *gentes*, to which privileged order were afterwards added the *equites* or knights 1835. **b.** *transf.* The common people; the mob 1647.

Plectognath (ple·ktǫgnæþ), *a.* and *sb.* 1835. [f. mod.L. *Plectognathi*, f. Gr. πλεκτός plaited, twisted + γνάθος jaw.] *Ichthyol.* **A.** *adj.* Of or pertaining to the *Plectognathi*, a suborder of teleostean fishes, having the upper jaw attached to the cranium, and the skeleton imperfectly ossified. **B.** *sb.* A fish of this suborder. So **Plectognathian** (-gnēⁱ·þiăn) *a.* and *sb.* **Plectognathik** (-gnæ·þik), **Plectognathous** (-ǫ·gnăþəs) *adjs.* = A.

Plectospondyl (plektǫspǫ·ndil), *a.* and *sb.* [f. mod. L. *Plectospondyli*, f. Gr. πλεκτός (see prec.) + σπόνδυλος vertebra.] *Ichthyol.* **A.** *adj.* Belonging to or having the characters of the *Plectospondyli*, teleostean fishes having some of the vertebræ co-ossified. **B.** *sb.* A fish of this order. So **Plectospo·ndylous** *a.*

‖ **Plectrum** (ple·ktrǒm). Pl. **-a.** 1626. Also anglicized **plectre** (1603). [L., a. Gr. πλῆκτρον anything to strike with, f. πλήσσειν to strike.] A small instrument of ivory, horn, quill, or metal, with which the strings of the cithara or lyre were plucked; now used for playing the zither, mandolin, etc.

Pledge (pledʒ), *sb.* [Late ME. a. OF. *plege* (mod.F. *pleige*) hostage, security, bail, pledge :—early Frankish L. *plevium, plibium, plebium*; app. deriv. sb. from med.L. *plevire, plebire, plivire* to warrant, assure, undertake for, engage; perh. repr. some form of WGer. **plehan*, or Goth. **plaihwan*, in sense 'to become responsible for'.] **1.** *Law* and *gen.* A person who becomes surety for another; a bail; a member of a frankpledge or frithborh (mod.L. *plegius*). *Obs.* exc. *Hist.* †**b.** A hostage -1633. **2.** Anything put in the possession of another, as security for the performance of a contract or payment of a debt, or as a guarantee of good faith, etc., and liable to forfeiture in case of failure (med.L. *plegium*) 1489. **b.** *spec.* A thing put in pawn 1800. **c.** A gage of battle 1590. **d.** *fig.* Applied to a child, as a token of mutual love and duty between parents, or as a hostage given to fortune 1590. **3.** Something given or taken as a sign of favour or the like, or as an earnest of something to come 1526. **4.** An assurance of allegiance or goodwill; e.g. the drinking of a health to a person, party, etc.; a toast 1635. **5.** A solemn engagement; a promise, vow 1814. **6.** The condition of being given or held as a pledge; the state of being pledged. late ME.

1. Petruchio patience, I am Grumio's p. SHAKS. 2. What P. haue we of thy firme Loyalty? SHAKS. b. Any time during which the said p. shall remain in pawn 1800. d. The first p. of their union, a fine little girl 1856. 5. He obtained them..under the p. of secrecy 1855. *The (temperance, total abstinence) p.*: a solemn engagement to abstain from intoxicating drink. *To take, sign, keep the p.* 6. Phr. *To be, lay, put in p., to give, have, lay, put to p., to take out of p.*, etc.

Pledge (pledʒ), *v.* [Late ME. *pleg(g)e*, f. prec. sb.] †**1.** *trans.* To make oneself responsible for (a person, thing, or statement) -1474. **2.** To deliver, deposit, or assign as security for the repayment of a loan or the performance of some action; to pawn 1515. **b.** *fig.* as in *to p. the future*; also, to plight or stake (one's life, honour, etc.) 1775. **3.** To bind by or as by a pledge 1571. **4. a.** To guarantee the performance of. **b.** To promise solemnly. 1593. **5.** To give assurance of friendship or fidelity to (any one) by or in the act of drinking. Also *absol.*, or with the drink as obj. †**a.** To drink in response to another; to drink to a health which has been proposed. **b.** To drink to the health of; to toast. 1546.

1. †*To p. out*: to redeem (a thing) from pawn; to ransom or bail (a person) from prison. 2. b. My vows are pledged to her SHERIDAN. 3. I p. myself, before God and my country..to make good my charge against you *Junius Lett.* 4. a. And heere to p. my Vow, I giue my hand SHAKS. 5. a. Drink to me, only with thine eyes, And I will p. with mine B. JONS. b. P. him in a bumper of port 1802. Hence **Ple·dgeable** *a.*

Pledgee (pledʒī·). 1766. [f. prec. + -EE.] One with whom a pledge is deposited.

Pledger (ple·dʒəɹ). Also (in legal use) **pledgor** (pledʒǭ·ɹ). 1576. [f. PLEDGE *v.* + -ER¹, -OR 2.] **1.** One who deposits something as a pledge. **2.** One who drinks in response to, or to the health of, another.

Pledget (ple·dʒėt). 1540. [Origin obsc.] A small compress or flattened mass of lint, etc. (often steeped in some medicament), for applying over a wound, sore, etc.

Pleiad (pləi·ăd). *Pl.* **Pleiads**; more commonly ‖**Pleiades** (pləi·ădīz). late ME. [a. L. *Plēïas*, pl. *Plēïades*, a. Gr. πλειάς, pl. -άδες; see -AD.] *Astron.* In *pl.*, A close group of small stars in the constellation Taurus, commonly spoken of as seven, though only six are visible to the average naked eye.

According to Greek Mythology, the Pleiades were the seven daughters of Atlas and Pleione, the eldest of whom, Electra, was 'the lost Pleiad', and not represented by a star.

b. *fig.* (*sing.*) A brilliant cluster of persons or things, esp. of seven, as the group of poets of the French Renaissance, called in French *La Pléiade* 1822.

Plein-air (also **plain-air**), from the Fr. phr. *en plein air* (anplęnę̄r) 'in the open air' used attrib. to denominate certain impressionist schools and styles of painting, which arose in France about 1870, and aimed at the representation of effects of atmosphere and light that cannot be observed in the studio 1894.

Pleio-, plio- (pləiǫ, pləio), **pleo-** (plīǫ), comb. forms of Gr. πλείων (poet. πλέων), πλεῖον more, compar. of πολύς, -ύ much; see POLY-. *Plio-*, which follows L. spelling, is chiefly used in generic names and their derivs., as *Pliosaurus, Pliosaurian*.

Pleiocene, Pleiohippus: see PLIO-.

Pleistocene (pləi·stŏsīn), *a.* (*sb.*) 1839. [f. Gr. πλεῖστος most + καινός new, recent.] *Geol.* Epithet applied at first to the newest division of the Pliocene or Upper Tertiary formation (as containing the greatest number of fossils of still existing species), also called Newer Pliocene; afterwards to the older division of the Post-tertiary or Quaternary, also called Post-Pliocene. Also applied to the animals, etc., of either of these periods. **B.** *ellipt.* as *sb.* = pleistocene division or formation.

Plenarty (plī·năɹti) [Late ME. a. AF. *plenerte*, OF. *plenierete* fullness, f. *plenier, plener* complete; see -TY.] *Eccl. Law.* Of a benefice: The state of being full or occupied.

Plenary (plī·nări), *a.* 1450. [ad. late L. *plenarius*, f. *plenus* full; see -ARY¹.] **1.** Of full scope or extent; complete or absolute in force or effect; as *p. indulgence, power, remission.* **2.** Of an assembly, etc.: Composed of all the members; fully constituted, fully attended 1532. Hence **Ple·narily** *adv.*

Plenilune (plī·nil\|ūn, ple·ni-). Chiefly *poet.* late ME. [ad. L. *plenilunium* full moon, prop. adj. of the full moon (sc. *tempus* time), f. *plenus* full + *luna* moon.] **a.** The time of full moon. **b.** A full moon. Hence **Plenilu·nal, -lu·nar, -lu·nary** *adjs.* belonging to or resembling the full moon.

Plenipo (ple·nipǫ). 1687. Colloq. shortening of PLENIPOTENTIARY.

Pleni·potency. *rare.* 1624. [f. L. **plenipotentia*, f. *plenipotens*; see next and -ENCY.] The quality of being plenipotent; full authority. So **Pleni·potence**, *rare*, full power or authority.

Plenipotent (plĭni·pǒtěnt), *a. rare.* 1658. [ad. late L. *plenipotens, -potentem*, f. L. *plenus* full + *potens* POTENT.] Invested with or possessing full power or authority. So **Plenipote·ntial** *a. rare*, possessed of full authority; of or belonging to a plenipotentiary.

Plenipotentiary (ple:nipǒte·nʃări). 1645. [ad. med. and law L. *plenipotentiarius*; see PLENIPOTENCY and -ARY¹.] **A.** *adj.* Invested with full power, esp. as the representative of a sovereign ruler; exercising absolute power or authority. **b.** Of or belonging to a plenipotentiary (see B); absolute, full 1648. **B.** *sb.* A person invested with full or discretionary powers, *esp.* in regard to a particular transaction; an envoy or ambassador deputed by his sovereign to act at his own discretion 1656.

I know not why the Character of P. may not agree with that of Envoy Extraordinary on all Hands 1668.

Plenish (ple·niʃ), *v.* Chiefly *Sc.* 1470. [ad. OF. *pleniss-*, lengthened stem of *plenir* to fill, f. stem *plen-* :—L. *plenus* full.] *trans.* To fill up, furnish, stock; to replenish. Orig. *Sc.* and *n. dial.* **b.** *spec.* To furnish (a house, etc.) *Sc.* and *n. dial.* 1578. Hence **Ple·nishing** *vbl. sb.* the action of filling up or furnishing; stock, furniture; the outfit of a bride.

Plenist (plī·nist). 1660. *Hist.* [f. L. PLENUM + -IST.] An adherent of the theory that all space is full of matter, and that no vacuum exists.

Plenitude (ple·nitiud). late ME. [a. OF., ad. L. *plenitudo*, f. *plenus* full; see -TUDE.] **1.** The condition of being absolutely full or complete; fullness, completeness, perfection. **b.** *Her.* Fullness (of the moon) 1864. **c.** Comparative fullness, abundance, amplitude 1653. **2.** The condition of being filled or full 1662. †**3.** *Med.* Repletion; plethora -1802.

1. Pawle sayth the plenytude of the lawe is loue and charyte CAXTON. c. P. of incident without confusion 1794.

Plenteous (ple·ntĭəs), *a.* Now chiefly *poet.* [ME. *plentifous, -ivous*, a. OF. *plentivous, plentevous*, etc., extended forms of *plentif*, f. *plenté* PLENTY; see -IVE, -OUS. Cf. BOUNTEOUS.] **1.** Present or existing in plenty; abundant, plentiful, copious. **2.** Bearing or yielding abundantly; fertile, productive. Const. *in, of.* ME. †**3.** Possessing abundance; rich -1643. †**4.** Giving abundantly; bountiful -1700.

1. A p. crop of such philosophers COLERIDGE. 2. The seasons had been p. in corn GEO. ELIOT. 4. P. of Grace, descend from high, Rich in thy Sevenfold Energy! DRYDEN. Hence **Ple·nteous-ly** *adv.*, **-ness.**

Plentiful (ple·ntifŭl), *a.* 1470. [f. next + -FUL.] **1.** Full of plenty; furnished with or yielding abundance; opulent. Now *rare.* **2.** Present or existing in plenty; abundant, ample 1510. †**3.** Generous, lavish -1625.

1. If it be a long winter, it is commonly a more p. year BACON. 2. They haue a plentifull lacke of Wit SHAKS. 3. He that is Plentifull in Expences of all Kindes, will hardly be preserved from Decay BACON. Hence **Ple·ntiful·ly** *adv.*, **-ness.**

Plenty (ple·nti), *sb.* (*a.*, *adv.*) [ME. *plenteð, plenteth, plenté*, a. OF. *plentet* :—L. *plenitatem* fullness, f. *plenus* FULL; see -TY.] **A.** *sb.* **1.** The state of abounding or being in abundance; plentifulness, abundance. **2.** A full supply; as much as one could desire; abundance *of* something ME. **b.** with *a*: an abundance (*of*). Now chiefly *U.S.* 1627. **3.** Abundance of the necessaries and comforts of life; a condition of general abundance. late ME. †**b.** *concr.* in *pl.* Things that constitute 'plenty'; provisions, possessions -1723.

1. *In p.*: plentiful; plentifully, abundantly; Compliments passed in p. 1852. 2. We were in p. of time 1885. 3. To scatter p. o'er a smiling land GRAY. *Horn of p.* = CORNUCOPIA. b. *Hen. V*, v. ii. 35.

B. *adj.* or quasi-*adj.* Existing or present in abundance; abundant, plentiful, numerous. Now chiefly *colloq.*, *arch.*, or *U.S.* ME.

Gold and syluer plente to spend MALORY. Where money is p., and land scarce 1656.

C. quasi-*adv.* Abundantly (*colloq.*) 1842.

They're p. large enough 1884.

‖ **Plenum** (plī·nǒm). 1678. [L., neut. of *plenus* adj. full (sc. *spatium* space); cf. *vacuum*.] **1.** *Physics.* A space completely filled with matter; *spec.* the whole of space regarded as being so filled; opp. to VACUUM. **b.** *transf.* A condition of fullness; a full place 1795. **2.** A full assembly; one at which all the members are expected to be present 1772.

attrib. P. method, system, a system of artificial ventilation in which fresh air, forced into the building to be ventilated, drives out the vitiated air.

Pleochroic (plī\|ǫkrōᵘ·ik), *a.* 1864. [f. *pleo-* PLEIO- + Gr. χρώς, -χροος + -IC; cf. DICHROIC.] *Cryst.* Showing different colours when viewed in two or in three different directions (*dichroic* or *trichroic*), as certain double-refracting crystals. So **Pleochroism** (plī\|ǫ·kro\|iz'm), the quality of thus exhibiting different colours; **Ple:ochroma·tic** *a.* = *pleochroic*; **Pleochro·matism** = *pleochroism*; **Pleochroous** (plī\|ǫ·kro\|əs) *a.* = *pleochroic.*

Pleomorphic (plī\|ǫmǭ·ɹfik), *a.* 1886. [f. as

prec. + Gr. μορφή form + -IC.] Having more than one form: (*a*) *Biol.* exhibiting different forms at different stages of the life-history, as certain bacteria and parasitic fungi; (*b*) *Chem.* and *Min.* crystallizing in two or more fundamentally different forms. So **Pleomo·rphism,** the fact or condition of exhibiting a plurality of forms. **Pleomo·rphous** *a.* = *pleomorphic.*

Pleon (plī·ǫn). 1855. [Arbitrarily ad. Gr. πλέων, pr. pple. of πλεῖν to swim, sail.] *Zool.* The abdomen in Crustacea, which bears the swimming limbs (see PLEOPOD).

Pleonasm (plī·ŏnæz'm). 1586. [ad. L. *pleonasmus* (also formerly used), a. Gr., f. πλεονάζειν to be superfluous, f. πλέον more, compar. of πολύ much.] 1. *Gram.* and *Rhet.* The use of more words in a sentence than are necessary to express the meaning; redundancy of expression; with *a* and *pl.*, an instance of this, or the superfluous word or phrase itself. 2. *gen.* Superfluity, redundancy; something superfluous or redundant. Now only *fig.* from 1617.

1. What the energetic p. of our ancestors denominated 'a false lie' 1860. Hence **Pleona·stic, †-al** *adjs.*; **-ly** *adv.*

Pleonaste (plī·ŏnæst). Also **pleonast.** 1804. [a. F. *pléonaste*, ad. Gr. πλεοναστός abundant.] *Min.* = CEYLONITE.

Pleopod (plī·ǒpǫd). 1855. [f. as PLEON + Gr. πούς, ποδ- foot.] *Zool.* One of the swimming limbs attached to the pleon in Crustacea.

‖ **Pleroma** (pliərōu·mă). 1765. [a. Gr. πλήρωμα that which fills, f. πληροῦν, f. πλήρης full.] Fullness, plenitude; in Gnostic theology, the spiritual universe as the abode of God and of the totality of the Divine powers and emanations. b. Used in ref. to Colossians ii. 9, where the Eng. versions from 1388 have 'fullness'.

Plerome (pliə·roum). 1875. [ad. G. *plerom*, ad. Gr. πλήρωμα; see prec.] *Bot.* The innermost layer of the primary tissue or meristem at a growing-point, which develops into the fibrovascular tissue, or into this and the pith.

Plerophory (pliərǫ·fŏri). Now *rare.* 1605. [ad. Gr. πληροφορία (Heb. vi. 11, x. 22, etc.) fullness of assurance, f. (ult.) πλήρης full + -φόρος bearing.] Full assurance or certainty.

A P. or full Assurance that I am forgiven WESLEY.

Plesance, -aunce, obs. ff. PLEASANCE.

Plesio-, comb. form from Gr. πλησίος near.

Plesiomorphous (plīːsiǫmǭ·ɪfəs), *a.* 1837. [f. PLESIO- + Gr. μορφή form + -OUS.] *Cryst.* Very near in form; crystallizing in forms closely resembling, but not identical with each other. So **Pleːsiomo·rphic** *a.* **Pleːsiomo·rphism,** the fact or condition of being p.

‖ **Plesiosaurus** (plīːsiosǭ·rŏs). *Pl.* **-i.** 1825. [mod.L., f. PLESIO- + Gr. σαῦρος lizard.] *Palæont.* A genus of extinct marine reptiles, having a long neck, a small head, a short tail, and four large paddles, found in the Lias and neighbouring formations. Hence **Ple·siosaur,** a reptile of the extinct genus *Plesiosaurus* or order *Plesiosauria.* **Pleːsiosau·rian** *a.* belonging to the order *Plesiosauria*; *sb.* a reptile of this order.

Plessimeter (plesi·mɪ̆tə.ɪ). 1857. [ad. F. *plessimètre.*] = PLEXIMETER.

Plethora (ple·þŏră, plĭþō·ră). See next. 1541. [a. med.L., a. Gr. πληθώρη fullness, f. πλήθειν to become full.] 1. *Path.* A morbid condition, characterized, according to older writers, by over-fullness of blood or of any other humour (or of juices in a plant), according to later writers, by an excess of red corpuscles in the blood. 2. *fig.* Any unhealthy repletion or excess 1700.

2. We are..suffering under a p. of capital 1835. So **Plethoric** (plĭþǫ·rik, ple·þŏrik) *a. Path.* characterized by p.; *fig.* full to excess; inflated, turgid. late ME. †**Pletho·rical** *a.*, **-ly** *adv.*

Plethory (ple·þŏri). Now *rare.* 1624. [irreg. f. PLETHORA] = PLETHORA.

‖ **Plethron** (ple·þrǫn). *Pl.* **-a.** 1623. [a. Gr. πλέθρον.] An ancient Greek measure of length, = 100 Greek, or about 101 English feet; also a square measure, in extent somewhat less than an imperial rood.

Plethysmograph (plĭþi·zmŏgraf). 1872. [f. Gr. πληθυσμός enlargement (ult. f. πληθύς fullness) + -GRAPH.] *Physiol.* An instrument for recording and measuring the variation in the volume of a part of the body, esp. as due to the changes in the circulation of the blood produced by emotion, etc. Hence **Plethysmogra·phic** *a.* **Plethysmo·graphy,** the use of the p.

‖ **Pleura** (plūə·ră). *Pl.* **-æ.** 1664. [med.L., a. Gr. πλευρά side of the body, rib.] *Anat.* and *Zool.* 1. One of the two serous membranes which line the thorax and envelop the lungs in mammals; each forms a closed sac, one side of which (*pulmonary p.*) invests the lung, while the other (*costal* or *parietal p.*) is attached to the inner wall of the chest. 2. In invertebrates: Name for a part of the body-wall on each side in arthropods 1826. b. In molluscs: The region on each side of the rachis of the lingual ribbon of the odontophore 1851. **Pleu·ral** *a.*[1] of or pertaining to the p.

Pleu·ral, *a.*[2] 1887. [f. PLEURON + -AL.] Of or pertaining to the pleuron; costal, lateral.

‖ **Pleuralgia** (pluræ·ldʒiă). 1822. [mod.L., f. Gr. πλευρά side + -αλγία, ἄλγος pain.] *Path.* Pleurodynia. Hence **Pleura·lgic** *a.*

‖ **Pleurapophysis** (plūəræpǫ·fisis). *Pl.* **-yses** (-isīz). 1854. [mod.L., f. Gr. πλευρά side + APOPHYSIS.] *Compar. Anat.* Each of the lateral processes of a typical vertebra, forming part of the hæmal arch. Hence **Pleuːrapophy·sial** *a.*

‖ **Pleurenchyma** (plure·ŋkimă). Also **pleure·nchym.** 1842. [mod.L., f. Gr. πλευρόν rib, πλευρά side + ἔγχυμα infusion, after *parenchyma*, etc.] *Bot.* The woody tissue, of which the woody parts of plants are mainly formed. Hence **Pleurenchy·matous** *a.*

Pleurisy (plūə·rĭsi). late ME. [a. OF. *pleurisie* (mod.F. *pleurésie*), f. late L. *pleurisis*, mod.L. *pleuresis*, substituted for *pleuritis*, a. Gr.; see PLEURITIS.] *Path.* Inflammation of the pleura, with or without effusion of fluid into the pleural cavity, and usu. characterized by pain in the chest or side. Formerly often with *a* and *pl.*

attrib. **P.-root,** name for *Asclepias tuberosa*, also called Butterfly-weed, a popular remedy for p.

Pleuritic (pluri·tik), *a.* 1570. [a. F. *pleurétique*, or ad. L. *pleuriticus*, a. Gr., f. πλευρῖτις PLEURITIS.] 1. Affected with or suffering from pleurisy. 2. Of or pertaining to pleurisy; symptomatic of pleurisy 1652.

‖ **Pleuritis** (plurəi·tis). *rare.* 1693. [L., a. Gr., f. πλευρά side, rib; see -ITIS.] *Path.* = PLEURISY.

Pleuro- (plūəro), bef. a vowel **pleur-,** comb. form of Gr. πλευρά side, PLEURA, πλευρόν rib; used chiefly in senses 'side' and 'pleura', occas. in that of 'rib'.

‖**Pleurobranchia** (-bræ·ŋkiă), also **pleu·robranch** (-bræŋk), *Zool.* a pleural branchia or gill, i.e. one attached to the epimeron of a thoracic somite, in Crustacea. **Pleurobra·nchial** *a.*, of or pertaining to a pleurobranchia. **Pleurobra·nchiate** *a.*, having pleurobranchiæ, as a crustacean; having gills along the sides, as a gastropod mollusc of the order *Pleurobranchiata.* **Pleuroca·rpous** [Gr. καρπός fruit] *a.*, *Bot.* lateral-fruited. ‖**Pleuroce·ntrum** (*pl.* -a), *Anat.* each lateral half of the centrum of a vertebra, a hemicentrum; hence **Pleuroce·ntral** *a.* **Pleurodiran** (-dəi·răn) [Gr. δειρή neck] *a.*, *Zool.* applied to those tortoises which bend the neck sideways in the shell (opp. to *cryptodirous*); *sb.* a p. tortoise. **Pleu·rodont** [Gr. ὀδούς, ὀδοντ-, tooth], *Zool.* a lizard having teeth fixed to the side of the jawbone; *a.* belonging to the *Pleurodontes*, a group of lizards having this character. **Pleuːro-perica·rdial** *a.*, belonging to the pleura and the pericardium; applied to a friction-sound heard in auscultation in cases of pleurisy. **Pleuːro-pericardi·tis** *Path.*, inflammation involving the pleura and pericardium. ‖**Pleuro·steon** (pl. -ea) [Gr. ὀστέον bone], *Zool.* a lateral part on each side of the sternum in birds, to which the ribs are attached; hence **Pleuro·steal** *a.* See also Main words.

‖**Pleurodynia** (plūərodi·niă). Also †**pleurodyne** (-ǫ·dinī), **pleurodyny** (-ǫ·dini). 1802. [f. PLEURO- + Gr. -οδυνία in comb., f. ὀδύνη pain.] *Path.* Pain in the side caused by rheumatism in the muscles of the chest.

‖ **Pleuron** (plūə·rǫn). *Pl.* **pleura.** 1706. [a. Gr. πλευρόν rib, side.] *Anat.* and *Zool.* The lateral part of the body-wall, the side; *spec.* in Arthropoda, the lateral part of each somite or section of the body (in insects, of each thoracic somite).

Pleuronect (plūə·rŏnekt). 1849. [ad. mod. L. *Pleuronectes*, f. Gr. πλευρά side + νήκτης swimmer.] *Ichthyol.* A fish of the genus *Pleuronectes* or family *Pleuronectidæ*; a flat-fish. So **Pleurone·ctid, -ne·ctoid** *sb.* a fish of the family *Pleuronectidæ*; *a.* belonging to this family.

‖ **Pleuːro-peritone·um, -æ·um.** 1875. [mod.L., f. PLEURO- + PERITONEUM.] *Anat.* The serous membrane lining the body-cavity and enveloping the viscera in vertebrates below mammals; corresponding to the pleuræ and peritoneum in mammals. Also called simply PERITONEUM. So **Pleuːro-peritone·al, -æ·al** *a.* of or belonging at once to the pleuræ and the peritoneum, or the pleuro-peritoneum 1872.

‖ **Pleuro-pneumonia** (plūəːroˌniumōu·niă). 1725. [mod.L., f. PLEURO- + PNEUMONIA.] *Path.* Inflammation involving the pleura and the lung; pneumonia complicated with pleurisy; *esp.* a contagious febrile disease peculiar to horned cattle.

‖ **Pleurothotonos** (plūərǫþǫ·tŏnǫs), **-us** (-ŏs). 1822. [mod.L., f. Gr. πλευρόθεν from the side (f. πλευρά side) + -τονος stretched, stretching.] *Path.* Tetanic bending of the body to one side.

Pleurotomid (plurǫ·tŏmid). [ad. mod.L. *Pleurotomidæ* pl., f. *Pleurotoma* name of the typical genus, f. Gr. πλευρά side + τομή cutting; see -ID.] *Zool.* A gastropod mollusc of the family *Pleurotomidæ.*

Plexiform (ple·ksifǭɪm), *a.* 1828. [f. PLEXUS + -FORM.] *Anat.* Of the form of a plexus; forming a plexus or plexuses.

Pleximeter (pleksi·mɪ̆təɪ). Also (irreg.) **plexometer.** 1842. [f. Gr. πλῆξις percussion (f. πλήσσειν to strike) + -METER (with the sense of 'estimating').] *Med.* A small thin plate of ivory, etc., which is placed firmly upon some part of the body and struck with a PLEXOR in medical percussion.

Plexor (ple·ksǭɪ). 1844. [irreg. f. Gr. πλῆξις or πλήσσειν (see prec.) + -OR, after *flexor*, etc.] *Med.* A small hammer, etc. used (with a PLEXIMETER) in medical percussion; a percussion-hammer.

Plexure (ple·ksiŭɪ). *rare.* 1671. [f. L. *plex-*, *plectere* to plait, etc.] A plaiting or interweaving; something plaited or interwoven.

‖ **Plexus** (ple·ksŏs). *Pl.* **plexuses,** rarely **plexus.** 1682. [a. L., f. *plex-*: see prec.] 1. *Anat.* A structure in the animal body consisting of a network of fibres or vessels closely interwoven and intercommunicating; as *gastric p.*, *solar p.*, etc. 2. *gen.* A network, complication 1769.

Pliable (pləi·ăb'l), *a.* 1483. [a. F., f. *plier* to bend; see PLY *v.*[1] and -ABLE.] 1. Easy to be bent; flexible, supple; †plastic. 2. *fig.* Flexible in disposition or character; yielding, docile; adaptable. Sometimes in bad sense. 1494.

1. A plyable flexure of joynts SIR T. BROWNE. 2. P. judges were previously chosen 1863. Hence **Pliabi·lity, Pli·ableness,** p. quality or property. **Pli·ably** *adv.*

Pliancy (pləi·ănsi). 1711. [f. next; see -ANCY.] The quality of being pliant; flexibility.

P. of mind 1810. The agile p. of youth 1835.

Pliant (pləi·ănt), *a.* ME. [a. F., pr. pple. of *plier* to PLY.] 1. Bending; supple, flexible; †plastic. 2. *fig.* Readily influenced for good or evil; compliant, complaisant. late ME. b. = FLEXIBLE 3. 1835.

1. The fisher, with his p. wand 1880. 2. A committee thus instructed was likely to be sufficiently p. 1860. Hence **Pli·ant-ly** *adv.*, **-ness** (now *rare*).

‖ **Plica** (pli·kă, pləi·kă). *Pl.* **plicæ.** 1684. [med.L., plait, f. *plicare* to fold; see PLY.] 1. *Path.* (More fully *pli·ca polo·nica.*) A matted filthy condition of the hair due to disease; Polish plait. 2. A fold or folding of any part, as of the skin or a membrane 1706.

Plicate (pləi·kĕt), *a.* 1760. [ad. L. *plicatus*, pa. pple. of *plicare* to fold.] Folded, pleated. So **Pli·cated** *ppl. a.* 1753. **Pli·cately** *adv.*

Plication (pli-, pləikēɪ·ʃən). late ME. [a. OF., f. L. *plicare* to fold.] 1. The action of folding; folded condition. 2. *concr.* A folding, a fold 1748. 3. *Geol.* The folding of strata; a fold in a stratum 1859.

Plicato- (pli-, pləikēi·to), comb. adv. form from L. *plicatus* plicate, prefixed to other adjs. in the sense 'plicately —', 'plicate and —', as *p.-contorted* (plicately contorted), *p.-papillose* (papillose with plications or wrinkles), etc.

Plicature (pli·kătiŭı). 1578. [ad. L. *plicatura* a folding.] = PLICATION.

Plicidentine (pliside·ntin). 1849. [f. med. L. *plica* fold + DENTINE.] A form of dentine in which it is folded on a series of vertical plates, causing the surface of the tooth to be fluted.

Plier (pləi·əı). 1490. [f. PLY *v.* + -ER 1.] 1. One who plies (see PLY *v.*) 1673. 2. *pl.* Pincers, usu. small, having long jaws mostly with parallel surfaces, sometimes toothed, for bending wire, handling small objects, etc.

Plight (pləit), *sb.*[1] [OE. *pliht* danger, risk; cf. MDu. *plicht*, *plecht* responsibility, duty; OHG., MHG. *pfliht* obligation, duty, care of or for; f. stem *pleh-*, *pleg-* of OE. *plēon* (with genitive) to risk the loss of, expose to danger.] †1. Peril, danger, risk. -late ME. †2. Sin, offence; guilt, blame. ME. only. 3. Undertaking (of a risk or obligation); pledge (under risk of forfeiture); engagement, plighting ME.

3. *Lear* I. i. 103.

Plight (pləit), *sb.*[2] [ME. *plit*, *plyt*, a. AF. *plit*, for ONF. **pleit*, OF. *ploit* fold, etc.; see PLAIT *sb.*, of which this is orig. a doublet.] I. Fold, manner of folding; plait. †1. = PLAIT *sb.* 1, 1 b. -1697. †2. = PLAIT *sb.* 2. -1800. †3. A recognized length or 'piece' of lawn -1535. II. Manner of being; condition, state. (Cf. *complexion.*) 1. Condition, state, trim. (Orig. neutral or good; now usually evil.) ME. 2. State as to health; now esp. of cattle. late ME. b. *absol.* Health 1450. †3. Mood. esp. *to do* something -1726. 4. State or position from a legal point of view 1540. 5. Attire, dress (*rare*) 1590.

1. Being in so excellent a p. DRAYTON. He was now in a woful p. GOLDSM. 3. 'Less Philomel will daign a Song, In her sweetest, saddest p. MILT.

Plight (pləit), *v.*[1] Now chiefly *poet.* or *rhet.* [OE. *plihtan*, f. *pliht* danger; see PLIGHT *sb.*[1]] †1. *trans.* To put (something) in danger or risk of forfeiture; to pledge or engage (one's faith, oath, etc.), esp. in ref. to betrothal or marriage ME. †2. To pledge oneself to do or give (something); to promise -1587. 3. To engage or bind (oneself); *pass.* to be engaged or bound *to* some one. late ME.

1. To p. faith to William, rightful and lawful King 1855. Hence **Pli·ghter** *rare*, one who or that which plights or pledges.

†Plight, *v.*[2] [ME. *plite*, etc., collateral form of PLAIT *v.*; later *plight*, going with PLIGHT *sb.*[2]] 1. *trans.* = PLAIT *v.* 1; also to contract into folds or wrinkles -1658. 2. = PLAIT *v.* 2; to knit, to tie in a knot -1633.

Plim (plim), *v.* Chiefly *dial.* 1654. [Etym. unkn.] a. *intr.* To swell, fill *out*. b. *trans.* To swell, inflate 1881.

Pli·msoll. 1881. [Name of S. *Plimsoll*, M.P. for Derby, to whom the Merchant Shipping Act of 1876 was largely due.] In *P. line*, (also *Plimsoll's*) *mark*: see MARK *sb.*[1] III. 3. b. *sb. pl.* A kind of rubber-soled canvas shoes 1927.

Plinth (plinþ). 1611. [ad. L. *plinthus* (also orig. used), a. Gr. πλίνθος tile, brick, etc.] 1. a. 'The lower square member of the base of a column or pedestal' (Gwilt). b. The projecting part of a wall immediately above the ground. Also *attrib.*, as *p.-stone*. 1823. c. *fig.* A plinth-like base 1803. 2. The uppermost projecting part of a cornice or wall. Now *rare*. 1613.

Pliocene (pləi·ŏsīn), *a.* (*sb.*) Also **pleio-** 1833. [f. Gr. πλείων, -ον more (see PLEIO-) + καινός new.] *Geol.* Epithet applied to the newest division of the Tertiary formation; called also Upper Tertiary. Also applied to animals, etc. of this period. b. *absol.* as *sb.* = Pliocene division or formation.

‖ **Pliosaurus** (pləi,osǭ·rŏs). Also **pleio-.** 1841. [f. Gr. πλεῖον more, PLEIO- + σαῦρος lizard; so called because more near to the saurian type than the ICHTHYOSAURUS.] *Palæont.* A genus of fossil marine reptiles, resembling *Plesiosaurus*; their remains are found in the Upper Oolite. Also **Pli·osaur.**

Pliotron (pləi·ŏtrǫn). *Wireless Telegr.* 1918. [irreg. f. *plio* -PLEIO- + *-tron* of ELECTRON.] A three-electrode valve the bulb of which is as highly evacuated of air as possible.

‖ **Ploce** (plǫ·sī). 1577. [Late L., a. Gr. πλοκή plaiting, f. πλέκειν to plait.] *Rhet.* The repetition of a word in an altered or pregnant sense, or for the sake of emphasis.

Ploce,..as, In that great victory Cæsar was Cæsar 1678.

Plod (plǫd), *v.* 1562. [app. echoic.] I. *intr.* To walk heavily; to move laboriously, to trudge. Also *p. on. lit.* and *fig.* 1566. b. *trans.* To trudge along, over, or through (a road, etc.) 1750. 2. *intr.* To work with steady laborious perseverance; to toil in a laborious, stolid, monotonous fashion. Const. *at, on, upon*. 1562.

1. Bare-foot p. I the cold ground vpon SHAKS. b. The plowman homeward plods his weary way GRAY. 2. The secret of good work—to p. on and still keep the passion fresh MEREDITH. Hence **Plod** *sb.*, an act or spell of plodding· a heavy tiring walk. **Plo·dder,** one who plods. **Plo·dding** *ppl. a.*; hence **Plo·dding-ly** *adv.*, **-ness.**

Plop (plǫp), *sb.* and *adv.* 1833. [Echoic.] A. *sb.* The sound made by a smooth object dropping into water without splashing, or the like; the act of falling with this sound. B. *adv.* or *int.* With a plop. So **Plop** *v.* to fall with or as with a plop. Also *trans.* in causative sense.

Plosion (plōu·ʒən). 1899. [Extracted from EXPLOSION and IMPLOSION.] *Phonetics.* The percussive shutting off or release of the breath, as in the pronunciation of stops such as (p), (b). Hence **Plos·ive** *a.* and *sb.* (a speech sound) characterized by this.

Plot (plǫt), *sb.* OE. [Origin unkn. See also the collateral form *plat* (PLAT *sb.*[2]).] I. †1. A small portion of any surface differing in character or aspect from the rest; a patch, spot -1834. 2. A piece (of small or moderate size) of ground, or of what grows or lies upon it; a patch, spot. Cf. PLAT *sb.*[2] 1. OE. †b. The site, situation, of a building, town, city, etc. -1603.

2. The grass p. before the door W. IRVING.

II. In these senses *plat* occurs earlier. 1. A ground plan of a building, field, farm, etc.; a map, a chart. *Obs.* or *arch.* exc. in *U.S.* 1551. †2. A sketch or outline of a literary work -1626. 3. The plan or scheme of a play, poem, work of fiction, etc. 1649.

1. The ruins of the cathedral of Elgin..Its whole p. is easily traced JOHNSON. 3. In every narrative, there is a certain connexion of events..which, in a work of fiction, is called a p. 1852.

III. Perh. infl. by COMPLOT. A plan or project, secretly contrived, to accomplish some wicked, criminal, or illegal purpose; a conspiracy; also later, *joc.*, a sly plan, an innocent scheme 1594.

The Powder-plot. Inuented by hellish Malice. 1617.

Plot (plǫt), *v.* 1588. [f. prec. sb.] I. *trans.* To make a plan, map, or diagram of (an existing object, as a building, etc.); to lay down on a map (as a ship's course, etc.); to represent by a plan or diagram (the course or result of any action or process). Also with *down*. 1590. 2. To make a plan of (something to be laid out, constructed, or made). Also with *out*. 1588. 3. To plan, contrive, or devise (something to be carried out or accomplished). Now always in evil sense. 1589. 4. *intr.* To scheme, lay plans, contrive, conspire 1607.

1. This treatise plotteth downe Cornwall, as it now standeth 1602. 3. They..plotted the..mercilesse, devilish, and damnable gunpowder-treason 1631. Had he plotted to dethrone a princess H. WALPOLE. 4. The wicked plotteth against the iust *Ps.* xxxvii. 12. Hence **Plo·tter,** one who plans or devises anything (now *rare*); *spec.* a conspirator.

Plotinian (ploti·niăn), *a.* 1678. [f. L. *Plotinus*, a. Gr. Πλωτῖνος, proper name.] Of or pertaining to Plotinus (A.D. 204-270), the most noted philosopher of the Neo-Platonic school. So **Ploti·nic, -al** *a.* **Plo·tinist,** a follower of Plotinus.

Plough (plau), *sb.*[1] Also *U.S.* **plow.** [Com. Teut. of obsc. origin: late OE. *plōh* (*plōg*) plough-land :—Teut. **plōgo-*, **plōho-* (which passed into the Baltic and Slavonic langs.).] 1. An agricultural implement, used to prepare the soil for sowing or planting, by cutting furrows in it and turning it up. It consists essentially of a cutting blade, fixed in a frame, drawn by oxen or horses (or, now, by steam, etc.), and guided by a man. Often used as the symbol of agriculture. ME. 2. Chiefly *s.w. dial.* A team of draught beasts harnessed to a wagon 1505. 3. †a. = PLOUGH-LAND 1. -1791. b. Ploughed land. (Chiefly *hunting slang.*) 1861. 4. *transf.* The group of seven stars, also called Charles's Wain, in the constellation *Ursa Major*; also, that constellation as a whole 1513. 5. Applied to various instruments, etc., resembling a plough in shape or action; *esp.* a. An instrument for cutting or trimming the edges of books 1688; b. A plane for cutting rabbets or grooves 1678. 6. An antler or branch on the horn of a caribou 1892.

1. I think that whosoever doth not maintain the P., destroys this Kingdom 1601. ICE-, SNOW-P., etc.: see those words. Phrases. *To be at the p.*, *to follow* or *hold the p.* *To put (lay, set) one's hand to the p.* (after Luke ix. 62): to undertake a task. *Under the p.*: (of land) in cultivation. 2. The driver of a p.,.. laden with tin, for Penzance coinage 1762.

attrib. and *Comb.*: **p.-beam,** the central longitudinal beam in a plough, to which the other principal parts are attached; **-cutter** = *plough-press*; **-iron,** any iron part of a p., *esp.* in *pl.*, the coulter and share; **-knife,** the knife of a bookbinder's plough-cutter; **-plane** = sense 5 b; **-point,** the point of a ploughshare; **-press,** in bookbinding, a press in which a book is held while the edges are cut or 'ploughed'; **-tree,** a plough-handle; **-wright,** a maker of ploughs. See also Main words. Hence **Plou·gher,** one who ploughs· a ploughman.

Plough, *sb.*[2] *slang.* 1863. [f. PLOUGH *v.* 8.] The act or fact of rejecting a candidate in an examination.

Plough (plau), *v.* late ME. Also *U.S.* **plow.** [f. PLOUGH *sb.*[1]] 1. a. *trans.* To make furrows in and turn up (the earth) with a plough, esp. as a preparation for sowing; also *absol.* to use a plough. b. To make (a furrow, ridge, line) by ploughing 1589. 2. *intr.* (or *absol.*) To use the plough, work as a ploughman, till the ground 1535. b. *intr.* in pass. sense (of land): To stand ploughing (well, etc.); to prove (tough, etc.) in the ploughing 1762. 3. *trans.* By extension: To furrow as by ploughing; to gash, tear up, scratch (any surface). Often *p. up*. 1588. b. *intr.* To move through soft ground, snow, etc., furrowing it 1847. 4. *fig.* Of a ship, boat, swimming animal, etc.: To cleave the surface of the water. Chiefly *poet.* *trans.* and *intr.* 1607. 5. *trans. fig.* To furrow (the face, brow, etc.) deeply with wrinkles; also with resultant object 1725. 6. In various fig. applications 1535. 7. a. *Bookbinding.* To cut with a 'plough' or plough-press 1873. b. *Carpentry.* To cut or plane (a groove, rabbet) with a 'plough'. Also *intr.* 1805. 8. *Univ. slang.* To reject (a candidate) in an examination 1853.

1. As much land as a yoke of oxen could p. in one day 1796. 2. That hee that ploweth, should plow in hope 1 *Cor.* ix. 10. 3. [He] Fell prone and plough'd the Dust 1740. The course which the river had ploughed for itself down the valley SCOTT. 4. *trans.* He and his eight hundred Shall p. the wave no more COWPER. 5. Italia!..On thy sweet brow is sorrow plough'd by shame BYRON. 6. Cromwell.. who through a cloud..To peace and truth thy glorious way hast plough'd MILT.

With advbs. *P. around*: *lit.* in ref. to stumps left in cultivated land; *fig.* to feel one's way. *P. in*, *p. into the land*: to embed or bury in the soil (manure, vegetation, etc.) by ploughing. *P. up*: to break up (ground) by ploughing; to throw or cast up (roots, weeds) with the plough; to cut up roughly, furrow or scratch deeply by any similar action.

Phrases. *To p. with any one's heifer* (*ox*, *†calf*) after Judges xiv. 18. *To p. the sands*: a type of fruitless labour. Also *to p. the air*. Hence **Plou·ghable** *a.* that can be ploughed; arable.

Plou·gh-boy. 1569. A boy who leads the team that draws a plough; hence, a young rustic.

Plough-head. 1453. [f. PLOUGH *sb.*[1] + HEAD *sb.*] †1. The share-beam of a plough; a wooden frame to which the share was fixed -1613. 2. The front part of a plough 1733.

Plough-land (plau·lænd). ME. [f. PLOUGH *sb.*[1] + LAND *sb.*] 1. *Hist.* The unit of assessment of land in the N. and E. counties of England, after the Norman Conquest, based upon the area capable of being tilled by one plough-team of eight oxen in the year; cf. HIDE *sb.* 2. Arable land 1530.

Ploughman (plau·mæ̆n). ME. A man who follows and guides the plough; hence, a farm-labourer or rustic.

Comb. **Ploughman's Spikenard**: see SPIKENARD.

Plough-Monday (plau:mʊ·ndeⁱ, mʊ·ndi). 1542. The first Monday after Epiphany, on which, esp. in the N. and E. of England, the commencement of the ploughing season was celebrated by a procession of disguised ploughmen and boys drawing a plough from door to door.

Ploughshare (plau·ʃēᵊɹ). late ME. 1. The large pointed blade of a plough, which, following the coulter, cuts a slice of earth, and passes it on to the mould-board. 2. *Anat.* The vomer.

attrib. and *Comb.* **p.-bone** *Anat.*, (*a*) the vomer; (*b*) the pygostyle of a bird.

Plou·gh-staff. ME. A staff, ending in a small spade or shovel, used to clear the coulter and mould-board from earth, roots, weeds, etc.

Plou·gh-tail. 1523. The rear or handles of a plough. Symbolically, farm-labour; as *at, from the plough-tail.*

Plover (plʊ·vəɹ). [ME. and AF., = OF. *plovier*:—late L. *plovarius* belonging to rain, f. L. *pluvia* rain. The connexion with rain has been variously explained: see N.E.D.] 1. The common name of several gregarious grallatorial (limicoline) birds of the family *Charadriidæ*, esp. those of the genera *Charadrius* and *Squatarola*; also popularly given to the Lapwing, the eggs of which are sold as 'Plovers' eggs'. 2. With defining words, applied to species of the family *Charadriidæ*, and extended to some of the allied *Thinocoridæ* and *Scolopacidæ* or Snipe family, and to the isolated genus *Dromas* (Crab Plover) 1538.

Plover-page, plover's page. *Sc.* 1837. [f. prec. + PAGE *sb.*¹] The dunlin (*Tringa alpina*), which is said to attend or follow the golden plover; applied also to other species of *Tringa*, and to the Jack Snipe.

Ploy (ploi). *Sc.* and *north.* 1722. [Origin unkn.] Anything in which one personally engages; a hobby; a game, pastime, or sport; an escapade; a trick.

Pluck (plʊk), *sb.* late ME. [f. next.] I. 1. An act of plucking; a tug, a jerk, a snatch. †b. *fig.* A bout; an attempt; a 'go' -1762. 2. In examinations: The act of plucking or rejecting a candidate; the fact of being plucked 1852.

1. b. They being come to By path Stile, have a mind to have a p. with Gyant Dispair BUNYAN.

II. 1. The heart, liver, and lungs (sometimes with other viscera) of a beast, as used for food 1611. b. In ref. to human beings 1710. 2. *colloq.* (orig. app. *pugilistic slang.*) The heart as the seat of courage; courage, spirit; determination not to yield but to keep up the fight in the face of danger or difficulty 1785.

1. b. It vexes me to the p. that I should lose walking this delicious day SWIFT. 2. The one thing the English value is p. EMERSON. Hence **Plucked** (plʊkt) *a.* having p. or courage; as in *good-p., rare-p.*, etc. (*colloq.* 1848.) **Plu·ckless** *a.* without p., courage, or spirit.

Pluck (plʊk), *v.* [Com. WGer.: late OE. *ploccian, pluccian.*] 1. *trans.* To pull off (a flower, fruit, hair, feather, etc.) from where it grows; to pick off or out; to cull, gather. 2. To drag; to snatch. With *away, in, out, off, on, up*, etc. *arch.* (Now usu. expressed by *pull.*) late ME. b. *absol.* or *intr.* To draw or drag; to snatch or take by force; to steal ME. 3. *trans. fig.* To pull, draw, or snatch something intangible, or something from or into a state or condition; to snatch *from* danger. Now *rare.* late ME. †b. With *down*, etc. To bring down, bring low -1672. 4. To give a pull at; to pull with a jerk; to sound (the strings of a musical instrument) by doing this, to twang. Also, to pull (a person, etc.) *by* some part of the body or dress. late ME. b. *intr.* To pull sharply or forcibly, to tug (*at* something). Also, to snatch *at.* late ME. 5. To strip or make bare; *esp.* to strip (a bird) of feathers by pulling them off. late ME. 6. *fig.* To rob; to plunder; to swindle, fleece. late ME. 7. To reject (a candidate) as below the required standard in an examination; usu. in pass. *To be plucked*, to fail to pass 1713.

1. Let him..From off this Bryer p. a white Rose with me SHAKS. 2. Yf thy right eye offende the plucke hym out and caste him from the TINDALE *Matt.* v. 29. They plucke downe townes; and leaue nothing stondynge 1551. 4. 'Tis most ignobly done To plucke me by the Beard SHAKS. Phr. *To p. the Proctor's gown*, the means formerly used (and still usable) for objecting to the granting of a degree to a person who has passed the requisite examinations. 5. Since I pluckt Geese, plaide Trewant, and whipt Top SHAKS. Phr. *A crow to p.*: see CROW *sb.*¹ 6. I did p. those Ganders, did rob them DEKKER. Phr. *To p. a pigeon*: see PIGEON *sb.* 3 b.

Pluck up. a. *To p. up (one's) heart, spirits, courage*, etc.: to summon up courage, rouse one's spirits, cheer up. b. To pull up; to uproot, eradicate; to raze, demolish. Now *rare* or *arch.* Hence **Plu·cker**, one who or that which plucks.

Plucky (plʊ·ki), *a. colloq.* 1826. [f. PLUCK *sb.* + -Y¹.] Characterized by pluck; showing determination to fight. b. *Photogr.* Of a print or negative: Bold, decided, clear 1885.

The pluckiest charge of all that hard fought day 1857. Hence **Plu·ckily** *adv.* **Plu·ckiness.**

Pluff (plʊf), *sb.* (*int.*) *Sc.* 1663. [Echoic.] 1. A strong puff or explosive emission of air, gas, or smoke (as in the firing of gunpowder), or of dust; hence, *colloq.* a shot of a musket, etc. 2. as *int.* or *adv. colloq.* 1860.

Plug (plʊg), *sb.* 1618. [app. a. MDu. *plugge* plug, bung, stopper, of unkn. origin.] 1. A piece of wood or other material, driven into or used to stop up a hole, to fill a gap, or act as a wedge; also *transf.* a natural or morbid concretion having a similar action. 2. *spec.* in technical applications; *esp.* a. A tapering block of wood driven into a wall between the stones or bricks so as to bear a nail. b. In railways, A wedge-pin driven between a rail and its chair. c. *Dentistry.* The filling of a hollow tooth. 1766. d. The release-mechanism of a water-closet flushing apparatus. 3. The cock on a public water-pipe; a fire-plug 1727. 4. a. Tobacco pressed into a flat oblong cake or stick. b. A piece of cake or twist tobacco cut off for chewing, etc. 1728. 5. Applied variously to inferior or defective persons, animals, or objects. *U.S.* and *Colonial.* 1872. 6. Short for *plug-hat* (see below). *U.S. slang.* 1864.

Comb.: **-basin**, a wash-hand basin having a plug-hole for letting the water out; **-hat** (*U.S. slang*), a silk, 'top', or 'chimney-pot' hat [perh. because the head fits in it like a p.]; **-hole**, an aperture fitted with a p. by which it can be closed; **-rod**, a contrivance attached to the beam of a steam-engine, for opening and closing the valves of the cylinder; **-switch** (*Electr.*), a switch in which connexion is made by inserting a metal p.; **-tobacco** = sense 4.

Plug (plʊg), *v.* 1630. [f. prec. sb.] 1. *trans.* To stop, close tightly, or fill (a hole) with or as with a plug; to drive a plug into. Chiefly with *up.* b. *intr.* with *in* (*Electr.*): To complete a circuit by inserting a key or plug between metal plates 1903. 2. *trans.* To put a bullet into, to shoot (*slang*) 1888. 3. To strike with the fist (*slang*) 1875. 4. *intr.* a. To 'stick to it' 1865. b. To labour with piston-like strokes against resistance (*slang*) 1898.

4. a. We plugged for all we were worth 1865. Hence **Plu·gger**, one who or that which plugs.

Plugging (plʊ·giŋ), *vbl. sb.* 1708. [-ING¹.] 1. The action of PLUG *v.* 2. *concr.* Plugs 1875.

Plug-ugly (plʊg,ʊ·gli). *U.S. slang.* 1860. [Origin obsc.] A city ruffian or rowdy.

Plum (plʊm), *sb.* [OE. *plūme* plum, a. late L. or Rom. **pruna* for L. *prunum* PRUNE, a. later Gr. προῦνον, for cl. Gr. προῦμνον plum.] 1. The fruit of the tree *Prunus domestica*, a roundish fleshy drupe, covered with a glaucous mealy bloom, and having a somewhat flat pointed stone and sweet pulp. 2. The tree bearing this fruit, *Prunus domestica* (N.O. *Rosaceæ*) OE. 3. With qualifying words. Applied to many species (and varieties) of the genus *Prunus.* 4. A dried grape or raisin as used for puddings, cakes, etc. 1660. b. *fig.* A 'good thing', a tit-bit; also, the pick or best of a collection of things, animals, etc. 1780. 5. The sum of £100,000. *slang*, now *rare.* 1689. †b. *transf.* One who is possessed of this sum -1774.

1. **Damascene**, †**Damasco**, or **Damson P.**: see DAMASK, DAMSON; **Wild P.**, in Britain, *P. insititia* or *spinosa*; in N. America, *P. americana* and *P. subcordata.* Also applied to trees resembling the p., esp. in fruit: **Australian P.** or **Black P. of Illawarra**, *Cargillia australis*, N.O. *Ebenaceæ*; **Blood P.** of Sierra Leone, *Hæmatostaphis Barteri*, N O. *Anacardiaceæ*; **Cocoa P.** of tropical America and Africa, *Chrysobalanus Icaco*; **Grey P.** or **Guinea P.**, of Sierra Leone, *Parinarium excelsum*, N.O. *Chrysobalanaceæ.* See also DATE-*p.*, GINGERBREAD-*p.*, etc. 1626. 4. b. The reviewer who picks all the 'plums' out of a book 1889. The posts named are justly regarded as plums of the Indian Civil Service 1901.

Comb. **p.-colour**, a shade of purple; so **-coloured** *a.*; **-gouger**, a weevil (*Coccotorus scutellaris*).

Plumage (plū·medʒ). 1481. [a. OF., f. *plume* PLUME; see -AGE.] 1. Feathers collectively; the covering of a bird. 2. A bunch or tuft of feathers used as an ornament; a plume. Now *rare.* 1656.

1. *fig.* All the strength and p. of thy youth WORDSW. Hence **Plu·maged** *a.* feathered; having p.

Plumassier (plūmăsīᵊ·ɹ). 1598. [a. F., f. obs. F. *plumasse* a great plume, f. *plume* + augm. suffix *-asse*:—L. *-acea* adj. suffix; see -IER.] One who works or trades in ornamental feathers or plumes.

Plumb (plʊm), *sb.* ME. [ad. F. *plomb*:—L. *plumbum* lead.] A mass or ball of lead; *esp.* the weight attached to a mason's plumb-line, to secure its perpendicularity. b. A sounding lead, a mariner's plummet 1440.

Plumb, plum (plʊm), *a.* and *adv.* late ME. [f. prec. sb.] A. *adj.* 1. Vertical, perpendicular 1460. 2. Downright; sheer (Now *U.S.*) 1748; in *Cricket*, (of the wicket) level, true 1902. B. *adv.* 1. Of motion or position: Vertically, perpendicularly; straight *down*; rarely, straight *up.* late ME. 2. *transf.* and *fig.* a. Exactly, directly, precisely 1601. b. As an intensive: Completely, absolutely, quite. Chiefly *U.S. slang.* 1587.

1. Fluttring his pennons vain p. down he drops MILT.

Plumb (plʊm), *v.* late ME. [f. PLUMB *sb.* and *a.*; perh. partly after F. *plomber.*] I. †1. *intr.* To sink or fall like a plummet; to fall or plump straight down. WYCLIF. II. a. *trans.* To sound (the sea, etc.) with a plummet; to measure (the depth) by sounding 1568. b. *fig.* To sound the depths of; to fathom 1599.

a. The depth having been carefully plumbed 1867.

III. 1. To render vertical, to adjust or test by a plumb-line 1711. 2. To place vertically above or below 1838. b. *intr.* To hang vertically 1867. IV. 1. *trans.* To weight with lead 1450. 2. To seal (luggage) with a leaden seal 1756. V. [Back-formation from *plumber.*] *intr.* To work in lead as a plumber. Also *trans.* 1889.

Plumbagin (plʊmbēⁱ·dʒin). 1830. [ad. F. *plombagine*, f. L. *plumbago* (see next) + *-ine*, -IN¹.] *Chem.* The acrid principle of the root of *Plumbago europæa.*

Plumbago (plʊmbēⁱ·go). 1612. [a. L., tr. Gr. μολύβδαινα of Dioscorides, deriv. of μόλυβδος lead.] †1. Applied to the yellow oxide of lead (litharge); also sometimes to the sulphide (galena) -1669. 2. *Min.* Black lead or graphite; one of the allotropic forms of carbon; used for pencils, etc., also, mixed with clay, for making crucibles 1712. 3. *Bot.* A genus of herbaceous plants, having spikes of subsessile flowers, with a tubular five-parted calyx; leadwort; so called from the colour of the flowers 1747. Hence **Plumba·ginous** *a.* of the nature of or pertaining to p. or graphite.

Plumb-bob (plʊ·m,bǫ:b). 1835 [BOB *sb.*¹] The leaden bob, usu. conoidal, forming the weight of a plumb-line.

Plumbeous (plʊ·mbiəs), *a.* 1578. [f. L. *plumbeus* leaden (f. *plumbum* lead) + -OUS.] Made of or resembling lead, leaden; lead-coloured. Chiefly in *Zool.* b. *Ceramics.* Lead-glazed 1875.

Plumber (plʊ·məɹ). ME. [a. OF. *plummier, plommier* (mod.F. *plombier*):—L. *plumbarius* plumber, f. *plumbum* lead.] An artisan who works in lead, zinc, and tin, fitting in, soldering, and repairing water and gas pipes, cisterns, boilers, and the like in buildings; orig., a man who dealt and worked in lead.

Plumber-block: see PLUMMER-BLOCK.

Plumbery (plʊ·məri). [ME., a. OF. *plommerie, plomberie*, f. *plommier* plumber; in med. L. *plumbaria.*] 1. A plumber's workshop. 2. Plumber's work, plumbing 1464.

Plumbic (plɒ·mbik), *a.* 1799. [f. L. *plumbum* lead + -IC.] Of or pertaining to lead. **a.** *Chem.* Combined with lead; applied to compounds in which lead has its higher valency (divalent), as *p. acid*, dioxide of lead, PbO_2. **b.** *Path.* Due to the presence of lead 1875.

Plumbi·ferous, *a.* 1796. [f. L. *plumbum* lead + -FEROUS.] Containing lead.

Plumbing (plɒ·miŋ), *vbl. sb.* 1666. [-ING [1].] The action of PLUMB *v.*; now *esp.* the work of a plumber. **b.** *concr.* That which is made by this action; plumber's work 1756. **c.** *attrib.*, as **p.-line, -rope,** a lead-line, sounding-line.

Plumbism (plɒ·mbiz'm). 1876. [f. L. *plumbum* lead + -ISM.] *Path.* Lead poisoning.

Plumb-line (plɒ·mləin). 1538. **1.** A line or cord having at one end a metal bob or plummet, for testing or determining vertical direction; occas. = PLUMB-RULE. †**2.** *Geom.* A vertical or perpendicular line; a straight line at right angles to another –1704. **3.** A mariner's sounding-line; also *fig.* 1648.

Plumbo-, bef. a vowel **plumb-,** comb. form of L. *plumbum* lead, forming chemical and mineralogical terms.

Plumbous (plɒ·mbəs), *a.* 1685. [ad. L. *plumbosus* full of lead; see -OUS.] †**1.** Leaden; *fig.* dull –1737. **2.** *Chem.* Applied to compounds in which lead has its lower valency. Cf. PLUMBIC a. 1895.

Plumb-rule (plɒ·m,rūl). late ME. [f. PLUMB *sb.* + RULE *sb.*] A plummet and line attached to and swinging freely on the surface of a narrow straight-edged board, marked with a longitudinal line which, when its position is vertical, coincides with the string. Used by builders, masons, carpenters, etc. for ensuring or testing the verticality of an erection.

Plum-cake. 1635. A cake containing raisins, currants, and other preserved fruits.

Plum-duff. Also **-dough.** 1840. [f. PLUM *sb.* 4 + DUFF *sb.* [1]] Plain flour pudding with raisins or currants in it, boiled in a cloth or bag.

Plume (plūm), *sb.* late ME. [a. OF. :—L. *pluma* a small soft feather, down.] **1.** A feather; now chiefly *poet.* and *rhet.*; also, a large or conspicuous ornamental feather, as a plume of an ostrich, etc.; in *Ornith.* a contour-feather, as dist. from a plumule. **b.** *fig.* with ref. to the feathers of birds as used in flight, displayed in pride, etc. 1591. **2.** Downy plumage, down; plumage generally 1552. **3.** An ornament, usu. symbolizing dignity or rank, consisting of a large feather or bunch of feathers, or a waving feather-like tuft or bunch of hair, etc.; esp. when attached to a helmet or hat, or worn in the hair, as the *court p.* of ostrich feathers; also used at funerals 1530. **b.** *fig.* (Cf. *a feather in one's cap.*) 1605. **4.** *transf.* Anything resembling the down of feathers or a feather, in form or lightness 1601. **b.** *Bot.* A plumose pappus or other appendage of a seed, by which it floats away 1578. **c.** *Zool.* A plumose or feather-like part or formation 1834.

1. With ruffled plumes and flagging wing GRAY. b. Our plumes fall, and we begin to be humble 1642. He is stripped of his borrowed plumes 1802. 3. These nodding plumes and dragging trains BYRON. b. Ambitious to win From me som P. MILT. 4. The long p. of smoke over the plain STEVENSON.

attrib. and *Comb.*, as **p.-bird,** a bird with conspicuous plumes, such as are used for ornament; *spec.* a bird of paradise of the subfamily *Epimachinæ*; **-grass,** a grass of the genus *Erianthus*, having a plume-like inflorescence, a Woolly Beard-grass; **-moth,** any species of the family *Pterophoridæ* (*Alucitidæ*), small moths whose wings are divided into feathery lobes. Hence **Plu·meless** *a.*

Plume (plūm), *v.* late ME. [a. OF. *plumer* to pluck (a bird), etc., f. *plume* PLUME *sb.* In branch II, f. PLUME *sb.* or ad. L. *plumare* to cover with feathers.] **I.** †**1.** *intr. Falconry.* To pluck the feathers of its prey, as a hawk; const. *upon, on.* Also *fig.* –1667. **2.** *trans.* To pluck (a bird); hence, to strip, bare. Now *rare.* 1599. †**b.** To pluck (feathers) from a bird –1681. †**c.** *fig.* To pluck, despoil, plunder –1760.

2. I will so pluck him as never hawk plumed a partridge SCOTT.

II. 1. *trans.* To furnish or cover with plumes, feathers, or plumage; to fledge, feather. late ME. **2.** *refl.* **a.** Of a bird: To dress its feathers. **b.** To dress oneself with borrowed plumes. Chiefly *fig.* 1702. **c.** *fig.* Usu. with *on, upon*: To pride oneself, show self-satisfaction, esp. regarding something trivial, ridiculous, or unworthy, or to which one has no just claim 1643. **3.** *trans.* To preen or dress (the feathers or wings); to prepare for flight 1821.

1. The Swan..is a Bird excellently plumed 1627. 2. c. Pluming and praising himself, and telling fulsome stories in his own commendation 1715. 3. *fig.* And calumny plumed her wings for a fresh attack MOTLEY. Hence **Plumed** *ppl. a.*, feathered 1526.

Plumelet (plū·mlėt). 1850. [f. PLUME *sb.* + -LET.] A minute plume.

Plu·me-like, *a.* 1847. [-LIKE.] Resembling a plume; feathery.

Plumet (plū·mėt). 1585. [ad. F. *plumet*, f. *plume*: see -ET.] A small plume.

Plu·micorn. 1884. [f. L. *pluma* plume + *cornu* horn.] *Ornith.* One of the pair of horn-like or ear-like feathers on the head of several species of owls, often called horns or ears.

Plumiform (plū·mifǫɹm), *a.* [f. L. *pluma* PLUME *sb.* + -(I)FORM.] Feather-shaped.

Plummer-block (plɒ·məɹ,blǫk). Also **plumber-.** 1814. [perh. from a surname + BLOCK *sb.* 5.] = *pillow-block* (PILLOW *sb.*).

Plummet (plɒ·mėt). [ME. a. OF. *plommet, plombet, plummet* ball of lead, plummet, dim. of *plomb* lead; see PLUMB *sb.* and -ET.] **1.** A ball of lead, or other weight, attached to a line, and used for determining the vertical; esp. the bob of a plumb-line used by masons, builders, carpenters, etc.; also, the whole instrument, bob, line, and board. late ME. **2.** A piece of lead, etc. attached to a line and used for sounding; a sounding-lead. late ME. †**3.** A ball or lump of lead used for various purposes –1612. **b.** *fig.* That which weighs down, like a dead weight 1625. **4.** *spec.* †**a.** A weight enclosed in a cestus –1661. †**b.** The weight of a clock; also *fig.* a spring of action –1697. **c.** In angling, a small piece of lead attached to a line, for various purposes 1616. †**5.** A pencil of lead, formerly used to rule lines –1828.

2. My Sonne i'th Ooze is bedded; and I'le seeke him deeper then ere p. sounded SHAKS. 3. b. Hang early Plummets upon the Heels of Pride SIR T. BROWNE. *Comb.*, as *p.-line*, etc.

Plummy (plɒ·mi), *a.* 1759. [f. PLUM *sb.* + -Y [1].] **1.** Consisting of, abounding in, or like plums. **2.** *fig.* Of the nature of a 'plum'; rich, good, desirable. *slang* or *colloq.* 1812.

2. Signing one's self over to wickedness for the sake of getting something p. GEO. ELIOT.

Plumose (plūmōu·s), *a.* 1697. [ad. L. *plumosus*, f. *pluma* PLUME *sb.*; see -OSE.] Furnished with feathers or plumes; feathery; resembling a feather or plume in having two series of fine filaments on opposite sides; *esp.* in *Zool.*, *Bot.*, and *Min.*

Plumosite (plū·mǒsəit). 1864. [ad. G. *plumosit*, f. L. *plumosus* downy + *-it* -ITE [1].] *Min.* = JAMESONITE.

Plump (plɒmp), *sb.* [1] Now *arch.* and *dial.* late ME. [Origin obsc.] A compact body of persons, animals, or things; a band, troop, company; a flock; a cluster, clump.

A p. of spears (arch.), a band of spearmen (revived by Scott).

Plump (plɒmp), *sb.* [2] 1450. [f. PLUMP *v.* [1]] **1.** An act of plumping (see PLUMP *v.* [1] 1); an abrupt plunge or heavy fall. *familiar.* **2.** A sudden heavy fall of rain. *Sc.* 1822.

Plump (plɒmp), *a.* [1] 1481. [Corresp. to MDu. *plomp* blunt, in both senses, 'not pointed', and 'not sharp'. Ult. origin unkn.] **I.** †**1.** Blunt (in manners); not 'sharp' in intellect; dull, clownish, rude –1620. †**2.** Of an arrow-head: Blunt and broad. ASCHAM. **II.** Of full and rounded form; chubby; having the skin well filled or elastically distended 1545. **b.** Of coins: Of full size and weight, not clipped 1867. **c.** *fig.* 'Fat', rich, abundant; well-supplied; full and round in tone; great, big; complete, round. Now *rare.* 1635.

The p. convivial parson COWPER. He..looked as p. as a pincushion MRS. CARLYLE. Hence **Plu·mp-ly** *adv.*, **-ness. Plu·mpy** *a.* plump.

Plump, *a.* [2]: see PLUMP *adv.*

Plump (plɒmp), *v.* [1] ME. [Com. LG. verb; prob. of echoic origin.] **1.** *intr.* To fall, drop, plunge, or come down (or against something) flatly or abruptly (usu. implying 'with full or direct impact'). **b.** *transf.* and *fig.* To come plump, i.e. all at once (into some place or condition); to plunge, burst (*in* or *out*). *familiar.* 1829. **2.** *trans.* To drop, throw down, plunge abruptly (into water, etc., or upon a flat surface); to pay *down* at once and in one lot; *refl.* to drop down abruptly and heavily. late ME. **3.** *transf.* and *fig.*: *esp.* To utter abruptly, to blurt *out. familiar.* 1579. **4.** *intr.* [Short for *to vote plump*, or *give a plumper.*] To vote at an election for one candidate alone (when one could vote for two or more). Also *loosely*, to 'vote for' (something). 1806.

1. It will give you a Notion how Dulcissa plumps into a Chair STEELE. b. With a convulsive gurgle, out plumped the words 1874. 2. She plumped down the money and walked out 1892. 4. We'll p. for Tarleton, to prove we are free 1806.

Plump, *v.* [2] 1533. [f. PLUMP *a.* [1] II.] **1.** *trans.* To make plump; to fill *out*, distend; to fatten *up.* **2.** *intr.* To swell *out* or *up* 1602.

1. Fowls..plumped for sale by the poulterers of London JOHNSON. 2. Her cheeks had plumped out 1882.

Plump (plɒmp), *int.*, *adv.*, and *a.* [2] 1594. [app. the stem of PLUMP *v.* [1]] **A.** †*int.* Imitative of the sound of a heavy body falling into water 1597. **B.** *adv.* (Mostly *familiar.*) **1.** With a sudden drop or fall into water 1610. **2.** With a sudden or abrupt fall or sinking down; with sudden direct impact, flat upon or against something; with a sudden encounter 1594. **3.** Directly, at once, straight; *esp.* With ref. to a statement, etc.: In plain terms, bluntly, flatly 1734.

2. Sitting p. on an unsuspected cat in your chair 1806. 3. Hayes first said no, p. THACKERAY.

C. *adj.* Now *rare.* **1. a.** Descending directly, vertical. **b.** Directly facing in position. 1611. **2.** *fig.* Of statements, etc.: Direct, blunt, straightforward, unqualified, 'flat'. 1789. **3.** Plumped down; paid down at once 1865.

2. P. assertion or p. denial for me MAR. EDGEWORTH.

Plumper [1] (plɒ·mpəɹ). 1690. [f. PLUMP *v.* [2] + -ER [1].] That which plumps or makes plump; as a small ball or disk sometimes carried in the mouth, to fill out hollow cheeks.

Plumper [2] (plɒ·mpəɹ). 1761. [f. PLUMP *v.* [1] or *adv.*] **1. a.** An act of plumping, as into water, or to the ground 1810. †**b.** *slang.* A heavy blow –1796. **2.** A vote given solely to one candidate at an election (when one has the right to vote for two or more). Also attrib. *p. vote.* 1761. **b.** A voter who 'plumps'. *rare* 1818. **3.** A downright lie. *vulgar.* 1812.

Plum-pie. 1660. [f. PLUM *sb.* + PIE.] †**1.** A pie containing raisins and currants; esp. a mince-pie. **2.** A pie containing plums or prunes 1830.

†**Plu·m-po·rridge.** 1591. Porridge containing prunes, raisins, currants, etc.; formerly in favour as a Christmas dish –1808. So †**Plu·m-po·ttage,** app. in same sense.

Plum pudding, plum-pudding (plɒ·m,pu·diŋ). 1711. A pudding containing plums. **a.** (= *Christmas p.*) *spec.* A boiled pudding now composed of flour, bread-crumbs, suet, raisins, currants, etc., with eggs, spices, etc., eaten at Christmas; also, an ordinary suet pudding with raisins. **b.** A pudding of fresh plums contained in a crust 1813.

attrib. and *Comb.*, as **plum-pudding breed, -dog,** the Dalmatian or Spotted Coach breed of dog; **plum-pudding stone** (*Geol.*), orig. a conglomerate of flint pebbles embedded in a siliceo-calcareous matrix; now, *loosely*, any conglomerate.

Plum-tree (plɒ·m,trī). OE. = PLUM *sb.* 2.

‖**Plumula** (plū·miŭlă). 1760. [L., dim. of *pluma* PLUME.] *Bot.* = PLUMULE 1.

Plumularia (plūmiulēᵊ·riă). 1859. [mod. L., f. *plumula* (see prec.).] *Zool.* A genus of hydroids having a plume-like form. Hence **Plumula·rian** *a.* of or pertaining to *P.*, or the family of which it is the type; *sb.* a member of this family.

Plumule (plū·miūl). 1727. [ad. L. *plumula.*] **1.** *Bot.* The rudimentary shoot, bud, or bunch of undeveloped leaves in a seed; the stem of the embryo plant. **2.** A little feather; *spec.* in *Ornith.*, a down-feather 1847.

Plumy (plū·mi), *a.* 1582. [f. PLUME *sb.* + -Y [1].] †**1.** Composed of down, downy

-1700. 2. Abounding in plumes; feathery, feathered 1597. 3. Adorned with a plume or plumes 1700. 4. Plume-like 1611.

1. Her head did on a p. pillow rest DRYDEN. 4. When the first sheaf its p. top uprears 1798.

Plunder (plɒ·ndəɹ), *sb.* 1643. [f. next.] 1. The action of plundering or taking as spoil; *spec.* as practised in war; pillage, spoliation, depredation. Now *rare* or *Obs.* b. *transf.* The acquisition of property by violent or questionable means; spoliation 1672. 2. Goods taken from an enemy by force; spoil, booty, loot 1647. b. *transf.* Property acquired by illegal or questionable means; also (*slang*), profit, gain 1790.

1. I abhorre all violence, p., rapine, and disorders in Souldiers 1643. 2. The instigator of the depredations..sharing in the p. 1844. b. A love of p. and of place 1865.

Plunder (plɒ·ndəɹ), *v.* 1632. [a. G. *plündern* to pillage, sack, lit. to rob of household effects, f. MG., MHG. *blunder, plunder* bedclothes, household stuff, etc.; in mod.G. *plunder* lumber, trash.] 1. *trans.* To rob (a place or person) of goods, etc., by forcible means, or as an enemy; esp. as done in war; to pillage, spoil; to rob systematically. 2. To take (goods, valuables, etc.) with illegal force, or as an enemy; to embezzle; to take by robbery, steal 1645. 3. *absol.* or *intr.* To commit depredations 1638.

1. Many Townes and Villages he [Prince Rupert] plundered, which is to say robb'd, for at that time first was the word p. used in England, being borne in Germany 1647. 2. If they..neither steal men or p. their goods 1869. Hence **Plu·nderer. Plu·nderous** *a. rare*, given to plundering.

Plunderage (plɒ·ndərėdʒ). 1796. [f. prec. + -AGE.] The action of plundering; pillage, spoliation; *spec.* in *Maritime Law*, embezzling goods on shipboard; *concr.* spoil obtained by such means.

Plunge (plɒndʒ), *sb.* late ME. [f. next.] I. 1. A place where one can plunge; a deep pool (*dial.*); a plunge-bath. 2. An act of plunging; a dive, dip; also *fig.* 1711. 3. *transf.* A sudden and heavy or violent pitching forward of the body 1496. 4. The fall or breaking of a wave; a heavy downpour of rain (*rare*) 1781.

2. After his first P. into the Sea ADDISON. 3. By directing the animal's plunges judiciously I got him also on *terra firma* 1889.

II. The point of being plunged or overwhelmed in trouble, difficulty, or danger; a crisis, strait; a dilemma; esp. in phr. *at* (*in*) *a p., to put to* or *into the p.* or *plunges*. *Obs.* exc. *dial.* 1535.

When I was in the greatest p. for money 1656.

attrib. and *Comb.*: **p.-bath**, a bath in which a plunge is taken, e.g. after exercise.

Plunge (plɒndʒ), *v.* [ME. *plunge(n, plonge*, a. OF. *plung(i)er*, etc., F. *plonger* :—late L. **plumbicare* to heave the lead, f. *plumbum* lead.] 1. *trans.* To put violently, thrust, or cast *into* a liquid, a penetrable substance, or a cavity; to immerse, submerge. 2. *fig.* To thrust, force, or drive *into* some thing, condition, state, or sphere of action. late ME. †3. *fig.* To overwhelm, esp. *with* trouble or difficulty; to put to straits -1681. 4. *Gardening.* To sink (a pot containing a plant, less usu., a plant itself) in the ground 1664. 5. *intr.* To throw or hurl oneself *into* water or the like; to dive head-foremost; to fall or sink (involuntarily) *into* a deep place (as a pit or abyss); also, to penetrate impetuously *into* any thing or place in which one is submerged or lost to view. late ME. b. *transf.* To enter impetuously or abruptly *into* (a place). Also with *upon*. 1834. c. *transf.* To descend abruptly and steeply; to dip suddenly (as a road or stratum) 1854. 6. To enter impetuously or determinedly *into* some state, condition, or affair; to involve oneself deeply 1694. 7. *transf.* To fling oneself violently forward, esp. with a diving action; of the chest: to expand with falling of the diaphragm 1530. 8. To spend money or bet recklessly; to speculate deeply; to run into debt. *colloq.* 1876.

1. The holy Man bid him p. his Head into the Water ADDISON. You have only to p. a lighted taper into it HUXLEY. 2. The Councels themselves.. plung'd into worldly ambition MILT. 5. I plunged in, And bad him follow SHAKS. He plunged into the thickest portion of the little wood DICKENS. 6. The character of their party is to be very ready to p. into difficult business BURKE. 7. Wounded, he rears aloft, And plunging, from his Back the Rider hurls Precipitant 1735.

Plunger (plɒ·ndʒəɹ). 1611. [f. prec. + -ER[1].] I. 1. One who plunges; a diver. 2. In techn. applications; an instrument or part which works with a plunging or thrusting motion; *esp.* a. Any solid piston, as that of a force-pump, *esp.* the piston of a Cornish pump. b. The firing pin in some breech-loading firearms. c. *Pottery.* A vessel in which clay is beaten to paste or slip. 1777. II. 1. *Mil. slang.* A cavalry man 1854. 2. *slang.* One who bets, gambles, or speculates wildly 1876.

attrib. and *Comb.*, as **p.-bucket, -lift**, in a pump, a bucket having no valve; also = next (*b*); **-piston**, (*a*) a solid cylindrical piston used in a plunger-pump; (*b*) a similar piston used in a pressure-gauge, steam-indicator, etc.; **-pump**, one with a solid piston, as a force-pump.

Plunging (plɒ·ndʒiŋ), *vbl. sb.* 1450. [-ING[1].] The action of PLUNGE *v.*; *spec.* †immersion in baptism.

attrib. and *Comb.*, as *p.-bath*, etc.; **p.-battery** (*Electr.*), a battery in which the plates may be plunged into or withdrawn from the fluid at pleasure. **Plu·nging**, *ppl. a.* [-ING[2].] In senses of the verb PLUNGE. p. fire (= F. *feu plongeant*), direct fire upon an enemy from a superior position. Hence **Plu·ngingly** *adv.*

Plunk (plɒŋk), *int., sb., v.* 1805. orig. *dial.* Imitative of the sound of the forcible plucking of the strings of a musical instrument, a heavy blow or plunge, the drawing of a cork, or the like.

Pluperfect (plupə̄·ɹfėkt, plū̆pə̄ɹfėkt), *a.* (*sb.*) Also †plus-. 1530. [Contr. from *plusquam-perfect*, ad. L. (*tempus præteritum*) *plus quam perfectum* '(past tense) more than perfect'; tr. Gr. (χρόνος) ὑπερσυντελικός.] 1. *Gram.* Applied to that tense of the verb which expresses a time or action completed prior to some past point of time, specified or implied. Also *absol.* or as *sb., ellipt.* for *p. tense*. 2. *gen.* More than perfect; *spec.* in *Mus.* (rarely) applied to an augmented (as dist. from a perfect) fourth or fifth 1802.

Plural (plū̆·răl), *a.* (*sb.*) late ME. [a. OF. *plurel*, or ad. L. *pluralis*, f. *plus, plur-* more; see -AL.] 1. *Gram.* Applied to the form of a word which denotes more than one (or, in languages having a dual form, more than two); opp. to *singular*. 2. More than one in number; consisting of, containing, pertaining to, or equivalent to, more than one 1591. B. *sb.* a. *Gram.* The plural number. b. The fact or condition of there being more than one. ME.

2. Better haue none Then plurall faith, which is too much by one SHAKS. *P. livings*: see PLURALITY. *P. vote*, the right of giving more than one vote, or of voting in more than one constituency; hence *p. voter, voting*. 3. *P. of excellence* or *majesty, p. intensive*, terms applied in Heb. Grammar to a p. sb. used as the name of a single person; as *ĕlōhīm*, lit. gods, used as the name of (the one) God. Hence **Plu·rally** *adv.*

Pluralism (plū̆·răliz'm). 1818. [f. prec. + -ISM.] 1. a. *Eccl.* The holding of more than one benefice at the same time by one person. b. The holding of two or more offices of any kind together. 2. *Philos.* A system of thought which recognizes more than one ultimate principle; opp. to MONISM 1887.

Pluralist (plū̆·rălist). 1626. [f. PLURAL + -IST.] *Eccl.* One who holds two or more benefices at the same time. b. *gen.* One who combines two or more offices, professions, or conditions.

The odious Names of Pluralists and Non-residents 1692. Hence **Plurali·stic** *a.* of or belonging to a p. or to pluralism, in any sense; **Plurali·stically** *adv.*

Plurality (pluræ·lĭti). late ME. [a. OF. *pluralite*, ad. late L. *pluralitas*, f. *pluralis* PLURAL.] I. Related in sense to *plural*. 1. The state of being plural, or denoting, comprising, or consisting of, more than one. b. The fact of there being many; numerousness; hence, a large number or quantity; a multitude. late ME. 2. *Eccl.* a. The holding of two or more benefices concurrently by one person. b. A benefice held concurrently with another or others; *pl.* two or more benefices held together. late ME. c. *transf.* and *gen.* 1678.

1. The p. of wives was by a special prerogative suffered to the fathers of the Old Testament 1563. b. Doe you count it lawfull to haue such pluralitie of seruants? B. JONS. 2. I do not reckon the holding poor livings that lie contiguous, a p. 1715.

II. Related in sense to L. *plus* more. 1. = MAJORITY 3. 1578. 2. *U.S. Politics.* An excess of votes polled by the leading candidate in an election above those polled by the one next to him, in cases where there are three or more candidates; as dist. from *majority*, which in such cases is applied to an absolute majority of all the votes given 1828.

Pluralize (plū̆·rălaiz), *v.* 1803. [a. F. *pluraliser*; see PLURAL and -IZE.] 1. *trans.* To make plural; to attribute plurality to; to express in the plural. 2. *intr.* To hold more than one benefice (or office) at one time; to be or become a pluralist 1842. Hence **Pluraliza·tion**, the act of pluralizing. **Plu·ralizer**, *spec.* = PLURALIST.

Pluri- (plū̆ri), comb. form of L. *plus, plur-* more, pl. *plures* several; as in: **Plurili·terai** *Heb. Gram.* [L. *littera* letter] *a.* containing more than three letters in the root; *sb.* a root consisting of more than three letters. **Pluri·se·rial** *a.* consisting of several series or rows; hence **Plurise·rially** *adv.* **Plurise·riate** *a.* arranged in several series.

‖ **Pluries** (plū̆·ri,iz), in full **P. capias**. 1444. [L. = '(thou mayest take) several times'.] *Law.* A third writ of attachment, issued when the CAPIAS and ALIAS prove ineffectual.

Pluripresence (plū̆ripre·zĕns). 1773. [f. L. *plus, plur-* more + PRESENCE.] Presence in more than one place at the same time.

Plus (plɒs). 1615. [a. L. = more.] I. quasi-*prep.* In mathematical use as the oral rendering of the symbol +. Hence *gen.* With the addition of; with . . . besides. (Opp. to MINUS 1.) 1668. b. *predicatively.* Having (something) in addition, having gained (opp. to MINUS 1 b) 1856. 2. As the oral rendering of the sign + in its algebraical use to denote a positive quantity, as $+ x$, read *plus x*. Hence *attrib.* or *adj.* in *p. quantity*, a quantity having the sign + prefixed (or not having the sign −), a positive quantity. (Only as opp. to MINUS 2, 2 b.) 1579. b. *Electr.* (*a*) *adv.* Positively. (*b*) *adj.* Positive; positively electrified. (Opp. to MINUS 2 d.) 1747. c. *adv.* And an indefinite quantity more, as £100,000 *plus*. (*colloq.*) 3. *adj.* Additional, extra 1756. 4. Applied to golfers whose handicap is denoted by 'plus 1', etc. 1909. 5. *sb.* a. The mathematical symbol +; also *plus sign*. b. A quantity added; an addition, a gain. c. A positive quantity (also *fig.*). Opp. to MINUS 3. 1654.

1. **Plus fours**, long wide knickerbockers, or a suit having such; so named because, to produce the overhang, the length was originally increased by four inches. c. *ellipt.*, indicating a fractional amount more (e.g. raising the school age to 15 plus), also indicating a slightly higher grade (*Beta plus*, β+).

Plush (plɒʃ). 1594. [ad. F. *pluche*, contr. f. of *peluche* a hairy fabric, shag, plush, f. late L. **piluceus, -ea*, f. L. *pilus* hair.] 1. A kind of cloth, of silk, cotton, wool, etc., having a nap softer and longer than that of velvet, used for upholstery, etc. b. *pl.* Plush breeches (as worn by footmen) 1844. 2. *transf.* A natural substance likened to these 1619. 3. *attrib.*, usu. in sense Made or consisting of plush; also, of or pertaining to plush 1629. **Plu·shy** *a.* soft and shaggy, like p.

Plushette (plɒʃe·t). 1910. [f. prec. + -ETTE.] An imitation plush.

Plutarchy (plū̆·tāɹki). 1643. [f. Gr. πλοῦτος wealth, riches + -αρχία rule; after *monarchy*, etc.] The rule or dominion of wealth, or of the wealthy; plutocracy.

‖ **Pluteus** (plū̆·ti,ɒs). *Pl.* **-ei** (-i,əi). 1832. [L.; see sense 1.] 1. *Rom. Antiq.*, etc. a. *Arch.* A barrier or light wall placed between columns. b. *Mil.* A kind of shed or penthouse for protection of the soldiers, sometimes running on wheels. c. A shelf for books, small statues, busts, etc. 2. *Zool.* The larva of an echinoid or ophiuroid; known from its shape as the 'painter's easel larva' 1877. Hence **Plu·teal** *a.*

Plutocracy (plutǫ·krăsi). Also **plout-**.

1652. [ad. Gr. πλουτοκρατία, f. πλοῦτος wealth + -κρατία power; see -CRACY.] 1. The rule or sovereignty of wealth or of the wealthy. 2. A ruling or influential class of wealthy persons 1832. So **Plu·tocrat**, a member of a p.; a person possessing power or influence over others in virtue of his wealth. **Plutocra·tic** *a.* of or pertaining to plutocrats; characterized by p.

Plutolatry (pl*ut*ǫ·lătri). 1889. [f. Gr. πλοῦτος wealth + -λατρεία -LATRY, after *idolatry*.] Worship of mere wealth.

Plutonian (pl*u*tōᵘ·niăn), *a.* (*sb.*) 1667. [f. L. *Plutonius* (ad. Gr. Πλουτώνιος, f. Πλούτων Pluto, god of the infernal regions) + -AN.] 1. Of or pertaining to Pluto; belonging to or suggestive of the infernal regions; infernal. 2. *Geol.* = PLUTONIC 1. 1828. B. *sb. Geol.* = PLUTONIST 1828.

Plutonic (pl*u*tǫ·nik), *a.* (*sb.*) 1796. [f. Gr. Πλούτων Pluto; see prec. and -IC.] 1. *Geol.* **a.** Pertaining to or involving the action of intense heat at great depths upon the rocks forming the earth's crust; igneous. Applied *spec.* to the theory that attributes most geological phenomena to the action of internal heat. 1796. **b.** *spec.* Applied to that class of igneous rocks, such as granite and syenite, which are supposed to have been formed by fusion and subsequent slow crystallization at great depths below the surface, as dist. from *volcanic* rocks 1833. 2. Belonging to or resembling Pluto; Plutonian 1819. **B.** *sb. Geol.* (*pl.*) Plutonic rocks 1856. So **Plutonism** (pl*ū*·tŏniz'm), the Plutonic theory. **Plu·tonist**, one who holds the P. theory (see 1 a).

Plutonomy (pl*u*tǫ·nŏmi). 1851. [f. Gr. πλοῦτος wealth + -νομία arrangement; after *economy*.] The science of the production and distribution of wealth; political economy. So **Plutono·mic** *a.* **Pluto·nomist**, a political economist.

Pluvial (pl*ū*·viăl), *sb. Obs.* exc. *Hist.* 1669. [ad. med.L. *pluviale*, prop. rain-cloak, orig. neut. of L. *pluvialis*.] *Eccl.* A long cloak worn by ecclesiastics as a ceremonial vestment; = COPE *sb.*[1] 2; also, a similar garment worn by monarchs as a robe of state.

Pluvial (pl*ū*·viăl), *a.* 1656. [ad. L. *pluvialis*, f. *pluvia* rain.] Of or pertaining to rain; rainy; characterized by much rain. **b.** *Geol.* Caused by rain 1859.

Pluviometer (pl*ū*viǫ·mĭtəɪ). 1791. [f. L. *pluvia* rain + -METER.] An instrument for measuring the rain; a rain-gauge. Hence **Pluviome·tric, -al** *adjs.*; **-ly** *adv.* **Pluvio·metry.**

Pluvious (pl*ū*·viəs), *a.* late ME. [a. OF. *pluvieus*, F. *pluvieux*, or ad. L. *pluviosus* rainy.] Of, pertaining to, or characterized by rain; bearing rain or moisture; rainy.

Ply (pləi), *sb.* 1470. [a. F. *pli* fold, etc.; altered from OF. *ploi*, vbl. sb. f. *ployer*, later *plier*; see PLY *v.*[1]] I. 1. A fold; each of the layers or thicknesses produced by folding cloth, etc.; a strand or twist of rope, yarn, or thread 1532. 2. A bend, crook, or curvature; *spec.* in *Falconry*, of a hawk's wing. Now *rare* or *Obs.* 1575. 3. The condition of being bent or turned to one side; a twist, turn; a bent, bias, inclination; esp. in phr. *to take a* (*the, one's*) *p.* Chiefly *fig.* 1605.

1. *Two-p., three-p., four-ply*: a fold of two, three, etc., layers; used *attrib.* to designate fingering or worsted, and carpets made of two or more interwoven webs; also of wood (cf. PLYWOOD). 3. It is true that late learners cannot so well take the plie BACON.

II. Plight, condition; esp. in phrases *in p.*, *in good p.*; so *out of p.* *Sc.* 1470.

Ply (pləi), *v.*[1] Now *rare* or *dial.* Pa. t. and pple. plied (pləid). [ME. *plien*, a. OF. *plier*, secondary form of *pleiier*, mod.F. *plier* and *ployer*:—L. *plicare* to fold.] 1. *trans.* To bend, bow; to fold or double (cloth or the like); to mould or shape (anything plastic). Now chiefly *dial.* †**b.** *fig.* To bend in will or disposition; to bend the sense of (words); to adapt, accommodate –1657. †2. *intr.* To bend or be bent; to yield, give (*to* pressure, etc.) –1753. 3. *fig.* To yield, give way *to*; to incline, tend; to submit, comply, consent; to be pliant. Now *rare* or *Obs.* ME.

1. Right as men may warm wex with handes plye CHAUCER. 3. With kindly indulgence plied into the daughter's will CARLYLE.

Ply (pləi), *v.*[2] Pa. t. and pple. **plied.** [ME. *plye*, aphet. f. ME. *aplie, aplye*, APPLY *v.*, q. v.] I. To apply, employ, work busily at. 1. *intr.* To employ or occupy oneself busily or steadily; to work *at* something; to apply closely *to*. Now *rare*. 2. *trans.* To use or wield vigorously (a tool, etc.); to exert (a faculty) ME. 3. **a.** To keep at work at; to attack or assail vigorously or repeatedly (*with* some instrument or process). **b.** To press (one) to take; to continue to supply *with* food, gifts, etc. 1548. 4. To importune, urge; to keep on at (a person) *with* questions, petitions, etc. 1587.

1. Ere half these Authors be read (which will soon be with plying hard and daily) MILT. 2. The town in which they plied their trade 1867. Together their oars they p. 1887. 3. **b.** To p. them more pressingly with food than with arguments 1856. 4. In vain did he p. Christ with questions 1883.

II. *Naut.*, etc. 1. *intr.* To beat up against the wind; to tack, work to windward 1556. **b.** *gen.* To direct one's course, steer. Now only *poet.* 1595. 2. *intr.* Of a vessel or its master: To sail or go periodically to and fro *between* certain places; also said of land-carriage 1803. 3. *intr.* Of a boatman, porter, cabman, omnibus, taxi, etc.: To attend regularly, to have one's stand *at* a certain place for hire or custom 1700.

1. Neither might wee plie up unto that iland, the winde was soe contrarie for our course 1595. Phr. *To p. about, off and on, to and again, up and down*, etc. **b.** Wee plied for Plimworth 1595. 3. He was ..forced to think of plying in the Streets as a Porter ADDISON.

Plyer: see PLIER.

Plymouth Brethren. 1842. [See *Brethren* in BROTHER *sb.* 3.] A religious body calling themselves 'the Brethren', recognizing no official order of ministers, and having no formal creed, which arose at Plymouth *c* 1830. **Plymouth brother** (also **Plymouth sister**), a member of this body. So **Ply·mouthism**, the system or doctrine of the Plymouth Brethren 1876.

†**Plymouth cloak.** *slang.* 1608. A cudgel or staff, carried by one who walked *in cuerpo*, and thus joc. assumed to serve as a cloak –1855.

Plymouth Rock (pli·məþ,rǫ·k). 1873. [The spot at which the passengers of the Mayflower landed in New England in 1620.] Name of a breed of domestic fowls of American origin, characterized by large size, ashen or grey plumage barred with blackish stripes, and yellow beak, legs, and feet.

Plywood (pləi·wud). orig. *U.S.* 1917. [f. PLY *sb.* 1 + WOOD.] A compound wood made of three (five, etc.) thin layers glued or cemented together under pressure, and arranged so that the grain of one layer runs at right angles to the grain of any adjacent layer.

P.M., abbrev. of POST MERIDIEM.

Pn-, an initial comb. occurring only in words from Greek; the *p* is usually mute in English.

Pneo- (pnī,o, nī,o), comb. element from Gr. πνέειν, πνεῖν to blow; as in **Pneo·meter** [-METER], an instrument for measuring the amount of air inspired and expired, a pneumatometer, spirometer; **Pneo·metry**; etc.

Pneum(e (pni*ū*m, ni*ū*m). 1879. [ad. Gr. πνεῦμα; see next.] *Mus.* = NEUME 2.

‖**Pneuma** (pni*ū*·mă, ni*ū*·mă). 1880. [a. Gr. πνεῦμα wind, breath, spirit, prop. that which is blown or breathed, f. πνέειν, πνεῖν to blow, breathe.] 1. The Greek word for 'spirit' or 'soul' 1884. 2. *Mediæval Mus.* **a.** = NEUME 1. **b.** = NEUME 2. 1880.

Pneumatic (niumæ·tik), *a.* (*sb.*) 1659. [ad. L. *pneumaticus* of or belonging to air or wind, a. Gr. πνευματικός.] 1. Pertaining to, or acting by means of, wind or air. **b.** Belonging to or transmitted by pneumatic dispatch 1903. 2. Of, or relating or belonging to, gases. Now *rare*, exc. in *p. trough*. 1793. 3. *Zool.*, *Anat.*, and *Phys.* **a.** Pertaining to breath or breathing; respiratory (*rare*) 1681. **b.** Containing or connected with air-cavities, as those in the bones of birds, etc. 1831. 4. Belonging or relating to spirit or spiritual existence; spiritual. (Usu. with direct ref. to Gr. πνευματικός.) 1797.

1. Phr. *P. dispatch*, a system by which parcels, etc. are conveyed along tubes by compression or exhaustion of air. *P. engine*, formerly applied spec. to the air-pump. *P. tires*, tires filled with compressed air 1890. 2. *P. trough*, a trough by means of which gases may be collected in jars over a surface of water or mercury. 4. †*P. philosophy*: = PNEUMATOLOGY 1.

B. *sb.* 1. = PNEUMATOLOGY 1 a. (*rare*) 1836. 2. Name in Gnostic theology for a spiritual being of a high order 1876. 3. A pneumatic tire, or a cycle having such tires 1890. So **Pneuma·tical** *a.* in senses 1, 2, 4; †*sb.* a gaseous substance. **Pneuma·tically** *adv.*

Pneumaticity (ni*ū*măti·sĭti). 1858. [f. PNEUMATIC + -ITY.] The quality or condition of being pneumatic.

Pneumatico-, comb. form from L. *pneumaticus* or Gr. πνευματικός PNEUMATIC.

Pneumatics (ni*u*mæ·tiks). 1660. [In form, pl. of PNEUMATIC *a.* = pneumatic treatises or matters; see -IC.] 1. That branch of physics which deals with the mechanical properties (as density, elasticity, pressure, etc.) of air, or other elastic fluids or gases. 2. = PNEUMATOLOGY 1 a, b. *Obs.* exc. *Hist.* 1695.

Pneumato- (ni*ū*·măt*o*, pni*ū*·-), bef. a vowel **pneumat-**, a. Gr. πνευματο-, comb. form of πνεῦμα air, breath, spirit.

Pneu·matocele [Gr. κήλη tumour], *Path.* a tumour or hernia containing air or gas. **Pneu·matocyst** *Zool.* (*a*) an air-sac serving as a float in certain 'colonial' or compound Hydrozoa; the pneumatophore, or the cavity contained in this; (*b*) an air-sac in the body of a bird. **Pneu·matogram**, a diagram or tracing of the movements of the chest in respiration, obtained by a pneumograph. **Pneumato·meter**, an instrument for measuring the amount of air breathed in or out at each inspiration or expiration, or for measuring the force of inspiration or expiration; so **Pneumato·metry.** **Pneu·matophore** [Gr. -φορος bearing], (*a*) *Zool.* in certain 'colonial' Hydrozoa of the order *Siphonophora*, a specialized part or individual of the 'colony', containing an air-cavity, and serving as a float; (*b*) *Bot.* a structure having numerous lenticels, and supposed to serve as a channel for air, arising from the roots of various tropical trees which grow in swampy places. **Pneu·matotho·rax** = PNEUMOTHORAX.

Pneumatology (ni*ū*mătǫ·lŏdʒi, pni*ū*-). 1678. [See PNEUMATO- and -LOGY.] 1. **a.** The science, doctrine, or theory of spirits or spiritual beings; considered as comprehending the doctrine of God as known by natural reason, of angels and demons, and of the human soul. **b.** Later, The science of the nature and functions of the human soul or mind, now called PSYCHOLOGY 1785. 2. *Theol.* The, or a, doctrine of the Holy Spirit 1881. 3. The science or theory of air or gases; pneumatics 1767. Hence **Pneu·matolo·gical** *a.* of or relating to p. **Pneumato·logist.**

Pneumatomachian (-mēᶦ·kiăn), *sb.* and *a.* 1707. [f. late Gr. πνευματομάχος (f. πνεῦμα spirit + -μάχος fighting, fighter) + -IAN.] **A.** *sb.* Name of a 4th c. sect who denied the divinity or personality of the Holy Spirit. **B.** *adj.* Belonging to such a sect or holding such a doctrine. Also **-o·machist** 1654.

Pneumo- (ni*ū*mo-, pni*ū*-), comb. form and verbal element. **a.** Gr. πνεῦμα wind, etc. (see PNEUMA), = PNEUMATO-, in some scientific terms. **b.** Short for PNEUMONO-, f. Gr. πνεύμων, -μον- lung; chiefly in terms of pathology.

‖**Pneumococcus** [Gr. κόκκος berry], name for two different micro-organisms of oval form which have been found in the rusty sputum of pneumonia, and supposed to be the cause of the disease; hence **Pneumococ·ccal, -co·ccic, -co·ccous** *adjs.* **Pneu·mograph**, an instrument for automatically recording the movements of the chest in respiration. **Pneumo·graphy**, (*a*) a description of the lungs; (*b*) the recording of the respiratory movements, as by a pneumograph. **Pneumo·logy** (*rare*), a treatise on, or the scientific description or knowledge of, the lungs. **Pneumo·meter** = PNEUMATOMETER; so **Pneumo·metry.** **Pneu·motho·rax** (also *pneumatothorax*) *Path.* the presence of air or gas in the cavity of the thorax, i.e. of the pleura, usu. caused by a wound or by perforation of the lung.

Pneumogastric (ni*ū*mogæ·strik, pni*ū*-), *a.* (*sb.*) 1831. [f. PNEUMO- b + GASTRIC.] *Anat.* **a.** Pertaining to the lungs and the stomach or abdomen. **b.** *ellipt.* as *sb.* The p. nerve 1874.

a. *P. nerve*, name for the tenth pair of cerebral nerves, which, with their branches, supply the lungs and other respiratory and vocal organs, stomach, œsophagus, spleen, liver, intestines, heart, etc.

Pneumonia (niumǭ·niă). 1603. [a. medical L. *pneumonia*, a. Gr. πνευμονία inflammation of the lungs, f. πνεύμων, πνευμον- lung.] *Path.* Inflammation of the substance of the lungs.

Called *single* or *double p.*, according as one or both lungs are affected. *attrib.*: p. **bacillus, coccus, microbe** = PNEUMOCOCCUS.

Pneumonic (niumǫ·nik), *a.* (*sb.*) 1675. [ad. medical L. *pneumonicus*, a. Gr. πνευμονικός of the lungs, etc.] †1. Pertaining to the lungs; pulmonary. *rare.* 2. Pertaining to, of the nature of, characterized by, or affected with pneumonia 1783. B. *sb.* †a. A person affected with lung-disease -1681. b. A remedy for lung-disease. *rare.* 1727.

‖ **Pneumonitis** (niūmŏnəi·tis, pniū-). 1822. [mod.L., f. Gr. πνεύμων lung + -ITIS.] *Path.* = PNEUMONIA. Hence **Pneumoni·tic** *a.* = PNEUMONIC 2.

Pneumono- (niūmŏno, pniū-), bef. a vowel **pneumon-**, comb. form of Gr. πνεύμων, πνευμον- lung (Often contracted to PNEUMO-.) **Pneumono·meter** [-METER] = PNEUMATOMETER. **Pneumonophorous** (-ǫ·fŏrəs) [Gr. -φόρος bearing] *a.*, bearing or having lungs.

‖ **Pnyx** (pniks). 1822. [a. Gr. Πνύξ.] The public place of assembly in Ancient Athens, a semicircular level cut out of the side of a little hill west of the Acropolis.

Po (pōu). *colloq.* = POT *sb.*[1] 1 e.

‖ **Poa** (pōu·ă). 1753. [mod.L., a. Gr. πόα grass.] *Bot.* A large genus of grasses widely distributed in temperate and cold regions; meadow-grass.

Poach (pōutʃ), *v.*[1] 1450. [a. OF. *pochier*, later *pocher* to enclose in a poke or bag; f. *poche* poke, bag; see POKE *sb.*[1]] *trans.* To cook (an egg) by dropping it, without the shell, into boiling water. Hence **Poached** *ppl. a.*

Poach (pōutʃ), *v.*[2] 1528. [In 16th c. *poche*; app. a palatalized collateral form of POKE *v.*[1]] I. 1. *trans.* = POKE *v.*[1] 1; also, to stir *up* by poking; to ram or roughly push (things) together; *fig.* to instigate. Now *dial.* 2. To thrust or push (a stick, a finger, a foot, etc.) into any hole or thing. Now chiefly *dial.* 1673. †3. To stab, pierce -1644. †b. To make a thrust *at* as in fencing (*rare*). Also *fig.* -1624.

1. He bid him beat abroad, and not p. up the Game in his Warren FIELDING. 3. b. *Cor.* I. x. 15. They have rather poached and offered at a number of enterprizes, than maintained any constantly BACON.

II. 1. *trans.* To thrust or stamp down with the feet; to trample (soft or sodden ground) into muddy holes; to cut *up* (turf, etc.) with hoofs 1677. 2. *intr.* To sink (into wet heavy ground) in walking; to tramp heavily or plungingly 1600. 3. Of land: To become sodden, miry, and full of holes by being trampled 1707. 4. *trans.* To make sodden 1881. 5. To mix with water and reduce to a uniform consistency. (Also *potch.*) 1873.

1. The cattle of the villagers..had poached into black mud the verdant turf SCOTT.

III. 1. *intr.* To encroach or trespass (*on* the land or rights of another) esp. in order to steal game; hence, to take game, etc. illegally, or by unsportsmanlike devices 1611. 2. *trans.* a. To trespass on (land or water), esp. in order to kill or catch game 1715. b. To catch and carry off (game or fish) illegally, or by unsportsmanlike methods. Also *fig.* 1862. c. *Sporting slang.* To filch (an advantage, e.g. at the start in a race) by unfair means; in tennis, to return a ball that should normally be dealt with by one's partner 1891.

1. The politician feels that he is poaching on the preserves of the geographer 1868. 2. b. You were always 'poaching' our best men 1895.

Poacher (pōu·tʃəɹ). 1667. [f. prec. + -ER[1].] 1. One who poaches; one who takes or kills game unlawfully. 2. a. *U.S.* The widgeon, *Mareca americana*. b. The sea-poacher, a fish of the family *Agonidæ*. 3. (Also **potcher.**) *Paper-making.* One of the series of engines by which rags, etc., are comminuted, washed, bleached, and reduced to pulp 1877.

Poachy (pōu·tʃi), *a.* 1707. [f. as prec. + -Y[1].] Of land: Spongy, retentive of moisture, and so liable to be trampled into muddy holes; sodden, swampy. Hence **Poa·chiness.**

Pob (pǫb). *Sc.* 1747. [Origin obsc.] The refuse of flax or jute.

Pocan (pōu·kăn). 1858. [app. native Amer. Indian name.] = POKE *sb.*[4] 2 a.

‖ **Pochade** (poʃa·d). 1872. [F., f. *pocher* to sketch in the rough, also to blur; see -ADE.] A rough, smudgy, or blurred sketch. BROWNING.

Po'chaise, -'chay, pochay. 1827. Colloq. contractions of POST-CHAISE.

Pochard (pōu·tʃ-, pōu·kăɹd, pǫ·kăɹd). 1552. [Origin obsc.] A European diving-bird, *Fuligula* or *Æthyia ferina*, of the family *Anatidæ*, characterized by the bright reddish-brown colour of the head and neck; also called *red-headed p.*, *poker*, *widgeon*, DUN-BIRD. Also applied to other species as the Red-crested P., *F.* or *Nyroca rufina*, of India; the Tufted P., *F. cristata*, of Europe and Asia; and in U. S. to the RED-HEAD, *Anas americana*.

Pochette (pǫʃe·t). 1923. [a. F., lit. 'little pocket'.] A lady's handbag in the shape of a flat pouch or envelope.

Pock (pǫk), *sb.* [OE. *poc*, *pocc-* pustule, ulcer = MDu., MLG. *pocke* (*poche*), etc.] 1. A pustule in any eruptive disease, esp. (since 1700) in small-pox. 2. A disease characterized by such pustules; *esp.* (*a*) small-pox; (*b*) 'great (French or Spanish) pox', syphilis. In *pl.* now written POX; in *sing.* now *dial.* and *vulgar.* ME. †Also *fig.* (*sing.*) -1607.

1. And it is hool anon, and forthermoor Of pokkes, and of scabbe, and euery soor CHAUCER.

attrib. and *Comb.*, as **p.-hole, -mark,** a scar, mark, or 'pit' left by a pustule, esp. of small-pox; **-broken, -frecken, -fret, -fretted** (-fretten), **-marked, -pitted** (-**pitten**) *adjs.*, scarred, marked, or 'pitted' with pustules, esp. of small-pox; **-lymph,** the lymph of cow-pox, as used in vaccination. Hence **Pock** *v. trans.* to mark with pocks, or with disfiguring spots.

Pocket (pǫ·kėt), *sb.* [ME. *poket*, a. Anglo-Norman *pokete*, dim. of ONF. *poke*, *poque* = F. *poche*, whence dim. *pochette*; see POKE *sb.*[1], POUCH *sb.*] 1. A bag or sack. Sometimes used as a measure of quantity; now chiefly for hops (= half a sack), or wool (= about 168 lbs.). 2. A small bag or pouch worn on the person; spec. one inserted in a garment, for carrying a purse, etc. late ME. b. *esp.* That in which money is carried; hence = one's purse or stock of cash; private means 1717. 3. *Billiards.* One of the open-mouthed pouches placed at the corners and on each side of the table, into which the balls are played 1753. 4. *Zool.* and *Anat.* A sac-shaped or pocket-like cavity in the body of an animal; as the abdominal pouch of a marsupial, etc. 1773. 5. a. *Mining.* A cavity in the earth filled with gold or other ore; also, an accumulation of alluvial gold 1850. b. A small cavity in a rock; esp. (*Geol.*) one filled up with foreign material 1850. c. A subterranean cavity containing water 1852. d. A hollow in the ground, or among hills, as a glen, etc. 1869. e. (More fully *air-p.*) a patch of rarefied air, or a downward eddy, which causes an aeroplane to lose altitude 1914. 6. A recess or cavity resembling a pocket in use or position; e.g. a receptacle in the cover of a book for a folded map, etc.; a small cabin or coal bunker on board ship; etc. 1881. 7. *Racing.* The position in which a competitor is hemmed in by others and so has no chance of winning 1890. 8. *attrib.* and *Comb.* a. Adapted or intended to be carried in the pocket, as *p.-comb*, *-lens*, etc. 1612. b. Small enough to be so carried; tiny, diminutive 1621. c. (from 2.) Having reference to money 1705.

2. A Prodigal is a P. with a Hole in the Bottom 1680. Phr. *To put in one's p.*, to put away, conceal, suppress; I put my pride in my p. 1885. *In (some one's) p.*, (*a*) in close attendance on (some one); (*b*) under the personal control of (some one). b. A gentleman can't consider his p. R. BRIDGES. *In p.*, (*a*) having money available; (*b*) having (so much) money left over or to profit, as 'to be ten shillings in p. by the transaction'. *Out of p.*, †out of funds; *to be out of p.*, to be a loser (by some transaction). Hence *attrib.* as *out-of-p. expenses*, (an allowance or payment for) expenses by which one would otherwise be out of p. 8. b. A p. Switzerland EMERSON.

Comb.: **p.-borough,** a borough of which the parliamentary representation was under the control of one person or family; **†-expenses,** small personal outlays; **-mouse,** a rodent of the family *Saccomyidæ*, a pouched mouse; **-piece,** a piece of money kept in the p. as a charm; often one which is damaged or spurious; **-pistol** (*a*) a small pistol to be carried in the p.; (*b*) *joc.* a pocket spirit-flask; **-sheriff,** a sheriff nominated by the sole authority of the crown; **-veto** *sb.* and *v. U.S.* (cf. next, 3 b).

Pocket (pǫ·kėt), *v.* 1589. [f. prec.] 1. *trans.* To put into one's pocket. Also with *up*. b. To confine or enclose as in a pocket. (Chiefly in *pass.*) 1681. c. *Racing.* To hem in (a competitor) in front and at the sides, so as to prevent him from winning 1890. 2. To appropriate; sometimes with implication of dishonesty 1637. 3. *fig.* a. To take or accept (an affront, etc.) without showing resentment; to submit to, 'swallow' 1589. b. To conceal, give no indication of (pride, anger, etc.); to refrain from publishing (a report, letter, etc.); in U. S. politics (of the President or the Governor of a State): To retain (a bill) unsigned, so as to prevent it from becoming law 1610. 4. *Billiards.* To play (a ball) into one of the pockets 1780. 5. To hold under private control; *esp.* the representation of a constituency 1882. 6. To furnish with pockets. (Chiefly in *pass.*) 1896. 7. *Path.* and *Surg.* To convert or form into a pouch, cavity, or depression 1885. 8. *intr.* To form pockets or bag-like recesses. b. *U.S.* To pucker or become bagged (*rare*). 1614.

2. These sums were pocketed by Edward VI, or rather by his advisers 1879. 3. a. I must p. vp these wrongs SHAKS. The United States must p. the rebuff with a pleasant diplomatic smile 1891. Hence **Po·cketable** *a.* that may be put or carried in the p.

Pocket-book (pǫ·kėt,buk). 1617. 1. A small book, to be carried in the pocket. Now usu. two words. 2. A note-book, to be carried in the pocket; also, a book-like case for papers, bank-notes, bills, etc. 1685. 3. *attrib.* 1819.

Pocketful (pǫ·kėt,ful). 1611. [-FUL.] As much as fills a pocket.

A whole p. of money THACKERAY.

Pocket-handkerchief (pǫ·kėt,hæ·ŋkəɹtʃif). 1781. A handkerchief to be carried in the pocket.

Pocket-knife (pǫ·kėt,nəif). 1727. A knife with one or more blades which fold into the handle, for carrying in the pocket.

Po·cket-mo·ney. 1632. Money carried in the pocket for occasional expenses; *esp.* that allowed to schoolboys or schoolgirls.

Pockety (pǫ·kėti), *a.* 1874. [f. POCKET *sb.* + -Y[1].] Of a mine or mineral deposit: Characterized by pockets; having the ore unevenly distributed.

†**Po·ckwood.** 1590. [f. POCK *sb.* + WOOD *sb.*] The wood of a tree of the genus *Guaiacum*, formerly used for the cure of syphilis; = GUAIACUM 2. -1764.

Pocky (pǫ·ki), *a.* Now *rare.* ME. [f. POCK *sb.* + -Y[1].] 1. Full of or marked with pocks or pustules; *spec.* infected with the pox (i. e., usu. syphilis). †b. As a coarse expression of dislike, or an intensive. (Cf. *mangy.*) -1663. 2. Pertaining to, or of the nature of, a pock or pustule, or the pox; syphilitic or variolous 1555.

1. b. These French villains have p. wits B. JONS. Hence **Po·ckiness.**

‖ **Poco-curante** (pō:ko,kura·nte), *a.* and *sb.* 1762. [It., f. *poco* little + *curante* caring, pr. pple. of *curare* :—L. *curare.*] Caring little; indifferent, nonchalant. Also *sb.* Hence **Po:co-cura·nt(e)ism,** indifference; indifferentism.

‖ **Pocosin, poquosin** (pŏkōu·sin). *U.S.* 1709. [Algonquin *poquosin.*] In Southern U. S., A tract of low swampy ground, usually wooded: a marsh, a swamp.

Poculiform (pǫ·kiū̆lifǭɹm), *a.* 1832. [ad. F., f. L. *poculum* cup + -(I)FORM.] *Nat. Hist.* Of the form of a cup or drinking-vessel.

Pod (pǫd), *sb.*[1] 1573. [Origin unkn.] Earlier form of PAD *sb.*[3] III.; the socket of a brace in which the end of a bit is inserted.

Comb. **p.-bit,** a boring-tool adapted to be used in a brace.

Pod (pǫd), *sb.*[2] 1688. [Origin unkn.] 1. A seed-vessel of a long form, usually dry and dehiscent; prop. of leguminous and cruciferous plants; a legume or siliqua. 2. *transf.* a. The cocoon of the silk-worm. b. The case of the eggs of a locust. 1753. 3. A purse net with a narrow neck for catching eels. Also *p.-net.* 1882. †4. The blade of a cricket-bat -1862.

Comb. p.-pepper, a common name for capsicum.

Pod, *sb.*³ orig. *U.S.* 1827. [Origin unkn.] A small herd or school of seals or whales, etc.; a small flock of birds.

Pod (pǫd), *v.*¹ 1734. [f. POD *sb.*²] 1. *intr.* To bear or produce pods. 2. *trans.* To hull or empty peas out of pods 1902.

Pod, *v.*² 1887. [f. POD *sb.*³] *trans.* To drive (seals, etc.) into a pod or bunch for the purpose of clubbing them.

‖**Podagra** (pǫ·dăgră, podæ·gră). late ME. [L., a. Gr. ποδάγρα lit. a trap for the feet, f. πούς, ποδ- foot + ἄγρα a catching.] *Med.* Gout in the feet; hence, gout generally. Hence **Po·dagral** *a.* of or pertaining to gout; gouty. **Poda·gric** *a.* podagral; *sb.* a sufferer from gout. †**Poda·grical** *a.* **Po·dagrous** *a.* gouty.

‖**Podalgia** (podæ·ldʒiă). 1842. [mod.L., f. Gr. πούς, ποδ- foot + ἄλγος pain.] Pain in the foot, as from gout, rheumatism, etc.

Podded (pǫ·dėd), *a.* 1753. [f. POD *sb.*² + -ED ².] 1. Bearing pods; leguminous; growing (as a seed) in pods. 2. *fig.* (transl. F. *cossu.*) Well-off, comfortable 1889.

Podder (pǫ·dəɹ). 1681. [f. POD *sb.*²] A person employed in gathering peas in the pod.

‖**Podestà** (podesta·). 1548. [It., :—L. *potestatem* power, authority, hence public officer, etc.] a. A governor appointed by the Emperor Frederick I (Barbarossa) over one or more cities of Lombardy. b. A chief magistrate elected annually in mediæval Italian towns. Also *transf.* c. A subordinate judge or magistrate in modern Italian municipalities.

‖**Podetium** (podī·ʃiŏm). *Pl.* **-ia.** 1857. [mod.L., arbitrary f. Gr. πούς, ποδ- foot.] *Bot.* In some lichens, a stalk-like or shrubby outgrowth of the thallus, bearing the apothecium or fruit; also, any stalk-like elevation.

‖**Podex** (pōᵘ·deks). Now only *Zool.* 1598. [L.] The fundament, the rump; also, the last dorsal segment of the abdomen of insects, the pygidium. Hence **Po·dical** *a. Zool.* pertaining to the p.; anal; *p. plates,* two or more small plates surrounding the p. in some insects.

Podge (pǫdʒ). *dial.* or *colloq.* 1833. [A parallel form of PUDGE *sb.*] Anything podgy; *spec.* a short fat man or woman; a short stout thick-set animal. Hence **Po·dgy** *a.* short, thick, and fat; squat. **Po·dgily** *adv.*

Podite (pǫ·dəit). 1875. [f. Gr. πούς, ποδ- foot + -ITE ¹.] *Zool.* A leg or ambulatory limb of an arthropod, esp. of a crustacean. Usu. in comb. Hence **Podi·tic** *a.*

‖**Podium** (pōᵘ·diŏm). *Pl.* **podia.** 1789. [L., ad. Gr. πόδιον, dim. of πούς, ποδ- foot.] 1. *Arch.* a. A continuous projecting base or pedestal, a stylobate. b. A raised platform surrounding the arena in an ancient amphitheatre. c. A continuous seat or bench round a room. 2. *Anat.* and *Zool.* The fore or hind foot of a vertebrate; in birds, the junction of the toes, or the toes collectively. Also in compounds, as EPIPODIUM, etc. 1858.

Podley: see POLLACK.

Podo- (pǫdo), bef. a vowel **pod-,** a. Gr. ποδο-, comb. form of πούς, ποδ- foot, as in:

‖**Podarthri·tis,** *Med.* inflammation of joints of the foot. **Po·dobranch** (-bræŋk) [Gr. βράγχια gills], *Zool.* a breathing organ of crustaceans attached to the legs; a foot-gill; so **Podobra·nchial** *a.* of or pertaining to foot-gills. **Po·docarp** [Gr. καρπός fruit], *Bot.* a footstalk bearing the fruit of a plant. **Podoce·phalous** [Gr. κεφαλή head], *a. Bot.* bearing a head of flowers on a long footstalk. ‖**Podogynium** (-dʒi·niŏm) [mod.L., f. Gr. γυνή female], *Bot.* = BASIGYNIUM. **Podophy·llous** [Gr. φύλλον leaf], *a.* (*a*) *Entom.* having, as some insects, compressed leaf-like locomotive organs or feet; (*b*) *Zool.* in *p. tissue,* the layer of tissue composed of leaf-like vascular lamellæ beneath the coronary cushion of a horse's hoof. **Po·doscaph** [Gr. σκάφος ship], a canoe-shaped float attached to the foot for moving on water; also, a water-velocipede. **Po·dosperm** [Gr. σπέρμα seed], *Bot.* the stalk of a seed. **Podosto·matous** [Gr. στόμα mouth], *a. Zool.* belonging to the *Podostomata,* a group of *Arthropoda* characterized by having a foot-like mouth. ‖**Podothe·ca** [mod. L., f. Gr. θήκη sheath], *Zool.* the scaly leg-covering of a bird or reptile; also, the sheath covering the leg of an insect in the pupa; hence **Podothe·cal** *a.*

Podophthalmate (pǫdǫfþæ·lmět), *a.* 1835. [f. Gr. πούς, ποδ- foot + ὀφθαλμός eye + -ATE ².] *Zool.* Having the eye at the end of a movable stalk, stalk-eyed; of or pertaining to the stalk-eyed crustaceans. So ‖**Podophtha·lmia,** an order of Crustacea, including those with eyes set on movable footstalks, as crabs and lobsters. **Podophtha·lmian** *a.*, pertaining to the *Podophthalmia*; *sb.* a member of the *Podophthalmia.* **Podophtha·lmic, Podophtha·lmous** *adjs.*

‖**Podophyllum** (pǫdofi·lŏm). 1760. [mod. L., f. Gr. ποδο- PODO- + φύλλον leaf.] a. *Bot.* A genus of *Ranunculaceæ* with two known species, *P. peltatum* of eastern N. America, and *P. Emodi* of the Himalayas, having long thick creeping rhizomes, large long-stalked palmately lobed leaves, and a solitary white flower. b. *Pharm.* The dried rootstock of *P. peltatum.* Also *attrib.* Hence **Podophy·llin** *Chem.*, a yellow bitter resin having cathartic properties, obtained from the dried rhizome of *P. peltatum*; = *resin of p.*

‖**Podura** (podiūᵊ·ră). 1797. [mod.L., f. Gr. πούς, ποδ- foot + οὐρά tail.] *Entom.* A genus of apterous insects, having a terminal forked springing organ; hence known as springtails. Hence **Podu·ran** *a.* of or pertaining to the genus *P.*; *sb.* an insect of this genus or of the family *Poduridæ*; so **Podu·rid** *a.* and *sb.*

Poë-bird (pōᵘ·iˌbɔ̄ɹd). 1777. [From the Otaheitan word for ear-rings; so named from the little tufts of curled hair under the throat.] A New Zealand bird, *Prosthemadera novæ-zelandiæ*, now called PARSON-BIRD.

‖**Pœcile** (pī·sili). 1819. [a. Gr. (ἡ) ποικίλη (στόα) the painted porch.] Name of a portico in the market-place of ancient Athens, adorned with a variety of paintings.

†**Pœcilite** (pī·siləit). 1832. [f. Gr. ποίκιλος variegated + -ITE ¹.] *Geol.* A name proposed for the Upper New Red Sandstone. Hence **Pœcilitic** (pīsili·tik) *a.* = POIKILITIC.

Pœcilo- (pī·silo), bef. a vowel **pœcil-** from Gr. ποικίλος many-coloured, various, a formative element in scientific terms; as in **Pœ·cilopod** [Gr. πούς, ποδ- foot], *Zool.* a member of the *Pœcilopoda,* a division, now abandoned, of *Crustacea,* distinguished by limbs of various forms and functions; hence **Pœcilo·podous** *a.*

Poem (pōᵘ·ėm). 1548. [a. F. *poème,* ad. L. *poema,* a. Gr. πόημα, early var. of ποίημα, thing made or created, f. ποεῖν, ποιεῖν to make.] 1. 'The work of a poet, a metrical composition' (J.); a composition of words, expressing facts, thoughts, or feelings in poetical form; a piece of poetry. b. *transf.* Applied to a composition which, without the form, has some quality or qualities in common with poetry 1581. 2. *fig.* Something (other than a composition of words) of a nature or quality akin or likened to that of poetry 1642. 3. *attrib.* 1806.

1. And may not I..say that the holy Dauids Psalmes are a diuine P. SIDNEY. 2. The Celts.. gave to the seas and mountains names which are poems EMERSON.

Poephagous (po,e·fāgəs), *a. rare.* 1839. [f. mod.L. *Poephaga,* neut. pl. (ad. Gr. ποηφάγος herbivorous, f. πόα grass + -φάγος eating) + -OUS.] *Zool.* Eating grass or herbs; *spec.* belonging to the division *Poephaga* of marsupials.

Poesy (pōᵘ·ėsi), *sb. arch.* ME. [a. OF. *poesie,* ad. Com. Rom. f. L. *poesis* poetry, poem, a. Gr. πόησις, var. of ποίησις a making, poetry, a poem.] 1. = POETRY. a. Poetical work or composition; poems collectively or generally; poetry in the concrete, or as a form of literature. Now an arch. or poet. synonym of *poetry.* b. Poetry in the abstract, or as an art. c. Faculty or skill of poetical composition. 1579. †2. (with *a* and *pl.*) A poetical (or, earlier, imaginative) composition; a poem -1843. †3. = POSY 1. -1602. †4. = POSY 2. -1688.

1. It is not ryming and versing, that maketh Poesie SIDNEY. b. The high-water mark of English P. 1879. 3. Is this a Prologue, or the Poesie of a Ring? SHAKS. Hence **Po·esy** *v. intr.* to speak or write poetically KEATS.

Poet (pōᵘ·ėt). [ME. *poete, poyete,* a. OF. *poete,* mod.F. *poète,* ad. L. *poeta,* ad. Gr. ποητής, var. of ποιητής maker, f. ποεῖν, ποιεῖν to make.] One who composes poetry; a writer in verse. (The ordinary current use.) †b. Formerly (after Gr. and L. use): An author, writer -1678. c. In emphatic sense: A writer in verse (or sometimes in elevated prose) distinguished by imaginative power, insight, sensibility, and faculty of expression 1530.

Fumbling baronets and poets small GRAY. *P.-laureate*: see LAUREATE *a.* c. The Poets eye in a fine frenzy rolling, Doth glance from heauen to earth, from earth to heauen SHAKS.

Comb. **Poets' Corner,** (*a*) a part of the south transept of Westminster Abbey, which contains the graves and monuments of many distinguished poets; (*b*) applied joc. to a part of a newspaper, etc., containing short poetical contributions. Hence **Po·etship,** the position or function of a p.; also with *poss. adj.* as a mock title for a p.

Poetaster (pōᵘ·ėtæstəɹ, pōᵘėtæ·stəɹ). 1599. [a. med. or mod.L. *poetaster*; see POET and -ASTER.] A paltry poet; a writer of trashy verse; a rimester.

There are always poetasters enough 1883. Hence **Poetastery, -try,** the work of a p.

Poetess (pōᵘ·ėtės). 1530. [f. POET + -ESS.] A female poet.

Poetic (po,e·tik). 1530. [a. F. *poëtique,* ad. L. *poeticus,* a. Gr. ποητικός, ποιητικός, f. πο(ι)ητής POET; see -IC.] A. *adj.* 1. Belonging or proper to poets or poetry. 2. a. That is a poet 1640. b. Of a poet or poets 1712. 3. = POETICAL 3. 1656. b. Having the style or character proper to poetry as a fine art 1826. 4. = POETICAL 4. 1704. 5. Celebrated in poetry; affording a subject for poetry 1742. 6. In sense of Gr. ποιητικός: Making, creative; relating to artistic creation (*rare*) 1872.

1. Poetique Fires DRYDEN. *P.* JUSTICE, LICENCE: see the sbs. 2. a. The p. Earl of Surrey D'ISRAELI. b. The p. tribe COWPER. 3. P. Prose 1749.

B. *sb.* 1. *sing.* and *pl.* That part of literary criticism which treats of poetry; also, a treatise on poetry; *esp.* that of Aristotle 1727. 2. *pl.* Poetic composition 1851.

Poetical (po,e·tikăl), *a.* late ME. [f. L. *poeticus* (see prec.) + -AL.] 1. = POETIC *a.* 1. 2. Characteristic of a poet or poets 1585. b. Having the character of a poet 1581. †c. That is a poet; composing in verse -1720. 3. Composed in poetry; written in verse 1549. b. Of the style or character proper to poetry as a fine art 1447. 4. Relating to or dealing with poetry; occupied with or fond of poetry 1779.

1. *P.* JUSTICE, LICENCE: see the sbs. 2. b. Truly, I would the Gods hadde made thee poeticall SHAKS. 4. A new p. philosophy 1851. Hence **Poe·tically** *adv.*

Poe·ticize (-səiz), *v.* 1804. [f. POETIC + -IZE.] 1. *trans.* To make poetic; to treat poetically; to put into poetry. 2. *intr.* To write or speak poetically or as a poet 1850.

Poetico- (po,e·tiko), comb. form of L. *poeticus* POETIC, to denote a combination of the poetic with another quality, as *p.-antiquarian.*

Poeticule (po,e·tikiul). 1872. [f. L. *poeta* POET + -CULE.] A petty or insignificant poet.

Poetize (pōᵘ·ėtəiz), *v.* 1581. [ad. F. *poétiser*; see POET and -IZE.] 1. *intr.* To play the poet; to compose poetry. †b. To deal in poetical fiction; to romance -1639. 2. *trans.* a. To make poetical; to turn into poetry 1762. b. To celebrate in poetry 1837.

1. Not onely to read others Poesies, but to poetise for others reading SIDNEY. b. I versifie the troth, not p. DANIEL. 2. b. To p. the moon 1884.

Poetry (pōᵘ·ėtri). [Late ME. = OF. *poetrie, poeterie*; ad. late and med.L. *poetria,* f. *poeta* POET.] I. In obsolete senses. †1. = med.L. *poetria* in sense of an *ars poetica* -1447. †2. Fable, fiction -1601.

2. Their profession of Poëtry, that is to say, of faining and deuising fables HOLLAND.

II. In existing use. 1. The art or work of the poet. a. Composition in verse or metrical language. late ME. b. The product of this art as a form of literature; the writings of a poet or poets; poems collectively or generally; verse. (Opp. to *prose.*) 1586. c. The expression of beautiful or elevated thought, imagination, or feeling, in appropriate language, such language containing a rhythmical element and having usu. a metrical form 1581. d. Extended to creative art in general (*rare*) RUSKIN. 2. *pl.*

Pieces of poetry; poems collectively (*rare*). late ME. 3. *fig.* Something compared to poetry; poetical quality, spirit, or feeling 1816. 4. A class in Roman Catholic schools and colleges intermediate between *Syntax* and *Rhetoric* 1629. 5. *attrib.* 1798.

1. b. The end of p...is to please 1807. c. I will proue those Verses to be very vnlearned, neither sauouring of Poetrie, Wit, nor Inuention SHAKS. *Prose-p.*, expression in non-metrical language having the harmonic and emotional qualities of p. 3. To live p., indeed, is always better than to write it 1874.

Poggy (pǫ·gi). 1874. [Origin unkn.] A small arctic whale; supposed to be the young of the common whale, *Balæna mysticetus.*

Pogo (pōu·gǫ). 1922. [Etym. unascertained.] In full *p.-stick*, a toy resembling a stilt with a spring on which the player jumps about.

‖ **Pogrom** (pǫgrǫ·m). 1905. [Russ. = destruction.] An organized massacre in Russia for the annihilation of any body or class; *esp.* one directed against the Jews.

Pogy (pōu·gi). local *U.S.* Also **-ie.** 1888. [Contraction of *pauhaugen.*] The menhaden.

Poh (pǫ), *int.* 1679. An exclam. of contemptuous rejection. (Cf. POOH.)

‖ **Poi** (poi). Also **poe.** 1840. [Hawaiian name.] A dish made in Hawaii from the root of the taro or kalo plant, by grinding, mixing, and allowing it to ferment; also, a dish made from the banana and pandanus fruit. Also *attrib.*

Poietic (poi,e·tik), *a. rare.* 1905. [ad. Gr. ποιητικός active, effective, f. ποιεῖν to do, make.] Creative, formative, productive, active.

Poignancy (poi·nⁱănsi). 1688. [f. POIGNANT; see -ANCY.] The quality or fact of being poignant.

A..p. of grief 1787. The p. of their wit 1838.

Poignant (poi·nⁱănt), *a.* [Late ME. a. OF. *puignant, poignant*, pr. pple. of *poindre* :—L. *pungere* to prick.] †1. Of weapons, etc.: Sharp-pointed, piercing -1695. b. *fig.* Of the eye or look: Piercing, keen 1787. 2. Sharp, pungent, piquant to the taste or smell. late ME. 3. Painfully sharp to the physical or mental feelings. late ME. b. Stimulating; piquant 1649. 4. Of words or expressions: Sharp, stinging; also, piquant 1542.

2. Poynaunt sauce CHAUCER. The rich, p. perfume 1864. 3. This pang is made more p. by exile 1887. b. A..p. felicity HAWTHORNE. 4. P. sarcasm DISRAELI. Hence **Poi·gnantly** *adv.*

Poikilitic (poikili·tik), *a.* 1836. [var. of PŒCILITIC.] *Geol.* A term formerly applied to the Triassic and Permian systems, as being mainly composed of variegated rocks.

Poi·kilo-, var. of PŒCILO-.

‖ **Poilu** (pwalü). 1916. [F. = hairy.] French slang for: A private soldier.

Poind (pūnd, pind), *sb. Sc.* 1563. [f. next.] a. An act of poinding, a distraint. b. A beast or chattel poinded.

Poind (pūnd, pind), *v. Sc.* late ME. [Sc. repr. of OE. *pyndan* to shut in, impound, = PIND.] 1. *trans.* To distrain upon (a person or his goods). b. *absol.* To distrain 1500. 2. *trans.* To impound 1450. Hence **Poi·nder**, a person who distrains goods or impounds cattle.

‖ **Poinsettia** (poinse·tiă). 1867. [mod.L.; after J. R. *Poinsett*, American Minister to Mexico.] A Mexican species of Euphorbia, *E.* (*Poinsettia*) *pulcherrima*, having large scarlet floral leaves surrounding small greenish-yellow flowers.

Point (point), *sb.*¹ ME. [Two, or perh. three, words. In A., a. F. *point* :—L. *punctum*, pa. pple. neut. of *pungere* to prick, pierce, used subst. In B., a. F. *pointe* :—Com. Rom. (and med.L.) *puncta* the action of piercing, etc.; ppl. sb. fem. from *pungere*. In C., app. from F. *poindre*, or *pointer*, or from POINT *v.*¹] **A.** = F. *point.* **I.** A prick, a dot. 1. A dot, a minute spot or speck, on a surface; also, anything appearing like a speck. late ME. 2. A dot or other small mark used in writing or printing. a. A punctuation-mark; *esp.* the *full p.* or full stop. late ME. b. In Semitic alphabets, any one of the dots, minute strokes, or groups of these used to indicate the vowels; in Hebrew also to indicate variation or doubling of the consonant, stress accent, punctuation, in Arabic and Persian to distinguish consonants otherwise identical in form 1614. c. A dot used in writing numbers: (*a*) In decimals, separating the integral from the fractional part; also, placed over a repeating decimal, or over the first and last figures of a circulating decimal. (*b*) A dot or stroke used to separate a line of figures into groups. 1794. 3. A dot or mark used in mediæval musical notation. a. A mark indicating a tone or sound; corresp. to the modern 'notes' 1674. b. = DOT *sb.*¹ 5 d. 1597.

1. As the fix'd Stars..appear but as so many points LAW. 2. a. The p. of Interrogation, ? The p. of Exclamation, ! 1824.

II. A separate or single article, item, or clause in an extended whole; a detail, a particular; †an instance (of some quality, etc.) ME.

This is the p. upon which the whole reasoning turns 1701. The 'six points' of modern Ritualism 1897. Phr. †*To stand* (*up*)*on* (*one's*) *points*, to be punctilious or scrupulous. *To strain* or *stretch a p.*; see the vbs.

III. A minute part or particle of anything; the smallest unit of measurement. †1. A jot, whit, particle of something -1477. †2. A moment, instant, of time -1533. †3. *Sensible p.*: the least discernible portion of matter or space (*rare*) -1704. 4. *Mus.* A short strain or snatch of melody ME. b. An important phrase or subject, usu. in a contrapuntal composition, esp. in relation to its entry in a particular part; the entry of such a phrase or subject 1597. †5. The twelfth part of the side or radius of a quadrant, etc.; *spec.* in *Astron.* One of the 24 (or, according to some, 12) equal divisions of the diameter of the sun or moon, by which the degree of obscuration in an eclipse was measured -1594. 6. *Nine* or *eleven points*, usu. in the saying 'Possession is nine (or eleven) points of the law', i.e. out of a supposed ten or twelve points (= a vast majority of the points) that may be raised in a legal action 1670. 7. A unit of count in the score of a game 1746. b. *spec.* in *Piquet*: The number of cards of the most numerous suit in one's hand after discarding; the number scored by the player who holds the highest number of one suit 1719. 8. A unit in appraising the qualities of a competitor, or of an exhibit in a competitive show. Also *fig.* 1777. 9. A recognized unit in quoting variations in the price of stocks, shares, commodities, etc. 10. *Printing.* A unit of measurement for type bodies; in the French or Didot system the seventy-second part of a French inch; in the U. S. system, ·0138 of an inch 1890.

1. †*No p.* (cf. F. *ne point*), not a bit, not at all. 4. Phr. *P. of war*, etc., a short phrase sounded on an instrument as a signal; To perform the beautiful and wild p. of war SCOTT. 7. Cumberland scored 14 points [at Football] 1895. Phr. *To give points to*, to allow (a rival) to count so many points at starting, to give odds to; *colloq.* to have the advantage of, be superior to; so *to gain a p., get points*, to gain an advantage. 8. All these were points against him 1886.

IV. Something having definite position, without extension. 1. *Geom.* That which has position, but not magnitude (as the extremity of a line). late ME. 2. A place having definite spatial position, but no extent, or of which the position alone is considered; a spot ME. b. *spec.* The spot at which a policeman is stationed 1888. c. *Hunting. colloq.* A spot to which a straight run is made; hence, a cross-country run 1875. 3. *Her.* Any of nine particular spots or places upon a shield, which serve to determine accurately the position a charge is to occupy. late ME. 4. A definite position in a scale of any kind; a step, stage, or degree in progress or development, or in increase or decrease, as of temperature (e.g. *boiling-p., freezing-p.*, etc.). late ME. b. A critical position in the course of affairs; a juncture; the precise moment for action. late ME. 5. In time, that which has position, but not duration; an instant, moment, as the moment of death. late ME. †6. Condition, plight -1732.

1. If a P. be supposed to be moved any way, it will by its Motion describe a Line 1704. CARDINAL, EQUINOCTIAL, SOLSTITIAL, VERTICAL *p.*: see those words. 2. c. Phr. *To make his p.* (of a fox), to run straight to a p. aimed at. d. (*colloq.*) A stopping-place on a tramway, omnibus, or other route, from which fare-stages are reckoned 1907.

V. fig. and transf. senses. †1. The highest part or degree; the height, summit, zenith, acme -1728. 2. A distinguishing mark or quality; a characteristic 1470. b. *spec.* A physical feature in an animal; *esp.* one by which excellence or purity of breed is judged. Hence *transf.* in ref. to a person or thing. 1546. 3. *The p.*: the precise matter in discussion; the important thing. late ME. 4. That at which one aims, or for which one contends; aim, object, end. Often in phr. *to carry one's p.* ME †5. A conclusion, culmination, 'period'. Also *full p.* -1833. †6. Decision, resolution -1738.

2. It is become..a p. of good fellowship..to take a pipe of Tobacco JAMES I. Description was not Lettice's strong p. 1889. b. Versed in the points of a horse 1841. 3. Phr. *To come to the p., to keep to the p.*, etc. *To make a p. of* (= F. *faire un point de*), to treat (something) as indispensable; to make (it) a special object. 4. *To make a p.*, to establish a proposition, to prove a contention; also *gen.* to attain something aimed at. 6. I begin to come to a p.; I intend to go along with this good man BUNYAN.

VI. (From 16th c. F. *point* = 15–16th c. It *punto*; derived from the sense 'prick', through that of 'stitch', 'work done with stitches' with the needle.) Thread lace made wholly with the needle (more fully *p. lace, needle-p. lace, needle-p.*); also improp. applied to pillow lace imitating that done with the needle, and occas. to lace generally 1662. †b. A piece of lace used as a kerchief or the like -1756.

B. = F. *pointe.* **I.** 1. A sharp end to which anything tapers; as of a weapon, tool, pin, pen, pointer ME. b. Short for *p. of the sword* (or other weapon) 1596. 2. The (or a) salient or projecting part of anything; a tip, apex; a sharp prominence. late ME. b. *spec.* A tapering promontory, or cape; often in names, as Start P., P. of Ardnamurchan. Also, a peak of a mountain or hill. 1553. c. *Mil.* The small leading party of an advanced guard 1589. d. *pl.* The extremities of a horse 1855. 3. An object or instrument consisting of or characterized by a point (in sense 1), or which pricks or pierces. †a. A dagger, pointed sword, or the like; also, a bodkin -1719. b. An etching-needle; a small punch or chisel used by stone-workers; etc. 1727. c. A tine of a deer's horn 1856. d. *Electr.* A metallic point at which electricity is discharged or collected; also, each of the carbon points or pencils in an electric light (see also below) 1836. e. On a railway: A tapering movable rail by which vehicles are directed from one line of rails to another. Usu. in *pl.* See also DIAMOND POINT 2. 1838. f. One of the twelve tapered divisions on each 'table' of a backgammon board 1588. g. In other applications, e.g. one of the pointed legs of a pair of compasses, an angular fragment of diamond adapted for glass-cutting 1545. 4. *Printing.* One of the short sharp pins fixed on the tympan of a press so as to perforate the sheet and serve to make register 1683. b. Short for *p.-plate* 1683.

1. *fig. To put too fine a p. upon*, to express with unnecessary delicacy. b. Phr. *To come to points*, to begin fighting (with swords). 2. d. A little bay with black points 1872. 3. d. Also, a socket connected by wiring to a source of electricity from which current can be obtained 1927.

II. 1. A tagged lace or cord, for attaching the hose to the doublet, lacing a bodice, etc.; often used as a type of something of small value (esp. *blue p.*) Now *arch.* or *Hist.* late ME. 2. *Naut.* One of the short pieces of flat braided cord attached near the lower edge of a sail for tying up a reef 1769. 3. A short buckling strap 1875. **III.** Each of the equidistant points on the circumference of the mariner's compass, indicated by one of the thirty-two rays drawn from the centre; also *transf.* the angular interval between two successive points (one-eighth of a right angle, or 11° 15'). Hence, any (corresponding) point of the horizon. (In ordinary use, usu. *p. of the compass.*) 1500. **IV.** a. The salient feature of a story, discourse, epigram, joke, etc.; effective or telling part. Also, a witty or ingenious turn of thought. 1728. b. That quality in speech or writing which arrests attention 1643.

a. The p. and cream of the joke DICKENS.

V. *Cricket.* The position of the fieldsman who is stationed more or less in a line with the popping-crease, a short distance on the off-side of the batsman (orig. close to the point of the bat); *transf.* the fieldsman himself 1833. b. In *Lacrosse*, The position of the player who stands a short distance in front of the goalkeeper, or the player himself; in *Baseball*, The positions occupied by the pitcher and catcher 1868.

C. Noun of action of French or English origin. †**1.** A feat; *esp.* a feat of arms, a deed of valour, an exploit; also, an encounter, skirmish. [OF. *pointe.*] –1602. **2.** *Falconry.* Of a hawk: The action of rising vertically in the air; esp. in phr. *to make* (*her*) *p.* 1651. **3.** Of a pointer or setter: The act of pointing (see POINT *v.*[1] IV. 3). Usu. in phr. *to make, come to a p.* Also *fig.* 1771. **4.** The act of pointing 1831. **5.** An indication; a hint, suggestion, direction 1882. **6.** *Arch.* An amount or degree of pointedness; in phr. *of the third* (or *fourth*) *p.*, tr. It. *di terzo* (or *quarto*) *acuto* 1703.

1. †*Points of war*, warlike exercises. 4. Phr. *Bread* or *potatoes and p.* (joc.), bread or potatoes only to eat, and the relish, such as bacon, fish, etc., merely to p. or look at. 5. Supposing that he could have given Solomon points about women 1892.

Phrases and Combs. (chiefly from A.). *With preps. **At p.** [= F. *à point.*] †**a.** Aptly, conveniently. †**b.** (Also *at a p.*) In readiness. **c.** *At (the) p. to* (with inf.), ready to, just about to (*arch.*). †**d.** *At a p.*, agreed; decided, resolved. **e.** *At all points*, in every part, in every respect. (Usu. with *armed.*) **f.** *At the p. of*, on the verge of, just about to do something. †*At the p. of day* [F. *au point du jour*], at daybreak. **From p. to p.** [OF. *de point en point.*] From one p. or detail to another, in every particular, in detail (*Obs.* or *arch.*). **In p.** †**a.** In order. **b.** *predic.* (Cf. F. *à point* = *à propos.*) Apposite; appropriate. **c.** *In p. of*, in the matter of; as regards. *In p. of fact*, see FACT 5. **On or upon the p. of.** [F. *sur le point de.*] On the very verge of, just about to do something. Formerly in reference to a specified time or number: Very near, close upon. **To p. a.** To the smallest detail; exactly, completely (*arch.*). **b.** *To the p.*, apposite, apt, pertinent. **With other sbs. **P. of honour** [F. *point d'honneur*]. A matter regarded as vitally affecting one's honour. Hence, the obligation to demand satisfaction (esp. by a duel) for a wrong or insult. **Point-to-point**, *a.* (Made, reckoned, etc.) from one point or place to another in a direct line; directly of a cross-country race; hence *ellipt.* as *sb.* a cross-country race, a steeple-chase. **P. of view** [F. *point de vue*]. The position from which anything is viewed or seen, or from which a picture is taken; also, the position or aspect in which anything is seen or regarded.

attrib. and *Comb.* **1.** General: as *p.-hole* (Printing), *-system*, etc. In Phonetics, used to describe a consonant articulated with the point of the tongue, as *t, d*; also in comb. as *p.-side* (as *l*), *p.-teeth* (as *þ*) adjs.

2. Special: **p.-bar**, in the Jacquard apparatus, one of the needles governing the warp-threads, by the motion of which the pattern is produced; **-constable**, a constable on point-duty; **-handle, -lever**, the lever by which a p. or railway-switch is moved; **-net**, simple p. lace; **-paper**, pricked paper for making, copying, or transferring designs; **-plate** (*Printing*), the adjustable plate carrying the points; **-policeman** = *p.-constable*.

‖**Point** (pwæ̃n), *sb.*[2] 1645. The French for POINT *sb.*[1] A., occurring in phrases used in English, as *p. d'appui*, point of support, fulcrum; *p. d'arrêt*, *p. saillant* (Geom.): see quots. **b.** *esp.* In names of kinds of lace, as (from the real or supposed place of manufacture) *p. d'Alençon*, *p. d'Espagne*, *p. de Venise*; also of various stitches in lace and embroidery.

A *p. d'arrêt* is a point at which a single branch of a curve suddenly stops. A *p. saillant* is a point at which two branches of a curve meet and stop without having a common tangent. 1871.

Point (point), *v.*[1] ME. [orig. a. OF. *pointer*, f. F. *point*, and *pointe*; in some senses, from POINT *sb.*[1]] **I.** †**1.** *trans.* To prick; to pierce, puncture –1570. †**2.** To mark with, or indicate by, pricks or dots; to jot down, note, write, describe –1669. **3.** To insert the proper points or stops in (writing); to make the proper pauses in (something read or spoken); to punctuate. Also *absol.* Now *rare.* late ME. **b.** To mark (the Psalms, etc.) for chanting, by means of points 1604. **c.** To insert the vowel (and other) points in the writing of Hebrew, etc.; also, in shorthand 1631. **d.** To mark *off* (figures) into groups by dots or points; *esp.* to mark *off* the decimal fraction from the integral part 1706.

3. When sentences be euill pointed, and the sence thereby depraued 1551.

II. 1. To furnish with a point or points; to work to a point, to sharpen. Also *fig.* ME. **2.** *fig.* To give point to (words, action, etc.) 1704. †**3.** To fasten or lace with tagged points or laces; to adorn with such points –1598.

1. Phr. *To p. a cable* or *rope*, to taper off the ends, and finish them neatly and securely. 2. To p. a moral, or adorn a tale JOHNSON.

III. 1. †To work or deepen with a point or graving-tool 1662. **2. a.** *Building.* To fill in the lines of joints of (brickwork) with mortar or cement, smoothed with the point of the trowel. late ME. **b.** *Gardening.* To prick *in* (manure, etc.) to a slight depth with the point of the spade; also, to turn *over* (the surface of the soil) in this way; to prick *over* 1828. **c.** *Naut.* To insert the point of (a mast or spar) through an eye or ring which secures its foot; to thread 1882. **IV. 1.** *intr.* To indicate position or direction by or as by extending the finger; to direct attention *to* or *at* something in this way 1470. **b.** *fig.* To direct the mind or thought in a certain direction; to indicate, hint *at*, allude *to*. late ME. **2.** *trans.* To indicate the place or direction of (something); to direct attention to, show. Now almost always *p. out.* 1489. **3.** Of a dog: To indicate the presence and position of (game) by standing rigidly looking towards it. *trans.* and *intr.* 1717. **4.** *trans.* To direct (the finger, a weapon, etc.) *at*; to direct (a person, his attention, or his course) *to*; to turn (the eyes or mind) *to* or *upon* 1547. **5.** *intr.* Of a line, etc.: To lie or be situated with its point or length directed *to* or *towards* something; to have a specified direction; also, of a house, etc., to look or face 1678. **b.** To aim *at*, have a motion or tendency *towards* or *to* (also with *inf.*) 1771. †**6.** To project or stick *out* in a point –1703. **7.** Of an abscess: To form a point or head; to come to a head 1876. **8.** *trans.* To place (a man) in Backgammon, etc., on a point 1680.

1. He shewed hym, pointyng with his finger, a man with a bottle Nose 1553. b. Everything pointed to the probability of a French protectorate being proclaimed 1886. 2. He pointed out that there were certain formalities to be observed (*mod.*). 3. Young pointers will p. birds' nests in hedges or trees JEFFERIES. 4. The fixed Figure for the time of Scorne To p. his slow, and mouing finger at SHAKS. 5. b. Our Ships endeavouring to form a junction, the Enemy pointing to separate us NELSON.

†**Point**, *v.*[2] 1440. [Aphetic f. APPOINT *v.*] **1.** *trans.* To fix (a time or place); to prescribe, ordain, decree; to nominate (a person) *to* an office –1711. **2.** To equip, furnish, fit up –1514.

Point-blank (poi·nt blæ·ŋk), *a.*, *sb.*, and *adv.* 1571. [app. f. POINT *v.*[1] + BLANK the white spot in the centre of a target, = F. *blanc.*] **A.** *adj.* **1.** That points or aims straight at the mark, esp. in shooting horizontally; hence, aimed or fired horizontally; level, direct, straight 1591. **2.** Straightforward, direct, plain, 'flat', blunt 1656.

1. Phr. *P. shot, fire, firing, trajectory. P. distance, range, reach*, the distance within which a gun may be fired horizontally at a mark; the distance the shot is carried before it drops appreciably below the horizontal plane of the bore. 2. A p. refusal to go into the division lobbies 1901.

B. *sb.* **1.** = *P. range* or *distance*: see A. 1. †Also *fig.* 1571. †**2.** A p. shooting or shot –1781.

1. *fig.* Within point-blanke of our Iurisdiction Regall SHAKS.

C. *adv.* **1.** With a direct aim; esp. in a horizontal line 1594. **2.** Directly, straight (in space) 1607. **b.** *fig.* Directly, exactly (in purport or effect). Now *rare* or *Obs.* 1621. **3.** *fig.* Of a statement, question, etc.: **a.** Without qualification or circumlocution; directly, flatly 1627. **b.** Straight away, offhand 1679.

2. b. So p. against the common sentiment 1704. 3. a. Origen point blanck denies the charge 1672. b. Called upon to deliver his judgement point-blank 1887.

Poi·nt-devi·ce, *phr.*, *a.*, *adv.* [Orig. in late ME. phrase *at point devis*, app. repr. an OF. or AF. phrase **à point devis* arranged properly or to perfection.] **A.** *phr.* †*At point device*, at or to the point of perfection, perfectly; precisely. late ME. only. **B.** *adj.* Perfectly correct; neat or nice in the extreme; extremely precise or scrupulous. *Obs.* or *arch.* 1526.

You are rather point deuice in your accoustrements SHAKS. Thus he grew up, in Logic p. LONGF.

C. *adv.* Completely, perfectly, to perfection; in every point; = A. *arch.* 1500.

Poi·nt-du·ty. 1888. The duty of a police constable stationed at a particular point in a thoroughfare, to regulate traffic.

Pointed (poi·nted), *ppl. a.* ME. [f. POINT *v.*[1] and *sb.*[1] + -ED.] In various senses of the verb; *spec.* **1.** Having a point or points; tapering to or ending in a point. **b.** *Arch.* In *p. arch*, an arch with a pointed crown; hence applied to the style of architecture having this feature; cf. GOTHIC A. 3 b. 1750. **2.** *fig.* Piercing, cutting, stinging, pungent, 'sharp'; having point 1665. **3.** Directed, aimed; *fig.* marked, emphasized, clearly defined, made evident 1578. **b.** Exact to a point; precise 1727.

1. I saw a row of p. rocks at some distance below me TYNDALL. 2. The most p. thing to say about a person is that he 'means well' 1897. 3. His attention,..is so p., that it always confuses me 1778. Hence **Poi·nted-ly** *adv.*, **-ness.**

Pointel (poi·ntĕl). Now *rare.* ME. [a. OF. *pointel* (mod. *pointeau*) point of a spear, etc. = It. *puntello*, dim. of *punto* point.] **1.** A small pointed instrument; a stylus, a pencil. *Obs.* exc. *Hist.* **2.** The pistil or style of a flower; formerly also applied to a stamen. Now *rare* or *Obs.* 1597. †**3.** A slender style-like organ on the body of an animal, as the 'horn' of a snail, etc. –1713.

2. White flowers with yellow pointels in the middle 1597.

Pointer (poi·ntəɹ). 1621. [f. POINT *v.*[1] + -ER[1].] One who or that which points; *spec.* **1.** A rod used to point to what is delineated or written on a map, blackboard, etc. 1658. **b.** The index-hand of a clock, balance, etc. 1667. **2.** A dog of a breed nearly allied to the true hounds, used by sportsmen to point at game, esp. birds; on scenting which the dog stands rigidly, with muzzle stretched towards the game, and usu. one foot raised 1717. **3.** *pl.* The two stars *α* and *γ* in the Great Bear, a straight line through which points nearly to the pole star 1574. **4.** *Naut.* (*pl.*) Timbers sometimes fixed diagonally across the hold, to support the beams 1769. **5.** *colloq.* A hint 1890.

Pointillism (pwæ̃ntiliz'm). Also ‖**-isme.** 1901. [ad. F. *pointillisme*, f. *pointiller* to mark with dots, f. *pointille*, ad. It. *puntiglio*, dim. of *punto* point; see -ISM.] A method invented by French impressionist painters, of producing luminous effects by crowding a surface with small spots of various colours, which are blended by the eye. So **Poi·ntillist**, an artist who follows this style; also *attrib.* 1893.

Pointing (poi·ntiŋ), *vbl. sb.* late ME. [f. POINT *v.*[1] + -ING[1].] The action of POINT *v.*[1], or its result. *spec.* **1.** The insertion of stops; punctuation 1440. **b.** In Semitic langs., the insertion of vowel points 1659. **2.** The removal of points from grain in preparing it for the mill 1879. **3.** The filling up with special strong mortar of the exterior face of the joints in brickwork; *concr.* the protective facing thus given to the joints 1483. **4.** The action of indicating or directing, as with the finger or the point of anything; also *fig.* a prompting; a hint in words 1553. **b.** Of a yacht, etc.: The action of sailing with its prow close to the wind 1899. **5.** The disposition of the points on a railway 1902.

Comb. †**p.-stock**, a person pointed at; an object of scorn, derision, or ridicule.

Poi·nt-la·ce. 1672. [f. POINT *sb.*[1] A. VI. + LACE *sb.* 5.] Lace made with the needle on a parchment pattern, as dist. from that made with bones or bobbins on a pillow. Also *attrib.*

Pointless (poi·ntlės), *a.* ME. [f. POINT *sb.*[1] + -LESS.] **1.** Without a point; blunt. **2.** Without point; ineffective, meaningless 1726. **3.** Of a competitor, side: Not having scored a point. Of a game, etc.: In which no point is scored. 1876.

1. A poincteless sword 1548. 2. P. wit POPE. 3. A p. draw 1892. Hence **Poi·ntless-ly** *adv.*, **-ness.**

Pointlet (poi·ntlėt). 1866. [f. as prec. + -LET.] A small point. So **Poi·ntleted** *a. Bot.* terminating in a small point; apiculate 1839.

Pointrel (poi·ntrĕl). *rare.* 1688. [dim. of POINT *sb.*[1] B.] **a.** = POINTEL 1. **b.** The pointed extremity of the lobe of a leaf.

Pointsman (poi·ntsmæ̆n). 1849. [f. POINT *sb.*[1] + MAN *sb.*] **1.** A man who has charge of the points on a railway. **2.** A police-constable stationed on point-duty 1883.

Poise (poiz), *sb.* [Late ME. *poys*, a. Central OF. *pois* (now *poids*), from earlier OF. *peis* weight:—late pop.L. *pesum* for cl. L. *pensum* weight, f. *pendere.*] **I.** Weight. †**1.** The quality of being heavy; weight. Also in semi-concr. sense. -1665. †**b.** *fig.* Gravity; burden; burdensomeness -1752. †**2.** Definite weight; the amount that a thing weighs -1706. †**b.** A standard of weight -1614. †**3.** A weight; e. g. a weight of a clock -1688. **b.** *fig.* Something that acts like a weight; a bias; one of the *halteres* of a fly. Now *rare* or *Obs.* 1615. †**4.** Forcible impact, as of a heavy body; momentum; a heavy blow or fall -1606.

3. b. Such a hint was likely enough to give an adverse p. to Gwendolen's own thought GEO. ELIOT. 4. *Tr. & Cr.* I. iii. 207.

II. Equality of weight, balance. **1.** *Equal* or *even p.*: The condition of being equally weighted on both sides; balance, equilibrium. *lit.* and *fig.* 1555. **2.** Hence *absol.*: Balance, equilibrium, stability 1711. **b.** Carriage (of the body, head, etc.) 1770. **c.** A balanced condition; a pause between two periods of motion or change 1867. **d.** Balanced condition; state of indecision; suspense 1713.

1. And that demands a mind in equal poize YOUNG. 2. d. The event was long on the p. 1787.

Poise (poiz), *v.* [Late ME. *poise* (parallel form to PEISE), repr. OF. *poise*, from earlier *peise*, stem-stressed form of *peser*:—late pop. L. *pesare* for cl. L. *pensare*, frequentative of *pendere* to weigh.] †**1.** *trans.* (or *intr.* with *compl.*) = PEISE *v.* 5. -1587. †**2.** = PEISE *v.* 1, 1 b. -1695. **3.** *fig.* = PEISE *v.* 2. Now *rare.* 1483. †**4.** To add weight to; to load, burden; to weigh *down*, oppress; to incline or sway as by weight. *lit.* and *fig.* -1711. †**b.** To steady or render stable, as by adding weight; to ballast -1710. **5.** To place or keep in equilibrium; to balance. *lit.* and *fig.* 1639. **b.** To weigh or balance (one thing *with* or *against* another, or two things against each other); to bring into mutual equilibrium; to equalize. Usu. *fig.* Now *rare.* 1592. †**c.** To be of equal weight with (usu. *fig.*); to counterbalance; to match -1742. **6.** To hold or carry in equilibrium; to carry steadily or evenly 1598. **7.** *intr.* for *refl.* To be balanced; to hang supported or suspended 1847.

3. A thousand resolutions..weighed, poised, and perpended STERNE. 4. When a man is biassed and poised by his heart to a thing 1677. b. That Sobriety of Thought which poises the Heart STEELE. 5. Where Earth now rests Upon her center pois'd MILT. 6. Their favourite mode of carrying things is to p. them on the top of the head 1870. 7. A butterfly.. Poising in sunshine GEO. ELIOT. Hence **Poi·ser**, that which poises or balances; an organ used for balancing; *spec.* in *Entom.*, each of the pair of appendages which replace the hind wings in dipterous insects; see HALTERES 2.

Poison (poi·z'n), *sb.* (*a.*) [ME. *puison*, *poison*, a. OF. *puison*, *poison* drink, draught, poisonous draught:—L. *potionem*, f. *potare*, *potum* to drink; see POTION.] †**1.** A potion -1579. **2.** Any substance which, when introduced into or absorbed by a living organism, destroys life or injures health: pop. applied to a substance which destroys life by rapid action, and when taken in a small quantity. late ME. **3.** *fig.* Any baneful principle, doctrine, or influence; any baneful element taken in from without 1470.

2. They hate each other like p. (*mod. colloq.*). *Slow p.*, a drug or agent having a cumulative deleterious effect when taken for a length of time. 3. The poyson of seditious doctrines HOBBES.

attrib. and *Comb.*, as *p.-fang*, *-gland*, *-sac*; **p.-cup**, (*a*) a cup containing p.; (*b*) a cup, etc., reputed to break on p. being poured into it; **-gas**, gas liberated from cylinders, a burst shell, etc., for the purpose of poisoning or asphyxiating enemy forces; **-ring**, a ring by which p. was communicated in the grasp of the hand. **b.** *esp.* in names of plants having poisonous qualities: **p.-ash**, **-dogwood**, **-elder** = *p.-sumac*; **-hemlock**, *U.S.* the common hemlock, *Conium maculatum*; **-ivy**, a trailing or climbing species of sumac, *Rhus Toxicodendron*, of N. America, having trifoliolate leaves, and producing poisonous effects when touched; **-nut**, (*a*) the violently poisonous seed of *Tanghinia venenifera* (N.O. *Apocynaceæ*), used by the natives of Madagascar in trial by ordeal; also the tree; (*b*) = NUX VOMICA; **-oak**, the low-growing variety of *Rhus Toxicodendron* (see *poison-ivy*); also the allied *R. diversiloba* of Pacific N. America; **-sumac**, *Rhus venenata*, a tall N. American shrub with pinnate leaves, also called *p.-ash* and *p.-elder*, and having properties resembling those of the allied *p.-ivy*; **-tree**, applied to various trees having poisonous properties.

†**B.** *adj.* Poisonous, poisoned -1822.

With what p., deadly, and venomous hate hateth a man his enemy TINDALE. Hence †**Poi·sonsome** *a.* poisonous -1688.

Poison (poi·z'n), *v.* [ME. *poisonen*, a. OF. *poisonner* to give to drink, f. *poison* POISON.] **1.** *trans.* To administer poison to; to kill or injure by means of poison, poisonous gases, etc. **b.** To produce morbid effects in (the blood, a wound, etc.) by impregnation or infusion of poison, ptomaine, etc. 1605. **2.** To infect (air, water, etc.) with poison; to charge or smear (a weapon) with poison. late ME. **3.** *fig.* To corrupt, pervert morally, to influence perversely. late ME. **b.** To prove destructive or fatal to (an action, state, etc.) 1605. **4.** *transf.* To render (a thing) foul and unfit for its purpose by some noxious addition or application 1500.

1. The Pope hireth men to poyson other 1560. b. Tooth that poysons if it bite SHAKS. The bite of some insects may p. the blood (*mod.*). 2. Poisoning the points of their arrows 1851. 3. Another voice ..ever ready to p. the royal mind 1868. b. A word of bitterness to p. the pleasure 1894. 4. The land will be poisoned with noxious roots and plants 1816. Hence **Poi·sonable** *a.* poisonous; capable of being poisoned. **Poi·soner**, one who or that which poisons (*lit.* and *fig.*).

Poisoning (poi·z'niŋ), *vbl. sb.* late ME. [-ING[1].] The action of the verb POISON. **b.** As the second element in combs. with words denoting (*a*) the agent or medium, as *beer-*, *food-*, *phosphorus-p.*, (*b*) the object, as **blood-poisoning**, applied to diseases caused by the introduction into the blood of decomposing organic matter; toxæmia.

Poisonous (poi·z'nəs), *a.* 1565. [f. POISON *sb.* + -OUS.] **1.** Containing or of the nature of, having the properties of, a poison; venomous. **2.** *fig.* Morally destructive or corrupting; malevolent, malignant. Also with *of.* 1586.

2. The falsehood of their p. lips SHELLEY. **Poi·sonous-ly** *adv.*, **-ness.**

Poi·sonwood. 1716. **a.** Name for certain poisonous species of *Rhus*, as *R. venenata*, and *R. Metopium.* **b.** *Sebastiana lucida* (N. O. *Euphorbiaceæ*), of the W. Indies.

‖**Poissarde** (pwasard). 1790. [F., fem. of †*poissard* pickpocket, rogue, f. *poix* pitch + -ARD (because things 'stick to his fingers'); also a fishwife (by association with *poisson*).] A Frenchwoman of the lowest class, *esp.* one of the Parisian market-women, who led riots during the first revolution. **b.** A French fishwife 1818.

Poitrel (poi·trĕl). Now *Hist.* and *arch.* 1489. [a. OF. *poitral*, orig. *peitral* PEITREL, now *poitrail*:—L. *pectorale* PECTORAL.] A piece of armour to protect the breast of a horse. **b.** A breast-plate; a stiff stomacher 1607.

‖**Poivrade** (pwavrad). 1699. [F., f. *poivre* pepper.] Pepper-sauce.

Poke (pōuk), *sb.*[1] Now chiefly *dial.* [ME. *poke* agrees in form with ONF. *poque*, *poke* = F. *poche.*] **1.** A bag; a small sack; applied usu. to a bag smaller than a *sack.* Now chiefly *dial.* **b.** A pocket worn on the person. *Obs.* or *arch.* 1600. **2.** A morbid bag-like swelling on the neck. †**a.** Goitre, also called *Bavarian p.* -1673. **b.** In sheep, a bag growing under the jaws, symptomatic of the rot; hence, the disease marked by this 1798. **3.** The stomach of a fish. *colloq.* or *dial.* 1773.

1. Phr. *To buy a pig in a p.*: see PIG *sb.*[1] b. Then he drew a diall from his poake SHAKS.

Poke, *sb.*[2] 1770. [perh. f. POKE *v.*[1]] **1.** A projecting brim or front of a woman's bonnet or hat. **2.** Short for POKE-BONNET 1815.

Poke, *sb.*[3] 1796. [f. POKE *v.*[1]] **1.** An act of poking; a thrust, push, nudge. **2.** A contrivance fastened upon cattle, pigs, etc., to prevent them from breaking through fences 1828. **3.** *U.S. colloq.* A lazy person; a dawdler 1860.

Poke, *sb.*[4] [N. Amer. Indian; in sense 1, app. = Narraganset *puck* smoke; in sense 2, app. shortened f. POCAN.] †**1.** Some plant smoked by the N. Amer. Indians, hence called *Indian tobacco* -1865. **2. a.** A name for American species of *Phytolacca*, esp. *P. decandra*, Virginian Poke, Poke-berry, Poke-weed. **b.** **Indian P.**, the Green Hellebore or Poke-root, *Veratrum viride.* 1731.

Comb.: **p.-berry**, the black berry of *Phytolacca decandra*, also the plant (2 a); **-root**, (*a*) the white hellebore of N. America, *Veratrum viride* (2 b), also its root; (*b*) the root of **poke-weed**, *Phytolacca* (2 a).

Poke (pōuk), *v.*[1] [ME. *poken* = late MDu., Du., LG. *pōken*, to poke, thrust; whence also OF. *poquer*, *pocher.*] **1.** *trans.* To thrust or push (anything) with one's hand or arm, the point of a stick, or the like. **b.** To shut *up* or confine in a poky place (*colloq.*) 1860. **c.** To make, find *out*, stir *up*, by poking 1646. **2.** *fig.* To urge, incite, stir up, excite, irritate. Now *rare* or *Obs.* ME. †**3.** To crimp (a ruff) with a poking-stick. Also *absol.* -1636. **4.** *intr.* or *absol.* To make a thrust or thrusts with a stick, the nose, etc. 1608. **5.** *trans.* To thrust forward (the finger, head, nose, etc.); *esp.* to thrust obtrusively 1700. **6.** *intr.* **a.** To poke one's nose, go prying into corners or looking about one; *fig.* to make curious investigation 1715. **b.** To potter 1796. **7.** trans. *To p. the head*, and absol. *to p.*; to carry the head thrust forward; to stoop 1811.

1. Aleyn the clerk..He poked John and seyde slepestow CHAUCER. *To p. through*, to thrust through (*with* a weapon). b. To be poked up in a town 1864. c. Children who p. a hole in a drum 1823. 4. To go and p. at the fire 1784. 5. *To p. fun* (*at*), to assail with jest, banter, or ridicule, esp. in a sly or indirect manner. 6. a. Having a lawyer to p. and pry into his accounts 1888. b. I should enjoy poking about a bit 1877. 7. 'A quarter's dancing' would be well bestowed on the young lady, as she certainly poked most terribly 1811.

Poke, *v.*[2] 1828. [f. POKE *sb.*[3] 2.] *trans.* To put a poke on (an ox, etc.).

Po·ke-bo·nnet. 1820. [See POKE *sb.*[2]] A bonnet with a projecting brim; *spec.* one of this shape worn in the early 19th c. **b.** Applied to the form of bonnet worn by Quakeresses, and later to that of Salvation Army women, etc.; hence, to the wearers of such 1848.

Po·ke-pu·dding. Also (*Sc.*) **pock-.** 1552. [f. POKE *sb.*[1] + PUDDING.] **1.** A pudding made in a bag. Now *Sc.* and *dial.* **2.** *Sc.* Applied contempt. to a corpulent or gluttonous person; a designation in Scotland for an Englishman. Now *joc.* 1730. **3.** A local name for the Long-tailed Titmouse 1856.

Poker (pōu·kəɹ), *sb.*[1] 1534. [f. POKE *v.*[1] + -ER.[1]] **1.** A stiff metal rod with a handle; used for poking or stirring a fire. **b.** *fig.* A person with a rigid stiff carriage or manner 1812. †**2.** = *Poking-stick*; see POKING *vbl. sb.* 2. -1606. **3.** *transf.* **a.** *joc.* The staff carried by a verger, bedel, etc. 1844. **b.** *Univ. slang.* One of the bedels at Oxford and Cambridge, who carry staves or maces ('pokers') before the Vice-Chancellor 1841. **4.** *Red-hot p.*, pop. name of a species of S. African liliaceous plants, bearing spikes of scarlet or yellow flowers; called also FLAME-*flower* 1884. **5.** The implement with which poker-work is done; hence, short for POKER-WORK. Also *attrib.* 1827. **6.** A person who pokes 1608.

Phr. *By the holy p.*, a humorous asseveration, of Irish origin and uncertain meaning.

Comb.: **p.-bearer**, a (University) bedel; **-drawing**, **-painting** = POKER-WORK; **-picture**, a picture made by poker-work. Hence **Po·kerish** *a.*[1] inclined to be 'stiff as a p.', esp. in manner.

Poker (pōu·kəɹ), *sb.*[2] Now *U.S. colloq.* 1598. [perh. from Norse; corresp. to Da. *pokker*, Swed. *pocker* the devil. Cf. also PUCK.] A hobgoblin, bugbear, demon. *Old P.*, the devil.

As if old p. was coming to take them away H. WALPOLE. Hence **Po·kerish** *a.*[2] (*U.S. colloq.*) ghostly, uncanny.

Poker (pōu·kəɹ), *sb.*[3] Chiefly *U.S.* 1848. [Origin obsc.] An American card game, a variety of BRAG, played by two or more persons, each of whom, if not bluffed into declaring his hand, bets on the value of it, the player with the highest combination of cards winning the pool.

Comb.: **p.-face**, an inscrutable face, not easily betraying emotion; hence applied *colloq.* to a person with such a face; **p.-faced**, *a.*

Poker, *sb.*[4], a kind of duck; see POCHARD.

Poker (pōu·kəɹ), *v.* 1787. [f. POKER *sb.*[1]] **1.** *trans.* **a.** To poke, stir, or strike with a poker. **b.** *P. up*: to make as stiff as a poker. *nonce-uses.* **2.** To draw in or adorn with poker-work 1897.

Po·ker-work. 1813. [f. POKER *sb.*[1] + WORK *sb.*] Ornamental work produced by burning a design on the surface of white wood, leather, etc. with a heated pointed implement.

Poking (pōu·kiŋ), *vbl. sb.* 1582. [f. POKE *v.*[1] + -ING[1].] 1. The action of POKE *v.* Also *attrib.* 2. **Po·king-stick** (-iron). A rod used for stiffening the plaits of ruffs; orig. of wood or bone, later of steel so as to be applied hot. *Hist.* 1592.

2. Pins, and poaking-stickes of steele SHAKS.

Poking (pōu·kiŋ), *ppl. a.* 1769. [f. POKE *v.*[1] + -ING[2].] 1. Projecting, thrust forward; esp. of the head 1799. 2. = POKY *a.*[1] 1 a, b. 1769.

2. Some p. little country-curacy KINGSLEY.

Poky (pōu·ki), *a.*[1] 1849. [f. POKE *v.*[1] + -Y[1].] 1. a. Of a person or his work: Pottering, peddling; hence petty, mean 1856. b. Of a place: Petty in size or accommodation; confined, mean, shabby 1849. c. Of dress, etc.: Shabby, dowdy 1854. 2. *Cricket.* Inclined to 'poke' in batting 1891.

Poky, *a.*[2] and *sb. rare.* 1861. [f. POKE *sb.*[2] + -Y[1].] In full *p. bonnet* = POKE-BONNET.

‖ **Polacca**[1] (polæ·kă. ‖polα·kka). 1813. [It., orig. adj. fem. of *polacco* POLISH, ad. G. *Polack*, a. Pol. *Polak* a Pole.] A Polish dance, a polonaise; also, the music for it.

Polack (pōu·lăk), *sb.* (*a.*) 1599. [a. Pol. *Polak* a Pole.] A Pole. B. *adj.* Polish. CARLYLE.

Polacre (polā·kəɹ), **polacca**[2] (polæ·kă). 1625. [a. F. *polacre, polaque.* Origin obsc.] A three-masted merchant vessel of the Mediterranean, usu. without either top-mast or top-gallant-mast. Also *attrib.*

Poland (pōu·lănd). 1564. [f. POLE *sb.*[4] + LAND *sb.*] A country of E. Europe; hence short for *P. oats* or *wheat, P. fowl.*

Comb.: **P. fowl,** one of a breed of domestic fowls, having black plumage and a white topknot; **P. wheat,** white cone wheat (*Triticum polonicum*). Hence **Po·lander,** a Pole (*obs.*); also a Poland fowl.

Polar (pōu·lăɹ), *a.* (*sb.*) 1551. [ad. med.L. *polaris*, f. L. *polus* POLE *sb.*[2]; see -AR[1].] 1. *Astron.* and *Geog.* Of or pertaining to the poles of the celestial sphere or of the earth; situated near or connected with either pole. 2. *Magn.* Having polarity; of or pertaining to a magnetic pole or poles (see POLE *sb.*[2] 5); magnetic 1692. 3. *Electr.* Pertaining to the poles of a voltaic battery; having positive and negative electricity 1836. 4. *Physics.* a. Of forces: Acting in two opposite directions. (Also in *fig.* uses.) 1809. b. Of molecules: Regularly or symmetrically arranged in a definite direction (as though under the action of a magnetic force) 1850. 5. *Biol.* Of or pertaining to the poles of a nerve-cell, an ovum, etc. (See POLE *sb.*[2] 7.) 1878. 6. *Geom.* Relating or referred to a pole (see POLE *sb.*[2] 8); *spec.* Reciprocal to a pole; of the nature of a polar (see B.) 1816. 7. *fig.* a. Analogous to the pole of the earth, or to the pole-star; of or pertaining to a central or directive principle 1799. b. Directly opposite in character, action, or tendency 1832.

1. P. Winds MILT. Cold as P. Ice 1711. *P. bear*, the white bear, *Ursus maritimus. P. circle*, each of the circles parallel to the equator at the distance of 23° 28′ from either pole, bounding the Arctic and Antarctic zones. *P. dial*, a dial having its gnomon in the plane of the earth's axis. *P. distance*, the angular distance of any point on a sphere from the nearer pole; the complement of declination or latitude. *P. hare*, the white hare, *Lepus arcticus. P. lights*, the aurora borealis or australis. *P. projection*: see PROJECTION. *P. star*, the POLE-STAR; also *fig.* = guiding-star, guide, cynosure. 6. *P. co-ordinates*: see CO-ORDINATE *sb.* 2. *P. equation*, an equation in p. co-ordinates. 7. a. A king over men; whose movements were p., and carried..those of the world along with them CARLYLE.

B. *sb. Geom.* A curve related in a particular way to a given curve and a fixed point called the pole; in conic sections, the straight line joining the points at which tangents from the fixed point touch the curve 1848.

Polari- (polæ·ri), comb. form. of med.L. *polaris* polar.

†**Po·larily,** *adv.* [f. POLARY *a.* + -LY[2].] Magnetically. SIR T. BROWNE.

Polarimeter (pōulări·mĭtəɹ). 1864. [f. med. L. *polaris* POLAR (with ref. to POLARIZATION) + -METER.] A form of polariscope for measuring the amount of rotation of the plane of polarization, or the amount of polarized light in a beam. Hence **Polarime·tric** *a.* **Polari·metry,** the art or process of measuring or analysing the polarization of light.

‖ **Polaris** (polēə·ris). *Astron.* Short for med.L. *stella polaris* = Polar star, POLE-STAR.

Polariscope (polæ·riskoup). 1842. [f. med. L. *polaris* POLAR + -SCOPE.] An instrument for showing the polarization of light, or viewing objects in polarized light. Also *attrib.* Hence **Polarisco·pic** *a.* of or pertaining to, made, obtained, or viewed by, a p. **Polari·scopy,** the art of using a p.

Polarity (polæ·rĭti). 1646. [f. POLAR *a.* + -ITY.] 1. *Magnetism.* The quality or property possessed by certain bodies, as a lodestone or magnetized bar, of turning (when free to move) so as to point with their two extremities to the two (magnetic) poles of the earth; the quality of being polar, or possessing magnetic poles. 2. Hence *gen.* A property of matter or force, analogous or compared to that of a magnet or magnetism. a. The disposition of a body or an elementary molecule to place its mathematical axis in a particular direction 1674. b. The possession of two points called poles having contrary qualities or tendencies 1818. c. Tendency to develop in two opposite directions in space, time, serial arrangement, etc. 1848. 3. *Electr.* The relation of a body to the poles or electrodes of an electric circuit; the electrical condition of a body as positive or negative 1849. 4. *Optics.* The quality of light which admits of its polarization; hence, the condition of being polarized. (An inaccurate use.) 1861. 5. *fig.* a. (from 1.) Direction (of thought, feeling) towards a single point; tendency or trend in a certain direction 1767. b. (from 2 b.) Possession or exhibition of two opposite or contrasted aspects, principles, or tendencies 1862.

2. b. P., or action and reaction, we meet in every part of nature EMERSON. 5. a. This p. of mind, this intellectual magnetism towards universal truth, has always been a characteristic of the greatest minds 1834.

Polarization (pōulărəizē·ʃən). 1812. [In sense 1, a. F. *polarisation.* In later uses, n. of action from the vb.] I. A modification of the condition of light or radiant heat, whereby the ray exhibits different properties on different sides, so that opposite sides are alike, while the maximum difference is between two sides at right angles to each other; the production of this condition, the action of polarizing.

Angle of p. = *polarizing angle* (POLARIZING *vbl. sb.*). *Plane of p.*, the plane which contains the incident ray and the reflected or refracted ray which is polarized.

II. 1. *Electr.* and *Magn.* a. See POLARIZE *v.* 2. 1866. b. In voltaic electricity, the production of an electromotive force at the electrodes, due to the presence of the products of electrolytic decomposition of the fluid between them, and acting in an opposite direction to the original current, thus producing an apparent increase of the resistance 1839. 2. The arrangement of molecules, etc., in a definite direction 1846.

Polarize (pōu·lărəiz), *v.* 1811. [In sense 1, a. F. *polariser*, f. F. *pôle* POLE *sb.*[2] In other senses, f. POLAR + -IZE.] 1. *Optics.* (*trans.*) To cause the vibrations of light (radiant heat, etc.) to be modified in a particular way, so that the ray exhibits different properties on different sides, opposite sides being alike, and those at right angles to each other showing the maximum of difference. 2. *Magn.* and *Electr.* To give polarity to; to give opposite magnetic properties to opposite ends of (a bar, coil, etc. of iron, etc.). Also *intr.* To acquire polarity. 1838. b. In voltaic electricity: see POLARIZATION 2 b. 1856. 3. *fig.* To give an arbitrary direction, or a special meaning or application, to 1860. b. To give unity of direction to 1868. Hence **Po·larizable** *a.* capable of being polarized.

Polarizer (pōu·lărəizəɹ). 1854. [f. prec. + -ER[1].] One who or that which polarizes; *spec.* that plate or prism in a polariscope which polarizes the incident ray of light (opp. to *analyser*).

Polarizing (pōu·lărəiziŋ), *vbl. sb.* 1812. [f. as prec. + -ING[1].] The action of POLARIZE *v.*

attrib. In *p. angle* (Optics), that angle of incidence (differing for different substances) at which the maximum polarization of the incident light takes place.

Polarly (pōu·lăɹli), *adv.* 1830. [f. POLAR *a.* + -LY[2].] In a polar direction, manner, or degree; with reference to poles.

†**Po·lary,** *a.* 1559. [ad. med.L. *polaris*, f. L. *polus* POLE *sb.*[2]; see -ARY[2].] 1. = POLAR *a.* 1. -1658. 2. POLAR *a.* 2. -1665.

‖ **Polatouche** (pǫlătūʃ). 1827. [F., ad. Russ. *poletuchiĭ* flying.] *Zool.* The small flying squirrel of Europe and N. Asia, *Sciuropterus volans.*

Poldavy (pǫldē¹·vi), **poldavis** (pǫldē¹·vis). Now *rare.* 1481. [app. f. *Poldavide*, on the coast of Brittany.] A coarse canvas or sacking, orig. woven in Brittany, and formerly much used for sailcloth. Also *attrib.*

Polder (pōu·ldəɹ). 1604. [a. Du. *polder.*] A piece of low-lying land reclaimed from the sea, a lake, or a river, from which it is protected by dikes. Also *attrib.*

Pole (pōul), *sb.*[1] [OE. *pál*, ad. L. *palus* stake, prop.] 1. orig., A stake, without ref. to length or thickness; now, a long, slender, and more or less cylindrical piece of wood (rarely metal); used as a support for a tent, hops or other climbing plants, telegraph or telephone wires, etc., for scaffolding, and for other purposes. 2. *spec.* a. A long tapering wooden shaft fitted to the fore-carriage of a vehicle and attached to the yokes or collars of the draught-animals 1619. b. Used as a tradesman's sign 1566. c. *Naut.* A ship's mast. Also, the upper end of a mast, rising above the rigging. 1669. 3. A pole (in sense 1) of definite length used as a measure; hence, a lineal measure; in statutory measure, = $5\frac{1}{2}$ yards; a PERCH, a ROD 1502. b. As a measure of area: A square rod or perch; $30\frac{1}{4}$ square yards 1637.

1. Slang phr. *Up the p.*, in great difficulties; crazy, 'dotty'; under the influence of drink. 2. b. By a statute still in force, the barbers and surgeons were each to use a p. 1797. c. Phr. *With* or *under* (*bare*) *poles*, with no sail set · with furled sails.

attrib. and *Comb.*: **p.-bean,** any climbing bean; **-cap,** the insulating cap of a telegraph pole; †**-clipt** *a.*, hedged in by poles; **-hedge** = ESPALIER 1; **-horse,** a horse harnessed alongside of the p., a wheeler; **-lathe,** a lathe in which the work is turned by a cord passing round it, and fastened at one end to the end of an elastic p., and at the other to a treadle; **-mast,** a mast formed of a single spar; so **-masted** *a.*; **-torpedo,** a torpedo carried on the end of a p., projecting from the bows of a vessel, a spar-torpedo; **-trap,** a circular steel trap set on the top of a post.

Pole, *sb.*[2] late ME. [ad. L. *polus* end of an axis, pole, the sky, a. Gr. πόλος pivot, axis, etc.] 1. Each of the two points in the celestial sphere (*north p.* and *south p.*) about which as fixed points the stars seem to revolve; being the points at which the earth's axis produced meets the celestial sphere. Sometimes also = POLE-STAR. 2. Each of the extremities (north and south) of the axis of the earth; also of any rotating spherical or spheroidal body (*p. of revolution*) 1551. 3. Geom. *P. of a circle of the sphere*: each of the two points on the surface of the sphere, in which the axis of that circle cuts the surface; as the poles of the ecliptic on the celestial sphere. late ME. b. Hence in *Cryst.*, the point at which a straight line perpendicular to a face or plane of a crystal meets the (ideal) sphere of projection 1878. 4. *poet.* The sky, the heavens. Also *pl. arch.* or *Obs.* 1572. 5. *Magn.* Each of the two opposite points or regions on the surface of a magnet at which the magnetic forces are manifested 1574. 6. *Electr.* Each of the two terminal points (positive and negative) of an electric cell, battery, or machine 1802. 7. *Biol.* Each extremity of the main axis of any organ of more or less spherical or oval form 1834. 8. *Geom.* a. A fixed point to which other points, lines, etc., are referred; as, the origin of polar co-ordinates; the point of which a curve is a polar. b. The point from which a pencil of lines diverges. 1849. 9. *fig.* Each of two opposed or complementary principles to which the parts of a system or group of phenomena, ideas, etc., are referable 1471.

2. Oh sleep! it is a gentle thing, Beloved from p. to p. COLERIDGE. We're as far apart as the Poles 1880. 4. Stars unnumber'd gild the glowing p. POPE. 5. *Magnetic p.*, each of the two points in the polar regions of the earth where the dipping needle takes a vertical position. 9. The..Nominalists and Realists each maintained opposite poles of the same truth COLERIDGE.

attrib. and *Comb.*, as **p.-cell** (sense 6); **-changer,** a switch or key for reversing the direction of an electric current; -**piece**, a mass of iron forming the end of an electromagnet, through which the lines of magnetic force are concentrated and directed. Hence **Po·leward** *adv.* towards or in the direction of the (north or south) p.; *adj.* directed or tending towards the p. **Po·lewards** *adv.*

Pole (pōul), *sb.*³ *rare.* 1668. [a. F. *pole.*] A species of deep-water flounder, *Pleuronectes* (*Glyptocephalus*) *cynoglossus.* Also *p.-dab, -flounder, -fluke.*

Pole, *sb.*⁴ 1533. [a. G. *Pole,* sing. of *Polen,* a. Polish *Poljane* lit. field-dwellers, f. *pole* field.] †1. Poland –1671. 2. A native of Poland 1656. b. A Poland fowl 1885.

Pole, *v.* 1573. [f. POLE *sb.*¹] 1. *trans.* To furnish with poles. 2. To attach (a horse) to the carriage-pole 1861. 3. To push, poke, or strike with a pole; to stir *up,* push *off,* with a pole 1753. b. To strike or pierce with a carriage pole 1728. 4. To propel (a boat or raft) with a pole. Also *intr.* or *absol.* 1774. 5. To stir (molten metal or glass) with a pole of green wood, to reduce the proportion of oxygen in the mass 1842.

4. *intr.* We poled and paddled up the river 1895.

-pole, comb. element from Gr. -πώλης a seller, dealer, f. πωλεῖν to sell, used rarely to designate a merchant, as in BIBLIOPOLE, etc.

Pole-axe, poleaxe (pōu·l,æks), *sb.* [ME. *pollax, polax,* f. *pol* POLL *sb.*¹ + AXE. Written later *pole-axe,* as if an axe upon a *pole* or long handle.] 1. A kind of axe formerly used as a weapon of war, a battle-axe; also, a short-handled form of this used later in naval warfare for boarding, resisting boarders, cutting ropes, etc. 2. A halbert or the like carried by the bodyguard of a king or great personage 1562. 3. An axe with a hammer at the back, used to fell or stun animals; a butcher's axe 1719. Hence **Po·leaxe** *v. trans.* to fell with a p.

Polecat, pole-cat (pōu·lkæt). [ME. *polcat, pulcatt,* the first element being perh. OF. *pole, poule* fowl, the second being CAT *sb.*¹] 1. A small dark-brown carnivorous quadruped, *Putorius fœtidus,* of the *Mustelidæ* or Weasel family, a native of Europe. Called also *fitchet, fitchew, foumart.* b. Applied to other species of *Putorius*; also to other *Mustelidæ,* esp. in *U.S.* the skunks 1688. 2. *fig.* Applied contempt. to a vile person; a courtesan, a prostitute 1598. 3. *attrib.* 1596.

Poleman (pōu·lmæ̆n). 1838. [f. POLE *sb.*¹ + MAN.] A man who uses, carries, or fights with a pole. b. At the Montem at Eton, a name for lower boys, who followed the Oppidans of the fifth form with long white poles 1844.

Polemarch (pǫ·lǐmāɹk). 1656. [ad. Gr. πολέμαρχος, f. πόλεμος war + -αρχος ruling, ruler.] *Anc. Hist.* An officer in ancient Greece, orig., a military commander-in-chief, but having also civil functions varying according to date and locality.

Polemic (pǒle·mik), *a.* and *sb.* 1638. [ad. Gr. πολεμικός, f. πόλεμος war.] A. *adj.* Of or pertaining to controversy; controversial, disputatious 1641.

Senseless questions of p. theology 1866.

B *sb.* 1. A controversial argument or discussion; aggressive controversy; in *pl.* the practice of this, esp. as a method of conducting theological controversy; opp. to *irenics* 1638. 2. A controversialist: esp. in theology 1680.

1. Religious polemics..have seldom formed a part of my studies 1800. 2. The divines of James I.'s court were all casuists and polemics 1886. So **Pole·mical** *a.* warlike, military; also = POLEMIC *a.*; *sb.* a polemical discussion, a controversy (*rare*); **-ly** *adv.* **Pole·micist** (-sist) a writer of polemics.

Polemist (pǫ·lǐmist). 1825. [ad. Gr. πολεμιστής.] = POLEMIC *sb.* 2.

Po·lemize, *v.* 1828. [ad. Gr. πολεμίζειν.] *intr.* To argue polemically; to carry on a controversy.

‖**Polenta** (pole·ntă). OE. [L.; in later use, repr. It. *polenta.*] †a. Pearl-barley. †b. A kind of barley meal. c. Porridge made from steeped and parched barley, or, later, of meal of chestnuts, maize flour, etc.; much used in Italy.

Poler (pōu·ləɹ). 1688. [f. POLE *sb.*¹ or *v.* + -ER¹.] †1. A stirring pole; used in tanning –1775. 2. One who sets up hop-poles 1848. 3. The horse harnessed alongside the pole; a wheeler 1881. 4. One who propels a barge, boat, or canoe by means of a pole 1895.

Pole star (pōu·lstāːɹ). 1555. [f. POLE *sb.*² + STAR *sb.*] 1. The star α *Ursæ Minoris,* at present about 1¼° distant from the northern pole of the heavens; also called *Polar star* and *Polaris.* 2. *fig.* A guide or director, a lodestar, a governing principle; a cynosure 1604.

Polewig (pōu·lwig). *local.* 1880. [See POLLIWOG.] 1. A tadpole 1882. 2. A small Thames fish, the Spotted or Freckled Goby 1880.

Poley, polley (pōu·li), *a.* *Eng. dial.* and *Austral.* 1844. [f. POLL *sb.*⁴ + -Y¹.] Hornless, polled.

Police (pǒlī·s), *sb.* 1530. [a. F. *police,* ad. med.L. *polītia* for earlier *polītia*; see POLITY, POLICY, and -ICE. Formerly pronounced (pǫ·lis), as it is still in Scotland and Ireland.] †I. = POLICY *sb.*¹ I. 3, 4, 4 b. –1768. II. †1. Civil organization; civilization –1845. 2. The regulation, discipline, and control of a community; civil administration; enforcement of law; public order 1716. See N.E.D. for historical details. †b. In commercial legislation, Public regulation or control of a trade; an economic policy –1866. c. The keeping clean of a camp or garrison; the condition of a camp or garrison in respect of cleanliness. *U.S.* 1893. 3. The department of government which is concerned with the maintenance of public order and safety and the enforcement of the law 1730. 4. The civil force to which is entrusted the duty of maintaining public order, enforcing regulations for the prevention and punishment of breaches of the law, and detecting crime; construed as *pl.* the members of a police force; the constabulary of a locality 1800. b. *transf.* Any body of men, officially employed to keep order, enforce regulations, or maintain a political or ecclesiastical system 1837.

1. A barbarous nation [the Turks], with a barbarous neglect of p., fatal to the human race BURKE. 2. The p. of the seas was imperfectly kept 1850. 3. The p. of Glasgow consists of three bodies; the magistrates with the town council, the merchants house, and the trades house 1774. 4. The entire success of the P. in London. It is impossible to see anything more respectable than they are. WELLINGTON. *Marine P.,* the force instituted *c* 1798 to protect the merchant shipping on the Thames in the Port of London. b. The railway p. 1837.

attrib. and *Comb.*: **p. captain,** a subordinate officer in the police force in large cities of U.S.; **magistrate,** a stipendiary magistrate who presides in a p. court; **p. officer,** a member of a p. force, a constable; †-**runner,** a p. officer of the lowest rank.

Police (pǒlī·s), *v.* 1589. [Partly a. F. *policer,* f. †*policie, police*; partly f. POLICE *sb.*] †1. *trans.* To keep in (civil) order, organize, regulate (a state or country). Chiefly in *pass.* –1791. b. To make or keep clean (a camp). *U.S.* 1862. 2. To control, regulate, or keep in order by means of the police, or a similar force 1841. b. To furnish, provide, or guard with a police force, or some similar force 1858. c. *fig.* To keep in order, administer, control 1886.

2. The navy which polices the seas 1891. b. They are building gunboats to p. their coasts 1868.

Poli·ce cou·rt. 1823. A court of summary jurisdiction for the trial or investigation of charges preferred by the police. (At first called POLICE OFFICE.) Also *attrib.*

Policed (pǒlī·st), *ppl. a.* 1591. [f. POLICE *v.* or *sb.* + -ED; orig. (pǫ·list).] †1. Politically organized, regulated, or ordered; governed, disciplined –1858. 2. Provided with or guarded by a police force 1897.

Policeman (pǒlī·smæ̆n). 1829. A member of the police force; a paid constable. Also *fig.* b. A soldier-ant 1877. So **Poli·cewo:man,** a woman member of the police force.

Poli·ce O·ffice. 1798. The head-quarters of the police force in a city or town, at which the police business is transacted.

These formerly included a court-room in which offenders were tried, and a place of detention; hence the name was formerly regularly applied to what is now called a POLICE COURT.

Poli·ce sta·tion. 1858. The office or head-quarters of a local police force, or of a police district.

Policy (pǫ·lǐsi), *sb.*¹ [In Branch I, late ME. *policie,* a. OF. *policie,* ad. L. *politia,* a. Gr. πολιτεία citizenship, government, etc., f. πολίτης, f. πόλις city, state. (See POLICE *sb.*) Branch II is due to the association of this Græco-L. word with L. *politus* polished, refined.] I. 1. A constitution, polity. Now *rare* or *Obs.* †b. An organized state, a commonwealth –1558. †2. Government, administration; political science –1796. 3. Political sagacity; statecraft; diplomacy; in bad sense, political cunning. late ME. 4. In ref. to conduct or action generally: Prudent, expedient, or advantageous procedure; prudent or politic course of action; as a quality of the agent: sagacity, shrewdness, artfulness; in bad sense, cunning, craftiness. late ME. †b. A device, expedient, contrivance; a crafty device, stratagem, trick –1849. 5. A course of action adopted and pursued by a government, party, ruler, statesman, etc.; any course of action adopted as advantageous or expedient. (The chief living sense.) late ME.

2. Turne him to any Cause of Pollicy The Gordian Knot of it he will vnloose SHAKS. *Court of P.,* the Legislative Council in British Guiana. 3. In this.. he was actuated by p. rather than sentiment FREEMAN. 4. Our grosse conceipts, who think honestie the best policie 1599. 5. Thys was the crafty polycye of the clergye 1544. Edward's foreign p. 1861.

II. Sc. senses influenced by L. *politus* polished, etc. †a. The improvement or embellishment of an estate, building, town, etc. –1555. †b. The improvements, etc., so made; property created by human skill and labour –1594. c. The (enclosed, planted, and partly embellished) park or demesne land lying around a country seat or gentleman's house 1775.

Policy (pǫ·lǐsi), *sb.*² 1565. [ad. F. *police* bill of lading, contract of insurance, etc., ad. Pr. *polissa,* prob. :—med.L. *apo·dissa, apo·dixa,* receipt or security for money paid, altered from L. *apodixis,* a. Gr. ἀπόδειξις a making known, evidence, proof.] 1. More fully *p. of assurance* or *insurance p.*: A document containing an undertaking, in consideration of a *premium* or *premiums,* to pay a specified amount or part thereof in the event of a specified contingency. b. A conditional promissory note, depending on the result of a wager 1623. c. A form of gambling in which bets are made on numbers to be drawn in a lottery. *U.S.* 1890. †2. [= It. *polizza* ticket.] A voting-paper; a voucher, warrant –1675.

1. *Floating p.,* a p. in which there is no limitation of the risk to a particular ship, as where goods 'on ship or ships' are insured for the same voyage. *Open p.,* one in which the value of the subject insured is left to be estimated in case of loss. *Wager* or *wagering p.,* a p. of insurance taken out where the insured has no real interest in the thing insured. now declared illegal as a species of gambling.

Comb.: **p.-shop,** *U.S.* a place for gambling by betting on the drawing of certain numbers in a lottery.

†**Po·licy,** *v.* 1565. [a. obs. F. *policier* to administer. f. obs. F. *policie*; see POLICY *sb.*¹, POLICE *v.*] = POLICE *v.* 1. –1824. Hence †**Po·licied** *ppl. a.* civilly organized.

Poling (pōu·liŋ), *vbl. sb.* 1573. [f. POLE *v.* + -ING¹.] 1. The action of POLE *v.,* in various senses. 2. *concr.* Poles collectively, as used for poling hops, or for lining the sides of a tunnel 1842.

‖**Poliomyelitis** (pǫ:lio,məi,ělǝi·tis). 1880. [mod.L., f. Gr. πολιός grey + μυελός marrow + -ITIS.] *Path.* Inflammation of the grey matter of the spinal cord.

-polis, repr. Gr. πόλις city, as in METROPOLIS, etc.; occas. used (in the form *-opolis*) to form nicknames of cities or towns, e.g. COTTONOPOLIS (Manchester), *Porkopolis* (Chicago).

Polish (pǫ·liʃ), *sb.* 1597. [f. POLISH *v.*] 1. The act of polishing or condition of being polished; smoothness and usu. glossiness of surface produced by friction 1704. 2. *fig.* Refinement 1597. 3. A substance used to produce smoothness or glossiness on any surface, as FRENCH P., etc. 1819.

1. Another Prism of clearer Glass and better P NEWTON. 2. This Roman p., and this smooth behaviour ADDISON.

Polish (pōu·liʃ), *a.* 1704. [f. POLE *sb.*⁴ + -ISH¹.] Of or pertaining to Poland or its inhabitants.

Polish (pǫ·liʃ), *v.* [ME. *polis-, -iss-, -issh-,* a. F. *poliss-,* lengthened stem of *polir* :—L.

polire to polish; see -ISH [2].] 1. *trans.* To make smooth and (usu.) glossy by friction. **b.** *intr.* for *pass.* †(*a*) To become bright. (*b*) To become smooth, take a smooth and (usu.) glossy surface. late ME. **2.** *fig. trans.* To free from roughness, rudeness, or coarseness; to make more elegant or cultured; to refine ME. **b.** *intr.* for *pass.* To become refined 1727. **3.** *trans.* To bring to a finished or complete state; to deck out, adorn. Const. *out, up.* 1581. **4.** *To p. off*: to finish off quickly; to do for or get rid of summarily. *colloq.* (orig. *Pugilistic slang*). 1829.

1. Hard Wood they p. with Bees-wax 1703. **b.** A kind of steel..which would p. almost as..bright as silver BACON. 2. Arts that p. Life MILT. Hence **Po·lishable** *a.* capable of being polished. **Po·lished-ly** *adv.*, **-ness.**

Polisher (pǫ·lisəɹ). ME. [f. prec. + -ER [1].] One who, or that which, polishes, *lit.* or *fig.*

Polishing (pǫ·lisiŋ), *vbl. sb.* 1530. [f. as prec. + -ING [1].] The action of POLISH *v.*; the fact of being polished.

attrib. in names of tools, appliances, etc., used in producing a polish; as *p.-block, -iron, -paste, -powder, -stick, -wheel*; **p.-mill,** a lap of metal or other material used by lapidaries in polishing gems (Knight); **-slate,** (*a*) a grey or yellow slate found in the coal-measures of Bohemia, etc., used for polishing; (*b*) a kind of whetstone; **-snake,** a kind of serpentine formerly used for polishing lithographic stones.

Polite (pŏləi·t), *a.* 1450. [ad. L. *politus* polished, prop. pa. pple. of *polire* to smooth, polish.] †1. *lit.* Smoothed, polished, burnished –1737. †**b.** Cleansed, trim, orderly –1703. **2.** *transf.* **a.** Of the arts, literature, etc.: Polished, refined, elegant; correct, scholarly. (Now only in certain collocations.) 1501. **b.** Of persons: Polished, refined, cultivated, well-bred, modish 1629. **c.** Of refined manners; courteous, mannerly, urbane. (The chief current use.) 1762.

1. P. Bodies, as Looking-Glasses 1678. 2. **a.** P. Learning BENTLEY. A p. education 1786. **b.** Whatever the French and learned may think MACAULAY. **c.** The French are the politest enemies in the world 1772. Hence **Poli·te·ly** *adv.*, **-ness.**

‖ **Politesse** (polite·s). 1717. [F., ad. It. *politezza*, f. *polito* polite.] Politeness; now usu. *depreciatory.*

Politic (pǫ·litik), *a.* and *sb.* late ME. [a. F. *politique*, ad L. *politicus*, a. Gr. πολιτικός, f. πολίτης citizen (f. πόλις); see -IC.] **A.** *adj.* †1. = POLITICAL *a.* 1 (by which it is now superseded) –1756. **b.** Pertaining to a constitutional state, as dist. from a despotism; constitutional (*rare*) 1449. **2.** Characterized by policy; (of persons) sagacious, prudent, shrewd; (of actions or things) judicious, expedient, skilfully contrived. late ME. **b.** In a sinister sense: Scheming, crafty, cunning; diplomatic, artfully contriving or contrived 1580.

1. †*P. body = body p.*: see BODY *sb.* IV. 1. 2. Enrich'd With politike graue Counsell SHAKS. A prudent and Politick Captain 1686. To learn of an enemy has always been accounted politick JOHNSON. **b.** These being the craftiest and politiquest sort of knaves 1667.

B. *sb.* †1. A politician –1738. †**b.** An indifferentist in matters of religion, a worldly-wise man; see POLITIQUE –1633. †**2.** Policy; politics –1715. **3.** *pl. Politics.* The science and art of government; the science dealing with the form, organization, and administration of a state or part of one, and with the regulation of its relations with other states (hence *imperial, national, domestic, municipal, parochial, foreign politics*, etc.). Also †*the politics*, that branch of moral philosophy dealing with the state or social organism as a whole. 1529. **b.** *The Politics*: name of Aristotle's treatise on political science, τὰ πολιτικά 1651. †**c.** Political actions or practice; policy –1741. **d.** Political affairs or business; political life 1693. **e.** The political principles, opinions, or sympathies *of* a person or party 1769. **f.** *fig.* Conduct of private affairs; politic management, scheming, planning 1693.

1. Amongst states men and politikes BACON. **b.** Worldlings, and Depraued Politickes, who are apt to contemne Holy Things BACON. 2. This did not suit with Popish P. BENTLEY. 3. Machiavelli..founded the science of politics for the modern world 1883. **c.** Confound their politicks, Frustrate their knavish tricks *God save the King.* **d.** She now agrees with me, that Politicks is not the Business of a Woman 1714. **e.** Most men's politics sit much too loosely about them *Junius Lett.* **f.** A lecture on prudence, and matrimonial politics FIELDING. Phr. *Not practical politics.* Hence **Po·liticly** *adv.*, in a politic manner; with policy; shrewdly; artfully 1477.

Political (pŏli·tikăl), *a.* (*sb.*) 1551. [f. L. *politicus*, a. Gr. πολιτικός (see prec.) + -AL.] **A.** *adj.* 1. Of, belonging or pertaining to, the state, its government and policy; public, civil; of or pertaining to the science or art of politics. **b.** Of persons: Engaged in civil administration; *spec.* in India, having, as a government official, the function of advising the ruler of a native state on political matters, as *p. agent, resident.* 1849. **2.** Having an organized government or polity. †Said also of bees, ants, etc. 1657. **3.** Concerned or dealing with politics or the science of government 1646. **4.** Belonging to or taking a side in politics; in a bad sense, partisan, factious 1769. †**5.** = POLITIC A. 2. –1817.

1. The true p. spirit; the faculty of nation-making GLADSTONE. 3. The highest positions in p. life 1885. 4. The malice of p. writers *Junius Lett.*

Phrases. *P. economy*: see ECONOMY 2. *P. geography*, that part of geography which deals with the boundaries, divisions, and possessions of states. *P. prisoner*, a person imprisoned for a p. offence. *P. verse* [Gr. πολιτικός popular], in Byzantine and mod. Gr. literature, verse composed by accent, not quantity, with an accent on the last syllable but one.

B. *sb.* (the adj. used ellipt.) 1. **a.** = Political agent, officer, resident; see above, 1 b. 1848. **b.** = *political prisoner*; see above 1888. †**2.** *pl.* Political matters, politics –1734. Hence **Poli·tically** *adv.* 1588.

Politicaster (pǫli·tikæstəɹ). *rare.* 1641. [ad. It. (or Sp.) *politicastro*; see POLITIC B. and -ASTER.] A petty, feeble, or contemptible politician.

Politician (pǫliti·ʃăn). 1588. [f. as POLITIC + -IAN.] †1. A politic person; *esp.* a crafty intriguer –1764. **2.** One versed in the theory of government or the art of governing; one practically engaged in conducting the business of the state; a statesman 1589. **b.** One interested in politics; one who engages in party politics, esp. as a profession; also (esp. in *U.S.*) in a sinister sense, one who lives by politics as a trade 1628. †**3.** = POLITIQUE –1681. **4.** *attrib.* 1638.

1. 1 *Hen. IV*, I. iii. 241. 2. That felicity Politisians search after, as being the end of civil life 1634. **b.** That insidious and crafty animal, vulgarly called a statesman or p. ADAM SMITH.

Politicize (pǫli·tisəiz), *v.* 1758. [f. as POLITIC + -IZE.] 1. *intr.* To act the politician; to engage in or talk politics. **2.** *trans.* To give a political character to 1846.

Poli·tico-, comb. form of Gr. πολιτικός civil, political, denoting **a.** 'politically, as applied to politics', as *p.-ethical, -geographical*, etc.; **p.-economical,** pertaining to political economy; **b.** 'political and ...' as *p.-commercial, -military, -theological*, etc.; **p.-religious,** pertaining to politics as influenced by or dependent on religion; at once political and religious; also used to form sbs., as **poli:ticopho·bia,** a horror of politics.

‖ **Politique** (politī·k). 1609. [F., prop. adj. 'political'.] One of an opportunist and moderate party, which arose in France *c* 1573, during the Huguenot wars, and regarded peace and political reform as more urgent than the decision by arms of the religious quarrel; also, a sympathizer with this party elsewhere, and opprobriously, an indifferentist, a temporizer.

Politize (pǫ·litəiz), *v. rare.* 1598. [f. POLITY + -IZE.] †1. **a.** *trans.* To deal with or treat (a matter) politicly, diplomatically, or craftily. **b.** *intr.* To deal politicly or diplomatically. –1641. **2.** †**a.** To have political relations. **b.** To deal in politics (*rare*). 1623.

†**Po·liture.** 1592. [a. obs. F. *politure* = It. *politura*, L. *politura* polishing, f. *polit-, polire*; see -URE.] Polishing; polish, smoothness –1776. **b.** Elegance of form; polish of style, manners, or habits; refinement –1720.

Polity (pǫ·liti). 1538. [a. obs. F. *politie*, ad. L. *politia*; see POLICY *sb.*[1]] 1. Civil order. **b.** Administration of a state; civil government 1715. **2. a.** A particular form of political organization 1597. **b.** An organized society; a state 1650. †**3.** = POLICY *sb.*[1] I. 2-4. –1843.

1. Nor is it possible that any form of politie, much less politie ecclesiasticall should be good, vnlesse God himselfe bee authour of it HOOKER. 2. **b.** The soul of man is intended to be a well-ordered p. 1840.

Politzerize (pǫli·tsĕrəiz), *v.* 1879. [f. Adam *Politzer*, a physician of Vienna, who introduced the method; see -IZE.] *trans.* To inflate the tympanic cavity of (a patient) through the Eustachian tube. Hence **Poli:tzeriza·tion.**

†**Polk,** *v.* 1845. [ad. F. *polker*, f. *polka.*] *intr.* To dance the polka –1876.

Polka (pǫ·lkă, pōu·lkă), *sb.*[1] 1844. [= F. and Ger. *polka*; origin obsc.] 1. A lively dance of Bohemian origin, the music for which is in duple time. **2.** A piece of music for this, or in its time or rhythm 1844. Hence **Po·lka** *v. intr.* to dance the p.

†**Po·lka,** *sb.*[2] 1844. [f. prec.] A woman's tight-fitting jacket, usu. knitted; more fully *p.-jacket* –1859.

Poll (pōul), *sb.*[1] [ME. *polle* = obs. Du. *polle* the top of the head, *polle, pol* the head, etc.] **I. 1.** The human head. (Not now in serious literary use.) **2.** *spec.* **a.** The part of the head on which the hair grows; the head as characterized by the colour or state of the hair 1602. **b.** The crown or top of the head. late ME. **c.** The nape of the neck 1671. **3.** = HEAD *sb.* I. 7, 7 b. *Obs.* exc. in legal phr. CHALLENGE *to the polls.* ME. **4.** Short for *p.-tax. Obs.* or *Hist.* 1684.

2. **a.** All Flaxen was his Pole SHAKS. **c.** The arrow pierced his neck from throat to p. HOBBES. 3. Twenty poule of pultrey 1544. *P. by p.*, one by one; Take them p. by p. PRYNNE.

II. From I. 3, app. infl. by POLL *v.* †1. **a.** Muster –1613. **b.** Counting of heads; census –1697. **2.** The counting of voters; the entering of votes, in order to their being counted; esp. at the election of parliamentary or other representatives 1625. **b.** The voting at an election 1832. **c.** The number of votes recorded 1853.

1. **a.** *Cor.* III. i. 134. 2. It is not a question to be decided by a p. 1857. **b.** The recent reverses at the p. 1877. **c.** He stood at the head of the p. 1853.

III. Transf. uses. **a.** The top or crown of a hat or cap 1704. **b.** The blunt end of the head of a miner's pick or hammer 1603.

attrib. and *Comb.*: **p.-book,** an official register, previous to the Ballot Act, of the votes given; now, of those qualified to vote; **-clerk,** a clerk who records the votes polled; **-evil,** an inflamed or ulcerous sore between the ligament and the first bone of the neck of a horse; **-pick,** a miner's pick with a p.; †**-money,** capitation, poll-tax; **-tax,** a capitation or head-tax.

Poll (pǫl), *sb.*[2] 1630. [Altered f. *Moll*, a familiar equivalent of *Mary.*] Used as the conventional proper name of any parrot; hence, = parrot. So **Poll-pa·rrot** (also used *fig.* and *attrib.*), whence **Poll-pa·rrot** *v. trans.* and *intr.* = PARROT *v.*

Poll (pǫl), *sb.*[3] *Camb. Univ. slang.* Also **pol.** 1831. [Explained as ad. Gr. οἱ πολλοί the many.] *The P.*: the passmen. *To go out in the P.*: to come out in the list of those who take a pass degree. Also *attrib.*

Poll (pōul), *a.* and *sb.*[4] late ME. [Short for *pold* POLLED *ppl. a.*] **A.** *adj.* 1. Polled or cut even at the edge (see POLL *v.* II. 2); as in DEED POLL, POLL DEED 1523. **2.** In *Comb.* **a.** In names of animals without horns, as *poll-sheep* 1773. †**b.** (Usu. *pol-.*) In names of beardless cereals, as *polbarley, polbere, polwheat* –1601. **B.** *sb.* Short for *p.-beast, -ox, -cow* (see A. 2 a); *esp.* one of a breed of hornless oxen 1789.

Poll (pōul), *v.* ME. [f. POLL *sb.*[1]] **I.** *trans.* To cut short the hair of (a person or animal); to crop, clip, shear; also with the head, hair, etc. as object. *Obs.* or *arch.* **II. 1.** To cut off the top of (a tree or plant); *esp.* to pollard; also, to lop the branches of. Also *transf.* and *fig.* 1577. †**b.** To behead –1661. **2.** To cut even the edge of (a sheet, as in a deed executed by one person) 1628. **3.** To cut off the horns of (cattle) 1607.

2. A deed made by one party only is not indented, but polled or shaved quite even BLACKSTONE.

III. *fig.* To plunder by or as by excessive taxation; to pillage, rob, fleece; to despoil (a person or place) of (anything). *arch.* †Also *absol.* or *intr.* 1489. **IV.** †1. To count heads –1711. **2.** To take the votes of; in *pass.* to have one's vote taken, to record a vote 1625. **b.** Of a candidate: To bring to the poll as voters; to receive (so many votes) 1846. **3.** *intr.* To vote at a poll 1678. **b.** *trans.* To give or record (a vote) 1717.

2. That more excellent way of polling by the Ballot BRIGHT. **b.** Birney polled just enough votes to defeat Clay 1892.

Pollack, pollock (pǫ·lək). Also †**podlok, podley.** 1602. [Origin obsc.] A sea-fish of the genus *Pollachius*, allied to the cod, but having the lower jaw protruding; *esp.* the true or whiting p., *Pollachius pollachius*, of European seas, also called *green-fish, lythe*, etc.; and the green p. or COAL-FISH, *Pollachius virens* or *carbonarius*, of the North Atlantic generally.

Pollan (pǫ·lăn). 1713. [perh. f. Ir. *poll* inland lake + *-an*, Celt. deriv. formative.] A species of freshwater fish, *Coregonus pollan*, found in the inland loughs of Ireland.

Po·llard, *sb.*[1] *Obs.* exc. *Hist.* ME. [app. f. POLL *sb.*[1] + -ARD (in ref. to its device, a head).] A base coin of foreign origin, current in England in the 13th c., as an equivalent of the penny; in 1299 declared illegal.

Pollard (pǫ·lărd), *sb.*[2] (*a.*) 1523. [f. POLL *v.* + -ARD.] **I. 1.** An animal that has cast or lost its horns, as a stag; also, an ox, sheep, or goat of a hornless variety 1546. **2.** A tree which has been polled or cut back, so as to produce a thick close growth of young branches, forming a rounded head or mass 1662. †**3.** Short for *pollard wheat* –1688. **II.** Bran sifted from flour; *techn.* a finer grade of bran containing some flour; also, flour or meal containing the finer bran. (Cf. TOPPINGS.) 1577. **B.** *attrib.* or *adj.* †**1.** Of wheat: Beardless, awnless –1765. **2.** That is a pollard (tree); polled, lopped 1669.

Pollard (pǫ·lărd), *v.* 1670. [f. prec.] *trans.* To cut off the branches of (a tree), leaving only the main trunk; to make a pollard of.

I hate to see trees pollarded—or nations 1836.

Po·ll deed. Now *rare.* 1523. [f. POLL *a.* + DEED.] = DEED POLL.

Polled (pōuld), *ppl. a.* ME. [f. POLL *v.* + -ED[1].] †**1.** Having the hair cut short; shorn, shaven; also of the hair: clipped –1650. **2.** Hornless 1607. **3.** Of trees: Pollarded 1611. †**4.** *P. deed* = POLL DEED –1706.

1. With pollid heed WYCLIF. P. lockes SIDNEY. **2.** A herd of Red P. Cattle 1902.

Pollen (pǫ·lėn), *sb.* 1523. [a. L. *pollen, -inem* fine flour, etc., in sense 2 from mod.L. (Linn.).] †**1.** Fine flour or meal; fine powder –1736. **2.** *Bot.* The fine powdery substance, produced by and discharged from the anther of a flower, constituting the male element that fecundates the ovules 1760.

Comb.: **p.-cell,** (*a*) a cell which develops into a pollen-grain, or forms part of one; (*b*) = *p.-sac*; (*c*) a cell in a honeycomb in which p. is stored; **-grain,** each of the grains of which p. consists; **-granule,** each of the ultimate granules contained in a pollen-grain; also = *p.-grain*; **-sac,** each of the (usu. four) cavities or loculi of an anther, in which the p. is contained; **-tube,** a tube formed by protrusion of the intine of a pollen-grain when deposited upon the stigma, which penetrates the style so as to convey the fecundating substance to the ovule. Hence **Po·llen** *v. trans.* to convey p. to, to pollinate.

†**Po·llenin.** 1816. [ad. F. *pollénine*, f. POLLEN; see -IN[1].] *Chem.* A supposed peculiar substance obtained from pollen, and from the spores of *Lycopodium* –1895.

Poller (pōu·lər). 1513. [f. POLL *v.* + -ER[1].] †**1.** A barber or hair-cutter –1688. **b.** One who polls trees 1828. †**2.** A plunderer, extortioner, despoiler –1674. **3. a.** A voter 1776. **b.** One who registers voters 1828.

‖**Pollex** (pǫ·leks). *Pl.* **pollices** (-isīz). 1835. [L., = thumb, great toe.] *Anat.* The innermost digit of the fore limb in air-breathing vertebrates; in man, etc. the thumb. Occas. including the corresponding digit of the hind limb (the great toe), distinctively called HALLUX.

Pollicitation (pǫlisitēⁱ·ʃən). 1528. [ad. L. *pollicitationem, pollicitari*, freq. of *polliceri* to promise; see -ATION.] The action of promising; a promise; a document containing a promise; *Civil Law*, a promise not formally accepted, and therefore in certain cases revocable.

Pollinate (pǫ·lineⁱt), *v.* 1875. [f. L. *pollen, pollin-* + -ATE[3].] *trans.* To besprinkle with pollen or shed pollen upon (the stigma, etc.) in order to fertilization. So **Pollina·tion,** the action of pollinating. **Po·llinator,** an insect which assists pollination.

†**Polli·nctor.** 1646. [a. L., from *pollingere.*] One who prepared a dead body for burning or embalming, by washing, etc. –1705.

Polling (pōu·liŋ), *vbl. sb.* late ME. [f. POLL *v.* + -ING[1].] The action of POLL *v.* *spec.* **1.** The cutting off of the top of a tree 1626. †**2.** Plundering, extortion, robbery –1665. **3.** The registering or casting of votes 1625.

attrib., as *p.-agent, -booth, -clerk*, etc.; †**p.-penny, -pence,** money exacted as poll-tax; hence, esp. in *pl.*, a poll-tax.

Polliniferous (pǫlini·fĕrəs), *a.* Also erron. pollen-. 1830. [f. L. *pollen, -inem* + -IFEROUS.] *Bot.* Bearing or producing pollen.

Pollinigerous (pǫlini·dʒĕrəs), *a.* 1819. [f. as prec. + -(I)GEROUS.] *Entom.* Carrying, or adapted for carrying, pollen.

‖**Pollinium** (pǫli·niŏm). *Pl.* **-ia.** 1862. [mod.L., f. *pollen, pollin-* POLLEN 2 + *-ium* as in *antheridium.*] *Bot.* A coherent mass of pollen grains in each cavity of the anther, characteristic of the *Orchidaceæ* and *Asclepiadaceæ*.

‖**Pollinodium** (pǫlinōu·diŏm). 1875. [mod. L., f. as prec. + *-odium*; see -ODE.] *Bot.* The antheridium or male reproductive organ in ascomycetous fungi. Hence **Pollino·dial** *a.* pertaining to or of the nature of a p.

Polliwog, pollywog (pǫ·liwǫg). *dial.* and *U.S.* [late ME. *polwygle*, f. POLL *sb.*[1] + WIGGLE *v.*] A tadpole.

Pollucite (pǫ·liusəit). 1868. [orig. named *Pollux*, being assoc. with *Castor* or CASTORITE.] *Min.* Silicate of aluminium and cæsium, found in brilliant transparent colourless crystals.

Pollute (pǫliū·t), *ppl. a.* *Obs.* exc. *poet.* late ME. [ad. L. *pollutus, polluere.*] = POLLUTED *ppl. a.*

Pollute (pǫliū·t), *v.* late ME. [f. L. *pollut-*, ppl. stem of *polluere* to soil, f. **por* (= *pro*) forth + *luere* to wash.] **1.** *trans.* To render ceremonially or morally impure; to profane, desecrate; to sully, corrupt. **2.** To make physically impure, foul, or filthy; to dirty, stain, taint, befoul 1548.

1. Churches and altars were polluted by atrocious murders GIBBON. **2.** Thei..with their proper bloud, embrued and polluted their awne handes HALL. Hence **Pollu·ted** *ppl. a.* defiled, rendered impure or unclean. **Pollu·ted-ly** *adv.*, **-ness. Pollu·ter,** one who pollutes.

Pollution (pǫliū·ʃən). ME. [ad. L. *pollutionem*, f. *polluere* to POLLUTE.] **1.** The action of polluting, or condition of being polluted; defilement; uncleanness or impurity. late ME. **2.** Ceremonial impurity or defilement; profanation. late ME. **3.** Seminal emission apart from coition ME.

2. Thir strife p. brings Upon the Temple MILT.

Pollux (pǫ·lŏks). 1526. [a. L. *Pollux*, earlier *Polluces*, ad. Gr. Πολυδεύκης.] *Gr. Myth.* Name of one of the twin sons of Tyndarus and Leda; hence in *Astron.* the second star in the constellation Gemini; see CASTOR[3].

Polly (pǫ·li). 1616. Dim. of POLL *sb.*[2]; as female name, and name for a parrot.

Polo (pōu·lo). 1872. [a. Baltī *polo*; cf. Tibetan *pulu.*] **1.** A game of Eastern origin resembling hockey, played on horseback with long-handled clubs and a wooden ball. **2.** A ball-game with goals played by swimmers (*water p.*); hockey played on skates (*rink p.*) 1884. **3.** *attrib.* as *p.-match, pony*, etc.

Polonaise (pǫlonēⁱ·z, pōul-), *sb.* 1773. [a. F. *polonaise*, prop. adj. fem. (scil. *robe*) of *polonais*: see next.] **1.** A dress or over-dress consisting of a bodice, with a skirt open from the waist downwards; orig. suggested by the dress of Polish women. **2.** A slow dance of Polish origin, consisting chiefly of an intricate march, procession, or promenade of the dancers in couples; also, the music for this, or any music written in its peculiar triple rhythm 1797. Hence **Polonai·se** *v. intr.* to dance a p.; to move in a slow and stately manner.

†**Polone·se,** *sb.* and *a.* 1755. [ad. F. *polonais* Polish, It. *Polonese*, f. med.L. *Polonia* Poland; see -ESE.] **A.** *sb.* **1.** = POLONAISE **1**, or the material for this –1774. **2.** A Pole –1810. **B.** *adj.* = POLISH *a.* –1744.

Polonian (pŏlōu·niăn), *a.* and *sb.* *Obs.* or *arch.* 1555. [f. med.L. *Polonia* Poland + -AN.] Polish; a Pole.

Polonium (pŏlōu·niŏm). 1898. [mod.L. and F., f. med.L. *Polonia* + -IUM. Named from the Polish nationality of Madame Curie.] *Chem.* A highly radio-active metallic element, discovered in 1898 by Prof. and Madame Curie in pitchblende.

Polony (pŏlōu·ni). 1661. [In full *P. sausage* (also †*Polonian sausage*), app. replacing †*Bologna* or †*Bolognian sausage*; cf. BOLOGNA.] A sausage made of partly cooked pork.

Polt (pōult). *Obs.* exc. *dial.* 1610. [Origin obsc.] **1.** A blow, a hard knock. Now *dial.* †**2.** A pestle or club –1612.

‖**Poltergeist** (pǫ·ltəɪ,geist). 1838. [G., f. *polter* noise + *geist* ghost.] A spirit which makes its presence known by noises; a noisy spirit.

Po·lt-foot. *arch.* 1579. [app. f. POLT 2 + FOOT *sb.*] **1.** A club-foot. **2.** *attrib.* (often poltfoot) = *polt-footed* 1589. Hence **Po·lt-footed** *a.* club-footed.

Poltroon (pǫltrū·n). 1529. [a. F. *poltron*, ad. It. *poltrone*, f. It. *poltro* idle, lazy + *-one*; see -OON. Orig. stressed *pu·ltron*; *poltroo·n* is after F.] A spiritless coward; a mean-spirited, worthless wretch; a craven. Also *attrib.* So **Poltroo·nery,** the behaviour of a p.; †laziness; pusillanimity, cowardice. **Poltroo·nish** *a.*

Poly, poley (pōu·li). 1578. [ad. L. *polium*, *polion* (Plin.), a. Gr. πόλιον an aromatic plant, perh. f. πολιός hoary.] †A species of Germander, *Teucrium Polium*, an aromatic herb of Southern Europe; also extended to other species of *Teucrium*, as Golden P. (*T. aureum*), Yellow P. (*T. flavescens*) –1608. **b. Poly-mountain,** also **poly of the mountain, mountain poly** [ad. L. *polium montanum*], name of an aromatic herb, variously identified 1578.

Poly- (pǫli), repr. Gr. πολυ-, comb. form of πολύς, πολύ much, in pl. πολλοί, -αί, -ά many, forming the first element in compounds, the second element of which is prop. of Greek origin, often of Latin, and occas. English.

1. General words. **Po·lyarch** [Gr. ἀρχή beginning], *a. Bot.* proceeding from many points of origin; said of the primary xylem or woody tissue of a stem or root. **Po·lyarchy** [Gr. -αρχία rule], the government of a state or city by many; *Bot.* the condition of being polyarch. †**Polyauto·graphy,** early name for LITHOGRAPHY, as applied to the production of numerous copies of autographs, etc. **Polyca·rpellary,** *a. Bot.* having or consisting of several carpels. **Polyca·rpic** (*rare*), **-ca·rpous** [Gr. καρπός fruit], *adjs. Bot.* †(*a*) bearing fruit many times, as a perennial plant; (*b*) = *polycarpellary*. **Polychro·ic** [Gr. χρόα colour], *a. Cryst.* = PLEOCHROIC. **Polycli·nic,** (*a*) an institution giving clinical instruction in all kinds of diseases; (*b*) a hospital for the treatment of all kinds of disease. **Polycotyle·don,** *Bot.* a plant of which the seed contains more than two cotyledons. **Po·lycrase** [Gr. κρᾶσις mixture], *Min.* a shining black mineral, consisting of columbate and titanate of uranium, zirconium, yttrium, etc. **Polyda·ctyl,** *a. Zool.* having more than the normal number of fingers or toes; *sb.* a polydactyl animal. **Polydi·psia,** morbid or abnormal thirst. **Polydyna·mic** [Gr. δύναμις power], *a.* relating to or possessing many forces or powers. **Polye·mbryonate,** *a. Bot.* containing more than one embryo, as a seed; so **Polyembryo·nic** *a.*; **Polye·mbryony,** the formation or presence of more than one embryo in a seed. **Polyga·stric,** *a.* having many stomachs or digestive cavities; belonging to certain infusorians formerly called *Polygastrica*; also as *sb.* **Polygoneu·tic** [Gr. γονεύειν to beget], *a. Zool.* producing several broods in a year. **Po·lygram** [Gr. γραμμή line], a figure consisting of many lines, with their points of intersection. ‖**Polyhæ·mia** [Gr. αἷμα blood], *Path.* fullness or excess of blood; plethora. **Polylogy** (pǫli·lŏdʒi) [-LOGY], much speaking, loquacity (*rare*). **Polymeni·scous** [MENISCUS], *a.* composed of many lenses, as the eye of an insect. ‖**Polyo·ptron** [Gr. -οπτρον, naming instruments of sight], an optical instrument through which objects appear multiplied. **Po·lypetal** (*rare*), **-pe·talous,** *adjs. Bot.* having many petals; usu. = having the petals distinct or separate, not coherent or united. ‖**Polypha·gia,** *Phys.* and *Path.* excessive eating; voracious or ravenous appetite; *Zool.* the habit of feeding on various kinds of food. **Poly·phagous** [Gr. -φάγος eating], *a.* eating much, voracious; *Zool.* feeding upon various kinds of food. **Polypha·rmacy,** *Med.* the use of many drugs or medicines in the treatment of disease. **Polyphyle·tic** [PHYLETIC], *a.* belonging to several tribes or families; polygenetic.

Polyphy·llous, *a. Bot.* having many leaves; usu., having the (perianth-) leaves separate, not united. **Polypragma·tic,** *a.* busying oneself about many affairs; meddlesome, officious; †also as *sb.*; so †**Polypragma·tical** *a.*; **Polypra·gmatism. Polyproto·dont** [Gr. πρῶτος first + ὀδούς, ὀδοντ- tooth], *a. Zool.* having more than two front or incisor teeth in the lower jaw; *sb.* a polyprotodont marsupial. **Polypsychical** (-psəi·kikăl) [Gr. ψυχή soul], *a.* having many souls, many-souled; so **Polypsy·chic** *a.*, **Polypsy·chism. Polyptych** (pǫ·liptik) [Gr. πτυχή fold], anything consisting of more than three leaves or panels folded together. ‖**Polysarcia** (-sā·ɹsiă) [Gr. σάρξ, σαρκ- flesh], *Path.* excessive growth of flesh (or, loosely, of fat); corpulence, obesity. **Polyse·palous** [mod.L. *sepalum* SEPAL], *a. Bot.* prop., having numerous sepals; but used for, having the sepals distinct or separate, not coherent or united. **Po·lysperm** [Gr. σπέρμα seed], *a. Bot.* having or producing many seeds (*rare*). **Po·lyspermy,** *Phys.* impregnation of an ovum by more than one spermatozoon. **Po·lyspore,** *Bot.* (*a*) a spore-case containing numerous spores; (*b*) a compound spore, as in certain algæ; so **Polyspo·rous,** *a.* having or producing numerous spores. **Polysto·matous** [Gr. στόμα, στοματ- mouth], having many or several mouths or suckers; *spec.* belonging to the *Polystomata*, a name for the Sponges, etc. **Po·lystome,** *a.* having many mouths; *sb.* an animal having many mouths or suckers, as a sponge, etc. **Polytha·lamous** [Gr. θάλαμος bed-chamber], *a. Nat. Hist.* having or consisting of several chambers or cells; many-chambered. **Poly·tocous,** *a. Zool.* producing several young at a birth; *Bot.* bearing fruit many times. **Polytro·pic** [Gr. τρόπος turn], *a.* capable of turning to various courses or expedients; *Math.* turning several times round a pole; also applied to a function which has several different values for one of the variable. **Poly·valent,** *a. Chem.* = MULTIVALENT; *Med.* having the property of counteracting many zymotic poisons. **Polyzo·nal,** *a.* applied to a form of lens composed of a number of annular segments or zones; chiefly used in lighthouses.

2. In *Chem.*, a prefix indicating generally the higher members of a series of *mono-*, *di-*, *tri-*, etc. compounds; sometimes including all except the *mono-* member.

a. Prefixed to sbs., forming sbs. used as the names of compounds formed by the combination of two or more atoms, molecules, or radicals (sometimes with elimination of hydrogen atoms, water molecules, etc.) as *pole·thylene* = $(C_2H_4)_n$, (e.g. hexethylene alcohol $(C_2H_4)_6 H_2O_7$); *polyo·xide*, a binary compound containing several oxygen atoms, as a pentoxide; so *polysu·lphide*, etc. **b.** Prefixed to adjs. or sbs., forming adjs., meaning 'containing or derived from two or more molecules of the substance expressed by the second element'; e.g. *polya·cid*, *polyca·rbic*, etc.

‖**Polyadelphia** (pǫ:liăde·lfiă). 1828. [mod. L., f. Gr. πολυ- POLY- + ἀδελφός brother + -IA [1].] *Bot.* The eighteenth class in the Linnæan Sexual System, comprising plants whose flowers have the stamens united in three or more bundles. Hence **Polyade·lphian, -ade·lphous** *adjs.* belonging to this class; having the stamens so united; also said of such stamens.

Polyandria (pǫli,æ·ndriă). 1753. [mod.L., a. Gr. πολυανδρία, f. πολύανδρος (f. πολυ- POLY- + ἀνδρ- man, male), employed by Linnæus in the sense 'having many stamens or male organs'.] **1.** *Bot.* The thirteenth class in the Linnæan Sexual System, comprising plants having twenty or more stamens inserted on the receptacle. Also the name of one of the orders in certain classes, as the *Monadelphia*, *Gynandria*, *Monœcia*, in which the number of stamens is used to subdivide them into orders. **2.** *Zool.* and *Anthropol.* = POLYANDRY 1876. So **Polya·ndrian, Polya·ndric** *adjs.* = POLYANDROUS.

Polyandrous (pǫli,æ·ndrəs), *a.* 1830. [f. Gr. πολύανδρος (see POLYANDRIA) + -OUS.] **1.** *Bot.* Having numerous stamens; *spec.* belonging to the class *Polyandria*. **2.** Having more than one, or several, husbands; practising, pertaining to, or involving polyandry. (Corresp. to POLYGYNOUS 2.) 1865.

Polyandry (pǫ·li,ændri). 1780. [ad. Gr. πολυανδρία; see POLYANDRIA.] That form of polygamy in which one woman has two or more husbands at the same time; plurality of husbands. (Corresp. to POLYGYNY.) **b.** *Zool.* The fact of a female animal having more than one mate 1871.

Polyanthus (pǫli,æ·nþŏs). 1727. [a. mod.L. *polyanthus*, f. Gr. πολυ- POLY- + ἄνθος flower.] **1.** A cultivated form of *Primula*, having flowers of various shades, chiefly brown or crimson with yellow eye and border, in an umbel on a common peduncle. **2.** *attrib.* or *adj. P. Narcissus*: any one of a group of species of Narcissus, as *N. Tazetta*, which have the flowers in an umbellate cluster on a common peduncle. So *P. Primrose* = sense 1. 1866.

Polyatomic (pǫli,ătǫ·mik), *a.* 1857. [f. POLY- + ATOMIC.] *Chem.* Containing or consisting of many atoms of some substance; *esp.* having many replaceable hydrogen atoms; also = multivalent.

Polybasic (pǫlibē·sik), *a.* 1842. [f. POLY- + BASIC.] *Chem.* Having more than two bases, or atoms of a base.

P. acid, an acid containing three or more atoms of replaceable hydrogen.

Polybasite (pǫli·băsəit). 1830. [ad. G. *polybasit*, f. Gr. πολυ- POLY- + βάσις; see -ITE [1]. According to Chester, alluding to the large amount of the base, sulphide of silver.] *Min.* A sulpharseno-antimonite of silver and copper, of an iron-black colour, and metallic lustre, occurring in short tabular hexagonal prisms, also massive and disseminated.

Polycephalic (pǫ:lisĭfæ·lik), *a. rare.* 1850. [f. Gr. πολυκέφαλος + -IC.] Many-headed. So **Polyce·phalous** *a.*

Polychæte, -chete (pǫ·likīt), *a.* and *sb.* 1886. [ad. mod.L. *Polychæta*, f. Gr. πολυχαίτης, f. πολυ- much + χαίτη mane (here 'bristle').] *Zool.* **A.** *adj.* Belonging to the *Polychæta*, one of the two divisions of the *Chætopoda*, a class of worms characterized by numerous bristles on the foot-stumps. **B.** *sb.* A worm of this division.

Polychord (pǫ·likǭɹd), *a.* and *sb.* 1674. [ad. Gr. πολύχορδος, f. πολυ- POLY- + χορδή CHORD.] **A.** *adj.* Having many strings, as a musical instrument. **B.** *sb.* **1.** An instrument having ten gut strings, resembling a double-bass without a neck, played with a bow or with the fingers 1838. **2.** Trade-name for a kind of octave-coupler 1858.

†**Polychrest** (pǫ·likrest). 1656. [a. med.L. *polychrestus*, a. Gr. f. πολυ- POLY- + χρηστός useful.] Something adapted to several different uses; *esp.* a drug or medicine serving to cure various diseases –1812.

attrib. †*P. salt* (also *salt p.*), neutral sulphate of potassium; also, sodio-potassic tartrate. So **Polychre·stic** *adj.* serving for various uses.

Polychroite (pǫ·likro,əit). 1815. [a. F. *polychroïte*, f. Gr. πολύχροος many-coloured; see -ITE [1].] *Chem.* Name for the colouring matter of saffron (also called SAFRANIN), which exhibits various colours under different reagents.

Polychromatic (pǫ:likromæ·tik), *a.* 1849. [f. POLY- + CHROMATIC.] Having or characterized by various colours; many-coloured.

P. acid (Chem.) = POLYCHROMIC *acid*.

Polychrome (pǫ·likrōᵘm), *a.* and *sb.* 1801. [a. F., ad. Gr. πολύχρωμος many-coloured, f. πολυ- POLY- + χρῶμα.] **A.** *adj.* Polychromatic; *esp.* painted, decorated, or printed in many colours 1837. **B.** *sb.* **1.** A work of art in several colours; *spec.* a coloured statue 1801. **2.** Varied colouring 1882. **3.** *Chem.* A name for ÆSCULIN, from the fluorescence of its solution and infusion 1838.

Polychromic (pǫlikrōᵘ·mik), *a.* 1825. [f. as prec. + -IC.] **1.** = prec. A. **2.** *Chem.* In *p. acid*, a name for aloetic acid, from the various colours it exhibits in powder, in solution, and in combination 1863. So **Po·lychro:mous** *a.*

Polychromy (pǫ·likrōᵘmi). 1854. [ad. F. *polychromie*, f. as POLYCHROME; see -Y [3].] The art of painting or decorating in several colours, esp. as used in pottery, architecture, etc.

†‖ **Polychro·nicon.** 1570. [med.L., f. Gr. πολυ- POLY- + χρονικόν, in pl. (sc. βιβλία books) annals.] A chronicle of many events or periods –1815.

Polyconic (pǫlikǫ·nik), *a.* 1864. [f. POLY- + CONIC.] Involving or based upon a number of cones; applied to a system of map-projection in which each parallel of latitude is represented by the development of a cone touching the earth's surface along that parallel. Also *sb.* a polyconic projection.

Polydæmonism, -demonism (pǫlidī·mŏniz'm). 1711. [f. Gr. πολυ- POLY- + δαίμον, divinity, demon + -ISM, after *polytheism*.] A belief in many divinities (i.e. simply, supernatural powers, or *spec.* evil spirits).

Polyedral, etc.: see POLYHEDRAL, etc.

‖ **Polygamia** (pǫligē·miă). 1753. [mod.L. (Linn.).] *Bot.* The twenty-third class in the Linnæan Sexual System, comprising species which bear both hermaphrodite and unisexual (male or female) flowers, on the same or different plants. Hence **Polyga·mian** *a.* belonging to the class *P.*; *sb.* a plant of this class. **Polyga·mious** *a.*

Polygamic (pǫligæ·mik), *a.* 1819. [f. late Gr. πολύγαμος often married + -IC.] Of or pertaining to polygamy; (less correctly) polygamous.

Polygamist (pǫli·gămist). 1637. [f. as prec. + -IST.] One who practises or favours polygamy; usu., a man who has several wives. **b.** *attrib.* Practising polygamy, polygamous 1875. Hence **Polygami·stic** *a.*

Poly·gamize, *v. rare.* 1598. [f. as prec. + -IZE.] *intr.* To practise polygamy.

Polygamous (pǫli·gaməs), *a.* 1613. [f. as prec. + -OUS.] **1.** Practising or addicted to polygamy; of, pertaining to, or involving polygamy. **2.** *Zool.* Having more than one, or several, mates of the opposite sex, as an animal; characterized by polygamy, as a species. Usu. = *polygynous*. 1834. **3.** *Bot.* Belonging to the Linnæan class *Polygamia* 1760.

2. The war is, perhaps, severest between the males of p. animals DARWIN. Hence **Poly·gamously** *adv.*

Polygamy (pǫli·gămi). 1591. [ad. F. *polygamie*, ad. eccl. Gr. πολυγαμία, f. πολύγαμος often married, f. πολυ- POLY- + γάμος.] **1.** Marriage with several, or more than one, at once; plurality of spouses; usu. the practice or custom according to which one man has several wives. **b.** *fig.*: esp. applied to plurality of benefices 1638. **2.** *Zool.* The habit of mating with more than one, or several, of the opposite sex; usu., one male with several females (*polygyny*), as in gallinaceous birds 1890.

Polygenesis (pǫli,dʒe·nĭsis). 1862. [f. POLY- + GENESIS.] *Biol.* (Theoretical) origination of a race or species from several independent ancestors or germs; in ref. to man usu. called POLYGENY.

Polygenetic (pǫ:li,dʒĭne·tik), *a.* 1861. [f. prec., after GENETIC.] **1.** *Biol.* Of or pertaining to polygenesis. **2.** *Geol.* Having more than one origin; formed in several different ways 1873. Hence **Polygene·tically** *adv.*

Polygenic (pǫli,dʒe·nik), *a.* 1858. [f. Gr. πολυ- POLY- + γενικός, f. γένος kind, or (in sense 2) from -GEN 1 + -IC.] **1.** *Geol.* = POLYGENOUS 1. **2.** *Chem.* Forming more than one compound with hydrogen or other monovalent element 1873.

Polygenism (pǫli·dʒĭniz'm). 1878. [f. POLYGENY + -ISM.] The doctrine of polygeny; the theory that mankind are descended from several independent pairs of ancestors, or that the human race consists of several independent species. So **Poly·genist,** an adherent of the theory of polygeny; also *attrib.* 1857.

Polygenous (pǫli·dʒĭnəs), *a.* 1799. [irreg. f. Gr. πολυγενής of many kinds (f. πολυ- POLY- + γένος) + -OUS.] **1.** Composed of constituents of different kinds; *spec.* in *Geol.* composed of various kinds of rocks. **2.** *Chem.* = POLYGENIC 2. 1870. **3.** Of or pertaining to, or involving polygeny 1860.

Polygeny (pǫli·dʒĭni). 1865. [f. POLY- + Gr. -γενεια birth.] The (theoretical) origination of mankind (or of any species) from several independent pairs of ancestors; *loosely*, the theory of such origination, polygenism.

Polyglot (pǫ·liglǫt), *a.* and *sb.* 1645. [ad. Gr. πολύγλωττος, f. πολυ- POLY- + γλῶττα tongue.] **A.** *adj.* **1.** Of a person: That speaks or writes several languages 1656. **2.** Of or relating to many languages: *esp.* of a book or writing: In many or several languages 1673.

1. P. waiters who can tell us when the train starts in four or five languages 1873. 2. The Polyglott Bible, a Polyglott Dictionary 1706.

B. *sb.* **1.** One who speaks or writes several languages 1645. †**b.** A bird that imitates the notes of other birds –1776. **2.** A book or writing (*esp.* a Bible) in several languages 1666. **b.** A mixture of several languages (*rare*) 1715.

1. A p. or good linguist 1645. b. It [sedge warbler] is a most entertaining p., or mocking bird PENNANT. 2. b. His wrath aired itself in a polyglott 1830. So **Polyglo·ttic, Polyglo·ttous** *adjs.* = *polyglot* A.

Polygon (pǫ·ligǫn), *sb.* and *a.* 1570. [ad. L. *polygonum*, a. Gr. πολύγωνον, prop. adj. neut. polygonal, f. πολυ- POLY- + -γωνος, from stem of γωνία angle. Used first in L. forms **polygo·num, polygo·nium.**] **A.** *sb.* **1.** *Geom.* A figure (usu. a plane rectilineal figure), having many, i. e. (usu.) more than four, angles (and sides); a many-sided figure 1571. **b.** *Arith.* A polygonal number: see POLYGONAL 2. Hence extended to higher orders of figurate numbers, as the PYRAMIDAL numbers, etc. 1842. **2.** A material object of the form of a polygon 1669.

1. *P. of forces*, a polygonal figure illustrating a theorem relating to a number of forces acting at one point, each of which is represented in magnitude and direction by one of the sides of the figure, analogous to the *parallelogram of forces*; hence, the theorem itself. So *p. of velocities*, etc. 2. *Funicular p.*: see FUNICULAR 2.

B. *adj.* Having many angles; polygonal. ? *Obs.* 1570.

Polygonaceous (pǫ:ligŏnē¹·ʃəs), *a.* 1874. [f. mod.L. *Polygonaceæ* (f. POLYGONUM) + -OUS; see -ACEOUS.] *Bot.* Belonging to the N.O. *Polygonaceæ*, of which the typical genus is POLYGONUM.

Polygonal (pǫli·gŏnăl), *a.* (*sb.*) 1704. [f. L. *polygonum* POLYGON + -AL.] **1.** Having the form of a polygon; many-sided. As applied to a solid body, denoting a prismatic or similar form whose base or section is a polygon. 1727. **2.** *Arith.* Applied to the first order of figurate numbers (see FIGURATE *ppl. a.* 3 b.) So called because each of these numbers, represented (e. g.) by dots, can be arranged according to a certain rule in the form of the corresponding regular polygon. 1704. **b.** as *sb.* A polygonal number (*rare*) 1795.

Polygonometry (pǫ:ligonǫ·mĕtri). *rare.* 1811. [f. as POLYGON + -METRY.] *Math.* A branch of mathematics dealing with the measurement and properties of polygons, as trigonometry with those of triangles.

Polygonous (pǫli·gŏnəs), *a.* Now *rare* or *Obs.* 1660. [f. L. *polygonum* + -OUS.] = POLYGONAL *a.*

‖ **Polygonum** (pǫli·gŏnŏm). 1706. [mod.L., a. Gr. πολύγονον knotgrass, etc., f. πολυ- POLY- + γόνυ knee, joint.] *Bot.* A large and widely distributed genus of plants, type of the N.O. *Polygonaceæ*, with swollen stem-joints, sheathed by the stipules, including knotgrass, snakeweed, persicaria, etc. Also *attrib.*

†**Poly·gony.** 1450. [ad. L. *polygonium*, f. Gr. πολύγονον.] A plant of the genus *Polygonum*; esp. Snakeweed, *P. Bistorta* –1706.

Polygraph (pǫ·ligraf). 1794. [ad. Gr. πολυγράφος, -ον adj. writing much.] **I. 1. a.** An apparatus for producing two or more identical drawings or writings simultaneously. **b.** A copying-machine; *esp.* a gelatine copying-pad. 1805. †**2.** *fig.* A person who imitates, or is a copy of, another; an imitator or imitation –1797. **3.** A myograph 1876. **II.** A writer of many works; a voluminous author 1883.

Polygraphic (pǫligræ·fik), *a.* (*sb.*) 1735. [f. POLYGRAPHY + -IC.] **1.** Writing much; treating of many subjects (*rare*). **2.** Applied to a method of mechanically copying pictures; see POLYGRAPHY III a. 1788. †**3.** *fig.* That is an exact copy or imitation of another –1824. **4.** Of or pertaining to a POLYGRAPH (sense 1); used for multiplying copies of a drawing or writing; produced by a polygraph 1828.

2. P. transparencies..to be had for next to nothing LANDOR. 4. A sheet of damped p. paper 1883. So **Polygra·phical** *a.* 1588.

Polygraphy (pǫli·grăfi). 1593. [ad. Gr. πολυγραφία; see POLY- and -GRAPHY.] †**I.** A kind of cipher or secret writing; also applied to a particular system of shorthand –1855. **II.** Much writing; copious or various literary work 1661. **III. a.** A method of producing copies of paintings, invented by Joseph Booth *c* 1788. **b.** The use of a POLYGRAPH (sense 1 a) 1828.

‖ **Polygynia** (pǫli,dʒi·niă). 1760. [f. mod.L. *polygynus*, f. Gr. πολυ- POLY- + γυνή woman, wife (here 'pistil').] **1.** *Bot.* An order in some classes of the Linnæan Sexual System, comprising plants having flowers with more than 12 styles. **2.** = POLYGYNY (*rare*) 1865. Hence **Polygy·nian** *a. rare* = POLYGYNOUS 1.

Polygynist (pǫli·dʒinist). 1876. [f. as POLYGYNY + -IST.] One who practises or favours polygyny.

Polygynous (pǫli·dʒinəs), *a.* 1841. [f. mod.L. *polygynus* (see POLYGYNIA) + -OUS.] **1.** *Bot.* Having many pistils, styles, or stigmas; *spec.* belonging to the order *Polygynia*. **2.** Having more than one, or several, wives (or concubines); practising, pertaining to, or involving polygyny 1874. **b.** *Zool.* Of a male animal: Having several mates; characterized by polygyny, as a species.

Polygyny (pǫli·dʒini). 1780. [f. POLY- + Gr. γυνή woman, wife.] That form of polygamy in which one man has several wives (or concubines). **b.** *Zool.* Of a male animal: The having more than one female mate.

Polyhalite (pǫlihæ·ləit). 1818. [ad. G. *polyhalit*, f. Gr. πολυ- POLY- + ἅλς salt; see -ITE [1].] *Min.* Hydrous sulphate of calcium, potassium, and magnesium, usu. occurring in fibrous masses of a red or yellowish colour.

Polyhedral (pǫlihī·drăl, -he·drăl), *a.* Also **polyedral.** 1811. [f. Gr. πολύεδρος (f. πολυ- POLY- + ἕδρα base, etc.) + -AL.] **1.** Of the form of a polyhedron; having many faces or sides, as a solid figure or body. **2.** Pertaining or relating to a polyhedron; in *Algebra* applied to a class of functions 1880. **3.** Of an angle: Formed by three or more planes meeting at a point. (Usu. called a *solid angle.*) 1864. So **Polyhe·dric, -al** *adjs.* = sense 1; also *fig.* many-sided. **Polyhe·drous** *a.* polyhedral.

Polyhedron (pǫlihī·drǫn, -he·drǫn). Also **polyedron.** *Pl.* **-a** (rarely **-ons**). 1570. [a. Gr. πολύεδρον a polyhedron, prop. adj. neut.; see prec.] *Geom.* A solid figure contained by many (i. e. usu. more than six) plane faces; a many-sided solid. Hence, a material body having such a form. **b.** *spec.* A lens having many facets, multiplying the image of an object; a multiplying-glass 1727.

Polyhistor (pǫlihi·stǫɹ). 1588. [a. Gr. πολυΐστωρ very learned, f. πολυ- POLY- + ἵστωρ (see HISTORY).] A man of much or varied learning; a great scholar. So **Polyhisto·rian,** polyhistor. **Polyhisto·ric** *a.* **Polyhi·story.**

Polymath (pǫ·limæþ), *sb.* (*a.*) 1621. [ad. Gr. πολυμαθής, f. πολυ- POLY- + μαθ-, stem of μανθάνειν to learn.] A person of much or varied learning; one acquainted with various subjects of study. Also *attrib.* So **Polyma·thic** *a.* pertaining to a p., characterized by varied learning. †**Poly·mathist** = *polymath.* **Poly·mathy** [ad. Gr. πολυμαθία], much or varied learning.

Polymer (pǫ·liməɹ). 1866. [mod. f. Gr. πολυμερής having many parts. See ISOMER.] *Chem.* A substance polymeric with another; any one of a series of polymeric compounds. So **Poly·meride** = *polymer.*

Polymeric (pǫlime·rik), *a.* 1847. [f. as prec. + -IC, after G. *polymerisch.*] *Chem.* Of two or more compounds, or of one compound in relation to another (const. *with*): Composed of the same elements in the same proportions, but so that the numbers of atoms of the several elements in the molecule in one substance are some multiple of those in another, and thus the molecular weight of the one is the same multiple of that of the other. (Dist. from ISOMERIC.)

Polymerism (pǫli·mĕriz'm). 1847. [f. as POLYMER + -ISM.] **1.** *Chem.* The condition of being polymeric. **2.** *Biol.* The condition of being polymerous 1849.

Polymerize (pǫ·limĕrəiz), *v.* 1865. [f. as prec. + -IZE.] **1.** *Chem.* **a.** *trans.* To render polymeric; to form a polymer of. **b.** *intr.* To become polymeric; to be converted into a polymer. **2.** *Biol.* (*trans.*) To render polymerous 1879. Hence **Poly:meriza·tion,** the action or process of polymerizing; formation of polymers.

Polymerous (pǫli·mĕrəs), *a.* 1858. [f. as prec. + -OUS.] *Nat. Hist.* Composed of many parts, members, or segments.

Polymorph (pǫ·limǫɹf). 1828. [mod. f. Gr. πολύμορφος, f. πολυ- POLY- + μορφή.] **1.** *Nat. Hist.* A polymorphous organism, or an individual of a polymorphous species. **2.** *Chem.* and *Min.* A substance that crystallizes in two or more different forms 1890. So **Polymo·rphic** *a.* = POLYMORPHOUS 1, 2.

Polymorphism (pǫlimǫ·ɹfiz'm). 1839. [f. as prec. + -ISM.] The condition or character of being polymorphous; the occurrence of something in several different forms.

Polymorpho-, comb. form repr. Gr. πολύμορφος multiform; as in **P.-nu·clear, -nu·cleate** *adjs.*, having several nuclei of various shapes.

Polymorphous (pǫlimǫ·ɹfəs), *a.* 1785. [f. Gr. πολύμορφος multiform + -OUS.] Having, assuming, or occurring in, many or various forms; multiform. **1.** *gen.* 1823. **2.** *Nat. Hist.*, *Biol.*, *Path.* **a.** Having many varieties; as a species of animal or plant, an eruptive disease, etc. **b.** Assuming various forms successively; as an amœba, infusorian, etc. **c.** Having several definitely marked metamorphoses. 1785. **3.** *Chem.* and *Min.* Crystallizing in two or more forms, esp. in forms belonging to different systems; dimorphous or trimorphous 1866.

Polymorphy (pǫ·limǫɹfi). 1846. [ad. Gr. πολυμορφία; see -Y [3].] = POLYMORPHISM.

Poly-mountain: see POLY b.

Polynesia (pǫlinī·ʃiă, -siă). 1766. [mod.L. form of F. *Polynésie*, f. Gr. πολυ- POLY- + νῆσος island.] Collective name for the numerous small islands in the Pacific Ocean, east of Australia and the Malay archipelago. Hence **Polyne·sian** *a.* belonging to P.; *sb.* a native or inhabitant of P., a South Sea islander.

‖ **Polynia** (poli·niă). 1853. [Russ. *polŭinya*, f. root of *pole, polyana* field.] A space of open water in the midst of ice, esp. in the arctic seas.

Polynomial (pǫlinōu·miăl), *a.* and *sb.* 1674. [Hybrid f. POLY- after BINOMIAL (irreg. f. L. *nomen* name).] **A.** *adj.* **1.** *Alg.* Consisting of many terms; multinomial 1704. **2.** Characteristic of a nomenclature in which the genus, species, sub-species, variety, etc. are indicated by more than two terms 1889.

1. *P. theorem* (also called *multinomial theorem*), an extension of the binomial theorem, for the expansion of any power of a polynomial expression.

B. *sb.* **1.** *Alg.* An expression consisting of many terms; a multinomial 1674. **2.** A scientific name consisting of many terms (see A. 2) 1885. Hence **Po·lynome** = B. 1.; *adj.* having many names.

Polyonymous (pǫli,ǫ·niməs), *a.* 1678. [f. Gr. πολυώνυμος (f. πολυ- POLY- + ὄνομα, Æol. ὄνυμα) + -OUS; cf. *anonymous.*] Having many names or titles; called or known by several different names. So **Po·lyonym** (*a*) = SYNONYM (*rare*); (*b*) used by Buck for a technical term consisting of two or more words, as *pia mater*, etc. **Polyony·mic** *a.* of the nature of a polyonym.

Polyonymy (pǫli,ǫ·nĭmi). 1678. [ad. Gr. πολυωνυμία, f. πολυώνυμος; see prec. and -Y [3].] **1.** The use of several different names for the same person or thing. **2.** Polynomial nomenclature 1889.

Polyp, polype (pǫ·lip). late ME. [a. F. *polype*, ad. L. *polypus*; see POLYPUS.] **1.** *Zool.* Prop., an animal having many feet or foot-like processes. †**a.** *orig.* A cephalopod having eight or ten arms, as an octopus or a cuttle-fish –1752. **b.** In later use, applied to various animals of low organization; chiefly to cœlenterates of different classes, esp. a hydra or other hydrozoan, a 'coral-insect' or other anthozoan; also to the polyzoa, to certain echinoderms, and loosely to rotifers, infusorians, etc. **c.** Many of these being 'colonial' organisms, the term is hence used *spec.* for a single individual, 'person', or zooid of the colony. 1742. **2.** *Path.* = POLYPUS 2 (*rare*). late ME.

Comb. **p.-stem, -stock,** = POLYPARY, POLYPIDOM. So **Poly·pean** *a. rare* pertaining to, or resembling that of, a p.

Polypary (pǫ·lipări). 1750. [ad. mod.L. *polyparium* (also used), f. *polypus* POLYP + -ARIUM.] The common stem, stock, or supporting structure of a colony of polyps, to which the individual zooids are attached, usu. each in a cell or cavity of its own; = POLYPIDOM.

Polypheme (pǫ·lifīm). 1641. [a. F. *Polyphème*, ad. L. POLYPHEMUS.] A one-eyed giant in Homer's *Odyssey* ix; hence *allusively*.

‖ **Polyphemus** (pǫlifī·mǒs). 1829. [L., ad. Gr. Πολύφημος; see prec.] **1.** = prec.; a Cyclops, a one-eyed giant. **2.** *Zool.* **a.** A one-eyed animal. **b.** A very large American silkworm-moth, *Telea polyphemus*. 1890.

Polyphone (pǫ·lifōun). 1655. [mod. ad. Gr. πολύφωνος having many tones, etc., f. πολυ- POLY- + φωνή voice, sound.] †**1.** A musical instrument, somewhat resembling a lute, but having a large number of wire strings –1789. **2.** *Philol.* A written character used to represent different sounds 1872.

Polyphonic (pǫlifǫ·nik), *a.* 1782. [f. Gr. πολύφωνος (see prec.) + -IC.] **1.** *Mus.* Composed or arranged for several voices or parts, each having a melody of its own; consisting of a number of melodies combined; contrapuntal; of or pertaining to polyphonic music. **2.** Producing many sounds; many-voiced 1864. **3.** *Philol.* Of a letter or other symbol: Having more than one phonetic value (as *c*, *g*, *s*) 1891.

2. A grand organ..called a p. organ 1890. So **Poly·phonous** *a.* = *polyphonic* 1677.

Polyphonism (pǫ·lifǫniz'm). *rare.* 1713. [f. as POLYPHONE + -ISM.] **1.** Multiplication of sound, as by echo. **2.** *Mus.* The use of polyphony; polyphonic style or composition 1864.

Polyphonist (pǫ·lifǫnist). *rare.* 1829. [f. as prec. + -IST.] **1.** A ventriloquist. **2.** *Mus.* One versed in polyphony; a contrapuntist 1864.

Polyphony (pǫli·fǫni, pǫ·lifǫuni). 1828. [ad. Gr. πολυφωνία, f. πολύφωνος; see POLYPHONE.] **1.** = POLYPHONISM **1.** **2.** *Mus.* The simultaneous combination of a number of parts, each forming an individual melody, and harmonizing with the others; polyphonic composition; counterpoint 1864. **3.** *Philol.* The symbolization of different vocal sounds by the same letter or character; the fact or quality of being polyphonic 1880.

Polypide (pǫ·lipəid). 1850. [f. POLYP + *-ide*; cf. -ID[3].] *Zool.* An individual or zooid of a compound polyzoan.

Polypidom (pǫli·pidǒm, pǫ·lip-). 1824. [f. L. *polypus* POLYP + *domus*, Gr. δόμος house.] = POLYPARY.

Polypier (pǫ·lipiəɹ). 1828. [a. F. *polypier*, f. *polype* POLYP + *-ier*, as in *poirier*, etc.] *Zool.* = POLYPARY; sometimes, a distinct part of this to which an individual zooid is attached.

Polypifer (pǫli·pifəɹ). 1822. [f. L. *polypus* POLYP + *-fer* bearing; after mod.L. *Polypifera*; see next.] *Zool.* A polypary or polypidom; also, the whole compound organism; usu. in pl. as an Eng. equivalent of L. *Polypifera*.

Polypiferous (pǫlipi·fĕrəs), *a.* 1775. [f. mod.L. *polypifer*, f. *polypus* + *-fer* (in *Polypifera*, a former division of Invertebrates) + -OUS.] *Zool.* Bearing polyps, as a polyp-stock or polypary.

Polypite (pǫ·lipəit). 1828. [f. L. *polypus* POLYP + -ITE[1].] **1.** *Palæont.* A fossil polyp. **2.** *Zool.* An individual or zooid of a compound polyp, esp. of a cœlenterate. Also sometimes applied to a free polyp, as a *Hydra*. 1867.

Polypod (pǫ·lipǫd), *sb.*[1] Now *rare.* late ME. [a. OF. *polipode* (mod.F. *polypode*), ad. L. POLYPODIUM.] = POLYPODY.

Po·lypod, *a.* and *sb.*[2] 1753. [a. F. *polypode* adj., f. Gr. πολυποδ-, stem of πολύπους many-footed; see POLYP.] **A.** *adj.* Having many feet or foot-like organs 1826. **B.** *sb.* An animal having many feet, e. g. a millepede 1753.

‖ **Polypodium** (pǫlipōu·diǒm). 1525. [L., a. Gr. πολυπόδιον, f. πολυ- many + πούς, ποδ- foot, with dim. suffix -ιον; from the many branches of the root-stock.] *Bot.* A large and widely distributed genus of ferns, of various forms.

Polypody (pǫ·lipǒdi). late ME. [ad. L. *polypodium*; see prec.] A fern of the genus *Polypodium*; esp. *P. vulgare*, the Common Polypody (formerly known as *p. of the oak* or *of the wall*).

Polypoid (pǫ·lipoid), *a.* 1842. [f. L. *polypus* POLYP + -OID.] **1.** *Zool.* Resembling or of the nature of a polyp 1850. **2.** *Path.* Resembling or of the nature of a polypus 1842.

Polypous (pǫ·lipəs), *a.* 1748. [f. L. *polypus* POLYP, POLYPUS + -OUS.] **1.** *Zool.* Pertaining to, or of the nature of, a polyp; also *fig.* like that of a polyp. **2.** *Path.* Pertaining to, or of the nature of, a polypus; characterized by polypi 1758. So **Po·lipose** *a.* 1731.

Polypterid (pǫli·ptĕrid). 1849. [f. mod.L. *Polypterus* generic name, a. Gr. πολύπτερος many-winged + -ID[3].] *Ichthyol.* A fish of the family *Polypteridæ* of crossopterygian ganoids, having the dorsal fin replaced by a series of spines with finlets attached; now represented only by the genus **Poly·pterus** of tropical African rivers. So **Poly·pteroid** *a.* akin in form to *Polypterus*, belonging to the sub-order *Polypteroidei*; *sb.* a polypteroid fish.

‖ **Polyptoton** (pǫliptōu·tǫn). 1586. [L., a. Gr. πολύπτωτον adj. neut., f. πολυ- POLY- + πτωτός falling, f. πίπτειν to fall.] *Rhet.* A figure consisting in the repetition of a word in different cases or inflexions in the same sentence.

Polypus (pǫ·lipǒs). *Pl.* **-pi** (-pəi). late ME. [a. L., a. Doric or Æolic Gr. πωλύπος = Attic πολύπους a cuttle-fish, etc., also polypus in the nose, f. πολυ- POLY- + πούς foot.] **1. a.** = POLYP **1 a.** (*Obs.* exc. in allusion to L. or Gr.) 1520. **b.** = POLYP **1 b, c.** Now *rare* or *Obs.* 1742. **2.** *Path.* A general term for tumours of various kinds, arising from a mucous or serous surface, usu. pedunculated, and having ramifications like the tentacles of a polyp. Also formerly applied to a fibrinous blood-clot in the heart or blood-vessels. late ME. **3.** *attrib.* 1607.

Polyscope (pǫ·liskoup). 1704. [f. POLY- + -SCOPE.] **1.** An optical instrument through which objects appear multiplied; a multiplying-glass. **2.** An apparatus for examining cavities of the body 1881.

Polysyllabic (pǫ:lisilæ·bik), *a.* 1782. [f. med.L. *polysyllabus*, Gr. πολυσύλλαβος (f. πολυ- POLY- + συλλαβή syllable) + -IC.] **a.** Of a word: Consisting of many (i. e., usu., more than three) syllables. **b.** Of language, etc.: Characterized by polysyllables. So **Pollysylla·bical** *a.* 1656, **-ly**, *adv.*

Polysyllable (pǫlisi·lăb'l), *sb.* and *a.* 1570. [f. med.L. *polysyllaba* adj. fem. (sc. *vox*), after SYLLABLE.] **A.** *sb.* A word of many (i. e., usu., more than three) syllables. **B.** *adj.* = POLYSYLLABIC. Now *rare.* 1589.

‖ **Polysyndeton** (pǫlisi·ndĭtǫn). 1589. [mod. L., a. Gr. *πολυσύνδετον, prop. neut. adj. (cf. ASYNDETON), f. πολυ- POLY- + σύνδετος, verbal adj. f. συνδεῖν to bind together.] *Rhet.* A figure consisting in the use of several conjunctions close together; usu., the repetition of the same conjunction (as *and*, *or*, *nor*).

Polysynthesis (pǫlisi·nþĭsis). 1869. [f. POLY- + SYNTHESIS.] Synthesis or composition of many elements; complex or multiple synthesis; *spec.* in *Philol.* = INCORPORATION 1 b.

Polysynthetic (pǫ:li,sinþe·tik), *a.* 1805. [f. Gr. πολυσύνθετος much compounded; see POLY- and SYNTHETIC.] Of the nature of or characterized by polysynthesis; combining numerous elements; complex. *spec.* **1.** *Cryst.* Applied to a compound crystal consisting of a series of twin crystals united so as to form a laminated structure. **2.** *Philol.* Characterized by combining several words of a sentence into one word 1821.

2. The Isolating, P., Agglutinative, Inflectional and Analytic forms of language 1889. Hence **Polysyn·the·tical** *a.*, **-ly** *adv.* **Polysynthe·ticism, Poly·sy·nthetism,** p. character or condition.

Polytechnic (pǫli,te·knik), *a.* and *sb.* 1805. [ad. F. *polytechnique*, f. Gr. πολύτεχνος skilled in many arts + *-ique* -IC; see POLY- and TECHNIC.] **A.** *adj.* Pertaining to, dealing with, or devoted to, various arts; esp. in *p. school*, an institution for giving instruction in various technical subjects.

P. Institution, an institution in London, opened in 1838, for the exhibition of objects connected with the industrial arts; now, a technical and recreative school. (After the *école polytechnique*, an engineering school in Paris, founded 1794.)

B. *sb.* Short for *P. Institution* (rarely for *p. school*); see A. Hence *gen.* 1881. So **Poly·te·chnical** *a.* = A.

Polytheism (pǫ·liþī,iz'm), 1613. [ad. F. *polythéisme*, f. Gr. πολύθεος (f. πολυ- POLY- + θεός god); see -ISM.] Belief in, or worship of, many gods (or more than one god).

Some Temples..furnisht with wooden gods for politheisme 1638.

Polytheist (pǫ·liþī,ist), *sb.* (*a.*) 1619. [f. as prec. + -IST.] One who believes in or worships many gods (or more than one); an adherent of polytheism. Also *attrib.* or as *adj.* Hence **Po:lythei·stic** *a.* of, pertaining to, holding, or characterized by polytheism 1770. **Poly·thei·stical** *a.* = polytheistic; having a polytheistic character or tendency 1678; **-ly** *adv.*

Polytomous (pǫli·tǒməs), *a.* 1858. [f. Gr. *πολύτομος (f. πολυ- POLY- + -τομος cut) + -OUS.] Divided, or involving division, into many parts. **1.** *Bot.* **a.** *spec.* Applied to a leaf having several divisions, but not articulated with the midrib so as to form leaflets. **b.** Applied to branching in which the axis divides into more than two secondary axes at the same point. **2.** *Logic.* Involving polytomy; see next, **2.**

Polytomy (pǫli·tǒmi). 1864. [f. Gr. πολυ- POLY- + -τομια, f. -τομος cut.] **1.** *Bot.* Division into several (more than two) branches at the same spot 1875. **2.** *Logic.* Division into several (usu., more than three) members 1864.

Polytype (pǫ·litəip). 1802. [a. F. *polytype*; see POLY- and TYPE.] A cast, or form of stereotype, made from an intaglio matrix obtained by pressing a woodcut or other plate into semi-fluid metal; a copy of an engraving, of printed matter, etc. made from such a cast. Also *attrib.* So **Po·lytype** *v. trans.* to produce a p. of.

‖ **Polyzoa** (pǫlizōu·ă), *sb. pl.* Sing. **polyzoon** (-zōu·ǫn). 1842. [mod.L., f. Gr. πολυ- POLY- + ζῷον an animal.] *Zool.* = BRYOZOA.

Polyzoan (pǫlizōu·ăn), *a.* and *sb.* 1864. [f. prec. + -AN.] **A.** *adj.* Belonging to or having the character of the *Polyzoa*. **B.** *sb.* A polyzoon; an individual of a polyzoan colony.

Polyzoary (pǫlizōu·ări). Also in L. form **polyzoarium** (pǫ:lizo,ēə·riǒm), pl. **-ia.** 1856. [ad. mod.L. *polyzoarium*, f. POLYZOA + *-arium* -ARY[1].] *Zool.* The polypary or polypidom of a colony of *Polyzoa*, or the colony as a whole.

Polyzoic (pǫlizōu·ik), *a.* 1855. [f. POLYZOA + -IC.] *Zool.* Pertaining to or of the nature of the *Polyzoa*; compound, colonial. **b.** In *Sporozoa*, Applied to a spore which produces many germs or sporozoites 1901.

Polyzoon, sing. of POLYZOA.

Pom (pǫm), abbrev. f. POMERANIAN *sb.* b.

Pomace (pv·mĕs). late ME. [A deriv. of L. *pomum* or F. *pomme* apple.] **1.** The mass of crushed apples in the process of making cider after or before the juice is pressed out. **2.** *transf.* **a.** Anything crushed or pounded to a pulp 1555. **b.** Any solid refuse whence oil has been expressed or extracted 1861.

Pomaceous (pomēi·ʃəs), *a.* 1706. [f. mod. L. *pomaceus* (f. L. *pomum*) + -OUS; see -ACEOUS.] **1.** Of, pertaining to, or consisting of apples. **2.** *Bot.* Of the nature of a pome or apple; of or pertaining to the *Pomeæ*, a division of rosaceous trees bearing pomes or pome-like fruits 1858.

Pomade (pǒmā·d, pǒmēi·d), *sb.* 1562. [a. F. *pommade.* See POMATUM.] A scented ointment (in which apples were perh. orig. an ingredient) for application to the skin; now used esp. for the skin of the head and the hair. Hence **Poma·de** *v. trans.* to anoint or dress with p.

Pomander (pōu·-, pǫ·măndeɹ, pǫmæ·ndəɹ). Now *Hist.* 1492. [Early mod.E. *pom(e)amber*, a. OF. **pome ambre*, *pomme d'embre*, f. *pome* apple + *ambre* AMBER.] **1.** A mixture of aromatic substances, usu. made into a ball, to be carried about with one, esp. as a safeguard against infection. **b.** *transf.* and *fig.* Something scented, or having a sweet odour 1599. **2.** The case in which the perfume was carried, usu. a hollow ball of gold, silver, ivory, etc. 1518. **3.** *attrib.*, as *p. box*, etc. 1599.

‖**Pom(m)ard** (pomā·ɹ). 1833. [Name of a village in the department of Côte d'Or, France.] A red Burgundy wine.

Pomarine (pǫ·mărəin), *a.* 1831. [ad. F. *pomarin*, arbitrary repr. of mod.L. *pomatorhi-*

nus.] *Ornith.* Having the nostrils partly covered with a scale; applied to a species of Skua.

Pomatum (pǒmēⁱ·tǒm), *sb.* 1562. [a. mod. L. *pomatum*, f. *pomum* apple + *-atum* -ATE [1].] = POMADE *sb.* Also *attrib.* Hence **Poma·tum** *v. trans.* = POMADE *v.*

Pome (pōᵘm), *sb.* late ME. [a. OF. *pome* (F. *pomme*) :—late L. or Rom. **poma* apple, orig. pl. of L. *pomum* 'fruit', later, 'apple'.] **1.** A fruit resembling an apple; now only *poet.* an apple. **b.** *Bot.* A succulent inferior fruit, consisting of a firm fleshy body formed of the enlarged calyx, enclosing two or more few-seeded carpels of cartilaginous or bony texture, forming the core; as an apple, quince, pear, haw, etc. 1816. †**2.** The heart or head of a cabbage, cauliflower, or broccoli -1664. **3.** *transf.* A ball or globe, esp. of metal; the royal globe or ball of dominion = *golden apple* (APPLE 5). late ME.

†**Pome,** *v.* 1658. [ad. F. *pommer*, f. *pomme*; see prec.] *intr.* To form a close compact head or heart, as a cabbage, lettuce, etc. -1727.

†**Pome-ci·tron.** 1555. [f. POME + CITRON.] = CITRON 1. -1802.

Pomegranate (pǫ·m-, pɒ·mgrænėt, pǫm-, pɒmgræ·nėt). [ME. a. OF. *pome* (*pomme*, *pume*) *grenate*, *-ade*, etc., f. *pomme* apple + *grenate*, in mod.F. *grenade* :—pop. L. or Com. Rom. **granata* for cl. L. *granatum* (= *malum granatum*), lit. an apple having many grains or seeds.] **1.** The fruit of the tree *Punica Granatum*, N. O. *Myrtaceæ*, a large roundish many-celled berry, with many seeds, each enveloped in a pleasantly acid juicy reddish pulp, enclosed in a tough rind of a golden colour tinged with red. **b.** The tree *Punica Granatum*, a native of northern Africa and western Asia. late ME. **c.** The flower of the pomegranate; usu. scarlet 1873. **2.** A representation of a pomegranate as an ornament or decoration. late ME. **3.** *attrib.*, as *p. apple*, etc.; **p.-tree** = 1 b. late ME.

Pomelo (pǫ·mělo, pɒ·mělo). 1858. [Origin obsc.] **a.** In the E. Indies, a synonym of POMPELMOOSE or SHADDOCK. **b.** In America, a variety of *Citrus*, also called 'grape-fruit'.

Pomeranian (pǫmĕrēⁱ·niăn). *a.* (*sb.*) 1760. [f. *Pomerania*, name of the province.] Of or pertaining to Pomerania, a district on the south coast of the Baltic Sea, now a province of Prussia. **B.** *sb.* **a.** An inhabitant of Pomerania. **b.** Short for *P. dog*, a small (black, white, or brown) breed of dog characterized by long silky hair forming a frill round the neck, bushy tail, sharp muzzle, and pointed ears.

Pomeridian (pōᵘměri·diăn), *a.* 1560. [ad. L. *pomeridianus*, f. *post* after + *meridianus* MERIDIAN.] †**a.** = POSTMERIDIAN *a.* -1653. **b.** *Entom.* Flying in the afternoon, as some lepidopterous insects. **c.** *Bot.* Opening or closing in the afternoon, as a flower. 1866.

Po·mewa·ter. *Obs.* exc. *dial.* late ME. [app. f. POME + WATER *sb.*] A large juicy kind of apple.

Pomeys, pomeis (pōᵘ·mis), *sb. pl.* 1562. [perh. old spelling of *pommes*.] *Her.* The name given to roundels when of a green colour.

Pomfret (pǫ·mfrėt). 1727. [app. f. Pg. *pampo*, F. *pample*.] A fish of the genus *Stromateoides*, inhabiting the Indian and Pacific Oceans, much esteemed for food, esp. *S. niger*, the *black p.*, and *S. sinensis*, the *white p.*, known when young as *silver p.* **b.** A species of sea-bream, *Brama Rayi*, found near Bermuda 1890.

Pomfret-cake (pǫ·mfrėt kēⁱk). 1838. [f. *Pomfret* (now spelt *Pontefract*), a town in Yorkshire.] A liquorice cake made at Pontefract.

Pomiculture (pōᵘ·mikɒltʃəɪ). 1876. [f. L. *pomum* + CULTURE.] The art or practice of fruit-growing.

Pomiferous (pomi·fĕrəs), *a.* 1656. [f. L. *pomifer* + -OUS.] Producing fruit, or specifically apples; *spec.* in *Bot.*, bearing pomes or pome-like fruits (formerly including cucumbers, melons, etc.).

Pommage (pǫ·mėdʒ). 1570. [Cf. F. *pommage* cider harvest or production; also, POMACE.] †**1.** Cider (*rare*) -1577. **2.** = POMACE 1. 1789.

‖**Pommé, -ee** (pome), *a.* 1727. [F. *pommé*, pa. pple of *pommer* to POME.] *Her.* = POMMETTY.

Pommel (pɒ·mĕl), *sb.*[1] [ME., a. OF. *pomel* (mod.F. *pommeau*) :—late L. type **pomellum*, dim. of *pomum* apple (see POME).] †**1.** A globular body or prominence; a ball; a round boss, knob, or button -1688. †**2.** A ball or spherical ornament forming a finial, or the like -1720. **3. a.** The knob terminating the hilt of a sword, dagger, or the like ME. †**b.** = CASCABEL 1. -1692. †**4.** A rounded or semi-globular projecting part; as the rounded top of the head, etc.; also, a bastion -1687. **5.** The upward projecting front part of a saddle; the saddle-bow 1450.

4. He pighte hym on the pomel of his heed CHAUCER. *Comb.* **p.-foot,** a club-foot.

Pommel (pɒ·mĕl), *sb.*[2] 1839. [ad. F. *paumelle*, f. *paume* PALM *sb.*[2]] A wooden block with a convex ribbed face for making leather supple.

Pommel (pɒ·mĕl), *v.* 1530. [f. POMMEL *sb.*[1] 3 a.] *trans.* To beat or strike repeatedly with or as with a pommel; to beat or pound with the fists; to bruise. See also PUMMEL.

†**Pomme·lion.** 1796. [Unexplained extension of POMMEL *sb.*[1] 3 b.] = CASCABEL 1. -1867.

Pommery (pǫ·mĕri). 1892. A brand of champagne.

Pommetty (pǫ·mĕti), *a.* 1611. [a. F. *pommetté*, f. *pommette*, dim. of *pomme* apple.] *Her.* Terminating in a knob or knobs, as the arms of a cross.

Pommy (pǫ·mi). *Australian.* 1922. [Of obsc. origin.] A newcomer from 'the old country'.

‖**Pomœrium** (pomīᵊ·riǒm). 1598. [L., f. *post* + *mœrus*, *murus* wall.] *Rom. Antiq.* The open space running inside and outside the walls of a city, which was consecrated by the pontifex and ordained to be left free from buildings. Hence *transf.*

Pomology (pomǫ·lŏdʒi). 1818. [ad. mod. L. *pomologia*; see POME and -LOGY.] The science and practice of fruit-culture; also, a treatise on this. Hence **Pomolo·gical** *a.* **Pomo·logist.**

Pomona (pǒmōᵘ·nă). 1584. [L.] *Rom. Myth.* The goddess of fruits and fruit-trees; hence, the fruit-trees of a country, or a treatise on them (cf. *flora*).

P. green, green in which yellow predominates.

Pomp (pǫmp), *sb.* ME. [a. F. *pompe* :—L. *pompa*, ad. Gr. πομπή a sending, procession, pomp, etc., f. πέμπειν to send.] **1.** Splendid display or celebration; splendour, magnificence. Also with *a* and *pl.* †**2.** A triumphal or ceremonial procession or train; a pageant -1807 †**b.** *fig.* -1712. †**3.** Ostentatious display; parade; vain glory; esp. in phr. *p. and pride* -1772. **b.** *pl.* ME.

1. The boast of heraldry, the p. of pow'r GRAY. *fig.* I saw the p. of day depart LONGF. 2. Here, while the proud their long-drawn pomps display GOLDSM. 3. b. The pomps and vanities of the wicked world *Bk. Comm. Prayer* (1603) *Catechism.* Hence †**Pomp** *v. intr.* to exhibit p. or splendour; to conduct oneself pompously. **Po·mpal** *a. rare*, splendid, showy.

Pompadour (pǫ·mpădūᵊɪ). 1752. Name of the Marquise de Pompadour, mistress of Louis XV (1721-64), used as sb. and attrib. to designate fashions, a colour, etc. **1.** Designating fashions of dress, hair-dressing, furniture, etc. **2.** A shade of crimson or pink; also, a fabric of this colour. Also *attrib.* 1756. **3.** Designating a pattern consisting of sprigs of flowers in pink, blue, and sometimes gold, scattered on a white ground 1807. **4.** A tropical S. Amer. bird (*Xipholena pompadora*), having brilliant crimson-purple plumage. Also *attrib.* 1759. **5.** A style of arranging women's hair, in which it is turned back off the forehead in a roll. Also *attrib.* 1899.

Pompano (pǫ·mpăno). Also **pompono.** 1863. [a. Sp. *pámpano*, applied to a stromateoid fish, *Stromateus fiatola*.] **1.** One of various W. Indian and N. American fishes, highly esteemed for the table; as **a.** In the W. Indies, *Trachynotus carolinus.* **b.** In California, *Stromateus simillimus.* **c.** In Florida, *Gerres olisthostoma*, known as the *Irish p.* **2. P.-shell.** A bivalve shell of the genus *Donax*; found on the coast of Florida 1890.

†**Pompa·tic,** *a.* 1535. [ad. late L. *pompaticus*, f. *pompare* to do (a thing) with pomp, f. *pompa* POMP *sb.*] Pompous, splendid, ostentatious -1677.

Pompeian (pǫmpī·ăn), *a.* †Also **Pompeiian.** 1834. [ad. L. *Pompeianus*, f. *Pompeii*; see -AN.] Of or pertaining to Pompeii, an Italian town, buried by an eruption of Mount Vesuvius in A.D. 79.

P. red, a shade of red resembling that found on the walls of houses in Pompeii.

Pompelmoose, pampelmouse (pǫ·mp-, pæ·mp'lˌmūs). 1696. [Du. *pompelmoes*, perh. repr. Du. *pompoen* pumpkin + Old Javanese *limoes*, borrowed from Pg. *limoes* pl. of *limão*, lemon; i.e. 'pumpkin-like citron'.] The large fruit of *Citrus decumana*, called also SHADDOCK; esp. the larger variety. Also the plant itself.

Pompey (pǫ·mpi), *v.* 1860. [Extended f. dial. *pomp* to pamper; a word of Dickens.] *trans.* To pamper.

‖**Pompholyx** (pǫ·mfǒliks). 1541. [a. Gr. πομφόλυξ bubble, slag of ore]. †**1.** *Chem.* Crude zinc oxide -1725. **2.** *Path.* A vesicle on the skin; also, an eruption of vesicles, without inflammation or fever, appearing chiefly on the palms of the hands and the soles of the feet 1818. Hence **Pompho·lygous** *a.* affected with p.

‖**Pompier** (pǫ·mpiəɪ). 1893. [F., f. *pompe* PUMP *sb.*; see -IER.] A fireman.

P. ladder, a fireman's scaling ladder, with a hook at the top to attach it to a building.

Pompion, pumpion (pɒ·mpiən). Now *rare.* 1545. [Orig. a. obs. F. *pompon*, nasalized form of *popon*, *poupon*, also *pepon*, ad. L. *pepo*, *-onem*, a. Gr. πέπων, -ον- PUMPKIN.] **1.** The large fruit of *Cucurbita Pepo*; a pumpkin; also the plant itself. †**2.** Occas. applied to the POMPELMOOSE -1704. †**3.** Applied in contempt to a (big) man -1625.

3. This vnwholsome humidity, this grosse-watry Pumpion SHAKS.

Pompoleon (pǫmpōᵘ·liǫn). 1837. [a. F. *pompoléon*; app. conn. w. *pompelmoose*.] The SHADDOCK or POMPELMOOSE (*Citrus decumana*).

Pom-pom (pǫ·mpǫm). 1899. [Echoic.] Name given to the Maxim automatic quick-firing gun; see MAXIM [2]. Also *fig.*, and *attrib.* as *p. gun* 1900.

Pompon (pǫ·mpǫn, ‖ poṅpoṅ). Also **pom-pom.** 1748. [a. F., a tuft, top-knot; origin unkn.] **1.** A jewel or ornament attached to a long pin; a tuft or bunch of ribbon, velvet, threads of silk, etc., formerly worn in the hair, or on the cap or dress; now worn on women's and children's hats and shoes, etc., and used to ornament the edge of curtains, etc.; also, the round tuft on a soldier's or sailor's cap, the front of a shako, etc. **2.** A variety of Chrysanthemum, and of Dahlia, bearing small globular flowers. Also *attrib.* 1861.

Pomposity (pǫmpǫ·sĭti). late ME. [ad. med.L. *pompositas*; see POMPOUS and -ITY.] The quality of being pompous; †pomp, solemnity; ostentatiousness in deportment or language.

Pompous (pǫ·mpəs), *a.* late ME. [= F. *pompeux*, ad. late L. *pomposus*, f. *pompa* POMP; see -OUS.] **1.** Characterized by pomp; magnificent, splendid; †processional. **2.** Characterized by an exaggerated display of self-importance or dignity; consequential, pretentious, ceremonious; of language: inflated, turgid. late ME.

1. Many processions and other p. shows 1841. 2. A well-meaning, civil, prosing, p. woman, who thought nothing of consequence, but as it related to her own ..concerns JANE AUSTEN. Hence **Po·mpous-ly** *adv.*, **-ness.**

‖**Ponceau** (poṅso). 1835. [F.] The bright red colour of the corn poppy. Also, a coal-tar dye of red colour.

Poncho (pǫ·ntʃo, pǫ·nʃo). 1748. [a. S. Amer.-Sp., a. Araucanian *poncho*, *pontho*.] A S. Amer. cloak, consisting of an oblong piece of cloth with a slit in the middle for the head.

Pond (pǫnd), *sb.* [ME. *ponde*, app. var. of POUND *sb.*[2]] 1. A small body of still water of artificial formation. Often distinguished as a *duck-p.*, *fish-p.*, *mill-p.*, *village p.*, etc. Formerly often *spec.* = fish-pond. b. Locally applied to a natural pool, tarn, mere, or small lake 1480. 2. Applied *fig.* or *joc.* to the sea, esp. the Atlantic Ocean; cf. HERRING-POND 1641. 3. In a canal: = POUND sb.[2] II. 1 b.

attrib. and *Comb.*: **p.-fish,** (*a*) a fish usu. reared in a pond, as a carp; (*b*) *spec.* in *U.S.*, a fish of the genus *Pomotis* or *Lepomis*, a sunfish; **-life,** the animals, esp. the invertebrata, that live in ponds or stagnant water; **-lily,** a water-lily, as the yellow *Nuphar lutea*, or the white *Nymphæa alba*; **-snail,** any freshwater snail inhabiting ponds; **-spice,** a N. Amer. shrub (*Tetranthera geniculata*) growing in sandy swamps; **-tortoise, -turtle** (*U.S.*), any freshwater tortoise of the family *Emydidæ*; a terrapin or mud-turtle.

Pond (pǫnd), *v.* 1673. [f. prec. Cf. POUND *v.*[2]] 1. *trans.* To hold *back* or dam *up* (a stream) into or as into a pond; to pound. 2. *intr.* Of water, etc.: To form a pool or pond; to collect by being held back 1857.

Pondage (pǫ·ndėdʒ). 1877. [f. POND *sb.* + -AGE.] Storage or ponding of water; the capacity of a pond or dam for holding water.

Ponder (pǫ·ndəɹ), *v.* [ME. a. OF. *ponderer*, F. *pondérer*, ad. L. *ponderare* to weigh, f. *pondus, ponder-* weight.] †1. *trans.* To weigh. Also *fig.* -1645. †2. To estimate the worth, value, or amount of; to appraise -1566. 3. To weigh (a matter, words, etc.) mentally; to give due weight to; to think over, meditate upon. late ME. 4. *intr.* To consider, meditate, reflect; to think deeply or seriously *on*, muse *over* 1605.

3. Consydre thys mater and p. my cause LYDG. Pondering only how he might save that monarch's crown 1848. 4. Pondering on his unhappy lot DICKENS. Hence †**Po·nder,** an act of pondering. **Po·nderable** *a.* capable of being weighed; having appreciable weight. **Ponderabi·lity, Po·nderableness,** weight, heaviness. **Po·nderer. Po·nderingly** *adv.*

Ponderal (pǫ·ndərăl), *a.* 1674. [f. L. *pondus, ponder-* + -AL.] Of or pertaining to weight; determined or estimated by weight.

Ponderance (pǫ·ndərăns). 1812. [f. L. *ponderare* + -ANCE.] Weight; gravity, importance. So **Po·nderary** *a.* = PONDERAL 1845.

Ponderate (pǫ·ndəreit), *v.* 1513. [f. L. *ponderat-*, *ponderare*; see PONDER *v.* and -ATE [3].] 1. *intr.* To have weight; to be heavy, to weigh 1659. †2. *trans.* To weigh down; to influence, bias -1709. †3. To estimate in the mind, ponder -1753. 4. To estimate the importance or value of; to appraise (*rare*) 1649. So **Pondera·tion,** weighing; balancing; also *fig.*

Ponderosity (pǫndərǫ·sĭti). 1450. [ad. med.L. *ponderositas*, f. L. *ponderosus* + -ITY.] 1. The quality of being ponderous; weightiness, weight. 2. *fig.* Weightiness, importance; heaviness, dullness 1589.

Ponderous (pǫ·ndərəs), *a.* late ME. [ad. F. *pondéreux*, ad. L. *ponderosus*; see -OUS.] 1. Having great weight; heavy; massive; clumsy, unwieldy. Also *fig.* †b. Having some weight; ponderable SIR T. BROWNE. †2. Of great weight in proportion to bulk -1800. †3. *fig.* Of grave import; weighty, important, profound -1794. †4. Given to weighing or pondering matters; deliberate -1647. 5. Of a task, etc.: Heavy, laborious. Of style: Laboured; grandiloquent; tedious. 1704.

1. Why the Sepulcher..Hath op'd his p. and Marble iawes SHAKS. 2. *P. earth, spar* = HEAVY SPAR. 5. Sir John Hawkins's p. labours BOSWELL. Hence **Po·nderous-ly** *adv.*, **-ness.**

Po·ndweed. 1578. [f. POND *sb.* + WEED *sb.*] An aquatic weed that grows in ponds and still waters; *spec.* in Great Britain, the species of *Potamogeton*.

American, Canadian, or Choke P., *Elodea canadensis* (*Anacharis Alsinastrum*); Horned or Triple-headed P., *Zannichellia palustris*.

†‖**Pone** [1] (pōu·nĭ). ME. [L. *pone*, imper. of *ponere* to place.] *Law.* a. A writ by which a suit was removed from an inferior court to the Court of Common Pleas. b. A writ requiring the sheriff to secure the appearance of the defendant by attaching his goods or by causing him to find sureties for his appearance. -1768.

Pone [2] (pōu·nĭ). 1890. [f. as prec.] The leader, or the leader's partner, in some card games. Also written *pony*.

Pone [3] (pōun). 1634. [ad. Algonkin *pone*, *apone*, *oppone* bread, perh. orig. pa. pple. = 'baked'.] Any bread made of maize; orig. that of the N. Amer. Indians, made in thin cakes, and cooked in hot ashes; also, very fine light bread, enriched with milk, eggs, and the like, and made in flat cakes. Also *attrib.* b. A cake or loaf of such bread 1796.

Ponent (pōu·nĕnt), *a.* (*sb.*) 1538. [ad. It. *ponente*, med.L. *ponens, ponentem* west, west wind, sunset, lit. setting, f. *ponere*.] †1. Situated in the west; occidental. Also as *sb.* The west; the occident. -1819. 2. *Geol.* Name for a subdivision of the Palæozoic strata of the Appalachian chain 1858. 3. *Logic.* That posits 1837.

1. Forth rush the Levant and the P. Windes MILT.

Pongee (pǫndʒī·). 1711. [perh. ad. N. Chinese *pŭn-chī* own loom, or ad. *pŭn-chəh* own weaving.] A soft unbleached kind of Chinese silk; known in the East as Chefoo silk; also *attrib.*

‖**Pongo** (pǫ·ŋgo). 1625. [Native name in Angola or Loango.] In early writers, a large anthropoid African ape; variously identified with the Chimpanzee, and the Gorilla. b. Transferred (erron.) to the Orang-outang 1834.

Poniard (pǫ·nyăɹd). 1588. [a. F. *poignard*, †*poingnart*, f. *poing* fist; see -ARD.] A short stabbing weapon; a dagger.

fig. Shee speakes poynyards, and euery word stabbes SHAKS. Hence **Po·niard** *v. trans.* to stab or pierce (esp. to stab to death) with a p. 1601.

‖**Pons** (pǫnz). The L. word for 'bridge', used in certain phrases. 1. **Pons asinorum** (= bridge of asses): a *joc.* name for the fifth proposition of the first book of Euclid, which beginners, etc., find difficulty in 'getting over'. Hence allusively. 1751. 2. **Pons Varolii** (= bridge of Varolius or Varoli, an Italian anatomist of the 16th c.), also **pons cerebri** or **cerebelli,** and often simply **pons:** a band of nerve fibres in the brain, just above the medulla oblongata, consisting of transverse fibres connecting the two hemispheres of the cerebellum, and longitudinal fibres connecting the medulla with the cerebrum 1693.

Pontage (pǫ·ntėdʒ). Now *Hist.* or *local.* 1447. [a. OF.:—med.L. *pontaticum* a bridge-toll, f. L. *pons, pontem* bridge + -*aticum* -AGE.] A toll paid for the use of a bridge; a tax paid for the maintenance and repair of a bridge or bridges; bridge-toll.

Pontic (pǫ·ntik), *a.* 1477. [ad. L. *Ponticus*, a. Gr. ποντικός, f. πόντος sea, spec. the Black Sea, hence the country of Pontus.] 1. Of, belonging to, found in, or obtained from the district of Pontus 1551. †2. Having a somewhat sour and astringent taste [? like Pontic rhubarb] -1684.

1. **P. nut,** the hazel nut. **P. rhubarb,** *Rheum rhaponticum*. **P. wormwood,** *Artemisia pontica*. **P. sea,** the Black Sea.

‖**Pontifex** (pǫ·ntifeks). *Pl.* **pontifices** (pǫnti·fisīz). 1579. [L. *pontifex, -icem*; perh. f. Osc.-Umb. *puntis* propitiatory offering, assim. to *pons, pontem* bridge + -*fic-* from *facere* to make.] 1. *Rom. Antiq.* A member of the principal college of priests in ancient Rome, the head of which was the *P. Maximus* or chief priest. 2. *Eccl.* = PONTIFF 2. 1651. 3. With allusion to the reputed etymological meaning = Bridge-maker 1831.

Pontiff (pǫ·ntif). 1610. [a. F. *pontife*, ad. L. *pontifex*; see prec.] 1. *Rom. Antiq.* = prec. 1. 1626. 2. A bishop; *spec.* and usu., the bishop of Rome, the pope (in full, *sovereign p.*) 1677. 3. *gen.* A chief or high priest. Also *fig.* 1610.

Pontific (pǫnti·fik), *a.* Now *rare* or *Obs.* 1644. [f. L. *pons, pontem* + -*ficus* making, but used in sense of *pontificius*; see PONTIFICIAL.] 1. *Rom. Antiq.* = PONTIFICAL *a.* II. 2. = PONTIFICAL *a.* I. 1–3. 1716. ¶3. *catachr.* Pertaining to a bridge (*joc.*) STERNE.

Pontifical (pǫnti·fikăl), *a.* and *sb.* ME. [ad. L. *pontificalis*, f. PONTIFEX; see -AL.] A. *adj.* I. 1. Pertaining or proper to a bishop or prelate; episcopal 1440. 2. *spec.* Of or pertaining to the pope; papal 1447. 3. *gen.* Of or pertaining to a chief or high priest; high-priestly 1440. 4. Characterized by the pomp, state, authority, or dogmatic character of a pontiff 1589.

4. Comte's arrogance, his p. airs, and his hatred of liberty 1892.

II. *Rom. Antiq.* Of or belonging to the *pontifices* of ancient Rome; see PONTIFEX 1. 1579. III. Bridge-making, bridge-building 1667.

B. *sb.* †1. a. *pl.* The offices or duties of a pontifex or pontiff. b. An office celebrated with pontifical ceremony. -1691. 2. (Now always *pl.*) = PONTIFICALIA ME. 3. An office-book in the Western Church, containing the forms for rites and ceremonies to be performed by bishops 1584. †4. a. A pontiff, a church dignitary. b. An adherent of the pontiffs or prelates. -1590. Hence **Ponti·fically** *adv.*

‖**Pontificalia** (pǫntifikēi·liă), *sb. pl.* 1577. [L., neut. pl. of *pontificalis* adj. PONTIFICAL.] The vestments and other insignia of a bishop (or of a priest). Also *transf.* Official robes.

In pontificalibus: see ‖IN 13; hence *pontificalibus* is occas. used as if an ordinary English noun. late ME.

Pontificality (pǫntifikæ·lĭti). 1556. [ad. obs. F. *pontificalité* pontifical dignity; see PONTIFICAL and -ITY.] 1. Pontifical office or dignity; esp. that of the pope. b. *transf.* or *gen.* Priesthood; high-priesthood 1593. †2. (Usu. in *pl.*) Pontifical robes, pontificals -1645. 3. A pontifical rite, ceremony, or function CARLYLE.

Pontificate (pǫnti·fikĕt), *sb.* 1581. [ad. L. *pontificatus*, the office or dignity of a pontifex; see -ATE [1].] a. The office of an ancient Roman *Pontifex*. b. The office, or period of office, of a bishop; usu. of the pope; papacy; popedom 1674. c. *gen.* High-priesthood 1727.

Pontificate (pǫnti·fikeit), *v.* 1818. [f. med. L. *pontificat-*, *pontificare* to perform pontifical functions, f. *pontificem* PONTIFEX; see -ATE [3].] 1. *intr.* To perform the functions of a pontiff or bishop; to officiate as a bishop, esp. at mass. 2. To act the pontiff, assume the airs of a pontiff. Also *fig.* to issue dogmatic decrees. 1825.

†**Po·ntifice.** [f. L. *pons, pont-* bridge, after *edifice*.] The edifice of a bridge; a bridge MILT.

†**Pontifi·cial,** *a.* and *sb.* 1591. [f. L. *pontificius* pertaining to a pontifex + -AL.] A. *adj.* 1. = PONTIFICAL *a.* I. 1, 2. -1769. 2. Popish, papistical -1684. 3. = PONTIFICAL *a.* I. 4. -1709. B. *sb.* An adherent of the prelates, or of the pontiff -1838.

A. 1. *P. law*, canon law. 2. P. Princes and Prelates, the sworn Enemies to the Protestant Religion 1641. Hence †**Pontifi·cially** *adv.* So †**Pontifi·cian** *a.* and *sb.*

Pontil (pǫ·ntil). 1832. [a. F., app. ad. It. *pontello, puntello*, dim. of *punto* point, etc.] *Glass-making.* An iron rod used for handling soft glass in the process of formation, esp. in the manufacture of crown-glass. Cf. PUNTY.

Pontine (pǫ·ntəin), *a.* 1899. [f. L. *pons, pont-* + -INE [1].] *Anat.* and *Path.* Pertaining to or occurring in the *pons Varolii*; see PONS.

‖**Pont-levis** (poṅləvi, pǫnt‚le·vis). 1489. [a. F., f. *pont* bridge + *levis*, OF. *leveïs* adj. movable up and down:—L. **levaticius*, f. *levare* to raise.] A drawbridge.

Pontoneer, -ier (pǫntonī^ə·ɹ). 1830. [ad. F. *pontonnier*:—med.L. *pontonarius* a ferryman, f. *ponto, -onem* PONTOON; see -EER.] *Mil.* One who has charge of pontoons, or of the construction of a pontoon-bridge.

Pontoon (pǫntū·n), *sb.*[1] 1676. [ad. F. *ponton*, f. L. *ponto, -onem* punt, floating bridge, pontoon, f. *pons, pontem*; see -OON.] 1. A flat-bottomed boat used as a lighter, ferry-boat, or the like; *spec.* in *Mil. Engineering*, such a boat, or other floating vessel (as a hollow metal cylinder), of which a number are used to support a temporary bridge over a river. 2. *Naut.* A large flat-bottomed barge or lighter furnished with cranes, capstans, and tackle, used for careening ships, raising weights, etc. 1769. 3. *Hydraulic Engineering* = CAISSON 2 b, c. 1875.

attrib. and *Comb.*: **p.-bridge,** a bridge constructed upon pontoons; **-train,** a train of wagons carrying pontoons. Hence **Pontoo·n** *v. trans.* to cross (a river) by means of pontoons; also *fig.*

Pontoo·n, *sb.*² 1900. Corruption (orig. soldiers') of the name of the card-game VINGT-UN.

Pony (pōu·ni), *sb.* 1659. [Sc. *powney*, prob. :—**poulney*, ad. F. *poulenet* little foal, dim. of *poulain*, *polain* foal, colt :—late L. *pullanus*, f. L. *pullus* young animal, foal.] **1.** A horse of any small breed; *spec.* a horse not more than 13 or (in pop. use) 14 hands high. **2.** *slang.* The sum of twenty-five pounds sterling 1797. **3.** *U.S. slang.* A school or college 'crib' 1832. **4.** *slang.* A small glass of liquor 1884.

attrib. and *Comb.*, as *p.-chaise*, etc.; also, **p. engine,** a small locomotive for shunting; **-truck,** a two-wheeled leading or trailing truck in some forms of locomotive; **-truss,** a truss so low that overhead bracing cannot be used.

‖**Pood** (pūd). 1554. [Russ. *pud*ᵘ, ad. LG. or Norse *pund* POUND.] A weight, equal to 40 lb. Russian, or about 36 lb. avoirdupois.

Poodle (pū·d'l), *sb.* 1825. [a. G. *pudel*, short for *pudelhund*, f. LG. *pud(d)eln* to splash in water, the poodle being a water-dog.] One of a breed of pet dogs with long curling hair, usu. black or white, which is often clipped or shaved in a fantastic manner. Also *attrib.*

Comb. **p.-faker,** one who cultivates female society; also **-faking.** Hence **Poo·dle** *v. trans.* to clip and shave the hair of (a dog).

Poof (puf), *int.* Also **pouf.** 1857. [Cf. F. *pouf.*] A sound imitating a short puff of the breath, as in blowing out a candle; hence an expression of contemptuous rejection.

Pooh (pū, puh), *interj.* (*sb.*) 1593. A 'vocal gesture' expressing the action of puffing anything away, and hence impatience or contemptuous disregard. **B.** as *sb.* 1667.

Affection, puh! You speake like a greene Girle SHAKS. Hence **Pooh** *v. intr.* and *trans.*

Pooh Bah (pū bā). 1888. [Name of a character in W. S. Gilbert's *Mikado*, joc. made up of the interjections *pooh* and *bah*.] One who holds many offices at one time.

Pooh pooh (pū·pū·), *int.* (*sb.*, *a.*) 1679. Reduplication of POOH *int.* **B.** *sb.* (*pooh-pooh*). An utterance of this exclam.; one who is addicted to using this exclam. 1798. **C.** *attrib.* or *adj.*, as in *pooh-pooh theory*, the theory that language is a development of natural interjections 1860. Hence **Pooh-pooh** *v. trans.* to express contempt or disdain for; to make light of 1827.

‖**Pookoo, puku** (pū·ku). 1890. [ad. Zulu *mpuku*.] A red water-buck or antelope (*Cobus vardoni*) of southern Central Africa.

Pool (pūl), *sb.*¹ [OE. *pól*; WGer. stem **pôlo-*.] **1.** A small body of standing or still water; usu., one of natural formation. **b.** A small shallow collection of any liquid; a puddle 1843. **c.** *transf.* and *fig.* 1587. **2.** A deep and still place in a river or stream OE.

1. The noisy geese that gabbled o'er the p. GOLDSM. **b.** Wallowing in a p. of blood MACAULAY. **c.** On the floor ..A little p. of sunlight 1875. **2.** *The P.*, the part of the Thames between London Bridge and Cuckold's Point.

Pool, *sb.*² 1693. [= F. *poule* in same sense. In Eng., assoc. w. prec., but prob. derived from F. *poule* hen, chicken, being at first perh. slang for 'booty, plunder'.] **1.** In certain card games, etc.: The collective amount of the stakes and fines of the players joining in the game 1711. **b.** The receptacle containing the stakes; the pool-dish 1770. †**2.** A party in a card-game in which there is a pool –1859. **3.** A game played on a billiard-table, in which each player has a ball of a distinctive colour with which he tries to pocket the balls of the other players in a certain order, each player contributing an agreed sum, the whole of which the winner takes; also, a similar game in U. S., played with balls numbered 1 to 15, the number of each ball a player pockets being added to his score 1848. **4. a.** *Rifle-Shooting.* A contest in which each competitor pays a certain sum for every shot he fires, the proceeds being divided among the winners. Also *attrib.* 1861. **b.** *Betting.* The collective stakes in an instance of PARI MUTUEL 1881. **5.** A common fund into or from which all gains or losses of the contributors are paid; hence, a 'combine' 1872. **6.** An arrangement between previously competing parties, by which rates or prices are fixed, and business or receipts divided, in order to do away with mutually injurious competition (orig. *U.S.*) 1881. **7.** *Fencing.* A contest between teams, in which each member of one side opposes each member of the other 1901.

2. Monday, when we played six pools 1801. *To make (up) a p.*, to form or make up the party. **5.** The fifty-million dollar p. in Union Pacific Preferred Stock 1906.

Pool (pūl), *v.*¹ 1793. [f. POOL *sb.*¹] *trans.* In quarrying granite: To sink or make (a hole) for the insertion of a wedge. In coal-mining: To undermine (coal) so as to cause it to fall.

Pool (pūl), *v.*² 1879. [f. POOL *sb.*²] *trans.* To throw into a common stock to be distributed according to agreement; to combine (capital or interests) for the common benefit; *spec.* of competing railway companies, etc.: To share or divide (traffic or receipts).

‖**Poon** (pūn). 1699. [Sinhalese *pūna*, Tamil *punnai*.] Any of several large E. Indian trees of the genus *Calophyllum*, esp. *C. Inophyllum*; also, their timber. Chiefly *attrib.*

‖**Poonac** (pū·næk). 1890. [Tamil *punnakku*, Sinhalese *punakku*.] The oil-cake or mass left after the oil has been expressed from coco-nut pulp; used as fodder or manure.

Poonah (pū·nă). 1821. Name of a city in the Bombay Presidency.

attrib.: **P. painting,** painting on rice (or other thin) paper, in imitation of oriental work, by the application of thick body-colour, with little or no shading, and without background.

‖**Poonga-oil** (pū·ŋgă,oil). 1866. [f. Tamil *punga*.] A dark-yellow oil expressed from the seeds of *Pongamia glabra*, used in India as lamp-oil and as a remedy in skin-diseases.

Poop (pūp), *sb.* 1489. [a. OF. *pupe*, *pope*, F. *poupe* :—late L. **puppa* for L. *puppis* poop, stern.] **1.** The aftermost part of a ship; the stern; also, the aftermost and highest deck, often forming the roof of the cabin built in the stern. †**2.** *transf.* The dickey or seat at the back of a coach; the hinder part of a man or animal. *colloq.* or *vulgar.*

1. The Poope was beaten Gold SHAKS.

Comb.: **p.-royal,** the deck forming the roof of the poop-cabin.

†**Poop** (pūp), *v.*¹ 1575. [Origin obsc.; cf. Du. *poep* a clown.] *trans.* To cheat, befool –1663.

Poop (pūp), *v.*² 1727. [f. POOP *sb.*] *Naut. trans.* Of a wave: To break over the stern of (a vessel). **b.** *transf.* Of a ship: To receive (a wave) over the stern; to ship (a sea) on the poop 1894.

Pooped (pūpt), *a.* 1879. [f. POOP *sb.* + -ED ².] Having a poop; chiefly in comb. as *high-p.*

Poor (pūᵊɹ), *a.* (*sb.*) [ME. *pov(e)re*, *pou(e)re*, a. OF. *povre*, *poure*, F. *pauvre* :—L. *pauper*.] **I. 1.** Having few, or no, material possessions; wanting means to procure the comforts, or the necessaries, of life; needy, destitute; *spec.* (esp. in legal use), so destitute as to be dependent on gifts or allowances for subsistence. In common use expressing various degrees of poverty. The opposite of *rich* or *wealthy*. **b.** Of, involving, or characterized by poverty ME. **2.** Ill-supplied, lacking (*in* some possession or quality). late ME. **b.** Of soil, ore, etc.: Yielding little, unproductive 1592. **3.** In lean or feeble condition from ill feeding 1539. **4.** Small in amount; less than is wanted or expected; scanty, inadequate ME. **5.** Not worth much; of inferior quality, paltry, sorry; mean, shabby. Usu. of abstract things. ME. **b.** Mentally or morally inferior; mean-spirited; despicable, 'small'; spiritless. late ME. **c.** Slight, insignificant 1603. **d.** In modest or apologetic use: Of little worth or pretension; humble, insignificant. late ME. **6.** Such, or so circumstanced, as to excite one's compassion or pity; unfortunate, hapless. In many parts of England regularly said of the dead whom one knew; = late, deceased. Chiefly *colloq.* ME.

1. If thou be'st as poore for a subiect, as hee's for a King, thou art poore enough SHAKS. *fig.* Blissed be þai þat er pouer in spirit 1400. *P. people*, the poor as a class; often connoting humble rank or station; They are almost like p. people's children! C. BRONTE. **b.** Forced..to take..p. and painful Employments FULLER. **2.** Stratified masses,..p. in mineral substances 1863. **b.** P. and hungry soils SIR H. DAVY. **4.** One poore peny-worth of Sugar-candie SHAKS. The crop of wheat would be thought p. MACAULAY. **5.** They made but p. work of it DE FOE. It was p. consolation to know [etc.] (*mod.*). **b.** A Man of a poore Minde, and not valiant 1627. He is a p. creature and more of a Genoese than an Englishman NELSON. **d.** For mine owne poore part, Looke you, Ile goe pray SHAKS. **6.** Till his book of p. Dr. Johnson's life is finished MME. D'ARBLAY. He looked dreadfully weak still, p. fellow! 1857.

II. *absol.* or as *sb.* (usu. in sense 1). **a.** *absol.* in *pl.* sense (usu. with *the*): poor people as a class; those in necessitous or humble circumstances; *spec.* those dependent upon charitable or parochial relief ME. **b.** possessive *poor's* (in sing. or pl. sense). Now *rare* exc. *dial.* late ME.

a. The short and simple annals of the p. GRAY. Money left to the p. of the parish (*mod.*).

Combs. and Phrases. **P. child,** a pupil at a charity school (CHILD *sb.* I. 4); **p.-chest** = POOR-BOX; **p. Clares,** the order of nuns of St. Clare; **p. relation,** a relative or kinsman in humble circumstances (also *transf.*); **p. white** (see WHITE *sb.*). Hence **Poo·rness,** the quality or condition of being p. ME.

Poo·r-box. Also †**poor's box.** 1621. A money-box (esp. in a church) for gifts towards the relief of the poor.

Poorhouse (pūᵊ·ɹhaus). Also **poorshouse** (*Sc.* and *U.S.*). 1781. A house in which poor people in receipt of public charity are lodged.

Poor John, poo·r-john. 1585. [f. POOR *a.* + JOHN.] Hake salted and dried for food; often a type of poor fare. *Obs.* exc. *Hist.*

Poore-Iohn and Apple-pyes are all our fare 1612.

Poor-law (pūᵊ·ɹlǭ). 1752. The law, or system of laws, relating to the support of paupers at the public expense. **b.** *attrib.*, as *p. bill*, *officer*, etc.; **p. parish**: see PARISH 2.

Poorly (pūᵊ·ɹli), *adv.* and *a.* ME. [f. POOR *a.* + -LY ².] In a poor manner or condition. **A.** *adv.* **1.** In a state of poverty or indigence; necessitously. Now somewhat *rare.* late ME. **2.** With deficiency of some desirable quality; scantily, defectively; in mean style, humbly; in an inferior way, rather badly; not highly, with low estimation ME. †**3.** Meanly, shabbily –1723. †**4.** Abjectly, humbly; despicably; mean-spiritedly –1811. **B.** *adj.* Chiefly *colloq.* In a poor state of health; unwell, indisposed. (Always *predicative.*) 1750.

A. 1. Poorely content is better then richlye couetous GREENE. **2.** Long lines of poorly-lighted streets DICKENS. **3.** 'Twas p. done, unworthy of your self OTWAY. **4.** He, instead of opposing..did p. go on board himself, to ask what De Ruyter would have PEPYS. **B.** His wife had..been p. MACAULAY. Hence **Poo·rlyish** *a.* somewhat p. (*rare*).

Poor man. ME. **1.** *lit.* A man who is poor (in any sense); *esp.* a man who is indigent or needy, or who belongs to the class of the poor. **2.** *Poor man of mutton* (Sc. colloq.): the remains of a shoulder of mutton, broiled 1818.

2. I think, landlord..I could eat a morsel of a poor man SCOTT.

Combs.: **poor man's mustard**: see MUSTARD 2 b; **poor man's weather-glass,** the pimpernel, *Anagallis arvensis*, from its closing its flowers before rain.

Poo·r-rate. Also †**poor's rate.** 1601. A rate or assessment for the relief or support of the poor.

Poor-spi·rited, *a.* 1648. Having or showing a poor spirit; deficient in spirit, cowardly. Hence **Poo·r-spi·ritedness.**

Poortith (pūᵊ·ɹtiþ). *Sc.* and *n. dial.* 1508. [a. OF. *povretet*, **povreteð* :—L. *paupertatem* POVERTY.] Poverty.

Poo·r-will. *U.S.* 1888. [In imitation of its note.] A bird of the N. American genus *Phalænoptilus*, esp. *P. nuttalli.* Cf. WHIP-POOR-WILL.

Pop (pǫp), *sb.*¹ late ME. [Echoic; goes with POP *v.*] **1.** An act of popping; now, a slight rap or tap. *Obs.* exc. *dial.* **2.** A short abrupt sound of explosion 1591. **3.** A shot with a fire-arm 1657. **b.** *slang.* A pistol 1728. **4.** A name for any effervescing beverage, esp. ginger-beer, from the sound made when the cork is drawn (*colloq.*) 1812. **5.** A mark made by a slight rapid touch; a dot; a spot, a speck. Also *fig.* 1718. **6.** *slang.* The act of pawning 1866.

3. *fig.* Prestige, you know, I always like to have a p. at FREEMAN. **6.** *In p.*, in pawn.

Pop (pǫp), *sb.*² 1862. Colloq. abbrev. of *popular concert.*

Pop (pǫp), *sb.*³ 1865. [perh. from L. *popina*

or Eng. *lollipop shop*, 'the rooms having orig. been in the house of Mrs. Hatton, who kept such a shop'.] A social club and debating society at Eton College, founded in 1811.

Pop, *sb.*4 *U.S.* 1840. Shortened f. POPPA.

Pop (pǫp), *v.* late ME. [Echoic; goes with POP *sb.*1, *int.*, *adv.*] **1.** *trans.* To strike with a slight rap or tap (*dial.*). **2.** *intr.* To make a small quick explosive sound; to burst or explode with a pop 1576. **3.** *trans.* To cause to go off with a pop; to fire, let off, as an explosive or fire-arm (also *fig.*) 1595. **4.** *intr.* To shoot, fire a gun (*colloq.*) 1725. **b.** *trans.* To shoot *down*; to pick *off* with a shot 1762. **5.** *trans.* To put promptly, suddenly, or unexpectedly; usu. with *down, in, on, out, up, into* or *out of* (a place), etc. 1529. **6.** To put (a question) abruptly; spec. *to p. the question* (*slang* or *colloq.*), to propose marriage 1593. **7.** *slang.* To put in pledge, to pawn 1731. **8.** *intr.* To pass, move, go or come promptly, suddenly, or unexpectedly (*up, down, in, out, between*, etc.) 1530. **b.** *To p. off* (also *off the hooks*): to die (*slang*) 1764.

2. When the chestnuts popped in the ashes 1859. 3. *To p. corn*, to parch or roast Indian corn until it 'pops' open. 4. Popping at pheasants BARHAM. 5. She..popt it into her mouth, and swallowed it all at once 1662. P. me down among your fashionable visitors DICKENS. 8. He that hath..Popt in betweene th' election and my hopes SHAKS. b. I am afraid I shall p. off just when my mind is able to run alone KEATS. Hence **Po·pping** *vbl. sb.* 1652.

Pop (pǫp), *int.*, *adv.* 1621. [See prec.] With (the action or sound of) a pop; instantaneously, abruptly; unexpectedly.

I heard it go p. (*mod.*). *P. goes the weasel*, name of a country dance in which these words were sung while one of the dancers darted under the arms of the others; also the name of the tune.

Pop-, usu. the verb in comb. with a sb. or adv., meaning something that pops; rarely the sb. or adv.: **p.-eye**, a bulging prominent eye; hence **-eyed** *a.*; **-valve** = PUPPET-VALVE; **-weed**, the Bladderwort; etc.

‖**Popadam** (pǫ·pădăm). 1820. [Tamil *pappadam*, contr. from *paruppu-adam* 'lentil cake' (Yule).] Small cakes eaten with curries.

Po·p-corn. *U.S.* 1858. [f. POP *v.* 3 + CORN *sb.*1 3.] **a.** Maize or Indian corn parched till it bursts open and exposes the white inner part of the grain. **b.** A variety of maize suitable for popping. Also *attrib.*

Pope 1 (pōup). [OE. *pápa*, a. eccl. L. *papa*, ad. late Gr. πάπας, παπᾶς, var. of πάππας father]. **I. 1.** The Bishop of Rome, as head of the Roman Catholic Church. **2.** An effigy of the pope burnt on the anniversary of the Gunpowder Plot (Nov. 5), or at other times. *Obs.* or *dial.* 1673. **3. a.** *transf.* Applied to the spiritual head of a non-Christian religion. late ME. **b.** *fig.* One who assumes, or is considered to have, a position or authority like that of the pope 1589. †**4.** In early times, A bishop of the Christian Church; *spec.* in the Eastern Church, the title of the Bishop or Patriarch of Alexandria -1850.

3. b. Dr. McMill..the present Low-Church p. of Liverpool 1854.

II. Transf. uses. **1.** A freshwater fish of the Perch family; the Ruff 1653. **2.** A local name for various birds (e.g. the Puffin, the Bullfinch), from their colouring or stout form 1674.

Comb. **pope's nose** = *parson's nose*.

Pope 2 (pōup). 1662. [a. Russ. *popŭ*, app. ad. WGer. **papo*, ad. later Gr. παπᾶς PAPA 2.] A parish priest of the Greek Church in Russia, Serbia, etc.

Popedom (pōu·pdəm). [Late OE. *pápdóm*, f. *pápa* POPE 1; see -DOM.] **1.** = PAPACY 1. **b.** *transf.* Applied to a position of supreme authority in any religious system; also *ironically* 1588. **2.** = PAPACY 2. 1641. **b.** An eccl. polity resembling the papacy 1545.

1. b. The p. of Paternoster-Row 1837.

†**Pope-holy** *a.* (*sb.*) late ME. [app. f. POPE 1 + HOLY *a.*, but taken to represent F. *papelard* hypocritical.] Pretending to great holiness; characterized by a show or pretence of piety. **B.** *sb.* Hypocrisy. late ME.

Pope Joan. 1590. [After the fabulous female pope Joan.] A card-game played by three or more persons, with a pack from which the eight of diamonds has been removed, the stakes being won by the players of certain cards.

Popeling (pōu·pliŋ). 1561. [f. POPE 1 + -LING 1 1, 2.] †**1.** An adherent of the pope; a papist -1705. **2.** A little or petty pope 1588.

Popery (pōu·pəri). 1534. [f. POPE 1 + -ERY.] The doctrines, practices, and ceremonial associated with the pope; the papal system; the Roman Catholic religion, or adherence to it. (A hostile term.)

The cry of 'No P.' is foolish enough in these days CARLYLE.

Pope's eye. 1673. The lymphatic gland surrounded with fat in the middle of a leg of mutton; regarded as a tit-bit.

Pope's head. 1609. [From its appearance.] **1.** A species of Cactus, *Melocactus communis*, producing its flowers on a woolly cushion or head, beset with bristles and spines. **2.** A round brush or broom with a long handle, for sweeping ceilings, etc.; called also *Turk's head* 1824.

Po·p-gun, po·pgun, *sb.* 1662. [f. POP *sb.*1 or *v.* + GUN *sb.*] **1.** A child's toy; a tube from the mouth of which a tight-fitting pellet is expelled with a pop by compressing the air in the tube with a piston. Also *attrib.* **2.** A small, inefficient, or antiquated fire-arm (*contempt.*) 1849.

Popinjay (pǫ·pin,dʒēi). [ME. *papegai*, *papejai*, a. OF. *papegai* (also F.), *papingay*. OF. had also *papegau* (F. *papegaut*) = med.L. *pap(p)agallus*, mod. Gr. παπαγάλλος. The form in *-gai, -gay*, is app. an assimilation to the name of the jay, med.L. *gaius*, Pr. and ONF. *gai*.] **1.** A parrot. *Obs.* or *arch.* **2.** A representation of a parrot; *esp.* as a heraldic charge or bearing ME. **3.** The figure of a parrot fixed on a pole as a mark to shoot at. *Obs.* exc. *Hist.* 1548. **4.** *fig.* Taken as a type of vanity or empty conceit, and thus applied contemptuously to a person; cf. PARROT 2. 1528. †**5.** The prevailing colour of the green parrot; a shade of green; also *attrib.* -1865. **6.** A local name of the green woodpecker 1833.

4. As pert and as proud as any p. SCOTT.

Popish (pōu·piʃ), *a.* 1528. [f. POPE 1 + -ISH.] †**1.** Of or pertaining to the pope; papal -1567. **2.** Of or pertaining to popery; of or belonging to the Church of Rome; papistical. (In hostile use.) 1528. Hence **Po·pish-ly** *adv.*, **-ness.**

Poplar (pǫ·plăɹ). [ME. *popler*, a. OF. *poplier*, F. *peuplier*, f. L. *populus* poplar + *-ier* (:—L. *-arius*) forming names of trees.] **1.** A tree of the genus *Populus*, comprising large trees of rapid growth, some species remarkable for tremulous leaves; also, the timber of this tree. The Black P., White P., Lombardy P., and Trembling P. or Aspen are the familiar European species. **2.** Applied to other trees resembling the poplar in some respect; *esp.* the Tulip-tree (also **Tulip-P.**) of N. America (*Liriodendron Tulipifera*) 1766. **3.** *attrib.* late ME.

Poplin (pǫ·plin). 1710. [ad. F. *popeline*, for earlier *papeline*, ad. It. *papalina* adj. fem. papal; so named because made at Avignon, a papal town until 1791.] A mixed woven fabric, consisting of a silk warp and worsted weft, and having a corded surface; now made chiefly in Ireland. Hence **Popline·tte**, a woollen or linen fabric in imitation of p. 1861.

Popliteal (pǫpli·tĭăl), *a.* 1786. [f. mod.L. *popliteus* + -AL.] *Anat.* Pertaining to, situated in, or connected with the ham, or the hollow at the back of the knee; as *p. artery, tendons* (= hamstrings), etc.

Po·ppa. *U.S. colloq.* 1902. = PAPA 1.

Popper (pǫ·pəɹ), *sb.* 1750. [f. POP *v.* + -ER 1.] **1.** A gun, fire-arm, or the like; *spec.* a pistol (*slang*). **2.** A utensil for popping 'corn' (maize). *U.S.* 1875.

Poppet (pǫ·pĕt). [ME. *popet*, *-ette* :—(ult.) dim. of Romanic **puppa* for L. *pupa* a girl; also, a doll, puppet. The earlier form of PUPPET.] **1.** A small or dainty person; now, usu., a term of endearment; darling, pet. †**2.** A doll -1729. †**3.** = PUPPET *sb.* 3, 3 b. -1745. **4.** One of the upright pieces in a turning-lathe, in which the centres are fixed on which the work turns; a lathe-head 1665. **b.** = PUPPET-VALVE 1875. **5.** *Naut.* Applied to short pieces of wood, used for various purposes; *esp.* **a.** stout vertical squared pieces placed beneath a ship's hull to support her in launching; **b.** pieces on the gunwale of a boat, forming the rowlocks 1792.

Po·ppet-hea·d. 1665. **1.** = prec. 4. **2.** *Mining.* = HEAD-GEAR 3. (Often in *pl.* in same sense.) 1874.

Poppied (pǫ·pid), *a.* 1805. [f. POPPY *sb.* + -ED 2.] **1.** Having, or affected by, the sleep-inducing quality of the poppy; slumberous, drowsy, narcotic. **2.** Filled or adorned with poppies 1818.

1. The p. sleep, the end of all SWINBURNE.

Po·pping-crease. 1774. [f. POPPING *vbl. sb.*, prob. in sense 'striking' + CREASE *sb.*2 2.] *Cricket.* A line drawn four feet in front of and parallel to the wicket, within which the batsman must stand.

Popple (pǫ·p'l), *sb.*1 Now *dial.* and *U.S.* [late OE. *popul-*, ME. *popul*, ad. L. *populus* poplar.] = POPLAR.

Popple (pǫ·p'l), *sb.*2 Now *local.* [late ME.; perh. a Rom. representative of L. *papaver*.] **1.** = COCKLE *sb.*1 1. †**b.** = COCKLE *sb.*1 2. -1644. **2.** Extended to the Corn Poppy, Charlock, etc., and their seeds 1855.

1. b. That malicious one did sow p. among the good Wheat 1644.

Popple (pǫ·p'l), *sb.*3 1875. [Goes with next.] An act or condition of poppling; a rolling or tossing of water in short tumultuous waves; a strong ripple. Hence **Po·pply** *a.* broken, choppy, ripply.

Popple (pǫ·p'l), *v.* ME. [Prob. imitative.] *intr.* To roll or tumble about; to bubble up; to ripple; to toss to and fro in short waves.

Poppy (pǫ·pi). [OE. *popæg*, app. repr. a WGer. **papāg*, **popāg*, altered from **papau* = pop. L. **papavum*, alteration of L. *papaver* poppy. The ending was subseq. weakened to *-ig*, whence ME. *popi, popy*.] **I. 1.** A plant (or flower) of the genus *Papaver*, having milky juice with narcotic properties, showy flowers with petals of various colours, and roundish capsules containing numerous small round seeds. **2.** With qualifying words, applied to various species of *Papaver* or other genera of *Papaveraceæ* ME. **3.** The plant or its extract used in pharmacy 1604. **4.** *fig.* With reference to the narcotic qualities of the plant 1591.

1. Sleepy poppies DRYDEN. The blushing p. with a crimson hue PRIOR. 2. **Californian P.**, *Platystemon californicus* and the genus *Eschscholtzia*; **Corn, Field P.**, the common wild p. of cornfields, *Papaver rhœas*, with bright scarlet flowers, or any other species growing in corn; **Horn P., Horned P.**, any plant of the genus *Glaucium*, distinguished by its long horn-like capsules; **Iceland P.**, see ICELAND 2; **Prickly P.**, *Argemone mexicana*, with yellow or white flowers and prickly leaves and capsules.

II. = POPPY-HEAD 2. late ME.

attrib. and *Comb.*: **p.-bee**, a kind of upholsterer-bee (*Anthocopa papaveris*) which lines its cells with the petals of poppies; **-colour**, a bright scarlet; **P. Day**, the anniversary of Armistice Day, 11 Nov. 1918, commemorated by wearing an artificial red poppy (a Flanders poppy) made by disabled ex-service men in aid of Earl Haig's British Legion Appeal Fund.

Poppycock (pǫ·pikǫk). *U.S. slang.* 1863. Nonsense, rubbish.

Po·ppy-hea·d. 1585. **1.** The capsule of the poppy. Also *attrib.* **2.** *Arch.* An ornamental finial, often richly carved, at the top of the end of a seat in a church. Also *attrib.* 1839.

Po·ppy-seed. late ME. **1.** The, or a, seed of the poppy. †**2.** As a measure of length, varying from $\frac{1}{12}$ to $\frac{1}{20}$ of an inch -1729.

Poppywort (pǫ·piwɔ̄ɹt). 1846. [f. POPPY *sb.* + WORT.] **a.** Lindley's name for plants of the N.O. *Papaveraceæ*. **b.** Satin P., *Meconopsis Wallichiana*.

Po·p-shop. *slang.* 1772. [f. POP *v.* 7 + SHOP *sb.*] A pawnbroker's shop. Also *attrib.*

Populace (pǫ·piŭlĕs). 1572. [a. F., ad. It. *popolaccio, -azzo*, f. *popolo* PEOPLE + pejorative suffix *-accio, -azzo* :—L. *-aceus*.] The mass of the people of a community, as dist. from the titled, wealthy, or educated classes; (*contempt.*) the mob, the rabble.

T'accommodate..the Peeres, and please the Populasse DANIEL. So †**Po·pulacy**, the p.; also, populousness; popular government, democracy.

Popular (pǫ·piŭlăɹ), *a.* (*sb.*) 1490. [ad. L. *popularis*, f. *populus* people.] **1.** *Law.* Affecting, concerning, or open to all or any of the people; public; esp. in *action p.* **2.** Of, pertaining to, or consisting of the common people, or the people as a whole; constituted or carried on by the people 1548. †**b.** Plebeian -1691. †**3.** Full of people; populous; crowded -1811. **4.** Adapted to the understanding, taste, or means of ordinary people 1573. †**5.** Studious of, or designed to gain, the favour of the common people; devoted to the cause of the people -1771. **6.** Finding favour with the people, or with many people; favourite, acceptable, pleasing 1608. **7.** Prevalent among, or accepted by, the people generally; common, general; †(of sickness) epidemic 1603.

1. *P. action*, brought by one of the public to recover some penalty given by statute to any one who chooses to sue for it WHARTON. 2. P. tumults HUME. A completely p. election 1833. 4. In a p. style which boys and women could comprehend MACAULAY. The foundation of the P. Concerts in 1859. 1902. All seats at p. prices (*mod.*). 5. The first acts of an usurper are always p. GOLDSM. 6. The p. Preachers 1812. 7. Sir, that 's a p. error, deceiues many B. JONS.

B. *absol.* or as *sb.* (from sense 2). †**a.** In collective sense, or *pl.*: the populace; the common people, the commons -1633. **b.** Short for *p. concert* 1885. Hence **Po·pular-ly** *adv.*, **-ness** (*rare*).

Popularity (pǫpiŭlæ·rĭti). 1548. [ad. F. *popularité*, ad. L. *popularitas*, f. *popularis* POPULAR; see -ITY.] †**1.** Popular or democratic government -1701. †**2.** The principle of popular government; democracy -1689. †**3.** The action or practice of courting popular favour -1715. **4.** The fact or condition of being admired, approved, or beloved by the people, or by many people 1601. †**5.** = POPULOUSNESS (*rare*) -1720.

2. The spirit of p. and republicanisme 1689. 3. P. is a courting the favour of the people by undue practices 1697. 4. His popularitie gained him a Consulship 1601.

Popularize (pǫ·piŭlărəiz), *v.* 1797. [f. POPULAR *a.* + -IZE.] *trans.* To make popular. **a.** To cause to be generally known and accepted, liked, or admired. **b.** To render democratic 1831. **c.** To present (a technical subject, etc.) in a popular form 1836.

a. To preserve their power they must popularise themselves 1835. c. Engaged in..popularising history or science 1871. Hence **Po·pularization.** **Po·pularizer.**

Po·pulate, *ppl. a. Obs.* exc. *poet.* 1574. [ad. late L. *populatus*, *populare* to inhabit.] Peopled.

Populate (pǫ·piŭlėⁱt), *v.* 1578. [f. L. *populat-* POPULATE *ppl. a.*: see -ATE³.] **1.** *trans.* **a.** To inhabit, form the population of (a country). **b.** To supply (a country) with inhabitants; to people. **2.** *intr.* Of people: To grow in numbers by propagation (*rare*) 1625. **3.** *intr.* (for *refl.*) To become populous. *U.S. rare.* 1796. Hence **Po·pulator,** one who or that which populates or peoples.

Population (pǫpiŭlē¹·ʃən). 1578. [ad. late L. *populationem* population, f. *populare* to POPULATE.] †**1.** *concr.* An inhabited place -1613. **2.** The degree in which a place is populated or inhabited; hence, the total number of its inhabitants. Also *transf.* 1612. **3.** The action or process of peopling a place or region; increase of people 1776.

2. P...increases in a geometrical ratio, subsistence in an arithmetical ratio MALTHUS. 3. The p. of the province was extremely rapid 1796.

Populin (pǫ·piŭlin). 1838. [ad. F. *populine*, f. L. *populus* poplar; see -IN¹.] *Chem.* A white crystalline substance, $C_{20}H_{22}O_8$, obtained from the aspen (*Populus tremula*).

Populist (pǫ·piŭlist). 1892. [f. L. *populus* people + -IST.] **1.** An adherent of a political party formed in the U.S. in Feb. 1892, having for its objects the public control of railways, limitation of private ownership of land, free coinage of silver and increased issue of paper-money, a graduated income-tax, etc. **2.** A member of a Russian socio-political party advocating a form of collectivism 1895.

1. A people's party,—Populists as..they are called 1893. So **Po·pulism,** the political doctrine or principle of the Populists 1893.

Populous (pǫ·piŭləs), *a.* 1449. [ad. L. *populosus*, f. *populus* people; see -OUS.] **1.** Full of people; thickly inhabited; fully occupied. **b.** Of a time or season: Productive, prolific 1789. †**2.** Of a body of people: Numerous, abundant -1662. **3.** = POPULAR *a.* in various senses. *Obs.* exc. *poet.* 1592.

1. A continuall p. Market PURCHAS. P. districts 1880. 2. Furnished with a p. army HALL. Hence **Po·pulous-ly** *adv.*, **-ness.** So †**Populo·sity,** populousness.

Porbeagle (pǭ·ɹ¹bīːg'l). 1758. [Origin unkn.; orig. Cornish dial.] A shark of the genus *Lamna*, esp. *L. cornubica*, sometimes 10 feet in length, and having a pointed snout; a mackerel-shark.

Porcelain (pǭ·ɹslĕn, pōᵊ·ɹ-). 1530. [a. F. *porcelaine*, ad. It. *porcellana*, f. *porcella*, dim. of *porca*; ult. etym. unkn.] **1.** A fine kind of earthenware, having a translucent body and a transparent glaze; = CHINA¹ II. **2.** An article or vessel made of porcelain; a piece of porcelain. Usu. in *pl.* 1604. **3.** The COWRIE (*Cypræa moneta*). Only in *p. shell.* 1601. **4.** *attrib.* or as *adj.* Made of porcelain or china 1598; *fig.* like porcelain; fine, fragile; superfine 1638.

1. *fig.* The precious p. of human clay BYRON. 4. A maid who had broken a p. cup JOHNSON.

attrib. and *Comb.*, as **p. cement,** a cement for mending china or glass; **-clay,** the clay used in the manufacture of p.; china-clay, kaolin; **-crab,** a crab of the genus *Porcellana*, so called from its smooth and polished shell; **p. jasper** = PORCELLANITE; **p. shell**: see sense 3; **p. tower,** a famous tower at Nankin in China, covered with p. tiles. Hence **Po·rcelainize** *v. trans.* to convert into p. or a substance of the same nature. **Po·rcelainous** *a.* = next.

Porcellaneous (pōᵊɹsĕlē¹·nĭəs), *a.* 1799. [f. It. *porcellana* PORCELAIN + -EOUS.] Of the nature of or resembling porcelain. So **Porcellanous** (poɹse·lănəs) *a.*

Porcellanite (poɹse·lănəit). 1796. [a. G. *porzellanit*, f. *porzellan* PORCELAIN + *-it* -ITE¹.] *Min.* A hard naturally-baked clay, somewhat resembling jasper; also called *porcelain jasper.*

Porch (pōᵊɹtʃ). ME. [a. F. *porche* :—L. *porticus* colonnade, gallery, porch.] **1.** An exterior structure forming a covered approach to the entrance of a building; sometimes applied to an interior space serving as a vestibule. Also *transf.* and *fig.* †**2.** A colonnade, portico, cloister -1687. **b.** *U.S.* A verandah 1840. **3.** spec. *The P.*, the Painted Porch (Gr. στοὰ ποικίλη), a public ambulatory in the agora of ancient Athens, to which Zeno the philosopher and his disciples resorted; hence (οἱ τῆς στοᾶς, those of the porch), the Stoic school, the Stoic philosophy 1670.

1. Of hewen stone the p. was fayrely wrought SPENSER. 2. They stay for me In Pompeyes P. SHAKS.

Porcine (pǭ·ɹsəin), *a.* 1656. [a. F. *porcin*, *-e*, ad. L. *porcinus* swinish.] **1.** Of or consisting of swine; related to or resembling the swine. **2.** Like that of a hog; swinish, hoggish 1660.

Porcupine (pǭ·ɹkiŭpəin), *sb.* [late ME. *porke despyne*, *porkepyn*, etc., a. OF. *porc espin*; f. *porc* :—L. *porcus* hog, pig + *espin*, *épin*, deriv. of L. *spina* thorn.] **1.** A rodent quadruped of the genus *Hystrix* or family *Hystricidæ*, having the body and tail covered with defensive erectile spines or quills; formerly supposed to shoot or dart its spines at an enemy. **b.** A figure of this animal, esp. as a device 1578. **2.** *fig.* 1594. **3.** Applied to machines having numerous projecting spikes or teeth; *esp.* an apparatus for heckling flax, worsted, or cotton; a kind of masher used in brewing 1869. **4. a.** = *P. ant-eater*; **b.** = *P. fish* 1875.

1. Like Quilles vpon the fretfull Porpentine SHAKS.

attrib. and *Comb.*, as **p. ant-eater,** an Australian monotremate mammal (*Echidna hystrix*), having spines; **p. crab,** a Japanese crab (*Lithodes hystrix*), having spiny carapace and limbs; **p. fish,** a fish having the skin covered with spines, as *Diodon hystrix*; a sea-porcupine; **p. grass,** (*a*) *Triodia irritans* and other species, of Australia, with stiff sharp-pointed leaves; (*b*) *Stipa spartea*, of the western U.S., with long stiff awns; **p.-wood,** the wood of the coco palm, which when cut across shows variegated markings like those of a porcupine-quill.

Pore (pōᵊɹ), *sb.* late ME. [a. F., ad. L. *porus*, a. Gr. πόρος passage, pore.] **1.** A minute opening or orifice (usu. one imperceptible to the unaided eye) through which fluids (rarely solids) pass or may pass. **a.** In an animal body esp. applied to those in the skin. **b.** *fig.*, esp. in phr. *at every p.* 1632. **c.** In a plant (or vegetable substance); as the stomata in the epidermis of leaves, etc. late ME. **d.** In inanimate bodies or substances. late ME. †**2.** A passage, channel, canal, duct (*rare*) -1615.

1. b. I see him chafe and fret at every p. DICKENS.

Pore (pōᵊɹ), *v.* [ME. *pūren*, *pouren*; origin unkn.] **1.** *intr.* **a.** To look intently or fixedly (*in, on, upon, at, over*); to search *for* or *into* something by gazing. (Now always with admixture of sense b.) **b.** To look at something (usu. a book) with fixed attention, in the way of study; to be absorbed in reading or study. (Const. *on, upon*, (now chiefly) *over*). late ME. **c.** To meditate, muse, or think intently upon something. Const. *on, upon, over.* late ME. †**2.** To look closely, as a near-sighted person; to peer -1862. **3.** *trans.* To bring into some state by poring 1593.

1. b. Instead of poaring on a booke, you shall holde the plough LYLY. 3. Phr. †*To p. one's eyes out*, to ruin one's eyes by close reading. Hence **Po·rer.** **Po·ringly** *adv.*

Po·rgo, pa·rgo. [Sp., Pg.] The sea bream.

Porgy (pǭ·ɹgi). Also **paugie.** 1725. [Of obsc. and app. various origin. Cf. prec.] *U.S.* Applied to various sea-fishes, chiefly N. Amer. species of *Sparidæ* or Sea Breams, but also locally to fishes of other families.

‖ **Porifera** (pori·fĕră), *sb. pl.* 1843. [mod.L., neut. pl. of *porifer*, f. L. *porus* PORE + *-fer* bearing.] *Zool.* The Sponges, reckoned as a class or main division of *Cœlenterata*, characterized by having the body-wall perforated by numerous inhalant pores. Hence **Pori·feran** *a.* belonging or relating to the *P.*; *sb.* a member of the *P.*

†**Po·riness.** 1653. [f. PORY + -NESS.] Porosity; also *concr.* a porous part -1676.

Porism (pōᵊ·riz'm, pǫ·r-). late ME. [ad. L. *porisma*, a. Gr. πόρισμα, f. πορίζειν to carry, deduce, f. πόρος way.] *Math.* A kind of geometrical proposition; app. one arising during the investigation of some other proposition, either by immediate deduction from it (= COROLLARY *sb.* 1), or by consideration of some special case in which it becomes indeterminate. So **Porism·atic** *a.* pertaining to or of the nature of a p. Also **Poristic** (pori·stik) *a.* 1704.

Porite (pōᵊ·rəit). 1828. [ad. mod.L. *Porites*, f. Gr. πόρος passage, pore, or πῶρος calcareous stone; see MADREPORE and -ITE¹.] *Zool.* A coral of the genus *Porites* or family *Poritidæ* of perforate sclerodermatous corals.

Pork (pōᵊɹk). ME. [a. F. *porc* :—L. *porcus* swine.] **1.** A swine, a hog, a pig. Sometimes dist. from a pig or young swine. *Obs.* exc. *Hist.* late ME. **2.** The (fresh) flesh of swine used as food ME. **3.** *U.S. slang.* Money, position, etc. for a district, obtained from the (Federal) government; also *transf.* Cf. *p.-barrel.* 1916.

Comb.: **p.-barrel** *spec.* (*U.S. slang*), the Federal treasury viewed as a source of grants for local purposes; **-butcher,** one who slaughters pigs for sale; **-pie,** a pie of pastry enclosing minced p.; (in full, *p.-pie hat*) a hat with a flat crown and a brim turned up all round, worn by women *c* 1855–65.

Porker (pōᵊ·ɹkəɹ). 1657. [f. prec. + -ER¹ 1.] A young hog fattened for pork; also, any pig raised for food.

Porket (pōᵊ·ɹkĕt). Now *dial.* 1554. [a. ONF. *porket*, OF. *porchet*, dim. of *porc* PORK.] A small or young pig or hog; *dial.* = prec.

Porkling (pōᵊ·ɹkliŋ). 1542. [f. PORK + -LING¹.] A small or young pig 1570. †**b.** Applied to a person. Also *attrib.* -1602.

Po·rkwood. 1880. [f. PORK + WOOD *sb.*] **a.** A bush or small tree (*Kigellaria capensis*) found in the warmer parts of Africa; **b.** *Pisonia obtusata*, the Pigeon-wood, Beef-wood, or Cork-wood of the W. Indies.

Pornocracy (pǫɹnǫ·krăsi). 1860. [f. Gr. πόρνη harlot + -CRACY.] Dominating influence of harlots; *spec.* the government of Rome during the first half of the tenth century.

Pornographer (pǫɹnǫ·grăfəɹ). 1850. [f. Gr. πορνογράφος writing of harlots + -ER¹.] One who writes of prostitutes or obscene matters.

Pornographic (pǭɹnŏgræ·fik), *a.* 1880. [f. as prec. + -IC.] Of, pertaining to, or of the nature of pornography; dealing in the obscene.

Pornography (pǭɪnǫ·grăfi). 1864. [f. as prec. + -Y.] Description of the life, manners, etc. of prostitutes and their patrons; hence, the expression or suggestion of obscene or unchaste subjects in literature or art.

Poroplastic (pǫro-, pōᵊroplæ·stik), *a.* 1879. [f. Gr. πόρος PORE + PLASTIC.] Both porous and plastic; applied to a kind of porous felt, plastic when heated, becoming stiff when cold, used for splints and other surgical appliances.

Poroscopy (porǫ·skŏpi). 1921. [f. PORE *sb.* + -(O)SCOPY.] The examination of the pores as a means of identification. Hence **Porosco·pic** *a.*

Porosity (porǫ·sĭti). late ME. [ad. med.L. *porositas*, f. L. type **porosus* POROUS; see -ITY.] The quality or fact of being porous; porous consistence. **b.** *concr.* A porous part or structure; an interstice or pore 1597.

Porous (pōᵊ·rəs), *a.* late ME. [ad. L. type **porosus*, f. *porus* PORE *sb.*; see -OUS.] Full of pores; having minute interstices through which water, air, light, etc. may pass. Also *fig.*

P. plaster, a plaster having numerous small holes pierced through it so as to enable it to lie smoothly. Hence **Po·rous-ly** *adv.*; **-ness**, porosity.

Porpentine, obs. f. PORCUPINE.

Porphyr-, porphyro-, repr. Gr. πορφυρ(ο-, comb. stem of πόρφυρος purple; a formative element in senses 'purple' and 'porphyry' as in **Porphyra·ceous**, *a.* (*rare*) of the nature of or allied to porphyry; porphyritic, etc. **Po:r·phyrogene·tic**, *a.* producing or generating porphyry.

Porphyrian (pǫɪfi·riăn), *a.* (*sb.*) 1593. [f. L. *Porphyrius* (a. Gr. Πορφύριος), proper name (f. πόρφυρος purple) + *-anus* -AN.] Of or pertaining to Porphyrius or Porphyry, the neo-Platonic philosopher and antagonist of Christianity (A.D. 233–*c* 306), or to his doctrines.

P. scale or *tree*, a definition of *man* in the form of a kind of genealogical table or tree, displaying the series of subaltern genera to which he may be assigned below the summum genus *substance*, and the differentiæ by which each subaltern genus is distinguished within the genus next above it.

B. *sb.* A disciple or follower of Porphyry 1678.

‖ **Porphyrio** (pǫɪfi·rio). 1609. [L., ad Gr. πορφυρίων the purple coot.] *Ornith.* A name given by the ancients to the purple coot; taken by Brisson as name of the genus *Rallidæ* including this.

Porphyrite (pǭ·ɪfĭrəit), *sb.* 1577. [ad. L. *porphyrites*, ad. Gr. πορφυρίτης adj. like purple, π. λίθος stone of this colour, porphyry, f. πόρφυρος purple; see -ITE¹ 2 b.] †**1.** = PORPHYRY 1. –1736. **2.** *Min.* = PORPHYRY 2. 1796.

Porphyritic (pǫɪfĭri·tik), *a.* late ME. [ad. med.L. *porphyriticus*, f. L. *porphyrites* PORPHYRITE.] Of or pertaining to the porphyry of the ancients; of the nature or structure of the porphyry of modern mineralogists; *spec.* containing distinct crystals or crystalline particles embedded in a compact ground-mass. So **Porphyri·tical** *a.*, **-ly** *adv.*

Porphyrogenite (-ǫ·dʒĕnəit). *Obs.* exc. in L. form. 1614. [ad. med.L. *porphyrogenitus*, ad. late Gr. πορφυρογέννητος, f. Gr. πορφυρο- PORPHYR(O- + γεννητός born.] Orig., one born of the imperial family at Constantinople, and (as is said) in a chamber called the *Porphyra* (πορφύρα). Hence, a child born after his father's accession to the throne; and, vaguely, one born 'in the purple'; see PURPLE *sb.*

Hence **Porphyroge·nitism**, the doctrine of succession in a royal family which prefers a son born after his father's accession to one born before. **Porphyroge·niture**, the condition of being born 'in the purple' (see above).

Porphyroid (pǭ·ɪfĭroid), *sb.* (*a.*) 1796. [f. PORPHYR(O- + -OID.] *Geol.*, etc. **A.** *sb.* A rock resembling porphyry or of porphyritic structure. **B.** *adj.* Resembling porphyry 1798.

Porphyry (pǭ·ɪfĭri). late ME. [ult. from Gr. πόρφυρος adj. purple, πορφύρα sb. the purple-whelk, and its dye; but the stone was called in Gr. πορφυρίτης, L. *porphyrites*, whence PORPHYRITE.] **1.** A beautiful and very hard rock quarried anciently in Egypt, composed of crystals of white or red plagioclase felspar embedded in a fine red ground-mass. By modern poets often used vaguely, in the sense of a beautiful red stone taking a high polish. **2.** *Geol.* and *Min.* **a.** A rock consisting of a compact base of felspathic or other unstratified rock containing scattered crystals of felspar of contemporary age 1796. **b.** *gen.* Any unstratified or igneous rock having a homogeneous base in which crystals of one or more minerals are disseminated 1813.

Comb.: **p. chamber**, a room in the palace of the Emperors at Byzantium; **p.-shell**, a shell of the genus *Murex*, esp. that from which the purple dye was obtained.

Porpoise (pǭ·ɪpəs). [ME. *porpays*, *-peys*, *-poys*, a. OF. *porpeis*, *-pois* = L. type **porcus piscis*, lit. hog-fish or fish-hog. In the 18th c. the form *porpus* was prevalent.] A small cetaceous mammal (*Phocæna communis*) about five feet in length, blackish above and paler beneath, having a blunt rounded snout not produced into a 'beak' as the dolphin's. Hence extended to other small cetaceans. (Formerly also, like *fish*, as collect. sing.) Hence **Po·rpoise** *v. intr.* spec. of aircraft: to make a series of plunges when taking off or landing 1920.

Porraceous (pǫrē¹·ʃəs), *a.* 1605. [f. L. *porraceus* f. *porrum* leek; see -ACEOUS.] Of the nature or colour of the leek; leek-green.

Porrect (pǫre·kt), *a.* 1819. [ad. L. *porrectus*; see next.] *Zool.* Stretched out or forth; extended, esp. forward.

Porrect (pǫre·kt), *v.* late ME. [f. L. *porrect-*, *porrigere*, f. *por-* = *pro-* forth + *regere* to stretch, direct.] **1.** *trans.* To stretch out, extend (usu., a part of the body). Now only in *Nat. Hist.* **2.** To put forward, tender (a document, etc.); to produce for examination or correction. *Obs.* exc. in eccl. law. 1774. So **Porre·ction**, †extension (*rare*); proffering; presentation (now only *Eccl.*)

Porret (pǫ·rĕt). Now only *dial.* [ME. *poret*, *-ette*, a. OF. *poret* leek, f. L. *porrum* leek + dim. suffix *-et* -ET.] A young leek or onion.

Porridge (pǫ·ridʒ), *sb.* 1532. [Altered f. POTTAGE. In Sc. and Eng. dial., usu. collective pl.] †**1.** Pottage made by stewing vegetables, herbs, or meat, often with a thickening of pot-barley, etc. –1805. **2.** A soft food made by stirring oatmeal (or other meal or cereal) into boiling water (or milk); often dist. as *oatmeal p.*, *wheatmeal p.*, *rice p.* 1643. **3.** *fig.* A conglomeration, a hotchpotch; unsubstantial stuff 1642.

Provb. phr. *To keep one's breath to cool one's p.*, to reserve one's advice, etc. for one's own use.

Comb.: **p.-pan**, a double pan in which p. is made; **-pot**, the pot in which p. is cooked; **-stick**, a stick used for stirring p.

‖ **Porrigo** (pǫrəi·go). 1706. [L., = 'scurf'.] *Path.* A name for several diseases of the scalp characterized by scaly eruptions. So **Porri·ginous** *a.* affected with p.

Porringer (pǫ·rindʒəɪ). 1522. [Alteration of *potager*, going with *porridge* from *potage*. For the *n* cf. *messenger*, *passenger*.] A small basin or the like, from which soup, porridge, children's food, etc. is eaten. **b.** A hat resembling a porringer (*joc.*) 1613.

Port (pōᵊɪt), *sb.*¹ [OE., ad. L. *portus* haven, harbour.] **1.** A place by the shore where ships may run in for shelter from storms, or to load and unload; a harbour, a haven. **2.** A town possessing a harbour to which vessels resort to load or unload, from which they start or at which they finish their voyages; *spec.* a place where customs officers are stationed to supervise the entry of goods OE. †**3.** *The five ports* = CINQUE PORTS. Also the barons of the Cinque Ports. –1631.

1. To set me safe ashore in the first p. where we arrived SWIFT. *fig.* Doubt was expressed..as to the possibility of the measure reaching p. this year 1879. **2.** *Free P.*, ..a p. open and free for merchants of all nations to load and unload their vessels in... *Free P.* is also used for a total exemption and franchise..for goods imported into a state, or those of the growth of the country exported. CHAMBERS. *Close ports*, those which lie up rivers SMYTH.

Comb.: **p.-bar**, (*a*) a shoal or bank across the entrance to a p.; (*b*) = BOOM *sb.*² 3; **-bound** *a.*, detained in p. by contrary winds, etc.; **-charge**, **-duty**, harbour-due (see HARBOUR *sb.*¹); **-pay**, wages due for time during which one's ship is detained in p.

Port, *sb.*² *Obs.* exc. *Hist.* or in *Comb.* [OE. *port* = MFl., MDu. *port* town, burgh, city. In origin, the same word either as prec. or as next.] †A town; perh. *spec.* a walled town, or a market town; but identified with *burh* as a rendering of L. *civitas* –ME. **b.** *attrib.* and *Comb.*, as PORT-REEVE, etc. OE.

Port (pōᵊɪt), *sb.*³ [ME. *porte*, *port*, a. F. *porte*:—L. *porta* door, gate. OE. had irregularly *port* m.] **1.** A gate or gateway; from 14th c., usu. that of a city or walled town. Now chiefly *Sc.* OE. **2.** *Naut.* **a.** An opening in the side of a ship for entrance and exit, and for the loading and discharge of cargo. **b.** Each of the apertures in a ship of war through which cannon were pointed; now, an aperture for the admission of light and air. late ME. **c.** The shutter of a port-hole; a port-lid 1627. **3.** *Mech.* An aperture for the passage of steam, gas, or water; *esp.* in a steam-engine, for the passage of steam into or out of the cylinder, a *steam-p.* 1839. **4.** The curved mouthpiece of some bridle-bits 1587.

1. Him I accuse: The City Ports by this hath enter'd SHAKS. *fig.* O pollish'd Perturbation!..that keep'st the Ports of Slumber open wide To many a watchfull Night SHAKS.

attrib. and *Comb.*, as **p.-bit** (sense 4), a bridle-bit of which the mouth is curved into an arch; also called **p.-mouth**; **-piece**, an obsolete kind of ship's gun; **-rope**, a rope for raising and lowering a port-lid; **-stopper**, a revolving shutter for closing a p. in a turret-ship; **-way** = sense 3. Hence **Po·rted** *a.* having ports or gates (*rare*).

Port (pōᵊɪt), *sb.*⁴ late ME. [a. F. *port* a carrying, etc., vbl. sb. f. *porter*; see PORT *v.*¹] **I. 1.** The manner in which one bears oneself; external deportment; carriage, bearing. **b.** *fig.* Bearing, purport (of a matter) 1568. **2.** Style of living; *esp.* a grand or expensive style; state; hence *transf.* social position, station. Now *rare* or *Obs.* 1523. †**b.** *transf.* A train of attendants; a retinue. Also *fig.* –1621.

1. With them comes a third of Regal p. MILT. **2.** The name and p. of gentlemen SCOTT.

II. †**1.** The action of carrying; the fee or price of carrying; carriage, postage –1692. **2.** *Mil.* [from phr. *Port arms.*] The position required by the order '*Port arms*'; see PORT *v.*¹ 2. 1833.

Port (pōᵊɪt), *sb.*⁵ (*a.*) 1543. [Origin obsc.] **1.** = LARBOARD 1. (Often in phr. *to p.*, A-PORT.) **2.** *attrib.* or as *adj.* = LARBOARD 2. 1857.

Port (pōᵊɪt), *sb.*⁶ 1691. [Shortened f. *O Porto* (*wine*), f. *Oporto* (Pg. *O Porto*, lit. 'the Port') a city of Portugal, the chief port of shipment for the wines of the country.] A strong dark-red wine of Portugal, having a sweet and slightly astringent taste. Also *attrib.*

Port (pōᵊɪt), *sb.*⁷ *Sc.* 1721. [a. Gael. *port* tune.] A lively tune, a catch, an air.

The pipe's shrill p. aroused each clan SCOTT.

Port (pōᵊɪt), *v.*¹ 1566. [a. F. *porter*:—L. *portare.*] †**1.** *trans.* To carry, bear, convey, bring –1711. **2.** *Mil.* To carry or hold (a pike, etc.) with both hands; *spec.* to carry (a rifle or other weapon) diagonally across and close to the body, so that the barrel or blade is opposite the middle of the left shoulder; esp. in the command *Port arms!* 1625.

1. To p. Books about to sell 1706. **2.** On the approach of any person, the sentry will p. Arms, and call out Halt, who comes there? 1877. Hence **Po·rted** *ppl. a.* held in the position of the port.

Port (pōᵊɪt), *v.*² 1580. [f. PORT *sb.*⁵] **1.** *trans.* In *to p. the helm*, to put or turn it to the left side of the ship; also ellipt. *to p.* **2.** *intr.* Of a ship: To turn or go to her port or left side 1890.

‖ **Porta** (pōᵊ·ɪtă). late ME. [L., a gate; also applied to a part of the liver. See PORT *sb.*³] *Anat.* **a.** The transverse fissure of the liver, at which the portal vein, hepatic artery, etc. enter it; the portal fissure. **b.** The *vena porta* or portal vein; see PORTAL *a.*

Portable (pōᵊ·ɪtăb'l), *a.* late ME. [a. F., ad. late L. *portabilis*; see PORT *v.*¹ and -ABLE.] **1.** Capable of being carried by hand or on the person; capable of being moved from place to place; easily carried or conveyed. **b.** Said of liquid substances congealed, and of gaseous substances liquefied, so as to be more conveniently carried or transported 1753. †**2.** *fig.*

Bearable; endurable -1653. †3. Capable of carrying ships or boats; navigable -1696.

1. A very convenient p. camera obscura 1831. *fig.* This p. Quality of Good-humour STEELE. *P. derrick, furnace, steam engine*, etc., modified movable forms of these. **b.** P. Soup..P. Milk 1849. **2.** How light and p. my pain seems now SHAKS. Hence **Portabi·lity, Po·rtableness,** the quality or state of being p.

Portage (pōᵊ·ɹtėdʒ), *sb.*[1] late ME. [a. F., = med.L. *portaticum*, also *portagium*, f. L. *portare* to carry; see PORT *v.*[1] and -AGE.] **I.** **1.** The action or work of carrying or transporting; carriage 1440. †**b.** That which is carried or transported; cargo; freight; baggage -1667. **2.** The cost of carriage; porterage; freight-charges; †also, a due levied in connexion with the transport of goods. *Obs.* exc. *Hist.* 1472. †**3.** *Naut.* Burden of a vessel; tonnage -1710. **4.** In full, *mariner's p.*: A mariner's venture, in the form of freight or cargo, which he was entitled to put on board, if he took part in the common adventure and did not receive wages; the space allowed to a mariner for his own venture or to be let by him for freight payable to him in lieu of wages; hence, in late use, a mariner's wages. *Obsol.* 1550.

2. The cheapest Letter, that ever I paid p. for DONNE. **4.** *fig. Per.* III. i. 35.

II. The carrying or transporting of boats and goods from one navigable water to another, as between two lakes or rivers. (Orig. *U.S.*) 1698. **b.** A place at or over which such portage is necessary 1698.

†**Po·rtage,** *sb.*[2] [f. PORT *sb.*[3] + -AGE.] Provision of ports or port-holes SHAKS.

Po·rtage (pōᵊ·ɹtėdʒ), *v.* 1864. [f. PORTAGE *sb.*[1]] *trans.* To carry or transport (boats, goods, etc.) overland between navigable waters; to convey over a portage. Also with the place (rapids, etc.) as obj.; also *absol.*

†**Portague, -igue.** 1532. [app. a false sing. deduced from *porta-, porteguse* (PORTUGUESE B. 3), taken as a pl., as if *portagues.*] A Portuguese gold coin, the great 'crusado', current in the 16th c.

Portail (pōᵊ·ɹtēl). 1483. [a. F. *portail* façade of a church:—L. **portaculum*, dim. of *porta* gate. Confused with next.] *Arch.* = next **1.**

Portal (pōᵊ·ɹtăl), *sb.* [ME. a. obs. F. *portal* gate, ad. med.L. *portale*, orig. adj. neut., f. L. *porta*; see PORT *sb.*[3] and -AL.] **1.** A door, gate, doorway, or gateway, of stately or elaborate construction; the entrance, esp. of a large or magnificent building. Hence often poet. for 'door' or 'gate'. †**2.** A space within the door of a room, partitioned off, and containing an inner door; also, such a partition itself -1703. **3.** *attrib* 1592.

1. The portals of Abbeville,..are some of the finest specimens of this style 1862. *fig.* As doth the blushing discontented Sunne, From out the fierie Portall of the East SHAKS.

Portal (pōᵊ·ɹtăl), *a.* 1845. [ad. med.L. *portalis*, f. *porta* gate.] *Anat.* Pertaining to the *porta* or transverse fissure of the liver.

P vein, the *vena porta*, or great vein formed by the union of the veins from the stomach, intestine, and spleen, conveying blood to the liver, where it divides again into branches. *Renal p.* or *reni-portal vein*, a vein similarly passing to the kidney and dividing into branches there, in many of the lower vertebrates.

‖ **Portame·nto.** 1774. [It., lit. a carrying.] *Mus.* A gliding or passing continuously from one pitch to another, in singing, or in playing a violin or similar instrument. Also *attrib.*

Portance (pōᵊ·ɹtăns). *arch.* 1590. [a. obs. F. *portance* action of carrying, etc., vbl. sb. f. *porter*, PORT *v.*[1]; see -ANCE.] Carriage, bearing, demeanour; conduct, behaviour.

Cor. II. iii. 232.

Portas, -eous, -es. Now only *Hist.* [late ME. *portehors, porthors*, a. OF. *portehors* (= med.L. *portiforium*) a portable breviary, f. *porte* carry + *hors* :—L. *foris* out of doors.] **1.** A portable breviary in the mediæval church. Also *attrib.* **2.** *Sc. Law.* (In later use *porteous roll.*) A roll of the names of offenders, prepared, by the old custom of the Justiciary court, by the Justice-Clerk. late ME.

1. Their Seruice bookes, Portesses, and Breuiaries BIBLE *Transl. Pref.*

Portate (pōᵊ·ɹtėt), *a.* 1562. [ad. L. *portatus*, pa. pple of *portare* to carry.] *Her.* In *cross p.*, a cross represented in a sloping position (*in bend*), as if carried on the shoulder.

Portative (pōᵊ·ɹtătiv), *a.* and *sb.* [late ME. *portatif*, a. F. *portatif, -ive*, f. L. *portatus, portare* + *-if*, -IVE.] **A.** *adj.* **1.** Portable; *spec.* applied to a kind of small organ. Now chiefly *Hist.* **2.** Having the function of carrying or supporting 1881. **B.** *sb.* (usu. *pl.*) A portative organ. *Obs.* exc. *Hist.* 1450.

Port-crayon (pōᵊɹtˌkrēˑɒn), ‖ **porte-crayon** (portˌkreyoṅ). 1720. [ad. F. *porte-crayon*; see PORTE- and CRAYON.] An instrument (e.g. a metal tube split at the end and held by a sliding ring) used to hold a crayon for drawing.

Portcullis (poɹtkɒ·lis), *sb.* [ME. a. OF. *porte coleïce* lit. sliding door or gate, f. *porte* + *col(e)ïce* (mod.F. *coulisse*), fem. of *couleïs* adj. gliding, sliding :—L. type **colaticius*, f. L. *colatus, colare* to strain, filter.] **1.** A strong and heavy frame or grating, suspended by chains, and made to slide up and down in vertical grooves at the sides of the gateway of a fortress or fortified town, so as to be quickly let down as a defence against assault. Also *fig.* **2.** A figure of a portcullis, as an ornament or a heraldic charge. In *Her.* also applied to a number of vertical and horizontal strips crossing each other over the field. 1485. **3.** *P. coins, money*, numismatists' name for the coins (crown, half-crown, shilling, and sixpence) struck by Queen Elizabeth in 1600–2 for the East India Company, having the figure of a portcullis on the reverse 1784. **4.** Title of one of the English Pursuivants of Arms, from his badge 1491.

1. And.., Forthwith the huge P. high up drew MILT. Hence **Portcu·llis** *v. trans.* to furnish with a p.; to close with or as with a p. **Portcu·llised** *a.* furnished with or having a p.; *Her.* latticed.

Porte (pōᵊɹt). 1609. [a. F., in full *la Sublime Porte*, transl. Turkish official title of the central office of the Ottoman Government.] (In full, *the Sublime* or *Ottoman P.*) The Ottoman court at Constantinople; hence *transf.* the Turkish Government.

‖ **Porte-** (port), stem of F. *porter* to bear, carry, occas. anglicized as *port.* **Porte-bonheur** (-bonōr) [F. *bonheur* good luck], an amulet, or a trinket worn like an amulet. **Porte-bouquet** (-bukė), a bouquet-holder. **Porte-feu** (-fö) [F. *feu* fire] = PORT-FIRE. **Portefeuille** (-fölʸ) [F. *feuille* leaf, sheet], = PORTFOLIO. **Porte-monnaie** (-monę) [F. *monnaie* MONEY], a flat leather purse or pocket-book.

‖ **Porte-cochère** (portˌkoʃę̄r). 1698. [F., f. *porte* PORT *sb.*[3] + *cochère* adj. fem. f. *coche* COACH *sb.*] A gateway for carriages, leading into a court-yard; a carriage-entrance.

Portend (poɹte·nd), *v.* [late ME. ad. L. *portendere*, arch. form of *protendere* to stretch forth, f. *por-* = *pro-* forth + *tendere* to stretch; see PROTEND.] **1.** *trans.* To presage as an omen; to foreshow, foreshadow. **b.** Hence: To point to beforehand; to give warning of 1592. **2.** Of a person: To foretell, prognosticate (*rare*) 1611. †**3.** To signify, symbolize, indicate -1782.

1. b. What portends thy cheerful countenance? KYD. **2.** Some great misfortune to p., No enemy can match a friend SWIFT. **3.** *Twel. N.* II. v. 130.

Portent (pōᵊ·ɹtent). 1563. [ad. L. *portentum*, f. *portendere* to PORTEND. Orig. stressed *porte·nt.*] **1.** That which portends or foretells something about to happen, esp. of a calamitous nature; an omen, significant sign. **b.** The fact or quality of portending; in phr. *of dire* (etc.) *p.* 1715. **2.** Something considered portentous; a prodigy, wonder, marvel 1741.

1. My Loss by dire Portents the Gods foretold DRYDEN. Lowering with portents of rain HAWTHORNE. **2.** What p. can be greater than a pious notary? GEO. ELIOT.

Portentous (poɹte·ntəs), *a.* 1540. [ad. L. *portentosus*, f. *portentum* PORTENT; see -OUS.] **1.** Of the nature of a portent; ominous, threatening, warning. **2.** Applied to any object exciting wonder, awe, or amazement; marvellous, monstrous, prodigious; hence as an intensive (sometimes *joc.*) = extraordinary 1553.

1. The p. blaze of comets MILT. **2.** A p. apple-dumpling 1823. Hence **Porte·ntously** *adv.*

Porter (pōᵊ·ɹtəɹ), *sb.*[1] [ME. and AF. *porter* = OF. *portier* :—late L. *portiarius* door-keeper, f. L. *porta* door; see -ER[2] 2.] One who has charge of a door or gate; a gate-keeper, door-keeper, janitor. Also *fig.*

Comb. **porter's lodge,** a lodge for the p. at the gate of a castle, park, etc. (formerly a place of corporal punishment for servants and dependants). Hence **Po·rter** *v.*[1] *intr.* to be or act as a p.

Porter (pōᵊ·ɹtəɹ), *sb.*[2] [late ME. *portour*, a. OF. *porteour* (mod.F. *-eur*) :—L. *portatorem*, f. L. *portare* to carry; see -ER[2] 3.] **1.** A person employed to carry burdens; now *esp.* a servant of a railway company who carries luggage at a station (in full, *railway p.*). **b.** *gen.* and *fig.* A bearer, carrier 1581. **2.** An iron bar attached to a heavy body to be forged, by which it may, when suspended from a crane, be guided beneath the hammer or into a furnace 1794.

Hence **Po·rter** *v.*[2] *trans.* to carry as a p. (sense 1).

Porter (pōᵊ·ɹtəɹ), *sb.*[3] 1727. [Short for *porter's ale, porter's beer*, or *porter beer*, app. because orig. made for porters and other labourers.] A kind of beer, of a dark-brown colour and bitterish taste, brewed from malt partly charred or browned by drying at a high temperature. Also *attrib.*

My electors shall have p. at threepence a pot 1781.

Porterage (pōᵊ·ɹtərėdʒ). late ME. [f. PORTER *sb.*[2] + -AGE.] The action or work of a porter; carriage or transportation of goods; also, the charge for this. Also *attrib.*

Po·rter-house. Chiefly *U.S.* 1800. [f. PORTER *sb.*[3] + HOUSE *sb.*] A house at which porter and other malt liquors are retailed; also, one where steaks, chops, etc. are served.

attrib. **porter-house steak** (*U.S.*), a thick juicy beef-steak cut from between the sirloin and the tenderloin, supposed to derive its name from a well-known porter-house in New York.

Portfire (pōᵊ·ɹtfəiᵊɹ). 1647. [After F. *porte-feu*, in same sense; see PORTE-.] A device used formerly for firing artillery, and now for firing rockets, etc., and for igniting an explosive in mining, etc.

Portfolio (poɹtfōᵘ·lio). 1722. [In 18th c. *porto folio*, ad. It. *portafogli*, f. *porta*, imper. of *portare* to carry + *fogli* leaves, sheets of paper, pl. of *foglio* :—L. *folium.*] **1.** A receptacle or case, usu. in the form of a large book-cover, for keeping loose sheets of paper, prints, drawings, maps, music, etc. **2.** *spec.* Such a receptacle containing the official documents of a state department; *fig.* the office of a minister of state. **3.** *U.S.* A list of the securities owned by a financial institution, a bill-broker, etc.

2. *Minister without p.* (F. *sans portefeuille*), a member of the Cabinet who is not in charge of any department of state.

Comb. **p.-stand,** a piece of furniture for holding portfolios, drawings, music, etc.

Port-hole (pōᵊ·ɹtˌhōᵘl). 1591. [f. PORT *sb.*[3] + HOLE *sb.*] **1.** *Naut.* = PORT *sb.*[3] 2 b. **2.** *transf.* **a.** An aperture in a wall for shooting through, etc.; an embrasure; **b.** a similar aperture in other structures, e.g. in the door of a furnace 1644. **3.** A steam port (PORT *sb.*[3] 3) 1875.

Porthors, early f. PORTAS.

Portico (pōᵊ·ɹtiko). *Pl.* **-os, -oes.** 1605. [a. It. *portico* :—L. *porticus*, colonnade, porch, etc., f. *porta* PORT *sb.*[3]] *Arch.* An ambulatory consisting of a roof supported by columns placed at regular intervals, usu. attached as a porch to a building; a colonnade. Also *transf.* and *fig.* **b.** *spec.* The Painted Porch at Athens; see PORCH 3; hence *fig.* the Stoic philosophy. Also *allus.* 1788.

b. From the p., the Roman civilians learned to live, to reason, and to die GIBBON. Hence **Po·rticoed** *a.* furnished with a p.

‖ **Portière** (portyę̄r). 1855. [Fr. :—med.L. *portaria*, prop. adj. fem. sing., belonging to a door or gate.] A curtain hung over a door or doorway, to prevent draught, to serve as a screen, or for ornament.

Portion (pōᵊ·ɹʃən), *sb.* [ME. *porciun, portion*, a. OF. *porcion*, ad. L. *portionem* share, part, proportion.] **I. 1.** The part (of anything) allotted to one person; a share. Also *fig.* **b.** An allowance of food allotted to, or enough for, one person 1484. **2.** The part or share of an estate given or passing by law to an heir, or to be distributed to him in the settlement of the estate. Also *fig.* ME. **3.** Dowry; a marriage portion 1511. **4.** That which is allotted a person by providence; lot, destiny, fate ME.

1. Giue me the p. of goods that falleth to me *Luke* xv. 12. 3. I married Mrs. Mary Burton..with whom I received four hundred pounds for a p. SWIFT. 4. When Labour was pronounced to be the P. of Man STEELE. Brief life is here our p. 1851.

II. **1.** = PART *sb.* I. 1. ME. **2.** A (limited) quantity or amount; some ME.

1. A p. of the pressure was transmitted laterally TYNDALL. 2. But grace, ye the leest porcyon of grace,..is sufficyent 1526. Hence **Po·rtionless** *a.* without a p.; dowerless.

Portion (pōᵊ·ɹʃən), *v.* ME. [ad. obs. F. *portionner*, f. F. *portion* PORTION.] **1.** *trans.* To divide into portions or shares; to share *out*. **b.** = APPORTION *v.* 1. 1871. **2.** To dower, endow 1712.

1. The petty chiefs among whom the country was portioned out 1859. 2. When I marry with their consent they will p. me most handsomely DICKENS.

Portional (pōᵊ·ɹʃənăl), *a. rare.* late ME. [ad. late L. *portionalis*; see -AL.] Pertaining to or of the nature of a portion or part. Hence **Po·rtionally** *adv.* by way of a portion or part; partly, in part.

Portioner (pōᵊ·ɹʃənəɹ). 1508. [f. PORTION *sb.* or *v.* + -ER [1, 2].] **1.** *Scots Law.* The proprietor of a small piece of land forming a portion of an original forty-merk land. **b.** *Heir-* or *heiress-p.*, one of two or more heirs female who succeed to equal portions of a heritage; or the male representative of such an heiress 1576. **†2.** *Eccl.* = PORTIONIST 2. –1848. **3.** *Eng. Law.* One of several persons among whom a settled fund is appointable (*rare*) 1884.

Po·rtionist. 1672. [ad. med.L. *portionista* a scholar receiving a defined portion of food, f. *portionem* portion; see -IST.] **1.** In ref. to Merton College, Oxford: A rendering of the L. term *portionista*, applied to the class of poor scholars usu. called *postmasters*. **2.** *Eccl.* One of two or more incumbents who share the duties and revenues of a benefice 1743.

Portland (pōᵊ·ɹtlænd). 1720. A peninsula or 'island' on the coast of Dorsetshire; *attrib.* in names of products of Portland Island, or of objects connected with it; as **P. cement,** a cement resembling *P. stone* in colour; also *attrib.*; **P. oolite,** a limestone of the Upper Oolite formation, especially developed in the Isle of Portland; **P. stone,** a valuable building stone quarried in the Isle of Portland; etc.

Portly (pōᵊ·ɹtli), *a.* 1529. [f. PORT *sb.*[4] + -LY [1].] Characterized by stateliness or dignity of bearing, appearance, and manner; stately, dignified; imposing. **b.** Now usu. connoting 'Large and bulky in person; stout, corpulent' 1598. **c.** Of things: Stately, magnificent, fine 1548.

b. He dwindled..from a p. and even corpulent man to a skeleton MACAULAY. Hence **Po·rtliness.**

Po·rtman. Now *local.* OE. [f. PORT *sb.* [2] + MAN *sb.*] In OE. use, a citizen of a town, a burgess or burgher; *spec.* (after the Conquest) = *capital* or *head p.*, one of a select number of citizens chosen to administer the affairs of a borough.

Portmanteau (poɹtmæ·nto), *sb.* 1584. [a. F.; see PORTE- and MANTEAU.] **1.** A case or bag for carrying clothing and other necessaries when travelling; now, an oblong stiff leather case, which opens like a book, with hinges in the middle of the back. ‖ **2.** A clothes-rack, an arrangement of pegs to hang clothes on 1727. **3.** *attrib.*, as in *p. horse*, etc.; **p. word,** a word like those invented by 'Lewis Carroll', made up of the blended sounds and combining the meanings of two distinct words (as *slithy*, meaning 'lithe and slimy').

Po·rtmote. *Obs.* exc. *Hist.* ME. [f. PORT *sb.*[1], [2] + ME. *imote* MOOT *sb.*] **1.** The court of a borough; a borough-mote. **2.** The court of a (legal) sea-port town 1598.

‖ **Portolano** (pōᵊɹtolā·no), **portulan** (pōᵊ·ɹtiŭlăn). 1850. [It. *portolano*, f. *porto* PORT *sb.*[1]; hence F. *portulan*.] A book of sailing directions, describing harbours, etc. and illustrated with charts.

Portrait (pōᵊ·ɹtrĕt), *sb.* 1570. [a. F. *portrait*, from *portrait* pa. pple. of *portraire* obs. to portray; see PORTRAY.] **1.** A figure drawn, painted, or carved upon a surface to represent some object; *spec.* (now almost always) a likeness of a person, esp. of the face, made from life by drawing, painting, photography, engraving, etc. **†b.** A solid image, a statue –1638. **2.** *fig.* An image, representation, type; likeness, similitude 1577. **b.** A verbal picture; a graphic description 1596.

1. The..Coines, the portracts whereof I have here shewed 1610. What 's here, the p. of a blinking idiot SHAKS. The gentleman who wanted to take your p. 1858. 2. Poetes terme sleepe an image, or pourtraite of death 1577.

Comb.: **p.-bust,** a bust giving an exact likeness; **-gallery,** a gallery containing a collection of portraits, or the collection itself; also *fig.*; **-lens,** a compound photographic lens adapted for taking portraits; **-painter**; **-painting.** Hence **Po·rtraitist,** one whose occupation it is to take portraits; esp. a p.-painter.

†Po·rtrait, *v.* 1548. [orig. as pa. pple. *portraited*, app. an extended form of the ME. (orig. F.) pa. pple. *portrait*.] **1.** *trans.* = PORTRAY *v.* 1. –1864. **2.** *fig.* = PORTRAY *v.* 4. –1665. **3.** *transf.* = PORTRAY *v.* 1 b. –1669.

Portraiture (pōᵊ·ɹtrĕtiŭɹ, -tʃəɹ). [late ME. a. OF. *portraiture*, f. *portrait* PORTRAIT *sb.* + -URE.] **1.** The action or art of portraying; delineation. Also in concr. or collective sense; esp. in phr. *in p.* = portrayed, delineated. **2.** *concr.* = PORTRAIT *sb.* 1. late ME. **†b.** = PORTRAIT *sb.* 1 b. –1720. **3.** *gen.* and *fig.* An image, representation; a mental image, idea; †a type. late ME. **4.** = PORTRAIT *sb.* 2 b. 1610. **†5.** Figure, likeness, appearance (as an attribute of a thing) –1797.

1. The Portraitures of insignificant People by ordinary Painters STEELE. 4. Shakespeare's p. of John of Gaunt 1863. Hence **†Po·rtraiture** *v. trans.* to make a p. or portrait of, to portray (*lit.* and *fig.*).

Portray (poɹtrē·), *v.* [ME. a. OF. *pourtrai-*, stem of *pourtraire* to portray :—L. *protrahere* to draw forth, in med.L. also to portray, f. *pro-* forth + *trahere*.] **1.** *trans.* To make a picture, image, or figure of. **†b.** *transf.* To make (a picture, image, or figure); to draw, paint, or carve; to trace –1604 **†2.** *transf.* To paint or adorn (a surface) *with* a picture or figure 1667. **3.** *fig.* **†a.** To picture to oneself; to fancy. **b.** To represent (e.g. dramatically). ME. **4.** *esp.* To represent in words, describe graphically, set forth. late ME.

2. Shields..with boastful Argument portraid MILT. 4. Well hast thou pourtray'd..The face and personage of a wondrous man MARLOWE. Hence **Po·rtray** *sb.* the act of portraying; portrayal; a portrait. **Portray·al,** *lit.* pictorial representation; *fig.* representation in general; *esp.* verbal picturing. **Portray·er.**

Portreeve (pōᵊ·ɹtˌrīv). [OE. *portgerēfa*, f. PORT *sb.*[2] + REEVE *sb.*[1]] **1.** *orig.* The ruler or chief officer of a town or borough; after the Norman Conquest often identified with the mayor; in later times, sometimes an officer inferior to the mayor; a bailiff. **2.** Erron. referred to PORT *sb.*[1] 2, as if the reeve of a seaport town 1607.

Portress (pōᵊ·ɹtrès), **porteress** (pōᵊ·ɹtərès). late ME. [f. PORTER *sb.*[1] + -ESS.] A female porter; esp. in a nunnery. Also *fig.*

Port-Royal (pōᵊɹtˌroi·ăl). 1692. Name of a convent near Versailles (*Port-Royal des Champs*) which in the 17th c. became the home of a lay community celebrated for its connexion with Jansenism and its educational work. Hence **Port-Roy·alist** 1727.

†Po·rt-sa·le. 1494. [f. PORT *sb.*[2] or *sb.*[3] + SALE.] Public sale to the highest bidder; sale by auction –1670.

Portsman (pōᵊ·ɹtsmæ̆n). 1626. [f. PORT *sb.*[1] 3 + MAN *sb.*] A citizen or inhabitant of one of the Cinque Ports. (Usu. in pl.)

Portuary (pōᵊ·ɹtiuˌări). *arch.* 1867. [mod. f. *portuas*, or other var. of PORTAS, perh. after *breviary*.] = PORTAS. Also *attrib.*

Portugal (pōᵊ·ɹtiŭgăl). late ME. [a. Pg. *Portugal*, earlier *Portucal*, ad. med.L. *Portus Cale*, the port of Gaya, Oporto.] **1.** A country in the west of the Iberian peninsula. **†2.** A native or inhabitant of Portugal –1707. **†3.** *attrib.* or as *adj.* = PORTUGUESE A. –1719.

1. A French Shallop which he tooke in the Bay of Portingall RALEIGH. 3. Great P. ships 1691.

Portuguese (pōᵊɹtiŭgī·z), *a.* and *sb.* 1586. [ad. Pg. *Portuguez*, in med.L. *Portugalensis*; see PORTUGAL and -ESE.] **A.** *adj.* Pertaining to Portugal or its people 1662.

P. man-of-war: see MAN-OF-WAR.

B. *sb.* **1.** A native of Portugal. [pl. *Portugueses* in 17th c.; now *Portuguese* sing. and pl.] 1622. **2.** The Portuguese language 1617. **†3.** = PORTAGUE –1668.

‖ **Portulaca** (pōᵊɹtiŭlē·kă). 1548. [L., purslain (*P. oleracea*); taken as a generic name.] *Bot.* A genus of plants, comprising low succulent herbs bearing white, yellow, red, or purple terminal flowers, expanding only once in direct sunshine; esp. a plant of a cultivated species of this. Hence **Portulaceous** (-ē·ʃəs) *a. Bot.* of or pertaining to the N.O. *Portulaceæ*, comprising succulent herbs or shrubs, chiefly American.

Po·rt-wi·ne. 1700. = PORT *sb.*[6]; *attrib.* in *p. mark* = NÆVUS.

†Po·ry, *a.* 1535. [f. PORE *sb.* + -Y.] Full of pores; porous –1826.

‖ **Posaune** (pozau·nĕ, pǫ̈zǭ·n). 1724. [G.] **†1.** A trombone –1814. **2.** A reed-stop on an organ 1843.

Pose (pōuz), *sb.* 1818. [a. F., f. *poser* to put; see POSE *v.*[1]] An act of posing. **1.** An attitude or posture of the body, or of a part of the body, esp. one deliberately assumed, or in which a figure is placed for effect, or for artistic purposes. **2.** *fig.* An attitude of mind, esp. one assumed for effect 1884.

Pose (pōuz), *v.*[1] *Pa. t.* and *pple.* **posed.** ME. [a. F. *poser* :—L. *pausare* PAUSE *v.*, subseq. confused with L. *ponere* (*posui, positum*).] **†1.** *trans.* To suppose for argument's sake –1528. **2. a.** To lay down, put forth (an assertion, claim, instance, etc.) ME. **b.** To propose (a question, problem) 1862. **3. a.** To place in an attitude (as an artist's model, etc.). 1859. **b.** *intr.* To assume a certain attitude, esp. for artistic purposes 1850. **c.** *fig.* To set up *as*, give oneself out *as*; to attitudinize 1840.

2. b. Hesiod poses the eternal problems: what is the origin and destiny of mankind? 1873. 3. a. In studied attitude, like one posed for a daguerreotype 1868. b. It is more easy to p. than to act 1885. c. Politicians have of late years begun to p. as the special friends of the working man 1888. Hence **Po·ser** [2], one who poses or attitudinizes.

Pose (pōuz), *v.*[2] 1526. [Aphetic f. APPOSE *v.*[1], or OPPOSE, which were confused.] **†1.** *trans.* = APPOSE *v.*[1] 1. –1722. **2.** To non-plus with a question or problem 1593.

2. A question wherewith a learned Pharisee thought to p. or puzzle him 1677.

‖ **Posé** (poze), *a.* 1725. [Fr., pa. pple. of *poser* to place.] *Her.* = STATANT.

Poser [1] (pōu·zəɹ). 1587. [Aphetic f. APPOSER; see POSE *v.*[2]] **1.** One who sets testing questions; an examiner. Now *rare.* **2.** A puzzling question or problem 1793.

‖ **Poseur** (pozö̆r). 1881. [Fr., f. *poser* POSE *v.*[1]] One who practises an affected mental or social attitude. Also ‖ **Poseuse** fem.

Posh (pǫʃ), *a. slang.* 1918. [Of obsc. origin; app. adj. use of *posh* sb. (1) money, (2) dandy.] Smart, 'swell'; fine, splendid.

Posied (pōu·zid), *a.* 1597. [f. POSY + -ED [2].] **1.** Inscribed with a posy or motto (*arch.*). **2.** Furnished with nosegays; flowery. *dial.* 1797.

1. Many a ring of P. gold SHAKS.

Posit (pǫ·zit), *v.* 1647. [f. L. *posit-*, ppl. stem of *ponere*.] **1.** *trans.* To put in position; to set, dispose, or situate; to place. (Chiefly in *pa. pple.* or *pass.*) **2.** To put down or assume as a fact; to postulate. Chiefly in *Logic* and *Philos.* 1697.

2. In so far as anything is a cause, it posits something different from itself as an effect 1877.

Position (pǫ̆zi·ʃən), *sb.* late ME. [a. F., ad. L. *positionem*, n. of action from *posit-*, *ponere* to put, place, set.] **I. 1.** The action of positing; the statement of a proposition or thesis; affirmation. Chiefly in *Logic* and *Philos.* **2.** Something posited; a statement, assertion, tenet 1451. **3.** *Arith.* A method of finding the value of an unknown quantity by positing one or more values for it, finding the error as indicated by the results, and then adjusting it. Also called *rule of* (*false*) *p.*, *rule of trial and error*, etc. 1551. **†4.** The action of positing or placing; disposition -1735. 5. The manner in which a body, or the several parts of it, are disposed or arranged; disposition, posture, attitude 1703. b. *fig.* Mental attitude 1905. 6. *Mus.* The arrangement of the constituent notes of a chord, with respect to their order, or to the intervals between them 1880.

2. It is a p. in the Mathematiques that there is no proportion betweene somewhat and nothing BACON. 5. *Eastward p.*, the p. of the officiating priest at the Eucharist, when he stands facing east with his back to the people.

II. 1. The place occupied by a thing, or in which it is put; situation, site, station 1541. b. *Mil.* A site chosen for occupation by an army, usu. as having a strategic value 1781. 2. *Phonology.* The situation of a vowel in an open or closed syllable; *spec.* in *Gr.* and *L. Prosody*, the situation of a short vowel before two consonants or their equivalent, making the syllable metrically long (phr. *in p.* said of such a vowel) 1580. 3. The situation which one metaphorically occupies in relation to others, to facts, or to circumstances 1827. b. Place in the social scale; status, rank 1865. c. An official situation, place, or employment 1890.

1. Phr. *In p.*, in its (his, etc.) proper place; so *out of p.* *Angle of p.*, (*a*) the angle between any two points subtended at the eye; (*b*) *Astron.* the angle between the circles of declination and latitude of a celestial body. *Circle of p.*, any one of six great circles of the celestial sphere passing through the north and south points of the horizon. *Gun of p.*, a heavy field gun, not designed for executing quick movements. 3. We are now in a p. to discuss the air thermometer 1871. b. A man of considerable p. 1868. c. A p. in a bank 1890.

attrib. and *Comb.*, as **p.-artillery**, heavy field-artillery; so **p.-battery**; **p. error**, the error of a watch when laid in certain positions; **-finder**, an apparatus by means of which a gunner is enabled to aim a gun at an object not visible to him.

Position (pǒzi·ʃən), *v.* 1817. [f. prec.] *trans.* To place in a particular or appropriate position. b. To determine the position of; to locate 1881.

Positional (pǒzi·ʃənăl), *a.* 1571. [f. POSITION *sb.* + -AL.] Of, pertaining to, or determined by position.

Positive (pǫ·zitiv), *a.* and *sb.* [ME. *positif*, a. F., ad. L. *positivus* (in grammar) positive, f. *posit-*, *ponere*; see -IVE.] **A.** *adj.* **I. 1.** Formally laid down or imposed; arbitrarily or artificially instituted; conventional; opp. to *natural*. 2. Explicitly laid down; admitting no question; express, definite, precise; emphatic; †objectively certain 1598. 3. Of persons: Confident in opinion or assertion; convinced; also, opinionated, cock-sure, dogmatic, dictatorial 1665.

1. Again, of p. laws some are human, some divine; and of human p. laws, some are distributive, some penal HOBBES. 2. P. orders oblige us to go tomorrow 1709. P. proof 1870. 3. Nor is Socrates p. of anything but the duty of enquiry JOWETT.

II. Unqualified, unrelated, absolute. 1. *Gram.* Applied to the primary form of an adjective or adverb, which expresses simple quality, without qualification, comparison, or relation to increase or diminution 1447. 2. Having no relation to or comparison with other things; absolute, unconditional; opp. to *relative* and *comparative* 1606. b. *colloq.* Nothing less than, downright; 'out-and-out' 1802.

2. Patroclus is a foole positiue SHAKS. Beauty is no p. thing, but depends on the different tastes of the people 1727. b. You are a p. enigma 1853.

III. 1. Dealing only with matters of fact; practical; not speculative or theoretical 1594. 2. Actual, real; sensible, concrete (*rare*) 1831.

1. *P. philosophy* = POSITIVISM 1. 2. *P. image* = real image; see REAL *a.*[2] I. 1 d.

IV. Having real existence; opp. to *negative*. 1. Characterized by the presence, and not merely by the absence, of features or qualities; of an affirmative nature 1618. b. Of a term, etc.: Denoting the presence, as opp. to the absence, of a quality 1725. 2. *Alg.* Of a quantity: Greater than zero; additive; the opp. of NEGATIVE *a.* II. 2. 1704. b. Hence, Reckoned or tending in the direction taken (naturally or arbitrarily) as that of increase, progress, or onward motion 1873. 3. *Electr.* Applied to that form of electricity which is produced by rubbing glass with silk; vitreous; opp. to NEGATIVE *a.* II. 3. 1755. b. Of, pertaining to, or marked by the presence or production of positive electricity; *spec.* denoting that member of a voltaic couple which is most acted upon by the solution, and from which a current of positive electricity proceeds 1808. 4. *Magnetism.* Applied to the north-seeking pole of a magnet, and the corresponding (south) pole of the earth 1849. 5. *Optics.* a. Of a double-refracting crystal: Having the index of refraction of the extraordinary ray greater than that of the ordinary ray 1831. 6. *Photogr.* Showing the lights and shades as seen in nature; opp. to NEGATIVE *a.* II. 5. 1840.

1. Ease from misery occasioning for some time the greatest p. enjoyment 1729. 2. *P. sign*, the sign +, used to mark a p. quantity. 5. *P. eyepiece*, an eyepiece consisting of two plano-convex lenses, having their convex sides facing each other, in which the object is viewed beyond both lenses.

V. Adapted to be placed or set down. *P. organ*, a small organ, orig. app. portable, but placed upon a stand when played 1727.

B. *sb.* (the adj. used absol. or ellipt.) 1. *Gram.* The positive degree (see A. II. 1); an adj. or adv. in the positive degree 1530. 2. That which has an actual existence, or is capable of being affirmed; a reality 1620. 3. Elliptically or contextually for *p. quantity* (see A. IV. 2); *p. plate*, *metal*, etc. (see A. IV. 3); *p. organ* (see A. V.); etc. 1706. 4. *Photogr.* A picture in which the lights and shades are the same as in nature; opp. to NEGATIVE *sb.* 4. 1853. Hence **Po·sitive-ly** *adv.*, **-ness**.

Positivism (pǫ·zitiviz'm). 1854. [ad. F. *positivisme*, f. *positif*, *-ive* POSITIVE; *la philosophie positive* being Comte's name for his system.] 1. A system of philosophy elaborated by Auguste Comte, which recognizes only positive facts and observable phenomena, with the objective relations of these and the laws which determine them, abandoning all inquiry into causes or ultimate origins; also, a religious system founded upon this philosophy, in which the object of worship is Humanity considered as a single corporate being. 2. a. Definiteness, peremptoriness; b. Certainty, assurance 1854.

Positivist (pǫ·zitivist). 1854. [ad. F. *positiviste*, f. as prec.; see -IST.] An adherent or supporter of POSITIVISM; a Comtist. Also *attrib.* or as *adj.* Hence **Positivi·stic** *a.* of or pertaining to positivists; of the nature of positivism.

Positivity (pǫziti·vĭti). 1659. [f. POSITIVE + -ITY.] The quality, character, or fact of being POSITIVE; positiveness.

Posnet (pǫ·snėt). Now *arch.* and *dial.* [ME. *possenet*, a. OF. *poçonnet*, dim. of *poçon* vase.] A small metal pot or vessel for boiling, having a handle and three feet.

Posology (posǫ·lŏdʒi). 1811. [ad. F. *posologie*, f. Gr. πόσος how much + -LOGY.] 1. That part of medicine which relates to the quantities or doses in which drugs should be administered 1823. 2. Used by Bentham for the science of quantity, i.e. mathematics 1811. Hence **Poso·lo·gical** *a.* pertaining to p. **Poso·logist**, one who compounds doses SYD. SMITH.

‖ **Pospolite** (pǫspǫ·litė). 1697. *Hist.* [Polish *pospolite* general, universal; as sb. = *pospolite ruszenie* general levy.] The Polish militia.

Poss (pǫs), *v.* Now only *dial.* late ME. [Origin obsc.] 1. *trans.* To drive or thrust; to dash or toss with a blow; to knock. Also *fig.* 2. To pound, beat down flat, squash; *spec.* to beat or stamp (clothes, etc.) in water, in the process of washing 1611.

2. Nasty women possing clothes with their feet THORESBY. Hence **Po·sser**, an implement for possing clothes. **Po·ss-tub**, a wash-tub.

Posse (pǫ·si). 1583. [a. L. *posse* to be able, in med.L. as sb., power, armed force; in scholastic L., potentiality.] 1. *Law.* = next. Now chiefly *U.S.* 1659. b. A force, *esp.* of constables 1697. c. *transf.* A company (*of* persons, animals, or things) 1645. ‖ 2. The fact or state of being possible; potentiality (opp. to *esse*); esp. in phr. *in p.* opp. to *in esse* 1583.

‖ **Posse comitatus** (pǫ·si kǫmitē·tǒs). 1626. [med. (Anglo-) L., force of the county; see prec. and COUNTY.] The body of men above the age of fifteen in a county (exclusive of peers, clergymen, and infirm persons), whom the sheriff may summon or raise to repress a riot or for other purposes; also, a body of men so raised and commanded by the sheriff. (See also prec. 1.) b. *transf.* = POSSE 1 c. 1819.

Possess (pǒze·s), *v.* 1465. [a. OF. *possessier*, f. L. *possess-*, ppl. stem of *possidere*.] **I.** †1. *trans.* To hold, occupy (a place or territory); to reside or be stationed in; to inhabit -1713. †b. Of a thing: To occupy (a space or region); to be situated at, on, or in -1755. †c. To occupy, engross the attention or thoughts of -1719. 2. To hold as property; to own 1500. b. *Law.* To have possession of, as distinct from ownership 1888. c. To have as a faculty, attribute, quality, etc. (Often = the simple *have*.) 1576. d. (after F. *posséder*.) To have knowledge of; to be master of or conversant with (a language) 1852. 3. To seize, take; to come into possession of, obtain, win (*arch.*) 1526. 4. To keep, maintain (oneself, one's mind, soul) *in* a state or condition (of patience, quiet, etc.); often in allusion to Luke xxi. 19 (the proper sense being misunderstood; see quot. in 3). Also (without *in*) to maintain control over. 1643. 5. Of a demon or (usu. evil) spirit: To occupy and dominate, control, or actuate 1596. 6. Of an idea, etc.: To take or have hold of (a person); to affect strongly and persistently. (Formerly also of bodily conditions.) 1591.

1. Dominion giv'n Over all other Creatures that possesse Earth, Aire, and Sea MILT. 2. He could not give to others what he did not himself p. 1881. c. The former may p. many times the intensity of the latter 1860. 3. With your pacience possesse your soules TINDALE, *Luke* xxi. 19. 4. All Christians.. are obliged..to p. their souls in patience 1654. 5. I am possest with the diuell and cannot sleepe DEKKER. 6. What can p. this young lord to be out of his bed at this hour? 1814.

II. Causal uses; = cause to possess. †1. To put in possession of (lands, etc.); to settle or establish *in* -1708. 2. To endow with, put in possession *of*; to give (something) to. Now *rare* or *Obs.* exc. as in b or c. 1549. b. *refl.* = sense I. 3. 1593. c. *pass.* To be in possession *of*; to possess 1495. 3. To cause to be possessed by (a feeling, idea, etc.); to imbue, inspire, permeate *with*; to cause to feel or entertain 1597. †b. Without const.: To prepossess -1681. 4. To put in possession *of*, furnish *with* (information, etc.); to instruct *in*; to acquaint *that*. *Obs.* or *arch.* 1596.

2. I will possesse you of that ship and Treasure SHAKS. b. All that the plaintiffs did was to p. themselves..of the securities 1885. c. *Possessed of* or *with*, having possession of, possessing; Every human being possessed of reason COLERIDGE. 3. What Devil possesses them with such wicked designs? 1670. b. In all causes the first tale possesseth much BACON. 4. I haue possest your grace of what I purpose SHAKS. Hence **Possessed** (pǒze·st) *ppl. a.* occupied, held as property; inhabited or controlled by a demon or spirit; lunatic, crazy.

Possession (pǒze·ʃən). ME. [a. OF., ad. L. *possessionem*, f. *possidere*; see POSSESS.] 1. The action or fact of possessing, or condition of being possessed; the holding something as one's own; actual occupancy, as dist. from ownership. b. *Law.* The visible possibility of exercising over a thing such control as attaches to lawful ownership; the detention or enjoyment of a thing by a person himself or by another in his name; the relation of a person to a thing over which he may at his pleasure exercise such control as the character of the thing admits, to the exclusion of other persons; *esp.* the having of such exclusive control over land, in early instances sometimes used in the technical sense of SEISIN 1535. 2. *concr.* That which is possessed or held as property; (with *a*, etc.) a thing possessed, a piece of property; *pl.* belongings, property, wealth ME. 3. A territory subject to a sovereign ruler or state; now chiefly applied to the foreign dominions of an independent country 1818. 4. The fact of a demon possessing a person; the fact of being possessed by a demon or spirit 1590. 5. The action of an idea or feeling possessing a person; *transf.* an idea or impulse that holds one strongly; †a prepossession 1621. 6. The action of keeping (oneself, one's mind, etc.) under control (*rare* exc. in SELF-POSSESSION) 1703.

1. Philosophy is the p. of knowledge JOWETT. **b.** Phr. *In p.*, said (*a*) of a thing, actually possessed or held; (*b*) of a person, usu. *in p. of*, actually possessing, holding, or occupying something. *Chose in p.*: see CHOSE 1. *Man in p.*, a duly authorized person who is placed in charge of chattels upon which there is a warrant for distress. *To take p. of*, to take for one's own or into one's control, to seize. Provb. *P. is nine points of the law*: see POINT *sb.*[1] III. 6. **2.** The ȝong man..wente awei sorewful, for he hadde many possessiouns WYCLIF *Matt.* xix. 22. **3.** Canada became a British p. in 1763. 1850. **4.** How long hath this p. held the man? SHAKS. Hence **Posse·ssional** *a. rare*, pertaining to p.; having possessions or property; propertied. **Posse·ssionary** *a.* constituted by p.; having, pertaining to, or relating to p.

Posse·ssioner. *Hist.* late ME. [f. POSSESSION *sb.* + -ER [2].] One who is in possession or holds possession *of* something; a holder, occupier; an owner; an owner of possessions. **b.** *spec.* A member of a religious order having possessions or endowments; an endowed clergyman or ecclesiastic. late ME.

Possessive (pǒze·siv), *a.* (*sb.*) 1530. [ad. L. *possessivus*; see POSSESS *v.* and -IVE.] **1.** *Gram.* Denoting possession; qualifying a thing (or person) as belonging to some other. **2.** Of or pertaining to possession; indicating possession 1560. **b.** Having the quality of being in possession 1838. **B.** *sb. Gram. ellipt.* (*a*) for *p. pronoun* or *adjective*; (*b*) for *p. case* 1591.

1. *P. pronoun* (*p. adjective*), a word derived from a personal or other pronoun, and expressing possession. *P. case*, a name for the genitive case in modern English, ending (in nouns) in *'s, s'*, and expressing possession. Hence **Posse·ssive-ly** *adv.* in a p. sense or relation; in the way of possession; **-ness.**

Possessor (pǒze·səɪ). [Late ME. and AF. *possessour* = F. *possesseur*, ad. L. *possessor, -orem*, f. *possidere*; see POSSESS *v.* and -OR [1].] One who possesses; one who holds something as property or in actual control; one who has something belonging to him; a holder; an owner, proprietor. Const. *of* or with *poss. pron.* **b.** *spec.* (mainly *Law*). One who takes, occupies, or holds something without ownership, or as dist. from the owner 1565.

The most hye God, p. of heauen and earth COVERDALE *Gen.* xiv. 19. This charm was too dangerous to its p. MRS. RADCLIFFE. **b.** The p. remains liable to the true owner 1800. Hence **Posse·ssorship.**

Possessory (pǒze·sŏri). *a.* late ME. [ad. late L. *possessorius*: see POSSESS *v.* and -ORY.] **1.** *Law.* **a.** Pertaining to a possessor; relating to possession. **b.** Arising from possession, as *p. interest, right, title* 1615. **2.** That is a possessor; holding something in possession 1633. **3.** Of, belonging to, or characterizing a possessor 1659.

1. a. *P. action*, an action in which the plaintiff's claim is founded upon his or his predecessor's possession, and not upon his right or title.

Posset (pǫ·sėt), *sb.* [Late ME. *poshote, possot*; origin unkn.] A drink composed of hot milk curdled with ale, wine, or other liquor, often with sugar, spices, etc.; formerly much used as a delicacy, and as a remedy for colds, etc. Also *attrib.* Hence **Po·sset** *v.* †*trans.* to curdle like a p.; *intr.* to make a p.

Possibilist (pǫsi·bilist). 1881. [ad. F. *possibiliste* or Sp. *posibilista*, f. L. *possibilis*; see POSSIBLE and -IST.] A member of a political party whose aims at reform are directed to what is immediately possible.

spec. (*a*) of a party of Republicans in Spain; (*b*) of a party of Socialists in France. Also *attrib.* or as *adj.*

Possibility (pǫsibi·lĭti). late ME. [a. F. *possibilité*, ad. L. *possibilitas*, f. *possibilis* POSSIBLE; see -ITY.] **1.** The state, condition, or fact of being possible; capability of being done, happening, or existing. **b.** The quality or character of representing or relating to something that is possible 1638. **2.** A possible thing or circumstance; something that may exist or happen. (Usu. with *a* or *pl.*) late ME. †**3.** Regarded as an attribute of the agent: The fact of something being possible to one, in virtue either of circumstances or of one's own powers; hence, Capacity, power, ability; pecuniary ability, means -1815. †**b.** *sing.* and *pl.* Pecuniary prospects -1637.

1. Science and Revelation come into..collision on the p. of miracles 1884. Phr. *By any p.*, in any possible way, by any existing means, possibly; so *by no p.* *In p.*, (*a*) = *in* POSSE; (*b*) in relation to something possible, but not actual; potentially. *After p.* (Law), ellipt. for *after p. of issue is extinct*, i. e. when there is no longer any p. of issue. **b.** To consult on the p. of certain views DISRAELI. **2.** Her clearer intellect saw possibilities which did not occur to him TROLLOPE. **3.** I haue speeded hither with the very extremest ynch of possibilitie SHAKS. **b.** *Merry W.* I. i. 65.

Possible (pǫ·sĭb'l), *a.* (*sb.*, *adv.*) ME. [a. F., or ad. L. *possibilis*, f. *posse* to be able; see -IBLE.] **1.** That may be (i. e. is capable of being); that may or can exist, be done, or happen; that is in one's power, that one can do, exert, use, etc. (const. *to* the agent). **b.** That can or may be or become (what is denoted by the sb.); as *a p. object of knowledge* = something that can or may be known 1736. **2.** That may be (i. e. is not known not to be); that is perhaps true or a fact; that perhaps exists. (Sometimes nearly = credible, thinkable.) 1582. **b.** That may be (what is denoted by the sb.); that perhaps is or will be 1882. †**3.** Having the power *to do* something; capable (*rare*) -1667. **4.** *Math.* = REAL *a.*[2] I. 1 c; opp. to IMPOSSIBLE A. 2. 1874. **5.** With ellipsis of some qualification: Possible to deal with, get on with, understand, etc. (*rare*) 1865.

1. All thynges are possyble to hym that belevith TINDALE *Mark* ix. 23. To express ourselves with all p. energy BURKE. Phr. *If p.*, if it be (or were) p., if it can (or could) be. *As much as p.*, as much as may (or might) be, as much as one can (or could). **2.** In such an age, it is p. some great genius may arise, to equal any of the ancients DRYDEN. **3.** Firm we subsist, yet p. to swerve MILT.

B. *absol.* or as *sb.* **1. a.** *absol.* (usu. with *the*): That which is possible 1646. **b.** as *sb.* A possible thing. (Almost always in *pl.*) 1657. ¶ **c.** *To do one's p.* (after F. *faire son possible*): to do what is possible to one, to do one's utmost 1797. **2.** *colloq.* (orig. *highest p.*), short for 'highest possible score or number of points' (esp. in rifle practice) 1866. †**C.** as *adv.* = POSSIBLY. (As an intensive qualification of *can* or *could.*) -1799.

Possibly (pǫ·sĭbli), *adv.* late ME. [f. POSSIBLE + -LY [2].] **1.** In a possible manner; according to what may or can be (in the nature of things); by any existing power or means. (Usu., now always, as an intensive qualification of *can* or *could.*) **2.** According to what may be (as far as one knows); perhaps, maybe. (Often as intensive qualification of *may* or *might.*) 1600.

1. He cannot p. live till Five in the Morning ADDISON. How could you p. think so? (*mod.*). **2.** P. I might have some poor low relations C. BRONTE.

Possum (pǫ·sŏm), *sb.* Now *colloq.* 1613. Aphetic form of OPOSSUM.

To play p. (U.S. colloq.), to feign; to pretend illness; in allusion to the opossum's habit of feigning death when threatened or attacked. Hence **Po·ssum** *v. intr.* to play p.; to hunt opossums.

Post (pōust), *sb.*[1] [OE., ad. L. *postis* post, door-post (in med.L. also rod, pole, beam).] **I. 1.** A stout piece of timber, etc., of considerable length, and usu. cylindrical or square, used in a vertical position, esp. in building as a support for a superstructure. **b.** As a type of lifelessness, stupidity, ignorance, deafness, or hardness. late ME. **2.** A stake, stout pole, or the like, set upright in or on the ground, for various purposes ME. †**b.** Formerly set up by the door of a mayor, sheriff, or other magistrate -1845. **3.** With prefixed words indicating special purpose 1643. **4.** Contextually for various specific kinds of posts: **a.** A door-post or gate-post ME. **b.** *Racing.* A starting-post or winning-post 1642. **c.** *Naut.* The upright timber on which the rudder is hung; the stern-post; †hence *transf.* the stern of a ship 1622. †**5.** The door-post on which the reckoning at a tavern was kept; hence, the score -1604.

1. b. Phr. *Between you and me and the p.* (*bed-p.*, *gate-p.*), as something that no one else is to hear or know; as a secret, in confidence. **2.** Like Posts of direction for Travellers MILT. **b.** *Twel. N.* I. v. 157. **3.** *Draw-p.*, a post used in wire fences, provided with winders for tightening the wires; *kerb-p.*, a post set at the edge of a pavement. See also BED-*p.*, DOOR-*p.*, GATE-P., GOAL-*p.*, KING-P., LAMP-P., SIGN-P. **4. a.** The Gates of Azza, P., and massie Bar MILT. **5.** *Com. Err.* I. ii. 64.

II. Transf. uses. **a.** A vertical mass or stack of stratified rock between two 'joints' or fissures 1712. **b.** Any thick compact stratum of sandstone or limestone 1794. **c.** = PILLAR *sb.* 6.

Phrases. *From p. to pillar*: see PILLAR *sb.* *To run one's head against a p.*: in fig. use. *On the right* or *the wrong side of the p.*, etc. (referring to posts marking the right course); hence *fig.*

Comb.: **p.-hole,** a hole made in the ground to receive the foot of a p.; also *attrib.*; **-mill,** a windmill pivoted on a p., so as to be turned round to catch the wind.

Post (pōust), *sb.*[2] 1506. [a. F. *poste*, ad. It. *posta*, orig. same as *posta* position, F. *poste* station, stand, late L. or Rom. *posta* sb. fem. from *postus* (Lucretius) = *positus*, pa. pple. of *ponere* to place.] **I.** †**1.** Orig. applied to men with horses stationed or appointed at intervals along the post-roads, the duty of each being to ride with, or forward to the next stage, the king's 'packet', and later the letters of other persons, and to furnish change of horses to messengers riding post -1628. **2.** One who travels express with letters, messages, etc., esp. on a fixed route; *orig.* a courier, a post-rider (now chiefly *Hist.*); a letter-carrier, a postman (now chiefly *dial.*). Also *transf.* and *fig.* 1507. **3.** A vehicle or vessel used in the conveyance of the mails; a mail-coach or cart; †a packet-boat. †Also, in early use, a post-horse. 1597. **4.** A single dispatch of letters, etc. from or to a place; also *concr.*, the letters, etc. collectively, as dispatched or conveyed, with that which carries them; the mail. Also *colloq.* the portion of a mail cleared from a receiving-box, or delivered at one house. 1674. **5.** = POST-OFFICE 1; the official conveyance of letters, books, parcels, etc. 1663. **b.** = POST-OFFICE 2; also the postal letter-box 1808.

1. In the 16th and 17th c., these 'posts' had also usu. the exclusive privilege of furnishing post-horses to ordinary travellers, and of conducting the business of a posting establishment N.E.D. Phr. *To lay posts*, to establish a chain of posts along a route for the speedy forwarding of dispatches. **2.** The Postes come tyring on, And not a man of them brings other newes SHAKS. Now my days are swifter than a p. *Job* ix. 25. **3.** I haue fowndred nine score and odde Postes SHAKS. **4.** The state of foreign affairs varied every p. 1715. **5.** *Book-p.*, *parcel-p.*, the departments of the post-office which carry books and parcels.

†**II.** One of a series of stations where post-horses are kept for relays; a posting-house; also, the distance between two successive posting-houses; a stage -1809.

'Twill scarce be ten posts out of my way STERNE.

III. Phrases and senses arising out of them.

a. *By p.*, †*orig.* by posting; by courier; by relays of post-horses; in current use, through the post-office. **b.** *By return of p.* (F. *par retour du courrier*), †*orig.* by return of the 'post' or courier who brought the dispatch; now, by the next mail in the opposite direction. †**c.** *In p.* (= F. *en poste*), in the manner or capacity of a courier or bearer of dispatches, as a post; hence, at express speed, in haste; whence *post* becomes = haste, full speed. **d.** *To ride p.* = *to ride in p.* (c); see POST *adv.* †**e.** *To take p.*, to start on a journey with post-horses.

IV. Transf. uses. **1.** A frequent title of newspapers 1681. **2.** A parlour game; short for *general post* 1868. **3.** orig. *post-paper*: A size of writing-paper, the half-sheet of which when folded forms the ordinary quarto letter-paper. So-called because its original water-mark was a postman's horn. 1711.

attrib. and *Comb.*, as **p.-bag,** a bag for carrying letters and other postal matter; *transf.* the letters delivered to or sent from any one house or person; **-boat,** a boat or ship engaged in the conveyance of mails; also, a boat which conveys travellers between certain points; **-box,** a box in which letters are posted or deposited for dispatch, a letter-box; **-cart,** a cart in which local mails are carried; **-chariot,** a chariot for travelling post; *spec.* a light four-wheeled carriage, differing from a p.-chaise in having a driver's seat in front; **-paid** *a.*, having the carriage prepaid; **-paper,** (see IV. 3); **-rider,** one who rides p.; a mounted letter-carrier; **p.-wagon** [Du., G. *postwagen*], a mail or stage coach in the Netherlands, etc.; **-woman,** a female letter-carrier.

Post (pōust), *sb.*[3] 1598. [a. F. *poste*, ad. It. *posto* post, station, employment:—L. *postum*, sb. neut. from *positum*, pa. pple. neut. of *ponere* to place.] **1.** *Mil.* The place where a soldier is stationed. **b.** *transf.* and *fig.* The appointed place; the place of duty 1692. **2.** *Mil.* A position taken; a place at which a body of soldiers is stationed, or the force occupying this; *esp.* a strategic position taken by a commander. Cf. OUTPOST. Also *transf.* and *fig.* 1692. **b.** A place where armed men are permanently quartered for defensive or other purposes; a fort 1703. **c.** *transf.* A place occupied for purposes of trade, esp. in an uncivilized or unsettled country 1837. **d.** *attrib.*, as *p.-adjutant*, etc. 1878. **3.** An office or situation to which any one is appointed; position, place; employment 1695. **4.** *Naval.* Position as a full-grade captain, i. e. commission as officer in command of a vessel of 20 guns or more; hence, position or order of seniority in the list of captains 1720.

1. Clive..was awakened by the alarm, and was instantly at his p. MACAULAY. **b.** My daily p. was by the bed of disease and suffering LYTTON. **2.** Phr. *To take p.*, to occupy a position; Richard..had taken p. at Nottingham HUME. **b.** This P. was Garisoned by 600 Men 1703. **c.** The trading p. of the Hudson's Bay Company 1837. **3.** Those posts in the public service supposed to be posts for gentlemen M. ARNOLD. **4.** Phr. *To give p.*, said of a ship of 20 guns or more, the officer in command of which had the rank of captain; *to take p.*, said of the officer, to receive the commission of captain of such a vessel; also *to be made p.*, to be appointed post captain. Now *arch.* or *Hist.* **Post captain**, a captain who 'takes post'; a designation formerly applied to a naval officer holding a commission to distinguish him from an officer having merely the courtesy title of captain. *Obs.* exc. *Hist.* †**P. ship**, a ship of not less than 20 guns, the commission to command which 'gave post' to a captain.

†**Post** (pōust), *sb.*4 1528. [app. ad. It. *posta* a stake laid down :—L. *posta, posita*, f. *ponere*.] **a.** Name of an obs. card game, app. the same as *p. and pair* -1688. **b.** *P. and pair*, a card-game, played with three cards each, in which the players bet on their own hands -1887.

Post, *sb.*5 1727. [app. ad. Ger. *posten* parcel, lot, etc., ad. It. *posto* :—L. *positum* that which is put; cf. POST *sb.*2, 3 and 4.] **1.** *Paper-making.* A pile of from four to eight quires of hand-made paper fresh from the mould, laid with alternate sheets of felt ready for pressing. **2.** *Metall.* A batch of ore for smelting at one time 1839.

Post (pōust), *sb.*6 1885. [app. from POST *sb.*3 1; short for 'call to post', or the like.] A bugle-call giving notice of the hour of retiring for the night. Usu. *first* or *last p.*

It is customary to sound the 'last p.' beside a soldier's grave after the interment.

Post (pōust), *v.*1 1533. [f. POST *sb.*2, or a. obs. F. *poster*.] **I. 1.** *intr.* To travel with relays of horses (orig. as a bearer of letters). **2.** To travel with speed or haste; to hasten, hurry 1558.

1. We posted from morning till night HAKLUYT. **2.** Gray haires come posting on 1632.

†**II.** *trans.* To cause to post or hasten; to hasten, hurry (a person) -1807. **III.** †**1.** To convey in the manner of a post; to convey swiftly -1682. **2.** †**a.** To send by special messenger -1724. **b.** To send through the post office; to put (a letter, etc.) into a post-office or letter-box for transmission by the post 1837.

1. *Cymb.* II. iv. 27. **2. b.** His letter was posted two days later 1870.

IV. *Book-keeping*, etc. **1.** To carry or transfer (an entry) from an auxiliary book to a more formal one, esp. from the day-book into the ledger; to carry (an item or entry) to the proper account; also, by extension, to enter (an item) in proper form in any of the books 1622. **b.** To complete (the ledger or other book) by transferring to it all the items in the auxiliary books, and entering them in their proper accounts; to make the proper entries in all the books; often *p. up* (i. e. up to date, or to completion) 1707. **2.** *fig.* (orig. *U.S. colloq.*) To supply with full information or latest news on a subject. Often *p. up.* Usu. in *pass.* 1847.

1. To see the crimes of new democracy posted as in a ledger against the crimes of old despotism BURKE. **b.** You have not posted your books these ten years 1718. **2.** To..keep myself 'posted up'..with the literature of the day THACKERAY.

Post (pōust), *v.*2 1520. [f. POST *sb.*1] **I.** *trans.* To square (timber) before sawing it, or in order to form it into posts. *Obs.* or *dial.* **II.** To attach or moor (a vessel) to a post 1868. **III. 1.** To affix (a paper, etc.) to a post or in a prominent position; to stick *up* in a public place 1650. **2.** To make known, advertise (some fact, thing, or person) by or as by posting a placard. Also with *up*. 1633. **b.** *spec.* To expose to ignominy, or ridicule, by this means. Now *rare*. 1642. **c.** In some colleges: To place in a list, which is posted up, the names of (students who fail to pass in the college examinations) 1852. **d.** To publish the name of (a ship) as overdue or missing 1886. **3.** To placard (a wall, etc.) with bills 1854.

1. The old bill-stickers went to Trafalgar Square to attempt to p. bills DICKENS. **2. b.** I'll p. you for a swindler and a coward THACKERAY.

Post (pōust), *v.*3 1683. [f. POST *sb.*3] **1.** *trans.* To place, station. **2.** *Mil.* and *Naval.* To appoint to a post or command; *spec.* to appoint to command a ship which 'gave post'; to commission as captain. Chiefly *pass.* 1800.

2. I am posted, and appointed to the *Semiramis* frigate 1833.

Post (pōust), *adv. Obs.* or *arch.* 1549. [Originating in the phr. *ride in post* (POST *sb.*2 III. c), abbrev. to *ride post*.] With post-horses; by post; express; with speed or haste.

To speake hastily.., to talke p., as they say 1632. He set out P. for Paris 1716.

‖**Post** (pōust). 1704. The L. prep. meaning 'after', occurring in phrases in Eng. use, as *p. meridiem, p. mortem*; also in **1. Post bellum,** after the war 1883. **2. Post hoc,** after this. *Post hoc, ergo propter hoc,* after this, therefore because of this; expressing the fallacy that a thing which follows another is therefore caused by it 1704. **3. Post partum,** after child-birth 1857. **4. Post terminum** (*Law*): see POST TERM.

Post- (pōust), *prefix*, repr. L. *post*, adv. and prep., after, behind. Widely used, esp. in the prepositional relation, not only in compounds formed on words from L., but also, in techn. terms, from Gr., and sometimes even on Eng. or other words, as *p.-war* a. etc. **A.** Words in which *post-* is adv. or adj. In compounds derived or formed from L., or on L. analogies, as POST-DATE, -PONE, -SCRIPT, etc.; also in nonce-wds.

1. Relating to time or order. **a.** In adverbial relation: = After, afterwards, subsequently; as *p.-determined* (opp. to *predetermined*). **Post-exi·st** *v.* (*rare*) to exist after; to live subsequently; so **Post-exi·stence.** **Postfi·x** *v.* to affix after, or at the end; to append, as a postfix. **b.** In *quasi*-adjectival relation to a sb. forming, or implied in, the second element: = Occurring or existing after, coming after, subsequent, later; as *p.-act, -legitimation*. †**Post-dissei·sin** *Old Law*, a second or subsequent disseisin; also a writ that lay for one who had a second time been disseised, after a recovery by novel disseisin; so **Post-dissei·sor.** **Po·st-entry,** a subsequent or late entry; *spec.* an additional or supplemental entry, in the manifest of a vessel, of an item or items of dutiable merchandise; the warrant issued on this is a **Post-warrant.** **Po·stfix** [after PREFIX *sb.*], a word, syllable, or letter affixed or added to the end of a word, a suffix. **Po·stlude** [after PRELUDE], a concluding piece or movement played at the end of an oratorio or the like. **Po·st-note** *U.S.* (*Obs.* exc. *Hist.*) a note issued by a bank, payable to order at a future specified date.

2. Of local position. **a.** In advb. relation to a vbl. sb.: = Behind, posteriorly; as *postjacent*, etc. **b.** In adjectival relation to a sb. expressed or implied; as **Post-abdo·men,** the posterior part of the abdomen; *esp.* in invertebrates, the portion posterior to the abdominal cavity; hence **Post-abdo·minal** *a.* **Postcava** (-kēi·vă), *Anat.* the inferior vena cava; so called as being behind or posterior in animals generally. **Postcla·vicle,** *Anat.* and *Zool.* the posterior bone of the scapular arch of some fishes. ‖**Post-fu·rca** [L. *furca* fork], the hindmost of the three apodemes in the thoracic somites of insects. ‖**Post-nares** (-nē·rīz) [L. *naris* nostril] *pl.*, the posterior nostrils, the openings of the nasal chamber into the pharynx. ‖**Postscute·llum,** *Entom.* the fourth sclerite of each of the segments of the thorax in an insect, situated behind the *scutellum*. **Postsphenoid** (-sfī·noid) *a.*, *Anat.* in *p. bone*, the posterior part of the sphenoid bone of the skull; also *ellipt.* as *sb.* **Post-zygapophesis** (-zigăpǫ·fisis), each of the two posterior or inferior processes on the neural arch of a vertebra.

B. Compounds in which *post-* is prepositional.

1. Relating to time or order: = After, subsequent to, following, succeeding, later than. **a.** With sbs., forming adjs. (or attrib. phrases), usu. of obvious meaning; as *p.-Asce·nsion, -Ea·ster, -ele·ction, -war* (esp. after the war of 1914–18), etc. **b.** With adjs., or formed from *post* + a L. or Gr. sb. with an adjectival ending, as *p.-Ada·mic, -bapti·smal, -Carte·sian* (see CARTESIAN), *-Darwi·nian, influe·nzal, na·tal, nu·ptial*, etc. **Post-exilian** (-egzi·liăn), of or pertaining to the period of Jewish history subsequent to the Babylonian exile. **Postmille·nnial,** of or belonging to the period following the millenium; so **Postmille·nialism,** the doctrine that the second Advent will follow the millennium. **c.** Rarely with sbs., forming sbs., as **Po·st-fine,** *Law* (*Obs.* exc. *Hist.*) a duty paid to the Crown for the royal licence to levy a fine. **2.** Relating to locality: = Behind, situated at the back of, posterior to. In many adjs. (rarely sbs.), chiefly *Anat.* and *Zool.*, indicating parts or organs situated behind (more rarely, in the hinder parts of) other parts or organs; as **Post-a·xial,** of, pertaining to, or situated on that side of a limb (in vertebrates) which is posterior to a line drawn at right angles to the body axis through the axis of the limb. **Post-fro·ntal** [L. *frons* forehead], (*a*) situated behind the forehead, or at the back of the frontal bone; (*b*) situated in the hinder part of the frontal lobe of the brain; *sb.* the external angular process of the frontal bone, which is situated at the back part of the brim of the orbit of the eye. **Posto·cular,** situated behind the eye; *sb.* a postocular scale, as in snakes. **Post-o·ral,** situated behind the mouth; applied to certain visceral arches in the embryo of vertebrates. **Postsca·pular,** situated behind or below the spine of the scapula, as in *p. fossa.* **Post-te·mporal,** situated behind the temporal region of the skull. **Post-tympa·nic,** behind the tympanic bone; applied to a bone, and a process of bone, in some Carnivora; also as *sb.* = *post-tympanic bone* or *process*.

Postage (pōu·stėdʒ). 1590. [f. POST *sb.*2 + -AGE.] †**1.** The conveyance of letters, etc., by post -1693. †**2.** The postal service; a postal service between particular points -1779. **3.** The amount charged for carrying a letter or postal packet; now usu. prepaid by means of a POSTAGE STAMP or stamps 1654. †**4.** Travelling by means of post-horses; posting; also *transf.* a rapid journey -1808.

Po·stage sta·mp. 1840. [f. prec. + STAMP *sb.*] An official stamp, either a stamp embossed on an envelope or impressed on a card or wrapper, or (now usu.) a small adhesive label having a specified face-value, sold by or on behalf of the Post Office, to be affixed to any letter or packet sent by post, as a means and evidence of prepayment of postage. Also *attrib.*

Postal (pōu·stăl), *a.* (*sb.*) 1843. [a. F. *postal(e*, f. *poste* POST *sb.*2; see -AL.] Of or pertaining to the post; relating to the carriage of mails. **B.** as *sb. U.S.* Short for *p. card, p. note*; also for *p. car, p.* (i. e. mail) *train*.

Comb.: **p. car,** a railway car for the carriage of mails (*U.S.*); **p. card** (*U.S.*) = POSTCARD, when issued by the post office itself; **p. note,** (*U.S.*) an order issued by a post office for any sum of less than five dollars payable at any other post office; **p. order,** a form of money order issued by a post office of the United Kingdom for one of a number of fixed sums, payable at any post office; **p. union,** a union of the governments of various countries for the regulation of international postage.

Po·st-boy. 1588. [f. POST *sb.*2 + BOY *sb.*] **1.** A boy or man who rides post; a letter-carrier. **2.** = POSTILION 2. 1707.

2. The post-boys cracked their whips LYTTON.

Post-captain: see POST *sb.*3 4.

Postcard (pōu·stkāɹd). 1870. [f. POST *sb.*2 + CARD *sb.*2] A pasteboard card of a regulation size, used for correspondence.

Pictorial or *picture p.*, a p. bearing a picture on the reverse side.

Post-chaise (pōu·st,ʃēⁱz), *sb.* Also *colloq.* **postchay, -shay,** PO'CHAISE, etc. 1712. [f. POST *sb.*2 + CHAISE.] A travelling carriage, either hired from stage to stage, or drawn by horses so hired. Also *attrib.*

Post-cla·ssical, *a.* 1867. [f. POST- B. 1 + CLASSICAL.] Occurring or existing subsequent to the classical period of any language, literature, or art; *spec.* of the Greek and Latin.

Post-commu·nion, *sb.* (*a.*) 1483. [ad. med.L. *postcommunio, -onem*; see POST- B. 1 c and COMMUNION. Earlier †*post-common.*] The or a part of the eucharistic office which follows the act of communion. **B.** *adj.* Following the act of communion; used after communion 1890.

Post-date (pōu·st,dēit), *sb.* 1611. [f. POST- A. 1 b + DATE *sb.*2] A date affixed to a document, or assigned to an event, later than the actual date.

Post-date (pōust,dēi·t), *v.* 1624. [f. POST- A. 1 a + DATE *v.*] *trans.* To affix or assign a date later than the actual date to (a document, book, event, etc.).

Post-dilu·vial, *a.* 1823. [f. as next + -AL.] **a.** *Geol.* Posterior to the diluvial or drift period. **b.** *gen.* = next A.

Post-diluvian (pōust,dili̱ū·viăn), *a.* and *sb.* 1680. [f. POST- B. 1 + L. *diluvium* a deluge + -AN.] **A.** *adj.* Existing or occurring after the Flood or Noachian deluge. **B.** *sb.* One who lived, or lives, after the Flood 1684.

‖**Postea** (pōu·sti,ă). 1596. [L. = afterwards;

being the first word of the usual beginning of the record.] *Law.* That part of the record of a civil process which sets forth the proceedings at the trial and the verdict given.

†**Po·stel.** ME. [a. OF. *postel*, mod.F. *poteau* post, dim. of OF. *post* POST *sb.*[1]; see -EL[2].] A door- or gate-post -1631.

Poster[1] (pōu·stəɹ). 1605. [f. POST *v.*[1] + -ER[1].] 1. One who travels 'post', expeditiously, or swiftly. Also *fig.* Now *rare* or *Obs.* 2. A post-horse 1817.

1. The weyward Sisters,..Posters of the Sea and Land SHAKS.

Poster[2] (pōu·stəɹ). 1838. [f. POST *v.*[2] + -ER[1].] 1. One who posts or sticks up bills; a bill-poster 1864. 2. A placard posted or displayed in a public place as an announcement or advertisement. Also *attrib.* 1838.

‖ **Poste restante** (post,rę̄stānt). 1768. [Fr., = letter(s) remaining (i. e. at the post office).] A direction written upon a letter which is to remain at the post office till called for; in Eng. use, transf. to the department in a post office in which letters for visitors or travellers are kept till applied for.

Posterior (pǫstīə·riəɹ), *a.* and *sb.* (*adv.*) 1534. [a. L., compar. of *posterus* or *poster* coming after, f. *post* prep., after.] A. *adj.* 1. Later, subsequent in time; opp. to *prior.* 2. Coming after in a series or order 1626. 3. Hinder; situated behind, or farther back than something else. Opp. to *anterior.* 1632.

1. The precepts of the art of poesy were p. to practise 1756. 3. The legs are called anterior, p., and intermediate 1868.

B. *sb.* 1. *pl.* Those who come after; descendants, posterity 1534. 2. *pl.* The hinder parts of the body; the buttocks 1605. †3. *pl.* The later part (*joc.*) SHAKS.

1. Neither he, nor his posteriors from generation to generation SCOTT.

C. *adv.* Subsequently 1826. Hence **Poste·riorly** *adv.*

Posteriority (pǫstīəri,ǫ·rĭti). late ME. [prob. a. AF. **posteriorité*, ad. med.L. *posterioritas*, f. L. *posterior*; see -ITY.] 1. The state or quality of being later or subsequent in time. Opp. to *priority.* †2. Inferiority in order, rank, or dignity -1704.

Posterity (pǫste·rĭti). [Late ME. *posterite*, a. F. *postérité*, ad. L. *posteritas*, f. *posterus* coming after; see -ITY.] 1. The descendants collectively of any person; all who have proceeded from a common ancestor. 2. †a. A later generation (with *pl.*). b. All succeeding generations (collectively). 1535.

1. Thy posterite shalbe as the grasse vpon the earth COVERDALE *Job* v. 25. 2. The ocean and the sun will last our time, and we may leave p. to shift for themselves JOHNSON.

Postern (pōu·stəɹn), *sb.* (*a.*) [ME. a. OF. *posterne* (mod.F. *poterne*), altered f. OF. *posterle* :—late L. *posterula* a back way, dim. of *posterus* that is behind.] 1. A back door; a private door; any door or gate distinct from the main entrance. b. *Fortif.* A tunnel serving as a means of access to the ditch and outworks 1704. 2. *fig.* A way of escape or of refuge. b. An entrance other than the usual and honourable one. c. An obscure passage. 1579. 3. *attrib.* or as *adj.* Placed at the back; private, side, inferior, esp. in *p. door* or *gate*; also *fig.* ME.

Postero- (pǫ·stërǫ), comb. form of L. *posterus* hind, hinder, prefixed to adjs., in the sense (*a*) hinder and —, as in *postero-external*, etc.; (*b*) on the back part of that which is —, as **postero-lateral,** placed at the posterior end of a lateral margin or part; etc.

Post-free, *a.* 1882. [f. POST *sb.*[2] + FREE *a.*] Free from charge for postage, either as being officially carried free of charge, or as being prepaid.

Post-glacial (-glē̆i·ʃiăl), *a.* 1855. [f. POST-B. 1 b + GLACIAL *a.*] *Geol.* Existing or occurring subsequent to the glacial period or ice age.

Post-gra·duate, *a.* (*sb.*) orig. *U.S.* 1858. [f. POST- B. 1 b + GRADUATE.] Pertaining or relating to a course of study carried on after graduation. B. *sb.* A student who takes a post-graduate course 1890.

Post-haste (pōu·sthē̆i·st), *sb.*, *adv.*, and *adj.* 1545. [From the old direction on letters 'Haste, post, haste'; taken subseq. as a comb. of POST *sb.*[2] and HASTE *sb.*] A. *sb.* Haste or speed like that of one travelling post; great speed in travelling (*arch.*). B. *adv.* With the speed of a post; with all possible expedition 1593. †C. *adj.* Done with all possible speed SHAKS.

B. Her Coach is order'd, and Post-haste she flies 1709. C. *Oth.* I. ii. 37.

Post-horn (pōu·sthǭɹn). 1675. [f. POST *sb.*[2] + HORN *sb.*] A horn formerly used by a postman or the guard of a mail-coach, to announce his arrival.

Post-horse (pōu·sthǭɹs). 1527. A horse kept at a post-house or inn for the use of post-riders, or for hire by travellers.

Post-house (pōu·sthaus). *Obs.* exc. *dial.* 1635. [f. POST *sb.*[2] + HOUSE *sb.*[1]] 1. A post office. *Obs.* or *dial.* †2. An inn or other house where horses are kept for the use of travellers; a posting-house -1833.

Posthumous (pǫ·stiŭməs), *a.* 1608. [f. L. *postumus* last, superl. f. *post* after; in late L. referred to *humus* the earth or *humare* to bury; see -OUS.] a. Of a child: Born after the death of its father 1619. b. Of a book or writing: Published after the death of the author 1668. c. Of an action, reputation, etc.: Occurring, arising, continuing after death 1608. Hence **Po·sthumously** *adv.*

‖ **Posthumus** (pǫ·stiŭmǒs), *a.* and *sb.* 1591. [L. *post(h)umus* POSTHUMOUS.] †A. *adj.* = POSTHUMOUS -1660. B. *sb.* †a. (*pl.* -i.) A posthumous child -1677. b. *neut.pl.* **posthuma.** Posthumous writings 1655.

†**Po·stic,** *a.* 1638. [ad. L. *posticus* hinder, f. *post* behind; cf. *anticus* ANTIQUE.] Hinder, posterior, 'back' -1664.

‖ **Postiche** (postiʃ), *a.* and *sb.* 1854. [F., adj., ad. It. *posticcio* counterfeit :—L. type **pos(i)ticius*, f. *pos(i)tus* placed, put.] A. *adj.* a. Counterfeit, artificial. b. Applied to an ornament superadded to a finished work of sculpture or architecture, esp. when inappropriate. B. *sb.* a. An imitation substituted for the real thing. b. Counterfeiting, feigning, pretence. 1876.

Posticous (pǫstəi·kəs), *a.* 1866. [f. L. *posticus* POSTIC + -OUS.] *Bot.* Posterior, hinder; applied variously to parts of a flower or inflorescence.

Postil (pǫ·stil), *sb.* Now only *Hist.* [Late ME. a. F. *postille*, ad. med.L. *postilla* a gloss on the gospel. Origin obsc.] 1. A marginal note or comment upon a text of Scripture or upon any passage. 2. A series of such comments; *spec.* an expository discourse or homily upon the Gospel or Epistle for the day, read or intended to be read in the church service 1483. b. A book of such homilies 1566. 3. *attrib.* 1635. So †**Po·stil,** †**Po·stillate** *vbs. trans.* to write comments or marginal notes on. †**Po·stiller.**

Postilion, postillion (pǫsti·lyən). 1565. [a. F. *postillon*, ad. It. *postiglione*, f. It. *posta* POST *sb.*[2] + *-iglione* compound suffix (cf. *vermilion*).] †1. A post-boy; a swift messenger. Also *fig.* -1708. 2. One who rides the near horse of the leaders when four or more are used in a carriage or post-chaise; one who rides the near horse when one pair only is used without a driver 1623.

Po:st-impre·ssionism. 1910. Art of a more 'advanced' style than IMPRESSIONISM, in which representation of form is subordinated to the subjective view of the artist.

Posting (pōu·stiŋ), *vbl. sb.* 1559. [f. POST *v.*[1] + -ING[1].] The action of POST *v.*[1] 1. †a. The dispatching of letters, etc., by a messenger riding post. b. Travelling by means of relays of horses. c. The keeping of post-horses, vehicles, etc., as a business. 2. The dispatching or conveying of letters and other postal matter through or by the post office 1871. 3. *Book-keeping.* The carrying of an entry from the journal or other auxiliary book into the ledger; the formal entry of an item in a book of accounts; the bringing of account books up to date 1682.

Postliminary (-li·minări), *a.* 1702. [f. L. *post* after + *limen, limin-* threshold + -ARY[1]; but in sense 1 assoc. w. POSTLIMINIUM.] 1. Pertaining to or involving the right of postliminium. 2. Subsequent; opp. to *preliminary* 1826.

Postliminious (-limi·niəs), *a.* 1656. [f. L. *postliminium* + -OUS.] 1. Of or pertaining to postliminium (*rare*). 2. = POSTLIMINOUS 1684.

‖ **Postliminium** (-limi·niŏm). 1638. [L., a return 'behind one's threshold', f. *post* POST-B. 2 + *limen, -in-* threshold.] *Rom. Law.* = POSTLIMINY.

Postliminous (-li·minəs), *a.* 1714. [f. L. *post* after + *limen, -in-* threshold + -OUS.] Subsequent; of the nature of an appendix; opp. to *preliminary.*

Postliminy (-li·mĭni). 1658. [Anglicized f. POSTLIMINIUM.] *Rom. Law.* The right of any person who had been banished or taken captive, to assume his former civic privileges on his return home. Hence, in *Internat. Law*, The restoration to their former state of persons and things taken in war, when they come again into the power of the nation to which they belonged.

Postman[1] (pōu·sᵗmæn). 1529. [f. POST *sb.*[2] + MAN *sb.*] 1. A bearer or carrier of letters or other postal matter; a letter-carrier. †2. A newsman, a news-writer -1709.

2. You want..some news: therefore let me be your p. PEPYS.

Postman[2]. *Obs.* exc. *Hist.* 1768. [f. POST *sb.*[1] + MAN *sb.*] A barrister in the Court of Exchequer, who had precedence in motions except in Crown business; the name was derived from the post, the measure of length in excise cases, beside which he took his stand.

Po·stmark, *sb.* 1678. [f. POST *sb.*[2] + MARK *sb.*[1]] A mark officially impressed upon letters or other postal packages; now, usu. a mark giving the place, date, and hour of dispatch, or of the arrival of the mail. Hence **Po·stmark** *v. trans.* to mark with the post-office stamp, esp. that showing date and place of posting.

Postmaster[1] (pōu·stmāstəɹ). 1513. [f. POST *sb.*[2] + MASTER *sb.*[1]] 1. †a. *orig.* A master of the posts; the officer who had the charge or direction of the post-messengers -1708. †b. In the 17th and 18th c.: The post-office servant at each of the stations or stages of a post-road; orig. called POST (*sb.*[2] 1). c. Now, The person who has official charge of a post office, and the superintendence of all business there transacted. 1603. 2. The keeper of a posting establishment 1581. Hence **Po·stma:stership**[1].

Postmaster[2] (pou·stmāstəɹ). 1593. The name given at Merton College, Oxford, to the class of poor scholars instituted in 1380 by John Wyllyot; now the equivalent in that college of the term 'scholar' in general collegiate use. Hence **Po·stma:stership**[2].

Po·stmaster ge·neral. 1626. [f. POSTMASTER[1] + GENERAL *a.*] The administrative head of the postal service of a country or state, who is in Great Britain often, and in U. S. always, a member of the cabinet. Hence **Po·stmaster-ge·neralship.**

Postmeridian (-mĕri·diăn), *a.* 1626. [ad. L. *postmeridianus* in the afternoon, f. *post* after + *meredianus* MERIDIAN *a.*] 1. Occurring after noon or midday; of or pertaining to the afternoon. Also *fig.* 2. *Geol.* Applied to a subdivision of the Palæozoic strata of the Appalachian chain 1858.

‖ **Post meridiem** (pōust mĕri·diĕm), *phr.* 1647. [L., after midday.] After midday; applied to the hours between noon and midnight; abbrev. P.M. or p.m.

Postmistress (pōu·stmi:strĕs). 1697. [f. POST *sb.*[2] + MISTRESS.] A woman who has charge of a post office. **Po·stmi:stress-ship.**

‖ **Post mortem, post-mortem,** *advb. phr.*, *a.*, and *sb.* 1734. [L., after death.] A. *advb. phr.* (*post mortem*). After death.

The fistulas are but rarely found post-mortem 1897.

B. *adj.* (*post-mortem*). Taking place, formed, or done after death 1835.

A *post mortem* examination 1837.

C. *sb.* Short for *post-mortem examination.* Also *attrib.* 1850. b. *transf.* Discussion of a game or match after it is finished **1922.**

Post-mortems show the cause of death 1903.

‖ **Postnatus** (-nē̆i·tǒs), pl. -i. 1609. [med.L., born after.] One born after a particular event; *spec.* in Scotland, one born after the Union of the Crowns.

Post-obit (pōᵘstˌǫᵘbit, -ōᵘ·bit). 1751. [Shortened from L. *post obitum* after decease.] **A.** *adj.* **1.** Taking effect after some one's death; esp. in *post-obit bond* 1788. **2.** Post-mortem. *rare.* 1822. **B.** *sb.* (Short for *post-obit bond.*) A bond given by a borrower, securing to the lender a sum of money to be paid on the death of a specified person from whom the borrower has expectations 1751.

Ready gold, to be paid back, post-obit fashion, on a father's coffin-lid 1851.

Post office, post-office (pōᵘ·stˌǫ:fis). 1652. [f. POST *sb.*² + OFFICE.] **1.** The public department charged with the conveyance of letters, etc. by post. **2.** A house or shop where postal business is carried on, where postage stamps are sold, letters are registered and posted for transmission, etc. 1657.

2. *General Post Office* (abbrev. *G.P.O.*), the central or head post office of a country or state, as that in London; also pop. applied to the head office in a city or town.

attrib. and *Comb.*, as *p. clerk*, etc.; **p. annuity, insurance,** a system whereby annuities can be purchased and lives insured through the post office; **p. car,** *U.S.* a mail-van or coach on a railway; **p. department** = sense 1; **p. order** (abbrev. P.O.O.), a money-order for a specified sum, issued at one post office and payable at another therein named, to a person whose name is officially communicated in a letter of advice; **p. savings-bank,** a bank having branches at local post offices where sums within fixed limits are received on government security, at a small rate of interest; **p. stamp,** a stamp officially imprinted on a letter by the post office; also the instrument used for stamping the postmark.

Postorbital (-ǭ·ɪbităl), *a.* (*sb.*) 1835. [f. POST- B. 2 + ORBITAL.] *Anat.* and *Zool.* Situated behind, or on the hinder part of, the orbit of the eye. Also *ellipt.* as *sb.* **a.** The postorbital bone or process. **b.** A scale behind the eye in snakes.

Post-pliocene (-plǝi·ŏsīn), *a.* (*sb.*) 1841. [f. POST- B. 1 b + PLIOCENE.] *Geol.* Applied to the lowest division of the Post-tertiary or Quaternary formation, immediately overlying the Pliocene or Upper Tertiary; also to the whole of the formations later than the Pliocene. Also applied to animals, etc. of this period. Also *ellipt.* as *sb.* = p. division or formation.

Postpone (poᵘsᵗpōᵘ·n, pǒs-), *v.* 1500. [ad. L. *postponere*, f. *post* after + *ponere* to place. In 16th c. Scotch only.] **1.** *trans.* To put off to a later time; to defer. **†b.** To 'put (a person) off', i. e. to keep him waiting for something expected –1705. **c.** *intr. Path.* Of ague or the like: To recur after a longer interval than is usual or expected 1843. **2.** To place after in serial order or arrangement; to put at, or nearer to, the end 1620. **†3.** To place after in order of precedence, rank, importance, or value; to subordinate –1893.

1. The project had to be postponed W. IRVING. **3.** You have postpon'd the publick interest to your own 1670. Hence **Postpo·nement,** the action or fact of postponing. **Postpo·nence** (*rare*), subordination. **Postpo·ner.**

†Postpo·se, *v.* 1598. [a. F. *postposer*: see POST- A, *poser* POSE *v.*¹] *trans.* = POSTPONE –1656.

Postposit (pōᵘstpǫ·zit), *v. rare.* 1661. [f. L. *postposit-*, ppl. stem of *postponere.*] *trans.* = POSTPONE 2, 3. Hence **Postpo·sited** *ppl. a.*

Postposition (pōᵘstpŏzi·ʃǝn). 1638. [f. L. *postponere, postposit-*; but in sense 2, after *preposition.*] **1.** The action of placing after; the condition or fact of being so placed. **2.** A particle or relational word placed after another word, usu. as an enclitic; esp. a word having the function of a preposition, which follows its object, as L. *versus* 1846. Hence **Postposi·tional** *a.* = next.

Postpositive (poᵘstpǫ·zĭtiv), *a.* (*sb.*) 1786. [f. L. *postposit-*, *postponere*; see POSTPONE.] Characterized by postposition; having the function of being suffixed; enclitic. **B.** *sb.* A postpositive particle or word 1846.

Postprandial (-præ·ndiăl), *a.* 1820. [f. POST- B. 1 b + L. *prandium* meal + -AL.] Done, made, taken, happening, etc. after dinner; after-dinner. (Chiefly *joc.*)

Men far advanced in post-prandial potations 1890.

Po·st-roa·d. 1657. A road on which a series of post-houses or stations for post-horses is (or was) established; a road on which the mails were carried.

‖**Postscenium** (pōᵘstˌsī·niǝ̆m). 1727. [L. *postscænium*, f. *post* after + *scæna*, a. Gr. σκηνή stage, scene.] *Class. Antiq.* The back part of a theatre, behind the scenes. Cf. PROSCENIUM.

Postscribe (pōᵘstˌskrǝi·b), *v.* 1614. [ad. L. *postscribere.*] *trans.* To write (something) after; to write as a postscript or appendix.

Postscript (pōᵘ·sᵗskript), *sb.* Also **post-scriptum,** pl. **-ta.** 1523. [ad. L. *postscriptum*, neut. pa. pple. of *postscribere*, used as sb.] Something written at the end of a letter, after the signature, containing additional matter (often expressing an afterthought). **b.** *transf.* A paragraph written or printed at the end of any composition, containing some appended matter 1638. So **Postscri·ptal** *a.* of the nature of, or relating to, a p.

Post term. 1607. *Law.* A partial rendering of L. phrase **post terminum** after the term, used *advb.*, as *adj.*, and as *sb.* for: The return of a writ after term, and the fee payable for its then being filed.

Po·st-te·rtiary, *a.* (*sb.*) 1854. [f. POST- B. 1 b + TERTIARY.] *Geol.* Applied to the formations, or the period, subsequent to the Tertiary, the most recent of the geological series; quaternary; hence to animals, etc. of this period. Also *ellipt.* as *sb.*

Po·st-town. 1635. [f. POST *sb.*² + TOWN.] **1.** A town having a (head) post office, or one that is not merely a sub-office of another. **†2.** A town at which post-horses are kept –1838.

Postulant (pǫ·stiŭlănt). 1753. [a. F., ad. L. *postulans*, *-antem*, pr. pple. of *postulare*; see POSTULATE *v.*] One who asks or petitions for something; a petitioner; a candidate; *esp.* a candidate for admission into a religious order or community. Hence **Po·stulancy,** the condition, or period, of being a p.

Postulate (pǫ·stiŭlėt), *sb.* 1588. [ad. L. *postulatum* (a thing) demanded; see POSTULATUM.] **I.** A demand, a request; *spec.* a demand of the nature of a stipulation. Now *rare.* **II.** **1.** *Logic* and *gen.* A proposition demanded or claimed to be granted; *esp.* something claimed or assumed as a basis of reasoning, discussion, or belief; hence, a fundamental condition or principle 1646. **b.** An unproved assumption, a hypothesis *rare.* 1646. **c.** A pre-requisite of some actual or supposed occurrence or state of things 1841. **3.** *spec.* in *Geom.* (or derived use). A claim to take for granted the possibility of a simple operation, e. g. that a straight line can be drawn between any two points; a simple problem of self-evident nature; dist. from AXIOM (a self-evident theorem) 1660.

1. Christianity is essentially miraculous. This is a p. of Biblical criticism. 1860.

Postulate (pǫ·stiŭleᵢt), *v.* 1533. [f. ppl. stem. of L. *postulare* to demand, request; see -ATE ³.] **1.** *trans.* To demand; to require; to claim 1593. **b.** *intr.* To make a request; to stipulate 1860. **2.** *trans. Eccl. Law.* To ask authority to admit (a nominee) by dispensation; hence, to nominate or elect to an ecclesiastical dignity, subject to the sanction of the superior authority 1533. **3.** To claim or take for granted the existence, fact, or truth of (something); *esp.* to assume as a basis of reasoning, discussion, or action 1646. **b.** To assume the possibility of (some construction or operation) 1817.

1. Logic..postulates to express in words what is already in the thoughts MILL. **2.** The chapter was then allowed to p. the bishop of Bath STUBBS. **3.** Reason postulates God, though it cannot prove him 1885. So **Postula·tion,** the action of postulating; a request, demand, claim; an assumption. **Po·stulator,** one who postulates; *spec.* in *R.C.Ch.* a pleader in favour of a candidate for beatification or canonization.

Postulatory (pǫ·stiŭlătǝri), *a.* Now *rare.* 1631. [ad. L. *postulatorius* adj.; see POSTULATE *v.* and -ORY ².] **1.** Making request; supplicatory. **2.** Of the nature of an assumption; hypothetical 1646.

†‖Postula·tum. *Pl.* **-a.** 1619. [L., sb. use of pa. pple. neut. of *postulare* to POSTULATE.] = POSTULATE *sb.* 1, 2. –1827.

Posture (pǫ·stiŭɪ, -tʃǝɪ), *sb.* 1605. [a. F., contr. from earlier *positure*, ad. L. *positura* position, posture.] **1.** The relative disposition of the various parts of anything; *esp.* the position and carriage of the limbs and the body as a whole; attitude, pose 1606. **†2.** Position, situation –1835. **3.** A state of being; a condition or situation in relation to circumstances 1642. **4.** *fig.* A mental or spiritual attitude or condition 1642.

1. Restlessness, which caused a constant variation of p. 1804. **2.** To give intelligence of the forces, or p. of the enemy GOLDSM. **3.** The present p. of affairs round Paris RUSKIN. **4.** Therewith we broke up, all in a sad p. PEPYS. A certain..p. of the soul 1866. Hence **Po·stural** *a.* pertaining or relating to p.

Posture (pǫ·stiŭɪ, -tʃǝɪ), *v.* 1628. [f. prec.] **†1.** *trans.* To place in position; to set –1677. **2.** To dispose the body or limbs of (a person) in a particular way 1628. **3.** *intr.* To assume a particular posture of body; also, to put the limbs, or body, in an artificial position 1851. **4.** *fig.* **a.** To pose for effect. **b.** To take up an artificial mental position. 1877.

2. And still these two were postured motionless, Like natural sculpture in cathedral cavern KEATS. **4.** Jewell..occasionally postured as a buffoon 1880. Hence **Po·sturer,** one who poses for effect.

Po·sture-ma·ker. 1711. **a.** One who makes postures; a contortionist; an acrobat. **b.** A teacher of postures or callisthenics.

Posy (pōᵘ·zi). Now *arch.* or *dial.* 1533. [Syncopated f. POESY.] **1.** A short motto, orig. a line or verse of poetry, inscribed on a knife, within a ring, as a heraldic motto, etc. **2.** A bunch of flowers; a nosegay, a bouquet. Now somewhat *arch.* or *rustic.* 1573. **b.** A collection of 'flowers' of poetry or rhetoric. Cf. ANTHOLOGY. *arch.* 1569.

1. Let this be your Posie rather,..Manners makes man 1569. **2.** I will make thee beds of roses, And a thousand fragrant posies MARLOWE.

Comb. **p.-ring,** a finger-ring with a motto inside.

Pot (pǫt), *sb.*¹ [Late OE. or early ME. *pott*, cogn. w. OFris. *pot*, MDu., MLG. *pot*; also with F. *pot*, obs. It. *potto*, pointing to a late L. **pottus*. Origin unkn.] **1.** A vessel of rounded form, and rather deep than broad, made of earthenware or metal (less commonly glass), used to hold liquids or solids, for various purposes. (Often with defining word as *glue-p.*, *ink-p.*, *jam-p.*, *water-p.*, etc.) **b.** *spec.* Such a vessel used for cooking or boiling. Hence *transf.* the vessel with the food boiling in it; also allus. = cooking, food (as in phr. *for the p.*); also in fig. allusions ME. **c.** Such a vessel used to contain wine, beer, coffee, tea, etc. 1440. **d.** A FLOWER-POT 1615. **e.** A chamber-pot 1705. **f.** Any of various receptacles used in manufactures, etc. 1676. **g.** *slang.* A vessel, usu. of silver, given as a prize in athletic sports. Also applied to any prize so given 1865. **2.** Such a vessel with its contents; hence, a potful 1450. **b.** *ellipt.* A pot of liquor; *transf.* liquor, drink; drinking, potation (also *pl.*) 1583. **3.** Used as a measure of various commodities 1530. **4.** A steel cap or small helmet, worn esp. by cavalry in the 17th c. *Obs.* exc. *Hist.* 1639. **5.** A wicker basket used as a trap for fish or crustaceans; a fish-pot, lobster-pot, etc. 1669. **6.** = CHIMNEY-*pot* 1845. **7.** A large sum of money (*colloq.*) 1871. **b.** *slang.* A large sum staked or betted 1823. **c.** *Racing.* 'A horse backed for a large amount, a favourite' (Farmer) 1823. **d.** A person of importance. (Usu. *big p.*) 1891. **8.** In full, **pot-paper:** A size of printing or writing paper; orig. bearing the watermark of a pot. Also *attrib.* as **p.-folio, -octavo, -quarto.** (Now usu. spelt **pott.**) 1579. **9.** As the name of a substance: Earthenware, stoneware; *attrib.* made of pot 1825.

1. b. Henry the Fourth [of France] wished that he might live to see a fowl in the p. of every peasant BURKE. Pots and pans 1875. **2.** A p. of ale and a piece of cheese SWIFT. **b.** He carries her into a public-house to give her a p. and a cake DE FOE. **7.** He went to India..and came back..with a p. of money TROLLOPE.

Phrases, etc. *The p. goes so long* (or *often*) *to the well that it is broken at last. The p. calls the kettle black* (etc.), said of a person who blames another for something of which he himself is also guilty. *A little p. is soon hot*, a little person is soon roused to anger. *To boil the p.*, *make the p. boil* (= F. *faire bouillir le pot*), to provide one's livelihood. So, *to keep the p. boiling*; also, to keep anything going briskly. *To go to p.* (formerly also *to the p.*), to be cut in pieces like meat for the p.; to be ruined or destroyed (*colloq.*).

attrib. and *Comb.*: **p.-ale**, the completely fermented wash in distillation; **-bank** *dial.*, a pottery; **-clay**, clay used for making earthenware; **p. cultivation, p. culture**, cultivation of plants in pots; **p. hat** (*colloq.*), a low-crowned stiff felt hat, a 'bowler'; **-paper** (see sense 8); **-sleeper**, a metal sleeper for railways, of dish-like form; **-still**, a still to which heat is applied directly as to a p., not by means of a steam-jacket; *attrib.*, applied to whisky distilled in a pot-still.

Pot (pǫt), *sb.*[2] *Sc.* and *dial.* ME. [perh. orig. same word as prec.] A deep hole; e.g. †the shaft or pit of a mine; a hole out of which peat has been dug.

Pot, *sb.*[3] 1888. Short for POT-SHOT.

Pot (pǫt), *v.* 1562. [f. POT *sb.*[1]] **I.** *intr.* To drink beer, etc. out of a pot; to tipple. *Obs.* or *arch.* 1594. **II. 1.** *trans.* To put up and preserve (flesh, butter, etc., usu. salted or seasoned) in a pot, jar, or other vessel. Also *absol.* Also *fig.* 1616. **b.** *Sugar manuf.* To transfer (crude sugar) from the coolers to perforated 'pots' or hogsheads, for the molasses to drain off 1740. **2.** To set (a plant) in earth in a flower-pot for cultivation; to plant in or transplant into a pot 1664. **3.** *Billiards* = POCKET *v.* 4. 1860. **4.** *colloq.* or *slang.* To shoot or kill (game) for the pot, i.e. for cooking; to 'bag'; *gen.* to bring down by a pot-shot (a man or animal) 1860. **b.** *intr.* To take a pot-shot (*at*) 1854. **c.** *trans.* To win, secure, 'bag' 1900.

4. He'll have to show himself, and if he does I'll p. him 1889. **b.** To be potted at like a woodcock 1861.

III. To outdo, outwit, deceive. Now *slang.* 1562. **IV.** To manufacture, as pottery, etc.; *esp.* to shape and fire, as a preliminary to decoration 1743.

Potable (pōᵘ·tăb'l), *a.* (*sb.*) 1572. [a. F., ad. late L. *potabilis*, f. *potare* to drink; see -ABLE.] **A.** *adj.* Drinkable. **B.** *sb. pl.* Things potable; drinkables, liquor 1623.

A. Sweet p. liquor 1645. *P. gold*, a preparation of nitro-muriate of gold deoxydized by some volatile oil, formerly esteemed as a cordial medicine; drinkable gold. So *p. Mars* (= iron). Hence **Potabi·lity, Po·tableness**, p. quality.

‖**Potage** (potāʒ). 1567. [F.; cf. POTTAGE.] Soup of any kind.

Potamian (potēⁱ·miăn, -æ·miăn), *a.* and *sb.* 1850. [f. Gr. ποταμός river + -IAN.] **A.** *adj.* Of or pertaining to the *Potamites* or *Trionychidæ*, the soft-shelled river tortoises. **B.** *sb.* A tortoise of this group, a mud turtle.

Potamic (potæ·mik), *a.* 1883. [f. as prec. + -IC.] Of or pertaining to rivers; fluviatile.

Potamo·logy. 1829. [f. as prec. + -LOGY.] The scientific study of rivers. Hence **Potamolo·gical** *a.* of or pertaining to p. **Potamo·logist**, one who studies or is versed in p.

Potash (pǫ·tæʃ), *sb.* 1648. [Early mod. E. *pot-ashes* pl., ad. early Du. *potasschen*, mod. *potasch*; in mod.L. *potassa.*] **1.** An alkaline substance obtained orig. by lixiviating the ashes of terrestrial vegetables, and evaporating the solution in large iron pans or pots (whence the name). Chemically, this is a crude form of potassium carbonate. **a.** *orig.* pl., *pot ashes, pot-ashes*: now applied to the crude substance. (When purified by calcination and re-crystallization, known as *pearl-ashes* or *pearl-ash.*) **b.** sing., *pot-ash, potash*: applied esp. to the purified carbonate 1751. **2.** *Chem.* The hydroxide or hydrate of potassium, KHO; a hard white brittle substance, soluble in water and deliquescent in air, having powerful caustic and alkaline properties; *caustic p.* 1800. **b.** Now sometimes applied to POTASSA; in non-chemical works vaguely to any compound of potassium 1843. **c.** In names of compounds = POTASSA, and now in chemical use mostly repl. by POTASSIUM 1791. **3.** Short for *p.-water* 1876.

2. **c.** *Carbonate of p.* = potassium carbonate; *sulphate of p.* = potassium sulphate.

Comb.: **p.-mica** = MUSCOVITE *sb.*[2]; **-water**, an aerated beverage; water impregnated with carbonic acid gas, to which is added potassium bicarbonate.

Potass (potæ·s, pǫ·tæs). Now *rare.* 1799. [ad. F. *potasse* POTASH.] *Chem.* An anglicized form, variously used for potash, potassa, and (in names of compounds) potassium.

‖**Potassa** (potæ·să). 1812. [mod.L.; see POTASH.] *Chem.* Davy's name for potassium monoxide, K_2O, also called *anhydrous potash*; sometimes also applied to the hydrate or hydroxide, KHO (= $K_2H_2O_2$), also called *potassa fusa* and *caustic potash.*

Liquor potassæ, an aqueous solution of potassium hydrate, containing about 5·84 per cent. of the hydrate.

Potassamide (potæ·sămǝid). 1838. [f. POTASS(IUM + AMIDE.] *Chem.* An amide of potassium formed by the substitution of one or more atoms of potassium for those of the hydrogen of ammonia (NH_3).

Potassic (potæ·sik), *a.* 1858. [f. POTASS(IUM + -IC.] *Chem.* Of, pertaining to, or containing potassium or potash; = *potassium* in comb.

Pota·ssio-, comb. form of POTASSIUM, in the names of double salts of potassium and another substance, as *p.-tarta·ric* adj., *p.-ta·rtrate*, etc.

Potassium (pǒtæ·siǒm). 1807. [In form, mod.L., f. POTASS or POTASH, after names of metals in -IUM.] *Chem.* One of the elements, an alkaline monad metal, the basis of POTASH; it is a highly lustrous white metal with a slight tinge of pink, soft at ordinary temperatures, of specific gravity 0·865, being the lightest solid body known except lithium; when exposed to the air it at once tarnishes or oxidizes, and when thrown upon water instantly decomposes it, uniting with the oxygen and causing the liberated hydrogen to burn with a characteristic violet flame. Symbol K (for *Kalium*); atomic weight 39·1. Also *attrib.* in names of chemical compounds, as *p. carbonate, permanganate*, etc.

Potation (potēⁱ·ʃǝn). [Late ME. a. OF. *potacion, -ation*, ad. L. *potationem.*] **1.** Drinking; a drinking, a drink, a draught 1479. †**b.** A drinking party, compotation -1574. **c.** Intemperate drinking 1800. **2.** Liquor for drinking; a drink, a beverage. late ME.

1. Potations, pottle-deepe SHAKS. Indulging in moderate potations 1875.

Potato (pǒtēⁱ·to), *sb.* 1565. [ad. Sp. *patata*, var. of BATATA.] **1.** = BATATA. Now known as *Sweet* or *Spanish p.* **2.** The plant *Solanum tuberosum*, a native of the Pacific slopes of S. America, now widely cultivated for its farinaceous tubers 1597. **b.** The tuber of this plant, of roundish or oblong shape; now a well-known article of food in most temperate climes 1663. **3.** With distinctive words. **a.** *Carolina, Spanish, Sweet p.* = sense 1. 1599. **b.** *Chilian p., Irish p.* (now U. S.), *White p.* (U. S.) = sense 2. 1664. **4.** Applied to other plants having tubers, mostly edible 1629.

1. Let the skie raine Potatoes SHAKS. **2. b.** As to potatoes, it would be idle to consider them..as an article of human food, which ninety-nine hundredths of the human species will not touch 1792. Phr. *Potatoes and point*: see POINT *sb.*[1] C. 4. **4. Sea-side p.**, *Ipomæa biloba* (*Pes-capræ*), N.O. *Convolvulaceæ*, a tropical creeping shore-plant of both hemispheres; **Wild p.**, (*a*) *Convolvulus panduratus*; (*b*) of Jamaica, *Ipomæa fastigiata.*

Phrases (colloq.). *Small potatoes* (orig. *U.S.*), 'no great things', said also of persons. *The p.*, the (very or real) thing, what is correct or excellent (*slang*).

Comb.: **p.-beetle**, (*a*) the COLORADO Beetle, *Doryphora decemlineata*; (*b*) the Three-lined Leaf Beetle, *Lema trilineata*, or its larva; **p. blight** = *p. disease*; **p. bug** = *p.-beetle*; **p.-chips**, potatoes sliced and fried crisp in fat or oil; **p. disease**, a very destructive disease of potatoes, caused by a parasitic fungus, *Phytophthora infestans*, which attacks the leaves, stems, and tubers; also called *p. blight, murrain, rot*; **-eye**, a bud of the potato tuber; see EYE *sb.*[1] III. 1; **-fly**, one of the various blister beetles of the genus *Lytta*, which are injurious to potato-plants in U. S. and Canada; **p. murrain** = *p. disease*; **p. pit**, a shallow pit, usu. covered with a mound of straw and earth, in which potatoes are stored in winter; **p. rot** = *p. disease*; **-spirit**, alcohol distilled from potatoes; **-stalk weevil, p. weevil**, an American beetle that injures p. crops, *Baridius trinotatus*; **-trap** (*slang*), the mouth. Hence **Pota·to** *v. trans.* to plant or crop with potatoes.

Potator (potēⁱ·tǝɹ). *rare.* 1660. [a. L.] A drinker, toper.

Potatory (pōᵘ·tătǝri), *a.* 1834. [ad. L. *potatorius*; see -ORY[2].] Of, pertaining to, or given to drinking.

Pot-bellied (pǫ·tˌbeːlid), *a.* 1657. [f. next + -ED[2].] Having a pot-belly. Also *transf.*

Pot-belly (pǫ·tˌbe·li). 1714. [f. POT *sb.*[1] + BELLY *sb.*] **1.** A swollen or protuberant belly. **2.** *transf.* A pot-bellied person 1871.

Po·t-boi·ler. 1803. [f. phr. *to make the pot boil*; see POT *sb.*[1]] **1.** One who boils a pot; *spec.* in *Eng. Politics* = POTWALLER (*rare*) 1824. **2.** *colloq.* Applied depreciatively to a work of literature or art executed for the purpose of 'boiling the pot'; a writing, picture, etc. made to sell 1803. **b.** One who produces 'pot-boilers' 1892. **3.** *Anthropol.* One of the rounded pebbles, with marks of fire upon them, which are supposed to have been heated for the purpose of boiling water 1874.

Po·t-bound, *a.* 1850. [f. POT *sb.*[1] 1 d + BOUND *ppl. a.*] Said of a plant when its roots fill a flower-pot and have no more room to expand. Also *fig.*

Po·t-boy. 1795. [f. POT *sb.*[1] + BOY *sb.*] A boy or young man employed at a public house to serve the customers with liquor; a publican's assistant.

Potch, Potcher, var. ff. POACH *v.*[2], POACHER, esp. in paper-making.

Pot-earth. 1644. [POT *sb.*[1]] Potter's earth; potter's clay; *Geol.* the BRICK-EARTH of the London basin.

Poteen, potheen (pǫtī·n, pǫþī·n). 1812. [a. Ir. *poitín* (potʸī·n) 'little pot', dim. of *pota*, *puite* POT *sb.*[1]; short for *uisge poitín* 'little-pot whisky'.] Whisky distilled in Ireland in small quantities, privately, i.e. the produce of an illicit still. Also *attrib.*

Potence[1] (pōᵘ·tĕns). late ME. [a. OF., ad. L. *potentia*, f. *potentem*, *posse*; see -ENCE.] **1.** Power, ability, strength. **2.** Degree of power or intensity 1817.

Potence[2] (pōᵘ·tĕns). 1500. [a. F. *potence* crutch, etc., ad. L. *potentia* power, POTENCE[1].] †**1.** A cross or gibbet -1816. **b.** *Engineering.* A supporting framework formed like a gallows 1853. **2.** *Watchmaking.* A stud screwed to the top plate in which is made the bearing for the lower pivot of the verge; any stud or fixture supporting a bearing 1678. †**3.** A military formation, in which a line is thrown out at right angles to the main body -1865.

Potencé (pōᵘ·tĕnseː), *a.* Also improp. **potence.** 1572. [a. F. *potencé*, f. *potence*; see POTENCE 2.] *Her.* = POTENT *a.*[2]

Potency (pōᵘ·tĕnsi). 1539. [ad. L. *potentia* power; see POTENCE[1] and -ENCY.] The quality of being potent. **1.** Power, ability to effect something; inherent capacity; authority. **b.** Power to affect one physically; of liquor, etc., strength 1637. **2.** *transf.* A person or body wielding power; a power 1645. **3.** Capability of active development; potentiality 1644. **4.** Degree of (latent) force 1691.

1. b. The p., vertue, and operation of our English Ale 1637. **3.** Books..doe contain a potencie of life in them to be as active as that soule was whose progeny they are MILTON.

Potent (pōᵘ·tĕnt), *sb.*[1] and *a.*[2] late ME. [app. a var. of F. *potence* POTENCE[2].] **A.** *sb.* †A crutch; a staff with a cross piece to lean upon; also *transf.* a crozier -1480. **b.** *fig.* A support, stay. *Obs.* or *arch.* late ME. **B.** *adj.* *Her.* Having the limbs terminating in potents or crutch-heads, as *cross-p.*; formed by a series of potents 1610.

Potent (pōᵘ·tĕnt), *a.*[1] and *sb.*[2] 1500. [ad. L. *potens, -entem*, pres. pple. of *posse.*] **1.** Powerful; mighty; used of persons and things, in many shades of meaning, as the power implied is political, military, social, moral, mental, etc. (Usu. a poet. or rhet. word, felt to be stronger than *powerful.*) **b.** Of reasons, motives, etc.: Cogent, effective, convincing 1606. **2.** Having strong physical or chemical properties, as a solvent, drug, etc. 1715. **3.** Possessing sexual power 1899.

1. The Doctor is well monied, and his friends P. at Court SHAKS.

†**B.** *sb.* **1.** Power; a power -1631. **2.** A potent person; a potentate -1642. **3.** A military warrant or order -1690. Hence **Po·tently** *adv.*

Potentate (pōᵘ·tĕntēⁱt). late ME. [ad. L. *potentatus* power, dominion, in late L. a potentate, f. *potens* POTENT *a.*[1]; see -ATE [1].] **1.** A person endowed with independent power; a prince, monarch, ruler. **2.** A powerful city, state, or body 1624.

1. But Kings and mightiest Potentates must die SHAKS.

Potential (pŏte·nʃăl), *a.* and *sb.* [Late ME. *potenciall*, ad. late L. *potentialis*, f. *potentia* POTENCY + -AL.] **A.** *adj.* **1.** Possessing potency or power; potent; commanding. Now *rare.* 1485. **2.** Possible as opp. to actual; existing *in posse*; capable of coming into being; latent. late ME. **3.** *Med. P. cautery*, an agent which produces the same effects on the skin as an *actual cautery* or red-hot iron. So *p. corrosive.* late ME. **4.** *Gram.* That expresses potentiality or possibility 1530. **5.** *Physics.* **a.** *P. function*: a mathematical function or quantity by the differentiation of which the force at any point in space arising from any system of bodies, etc. can be expressed 1828. **b.** *P. energy*: energy existing in a positional form, not as motion; *see* ENERGY 6. 1853.

1. *Oth.* I. ii. 13. 4. *P. mood*, a name sometimes given to the subjunctive mood when used to express possibility. Hence **Pote·ntial·ly** *adv.*, **-ness.**

B. *sb.* That which is possible; a possibility 1817. **2.** *Gram.* Short for *potential mood*; see A. 4. **3.** *Physics.* Short for *potential function*; see A. 5a. Hence, the amount of energy or quantity of work denoted by this, considered as a quality of the matter, electricity, etc. in question. Also *attrib.* 1828.

Potentiality (pŏtenʃiæ·lĭti). 1625. [ad. med.L. *potentialitas*, f. *potentialis*; see prec. and -ITY.] **1.** The quality of being powerful or having power 1627. **2.** *esp.* The state or quality of possessing latent power or capacity capable of development into activity; possibility of action or active existence; opp. to *actuality* 1625. **b.** With *a* and *pl.*: An instance of this quality; a capacity or possibility, or that in which it is embodied 1668.

2. We are not here to sell a parcel of boilers and vats, but the p. of growing rich beyond the dreams of avarice JOHNSON. **b.** The seed is the p. of the plant 1875.

Potentialize (pŏte·nʃăləiz), *v.* 1856. [f. POTENTIAL + -IZE.] *trans.* To make potential; *spec.* to convert (energy) into a potential condition.

Potentiate (pote·nʃiˌeit), *v.* 1817. [f. L. *potentia* + -ATE [3].] **1.** *trans.* To endow with power or potency. **2.** To make possible 1865.

‖**Potentilla** (pōutĕnti·lă). 1548. [med.L., f. L. *potens, -ent-* POTENT *a.*[1] + dim. *-illa.*] *Bot.* An extensive genus of *Rosaceæ*, comprising herbs and undershrubs, of which the Silverweed, Cinquefoil, and Tormentil are common British species.

Potentiometer (potenʃiǫ·mĭtəɹ). 1881. [f. L. *potentia* + -OMETER.] An instrument for measuring differences of electrical potential.

Po·tentize, *v.* 1857. [f. L. *potentem* + -IZE, after G. *potenzi(e)ren* to potentiate.] *trans.* To make potent; *spec.* to develop the power of (a medicine) by trituration or succussion.

‖**Potestas** (pote·stæs). 1870. [L., power.] *Rom. Law.* The power or authority of the head of a family over those depending on him; *esp.* parental authority.

†**Po·testate.** late ME. [ad. L. *potestas, -atem.*] †**1.** A person possessed of power over others; a superior, potentate –1678. **2.** Rendering *potestas* in the Vulgate (Eph. vi. 12, Pet. iii. 22); cf. POWER II. 3. –1610. **3.** = PODESTA b; *transf.* a chief magistrate in certain Turkish towns –1603.

1. Lawfull for the potestates, the nobilitie, the gentrie 1583.

Potestative (pōu·testeⁱtiv), *a.* 1630. [ad. F. *potestatif*, ad. late L. *potestativus*, f. L. *potestatem* power; see -IVE.] Befitting a potestate; having power or authority; authoritative.

P. condition, a condition within the power or control of one of the parties concerned.

†**Po·t-gu·n, po·tgun.** 1549. [f. POT *sb.*[1] + GUN *sb.*] **1.** A short piece of ordnance with a large bore, a mortar; so called from its shape –1599. **2.** = POP-GUN 1, 2. –1801. **3.** *fig.* A loud talker, a braggart –1693.

2. How! fright me with your p.? 1619. 3. That sign of a man there, that p. charged with wind CONGREVE.

Po·thecary. Now only *dial.* late ME. Aphet. f. APOTHECARY, formerly in common use. Also *attrib.*

Pother (pǫ·ðəɹ, pɒ·ðəɹ), *sb.* 1591. [app. differentiated form, with shortened vowel, of POWDER *sb.*, earlier *pouder, pouther.*] **1.** A choking smoke or atmosphere of dust 1627. **2.** Disturbance, commotion; a tumult; a noise, din. Cf. DUST *sb.* 4. 1591. **b.** *transf.* A verbal commotion, fuss 1609. **3.** Mental perturbation; display of sorrow or grief 1641.

1. *To kick up a p.*, to raise a choking dust. 2. The great Goddes, That keepe this dreadfull pudder o're our heads SHAKS. **b.** All this p. for an apple! MASSINGER. 3. Well! if all husbands keep so great a p., I'll live unmarried—till I get another 1738.

Pother (pǫ·ðəɹ, pɒ·ðəɹ), *v.* 1692. [app. f. POTHER *sb.*; but occas. assoc. w. BOTHER *v.*] **1.** *trans.* To put into a fuss; to fluster, worry. **2.** *intr.* To make a fuss; to fuss, to worry 1735.

2. I found the old Gentleman..pothering over the Newspaper 1778.

Pot-herb (pǫ·thəɹb). 1538. [f. POT *sb.*[1] + HERB.] A herb grown for boiling in the pot; any of the herbs cultivated in a kitchen-garden.

Po·t-hole [1]. 1839. [f. POT *sb.*[1] + HOLE *sb.*] *Geol.* A deep hole of more or less cylindrical shape; esp. one formed by the wearing away of rock by the rotation of a stone, or gravel, in an eddy of running water, or in the bed of a glacier. **b.** *Archæol.* A hole from which clay for pottery has been taken 1898.

Po·t-hole [2]. = POT *sb.*[2]; now *esp.* a deep hole in the surface of a road.

Pot-hook (pǫ·thuk). 1467. [f. POT *sb.*[1] + HOOK *sb.*] **1. a.** A hook suspended over a fireplace, for hanging a pot or kettle on; a crook. **b.** An iron rod with a hook at the end, for lifting a heated pot, stove-lid, etc. **2.** A curved or hooked stroke made in writing; now usu. a hooked stroke as made by children in learning to write. (Often with *hanger*; cf. HANGER [2] 4 c.). 1611.

2. She 's scrawling pothooks and hangers on a dirty sheet of paper 1887.

Pot-house (pǫ·thaus). 1697. [f. POT *sb.*[1] + HOUSE *sb.*[1]] †**1.** A house where pottery is made (*rare*) –1761. **2.** An ale-house; a small, unpretentious, or low public-house 1724. **b.** *attrib.* Belonging to or characteristic of a pot-house; low, vulgar 1816.

2. b. Reeking yet with p. odours DICKENS.

Po·t-hu·nter. 1592. [f. POT *sb.*[1] + HUNTER.] †**1.** An opprobrious appellation; perh. a sycophant, parasite. **2.** 'A sportsman who shoots anything he comes across, having more regard to filling his bag than to the rules which regulate the sport' 1781. **3.** *slang.* One who takes part in any contest merely for the sake of winning a prize 1873. So **Po·t-hu·nting** *sb.* and *a.*

Potichomania (pǫtiːʃoˌmēⁱ·niă). 1855. [ad. F. *potichomanie* (also used), irreg. f. *potiche* an oriental porcelain vase + *-manie* -MANIA.] The craze for imitating Japanese or other porcelain by covering the inner surface of glass vessels, etc., with designs on paper or sheet gelatine; the process of doing this.

Potion (pōu·ʃən), *sb.* ME. [a. OF. *pocion, potion*, mod.F. *potion*, ad. L. *potionem*, f. *potum, potare* to drink.] A dose of liquid medicine or of poison; a draught.

fig. Your Lordship may minister the P. of imprisonment to me SHAKS. Hence **Po·tion** *v. trans.* to treat or dose with potions; to drug.

Pot-lead (pǫ·tled), *sb.* 1890. [ad. Du. *potlood*, f. *pot* POT *sb.*[1] + *lood* lead.] Black-lead or graphite. Hence **Po·tlea·d** *v. trans.* to coat with pot-lead.

Pot-lid. late ME. [f. POT *sb.*[1] + LID *sb.*] **1.** The lid of a pot. **2.** *Geol.* Pop. name for a concretion occurring in various sandstones and shales 1827.

Po·t-lu·ck. 1592. [f. POT *sb.*[1] + LUCK *sb.*] One's luck or chance as to what may be in the pot, i.e. cooked for a meal; used in ref. to a person invited to a meal without any special preparation having been made for him; chiefly in phr. *to take p.* (= Fr. *courir la fortune du pot*). Also *transf.* or *gen.*

Potman (pǫ·tmæ̆n). 1589. [f. POT *sb.*[1] + MAN *sb.*] †**1.** A toper –1685. **2.** A man employed at a public-house to attend to the pots and serve the liquor 1846.

Pot-metal (pǫ·tmeːtăl). 1693. [f. POT *sb.*[1]] **1.** An alloy of lead and copper of which pots were formerly made. **2.** Stained glass coloured in the melting-pot, so that the colour pervades the whole substance 1832. **3.** A kind of cast iron suitable for making pots 1864.

‖**Potoo** (potū·). 1847. [Echoic; from its cry.] Name in Jamaica for one of the Night-jars (*Nyctibius jamaicensis*).

‖**Potoroo** (pǫtŏrū·). 1790. [Native name in New South Wales.] = KANGAROO-RAT.

Pot-pie. Chiefly *U.S.* 1823. [f. POT *sb.*[1] + PIE *sb.*[2]] A meat pie made in a pot.

‖**Pot-pourri** (pōu·pu·ri, ‖popuri). 1611. [F., lit. 'rotten pot', f. *pot* POT *sb.*[1] + *pourri*, pa. pple. of *pourrir*:—L. *putrere* to be rotten; tr. Sp. OLLA PODRIDA.] †**1.** A stew, a hotchpotch –1725. **2.** A mixture of dried petals of different flowers mixed with spices, kept in a jar for its perfume 1749. **3.** *fig.* A musical or literary medley 1864.

Potsherd (pǫ·tˌʃəɹd). Now somewhat *arch.* ME. [f. POT *sb.*[1] + *sherd* SHARD, OE. *sceard* fragment.] A fragment of a broken earthenware pot; a broken piece of earthenware.

Po·t-sho·t. 1858. [POT *sb.*[1]] A shot taken at game merely for the purpose of filling the pot for a meal. Hence *transf.* A shot aimed at a person or animal that happens to be within easy reach, without giving any chance of self-defence; e.g. at an enemy from ambush.

Potstone (pǫ·tˌstōun). 1771. [f. POT *sb.*[1] + STONE *sb.*; tr. L. *lapis ollaris.*] A granular variety of STEATITE or SOAPSTONE.

Pottage (pǫ·tėdʒ). [ME. *potage*, a. F. *potage*, lit. that which is put in a pot; see POT *sb.*[1] and -AGE. Orig. stressed *pota·ge.*] **1.** A dish composed of vegetables, alone or with meat, boiled to softness in water, and seasoned; soup, *esp.* a thick soup. **b.** *fig.* Often with ref. to Esau's 'mess of pottage' (see MESS *sb.* I. 2 quots.) late ME. †**2.** Oatmeal porridge –1797.

1. Potage is not so moche vsed in al Crystendom as it is vsed in Englande 1542.

Potted (pǫ·tėd), *ppl. a.* 1646. [f. POT *v.* + -ED [1].] **1.** Of meat, fish, etc.: Minced or pounded and preserved in a closed pot or other vessel. **2.** Of a plant: Planted or grown in a pot 1849.

1. *fig. P.* learning in the form of popular abridgments 1883.

Potter (pǫ·təɹ), *sb.*[1] [Late OE. *pottere*, f. POT *sb.*[1] + -ER [1].] **1.** A maker of pots or of earthenware vessels. **2.** A vendor or hawker of earthenware. *n. dial.* 1500.

1. Thou and all mankind are as clay in the hand of the p. 1720. *attrib.* and *Comb.* (also with *potter's*): **potter's asthma**, a form of fibroid phthisis to which persons exposed to the dust of pottery making are subject; **potter's clay, potter's earth,** any plastic clay free from iron; **potter's field,** a name given (after Matt. xxvii. 7) to a piece of ground used as a burial place for the poor and for strangers; **potter's lead, potter's ore,** lead ore used for glazing pottery, galena; **p. wasp,** a wasp which builds a cell or cells of clay in a cylindrical cavity, as *Eumenes fraterna*; **potter's wheel,** the horizontal revolving disk of the lathe used by potters, on which the prepared clay is moulded into shape.

Potter (pǫ·təɹ), *v.* 1530. [app. freq. of obs. *pote* push, OE. *potian* (see PUT *v.*[1]).] **1.** *intr.* To poke again and again. Now only *dial.* **2.** *trans.* To trouble, perplex, bother (*dial.*) 1746. **3.** *intr.* To meddle, interfere; to tamper (*with*). Now *dial.* 1655. **4.** To occupy oneself in an ineffectual or trifling way; to work or act in a feeble or desultory manner; to trifle; to dabble (*in* something) 1740. **5. a.** To move or go about poking or prying into things in an unsystematic way, or doing slight and desultory work 1840. **b.** To saunter, dawdle, loiter 1829.

4. I suppose your husband is pottering on in his old way MANNING. 5. **a.** Pottering about in the Bodleian, and fancying I should like to be a great scholar 1861. **b.** The slowest of Sunday trains, pottering up to London 1888. Hence **Po·tter** *sb.*[2] trifling action or (in Scott) talk. **Po·tterer. Po·ttering** *vbl. sb.* and *ppl. a.*

Pottery (pǫ·təri). 1483. [orig. a. F. *poterie*, f. *potier* POTTER *sb.*[1]; in later use referred to POT *sb.*[1]; cf. *crockery.*] **1.** A potter's workshop or factory. 2. The potter's art, ceramics; the manufacture of earthen vessels 1727. 3. Pottery-ware, earthenware 1785. 4. *attrib.*, as *p. trade*, etc. 1839.

1. *The Potteries*, a district in N. Staffordshire, including Hanley and Stoke-upon-Trent, the chief seat of the English p. industry.

Potting (pǫ·tiŋ), *vbl. sb.* 1594. [f. POT *v.* + -ING[1].] 1. Drinking (of ale, etc.); tippling (*arch.*). 2. The making of pottery or earthenware 1743. 3. The preserving of butter, meat, fish, etc. in pots or other vessels 1615. 4. Planting in, or transplanting into, a pot 1845.

1. I learn'd it in England; where indeed they are most potent in P. SHAKS.

Comb.: **p.-shed**, a shed in which delicate plants are reared in pots for planting out later.

Pottinger (pǫ·tindʒəɹ). Now *dial.* 1466. [orig. *potager*, a. F. *potager*, f. *potage* POTTAGE; cf. *passenger*, etc.] A vessel of metal, earthenware, or wood, for holding soup, broth, etc.; a small basin, porringer.

Pottle (pǫ·t'l). [ME. *potel*, a. OF., f. *pot* POT *sb.*[1] + *-el* -LE 2.] 1. A measure of capacity for liquids, etc., equal to half a gallon: now abolished. b. A pot or vessel of about this capacity 1698. c. *ellipt.* A pottle of wine, etc.; hence, drink, liquor 1700. 2. A small wicker or 'chip' basket, esp. a conical one used for strawberries 1771.

1. b. By his elbow stood a p. of spiced ale 1888. 2. One never sees a p. of strawberries now 1880.

Comb.: **p.-pot**, a two-quart pot or tankard *transf.* a heavy drinker.

Potto (pǫ·to). 1705. [Alleged to be from a Guinea dial.] 1. A W. African lemur (*Perodicticus potto*), commonly called a 'sloth'. b. *Calabar p.*, a species of lemur (*Arctocebus calabarensis*), inhabiting the district of Old Calabar. 2. The kinkajou 1790.

Potty (pǫ·ti), *a.* *slang.* 1899. [Origin unkn.; perh. connected with POTTER *v.*] Of no importance; petty, trivial, insignificant. Also, silly, crazy.

Po·t-va:liant, *a.* 1641. [f. POT *sb.*[1] + VALIANT.] Valiant or courageous through drink. So **Po·t-va:lour**, courage induced by drink; 'Dutch courage'.

Potwaller (pǫ·twǫ:ləɹ). 1701. [f. POT *sb.*[1] + *waller*, f. WALL *v.*[1], OE. *weallan* to boil.] In some English boroughs, before 1832, a man qualified for a parliamentary vote as a householder; the test being his having a separate fire-place, on which food was cooked for himself and his family.

Potwalloper (pǫ·twǫ:ləpəɹ). 1725. [pop. alteration of prec. (after WALLOP *v.* to boil with agitation).] 1. = POTWALLER. b. Used as a term of reproach 1820. 2. A scullion; also, a cook, esp. on board a whaler 1860.

Pouch (pautʃ), *sb.* [Late ME. *pouche*, a. ONF. *pouche*, parallel form of OF. *poche* bag, pouch; see POKE *sb.*[1]] 1. A bag, sack, or receptacle of moderate size; a pocket worn outside the dress. b. *spec.* A small bag in which money is carried; a purse. Now chiefly *arch.* or *literary.* late ME. c. A leathern bag or case used by soldiers for carrying ammunition 1627. d. A small flat bag of leather, rubber, etc. for carrying tobacco; a *tobacco-p.* 1687. 2. *Naut.* One of a number of divisions made by small bulkheads or partitions in a ship's hold, for stowing corn or other loose cargo 1627. 3. Applied to a natural receptacle resembling a bag or pocket. a. *Anat.*, *Zool.*, *Path.* A cavity like a bag; a sac, cyst. *spec.* †(*a*) the stomach of a fish; (*b*) the distensible gular sac beneath the bill in pelicans, cormorants, etc.; (*c*) a cheek-pouch in certain mammals; (*d*) the receptacle in which marsupial mammals carry their undeveloped young; the marsupium. 1450. b. *Bot.* A bag-like cavity, sac, or cyst, in a plant; *spec.* a seed-vessel resembling a bag or purse, a pod, a silicle 1577.

Pouch (pautʃ), *v.* 1566. [f. prec.] I. *trans.* To put into or enclose in a pouch; usu., to pocket; also *fig.* to 'bag'; to 'pocket', put up with. 2. To take into the stomach, to swallow: said of fishes, and of certain birds 1653. 3. To supply the purse or pocket of; to 'tip'. *slang* or *colloq.* 1810. 4. *Dressmaking.* To make or arrange (a part of dress) so as to hang loosely in a pouch-like form. b. *intr.* said of the dress. 1897. 5. To form a pouch or pouch-like cavity 1698.

3. To p. those venal villains, the reviewers 1810.

Pouched (pautʃt), *a.* 1834. [f. POUCH + -ED.] 1. Furnished with or having a pouch or pouches. 2. Put or enclosed in a pouch 1905.

1. A..p. bodice of mauve and white foulard 1897.

‖ **Poudrette** (pudret). 1840. [F., dim. of *poudre* POWDER; see -ETTE.] A manure made from night-soil dried and mixed with charcoal, gypsum, etc.

‖ **Pouffe** (puf). Also **pouf**(f. 1817. [F.; cf. PUFF *sb.*] 1. a. A kind of elaborate female head-dress fashionable late in the 18th c. b. A high roll or pad of hair worn by women. 2. *Dressmaking.* A part of a dress gathered up in a projection or bunch 1869. 3. A very soft stuffed ottoman or couch; a large soft cushion used as a low seat 1884.

‖ **Poulaine** (pulē·n). 1464. [OF. *Poulaine* Poland, *souliers à la Poulaine* shoes in Polish fashion, crakows; hence the pointed beak of such shoes.] The long pointed toe of a shoe.

Poulard (pulā·ɹd). 1732. [a. F. *poularde*, f. *poule* hen + *-arde*; see -ARD.] A young hen fattened for the table; a spayed hen.

Pouldron (pōu·ldrən), **pauldron** (pǭ·ldrən). *Obs.* exc. *Hist.* 1465. [ult. aphetic f. OF. *espauleron*, f. *espaule*, mod.F. *épaule* shoulder; with parasitic *d.*] A piece of armour covering the shoulder; a shoulder-plate.

‖ **Poulet** (pulę). 1848. [F. = PULLET, also a love-letter, sometimes folded in the shape of a wing.] A love-letter, a (neatly-folded) note.

Poulp(e (pūlp). 1601. [a. F. *poulpe* :—L. *polypus* POLYPUS.] An octopus, cuttle-fish, or other cephalopod.

Poult (pōult). [Late ME. contr. f. *polet*, *poullet*, a. F. *poulet* PULLET, dim. of *poule* hen.] The young of the domestic fowl, turkey, pheasant, guinea-fowl, or various game-birds. Also *attrib.* b. *transf.* A child; a youth. *colloq.* or *dial.* 1739.

‖ **Poult-de-soie** (pudəswa). 1850. [F., of unkn. origin; see PADUASOY.] A fine corded silk; 'a plain silk of rich quality in a soft and bright *grosgrain* make' (see GROGRAM); now usu. applied to coloured goods.

Poulter (pōu·ltəɹ). *arch.* ME. [ad. OF. *pouletier*, f. *poulet* + *-ier* -ER[2].] 1. = POULTERER. *Obs.* exc. as name of a London City Company †2. An officer in a great household, who attended to the purchase of poultry, etc. –1601.

Poulterer (pōu·ltərəɹ). 1638. [Extended f. POULTER; see -ER[1] 3.] One whose business is the sale of poultry (and usu. hares and other game); a dealer in poultry.

Poultice (pōu·ltis), *sb.* 1542. [ult. from L. *puls, pultem* thick pap (= Gr. πόλτος). The earliest form *pultes* was app. the L. pl. *pultes*, soon pop. taken as a sing.] A soft mass of bread, meal, bran, linseed, etc., usu. made with boiling water, and spread upon muslin, linen, etc., applied to the skin as an emollient for a sore or inflamed part, or as a counter-irritant (e.g. a mustard-poultice); a cataplasm. Also *attrib.* Hence **Pou·ltice** *v. trans.* to apply a p. to; to treat with a p.

Poultry (pōu·ltri). [Late ME. *pult(e)rie*, a. OF. *poul(l)etrie*, f. *poul(l)etier* POULTER; see -ERY 1.] †1. The office of a POULTER (sense 2); the superintendence of the purchase of fowls and other provisions; also, the room in which such provisions were stored –1601. 2. †a. A place where fowls are reared; a poultry-farm. †b. A poultry-market. –1570. c. Hence, the name of a street at the east end of Cheapside in London, where there was formerly a poultry-market. late ME. 3. Domestic fowls collectively; those tame birds which are reared for their flesh, eggs, or feathers, as barndoor fowls, ducks, geese, turkeys, guinea-fowls (excluding pigeons, pheasants, etc.); sometimes limited to the barndoor fowl with its varieties; also applied to the birds as dressed for market or prepared for food. (Usu. collect. pl.; formerly also as individual pl. after a numeral.) late ME.

attrib. and *Comb.* as *p.-fancier*, *farm*, etc.

Pounce (pauns), *sb.*[1] 1486. [Cf. PUNCH *sb.*[1] *Pounce* and *punch* seem to be shortened forms of *ponson*, *ponchon* PUNCHEON.] The claw or talon of a bird of prey; rarely of other animals. b. *fig.* in ref. to persons 1641.

In his pounces strong A fawn he bore COWPER. b. The King and the Duke (which latter they thought already in their Pounces) 1734.

Pounce (pauns), *sb.*[2] 1706. [ad. F. *ponce* pumice, also pounce :—L. *pumicem*, *-ex* PUMICE *sb.*] 1. A fine powder, as pulverized sandarac, etc., used to prevent the ink from spreading in writing over an erasure or on unsized paper, and also to prepare the surface of parchment to receive writing. 2. A fine powder, as powdered sandarac, pipeclay, or charcoal, dusted over a perforated pattern sheet to transfer the design to the object beneath; stamping-powder 1727.

attrib. and *Comb.* as *p.-box*, etc.; **p.-paper**, a transparent paper for drawing, tracing, etc.

Pounce, *sb.*[3] 1841. [f. POUNCE *v.*[2]] An act of pouncing; a sudden swoop or spring; quick or eager movement to an object. *On the p.*, watching for an opportunity to pounce.

Pounce (pauns), *v.*[1] late ME. [Cf. PUNCH *v.*] I. 1. *trans.* To emboss (metal-work) as a decoration, by raising the surface with blows struck on the under side, as in *repoussé* work. *Obs.* exc. *Hist.* 2. = PINK *v.*[1] 3. Also *p. out* *Obs.* exc. *Hist.* late ME. b. To cut the edges of (a garment) into points and scallops; to jag; chiefly pass. of the cloth or garment. *Obs.* exc. *Hist.* 1542. II. †1. To bruise with blows; *esp.* to bruise, stamp, pound, or beat small –1662. 2. To beat, thump, thrash (a person) 1827. III. †1. To prick, puncture, pierce, stab –1678. †2. To tattoo –1650.

Pounce (pauns), *v.*[2] 1686. [f. POUNCE *sb.*[1]] 1. *trans.* To seize, as a bird of prey, with the pounces or talons; to swoop down upon and lay hold of suddenly. 2. *intr.* To make a pounce; to spring suddenly *upon* or *at* in the way of attack 1744. 3. To spring or jump unexpectedly; to 'come down' 1836.

1. They cannot p. the quarry on the ground G. WHITE. 2. *To p. on* or *upon* (transf.) to seize upon suddenly; *fig.* to 'lay hold of' eagerly, suddenly, or promptly. 3. At a quarter past seven Mr. Smith 'pounced', and the Closure was carried 1890.

Pounce (pauns), *v.*[3] 1580. [ad. F. *poncer* :—L. *pumicare*, f. *pumicem*, *pumex* PUMICE, POUNCE *sb.*[2]] 1. *trans.* To smooth down by rubbing with pumice or pounce; *spec.* to smooth or finish (the surface of a hat) with pumice, sand-paper, or the like. 2. To trace or transfer (a design) on or to a surface by dusting a perforated pattern with pounce; also, to copy a design upon (a surface) by means of pounce 1594. †3. To sprinkle with powder; to powder, dust; *esp.* to powder (the face) with a cosmetic. b. To sprinkle with specks, spots, or the like. –1685.

3. b. Thy azure robe..pounc't with stars..Like a celestial canopie HERRICK.

Pou·ncet-box. 1596. [perh. orig. misprint for *pounced-box* = perforated box.] app. A small box with perforated lid for perfumes. (A Shaksperian word revived by Scott.)

Pound (paund), *sb.*[1] [OE. *pund* :—WGer. stem **pundo-*, a. L. *pondo* indecl. a pound (weight), orig. instr. abl. of **pondus*, *-um* = *pondus*, *-er-* weight, used as short for *libra pondo* a pound by weight.] I. A measure of weight derived from the ancient Roman *libra*, but very variously modified in different countries; in the British Empire now = 16 ounces avoirdupois, and 12 ounces troy; fixed for use in trade by a Parliamentary standard. Denoted by *lb.* (L. *libra*). Formerly, and still *dial.* and *colloq.* uninflected in pl.; also in *comb.*, as *a twenty p. shot.* b. *One's p. of flesh*: used proverbially, with ref. to Shaks. *Merch. V.*

b. All the other Great Powers want their p. of flesh from Turkey 1887.

II. 1. An English money of account (orig. a pound weight of silver), of the value of 20 shillings or 240 pence, and now represented by the gold sovereign. Denoted by £ before the numeral (occas. by *l.* after it), and dist. by the epithet *sterling*. OE. †b. The 'pound Scots', orig. the same as the English, was at the Union of the Crowns equal to one-twelfth of a pound sterling, being divided into 20 shillings each of the value of an English penny –1814. **c.** Applied to the Turkish and Egyptian gold pieces of 100 piastres, the former of 111·36 grains, the latter of 131·18 grains 1883.

Phrases. *In the p.*, reckoned at so much for each p. *Pounds, shillings, and pence*: = money; also *attrib.* = monetary; *fig.* = concerned chiefly with the money value of things; matter-of-fact, realistic; Even in this low, pounds-shillings-and-pence point of view SOUTHEY.

Comb.: **p. note**, a bank-note for one p.; also an English treasury-note of the value of one p.; **-rate**, a rate of so much in the p.; **-velo**, a unit of momentum; the momentum of a body of mass 1 lb. moving with a velocity of 1 foot per second; **-worth, pound's-worth**, as much of anything as is worth or may be bought for a p.

Pound (paund), *sb.*[2] [Late ME. :—OE. **pund*, known only in comb. *pundfald* PINFOLD, and early ME. *pundbreche* POUNDBREACH. POND *sb.* is app. an anomalous parallel form.] **I. 1.** An enclosure maintained by authority, for the detention of stray or trespassing cattle, and for the keeping of distrained cattle or goods until redeemed; a pinfold. **b.** An enclosure for sheltering or dealing with sheep or cattle in the aggregate. **2.** *transf.* and *fig.* A place of confinement; a pen, a pent-up position; a trap; a spiritual 'fold'; in *Hunting*, a position from which escape is impossible or difficult. late ME.

1. *P. close* or *covert*, a p. to which the owner of impounded animals may not have access; *p. open* or *overt*, one which is not roofed, and to which the owner may have access to feed his beasts.

II. 1. a. = POND *sb.* 1. Now *dial.* **b.** *esp.* A body of water held up or confined by a dam or the like, as the reach of a canal above a lock, etc. late ME. **2.** An enclosure for fish; *spec.* the last compartment of a p. net, in which the fish are finally caught; the bowl or pocket 1809.

Comb.: **p.-fee**, a fee paid for the release of cattle or goods from the p.; **-keeper**, one who has charge of a public p.; a pinder; **-lock**, a lock on a river for pounding up the water; **p. net** *U.S.*, an enclosure formed by nets in the sea near the shore, consisting of a long straight wall or leader, a first enclosure (the 'heart') into which the fish are conducted by the leader, and a second enclosure (the p., bowl, or pocket) from which they cannot escape.

Pound (paund), *sb.*[3] 1832. [f. POUND *v.*[1]] **1.** An apparatus for pounding or crushing apples for cider; a cider-mill. **2.** A heavy beating blow; a thump, also, the sound caused by this, a thud 1890.

Pound (paund), *v.*[1] [OE. *pūnian* :—WGer. **pūnōjan*. For the final *d*, cf. ASTOUND *v.*, etc.] **1.** *trans.* To break down and crush by beating, as with a pestle; to reduce to pulp or powder; to bray, bruise, pulverize. **2.** To strike or beat with repeated heavy blows; to thump, to pummel 1700. †**3.** With inverted construction: To deliver (heavy blows) *on* some one SPENSER. **4.** *intr.* To deliver heavy blows, fire heavy shot (*at, on*) 1815. **b.** Of a ship or boat: To beat the water, rise and fall heavily 1903. **5.** To walk, run, or dance with heavy steps; to ride hard and heavily; *transf.* of a steamer, to paddle or steam along forcibly 1802.

1. The Peasant..who pounds with Rakes The crumbling Clods DRYDEN. *fig.* The Lord Advocate ..pounded it [the Bill] to powder 1884. **2.** I.. pounded a piano, and sang a little 1875. The fortifications might be pounded to pieces 1884. **4.** *To p. away*, to continue delivering blows. **b.** The vessel is lying far inside the reef, and is pounding heavily 1906. **5.** A fat farmer sedulously pounding through the mud KINGSLEY.

Pound (paund), *v.*[2] 1450. [f. POUND *sb.*[2] Cf. PIND *v.*, POIND *v.*] **1.** *trans.* To place or shut *up* (trespassing or straying cattle) in a pound; to impound. **2.** To shut up or confine in any enclosure, material or otherwise. Also with *up.* 1589. **b.** *spec.* in *Fox-hunting* (*pass.*), said of a rider who gets into an enclosed place from which he cannot get out. *To p. the field*: see quot. 1827. **3.** To dam (water); to dam *up.* Now chiefly *dial.* 1649.

2. b. In hunting, an impassable barrier is said 'to p. the field'. So also a bold rider who clears a fence which others cannot do is said 'to p. the lot'. 1886.

Pound, *v.*[3] 1890. [f. POUND *sb.*[1] I.] *Coining.* To test the weight of coins (or blanks to be minted) by weighing the number of these which ought to make a pound weight (or so many pounds), and ascertaining how much they vary from the standard.

Poundage[1] (pau·ndėdʒ). ME. [f. POUND *sb.*[1] + -AGE.] **1.** An impost, duty, or tax of so much per pound sterling; *spec.* a subsidy, usu. of 12 pence in the pound, formerly granted by Parliament to the Crown, on all imports and exports except bullion and commodities paying tonnage. Now *Hist.* **2.** A payment of so much per pound sterling upon the amount of any transaction in which money passes 1599. **b.** A percentage of the total earnings of any concern, paid as wages to those engaged in it, sometimes in addition to a fixed wage 1892. **3.** A payment or charge of so much per pound weight; payment by weight 1500. **4.** *Betting.* Extravagant odds 1816. Hence **Pou·ndage** *v.*

Poundage[2] (pau·ndėdʒ). 1554. [f. POUND *v.*[2], *sb.*[2] + -AGE.] †The action or right of pounding stray cattle (*obs.*); the charge levied upon the owner. **b.** The keeping of cattle in a pound or enclosure; also, the enclosure 1866.

Poundal (pau·ndăl). 1879. [f. POUND *sb.*[1]] The force which, acting on one pound of matter for one second, generates a velocity of one foot per second.

Poundbreach (pau·ndbrītʃ). ME. [f. POUND *sb.*[2] + BREACH *sb.*] *Law.* The breaking open of a pound; hence, the illegal removal or recovery by the owner of goods lawfully impounded.

Pou·nd-cake. 1841. [f. POUND *sb.*[1] + CAKE *sb.*] A rich cake so called as containing a pound of each of the principal ingredients, flour, butter, sugar, fruit, etc.

Pounder[1] (pau·ndəɹ). 1533. [f. POUND *v.*[1] + -ER[1]; cf. OE. *pūnere*, f. *pūnian* POUND *v.*[1]] **1.** An instrument for pounding; a pestle, a crushing beetle; a beater 1564. **b.** A mortar 1891. **2.** A person who pounds 1533.

Pounder[2] (pau·ndəɹ). 1695. [f. POUND *sb.*[1] + -ER[1].] **I.** Something of a pound weight, e.g. a fish 1834. **II.** In comb. with prefixed numeral. **1.** Something weighing so many pounds; *spec.* a gun carrying a shot of a specified weight; *rarely*, a projectile of a specified weight 1695. **2.** A person possessing, having an income of, or paying (e.g. as rent) so many pounds sterling; a woman having a marriage-portion of so many pounds 1706. **b.** Any article of the value of a specified number of pounds sterling 1755.

1. A battery of twenty-four sixty pounders 1756. **2.** Rich Miss Dripping, the twenty-thousand-p. from London THACKERAY.

Pou·nd-foo·lish, *a.* Foolish in dealing with large sums; antithetical to PENNY-WISE.

Pounding (pau·ndiŋ), *vbl. sb.* 1591. [-ING[1].] The action of POUND *v.*[1] **1.** Crushing or bruising into pulp or powder; trituration, pulverizing. **b.** *concr.* Pounded substance; the quantity pounded at one time 1872. **2.** Striking or beating with or as with the fist; beating, knocking, thumping; heavy firing; an instance of this 1815. **3.** Heavy riding 1833.

Comb. **p.-match** (*nonce-wd.*), a battle.

Pou·nd-wei·ght, *sb.* 1538. [f. POUND *sb.*[1] + WEIGHT *sb.*] A weight of one pound; *spec.* a piece of metal of the weight of a pound avoirdupois, and stamped to that effect, used in weighing.

Pour (pōᵊɹ), *sb.* 1790. [f. next.] **1.** A pouring stream (*lit.* and *fig.*). *rare.* **2.** A heavy fall of rain; a downpour 1814. **3.** *Founding.* **a.** The act, process, or operation of pouring melted metal. **b.** The amount of melted metal poured at one time. 1884.

Pour (pōᵊɹ), *v.* [ME. *pouren*; origin obsc. In ME. pronounced (pūr); in mod. Eng. till 19th c., and still dial. (pauᵊɹ).] **I.** *trans.* **1.** To emit in a stream; to cause (a liquid or granular substance) to flow out of a vessel or receptacle; to discharge copiously; also, to emit (rays of light). Often with advs., *forth, out, in, down, off*, etc. **2.** Said of a river, etc.: To cause the water to flow in a flood; *refl.* to flow with strong current; to fall *into* the sea, etc. 1665. **3.** *transf.* and *fig.* To send forth as in a stream; to discharge copiously or in rapid succession; to bestow profusely 1451.

1. Drynke my wyne, which I haue poured out for you COVERDALE *Prov.* ix. 5. Trying to p. oil on the troubled waters KINGSLEY. To p. cold water..upon the zeal of his Irish friends 1893. *absol.* Poure out for the people, that they may eat BIBLE (Genev.) 2 *Kings* iv. 41. **3.** How London doth powre out her Citizens SHAKS. He..poured forth..torrents of frantic abuse MACAULAY.

II. *intr.* (for *refl.*) **1.** Of liquids, etc.: To flow in a stream; of rain: to fall heavily 1538. **b.** *impers.* To rain heavily or copiously 1726. **2.** *transf.* and *fig.* To run or rush in a stream or crowd; to stream, to swarm 1573.

1. *Lear* III. iv. 18. The torrent brooks..From craggy hollows pouring,..Sound all night long TENNYSON. **b.** Prov. *It never rains but it pours*, events (esp. misfortunes) come all together or happen in rapid succession. **2.** Troops poured towards the Rhine MACAULAY. Business prospered, and money came pouring in 1891.

‖**Pourboire** (purbwār). 1836. [F., prop. *pour boire* for drinking.] A gratuity to be spent on drinking; hence *gen.* a gratuity, 'tip'.

Pourer (pōᵊ·rəɹ). 1594. [f. POUR *v.* + -ER[1].] One who or that which pours; a vessel used in pouring anything.

This..teapot..is not a good p. 1881.

‖**Pourparler** (purparle). 1795. [F., f. *pour-* for, before + *parler* to speak.] An informal discussion preliminary to actual negotiation.

Pourpoint (pūᵊ·ɹpoint), **purpoint** (pɔ̄·ɹpoint). *Obs.* exc. *Hist.* late ME. [a. OF. *po(u)rpoint*, prop. pa. pple. of *pourpoindre* to perforate, f. *pour-* (for *par-* :—L. *per* through) + *poindre* :—L. *pungere* to prick.] Something quilted. **a.** A doublet, stuffed and quilted, worn by men in the 14th and 15th centuries, as part both of civil costume and of armour. †**b.** A quilt, as a bed-covering –1459.

Poussette (puse·t), *sb.* 1814. [a. F., dim. of *pousse* a push; see -ETTE.] An act of poussetting; see next.

Poussette (puse·t), *v.* 1812. [f. prec.] *intr.* To dance round and round with hands joined, as a couple in a country dance.

‖**Pou sto** (pau stōu). 1847. [a. Gr. ποῦ στῶ 'where I may stand', from the saying of Archimedes, δός μοι ποῦ στῶ, καὶ κινῶ τὴν γῆν 'give me (a place) where I may stand, and I will move the earth'.] A place to stand on; *fig.* a basis of operation.

Pout (paut), *sb.*[1] [OE. **pūta* in *ǣle-pūta* EEL-POUT; app. from a verbal stem **put-* to inflate.] A name for several kinds of fish, esp. the BIB or *whiting-p.*

Pout (paut), *sb.*[2] 1591. [f. POUT *v.*] A protrusion of the lips, expressive of pique or annoyance. Also *transf.*

In the pouts, in a pouting mood, sulky.

Pout, *sb.*[3] Sc. and dial. f. POULT *sb.*

Pout (paut), *v.* ME. [perh. repr. OE. **pūtian*, from a vbl. stem **put-* to be inflated, to swell; cf. POUT *sb.*[1]] **1.** *intr.* To protrude the lips, esp. in expression of displeasure or sullenness; hence, to show displeasure. **b.** Without implication of displeasure: To swell out, to protrude, as lips 1598. **2.** *trans.* To protrude (esp. the lips) 1784. **b.** To say with a pout 1877.

1. Like a misbehav'd and sullen wench, Thou pout'st upon thy fortune and thy love SHAKS. Hence **Pou·tingly** *adv.*

Pouter (pau·təɹ), *sb.* 1725. [f. POUT *v.* + -ER[1].] **1.** One who pouts 1809. **2.** A breed of the domestic pigeon with a great power of inflating the crop 1725. **3.** The whiting-pout 1889.

attrib.; **p.-fish** = 3; **p.-pigeon** = 2.

Poverty (pǫ·vəɹti). [ME. *povert(e* and *poverté*; (α) OF. *poverte* or *pouerte* :—L. *paupertas* nom., and (β) OF. *poverté, pouerté, pourelé* (see POORTITH), F. *pauvreté* :—L. *paupertatem*, accus., f. *pauper*; see -TY.] The quality or condition of being poor. **I.** The condition of having little or no wealth or material possessions; indigence, destitution, want (in various degrees). **b.** *fig.* in allusion to Matt. v. 3. ME. **c.** Personified and applied to a person, or persons gen., in whom it is exemplified 1813.

Ther is no warre but it causeth pouerte LD. BERNERS. **c.** Alike must Wealth and P. Pass heedless and unheeding by BYRON.

II. 1. Deficiency, dearth, scarcity; smallness of amount. late ME. **2.** Deficiency in the proper or desired quality; inferiority, meanness. late ME. **3.** Deficiency *in* some property, quality, or ingredient; (of soil, etc.) unproductiveness. late ME. 4. Poor condition of body; leanness or feebleness resulting from insufficient nourishment, etc. 1523.

1. The p. of modern literature 1838. 2. The p. of your understanding WATTS. 3. The..p. of north and north-eastern Africa in river-producing power 1880.

Comb.: **p.-grass,** (*a*) a N. American grass, *Aristida dichotoma*; (*b*) = **p.-plant,** a small N. American heath-like shrub, *Hudsonia tomentosa* (N.O. *Cistaceæ*); both plants growing in poor soil.

Po·verty-stri:cken, *a.* 1844. Stricken or afflicted with poverty; extremely poor or destitute. Earlier **Po·verty-struck** *a.* (now *rare* or *Obs.*) 1813.

Powan (pō̆u·wăn, pō̆u·ăn). 1633. [Sc. form of POLLAN.] A species of freshwater fish, *Coregonus clupeoides*, belonging to the same genus as the vendace and the pollan, with which it was formerly identified, and is still often confused, under the name of *freshwater herring*.

Powder (pau·dəɹ), *sb.*[1] [ME. a. F. *poudre* :—OF. *poldre, puldre* :—L. *pulverem* dust. In 15–17th c. usu. spelt *poulder*.] 1. The mass of dry impalpable particles or granules produced by the grinding, crushing or disintegration of any solid substance; dust. **b.** Applied to the pollen of flowers, or the spores of *Lycopodium* 1676. 2. A preparation in the form of powder, for some special use or purpose, e.g. in medicine, for the face or hair, etc. ME. 3. = GUNPOWDER 1. late ME.

1. He shall grynd him to p. TINDALE *Matt.* xxi. 44. 2. Such an one has great faith in Ward's pill, or James' p. 1768. We wore p. in those days THACKERAY. 3. Bothwell with pulder blew him in the air 1570. *P. and shot*, the matériel expended in warfare; hence, the cost or effort expended for some result. *Food for p.*: see FOOD *sb.* 1. *The smell of p.*, actual experience of fighting. *To keep one's p. dry*, to be prepared for action in any emergency.

attrib. and *Comb.*: **p.-flag,** the red flag carried by a *p.-hoy*, or hoisted on a ship when taking in or discharging gunpowder; **-house,** a building for storing gunpowder; **-hoy,** an ordnance vessel expressly fitted to convey p. from the land magazine to a ship; **-magazine,** a place where gunpowder is stored in a fort or on board ship; **-mill,** a mill for making gunpowder; **-tax,** a tax upon hair-powder.

Powder (pau·dəɹ), *sb.*[2] *Obs.* exc. *dial.* 1600. [Origin unkn.] An impetus, a rush; force, impetuosity. Chiefly in phr. *with* (dial. *at, in*) *a p.*, impetuously, violently.

Jordan..comes down with a p., and at set times overflowes all his bankes 1650.

Powder (pau·dəɹ), *v.*[1] ME. [a. F. *poudrer*, f. *poudre* POWDER *sb.*[1]] I. †1. *trans.* To sprinkle (food) with a condiment of powdery nature; to season, spice –1440. †**b.** *fig.* To mix with some modifying ingredient; to 'season'; to 'alloy' –1790. 2. To sprinkle (meat) with salt or powdered spice; to salt; to cure. *Obs.* exc. *dial.* late ME. 3. To sprinkle powder upon; to cover *with* or as *with* some powdery substance ME. **b.** To apply powder to (the hair, etc.) as a cosmetic. Also with the person as obj.; also *absol.* or *intr.* for *refl.* 1599. 4. To ornament with spots or small devices scattered over the surface; to sprinkle or spangle (a surface) with. Usu. in *pa. pple.* ME.

1. b. Powdering their lives with improbable passages to the great prejudice of truth 1661. 2. She roasted red veal, and she powder'd lean beef 1715. 3. That Milky way Which nightly as a circling Zone thou seest Pouderd with Starrs MILT. b. 'A red nose..she can always p. it.' 'She would scorn to p. it', says Edwin. DICKENS. 4. Gold shoes powdered with pearls 1766.

II. To sprinkle or scatter like powder; to disperse here and there upon a surface. Usu. in *pa. pple.* ME.

To p. violets on a silk ground 1890.

III. 1. To reduce to powder; to pulverize 15.. 2. *intr.* To fall to powder, become pulverized 1846. Hence **Pow·derable** *a. rare.*

Pow·der, *v.*[2] *colloq.* and *dial.* 1632. [f. POWDER *sb.*[2]] *intr.* To rush; to hurry with rushing speed: said esp. of a rider.

Pow:der-blue·, *sb.* and *a.* 1707. [f. POWDER *sb.*[1]] A. *sb.* Powdered smalt, esp. for use in the laundry. B. *adj.* Having the deep blue colour of smalt. **b.** *sb.* A name for this colour. 1894.

Pow·der-dow:n. 1861. [f. POWDER *sb.*[1] + DOWN *sb.*[2]] Name for peculiar down-feathers or plumules, found in various birds in definite tracts or patches; so called from the bluish-white powdery or scurfy substance into which they disintegrate. Also *attrib.*, as in *p. patch*, etc.

Powdered (pau·dəɹd), *ppl. a.* late ME. [f. POWDER *v.*[1]] 1. Preserved; cured; corned. *Obs.* exc. *dial.* 2. Decorated with a multitude of spots or small figures scattered over the surface. late ME. **b.** *Zool.* Marked as if dusted over with powder. Said esp. of moths. 1832. 3. Of the hair or skin: Dressed with powder as a cosmetic. Also said of the person. 1655. 4. Reduced to powder or dust 1591.

3. The powder'd footman GAY. 4. P. glasse 1646.

Pow·der-fla:sk. 1753. A case for carrying gunpowder, orig. of horn, later of leather or metal.

Pow·der-ho:rn. 1533. A powder-flask made of the horn of an ox or a cow with a wooden or metal bottom at the larger end.

Powdering (pau·dəriŋ), *vbl. sb.* late ME. [f. POWDER *v.*[1] + -ING[1].] The action of POWDER *v.*[1], or the result of this.

Comb. **p.-closet, -room,** a room appropriated to powdering the hair; **-tub,** a tub in which the flesh of animals is powdered, or salted and pickled; †also *joc.*, a sweating-tub used for the cure of venereal disease.

Pow·der-mo:nkey. 1682. Joc. term for a boy employed on board ship to carry powder to the guns.

Pow·der-puff. 1704. A soft pad, usu. of down, for applying powder to the skin. **b.** An instrument like a small bellows formerly used for powdering the hair.

Powdery (pau·dəri), *a.* late ME. [f. POWDER *sb.*[1] + -Y[1].] 1. Of the nature or consistence of powder; pulverulent; dusty. **b.** Easily disintegrated into powder; friable 1728. 2. Covered with or full of powder; dusty 1708.

1. The p. snow WORDSW. b. A brown, p. Spar 1728. 2. Auriculas with p. leaves and stems 1874.

Power (pau·əɹ, pauᵊɹ). [ME. *poër, poeir, pouer*, a. AF. *poër, poair, pouair*, sb. use of vb. inf. *poeir, pouoir* :—late pop. L. *potere*, repl. *posse* to be able.] I. As a quality or property. 1. Ability to do something or anything, or to act upon a person or thing. **b.** With *a* and *pl.* A particular faculty of body or mind 1483. **c.** *pl.* Power put forth in various directions or on various occasions 1586. 2. Ability to act or affect something strongly; physical or mental strength; vigour, energy; force of character; effect 1440. **b.** Political or national strength 1701. 3. Of things: Active property; capacity of producing some effect 1592. **b.** The sound expressed by a character or symbol; the meaning expressed by a word or phrase in a particular context 1727. 4. Possession of control or command over others; dominion; government, sway; authority *over* ME. **b.** Liberty or permission to act ME. **c.** Personal or social ascendancy, influence 1535. **d.** Political ascendancy or influence 1833. 5. Legal ability, capacity, or authority to act; *esp.* delegated authority 1486. **b.** A document, or clause in a document, giving legal authority 1483.

1. Is it not in your p. to open your eyes? 1713. Money is p. 1853. b. Memory, reason, & wyll. And these ben the thre powers of the soule. 1526. c. His powers of attention 1852. 2. More p. to your elbow LOWELL. b. *Balance of p.*: see BALANCE *sb.* 12. 3. The P. of Herbs can other Harms remove GRAY. The p. of heat to burn JOWETT. 4. The p. and jurisdiction of the Parliament COKE. b. The bishops,..had no p. to imprison priests 1856. c. A man's p. means the readiness of other men to obey him MILL. d. The governing party has always come into p. by means of revolution 1878. 5. The borrowing powers of the company 1891. b. *P. of attorney*, a document appointing a person or persons to act as the attorney or attorneys of the appointer.

II. As a person, body, or thing. 1. An influential or governing person, body, or thing; in early use, one in authority, a ruler, governor. late ME. **b.** In late use, A state or nation from the point of view of its international authority or influence 1726. 2. A celestial or spiritual being having control or influence; a divinity. Chiefly in pl.; often in exclams., etc., as *by (all) the powers! merciful powers!* 1596. 3. In med. angelology, the sixth order of angels in the celestial hierarchy; see ORDER *sb.* II. 1. 1667. 4. A force of armed men; a host, an army; in pl. = *forces*, i.e. distinct hosts, or different kinds of troops composing an army. Orig. less concrete, without *a* or *pl.* Now *rare* or *arch.* ME. 5. A large number of persons; a large number, quantity, or amount of things; 'a lot'. Now *dial.* or *vulgar colloq.* 1661.

1. The powers that be *Rom.* xiii. 1. This..banker who was..something of a p. in Greece 1874. b. There was no talk then of being a World P. 1901. 3. Thrones, Dominations, Princedoms, Vertues, Powers MILT. 4. Brutus and Cassius are leuying Powers; We must straight make head SHAKS. *P. of the county*, POSSE COMITATUS. 5. It has done a p. of work DICKENS.

III. Techn. uses. 1. *Math.* The result of taking a quantity (*a*) a given number of times (*x*) as a factor, the number of times being indicated by an exponent (except in the case of 1), thus a^x; *gen.* the result of operating on a quantity by any exponent, positive or negative, integral or fractional 1674. **b.** *P. of a point* with regard to a circle: the square of the distance from that point to the point of contact of the tangent drawn from it 1885. 2. *Mech.* An instrument by means of which energy may be applied to mechanical purposes 1671. 3. Any form of energy or force available for application to work. *spec.* **a.** Mechanical energy (as that of running water, wind, steam, electricity, etc.). **b.** Force applied to produce motion or pressure; the acting force in a lever, etc., as opp. to the *weight*. **c.** The mechanical advantage gained by the use of a machine. 1727. 4. Capacity for exerting mechanical force, as measured by the rate at which it is exerted, or the work done by it (cf. HORSE-POWER); also applied to a measurable capacity for producing some other physical effect 1806. 5. *Optics.* The capacity of a lens (or combination of lenses) for magnifying the apparent size of an object; also *ellipt.*, the lens itself 1727.

1. 2 is the root, or 1st p. of 2. 4 is the 2d p., or square of 2. 1827. 2. *Mechanical* (†*mathematical*, †*mechanic*) *powers*, the simple machines by means of which energy may be advantageously applied; now reckoned as six, viz. the lever, wheel and axle, pulley, wedge, inclined plane, and screw. 3. Plans..for..working the weaving loom by the application of p. 1808.

Phrases. *In p.*, in a position of authority. *In one's p.*, within one's ability, under one's control. *To the best, uttermost*, or *extent of one's p.*, as far as one is able. *P. of pit and gallows*: see PIT *sb.* I. 7.

Comb.: **p.-gas,** coal-gas used for supplying power, not illumination; **p. house, p. station,** a building in which power (esp. electrical or mechanical) is generated; **-load** *Electr.*, the amount of current delivered for use in driving machinery, as dist. from that used for lighting. Hence **Power** *v.*, to supply the power for (an engine, etc.) 1899.

†**Pow·erable,** *a.* 1584. [f. POWER *sb.*[1] + -ABLE; cf. *comfortable*, etc.] 1. = POWERFUL –1632. 2. Extreme, excessive (*rare*) –1598.

Powerful (pau·əɹ-, pauᵊ·ɹfŭl), *a.* (*adv.*) late ME. [f. POWER *sb.*[1] + -FUL.] 1. Having, or capable of exerting, great (moral, physical, or other) power; potent. 2. Producing great effect. **b.** Having power to influence greatly; impressive, convincing, telling. 1596. 3. Great in quantity or number. *dial.* or *vulgar.* 1852. B. as *adv.* Powerfully, exceedingly. *dial.* or *vulgar.* 1835.

1. The powerfullest King on the Sea-coast of Malabar 1727. P. stimulants 1802. 2. There is a p. force in a father's command DE FOE. B. He was p. tired W. IRVING. Hence **Pow·erful·ly** *adv.*, **-ness.**

Powerless (pau·əɹ-, pauᵊ·ɹlės), *a.* 1552. [f. POWER *sb.* + -LESS.] Without power; devoid of power or ability; helpless. Hence **Pow·erless·ly** *adv.*, **-ness.**

Pow·er-loo:m. 1808. A weaving loom worked by mechanical power (water, steam, etc.), as dist. from a hand-loom.

Powwow, pow-wow (pau·wau), **pawaw** (pawǭ·), *sb.* 1624. [Algonkin *powwaw·* or *powah·*.] 1. A priest, sorcerer, or medicine-man of the N. Amer. Indians. 2. A ceremony of the N. Amer. Indians, esp. one where magic was practised and feasting indulged in; also, a council of Indians, or conference with them 1663. 3. *transf.* A political or other meeting, a friendly consultation, or a merry-making; a 'palaver' of any kind. (Chiefly *U.S.*) 1812.

2. To find the thief the Indians held the Pow-wow 1887. 3. I was not at the Cambridge pow-wow HUXLEY.

Powwow (pau:wau·), *v.* 1642. [f. prec.]

1. *intr.* Of N. Amer. Indians: To practise medicine or sorcery; to hold a powwow. **b.** *transf.* To confer, deliberate, talk, hold palaver. (Chiefly *U.S.*) 1780. **2.** *trans.* To doctor, to treat with magic 1856.

Pox (pǫks), *sb.* 1476. [Altered spelling of *pocks*, pl. of POCK *sb.*, used collectively (cf. *mumps*, etc.), and at length as a sing.] **1.** Name for different diseases characterized by 'pocks' or eruptive pustules on the skin; see POCK *sb.* 2. †**a.** = SMALL-POX –1819. **b.** With qualifying words: (*a*) See CHICKEN-*p.*, COW-POX, SMALL-POX; (*b*) *Great, French*, or *Spanish p.*, syphilis 1503. †**2.** In imprecations, etc. –1820.

2. A P. of that iest SHAKS. Hence **Pox** *v. trans.* to infect with the p. (usu. syphilis). Also in imprecations. *Obs.* or only in vulgar use.

†**Poz** (pǫz). *colloq.* 1710. [abbrev. of POSITIVE.] Positive, certain; esp. in phr. *that's p.* Also as *adv.* = positively. –1839.

‖ **Pozzolana, pozzuolana** (pǫttsǫ-, pǫttswǫlā·nă). 1706. [It. *pozz(u)olana*, prop. adj. (sc. *terra* earth) 'belonging to Pozzuoli' (L. *Puteoli* little springs), a town near Naples.] A volcanic ash, containing silica, alumina, lime, etc., found near Pozzuoli, etc., much used in the preparation of hydraulic cement. Also, a name for similar artificial preparations.

Prabble: see PRIBBLE.

Practic (præ·ktik), *sb.*[1] *arch.* [Late ME. *practik(e*, a. OF., ad. med.L. *practica*, a. Gr. πρακτική (also πρακτικὴ ἐπιστήμη, Plato) practical science, fem. sing. of πρακτικός adj.: see next.] The earlier Eng. and esp. Sc. equivalent of PRACTICE. **1.** = PRACTICE 1. **b.** An action, deed; *pl.* doings, practices; practical matters 1641. †**2.** = PRACTICE 2 c. –1653. **3.** Legal usage; case-law; esp. in Scots Law 1533. †**4.** = PRACTICE 3. –1734. †**5.** Artful dealing, contrivance, cunning, policy; also with *a* and *pl.* –1693.

Practic (præ·ktik), *a.* (*sb.*[2]) *arch.* late ME. [a. obs. F. *practique*, var. of *pratique*, ad. late L. *practicus*, a. Gr. πρακτικός, f. πράττειν to do, act; see -IC.] **1.** = PRACTICAL 1. 1551. **b.** Opp. to *theoretic, speculative, contemplative. arch.* or *Obs.* late ME. †**2.** = PRACTICAL *a.* 2, 4. –1642. †**3.** Experienced, practised –1639. †**4.** Artful, cunning –1590. †**B.** *sb.*[2] (absol. use of the adj.) A practical man, as opp. to a theorist; *spec.* a member of the Jewish sect of the Essenes who took part in the active affairs of life –1650.

1. b. The Art and Practique part of Life, Must be the Mistresse to this Theorique SHAKS.

Practicable (præ·ktikăb'l), *a.* 1670. [ad. F. *praticable*, f. *pratiquer* to practise; see prec. and -ABLE.] **1.** Capable of being carried out in action; feasible. **2.** Capable of being used or traversed, as a road, ford, etc. 1710. **b.** *Theatr.* Said of windows, doors, etc., which are capable of actual use in the play. Also (*colloq.*) *ellipt.* as *sb.* 1838.

1. Ascended the glacier as far as p. 1860. 2. The road to Cadiz is likewise very p. for ladies W. IRVING. Hence **Pra·cticabi·lity, Pra·cticableness**, the quality of being p. **Pra·cticably** *adv.*

Practical (præ·ktikăl), *a.* 1570. [f. as PRACTIC *a.* + -AL.] **1.** Of, pertaining, or relating to practice; exhibited in practice or action. Opp. to *speculative, theoretical*, or *ideal.* 1617. **b.** Applicable in practice; practically useful 1642. **2.** Engaged in practice; practising, working 1604. **3.** Inclined to action (as opp. to speculation, etc.); also, having ability for action 1667. **4.** That is such in practice; that is such in effect, though not nominally or professedly so; virtual 1642. †**5.** Crafty, scheming, artful FOXE.

1. *P. agriculture, chemistry, logic*, etc. *P. joke*: see JOKE *sb.* 1; He said solemnly that he did not approve of p. jokes THACKERAY. **b.** A p. work for p. men 1858. P. politics is to do what you can, and not what you ought 1897. 2. The p. iron men are much better judges than we theorists 1788. 3. The p. man, who relies on his own experience 1875. 4. In a word, if he was not a practicall Atheist, I know not who was FULLER. Hence **Practica·lity**, the quality of being p.; also, a p. matter or affair (chiefly in *pl.*). **Pra·cticalize** *v. trans. rare*, to render p. **Pra·ctical·ly** *adv.*, **-ness.**

Practice (præ·ktis). 1494. [Formerly *practyse, -ize*, f. PRACTISE *v.*; later assimilated in spelling to words in -ICE. Supplanted PRACTIC *sb.*[1]] The action, or an action, of practising, etc. **1.** The action *of* doing something; performance; working, operation; method of working. *Obs.* or merged in 2. 1553. **b.** An action, a deed; *pl.* doings. *Obs.* or merged in 2. 1565. **2.** The habitual doing or carrying on *of* something; customary or constant action; action as dist. from profession, theory, knowledge, etc.; conduct 1509. **b.** *Law.* The method of procedure used in the law-courts 1623. **c.** A habit, custom; (with *pl.*) a habitual action 1568. **3.** Exercise in any art, handicraft, etc., for the purpose of attaining proficiency 1525. †**4.** An exercise; a practical treatise –1712. **5.** *spec.* The exercise of a profession or occupation; the professional work or business of a lawyer or medical man 1576. **6.** The action of scheming, esp. (now only) in an underhand way and for an evil purpose; machination, treachery; artifice. *arch.* 1494. **b.** Dealings; *esp.* in evil sense, Conspiracy, intrigue, collusion (*with* a person, *between* persons). *arch.* 1540. **c.** (with *pl.*) A scheme, plot, intrigue, manœuvre, artifice 1539. **7.** The action, or an act, of practising *on* or *upon* a person, etc.: see PRACTISE 11. *rare.* 1614. **8.** *Arith.* A compendious method of performing multiplication by means of aliquot parts, in cases where one or both quantities are expressed in several denominations; e. g. in finding the value of so many articles at so many pounds, shillings, and pence each 1574.

1. *Much Ado* v. i. 255. 2. His P. of Religious Severities 1717. To stoop from speculation to p. MACAULAY. **c.** A man of free principles, shewn by practices as free RICHARDSON. 3. Through practise made perfect 1553. A pleasant bit of mountain p. 1860. 5. The mysteries of mingled medicines, and the practise of Physicke 1576. He sold this p. and removed into Dunchester 1898. 6. The Practise of the Deuill 1560. He..died a martyr's death, through the p. of the Lady Ælfthryth FREEMAN. **c.** Plots and practises of the popish faction 1645. 7. Another piece of p. on the fears of the assembly 1759.

Phrases. *In practice.* **a.** In the realm of action; practically, as a fact. **b.** In the condition of being exercised so as to maintain skill or ability. **c.** Of a lawyer, doctor, etc.: Engaged in practising his profession. *To put in* (or *into*) *p.*, to exercise, carry out in action. *To make a p. of* (something), to do it habitually and of purpose.

Practician (prækti·ʃăn). 1500. [a. obs. F. *practicien*, var. of *praticien*, f. med.L. *practica* PRACTIC *sb.*[1] + *-ien* -IAN.] One who practises any art, profession, or occupation; a practitioner; a practical man.

Practise (præ·ktis), *v.* late ME. [a. OF. *pra(c)tiser*, f. *pra(c)tiquer*, med.L. *pra(c)ticare*. The stress, orig. on *-ize* (praktī·z, -əi·z), was subseq. shifted to the first syllable, whence also the change of z to s.] **1.** *trans.* To perform, execute, carry on, exercise (any action or process). Now *rare*, or merged in 2. 1460. †**b.** To work out (a problem, etc.); to perform, act (a play) –1685. **c.** *intr.* To act, work, proceed, operate 1553. **2.** *trans.* To carry on, or do, habitually or constantly; to make a practice of; to carry out in action 1526. **b.** With *inf.* To be wont (*arch.*) 1674. **c.** *intr.* To act habitually 1681. **3.** *trans.* To exercise, pursue (an occupation, profession, or art) 1560. **b.** *spec. intr.* To exercise the profession of law or of medicine 1538. †**4.** *trans.* To put into practice, execute (a law, command, etc.) –1771. **5.** To exercise oneself in (any art, process, or act) for the purpose of attaining proficiency. Also with *obj. inf.* late ME. **b.** *absol.* or *intr.* To exercise oneself in the performance of music, etc. with the view of acquiring skill 1596. **6.** *trans.* To exercise (any one) *in* some action; to train, drill 1598. **b.** *pa. pple.* Experienced by practice; skilled, versed, proficient (*in*) 1542. †**7.** To put to practical use; to make use of, employ –1740. †**b.** To frequent, haunt [after F. *pratiquer*] –1718. †**8.** To bring about, compass, effect –1736. †**b.** To devise means to bring about (a result); to plan, intend (something to be done). With *simple obj.* or *obj. clause.* –1711. **9.** *intr.* To lay schemes or plans, esp. for an evil purpose; to scheme, plot, conspire, intrigue (*with* or *against* a person, *to do* something). Now *rare.* 1537. †**b.** *trans.* To plot, conspire (some evil) –1634. **10.** *intr.* To have dealings, to negotiate or treat *with* a person; *esp.* to deal *with* so as to gain over to some course of action. *Obs.* or *arch.* 1538. †**b.** *trans.* To influence (a person) by underhand dealings, win over, 'get at', corrupt –1715. **11.** *To p. upon*: To practise tricks or artifices upon; to act upon, by artifice, so as to induce to do or believe something; to impose upon, delude; to work upon (a person or his feelings, etc.) 1596. †**12.** To make trial of practically –1802.

1. To thinke, that you haue ought but Talbots shadow, Whereon to p. your seueritie SHAKS. **c.** Being little inclined to p. upon others, and as little that others should p. upon me TEMPLE. 2. Practice as much of Religion as you Talk 1698. Phr. *To p. religion*, to perform the religious duties which the Church requires of its members; to be a practising and not merely a nominal member (esp. in *R.C.Ch.*); also *absol.* and *intr.* **c.** If he practises as well as he preaches, he must be a paragon (*mod.*). 3. They admit of no Trade, but p. Piracy 1727. **b.** A counsel practising at the bar 1883. 5. Ere I learne loue, Ile p. to obey SHAKS. The young people..practised hymns 1863. **b.** She will never play really well unless she practises more JANE AUSTEN. 6. The captain practises his company in all the phases of war 1888. 9. Hee will p. against thee by poyson SHAKS. 11. I ..will so p. upon Benedicke, that..hee shall fall in loue with Beatrice SHAKS.

Practised (præ·ktist), *ppl. a.* 1568. [f. prec. + -ED[1].] **1.** That has had practice; experienced, skilled. **2.** Put into practice; exercised 1590.

1. A companie of..p. souldiours 1568.

Practiser (præ·ktisəɹ). [ME. *practisour*; see PRACTISE *v.* and -OUR; the suffix was weakened later to -ER[2] 3.] One who exercises a profession or occupation; a practitioner. **b.** *gen.* One who practises any art, science, manner of life, course of action, etc.; one who carries out a theory, etc., in action 1540.

Practitioner (prækti·ʃənəɹ). 1544. [Extended f. †*practitian* PRACTICIAN; see -ER[1].] **1.** One engaged in the practice of any art, profession, or occupation; esp. in medicine, surgery, or law. †**2.** A learner, novice, beginner; a probationer –1801. **3.** One who practises anything; a habitual doer 1548.

1. *General p.*, one who practises both medicine and surgery; also opp. to *specialist* in either branch.

†**Pra·ctive**, *a.* (*sb.*) late ME. [f. stem *pract-* in PRACTIC + -IVE.] **1. a.** Devoted to practice or action –1610. **b.** Adept, skilful, dexterous –1594. **2.** Belonging to practice; practical –1658. **B.** *sb.* Practice; actual doing or working –1523.

Prad (præd). *slang.* 1798. [By metathesis from Du. *paard* a horse:—late L. *paraveredus* (see PALFREY).] A horse.

He's in the gig, a-minding the p. DICKENS.

Præ- in med.L. also PRE-. a. L. prep. and adv., meaning 'before'. In Eng. the L. spelling is now usual only in words that are still regarded as Latin, as *præmunire*, or that belong to Roman antiquities, as *prætor.*

‖ **Præcipe** (prī·sipi). 1500. [L., imper. of *præcipere* to admonish, enjoin (see PRECEPT). The opening word of the writ, *præcipe quod reddat*, enjoin (him) that he render.] *Law.* **1.** A writ requiring something to be done, or demanding a reason for its non-performance. **2.** A note containing particulars of a writ which must be filed with the officer of the Court from which the writ issues, by the party asking for the writ, or by his solicitor 1848.

Præcocial (prīkōu·ʃiăl), *a.* 1872. [f. L. *præcoces* (pl. of *præcox* early mature: see PRECOCIOUS).] *Ornith.* Of or pertaining to the *Præcoces*, applied to those birds whose young are able to leave the nest and to feed themselves as soon as they are hatched.

‖ **Præcognitum** (prīkǫ·gnitǒm). *Pl.* **-a.** 1634. [L., f. *præ* before + *cognitum, cognoscere* to know.] Something known beforehand; *esp.* something necessary to be known as a basis of reasoning, investigation, or study; a principle.

‖ **Præcordia** (prīkǭ·ɹdiă). 1681. [L. pl., f. *præ* before + *cor, cord-* heart.] *Anat.* The forepart of the thoracic region; the parts or region of the body about the heart.

Præcordial, etc.: see PRECORDIAL, etc.

‖ **Præmunientes** (prīmiūni‚e·ntīz). 1700.

[med.L., for L. *præmonentes*, pres. pple. pl. of *præmonere* (see next).] *Law. P. clause*: the clause of the writ of Edw. I, 1295, in which the bishops and abbots summoned to parliament are ordered to summon representatives of the minor clergy to attend with them. So *p. writ.*

‖ **Præmunire** (prīmiunəi·ri), *sb.* late ME. [L., used in med.L. for *præmonere* to forewarn, f. *præ* PRE- A. I. 1 + *monere*. Occurring in the text of the writ.] 1. (More fully *p. facias.*) A writ by which the sheriff is charged to summon a person accused, orig., of prosecuting in a foreign court a suit cognizable by the law of England, and later, of asserting or maintaining papal jurisdiction in England; also, the statute of 16 Richard II (*Statute of P.*), on which this writ is based 1449. †2. *transf.* a. An offence against the statute of præmunire; also, any offence incurring the same penalties –1678. b. The penalties incurred by an offender against the statute of præmunire, which was subseq. applied to various offences not connected with its original purpose –1724. †3. A difficulty, predicament. (Often *joc.*) –1814.

3. If the law finds you with two wives at once, There's a shrewd premunire 1599. Hence **Præmunire** (-əi·ɹ) *v. trans.* to issue a writ of p. against; to convict of breach of the statute of p. *Obs.* exc. *Hist.*

‖ **Prænomen** (prīnōu·men). Also **pre-**. 1706. [L., a forename, f. *præ* before + *nomen* name.] *Rom. Antiq.* The first name, preceding the nomen and cognomen; the personal name, as Marcus in Marcus Tullius Cicero. Hence, the Christian name.

‖ **Præpostor, pre-** (prīpǫ·stǫɹ). 1518. [Syncopated f. *præpositor* PREPOSITOR.] In some English public schools, the term for those senior pupils elsewhere called prefects or monitors.

‖ **Prætexta** (prīte·kstă). Also **pre-**. 1601. [L., short for *toga prætexta* gown bordered in front; pa. pple. fem. of *prætexere* to weave before.] *Rom. Antiq.* A long white robe with a purple border, worn orig. by the magistrates and some of the priests, but afterwards by the children of the higher classes, viz. by boys till they were entitled to assume the *toga virilis*, and by girls till marriage.

Prætor (prī·tǫɹ). late ME. Also (*U.S.*) **pretor.** [ad. L. *prætor, -orem*, contr. f. **præitor*, lit. one who goes before, f. *præ* + *ire* to go.] Orig., The title of a Roman consul as leader of the army; later, that of an annually elected curule magistrate who performed some of the duties of the consuls. Of these magistrates there were at first one, later two (*p. urbanus, p. peregrinus*), and eventually eighteen. b. *transf.* One holding high civic office, as a mayor or chief magistrate 1494. Hence **Præto·rial, pre-**, *a.* of or pertaining to a Roman p.; prætorian. **Præ·torship, pre·torship,** the office, or term of office, of a Roman p.

Prætorian (prītōə·riăn), *a.* and *sb.* late ME. Also (*U.S.*) **pre-**. [ad. L. *prætorianus*; see prec. and -IAN.] A. *adj.* 1. Of, belonging or pertaining to a Roman prætor or to the office or rank of prætor 1598. 2. Of or belonging to the bodyguard of a Roman military commander or of the emperor. late ME. b. Of or pertaining to the prætorian soldiers 1741. c. *fig.* Like the prætorian cohort in venality 1907.

2. Augustus set up the P. Guard of 10000 men 1651. c. The calling into existence of a Pretorian band of pauper labour through doles for the encouragement of the unemployed 1907.

B. *sb.* 1. A man of prætorian rank; as an ex-prætor, etc. 1756. 2. A soldier of the prætorian guard 1625. b. *fig.* One of a company whose function or interest is to defend an established power or system 1647. Hence **Prætorianism,** military despotism, esp. when venal.

‖ **Prætorium** (prītōə·riŏm). 1600. Also (*U.S.*) **pre-**. [L., a general's tent, etc.; sb. use of neut. of *prætorius* adj., belonging to a prætor.] 1. The tent of the commanding general in a Roman camp; the space where this was placed. 2. The palace or court of the governor of a Roman province 1611. b. By extension: The court or palace of an ancient king; also, a town-hall, etc. 1611. 3. The quarters of the Prætorian Guard in Rome 1670.

Pragmatic (prægmæ·tik), *a.* and *sb.* 1587. [ad. L. *pragmaticus*, a. Gr. πραγματικός active, business-like, etc., f. πρᾶγμα, πραγματ- deed, act, business, affair, f. πράττειν to do.] A. *adj.* 1. Relating to the affairs of a state or community 1643. 2. Busy, active; *esp.* officiously busy in other people's affairs; interfering, meddling 1616. 3. Opinionated; dictatorial, dogmatic 1638. 4. Treating the facts of history in their connexion with each other as cause and effect, and with ref. to their practical lessons. [= G. *pragmatisch.*] 1853. 5. = PRAGMATICAL *a.* 2. 1853. 6. Belonging or relating to philosophical pragmatism 1902.

1. *P. sanction*, 'an imperial decree relating to the affairs of a community', the technical name given to some imperial and royal ordinances issued as fundamental laws: applied esp. to the edict of Charles VII of France in 1438, which was the basis of the liberties of the Gallican church; and to the ordinance of the emperor Charles VI, in 1724, settling the succession to the Austrian throne. 2. Common estimation puts an ill character upon p. medling people 1674. 3. She is as p. and proud as the Pope 1771. 5. A strict and p. people, like the mass of the Scotch 1853.

B. *sb.* 1. = *p. sanction*; see A. 1. 1587. †2. One versed in business; an agent –1625. 3. An officious or meddlesome person; a conceited person 1645.

Pragmatical (prægmæ·tikăl), *a.* 1543. [f. as PRAGMATIC + -AL; see -ICAL.] 1. = PRAGMATIC *a.* 1. Now *rare.* 2. Of, pertaining to, or dealing with practice; practical. *Obs.* exc. as used after G. *pragmatisch.* 1597. †3. Actively engaged; active, busy; methodical; energetic –1661. b. Experienced in affairs; expert; shrewd. Now *rare.* 1656. 4. = PRAGMATIC *a.* 2. Now *rare.* 1611. b. Self-important; opinionated, dogmatic; doctrinaire; crotchety 1704. 5. = PRAGMATIC *a.* 6. 1903.

2. The practical or p. form of Christianity associated with the name of James 1906. 4. A wise man is not p., for he declines the doing of any thing that is beyond his office 1656. b. Which..may perhaps give me the title of p. and overweening SWIFT. Hence **Pragma·tical·ly** *adv.*, **-ness.**

Pragmatism (præ·gmătiz'm). 1863. [f. Gr. πρᾶγμα, πραγματ- deed, act + -ISM. Cf. G. *pragmatismus.*] 1. Officiousness; pedantry; an instance of this. 2. Matter-of-fact treatment of things 1872. †3. A method of treating history in which the phenomena are considered with special ref. to their causes, antecedent conditions, and results, and to their practical lessons –1884. 4. *Philos.* The doctrine that the whole meaning of a conception expresses itself in practical consequences 1898.

3. I have drawn attention..to the prophetic p. of Matthew 1865. So **Pra·gmatist,** a pragmatical person; an adherent of the doctrine called p.

Pragmatize (præ·gmătəiz), *v.* 1831. [f. Gr. πρᾶγμα, πραγματ- + -IZE.] *trans.* To represent (what is imaginary or subjective) as real or actual; to materialize or rationalize (a myth). Hence **Pra·gmatizer.**

Prairie (prēə·ri). 1773. [a. F.:—Rom. **prataria*, f. L. *pratum* meadow; see -RY.] A tract of level or undulating grass-land, without trees, and usu. of great extent; applied chiefly to the grassy plains of North America.

The P., or meadow ground on the eastern side, is at least twenty miles wide 1773.

attrib. and *Comb.*: **p.-chicken,** the Pinnated Grouse, *Cupidonia* or *Tympanuchus cupido*, a gallinaceous bird of N. America; **-dog,** a N. Amer. rodent animal, genus *Cynomys*, of the squirrel family; *spec. C. Ludovicianus*, the Louisiana Marmot, having a cry like the bark of a dog; **-grouse** = *p.-chicken*; **-hawk,** the American Sparrow-hawk, *Tinnunculus* or *Falco sparverius*; **-hen** = *p.-chicken*; **-marmot** = *p.-dog*; **-mole,** a silvery mole, *Scalops argentatus*, found on the western prairies; **p. rattler** or **rattlesnake,** one of various rattlesnakes of the prairies, as *Sistrurus catenatus*, or *Crotalus confluentus*; **-rent**: see *p. value*; **-squirrel,** a N. Amer. ground-squirrel of the genus *Spermophilus*, inhabiting the prairies; **P. State,** the state of Illinois, U.S.; in pl. more general, including Wisconsin, Iowa, Minnesota, and States to the south of these; **-turnip,** a hairy herbaceous plant (*Psoralea esculenta*) of N. W. America, or its edible farinaceous tuber; **p. value** *Pol. Econ.*, the rental value of p. land, or of any waste land; **-warbler,** a small warbler, *Dendrœca discolor*, of eastern N. America; **-wolf** = COYOTE.

Praisable (prē·zăb'l), *a.* Now *rare.* ME. [f. PRAISE *v.* + -ABLE.] Praiseworthy, laudable. Hence **Prai·sableness. Prai·sably** *adv.*

Praise (prēz), *sb.* late ME. [f. next. Not common till after 1500.] 1. The action or fact of praising; commendation of the worth or excellence of a person or thing; eulogy. b. The fact or condition of being praised 1533. 2. The expression of admiration and ascribing of glory, as an act of worship; hence, worship by song. late ME. 3. *transf.* The ground of praise; praiseworthiness; merit, virtue. *arch.* 1526. †b. An object or subject of praise –1787.

1. For they loved the prayse that is geven off men, more then the prayse, that commeth of god TINDALE *John* xii. 43. b. The p. of politeness and vivacity could now scarcely be obtained except by some violation of decorum MACAULAY. 2. The pealing anthem swells the note of p. GRAY. 3. A restless crowd,.. Whose highest p. is that they live in vain COWPER. b. He is thy prayse, & thy God COVERDALE *Deut.* x. 21. Hence **Prai·seless** *a.* without p. or honour; undeserving of p.

Praise (prēz), *v.* ME. [a. OF. *preisier* :—late L. *preciare*, earlier *pretiare* to price, value, prize, f. *pretium* price. Cf. PRIZE *v.*] I. 1. *trans.* To set a price or value upon; to value, appraise. *Obs.* or *dial.* †2. To value, esteem; to PRIZE –1567.

2. They preysed nothing the thinges that were erthely CAXTON.

II. 1. To commend the worth, excellence, or merits of; to express warm approbation of; to laud, extol. (The leading current sense.) ME. 2. To extol the glorious attributes of (God, or a deity), esp., to sing the praises of; to glorify, magnify, laud ME.

1. They extolled and praysed him farre above the Starres 1513. P. the sea, but keep on land G. HERBERT. 2. Let the people prayse the (o God) let all people prayse the COVERDALE *Ps.* lxvii. 5.

Praiseful (prē·zfŭl), *a.* late ME. [f. PRAISE *v.* or *sb.* + -FUL.] †1. Praiseworthy –1818. 2. Eulogistic, laudatory 1613. Hence **Prai·seful·ly** *adv.*, **-ness.**

Praiser (prē·zəɹ). late ME. [f. PRAISE *v.* + -ER[1].] †1. One who appraises; a valuer –1707. 2. One who praises, commends, or extols. late ME.

2. The sweete wordes of flaterynge preiseres CHAUCER.

Praiseworthy (prē·z₁wɒ̄:ɹði), *a.* 1538. [f. PRAISE *sb.* + WORTHY *a.*] Worthy of praise; laudable, commendable.

That right good and praise-worthy man 1610. Hence **Prai·sewo:rthily** *adv.* **Prai·sewo:rthiness.**

Prakrit (prā·krit). 1786. [ad. Skr. *prākṛta* natural, unrefined, vulgar; opp. to *saṅskṛta* prepared, refined, polished (SANSKRIT).] A general name for those popular langs. or dialects of Northern and Central India which existed alongside of or grew out of Sanskrit. Hence **Prakri·tic** *a.*

Praline (prā·līn), **prawlin** (prǭ·lin). Chiefly *U.S.* 1727. [a. F. *praline*, f. the name of Marshal Duplessis-Praslin, whose cook invented the confection.] Almonds or nuts browned in boiling sugar; also *transf.*

‖ **Pram**[1], **praam** (prām). 1548. [Du. *praam*, from Slav.] A flat-bottomed boat or lighter, used esp. in the Baltic or the Netherlands for shipping cargo, etc.

Pram[2] (præm). *colloq.* 1884. [See sense 1.] 1. Abbrev. of PERAMBULATOR 3. 2. A milkman's hand-cart; also *attrib.* as *p.-round* 1897.

Pramnian (præ·mniăn), *a.* 1601. [f. L. *Pramnium* (*vinum*), Gr. Πράμνιος (οἶνος) + -AN.] *Gr.* and *Rom. Antiq.* In *P. wine*, a wine from the neighbourhood of Smyrna.

‖ **Prana** (prā·na). 1913. [Skr. = breath of life.] *Theosophy.* The life-principle. Hence **Pra·nic** *a.*

Prance (prɑns), *sb.* 1751. [f. next.] The act of prancing; a prancing movement or walk.

Prance (prɑns), *v.* late ME. [Origin obsc.] 1. *intr.* Of a horse: 'To spring and bound in high mettle' (J.); to rise by springing from the hind legs; to move by a succession of such springs. b. *trans.* To cause (a horse) to prance 1530. 2. *intr.* To ride (or drive) with the horse prancing; to ride ostentatiously; to ride gaily, proudly, or insolently. late ME. 3. To move or walk in a manner suggestive of a prancing horse, or (more gen.) an elated or arrogant manner; to swagger. late ME.

1. I have a little white favourite [horse]..he prances under me with so much fire 1717. 2. His Majesty

prancing in person at the head of them all THACKERAY. 3. Rawdon..pranced off to engage lodgings THACKERAY. Hence **Pra·ncer**, one who or that which prances; *esp.* a mettled or prancing horse; *slang*, a cavalry officer.

Prandial (præ·ndiăl), *a.* *affected* or *joc.* 1820. [f. L. *prandium* late breakfast + -AL.] Pertaining or relating to dinner. Hence **Pra·ndially** *adv.* in connexion with dinner.

Prank (præŋk), *sb.* 1525. [Allied to PRANK *v.*²] A trick, a frolic. †**a.** In early use, a trick of malicious or mischievous nature; sometimes rendering L. *scelus* or *facinus* –1737. †**b.** A trick of magic, conjuring, or the like –1840. **c.** A mad frolic, a practical joke 1576. **d.** Said of capricious or frolicsome movements of animals, and of erratic actions of machines 1692.

a. Infamous..for many lewd pranks (as that he killed his brother, and then his owne sister) 1654. b. Like those priests of Bel, whose pranks Daniel found out MILT. c. The pranks..of healthy schoolboys 1884. Hence **Pra·nkish** *a.* of the nature of a p.; inclined to pranks. **Pra·nksome** *a.* addicted to pranks; frolicsome.

Prank, *v.*¹ *Obs.* or *dial.* 1519. [Origin obsc.] *intr.* = PRANCE *v.* (in various senses); to caper; to dance.

Prank (præŋk), *v.*² 1546. [Cogn. w. Du. *pronken* to strut, parade.] **1.** *trans.* To dress or deck in a gay, bright, or showy manner; *refl.* to deck oneself *out*, dress oneself *up*. **b.** *fig.* To dress up 1607. **c.** *transf.* To dress, adorn; to set out with colours; to spangle 1591. **2.** *intr.* (for *refl.*) To show oneself off, make display. Also *to p. it.* 1567.

1. She..spends halfe a day in pranking her selfe if she be inuited to any strange place 1592. c. Broad flag-flowers, purple prankt with white SHELLEY. 2. White houses p. where once were huts M. ARNOLD.

Prase (prēⁱz). late ME. [a. F., ad. L. *prasius* (also formerly used), a. Gr. πράσιος leek-green, f. πράσον leek.] *Min.* A cryptocrystalline or crystalline variety of translucent quartz, of a leek-green colour.

Praseolite (prēⁱ·ziŏləit). 1864. [ad. Sw. *praseolith*, irreg. f. Gr. πράσον or πράσιος (see prec.) + -LITE.] *Min.* A form of iolite.

Prasine (prēⁱ·zin), *sb.* and *a.* ME. [ad. late L. *prasina* green chalk, fem. of L. *prasinus* adj., a. Gr. πράσινος leek-green.] **A.** *sb.* A green-coloured mineral; now a synonym of pseudo-malachite. **B.** *adj.* Leek-like; leek-green in colour. *rare.* 1528.

Praso-, repr. Gr. πράσον leek; as in **Praso·phagous** [Gr. -φαγος] *a.*, eating leeks.

Prate (prēⁱt), *sb.* 1569. [f. next.] The act or action of prating; talk; now *esp.* idle talk; chatter.

Prate (prēⁱt), *v.* late ME. [= (M)Du. *praten*; perh. onomatopœic.] **1.** *intr.* To talk, to chatter: usu. dyslogistic, implying speaking much or long to little purpose; to tell tales, blab. **2.** *trans.* To utter or tell in a prating manner; to repeat to little purpose 1489.

1. Sober wretches, who p. whole evenings over coffee 1713. 2. What Nonsense wou'd the Fool thy Master p. DRYDEN. **Pra·ter**, one who prates; a chatterer; formerly also, a boaster, an evil-speaker.

Pratincole (præ·tiŋkoul). 1773. [ad. mod. L. *pratincola*, f. L. *pratum* meadow + *incola* inhabitant.] *Ornith.* One of several species of the genus *Glareola*, grallatorial (limicoline) birds allied to the plovers.

‖ **Pratique** (præ·tik, ‖ pratīk). 1609. [a. F. = practice, etc., ad. L. *practica* (see PRACTIC *sb.*¹).] Permission or licence granted to a ship to hold intercourse with a port after quarantine, or on showing a clean bill of health. Used esp. in connexion with the south of Europe.

attrib. **p. boat, house,** the boat, house, of the quarantine officer.

Prattle (præ·t'l), *sb.* 1555. [f. next.] The act or action of prattling; that which is prattled; idle or childish chatter, small talk.

Let him..keep his babble and p. to himselfe 1600.

Prattle (præ·t'l), *v.* 1532. [dim. and freq. of PRATE *v.*; see -LE 3.] **1.** *intr.* To chatter in a childish or artless fashion; to be loquacious about trifles; formerly equivalent to PRATE; now chiefly said, without contempt, of the talk of young children. Also *transf.* and *fig.* **2.** *trans.* To utter in an idle, garrulous, or (now usu.) childish way 1560.

1. He had the Mastery of his Parents ever since he could P. 1692. The light leaves prattled to neighbour ears MEREDITH. 2. Ambling and prattling scandal as he goes COWPER. **Prattlement** (præ·t'lmĕnt), idle talk, prattle, prattling. *rare.* **Pra·ttler**, one who prattles; now *esp.* a prattling child.

Pravity (præ·vĭti). 1550. [ad. L. *pravitas*, f. *pravus* crooked, perverse.] **1.** Moral perversion or corruption; depravity. Now *rare* or *Obs.* **2.** *gen.* Corrupt or evil quality 1620.

1. The natural p. of man 1847. 2. Scarcity or p. of food 1822.

Prawn (prǭn), *sb.* [Late ME. *prayne*, *prane*; origin unkn.] A small long-tailed decapod marine crustacean (*Palæmon senatus*), larger than a shrimp, common off the coasts of Britain, and used as food.

Praxinoscope (præ·ksino₁skōᵘp). 1882. [a. F., irreg. f. Gr. πρᾶξις action + -SCOPE.] A scientific toy resembling the zoetrope, in which the reflexions of a series of pictures produce the impression of an actually moving object.

‖ **Praxis** (præ·ksis). 1581. [a. Gr. πρᾶξις doing, f. πράττειν to do.] **1.** Action, practice; *esp.* accepted practice, custom. **2.** An example or collection of examples to serve for practice in a subject, esp. in grammar 1612. †**b.** A means or instrument of practice in a subject; a practical specimen or model –1800.

1. For as Aristotle sayth, it is not *Gnosis*, but *P.* must be the fruit SIDNEY.

Pray (prēⁱ), *v.* [ME. *preien*, a. OF. *preier* :—late L. *precare*, cl. L. *precari* to entreat, pray.] **I.** *trans.* with personal obj. **1.** To ask earnestly, humbly, or supplicatingly, to beseech; *esp.* in religious use, to make devout and humble supplication to (God, or an object of worship). *arch.* †**2.** To entreat (a person) to come to a feast, or the like; to invite –1603.

1. I will p. the Father, and hee shall giue you another Comforter *John* xiv. 16. I p. God your friends..stick as well to you 1613. Praying their Lordships to relieve him from the expenses..of a law-suit NELSON.

II. With the thing asked as object. To ask (something) earnestly in prayer; to ask or beg (a thing) with supplication; to crave. late ME.

They were inforced to p. his aid 1594. Ile p. a thousand praiers for thy death SHAKS. [They] prayed to be exempted from the operation of the law 1844.

III. *intr.* To make earnest request or petition; *esp.* to present petitions to God, or to an object of worship ME. **b.** In the formal ending of a petition to the Sovereign, to Parliament, a petition in Chancery, etc. The words after 'pray' were at length reduced to 'etc.', which is now usu. omitted. late ME.

How I perswaded, how I praid, and kneel'd SHAKS. That will duly and truly prea for yee 1641. Shall we believe a God, and not p. to him for future benefits? 1732. b. The familiar expression 'and your petitioner[s] shall ever p., &c.'.. came in about the middle of the fifteenth century 1896.

Phrases, etc. *To p. in aid*, to crave the assistance *of* some one. †*I p. you (thee)*, used parenthetically to add instance or deference to a question or request; so *p. you*, *p. thee*, etc.; also contracted to *pray*.

Pray, -e, obs. ff. PREY.

Prayer¹ (prēᵊɹ). [ME. a. OF. *preiere*, mod. F. *prière* :—Rom. and med.L. *precaria* fem. sing., orig. neut. pl. of L. *precarius* obtained by prayer, PRECARIOUS.] **1.** A solemn and humble request to God, or to an object of worship; a supplication, petition, or thanksgiving, usu. expressed in words. **b.** The action or practice of praying to the Divine Being ME. **c.** *pl.* Petitions to God for His blessing upon some one; hence, earnest good wishes 1597. **2.** A formula used in praying; e.g. *the Lord's P.* (LORD *sb.* I. 7). late ME. **3.** A religious observance, public or private, of which prayer to God forms a principal part; in *pl.* with possessive, one's private devotions ME. **4.** An entreaty made to a person ME. **5.** The thing prayed for or entreated; *spec.* that part of a memorial or petition that specifies this. late ME.

1. And so would I..make my speciall prayour to God 1529. b. More things are wrought by p. Than this world dreams of TENNYSON. c. He..shall haue my Prayers While I shall haue my life SHAKS. 3. The Assassinates found him at his prayers 1678. Phr. *Morning* or *Evening P.*, *family prayers*. 4. I held it in spite of..her prayers, and, at last, her tears 1858. 5. His p. was granted by the Deity HOBBES.

Comb.: **p.-carpet, -mat, -rug,** a small carpet, mat, or rug used, esp. by a Moslem, when engaged in p.; **-meeting,** a religious meeting for devotion, in which several of those present offer p.; **-tower,** a minaret; **-wheel,** a cylindrical box inscribed with or containing prayers, revolving on a spindle: used esp. by the Buddhists of Tibet.

Prayer² (prēⁱ·əɹ). Also **pray-er.** 1440. [f. PRAY *v.* + -ER¹.] One who prays.

Pray·er-book. 1595. A book of forms of prayer; *spec.* the Book of Common Prayer, containing the public liturgy of the Church of England.

Prayerful (prēᵊ·ɹfŭl), *a.* 1626. [f. PRAYER¹ + -FUL.] **1.** Much given to prayer; devout. **2.** Characterized by or expressive of prayer 1652.

2. With p. earnest eyes 1871. Hence **Pray·erful·ly** *adv.*, **-ness.**

Pray·erless, *a.* 1631. [f. PRAYER¹ + -LESS.] Without prayer; not having the habit of prayer. **b.** *transf.* (Of times, places, states, etc.) 1816.

Untaught, ungoverned p. families 1653. b. Scarce a lamp Burnt on the p. shrines 1826. Hence **Pray·erless·ly** *adv.*, **-ness.**

Pray·ing, *vbl. sb.* ME. [f. PRAY *v.* + -ING¹.] The action of PRAY *v.*; prayer, earnest request.

attrib. and *Comb.* = Used for or in prayer, as **p.-carpet, -mat, -rug** = PRAYER-*carpet*; **-cylinder, -drum, -jenny, -machine, -wheel** = PRAYER-*wheel.*

Pray·ing, *ppl. a.* 1483. [-ING².] That prays.

p.-insect, the MANTIS (*p. mantis*, or *p. locust*). Hence **Pray·ingly** *adv.* in a p. manner.

Pre- (prī, pri, prĭ) *prefix*, repr. L. *præ* adv. and prep. (of place, rank, and time) before, in front, in advance. In Eng. sometimes written *præ-* after the Revival of Learning, but now regularly *pre-*. See PRÆ-.

In English many Latin verbs and their derivs. in *præ-* have their representatives in *pre-*, which is also sometimes prefixed to words of English or modern origin, as *pre-embody*, *pre-plot*, etc. The prepositional construction has in English become the second great living use, *pre-* being preferred to *ante-* as the opposite of *post-* in new formations, and often substituted for it, as in *pre-Christian*, *prehistoric*, etc.

Nonce-words and casual compounds of English formation in *pre-* are usu. hyphened; other compounds, as *precaution*, *predestination*, are regularly written *indivisim*, except where the hyphen adds clearness, or emphasizes the function of the prefix.

A. Combinations in which *pre-* is adverbial or adjectival.

I. Of time or order of succession. **1.** With vbs., or ppl. adjs. and vbl. sbs. derived from them, in sense 'fore-, before, beforehand, previously, in advance', as *pre-acquaint*, *-admonish*, *-act*, *-cogitate*, *-condemn*, *-conform*, *-elect*, *-intimate*, *-limit*, *-warn*, etc., and in many others of obvious meaning. **2.** With a sb., this being usu. a deriv. from a vb. to which *pre-* is in adverbial relation: = Existing or taking place previously, placed before (something else), previous, preceding, earlier; as *pre-accusation*, *-adjustment*, *-connexion*, *-condition*, etc. Also with other sbs.: **Pre-anti·quity,** previous antiquity; **Pre-bo·ding,** foreboding; **Pre-de·stiny,** preappointed destiny or fate; **Pre-ete·rnity,** previous eternity, eternal previous existence; **Pre-name,** a forename, 'Christian' name. **3.** With an adj.: as *precognizant*, *pre-essential*, etc.

II. Of local position. (Chiefly *Anat.*) Usu. without hyphen. **a.** In adverbial relation to an adj.: = Before, anteriorly, in front; as **Prede·ntate,** having teeth in the fore part of the upper jaw only, as some cetaceans. Also in adjs. = 'anterior', as **Pre·cerebellar** = anterior cerebellar (artery), etc. **b.** In quasi-adjectival relation to a sb.: = 'Situated in front, anterior, fore-', with derivative adjs.; as **Pre·abdo·men,** Latreille's name for the first five segments of the abdomen of Crustacea; etc. **c.** In advb. relation to a vb.; in compounds formed in L., as PRECLUDE, PREFIX.

III. Of order, rank, importance, quality, degree. In sense 'before in order or importance, above, in preference to, superior to, more than, beyond'; as in PRECEDE *v.*, PREDOMINATE *v.*, PREPONDERATE *v.*, etc.

B. Combinations in which *pre-* is prepositional, having as its object the sb. forming, or implied in, the second element.

I. Relating to time or order of succession; in which *pre-* = before; anterior, prior, or previous to; preceding, earlier than. These are properly hyphened. **1.** With adjs. (and their derivative advs. and sbs.), or f. *pre-* + a (Lat.) sb. + adjectival ending, as *pre-reformational*; forming adjs., with derivative advs. and sbs. **a.** Formed on proper nouns (or their adjs.), esp. on names of persons, races, nations, dynasties, and religions, as *pre-Alfredian*, *-Darwinian*, *-Messianic*; *pre-Aryan*, *-Hellenic*, *-Islamic*, *-ite*, *-Norman*; etc. **b.** In names of geological formations and of prehistoric periods, as *pre-Cambrian* (earlier than the

Cambrian); *pre-metallic* (before the knowledge of metals); etc. **c.** In pathological terms, as *pre-albuminuric* (previous to the appearance of albuminuria); so *pre-phthisical*, etc. **d.** Formed on other adjs. (or the L. or other sbs. to which these belong); as *pre-anæsthetic* (before the use of anæsthetics), *pre-artistic* (before the cultivation of art), *-classical, -critical, -lingual, -monarchical, -prophetic, -telegraphic*, etc. **2.** With sbs. or phrases (adj. + sb.) forming *quasi*-adjs., or attrib. phrases of obvious meaning; as *pre-advertisement, -advertising* (belonging to the days before advertising was usual), *-civilization, -Conquest, -marriage, -Mutiny, -war* (esp. before the war of 1914–18), etc. **b.** with personal names, meaning 'before the time or public work of'; as *pre-Chamberlain, pre-Conqueror, pre-Jenner*, etc.

II. Denoting local position; in which *pre-* = before, in front of, anterior to. These are usu. written without the hyphen. In adjs. (also sometimes used as sbs.), chiefly *Anat.* and *Zool.*, denoting parts or organs situated in front of (or, rarely, in the front part of) other parts or organs; as *pre-aortic, prebronchial*, PREOCULAR, *pre-oral*, etc.

Preace, obs. by-form of Press *sb.*[1] and *v.*[1]

Preach (prīt∫), *v.* [ME. *prechen*, a. F. *prêcher*, OF. *prechier*, ad. L. *prædicare* to proclaim publicly, f. PRÆ- + *dicare* to proclaim.] **1.** *intr.* 'To pronounce a public discourse upon sacred subjects' (J.); to deliver a sermon or religious address. **b.** To utter an earnest exhortation, esp. moral or religious. Now usu. dyslogistic: To give moral or religious advice in an obtrusive or tiresome way. 1523. **2.** *trans.* To proclaim by public discourse (the gospel, something sacred or religious). Also with *obj. cl.* ME. **b.** To set forth or teach (anything) in the way of exhortation; to advocate by discourse or writing; to exhort people to (some act or practice). Also with *obj. cl.* ME. **3.** To utter or speak publicly, deliver (a sermon, a religious or moral discourse). late ME. †**4.** To preach to; to exhort –1709. **5.** To affect in some way by preaching 1609.

1. On Sunday morneing I went to hear on Bayly of Maudlins p. 1674. **b.** Why do you p. to me in that manner? 1875. **2.** Ye Lorde hath anoynted me, and sent me, to p. good tydinges vnto the poore COVERDALE *Isa.* lxi. 1. **b.** My Mr preaches patience to him SHAKS. *P. up*, to extol by preaching; to discourse in praise of. *P. down*, to decry, oppose, or put down by preaching. **5.** We had a Preacher that would p. folke asleepe still B. JONS.

Hence **Preach** *sb.* (*colloq.*) an act of preaching; preachment. **Prea·chable** *a.* capable of being preached, or preached about or from. **Prea·chy** *a.* (*colloq.*) given to preaching; characterized by a preaching style.

Preacher (prī·t∫əɹ). [ME. *precho(u)r*, a. OF. *prech(e)or* :—L. *predicatorem*; see prec. and -ER[2].] One who preaches. **1.** One who proclaims religious doctrine by public discourse; *esp.* a minister of religion; *spec.* one licensed to preach. **b.** One who exhorts earnestly; one who inculcates something by speech or writing. late ME. **c.** With *of*: One who preaches (something specified). late ME. **2.** *spec.* A name for Solomon as supposed speaker in the Book of Ecclesiastes; hence, that book itself 1535.

1. To church, and there being a lazy p. I slept out the sermon PEPYS. *Friars Preachers*: see FRIAR 2. **b.** No p. is listened to but Time SWIFT. **c.** A perpetual p. of his own virtues MILT. **2.** All is but vanite, saieth ye p. COVERDALE *Eccl.* i. 2. Hence **Prea·chership**, the office of a p.

Preachify (prī·t∫ifəi), *v. colloq.* 1775. [f. PREACH *v.* + -(I)FY; cf. *speechify*.] *intr.* To preach in a factitious or tedious way; to make a preachment. Often merely contempt. for *preach*.

Preaching (prī·t∫iŋ), *vbl. sb.* ME. [-ING[1].] **1.** The action of PREACH *v.* **2.** With *a* and *pl.* The delivering of a sermon, that which is preached, a sermon or discourse 1449.

attrib. and *Comb.*, as **p.-cross**, a kind of cross formerly erected on a highway or in an open place, at which monks and others used to preach.

Prea·ching, *ppl. a.* 1583. [-ING[2].] That preaches.

P. friar (spec.) a Dominican.

Prea·ching-house. 1760. [f. PREACHING *vbl. sb.* + HOUSE *sb.*] A house devoted to preaching; *spec.* Wesley's name for a Methodist place of worship.

Preachment (prī·t∫měnt). [ME., a. OF. *prechement*, ad. L. *prædicamentum* PREDICAMENT.] **1.** The action or fact of preaching; delivery of a sermon or exhortation, now esp. of a tedious character. **2.** A sermon or hortatory discourse: usu. *contemptuous*. late ME.

Pre-adamite (prī͵æ·dămait), *sb.* and *a.* Also unhyphened, and with capital A. 1662. [ad. mod.L. *præadamita*; see PRE- B. I. 1, ADAM, -ITE[1].] **A.** *sb.* **1.** One who lived (or one of a race held to have existed) before the time of Adam. †**2.** A believer in the existence of men before Adam –1774. **B.** *adj.* **1.** That existed before Adam; prehuman 1786. **2.** Relating to the time, or to a race, previous to Adam; belonging to the Pre-adamites (sense A. 1) 1882.

Hence **Pre-adami·tic, -al** *adjs.* = B. 1. So **Pre-ada·mic** *a.*

Pre͵admi·ssion. 1887. [PRE- A. I. 2.] Admission beforehand; *spec.* the admission of a certain amount of steam into the cylinder of a steam-engine before the end of the back stroke.

Preamble (prī·æmb'l, prī͵æ·mb'l), *sb.* late ME. [ad. F. *préambule*, ad. med.L. *præambulum*, prop. neut. sing. of L. *præambulus* adj. going before, f. *præambulare* to walk before (PRE- A. I. 1, AMBLE *v.*).] **1.** A preliminary statement, in speech or writing; a preface, prologue, introduction. **b.** *spec.* An introductory paragraph or part in a statute, deed, etc., setting forth the grounds and intention of it 1628. **c.** A (musical) prelude (*poet.*) 1667. **2.** *gen.* An introductory fact; a preliminary; *esp.* a presage, prognostic 1548.

1. **c.** With Præamble sweet Of charming symphonie they introduce Thir sacred Song MILT. **2.** This was the p. of the great troubles that after followed 1663.

Preamble (prī͵æ·mb'l), *v.* 1621. [f. prec.] **a.** *trans.* To state by way of preamble. Also, to make a preamble to. **b.** *intr.* To make a preamble or introductory statement 1641.

Preambular (prī͵æ·mbiŭlăɹ), *a. rare.* 1645. [f. med.L. *præambulum* + -AR.] Preambulatory. So **Prea·mbulary** *a.*

Preambulate (prī͵æ·mbiŭleit), *v. rare.* 1608. [f. L. *præambulat-*, *præambulare* to walk before; see -ATE[3].] †**1.** *intr.* To walk or go before or in front –1660. **2.** = PREAMBLE *v.* b. 1608. So **Preambula·tion**, the making of a preamble. late ME. **Preambulatory** (prī͵æ·mbiŭlătəri) *a.* having the character of a preamble; prefatory, preliminary 1608.

Preapprehension (prī:æprĭhe·n∫ən). 1633. [PRE- A. I. 2.] **1.** A conception formed beforehand; a preconceived idea 1646. **2.** A preconceived fear of what may happen; foreboding 1633.

Prearrange (prī͵ărēi·ndʒ), *v.* 1851. [PRE- A. I. 1.] *trans.* To arrange beforehand. Hence **Pre͵arra·ngement**, previous arrangement.

Preassurance (prī͵ă∫ūə·răns). 1635. [PRE- A. I. 2.] **1.** An assurance given or received beforehand. **2.** A previous feeling of certainty in one's own mind; an assured presentiment 1671. So **Preassu·re** *v. trans.* to assure or make certain beforehand.

Preaudience (prī͵ǭ·diěns). 1768. [PRE- A. I. 2.] The right to be heard before another; precedence or relative rank (of lawyers at the Bar).

Pre-a·xial, *a.* 1872. [f. PRE- B. II. + L. *axis*; cf. AXIAL.] *Anat.* Situated in front of the axis of the body or of a limb. Hence **Pre-a·xially** *adv.*

Prebend (pre·bĕnd). late ME. [a. OF. *prebende*, mod.F. *prébende*, ad. med.L. *præbenda* a pension, a living, prop. 'things to be supplied', f. L. *præbere*, for *præhibere*, f. *præ* before, forth + *habere* to hold.] **1.** The portion of the revenues of a cathedral or collegiate church granted to a canon or member of the chapter as his stipend. **2.** The separate portion of land or tithe from which the stipend is gathered (hence known as the *corps of the p.*); the tenure of this as a benefice. late ME. **3.** = PREBENDARY 1. 1556.

Prebendal (prībe·ndăl), *a.* 1751. [ad. med. L. *præbendalis*, f. *præbenda* PREBEND; see -AL.] Of or pertaining to a prebend or prebendary.

P. stall, the stall of a prebendary in a cathedral; hence, the benefice of a prebendary.

Prebendary (pre·bĕndări), *sb.* (*a.*) late ME. [ad. med.L. *præbendarius*, f. *præbenda*; see PREBEND and -ARY[1].] **1.** The holder of a prebend; a canon of a cathedral or collegiate church who holds a prebend. †**2.** The office of a prebendary; a prebend –1725. **3.** *attrib.* or *adj.* = PREBENDAL 1731. **Pre·bendaryship**, the office or benefice of a p.; a prebend.

Precalculate (prīkæ·lkiŭleit), *v.* 1841. [PRE- A. I. 1.] *trans.* To calculate or reckon beforehand. **Preca·lculable** *a.* **Precalcula·tion.**

Preca·ncel, *v.* 1905. [PRE- A. I. 1.] (orig. and esp. in U.S.) To cancel (postage stamps) in advance of use, usu. with the name of the city (and state), for business firms, etc. sending postal matter in bulk. So **Preca·ncel** *sb.* **Precancella·tion.**

Precarious (prĭkēə·riəs), *a.* 1646. [f. L. *precarius* (f. *prec-*, **prex* prayer, entreaty + *-arius* -ARY[1]) + -OUS.] **1.** Held by the favour and at the pleasure of another; hence, uncertain. **2.** Question-begging, taken for granted; unfounded, doubtful 1659. **3.** Dependent on circumstances or chance; unstable 1687. **4.** Perilous 1727. †**5.** Suppliant; importunate –1697.

1. *P. tenure*, a tenure held during the pleasure of the superior. **3.** A scanty and p. support 1794. **4.** The p. track through the morass SCOTT. **Preca·rious-ly** *adv.*, **-ness.**

Precative (pre·kătiv), *a.* 1662. [ad. late L. *precativus*, f. *precari* to entreat; see -ATIVE.] Expressing entreaty or desire; supplicatory.

In *Gram.* applied to a word, particle, or form, expressing entreaty, or the like.

Precatory (pre·kătəri), *a.* 1636. [ad. late L. *precatorius*, f. *precatorem* one who prays.] Of, pertaining to, of the nature of, or expressing entreaty or supplication. In *Gram.*, = prec.

P. words, words in a will praying or expressing a desire that a thing be done. When these are deemed to have an imperative force, they constitute a *p. trust*.

Precaution (prĭkǭ·∫ən). 1603. [a. F. *précaution*, ad. late L. *præcautionem*, f. L. *præcavere*, f. *præ* PRE- + *cavere* to beware of; see CAUTION *sb.*] **1.** Caution exercised beforehand to provide against mischief or secure good results; prudent foresight. **2.** An instance of this; a measure taken beforehand to ward off an evil or to ensure a good result. (With *a* and *pl.*) 1603.

1. I have used all the care and p. that I could 1782. **2.** The Governor..had taken several precautions to prevent us from forcing our way into the harbour 1748. Hence **Precau·tional, Precau·tionary** *adjs.* suggesting provident caution; of the nature of p.

†**Precau·tion**, *v.* 1654. [a. F. *précautionner*, f. *précaution* sb.] **1.** *trans.* To forewarn (any one) *against* something –1768. **2.** To put (any one) upon his guard *against* something; esp. *refl.* to be on one's guard *against* –1805. **3.** To say beforehand by way of caution –1690.

Precautious (prĭkǭ·∫əs), *a.* 1711. [f. PRECAUTION; see -OUS and CAUTIOUS.] Using precaution; displaying previous caution or care.

‖**Precava, præ-** (prī͵kēi·vă). 1866. [f. PRE- A. II. b. + CAVA for *vena cava*; cf. *postcava* (POST- A. 2 b.)] *Anat.* The superior or anterior vena cava. Hence **Pre-, præca·val** *a.* (*sb.*).

Precede (prĭsī·d), *v.* late ME. [a. F. *précéder*, ad. L. *præcedere* to go before; see PRE- A. III. and CEDE.] †**1.** *trans.* To go before or beyond (another) in quality or degree; to surpass; to exceed. **2.** To go before in rank or importance; to take precedence of 1485. **3.** To come or go before in order or arrangement 1494. **4.** To go before; to walk or proceed in advance of 1530. **5.** To come before in time; to happen, occur, or exist before; to be earlier than 1540. **6.** *intr.* or (now only) *absol.* (in senses 2–5) 1540. **7.** *trans.* To cause to be preceded (*by*); to preface (*with, by*) 1718.

2. All the sons of viscounts and barons are allowed to p. baronets 1819. **4.** As harbingers preceding still the fates SHAKS. **5.** He told them of signes which should preceed the day of Judgement 1653. **6.** A statement different from anything that precedes or follows (*mod.*). **7.** The emperor precedes his visit by a royal present 1718.

Precedence (pre·sĭděns, prĭsī·děns). 1484. [prob. f. PRECEDENT *a.*; see -ENCE.] †**1.** = PRECEDENT *sb.* 2, 3. –1546. †**2.** = PRECEDENT *sb.* 1. –1610. **3.** The fact of preceding another or others in time or succession; priority 1605. **4.** The fact of preceding another or others in order, rank, importance, estimation, or dignity; higher position; pre-eminence, supremacy 1658. **b.** *spec.* The right of preceding others in ceremonies and social formalities. Hence:

The order to be ceremonially observed by persons of different ranks. 1598.

2. *Ant. & Cl.* II. v. 51. **3.** The payment of interest ..will take p. of other Egyptian obligations 1884. **4.** The Andalucian horse takes p. of all 1845. **b.** Disputes concerning Rank and P. ADDISON.

Precedency (pre·sĭdĕnsi, prĭsī·dĕnsi). 1599. [f. as prec. + -ENCY.] †**1.** The being or serving as a precedent –1657. **2.** = prec. 3. 1612. **b.** *spec.* = prec. 4 b. 1599.

Precedent (pre·sĭdĕnt), *sb.* late ME. [a. F. *précédent*, sb. use of the adj.; see next.] **1.** A thing or person that precedes or goes before another. †**a.** That which has been mentioned just before. Usu. in *pl.* –1607. †**b.** That which precedes in time; an antecedent –1788. **2.** A previous instance or case taken as an example or rule for subsequent cases or as supporting or justifying some similar act or circumstance. (The prevailing sense.) late ME. **b.** *Law.* A previous judicial decision, method of proceeding, or draft of a document which serves as an authoritative rule or pattern in similar or analogous cases 1523. **c.** *collect.* or *gen.* (without article or *pl.*) *Without p.*, unprecedented. 1622. †**3.** *transf.* A written or printed record of some past proceeding or proceedings, serving as a guide or rule for subsequent cases –1650. †**4.** A pattern, model, exemplar –1709. †**b.** An example, illustration, specimen –1695.

1. The president were to yvel to be admytted CROMWELL. **b.** One p. creates another.—They soon accumulate, and constitute law. 1772. **c.** Each comforts himself that his faults are not without p. JOHNSON.

Precedent (prĭsī·dĕnt), *a.* Now *rare*; largely repl. by PRECEDING. late ME. [a. F. *précédent*, ad. L. *præcedens, -dentem.*] **1.** Existing or occurring before something else; previous, former. **2.** Coming or placed before 1483. **b.** Mentioned or said just before; preceding 1530. **3.** Having or taking precedence 1613.

1. Phr. *The p.*, that coming immediately before, the foregoing. Hence **Prece·dently** *adv.* previously, beforehand.

Precedent (pre·sĭdĕnt), *v.* 1614. [f. PRECEDENT *sb.*] *trans.* To be a precedent for; to support or justify by a precedent. Now only in *pa. pple.*: see next.

Precedented (pre·sĭdented), *ppl. a.* 1653. [f. PRECEDENT *sb.* or *v.* + -ED.] Furnished with or having a precedent; in accordance with precedent; usu. *predic.*

Precedential (presĭde·nʃăl). *a.* Now *rare.* 1641. [f. PRECEDENT *sb.* or PRECEDENCE.] **1.** Of the nature of, constituting, or furnishing a precedent. **2.** Having precedence, preceding, preliminary 1661.

Preceding (prĭsī·diŋ), *ppl.a.* 1494. [f. PRECEDE + -ING².] That precedes in order, time, or movement; *spec.* in *Astr.* said of a heavenly body, etc. situated to the west of another, and therefore moving in front of it in the apparent diurnal rotation of the heavens.

Precent (prĭse·nt), *v.* 1732. [ad. L. *præcentare* to sing before.] *intr.* To officiate as precentor. **b.** *trans.* To lead in singing (a psalm, antiphon, etc.).

Precentor (prĭse·ntǫ̈ı). 1613. [a. late L. *præcentor*, f. L. *præcinere, -cent-* to sing or play before (a person, etc.), f. *præ* PRE- + *canere.*] One who leads or directs the singing of a choir or congregation; *spec.* **a.** in cathedrals of the Old Foundation, a member of the chapter (ranking next to the dean), whose duties as precentor are now commonly discharged by the succentor; **b.** in those of the New Foundation, one of the minor canons or a chaplain, who performs the duties in person; **c.** the leader of the congregational singing in churches which have no choir, and esp. in those in which there is no instrumental accompaniment. **Prece·ntorship.** So **Prece·ntrix**, a female p.

Precept (prī·sept). late ME. [ad. L. *præceptum* maxim, command, f. *præcipere* to advise, instruct, f. *præ* PRE- A. + *capere* to take.] †**1.** An authoritative command to do some particular act; an order, mandate –1513. **2.** A general command or injunction; *esp.* an injunction as to moral conduct; a maxim. Usu. applied to divine commands. late ME. **b.** One of the practical rules of an art; a direction 1553. †**3.** A written order or mandate authorizing a person to do something; a warrant –1771. **4.** *spec.* **a.** A written or printed order issued by the King, a court, or a judge, to require the attendance of members of parliament, a court, or a jury, to direct the holding of an assize, to procure the appearance, arrest, or imprisonment of a delinquent, etc.; a writ, warrant 1444. **b.** A written order to arrange for and hold an election; usu. that issued by the sheriff to the returning officer 1684. **c.** An order for collection or demand for payment of money due under a rate 1877.

2. Example draws where p. fails 1708. **4. b.** The p. for the election has arrived 1865. **c.** The amount of the p. has been thus reduced 1888.

Preception (prĭse·pʃən). 1619. [ad. L. *præceptionem*, f. *præcipere*; see prec.] †**1.** A previous conception; a preconception, presumption (*rare*) –1640. **2.** *Rom. Law.* The right of receiving beforehand, as a part of an inheritance before partition 1875.

Preceptive (prĭse·ptiv), *a.* 1456. [ad. late L. *præceptivus*; see PRECEPT *sb.* and -IVE.] Of the nature of, pertaining to, or conveying a precept; mandatory; didactic, instructive.

The Law hath two parts,..the P. and the Punitive 1672. The didactive or p. Manner 1711.

Preceptor (prĭse·ptəı). 1440. [a. L. *præceptor* teacher; see PRECEPT and -OR 2.] **1.** One who instructs; a teacher, tutor. **2.** The head of a preceptory of Knights Templars 1710. So **Precepto·rial** *a.* of or pertaining to a p. **Prece·ptress**, a female p.

Preceptory (prĭse·ptəri). 1540. [ad. med. L. *præceptoria*; see PRECEPTOR and -ORY².] A subordinate community of the Knights Templars; the estate or manor supporting this, or its buildings. Cf. COMMANDERY.

‖ **Preces** (prī·sīz), *sb. pl.* 1450. [L., pl. of **prex, prec-* prayer.] *Liturg.* The short petitions which are said as verse and response by the minister and the congregation alternately.

Precession (prĭse·ʃən). ME. [ad. late L. *præcessionem*, f. *præcedere* to PRECEDE.] †¶**1.** An error for *procession* –1529. **2.** The action or fact of preceding; precedence 1628. **3.** *Phonetics.* Advance in oral position 1844.

P. of the equinoxes, often ellipt. *precession* (Astr.): the earlier occurrence of the equinoxes in each successive sidereal year, due to the retrograde motion of the equinoctial points along the ecliptic, produced by the slow change of direction in space of the earth's axis, which moves so that the pole of the equator describes a circle (see NUTATION) around the pole of the ecliptic once in about 25,800 years. Hence commonly used to denote this motion of the equinoctial points, of the earth's axis, or of the celestial pole or equator. *Lunisolar p.*, that part of the p. which is caused by the combined attractions of the moon and sun upon the mass of the earth. Hence **Prece·ssional** *a.* (*Astron.*).

Pre-Christian (prīkri·styăn, -tʃən), *a.* 1828. [PRE- B. I. 1.] **1.** Of or pertaining to times prior to the birth of Christ or the Christian era. **2.** Prior to the introduction of Christianity 1861.

‖ **Précieuse** (presyöz), *sb.* (*a.*). 1727. [F., fem. of *précieux* PRECIOUS (sense 3), used as sb. See Molière's *Les Précieuses ridicules.*] A woman affecting a refined delicacy of language and taste; usu. connoting ridiculous over-fastidiousness. **B.** *adj.* Affected after the style of *les précieuses* 1785.

Precinct (prī·siŋkt), *sb.* late ME. [ad. med. L. *præcinctum*, sb. use of neut. pa. pple. of *præcingere* to gird (in front), encircle, f. *præ* PRE- A. II. c + *cingere* to gird.] **1.** The space enclosed by the walls or other boundaries of a particular place or building, or by an imaginary line drawn around it; *esp.* the ground immediately surrounding a religious house or place of worship 1547. **b.** *esp.* in *pl.* The environs 1464. **2.** A girding or enclosing line or surface; a boundary, a compass. Also *fig.* 1542. **3.** A district defined for purposes of government or representation; *spec.* in U.S., a subdivision of a county or ward for election and police purposes. late ME.

1. b. Ye citie of York, suburbs, or precinctes of ye same 1485. *fig.* The warm precincts of the chearful day GRAY. **2.** Within the precincts of a petty island 1843. **3.** The smallest P. was that of the Parish 1647.

Precinct (prĭsi·ŋkt), *pa. pple.* and *ppl. a. rare.* 1641. [ad. L. *præcinctus, -cingere*; see prec.] Girt about; engirdled, encompassed.

Preciosity (preʃiǫ·sĭti). late ME. [a. OF. *preciosité*, ad. L. *pretiositas*, f. *pretiosus* PRECIOUS; see -ITY.] **1.** The quality of being precious or costly; preciousness. Now *rare* or *Obs.* **2.** Anything very costly. Now *rare* or *Obs.* 1485. **3.** Affectation of refinement or distinction, esp. in the use of language 1866.

3. The circles of Oxford p. 1887.

Precious (pre·ʃəs), *a.* (*sb.*, *adv.*) [ME. a. OF. *precios*, mod.F. *précieux*, ad. L. *pretiosus* costly, f. *pretium* price, value; see -OUS.] **1.** Of great price; valuable; costly. **b.** Used ironically; cf. FINE *a.* III. 1. 1619. **2.** Of great moral, spiritual, or non-material worth; held in high esteem ME. **3.** Affecting distinction in conduct, manners, language, etc.; fastidious; *esp.* in mod. use (after F.), affecting fastidious refinement in language, workmanship, etc.; often with an implication of over-refinement. late ME. **4.** *colloq.* As an intensive: Egregious, out-and-out, arrant; in some uses, a mere emotional intensive. late ME.

1. The Generalls pretious Jewel, or his Treasure HOBBES. *P. metals*: gold and silver; sometimes including platinum, and rarely mercury. *P. stone*, a gem; *p.* GARNET, OPAL, etc.: see those words. **b.** Are not these p. instructers of youth? WESLEY. **2.** Justice, which is a treasure far more p. than gold JOWETT. *P. blood*, the blood of Christ shed for man's redemption. So *p. body*. **3.** Elaborate embroidery of p. language 1887. **4.** It's hard enough to see one's way, a p. sight harder than I thought 1857.

B. *sb.* Precious one, dear 1706. **C.** *adv.* (qualifying adj. or adv.) **a.** = Preciously 1595. **b.** With intensive force: Extremely, very: *p. few*, few indeed. *colloq.* 1837. Hence **Pre·ciously** *adv.*, **-ness.**

Precipice (pre·sipis), *sb.* 1598. [= F. *précipice*, ad. L. *præcipitium*, f. *præceps, -cipit-* headlong, steep, precipitous.] †**1.** A headlong fall or descent, esp. to a great depth –1650. **2.** A vertical or very steep face of rock, etc.; a cliff, crag, or steep mountain side 1632. **b.** *fig.* A perilous situation 1651.

2. A Torrent, rowling down a P. DRYDEN. **b.** The precipices which environ beauty 1651. Hence **Pre·cipiced** (-ist) *ppl. a.* having, furnished, or formed with precipices.

Precipitable (prĭsi·pităb'l), *a.* 1670. [f. L. *præcipitare* to PRECIPITATE + -ABLE.] Capable of being precipitated from solution in a liquid, or from a state of vapour. Hence **Preci·pitabi·lity**, capability of being precipitated.

Precipitancy (prĭsi·pitănsi). 1619. [f. PRECIPITANT *a.*; see -ANCY.] The quality of being precipitant. **1.** Headlong speed, violent hurry 1646. **2.** Great want of deliberation; hastiness, rashness; an instance of this 1619. So **Preci·pitance** 1667.

Precipitant (prĭsi·pitănt), *a.* and *sb.* 1608. [ad. L. *præcipitantem*, pres. pple. of *præcipitare* to PRECIPITATE.] **A.** *adj.* (Now *rare*; usu. repl. by PRECIPITATE *a.*) **1.** Falling headlong; descending vertically or steeply; headlong; falling to the bottom as a precipitate or sediment 1620. **2.** Rushing headlong; moving hurriedly or very swiftly onwards 1671. **3.** Acting or taking place with great hurry, rapidity, or suddenness; very sudden or unexpected, abrupt 1641. **4.** Hasty, rash, headstrong 1608.

1. He..plunging, from his Back the Rider hurls P. 1735. **2.** That troop so blithe and bold,..P. in fear, wou'd wing their flight POPE. **3.** I was hard..either to discern the Rise, or apply a Remedy to that p. Rebellion 1641.

B. *sb. Chem.* A substance that causes precipitation. Sometimes const. *of* (the substance precipitated). 1684. Hence **Preci·pitantly** *adv.*

Precipitate (prĭsi·pitĕt), *sb.* 1563. [ad. mod.L. *præcipitatum*, sb. use of neut. pa. pple. of L. *præcipitare*; see PRECIPITATE *v.*] That which is precipitated; the product of precipitation. **a.** *Chem.* A body precipitated from any solution; any substance which, by the action of a chemical reagent, or of heat, etc., is separated from the liquid in which it was previously dissolved, and deposited in the solid state 1594. **b.** *Old Chem.* and *Pharm.*, applied *spec.* to certain preparations of mercury obtained by precipitation 1563. **c.** *Physics*, etc. Moisture condensed from the state of vapour by cooling, and deposited in drops, as rain, dew, etc. 1832.

b. *P. per se*, or *red p.*, mercuric oxide or red oxide of mercury, HgO; *white p.*, mercurammonium chloride, $HgH_6N_2Cl_2$ (*fusible white p.*), or dimercurammonium chloride, $Hg_2H_4N_2Cl_2$ (*infusible white p.*).

Precipitate (prĭsi·pitět), *a.* 1607. [ad. L. *præcipitatus*; see prec.] **1.** Hurled headlong; descending steeply or directly downwards; headlong 1614. †**b.** Of a place, etc.: Very steep, precipitous –1630. **2.** Moving or moved with excessive haste or speed; violently hurried 1654. **3.** Performed, taking place, acting, or passing with very great rapidity; greatly hurried; exceedingly sudden or abrupt 1658. **4. a.** Of persons, their dispositions, etc.: Over-hasty, rash, inconsiderate, headstrong 1607. **b.** Of acts, etc.: Done in sudden haste; hurried, rash, unconsidered 1618.

1. On the Shepherd's Fold He [an Eagle] darts p. 1703. 2. The general escaped by a p. flight GIBBON. 3. Their service consisted in p., and very irreverent chattering of certain Prayers and Hymns 1703. 4. a. If I could perswade these p. young Gentlemen to compose this Restlessness of Mind STEELE. b. A p. burning of his papers a few days before his death BOSWELL. Hence **Preci·pitately** *adv.*

Precipitate (prĭsi·pitēit), *v.* 1528. [f. L. *præcipitare*, f. *præceps*, *-cipitem* headlong, f. *præ* before + *caput* head; see -ATE[3].] **I. 1.** *trans.* To throw down headlong; to hurl or fling down. (Often *refl.*) 1575. **b.** *fig.* To hurl, fling (*into* some condition, or *upon* an object of attack) 1528. †**2.** *intr.* (for *refl.* or *pass.*) To fall headlong; to fall, gravitate –1785. †**b.** To descend steeply, as a river –1793. †**c.** *fig.* To 'plunge' *into* some condition or act; to fall or come suddenly to ruin or destruction –1758.

1. The garrison had no alternative but to perish by the..sword, or to p. themselves into the ocean 1774. b. Precipitated from the height of prosperity, into the depth of adversity 1662. 2. *Lear* IV. vi. 50.

II. 1. *trans.* To cause to move, pass, act, or proceed very rapidly; to hasten, hurry, urge on 1558. **b.** To bring on quickly, suddenly, or unexpectedly; to hasten the occurrence of 1625. **2.** *intr.* To rush headlong; to hurry; to move, act, or proceed very quickly 1622. †**b.** To be precipitate in action –1670.

1. Men are impatient, and for precipitating things 1736. b. They could not p. his departure 1748.

III. 1. *Chem. trans.* To deposit, or cause to be deposited, in a solid form from solution in a liquid, by chemical action; see PRECIPITATE *sb.* Also occas. to produce precipitation in (the solution); †to deposit from suspension or admixture in a liquid, as sediment, etc. 1644. **b.** *Physics*, etc. To condense (moisture) into drops from a state of vapour, and so deposit or cause to fall, as dew, rain, etc. 1863. **c.** *transf.* and *fig.*; *spec.* in *Spiritualism* = MATERIALIZE 2. 1825. **2.** *intr.* (for *refl.*) To be deposited from solution (or from suspension); to settle as a precipitate 1626.

1. b. The mass of ice cools the surrounding air, and thus precipitates its moisture HUXLEY. c. The world is mind precipitated EMERSON. 2. By what strong water every metal will p. BACON.

Precipitation (prĭsipitēi·ʃən). 1502. [a. F. *précipitation*, ad. L. *præcipitationem*; see prec.] **I.** The action of precipitating from a height; the fact of being precipitated; headlong fall or descent 1607. **b.** Precipitousness (*rare*) 1607.

In perill of p. From off the Rocke Tarpeian SHAKS.

II. 1. Violent onward motion 1624. **2.** Sudden and hurried action; hurry 1502. **b.** Unduly hurried action; inconsiderate haste 1629. **3.** Hastening, hurrying; acceleration 1621.

2. The lady having seized it, with great p., they retired DICKENS. b. We must not act with p. DISRAELI. 3. This..gave p. to his own downfall GOLDSM.

III. 1. *Chem.* Separation and deposition of a substance in a solid form from solution in a liquid, by the action of a chemical reagent, or of electricity, heat, etc. 1612. **b.** *concr.* The product of this process; a precipitate 1605. **2.** *Physics.* and *Meteorol.* Condensation and deposition of moisture from the state of vapour, as by cooling; *esp.* in the formation of dew, rain, snow, etc. **b.** *concr.* That which is so deposited. 1675. **3.** *fig.*; *spec.* in *Spiritualism* = MATERIALIZATION 1891.

Precipitator (prĭsi·pitēitəɹ). 1660. [a. late L. *præcipitator*; see PRECIPITATE *v.* and -OR.] **1.** One who precipitates something; a hastener. **2.** *Chem.* and *Physics.* A precipitant 1681. **b.** An apparatus for precipitation; *spec.* a tank for purifying hard water or sewage 1883.

Precipitin (prĭsi·pitin). 1900. [irreg. f. PRECIPIT(ATE + -IN[1].] *Biol. Chem.* A substance that causes precipitation from a solution.

Precipitous (prĭsi·pitəs), *a.* 1646. [ad. obs. F. *precipiteux*, ad. late L. **præcipitosus*, f. *præceps*, *-cipit-* headlong; see -OUS.] **I.** †**1.** = PRECIPITATE *a.* 4. –1734. †**2.** = PRECIPITATE *a.* 3. –1666. **3.** = PRECIPITATE *a.* 2. *rare.* 1774. **II.** Of the nature of a precipice; consisting of or characterized by precipices. (The usual sense.) 1806.

Salisbury Craig..is noted chiefly for its steep p. front 1806. Hence **Preci·pitous-ly** *adv.*, **-ness.**

‖**Précis** (prēi·si). 1760. [F. (presi), sb. use of *précis*; see next.] A concise or abridged statement; a summary; an abstract. **b.** *attrib.*, as *p.-writing*, etc. 1809. Hence **Pré·cis** *v. trans.*

Precise (prĭsəi·s), *a.* 1526. [= F. *précis*, *-ise*, ad. L. *præcisus*, pa. pple of *præcidere* to cut short, abridge, f. *præ* PRE- A. II. c + *cædere* to cut.] **1.** Strictly expressed; exactly defined; (of a person) definite and exact in statement. **b.** Of the voice or tone: Distinctly uttered 1848. **2.** Strict in the observance of rule, form, or usage; correct; punctilious, particular; occas., over-exact, fastidious; (of a practice or action): strictly observed 1530. **b.** *esp.* Strict in religious observance; in 16–17th c., puritanical 1566. **3.** Exact; neither more nor less than; perfect, complete; opp. to *approximate* 1571. **4.** Distinguished with precision from all others; identified, or stated, with exactness; *the p.*, the very, the exact 1628.

1. It is in a sense less strict and p., that we take the word 1775. He is very p. about dates and facts 1875. 2. Learned without pride, Exact, yet not p. COWPER. b. Men are now called 'precise', who will not connive at sin PUSEY. 3. A definition..should be P., that is, contain nothing unessential, nothing superfluous 1837. 4. The p. moment at which a traveller is passing 1860. Hence **Preci·se-ly** *adv.*, **-ness.**

Precise (prĭsəi·s), *v.* 1866. [a. F. *préciser* to determine exactly, f. *précis*: see prec.] *trans.* To make precise; to define precisely or exactly; to particularize.

Precisian (prĭsi·ʒăn). 1571. [f. PRECISE *a.* + -IAN.] One who is rigidly precise in the observance of rules or forms. **b.** *spec.* One who is precise in religious observances; in the 16–17th c. synonymous with *Puritan*.

A man may dwell upon words till he becomes.. a mere p. in speech 1834. b. A profane person calls a man of piety a p. 1725. Hence **Preci·sianism**, the practice of a p.; orig. applied to Puritanism.

Precision (prĭsi·ʒən). 1640. [a. F. *précision*, or ad. L. *præcisionem* a cutting off abruptly, f. *præcidere*; see PRECISE *a.*] **1.** The fact, condition, or quality of being precise; exactness, definiteness; distinctness, accuracy 1740. †**2.** The cutting off of one thing from another; *esp.* the mental separation of a fact or idea; abstraction. (App. used for *prescission*.) –1710.

1. The p. of statement, which..distinguishes science from common information HUXLEY. Hence **Preci·sionist** (also *erron.* (after *precisian*) **-anist**) one who makes a profession or practice of precision in observance or expression; a purist.

Precisive (prĭsəi·siv), *a. rare.* 1679. [f. L. *præcis-*, ppl. stem (see PRECISE *a.*) + -IVE.] **1.** That cuts off, separates, or defines one (person or thing) from another or others, as in *p. abstraction.* (app. for *prescissive*). **2.** Characterized by precision 1881.

Preclude (prĭklū·d), *v.* 1618. [ad. L. *præcludere*, f. *præ* PRE- A. II. c + *claudere* to shut.] **1.** *trans.* = FORECLOSE 2, 5. 1629. **2.** To close the door against, shut out; to exclude, prevent; to render impracticable by anticipatory action 1618. **3.** = FORECLOSE 3. 1736.

1. Every intellect was precluded by Prejudice JOHNSON. 2. They hesitated till death precluded the decision JOHNSON. 3. Employed in staff offices which p. them from the performance of regimental duties 1800. Hence **Preclu·sion** (now *rare*), the action of precluding; prevention by previous action. **Preclu·sive** *a.* that tends to p.; shutting out beforehand; preventive (*of*). **Preclu·sively** *adv.*

Precoce (prĭkōu·s), *a.* (*sb.*) *rare.* 1664. [a. F. *précoce*, ad. L. *præcocem*, *-cox*, f. *præcoquere*, f. *præ* PRE- A. I. 1 + *coquere* to cook.] **1.** Of plants: Early flowering. **2.** = PRECOCIOUS 2. 1689. **B.** *sb.* An early plant; *spec.* = *p. tulip* 1699.

Precocious (prĭkōu·ʃəs), *a.* 1650. [f. L. *præcox*, *-cocem* PRECOCE; see -IOUS.] **1.** Of a plant: Flowering or fruiting early; *spec.* having blossoms before the leaves; also said of the blossoms or fruit. **2.** *fig.* Of persons: Prematurely developed in some faculty or proclivity 1678. **b.** Of, pertaining to, or indicating precocity 1672. **c.** Of things: Of early development 1838.

1. Some expressions in Scripture concerning p. Figgs SIR T. BROWNE. 2. She was somewhat p. in love matters 1868. b. Untimely decrepitude was the penalty of p. maturity 1827. Hence **Preco·cious-ly** *adv.*, **-ness.**

Precocity (prĭkǫ·sĭti). 1640. [ad. F. *précocité*, f. (ult.) L. *præcox* PRECOCE.] The quality of being precocious. **1.** Of plants: Early flowering or ripeness 1656. **2.** Early maturity, premature development 1640. **b.** *transf.* A precocious child 1882.

2. Their productions..bear the marks of p. and premature decay HAZLITT.

Precognition (prĭkǫgni·ʃən). 1611. [ad. late L. *præcognitionem*, n. of action f. *præcognoscere* to foreknow, foresee.] **1.** Antecedent cognition or knowledge; foreknowledge. **2.** *Scots Law.* The preliminary examination of witnesses likely to know about the facts of a case, in order to obtain, with a view to trial, a general knowledge of the available evidence; a statement taken from such a witness 1661.

Precognosce (prĭkǫgnǫ·s), *v.* 1753. [f. PRE- A. I. 1 + COGNOSCE.] *Sc. Law. trans.* To make a preliminary examination of (witnesses); cf. prec. 2.

Preconceive (prĭkǫnsī·v), *v.* 1580. [PRE- A. I. 1.] *trans.* To conceive or imagine beforehand; to anticipate in thought. Hence **Preconcei·ved** *ppl. a.*

Preconception (prĭkǫnse·pʃən). 1625. [f. PRE- A. I. 2 + CONCEPTION.] The action of preconceiving; usu. (with *a* and *pl.*), a conception or opinion entertained prior to actual knowledge; a prepossession; an anticipation.

Preconce·rt, *v.* 1748. [f. PRE- A. I. 1 + CONCERT *v.*] *trans.* To concert or arrange beforehand. Hence **Preconce·rted** *ppl. a.*; **-ly** *adv.*, **-ness.**

Preconization (prĭkǫnəizēi·ʃən). 1644. [ad. med.L. *præconizationem*; see next.] **1.** Public proclamation. **2.** *spec.* in *R. C. Ch.* The public confirmation of an appointment (as that of a bishop) by the pope 1692.

Preconize (prī·kǫnəiz), *v.* Also **præ-**. late ME. [ad. med.L. *præconizare*, f. L. *præconem* public crier; see -IZE.] **1.** *trans.* To proclaim publicly; to commend or extol publicly, to cry up. **b.** To summon by name 1863. **2.** *spec.* in *R. C. Ch.* Of the pope: To approve publicly the appointment of (a bishop) 1692.

Pre:-conque·stal, -conque·stual, *a.* 1878. [PRE- B. I. 1.] Existing in, or belonging to, times preceding the (Norman) Conquest.

Preconscious (prĭkǫ·nʃəs), *a.* 1870. [PRE- B. I. 1.] Antecedent to consciousness, or to conscious action of some specified kind.

Preconsider (prĭkǫnsi·dəɹ), *v.* 1647. [PRE- A. I. 1.] *trans.* To consider beforehand or previously. So **Pre:considera·tion**, previous consideration; a preliminary consideration 1598.

Pre-contract (prĭkǫ·ntrækt), *sb.* 1483. [PRE- A. I. 2.] A pre-existing contract; a contract or agreement previously entered into: **a.** of marriage; **b.** *gen.* 1610.

a. He is your husband on a p. SHAKS.

Pre-contract (prĭkǫntræ·kt), *v.* 1579. [PRE- A. I. 1.] *trans.* **a.** To affiance or betroth beforehand. **b.** To establish (an agreement, etc.) by contract in advance. **c.** To acquire (habits, etc.) beforehand.

a. Nor could a contract with Percy have invalidated her marriage with the king..Percy having been pre-contracted to another person FROUDE.

Preco·racoid, *a.* and *sb.* 1870. [PRE- B. II.] **A.** *adj.* Situated anterior to the coracoid 1872. **B.** *sb.* A precoracoid bone or cartilage.

Precordial, præ- (prĭkǫ·ɹdiăl), *a.* 1562. [f. PRAECORDIA + -AL.] Situated in front of or about the heart; of or pertaining to the PRÆCORDIA.

‖**Precuneus, præ-** (prĭkiū·niǝ̆s). 1890. [f.

L. *præ* PRE- B. II. + *cuneus* wedge.] *Anat.* The quadrate lobule of the brain, situated immediately in front of the cuneate.

Precursive (prĭkɒ̄·ɹsiv), *a.* 1814. [f. L. *præcurs-*, *præcurrere* + -IVE.] = PRECURSORY.

Precursor (prĭkɒ̄·ɹsəɹ). 1504. [a. L. *præcursor*, agent-n. from *præcurrere* to run before.] **1.** One who or that which runs or goes before; a forerunner; *esp.* a harbinger; *spec.* applied to John the Baptist. **2.** One who precedes in some course or office 1792.

1. Shame, the p. of saving penitence 1856. 2. Cowper..by his genuine love of nature was a p. of Wordsworth 1879. Hence **Precu·rsorship**, the office or function of a p.; prior occurrence.

Precursory (prĭkɒ̄·ɹsəri), *a.* (*sb.*) 1599. [ad. L. *præcursorius*; see prec. and -ORY [2].] Having the character of a precursor; preceding, esp. as the harbinger or presage of something to follow; preliminary, introductory. **b.** as *sb.* A precursory fact, condition or symptom; an antecedent 1660.

Another symptom which is sometimes p. of exophthalmic goitre 1899.

Predacious (prĭdēⁱ·ʃəs), *a.* 1713. [f. L. **prædax*, *-ac-* (f. L. *prædari* to prey upon) + -OUS; see -ACIOUS.] **1.** Of animals: Naturally preying upon other animals; predatory, raptorial. Also of cells and organisms. **2.** Of or pertaining to predatory animals 1822. Hence **Preda·city.**

Predate (prīdēⁱ·t), *v.* 1864. [f. PRE- A. I. 1 + DATE *v.*] **1.** *trans.* To date before the actual time; to antedate. **2.** To precede in date 1889.

Predatory (pre·dătəri), *a.* 1589. [ad. L. *prædatorius*, f. *prædator*, f. *prædari* to plunder, spoil; see -ORY [2].] **1.** Of, pertaining to, characterized by, or consisting in plundering, pillaging, or robbery. **2.** Addicted to, or living by, plunder; plundering, marauding, thieving 1781. †**3.** Destructive, wasteful, deleterious –1711. **4.** Of an animal: That preys upon other animals; carnivorous. Also, of its organs of capture. 1668.

1. Prædatory excursions by sea and land GIBBON. 2. A p. and formidable race, the Mahrattas WELLINGTON. 3. Exercise..maketh the Spirits more hot and p. BACON. Hence **Pre·datorily** *adv.* **Pre·datoriness.**

Predecease (prīdĭsī·s), *v.* 1593. [f. PRE- A. I. 1 + DECEASE *v.*] *trans.* To die before (some person, or, rarely, some event). So **Predecea·se** *sb.* the death of one person before another 1765.

Predecessor (prī·dĭsesəɹ, prīdĭse·səɹ). [ME. *-our*, ad. F. *prédécesseur* or late L. *prædecessor*, f. *præ* PRE- A. + *decessor*, f. *decess-*, *decedere* to depart.] **1.** One who has preceded another in any office or position. **b.** A thing to which another has succeeded 1742. **2.** An ancestor, a forefather (now *rare*). late ME.

1. Eadmer's immediate p. in the see of St. Andrews was Turgot 1861. b. To-day is Yesterday return'd; ..Let it not share its predecessor's fate 1742.

Predefine (prīdĭfəi·n), *v.* 1542. [PRE- A. I. 1.] *trans.* To define, limit, appoint, or settle previously; to predetermine. So **Prede·finite** *a.* predetermined. **Predefini·tion,** predetermination.

Predella (prĭde·lă). 1848. [a. It. (prede·lla) kneeling-stool; prob. f. OHG. *pret* board + *-ella* dim. suffix.] **1.** The step or platform upon which an altar is placed, an altar-step, footpace; also, a painting or sculpture upon the vertical face of this 1853. **2.** = GRADINO 1848. **b.** *attrib.*, as *p. panel*, *picture* 1884.

Predesignate (prĭde·zignĕt, -de·s-), *a.* 1837. [f. PRE- A. I. 1 + DESIGNATE *ppl. a.*] **a.** Designated or specified beforehand. **b.** *Logic.* Of a proposition or term: Having a sign of quantity prefixed.

Predesignation (prīdezignēⁱ·ʃən, -des-). 1641. [PRE- A. I. 2; see -ATION.] **1.** Previous designation, appointment, or specification. **2.** *Logic.* A sign of quantity prefixed to a term or preposition 1840.

Predestinarian (prĭdestinē·riăn, prī-), *sb.* and *a.* 1638. [f. PREDESTINE *v.* + *-arian* (in *Trinitarian*, etc.).] **A.** *sb.* One who believes or maintains the theological doctrine of predestination; a fatalist 1667. **B.** *adj.* Of, pertaining to, concerning, or relating to predestination; holding or maintaining the doctrine of predestination.

b. Every Fatalist or P. scheme destroys merit J. MARTINEAU. Hence **Predestina·rianism,** the doctrine of predestinarians.

Predestinate (prĭde·stinĕt), *ppl. a.* and *sb.* late ME. [ad. L. *prædestinatus* pa. pple.; see next.] **A.** *ppl. a.* (as *adj.* or *pple.*) **1.** *Theol.* Foreordained by the eternal purpose of God to eternal life, or to any specified fate or lot. Also of things: Foreordained by divine decree. Const. *to*, or inf. with *to*. **2.** In more general sense: Destined beforehand; fated 1500.

1. Can the p. be lost, or the reprobate saved? 1833. 2. So some Gentleman or other shall scape a p. scratcht face SHAKS.

B. *sb. Theol.* A person predestinated to eternal life; one of the elect 1529.

Predestinate (prĭde·stineⁱt), *v.* 1450. [f. L. *prædestinat-*, *prædestinare*, in Chr. L. rendering Gr. προορίζειν to determine beforehand; f. L. *præ* PRE- A. I. 1 + *destinare* to make fast, appoint, etc. In Eng. the vb. was first PREDESTINE (q.v.).] **1.** *Theol.* Of God: To foreordain: **a.** to eternal life; **b.** to any fate or lot; to foreordain everything that comes to pass. **2.** To destine (as by fate); to fix beforehand by human (or animal) determination 1593.

1. a. He that is predestynate is written in the boke of lyfe 1530. b. These..taught that certain were by God's foreknowledge so predestinated to death that neither Christ's passion nor baptism..could help them 1887.

Predestination (prĭdestinēⁱ·ʃən, prī-). ME. ad. late L. *prædestinationem*, f. *prædestinare* to PREDESTINE; see -ATION.] **1.** *Theol.*, etc. The action by which God is held to have immutably determined all (or some particular) events by an eternal decree or purpose. **a.** The action of God in foreordaining certain of mankind through grace to salvation or eternal life (= *election*, and opp. to *reprobation*). **b.** The action of God in foreordaining whatever comes to pass; *esp.* the lot and fate of all men. late ME. **2.** *gen.* Previous determination or appointment; fate, destiny 1631.

1. a. The most blessed and comfortable doctrine of P. 1579. b. P. is as well to the reprobate, as to the Elect. Election pertaineth only to them that be saved. P., in that it respecteth the Reprobate, is called Reprobation: in that it respecteth the saved, is called Election. 1563. 2. A kind of moral p., or over-ruling principle which cannot be resisted JOHNSON.

Predestine (prĭde·stin), *v.* late ME. [a. F. *prédestiner*, or ad. L. *prædestinare*; see PREDESTINATE *v.*] *trans.* To destine beforehand; to ordain or decree previously. (Usu. *pass.*)

Predetermination (prīdĭtɜ̄ɹminēⁱ·ʃən). 1646. [f. next or (in some uses) f. PRE- A. I. 2 + DETERMINATION.] The action of predetermining; the fact or condition of being predetermined; previous determination.

The Calvinists are fierce in the matters of absolute P. JER. TAYLOR. Hear me, then, I beg of you, with no pre-determination to disregard me MISS BURNEY.

Predetermine (prīdĭtɜ̄·ɹmin), *v.* 1625. [ad. Chr. L. *prædeterminare*, f. *præ* PRE- A. I. 1 + *determinare* to DETERMINE.] To determine beforehand. **1.** *trans.* To fix beforehand; to decree beforehand, to predestine. Also with *obj. cl.* or *inf.* **2.** To direct or impel beforehand (*to* something) 1667. **3.** *intr.* To determine beforehand or previously (*to do* something) 1823.

1. Every man's end being predetermined, and unalterably..decreed DE FOE. 3. He had almost predetermined to assent to his brother's prayer LYTTON. Hence **Predete·rminable** *a. rare*, determinable beforehand. **Predete·rminate** *a.* determined beforehand.

Predial (prī·diăl), *a.* (*sb.*) Also **prædial.** 1464. [ad. med.L. *prædialis*, f. L. *prædium* a farm, etc.; see -AL.] **1.** Consisting of or pertaining to land or farms; 'real', landed; rural; agrarian 1529. **2.** Arising from the occupation of farms or lands: agrarian 1641. **3.** Attached to farms or to the land; owing service as tenanting land 1754. **B.** *sb.* [adj. used ellipt.] †A predial tithe; a predial slave 1531.

2. The p. or rural disorders of Ireland 1833. *P. tithe*: tithe derived from the produce of the soil. 3. *P. serf, slave, labour, servitude, villeinage*, etc.

Predicable (pre·dikăb'l), *a.* and *sb.* 1551. [a. F. *prédicable* adj. and sb., or ad. L. *prædicabilis*, f. *prædicare* to PREDICATE; see -ABLE.] **A.** *adj.* That may be predicated or affirmed; capable of being asserted 1598.

A people of whom great good is p. CARLYLE. Hence **Pre:dicabi·lity.**

B. *sb. gen.* That which may be predicated 1785. **b.** *spec.* in Aristotelian Logic (in *pl.*, tr. Gr. κατηγορικά): The classes or kinds of predicates viewed relatively to their subjects, to one or other of which classes every predicated thing may be referred; second intentions of predicates in relation to subjects 1551.

Of these relations Aristotle (*Topica* I. iv. v) recognized four, viz. *genus* (γένος), *definition* (ὅρος), *property* (ἴδιον), *accident* (συμβεβηκός). The 'Five Predicables', *genus, species, difference, property, accident*, are due to Porphyry and the Schoolmen, who substituted *species* for *definition*.

Predicament (prĭdi·kămĕnt). late ME. [ad. late L. *prædicamentum*, f. *prædicare*; see PREDICATE *v.* and -MENT.] **1.** That which is predicated or asserted; *spec.* in *Logic.* (in *pl.*) the ten categories formed by Aristotle; see CATEGORY 1. **2.** A class about which a statement is made 1548. **3.** State of being; condition, situation, position; *esp.* an unpleasant, trying, or dangerous situation 1586.

3. His deep sense of..the cruel p. to which he was reduced SCOTT. Hence **Predicame·ntal** *a.*; -ly *adv.*

Predicant (pre·dikănt), *a.* and *sb.* 1590. [ad. L. *prædicans*, *-antem*, *prædicare* to proclaim, f. *præ* forth + *dicare* to make known; as *sb.*, a. F. *prédicant* or Du. *predikant* a Protestant preacher.] **A.** *adj.* Given to or characterized by preaching; applied esp. to the Dominicans or Black Friars 1629. **B.** *sb.* A preacher; *spec.* a member of a predicant religious order. Now *rare* or *Obs.* 1590. **b.** = PREDIKANT.

These stipendiary, roving predicants 1590.

Predicate (pre·dikĕt), *sb.* 1532. [ad. late and med.L. *prædicatum* that which is said of the subject, sb. use of neut. pa. pple. of *prædicare* (see next.)] **1.** *Logic.* That which is predicated or said of the subject in a proposition; the second term of a proposition, which is affirmed or denied of the first term by means of the copula. (At first used in L. form, *prædicatum.*) **2.** *Gram.* The statement made about a subject, including the logical copula (which in a verb is expressed by the personal suffix) 1638. **b.** An appellation that asserts something 1882. **c.** A quality, an attribute 1872.

1. Existence is its own p. [i. e. The word *is* when it means *exists* is a p. as well as a copula] COLERIDGE. 2. Thus in the sentence 'Time flies', *time* is called the subject, and *flies* the p...In using the word *predicate*, we mean the p. and copula combined. 1858.

Predicate (pre·dikeⁱt), *v.* 1552. [f. ppl. stem of L. *prædicare* to cry in public, proclaim, hence, to declare, in med.L. to preach, and in Logic, to assert, f. *præ* forth + *dicare* to proclaim; see -ATE [3].] **1.** *trans.* To proclaim, declare; to affirm, assert; also, to preach; to preach up, extol (*rare* or *obs.*) **b.** *intr.* or *absol.* To assert, affirm; to make a statement 1827. **2.** *spec. trans.* To assert or affirm as a quality, property, or attribute (*of* something) 1614. **b.** *Logic.* To state or assert (something) about the subject of a proposition 1570. **3.** To affirm (a statement or the like) *on* some given grounds; hence, 'to found a proposition, argument, etc. *on* some basis or data' (Bartlett); and *transf.* to found or base (anything) *on* or *upon* stated facts or conditions. *U.S.* 1766. ¶**4.** *erron.* = PREDICT *v.* 1623.

1. b. To think is mentally to p. 1866. 2. b. The famous..*Dictum de omni et nullo*, that whatever is predicated..universally of any Class. may be also predicated of any part of that Class 1864. 3. This.. is predicated upon my confidence in his ability 1839.

Predication (predikēⁱ·ʃən). [ME. a. OF. *predicaciun*, mod.F. *prédication*, ad. L. *prædicationem*; see prec.] **1.** The action of publicly or loudly proclaiming; preaching; an instance of this; a sermon, discourse. *Obs.* or *arch.* **2.** The action of predicating or asserting, or an instance of this; assertion, affirmation 1579. **b.** *spec.* in *Logic*: The assertion of something of or about a subject 1638.

Predicative (prĭdi·kătiv), *a.* 1846. [ad. L. *prædicativus*; see PREDICATE *v.* and -IVE.] Having the quality of predicating, affirming, or asserting. Hence **Predi·catively** *adv.*

Predicator (pre·dikeⁱtəɹ). Now *rare.* 1483.

[a. OF. *predicatour*, ad. L. *prædicator*, f. *prædicare* to PREDICATE.] One who or that which predicates; *spec.* a preacher, a preaching friar. So Predicatory (pre·dikĕtəri, -keⁱ·təri) *a.*

Predict (pri̅di·kt), *v.* 1546. [f. L. *prædict-*, *prædicere* to foretell, etc., f. *præ* PRE- A. I. 1 + *dicere* to say, tell.] †1. *trans.* To mention previously –1599. 2. To foretell, prophesy, announce beforehand (an event, etc.) 1623. 3. *intr.* To utter prediction; to prophesy 1652.

2. How often an observer can p. a man's actions 1884. 3. No one can p. as to the length of her life MRS. CARLYLE. Hence **Predi·ctable** *a.* **Predictabi·lity.** **Predi·ctive** *a.* having the quality of predicting; **-ly** *adv.*; **-ness.** **Predi·ctor, -er,** one who or that which predicts. **Predi·ctory** *a.* of or pertaining to a predictor; predictive.

Prediction (pri̅di·kʃən), *sb.* 1561. [ad. L. *prædictionem.*] The action of predicting; also, an instance of this, a prophecy.

Dreames, and Predictions of Astrologie BACON.

Predigest (pri̅didʒe·st, -dəi-), *v.* 1663. [f. PRE- A. I. 1 + DIGEST *v.*] *trans.* To digest beforehand; *spec.* to treat (food), before its introduction into the body, by a process similar to digestion.

Predigestion (pri̅didʒe·styən, -tʃən, -dəi-). 1607. [f. PRE- A. I. 2 + DIGESTION.] †1. Over-hasty digestion –1698. 2. Digestion by artificial means before introduction into the stomach 1890.

‖ **Predikant** (predika·nt). Also **predicant.** 1849. [Du.; see PREDICANT.] A minister of the Dutch Protestant Church, esp. in S. Africa.

Predilection (pri̅dile·kʃən). 1742. [a. F. *prédilection*, f. (ult.) med.L. *prædiligere* to choose or love before others; see DILECTION.] A mental preference or partiality; a favourable predisposition or prepossession.

Robert had never testified much p. for violent exertion SCOTT.

Predisponent (pri̅dispōu·nĕnt), *a.* and *sb.* 1649. [f. PRE- A. I. 1, 2 + DISPONENT.] A. *adj.* Predisposing. Now *rare.* B. *sb.* A predisposing influence or cause 1771.

Predispose (pri̅dispōu·z), *v.* 1646. [PRE- A. I. 1.] 1. *trans.* To dispose (a person, etc.) beforehand; to render subject or liable *to* something; to incline or adapt previously. Also *absol.* 2. To dispose of before 1666.

1. The majority of his judges..came predisposed to condemn him 1871. So **Predispo·sal,** previous disposal. **Predispo·sed** *ppl. a.* disposed or inclined beforehand; previously or already liable or subject.

Predisposition (pri̅dispŏzi·ʃən). 1622. [PRE- A. I. 2.] 1. The condition of being predisposed or inclined beforehand (*to* or *to do* something); a previous inclination or favourable state of mind 1626. 2. *spec.* A physical condition which renders its possessor liable to the attack of certain diseases 1622.

1. A p. to heresy MACAULAY. 2. P. to Small-pox 1801.

Predominance (pri̅dǫ·minăns). 1602. [f. as next + -ANCE.] The fact or position of being predominant: a. *Astrol.* Ascendancy, superior influence 1605. b. *gen.* Prevailing or superior influence; prevalence, preponderance 1602.

b. The early p. of intellectual vigour BOSWELL. So **Predo·minancy,** the quality or fact of being predominant.

Predominant (pri̅dǫ·minănt), *a.* and *sb.* 1576. [a. F. *prédominant*, ad. L. **prædominantem*, pres. pple. of **prædominari, -are*, f. *præ* PRE- A. III. + *dominari, -are* to be master, rule.] A. *adj.* Having ascendancy, power, influence, or authority over others; superior, ascendant, prevalent. b. More vaguely: More abundant; more frequent; prevailing 1601. c. *fig.* Superior in position 1797.

The temporary effect of a p. passion JOHNSON. *P. partner*: applied (after Lord Rosebery) to England among the several constituents of the United Kingdom. b. The p. winds HUXLEY. c. Made the roofs boldly p. 1867.

B. *sb.* That which predominates; a predominating person, influence, power, or authority; a predominating quality, fact, or feature 1589. Hence **Predo·minantly** *adv.*

Predo·minate, *a.* mistaken form for prec.

Predominate (pri̅dǫ·mineⁱt), *v.* 1594. [f. med.L. **prædominare*, f. *præ* PRE- A. III. + *dominari, -are* to rule: see -ATE [3].] †1. *intr. Astrol.* To have ascendancy, to exert controlling influence –1633. 2. *gen.* a. To have or exert controlling power, to lord it *over*; to be superior 1618. b. To be the stronger, main, or leading element; to preponderate 1594. c. To tower *over* 1814. 3. *trans.* To dominate over, control. Now *rare.* 1607.

1. *Merry W.* II. ii. 294. 2. a. The women in those parts never p. 1638. b. The desires that p. in our hearts JOHNSON. 3. *Timon* IV. iii. 142. So **Predomina·tion,** the action, fact, or condition of predominating; predominance; ascendancy 1586.

Predoom (pri̅dū·m), *v.* 1618. [PRE- A. I. 1.] *trans.* a. To pronounce the doom of beforehand. b. To foreordain (some doom) *to.*

Pre-election (pri̅ˌi̅le·kʃən), *sb.* Also **præ-.** 1589. [PRE- A. I. 1.] †1. Selection, preference –1629. 2. Previous choice; an anticipatory election 1611.

Pre-election (pri̅ˌi̅le·kʃən), *adj. phr.* 1893. [f. PRE- B. I. 1 + ELECTION.] Occurring or given before a parliamentary (or other) election.

Pre-eminence (priˌe·minĕns). Also †**preh-** (*h* inserted to avoid hiatus). ME. [ad. late L. *præeminentia*, f. L. *præeminentem*; see -ENCE.] Surpassing eminence. 1. Higher rank or distinction; precedence; superiority. 2. Superiority in any quality; the possession or existence of a quality or attribute in a pre-eminent degree. late ME. 3. With *a* and *pl.* An individual case or instance of pre-eminence. Now *rare.* ME.

1. They allowed p. to their Magistrates rather than Supremacy 1647. 2. Shakspere's p. consists chiefly in this, that he did supremely well what all were doing 1883. 3. The office, the powers and preheminences annexed to it, differ very widely BURKE. So **Pre-e·minency** (now *rare*).

Pre-eminent (priˌe·minĕnt), *a.* Also †**preh-.** late ME. [ad. L. *præeminentem*, *præeminere* to excel, f. *præ* PRE- A. III. + *eminere*; see EMINENT.] Eminent before or above others; excelling others; distinguished beyond others. MILT. *P. L.* VIII. 279. Hence **Pre-e·minently** *adv.*

Pre-empt (priˌe·mᵖt), *v.* Chiefly *U.S.* 1857. [Back-formation from next.] *trans.* To obtain by pre-emption; hence (*U.S.*), to occupy (public land) so as to establish a pre-emptive title. Also *absol.* b. *fig.* To appropriate beforehand, pre-engage. Also *intr.* 1872. c. *Auction Bridge.* To make a pre-emptive bid 1914. So **Pre-e·mptive** *a.* relating or belonging to, or of the nature of pre-emption. **Pre-e·mptor** (*U.S.*), one who acquires land by pre-emption.

Pre-emptive bid (Auction Bridge): a bid intended to be high enough to prevent further bidding.

Pre-emption (priˌe·mᵖʃən). 1602. [ad. med.L. **præemptionem*, f. **præemere*; see PRE- A. I. 2 and EMPTION.] Purchase by one person or corporation before an opportunity is offered to others; also, the right to make such purchase; *spec.*

a. Formerly in England, the prerogative of the sovereign of buying household provisions in preference to other persons, and at special rates. b. In U.S., Australia, etc., the purchase, or right of purchase, in preference and at a nominal price, of public land by an actual occupant, on condition of his improving it.

Preen (pri̅n), *sb.* Now *Sc.* and *n. dial.* [OE. *préon.*] a. A pin, a brooch. b. As type of a thing of small value 1470.

Preen (pri̅n), *v.*[1] Now *Sc.* and *n. dial.* ME. [f. prec. sb.] †1. *trans.* To sew; to stitch up –1513. †2. To pierce; to transfix –1460. 3. To fasten with a pin; to pin 1572.

Preen (pri̅n), *v.*[2] late ME. [app. orig. var. of PRUNE *v.*[1], assim. to PREEN *v.*[1]] 1. *trans.* Of a bird: To trim (the feathers) with the beak 1486. 2. *refl.* Of a person: To trim oneself up; to smooth and adorn oneself. late ME.

Pre-engage (pri̅·ĕngeⁱ·dʒ), *v.* 1646. [PRE- A. I. 1.] 1. *trans.* To bind in advance by a pledge or promise; to put under obligation beforehand 1649. b. *spec.* To betroth beforehand. Usu. *pass.* or *refl.* 1673. c. *intr.* To guarantee or engage beforehand. (With *inf.* or *subord. cl.*) 1654. 2. *trans.* a. To win over beforehand, to prepossess 1646. b. To bespeak for oneself beforehand 1683. 3. To preoccupy. Now *rare.* 1656.

1. She pressed me to stay dinner, but..I informed her that I was pre-engaged 1785. 2. b. To pre-ingage his Vote 1712.

Pre-engagement (pri̅·ĕngeⁱ·dʒmĕnt). 1647. [PRE- A. I. 2.] 1. The act of pre-engaging, or fact of being already engaged. 2. An engagement previously given or made 1647. b. *spec.* A prior marriage engagement 1684.

1. Two chairs had been tilted up in token of pre-engagement 1896.

Pre-establish (pri̅ˌĕstæ·bliʃ), *v.* 1643. [PRE- A. I. 1.] *trans.* To establish beforehand.

Pre-established harmony (after F. *harmonie préétablie* Leibnitz): see HARMONY 1.

Pre-exilian (pri̅ˌĕgzi·liăn, -ĕks-), *a.* 1863. [f. PRE- B. I. 1 + L. *exilium* EXILE + -AN.] Before exile; *spec.* of or belonging to the period of Jewish history before the Babylonian exile. So **Pre-exi·lic, Pre-e·xile** *adjs.*

Pre-exist (pri̅ˌĕgzi·st), *v.* 1599. [PRE- A. I. 1.] 1. *intr.* To exist before. b. To exist before the present life 1647. c. To exist ideally, before material embodiment 1775. 2. *trans.* To exist before (something) 1778.

Pre-exi·stence. 1652. [PRE- A. I. 2.] Previous existence; *esp.* of the soul before its union with the body.

Pre-existent (pri̅ˌĕgzi·stĕnt), *a.* 1624. [PRE- A. I. 3.] Existing beforehand, or before some person, thing, or event.

Preface (pre·fĕs), *sb.* late ME. [a. F. *préface*, app. ad. med.L. *prefatia*, substituted for L. *præfatio*, f. *præfari*; see PREFATORY.] I. In the liturgies of Christian Churches: The introduction or prelude to the central part of the Eucharistic service (the consecration, etc.) concluding with the Sanctus.

Proper P., a variation of the Common P., to be used at certain seasons, including a special part proper to the particular occasion.

II. 1. The introduction to a literary work, usu. explaining its subject, purpose, scope, and method. late ME. 2. The introductory part of a speech; an introduction 1530. 3. *fig.* Something preliminary or introductory 1594.

1. I have run into a p., while I professed to write a dedication FIELDING. 2. This superficiall tale, Is but a p. of her worthy praise SHAKS.

Preface (pre·fĕs), *v.* 1616. [f. prec. sb.] 1. *intr.* To make introductory remarks 1619. 2. *trans.* To write or say (something) as a preface; to state beforehand. Now *rare* or *Obs.* 1628. †3. *fig.* To introduce, precede, herald –1807. 4. To furnish (a book, etc.) with a preface; to commence (a writing or speech) with a preface or introduction 1691. 5. *fig.* To place in front of; to face (*with* something) 1658. 6. To come before as an introduction 1843.

1. I will p. no longer, but proceed WALTON. 4. I must p. this letter with an honest declaration SWIFT. 5. Not prefacing old Rags with Plush 1658. 6. A depressing..passage has prefaced every new page I have turned in life C. BRONTË. Hence **Pre·facer,** one who makes or writes a p.

Prefatorial (prefătōᵊ·riăl), *a.* 1799. [f. as next + -AL.] Of or pertaining to a prefacer or a preface; prefatory. Hence **Prefato·rially** *adv.*

Prefatory (pre·fătəri), *a.* 1671. [f. L. **præfatorius*, f. **præfator*, f. *præfari*, f. *præ* PRE- A. I. 1 + *fari* to speak; see -ORY [2].] Of the nature of a preface; introductory, preliminary.

The P. Note which precedes the volume 1860. Hence **Pre·fatorily** *adv.*

Prefect, præfect (pri̅·fekt). ME. [a. OF. *prefect*, mod.F. *préfet*, ad. L. *præfectus* an overseer, etc.; sb. use of pa. pple. of *præficere* to set over, f. *præ* PRE- A. III + *facere* to appoint.] 1. A person appointed to a position of command. Applied as a title to various officers in ancient or modern times. a. Repr. L. *præfectus*, In ancient Rome and the Roman empire, the title of various officers civil and military, e.g. the prefect or chief magistrate of the city, *præfectus urbi*, the civil governor of a province, a colony, or provincial city, the commander of the pretorian troops, *præfectus prætorio*, etc. ME. b. *esp.* (repr. F. *préfet.*) The chief administrative officer of a department of France. *P. of Police*, the head of the police administration in Paris and the department of the Seine. 1827. 2. *transf.* In some English Schools, one of the body of senior pupils to whom authority is delegated for the maintenance of order and discipline 1629. So **Prefe·ctoral, Prefecto·rial** *adjs.* of or pertaining to a p. or prefects; *esp.* in the English Public School system. **Pre·fectship** = next 1.

Prefecture (pri̅·fektiŭɹ). 1577. [ad. L. *præfectura*; see prec. and -URE.] 1. The office or position of prefect, ancient or modern; the period during which such office is held 1608. **2.** A district under the government of a prefect 1577. **b.** = Chinese *fu*, an administrative district of a province; also a corresponding district in Japan 1885. **3.** The official residence of a prefect or French *préfet* 1848. Hence **Pre·fe·ctural** *a.* So **Prefe·ctureship** 1559.

Prefer (prɪ̆fɔ̄·ɪ), *v.* late ME. [a. F. *préférer*, ad. L. *præferre*, f. *præ* PRE- A. II, III + *ferre* to bear.] **I. 1.** *trans.* To put forward, in status, rank, or fortune; to promote (*to* a position or office). **b.** *transf.* To promote (in various uses) 1533. **†2.** To forward, advance, promote (a result); to assist in bringing about –1647.

1. Happy..that he never preferred a Man who has not proved remarkably serviceable to his Country STEELE. **b.** All Grasiers preferre their Cattell from meaner Pastures to better BACON. **2.** Thus fingring money to preferre the case 1600.

II. †1. *trans.* To put or set in front or before –1575. **2.** To put (something) before any one for acceptance; to hold out, offer; to introduce or recommend. *Obs.* or *arch.* 1573. **3.** To lay (a matter) before any one formally for consideration, approval, or sanction; to bring forward (a statement, bill, indictment, etc.) 1559.

2. He spake, and to her hand preferr'd the bowl POPE. **3.** Preferring an indictment against her for stealing his goods 1884.

III. To set or hold (one thing) before another in favour or esteem; to choose rather; to like better. Now the chief sense. late ME. **b.** *Law.* To give preference to as a creditor. late ME.

Afore all worldly thynges prefarre thou the honour & medytacion of god 1502. Hence **Pre·ferable** *a.* worthy to be preferred; more desirable; whence **Pre·ferabi·lity, Pre·ferableness,** the quality of being preferable. **Pre·ferably** *adv.* **Prefe·rred** *ppl. a.* in senses of the vb.; *Preferred share, stock* = PREFERENCE *share, stock.*

Preference (pre·fĕrĕns). 1603. [a. F. *préférence*, ad. med.L. *præferentia*, f. L. *præferent-*, *præferre* to PREFER; see -ENCE.] **1.** The action of preferring or the fact of being preferred; liking for one thing before another; prior favour or choice 1656. **†2.** Precedence, superiority –1793. **3.** That which one prefers; the favourite 1864. **4.** Preferment; promotion. Now *rare.* 1656. **5.** A prior claim to something; *spec.* priority of payment given to a certain debt or class of debts; a prior right to payment 1665. **b.** Short for *p. share* 1890. **6.** *Pol. Econ.* The practical favouring of one customer before others in business relations; *spec.* the favouring of one country by admitting its products at a lower import duty than that levied on those of others or of foreigners generally, or by levying a duty on the latter while admitting the former free 1887.

1. [It] can't be that the mind is indifferent before it comes to have a choice, or till it has a P. 1754. **3.** Of the two, this is my p. (*mod. colloq.*). **5.** *Fraudulent p.*, prior payment made by a bankrupt with the object of preventing the equal distribution of his assets among all his creditors. **6.** Still less am I afraid to preach to you p. with our Colonies J. CHAMBERLAIN. *attrib.* and *Comb.*, as **p. bond, share, stock,** i. e. on which dividend or interest is payable before any is paid on ordinary stock.

Pre·ferent, *a.* 1883. [ad. L. *præferentem*, pr. pple. of *præferre* to PREFER.] Having preference or precedence; having a right to priority of payment or consideration.

Preferential (prefĕre·nʃăl), *a.* 1849. [f. med.L. *præferentia* PREFERENCE + -AL.] Of, pertaining to, or of the nature of preference; showing or giving, receiving or enjoying, a preference. **b.** *Pol. Econ.* Of the nature of or characterized by import duties favouring particular countries, *spec.* in favour of trade between Great Britain and her colonies 1903.

The king was allowed a 'p.' claim on the public revenue STUBBS. **b.** A p. treatment of 12½ per cent. 1903. Hence **Prefere·ntialism,** the system of giving preference in the fixing of a tariff. **Prefere·ntialist,** an advocate of preference in tariff relations. **Prefere·ntially** *adv.*

Preferment (prɪ̆fɔ̄·ɪmĕnt). 1451. [f. PREFER + -MENT.] **I. †1.** Furtherance, promotion –1581. **2.** Advancement in condition, status, or position in life; in early use, also, that which is done or given towards the advancement of the children of a family 1478. **3.** A post which gives social or pecuniary advancement; usu. an eccl. appointment 1536.

2. Vpon hope of p. to the diuinitie lecture in Oxforde 1553.

II. †a. The action or fact of preferring as more desirable; the giving of preference; preference, advantage –1754. **b.** *spec.* Priority of right, claim, or privilege; *esp.* prior right to receive payment, or to purchase or offer for anything to be sold or let. *arch.* 1451.

Prefigurate (prɪ̆fi·giŭreɪt), *v.* Now *rare.* 1530. [f. ppl. stem of late L. *præfigurare* to PREFIGURE; see -ATE[3].] = PREFIGURE. So **Prefi·gurate** *ppl. a.* prefigured.

Prefiguration (prɪ̆figiŭrē·ʃən). late ME. [ad. L. *præfigurationem*, n. of action f. *præfigurare* to PREFIGURE.] **1.** The action of prefiguring; representation beforehand by a figure or type. **2.** That in which something is prefigured; a prototype 1600.

Prefigurative (prɪ̆fi·giŭrĕtiv), *a.* 1504. [ad. med.L. *præfigurativus*; see PREFIGURATE *v.* and -IVE.] Prefiguring, foreshadowing by a figure or type.

Prefigure (prɪ̆fi·gəɪ, -iŭɪ), *v.* 1450. [ad. late L. *præfigurare*; see PRE- A. I. 1 and FIGURE *v.*] **1.** *trans.* To represent beforehand by a figure or type. **2.** To figure or picture to oneself beforehand 1626.

1. The Jews Baptisme prefigured our spiritual washing 1651. Hence **Prefi·gurement,** the action or fact of prefiguring; the embodiment of this.

Prefix (prī·fiks), *sb.* 1646. [ad. mod.L. *præfixum*, sb. use of neut. of *præfixus*, *præfigere*; see PRE- A. II. c and FIX *v.*] **1.** *Gram.* A verbal element placed before and joined to a word or stem to add to or qualify its meaning, or (in some languages) as an inflexional formative. **2.** A title prefixed to a person's name, as *Mr.*, *Dr.*, etc. 1836. **3.** The act of prefixing (*rare*) 1793.

Prefix (prɪ̆fi·ks, *in* I. 1 *also* prī·fi·ks), *v.* late ME. [a. OF. *prefixer*; see PRE- A. I. 1, II. c, and FIX *v.*] **I.** In ref. to time. **1.** *trans.* To fix beforehand (esp. a time). Now *rare.* **†2.** To fix or determine in one's mind beforehand; to resolve on; to make up (the mind) beforehand –1652. **II.** In ref. to order or place. **1.** To place at the beginning of a book or writing, esp. as an introduction or title 1538. **2.** *Gram.* To place (a word or particle) before a word, esp. in combination with it; cf. PREFIX *sb.* 1. Const. *before* (rare), *to.* 1605.

1. The legislator..will p. preambles to his principal laws 1875. **2.** In English, we generally p. the relative Article to the names of our rivers 1845.

Prefixion (prɪ̆fi·kʃən). 1526. [a. F. *préfixion*, ad. L. *præfixionem, n. of action f. *præficere* to PREFIX.] **†1.** Preappointment –1754. **2.** *Gram.* Employment of a prefix 1811.

Prefixture (prɪ̆fi·kstiŭɪ). Also **præ-**. 1821. [f. PREFIX *v.* after FIXTURE.] **1.** The action of prefixing, esp. in grammar 1824. **2.** A word prefixed; a prefix 1821.

Prefloration (prɪ̆florē·ʃən). 1832. [ad. F. *préfloraison*, f. *pré-* PRE- B, + L. *flos, florem*; see -ATION.] = ÆSTIVATION 3.

Prefoliation (prɪ̆fōuliˌē·ʃən). Also **præ-**. 1856. [a. F. *préfoliation*; see PRE- B. and FOLIATION.] = VERNATION.

Preform (prī-, prɪ̆fǭ·ɪm), *v.* 1601. [ad. L. *præformare*; see PRE- A. I. 1 and FORM *v.*[1]] *trans.* To form or shape beforehand. Hence **Preformed** (prī·fǭ·ɪmd) *ppl. a.* formed beforehand, previously formed.

Preformation (prīfǭɪmē·ʃən). Also **præ-**. 1732. [f. PRE- A. I. 2 + FORMATION.] The action or process of forming or shaping beforehand; previous formation.

Theory of p. (Biol.): the theory, formerly prevalent, that all the parts of the perfect organism exist previously formed in the germ, and are merely 'developed' in the process of reproduction; opp. to *theory of* EPIGENESIS.

Preformative (prɪ̆fǭ·ɪmătiv), *a.* (*sb.*) Also **præ-**. 1821. [PRE- A. I. 3, II.] **1.** Having the quality or capacity of forming beforehand 1841. **2.** *Philol.* Prefixed as a formative element; said of a letter, syllable, etc. 1821. **B.** *sb. Philol.* A preformative particle; a prefix (esp. in Semitic langs.) 1821.

Prefrontal (prīfrɒ·ntăl), *a.* (*sb.*) Also **præ-**. 1854. [f. PRE- A., B. + L. *frons, front-* forehead + -AL.] *Anat.*, etc. **a.** Situated in front of the frontal bone of the skull. **b.** Situated in the fore part of the frontal lobe of the brain. **B.** *sb.* (*ellipt.* for *p. bone.*) A portion of the ethmoid, which forms a distinct bone in some reptiles, batrachians, and fishes 1854.

Pre-glacial (prīglē·ʃiăl), *a.* 1855. [PRE- B. I. 1 b.] Existing or occurring previous to the glacial period.

Pregnable (pre·gnăb'l), *a.* [Late ME. *prenable*, a. F., f. *prendre* :—L. *prendere* = *prehendere* to seize.] Of a fortress: Capable of being taken by assault. Also *transf.* **b.** *fig.* Open to attack; vulnerable 1836.

A strong hold kept by a coward is p. HOLLAND. **b.** A hard-headed English infidel, p. to neither religion nor common-sense 1837.

Pregnancy[1] (pre·gnănsi). 1529. [f. PREGNANT *a.*[2]; see -ANCY.] **1.** The condition of being pregnant, or with child or young; gestation. **2.** *transf.* Of the soil, etc.: Fertility, fruitfulness; abundance 1615. **3.** *fig.* In ref. to the mind: Fertility, productiveness, inventiveness, imaginative power; quickness of wit 1550. **4.** In ref. to speech, words, actions, etc.: Latent capacity to produce results, potentiality 1818.

3. Pregnancie is made a Tapster, and hath his quicke wit wasted in giuing Recknings SHAKS. **4.** The political p. of certain words in these had excited my interest 1884.

†Pre·gnancy[2]. 1649. [f. next; see -ANCY.] Cogency, force of an argument; clearness of evidence or proof; a weighty reason –1677.

†Pre·gnant, *a.*[1] late ME. [a. OF. *preignant*, pr. pple. of *preindre*, earlier *priembre*, *prembre* to press :—L. *premere.*] Of an argument, proof, etc.: Pressing, weighty; cogent, convincing; hence, clear, obvious –1766.

The Proofs were so P. and the Crime so black 1718. Hence **†Pre·gnantly** *adv.*[1]

Pregnant (pre·gnănt), *a.*[2] late ME. [ad. L. *prægnans*, -*antem* with child, pregnant; usu. explained as a ppl. form, f. *præ* before + root *gna-* of *gnascor, gnatus* to be born.] **I. 1.** With child or with young. Const. *with*, *of* (the offspring), *by* (the male parent). 1545. **†2.** *transf.* **a.** Of a plant or seed: Fertilized; fruitful –1769. **b.** Of the soil, etc.: Fertile, fruitful; prolific, teeming. Const. *with.* –1796.

1. *fig.* The p. quarry teem'd with human form GOLDSM. **2. b.** An Isle..call'd Marmora, very p. with Metals 1715.

II. In non-physical uses. **1. a.** Of a person or his mind: Teeming with ideas, imaginative, resourceful, ready. Const. *of*, *in*, or *to* with *inf. arch.* or *Obs.* late ME. **†b.** *esp.* of young persons, or their faculties: Apt to conceive or apprehend, quick-witted, promising –1707. **†c.** Apt to be influenced; receptive; ready. (Chiefly in Shaks.) –1628. **2.** Of words, symbolic acts, etc.: Full of meaning; suggesting more than is expressed; also, †full *of*, replete *with* (something significant) 1450. **3.** Fertile or fruitful in results; big *with* consequences 1591.

1. That Oxford scholar poor Of p. parts and quick inventive brain M. ARNOLD. **b.** She was a very p. Lady above her age, and died..when not full four years old FULLER. **c.** *Twel. N.* III. i. 100. **2.** The style is what was called p., leaving much to be filled up by the reader's reflection 1838. *P. construction*, in *Gram.* or *Rhet.*, a construction in which more is implied than the words express. *Negative p.*, in *Law*, a negative implying or involving an affirmative. **3.** They hold a p. lie well told, Is worth at least its weight in gold 1820. Hence **Pre·gnantly** *adv.*[2]

‖**Prehallux, præ-** (prɪ̆hæ·lɒ̆ks). 1888. [mod. L., f. *præ* PRE- B. II. + HALLUX.] *Anat.* etc. A rudimentary structure, found on the inner side of the tarsus of some Mammalia, Reptilia, and Batrachia, and supposed to represent an additional digit.

Prehensile (prɪ̆he·nsəil, -sil), *a.* 1781. [a. F. *préhensile*, f. as prec. + *-ile* -ILE.] Chiefly *Zool.* Capable of prehension; having the capacity of laying hold of anything.

Not any of the limbs of fishes are p. 1854. Hence **Prehensi·lity,** p. quality.

Prehension (prɪ̆he·nʃən). 1534. [ad. L. *prehensionem*, n. of action f. *prehendere* to grasp, seize.] **1.** The action of taking hold (physically); grasping, seizing. Chiefly *Zool.* 1828. **†2.** Seizure or arrest in the name of justice or authority; apprehension -1802. 3. Mental apprehension 1836.

Prehistoric (prīhistǫ·rik), *a.* 1851. [f. PRE- B. I. 1 + HISTORIC *a.*] Of, belonging to, or existing in the period antecedent to history, or to the first historical accounts of a people.
Homer and Troy lie far back in the p. period GLADSTONE. So **Prehisto·rical** *a.*, **-ly** *adv.*

Prehistory (prīhi·stŏri). 1871. [f. PRE- + HISTORY, after prec.] The account of events or conditions prior to written or recorded history.

Prehnite (prēⁱ·nəit). 1795. [ad. G. *prehnit*, f. Colonel von *Prehn*, who brought it from the Cape of Good Hope; see -ITE¹ 2 b.] *Min.* A hydrous silicate of aluminium and calcium, found in more or less globular masses of a pale green colour and vitreous lustre. Hence **Prehni·tic** *a. Chem.*, in *Prehnitic acid*, $C_{10}H_6O_8$, crystallizing in large prisms resembling the mineral p.

Prejacent (prīdʒēⁱ·sĕnt), *a.* (*sb.*) 1546. [a. OF., ad. L. *præjacentem*, pr. pple. of *præjacere* to lie in front, f. *præ* + *jacere* to lie.] †1. Pre-existent -1703. 2. *Logic.* Laid down previously; constituting the original proposition from which another is inferred. Hence *ellipt.* as *sb.* 1840.

Prejudge (prīdʒɒ·dʒ), *v.* 1579. [ad. F. *préjuger*, after L. *præjudicare* to PREJUDICATE; see PRE- A. I. 1 and JUDGE *v.*] 1. *trans.* To pass judgement, or pronounce sentence on, before trial, or without proper inquiry; hence, to judge (a person, cause, opinion, action, etc.) prematurely and without due consideration. †b. To judge unfavourably in advance BACON. †2. To anticipate (another) in judging -1719.
1. An unauthorised attempt to p. the very question to be inquired into 1845. So **Preju·dg(e)ment**, the action of prejudging; a conclusion formed before examination of the facts; prejudice.

†**Preju·dicate**, *ppl. a.* 1570. [ad. L. *præjudicatus*, *præjudicare*; see next.] 1. Judged, or decided beforehand (*rare*) -1677. 2. Formed (as an opinion) prior to knowledge of the case; preconceived -1725. 3. Affected by a preconceived opinion; prejudiced, biased -1716.
1. Neither were ignorant..how yᵉ cause was preiudicate before 1570. 2. A..preiudicate opinion 1583. 3. Their reasons enforce beliefe even from p. Readers SIR T. BROWNE.

†**Preju·dicate**, *v.* 1553. [f. L. *præjudicat-*, *præjudicare*, f. *præ* PRE- A. I. 1 + *judicare*, f. *judex* JUDGE.] 1. *trans.* = PREJUDICE *v.* I. -1670. 2. = PREJUDGE 1. -1734. Also *intr.* or *absol.* 3. = PREJUDICE *v.* II. 2. -1698.
1. It is euident, that the fault of the father may preiudicate the sonnes 1594. 2. If that Vote had not prejudicated the Matter 1734.

Prejudication (prīdʒūdikēⁱ·ʃən). 1616. [f. L. *præjudicare*: see prec.] The action of prejudicating; a judging beforehand; a previously formed decision or opinion.

Prejudice (pre·dʒŭdis), *sb.* ME. [a. F. *préjudice*, ad. L. *præjudicium*, f. *præ* PRE- A. I. 2 + *judicium* judgement.] I. Injury, detriment, or damage, caused to a person by judgement or action in which his rights are disregarded; hence, injury to a person or thing likely to be the consequence of some action. †b. *gen.* Injury, damage, loss -1790.
Phr. *In p. of*, to the (intended or consequent) detriment or injury of. *To the p. of*, to the (resulting) injury of. *Without p.*, without detriment to any existing right or claim; *esp.* in *Law*, without detracting from one's own rights or claims.
II. †1. A previous judgement; *esp.* a premature or hasty judgement -1835. 2. Preconceived opinion; bias favourable or unfavourable; prepossession; when used *absol.*, usu. with unfavourable connotation 1643. b. With *a* and *pl.*: An instance of this; a prepossession; an unreasoning predilection or objection 1654. †3. A preliminary or anticipatory judgement; an anticipation -1771.
2. P. renders a man's virtue his habit BURKE. Ignorance is the mother of p., whether among nations or individuals 1861. b. A historian dares not have a p., but he cannot escape a purpose 1894.

Prejudice (pre·dʒŭdis), *v.* 1472. [a. F. *préjudicier* to prejudice, f. *préjudice*; see prec.] I. *trans.* To affect injuriously or unfavourably; to injure or impair the validity of (a right, claim, statement, etc.). b. To injure materially; to damage. Now *rare.* 1591.
Yet no prescription of time could p. the title of the King of Heaven 1639. b. A wicket very much prejudiced by the rain 1884.
II. †1. To prejudge, *esp.* unfavourably (*rare*) -1642. 2. To affect or fill with a prejudice; to give a bias or bent to, influence the mind or judgement of beforehand (often, unfairly). Const. *against*, *in favour of*, †*to*. 1610.
2. I wished..to p. my readers' minds in their favour rather than against them KINGSLEY.

Prejudicial (predʒŭdi·ʃăl), *a.*¹ late ME. [In form corresp. to F. *préjudicial*, *-el* preceding judgement; but in sense belonging to PREJUDICE *sb.*; see -AL.] 1. Causing prejudice; detrimental, damaging (to rights, interests, etc.). †2. Of the nature of prejudice; prejudiced (*to* = against), unfavourably prepossessed -1643.
1. The existing system..was p. both to commerce and to learning MACAULAY. 2. It was no time then to contend with their slow and prejudiciall belief MILT. Hence **Prejudi·cial-ly** *adv.*, **-ness.** So **Prejudi·cious** *a.* (now *rare*), in sense 1.

Pre-judicial (prīdʒŭdi·ʃăl), *a.*² 1651. [ad. L. *præjudicialis*, f. *præjudicium* a judicial examination previous to trial (f. *præ* before + *judicium* judgement); see -AL.] *Rom. Law.* Applied to a class of actions, whereby questions of right or fact, esp. as regards status, were determined, usu. with a view to further proceedings.

Prelacy (pre·lăsi). ME. [a. AF. *prelacie*, ad. med.L. *prelatia*, f. *prælatus* PRELATE.] 1. The office, position, or dignity of a prelate; a prelatic benefice or see. 2. The order or rank of prelates; the body of prelates or of bishops collectively ME. †3. The authority of a prelate; ecclesiastical power -1577. 4. The system of church government by prelates or bishops of lordly rank; a term, chiefly hostile, for EPISCOPACY 2. late ME.
1. Nominated by the king to titular bishoprics and other prelacies 1827. 4. The Cleere Antithesis..betweene Presbytery and P. 1644. Others..began to associate p. with popery 1850.

Prelate (pre·lĕt), *sb.* [ME. *prelat*, a. OF. *prélat*, ad. L. *prælatus*, sb. use of pa. pple. of *præferre* to PREFER.] 1. An eccl. dignitary of exalted rank, as a bishop, archbishop, metropolitan, or patriarch. †b. Applied to a chief priest of a non-Christian religion -1601. †2. A person having superiority, a chief, head, principal, superior -1780.
1. The curates are ill-paid, and the prelates are overpaid 1856. b. The kepers..shewed vnto the prelattes all thinges whych had hapened TINDALE *Matt.* xxviii. 11. 2. The humble subieccyon of the subiecte to the p. 1502. Hence **Pre·lateship**, the office, or tenure of office, of a p. **Pre·latess**, a female p.; an abbess or prioress; also, the wife of a p. (*joc.*). **Prela·tial** *a. rare*, of, pertaining to, or proper to a p. or prelacy. **Prela·tic**, **-al** *a.* of, pertaining to, or like a p.; governed by or adhering to prelates or prelacy; episcopal; episcopalian; **-ly** *adv.* **Pre·latism**, prelacy, lordly episcopacy; adherence to this; so **Pre·latist.**

†**Pre·late**, *v.* 1548. [f. prec. sb.] *intr.* To act the prelate; to perform the office of a prelate -1656.

Prelation (prĭlēⁱ·ʃən). Now *rare* or *Obs.* [ME. *prelacioune*, a. OF. *prelacion*, F. *prélation*, ad. L. *prælationem* a preferring, preference.] †1. Uttering, pronunciation (*rare*) -1659. 2. The action of preferring or condition of being preferred; preferment; pre-eminence, superiority, dignity; preference. late ME.

Prelatize (pre·lătəiz), *v.* 1641. [f. PRELATE *sb.* + -IZE.] †1. *intr.* To be or become prelatical MILT. 2. *trans.* To make prelatical; to bring under prelatic government 1864.

Prelatry (pre·lătri). 1641. [f. as prec. + -RY.] Prelacy.

Prelature (pre·lătiŭɹ). 1607. [a. F. *prélature*, ad. med.L. *prælatura*; see PRELATE *sb.* and -URE.] = PRELACY 1, 2.

†**Pre·laty.** *rare.* 1641. [ad. med.L. *prælatia*; see PRELACY.] 1. = PRELACY 4. -1644. 2. The office or superiority of a prelate -1642.

Prelect, præ- (prĭle·kt), *v.* 1620. [f. L. *prælect-*, *prælegere* to read to others, f. *præ* + *legere* to choose, read.] †1. *trans.* To choose in preference to others -1656. 2. *intr.* To lecture or discourse (*to* an audience, *on* or *upon* a subject); to deliver a lecture 1785.

Prelection, præ- (prĭle·kʃən). 1587. [ad. L. *prælectionem*, f. *prælegere*; see prec.] 1. A public lecture or discourse; *esp.* a lecture by a teacher to students at a college or university. 2. A previous reading 1655.

Prelector, præ- (prĭle·ktəɹ). 1586. [a. L. *prælector*, f. *prælegere*; see PRELECT.] A public reader or lecturer, esp. in a college or university Hence **Prele·ctorship.**

Prelibation (prīləibēⁱ·ʃən). 1526. [ad. late L. *prælibationem*, f. *prælibare* (f. *præ* PRE- A. I. 2 + *libare* to taste).] 1. A foretaste. Chiefly *fig.* 2. An offering of firstfruits, or of the first taste, of anything. Now *rare.* 1635.
1. The wicked have a p. of that darkness they shall go unto hereafter 1633.

Prelim., abbrev. f. PRELIMINARY (examination, etc.).

Preliminary (prĭli·minări), *sb.* and *a.* 1656. A. *sb.* A preparatory step, measure or arrangement. Chiefly in *pl.* b. *ellipt.* Preliminary examination. (In student slang, often *prelim.*) 1882. B. *adj.* Preceding and leading up to the main subject or business; introductory; preparatory 1667.
A. The preliminaries for the lord Mohuns tryall 1693. B. It is for want of this p. knowledge 1890. Hence **Preli·minarily** *adv.*

Prelude (pre·liūd), *sb.* 1561. [a. F. *prélude*, ad. late or med.L. *præludium*, f. *præludere*; see next.] 1. An introductory performance, action, event, or condition, coming before one of more importance; an introduction, preface. 2. *Mus.* A movement or piece forming the introduction to a musical work; *esp.* one preceding a fugue or forming the first piece of a suite 1658.
1. A sort of p. to the still greater work which he had to do 1869. 2. *attrib.* So the hoarse thunder Growl'd long—but low—a p. note of death HOOD.

Prelude (pre·liūd), *v.* 1640. [ad. L. *præludere*, f. *præ* PRE- A. I. 1 + *ludere* to play; so F. *préluder.* Till c 1830 (prĭliū·d).] 1. *trans.* To serve as a prelude to; to prepare the way for, introduce; to foreshadow 1655. b. Of an agent: To introduce with a prelude or preliminary action 1697. 2. *intr.* To give a prelude or introductory performance *to* some later action 1640. b. To be introductory (*to*) 1838. 3. *Mus.* a. *intr.* To play a prelude before the main composition 1678. b. *trans.* (*a*) To play as a prelude; (*b*) to introduce with a prelude 1795.
1. When the gray Of morn preludes the splendour of the day DRYDEN. 2. He..was even in his Youth preluding to his Georgics, and his Æneis DRYDEN. 3. b. And I—my harp would p. woe—I cannot all command the strings TENNYSON. Hence **Pre·luder**, one who plays or performs a prelude.

Preludial (prĭliū·diăl), *a.* 1649. [f. late or med.L. *præludium* PRELUDE *sb.* + -AL.] Pertaining to, or of the nature of, a prelude; serving to introduce. So **Prelu·dious** *a.*

‖**Preludium, præ-** (prĭliū·diŏm). Now *rare.* 1570. [Late or med.L.] A prelude or introduction; a preliminary.

Prelusion (prĭliū·ʒən). 1597. [ad. L. *prælusionem*; see PRELUDE *v.*] The performance of a prelude; an introduction.

Prelusive (prĭliū·siv), *a.* 1605. [f. L. *prælus-*, *præludere* to PRELUDE + -IVE.] Of the nature of or serving as a prelude; introductory to what is to follow. Hence **Prelu·sively** *adv.*

Prelusory (prĭliū·səri), *a.* 1640. [f. as prec. + -ORY².] = prec.

Premature (prī·-, pre·mătiŭɹ, prīmătiūᵊ·ɹ), *a.* 1529. [ad. L. *præmaturus* very early, f. *præ* PRE- A. + *maturus* MATURE *a.*] Occurring, existing, or done before the proper time; too early; over-hasty.
His birth was p. 1838. The advance of p. age 1874. Hence **Premature-ly** *adv.*, **-ness.**

Prematurity (prī-, premătiūᵊ·rĭti). 1611. [ad. F. *prématurité*; see PRE- A. I. 2 and MATURITY.] †1. Of plants: Early ripening or flowering -1707. 2. = PRECOCITY 2. 1778. 3. Undue earliness or haste (of any action or event); precipitancy 1706.
2. P. of thought and feeling has often an early grave 1907.

‖**Premaxi·lla, præ-.** 1866. [mod.L., f. PRE- B. + MAXILLA, after next.] *Zool.* The premaxillary bone.

Premaxillary (prīmæksi·lări), *a.* and *sb.*

1854. [f. PRE- B. II. + MAXILLARY.] *Anat.* A. *adj.* Situated in front of the maxilla or upper jaw. B. *sb.* The premaxillary bone.

Premeditate (prime·diteit), *v.* 1548. [f. PRE- A. I. 1 + MEDITATE *v.*] To meditate beforehand. 1. *trans.* To study with a view to subsequent action, to think out beforehand; now *esp.* to plan or contrive previously. 2. *intr.* To think deliberately beforehand or in advance (*on* or *of* something) 1586.

1. I began now to p. the Destruction of the next that I saw there DE FOE. 2. I never p., dear lady 1849. Hence **Preme·ditated** *ppl. a.* previously contrived or planned. **Preme·ditatedly** *adv.* with premeditation.

Premeditation (prī-, primeditē·ʃən). Also †præ-. late ME. [ad. L. *præmeditationem*, f. *præmeditari.*] The action of premeditating; previous thinking out of something to be done; now *esp.* designing, planning, or contrivance to do something.

Premiate (prī·mieit), *v. rare.* 1537. [f. ppl. stem of L. *præmiari* to stipulate for a reward.] *trans.* To reward; to award a prize to. Hence **Pre·miated** *ppl. a.*

Premier (pre·miəɹ, prī·miəɹ), *a.* and *sb.*[1] 1470. [a. F., = first :—L. *primarius* PRIMARY, f. *primus* first.] A. *adj.* 1. First in position, importance, or rank; chief, leading, foremost. 2. First in time; earliest 1652.

1. One of the p. knights of the order of the garter 1630. †*P. minister, Minister p.* [cf. F. *premier ministre*], = B. 2. The p. advertisement of opera in England 1882.

B. *sb.* [short for *p. minister.*] a. *gen.* The first or chief minister of any ruler; the chief officer of an institution 1711. b. The first minister of the Crown, the PRIME MINISTER of Great Britain or one of its colonies 1726. c. *U.S.* The Secretary of State 1905. **Pre·miership.**

Premier (prəmye), *sb.*[2] 1865. [F., sc. *étage.*] The first floor, in a hotel, etc.

‖**Première** (prəmyēr). 1895. [F., short for *première représentation.*] A first performance of a play; a 'first night'.

Premillennial (prī:mile·niăl), *a.* 1846. [f. PRE- B. I. 1 + MILLENNIAL *a.*] Occurring before the millennium; said particularly of the Second Advent of Christ; also, pertaining to the world as it now is before the millennium. So **Premille·nnian** *a.*

Premise, premiss (pre·mis), *sb.* late ME. [a. F. *prémisse*, also obs. *premise*, ad. med.L. *præmissa* (*propositio, sententia*), pa. pple. of *præmittere* to put before; see PREMIT.] I. in *Logic.* (Often *premiss.*) A previous proposition from which another follows as a conclusion; *spec.* in *pl.* the two propositions from which the conclusion is derived in a syllogism.

Her foe's conclusions were not sound, From premisses erroneous brought SWIFT.

II. in *Law* and *gen.* (Now always *premise(s).*) 1. *pl.* The matters or things stated or mentioned previously; the aforesaid, the foregoing. Rarely in *sing.* Now *rare* or *Obs.* exc. in techn. use. late ME. 2. *Law.* (*pl.*) That part in the beginning of a deed or conveyance which sets forth the names of the grantor, grantee, and things granted, together with the consideration or reason of the grant 1641. 3. *Law.* (*pl.*) (*spec.* use of 1.) The subject of a conveyance or bequest, specified in the premises of the deed; = the houses, lands, or tenements beforementioned 1480. 4. (*pl.*) A house or building with its grounds or other appurtenances 1730. †5. Previous circumstances or events –1759.

1. To discuss questions conformably to the premises thus agreed on 1830. 3. Alice Higgins devised the premises, being a term for 999 years, to trustees 1818. 4. Nor shall any coroner's inquest be held on such licensed premises 1902.

Premise (primai·z), *v.* 1526. [f. prec. sb.; cf. PREMIT.] 1. *trans.* To state before something else; to say or write by way of introduction. (With *simple obj.* or, now usu., *obj. cl.*) b. *Logic.* To state in the premises. Also *absol.* 1684. †2. To make, do, perform, or use beforehand –1836. 3. *transf.* To preface or introduce (*with, by* something else) 1823.

1. b. For if only *some* is premised, we cannot conclude *all* 1864. 2. In the first case, of ulcers, I premised a seton in the arm 1836.

†**Premi·t**, *v.* 1540. [ad. L. *præmittere*, f. *præ* PRE- A. + *mittere* to send.] 1. *trans.* = PREMISE *v.* 1. –1784. 2. = PREMISE *v.* 2. –1670.

Premium (prī·miəm). *Pl.* **-iums,** formerly **-ia.** 1601. [a. L. *præmium* booty, profit, reward, f. *præ* PRE- A. I. 1 + *emere* to buy, orig. to take.] 1. A reward given for some specific act or as an incentive; a prize. 2. The amount agreed on, in an insurance policy, to be paid at one time or from time to time in consideration of a contract of insurance 1661. 3. A bonus; a bounty on the production or exportation of goods 1695. 4. A fee paid for instruction in a profession or trade 1765. 5. The charge made for changing one currency into another of greater value; agio; hence, the excess value of one currency over another 1717.

1. He knew the p. set upon his head 1765. 2. The conditions of insurance are 2s. per cent. premium 1766. 3. If no p. were allowed for the hire of money, few persons would care to lend it 1766. 5. *At a p.*: at more than the nominal or usual value; above par; *fig.* in high esteem; When the exchange is unfavourable, and bills at a p., this p. . . varies from day to day 1863.

Comb.: **p. bonus system, p. system,** a system by which a bonus is paid in addition to wages in proportion to the amount or value of work done.

Premolar (prīmōu·lăɹ), *sb.* (*a.*) 1842. [f. PRE- B. II. + MOLAR.] One of the set of molar teeth in front of the true molars, replacing the molars or grinders of the milk dentition; a false molar, in man called 'bicuspid'. B. *adj.* That is a premolar 1880.

Premonish (primǫ·niʃ), *v.* Now *rare.* 1526. [f. L. *præmonere* to forewarn (f. *præ* PRE- A. I. 1 + *monere* to warn), after ADMONISH.] *trans.* To forewarn; to admonish beforehand. b. *intr.* or *absol.* 1550.

Premonition (prīmoni·ʃən). 1456. [ad. obs. F. *premonicion, -ition*, ad. late L. *præmonitio*, f. L. *præmonere.* See also PREMUNITION.] The action of premonishing; a previous notification or warning of subsequent events; a forewarning.

Premonitor (primǫ·nitəɹ). 1656. [a. L., f. *præmonere.*] One who or that which forewarns. So **Premo·nitory** *a.* giving or conveying premonition. **Premo·nitorily** *adv.*

Premonstrant (primǫ·nstrănt), *sb.* and *a.* 1700. [pres. pple. of OF. *premonstrer* to foreshow.] *Eccl. Hist.* A. *sb.* = next A. B. *adj.* = next B. 1872.

Premonstratensian (primǫnstrăte·nsiăn), *sb.* and *a.* Also †præ-. 1695. [f. med.L. *Præmonstratensis* (see next) + -AN.] A. *sb.* A member of the order of regular canons founded by St. Norbert at Prémontré, near Laon, in 1119. Also, a member of a corresponding order of nuns. B. *adj.* Belonging to this order 1695.

‖**Premonstrate·nsis, præ-,** *a.* and *sb.* late ME. [med.L. = belonging to Prémontré, (*locus*) *Præmonstratus* lit. the place foreshown, so called because prophetically pointed out by St. Norbert.] = prec. *a.* and *sb.*

†**Premonstra·tion.** 1450. [ad. late L. *præmonstrationem*, f. *præmonstrare*, to show beforehand.] The action of making known beforehand; a showing forth beforehand –1623. So **Pre·monstrator** 1660.

Premorse (primǭ·ɹs), *a.* Also **præ-.** 1753. [ad. L. *præmorsus, præmordere* to bite (off) in front, f. *præ* PRE- A. II. c + *mordere* to bite.] *Bot.* and *Entom.* Having the end abruptly truncate, as if bitten or broken off.

Premotion (prīmōu·ʃən). 1643. [ad. med.L. *præmotionem*, f. late L. *præmovere* to move (anything) beforehand.] Motion or impulse given beforehand; *esp.* applied to divine action held to determine the will of the creature. So **Premove** *v. trans.* 1598.

Premunire: see PRÆMUNIRE.

Premunition (prīmiuni·ʃən). Now *rare.* 1456. [ad. late L. *præmunitionem*, f. *præmunire*, f. *præ* PRE- A. II. c + *munire* to fortify, defend. (Cf. PRÆMUNIRE.)] 1. The action of fortifying or guarding beforehand; a forearming 1607. 2. By confusion, = PREMONITION. (The earlier use.) *Obs.* exc. as referring to PRÆMUNIENTES. So **Premu·nitory** *a.* = PREMONITORY *a.*

Prenatal (prīnē·tăl), *a.* 1826. [f. PRE- B. I. 1 d + NATAL *a.*] Existing or occurring before birth; antenatal.

Prender (pre·ndəɹ). 1597. [sb. use of AF. *prender*, F. *prendre* to take.] *Law.* The power or right of taking a thing without its being offered.

Prenominal (prinǫ·minăl), *a.* 1646. [f. L. *prænomin-*, stem of PRÆNOMEN + -AL.] Pertaining to the *prænomen* or personal name; also, to the first word in binominal specific names.

Prenotion (prīnōu·ʃən). Now *rare.* 1588. [ad. L. *prænotio*, tr. Gr. πρόληψις of the Epicureans; see PRE- A. I. 2.] 1. A mental perception of something before it exists or happens. Also, prescience. 2. A previous notion; a preconceived idea 1605.

Prentice (pre·ntis), *sb.* Now *arch.* or *dial.* ME. [Aphet. f. APPRENTICE.] 1. = APPRENTICE *sb.* 1. †2. *Law.* = APPRENTICE *sb.* 2. –1530. †3. *fig.* = APPRENTICE *sb.* 3. –1586. 4. *attrib.*, as *p.-boy, ear, hand*, etc. 1594. Hence **Pre·ntice** *v. trans.* (*arch.* or *dial.*) = APPRENTICE *v.* †**Pre·nticehood** = APPRENTICESHIP 1. **Pre·nticeship** = APPRENTICESHIP 1–3.

†**Prenu·nciate, -tiate,** *v.* 1623. [f. ppl. stem of L. *prænuntiare*, f. *præ* PRE- A. I. 1 + *nunciare* to announce.] *trans.* To announce beforehand; to foretell, predict –1652. So †**Prenuncia·tion,** announcement beforehand, prediction.

Preoccupancy (pri,ǫ·kiŭpănsi). 1755. [f. PRE- A. I. 2 + OCCUPANCY.] 1. = PREOCCUPATION 3. 2. The state of being preoccupied or engaged 1893.

†**Preo·ccupate,** *v.* 1582. [f. ppl. stem of L. *præoccupare* to PREOCCUPY.] 1. *trans.* To take possession of beforehand or before another; to usurp –1727. 2. To take at unawares, surprise, overtake –1654. 3. To prepossess; to influence, bias, prejudice –1681. 4. To anticipate, forestall –1678.

4. Revenge triumphes over death, . . greif flyeth to it, feare preoccupateth it BACON.

Preoccupation (pri,ǫkiŭpē·ʃən). 1552. [ad. L. *præoccupationem* f. *præoccupare*; see prec.] The action of preoccupying. †1. The meeting of objections beforehand. In *Rhet.* A figure of speech in which objections are anticipated and prevented; prolepsis. –1683. 2. Prepossession; bias; prejudice 1603. 3. Actual occupation (of a place) beforehand 1658. 4. Occupation that takes precedence of all other 1873. 5. Mental absorption 1854.

4. Marrying and giving in marriage is now and always has been the great p. of man and womankind 1885. 5. The p. of men's minds with this absorbing subject 1854.

Preoccupied (pri,ǫ·kiŭpəid), *ppl. a.* 1849. [f. next + -ED[1].] Occupied previously. a. Absorbed in thought. b. *Zool.* and *Bot.* Of a name: already used for something else. Hence **Preo·ccupiedly** *adv.*

Preoccupy (pri,ǫ·kiŭpəi), *v.* 1567. [f. PRE- A. I. 1 + OCCUPY, after L. *præoccupare* to seize beforehand.] 1. *trans.* To occupy or engage beforehand; to engross; †to prepossess, to bias. 2. To take possession of before another; to appropriate for use in advance 1622.

1. *Cor.* II. iii. 240. 2. The name of Antoninus being preoccupied by Antoninus Pius M. ARNOLD.

Preocular (pri,ǫ·kiŭlăɹ), *a.* (*sb.*) 1826. [PRE- B. II. + L. *oculus* + -AR[1].] Situated in front of the eye; *spec.* applied to certain plates in the head of a reptile.

Pre-operculum, præ- (prī,opə̄·ɹkiŭlə̆m). 1828. [f. L. *præ* PRE- A. II. + OPERCULUM.] 1. *Ichthyol.* The foremost of the four bones forming the operculum in fishes. 2. *Bot.* = OPERCULUM 2. 1864. So **Pre-ope·rcular** *a.* of or pertaining to the p.; also *absol.* or as *sb.*, the p.

Pre-option (pri,ǫ·pʃən). 1666. [PRE- A. I. 2.] An option before any one else; right of first choice.

Pre-orbital (pri,ǭ·ɹbităl), *a.* (*sb.*) Also præ-. 1852. [f. PRE- B. II. + ORBIT + -AL[1].] *Zool.* Situated in front of the orbit or eye-socket. B. *sb.* The pre-orbital bone or process 1897.

Pre-ordain (prī,ǫɹdē·n), *v.* 1533. [PRE- A. I. 1.] *trans.* To ordain or appoint beforehand; in *Theol.* to foreordain. So **Pre-ordina·tion** (*rare*).

Pre-o·rdinate, *ppl. a. arch.* late ME. [ad. late L. *præordinatus, præordinare* to pre-ordain.] Foreordained, predestined.

Prep (prep). 1862. *School slang.* **1.** Short for PREPARATION (sense 1 c). **2.** Short for PREPARATORY *a.* (sense 2) 1905.

Preparation (prepărēⁱ·ʃən). late ME. [a. F. *préparation*. ad. L. *præparationem*, f. *præparare* to PREPARE.] **1.** The action of preparing, or condition of being prepared; making or getting ready; fitting out, equipment. **b.** A preparatory act or proceeding; usu. in *pl.* Things done to make ready *for* something 1560. **c.** *spec.* The preparing of lessons, as a part of the routine of school work (abbrev. *prep*) 1862. **2.** The action or special process of putting something into proper condition for use; dressing and serving up (*of* food); composition, manufacture (*of* a chemical, medicinal, or other substance); drawing up (*of* a document) 1495. †**3.** *concr.* That which is prepared, esp. for warfare; an equipment; an armament –1781. **4.** *concr.* A substance specially prepared, e. g. as food or medicine, or in the arts or sciences. late ME. **b.** A specimen of a natural object specially prepared for some scientific purpose; *esp.* an animal body or part of one prepared for dissection, or preserved for examination 1753. **5.** The observances preliminary to the celebration of the Jewish sabbath or other festival; hence *transf.* (= *day of p.*) the day before the sabbath, etc. 1557. **6.** In devotional use: The action of preparing for Holy Communion; a set of prayers used before a celebration by the officiant and his ministers, or by a person intending to communicate; also, the first part of the Communion Office 1650. **7.** *Mus.* The preparing of a discord (see PREPARE *v.* 8 a); opp. to *percussion* and *resolution* 1727.

1. Be yare in thy p., for thy assaylant is quick, skilfull, and deadly SHAKS. **b.** The preparations for the marriage were commenced 1856. **2.** A new edition is in active p. 1895. **3.** The Turke with a most mighty P. makes for Cyprus SHAKS. **4.** The most commonly used preparations of opium 1836. **5.** And it was the p. of the Passeouer *John* xix. 14. *attrib.* and *Comb.* **p. day**: see 5.

Preparative (prĭpæ·rătiv), *a.* and *sb.* [15th c. *preparatif*, a. F. *préparatif*, *-ive* adj. and sb., ad. med.L. *præparativus*; see PREPARE *v.* and -ATIVE.] **A.** *adj.* **1.** Having the function or quality of preparing; serving as a preparation; preliminary; preparatory 1530. †**b.** *spec.* Of medicine: Serving to prepare the system for a course of treatment –1747. **c.** quasi-*adv.* In preparation 1632. **2.** Used in or for preparing (*rare*) 1745.

1. **c.** Such notes as she had taken p. to her trial GOLDSM.

B. *sb.* **1.** Something that prepares the way for something else; a preliminary; a preparation 1440. †**b.** *Med.* Something to prepare the system for medicine, or for a course of treatment. Often *fig.* –1778. **2.** A military or nautical signal sounded on a drum, bugle, etc., as an order to make ready 1635.

1. The preparatives against France are so terrible in Italy 1707. Hence **Prepa·ratively** *adv.*

Preparator (pre·pǎreⁱtəɹ). *rare.* 1762. [a. late L. *præparator*.] One who makes a preparation; a preparer (of medicine, etc.).

Preparatory (prĭpæ·rătəri), *a.* and *sb.* late ME. [ad. med.L. *præparatorius*; see prec. and -ORY[2].] **A.** *adj.* **1.** That prepares for something following; preliminary, introductory. **b.** quasi-*adv.* = Preparatorily. Const. *to.* 1649. **2.** Applied to a junior school in which pupils are prepared for a higher school 1828; or in U.S. in which older boys are prepared for college.

1. **b.** They were weighing it p. to sending it to town 1877. **2.** The children of the rich are sent to p. schools 1828.

B. *sb.* **1.** = PREPARATIVE *sb.* 1. Now *rare* or *Obs.* 1620. **2.** Short for *p. school* 1907. Hence **Prepa·ratorily** *adv.* in a p. manner.

Prepa·re, *sb.* 1535. [f. next.] **1.** The act of preparing; preparation. *Obs.* or *dial.* **2.** A substance used to prepare stuff for a dye 1874.

Prepare (prĭpēᵊ·ɹ), *v.* 1466. [a. F. *préparer*, ad. L. *præparare*, f. *præ* PRE- A. I. 1 + *parare* to make ready.] **1.** *trans.* To get ready, make ready, to fit or put in order beforehand for something. **2.** *intr.* for *refl.* To put oneself, or things, in readiness; to get ready, make preparation 1509. †**3.** *refl.* and *intr.* To make preparation for a journey; to get ready to go (*to, into*, etc. a place); hence, to go, repair –1784. **4.** *trans.* To get or have in readiness beforehand; to provide. Now *arch.* or merged in 1. 1535. **5.** To make ready (food, a meal) for eating 1490. **6.** To bring into proper state for use by some special or technical process; to work up; to dress 1722. **7.** To manufacture, to make or compound (a chemical product, a 'preparation', etc.) 1535. **b.** To draw up (a writing or document) 1797. **8.** *Mus.* **a.** To lead up to (a discord) by sounding the dissonant note in it as a consonant note in the preceding chord. **b.** To lead up to (a shake or other grace) by a preliminary note, turn, etc. 1727.

1. P. my Horses SHAKS. And now p. thee for another sight MILT. In this manner I prepared almost all my sermons that summer 1866. For ten years he has 'prepared'..pupils for Army and other examinations 1900. Phr. *To be prepared*: to be ready, inclined, disposed (*for, to do* something). **2.** P. to meete thy God, O Israel *Amos* iv. 12. **5.** Goo and p. vs the ester lambe, that we maye eate TINDALE *Luke* xxii. 8. **6.** Sheep-skins are sometimes prepared to imitate morocco 1879. **7.** Writing Ink may be..prepared in many different ways 1875. **b.** A code is preparing for the regulation of commerce 1854. Hence **Pre·parable** *a. rare*, capable of being prepared. **Prepa·red·ly** *adv.*, **-ness. Prepa·rer**, one who or that which prepares.

Prepay (prīpēⁱ·), *v.* 1839. [f. PRE- A. I. 1 + PAY *v.*[1]] *trans.* To pay (a charge) beforehand; *esp.* to pay (the postage of a letter or parcel) before dispatching it (as by affixing a postage stamp). Also *transf.* with the letter, etc. as obj.

Pre-paying a letter..used to be thought little short of an insult 1858. Hence **Prepay·able** *a.* that may or must be prepaid. **Prepay·ment**, payment in advance; also *attrib.*

Prepense (prĭpe·ns), *a.* 1702. [For earlier *prepenst* PREPENSED (orig. *purpensed*, OF. *purpense*).] Considered and planned beforehand; premeditated; intentional. **a.** in *Malice p.* (Law): malice premeditated or planned beforehand; wrong or injury purposely done. Also *joc.* **b.** *gen.* 1770.

a. He..plunges into slang, not irreverently..but of malice p. L. STEPHEN. Hence **Prepe·nsely** *adv.*

†**Prepe·nse**, *v.* 1509. [Altered from earlier *purpense*, OF. *purpenser*, after words in PRE-.] **1.** *trans.* To plan or contrive beforehand –1633. **2.** To consider beforehand –1656.

†**Prepe·nsed**, *ppl. a.* 1529. [f. prec. vb. + -ED[1]; subseq. reduced to PREPENSE *a.*] **a.** esp. in legal phr. *malice p.*, *p. malice*: see PREPENSE *a.* –1704. **b.** = PREPENSE *a.* b. –1670.

Pre:perce·ption. 1871. [PRE- A. I. 2.] Previous perception; a condition preceding perception.

Prepollent (prĭpǫ·lĕnt), *a.* Now *rare.* Also præ-. 1657. [ad. L. *præpollentem*, *præpollere*, f. PRE- A. III. + *pollere* to be strong.] Having superior power, weight, or influence; predominating, prevailing.

‖**Prepo·llex, præ-.** 1889. [mod.L., f. *præ* PRE- B. II. + POLLEX.] *Anat.*, etc. A rudimentary structure found in certain animals on the radial border of the hand or fore-foot, and supposed to represent an additional digit.

Preponder (prĭpǫ·ndəɹ), *v.* Now *rare.* 1624. [a. OF. *prépondérer*, or L. *præponderare* to outweigh; see PRE- A. III. and PONDER *v.*] **1.** *trans.* To outweigh in importance. **2.** *intr.* = PREPONDERATE *v.*[1] 1. 1676.

Preponderance (prĭpǫ·ndərăns). 1681. [f. next; see -ANCE.] **1.** The fact of exceeding in weight; greater heaviness. **b.** *Gunnery.* The excess of weight of that part of a gun which is to the rear of the trunnions over that in front of them 1864. **2.** Superiority or excess in moral weight, power, influence, or importance 1780. **3.** Superiority in number or amount 1845.

2. The good would have an incontestible p. over the evil 1780. **3.** Their immense p. in point of numbers 1845. So **Prepo·nderancy** (now *rare*), the quality or fact of being preponderant 1646.

Preponderant (prĭpǫ·ndərănt), *a.* 1660. [ad. L. *præponderantem*, *præponderare*; see PREPONDER.] **1.** Surpassing in weight; heavier 1664. **2.** Surpassing in influence, power, or importance, predominant 1660.

2. The Roundhead party was now decidedly p. MACAULAY. Hence **Prepo·nderantly** *adv.*

Preponderate (prĭpǫ·ndəreⁱt), *v.*[1] 1611. [f. ppl. stem of L. *præponderare*; see PREPONDER *v.* and -ATE[3].] **I.** *intr.* **1.** To weigh more; to be heavier; to turn the scale 1623. **b.** *fig.* To have the greater moral or intellectual weight 1659. **c.** To exceed in power, force, or influence; to exceed in amount, number, etc.; to predominate 1799. **2.** To incline downwards, as one scale of a balance, on account of greater weight; to weigh or be weighed down; to show a preponderance 1678.

1. Where neither side doth p., the balance should hang even 1672. **b.** These last reasons did p. with me FULLER. **c.** The good in this state of existence preponderates over the bad DICKENS.

II. *trans.* †**1.** To weigh more than; to turn the scale when weighed against (something else); to outweigh –1774. †**2.** To cause to descend, as one scale of a balance, by reason of greater weight; to weigh down. Also *fig.* –1796. Hence **Prepo·nderatingly** *adv.*

†**Pre-po·nderate**, *v.*[2] 1599. [f. PRE- A. I. 1 + PONDERATE *v.*] *trans.* and *intr.* To ponder previously; to weigh mentally or consider beforehand –1838.

Prepondera·tion. Now *rare* or *Obs.* 1653. [f. L. *præponderare*.] **1.** The action or fact of preponderating; preponderance. **2.** The adding of weight to one side; greater inclination or bias 1653.

†**Prepo·se**, *v.* 1491. [a. F. *préposer*, after L. *præponere* to put before; see PRE- A. and POSE *v.*[1]] **1.** *trans.* To set over; to appoint as chief or superior –1655. **2.** To preface, prefix –1850. **3.** To propose, purpose, or intend –1635.

Preposition (prepǒzi·ʃən). late ME. [ad. L. *præpositionem*, f. *præponere* to put before; see PRE- A. II and POSITION.] **1.** *Gram.* One of the parts of speech; an indeclinable word or particle serving to mark the relation between two notional words, the latter of which is usu. a sb. or a pronoun; as, sow *in* hope, good *for* food, etc. The following sb. or pron. is said to be 'governed' by the preposition. †**2.** More widely: Any word or particle prefixed to another word; a prefix –1661. **3.** The action of placing before; position before or in front (*rare*) 1586.

1. *Inseparable p.*: a p. when combined as prefix with a verb or other part of speech. Hence **Preposi·tional** *a.* of, pertaining to, or expressed by a p. **Preposi·tionally** *adv.*

Prepositive (prĭpǫ·zĭtiv), *a.* (*sb.*) 1583. [ad. late L. *præpositivus*, f. ppl. stem of *præponere* to put before; see -IVE.] Proper to be placed before or prefixed. **B.** *sb.* A prepositive word or particle 1693.

Prepositor, præ- (prĭpǫ·zitǫɹ). 1518. [Alteration of L. *præpositus*.] = PRÆPOSTOR.

Prepossess (prīpǒze·s), *v.* 1614. [f. PRE- A. I. 1 + POSSESS.] **1.** *trans.* To take or get possession of beforehand, or before another; to have prior possession of. Now *rare.* **2.** To possess (a person) beforehand *with* or *by* a feeling, notion, etc.; to imbue, inspire, or affect strongly beforehand. Chiefly in *pass.* 1639. **3.** *spec.* To bias, prejudice (a person) against or in favour of a person or thing; now chiefly, To impress favourably beforehand 1647.

1. Hope is that which antedates and prepossesses a future good 1716. **2.** They were..prepossest with an ill opinion of him 1657. **3.** His talk prepossessed me still more in his favour 1866.

Prepossе·ssing, *ppl. a.* 1642. [-ING[2].] **1.** Biasing; causing prejudice. **2.** *spec.* That predisposes favourably; causing an agreeable first impression; pleasing 1805.

1. This awkward p. visage of mine GOLDSM. **2.** Its expression was eminently gentle and prepossessing LYTTON. Hence **Preposse·ssing-ly** *adv.*, **-ness.**

Prepossession (prīpǒze·ʃən). 1648. [f. PREPOSSESS *v.*, after POSSESSION.] **1.** The having or taking of possession beforehand; prior possession or occupancy. Now *rare.* **2.** The condition of being mentally prepossessed; a preconceived opinion which tends to bias the mind; unfavourable or favourable antecedent opinion; prejudice, predisposition 1649.

2. The prepossessions of the Vulgar for men in power and authority are blind 1702.

Preposterous (prĭpǫ·stərəs), *a.* 1542. [f. L. *præposterus* reversed (f. *præ* before and *posterus* coming after) + -OUS.] **1.** Having last that which should be first; inverted in order. Now *rare.* 1552. **2.** Contrary to nature, or to reason or common sense; monstrous; perverse, nonsensical; in later use, utterly absurd 1542.

1. The fatal effects of this p...procedure 1856. 2. The muff and fur are p. in June 1713. The p. idea of convincing the mind by tormenting the body 1809. Hence **Prepo·sterous-ly** *adv.*, **-ness.**

Prepostor, var. of PRÆPOSTOR.

Prepotency (prĭpōu·tĕnsi). 1646. [ad. L. *præpotentia*; see next and -ENCY.] **1.** The quality of being prepotent; predominance, prevalence. **2.** *Biol.* The prepotent power of a parent organism to transmit special characteristics to offspring 1859. So **Prepo·tence** (in sense 1).

Prepotent (prĭpōu·tĕnt), *a.* 1450. [ad. L. *præpotentem*, pr. pple. of *præposse* to be very powerful, f. *præ* PRE- A. III. + *posse* to be able; see POTENT.] **1.** Having great power, force, influence, or authority; pre-eminent in power. **b.** Predominant 1641. **2.** *Biol.* Having a greater power of transmitting hereditary features or qualities; having a stronger fertilizing influence 1859.

2. When two species are crossed, one has sometimes a p. power of impressing its likeness on the hybrid DARWIN.

Preprandial (prīpræ·ndiăl), *a.* 1822. [f. PRE- B. I. 1 + L. *prandium* luncheon.] Done or happening before dinner.

Pre-pre·ference, *a.* 1882. [PRE- B. I. 2.] Ranking before preference bonds, shares, claims, etc., in security, payment of dividend or interest. So **Pre-prefere·ntial** *a.*

‖ **Prepubis, præ-** (prīpiū·bis). Also **-es.** 1888. [PRE- A. II.] *Anat.* The pre-acetabular portion of the pubis, esp. in Dinosaurs. So **Prepu·bic** *a.* pertaining to the p.; situated in front of the pubis.

Prepuce (prī·piūs). late ME. [a. F. *prépuce* :—L. *præputium.*] The loose fold of integument which covers the glans penis (or the glans clitoridis); the foreskin. †**b.** *transf.* The state of the uncircumcised, uncircumcision –1582. So **Prepu·tial** *a.*

Pre-Raphael (prīræ·fĕ,ĕl), *a.* (*sb.*) 1850. [PRE- B. I. 2.] Previous to Raphael; a painter (or painting) before the time of Raphael. **b.** = Pre-Raphaelite. So **Pre-Ra·phaelism, prera·ph-, præ-**, = PRE-RAPHAELITISM; by Ruskin and others applied to the art of the painters who preceded Raphael.

Pre-Raphaelite, preraphaelite, præ- (prīræ·fĕ,ĕləit), *sb.* and *a.* Also **-Raffael-.** 1849. [f. PRE- B. I. 1 + RAPHAEL (It. *Raffaelo, Raffaele*) + -ITE [1].] **A.** *sb.* **1.** An artist who aims at producing work in the spirit which generally imbued art before the time of Raphael; *spec.* one of the group of English artists, including Holman Hunt, Millais, and D. G. Rossetti, who called themselves the 'Pre-Raphaelite Brotherhood' (P.R.B.). **2.** One of the painters who preceded Raphael 1850.

1. The Pre-Raphaelites imitate no pictures: they paint from nature only RUSKIN.

B. *adj.* (or attrib. use of sb.) **1.** Of, belonging to, or characteristic of the Pre-Raphaelites, or their principles and style 1849. **2.** Existing before Raphael 1855.

1. The P. movement 1873. 2. In these p. productions Florence is very rich 1855.

Pre-Ra·phaelitism, preraph-, præ-. 1851. [f. prec. + -ISM.] The principles, methods, or style of painting adopted by the Pre-Raphaelite Brotherhood and their followers; sometimes applied to a similar tendency in poetry and other arts.

Prerequisite (prīre·kwizit), *a.* and *sb.* 1633. [PRE- A. I. 3.] **A.** *adj.* Required beforehand; requisite as a previous condition 1651. **B.** *sb.* That which is required beforehand; a condition previously necessary 1633.

Prerogative (prĭrǫ·gătiv), *sb.* late ME. [a. F. *prérogative*, ad. L. *prærogativa* a previous choice or election, etc.; prop. fem. sing. of *prærogativus* adj. (see next), agreeing with *tribus* or *centuria*, applied to the tribe or century to which it fell by lot to give its vote first in the Roman comitia.] **1.** A prior, exclusive, or peculiar right or privilege. **a.** *esp.* in *Constitutional Hist.* That special pre-eminence which the sovereign, by right of regal dignity, has over all other persons and out of the course of the common law, the *royal p.*, a sovereign right (in theory) subject to no restriction or interference. **b.** *gen.* The peculiar right or privilege of any person, class, or body of persons. late ME. **2.** *fig.* A natural or divinely-given advantage or privilege. late ME. †**b.** Precedence, superiority –1671. **3.** The right of giving the first vote and thus of serving as a guide or precedent to the votes that follow. (Only an etym. use in English.) 1600.

1. The parliament by perseverance, and by taking advantage of foreign wars, disputed successions and other circumstances, gradually set limits to p. 1839. b. Freedom, an English subjects sole p. DRYDEN. 2. Rare Qualities may sometimes be Prerogatives, without being Advantages 1665.

attrib. and *Comb.*: **p. court,** the court of an archbishop for the probate of wills and trial of testamentary causes in which effects to the value of five pounds had been left in each of two (or more) dioceses within his province, its jurisdiction was transferred in 1857 to the Court of Probate; **p. lawyer,** a lawyer retained in behalf of the royal p.; **p. writ,** a writ issued on extraordinary occasions in the exercise of the royal p. Hence **Prero·gatived** *ppl. a.* endowed with or possessed of a p.

Prerogative (prĭrǫ·gătiv), *a.* late ME. [ad. L. *prærogativus*, f. *prærogatus*, *prærogare* to ask before (others), f. *præ* PRE- A. I. 1 + *rogare*; see -IVE.] **1.** *Rom. Hist.* Characterized by having the right to vote first. Of a vote: Given first and serving as a precedent for those that follow. 1600. **2.** Of, pertaining to, or arising from prerogative; enjoyed by exclusive privilege; privileged. late ME. **3.** Having precedence or priority; pre-eminent (*rare*) 1646.

2. Such p. modes of process, as are peculiarly confined to the crown 1768. Hence **Prero·gatively** *adv.* as a prerogative.

Prerupt (prĭrv·pt), *a. rare.* 1603. [ad. L. *præruptus*, *prærumpere* to break off before (the point), f. *præ* + *rumpere* to break.] = ABRUPT *a.* 4.

Presage (pre·sĕdʒ, formerly prĭsē¹·dʒ), *sb.* late ME. [a. F. *présage*, ad. L. *præsagium*, f. *præsagire* to forebode, f. (ult.) *præ* PRE- A. I. 3 + *sagus* predicting, divining.] **1.** An indication of a future event; an omen, sign, portent. **b.** Without *pl.* Indication of the future; chiefly in phr. *of evil* (etc.) *p.* 1671. **2.** A prediction, prognostication. Now *rare.* 1595. **3.** A presentiment, a foreboding; an intuition of the future 1593.

1. A very euil signe and p. for him, to enter into Rome with such bloudshed 1579. b. If there be aught of p. in the mind, This day will be remarkable in my life By some great act MILT. 3. He had a strong p. upon his mind that he had only a very short time to live 1812.

Presage (pre·sĕdʒ, prĭsē¹·dʒ), *v.* 1562. [a. F. *présager*, f. *présage* PRESAGE *sb.*] **1.** *trans.* To signify beforehand (supernaturally); to portend. **b.** *transf.* To give warning of (by natural means) 1591. **2.** Of a person: To augur, predict, forecast. †In Spenser: To make known. 1578. **b.** *intr.* To form or utter a presage or prediction 1592. **3.** *trans.* To have a presentiment or prevision of 1594. **b.** *intr.* To have a presentiment 1586.

1. Have not eclipses been esteemed as omens presaging some direful calamity? 1816. b. The rising of the mercury presages, in general, fair weather 1822. 2. Lands he could measure, terms and tides p. GOLDSM. Hence **Presager,** one who or that which presages or portends. **Presa·gingly** *adv.*

Presageful (stress var.), *a.* 1591. [f. PRESAGE *sb.* + -FUL.] **1.** Full of presage; ominous. **2.** Full of presentiment 1729.

2. Dark remembrance and p. fear COLERIDGE.

†**Presa·gement.** 1595. [f. PRESAGE *v.* + -MENT.] The action or fact of presaging. **a.** Prognostication; an omen, a portent –1646. **b.** Presentiment; foretelling power –1646.

a. The falling of Salt is an authenticke p. of ill lucke SIR T. BROWNE.

Presanctified (prīsæ·ŋktifəid), *ppl. a.* [PRE- A. I. 1.] *Liturg.* In *mass* or *liturgy of the p.* [tr. med.L. *missa præsanctificatorum*], a celebration of the Eucharist at which the elements used have been consecrated at a previous celebration, used in the Eastern Church during Lent and in the Western Church on Good Friday.

‖ **Presbyopia** (prezbi,ōu·piă). Rarely **pre·sbyopy.** 1793. [mod.L., f. Gr. πρέσβυς an old man + -ωπία, f. ὤψ, ὠπ- eye.] An affection of the eyes incident to advancing age, in which the power of accommodation to near objects is lost, and only distant objects are seen distinctly; a form of long-sightedness. So **Presby,opic** (-ǫ·pik) *a.* pertaining to or affected with p.

Presbyter (pre·zbitəɹ, *Sc.* and *U.S.* pres-). 1597. [a. late L., ad. Gr. πρεσβύτερος, prop. adj. 'older, elder', compar. of πρέσβυς an old man; see PRIEST.] **1.** An elder in the Christian church. **a.** In the early church: One of a number of officers who had the oversight and management of the affairs of a local church or congregation, some of them having also the function of teaching. **b.** In Episcopal churches: A minister of the second order; a priest 1597. **c.** In Presbyterian churches: Occasional name for an elder; *esp.* one who is a member of a PRESBYTERY 1615. †**2.** A Presbyterian –1827.

1. b. In truth the word P. doth seeme more..agreeable than Priest with the drift of the whole Gospell of Iesus Christ HOOKER. c. New P. is but Old Priest writ large MILT.

Presbyteral (prezbi·tərăl), *a.* 1611. [a. F. *presbytéral*, ad. med.L. *presbyteralis*; see prec. and -AL.] **1.** Of or pertaining to a presbyter or priest; consisting of presbyters. **2.** = PRESBYTERIAN *a.* 1651.

Presbyterate (prezbi·tərĕt), *sb.* 1641. [ad. med.L. *presbyteratus*; see PRESBYTER and -ATE [1].] **1.** The office of presbyter; presbytership, eldership 1642. **2.** A body of presbyters; the order of presbyters 1641.

†**Pre·sbyteress.** 1546. [ad. med.L. *presbyterissa*; in sense 2 for earlier L. *presbytera*; see PRESBYTER and -ESS.] **1.** The wife of a presbyter or priest –1675. **2.** A female presbyter; one of an order of women in the early church, having some of the functions of presbyters –1682.

Presbyterial (prezbitī°·riăl), *a.* (*sb.*) 1592. [f. late L. *presbyterium* PRESBYTERY + -AL.] **1.** Of or pertaining to a presbytery or body of elders 1600. **2.** = PRESBYTERIAN *a.* 1592.

Presbyterian (prezbitī°·riăn, *Sc.* and *U.S.* pres-), *a.* and *sb.* Now usu. w. capital *P.* 1641. [f. L. *presbyterium* + -AN.] **A.** *adj.* Pertaining to or characterized by government by presbyters or presbyteries; applied to a system of church polity; belonging to or maintaining this system; see next.

1. *Reformed P.*, of or pertaining to those Presbyterians who protested against the constitution of Church and State in Scotland at the Revolution Settlement in 1689; also pop. called CAMERONIAN. *United P.*, of or pertaining to the united church or denomination formed in Scotland in 1847 by the union of the United Secession and Relief churches. (Abbrev. U.P.) In 1900 this body united with the Free Church of Scotland, to form the denomination then named the United Free Church of Scotland.

B. *sb.* One who maintains the Presbyterian system of church government; a member or adherent of a Presbyterian church 1641.

Presbyterianism (prezbitī°·riăniz'm, *Sc.* and *U.S.* pres-). 1644. [f. prec. + -ISM.] The Presbyterian system of church government, in which no higher order than that of presbyter or elder is recognized, the 'bishop' and 'elder' of the N. T. being held to be identical and all elders being ecclesiastically of equal rank.

Presbyte·rianize, *v.* 1843. [f. as prec. + -IZE.] **a.** *trans.* To make Presbyterian; to organize on Presbyterian lines. **b.** *intr.* To act as a Presbyterian or in a way tending towards Presbyterianism.

‖ **Presbyte·rium, -ion.** 1565. [Christian L., ad. Gr. πρεσβυτέριον, -τερεῖον (N.T.)] **1.** = PRESBYTERY 1. **2.** = PRESBYTERY 3. 1886.

Pre·sbytership. 1597. [-SHIP.] = PRESBYTERATE 1.

Presbytery (pre·zbitəri, *Sc.* and *U.S.* pres-). late ME. [a. OF. *presbiterie* a priest's house, ad. late L. *presbyterium*.] **1.** A part of a church reserved for the clergy; the eastern part of the chancel beyond the choir, in which the altar is placed; the sanctuary. †**2.** = PRESBYTERATE 1. –1704. **3.** A body of presbyters or elders 1611. **4.** In the Presbyterian system: A body or assembly of presbyters or elders, consisting of all the ministers, and one ruling elder (or sometimes two) from each parish or congregation within a particular local area, constituting the eccl. court next above the kirk-session and below the synod 1578. **b.** *transf.* The district comprising the parishes or congregations represented by a presbytery 1581. **5.** The Presbyterian polity or system; Presbyterianism. (Contrasted with *episcopacy* or *prelacy*, and with *independency*.) Now *rare.* 1590. **6.** A presbyter's or priest's house; a parsonage. (Now only in *R. C. Ch.*) 1825.

‖ **Prescapula** (prīˌskæ·piŭlă). 1890. [PRE- A. II. b.] *Anat.* That part of the scapula or shoulder-blade above (or in quadrupeds, anterior to) its spine or median axis. Hence **Presca·pular** *a.* anterior to the spine or long axis of the shoulder-blade.

Prescience (pre·ʃiĕns, -s-). late ME. [a. F., ad. late L. *præscientia*: see PRESCIENT *a.* and -ENCE.] Knowledge of events before they happen; foreknowledge; esp. as a divine attribute. **b.** as a human quality: Foresight. late ME.

Predestination..cannot be avoided, if we hold an universal p. in the Deity BOSWELL. **b.** Statesmen of a more judicious p., look for the fortunate moment too BURKE.

Prescient (pre·ʃiĕnt,-s-), *a.* 1626. [a. F., ad. L. *præscientem, præscire* to know before, f. *præ* PRE- A. I. 1 + *scire* to know.] Having foreknowledge or foresight; foreseeing.

James Harrington, one of the most p. minds of that great age 1888. Hence **Pre·sciently** *adv.*

Prescientific (prīsəiˌĕnti·fik), *a.* 1858. [f. PRE- B. I. 1 + SCIENTIFIC.] Of or pertaining to times prior to the rise of modern science, or to the application of the scientific method.

Prescind (prĭsi·nd), *v.* 1636. [ad. L. *præscindere, præsciss-* to cut off in front, f. *præ* PRE- A. + *scindere.*] **1.** *trans.* To cut off prematurely or abruptly; to cut away at once. **2.** To cut off *from*; to abstract 1660. **3.** *intr.* (for *refl.*): To withdraw the attention *from*; to leave out of consideration 1890.

2. An abstract idea of happiness, prescinded from all particular pleasure 1710.

Prescribe (prĭskrəi·b), *v.* 1531. [ad. L. *præscribere* to write before, etc., f. *præ* PRE- A. + *scribere* to write.] **I.** †**1.** *trans.* To write first or beforehand; also, to describe beforehand -1653. **2.** To write or lay down as a rule or direction to be followed; to appoint, ordain, direct, enjoin. Const. *to* or dative. 1535. †**b.** *absol.* or *intr.* To lay down a rule; to dictate, appoint, direct. Of a law or custom: To be of force. -1716. **3.** *Med. trans.* To advise or order the use of (a medicine, etc.) with directions for the manner of using it 1581. **b.** *absol.* or *intr.* Also *fig.* 1598. †**4.** *trans.* To limit; to confine within bounds -1726.

2. Wood prescribes to the news mongers in London what they are to write SWIFT. And ten were prescribed the whip BROWNING. **3.** To leech his head and p. tartar emetic 1843. **b.** His motto was that no statesman should p. until he was called in 1899.

II. *Law.* **1.** *intr.* To make a claim by prescription; to assert a prescriptive right or claim (to or *for* something; also with *inf.* or *clause*) 1531. †**2.** To plead prescription of time (PRESCRIPTION II. 1) *against* an action, statute, or penalty; to cease to be liable on account of the lapse of the prescribed time -1672.

1. A man might..p. that he and his ancestors had from time immemorial exercised a certain right in gross 1844.

Prescript (prī·skript, †prĭskri·pt), *sb.* 1540. [ad. L. *præscriptum, præscribere* to PRESCRIBE.] **1.** That which is prescribed or laid down as a rule; an ordinance, law, command; a regulation, direction. **2.** Medicine prescribed; also *transf.* a medical prescription. Now *rare.* 1603.

Prescript (prĭskri·pt), *a.* 1460. [ad. L. *præscriptus*, pa. pple. of *præscribere*; see prec.] Prescribed or laid down beforehand as a rule; ordained, appointed. Now *rare.*

Prescription (prĭskri·pʃən). late ME. [a. F., or ad. L. *præscriptionem*, f. *præscribere, præscript-* to PRESCRIBE.] **I. 1.** The action of prescribing or appointing beforehand; that which is prescribed; written or explicit direction or injunction 1549. **2.** A direction or formula (usu.) written by a physician for the composition and use of a medicine; *transf.* the medicine prescribed. In early use, more widely, 'doctor's orders'. 1579. †**3.** Restriction, limitation -1718.

1. In the recognition of conduct as 'right' is involved an authoritative p. to do it 1874. **2.** This P. the Sub-prior faithfully made up, and put into Phials for use 1679.

II. *Law.* **1.** Limitation of the time within which an action or claim can be raised. Now commonly called *negative p.* 1474. **b.** Uninterrupted use or possession from time immemorial, or for a period fixed by law as giving a title or right; hence, title or right acquired by such use or possession; sometimes called *positive p.* late ME. **c.** *transf.* and *fig.* (*a*) Ancient or continued custom, esp. when viewed as authoritative 1589. (*b*) Claim founded upon long use 1625. †**2.** The action of prescribing or claiming by prescription -1818.

1. There's no p. to inthrall a King 1605. **b.** 'Tis said in our Law Books, that the Publick acquires a Right by Custom, but only private Persons acquire it by P. 1726. **c.** (*b*) Narrow self-ended Souls make p. of good Offices SIR T. BROWNE.

Prescriptive (prĭskri·ptiv), *a.* 1748. [ad. late L. *præscriptivus* pertaining to a legal exception or demurrer; see PRESCRIPT *sb.* and -IVE.] **1.** That prescribes or directs; †appointed by prescription. **2.** Derived from or founded on prescription or lapse of time, as *p. right* or *title* 1766. **3.** Arising from or recognized by long-standing custom or usage; prescribed by custom 1775. **4.** Giving or recognizing prescription or prescriptive right. BURKE.

1. P. rules for the preservation of health 1788. **3.** To have his regular score at the bar..and his p. corner at the winter's fireside 1837. **Prescri·ptive·ly** *adv.*, **-ness.**

Presence (pre·zĕns). ME. [a. OF. (mod.F. *présence*):—L. *præsentia*, f. *præsens* PRESENT *a.*; see -ENCE.] **1.** The fact or condition of being present; the state of being before, in front of, or in the same place with a person or thing; being there. **b.** In ref. to the manner in which Christ is held to be present in the Eucharist (see REAL *a.* I. 2) 1552. **2.** In certain connexions, used with a vague sense of the place or space in front of a person, or which immediately surrounds him ME. **b.** Without *of* or possessive; usu. preceded by prep., as *in (the) p., to (the) p.*, etc.; *spec.* (now only) in ref. to ceremonial attendance upon a person of superior, esp. royal, rank; formerly also = 'company', 'polite society'. late ME. †**c.** Hence, a presence-chamber -1735. †**3.** *concr.* Those who are present; an assembly, a company -1788. **4.** With possessive, denoting the actual person (or thing) that is present; hence occas. = embodied self, objective personality. Chiefly *poet.* late ME. **b.** Hence, a person who is corporally present; usu. with implication of impressive appearance or aspect 1826. **5.** Demeanour, carriage, or aspect of a person, esp. when stately or impressive 1579. **6.** Something present; a present being; a divine, spiritual, or incorporeal being or influence felt or conceived as present 1667. **7.** *P. of mind*: the state or quality of having one's wits about one; calmness in exacting circumstances; freedom from embarrassment, agitation, or panic 1665.

1. Our Law forbids at thir Religious Rites My p. MILT. **b.** The doctrine of the objective p. in, under, or with, the consecrated elements 1901. **2.** He was always very collected in the p. of danger (*mod.*). *In his p.* = before or with him, where he is, in his company; *from his p.* = from being with him, from where he is, out of his company, etc.; also *poet.* and *rhet.* with demonstrative or other adjs.; e. g. *in this (august) p.* = in the presence of this (august) personage. **b.** 'Tis very true: You were in p. (= present) then, And you can witness with me, this is true SHAKS. **c.** *Hen. VIII*, III. i. 17. **4.** As in a fiery column charioting His Godlike p. MILT. **b.** And over him who stood but Herakles? There smiled the mighty p., all one smile. BROWNING. **5.** More was a man of a stately and handsome p. H. WALPOLE. **6.** And I have felt A p. that disturbs me with the joy Of elevated thoughts WORDSW.

attrib. and *Comb.*: **p.-lobby**, the lobby or ante-room of a presence-chamber; **-room** = next.

Pre·sence-chamber. 1575. [Cf. prec. 2 c.] The chamber in which a sovereign or other great personage receives guests, or persons entitled to appear before him; a reception-room in a palace or great house.

Presensation (prīˌsensēⁱ·ʃən). 1653. [PRE- A. I. 2.] = next.

Presension (prīse·nʃən). Now *rare* or *Obs.* 1597. [ad. L. *præsensionem* a foreboding, f. *præsentire, præsens-* to feel beforehand.] Feeling or perception of something before it exists, occurs, or manifests itself; foreknowledge, foresight; presentiment.

Present (pre·zĕnt), *sb.*[1] ME. [PRESENT *a.* used ellipt. or absol. In ME. orig. *prese·nt.*] †**1.** = PRESENCE 1, 2, 2 b. -1470. †**2.** The thing or person that is present; affair in hand; present occasion; *pl.* things present, circumstances -1764. **b.** *This p.*, more commonly *these presents*: the present document or writing; these words or statements. Chiefly, now only, in legal use. late ME. **3.** The present time, the time that now is 1600. †**b.** With ellipsis of *month* (usu. *this p.*) -1661. **c.** *Gram.* Short for *present tense*: see PRESENT *a.* II. 2. *P. stem*, the stem of the present tense. 1530.

2. Shall I be charg'd no further then this p.? Must all determine heere? SHAKS. **b.** Know all men by these presents, that I [etc.] 1752. **3.** Better this p. than a past like that BROWNING.

Phrases with preps. †**In present**, (*a*) now; (*b*) immediately; (*c*) at that time, then. So *in this p.* = (*a*). **At p.**, at the present time, now. **For the p.**, for the time; †for that time, just then; in mod. use, for this time, just now. **Until the p., up to the p.**, until now, up to now.

Present (pre·zĕnt), *sb.*[2] ME. [a. OF., an offering, a gift. In OF. orig. in phr. *mettre (une chose) en present à* (quelqu'un), to put a thing before any one, in which *en present* was in effect = *en don* 'in the form of, or as a gift'.] a. = GIFT *sb.* II. 1. (The ordinary current sense.) **b.** = GIFT *sb.* I. 1. Usu. in phr. *to make a p. of* = to present, give, bestow. ME. †**c.** An offering to God or a deity -1707.

c. Were the whole realm of nature mine, That were a p. far too small WATTS.

Present (prĭze·nt), *sb.*[3] 1833. [f. PRESENT *v.*] The act of presenting or aiming a weapon, esp. a fire-arm; the position of the weapon when presented; *esp.* the position from which a rifle is fired.

Bring the carbine down to the 'P.' 1833.

Present (pre·zĕnt), *a.* (*adv.*) ME. [a. OF., mod.F. *présent*:—L. *præsens, præsentem*, prop. pres. pple. of *præesse* to be before, to be at hand.] An adj. of relation; expressing a local or temporary relation to a person or thing which is the point of reference. **I.** Senses relating to place, etc. **1.** Being in the place considered or mentioned; that is here (or there). Chiefly in predicate. Opp. to ABSENT *a.* 1. **b.** Existing in the thing, class, or case mentioned or under consideration; not wanting; 'found'. Opp. to ABSENT *a.* 1. 1809. **2.** That is actually being dealt with, written, discussed, or considered; often used in a writing to denote the writer himself. late ME. **3.** Of which one is conscious; directly thought of, remembered, or imagined. Usu. const. *to.* 1500. **4.** Attentive (opp. to ABSENT *a.* 2); having presence of mind, collected, self-possessed (in this sense usu. *p. to oneself*); prompt to perceive or act, ready, quick. Now *rare* or *Obs.* 1451. **5.** Ready at hand; *esp.* ready with assistance, 'favourably attentive, not neglectful, propitious' (J.). *arch.* 1539.

1. A p. deity, they shout around DRYDEN. P. at his burial 1839. **b.** In the Hemiptera..wings may be p. or absent HUXLEY. **2.** The said parties to these p. Indentures 1592. The entire subject..cannot be fully considered in such a paper as the p. 1895. **3.** The legends of the place are p. to the imagination throughout the discourse 1875. **5.** God is our hope & strength: a very p. helpe in trouble BIBLE (Great) *Ps.* xlvi. 1.

II. Senses relating to *time.* **1.** That is, or that is so, at this time or now; current, contemporary; modern. Opp. to *past* and *future.* ME. **b.** Actually existing, actual 1774. **2.** *Gram.* Applied to that tense of a verb which denotes an action now going on or a condition now existing (or one considered generally). Opp. to *past* (or *preterite*) and *future.* late ME. **3.** That was, or that was so, at that time. Now *rare.* 1450. †**4.** Without delay; immediate, instant -1836. †**b.** Of a remedy or poison: Taking immediate effect, acting speedily -1694.

1. All things, past, p., and to come, are p. before God PUSEY. **b.** In the p. state of nature, the means of safety are rather superior to those of offence GOLDSM. *P. value* or *worth* of a sum due at a definite future date (*Comm.*): that sum which, together with compound interest upon it from now until that date, will amount to the sum then due. 2. The..P. Perfect ONIONS. 3. The p. business was to attend to p. needs (*mod.*). 4. Peter stroke Ananias ..with p. death BACON.

†B. as *adv.* 1. = PRESENTLY *adv.* 2. -1654. 2. In or into the presence of some one; in the (or this) very place, there (or here) -1554.

1. Or let me deye p. in this place CHAUCER.

Present (prĭze·nt), *v.* ME. [a. OF. *presenter* (mod.F. *présenter*) :—L. *præsentare* to place before, etc., in late and med.L. to present to a person as a gift, f. *præsentem* PRESENT *a.*] I. To make present *to*, bring into the presence of. 1. *trans.* To bring or place (a person) before, into the presence of, or under the notice of, another; to introduce; *spec.* to introduce at court, or before a sovereign, etc. b. To bring before or into the presence of God; to dedicate by so bringing ME. †c. To give greeting from, to 'remember' (any one) *to* -1792. 2. *refl.* *To p. oneself*: to appear, attend. late ME. 3. *trans.* a. To name and recommend (a clergyman) to the bishop for institution to a benefice. Often *absol.* ME. b. To nominate to the benefits of any foundation 1820. 4. To show, exhibit, display; also (in recent use), to exhibit, be characterized by (some quality or attribute) 1500. b. *P. arms* (Mil.), to hold a fire-arm, etc. in a position expressing honour or deference, in saluting a person of superior rank 1759. 5. To make present or suggest to the mind; to set forth or describe; to represent (*as* or *to be*); to set forth 1579. 6. *refl.* (from 4, 5) To show itself, appear; to suggest itself, come into one's mind; to occur 1590. Also *intr.* (now *rare*). 7. *trans.* To symbolize; to represent; to stand for, denote; to be a picture of (*arch.*) late ME. b. To represent (a character) on the stage; to act; to personate (*arch.*) 1588. †c. To act (a play, or scene in a play) -1637. 8. *Law.* To make presentment of. a. To make a formal statement of; to submit (a fact, or a request, etc.). Also *absol.* late ME. b. To bring (an offence, etc.) formally under the notice of the proper authority, for inquiry or action. late ME. c. To charge (a person) formally; to report or bring up for trial 1526. 9. To place (a thing) in, or give to (it), a particular direction or position. a. To point (a fire-arm, etc.) at something; to hold (it) out in the position of taking aim. Also *absol.* (esp. as word of command). 1579. b. *Obstetrics.* Of the fœtus: To direct (a particular part) towards the *os uteri* during labour; usu. *intr.* for *refl.* said of the part so directed 1597. c. To point, direct, or turn (a thing) to face something, or in a specified direction. Also *intr.* 1793. 10. To bring (a substance) into the presence of or into close contact with another 1758.

1. The Dutchesse..presented mee to kisse the Queene's hand 1670. A candidate is said to present himself for examination; one who has qualified for, or is honoured with a degree, is presented for the degree; a theatrical manager is said (in recent use) to present an actor, etc. N.E.D. b. They brought hym to hierusalem, to p. hym to the lorde TINDALE *Luke* ii. 22. c. P. me cordially to Mrs. Champion BURKE. 2. Now there was a day, when the sons of God came to p. themselues before the Lord *Job* i. 6. 3. A lunatic cannot p. to a church, nor his committee 1818. 4. The few points which p. any difficulty 1885. 5. Hear what to my mind first thoughts p. MILT. 6. A remedie presents it selfe SHAKS. 7. b. He presents Hector of Troy SHAKS. c. A Maske presented at Ludlow Castle MILT. (*title*). 9. a. He sees me cock and p. DE FOE. 10. If a pure Alkali be presented to a pure Acid, they rush together with violence 1758.

II. To offer, deliver, give. 1. *trans.* To bring or place (a thing) before or into the presence of a person, or to put (it) into his hands, for acceptance; to offer, hand over, bestow, give (usu. in a formal or ceremonious manner) ME. b. To deliver, convey, give (a message, greeting, etc.); to offer (compliments, regards, etc.) ME. c. To deliver (a document, as a written address, petition, bill, etc.) to the proper quarter, for acceptance, or to be dealt with according to its tenor 1509. d. Of things: To offer, furnish, afford, supply 1604. †2. To make presentation of (a benefice) *to* a clergyman -1796. 3. a. *To p.* a person *with* a thing = *to present* a thing *to* a person (sense II. 1). Also *fig.* to furnish or supply *with* something. ME. †b. With personal obj. only; rarely *absol.* -1712.

1. I beseech you therefore, brethren,..that ye p. your bodies a liuing sacrifice, holy, acceptable vnto God *Rom.* xii. 1. [They] presented vnto him a mulet 1585. To p. to the world..a full and clear Narration CLARENDON. b. To p. you my complements 1638. c. My Soul more bent To serve therewith my Maker, and p. My true account MILTON. 3. a. Yesterday week Mrs. Morse presented me with a fine daughter 1803.

Presentable (prĭze·ntăb'l), *a.* 1540. [f. prec. + -ABLE.] 1. Capable of, or suitable for, presentation 1626. 2. *Law.* That may or should be formally brought up or charged, as an offence, an offender, etc. 1540. 3. *Eccl.* Of a benefice: = PRESENTATIVE 1. 1636. 4. Suitable, by attire and appearance, to be introduced into society or company; of decent appearance, fit to be seen. (Properly of persons; often also of things.) The usual current sense. 1827.

1. A p. claim 1868. 4. Is he a p. sort of a person? THACKERAY. This table looks very fine.., but only the ends are of mahogany and have p. legs 1898. Hence **Presentabi·lity. Prese·ntably** *adv.*

Presentation (prezĕntē¹·ʃən). [ME. a. OF. *presentacion*, or ad. late L. *præsentationem.*] I. 1. The action of presenting or introducing a person: see PRESENT *v.* I. 1. 2. *Eccl.* The action, or the right, of presenting a clergyman to a benefice, or to the bishop for institution; see PRESENT *v.* I. 3. late ME. †3. *Law.* = PRESENTMENT 2. -1610.

1. His p. at St. James's JANE AUSTEN. The P. for Doctor's Degrees 1883. *The P. of Christ in the Temple*: see Luke ii. 22-39. *The P. of the Virgin Mary* as a child, as narrated in the Apocryphal Gospels. Also in *Art*, a representation of either of these incidents. 2. Locke..was made Secretary of Presentations—that is, of the Chancellor's church patronage 1880.

II. The action of offering for acceptance; handing over, delivery; bestowal, gift, offering. late ME. b. Something offered for acceptance; a present, gift, donation; an address 1619.

Prayers..are..sometimes a p. of mere desires HOOKER.

III. 1. Theatrical, pictorial, or symbolic representation; a display, show, exhibition 1600. b. An image, likeness, semblance; a representation, a symbol 1594. 2. A setting forth, a statement 1597. 3. *Metaph.* and *Psychol.* (tr. G. *Vorstellung*). All the modification of consciousness directly involved in the knowing or being aware of an object in a single moment of thought 1842. 4. The action of placing, or condition of being placed, in a particular direction or position with respect to something else or to an observer; the mode in which a thing is presented or presents itself; *spec.* in *Obstetrics* (see PRESENT *v.* I. 9 b) 1754.

1. He vses his folly like a stalking-horse, and vnder the p. of that he shoots his wit SHAKS. b. *Rich. III*, IV. iv. 84. 2. I have not further to trouble yr Excellcy then wt the p. of my reall desires to serve you 1674.

attrib. in sense II., as *p. copy, clock*, etc. Hence **Presenta·tional** *a.* of or pertaining to p. (sense III. 3). **Presenta·tionalism, Presenta·tionism,** the doctrine that in perception the mind has an immediate cognition of the object; **Presenta·tionalist, Presenta·tionist,** one who holds this doctrine.

Presentative (prĭze·ntătiv), *a.* late ME. [See PRESENT *v.* and -ATIVE.] 1. *Eccl.* Of a benefice: To or for which a patron has the right of presentation. Also said of the advowson, the tithes, etc. connected with such a benefice. Opp. to APPROPRIATE, COLLATIVE, DONATIVE, IMPROPRIATE. 1559. †2. = REPRESENTATIVE *a.* 1, 2. -1653. 3. Having the function or power of presenting an idea or notion to the mind 1855. 4. *Metaph.* and *Psychol.* Of, pertaining or relating to, or of the nature of presentation (sense III. 3) 1842.

Presentee (prezĕntī·). ME. [a. AF. = F. *présenté*, pa. pple. of *présenter* to PRESENT; see -EE.] 1. A person presented; *spec.* a clergyman presented (for institution) to a benefice. 2. One to whom something is presented 1854.

Presenter (prĭze·ntəɹ). 1544. [f. PRESENT *v.* + -ER¹. See also PRESENTOR.] One who presents (in various senses).

Presential (prĭze·nʃăl), *a.* Now *rare.* Also præ-. 1635. [ad. med.L. *præsentialis* present, f. L. *præsentia* PRESENCE; see -AL.] 1. Of or pertaining to presence; having or implying actual presence with a person or in a place; present. 2. = PRESENT *a.* I. 4. 1649. 3. Pertaining to present time 1846. b. *Gram.* Applied to those tenses formed on the present stem 1898.

1. To see the presentiall countenance of God 1635. So **Presentia·lity** (now *rare*), presentness (in time); the being present in place, presence.

Presentiate (prĭze·nʃi,eⁱt), *v.* Now *rare.* 1659. [f. L. *præsentia* + -ATE³; cf. *substantiate*, etc.] *trans.* To make present in time or place.

Presentient (prĭse·nʃiĕnt), *a.* 1814. [ad. L. *præsentientem, præsentire*; see PRE- A. I. 3 and SENTIENT.] Feeling or perceiving beforehand; having a presentiment; scenting beforehand.

Presentiment (prĭze·ntimĕnt, pris-). 1714. [a. obs. F.; see PRE- A. I. 2 and SENTIMENT.] 1. A mental impression or feeling of some future event; a vague expectation, seeming like a direct perception of something about to happen; an anticipation, foreboding (usu. of something evil). 2. A previously conceived sentiment or opinion; a prepossession (*rare*) 1751. Hence **Presentime·ntal** *a.*

Presentive (prĭze·ntiv), *a.* (*sb.*) 1871. [irreg. f. PRESENT *v.* + -IVE; used in distinction from *presentative.*] Presenting an object or conception directly to the mind (opp. to *symbolic*); also *sb.*, a presentive word. Hence **Prese·ntive·ly** *adv.*, **-ness.**

Presently (pre·zĕntli), *adv.* late ME. [f. PRESENT *a.* + -LY².] †1. So as to be, or as being, present; on the spot; in person, personally -1579. 2. At the present time; now. *Obs.* or *dial.* 1485. †b. At the time referred to; just then -1740. 3. At the very time; at once; immediately, instantly, quickly, promptly. *Obs.* or *arch.* late ME. 4. In blunted sense (from 3): In the space of time that immediately follows, in a little while, before long, soon, shortly. Now the ordinary use. 1566. †5. Immediately (in space or relation); directly, closely -1661. 6. As a direct result or conclusion; consequently, thereupon; necessarily, *ipso facto. Obs.* or *arch.* 1634.

2. A reward to be rendred hereafter, not p. 1637. 3. Go p., and take this Ring with thee SHAKS. 4. Toys..which are p. put out of order 1699. The struggle, as we shall p. see, lasted two generations 1857. I cannot attend to it at once; I will do so p. (*mod.*). 6. We do not infer, nor doth it p. follow, that the present reading is corrupt and false 1659.

Presentment (prĭze·ntmĕnt). ME. [a. OF. *presentement*; see PRESENT *v.* and -MENT.] The act of presenting or fact of being presented, presentation; an instance or embodiment of this; chiefly in techn. or spec. uses. 1. The act of presenting a person to or for any office, esp. a clergyman for institution to a benefice. *Obs.* exc. *Hist.* 2. *Law.* The act of presenting or laying before a court or person in authority a formal statement of some matter to be legally dealt with. a. A statement on oath by a jury of a fact within their knowledge. late ME. †b. A similar statement (formerly) made by a magistrate or justice of the peace, or by a constable -1875. c. *Eccl.* A formal complaint or report of some offence or fault, made by the churchwardens, etc., to the bishop or archdeacon at his visitation 1576. 3. = PRESENTATION II, I. 1. Now *rare.* 1607. 4. = PRESENTATION III. 1. 1605. b. Delineation; usu. quasi-*concr.* a picture, portrait, image, likeness 1602. c. The appearance, aspect, form, or mode in which anything is presented; exhibition, display 1634. 5. Statement, setting forth, description; the form or mode of so stating 1611. 6. The act of presenting to consciousness, or to the imagination; suggestion; the conception thus given 1633. b. *Metaph.* and *Psychol.* = PRESENTATION III. 3. 1842.

4. An honored guest at the p. of a burlesque masque 1834. b. The counterfet p. of two Brothers SHAKS. c. To cheat the eye with blear illusion, And give it false presentments MILT. 5. A scientific and exact p. of religious things M. ARNOLD.

Presentness (pre·zĕntnĕs). 1530. [f. PRESENT *a.* + -NESS.] The quality or condition of being present in place, time, or thought.

Presentor (prĭze·ntǫɹ). 1532. [a. AF. *presentour*, f. *présenter*; see -OR. Cf. PRESENTER.] One who makes a presentment. b. One who presents to a benefice 1865.

Preservation (prezəɹvēⁱ·ʃən). 1472. [a. F. *préservation*, ad. med.L. *præservatio*, f. late L.

præservare to PRESERVE.] **1.** The action of preserving or keeping from injury or destruction; the fact of being preserved. **2.** The state of being (well or ill) preserved; state of keeping 1751. †**3.** A preservative -1617.

1. We bless thee for our creation, p., and all the blessings of this life *Bk. Com. Prayer.* 2. The foxtails are still in great p. 1816.

Preservative (prĭzɔ̄·ɪvătiv), *a.* and *sb.* late ME. [ad. F. *préservatif* adj. and sb., ad. med. L. *præservativus*; see PRESERVE *v.* and -ATIVE.] **A.** *adj.* Having the quality of preserving; tending to preserve; protective. **B.** *sb.* (absol. use of adj.) **1. a.** A medicine that preserves health, protecting from or preventing disease; a safeguard against poison or infection; a prophylactic. Now *rare.* 1466. **b.** *gen.* A safeguard *from* (or *against*) any danger or injury 1526. **2.** That which preserves, or tends to preserve or protect from decay, loss, or destruction 1503. **3.** *spec.* A chemical substance or preparation used to preserve perishable food-stuffs, etc. 1875.

1. a. To swallow a Vipers head was a most certain P. and Remedy against the biting of a Viper 1672. 3. The introduction of preservatives into articles of food 1898.

Preservatory (prĭzɔ̄·ɪvătəri), *a.* and *sb. rare.* 1649. [f. L. *præservare* to PRESERVE; see -ORY; cf. *conservatory*, etc.] **A.** *adj.* Tending to preserve; preservative. **B.** *sb.* (absol. use of *adj.*) **1.** A preservative 1654. **2.** = PRESERVE *sb.* 3. 1823. **3.** *U.S.* An apparatus for preserving substances for food 1875.

Preserve (prĭzɔ̄·ɪv), *sb.* 1552. [f. next.] †**1.** A preserving agent; a preservative -1677. **b.** *pl.* Goggles used to protect the eyes from dust, excess of light, etc. 1887. **2.** A confectionary preparation of fruit, etc., preserved with sugar; jam; often in *pl.* 1600. **3.** A wood or other ground set apart for the protection and rearing of game; a piece of water for fish; a vivarium 1807. **b.** *transf.* and *fig.* (often *pl.*) A thing over which one claims special rights 1829.

3. b. In the Colonies..we have not so much neutral markets, as preserves 1897.

Preserve (prĭzɔ̄·ɪv), *v.* late ME. [a. F. *préserver*, ad. late L. *præservare*, f. *præ* before + *servare* to keep, protect.] **1.** *trans.* To keep safe from harm or injury; to take care of, guard. Const. *from* (†*of, out of*). **2.** To keep alive (*arch.*); to keep from decay, make lasting (a material thing, a name, a memory) 1560. **b.** To maintain (a state of things) 1676. **c.** To keep in one's possession; to retain (a possession, acquisition, quality, etc.) 1617. **3. a.** To prepare (fruit, meat, etc.) by boiling with sugar, salting, or pickling, so as to prevent its decomposition or fermentation. Also *absol.* 1579. **b.** To keep (organic bodies) from decomposition, by chemical treatment, freezing, etc. 1613. **4.** To keep (game) undisturbed for personal use in hunting, shooting, or fishing; to keep (game runs, fishing rivers, etc.) for private use 1807.

1. Forto kepe and to p. The bodi fro siknesses alle GOWER. Oh, the Lord preserue thy good Grace SHAKS. See also WELL-PRESERVED. 2. A tiny little village preserves the name of the Percy 1874. b. Means..effectual in preserving discipline 1810. c. In politics they often yield the name while they p. the thing 1828. 3. a. Hast thou not learn'd me how To make Perfumes? Distill? Preserue? SHAKS. 4. A man who preserves is always respected by the poachers TROLLOPE. Hence **Prese·rvable** *a.* **Prese·rval,** preservation. **Prese·rver,** one who or that which preserves; *esp.* one who keeps safe from destruction or injury; a saviour.

Preside (prĭzəi·d), *v.* 1611. [a. F. *présider*, ad. L. *præsidere* to sit before, f. *præ* PRE- + *sedere* to sit.] **1.** *intr.* To occupy the chair or seat of authority in any assembly, or at the ordinary meetings of a society or company; to act as chairman or president. **b.** To sit at the head of the table 1871. **2.** To exercise superintendence, direction, or control. Also *fig.* to sit or reign supreme. 1656. **3.** *trans.* To control, direct (*rare*) 1665. **4.** *intr. To p. at the organ*, or *piano*, etc. *orig.* To conduct the band on the instrument in question; now, in pop. use, To be (or act as) organist or pianist during any social, religious, or musical assembly 1799.

1. By his place, he presided in all Publick Councils CLARENDON. 2. In none of their meetings have they [Quakers] a President; as they believe Divine Wisdom alone ought to p. 1796. Hence **Presi·der,** one who presides.

Presidence (pre·zidĕns). 1595. [a. F. *présidence*, ad. med.L. *præsidentia*; see next.] **1.** The action or fact of presiding; superintendence, direction. **2.** = next **1.** Now *rare.* 1606.

Presidency (pre·zidĕnsi). 1591. [= med. L. *præsidentia*, f. L. *præsidens, -entem*; see next and -ENCY.] **1.** The office or function of president; presidentship, chairmanship; superintendence, direction; also, the term during which a president holds office. **2.** A district under the administration of a president; *spec.* in India, Each of the three divisions of the East India Company's territory, which were orig. governed by the Presidents of the Company's three factories. Loosely, the seat of government of each of these. *Obs.* in official use. 1698.

1. In the days of the p. of Washington CANNING. 2. The term 'P.'..applied to the Provinces or Governments of Bengal, Madras, and Bombay, is no longer applicable to the present condition of things, and in the case of Bengal is positively misleading 1872.

President (pre·zidĕnt), *sb.* late ME. [a. F. *président*, ad. L. *præsidens, -dentem*, sb. use of pres. pple. of *præsidere* to PRESIDE.] **1.** The appointed governor or lieutenant of a province, or division of a country, a dependency, colony, city, etc. Now chiefly *Hist.* **b.** *fig.* A presiding deity, patron, or guardian 1611. **2.** The head of a temporary or permanent body of persons, who presides over their meetings and proceedings. **a.** *gen.* late ME. **b.** The title often born by the head of a college in a university, or in U.S. of a university consisting of a single college 1464. **c.** The person elected to preside over the meetings and proceedings of an academy, society, or institution, literary, scientific, artistic, or the like 1660. **d.** In U.S. the title of one who presides over the proceedings of a financial, commercial, or industrial company, as a bank, railway, mining company, etc. 1781. **3.** The head of an advisory council, or administrative board or department of government, as, in Great Britain, the (Lord) P. of the Council, the P. of the Board of Agriculture, of Education, of Trade, etc.; also of certain courts of justice, as the Court of Session in Scotland, the Court of Probate in England, etc. 1530. †**b.** Formerly the title of the chief magistrate in some of the British North American colonies, and in the States to which they gave rise -1817. **4.** The officer in whom the executive power is vested in a modern republic, the elected head of the government 1783.

2. a. He receiv'd publick thanks from the Convocation, of which he was P. 1663 b. He..was ons ellect presydent of Maudlen Colledge 1530. 3. *Lord P. of the Council*: an officer of the English crown whose duty is to preside at the meetings of the Privy Council, and to report to the King the business transacted there. 4. Four Presidents (Harrison, Taylor, Lincoln, Garfield) have died in office, and been succeeded by Vice-Presidents 1889.

President (pre·zidĕnt), *a.* Now *rare.* late ME. [ad. L. *præsidentem.*] That presides or occupies the chief place; superintending.

Pre·sidentess. 1782. [f. PRESIDENT *sb.* + -ESS [1].] **a.** A female president. **b.** The wife of a president.

Presidential (prezide·nʃăl), *a.* 1603. [ad. med.L. *præsidentialis*, f. *præsidentia* PRESIDENCY; see -AL.] **1.** Of or pertaining to a president or his office. **2.** Of the nature of a president; presiding 1650.

2. The next P. Election looms always in advance 1860. Hence **Preside·ntially** *adv.*

Pre·sidentship. 1525. [-SHIP.] The office or function of a president; the period of this.

Presidial (prĭsi·diăl), *a.* and *sb.* 1598. [a. F. *présidial* sb. and adj., ad. late L. *præsidialis*, f. *præses, -idem* the governor of a province; see -AL. In sense 4, f. L. *præsidium* garrison, fort.] **A.** *adj.* **1.** *French Hist.* Of or pertaining to a province, provincial 1611. †**2.** Of a Roman province: Under a *præses* or president -1771. **3.** Of or pertaining to a president or the action or function of presiding (*rare*) 1598. **4.** †**a.** = PRESIDIARY *a.* **b.** Of or pertaining to a presidio. 1598. **B.** *sb. French Hist.* A presidial court of justice in France 1683.

Presidiary (prĭsi·diări), *a.* and *sb.* 1594. [ad. L. *præsidiarius* that serves for defence, f. *præsidium* garrison, f. *præsidere* to PRESIDE; see -ARY [1].] **A.** *adj.* Of, pertaining to, or serving as a garrison; garrisoned. **B.** *sb.* A guard, a protection 1623.

Presi·ding, *ppl. a.* 1667. [-ING [2].] That presides. *P. officer*, an official appointed to superintend the counting of votes at an election.

‖ **Presidio** (prĭsi·dio). 1808. [Sp., garrison, fort:—L. *præsidium.*] In Spain and the s.w. U.S., etc.: A fort, a fortified settlement, a military station, a garrison town. Also a Sp. penal settlement in a foreign country.

Presignification (prĭsi:gnifikē̆ⁱ·ʃən). Now *rare.* 1603. [ad. L. *præsignificationem.*] The action of signifying or indicating beforehand; an indication or sign (of what is coming).

Presignify (prĭsi·gnifəi), *v.* 1586. [ad. L. *præsignificare*, f. *præ* PRE- A. I. 1 + *significare.*] *trans.* To signify or intimate beforehand.

Presphenoid (-sfī·noid). 1854. [f. PRE- A. II. + SPHENOID.] *Anat.* The anterior part of the sphenoid bone of the skull, which forms a separate bone in (human) infancy. Hence **Presphenoidal** (prī:sfĭnoi·dăl) *a.*

Press (pres), *sb.*[1] [Two forms: *a.* ME. *presse*, a. F. *presse*, f. F. *presser* PRESS *v.*[1] *β.* ME. *prēs, prees*, in 16–17th c. *prese, preas(e, preace*, only in early senses.] **I. 1.** The condition of being crowded or thronged; a crowd, a throng, a multitude (*arch.*). **b.** A throng or crush in battle; the thick of the fight; a mêlée. late ME. **2.** A crowding or thronging together ME. †**3.** The condition of being hard pressed; a critical situation; straits, distress -1677. **4.** Pressure of affairs; urgency, hurry. late ME.

1. Who is it in the presse, that calles on me? SHAKS. b. He..fought, sword in hand, in the thickest p. MACAULAY. 2. Give gently way, when there 's too great a p. BYRON. 4. Amid the flame and armes ran I in preasse 1547. The eager p. of our modern life 1883.

II. 1. The act of pressing (something); pressure 1513. **2.** A mark made by pressing; a crease; *fig.* an impression 1601. **3.** The action of pressing (forward) 1893. **4.** Naut. *P. of sail, canvas* (formerly *p. sail, prest sail, pressing sail*): 'as much sail as the state of the wind, etc., will permit a ship to carry' (Smyth) 1592.

4. He bore away with a p. of sail for Malta 1806.

III. An instrument or machine by which pressure is communicated. **1.** An instrument used to compress a substance into smaller compass, denser consistency, a flatter shape, or a required form; as *coining, copying p.*, etc.; *cheese, clothes p.*, etc.; *cam, hydraulic, screw, toggle p.*; etc. late ME. **b.** The apparatus for inflicting the torture of *peine forte et dure. Obs.* exc. *Hist.* 1734. **2.** An apparatus for expressing or extracting the juice, or the like, out of anything; as *wine, oil, cider, sugar p.*, etc. late ME. **3.** A machine for printing, a printing-press 1535. **b.** A printing-house or printing-office. Often used in the names of printing establishments, e.g. the Clarendon P., Oxford, the Pitt P., Cambridge, etc. Hence, contextually, for the *personnel* of such an establishment. 1579. **c.** The printing-press in operation, the work or function of the press; the art or practice of printing 1579. **d.** (Also *periodical* or *public p., daily p.*, etc.) The newspapers, journals, and periodical literature generally; the newspapers and journals of a country, district, party, etc., as the French P., the London P., the Conservative P., the religious p., etc. Hence sometimes the title of a newspaper. 1797.

3. b. The Presses swell'd with the most virulent Invectives against them CLARENDON. c. These are the new dark ages, you see, of the popular p. TENNYSON. d. I seldom..read..the ordinary animadversions of the p. RUSKIN.

Phrases. *At, in*, †*under (the) p.*, in the process of printing, being printed. *Off the p.*, finally printed, issued. †*Out of p.*, = prec., also out of print. *To pass the p.*, etc. *To correct the p.*, i.e. the printing, or the errors in composing the type. Now *rare. Freedom* or *liberty of the p.*, free use of the printing-press; the right to print and publish anything without submitting it to previous official censorship. So in *free p., unfettered p.*, etc. *A good* or *bad press*, favourable or unfavourable reception by the newspapers.

IV. A large (usu. shelved) cupboard, esp.

one placed in a recess in the wall, for holding clothes, books, etc.; in Scotland, also for victuals, plates, dishes, and other table requisites. Cf. CLOTHES-*p.* late ME.

attrib. and *Comb.* **a.** **p.-copy** *sb.*, a copy of a writing made by transfer in a copying-press; hence **-copy** *v.*; **-pack** *v.*, to pack or compress (something) into small compass by means of a p.; **-printing,** printing by a p.; a method of printing porcelain. **b.** (connected with printing and journalism): **p. agent,** a man employed in connexion with a theatre or the like to attend to the advertising, and the reporting of the performances; **-box,** a shelter for newspaper reporters in the open air, as at a cricket or football match; **p. cutting,** a paragraph, article, or notice, cut from a newspaper; also *attrib.* as *p.-cutting agency*; **-gallery,** a gallery or part of the house at any public meeting, set apart for reporters; esp. that in the House of Commons; **-proof, -revise,** the last proof examined before printed matter goes to p.

Press (pres), *sb.*[2] Now *rare.* 1596. [Altered from PREST sb. 5.] **1.** The impressing of men for service in the navy or (less frequently) the army. Now *Hist.* 1599. **b.** A warrant giving authority to impress recruits. *Obs.* exc. *Hist.* 1596. **2.** *transf.* and *fig.* Impressment into service of any kind; a requisition 1667. **3.** *attrib.*, as PRESS-GANG, PRESS-MONEY, etc. 1688.

1. b. I haue mis-vs'd the Kings Presse SHAKS.

Press (pres), *v.*[1] [Two forms: *a.* ME. *pressen*, a. OF. *presser* :—L. *pressare*, freq. of *premere, pressum* to press. *β.* ME. *prēse(n, prēce(n*, with lengthened vowel; cf. PRESS sb.[1] The latter form was rare in branches I and II.] I. Literal and directly connected senses. **1.** *trans.* To exert a steady force against (something in contact), e. g. by weight (downwards), or by other physical agency (in any direction); to subject to pressure. **b.** *To p.* (*to death*): to execute the punishment of *peine forte et dure* upon (a person arraigned for felony who stood mute and would not plead); see PEINE. *Obs.* exc. *Hist.* 1544. **c.** As a sign of affection or courtesy (with a person, the hand, etc., as object) 1700. **d.** *intr.* To exert pressure; to bear with weight or force *on, upon, against* 1815. **2.** *trans.* To cause to move by pressure; to push, drive, thrust. (With abvbs. and preps.) late ME. **b.** *fig.* (usu. with *down*) ME. **3.** To extract by pressure; to express; to squeeze (juice, etc.) *out of* or *from* something. late ME. **4.** To subject to pressure so as to reduce to a particular shape, consistence, smoothness, thinness, or bulk, or so as to extract juice, etc., from; to compress, squeeze. late ME. **5.** To print. *Obs.* or *arch.* 1579.

1. Her step seemed to pity the grass it prest SHELLEY. *To p. the button* (fig.): to set things in motion. **c.** The Minstrel's hand he kindly pressed SCOTT. **d.** Since air possesses weight, it necessarily presses upon any object exposed to its influence HUXLEY. **2.** Good measure, pressed doune..and runnynge ouer TINDALE *Luke* vi. 38. **3.** Wine is pressed from the grape 1744. **4.** P. them as long as there is any milk in the almonds 1796.

II. Figurative senses. **1.** *trans.* (fig. of I. 1.) Of an enemy, etc.: To bear heavily on; to reduce to straits; to beset, harass. Now chiefly in *hard pressed.* late ME. †**b.** Of a tyrant, circumstances, etc.: To oppress; to crush; to distress, afflict –1793. **c.** To weigh down, burden, oppress (the feelings, mind, spirits, etc.) 1604. **d.** To put to straits, as by want of time, means, etc.; in passive, usu. with *for* 1678. **2.** *intr.* To produce a strong mental or moral impression *upon*; now usu., to bear heavily, weigh *upon* (the mind, etc.) 1561. **3.** *trans.* To urge on; to constrain, compel, force. late ME. **b.** Said of danger, business, etc., or of time. Now only *absol.* or *intr.* To compel dispatch; to be pressing; to demand immediate action. 1440. **c.** To urge on, drive quickly (*rare*) 1611. **d.** With the movement as obj. 1742. **4.** To urge on by words or arguments; to importune, beg, entreat (a person *to do* something or *for* something) 1593. **b.** *intr.* or *absol.* To ask or seek importunately. Const. *for* or *inf.* late ME. **5.** *trans.* To urge, insist on the doing of (something); to solicit, request (a thing) earnestly. Const. *on, upon* (a person). 1625. **6.** To urge, insist on the belief, admission, or mental acceptance (of something); to impress (a thing) on the mind; to plead with insistence (a claim, etc.). Const. *on, upon* (a person, his attention, etc.) 1625. **7.** To urge, thrust (something to be taken or accepted) *upon* a person 1797. **8.** To push forward (arguments, views, positions, etc.) 1665.

1. Although hard pressed at first, the force eventually gained a..victory 1893. **c.** I haue this while with leaden thoughts beene prest SHAKS. **d.** In writing the last Number I was pressed for time 1817. **3.** Why should hee stay whom Loue doth presse to go? SHAKS. **b.** Let it be done with Dispatch, for the time presses 1746. **d.** Fast as they prest their flight 1742. **4.** To avoid being pressed..to stay another day DE QUINCEY. **b.** Don't p. for an answer yet 1833. **6.** Remember, if you mean to please, To p. your point with modesty and ease COWPER. **8.** Stephen pressed his advantage 1874.

III. Senses connected with the notion of a throng, or of pushing one's way as in a throng. Primarily *intr.* **1.** *intr.* To crowd, throng about a person or place ME. **b.** *trans.* To crowd upon, throng. *Obs* or *arch.* 1549. **2.** *intr.* To push or strain forward; to hasten onward, urge one's way ME. **3.** To push one's way into a person's presence, or into a place, boldly, presumptuously, or insistently; to venture; to obtrude oneself, intrude. late ME. †**4.** To strive, try hard, attempt *to do* something (usu. with eagerness or haste); to aim at, endeavour after something. Also in weaker sense: To essay, undertake. –1642. **5.** To strive, contend, make resistance (*rare*). late ME.

1. No humble suters prease to speake for right SHAKS. The enemy presseth harde upon us 1648. **2.** I..preace vnto the marke apoynted TINDALE *Phil.* iii. 14. Pressing forward like the wind SCOTT. **3.** Prease not into yͤ place of greate men COVERDALE *Prov.* xxv. 6.

IV. *Comb.*: **p.-stud,** a stud which is fastened by pressing.

Hence **Pressed** (prest) *ppl.a.*, subjected to pressure; compacted or moulded by pressure; often qualifying articles in the preparation of which pressure is specially used, as *p. beef, brick, glass,* etc.

Press (pres), *v.*[2] *Pa. t.* and *pple.* **pressed;** †**prest.** 1543. [Altered from PREST *v.*[2], by assoc. with PRESS *v.*[1]; see PRESS-MONEY.] *trans.* To force (a man) to serve in the army or navy; cf. IMPRESS *v.*[2], PREST *v.*[2] **b.** *intr.* or *absol.* 1625. **c.** *trans.* To take authoritatively for royal or public use 1633. **d.** *transf.* To seize and force into some service 1598.

The peaceful Peasant to the Wars is prest DRYDEN. **b.** The King is fain to p. now MARVELL.

Press-bed. *Obs.* exc. *dial.* 1660. A bed constructed to fold up, when not in use, into a press (PRESS *sb.*[1] IV) closed by a door or doors; sometimes less correctly applied to a box-bed shut in by folding doors.

The Judge and I..lay in one press bed PEPYS.

Presser (pre·səɹ). 1545. [f. PRESS *v.*[1] + -ER[1].] **1.** One who presses, or works a press of any kind. **2.** An instrument, machine, etc., which applies pressure 1725.

Comb.: **p.-bar,** (*a*) the presser in a knitting-machine, which drives the barb of the needle into the groove of the shank; (*b*) the vertical bar in a sewing-machine which bears the presser-foot; **-foot,** the foot-plate of a sewing-machine which holds the cloth down to the feed-plate.

Pre·ss-gang, *sb.* 1693. [f. PRESS *sb.*[2] or *v.*[2] + GANG *sb.*] A body of men employed, under the command of an officer, to press men for service in the army or navy. Hence **Pre·ss-gang** *v. trans.* and *intr.* = PRESS *v.*[2]

Pre·ssing, *ppl. a.* 1591. [f. PRESS *v.*[1] + -ING[2].] That presses, in the senses of the verb; *esp.* calling for immediate attention, urgent. **b.** Of a request, etc., expressed with an earnest desire for compliance; also of the person, persistent, importunate 1705.

Discharging the most p. and crying debts 1616. **b.** My Mother..is very p. with me to marry STEELE. A p. summons 1855. Hence **Pre·ssing-ly** *adv.*, **-ness.**

Pression (pre·ʃən). Now *rare.* 1661. [a. F., ad. L. *pressionem*, f. *premere*: see PRESS *v.*[1]] **1.** The action of pressing; pressure. Sometimes applied *spec.* to a particular pressure used in massage. †**2.** In the Cartesian physics: Pressure or impulse communicated to and propagated through a fluid medium –1756.

Pressiroster (presirǫ·stəɹ). 1842. [ad. F. *pressirostre* (Cuvier), ad. mod.L. *pressirostris* adj., f. L. *pressus* pressed + *rostrum* beak, bill.] *Ornith.* A bird of the *Pressirostres* of Cuvier, now included in the *Charadriomorphæ* or plover-snipe group. So **Pressiro·stral** *a.* having the characteristics of the *Pressirostres.*

Pressive (pre·siv), *a.* 1619. [ad. obs. F. *pressif, -ive*; see PRESS *v.*[1] and -IVE.] †**1.** Pressing, oppressive. *rare.* –1623. **2.** Characterized by pressure 1822.

Pre·ssman. 1598. [f. PRESS *sb.*[1] + MAN *sb.*] **1.** A man who operates a printing-press; *esp.* a hand-press printer. **2.** One who writes or reports for the press; a reporter, journalist 1859. **3.** In shoemaking: A workman who stamps out the sole-leather for boots or shoes with a press 1895.

Pre·ss-mark. 1802. [PRESS *sb.*[1] IV.] In libraries, a mark or number written or stamped in or on each book, and also given in the library catalogue, specifying the room, shelf, etc., where the book is kept. Hence as vb.

Pre·ss-mo:ney, †**pre·st-mo:ney.** Now only *Hist.* late ME. [orig. *prest-money*, f. PREST *sb.* + MONEY.] = PREST *sb.* 1, 3, 4.

Pressor (pre·sǭɹ), *a.* 1890. [Agent-n. in L. form from *premere* to press, used attrib.] *Phys.* That presses; stimulating, exciting.

P. nerves, nerves whose stimulation increases activity of vaso-motor centres 1890.

Pre·ss-room. 1683. [f. PRESS *sb.*[1] + ROOM *sb.*] **1.** The room in a printing-office in which the presses stand, and where the printing is done. **2.** A room in which a press of any kind is kept 1696.

Pressure (pre·ʃiūɹ, pre·ʃəɹ). late ME. [a. obs. F., ad. L. *pressura*, f. *press-*, ppl. stem of *premere* to press; see -URE.] **I. 1.** The action or fact of pressing; the fact or condition of being pressed (see PRESS *v.*[1]); compression, squeezing, crushing, etc. 1601. **2.** *Physics.* The force exerted by one body on another by its weight, or by the continued application of power, viewed as a measurable quantity, the amount being expressed by the weight upon a unit area 1660. **b.** *Electr.* 'That which causes or tends to cause an electric current' (Trotter) 1889. †**3.** The mark, form, or character impressed; impression, stamp, image –1809.

1. The soft p. of a melting kisse 1602. **2.** *Absolute p.*, the total p. (of steam, etc.), found by adding the amount of the atmospheric p. to that indicated by the ordinary steam-gauge (which shows the *relative p.*, or p. above that of the atmosphere). *Centre of p.*: see CENTRE. *P. of the atmosphere*; The weight or p. of the atmosphere is about 15 lbs. in every square inch HUXLEY. **3.** *Haml.* I. v. 100, III. ii. 27.

II. 1. The condition of being painfully oppressed in body or mind; affliction, oppression. late ME. †**2.** The action of political or economic burdens; a heavy charge; the condition of being weighed down by these –1719. **b.** A state of trouble or embarrassment; *pl.* straits 1648. **c.** Urgency of affairs 1845. **3.** The action of anything that influences the mind or will; constraining influence 1625.

1. In presure and in paine My joyes thy preceptes give 1586. The p. of grief 1794. **2. b.** A period of financial p. 1868. **c.** Writing hastily and under p. 1885. **3.** His virtue, such as it was, could not stand the p. of occasion 1791.

Phrases. **High p.** *orig.* A p. higher than that of the atmosphere, but now only a relative term without any absolute limits; esp. in ref. to compound engines in which the steam is used at different pressures in the different cylinders; mostly *attrib.*, as in *high-p. engine, steam,* etc. **b.** *transf.* of speed, work, business, etc., and in *Path.*, as a *high-p. pulse.* **c.** In *Meteorol.* said of a dense condition of the atmosphere over a certain region, as in *high-pressure area, system* (of winds). So **low p.**

Comb. **p.-button,** a 'button' or stud, by pressing which a spring is liberated or an electric bell rung; **-gauge, -gage,** an instrument for showing the p. of an elastic agent, as steam or gas; also, one for showing the p. in a cannon or fire-arm at the instant of explosion of the charge; **-paralysis,** paralysis caused by p. on part of the brain; **-pipe,** the pipe of the p.-gauge of a steam-engine.

Pre·ss-wa:rrant. Now *Hist.* 1688. [f. PRESS *sb.*[2] + WARRANT *sb.*] A warrant giving authority to impress men for the service of the army or navy.

Pre·ss-work. 1771. [f. PRESS *sb.*[1] + WORK *sb.*] **1.** The work and management of a printing-press; the printing off on paper, etc., of what has been 'composed' or set up in type; the work so turned out, esp. from the point of view of its quality. **2.** Literary work done for the press 1888. 3. *Pottery.* The making of ware by pressing the clay into moulds 1839.

Pre·ss-yard. *Obs.* exc. *Hist.* 1654. [f. PRESS *v.*[1] I. 1 b + YARD.] Name of a yard or court of old Newgate Prison, in which the torture of *peine forte et dure* (PEINE) is supposed to have orig. been carried out; and from which, later, prisoners started for the place of execution.

†Prest, *sb.* late ME. [a. OF., mod.F. *prêt*, a loan, etc.; vbl. sb. f. OF. *prester*, mod.F. *prêter* PREST *v.*[1]] 1. An advance of money, a loan; *esp.* one made to the sovereign in an emergency; a forced loan; a grant, gift, bequest –1643. 2. A charge, duty, or impost; a deduction made from or in connexion with any payment –1548. 3. A payment or wages in advance –1657. 4. *esp.* Earnest-money paid to a sailor or soldier on enlistment –1588. 5. An enlistment of soldiers or sailors –1602. 6. *In p.*: as a prest or loan; in advance; on account; as earnest-money –1603.

Comb. **p.-warrant,** a warrant for paying prest money.

†Prest, *a.* and *adv.* ME. [a. OF., mod.F. *prêt*:—late or pop. L. *præstus* ready, f. earlier L. *præsto* (*præstu*) adv., near at hand; perh. contr. from **præsito*, f. *præ* before + abl. or dat. of *situs* placed; or from **præsitu*, f. *præ* + *situ*, abl. of *situs* situation.] A. *adj.* 1. Ready; at hand; prepared –1697. 2. Ready in mind, disposition, or will; willing; prompt, eager, keen –1697. b. Alert, sprightly, brisk –1573. 3. Close at hand –1589. B. *adv.* Readily, quickly 1558. Hence †**Pre·st-ly** *adv.*

A. 1. A huge Nauy p. at all Essayes 1635. 2. Every Knight is..P. for their Country's Honour DRYDEN.

†Prest, *v.*[1] 1539. [a. OF. *prester*, mod.F. *prêter* to lend, pay in advance, etc.:—L. *præstare*; f. *præ* before + *stare* to stand.] 1. *trans.* To lend (money); to advance on loan –1561. 2. To advance (money) on account of work to be done or not yet completed –1586.

†Prest, *v.*[2] 1513. [f. PREST *sb.*] 1. *trans.* To hire the services of (a person) or the use of (a ship, etc.) by part-payment in advance –1545. 2. *esp.* To engage (men) for military service on land or sea by giving part-payment or earnest-money in advance; to enlist, levy (generally); to press –1600.

Pre·stable, *a.* *Sc.* Now *rare.* 1650. [a. obs. F., (mod.F. *prêtable*), f. *prester*; see PREST *v.*[1] and -ABLE.] Capable of being paid or advanced; capable of being performed or discharged.

To offer my fortune so far as it was p..., to make good all claims upon Ballantyne & Co. SCOTT.

Prestate (pre·steɪt), *v.* 1880. [f. ppl. stem of L. *præstare* to stand before, vouch for, answer for; see PREST *v.*[1] and -ATE [3].] *Rom. Law. trans.* To undertake, take upon oneself, become responsible for; to furnish, manifest.

Prestation (prestēɪ·ʃən). 1473. [a. F., ad. L. *præstationem*, f. *præstare*; see PREST *v.*[1], PRESTATE.] The action of paying, in money or service, what is due by law or custom, or feudally; a payment or the performance of a service so imposed or exacted; also, the performance of something promised.

†Pre·ster. late ME. [a. L., a. Gr. πρηστήρ, f. πιμπράναι, πρήθειν (root *pra-*) to burn, also to inflate.] 1. A serpent, the bite of which was fabled to cause death by swelling –1847. 2. A burning or scorching whirlwind –1797.

Pre·ster Jo·hn. [ME. *Prestre Johan*, a. OF. *prestre Jehan*, mod.F. *prêtre-Jean*, med.L. *presbyter Iohannes* 'Priest John'.] The name given in the Middle Ages to an alleged Christian priest and king, orig. supposed to reign in the extreme Orient, but generally identified later with the king of Ethiopia or Abyssinia.

‖**Pre·ste·rnum, præste·rnum.** 1828. [PRE- A. II. b.] 1. *Entom.* = PROSTERNUM. 2. *Comp. Anat.* The front part of the sternum; the part corresponding to the first segment of the human sternum 1872. Hence **Pre·ste·rnal** *a.* of or pertaining to the pre-sternum, as *presternal bone, region*, etc.

Prestidigitator (pre:stiˌdi·dʒiteɪtəɹ). Also in F. form ‖ **prestidigitateur** (prĕstidiʒitatœr). 1843. [ad. F. *prestidigitateur*, f. *preste* nimble (ad. It. *presto*, L. *præstus*) + L. *digitus* a finger + -*ateur*, L. -*ator* agent-suffix.] One who practises sleight of hand or legerdemain; a juggler, a conjurer; hence *fig.* a juggler with words, a trickster. So **Prestidigitation** (pre:stiˌdidʒitēɪ·ʃən), sleight of hand, legerdemain.

Prestige (prestī·ʒ). 1656. [a. F., ad. L. *præstigium* a delusion, illusion, usu. in pl. *præstigiæ* juggler's tricks, for **præstrigium*, f. *præstringere* to bind fast (*præstringere oculos* to blindfold; hence, to dazzle the eyes); see PERSTRINGE.] †1. An illusion; a conjuring trick; a deception, an imposture. Usu. *pl.* –1881. 2. *transf.* Blinding or dazzling influence; 'magic', glamour; influence or reputation derived from previous character, achievements, or success 1829.

2. Such is the p. of broad cloth 1845.

Prestigia·tion. Now *rare.* 1540. [f. late L. *præstigiare* (f. *præstigium*: see prec.)] The practice of juggling, sorcery, or magic; conjuring.

Prestigiator (presti·dʒiˌeɪtəɹ). 1614. [a. L. *præstigiator*; see prec.] A juggler; a conjurer; †a cheat.

Prestigious (presti·dʒəs), *a.* Now *rare.* 1546. [ad. late L. *præstigiosus*, f. *præstigium* PRESTIGE + -OUS.] Practising juggling or legerdemain; cheating; deceptive, illusory. Hence **Presti·gious-ly** *adv.*, **-ness.**

‖**Prestissimo** (prestī·ssimo), *a.*, *adv.*, *sb.* 1724. [It., superl. of *presto* adj. and adv.; see PRESTO.] *Mus.* A direction: Very quick; very fast; as *sb.* a very quick piece or movement.

Prest-money, earlier form of PRESS-MONEY.

‖**Presto** (pre·sto), *a.*[1], *adv.*[1], *sb.*[1] 1683. [It. = quick, quickly (*tempo presto* quick time):—late L. *præstus*; see PREST *a.*] *Mus.* **A.** *adj.* or *adv.* A direction: In quick time, fast. **B.** *sb.* A movement or piece in quick time 1869.

Presto (pre·sto), *adv.*[2], *a.*[2], *sb.*[2] 1598. [a. It.; the same word as prec.] **A.** *adv.* (interj.) Quickly, immediately, at once; used by conjurers and jugglers in various phrases of command, esp. *P.*, *be gone, Hey p.*, *pass*, etc.; hence, = immediately, instanter. Also interjectionally. **B.** *sb.* An exclam. of 'presto!' 1622. **C.** *adj.* or *attrib.* At hand, in readiness; active, ready, quick, instantaneous; of the nature of a magical transformation; juggling 1644.

A. Put in your money..; P. be gone—'Tis here agen SWIFT. Hence **Pre·sto** *v. trans.* to conjure.

Presume (prĭziū·m), *v.* late ME. [a. F. *présumer*, or ad. L. *præsumere* to anticipate, assume, suppose, f. *præ* PRE- A. I. 1 + *sumere* to take.] †1. *trans.* To take possession of without right; to usurp. late ME. only. 2. To take upon oneself, undertake without adequate authority or permission; to venture upon. late ME. b. with *inf.* To take the liberty; to venture, dare (*to do* something). late ME. †3. *trans.* (with *inf.* or *cl.*) To profess, pretend –1652. 4. To assume or take for granted; to presuppose; to count upon. *spec.* in *Law*: To take as proved until evidence to the contrary is forthcoming. late ME. 5. *intr.* To act on the assumption of right or permission; to be presumptuous, take liberties. Often *p. on, upon* (†*of*): to act presumptuously on the strength of; also in neutral sense, to take advantage of. late ME. 6. To press forward presumptuously; to aspire presumptuously; to presume to go. Now *rare* or *Obs.* late ME. 7. *P. on, upon* (†*of*): to rely upon, count upon, take for granted; to look for. Now *rare* or *Obs.* 1586.

2. Hopes of excellence which I once presumed, and never have attained JOHNSON. b. Know then thyself, p. not God to scan POPE. 4. At any time beyond the first seven years they might fairly p. him dead 1805. 5. To take no care, is to p. upon providence 1708. 6. Up led by thee, Into the Heaven of Heavens I have presumed, An earthly guest MILT. 7. How uncertain our lives are, and how little to be presumed of PEPYS. Hence **Presu·mable** *a.* probable, likely; to be counted on beforehand; **Presu·mably** *adv.* **Presu·medly** *adv.* **Pre·sumer,** a presumptuous person; one who assumes something without proof. **Presu·mingly** *adv.* presumptuously.

Presumption (prĭzɒ·mpʃən). [ME. a. OF. *presumpcion, presompcion*, ad. L. *præsumption-*, f. *præsumere* to PRESUME.] †1. Seizure and occupation without right; usurpation (*of* an office). *rare.* –1810. 2. The taking upon oneself of more than is warranted; forward or overconfident opinion or conduct; arrogance, pride, effrontery, assurance ME. 3. The taking of something for granted; also, that which is presumed; assumption, assumed probability, supposition, expectation ME. b. *spec.* in *Law.* (See quots.) 1596. 4. A ground for presuming or believing; presumptive evidence 1586.

2. God smote him there because of his presumpcion, so that he dyed there besyde the Arke of God COVERDALE *2 Sam.* vi. 7. 3. The..p. that a relatively late text is likely to be a relatively corrupt text 1881. b. *P. of fact* (Law), the inference of a fact not certainly known, from known facts. *P. of law*, (*a*) the assumption of the truth of anything until the contrary is proved; (*b*) an inference established by the law as universally applicable to certain circumstances. 4. There seems strong internal p. against the authenticity of these epistles 1838.

Presumptive (prĭzɒ·mptiv), *a.* 1561. [a. F. *présomptif, -ive*, ad. late L. *præsumptivus*, f. *præsumpt-*, *præsumere* to PRESUME; see -IVE.] 1. = next 1. Now *rare* or *Obs.* 1609. 2. Giving reasonable grounds for presumption or belief 1561. 3. Based on presumption; presumed, inferred 1628.

2. This is strong p. evidence, but we have positive proof—the evidence of our own senses DICKENS. 3. *Heir p.*: see HEIR *sb.* 1. Hence **Presu·mptively** *adv.*

Presumptuous (prĭzɒ·mptiuəs), *a.* ME. [a. OF. *presuntuex, presumptuoux*, mod.F. *présomptueux*, ad. L. *præsumptuosus*, late var. of the regular *præsumptiosus.*] 1. Characterized by presumption; unduly confident; arrogant, presuming; forward, impertinent. †2. = PRESUMPTIVE 2. *rare.* –1653.

1. A mouth speakynge p. thinges COVERDALE *Dan.* vii. 20. That glorious, that p. thing, call'd man 1635. No less brave in action than p. in conduct 1777. Hence **Presu·mptuous-ly** *adv.*, **-ness.**

Presupposal (prīsŏpōu·zăl). Now *rare.* 1589. [f. next + -AL.] A presupposition.

Presuppose (prīsŏpōu·z), *v.* late ME. [a. F. *présupposer*, after med.L. *præsupponere*; see PRE- A. I. 1 and SUPPOSE *v.*] 1. *trans.* Of a person: To suppose, lay down, or postulate beforehand; hence, to assume to start with; to presume. 2. To suppose beforehand or *a priori* 1530. 3. Of a thing: To involve or imply as an antecedent 1526. 4. *pass.* (from 1 or 3). To be implied or involved as something previously or already present or in existence. Formerly with *to.* 1526.

1. Pre-supposing such a desire to please 1809. 2. Men of corrupted minds p. that honesty groweth out of simplicity of manners BACON. 3. An effect presupposes a cause 1877.

Presupposition (prīsŏpŏzi·ʃən). 1533. [ad. med.L. *præsuppositionem*, f. *præsupponere*, f. *præ* PRE- A. I. 1 + *supponere* to SUPPOSE.] 1. The action or an act of presupposing; a supposition antecedent to knowledge. 2. That which is presupposed; a supposition, notion, or idea assumed as a basis of argument, action, etc.; a preliminary assumption 1579.

‖**Presystole** (prīsi·stŏli). 1884. [mod.L., f. PRE- B. I. 1 + SYSTOLE.] *Physiol.* The interval immediately preceding the systole. So **Presysto·lic** *a.*

Pretaxation (prītæksēɪ·ʃən). *Hist.* Also præ-. 1769. [ad. med.L. **prætaxationem*, f. med.L. *prætaxare* to count beforehand; see PRE- A. I. 2 and TAXATION.] The action of giving a vote before others; prior election.

Prete·mporal (prī-), *a.* (*sb.*) 1866. [ad. mod.L. *prætemporalis*; see PRE- B. II. and TEMPORAL.] Situated in front of the temporal region of the skull: applied to a muscle. Also *ellipt.* as *sb.*

Pretence (prĭte·ns). late ME. Also (now U.S.) **pretense.** [= AF. *pretensse*, ad. med.L. **prætensa* vbl. sb., f. *prætensus* for class. L. *prætentus*, pa. pple. of *prætendere*; see PRETEND. The sp. *pretense* is now usual in the U.S.; cf. *defense.*] 1. The putting forth of a claim; a claim. Now *rare.* b. *Her. In p.*, borne on an inescutcheon to indicate a pretension or claim, e.g. that of a husband to the estates of his wife. *Escutcheon of p.*, such an inescutcheon. 1562. 2. The putting forth of a claim to merit, dignity, etc.; pretension, profession; ostentation, display 1526. †3. An expressed intention, purpose, or design; an intending or purposing; the end purposed –1783. b. *esp.* A false or hypocritical profession or pretension 1545. 4. A profession of purpose;

esp. a pretext, a cloak 1538. 5. A (false or misleading) assertion, allegation, or statement as to fact 1608. b. Make-believe, as in children's play 1863. 6. The assertion of a ground, cause, or reason for any action; an alleged ground or reason, a plea; now usu., a trivial, groundless, or fallacious plea or reason, a pretext 1560.

1. Spirits that in our just pretenses arm'd Fell with us from on high MILT. 2. Persons..who yet make great pretences to religion 1729. 3. b. How often do we see p. cultivated in proportion as virtue is neglected 1763. 4. He had some other object—this is all a p. 1845. 5. The p. is that the noble is of unbroken descent from the Norman...But the fact is otherwise. EMERSON. b. This is a fairy tale and all fun and p. KINGSLEY. 6. And ring for the servants on the smallest pretense 1880.

Pretenced, pretensed (-e·nst), *ppl. a.* late ME. [orig. *pretensed*, f. L. *prætensus* + -ED[1] 2.] 1. = PRETENDED 1. *arch.* †2. Intended, purposed, designed –1596. Hence **Prete·ncedly, prete·nsedly** *adv. rare.*

Pretend (prĭte·nd), *v.* late ME. [ad. L. *prætendere* to stretch forth, etc., f. *præ* PRE- A. + *tendere* to stretch, extend, TEND.] I. †1. *trans.* To stretch, or hold (something) before, in front of, or over a person or thing (e.g. as a covering or defence) –1670. †2. To proffer, present; to bring (a charge, an action at law) –1690. 3. †a. *refl.* To put oneself forward in some character; to profess or claim (with *inf.* or *compl.*) –1680. b. Without refl. pron., in same sense as a; whence: To put forth an assertion or statement (expressed by an *inf.*) about oneself; now usu., to feign *to be* or *do* something. (A leading mod. sense.) late ME. c. To feign in play; to make believe 1865. 4. *trans.* To give oneself out as having (something); now always, To profess falsely, to feign (some quality). Now *rare.* late ME. †b. *esp.* To claim to have (a right, title, power, etc.); to claim –1784. †5. To put forth or lay a claim to (a thing); to claim –1761. †6. To put forward as a reason or excuse; to use as a pretext –1776. 7. To allege; now *esp.* to allege or declare with intent to deceive. (A leading current sense.) 1610. †8. To intend, purpose, design, plan –1728. 9. To aspire to; to take upon one; to venture, presume; to attempt, endeavour, try. Const. with *inf.* 1482. †10. To portend, presage, foreshow –1634. †11. To indicate, signify, import, mean –1639.

3. a. Poor, petty, pitiful persons, who pretended themselves princes 1660. b. He was ignorant, or at least pretended to be so FIELDING. 4. The enchantress then related..how she pretended illness 1850. 5. As both the archbishops pretended to sit on his right hand, this question of precedency begat a controversy between them HUME. 7. Pretending that he was sickly 1610. To p. difficulties and inconsistencies BERKELEY. 8. Women when they be most pleasaunt, p. most mischiefe 1579. 9. The people offered to fire at them, if they pretended to go forward DE FOE.

II. *intr.* (from prec. senses.) †1. To stretch forward; to move or go forward; to extend, tend; to make *for* –1650. 2. *To p. to.* †a. To aspire to, aim at; to be a suitor or candidate for –1672. b. *spec.* [= F. *prétendre à.*] To make suit for, try to win in marriage. Now *rare.* 1650. c. To lay claim to 1647. d. To claim or profess to have; to affect 1659. †e. To make pretensions on behalf of –1670. 3. To make pretence; to make believe; to feign 1526. b. In imagination or play: *absol.* of I. 3 c.

1. Who pretendeth to god, God attendeth to hym CAXTON. 2. a. When that my friend pretendeth to a place, I quit my interest, and leave it free G. HERBERT. b. He might p. surely to his kinswoman's hand THACKERAY. c. Yet they pretended to no Share of the Spoil 1683. d. People who p. to supernatural wisdom 1868. 3. Weak to perform, though mighty to p. COWPER. b. *Let's p.*, a child's game of 'make-believe'. Hence **Prete·ndingly** *adv.*

Pretendant, -ent (prĭte·ndănt, -ĕnt), *sb.* and *a.* 1594. [a. F. *prétendant*, f. *prétendre* PRETEND *v.*] A. *sb.* A claimant; esp. to a throne. Now *rare.* 1600. b. A mere pretender 1826. 2. A suitor: a. at law; b. a wooer 1652. †B. *adj.* That claims to be (somebody); of or pertaining to a claimant –1620.

Prete·nded, *ppl. a.* 1461. [f. PRETEND *v.* + -ED[1].] 1. Alleged, asserted; claimed to be such. a. Reputed, so-called 1461. b. Applied to things of which the speaker does not admit the existence, reality, or validity 1500. c. Professed falsely or insincerely 1643. 2. Hence, Fictitious, counterfeit, feigned 1727. †3. Intended, designed, purposed, proposed –1703.

1. a. One Isaac Bickerstaff, a P. Esquire STEELE. 2. An open foe may prove a curse, But a p. friend is worse GAY. Hence **Prete·ndedly** *adv.*

Pretender (prĭte·ndəɹ). 1612. [f. PRETEND *v.* + -ER[1].] 1. One who puts forth a claim, or who aims at something; a claimant, candidate, aspirant; now, one who makes baseless pretensions 1622. †b. A suitor, wooer –1728. c. A claimant to a throne or the office of a ruler; *orig.* in a neutral sense, but now always applied to a claimant who is held to have no just title 1697. 2. One who makes a profession, show, or assertion, esp. on inadequate grounds, or with intent to deceive; a deceiver, charlatan 1631.

1. c. *The Old* and *the Young P.* (Eng. Hist.), the designation of the son and grandson of James II of England, who successively asserted their claim to the British throne against the house of Hanover. 2. To distinguish the p. in medicine from the true physician 1871. Hence **Prete·ndership,** the position or character of a p.

Pretension (prĭte·nʃən). Also †-tion. 1600. [app. ad. med.L. *prætensio*, f. *prætendere*, also med.L. *prætentio.*] The action of pretending. 1. An allegation or assertion the truth of which is not proved or admitted; hence, a pretext, pretence 1609. 2. The assertion of a claim as of right; a claim put forth, a demand 1600. b. A rightful claim, a title 1710. 3. The claim that one is or has something; profession. Also of things. Const. *to.* 1662. b. Pretentiousness, ostentation 1727. †4. An intention, a design; aim, aspiration –1782.

1. Miss Bird..declares all the viands of Japan to be uneatable—a staggering p. 1894. 2. Ecclesiastical pretensions were still formidable under the Tudors FROUDE. 3. I..have little or no Pretensions to Beauty 1718. b. Good without noise, without p. great POPE.

Pretentious (prĭte·nʃəs), *a.* 1845. [ad. F. *prétentieux*, ad. L. **prætentiosus*, f. *prætentionem* PRETENSION; see -IOUS.] Full of pretension; making claim to great merit or importance, esp. when unwarranted; showy, ostentatious. Hence **Prete·ntious-ly** *adv.*, **-ness.**

†**Pre·ter,** *a.* (*sb.*) 1530. [The contraction *præter* for *præteritum* preterite, in *preterperfect*, etc., prefixed in the same way to *tense*, and at length treated as a separate word.] A. *adj. Gram.* = PRETERITE, past –1747. B. *sb.* a. *ellipt.* for *p. tense.* b. Past time, the past. –1675.

Preter-, præter- (prī·təɹ), *prefix.* The L. adv. and prep. *præter* past, by, beyond, above, more than; in addition to, besides; comparative of *præ* before, = further forward.

1. In Latin *præter* adv. was prefixed only to verbs and their derivative sbs. and adjs., as *præterire* to go or pass by, etc., whence *preterite, preterition*, etc. 2. In Scholastic Latin, adjs. began to be formed from L. phrases with *præter* prep. + sb., e.g. *præternaturalis*, from *præter naturam* beyond or outside nature. From these adjs., advs. and nouns of quality, as *preternaturally, preternaturalism*, are always possible.

Preterhuman (prītəɹhiū·măn), *a.* 1811. [f. PRETER- + HUMAN.] Beyond or outside of what is human; often = *superhuman.*

Pre:terimpe·rfect, *a.* (*sb.*) Now *rare.* 1530. [ad. L. *præteritum imperfectum*; see PRETER and IMPERFECT.] *Gram.* = IMPERFECT II. 1. Also *absol.* as *sb.*

Preterist (pre·tĕrist), *sb.* (*a.*) Also **præ-.** 1843. [f. PRETER + -IST.] *Theol.* One who holds that the prophecies of the Apocalypse have been already fulfilled.

Preterite, -it (pre·tĕrit), *a.* (*sb.*) ME. [ad. L. *præteritus* gone by, past, pa. pple. of *præterire*, f. *præter* PRETER- + *ire* to go.] A. *adj.* 1. = PAST *a.* II. 1. 2. *Gram.* Expressing past action or state; past; as *p. tense, p. participle.*

1. Things and persons as thoroughly p. as Romulus or Numa LOWELL.

B. *sb.* [the adj. used ellipt.] †1. Past time, the past; also *pl.* past times or events. *rare.* late ME. only. 2. *Gram.* = Preterite tense 1530. Hence **Pre·teriteness,** the state or condition of being past.

Pre·terite-pre·sent, *a.* (*sb.*) 1874. [ad. mod.L. *præterito-præsens*, neut. pl. *-præsentia*, f. *præteritus* PRETERITE + *præsens* PRESENT.] *Gram.* Applied to verbs of which the tense now used as present was orig. a preterite (or to this tense); e.g. *can, may, must, shall, will.*

Preterition (prītəri·ʃən). Also **præ-.** 1609. [ad. late L. *præteritionem* a passing over, f. *præterire* to go by, pass.] †1. Passing by, passage (of time) –1647. 2. The action of passing over or fact of being passed by or over, without notice; omission, neglect; with *a* and *pl.* an instance of this 1609. 3. *Rhet.* A figure by which summary mention is made of a thing, in professing to omit it 1612. 4. *Theol.* The passing over of the non-elect; non-election to salvation 1621. 5. *Rom. Law.* The omission by a testator to mention in his will one of his children or natural heirs 1722.

Preteritive (prĭte·ritiv), *a. rare.* 1885. [f. L. *præterit-, præterire*; cf. PRETERITE and -IVE.] *Gram.* Used only in the preterite forms 1847; *p. present* = next 1885.

Preterito-present (prĭte·rito,pre·zĕnt), *a.* = PRETERITE-PRESENT.

Preterlabent (prītəɹlǣ·bĕnt), *a. rare.* Also præter-. 1670. [ad. L. *præterlabentem, -labi* to glide or flow by.] Gliding or flowing past.

Pretermission (prītəɹmi·ʃən). Also **præter-.** 1583. [ad. L. *prætermissionem*, f. *prætermittere* (see next).] 1. The passing over, overlooking, or disregarding of anything; omission of anything. 2. Ceasing to do something (for a time); leaving off the practice of anything 1677. 3. *Rhet.* = PRETERITION 3. 1727. 4. *Rom. Law.* = PRETERITION 5. 1795.

Pretermit (prītəɹmi·t), *v.* Also **præter-.** 1513. [ad. L. *prætermittere*, f. *præter* PRETER- + *mittere* to let go, send.] 1. *trans.* To leave out of a narrative; to omit 1538. b. *Rom. Law.* To omit mention of (a descendant or natural heir) in a will 1875. 2. To allow to pass without notice; to overlook intentionally 1542. 3. To fail to do; to leave undone, neglect, omit 1513. 4. To neglect to avail oneself of (time or opportunity); to miss, lose. Now *rare.* 1538. 5. To leave off for the time or for a time; *erron.*, to leave off, cease 1828.

1. The recitall whereof I p. for breuitie 1598. 5. Some customs..have been fortunately pretermitted STEVENSON. Hence **Pretermi·ttently** *adv.*, erron. for INTERMITTENTLY.

Preternatural (prītəɹnæ·tiŭrăl, -tʃərăl), *a.* Also præter-. 1580. [ad. med.L. *præternaturalis*, f. L. phr. *præter naturam*; see PRETER-.] That is out of the ordinary course of nature; beyond, surpassing, or differing from what is natural; non-natural; formerly = abnormal, exceptional, unusual; sometimes = UNNATURAL. b. Used as = SUPERNATURAL 1774.

A preternaturall, or supernaturall ominous worke of God 1580. Mrs. Transome..seemed to hear and see what they said and did with p. acuteness GEO. ELIOT. b. P. impressions are sometimes communicated to us for wise purposes 1829. Hence **Preterna·turalness,** p. quality. **Preterna·turally** *adv.*

Preterna·turalism. 1834. [f. prec. + -ISM.] 1. The character of being preternatural; that which is preternatural; with *a* and *pl.* a preternatural occurrence. 2. A recognition of the preternatural; a system or doctrine of the preternatural 1864.

2. A religion of p. is doomed M. ARNOLD.

Preterperfect (prītəɹpɔ̄·ɹfekt), *a.* (*sb.*) 1534. [ad. late L. *præteritum perfectum* 'complete past', with contraction; see PRETER and PERFECT.] *Gram.* Past perfect; applied to a tense which indicates a past or completed state or action. Also as *sb.* Now *rare* or *Obs.*

Pre:terplupe·rfect, *a.* (*sb.*) 1530. [ad. late L. *præteritum plusquamperfectum*; see PRETER and PLUPERFECT.] 1. *Gram.* = PLUPERFECT *a.* 1. Also *ellipt.* as *sb.* Now *rare* or *Obs.* 2. *gen.* or *allusively.* More than pluperfect; superlatively perfect. (Chiefly *joc.*) 1599.

Pretext (prī·tekst), *sb.* 1513. [ad. L. *prætextus* outward display, f. ppl. stem of *prætexere* to cloak, disguise, pretend. Formerly stressed *prete·xt.*] That which is put forward to cover the real purpose or object; the ostensible reason or motive of action; an excuse, specious plea.

Publick benefit would soon become the p., and perfidy and murder the end BURKE.

Pretext (prĭte·kst), *v.* 1606. [a. F. *prétexter* to take as a pretext, f. *prétexte* PRETEXT *sb.*] *trans.* To use or assign as a pretext; to allege as an excuse; to pretend. Also *absol.*

Pretone (prī·tōun). 1864. [f. PRE- B. +

TONE.] *Phonology.* The syllable or vowel preceding the stressed or tonic syllable. So **Pre-to·nic** *a.* coming immediately before the stressed or tonic syllable.

Prettify (pri·tifəi), *v. colloq.* 1850. [f. PRETTY *a.* + -FY.] *trans.* To make pretty; to represent prettily in a painting or writing.

Prettily (pri·tili), *adv.* late ME. [f. PRETTY *a.* + -LY [2].] In a pretty manner. †1. Cleverly, ingeniously; aptly –1776. 2. In a way that pleases the eye, ear, or æsthetic sense; 'nicely'. late ME. †3. Considerably, fairly –1826.

1. I find how p. this cunning Lord can be partial and dissemble it in this case PEPYS. 2. *Eat, ask, behave p.* (nursery language). 3. I..had an ear that served me p. BYRON.

Prettiness (pri·tinės). 1530. [f. next + -NESS.] The quality of being pretty. 1. Beauty of a slight, diminutive, dainty, or childish kind, without stateliness. †2. Pleasantness, agreeableness –1658. 3. With *a* and *pl.* That which is pretty; a pretty act, thing, feature, etc. 1649. 4. Affected or trivial beauty of expression, style, or execution in literature or art. Also, an instance of this. 1660.

1. The feeble p. of Worcester Chapel 1874. 2. *Haml.* IV. v. 189. 4. He..uttered a thousand prettinesses in the way of compliment SMOLLETT.

Pretty (pri·ti), *a.* (*sb.*) [OE. *prættig*, f. *prætt* trick, wile, craft :—WGer. **pratti-* or **pratta.* The prevailing pronunc. is (pri·ti), but (pru·ti) also is widely current.] †I. In OE. Cunning, crafty, artful, astute. II. From 15th c. 1. a. Of persons: Clever, skilful; apt. *Obs.* or *arch.* late ME. b. Of things: Ingenious, artful, clever. *Obs.* or *arch.* 1440. 2. A general epithet of admiration or appreciation. a. Of persons: Having the proper appearance, manners, or qualities of a man, etc.; conventionally applied to soldiers: Brave, gallant, stout (chiefly *Sc.*). *P. fellow*, a fine fellow, a 'swell', a fop: common in 18th c. Now *arch.* late ME. b. Of things: Fine, nice; proper 1566. c. Used ironically: cf. FINE *a.* III. 1. 1538. 3. Beautiful in a slight, dainty, or diminutive way, as opp. to *handsome*; usu. of women or children 1440. b. Of things: Pleasing to the eye, the ear, or the æsthetic sense 1472. c. Often conjoined with *little*; see LITTLE A. I. 3. late ME. 4. Considerable in number, quantity, or extent, as in *a p. deal, while, way*, etc. Now *arch.* or *dial.* 1485. †b. *P. and* (with another adj.) = PRETTY *adv.* 1. –1633.

1. a. 'There goes the prettiest fellow in the world.. for managing a jury' 1712. 2. a. A p. fellow—that is a fine dress'd man with little sense and a great deal of assurance GAY. He gaed out with other p. men in the Forty-five SCOTT. b. He has a p. wit SHERIDAN. c. A p. pass things are come to, when hussies like this are to be..bepitied THACKERAY. 3. She was a very p. Woman, and is so still, only too fat 1722. While my little one, While my p. one, sleeps TENNYSON. b. She can have a prettier room at the Hook 1888. 4. The transfer of his commission, which brought a p. sum into his pocket THACKERAY. Phr. *A p. penny*, a considerable sum. b. The weather.. was p. and warme 1633.

B. *sb.* (The adj. used absol.) a. A pretty man, woman, or child; a pretty one; in phr. *my p.! my pretties!* 1599. b. A pretty thing; an ornament 1882. c. The fluted or ornamented part of a glass or tumbler 1890. d. The fairway of a golf course 1907.

Pretty (pri·ti), *adv.* 1565. [The adj. in advb. use.] 1. To a considerable extent; fairly, moderately, tolerably; rather. (Qualifying an adj. or adv.). 2. = PRETTILY. Now *rare* and *illiterate.* 1667.

1. It is p. like a young Willow 1727. The other men..lived p. much as they did 1861. *Comb.*: **p.-behaved** = prettily-behaved; **-spoken** = speaking prettily. *colloq.*

Prettyish (pri·ti,iʃ), *a. colloq.* 1741. [-ISH [1].] Somewhat pretty, rather pretty.

Prettyism (pri·ti,iz'm). 1806. [-ISM.] Studied prettiness of style or manner; an instance of this.

Pre·tty-pre·tty, *a.* and *sb.* 1875. [Redupl. of PRETTY *a.*] A. *adj.* That overdoes the pretty; in which the aim at prettiness is overdone 1897. B. *sb.* (*pl.*) Pretty things; ornaments, knick-knacks 1875.

‖**Pretzel** (pre·tsĕl), **bretzel** (bre·tsĕl). *U.S.* 1879. [G.; usu. taken as ad. med.L. *bracellus* a bracelet.] A crisp biscuit baked in the form of a knot and flavoured with salt; used by Germans as a relish with beer.

‖**Preux** (prȫ), *a.* 1771. [F. :—late L. *prodis.*] Brave, valiant, gallant; chiefly in *p. chevalier*, gallant knight.

Prevail (prĭvēⁱ·l), *v.* [Late ME. *prevaylle*, *-vaile*, ad. L. *prævalere* to be very able, prevail (see PRE- and VAIL *v.*).] †1. *intr.* To become very strong; to increase in vigour or force (*rare*) –1755. 2. To be superior in strength or influence; to have or gain the superiority or advantage; to gain the mastery or ascendancy; to be victorious. Const. *against, over*, †*of*, †*upon.* 1450. 3. To be effectual or efficacious; to succeed. late ME. †b. *trans.* To persuade, induce –1834. †4. *intr.* = AVAIL *v.* 2. –1584. †b. *trans.* = AVAIL *v.* 3. –1593. †c. = AVAIL *v.* 5. Usu. *refl.* –1681. 5. *intr.* To be or become the stronger, more wide-spread, or more frequent usage or feature; to predominate. (A weakening of sense 2.) 1628. b. Hence, To be in general use or practice; to be prevalent or current 1776.

2. Hell gates shall not prevayle ageinste them 1529. Great is truth, and it shall prevaile 1650. 3. But why Prevailed not thy pure prayers? TENNYSON. Phr. †*To p. to* (a thing) or *to do* (something), to succeed in doing, attaining, etc. (*rare*). *To p. on, upon*, †*with*, to succeed in persuading, inducing, or influencing. 4. c. P. yourself of what occasion gives DRYDEN. 5. Soon as the Evening Shades p., The Moon takes up the wondrous Tale ADDISON. b. Their way of thinking is far better than any other which now prevails in the world JOWETT. Hence **Prevai·ling** *ppl. a.* **Prevai·lingly** *adv.* in a prevailing manner or degree.

Prevalence (pre·vălĕns). 1592. [a. F. *prévalence*, ad. med.L. *prævalentia* superior force, f. *prævalere* to PREVAIL; see -ENCE.] 1. The fact or action of prevailing; the having or obtaining of predominance or mastery. Now *rare.* 2. Effective force or power; influence, weight; efficacy; prevailingness. Now *rare.* 1631. 3. The condition of being prevalent, or of general occurrence or existence; common practice or acceptance. (The ordinary current sense.) 1713.

1. The final p. of the good over the evil 1833. 2. Example has great p., whether good or bad 1802. 3. The p. of ambition STEELE. The steady p. of winds in the westerly quarter BURKE. So **Pre·valency** (now *rare*), in all senses.

Prevalent (pre·vălĕnt), *a.* 1576. [ad. L. *prævalens, -entem, prævalere*; see PREVAIL *v.*] 1. Having great power or force; effective; efficacious, potent. Now *rare.* 2. Having the superiority or ascendancy; predominant, victorious. Now *rare.* 1614. 3. Most extensively used or practised; generally accepted; of frequent occurrence; extensively existing; in general use 1658.

1. Ill-affected persons, who are so p. with His Majestie 1642. Cider..is also p. against the stone 1676. 2. The Puritans, though then p., did not think proper to dispute this great constitutional point HUME. 3. The cholera was p. in that year 1870. Hence **Pre·valently** *adv.*

Prevaricate (prĭvæ·rikēⁱt), *v.* 1582. [f. L. *prævaricari* to walk crookedly, hence, to deviate from the path of duty; in eccl. L. to transgress, f. *præ* PRE- A. + *varicare* to straddle (f. *varicus*, f. *varus* bent, knock-kneed + *-icus* -IC); see -ATE [3].] I. *intr.* †1. To go aside from the right course, method, or mode of action; to deviate, go astray, transgress –1681. 2. To deviate from straightforwardness; to act or speak evasively; to quibble, shuffle, equivocate 1631. †3. *Law.* a. To betray the cause of a client by collusion with an opponent. b. To undertake a matter falsely and deceitfully in order to defeat the object professed to be promoted. –1716.

2. Do not hesitate nor p.; but answer faithfully and truly to every question I ask FIELDING.

II. *trans.* †1. To deviate from, transgress (a 'law', etc.) –1604. †2. To turn (anything) from the straight course, application, or meaning; to pervert –1705.

2. He may not p. this duty of a judge JER. TAYLOR.

Prevarication (prĭværikēⁱ·ʃən). late ME. [ad. L. *prævaricationem*; see prec.] †1. Divergence from the right course, method, or mode of action –1701. †2. Deviation from duty; violation of trust; corrupt action, esp. in a court of law –1741. †b. *Law.* See PREVARICATE *v.* 3. –1710. 3. Avoidance of plain dealing; evasion, quibbling, equivocation, double-dealing, deception 1655.

1. That all Men do not die through the Death and P. of Adam 1701. 2. *P.* is also used for a secret abuse committed in the exercise of a public office, or of a commission given by a private person 1727. 3. Hume..was a man..utterly incapable of falsehood, or of p. of any kind 1862.

Prevaricator (prĭvæ·rikēⁱtəɹ). 1542. [a. L. *prævaricator*, f. *prævaricari* to PREVARICATE; see -OR.] †1. One who prevaricates; a transgressor –1755. †b. One who betrays a cause or violates a trust –1637. †2. One who diverts something from its proper use; a perverter –1907. 3. A quibbler, shuffler, equivocator 1650. 4. At Cambridge University: An orator who made a jocose or satirical speech at Commencement; called also *varier. Obs.* exc. *Hist.* 1614. †5. *Law.* (See PREVARICATE *v.* 3.) –1793. So **Preva·ricatory** *a.* (*rare*), prevaricating; evasive.

Preve, obs. f. PROOF, PROVE.

Prevenance (pre·vĭnăns). 1823. [a. F. *prévenance* (prevənāns), which is also in Eng. use, f. *prévenir* to anticipate, prepossess; see PREVENE and -ANCE.] Courteous anticipation of the desires or needs of others; an obliging manner; complaisance.

She did everything he asked carefully and well, but the sweet p. was gone 1876.

†**Preve·ne,** *v.* Chiefly *Sc.* 1456. [ad. L. *prævenire*, f. *præ* PRE- A. + *venire* to come.] *trans.* To take action before or in anticipation of (a person or thing) –1708.

Prevenient (prĭvī·niĕnt), *a.* 1607. [ad. L. *prævenientem*; see prec.] 1. Coming before, preceding, previous 1656. b. Hence, Anticipatory, expectant. Const. *of.* 1814. 2. Antecedent to human action 1607.

2. *P. grace* (Theol.), the grace of God which precedes repentance and conversion, predisposing the heart to seek God, previously to any desire or motion on the part of the recipient. Hence **Preve·niently** *adv.* previously (*rare*).

Prevent (prĭve·nt), *v.* late ME. [f. L. *prævent-*, ppl. stem of *prævenire*; see PREVENE.] I. †1. *trans.* To act in anticipation of or in preparation for (a future event, or a point of time); to act as if the event or time had already come –1813. b. To meet beforehand (an objection, question, command, desire, want, etc.). *arch.* 1533. †c. *intr.* or *absol.* To come, appear, or act before the time –1626. 2. *trans.* To act before or more quickly than (another person or agent); to anticipate in action. Now *rare* and *arch.* 1523. 3. To come, arrive, or appear before, to precede; to outrun, outstrip. Now *rare* and *arch.* 1523. 4. *Theol.* To go before with spiritual guidance and help; said of God, or of his grace anticipating human action or need. *arch.* 1531. b. Said of the action of God's grace; see PREVENIENT 2. *arch.* 1548. †c. To come in front of; to meet –1611.

1. Thus we p. the last great day, And judge our selves 1633. b. Your goodness still prevents my wishes DRYDEN. 3. I went..to Geneva, where I found..my fame had prevented my coming 1648. 4. That thy grace maye alwayes preuente and folowe us *Bk. Com. Prayer.* c. The euill shall not ouertake nor preuent vs *Amos* ix. 10.

II. †1. To forestall, balk, or baffle by previous measures –1737. 2. To cut off beforehand, debar, preclude *from*, deprive *of* a purpose, expectation, etc. Now *rare.* 1549. 3. To stop, keep, or hinder *from* doing something. Often with const. omitted. 1663. 4. To provide beforehand against the occurrence of (something); to preclude, stop, hinder 1548. †5. To keep (something) from befalling oneself; to escape by timely action –1710. †6. To frustrate, defeat, bring to nought (an expectation, plan, etc.) –1652. †7. *intr.* or *absol.* To use preventive measures –1723.

2. A wall prevents me from this sight L. HUNT. 3. To..p. the enemy from erecting their magazines SWIFT. To p. this becoming a serious affair MORLEY. 4. Should any thing occur..to p. his return W. IRVING. I shall not p. your going 1847. 7. *Jul. C.* II. i. 28.

†III. 1. *causative.* To bring about or put before the time or prematurely; to anticipate –1683. 2. To preoccupy, prejudice (a person's mind) –1718.

2. Endeavouring to p. your Lordship in Favour of my Author 1718. Hence **Preve·ntable** 1640,

-ible 1850, *adjs.* that may be prevented. **Preventa·bi·lity, -ibi·lity.**

Preventative (prĭve·ntătiv), *a.* and *sb.* 1654. [f. PREVENT *v.* + -ATIVE.] = PREVENTIVE *a.* 2, 2 b, 2 c, and *sb.*

Preventer (prĭve·ntəɹ). 1587. [f. as prec. + -ER[1].] †1. One who goes or acts before another; an anticipator BACON. 2. A person or thing that hinders, restrains, or keeps something from occurring or being done 1587. 3. *Naut.* orig. *p.-rope*, an auxiliary rope to support spars, etc., during a strong gale; later, applied to any additional rope, etc. used to strengthen or take the place of another 1711.

attrib. and *Comb.*, as *p.-backstay, -brace, -rope, -stay*, etc.; also, denoting other secondary or additional parts serving to strengthen or take the place of the main ones, as *p.-bolt, -plate*, etc.

Prevention (prĭve·nʃən). 1528. [ad. late L. *præventionem*, f. *prævenire* to PREVENT.] †1. Previous occurrence, anticipation; in *Theol.* the action of prevenient grace -1705. 2. *Canon Law.* The privilege claimed by an ecclesiastical superior of forestalling an inferior in the execution of an official act regularly pertaining to the latter 1528. †3. Action or occurrence before the expected, appointed, or normal time; anticipation -1711. 4. †a. The action of forestalling -1667. †b. Precaution; a precaution, a defensive measure -1774. c. The action of keeping from happening or of rendering impossible an anticipated event or an intended act 1661. †d. A means of preventing; a safeguard; an obstacle, obstruction -1821. †5. A mental anticipation; a presentiment -1801. †6. Prepossession, bias, prejudice -1829.

4. a. Caska be sodaine, for we feare preuention SHAKS. c. Lord Erskine's Bill for the P. of Cruelty towards Animals 1813. *Prov.* P. is better than cure.

Preventive (prĭve·ntiv), *a.* and *sb.* 1639. [f. L. *prævent-, prævenire*; see PREVENE and -IVE.] A. *adj.* †1. That comes or goes before something else; antecedent, anticipatory -1698. 2. That anticipates in order to ward against; that acts as a hindrance or obstacle 1639. b. *Med.* Having the quality of keeping off disease; prophylactic 1646. c. Belonging to that department of the Customs which is concerned with the prevention of smuggling; *spec.* of or belonging to the Coast Guard 1827.

2. A p. war, grounded on a just fear of an invasion FULLER. Statutes p. of blasphemy and profaneness 1822. b. Physicke is either curative or p. SIR T. BROWNE.

B. *sb.* A preventive agent or measure; a hindrance, obstacle, obstruction 1639. b. *Med.* A prophylactic 1674. Hence **Preve·ntively** *adv.*

Previous (prī·viəs), *a.* (*adv.*) 1625. [f. L. *prævius* going before, leading the way (f. *præ* PRE- A. + *via* way) + -OUS.] †1. Going before or in front; leading the way. Also *fig.* -1678. 2. Coming or going before (in time or order); preceding, prior. Also with *to* (now *rare*). 1625. 3. *slang* or *colloq.* (orig. *U. S.*) Coming too soon, hasty, premature. (Usu. with *too.*) 1885.

2. A p. blast foretels the rising storm YOUNG. Phr. *P. question* (in parliamentary procedure), the question whether a vote shall be taken on the main question or issue, moved before the main question is put. *P. Examination* (Cambridge Univ.), the first examination for the B.A. degree; colloq. called *Little-go.* (Also ellipt. as *sb.*)

B. as *adv.* Previously; usu. *p. to* = before, prior to 1719.

P. to Ordination, they may be subjected to some literary ordeal 1849. Hence **Pre·vious·ly** *adv.*, **-ness.**

Previse (prĭvəi·z), *v.* 1597. [f. L. *prævis-, prævidere* to foresee, anticipate.] 1. *trans.* To foresee; to forecast. Also *absol.* 2. To inform beforehand LYTTON.

Prevision (prĭvi·ʒən), *sb.* 1612. [ad. L. **prævisionem*, f. *prævidere.*] The action or faculty of foreseeing; knowledge of or insight into the future; an instance of this. Hence **Previ·sion** *v. trans.*, (*a*) to endow with p.; (*b*) to have p. of, to foresee. **Previ·sional** *a.* relating to, depending on, characterized by, or exhibiting p.; **-ly** *adv.*

Prey (prē̆i), *sb.* [ME. *preye*, a. OF. *preie* booty, prey, F. *proie*, earlier OF. **preide* :—L. *præda.*] 1. That which is taken in war, or by pillage or violence; booty, spoil, plunder. Formerly, often with *pl. arch. rare.* b. *fig.* (In Scriptural use.) That which one brings away or saves from any contest, etc. late ME. 2. An animal hunted or killed by carnivorous animals for food; quarry. Now only *collect.* ME. 3. One who or that which falls or is given into the power of a hostile person or an injurious influence; a victim; esp. in const. *to be* or *become a p. to* ME. 4. The action of preying; seizing or taking by force or violence, or (of an animal) in order to devour; depredation, pillage, capture. Now *rare.* 1523.

1. b. He shall have his life for a p., and shall live *Jer.* xxxviii. 2. 2. As the Tigre his time awaiteth In hope forto cacche his preie GOWER. 3. Jerusalem fell an easy p. to his arms BURKE. To dumb Forgetfulness a p. GRAY. 4. The whole little wood..is a world of plunder and p. TENNYSON. *Beast, bird, fish*, etc., *of p.*, one that kills and devours other animals. Hence †**Prey·ful** *a.* (*rare*), killing much p., prone to prey.

Prey (prē̆i), *v.* [ME. a. OF. *preer, preier* :—late L. *prædare*, collateral f. *prædari* to plunder, etc., f. *præda* PREY *sb.*] †1. *trans.* To plunder, pillage, spoil; to rob, ravage (a place, person, etc.) -1654. 2. *intr.* To take booty; to pillage, plunder; *to p. on, upon* = sense 1. ME. 3. To seek for or take prey, as an animal; esp. with *on, upon*: To seize and kill as prey; to kill and devour, to feed on ME. 4. To exert a baneful, wasting, or destructive influence *on, upon*; to destroy gradually 1713.

2. The buccaneers preying upon Spanish commerce 1872. 3. *fig.* Brokers I meane and Vsurers, that like vultures p. vpon the simple 1610. 4. The secret which preyed upon his mind 1798. Hence **Prey·er**, one who or that which preys.

Priapean (prəiˌăpī·ăn), *a.* 1693. [ad. F. *priapéen*, f. L. *Priapeius* (a. Gr. Πριάπειος adj., f. Πρίαπος) + -*en* -AN.] 1. Priapic. 2. *Anc. Pros.* Applied to a logaœdic metre consisting of a catalectic Glyconic and a Pherecratean, associated with poems to Priapus.

Priapic (prəiˌæ·pik), *a.* 1786. [f. PRIAPUS + -IC.] Of or relating to Priapus or his cult.

Priapism (prəi·ăpiz'm). 1598. [ad. late L. *Priapismus*, a. Gr. Πριαπισμός, f. Πριαπίζειν to act Priapus; see next and -ISM.] 1. *Path.* Persistent erection of the penis. 2. = PRIAPUS 3. 1662. 3. Licentiousness; intentional indecency. Also *fig.* 1758.

Priapus (prəiˌē̆i·pɒs). late ME. [a. L., a. Gr. Πρίαπος.] 1. The Greek and Roman god of procreation, (and so) of gardens, vineyards, etc. 2. A statue or image of the god Priapus; often placed in gardens to protect them from depredators or as a scarecrow 1632. 3. A phallus. b. A drinking vessel of phallic shape. 1613.

Pri·bble. 1598. Weakened echo of PRABBLE, dial. var. of BRABBLE.

P. and prabble (SHAKS.), *p.-prabble*, petty disputation, vain chatter.

Price (prəis), *sb.* [ME. a. OF. *pris* (F. *prix*) :—late L. *precium*, orig. *pretium.*] I. Money, or the like, paid for something. 1. The money (or other equivalent) for which anything is bought or sold; the rate at which this is done or proposed; also, less usu., wages; rate of wages. b. Payment of money in purchase of something. *Obs.* exc. in phr. *without p.* = without payment, gratis (*arch.*). late ME. c. Estimation of value 1582. 2. A sum of money offered for the capture, apprehension, or death of a person 1766. 3. *Betting.* = ODDS 5. 1882. 4. The amount of money, or other consideration, by which a man's support or interest may be purchased 1780. 5. *fig.* What it costs to obtain some advantage. late ME.

1. To haue vytaylles at resonable prys CAXTON. Labour was the first p., the original purchase-money that was paid for all things ADAM SMITH. Slang phr. *What price..?*, a taunting questioning of the vaunted value of something. b. Come, buy wine and milke without money, and without p. *Isa.* lv. 1. c. *Above, beyond, without p.* = PRICELESS 1. 2. *To set* (*put*) *a p. on* (*the head of*, etc.). 3. The starting p. of Mr. Perkin's horse was 5 to 1. 1882. 4. Every man has his p. BENTHAM. 5. *At any p.*, whatever it may cost, whatever loss or disadvantage is or may be entailed; He determined to bring his design to pass at any p. whatsoever 1653.

II. Value, worth. *Obs.* or *arch.* 1. Preciousness, value, worth. Usu. qualified as *great, dear, little, no*, etc. *arch.* ME. 2. *Of p.*, of great value, worth, or excellence. *arch.* ME. †3. Esteem, estimation, regard -1662. †b. Valuation, appraisement SHAKS.

2. Faire pillars of marble..and other stones of p. 1615. 3. Wel biloued and holden in greet prys CHAUCER. Phr. *To have* or *hold in p.*, to value highly. b. Cæsars no Merchant, to make prize with you Of things that Merchants sold SHAKS.

†III. 1. Honour, glory, renown -1600. 2. = PRAISE *sb.* 1. -1567. †IV. 1. The position of excelling others; first or highest place; preeminence. Usu. in phr. *to bear* or *have the p.*, to have the pre-eminence. -1573. †2. The position of excelling in a match or struggle; superiority, victory -1542. †3. = PRIZE *sb.*[1] ME.

2. If yᵉ flemynges had achyued the prise ouer them 1523. *attrib.* and *Comb.*: **p.-current**, a list of current prices of commodities; a price-list; **-cutting**, the action of 'cutting down' or lowering prices, esp. in or by way of competition; also *attrib.*; **-list**, (*a*) a list of the prices of commodities offered for sale; (*b*) a list of the 'prices' or odds in betting.

Price (prəis), *v.* 1490. [var., assimilated to prec. sb., of the earlier *prise*, now PRIZE *v.*[1]] 1. *trans.* To fix the price of (a thing for sale); to state the price of. †2. To pay the price for, pay for -1590. 3. To enquire the price of, bargain for 1845. †4. = PRIZE *v.*[1] 3. -1643.

1. London ale was priced 5*s.* a barrel more than that of Kent 1845. 2. So that thi confessioun ma thi synnes pryce DUNBAR. 4. Men p. the thing ungained more then it is SHAKS.

Priced (prəist), *ppl. a.* 1552. [f. PRICE *sb.* or *v.* + -ED.] 1. Having the price fixed or stated; containing a statement of prices. 2. Having a (specified or indicated) price; in parasynthetic combs., as *high-, low-p.*

Priceite (prəi·səit). 1873. [f. name of Thomas *Price*, an American metallurgist.] *Min.* Hydrous borate of calcium.

Priceless (prəi·slės), *a.* 1593. [f. PRICE *sb.* + -LESS.] 1. Having a value beyond all price or equivalent; invaluable. b. Having no market price; that cannot be obtained for money 1884. 2. Having no value; worthless 1771. 3 Incredibly amusing or absurd (*slang*) 1907.

Prick (prik), *sb.* [OE. *pric*(*c*)*a*, *price*, = LG. *prik* a sharp point; cf. PRICK *v.*] I. 1. A minute hole or impression made by pricking; a puncture. b. *spec.* in *Farriery.* A puncture or wound in the quick or sole of the foot of a horse 1607. c. The track of a hare 1598. 2. A minute mark made by slightly pricking or indenting a surface with a pointed tool; a dot, tick, point. OE. †b. Each of the marks dividing the circumference of a dial, or any scale -1593. †3. = POINT *sb.*[1] I. 2, 3. -1749.

1. The less credulous tooke the pricke of a pinne for a Saintes marke 1638. 2. Set ther a prikke of ynke CHAUCER. b. *Rom. & Jul.* II. iv. 119.

†II. A minute particle. 1. A point of space (or particle of matter), in ref. to its minuteness, a mere point -1616. 2. = POINT *sb.*[1] III. 1. -1645. 3. = POINT *sb.*[1] III. 2. -1579.

1. This little pricke of the world (for surely the earth is nothing else in comparison of the whole) HOLLAND. 2. Not one jot or p. of the Law shall perish 1645.

†III. A point in ref. to position. 1. A point in space, a geometrical point -1619. 2. A point marking a stage in progression; degree, pitch -1606. †IV. In archery. The mark aimed at in shooting; the spot in the centre of a target; hence, a target -1845. V. Anything that pricks or pierces. 1. A small sharp projecting organ or part; a thorn or prickle; a spine on the skin of an animal, or the like. Also †*fig.* Now *rare* or *Obs.* ME. 2. A goad for oxen ME. †3. A slender piece of wood or metal tapering to a sharp point; a skewer; a pin for fastening one's clothes; a thatcher's broach -1721. 4. A pointed weapon or implement; e.g. †a dagger; a chisel; etc. 1552. 5. The penis. (Not now in polite use.) 1592. 6. A small roll (of tobacco). 1666.

1. As pricks be hidden under Roses 1579. *fig.* Forsoth the pricke of deeth is synne WYCLIF 1 *Cor.* xv. 55. 2. *To kick against the pricks*, said of oxen; now *arch.* and usu. *fig.* (after Acts ix. 5).

VI. The act of pricking, or the fact of being pricked; a puncture. Also *fig.*, esp. in *p. of conscience* (med.L. *stimulus conscientiæ*), stinging compunction, remorse; in earlier use, that which pricks the conscience or causes remorse. ME.

Gentlewomen that liue honestly by the pricke of their Needles SHAKS. A p. with a Catfishes Fin 1699. *attrib.* and *Comb.*: **p.-hedge**, a thorn hedge; **-line**, a dotted line; **-spur**, a spur having a single point;

-tobacco, tobacco made up into a small roll; see V. 6; **-wheel**, a toothed wheel mounted on a handle, used by saddlers for marking places for stitches at regular intervals. Hence **Pri·cky** *a. dial.* prickly.

Prick (prik), *v.* [Late OE. *prician*, ME. *prikie(n, prike*; cogn. with OE. *prica* PRICK *sb.*; perh. from an onomatopœic root.] **I.** To pierce, or indent with a sharp point. **1.** *trans.* To pierce slightly, make a minute hole in (a surface or body) with a fine or sharp point; to puncture; hence, to wound (or hurt) with or as with a pointed instrument. Said also of the instrument. **b.** To make (a hole or mark) by pricking 1680. **c.** *Farriery.* To pierce the foot of (a horse) to the quick in shoeing, causing lameness 1591. **d.** To affect with a sensation as of pricking. late ME. **2.** *fig.* To cause sharp mental pain to; to sting with sorrow or remorse; to grieve, pain, vex. Also *absol.* OE. **3.** *intr.* To perform the action of pricking or piercing; to cause a pricking sensation; also, to have the quality of pricking, to be sharp OE. **4.** To thrust *at* something as if to pierce it; to make a thrust or stab *at* 1470. †**b.** *Archery.* To shoot at a 'prick' or target; hence *fig.* to aim *at* –1622. **5.** *intr.* or *absol.* Of a hare: To make a track in running. late ME. **b.** *trans.* To look for or find the 'pricks' of (a hare); to trace or track (a hare) by its footprints. Also *absol.* or *intr.* late ME. **6.** *intr.* To have a sensation of being pricked; to tingle 1850. **7.** Of wine, beer, etc.: To become or begin to be sour; to be touched or tainted with acetous fermentation; = F. *se piquer* 1594.

1. I could perceive her to take pins out of her pocket to p. me PEPYS. Phr. *To prick a* or *the bladder* or *bubble*, to show the emptiness of a person or thing that has passed for important or formidable. 2. His conscience pricks him so much that he cannot rest 1874. 3. The Thorn, or Bryar, which p., and scratch BACON. Phr. *To p. for*, to try, choose, or decide for something by pricking; also *fig. To p.* (*in*) *the belt, garter, loop*, to play at FAST-AND-LOOSE. 5. b. You have been pricking up and down here upon a cold scent DRYDEN. 6. When the blood creeps, and the nerves p. And tingle TENNYSON.

II. 1. *trans.* †To urge forward (a beast) with a goad; to spur (a horse) (*arch.*) ME. **2.** *fig.* To drive or urge as with a spur; to incite, stimulate, provoke ME. **3.** *intr.* To spur or urge a horse on; to ride fast; hence, to ride ME.

2. So priketh hem nature in hir corages CHAUCER. 3. A gentle Knight was pricking on the plaine SPENSER.

III. To mark by or with pricks or dots. †**1.** *trans.* To write or set down (music) by means of 'pricks' or notes –1826. **2.** To mark or indicate by a 'prick'; *esp.* to mark (a name, or an item) in a list by making a 'prick' through or against it; hence, to mark off or tick off in this way; *spec.* (of the sovereign) to select (persons) for the office of sheriff from a list by this means; also, to appoint, choose, pick *out*. Also *p. down, off.* etc. 1557. **3.** To mark or trace something on (a surface) by pricks or dots; also, to mark or trace (a position, direction, design, etc.) on a surface by pricks or dots. Also *p. off, out*. 1598.

1. To my chamber, to p. out my song 'It is Decreed' PEPYS. 2. My friend was pricked as High Sheriff of the county 1853. 3. To p. the Chart..at Sea, signifies to make a Point in their Chart whereabout the Ship is now 1704.

IV. To put into some position or condition by piercing or transfixing. †**1.** To secure or fasten with a pin or skewer, or the like –1819. **2.** To attire (a person) elaborately with the aid of pins, bodkins, etc.; to dress *up*. Now *dial.* ME. †**3.** To remove, or bring into some position, by pricking –1683. **4.** To plant (seedlings) in small holes made by piercing the ground at suitable intervals. Const. *in, out, off*. Also, to *p. in* (manure). 1608. **5.** *To p. up* (in plastering on laths): to scratch or score the surface of the first coat so as to afford a hold for the next; hence, to lay on the first coat 1778.

1. *Tam. Shr.* III. ii. 70. 3. *Rom. & Jul.* I. iv. 66. 4. Cabbage plants are pricked in in March 1854.

V. To insert or stick as a point. †**1.** To thrust or stick (a pointed object) *into* something; to set, fix, or insert by the point; to stick *in, on* –1669. †**2.** To stick (something) *full of*, or set (it) *with* pointed objects or points; hence, to stud, mark, or dot *with* something. 1530. **VI.** To stick up as or in a point. **1.** To raise or erect, as the ears of an animal when listening; hence, of a person, *to p. up one's ears*, to become attentive 1587. **2.** *intr. P. up*, to rise or stand erect with the point directed upward; to point or stick up 1610.

1. At this the town of Mansoul began to p. up its ears BUNYAN. 2. His ears..p. up at the sound of a fiddle 1887.

Pri·ck-ea:r, prick ear. 1634. [app. back-formation from next.] **1.** *pl.* The erect pointed ears of some beasts, *spec.* of dogs; ears that are pricked up or stand erect; hence *fig.* those of a person on the alert to hear. **b.** Applied to the ears of a 'Roundhead'; cf. next 2. 1641. †**2.** A person having prick-ears; one whose ears are conspicuous; a nickname for a Puritan –1642.

Prick-eared (pri·kˌīəːɹd), *a.* late ME. [app. f. PRICK *sb.* (branch V) + EARED.] **1.** Having erect ears; *spec.* of dogs. **b.** *fig.* Having the ears pricked or erected in attention; hence, attentive, alert 1550. **2.** Of a man: Having the hair cut short and close, so that the ears are prominent; applied to Puritans or 'Roundheads'; whence opprobriously, priggish 1641.

1. b. Jealousy is p., and will hear the wagging of a hair MIDDLETON. 2. These Prickear'd, starch, sanctify'd Fellows 1707.

Pricker (pri·kəɹ). late ME. [f. PRICK *v.* + -ER[1].] One who or that which pricks. **1.** One who pricks or goads. Also *fig.* **2.** One who spurs or rides a horse; a horseman; hence, a mounted soldier, *esp.* a light horseman employed as a skirmisher or scout. *arch.* and *Hist.* late ME. **3.** *spec.* A mounted attendant at a hunt, a huntsman. Now chiefly in YEOMAN *p.* 1575. **4.** An instrument or tool for pricking or piercing. late ME.

Pricket (pri·kėt). late ME. [app. ad. med. (Anglo-) L. *prikettus*, f. Eng. *prike* PRICK *sb.* + Rom. suffix *-ettus, -etto* -ET.] **1.** A buck in its second year, having straight unbranched horns 1440. **2.** A spike on which to stick a candle; hence, *p. candlestick*, a candlestick having one or more of these. late ME.

Pricking (pri·kiŋ), *vbl. sb.* ME. [f. PRICK *v.* + -ING[1].] The action of PRICK *v.* *esp.* **1.** Piercing, puncturing, wounding. With *a* and *pl.*, an instance of this. late ME. **b.** The sensation of, or as of, being pricked; smarting, tingling ME. **2.** The footprint or track of a hare (rarely of other beasts). Hence, the tracking of a hare by its pricks. late ME. **4.** *P. up* (Plastering): see PRICK *v.* IV. 5. 1778.

1. b. By the p. of my Thumbes, Something wicked this way comes SHAKS.

Prickle (pri·k'l), *sb.*[1] [OE. *pricel*, later form of *pricels*, f. stem *pric-* of *prician* to PRICK + instr. suffix *-els*.] †**1.** A thing to prick with; a goad –1609. **2.** A rigid sharp-pointed process developed from the bark or any part of the epidermis of a plant, consisting of a compound hair 1580. **3.** A hard-pointed spine or outgrowth of the epidermis of an animal, as in the hedgehog, etc. 1567. **4.** *fig.* Something that pricks the mind or feelings. (Chiefly in *pl.*) 1638.

4. The Rose has prickles, so has Love, Though these a little sharper prove 1705.

Prickle (pri·k'l), *sb.*[2] 1609. *Obs.* or *local.* [Origin obsc.] A wicker basket, esp. for fruit or flowers. **b.** *spec.* As a measure 1674.

Prickle (pri·k'l), *v.* 1513. [Partly from PRICKLE *sb.*[1]; partly dim. of PRICK *v.*] **1.** *trans.* (or *absol.*) To prick, as with a goad, etc.; hence, to goad, instigate. **b.** *transf.* To affect with a prickling sensation 1855. **2.** *intr.* To tingle as if pricked 1634.

Pri·ckle-back. 1711. [f. PRICKLE *sb.*[1] + BACK *sb.*[1]] The three-spined stickleback.

Pricklouse (pri·kˌlaus). Now *dial.* 1500. A derisive name for a tailor.

Prickly (pri·kli), *a.* 1578. [f. PRICKLE *sb.*[1] + -Y[1].] **1.** Having, armed with, or full of prickles; aculeate. Also *fig.* **2.** Having a sensation as of many pricking points; smarting; tingling 1836

Special collocations **p. ash**, an aromatic N. Amer. shrub, *Xanthoxylum americanum*; **p. palm, pole**, a West Indian palm, *Bactris Plumierana*; **p. rat**, any one of the species of *Ctenomys* and allied genera of S. Amer. burrowing rodents, the hair of which is usu. intermingled with sharp spines. Hence **Pri·ckliness.**

Prickly heat. 1736. A common name for *Lichen tropicus*, an inflammatory disorder of the sweat glands, prevalent in hot countries, characterized by eruption of small papules or vesicles, accompanied by a sense of pricking or burning.

Prickly pear. 1760. Any species of the cactaceous genus *Opuntia*, prickly plants with pear-shaped fleshy edible fruit; also the fruit.

†**Pri·ck-ma·dam.** 1545. [Altered from F. *trique-madame*.] *Herb.* An old name of the Stone-crops, esp. *Sedum acre*; also *S. album* and *S. reflexum* –1883.

Pri·ck-seam. 1632. [f. PRICK *sb.* or *v.* + SEAM.] A particular stitch used in glove-sewing. Also *attrib.*

Prick-song (pri·kˌsǫŋ). *Obs.* exc. *Hist.* 1463. [Shortened from *pricked song, prickt song*; cf. PRICK *v.* III. 1.] *Mus.* **1.** Music sung from notes written or 'pricked'; written vocal music. **2.** *esp.* A written descant; hence, *gen.* descant or 'counterpoint' accompanying a simple melody (also *fig.*) 1501.

Pri·ckwood. 1661. [PRICK *sb.* V. 3.] **a.** The Spindle-tree. **b.** The Wild Cornel 1869.

Pride (prəid), *sb.*[1] [Late OE. *prȳtu, prȳte*, also *prȳde*, f. *prūt, prūd* PROUD.] The quality of being proud. **I. 1.** A high or overweening opinion of one's own qualities, attainments, or estate; inordinate self-esteem. **b.** in pl. *rare.* OE. **c.** Personified, esp. as the first of the seven deadly sins. late ME. **2.** The exhibition of this quality in attitude, bearing, conduct, etc.; arrogance, haughtiness ME. **3.** A consciousness of what is befitting or due to oneself or one's position; as a good quality, 'honest' or 'proper pride'; also as a misapplied feeling, 'false pride' ME. **4.** A feeling of elation or high satisfaction derived from some action or possession; esp. in *to take a p. in* 1597. **5.** That of which any person or body of persons is proud; hence, the flower, the best, of a class, country, etc. late ME. **b.** In names of plants 1629.

1. P. goeth before destruction *Prov.* xvi. 18. Spiritual p. JER. TAYLOR. P. must have a fall JOHNSON. P. of birth 1797. 2. P. in their port, defiance in their eye, I see the lords of human kind pass by GOLDSM. 3. Chatterton, the marvellous Boy, The sleepless Soul that perished in his p. WORDSW. 4. My Grauitie Wherein..I take p. SHAKS. 5. A bold peasantry, their country's p. GOLDSM. **b. P. of China, p. of India**, a tree, the AZEDARAC; **p. of London** = LONDON PRIDE.

II. 1. Magnificence, splendour; pomp, display. *poet* and *rhet.* ME. †**b.** Love of display or ostentation –1680. **2.** Magnificent, splendid, or ostentatious adornment or ornamentation (*arch.*) ME. †**3.** Honour, glory –1591. **4.** The best, highest, most excellent or flourishing state or condition; the prime; the flower. late ME. **5.** Mettle or spirit in a horse 1592. †**6.** Sexual desire, 'heat'; esp. in female animals –1604. **7.** *Falconry. P. of place*: see PLACE *sb.* I. 6 b. **8.** A 'company' of lions in the wild state *c* 1452 (taken up latterly by writers on big game).

1. Oh farewell..all Qualitie, Pride, Pompe, and Circumstance of glorious Warre SHAKS. *P. of life, p. of the world*, worldly p. or ostentation, vainglory (*arch.*). *In his p.* (Her.), applied to a peacock represented with the tail expanded and the wings drooping. 2. Loftie trees, yclad with sommers p. SPENSER. 3. 1 *Hen. VI*, IV. vi. 57. 4. Since we have seen the p. of Nature's works..Let us depart MARLOWE. Hence **Pri·deful** *a.* full of p., arrogant. (Chiefly *Sc.*) **Pri·deless** *a.* devoid of p.

Pride (prəid), *sb.*[2] *local.* 1490. [perh. abbrev. from †*lampride* = med.L. *lampreda, lamprida* LAMPREY.] The fresh-water or river lamprey; also called *sand-pride*.

Pride (prəid), *v.* [Early ME. *pruden, priden*, f. *prude* PRIDE *sb.*[1]] †**1.** *intr.* To be or become proud –1802. **2.** *trans.* To make proud. Chiefly in *pass.* ME. **3.** *refl.* To make or show oneself proud; to plume oneself. Const. *on, upon, in, that*, etc. ME. **b.** *intr.* in same sense. Now *rare.* 1470.

3. He prided himself on his punctuality 1882.

Pridian (pri·diăn), *a. rare.* 1656. [ad. L. *pridianus*, f. *pridie* adv., on the day before; see -AN.] Of or pertaining to the previous day.

‖ **Prie-dieu** (prīdyö). 1760. [F., lit. 'pray God'.] **a.** A praying-desk, kneeling-desk. **b.** A chair with tall sloping back for use in praying; also, a chair of this form for ordinary use. Also *p. chair*.

Priest (prīst), *sb.* [OE. *prēost,* (ult.) from L. *presbyter,* a. Gr. πρεσβύτερος elder; see PRESBYTER.] †1. A PRESBYTER or elder of the early church (*rare*) –1582. 2. In hierarchical Christian churches: A clergyman in the second of the holy orders (above a deacon and below a bishop) having authority to administer the sacraments and pronounce absolution. 3. *gen.* A clergyman, a member of the clerical profession, a minister of religion OE. b. *fig.* as in *a p. of nature, of science,* etc. 1697. 4. A sacrificing priest, a minister of the altar. a. In the Jewish Church, and other pre-Christian systems ME. b. In specific Christian use, The officiant at the Eucharist and other sacerdotal offices OE. c. Applied (*a*) to Christ in his sacrificial or mediatorial character. (After Heb. v. 6, vii. 15–21.) ME.; (*b*) to all believers (after Rev. i. 6), and to the Christian Church. late ME. 5. An official minister of a pagan or non-Christian religion ME. †b. Applied to a priestess (*rare*) –1614. †6. Allus., *To be* (a person's) *p.*: to kill him. (In allusion to the function of a priest in performing the last offices to the dying.) –1800.

2. The Priests and Deacons (whom we usually class together under the common name of Clergymen) 1833. In every Catholic parish the p. is at the very heart of things 1901. 3. b. Ye sacred Muses..Whose P. I am DRYDEN. 5. Mathan..the prest of Baal, thei slewen before the auter WYCLIF 2 *Kings* xi. 18. Orthodox Islam has never had real priests 1885. b. *Per.* v. i. 243. 6. 2 *Hen. VI,* III. i. 272.

attrib. and *Comb.*: **p.-cap, priest's cap,** (*a*) *lit.* a cap worn by a p.; (*b*) *Fortif.* an outwork with three salient and two re-entrant angles; **priest's hole,** a hiding-place for a (R. C.) p. (in times of the penal laws); **priest's hood,** the wild Arum (*A. maculatum*), from the form of the spathe; **-vicar,** in some cathedrals, a vicar choral who is a priest; a minor canon. Hence **Prie·stdom,** †the office of p.; the rule or dominion of priests. †**Prie·stery,** a body or company of priests (*contempt.*) MILT. **Prie·stism,** the system, spirit, methods, or practices of priests (in hostile use). **Prie·stless** *a.* not having, or not attended by, a p. **Prie·stling,** a little, young, or insignificant p. (usu. *contempt.*).

Priest (prīst), *v.* late ME. [f. prec.] †1. *intr.* To exercise the ministry or functions of a priest –1642. 2. *trans.* usu. *pass.* To make a priest; to ordain to the priesthood 1504.

Priestcraft (prī·stkraft). 1681. Priestly craft or policy; the arts used by ambitious and worldly priests to impose upon the multitude or further their own interests.

Priestess (prī·stės). 1693. [f. PRIEST *sb.* + -ESS¹.] 1. A female priest; a woman who holds the office and performs the functions of a priest, or (loosely) of a minister of religion. Also *fig.* and *transf.* 2. A priest's wife (*colloq.*) 1709.

Priesthood (prī·st,hud). [OE. *prēosthād,* f. *prēost* PRIEST *sb.* + *-hād* -HOOD.] 1. The office or function of a priest; the condition of being a priest; the order of priest. b. The priestly office of Christ, of his Church, or of believers OE. 2. The system of priests; the or a body of priests. Also *transf.* and *fig.* late ME.

Priestlike (prī·stləik), *a.* (*adv.*) 1470. [f. PRIEST *sb.* + -LIKE.] Like, or like that of, a priest; characteristic of or befitting a priest; priestly, sacerdotal. B. *adv.* Like a priest; in the character or manner of a priest 1565.

A. The moving waters at their p. task Of pure ablution round earth's human shores KEATS.

Priestly (prī·stli), *a.* OE. [f. PRIEST *sb.* + -LY¹; in OE. *prēostlic.*] 1. Of or pertaining to a priest or priests; sacerdotal. 2. = PRIESTLIKE *a.* 1465. 3. That is a priest 1817.

2. A prystly man and vertusly dysposyd 1465. *Per.* III. i. 70. Hence **Prie·stliness,** p. quality or character.

Priest-ridden (prī·st,ri:d'n), *ppl. a.* Also -rid (*obs.* or *arch.*). 1653. [f. PRIEST *sb.* + RIDDEN *ppl. a.*] 'Ridden', i.e. managed or controlled by a priest or priests; held in subjection by priestly authority.

I..know better than to be p. SCOTT.

Prig (prig), *sb.* 1567. [Origin unkn.] I. †1. *Rogues' Cant.* A tinker. 2. *slang.* A (petty) thief 1610.

2. *Wint. T.* IV. iii. 108.

II. *slang* and *colloq.* †1. A spruce fellow, a fop; a coxcomb –1835. †2. A vague term of dislike or disrespect –1749. †3. In late 17th and early 18th c.: Applied to a precisian in religion, *esp.* a nonconformist minister –1752. 4. A precisian in speech or manners; one who cultivates or affects a propriety of culture, learning, or morals, which offends or bores others; a conceited or didactic person. (Only in later use including women.) 1753.

1. A Cane is Part of the Dress of a P., and always worn upon a Button STEELE. 2. What does the old p. threaten then? CHESTERF. 4. A p. is a fellow who is always making you a present of his opinions GEO. ELIOT. Hence **Pri·ggery,** the action or conduct of a p. **Pri·ggism,** †professional thievery or roguery; priggishness.

Prig (prig), *v.* 1513. [Goes w. prec.] I. *trans.* To steal. (*Thieves' Cant.*) Now usu. said of petty theft. 1561. II. 1. *intr.* To chaffer, to haggle about the price of anything. *Sc.* and *n. dial.* 1513. b. *fig.* To try to drive a hard bargain 1632. 2. To beg, importune 1714. Hence **Pri·gger** (*slang*), a thief.

Priggish (pri·giʃ), *a.* 1700. [f. PRIG *sb.* + -ISH.] Having the character of a prig; †thievish; †coxcombical –1835; conceited, pragmatical 1752. Hence **Pri·ggish-ly** *adv.*, **-ness.**

Prill¹ (pril). Now *local.* 1603. [var. of *pirle* PURL, a small rill.] A small stream of running water; a rill.

Prill². 1778. [Local term in Cornwall.] *Mining.* 1. In Cornish copper-mining: The rich copper ore which remains after cobbing and separating the inferior pieces. 2. Hence, A button or globule of metal obtained by assaying a specimen of ore in the cupel. *U.S.* and *Colonies.* 1864.

Prim, *a.* 1709. [Cognate w. next.] Of persons, their manner, speech, etc.: Consciously or affectedly strict or precise; formal, stiff, demure. b. Of things: Formal, regular, stiff 1771.

A p. Quakeress 1838. b. A square prim garden, arranged in parallelograms TROLLOPE. Hence **Pri·m-ly** *adv.*, **-ness.**

Prim, *v.* 1684. [Of obsc. origin.] 1. *intr.* To assume a formal, precise, or demure air. 2. *trans.* To form (the face or mouth) into an expression of preciseness or demureness; to close (the lips) primly 1706. b. 'To deck up precisely' (J.); chiefly with *up, out.* In later use, to make prim. 1721.

1. They mince and p. and pout, and are sigh-away and dying-ducky G. MEREDITH. *To p. up,* to bridle up, set the face or mouth firmly, as if to repel familiarities Tell dear Kitty not to p. up as if we had never met before MME. D'ARBLAY.

‖**Prima**¹ (prəi·mă). 1880. [a. L. *prima,* adj. fem., 'first'.] *Typogr.* The page of printer's copy on which a new sheet begins and on which the first word of the sheet is marked.

‖**Prima**² (prī·mă). It. fem. of *primo* first, used in PRIMA DONNA, and other phrases (chiefly musical).

Primacy (prəi·măsi). late ME. [a. OF. *primacie* (F. *primatie*), ad. med.L. *primatia*; see PRIMATE *sb.*] 1. The state or position of being 'prime' or first in order, rank, importance, or authority; the first or chief place; pre-eminence, superiority. 2. *Eccl.* The first place or leadership in spiritual matters; the office, dignity, or authority of a primate; *spec.* the chief dignity in an eccl. province 1470.

2. They yeild a Primacie to the Pope, if he be Orthodox, but no Supremacie 1635.

‖**Prima donna** (prī·mă, prəi·mă dǫ·nă). *Pl.* prime donne, prima donnas. 1812. [It., 'first lady'.] The first or principal female singer in an opera.

‖**Prima facie** (prəi·mă fē·ʃi,ī), *adv.* and *adj. phr.* late ME. [L., at first sight.] A. *adv.* At first sight; on the face of it. B. *adj.* Arising at first sight; based on the first impression 1800.

A. And indeed, *prima facie* they have reason 1624. B. *Prima facie case* (Law), a case resting on *prima facie* evidence. So ‖**Prima fronte** (prəi·mă frǫ·ntī) *adv. phr.*, at first appearance, on the face of it 1790.

Primage¹ (prəi·mėdʒ). 1540. [Origin obsc.] A customary allowance formerly made by the shipper to the master and crew of a vessel for the loading and care of the cargo; now, a percentage addition to the freight, paid to the owners or freighters of the vessel.

Pri·mage². 1881. [f. PRIME *v.*¹ 5.] *Engineering.* The amount of water carried off suspended in the steam from a boiler.

Primal (prəi·măl), *a.* 1602. [ad. med.L. *primalis,* f. L. *primus*; see -AL.] 1. Belonging to the first age or earliest stage; original; primitive, primeval. 2. Of first rank, standing, or importance 1812. 3. *Geol.* Applied to the earliest or lowest member of the palæozoic strata of the Appalachian chain, and to the period at which this was deposited 1858.

1. My offence..hath the primall eldest curse vpon 't, A Brothers murther SHAKS. Hence **Prima·lity** (*rare*), p. quality or condition. **Pri·mally** *adv.*

Primary (prəi·mări), *a.* and *sb.* 1471. [ad. L. *primarius* chief, f. *primus* first; see PRIME *a.* and -ARY¹.] A. *adj.* 1. Of the first order in time or temporal sequence; earliest, primitive, original. b. *Geol.* Of the first or earliest formation; formerly applied to crystalline rocks, as having been formed before the appearance of life on the earth; now = PALÆOZOIC 1. 1813. c. *Biol.* Belonging to or directly derived from the first stage of development or growth 1848. 2. Of the first importance; principal, chief 1565. 3. Of the first order in any sequence or process, esp. of derivation or causation 1621. b. *Cryst.* = PRIMITIVE *a.* II. 2 b. 1823.

1. *P. amputation* (Surg.), amputation performed at the earliest possible stage, before inflammation supervenes. *P. education* or *instruction,* that which begins with the rudiments or elements of knowledge; *P. school,* one at which such instruction is given; so *p. scholar* 1802. *P. assembly* or *meeting,* a gathering at which a preliminary selection of candidates, or of delegates, is effected; *spec.* in *U. S.,* a meeting of the voters belonging to a party in an election district, for this purpose. 2. Every apostle..assigns to faith a p. importance 1850. *P. feather,* one of the large flight-feathers of a bird's wing, growing from the manus. †*P. humours,* the 'cardinal humours'; see HUMOUR *sb.* 2 b. 3. The large p. branches of the carotid artery ABERNETHY. The Sun..gives us the p. division of time into day and night 1868. Poverty, due to absolute deficiency of money income, is called 'p.' 1901. *P. colours*: see COLOUR *sb.* 2. *P. qualities* (Philos.), the extension, the figure, and the solidity of external objects. *P. planets,* those planets which revolve directly around the sun as centre. *P. rainbow,* the rainbow produced by the simplest series of refractions and reflexions; the inner and usu. brighter when two are seen. *P. battery* (Electr.), a battery in which a current is produced. *P. coil, wire,* that which conveys the current from the battery, and induces a current in the secondary coil or wire.

B. *sb.* [ellipt. use of adj. Mostly in *pl.*] 1. That which (or one who) is first in order, rank, or importance; anything from which something else arises or is derived. Usu. *pl.* = Primary things; first principles. 1760. 2. Short for *p. planet*: see A. 3. 1721. 3. A primary feather: see A. 2. 1776. 4. *U.S.* Short for *p. meeting* or *assembly,* a caucus: see A. 1; so *p. election a* 1861. Hence **Pri·marily** *adv.* 1617.

Primate (prəi·mėt). ME. [ad. late L. *primas, -atem* adj., in med.L. sb. a primate; f. *primus* first.] 1. One who is first in rank or importance; a chief, superior, leader. Now *rare.* 2. *Eccl.* An archbishop, or †sometimes a bishop, holding the first place among the bishops of a province; also applied to a patriarch or exarch of the Eastern Church ME. 3. *Zool.* Anglicized sing. of next.

‖**Primates** (prəimēi·tīz, prəi·mėts), *sb. pl. Sing.* primas (prəi·mæs), also anglicized primate. 1774. [L. *primates,* pl. of *primas* PRIMATE.] *Zool.* The highest order of the *Mammalia,* including man, monkeys, and lemurs, and, in the Linnæan order, bats.

Pri·mateship. 1631. [f. PRIMATE + -SHIP.] The office or position of primate.

Primatial (prəimēi·ʃăl), *a.* 1623. [a. F., f. L. *primatia* PRIMACY; see -AL.] 1. Of, pertaining to, or having ecclesiastical primacy; pertaining to a primate. 2. *Zool.* Of or pertaining to the mammalian order *Primates* 1864.

Primatic (prəimæ·tik), *a.* 1687. [f. PRIMATE + -IC.] †1. = PRIMATIAL *a.* 1. –1826. 2. = PRIMATIAL 2. 1890. So **Prima·tical** *a.,* in sense 1. 1677.

‖**Prima vista** (prī·ma vī·sta). 1591. [It., = first sight.] †1. An old game at cards –1652. 2. *Mus.* At sight; as, to play or sing *prima vista.*

Prime (prəim), *sb.*¹ [OE. *prim,* ad. L. *prima,* for *prima hora* the first hour (in Roman reckoning); see PRIME *a.*] I. In eccl. and connected senses. 1. One of the day hours of the Western Church: a canonical hour of the

Divine Office, appointed for the first hour of the day, i.e. 6 A.M. (or, sometimes, sunrise); also, the hour or time of this office. **2.** Hence *gen.*, The first hour of the day, beginning either at six o'clock throughout the year, or at sunrise; also sometimes used for the period between the first hour and terce ME.

2. *High p.* or *p. large*, perh. the end of the period between p. and terce; Then to Westmynster-Gate I presently went, When the sonn was at hyghe pryme LYDG. *Comb.* **p.-song** *Hist.* [repr. OE. *primsang*], the office or service of prime (= sense 1).

II. The beginning of a period or cycle. **1.** The Golden Number: see GOLDEN 5 (*arch.*) ME. †**2.** The beginning or first appearance of the new moon –1704. **3.** *fig.* The beginning or first age of anything. late ME. **b.** The beginning or first age of the world 1616. **4.** The first season of the year (when this began at the vernal equinox); spring 1541. **5.** The 'springtime' of human life; the time of early manhood or womanhood, from about 21 to 28 years of age. Now *rare.* 1592.

3. b. Thou, thou art not a Child of Time, But Daughter of the Eternal P. WORDSW. 4. The teeming Autumne big with ritch increase, Bearing the wanton burthen of the p. SHAKS. 5. Lady that in the p. of earliest youth, Wisely hath shun'd the broad way and the green MILT.

III. That which is first in quality or character. **1.** Of human life: The period of greatest perfection or vigour 1615. **b.** Of things, material or immaterial: The best stage or state; the state of full perfection 1536. **2.** The chief or best one of a group 1579. **b.** The best part of anything 1635.

1. He was still in the p. of life, not more than four-and-forty GEO. ELIOT. b. Where the summer's p. Never fades away BLAKE. 2. b. [He] always chused to have the p. of everything MISS BURNEY.

Prime (prəim), *sb.*[2] 1594. [absol. use of PRIME *a.*, or of its Lat. or Fr. equivalent.] **I. 1.** *Arith.* A prime number; see PRIME *a.* 7. **2.** A subdivision of any standard measure or dimension, which is itself subdivided in the same ratio into seconds, and so on; e.g. $\frac{1}{60}$ of a degree, a minute ($\frac{1}{60}$ of which is in its turn a *second*); the twelfth part of a foot, an inch 1604. **b.** *Printing.* The symbol ′ or [1], written above and to the right of a letter or figure, to denote primes, or merely to distinguish it from another not so marked 1875. **3.** *Fencing.* The first of the chief guards 1710. **4.** *Mus.* **a.** A tone represented by the same staff degree as a given tone; the pitch relation between two such tones. **b.** The tonic, or first tone, of a scale. **c.** Short for *p. tone* (see next). 1788. †**II.** Related to PRIMA VISTA, PRIMERO. *Cards.* A hand in primero consisting of a card from each of the four suits. Also, an old game of cards. –1816.

Prime (prəim), *a.* (*adv.*) late ME. [a. F. *prime*, or ad. L. *primus.*] **1.** First in order of time or occurrence; early, youthful; primitive, primary. **2.** Of persons: First in rank, authority, or dignity; highest in degree; principal, chief 1610. **3.** First in importance, excellence, or value; principal, chief, main 1610. **4.** 'First-class', 'first-rate'; of the best quality; now esp. of cattle and provisions 1628. †**5.** Ruttish SHAKS. **6.** Primary, original, fundamental; from which others are derived, or on which they depend 1639. **7.** *Arith.* Of a number: Having no integral factors except itself and unity. So *p. divisor, factor, quotient*, etc. **b.** Of two or more numbers in relation to each other: Having no common measure except unity. 1570. **8.** First in numerical order, as in *p. meridian*, the first meridian (of any system of reckoning) 1878.

1. It befell in the p. time of the world 1587. 2. The nobility and p. gentry of the nation HUME. 3. That p. ill, a talking wife PRIOR. 4. *P. fish*, the more valuable kinds of fish caught for food; opp. to OFFAL 3. 6. *P. feathers*, primary feathers; see PRIMARY *a.* 2.

Spec. collocations: **p. entry,** an entry of two-thirds of a ship's cargo liable to duty, made before discharge (on which an estimate of the duty is paid); **p. ratio,** the initial limiting ratio between two variable quantities which simultaneously recede from definite fixed values or limits; **p. tone** (*Mus.*), the fundamental note of a compound tone; **p. vertical,** (*a*) in full *p. vertical circle*, a great circle of the heavens passing through the east and west points of the horizon, and through the zenith; (*b*) short for *p. vertical dial*, a dial the plane of which lies in that of the prime vertical circle, a north and south dial. Also *p.* CONDUCTOR, COST, MOVER, etc.: see the sbs.

B. as *adv.* In prime order, excellently (*dial.*) 1648. Hence **Pri·me·ly** *adv.*, **-ness.**

Prime (prəim), *v.*[1] 1513. [Origin obsc.] **1.** *trans.* To fill, charge, load. Now chiefly *dial.* **2.** To supply (a fire-arm of old-fashioned type, or more strictly its pan) with gunpowder for firing a charge. Also *intr.* or *absol.* 1598. **3.** *fig.* and *transf.* **a.** To charge, fill, or fully furnish (a person) beforehand *with* information, etc. 1791. **b.** To fill with liquor 1823. **4.** To cover (a surface) with a ground or first colour or coat of paint, or with size, oil, etc. to prevent the paint from being absorbed 1609. †**b.** *transf.* To 'make up' (the face, etc.) with cosmetics –1782. **5.** *intr. Engineering.* Of an engine boiler: To let water pass to the cylinder in the form of spray along with the steam 1832.

3. a. Every man present..is primed with a speech 1884. b. A fat little man, primed with port 1854.

Prime (prəim), *v.*[2] 1756. [f. PRIME *a.* or *sb.*[1]] †**1.** To be first; to domineer; to lord it –1821. **2.** Of a tide: To come at a shorter interval. (So F. *primer.*) 1890.

Prime (prəim), *v.*[3] Now only *dial.* 1565. [Origin obsc.] *trans.* To prune or trim (trees).

Prime (prəim), *v.*[4] 1787. [Origin unkn.] *intr.* Of a fish: To leap or 'rise'.

Pri·me Mi·nister. 1646. [PRIME *a.* 2.] †**1.** *gen.* A principal or chief minister, servant, or agent. Often in *pl.* –1713. **2.** The first or principal minister or servant of any sovereign, ruler, or state, or more vaguely of any person of rank or position 1655. **3.** In Great Britain (orig. *prime minister of state*): A descriptive designation which is now the official title of the First Minister of State or leader of the administration 1694. **b.** Also used in some of the self-governing British colonies 1901.

Primer (pri·mər, prəi·məɪ), *sb.*[1] late ME. [= med.L. *primarius, -arium*, f. L. *primus* first; see -ARIUM and cf. PRIMER *a.*] **1.** A prayer-book or devotional manual for the use of the laity, before, and for some time after, the Reformation. **2.** An elementary school-book for teaching children to read. late ME. **b.** Hence, a small introductory book on any subject 1807. **c.** *fig.* That which serves as a first means of instruction 1640. **3.** *Typogr.* **a.** *Great P.*, a size of type between Paragon and English, of 51 ems to a foot.

Great Primer type.

b. *Long P.*, a size between Small Pica and Bourgeois, of 89 ems to a foot. *Two-line long p.* = PARAGON II. 4. 1598.

Long Primer type.

2. Horne bookes and primers to be giuen to poore children of the said parish 1639. c. Spell in lovers' primers sweetly 1871.

Primer (prəi·məɪ), *sb.*[2] 1497. [f. PRIME *v.*[1] + -ER [1].] **1.** A priming-wire; see PRIMING *vbl. sb.*[1] **2.** A cap, wafer, cylinder, etc., containing fulminating powder or other compound, for igniting a charge of gunpowder when exploded 1819. **3.** A person who primes 1890.

Primer (pri·məɪ, prəi·məɪ), *a.* 1448. [a. AF. *primer* = OF. *primier*, var. of OF. and mod.F. *premier*:—L. *primarius* PRIMARY; cf. PREMIER.] †**1.** First in time; early; primitive –1622. †**2.** First in position or rank; chief, premier –1747. **3. a. P. fine,** in *Feudal Law*, the sum paid to the crown by a plaintiff who sued for the recovery of lands by a writ of covenant. Now only *Hist.* 1634. **b. P. seisin,** in *Feudal Law*, a right of the English Crown to receive from the heir of a knight of a tenant *in capite* who died seised of a knight's fee the profits of his estate for the first year. Now only *Hist.* 1488.

‖ **Primero** (primē·ro). *Hist.* 1533. [Altered from Sp. *primera* adj. fem. :—L. *primaria*; see prec.] A gambling card-game, in which four cards were dealt to each player, each card having thrice its ordinary value.

Primeval, primæval (prəimī·văl), *a.* 1662. [f. L. *primævus* + -AL.] Of or pertaining to the first age of the world or of anything ancient; primitive.

With Night primæval, and with Chaos old POPE. This is the forest primeval LONGF. Hence **Prime·vally** *adv.* in the first age of the world, also, in a p. manner or degree. So †**Prime·vous, -æ·vous** *a.* 1656.

Primigenial (prəimiˌdʒī·niăl), *a.* Now *rare.* 1602. [f. L. *primigenius* first of its kind (f. *primi-*, comb. f. *primus* + *genus*, or *gen-*, stem of *gignere*) + -AL.] †**1.** First generated or produced; earliest formed; original, primitive, primary –1822. **2.** *Zool.* Applied to species belonging to a primitive type (rendering the specific name *primigenius*, as in *Bos primigenius*, etc.) 1851. So **Pri·migene** (*rare*), **Primige·nian** (*rare*), †**Primige·nious** *adjs.*

Primine (prəi·min). 1832. [= F. *primine*, f. L. *primus* + -INE [1].] *Bot.* The first of the two coats or integuments of an ovule; i.e. **a.** (orig.) the outer one; but subseq. **b.** the inner, as being formed first 1875.

Priming (prəi·miŋ), *vbl. sb.*[1] 1598. [f. PRIME *v.*[1] + -ING [1].] The action of PRIME *v.*[1] **1.** The putting of gunpowder in the pan of an old-fashioned fire-arm. **2.** *concr.* The gunpowder so placed; also, the train of powder connecting a fuse with a charge in blasting, etc. 1625. **3.** The preparing of (a surface) for painting, by coating it with a body colour, etc. Also *transf.* 1609. **4.** *concr.* **a.** The mixture used by painters for the preparatory coat. **b.** A coat or layer of the substance. 1625. **5.** The hasty imparting of knowledge; cramming 1859. **6.** *Engineering.* (See PRIME *v.*[1] 5.) 1841.

attrib. and *Comb.*: **p.-horn,** (*a*) a horn containing priming-powder formerly carried by gunners; (*b*) the powder-horn carried by miners and quarry-men; **-iron, -wire,** a sharp pointed wire used in gunnery and blasting to ascertain whether the touch-hole or vent is free and to pierce the cartridge.

Priming (prəi·miŋ), *vbl. sb.*[2] 1833. [f. PRIME *v.*[2] 2 + -ING [1].] *P. of the tides*: the acceleration of the tides, taking place from the neap to the spring tides; opp. to *lagging.*

‖ **Primipara** (prəimi·pără). 1842. [L., f. *primus* first + *-parus*, from *parere* to bring forth.] A female that brings forth for the first time. Hence **Primi·parous** *a.* bearing a child (or young) for the first time.

Primipilar (prəimipəi·lăɪ), *a.* 1600. [ad. L. *primipilaris*, f. *primipilus* chief centurion of the *triarii* in a legion, f. *primus* first, *pilus* a body of pikemen, f. *pilum* javelin.] *Rom. Antiq.* Belonging to, or that is, a *primipilus.*

Primitive (pri·mĭtiv), *a.* and *sb.* [Late ME. *primitif*, a. F., ad. L. *primitivus* first or earliest of its kind, f. *primus.*] **A.** *adj.* **I.** *gen.* **1.** Of or belonging to the first age, period, or stage; original; early, ancient 1486. **2.** Having the quality or style of that which is early or ancient; simple, rude, or rough like that of early times; old-fashioned 1685. **3.** Original as opp. to derivative; primary; radical. late ME.

1. The p. pastoral ages LONGF. *P. Church*, the Christian Church in its earliest times. 2. A poor good p. creature H. WALPOLE. Her very p. wardrobe 1838. 3. God is the p...cause 1628.

II. *spec.* and *techn.* **1.** *Gram.* and *Philol.* Of a word or language: Original, radical: opp., or correl. to *derivative* 1530. **2.** *Math.*, etc. Applied to a line or figure from which some construction or reckoning begins; or to a curve, surface, magnitude, equation, operation, etc., which is not derived from another 1690. **b.** *Cryst.* Applied to a fundamental crystalline form from which all the other forms may be derived by geometrical processes 1805. **3.** Of colours: see PRIMARY *a.* 3. 1759. **4.** *Geol.* Belonging to the earliest geological period; primary 1777. **5.** *Biol.*, *Anat.*, etc. **a.** Applied to a part or structure in the first or a very early stage of formation; rudimentary, primordial. **b.** Applied to the minute or ultimate elements of a structure, or to some part connected with these; as the *p. fibrillæ* of a nerve; the *p. sheath* investing each of these. 1857. **6.** *P. Methodist Connexion*: a society of Methodists founded by Hugh Bourne in 1810 by secession from the main body; so called as adhering to the original methods of preaching, etc., practised by the Wesleys and Whitefield 1812.

2. *P. circle* or *plane*, the circle or plane upon which projection is made. 5. a. *P. streak* or *trace*, the faint streak which constitutes the earliest trace of the embryo in the fertilized ovum; *p. groove*, (*a*) = *p. streak*; (*b*) a groove or furrow which appears (in vertebrates) in the upper surface of the p. streak, and marks the beginning of the vertebral column. 6. *P. Methodist*, a member or adherent of the P. Methodist

Connexion. *P. Methodism*, the principles of this society, or adherence to it.

B. *sb.* **I. 1.** †**a.** A primitive Christian; a member of the early Church -1686. **b.** An aboriginal; a man of primitive (esp. prehistoric) times 1779. **2.** Short for *P. Methodist* (see A. II. 6). **3.** In art criticism: **a.** A painter of the period before the Renaissance; also *transf.* a modern who imitates the style of these. **b.** A picture painted by any of these. 1892. **II. 1.** *Gram.* A word from which another or others are derived; a root-word. Opp. to *derivative*. 1565. **2.** *Math.* Any algebraical or geometrical form in relation to another derived from it. (Short for *p. expression, equation, curve*, etc.: see A. II. 2.) Hence **Pri·mitive·ly** *adv.*, **·ness. Primiti·vity,** p. quality, character, or condition.

Primogenital (prəimo͵dʒe·nităl), *a.* 1657. [ad. late L. *primogenitalis*, f. *primogenitus* (taken as sb.); see -AL.] Of or pertaining to the first-born or to primogeniture. So **Primoge·nitary** *a.* **Primoge·nitive** *a.*; †also as *sb.* = PRIMOGENITURE 2. SHAKS.

Primogenitor (prəimodʒe·nitǫ̈ɹ). 1475. [a. med.L., f. L. *primo* adv., at first + *genitor* GENITOR [2].] First parent, earliest ancestor; *loosely*, ancestor, progenitor.

Primogeniture (prəimodʒe·nitiŭɹ, -tʃəɹ). 1602. [ad. med.L. *primogenitura*, f. L. *primo* adv., first + *genitura* GENITURE; after L. *primogenitus*.] **1.** The fact or condition of being the first-born of the children of the same parents. **2.** The right of succession or inheritance belonging to the first-born; the principle, custom, or law by which the property or title descends to the eldest son (or eldest child); *spec.* the feudal rule of inheritance by which the whole of the real estate of an intestate passes to the eldest son 1631.

1. *Right of p.*, the right (of succession, etc.) of the first-born; In the division of personal estates,..no right of p. is allowed BLACKSTONE. Hence **Primoge·nitureship** (now *rare*) = sense 2.

Primordial (prəimǭ·ɹdiăl), *a.* (*sb.*) late ME. [ad. late L. *primordialis* that is first of all, f. PRIMORDIUM; see -AL.] **1.** Of, pertaining to, or existing at (or from) the very beginning; first in time, original, primitive, primeval. **2.** Constituting the beginning or starting-point; original, not derivative; fundamental; elementary 1529. **3.** *Anat.* and *Zool.* = PRIMITIVE *a.* II. 5 a. 1786. **4.** *Bot.* **a.** Earliest formed in the course of growth; said of leaves, fruit, etc. 1785. **b.** Applied to tissues, etc., in their rudimentary stage or condition 1849. **5.** *Geol.* and *Palæont.* †**a.** = PRIMITIVE *a.* II. 4. -1802. **b.** Applied to a series of strata in Bohemia, containing the earliest fossil remains there found; hence to corresponding strata elsewhere, forming part of the Cambrian system; also applied to fossils found in these strata 1885.

1. The p. tenets of the Tory party DISRAELI. **4. b.** *P. cell*, a cell in its simplest form, consisting merely of a mass of protoplasm, without cell-wall, cell-sap, etc. *P. utricle*, the layer of denser protoplasm lining the wall of a vacuolate cell.

B. *sb.* Something primordial; beginning, origin; a first principle, an element (*rare*) 1522. Hence **Primo·rdialism,** p. nature or condition. **Primo·rdially** *adv.* in a p. way.

‖**Primordium** (prəimǭ·ɹdiǒm). *Pl.* **-ia.** 1671. [L., orig. neut. of *primordius* adj. original, f. *primus* first + *ordiri* to begin.] The very beginning, the earliest stage; introduction, opening part; primitive source, origin. **b.** *Biol.* The first rudiment of an organ or structure 1890.

Primrose (pri·mrōuz), *sb.* (*a.*) [Late ME. *primerose*, corresp. to early OF. *primerose*, and to med.L. *prima rosa*, lit. 'earliest rose'.] **1.** A plant (*Primula veris*) bearing pale yellowish flowers in early spring, growing wild in woods and hedges, and on banks. Also, the flower of this plant. Occas. extended to include other species of the genus PRIMULA. **2.** Applied to some other plants having flowers resembling those of the common p.; as **Evening (Night,** †**Nightly) P.,** the genus *Œnothera*; **Peerless P.** = P. PEERLESS 1760. †**3.** *fig.* The first or best; the finest, or a fine, example; the 'flower', 'pearl' -1664. **4.** Ellipt. for *p. colour*: A pale greenish yellow or lemon colour 1882.

1. The rathe P. that forsaken dies MILT.

Comb.: **P. day,** the anniversary of the death (19th April, 1881) of Benjamin Disraeli, Earl of Beaconsfield, with whose memory the p. is associated; **P. League,** a political association formed in 1883 in support of the principles of Conservatism as represented by Lord Beaconsfield; **p. path, way,** a path abounding in primroses; *fig.* the path of pleasure (*Ham.* I. iii. 50, *Macb.* II. iii. 21). Hence **Pri·mrosy** *a.*

Pri·mrose pee·rless. 1578. A name formerly given to the species of Narcissus, including the wild daffodil; now spec. to *Narcissus biflorus*, the two-flowered narcissus.

Primula (pri·miŭlă). 1753. [a. med.L. *primula*, fem. of *primulus*, dim. of *primus* first; orig. in *primula veris*, applied first app. to the cowslip, and at an early date also to the field daisy.] *Bot.* A genus of herbaceous perennial plants, of low-growing habit, having radical leaves, and yellow, white, pink, or purple flowers mostly borne in umbels. Hence **Primula·ceous** *a.* belonging to the natural order *Primulaceæ*, of which *P.* is the typical genus.

‖**Primum mobile** (prəi·mǒm mōu·bili). 1460. [med.L., lit. 'first moving thing', f. L. *primus* first, *mobilis* movable; see PRIME *a.* and MOBILE *sb.*[1]] **1.** The supposed outermost sphere, added in the Middle Ages to the Ptolemaic system of astronomy, and supposed to revolve round the earth from east to west in 24 hours, carrying with it the (eight or nine) contained spheres. **2.** *transf.* and *fig.* A prime source of motion or action; a prime mover, mainspring 1612.

‖**Primus** (prəi·mǒs), *a.* and *sb.* 1592. [L., 'first'; see PRIME *a.*] **A.** *adj.* **1.** In L. phrases, as *primus inter pares*, first among equals; *primus motor*, prime mover. **2.** In some boys' schools, used to distinguish the oldest (or senior) of those having the same surname 1796. **B.** *sb.* **1.** In the Scottish Episcopal Church: The presiding bishop, who has certain ceremonial privileges, but no metropolitan authority 1860. **2.** (In full *primus stove*.) Trade name of a stove burning vaporized paraffin oil 1907.

Primy (prəi·mi), *a. rare.* 1602. [f. PRIME *sb.* + -Y [1].] That is in its prime.

A Violet in the youth of P. Nature SHAKS.

Prince (prins), *sb.* ME. [a. F., ad. L. *princeps, -cipem* PRINCEPS.] **I. 1.** A sovereign ruler; a monarch, king. Now *arch.* or *rhet.* †**b.** Applied to a female sovereign -1650. †**2.** One who has the chief authority; a ruler, commander, governor -1611. **3.** One who or that which is first or pre-eminent in a specified class or sphere; the chief, the greatest ME. **4. a.** Applied to Christ, *esp.* in *p. of peace*. **b.** = PRINCIPALITY 5. **c.** Applied to Satan in the phrases *p. of the air, darkness, evil, the world*, etc. ME.

1. Phr. *To live like a p.*; The iolly fellowes that once in England liued like Princes in their Abbeies GREENE. 4. c. WYCLIF *John* xii. 31.

II. Spec. uses. **1.** The ruler of a principality, actually, nominally, or orig. a feudatory of a king or emperor ME. **2.** A male member of a royal family; *esp.* in Great Britain, a son or grandson of a king or queen. Also called *p. of the blood* (*royal*). **3.** The English rendering of a title of nobility in some foreign countries 1727. **b.** Applied as a title of courtesy in certain connexions to a duke, marquis, or earl 1707. **c.** *P. of the* (*Holy Roman*) *Church*, a title applied to a Cardinal 1674.

2. *P. Albert* (*coat*) [f. *Prince Albert* Edward, afterwards Edward VII] (*U.S. colloq.*), a frock-coat. *P. Consort*, the husband of a reigning female sovereign being himself a p. *P. Rupert's drops*: see DROP *sb.* I. 8. *P. of Wales's feathers*: see FEATHER *sb.* II. 3.

Comb. with *prince's*: **prince's metal,** also **Prince Rupert's metal,** an alloy of about three parts of copper and one of zinc, in colour resembling gold; **prince's pine,** (*a*) the Grey Pine, *Pinus Banksiana*; (*b*) = PIPSISSEWA. Hence **Prince** *v. intr.* with *it*, to play the p., carry oneself as a p. **Pri·ncehood** (now *rare*). **Pri·ncekin** (*joc.*), a little, young, or diminutive p. **Pri·ncelet, -ling,** a little or petty p.; the ruler of a small principality. **Pri·ncelike** *a.* and †*adv.*

Pri·nce-bi·shop. 1849. A bishop who is also a prince (sense II. 1); also, one who enjoyed the temporal possessions and authority of a bishopric, with princely rank.

Princedom (pri·nsdəm). 1560. [f. PRINCE *sb.* + -DOM.] = PRINCIPALITY 2, 4, 5.

Thrones, Princedoms, Powers, Dominions MILT.

Pri·nce-ele·ctor. 1560. (= G. *Kurfürst*.) One of the princes who elected the Holy Roman (German) Emperor.

Princely (pri·nsli), *a.* 1500. [f. PRINCE *sb.* + -LY [1].] **1.** Of, pertaining, or belonging to a prince or princes; held or exercised by a prince; royal, regal, kingly 1503. **2.** That is a prince; royal, kingly 1582. **3.** Princelike; dignified, stately, noble 1500. **4.** Like that of a prince; sumptuous, magnificent, munificent 1539.

1. The p. houses of Western Europe 1869. 3. I see him yet, the p. boy! SCOTT. 4. Sir E— G—'s gift.. is 'p.' 1889. Hence **Pri·nceliness,** the quality of being p. **Pri·ncely** *adv.* (now *rare*) in a p. manner.

‖**Princeps** (pri·nseps), *a.* and *sb.* Pl. **pri·ncipes** (-sipīz). 1809. [L. *princeps* adj., first, chief; f. *primus* + *-ceps, -cip-*, f. *capere* to take.] **A.** *adj.* First, original; *spec.* of a book, from L. phrase *editio princeps* original edition. **b.** Also frequent in L. phr. *facile princeps*, easily the first or chief. **B.** *sb.* **1.** The title under which Augustus Cæsar and his successors exercised supreme authority in the Roman Empire; now gen. used by historians to describe the constitutional position of the head of the state 1837. **2.** *ellipt.* for *editio princeps*; see A.

Pri·nce Re·gent. 1789. A prince who is regent of a country, during a minority, or in the absence or disability of the sovereign; *spec.* the title commonly given to George Prince of Wales (afterwards George IV) during the mental incapacity of George III, 1811–20.

Prince royal. 1702. [a. F., 'royal prince'; see PRINCE *sb.* ROYAL *a.*] The eldest son of a reigning monarch; *spec.* of the king of Prussia.

Prince's feather. 1629. **a.** London Pride (*Saxifraga umbrosa*). Now *dial.* **b.** A garden plant, *Amaranthus hypochondriacus*, bearing feathery spikes of small red flowers; also *A. speciosus*, a larger species 1721.

Princess (prinse·s, pri·nses). [Late ME. *princesse*, a. F., fem. of *prince*; see -ESS [1].] **1.** A female sovereign or ruler; a queen (*arch.*). **2.** The wife of a prince. late ME. **3.** The daughter or grand-daughter of a sovereign; a female member of a royal or princely family. 1508. **4.** Applied to a female, or anything personified as feminine, that is likened to a princess in pre-eminence or authority; formerly often to the Virgin Mary. late ME.

1. So excellent a p., as the present queen SWIFT. 2. *P. dowager*: see DOWAGER. 3. *P. of the blood*: see BLOOD *sb.* III. 2. *P. royal*, the eldest daughter of the sovereign in Great Britain; also formerly in Prussia.

Comb. **p. dress,** a lady's dress of which the lengths of the bodice and skirt are cut in one piece; also applied to modifications of this shape; so *p.-shape, p. frock, petticoat*, etc.; also *p.-shaped* adj., and *p.* adj. or ellipt. = p.-shaped.

Pri·nce-wood. Also **prince's wood.** 1686. A dark-coloured and light-veined timber produced by two W. Indian trees, *Cordia gerascanthoides* and *Hamelia ventricosa*; also called *Spanish elm*.

Principal (pri·nsĭpăl), *a.* and *sb.* ME. [ad. L. *principalis*, f. *princeps, -ipem*; see PRINCE *sb.* and -AL.] **A.** *adj.* **I.** *gen.* **1.** First in rank or importance. **2.** Less definitely: Belonging to the first or highest group in rank or importance; prominent, leading. ME. **3.** Specially great; of high degree or importance; special, eminent. Now *rare* or *Obs.* late ME. †**4.** Princely, royal -1591.

1. He was the p. projector of the fund for decayed musicians 1795. Their p. food is flour and meal JOWETT. *P. boy*, the principal male character in a pantomime (usu. played by a woman); so *p. girl*. **2.** Certaine of the Principallest Gentlemen of the citie 1598. Character is..a p. source of interest..employed by the drama 1874. **3.** A principall portion of Gods spirit 1611.

II. *spec.* and *techn.* **1.** Of money: Constituting the original sum; that is the capital sum invested or lent, and yielding interest; capital, capitalized ME. **2.** *Law.* **a.** That is the chief person concerned in some action or proceeding; *esp.* that is the actual perpetrator of, or directly responsible for, a crime. **b.** *P. challenge*: a challenge against a jury, or against a particular juror, alleging a fact such as, if proved, would disqualify such jury or juror as a matter of law. 1448. **3.** *Gram.* Said of a sentence or clause, or of a word, in relation to another which is auxiliary to or dependent upon it; opp. to *subordinate* or *dependent*. *P. parts* (of a verb), those from which the other parts can be derived, or which contain the different stems in the simplest forms. 1590. 4. *Building.* Applied to the main rafters, posts, or braces in the wooden framework of a building, which support the chief strain 1594. 5. *Math.*, etc. 1704.

5. *P. axis*, (*a*) of a conic, that axis which passes through the foci, the transverse axis (opp. to *conjugate axis*); (*b*) each of three lines in a body or system used as the chief lines of reference in relation to forces operating upon it. *P. plane*, of a symmetrical body, an imaginary plane of symmetry, as, in an oblate or prolate spheroid, the plane passing through the centre at right angles to the axis of revolution. *P. point*, in *Perspective*, the point where the *p. ray* meets the plane of delineation. *P. ray*, in *Perspective*, the straight line from the point of sight perpendicular to the plane of delineation. *P. section* of a crystal, any section passing through the optical axis.

B. *sb.* **I. 1.** A head man or woman; a chief, ruler, superior; a governor, a presiding officer, as the head of a religious or educational institution, the manager of a house of business, etc.; †the master or mistress of a household. late ME. **b.** In Great Britain, outside Oxford and Cambridge, the most usual designation of a head of a college or hall 1438. **2.** A chief actor or doer; the person for whom and by whose authority another acts 1625. **b.** A person directly responsible for a crime, either as the actual perpetrator (*p. in the first degree*), or as present, aiding and abetting, at the commission of it (*p. in the second degree*) 1594. **c.** A person for whom another is surety 1576. **d.** Each of the combatants in a duel, as dist. from their *seconds* 1709.

2. We were not principals, but auxiliaries in the war SWIFT.

II. †1. The chief, main, or most important thing, part, point, or element. –1845. **†2.** The original document, drawing, painting, etc., from which a copy is made –1660. **3.** A principal rafter or post; any one of the rafters upon which rest the purlins which support the common rafters. Also applied to a main iron girder. 1448. **†5.** An upright pillar or stem having branches to bear tapers; formerly used on a hearse –1849. **6.** The original sum dealt with in any transaction, as dist. from any later accretions; the capital sum as dist. from the interest; also, capital as dist. from income. late ME. **7.** *Mus.* An organ-stop of the same quality as the Open Diapason, but an octave higher in pitch 1613. Hence **Pri·ncipally** *adv.* in the chief place, mainly, above all; for the most part, in most cases. **Pri·ncipalship**, the office of p. (of a college, etc.).

Principality (prinsipæ·liti). [Late ME. *principal(i)te*, a. OF. *principalite, principaltee*, ad. late L. *principalitatem*, f. *principalis* PRINCIPAL *a.*; see -ITY.] **1.** The quality, condition, or fact of being principal; chief place or rank; pre-eminence. Now *rare.* **2.** The position, dignity, or dominion of a prince or chief ruler; sovereignty; supreme authority. late ME. **3.** The sovereignty, rule, or government of the prince of a small or dependent state 1459. **4.** A region or state ruled by a prince. late ME. **5.** A spiritual being (evil or good) of a high order; *spec.* in *pl.*, in mediæval angelology, one of the nine orders of angels (see ORDER *sb.* II. 1.) (Repr. L. *principatus*, Gr. ἀρχαί.) 1560. **6.** The office of principal of a college, university, etc.; principalship. Now *rare.* 1641.

4. Samos...A p. of the Ottoman Empire, more or less independent 1905. *The P.*, Wales. 5. Nisroc, of Principalities the prime MILT.

Principate (pri·nsipĕt). ME. [ad. L. *principatus* the first place, etc., f. *princeps, princip-*; see PRINCE *sb.* and -ATE [1].] **1.** = PRINCIPALITY 1, 2. Now *rare.* **b.** *Rom. Hist.* The rule of the PRINCEPS; the imperial power of Augustus and his successors, while some of the republican forms were still retained; the period of rule of a princeps 1862. **2.** = PRINCIPALITY 4. 1494.

‖**Principia**, L. pl. of PRINCIPIUM.

†**Princi·pial**, *a.* [f. L. *principium* + -AL.] Standing at the beginning; initial BACON.

†**Princi·piant**, *a.* 1615. [a. F. †*principiant*, f. *principier*, ad. L. *principiare*; see -ANT [1].] Constituting the beginning of something; originating; primary –1675.

‖**Principium** (prinsi·pi*ŏ*m). *Pl.* **-ia.** 1600. [L., f. *princeps, -ipem* first in time or order.] **1.** = PRINCIPLE *sb.* in various senses. **b.** *pl. Principia*: abbreviated title of a work by Sir Isaac Newton, setting forth the principles of natural philosophy or physics 1727. **2.** *Rom. Antiq.* (*pl.*) The general's quarters in a camp 1581.

Principle (pri·nsĭp'l), *sb.* late ME. [ad. F. *principe*, or f. L. *principium* (see prec.).] Often emphasized by prefixing *first*. **I.** Origin, source; source of action. **†1.** Beginning; fountain-head; original or initial state –1674. **†2.** That from which something takes its rise, originates, or is derived. *Obs.* (exc. as in 3.) –1697. **3.** In gen. sense: a fundamental source; a primary element, force, or law which produces or determines particular results; the ultimate basis of the existence of something; cause. late ME. **4.** An original tendency or faculty; a natural disposition. late ME.

3. Those Idolaters adore two Principles; the P. of Good, and that of Evil SWIFT. 4. Of verray wommanly benignytee That nature in youre principles hath yset CHAUCER. Out of a P. of good will I have to you 1669.

II. Fundamental truth, law, or motive force. **1.** A fundamental truth or proposition, on which many others depend; a fundamental assumption forming the basis of a chain of reasoning. late ME. **b.** *Physics*, etc. A highly general or inclusive theorem or 'law', exemplified in a multitude of cases 1710. **2.** A fundamental quality or attribute; essential characteristic or character; essence 1662. **3.** A general law or rule as a guide to action; a fundamental motive or reason of action, esp. one consciously recognized and followed 1532. **b.** Used *absol.* for *good, right,* or *moral p.* (Also in *pl.*) 1653. **4.** A general fact or law of nature by virtue of which a machine or instrument operates; hence, the general mode of construction or operation of a machine, etc. 1802.

1. Principles of political economy 1825. First principles..should be carefully considered JOWETT. 3. The barbarian lives without p. and without aim J. H. NEWMAN. **b.** If I were to choose any servant..I would choose a godly man that hath principles CROMWELL. Thus my pride, not my p...kept me honest DE FOE. *On p.*, as a matter of (moral) p.; from a settled (conscientious) motive. 4. This thermometer is sometimes varied in its form and arrangement, but the p. remains the same 1858.

III. Rudiment, element. **†1. a.** *pl.* The earliest parts of a subject of study; elements, rudiments –1706. **†b.** *concr.* A germ, embryo, bud (of a natural structure) –1732. **†2.** A component part, ingredient, constituent, element –1732. **†b.** *Old Chem.* Chiefly in *pl.*: The five supposed simple substances or elements of which all bodies were believed to be composed –1799. **c.** *Chem.* One of the constituents of a substance as obtained by chemical analysis; usu., one which gives rise to some characteristic quality, or causes some special action or effect, as *active, bitter, neutral p.* 1732.

2. A confluence of buyers, sellers, and lookers-on, which are the three principles of a fair 1655. Hence †**Principle** *v. trans.* to ground (any one) in the principles or elements of a subject, to impress with principles of action; to be the principle, source, or basis of; to originate –1760.

Principled (pri·nsipl'd), *ppl. a.* Now *rare* (exc. in comb.). 1642. [f. PRINCIPLE *v.* + -ED [1].] **1.** Established in principles; holding or habitually actuated by particular principles; that is so or such on principle. Often in comb., as *high-, well-p.* **2.** Having good or right principles. (Opp. to *unprincipled.*) 1697. **3.** Founded on a principle; instilled into the mind as a principle 1784.

Pri·ncock, -cox. *Obs.* exc. *dial.* 1540. [Etym. unkn.] A pert, forward, saucy boy or youth; a coxcomb. (*joc.* or *contempt.*) **b.** *attrib.* or as *adj.*, esp. in *p.-boy* 1595.

Prink (priŋk), *v.* 1576. [app. related to PRANK *v.*[2]] **1.** *trans.* To make spruce or smart; to dress *up*; esp. *refl.* to dress oneself *up. colloq.* **b.** *intr.* To dress oneself up; make oneself look smart. *colloq.* 1709. **2.** *trans.* Of a bird: To trim (the feathers); to preen. Also *intr.* 1575.

1. To gather king-cups in the yellow mead, And p. their hair with daisies COWPER.

Print (print), *sb.* [ME. a. OF. *priente, preinte* impression of a seal, etc., f. pa pple. of *preindre* to press, stamp:—L. *premere.*] **I. 1.** The impress made in a plastic material by a stamp, seal, die, or the like; a distinctive stamped or printed mark or design, as on a coin. **2.** *fig.* **a.** An image or character stamped upon the mind or soul; a mental impression. Now *rare.* ME. **b.** An image or likeness of anything. late ME. **3.** *gen.* Any indentation in a surface preserving the form left by the pressure of some body; also, a mark, spot, or stain produced on any surface by another substance. late ME. **4.** An instrument, etc. which produces a mark or figure by pressing; a stamp or die; a mould. Also *fig.* late ME. **b.** *Founding.* A support for the core of a casting 1864. **5.** A pat of butter, moulded to a shape 1754. **6.** A printed cotton fabric; a piece of printed cotton cloth. Often *attrib.* 1824.

2. **b.** Y[e] fathers owne figure,..y[e] very prent of his visage MORE. 3. The prynte of the hors shoo and nayles abode euer in his vysage CAXTON. The recent prints of a bear and two cubs 1853. 6. He chose the p. stuff for his wife's dresses STEVENSON.

II. Typographical uses. **1.** The state of being printed; printed form 1482. **2.** *concr.* Language embodied in a printed form; typography; esp. with ref. to size, form, or style, as *small p., clear p.* 1623. **†3.** A printing-press (with its accessories). Hence, the work of the press, the process of printing. –1691. **4.** An impression of a work printed at one time; an edition 1535. **5.** A printed publication; *esp.* a printed sheet, news sheet, newspaper (now chiefly *U.S.*) 1570. **6.** A picture or design printed from a block or plate 1662. **7.** *Photogr.* A picture produced from a negative 1851.

1. Rush like a hero into p. PRAED. *In p.*, (*a*) in printed form; (*b*) of a book or edition, not yet sold out. *Out of p.* (of a book or edition), sold out. 2. *fig.* All the wickedness of the world is P. to him DICKENS. 5. I have often admired your talents in the daily prints SHERIDAN. 6. There is a p. of him, painted by John Lyvyus, and engraved by Vosterman H. WALPOLE.

III. Transf. uses, of uncertain origin. *In p.* **a.** In a precise and perfect way or manner; with exactness; to a nicety. Now *dial.* 1576. **†b.** With a sb.: *A man, fool* (etc.) *in p.*, a perfect or thorough man, fool, etc. –1633. **†c.** Applied to the exact crimping of the pleats of a ruff –1641. **d.** Said of the beard or hair. So also *out of p.*, out of proper order. *Obs.* or *dial.* 1605.

attrib. and *Comb.*: **p. hand**, handwriting imitating p.; so **p. letters**; **-holder**, a small frame for holding a photograph or engraving; **-room**, a room in a museum or the like, containing a collection of prints; **-seller**, one who sells prints or engravings; **-shop**, a p.-seller's shop; **-washer**, an apparatus for washing photographic prints after fixing; **-work(s**, a factory in which cotton fabrics are printed. Hence **Pri·ntless** *a.* making or leaving no p. or trace; that has received, or that retains, no p.

Print (print), *v.* [ME. *prenten, printe*, f. *prente, printe* PRINT *sb.*] **I. 1.** *trans.* To impress or stamp (a surface) with a seal, die, or the like; to mark with any figure or pattern; to brand. Said also of footsteps upon soft or yielding ground. **2.** To impress or stamp (a form, figure, mark, etc.) in or on a yielding substance; also, by extension, to set or trace (a mark, figure, etc.) on any surface, by carving, writing, or otherwise. late ME. **b.** *fig.* To impress (an image, thought, saying, etc.) upon the heart, mind, or memory; to fix in the mind. late ME. **3.** To press (anything hard) into or upon a yielding substance, so as to leave an indentation or imprint. Also with *in.* late ME. **†4.** To commit (anything) to writing; to express in written words; to inscribe –1588.

1. Little footsteps lightly p. the ground GRAY. 2. The child prints many a playful kiss Upon their hands 1812. **b.** This sentence is very meet for women to p. in their remembrance 1563. 3. Horses..Printing their prowd Hoofes i' the receiuing Earth SHAKS. *Tit. A.* IV. i. 75.

II. Senses relating to typography. **1.** To produce (a book, picture, etc.) by applying to paper, vellum, etc., in a press or machine, inked types, blocks, or plates, bearing characters or designs 1511. **2.** Said of an author or editor: **a.** To cause (a manuscript, book, etc.) to be printed; to give to the press 1530. **b.** To express or publish in print (ideas, etc.) 1638. **3.** *intr.* or *absol.* To exercise the vocation of a printer; to employ the press in printing 1699. 4. *trans.* To take an impression from (a forme of type, a plate, block, etc.); to use in printing 1727. 5. To form (letters) in the style of printed letters; also *absol.* 1837.

1. 160 Englishe Bibles were printed at Paris 1560. His Majesty's Picture, printed in natural Colours 1720. 2. a. Some said, John, p. it; others said, Not so BUNYAN. 4. The stone is then etched, washed out, and printed 1875.

III. Techn. senses analogous to II. 1. *trans.* To mark (a textile fabric) by hand or machinery with a pattern or design in colours. Also *absol.* 1588. 2. *Pottery.* To transfer to the unglazed surface a decorative design in colour from paper, or in oil from a gelatine sheet or bat. With the pottery, or the design, as obj. 1839. 3. *Photogr.* To produce (a positive picture) by the transmission of light through a negative placed immediately upon the sensitized surface, or, in an enlarging camera, before it. Also with *off*, *out.* 1851. b. *intr.* Of a negative: To produce a photograph (*well, badly*, etc.) 1852. 4. See NATURE-PRINTING.

Hence **Pri·ntable** *a.* capable of being printed, or printed from.

Printer (pri·ntəɹ). 1504. [f. PRINT *v.* + -ER [1].] 1. A person who prints, in any sense of the word 1567. b. *spec.* One whose business is the printing of books, etc.; the owner of a printing business; a workman in a printing-office 1504. 2. An instrument or appliance used for printing 1890. 3. *Trade.* A cotton cloth made to be printed on 1864. 4. *attrib.*, as *p.-author, -journalist* 1663.

Comb. with *printer's*: **printer's devil**: see DEVIL *sb.* 5; **printer's mark**, a monogram or other device used by a p. as a trade-mark. b. With *printers'*, as *printers' ink* (see INK *sb.*[1]), *pie* (see PIE *sb.*[4]); **printers' bible**, the Bible which contains the misreading 'Printers have persecuted me without a cause' (Ps. cxix. 161).

Printery (pri·ntəri). Chiefly *U.S.* 1638. [f. prec.; see -ERY.] 1. A printing-office. 2. A cotton-printing factory 1846.

Printing (pri·ntiŋ), *vbl. sb.* late ME. [f. PRINT *v.* + -ING [1].] The action of PRINT *v.*, in various senses; an instance of this.

attrib. and *Comb.*, as **p.-cloth**, cotton cloth made specially for printing; **-frame** (*Photogr.*), a frame in which sensitized paper is placed beneath a negative and exposed to light; **-ink** = *printers' ink*; **-machine**, a printing-press for rapid work on a large scale, usu. one in which mechanical power is employed; **-office**, an establishment in which books, newspapers, etc. are printed; **-paper**, (*a*) paper used for printing on; (*b*) in *Photogr.* sensitized paper on which pictures are printed (also *printing-out paper*, abbrev. P.O.P.).

Pri·nting-house. Now only *Hist.* 1576. A building in which printing is carried on, a printing-office.

Printing House Square, a small square in London, the site of the office of the *Times* newspaper.

Pri·nting-press. 1587. An instrument or machine for printing on paper, etc., from types, blocks, or plates; sometimes restricted to a hand-press, as dist. from a *printing-machine*.

Prior (prəi·əɹ), *sb.* [Late OE. a. L. *prior*, *-orem* PRIOR *a.*; in med.L. as sb., spec. a prior.] 1. A superior officer of a religious house or order. 2. a. In foreign countries, the title of the elected head of a guild of merchants or craftsmen. b. The title of a chief magistrate in some of the former Italian republics, e. g. Florence. *Obs.* exc. *Hist.* 1604. 3. *Commerce.* The head of a firm. Now *rare.* 1853.

1. *Grand P.*, the commander of a priory of the knights of St. John of Jerusalem, or of Malta. Hence **Pri·oral** *a.* **Pri·orship**, the office or dignity of p.

Prior (prəi·əɹ), *a.* (*adv.*) 1714. [a. L., former, earlier, superior, f. OL. prep. *pri* before.] Preceding (in time or order); earlier, former, anterior, antecedent. B. as *adv.* with *to*: Previously to, before 1736.

The sin is p. to..the action 1714. A p. marriage 1765.

Priorate (prəi·ŏrĕt). late ME. [ad. late L. *prioratus*, f. *prior* PRIOR *a.*; see -ATE [1].] 1. The office and dignity of a prior; also, the term of office of a prior. 2. A priory; also, the inmates as a community 1749.

Prioress (prəi·ŏrĕs). [ME. a. OF. *prioresse, prieuresse*; see PRIOR *sb.* and -ESS [1].] A nun holding a position similar to that of a prior.

Priority (prəiˌǫ·rĭti). [Late ME. a. F. *priorité*, ad. med.L. *prioritas*, f. L. *prior* PRIOR *a.*; see -ITY.] 1. The condition or quality of being earlier in time, or of preceding something else. 2. Precedence in order, rank, or dignity. late ME. 3. *Law.* A precedence among claims, or a preference in order of payment 1766.

1. The preeminence of prioritie in birth HOOKER. 2. *Tr. & Cr.* I. iii. 86.

attrib. **p.-bond** = *preference bond.*

Priory (prəi·ŏri). [ME. a. AF. *priorie*; see PRIOR *sb.* and -Y [3].] A monastery or nunnery governed by a prior or prioress; usu. an offshoot of an abbey on which it was dependent; also, a house of Canons Regular.

Alien p.: see ALIEN *a.* 1.

Prisage (prəi·zĕdʒ). Now *Hist.* 1505. [f. AF. *prise* PRISE *sb.* + -AGE.] An ancient custom levied upon imported wine; in later times correlated to and often identified with BUTLERAGE 1. (Abolished 1809.) b. *attrib.*, as *p. fund, lease, wine* 1586.

Priscian (pri·ʃiăn). 1525. [ad. L. *Priscianus.*] Name of a celebrated Roman grammarian, *c* 500–530.

Phr. *To break Priscian's head*, to violate the rules of grammar.

Priscillianist (prisi·liănist), *sb.* and *a.* 1574. [ad. med.L. *Priscillianista*, f. *Priscillianus* Priscillian; see -IST.] A. *sb.* A disciple of Priscillian, bishop of Avila, in Spain, in the 4th c., who taught doctrines alleged to be Gnostic or Manichæan. B. *adj.* Of or pertaining to the Priscillianists or their doctrines 1887.

Prise (prəiz, ‖prīz). *Obs.* or *Hist.* ME. [a. F. *prise* a taking, f. pa. pple. *pris* of *prendre*; cf. PRIZE *sb.*[3]] 1. The taking or seizing of anything by a lord for his own use from his feudal tenants or dependants; a thing requisitioned for the king's use, or for the use of the garrisons in his castles; the right of such seizure. *Obs.* exc. *Hist.* 2. *pl.* (rarely *sing.*) The king's customs; that is, portions taken by him from goods brought into the realm, or duties levied in lieu thereof 1455.

Prism (priz'm). 1570. [ad. late L. *prisma*, a. Gr. πρίσμα a thing sawn, f. πρίζειν to saw.] 1. *Geom.* A solid figure of which the two ends are similar, equal, and parallel rectilineal figures, and the sides parallelograms. 2. Any body or object of this form 1661. 3. *Optics.* A transparent body of this form, usu. a triangular geometrical prism, of which the refracting surfaces are at an acute angle with each other 1612. b. Loosely used for a spectrum produced by refraction through a prism; *pl.* prismatic colours 1840. 4. *Cryst.* A 'form' consisting of three or more planes parallel to the vertical axis of the crystal 1878.

3. *Nicol('s) p.* = NICOL. Hence **Pri·smal** *a.* = next.

Prismatic (prizmæ·tik), *a.* 1709. [f. Gr. πρισματ-, πρίσμα; see prec. and -IC.] 1. Of or pertaining to a prism; prism-like. 2. Of or pertaining to the optical prism; formed, effected, separated, or distributed by or as by a transparent prism; hence, of varied colours, bright-coloured, brilliant 1728. 3. *Cryst.* = ORTHORHOMBIC *a.* 1858.

1. *P. powder*, a gunpowder the grains of which are hexagonal prisms. 2. *P. colours*, the seven colours into which a ray of white light is separated by a prism. *P. compass*, a surveying compass so arranged that by means of a prism the angle of position of the object sighted can be read at the same time as the object itself is seen. So **Prisma·tical** *a.* 1654; **-ly** *adv.*

Prismatoid (pri·zmătoid), *a.* and *sb.* 1858. [ad. Gr. πρισματοειδής prism-shaped, f. πρισματο- πρίσμα PRISM; see -OID.] A. *adj. Cryst.* Applied to any plane, in a crystallographic system, parallel to one of the three axes of coordinates and intersecting the other two; so called because a group of eight such planes would form a prism. B. *sb. Geom.* A solid figure having parallel polygonal ends connected by triangular sides 1890. So **Prismatoi·dal** *a.* resembling a prism; also, = PRISMOIDAL.

Prismoid (pri·zmoid). 1704. [= F. *prismoïde*, f. *prisme* PRISM; see -OID.] A body approaching in form to a prism, with similar but unequal parallel polygonal bases. Hence **Prismoi·dal** *a.* of the form of, or pertaining to, a p.

Prison (pri·z'n), *sb.* [Early ME. *prisun, -on*, a. OF. *prisun, prison* the action of taking, etc.:—L. *prensionem*, contr. from *prehensionem*, f. *prehendere, prendere* to seize.] *orig.* The condition of being kept in captivity or confinement; imprisonment; hence, a place in which such confinement is ensured; *spec.* a jail. a. Without article. b. with *a, the*, etc., or in *pl.* ME. c. *transf.* and *fig.* ME.

a. Phr. *To break p.* (BREAK *v.* IV. 3); *to cast, put, set in p.*; *to keep, lay, lie in p.* b. There are no prisons in al his empire: for..iustice is executed out of hand 1600. Stone Walls doe not a P. make Nor Iron bars a Cage LOVELACE. *State p.*, (*a*) a p. for the confinement of political offenders; (*b*) *U.S.* a p. under the control of the authorities of a State. c. The Island was certainly a P. to me DE FOE.

attrib. and *Comb.*, as *p.-accommodation, camp, -industry*, etc.; also **p.-bars**, the iron bars by which a prison, its door, windows, etc., are made fast; bars which imprison; **-crop**, hair cut very short; **p. editor**, an editor (of a newspaper) who takes the legal responsibility for what appears in the newspaper, and serves the terms of imprisonment that conviction for an offence may entail; **-fever** = JAIL-FEVER; **-van**, a close carriage for the conveyance of prisoners.

Prison (pri·z'n), *v.* ME. [f. prec.] *trans.* To put in prison, make a prisoner of; to keep in a place of confinement; to detain in custody. Now *poet.* or *rhet.*, and *n. dial.* b. *transf.* and *fig.* To confine. late ME.

b. His true respect will p. false desire SHAKS.

Prisoner (pri·z'nəɹ). [ME. a. F. *prisonnier*; see PRISON *sb.* and -ER [2] 2.] 1. One who is kept in prison or in custody; *spec.* one who is in custody as the result of a legal process. 2. One who has been captured in war; a captive. Now often *p. of war.* ME. 3. *transf.* and *fig.* One who or that which is confined to a place or position. late ME. 4. *attrib.* Of or pertaining to a prisoner; that is a prisoner 1846.

1. Phr. *P. at the bar*, a person in custody upon a criminal charge, and on trial in a court of justice. *P. of state, state p.*, one confined for political or state reasons. 2. *To take* (a person) *p.*, to seize and hold as a p., esp. in war. 3. An vntimely Ague Staid me a P. in my Chamber SHAKS.

Prisoners' bars, base. 1801. Earlier †prison-bars (1611), -base (1598). [See PRISONER and BAR *sb.*[1], BASE *sb.*[2]] = BASE *sb.*[2]

Pri·son-house. late ME. A house of imprisonment; a building that is or serves as a prison. Often *fig.*

Pristine (pri·stəin, *U.S.* -in), *a.* 1534. [ad. L. *pristinus* former.] Of or pertaining to the earliest period or state; original, former; primitive, ancient.

To restore it to its p. purity 1782. The p. simplicity of our Saxon-English 1841.

Pritchel (pri·tʃ'l). *dial.* late ME. [Southern form of PRICKLE *sb.*[1]] A sharp-pointed instrument or tool; esp. for punching the nail-holes in horse-shoes.

Prithee (pri·ði), *int. phr.* 1577. Archaic colloquialism for '(I) pray thee'.

Pr'ythee don't send us up any more Stories of a Cock and a Bull ADDISON.

Prittle-prattle (pri·t'lˌpræ:t'l). Now *rare.* 1556. [Reduplicated extension of PRATTLE *sb.*] Trivial, worthless, or idle talk; also, small talk; chatter; childish prattle.

‖**Prius** (prəi·ŏs). 1891. [L., neut. of *prior.*] a. That which takes precedence. b. That which is prior, *esp.* that which is a necessary prior condition.

Privacy (prəi·văsi, pri·v-). 1450. [f. PRIVATE *a.*; see -CY.] 1. The state or condition of being withdrawn from the society of others, or from public interest; seclusion. 2. *pl.* Private or retired places; private apartments; places of retreat. Now *rare.* 1678. 3. Absence or avoidance of publicity or display 1598. 4. A private matter, a secret; *pl.* private or personal matters or relations. Now *rare.* 1591. 5. = PRIVITY 4 (*rare*) 1719.

1. To guard the independence and p. of their homes EMERSON. 3. A marriage..solemnised with strict p. in the chapel of Leigh Court 1876.

Private (prəi·vĕt), *a.* and *sb.* late ME. [ad. L. *privatus*, properly pa. pple. of *privare* to bereave, deprive.] A. *adj.* 1. Of a person: Not holding public office or official position. b. *P. soldier*: a soldier below the rank of a non-commissioned officer 1579. **c.** *P. member*, a member of the House of Commons who is not a member of the Ministry 1863. **2.** Kept or removed from public view or knowledge; not within the cognizance of people generally 1472. **b.** *P. parts*, the pudenda 1885. **3.** Not open to the public; intended only for the use of particular and privileged persons. late ME. **b.** Not open to the public, or not publicly done or performed, dist. from a thing of the same kind that is 'public' 1560. **4.** That belongs to or is the property of a particular individual; belonging to oneself, one's own 1502. **5.** Of or pertaining to a person in a non-official capacity 1613. **6.** Of, pertaining or relating to, or affecting a person, or a small group of persons apart from the general community; individual, personal 1526. **7.** By one's self, alone; without the presence of any one else 1592. **8.** Of a conversation, etc.: Intended only for the person or persons directly concerned 1560. **9.** Retiring; retired; secluded 1494. †**10.** quasi-*adv.* Privately, secretly –1704.

1. A Woman of Quality; married to a p. Gentleman STEELE. **2.** Lady Alethea's privet wedding 1677. **3.** A p. staircase conducted into the gardens LYTTON. News which reached him through p. channels MACAULAY. **b.** He resygned his crowne, & lyued a holy pryuate lyfe 1526. *P. assembly, function, meeting*, etc.; *p. baptism, communion, education, funeral, marriage*, etc.; *p. boarding-house, brougham, carriage, chapel, hotel, theatricals*, etc. *P. view* (e. g. of an exhibition of pictures or the like). **4.** The institution of p. property 1845. *P. house*, the dwelling-house of a p. person, or of a person in his p. capacity. *P. family*, the family occupying a p. house. *P. school*, a school owned and carried on by a person or persons for their own profit. *P. judgement*: see JUDGEMENT 7. **5.** A tribute to p. worth and public usefulness 1864. **6.** For your priuate satisfaction..I will let you know SHAKS. Phr. *P. bill, act*, a parliamentary bill or act affecting the interests of a particular individual or corporation only. **8.** P. Confession is retained in the reformed churches 1650. A letter..marked 'p.' TROLLOPE. **10.** Every body now drink the King's health..whereas before, it was very p. that a man dare do it PEPYS.

B. *sb.* **I.** Of a person. †**1.** A private person –1671. †**b.** *The p.*: private people, opp. to *the public* –1734. †**2.** An intimate, a favourite. (With play on sense II. 3) SHAKS. **3.** A private soldier 1781. **II.** Of things or affairs. †**1.** A private matter, business, or interest; *pl.* private affairs –1642. †**2.** Retirement, privacy –1653. **b.** *In p.*, privately, not publicly; in private company; in private life 1581. **3.** *pl.* The private parts.

2. Go off, I discard you: let me enioy my priuate SHAKS. **b.** Laugh and spare not So't be in priuate 1615. Hence **Pri·vate·ly** *adv.*, **-ness** (now *rare*).

Privateer (prəivătī³ɹ), *sb.* 1664. [f. PRIVATE *a.* + -EER, prob. after *volunteer*; in sense 1, app. orig. colloq. for *private man of war*, the earliest name.] **1.** An armed vessel owned and officered by private persons, and holding a commission from the government, called 'letters of marque', authorizing the owners to use it against a hostile nation, and esp. in the capture of merchant shipping. **2.** The commander, or *pl.* the crew, of such a vessel 1674. **3.** *attrib.*, as *p. brig*, etc. 1675.

2. Privateers were little scrupulous as to what kind of victim they pounced upon 1883. Hence **Privatee·r** *v. rare, intr.* to practise privateering. **Privatee·ring** *vbl. sb.* the occupation of a p.; often *attrib.*; also *fig.* **Privatee·rsman** (*U.S.*), an officer or seaman of a p.

Privation (prəivē¹·ʃən). ME. [ad. L. *privationem*, f. *privare* to bereave, deprive.] **1.** The action of depriving or taking away; the fact or condition of being deprived *of* or †cut off *from* something; deprivation. Now *rare*. **b.** *Law.* = DEPRIVATION 2; in *R. C. Ch.* = SUSPENSION. Now *rare* or *Obs.* late ME. **2.** *Logic.* The condition of being without some attribute formerly or properly possessed; the loss, or (loosely) the mere absence of a quality, a negative quality. late ME. **3.** Want of the usual comforts, or esp. of some of the necessaries of life 1790.

1. All general privations are great because they are all terrible; Vacuity, Darkness, Solitude, and Silence BURKE. **2.** Cold, which is the p. of heat EMERSON. **3.** A needy band of mercenaries, urged by hunger and p. 1845.

Privative (pri·vătiv), *a.* (*sb.*) 1588. [ad. L. *privativus*, f. ppl. stem of *privare*; see -IVE. So F. *privatif, -ive.*] **1.** Having the quality of depriving; tending to take away 1600. **2.** Consisting in or characterized by the taking away or removal of something, or by the loss or (loosely) absence of some quality or attribute normally or presumably present 1598. **3.** Of terms: Denoting or predicating privation, or (loosely) absence of a quality or attribute 1646. **4.** *Gram.* Expressing privation or negation; esp. applied to a particle or affix (e. g. the Greek prefix *a-*) 1590. **B.** *sb.* A privative attribute, quality, proposition, word, or particle 1588.

1. If the thing sworn should become p. of, or opposite to, the publick good 1650. Hence **Pri·vative·ly** *adv.*, **-ness** (*rare*).

Privet (pri·vėt). 1542. [Origin unkn.] **1.** A bushy evergreen shrub, *Ligustrum vulgare* (N.O. *Oleaceæ*), a native of Europe, having elliptic-lanceolate smooth dark-green leaves, and clusters of small white flowers, succeeded by small shining black berries; much used for garden hedges. **2.** Applied to other species of *Ligustrum*, and other shrubs resembling p. 1597.

2. **Egyptian p.** = HENNA; **Evergreen p.**, any evergreen species of the genus *Rhamnus*; **Mock p.**, the evergreen genus PHILLYREA, N.O. *Oleaceæ*. *Comb.* **p. hawk (-moth)**, a large species of hawk-moth which deposits its eggs on the p.

Privilege (pri·vĭlėdʒ), *sb.* ME. [ad. L. *privilegium* a bill or law in favour of or against an individual, f. *privus* + *lex, legem.*] **1.** *Rom. Antiq.* A special ordinance having reference to an individual 1483. **2.** A right, advantage, or immunity granted to or enjoyed by a person, or class of persons, beyond the common advantages of others ME. **b.** In extended sense: A special advantage, with ref. to divine dispensations, gifts of fortune, etc. ME. †**c.** Advantage yielded, superiority SHAKS. **3.** A privileged position; the possession of an advantage over others or another. late ME. **4.** The special right or immunity attaching to some office, rank, or station; prerogative ME. **5.** *R. C. Ch.* A special ordinance issued by the pope, granting exemption from all such acts as are necessary for the purpose for which it is obtained. late ME. **6.** A grant of special rights or immunities to an individual, corporation, community, or place; a franchise, monopoly, patent; †*spec.* the sole right of printing or publishing a book or the like. late ME. †**7.** The right of affording security from arrest, attached to certain places; the right of asylum or sanctuary –1683.

2. A monopoly of privileges is always invidious 1879. **b.** All the greater Prophets claimed..the p. of married life 1862. **3.** Inequalities of legal p. between individuals or classes MILL. **4.** *The p.*, the royal prerogative. *P. of clergy* = *benefit of clergy*: see CLERGY 5. *P. of Parliament*, the immunities enjoyed by either house of parliament, or by individual members, as such. *Bill of p.*, a petition of a peer demanding to be tried by his peers. *Writ of p.*, a writ to deliver a privileged person from custody when arrested in a civil suit.

Privilege (pri·vĭlėdʒ), *v.* ME. [ad. F. *privilégier*, ad. med.L. *privilegiare*, f. *privilegium*; see prec.] **1.** *trans.* To invest with a privilege or privileges; to invest (a thing) with special honourable distinctions. **2.** To authorize, license (what is otherwise forbidden); to justify, excuse 1592. **3.** To exempt *from* a liability or burden to which others are subject 1542.

2. Kings cannot p. what God forbade DANIEL. **3.** Some thinges are priuiledged from iest BACON.

Privileged (pri·vĭlėdʒd), *ppl. a.* late ME. [f. prec. vb. or sb. + -ED.] Invested with or enjoying certain privileges or immunities.

P. communication, in *Law*, (*a*) a communication which a witness cannot be legally compelled to divulge; (*b*) a communication made between such persons and in such circumstances that it is not actionable, unless made with malice. **P. debt**, a debt having a prior claim to satisfaction. **P. share, stock**, preference stock.

Privity (pri·vĭti). Now chiefly *techn.* (in Law, etc.). [ME. *privete, -ite*, a. OF., ad. L. **privitas, -atem*, f. *privus* private, peculiar; see -ITY.] †**1.** A thing that is kept hidden or secret –1625. †**2.** The condition of being private; privacy, seclusion –1661. **3.** The private parts. Chiefly in *pl.* Now *rare*. late ME. **4.** The fact of being privy to something; participation in the knowledge of something private or secret, usu. implying concurrence or consent; private knowledge or cognizance 1560. **5.** *Law.* Any relation between two parties recognized by law, e. g. that of blood, covenant, tenure, service, etc.; mutual interest in any transaction or thing 1523.

1. Yet neither shewed to other their hearts p. SPENSER.

Privy (pri·vi), *a.* and *sb. arch.* or *techn.* (in Law, etc.). [ME. *prive, privy*, etc., a. F. *privé*:—L. *privatus*; see PRIVATE.] **A.** *adj.* **I.** †**1.** That is of one's own private circle or companionship; intimate, familiar –1645. **2.** = PRIVATE *a.* 4. *Obs.* exc. in P. CHAMBER, COUNCIL, COUNCILLOR, SEAL. ME. **3.** Participating in the knowledge of something secret or private; in the secret; accessory to some secret transaction. late ME.

3. The clergy believed that they alone were p. to the counsels of the Almighty 1862.

II. **1.** Withdrawn from public sight, knowledge, or use; kept secret; hidden; secluded. *arch.* ME. **2.** Acting or done in secret or by stealth; clandestine, furtive, surreptitious, sly. *arch.* ME.

1. In at a preuy posterne gate, By night she stale 1440. **2.** From all sedicion and priuye conspiracie.. Good lorde deliuer us *Bk. Com. Prayer*.

Collocations with sbs. **P. parts** (see PRIVATE *a.* 2 b). **P. purse. a.** The allowance from the public revenue for the private expenses of the monarch. **b.** Short for *Keeper of the P. Purse*, an officer of the royal household charged with the payment of the private expenses of the sovereign. **P. signet**: see SIGNET. **P. verdict**, a verdict given to the judge out of court.

B. *sb.* [The adj. used absol. or ellipt.] **I.** *Law.* One who is a partaker or has any part or interest in any action, matter, or thing 1483. **II.** **1.** A private place of ease, a latrine. late ME. †**2.** That which is secret, secrecy; in phr. *in p.*, in secret, covertly –1569. Hence **Pri·vily** *adv.* (now *arch.* or *literary*).

Pri·vy cha·mber. Now *Hist.* late ME. [PRIVY *a.* I. 2.] **1.** *gen.* A private room, in which one is not liable to interruption or disturbance. Also *fig. Obs.* or *arch.* **2.** *spec.* A private apartment in a royal residence 1540.

Pri·vy cou·ncil. [ME. *prive counseil*: see PRIVY *a.* I. 2, COUNCIL *sb.*).] †**1.** *gen.* A private consultation or assembly for consultation –1825. **2.** The private counsellors of the sovereign; *spec.* in Great Britain a body of advisers selected by the sovereign, together with certain persons who are members by usage, as the princes of the blood, the archbishops, and the chief officers of the present and past ministries of state 1450. **b.** Applied to a council of state in a foreign country, etc. 1450. **c.** A similar body formed to assist the Lord Lieutenant of Ireland, and the governors of some British colonies or dominions 1765.

Pri·vy cou·nsellor, cou·ncillor. [ME. *prive counseiller*; see PRIVY *a.* I. 2 and COUNSELLOR; often spelt *councillor* after prec.; but *counsellor* is the official form.] **1.** A private or confidential adviser. **2.** *spec.* in Great Britain: One of the private counsellors of the sovereign; a member of the Privy Council 1647. Hence **Pri·vy-Cou·nsellorship, -Cou·ncillorship.**

Pri·vy sea·l. late ME. [PRIVY *a.* I. 2.] **1.** The seal affixed to documents that are afterwards to pass the Great Seal; also to documents of less importance which do not require the Great Seal. **2.** A document to which the privy seal is affixed; *spec.* a warrant, under the privy seal, demanding a loan; hence *transf.* a forced loan, a benevolence. Now only *Hist.* late ME. **3.** The keeper of the privy seal; now *Lord Privy Seal*. late ME.

1. *Keeper of the privy seal*: see KEEPER 1.

Prizable, prizeable (prəi·zăb'l), *a.* Now chiefly *dial.* 1569. [f. PRIZE *v.*[1] + -ABLE.] Worthy to be prized; valuable.

Prize (prəiz), *sb.*[1] ME. [Variant, now differentiated in spelling and pronunciation, of ME. *pris, prise* PRICE *sb.* (The mod. spelling appears *c* 1600.)] **1.** A reward, trophy, or symbol of victory or superiority in any contest or competition. **b.** In colleges, schools, etc.: A reward in the form of money, books, or the like, given to the pupil who excels in attainments 1752. **c.** A premium offered to the person who exhibits the best specimens of natural productions, works of art, or manufactures, at a competition, or at an exhibition 1775. **2.** A sum of money or a thing of value, offered for competition by chance or hazard 1567. **3.** *fig.* Anything striven for or worth striving for; a thing of value won by or inspiring effort 1606. †**b.** An advantage, privilege; something prized -1638 **4.** *attrib.* That gains a prize; *fig.* such as would or might gain a prize; first-class 1803.

1. We overvalue the p. for which we contend HUME. *Consolation p.*, a p. won in a consolation match; see CONSOLATION 1. c. The first p. for 12 Ranunculuses 1845. 2. A twenty thousand p. in the lottery 1842. 3. Place, ritches, and fauour, Prizes of accident as oft as merit SHAKS. b. Tis warres prise to take all aduantages SHAKS. 4. A P. Essay 1803. There was a p. ox, a p. pig, and ploughman BYRON.

Comb.: **p.-fellowship**, a fellowship in a college given as a reward for eminence in an examination; hence **-fellow**; **-list**, a list of the winners of prizes in any competition; **-medal**, a medal offered or gained as a p.

†**Prize**, *sb.*[2] 1565. [perh. transf. use of prec.; cf. Gr. ἆθλον 'prize', also 'contest'.] A contest, match; a public athletic contest; *pl.* the public games of the Greeks and Romans; in late use, a prize-fight. -1715.

Here we saw a p. fought between a soldier and a country fellow PEPYS. Phr. *To play a p.*, to engage in a match, esp. a fencing-match; also (*fig.*) *to play one's p.*, to play one's part.

Prize (prəiz), *sb.*[3] late ME. [Orig. special sense of PRISE *sb.*, identified later with PRIZE *sb.*[1]] †**1.** The action of taking; capture, seizure -1721. **2.** Anything seized or captured, esp. in war; booty, plunder; a captive of war. *Obs.* exc. as in b. late ME. **b.** *esp.* A ship or property captured at sea in virtue of the rights of war 1512. **c.** without *a* or *pl.* Property seized as in war; esp. in the phr. *to make p.* 1594. **d.** In *good, fair, free, just, lawful p.*, with ref. to the legality of the seizure 1550.

2. b. They took a p. of nine hundred tunnes PURCHAS. c. P. or not P., must be determined by Courts of Admiralty 1755.

Comb.: **p. court**, a department of the admiralty court, which adjudicates concerning prizes; **p. crew**, a crew of seamen put on board a prize ship to bring her into port; **-list**, a list of persons entitled to receive prize-money on the capture of a ship; **-money**, money realized by the sale of a p., and distributed among the captors.

Prize, prise (prəiz), *sb.*[4] [ME. *prise*, a. F. *prise* a taking hold.] **1.** An instrument for prizing; a lever. Now *dial.* **2.** The act of prizing; leverage, purchase 1835.

Prize (prəiz), *v.*[1] [ME. a. OF. *prisier*, F. *priser*, levelled form of OF. *preisier*, PRAISE *v.*] †**1.** *trans.* To value; to account as worth (so much); to account, reckon -1724. †**2.** To fix the money value of; to appraise; to fix the price of (a thing for sale). Now PRICE. -1755. **3.** To value or esteem highly; to think much of. late ME.

3. P. your time now, while you have it 1720. Hence **Pri·zer** [1], one who prizes (now *rare*).

Prize, *v.*[2] 1535. [f. PRIZE *sb.*[3]] *trans.* To seize, take, capture; to seize as forfeited, to confiscate. *Obs.* exc. as in b. **b.** *spec.* To seize (a ship or her cargo) as a prize of war 1568.

Prize, prise (prəiz), *v.*[3] 1686. [f. PRIZE *sb.*[4]] *trans.* To raise or move by force of leverage; *esp.* to force open in this way.

Prize-fight (prəi·zfəi:t). 1824. [Back-formation from next.] A public contest between prize-fighters; a boxing-match for money.

Prize-fighter (prəi·zfəi:tə1). 1703. [orig. f. PRIZE *sb.*[2] + FIGHTER, from the phr. 'to fight a prize'; now assoc. with PRIZE *sb.*[1]] †**a.** *orig.* One who engaged in a public fighting-match or contest. **b.** A professional pugilist or boxer, who fights publicly for a prize or stake. So **Pri·ze-fi:ghting** *sb.* and *a.*

Prizeman (prəi·zmæ̆n). 1800. [f. PRIZE *sb.*[1] + MAN *sb.*] A man who wins a prize.

Pri·zer[2]. *arch.* 1599. [f. PRIZE *sb.*[2] + -ER[1].] One who engages in a 'prize' or contest; a prize-fighter.

And fought like prizers, not as angry rivals 1679.

Prize-ring (prəi·z,ri:ŋ). 1840. [f. after PRIZE-FIGHT; see RING *sb.*[1]] A ring or enclosed space (now a square area enclosed by poles and ropes) for prize-fighting; hence *transf.* the practice of prize-fighting.

‖**Pro**[1] (prōu). late ME. The L. prep. *pro* before, in front of, for, on behalf of, instead of, in return for, on account of, etc. **A.** as *prep.* in various L. phrases, used in Eng.

1. **pro aris et focis** (ēᵊris et fōu·sis), for altars and hearths; for the sake of, or on behalf of, religion and home 1621. 2. **pro bono publico** (bōu·no pɒ·bliko) for the public good 1726. 3. **pro fo·rma**, for form's sake; as a matter of form. Also *attrib.* 1573. 4. **pro hac vice** (hæk vəi·si), for this turn or occasion (only) 1653. 5. **pro rata** (rē̆i·tă) [= 'according to the rate': RATE *sb.*[1] 2], in proportion to the value or extent (of his interest); proportionally. Also *attrib.* or as *adj.*, proportional. 1575. 6. **pro re nata** (rī nē̆i·tă), 'for the affair born, i. e. arisen'; for an occasion as it arises. Also *attrib.* 1578. 7. **pro tanto** (tæ·ntə), 'for so much', so far, to such an extent. Also *attrib.* 1780. 8. **pro tempore** (te·mpŏri), for the time, temporarily; *attrib.* or as *adj.* temporary. (Abbreviated *pro tem.*)

B. as *sb.* An argument for or in favour of something, as opp. to one against it. (Now usu. in PRO AND CON.) **b.** A person who sides or votes in favour of some proposal. late ME.

Pro.[2] 1848. Familiar abbrev. of various compounds of PRO- *prefix* [1], esp. *proproctor* and *professional.*

Pro-, *prefix* [1]. The L. adv. and prep. (see above) used in comb. with verbs and their derivs., and occas. with other words not of verbal derivation.

A large number of L. wds. so formed were taken into English through French. In later times words of this kind have been adopted or adapted in Eng. directly from L., or have been formed from L. elements.

I. As an etymological element.

1. a. Forward, to or towards the front, from a position in the rear, forth, out, into a public position; as PROCLAIM, PRODUCE, PROJECT, PROMINENT, etc. b. To the front of, down before (the face of), forward and down; as PROCUMBENT, PROFLIGATE, PROSTRATE, etc. c. Forth from its place, away; as PRODIGAL, etc. d. Forward, onward, in a course or in time; as PROCEED, PROCRASTINATE, PROGRESS, PROPEL, etc. e. Out, with outward extension; as PROLIX, PROPAGATE, PROTRACT, etc. f. Before in place, in front of; as PROSCRIBE, PROTECT. g. Before in time, in anticipation of, in provision for; as PRODIGY, PROVIDE, etc. h. For, in preparation for, on behalf of; as PROCURE, PROFIT, etc. i. With worn-down or obscure force; as PROFANE, PROFOUND, PROMISCUOUS, PROVERB, PROVINCE, etc.

2. Freq. prefixed in L. to names of relationship, answering to Eng. 'great' or 'grand'; as *avus* grandfather, *pro-avus* great-grandfather; etc. So †**pro·nephew** (*Sc.*), a great-grandson.

II. As a living prefix.

1. In Latin, *pro-*, in the sense 'for', 'instead of', 'in place of', was prefixed to a sb., app. orig. in prepositional construction, as *pro consule* (one acting) for a consul, subseq. combined with the sb., as *proconsul* = deputy-consul; etc.; so in a few names of things, as *pronomen* PRONOUN, etc. English has examples of *pro-* prefixed a. to names of persons, 'acting as deputy', as PROCONSUL, PROPROCTOR, etc. b. to names of things, as PRO-CATHEDRAL, etc. 2. In sense 'for, in favour of, on the side of'. This use has no precedent or analogy in Latin, and appears to have arisen from the use of *pro* in PRO B. b. a. Prefixed to a sb., sb. phr., or adj., forming adjs. with sense 'favouring or siding with (what is indicated by the second element)'; as *pro-Boer, -clerical, -tariff reform*, etc. Some of these are also used as sbs., as *pro-Boer* = 'one who is on the side of the Boers'. b. In comb. with a sb. (or verb-stem) + -ER or -ITE, forming a nonce-sb., in sense 'one who sides with..'; as *pro-flogger* (one who favours flogging), *pro-liquorite* (one in favour of the unrestricted sale of alcoholic drinks). c. In comb. with a sb. or adj. + -ISM, forming abstract sbs. = 'the principle or character of being in favour of..', as *pro-Boerism, -clericalism*, etc.

Pro- (prou), *prefix* [2], repr. Gr. prep. πρό before (of time, position, preference, priority, etc.), forming in Gr. many compounds—vbs., sbs., and adjs. Many of these forms, as latinized, have been adopted or adapted in the modern languages generally, in the nomenclature of modern science and philosophy.

1. In sense 'Before in time': forming (*a*) sbs., chiefly scientific terms denominating the earlier, or (supposed) primitive type of an animal, plant, organ, or structure (with derived adjs.); (*b*) adjs. meaning 'previous to or preceding that which is expressed by the second element'. **Probouleu·tic** *a. Gr. Hist.* that deliberates preliminarily; *spec.* applied to the Athenian senate, which discussed measures before they were submitted to the Assembly. ‖**Proca·mbium** [CAMBIUM], *Bot.* the young tissue of a fibrovascular bundle, before its differentiation into permanent cells of wood, bast, etc. ‖**Proempto·sis** [Gr. ἔμπτωσις] an anticipation or occurrence of a natural event earlier than the time given by a rule; esp. the occurrence of the new moon earlier than the Metonic cycle would make it. **Promorpho·logy,** *Biol.* the morphology of fundamental forms; the branch of morphology that treats of organic forms from a mathematical standpoint. **Pro·ode,** an introductory ode in a Greek chorus; an overture or prelude. **Proparo·xytone** *a. Gram.* having an acute accent on the antepenult; *sb.* a word so accented. **Pro·plasm** [PLASM], a mould, a matrix (*rare*). **Prosi·phon** [SIPHON], *Zool.* the primitive siphon in an embryonic ammonite, a kind of ligament attached to the protoconch. ‖**Protha·llium, -tha·llus,** *Bot.* in vascular cryptogams, a minute cellular structure or thallus, bearing the sexual organs, forming the first of the two alternate generations, much simpler than the fully-developed (asexual) plant. ‖**Protrachea·ta** *sb. pl., Zool.* a class of arthropodous animals (representing the supposed ancestral form of all the tracheate *Arthropoda*), represented by the single genus *Peripatus.*

2. Of local position; forming sbs. and adjs., chiefly anatomical and zoological terms (often correlated with words in META- and MESO-); (*a*) in adjectival relation to the second element, denoting either 'an anterior or front (thing of the kind)', or 'an anterior or front part (of the thing)'; (*b*) in prepositional relation to the second element = 'lying before or in front of (the thing)'. **Procepha·lic** [Gr. κεφαλή] *a., Zool.* belonging to the fore part of the head; applied to certain lobes or processes in Crustacea and other Arthropoda. **Pro·cerite** [Gr. κέρας horn], *Zool.* the many-jointed terminal segment of the antenna in certain Crustacea, as lobsters. **Procho·rdal** *a., Embryol.* anterior to the notochord. **Procœ·lian** [Gr. κοῖλος hollow] *a.*, having procœlous vertebræ; pertaining to the *Procœlia*, a suborder of *Crocodilia.* **Procœlous** (-sī·ləs) *a.*, concave or cupped in front: applied to vertebræ. ‖**Proglo·ttis** [Gr. προγλωσσίς point of the tongue], a sexually mature segment or joint of a tapeworm. ‖**Prone·phron, -ne·phros** [Gr. νεφρός kidney], the anterior division of the primitive kidney or segmental organ in the embryos of lower vertebrates. ‖**Prono·tum** [NOTUM], *Entom.* the dorsal part of the prothorax of an insect; the anterior division of the notum. ‖**Pro-o·stracum** [Gr. ὄστρακον potsherd], *Palæont.* the anterior prolongation, usu. lamellar, of the guard or rostrum of a fossil cephalopod. **Pro-o·tic** *a.*, that is in front of the ear; applied distinctively to one of the three bones which together form the periotic capsule; *sb.* the pro-otic bone. **Pro·podite** [Gr. ποδ- foot], *Zool.* the penultimate joint of a developed endapodite limb, as of a crustacean. ‖**Propo·dium,** the anterior lobe of the foot in some molluscs; hence **Propo·dial** *a.* ‖**Pro-pterygium,** *Ichthyol.* the anterior cartilaginous portion of the fin in elasmobranch fishes. ‖**Proso·ma** [Gr. σῶμα body], *Zool.* the anterior or cephalic segment of the body in certain animals, as cephalopods, etc. ‖**Prosto·mium,** *Zool.* the part of the body situated in front of the mouth in certain invertebrates.

Proa (prōu·ă), ‖**prahu** (prā·*u*). 1582. [ad. Malay *p*(*ă*)*rā*(*h*)*ū* a boat.] A Malay boat propelled by sails or by oars; *spec.* a sailing boat of the type used in the Malay archipelago.

Pro and con. late ME. [abbrev. of L. *pro et contra* for and against.] **A.** *adv. phr.* For and against; on both sides. So *pro or con.*

The matter throughly handled *Pro* and *Con* 1572.

B. *sb. phr.* (now always, in pl., *pros and cons.*) Reasons for and against; reasonings, arguments, statements, or votes on both sides of a question 1589.

Stating all the pros and cons of the case 1880.

C. *vb.* To weigh the arguments for and against; to debate both sides of a question 1694.

Wasted a precious minute in pro-and-conning 1835.

Probabiliorism (prǫbăbi·liŏriz'm). 1845. [f. L. *probabilior* more probable + -ISM]. The doctrine of the probabiliorists; according to which it is claimed, in opposition to probabilism, that that side on which the evidence preponderates is more probably right and therefore ought to be followed. So **Probabi·liorist,** one who holds the doctrine of p. 1727.

Probabilism (prǫ·băbiliz'm). 1842. [f. L. *probabilis* PROBABLE + -ISM.] **1.** *R. C. Casuistry.* The doctrine that in matters of conscience on which authorities differ, it is lawful to follow any course in support of which the authority of a recognized doctor of the Church can be cited. **2.** *Philos.* The theory that there is no absolutely certain knowledge, but that there may be grounds of belief sufficient for practical life 1902. So **Pro·babilist,** one who holds the casuistic doctrine of probabilism 1657; one who holds the philosophical theory of probabilism 1847.

Probability (prǫbăbi·lĭti). 1551. [ad. F. *probabilité*, ad. L. *probabilitatem*, f. *probabilis*; see -ITY.] **1.** The quality or fact of being probable; likelihood. **2.** A probable event, circumstance, belief, etc.; something which, judged by present evidence, is likely to be true, to exist, or to happen 1576. **3.** *Math.* As a measurable quantity: The amount of antecedent likelihood of a particular event, as measured by the relative frequency of occurrence of events of the same kind in the whole course of experience 1718.

1. Phr. *In p.*, probably; considering what is probable. (Now always *in all p.*) 2. Wolsey's return to power was discussed openly as a p. 1856.

Probabilize (prǫ·băbiləiz), *v.* 1802. [f. L. *probabilis* + -IZE.] *trans.* To render probable.

Probable (prǫ·băb'l), *a.* (*sb.*) late ME. [a. F., or ad. L. *probabilis*, f. *probare* to try, test, make good; f. *probus* good; see -ABLE.] **1.** Capable of being proved; demonstrable, provable. Now *rare.* 1485. †**2.** Such as to approve itself to the mind; worthy of acceptance or belief; rarely in bad sense, specious, colourable. (Now merged in 3.) –1872. **3.** Having an appearance of truth; that may reasonably be expected to happen, or to prove true; likely 1606. **B.** as *sb.* †Something p., a probability; a probable (member, candidate, etc.) 1647.

1. Neither proved nor p. GROTE. 2. He assigns the most p. reasons for that opinion 1780. 3. This was the more p. solution 1891. Hence **Pro·bably** *adv.*

Probang (prōu·bæŋ). 1657. [The inventor's name was *provang*, of unkn. origin; subseq. altered, prob. after PROBE *sb.*] *Surg.* A long slender strip of whalebone with a sponge, ball, button, etc. at the end, for introducing into the throat to apply a remedy or to remove a foreign body.

Probate (prōu·bĕt), *sb.* late ME. [ad. L. *probatum* a thing proved, sb. use of pa. pple. neut. of *probare* to PROVE.] †**1.** The act of proving or fact of being proved; that which proves; proof; evidence –1842. **2.** *Law.* The official proving of a will; also, the officially verified copy of a will together with the certificate of its having been proved, which are delivered to the executors 1463.

attrib. **P. Act**, an English statute passed in 1857, by which the jurisdiction of p. and administration was removed from eccl. and other courts, and transferred to a new Court of P. **P. court**, a court having jurisdiction of p. and administration. **P. judge**, a judge having jurisdiction in probate and testamentary causes.

Probate (prōu·beit), *v.* 1792. [f. L. *probat-*, *probare* to PROVE.] *trans.* To obtain probate of, to prove (a will). Now chiefly *U.S.*

Probation (prŏbē¹·ʃən). [Late ME. a. OF. *probacion*, ad. L. *probationem*, f. *probare* to prove, test.] **I.** †**1.** The action or process of testing or putting to the proof; trial, experiment; investigation, examination. *Obs.* (exc. as in 2). –1865. **2.** The testing or trial of a person's conduct, character, or moral qualifications; a proceeding designed to ascertain these: esp. in ref. to the period or state of trial. **a.** Of a candidate for membership in a religious body, order, or society, for holy orders, for fellowship in a college, etc. late ME. **b.** In theological and religious use: Moral trial or discipline; the divinely appointed testing of character and principle, esp. as taking place in this life in view of a future state of rewards and punishments 1526. **c.** *gen.* 1616. **3.** In criminal jurisdiction: A system of releasing on suspended sentence during good behaviour young persons, and esp. first offenders, and placing them under the supervision of a *p. officer*, who acts as a friend and adviser 1897.

2. b. Of the various views under which human life has been considered, no one seems so reasonable as that which regards it as a state of p. PALEY. c. For a yeare of probacion of his manners and good behavior 1616.

II. The action of proving or showing to be true; proof, demonstration; an instance of this. Now *rare* or *Obs.* exc. *Sc.* 1475. †**b.** = PROBATE *sb.* 2. –1590.

attrib. and *Comb.*, as *p. sermon*; *p.-state*; *p. law*, *officer*, *system*; etc. Hence **Proba·tionship**, a state or condition of p.; a term or period of p. (*rare*).

Probationary (prŏbē¹·ʃənări), *a.* 1664. [f. as prec. + -ARY¹.] **1.** Of, pertaining or relating to, or serving for probation; made, performed, or observed in the way of probation. **2.** Undergoing probation; that is a probationer; consisting of probationers 1818.

Probationer (prŏbē¹·ʃənəɹ). 1603. [f. as prec. + -ER¹.] A person on probation or trial; a candidate; a novice. **b.** *spec.* (*a*) A candidate for a fellowship in a college, admitted on probation 1609. (*b*) A novice in a religious house or order 1629. (*c*) A candidate for the ministry of a church, etc.; one licensed to preach but not yet ordained 1645. (*d*) In criminal jurisdiction, an offender under probation 1907. **c.** *transf.* and *fig.* 1642. **d.** *attrib.*: chiefly *appositive* = that is a probationer 1649.

He is still a Prentise and a p. FLORIO. c. To make my selfe a canting P. of orisons MILT. d. A p. nurse at Poplar Hospital 1905. Hence **Proba·tionership**, the position or condition of a p.

Probative (prōu·bătiv), *a.* 1453. [ad. L. *probativus* belonging to proof; see -IVE.] **1.** Having the quality or function of testing; serving for trial or probation; probationary. Now *rare.* **2.** Having the quality or function of proving or demonstrating; affording proof or evidence 1681.

Probatory (prōu·bătŏri), *a.* 1593. [ad. med.L. *probatorius*, f. *probat-*, *probare*; see -ORY².] = PROBATIVE. Now *rare.*

Probe (prōub), *sb.* 1580. [ad. late L. *proba* a proof, f. *probare* to PROVE.] **1.** A surgical instrument, commonly of silver, with a blunt end, for exploring the direction and depth of wounds and sinuses. **2.** *transf.* **a.** The proboscis of an insect 1664. **b.** *Angling.* A baiting-needle 1681. **3.** [f. PROBE *v.*] An act of probing; a piercing or boring 1890. **b.** *fig.* (*U.S.*) An inquiry, investigation 1921.

attrib. and *Comb.*: **p.-needle**, a needle used in the manner of a p.; **-scissors**, scissors used for opening wounds, having a button on the point of the blade.

Probe (prōub), *v.* 1649. [f. PROBE *sb.*; occas. infl. by L. *probare.*] **1.** *trans.* To explore (a wound or cavity of the body) with a probe. Also with the person as obj. 1687. **2.** *fig.* To search into, so as thoroughly to explore, or to discover or ascertain something; to try, prove, sound; to interrogate closely 1649. **3.** *transf.* To pierce or penetrate with something sharp, esp. in order to test or explore 1789. **4.** *intr.* To perform the action of piercing with or as with a probe; to penetrate, as a probe 1835.

1. I probed him carefully, and found no Stone 1758. 2. Stand firm, while I p. your prejudices BERKELEY.

Probity (prǫ·biti, prōu·b-). 1514. [ad. L. *probitas*, *-atem*, f. *probus*; see -ITY.] Moral excellence, integrity, rectitude, uprightness; conscientiousness, honesty, sincerity.

Of much reputation for p. and integrity of life CLARENDON.

Problem (prǫ·blĕm, -əm). [Late ME. *probleme*, a. F. *problème*, ad. L. *problema*, a. Gr. πρόβλημα lit. a thing thrown or put forward, f. προβάλλειν, f. πρό PRO-² + βάλλειν to throw.] †**1.** A difficult question proposed for solution; a riddle; an enigmatic statement –1602. **2.** A question proposed for academic discussion or scholastic disputation. *Obs.* exc. *Hist.* 1529. **b.** *Logic.* The question involved in a syllogism, and of which the conclusion is the solution or answer 1656. **3.** A doubtful or difficult question; a matter of inquiry, discussion, or thought 1594. **4.** *Geom.* A proposition in which something is required to be done; opp. to *theorem* 1570. **5.** *Physics* and *Math.* A question or inquiry which starting from some given conditions investigates some fact, result, or law 1570. **6.** *Chess.* An arrangement of pieces upon the chessboard, in which the player is challenged to discover the method of accomplishing a specified result 1817. **7.** *attrib.*, as *p. drama*, *novel*, *play*, etc.

3. Elizabeth..had hardly mounted the throne.. when she faced the p. of social discontent 1874. Hence **Pro·blemist**, one who devotes himself to, studies, or composes problems 1615.

Problematic (prǫblĕmæ·tik, -bləm-), *a.* 1609. [a. F. *problématique*; see PROBLEM and -ATIC.] **1.** Of the nature of a problem; presenting a problem; difficult of solution or decision; doubtful, questionable. **2.** *Logic.* Enunciating or supporting what is possible but not necessarily true 1610. **3.** *Chess.* Of or relating to problems 1890.

Problematical (prǫblĕmæ·tikăl, -bləm-), *a.* 1588. [f. as prec. + -AL.] **1.** = prec. **1.** 1611. **2.** = prec. **2.** 1588.

1. A very p. assertion 1815. A dialect of peculiar and p. character 1875. 2. *P. question*, a question put forth merely for discussion, but not of any practical bearing; an academic question. Hence **Problema·tically** *adv.*

Problematist (prǫ·blĕmătist). 1668. [f. Gr. πρόβλημα, -ατ- + -IST.] One who occupies himself with problems.

‖**Proboscidea** (prǫbǫsi·dĭă), *sb. pl.* 1836. [mod.L. neut. pl., f. L. *proboscidem.*] *Zool.* An order of mammalia containing the elephant and its extinct allies; characterized by having a long flexible proboscis and the incisors developed into long tusks.

Proboscidean, -ian (prǫbǫsi·dĭăn, -iăn), *a.* and *sb.* 1835. [f. prec. + -AN.] **A.** *adj.* **1.** Of or belonging to the *Proboscidea* 1839. **2.** Having a proboscis 1836. **3.** Of, pertaining to, or resembling a proboscis 1875. **B.** *sb.* A mammal of the order *Proboscidea* 1835.

Proboscidiferous (prǫbǫsidi·fĕrəs), *a.* 1828. [f. L. *proboscidem* + -(I)FEROUS.] Bearing or having a proboscis; *spec.* in *Conch.*, belonging to a division of pectinibranchiate gastropods (*Proboscidifera*) characterized by a long retractile snout.

Proboscidiform (prǫbǫsi·difǭɹm), *a.* 1837. [f. as prec. + -(I)FORM.] Having the form or shape of a proboscis; proboscis-like. So **Probo·sciformed** *a.*

Proboscis (prŏbǫ·sis). *Pl.* **probo·scides** (-idīz), **probo·scises** (-isĕz). 1609. [a. L., a. Gr. προβοσκίς, -κιδ- an elephant's trunk, f. πρό PRO-² + βόσκειν to feed.] **1.** An elephant's trunk; also applied to the long flexible snout of the tapir, the proboscis-monkey, etc. **2.** *joc.* The human nose 1630. **3.** *Entom.* Applied to various elongated, often tubular and flexible, parts of the mouth of insects 1645. **4.** An extensible tubular structure in other invertebrates, *esp.* a sucking organ in various worms, and the tongue of some molluscs 1796.

Comb. **p.-monkey**, a large semnopithecine ape, *Nasalis larvatus*: = KAHAU.

Procacity (prokæ·siti). Now *rare.* 1621. [ad. F. *procacité*, ad. L. *procacitas*, *-atem*, f. *procax*, *-acem* forward, bold, insolent, f. *procare*, *-ari* to ask, demand.] Forwardness, petulance; sauciness, pertness.

‖**Procatalepsis** (prōukætăle·psis). 1586. [med.L., a. Gr. προκατάληψις, f. προκαταλαμβάνειν to take up beforehand.] *Rhet.* A figure by which an opponent's objections are anticipated and answered.

Pro-cathedral (prōuˌkăþī·drăl), *a.* and *sb.* 1868. [f. PRO-¹ II. 1 + CATHEDRAL *sb.*] **A.** *adj.* Used as the substitute for a cathedral. **B.** *sb.* A church used instead of, or as a substitute for a cathedral church.

‖**Procedendo** (prōusĭde·ndo). 1593. [L. (*de*) *procedendo* (*ad judicium*) 'of proceeding (to judgement)'; see PROCEED *v.*] *Law.* A writ which formerly issued out of the common law jurisdiction of the Court of Chancery, commanding a subordinate court to proceed to judgement, either when judgement had been wrongfully delayed, or when the action had been removed to a superior court on insufficient grounds.

Procedure (prŏsī·diŭɹ, -dʒəɹ). 1611. [a. F. *procédure*, f. *procéder* to PROCEED; see -URE.] **1.** The fact or manner of proceeding or going on; proceeding, in ref. to its mode or method; conduct, behaviour. **b.** With *a* and *pl.* A particular action or mode of action 1677. **c.** *spec.* Legal action or proceeding; the mode or form of conducting judicial proceedings 1676. **d.** The mode of conducting business in Parliament 1839. †**2.** Progress, course of an action or process –1716.

1. b. This was, indeed, a p. truly Roman COTTON. 2. The hindrance of the P. of the Work 1703.

Proceed (prōu·sīd), *sb.* 1628. [f. next.] †**1.** Procedure; course –1674. **2.** That which proceeds from something; produce, outcome, profit. Now usu. in *pl.* **proceeds.** 1643.

2. The only procede..you can expect is thanks 1645. Handing over the proceeds of sale 1885.

Proceed (prŏsī·d), *v.* [Late ME. *proceden*,

a. F. *procéder*, a. L. *procedere* to go on; see PRO-[1] and CEDE.] **1.** *intr.* To go, move or travel forward; to make one's way onward; *esp.* to move onward after interruption or stoppage. **2.** To go on with an action, a discourse, an investigation, etc. late ME. **b.** To deal *with*; to treat, act (esp. judicially) with regard to. late ME. **c.** *spec.* To take legal proceedings (*against* a person) 1440. **3.** With stress on the progress or continuance of the action: **a.** To go on with or continue what one has begun; to advance from the point already reached; to go on after interruption. late ME. **b.** To go on *to do* something; to advance *to* another action, subject, etc. late ME. **c.** *absol.* To continue or pursue one's discourse 1509. †**d.** In emphatic sense: To make progress, get on; to prosper –1777. **4.** *intr.* To advance, in one's university course, from graduation as B.A. to some higher degree, as master or doctor. In the Inns of Court, to be admitted a barrister. 1479. **b.** *transf.* and *fig.* To advance to some status or function; to become 1579. **5.** Of an action, process, etc.: **a.** To go on, take place; to take effect 1440. **b.** To go on to a certain point; to continue 1670. **6.** To go or come forth; to issue (*lit.* and *fig.*). late ME. **b.** *spec.* To be the issue or descendant *of*; to spring *from* (a parent, ancestor, or stock). Now *rare* or *Obs.* 1480.

1. Before we procede on our iourney 1526. 2. The true Philosopher must always p. with a sober Pace 1718. c. In what manner he should p. against such as refused CLARENDON. 3. a. Exhorting him to procede as he hath begonne 1560. b. Then shal the Bisshop procede to the Communion *Bk. Com. Prayer*. c. To p., the land of Egypt is highly renowned 1660. 4. b. As you haue proued learned Philosophers, you will also proceede excellent diuines LYLY. 5. a. He will..tell you What hath proceeded worthy note to day SHAKS. 6. a. Every worde that proceadeth out off the mouth off God TINDALE *Matt.* iv. 4. b. We all p. from the loins of Adam 1768. Hence **Procee·der** (now *rare*).

Proceeding (prŏsī·diŋ), *vbl. sb.* 1517. [f. prec. + -ING[1].] The action of PROCEED *v.* **1.** The action of going onward; advance. **2.** = PROCEDURE 1. 1553. **b.** A particular action or course of action; a piece of conduct or behaviour; a transaction. Usu. in *pl.*: Doings, actions, transactions. 1553. **c.** *pl.* A record of the doings of a society; sometimes *spec.* a record of the business done, with abstracts of the less important papers not included in the *Transactions* 1830. **3.** *spec.* The instituting or carrying on of an action at law; a legal action or process; any act done by authority of a court of law; any step taken in a cause by either party 1546.

2. b. The..Dayly Proceedings of Both Houses, in this Great and Happy Parliament 1641. 3. Proceedings were begun against the Papists 1643.

Proceleusmatic (prǫ·sĭliūsmæ·tik), *a.* (*sb.*) 1751. [ad. late L. *proceleusmaticus*, a. Gr. προκελευσματικός, f. προκέλευσμα incitement, f. προκελεύειν.] **1.** Serving for incitement; animating, inspiriting 1773. **2.** *Pros.* **a.** Epithet of a metrical foot of four short syllables; pertaining to or consisting of such feet. **b.** *sb.* A proceleusmatic foot 1751.

Procellarian (prǫselē·riăn), *a.* and *sb.* 1864. [f. mod.L. *Procellaria* (f. *procella* storm) + -AN.] *Ornith.* **A.** *adj.* Belonging to or resembling the genus *Procellaria* or family *Procellariidæ* of sea-birds. **B.** *sb.* A bird of this family, a petrel.

Procerity (prose·rĭti). Now *rare.* 1550. [ad. L. *proceritatem*, f. *procerus*; see -ITY.] Tallness, loftiness, height; length.

Process (prōu·sės, prǫ·sės), *sb.* [ME. *proces*, a. F. *procès*, ad. L. *processus*, f. ppl. stem of *procedere*.] **1.** The fact of going on or being carried on; progress, course. **2.** Course, lapse (of time). Chiefly in *in p. of time.* ME. †**3.** Course (of a narrative, etc.); drift, tenor, gist –1643. †**4.** A narrative; a discourse or treatise; a discussion –1784. **5.** Something that goes on or is carried on; proceeding, procedure ME. **6.** A continuous and regular action or succession of actions, taking place or carried on in a definite manner; a continuous (natural or artificial) operation or series of operations 1627. **b.** A particular method of operation in any manufacture, as *Bessemer p.*, *collodion p.*, etc.; in recent use *spec.* applied to methods other than simple engraving by hand of producing blocks for printing from; *ellipt.* a print from such a block 1839. **7.** *Law.* **a.** The whole of the proceedings in any action at law; the course or method of carrying on an action; an action, suit ME. **b.** *spec.* The formal commencement of any action at law; the mandate, summons, or writ by which a person or thing is brought into court for litigation. late ME. **8.** *fig.* Of action, time, etc.: Progress, advance; development. Now *rare.* 1638. **b.** *Logic.* The act of proceeding from a term in one of the premisses to the corresponding term in the conclusion; only in ILLICIT *p.* 1864. †**9.** A formal command or mandate. SHAKS. **10.** A projection from the main body of something; esp. a natural appendage, extension, or outgrowth 1578.

1. New edifices..are in p. of erection HAWTHORNE. 2. Three beautious springs to yellow Autumne turn'd In processe of the seasons haue I seene SHAKS. 4. *Haml.* I. v. 37. 5. Behinde the Arras I'le conuey my selfe To heare the Processe SHAKS. 6. Such are the different processes for procuring carbonic oxide 1807. 7. b. They..had servid proces upon him 1577.

attrib. and *Comb.*, as **p. block**, a block to print from, produced by some p. other than simple engraving by hand; **p. printing**, a method of printing, from half-tone plates, in three colours, yellow, red, and blue (and, usu., black); **-server**, a sheriff's officer who serves processes or summonses; **-serving**.

Process (prōu·sės, prǫ·sės), *v.*[1] 1532. [In sense 1, a. OF. *processer* to prosecute, f. *procès*; in 2, f. prec.] **1.** *trans.* To institute a process or action against; to sue, prosecute; to obtain a summons against (a person); to serve a process on. orig. *Sc.* **2.** To treat by a special process; e. g. to reproduce (a drawing, etc.) by a mechanical or photographic process 1884.

Hence **Pro·cessing** *vbl. sb.*, *attrib.* **p. tax** (*U.S.*), a tax imposed on agricultural commodities while going through the first process after leaving the farmer.

Process (prǒse·s), *v.*[2] *colloq.* or *joc.* 1814. [Back-formation from next, after *progress*, etc.] *intr.* To go, walk, or march in procession.

Procession (prǒse·ʃən), *sb.* [Early ME. a. F. *procession*, ad. L. *processionem*, f. *procedere.*] The action of proceeding. **1.** The action of a body of persons going or marching along in orderly succession, esp. as a religious ceremony or on a festive occasion. **b.** *transf.* Of boats, barges, etc. 1843. **2.** *concr.* A body of persons marching in this way. late ME. **3.** *transf.* A litany, form of prayer, or office, said or sung in a religious procession. *Obs.* exc. *Hist.* 1543. **4.** The action of proceeding, issuing, or coming forth from a source; emanation. Chiefly *Theol.* in ref. to the Holy Spirit. late ME. **5.** Onward movement, progression, advance (now *rare*). 1585.

1. Phr. *To go, walk* (etc.) *in p.*; The Commons went in p. to Whitehall with their address on the subject of the test MACAULAY. b. From Fawley it was simply a p., the London pair winning anyhow 1902. 4. The Greeks..maintain the p. of the Holy Spirit from the Father alone FULLER.

attrib. and *Comb.*: **p. caterpillar, moth** (PROCESSIONARY *a.* 2); **-day**, a day on which a p. is made; *spec.* (*pl.*) the Rogation days; **-week**, Rogation week, so named for the processions then made. Hence **Proce·ssioner,** a person going in p.; a processionary caterpillar. **Proce·ssionist,** one who goes in a p. **Proce·ssionize** *v. intr.* to go in p.

Procession (prǒse·ʃən), *v.* 1546. [f. prec.] **1.** *trans.* To honour by a procession; to carry in procession. **2.** *intr.* To go in procession 1671. **3.** *trans.* To go round (something) in procession; *spec.* (*local* in *U.S.*), to make a procession around a piece of land in order formally to determine its bounds (with the land, or bounds, as obj.). Also, to walk along (a street, etc.) in procession. 1710.

Processional (prǒse·ʃənăl), *sb.* late ME. [ad. med.L. *processionale* adj. neut.; see next.] *Eccl.* An office-book containing litanies, hymns, etc., for use in religious processions. **b.** A processional hymn; see the adj. 1884.

Processional (prǒse·ʃənăl), *a.* 1611. [ad. med.L. *processionalis*; see PROCESSION *sb.* and -AL.] Of, pertaining to, or of the nature of a procession; characterized by processions. Of a hymn, psalm, litany, etc.: sung or recited in procession. **b.** Used or carried in processions 1846. **c.** Walking or going in procession; forming a procession 1855.

The ceremonial of Egyptian worship was essentially p. 1877. c. *P. caterpillar*: see next. Hence **Proce·ssionalist**, a processionist. **Proce·ssionally** *adv.*

Processionary (prǒse·ʃənări), *a.* 1597. [ad. med.L. **processionarius*; see PROCESSION *sb.* and -ARY[1].] = PROCESSIONAL *a.*; *Entom.* applied to caterpillars which go in procession, esp. those of the moth *Cnethocampa processionea*; hence, *p. moth* 1765.

Processive (prǒse·siv), *a.* *rare.* 1819. [f. L. *process-*, *procedere* to PROCEED.] Having the quality of proceeding; progressive.

‖**Procès verbal** (prosę vęrbal). *Pl.* **procès verbaux** (-bo). 1635. [F.] A detailed written report of proceedings; minutes; in *Fr. Law*, an authenticated written statement of facts in support of a criminal or other charge.

‖**Prochain** (proʃęñ), *a.* 1473. [F., f. *proche* near:—L. *propius* adv.] *Law.* In *p. ami* = next friend (see NEXT *a.* 3).

Prochronism (prōu·krŏniz'm). 1646. [f. PRO-[2] + Gr. χρόνος time + -ISM; cf. ANACHRONISM.] The referring of an event, etc., to an earlier date than the true one.

†**Proci·nct.** 1611. [ad. L. *procinctus*, *procingere* to gird up, in phr. *in procinctu.*] *In p.*, in readiness for action, ready, prepared –1839.

Proclaim (prŏ͵klē^i·m), *v.* [Late ME. *proclame*, ad. L. *proclamare* to cry out; see PRO-[1] and CLAIM *v.*] **1.** *trans.* To make official announcement of (something) by word of mouth in some public place; also, to cause this to be done. **b.** To publish (the banns of marriage) 1596. **2.** To make official announcement of or concerning (a person or thing) 1494. **b.** Short for 'to proclaim (a person) as a rebel or outlaw'. Also, to denounce (a person or thing). 1500. **c.** To proclaim the accession of (a sovereign) 1714. **d.** To place (a district, country, etc.) under legal restrictions by proclamation 1881. **3.** *transf.* To declare publicly; to publish. late ME. **4.** *fig.* Of things: To make known or manifest; to intimate, prove 1597. **5.** *intr.* To make proclamation or public announcement 1470.

1. He caused it to be proclamed thorow out all his empyre COVERDALE *2 Chron.* xxxvi. 22. Phr. *To p. war*, to make public declaration of war *against* another power; to declare war. 2. When he found himself proclaimed a traitor 1858. b. *Lear* II. iii. 1. 4. The Apparell oft proclaimes the man SHAKS. Hence **Proclai·mer.**

Proclamation (prǫklămē^i·ʃən). late ME. [a. F., ad. L. *proclamationem*, f. *proclamare* to PROCLAIM.] **1.** The action of proclaiming; the official giving of public notice. **b.** *spec.* The formal announcement of the accession of a king or ruler; the fact of being proclaimed king 1593. **c.** The action of denouncing by a public notice; the fact of being so proclaimed; proscription 1561. **2.** That which is proclaimed, publicly announced, or posted up in public places. late ME. †**3.** *transf.* Open declaration; manifestation; favourable or unfavourable notice –1607.

2. They say the King hath put out a P. to forbid maskerades 1671.

Proclitic (pro͵kli·tik), *a.* and *sb.* 1846. [ad. mod.L. *procliticus*, f. Gr. *προκλιτικός, f. προκλίνειν, f. πρό PRO-[2] + κλίνειν to bend.] **A.** *adj.* In *Gr. Gram.*, used of a monosyllabic word that is so closely attached in pronunciation to the following word as to have no accent of its own; applied gen. to a similar word in any language. **B.** *sb.* A proclitic word 1864.

Proclivity (pro͵kli·vĭti). 1591. [ad. L. *proclivitas* propensity, f. *proclivis*; see -ITY.] A condition of being inclined to something; an instance of such condition; inclination, tendency, leaning, propensity.

This naturall p. of men, to hurt each other HOBBES. Persons with Jacobite proclivities 1708.

Proconsul (prōu·kǫ·nsŭl). late ME. [a. L., from earlier *pro consule* '(one acting) for the consul'; see PRO-[1] II. 1 and CONSUL.] *Rom. Hist.* An officer who acting as governor or military commander in a Roman province discharged the duties and had most of the authority of a consul. **b.** *transf.* Applied rhet. to a governor of a modern colony, etc. 1827. Hence

Proco·nsular *a.* of or pertaining to a p.; of a province, under the administration of a Roman p. **Proco·nsulship.**

Proconsulate (prǫkǫ·nsiŭlět). 1656. [ad. L. *proconsulatus*; see prec. and -ATE [1].] The office of a proconsul; the district under the government of a proconsul.

Procrastinate (pro͵kræ·stineᵗt), *v.* 1588. [f. L. *procrastinare*, f. *pro* PRO-[1] I. 1. d + *crastinus* belonging to to-morrow (f. *cras* to-morrow); see -ATE [3].] **1.** *trans.* To postpone till another day; to put off from day to day; to defer, delay. Now *rare.* **2.** *intr.* To defer action, delay; to be dilatory 1638.

1. Many such deuices they fained to p. the time 1624. Hence **Procra·stinatingly** *adv.* **Procra·stinative** *a.* that tends to p. **Procra·stinator,** one who procrastinates. **Procra·stinatory** *a.* given to or implying procrastination; dilatory.

Procrastination (pro͵kræstinēⁱ·ʃən). 1548. [ad. L. *procrastinationem*; see prec.] The action or habit of procrastinating or putting off; delay, dilatoriness. Also with *of.*

P. is the thief of time YOUNG.

Procreant (prōu·kriǎnt), *a.* (*sb.*) 1588. [ad. L. *procreantem, procreare*; see next.] **1.** That procreates or begets; producing young; generating. **2.** Of, pertaining or subservient to procreation 1605. **†B.** *sb.* One who or that which procreates; a generator -1641.

Procreate (prōu·kri͵eᵗt), *v.* Now *rare.* 1536. [f. L. *procreat-, procreare*, f. *pro* PRO-[1] + *creare* to create.] *trans.* To beget, engender, generate. Also *transf.* and *fig.* **b.** *absol.* or *intr.* To produce offspring 1646.

b. Couples marry and p. on the idea, not the reality, of a maintenance 1792. Hence **Pro·creative** *a.* pertaining to procreation; having the power of producing offspring. **Pro·creativeness. Pro·creator,** a parent.

Procreation (prōu͵kri͵ēⁱ·ʃən). late ME. [a. OF. *procreacion*, ad. L. *procreationem*, f. *procreare* to PROCREATE.] The action of procreating or begetting; generation; the fact of being begotten. Also *transf.* and *fig.*

Procrustean (prokrʊ·stiǎn), *a.* 1846. [f. PROCRUSTES + -AN.] Of or pertaining to Procrustes; aiming or tending to produce uniformity by violent and arbitrary methods.

Procrustes (prokrʊ·stīz). 1583. [a. Gr. Προκρούστης, personal name, lit. 'one that stretches', f. προκρούειν to beat or hammer out.] A fabulous robber of Attica who made his victims conform to the length of his bed by stretching or mutilation. Also *attrib.*

Procryptic (prokri·ptik), *a.* 1891. [f. PRO-[1] or [2] + Gr. κρυπτικός fit for concealing, f. κρύπτειν to hide.]. *Zool.* Having the function of protectively concealing; applied to the protective mimicry of colour and form, observed in insects and some other animals. Hence **Procry·ptically** *adv.*

Procto- (prǫ·ktǫ), bef. a vowel **proct-,** comb. form of Gr. πρωκτός anus; used to form modern scientific terms, chiefly medical and surgical. **Procti·tis** [-ITIS], inflammation of the rectum and anus. ‖**Proctodæ·um** [Gr. ὁδαῖος that is on or by the road], *Embryol.* the posterior portion of the digestive tract, beginning as an invagination of the epiblast; hence **Proctodæ·al** *a.* **Proctu·chous** *a.* [Gr. ἔχειν to have], having an anus; applied to one division of turbellarians, the *Proctucha*, as dist. from the *Aprocta.*

Proctor (prǫ·ktəɹ), *sb.* late ME. [A syncopated form of *procuratour* PROCURATOR.] **1.** = PROCURATOR 2. *Obs.* or *arch.* exc. in techn. use. 1449. **†b.** A steward -1578. **c.** An agent for the collection of tithes and other church dues; a tithe-farmer. In full *tithe-p.* 1607. **2.** At Oxford and Cambridge, each of two officers (*Senior* and *Junior P.*) appointed annually by the colleges in rotation, and charged with various functions, esp. with the discipline of all persons *in statu pupillari*, and the summary punishment of minor offences 1536. **3.** *Law.* One whose profession is to manage the causes of others in a court administering civil or canon law; corresponding to an attorney or solicitor in courts of equity and common law. (Now retained chiefly in courts of eccl. jurisdiction.) late ME. **4.** A deputy elected to represent the chapter of a cathedral or collegiate church, or the clergy of a diocese or archdeaconry (*p. of the clergy*), in the Lower House of Convocation of either province 1586. **†5.** One who collected alms on behalf of lepers or others who were debarred from begging for themselves; *esp.* one having a licence to do this for the occupants of a 'spital-house' 1529.

2. *Proctors' dogs* or *bulldogs* (Univ. slang), the sworn constables who accompany the proctors in their nightly perambulation of the streets. **3.** *King's* (*Queen's*) *P.*, an official of the Probate, Divorce, and Admiralty Division of the High Court of Justice, who has the right to intervene in probate, divorce, and nullity cases, when collusion or suppression of material facts is alleged. Hence **Pro·ctorage,** management by a p. **Procto·rial** *a.* of or pertaining to a p. (at the Universities, or in the eccl. courts). **Pro·ctorize** *v. trans.* to exercise the proctorial authority on (an undergraduate, etc.). **Pro·ctorship,** the office, position, or function of a p.

Procumbent (prokʊ·mběnt), *a.* 1668. [ad. L. *procumbentem, procumbere* to fall forwards, bend down, f. *pro* PRO-[1] + *cumbere* to lay oneself.] **1.** Lying on the face; prone, prostrate 1721. **2.** *Bot.* Of a plant or stem: Lying flat on the ground without throwing out roots; having a prostrate or trailing stem 1668.

Procurable (prǒkiūᵊ·rǎb'l), *a.* 1611. [f. PROCURE *v.* + -ABLE.] That can be procured or obtained.

†**Pro·curacy.** late ME. [ad. med. L. *procuratia*, for cl. L. *procuratio* PROCURATION.] **1.** The office or action of a procurator; management or action for another -1762. **2.** A document empowering a person to act for another; a proxy, a letter of attorney -1607.

1. *Letters of p.* = **2.**

Procurance (prǫkiūᵊ·rǎns). 1553. [f. PROCURE *v.* + -ANCE.] The action of procuring; the action by which something is attained or brought about; agency.

Procuration (prǫkiūᵊrēⁱ·ʃən). [Late ME., a. F., ad. L. *procurationem*, f. *procurare*; see -ATION.] **†1.** The action of taking care of, looking after, or managing -1677. **2.** The appointment of a procurator or attorney; the power thus delegated; also, the authorized action of one's agent; the function of an attorney or representative 1489. **b.** A formal document whereby a person gives legal authority to another to act for him; a letter or power of attorney. Now *rare.* late ME. **3.** *Eccl.* The provision of entertainment for the bishop, archdeacon, or other visitor by the incumbent, parish, etc., visited; later commuted to a payment in money 1450. **4.** The action of procuring; procurement 1533. **b.** *spec.* The negotiating of a loan for a client; also, the fee for this 1678. **c.** The action of a procurer or procuress; pimping 1696.

2. *Letters of p.* = **2 b.** *By p.*, by attorney or proxy (cf. p. p. s.v. P II).

attrib. **P. fee, money,** a fee paid for procuring a loan.

Procurator (prǫ·kiŭreᵗtəɹ). ME. [a. OF. *procuratour*, or ad. L. *procuratorem.*] **1.** *Rom. Hist.* An officer who collected the taxes, paid the troops, and had charge of the interests of the imperial treasury, in an imperial province. **2.** One who manages the affairs of another; an agent, an attorney ME. **3.** *Law.* An agent in a court of law: = PROCTOR 3; *spec.* in Scotland, a law-agent practising before the inferior courts, an attorney. (Now *rare.*) late ME. **4.** (repr. It. *procuratore.*) In some Italian cities, A public administrator or magistrate; also repr. F. *procureur* (see PROCUREUR) 1618.

2. *P. general*, an agent-general. **4.** *P. of St. Mark*, a senator, afterwards each of two senators, of the Venetian Republic, charged with high administrative functions. Hence **Procurato·rial** *a.* of or pertaining to a p. or proctor. **Pro·curatorship,** the office, function, or period of office of a p.

Pro·curator-fi·scal. [See FISCAL *a.*] 1583. In Scotland, the public prosecutor of a shire or other local district.

Procuratory (prǫ·kiŭrětəri), *a.* and *sb.* 1459. [ad. late L. *procuratorius*; see -ORY [2].] **A.** *adj.* Of or pertaining to a procurator or procurators, or to procuration. Now *rare* or *Obs.* **B.** *sb. Civil* and *Sc. Law.* Authorization of one person to act for another; an instrument or clause giving such power; esp. in *letters of p.* 1540.

Procuratrix (prǫkiŭrēⁱ·triks). 1660. [a. L.] The inmate who attends to the temporal concerns of a nunnery.

Procure (prǒkiūᵊ·ɹ), *v.* ME. [a. F. *procurer*, ad. L. *procurare*; see PRO-[1] and CURE *v.*] **1.** *trans.* To bring about by care or pains; also (more vaguely) to bring about, cause, effect, produce. *rare* or *arch.* **2.** To obtain by care or effort; to acquire ME. **b.** To obtain (women) for the gratification of lust. Usu. *absol.* or *intr.* To act as a procurer or procuress. 1603. **3.** To prevail upon, induce, persuade (a person) *to do* something. *Obs.* or *arch.* ME. †Also with adv. of place or without const. -1625.

1. A drinke called Coffa..which helpeth..digestion, and procureth alacrity 1615. An ingenious lover procured his..rival to be arrested for lunacy 1866. **2.** She endeavoured to p. employment as a needlewoman 1776. Books were..impossible to p. 1874. **3. b.** What vnaccustom'd cause procures her hither? SHAKS. Hence **Procu·rement,** the action of procuring; management; contrivance; acquisition, getting, gaining.

Procurer (prǒkiūᵊ·rəɹ). [Late ME. and AF. *procurour* = OF. *procurëur* :—L. *procuratorem* PROCURATOR; see -ER [1].] **†1.** = PROCURATOR, in various uses -1658. **2.** One who or that which brings about, effects, or induces something; *esp.* a promotor, prime mover, ultimate author. Now *rare* or *Obs.* 1451. **3.** One who procures or obtains 1538. **4.** A pander; a procuress 1632.

Procuress (prǒkiūᵊ·rěs). 1712. [Syncopated from OF. *procureresse*, fem. of F. *procureur* PROCURER.] A woman who makes it her trade to procure women for the gratification of lust; a bawd.

‖**Procureur** (prokürǒ̈r). 1598. [F. :—L. *procuratorem* PROCURATOR.] A procurator (esp. in sense 3); an attorney, agent, or legal representative.

Procyon (prōu·siǫn). 1658. [a. L., a. Gr. Προκύων (in sense 1), f. πρό before + κύων dog; so called as rising before the dog-star Sirius.] **1.** The principal star in the constellation *Canis Minor.* **2.** *Zool.* A genus of plantigrade carnivorous mammals, including the racoons, typical of the family *Procyonidæ* 1843.

Prod (prǫd), *sb.* 1787. [f. next.] **1.** An act of prodding; a thrust with some pointed instrument; a poke, a stab 1802. **2.** A name for various pointed instruments, as a goad, a skewer, a brad, etc. 1787.

Prod (prǫd), *v.* 1535. [perh. orig. onomatopœic.] **1.** *trans.* To thrust or stab; to poke with a pointed instrument, or with the end of a stick. **b.** *fig.* To goad mentally; to stir up; to irritate 1871. **2.** *intr.* To thrust, to poke 1696. **3.** *trans.* To make by prodding 1865.

1. I..have vitality enough to kick..when prodded HUXLEY. Hence **Pro·dder.**

Prodigal (prǫ·digǎl), *a.* and *sb.* (*adv.*) 1450. [a. obs. F. *prodigal*, ad. late L. **prodigalis*, f. *prodigus* wasteful, lavish; see -AL.] **A.** *adj.* **1.** Given to extravagant expenditure; recklessly wasteful. **2.** Of things or actions: Wastefully lavish 1500. **3.** Lavish in the bestowal or disposal of things 1595. **b.** with *of*; also with *in* (*rare*) 1588.

1. The nobility is..prodigall in expenses, spending more than their reuenues in diet and apparell 1601. Nature is p. of human life 1864. *P. son, child*, in ref. or allusion to the parable, in Luke xv. 11-32. **2.** Our little suppers they traduce as p. 1672. **3.** P. veins of Gold and Silver 1652. **b.** When..May is p. of flowers 1778.

B. *sb.* **1.** One who spends his money extravagantly and wastefully; a spendthrift, waster 1596. **2.** In pregnant sense, with allusion to the career of 'the Prodigal Son' (A. 1). 1596.

1. A bankrout, a prodigall, who dare scarce shew his head on the Ryalto SHAKS. Phr. *To play the p.*, to act prodigally; to act like 'the p. son'.

C. as *adv.* Prodigally, lavishly SHAKS. Hence **Pro·digalize** *v. trans.* to spend profusely or lavishly. **Pro·digally** *adv.* 1530.

Prodigality (prǫdigæ·liti). [ME. *prodigalite*, a. F. *prodigalité*, ad. med.L. *prodigalitas*, f. **prodigalis*; see prec.] **1.** Reckless extravagance in expenditure, wastefulness; esp.

of money. **2.** Lavishness, profuseness; lavish display, profuse supply 1594.

2. *Rich. III.* I. ii. 244.

Prodigious (prǫdi·dʒəs), *a.* (*adv.*) 1552. [ad. L. *prodigiosus*; see next and -OUS.] †**1.** Of the nature of a prodigy; ominous, portentous –1705. **2.** Having the appearance of a prodigy; unnatural, abnormal 1579. **3.** Causing wonder; marvellous, amazing; (in bad sense) monstrous 1568. **4.** Of extraordinary size, extent, power, or amount; vast, enormous. (Often hyperbolical.) 1601. **b.** As an exclam. 1730. **B.** quasi-*adv.* Amazingly, exceedingly, 'mightily'. *arch.* 1676.

1. *Mids. N.* v. i. 419. **2.** All p. things..Gorgons and Hydra's, and Chimera's dire MILT. **4.** Five thousand Marks, a p. sum in that age FULLER. Satan, who that day P. power had shewn MILT. At great depths, the pressure must be p. HUXLEY. **B.** The Sea running p. high 1676. Hence **Prodi·gious-ly** *adv.*, **-ness.**

Prodigy (prǫ·didʒi). 1494. [ad. L. *prodigium*, f. *prod-*, early form of *pro* PRO-[1] + (?) prim. L. **agiom* a thing said.] **1.** Something extraordinary from which omens are drawn; an omen, portent. Now *rare.* **2.** An amazing or marvellous thing; *esp.* something abnormal or monstrous 1626. **3.** Anything that causes wonder, astonishment, or surprise; a wonder, a marvel 1660. **b.** A wonderful example *of* (some quality) 1646. **c.** A person endowed with some quality which excites wonder; *esp.* a child of precocious genius 1658.

1. Omens and prodigies have lost their terrors JOHNSON. **2.** A climate, where rain is considered as a p. 1748. **3.** Monstrous untruths, and prodigies of lies 1660. **b.** This bird..is a p. of understanding GOLDSM. **c.** This infant p. 1831.

Prodition (prǫdi·ʃən). Now *rare.* [Late ME. *prodycyon*, a. OF. *prodicion*, ad. L. *proditionem*, f. *prodere* to betray, f. *pro* PRO-[1] + *dare.*] Betrayal, treason, treachery.

†**Pro·ditor.** late ME. [ad. L. *proditorem*; see prec.] A betrayer; a traitor –1678. Hence **Prodito·rious** *a.* traitorous, perfidious; *fig.* apt to betray what is hidden or in the mind. (*Obs.* or *arch.*) †**Pro·ditory** *a.* traitorous.

Prodrome (prǫ·drǫm). 1822. [a. F., ad. mod.L. PRODROMUS.] **1.** A preliminary or introductory treatise or book 1866. **2.** *Path.* A premonitory symptom 1822. So **Pro·dromal, Prodro·mic** *adjs.* forerunning; introductory, preliminary; in *Path.* premonitory (of disease).

‖**Prodromus** (prǫ·drǫmǒs). *Pl.* **prodromi.** 1645. [mod.L., a. Gr. πρόδρομος adj., running before, as *sb.* precursor, f. πρό PRO-[2] + δραμεῖν, δρόμος.] **1.** A forerunner, a precursor, a premonitory event. **2.** A book or treatise which is introductory to some larger work 1672. **3.** *Path.* = PRODROME 2. 1693.

Produce (prǫ·diūs), *sb.* 1699. [f. PRODUCE *v.*] **1.** The amount produced, yielded, or derived; the proceeds; the return, yield. Now chiefly in the assay of ore. 1707. **2.** The thing (or things collectively) produced; product, fruit 1699. **b.** Result, effect, consequence 1730. **c.** Offspring, progeny (*rare*) 1845. **3.** Agricultural and natural products collectively, as dist. from manufactured goods. Also *raw p.* 1745. **4.** *techn.* Materials produced from breaking up ordnance or other military or naval stores 1904.

3. Raw p., wool and hides, corn, beer, and cheese 1861. **4.** Phr. *Brought to p.*, broken up, and the material assorted into various kinds or classes.

Produce (prǒdiū·s), *v.* 1499. [ad. L. *producere* to lead or bring forth, extend, produce, f. *pro* PRO-[1] + *ducere.*] **1.** *trans.* To bring forward, bring forth or out; to offer for inspection or consideration, exhibit. **b.** To introduce; now *spec.* to bring (a performer or performance) before the public; to put (a play) on the stage before the public with the necessary complement of actors and scenic apparatus 1585. †**c.** To bring (to a specified condition) –1741. **2.** *Geom.* To extend (a line) in length; to continue; hence *gen.* to lengthen (anything) out; to extend longitudinally 1570. **3.** To bring forth, bring into being or existence. **a.** *gen.* To bring (a thing) into existence from its raw materials or elements; to give rise to, bring about, effect (an action, condition, etc.) 1513. **b.** Of an animal or plant: To generate, bring forth, yield (offspring, seed, fruit, etc.) 1526. **c.** Of a country, river, mine, process, etc.: To give forth, yield, furnish, supply 1585. **d.** To compose or bring out (a work of literature or art); to work up from raw material, manufacture (material objects); in *Pol. Econ.* often blending with sense c. 1638.

1. P. your cause, saith the Lord, bring foorth your strong reasons *Isa.* xli. 21. The books must be produced, as we cannot receive parole evidence of their contents 1776. **3. a.** Art may make a Suit of Clothes. But Nature must p. a Man. HUME. **b.** The goat produces but two at a time GOLDSM. Flowers..capable of producing seeds 1857. **c.** England hath of late produced great philosophers BERKELEY. **d.** Nectar that the bees p. GRAY. Such volumes..were here multiplied as fast as the press could p. them 1856. Hence †**Produ·cement,** production. **Producibi·lity,** the capability of being produced. **Produ·cible, -eable** *a.* capable of being, fit to be, produced.

Producent (prodiū·sĕnt), *a.* and *sb.* Now *rare.* 1604. [ad. L. *producens, -entem.*] **A.** *adj.* That produces; in *Eccl. Law*, that brings forward a witness or document. **B.** *sb.* One who or that which produces; a producer; the party producing a witness or document 1622.

Producer (prǒdiū·səɪ). 1513. [f. PRODUCE *v.* + -ER[1].] **1.** One who or that which produces; *spec.* one who 'produces' a play; *U.S.* the manager or proprietor of a theatre. **2.** *Pol. Econ.* One who produces (grows, makes) an article of consumption: opp. to *consumer* 1790. **3.** Short for *gas p.*, a furnace in which carbon monoxide gas is produced for use as fuel; hence *p.-gas*, gas so produced 1881.

Product (prǫ·dǒkt), *sb.* late ME. [ad. L. *productum*, sb. use of pa. pple. neut. of *producere* to PRODUCE.] **1.** *Math.* The quantity obtained by multiplying two or more quantities together. **2.** A thing produced by nature or a natural process; also *collect.* = produce, fruit 1653. **3.** That which is produced by any action, operation, or work; a production; the result 1575. **4.** That which results from the operation of a cause 1651. **5.** *Chem.* A compound not previously existing in a body, but formed during its decomposition 1805.

2. These are the p. Of those ill-mated Marriages thou saw'st MILT. The products of distant countries JOHNSON. **3.** The fruit and p. of his labours past DRYDEN.

Produ·ctible, *a. rare.* 1830. [f. L. *product-*, *producere* + -IBLE.] = PRODUCIBLE. Hence **Produ:ctibi·lity,** the quality or fact of being producible.

Production (prǒdv·kʃən). [Late ME. a. F., ad. L. *productionem.*] **I. 1.** The action of producing; the fact or condition of being produced; with *a* and *pl.*, an act of producing 1483. **2.** That which is produced; a thing that results from any action, process, or effort. late ME. **b.** *spec.* A literary or artistic work. Chiefly in *pl.* 1651.

1. The P. and Modulation of the Voice BOYLE. **2. b.** The finest productions of Praxiteles 1879.

II. The action of bringing forward or exhibiting; in *Law*, the exhibiting of a document in court 1562. **III.** Drawing out, extending, or lengthening in †time or space; prolongation, extension 1536.

Productive (prǒdv·ktiv), *a.* 1612. [ad. F. *productif, -ive*, or med.L. *productivus*; see -IVE.] **1.** Having the quality of producing or bringing forth; tending to produce; creative, generative. Also with *of.* **2.** That causes or brings about; causative. Always with *of.* 1647. **3.** *Pol. Econ.* That produces or increases wealth or value; producing commodities of exchangeable value; esp. in *p. labour, classes* 1776. **4.** That produces abundantly; prolific, fertile 1846.

1. Shakespeare..during his p. period 1870. Oak trees..p. of gall nuts 1870. **2.** It may be p...of incalculable good 1806. Hence **Produ·ctive-ly** *adv.*, **-ness. Producti·vity.**

Productor (prǒdv·ktəɪ). 1624. [a. late L., f. *producere*; see -OR.] One who or that which produces; a producer. So **Produ·ctress,** a female p. or producer. Chiefly *fig.*

Proem (prōu·ĕm). [Late ME. *proheme*, a. OF. *pro(h)eme*, ad. L. *proœmium*, ad. Gr. προοίμιον an opening, prelude, f. πρό PRO-[2] + οἶμος way, road.] An introductory discourse to a book or other writing; a preface, preamble. **b.** The prefatory part of a speech or discourse; an exordium 1541. **c.** *fig.* A beginning, prelude 1641.

Thus much may serve by way of p.: Proceed we therefore to our poem SWIFT. Hence **Proe·mial** *a.* prefatory, introductory.

†**Profa·ce,** *int.* 1515. [a. obs. F. *prou fasse!* in full *bon prou vous fasse!* 'may it do you good'.] A formula of welcome or good wishes at a meal, = 'may it do you good' –1638.

Master Page, good M. Page, sit: P. SHAKS.

Profanation (prǫfănē·ʃən). 1552. [a. OF. *prophanation*, or ad. late L. *profanationem*, f. *profanare.*] The action of profaning; desecration or violation of that which is sacred; defilement, pollution. **b.** By extension: The degradation or vulgarization of anything worthy of being held in reverence or respect; cheapening by familiarity 1588.

A wall was built round the tomb to protect it from p. 1877. **b.** 'Twere prophanation of our joyes To tell the layitie our love DONNE.

Profane (prǒfē·n), *a.* (*sb.*) 1483. [a. obs. F. *prophane*, mod.F. *profane*, ad. L. *profanus*, lit. 'before (i.e. outside) the temple', hence 'not sacred, common', also 'impious'; see PRO-[1] and FANE[2].] **1.** Not pertaining or devoted to what is sacred or biblical, esp. in *p. history, literature*: secular, lay, common; civil, as dist. from ecclesiastical. **b.** Of persons: *orig.* Not initiated into the religious rites or sacred mysteries; *transf.* not admitted to some esoteric knowledge; uninitiated 1616. **2.** Unhallowed; ritually unclean or polluted; esp. said of the rites of an alien religion; heathen, pagan 1500. **3.** Characterized by disregard or contempt of sacred things; irreverent, blasphemous; impious, irreligious, wicked 1560. **4.** *absol.* or as *sb.* One who is profane 1529.

1. b. Hence, ye Prophane; I hate ye all; Both the Great Vulgar, and the Small COWLEY. **2.** Nothing p. can dwell with Thee WESLEY. **3.** The Bill against Atheism and prophane Swearing we have sent up to the Lords MARVELL. Hence **Profa·ne-ly** *adv.*, **-ness.**

Profane (prǒfē·n), *v.* [Late ME. *prophane* = OF. *prophaner*, ad. L. *profanare*, f. *profanus* PROFANE *a.*] *trans.* To treat (what is sacred) with irreverence, contempt, or disregard; to desecrate, violate. **b.** To misuse, abuse (what ought to be reverenced or respected); to violate, defile, pollute 1563.

Neither shalt thou prophane the Name of thy God: I am the Lord *Lev.* xix. 12. Guilty of profaning the Lord's day DE FOE. **b.** So idly to prophane the precious time SHAKS. No callous chatter to p. his ear DISRAELI. Hence **Profa·ner,** one who profanes.

Profanity (prǒfæ·nĭti). 1607. [ad. late L. *profanitas*; see PROFANE *a.* and -ITY.] The quality or condition of being profane; profaneness; profane conduct or speech; in *pl.* profane words or acts.

Profection (profe·kʃən). Now *rare.* 1540. [Partly a. F., f. L. *profect-*, *proficere* to put forward, go forward; partly ad. L. *profectionem* a setting out, f. *proficisci.*] **1.** The action or fact of going forward; progression, advance. *Obs.* exc. *Astrol.* 1597. †**b.** The degree of advancement attained; proficiency –1631. †**2.** Advancement in process or rank –1657.

Profecti·tious, *a.* 1656. [f. late L. *profecticius, -itius* that proceeds from some one (f. *profect-*, *proficisci*) + -OUS.] *Rom. Law.* That proceeds or is derived from a parent or ancestor.

Profe·r, *v.* *Obs.* or *rare arch.* late ME. [app. a. F. *proférer*, ad. L. *proferre* to bring forth.] †**1.** To produce, yield –1600. **2.** To bring out (words), utter, pronounce. late ME.

Profert (prōu·fəɪt). *Obs.* exc. *Hist.* 1719. [f. L. *profert* (*in curia*) 'he produces (in court)', f. *proferre.*] *Law.* The production or exhibition of a deed in court.

Profess (prǒfe·s), *v.* ME. [f. L. *profess-*, *profiteri*, f. PRO-[1] + *fass-*, *fateri* to confess, own.] **1.** *trans.* **a.** Orig. in pass. form, *to be professed*, to have made one's profession of religion; to make one's profession, to take the vows of some religious order, *esp.* to become a monk or nun; later app. viewed as passive in sense, whence **b.** in active use, to receive the profession of, to receive into a religious order. **c.** *refl.* and *intr.* To make one's profession (*rare*) 1510. **2.** *trans.* To declare openly, announce, affirm; to avow, acknowledge, confess 1526. 3. To make profession of, to lay claim to (some quality, feeling, etc.); often implying insincerity; to pretend to 1530. b. *refl.* and *intr.* To make a profession or professions; *esp.* to profess friendship or attachment 1601. 4. *trans.* To affirm or declare one's faith in or allegiance to (a religion, principle; God, a saint, etc.) 1560. 5. To make profession of (some art or science); to declare oneself expert or proficient in; to make (a thing) one's profession or business. *Obs.* or *arch.* 1577. 6. To teach (some subject) as a professor 1560. b. *intr.* To perform the duties of a professor 1610.

1. c. The young man went back to France, and professed there in some religious order SOUTHEY. 2. All who p. and call themselves Christians *Bk. Com. Prayer.* They one by one professed their faith in Christ J. H. NEWMAN. 3. That love of truth which ye eminently professe MILT. b. *Wint. T.* I. ii. 456. 4. The God..whom Israel still professed 1631. 5. War was the only art which he professed GIBBON.

Professed (prŏfe·st, profe·sėd), *ppl. a.* late ME. [f. prec. + -ED¹.] 1. That has taken the vows of a religious order. b. *transf.* Of or pertaining to professed persons 1526. 2. Self-acknowledged; openly declared by oneself; sometimes = Alleged, ostensible, pretended 1569. 3. That professes to be duly qualified; professional 1675.

1. b. The Profess'd House of the Jesuits 1662. 2. My Friend profest SHAKS. 3. I do not pretend to teach p. cooks MRS. GLASSE. Hence **Professedly** (prŏfe·sėdli) *adv.* avowedly; ostensibly.

Profession (prŏfe·ʃən). [ME. a. F., ad. L. *professionem* public declaration, etc., f. *profiteri.*] The act or fact of professing; that which is professed. I. 1. The declaration, promise, or vow made on entering a religious order; hence, the action of entering such an order; the fact of being professed in a religious order. 2. The action of declaring or avowing (truly or falsely) an opinion, belief, intention, practice, etc. 1526. b. with *a* and *pl.* An act of professing; a declaration 1674. 3. The profession of religion; the declaration of belief in and obedience to religion or a religion; hence, the faith or religion which one professes 1526. b. A religious system, communion, or body. Now *rare* or *Obs.* 1600.

1. The novice kneeling before him made her p. 1797. 2. Here, too, p. was at variance with fact 1817. b. Professions of friendship 1755.

II. The occupation which one professes to be skilled in and to follow. a. A vocation in which a professed knowledge of some department of learning is used in its application to the affairs of others, or in the practice of an art founded upon it. Applied *spec.* to the three learned professions of divinity, law, and medicine; also to the military profession. 1541. b. In wider sense: Any calling or occupation by which a person habitually earns his living 1576. c. The body of persons engaged in a calling 1610.

The Captain looks upon himself in the military capacity as a gentleman by p. GAY. b. Joseph her Spouse, by P. a Carpenter 1733. c. *The p.*, in theatrical use, actors as a body; public performers generally.

Professional (prŏfe·ʃənăl), *a.* (*sb.*) 1747. [f. prec. + -AL.] 1. Pertaining to, proper to, or connected with a or one's profession or calling. 2. Engaged in one of the learned or skilled professions 1793. 3. That follows an occupation as his (or her) profession, life-work, or means of livelihood; *spec.* applied to one who follows, by way of profession, what is generally followed as a pastime, as a *p. cricketer*, etc. Disparagingly applied to one who 'makes a trade' of politics, etc. 1805. b. Of play, sports, etc.: Engaged in for money; engaged in by professionals (as dist. from amateurs) 1884. 4. That is skilled in the theoretic or scientific parts of a trade; that raises his trade to the dignity of a learned profession 1860.

1. As perfectly p. as the mourning of an undertaker 1870. 2. There has been a great upward movement of the p. class 1888. 3. Ladies raised..to the..position of 'p. beauty' 1887.

B. *sb.* 1. One who belongs to one of the learned or skilled professions 1848. 2. One who makes a profession or business of what is ordinarily followed as a pastime; see A. 3. 1811. Hence **Profe·ssionally** *adv.*

Professionalism (prŏfe·ʃənăliz'm). 1856. [f. prec. + -ISM.] 1. Professional quality, character, method, or conduct; the stamp of a particular profession. 2. The position of a professional as dist. from an amateur; the class of professionals 1884. So **Profe·ssionalist,** one who follows an occupation as a profession; a representative of professionalism. **Profe·ssionalize** *v.* to render or become professional.

Professor (prŏfe·səɹ). late ME. [ad. L., f. *profiteri* to PROFESS.] I. One who makes open declaration of his sentiments, beliefs, etc.; one who professes (sometimes opp. to one who practises) 1538. b. A professing Christian. Now chiefly *Sc.* and *U.S.* 1597.

There is no Error to be named, which has not had its Professors LOCKE. b. As he was a p., he would drive a nail for no man on the Sabbath SCOTT.

II. 1. A public teacher of the highest rank in a specific faculty or branch of learning; *spec.* one who holds a 'chair' in a university or one of its colleges. late ME. b. Prefixed as title to the name (sometimes abbrev. *Prof.*) 1706. 2. One who makes a profession of any art or science. Also, in mod. use, a 'professional' as opp. to an 'amateur' in any branch of sport. 1563. b. Assumed as a grandiose title by teachers and exponents of dancing, jugglery, phrenology, etc. 1864.

1. Our Regius Professour of Physick BURTON. 2. Asbolius, a p. of wrestling HOLLAND. Hence **Profe·ssorate**, professorship; a body of professors. **Profe·ssoress**, a female p. **Professo·rial** *a.* of or pertaining to a p.; pedagogic, dogmatic; **-ly** *adv.* **Professoriate** (prǫfesōᵊ·riĕt), a body of professors; the professorial staff of a university; the office of p. **Profe·ssorship,** the office or function of a p.

Proffer (prǫ·fəɹ), *sb.* [ME. *profre*, a. AF. *profre*, OF. **poroffre*, vbl. sb. f. *poroffrir*; see next.] 1. The act of offering something, or of proposing to do something; an offer, a proposal. Now chiefly *literary.* †2. An act or movement as in beginning something; a show of intention to do something; an essay, attempt -1703. 3. *Law.* A provisional payment of estimated dues into the Exchequer by a sheriff or other officer at certain appointed times 1450.

1. Hoping that the enemy..would make a p. of peace BURKE.

Proffer (prǫ·fəɹ), *v.* [ME. *profren*, *proffre*, a. AF., OF. *proffrir* = OF. *poroffrir*, f. OF. *por* :—L. *pro* PRO-¹ + *offrir* :—L. *offerre* to OFFER.] 1. *trans.* To put before a person for acceptance; to offer, present, tender. Now *literary.* Also *absol.* 2. with *inf.* To propose or offer (to do something). *Obs.* or *arch.* ME. †3. with *inf.* To attempt, essay -1655. †b. *absol.* or *intr.* To begin to act or move, and then stop or turn back; *spec.* of a stag -1650.

1. Mr. Winkle seized the wicker bottle which his friend proffered DICKENS. 2. He proffereth to go for a coach and lets the servant go LAMB. Hence **Pro·fferer.**

Proficiency (prŏfi·ʃĕnsi). 1544. [f. next; see -ENCY.] †1. Advance towards completeness or perfection; improvement in skill or knowledge -1855. 2. The state or degree of improvement attained; the quality or fact of being proficient; adeptness, expertness 1639.

1. We are now in a State of P., not of Perfection 1690. 2. His P. in the noble Science of Detraction 1699. So †**Profi·cience.**

Proficient (prŏfi·ʃĕnt), *a.* and *sb.* 1590. [ad. L. *proficiens*, *-entem*, pres. pple. of *proficere* to advance, profit, f. *pro* PRO-¹ + *facere*, *-ficere* to do, make.] A. *adj.* Advanced in the acquirement of some kind of skill; skilled; expert 1590.

2. To become p. in the use of the gun 1892.

B. *sb.* †1. A learner who makes progress in something; opp. to one who is perfect -1742. 2. One who has made good progress in some art or branch of learning; an advanced pupil; an expert, an adept 1610. Hence **Profi·ciently** *adv.* skilfully.

Profile (prōᵘ·fəil, -fīl, -fil), *sb.* 1656. [ad. It. *profilo*, f. *profilare*: see next. Cf. F. *profil*, whence perh. some of the Engl. senses.] 1. A drawing or other representation of the outline of anything; esp. of the human face, outlined by the median line. 2. The actual outline or contour of anything, esp. of the human face 1664. 3. *Arch.*, *Surveying*, and *Engineering.* A sectional drawing, usu. vertical; *esp.* in *Fortif.*, a transverse vertical section of a fort 1669. b. *transf.* The comparative thickness of an earthwork or the like 1810. 4. In *Pottery* (and *Bell-founding*). A plate in which is cut the exterior or interior outline of one side of the object to be made 1756. 5. *Theatr.* A flat piece of scenery or property on the stage of a theatre, cut out in outline 1904.

1. *In p.*, as seen from one side. *Comb.* **p. paper**, paper ruled with equidistant vertical and horizontal lines, for convenience in drawing to scale. Hence **Pro·filist,** one who produces silhouettes.

Profile (prōᵘ·fəil, -fīl, -fil), *v.* 1715. [ad. It. *profilare*, f. *pro* :—L. *pro* PRO-¹ + *filare* to spin, †to draw a line :—late L. *filare* to spin, f. L. *filum* a thread.] 1. *trans.* To represent in profile; to outline. 2. To furnish with a profile (of a specified nature); also, to cause to form a profile 1823.

Profit (prǫ·fit), *sb.* ME. [a. OF., mod.F. *profit* :—L. *profectus* advance, etc., f. *proficere*, *profect-* to advance; see PROFICIENT.] 1. The advantage or benefit (of a person, community, or thing); use, interest; the gain, good, well-being. Formerly sometimes *pl.* b. *transf.* Something advantageous or profitable SHAKS. †2. The advantage or benefit of or resulting from something -1628. †3. = PROFICIENCY 1. SHAKS. 4. That which is derived from or produced by some source of revenue; proceeds, returns. Chiefly *pl.* late ME. 5. The pecuniary gain in any transaction; the excess of returns over the outlay of capital; in commercial use chiefly in pl. In *Pol. Econ.*, The surplus product of industry after deducting wages, cost of raw material, rent, and charges. 1604.

1. Posts of Honour, Dignity, and P. ADDISON. b. *Oth.* III. iii. 379. 5. Nobody would be an innkeeper if it were not for the p. 1845. His profits diminished at the rate of 60 per cent 1893.

Phrase. **P. and loss,** an inclusive expression for the gain and loss made in a series of transactions, and the gain or loss made in one transaction; esp. in *p. and loss account*, an account in book-keeping to which all gains are credited and all losses debited, so as to ascertain the net gain or loss at any time. In *Arith.*, a rule by which the gains or losses on commercial transactions are calculated.

Comb.: **p.-rent**, a rent of which the amount is due to a tenant's improvements; **-sharing,** the sharing of profits, *spec.* between employer and employed, or between capital and labour; so *profit-sharer*; **-taking** (*Stock-exchange*), the act of realizing the profit obtainable by the sale of stock, etc., in which a rise in price has taken place. Hence **Pro·fitless** *a.* void of p.; improfitable, useless.

Profit (prǫ·fit), *v.* [ME. a. F. *profiter*, earlier OF. *prufiter*, f. *prufit*, *profit* PROFIT *sb.*] †I. *intr.* To make progress; to advance; to improve (in some respect) -1612.

My husband saies my sonne profits nothing in the world at his Booke SHAKS.

II. 1. *trans.* Of a thing: To be of advantage, use, or good to; to benefit, further, promote. (Orig. *intr.*, with indirect (dative.) obj.) ME. b. *intr.* To be of advantage, use, or benefit; avail. Const. *to.* ME. 2. *intr.* (for *refl.*) To be benefited. late ME. b. *esp.* with preps. †*with*, *by*, *of*, *from*: To derive benefit from; to avail oneself of; to take advantage of. late ME.

1. Whatt shall hit proffet a man, yf he shulde wyn all the whoole worlde: so he loose hys owne soule? TINDALE *Matt.* xvi. 26. 2. b. Mrs. Burke..has not profited of the bathing BURKE. All of these..profited by the opportunity to effect their escape 1797.

Profitable (prǫ·fităb'l), *a.* ME. [a. F.; see PROFIT and -ABLE.] 1. Yielding profit or advantage; beneficial, useful, valuable. (Rarely of persons.) Formerly, also, useful as a remedy. 2. Yielding pecuniary profit; lucrative, remunerative 1758.

1. Silence or flight were much profitabler for you 1627. 2. The p. employment of millions upon millions of capital 1825. A p. voyage 1845. Hence **Profitabi·lity, Pro·fitableness,** the quality of being p. **Pro·fitably** *adv.* in a p. manner.

Profiteer (prǫfitīᵊ·ɹ), *sb.* 1797. [f. PROFIT *sb.* + -EER.] One who profits; *spec.* one who makes or attempts to make excessive profit on the sale of necessaries during a period of scarcity, e.g. in war-time. Hence **Profitee·r** *v. intr.* to make excessive profits; to act like a p.

Profligacy (prǫ·fligăsi). 1738. [f. next; see -ACY 3.] The quality or condition of being profligate.

Profligate (prǫ·figĕt), *a.* and *sb.* 1535. [ad. L. *profligatus* overthrown, pa. pple. of *profligare* to dash to the ground, f. *pro* PRO-¹ + *-fligare* for *fligere* to strike down, dash.] †1. (Const. as *pa. pple.*) Overthrown, overwhelmed, routed –1663. 2. Abandoned to vice or vicious indulgence; recklessly licentious or debauched; dissolute; shamelessly vicious 1647. b. Recklessly prodigal, extravagant, or profuse 1779. B. *sb.* A profligate or dissipated person 1709.

2. P. in their lives, and licentious in their compositions JOHNSON. Hence **Pro·fligate·ly** *adv.*, **-ness** (now *rare*).

†**Profligate** (prǫ·fligeⁱt), *v.* 1542. [f. L. *profligat-, profligare*; see prec.] *trans.* To overcome in battle or conflict, to rout; to put to flight; disperse (*lit.* and *fig.*) –1845.

Profluence (prōu·fluĕns). Now *rare.* 1568. [ad. L. *profluentia*, f. *profluere* to flow forth; see -ENCE.] †A flowing forth or onward; current, stream –1693. b. *fig.* The onward flow (of events, etc.). *rare.* 1639.

Profluent (prōu·fluĕnt), *a.* late ME. [ad. L. *profluentem, profluere*, f. *pro* PRO-¹ + *fluere*.] Flowing forth or onward; flowing in a full stream. Also *fig.*

‖**Profluvium** (proflū·viŏm). *Pl.* **-ia.** 1603. [L., f. *profluere*; see prec.] A flowing forth; a copious flow or discharge. (Chiefly *Path.*)

Profound (prŏfau·nd), *a.* (*sb.*) ME. [a. OF. *profund, profond*, ad. L. *profundus*, f. *pro* PRO-¹ + *fundus* bottom.] 1. Deep (as a physical or material quality). a. Having great or considerable downward (or inward) measurement. late ME. b. Deep-seated, deep-reaching. late ME. c. Originating in, or coming from, a depth; carried far down (as an inclination of the body) 1550. 2. a. Of a person: Characterized by intellectual depth; that has penetrated deeply into a subject of knowledge; very learned ME. b. Of personal attributes, actions, or works: Showing depth of insight or knowledge; marked by great learning. late ME. 3. Of non-material things figured as having depth. a. Of a subject of thought: Deep in meaning; abstruse, recondite; *occas.*, Difficult to understand; having a meaning that does not lie on the surface. late ME. b. Of a condition, state, or quality: Having depth or intensity; in which one may be intensely immersed or engaged; unbroken or undisturbed (as *p. silence, sleep, peace*); deep-seated; deeply-buried, hence, concealed (as a *p. secret*) 1599. c. Said of reverence, respect, submission, or the like: often with some ref. to the notion of bowing low 1526.

1. Profoundest Hell MILT. c. A sigh, so pittious and p. SHAKS. The three ambassadors..made a p. reverence 1732. 2. a. Their Abbot..was pious, painfull, and a p. Schollar FULLER. b. Their profoundest Speculations 1664. 3. a. A higher and profounder doctrine 1583. b. Profoundest ignorance 1853. c. They treat themselves with most p. respect POPE.

B. *sb.* That which is profound; a vast depth; an abyss (chiefly *poet.*) 1640. b. *spec.* The depth of the sea or other deep water; 'the deep' (*poet.*) 1621.

b. Expert to try The vast p., and bid the vessel fly POPE. Hence **Profou·nd-ly** *adv.*, **-ness.**

Profulgent (profʊ·ldʒĕnt), *a. rare.* 1500. [f. PRO-¹ + L. *fulgentem* FULGENT.] Shining forth, effulgent, radiant.

Profundity (prŏfʊ·ndĭti). [Late ME. *profundite*, a. OF., ad. late L. *profunditas*, f. *profundus* PROFOUND; see -ITY.] 1. Depth, in a physical sense. †a. *gen.* = DEPTH 1. –1696. b. The quality of being (very) deep; deepness; extreme lowness (of a bow) 1604. c. *concr.* or quasi-*concr.* A very deep place; the deepest part *of* something; a (vast) depth, an abyss. Also *fig.* late ME. 2. Intellectual depth; depth of meaning or content; abstruseness 1450. b. *pl.* Depths of thought or meaning; 'deep things' 1582. 3. Intensity, thoroughness, extremeness of degree 1576.

1. c. Through the vast profunditie obscure MILT. 2. The profoundity of the scripture 1679. b. The Spirit searcheth al things, yea the profoundities of God N.T. (Rhem.) 1 *Cor.* ii. 10.

Profuse (prŏfiū·s), *a.* late ME. [ad. L. *profusus*, prop. pa. pple. of *profundere* to pour forth, f. *pro* PRO-¹ + *fundere* to pour.] 1. Expending, bestowing, or producing abundantly; lavish; wasteful, prodigal. Const. *in, of.* 2. Of actions, conditions, or things: Very abundant; exuberant; copious; excessive 1610.

1. Justinian was so p. that he could not be liberal GIBBON. *fig.* On a green shadie Bank p. of Flours MILT. 2. The kisses of an enemy are p. R.V. *Prov.* xxvii. 6. Hence **Profu·se-ly** *adv.*, **-ness.**

†**Profu·se,** *v.* 1611. [f. L. *profus-, profundere*; see prec.] *trans.* To pour forth; to expend, bestow, or produce freely; to lavish, squander, waste –1771.

Profusion (prŏfiū·ʒən). 1545. [a. F., ad. L. *profusionem*, f. *profundere.*] 1. The action of pouring forth; outpouring (of a liquid); spilling, shedding. Now *rare.* 1604. 2. Lavish or wasteful expenditure *of* money, etc. 1545. 3. The fact, condition, or quality of being profuse; lavishness, wastefulness 1692. 4. Abundance; lavish or copious supply 1705.

2. A wanton p. of the public wealth D'ISRAELI. 3. The p...with which he lavished his gold 1838. 4. Fields, where summer spreads p. round GOLDSM.

Profusive (prŏfiū·siv), *a.* 1638. [f. L. *profus-, profundere* + -IVE.] Marked by or tending to profusion or lavishness. Hence **Profu·sive-ly** *adv.*, **-ness.**

Prog (prǫg), *sb.*¹ 1615. [Origin unkn.] A piercing instrument or weapon; a spike; a skewer; a stiletto.

Prog (prǫg), *sb.*² 1655. [perh. f. PROG *v.*¹, = that which is got by progging.] Food, victuals, provender; esp. *colloq.* provisions for a journey or excursion; *slang.* food generally. b. *fig.* Food for the mind 1770.

Rings, watch, and so forth, fairly went for p. 1704.

Prog, *sb.*³ *Undergraduates' slang.* Also **proggins.** 1898. [Perversion of PROCTOR.] A proctor at Oxford or Cambridge. Hence **Prog** *v.*³ = PROCTORIZE *v.*

Prog (prǫg), *v.*¹ *Obs.* exc. *dial.* 1622. [Origin unkn.] 1. *intr.* To poke about *for* anything that may be laid hold of; to hunt about, *esp.* for food; to forage; also, to beg, to go about begging. †2. *trans.* To search or hunt out; to poke out –1656.

Prog, *v.*² *dial.* 1811. [f. PROG *sb.*¹] *trans.* To prick, stab, pierce; to prod.

†**Proge·nerate,** *v. rare.* 1611. [f. ppl. stem of L. *progenerare* to beget, engender; see PRO-¹ and GENERATE *v.*] *trans.* To beget, propagate, procreate –1824.

To p. a..far better race LANDOR. So †**Progenera·tion,** procreation, propagation, begetting.

Progenitive (proˌdʒe·nĭtiv), *a.* 1838. [f. L. *progenit-, progignere*; see next and -IVE.] Having the quality of producing offspring; possessed of reproductive power or properties.

Progenitor (proˌdʒe·nitəɹ). [Late ME. *progenitour*, a. obs. F. *progeniteur*, ad. L. *progenitorem* ancestor, f. *progignere*, f. *pro* PRO-¹ + *gignere.*] 1. An ancestor, a forefather. b. *Biol.* An ancestor or ancestral species of animals or plants 1859. 2. *fig.* A spiritual, political, or intellectual 'ancestor' or predecessor 1577.

1. The most renommed of alle his noble progenytours CAXTON. Hence **Progenito·rial** *a.* of or pertaining to progenitors; ancestral. **Proge·nitorship,** the position or fact of being a p. **Proge·nitress, -trix,** a female p.

Progeniture (proˌdʒe·nitiŭɹ, -tʃəɹ). 1801. [f. L. *progenit-, progignere* to beget + -URE.] 1. Begetting of offspring; generation. 2. Offspring, progeny 1893.

Progeny (prǫ·dʒĭni). [ME. a. obs. F. *progenie*, ad. L. *progenies*, f. *progignere* to beget.] 1. The offspring (of a father or mother, or of both); issue, children collectively; descendants. b. Of lower animals, and plants 1697. c. *fig.* Spiritual or intellectual descendants, followers, disciples 1451. 2. *fig.* That which originates from something; issue, product, outcome, result. late ME. †3. A race, stock, or line descended from a common ancestor –1697. †4. Lineage; descent –1775.

1. From this union sprang a vigorous p. HAWTHORNE. c. The Lutherans, and all their p. 1616.

Prognathic (prǫgnæ·þik), *a.* 1850. [f. as PROGNATHOUS + -IC.] = PROGNATHOUS *a.*

Prognathism (prǫ·gnăþiz'm). 1864. [f. as next + -ISM.] The condition of being prognathous. So **Pro·gnathy.**

Prognathous (prǫ·gnăþəs), *a.* 1836. [f. PRO-² + Gr. γνάθος jaw + -OUS.] Having projecting jaws; having a low facial angle; also, of the jaws: prominent, protruding. Opp. to *opisthognathous* and *orthognathous.*

‖**Progne** (prǫ·gnī). late ME. [L. *Progne*, var. of *Procne*, Gr. Πρόκνη, name of Philomela's sister, transformed into a swallow.] 1. A poetic name for the swallow. 2. *Ornith.* An Amer. genus of *Hirundinidæ* or Swallows, including the common Purple Martin of the United States (*P. purpurea* or *subis*).

‖**Prognosis** (prǫgnōu·sis). *Pl.* **-oses** (-ōu·sīz). 1655. [L., a. Gr. πρόγνωσις, f. προγιγνώσκειν to know beforehand; see PRO-².] 1. *Med.* A forecast of the probable course of a case of disease; also, the action or art of making such a forecast. 2. *gen.* Prognostication, anticipation 1706.

Prognostic (prǫgnǫ·stik), *sb.* [Late ME. *pronostike*, a. OF. *pronostique*, ad. L. *prognosticon* (*-cum*), a. Gr. προγνωστικόν, adj. neut. sing. used subst.] 1. That from which the future may be foreknown; a pre-indication, token, omen. 2. A prediction of the future drawn from such an indication; a forecast, prophecy 1634. 3. *Med.* A symptom or indication on which prognosis is based 1621.

1. A..comet appeared about the time of her death, and the vulgar esteemed it the p. of that event 1761.

Prognostic (prǫgnǫ·stik), *a.* 1603. [ad. med.L. *prognosticus*, a. Gr., f. προγιγνώσκειν; see -IC.] Characterized by prognosticating; foreshowing, predictive. b. *Med.* Of a pertaining to prognosis 1648. So **Progno·stically** *adv.*

Prognosticate (prǫgnǫ·stikeⁱt), *v.* 1529. [f. ppl. stem of mod.L. *pro(g)nosticare*, f. L. *prognosticum.*] *trans.* To know or tell of (an event, etc.) beforehand; to predict, prophecy, forecast. b. Of things: To betoken; to indicate beforehand 1533.

Prudent men prognosticated evil 1842. b. Everything seems to p. a hard winter COBBETT. So **Progno·sticative** *a.* characterized by prognosticating; tending to p. **Progno·sticator,** one who or that which prognosticates; †a maker or publisher of almanacs containing forecasts for the ensuing year; also, such an almanac. **Progno·sticatory** *a.* of the nature of a prognostication; serving to p.

Prognostication (prǫgnǫstikēⁱ·ʃən). [Late ME. a. OF. *pronosticacion*, f. med.L. *prognosticare.*] 1. The action or fact of prognosticating; prediction, prophecy 1490. b. with *a* and *pl.* A forecast, prediction, prophecy 1440. c. A presentiment, foreboding 1760. †2. An astrological or astrometeorological forecast for the year, published in (or as) an almanac; hence, an almanac containing this –1643. 3. An indication of something about to happen; a sign, token, portent, prognostic. Now *rare.* late ME.

3. *Ant. & Cl.* I. ii. 54.

Program, programme (prōu·græm). 1633. [Orig., in spelling *program*, ad. Gr.-L. *programma* (see next); subseq. reintroduced from F. *programme*, and now more usu. so spelt.] †1. A public notice. *Sc.* –1824. 2. A descriptive notice, issued beforehand, of any formal series of proceedings, as a festive celebration, a course of study, etc.; a prospectus, syllabus; now *esp.* a list of the items or 'numbers' of a concert, etc., in the order of performance; hence *transf.* the items themselves collectively, the performance as a whole 1805. b. *gen.* and *fig.* A definite plan of any intended proceedings 1837. 3. = PROGRAMMA 2. 1831.

Comb. **p.-music,** music intended to convey the impression of a definite series of objects, scenes, or events; descriptive music.

‖**Programma** (prograe·mă). *Pl.* **-gra·mmata.** 1661. [Late L., a. Gr. πρόγραμμα, f. προγράφειν to write publicly, f. πρό (see PRO-²) + γράφειν to write.] 1. A public notice. (In *Gr.* and *Rom. Antiq.*, and formerly in universities.) –1820. Hence b. = PROGRAM 2. –1820. 2. A written preface or introduction; in *pl.*, = prolegomena 1711.

Progress (prōu·grĕs, prǫ·grĕs), *sb.* late ME. [(ult.) f. L. *progress-, progredi* to go forward, f. *pro* PRO-¹ + *gradi* to step.] 1. The action of stepping or moving forward or onward; travel;

a journey, an expedition. Now *rare*. 1475. 2. *spec.* A state journey made by a royal or noble personage, or by a church dignitary; also, an official tour; a circuit. Now somewhat *arch.* 1461. 3. a. Onward movement in space; course, way 1595. b. *fig.* Going on; course or process (of action, events, narrative, time, etc.) late ME. 4. a. Forward movement in space; advance 1500. b. *fig.* Advance, advancement; growth, development; usu. in good sense, continuous improvement 1603.

1. The Pilgrim's P. from this world, to that which is to come BUNYAN (*title*). 2. His official tours..were scarcely inferior in pomp to royal progresses MACAULAY. 3. a. For see the Morn..begins Her rosie p. smiling MILT. b. *In p.*, proceeding, taking place; While these changes were in p. MACAULAY. 4. b. The p. of manufactures greatly outstrips the p. of agriculture 1862.

Progress (prǒgre·s), *v.* 1590. [f. prec.] 1. *intr.* To make a 'progress' or journey; to travel; *spec.* to make a state journey. Now *rare* or *Obs.*, or merged in 2. †b. *trans.* To travel through –1641. 2. *intr.* To go or move forward or onward; to make one's way, advance 1595. 3. *fig.* Of action or an agent: To go on, proceed, advance; to be carried on as an action; to carry on an action 1607. 4. *fig.* To make progress; to advance, get on; to develop; usu., to improve continuously 1610. 5. *trans.* To cause to advance; to push forward. *lit.* and *fig.* 1875.

1. b. Progressing the datelesse and irrevoluble Circle of Eternity MILT. 2. This honourable dewe, That siluerly doth progresse on thy cheekes SHAKS. 3. The controversy is progressing 1906. 4. Our country ..is fast progressing in its political importance and social happiness WASHINGTON. Her convalescence had so far progressed HAWTHORNE.

Progression (prǒgre·ʃən). [Late ME. a. F., ad. L. *progressionem* a going forward, f. *progredi*; see PROGRESS *sb.*] 1. The action of stepping or moving forward or onward. †a. = PROGRESS *sb.* 1. –1548. b. = PROGRESS *sb.* 3 a, 4 a. 1588. 2. *fig.* Continuous action conceived as onward movement; going on (of action, life, time, etc.), proceeding, process. Now *rare* or merged in 4. 1474. 3. *fig.* The action of passing successively from each item or term of a series to the next; succession; a series 1549. 4. *fig.* = PROGRESS *sb.* 4 b. 1586. 5. *Math.* The succession of a series of quantities, between every two successive terms of which there is some particular constant relation; such a series itself. late ME. 6. *Mus.* a. The action of passing (in melody) from one note to another, or (in harmony) from one chord to another; a succession of notes or chords. b. Sometimes = SEQUENCE. 1609.

2. There is a p.—I cannot call it a progress—in his work toward a more and more strictly prosaic level STEVENSON. 4. The p. and retrogression of the arts 1877. Hence **Progre·ssional** *a.* of, pertaining to, or involving p.

Progressionist (prǒgre·ʃənist). 1849. [-IST.] 1. An advocate of progression or progress; a progressive. 2. One who holds that life on the earth has been marked by gradual progression from lower to higher forms 1859. 3. *attrib.* or as *adj.* 1871. So **Progre·ssionism,** the theory or principles of a p.

Progressist (prōᵘ·grĕsist, prǫ·g-). 1848. [ad. F. *progressiste*; see PROGRESS *sb.* and -IST.] One who advocates progress, esp. in political or social matters; a reformer, a progressive. b. *attrib.* or as *adj.* 1889. So **Pro·gressism,** the principles of a p.

Progressive (prǒgre·siv), *a.* (*sb.*) 1607. [a. F. *progressif, -ive*, f. L. *progress-*; see PROGRESS *v.* and -IVE.] 1. a. Characterized by moving onward, as in the locomotion of men and animals generally 1644. b. *gen.* Moving forward (in space); of the nature of onward motion 1667. 2. Proceeding step by step; occurring one after another, successive 1620. b. Applied to certain games at cards, when played by several sets of players simultaneously at different tables, certain players passing after each round to the next table 1890. 3. Characterized by progress or advance 1607. b. *Path.* Of a disease: Continuously increasing in severity or extent 1736. 4. Advocating progress or reform, esp. in political, municipal, or social matters 1884.

1. b. Thir wandring course.. P., retrograde, or standing still MILT. 3. A people..may be p. for a certain length of time, and then stop MILL. He had to teach that the creation was not merely orderly, but p. 1884. 4. P. Conservatism is to adopt Liberal principles, and say they were always your own 1897.

B. *sb.* One who advocates or aims at progress or reform 1865. Hence **Progre·ssive-ly** *adv.*, **-ness.** **Progre·ssivism,** the principles of a p.; advocacy of progress or reform.

Prohibit (prǒhi·bit), *v.* late ME. [f. L. *prohibit-, prohibere* to hold back, f. *pro-* in front + *habere* to hold.] 1. *trans.* To forbid (an action or thing) by or as by a command or statute; to interdict. 2. To prevent, hinder, or debar (an action or thing) by physical means 1548. 3. To forbid or prevent (a person) *from* doing something; also with inf. (*arch.*) 1523.

1. They altogether prohibite the use of wine in fevers 1669. 2. Gates of burning Adamant Barr'd over us p. all egress MILT. 3. There is no Act..prohibiting the Secretary of State for Foreign Affairs from being in the pay of continental powers MACAULAY. Hence **Prohi·biter, Prohi·bitor,** one who prohibits.

Prohibition (prōᵘhibi·ʃən). late ME. [a. F., ad. L. *prohibitionem*, f. *prohibere.*] 1. The action of forbidding or by as by authority; an edict, decree, or order that forbids; a negative command. 2. *Law.* A writ issuing from a superior court, forbidding some court, and the parties engaged in it, from proceeding in a suit, on the ground that this is beyond the cognizance of the court in question 1548. 3. The interdiction by law of the importation of some foreign article of commerce 1670. 4. *spec.* The forbidding by law of the manufacture and sale of alcoholic drinks for common consumption 1851.

3. Manufacturers in want of customers cried out for trade prohibitions 1872.

attrib. P. party, a political party in U.S., formed in Sept. 1869 to nominate or support only persons pledged to vote for the p. of the liquor traffic. Hence **Prohibi·tionist,** one who favours p., *spec.* of the manufacture and sale of alcoholic drinks; also *attrib.*

Prohibitive (prǒhi·bitiv), *a.* late ME. [a. F. *prohibitif, -ive*; see -IVE.] 1. Having the quality of prohibiting; that forbids or restrains from some course of action. 2. Of taxes, prices, etc.: Such as serve to prevent the use or abuse of something 1886. 3. *Gram.* That expresses prohibition 1875.

2. The cab-rates are p. M. ARNOLD. A well-nigh p. price 1898. Hence **Prohi·bitive-ly** *adv.*, **-ness.**

Prohibitory (prohi·bitəri), *a.* 1591. [ad. L. *prohibitorius* restraining; see -ORY.] 1. = prec. 1; esp. with ref. to the liquor traffic, as in *p. law, party*, etc. 2. = prec. 2. 1849.

Project (prǫ·dʒĕkt, prōᵘ·dʒĕkt), *sb.* late ME. [ad. L. *projectum*, neut. sing. of pa. pple. *projectus*; see next.] †1. A plan, draft, scheme, or table of something; a tabulated statement; a design or pattern –1627. †2. A mental conception or idea; speculation –1727. 3. Something projected for execution; a plan, scheme, purpose; a proposal 1601.

2. 2 *Hen. IV*, I. iii. 29. 3. Proiects of draining surrounded grounds 1623. New Projects were every day set on foot for Money, which serv'd only to..incense the People CLARENDON.

Project (prǒ₁dʒe·kt), *v.* 1477. [f. L. *project-, projicere* to throw forth, f. *pro* PRO-¹ + *jacere* to throw.] I. 1. *trans.* To plan, contrive, or design (something to be done, or some action to be carried out); to form a project of. Also with *inf.* (now *rare* or *Obs.*). †2. To set forth, exhibit; to present to expectation –1697.

1. I projected and drew up a plan for the union FRANKLIN. Sketches projected but abandoned 1865. 2. I cannot proiect mine owne cause so well To make it cleare SHAKS.

II. Of physical operations. †1. *trans.* To throw or cast away (*lit.* and *fig.*) –1603. 2. To cast, throw, hurl, shoot, impel, or cause to move forward, or onward in any direction. Also *fig.* 1596. b. To throw or cast (a substance) *in, into, on, upon* something. (Chiefly in *Alchemy* and *Chem.*) 1599. 3. To place (a thing) so that it protrudes or juts out. Now *rare.* 1624. 4. *intr.* To jut out; to protrude beyond the adjacent parts 1718. 5. *trans.* To throw or cause to fall (light or shadow) upon a surface or into space. Also *fig.* 1664. b. To cause (a figure or image) to appear or 'stand out' *on* or *against* a background 1831. 6. *Geom.* To draw straight lines or 'rays' from a centre through every point of a given figure, so that they fall upon or intersect a surface and produce upon it a new figure of which each point corresponds to a point of the original. (With either the rays, the resulting figure, or the original figure as obj.) Hence, to represent or delineate (a figure) according to any system of correspondence between its points and the points of the surface on which it is delineated. 1679. b. *Chartography.* To make a geometrical or other projection or representation on a plane surface of (the earth, sky, etc.) 1855.

2. Before his feet her selfe she did p. SPENSER. *fig.* Can we not p. ourselves..into the future? 1878. b. When projected on red-hot nitre, it [plumbago] should detonate 1800. 4. The booths..projected far into the streets MACAULAY. 5. The Shade my Body projected, near Noon BOYLE. b. He..saw Huxley's form projected against the sky 1860.

Projectile (prǒ₁dʒe·ktəil, -il), *a.* and *sb.* 1665. [ad. mod.L. *projectilis*, f. ppl. stem of *projicere.*] A. *adj.* 1. Of motion or velocity: Caused by impulse or projection. Now *rare* or *Obs.* 1696. 2. Of force, etc.: Impelling forward or onward; projecting 1715. 3. Capable of being projected by force, esp. of being thrown as a missile 1865.

3. *P. anchor*, in life-saving apparatus, an anchor adapted to be shot out of a tube towards the place where it is intended to grapple.

B. *sb.* A projectile object; *spec.* a missile adapted to be discharged from a cannon by the force of some explosive 1665.

Comb.: p. theory, (*a*) that branch of mechanics which treats of the motion of projectiles, as affected by gravity and the resistance of the air; (*b*) = the emission theory of light: see EMISSION 4.

Projection (prǒ₁dʒe·kʃən). 1557. [ad. L. *projectionem*, f. *projicere*, or a. F.] I. 1. The action of projecting; the fact of being projected; throwing or casting forth or forward 1599. 2. The casting of some ingredient into a crucible; esp. in *Alchemy*, the casting of the powder of philosopher's stone (*powder of p.*) upon a metal in fusion to transmute it into gold or silver; the transmutation of metals 1594. b. *fig.* Change from one thing to another; transmutation 1630. II. 1. The forming of mental projects; scheming, planning 1599. †2. That which is projected; a project; a proposal –1804.

II. 1. The p. of a canal 1838.

III. The action of placing a thing or part so that it sticks or stands out beyond the general line or surface; the fact or condition of being so placed as to project 1644. b. *concr.* Anything which projects; a projecting part 1756.

b. The projections at the corners..are called buttresses 1815.

IV. 1. *Geom.* The drawing of straight lines or 'rays' through every point of a given figure, usu. so as to fall upon a surface and produce upon it a new figure each point of which corresponds to a point of the original figure. Hence, each of such rays, or of such points of the resulting figure, is said to be the p. of a point of the original one; or the whole resulting figure is said to be a p. of the original. 1731. 2. The drawing according to scale, and on mathematical principles, of a plan, chart, or map of a surface, or a diagram on the flat of a machine or the like; *spec.* the representation of any spherical surface on the flat, e. g. of the whole or any part of the earth, more fully called *map-p.* 1557. b. *Chartography.* A representation on a plane surface of the whole or any part of the surface of the earth, or of the celestial sphere; any one of the modes in which this is done 1570. c. *Cryst.* The projection of a point in each face of a crystal upon an imaginary containing sphere, called the *sphere of p.* 1878. 3. The action of projecting, or fact of being optically projected, as a figure or image, against a background 1881. 4. A mental image visualized and regarded as an objective reality 1836.

2. b. CYLINDRICAL, GNOMONIC, ORTHOGRAPHIC, etc. *p.*: see the adjs. 4. The youth, intoxicated with his admiration of a hero, fails to see that it is only a p. of his own soul which he admires EMERSON.

Projective (prǒ₁dʒe·ktiv), *a.* 1682. [f. L. *project-* (see PROJECT *v.*) + -IVE.] 1. *Geom.*, etc. Of, pertaining to, or produced by the projection of lines or figures on a surface. 2. Jutting out, projecting (*rare*) 1703. 3. Having the quality of being mentally projected, or the power of projecting 1834.

1. *P. property*, a property (of a figure) which remains unchanged after projection. *P. Geometry*, that branch which deals with p. properties. Hence **Proje·ctively** *adv.*

Projector (prǒ₁dʒe·ktəɪ). 1596. [a. L. type **projector*, f. *projicere*; see -OR.] 1. One who forms a project, who plans or designs some enterprise or undertaking. b. A schemer; one who lives by his wits; a promoter of bubble companies; a speculator, a cheat 1616. 2. One who or that which projects or throws something forward 1674. 3. An apparatus for projecting rays of light; a parabolic reflector or a combination of lenses 1887. b. A camera for throwing an image upon a screen 1884.

1. b. Let not the P. pretend the publike good, when he intends but to robbe the riche and to cheat the poore 1636.

Projecture (prǒ₁dʒe·ktiŭɹ, -tʃəɹ). Now *rare.* 1563. [ad. L. *projectura*, f. *project-*; see PROJECT *v.* and -IVE.] The fact or state of projecting beyond the general line; in *Arch.*, a projecting architectural member or moulding.

‖**Projet** (proʒe). 1808. [F., ad. L. *projectum.*] A proposition, proposal; the draft of a proposed treaty, etc.

Prolapse (prolæ·ps), *sb.* 1822. [ad. late L. *prolapsus.*] *Path.* = PROLAPSUS.

Prolapse (prolæ·ps), *v.* 1736. [f. L. *prolaps-, prolabi*; see next.] *Path. intr.* To slip forward or down out of place.

‖**Prolapsus** (prolæ·psǒs). 1797. [Late L., f. L. *prolabi, prolaps-*; see PRO-[1] and LAPSE *sb.*] *Path.* A slipping forward or down of a part or organ, esp. of a part of the viscera, from its normal position into a cavity or through an opening; *spec.* that of the uterus or of the rectum.

Prolate (prōu·leɪt), *a.* 1694. [ad. L. *prolatus*, pa. pple. of *proferre*, f. *pro* PRO-[1] + *ferre* to carry.] 1. *Geom.* Lengthened in the direction of the polar diameter: said of a spheroid formed by the revolution of an ellipse about its longer axis. Cf. OBLATE *a.* 2. Extended or extending in width; *fig.* widely spread 1846.

Prolation (prolē·ʃən). late ME. [ad. L. *prolationem*, f. *prolat-, proferre*; see prec.] †1. The bringing forth of words; utterance -1734. 2. In mediæval music, A term used to indicate the relative duration or time-value of the minim to the semibreve in the rhythm of a piece. late ME. †3. *Theol.* The 'emission', origination, or procession of the Logos -1721.

Prolative (prolē·tiv), *a.* 1867. [ad. late L. *prolativus*, f. *prolatus* PROLATE *a.*; see -IVE.] *Gram.* Having the function of extending or completing the predication.

‖**Prolegomenon** (prōulegǫ·menǫn). *Pl.* **-mena** (-ă). 1652. [a. Gr. προλεγόμενον, neut. of pres. pple. pass. of προλέγειν to say beforehand, f. πρό PRO-[2] + λέγειν.] A preliminary discourse prefixed to a literary work; esp. a learned preamble; chiefly in *pl.* introductory observations on the subject of a book. Hence **Prolego·menal, Prolego·menary** *adjs.* introductory, preliminary.

‖**Prolepsis** (prole·psis, -lī·psis). *Pl.* **-ses** (-sīz). 1577. [L., a. Gr. πρόληψις a preconception, f. προλαμβάνειν.] 1. The taking of something future as already done or existing; also, the assignment of an event, a name, etc. to a too early date; an anachronism, prochronism. 2. *Rhet.* and *Gram.* a. = PROCATALEPSIS 1611. b. The anticipatory use of an attribute 1850.

2. b. P. or anticipation..an effect to be produced represented as already produced, by the insertion of an epithet:..'Hang his poison in the sick air' 1875.

Proleptic (prole·ptik, -lī·ptik), *a.* 1656. [ad. Gr. προληπτικός, f. προλαμβάνειν; see prec. and -IC.] 1. Of, pertaining to, or characterized by prolepsis; anticipative. 2. *Gram.* Of, pertaining to, or exemplifying prolepsis; see prec. 2. b. 1866. So **Prole·ptical** *a.* (*rare*) 1627. **-ly** *adv.*

Proletaire (prōulĭtēə·ɪ). Also as F. **prolétaire.** 1820. [ad. F. *prolétaire*, ad. L. *proletarius* a Roman citizen of the lowest class who served the state only with his offspring; f. *proles, -em* offspring.] = PROLETARIAN *sb.*

Proletarian (prōulĭtēə·riăn), *a.* and *sb.* 1658. [f. L. *proletarius* PROLETAIRE + -AN.] A. *adj.* Of or pertaining to the lowest class of the people. †a. In hostile use: Vile, low, vulgar -1734. b. Of or pertaining to the proletariate in the modern sense 1851. B. *sb.* One of the proletariate 1658. Hence **Proleta·rianism**, the condition of a p.; the political principles and practice of the proletarians.

Proletariate, -at (prōulĭtēə·riĕt, -ăt). 1853. [ad. mod.F. *prolétariat*, f. L. *proletarius* PROLETAIRE + F. *-at* -ATE[1].] 1. *Anc. Hist.* The lowest class of the community in ancient Rome, regarded as contributing nothing to the state but offspring. Also with ref. to other ancient states. 1861. 2. In ref. to modern society. a. Applied to the lowest class of the community. (Often *hostile.*) 1853. b. *Pol. Econ.* The class of wage-earners who have no reserve or capital; sometimes extended to include all wage-earners; working men 1858.

2. b. The proletariat or hand-to-mouth wage-earners 1883.

Proletary (prōu·l-, prǫ·lĭtări), *a.* and *sb.* 1579. [ad. L. *proletarius.*] = PROLETARIAN.

Proliferate (proli·fĕreɪt), *v.* 1873. [Back-formation from next.] 1. *intr.* To reproduce itself by proliferation; to grow by multiplication of elementary parts. b. *Zool.* To produce new individuals, esp. sexual as dist. from nutritive zooids 1878. 2. *trans.* To produce or form by proliferation 1885. So **Proli·ferative** *a.* characterized by or tending to proliferation. (Chiefly *Path.*)

Proliferation (proliferē·ʃən). 1858. [a. F. *prolifération*; f. *prolifère* PROLIFEROUS; see -ATION.] 1. *Path.*, etc. The formation or development of cells by budding or division 1867. b. *Zool.* The production of (sexual) zooids, by some hydrozoans 1894. 2. *Bot.* The condition or fact of being PROLIFEROUS (3 a) 1858.

Proliferous (proli·fĕrəs), *a.* 1654. [f. med. L. *prolifer* (f. L. *proles* + *-fer* bearing) + -OUS.] †1. Producing offspring; prolific -1692. 2. Producing many flowers; prolific (*rare*) 1682. 3. Of, pertaining to, or characterized by proliferation. a. *Bot.* Producing leaf- or flower-buds from a leaf or flower, or other part which is normally terminal; also, Producing new individuals from buds 1702. b. *Zool.* Reproducing itself by budding; *spec.* producing sexual or generative (as opp. to nutritive) zooids 1856. c. *Path.* Spreading by proliferation 1874. Hence **Proli·ferously** *adv.*

Prolific (prǒli·fik), *a.* 1650. [ad. med.L. *prolificus*, f. *proles*; see -FIC; or ad. F. *prolifique.*] 1. Generating or producing offspring; fertile, not barren. b. *Bot.* Producing fertile seed 1828. 2. a. Producing much offspring or fruit; abundantly productive 1653. b. Abundantly productive *of*; abounding *in* 1693. 3. Causing abundant production; fertilizing 1669. b. Characterized by abundant production 1695.

2. a. *fig.* The public lands—that p. source of corruption in the hands of the profligate 1850. b. This age being not very prolifique of customers for such a commodity PEPYS. 3. By Nile's p. torrents delug'd o'er 1738. b. A p. year for apples (*mod.*) So **Proli·ficacy**, p. quality or state. †**Proli·fical** *a.* = PROLIFIC *a.* 1, 2. 1608. **Proli·fically** *adv.* **Proli·fic·ly** *adv.*, **-ness.**

Prolificate (proli·fikeɪt), *v. rare.* 1658. [f. med.L. *prolificare* + -ATE[3].] *trans.* To render prolific or fruitful; to fertilize.

Prolification (prolifikē·ʃən). late ME. [ad. med.L. *prolificationem.*] 1. The generation or production of offspring; also, reproductive power; fecundity, fertility. 2. a. *Bot.* = PROLIFERATION 2. 1760. b. *Zool.* = PROLIFERATION 1 b. 1865.

Prolificity (prōulifi·sĭti). 1725. [f. med.L. *prolificus* + -ITY.] The quality of being prolific.

Proligerous (proli·dʒĕrəs), *a.* 1836. [f. L. *proles* + -GEROUS.] 1. Bearing offspring; generative; germinative. 2. *Bot.* = PROLIFEROUS *a.* 3 a. 1890.

Prolix (prōu·liks, proli·ks), *a.* late ME. [a. F. *prolixe*, or ad. L. *prolixus*, app. f. *pro* PRO-[1] + **lixus*, pa. pple. of *liquere* to flow, be liquid.] 1. Of long duration, lengthy; of a speech or writing, wordy, tedious. 2. Of a person: Given to lengthy tediousness in speech or writing; long-winded 1527. 3. Long in measurement or extent. Now *rare.* 1650.

1. Prolixe prayers, hindering the preaching of the Word 1651. 2. Conscious dulness has little right to be p. JOHNSON. 3. With wig p., down flowing to his waist COWPER. Hence **Prolix·ly** *adv.*, **-ness.**

†**Proli·xious**, *a.* 1527. [irreg. f. L. *prolixus* + -OUS.] 1. = PROLIX *a.* 1, 2. -1632. 2. Long in extent or duration -1604.

2. Lay by all nicetie, and p. blushes SHAKS.

Prolixity (proli·ksĭti). late ME. [a. F. *prolixité*, ad. late L. *prolixitas*, f. *prolixus* PROLIX; see -ITY.] 1. The quality or state of being prolix; length of discourse; copiousness of detail; *esp.* tedious or tiresome lengthiness. 2. Material length. Now *joc.* 1543.

1. The..verbose p. of the narrative 1864. 2. The monkey..with a thick tail curling out into preposterous p. HAWTHORNE.

Prolocution (prǫ·l-, prōulǒkiū·ʃən). 1597. [Partly ad. late L. *prolocutio* a preamble, f. *proloqui*, here identified with *præloqui* to speak before; partly f. PRO-[1] + LOCUTION.] 1. A preliminary speech or remark (*rare*). †2. The use of ambiguous language so as to mislead -1716. 3. Acting as spokesman (*rare*) 1826.

Prolocutor (prōu·lǒkiūtǫɹ, prolǫ·kiŭtəɹ). 1475. [a. L., f. *proloqui* to speak out.] One who speaks for another or others; a spokesman. Now *rare* in gen. sense. b. The chairman of the Lower House of Convocation of either province of the Church of England; he is spokesman of that body in the Upper House 1560. c. The presiding officer of an assembly; a chairman, 'speaker' 1591. Hence **Prolocutorship**, the office of p.

Prologize (prǫ·lǒdʒəiz, prōu·l-), *v.* See also PROLOGUIZE. 1608. [ad. Gr. προλογίζειν to speak the prologue; see PROLOGUE *sb.* and -IZE.] *intr.* To compose or speak a prologue. Hence **Pro·logizer.**

Prologue (prōu·lǫg), *sb.* [ME. *prolog*, a. F. *prologue*, ad. L. *prologus*, a. Gr. πρόλογος prologue of a play, also its speaker, f. πρό PRO-[2] + λόγος.] 1. The preface or introduction to a discourse or performance; *esp.* a discourse or poem introducing a dramatic performance. b. *transf.* and *fig.* An introductory or preliminary act, proceeding, or event 1593. 2. One who speaks the prologue to a play 1579.

1. b. My death..is made the P. to their Play SHAKS. Hence **Pro·logue** *v. trans.* to introduce or furnish with a p.; also *fig.*

Prologuize (prōu·lǒgəiz), *v.* 1761. [f. prec. + -IZE.] *intr.* To write or deliver a prologue.

Prolong (prǒlǫ·ŋ), *v.* [Late ME. *prolonge*, a. OF. *prolonguer*, var. of F. *prolonger*, ad. late L. *prolongare* to lengthen (f. *pro* PRO-[1] + *longus*).] 1. *trans.* To lengthen out in time; to extend in duration; to continue, carry on. †2. To delay, postpone -1785. †b. To prorogue (parliament) -1649. †3. *intr.* To delay, put off. Also with *inf.* -1623. 4. *trans.* To lengthen the pronunciation of (a word or syllable); to draw out (a sound) 1560. 5. To extend in spatial length; to make longer 1573.

1. To sing thy Praise, wou'd Heav'n my Breath p. DRYDEN. 2. But wherto now shold I p. my death? SURREY. 5. Up to which the fault..had prolonged itself as a crevasse TYNDALL. Hence **Prolo·ngable** *a.* **Prolonger** (-ǫ·ŋgəɹ). **Prolo·ngment** (*rare*), prolongation.

Prolongate (prōu·lǫŋgeɪt), *v. rare.* 1597. [f. ppl. stem of late L. *prolongare* to PROLONG; see -ATE[3].] *trans.* To prolong, lengthen.

Prolongation (prōulǫŋgē·ʃən). late ME. [a. F., ad. late L. **prolongationem*, f. *prolongare.*] 1. Lengthening or extension in time; extension of the duration of anything. †2. Delay, postponement -1622. 3. The lengthening or prolonging of a syllable, note, etc. 1589. 4. Linear extension in space; with *a* and *pl.*, an instance of this; an addition by which the length is increased 1671.

‖**Prolonge** (prolōnʒ). 1858. [F., f. *prolonger.*] *Mil.* A rope composed of three pieces joined by two open rings, and having a hook at one end and a toggle at the other, used for moving a gun when unlimbered, and for various other purposes.

Prolusion (prol^{i}ū·ʒən). 1601. [ad. L. *prolusionem*, f. *proludere* to play or practise beforehand.] **1.** A display introductory to a game, performance, or entertainment; a preliminary attempt. **2.** A preliminary essay or article; a slight literary production 1627.

2. My Treatise..was intended but for a p. EVELYN. So **Prolu·sory** *a.* preliminary, introductory.

Prom, colloq. abbrev. of PROMENADE *sb.* 2, b. and PROMENADE *concert*.

Promenade (prǫmĕnā·d, -ən-, -ā·d), *sb.* 1567. [a. F., f. *promener* to take for a walk :—late L. *prominare* to drive onward (a beast), f. *pro* forth + *minare* to threaten.] **1.** A walk taken (usu. at a leisurely pace) for exercise or amusement, or (esp.) to and fro for display, or as part of a social ceremony. Also *transf.* **2.** A place for promenading; *esp.* a paved public walk for social promenades 1648. **b.** *U.S.* A ball or dance at a school or college 1905.

1. To see the exhibition lit up for a p. SCOTT.

attrib.: *p. deck*; p. **band,** a band that performs at a p. concert; p. **concert,** a concert at which the audience walk about instead of being seated.

Promenade (prǫmĕnā·d, -ən-, -ā·d), *v.* 1588. [f. prec.] **1.** *intr.* To make a promenade; to walk about (or ride, etc.), esp. for amusement or display; to parade. **2.** *trans.* To make a promenade through, to walk about (a place) 1837. **3.** (= F. *promener*): To lead (a person, etc.) about a place, esp. in the way of display. Also *fig.* 1850.

1. Promenading gently on horseback CARLYLE. Hence **Promena·der.**

‖**Promerops** (prǫ·mĕrǫps). *Pl.* **promeropes** (-me·ropīz). 1827. [mod.L., f. Gr. πρό before + μέροψ bee-eater.] *Ornith.* A South African genus of birds, including the Cape Promerops, *P. cafer*, a small bird with a long curved slender bill and a very long tail, and the Natal species, *P. gurneyi*.

Promethean (prǒmī·þiăn), *a.* (*sb.*) 1588. [f. PROMETHEUS + -AN.] **1.** Of, pertaining to, or resembling Prometheus, in his skill, art, or punishment. †**2.** Applied to a contrivance invented in 1828 and used before the introduction of phosphorus or lucifer matches for obtaining a light readily –1889.

1. *L.L.L.* IV. iii. 304.

Prometheus (prǒmī·þiūs). 1588. [L. *Prometheus*, Gr. Προμηθεύς.] *Gr. Myth.* A demigod (son of the Titan Iapetus), who made man out of clay, stole fire from Olympus, and taught men the use of it and various arts, for which he was chained by Zeus to a rock in the Caucasus, where his liver was preyed upon every day by a vulture. Hence allusively.

Prominence (prǫ·minĕns). 1598. [a. obs. F. *prominence*, ad. L. *prominentia* a jutting out; see PROMINENT and -ENCE.] **1.** The fact or condition of being physically prominent 1611. **2.** That which is prominent; a projection, protuberance 1598. **3.** The quality or state of being conspicuous or plainly apparent 1828. **4.** Any conspicuous or salient point or matter 1827.

2. *Solar p.*, a projecting cloud of incandescent hydrogen, etc., above the chromosphere of the sun, best seen during an eclipse. Also *attrib.*, as *p.-spectrum*. **3.** Its importance comes into historical p. STUBBS. So **Pro·minency.**

Prominent (prǫ·minĕnt), *a.* (*sb.*) 1545. [ad. L. *prominens, -entem, prominere*; f. *pro* PRO-[1] + **minere*, f. root of *minæ* projecting points.] **1.** Jutting or standing out; projecting, protuberant. **2.** Conspicuous 1759. **b.** *fig.* Standing out so as to strike the attention; conspicuous; distinguished above others 1849.

1. An orifice with p. tumid lips 1870. **2.** The most p. object was a mountain on the other side of the valley 1883. **b.** Attachment to France had been p. among the crimes imputed by the Commons to Clarendon MACAULAY.

B. *sb.* Any cuspidate moth of the genus *Notodonta* 1819. Hence **Pro·minent-ly** *adv.*, **-ness.**

Promiscuity (prǫmiskiū·iti). 1849. [ad. F. *promiscuité*, f. L. *promiscuus* (see next) + *-ité* -ITY.] **1.** The condition of being promiscuous; indiscriminate mixture; promiscuousness. **2.** Promiscuous sexual union 1865.

Promiscuous (prǒmi·skiu,əs), *a.* 1603. [f. L. *promiscuus* (f. *pro* PRO-[1] + *miscere* to mix) + -OUS.] **1.** Consisting of members or elements of different kinds massed together without order; of mixed and disorderly composition or character; also, with *pl. sb.*, of various kinds mixed together. **b.** Rarely of a single thing 1663. **2.** That is without discrimination or method; confusedly mingled, indiscriminate 1605. **b.** Of an agent or agency: Making no distinctions; undiscriminating 1633. **3.** Casual, carelessly irregular (*vulgar* or *colloq.*) 1837. **5.** quasi-*adv.* Promiscuously 1671.

1. While the p. croud stood yet aloof MILT. **b.** A wild p. sound POPE. **2.** To forbid the p. Use of Women 1650. Hence **Promi·scuous-ly** *adv.* in a p. manner; **-ness** (*rare*).

Promise (prǫ·mis), *sb.* late ME. [ad. L. *promissum*, neut. pa. pple. of *promittere* used subst.] **1.** A declaration made to another person with respect to the future, stating that one will do, or refrain from, some specified act, or that one will give some specified thing. (Usu. in good sense.) **2.** In religious use: A Divine assurance of future good or blessing; *spec.* that made to Abraham with respect to his posterity (Gen. xii. 2, etc.) 1502. **3.** *transf.* The thing promised; *contextually* (with *claim*) = the fulfilment of a promise 1526. **4.** *fig.* That which affords a ground of expectation of something to come, esp. of future good; a pledge, earnest, pre-indication (*of* something) 1532.

1. Geuyng them faire wordes, and makyng large promises 1548. *Breach of p.* = breach of a p. to marry; also *attrib.* as in *breach-of-p. case*. **2.** *Land of p.* (tr. τὴν γῆν τῆς ἐπαγγελίας, Heb. xi. 9) : = PROMISED *land*; also *fig. Bow of p.*, the rainbow (see Gen. ix. 12–17). **3.** He stood once more before her face, Claiming her p. TENNYSON. **4.** Phr. *To give* (*afford, show*, etc.) *p.*, to afford expectation *of* something, esp. good. *Of great* (*high*, etc.) *p.*, such as leads one to expect future excellence; very promising.

Promise (prǫ·mis), *v.* late ME. [f. prec.] **1.** *trans.* To make promise of; to undertake or engage, by word or writing addressed to another person, to do or refrain from (some specified act), or to give (some specified thing): usu. to the advantage of the person concerned. Often with dative (with or without *to*) of the promisee. **2.** *absol.* or *intr.* To make a promise; to engage to do or give something 1447. **3.** *spec. trans.* To engage to give (e. g. a daughter) in marriage to another; to betroth 1548. **4.** *To p. oneself* (something): to entertain the (pleasing) expectation of 1617. **5.** *colloq.* With *obj. cl.* or *parenthetically*, and with *dat.* of person: To assert confidently, to declare; chiefly in phr. *I p. you* = I assure you, I tell you plainly 1440. **6.** *fig.* To afford ground of expectation of; to lead one to expect (something good or bad); to give pre-indication of 1594. **b.** *absol.* or *intr.* To encourage expectation, to give tokens; usu. with adv., as *fair, well* 1601.

1. They did p. and vowe three thinges in my name *Bk. Com. Prayer, Catechism.* He promis'd to meete me two howres since SHAKS. **3.** Her father..will not p. her to any man, Vntill the elder sister first be wed SHAKS. **5.** You wont get a lamb out of our fold, I. p. you 1777. Magnificent dandies, I p. you, some of us were THACKERAY. **6.** He..promised to be stout when grown up DE FOE. **b.** The weather promising fair 1687. Hence **Pro·missee·**, the person to whom a promise is made. **Pro·miser, -or,** the person who makes a promise.

Promised (prǫ·mist), *ppl. a.* 1538. [f. prec. + -ED[1].] Undertaken to be done or given; of which promise is made.

P. land, the land of Canaan, as promised to Abraham and his posterity (Gen. xii. 7, xiii. 15, etc.); hence applied to heaven or any place of felicity.

Promising (prǫ·misiŋ), *ppl. a.* 1601. [f. as prec. + -ING[2].] **1.** *lit.* That makes a promise or promises 1720. **2.** *fig.* Affording expectation of good; showing signs of future excellence or success; likely to turn out well 1601.

Promissive (promi·siv), *a.* Now *rare.* 1635. [ad. late L. *promissivus* promising, applied to the future tense; see PROMISE and -IVE.] Conveying, implying, or having the character of a promise; promissory.

Promissory (prǫ·misəri), *a.* 1649. [ad. med.L. *promissorius*, f. L. *promissor*; see -ORY[2].] Conveying, containing, or implying a promise; of, pertaining to, or of the nature of a promise. Also *fig.*

P. note, a signed document containing a written promise to pay a stated sum to a particular person (or to the bearer), either at a date specified, or on demand. Hence **Pro·missorily** *adv. rare*, in the way of a promise.

Promontory (prǫ·mǫntəri). 1548. [ad. med.L. *promontorium*, alteration of L. *promunturium* headland, etc.; perh. f. *prominere* to jut forward.] **1.** A point of high land which juts out into the sea or other expanse of water; a headland. Also *transf.* and *fig.* **2.** *Anat.* Applied to certain prominences of the body 1831. **3.** *attrib.* (or *adj.*) Resembling a promontory, projecting, outstanding 1579.

1. Monaco stands on a p. of rock which falls in bold cliffs into the sea 1876. **2.** *P. of the sacrum*, an angular prominence formed by the junction of the last lumbar vertebra with the sacrum. *P. of the tympanum*, a protuberance of the inner ear caused by the projection of the cochlea. **3.** Each bold and p. mound CAMPBELL. Hence **Pro·montoried** *a.* formed into or furnished with a p. or projection.

Promote (prǒmōu·t), *v.* late ME. [f. L. *promot-, promovere*; see PRO-[1] and MOVE *v.*] **I. 1.** *trans.* To advance (a person) *to* a position of honour, dignity, or emolument; *esp.* to raise to a higher grade or office; to prefer. **b.** *Chess.* To raise (a pawn) to the rank of a piece 1803. **2.** To further the growth, development, progress, or establishment of (anything); to further, advance, encourage 1515. **b.** To support actively the passing of (a law or measure); now *spec.* to take the necessary steps for obtaining the passing of (a local or private act of parliament) 1721.

1. Boniface..was promoted to..the Archbishopric of Canterbury 1874. **2.** The Hon[ble] Society for Promoting Christian Knowledge 1698.

II. †**1.** To put forth into notice; to publish; to assert, advance (a claim) –1683. **2.** To cause to move forward in space or extent; to extend. *Obs.* exc. *dial.* 1652. **III.** †**1.** To inform against (a person); to lay an information of (a delinquency, etc.); also *intr.* or *absol.* to act as informer –1623. **2.** *Eccl. Law.* To set in motion (the office of the ordinary or judge) in a criminal suit in an ecclesiastical court; to institute (a suit *ex officio promoto*) by permission of the ordinary 1681. Hence **Promo·table** *a.* that may be or is to be promoted.

Promoter (prǒmōu·təɹ). 1450. [AF. and early mod.E. *promotour* = F. *promoteur*, ad. med.L. *promotor*, agent-n. f. *promovere* to PROMOTE. From 16th c. usu. spelt with *-er*, as if f. PROMOTE *v.* + -ER[1].] **I. 1.** One who or that which promotes or furthers any movement or project. **b.** *Legisl.* One who takes steps for, or actively supports, the passing of a law; now *spec.* of a local or private act of parliament 1741. **c.** *Finance.* One who promotes the formation of a joint-stock company; one who is a party to the preparation or issue of the prospectus; a company-promoter. (Usu. in an opprobrious sense.) 1876. **2.** One who advances another in dignity or position 1425.

1. c. A p., *quoad* p., is not necessarily a bad man 1876.

II. †**a.** One whose business was to prosecute or denounce offenders against the law; a professional accuser, an informer –1670. **b.** *Eccl. Law.* The prosecutor of a suit in an ecclesiastical court 1754.

Promotion (prǒmōu·ʃən). late ME. [a. F., ad. L. *promotionem*, f. *promovere.*] **1.** Advancement in position; preferment. **b.** *Chess.* The elevation of a pawn to the rank of a higher piece 1803. **2.** The action of helping forward; the fact or state of being helped forward; furtherance, advancement 1483. **b.** The getting up of a joint-stock company 1886.

1. Phr. *On p.*, on the way to p., on trial; *to be on one's p.*, to conduct oneself with a view to p. (also *colloq.* to marriage). **2.** Institutions for the p. of learning 1845. Hence **Promo·tional** *a.* of or pertaining to p.

Promotive (prǒmōu·tiv), *a.* 1644. [f. as PROMOTE *v.* + -IVE.] Having the quality of promoting; tending to the promotion (*of* a thing). Hence **Promo·tiveness.**

†**Promo·ve,** *v.* late ME. [ad. L. *promovere*; see PRO-[1] and MOVE *v.*] **1.** *trans.* = PROMOTE *v.* I, 2. –1702. **2.** To move mentally, provoke, incite –1637. **3.** *intr.* To advance, make progress –1655. Hence †**Promo·ver** = PROMOTER I.

Prompt (prǫm^{p}t), *sb.* 1597. [In branch I.

f. PROMPT *v.*; in II. f. PROMPT *a.*] **I.** An act of prompting; instigation; something said to incite to action, or to help the memory. **b.** *Theatr.* The act of the prompter 1784.

Comb.: **p.-bell**, the bell used by a prompter to call an actor; **-book**, a copy of a play prepared for the prompter's use; **-box**, the prompter's box on a stage; **-copy** = *prompt-book*: **-side**, the side of the stage on the actors' left (in England), right (in U.S.).

II. *Commerce* (ellipt. for *p. date, day, time*). A limit of time given for payment of the account for produce purchased; the limit being stated on a note of reminder called a *p.-note*; hence = due-date 1755. **b.** ellipt. for *prompt goods*, goods sold under an agreement as to a p. or time-limit.

Prompt (prǫmᵖt), *a.* (*adv.*) late ME. [a. F., or ad. L. *promptus* brought forth, at hand; pa. pple. of *promere*, f. *pro* PRO-¹ + *emere* to take, to buy.] **1.** Ready in action; quick to act when occasion arises; acting with alacrity; ready and willing. †**b.** Ready in mind; inclined, disposed SHAKS. **2.** Of action, speech, etc.: Characterized by readiness or quickness; done, performed, etc. at once, at the moment, or on the spot 1526. **3.** *Commerce.* For immediate delivery (and payment); also, due at once, or at the date fixed 1879. **4.** as *adv.* Promptly; sharp (*mod.*).

1. A man of p. wytte 1555. Tell him, I am p. To lay my Crowne at 's feete, and there to kneele SHAKS. 2. Such p. eloquence Flowed from their lips, in prose or numerous verse MILT. We deduct 10 per cent for p. cash 1897. 4. She must be called p. at seven o'clock (*mod.*). Hence **Pro·mpt-ly** *adv.*, **-ness.**

Prompt (prǫmᵖt), *v.* ME. [f. prec. or its F. or L. original in sense 'to make prompt or ready to do something'.] **1.** *trans.* To incite to action; to move (a person, etc.) *to do* or *to* something. **2.** To assist (a speaker when at a loss) by suggesting something to be said, or (a reciter) by supplying the words that come next. late ME. †**b.** To put (one) in mind SHAKS. **3.** To urge, suggest, or dictate (a thing); to inspire, give rise to (thought, action) 1602.

1. Defer what your passion promts you to do 1673. *absol.* They migrate..as their necessities p. 1856. 3. Whisp'ring Angels p. her golden dreams POPE.

Prompter (prǫ·mᵖtəɹ). 1440. [f. prec. + -ER¹.] **1.** One who prompts or incites to action. **2.** One who helps a speaker or reciter by prompting him when at a loss 1592. **b.** *spec. Theatr.* A person stationed out of sight of the audience, to prompt any actor at a loss in remembering his part 1604.

Promptitude (prǫ·mᵖtitiūd). 1450. [a. F., or ad. late L. *promptitudo*; see PROMPT *a.* and -TUDE.] Quickness or readiness of action; promptness. †**b.** Inclination –1712.

Assurance of address, and p. of reply JOHNSON.

Promptuary (prǫ·mᵖtiuări), *sb.* Now *rare.* late ME. [ad. late L. *promptuarium* storehouse.] †**1.** A place where supplies, etc. are kept in readiness for use; a storehouse, a repository; the source whence anything is derived –1774. **2.** Applied to a handbook or note-book containing a digest of information, etc. 1577.

Prompture (prǫ·mᵖtiŭɹ). *rare.* 1603. [f. L. ppl. stem *prompt-* (taken in sense of PROMPT *v.*) + -URE.] Prompting.

Promulgate (prǫ·mǒlgeᶦt, prōᵘ-, *formerly* promʊ·lgeᶦt), *v.* 1530. [f. L. *promulgat-*, *promulgare* to expose to public view; see PROMULGE.] *trans.* To make known by public declaration; to publish; *esp.* to disseminate (some creed or belief), or to proclaim (some law, decree, or tidings).

The arrogant pedant does not communicate, but promulgates his knowledge CHESTERF. Hence **Pro·mulgator**, one who promulgates or publishes.

Promulgation (prǫmǒlgēᶦ·ʃən, prōᵘ-). 1604. [a. F., ad. L. *promulgationem*, f. *promulgare* PROMULGE *v.*] The action of promulgating or fact of being promulgated; publication. **b.** *spec.* The official publication of a new law, ordinance, etc., putting it into effect 1618.

b. The p...of the celebrated Edict of Nantes 1867.

Promulge (promʊ·ldʒ), *v. arch.* 1488. [ad. L. *promulgare*; perh. altered from *provulgare* in same sense.] **1.** *trans.* To publish or proclaim formally (a law or decree). Now chiefly an *official archaism.* **2.** To set forth, declare, or teach publicly (a creed, doctrine, opinion, etc.); to bring before the public, to publish (a book, etc.) 1614. Hence **Promu·lger.**

‖**Promuscis** (promʊ·sis). 1576. [L., altered f. *proboscis.*] †**1.** The proboscis or trunk of an elephant –1709. **2.** *Entom.* The proboscis in certain orders of insects; *spec.* that of the Hymenoptera 1658.

‖**Pronaos** (pronēᶦ·ǫs). 1613. [L., a. Gr. πρόναος (-ον) the hall of a temple, prop. adj.; see PRO-² and NAOS.] *Gr.* and *L. Antiq.* The space in front of the body of a temple, enclosed by the portico and the projecting side walls; the vestibule. Also, = NARTHEX.

Pronate (prōᵘ·neᶦt), *v.* 1836. [f. late L. *pronat-*, *pronare* to bend forward, f. *pronus* PRONE *a.*] *Physiol. trans.* To render prone; to put (the hand, or the fore limb) into the prone position; to turn the palm downwards: opp. to SUPINATE. So **Pro·nate** *ppl. a.* bent forward and downward (*rare*).

Pronation (prōᵘnēᶦ·ʃən). 1666. [ad. med.L. *pronationem*, f. *pronare*; see prec.] *Physiol.* The putting of the hand or fore limb into the prone position, i. e. with the palmar surface downwards (or backwards); the position or condition of being pronated: opp. to SUPINATION.

Pronator (prōᵘnēᶦ·tǫɹ). 1727. [a. med.L.; see PRONATE *v.*] *Anat.* A muscle that effects or assists in pronation *spec.* one of two muscles of the fore limb, *p.* (*radii*) *teres* and *p.* (*radii*) *quadratus*: opp. to SUPINATOR.

Prone (prōᵘn), *a.* late ME. [ad. L. *pronus.*] **1.** Having the front or ventral part downwards; bending forward or downward; situated or lying face downwards, or on the belly. Of the hand: with the palm downwards (or backwards); also, of the fore-arm, or the radius, in the corresponding position. 1578. **2.** *loosely* (as if opp. to *erect*): Lying (or so as to lie) flat; in (or into) a horizontal posture; prostrate. Often predicative or quasi-advb., with *lie, fall*, etc. = flat down. 1697. **3.** Having a downward aspect or direction; having a downward slope. Also *loosely*, steeply descending, headlong. Often predic. or quasi-advb. 1627. **4.** *fig.* Directed 'downwards', or towards what is base; grovelling, abject 1645. **5.** Having a natural inclination or tendency to something; inclined, disposed, apt, liable. Const. *to* with sb. or inf. late ME. **6.** Ready in mind (for some action); eager. *Obs.* or *arch.* 1553.

1. A Creature who not p. And Brute as other Creatures,..might erect His Stature MILT. 2. The broken column, vast and p. 1835. 3. From high Olympus p. her flight she bends POPE. 4. Erect in stature, p. in appetite! YOUNG. 5. I am not p. to weeping SHAKS. More p. to concord 1665. Not being p. to inflammation ABERNETHY. 7. *Cymb.* v. iv. 208. Hence **Pro·ne-ly** *adv.*, **-ness.**

Prong (prǫŋ), *sb.* 1492. [Origin obsc.] **1.** An instrument with two, three, or more points or tines; a forked instrument, a fork. **b.** Any forked object, appendage, or part 1846. **2.** Each pointed tine or division of a fork 1697. **b.** A projecting spur of any natural object, as a tooth, a deer's horn, a rock, etc. 1802.

Comb.: **p.-hoe**, an agricultural implement with two curving prongs, used like a hoe; hence **-hoe**, *v. trans.*, to break up or dig with a prong-hoe. Hence **Prong** *v. trans.* to pierce with a p.; to turn up the soil with a p.; to fork; to furnish with prongs or prong-like points.

Prongbuck (prǫ·ŋbʊk). 1834. [f. PRONG *sb.* + BUCK *sb.*¹] = PRONGHORN (strictly, the male).

Pronged (prǫŋd), *a.* 1767. [f. as prec. + -ED².] Furnished with or having prongs.

Pronghorn (prǫ·ŋ,hǭɹn). Short for *prong-horn*(*ed antelope*: see next.

Prong-horned (prǫ·ŋ,hǭɹnd), *a.* 1815. [f. PRONG *sb.* + HORNED *a.*] In *prong-horned antelope*: A North Amer. ruminant (*Antilocapra americana*), resembling a deer, the male of which has hollow deciduous horns with a short 'prong' or snag in front. Also called CABRIE.

Pronominal (prǒnǫ·minăl), *a.* (*sb.*) 1680. [ad. late L. *pronominalis*, f. L. *pronomen* PRONOUN; see -AL.] **A.** *adj.* Of, pertaining to, or of the nature of a pronoun. **B.** *sb.* A pronominal word 1871. Hence **Prono·minalize** *v. trans.* to render p. **Prono·minally** *adv.*

Pronoun (prōᵘ·naun). 1530. [f. PRO-¹ + NOUN, after F. *pronom*, L. *pronomen.*] One of the parts of speech: a word used instead of a noun substantive, to designate an object without naming it, when that which is referred to is known from context or usage, has been already mentioned or indicated, or, being unknown, is the subject or object of inquiry.

Pronounce (prǒnau·ns), *v.* [ME. *pro-n*(*o*)*unce*, a. OF. *pronuncier* (mod.F. *prononcer*) :—late L. *pronunciare* for *pronuntiare* to proclaim, etc., f. *pro* PRO-¹ + *nuntiare.*] **I. 1.** *trans.* To utter, declare, or deliver (a sentence or statement) formally or solemnly; to proclaim authoritatively or officially. **2.** To declare aloud, make known; to tell, narrate, report. *Obs.* or merged in **1.** late ME. **3.** To state definitely; to declare as one's opinion or judgement, or as a known fact. late ME. **4.** *intr.* To make a statement or assertion, now always, an authoritative or definite one; to pass judgement, give one's opinion or decision. Now usu. const. *on* or *upon*; also *for* or *against.* late ME. **b.** *refl.* To declare oneself 1837.

1. The absolucion to be pronounced by the Minister alone *Bk. Com. Prayer.* The pronouncing of Sentence of Death LOCKE. 3. Pronouncing you a Genteel, Fine, Beautiful Woman 1718. The child was pronounced out of danger (*mod.*). 4. The majority ..pronounced in favour of William's undertaking MACAULAY.

II. 1. *trans.* To utter, speak, articulate. late ME. **b.** With ref. to the mode of pronunciation 1620. **2.** To deliver, declaim, in a certain manner. *Obs.* or passing into I. 1. 1560. (All also *absol.*)

1. Language of Man pronounc't By Tongue Of Brute MILT. **b.** The word is sometimes pronounc'd with a *b* 1686. He pronounces English quite different from other foreigners 1775. 2. Speake the Speech I pray you, as I pronounc'd it to you trippingly on the Tongue SHAKS. Hence **Pronou·nceable** *a.* that can be pronounced. **Pronou·nced** *ppl. a.* spoken, articulated; *fig.* clearly expressed, strongly marked; decided. **Pronou·ncedly** *adv.* **Pronou·ncement**, the action or an act of pronouncing; a formal statement; a decision or opinion given. **Pronou·ncer.**

Pronou·ncing, *vbl. sb.* late ME. [-ING¹.] The action of the verb PRONOUNCE.

attrib.: **p. dictionary**, a dictionary in which the received pronunciation of the words is indicated.

Pronto (prǫ·nto), *adv. U.S. slang.* 1918. [Sp. :—L. *promptus* PROMPT.] Quickly.

‖**Pronucleus** (proniū·kliǒs). 1880. [mod. L., f. Gr. πρό PRO-² + NUCLEUS.] *Biol.* A primitive or prior nucleus; in *Zool.* the nucleus of a spermatozoön or of an ovule, before these unite to form the definitive nucleus of the fertilized ovum; in *Bot.* the nucleus of a gamete, which, by coalescing with another of the opposite sex, forms the germ nucleus.

Pronunciamento (pronʊnsiămeˑnto). 1843. [ad. Sp. *pronunciamiento* pronouncement, f. L. *pronuntiare*; see -MENT.] A proclamation, a manifesto; often applied to one issued by insurrectionists, esp. in Spanish-speaking countries.

Pronunciation (prǒnʊnsi,ēᶦ·ʃən). late ME. [ad. L. *pronuntiationem*, f. *pronuntiare* to PRONOUNCE.] **1.** The pronouncing of a word or words; the mode in which a word is pronounced. †**2.** Oratorical utterance; elocution; delivery –1748. †**3.** Declaration, promulgation; a pronouncement –1674.

1. They have utterly neglected the frenche mennes manner of pronounciation, and so rede frenche as theyr fantasy..dyde lede them PALSGR. 2. By P., the Antients understood both Elocution and Action 1748.

Pronunciator (prǒnʊ·nsi,eᶦtəɹ, -nʊ·nʃi,eᶦtəɹ). *rare.* 1846. [a. L.] One who pronounces. So **Pronu·nciatory** *a.* of or pertaining to pronunciation; of the nature of a pronouncement 1806.

‖**Prooemium** (pro,ī·miǒm). 1456. [L., a. Gr. προοίμιον PROEM.] = PROEM *sb.*

Proof (prūf), *sb. Pl.* **proofs.** [ME. *preove*, *proeve preve*, etc., a. OF. *prueve, proeve*, etc. :—late L. *proba* proof, f. *probare* to PROVE.] **I. 1.** That which makes good or proves a statement; evidence sufficient (or contributing) to establish a fact or produce belief. **b.** *Law.*

(*gen.*) Evidence such as determines the judgement of a tribunal. Also *spec.* (*a*) A written document so attested as to form legal evidence. (*b*) A written statement of what a witness is prepared to swear to. (*c*) The evidence given in a particular case, and entered on the court records. 1481. **2.** The action, process, or fact of proving a statement; the action of evidence in convincing the mind; demonstration ME.

1. As a p. of his esteem and confidence 1832. P. positive that he had thought better of his intention 1833. b. Every creditor who has lodged a p. shall be entitled to see and examine the proofs of other creditors 1883. 2. The burthen of p. was of course thrown on the heresiarch KEBLE. Capable of experimental p. 1860.

II. 1. The action or an act of making trial of anything, or the condition of being tried; test, experiment; examination, probation; assay. late ME. **b.** *Arith.* An operation serving to check the correctness of a calculation. late ME. **†2.** The action of experiencing; also, knowledge derived from this; experience -1613. **†3.** That which anything proves to be; the issue, result, effect, fulfilment; esp. in phr. *to come to p.* -1612. **4.** *esp.* The fact, condition, or quality of turning out well or producing good results; thriving; good condition, good quality; goodness, substance. Now only *dial.* 1616. **5.** The testing of cannon or small fire-arms by firing a heavy charge, or by hydraulic pressure 1669. **b.** A place for testing fire-arms or explosives 1760. **6.** Proved or tested power; *orig.* of armour and arms, whence *transf.* and *fig.*: impenetrability, invulnerability (*arch.*) 1456. **7.** The standard of strength of distilled alcoholic liquors (or of vinegar); now, the strength of a mixture of alcohol and water having a specific gravity of 0·91984, and containing 0·495 of its weight, or 0·5727 of its volume, of absolute alcohol. Also *transf.* Spirit of this strength. 1705.

1. The P. of the Pudding is in eating it 1727. Phr. *To bring, put, set,* etc. (something) *in, on, to p.* 3. The proofe is best, when Men keepe their authoritye towardes theire Children, but not theire purse BACON. 6. Phr. *Armour* (etc.) *of p.*; I was cloathed with Armour of p. BUNYAN.

III. 1. A means or instrument for testing. **1.** *Typog.* A trial impression taken from composed type 1563. **2.** *Engraving.* Orig., An impression taken by the engraver from an engraved plate, stone, or block, to examine its state during the progress of his work; now, each of an arbitrary number of careful impressions made from the finished plate before the printing of the ordinary issue, and usu. before the inscription is added (*p. before letter(s)* 1797. **3.** †A coin or medal struck as a test of the die; also, one of a limited number of early impressions of coins struck as specimens 1762. **4.** An instrument or vessel for testing. (*a*) A test-tube. (*b*) An apparatus for testing the strength of gunpowder. 1790. **5.** *Bookbinding.* The rough uncut edges of the shorter or narrower leaves of a book, left in trimming it to show that it has not been cut down 1890.

2. *Artist's* or *engraver's p.*, a p. taken for examination or alteration by the artist or engraver; *signed p.*, an early p. signed by the artist. *Letter* or *lettered p.*, a p. with the signatures of the artist and engraver, and the inscription.

Comb.: **p.-gallon**, a gallon of proof-spirit; **-glass**, a deep cylindrical glass for holding liquids while under test; **-mark**, a mark impressed on a fire-arm to show that it has passed the p.; **-plane**, a small flat or disk-shaped conductor fixed on an insulating handle, used in measuring the electrification of any body; **-press**, a press used for taking proofs of type; **-reader**, one whose business is to read through printer's proofs and mark errors for correction; so **-reading**; **-sheet**, a sheet printed from a forme of type for the purpose of examination and correction; **p. strength** = sense II. 7; **p. vinegar**, vinegar of standard strength. Hence **Proo·fless** *a.* unsupported by p. or evidence.

Proof (prūf), *a.* 1592. [The sb. used as adj., app. by ellipsis of *of.*] **1.** Of tried strength or quality; *esp.* of armour: of tested power of resistance; hence *transf.* and *fig.* strong, impenetrable, invulnerable. Const. *against, to.* **b.** Often as the second element in compounds, as *fire-p., fool-p., water-p.* etc. **2.** Of distilled alcoholic liquors: Of standard strength; cf. PROOF *sb.* II. 7. 1709.

1. Not incorruptible of Faith, not prooff Against temptation MILT.

Proof (prūf), *v.* 1834. [f. PROOF *sb.* or *a.*] **1.** *trans.* To test, prove; to take a proof impression of (an engraved plate, or the like). **2.** To render proof against or impervious to something; *esp.* to render (a fabric) impervious to water, to waterproof 1885.

Proof-spirit. 1790. Spirit of wine, or any distilled alcoholic liquor, of proof strength; see PROOF *sb.* II. 7.

Prop (prǫp), *sb.*[1] 1440. [= MDu. *proppe* vine-prop, support; origin unkn.] A stick, rod, pole, stake, beam, or other rigid support, used to sustain an incumbent weight; esp. when such an appliance is auxiliary, or does not form a structural part of the thing supported. **b.** *spec.* in *Coal-mining*: A piece of timber set upright to support the roof or keep up the strata. (Also *pit-p.*) 1756. **c.** *dial.* or *slang.* The leg; also, the arm extended in boxing; hence, a straight hit (usu. in *pl.*) 1793. **d.** *fig.* Any person or thing that serves as a support or stay; *esp.* one who upholds some institution 1571.

The vine must be set vp with props 1573. d. The boy was the verie staffe of my age, my verie p. SHAKS.

Prop (prǫp), *sb.*[2] 1850. [= MDu. *proppe*, Du. *prop.*] *Thieves' slang.* A scarf-pin.

Prop, *sb.*[3] 1871. *colloq.* or *School slang.* Short for PROPOSITION.

Prop, *sb.*[4] *U.S.* 1833. [Origin unkn.] (Usu. in *pl.*) Cowrie shells, used in a gambling game; hence the game itself.

Prop (prǫp), *sb.*[5] 1865. *Theatr. slang.* Short for PROPERTY *sb.* 3. (Usu. *pl.*)

Prop (prǫp), *v.* 1492. [f. PROP *sb.*[1]] **1.** *trans.* To support or keep from falling by or as by means of a prop; to hold up: said both of the prop and of the person who places it. Also with *up.* **2.** *fig.* To support, sustain, esp. a failing cause or institution 1549. **3.** To hit straight; to knock down (*slang*) 1851.

1. To p. the Ruins, lest the Fabrick fall DRYDEN. Propt on a staff, a beggar old and bare POPE. 2. *Hen. VIII*, I. i. 59.

Propædeutic (prōupīdiū·tik), *a.* and *sb.* 1836. [f. Gr. προπαιδεύειν to teach beforehand, f. πρό PRO-[2] + παιδεύειν; see PÆDEUTICS.] **A.** *adj.* Pertaining to or of the nature of preliminary instruction; preliminarily educational 1849. **B.** *sb.* **1.** A subject or study which forms an introduction to an art or science, or to more advanced study generally 1836. **2.** *pl.* **Propædeutics.** The body of principles or rules introductory to any art, science, or subject of special study; preliminary learning 1842. Hence **Propædeu·tical** *a.* = A.

Propagable (prǫ·păgăb'l), *a.* 1651. [f. L. *propagare* to PROPAGATE + -ABLE.] Capable of being propagated. Hence **Pro:pagabi·lity, Pro·pagableness.**

Propagand (prǫpăgæ·nd), *v.* 1901. [Back-formation from next.] *intr.* To carry on a propaganda.

Propaganda (prǫpăgæ·ndă). 1718. [a. It. *propaganda*, from the mod.L. title *Congregatio de propaganda fide*; see sense 1.] **1.** (More fully, *Congregation* or *College of the P.*) A committee of Cardinals of the R. C. Church having the care and oversight of foreign missions, founded in 1622. **2.** Any association, systematic scheme, or concerted movement for the propagation of a particular doctrine or practice. Sometimes erroneously treated as a plural. 1842.

Propagandism (prǫpăgæ·ndiz'm). 1818. [f. as prec. + -ISM.] The practice of a propaganda; systematic work at propagating any opinion, creed, or practice.

Propagandist (prǫpăgæ·ndist), *sb.* (*a.*) 1829. [f. as prec. + -IST.] **1.** A member or agent of a propaganda; one who devotes himself to the propagation of some creed or doctrine. **2.** *spec.* A missionary or convert of the R. C. Congregation of the Propaganda 1833. **B.** *adj.* Given or inclined to propagandism 1856.

Propagandize (prǫpăgæ·ndəiz), *v.* 1844. [f. as prec. + -IZE.] *trans.* To disseminate (principles) by organized effort; to subject to a propaganda. Also *intr.*

Propagate (prǫ·păgēit), *v.* 1570. [f. ppl. stem of L. *propagare* to multiply (plants) by means of layers, cogn. w. *propago, -aginem* a layer, f. PRO-[1].] **1.** *trans.* To multiply specimens of (a plant, animal, disease, etc.) by any process of natural reproduction from the parent stock; to procreate, reproduce, breed; to cause to breed; *refl.* to reproduce its kind. **b.** *absol.*, or *intr.* for *refl.* To breed, to produce offspring; to reproduce its kind 1601. **c.** *transf.* (*trans.*) To hand down from one generation to another; to reproduce in the offspring 1601. **2. a.** *fig.* To cause to increase or multiply 1592. **b.** To extend (anything material or immaterial) 1647. **c.** *intr.* for *refl.* To increase, multiply itself 1670. **3.** *trans.* To spread from person to person, or from place to place; to disseminate, diffuse (a statement, belief, practice, etc.) 1600. **4.** To extend the action or operation of; to transmit, spread, convey (motion, light, sound, etc.) in some direction, or through some medium 1656.

1. Men..are often content to p. a race of slaves GOLDSM. c. *All's Well* II. i. 200. 2. a. *Rom. & Jul.* I. i. 193. c. As Heresie did p. and increase 1670. 3. To p. the Gospel in foreign parts 1725. Men who made and propagated false rumours 1868. 4. The manner in which an earthquake is propagated from place to place HERSCHEL. Hence **Pro·pagative** *a.* having the quality of propagating; tending to propagation. **Pro·pagator,** one who or that which propagates.

Propagation (prǫpăgēi·ʃən). 1450. [a. F., or ad. L. *propagationem*, f. *propagare* to PROPAGATE.] **1.** The action of propagating; procreation, generation, reproduction. **†2.** *fig.* Increase; enlargement; extension in space or time -1741. **3.** Dissemination, diffusion, esp. of some principle, belief, or practice 1588. **4.** Transmission of some action or form of energy, as motion, light, sound, etc. 1656.

1. Of þe erth & of þe cley we haue owur propagacyon 1450. 2. *Meas. for M.* I. ii. 154. 3. The p. of error MILL. 4. The Nature and P. of Heat 1804.

Propane (prōu·pēin). 1866. [f. PROP(IONIC + -ANE 2.] *Chem.* The paraffin or saturated hydrocarbon C_3H_8, the third member of the series C_nH_{2n+2}; a colourless gas occurring in petroleum.

Propargyl (propā·ɹdʒil). 1866. [f. PROP(IONIC + *arg-* (one of its proportions of hydrogen being characteristically replaceable by silver, *argentum*) + -YL.] *Chem.* A hydrocarbon radical, C_3H_3, = $CH \equiv C{\cdot}CH_2$.

Propel (prŏpe·l), *v.* 1658. [ad. L. *propellere* to drive before one, f. *pro* PRO-[1] + *pellere.*] *trans.* To drive forward or onward; to impart an onward motion to. **b.** *fig.* To give a forward impulse to 1762.

Treatise on propelling Vessels by Steam 1816.

Propellent (prŏpe·lĕnt), *a.* and *sb.* 1644. [ad. L. *propellentem*; see PROPEL and -ENT.] **A.** *adj.* Propelling, driving forward; *spec.* (of an explosive) Adapted for propelling a bullet, etc. from a fire-arm. **B.** *sb.* Something that propels; *fig.* an incentive, a stimulus; *spec.* an explosive for use in fire-arms 1814.

Propeller (prŏpe·ləɹ). 1780. [f. PROPEL + -ER[1].] **1.** *gen.* One who or that which propels. **2.** *spec.* An appliance or mechanism for propelling a ship, aeroplane, or other vessel; most commonly a revolving shaft with blades, often set at an angle and twisted like the thread of a screw 1809. **b.** *transf.* A steamer with a screw propeller 1860.

†**Prope·nd,** *v.* 1545. [ad. L. *propendere* to hang forward or down, f. *pro* PRO-[1] + *pendere.*] **1.** *intr.* To hang or lean forward or downward; to incline in a particular direction; of a scale, to weigh down, to preponderate -1691. **2.** *fig.* To incline, be disposed, tend (*to* or *towards* something, or *to do* something) -1844.

2. Some sports..more p. to be ill than well used FULLER.

Propendent (prope·ndĕnt), *a.* 1593. [ad. L. *propendentem*; see PROPEND and -ENT.] Hanging forward, outward, or downward.

Propene (prōu·pīn). 1866. [f. as PROPANE + -ENE.] *Chem.* The olefine C_3H_6, more commonly called PROPYLENE.

Propense (prŏpe·ns), *a.* Now *rare.* 1528. [ad. L. *propensus* hanging toward; pa. pple. of *propendere*; see PROPEND.] Having an inclination, bias, or propensity to something;

disposed, prone; ready, willing. Const. *to* with *sb.* or *inf.* †b. Biased in favour of some person, cause, etc.; favourable, partial -1797.

He appears always p. towards the side of mercy JOHNSON. Hence **Prope·nse·ly** *adv.*, **-ness** (now *rare*).

Propension (prǒpe·nʃən). Now *rare.* 1530. [ad. L. *propensionem* inclination, f. *propendere*; see PROPEND.] 1. = PROPENSITY. †2. Tendency to move in some direction or to take some position; inclination, as of the scale of a balance -1709.

1. I feele A strong p. in my braine, to court Sleepe 1640. 2. He defines Gravity to be a Natural p. towards the Centre of the Earth HOBBES.

Propensity (prǒpe·nsĭti). 1570. [f. as prec. + -ITY.] The quality or character of being 'propense' or inclined to something; inclination, tendency, bent. Const. *to, towards*, (rarely *for, of*) with *sb.*, or *to* with *inf.*

A natural p. in us to do evil DE FOE.

Propenyl (prōu·pĭnil). 1866. [f. PROPENE + -YL.] *Chem.* The hypothetical hydrocarbon radical C_3H_5, the trivalent hydrocarbon radical of the propyl or trityl series.

Proper (prǫ·pəɹ), *a.* (*adv.*, *sb.*) [ME. *propre*, a. F. *propre*:—L. *proprius* one's own.] A. *adj.* I. 1. Belonging to oneself or itself; (one's or it's) own; owned as property; intrinsic, inherent. Usu. preceded by a possessive; sometimes also by *own. arch.* exc. in special connexions. 2. Belonging or relating to the person or thing in question distinctively or exclusively; special, particular, distinctive; peculiar, restricted; individual; of its own. Const. *to*. ME. b. *Gram.* Applied to a name or noun (written with an initial capital letter) which is used to designate a particular individual object. Opp. to COMMON *a.* III. 2. ME. 3. *Her.* Represented in the natural colouring, not in any of the conventional tinctures 1572.

1. With his own propre Swerd he was slayn 1400. To judge.. with my p. eyes 1877. Phr. *P. motion* (Astron.), that part of the apparent motion of a heavenly body (now usu. of a 'fixed' star) supposed to be due to its actual movement in space. 2. Local Infirmities p. unto certain Regions SIR T. BROWNE. *P. psalms, lessons*, etc., in liturgies, those specially appointed for a particular day or season. b. P. names have strictly no meaning: they are mere marks for individual objects MILL.

II. 1. Strictly belonging or applicable; accurate, exact, correct 1449. 2. To which the name accurately belongs; strictly so called; genuine, real; normal. In mod. use often following its noun. late ME. b. *Arith. P. fraction*, a fraction whose value is less than unity, the numerator being less than the denominator 1656. 3. Answering fully to the description; thorough, complete, out-and-out. Now *arch.* or *dial.* late ME. 4. Such as a thing of the kind should be; excellent, admirable, of high quality. Now *arch.* or *vulgar.* late ME. b. Of good character or standing; respectable, worthy. *Obs.* or merged in III. 2 b. 1597. 5. Of goodly appearance or make; 'fine', good-looking, handsome. *arch.* and *dial.* late ME.

1. As I was walking along the common—blown along would be the properer phrase 1828. 2. The earths p. do not unite with oxygen 1807. 3. Old Markham seems in a p. taking 1853. 4. She had a p. wytte & coulde both reade and wryte 1548. b. A p. Gentlewoman SHAKS. 5. These Indians..were very p., tall and lusty men 1648.

III. 1. Adapted to some purpose or requirement; fit, apt, suitable; fitting, befitting; *esp.* appropriate to the circumstances; right ME. 2. In conformity with the demands or usages of society; decent, decorous, respectable, 'correct' 1738. b. *transf.* of persons. (Somewhat *colloq.*) 1818.

1. Choose not alone a p. mate, But p. time to marry COWPER. 2. b. You hear very p. people..cry out against some of us 1880.

B. *adv.* Properly. 1. Excellently; genuinely, thoroughly. Now *dial.*, *vulgar*, or *slang.* 1450. †2. Suitably, appropriately -1774.

1. 'Had 'em that time—had 'em p.!' said he 1898.

C. *sb.* or quasi-*sb.* †1. That which is one's own; private possession, private property -1550. 2. *Eccl.* An office, or some part of an office, as a psalm, etc., appointed for a particular occasion or season. Opp. to COMMON *sb.* 5. 1548.

1. How moche thou mayste despende of thyn owyn propyr 1422. †*In p.*, in individual possession; as one's own (opp. to *in common*); They haue their lands and gardens in p. PURCHAS. Hence **Pro·per·ly** *adv.*, **-ness** (now *rare*).

Properispome (propeˑrispōᵘm), *a.* and *sb.* 1818. [abbrev. of **properispo·menon** (also in use) = Gr. προπερισπώμενον, neut. pr. pple. pass. of προπερισπᾶν, f. πρό PRO-² + περισπᾶν; see PERISPOME.] *Gr. Gram.* A. *adj.* Having a circumflex accent on the penultimate syllable. B. *sb.* A word so accented.

Propertied (prǫ·pəɹtid), *a.* 1606. [f. next + -ED².] †1. Having a specified property, quality, nature, or disposition -1633. 2. Possessed of, owning, or holding property 1760.

2. The p. and satisfied classes M. ARNOLD.

Property (prǫ·pəɹti), *sb.* [ME. *proprete*, modification of OF. *proprieté*, ad. L. *proprietatem*, f. *proprius* own, proper.] 1. The condition of being owned by or belonging to some person or persons; hence, the fact of owning a thing; the holding of something as one's own; the right (*esp.* the exclusive right) to the possession, use, or disposal of anything; ownership, proprietorship. 2. That which one owns; a possession or possessions collectively, (one's) wealth or goods ME. b. A piece of land owned; a landed estate 1719. 3. *Theatr.* Any portable article, as an article of costume or furniture, used in acting a play; a stage requisite. Chiefly *pl.* late ME. †4. *fig.* A mere means to an end; an instrument, a tool, a cat's-paw -1764. 5. An attribute or quality belonging to a thing or person ME. b. *Logic.* Reckoned as one of the PREDICABLES 1551. †6. Usu. with *the*: The characteristic quality of a person or thing; character, nature -1703.

2. They..had no p., but all was in commune 1526. The personal p. of 24 English Bishops 1838. Real p. always falls in value in the vicinity of barracks COBDEN. b. Small properties, much divided 1792. 3. I wil draw a bil of properties, such as our play wants SHAKS. 5. The philosophers had suche..desyre to knowe the natures & propertees of thynges 1526. He hath this p. of an honest man, that his word is as good as his hand FULLER. b. P...may perhaps be best described as any quality which is common to the whole of a class, but is not necessary to mark out that class from other classes 1870. 6. It is the p. of error to contradict it self 1651.

Comb.: **p. qualification**, a qualification for office (e.g. of a member of parliament), or for the exercise of a right (e.g. of voting), based on the possession of p. to a certain amount; **p. tax**, a direct tax levied on p. b. In sense 3 (*Theatr.*): **p.-man**, **-master**, a man who furnishes and has the charge of stage-properties at a theatre; **-room**, the room in which the properties are kept.

Pro·perty, *v.* *Obs.* or *rare.* 1595. [f. prec.] †1. *trans.* To make a 'property' or tool of, to use for one's own ends -1758. 2. To make one's own property, to appropriate 1607.

1. *John* v. ii. 79. 2. His large Fortune..Subdues and properties to his loue and tendance All sorts of hearts SHAKS.

Prophecy (prǫ·fĭsi). ME. [a. OF. *profecie*, ad. late L. *prophetia*, *-ecia*, a. Gr. προφητεία prophecy, f. προφήτης.] 1. The action, function, or faculty of a prophet; divinely inspired utterance. 2. The spoken, or esp., the written utterance of a prophet, or of the prophets ME. 3. The foretelling of future events; orig. as an inspired action; extended to foretelling by any means; an instance of this ME. 4. The interpretation and expounding of Scripture or of divine mysteries; applied in the 16th and 17th centuries, and sometimes later to exposition of the Scriptures, esp. in conferences, and to preaching. late ME.

1. P., or the authorized declaration of God's will KEBLE. 2. The 53rd Chapter of the Prophesie of Isaiah BURNET. 3. Until the prophesies of Merlin should be fulfilled 1584. Of all forms of error p. is the most gratuitous 1897.

Prophesier (pro·fĭsəi,əɹ). 1477. [f. next + -ER¹.] One who or that which prophesies; *esp.* one who predicts or foreshows.

Prophesy (prǫ·fĭsəi), *v.* [Late ME. a. OF. *prophecier*, *-phesier*, f. *prophecie* PROPHECY.] 1. *intr.* To speak by (or as by) divine inspiration, or in the name of a deity; to speak as a prophet. b. *spec.* To foretell future events. late ME. c. In the Apostolic churches, To interpret or expound the Scriptures, to utter divine mysteries (as moved by the Holy Spirit); hence, later, to preach the Gospel. late ME. 2. *trans.* To utter by (or as by) divine inspiration; *esp.* so to announce (a future event); to predict, to foretell. late ME. †b. *fig.* To foreshow SHAKS.

1. Sone of man, prophecy thou, and sey, Thes thingis seith the Lord God WYCLIF *Ezek.* xxx. 2. b. Half-extinguished words, which prophesied of change SHELLEY. 2. I p. you will not succeed better than I have 1802. b. Me thought thy very gate did prophesie A Royall Noblenesse *Lear* v. iii. 177.

Prophet (prǫ·fĕt). [ME. *prophete*, *-fete*, a. F. *prophète*, ad. L. *propheta*, ad. Gr. προφήτης; f. πρό forth, before, for + -φητης speaker, f. φάναι.] 1. One who speaks for God or for any deity, as the inspired revealer or interpreter of his will; *loosely*, one who claims to have this function; an inspired or quasi-inspired teacher. †b. As tr. L. *vates* or *poeta*, an 'inspired' bard -1840. c. Sometimes applied to those who preach or 'hold forth' in a religious meeting 1560. d. *fig.* (In non-religious sense.) The accredited spokesman, proclaimer, or preacher of some principle, cause, or movement 1848. 2. *spec. The P.*: a. Mohammed, the founder of Islam 1615. b. Applied by (or after) the Mormons to the founder of their system, and his successors 1844. 3. *pl.* The prophetical writers or writings of the Old Testament. late ME. 4. One who foretells what is going to happen; a prognosticator ME. b. An omen, a portent 1591. c. *slang.* One who predicts the result of a race; a tipster 1884.

1. Elisee þe profete WYCLIF. A certayne sorserer, a falce p. which was a iewe TINDALE *Acts* xiii. 6. 4. I protest, I know no more than a p. what is to come H. WALPOLE. b. 1 *Hen. VI*, III. ii. 32. Hence **Pro·phetess**, a female p.; *spec.* a woman who foretells events. **Pro·phethood**. **Pro·phetship**.

Prophetic (prǒfe·tik), *a.* 1595. [a. F. *prophétique*, or ad. late L. *propheticus*, a. Gr. προφητικός; see PROPHET and -IC.] 1. Of, pertaining or proper to a prophet or prophecy; having the character or function of a prophet 1604. 2. Characterized by, containing, or of the nature of prophecy; predictive, 1595. 3. Spoken of in prophecy; predicted 1651.

1. Till old experience do attain To something like P. strain MILT. Phr. *P. present, perfect*, the present or perfect tense used to express a certain future. 2. Now heare me speake with a propheticke spirit SHAKS. So **Prophe·tical** *a.* 1456, **-ly** *adv.*

Prophetism (prǫ·fĕtiz'm). 1701. [f. PROPHET + -ISM.] The action or practice of a prophet or prophets; the system or principles of the Hebrew prophets.

Prophylactic (prǫfilæ·ktik), *a.* and *sb.* 1574. [ad. Gr. προφυλακτικός; see PRO-².] *Med.* A. *adj.* That defends from or tends to prevent disease; also *transf.* preservative, precautionary. B. *sb.* A p. medicine 1642. So †**Prophyla·ctical** *a.*, **-ly** *adv.*

‖**Prophylaxis** (prǫfilæ·ksis). 1842. [mod. L., f. Gr. πρό PRO-² + φύλαξις a guarding, after prec.] *Med.* The preventive treatment of disease. Also *transf.* So **Prophylaxy** (prǫ·filæksi).

Propine (prōᵘ·pəin), *sb.* 1866. [f. as PROPANE + -INE⁵ 2.] *Chem.* = ALLYLENE.

Propine (propəi·n), *v.* Chiefly *Sc.* *Obs.* or *arch.* late ME. [ad. L. *propinare* to pledge; ad. Gr. προπίνειν, lit. to drink before or above, f. πρό PRO-² + πίνειν.] 1. *trans.* To offer or give to drink; to present with (drink). 2. To offer for acceptance; to present; to put before one, propose 1450. 3. To present (a person) *with* something 1450.

Propinquity (propi·ŋkwĭti). [Late ME. *propinquite*, a. obs. F. *propinquité*, ad. L. *propinquitas*, *-tatem*, f. *propinquus* near, deriv. of *prope* near.] Nearness, closeness, proximity: a. in space: Neighbourhood 1460. b. in blood or relationship: Near or close kinship. late ME. c. in nature, belief, etc.: Similarity, affinity 1586. d. in time: Near approach, nearness 1646.

Propio-, propion-. *Chem.* A formative derived from PROPIONIC, entering into the names of compounds related to propionic acid.

Propionic (prōᵘpiǫ·nik), *a.* 1851. [ad. F. *propionique*, f. Gr. πρό PRO-² + πίων fat, in ref. to its being the first in order of the fatty acids.] *Chem.* **P. acid**, the monatomic monobasic acid of the propyl or tri-carbon series, the third acid of the fatty series, $C_3H_6O_2$.

Propitiable (prŏpi·ʃi,ăb'l), *a.* 1557. [ad. L. *propitiabilis*; see next and -ABLE.] Capable of being propitiated or made propitious.

Propitiate (prŏpi·ʃi,ēɪt), *v.* 1645. [f. ppl. stem of L. *propitiare* to render favourable (f. *propitius*); see -ATE [3].] *trans.* To render propitious or favourably inclined; to appease, conciliate (one offended).

That they [the Gods] can be propitiated..is not to be allowed or admitted for an instant JOWETT. So **Propi·tiator**, one who propitiates.

Propitiation (prŏpiʃi,ēɪ·ʃən). late ME. [ad. late L. *propitiationem*, f. *propitiare* to PROPITIATE.] The action or an act of propitiating; appeasement, conciliation; atonement, expiation. **b.** A propitiatory offering or sacrifice (*arch.*) 1552.

b. He is the propiciation for our synnes *Bk. Com. Prayer, Communion.*

Propitiatory (prŏpi·ʃiătəri), *sb.* and *a.* ME. [As sb. ad. late L. *propitiatorium*, rendering Gr. ἱλαστήριον; sb. use of neut. sing. of late L. *propitiatorius* adj. (whence the adj. B.), f. *propitiator*; see -ORY.] **A.** *sb.* **1.** The mercy-seat. **b.** *transf.* and *fig.*, esp. applied to Christ 1549. **†2.** *Theol.* A propitiation; an offering of atonement; esp. said of Christ –1726. **B.** *adj.* That propitiates or tends to propitiate; of or pertaining to propitiation; appeasing, atoning, conciliating, expiatory; ingratiating 1551.

Looking about him with a p. smile DICKENS.

Propitious (prŏpi·ʃəs), *a.* 1447. [a. OF. *propicius*, *-eux*, f. L. *propitius* see -OUS.] **1.** Disposed to be favourable; favourably inclined; gracious. **b.** Indicative of, or characterized by, favour; of favourable import; boding well 1586. **2.** Presenting favourable conditions; favourable, advantageous 1601.

1. Astrology considers some of the Planets in their Influences as p. to Mankind 1681. **b.** The auspices were not p. 1734. **2.** The circumstances were p. to the designs of an usurper GIBBON. Hence **Propi·tious·ly** *adv.*, **-ness.**

‖**Propolis** (prǫ·pŏlis). 1601. [L. (Plin.) a. Gr. πρόπολις a suburb, also bee-glue, f. πρό PRO- [2] + πόλις.] A red, resinous, aromatic substance collected by bees from the viscid buds of trees, as the horse-chestnut; used to stop up crevices, and fix the combs to the hives; bee-glue.

Propone (prŏpōᵘ·n), *v.* Now only *Sc.* late ME. [ad. L. *proponere* to put or set forth, f. *pro* PRO- [1] + *ponere.*] **1.** *trans.* To propound as a question or matter for decision. **†2.** To set before any one as an example or aim; to propose or offer as a reward –1653.

Proponent (prŏpōᵘ·nĕnt), *a.* and *sb.* 1588. [ad. L. *proponentem*, *proponere*; see prec.] **A.** *adj.* That brings forward or proposes 1687. **B.** *sb.* One who brings forward a proposition or argument; a propounder, a proposer 1588.

‖**Propontis** (propǫ·ntis). 1642. [L., a. Gr. προποντίς, lit. 'the fore-sea', f. πρό PRO- [2] + πόντος a sea, spec. the Euxine.] Ancient name of the Sea of Marmora. Hence **Propo·ntic** *a.* of or pertaining to the P.; *sb.* the Propontic Sea, Sea of Marmora.

Proportion (prŏpōᵊ·ɹʃən), *sb.* [Late ME. *proporcioun*, a. F. *proportion*, ad. L. *proportionem*, app. from *pro portione* for or in respect of (his or its) share; see PORTION.] **I.** *gen.* **1.** A portion or part in its relation to the whole; a comparative part, a share; *occas.*, a portion, division, part. **2.** The relation existing between things or magnitudes as to size, quantity, number, etc.; comparative relation, ratio. Also *fig.* late ME. **3.** *transf.* A relation, other than that of quantity, between things; comparison; analogy 1538. **4.** (= *due* or *proper p.*) Due relation of one part to another; such relation of size, etc., between things or parts of a thing as renders the whole harmonious; balance, symmetry, agreement, harmony. late ME. **5.** Size or extent, relatively to some standard; also *fig.* extent, degree. late ME. **b.** Now only in *pl.* Dimensions 1638. **†6.** The action of making proportionate; proportionate estimate, reckoning, or adjustment –1605. **7.** Configuration, form, shape; a figure or image of anything. Now only *poet.* late ME.

1. Therefore let our proportions for these Warres Be soone collected SHAKS. The sea which covers so large a p. of the earth's surface HUXLEY. **2.** The p. of Births to Burials BENTLEY. Phr. *In p.*; The rooms large, but some of them not lofty in p. H. WALPOLE. **4.** Let thy recreations..bear p. with thine age FULLER. *Out of p.*, having no due relation in size, amount, etc. (usu. implying excess). **5. b.** The ice-crags..seemed of gigantic proportions TYNDALL. **6.** *Macb.* I. iv. 19.

II. In techn. senses. **1.** *Math.* An equality of ratios, esp. of geometrical ratios; a relation among quantities such that the quotient of the first divided by the second is equal to that of the third divided by the fourth. late ME. **b.** *Arith.* The rule or process by which, three quantities being given, a fourth may be found which is in the same ratio to the third as the second is to the first 1542. **2.** *Mus.* Ratio (of duration of notes, rates of vibration, lengths of strings, etc.): = sense I. 2, in specific applications 1609. Hence **Propo·rtionless** *a.* that is wanting in p.; disproportionate.

Proportion (prŏpōᵊ·ɹʃən), *v.* [Late ME. a. OF. *proporcioner*, ad. med.L. *proportionare*, f. *proportio*; see prec.] **1.** *trans.* To adjust in proper proportion *to* something else; to make proportionate. Const. *to*, *with.* 1449. **2.** To adjust the proportions of; to fashion, form, shape. *Obs.* exc. in *ppl. a.* late ME. **†3.** To be in proportion to; to correspond to, to equal –1666. **†4.** To divide into proportionate parts; to mete out –1724. **†5.** To estimate the relative proportions of –1711.

1. The punishment should be proportioned to the offence MILL. **3.** *Hen. V*, III. vi. 134. **4.** Proportioning the Glory of a Battle among the whole Army STEELE. Hence **Propo·rtioned** *ppl. a.* adjusted in due proportion, measure, or relation to something else; formed with 'proportions', composed; also in *comb.* as *well-proportioned.* **Propo·rtionment**, the act or fact of proportioning.

Proportionable (prŏpōᵊ·ɹʃənăb'l), *a.* late ME. [f. (ult.) med.L. *proportionare* (see PROPORTION *v.*) + *-abilis* -ABLE.] **1.** That is in due proportion; corresponding, agreeable, commensurate, proportional. **2.** Well-proportioned; symmetrical. *Obs.* or *arch.* 1625.

1. For vs to leuy power P. to th' enemy, is all impossible SHAKS. **2.** Nature having done her part in giving him p. lineaments 1625. Hence **Propo·rtionableness. Propo·rtionably** *adv.*

Proportional (prŏpōᵊ·ɹʃənăl), *a.* and *sb.* late ME. [ad. L. *proportionalis*; see PROPORTION *sb.* and -AL.] **A.** *adj.* **1.** Of or pertaining to proportion; relative; also, used in obtaining proportions 1561. **2.** That is in proportion, or in due proportion; corresponding, esp. in degree or amount. late ME. **3.** *Math.* That is in proportion (sense II. 1); having the same or a constant ratio 1570.

1. *P. compasses*, compasses having two opposite pairs of legs turning on a common pivot, which is adjustable so as to vary the distance apart of the points at each end in any desired ratio. **2.** P. Representation finds little favour with the caucuses 1884. **3.** The heat is p. to the square of the velocity TYNDALL.

B. *sb.* **1.** *Math.* One of the terms of a proportion 1570. **†2.** *Chem.* A combining equivalent; the proportional weight of an atom or molecule –1855. Hence **Propo·rtionalism,** *Chem.* the system, doctrine, or fact of the combination of elements in definite proportions; the theory or practice of p. representation. **Proportiona·lity,** the quality, character, or fact of being p. **Propo·rtionally** *adv.*

Proportionate (prŏpōᵊ·ɹʃənĕt), *a.* late ME. [ad. late L. *proportionatus* proportioned, f. *proportionem* + *-atus*; see -ATE [2].] Proportioned; that is in due proportion. **†b.** Adequately adapted –1680.

No more is your giuing p. to my liking 1576. Hence **Propo·rtionate·ly** *adv.*, **-ness.**

Proportionate (prŏpōᵊ·ɹʃəneᶦt), *v.* 1570. [f. prec.; see -ATE [3].] **1.** *trans.* = PROPORTION *v.* 1. **†2.** = PROPORTION *v.* 3. –1666.

Proposal (prŏpōᵘ·zăl). 1653. [f. next + -AL.] **†1.** The action, or an act, of putting before the mind; setting forth, propounding, statement –1678. **2.** *spec.* An offer of marriage 1749. **3.** The action, or an act, of proposing something to be done; an offer to do something; a scheme or plan proposed 1657. **b.** *U.S.* An offer or tender 1914.

2. Dearest Mamma,—I have had a p.! 1900. **3.** Proposals for doing the whole work 1748.

Propose (prŏpōᵘ·z), *v.* ME. [a. F. *proposer*, f. *pro-* PRO- [1] + *poser* POSE *v.*[1]; substituted for L. *proponere.*] **1.** *trans.* To put forward for consideration, discussion, solution, etc.; to put before the mind; to state, propound. late ME. **†b.** To set before one's mind as something to be expected; to anticipate –1749. **c.** To put forward as something to be attained 1601. **†d.** To contemplate as a supposition SHAKS. **2.** To put forward for acceptance 1586. **b.** *absol.* To make an offer of marriage (*colloq.*) 1764. **3.** *trans. spec.* with an action as obj. **a.** To lay before another or others as something which one offers to do or wishes to be done 1647. **b.** To put before one's own mind as something that one is going to do; to design, purpose, intend 1500. **c.** *absol.* To make a proposal or motion; to form a design or purpose ME. **†4.** *intr.* To carry on a discussion; to confer, converse, discourse SHAKS.

1. Nature herself does not give an answer to the riddles which she proposes 1892. **b.** *Tr. & Cr.* II. ii. 146. **c.** *Ham.* III. ii. 204. **2.** P. the Oath my Lord SHAKS. I p. the head boy..for chief 1871. The second part of his duty was to p. the health of the honorary Fellows 1892. **3. a.** The king proposed the marching to London DE FOE. **b.** He had proposed to conquer Jerusalem 1853. **c.** Prov. *Man proposes, God disposes.* **4.** *Much Ado* III. i. 3. Hence **Propo·ser**, one who proposes.

Proposition (prǫpŏzi·ʃən). [ME. *proposicioun*, a. F. *proposition*, ad. L. *propositionem* a setting forth, etc., f. *proponere*; see PROPONE.] **1.** The action of setting forth or presenting to view or perception; presentation, exhibition. Now *rare.* late ME. **†2.** The action of offering for acceptance; an offer –1649. **3.** The action of propounding something, or that which is propounded; something proposed for discussion, or as a basis of argument; *spec.* an introductory part of a speech or literary work in which is set forth the subject to be treated. Now *rare* or *Obs.* ME. **†b.** A question proposed for solution; a problem –1600. **4.** The making of a statement about something; a statement, an assertion. (*b*) In *Logic*, a form of words in which something (the PREDICATE) is affirmed or denied of something (the SUBJECT), the relation between them being expressed by the COPULA. late ME. **b.** *spec.* Either of the premisses of a syllogism; *esp.* the major premiss (opp. to ASSUMPTION 9). Now *rare* or *Obs.* 1551. **5.** *Math.* A formal statement of a truth to be demonstrated (*theorem*) or of an operation to be performed (*problem*); in common use often including the demonstration 1570. **6.** The action of proposing something to be done; something put forward as a scheme or plan of action; a proposal. late ME. **b.** A problem, task, or undertaking (*transf.* a person) to be dealt with (orig. *U.S.*) 1893.

2. *Tr. & Cr.* I. iii. 3. **3.** The custom of beginning all Poems, with a P. of the whole work COWLEY. **b.** *A.Y.L.* III. ii. 246. **6.** When the protector had harde the proposicion, he loked very strangely therat HALL. Hence **Proposi·tional** *a.*, **-ly** *adv.*

Propound (prŏpau·nd), *v.* 1537. [Later form of PROPONE; cf. COMPOUND.] **1.** *trans.* To set forth, propose, or offer for consideration, discussion, acceptance, or adoption; to put forward as a question for solution. **b.** *Eccl. Law.* To bring forward (an allegation, etc.) in a cause 1685. **c.** *absol.* or *intr.* To make a proposal 1570. **2.** *trans.* To propose or nominate for an office or position, as a member of a society, etc. Now *U.S.* 1573. **†3.** To set before one as an example, reward, aim, etc. –1719. **†4.** To propose (to do or the doing of something) –1709. **†b.** To purpose (something) –1692. **5.** *Law.* To put forth or produce (a will, or other testamentary document) before the proper authority, in order to have its legality established 1753.

1. They propounded Articles of peace and friendship 1634. To answer such questions as they shall p. to you 1720. This theory is formally propounded 1836. **4.** After dinner propounds to me my lending him 500*l.* PEPYS. Hence **Propou·nder,** one who propounds, *esp.* in sense 1.

Proprætor (prōᵘ,prī·tǫɹ). 1579. [a. L., orig. *pro prætore* (one acting) for the prætor.] *Rom. Antiq.* A magistrate who after holding the office of prætor was given the administration of a province not under military control, with the authority of a prætor. Also, one who acted in place of a prætor. Hence **Propræto·rial, Propræto·rian** *adjs.*

Proprietary (prŏprəi·ĕtări), *sb.* and *a.* 1450. [ad. late L. *proprietarius*, f. *proprietas* PROPERTY; see -ARY [1].] A. *sb.* †1. = PROPRIETOR 2. –1790. 2. *Amer. Hist.* The grantee or owner, or one of the grantees or owners, of any one of certain N. American colonies. Also *Lord P.* 1637. 3. A proprietary body; proprietors collectively 1803. 4. Proprietorship 1624. †5. Something held as property; *esp.* a landed property –1846.

3. Certain burdens..borne exclusively by the landed p...of this country 1849. 4. 'Peasant p.' or 'occupying ownership' 1886.

B. *adj.* 1. Belonging to a proprietor or proprietors; owned or held as property; held in private ownership 1589. 2. Holding property; that is a proprietor, or consisting of proprietors 1709. 3. *Amer. Hist.* Pertaining or subject to the proprietor or owner of any one of certain N. American colonies, which were granted by the Crown to particular persons; being such a proprietor; see A. 2. 1704. 4. Of or relating to property or proprietorship 1832.

1. Certain well-known p. tobacco 1900. 2. The p. classes 1844. 4. The p. rights of the Crown 1855. Hence **Propri·etarily** *adv.*

Proprietor (prŏ͵prəi·ĕtəɹ). 1639. [Anomalously formed and substituted for prec.] 1. *Amer. Hist.* = prec. A. 2. Also *Lord P.* 2. One who holds something as property; one who has the exclusive right or title to the use or disposal of a thing; an owner 1645.

2. *Peasant p.*, a man of the peasant class who is the owner of the land he cultivates. Hence **Proprieto·rial** *a.* of or pertaining to a p.; that is a p.; consisting of proprietors; **-ly** *adv.* **Propri·etorship**, the position or condition of a p.; ownership. **Propri·etory** *sb.* = prec. A. 3 *adj.* = prec. B. **Propri·etress**, a female p.

Propriety (prŏ͵prəi·ĕti). 1456. [15th c. *propriete*, a. F. *propriété*, ad. L. *proprietatem*; see PROPERTY.] †1. = PROPERTY *sb.* 1. –1827. †2. = PROPERTY *sb.* 2. –1711. b. = PROPERTY *sb.* 2 b. Now only *Amer. Hist.* 1661. 3. Proper or particular character; own nature, disposition; essence, individuality; *occas.*, proper state or condition. Now *rare.* 1456. †4. = PROPERTY *sb.* 5. –1868. 5. Fitness, suitability; conformity with requirement, rule, or principle; rightness, correctness 1615. 6. Conformity with good manners or polite usage; correctness of behaviour or morals 1782.

1. When men give, they transfer P. to another 1671. 3. Silence that dreadfull Bell, it frights the Isle, From her p. SHAKS. This p., or characteristic in the individual 1876. 4. The several proprieties of the Magnet HOBBES. 5. They..appointed a committee to consider the p. of impeaching Arlington MACAULAY. 6. Propriety's cold cautious rules Warm fervour may o'erlook BURNS. *The proprieties*, the details of conventionally correct or proper conduct.

‖**Proprium** (prōu·priŏm). *Pl.* **-ia.** 1551. [L., neut. sing. of *proprius* PROPER.] a. *Logic.* = PROPERTY *sb.* 5 b. b. A distinctive characteristic; the essential nature, selfhood 1795.

Pro-proctor (prōu:prǫ·ktəɹ). 1650. [f. PRO-[1] + PROCTOR.] orig. One who acted for the proctor of a university; now, an assistant or deputy proctor in the universities.

‖**Proptosis** (prǫptōu·sis). 1676. [late L., a. Gr. πρόπτωσις, f. προπίπτειν to fall forwards.] *Path.* Prolapse or protrusion of some bodily part, esp. of the eye.

†**Propu·gn**, *v.* 1555. [ad. L. *propugnare* to go forth to fight, f. *pro* PRO-[1] + *pugnare.*] *trans.* To contend for; to defend, vindicate (an opinion, doctrine, etc.) –1676.

†**Propugna·tion.** 1586. [ad. L. *propugnationem*, f. *propugnare*; see PROPUGN.] Defence, protection, vindication –1647.

Propugnator (prōu·pŭgnēⁱtəɹ). 1450. [ad. L. *propugnatorem*; see PROPUGN.] A defender, champion.

Propulsion (prŏpʊ·lʃən). 1611. [a. F., f. L. *propellere* to PROPEL.] †1. The action of driving forth or away; expulsion, repulsion –1756. 2. The action of driving or pushing forward or onward; the condition of being impelled onward; propulsive force or effort 1799. b. *fig.* Impelling influence, impulse 1800.

2. b. I set to, with an unconquerable p. to write, with a lamentable want of what to write LAMB.

Propulsive (prŏpʊ·lsiv), *a.* 1758. [f. L. *propuls-*, *propellere* to PROPEL + -IVE.] Having the quality of propelling, or the tendency to propel; that drives forward or onward.

The p. movement of the foot in walking 1874. So **Propu·lsory** *a. rare.*

Propyl (prōu·pil). 1859. [f. PROP(IONIC + -YL; so called as being the radical of propionic acid.] *Chem.* The hypothetical alcohol radical of the tricarbon series, C_3H_7; also called *trityl.* Chiefly *attrib.* = PROPYLIC.

‖**Propylæum** (prǫpilī·ŏm). *Pl.* **-æa.** 1706. [L., ad. Gr. προπύλαιον, sb. use of neut. adj. 'before the gate', f. πρό PRO-[2] + πύλη.] The entrance to a temple or other sacred enclosure; *spec.* the entrance to the Acropolis at Athens. Hence, A gateway, porch, or vestibule. b. *fig.* An introduction; *pl.* prolegomena 1727.

Propylene (prōu·pilīn). 1850. [f. PROPYL + -ENE.] *Chem.* The olefine of the tricarbon or propyl series, C_3H_6, a colourless gas.

Propylic (prǫpi·lik), *a.* 1850. [f. as prec. + -IC.] *Chem.* Of or belonging to propyl, containing propyl.

Propylite (prǫ·piləit). 1867. [f. Gr. πρόπυλον (see next) + -ITE [1]. So named as opening the Tertiary volcanic epoch.] A volcanic rock occurring in and considered to be characteristic of various silver-mining regions.

‖**Propylon** (prǫ·pilǫn). 1831. [L., a. Gr. πρόπυλον, f. πρό PRO-[2] + πύλη gate.] = PROPYLÆUM. Also *transf.*

Pro-rate (prōu͵rēⁱ·t), *v.* Chiefly *U.S.* 1864 [f. *pro rata* (PRO[1] 5).] *trans.* To divide or assess *pro rata*; to distribute proportionally. b. *intr.* To make arrangement or agreement on a basis of proportional distribution 1867.

Prore (prōᵊɹ). Now *poet.* and *rare.* 1489. [a. obs. F. *prore*, ad. L. *prora* PROW *sb.*] The prow of a ship or boat. b. *poet.* A ship 1645.

Pro-rector (prōu:͵re·ktəɹ). 1618. [f. PRO-[1] + RECTOR; also mod. L.] The deputy or substitute of a rector in a university, college, etc.; a vice-rector. Now chiefly in German use. Hence **Prore·ctorate**, the office of a pro-rector.

†‖**Pro·-rex.** 1586. [f. L. *pro* PRO-[1] + *rex.*] A deputy king, a viceroy –1679.

Prorogate (prōu·rŏgeⁱt), *v.* Chiefly *Sc.*: now only *Sc. Law.* late ME. [f. ppl. stem of L. *prorogare*; see PROROGUE.] †1. *trans.* = PROROGUE 1. –1693. 2. = PROROGUE 2, 3. 1569. 3. *Sc.* and *Civil Law.* To extend (the jurisdiction of a judge or court) to a cause in which it would otherwise be incompetent 1601.

Prorogation (prōurŏgēⁱ·ʃən, prǫro-). [Late ME. a. OF. *prorogacion*, f. (ult.) L. *prorogare* to PROROGUE.] 1. The action of lengthening in duration; extension of time; further continuance. Now *rare* or *Obs.* exc. in *Sc. Law.* 2. The action of proroguing an assembly, esp. Parliament 1472. b. *transf.* The time during which Parliament stands prorogued 1548. 3. *Sc. Law.* The extension of the jurisdiction of a judge or court to causes which do not properly come within it 1838.

Prorogue (prorōu·g), *v.* [Late ME. *proroge*, a. F. *proroger*, ad. L. *prorogare*, lit. to ask publicly, f. *pro* PRO-[1] + *rogare* to ask.] 1. *trans.* To prolong, extend (in time or duration); to continue, protract. (*Obs.* exc. as a Latinism.) †2. To defer, postpone –1716. 3. To discontinue the meetings of (a legislative or other assembly) for a time without dissolving it; to dismiss by authority until the next session. Orig. and chiefly in ref. to the British Parliament. 1455. b. *intr.* in *pass.* sense: To be prorogued; to discontinue meeting until the next session 1642.

2. The Kinges journey into Scotland must be prorogued untill another yeare 1632. 3. b. No opportunity was afforded..of discussing the question before Parliament prorogued 1896.

Prosaic (prŏzē·ik), *a.* 1656. [ad. med.L. *prosaicus*, f. *prosa* PROSE; see -IC.] 1. Of, pertaining to, or written in prose; (of an author) writing in prose. Now *rare* or *Obs.* 2. Having the character, style, or diction of prose as opp. to poetry; lacking poetic beauty, feeling, or imagination; plain, matter-of-fact 1746. Hence b. *transf.* Unpoetic, unromantic; commonplace, dull, tame 1813.

2. The verses were easy and..p. enough to be intelligible to the meanest capacity 1795. b. Marriage settlements are very p things 1877. So **Prosa·ical** *a.*, **-ly** *adv.*, **-ness.** **Prosa·icism** = next.

Prosaism (prōu·ze͵iz'm). 1787. [ad. F. *prosaïsme*, f. L. *prosa* PROSE; see -ISM.] 1. Prosaic character or style. 2. (with *pl.*) A prosaic expression 1817. So **Pro·saist**, one who writes in prose; a prosaic person.

‖**Proscenium** (prosī·niŏm). *Pl.* **-a.** 1606. [a. L., ad. Gr. προσκήνιον, f. πρό PRO-[2] + σκηνή SCENE.] 1. a. In the ancient theatre, The space between the 'scene' or background and the orchestra, on which the action took place; the stage. b. In the modern theatre, The space between the curtain or drop-scene and the orchestra 1807. 2. *transf.* and *fig.* The front, the foreground 1648.

attrib. as *p. arch*, *box*, etc.

‖**Proscholium, -ion** (proskōu·liŏm, -iǫn). 1676. [med.L. *proscholium*, f. Gr. πρό PRO-[2] + L. *schola*, ad. Gr. σχολή school.] The 'vaulted walk' fronting the eastern end of the Divinity School at Oxford.

Proscribe (prŏskrəi·b), *v.* 1560. [ad. L. *proscribere* to write in front of, f. *pro* PRO-[1] + *scribere.*] 1. To write up or publish the name of (a person) as condemned to death and confiscation of property; to put out of the protection of the law, to outlaw; to banish, exile. 2. To denounce (a thing) as useless or dangerous; to interdict; to proclaim (a district or practice) 1622.

1. Ro. Vere, Earle of Oxford, was..banished the realme and proscribed SPENSER. 2. Before their religion was proscribed and their country confiscated 1850. Hence **Proscri·ber.**

Proscript, *a.* and *sb.* 1576. [ad. L. *proscriptus*, *proscribere.*] †A. *adj.* (pro͵skri·pt). Proscribed –1628. B. *sb.* (prōu·skript). One who is proscribed 1576.

Proscription (pro͵skri·pʃən). late ME. [ad. L. *proscriptionem.*] 1. The action of proscribing; the condition or fact of being proscribed; decree of condemnation to death or banishment; outlawry. 2. Denunciation, interdiction, prohibition by authority; exclusion or rejection by public order 1659.

1. This cuntry..was very well quieted by a p. of the O'Connors made by the erle of Kildare 1600.

Proscriptive (pro͵skri·ptiv), *a.* 1757. [f. L. *proscript-*, *proscribere* + -IVE.] Characterized by proscribing; tending to proscribe; of the nature or character of proscription. Hence **Proscri·ptive·ly** *adv.*, **-ness.**

Prose (prōuz), *sb.* ME. [a. F. *prose*, ad. L. *prosa* (*oratio*), lit. straightforward discourse, sb. use of fem. of *prosus*, for earlier *prorsus.*] 1. The ordinary form of written or spoken language, without metrical structure; esp. as a division of literature. Opp. to *poetry*, *verse*, *rime*, or *metre.* b. with *a* and *pl.* A piece of prose; a prose exercise. Now only in school or college use. 1589. 2. *Eccl.* A piece of rhythmical prose or rimed accentual verse, sung or said between the epistle and gospel at certain masses; also called a *sequence* 1449. 3. *fig.* Plain, simple, matter-of-fact, (and hence) dull or commonplace expression, quality, spirit, etc. 1561. 4. a. A prosy discourse or piece of writing 1688. b. *Old colloq.* Familiar talk, chat; a talk 1805. 5. *attrib.* (often hyphened). a. Consisting of, composed or written in prose 1711. b. Composing or writing in prose 1668. c. *fig.* = PROSAIC 2. 1818.

1. Things unattempted yet in P. or Rhime MILT. The definition of good p. is—proper words in their proper places COLERIDGE. b. When my tutor fond supposes I am writing Latin proses 1901. 3. A broad embodiment of the p. and commonplace of her class 1900. 4. b. Long p. with the Duke of Portland till one in the morning 1807. 5. a. Bunyan..is the Ulysses of his own prose-epic 1875. b. Poets and prose-authors in every kind SHAFTESB.

Comb.: **p.-poem**, a p. work having the style or character of a poem; so **-poet, -poetry; -writer**, an author who writes in p.

Prose (prōuz), *v.* late ME. [f. prec.] 1. *trans.* To express in prose; to translate or turn into prose. b. *intr.* To compose or write prose 1805. 2. To talk or write prosily; *old colloq.* and *dial.* to chat, gossip 1797.

1. Al schal passyn þat men p. or ryme CHAUCER. b. I've rhymed, I've prosed.. In short done everything 1834. 2. Eternally prosing about the weather 1879.

Prosector (prose·ktəɪ). 1857. [a. late L., f. L. *prosecare* to cut up.] One whose business is to dissect dead bodies in preparation for anatomical research or demonstration, as assistant to a lecturer on anatomy, or the like.

Prosecute (prǫ·sǐkiut), *v.* late ME. [f. L. *prosecut-*, *prosequi*, f. *pro* PRO-[1] + *sequi* to follow.] 1. *trans.* To follow up, pursue (some action, undertaking, etc.) with a view to completing it. 2. To carry out, perform; to engage in, practise, exercise, follow 1576. 3. To follow out in detail; to go into the particulars of, investigate; to deal with in greater detail 1538. †4. = PURSUE -1697. 5. *Law.* a. To institute legal proceedings against (a person) for some offence; to arraign before a court of justice for some crime or wrong. Also with the crime or offence as obj. 1579. b. *intr.* or *absol.* To institute or carry on a prosecution, to be prosecutor 1611. †6. To follow (*fig.*) *with* honour, regard, execration, or other feeling or its expression -1741. †7. To persecute -1704.

1. Determined to p. their intended tour 1754. 3. I do not further p. this subject 1873. 4. We..prosecuted them home to Warrington Town CROMWELL. 5. a. Trespassers will be prosecuted (*mod.*) Phr. *To p. an action, a claim, †the law.* Hence **Pro·secutable** *a.* that may be prosecuted.

Prosecution (prǫsǐkiū·ʃən). 1567. [a. OF., or ad. late L. *prosecutionem*, f. *prosequi* to PROSECUTE.] The action of prosecuting. 1. The following up, continuing, or carrying out *of* any action, scheme, or purpose, with a view to its accomplishment or attainment. 2. The carrying on, exercise, performance, or plying *of* a pursuit, occupation, etc. 1631. †3. The action of pursuing; a literal pursuit, chase, or hunting -1649. 4. *Law.* a. A proceeding by way either of indictment or of information in the criminal courts, in order to put an offender on his trial; the exhibition of a criminal charge against a person before a court of justice. b. *gen.* The institution and carrying on of legal proceedings against a person. c. Loosely: The party by whom criminal proceedings are instituted and carried on. Also *attrib.* 1631.

1. Nothing was to be gained by the further p. of the war 1884. 3. *fig. Ant. & Cl.* IV. xiv. 65. 4. *Director of public prosecutions*, an English law officer, appointed in 1879, to institute and conduct criminal proceedings in the public interest.

Prosecutor (prǫ·sǐkiutəɪ). 1599. [a. med. L., f. *prosequi.*] 1. One who follows up or carries out any action, project, or business. 2. One who institutes and carries on proceedings in a court of law, esp. in a criminal court 1670.

2. *Public p.*, a law officer appointed to conduct criminal prosecutions on behalf of the crown or state or in the public interest; *spec.* in Scotland, the Procurator fiscal in each county, etc. So **Prosecu·trix**, *pl.* -**trices**, a female p.

Proseity (prǫ͵sī·iti). 1899. [f. L. *pro se* for oneself + -ITY.] *Metaph.* The quality or condition of existing for itself, or of having itself for its own end.

Proselyte (prǫ·sǐləit), *sb.* late ME. [ad. late L. *proselytus*, a. Gr. προσήλυτος one who has come to a place, prop. adj. f. προσηλυθ-, προσέρχεσθαι.] 1. One who has come over from one opinion, belief, creed, or party to another; a convert. 2. *spec.* A Gentile convert to the Jewish faith. late ME.

1. *Wint. T.* v. i. 108. 2. Jewis, and proselitis, men of Crete and Arabye WYCLIF *Acts* ii. 10. Hence **Pro·selyte** *v. trans.* to make a p. of; to proselytize. Also *absol.*

Proselytism (prǫ·sǐləit-, -litiz'm). 1660. [In sense 1, f. prec. + -ISM; in 2 f. PROSELYTIZE.] 1. The fact of becoming or being a proselyte; the state or condition of a proselyte. 2. The practice of proselytizing 1763.

Proselytize (prǫ·sǐlitəiz), *v.* 1679. [f. PROSELYTE *sb.* + -IZE.] 1. *intr.* To make proselytes. 2. *trans.* To make a proselyte of 1796.

2. One of these whom they endeavour to p. BURKE. Hence **Pro·selytizer.**

Proseminary (prose·minări). 1774. [f. PRO-[2] + SEMINARY *sb.*] A preparatory seminary or school.

‖**Prosencephalon** (prǫs͵ense·fălǫn). *Pl.* -**a.** 1846. [mod.L., f. Gr. πρός + ἐγκέφαλον ENCEPHALON.] *Anat.* The anterior part of the brain, consisting of the cerebral hemispheres and other structures; the fore-brain. Hence **Prosencepha·lic** *a.* pertaining to or connected with the p.

Prosenchyma (prǫs͵e·ŋkimă). 1832. [mod. f. Gr. πρός to, toward + ἔγχυμα infusion, after PARENCHYMA.] *Bot.* Tissue consisting of elongated cells closely packed with their ends interpenetrating, and often with the terminal partitions obliterated so as to form ducts or vessels. Also *attrib.* Hence **Prosenchy·matous** *a.* belonging to, consisting of, or having the nature of p.

Proser (prōu·zəɪ). 1627. [f. PROSE *v.* + -ER[1].] 1. A writer of prose. 2. One who proses; one who talks or writes in a prosy, dull, or tiresome way 1769.

Prosily (prōu·zili), *adv.* 1849. [f. PROSY *a.* + -LY[2].] In a prosy manner.

Prosiness (prōu·zinės). 1814. [f. PROSY *a.* + -NESS.] Prosy or prosaic quality; commonplaceness; tediousness of writing or speech.

Prosobranch (prǫ·sobræŋk), *sb.* (*a.*) 1851. [ad. mod.L. *Prosobranchia*, neut. pl., f. Gr. πρόσω forwards + βράγχια gills.] *Zool.* A prosobranchiate gastropod. B. *adj.* = next.

Prosobranchiate (-bræ·ŋkiět), *a.* (*sb.*) 1877. [f. mod.L. *Prosobranchiata* = *Prosobranchia*; see prec. and -ATE[2].] *Zool.* Having the gills in front of the heart, as some aquatic gastropod molluscs. B. *sb.* = prec.

Prosodiacal (prǫsodəi·ăkăl), *a.* 1774. [f. late L. *prosodiacus* (= Gr. προσῳδιακός) + -AL.] = PROSODIC. Hence **Prosodi·acally** *adv.*

Prosodial (prosōu·diăl), *a.* 1775. [f. L. *prosodia* PROSODY + -AL.] = PROSODIC.

Prosodian (prosōu·diăn), *sb.* and *a.* 1623. [f. L. *prosodia*, Gr. προσῳδία + -AN.] A. *sb.* = PROSODIST. B. *adj.* = next 1817.

Prosodic (prosǫ·dik), *a.* 1774. [f. L. *prosodia* PROSODY + -IC.] Of, pertaining or relating to prosody. So **Proso·dical** *a.*, -**ly** *adv.*

Prosodist (prǫ·sŏdist). 1779. [f. as prec. + -IST.] One skilled or learned in prosody.

Prosody (prǫ·sŏdi). 1450. [ad. L. *prosodia* the accent of a syllable, a. Gr. προσῳδία, f. πρός to + ᾠδή song, ODE.] 1. The science of versification; that part of the study of language which deals with the forms of metrical composition; formerly reckoned as a part of grammar, and including also *phonology* or *phonetics*, esp. in relation to versification. Also, a treatise on this. 2. Correct pronunciation of words; observance of the laws of prosody (*rare*) 1616.

‖**Prosopalgia** (prǫsopæ·ldʒiă). 1831. [mod. L., f. Gr. πρόσωπον a face (f. πρός to + ὤψ, ὠπ- eye, face) + ἄλγος pain.] *Path.* Facial neuralgia; face-ache.

†**Proso·pole:psy.** 1646. [ad. Gr. προσωποληψία, f. προσωπολήπτης, f. πρόσωπον + λαμβάνειν.] Acceptance or 'acception' of the person of any one (see ACCEPTION 2); respect of persons; partiality -1849.

‖**Prosopopœia** (prǫsŏpŏpī·ă). 1561. [L., a. Gr. προσωποποιία, f. πρόσωπον face, person + ποιεῖν to make.] 1. *Rhet.* A figure by which an imaginary or absent person is represented as speaking or acting; the introduction of a pretended speaker. 2. *Rhet.* = PERSONIFICATION 1. 1578. b. *transf.* An impersonation, embodiment *of* some quality or abstraction 1826. Hence **Prosopopœ·ic**, -**al** *adjs.*

Prospect (prǫ·spekt), *sb.* late ME. [ad. L. *prospectus* view, f. *prospicere*, f. *pro* PRO-[1] + *specere* to look.] I. †1. The action or fact of looking forth or out; the condition of facing in a specified direction; outlook, aspect, exposure -1845. †b. A place which affords an open view; a look-out -1885. 2. An extensive sight or view; the view of the landscape from any position 1538. 3. That which is seen from any point of view; a spectacle, a scene; the visible landscape 1633. †4. The appearance presented by anything; aspect (*rare*) -1715. †5. A picture, a sketch of a scene or the like -1771.

1. [Armenia] hath a p. to the Caspian sea HOLLAND. b. Him God beholding from his p. high,..Thus..spake MILT. 2. Phr. †*In* (*within*) or *into p.*, in or into sight or view; within view. 3. A goodly p...of hills, and dales, and woods, and lawns, and spires THOMSON. 4. *Oth.* III. iii. 398. 5. I went to Putney ..to take prospects in crayon EVELYN.

II. †1. A mental view or survey; also, a description -1764. 2. A scene presented to the mental vision, esp. of something future 1641. 3. A mental looking forward 1605. b. *esp.* Expectation, or reason to look for something to come; that which one has to look forward to. Often *pl.* 1665. c. A possible or likely purchaser, subscriber, or customer 1923.

1. The Traveller; or, a P. of Society GOLDSM. 2. The surmounting of one difficulty is wont still to give us the p. of another 1672. 3. *Macb.* I. iii. 74. b. Seeing no p. of fine weather, I descended to Saas 1860. Phr. *In p.*, expected, or to be expected.

III. *Mining.* a. A spot giving prospects of the presence of a mineral deposit 1839. b. A sample of ore or 'dirt' for testing; also, the resulting yield of ore 1879.

Comb. **p.-glass**, a 'prospective glass', telescope, field glass. Hence **Pro·spectless** *a.* having no p. or outlook; without prospects for the future.

Prospect (prǫspe·kt, prǫ·spekt), *v.* 1555. [In branch I, ad. L. *prospectare*, frequent. of *prospicere* (see prec.); in II, a new formation from PROSPECT *sb.* III.] †I. 1. *intr.* To look forth or out; to face; to afford a prospect in some direction -1613. 2. *trans.* To look out upon or towards; to look at, view -1698. II. *Mining*, etc. Orig. U.S. 1. *intr.* To explore a region *for* gold or other minerals 1848. b. *fig.* To search about *for* something 1867. 2. *trans.* a. To explore (a region) for gold, etc. b. To work (a mine or lode) experimentally so as to test its richness. 1858. c. *fig.* To survey as to prospects 1864. 3. *intr.* Of a mine, reef, or ore: To give (good or bad) indications of future returns; to 'promise' (well or ill). Also, to prove (rich or poor) on actual trial. 1868.

1. I've sent my mate to p. for a new claim 1885. 2. A shaft is being sunk to p. the ground RAYMOND. 3. Some of it prospects fully 20 ounces to the ton 1897.

Prospecting, *vbl. sb.* 1677. [-ING[1].] The action of PROSPECT *v.*

attrib., as *p. drill, shaft, work*; **p. claim**, the first claim, marked out by the discoverer of the deposit.

Prospection (prŏ͵spe·kʃən). Now *rare.* 1668. [f. L. *prospicere*; see PROSPECT *sb.*] The action of looking forward; anticipation; regard to the future; foresight.

Prospective (prŏ͵spe·ktiv), *a.* and *sb.* 1588. [As adj. ad. obs. F. *prospectif*, f. L. *prospect-*, *prospicere*; see PROSPECT *sb.* and -IVE. As sb. a. obs. F. *prospective*; but in senses 1 and 2 short for *p. glass.*] A. *adj.* 1. Characterized by looking forward into the future 1590. †2. Used or suitable for viewing at a distance (*lit.* and *fig.*) -1652. †3. Fitted to afford a fine prospect -1817. 4. That looks or has regard to the future; operative with regard to the future 1800. 5. That looks forward or is looked forward to; that is in prospect; future 1829.

4. The language..is entirely p. and not retrospective 1884. 5. All the pupils above fourteen knew of some p. bridegroom C. BRONTË.

B. *sb.* †1. = next 1. -1626. †2. = next 2. -1727. 3. The action of looking out (*lit.* or *fig.*). Now *rare.* 1599. †4. A scene, a view -1745. †5. The art of drawing in perspective; also, a perspective view -1684.

3. *In p.*, in view; in prospect or anticipation. Hence **Prospe·ctive·ly** *adv.*, -**ness.**

†**Prospe·ctive glass.** 1584. 1. A magic crystal, in which it was supposed that distant or future events could be seen -1628. 2. A spy-glass, field-glass, telescope. Also *pl.* spectacles, binocular glasses. -1738.

Prospector (prŏspe·ktəɪ, prǫ·spektəɪ). 1857. [a. late L., f. *prospicere*; see PROSPECT *sb.*] One who prospects; *esp.* one who explores a region for gold or the like.

Prospectus (prŏspe·ktŏs). *Pl.* -**uses.** 1777. [a. L.] A description or account of the chief features of a forthcoming work or proposed enterprise, circulated for the purpose of obtaining support.

The plaintiff applied for shares in this company on the faith of the p. 1890.

Prosper (prǫ·spəɪ), *v.* 1460. [a. F. *prospérer*, ad. L. *prosperare* to cause (a thing) to succeed, also absol., f. *prosper*, *prosperus.*] 1. *intr.* To be prosperous, fortunate, or successful; to thrive, succeed, do well. **2.** *trans.* To cause to flourish; to be propitious to 1530.

1. What soeuer he doth, it shal prospere COVERDALE *Ps.* i. 3. Why wicked men have often prospered in this world HOBBES. Where such Plants grow and p. 1682. 2. O prospere thou oure hondy worke COVERDALE Ps. lxxxix (= xc of A.V.) 17. If Heaven prospered them, they might seize a Spanish ship 1855.

Prosperity (prǫspe·rĭti). [ME. a. F. *prospérité*, ad. L. *prosperitas, -tatem*, f. *prosper, prosperus*; see -ITY.] The condition of being prosperous; good-fortune, success, well-being. **b.** *pl.* Instances of prosperity, prosperous circumstances ME.

P. is not apt to receive good lessons, nor always to give them BURKE. b. The vitious and bad triumph with so great prosperities 1598.

Prosperous (prǫ·spərəs), *a.* 1445. [a. obs. F. *prospereus*, f. L. *prosper*; see -OUS.] **1.** Having continued success or good fortune; flourishing 1472. **2.** Promoting or conducing to success; favourable, propitious 1445.

1. The Churches Prayers made him so p. SHAKS. The causes which make one nation more rich and p. than another 1878. 2. We sayled euer with p. wynde 1555. Hence **Pro·sperous-ly** *adv.*, **-ness.**

Prosphysis (prǫ·sfisis), *a.* 1693. [mod.L., a. Gr. πρόσφυσις, f. πρός to + φύσις growth.] *Path.* An adhesion; morbid adhesion of parts.

Prostate (prǫ·steᵢt), *sb.* (*a.*) 1646. [ad. med.L. *prostata*, ad. Gr. προστάτης one who stands before, f. προϊστάναι.] *Anat.* A large gland, or each of a number of small glands, accessory to the male generative organs, surrounding the neck of the bladder and the commencement of the urethra, in man and other Mammalia. **b.** *attrib.* or *adj.*, esp. in *p. gland* 1754. Hence **Prosta·tic** *a.* pertaining to, produced by, or connected with the p.; *prostatic body, gland*, the p. ‖**Prostati·tis,** inflammation of the p.

‖**Prosternum** (proˌstɜ·ɹnɒ̈m). 1826. [mod. L., f. PRO-[2] 2 + STERNUM.] *Entom.* The sternal, ventral, or under segment of the prothorax of an insect.

‖**Prostheca** (prǫsˌþī·kă). 1826. [mod.L., ad. Gr. προσθήκη, f. προστιθέναι to put to, add.] *Entom.* A process on the mandibles in certain coleopterous insects.

‖ **Prosthesis** (prǫ·sþĭsis). 1553. [L., a. Gr. πρόσθεσις, f. προστιθέναι.] **1.** *Gram.* The addition of a letter or syllable at the beginning of a word. **2.** *Surg.* That part of surgery which consists in supplying deficiencies, as by artificial limbs, teeth, etc. 1706.

Prosthetic (prǫsþe·tik), *a.* 1837. [ad. mod. L. **prostheticus*, ad. Gr. προσθετικός of the nature of addition, f. πρόσθετος added, vbl. adj. of προστιθέναι; see prec. and -IC.] **1.** *Gram.* Pertaining to, or of the nature of prosthesis; prefixed, as a letter or syllable. **2.** *Surg.* Pertaining to or of the nature of prosthesis 1902.

Prostitute (prǫ·stitiūt), *ppl. a.* and *sb.* 1563. [ad. L. *prostitutus*, pa. pple. of *prostituere*, f. *pro* PRO-[1] + *statuere* to cause to stand, place.] **A.** *adj.* **1.** Offered or exposed to lust (as a woman), prostituted; also, licentious. (Sometimes const. as *pa. pple.*) Now *rare* or *Obs.* 1572. **2.** *fig.* Debased or debasing; abandoned; corrupt. Now *rare.* 1563. †**3.** Given over, devoted; exposed, subjected (*to* something, usu. evil) -1708.

1. Made bold by want, and p. for bread PRIOR. 2. No courtier, even the most p., could go farther than the parliament itself 1754.

B. *sb.* **1.** A woman who is devoted, or (usu.) offers her body to indiscriminate sexual intercourse, esp. for hire; a common harlot 1613. **2.** A person given over to infamous practices; an abandoned person; *esp.* a base hireling, a corrupt and venal politician. Now *rare.* 1647.

1. Your friendship as common as a prostitute's favours GOLDSM. 2. He [Lord Brougham] is a notorious p., and is setting himself up to sale 1804.

Prostitute (prǫ·stitiūt), *v.* 1530. [f. L. *prostitut-, prostituere*; see prec.] **1.** *trans.* To offer (oneself, or another) to unlawful, esp. indiscriminate, sexual intercourse, usu. for hire; to devote or expose to lewdness. (Chiefly *refl.* of a woman.) **b.** To seduce, debauch (a woman). *rare.* 1658. **2.** *fig.* To surrender or put to an unworthy or infamous use; to sell for base gain or hire 1593.

1. *Lev.* xix. 29. He recovered his liberty by prostituting the honour of his wife GIBBON. 2. Justice was prostituted in the ordinary courts to the royal will GREEN. So **Pro·stitutor,** one who prostitutes (usu. *fig.*) 1611.

Prostitution (prǫstitiū·ʃən). 1553. [ad. late L. *prostitutionem*, f. *prostituere* to PROSTITUTE.] **1.** Of women: The offering of the body to indiscriminate lewdness for hire (esp. as a practice or institution); whoredom, harlotry. **2.** *fig.* Devotion to an unworthy use; degradation, debasement, corruption 1647.

1. P. seems never to have been recognized at Rome as a legal institution 1878. 2. The p. of their talents to gratify..personal animosities 1874.

Prostrate (prǫ·strĕt, -eᵢt), *a.* late ME. [ad. L. *prostratus*, pa. pple. of *prosternere.*] **1.** In strict use, Lying with the face to the ground in token of submission or humility; more loosely, Lying at full length (on the ground or other surface). **b.** Of things usu. erect, as trees, pillars, etc.: Levelled with the ground, overthrown 1677. **2.** *fig.* Laid low in mind or spirit; submissive; overcome, powerless 1591. **b.** In a state of physical exhaustion or complete weakness; unable to rise or exert oneself 1871. **3.** *Bot.* In its habit of growth, lying flat upon the ground; procumbent 1776. **b.** Closely appressed to the surface; lying flat: as, p. hairs or setæ.

1. Whiles we on grassie bed did lie p. 1642. b. The mournful waste Of p. altars WORDSW. 2. The violent reaction which had laid the Whig party p. MACAULAY. Hence **Pro·strately** *adv.*

Prostrate (prǫ·streᵢt), *v.* *Pa. t.* and *pple.* prostrated. late ME. [f. L. ppl. stem *prostrat-*; see prec.] †**1.** *intr.* To become prostrate; = sense 3. -1755. **2.** *trans.* To lay flat on the ground, etc.; to throw down, level with the ground, overthrow (something erect) 1483. **3.** *refl.* To cast oneself down prostrate; to bow to the ground in reverence or submission 1530. **4.** *trans. fig.* To lay low, overcome; to make submissive or helpless 1562. **b.** To reduce to extreme physical weakness: said of disease, fatigue, and the like 1829.

2. A storme, that all things doth p. SPENSER. 3. Sethos, upon entring, prostrated himself at his feet 1732. 4. You are to p. your reason to divine revelation KEN. b. He appeared exceedingly low and prostrated 1843.

Prostration (prǫstreᵢ·ʃən). 1526. [a. F., or ad. late L. *prostrationem*, f. *prosternere.*] **1.** The action of prostrating oneself or one's body, esp. as a sign of humility, adoration, or servility; the condition of being prostrated, or lying prostrate. **2.** *fig.* Veneration; abject submission, adulation; humiliation, abasement 1646. **3.** *fig.* Debasement of any exalted principle or faculty 1647. **4.** Extreme physical weakness or exhaustion; also extreme dejection 1651. **5.** The reduction of a country, party, or organization to a prostrate or powerless condition 1844.

1. The comely prostrations of the body..in time of Divine Service 1645. 2. The p. of the intellect 1823. 4. Nervous p. 1887. 5. The p. of Greece under the Turkish yoke 1844.

Prostrative (prǫ·strĕtiv), *a.* *rare.* 1817. [f. L. ppl. stem *prostrat-* + -IVE.] **a.** Having the quality or faculty of prostrating. **b.** Characterized by prostration or abjectness.

Prostyle (prōᵘ·stəil), *sb.* and *a.* 1696. [ad. L. *prostylos* adj. having pillars in front, also sb.; see PRO-[2] and STYLE *sb.*] *Anc. Arch.* **A.** *sb.* A portico in front of a Greek temple, of which the columns stood in front of the building 1697. **B.** *adj.* Having a prostyle 1696.

Prosy (prōᵘ·zi), *a.* 1821. [f. PROSE *sb.* + -Y[1].] **1.** Resembling, or having the character of, prose. Sometimes = PROSAIC 2; commonplace and tedious; dull and wearisome. **2.** Of persons: Given to talking or writing in a commonplace, dull, or tedious way 1838.

Prosyllogism (proˌsi·lŏdʒiz'm). 1584. [ad. med.L. *prosyllogismus*, ad. Gr. προσυλλογισμός; see PRO-[2] and SYLLOGISM.] *Logic.* A syllogism of which the conclusion forms the major or minor premiss of another syllogism.

Protagon (prōᵘ·tăgǫn). 1869. [a. G., f. Gr. πρῶτος first + ἄγον, neut. pres. pple. of ἄγειν to lead.] *Physiol. Chem.* A highly complex crystalline substance, containing nitrogen and phosphorus, found in brain and nerve tissue.

Protagonist (protæ·gŏnist). 1671. [ad. Gr. πρωταγωνιστής, f. πρῶτος first + ἀγωνιστής combatant, actor.] **1.** The chief personage in a drama; the principal character in the plot of a story, etc. **2.** A leading personage in any contest; a champion of any cause 1839.

1. 'Tis charg'd upon me that I make debauch'd Persons..my protagonists, or the chief persons of the drama DRYDEN.

Protamine (prōᵘ·tăməin). 1895. [f. Gr. πρωτο- PROTO- 3 c + AMINE.] *Physiol. Chem.* One of the simple proteins, a basic organic substance $C_{16}H_{32}N_9O_2$.

Protandrous (protæ·ndrəs), *a.* 1875. [f. PROT(O)- + -ANDROUS.] *Bot.* = PROTERANDROUS. So **Prota·ndric** *a.*

‖**Protasis** (prǫ·tăsis). 1616. [Late L., a. Gr. πρότασις a stretching forward, etc., f. πρό PRO-[2] + τάσις, f. τείνειν to stretch.] **1.** That which is put forward; a proposition, a maxim (*rare*) 1656. **2.** In the ancient drama, The first part of a play, in which the characters are introduced, as opp. to the *epitasis* and *catastrophe* 1616. **3.** *Gram.* and *Rhet.* The first or introductory clause in a sentence, *esp.* in a conditional sentence; opp. to the *apodosis* 1638.

Protatic (protæ·tik), *a.* 1668. [ad. late L. *protaticus*, a. Gr. προτατικός, f. πρότασις PROTASIS.] Of or pertaining to the or a protasis; in *p. character, person*, appearing only in the protasis (sense 2).

‖ **Protea** (prōᵘ·tiă). 1753. [mod.L., generic name (Linn.), f. PROTEUS, in allusion to the great variety of the species.] *Bot.* A large genus of shrubs or small trees, type of the *Proteaceæ*, chiefly natives of S. Africa, bearing large cone-like heads of flowers; also, a plant of this genus.

Proteaceous (prōᵘtiˌeᵢ·ʃəs), *a.* 1835. [f. mod.L. *Proteaceæ*, f. prec.; see -ACEOUS.] Of or pertaining to the *Proteaceæ*, a natural order of trees, shrubs, or (rarely) perennial herbs, mainly S. African and Australian, typified by the genus *Protea.*

Protean (prōᵘ·tiˌăn), *a.* 1598. [f. PROTEUS + -AN.] Of or pertaining to Proteus; like that of Proteus; hence, variable in form; characterized by variability or variation; changing, varying. **b.** *spec. Zool.* Varying in shape; of or pertaining to the proteus-animalcule; amœboid, proteiform 1802. Hence **Pro·teanly** *adv. rare*, with variation of form.

Protect (prŏte·kt), *v.* 1526. [f. ppl. stem of L. *protegere*, f. *pro* PRO-[1] + *tegere* to cover.] **1.** *trans.* To defend or guard from injury or danger; to shield; to keep safe, take care of; to extend patronage to. **b.** To act as official or legal protector or guardian of SHAKS. **2.** *Pol. Econ.* To assist or guard (a home industry) against the competition of foreign productions by means of imposts on the latter 1827. **3.** *Comm.* To provide funds to meet (a draft or bill of exchange) 1884. **4. a.** To furnish (*spec.* war-ships) with a protective covering 1839. **b.** To provide (machinery, etc.) with appliances to prevent injury from it 1900.

1. To every man remaineth..the right of protecting himselfe HOBBES. To p. the eyes from..excessive light 1879. b. 2 *Hen. VI*, II. iii. 29. 2. Their industries were protected and ours were not 1885. Hence **Prote·ctingly** *adv.*

Protectee (prŏtektī·). 1602. [f. PROTECT *v.* + -EE.] One who is under protection; *spec.* in 16–17th c., †an Irishman who had accepted the protection of the English government.

Protection (prŏte·kʃən). [Late ME. a. F., ad. late L. *protectionem*, f. *protegere.*] **1.** The action of protecting; the fact or condition of being protected; defence from harm, danger, or evil; patronage, tutelage. **b.** *euphem.* The keeping of a mistress in a separate establishment 1677. **2.** A thing or person that protects. late ME. **3.** A writing that protects or secures from molestation; a safe-conduct, passport, pass. In U.S. a certificate of American citizenship issued by the customs authorities to seamen. 1450. **4.** *Pol. Econ.* The theory or system of protecting home industries against foreign competition by imposing duties or the like on foreign productions 1828.

1. I leve this castel in your proteccyon & sauff garde CAXTON. Ireland..must be protected, and there is no p. to be found for her, but either from France or England BURKE. 2. His quiver and his laurel 'Gainst four such eyes were no p. GRAY. 3. Moved that the speaker sign protections for such persons as are called before the Committee for inspecting Treasury and Revenue 1658. Hence **Prote·ctionism,** the economic doctrine, policy, or system of p. **Prote·ctionist,** an advocate of protectionism; as *adj.* supporting p.

Protective (prŏte·ktiv), *a.* (*sb.*) 1661. [f. PROTECT *v.* + -IVE.] 1. Protecting; tending to protect; defensive; preservative. 2. *Pol. Econ.* Of or relating to the economic doctrine or system of protection 1829. B. *sb.* Anything employed to protect; e.g. in *Surgery*, carbolized oiled silk used for the protection of wounds 1875.

1. The favour of p. Providence 1661. Examples of p. colouring among insects (*mod.*). Hence **Prote·ctive-ly** *adv.*, **-ness.**

Protector (prŏte·ktəɹ). [Late ME. a. OF. *protectour*, ad. post-cl. L. *protector, -orem*, f. *protegere.*] 1. One who protects; a defender; a guardian, a patron. b. A thing that protects; a guard; *esp.* a device to prevent injury to or from something; e.g. *chest-p., cuff-p.*, etc. 1849. 2. *Eng. Hist.* a. One in charge of the kingdom during the minority, absence, or incapacity of the sovereign; a regent. late ME. b. The official title, in full *Lord P. of the Commonwealth*, borne by Oliver Cromwell 1653–8, and by his son Richard 1658–9.

1. The wulues kyld the dogges whiche were capytayns and protectours of the sheep CAXTON. 2. a. The p., Humphry, Duke of Gloucester GRAY. b. Saw the superb funerall of the P. EVELYN. Hence **Prote·ctoral** *a.* of or pertaining to a p., *esp. Hist.* to the p. of a kingdom or commonwealth. So **Protecto·rial** *a.* **Prote·ctress,** ‖**Prote·ctrix,** a female p.; a patroness.

Protectorate (prŏte·ktŏrět), *sb.* 1692. [f. PROTECTOR + -ATE [1].] 1. The office, position, or government of the Protector of a kingdom or state; *spec.* the period (1653–9) during which Oliver and Richard Cromwell held the title of Lord Protector. 2. The office, position, or function of a protector or guardian. *Internat. Law*: a. orig., The relation of a strong to a weaker state which it protects. b. The relation of a suzerain to a vassal state; suzerainty. c. now *spec.* The relation of a European power to a territory inhabited by native tribes, and not ranking as a state. 1836. 3. A state or territory placed or taken under the protection of a superior power; *esp.* a protected territory inhabited by native tribes 1884.

Protectorship (prŏte·ktəɹʃip). 1460. [-SHIP.] 1. = PROTECTORATE 1. 2. The position, character, or function of a protector; guardianship, patronage 1576.

‖**Protégé** *masc.*, **protégée** *fem.* (prǫ·tęʒe¹, ‖proteʒe). 1778. [F., pa. pple. of *protéger*, ad. L. *protegere.*] One who is under the protection or care of another, esp. of a person of superior position or influence.

Proteid (prōu·tiˌid). 1871. [f. PROTE(IN; see -ID [4].] *Chem.* One of a class of organic compounds previously known as 'protein bodies', and now by preference called 'proteins'; see PROTEIN.

Proteiform (prōu·tiˌifǭɹm), *a.* 1833. [f. PROTEUS + -(I)FORM.] Changeable in form, or assuming many various forms; protean.

Protein (prōu·tiˌin). 1868. [a. F. *protéine*, G. *proteïn*, f. Gr. πρωτεῖος primary, prime (so named as a fundamental material of the bodies of animals and plants); see -IN [1].] *Chem.* Any one of a class of organic compounds, consisting of carbon, hydrogen, oxygen, and nitrogen, with a little sulphur, in more or less unstable combination; forming an important part of all living organisms, and the essential nitrogenous constituents of the food of animals. Also called *albuminoids*, and *proteids*.

The name was applied earlier by Mulder to a residual substance obtained from casein, etc. and regarded by him as the essential constituent of organized bodies. Hence **Proteˌinaceous** (-ē¹·ʃəs), **Proteˌinic** (-i·nik), **Proteinous** (protī·nəs) *adjs.* of the nature of, or consisting of, p.

Protend (prote·nd), *v.* Now *rare.* [Late ME. ad. L. *protendere* to stretch forth; f. PRO-[1] + *tendere.*] 1. *trans.* To stretch forth; to hold out in front of one. b. *intr.* for *refl.* To stick out, protrude 1726. 2. *trans.* To extend in length, or in one dimension of space; to produce (a line); usu. *pass.* to extend (from one point to another). late ME. 3. To extend in duration. late ME.

1. [Ajax] Now shakes his spear, now lifts, and now protends POPE.

Protension (prote·nʃən). *rare.* 1681. [ad. late L. *protensionem*, f. *protendere.*] A stretching or reaching forward; length; duration.

Protensive (prote·nsiv), *a. rare.* 1643. [f. L. *protens-, protendere* + -IVE.] 1. Continuing, lasting, enduring. 2. Extending lengthwise 1836. Hence **Prote·nsively** *adv.*

‖**Proteolysis** (prōutiˌǫ·lisis). 1880. [mod. L., f. **proteo-*, assumed comb. form of PROTEIN + Gr. λύσις a loosening.] *Phys. Chem.* a. The separation of the proteins from a protein-containing mixture; b. The splitting up of proteins by ferments. Hence **Pro·teolyse** *v. trans.* to decompose or split up (proteins). **Proteoly·tic** *a.* having the quality of decomposing proteins.

Proteose (prōu·tiˌōus). 1890. [f. PROTE(IN + -OSE [2].] *Phys. Chem.* One of a class of products of protein-hydrolysis, including albumose, globulose, gelatose, etc.

Proterandrous (prǫtěræ·ndrəs), *a.* 1875. [f. PROTERO- + -ANDROUS.] 1. *Bot.* Having the stamens or male organs mature before the pistil or female organ. 2. *Zool.* Of a hermaphrodite animal or a colony of zooids: Having the male organs, or individuals, sexually mature before the female. Hence **Protera·ndry,** p. quality.

Proteranthous (prǫtěræ·nþəs), *a.* 1832. [f. as prec. + Gr. ἄνθος flower + -OUS.] *Bot.* Having flowers appearing before the leaves.

Protero- (prǫtěro), bef. a vowel **proter-** (prǫtěr), comb. form from Gr. πρότερος fore, former, anterior, in place, time, order, rank; used in a few scientific terms; as **Pro·terosaur** (-sǭr) [Gr. σαῦρος lizard], a saurian of the extinct genus *Proterosaurus* or group *Proterosauria*, comprising some of the oldest reptiles.

Proterogynous (prǫtěrǫ·dʒinəs), *a.* 1875. [f. PROTERO + -GYNOUS.] 1. *Bot.* Having the pistil or female organ mature before the stamens or male organs. 2. *Zool.* Of a hermaphrodite animal, or a colony of zooids: Having the female organs, or individuals, sexually mature before the male. So **Protero·gyny,** p. quality or state.

Protervity (protɔ̄·ɹviti). Now *rare.* 1500. [ad. obs. F. *protervité*, ad. L. *protervitatem*; etym. dub.] Waywardness, frowardness; stubbornness; pertness, insolence; petulance; an instance of this.

Protest (prōu·test), *sb.* [ME. = OF. *protest*, f. *protester* to PROTEST.] An act of protesting. 1. = PROTESTATION 1. 2. The action taken to fix the liability for the payment of a dishonoured bill; *spec.* a formal declaration in writing, usu. by a notary-public, that a bill has been duly presented and payment or acceptance refused 1622. 3. A written declaration made by the master of a ship, attested by a justice of the peace or a consul, stating the circumstances under which injury has happened to the ship or cargo, or under which officers or crew have incurred any liability 1755. 4. A formal declaration of dissent from, or of consent under certain conditions only to, some action or proceeding; a remonstrance 1751. b. A written statement of dissent from any motion carried in the House of Lords, recorded and signed by any Peer of the minority 1712.

4. The husband appeared under p. 1822. Paying under p. 1885.

Protest (prŏte·st), *v.* 1440. [a. F. *protester*, ad. L. *protestari*, f. PRO-[1] + *testari* to be or speak as a witness, to aver.] 1. *trans.* To state formally or solemnly (something about which a doubt is stated or implied). b. *intr.* To make protestation or solemn affirmation 1560. c. As a mere asseveration 1587. 2. *trans.* To make a formal written declaration of the non-acceptance or non-payment of (a bill of exchange) when duly presented 1655. †3. To assert publicly; to proclaim; to declare, show forth –1644. †4. To vow –1660. †5. To call to witness; to appeal to –1675. 6. *intr.* To give formal expression to objection, dissent, or disapproval; to make a formal (often written) declaration *against* some proposal, decision, or action; to remonstrate 1608.

1. I p. to you, the Gentleman has not spoken to me STEELE. She then..solemnly protested her innocence 1839. b. The Lady protests to much, me thinkes SHAKS. c. I will doe it I p. DEKKER. 2. b. *U.S.* To protest against 1904. 3. *Much Ado* V. i. 149. 4. On Dianaes Altar to p. For aie, austerity, and single life SHAKS. 6. A minister of religion may fairly p. against being made a politician J. H. NEWMAN.

Protestant (prǫ·těstănt), *sb.* and *a.* 1539. [a. G. or F. *protestant*, ad. L. *protestans, protestari* to PROTEST.] A. *sb.* I. *Eccl.* 1. *Hist.*, usu. *pl.* Those German princes and free cities who made a declaration of dissent from the decision of the Diet of Spires (1529), which reaffirmed the edict of the Diet of Worms against the Reformation; hence, the adherents of the Reformed doctrines and worship in Germany. 2. A member or adherent of any Christian church or body severed from the Roman communion in the Reformation of the 16th c.; hence, gen. any member of a Western church outside the Roman communion 1553. b. *spec.* In the 17th c., *Protestant* was generally accepted and used by members of the Established Church, and was even so applied to the exclusion of Presbyterians, Quakers, and Separatists 1608. II. *General.* Often pron. (prote·stănt). One who protests. a. One who protests devotion; a suitor (*rare*) 1648. b. One who protests against error 1836. c. One who makes a protest *against* any decision, proceeding, practice, custom, or the like; a protester 1853.

a. Bid me to live, and I will live Thy P. to be HERRICK.

B. *adj.* 1. Of, pertaining to, or of the nature of Protestants or Protestantism 1539. 2. Also (prote·stănt). Protesting; making a protest 1844.

1. To heare & see the manner of the French P. Churches service EVELYN. **P. Episcopal,** official title of the church in U.S. descended from and in communion with the Church of England. Hence **Pro·testantize** *v. trans.* to render P.; *intr.* to follow P. practices.

Protestantism (prǫ·těstănti:z'm). 1649. [f. prec. + -ISM.] 1. The religion of Protestants, as opp. to Roman Catholicism; the condition of being Protestant; adherence to Protestant principles. 2. Protestants, or the Protestant churches, collectively 1662. 3. An attitude of protest (*rare*) 1854.

3. There needs, then, a p. in social usages 1854.

Protestation (prǫtěstē¹·ʃən). ME. [a. F., ad. late L. *protestatio*, f. *protestari* to PROTEST.] The action of protesting; that which is protested. 1. A solemn affirmation of a fact, opinion, or resolution; a formal public assertion or asseveration. †2. *Law.* In pleading, an affirmation or denial, introduced in form of a protest, of some allegation the truth of which the pleader cannot directly affirm or deny without duplicating his plea, and which he cannot pass over lest he should be held to have tacitly waived or admitted it –1797. 3. = PROTEST *sb.* 4, 4 b. 1624.

1. If there had been any faith in mens vows and protestations COWLEY. *To make p.*, to protest in a solemn or formal manner.

Protester (prŏte·stəɹ). 1601. [f. PROTEST *v.* + -ER [1].] 1. One who makes a protestation or solemn affirmation. 2. One who makes a protest or remonstrance 1651. 3. One who protests a bill or other commercial document 1849. So **Prote·stor** 1550.

‖**Proteus** (prōu·tius, prōu·tiŭs). late ME. [L., a. Gr. Πρωτεύς proper name.] 1. *Gr.* and *Rom. Myth.* A sea-god, the son of Oceanus and Tethys, fabled to assume various shapes. 2. Hence allus., One who, or that which, assumes various forms, or characters; a changing, varying, or inconstant person or thing 1585. 3. *Zool.* and *Biol.* a. An AMŒBA. (Now disused as a generic name.) Also *p. animalcule.* 1802. b. A genus of tailed amphibians with persistent gills, having four short slender legs and a long eel-like body, found in subterranean caves in Austria 1835. 4. *attrib.* Changeable like Proteus, protean 1687.

4. O P. Conscience, never to be tied! DRYDEN.

‖ **Prothalamion** (prōuþǣlǣ·miǫn). Also **-ium.** 1597. [Coined by Spenser, after *epithalamion*; see PRO-[2].] A song sung before a wedding.

‖ **Prothesis** (prǫ·þĭsis). 1577. [a. Gr. πρόθεσις a placing before or in public, f. PRO-[2] + θέσις placing.] 1. *Eccl.* The placing of the elements, etc., in readiness for use in the eucharistic office; hence, a credence-table, or the part of the church where this stands. 2. *Gram.* = PROSTHESIS 1. 1870. Hence **Prothe·tic** *a.* **Prothe·tically** *adv.*

Prothoracic (prōuþoræ·sik), *a.* 1826. [f. mod.L. *prothorax*, *-thoracem* (see next) + -IC; see PRO-[2].] *Entom.* Of or pertaining to the front of the thorax; pertaining to or situated on the prothorax.

‖ **Prothorax** (proþōə·ræks). 1826. [mod.L.; see PRO-[2] 2 and THORAX.] *Entom.* The first of the three thoracic somites, or divisions of the thorax of an insect, which bears the first pair of legs.

‖ **Protista** (proti·stă), *sb. pl.* 1878. [mod.L., a. Gr. πρώτιστα, neut. pl. of πρώτιστος the very first.] *Biol.* A third kingdom of organized beings, not definitely distinguished as either animals or plants (thus comprising the Protozoa and Protophyta, with those forms indeterminately assigned to either group). Hence **Protist** (prōu·tist), one of the P.; also *attrib.* **Proti·stan** *a.* of or belonging to the P.; *sb.* = *protist.*

Proto- (prōuto), bef. a vowel or *h* properly **prot-** (prōut), or with *h* (prōuþ), repr. Gr. πρωτο-, comb. form of πρῶτος first.

In modern formations, esp. in group 1 below, the tendency is to leave *proto-* unchanged; e.g. *proto-apostate*, *proto-hippus*.

1. In words of rare occurrence, often self-explaining: *proto-* (which, when prefixed to a word already in English, is usu. hyphened) denoting (*a*) 'First in time, earliest, original, primitive', as in *proto-historian*, *-apostate*, *-chemistry*, etc.; (*b*) 'First in rank or importance, chief, principal', as in *proto-architect*, *-chemist*, *-rebel*, *-traitor*, etc.

2. In many mod. scientific and techn. terms (sbs. and adjs.). a. Prefixed to adjs. from names of countries or races, forming adjs. denominating primitive or original tribes, languages, writings, works of art or manufacture, styles of architecture, etc.; as *proto-Arabic*, *-Babylonian*, *-Celtic*, *-Doric*, etc. b. In terms, chiefly of Zoology or Biology: usu. designating an (actual or hypothetical) original or primitive form, type, organism, structure, etc. **Pro·toconch** [see CONCH], the embryonic shell in certain cephalopods; hence **Protoco·nchal** *a.* **Pro·tomorph** [Gr. μορφή form], a primitive or original form; so **Protomo·rphic** *a.*, having the primitive or simplest form or structure. ‖ **Protone·ma** [Gr. νῆμα thread], in mosses, the confervoid or filamentous thallus which produces the full-grown plant by lateral branching. **Proto-o·rganism,** a primitive or unicellular organism, animal or vegetable; a protozoön or protophyte. **Proto·pathy** [-PATHY], primary pain or suffering; *Path.* a primary disease or affection. **Proto·podite** [see PODITE], in Crustacea, the first or basal joint of a limb, which articulates with its somite hence **Protopodi·tic** *a.* ‖ **Proto·pterus,** a genus of dipnoan fishes, containing only the African mud-fish, having the pectoral and ventral fins reduced to long fringed filaments. **Protoso·mite,** each of the rudimentary somites of the embryo in arthropods and annelids.

3. In Chemistry. a. With names of binary compounds in -IDE (formerly *-uret*), designating that in which the element or radical combines in the first or smallest proportion with another element. **Protochlo·ride,** a compound of chlorine with another element or radical, containing the minimum proportion of chlorine; so **Protosu·lphide, Proto·xide. Pro·tosalt,** a salt formed by combination of an acid with the protoxide of a metal. Hence in derived vbs., ppl. adjs., etc. b. In ternary compounds *proto-* was formerly used to designate salts produced from protoxides (cf. PROTOSALT), which thus contain the smallest (or smaller) proportion of the acid radical. c. In Organic and Physiological Chemistry, *proto-* occurs in senses rather akin to its use in 1 or 2. Thus in *proto-catechuic acid* ($C_7H_6O_4$) the name was given because the substance has some resemblance to *catechuic* acid or *catechu*, but has a simpler composition.

Protocanonical (prou:tokănǫ·nikăl), *a.* 1629. [f. mod.L. *protocanonicus* (see PROTO- 1 and CANON) + -AL.] Of the books of Scripture: Canonical of the first order. Opp. to DEUTEROCANONICAL.

‖ **Protococcus** (prōutokǫ·kǒs). *Pl.* **-cocci** (-kǫ·ksəi). 1842. [f. PROTO- + Gr. κόκκος grain, seed.] *Bot.* A genus of microscopic unicellular algæ, of spheroidal form.

Protocol (prōu·tǒkǫl), *sb.* 1541. [Early mod.E. *prothocoll*, a. OF. *prothocole*, ad. med. L. *protocollum*, ad. Gr. πρωτόκολλον the first leaf of a volume, a fly-leaf glued to the case and containing an account of the MS., f. πρωτο- PROTO- + κόλλα glue.] 1. The original note or minute of a negotiation, agreement, or the like, drawn up by a notary, etc. and duly attested, which forms the legal authority for any subsequent deed, agreement, or the like based upon it. 2. *spec.* The original draught, minute, or record of a dispatch, negotiation, treaty or other diplomatic document or instrument; *esp.* a record of the propositions agreed to in a conference, signed by the parties, to be embodied in a formal treaty 1697. 3. A formal or official statement of a transaction or proceeding 1880. 4. In France, The formulary of the etiquette to be observed by the Head of the State in official ceremonies, etc.; the etiquette department of the Ministry of Foreign Affairs; the office of the Master of the Ceremonies 1896. 5. *Diplomatics.* The official formulas used at the beginning and end of a charter, papal bull, etc., as distinct from the *text*, which contains its subject-matter 1908. Hence **Pro·tocolist,** one who draws up a p.

Pro·tocol, *v.* 1832. [f. prec.] *intr.* and *trans.* To draw up, or record in, a protocol.

Protogine (prōu·tŏdʒin). 1832. [a. F., irreg. f. Gr. πρῶτος first + γίνεσθαι to be born or produced.] *Geol.* A variety of granite occurring in the Alps, in which chlorite often takes the place of biotite, and in which a foliated structure has frequently been produced by dynamic action.

Protogynous (protǫ·dʒinəs), *a.* 1875. [f. PROTO- + -GYNOUS.] *Bot.* = PROTEROGYNOUS. Hence **Proto·gyny** = PROTEROGYNY.

‖ **Protohippus** (prōuto₁hi·pǒs). 1876. [mod. L., f. Gr. πρωτο- PROTO- + ἵππος horse.] *Palæont.* An extinct genus of quadrupeds, ancestrally related to the horse.

Protomartyr (prōu·to₁mā:ɪtəɹ). [Late ME. *prothomartir*, a. OF.; see PROTO- and MARTYR *sb.*] The first martyr; the earliest of any series of martyrs; *spec.* applied to St. Stephen.

‖ **Proton** (prōu·tǫn). 1920. [neut. of Gr. πρῶτος first.] *Physics.* A unit constituent of matter associated with (or consisting of) an invariable charge of positive electricity.

Protonotary, prothonotary (prōu:to₁-, prōu:þonōu·tări; protǫ·n-, proþǫ·nŏtări). 1447. [ad. late L. *protonotarius*, in med.L. also *protho-*; a. Gr. πρωτονοτάριος, f. πρωτο- PROTO- + νοτάριος, ad. L. *notarius* NOTARY *sb.*] 1. A principal notary, chief clerk, or recorder of a court; orig., the holder of that office in the Byzantine court. 2. In England, formerly, The chief clerk or registrar in the Courts of Chancery, of Common Pleas, and of the King's Bench 1460. 3. *R. C. Ch.* A member of the college of twelve (formerly seven) prelates called *Protonotaries Apostolic(al*, whose function is to register the papal acts, to make and keep records of beatifications, to direct the canonization of saints, etc. 1494. b. *Gr. Ch.* The principal secretary of the Patriarch of Constantinople 1835. 4. A chief secretary in some foreign courts; also *transf.* and *fig.* 1502. Hence **Proto-, Prothono·taryship.**

‖ **Protopapas** (prōu·topæ:păs). 1682. [a. eccl. Gr. πρωτοπαπᾶς chief priest, f. πρωτο- PROTO- + παπᾶς priest.] = PROTOPOPE.

‖ **Protophyta** (protǫ·fĭtă), *sb. pl.* 1855. [mod.L., pl. of *protophytum*, f. Gr. πρῶτος PROTO- + φυτόν plant.] *Bot.* A primary division of the vegetable kingdom, comprising the most simply organized plants (usu. of microscopic size), each individual consisting of a single cell. So **Protophyte** (prōu·tofəit), a plant belonging to the division *Protophyta.*

Protoplasm (prōu·tŏplæz'm). 1848. [ad. G. *protoplasma*, f. Gr. πρωτο- PROTO- + πλάσμα moulded thing, figure, form.] *Biol.* A viscid, semifluid, semitransparent, colourless or whitish substance, consisting of oxygen, hydrogen, carbon, and nitrogen (often with a small amount of some other elements) in extremely complex and unstable combination, and manifesting 'vital properties'; constituting the physical basis of life in all plants and animals. Hence **Pro·toplasma·tic, Protopla·smic** *adjs.* of, pertaining to, or having the nature of p.; relating to p.; acting upon p.

Protoplast[1] (prōu·tŏ₁plæst). 1532. [a. F. *protoplaste*, or ad. late L. *protoplastus*, ad. Gr. πρωτόπλαστος, f. πρωτο- PROTO- + πλαστός, vbl. adj. f. πλάσσειν to form, mould.] 1. That which is first formed, fashioned, or created; the first-made thing or being of its kind; the original, archetype. 2. *Biol.* A unit or mass of protoplasm, such as constitutes a single cell; a bioplast. Sometimes applied to a unicellular organism; *spec.* one of the suborder *Protoplasta* of rhizopods. 1884.

1. In Salem citie was Adam our p. created 1600.

Pro·toplast[2]. 1600. [ad. med.L. *protoplastes*, a. Gr. *πρωτοπλάστης, f. πρωτο- PROTO- + πλάστης, f. πλάσσειν.] The first former, fashioner, or creator.

Protoplastic (prōuto₁plæ·stik), *a.* 1652. [f. PROTOPLAST[1] + -IC.] 1. Of the nature of a protoplast; first formed; original, archetypal. 2. *Biol.* = PROTOPLASMIC 1855.

Protopope (prōu·topōup). 1662. [ad. Russ. *protopopŭ*; see PROTO- and POPE *sb.*[2]; after eccl. Gr. πρωτοπαπᾶς.] A chief priest, or priest of higher rank, in the Greek Church.

‖ **Prototheria** (prōutoþī·riă), *sb. pl.* 1880. [mod.L., f. Gr. πρωτο- PROTO- + θηρία beasts.] *Zool.* The lowest subclass of Mammals, comprising the single order *Monotremata*, with their hypothetical ancestors. Hence **Pro·tothere,** a member of the P. **Protothe·rian** *a.* belonging to the P.; *sb.* a protothere.

Prototype (prōu·tŏtəip). 1603. [a. F., f. mod.L. *prototypon*, a. Gr. πρωτότυπον; see PROTO- and TYPE *sb.*] The first or primary type of anything; a pattern, model, standard, exemplar, archetype. Hence **Pro·totypal** *a.* of the nature of, or constituting, a p.; of or pertaining to a p.; archetypal.

‖ **Protozoa** (prōuto₁zōu·ă), *sb. pl.* 1834. [mod.L., f. Gr. πρωτο- PROTO- + ζῷα animals.] *Zool.* One of the two (or three) great divisions of the animal kingdom, comprising animals of the simplest or most primitive type, each consisting of a single cell, usu. of microscopic size: correlated with METAZOA. Also in sing. **Protozoon** (-zōu·ǫn), a member of the division *P.* Hence **Protozo·al** *a.* of, pertaining to, or connected with protozoa; in *Path.* caused, as a disease, by a parasitic protozoon.

Protozoan (prōuto₁zōu·ăn), *a.* and *sb.* 1864. [f. prec. + -AN.] A. *adj.* Of or belonging to the *Protozoa* or a protozoon; also = PROTOZOAL. B. *sb.* A protozoon.

Protozoic (prōuto₁zōu·ik), *a.* 1838. [In sense 1, f. Gr. πρωτο- PROTO- + ζωή life + -IC; in 2, f. PROTOZOA + -IC.] 1. *Geol.* and *Palæont.* Applied to those strata which contain the earliest remains or traces of living beings; also to fossils found in such strata. 2. *Zool.* and *Path.* = PROTOZOAN *a.* 1864.

Protozoology (prōu:to₁zo₁ǫ·lŏdʒi). 1904. [f. PROTOZOA + -(O)LOGY.] That department of zoology, or of pathology, which deals with protozoa, esp. with parasitic disease-producing protozoa.

Protract (prŏtræ·kt), *v.* 1548. [f. L. *protract-*, *protrahere* to prolong, etc., f. *pro* PRO-[1] + *trahere* to draw.] I. †1. *trans.* To prolong (time) so as to cause delay; to waste (time) -1769. 2. To lengthen out (an action); to cause to last longer; to prolong 1563. †3. To put off, postpone (an action) -1808. †4. *intr.* To make delay, to delay -1677.

1. This they did merely to p. time ROBERTSON. 2. Ne're could he so long p. his speech SHAKS. Their stay was protracted for some weeks 1838. 3. He attempted, however, to prevent, or at least to p., his ruin GIBBON.

II. *trans.* To extend in space or position 1658. III. To draw, represent by a drawing; *spec.* to draw to scale; to delineate by means of a protractor and scale; to plot out 1563. Hence Protra·cted·ly *adv.*, -ness.

Protractile (protræ·ktil, -əil), *a.* 1828. [f. as prec. + -ILE.] *Zool.* Capable of being lengthened out or extended.

Protraction (prŏtræ·kʃən). 1535. [a. F., f. L. *protrahere* PROTRACT *v.*] The action of protracting. I. 1. The lengthening out of time or of the duration of anything; prolongation. 2. A stretching out or extension; the action of a protractor (muscle) 1890.

1. The long p. of the suit 1868.

II. The drawing to scale or laying down of the figure of any surface, esp. of a piece of land 1607. b. A chart or plan drawn or laid down to scale; a survey 1669.

†**Protra·ctive,** *a.* 1606. [f. L. *protract-* (see PROTRACT *v.*) + -IVE.] Characterized by protraction; lengthening out, delaying -1819.

Protractor (prŏtræ·ktəɹ). 1611. [a. med. L. *protractor*, f. *protrahere* to PROTRACT.] One who or that which protracts. 1. One who lengthens out time or any action; †one who puts off or delays action. 2. An instrument, usu. having the form of a graduated semicircle, used in setting off and measuring angles 1658. 3. *Surg.* An instrument for extracting foreign bodies from wounds 1727. 4. *Anat.* A muscle which serves to protract or extend a limb or member. Also *p. muscle.* 1861.

Protreptic (protre·ptik), *a.* and *sb.* 1656. [As adj. ad. Gr. προτρεπτικός, f. πρό PRO-[2] + τρέπειν to turn; as sb. ad. late L. *protrepticon* (*-um*) = Gr. προτρεπτικόν, neut. of the adj.] A. *adj.* Directive, instructive, didactic 1658. B. *sb.* A book, writing, or speech intended to exhort or instruct 1656. So **Protre·ptical** *a.*

Protrude (prŏtrū·d), *v.* 1620. [ad. L. *protrudere*, f. *pro* PRO-[1] + *trudere* to thrust.] †1. *trans.* To thrust forward; to push or drive onward -1834. 2. To push or thrust into any position; to cause to project; to extend 1646. b. *fig.* To obtrude 1840. 3. *intr.* To stick out 1626.

2. When young Spring protrudes the bursting gems THOMSON. b. Critics, who..p. their nonsense upon the town THACKERAY. 3. A pair of feet protruding from under the curtains 1868. Hence **Protru·dable** *a.* capable of being protruded; so **Protru·sible.**

Protrusile (protrū·sil, -əil), *a.* 1847. [f. L. *protrus-*, *protrudere* + -ILE.] Adapted to be extended or thrust out, as a limb, tentacle, etc.

Protrusion (prŏtrū·ʒən). 1646. [a. F., f. L. *protrudere* to PROTRUDE.] 1. The action of protruding; the fact or condition of being protruded. 2. *concr.* That which protrudes or juts out; a protruding part, a protuberance, a prominence 1704.

2. The fantastic gables, pinnacles, and protrusions, which intercepted the light 1862.

Protrusive (prŏtrū·siv), *a.* 1676. [f. L. *protrus-*, *protrudere* to PROTRUDE + -IVE.] 1. Thrusting forward or onward; propulsive. 2. Obtrusive 1840. 3. Protruding, projecting, protuberant 1858. Hence **Protru·sive-ly** *adv.*, -ness.

Protuberance (prŏtiū·bĕrăns). 1646. [f. PROTUBERANT; see -ANCE.] 1. The fact or condition of being protuberant; bulging out or projecting in a rounded form 1681. 2. That which is protuberant; a rounded prominence, projection, or swelling; a knob, a bump 1646.

2. *Solar p.* = solar PROMINENCE. So **Protu·berancy.**

Protuberant (prŏtiū·bĕrănt), *a.* 1646. [ad. late L. *protuberantem*, *protuberare*, f. L. *pro* PRO-[1] + *tuber* a hump, swelling.] Bulging or swelling out beyond the surrounding surface; prominent.

Eocha III...is remembered for his p. nose 1807. Hence **Protu·berantly** *adv.*

Protuberate (prŏtiū·bĕreⁱt), *v. rare.* 1578. [f. late L. *protuberat-*, *protuberare*; see prec.] *intr.* To bulge out, to form a rounded prominence.

‖ **Protyle** (prōᵘ·təil). Also **prothyl.** 1886. [irreg. f. Gr. πρωτ(ο- PROTO- + ὕλη HYLE.] Proposed name for the hypothetical original undifferentiated matter, of which the chemical substances provisionally regarded as elements may be composed.

Proud (praud), *a.* (*adv.*) [Late OE. *prūt*, *prūd*, a. OF. *prud*, *prod* :—late L. **prodis* profitable, useful (cf. L. *prodesse* to be of value, be good; see also PREUX, PROW *a.*, and cf. PRIDE).] I. 1. Having a high or lofty opinion of oneself; valuing oneself highly on account of one's position, rank, attainments, possessions, etc. Usu. in bad sense, implying arrogance or hauteur. 2. Highly sensible of, or elated by, some honour done to one; taking pride or having high satisfaction in something; in early use sometimes merely = highly gratified or pleased; *colloq.* feeling highly honoured. Often const. *of*, or inf. ME. 3. Having a becoming sense of what is due to or worthy of oneself or one's position; feeling or showing a proper pride 1738. 4. *transf.* Of actions, etc.: Proceeding from or indicating pride; arrogant, presumptuous; arising from lofty self-respect. late ME. 5. That is a ground or cause of pride; of which one is or may be proud (now usu. in good sense) ME.

1. They are as bragge and as proude as pecockes 1560. Hee was a p. insolent Delegate 1613. Most of our women are extreamly p. Of their faire lookes 1616. They say he 's as p. as Lucifer 1782. 2. The author of the *Plain Dealer*, whom I am p. to call my friend DRYDEN. 4. There be sixe thinges, which the Lorde hateth..A proude loke [etc.] COVERDALE *Prov.* vi. 17. 5. The p. inheritance of their stainless loyalty 1868.

II. 1. As a poetic or rhetorical epithet. a. Of exalted station, of high degree, of lofty dignity; lordly ME. b. Of things: Stately, magnificent, 'gallant', splendid ME. 2. Characterized by great vigour, force, or vitality, such as indicates or suggests pride; in various applications. †a. Of warriors (or their acts): Valiant, brave; mighty -1697. b. Of animals: Spirited, high-mettled; moving with force and dignity. (Chiefly *poet.*) late ME. c. Of the sea or a stream: Swelling, swollen, strong, in flood 1535. d. Of organic structures: Overgrown, exuberant; swelling or swollen, tumid. (*b*) Applied to overgrown flesh in a healing wound; see also PROUD FLESH. 1593. †3. Sensually excited; 'swelling', lascivious -1641. †b. *spec.* Of certain female animals: In a state of sexual excitement -1781.

1. a. High though his titles, p. his name, Boundless his wealth SCOTT. b. View..The p. ships sail, and gay clouds move 1794. One of the proudest cities of the ancient world THIRLWALL. 2. b. Like a p. Steed reind MILT. c. Then the p. waters had gone ouer our soule *Ps.* cxxiv. 5.

Phr. *To do* (a person) *p.* (colloq.), to make p., gratify highly, do honour to.

B. as *adv.* Proudly, in a proud manner ME. Hence **Prou·dish** *a.* somewhat p. **Prou·d-ly** *adv.*, -ness.

Proud flesh. late ME. [See prec. II. 2 d.] Overgrown flesh arising from excessive granulation upon, or around the edges of, a healing wound.

Prou·d-hea·rted, *a.* late ME. Having a proud heart or spirit; proud, haughty.

Proustite (prū·stəit). 1835. [a. F., after J. L. *Proust*, a French chemist; see -ITE[1].] *Min.* Native sulpharsenide of silver, occurring in crystals or granular masses of a cochineal-red colour.

Provand (prǫ·vănd). ME. [app. ad. F. *provende*; see PROVEND *sb.*] Provisions, provender; *esp.* the food and fodder provided for an army.

Provant (prǫ·vănt), *sb.* (*a.*) 1450. [app. a. MLG. *provant* PROVAND.] 1. Provand, provender; an allowance of food. 2. *attrib.* or as *adj.* Of or belonging to the p. or soldier's allowance; hence, of inferior quality. *arch.* 1598.

Prove (prūv), *v.* Infl. **proved, proving;** pa. pple. also (orig. in Sc. legal use) proven. ME. [a. OF. *prover* :—L. *probare* to test (a thing) as to its goodness, f. *probus* good.] I. To make trial of, try, test. 1. *trans.* To make trial of; to try the genuineness or qualities of; to test. *arch.* exc. in techn. uses. b. To subject to a testing process (any natural, prepared, or manufactured substance or object) ME. c. *Arith.* To test the correctness of (a calculation) 1806. d. To take a proof impression of (composed type or an electro- or stereotype plate) 1797. 2. To find out, learn, or know by experience; to experience, 'go through', suffer; also, to find by experience (a person or thing) to be (something) ME.

1. Proue all things: hold fast that which is good 1 *Thess.* v. 21. c. Multiplication is also very naturally proved by Division 1806. 2. They only shall his Mercy p. WESLEY.

II. To make good, establish. 1. *trans.* To establish (a thing) as true; to demonstrate the truth of by evidence or argument ME. 2. To show the existence or reality of; to give proof of by action; to evince ME. 3. To establish the genuineness or validity of (a thing or person); to show to be such as is asserted or claimed 1517. b. *spec.* To establish the genuineness and validity of (a will); to obtain probate of. late ME. 4. *intr.* for *refl.* To be shown or found by experience or trial to be (so and so); to turn out (to be). late ME. 5. To come to be, become, grow (*arch.*) 1560.

1. He went about also to proue hym selfe a Germayne 1560. 3. It is very hard to p. a Witch FULLER. 6. **P. up** (*U.S.*): to adduce or complete the proof of right to (something); *spec.* to show that one has fulfilled the requirements for receiving a patent for (government land) 1867. Hence **Pro·v(e)able** *a.* capable of being proved. **Pro·v(e)ableness.** **Pro·v(e)ably** *adv.*

Provect (prove·kt), *v.* 1652. [f. L. *provect-*, *provehere*, f. *pro* PRO-[1] + *vehere* to carry.] †1. *trans.* To carry forward or onward -1776. 2. *Philol.* To change or 'mutate' a consonant in the direction of the sound-shift formulated for Germanic in Grimm's Law; *esp.* in Celtic, to change a voice consonant into a breath consonant of the same series 1861.

Provection (prove·kʃən). 1652. [ad. late L. *provectionem*, f. *provehere*; see prec.] †1. Advance, proficiency; advancement -1660. 2. *Philol.* a. The sound-shift formulated for Germanic langs. in Grimm's Law; also in Celtic, the mutation of voice consonants to breath consonants 1861. b. The carrying on of the final letter of a word to the succeeding one 1868.

Proveditor (prove·ditǫɹ), also in It. form ‖**Proveditore** (proveditō·re). 1549. [ad. obs. It. *proved-*, mod. *provveditore* provider, purveyor, f. *provedere* to PROVIDE.] 1. The title of certain officers of the Venetian republic; a governor, overseer, inspector. 2. A purveyor, caterer, steward 1599.

Provedore (prǫvīdōᵊ·ɹ). 1578. [ad. various Rom. forms, all the agent-n. from the vb. repr. L. *providere* to PROVIDE; cf. prec.] = prec.

Proven (prū·v'n, *Sc.* prōᵘ·v'n), *ppl. a.* 1653. [pa. pple., orig. Sc. (*provin*, *c.* 1536) of *preve*, early var. of PROVE *v.*, after str. vbs. like *cleave, cloven.*] 1. Shown to be true, or to be as stated; demonstrated by evidence. 2. Tried, tested (pseudo-*arch.*) 1870.

1. A p. falsehood LANDOR. *Not proven*, a form of verdict in criminal trials in Sc. Law, which is admitted beside 'Guilty' and 'Not guilty'.

Provenance (prǫ·vĕnăns). 1861. [a. F., f. *provenant*, pres. pple. of *provenir*, ad. L. *provenire.*] The fact of coming from some particular source or quarter; derivation.

The date and p. of Jewish apocalypses 1906.

Provençal (provaṅsal), *a.* and *sb.* 1589. [a. F., = of Provence :—L. *provincialis*; see PROVENCE.] A. *adj.* Of or pertaining to Provence and its inhabitants.

Dance, and P. song, and sunburnt mirth! KEATS.

B. *sb.* 1. An inhabitant of Provence 1600. 2. The Romanic language spoken there 1671.

Provence (‖provā·ṅs, prǫ·vĕns). 1578. [a. F., :—L. *provincia* PROVINCE.] The name of a former province in the south-east of France east of the Rhone; used *attrib.*, as in *P. oil*, olive oil from P.

Provend (prǫ·vĕnd), *sb. Obs.* or *arch.* ME. [a. F. *provende* :—Rom. type **provenda*; altered f. L. *præbenda*, *prebenda* PREBEND.] 1. = PREBEND 1; also, the portion or allowance of food supplied to each inmate of a monastery. 2. = next. ME.

Provender (prǫ·vĕndəɹ), *sb.* ME. [a. OF. *provendre*, var. of *provende* PROVEND.] Food, provisions; *esp.* dry food, as corn or hay for horses, etc.; fodder, forage. In ref. to human beings, now *joc.*

They must be dyeted like Mules, And haue their Prouender ty'd to their mouthes SHAKS. Hence **Pro·vender** *v. trans.* to provide (horses, etc.) with provender to fodder.

Provenience (prǒvīˈniĕns). 1882. (Common in U.S.) [f. L. *provenientem*; see -ENCE.] = PROVENANCE.

|| **Proventriculus** (prōuventriˈkiŭlǒs). 1835. [mod.L., f. *pro* PRO-[1] + *ventriculus* VENTRICLE.] **a.** *Ornith.* The glandular or true stomach of birds, which lies between the crop and the gizzard. **b.** In some insects, the crop or ingluvies, an expansion of the œsophagus; in worms, a muscular crop 1877.

Prover (prūˈvəɹ). late ME. [In sense 1, f. PROVE + -ER[1]; in 2 = Anglo-L. *probator*, AF. *provour, pruvour.*] **1.** One who tries, tests, or puts to the proof. *Obs.* or *arch.* **b.** An instrument or apparatus for testing 1751. **c.** *Engraving.* A skilled workman employed to print proof impressions 1875. †**2.** = APPROVER[1] 1. -1769.

Proverb (prǫˈvəɹb), *sb.* [ME. a. F. *proverbe*, ad. L. *proverbium*, f. *pro* PRO-[1] + *verbum* + *-ium*, collective suffix.] **1.** A short pithy saying in common use; a concise sentence, which is held to express some truth ascertained by experience or observation and familiar to all; an adage, a wise saw. **2.** †**a.** = BYWORD 2 -1791. **b.** *transf.* A thing that is proverbial or a matter of common talk 1655. †**3.** An oracular or enigmatical saying that requires interpretation; an allegory, a parable -1841. **4.** A play of which a proverb is taken as the foundation of the plot 1842. **5.** *pl.* Any of various round games played with popular sayings.

1. *The Book of Proverbs*, a book of the O.T., consisting of maxims ascribed to Solomon and others. Phr. *To a p.*, to an extent that has become proverbial; The new chief justice, Sir Robert Wright, was ignorant to a p. MACAULAY. 2. a. And thou shalt be a wonder, a prouerbe & a commune talke among all people BIBLE (Genev.) *Deut.* xxviii. 37. 3. To vnderstand a prouerbe, and the interpretation; the wordes of the wise, and their darke sayings *Prov.* i. 6.

Proverb (prǫˈvəɹb), *v.* late ME. [f. prec.] **1.** *trans.* To utter in the form of a proverb; to make a byword of. **2.** To furnish or provide with a proverb SHAKS. **3.** *intr.* To utter or compose proverbs MILT.

1. Am I not sung and proverbd for a Fool In every street? MILT. 2. I am prouerb'd with a Grandsier Phrase SHAKS.

Proverbial (prǒvǭˈɹbiăl), *a.* late ME. [ad. late L. *proverbialis*, f. *proverbium* PROVERB; see -AL.] **1.** Like, characteristic of, or of the nature of a proverb; expressed in a proverb or proverbs. **2.** That has passed into a proverb; current as a proverb; notorious 1571.

1. Yet is not all true that is proverbiall SIR T. BROWNE. 2. The p. London fog HUXLEY. Hence **Proveˈrbialism**, a p. saying. **Proveˈrbialist**, one who originates, uses, or records p. sayings. **Proverbiaˈlity**, the quality of being p. **Proveˈrbialize** *v. intr.* to make or utter proverbs. **Proveˈrbially** *adv.* in a p. manner; to a p. degree.

Proviant (prǫˈviănt). 1637. [a. G. *proviant*, Du. *proviand*, app. a var. of *provenda* PROVEND. Brought into Eng. by soldiers who served in the Thirty Years' War, 1618-48.] Food supply, esp. for an army; commissariat.

Pro:-vice-chaˈncellor. 1660. [See PRO-[1]] One of the deputies appointed by the vice-chancellor of a university on his election.

Provide (prǒvəiˈd), *v.* late ME. [ad. L. *providere* to see before, etc., f. *pro* PRO-[1] + *videre.*] **I.** †**1.** *trans.* To foresee -1640. **2.** *intr.* To exercise foresight in taking due measures in view of a possible event. Const. *for*, *against.* late ME. **b.** To lay it down as a provision; to stipulate *that.* late ME.

2. In tyme of peace, prouide for war GRAFTON. b. The Mayers wyfe..prouided in her wyll, that she would be buried without any pompe or noyse 1560.

II. 1. *trans.* To prepare, get ready, or arrange (something) beforehand. Now *rare.* late ME. †**2.** *intr.* To make preparation, get ready -1727. †**b.** *trans.* with *vbl. sb.* SHAKS. **3.** *trans.* To supply or furnish for use; to yield, afford 1447. **4.** To furnish or appoint (an incumbent) *to* a vacant benefice; *esp.* of the pope: To appoint (a person as successor) *to* a benefice not yet vacant, thus setting aside the right of the patron. Now only *Hist.* late ME.

1. The wise Ant her wintry Store provides DRYDEN. 2. Very few men..live at present, but are providing to live another time POPE. 3. Prouide me ynke and paper, and I will write 1581.

III. 1. To fit out (a person, etc.) with what is necessary for a certain purpose; to furnish or supply with something implied 1465. †**b.** *refl.* To equip oneself, to make oneself ready, prepare (*to do* something, *for* or *against* something) -1652. **2.** To furnish (a person, etc.) with something. Often in indirect passive. late ME. **3.** *intr.* To make provision *for* a person, his needs, etc. Often in indirect passive. 1535.

1. b. Neice prouide your selfe SHAKS. 2. Prouided with all complete prouisions of Warre CAMDEN. 3. His wonted Followers Shall all be very well prouided for SHAKS.

Provided (prǒvəiˈdĕd), *ppl. a.* and quasi-*conj.* 1460. [pa. pple. of PROVIDE *v.*] **I.** *ppl. a.* In senses of PROVIDE *v.* 1579. **II.** *pa. pple.* and quasi-*conj.* With the provision or condition (that); it being provided or stipulated (that); used chiefly in legal and formal statements; also, in general use: On the condition, supposition, or understanding (that) 1460. **b.** without *that*: = if only 1604.

I. *P. school*, a public elementary school provided by the local education authority. II. P. that all is safe, you may go 1879. b. Now or whensoeuer, prouided I be so able as now SHAKS.

Providence (prǫˈvidĕns). ME. [a. F., ad. L. *providentia*, f. *providere* to PROVIDE; see -ENCE.] **1.** The action of providing; provision, preparation, arrangement. Now *dial.* late ME. **b.** That which is provided; a supply, a provision. Now *dial.* 1475. **2.** Foresight, prevision; *esp.* anticipation of and preparation for the future; hence, prudent or wise management, government, or guidance. Also, an instance of this. late ME. **b.** Regard to future needs in the management of resources; thrift 1608. **3.** In full, *p. of God* (etc.), *divine p.*: The foreknowing and beneficent care and government of God (or of nature, etc.); divine direction, control, or guidance ME. **4.** Hence applied to the Deity as exercising prescient power and direction 1602. **b.** *transf.* A person who acts or appears in the character of Providence (*colloq.*) 1856. **5.** An instance or act of divine intervention; an event or circumstance which indicates divine dispensation 1643.

2. In this matter the p. of king Henry the seventh was in all men's mouths BACON. b. When there should have been p. there has been waste RUSKIN. 3. Almyȝty god, whos prouidence in hys ordinaunce faileþ noȝt 1400. 4. What P. has reserved for me he only knows DE FOE. 5. *Special p.*, a particular act of direct divine intervention.

Provident (prǫˈvidĕnt), *a.* late ME. [ad. L. *providens, -entem*, pres. pple. of *providere* to PROVIDE.] **1.** Foreseeing; that has foresight of and provides for the future, or for some future event. **2.** Economical; frugal, thrifty, saving 1596.

1. By Solomon God sends the Sluggard to school to the Ant, to learn a p. Industry BOYLE. *P. society* = FRIENDLY *society*. 2. He will always be poor, because he never was a p. man 1888. Hence **Proˈvidently** *adv.*, **-ness** (*rare*).

Providential (prǫvideˈnʃăl), *a.* 1648. [f. L. *providentia* PROVIDENCE + -AL.] †**1.** Of the nature of providence; provident, prudent -1845. **2.** Of, pertaining to, or ordained by divine providence 1648. **b.** That is, or is thought to be, by special interposition of providence; opportune, lucky, fortunate 1719.

2. A p. disposition of things 1736. b. [It] was by them considered as a p. escape BURKE. Hence **Provideˈntially** *adv.*

Provider (prǒvəiˈdəɹ). 1523. [f. PROVIDE *v.* + -ER[1].] One who provides or supplies; a purveyor. *Lion's p.*: see LION I.

Province (prǫˈvins). ME. [a. F., ad. L. *provincia*; etym. unkn.] **I. 1.** *Rom. Hist.* A country or territory outside Italy, under Roman dominion, and administered by a governor sent from Rome. late ME. **2.** An administrative division of a country or state; any principal division of a kingdom or empire. Formerly sometimes applied to the shires of England. late ME. **b.** Applied to the N. American colonies of Great Britain, now provinces of the Dominion of Canada; also formerly to several of those which afterwards united to form the United States of America 1622. **c.** *fig.* A main division of any 'realm' 1869. **3.** *Eccl.* The district within the jurisdiction of an archbishop or a metropolitan. late ME. **b.** One of the territorial divisions of the Knights Templars, the Franciscans, the Jesuits, or any similar order 1727. **4.** More vaguely, A country, territory, district, or region; a part of the world, or of one of its continents ME. **5.** *pl.* A comprehensive designation for all parts of a country outside the capital; e. g. of England apart from London 1804. **6.** *Nat. Hist.* A faunal or floral area less extensive than a 'region'; a sub-region 1877.

2. They divided the country into four provinces, viz. Ulster, Leinster, Munster, and Connaught, each of which had its King 1804. c. Our earth is but a p. of a wider realm 1869. 4. Some had long moved to distant provinces JOHNSON. 5. She had..starred the provinces with great eclat and had come back to London THACKERAY.

II. The sphere of action of a person or body of persons; duty, office, business, function, department 1626.

My p. was..to carry home the goods 1775. How he had secured an entrance..it is not our p. to inquire 1888.

III. *fig.* from I. A department, division, or branch of learning, science, art, government, or any subject 1709.

In the provinces of Æsthetics and Morals 1874.

Provincial (prǒviˈnʃăl), *a.* and *sb.* late ME. [a. F., or ad. L. *provincialis*, f. *provincia*; see prec. and -AL.] **A.** *adj.* **1.** Of or pertaining to a province or provinces. †**2.** Having the relation of a province to a sovereign state -1708. **3.** Of or belonging to a province or provinces as dist. from the nation or state of which they form a part; local; hence, of the 'provinces' as dist. from the capital; situated in 'the provinces' 1638. **b.** *transf.* Said of foxhunting outside the 'shires' 1861. **4.** Having the manners or speech, *esp.* the narrow views, etc., of a province or 'the provinces'; wanting the culture or polish of the capital 1755. †**5.** Of roses of Provence -1633.

2. The other parts of it..are still as much p. to Italy, as..in the time of the Roman Empire DRYDEN. 3. Those many barbarisms which characterize a p. education 1772. P. or local words 1787. Paris and the great p. towns 1844. 4. *Provincial*,..rude; unpolished JOHNSON. 5. *Haml.* III. ii. 288.

B. *sb.* [the adj. used absol. or ellipt.] **1.** *Eccl.* The ecclesiastical head of a province; the chief of a religious order in a district or province. late ME. **2.** A native or inhabitant of a province (Roman or modern); in *pl.* auxiliary troops raised in a province; formerly applied to the native Irish 1605. **b.** An inhabitant of the N. American colonies before the revolution; applied esp. to those engaged in military service 1758. **3.** One who dwells in or comes from the 'provinces' as dist. from the capital; hence, a 'countrified' person 1711.

3. Provincials, narrow in thought, in culture, in creed 1865. Hence **Proviˈncialist**, a native or inhabitant of a province or of the provinces, as dist. from the capital. **Provinciaˈlity**, the quality or condition of being p.; a p. trait. **Proviˈncialize** *v. trans.* and *intr.* to make or become p. **Proviˈncially** *adv.* in a p. manner or capacity.

Provincialism (prǒviˈnʃăliz'm). 1793. [f. prec. + -ISM.] **1.** *Politics.* Attachment to one's own province, its institutions, interests, etc., before those of the nation or state; desire for the autonomy of the province or provinces rather than national unity 1820. **2.** Provincial manner, fashion, mode of thought, etc. as dist. from that which is (or is held to be) national, or which is the fashion of the capital; hence, narrowness of view, thought, or interests, unpolished speech or manners 1836. **b.** with *a* and *pl.* A local peculiarity or variety 1845. **3.** *esp.* The manner of speech characteristic of a particular province; with *pl.*, A local word, phrase, or peculiarity of pronunciation 1793.

Provinciate (prǒviˈnʃiˌēit), *v.* 1629. [f. L. *provincia* PROVINCE + -ATE[3].] *trans.* To reduce to the condition of a province or of provincials.

Provine (provəiˈn), *v.* 1440. [ad. F. *provignier*, f. OF. *provain* :—L. *propaginem* young shoot, slip, or layer.] *trans.* To propagate (a vine or the like) by layering. Also *absol.*, and *intr.* in *pass.* sense.

Provision (prǒviˈʒən), *sb.* late ME. [a. F., ad. L. *provisionem*, f. *providere* to PROVIDE.] **1.** The action of providing; seeing to things beforehand; the fact or condition of being made ready beforehand 1456. b. *esp.* The providing or supplying of necessaries for a household, an expedition, etc. 1484. 2. *Eccl.* Appointment to a see or benefice not yet vacant; *esp.* such appointment made by the pope in derogation of the right of the regular patron. Now *Hist.* late ME. 3. Something prepared or arranged in advance; a preparation, a previous arrangement; a measure provided to meet a need; a precaution 1494. 4. A supply of necessaries or materials provided; a store of something 1451. 5. *spec.* A supply of food; now chiefly *pl.* supplies of food, victuals, eatables and drinkables 1610. 6. Each of the clauses or divisions of a legal or formal statement, or such a statement itself, providing for some particular matter; also, a clause in such a statement which makes an express stipulation; a proviso 1473.

1. Due p. for education..is..a duty of the state HUXLEY. Phr. *To make p.*, to provide *for*. 3. There was no..p. for a rudder 1832. 4. Here they deposit their p. of nuts and acorns 1796. 5. The English for want of provisions were forced to breake up Siege HOLLAND. The price of provisions is exorbitant 1773. 6. *Provisions of Oxford*, ordinances for checking the king's misrule, drawn up at a meeting of the barons under Simon de Montfort, held at Oxford in 1258.

Provision (prŏvi·ʒən), *v.* 1805. [f. prec.] *trans.* To supply with provisions or stores. b. *intr.* (for *refl.*) To supply oneself with provisions; to lay in provisions.

He raised a regiment of horse and provisioned it 1859.

Provisional (prŏvi·ʒənăl), *a.* 1601. [f. PROVISION *sb.* + -AL.] 1. Of, belonging to, or of the nature of a temporary provision or arrangement; provided or adopted for present needs or for the time being; also, accepted or used in default of something better. †2. Provident (*rare*) –1763.

1. To come to a prouisionall agreement 1601. The Church should not be without a p. Pastor 1726. Hence **Provi·sional-ly** *adv.*, **-ness.**

Provisionary (prŏvi·ʒənări), *a.* Now *rare.* 1617. [f. as prec. + -ARY [1].] 1. = prec. 1. †2. = prec. 2. –1784. 3. Of or pertaining to papal provisions; see PROVISION *sb.* 2. 1736. 4. Of, pertaining to, or of the nature of a proviso, a provision, or provisions (in a law, etc.) 1774.

Proviso (prŏvəi·zo). *Pl.* **-oes.** 1467. [a. L., abl. neut. pa. pple. of *providere*, as used in med.L. legal phrase *proviso quod* 'it being provided that'.] A clause inserted in a legal or formal document, making some condition, stipulation, exception, or limitation, or upon the observance of which the operation or validity of the instrument depends; a condition; hence *gen.*, a stipulation, provision.

Provisor (prŏvəi·zəɪ, -ǭɪ). [Late ME. *provisour*, a. AF., ad. L. *provisorem* provider, f. *providere.*] I. The holder of a provision or grant (esp. from the pope) giving him the right to be presented to a benefice when next vacant. Now *Hist.*

Statute of Provisors, the Act 25 Edw. III, 1350–1, enacted to prevent the granting of these provisions by the pope.

II. †1. One who is in charge; a supervisor; an agent, deputy –1533. †2. One who provides for another; a guardian, protector –1730. 3. A purveyor; the steward or treasurer of an establishment. Now *Hist.* 1498. 4. *R. C. Ch.* A vicar-general; a deputy-inquisitor 1560.

3. P. General of Pork for the Army 1683. Hence **Provi·sorship** (*rare*), the office or position of a p.

Provisory (prŏvəi·zəri), *a.* 1611. [ad. F. *provisoire.*] 1. Subject to a provision or proviso; conditional. 2. = PROVISIONAL *a.* 1. 1788. Hence **Provi·sorily** *adv.* in a p. manner; provisionally.

Provocation (prǫvŏkēⁱ·ʃən). late ME. [a. F., ad. L. *provocationem*, f. *provocare* to PROVOKE.] I. †1. The action of invoking the office of a court or judge; *esp.* an appeal to a higher ecclesiastical court –1726. 2. The action of calling; invitation, summons 1548. II. 1. The action of inciting; impulse; instigation; an incentive, a stimulus. late ME. 2. The action or an act of exciting anger, resentment, or irritation 1539. b. A cause of anger, resentment, or irritation 1716.

2. To the..prouocacion of the terrible wrath of god 1540. You ought not to give way to your temper, under whatever p. 1876.

Provocative (prŏvǫ·kătiv), *a.* and *sb.* late ME. [As adj. a. F. †*provocatif* or ad. late L. *provocativus*; as sb. ad. L. neut. sing.] A. *adj.* 1. Having the quality of provoking, calling forth, or giving rise to (const. *of*); *spec.* stimulating, irritating 1649. 2. *spec.* Serving to excite appetite or lust 1621. B. *sb.* 1. That which provokes, excites, or draws forth; an incentive 1638. 2. *spec.* Anything that excites appetite or lust; *esp.* an aphrodisiac. late ME. Hence **Provo·catively** *adv.*

Provokable (prŏvōᵘ·kăb'l), *a.* 1678. [f. PROVOKE *v.* + -ABLE.] Capable of being provoked.

Provoke (prŏvōᵘ·k), *v.* late ME. [a. OF. *provoker*, ad. L. *provocare*, f. *pro* PRO-[1] + *vocare.*] I. †1. *trans.* To call forth, invoke; to summon, invite. Also *absol.* –1708. †2. *intr.* To call to a judge or court to take up one's cause; to appeal (*from* a lower *to* a higher eccl. tribunal) –1682. †3. *trans.* To call out to a fight; to challenge, to defy –1697.

3. Tertullian..provokes all the world to contradict it, if they could EVELYN.

II. 1. To incite or urge (a person or animal) *to* some act or *to do* something; to stimulate to action. Now *arch.* exc. as infl. by next. late ME. 2. To incite to anger (a person or animal); to enrage, irritate. Also *absol.* late ME. 3. To excite, stir up (feeling, action, etc.); to give rise to, call forth 1533.

1. Beautie prouoketh theeues sooner then gold SHAKS. 2. You are really enough to p. a saint 1800. 3. My Tale prouokes that question SHAKS. Hence **Provo·ked** *ppl. a.* having received provocation; irritated, annoyed. †**Provo·kement**, the action of provoking; a provocation. **Provo·ker**, one who or that which provokes. **Provo·kingly** *adv.*

Provost (prǫ·vəst). [OE. *prafost*, *profost*, OF. and AF. *provost* (mod.F. *prévôt*); repr. med.L. *propositus*, *præpositus*, sb. use of *præpositus*, pa. pple. of *præponere*, f. *præ* before + *ponere* to place.] I. In eccl. and scholastic use. 1. The head or president of a chapter, or of a community of religious persons; in conventual bodies prop. the official next in rank to the abbot. Now chiefly *Hist.* b. In mod. use, tr. Ger. *propst*, Da. *provst*, etc., as the title of the Protestant clergyman in charge of the principal church of a town or district 1560. 2. The specific title of the heads of certain colleges 1442. II. A secular officer, etc. †1. One appointed to preside over or superintend something; usu. the representative of the supreme power in a district or sphere of action. Sometimes, without explicit ref. to his delegated or appointed position, = Ruler, chief, head, captain, etc. –1631. 2. An officer or official in charge of some establishment, undertaking, or body of men; a ruler, manager, steward, overseer, keeper. Now *Hist.* ME. 3. †The chief magistrate of a town; *spec.* the head of a Scottish municipal corporation or burgh ME. †4. An officer charged with the apprehension, custody, and punishment of offenders –1873. 5. *spec. Mil.* An officer of the military police in a garrison or camp, or in the field: see next. (In this sense usu. pronounced prŏvōᵘ·.) 1692.

4. Here comes Signior Claudio, led by the Prouost to prison SHAKS.

Comb.: **p.-cell**, a cell for confining military prisoners; **-sergeant**, a sergeant of the military police. Hence **Pro·vostship**, the office or position of a p.

Provost-marshal (prŏvōᵘ:mā·ɹʃăl). 1513. [f. prec. + MARSHAL *sb.*] In the army, An officer appointed to a force in camp or on active service, as the head of the military police. In the navy, the 'Master-at-arms' of the ship in which a court martial is to be held (being the Chief Petty Officer in charge of the ship's police) is appointed by warrant Provost-marshal for the occasion.

Prow (prau), *sb.*[1] Now chiefly *literary.* 1555. [a. F. *proue*, prob. ult. f. L. *prora*, a. Gr. πρῷρα.] 1. The fore-part of a ship or boat; the part about the stem. 2. A point or pointed part projecting in front, like the prow of a ship; *spec.* in *Zool.* either of the two points of a cymba or C-shaped sponge-spicule 1656. 3. *transf.* A ship (*poet.*) 1738.

3. Prows, that late in fierce Encounter mett GRAY. Hence **Prowed** (praud) *a.* having a p.

†**Prow**, *sb.*[2] [ME. *pru*, *prou*, a. OF. *pru*, *prou*, subst. use of *pru*, *prou* adj.; see next.] Advantage, profit, benefit, weal, good –1570.

It maye bee for his prowe, To thynke on it HARDING.

Prow (prau), *a. arch.* [ME. a. OF. *prou* :—late L. **prodis.*] Doughty, valiant.

The prowest knight that ever field did fight SPENSER.

Prowess (prau·ės). Now chiefly *literary.* [ME. *prowesse*, a. OF. *proece*, f. *pro*, *prou* PROW *a.* + -ESS [2].] Valour, bravery, gallantry, martial daring; manly courage, active fortitude. b. An act of bravery; a valiant deed. (Chiefly in *pl.* = deeds of valour.) ME.

His hye prowes was suche that no paynym durst abyde him 1533.

Prowl (praul), *v.* [ME. *prollen*; origin unkn.] 1. *intr.* Orig., To go or move about, esp. in search of something; hence, to rove, roam, or wander about in search of plunder, prey, etc., or with predatory intent. In mod. use, chiefly of wild beasts, or of men acting like them. †b. *fig.* To seek for advantage in an underhand way; to 'cadge' –1669. †2. *trans.* To obtain (something) in a clandestine way; to pilfer, filch –1677. 3. To traverse (a place or region) esp. on the look out for prey; to traverse stealthily 1586.

1. [Wolves] Priuely prolling two and froe SPENSER. How the troops of Midian P. and p. around 1850. b. An other pretie practise of the pope to proll for monie, was this FOXE. Hence **Prowl** *sb.* an act or the action of prowling; *on* or *upon the prowl*, prowling about. **Prow·ler**, one who prowls; a parasite; †a pilferer, cheat, plunderer. **Prow·lingly** *adv.*

‖**Proxenus** (prǫ·ksėnŏs). Also **proxenos.** *Pl.* **-i** (-əi). 1838. [mod.L., a. Gr. πρόξενος, f. πρό PRO-[2] + ξένος guest, stranger.] *Gr. Antiq.* A resident citizen of a state appointed by another state to represent and protect its interests there. So **Pro·xeny**, the office or function of a p.; the system of *proxeni.*

Proximad (prǫ·ksimæ̆d), *adv.* 1803. [f. as next + *-ad*; see DEXTRAD.] *Anat.* In the direction of its point of attachment: opp. to DISTAD.

Proximal (prǫ·ksimăl), *a.* 1803. [f. L. *proximus* + -AL.] *Anat.* Situated towards the centre of the body, or the point of origin or attachment of a limb, bone, etc.: opp. to DISTAL. Hence **Pro·ximally** *adv.* in a p. position; towards or near the p. end or part.

Proximate (prǫ·ksimět), *a.* 1597. [ad. late L. *proximatus*, *proximare* to approach, f. *proximus.*] 1. Next, nearest (in space, serial order, quality, etc.); close. b. Coming next or very near in time 1845. 2. Coming next (before or after) in a chain of causation, agency, reasoning, etc.; immediate: opp. to *remote* or *ultimate* 1661. 3. Approximate 1796.

2. *P. principle, constituent*, or *element* (Chem.), one of those compounds of which a more complex body is directly made up, and which are therefore first arrived at in the process of analysis; so *p. analysis.* 3. A p. notion of the extent of the carnage KINGLAKE. Hence **Pro·ximately** *adv.* in a p. position or manner; approximately.

‖**Proxime accessit** (prǫ·ksimi ækse·sit). 1878. [L. phr. = 'he has come very near (or next)'.] Phr. indicating that the person in question has come next to the winner of a prize, scholarship, etc.; hence as *sb.* applied to the person himself or his position. Also *colloq.* abbrev. *proxime.*

Proximity (prǫksi·mĭti). 1480. [a. F. *proximité*, ad. L. *proximitatem*, f. *proximus*, superl. adj. f. *prope* near.] The fact, condition, or position of being near or close by; nearness: a. in space 1579; b. in kinship, affinity of nature, time, etc. 1480.

b. Marriages in p. of blood are amongst us forbidden FLORIO.

‖**Proximo** (prǫ·ksimo). 1855. [L. *proximo* (sc. *mense*) in the next (month).] In or of next month, as *on the 3d p.* Abbrev. *prox.*

Proxy (prǫ·ksi). 1440. [contr. from PROCURACY, as *proctor* from *procurator.*] 1. = PROCURACY 1, PROCURATION 2; chiefly in phr. *by p.* 2. A letter of attorney. *Obs.* exc. as in b. 1460. b. *spec.* A writing authorizing a person to vote instead of another, at a meeting, etc., or formerly in the House of Lords; a vote so given 1587. 3. A person appointed to act instead of another; an attorney, agent, representative 1614. Also *fig.* of things. †4. *Eccl.* Provision or entertainment for a visiting bishop or his representative; an annual payment in commutation of this -1725.

1. Not content to acquire glory by p. H. WALPOLE. 3. Another privilege is, that every peer..may make another lord of parliament his p., to vote for him in his absence BLACKSTONE. Hence **Pro·xyhood, Pro·xyship,** the office or function of a p.

Prude (prūd), *a.* and *sb.* 1704. [a. mod.F. *prude*, in OF. *prude, prode*; either a back-formation from *prudefemme*, or a later fem. form of *prod*; see PREUX.] A. *adj.* That maintains or affects extreme propriety of speech and behaviour, esp. in regard to the relations of the sexes; excessively modest, demure, or prim; prudish; usu. applied adversely. Now *rare.* 1709. B. *sb.* A woman who is of extreme propriety in conduct or speech; usu. applied adversely with implication of affectation. Hence **Pru·dish** *a.* having the character of or resembling a p.; **-ly** *adv.*, **-ness.**

Prudence (prū·dĕns). ME. [a. F., ad. L. *prudentia*, contr. from *providentia* PROVIDENCE.] The quality of being prudent. 1. Ability to discern the most suitable, politic, or profitable course of action, esp. as regards conduct; practical wisdom, discretion. b. An instance of this; a prudent act 1667. †2. Wisdom; knowledge of or skill in a matter -1859.

1. Beyond all bounds of p. and discretion HUME. 2. Harken with your eares, that you may know p. BIBLE (Douay) *Baruch* iii. 9. So †**Pru·dency.**

Prudent (prū·dĕnt), *a.* late ME. [a. F., or ad. L. *prudens, -entem*, contr. from *providens* PROVIDENT, with weakening of the notion of 'foreseeing'.] 1. Of persons, etc.: Sagacious in adapting means to ends; having sound judgement in practical affairs; circumspect, discreet, worldly-wise. †2. Wise, discerning -1579. 3. Of conduct, action, etc.: Characterized by, exhibiting, or proceeding from prudence; politic, judicious. late ME.

1. So stears the p. Crane Her annual Voiage MILT. 2. Thou hast hyd these thynges from the wyse and p., and hast opened them vnto babes TINDALE *Matt.* xi. 25. Hence **Pru·dently** *adv.*

Prudential (prude·nʃăl), *a.* and *sb.* 1641. [f. L. *prudentia* PRUDENCE + -AL.] A. *adj.* 1. Of, of the nature of, or involving prudence; characterized by forethought and deliberation. 2. Of persons: Exercising prudence; (in New England) appointed to conduct the affairs of a town, society, etc. 1642.

1. Cultivating p. habits 1863. More thinking and p. persons SCOTT.

B. *sb.* 1. *pl.* a. Matters that fall within the scope of prudence; *esp.* (in *U.S.*) matters of local government and administration for which there is no need to go to the law courts 1646. b. Prudential considerations 1658. †2. A prudential maxim or precept -1734. Hence **Prude·ntialism,** a system or theory of life based upon p. considerations. **Prude·ntialist. Prudentia·lity,** p. quality, nature, or character. **Prude·ntial·ly** *adv.*, **-ness.**

Prudery (prū·dəri). 1709. [ad. F. *pruderie*, f. *prude* PRUDE; see -ERY.] The quality or character of being prudish; excessive regard for the proprieties in speech or behaviour; extreme or affected modesty or demureness.

A lady..has carried her p. so far, as to separate the writings of male and female authors in her library 1813.

Prudho·mme. 1701. [a. F. *prud'homme* :—OF. *prod(h)ome* = *prouz d'ome* a fine thing of a man, f. *prouz* PROW *a.* + *de* of †*(h)ome* man.] 1. *Hist.* A man of valour and discretion; a knight or freeholder who was summoned to sit on the jury or to serve in the king's council. ‖2. A member of a French tribunal appointed to decide labour disputes 1887.

Pruinose (prū·inōᵘs), *a.* 1826. [ad. L. *pruinosus*, f. *pruina* hoar-frost; see -OSE.] *Nat. Hist.* Covered with a fine whitish powdery substance giving the appearance of hoar-frost.

Prune (prūn), *sb.* ME. [a. F., :—med.L. *pruna*, fem. sing. from *pruna*, neut. pl. of L. *prunum*, a. Gr. προῦνον.] †1. The fruit of the plum-tree; a plum; also the tree, *Prunus domestica* -1698. b. *U.S.* A variety of plum suitable for drying 1902. 2. The dried fruit of several varieties of the common plum-tree, largely used for eating, raw or stewed; a dried plum. Formerly dist. as *dry p.* ME. 3. *transf.* The dark reddish purple colour of the juice of prunes; also called *p.-purple* 1884. 4. Phr. *Prunes and prism(s*: see Dickens, *Little Dorrit* II. v. Thence, applied to a prim and mincing manner of speech, and to superficial 'accomplishments'. 1855.

Comb. **p.-tree,** (*a*) a plum-tree; (*b*) *Prunus occidentalis*, a West Indian timber-tree.

Prune (prūn), *v.*[1] *Obsol.* [Late ME. *prune*, *pruyne, proyne*, of uncertain origin.] 1. *trans.* and *intr.* for *refl.* Of a bird, etc.: = PREEN *v.*[2] 1. 2. Of a person: To trim, dress up with minute nicety; to prink, deck out, adorn. late ME. †3. *refl. fig.* To plume oneself, pride oneself -1672.

Prune (prūn), *v.*[2] [Late ME. *prouyne*, 16th c. *provine*, a. OF. *proöing(n)ier, proögnier*, later *proignier* to prune or cut back the vine; origin unkn.] 1. *trans.* To cut or lop superfluous branches or twigs from (a vine, tree, or shrub) in order to promote fruitfulness, induce regular growth, etc.; to trim. Also *absol.* 1547. 2. To cut or lop off (branches, boughs, shoots) 1572. 3. *fig.* To 'cut down', mutilate; *esp.* to cut down or reduce by rejecting superfluities; also to rid *of* what is superfluous or undesirable. late ME. b. To remove (superfluities, deformities) 1680.

1. Sixe yeeres thou shalt p. thy Vineyard *Lev.* xxv. 3. 3. Some..Authors..began to p. their Words of all superfluous Letters ADDISON. Hence **Pru·ner,** one who prunes trees or shrubs.

Prunella[1] (prune·lă). 1656. [= mod.F. *prunelle*; origin obsc.] 1. A strong stuff, orig. silk, afterwards worsted, formerly used for graduates', clergymen's, and barristers' gowns; later, for the uppers of women's shoes. 2. *attrib.* Made or consisting of prunella 1706.

1. *Leather and p.*: see LEATHER *sb.* 1.

‖**Prune·lla**[2]. 1599. [Bot.L., alteration of *Brunella*.] *Bot.* A genus of herbaceous labiates, including *P. vulgaris*, Self-heal.

†‖**Prune·lla**[3]. 1627. [mod.L., earlier *brunella*, dim. of med.L. *brunus* brown.] 1. *Path.* The Hungarian or camp-fever which prevailed among the imperial troops in Germany in 1547 and 1566. In later times applied to quinsy, and other disorders of the throat or fauces -1895. 2. *Pharmacy.* Chiefly in comb. **p. salt, prunelle salt,** a preparation of fused nitre, so called as used for the disorder of the throat -1868.

Prunello (prune·lo). 1616. [Altered from obs. It. *prunella*, dim. of *pruna* plum, prune.] †a. A variety of plum or prune. b. The finest kind of prunes or dried plums, made from the greengage and other varieties.

Pruni·ferous, *a. rare.* 1668. [f. L. *prunum* PRUNE *sb.* + -(I)FEROUS.] Bearing plums or stone-fruits; drupiferous.

Pru·ning, *vbl. sb.* 1548. [-ING[1].] The action of PRUNE *v.*[2] Also *fig.* b. *concr.* (*pl.*) Portions cut off in pruning 1832.

Comb., esp. in the names of tools, etc., used in pruning, as *p.-bill*; **p.-hook,** a curved cutting instrument used in pruning; **-knife.**

Prunt (prʊnt). 1891. [perh. a provincial form of *print*.] A piece of ornamental glass, laid on to a body of glass, as a vase; also the tool with which this ornament is moulded or impressed with its pattern. Hence **Pru·nted** *a.* ornamented with prunts.

‖**Prunus** (prū·nʊs). 1706. [L., = plum-tree, ad. Gr. προῦνος = προύμνη; also, a sloe-bush.] 1. *Bot.* A genus of trees and shrubs, N.O. *Rosaceæ*, containing the common sloe, bullace, plum, apricot, and other species, bearing drupaceous fruits. 2. In *Oriental Pottery.* A representation of a Chinese and Japanese species, *P. mume*, on porcelain, etc. Hence *p. decoration.* 1878.

Prurience (prūᵊ·riĕns). 1688. [f. as PRURIENT; see -ENCE.] 1. The fact or sensation of itching. 2. *fig.* Mental itching or craving 1829. 3. = next 3. 1781.

Pruriency (prūᵊ·riĕnsi). 1669. [f. as prec.; see -ENCY.] 1. The quality of itching; itchingness (*rare*). 2. *fig.* The quality or condition of mental itching 1711. 3. Tendency towards lascivious or impure thought; an instance of this 1795.

2. A constant P. of inordinate Desire STEELE.

Prurient (prūᵊ·riĕnt), *a.* 1639. [ad. L. *pruriens, -entem, prurire* to itch.] 1. That itches physically, itching. *rare.* 2. *fig.* Having an uneasy or morbid desire or curiosity. *rare.* 1653. 3. Given to the indulgence of lewd ideas; impure-minded 1746. 4. Unduly forward or excessive in growth 1822. 5. *Bot.* Applied to plants which cause a slightly stinging sensation (*rare*) 1858.

2. The reading public..in its usual p. longing after anything like personal gossip KINGSLEY. Hence **Pru·riently** *adv.* in a p. manner.

Pruriginous (pruri·dʒinəs), *a.* 1609. [ad. F. *prurigineux*, ad. late L. *pruriginosus*, f. *prurigo, -inem*; see next and -OUS.] Affected by or liable to prurigo or itching; pertaining to or of the nature of prurigo; †prurient.

‖**Prurigo** (prurəi·go). 1846. [L., an itching, lasciviousness, f. *prurire*.] An itching; *spec.* in *Path.*, a diseased condition of the skin attended by a violent and chronic itching, and characterized by the presence of flat slightly red papules, and a thickening of the part affected. Also *attrib.*

‖**Pruritus** (prurəi·tʊs). 1653. [L., f. *prurire*.] Itching; *esp.* itching of the skin without visible eruption. Also *fig.*

Prussian (prʊ·ʃăn), *a.* and *sb.* 1677. [ad mod.L. *Prussianus* adj., f. *Prussia*.] A. *adj.* Of or pertaining to Prussia or its inhabitants; also designating things actually or reputedly coming from Prussia 1702.

P. carp, a smaller form of the common carp. *P. blue*, a deep blue pigment, consisting essentially of hydrated ferric ferrocyanide, usu. mixed with varying quantities of potassioferrous ferricyanide. (Called *Prussian* from being discovered by a colour-maker in Berlin.) Also, a variety of pea. *P. brown, P. green*, pigments derived from or allied to Prussian blue.

B. *sb.* A native or inhabitant of Prussia (the ethnic territory, the duchy, or the kingdom) 1677. Hence **Pru·ssianize** *v. trans.* to render P. or like Prussia in organization or character.

Prussiate (prʊ·s-, prʊ·ʃiĕt). 1790. [a. F., f. *prussique* PRUSSIC + -ATE[1].] *Chem.* A salt of prussic acid; a cyanide. Also, a ferro- or ferri-cyanide.

Prussic (prʊ·sik), *a.* 1790. [ad. F. *prussique*, f. *Prusse* Prussia + *-ique* -IC.] *Chem.* Of, pertaining to, or derived from Prussian blue. Chiefly in *P. acid* = HYDROCYANIC *acid.*

Prut (prʊt), *int.* and *sb.* ME. [Echoic, repr. a slight explosive sound.] 1. An exclam. of contempt. 2. The sound of a rifle shot 1898.

†**Prute·nic,** *a.* (*sb.*) 1615. [ad. med.L. *Prutenicus*, f. *Prut(h)eni* Prussians; see -IC.] Prussian; in *P. tables*, the Copernican planetary tables published in 1551 by Erasmus Reinhold; so named in compliment to Albert, Duke of Prussia. Also as *sb.* in *pl.*, the P. tables. So †**Prute·nical** *a.* 1594.

Pry (prəi), *sb.*[1] 1750. [f. PRY *v.*[1]] 1. An act or the action of prying. 2. An inquisitive person. Cf. *Paul Pry* (PAUL 3). 1845.

Pry (prəi), *sb.*[2] *dial.* and *U.S.* 1823. [f. PRIZE *sb.*[4]; cf. PRY *v.*[2]] A lever or crow-bar for prizing.

Pry (prəi), *v.*[1] [ME. *prien*; origin unkn.] 1. *intr.* To look, *esp.* to look closely or curiously; to peer inquisitively or impertinently; to spy. †2. *trans.* To look for, look through, or look at closely; to observe narrowly -1632.

1. Thus..glide obscure, and prie In every Bush and Brake MILT. Endeavour to p. into the nature..of the Almighty 1754. He pries into all the stratagems of Camillus MOTLEY. Hence **Pry·ingly** *adv.*

Pry (prəi), *v.*[2] *dial.* and *U.S.* 1823. [Shortened from PRIZE *v.*[3]; cf. PRY *sb.*[2]] *trans.* To force or prize up, etc.

Pryse, pryce. *arch.* [ME. a. OF. or AF. *pris* taken, or OF. *prise* taking, capture.] *Hunting.* In phr. *to blow the pryse*, to sound a blast on the hunting-horn as a signal that the stag is taken.

‖**Prytaneum** (pritănī·ʊm). 1600. [L., a. Gr. πρυτανεῖον, f. πρύτανις; see next.] *Gr. Antiq.* The public hall of a Greek state or city, in which the sacred fire was kept burning; *esp.* in ancient Athens, the hall in which distinguished citizens, foreign ambassadors, and the successive presidents of the senate were entertained at the public charge.

‖ **Prytanis** (pri·tănis). *Pl.* **-nes** (-nīz). 1656. [L., a. Gr. πρύτανις a prince, ruler, at Athens a president.] **1.** In ancient Athens, A member of that division of the Council of Five Hundred which was presiding at the time. **2.** The chief magistrate of a Greek state, as of Rhodes, Lycia, or Miletus 1682. **3.** *transf.* A president 1847. So **Pry·tany,** each of the ten divisions of the Athenian Council of Five Hundred during its presidency; also the period of five weeks during which each division presided.

P. S., abbrev. of L. *post scriptum* POSTSCRIPT, often pronounced (pī·e·s).

Psalm (sām), *sb.* [OE. (*p*)*sealm*, ad. L. *psalmus*, a. Gr. ψαλμός a twitching (of the strings of the harp), a song sung to the harp, f. ψάλλειν to twitch, twang, sing to the harp (in LXX and N.T.).] **1.** *gen.* Any sacred song sung in religious worship; a hymn; esp. in biblical use. **2.** *spec.* Any one of the sacred songs or hymns which together form the 'Book of Psalms'; a version or paraphrase of any of these, esp. as read or sung in public or private worship OE. **3.** *attrib.* OE.

1. Hymns devout and holy Psalms Singing everlastingly MILT. 2. *Proper psalms*, see PROPER *a.* 2. *The Psalms, the Book of Psalms*, one of the books of the O.T., forming the hymn-book of the Jewish church, and used also in Christian worship from the earliest times; the Psalter; often called *the Psalms of David*, from the belief that David, king of Israel, composed them or some of them.

Psalm, *v.* [OE. *sealmian*; f. prec.] **1.** †**a.** *intr.* To sing psalms. **b.** *trans.* To sing or celebrate in psalms. **2.** To say or sing a psalm to or over (*rare*) 1800.

Psalmist (sā·mist). 1483. [ad. late L. *psalmista*, f. *psalmus*; see -IST.] **1.** The author of a psalm or psalms; almost always with def. art. as a title for David considered as the author of the Psalms, or as a designation of the author of any one of them. **2.** *Eccl. Hist.* A member of one of the minor clerical orders, discharging the functions of a chorister or cantor 1565. Hence †**Psa·lmistry,** the office or work of a p.

Psalmodic (sælmǫ·dik), *a.* 1749. [See PSALMODY and -IC.] Of or pertaining to psalmody; having the style or character of psalmody. So **Psalmo·dial, Psalmo·dical** *adjs.*

Psalmodist (sā·mǒdist, sæ·lm-). 1652. [f. PSALMODY + -IST.] **1.** One who practises or is skilled in psalmody; a singer of psalms 1659. †**b.** = PSALMIST 2. 1726. †**2.** A writer of psalms -1886

Psalmodize (sā·mǒdəiz, sæ·lm-), *v.* 1513. [ad. med.L. *psalmodizare*, f. *psalmodia*; see -IZE.] *intr.* To practise psalmody; to sing psalms.

Psalmody (sā·mǒdi, sæ·lm-), *sb.* ME. [ad. late L. *psalmodia*, a. Gr. ψαλμῳδία, f. ψαλμῳδός psalmist, f. ψαλμός psalm + ᾠδή song.] The action, practice, or art of singing psalms (or sacred vocal music in general), esp. in public worship. **b.** The arrangement of psalms for singing; hence, psalms and hymns so arranged, collectively 1554. Hence **Psa·lmody** *v. trans.* to celebrate as in psalmody; to hymn (*rare*).

†**Psa·lmograph.** 1542. [ad. late L. *psalmographus*, a. Gr. ψαλμογράφος, f. ψαλμός psalm + -γραφος -GRAPH.] = PSALMIST 1. -1657.

Psalter (sǭ·ltəɹ). [OE. (*p*)*saltere*, ad. L. *psalterium*. In ME. *sauter*, a. AF. *sauter*:—L. *psalterium*, a. Gr. ψαλτήριον a stringed instrument played by twanging, f. ψάλλειν to twang.] **I. 1.** The Book of Psalms. **b.** A translation or particular version of the Book of Psalms: e.g. a Latin, English, metrical P.; the Prayer-book P., etc. OE. **c.** A copy of the Psalms, esp. as arranged for liturgical or devotional use OE. **2.** *transf. Our Lady's p.*, the rosary (because it contains the same number (150) of Aves as there are psalms in the Psalter); also, a book containing this. late ME. **4.** Applied to certain old Irish chronicles in verse (*P. of Cashel*, etc.) 1685. **II.** = PSALTERY 1. *Obs.* or *arch.* OE.

Psalterial (sǫltīə·riăl), *a.* 1865. [f. PSALTERIUM + -AL.] *Anat.* and *Zool.* Pertaining to the psalterium.

Psalterian (sǫltīə·riăn), *a.* 1819. [f. L. *psalterium* PSALTERY + -AN.] Of, like, or having a sound like that of, a psaltery.

‖ **Psalterion** (sǫltīə·riǒn). [In ME. a. OF. *salterion*, ad. L. *psalterium*; in mod. use a transliteration of Gr. ψαλτήριον.] **1.** = PSALTERY 1.

‖**Psalterium** (sǫltīə·riǒm). 1857. [L.] *Anat.* and *Zool.* **a.** = LYRA 3. **b.** The third stomach of a ruminant; the omasum or manyplies.

Psaltery (sǭ·ltəri). ME. [a. OF. *psal-*, *sauterie*, ad. L. *psalterium*, ad. Gr. ψαλτήριον.] **1.** An ancient and mediæval stringed instrument, resembling the dulcimer but played by plucking the strings with the fingers or a plectrum. †**2.** = PSALTER 1. *rare.* -1890.

1. Bothe his harpe and sawtrey 1557.

Psammo- (psæmo, sæmo), bef. a vowel **psamm-**, repr. Gr. ψαμμο-, comb. form of ψάμμος sand, entering into some scientific terms, as **Psammoli·thic** *a.*, *Geol.* consisting of sandstone. **Psammo·philous** *a.*, *Bot.* sand-loving, growing in sandy soil.

Psarolite (psæ·roləit). 1859. [f. Gr. ψάρ starling (or ψαρός speckled) + λίθος stone (see -LITE); app. rendering Ger. *starstein*.] *Palæont.* Name for the silicified stems of tree-ferns found in the Permian or Lower New Red Sandstone, from the speckled markings they exhibit in section.

Psephism (ps-, sī·fiz'm). 1656. [ad. Gr. ψήφισμα, f. ψηφίζειν to vote, prop. with pebbles, f. ψῆφος pebble.] *Gr. Antiq.* A decree enacted by a vote of a public assembly, esp. of the Athenians.

‖ **Pseudepigrapha** (siūdėpi·grăfă, ps-), *sb. pl.* 1692. [a. Gr. neut. pl. of ψευδεπίγραφος 'with false title', f. ψευδ- PSEUD(O + ἐπιγράφειν to inscribe (see EPIGRAPH).] A collective term for books or writings bearing a false title, or ascribed to another than the true author; *spec.* applied to certain Jewish writings ascribed to various patriarchs and prophets of the O.T. Also *sing.* in anglicized form **Pseude·pigraph.** Hence **Pseudepi·graphal, Pseudepigra·phic, -al, Pseudepi·graphous** *adjs.* pertaining to or having the character of p.; spurious. **Pseudepi·graphy,** false ascription of authorship.

Pseudo (siū·do, ps-), quasi-*adj.*, (*sb.*) late ME. [The comb. element PSEUDO- as a separate word.] False, counterfeit, pretended, spurious. (Now usu. hyphened to the following noun; see PSEUDO- 1.) †**B.** *sb.* (with *pl.*) A false person, a pretender.

Luxuries which, when long gratified, become a sort of p. necessaries SCOTT.

Pseudo- (siūdo, ps-), before a vowel usu. **pseud-**, repr. Gr. comb. element ψευδο-, ψευδ- 'false, falsely', from stem of ψευδής false, ψεῦδος falsehood.

1. Prefixed to any noun or adj., forming combs., mostly nonce-wds., with the sense 'false, pretended, counterfeit, spurious, sham, falsely so called or represented; falsely, spuriously, apparently but not really'; as *pseudo-archaic*, *-classic(al*, *-Gothic*, *-patriotic*; *pseudo-philanthropist*, *-prophet*. Here *pseudo-* is properly hyphened. 2. Special combs.: nearly all terms of modern science, (*a*) indicating close or deceptive resemblance to the thing denoted by the second element, without real identity or affinity with it; or sometimes simply denoting an abnormal or erratic form or kind of the thing; (*b*) denoting something which does not correspond with the reality, or to which no reality corresponds, as false perceptions, errors of judgement or statement. ‖ **Pseudæsthe·sia** [mod.L.; cf. ANÆSTHESIA], *Path.* false or depraved sensation, as that occurring apparently in an amputated limb. **Pseude·lephant,** *Zool.* an animal resembling an elephant, as a mastodon. **Pseude·mbryo,** *Zool.* a spurious embryo; a term applied to various larval forms in sea-urchins, star-fishes, and sponges; hence **Pseudembryo·nic** *a.* **Pseu·docœle** (-sīl) [Gr. κοῖλος hollow], *Anat.*, (*a*) applied to the body-cavity of certain invertebrates, derived from spaces developed secondarily in the mesoblast, not directly from the blastocœle or original cavity of the embryo; (*b*) applied to the fifth ventricle of the brain. ‖ **Pseudofila·ria,** *Zool.* a stage in the development of certain *Gregarinida*, resembling a thread-worm of the genus *Filaria*. **Pseudogale·na,** *Min.* native zinc sulphide, resembling black lead sulphide or galena. **Pseudo-hype·rtrophy,** *Path.* enlargement of an organ by growth of fat or connective tissue, with atrophy of its proper substance; so **Pseudo-hypertro·phic** *a.*, applied to a form of paralysis caused by pseudo-hypertrophy of the muscles. **Pseudo-meta·llic** *a.*, resembling, but not of the nature of, a metal; said of lustre which is perceptible only when held towards the light. **Pseu·doscope,** an optical instrument containing two reflecting prisms which can be so adjusted as to produce an apparent reversal of the convexity or concavity of an object. **Pseu·dosphere,** *Geom.*, (*a*) a surface having constant negative curvature (as a sphere has positive); (*b*) a sphere in non-Euclidean geometry; so **Pseudosphe·rical** *a.* ‖ **Pseudo·stoma** [Gr. στόμα mouth], *Anat.* a point on the surface of a serous membrane, regarded by some as the mouth of one of the absorbents or lymphatic vessels which begin in such membranes. **Pseu·dostome,** *Zool.* in a sponge, a false osculum or excurrent opening, the mouth of a secondary canal arising from fusion. **Pseudo·vary,** *Zool.* the ovary or generative gland of certain imperfect female insects which reproduce parthenogenetically.

Pseudo-carp (siū·dokāɹp, ps-). 1835. [f. PSEUDO- + Gr. καρπός fruit.] *Bot.* A fruit formed by the modification and enlargement of other parts of the flower besides the ovary, or of parts not belonging to the flower.

Pseudo-ca·tholic, *a.* and *sb.* 1601. [PSEUDO- 1.] **A.** *adj.* Falsely or erroneously called or claiming to be catholic 1605. **B.** *sb.* A Catholic falsely so called 1601.

Pseudo-Christ (siū·doˌkrəist, ps-). late ME. [ad. late L. *pseudochristus*, Gr. ψευδόχριστος (Mark xiii. 22); see PSEUDO-.] A false Christ; one pretending to be the Christ or Messiah. So **Pseudo-Chri·stian** *a.* falsely called or professing to be Christian; also as *sb.* 1579.

Pseudodipteral (siūdoˌdi·ptĕrăl, ps-), *a.* 1696. [f. late Gr. ψευδοδίπτερος + -AL; see PSEUDO- and DIPTEROS.] *Anc. Arch.* Having, as a temple, etc., a single peristyle or surrounding row of columns, placed at the same distance from the walls as the outer of the two rows in the dipteros. So ‖**Pseudodi·pteron,** a building of this type.

Pseudodox (siū·dǒdǫks, ps-). 1615. [ad. Gr. ψευδόδοξος, ψευδοδοξία; f. ψευδο- PSEUDO- + δόξα opinion.] A false or erroneous opinion.

Pseudograph (siū·dograf, ps-). 1828. [ad. late L. *pseudographus*, a. Gr. ψευδογράφος; see PSEUDO- and -GRAPH.] A spurious writing; a literary work purporting to be by another than the real author. So **Pseudo·graphy,** the writing of words falsely; false, incorrect, or bad spelling; an instance of this.

Pseudology (siudǫ·lŏdʒi, ps-). 1658. [ad. Gr. ψευδολογία, f. ψευδολόγος; see -LOGY.] False speaking; the making of false statements; the 'art of lying'. So **Pseudo·loger, Pseudo·logist,** a maker of false statements, a (systematic) liar.

Pseudomorph (siū·domǭɹf, ps-). 1849. [f. Gr. ψευδο- PSEUDO- + μορφή form.] A false or deceptive form; *spec.* in *Min.* a crystal or other body consisting of one mineral but having the form proper to another. So **Pseudomo·rphic** *a.* **Pseudomo·rphism,** the formation or occurrence of pseudomorphs, or the condition of a p. **Pseudomo·rphous** *a.*

Pseudonym (siū·dŏnim, ps-). 1846. [(ult.) a. Gr. ψευδώνυμον, neut. of ψευδώνυμος, f. ψευδο- PSEUDO- + ὄνομα name.] A false or fictitious name, *esp.* one assumed by an author.

Pseudonymous (siudǫ·niməs, ps-), *a.* 1706. [f. med. or mod.L. *pseudonymus* (a. Gr. ψευδώνυμος) + -OUS.] **1.** Bearing or assuming, esp. writing under, a false or fictitious name; belonging to or characterizing one who does this. **2.** Written under an assumed or fictitious name; bearing the name of another than the real author 1727. So **Pseudony·mity,** the condition of being p.; the use of a pseudonym. **Pseudo·nymously** *adv.*

‖ **Pseudoperipteros, -on** (psiūdopĕri·ptĕrǫs, -ǫn). 1696. [a. late Gr. ψευδοπερίπτερος, f. ψευδο- PSEUDO- + περίπτερος PERIPTER.] *Anc. Arch.* A form of temple or other building with free columns forming a portico in front (and sometimes in rear) as in a peripteral building, but the rest of the columns engaged in the walls instead of standing free. Hence **Pseudoperi·pteral** *a.*

‖ **Pseudopodium** (siūdopōu·diə̆m, ps-). *Pl.* **-ia.** 1854. [mod.L., f. Gr. ψευδο- PSEUDO- + *-podium*, ad. Gr. πόδιον, dim. of πούς foot.] **1.** *Zool.* In certain Protozoa (esp. Rhizopoda), Each of a number of processes temporarily formed by protrusion of any part of the protoplasm of the body, and serving for locomotion, prehension, or ingestion of food. Also, a similar formation in an amœboid cell, as a leucocyte. **2.** *Bot.* A false pedicel or footstalk; applied to certain elongations of the stem in mosses 1861. **Pseu·dopod, -po·dial** *a.*

Pshaw (ʃǭ, pʃǭ), *int.* and *sb.* 1673. [A natural expression of rejection.] An exclam. expressing contempt, impatience, or disgust.

Pshah, how silly that is SWIFT. *sb.* Pishes and Pshaws, or other well-bred Interjections STEELE. Hence **Pshaw** *v. intr.* to say 'pshaw!'; *trans.* to show contempt for by saying 'pshaw!'

Psilanthropism (psəilæ·nþrǒpiz'm). 1810. [f. eccl. Gr. ψιλάνθρωπος merely human (f. ψιλός bare, mere + ἄνθρωπος) + -ISM.] The doctrine that Jesus Christ was a mere man. So **Psilanthro·pic** *a.* of, pertaining to, or in accordance with p. **Psila·nthropist,** one who holds this doctrine. **Psila·nthropy.**

Psilo- (psəilo, səilo), bef. a vowel **psil-**, comb. form of Gr. ψιλός bare, smooth, mere, as in: Psilopædic (-pī·dik) [Gr. παῖς, παιδ- + -IC] *a.*, *Ornith.* of a bird: hatched naked or without down. **Psilo·sophy** [see -SOPHY], shallow philosophy; so **Psilo·sopher.**

Psilomelane (psəilǫ·mĕlėⁱn). 1883. [f. PSILO- + Gr. μέλαν, neut. of μέλας black.] *Min.* A common ore of manganese, occurring in smooth black amorphous masses, or in botryoidal or stalactitic shapes.

‖ **Psilosis** (psəilōu·sis). 1904. [a. Gr. ψίλωσις, f. ψιλοῦν to strip bare; see -OSIS.] *Greek Gram.* The substitution of a *tenuis* for an aspirate (as in ῥάπυς for ῥάφυς), or of the *spiritus lenis* for the *spiritus asper.*

Psittaceous (psitēⁱ·ʃəs), *a.* 1835. [f. L. *psittacus* (a. Gr. ψιττακός parrot) + -EOUS.] *Ornith.* Of or belonging to the parrot family of birds, *Psittacidæ.* So **Psi·ttacid** *a.*

Psittacine (psi·tăsəin), *a.* (*sb.*) 1888. [ad. L. *psittacinus*, f. *psittacus.*] Of parrots; *fig.* parrot-like. B. *sb.* A bird of the parrot family.

‖ **Psittacosis** (sităkōu·sis). 1897. [mod L., f. Gr. ψιττακός parrot + -OSIS.] A contagious disease of birds, esp. parrots, characterized by diarrhœa and wasting, and causing bronchial pneumonia when communicated to human beings.

Psoas (psōu·æs). 1681. [Prop. pl. of *psoa*, a. Gr. ψόα, usu. in pl. ψόαι, acc. ψόας, the muscles of the loins.] *Anat.* The name of two muscles of the hip: (*a*) *P. magnus*, a large flexor muscle of the hip-joint which arises from the lumbar vertebræ and sacrum. (*b*) *P. parvus* or *minor*, a muscle which in many animals forms a powerful flexor of the pelvis upon the spine.

‖ **Psora** (psōᵊ·ră). 1681. [L., a. Gr. ψώρα.] A contagious skin disease; scabies, the itch.

‖ **Psoriasis** (sorəi·ăsis, ps-). 1684. [mod.L., a. Gr. ψωρίασις, f. ψωριᾶν to have the itch, f. ψώρα.] A disease of the skin, marked by dry reddish patches covered with scales.

Psoric (psōᵊ·rik), *a.* and *sb.* 1822. [ad. Gr. ψωρικός f. ψώρα.] Of or pertaining to, a remedy for, psora.

‖ **Psorophthalmia** (psōᵊrǫfþæ·lmiă). 1656. [mod.L., f. Gr. ψώρα + OPHTHALMIA.] *Path.* Scurfy inflammation of the eyes.

Psorosperm (psōᵊ·rospə̄ɹm). 1866. [f. Gr. ψώρα + σπέρμα.] An individual of a group of Sporozoa (*Psorospermiæ*), parasitic protozoa found in the mucous membranes, muscles, and liver of domestic animals, and occas. in man.

Psychagogue (səikăgǫg). 1843. [f. Gr. ψυχή PSYCHE + ἀγωγός leading, leader.] **1.** One who directs or leads the mind (*rare*) 1847. **2.** One who calls up departed spirits; a necromancer 1843. So **Psychagogic** (-ăgǫ·dʒik) *a.* influencing or leading the mind or soul; evoking the spirits of the dead (*rare*).

Psy·chal, *a. rare.* 1844. [f. Gr. ψυχή PSYCHE + -AL.] Of or pertaining to the soul; spiritual; psychical.

Psyche (səi·kĭ, ps-). 1647. [a. Gr. ψυχή breath, f. ψύχειν to breathe; hence, life, soul, spirit.] **1.** The soul, or spirit, as dist. from the body; the mind 1658. **b.** In later *Gr. Myth.*, personified as the beloved of Eros (Cupid or Love), and represented as having butterfly wings, or as a butterfly. Hence *attrib.* in sense 'like that of Psyche'. 1876. **2.** a. (After Gr.) A butterfly 1878. **b.** *Entom.* A genus of day-flying bombycid moths, typical of the family *Psychidæ* 1832. **3.** A cheval-glass. [Mod.F.] 1838.

Psychiater (səikəi·ătəɹ, ps-). 1857. [f. Gr. ψυχή PSYCHE + ἰατήρ, ἰατρός healer.] One who treats mental disease; an alienist.

Psychiatric (-iæ·trik), *a.* (*sb.*) 1847. [f. as prec. + -IC.] Of or pertaining to psychiatry. B. *sb. pl.* **Psychia·trics.** The theory or practice of psychiatry 1847.

Psychiatry (-əi·ătri). 1846. [f. Gr. ψυχή PSYCHE + ἰατρεία (f. ἰατρός).] The medical treatment of diseases of the mind. Hence **Psychi·atrist,** a student of p.

Psychic (səi·kik, ps-), *a.* (*sb.*) 1858. [ad. Gr. ψυχικός of the soul or life.] **1.** = PSYCHICAL *a.* 1. 1873. **b.** Characterized by being susceptible to psychic or spiritual influence 1905. **2.** Pertaining to, or characterized by, the 'lower soul' or animal principle, as dist. from the spirit or 'higher soul'; natural, animal. (After St. Paul's use of ψυχικός, 1 Cor. ii. 14, etc.) 1858. **3.** = PSYCHICAL *a.* 3. 1887. B. *sb.* One who is particularly susceptible to 'psychic' influence (see PSYCHICAL 3); a medium 1871.

1. The varied stimuli, p. and physical 1883. 3. *P. force*, a supposed force, power, or influence, not physical or mechanical, exhibiting intelligence or volition, and assumed as the cause of certain so-called spiritualistic phenomena. Hence **Psy·chicism,** the theory or study of psychical or spiritistic phenomena.

Psychical (səi·kikăl, ps-), *a.* 1642. [f. as prec. + -AL.] **1.** Of or pertaining to the soul or the mind; mental, as dist. from *physical*; *spec.* in *Path.*, due to mental affection or influence. **2.** Repr. Gr. ψυχικός: Of or pertaining to the animal or natural life of man, as opp. to the spiritual (πνευματικός) 1708. **3.** Of or pertaining to phenomena and conditions which appear to lie outside the domain of physical law, and are therefore attributed by some to spiritual or hyperphysical agency. *P. research*, investigation of such phenomena. 1878.

1. *P. blindness, deafness*, inability of the brain to interpret impressions received by the visual or auditory organs. 3. Why, he asks, call the subject matter of their investigation 'p. research', when it is really, ..only a branch of morbid psychology? 1901. Hence **Psy·chically** *adv.* with reference to the soul or mind; mentally.

Psychics (səi·kiks, ps-). 1811. [f. PSYCHIC *a.*, after sbs. in *-ics* = Gr. -ικά; see -IC 2.] The science of psychical or mental phenomena; psychology.

Psychism (səi·kiz'm, ps-). 1871. [f. Gr. ψυχή PSYCHE + -ISM.] **1.** ANIMISM 1890. **2.** The doctrine or theory of the existence of forces unexplainable by physical science in connexion with spiritistic phenomena 1871. So **Psy·chist,** a psychologist; also, one who engages in psychical research.

Psycho- (səi·ko, ps-), bef. a vowel regularly **psych-**, repr. Gr. ψυχο-, ψυχ-, comb. form of ψυχή PSYCHE. In mod. use, taken in the sense of 'mind', 'psychic organism', 'mental', 'psychical', mainly in scientific compounds.

Psy:chodyna·mic *a.*, of or pertaining to mental powers or activities; hence **Psy:chodyna·mics,** the science of the laws of mental action. **Psychoge·nesis,** (*a*) the genesis or origin of the soul or mind; (*b*) origin or evolution due to the activity of the soul or mind itself. **Psy·chogram,** a 'spirit-writing'; a writing or message supposed to come from a spirit; so **Psy·chograph,** an instrument by means of which pyschograms are written; also = *psychogram.* **Psycho·graphy,** the history, description, or delineation of the mind or soul, or of mind in the abstract; also, supposed 'spirit-writing' by the hand or intervention of a medium. **Psy·chomancy,** †(*a*) divination through communication with the spirits of the dead; (*b*) occult intercommunication between souls or with spirits. **Psy·cho-mo:tor** *a.*, inducing movement by psychic or mental action; involving such movement. **Psy:cho-physio·logy,** the department of physiology which deals with mental phenomena; experimental psychology. **Psy·choplasm,** the basis of consciousness conceived as a substance corresponding and correlative to PROTOPLASM. **Psychozo·ic** *a.*, of the geological period of living creatures having souls or minds, i.e. the human period.

Psychoanalysis (səi:ko,ănæ·lĭsis). 1910. [f. PSYCHO- + ANALYSIS; after G. *psychoanalyse.*] The name given (1896) by Dr. Sigmund Freud of Vienna to the theory and practice of his method of treating psychopathic disorders; analysis of the unconscious mind by the method of 'free association'. So **Psychoa·nalyst,** one who practises p. **Psychoanaly·tic(al** *a.* of or pertaining to p. **Psychoa·nalyse** *v. trans.* to treat by p.; to analyse the mind of (a person) by the method of p.

Psychologic (-ǒlǫ·dʒik), *a.* 1787. [f. as PSYCHOLOGY + -IC.] Of or belonging to psychology.

Psychological (səikǒlǫ·dʒikăl, ps-), *a.* 1776. [f. as PSYCHOLOGY + -ICAL.] **1.** Of, pertaining to, or of the nature of psychology; dealing with or relating to psychology 1812. **2.** Loosely used for PSYCHICAL: Of or pertaining to the mind, mental; opp. to *physical* 1776.

P. moment = F. *moment psychologique*, applied to 'the moment in which the mind is in actual expectation of something that is to happen'; the psychologically appropriate moment; often misused for 'the critical moment', 'the very nick of time'. (The Fr. use was orig. due to G. *das psychologische Moment* the psychological 'momentum' or factor being mistaken for *der psychologische Moment* the psychological moment of time.) Hence **Psycholo·gically** *adv.*

Psychologism (səikǫ·lŏdʒiz'm, ps-). 1858. [f. PSYCHOLOGY + -ISM.] *Philos.* Idealism as opp. to sensationalism.

Psychologist (səikǫ·lŏdʒist, ps-). 1727. [f. as prec. + -IST.] One who makes a study of or is versed in psychology.

Psychologize (səikǫ·lŏdʒeiz, ps-), *v.* 1836. [f. as prec. + -IZE.] **1.** *intr.* To study or treat of psychology; to theorize or reason psychologically. **2.** *trans.* To analyse or describe psychologically 1856. **3.** To subject to 'psychical' influence 1885.

Psy·chologue (-ǒlǫg). *rare.* 1872. [a. F. *psychologue*, f. L. type **psychologus*; see next.] = PSYCHOLOGIST.

Psychology (səikǫ·lŏdʒi, ps-). 1693. [ad. mod.L. *psychologia*, f. Gr. ψυχο- PSYCHO- + -LOGY.] The science of the nature, functions, and phenomena of the human soul or mind. **b.** A treatise on, or system of, psychology 1791.

Psychometry (səikǫ·mĕtri, ps-). 1854. [f. Gr. ψυχο- PSYCHO- + -μετρία measuring.] **1.** The (alleged) faculty of divining, from physical contact or proximity only, the qualities or properties of an object, or of persons or things that have been in contact with it. **2.** The measurement of the duration and intensity of mental states or processes 1883. So **Psycho·meter,** one who practises p. **Psychome·tric, -al** *adjs.* of, pertaining to, or of the nature of p.; **-ly** *adv.* **Psycho·metrist.**

Psychopannychy (psəiko,pæ·niki). 1642. [ad. med.L. *psychopannychia*, f. Gr. ψυχο- + παννύχιος lasting all night.] All-night sleep of the soul; a state in which (according to some) the soul sleeps between death and the day of judgement. So **Psychopa·nnychist,** one holding this doctrine; **-pa·nnychism.**

Psychopath (səi·kopæþ, ps-). 1885. [f. PSYCHO- + Gr. -παθής, f. πάθος suffering.] One affected with psychopathy; a mentally deranged person; also = PSYCHOPATHIST.

Psychopathy (səikǫ·păþi, ps-). 1847. [f. Gr. ψυχο- PSYCHO- + -πάθεια from πάθος.] *Path.* **1.** Mental disease or disorder; mental disorder considered apart from cerebral disease. **2.** The treatment of disease by 'psychical' influence, e.g. by hypnotism 1891. Hence **Psychopa·thic** *a.* **Psycho·pathist,** one who studies or treats psychopathy or mental disease. **Psy:cho-patho·logy,** the science of mental disease.

Psycho-physic (səikoˌfiˑzik, ps-), *a.* and *sb.* 1879. [f. Gr. ψυχο- PSYCHO- + φυσικός physical.] **A.** *adj.* = next 1890. **B.** *sb.* Commonly in pl. **Psycho-phyˑsics.** The science of the general relations between mind and body; *spec.* the investigation of the relations between physical stimuli and psychic action in the production of sensations 1879.

Psycho-phyˑsical, *a.* 1879. [f. as prec. + -AL.] Of or pertaining to psycho-physics; having to do with psychology and physics, or the connexion of the psychical and the physical.

Psychopomp (səiˑkǫpǫmp, ps-). 1863. [ad. Gr. ψυχοπομπός, f. ψυχή soul + πομπός conductor.] A conductor of souls to the place of the dead.

‖**Psychosis** (səikōᵘˑsis, ps-). *Pl.* **-oses** (-ōᵘˑsīz). 1847. [a. late Gr. ψύχωσις animation, principle of life, f. ψυχόω I give soul or life to.] **1.** *Path.* Any kind of mental affection or derangement; esp. one which cannot be ascribed to organic lesion or neurosis. **2.** *Psychol.* An activity or movement of the psychic organism, as dist. from neurosis (NEUROSIS 2) 1871.

Psychostasy (-ǫˑstăsi). 1850. [ad. Gr. ψυχοστασία, f. ψυχή soul + στάσις weighing.] A weighing of souls; in *Anc. Myth.* supposed to take place during a combat, the combatant having the lighter soul being slain.

Psycho-therapeutic (səiːkoþerăpiūˑtik, ps-), *a.* and *sb.* 1887. [f. PSYCHO- + THERAPEUTIC.] **A.** *adj.* Of or pertaining to the treatment of mental or psychic disease 1890. **B.** *sb.* in pl. form **Psyːcho-therapeuˑtics.** The subject of the treatment of psychic disease 1887.

Psychrometer (-ǫˑmĭtər). 1727. [f. Gr. ψυχρός cold + -METER; lit. a measurer of cold.] *Meteorol.* orig., A thermometer; now, an instrument for measuring the relative humidity of the air; a wet-and-dry bulb thermometer. Hence **Psychromeˑtric, -al** *adjs.* of or pertaining to the p. or to psychrometry. **Psychroˑmetry,** the measurement of the humidity of the atmosphere by means of a p.

Ptarmigan (tāˑɹmigăn). 1599. [= Gael. *tàrmachan*; history and origin unkn. The spelling with *pt-* arises from false analogy.] A bird of the grouse family (*Lagopus alpinus* or *mutus*) which inhabits high altitudes in Scotland and northern Europe, the Alps and Pyrenees. **b.** Also extended to other species of *Lagopus*, as *L. albus* of Europe and Asia, *L. rupestris* of N. America, etc.

Ptenoglossate (tīːnoglǫˑsĕt, pt-), *a.* [f. Gr. πτηνός feathered + γλῶσσα tongue + -ATE [2].] *Zool.* Of certain molluscs: Having no median teeth on the odontophore, but a large number of lateral teeth resembling the barbs of a feather.

Pterichthys (tĕriˑkþis, pt-). 1842. [mod.L., f. Gr. πτερόν wing + ἰχθύς fish.] *Palæont.* A fossil genus of fishes of the Devonian period, having a pair of wing-shaped lateral appendages.

Pterido- (terido, pt-), bef. a vowel **pterid-**, comb. form of Gr. πτερίς, πτεριδ- fern. **Pteridoˑgraphy,** a description of ferns. **Pteridoˑlogy** [-(O)LOGY], that branch of botany which treats of ferns; hence **Pteːridoloˑgical** *a.*, **Pteridoˑlogist.** **Pteˑridophyte** [Gr. φυτόν plant], a member of the *Pteridophyta*, a division of plants including the ferns and their allies; a vascular cryptogam.

Ptero- (tero, pt-), bef. a vowel **pter-,** comb. form of Gr. πτερόν feather, wing.

Pterogloˑssal [Gr. γλῶσσα tongue] *a.*, having a tongue finely notched or divided like a feather, as a toucan of the genus *Pteroglossus*. ‖ **Pteroˑpoda** *sb. pl.*, a class or division of *Mollusca*, having the mesopodium or middle part of the foot expanded into a pair of lobes, like wings or flippers (the **Pteropoˑdium**), with which the animal swims; hence **Pteˑropod,** a mollusc of the class *Pteropoda*. **Pterostiˑgma** [Gr. στίγμα spot, mark], *Entom.* a peculiar mark or spot on the wings of some insects, esp. Hymenoptera.

Pterodactyl (terodæˑktil, pt-). 1830. [ad. mod.L. *Pterodactylus*, f. Gr. πτερόν wing + δάκτυλος finger.] *Palæont.* A winged reptile or pterosaur of the extinct genus *Pterodactylus*.

‖**Pteropus** (teˑrǫpŭs, pt-). *Pl.* **-i.** 1835. [mod.L., ad. Gr. πτερόπους wing-footed.] *Zool.* A genus of tropical and subtropical bats having membranous wings, known as flying foxes or fruit-bats; an animal of this genus. Hence **Pteˑropid, Pteˑropine** *adjs.* belonging to or having the characteristics of the *Pteropidæ* or flying-fox family.

Pterosaur (teˑrosǭɹ, pt-). 1862. [ad. mod.L. *Pterosaurus*, f. PTERO- + Gr. σαῦρος (= σαύρα) lizard.] *Palæont.* A member of the *Pterosauria*, an extinct order of Mesozoic saurian reptiles, having the fifth digit of each fore-foot prolonged for the purpose of supporting a membrane for flight. Hence **Pterosauˑrian** *a.* of the nature of a p.; of or belonging to the *Pterosauria*; also *sb.*

Pterotic (tĕrōᵘˑtik, pt-), *a.* (*sb.*) 1870. [f. Gr. πτερόν wing + *-otic* in *periotic*, etc.] *Anat.* Applied to a wing-like expansion of the petrosal bone or periotic capsule, occurring in some vertebrates. **b.** as *sb.* The p. bone or expansion.

‖**Pterygium** (ptĕriˑdʒiŏm). 1657. [L., a. Gr. πτερύγιον little wing, fin, dim. of πτέρυξ wing.] **1.** *Path.* A diseased condition of the conjunctiva of the eye. **2.** *Bot.* Term applied to petals, etc. when shaped like wings 1895.

Pterygo- (teˑrigo, pt-), bef. a vowel **pteryg-,** comb. form of Gr. πτέρυξ, πτερυγ- wing, fin.

1. In general sense of 'wing', 'fin', or 'wing-like appendage'. **Pteˑrygoblaːst** [Gr. βλαστός germ], *Ichth.* a germinal fin-ray. ‖ **Pteːrygopoˑdium** [Gr. πούς, ποδ-], *Ichth.* one of the claspers of a shark, etc. **Pteˑrygostoːme** [Gr. στόμα mouth], the space between the anterior edges of the carapace in crabs and other crustacea.

2. Used as comb. form of PTERYGOID, denoting attachment or relation to the pterygoid processes of the sphenoid bone. **P.-maˑxillary** [L. *maxilla* jaw] *a.*, belonging to or connected with the pterygoid processes and the superior maxillary bone. **P.-paˑlatal, -paˑlatine** *adjs.*, of or belonging to the pterygoid and the palatine bones. **P.-quadrate** (-kwǫˑdrĕt) *a.*, pertaining to or combining the pterygoid and quadrate bones.

Pterygoid (teˑrigoid, pt-), *a.* (*sb.*) 1722. [ad. Gr. πτερυγοειδής like a wing, f. πτέρυξ, -υγ- wing; see -OID.] *Anat.* Having the form or appearance of a wing, wing-like, wing-shaped. *P. process*: Each of two processes of bone descending (on each side) from the junction of the body and great wing of the sphenoid bone. **b.** Connected with the pterygoid processes 1746. **B.** *sb.* **a.** The pterygoid bone. **b.** Each of the pterygoid muscles. 1831.

‖**Pteryla** (teˑrilă, pt-). *Pl.* **-æ.** 1867. [mod.L., f. Gr. πτερόν feather + ὕλη wood.] *Ornith.* A definite clump, patch, or area of feathers, one of a number on the skin of a bird, separated by *apteria* or featherless spaces. Hence **Pteryloˑgraphy,** the scientific description of, or a treatise on, pterylosis. **Pteryloˑsis,** the arrangement of the pterylæ, or of the feathers of birds.

Ptilo- (tilo, pt-), bef. a vowel **ptil-.** comb. form of Gr. πτίλον a soft feather, a plumelet. **Ptiˑlocerque** (-sɔ̄ɹk) [Gr. κέρκος tail], *Zool.* an elephant shrew of the genus *Ptilocercus*, having a long tail with distichous hairs towards the end; the pen-tailed shrew. **Ptilopædic** (-pīˑdik) [Gr. παῖς, παιδ- child] *a.*, *Ornith.* of birds: hatched with a complete covering of down.

Ptisan (tiˑzăn, tizæˑn). late ME. [a. F. *tisane*, ad. L. *ptisana*, a. Gr. πτισάνη peeled or pearl barley, also a drink made from this, f. πτίσσειν to peel.] A nourishing decoction of slightly medicinal quality; orig. barley-water; now often applied more widely.

Ptochogony (tōᵘkǫˑgŏni, pt-). 1839. [f. Gr. πτωχός poor + -γονία begetting.] The begetting or production of beggars.

Ptolemæan (tǫlĕmīˑăn), *a.* and *sb.* 1647. [f. L. *Ptolemæus* + -AN.] = next *a.* 1 and *sb.*

Ptolemaic (tǫlĕmēⁱˑik), *a.* and *sb.* 1674. [f. Gr. Πτολεμαῖος (L. *Ptolemæus*) Ptolemy + -IC.] **A.** *adj.* **1.** Of or pertaining to Ptolemy, a celebrated astronomer who lived at Alexandria in the second century A.D. **2.** Of or pertaining to the Ptolemies, the Macedonian Greek rulers of ancient Egypt from the death of Alexander the Great to Cleopatra 1771.

1. *P. system or theory*, the astronomical system or theory elaborated by Ptolemy, in which the relative motions of the sun, moon, and planets were explained to take place round the earth, which was supposed to be stationary.

B. *sb.* An adherent of the P. theory; a Ptolemaist 1751. Hence **Ptolemaˑist,** one who holds the P. theory.

Ptomaine (tōᵘˑmeⁱn, tomēⁱˑn, tōᵘˑmeˌəin). 1880. [ad. It. *ptomaina* (Selmi, 1878), f. Gr. πτῶμα, πτωματ- corpse; see -INE [5].] *Chem.* The generic name of certain alkaloid bodies found in putrefying animal and vegetable matter, some of which are very poisonous. Also *attrib.*, as *p. poisoning*.

‖**Ptosis** (ptōᵘˑsis). 1743. [a. Gr. πτῶσις falling.] **a.** Drooping of the upper eyelid from paralysis of the elevator muscle. **b.** Prolapsus of any of the viscera (*rare*) 1897.

Ptyalin (təiˑălin, pt-). 1845. [f. Gr. πτύαλον spittle + -IN [2]] *Physiol. Chem.* An amylolytic ferment in saliva.

Ptyalism (təiˑăliz'm, pt-). 1684. [ad. Gr. πτυαλισμός, f. πτυαλίζειν to expectorate, f. πτύαλον.] Excessive secretion or flow of saliva; salivation.

Pub (pɒb). *colloq.* 1865. Shortened f. PUBLIC *sb.* 4. Also *attrib.*, as *p.-crawl*.

Puberal (piūˑbĕrăl), *a.* 1836. [ad. late L. *puberalis*, f. *puber*; see -AL.] Of or at the age of puberty.

Pubertal (piūˑbəɹtăl), *a.* 1897. [irreg. f. next + -AL.] Of or pertaining to puberty.

Puberty (piūˑbəɹti). [Late ME. *puberte* = F. *puberté*, ad. L. *pubertas, -tat-*, f. *puber* or *pubes*.] The state or condition of having become functionally capable of procreating offspring. (In England the legal age of puberty is fourteen in boys and twelve in girls.)

Puberulent (piubeˑrŭlĕnt), *a.* 1864. [f. L. *puber* downy + -ULENT.] Covered with down pubescent. So **Pubeˑrulous** *a.*

‖**Pubes** (piūˑbīz). 1570. [L. *pubes, -is.*] **1.** The pubic hair. **2.** The hypogastric region, which in the adult becomes covered with hair 1682. **3.** *Zool.* and *Bot.* = next 2, 3. 1826.

Pubescence (piubeˑsĕns). 1646. [a. F.; see next and -ENCE.] **1.** The fact or condition of arriving at puberty; also = PUBERTY. **2.** *Bot.* The soft down which grows on the leaves and stems of many plants; the character or condition of being pubescent 1760. **3.** *Zool.* The soft down which occurs on certain parts of various animals, esp. insects 1826. So †**Pubeˑscency,** the quality or state of being pubescent.

Pubescent (piubeˑsĕnt), *a.* (*sb.*) 1646. [a. F., or ad. L. *pubescens, -ent-, pubescere*, inceptive verb f. *pubes* PUBES.] **1.** Arriving or arrived at the age of puberty. **2.** *Bot.* and *Zool.* Having pubescence; covered with short soft hair; downy 1760. **B.** *sb.* A youth at the age of puberty 1894.

Pubic (piūˑbik), *a.* 1831. [f. PUBES + -IC.] Of, pertaining to, or connected with the pubes or pubis.

Pubis (piūˑbis). 1597. [Short for L. *os pubis* the bone of the groin.] **1.** That portion of the innominate bone which forms the anterior wall of the pelvis. ¶ **2.** *erron.* = PUBES 2. 1681.

Public (pɒˑblik), *a.* and *sb.* [Late ME. *publike, -ique*, a. F. *public*, ad. L. *publicus*, early L. *poplicus*, f. *poplus* (later *populus*) PEOPLE.] Usu. opp. to PRIVATE. **A.** *adj.* **I.** Pertaining to the people of a country or locality. **1.** Of or pertaining to the people as a whole; common, national, popular. late ME. **2.** Done or made by or on behalf of the community as a whole; representing the community 1560. **b.** In the old universities: Belonging to, made or authorized by, acting for or on behalf of, the whole university (as dist. from the colleges, etc.) 1550. **3.** That is open to, may be used by, or may or must be shared by, all members of the community; generally accessible or available; generally levied (as a rate or tax). Also (in narrower sense), That may be used, enjoyed, shared, or competed for, by all persons legally or properly qualified. 1542. **4.** Open to general observation; existing, done, or made in public; manifest; not concealed. Also of an agent: Acting in public. 1548. **b.** Of a book, writing, etc.: (chiefly in phr. *made p.*) Made accessible to all, published, in print 1641. **5.** Of, pertaining to, or engaged in the affairs or service of the community 1571. **6.** Of or pertaining to a person in the capacity in which he comes in contact with the community; official 1538. **7.** Devoted or directed to the promotion of the general welfare; public-spirited, patriotic. Now chiefly in phr. *p. spirit.* 1607.

1. Well employed..in the publique service 1570. The event was celebrated by a p. holiday (*mod.*). Phr. *p. good, weal, p. wealth*, the common or national good or well-being. *P. act, bill, statute*, a parliamentary act or bill which affects the community at large. *P. office*, a building used for various departments of civic business, including the judicial, police, and coroner's courts, the meeting place of the local authority, the departments of municipal officials, etc. **2.** *P. utilities*, the services or supplies commonly available in large towns, such as omnibuses, electricity, water, etc. **b.** *P. examination, lecture, schools; p. orator, reader*, etc. (In some collocations now apprehended as = 'performed publicly', 'open to the public'.) **3.** *P. baths, library, park*, etc. *P. worship, meeting.* **4.** A publike exemple of infamie N.T. (Genev.) *Matt.* i. 19. **b.** The first of his dispatches has never been made p. 1777. **5.** When I embarked in p. life 1861. *P. notary, notary p.*: see NOTARY 2 b. **7.** The greatest Instances of publick Spirit the Age has produced STEELE.

II. With extended, international, or universal ref. **a.** Of or pertaining to the nations generally, or to the European, Christian, or civilized nations, regarded as a single community; general; international; esp. in *p. law* 1560. **b.** Of, pertaining or common to, the whole human race (*rare*) 1653.

a. The publique Quarrels in Christendome 1665.

B. *sb.* (the adj. used absol. or ellipt.) **1.** †**a.** The nation, the state; the commonwealth; the well-being of the community; = L. *res publica*. Usu. construed as sing. –1783. **b.** The community as an aggregate, but not as organized; hence, the members of the community (now usu. const. as pl.) 1665. **2.** With *a* and *pl.* A particular section, group, or portion of a community, or of mankind 1709. **3.** *In public*: In a situation, condition, or state open to public view or access; openly, publicly: opp. to *in private* 1450. **4.** Short for PUBLIC HOUSE. *colloq.* 1709. **b.** *attrib.* Of the public house 1756.

1. a. Hee's scarce a friend vnto the publike B. JONSON. **b.** The publick is the theatre for mountebanks and impostors BURKE. **2.** There is a separate p. for every picture, and for every book RUSKIN. **4.** He is a statesman, though he keeps a p. SCOTT. **b.** I suppose it was something in the p. line DICKENS. Hence **Pu·blic-ly** *adv.*, **-ness.**

Publican (pʊ·blikăn). ME. [a. F. *publicain*, ad. L. *publicanus*, f. *publicum* the public revenue, neut. of *publicus* PUBLIC.] **1.** *Rom. Hist.* One who farmed the public taxes; hence, a tax-gatherer. (Chiefly in Scriptural quots. and allusions.) **b.** *transf.* Any collector of toll, tribute, customs, or the like 1644. **2.** One who keeps a public house; a licensed victualler; a keeper of an ale-house or tavern 1728.

1. Whi etiþ your Maistir wiþ puplicans? WYCLIF.

†**Pu·blicate,** *v.* 1540. [f. L. *publicat-*, *publicare* to PUBLISH.] *trans.* To publish, make publicly known –1808.

Publication (pʊblikēⁱ·ʃən). [Late ME. *publicacion*, a. OF., f. L. *publicare* to PUBLISH.] The action of publishing or that which is published. **1.** The action of making publicly known; public notification or announcement; promulgation. **b.** *spec.* in *Law.* Notification or communication to those concerned, or to a limited number regarded as representing the public 1590. **2.** The issuing, or offering to the public, of a book, map, engraving, piece of music, etc.; also the work or business of producing and issuing copies of such works 1576. **b.** A work published; a book or the like printed or otherwise produced and issued for public sale 1656.

1. The P. of the Gospel to us Gentiles 1748. **b.** A man may tell his wife a thing, and that is not p.; or he may tell his next door neighbour, and that is 1897. **b.** The periodical publications of the day 1831.

Public house. (Now often with hyphen.) 1574. **1.** A public building. *Obs.* exc. with allusion to sense 2. **2. a.** An inn or hostelry providing food and lodging, or light refreshments for members of the general public; usu. licensed for the supply of ales, wines, and spirits. Now commonly merged in b. 1669. **b.** A house in which the principal business is the sale of alcoholic liquors to be consumed on the premises; a tavern 1768.

Publicist (pʊ·blisist). 1792. [a. F. *publiciste*, f. L. (*jus*) *publicum* public law; see -IST.] **1.** One who is learned in 'public' or international law; a writer on the law of nations. **2.** *loosely.* A writer on current public topics; a political journalist 1833. **3.** A publicity agent 1930.

1. Problems which baffle the p. 1868.

Publicity (pʊbli·sĭti). 1791. [ad. F. *publicité*, ad. med.L. *publicitas, -tatem*, f. L. *publicus* PUBLIC.] The quality of being public; the condition or fact of being open to public observation or knowledge. **b.** The business of making goods or persons publicly known 1904.

attrib.: **p. agent**, one employed to ensure that an actor, etc. is frequently brought into, or kept prominently in, public notice, by means of newspaper articles or the like.

Public school. 1580. A school which is public. **1.** In England, orig., A grammar-school, endowed for the use or benefit of the public, and carried on under some kind of public management or control; often contrasted with a 'private school'. In modern use, applied esp. to such of these as have developed into large boarding-schools, drawing, from the well-to-do classes, pupils who are prepared mainly for the ancient universities or for the public services, and also to some large modern schools with similar aims. **b.** *attrib.* as *public school boy, system*, etc. 1843. **2.** In Scotland, British colonies, and U.S.: A school provided at the public expense and managed by public authority, as part of a system of public (and usu. free) education 1644.

Public-spirited (stress var.), *a.* 1654. Characterized by public spirit animated by zeal for the public good; directed to the common welfare. Hence **Pu:blic-spi·rited-ly** *adv.*, **-ness.**

Publish (pʊ·bliʃ), *v.* [ME. *puplise, -ish*, and *publisshe, publisce*, f. OF. *puplier, publier*, ad. L. *publicare*, f. *publicus* PUBLIC: see -ISH *suffix* ².] **1.** *trans.* To make publicly or generally known; to declare openly or publicly; to tell or noise abroad; also, to propagate (a creed or system). **2.** *esp.* To announce in a formal or official manner; to pronounce (a judicial sentence), to promulgate (a law or edict); to proclaim. late ME. **b.** To ask (the banns of marriage) 1488. †**3.** To proclaim (a person) publicly as something, or in some capacity or connexion; also, (without compl.) to denounce, to 'show up' –1733. †**b.** To give public notice of –1710. **4.** *spec.* To issue or cause to be issued for sale to the public (copies of a book, engraving, etc.); said of an author, editor, or *spec.* of a professional publisher 1529. **b.** To make generally accessible or available; to place before or offer to the public. *Obs.* exc. as said of doing this by literary means. 1638.

1. Do not p. Your shame 1896. Phr. *To p. one's will*, to execute it properly before witnesses. *To p. a libel*, to communicate a libel to one or more persons. **3.** *Wint. T.* II. i. 98. **4. b.** The celebrated Leonard Euler had published a somewhat similar theory 1842. Hence **Pu·blishable** *a.* that may be published.

Publisher (pʊ·bliʃəɹ). 1453. [f. prec. + -ER ¹.] **1.** One who makes something public. Now *rare.* **2.** One whose business is the issuing of books, periodicals, music, etc., as the agent of the author or owner; one who produces copies of such works, and distributes them to the booksellers and other dealers, or to the public. (Without qualification, usu. a *book-publisher.*) 1740.

1. The Authors and Publishers of these vain Prophesies 1554. **2.** Petty dealers, or venders of small ware, like our publishers 1797. So **Pu·blishing** *vbl. sb. spec.* = PUBLICATION 2.

Publishment (pʊ·bliʃmĕnt). Now *rare.* 1494. [f. PUBLISH + -MENT.] The action of publishing; publication, proclamation, announcement; *esp.* in *U.S.*, publication of the banns of marriage.

Pubo-, assumed comb. form of L. *pubes*, used in the sense 'of or belonging to the pubes or *os pubis* and (some other part)'; as **p.-femoral** *a.*, belonging to the pubes and the femur; etc.

Puccoon (pʊkū·n). 1612. The Virginian Indian name of a N. Amer. plant or plants yielding a red dye: orig., of the Red P. or Blood-root, *Sanguinaria canadensis*, and Hoary P., *Lithospermum canescens.*

Puce (piŭs), *a.* (*sb.*) 1787. [a. F., :—L. *pulex, -icem* a flea.] Of a flea colour; purple brown or brownish purple. **b.** as *sb.* = puce colour 1882.

Pucelle. late ME. [a. F. *pucelle*, OF. *pucele* :—late L. *pulicella.*] **1.** A girl, a maid. *Obs.* (exc. as Fr.). **b.** *spec.* The Maid of Orleans, Joan of Arc. *Obs.* exc. *Hist.* 1450. †**2.** A drab, a slut, a courtesan –1700.

1. Three prety puzels az bright az a breast of bacon 1575.

‖**Puceron** (püsəroṅ, püsroṅ). 1752. [F., deriv. of *puce* flea.] A plant-louse or aphis.

Puck (pʊk), **pook** (puk), *sb.*¹ [OE. *púca* = ON. *púki* mischievous demon.] An evil or mischievous spirit. **a.** From the 16th c. (with capital P) the name of a fancied mischievous or tricksy goblin or sprite, called also Robin Goodfellow and Hobgoblin. **b.** with *a* and *pl.* One of a class of such demons, goblins, or sprites OE. **c.** *transf.* One given to mischievous tricks, esp. a mischievous child or youngster 1852. Hence **Pu·ckish** *a.* of the nature of or characteristic of Puck; impish, mischievous. **-ly** *adv.*, **-ness.**

Puck, *sb.*² 1834. [Origin obsc.] **1.** (Also *p. bird.*) The nightjar or goatsucker 1883. **2.** A disease in cattle attributed to the nightjar 1834.

Puck (pʊk), *sb.*³ 1891. [Origin unkn.] A flat india-rubber disk used for a ball in ice-hockey.

Pucka: see PUKKA.

Pucker (pʊ·kəɹ), *sb.* 1741. [f. next.] **1.** A ridge, wrinkle, or corrugation of the skin or other substance, or a number of small wrinkles running across and into one another 1744. **2.** *fig.* A state of agitation or excitement (*colloq.*) 1741. Hence **Pu·ckery** *a.* given to puckering, marked with puckers; that draws the mouth together, astringent.

Pucker (pʊ·kəɹ), *v.* 1598. [prob. f. root of POKE *sb.*¹, POCKET; see -ER ⁵.] **1.** *intr.* To contract or gather into wrinkles, small folds, cockles, or bulges; to cockle. Often with *up.* **2.** *trans.* To draw together or contract into wrinkles, bulges, or fullnesses; to draw (the skin, lips, etc.) into ridges and furrows; to gather one side of (a seam) more fully than the other, either as a fault in sewing, or intentionally for some purpose. Often with *up.* 1616. **b.** *absol.* To make puckers or bulges in sewing 1862.

1. His waistcoat..had a propensity to p. up over his chest 1847.

Puckfist (pʊ·kfist). 1599. [app. f. PUCK *sb.*¹] **1.** The puff-ball, *Lycoperdon Bovista.* Also abbrev. *puck.* 1601. **2.** An empty braggart 1599.

2. A base besognio, and a p. SCOTT.

Pud (pʊd). 1654. [Origin unkn.] A nursery word for the hand of a child or for the fore-foot of some animals.

Pudder (pʊ·dəɹ), *v.* *Obs.* or *dial.* ME. [Origin unkn.] **1.** *intr.* To poke or stir about with the hand or a stick; (of an animal) to poke or rout; to dabble in water, mud, or dust. **2.** To go 'poking' *about*; to potter; to meddle and muddle, to dabble (*in*) 1624.

Pudding (pu·diŋ), *sb.* [ME. *poding, puddyng*; deriv. unkn.] **I. 1.** The stomach or one of the entrails of a pig, sheep, or other animal, stuffed with minced meat, suet, seasoning, etc., boiled and kept till needed; a kind of sausage. Now chiefly *Sc.* and *dial.* **2.** (Chiefly *pl.*) The bowels, entrails, guts. Now *dial.* and *Sc.* 1444. **3.** *Naut.* **a.** A wreath of plaited cordage placed round the mast and yards of a ship as a support; a dolphin. **b.** A pad to prevent damage to the gunwale of a boat; a fender. **c.** The binding on rings, etc., to prevent the chafing of cables or hawsers. 1625.

1. P. which is called the Haggas..of whose goodnesse it is vain to boast 1615. He had sent a string of Hogs-puddings..to every poor Family in the Parish ADDISON.

II. 1. A preparation of food of a soft or moderately firm consistency, in which the ingredients, animal or vegetable, are either mingled in a farinaceous basis, or are enclosed in a farinaceous crust, and cooked by boiling or steaming. Preparations of batter, milk and eggs, rice, sago, and other farinaceous substances, suitably seasoned, and cooked by baking, are now also called puddings. **2.** *fig.* Material reward or advantage; esp. in allit. antithesis to *praise* 1728. **3.** *transf.* Anything of the consistency or appearance of a pudding 1731. †4. = JACK-PUDDING -1680.

1. Mr. Carter of Norwich, that used to eat such abundance of pudden 1670. One solid dish his week-day meal affords, An added p. solemniz'd the Lord's POPE. *Prov.* The proof of the p. is in the eating. 2. He turn'd, preferring p. to *no* praise BYRON.

attrib. and *Comb.*, as *p.-bowl, -cloth*, etc.; **p.-face,** a large fat face; hence **-faced** *a.*; **-head,** a stupid person; hence **-headed** *a.*; †**-sleeve,** a large bulging sleeve drawn in at the wrist or above; hence **-sleeved** *a.*; **-stone,** = CONGLOMERATE *sb.* 1; †**-time,** the time when p. is to be had; hence *fig.*, a time when one is in luck; a favourable time. Hence **Pu·dding** *v. trans.* to supply or treat with pudding or a pudding-like substance; *Naut.* to wrap with tow as a protection against chafing.

Pudding-pie. 1593. A name for various forms of pastry; *esp.* a dough pudding containing meat, baked in a dish. Also *attrib.*

Puddle (pɒ·d'l), *sb.* [ME. *podel, puddel*, app. dim. from OE. *pudd* ditch, furrow.] 1. A small body of standing water, foul with mud, etc., or with a muddy bottom; a small dirty pool. †Formerly including a pond, a pit full of water, or even an extensive slough or swamp. 2. *fig.*, esp. with ref. to moral defilement, or to false doctrine, etc., regarded as polluting 1533. b. *fig.* A confused collection or heap; a muddle, mess. Now only *colloq.* or *dial.* 1587. 3. Foul or muddy water such as is found in puddles. Chiefly *fig.* Now *dial.* 1555. 4. A preparation of clay, or of clay and sand, mixed with water and tempered, used as a water-tight covering for embankments, lining for canals, etc. Also called *puddling.* 1795. Hence **Pu·ddly** *a.* having the quality of a p.; muddy, turbid; more gen. foul, dirty; also, full of puddles.

Puddle (pɒ·d'l), *v.* 1440. [f. prec.; cf. Du. *poedelen*, LG. *pud(d)eln* to dabble or splash in water, etc.] 1. *intr.* To dabble or poke about, esp. in mud or shallow water; to wallow in mire; *fig.* to 'muddle' or 'mess' about. 2. *trans.* To bemire; to wet with mud or dirty water 1535. 3. To make (water) muddy or dirty 1593. b. To muddle, confuse; to sully the purity or clearness of 1604. 4. To reduce the surface of the ground, earth, clay, etc., into mud or puddle; *spec.* to knead and temper a mixture of wet clay and sand so as to form puddle (see prec. 4) 1762. b. To cover or line with puddle; to render water-tight by the application of puddle 1810. 5. *Iron Manuf.* To stir about and turn over (molten iron) in a reverberatory furnace, so as to expel the carbon and convert it into malleable iron 1798.

1. Children..are playing and puddling about in the dirt everywhere THACKERAY. 3. b. Something sure of State,.. Hath pudled his cleare Spirit SHAKS.

Comb.: **p.-ball,** a rounded mass of iron formed in puddling; **-bar,** a flat bar formed by passing a *puddle-ball* between *puddle-rolls*; **-roll,** each of a pair of large heavy rollers with grooved surfaces, between which puddled iron is passed to be flattened into bars; **-steel,** steel made by puddling. Hence **Pu·ddler,** one who puddles, chiefly in techn. senses. **Pu·ddling,** the action of the verb; also *concr.* = prec. 4; also *attrib.* as *puddling-furnace*, etc.

Pudency (piū·dĕnsi). 1611. [ad. late L. *pudentia*, f. *pudens, -entem, pudere* to make or be ashamed: see -ENCY.] Susceptibility to the feeling of shame; modesty, bashfulness.

‖ **Pudendum** (piude·ndɒm). Usu. in pl. **pudenda.** 1634. [L., lit. 'that of which one ought to be ashamed'.] The privy parts; the external genital organs. Hence **Pude·ndal** *a.* of or pertaining to the pudenda; pudic.

Pudge (pɒdʒ). *dial.* and *colloq.* 1808. [Cf. PODGE.] A short thick-set or fat person or animal; anything short and thick. Hence **Pu·dgy** *a.* short and thick or fat.

Pudic (piū·dik), *a.* (*sb.*) 1490. [a. F. *pudique*, ad. L. *pudicus* shamefaced, f. *pudere.*] †1. Modest, chaste -1610. 2. *Anat.* = PUDENDAL 1807. B. *sb. Anat.* The pudic artery 1827.

Pudicity (piudi·sĭti). Now *rare.* 1567. [ad. F. *pudicité*, ad. L. *pudicitia*, f. *pudicus* PUDIC.] Modesty, chastity.

Pudsy (pɒ·dzi), *a.* 1754. [perh. conn. w. PUD.] Plump.

‖ **Pudu** (pu·du). 1886. [Native Chilian.] The venada, *Pudua humilis* or *Cervus pudu*, a very small species of deer, native to Chili.

‖ **Pueblo** (pue·blo, pwe·blo). 1818. [Sp., = people:—L. *populus* PEOPLE.] 1. A town or village in Spain or Spanish America; esp. a communal village or settlement of Indians. 2. Short for *P. Indian* 1850.

1. *P. Indians*, partly civilized and self-governing Indians, dwelling in pueblos, in New Mexico and Arizona.

Puerile (piū·ĕrəil), *a.* 1661. [ad. L. *puerilis*, f. *puer*; see -ILE.] 1. Of, pertaining or proper to a boy or child; youthful, boyish, juvenile. Now *rare* exc. as in 2. b. Of respiration: Characterized by the louder pulmonary murmur found in children, which in adults is usu. a sign of disease 1822. 2. Merely boyish or childish; immature, trivial 1685.

2. Mere p. declamation COLERIDGE. Hence **Pu·erile·ly** *adv.*, **-ness.**

Puerility (piū,ĕri·lĭti). 1450. [a. F. *puérilité*, or ad. L. *puerilitas, -tatem*, f. *puerilis*; see prec.] 1. The condition of being a child; childhood; in *Civil Law*, the age between seven and fourteen 1512. 2. The quality of being puerile; (mere) childishness, triviality 1576. b. With *a* and *pl.* An instance of childishness 1450.

2. b. Those..Puerilities that are so often to be met with in Ovid ADDISON.

Puerperal (piu,ɔ̄·ɪpĕrăl), *a.* 1768. [f. L. *puerperus* (f. *puer* a child + *-parus* bringing forth) + -AL.] Of, pertaining to, accompanying, or ensuing upon parturition.

Pue·rpery. *rare.* 1602. [ad. L. *puerperium*, f. *puerperus*; see prec.] Childbirth 'confinement'.

Puff (pɒf), *sb.* ME. [cogn. with next.] 1. An act of puffing; a short impulsive blast of breath or wind; an abrupt emission of air, vapour, or smoke; a whiff. b. The sound of such an emission of air or the like 1834. c. *concr.* A small quantity of vapour, smoke, etc., emitted at one momentary blast; a whiff 1839. 2. A swelling caused by inflation or otherwise; a blister, tumour, protuberance, excrescence 1538. b. In costume, A rounded soft protuberant mass formed by gathering in the stuff at the edges and leaving it full in the middle as if inflated. Also, a similar mass formed of ribbons or small feathers, or of hair on the head 1601. 3. †a. An instrument like a small bellows, formerly used for blowing powder on the hair. b. A small pad of down or the like, for applying powder to the hair or skin; a POWDER-PUFF. 1658. 4. A name for various kinds of very light pastry or confectionery; now *esp.* a piece of puff-paste inclosing jam or the like. late ME. †5. *fig.* An inflated speech or piece of display; vainglory or pride; vain show; bombast; brag, bluff -1821. 6. Undue or inflated commendation; an extravagantly laudatory advertisement or review of a book, a performer or performance, a tradesman's goods, or the like 1732. 7. Applied to a person. a. A boaster, braggart. *arch.* 1599. †b. A writer of puffs -1789 c. *slang.* A decoy in a gambling-house 1731.

1. A lityl puffe of wynde..sholde soone caste hym downe 1400. c. Puffs of vapour were rising at various points 1869. 2. b. Mrs. Steward, very fine, with her locks done up with puffes, as my wife calls them PEPYS. P. of muslin, forming a panier 1889. 5. Any thing like p., or verbal ornament, I cannot bring myself to 1821. 6. The last puffs written for a morning concert RUSKIN.

Comb.: **p.-box,** a box to hold toilet-powder and a powder-puff; **-breeches,** puffed or inflated breeches; **-leg,** a humming bird of the genus *Eriocnemis*, having tufts of down upon the legs **-stone,** local name for the soft porous marlstone of the Middle Lias.

Puff (pɒf), *v.* Pa. t. and pple. **puffed** (pɒft). [ME. *puffen*, of onomatopœic origin.] 1. *intr.* To emit a puff of air or breath; to escape as a puff. *To p. out, up*, to issue, arise in puffs. b. To breathe hard, pant violently; often *to p. and blow*; hence, to run or go with puffing or panting. late ME. c. To send forth puffs of vapour or smoke, as a steam-engine, or a person smoking tobacco; to move *away, in*, or *out*, with puffing, as a locomotive or steamboat 1781. †2. To say 'pooh!' or the like; to speak or behave scornfully or insolently, to swagger. *P. at*, to pooh-pooh. -1677. 3. *trans.* To drive, impel, or agitate by puffing; to blow *away, down, up*, etc. with a quick short blast; to emit (smoke, steam, etc.) in puffs ME. b. To blow *out* 1547. c. To smoke (a pipe or cigar) in puffs 1809. d. To apply powder with a powder-puff 1838. 4. To cause (something) to swell by puffing air into it; to blow *out* or *up*; to inflate; to distend by inflation, or in any way 1539. b. *intr.* To swell *up* 1725. 5. *fig.* (*trans.*) To inflate with vanity, pride, ambition, or the like; to elate; *rarely*, to cause to swell with anger, to enrage. Usu. in pa. pple. with *up.* 1526. 6. To commend in extravagant terms; *esp.* to advertise with exaggerated or falsified praise 1735. b. *intr.* To bid at an auction for the purpose of inflating the price 1760.

1. Like foggy South, puffing with winde and raine SHAKS. b. Puffing and blowing as if..very much out of Breath ADDISON. c. Sanders..puffed away at his cigar 1861. Where the trains now go puffing in and out of Cannon Street Terminus 1870. 2. As for all his enemies, he puffeth at them *Ps.* x. 5. 3. The clearing North will p. the Clouds away DRYDEN. b. Yet we go out, Like candles puffed 1879. 5. Not stain'd with cruelty, nor puft with pride DRYDEN. Hence **Pu·ffer,** one who or that which puffs; *spec.* a person employed by a vendor to bid at an auction for the purpose of running up the price and inciting others to buy; also, a child's name for a railway engine or train. So **Pu·ffery,** the practice of a 'puffer'; inflated laudation, esp. by way of advertisement.

Pu·ff-adder. 1824. [a. S. Afr. Du. *pofadder.*] A large and very venomous African viper (*Bitis* or *Clotho arietans*), which puffs out the upper part of its body when excited.

Pu·ff-ball. 1649. [f. PUFF *sb.* or *v.* + BALL *sb.*[1]] A fungus of the genus *Lycoperdon* or of some allied genus; so called from the ball-like shape of the ripe spore-case, and its emission of the spores in a cloud of fine powder when broken.

Pu·ff-bird. 1821. Any bird of the family *Bucconidæ* or fissirostral barbets, so called from their habit of puffing out their feathers.

Puffin (pɒ·fin). [ME. *poffin, pophyn*; in latinized form, pl. *puffones.* Origin unkn.] A sea-bird of the genus *Fratercula*, of the family *Alcidæ* or Auks; *esp.* the common *F. arctica*, found on the coasts of the N. Atlantic, having a very large furrowed and parti-coloured bill. b. Erron. applied to a species of Shearwater (*Puffinus anglorum*), found in the Isle of Man and the Scilly Islands 1674. c. Applied locally in Ireland to the Razor-bill 1885.

Pu·ff-paste. 1602. [f. PUFF *sb.* or vb.-stem.] *Cookery.* A fine kind of flour paste, made very light and flaky by successive rollings and butterings 1611. b. *fig.* Applied to persons or things of a light, flimsy, or unsubstantial character 1602. So **Pu:ff-pa·stry,** fine pastry made with puff-paste.

Pu·ff-puff. 1870. [Echoic.] An imitation of the puffing of a steam-engine; hence, a nursery name for a locomotive, or a railway train.

Puffy (pɒ·fi), *a.* 1599. [f. PUFF *v.* or *sb.* + -Y[1].] 1. a. Of wind: Blowing in puffs, gusty; also, characterized by such wind. b. Of a person or animal: Easily caused to puff; short-winded. c. Of a sound: Dull, muffled. 1616. 2. Swollen or inclined to swell, by or as by puffing or inflation; turgid, tumid, puffed out; of persons, fat, corpulent and flabby 1664. 3. *fig.* Puffed up, vain, inflated, bombastic (*rare*) 1599.

1. I am too p. to enjoy hill-climbing 1844. 2. The [owl's] round p. head 1874. The p. sleeve 1899. 3. A rather p. and consequential man 1853. Hence **Pu·ffiness,** p. quality or condition.

Pug (pɒg), *sb.*[1] Now only *dial.* 1440. [Origin unkn.] The chaff of wheat or oats, the awns of barley, etc.; the refuse corn separated in winnowing.

Pug (pɒg), *sb.*[2] 1566. [Origin unkn.] I. Applied to a person, etc. †1. A term of endearment -1611. †2. A courtesan, mistress, harlot, punk -1719. †3. A bargeman -1611. 4. In servants' use: An upper servant in a large establishment 1847. II. An imp, a dwarf animal, etc. †1. A small demon or imp; a sprite; Puck -1678. 2. A monkey, an ape. Also applied to a child. Now *dial.* 1664. 3. orig. *pug-dog*: A dwarf breed of dog, resembling a bull-dog in miniature; much kept as a pet 1749. 4. A *quasi*-proper name for a fox 1809. 5. Also *p.-moth*: Collectors' name for geometrid moths of the genus *Eupithecia* 1819. 6. In full *p.-engine*: A small locomotive used chiefly for station or shunting purposes; a contractor's engine 1880.

attrib. and *Comb.*: **p.-face,** a face compared to that of a monkey; a squat flat-nosed face; **-fox,** a small-sized, blunt-nosed variety of fox; **-peal,** a young grilse or salmon; **-trout,** a sea-trout. Hence **Pu·ggish** *a.* resembling or characteristic of a pug or a pug-nose.

Pug (pvg), *sb.*[3] 1872. [See PUG *v.*[2]] Loam or clay comminuted, thoroughly mixed, kneaded, and prepared for brickmaking, etc.

Comb.: **p.-cylinder,** the cylinder of a pug-mill; **-mill,** a machine for making clay into pug.

||**Pug** (pvg), *sb.*[4] *Anglo-Ind.* 1865. [Hindī *pag* footprint.] The footprint of a beast.

Pug (pvg), *v.*[1] Now *dial.* 1575. [Origin obsc.] *trans.* To pull, tug.

Pug (pvg), *v.*[2] 1823. [Origin obsc.] **1.** *trans.* To temper (clay) for brickmaking, by kneading and working it into a soft and plastic condition, as in a pug-mill 1843. **2.** To pack or fill up (a space) with pug, cement, etc.; *esp.* to pack the space under a floor with earth, old mortar, sawdust, etc. to prevent the passage of sound 1823. Hence **Pu·gging,** the materials used to pug the space under a floor.

Pug (pvg), *v.*[3] *Anglo-Ind.* 1866. [f. PUG *sb.*[4]] *trans.* To track by footprints.

Puggree, puggaree (pv·gri, pv·gări). 1665. [a. Hind. *pagrī* a turban.] **1.** A light turban worn by Indian natives. **2.** A scarf of thin muslin or a silk veil wound round the crown of a sun-helmet and falling down behind as a shade 1859.

Pugil (piū·dʒil). *arch.* 1576. [ad. L. *pugillus*, f. root *pug-* as in *pugnus* fist.] Strictly, A handful; but now, as much as can be taken up between the thumb and the next two (or sometimes three) fingers; a little handful or big pinch.

Pugilism (piū·dʒiliz'm). 1791. [f. L. *pugil* boxer + -ISM.] The art or practice of fighting with fists; boxing.

Pugilist (piū·dʒilist). 1790. [f. as prec. + -IST.] A boxer, a fighter; *fig.* a vigorous controversialist. Hence **Pugili·stic** *a.* of or pertaining to pugilists or pugilism. **Pugili·stical** *a. rare*, **-ly** *adv.*

Pugnacious (pvgnē·ʃəs), *a.* 1642. [f. L. *pugnax, -aci-* (f. *pugnare* to fight, f. *pugnus* fist) + -OUS; see -ACIOUS.] Disposed to fight; given to fighting; quarrelsome; contentious. Hence **Pugna·cious-ly** *adv.*, **-ness.**

Pugnacity (pvgnæ·sĭti). 1605. [ad. L. *pugnacitas*, f. *pugnax*; see prec.] Tendency or inclination to fight; quarrelsomeness.

Pug nose, pug-nose (pv·gnōu·z). 1778. [f. PUG *sb.*[2] II. 2 or 3 + NOSE *sb.*] A short nose with a wide base sloping upward; a short squat or snub nose.

Pug-nose(d eel, a deep-sea species of eel, *Simenchelys parasiticus,* found off the Newfoundland bank, having a short and blunt nose. Hence **Pu·g-no:sed** *a.*

Puisne (piū·ni), *a.* and *sb.* 1598. [a. OF., mod.F. *puîné* (see PUNY), f. *puis* (:—L. *postea*, or Rom. **postius, -um*) + *né* (:—L. *natus* born).] **A.** *adj.* **1.** Born later, younger; junior (in appointment, etc.). Now only in legal use. 1613. **b.** Applied to an inferior or junior judge in the superior courts of common law 1688. **2.** Later, more recent, of subsequent date. Now only in legal use. 1655. †**3.** Small, insignificant, petty; now spelt PUNY –1782.

2. They were incumbrancers p. to the plaintiffs 1885. **3.** *A. Y. L.* III. iv. 46.

B. *sb.* †**1.** A junior; an inferior or underling; a novice –1663. **2.** *spec.* A puisne judge 1810.

Puissance (piū·isăns, piu̦i·săns, pwi·săns). *arch.* late ME. [a. F., f. *puissant* PUISSANT; see -ANCE.] **1.** Power, strength, force, might; influence. †**2.** *concr.* An armed force –1595.

1. To prove his p. in battell brave SPENSER. Our p. is our own, our own right hand Shall teach us highest deeds MILT. **2.** *John* III. i. 339.

Puissant (piū·isănt, piu̦i·sănt, pwi·sănt), *a. arch.* 1450. [a. F.:—Rom. type **possentem*, pr. pple. of L. *posse* to be able, repl. L. *potentem.*] Possessed of or wielding power; having great authority or influence; mighty, potent, powerful.

Or who from France a puisant Armie brings? DRAYTON. And with p. stroke the head to bruize 1642. The p. crowned, the weak laid low M. ARNOLD. Hence **Puissant-ly** *adv.*, **-ness** (*rare*).

†**Puke,** *sb.*[1] 1466. [15th c. *pewke, puke*, a. MDu. *puuc, puyck*; origin unkn.] **1.** A superior kind of woollen cloth, of which gowns were made –1612. **2.** A colour formerly used for woollen goods; app. a bluish black or inky colour –1725.

Puke (piūk), *sb.*[2] 1737. [f. PUKE *v.*] **1.** An act of vomiting, a vomit. **2.** An emetic, a vomit 1743.

Puke (piūk), *v.* 1600. [Origin unkn.] **1.** *intr.* To eject food from the stomach; to vomit. **2.** *trans.* To eject by vomiting; to vomit 1601.

1. At first the Infant, Mewling, and puking in the Nurses armes SHAKS. Hence **Pu·ker,** one who vomits; †a medicine causing vomiting.

||**Pukka** (pv·kă), *a.* 1698. [a. Hindī *pakkā*.] **a.** Applied to the larger of two weights of the same name: Of full weight, full, good; also, genuine, thorough. **b.** Sure, certain; thorough, out-and-out 1776. **c.** Permanent, as an appointment, a building, etc. 1784.

Pulchritude (pv·lkritiūd). late ME. [ad. L. *pulchri-, pulcritudo*, f. *pulcher, pulcer* beautiful; see -TUDE.] Beauty.

Pule (piūl), *v.* 1534. [Of echoic origin; perh. ad. F. *piauler.*] **1.** *intr.* To cry in a thin or weak voice, as a child; to whine, to cry in a querulous tone. **2.** To pipe plaintively, as a chicken, etc.; also said of the cry of the kite 1598. **3.** *trans.* To utter (something) in a whining or querulous tone 1535.

1. Don't come puling to me when it 's too late 1877. Hence **Pu·ler,** one who pules or whines; †a fledgeling.

Pulicine (piū·lisəin), *a. rare.* 1656. [f. L. *pulex, pulicem* flea + -INE[1].] Of or relating to fleas.

Pulicous (piū·likəs), *a. rare.* 1658. [ad. L. *pulicosus*, f. *pulex* flea; see -OUS.] Abounding in fleas. So **Pu·licose** *a.* infested with fleas, flea-bitten; *Path.* resembling flea-bites.

Puling (piū·liŋ), *ppl. a.* 1529. [-ING[2].] **1.** Crying as a child, whining, feebly wailing; weakly querulous. †**2.** Pining, weakly –1706.

1. The unmaskuline Rhetorick of any p. Priest MILT. Hence **Pu·lingly** *adv.*

||**Pulka** (pv·lkă). 1796. [a. Finnish *pulkka*, Lapp. *pulkke.*] A Lapland travelling-sledge in shape like the front half of a boat, drawn by a single reindeer.

Pull (pul), *sb.* ME. [f. next.] **I.** The act, action, or faculty of pulling. **1.** An act of pulling or drawing towards oneself with force 1440. **b.** The force expended in pulling or drawing; pulling power or force; draught, traction, strain; the force of attraction 1833. **c.** The drawing or dragging of a weight; the exertion of carrying one's own weight up an ascent 1841. **2.** *spec.* or *techn.* **a.** *Printing.* A pull of the bar of the hand-press; hence, an impression taken by this; now *spec.* a rough 'proof' 1683. **b.** A pull at the bridle in order to check a horse; *spec.* in *Racing*, a check dishonestly given to a horse to prevent his winning 1737. **c.** A pull at an oar; hence, a short spell at rowing 1793. **d.** The act of pulling the trigger of a fire-arm; also, the force required for this 1888. **e.** *Cricket.* A hit which brings a ball pitched to the off side round to leg. So in *Golf*, a hit which causes the ball to swerve in its flight towards the left (i. e. of a right-handed player). 1892. **f.** *Long p.* (in public-house use): the supply of an amount of beer, etc. exceeding that asked for 1908. †**3.** A trial of strength; a bout, a set-to; often in *to stand* or *wrestle a p.* –1747. **4.** Advantage possessed by one party, course, or method over another; esp. in phr. *to have a* or *the p. of, on, upon,* or *over* some one 1584. **b.** *spec.* Personal or private influence capable of being brought to bear to one's advantage. orig. *U.S. slang.* 1889. **5.** A long or deep draught of liquor 1575.

1. A long p., a strong p., and a p. all together 1883. **b.** The amount of this magnetic p. may be very considerable 1900. **c.** A stiff p...that brought us to the top 1861. **4.** Phr. *The p. of the table*, in gambling games, the advantage possessed by the dealer or banker. **b.** I have got a p., and any one who has got a p. can do a great deal 1894.

II. Concrete senses. **1.** That part of a mechanism with which a pull is exerted; a handle or the like; often in comb. as *beer-p.*, *bell-p.*; also, an instrument or device for pulling 1810. **2.** A part of a road where extra effort is necessary; *esp.* a steep ascent 1798.

Pull (pul), *v.* [OE. *pullian*; etym. unkn.] **I.** In senses akin to *pluck.* **1.** *trans.* = PLUCK *v.* 1. **a.** To pluck or draw out (feathers, hair, etc.). *Obs.* or *dial.* **b.** To pluck or draw up by the root (plants, e. g. carrots, etc.) ME. **c.** To pluck, gather (fruit, flowers, or leaves) from the trees, etc., on which they grow. Now chiefly *Sc.* ME. **2.** *trans. To p. caps*: to snatch off one another's caps; hence, to scuffle, to quarrel. So *to p. wigs.* 1778. **3.** *intr.* To snatch or tear *at* something; *spec.* of a hawk: To tear or pluck at food 1826. **4.** *trans.* = PLUCK *v.* 5. Now *rare* or *dial.* OE.

1. a. Wee'le p. his Plumes SHAKS. **c.** We'll pou the daisies on the green RAMSAY. **2.** A man..for whom half the females of Paris were pulling caps 1823.

II. To draw with force, etc. **1.** *trans.* To exert upon (anything) a force that tends to snatch, draw, or drag it away; to drag or tug at OE. **2.** To draw, drag, or haul with force or effort towards oneself (or into some position so pictured) ME. **3.** *intr.* To perform the action of pulling; to exert drawing, dragging, or tugging force. Often with *at.* late ME. **b.** *spec.* Of a horse: To strain (esp. habitually) against the bit 1791. **c.** To move, go, or proceed by pulling or by some exertion of force 1877. †**4.** *trans.* To take away with difficulty; to tear off, to wrench away –1625. **5.** *fig.* To bring forcibly into or out of some state or condition. *rare* or *Obs.* late ME. **6.** To take a draught of (liquor); to draw or suck (a draught of liquor) into the mouth; †to drink from (a vessel). late ME. **b.** *intr.* To draw or suck *at* (a pipe, cigar, etc.) 1861. †**7.** Implying an adv. = *pull down* –1655.

1. Phr. *To p. by the ear, nose, sleeve*, etc., to gain attention, or to punish or insult, by pulling at these parts. *To p. a bell*, to p. the bell-rope or handle in order to ring the bell. *To p. one's leg*: see LEG *sb.* 1 a. *To p. the strings, wires*: see the sbs. **2.** He placidly pulled his nightcap over his ears THACKERAY. Phr. *To p. in* or *to pieces*, etc., to separate the parts of (anything) forcibly; to demolish; also *fig.* to analyse and criticize unfavourably. **3.** Phr. *P. devil, p. baker* (†*parson*), an incitement to effort in a contest or the possession of something. **6.** To p. the tankards cheerfully 1595. **b.** Joe..pulled hard at his pipe DICKENS. **7.** Let them p. all about mine Eares SHAKS.

III. In techn. senses, with specific objects expressed or understood. **1.** *trans. Printing.* In the old hand-press, To draw the bar of the press) towards one, so as to press down the platen upon the sheet or forme; also *intr.* or *absol.* Hence, To print upon (a sheet) or from (a forme) in this way; to make or take (an impression, proof, or copy) by printing; to print off 1653. **2.** *intr.* or *absol.* To pull an oar so as to move a boat; to row; to proceed by rowing 1676. **b.** *trans.* To pull (an oar or sculls); hence, to row, to propel (a boat) by rowing; to transport in a boat by rowing 1820. **3.** To arrest in the name of justice (*slang*) 1811. **4.** *Racing.* To hold in or check (a horse), *esp.* so as to cause him to lose a race. Also *absol.* 1800. **5.** *Cricket.* To strike (a ball) from the off to the leg; *Golf*, to drive a ball so that it swerves to the left. Also *absol.* 1884.

1. A few copies were pulled before the disaster occurred 1900. **2. b.** Phr. *To p. one's weight*, to row with effect in proportion to one's weight; also *transf* to perform one's share of work, etc.

Phrases. *To p. a face, faces*, to draw the countenance into a grimace, to distort the features. *To p. a* (*sanctimonious*, etc.) *face*, to put on a (sanctimonious, etc.) expression. *To p. a long face*: see LONG *a.*[1] 1.

IV. With adverbs. **Pull about.** *trans.* To p. this way and that way *colloq.* to treat roughly or unceremoniously. **P. back. a.** See simple senses and BACK *adv.* **b.** *trans.* To draw or keep back (in space or progress). **P. down. a.** See simple senses and DOWN *adv.* **b.** *trans.* To demolish (a building). **c.** To seize and bring to the ground; to overcome (a hunted animal). **d.** To lower or depress in health, spirits, size, strength, value, etc.; also, to 'bring low', humble. **e.** To depose (a sovereign) violently; to overthrow (a government) by force. **P. in. a.** See simple senses and IN *adv.* **b.** *trans.* To rein in (one's horse); hence *fig.* Also *intr.* or *absol.* To check oneself in any course. **P. off. a.** See simple senses and OFF *adv.* **b.** *Sporting.* (*trans.*) To win (a prize or contest); hence to succeed in gaining or effecting (something). **P. out. a.** See simple senses and OUT *adv.* **b.** *absol.* or *intr.* Of a locomotive engine or train: To move out of a station; to draw out; hence, of a person: To go away, take his departure. Also, to 'get out' of an undertaking. Chiefly *U.S.* **P. through.** **a.** See simple senses and THROUGH *adv.* **b.** *trans.* To get (a person) through a difficult, dangerous, or critical condition or situation; to bring (a thing) to a successful issue. **c.** *intr.* To get through sickness, a trial, etc. with effort or difficulty. **P. together.** **a.** See sense II. 2 and TOGETHER. **b.** *To p. oneself together*, to rouse or recover oneself; to rally. **c.** *intr.* To work in harmony; also, to 'get on' together. **P. up.** **a.** See simple senses and UP *adv.* **b.** *trans.* To root out, demolish. **c.** To cause to stop; to stop; to arrest, to apprehend; *esp.* to apprehend and take before a magistrate; hence, to reprimand, reprove. **d.** To tighten (reins) by drawing them towards oneself; to bring (a horse) to a standstill by doing this; also *transf.* to check (a person) in any course of action, esp. a bad course. **e.** *absol.* Of a driver, etc.: To bring a horse or vehicle to a stop; also, of a horse or vehicle: To come to a standstill. **f.** *refl.* and *intr.* for *refl.* To check or stop oneself in any course of action. **g.** *intr.* To advance one's position in a race, etc.

Pull-, the stem of PULL *v.* (or PULL *sb.*) in comb.

1. With advbs., forming sbs. or adjs., in senses (*a*) *sb.* the act of pulling in the direction specified; (*b*) *adj.* that pulls or is pulled in the direction specified. **Pull-on:** see PULL-OVER 3. **Pu·ll-through,** a piece of gimp, etc. with which the tow or rag for cleaning the barrel is pulled through from breech to muzzle of a rifle. 2. With sbs. used *attrib.* in sense used by, for, or in pulling'.

Pu·ll-back. 1591. [f. phr. *to pull back.*] 1. The action or an act of pulling back 1668. 2. That which pulls back; a retarding influence; a check. Now *colloq.* and *dial.* 1591. 3. A contrivance for pulling something back 1703.

Pu·ll-down. 1588. [f. phr. *to pull down.*] 1. The act of pulling down, or fact of being pulled down. 2. In the organ, a wire which pulls down a pallet or valve when the key is depressed, thus admitting wind to the pipe 1852.

Pulled (puld), *ppl. a.* late ME. [f. PULL *v.* + -ED [1].] 1. In the senses of PULL *v.* *esp.* 2. Denuded of feathers, plucked; stripped of wool or hair. late ME.

P. bread, the inside of a loaf pulled out and lightly browned. *P. chicken, fowl*, chicken or fowl cooked, skinned, and boned, and the flesh cut up and put into a rich white sauce. *P. figs*, dried figs manipulated so that the eye is in the centre, and packed flat. *P. wool*, inferior wool separated from the skin by the aid of chemicals.

Pullen (pu·lėn). *Obs.* exc. *dial.* ME. [app. a. OF. *poulain* young of any animal, identified in Eng. with *poulaille* poultry.] 1. Poultry; the flesh of poultry as food. 2. Chickens collectively; young; rarely, a chicken; *fig.* a child 1631.

Puller (pu·ləɹ). late ME. [f. PULL *v.* + -ER [1].] One who or that which pulls.

Proud setter vp, and p. downe of Kings SHAKS.

Pullet (pu·lėt). ME. [a. F. *poulet* chicken, dim. of *poule.*] 1. A young (domestic) fowl; *spec.* and *techn.* a young hen from the time she begins to lay till the first moult. 2. In full, *P. Carpet-shell*: a bivalve mollusc, *Tapes pullastra* 1890.

Pulley (pu·li), *sb.* [ME. a. OF. *polie*, mod. F. *poulie*, prob. :—Gr. *πολίδιον little pivot or axis, dim. of πόλος POLE *sb.*[2]] 1. One of the simple mechanical powers, consisting of a grooved wheel mounted in a block, so that a cord or the like may pass over it; used for changing the direction of power, esp. for raising weights by pulling downwards. Also, a combination of such wheels in a BLOCK (*sb.* 4), or system of blocks in a TACKLE, by means of which the power is increased. 2. A wheel or drum fixed on a shaft and turned by a belt or the like for the application or transmission of power; usu. to increase speed or power 1619.

1. *Fixed p.*, a p. the block of which is fixed. *Frame p.*, a p. in which the wheels or sheaves are fixed in a frame.

attrib. and *Comb.*, as *p.-block*, etc.; also **p.-drum,** the block or shell in which the sheave or sheaves are mounted; **-frame,** the gearing above a pit, upon which the pulleys are supported; **-stile,** one of the vertical side-pieces of a window sash-frame, in which the pulleys are pivoted.

Pu·lley, *v.* 1599. [f. prec.] 1. *trans.* To raise or hoist with or as with a pulley. 2. To furnish or fit with a pulley; to work by means of a pulley 1767.

†**Pu·llicate.** 1794. [f. *Pulicat*, a town on the Madras coast.] **a.** A coloured handkerchief, orig. made at Pulicat -1839. **b.** A material made in imitation of these, woven from dyed yarn -1891.

Pullman (pu·lmăn). 1874. [f. George M. *Pullman*, the designer.] In full, *P. car* (*saloon*): a railway carriage constructed and arranged as a saloon, and (usu.) with special arrangements for use as a sleeping-car.

Pu·ll-on. 1923. Used chiefly *attrib.* of garments, boots, and the like, which are pulled on without fastening.

Pu·ll-o:ver. 1883. [f. phr. *to pull over.*] 1. The action or an act of pulling over or from side to side; also *attrib.* or as *adj.* having the function of pulling over 1894. 2. A knitted jumper or sweater, made without fastenings, so that it must be pulled over the head 1925.

Pullulant (pʊ·liŭlănt), *a.* 1889. [ad. L. *pullulantem*; see next.] Budding.

Pullulate (pʊ·liŭleᶦt), *v.* 1619. [f. L. *pullulat-*, *pullulare* to sprout out, etc., f. *pullulus*, dim. of *pullus* young of an animal.] 1. *intr.* Of a growing part, shoot, or bud: To sprout out, bud. **b.** Of a seed: To sprout, to germinate. Of a plant or animal: To propagate itself by budding; to breed, to multiply; now usu. with the connotation of rapid increase 1621. 2. *intr. transf.* and *fig.* **a.** To be produced as offspring, to spring up abundantly 1657. **b.** To teem, to swarm 1835.

2. b. As to the beggars, they p. in the place 1883.

Pullulation (pʊliulēᶦ·ʃən). 1641. [f. prec.; see -ATION.] The action of pullulating. Also, the product of this offspring, progeny. **b.** *spec.* in *Biol.* Generation or reproduction by budding 1822.

Pu·ll-up. 1854. [f. phr. *to pull up.*] 1. The act of pulling up a horse or vehicle; a sudden stop; hence *fig.* 2. A stopping-place for riders or drivers 1887.

Pulmo- (pʊ·lmo), shortened from PULMONI-, comb. form of L. *pulmo, pulmonem* lung; as in ‖**Pulmobranchiæ** (-bræ·ŋki,ī) *sb. pl.*, lung-sacs; hence **Pulmobra·nchial, Pulmobra·nchiate** *adjs.*, having, or breathing by means of pulmobranchiæ. **Pulmoga·stero-pod, -ga·stropod** *a.*, belonging to the *Pulmogastero·poda*, the pulmonate or air-breathing gastropods; *sb.* one of these.

‖**Pulmonaria** (pʊlmŏnē·riă). 1578. [med. L. fem. (sc. *herba*) of L. *pulmonarius* beneficial to the lungs, f. *pulmo, pulmonem* lung; so called from its assumed virtue in curing disease of the lungs, as supposed to be indicated by the spotted leaves resembling the lungs.] *Bot.* A genus of boraginaceous plants; lungwort.

Pulmonary (pʊ·lmŏnări), *a.* (*sb.*) 1704. [ad. L. *pulmonarius*, f. *pulmo, pulmonem*; see -ARY [1].] 1. Of, pertaining to, situated in, or connected with the lungs. (Chiefly *Anat.*) **b.** Constituting a lung or lung-like organ; of the nature of a lung 1834. **c.** Carried on by means of lungs 1826. 2. Occurring in or affecting the lungs (chiefly *Path.*); of or pertaining to disease of the lungs 1727. **b.** Affected with or subject to lung-disease; consumptive. Also *transf.* 1843. 3. *Zool.* Having lungs, lung-sacs, or pulmonary organs 1833. **B.** *sb.* *Zool.* A pulmonary arachnidan, as a spider or a scorpion 1835.

Pulmonate (pʊ·lmŏnĕt), *a.* (*sb.*) 1842. [ad. mod.L. *pulmonatus*, f. *pulmo, -monem*; see -ATE [2] 2.] *Zool.* Having lungs, as the higher vertebrates, or lung-like respiratory organs, as the orders *Pulmonata* of gastropod molluscs and *Pulmonaria* of arachnids. **B.** *sb.* A pulmonate mollusc (or, less usu., arachnid). So **Pu·lmonated** *a.*

Pulmoni- (pʊlmōᵘ·ni), comb. form of L. *pulmo, pulmonem*, as in **Pulmonibra·nchiate** *a.* and *sb.*; see *pulmobranchiate* (PULMO-).

Pulmonic (pʊlmŏ·nik), *a.* (*sb.*) 1661. [a. F. *pulmonique*, f. L. *pulmonem*; see -IC.] 1. = PULMONARY *a.* 1. 1702. 2. = PULMONARY *a.* 2. 1661. **B.** *sb.* A person subject to or affected with disease of the lungs 1735. So †**Pulmo·nical** *a.* 1597.

Pulmoniferous (pʊlmŏni·fĕrəs), *a.* 1835. [f. L. *pulmonem* + -FEROUS.] *Zool.* Bearing or having lungs (or lung-like organs); pulmonate; *spec.* belonging to the group *Pulmonifera* (= *Pulmonata*) of gastropod molluscs. So Pulmo·nifer, a p. gastropod.

Pulmono-, irreg. comb. form of L. *pulmo, -onem* lung, occas. used instead of PULMONI- or PULMO-.

Pulp (pʊlp), *sb.* 1563. [ad. L. *pulpa.*] A soft, moist, homogeneous or formless substance or mass. 1. The fleshy succulent part of a fruit; the soft pith in the interior of the stem of a plant. 2. Any soft muscular or fleshy part of an animal body; *esp.* the soft nervous substance which fills the interior cavity of a tooth 1611. 3. A soft formless mass, esp. of disintegrated organic matter 1676; *spec.* the fibrous material, as linen, wood, etc., reduced to a soft uniform mass, from which paper is made; paper-pulp 1727. **b.** Ore pulverized and mixed with water; slimes. *Dry p.*, dry crushed ore. 1837.

attrib. and *Comb.*, as **p.-canal, -cavity, -chamber,** the space in the interior of a tooth which contains the p.; **-digester,** a machine for reducing paper-stock and obtaining the fibre free from extraneous matter; **-mill,** a mill in which wood is reduced to paper-pulp; also, a factory in which pulping is carried on; **-wood,** wood suitable for making paper-pulp.

Pulp, *v.* 1662. [f. prec.] 1. *trans.* To reduce to pulp or to a pulpy mass. 2. To remove the surrounding pulp from (coffee-beans, etc.) 1791. 3. *intr.* To become pulpy, to swell with juice 1818. Hence **Pu·lper,** a machine for reducing fruit, paper-stock, etc. to pulp; a machine for removing the pulp from the coffee bean.

Pu·lpiness. 1846. [f. PULPY *a.* + -NESS.] The quality or state of being pulpy; softness, flabbiness.

Pulpit (pu·lpit), *sb.* ME. [ad. L. *pulpitum.*] 1. In ref. to ancient times: A scaffold, stage, or platform for public shows, speeches, or disputations. *Obs.* or *arch.* late ME. 2. A raised structure or enclosed platform, usu. supplied with a desk, seat, etc., from which the preacher in a church or chapel delivers the sermon. **b.** *fig.* The place from which anything of the nature of a sermon, as a moral lecture, is delivered 1616. 3. *transf.* The occupants of the pulpit; Christian ministers or the Christian ministry as occupied with preaching 1570. 4. Applied to other places elevated so as to give the occupant a conspicuous position, etc.; e.g. an auctioneer's desk or platform (now *local*). late ME.

1. *Jul. C.* III. i. 229. 2. Phr. *To occupy the p.*, to preach, or to conduct divine service. 3. The Bar, the P. and the Press Nefariously combine To cry up an usurped Pow'r And stamp it right divine 1695. 4. Come, get to your p., Mr. Auctioneer SHERIDAN. Hence **Pu·lpit** *v. trans.* to provide with a pulpit, or place in the pulpit; *intr.* to officiate in the pulpit, to preach. **Pu·lpiter** = PULPITEER. **Pulpi·tic, -al,** *adjs.*, **-ly** *adv.* **Pu·lpitish** *a.*

Pulpiteer (pulpitīᵊ·ɹ), *sb.* 1642. [f. prec. + -EER.] A preacher by profession; usu. *contempt.* Hence **Pulpitee·r** *v. intr.* to preach.

Pu·lpitry. 1606. [f. as prec. + -RY.] The work or service of the pulpit; preaching; the conventional talk of the pulpit; sermonizing.

Pulpous (pʊ·lpəs), *a.* 1601. [ad. L. *pulposus*, f. *pulpa* PULP.] Of the nature of or consisting of pulp; resembling pulp; pulpy. Hence **Pu·lpousness** (*rare*).

Pulpy (pʊ·lpi), *a.* 1591. [f. PULP *sb.* + -Y [1].] Of the nature of, consisting of, or resembling pulp; soft, fleshy, succulent; also *fig.* flabby.

‖**Pulque** (pu·lke). 1693. [Sp. Amer.; origin unkn.] A fermented drink made in Mexico from the sap of the agave or maguey (*Agave americana*).

Pulsate (pʊ·lseᶦt, pʊlsēᶦ·t), *v.* 1794. [f. L. *pulsat-*, *pulsare*, freq. of *pellere*, *puls-* to drive, strike, beat.] 1. *intr.* To expand and contract rhythmically, as the heart or an artery; to exhibit a pulse; to beat, throb. (Chiefly in scientific use.) 2. *gen.* To strike upon something with a rhythmical succession of strokes; to move with a regular alternating motion; to exhibit such a movement; to beat, vibrate, quiver, thrill 1861.

1. *fig.* Life pulsates in rock or tree EMERSON. 2. The air pulsates with the flash of arms 1861.

Pulsatile (pv·lsătil, -əil), *a.* 1541. [f. as prec. + -ILE.] 1. *Anat.* and *Phys.* Having the capacity or property of pulsating or throbbing, as the heart, etc.; exhibiting pulsation. b. Of, or characterized by, pulsation 1684. 2. Of a musical instrument: Played by percussion; percussive 1769.

‖**Pulsatilla** (pvlsăti·lă). 1597. [med.L., dim. of *pulsata* beaten, driven about.] *Bot.*, *Pharm.* The Pasque-flower, a species of Anemone (*A. Pulsatilla*); earlier, a generic name; now in *Bot.* a subgenus including this and other species; also, the extract or tincture of this plant.

Pulsation (pvlsēⁱ·ʃən). 1541. [ad. L. *pulsationem*, f. *pulsare*; see PULSATE.] 1. The movement of the pulse in a living animal body; rhythmic dilatation and contraction, as of the heart, an artery, etc.; beating, throbbing. b. with *pl.* = PULSE *sb.*¹ 1 b. 1645. 2. *gen.* Rhythmical beating, vibration, or undulation. Also with *a* and *pl.* 1658. 3. The action of striking, knocking, or beating; with *pl.* A stroke, knock, blow 1656.

2. A dove..Some..message knit below The wild p. of her wings TENNYSON.

Pulsative (pv·lsătiv), *a.* Now *rare.* late ME. [f. L. *pulsat-*, *pulsare*; see -ATIVE.] = PULSATILE 1.

Pulsator (pv·lseⁱtəɹ, pvlsēⁱ·təɹ). 1656. [f. L. *pulsare*; see PULSATE and -OR.] 1. One who or that which knocks or strikes (*rare*). 2. A machine, working on the principle of the jigger, for separating diamonds from the earth in which they are found 1890. 3. = PULSOMETER 1884.

Pulsatory (pv·lsătəri), *a.* 1613. [f. PULSATE; see -ORY ².] Having the quality of pulsating; characterized by or of the nature of pulsation. b. = PULSATILE 1. 1802.

Pulse (pvls), *sb.*¹ [ME. *pous*, *pouce*, a. OF. *pous*, *pousse*:—L. *pulsus* (*venarum*) the beating of the veins, f. *puls-*, *pellere* to drive, beat; altered in late ME. to *pulse* after L.] 1. The 'beating', throbbing, or rhythmical dilatation of the arteries as the blood is propelled along them by the contractions of the heart in the living body; esp. as felt in arteries near the surface of the body; usu. in ref. to its rate and character as indicating the person's state of health; often in phr. *to feel one's p.* b. Each successive beat or throb of the arteries, or of the heart. Usu. in *pl.* late ME. 2. *fig.* and *allus.*, denoting life, vitality, energy, feeling, sentiment, tendency, drift, inclination, etc.; with *pl.* a throb or thrill of life, emotion, etc. 1540. 3. The rhythmical recurrence of strokes, vibrations, or undulations; beating, vibration 1657. b. A single vibration or wave; a beat 1673. c. *Pros.* and *Mus.* A beat or stress in the rhythm of a verse or piece of music 1885.

1. Giue me your hand, and let mee feele your p. SHAKS. 2. And now I see with eye serene The very p. of the machine WORDSW. Phr. *To feel the p. of*, fig. to try to discover the sentiments, tendency, drift, etc. of; to 'sound'; With whom my Lord had occasion to talk and to feel his P. 1707. 3. b. The last faint p. of quivering light KEBLE.

attrib. and *Comb.*: **p.-curve**, **-tracing**, the curve traced by a sphygmograph, indicating the character of a pulse-wave; **-wave**, any of the component elements of the apparently simple movement of the pulsating artery. Hence **Pu·lseless** *a.* having or exhibiting no pulsation; devoid of life energy or movement; **-ness.**

Pulse (pvls), *sb.*² ME. [a. OF. *po(u)ls*:—L. *puls* pottage made of meal, pulse, etc.] 1. The edible seeds of leguminous plants, as peas, beans, lentils, etc. a. *collect. sing.*; sometimes const. as *pl.* b. with *a* and *pl.* A kind or sort of such seeds 1555. 2. *collect. sing.* (sometimes const. as *pl.*) Plants yielding pulse; esculent leguminous plants. late ME.

Pulse (pvls), *v.* 1549. [ad. L. *pulsare*, freq. of *pellere* to drive, strike, beat.] 1. *trans.* To drive, impel; to drive *forth*, expel. *Obs.* (exc. as in 4). 2. *intr.* = PULSATE 1 (now only literary) 1559. 3. *gen.* = PULSATE 2. 1851. 4. *trans.* To drive or send out in or by pulses or rhythmic beats 1819.

Pulsi·fic, *a.* Now *rare.* 1634. [f. L. *pulsus* PULSE *sb.*¹ + -FIC.] Producing or causing the pulsation of the arteries; also, pulsatory, throbbing.

Pulsimeter (pvlsi·mǐtəɹ). 1842. [f. L. *pulsus* PULSE *sb.*¹ + -METER.] An instrument for measuring the rate or force of the pulse. Also *attrib.*, as *p. watch.*

Pulsion (pv·lʃən). Now *rare.* 1634. [ad. L. *pulsio*, *-onem*, f. *puls-*, *pellere* to drive, push.] The action of driving or pushing.

Pulsive (pv·lsiv), *a.* Now *rare.* 1602. [f. L. *puls-*, *pellere* + -IVE.] Having the quality of driving or impelling; compelling; impulsive; propulsive.

Pulsometer (pvlsǫ·mǐtəɹ). 1875. [f. L. *pulsus* PULSE *sb.*¹ + -OMETER.] A steam-condensing vacuum-pump with two chambers so arranged that the steam is condensed in and the water admitted to each alternately; so called from the pulsatory action of the steam. (Proprietary term.) Also *p. pump.*

Pultaceous (pvltēⁱ·ʃəs), *a.* 1668. [f. L. *puls-*, *pultem* pap, pottage + -ACEOUS.] 1. Of the nature or consistency of pap; soft, semifluid, pulpy. 2. Of the nature or class of pulse 1762.

‖**Pulu** (pū·lū). 1858. [Hawaiian.] A fine yellowish silky vegetable wool obtained from the base of the leaf-stalks of the Hawaiian tree-ferns, *Cibotium menziesii*, *C. chamissoi*, and *C. glaucum.*

Pulverable (pv·lvĕrăb'l), *a.* 1657. [f. L. *pulverare*, f. *pulverem* + -ABLE.] Capable of being reduced to powder; pulverizable.

Pulveration (pvlvĕrēⁱ·ʃən). 1623. [ad. L. *pulverationem*, f. *pulverare.*] Reduction to powder or dust; pulverization.

Pulverescent (pvlvĕre·sĕnt), *a.* 1805. [f. L. *pulver-* dust + -ESCENT.] Tending to fall to powder or to be powder. So **Pulvere·scence.**

Pulverine (pv·lvĕrin). 1836. [Cf. It. *polverina* fine powder.] Ashes of barilla.

Pulverization (pv:lvĕrəizēⁱ·ʃən). 1658. [f. late L. *pulverizare* to pulverize.] The action of pulverizing; reduction to the state of powder or dust. b. *techn.* The separation (of a liquid) into minute particles, as spray 1861.

fig. The complete p. of their case by the Minister whom they approached 1884.

Pulverize (pv·lvĕrəiz), *v.* late ME. [ad. late L. *pulverizare*, f. L. *pulverem.*] 1. *trans.* To reduce to powder or dust; to comminute, to triturate. b. *techn.* To divide (a liquid) into minute particles or spray 1807. 2. *fig.* To demolish, to break down utterly 1631. 3. *intr.* To crumble or fall to dust; to become disintegrated 1801. 4. Of a bird: To roll in the dust (*rare*) 1890.

1. Cultivable land must be pulverised and watered 1868. 2. We have iron hammers To p. rebellion MASSINGER. 3. *fig.* The stern old faiths have all pulverized EMERSON. Hence **Pu·lverizable** *a.* capable of being pulverized. **Pu·lverizer,** one who or that which pulverizes; an instrument that reduces to powder; also *techn.* one that reduces a liquid to spray.

Pulverous (pv·lvĕrəs), *a.* 1778. [f. L. *pulver-* dust + -OUS.] Powdery; dusty.

Pulverulent (pvlve·rǐŭlĕnt), *a.* 1656. [f. L. *pulverulentus* dusty, f. *pulver-*; see -LENT.] 1. Consisting of or having the form of powder or dust; powdery. 2. Covered with powder or dust; dusty; spec. in *Entom.* and *Bot.* 1744. 3. Of very slight cohesion; crumbling to dust 1794. 4. Of birds: Addicted to lying or rolling in the dust 1828. So **Pulve·rulence**, dustiness, powder.

Pulvil (pv·lvil), *sb. arch.* 1691. [ad. It. *polviglio*; see next.] Cosmetic or perfumed powder for powdering the wig or perfuming the person. Hence †**Pu·lvil** *v. trans.* to powder or perfume with p.

‖**Pulvilio, -villio** (pvlvi·lyo). Now *Hist.* 1675. [a. It. *polviglio* fine powder, f. *polve*, *polvere* powder.] = prec.

‖**Pulvillus** (pvlvi·lɒs). 1706. [L., contr. from *pulvinulus*, dim. of *pulvinus* cushion.] 1. A little cushion; in *Surg.*, a small mass of lint used for plugging deep wounds. 2. *Entom.* A cushion-like process on the feet of an insect; a foot-cushion 1826.

‖**Pulvinar** (pvlvəi·năɹ). 1599. [a. L. *pulvinar* couch, f. *pulvinus* cushion, pillow.] 1. *Rom. Antiq.* A couch or cushioned seat of the gods; also, the cushioned seat in the circus 1600. 2. *Anat.* The posterior inner tubercle of the optic thalamus 1886.

Pulvinate (pv·lvinĕt), *a.* 1824. [ad. L. *pulvinatus*, f. *pulvinus* cushion; see -ATE ².] Pillowy, cushion-like; in *Bot.* and *Entom.*, cushion-shaped, swelling or bulging like a cushion. Hence **Pu·lvinately** *adv.*

Pulvinated (pv·lvineⁱtĕd), *a.* 1773. [f. as prec. + -ED.] 1. *Arch.* Swelling or bulging; esp. applied to a frieze having a convex face. 2. *Bot.* Having a pulvinus 1880. 3. *Entom.* = prec. 1858.

‖**Pulvinus** (pvlvəi·nɒs). 1857. [L., cushion, pillow.] *Bot.* Any cushion-like swelling or expansion of a stem or petiole; *esp.* one forming a special organ for movement of some leaves.

Puma (piū·mă). 1777. [a. Sp., a. Peruv. *puma.*] A large American feline quadruped, *Felis concolor*, also called COUGAR. b. The flesh of this animal 1845.

Pumice (pv·mis), *sb.* [Late ME. *pomis*, a. OF. *pomis*, *pumis*, ad. late L. *pumicem*; in 16th c. assim. to the L. form.] 1. a. A light kind of lava, usu. consisting of obsidian made spongy or porous by the escape of steam or gas during the process of cooling. b. with *pl.* A piece of this 1483. c. As a material used for smoothing or polishing (parchment, etc.), or removing stains; as an absorbent of ink, moisture, etc.; as proverbial for its dryness. late ME. 2. *attrib.* Consisting of or resembling pumice 1592. Hence **Pu·mice** *v. trans.* to rub, smooth, polish, clean with p. **Pu·miced** *ppl. a.* rubbed smooth with pumice; also, applied to a horse's hoof that has become spongy from disease.

Pumiceous (piumi·ʃəs), *a.* 1676. [f. L. *pumiceus* (f. *pumex*, *-icem*) + -OUS.] Consisting of pumice; having the character or texture of pumice.

Pumice-stone (pv·misˌstoᵘn, pv·mistoᵘn), *sb.* 1550. = PUMICE *sb.* Hence **Pu·mice-stone** *v. trans.* = PUMICE *v.*

Pummel (pv·m'l), *v.* 1548. [Alteration of POMMEL *v.*] *trans.* To beat or strike repeatedly, esp. with the fist; to pound, thump. Also *intr.*

Pump (pvmp), *sb.*¹ late ME. [= early mod. Du. *pompe*, L.G. *pump*, etc.; prob. an echoic formation from the sound of the plunger striking the water.] I. A mechanical device, commonly consisting of a tube or cylinder, in which a piston, sucker, or plunger is moved up and down by means of a rod, or rod and lever, so as to raise water by lifting, suction, or pressure, the movement of the water being regulated by a suitable arrangement of valves or clacks; now, a generic term for a great variety of machines and mechanical devices for the raising or moving of liquids, compressing or rarefying of gases, etc. b. *fig.* or *allus.* 1602. c. As employed in medical treatment, esp. at a place where a mineral spring is used; cf. PUMP-ROOM, etc. 1631. d. *transf.* Applied to the heart, the sucker or proboscis of an insect, the lachrymal glands 1796.

Pumps are variously qualified according to the principle of action, manner of construction, means of operating, purpose, etc., as *force, suction p.*; *centrifugal, centripetal, chain-, rotary p.*; *hand-, steam-p.*; *air-, beer-, bicycle-, feed-, oil-, stomach-p.*, etc.

II. [from the vb.] 1. An act of pumping; a stroke of the pump. Also *transf.* 1676. 2. a. An attempt at extracting information from any one by skilful questioning. b. One who is clever at this. 1741.

attrib. and *Comb.* as *p.-gear*, *-tube*, *-valve*, etc.; also **p.-brake,** the handle of a (ship's) p., esp. one having a transverse bar for several persons to work at it; **-house,** (*a*) the p.-room of a spa; (*b*) a place in which pumps are made; (*c*) a pumping station; **-rod,** a rod connecting the piston or plunger of a p. with the motive power; in mines a heavy iron or wooden beam or system of beams; **-stock,** the body of a p.

Pump (pvmp), *sb.*² 1555. [Origin unkn.] A kind of light shoe; a slipper for indoor wear; now *spec.*, a light, low-heeled shoe, usu. of patent leather and without fastening, worn with evening dress and for dancing.

Pump (pvmp), *v.* 1508. [f. PUMP *sb.*¹] I. Literal senses. 1. *intr.* To work a pump (in early use, always a ship's pump); to raise or move water or other fluid by means of a pump. **2.** *trans.* To raise or remove (water or other fluid) by means of a pump. Chiefly with *out, up.* 1530. **3.** To free from water, etc. by means of a pump or pumps. Said simply in ref. to a ship; of other things with *dry, empty,* etc. 1650. †**4.** To put (any one) under a stream of water from a pump –1840. **5.** *To p. up*: to inflate (a pneumatic tyre, or the like) by pumping air into it 1892.

3. They pumped the well dry 1890. 4. P. him soundly, impudent fellow! SHADWELL.

II. Transferred and *fig.* senses. **1.** To draw or force up or out, in a manner likened to the working of a pump; to move up, draw out, pour forth, or eject: said of the shedding of tears, the motion of the blood, the firing of projectiles from a gun (esp. a machine-gun), etc. Also *absol.* or *intr.* 1604. **2.** *trans.* To subject (a person or thing) to a process likened to pumping, with the object of extracting something; to obtain something by persistent effort; also, to drain, exhaust 1610. **b.** *spec.* To subject (a person) to such a process in order to elicit information; to ply with questions in an artful or persistent manner 1656. **3.** To extract, raise, or bring forth by persistent or factitious effort or art 1663. **b.** To elicit (information, etc.) by such means. Const. *out of* a person. 1633. **4.** *intr.* To labour or strive a. *for* the obtaining of something 1633; b. for the eliciting of information 1669. **5.** *trans.* and *intr.* To work with action like that of the handle or piston of a pump 1803. **6.** *trans.* To put completely out of breath from excessive exertion. Also with *out.* Usu. *pass.* 1858. **7.** *intr.* Of the mercury in a barometer: To rise and fall instantaneously in the tube as the result of sudden local alterations of pressure or of mechanical disturbance 1875.

1. *absol.* Our men were exposed to fearful odds, especially with two quick-firers pumping at them 1899. 2. b. I am going to p. Mr. Bentley for designs H. WALPOLE.

Comb. Pump- is used to qualify names of mechanical contrivances in which an essential part moves out and in, like the plunger of a force-pump, as *p.-cylinder, -screw,* etc. Hence **Pu·mpage,** the work done at pumping, the quantity pumped. **Pu·mper,** one who or that which pumps or works a pump; *U.S.* an oil well from which the oil is pumped, as dist. from a natural spring.

‖**Pumpernickel** (pu·mpəɹnik'l). 1756. [G. Origin unkn.] Bread made from coarsely ground unbolted rye; wholemeal rye bread: associated esp. with Westphalia.

Pu·mp-handle, *sb.* 1794. The handle by which a pump, esp. the ordinary hand- or house-pump, is worked. **b.** *attrib.,* as in *p. movement,* etc. 1820. Hence **Pu·mp-handle** *v. trans.* (*colloq.*), to shake (a person's hand, or a person by the hand) as if working a p.

Pu·mping, *vbl. sb.* 1598. [f. PUMP *v.* + -ING^{1}.] The action of PUMP *v.*

attrib. and *Comb.,* as *p.-well*; esp. in ref. to the machinery used in raising or moving water in mines and waterworks, air in refrigerators, etc., as *p.-engine, -station,* etc.

Pumpkin (pʊ·mᵖkin). Also (*U.S.*) **punkin.** 1647. [Altered f. *pumpion* (see POMPION), with the ending conformed to the suffix -KIN.] **1.** The large fruit of a cucurbitaceous plant (*Cucurbita Pepo*), egg-shaped or nearly globular with flattened ends; cultivated for the fleshy edible layer next the rind, used for pies, and as a food for cattle. **b.** The plant producing this fruit. Also called *p.-vine.* 1698. **2.** *fig.* a. A stupid self-important person 1830. **b.** *U.S. slang.* A person or matter of importance; esp. in phr. *some pumpkins* 1848.

2. b. Afore I left the settlements I know'd a white gal, and she was some punkins 1848.

Comb. **p.-pie,** a pie of which the p. is a chief ingredient; in U.S. considered especially appropriate to Thanksgiving day. Hence **Pumpkinifica·tion,** suggested by the travesty (ascribed to Seneca) of the apotheosis of the emperor Claudius, under the title of ἀποκολοκύντωσις transformation into a p.

Pu·mpkin-seed. 1781. **a.** The flattish oval seed of the pumpkin. **b.** A fresh-water fish of N. America, *Lepomis gibbosus,* the sunfish, pond-perch 1889.

Pu·mp-room. 1742. A room or building where a pump is worked; *spec.* a place at a spa where the medicinal water is dispensed for drinking, etc.

Pu·mp-well. 1769. **a.** The well of a ship, in which the pumps work. **b.** A well having a pump combined with it 1812.

Pun (pʊn), *sb.* 1662. [Origin obsc.] The use of a word in such a way as to suggest two or more meanings, or the use of two or more words of the same sound with different meanings, so as to produce a humorous effect; a play on words. Also *attrib.*

Laud..turned out Archy, the King's fool, for a p. [viz. for saying as grace 'Great praise be to God, and little Laud to the devil', or words to that effect] D'ISRAELI. Hence **Punno·logy,** the subject or study of puns.

Pun (pʊn), *v.*^{1} 1670. [Goes with PUN *sb.*] **1.** *intr.* To make puns; to play on words. **2.** *trans.* To bring or drive by punning 1711.

1. He that would p. would pick a Pocket 1729. 2. The Sinner was punned into Repentance ADDISON.

Pun, *v.*^{2} 1559. [Early and dial. var. of POUND *v.*^{1}] **1.** *trans.* = POUND *v.*^{1} in various senses. **2.** *spec.* (in techn. use). To consolidate by pounding or ramming down (as earth or rubble, in making a roadway, etc.) 1838. **b.** To work *up* to a proper consistency with a punner 1825.

‖**Puna** (pū·nă). 1613. [Peruv., in sense 1.] **1.** A high bleak plateau in the Peruvian Andes. **2.** Difficulty of breathing arising from a too rarefied atmosphere; mountain sickness 1842.

Punch (pʊnʃ), *sb.*^{1} 1462. [app. a collateral form of POUNCE *sb.*^{1}; or shortened from PUNCHEON^{1}.] **1.** An instrument or tool for pricking, piercing, or making a hole in anything; also for enlarging a hole already made, driving a bolt, etc. out of a hole (*starting p.*), or forcing a nail beneath the surface after it has been driven (*driving p.*) 1505. **2.** A tool or machine for impressing a design or stamping a die upon or into some material; in *Coining* and *Die-sinking,* a hardened steel cameo for forming a die; in *Type-founding,* a steel die having a letter cut in relief on its face, for making the intaglio impression in the copper matrix from which types are cast; in *Plastic Art,* a rod, handle, or wheel-rim having a figure or pattern upon it in relief for impressing a design on clay, etc. 1628. **3.** A post supporting the roof in a coal-mine 1462. **4.** *Hydraulic Engin.* A lengthening block or extension piece placed on a pile that has been driven too low to be reached by the ram; a dolly 1875.

1. **Bell-p.,** a conductor's or ticket p. having a signal bell which announces the punching of a ticket; **cold-p.,** a p. used for perforating cold metal; **ratchet-p.,** a screw punching machine operated by a lever, pawl, and ratchet-wheel; etc.

Punch (pʊnʃ), *sb.*^{2} late ME. [f. PUNCH *v.*] An act of punching; a thrusting blow, now usu. one delivered with the fist; also (*obs.* or *dial.*) a kick. **b.** Force, vigour (orig. *U.S.*) 1911.

Punch (pʊnʃ), *sb.*^{3} 1632. [Origin unkn. See N.E.D. Note.] **1.** A beverage now usu. composed of wine or spirits mixed with hot water or milk and flavoured with sugar, lemons, and some spice or cordial. Usu. qualified as *brandy, gin, rum, tea, whisky,* etc. *p.* **2.** With *a* and *pl.* **a.** A bowl or drink of punch. **b.** A party at which punch is drunk. 1682.

Punch (pʊnʃ), *sb.*^{4} and *a.* Now chiefly *dial.* 1669. [prob. short for PUNCHINELLO.] **A.** *sb.* †**1.** A short fat man, or anything short and thick –1836. **2.** One of a breed of heavy draught horses (in full *Suffolk Punches*), characterized by a short and very thick-set body and neck, and short legs 1813. **B.** *adj.* Short and thick, stout. Now only *dial.* Said esp. of horses. 1679.

Punch (pʊnʃ), *sb.*^{5} 1709. [Short for PUNCHINELLO.] **1.** Name of a grotesque hump-backed figure in the puppet-show called Punch and Judy. Also *attrib.* in *P. and Judy show,* etc. **2.** The title of a comic weekly journal published in London, of which 'Mr. P.' is the assumed editor. Also *attrib.* 1841.

1. Phr. *As pleased, as proud as P.*

Punch (pʊnʃ), *v.* late ME. [app. a collateral form of POUNCE *v.*^{1}] **I.** †**1.** *trans.* = POUNCE *v.*^{1} III. 1. –1664. **2.** To poke or prod, esp. with a stick or other blunt instrument. Now *U.S.* and *Colonial*: To drive cattle (by prodding them on). late ME. **b.** To put *out* or stir *up* by punching or poking 1863. **3.** To deliver a sharp blow or forward thrust at; *esp.* to strike with the closed fist; to beat, thump 1530. **b.** To strike with the foot; to kick. *n. dial.* 1538. **II. 1.** To pierce or cut (anything) in the manner of a punch, so as to make a hole or holes in or through it; to perforate (a plate of metal, a sheet of cloth or paper, etc.) 1594. **b.** With the hole as obj. 1677. **c.** To take *out* (a piece) by punching 1827. **2.** *intr.* To penetrate, pierce, or cut (as a punch) 1683.

1. My Annointed body By thee was punched full of holes SHAKS. To p. a railway ticket (*mod.*).

Punch-ball: see PUNCHING-*ball.*

Pu·nch-bowl. 1692. [f. PUNCH *sb.*^{3} + BOWL *sb.*^{1}] **1.** A bowl in which the ingredients of punch are mixed, and from which it is served with a ladle. **2.** *attrib.* Resembling a punch-bowl. Hence *sb.* A round deep hollow between hills or in a hill-side. 1855.

Puncheon^{1} (pʊ·nʃən). ME. [a. OF. *poinçon, poinchon* :—late L. or Com. Rom. **punctionem,* f. *puncta* point, or late L. **punctiare* to prick, etc.] **I. 1.** A pointed tool for piercing; a bodkin. †**b.** A graving tool, a burin. late ME. **2.** = PUNCH *sb.*^{1} 2. Now *rare* or *Obs.* 1504. **II.** In building and carpentry. **1.** A short upright piece of timber in a wooden framing which serves to stiffen one or more long timbers or to support or transmit a load; a supporting post; a post supporting the roof in a coal-mine 1466. **2.** A piece of timber with one face roughly dressed, or a split trunk, used for flooring and rough building. *U.S.* 1807.

Puncheon^{2} (pʊ·nʃən). Now *rare* exc. *Hist.* 1479. [a. OF. *ponçon, poinchon,* etc.] A large cask for liquids, fish, etc.; *spec.* one of a definite capacity, varying for different liquids and commodities.

Puncher (pʊ·nʃəɹ). 1681. [f. PUNCH *v.*^{1} + -ER^{1}.] One who or that which punches; an instrument for doing this. **b.** *U.S.* Short for Cow-*p.* 1894.

Punchinello (pʊnᵗʃine·lo). Also **polichinello.** 1666. [app. ad. Neapolitan dial. *Polecenella.* Origin obsc.] **1.** Name of the principal character in a puppet-show of Italian origin, the prototype of Punch; hence applied to the show; sometimes to a living performer. **2.** *transf.* Applied to any person, animal, or thing, thought to resemble the puppet, esp. in being short and stout. (Cf. PUNCH *sb.*^{4}) 1669.

2. His gun, which, from the shortness and bigness, they do call P. PEPYS.

Punching, *vbl. sb.* 1440. [-ING^{1}.] The action of PUNCH *vb.*

Comb.: **P.-ball,** an inflated ball held in position by elastic bands or supported on a flexible rod, which is punched by the fists as an athletic exercise (also *punch-ball*).

Punchy (pʊ·nʃi), *a.* 1791. [f. PUNCH *sb.*^{4} + -Y^{1}.] Short and stout, squat, stumpy.

Punctate (pʊ·ŋkteᵢt), *a.* 1760. [ad. mod.L. *punctatus,* f. L. *punctum* point; see -ATE^{2} 2.] **1.** *Nat. Hist.* and *Path.* Marked or studded with points, dots, spots, or (esp.) depressions resembling punctures; of the nature of or characterized by such markings. **2.** *Path.* Having or coming to a definite point 1899. So **Pu·nctated** *a.* (in sense 1).

Punctation (pʊŋktēⁱ·ʃən). 1617. [f. med. L. *punctare* to point.] **1.** †**a.** = PUNCTUATION 3, 3 b. –1748. **2.** *Nat. Hist.,* etc. The action of marking or fact of being marked with points or dots; the condition of being punctate, also *concr.* one, or a series, of such dots 1852. ‖**3.** [repr. G. *punktation.*] A laying down of points; a stipulation; a contract or agreement 1864.

Punctiform (pʊ·ŋktifǭɹm), *a.* 1822. [f. L. *punctum* point; see -FORM.] *Nat. Hist.,* etc. **1.** Having the form of a puncture, point, or dot. **2.** Punctate: esp. in pathology, of eruptions, etc. 1839.

Punctilio (pʊŋkti·lio). 1596. [a. It. *puntiglio* and Sp. *puntillo,* dim. of *punto* point; later with *punct-* after L.] †**1.** A small or fine point or mark, esp. one of those on a dial (*rare*) –1599. †**2.** A minute point, detail, or particular; a jot; a trifle -1815. 3. A minute detail of action or conduct; a nice point of behaviour, ceremony, or honour; a petty formality 1599. b. (without *pl.*) Petty formality in behaviour; punctiliousness 1596.

1. He shall finde the Puntilio of his honour blunted 1596. 2. When one of the parties..will not..abate a single p. BURKE. 3. The Bishop stood upon his punctilios 1626. b. The preliminaries had been conducted with proper p. 1820.

Punctilious (pɒŋkti·liəs), *a.* 1634. [ad. F. *pointilleux*, f. *pointille*, ad. It. *puntiglio.*] Attentive to punctilios; strictly observant of nice points or details of action or behaviour.

The p. honour of a Spanish gentleman has passed into a byeword 1858. Hence **Puncti·lious·ly** *adv.*, **-ness.**

Punctist (pɒ·ŋktist). 1859. [f. L. *punctum* POINT + -IST.] One who holds the vowel-points in the Hebrew Scriptures to be authoritative.

Punctual (pɒ·ŋktiuăl, -tʃuăl), *a.* (*sb.*) late ME. [ad. med.L. *punctualis*, f. L. *punctus* pricking, point; see -AL.] †I. *Surg.* a. Of the nature of a point or puncture. b. Used for making punctures, sharp-pointed. -1597. II. 1. Of, pertaining to, or made by, a point or dot; of or belonging to punctuation (*rare*) 1609. b. *Geom.* Of or pertaining to a point: as *p. co-ordinates*, the co-ordinates of a point. †2. Like a point or speck; small, minute -1667.

2. This opacous Earth, this p. spot MILT.

III. †Bearing directly on the point; to the point, apposite, apt -1642. b. Express, direct; explicit, definite (*arch.*) 1615.

b. A plain and p. testimony BENTLEY.

IV. 1. Exact in every point; precise, accurate. Now *rare* or *arch.* 1620. b. Of time or date: Exact. Now *rare* or *arch.* 1639. c. Exactly or aptly timed; timely (*rare*) 1611. d. Of or belonging to a precise place (*rare*) 1805. †2. Dealing with a matter point by point; minute, detailed -1772.

1. The p. accuracy of our statement 1852. 2. A p. relation of all the circumstances HOWELL.

V. 1. (Of persons, or their actions, etc.) Attentive to, or insisting upon, points or details of conduct; punctilious 1598. 2. *spec.* Exactly observant of an appointed time; up to time, in good time; not late 1675.

1. So much on p. niceties they stand 1725. His p. discharge of his duties FROUDE. 2. The undeviating and p. sun COWPER. Hence **Pu·nctual·ly** *adv.*, **-ness** (now *rare*).

†Pu·nctualist. 1641. [f. prec. + -IST.] One who discusses or treats of points of conduct or ceremony MILT.

Punctuality (pɒŋktiu,æ·lĭti, -tʃu-). 1620. [f. PUNCTUAL + -ITY.] 1. The quality or character of being punctual (in various senses); an instance of this. *esp.* 2. Exact observance of an appointed time; the fact or habit of being in good time 1777.

Punctuate (pɒ·ŋktiu,eᶦt, -tʃu,eᶦt), *v.* 1818. [f. med.L. *punctuare* to prick, point, etc., f. L. *punctus* (*u*-stem) pointing, point.] 1. *Nat. Hist.* To mark with points or dots, esp. with small depressions resembling punctures (*rare*). 2. To insert the punctuation-marks in (a sentence, etc.); to mark or divide with points or stops. Also *absol.* 1818. b. *fig.* To interrupt at intervals (as a speech) by exclamations, etc. 1882. 3. To give point to; to emphasize, accentuate 1883.

2. b. Mr. Gladstone's speech was..punctuated by cheers 1892.

Pu·nctuated, *ppl. a.* 1818. [f. prec. + -ED [1].] 1. = PUNCTATE 1. 2. Having the punctuation marks inserted 1841.

Punctuation (pɒŋktiu,ēᶦ·ʃən, -tʃu-). 1539. [ad. med.L. *punctuationem*, f. *punctuare* to PUNCTUATE.] †1. The pointing of the psalms; the pause at the mediation -1782. 2. = POINTING *vbl. sb.* 1 b. 1659. 3. The practice, art, method, or system of inserting points or 'stops' to aid the sense, in writing or printing; division into sentences, clauses, etc. by means of points or stops 1661. b. *transf.* Observance of the pauses, as indicated by the points or stops, in reading or speaking 1807.

3. On the p. of this..verse [Rom. ix. 5] a great controversy has arisen FARRAR. *attrib.* as *p. mark*, etc.

Punctuative (pɒ·ŋktiu,ĕᶦtiv), *a.* 1855. [f. as PUNCTUATE *v.* + -IVE; see -ATIVE.] Of, pertaining to, or serving for punctuation.

Punctuator (pɒ·ŋktiu,ēᶦtəɹ). 1659. [a. med.L., f. *punctuare* to PUNCTUATE.] 1. *Heb. Gram.* One who inserts the vowel (and other) points in writing. 2. One who inserts the stops in writing or printing 1846.

Punctulate (pɒ·ŋktiŭlĕt), *a.* 1847. [ad. mod.L. *punctulatus*, f. *punctulum* PUNCTULE.] *Nat. Hist.* Marked or studded with punctules; minutely punctate. So **Pu·nctulated** *ppl. a.* **Punctula·tion,** the condition of being p.; also *concr.* a number or mass of punctules.

Punctule (pɒ·ŋktiul). 1640. [ad. L. *punctulum*, dim. of *punctum* point.] A small point. *Nat. Hist.*, etc., a small punctum.

‖**Punctum** (pɒ·ŋktŏm). *Pl.* **-ta.** 1590. [L., orig. neut. of *punctus*, pa. pple. of *pungere* to prick.] †1. A point, in various fig. senses -1683. 2. *Nat. Hist.* and *Path.* A minute rounded mark or visible object; a speck, dot; a minute rounded spot of colour, or of elevation or depression (esp. the latter) upon a surface 1665. 3. In mediæval music: An inflexion used in singing collects, etc.; a grave accent denoting a descending note; a square note 1853.

2. *P. lachrymale* (also *lachrymal p.*, or simply *p.*), the minute orifice of each of the two lachrymal canals at the corner of the eye. *P. saliens* (cf. τοῦτο δὲ τὸ σημεῖον πηδᾷ, Aristotle), the first trace of the heart in an embryo, appearing as a pulsating point or speck.

Puncturation (pɒŋktiŭrēᶦ·ʃən). 1733. [f. PUNCTURE *v.*; see -ATION.] 1. The action or operation of puncturing (*rare*). 2. *Nat. Hist.* = PUNCTATION 2. 1890.

Puncture (pɒ·ŋktiŭɹ, -tʃəɹ), *sb.* late ME. [ad. L. *punctura*, f. *punct-*, *pungere* to prick; see -URE.] 1. An act, or the action, of pricking; a prick; perforation; in recent use *spec.* an accidental perforation of a pneumatic tyre. 2. A mark, hole, or wound made by pricking 1565.

Pu·ncture, *v.* 1699. [f. prec.] I. *trans.* To subject to puncture; to prick; to perforate; esp. in *Surgery*. b. *spec.* To mark (the skin) with punctures; to tattoo 1784. c. *Nat. Hist.* To mark with spots or dots resembling punctures: chiefly in *pa. pple.* 1847. 2. To make (a hole, etc.) by pricking 1831. 3. *pass.* and *intr.* or *absol.* To get a puncture; said of a pneumatic tyre, or *transf.* of the cycle or rider. (*colloq.*) 1893.

1. I punctured the tire within one mile of the start 1896. Hence **Punctured** (pɒ·ŋktiŭɹ'd, -tʃəɹd), *ppl. a.* pricked, pierced, perforated; made by puncturing; composed of punctures.

‖**Pundit** (pɒ·ndit). 1672. [a. Hindī *paṇḍit* :—Skr. *paṇḍita* learned, skilled.] A learned Hindu; one versed in Sanskrit and in the philosophy, religion, and jurisprudence of India. b. *transf.* A learned expert or teacher (*joc.*) 1816.

Pung (pɒŋ), *sb.* *U.S.* 1840. [Shortened from *tom-pung*, corrupt f. an Indian word meaning 'instrument for drawing'.] A one-horse sleigh or sledge used in New England; also, a toboggan. Hence **Pung** *v. intr.*, to 'coast' on a sleigh, to toboggan.

Pungency (pɒ·ndʒĕnsi). 1649. [f. L. *pungentem* PUNGENT; see -ENCY.] 1. The quality or property of pricking; the fact of having a sharp point or points (*rare*) 1656. 2. The quality of having a pungent smell or taste; such smell or taste itself; a stinging, irritant, or caustic property. Also *fig.* 1649.

2. The air had a perceptible p. upon inspiration 1856.

Pungent (pɒ·ndʒĕnt), *a.* (*sb.*) 1597. [ad. L. *pungentem*, *pungere* to prick, etc.] 1. Pricking, piercing, sharp-pointed. Now only in *Nat. Hist.* 1601. 2. *fig.* (of pain or grief). Sharp, keen, acute, poignant; causing or inflicting sharp pain; keenly distressing 1597. b. Of appetite or desire: Keen, eager; piercing. Now *rare* or *Obs.* 1710. 3. Keenly or strongly affecting the mind or feelings (now usu. with allusion to sense 4) 1637. 4. Affecting the organs of smell or taste (or the skin, etc.) with a sensation resembling that produced by pricking; penetrating and irritant 1668. 5. as *sb.* (or *absol.*) A pungent substance; an irritant 1822.

1. Terminating in a very sharp-pointed p. leaf 1787. 2. Intolerably p. grief and sorrow 1684. 3. A very good and p. sermon PEPYS. A few p. epigrams 1874. 4. P. radish, biting infant's tongue SHENSTONE. Hence **Pun·gent·ly** *adv.*, **-ness.**

Punic (piū·nik), *a.* and *sb.* 1533. [ad. L. *Punicus*, earlier *Pœnicus*, f. *Pœnus* a Carthaginian; f. Gr. Φοῖνιξ PHŒNICIAN; also purple. Cf. F. *punique.*] A. *adj.* 1. Belonging to Carthage; Carthaginian. b. †*P. apple* (L. *Punicum malum*), the pomegranate 1601. c. Having the character attributed by the Romans to the Carthaginians; treacherous, perfidious 1600. †2. Purple 1501-1607.

1. *P. wars*, the three wars between the Romans and Carthaginians waged between B.C. 264 and 146. c. *P. faith*: see FAITH *sb.* III. 2; Yes, yes, his faith attesting nations own; 'Tis P. all, and to a proverb known! 1738.

B. *sb.* †1. An inhabitant of Carthage, a Carthaginian -1696. 2. The Carthaginian tongue, an offshoot of Phœnician and allied to Hebrew 1813.

Puniceous (piuni·ʃiəs), *a.* 1730. [f. L. *puniceus* Punic (f. *Punicus* Punic + *-eus*) + -OUS.] Of a bright red, purplish-red, or red-dish-yellow colour.

Punish (pɒ·niʃ), *v.* ME. [a. F. *puniss-*, *punir* :—L. *punire* to punish, f. *pœna* = Gr. ποινή fine, penalty, PAIN *sb.*] 1. a. *trans.* To cause (an offender) to suffer for an offence; to subject to judicial chastisement as retribution or requital, or as a caution against further transgression; to inflict a penalty on. b. To inflict a penalty for (something) ME. c. *absol.* To inflict punishment. late ME. 2. *transf.* (*trans.*) To handle severely; to inflict heavy damage, injury, or loss on. Also *absol.* 1812.

1. 'Tis against the Law of Nature, To p. the Innocent HOBBES. c. God does not p. that way DE FOE. 2. We..drank freely—punished his claret 1825. The Oxonian's [bowling] was..severely punished 1883. Hence **Pu·nisher,** one who punishes; *Boxing slang*, a hard hitter; *transf.* a thing that hits one hard, a heavy or severe task.

Punishable (pɒ·niʃăb'l), *a.* 1531. [f. prec. + -ABLE.] Liable to punishment; capable of being punished. b. Of an offence: Entailing punishment 1548.

It is a pity these hags are not p. by law FIELDING. b. Wherfore emonge the Jewes, onely periury is punyshable 1548. Hence **Punishabi·lity, Pu·nishableness,** the quality of being p. **Pu·nishably** *adv.* in a p. manner or to a p. degree.

Punishment (pɒ·niʃmĕnt). late ME. [a. AF., OF. *punissement*, f. *punir* to PUNISH; see -MENT.] 1. The act of punishing or the fact of being punished; also, that which is inflicted as a penalty; a penalty imposed to ensure the application and enforcement of a law. 2. *slang* and *colloq.* Severe handling; belabouring, mauling; orig. that inflicted by a pugilist upon his opponent; pain, damage, or loss inflicted (without any retributive or judicial character) 1856.

1. We must, wherever we suppose a Law, suppose also some Reward or P. annexed to that Rule LOCKE. 2. Tom Sayers could not take p. more gaily than they do THACKERAY.

Punition (piuni·ʃən). Now *rare.* late ME. [a. F., ad. late L. *punitionem*, f. *punire* to PUNISH.] The action of punishing.

Punitive (piū·nitiv), *a.* 1624. [a. F. *punitif*, *-ive*, f. L. *punit-*, *punire*; see -IVE.] Awarding, inflicting, or involving punishment; retributive.

A British P. Expedition captured Benin City 1897. Hence **Pu·nitive·ly** *adv.*, **-ness.**

Punitory (piū·nitəri), *a.* 1710. [f. L. *punitor* a punisher; see -ORY [2].] = prec.

Punk [1] (pɒŋk). *Obs.* or *rare arch.* 1596. [Origin unkn.] A prostitute, strumpet, harlot.

Punk [2] (pɒŋk). Chiefly *U.S.* 1707. [Origin obsc.] 1. Rotten wood, or a fungus growing on wood, used in a dry state for tinder; touchwood, amadou. 2. A composition that will smoulder when ignited, used to touch off fireworks 1869. 3. Chinese incense 1890. Hence **Punk** *a.*, **Pu·nky** *a.* (chiefly *U.S.*), rotten.

‖**Punkah, punka** (pɒ·ŋkă). 1625. [a. Hindī *pankhā* fan :—Skr. *pakshaka*, f. *paksha* wing.] 1. A large fan, usu. made from the leaf of the palmyra. 2. A large swinging fan made of cloth stretched on a rectangular frame, suspended from the ceiling or rafters, and worked by a cord 1807.

Comb.: **p.-coolie, -wallah,** a native Indian servant who works a p.

Punner¹ (pʊ·nəɹ). Now *rare.* 1689. [f. PUN *v.*¹ + -ER ¹.] A punster.

Punner² (pʊ·nəɹ). 1611. [f. PUN *v.*²] One who or that which puns or rams earth, etc.; *spec.* a tool for ramming earth about a post, etc. Hence **p.-bar,** a p. and crow-bar combined.

Punnet (pʊ·nėt). *local.* 1822. [Origin obsc.] A small round shallow chip basket, used chiefly for fruit or vegetables.

Punster (pʊ·nstəɹ). 1700. [f. PUN *v.*¹ + -STER.] A professed maker of puns; one skilled in punning.

Punt (pɒnt), *sb.*¹ [OE. *punt*, ad. L. *ponto* a kind of Gallic transport, also a pontoon.] A flat-bottomed shallow boat, broad and square at both ends; also = PONTOON 2; now *spec.*, a boat of this kind propelled by means of a long pole thrust against the bottom of a river, or shallow water.

attrib. and *Comb.*: **p.-fisher,** one who fishes from a p.; so **-fishing; -gun,** a gun used for shooting water-fowl from a p.. so **-gunner, -gunning; -pole,** the long pole used in propelling a p. Hence **Pu·nter**², one who goes fishing or shooting in a p.; later, one who punts, or manages a p.

Punt, *sb.*² **1845.** [Goes w. PUNT *v.*³] *Football* (Rugby). An act of punting; a kick given to the ball dropped from the hands, before it reaches the ground.

Punt, *sb.*³ 1832. *Glass-making.* = PONTIL.

Punt (pɒnt), *v.*¹ 1706. [ad. F. *ponter.*] *intr.* At basset, faro, baccarat, etc.: To lay a stake against the bank. **b.** *slang.* and *colloq.* To bet upon a horse, etc. 1873.

Punt, *v.*² 1816. [f. PUNT *sb.*¹] **1.** *trans.* To propel (a punt or other boat) by thrusting a pole against the bottom of the river, etc.; to propel or shove off, in the manner of a punt. **b.** *intr.* or *absol.* To propel a punt, or any boat in the manner of a punt 1846. **2.** *trans.* To convey in a punt, or by punting 1853.

Punt, *v.*³ 1845. [Goes w. PUNT *sb.*² Prob. of dial. origin.] **1.** *Football* (Rugby). *trans.* To kick (the ball), after dropping it from the hands, before it reaches the ground. Also *absol.* **2.** To strike, hit, knock (*rare*) 1886.

Punter¹ (pʊ·ntəɹ). 1706. [f. PUNT *v.*¹ + -ER ¹.] **1.** A player who 'punts' or plays against the bank at faro, etc. **2.** *transf.* A small professional backer of horses; also, a gambler in stocks and shares 1873.

Punter²: see PUNT *sb.*²

Punto¹ (pʊ·nto). 1591. [a. It. or Sp.:— L. PUNCTUM.] †**1.** A small point or detail; a particle, a jot; a moment, instant -1706. †**2.** = PUNCTILIO 3. -1766. †**3.** *Fencing.* A stroke or thrust with the point of the sword or foil -1624. **4.** *Glass-making.* = PONTIL 1839.

3. *P. dritto*, a direct thrust. *P. riverso*, a back-handed thrust; Ah the immortall Passado the P. reuerso, the Hay SHAKS.

Punto² (pu·nto). 1728. [Sp. = point.] *Card-playing.* The ace of trumps, when the trump suit is diamonds or hearts.

Punty, ponty (pʊ·nti). 1662. [app. ad. F. *pontil* PONTIL.] **1.** An iron rod used in glass-blowing. **2.** A round hollow made on a glass object to remove the mark made in breaking off the p.-rod; a small circular or oval hollow made as an ornamentation on glass 1884.

Comb., as *p.-mark*; **p.-iron, -rod** = sense 1.

Puny (piū·ni), *a.* and *sb.* 1548. [Phonetic spelling of PUISNE.] **A.** *adj.* †**1.** = PUISNE *a.* 1, 1 b. -1733. †**2.** Raw, inexperienced; that is a novice or tyro -1712. **3.** Of inferior size, force, or importance; minor; petty, weak; diminutive, tiny 1593. **b.** esp. of human beings and animals: Undersized and weakly 1604.

2. 1 *Hen. VI*, IV. vii. 36. 3. A punie subiect strikes At thy great glory SHAKS. b. He was a very P. Man, yet he had often done things beyond the strength of a Giant 1693.

†**B.** *sb.* **1.** A junior pupil or student in a school or university, or in the Inns of Court -1678. **2.** A raw or inexperienced person; a novice, tyro -1688. **3.** A person of small account; a subordinate -1711.

Pup (pʊp), *sb.*¹ 1773. [Short for PUPPY *sb.*] **1.** A young dog, a whelp, a young puppy. **2.** Applied to the young of the fur seal 1858.

1. Phr. *To sell* (any one) *a p.*, to swindle, esp. by selling something on its prospective value.

Pup, *sb.*² 1871. *College slang.* Abbrev. of PUPIL, joc. associated with prec.

Pup, *v.* 1725. [Shortened f. PUPPY *v.*] *trans.* and *intr.* To bring forth pups, to litter.

‖**Pupa** (piū·pă). *Pl.* **-æ.** 1815. [mod.L., a use of L. *pupa* girl, doll.] **1.** An insect in the third and usu. quiescent state (of complete metamorphosis), preceding that of the imago; a chrysalis. **b.** A stage in the development of some other invertebrates, as cirripeds, holothurians 1877. **2.** *Conch.* Name of a genus of pulmonate molluscs; a chrysalis-shell.

attrib.: **p.-case,** the horny case of a p. or chrysalis Hence **Pu·pal** *a.* of, pertaining to, or characteristic of a p.; nymphal. **Pu·pate** *v. intr.* to become a p. or chrysalis. **Pupa·tion,** the formation of the p.

‖**Puparium** (piupēᵊ·riŏm). 1815. [mod.L., f. prec. + -ARIUM, after *herbarium*, etc.] The coarctate pupa of some Diptera and other insects, the case of which is formed by the last larval skin.

Pupigerous (piupi·dʒĕrəs), *a.* 1884. [f. PUPA; see -GEROUS.] Of a larva: Forming a PUPARIUM; having the pupa enclosed within the last larval skin.

Pupil¹ (piū·pĭl). late ME. [a. F. *pupille*, ad. L. *pupillus, pupilla.*] **1.** An orphan who is a minor and hence a ward; in *Civil* and *Sc. Law*, a person below the age of puberty who is under the care of a guardian. **2.** One who is taught by another; a scholar; a disciple 1563.

2. He took pupils to increase his income 1891.

Comb.: **p.-room** (at Eton), the room in which a tutor takes his pupils; the work done there by a p.

Pupil² (piū·pĭl). 1567. [a. OF. *pupille*, ad. L. *pupilla.*] **1.** The circular opening (appearing as a black spot) in the centre of the iris of the eye, which expands or contracts in regulating the passage of light through it to the retina; the apple of the eye. **2.** *fig.* and *transf.*; in *Entom.* The dark central spot of an ocellus 1599.

Pupil(l)age (piū·pilėdʒ). 1590. [f. PUPIL¹ + -AGE.] **1.** The condition of being a minor or ward; the period of this; nonage, minority. **2.** The condition or position of being a pupil or scholar 1658.

1. *fig.* Thus the colonies are kept in a state of perpetual pupillage 1777. 2. In the days of my medical pupillage 1882.

Pupil age. 1596. [f. PUPIL¹ + AGE *sb.*; app. due to erron. analysis of prec.] The age during which one is a pupil; minority.

His Pupill age Man-entred thus, he waxed like a Sea SHAKS.

Pupil(l)arity (piūpilæ·rĭti). 1583. [a. F. *pupillarité*, ad. med.L. **pupillaritas*, f. L. *pupillaris* belonging to a pupil; see -ITY.] *Civil* and *Sc. Law.* The state of being below the age of puberty; the period of this.

Pupil(l)ary (piū·pilări), *a.*¹ 1611. [ad. F. *pupillaire*, or L. *pupillaris.*] **a.** Of or pertaining to a person in pupillarity. **b.** Belonging to a pupil or scholar 1848.

Pu·pil(l)ary, *a.*² 1793. [f. L. *pupilla* PUPIL² + -ARY.] Of or pertaining to the pupil of the eye.

Pupil teacher (piū·pĭl,tī·tʃəɹ). 1838. A boy or girl preparing to be a teacher, who spent part of the period of preliminary education as a teacher in an elementary school under the supervision of the head teacher, and concurrently received general education either from him or in some place of higher education.

‖**Pupipara** (piupi·pără), *sb. pl.* 1874. [mod.L., neut. pl. of *pupiparus* bringing forth pupæ (f. *parere*).] *Entom.* A division of *Diptera* in which the young are born in, or ready to pass into, the pupal state. Hence **Pupi·parous** *a.* of or pertaining to the *P.*; producing or bringing forth young already advanced to the pupal state.

‖**Pupivora** (piupi·vŏră), *sb. pl.* 1836. [mod.L., neut. pl. of *pupivorus* devouring pupæ.] *Entom.* A division of hymenopterous insects containing those, such as the Ichneumon flies, which deposit their eggs in the larvæ of other insects. Hence **Pu·pivore,** one of the *P.* **Pupi·vorous** *a.* of or pertaining to the *P.*; devouring the pupæ of other insects; parasitic on pupæ.

Puppet (pʊ·pėt), *sb.* 1538. [Later f. POPPET.] **1.** A contemptuous term for a person (usu. a woman) 1586. **2.** A figure (usu. small) representing a human being; a child's doll. *Obs.* or *arch.* 1562. **3.** A human figure, with jointed limbs, moved by means of strings or wires; *esp.* one of the figures in a puppet-show 1538. **b.** *fig.* A person whose acts are suggested and controlled by another 1550. †**c.** A living personator in dramatic action; an actor in a pantomime -1668. **4.** A lathe-head 1680.

3. You look like a p. moved by clockwork! ARBUTHNOT. b. Charles remained for some while a p. in the hands of Herbert 1867. c. *Lear* II. ii. 39.

attrib., as *p.-stage, -theatre*, etc.; **p.-clack** = P.-VALVE. Hence †**Pu·ppet** *v. intr.* to play the p. **Puppetee·r. Pu·ppetish** *a.* (*rare*) pertaining to or of the nature of a p.

Pu·ppet-play. 1591. **1.** A play or dramatic performance acted by means, or with the aid, of puppets 1599. **2.** The playing or acting of puppets 1591. So **Pu·ppet-pla·yer,** †**a** performer in a pantomime; one who manages or exhibits a p.

Puppetry (pʊ·pėtri). 1528. [f. PUPPET *sb.* + -RY.] **1.** Mimic action or representation as of puppets; masquerade, mummery; make-believe; *spec.* applied to idolatrous or superstitious observances. **2.** Puppet-play; debased dramatic action 1613. †**3.** Appearance or dress as of a puppet -1638. **4.** Something compared to a puppet or a set of puppets; *esp.* an unreal character in fiction; a set of such characters 1610.

1. The pupetry in the Church of the Minerva, representing the Nativity EVELYN. 4. The stage-properties and p. of a Highland romance 1898.

Pu·ppet-show. 1650. [f. as prec. + SHOW *sb.*] A show, display, or exhibition of puppets; *esp.* a puppet-play.

Pu·ppet-va·lve. Also **poppet-valve.** 1829. [f. as prec. + VALVE; in allusion to its movement.] A disk valve which is opened by being bodily lifted from its seat, not by turning upon a hinge.

Puppy (pʊ·pi), *sb.* 1486. [perh. a. F. *poupée* doll, doll-like woman, plaything, toy, whence app. in Eng. toy dog.] †**1.** A small dog kept as a lady's pet or plaything -1655. **2.** A young dog, a whelp 1591. **b.** A young seal 1890. **3.** Applied to a person as a term of contempt; esp. a vain, empty-headed, impertinent young man; a fop, a coxcomb 1589. **4.** A white bowl or buoy used in the herring-fishery to mark the position of the net nearest the fishing-boat 1890.

1. A foolish woman may..dote upon a p. more than on her gold 1655. 3. Has no conceit about him like the puppies of our day 1849. Hence **Pu·ppydom,** puppyhood; puppies collectively. **Pu·ppyhood,** the state or time of being a p. **Pu·ppyish** *a.* of the nature or character of a p. (sense 3). **Pu·ppyism,** the character, style, or manners of a p. (sense 3); impertinent conceit, affectation, 'side'.

Puppy (pʊ·pi), *v.* 1589. [f. prec.] *intr.* and *trans.* To bring forth puppies; to whelp, litter; to pup.

Pur-, *prefix.* The usual AF. form of OF. *por-, pur-* :—L. *por-, pro-*, prep. and prefix; as in *purchase, purlieu, purloin*, etc.

‖**Purana** (purā·nă). 1696. [Skr. *purāṇá* belonging to former times, f. *purā* formerly.] One of a class of sacred poetical works in Sanskrit, containing the mythology of the Hindus. Hence **Pura·nic** *a.* of or pertaining to the Puranas; also *absol.* as *sb.* a Puranic work or author; a believer in the Puranas.

Purbeck (pɔ̄·ɹbek). 1691. Name of a peninsula on the Dorset coast; in full, Isle of Purbeck; used *attrib.*

P. beds. *Geol.*, the three strata of the P. series, reckoned as the uppermost members of the Oolite formation, or the lowest of the Wealden. **P. marble,** the finer qualities of P. stone. **P. stone,** a hard limestone obtained from P., and used in building and paving.

Purblind (pɔ̄·ɹbləind), *a.* ME. [orig. as

two words, perh. *pure* adv. entirely, or OF. *pur-*, *pour-* intensive.] †1. Quite or totally blind –1615. 2. Of impaired or defective vision: †a. Blind of one eye –1617. b. Near-sighted 1523. c. Partially blind; almost blind; *gen.* dim-sighted 1531. 3. *fig.* Stupid, obtuse, dull 1533.

1. *L. L. L.* III. i. 181. 3. Man is such a pur-blind creature, that he cannot unerringly see a day before him 1660. Hence **Purbli·nd** *v. trans.* to make p.; to impair the sight of. **Pu·rblind·ly** *adv.* (*rare*) **-ness.**

Purchasable (pɒ̄·ɹtʃĕsăb'l), *a.* 1611. [f. PURCHASE *v.* + -ABLE.] That may be purchased.

Purchase (pɒ̄·ɹtʃĕs, -ăs), *sb.* [ME. a. OF. *por-*, *purchas*, f. *porchacier* to PURCHASE.] I. The act or action of purchasing. †1. The action of hunting; the chase; the catching or seizing of prey; hence, seizing forcibly; pillage, plunder, robbery, capture –1725. †2. The action or process of procuring, obtaining, or acquiring for oneself in any way; acquisition, gain, attainment –1589. 3. The action of making one's profit or gaining one's sustenance in any way; esp. irregularly, as by begging, or by shifts of any kind; shifting for oneself. late ME. 4. *Law.* The acquirement of property by one's personal action, as dist. from inheritance 1460. 5. *spec.* Acquisition by payment of money or an equivalent; buying 1611. b. The action or system of buying commissions in the army; payment made for an appointment or promotion in the commissioned ranks 1796. 6. *fig.* Acquisition at the cost of something immaterial, as effort or suffering, sacrifice 1651.

1. We were bound now upon traffick, and not for p. DE FOE. 3. His purchas was wel bettre than his rente CHAUCER. 5. Miss Black's shop, where I wanted to make a p. 1833. 6. They that pay thus dear for damnation well deserve to enjoy the purchace 1658.

II. That which is purchased or acquired. †1. That which is obtained, gained, or acquired; gains, winnings, acquisitions; in later use, chiefly, a prize, or booty, taken by a privateer –1725. 2. The annual return or rent from land; in the phr. *at so many years' p.*, used in stating the price of land 1584. 3. That which is purchased or bought 1587. †b. A (good, bad, dear, etc.) bargain –1857. †4. The purchase-money –1742.

1. A..distressed Widow,..Made prize and p. of his wanton Eye SHAKS. 2. *fig.* The life of General Walpole would not have been worth half an hour's p. 1893. 3. *Ham.* V. i. 117. b. This might..be thought a dear p. 1812.

III. [f. PURCHASE *v.* III.] 1. Hold or position for advantageously exerting or applying power; mechanical advantage, leverage, fulcrum 1711. 2. Any contrivance for increasing applied power; esp. *Naut.* such a device consisting of a rope, pulley, windlass, or the like 1711. 3. *fig.* A hold or position of advantage for accomplishing something; a means by which one's power or influence is increased 1790.

1. If I could have calculated on a safe p. for my foot TYNDALL.

Purchase (pɒ̄·ɹtʃĕs, -ăs), *v.* [ME. a. AF. *purchacer* to seek for, procure, or bring about, f. *por*, *pur* :—L. *pro* for + *chacier*, *chasser* :— pop. L. *captiare* to CHASE.] I. †1. *trans.* To try to procure or bring about; to contrive (esp. something evil) *to* or *for* a person –1549. †2. *intr.* To exert oneself for the attainment of some object; to endeavour; to strive –1674. †3. *trans.* To bring about, cause, effect, produce; to procure, manage –1678.

2. *Timon* III. ii. 52.

II. †1. *trans.* To procure for oneself, acquire, get possession of; to gain –1703. b. To obtain from a constituted authority (a brief, a licence, etc.); *spec.* in *Law*, *To p. a writ*, to sue out, to obtain and issue a writ; hence, to commence an action. Now *Hist.* ME. 2. *spec. Law.* To acquire (property, esp. land) otherwise than by inheritance or descent; occas., to get by conquest in war. *Obs.* or *arch.* ME. 3. To acquire by the payment of money or its equivalent; to buy. late ME. b. *fig.* To acquire at the cost of toil, suffering, danger, or the like; to earn, win; to bring upon oneself, incur (mischief). late ME.

2. His faults in him..Hereditarie, Rather then purchaste SHAKS. 3. The field which Abraham purchased of the sonnes of Heth *Gen.* xxv. 10. b. Dearly, indeed, do I p. experience! MISS BURNEY.

III. *Naut.* To haul in, draw in (a rope or cable); *spec.* to haul up (the anchor) by means of the capstan; hence, to haul up, hoist, or raise (anything) by the aid of a mechanical power, as the pulley, lever, etc. 1567.

Pu·rchase-mo:ney. 1763. The sum for which anything is or may be purchased.

Purchaser (pɒ̄·ɹtʃĕsəɹ). [ME., a. AF. *purchasour* = OF. *porchaceor*; see prec.] †1. One who acquires or aims at acquiring possessions –1591. 2. *Law.* One who acquires land or property in any way other than by inheritance ME. 3. One who purchases for money; a buyer 1625.

2. If I give land freely to another, he is in the eye of the law a purchasor BLACKSTONE.

‖**Purdah** (pɒ̄·ɹdă). *E. Ind.* 1800. [a. Urdū and Pers. *pardah* veil, curtain.] A curtain; *esp.* one serving to screen women from the sight of men or strangers. b. As typical of the seclusion of Indian women of rank; hence, the system of such seclusion 1865.

Pure (piūəɹ), *a.* (*sb.*, *adv.*) ME. [a. OF. *pur* :—L. *purus.*] I. In physical sense. a. Unmixed; free from admixture or adulteration. b. *esp.* Not mixed with, or not having in or upon it, anything that defiles, corrupts, or impairs; unsullied, untainted, clean. c. Visibly or optically clear, spotless, stainless. d. Of a sound or voice: Free from discordant quality; clear; *spec.* in *Mus.* and *Acoustics*, said of tones that are perfectly in tune: esp. as opp. to *tempered* 1872.

The morning air p. from the city's smoke 1804. The snow was of the purest white 1860. d. A perfectly clear and p. tenor 1873.

II. In non-physical or general sense. 1. Without foreign or extraneous admixture; simple, homogeneous, unmixed, unalloyed. late ME. b. Of unmixed descent, pure-blooded 1475. c. *Law.* Having no condition annexed; absolute 1536. d. Of a subject of study or practice: Restricted to that which essentially belongs to it. (Often denoting the simply theoretical part of a subject, as in *p. mathematics*; opp. to APPLIED 2, MIXED 4.) Also said of a student who confines himself to one subject or branch of a subject. 1641. e. *Logic.* Of a proposition or syllogism; opp. to MODAL *a.* 4. 1697. f. *Gram.* (*a*) In Greek (καθαρός), of a vowel: Preceded by another vowel. Of the stem of a word: Ending in a vowel. Of a consonant (as *s*): Not accompanied by another consonant. (*b*) In Arabic, etc., of a syllable: Ending in a vowel, open. 1650. 2. Taken by itself, with nothing added; . . . and nothing else; mere, simple. Often in phr. *p. and simple*, following the sb. ME. b. Nothing short of .., absolute, sheer, utter, complete ME.

1. An act of P. Thought 1864. *P. naturals*: see NATURAL *sb.* II. 2. b. That horse..is very nearly a p. Arab 1866. d. He is a p. physicist; he does not know chemistry (*mod.*). 2. Alas Sir, we did it for p. need SHAKS. P. procrastination and dilatoriness 1861. b. A lot of p. nonsense 1902.

III. Free from corruption or defilement. 1. Unadulterated, uncorrupted, uncontaminated; conforming accurately to a standard of quality or style; faultless, correct ME. 2. Free from moral defilement or corruption; guiltless, innocent; guileless, sincere. Often absol., *the p.* (*sc.* persons). ME. 3. Sexually undefiled; chaste. late ME. 4. Free from ceremonial defilement; fit for sacred service or use 1611.

1. In suche places..as the pureste englyshe is spoken 1540. 2. Blessed are the p. in herte TINDALE *Matt.* v. 8.

IV. *slang* or *colloq.* A general term of appreciation: Fine, excellent, capital, nice, splendid. Now *rare* or *Obs.* 1675. b. In conjunction with another adj.: *P. and* .. = nice and .., fine and ..; excellently; thoroughly. Now *dial.* 1742.

Is it not p. that we shall meet in a fortnight? 1734.

B. *sb.* (or *absol.*) 1. That which is pure; purity. *poet.* 1625. 2. A 'pure' physician or surgeon (see II. 1 d). *Med. colloq.* 1827.

1. Her eies shrowd pitie, pietie, and p. LODGE.

C. *adv.* 1. Absolutely, entirely, thoroughly, quite. Now *dial.* or *Obs.* ME. 2. Purely; simply, merely; rightly; chastely. *poet. rare.* 1460. 3. Qualifying an adj. of colour (chiefly *white*): Purely, with no admixture ME.

2. For his sake, Did I expose my selfe (p. for his loue) Into the danger SHAKS. Hence **Pu·re-ly** *adv.*, **-ness.**

Pure, *v.* ME. [a. OF. *purer* :—L. *purare* to purify (with religious rites), f. *purus.*] †*trans.* To make pure; to cleanse, purify, refine (*lit.* and *fig.*) –1635. b. *Tanning.* To cleanse (hides) by steeping them in a bate or alkaline lye 1883. Hence †**Pured** *ppl. a.* purified, cleansed; refined; of fur: trimmed or cut down so as to show one colour only.

‖**Purée** (püre). 1824. [F., origin obsc.] A broth or soup made of vegetables, meat, or fish, boiled to a pulp and passed through a sieve.

Purfle (pɒ̄·ɹf'l), *sb.* late ME. [a. OF. *porfil* = med.L. *perfilum*; vbl. sb. from *profilare*, *perfilare*; see next and PROFILE.] A border; *esp.* the embroidered border or edge of a garment.

Purfle (pɒ̄·ɹf'l), *v.* ME. [a. OF. *porfiler* = It. *profilare*, med.L. *perfilare*, f. L. *pro* or *per* + *filum* thread; see PROFILE *v.*] 1. To border; *esp.* to adorn (a robe) with a border of thread work or embroidery; to trim with gold or silver lace, pearls, fur, etc. *arch.* b. *intr.* or *absol.* To do purfling 1890. †2. *trans.* To give to (leaves, flowers, etc.) a border or edge of a particular kind; in *pa. pple.*, denoting the outline, contour, or distinctive colouring of the edge –1640. 3. a. *Arch.* To ornament (the edge or ridge of any structure) *with* crockets, etc. 1849. b. To adorn (the back or belly of a violin, etc.) with a border of inlaid work 1848. 4. To adorn, ornament, beautify 1470.

1. A robe of scarlet, open before, and purfled with minever 1840. Hence **Purfled** (pɒ̄·ɹf'ld) *ppl. a.* in senses of the vb.; *transf.* of a person: decorated with purfling; *Arch.*, etc. ornamented in a manner resembling drapery, embroidery, or lace-work. **Pu·rfling** *vbl. sb.*, the action of the vb.; (*b*) *Arch.* the ornamentation of an edge or ridge; (*c*) the inlaid bordering of the backs and bellies of violins, etc.

Purgation (pɒɹgēⁱ·ʃən). late ME. [a. OF. *purgacion*, ad. L. *purgationem*, f. *purgare* to PURGE.] The action of purging. 1. The clearing away of impurities or extraneous matter; purification. b. *spec.* The discharge of waste matter from the body; now only the evacuation of the bowels, esp. by means of a cathartic; the administration of cathartics; purging. †c. Menstruation; *pl.* catamenia –1737. 2. Ceremonial or ritual cleansing from defilement. late ME. 3. Moral or spiritual cleansing; *spec.* in *R. C. Ch.*, the purification of the soul in purgatory. late ME. 4. The action of clearing oneself from the accusation or suspicion of crime or guilt. Now *Hist.* late ME.

2. Even the slaughter of enemies required a solemn p. among the Jews BLACKSTONE. 4. If any man doubt that, let him put mee to my p. SHAKS. *Canonical p.*, the affirmation on oath of his innocence by the accused in a spiritual court, confirmed by the oaths of several of his peers. *Vulgar p.*, a test by the ordeal of fire or water, or by wager of battle.

Purgative (pɒ̄·ɹgătiv), *a.* and *sb.* late ME. [a. F. *purgatif*, ad. late L. *purgativus*, f. *purgat-*, *purgare*; see -IVE, -ATIVE.] A. *adj.* Having the quality of purging; cathartic; cleansing or freeing from defilement. B. *sb.* A cathartic; any cleansing or purifying agent or means 1626. Hence **Pu·rgative-ly** *adv.*, **-ness.**

Purgatorial (pɒɹgătō³·riăl), *a.* 1450. [f. late L. *purgatorius* + -AL.] Of a spiritually purifying quality; also, of, pertaining to, or of the nature of purgatory.

Purgatorian (pɒɹgătō³·riăn), *a.* and *sb.* *rare.* 1550. [f. med.L. *purgatorium* PURGATORY *sb.* + -AN.] A. *adj.* Of, pertaining to, or relating to purgatory; purgatorial 1624. B. *sb.* A believer in purgatory 1550.

Purgatory (pɒ̄·ɹgătəri), *sb.* ME. [ad. med.L. *purgatorium*, absol. use of neut. of *purgatorius* adj. purifying, f. *purgare* to PURGE.] 1. A condition or place of spiritual purging and purification; *spec.*, a state in which souls who have departed this life in the grace of God are cleansed by suffering and are thereby prepared for heaven. 2. *fig.* Any place or state of temporary suffering, expiation, etc. late ME. 3. *U.S.* a. A cavern. b. A deep narrow gorge or ravine, with vertical or steep sides; also, a brook flowing through such a gorge. (Usu. as a place-name.) 1766.

Purgatory (pɔ̄·ɹgătəri), *a.* late ME. [ad. post-cl. L. *purgatorius*, f. *purgatorem* cleanser; see -ORY [2].] Having the quality of cleansing or purifying; of or pertaining to purgation.

Purge (pɔ̄ɹdʒ), *sb.* 1563. [f. next, or (in sense 2) a. F. *purge*.] **1.** That which purges; *spec.* an aperient medicine, a purgative. **2.** The act of purging; purgation; ridding of objectionable or hostile elements 1598.

2. *Pride's P.* (Eng. Hist.), the exclusion by Colonel Pride, on the 6th of December, 1648, of those members of the Long Parliament who were suspected of Presbyterian and Royalist leanings.

Purge (pɔ̄ɹdʒ), *v.* ME. [a. OF. *purg(i)er* :—L. *purgare* to cleanse, f. *purus* PURE.] **1.** *trans.* To make physically pure or clean; to rid of anything impure or extraneous; to clear or free *of, from.* **2.** = PURIFY 2, 4. ME. †**b.** = PURIFY 3. –1600. **3.** *transf.* To remove by some cleansing or purifying process (*lit.* or *fig.*); to clear *away, off, out*; to expel or exclude; to void. Also *intr.* for *refl.* ME. **4.** *Med.* To empty (the stomach, bowels, etc.); to deplete or relieve (the bowels) by evacuation. Also *refl.* and *intr.* late ME. **b.** *absol.* To induce purgation; (of a drug) to act as a purge 1606. **5.** *trans.* and *refl.* To clear (oneself or another, one's character, etc.) of a charge or suspicion of guilt; to exculpate; *spec.* in *Law*, by assertion on oath, with the support of compurgators, or by wager of battle ME. **6.** *Law.* To atone for (an offence, etc.) by expiation and submission, with the prospect of relief from penalties; to 'wipe out' (the offence or sentence) 1681. †**7.** *refl.* and *intr.* (also *pass.*). Of a liquid: To clear itself, to be made clear or pure by settlement or defecation –1833.

1. They p. the barley from the bran 1737. **2.** From mental mists to p. a nation's eyes 1798. He insisted that the Senate must be purged of its corrupt members FROUDE. **3.** I shal..purely p. away thy drosse BIBLE (Bishops') *Isa.* i. 25. **5.** He so well purged himself, that he was again restored to his Office CLARENDON. Hence **Pu·rgeable** *a.* capable of being purged. **Pu·rger**, one who or that which purges; †*spec.* a cathartic. **Pu·rging** *vbl. sb.* the action of the vb.; *spec.* = PURGATION 1 b. **Pu·rging** *ppl. a.* that purges; often in names of plants having cathartic qualities, as **purging flax**, *Linum catharticum*.

Purgery (pɔ̄·ɹdʒĕri). 1864. [a. F. *purgerie*, f. *purger*; see -ERY.] A bleaching or refining room for sugar.

Purification (piūᵊrifikēⁱ·ʃən). late ME. [a. F., or ad. L. *purificationem*, f. *purificare* to PURIFY.] **1.** Freeing from dirt or defilement; cleansing; separation of dross, dregs, refuse, etc. so as to obtain the substance in a pure condition 1598. **2.** Ceremonial or ritual cleansing; *spec.* the observances enjoined upon a woman after child-birth by the Jewish law; hence formerly applied to the churching of women. late ME. **3.** Moral or spiritual cleansing; clearing from taint of guilt 1660. **4.** Freeing from fault or blemish (in ideal or general sense); the action of clearing from debasing or corrupting elements 1753.

2. *The P. of St. Mary* (*of our Lady*, etc.), also simply *the P.*, a name in the Western Church for the festival (Feb. 2) of the Presentation of Christ in the Temple by the Virgin Mary (*Luke* ii. 22); also called CANDLEMAS.

Purificator (piūᵊ·rifikeⁱtəɹ). 1853. [f. L. *purificare*; see -OR.] **1.** *Eccl.* A cloth used at communion for wiping the chalice and paten, and the fingers and lips of the celebrant. **2.** One who or that which purifies (*rare*) 1866.

Purificatory (piūᵊ·rifikeⁱ:təri), *sb.* 1670. [ad. med.L. *purificatorium*; see next and -ORY [1].] = prec. **1.**

Pu·rificatory, *a.* 1610. [ad. late L. *purificatorius*, f. ppl. stem of L. *purificare* to PURIFY; see -ORY [2].] Having the quality of purifying; tending to purification.

Purifier (piūᵊ·rifəiˌəɹ). 1471. [f. PURIFY + -ER [1].] **1.** One who or that which purifies; a cleanser; a refiner. **2.** An apparatus for purifying. *spec.* **a.** A gas-purifier. **b.** A separator to remove bran scales and flour from grits or middlings. 1834.

Puriform (piūᵊ·rifɔɹm), *a.* 1797. [f. L. *pus, pur-* PUS + -(I)FORM.] *Path.* Having the form or character of pus; resembling pus.

Purify (piūᵊ·rifəi), *v.* ME. [a. F. *purifier*, ad. late L. *purificare*, f. L. *purus* pure; see -FY.] **1.** *trans.* To free from extraneous matter, esp. such as pollutes or deteriorates; to rid of (material) defilement or taint; to cleanse 1440. **2.** To cleanse from moral or spiritual defilement ME. **3.** To make ceremonially clean; to free from ceremonial uncleanness. Formerly *spec.* of the churching of women (mostly in *pass.*). ME. **4.** To free from blemish or corruption (in ideal or general sense); to clear of foreign or alien elements 1548. **5.** *Law.* To make (a contract, etc.) 'pure' by freeing it from conditions; also, to fulfil (a condition) so as to render the obligation 'pure' 1590. **6.** *intr.* for *refl.* To become pure 1668.

1. Fires..to purifie the aire HOBBES. **3.** In the Consecrated stream..to wash off sin, and fit them so Purified to receive him pure MILT. **4.** He saw the French Tongue abundantly purifi'd 1665. **6.** He does not put it in water to p. 1800.

‖**Purim** (piūᵊ·rim, ‖pūrī·m). late ME. [Heb., pl. of *pūr*, a foreign word, explained in Esther iii. 7, ix. 24, as = Heb. *gōrā·l* lot.] A Jewish festival observed in commemoration of the defeat of Haman's plot to massacre the Jews.

Purine (piūᵊ·rəin). 1899. [ad. G. *purin*, f. L. *purum* pure, and *uricum* URIC; see -INE [3].] *Chem.* A white crystalline basic substance $C_5H_4N_4$, of very complicated structure, which when oxidized forms uric acid ($C_5H_4N_4O_3$).

Purism (piūᵊ·riz'm). 1803. [ad. F. *purisme*, f. *pur* pure; see -ISM.] Scrupulous or exaggerated observance of, or insistence upon, purity or correctness, esp. in language or style 1804. **b.** with *pl.* An instance of this 1803.

Purist (piūᵊ·rist). 1706. [ad. F. *puriste*, f. *pur* PURE + -IST.] **1.** One who aims at, affects, or insists on scrupulous or excessive purity, esp. in language or style; a stickler for correctness. **2.** One who maintained that the New Testament was written in pure Greek 1835. Hence **Puri·stic, -al** *adjs.*

Puritan (piūᵊ·rităn), *sb.* and *a.* 1572. [f. L. *purus* pure, or *puritas* PURITY + -AN. Cf. F. *puritain* (Ronsard, 1564), mod.L. *puritani*.] **A.** *sb.* **1.** *Hist.* A member of that party of English Protestants who regarded the reformation of the church under Elizabeth as incomplete, and called for its further 'purification' from unscriptural and corrupt forms and ceremonies retained from the unreformed church; subsequently, often applied to those who separated from the established church on points of ritual, polity, or doctrine. **b.** *transf.* A member of any religious sect or party that advocates special purity of doctrine or practice 1577. **c.** A member of any (non-religious) party or school who practises extreme adherence to its principles; a purist 1885. **2.** Applied, chiefly in ridicule, to one who is, affects to be, or is accounted extremely strict, precise, or scrupulous in religion or morals 1592.

1. But one P. amongst them, and he sings Psalmes to horne-pipes SHAKS. Branded with the odious names of Puritanes FULLER. **c.** The Puritans of 'economic principle' 1885. **2.** He that hath not for euery word an oath..they say hee is a p., a precise foole, not fitte to hold a gentleman company RICH.

B. *adj.* **a.** Of, pertaining to, or characteristic of the Puritans; strict and scrupulous in religious matters. **b.** That is a Puritan. 1589.

Puritanic (piūᵊritæ·nik), *a.* 1606. [f. prec. + -IC; after *Satanic*, etc.] = PURITAN *a.* (now *rare*); having the character or manner of a puritan.

Puritanical (piūᵊritæ·nikăl), *a.* 1607. [f. as prec. + -ICAL.] Pertaining to or characteristic of the Puritans, or of puritans generally; having the character or qualities of puritans. (Chiefly *disparaging*.)

I do not want to be thought queer or p. 1878. Hence **Purita·nically** *adv.*

Puritanism (piūᵊ·rităniz'm). 1573. [f. as prec. + -ISM.] **1.** The Puritan system; the doctrines and principles of the Puritans; Puritan opinion or practice. Also *transf.* **2.** Excessive (or affected) strictness or preciseness like that of the Puritans; puritanical behaviour or principles; precisianism 1592.

2. That moderate austerity..which may, without p., be recommended 1832.

Puritanize (piūᵊ·ritănəiz), *v.* 1625. [f. as prec. + -IZE.] **1.** *intr.* (with *it*). To act the puritan; to practise, conform to, or affect puritanism. **2.** *trans.* To make puritan, imbue with puritanism 1648.

2. He has been puritanized till he is good for nothing 1853. Hence **Pu·ritanizer.**

Purity (piūᵊ·rĭti). [ME. *purte* (rare), a. OF. *purte*; later conformed to L. *puritas*, *-tatem* (f. *purus* PURE; see -ITY).] The quality or condition of being pure. **1.** The state of being unmixed; freedom from admixture of any foreign substance or matter, *esp.* from matter that corrupts or debases; physical cleanness 1526. **2.** In non-physical or general sense: Freedom from any foreign or extraneous element, esp. from such as corrupt or debase; unalloyed or unadulterated condition; faultlessness, correctness 1561. **3.** Freedom from moral corruption, from ceremonial or sexual uncleanness, or pollution; innocence, chastity, ceremonial cleanness ME.

1. The puritie and whitenesse of my Sheetes SHAKS. Snow of perfect p. TYNDALL. **2.** From Chaucer the p. of the English tongue began DRYDEN. **3.** Clennesse of vertue & purite of lyfe 1526.

Purkinjean (pɔɹki·ndʒĭăn), *a.* 1835. [f. name of J. E. *Purkinje*, Bohemian physiologist (1787–1869) + -AN.] *Anat.* and *Phys.* Pertaining to or named after Purkinje.

P. capsules in the cement of a tooth; *P. vesicle*, the nucleus of the ovum. So *Purkinje's cells*, large branching cells in the cortex of the brain; etc.

Purl (pɔ̄ɹl), *sb.*[1] 1535. [In senses 1, 2, app. orig. *pyrl(e*, f. PIRL *v.* to twist. In senses 3, 4, it is often spelt *pearl* (PEARL *sb.*[2]) and may have a different origin.] **1.** Thread or cord made of twisted gold or silver wire, used for bordering and embroidering. **2.** Each of the minute loops or twists used to ornament the edges of lace, braid, ribbon, etc.; hence, collectively, a series or chain of such loops 1611. **3.** †'The pleat or fold of a ruff or band', as worn about 1600; a frill. Also *transf.* 1593. **4.** *Knitting.* (Formerly often *pearl*.) An inversion of the stitches, producing a ribbed appearance of the surface; as in *p.-knitting, -stitch* 1825.

Purl (pɔ̄rl), *sb.*[2] 1552. [Akin to PURL *v.*[2]] †**1.** A small rill in which the particles of water are in a whirl of agitation –1651. **2.** The action or sound of purling as a rill 1650.

1. Receiving sundry pirles to it and many a running rill HOLLAND. **2.** The p. of waters through the weirs T. HARDY.

Purl (pɔ̄ɹl), *sb.*[3] *Hist.* 1659. [Origin unkn.] orig. A liquor made by infusing wormwood or other bitter herbs in ale or beer; later, a mixture of hot beer with gin (also called *dog's nose*), sometimes also with ginger and sugar; in repute as a morning draught.

Drank a Glass of P. to recover Appetite ADDISON.

Purl, *sb.*[4] *slang* or *colloq.* 1825. [Goes w. PURL *v.*[3] 3.] An act of whirling, hurling, or pitching head-over-heels or head-foremost; a header or cropper; a spill; an upset.

Mr. Tollemarsh got an awful p. over a Gate 1829.

Purl, *v.*[1] 1526. [f. PURL *sb.*[1]] †**1.** *trans.* To embroider with gold or silver thread; to edge embroidered figures with gold or silver thread. Chiefly in *pa. pple.* and *ppl. a.* –1688. **2.** *absol.* To border or edge with or as with purls (PURL *sb.*[1] 2). Chiefly in *pa. pple.* and *ppl. a.* 1766. †**3.** To pleat or frill like a ruff; to frill the edge of; also *transf.* –1653. **4.** *Knitting.* To invert the stitches so as to produce a furrow or 'seam' 1825.

Purl (pɔ̄ɹl), *v.*[2] See also PIRL *v.* 1586. [Goes w. PURL *sb.*[2]; cf. also Norw. *purla* to bubble up, gush out as water.] **1.** *intr.* Of water, a brook: To flow with whirling motion of its particles, or twisting round small obstacles: often with ref. to the murmuring sound of a rill. **2.** *transf.* Said of a stream of air, breath, wind, etc. 1593. **b.** *trans.* To utter with 'purling'. HERRICK.

1. The gravel-paved brook..He often sat to see it p. along CLARE.

Purl, *v.*[3] 1791. [In sense 1, app. a var. of PIRL *v.* (sense 2).] **1.** *intr.* To whirl round rapidly, as a wheel; to spin round, as a peg-top, etc. **2.** To wheel *round* suddenly, as a horse 1857. **3.** *trans.* and *intr.* To turn upside down, overturn, upset, capsize; to turn head over heels. *dial.* and *colloq.* 1856.

3. He hit the fence, and then purled over 1874.

Purler (pɒ̄·ɹləɹ). *colloq.* 1869. [f. prec. + -ER [1].] A throw or blow that hurls any one head-foremost; a knock-down blow.

Purlieu (pɒ̄·rliū). 1482. [Formerly *purlew(e*, app. alteration (by assoc. w. LIEU) of *purley*, **puraley*, a. AF. *puralé(e*.] 1. A piece or tract of land on the fringe or border of a forest; orig., one that, after having been included in the forest, was disafforested by a new perambulation, but still remained in some respects subject to provisions of the Forest Laws. 2. *transf.* and *fig.* A place where one has the right to range at large; a haunt; one's bounds, limits, beat 1643. 3. *pl. transf.* The parts about the border of any place; the outskirts (*arch.*) 1650. 4. †A suburb; also, the meaner streets about some main thoroughfare; a mean, squalid, or disreputable street or quarter 1618.

1. Where in the Purlews of this Forrest, stands A sheep-coat? SHAKS. 2. Wit has its walks and its purlieus, out of which it may not stray the breadth of an hair SWIFT. †*To hunt in p., in the purlieus*, to pursue illicit love. 3. A wolf..was skulking about the purlieus of the camp 1835. 4. A wretched shed in the most beggarly p. of Bethnal Green LAMB.

Purlieu-man, purley-man (pɒ̄·ɹlimæ̆n). 1574. [f. prec. + MAN *sb.*] The owner of freehold land within the purlieu of a forest.

Purlin (pɒ̄·ɹlin). 1447. [Origin obsc.] A horizontal beam, usu. one of two or more which run along the length of a roof, resting upon the principal rafters, and lending support to the common rafters or boards of the roof.

Purloin (pɒɹloi·n), *v.* 1440. [a. AF. *purloigner*, f. *por-*, *pur-* :—L. *pro-* + *loing, loin* :—L. *longe* far; hence, 'to put far off or far away'.] †1. *trans.* To put far away; to remove; to put away; to do away with; to make of no effect –1660. 2. To make away with; to steal, esp. under circumstances which involve a breach of trust; to pilfer, filch 1548. 3. *transf.* and *fig.* 1593.

2. I took..an opportunity of purloining his key from his breeches-pocket FIELDING. 3. Galleries purloined from the first floor of each house PENNANT. Hence **Purloi·ner**, a petty thief, a pilferer.

Puro- (piūᵊ·ro), comb. f. L. *pur-* PUS, used instead of the more usual PYO- of Greek origin.

Purpa·rty. *arch.* ME. [a. AF. *purpartie*, f. *por-*, *pour-* :—L. *pro-* + *partie* division, part; see PARTY.] *Law.* A proportion, a share, esp. in an inheritance.

Purple (pɒ̄·ɹp'l), *a.* and *sb.* [Late OE. *purple*, early ME. *purpel*, *-ul*, altered from *purpre*, *purper* PURPURE. Cf. *marble* for *marbre*.] A. *adj.* 1. Of the distinguishing colour of the dress of emperors, kings, etc.; = L. *purpureus*, Gr. πορφύρεος, in early use meaning crimson; hence, imperial, royal. b. Of persons: Clad in purple; of imperial or royal rank. *poet.* or *rhet.* 1704. 2. Of the colour described in B. 1 b, c. late ME. b. Of this colour as being the hue of mourning (esp. royal or eccl. mourning), or of penitence 1466. c. Used *poet.* to describe the colour of blood. Hence, Bloody, blood-stained. 1590. 3. *rhet.* Bright-hued, brilliant, splendid, gaudy, gay; (of sin) deep-dyed, grave, heinous 1598.

1. They did put on hym a p. garment TINDALE *John* xix. 2. b. P. tyrants vainly groan GRAY. 2. Heath-bell with her p. bloom SCOTT. That lovely dark p. colour of our Welsh and Highland hills RUSKIN. c. His p. spear GRAY. When Mathouse-burn to Melrose ran All p. with their blood SCOTT. 3. All the Glories of the P. Spring DRYDEN. I never said bridge was a p. sin 1905. *P. patch, passage, piece*, an ornate passage in a literary composition (after L. *purpureus pannus*, Horace).

B. *sb.* 1. The name of a colour. a. Anciently, that of the dye obtained from species of molluscs (*Purpura* and *Murex*), commonly called *Tyrian p.*, which was a crimson; b. in the Middle Ages applied vaguely to many shades of red; c. now applied to mixtures of red and blue in various proportions, usu. containing also some black or white, or both 1440. d. The Tyrian dye, or any pigment of the above-mentioned colours 1638. 2. Purple cloth or clothing; a purple robe 1460. b. As the distinguishing dress of emperors, kings, consuls, and chief magistrates; hence *fig.*; spec. *the p.*, imperial, royal, or consular rank, power, or office. Also the colour of imperial and royal mourning. 1440. c. *The p.*: in ref. to the scarlet colour of the official dress of a cardinal; hence the rank, state, or office of a cardinal; the cardinalate 1685. d. In phr. *born, cradled in (the) p.*: said of a child of an imperial or royal reigning family; hence *transf.* (Commonly assoc. w. sense 2, but see PORPHYROGENITE *a.*) 1790. 3. Any of the molluscs which yielded the Tyrian purple; now, a mollusc of the genus *Purpura* 1580. 4. *pl.* a. A disease characterized by an eruption of purplish pustules; esp. PURPURA 1533. b. Swine fever 1887. c. A disease in wheat caused by *Vibrio tritici* 1808. 5. A purple flower 1840.

2. *P. and pall*, an alliterative collocation in which *pall* has the more general sense of 'rich clothing'. b. Diocletian and Maximian had resigned the p. GIBBON. c. He was raised to the p. 1898.

Combs. and collocations. 1. Of the adjective: **p. chamber**: see PORPHYROGENITE; **p. copper (ore)**, *Min.* a native sulphide of copper and iron; **p. powder of Cassius** = GOLD-*p.*; named after Andreas Cassius (died 1673). b. In names of species or varieties of animals or plants characterized by a purple or purplish colouring, as *p. beech, heron, martin, sandpiper*, etc.; **p.-bird, p. coot**, the purple gallinule of Europe (see PORPHYRIO); **p.-shell**, (*a*) = B. 3; (*b*) an ocean snail of the genus *Ianthina*. 2. Of the sb.: **p.-gland**, the gland in some gastropods which yields the purple dye.

Purple (pɒ̄·ɹp'l), *v.* late ME. [f. PURPLE *a.*] 1. *trans.* To make purple; to colour or dye with purple. 2. *intr.* To become purple 1646.

1. When Morn Purples the East MILT. We purpled the seas with our blood 1783.

Pu·rple-re·d, *a.* and *sb.* 1578. Red inclining to or tinged with purple.

Purplish (pɒ̄·ɹpliʃ), *a.* 1562. [-ISH [1].] Somewhat purple; tinged with purple.

Purply (pɒ̄·ɹpli), *a.* 1725. [f. PURPLE *a.* or *sb.* + -Y [1].] Purplish.

Purport (pɒ̄·ɹpōɹt), *sb.* 1455. [a. AF. = OF. *por-*, *purport* produce, contents, f. *purporter*; see next.] 1. That which is conveyed or expressed, esp. by a formal document; bearing, tenor, import, effect; meaning, sense. †b. Outward bearing. SPENSER. 2. That which is intended to be done or effected by something; object, purpose, intention. Now *rare*. 1654.

1. And with a looke so pitious in p., As if he had been loosed out of hell SHAKS. **Pu·rportless** *a.*

Purport (pɒɹpōᵊ·ɹt, pɒ̄·ɹpōɹt), *v.* 1528. [a. AF., OF. *purporter* :—pop.L. **proportare* to carry forth.] 1. *trans.* To have as its purport; to convey to the mind; to mean, imply. b. Const. inf.: To profess or claim by its tenor 1790. 2. To purpose (*rare*) 1803.

1. b. This epistle purports to be written after St. Paul had been at Corinth PALEY.

Purpose (pɒ̄·ɹpəs), *sb.* ME. [a. AF. = OF. *porpos*, *purpos*, f. *porposer* to PURPOSE.] 1. The object which one has in view. 2. Without *a* or *pl.* The action or fact of intending or meaning to do something; intention, resolution, determination ME. 3. The object for which anything is done or made, or for which it exists; end, aim. late ME. †4. That which one propounds; a proposition, question, or argument; a riddle; *pl.* a game of questions and answers –1611. †b. Discourse, conversation; = F. *propos* –1599. 5. That which forms the subject of discourse; the matter in hand; the point at issue. Now only in phr. *to, from, the p.* late ME. 6. = PURPORT *sb.* 1. 1606.

1. The diuell can cite Scripture for his p. SHAKS. Phr. *To answer* or *serve one's p.*, to be of service in affecting one's object; to do what one wants. 2. Infirme of p.: Giue me the Daggers SHAKS. 3. To what p. is this waste? *Matt.* xxvi. 8. *To little, some, no p.*: with such result or effect. *For practical purposes*: in relation to actual performance or achievement. 4. b. *Much Ado* III. i. 12. 5. Come; you are a tedious foole: to the p. SHAKS. 6. Other common topics to the same p. SWIFT.

Phr. **In p.** *To be in p.*, to be minded, to intend (*to do* something). Also occas. *to have in p.* (*arch.*). **Of p.** = *on p.* Now *rare* or *arch.* exc. in *of set p.* **On p.** a. By design; purposely, intentionally. b. With *inf.* or *that*: With the express purpose mentioned; in order *to do* something; with the design or aim *that*. Also with *for*, †*to*: Expressly for. Hence **Pu·rpose-like** *a.* having the appearance of being efficient, suitable, or fit for a p. (*Sc.*); having a definite p.

Purpose (pɒ̄·ɹpəs), *v.* late ME. [a. OF. *porposer*, *purposer*, parallel forms of *proposer* to PROPOSE, with *por-*, *pur-* for L. *pro-*.] †I. *trans.* = PROPOSE *v.* 1. –1633. †b. *absol.* or *intr.* To discourse, talk. Also with *it*. –1598. II. 1. *trans.* To place before oneself as a thing to be done or attained; to form a purpose of doing (something); to resolve upon the performance of. Const. chiefly *inf.*; also *that* and *cl.*, *vbl. sb.*, and ordinary *sb.* late ME. b. *pass.* To be resolved. late ME. †2. *intr.*, *refl.*, and *pass.* ellipt. for *to p. to go*: To be bound *for* a place –1632. †3. *absol.* or *intr.* To have a purpose, plan, or design; esp. in *Man purposes* (now *proposes*), *God disposes*. Also, To mean (well or ill) *to* any one. –1656.

1. It is a capitall crime to devise or p. the death of the King SPENSER. My friend purposes to open an office JOHNSON. b. I am purposed instantly to return SCOTT. 2. He purposeth to Athens SHAKS. Hence **Pu·rposer**, †one who states a proposition or propounds a question or argument (*rare*); one who intends or plans anything.

Purposeful (pɒ̄·ɹpəsfŭl), *a.* 1853. [f. PURPOSE *sb.* + -FUL.] Having a purpose or meaning; indicating purpose; designed, intentional. b. Having a definite purpose in view 1865. Hence **Pu·rposeful-ly** *adv.*, **-ness.**

Purposeless (pɒ̄·ɹpəslės), *a.* 1552. [-LESS.] a. Devoid of purpose or design. b. Having no purposes, plans, or aims 1868. Hence **Pu·rposeless-ly** *adv.*, **-ness.**

Purposely (pɒ̄·ɹpəsli), *adv.* 1495. [f. PURPOSE *sb.* + -LY [2].] 1. Of set purpose; designedly. 2. With the particular object specified; on purpose; expressly 1528.

1. If the throng By chance go right, they [the learned] p. go wrong POPE. 2. The Queen herself came..p. to see him 1787.

Purposive (pɒ̄·ɹpəsiv), *a.* 1855. [f. PURPOSE *sb.* or *v.* + -IVE.] 1. Serving or tending to serve some purpose, esp. in the animal or vegetable economy. 2. Acting or performed with conscious purpose or design 1863. 3. Of or pertaining to purpose 1899. 4. Characterized by purpose and resolution 1903.

1. The stings of nettles are p., as stings. They act as protectors. 1894. 2. We have..p. intelligence distinctly opposed to natural selection 1884. 4. They are strong in mind and body, truthful and p. 1903. Hence **Pu·rposive-ly** *adv.*, **-ness.**

Purpresture (pɒɹpre·stiŭɹ, -tʃəɹ). late ME. [a. OF. *pur-*, *pourpresture*, altered from *por-*, *pourpresure*, f. *pourprendre* to occupy, enclose, encroach upon, etc. f. *por-* (:—L. *pro-*) + *prendre* (:—L. *præhendere*) to seize, take.] *Law.* An illegal enclosure of or encroachment upon the land or property of another or (now only) of the public; as by an enclosure or building in royal, manorial, or common lands, or in the royal forests, an encroachment on a highway, public water-way, etc. b. A payment or rent paid to a feudal superior for liberty to enclose land or erect any building upon it. late ME.

‖**Purpura** (pɒ̄·ɹpiŭră). 1753. [L., ad. Gr. πορφύρα purple shell-fish, purple.] 1. *Path.* A disease due to a morbid state of the blood or blood-vessels, characterized by purple or livid spots scattered irregularly over the skin. 2. *Zool.* A genus of gastropods, including some of those from which the ancient purple dye was obtained; a mollusc of this genus 1753.

Purpurate (pɒ̄·ɹpiŭrět), *sb.* 1818. [f. as PURPURIC + -ATE [1] 1 c.] *Chem.* A salt of purpuric acid.

Purpurate (pɒ̄·ɹpiŭrět), *a.* late ME. [ad. L. *purpuratus*, *purpurare*, f. *purpura* PURPURE.] 1. Purple-coloured, purple; also, clothed in purple. *Obs.* or *arch.* 2. Of or pertaining to the disease purpura 1846.

Purpure (pɒ̄·ɹpiŭɹ), *sb.* and *a. arch.* [OE. *purpure*, ad. L. *purpura*, ad. Gr. πορφύρα name of the shell-fish which yielded the Tyrian purple, hence the purple dye, and cloth dyed with it.] A. *sb.* †1. Purple cloth or clothing; a purple robe or garment; *spec.* as the dress of an emperor or king –1614. †2. = PURPLE *sb.* 1. –1496. b. *Her.* Purple as a colour or tincture; in engraving represented by diagonal lines from sinister to dexter 1535. B. *adj.* †1.

= PURPLE *a.* 2. -1614. 2. *Her.* Of the colour called purpure; see A. 2 b. 1562.

Purpureal (pɒɹpiū°·rĭăl), *a.* Chiefly *poet.* 1712. [f. L. *purpureus* + -AL.] Of purple colour; purple. So **Purpu·rean** *a.* (*rare*) 1615.

Purpureo- (pɒɹpiū°·rio), comb. f. L. *purpureus* adj. purple; as *p.-cobalt*, *-cobaltic* adj.

Purpuric (pɒɹpiū°·rik), *a.* 1818. [f. L. *purpura* PURPLE + -IC.] 1. *Chem.* Applied to a hypothetical acid ($C_8H_5N_5O_6$), the salts of which are purple or red. 2. *Path.* Of, pertaining to, or of the nature of purpura or purples; marked by a purple rash 1839.

Purpurin (pɒ̄·ɹpiŭrin). 1839. [f. L. *purpura* + -IN [1].] *Chem.* A red colouring matter, $C_{14}H_5O_2(OH)_3$, used in dyeing, orig. extracted from madder, hence called *madder-purple*; also prepared artificially by oxidation of alizarin.

Purr (pɒ̄ɹ), *sb.* 1601. [Cogn. w. next.] An act of purring; the soft murmuring sound made by a cat when pleased; also, any similar sound.

Purr (pɒ̄ɹ), *v.* 1620. [Echoic.] 1. *intr.* Of a cat, etc.: To make a low continuous vibratory sound expressive of satisfaction or pleasure. 2. *transf.* a. Of persons: To show satisfaction by low murmuring sounds, or by one's behaviour or attitude; also, to talk on in a quiet self-satisfied way 1668. b. Of things: To make a sound suggestive of the purring of a cat, as that caused by the boiling or bubbling of a liquid, etc. 1657. 3. *trans.* To utter or express by purring 1740.

1. It is said that the lion, jaguar, and leopard do not p. DARWIN.

Purre (pɒ̄ɹ). 1611. [From the voice of the bird.] A local name of the Dunlin (*Tringa variabilis*).

‖**Purree** (pɒ·rī). 1852. [Hindi *peorī.*] A yellow colouring matter, from which INDIAN *yellow* is prepared.

Purse (pɒ̄ɹs), *sb.* [OE. and ME. *purs*, app. ad. late L. *bursa* purse.] I. A money-bag or -receptacle and its contents. 1. A small pouch or bag of leather or other flexible material, used for carrying money on the person; orig. a small bag drawn together at the mouth with a thong or strings. 2. A purse with its contents; hence *transf.* money, funds ME. 3. A sum of money collected as a present or the like; a sum subscribed as a prize for the winner in a contest 1650. 4. As tr. Arab., Pers., Turkish *kīsah*, *kīseh* 'purse', used in the Turkish empire for a definite sum of money 1686. 5. A fragment of live coal starting out of the fire with a report: regarded as a prognostic of good fortune 1766.

1. Put Money in thy p. SHAKS. A heavy p. makes a light heart B. JONSON. 2. Phr. *A common p.*, funds possessed and shared by a number of people in common. *A heavy* or *long p.*, wealth. *A light p.*, poverty. *The public p.*, the national treasury or wealth. *Privy p.*: see PRIVY *a.* 3. His Friends made a P. for him, when he was to travel to Ægypt BENTLEY. 4. *The p.* (*of silver*) = 500 piastres. *The p. of gold* = 10,000 piastres.

II. A bag or bag-like receptacle. †1. A wallet, scrip, pouch -1771. 2. *transf. Organ-building.* A small leather bag formerly used in connexion with the pull-downs which passed through the bottom board of the wind-chest, to prevent the escape of wind 1852. 3. Applied to various natural receptacles (in animals or plants) resembling a bag; e. g. a marsupium, a cyst 1528. b. *spec.* The scrotum 1440.

3. With a naturall p. vnder her belly, wherein she putteth her young PURCHAS.

attrib. and *Comb.*: **p.-crab**, a crab of the genus *Birgus* living in burrows on the E. Indian islands; **-net**, a bag-shaped net, the mouth of which can be drawn together with cords **-seine**, a fishing-net or seine which may be pursed or drawn into the shape of a bag, used for catching shoal-fish.

Purse (pɒ̄ɹs), *v.* ME. [f. prec.] 1. *trans.* To put into one's purse; to pocket. Also with *up*. Now *rare*. †2. *fig.* To pocket (an affront); to withdraw or keep back (a boast); to take possession of, shut up -1691. 3. *trans.* To draw together (the lips, brow, etc.) in wrinkles or puckers, like the drawn-in mouth of a purse. Often with *up* 1604. b. *intr.* and *absol.* To become wrinkled, to pucker 1709. 4. *trans.* To close *up* like a purse (*rare*) 1823. †5. To steal purses, to rob -1616. 6. *U.S. trans.* To draw a purse-seine into the shape of a bag so as to close it.

1. I never p. one penny of it 1659. 2. *Ant. & Cl.* II. ii. 192. 3. Their Action is only to p. up the Mouth, as in whistling and blowing 1746. 5. I'll p.; if that raise me not, I'll bet at bowling-alleys BEAUM. & FLETCHER. Hence **Pu·rsing** *vbl. sb.* (also attrib.) and *ppl. a.*, as **pursing-block, -gear, -line, -weight,** the block, etc., used in working a purse-seine.

Pu·rse-bea:rer. ME. 1. The carrier of a purse; one who has charge of the money of another or of a company; a treasurer, bursar. 2. *spec.* The official who carries the Great Seal in front of the Lord Chancellor in a receptacle called 'purse' or 'burse' 1688. 3. A marsupial 1851.

Pu·rse-proud, *a.* 1681. Proud of wealth; puffed up on account of one's wealth. So **Pu·rse-pride** 1606.

Purser (pɒ̄·ɹsəɹ). ME. [f. PURSE *sb.* + -ER [1].] †1. A maker of purses -1638. †2. An officer charged with managing money matters and keeping accounts. *Obs.* in gen. sense. -1816. b. The officer on board a ship who keeps the accounts, and usu. has charge of the provisions 1458. c. In Cornwall, the treasurer of a mine, esp. one worked on the cost-book principle 1832. Hence **Pu·rsership.**

Pu·rse-string. late ME. Usu. in *pl.*: The two threaded strings by drawing which the mouth of a purse is closed; hence *fig.*

Phr. *To hold the purse-strings*, to control the expenditure of money. *To tighten* or *loosen the purse-strings*, to be sparing, or generous, in spending money. *attrib.* **purse-string suture** (*Surgical*), a suture running in and out.

Pursiness (pɒ̄·ɹsinės). late ME. [f. PURSY *a.*[1] + -NESS.] Short-windedness, dyspnœa.

Pursive (pɒ̄·ɹsiv), *a. arch.* late ME. [a. AF. *porsif*, app. var. of OF. *polsif*, mod.F. *poussif*, f. OF. *polser* to breathe with labour or difficulty:—L. *pulsare*, freq. of *pellere* to drive.] Short-winded, broken-winded, asthmatic; orig. said esp. of a horse. **Pu·rsiveness** = prec.

Purslane (pɒ̄·ɹslĕn). late ME. [a. OF. *porcelaine* = It. *porcellana*; altered from L. *porcil(l)aca*, used for the more usual L. *portulaca.*] 1. A low succulent herb, *Portulaca oleracea*, used in salads, and sometimes as a pot-herb, or for pickling. Also called *Common* or *Garden P.* 2. With qualification, denoting other species of *Portulaca* 1578.

2. **Crimson-flowered P.**, *Portulaca Thellussoni.* **Red-flowered P.**, *Portulaca splendens.* **Yellow-flowered P.**, *Portulaca aurea.* **Sea-P.**, *Atriplex portulacoides*, and *Arenaria peploides.* **Water-P.**, *Peplis Portula*, and *Isnardia palustris.*

Comb. **p.-tree**, a S. African shrub, *Portulacaria afra.*

Pursual (pɒ̄ɹsiū·ăl). *rare.* 1814. [f. PURSUE *v.* + -AL.] The action or fact of pursuing; pursuance.

Pursuance (pɒ̄ɹsiū·ăns). 1596. [f. as PURSUANT; see -ANCE.] †1. = PURSUIT I. 2. -1693. 2. = PURSUIT II. 1. (Now with *end, object*, or the like.) 1640. 3. The action of following out (a process); continuation, prosecution 1605. 4. The action of proceeding in accordance with a plan, direction, or order; prosecution, following out, carrying out 1660.

2. To start in p. of that object 1878. 3. In p. of some train of thought 1859. 4. When they reached London in p. of their little plan DICKENS.

Pursuant (pɒ̄ɹsiū·ănt), *sb.* and *a.* [Late ME. a. OF. *por-*, *poursuiant*, *poursuir* to PURSUE.] †A. *sb.* One who prosecutes an action (at law); a suitor; a prosecutor -1657. B. *adj.* †1. Prosecuting (in a court of law) -1543. 2. With *to*, rarely *upon*: Following upon, consequent on and conformable to; in accordance with. *Obs.* exc. as in b. 1648. b. quasi-*adv.* = PURSUANTLY 1675. 3. Going in pursuit; following after, pursuing 1691.

2. If..the fine is levied p. to the deed CRUISE. b. P. to our method..we have concluded it necessary 1675. Hence **Pursu·antly** *adv.* in a way that is p. or consequent *to.*

Pursue (pɒ̄ɹsiū·), *v.* [ME. a. AF. *pursiwer*, *pursuer* = OF. *porsieure*, *porsiure*, mod. F. *poursuivre* :—L. *prosequere*, *persequere*, pop. forms of *prosequi* and *persequi.*] I. *trans.* 1. To follow with hostility or enmity; to seek to injure (a person); to persecute; to harass, worry, torment. Now *rare* or *Obs.* exc. as in 2. †b. To follow with punishment -1697. 2. To follow with intent to capture or kill; to chase, hunt. late ME. 3. To prosecute in a court of law, to sue (a person). Chiefly *Sc.* 1580. 4. To follow, as an attendant; to come after in order, or in time. Now *rare* or *Obs.* 1470. b. To follow the course of (in description, etc.); to trace. *poet.* 1697. 5. To sue for, to seek after; to aim at. late ME. †6. To seek to attain to, to make one's way to -1681. 7. To follow (a path, way, course); to proceed along. Now chiefly *fig.* late ME. 8. To proceed in compliance or accordance with. Now only with *method, plan*, and the like. late ME. 9. To follow up (a course of action, etc. begun) 1456. b. *Law.* To carry on (an action); to lay (information); to present (a libel). Chiefly *Sc.* late ME. 10. To follow as an occupation or profession; to make a pursuit of 1523.

1. Those may justly be pursued as enemies to the community of nature JOHNSON. b. *Meas. for M.* v. i. 109. 2. P. and take him, for there is none to deliuer him BIBLE (Genev.) *Ps.* lxxi. 11. *fig.* The cold still pursued me BORROW. 5. He pursued Pleasure more than Ambition STEELE. 7. We too far the pleasing Path p. DRYDEN. 8. As we were going to p. this advice SMOLLETT. 9. The subject was pursued no farther JANE AUSTEN. 10. He persued..his studies..without persecution 1779.

II. *absol.* and *intr.* 1. To go in chase or pursuit ME. b. *To p. after* = sense I. 2. late ME. 2. To sue in a court of law; to make suit as plaintiff or pursuer. In later use chiefly *Sc.* late ME. 3. To continue (to do or say something); to go on (speaking). Also with *on.* 1500.

1. The wicked flee when no man pursueth *Prov.* xxviii. 1. Hence **Pursu·ingly** *adv.*

Pursuer (pɒ̄ɹsiū·əɹ). late ME. [f. prec. + -ER [1].] One who pursues; *spec. Civil* and *Sc. Law*, a suitor; a plaintiff, a petitioner; a prosecutor.

Pursuit (pɒ̄ɹsiū·t). late ME. [a. AF. *purs(e)ute*, OF. *por-*, *poursuite*, deriv. of *poursuivre*, after *suite* (:—pop.L. **sequita*) from *suivre.*] I. †1. Persecution, annoyance -1639. 2. The action of pursuing a fleeing object, as a hunted animal or an enemy. late ME. †3. The action of suing or entreating; a suit, request, petition, instance -1701. 4. *Law.* An action at law; a suit; prosecution. In later use chiefly *Sc.* late ME.

2. Each that passed that way Did join in the p. COWPER. *In p.* (*of*), said of the pursuer; *in p.* formerly sometimes of the pursued, = in flight.

II. 1. The action of seeking, or striving to obtain, attain, or accomplish something; search; †endeavour, attempt (*to do* something) 1606. b. *transf.* The object aimed at; aim 1592. 2. The action of following or engaging in something, as a profession, business, recreation, etc.; that which one engages in or follows 1529. †3. The pursuing *of* a plan, etc. -1655. †4. A continuation, a sequel -1725.

1. You may hear men talk as if the p. of wealth was the business of life J. H. NEWMAN. b. Be love my youth's p., and science crown my Age GRAY. 2. In our daily pursuits 1862. 4. I return now to the p. of our voyage DE FOE.

Pursuivant (pɒ̄·ɹswivănt), *sb.* [Late ME. a. OF. *por-*, *poursivant*, pr. pple. of *pours(u)ivre*, also used subst.] 1. Formerly, A junior heraldic officer attendant on the heralds; also one attached to a particular nobleman. Now, an officer of the College of Arms, ranking below a Herald. Also *p. at* (*of*) *arms.* †2. A royal or state messenger with power to execute warrants; a warrant-officer -1823. †b. *transf.* and *fig.* = 'messenger' -1631. 3. A follower; an attendant 1513.

1. Pursevantes and herauldes That crien ryche folkes laudes CHAUCER. 2. b. That great pursueaunt, Johan Baptist 1530. Hence †**Pu·rsuivant** *v. trans.* to send a p. after; to summon or arrest by a p.

Pursy (pɒ̄·ɹsi), *a.*[1] 1440. [Later form of *pursif* PURSIVE.] 1. = PURSIVE. 2. Fat, corpulent 1576.

2. *fig. Haml.* III. iv. 153.

Pursy (pɒ̄·ɹsi), *a.*[2] 1552. [f. PURSE *sb.* + -Y [1].] 1. Of cloth, the skin, etc.: Having puckers, puckered; drawn together like a purse-mouth. 2. Having a full purse; wealthy; purse-proud 1602.

Purtenance (pɒ̄·ɹtĭnăns). *arch.* [ME. a. AF. **purtinaunce*, for OF. *pertinance* PERTI-

NENCE.] That which pertains or appertains, or forms an appendage, to that which is the principal thing. †1. *Law.* That which pertains or is an appendage to a possession or estate –1525. 2. The 'inwards' of an animal 1440.

Purulence (piūᵊ·rĭ̆ŭlĕns). 1597. [ad. post-cl. L. *purulentia*, f. *purulentus* PURULENT; see -ENCE.] **a.** The fact of being purulent; the formation of pus; suppuration, festering. **b.** Purulent matter, pus. So **Pu·rulency,** the quality or state of being purulent.

Purulent (piūᵊ·rĭ̆ŭlĕnt), *a.* 1597. [ad. L. *purulentus*, f. *pus, pur-* PUS; see -LENT.] **1.** Consisting of, of the nature of, or resembling pus, or corrupt matter; also *gen.* corrupt, putrid (*rare*). **2.** Full of, forming, or discharging pus; suppurating, festering 1615. **b.** Characterized by or accompanied with the formation of pus 1834. Hence **Pu·rulent-ly** *adv.*, **-ness.**

Purvey (pɒ̈ɪvēⁱ·), *v.* [ME. a. AF. *por-, purveier*:—L. *providere* to PROVIDE, f. *pro-* for + *videre* to see.] **I.** †**1.** *trans.* = PROVIDE *v.* II. 1. –1548. †**2.** *intr.* To take measures, arrange, or prepare beforehand. Const. *inf.* or *that.* –1612. †**3.** To make provision for some event or action, or for the supply of something needed. Const. *for, of.* –1658. **II. 1.** *trans.* To provide, furnish, supply (something) ME. **b.** Now in ref. to articles of food, and as the act of a purveyor ME. †**2.** = To furnish or supply (a person) *with* something –1843. **3.** *intr.* To furnish or procure material necessaries or the like; to act as purveyor; *esp.* to make provision *for* a person, his needs, etc. 1440. **b.** Const. *to* (*rare*). late ME.

1. Get thy wounds healed, p. thee a better horse SCOTT. **b.** Purueying victuals for her nourishment 1576. 3. Purveying for the troops 1872. **b.** Their turpitude purveys to their malice BURKE. Hence **Purvey·able** *a.* (*rare*) provident; procurable.

Purveyance (pɒ̈ɪvēⁱ·ăns). [ME. a. OF. *por-, purvea(u)nce*:—L. *providentia*; see PROVIDENCE. Subseq. conformed to prec. vb.] †**1.** = PROVIDENCE 1, 2, 3. –1607. **2.** The providing (of some necessary), *esp.* the purveying of victuals. late ME. **3.** *spec.* The requisition and collection of victuals, etc., as a right or prerogative; *esp.* the right formerly appertaining to the crown of buying whatever was needed for the royal household at a price fixed by the PURVEYOR, and of exacting the use of horses and vehicles for the king's journeys ME. †**4.** That which is purveyed; a supply, stock, provision –1599.

Purveyor (pɒ̈ɪvēⁱ·əɪ). ME. [a. AF. *purveür, -our*, mod.F. *pourvoyeur*, f. OF. *porveeir*, to PURVEY; see -OR.] †**1.** One who makes preparation or prearrangement; a manager, director, steward –1448. **2.** One who procures or supplies anything necessary, or something specified, *to* or *for* others. In *commercial use*, One who makes it his business to provide victuals, etc., esp. luncheons, dinners, etc., on a large scale. ME. **b.** An official charged with the supply of requisites or of some necessary to a garrison, army, city, or the like 1475. **3.** A domestic officer who made purveyance of necessaries, transport, and the like for the sovereign (*king's* or *queen's p.*), or for some other great personage. Also *transf.* one who exacts supplies or contributions. Now *Hist.* late ME.

Purview (pɒ̈·ɪviu). 1442. [a. AF. *purview* provided = OF. *porveu*; see PURVEY. The word was used in the AF. statutes (*a*) in the phrase *purveu est* 'it is provided', and (*b*) *purveu que* 'provided that'; hence as sb., the provision or proviso.] **1.** The body of a statute, following next after the preamble, and beginning with the words 'Be it enacted'; the enacting clauses; hence, the provision, scope, or intention of an act or bill 1461. †**b.** A provisional clause; a proviso –1755. **2.** By extension, The scope or limits of any document, statement, scheme, subject, book, etc.; also, the range, sphere, or field of a person's labour or occupation 1788. **3.** Infl. by VIEW: Range of vision, physical or mental; outlook; contemplation, consideration 1837.

2. The objects of instruction, so far as they lie within the p. of a school-teacher 1881.

Pus (pɒs). 1541. [a. L. *pus*, stem *pur-*; cf. PURULENT.] *Path.* A yellowish-white, opaque, somewhat viscid matter, produced by suppuration; it consists of a colourless fluid in which white corpuscles are suspended. Also *attrib.*

Puseyism (piū̆·zi,iz'm). 1838. [f. name of E. B. *Pusey* (1800–82), professor of Hebrew and Canon of Christ Church at Oxford + -ISM.] A hostile term for the theological and ecclesiastical principles and doctrines of Pusey and those with whom he was associated in the 'Oxford Movement' for the revival of Catholic doctrine and observance in the Church of England. Now chiefly *Hist.* So **Pu·seyist** = PUSEYITE; also **Puseyi·stic, -al** *a.* of or pertaining to P. or Puseyites.

Puseyite (piū̆·zi,əit). 1838. [f. as prec. + -ITE.] A follower of Pusey; a supporter or promoter of Puseyism. Also *attrib.* or as *adj.* Hence **Puseyi·tical** *a.*

Push (puʃ), *sb.*[1] 1563. [f. PUSH *v.*] **I.** An act of pushing; a shove, thrust; †a blow, stroke, knock 1582. **b.** *spec.* in *Billiards.* A stroke in which the ball is pushed instead of being struck with the cue, or in which the cue, the cue ball, and the object ball are all in contact at the time the stroke is made; also, in *Cricket* and *Golf*, a push-stroke 1873. **c.** *fig.* An exertion of influence to promote a person's advancement by one who is 'at his back' 1655. **2.** A thrust of a weapon, or of the horn of a beast 1577. †**3.** An attack, a vigorous onset. Also *fig.* –1800. **4.** An effort, a vigorous attempt; a turn, bout, 'go' 1596. **b.** A determined advance; in phr. *to make a p.* Const. *at* or *for.* 1803. **5.** Pressure; *esp.* in *Building*, the thrust of an arch or the like 1715. **6.** *fig.* The pressure of affairs or circumstances; the condition of being 'pushed'; a case or time of stress or urgency; an extremity, a 'pinch' 1570. **7.** Determined effort to get on; enterprise, esp. that which is inconsiderate of the rights of others 1855.

1. **c.** It is money or 'push' which secured the place that should have been awarded to merit 1889. 4. Phr. *At one p., at the first p., to make a p.* (*at, for, to do* something). **b.** Making a 'push' of 400 miles 1828. 7. Like what is called 'push' in a practical man, Sidney Smith's style goes straight to its object 1855.

II. Concrete senses. **1.** A 'press' of people; a crowd, throng. Now *rare* exc. as *slang.* 1718. **2.** *slang.* A 'crowd' or band of thieves; a gang of convicts at penal labour; *esp.* in *Australia*, A gang of larrikins; hence, Any company or party; a 'crowd', 'set', 'lot' 1884. **4.** A contrivance which is pushed or pressed in order to operate a mechanism; as in *bell-p.* 1889.

Push (puʃ), *sb.*[2] *Obs.* exc. *dial.* late ME. [Origin obsc.] A pustule, pimple, boil.

Push (puʃ), *v.* ME. [a. F. *pousser*, with palatalization of *s* (cf. *brush*, etc.); in OF. *po(u)lser*:—L. *pulsare*, freq. of *pellere.*] **I.** Of physical action. **1.** *trans.* To exert force upon or against (a body) so as to move it away; to move by such exertion of force; to shove, thrust, drive (opp. to *draw* or *pull*). **b.** with an adverb or advb. phr., e. g. *to p. back, down*, etc. 1450. **c.** To drive or repulse by force of arms; to drive in the chase 1634. **d.** To move (a force) against opposition or difficulty 1748. **e.** *absol.* 1735. **f.** *trans.* or *absol.* in *Billiards.* To make a push-stroke 1873. **g.** (*absol.*) *P. off.* Of a person in a boat (and *transf.* of the boat): To push oneself away from the bank or the like; to shove off; hence (*slang*), to go away. 1726. **h.** *intr.* To sit abaft an oar and propel a boat with forward strokes. **2.** To thrust with a pointed weapon, stick, or the like (const. *at*); to tilt, fence; to use a spear, short sword, poniard, etc. *Obs.* or *arch.* 1599. **3.** To thrust or butt with the horns; chiefly biblical. Also *trans.* Now *dial.* 1535. **4.** *trans.* To thrust (a weapon); to thrust (a limb, organ, root, etc.) into some position; to put (anything) out in a projecting manner 1692. **5.** To thrust *out*, stick *out* (an organ or part). Of a plant: To send forth (a shoot, runner, root); also, to put *forth* (fruit). 1614. **b.** *intr.* To stick out, project. Of a plant or stem: To shoot out or grow; to sprout, bud. 1720. **6.** To exert pressure upon something in the way described in 1. 1613. **7.** To make one's way with force or persistence; esp. in *to p. on*, to press forward 1718. **b.** *To p. one's way*, to make one's way by thrusting obstacles or opponents aside 1781.

1. The tram. .is sometimes pushed by the boy, and sometimes pulled by a pony 1893. **b.** She turned the key and pushed open the door 1898. **c.** After we had thus pushed the enemy's cavalry DE FOE. **d.** Henry pushed his scouts along the road towards Windsor 1879. 2. As manhood shal compound: p. home SHAKS. 3. If the ox shall p. a manservant or a maidservant *Exod.* xxi. 32. 4. Some. .weeds. .p. their roots among the stones 1765. 5. To encourage the plants to p. fresh roots 1849. 6. We may as well p. against Powles as stirre 'em SHAKS. 7. Cæsar, after a short rest, pushed on and came under their walls FROUDE.

II. Of action other than physical. **1.** *intr.* To put forth vigorous effort or endeavour; to press; to aim *at* with endeavour to attain; to press *for*; to seek actively, labour *after.* Now *rare.* 1595. **2.** *trans.* To urge, press, impel (a person, etc.) *to do* something, or *to* some course; to urge or egg *on* 1578. **3.** To impel (a horse, etc.) to greater speed; *spec.* to urge (it) forward beyond its natural speed or endurance; also in ref. to other animals, a steamship, etc. 1727. **b.** To force (a thing) into more intense action. Now *rare.* 1756. **4.** To press forward, press with vigour (some action or operation); to urge, press (a claim, etc.) 1611. **b.** Phr. *To p. one's fortune*, to engage actively in making one's fortune 1657. **c.** To extend operations vigorously forward in space, or to more distant places 1842. **5.** To carry out (a matter, action, principle, etc.) to a farther point, or to the farthest limit 1713. **6.** To advance or try to advance or promote; to press the adoption, use, practice, sale, etc. of (a thing); to exert oneself for the advancement of (a person); also with *forward, on* 1714. **b.** To press (something) *on* or *upon* a person for attention, acceptance, or adoption 1723. **7.** To press or bear hard upon (a person) in dealing with him; *esp.* in *passive*, To be hard pressed or put to straits, as by lack of time, means, etc.; often with *for* 1761.

1. The manner in which the manufacturers 'pushed' for orders 1844. 2. Wild-Beasts. .pushed on to fight 1730. 4. Since the churchmen pushed on so wicked a business 1720. **c.** They pushed their trade to still more distant parts 1872. 5. *To p. through*, to press or carry by force to a conclusion. 6. Pushing the sale of British goods 1888. **b.** Physicians are too apt to p. their prescriptions upon the healthy 1869. 7. I'm a little pushed for time 1890.

Push-, stem of PUSH *v.*, or PUSH *sb.*[1], in comb.

a. General: in the senses (*a*) moved or actuated by a push, or by pushing, as *p.-pick, -tap*, etc.; (*b*) used for pushing, communicating a push, as *p.-pedal, -rod*, etc. **b.** Special: **p.-ball,** a game in which a very large ball is pushed by the hands and bodies of the players towards the opponents' goal; also *attrib.*; **-barred** *a.* (*Billiards*), in which a PUSH is barred or forbidden; **-bike** (*colloq.*), = *push-cycle*; **-car** *U.S.* (*a*) a hand-car; (*b*) a bogie car used to connect an engine with a train which is on a ferry-boat; (*c*) a plate-layers' trolley; **-cart,** a hand-cart or perambulator; **-chair,** a conveyance for a child, of the form of a chair on wheels, propelled by hand; **-cycle** (*colloq.*), a pedal-propelled bicycle as dist. from a motor-cycle; so **-cyclist; -stroke,** in *Billiards, Cricket, Golf*, etc. a stroke in which the ball is pushed instead of being hit.

Pusher (pu·ʃəɪ). 1591. [f. PUSH *v.* + -ER[1].] One who or that which pushes (*lit.* and *fig.*). Also in various techn. uses.

attrib.: **p. aeroplane,** one in which the propeller is behind the pilot; called also **p.** 1914.

Pushful (pu·ʃfŭl), *a.* 1896. [f. PUSH *sb.*[1] + -FUL.] Full of 'push' (see PUSH *sb.*[1] I. 7); active and energetic in prosecuting one's affairs; self-assertive; aggressively enterprising. Hence **Pu·shful-ly** *adv.*, **-ness.**

Pu·shing, *ppl. a.* 1692. [f. PUSH *v.* + -ING[2].] **a.** Thrusting, shoving, driving 1693. **b.** *fig.* That pushes forward; enterprising, keen to do business; also, self-assertive, officious 1692. Hence **Pu·shing-ly** *adv.*, **-ness.**

Push-pin (pu·ʃpin). 1588. [f. PUSH- + PIN *sb.*[1]] A child's game, in which each player pushes his pin with the object of crossing that of another player. **b.** *fig.* Child's play 1672. **c.** *U.S.* A drawing-pin.

‖**Pushtu** (pɒ·ʃtū̆), *sb.* and *a.* 1815. [a. Pers. *paṣ̌tō*, Afghan *păχtō.*] The native name of the language of the Afghans.

Pusillanimity (piū̆:silæni·mĭti). late ME. [a. F. *pusillanimité*, ad. eccl. L. *pusillanimitas*,

f. *pusillanimis*; see next.] The quality or character of being pusillanimous; pettiness of spirit; cowardliness, timidity.

Pusillanimous (piū̆silæ·nimǝs), *a.* 1586. [f. eccl. L. *pusillanimis* (tr. Gr. ὀλιγόψυχος), f. *pusillus* very small + *animus* soul, mind + -OUS.] **1.** Lacking in courage and strength of mind; faint-hearted, mean-spirited, cowardly. **2.** Of qualities, actions, etc.: Proceeding from or manifesting a want of courage 1611.

1. Where didst thou learne to be so agueish, so p.? MILT. 2. Excuses..for a conduct so p. 1797. Hence **Pusilla·nimous-ly** *adv.*, **-ness**.

Puss (pus). 1530. [Etym. unkn.; perh. orig. a call to attract a cat.] **1.** A conventional proper name of a cat; usu., a call-name. **b.** A nursery or pet-name for 'cat' 1605. **2.** Quasi-proper name for: **a.** A hare 1668; **b.** A tiger 1837. **3.** Used playfully of a girl or woman, as a term of endearment, often connoting slyness 1610. **4.** Short for PUSS-MOTH 1819.

P. in the corner, a game played by children, of whom one stands in the centre and tries to capture one of the 'dens' or 'bases' as the others change places; also, a sailors' game in the British Navy.

Pu·ss-cat. 1565. = PUSSY-CAT.

Pussley, -ly (pɒ·sli). 1861. A corruption of PURSLANE, common in U.S.

Pu·ss-moth. 1806. [f. PUSS + MOTH, from its downy appearance.] A large European bombycid moth, *Dicranura vinula*, having the fore-wings of a whitish or light grey colour with darker markings and spots.

Pussy (pu·si). 1583. [f. PUSS + -Y 6.] **1.** A cat: used much in the same way as PUSS 1726. **2.** A proper name for the hare 1785. **3.** Applied to a girl or woman 1583. **4.** In nursery use, anything soft and furry, as a fur necklet, a willow or hazel catkin, etc. 1858. Hence **Pu·ssy-cat**, nursery name for a cat.

Comb. **p.-willow** *U.S.*, any willow having silky catkins, esp. the American *Salix discolor* 1869.

Pu·ssy-foot, *v. U.S.* 1905. [f. prec.] *intr.* To tread softly or lightly; to proceed stealthily. Hence **Pu·ssyfoot** *sb.*, nickname of W. E. Johnson (1862–), American prohibition lecturer; hence, an advocate or supporter of prohibition; also *attrib.* and allusively 1919. **Pu·ssy-footer, -footing** *vbl. sb.* and *ppl. a.*

He pussy-footed in and got his things out 1919.

Pustulant (pɒ·stiŭlănt), *a.* and *sb.* 1871. [ad. late L. *pustulantem*, *pustulare* to PUSTULATE.] (An irritant) giving rise to the formation of pustules.

Pustular (pɒ·stiŭlăɪ), *a.* 1739. [ad. mod. L. *pustularis*, f. *pustula* PUSTULE; see -AR.] **1.** Of, pertaining to, of the nature of pustules; characterized by pustules. **2.** *Bot.* and *Zool.* Having low glandular excrescences like blisters or pustules 1776.

Pustulate (pɒ·stiŭlět), *a.* 1607. [ad. late L. *pustulatus*; see next.] Furnished with, or having pustules; pustulous, pustular.

Pustulate (pɒ·stiŭleᶦt), *v.* 1732. [f. late L. *pustulat-*, *pustulare*, f. *pustula* PUSTULE.] **a.** *trans.* To form into pustules. **b.** *intr.* To form pustules. Hence **Pustula·tion,** formation of pustules; occas., also, blistering.

Pustule (pɒ·stiul). late ME. [ad. L. *pustula.*] **1.** A small rounded elevation of the cuticle, with erosion of the cutis, inflammatory at the base and containing pus; a pimple; formerly, occas., a blister. **b.** *Malignant p.*, the carbuncular disease produced by the anthrax bacillus 1864. **2.** *Bot.* A small wart or swelling, natural or caused by parasitic influences. **b.** *Zool.* A warty excrescence of the skin, as in the toad; a pimple. 1776. **3.** *transf.* An eruptive swelling of the ground 1849.

Pustulous (pɒ·stiŭlǝs), *a.* 1543. [ad. post-cl. L. *pustulosus*, f. *pustula*; see -OUS.] Abounding in or characterized by pustules.

‖**Puszta** (pu·stă). 1842. [Magyar.] The Hungarian prairie land.

Put (put), *sb.*¹ ME. [f. PUT *v.*] An act of putting. **1.** An act of thrusting or pushing; a push. Now *dial.* late ME. **2.** The act of casting a heavy stone or weight overhand, as a trial of strength ME. **3.** *Stock-jobbing*, etc. The option of delivering a specified amount of a particular stock or produce at a certain price within a specified time: see OPTION 4. 1717.

Put, *sb.*²: see PUTT.

Put(t (pɒt), *sb.*³ *Obs.* or *arch.* 1680. [app. f. PUT *v.*] An old game at cards for two, three, or four players, somewhat resembling nap, three cards being dealt to each player; the score at this game.

Put (pɒt), *sb.*⁴ *Obs.* or *arch.* 1688. [Origin unkn.] A stupid man, blockhead, 'duffer'; *country p.*, a lout, a bumpkin (*slang* or *colloq.*).

Put (put), *v.*¹ Pa. t. and pple. **put** (put). [Late OE. **putian*; thence early ME. *puten*, later *putte(n*, *putt*, *put.*] **I.** To thrust, push, and allied senses. †**1.** *trans.* To thrust, push, shove; to knock –1440. **b.** To butt with the head or horns. Now *n. dial.* late ME. †**c.** *absol.* or *intr.* To give a push or knock; to push, knock (*at*, *on*, etc.) –1785. **2.** *trans.* To propel (a stone or weight) mainly by the swing of the body from the right hand raised and placed close to the shoulder: as an athletic exercise. Usu. in phr. *putting the stone* (*shot*, *weight*). ME. **3.** To thrust or plunge (a weapon) †*home* or *into* a body; to drive or send (a missile) *through* ME. **4.** *Coal-mining.* To propel (a tram or barrow of coal), orig. by pushing behind; now also by means of a pony, a stationary engine, etc. Also *absol.* 1708. †**5.** *Naut.* Of the wind or a storm: To drive or cast (a ship) on or from shore, to sea, etc. –1780. **6.** To launch (persons, a boat, a fleet, etc.). Now chiefly *p. off, out.* 1470. **7.** *Naut. intr.* To set out, set forth, proceed, take one's course (to sea, into harbour, etc.) 1590. **b.** To set out; to start; to pass, make one's way. *Obs.* exc. *U.S. colloq.*, to make off, be off, 'clear out'. late ME. †**c.** Of a stream, etc.: To make its way, to flow (*into* or *out of* a larger piece of water). *U.S.* Also of sap: to flow (in some direction). –1807. **8.** Of a plant: To shoot out or grow; to sprout, bud. Now *dial.* 1615.

3. *To p. a knife into*, to stab; *to p. a bullet through*, to shoot. 5. One..on her voyage was put ashore at Black Sod 1780. 7. *Erin*..was among the first vessels to p. down the bay this morning 1899. 8. The roots of trees do some of them p. downwards deep into the ground BACON.

II. To move (a thing or person) physically into or out of some place or local position. **a.** *trans.* To move (a thing) so as to place it in some situation; to place, lay, set ME. **b.** To remove, send away; to turn away or divert *from*. *Obs.* or *arch.* ME. **c.** To place (a garment, etc.) *on*, *upon* (also †*off*) the body. late ME. **d.** *spec.* To place upon or affix *to* a writing or document (a title, seal, signature, etc.) 1449. **e.** To harness (a draught animal) *to* a vehicle; to place *in* the shafts of a cart, etc. 1565. **f.** To introduce (a male animal *to* a female, or vice versa) for breeding 1523. **g.** To convey (a person, etc.) across a river, etc.; to set down on the other side 1649. **h.** *Stock-jobbing.* To deliver (stock or produce) at a specified price within a specified time 1814. **i.** with abstract obj. late ME.

a. This Figure, that thou heere seest put, It was for gentle Shakespeare cut B. JONS. P. your Hand to your Heart and tell me fairly 1699. P. about an ounce of butter into a frying-pan 1756. *To stay put* (U.S.), to remain in one's or its place. c. Bring foorth the best robe, and p. it on him *Luke* xv. 22. d. To this number..I also put my initials J. H. NEWMAN. i. Your Excellencies..conduct..has..put new lives into the Ministers 1707. The thing had been put before her in such vivid reality 1889. Phr. *To p. it across*, to administer chastisement or rebuke to.

III. To place or bring (a thing or person) in or into some condition, state, mode, or form. **1.** To place (a thing or person) *in* or *into* the hands or power of, *in* or *under* the care of a person. late ME. †**b.** To place with (a person); to apprentice *to* –1772. **2.** To place, set, or cause to be in some place or position, in a general or figurative sense, or when the name of a thing or place stands for its purpose, as *to p.* a person *to bed, to school, in prison*, etc. late ME. **3.** To place with or in, by way of addition; to add. Const. *to*, *in*. late ME. **4.** To place, insert, or enter (a name or an item) in a list, account, or table. Now usu. *p. down*. 1513. **5.** To place (a thing or person) in a scale of estimation or a classification. late ME. **6.** †To convert or change *into* something else; *esp.* to translate or render *into* another language or form of expression. late ME. **b.** To express (something) *in* spoken or written words; to turn *into* speech or writing ME. **c.** To express or state (in a particular way) 1699. **7.** To assign or attribute one thing to another in some relation. **a.** To assign or set (a quality, meaning, value, price) *on*, *upon*, *to* a thing. late ME. **b.** To assign or ascribe (a thing) to something else as cause, reason, or basis; to base, found, rest *upon* 1722. **8.** To apply *to* a use or purpose. late ME. **9.** To set mentally or conceptually *in the place of* (something else); to substitute (one thing) *for* another, in thought or expression 1483. **10.** To establish or introduce and bring to bear (a state, condition, relation, or alteration) *in*, *on*, or *to* an existing thing, action, or state of things. late ME. **b.** To place, repose (trust, confidence, etc.) *in* 1526. **11.** To commit (the fate of something) *to* a risk or hazard; to stake *on*, *upon* 1611. **b.** To invest or venture (one's money) in 1604. **c.** *To p. oneself on* or *upon*: to entrust or commit oneself to the ruling or verdict of 1660. **12.** To place before a person for consideration or answer; to propound (a question, supposition, etc.) ME. **b.** *spec.* To submit (a point for decision) formally to the vote of an assembly 1683. **c.** *To p. it*: to present a question, statement, etc. *to* a person for consideration or by way of appeal 1747. **13.** To impose (something) *on*, *upon* a person, etc. late ME. **b.** *absol.* *To p. upon*: †(*a*) to play a trick upon, befool; (*b*) to oppress, victimize. Chiefly in indirect passive. 1693. **14.** To lay the blame of (something) *on* or *upon*; to tax with; to charge *against*, impute *to*. late ME. **15.** To place *in*, bring *into*, or reduce (a person or thing) *to* some state or condition ME. **b.** With complement: To cause to be or become something; to make, render so-and-so. late ME. **16.** To subject (a person, etc.) *to* the suffering or endurance of something ME. **b.** *spec.* To subject (a piece of ground) to the plough, or to the raising of a particular crop. Const. *to*, *into*, *under* the crop, etc. 1845. **17.** To set (a person or animal) to do something, or upon some course of action. late ME. **b.** To set to learn, study, or practise. Const. *to*, †*on*, †*upon* (something). late ME. **c.** To direct or urge (a horse) towards something, esp. an obstacle to be cleared; also, to cause (a horse) to perform a particular pace, a leap, etc.; const. *to*, *at*, etc. 1589. **d.** To set (cattle) to feed upon; to restrict (a person) to a diet or regimen of. Const. *to*, *on*, *upon*. 1620. **18.** To force or drive (a person, etc.) to the performance of some action, e. g. of making a choice, etc. late ME. **b.** Const. *inf.* To oblige, compel, require *to do* something. *Obs.* or *arch.* 1603. **c.** *To p.* (a person) *to it*. (*a*) To force, urge, challenge, or call upon (him) to do what is indicated by the context. Chiefly *pass.* 1581. (*b*) *spec.* To force (one) to do one's utmost; to reduce to straits; to hamper or embarrass. Now always *pass.* 1603. †**19.** To posit, suppose, assume. With obj. cl. or simple obj. –1654. †**20.** To 'lay down'; to state, affirm as a fact –1607.

1. Will ye putte yourselfe nowe wholye into my handes? 1553. A very fine healthy young man put himself under my care 1843. 2. Having others put over their heads 1698. 3. P. no rum in thy tea 1849. 4. You are like to be put in the black List 1692. 5. *To p. at*, to estimate or price at; A circulation which a competent authority puts at three millions 1890. 6. b. Fables That..other poetes p. in ryme CHAUCER. c. A good story well put 1889. 7. a. Putting the best construction upon all men's words and actions 1708. 8. O glorious strength Put to the labour of a Beast MILT. 9. P. yourself in his place 1870. 10. *To p. an end, stop, period to*, to bring to an end, stop; so *to p. a stopper, veto on*, etc. b. P. not youre trust in prynces COVERDALE *Ps.* clxv[i]. 3. 11. *Cymb.* I. iv. 133. A Frenchman who had..put his money on Reluisant 1885. 12. *To p.* (*the*) *case*, to propound a hypothetical instance or illustration. b. The resolution was put and carried 1830. Let us p. it to the vote 1888. 13. If I p. any trickes vpon em SHAKS. The obligation he had put upon us DE FOE. She put herself upon him for a saint 1752. Putting upon you gifts of no real value 1825. 14. *Macb.* I. vii. 70. 15. *To p. at ease, at rest*; *to p. in doubt, fear, mind*; *to*

p. in (into) action, communication, force, motion, possession, shape; to p. on one's guard, one's honour, on oath, record, to rights, silence, sleep, in the wrong; see also the sbs. **b.** The least mistake..would p. the calculation all wrong 1892. **16.** *To p. to torture; to p. to death; to p. to ransom; to p. to expense, loss, trouble; to p. to the rack, the sword; to p. to confusion, shame; to p. upon one's trial*; see also the sbs. **17.** 'Tis they haue put him on the old mans death SHAKS. I suppose they'll p. me to herd the swine 1889. **c.** *To p. through*, to cause (a horse) to perform (a particular movement); *transf.* to cause (a person) to go through an exercise, course of study, etc.; Mr. Pumblechook then put me through my pence-table DICKENS. **18.** *To p. to flight*, etc.; see also the sbs. **c.** There is nothing a man of the world can't do when he 's put to it 1868. We were hard put to it..to get it done in so short a time DICKENS. **19.** P. that Christ did not dye for them 1626. **20.** As common bruite doth p. it SHAKS.

Comb. with adverbs in special senses. **Put about. a.** *Naut. trans.* To lay (a sailing vessel) on the opposite tack. Also *transf.* to cause (a horse, a body of men, etc.) to turn round so as to face in another direction. **b.** *Naut. absol.* or *intr.* To turn on to the other tack; to go about. Also *transf.* **c.** *trans.* To circulate, publish (a statement). **d.** To trouble; to distress. (Chiefly *Sc.* and *n. dial.*) **P. asunder.** *trans.* To separate. **P. away. a.** *trans.* To send away, get rid of; to reject; *spec.* to divorce. Somewhat *arch.* †**b.** To drive away, dispel; to put an end to. **c.** To stow away; also, to lay by for future use (money, etc.); = *put by*. **d.** *slang* or *colloq.* (*a*) To consume as food or drink; (*b*) to put in jail; (*c*) to pawn; (*d*) *dial.* to put in the grave. **P. back.** †**a.** *trans.* To repulse; to refuse, reject. **b.** To reduce to a lower position or condition; to retard, or check the advance of. **c.** To move (the hands of a clock) back; to set back; also *fig.* **d.** To defer; = *put off*. **e.** To restore to its former place or position. **f.** *Naut. intr.* To reverse one's course. **P. by. a.** *trans.* To thrust or set aside; to reject; to neglect. †**b.** To turn aside, avert (a blow, or *fig.* a calamity, etc.). Also *absol.* **c.** To turn aside, evade (a question, argument, etc.); to p. off (a person) with an excuse or evasion. †**d.** To divert *from* something. **e.** To lay aside (something out of use); to stow away; to lay by (money, etc.) for future use. **P. down. a.** *trans.* To suppress by force or authority; †to abolish. **b.** To depose from office, authority, or dignity; to dethrone, degrade. Somewhat *arch.* **c.** To 'take down'; to snub; to refute, put to silence. †**d.** To excel, surpass, 'beat' by comparison. **e.** To cease to keep up (something expensive). **f.** To write down; to enter in a written account, list, etc. **g.** *fig.* To account or reckon; to estimate *as, at*; to take *for*; to count or attribute *to*. **h.** To sink (a shaft, pit, etc.). **i.** *To p. one's foot down*: see FOOT *sb.* **P. forth. a.** *trans.* To stretch forth, extend (the hand or other member of the body, etc.). Now *rare* or *arch.* **b.** To set forth; *fig.* to display, exhibit. **c.** To set forth in words, propound. †**d.** To thrust, push, or send into view or prominence; to put out to service, etc.; *refl.* to come forward; to offer oneself. **e.** To put in operation; to exert (one's strength), lift up (one's voice). **f.** To issue, put in circulation. **g.** Of a plant: To send out (buds or leaves). Also *intr.* or *absol.* (*b*) *intr.* for *refl.* Of buds, leaves, etc.: To sprout out, shoot out, come out. †**h.** To lay out (money) to profit. **i.** *intr.* To start on one's way, esp. to sea; to make one's way forward. *arch.* **P. forward. a.** *trans.* To push into view or prominence. **b.** To advance for consideration or acceptance; to propound, advance, urge; to allege; to represent *as*. †**c.** *intr.* To press forward; to come forward. **P. in. a.** *trans.* To install in or appoint to an office or position; sometimes with mixture of literal sense, as *to p. in a caretaker, a bailiff*; so *to p. in a distress, an execution*. **b.** To present, or formally tender, as in a law court (a document, evidence, a plea, a claim, surety, an APPEARANCE, etc.). **c.** *intr.* To make a claim, plea, or offer; (*a*) to apply *for*; to enter *for*, bid *for*; (*b*) to plead or intercede *for* some one or something. **d.** *trans.* To drive in: (*a*) *Naut.* (a ship) into a port or haven; (*b*) *Falconry*. (the game) into covert. **e.** *intr.* To go in, enter. **f.** *trans.* To interpose (a blow, shot, etc.; a word or remark; also, the actual words); to get in (a word). *To p. in one's oar*: see OAR *sb.* 1. †**g.** *intr.* or *absol.* To intervene. **h.** *trans.* To 'throw in'; to insert as an addition or supplement. **i.** To perform (a piece of work, etc.) as part of a whole, or in the midst of other occupations. **j.** *colloq.* To pass, spend (a portion or period of time), usu. by means of some occupation. **P. off. a.** *trans.* To postpone to a later time; to defer. Also *absol.* **b.** To divest oneself (rarely another) of (clothes, etc.). †**c.** To dismiss, put away: (*a*) from one's mind; (*b*) from one's service or employment. **d.** To get rid of (as an importunate person or demand) by evasion or the like; to baffle by giving something less acceptable (const. *with*); *occas.*, to bid to wait. **e.** To divert *from* one's purpose; to hinder; to dissuade *from* doing something. Now usu. (without const.), to hinder (a person) from performing some act by diverting his attention or exciting his aversion. **f.** To pass, get through (time). *Obs.* or *dial.* **g.** To make to 'go off', to sell. Now *dial.* **h.** To pass off for what it is not; (now *rarely*) to palm off or foist upon some one. **i.** (*a*) *Naut. intr.* To leave the land; to start on a voyage; also, to leave a ship, as a boat. (*b*) To depart, make off. Now only *U.S.* (*c*) *trans.* To push off, send off (a boat) from the land, or from a ship. **P. on. a.** *trans.* To impose or inflict as a burden or charge. *To p. it on*, to add to the price, to overcharge. **b.** To don; to clothe oneself (or another) with. Also *fig.* in scriptural language; of a plant, to 'clothe itself' with (leaves or blossoms). †(*b*) *absol.* To put on one's hat, to 'be covered'. **c.** *fig.* To take upon oneself, assume (a character or quality, real or feigned). **d.** In mod. emphatic use: To assume deceptively or falsely; to affect, pretend. *To p. it on*, to pretend to something more than the fact. **e.** To add. (*a*) To develop additional (flesh or weight). (*b*) To add (so much) to the charge or price. (*c*) To add (runs, a goal, etc.) to the score. **f.** To lay, stake, bet (a sum of money). †**g.** To urge onward; to incite, impel; to promote (a state of things). †**h.** *intr.* To go faster; to push on; to go on, proceed. **i.** *trans.* To push forward (the hands of a clock, the time) so as to make it appear later. **j.** To bring into action or operation, as a brake, pressure, etc.; to apply; to exert. **k.** To set or appoint (a person) to do something; in *Cricket*, to set (a person) on to bowl; to set (a train, steamer, etc.) to make regular journeys or voyages; to lay (a hound) on the scent. **P. out.** *trans.* **a.** To thrust, drive, or send out of a place; to eject, turn out. (*b*) To blind (an eye), either by literally gouging it out or otherwise. (*c*) To put out of joint; to dislocate. **b.** To turn out of office, dignity, possession, etc.; to depose, dismiss. Now *rare* or *arch.*, exc. in sense 'to put out of play', in games, etc.; esp. in *Cricket*, to cause (a batsman) to be out. **c.** To extinguish, put an end to, destroy, abolish. **d.** To extinguish (fire, light, etc.). **e.** To disconcert, confuse, embarrass; (*b*) to distress, 'upset' (mentally); in mod. use, to put out of temper, annoy, vex; (*c*) to put to inconvenience. **e.** = *put forth* e. **f.** = *put forth* f. Now *rare*. **g.** (*a*) *Naut.* To send or take (a vessel) out to sea (*rare*). (*b*) *intr.* To go out to sea; to set out on a voyage. (*c*) To depart, make off; to set out. (Chiefly *U.S.*) **h.** To stretch forth, extend, protrude (the hand, etc.) to cause to stick out or project; to display, hang out. **i.** = *put forth* g. Now *rare*. **j.** (*a*) To place (a person) away from home under the care of some one, or in some employment; to turn out (a beast) to graze or feed; to plant out (seedlings, etc.). (*b*) To lend (money) at interest, or lay it out to profit. (*c*) To give (work) to be done off the premises, or by some one not in one's regular employment. **P. over.** orig. *U.S.* To secure a hearing for (a dramatic production); hence *gen.* to get accepted or favourably received. **P. through. a.** To cause to pass through any process; to carry (successfully) through; to get done with. (Chiefly *U.S.*) **b.** To place a person in telephonic connexion with another through one or more exchanges. **P. to.** †**a.** *trans.* To add (actually or mentally). Also *absol.* **b.** To exert, apply, put forth. *To p. one's hand to*: to set to work at something; to render assistance. Now *rare* or *arch.* **c.** To attach (a horse, etc.) to a vehicle; *transf.* (an engine) to a train. **d.** To shut. Now *arch.* and *dial.* **e.** *Naut. intr.* To put in to shore; to take shelter. **f.** *pass.* = *to be put to it*; see III. 18 c. **P. together. a.** To combine, unite (parts) into a whole; to join, e.g. in marriage. **b.** To form (a whole) by combination of parts. **c.** To combine mentally; to add together; often in *pa. pple.* taken together, collectively. *To p. this and that together*, to consider two facts together and draw a conclusion from them. So *to p. two and two together*: see TWO. **d.** *Cricket.* To make up, 'compile', as a score. **P. up. a.** *trans.* To raise; to lift; see also the sbs. BACK, HAIR, SHUTTER, etc. (*b*) To set up or mount (a person, esp. a jockey) on horseback, to employ as a jockey. (*c*) To put (a play, etc.) on the stage for performance. **b.** *Hunting.* To cause (game) to rise from cover. **c.** To raise in amount. **d.** *colloq.* To show, exhibit (a game, play); phr. *to p. up a good fight*. **e.** To offer (prayer or worship) to God or a divine being 'on high'; to present a petition to any exalted personage. **f.** To propose for election or adoption. (*b*) *trans.* (with mixture of lit. sense): To bring forward (a person) to stand up and speak. **g.** To hand in (a communication) to be published in a church in the course of the service; also, to publish (banns). **h.** To offer for sale by auction, or for competition. **i.** To place in a receptacle for safe keeping; to stow away; to pack up, do up, make up into a parcel, or place in small vessels, etc., so as to be ready for use. (*b*) To put into the sheath, to sheathe (a sword); also *absol.* *arch.* (*c*) To shut up, enclose (a beast for fattening, a meadow for hay). (*d*) To settle (any one) to rest or repose; to settle (a patient) in bed (*rare*). (*e*) To deposit, stake (a sum of money); to pay up. Also *absol.* orig. *U.S.* and *Colonial*. **j.** (*a*) To lodge and entertain (man or beast). (*b*) *intr.* for *refl.* or *pass.* To take up one's lodging, to 'stop' (at an inn, etc.). **k.** *fig.* †(*a*) *trans.* To 'pocket', submit to (an affront or injury). Now (*b*) *To p. up with*, to submit to (an injury), to suffer without resentment; in wider sense, To bear, endure, tolerate, do with (anything inconvenient or disagreeable). **l.** *trans.* *To p.* (a person) *up to* (colloq.): (*a*) To make conversant with or aware of; to inform of, instruct in (something, orig. some artifice or expedient). (*b*) To stir up, instigate (*to* some action, etc., or *to do* something). **m.** To erect, set up (a building, etc.); to construct, build. **n.** To concoct or plan in combination with others; to preconcert (a robbery or underhand piece of work): orig. and chiefly *Thieves' slang*.

Put, *v.*[2]: see PUTT *v.*

‖ **Putamen** (piutēⁱ·mėn). 1830. [L., f. *putare* to prune.] *Bot.* The endocarp of a fruit when hard and woody, as the 'stone' of a plum, etc.; rarely, the shell of a nut. **b.** *Anat.* A structure at the base of the brain 1890.

Putative (piū·tătiv), *a.* late ME. [a. F. *putatif*, or ad. late L. *putativus*, f. *putatus*, *putare* to think; -IVE.] That is such by supposition; reputed, supposed.

P. marriage, in *Canon law*, a marriage which though legally invalid was contracted in good faith by at least one of the parties. Hence **Pu·tatively** *adv.*

‖ **Putchuk, putchock** (pɒ·tʃɒ̆k). 1617. [Southern Hind. *pachak*; origin doubtful.] The root of the plant *Aplotaxis auriculata*, a native of Kashmir, used as a medicine and for making the Chinese joss-sticks.

Puteal (piū·tĭăl). 1850. [a. L. *puteal*, orig. neut. of *putealis*, f. *puteus* well.] *Rom. Antiq.* The stone curb surrounding a well.

Putid (piū·tid), *a.* Now *rare.* 1580. [ad. L. *putidus*, f. *putere* to stink; see -ID[1].] Foul, base; rotten or worthless. Hence **Puti·dity, Pu·tidness,** p. quality. **Pu·tidly** *adv.*

Putlog, putlock (pɒ·tlǫg, -lǫk). 1645. [Origin obsc.] One of the short horizontal timbers on which the scaffold-boards rest.

Pu·t-off. Pl. **put-offs.** 1549. [f. the phr. *put off*.] An act of putting off. **1.** An evasion, a shift. **2.** An act of postponing something; a putting a person off to a later time 1623.

Put-on, (stress var.), *ppl. a.* 1621. [pa. pple. of *to put on*.] *fig.* Assumed, affected, feigned, pretended.

Putrefaction (piūtrĭfæ·kʃən). late ME. [a. OF., or ad. L. *putrefactionem*, f. *putrefacere*, f. *putrere* + *facere*.] **1.** The action or process of putrefying; the decomposition of animal and vegetable substances, with its attendant loathsomeness of smell and appearance; rotting; corruption. **b.** Decomposition of tissues or fluids in a living body, as in ulceration, suppuration, or gangrene. late ME. †**2.** *Alchemy* and *Old Chem.* The disintegration of a substance by chemical or other action; also, the oxidation or corrosion of metals, etc. -1671. **3.** *concr.* Decomposed or putrid matter 1605. **4.** *fig.* Moral corruption and decay 1631.

Putrefactive (piūtrĭfæ·ktiv), *a.* late ME. [a. F. *putréfactif*, f. L. *putrefact-*; see -IVE.] **1.** Causing or inducing putrefaction; putrefying. **2.** Of, pertaining to, or characterized by putrefaction; indicative of putrefaction 1646.

2. *P. fermentation*, putrefaction scientifically viewed as a species of fermentation. Hence **Putrefa·ctiveness.**

Putrefy (piū·trĭfəi), *v.* late ME. [a. F. *putréfier*, ad. L. *putrefacere*, with ending -FY, as if from L. **putrificare*.] **1.** *trans.* To render putrid; to cause to rot or decay with a fetid smell. Now *rare*. †**b.** *Alchemy* and *Old Chem.* To decompose chemically; e.g. to oxidize -1651. **2.** *intr.* To become putrid; to decay with an offensive smell; to rot, 'go bad'. late ME. **b.** Of the tissues or fluids in a living body: To become putrid or gangrenous; to fester, suppurate 1500. **c.** *fig.* To become corrupt or decay morally, socially, etc. 1526.

1. They would but stinke, and putrifie the ayre SHAKS. **2. c.** The name of vnrighteous persons shall putrifie HOOKER. Hence **Pu·trefiable** *a.*

Putrescence (piutre·sěns). 1646. [f. L. *putrescentem*; see -ENCE.] The action or process of rotting or becoming putrid; incipient or advancing rottenness. **b.** *concr.* Putrescent matter 1843. **c.** *fig.*; esp. Moral rottenness 1840. So **Putre·scency,** the state of being putrescent.

Putrescent (piutre·sěnt), *a.* 1732. [ad. L. *putrescentem*, *putrescere*, inceptive of *putrere*.] **1.** Becoming putrid; in process of putrefaction. **2.** Of, pertaining to, or accompanying putrescence 1775.

1. P. manures 1834. **2.** We find game, in a p. state, eaten as a luxury 1849.

Putrescible (piutre·sĭb'l), *a.* 1797. [f. L. *putrescere* + -IBLE.] Liable to rot; subject to putrefaction. Hence **Putrescibi·lity.**

Putrescine (piutre·səin). 1887. [f. as prec. + -INE [5].] *Physiol. Chem.* One of the ptomaines or cadaveric alkaloids.

Putrid (piū·trid), *a.* 1598. [a. L. *putridus* rotten, f. *putrere* to rot, f. *puter, putr-* rotten.] **1.** Of organic bodies: Decomposed, rotten. **2.** Pertaining to, causing, proceeding from, accompanying, or infected with putrefaction; foul 1610. **3.** *fig.* (*a*) Morally, socially, or politically corrupt; æsthetically abominable. (*b*) Corrupting, noxious, noisome. 1628. (*c*) Of poor quality, 'rotten' (*slang*) 1902. †**4.** Of soil: Loose, friable –1780.

1. Stagnant sea-water, like fresh, soon grows p. GOLDSM. 2. *P. fever*, typhus fever. *P. sore throat*, gangrenous pharyngitis; sometimes applied to diphtheria. 3. In respect to electoral morality, Pontefract is p. 1893. Hence **Pu·trid·ly** *adv.*, **-ness.**

Putridity (piutri·dĭti). 1639. [f. as prec. + -ITY.] **1.** The condition of being putrid; rottenness. **b.** *fig.* Moral or metaphorical rottenness 1823. **2.** *concr.* Putrid matter 1790.

Putrilage (piū·triledʒ). 1657. [ad. L. *putrilago, -laginem* rottenness, f. *puter, putris.*] Putrid matter. Hence **Putrila·ginous** *a.*

Putt, put (pɒt), *sb.* 1743. [Differentiated f. PUT *sb.*[1]; orig. Sc.] *Golf.* An act of putting (see next 2); a gentle stroke given to the ball to make it roll along the putting-green, with the purpose of getting it into the hole.

Putt, put (pɒt), *v.* Pa. t. and pa. pple. **putted.** ME. [Differentiated f. PUT *v.*[1]] **1.** *trans.* = PUT *v.* I. 2. *Sc.* **2.** *Golf.* To strike the ball gently and carefully (with the PUTTER), so as to make it roll along the putting-green, with the object of getting it into the hole: orig. *Sc.* 1743.

‖ **Puttee** (pɒ·tī). 1886. [Hindī *paṭṭī* band, bandage.] A long strip of cloth wound spirally round the leg from the ankle to the knee, worn as a protection and support to the leg.

Putter (pu·təɹ), *sb.*[1] late ME. [f. PUT *v.*[1] + -ER [1].] **1.** One who or that which puts (in current senses of the vb.). **2.** *Coal-mining.* A man or boy employed in 'putting' or propelling the trams or barrows of coal from the workings; a haulier; see PUT *v.*[1] I. 4. 1708.

Putter (pɒ·təɹ), *sb.*[2] 1743. [f. PUTT *v.* + -ER [1].] **1.** One who 'puts' or throws a heavy stone or other weight; see PUTT *v.* Chiefly *Sc.* 1820. **2.** *Golf.* **a.** A club used in 'putting' 1743. **b.** A player who 'puts' 1857.

Putting (pu·tiŋ), *vbl. sb.*[1] [f. OE. **putian* PUT *v.*[1] + -ING [1].] The action of PUT *v.*[1], in various senses; *esp.* the exercise of throwing a heavy stone or weight from the shoulder.

Putting (pɒ·tiŋ), *vbl. sb.*[2] 1805. [f. PUTT *v.*] *Golf.* The action of striking the ball with the putter in order to get it into the hole.

Comb.: **p. cleek,** a cleek used in p.; **-green,** the part of the ground around each **p.-hole,** where the ball is 'putted'; **-iron,** an iron putter.

Putting-stone (pu·tiŋ-, *Sc.* pɒ·tiŋˌstōun). 17.. [f. PUTTING *vbl. sb.*[1]] A heavy stone used in the athletic exercise of putting.

‖**Putto** (pu·tto). Usu. in pl. **putti** (pu·tti). 1644. [It., pl. *putti* boy, ad. L. *putus* boy, child.] In *pl.*, Representations of children, nude or in swaddling bands, used in art, esp. in Italy in the 15th–17th c.

Puttock [1] (pɒ·tək). *Obs.* exc. *dial.* late ME. [Origin obsc.] A bird of prey; usu. applied to the Kite or Glede (*Milvus ictinus* or *regalis*); sometimes to the Common Buzzard (*Buteo vulgaris*).

†**Puttock** [2]. ME. [Origin obsc.] *Naut.* Original name of the small or short shrouds connecting the lower shrouds with the top; also, where there is a top-gallant mast, the similar set connecting the topmast shrouds with the top-gallant top. After 1700 usu. called **p. shrouds,** and now *futtock-shrouds*, from confusion with FUTTOCK.

Putty (pɒ·ti), *sb.* 1633. [a. F. *potée*; orig. a potful, f. *pot* POT *sb.*[1]] **1.** A powder of calcined tin (amorphous stannic oxide), or of calcined tin and lead, used for polishing glass or metals; dist. as *jeweller's p.*; also *p. powder* 1663. **2.** A fine mortar or cement made of lime and water without sand; dist. as *plasterers' p.* 1633. **3.** A stiff paste composed of powdered whiting, raw linseed oil, etc., used in fixing panes of glass, and for making up inequalities in woodwork, etc. before painting; dist. as *glaziers' p.* 1706. **b.** In full *p. colour*, a light shade of yellowish-grey 1886.

Comb.: **p.-knife,** a knife with a blunt flexible spatulate blade for spreading p. (sense 3); **p. medal,** a fit reward for a small achievement or service; **-root,** a N. American orchid (*Aplectrum hyemale*), the corm of which contains a glutinous matter sometimes used as a cement.

Putty (pɒ·ti), *v.* 1734. [f. prec.] *trans.* To cover, smear, fix, mend, or join with putty; to fill up with putty. Hence **Pu·ttier.**

Put-up, *ppl. a.* 1810. [pa. pple. of *to put up.*] **1.** (Orig. *Thieves' slang.*) Arranged or concocted beforehand, as a burglary, by conspiracy with other persons, as servants in the house; planned in an underhand manner. Often in phr. *a put-up job.* **2.** *transf. Put-up price*, the up-set price at or above which something will be sold at an auction 1895.

‖**Puy** (pwī). 1839. [F., hill, mount, hillock:—L. *podium* elevation, height.] A small volcanic cone; *spec.* one of those in Auvergne, France; also, in *Geol.*, generalized.

‖**Puya** (pū·yă). 1866. [mod.L. from the Chilean native name.] (A plant of) a genus of tropical and subtropical plants of Chili and Peru bearing spiny leaves and showy flowers.

Puzzle (pɒ·z'l), *sb.* 1599. [app. f. next.] **1.** The state of being puzzled; bewilderment, confusion. **2.** A puzzling question; a poser, 'problem', 'enigma' 1655. **3.** A toy or problem contrived for the purpose of exercising one's ingenuity and patience 1814. **b.** = *p.-peg*, a piece of wood, about a foot long, pointed at one end and fastened to the lower jaw of a dog or horse so that the pointed end projects in front, and prevents him from putting his nose close to the ground 1791.

3. *Chinese p.*, one of the ingenious puzzles made by the Chinese, in which the problem is to fit together the dissected pieces of a geometrical or other figure, to disentangle interlocked rings, etc. Hence *fig.* Any specially intricate p. or problem. Hence **Pu·zzledom,** the realm of p.; the state of being puzzled.

Puzzle (pɒ·z'l), *v.* 1595. [Etym. obsc. See N.E.D.] **1.** *trans.* †**a.** *orig.* To cause (any one) to be at a loss what to do or where to turn; to perplex, bewilder, confound; said of circumstances, material obstacles, etc. –1735. **b.** To perplex, bewilder (the brain, mind, understanding, will, wit) 1602. **c.** To perplex or embarrass mentally, as or by a difficult problem or question; to pose 1634. **2.** *intr.* To be at a loss how to act or decide; to ponder perplexedly; to exercise oneself with the solution of a puzzle. Const. *over*, formerly *about, upon.* 1605. **b.** To search in a bewildered way; to grope *for* something; to get *through* by perplexed searching 1817. Now *rare.* **3.** *trans.* To make puzzling; to confuse. Now *rare.* 1647. **4.** *To p. out*: to make out by the exercise of ingenuity and patience 1781.

1. The panting Throng In their own Footsteps puzzled, foil'd, and lost 1735. **b.** The dread of something after death..Puzels the will SHAKS. **c.** Men are annoyed at what puzzles them JOWETT. 2. I my selfe.. have pored and pusled vpon many an old Record CAMDEN. 3. The ways of Heaven are dark and intricate, Puzzled in mazes ADDISON.

Comb.: **p.-mo·nkey,** the Chilian tree *Araucaria imbricata*, from the difficulty which a monkey would have in climbing it. Hence **Pu·zzlingly** *adv.* **Pu·zzle-pate** = PUZZLE-HEAD; so **Pu·zzle-pated** *a.*, **-ness.**

Pu·zzle-hea·ded, *a.* 1784. [f. PUZZLE *sb.*, or put for *puzzled* + HEAD *sb.* + -ED [2].] Having a puzzled head; having confused ideas. Hence **Puzzlehea·dedness;** so also **Pu·zzlehead,** a p. person.

Puzzlement (pɒ·z'lmĕnt). 1822. [f. PUZZLE *v.* + -MENT.] The fact or condition of being puzzled; perplexity, bewilderment. **b.** A puzzle 1842.

Puzzler (pɒ·zləɹ). 1652. [f. PUZZLE *v.* + -ER [1].] One who or that which puzzles; also, one who occupies himself with puzzles.

‖**Pyæmia** (pəiˌī·miă). Also **pyemia.** 1857. [mod.L., f. Gr. πύον pus + αἷμα blood.] *Path.* A condition of blood-poisoning accompanied by fever, caused by the presence in the blood of pathogenic bacteria and their toxic products, and characterized by the formation of pus-foci; septicæmia. Hence **Pyæ·mic** *a.* of, pertaining to, or of the nature of p.; affected with p.

‖**Pycnidium** (pikni·diŏm). *Pl.* **-ia.** 1857. [mod.L., f. Gr. πυκνός thick + dim. suff. -ίδιον.] *Bot.* The special receptacle in certain ascomycetous fungi in which the stylospores are produced.

Pycnite (pi·knəit). 1802. [f. Gr. πυκνός + -ITE [1].] *Min.* A variety of topaz occurring in columnar aggregations.

Pycno- (pikno), bef. a vowel **pycn-,** comb. form of Gr. πυκνός thick, dense.

‖**Pycnaspi·deæ** [Gr. ἀσπίς, ἀσπιδ- shield] *Ornith.*, a cohort of scutelliplantar passerine birds, having the planta or back of the tarsus studded with small irregular scales or plates; hence **Pycnaspi·dean** *a.* **Py·cnodont** [Gr. ὀδούς, ὀδοντ- tooth] *a. Ichthyol.*, pertaining to or having the characteristics of the *Pycnodontidæ*, an extinct family of ganoid fishes; *sb.* a pycnodont fish. **Pycno·gonid** [Gr. γόνυ knee] *Zool.*, a marine arthropod of the group *Pycnogonida*, typified by the parasitic genus *Pycnogonum*; a sea-spider. **Pycno·meter,** an instrument for determining the specific gravity of a liquid; a specific gravity flask.

Pycnostyle (pi·knostəil), *a.* and *sb.* 1697. [ad. L. *pycnostylos*, a. Gr., f. πυκνός dense + στῦλος column.] *Arch.* **A.** *adj.* Having close intercolumniation; having the space between the columns equal to one diameter and a half of a column. **B.** *sb.* A building having such intercolumniation.

Pycnotic (piknǫ·tik), *a.* 1900. [ad. Gr. πυκνωτικός, f. πυκνόειν to condense.] Pertaining or relating to condensation; applied to a theory of the formation of matter.

‖**Pyelitis** (pəiˌeləi·tis). 1842. [mod.L., f. Gr. πύελος trough + -ITIS.] *Path.* Inflammation of the mucous membrane of the pelvis of the kidney. Hence **Pyeli·tic** *a.*

Pygal (pəi·găl), *a.* (*sb.*) 1838. [f. Gr. πυγή rump + -AL.] *Zool.* Of or pertaining to the rump or hinder quarters of an animal. **B.** *sb.* (Short for *p. plate* or *shield.*) The posterior median plate of the carapace of a turtle 1889.

Pygarg (pəi·gaɹg). late ME. [ad. L. *pygargus*, a. Gr. πύγαργος 'white-rump'; f. πυγή rump + ἀργός white.] **1.** A kind of antelope mentioned by Herodotus and Pliny; by some supposed to be the addax. (In the LXX, etc., used to render Heb. *dīshōn.*) **2.** (In L. form *pygargus.*) The osprey or sea-eagle. late ME.

‖**Pygidium** (pəidʒi·diŏm, pəigi·diŏm). 1849. [mod.L., f. Gr. πυγή rump + dim. suff. -ίδιον.] *Zool.* The posterior part of the body in certain invertebrates, when forming a distinct segment or division; the caudal or pygal segment. Hence **Pygi·dial** *a.*

Pygmæan, -mean (pigmī·ăn), *sb.* and *a.* 1555. [f. L. *pygmæus* PYGMY + -AN.] †**A.** *sb.* = PYGMY *sb.* 1. **B.** *adj.* Of or pertaining to the pygmies; of the nature or size of a pygmy; diminutive, dwarfish 1667.

Pygmy, pigmy (pi·gmi), *sb.* and *a.* late ME. [ad. L. *pygmæus*, a. Gr. πυγμαῖος adj., f. πυγμή measure of length from the elbow to the knuckles, also the fist.] **A.** *sb.* **1.** One of a race (or several races) of men of very small size, mentioned in ancient history and tradition as inhabiting parts of Ethiopia or India. *The Pygmies*, the dwarf races existing in equatorial Africa. †**b.** Formerly applied to the chimpanzee and other anthropoid apes –1863. **2.** *gen.* A dwarf 1520. **b.** *fig.* A person of very small importance, or having some specified quality in a very small degree 1592. **c.** *transf.* A thing that is very small of its kind 1838. **3.** An elf, puck, pixy 1611.

2. As very a manne is..a Pigmay as a Geaunt 1532. **b.** These are heathen arts, and we are but pigmies at them 1860.

B. *adj.* **1.** Of or pertaining to the race of pygmies 1661. **2. a.** Of persons and animals: Of very small size or stature, dwarf 1591. **b.** *gen.* Very small, diminutive. In *Nat. Hist.* often used in the names of species of animals that are very small of their kind. 1595.

2. **b.** A six years' Darling of a pigmy size WORDSW.

Pygo- (pəigo), repr. Gr. πυγο-, comb. form of πυγή rump.

Pygobra·nchiate [Gr. βράγχια gills] *a.*, belonging to the *Pygobranchia*, a group of gastropods having the gills arranged round the anus. **Py·gopod** [Gr. πούς, ποδ- foot], **a.** *adj.* of or pertaining to the *Pygopodes*, an order of aquatic birds, including the auks, grebes, and loons, having the legs set very far back; **b.** *adj.* of or belonging to the genus *Pygopus* of Australian lizards having rudimentary hind legs; *sb.* a lizard of this family; hence **Pygo·podous** *a.*

Pyin (pəi·in). 1845. [f. Gr. πύον pus + -IN [1].] An albuminoid substance found in pus.

Pyjamas, *U.S.* **pajamas** (pidʒā·măs, pă-, pəi-), *sb. pl.* 1800. [a. Pers. and Urdū *pāē jāmah*, f. Pers. *pāē* foot, leg + *jāmah* clothing, garment.] Loose drawers or trousers, usu. of silk or cotton, tied round the waist, worn by both sexes among the Mohammedans, and adopted for night wear by Europeans; in England often applied to a sleeping suit of loose trousers and jacket. Also *attrib.* (in sing. form) **Pyja·ma.**

Pylagore (pi·lăgoəɹ). Also **pylagoras.** 1753. [ad. Gr. πυλαγόρας, f. Πύλαι, Thermopylæ + ἀγορά.] *Gr. Antiq.* The title of one of the two deputies sent by each constituent tribe to the Amphictyonic Council.

Pylangium (pəilændʒəi·ŏm). 1875. [mod. L., f. Gr. πύλη gate + ἀγγεῖον vessel.] *Anat.* The undivided portion of the arterial trunk next the ventricle in the lower vertebrates. Hence **Pyla·ngial** *a.*

‖**Pylon** (pəi·lǫn). 1823. [a. Gr. πυλών a gateway, f. πύλη gate.] **1.** *Arch.* A gateway, a gate-tower; *spec.* in recent use, the monumental gateway to an Egyptian temple, usu. formed by two truncated pyramidal towers connected by a lower architectural member containing the gate. **2.** A tower, mast, or post such as is used to mark the course in an aerodrome, to support a long span of telegraph wire, or the like 1909.

Pyloric (pəilǫ·rik), *a.* 1807. [f. PYLORUS + -IC.] *Anat.* Of or pertaining to the pylorus.

Pyloro- (pəilōə·ro), comb. f. next, as in **Pylo·ropla·sty,** plastic surgery of the pylorus 1895.

‖**Pylorus** (pəilōə·rŏs). 1615. [Late L., a. Gr. πυλωρός, πυλουρός gatekeeper, f. πύλη gate + οὖρος warder.] *Anat.* The opening from the stomach into the duodenum, which is guarded by a strong sphincter muscle; also, that part of the stomach where it is situated. **b.** An analogous part in invertebrates, as the posterior opening of the stomach in insects 1828.

Pyo- (pəi‚o), bef. a vowel **py-,** repr. Gr. πυο-, comb. form of πύον pus.

Pyoco·ccal [Gr. κόκκος grain] *a.*, pertaining to the ‖**Pyoco·ccus,** a microbe or coccus causing suppuration. **Pyocy·anin,** a blue colouring matter, $C_{14}H_{14}NO_2$, obtained from blue or lead-coloured pus; so **Pyocya·nic** *a.* **Pyoge·nesis,** the formation of pus; suppuration; so **Pyogene·tic, Pyoge·nic** *adjs.*, of or pertaining to pyogenesis; producing pus. ‖**Pyopneumotho·rax,** the presence of pus and air in the pleural cavities. **Pyoxa·nthin, Pyoxa·nthose** [Gr. ξανθός yellow], a yellow colouring matter found with pyocyanin in blue suppuration.

Pyoid (pəi·oid), *a.* 1853. [ad. Gr. πυοειδής like pus, f. πύον; see -OID.] Of the nature of or resembling pus; purulent.

Pyorrhœa (pəi‚ǒrī·ă). 1800. [f. PYO- + Gr. ῥοία flux.] Discharge of pus; *spec.* from the gums.

Pyracanth (pəiə·răkænþ), **pyracantha** (pəiərăkæ·nþă). 1664. [ad. L. *pyracantha*, a. Gr. πυράκανθα, an unidentified shrub or plant.] An evergreen thorny shrub, *Cratægus Pyracantha*, a native of southern Europe, bearing clusters of white flowers and scarlet berries; also called Christ's, Egyptian, or Evergreen Thorn. Hence **Pyraca·nthine** *a.*

Pyral (pəiə·răl), *a. rare.* 1658. [f. L. *pyra* PYRE + -AL.] Of or pertaining to a pyre.

‖**Pyralis** (pi·rălis). *Pl.* **pyralides** (piræ·lidīz). 1588. [ad. Gr. πυραλίς, f. πῦρ fire.] †**1.** A fabulous fly supposed to live in or be generated by fire –1684. **2.** *Entom.* [mod.L.] A genus of moths typical of the family *Pyralidæ* So **Py·ralid** *a.* resembling or belonging to the *Pyralidæ*; *sb.* a moth of this family.

Pyramid (pi·rămid), *sb.* late ME. [orig. in form *pyramis*; a. L. *pyramis*, pl. *pyramides*, a. Gr. πυραμίς, pl. πυραμίδες (perh. of Egyptian origin).] **1.** A monumental structure built of stone or the like, with a polygonal (usu. square) base, and sloping sides meeting at an apex; *orig.* and *esp.* one of the ancient structures of this kind in Egypt 1555. **2.** The form of a pyramid; in *Geom.* a solid figure bounded by plane surfaces, of which one (the base) is a polygon of any number of sides, and the other surfaces triangles having as bases the sides of the polygon, and meeting at a point (the vertex) outside the plane of the polygon. late ME †**3.** *Arch.* Any structure of pyramidal form, as a spire, pinnacle, obelisk, etc. Also applied to a gable. –1716. **4.** Any material thing, or pile of things, of pyramidal form 1570. **b.** *Gardening.* Applied (orig. *attrib.*, hence also *simply*) to a fruit-tree, etc., trained in a pyramidal form 1712. **5.** *fig.* (from prec. senses) 1593. **6.** *Cryst.* A set of faces belonging to a single crystallographic form, and, if symmetrically developed, meeting in a point 1748. **7.** *loosely.* A plane figure or formation suggesting the profile of a p. 1589. **b.** *Billiards. pl.* A game played (usu.) with fifteen coloured balls arranged in a triangle, and one cue-ball 1850.

3. What needs my Shakespear..that his hallow'd reliques should be hid Under a Star-ypointing P.? MILT. 4. Smithfield blazing with pyramids of law-books SWIFT. 5. An unsteddy and sharp-pointed Pyramis of power 1628.

Comb.: **p.-rest** (*Billiards*), a cue-rest the head of which is arched so as to allow it to be placed over a ball which would otherwise be in the way; **-spot,** the spot on a billiard-table where the apex of the p. is placed, between the centre and the top spot. Hence **Py·ramidist,** one who investigates or is specially versed in the structure and history of the Egyptian pyramids.

Pyramidal (piræ·midăl), *a.* (*sb.*) 1571. [ad. med.L. *pyramidalis*; see prec. and -AL.] **1.** Of or pertaining to a pyramid; sloping, as an edge or face of a pyramid (*rare*). **2.** Of the nature or shape of a pyramid; resembling a pyramid 1599. **3.** *Cryst.* Used in senses 1 and 2; also applied to the TETRAGONAL system, of which the square pyramid is a characteristic form 1789. **4.** *Arith.* Applied to the several series of numbers, each beginning with unity, obtained by continued summation of the several series of POLYGONAL numbers; so called because each of these numbers, represented (e.g.) by balls, can be arranged according to a certain rule in the form of the corresponding pyramid (on a triangular, square, or polygonal base) 1674. **B.** (as *sb.*) A p. number 1706. Hence **Pyra·midally** *adv.* in a p. manner or form; †*fig.* in allusion to the embalmed bodies of the dead preserved in the pyramids: after the manner of a mummy.

Pyramidic (pirămi·dik), *a. rare.* 1743. [f. PYRAMID + -IC.] Of, like, or proper to a pyramid; heaped up, or lofty and massive, like a pyramid. So **Pyrami·dical** *a.* (now *rare*). = prec. **Pyrami·dically** *adv.*

‖**Pyramidion** (pirămi·diǫn). *Pl.* **-ia, -ions.** 1840. [mod.L., a. Gr. type *πυραμίδιον, dim. of πυραμίς PYRAMID.] A small pyramid; *spec.* in *Arch.*, the pointed pyramidal portion forming the apex of an obelisk.

Pyramidoid (piræ·midoid). *rare.* 1704. [ad. mod.L. *pyramidoides* (sc. *schema*): see PYRAMID and -OID.] *Geom.* A solid figure in form approaching a pyramid, but of which the edges that meet at the vertex are curves.

Pyramoid (pi·rămoid). *rare.* [ad. Gr. πυραμοειδής, f. πυραμίς; see -OID.] = prec.

Pyrargyrite: see PYRO- 2.

Pyre (pəiəɹ). 1658. [ad. L. *pyra*, a. Gr. πυρά.] A pile of combustible material, esp. wood; usu., a funeral pile for burning the dead.

When the Funeral P. was out, and the last Valediction over SIR T. BROWNE.

Pyrene [1] (pəiə·rīn). 1837. [ad. mod.L. *pyrena*, f. Gr. πυρήν fruit-stone.] *Bot.* The stone of a fruit; *esp.* one of those in a drupaceous pome.

Pyrene [2] (pəiə·rīn). 1839. [f. Gr. πῦρ fire + -ENE.] *Chem.* A solid hydrocarbon ($C_{16}H_{10}$) obtained from the dry distillation of coal, crystallizing in microscopic laminæ. Hence **Pyrenic** (pəire·nik) *a.* designating a yellow crystalline dibasic acid formed by the oxidation of p.

Pyrenean, -æan (pirĕnī·ăn), *a.* and *sb.* 1592. [f. L. *Pyrenæus* (f. *Pyrene*, a. Gr. Πυρήνη, daughter of Bebryx, beloved of Hercules, said to be buried on these mountains) + -AN.] **A.** *adj.* Of or belonging to the Pyrenees. **B.** *sb.* A native of the Pyrenees.

Pyrenoid (pəirī·noid). 1883. [f. Gr. πυρήν fruit-stone; see -OID.] A small colourless proteid body, resembling a nucleus, found in certain algæ and protozoa.

Pyrethrine (pəire·þrəin). 1838. [ad. F. *pyrétrine*; see next and -INE [5].] *Chem.* The substance to which the sialagogic action of pyrethrum root is due. Hence **Pyre·thric** *a.* as in *p. acid.*

‖**Pyrethrum** (pəirī·þrŏm). 1562. [L., a. Gr. πύρεθρον feverfew.] **1.** orig., The plant *Anacyclus Pyrethrum*, N.O. *Compositæ*, also called Pellitory of Spain, having a pungent root (*radix pyrethri*) used in medicine. Now so called only in pharmacy. **2.** *Bot.* A genus of composite plants; a plant of this genus, a feverfew 1882. **b.** In full, *P. powder*: an insecticide made of the powdered flower-heads of some species of P. 1876.

Pyretic (pəir-, pire·tik), *a.* and *sb.* 1728. [ad. mod.L. *pyreticus*, f. Gr. πυρετός fever; see -IC.] **A.** *adj.* **1.** Of or pertaining to fever; producing feverish symptoms 1858. **2.** Used for the cure of fever, antipyretic 1868. **B.** *sb.* A febrifuge, an antipyretic 1728.

Pyreto- (pəiə·r-, pi·rėto), bef. a vowel **pyret-,** comb. form of Gr. πυρετός fever; as in **Pyreto·logy** [-LOGY], the branch of medical science which treats of fevers; etc.

‖**Pyrexia** (pəir-, pire·ksiă). *Pl.* **-iæ.** 1769. [mod.L., f. Gr. πύρεξις, f. πυρέσσειν.] *Path.* Febrile disease; fever. Hence **Pyre·xial, Pyre·xic, -al** *adjs.* febrile.

Pyrheliometer (pəɹhīliǫ·mĭtəɹ). 1855. [f. Gr. πῦρ fire + ἥλιος sun + -METER.] An instrument for measuring the amount of heat given off by the sun.

Pyridine (pəiə·ridəin, piə·r-). 1851. [f. Gr. πῦρ, πυρ- fire + -ID [4] + -INE [5].] *Chem.* A colourless volatile liquid alkaloid of offensive odour and poisonous quality, produced in the dry distillation of bone-oil or coal-tar. Hence **Pyri·dic** *a.* of or related to p. **Py·ridyl,** the radical C_5H_4N of p.

Pyriform (pəiə·ri-, pi·rifǭm), *a.* 1704. [ad. mod.L. *pyriformis*, f. *pyrum*, misspelling of *pirum* pear + -FORM.] Pear-shaped; obconic. (Chiefly in scientific and techn. use.)

Pyritaceous (pəiər-, piritēi·ʃəs), *a. rare.* 1794. [f. PYRITES + -ACEOUS.] Of the nature of or containing pyrites.

Pyrite (pəiə·rəit). 1567. [f. L. *pyrites*; see next.] †**1.** = PYRITES 1. –1791. **2.** *Min.* Native disulphide of iron (FeS_2), crystallizing in isometric forms, esp. in cubes and pyritohedra: one of the forms of *iron pyrites* 1868.

‖**Pyrites** (pirəi·tīz). 1567. [L., fire-stone, a. Gr. πυρίτης of or in fire (f. πῦρ).] †**1.** Vaguely, a 'fire-stone' or mineral which strikes fire –1796. **2.** Either of the two sulphides of iron (FeS_2), pyrite and marcasite, also dist. as *iron p.*; also, the double sulphide of copper and iron ($Cu_2S \cdot Fe_2S_3$), chalcopyrite or *copper p.*

Used also generically to include many related sulphides and arsenides of iron, cobalt, nickel, etc., or of iron with another metal; e.g. **capillary p.,** native sulphide of nickel; **spear p., white iron p.,** varieties of MARCASITE; also HEPATIC *P.* Hence **Pyri·tic, -al** *a.* of or pertaining to p., containing or resembling p. **Pyriti·ferous** *a.* yielding p. **Py·ritous** *a.* of, of the nature of, or containing p.; characterizing, or characterized by the presence of, p.

Pyritize (pəiə·r-, pi·ritəiz), *v.* 1804. [f. prec. + -IZE.] *trans.* To convert into pyrites; to impregnate with pyrites.

Pyrito- (pirəi·to, pəiə·rito), comb. form of PYRITES; as in **Pyritohedron** (-hī·drǫn, -he·drǫn), pl. **-he·dra** [Gr. ἕδρα side], *Cryst.* a form of pentagonal dodecahedron common in crystals of pyrite; hence **Pyritohe·dral** *a.*, pertaining to or of the form of a pyritohedron. **Pyrito·logy** [-LOGY], a treatise on, or the study of, pyrites.

Pyritoid (pirəi·toid), *a.* 1895. [f. PYRITES + -OID.] Resembling or allied to pyrites.

Pyro (pəi°·ro). 1879. *Photogr.* Abbrev. of *pyrogallic acid* (see PYRO- 3), used as a developing agent. Often *attrib.*

Pyro- (pəi°ro, piro), bef. a vowel or *h* sometimes pyr-, repr. Gr. πυρο-, πυρ- comb. form of πῦρ fire.

1. In various terms, chiefly scientific or techn., in the sense: Of, relating to, done with, caused or produced by fire. **Pyro-ele·ctric** *a. Min.*, applied to certain crystals which on being heated become electrically polar. **Pyrognostic** (-gnǫ·stik) [Gr. γνωστικός] *a. Min.*, applied to or relating to those characters of a mineral that are ascertained by means of the flame of a blow-pipe or of a Bunsen burner; so **Pyrogno·stics** *sb. pl.*, pyrognostic characters, or the branch of mineralogy that deals with them. **Pyro·graphy** = POKER-WORK. **Pyrolu·site** [Gr. λοῦσις washing, from its use, when heated, for discharging colour from glass], *Min.* native dioxide of manganese, MnO_2. **Pyromagne·tic** *a.*, applied to a dynamo invented by Edison, the working of which depends on the magnetization of iron with increase of temperature. **Pyroma·nia**, insanity characterized by an impulse to set things on fire. **Pyromo·rphous** [Gr. μορφή] *a. Min.*, having the property of crystallizing after fusion by heat. **Pyrophanous** (pəirǫ·fănəs) [Gr. -φανης appearing] *a. Min.*, having the property of becoming transparent or translucent when heated. **Pyro-pho·tograph**, a photographic picture burnt in on glass or porcelain; hence **Pyro-photogra·phic** *a.*; **Pyro-photo·graphy**. **Py·roscope** [-SCOPE], an instrument for measuring the intensity of radiant heat, consisting of a differential thermometer having one bulb covered with silver.

2. In names of minerals and rocks, usu. indicating some property exhibited or alteration produced by the action of fire or heat; sometimes denoting a fiery red or yellow colour. **Pyrargyrite** (-ā·ɹdʒirəit) [Gr. ἄργυρον], a dark-red silver ore, a native sulphide of silver and antimony. **Py·rochlore** [Gr. χλωρός greenish-yellow], a niobo-titanate of calcium, cerium, and other bases, occurring in octahedral crystals of a brown colour, becoming greenish-yellow when strongly heated. **Pyromo·rphite** [Gr. μορφή], chlorophosphate of lead, occurring in green, yellow, or brown crystals; so called because the globule produced by melting assumes a crystalline form on cooling. †**Py·rophane** (-fēⁱn) [Gr. -φανής appearing], a variety of opal which absorbs melted wax, and becomes translucent when heated; also sometimes = FIRE-*opal*.

3. In Chemistry, *pyro-* is prefixed to the name of a substance or to an adj. forming part thereof, in order to name a new substance formed by a destructive distillation or other application of heat.

a. Prefixed to the adj. denominating an acid, to form the name of a new acid, etc. **Pyroga·llic** *acid*, a substance, $C_6H_6O_3$, much used as a reducing agent in photography, etc. **Pyromeco·nic** *acid*, a crystalline bitter acid, $C_5H_4O_3$, obtained by the dry distillation of meconic acid. **Pyromu·cic** *acid*, an acid, $C_5H_4O_3$, metameric with pyromeconic acid, produced by the dry distillation of mucic acid. **Pyrophospho·ric** *acid*, $H_4P_2O_7$, a tetrabasic acid, produced as a glass-like solid, by the action of heat on phosphoric acid. **Pyrotarta·ric** *acid*, $C_5H_8O_4$, obtained by the dry distillation of tartaric acid. **Pyru·vic** *acid* [L. *uva* grape], $C_3H_4O_3$, produced by dry distillation of racemic or tartaric acid. Also in the names of salts of these acids, as **Pyrota·rtrate**, etc.

b. Prefixed to a sb. (Now often superseded by other names.) **Pyrocatechin** (pəi:ro,kæ·tītʃin), also called *catechol*, *pyro-catechuic acid*, and *oxyphenic acid*, $C_6H_6O_2$, produced by the dry distillation of catechu, kino, etc., forming broad white strongly shining laminæ, and rhombic or small rectangular prisms. **Py·rocoll** [Gr. κόλλα glue], $C_{10}H_6N_2O_2$, a product of the distillation of gelatin when free from fat but containing albumen, casein or gluten. **Pyroxa·nthin** [Gr. ξανθός yellow], a yellow crystalline substance, produced by the action of potash on one of the constituents of the heavy oil of wood-tar.

c. Also in the derivative names of certain hydrocarbon compounds and groups, as **Py·razine, Py·rone.**

Pyro-acid (pəi·ro,æ·sid). 1835. *Chem.* An acid formed from another acid by dry or destructive distillation; see PYRO- 3.

Pyrogen (pəi°·rǫdʒen). *rare.* 1858. [f. PYRO- + -GEN; lit. 'fire-producer', or 'fire-produced'.] †**a.** The 'electric fluid' –1864. **b.** A substance which, when introduced into the blood, produces fever; a pyrogenetic agent 1896.

Pyrogenetic (pəi°:ro,dʒīne·tik), *a.* 1858. [f. PYRO- 1 + -GENETIC.] **a.** Having the property of producing heat, esp. in the body; thermogenetic. **b.** Having the property of producing fever. So **Pyroge·nic** *a.* = b.

Pyrogenous (-ǫ·dʒĭnəs), *a.* 1839. [f. as PYROGEN + -OUS.] 1. Produced by fire or heat. **a.** *Geol.* Of rocks: = IGNEOUS *a.* 2. **b.** *Chem.* Applied to a substance produced by the combustion of another substance. **2.** = prec. 1890.

Pyrolatry (pəirǫ·lătri). 1669. [f. PYRO- + Gr. λατρεία.] Fire-worship. Hence **Pyro·later** (-or), a fire-worshipper.

Pyroligneous (pəi°ro,li·gnīəs), *a.* 1790. [a. F. *pyroligneux*, f. PYRO- + L. *lignum*.] Produced by the action of fire or heat upon wood.

P. acid, a crude acetic acid (wood vinegar) obtained by the destructive distillation of wood; so *p. alcohol*, *ether*, *spirit*, methyl alcohol. So †**Pyroli·gnic**, †**Pyroli·gnous** *adjs.* **Pyroli·gnate**, a salt of p. acid.

Pyrology (pəirǫ·lŏdʒi). *rare.* 1731. [See PYRO- 1 and -LOGY.] The science of fire or heat; *spec.* that branch of chemistry which deals with the application of fire to chemical analysis, etc. Hence **Pyro·logist**, one versed in p.

Pyromancy (pəi°·romænsi, pi·ro-). Now *rare.* late ME. [a. OF. *pyromancie*, ad. late L. *pyromantia*, a. Gr. πυρομαντεία; see PYRO- and -MANCY.] Divination by fire or signs derived from fire. So **Pyroma·ntic** *a.* pertaining to or practising p.; *sb.* one who divines by fire.

Pyrometer (pəirǫ·mĭtəɹ). 1749. [f. PYRO- + -METER.] †**a.** *orig.* An instrument for measuring the expansion of solid bodies under the influence of heat. **b.** Any instrument for measuring high temperatures, usu. those higher than can be measured by the mercurial thermometer. Hence **Pyrome·tric, -al** *adjs.* pertaining to a p. or to pyrometry; of the nature of, or measurable by, a p. **Pyrome·trically** *adv.* **Pyro·metry**, the measurement of very high temperatures.

Pyrope (pəi°·rōᵘp). ME. [a. OF. *pirope*, ad. L. *pyropus*, a. Gr. πυρωπός gold-bronze, lit. fiery-eyed, f. πῦρ, πυρ- fire + ὤψ eye, face.] †1. Applied vaguely to a red or fiery gem, as ruby or carbuncle –1795. **2.** *Min.* The Bohemian garnet or fire-garnet, a deep-red gem 1804.

Pyrophoric (-fǫ·rik), *a.* 1828. [f. next + -IC.] Of, pertaining to, or of the nature of a pyrophorous; having the property of taking fire on exposure to air. Also **Pyro·phorous** *a.*

‖ **Pyrophorus** (pəirǫ·fŏrŭs). *Pl.* **-i** (-əi). 1778. [mod.L., ad. Gr. πυροφόρος fire-bearing.] **1.** *Chem.* Any substance capable (esp. in a finely divided state) of taking fire spontaneously on exposure to air. **2.** *Entom.* A genus of beetles of the family *Elateridæ*, found in tropical America, containing the most brilliantly luminous 'fire-flies' 1809.

‖ **Pyrosis** (pəirōᵘ·sis). 1789. [mod.L., a. Gr. πύρωσις, f. πυροῦν to set on fire.] *Path.* An affection characterized by a burning sensation in the stomach and œsophagus, with eructation of watery fluid; water-brash.

Pyrosome (pəi°·rosōᵘm). 1812. [ad. mod. L. *Pyrosoma*, f. Gr. πῦρ fire (PYRO-) + σῶμα body.] *Zool.* An animal of the genus *Pyrosoma*, consisting of highly phosphorescent compound ascidians, the individuals being united into a free-swimming colony in the form of a hollow cylinder closed at one end.

Pyrotechnic (pəi°ro,te·knik), *a.* and *sb.* 1704. [f. Gr. πυρο- PYRO- + τεχνικός, f. τέχνη art.] **A.** *adj.* †1. Of or pertaining to the use of fire in chemistry, metallurgy, or gunnery –1731. **2.** Of or pertaining to fireworks, or the art of making them; of the nature of a firework 1825. **b.** *fig.*, esp. said of a brilliant display of wit, rhetoric, etc. 1849. **B.** *sb. pl.* **a.** = PYROTECHNY 1, 3. 1729. **b.** A display of fireworks; also *transf.* of lightning 1840. **c.** *fig.* Brilliant displays 1901. So **Pyrote·chnical** *a.*; **-ly** *adv.*

Pyrotechnist (pəi°rote·knist). 1791. [f. next + -IST.] One employed or skilled in pyrotechny; a maker or displayer of fireworks.

Pyrotechny (pəi°·rǫtekni). 1579. [a. F. *pyrotechnie*, or mod.L. *pyrotechnia*, f. Gr. πυρο- PYRO- + τέχνη art.] The art of employing fire. †1. (*Military p.*) The manufacture and use of gunpowder, bombs, fire-arms, etc. –1728. †2. The use of fire in chemical operations or in metallurgy –1728. **3.** The making and managing of fireworks for scenic display, for military use, or as signals, etc. 1635.

Pyroxene (pəi°·rǫksīn). 1800. [f. Gr. πῦρ, πυρο- fire + ξένος stranger; so named because it was thought alien to igneous rocks.] *Min.* A species including a large variety of minerals, all bisilicates of lime with one or more of various other bases, most usu. magnesia and iron oxide, but also manganese, potash, soda, and zinc. Hence **Pyroxenic** (-e·nik) *a.* pertaining to, having the character of, consisting of, or containing p. **Pyroxenite** (-ǫ·ksenəit), also -yte, a metamorphic rock consisting chiefly of p.

Pyroxyle (pəirǫ·ksil). 1847. [a. F., f. Gr. πυρ(ο- PYRO- + ξύλον wood.] *Chem.* = PYROXYLIN. So **Pyroxy·lic** *a.*, *Chem.* obtained from wood by means of fire, i. e. by dry distillation; chiefly in *p.-spirit*, wood-spirit.

Pyroxylin (pəirǫ·ksilin). 1839. [ad. F. *pyroxyline*, f. as prec. + *ine*, -IN [1].] *Chem.* Any one of the class of explosive compounds, including gun-cotton, produced by treating vegetable fibre with nitric acid, or with a mixture of nitric and sulphuric acids; and used in solution for making lacquers, etc.

Pyrrhic (pi·rik), *sb.*[1] and *a.*[1] 1597. [ad. L. *pyrrhicha* or Gr. πυρρίχη a dance in armour, said to have been so named from one Πύρριχος the inventor; prop. an adj. (sc. ὄρχησις).] **A.** *sb.* The war-dance of the ancient Greeks, in which the motions of actual warfare were gone through, in armour, to a musical accompaniment. **B.** *adj.* Epithet of this dance; of or pertaining to this dance 1630.

Pyrrhic (pi·rik), *sb.*[2] and *a.*[2] 1626. [ad. L. *pyrrhichius*, a. Gr. πυρρίχιος of or pertaining to the Pyrrhic (dance); as sb., short for *pes pyrrhichius*, πούς πυρρίχιος pyrrhic foot, a metrical foot used in the war-song.] *Prosody.* **A.** *sb.* A metrical foot, consisting of two short syllables. **B.** *adj.* Consisting of two short syllables; composed of or pertaining to pyrrhics 1749.

Pyrrhic (pi·rik), *a.*[3] 1885. [ad. Gr. πυρρικός, f. Πυρρός, L. *Pyrrhus*, king of Epirus.] Of, pertaining to, or like that of Pyrrhus.

P. victory, a victory gained at too great a cost; in allusion to the exclamation of Pyrrhus after the battle of Asculum in Apulia, 'One more such victory and we are lost'.

Pyrrhonian (pirōᵘ·niăn), *a.* and *sb.* 1638. [a. F. *pyrrhonien*, f. L. *pyrrhonius*, *-eus* (f. *Pyrrho*, Gr. Πύρρων, sceptic philosopher of Elis); see -AN.] **A.** *adj.* = PYRRHONIC *a.* 1651. **B.** *sb.* = PYRRHONIST 1638.

Pyrrhonic (pirǫ·nik), *sb.* and *a.* 1593. [f. Gr. Πύρρων (see prec.) + -IC.] **A.** *sb.* = PYRRHONIST. **B.** *adj.* Of or pertaining to Pyrrho, or to his doctrines; purely sceptical.

Pyrrhonism (pi·rŏniz'm). 1670. [f. as prec. + -ISM.] A system of sceptic philosophy taught by Pyrrho of Elis (*c* 300 B. C.); the doctrine of the impossibility of attaining certainty of knowledge; absolute or universal scepticism; hence *gen.*, scepticism, incredulity, philosophic doubt. So **Py·rrhonist**, a follower or disciple of Pyrrho; a professor of P.; a sceptic. **Py·rrhonize** *v. intr.* to practise P.; *trans.* to treat or transform sceptically (*rare*).

Pyrrhotine (pi·rǫtəin). 1849. [f. Gr. πυρρότης redness + -INE [5].] *Min.* = next.

Pyrrhotite (pi·rǫtəit). 1868. [Altered from prec.; see -ITE [1] 2 b.] *Min.* A magnetic sulphide of iron, occurring massive and amorphous, having a granular structure, and a colour between bronze and copper-red.

Pyrrol (pi·rǫl). 1835. [f. Gr. πυρρός reddish + L. *oleum*.] *Chem.* A feebly basic, colourless transparent liquid, C_4H_5N, contained in bone-oil and coal-tar, having an odour like chloroform. Hence **Py·rroline** = p.

Pyruline (pi·riŭləin), *a.* [f. mod.L. *Pyrula*, generic name (f. L. *pirum*, *pyrum* pear) + -INE [1].] *Zool.* Related to the gastropod genus *Pyrula* or sub-family *Pyrulinæ*, having a pear-shaped shell, the pear-shells or fig-shells.

‖ **Pyrus** (pəi°·rŭs). 1894. [med. and mod.L. erron. spelling of L. *pirus*.] *Bot.* The genus of rosaceous trees and shrubs which includes the pear, apple, and their congeners; occas. used as the English name of foreign species, esp. the scarlet pyrus, *Pyrus japonica*.

Pythagorean (pəiþægōrī·ăn), *a.* and *sb.* 1550. [f. L. *Pythagoreus, -ius*, a. Gr. Πυθαγόρειος, f. proper name Πυθαγόρας Pythagoras + -AN.] **A.** *adj.* Of or pertaining to Pythagoras, an ancient Greek philosopher and mathematician of Samos (6th c. B.C.), or to his system or school. Often with allusion to his belief in the transmigration of souls, or to his abstinence from flesh as food. 1579.

There, love the Fork, thy Garden cultivate, And give thy frugal Frinds a P. Treat DRYDEN. *P. letter*, the Greek Y, used by Pythagoras as a symbol of the two divergent paths of virtue and of vice. *P. proposition* or *theorem*, the 47th of the first book of Euclid, namely, that the square on the hypotenuse of a right-angled triangle is equal to the sum of the squares on the other two sides.

B. *sb.* A disciple or follower of Pythagoras 1550. **b.** *transf.* or *allus.* A person whose doctrine or practice agrees with that of Pythagoras 1599. Hence **Pythagore·anism**, the P. philosophy.

Pythagoric (pəiþăgǫ·rik), *a.* Now *rare.* 1653. [ad. L. *Pythagoricus*, a. Gr. Πυθαγορικός.] = PYTHAGOREAN *a.* 1653. So †**Pythago·rical** *a.*

Pythagorize (pəiþæ·gŏrəiz), *v.* 1610. [ad. Gr. πυθαγορίζειν to be a disciple of Pythagoras.] **1.** *intr.* To speculate after the manner of Pythagoras. †**2.** *trans.* To change (one person or thing) into another as by transmigration of souls –1721.

‖**Pythia** (pi·þiă). 1842. [a. Gr. Πυθία (sc. ἱέρεια) the priestess of Pythian Apollo at Delphi, fem. of Πύθιος adj. Delphic, f. Πυθώ, place-name.] **1.** *Gr. Antiq.* The priestess of Apollo at Delphi, who delivered the oracles. **2.** *Zool.* A genus of gastropod molluscs.

Pythiad (pi·þiæd). 1842. [a. Gr. Πυθιάς, Πυθιαδ-, f. Πύθια pl. (sc. ἱερά) the Pythian games.] The period between two celebrations of the Pythian games.

Pythian (pi·þiăn), *a.* (*sb.*) 1598. [f. L. *Pythius* (a. Gr. Πύθιος of Delphi or the Delphic Apollo) + -AN.] **A.** *adj.* Of or pertaining to Delphi, or to the oracle and priestess of Apollo there; also, of or pertaining to the games held near Delphi.

P games, one of the four national festivals of the Greeks, held near Delphi. *P. meter* or *verse* (L. *versus Pythius*), the dactylic hexameter, perh. so called from its use in the Pythian oracles.

B. *sb.* A native or inhabitant of Delphi; *spec.* the Delphic priestess; hence, one who is ecstatic or frenzied like the priestess; also, an appellation of the Delphic Apollo; hence *transf.* Hence **Py·thic** *a.* = A.

Pythogenic (pəiþo₍dʒe·nik), *a.* 1862. [f. Gr. πύθειν to rot + -γεν- producing + -IC.] Generated by or from corruption or filth; esp. in *p. fever*, a name for typhoid or enteric fever.

Python[1] (pəi·þǫn). 1590. [a. L. *Python*, a. Gr. Πύθων.] **1.** *Gr. Myth.* The huge serpent or monster slain near Delphi by Apollo; hence *poet.* any monster or pestilential scourge. **2.** *Zool.* A genus of large non-venomous snakes inhabiting the tropical regions of the Old World, which kill their prey by constriction; the rock-snakes; pop., any large snake which crushes its prey 1836. Hence **Pytho·nic** *a.*[1] of, pertaining to, or resembling the p.; monstrous, huge.

Python[2] (pəi·þǫn). 1603. [ad. late L. *pytho, pythonem*, or late Gr. πύθων familiar spirit.] A familiar or possessing spirit; also, one possessed by such a spirit and acting as its mouthpiece. Hence **Pytho·nic** *a.*[2] prophetic, oracular; **-al** *a.* (now *rare*).

Pythoness (pəi·þŏnės). late ME. [a. OF. *phitonise*, ad. med.L. *phitonissa*; later F. *pythonisse*, ad. late L. PYTHONISSA.] A woman supposed to have a familiar spirit, and to utter his words; a woman having the power of soothsaying; a witch.

Pythonism (pəi·þŏniz'm). *rare.* 1662. [f. PYTHON[2] + -ISM.] Possession by a pythonic spirit; occult power thence derived; divination.

‖**Pythonissa** (pəiþŏni·să). Now *rare.* late ME. [Late L., fem. of *pytho* PYTHON[2].] = PYTHONESS. (Often treated as the proper name of the witch of Endor.)

Pythonomorph (pəiþō̆ᵘ·nǫmǭɹf). 1880. [ad. mod.L. *Pythonomorpha* pl., f. PYTHON[1] 2 + Gr. μορφή form.] *Palæont.* One of the *Pythonomorpha*, a division of extinct reptiles allied to the existing *Pythonoidea* (the peropodous snakes); a MOSASAURIAN.

Pyuria (pəiyūᵊ·riă). 1811. [f. PYO- + -URIA.] *Path.* Discharge of pus with urine.

Pyx (piks), *sb.* late ME. [ad. L. *pyxis*, a. Gr. πυξίς a box, f. πύξος box-tree.] **1.** A box; a coffer; a vase (*rare*) 1604. **2.** *Eccl.* The vessel in which the host or consecrated bread of the Sacrament is reserved. late ME. **3.** At the Royal Mint, London, the box or chest in which specimen gold and silver coins are deposited to be tested at the *trial of the p.*, i.e. the final official trial of the purity and weight of the coins, now conducted annually by a jury of the Goldsmiths' Company 1598. **4.** *Anat.* = PYXIS 2. 1864.

Comb. **p.-cloth**, a cloth used to veil the p.

Pyx (piks), *v.* 1546. [f. prec.] *trans.* To place in a pyx. **a.** To reserve (the host) in a pyx. **b.** To deposit (specimen coins) in the pyx (PYX *sb.* 3); hence, To test (coin) by weight and assay 1561.

Pyxidate (pi·ksideᶦt), *a.* 1753. [ad. mod. L. *pyxidatus*, f. *pyxis, -idem* box; see -ATE[2] 2.] *Bot.* Having the form of a pyxis or pyxidium; opening, as a capsule, with a transverse slit; also, bearing pyxidia.

‖**Pyxidium** (piksi·diɒ̆m). *Pl.* **-ia.** 1832. [mod.L., ad. Gr. πυξίδιον, dim. of πυξίς a box; see PYX.] *Bot.* A capsule opening by transverse dehiscence, so that the top comes off like the lid of a box.

‖**Pyxis** (pi·ksis). *Pl.* **pyxides** (pi·ksidīz). late ME. [L.] **1.** = PYX 1, 2. 1536. **2.** *Anat.* The acetabulum or socket of the hipbone, into which the head of the thigh-bone is inserted. late ME. **3.** (In full *p. nautica*.) The mariners' compass 1686. **4.** *Bot.* **a.** = prec. **b.** A cup-like dilatation of the podetium in lichens, having shields on its edge. 1845.

Q

Q (kiū), the seventeenth letter of the English and the sixteenth of the Roman alphabet, was in the latter an adoption of the Ϙ (κόππα, *koppa*) of some of the early Greek alphabets. The Phœnician letter from which this was derived had the forms φ, φ, ϕ, and was used as the sign for the more guttural of the two *k*-sounds which exist in the Semitic tongues. In OE. orthography the ordinary symbol for the Com.Teut. initial combination *kw-* was *cw-* (in early use also *cu-*). By the end of the 13th c. *cw-* was entirely discontinued, and *qu-* (or its variants *qv-*, *qw-*) was the established spelling for all cases of the sound (kw), whether of English, French, or Latin origin. In ordinary mod. English words *q* is employed only in the combination *qu*, whether this is initial as in *quality*, etc., medial as in *equal*, etc., or representing a final (k), as in *cheque, grotesque*, etc.

I. Used to denote serial order, as 'Q Battery', 'Section Q', etc., or as a symbol of some thing or person, a point in a diagram, etc.

II. Abbreviations. **1.** Of Latin words or phrases. **a.** q.v. = *quod vide* 'which see'. †**b.** From the language of medical prescriptions: q.l. = *quantum libet*, q.pl. = *quantum placet* 'as much as one pleases'; q.s. = QUANTUM SUFFICIT; q.v. = *quantum vis* 'as much as you wish'. **c.** Formulæ placed at the end of mathematical problems or theorems: Q.E.D., Q.E.F., Q.E.I., = *quod erat demonstrandum, faciendum, inveniendum*, 'which was to be demonstrated, done, found'.

2. Of English words or phrases. **a.** Q. = Queen; Q., q. = query, question; q. (in a ship's log) = squalls. **b.** Q.B. = Queen's Bench; Q.C. = Queen's Counsel; Q.M. = Quartermaster; Q.M.G. = Quartermaster-General; Q.T., q.t. = quiet (*slang*); phr. *on the q. t.* **c.** qr. = quarter, quire; qt. = quart, quantity; qu. = query.

Q-boat, Q-ship. 1919. = MYSTERY-*ship*.

‖**Qua** (kwēᶦ), *adv.* Also **quà, quâ.** 1647. [L., abl. sing. fem. of *qui* who.] In so far as; in the capacity of.

The Apostle commands Wives to submit to their Husbands, surely *quà* Husbands, not *quà* men 1649.

Qua-bird (kwā·bəɹd). *U.S.* 1789. [f. *qua*, imitative of its note + BIRD *sb.*] The Night Heron of N. America, *Nycticorax Gardeni*.

Quack (kwæk), *sb.*[1] 1638. [Abbrev. of QUACKSALVER.] **1.** An ignorant pretender to medical skill; one who boasts to have a knowledge of wonderful remedies; an empiric or imposter in medicine 1659. **2.** *transf.* One who professes a knowledge or skill concerning subjects of which he is ignorant 1638. **3.** *attrib.*, as *quack-doctor*, etc. 1653.

1. Running after Quacks and Mountebanks..for Medicines and Remedies DE FOE. Hence **Qua·ckish** *a.* of the nature of a q. or quackery. **Qua·ckism**, quackery.

Quack (kwæk), *sb.*[2] 1839. [Imitative.] The harsh cry characteristic of a duck; a sound resembling this.

Quack (kwæk), *v.*[1] 1628. [f. QUACK *sb.*[1]] **1.** *intr.* To play the quack; to talk pretentiously and ignorantly, like a quack. **2.** *trans.* To puff or palm off with fraudulent and boastful pretensions, as a quack-medicine 1651. **3.** To treat after the fashion of a quack; to administer quack medicines to; to seek to remedy by empirical or ignorant treatment 1746.

2. The Politician must be quacked, paragraphed,.. and coteried into notoriety 1830. **3.** A Valetudinarian, who quacked himself to death BENTHAM.

Quack (kwæk), *v.*[2] 1617. [Imitative.] **1.** *intr.* Of a duck: To utter its characteristic note. **b.** Of a raven or frog: To croak (*rare*) 1727. **2.** *transf.* To make a harsh sound like the note of a duck, make a noisy outcry 1624.

Quackery (kwæ·kəri). 1709. [f. QUACK *sb.*[1] + -ERY.] The characteristic practices or methods of a quack; charlatanry.

Quackle (kwæ·k'l), *v.* 1564. [In form a deriv. of QUACK *v.*[2], but earlier.] *intr.* To quack, as a duck.

Quack-quack (kwæk₁kwæk). 1865. [Imitative; see QUACK *sb.*[2]] An imitation of the note of a duck; a nursery name for a duck.

Quacksalver (kwæ·ksælvəɹ). 1579. [a. early mod.Du. *quacksalver*, perh. f. *quack-*, stem of *quacken* to quack + *salf, zalf* salve, ointment.] **1.** = QUACK *sb.*[1] 1. **2.** *transf.* = QUACK *sb.*[1] 2. 1611. So †**Qua·cksalving** *ppl. a.* belonging to or characteristic of a q.; resembling, acting like, a q.

Quad (kwǫd), *sb.*[1] 1820. Abbrev. (orig. in Oxford slang) of QUADRANGLE 2.

Quad (kwǫd), *sb.*[2] 1880. Abbrev. of QUADRAT 2.

Quad (kwǫd), *a.* 1888. Abbrev. of QUADRUPLE *a.* c.

Quad (kwǫd), *v.* 1888. [f. QUAD *sb.*[2]] *Printing.* To insert quadrats in (a line of type); to fill with quadrats.

Quadrable (kwǫ·drăb'l), *a.* 1695. [f. L. *quadrare* QUADRATE *v.*; see -ABLE.] *Math.* Capable of being represented by an equivalent square, or of being expressed in a finite number of algebraic terms.

Quadragenarian (kwǫ:drădʒĭnēᵊ·riăn), *a.* and *sb.* 1839. [f. L. *quadragenarius* (f. *quadrageni*) + -AN.] **A.** *adj.* Forty years old. **B.** *sb.* A person forty years of age. So **Qua:dragena·rious** *a.* 1656.

‖**Quadragesima** (kwǫdrădʒe·simă). 1581. [med.L., fem. (sc. *dies*) of L. *quadragesimus* fortieth, f. *quadraginta* forty.] *Eccl.* †**a.** The forty days of Lent. **b.** (Also *Q. Sunday*.) The first Sunday in Lent. Hence **Quadrage·simal** *a.* of a fast (*esp.* that of Lent), lasting for forty days; belonging or appropriate to the period of Lent.

Quadrangle (kwǫ·dræŋg'l). late ME. [a. F., ad. late L. *quadrangulum*, neut. of *quadrangulus* four-cornered, f. *quadr-* QUADRI- + *angulus*.] **1.** *Geom.* A figure having four angles, and therefore four sides. **2.** A square or rectangular space or court, the sides of which are occupied by parts of a large building, as a palace, college, etc. 1593. **3.** A building containing a quadrangle 1620. Hence **Quadra·ngular** *a.* shaped like a q.; having four angles; **-ly** *adv.*

Quadrant (kwǫ·drănt), *sb.*[1] late ME. [ad. L. *quadrans, -antem* fourth part, quarter, f. *quadr-* QUADRI-.] †1. A quarter of a day; six hours –1646. 2. A quarter of a circle or circular body, viz. (*a*) an arc of a circle, forming one fourth of the circumference; (*b*) one fourth of the area of a circle, contained within two radii at right angles 1571. **b.** A thing having the form of a quarter-circle 1638. 3. An instrument, properly having the form of a graduated quarter-circle, used for making angular measurements, *esp.* for taking altitudes in astronomy and navigation. late ME.

2. b. *Q. of altitude*, a graduated strip of brass on an artificial globe, fixed at one end to some point of the meridian, round which it revolves, and extending round one fourth of the circumference.

†**Quadrant**, *sb.*[2] 1443. [app. alteration of QUADRAT or QUADRATE *sb.*[1], through assoc. with prec.] 1. = QUADRANGLE 2, 3. –1655. 2. A square; a square thing or piece (also *fig.*); a square picture –1670.

†**Qua·drant**, *a.* 1509. [ad. L. *quadrantem*, *quadrare* to square; cf. prec.] Square –1618.

Quadrantal (kwǫdræ·ntăl), *a.* 1678. [ad. L. *quadrantalis*; see QUADRANT *sb.*[1] and -AL.] Having the shape of, consisting of, connected with a quadrant or quarter-circle; esp. *q. arc.*

Quadrat (kwǫ·drăt). late ME. [var. of QUADRATE *sb.*, in special senses.] †1. An instrument formerly used for measuring altitudes or distances, consisting of a square plate with two graduated sides, sights, etc. –1617. 2. *Printing.* A small block of metal, lower than the face of the type, used by printers for spacing; abbrev. QUAD *sb.*[2]

Quadrate (kwǫ·drė̆t), *sb.* 1471. [ad. L. *quadratum* sb., neut. sing. of *quadratus* QUADRATE *a.*] †1. A square; a square area or space; also, a rectangle or rectangular space –1680. †**b.** A square number; the square *of* a number –1646. 2. A square or rectangular plate or block (*rare*) 1647. †3. *Astron.* Quadrate aspect; quadrature –1695. 4. *Anat.* **a.** The quadrate bone. **b.** A quadrate muscle. 1872.

1. The Powers Militant, That stood for Heav'n, in mighty Q. joyn'd MILT. 2. His person was a q., his step massy and elephantine LAMB.

Quadrate (kwǫ·drĕ̄t), *a.* late ME. [ad. L. *quadratus*, *quadrare* to square.] 1. Square, rectangular. Now *rare.* †**b.** *Math.* Of numbers or roots: Square –1660. **c.** *Anat.* In the names of parts of the body having an approximately square shape 1856. †2. *Astron.* = QUARTILE *a.* –1685.

1. A strong Castel q. having at eche corner a great Round Tower LELAND. **c.** *Q. bone*, a special bone in the head of birds and reptiles, by which the lower jaw is articulated to the skull.

Quadrate (kwǫ·dreit), *v.* 1560. [f. L. *quadrat-*, *quadrare* to square.] 1. *trans.* To make (a thing) square (*rare*). **b.** *Math.* To square (a circle, etc.) (*rare*) 1645. 2. *intr.* To square, agree, correspond, conform *with* (rarely *to*) 1610. **b.** Without const.: To be fitting, suitable, or consistent. Also of two things: To harmonize with each other. Now *rare.* 1664. **c.** *trans.* To make conformable (*to*). *rare.* 1669. 3. *Artillery.* **a.** *trans.* To adjust (a gun) on its carriage. **b.** *intr.* Of a gun: To lie properly on the carriage. 1706.

2. He had to make a creed which would q. with his immorality 1876.

Quadratic (kwǫdræ·tik), *a.* and *sb.* 1656. [See QUADRATE *sb.* and -IC.] **A.** *adj.* 1. Square (*rare*). **b.** *Cryst.* Of square section through the lateral or secondary axes; characterized by this form 1871. 2. *Math.* Involving the second and no higher power of an unknown quantity or of a variable; esp. in *q. equation* 1668. **B.** *sb.* **a.** A quadratic equation. **b.** *pl.* The branch of algebra dealing with quadratic equations. 1684. So **Quadra·tical** *a.*

Quadrato- (kwǫdrē̆i·to), comb. form of L. *quadratus* or *quadratum*; *spec.* in *Zool.*, connected with or pertaining to the quadrate together with some other bone, as **Quadra:to-ju·gal** *a.*

Quadratrix (kwǫdrē̆i·triks). *Pl.* **-trices.** 1656. [mod.L. fem. agent-n. from *quadrare.*] A curve used in the process of squaring other curves.

Quadrature (kwǫ·drătiŭɹ). 1563. [ad. L. *quadratura* a square, the act of squaring; see QUADRATE *v.* and -URE.] †1. Square shape, squareness –1667. 2. *Math.* The action or process of squaring; *spec.* the expression of an area bounded by a curve, esp. of a circle, by means of an equivalent square 1596. 3. *Astron.* **a.** One of the two points (in space or time) at which the moon is 90° distant from the sun, or midway between the points of conjunction and opposition 1685. **b.** The position of one heavenly body relative to another when they are 90° apart, *esp.* of the moon to the sun when they are at the quadratures 1591.

Quadrennial (kwǫ̆dre·niăl), *a.* and *sb.* Also quadriennial. 1646. [See next and -AL.] **A.** *adj.* 1. Occurring every fourth year 1700. 2. Lasting for four years 1656. **B.** *sb.* †**a.** A period of four years (*rare*). **b.** An event happening every four years. 1646. Hence **Quadre·nnially** *adv.*

‖**Quadrennium** (kwǫ̆dre·niŏ̆m). Also quadriennium. 1797. [a. L. *quadriennium*, f. *quadri-* + *annus.*] A period of four years.

Quadri- (kwǫ·dri), also, before a *vowel*, *quadr-*, a comb. element (= L. *quattuor* four) with the sense 'having, consisting of, connected with, etc. four (things specified)'.

I. Adjs. with the sense 'having or consisting of four—', 'characterized by the number four', as **qua·driform**, having four forms or aspects; **quadri·li·ngual** [late L. *-linguis*], using, written in, etc., four languages; **quadrino·mial, -no·mical, -no·minal**, consisting of four (algebraic) terms.
b. *Bot.* and *Zool.*, as **quadrica·psular, ca·psulate; quadrici·pital**, having four heads or points of origin, as the quadriceps muscle; **quadride·ntate(d)**, having four serrations or indentations; **qua·drifid**, cleft into four divisions or lobes; **quadrifo·liate**, consisting of four leaves; **quadrige·minal, -ous**, belonging to the *corpora quadrigemina* at the base of the brain; **quadrilo·bate, -lobed; quadriva·lve, -va·lvular.**
II. Sbs., vbs., and advs., chiefly from adjs. in I: **quadriceps** (extensor) [cf. BICEPS], a large muscle of the leg, having four heads; **qua·dricy:cle**, a four-wheeled cycle; **qua·drifoil** = QUATREFOIL; **quadrise·ction**, a division into four equal parts; **quadrisy·llable**, a word of four syllables; **qua·drivalve**, a plant with a quadrivalvular seed-pod; an instrument, *esp.* a speculum, with four valves.
b. *Math.* Chiefly in sense 'quadric', 'of the second degree or order', as **qua·dricone**, etc.; also **quadrino·mial**, an expression consisting of four terms.
c. *Chem.* In the names of chemical compounds (now superseded by) TETRA-.

Quadric (kwǫ·drik), *a.* and *sb.* 1856. [f. L. *quadra* square; see -IC.] *Math.* **A.** *adj.* Of the second degree. (Used in solid geometry where the variables are more than two.) 1858. **B.** *sb.* A quantic of the second degree; a surface or curve whose equation in three variables is of the second degree 1856.

‖**Quadriga** (kwǫ̆drəi·gă). 1727. [L.; sing. form for pl. *quadrigæ* contr. of *quadrijugæ*, f. QUADRI- + *jugum* yoke.] A chariot drawn by four horses harnessed abreast; esp. as represented in sculpture or on coins.

Quadrilateral (kwǫdrilæ·tĕrăl), *a.* and *sb.* 1650. [f. L. *quadrilaterus* + -AL.] **A.** *adj.* Four-sided; having a four-sided base or section 1656. **B.** *sb.* A figure bounded by four straight lines; a space or area having four sides 1650. **b.** The space lying between, and defended by, four fortresses; *spec.* that in North Italy formed by the fortresses of Mantua, Verona, Peschiera, and Legnano 1859.

Quadriliteral (kwǫdrili·tĕrăl), *a.* and *sb.* 1771. [f. QUADRI- + LITERAL.] **A.** *adj.* Consisting of four letters; *spec.* of Semitic roots which have four consonants instead of the usual three. **B.** *sb.* A word of four letters; a root containing four consonants 1787.

Quadrille (kwǫ̆dri·l, kă-), *sb.*[1] 1726. [a. F., perh. ad. Sp. *cuartillo*, the form in F. being due to association w. next.] A card game played by four persons with forty cards, the eights, nines, and tens of the ordinary pack being discarded.

Quadrille (kwǫ̆dri·l, k(w)ă-), *sb.*[2] 1738. [a. F., ad. Sp. *cuadrilla*, It. *quadriglia* a band, troop, company, app. f. *cuadra, quadra* square.] 1. One of four groups of horsemen taking part in a tournament or carousel, each being distinguished by special costume or colours. 2. A square dance, of French origin, usu. performed by four couples, and containing five sections or figures, each of which is a complete dance in itself. Also called 'a set of quadrilles'. **b.** A piece of music for such a dance. 1773.

Quadrillion (kwǫ̆dri·lyən). 1674. [a. F., f. *quadri-* + (*m*)*illion*; see BILLION.] **a.** In Great Britain: The fourth power of a million (1 followed by 24 ciphers). **b.** In U. S. (as in France): The fifth power of a thousand (1 followed by 15 ciphers).

Quadripartite (kwǫdripā·ɹtəit), *a.* and *sb.* late ME. [ad. L. *quadripartitus*, f. *quadri-* QUADRI- + pa. pple. of *partiri* to divide.] **A.** *adj.* 1. Divided into, or consisting of, four parts. Now chiefly in *Bot.*, *Zool.*, and *Arch.* **b.** *spec.* Of a contract, indenture, etc.: Drawn up in four corresponding parts, one for each party 1527. 2. Divided among or shared by four persons or parties 1594. **B.** *sb.* The Tetrabiblos of Ptolemy 1477. Hence **Quadripa·rtitely** *adv.* So **Qua:driparti·tion**, division into or by four.

Quadrireme (kwǫ·drirīm), *a.* and *sb.* 1600. [ad. L. *quadriremis*, f. *quadri-* QUADRI- + *remus* oar.] **A.** *adj.* Of ancient ships: Having four banks of oars. **B.** *sb.* A vessel having four banks of oars 1656.

Quadrivial (kwǫ̆dri·viăl), *a.* and *sb.* late ME. [ad. med.L. *quadrivialis*; see next and -AL.] **A.** *adj.* 1. Having four ways meeting in a point. Of roads: Leading in four directions. 1490. 2. Belonging to the QUADRIVIUM. **B.** *sb. pl.* The four sciences constituting the QUADRIVIUM. Now *Hist.* 1522.

‖**Quadrivium** (kwǫ̆dri·viŏ̆m). 1804. [L. (f. *quadri-* QUADRI- + *via* way), a place where four ways meet.] In the Middle Ages, the higher division of the seven liberal arts, comprising the mathematical sciences (arithmetic, geometry, astronomy, and music).

Quadroon (kwǫ̆drū̆·n). 1707. [ad. Sp. *cuarteron*, f. *cuarto* fourth, quarter; perh. assoc. with other words in *quadr-*.] 1. **a.** The offspring of a white person and a mulatto; one who has a quarter of negro blood. **b.** *rarely.* One who is fourth in descent from a negro, one of the parents in each generation being white. Also *transf.* 1796. 2. *attrib.* or as *adj.* 1748.

1. b. *transf.* Koelreuter artificially fertilised hybrid flowers..and thus obtained a vegetable q. 1879.

Quadru- (kwǫ·dru), var. of QUADRI-; in L. used only in formations where the second element begins with *p*, as *quadrupes, quadruplex*, etc. Apart from words based on these L. forms, Eng. has *quadru-* only in *quadrumanous*, etc., and a few 16–17th c. examples.

‖**Quadrumana** (kwǫ̆drū̆·mănă), *sb. pl.* 1819. [neut. pl. (sc. *animalia*) of mod.L. *quadrumanus* four-handed, f. *quadru-* QUADRU- + *manus.*] *Zool.* An order of mammals, including monkeys, apes, baboons, and lemurs, of which the hind as well as the fore feet have an opposable digit, so that they can be used as hands. Hence **Quadru·manal, Quadru·manous** *adjs.* belonging to the Q.; four-handed.

Quadrumane (kwǫ·drumein), *a.* and *sb.* Also quadruman (-mæn). 1828. [a. F. *quadrumane*; see prec.] **A.** *adj.* = QUADRUMANOUS 1835. **B.** *sb.* One of the QUADRUMANA 1828.

Quadruped (kwǫ·drŭped), *sb.* (*a.*) 1646. [ad. L. *quadrupes, -pedis* four-footed, also as sb., f. *quadru-* QUADRU- + *pes.*] 1. An animal which has four feet. (Usu. confined to mammals, and excluding four-footed reptiles.) **b.** Applied *spec.* to the horse 1660. 2. *attrib.* or *adj.* Four-footed 1741. **b.** Belonging to, or connected with, four-footed animals 1835. Hence **Quadru·pedal** *a.* four-footed; of, belonging or appropriate to a q.

Quadruple (kwǫ·drup'l), *a.*, *sb.*, and *adv.* late ME. [a. F., ad. L. *quadruplus*, f. *quadru-* QUADRU- + *-plus* as in *duplus* DOUBLE.] **A.** *adj.* Fourfold; consisting of four parts; four times as great or as many as. Const. *of, to,* or without prep. 1557. **b.** *Q. alliance*, an alliance of four powers, *esp.* that of Britain, France, Germany, and Holland in 1718, and of Britain, France, Spain, and Portugal in 1834. 1735. **c.** Applied to printing-papers which are four times the usual size, as *q. crown*, etc. 1889.

Q. rhythm, time, in *Mus.*, rhythm or time having four beats in a measure.

B. *sb.* **1.** Anything fourfold; a sum or quantity four times as great as another. late ME. **2.** *spec.* †**a.** A coin of the value of four pistoles –1695. **b.** A printing machine which prints four copies at once 1890. **C.** *adv.* In a fourfold manner 1840. Hence **Qua·druply** *adv.*

Quadruple (kwǫ·drup'l), *v.* late ME. [ad. F. *quadrupler* or L. *quadruplare*, f. *quadruplus*; see prec.] **1.** *trans.* To make four times as great or as many; to multiply by four. **2.** To amount to four times as many as 1832. **3.** *intr.* (for *refl.*) To grow to four times as many or as much 1776.

3. The exports..have quadrupled since the relaxation of the monopoly 1833.

Quadruplet (kwǫ·druplet). 1787. [f. QUADRUPLE + -ET; after *triplet*.] **1.** *pl.* Four children born at a birth. **2.** Any combination of four things or parts united or working together 1852.

Quadruplex (kwǫ·druplex), *a.* and *sb.* 1875. [a. L., f. QUADRU- + *plic-*, to fold.] **A.** *adj.* **1.** *Electric Telegr.* Applied to a system by which four messages can be sent over one wire at one time. **2.** *Engineering.* Applied to an engine in which the expansion of the steam is used four times in cylinders of increasing diameter 1896. **B.** *sb.* A telegraphic instrument by means of which four simultaneous messages can be sent over the same wire 1889. Hence **Qua·druplex** *v. trans.* to make (a telegraph circuit, etc.) q.

Quadruplicate (kwǫdrū·plikĕt), *a.* and *sb.* 1657. [ad. L. *quadruplicatus*, *quadruplicare* to quadruple, f. *quadruplex*; see prec.] **A.** *adj.* **1.** Fourfold; four times repeated. **2.** Forming four exactly similar copies 1807.

1. *Q. proportion, ratio*, the proportion or ratio of fourth powers in relation to that of the radical quantities.

B. *sb.* **1.** *In q.*: in four exactly corresponding copies or transcripts 1790. **2.** *pl.* Four things, *esp.* copies of a document, exactly alike 1883.

Quadruplicate (kwǫdrū·plikeit), *v.* 1661. [f. ppl. stem of L. *quadruplicare*; see prec.] **1.** *trans.* To multiply by four; to quadruple. **2.** To make or provide in quadruplicate 1879. Hence **Quadruplica·tion**, the action of making fourfold, of multiplying by four; also, the result of this.

Quadruplicity (kwǫdrupli·sĭti). 1590. [ad. L. *quadruplicitas*, f. *quadruplex*; see -ITY.] Fourfold nature; the condition of being fourfold, or of forming a set of four.

‖**Quære** (kwīə·rī), *v. imper.* and *sb.* 1535. [L., imper. of *quærere* to ask, inquire. Now usu. QUERY.] **A.** *v. imper.* Ask, inquire; hence, 'one may ask', 'it is a question' (*whether*, etc.). **B.** *sb.* A question, QUERY 1589.

A. Q. more about this HEARNE. Hence †**Quære** *v. trans.* to query –1756.

Quæstor (kwī·stǫɹ). late ME. [a. L., f. *quærere*.] *Rom. Antiq.* **a.** One of a number of Roman officials who had charge of the public revenue and expenditure. **b.** In early times: A public prosecutor in certain criminal cases. Hence **Quæsto·rial** *a.* **Quæ·storship.**

Quaff (kwɑf), *sb.* 1579. [f. next.] An act of quaffing, or the liquor quaffed; a deep draught.

Quaff (kwɑf), *v.* Also †**quaft.** 1523. [prob. onomatopœic.] **1.** *intr.* To drink deeply; to take a long draught; also, to drink repeatedly in this manner. Const. *of* (†*in*). 1529. **2.** *trans.* To drink (liquor) copiously or in a large draught 1555. **3.** To drain (a cup, etc.) in a copious draught or draughts. Also with *off, out, up.* 1523. **4.** To drive *away*, to bring *down to* or *into* (a certain state) by copious drinking (*rare*) 1714.

1. To day we feast, and quaffe in frolique Bowles; To morrow fast QUARLES. **2.** *fig.* They drink, and in communion sweet Q. immortalitie and joy MILT. **3.** I quaffe full bowles of strong enchanting wines DEKKER. Hence **Qua·ffer.**

Quag (kwæg, kwǫg), *sb.* 1589. [Related to next.] A marshy or boggy spot, *esp.* one covered with a layer of turf which shakes or yields when walked on.

Quag (kwæg, kwǫg), *v.* *Obs.* exc. *dial.* 1611. [Onomatopœic.] *intr.* To shake; said of something soft or flabby.

Quagga (kwæ·gă). 1785. [S. Afr.] **a.** A S. African equine quadruped (*Equus* or *Hippotigris Q.*), related to the ass and the zebra, but less fully striped than the latter. **b.** Burchell's zebra.

Quaggy (kwæ·gi, kwǫ·gi), *a.* 1610. [f. QUAG *sb.* or *v.* + -Y[1].] **1.** Of ground: That shakes under the foot; full of quags; boggy, soft. Also of streams: Flowing through boggy soil. **2.** Of things, esp. of the body: Soft, yielding, flabby. Also of persons in respect of their flesh, and *fig.* 1611.

1. O'er the watery strath or q. moss COLLINS.

Quagmire (kwæ·gməiəɹ, kwǫ·g-). 1579. [app. f. QUAG *sb.* or *v.* + MIRE.] **1.** A piece of wet and boggy ground, which quakes or yields under the feet; a quaking bog; a fen, marsh. **2.** *transf.* and *fig.*; *esp.* a position or situation from which extrication is difficult 1635.

2. I have followed Cupid's Jack-a-lantern, and find my self in a q. at last SHERIDAN.

Quahaug, quahog (kwăhǭ·g, kwǭ·hǫg). *U.S.* 1794. [Narraganset Indian.] The common round clam (*Venus mercenaria*) of the Atlantic coast of N. America.

Quaich, quaigh (kwēχ). *Sc.* 1673. [a. Gael. *cuach* cup, OIr. *cúach*, prob. ad. L. *caucus* (Gr. καῦκα).] A kind of shallow drinking-cup formerly common in Scotland, usu. made of small wooden staves hooped together and having two ears or handles.

Quail (kwēl), *sb.* ME. [a. OF. *quaille* (F. *caille*); prob. of Teut. origin.] **1.** A migratory bird allied to the partridge (family *Perdicidæ*), found in the Old World and Australia; *esp.* the European species, *Coturnix communis* or *dactylisonans*, much esteemed for the table. **2.** One of several American gallinaceous birds resembling the European quail, *esp.* the Virginian Quail or colin (*Ortyx virginianus*), and the Californian or Crested Quail (*Lophortyx californicus*) 1817. †**3.** *fig.* A courtesan. (In allusion to the supposed amorous disposition of the bird.) –1694.

attrib. and *Comb.*, as **q.-call** = *q.-pipe*; **-dove,** a dove of the West Indies and Florida (*Starnœnas cyanocephalus*); **-hawk,** a New Zealand species of falcon; **-pigeon,** a pigeon of the genus *Geophaps*; **-pipe,** a pipe on which the note of the q. (usu. the female) can be imitated, in order to lure the birds into a net; †*transf.* the throat; **-snipe,** a S. American plover of the genus *Thinocorys*.

Quail (kwēl), *v.* ME. [Origin unkn. Common in literary use 1520–1650, after which it becomes rare until revived, app. by Scott.] **I.** *intr.* **1.** Of material things: To decline; to fail or give way; to fade, wither, etc. *Obs.* exc. *dial.* 1440. **2.** Of immaterial things. **a.** Of an action, undertaking, etc.: †To fail, break down. In mod. use (transf. from 3): To give way, yield *to* or *before*. ME. **b.** Of courage, etc.: To fail, give way, become faint 1557. **3.** Of persons: To lose heart, be cowed; to give way through fear (*to* or *before*) 1555. **b.** Of the heart or spirit; also of the eyes 1563.

1. Length of time, causeth man and beast to quaile 1568. **2. b.** Perils, which make the courage of the hardiest q. THIRLWALL. **3. b.** Their sharp eyes quailed..before his savage glances BORROW.

II. *trans.* †**1.** To spoil, impair; to overpower, destroy –1669. **2.** To daunt or cow (a person), to bring into subjection by fear; to cause to quail 1526. **b.** To daunt (the heart, courage) with fear or dejection 1567.

1. *Mids. N.* v. i. 292. **2.** He is a stout man whom adversity doth not quaile 1642. Hence **Quai·ler.**

Quaint (kwēint), *a.* ME. [a. OF. *queinte*, *cointe*:—L. *cognitum* known, pa. pple. of *cognoscere*.] **I.** †**1.** Of persons: Wise, knowing; skilled, clever, ingenious –1728. †**b.** In bad sense: Cunning, crafty, scheming –1680. †**2.** Of actions, schemes, etc.: Ingenious, clever, cunning –1641. †**3.** Of things: Ingeniously or cunningly designed or contrived; elaborate –1631. †**4.** Of things: Skilfully made, so as to have a good appearance; hence, beautiful, pretty, fine, dainty –1671. †**b.** Of dress: Fine, fashionable, elegant –1627. †**5.** Of persons: Beautiful or handsome in appearance; finely dressed; elegant, foppish –1784. †**6.** Of speech, modes of expression, etc.: Carefully or ingeniously elaborated; highly elegant or refined; clever, smart; affected –1783. †**7.** Strange, odd, curious (in character or appearance) –1808. **8.** Unusual or uncommon in character or appearance, but agreeable or attractive, esp. having an old-fashioned prettiness or daintiness 1795.

1. *Tam. Shr.* III. ii. 149. **b.** Sly, queynt, and fals HOCCLEVE. **4.** In his hand A Scepter or q. staff he bears MILT. **5.** He made himselfe as neate and q. as might be GREENE. **7.** The Flamins at their service q. MILT. **8.** He..knew many a merry ballad and q. tale SOUTHEY.

†**II.** Dainty, fastidious, prim –1678.

Too Queint and Finical in his Expressions 1678. Hence **Quai·ntly** *adv.*, **-ness.**

Quake (kwēⁱk), *sb.* ME. [f. the vb.] The act of quaking or trembling; *spec.* in mod. use, an earthquake.

Quake (kwēⁱk), *v.* [OE. *cwacian*, not found in the cognate langs.] **1.** *intr.* Of things: To shake, tremble, be agitated, as the result of external shock, internal convulsion, or natural instability. **2.** Of persons, etc., or parts of the body: To shake, tremble, through cold, fear, etc. OE. †**3.** *trans.* To cause to quake –1639.

1. With boughs that quaked at every breath, Grey birch and aspen wept beneath SCOTT. **2.** They reuerence them, and qwake at their presence KNOX. *Cymb.* II. iv. 5. Hence **Qua·kingly** *adv.* with quaking or fear.

Quaker (kwēⁱ·kəɹ). 1653. [f. QUAKE *v.* + -ER[1].] A member of the religious society (the Society of Friends) founded by George Fox in 1648–50, distinguished by peaceful principles and plainness of dress and manners. **b.** *transf.* Applied to various plain-coloured birds and moths, with allusion to the colour of the dress usu. worn by Quakers 1775.

attrib. and *Comb.*: **q.-bird,** the sooty albatross; **-buttons** *U.S.*, the seeds of nux vomica; **q. gun** *U.S.*, a dummy gun in a ship or fort; **-ladies** *U.S.*, the small pale-blue flowers of the American plant *Houstonia cærulea*. Hence **Qua·keress,** a female Q. **Qua·kerish** *a.* resembling, characteristic of, or appropriate to, Quakers; **-ly** *adv.* **Qua·kerism,** the principles or practice of the Quakers. **Qua·kerly** *a.* and *adv.* †**Qua·kery,** Quakerism.

Qua·king-grass. 1597. [f. *quaking* ppl. a. of QUAKE *v.*] A pop. name for grasses of the genus *Briza*, esp. *B. media*.

Quaky (kwēⁱ·ki), *a.* 1864. [f. QUAKE *v.* + -Y[1].] Inclined to quake; of the nature of quaking.

‖**Quale** (kwēⁱ·lī). 1675. [L., neut. sing. of *qualis* of what kind.] The quality of a thing; a thing having certain qualities.

Qua·lifiable, *a. rare.* 1611. [f. QUALIFY *v.* + -ABLE.] That may be qualified or modified.

Qualification (kwǫ:lifikēⁱ·ʃən). 1543. [ad. med.L. *qualificatio*, f. *qualificare* to QUALIFY; see -ATION.] The action of qualifying; the condition or fact of being qualified; that which qualifies. **1.** Modification, limitation, restriction; a modifying or limiting element or circumstance. †**2.** The distinctive quality *of* a person or thing; condition, character, nature –1745. †**3.** A quality, attribute, or property (*of*) –1799. †**b.** An accomplishment –1796. **4.** A quality, accomplishment, etc., which qualifies or fits a person *for* some office or function. Also *absol.* 1669. **5.** A necessary condition, which must be fulfilled before a certain right can be acquired, an office held, or the like 1723. **6.** The act of determining the quality or nature of a thing; *spec.* in *Logic*, the expression of quality, or the distinction of affirmative and negative, in a proposition 1891.

1. A promise that hath a q. or condition expressed 1651. **2.** *Oth.* II. i. 282. **4.** Besides his general qualifications for that trust 1669. **5.** A law which fixes a sum of money as the q. of citizenship JOWETT.

Comb. **q. shares,** shares which one must hold in order to be qualified for a directorship in a company.

Qualificative (kwǫ·lifikēⁱtiv), *a.* and *sb.* *rare.* 1661. [f. QUALIFY *v.*; see prec. and -ATIVE.] **A.** *adj.* Qualifying; denoting some quality. **B.** *sb.* A qualifying word or phrase.

Qualificator (kwǫ·lifikēⁱtəɹ). 1688. [a.

med.L., f. *qualificare.*] One of a board of theologians attached to the Holy Office, who report on the character (heretical or otherwise) of propositions submitted to them.

Qualificatory (kwǫ·lifikēᵢtəri), *a.* 1805. [Cf. prec. and -ORY [2].] Having the character of qualifying or modifying; tending to qualify.

Qualified (kwǫ·lifəid), *ppl. a.* 1558. [f. QUALIFY *v.* + -ED [1].] †1. Furnished with, possessed of (certain) qualities -1681. 2. Endowed with qualities, or possessed of accomplishments, which fit one for a certain end, office, or function; fit, competent 1558. 3. Legally, properly, or by custom, capable of doing or being something specified or implied 1559. 4. Limited, modified, or restricted in some respect; *spec.* in *q. acceptance, fee* (= *base fee*), *negative, oath, property,* etc. 1599. Hence **Qua·lified-ly** *adv.*, **-ness.**

Qualify (kwǫ·lifəi), *v.* 1540. [a. F. *qualifier*, or ad. med.L. *qualificare* to attribute a quality to, f. *qualis* of such a kind + *-ficare*; see -FY.] I. To invest with a quality or qualities. 1. *trans.* To attribute a certain quality or qualities to; to designate in a particular way. (Now current as a gallicism.) 1549. b. *Gram.* Of an adj.: To express some quality belonging to (a noun). Of an adv.: To modify. 1837. 2. To invest (a person) with proper qualities (*for* being something) 1581. b. To make fit or competent *for* doing (or *to do*) something, or *for* something. Chiefly *refl.* 1665. 3. To make legally capable; to give a recognized status to (a person) 1583. 4. *intr.* (for *refl.*) To make oneself competent *for* something *by* fulfilling some necessary condition 1588.

1. The propositions..have been qualified as heretical 1826. 2. b. I am qualifying myself to give lessons DICKENS. 4. All the ministers of state must q., and take this test BURKE.

II. To modify in some respect. 1. To modify (a statement, opinion, etc.) by any limitation or reservation; to make less strong or positive 1553. 2. To moderate or mitigate; *esp.* to render less violent, severe, or unpleasant; to lessen the effect of (something disagreeable) 1543. †b. To make less wrong -1776. †3. To appease, calm, pacify (a person) -1679. †4. To bring into, or keep in, a proper condition -1688. 5. To modify the strength or flavour of (a liquid) 1591. 6. †a. To affect (a person or thing) injuriously. b. To abate or diminish (something good); to make less perfect or complete. 1584.

1. Reasons to change or to q. some of my first sentiments BURKE. 2. b. A falsehood, however qualified by circumstances FIELDING. 5. Tea, which he drank.. qualified with brandy SMOLLETT. 6. b. *Haml.* IV. vii. 114. Hence **Qua·lifier**, one who, or that which, qualifies; *R. C. Ch.* = QUALIFICATOR.

Qualitative (kwǫ·litĕtiv), *a.* 1607. [ad. late L. *qualitativus*; see QUALITY and -IVE.] Relating to, connected or concerned with, quality or qualities. Now usu. opp. to QUANTITATIVE. Hence **Qua·litatively** *adv.*

Qualitied (kwǫ·litid), *a.* 1600. [f. next + -ED.] Furnished with a quality or qualities.

Quality (kwǫ·lĭti). [ME. *qualite*, a. F. *qualité*, ad. L. *qualitatem*, f. *qualis* of what kind; see -ITY.] I. Of persons (in 1 and 2 occas. of animals). 1. Character, disposition, nature. Now *rare.* b. Capacity, ability, or skill, in some respect. (An echo of Shaks. (*Ham.* II. ii. 452), who prob. intended the word in sense 5.) 1856. c. Without article or poss. pron.: Excellence of disposition; good natural gifts 1606. 2. A mental or moral attribute, trait, or characteristic 1533. b. An accomplishment or attainment 1584. 3. Rank or position in (a) society. Now *rare.* late ME. 4. Nobility, high birth or rank, good social position. Now *arch.* 1579. b. *concr.* People of good social position. Now *arch.* or *vulgar* and *dial.* 1693. †5. Profession, occupation, business, *esp.* that of an actor. b. Fraternity; those of the same profession; *esp.* actors as a body. -1633. c. Party, side. SHAKS. 6. Title, description, character, capacity. Freq. in phr. *in* (*the*) *q. of*: in the character of, as. Now chiefly as a gallicism. ME.

1. b. Hans had given me a touch of his q. by spearing a bird on the wing 1856. c. O, sir,..You are full of q. and faire desert HEYWOOD. 2. Youre godlye dysposytyon, and vertuous qualytyes 1551. b. *Timon* I. i. 125. 4. He had all the men of qualitie his sworne enemies NORTH. b. I have looked out among the q. for a future husband for her RICHARDSON. 5. *Two Gent.* IV. i. 58. 6. He serv'd his Master In q. of Poetaster 1664.

II. Of things. 1. An attribute, property, special feature ME. †b. A manner, style -1651. †c. *concretely.* A substance of a certain nature; an essence (*rare*) -1823. 2. The nature, kind, or character (*of* something); hence, the degree or grade of excellence, etc. possessed by a thing. late ME. †b. Nature, with ref. to origin; hence, cause, occasion SHAKS. 3. Without article: a. That aspect of things under which they are considered in thinking or speaking of their nature, condition, or properties 1533. b. *Gram.* Manner of action, as denoted by an adverb; chiefly in phr. *adverb of q.* 1530. c. Peculiar excellence or superiority 1874. 4. a. *Logic.* Of propositions: The condition of being affirmative or negative. Of concepts: Comparative clearness or distinctness. 1594. b. *Acoustics* = TIMBRE 1865. 5. A particular class, kind, or grade of anything, as determined by its quality 1656.

1. *Primary, secondary,* etc. *qualities*: see the adjs. 2. There is more difference in the q. of our pleasures than in the amount EMERSON. b. *Timon* III. vi. 117.

Qualm (kwām, kwǭm). 1530. [Origin obsc.] 1. A (sudden) feeling or fit of faintness, illness, or sickness. (Now restricted to cases in which the seat of disorder is in the stomach.) 2. *transf.* a. A fit of sickening fear, misgiving, or depression; a sudden sinking of heart. Now *rare.* 1555. b. A painful doubt or consciousness of acting wrongly 1649. c. A fit or sudden access *of* some quality, etc. (Now only with suggestion of prec.) 1626.

1. It makes the Stomach sick..and sickish Qualms to arise 1683. 2. b. It was absurd..to affect any qualms about this trifle FIELDING. c. Violent qualms of economy W. IRVING.

Qualmish (kwā·miʃ, kwǭ·miʃ), *a.* 1548. [f. QUALM + -ISH [1].] 1. Of persons: Affected with a qualm or qualms; tending or liable to be so affected. 2. Of feelings, etc.: Of the nature of a qualm 1798. Hence **Qua·lmish-ly** *adv.*, **-ness.** So **Qua·lmy** *a.*

Quamash (kwămæ·ʃ, kwǫ·mæʃ). See also CAMAS. 1814. [N.Amer. Indian.] A N.Amer. liliaceous plant (*Camassia esculenta*), the bulbs of which are used for food by the American Indians.

Quamoclit (kwæ·mǒklit). 1731. [Corruption of Mexican *quamo·chitl* f. *qua-*, comb. form of *quaiutl* tree.] A subgenus of climbing plants with brilliant flowers found in the tropical parts of America and Asia, belonging to the genus *Ipomœa.*

Quandary (kwǫ·ndări, kwǫndē·ri), *sb.* 1579. [Origin obsc.; prob. f. L. *quando* when?, with inf. ending *-are.*] A state of extreme perplexity or uncertainty; a dilemma causing (great) mental agitation or distress; † a ticklish plight.

Quannet (kwǫ·nĕt). 1842. [Origin obsc.] A flat file set in a frame, and used as a plane in filing flat surfaces, as in comb-making.

Quant (kwænt, kwǫnt), *sb.* 1440. [perh. ad. L. *contus* (Gr. κοντός) boat-pole.] A pole for propelling a boat, esp. one with a flat cap to prevent it sinking in the mud, used by bargemen on the east coast. Hence **Quant** *v. trans.* to propel a boat with a q.; also *absol.*

Quantic (kwǫ·ntik). 1854. [f. L. *quantus* + -IC.] *Math.* A rational, integral, homogeneous function of two or more variables.

Quantification (kwǫ:ntifikēᵢ·ʃən). 1840. [f. next; see -FICATION.] The action of quantifying.

Q. of the predicate, the expression of the logical quantity of the predicate of a proposition, by applying to the predicate the sign *all*, or *some*, or an equivalent.

Quantify (kwǫ·ntifəi), *v.* 1840. [ad. med.L. *quantificare*, f. *quantus*; see QUANTITY and -FY.] 1. *Logic. trans.* To express the quantity of a term in a proposition, by prefixing *all* or *some* or the like to the term. 2. To determine the quantity of, to measure 1878.

Quantitative (kwǫ·ntitĕtiv), *a.* 1581. [ad. med.L. *quantitativus*; see QUANTITY and -IVE.] 1. Possessing quantity, magnitude, or spacial extent. Now *rare.* 2. Estimated or estimable by quantity 1656. 3. Relating to or concerned with quantity or its measurement; ascertaining or expressing quantity 1668. 4. Pertaining to or based on vowel-quantity, as *q. verse* 1799. Hence **Qua·ntitative-ly** *adv.*, **-ness.** So **Qua·ntitive** *a.*, **-ly** *adv.*

Quantity (kwǫ·ntĭti). late ME. [a. OF. *quantité*, ad. L. *quantitas, -atem*, f. *quantus*; see -ITY.] I. 1. Size, magnitude, dimensions. *Obs.* in gen. sense. 2. Amount, sum. a. Of material things not usu. estimated by spatial measurement. late ME. b. Of immaterial things. late ME. †c. Of money, payment, etc. -1775. 3. Length or duration in time. Now only in the legal phr. *q. of estate*, the length of time during which the right of enjoyment of an estate is to continue. late ME. b. *Pros.* Length or shortness of sounds or syllables, determined by the time required to pronounce them 1563. c. *Mus.* Length or duration of notes 1597. 4. *esp.* as the subject of mathematics: That property of things which is involved in the questions 'how great?' or 'how much?' and is determinable, or regarded as being so, by measurement of some kind; a system of relationships by virtue of which one thing is said to be greater or less than another 1530. 5. *Logic.* a. The extension or intension of a term, dist. as *extensive* and *intensive q.* b. The degree of extension which a proposition gives to the term forming its subject. 1668. †6. Relative size or amount, proportion (*rare*) -1602. 7. Great or considerable amount or bulk 1753. 8. *Electr.* The strength of a current as dist. from intensity or potential 1837.

1. The q. of a surface is called its area; and the q. of a line..its length 1830. 2. a. Fern..grew in great Q. there DE FOE. 3. b. *False q.*, an incorrect use of a long for a short vowel or syllable, or *vice versa.* 4. *Continuous* and *discrete q.*: see DISCRETE *a.* 2. 6. *Haml.* III. ii. 177. 7. Windsor Castle is a noble instance of the effect of q. HOGARTH.

II. 1. A (specified) portion or amount *of* an article or commodity. Also *transf.* of immaterial things. ME. b. An indefinite (usu. a fair or considerable) portion or amount; †a small piece, a fragment ME. c. With def. article: The portion or amount (*of* something) present in a particular thing or instance 1611. 2. A specified, or indefinite, number of persons or things. late ME. b. *pregnantly.* A great number or amount; also *pl.* 3. A certain space or surface. Const. *of.* Now *rare.* late ME. 4. *Math.* A thing having q. (I. 4), the number or extension of which is expressible by means of symbols; the symbol itself 1570.

1. A sufficient q. of illusion for the purposes of dramatic interest LAMB. b. Away thou Ragge, thou quantitie, thou remnant SHAKS. A q. of wreckage was cast up at Southport 1883. c. The q. of sensible heat in a human body BENTHAM. 3. You would make them a grant of a sufficient q. of your land BURKE. 4. *transf.* Her husband was an unknown quantity STEVENSON. *Imaginary q.*: see IMAGINARY *a.* 1 c. *Negligible q.* (after F. *quantité négligeable*), often *fig.* a person or thing of next to no account, a nonentity. *Comb.*: **q.-mark**, a mark indicating the q. of a vowel or syllable; **-surveyor**, a surveyor who estimates the quantities of the materials and labour required for any work.

Quantivalence (kwǫnti·vălĕns). 1871. [f. L. *quanti-*, comb. form of *quantum* how much + *-valence*, after *equivalence.*] = VALENCY 2. **Quanti·valency. Quanti·valent** *a.*

Qua·ntize, *v.* 1921. [f. next + -IZE.] *trans.* To apply quantum mechanics or the quantum theory to; to measure (energy) in quanta. Hence **Quantiza·tion.**

‖**Quantum** (kwǫ·ntǒm). Pl. **quanta.** 1619. [L., neut. of *quantus* how much.] 1. = QUANTITY, in various senses, e.g. I. 2, II. 1, 1 c, 4. 2. *Physics.* A discrete unit quantity of energy, proportional to the frequency of radiation, emitted from or absorbed by an atom 1910.

1. Is there not a sufficient q. of distress and misfortune? 1789. 2. *Q. theory*, the hypothesis that in radiation the energy of the electrons is discharged in discrete amounts or quanta.

Quantum sufficit (kwǫ·ntǒm sʊ·fisit). Also abbrev. **quantum suff., quant. suff.** (**suf.**). 1699. [L., a formula used in medical prescriptions.] 'As much as suffices'; hence, a sufficient quantity, to a sufficient extent, etc.

Quaquaversal (kwēᵢkwăvɜ̄·ɹsăl), *a.* 1728. [f. late L. *quaquaversus, -versum*, f. *quaqua* where-, whithersoever + *versus* towards.] Turned or pointing in every direction; chiefly *Geol.* in *q. dip.* Hence **Quaquave·rsally** *adv.*

Quarantine (kwǫ·răntīn), *sb.* 1609. [In sense 1, ad. med.L. *quarentena*; in 2, prob. ad. It. *quarant-*, *quarentina*, f. *quaranta* forty.] 1. *Law.* A period of forty days during which a widow, entitled to dower, had the right to remain in the chief mansion-house of her deceased husband; hence, the right of a widow to remain in the house during this period. 2. A period (orig. of forty days) during which persons who might spread a contagious disease (esp. travellers) are kept isolated; commonly, the period during which a ship, suspected of carrying contagion, is kept isolated on its arrival at a port. Hence, the fact or practice of isolating or of being isolated in this way; the place where infected or isolated ships are stationed. 1663. b. *fig.* Any period, instance, etc., of detention or seclusion compared to the above 1680. 3. A period of forty days; a set of forty (days) 1639.

1. If she marry within the forty days she loseth her quarentine COKE. 2. Anchored off q. (*mod.*).

Quarantine (kwǫ·răntīn), *v.* 1804. [f. prec.] *trans.* To put in quarantine.

‖ **Quare impedit** (kwēə·ri i·mpĭdit). late ME. [L., 'Why he impedes or hinders'.] *Law.* A form of writ issued in cases of disputed presentation to a benefice, requiring the defendant to state why he hinders the plaintiff from making the presentation.

Quarenden, quarender (kwǫ·rĕnd'n, -dəɹ). late ME. [Origin obsc.] A variety of apple common in Somerset and Devon. Also *attrib.*

Quarrel (kwǫ·rĕl), *sb.*[1] ME. [a. OF. *quar(r)el*, mod.F. *carreau*, = med.L. *quadrellus*, dim. of med.L. *quadrus* a square.] 1. A short, heavy, square-headed arrow or bolt formerly used with the cross-bow or arbalest. 2. A square or (more usu.) diamond-shaped pane of glass, of the kind used in making lattice-windows. Now *rare* exc. *dial.* 1447. 3. *techn.* a. A glazier's diamond 1807. b. A four-sided graver 1882. c. A stonemason's chisel 1882.

Quarrel (kwǫ·rĕl), *sb.*[2] ME. [a. OF. *querel(l)e* :—L. *querela*, *-ella* complaint, f. *queri* to complain.] †1. A complaint; esp. a complaint against a person; esp. in legal use, an accusation or charge; an action or suit –1641. 2. A ground or occasion of complaint against a person, leading to hostile feeling or action; also, the state or course of hostility resulting from this. Const. *against*, †*to*, later *with*. Now *rare*. ME. b. With poss. pron. or genitive: One's cause, side, or party in a complaint or contest. late ME. †c. *transf.* Cause, reason, ground, plea –1633. 3. A violent contention or altercation *between* persons, or of one *with* another; a rupture of friendly relations 1572. †b. Quarrelling; quarrelsomeness (*rare*) –1605.

2. Phr. *To pick a q.*: see PICK *v.*[1] IV. 2. All the q. the squire hath to me is for taking your part FIELDING. b. 2 *Hen. VI*, III. ii. 233. In our own q. we can see nothing truly STEVENSON. c. So as a Man may have a quarrell to marrye when he will BACON. 3. A man very valiant of his hands, but hot brained, he had had many quarrels 1639. b. *Oth.* II. iii. 52.

Quarrel (kwǫ·rĕl), *v.* late ME. [orig., a. OF. *quereler* (F. *quereller*), f. *querele* (see prec.); in later use prob. f. the sb.] 1. *intr.* To raise a complaint, protest, or objection; to find fault; to take exception. 2. To contend violently, fall out, break off friendly relations, become inimical or hostile. Const. *with* (a person) *for* or *about* (a thing). 1530. †3. To dispute, call in question, object to (an act, word, etc.) –1786. 4. To find fault with (a person); to reprove angrily. *Obs.* exc. *Sc.* 1598. †5. With complement: To force or bring by quarrelling –1678.

1. I must not q. with the will Of highest dispensation MILT. Phr. *To q. with one's bread and butter*, to find fault with or give up a means of livelihood for insufficient reasons. 2. She quarrelled with me for supping with St. John 1829. 3. I hope you will not q. the words 1745. 4. I had quarrell'd My brother purposely B. JONS. 5. You must q. him out o' the house B. JONS. Hence **Qua·rreller**, one who quarrels.

†**Qua·rrelet.** [f. QUARREL *sb.*[1] 2.] A small square HERRICK.

Quarrelsome (kwǫ·rĕlsǝm), *a.* 1596. [f. QUARREL *sb.*[2] + -SOME.] Inclined to quarrel; given to, or characterized by, quarrelling.

Men who are..q. when they are drunk FIELDING. Hence **Qua·rrelsome-ly** *adv.*, **-ness**.

Quarrier (kwǫ·riəɹ). late ME. [a. OF. *quarreour*, *-ieur* (mod.F. *carrier*), f. *quarrer* (mod.F. *carrer*) :—L. *quadrare* to square (stones).] One who quarries stone; a quarryman.

Quarry (kwǫ·ri), *sb.*[1] ME. [a. OF. *cuirée*, *curée*, f. *cuir* (:—L. *corium*) skin.] †1. Certain parts of a deer placed on the hide and given to the hounds as a reward –1576. †2. A heap made of the deer killed at a hunting –1605. †b. *transf.* A heap of dead men –1633. 3. a. The bird flown at by a hawk, etc. 1486. b. The animal pursued by hounds or hunters 1612. c. *fig.* An intended prey or victim 1615.

2. *Macb.* IV. iii. 206. 3. a. As when Joue's..bird from hye Stoupes at a flying heron..The stone dead quarrey falls SPENSER. c. Folly was the proper Q. of Horace DRYDEN.

Quarry (kwǫ·ri), *sb.*[2] late ME. [ad. med.L. *quareia*, var. of *quareria*, etc.] 1. An excavation from which stone for building, etc. is obtained by cutting, blasting, or the like. b. *transf.* Any place from which stones may be obtained as from a quarry 1838. †2. A large mass of stone or rock in its natural state, capable of being quarried –1764.

1. b. Houses, temples, the monuments of the dead, were the quarries from which they drew THIRLWALL. Hence **Qua·rryman**, one employed in quarrying; one who works in a q.

Quarry (kwǫ·ri), *sb.*[3] 1555. [Later form of QUARREL *sb.*[1]] †1. = QUARREL *sb.*[1] 1. –1627. 2. = QUARREL *sb.*[1] 2. 1611. 3. A square stone, tile, or brick 1555.

Quarry (kwǫ·ri), *v.*[1] 1575. [f. QUARRY *sb.*[1]] †1. *trans.* To teach (a hawk) to seize its quarry –1618. †2. *intr.* To pounce *on*, as a hawk on its quarry; to prey or feed *on* –1709. 3. *trans.* To hunt down or kill (a beast of chase) 1820.

Quarry (kwǫ·ri), *v.*[2] 1774. [f. QUARRY *sb.*[2]] 1. *trans.* To obtain (stone, etc.) by the processes employed in a quarry. Also with *out*. b. *fig.* To extract by laborious methods 1860. 2. To form a quarry in; to cut into (rock, etc.) 1847. 3. *intr.* To cut or dig in, or as in, a quarry 1848.

1. b. To q. gold and silver out of the monastic treasuries 1868.

Quart (kwǭɹt), *sb.*[1] ME. [a. F. *quarte* fem., *quart* masc., repr. L. *quarta*, *-tum*, fem. and neut. of *quartus* fourth.] 1. An English measure of capacity, one-fourth of a gallon, or two pints. b. A vessel holding a quart; a quart-pot or quart-bottle 1450. †2. A quarter, region SPENSER.

1. *attrib.* To sende hom wyn and ij. q. botelys 1454.

Quart (kāɹt), *sb.*[2] 1674. [ad. F. *quarte*; see prec.] 1. A position in fencing: = QUARTE, CARTE[2] 1692. 2. A sequence of four cards, in piquet and other card-games 1674.

2. *Q. major*, the ace, king, queen, and knave of a suit.

Quart (kāɹt), *v.* 1692. [ad. F. *quarter*, f. *quarte* QUART *sb.*[2]] a. *intr.* To use the position 'quart' in fencing. b. *trans.* To draw back (the head and shoulders) in doing so.

Quartan (kwǭ·ɹtăn), *a.* and *sb.* ME. [a. F. (*fièvre*) *quartaine*, ad. L. (*febris*) *quartana* fem. of *quartanus*, f. *quartus* fourth.] A. *adj. Path.* Of a fever or ague: Characterized by the occurrence of a paroxysm every fourth (in mod. reckoning, every third) day.

Ageyn feuerys quarteyn It is medicyn souereyn 1400.

B. *sb.* A (*or* the) quartan ague or fever. late ME.

Quartation (kwǫɹtēⁱ·ʃən). 1612. [f. L. *quartus* fourth + -ATION.] The operation of combining three parts of silver with one of gold, as a preliminary to separating and purifying the gold by means of nitric acid.

‖ **Quarte** (kāɹt, ‖ kart). 1700. [a. F. *quarte*; see QUART *sb.*[2]] = CARTE.[2]

Quarter (kwǭ·ɹtəɹ), *sb.* ME. [a. OF. *quarter*, *-ier* :—L. *quartarius* a fourth part (of a measure), f. *quartus* fourth; see -ER[2] 2.] I. One of four equal or corresponding parts into which anything is or may be divided. 1. Of things generally. b. Const. with sbs. without *of* 1866. c. *ellipt.* in contextual uses, as, a *quarter-mile race* 1508. 2. One of the four parts, each including a leg, into which the carcases of quadrupeds are commonly divided; also of fowls, a part containing a leg or wing ME. b. *pl.* The four parts of a human body similarly divided, as in the case of those executed for treason ME. c. Of a live person or animal; also freq. = hind-quarter, haunch. late ME. 3. *Her.* One of the four parts into which a shield is divided by quartering (see QUARTER *v.* 3 b) 1486. b. A charge occupying one fourth of the shield, placed in chief 1592. c. = QUARTERING *vbl sb.* 2 b. 1727.

1. The four quarters of the rolling year DRYDEN. Garnish with a Seville orange cut in quarters MRS. GLASSE. Phr. *A bad q. of an hour* [tr. F. *un mauvais quart d'heure*], a short but very unpleasant experience. b. There is not one-quarter the amount of drunkenness 1897. 2. They bought a Q. of Lamb PEPYS. *Fifth q.*, the hide and fat of a slaughtered animal. b. This morning Mr. Carew was hanged and quartered..but his quarters..are not to be hanged up PEPYS. c. Two..walked at each side of the horse's quarter 1806. 3. c. A baron of sixteen quarters SCOTT.

II. The fourth part of some usual measure or standard. 1. As a measure of capacity for grain, etc. a. The British imperial quarter = 8 bushels; the fifth part of a wey or load; also, local varieties of this ME. b. The fourth part of a chaldron. late ME. 2. As a weight. The fourth part of a hundredweight = 28 lbs. (*U.S.* commonly 25 lbs.). Abbrev. qr. 1481. 3. As a measure of length or area. a. The fourth part of a yard; nine inches. late ME. b. *Naut.* The fourth part of a fathom 1769. 4. As a measure of time. a. The fourth part of a year, esp. as divided by the QUARTER-DAYS. Also (esp. in Scotland), the fourth part of the school-year, or of the period during which instruction is usually given, containing about eleven weeks. late ME. b. A fourth part of the lunar period. Also, the moon's position when between the first and second or third and fourth quarters; quadrature. late ME. c. The fourth part of an hour; the space of fifteen minutes. Also, the moment, as denoted by a mark on the dial, the sound of a bell, etc., at which one quarter of an hour ends and the next begins. late ME. 5. *U.S.* A silver coin = one fourth of a dollar 1856. 6. *Naut.* The fourth part of a point on the compass; 2° 48′ 45″. Also *q. point*. 1795. 7. A quarterly instalment of an allowance or payment 1679.

3. a. *Tam. Shr.* IV. iii. 109. 4. c. I shall die to-night, A quarter before twelve TENNYSON. 'The quarter 's gone!' cried Mr. Tapley DICKENS. 7. Pay me down the first q. now THACKERAY.

III. Senses denoting locality, and transf. uses of these. 1. The region lying about or under one of the four principal points of the compass or divisions of the horizon; the point or division itself. late ME. †b. Boundary or limit towards one of the cardinal points; side –1611. c. A direction or point of the compass when more than four are mentioned or may be implied 1604. 2. Region, district, place, locality ME. b. Indicating a certain portion or member of a community, or some thing or things, without ref. to actual locality 1777. 3. A particular division or district of a town or city, *esp.* that appropriated to a particular class or race of people 1526. †b. A part of a gathering or assembly, army, camp, etc. –1599. 4. Place of stay or residence; dwelling-place, lodgings, *esp.* of soldiers. Now usu. in *pl.* 1591. 5. Assigned or appropriate position 1549. †6. Relations with, or conduct towards, another; *esp.* in phr. *to keep good* (or *fair*) *quarter(s) with* –1674. b. (Good or fair) treatment or terms. *Obs.* exc. *arch.* 1648. 7. Exemption from being immediately put to death, granted to a vanquished opponent in a battle or fight; clemency shown in sparing the life of one who surrenders 1611. b. *transf.* and *fig.* 1647.

1. Vpon Elam I wil bringe the foure wyndes from yᵉ foure quarters of heauen COVERDALE *Jer.* xlix. 34. c. Winds from all quarters agitate the air COWPER. 2. A visit to a distant q. 1855. b. Even in the highest quarters justice had ceased to be much considered 1856. 3. b. 1 *Hen. VI*, II. i. 63. Phr. †*To keep good q.*, to keep good watch; to preserve good order. 4. *Free quarter(s)*: see FREE-QUARTER. *Head-*, *summer-*, *winter-quarters*: see the first element. *To beat up the quarters of*, see BEAT *v.*[1] II. 8. *To take up one's quarters*, to establish oneself (in a place). 5. Swift to thir several Quarters hasted then The cumbrous Elements MILT. *Quarters*, a name given, at sea, to the several stations where the officers and crew of the ship of war are posted in action FALCONER. 6. *Com. Err.* II. i. 108. 7. Many were cut down, the Swedes giving no q. 1659. Phr. †*To cry q.*, to call for q.

IV. Techn. uses, in many of which the original sense is much obscured. 1. *Carpentry.* A piece of wood, four inches wide by two or four inches thick, used as an upright stud or scantling in partitions and other framing. Chiefly in *pl.*

1497. **2.** *Farriery.* One side of a horse's hoof; one half of the coffin, extending between heel and toe. **b.** The corresponding part of a horse-shoe. 1523. **c.** That part of a shoe or boot lying immediately in front of the back-line, on either side of the foot; the piece of leather, or other stuff, forming this part of the shoe from the heel to the vamp 1753. **3.** *Naut.* **a.** The upper part of a ship's side between the after part of the main chains and the stern 1599. **b.** Of a yard: The part between the slings and the yard-arm 1769. **4.** One of the four parts into which a road is divided by the horse-track and the wheel-ruts 1767.

3. **a.** The French Admiral's Ship under our q. had lost her foremast 1805. *On the q.*, in a direction about midway between astern and on the beam.

Comb.: **q.-aspect**, quartile aspect; **-back**, in American football, a player stationed between the forwards and half-backs; **-bell**, a bell in a clock which sounds the quarters; **-bend**, a section of pipe bent into a quarter-circle; **-binding**, a style of book-binding with narrow leather back and no leather corners; **-block** *Naut.*, a block fitted under the q. of a yard; **-cask**, (*a*) a quarter-hogshead; (*b*) a quarter-butt; **-gallery**, a kind of balcony with windows projecting from the q. of a large vessel; **-guard** *Mil.*, a small guard mounted in front of each battalion in a camp; **-gunner** *Naut.*, an officer subordinate to the gunner; **-ill**, an inflammatory disease of cattle and sheep (*symptomatic anthrax*), causing putrefaction in one or more of the quarters; **-miler**, one who is good at running a quarter-mile race; **-note** *Mus.*, (*a*) = q.-tone; (*b*) *U.S.* a crotchet; **-plate**, a photographic plate measuring $3\frac{1}{4}\times4\frac{1}{4}$ inches; also, a photograph taken on a plate of this size; **-section** (U.S. and Canada), a quarter of a square mile of land, 160 acres; **-tone** *Mus.*, (the interval of) one half of a semitone; **-track**, a quarter-mile racing course; **-turn**, (*a*) a rifle in which the shot makes a quarter of a revolution in the length of the barrel; (*b*) a bend of a quarter of a circle; **-watch** *Naut.*, a ship's watch composed of one quarter of the crew; **-wheeling**, turning through a quarter of a circle; **-wind**, a wind blowing on a vessel's quarter.

Quarter (kwǭ·ɹtəɹ), *v.* late ME. [f. prec.] **1.** *trans.* To cut into quarters; to divide into four equal or equivalent parts. Also with *out.* **2.** To divide into parts fewer or more than four. Also with *out.* late ME. **3.** *Her.* **a.** To place or bear (charges or coats of arms) quarterly upon a shield; to add (another's coat) to one's hereditary arms; to place in alternate quarters *with.* late ME. **b.** To divide (a shield) into quarters, or into any number of divisions formed by vertical and horizontal lines 1590. **4.** To put (soldiers or others) into quarters; to station, place, or lodge in a particular place. Also *pass.* = to have one's abode, lodging, etc. 1594. **b.** With *on, upon*: To impose (soldiers) upon (a householder, town, etc.) to be lodged and fed. Also *transf.* and *fig.* 1683. **5.** *intr.* To take up (one's) quarters; to stay, reside, lodge 1581. †**6.** *trans.* To give quarters to; to furnish with quarters or lodgings -1682. **7.** *Naut.* To assign (men) to a particular quarter on board ship; to place or station for action 1695. **8.** *Naut. intr.* To sail with the wind on the quarter, *i.e.* between beam and stern 1627. **9.** *trans.* To range or traverse (ground, etc.) in every direction. Said esp. of dogs in search of game. 1698. **b.** *intr.* To range to and fro 1857. **10.** To drive a cart or carriage so that the right and left wheels are on (two of) the quarters of a road, with a rut between. Also, of a horse: To walk with the feet thus placed; hence, to walk in front of the wheel. 1800. **b.** To drive to the side in order to allow another vehicle to pass 1849. **11.** Of the moon: To begin a fresh quarter 1789.

1. Being discovered, betrayed,..hanged, quartered, etc. DE FOE. Pare and q. your apples and take out the cores MRS. GLASSE. *fig. John* II. i. 506. 2. Here is a sword..Will q. you in three 1800. 3. a. The royal banner of England, quartering the lion, the leopard, and the harp HAWTHORNE. 4. He was then quartered in Edinburgh as a lieutenant 1882. Soldiers were quartered on recalcitrant boroughs GREEN. 7. The Captain quartered his Men, and the Decks were cleared 1695. 9. Just like a Pointer quartering well his ground 1788. 10. b. Every creature that met us would rely on us for quartering DE QUINCEY. 11. They would have bad weather until the moon quartered 1789.

Quarterage (kwǭ·ɹtərėdʒ). late ME. [f. QUARTER *sb.* + -AGE.] **1.** A quarterly contribution, allowance, pension, or other payment. **2.** Quarters, place of abode; quartering of troops, or the expense of this (*rare*) 1577.

Qua·rter-day·. 1480. One of the four days fixed by custom as marking off the quarters of the year, on which the tenancy of houses usu. begins and ends, and the payment of rent and other quarterly charges falls due.

In England and Ireland the quarter-days are Lady Day (March 25), Midsummer Day (June 24), Michaelmas (Sept. 29), and Christmas (Dec. 25).

Qua·rter-deck. 1627. *Naut.* †**a.** Orig., a smaller deck situated above the HALF-DECK, covering about a quarter of the vessel. **b.** In later use: That part of the upper or spar-deck which extends between the stern and after-mast, and is used as a promenade by the superior officers or cabin-passengers.

Quartering (kwǭ·ɹtəriŋ), *vbl. sb.* 1592. [f. QUARTER *v.* + -ING[1].] **1.** Division into four equal parts; also, division in general 1610. **2.** *Her.* **a.** The dividing of a shield into quarters; the marshalling or bringing in of various coats upon one shield, to denote the alliances of one family with the heiresses of others 1592. **b.** *pl.* The various coats marshalled upon a shield; rarely *sing.*, one of these coats 1719. **3.** The assigning of quarters to a person; the action of taking up quarters; †a place in which one is or may be quartered 1625. **b.** *spec.* The billeting of soldiers; the fact of having soldiers quartered upon one 1646. **4.** *Build.* **a.** The placing or using of quarters in construction. **b.** Work formed of quarters. **c.** Wood in the form, or of the size, of quarters. 1703. **5.** Driving on the quarters of a road 1815. **6.** The moon's passage from one quarter to another 1854.

attrib. and *Comb.*, as *q.-block, -knife.* etc.

Quarterly (kwǭ·ɹtəɹli), *a.* and *sb.* 1563. [f. QUARTER *sb.* + -LY[1].] **A.** *adj.* **1.** That takes place, is done, etc., every quarter of a year; relating to, or covering, a quarter of a year. **2.** Pertaining or relating to a quarter (in other senses) 1769. **B.** *sb.* A quarterly review, magazine, etc. 1818.

A. 1. Q...payments 1802. The q. Seasons of Devotion, called the Ember-weeks 1688. 2. *Q. wind*, a wind on the quarter.

Quarterly (kwǭ·ɹtəɹli), *adv.* (*a.*, *sb.*) 1450. [-LY[2].] **1.** Every quarter of a year; once in a quarter 1458. **2.** *Her.* **a.** In the four divisions of a shield formed by a vertical and a horizontal line drawn through the fess point; usu. with ref. to two tinctures, charges, or coats of arms, placed in the diagonally opposite quarters 1450. **b.** With ref. to the division of the shield into quarters, or to blazoning it by quarters 1610. **c.** *ellipt.* as *adj.* = divided quarterly, or (by extension) into any number of parts at right angles to each other, as *q. of eight*; also as *sb.* = a shield divided or charged quarterly 1869.

2. b. *Q.-quartered*, having one or more quarters divided in four; so *q.-quartering.*

Quartermaster (kwǭ·ɹtəɹmɑːstəɹ). late ME. [In sense 1, app. f. QUARTER *sb.* III. 5; in sense 2, f. QUARTER *sb.* III. 4.] **1.** *Naut.* **a.** A petty officer who attends to the steering of the ship, the binnacle, signals, stowing of the hold, etc. **b.** *transf.* Steering-gear 1882. **2.** *Mil.* An officer attached to each regiment, with the duties of providing quarters for the soldiers, laying out the camp, and looking after the rations, ammunition, and other supplies of the regiment 1600. †**3.** One who shares authority with another to the extent of a fourth -1685.

2. **Q.-general**, a staff-officer who is chief of the department exercising control over all matters relating to the quartering, encamping, marching, and equipment of troops. **Q.-sergeant**, a non-commissioned officer, ranking as a staff-sergeant, who assists the q. in his duties. Hence **Qua·rterma·ster** *v. intr.* to perform the duties of a q. **Qua·rtermastership.**

Quartern (kwǭ·ɹtəɹn), *sb.* ME. [a. AF. *quartrun*, OF. *quart(e)ron*, f. *quart(e* fourth, fourth part.] **1.** A quarter *of* anything. *Obs.* exc. *dial.* **2.** A quarter of various weights and measures. late ME. **3.** A quartern-loaf 1844.

Comb. **q.-loaf**, a loaf made of a q. of flour; a four-pound loaf.

Quarter-sessions. 1577. [QUARTER *sb.* II. 4. a.] **1.** In England and Ireland: A court of limited criminal and civil jurisdiction, and of appeal, held quarterly by the justices of peace in the counties (in Ireland by county-court judges), and by the recorder in boroughs. **2.** In Scotland: A court of review and appeal held quarterly by the justices of the peace on days appointed by statute 1661.

Qua·rterstaff. 1550. **1.** A stout pole, from 6 to 8 feet long and tipped with iron, formerly used as a weapon by the English peasantry. **2.** Fighting or exercise with the quarterstaff 1712.

1. My owne Country weapon. What? A Quarter staffe 1626.

Quartet(te (kwǫɹte·t). 1790. [a. F. *quartette*, ad. It. *quartetto*; see next.] **1.** *Mus.* A composition for four voices or instruments, *esp.* for four stringed instruments. **2. a.** *Mus.* A set of four singers or players who render a quartette. **b.** *transf.* A set of four persons. 1814. **3.** A set of four things; e. g. of lines in a sonnet, of runs at cricket, etc. 1837.

†‖**Quartetto** (kwǫɹte·to). 1775. [a. It. f. *quarto* fourth.] = prec. -1842.

Quartic (kwǭ·ɹtik), *a.* and *sb.* 1856. [f. L. *quartus* + -IC.] *Math.* **A.** *adj.* Of the fourth degree. **B.** *sb.* A quantic, curve, or surface of the fourth degree.

Quartile (kwǭ·ɹtil), *a.* and *sb.* 1509. [ad. med.L. *quartilis*, f. *quartus* fourth; cf. *sextile*, etc.] *Astr.* and *Astrol.* **A.** *adj.* *Q. aspect*, the aspect of two heavenly bodies which are 90° distant from each other. **b.** Connected with, relating to, a quartile aspect. 1585. **B.** *sb.* A quartile aspect; a quadrature 1509.

Quarto (kwǭ·ɹto). Also written 4to, 4°. 1589. [L. (*in*) *quarto*, (in) the fourth (of a sheet), abl. sing. of *quartus* fourth.] **1.** The size of paper obtained by folding a whole sheet twice, so as to form four leaves, which, as a rule, are nearly square. Orig. and chiefly in phr. *in q.* **2.** A book composed of paper in this form; a quarto-volume 1642. **3.** *attrib.* or as *adj.* Of paper: Folded so as to form four leaves out of the original sheet; having the size or shape of a quarter-sheet. Of books: Printed on paper thus folded. Of works: Published in q. 1633.

2. The form and magnitude of a q. imposes upon the mind 1769.

Quart-pot. late ME. A pot capable of containing the measure of a quart.

Quartz (kwǭɹts). 1756. [a. G *quarz*; origin unkn.] *Min.* A widely diffused mineral, massive or crystallizing in hexagonal prisms; in a pure form consisting of silica or silicon dioxide (SiO_2), but varying greatly in colour, lustre, etc. Also *attrib.* Hence **Quartzi·ferous** *a.* bearing or containing q. **Qua·rtzoid**, a crystal having the form of a double six-sided pyramid. **Qua·rtzose** *a.* mainly or entirely composed of q.; of the nature of q. **Qua·rtzy** *a.* of the nature of q.; resembling q.

Quartzite (kwǭ·ɹtsəit). 1849. [f. prec. + -ITE 2 b.] *Min.* An extremely compact, granular rock, consisting essentially of quartz.

Quash (kwǫʃ), *v.* ME. [ad. OF. *quasser* = *casser* to annul, ad. late L. *cassare*, f. *cassus* null.] **1.** *trans.* To annul, to make null or void (a law, decision, election, etc.); to throw out (a writ, etc.) as invalid; to put an end to (legal proceedings). **2.** To bring to nothing; to crush or destroy; to put down completely; to stifle (a feeling, idea, scheme, etc.) 1609. **3.** To crush, quell, or utterly subdue (a person); to squash. Now *rare.* 1639.

3. This..resolution..would in all probability have quashed their enemies HANWAY.

Quashee (kwǫ·ʃi), **quashie** (kwǫ·ʃi). 1833. [Ashantee or Fantee *Kwasi*, a name given to a child born on Sunday.] A negro personal name, used as a general name for any negro.

‖**Quasi** (kwē¹·səi), *adv.* and *pref.* late ME. [L. = as if, almost.] **1.** Used parenthetically = 'as it were', 'almost', 'virtually' (*rare*) 1485. **2.** Treated (usu.) as a prefix and hyphened: **a.** With sbs.: (A) kind of; resembling or simulating, but not really the same as, that properly so termed 1643. **b.** With adjs., more rarely with advbs. or vbs.: Seemingly, but not really; almost, virtually 1802. **3.** Introducing an etymological explanation of a word: 'As if it were'. Abbrev. *q.*, *qu.* late ME.

2. a. An Empyriall Heaven, a *q. vacuitie* SIR T. BROWNE. b. Public or q.-public organisms BRYCE. 3. *L. L. L.* IV. ii. 85.

‖**Quasimodo** (kwē¹səi,mōᵘ·doᵘ). 1706. [f. L. *quasi modo*, the first words of the introit for the first Sunday after Easter.] In *Q. Sunday* = LOW SUNDAY.

Quassia (kwæ·siă, kwæ·ʃ-, kwǫ·ʃiă). 1765. [f. name of a Surinam negro, Graman (= grand man) *Quassi* or *Quacy* (= QUASHEE), who discovered the virtues of the root.] **1.** The wood, bark, or root of a S. Amer. tree (*Quassia amara*), found esp. in Surinam, also of the bitter ash (*Picræna excelsa*) of Jamaica, and the bitter damson (*Simaruba amara*) of the W. Indies and S. America. **b.** The bitter decoction prepared from this, used for medicinal and other purposes. **2.** Any of the trees yielding quassia, esp. the *Q. amara* of Surinam 1766.

Quassin (kwæ·sin). 1819. [f. prec. + -IN [1].] The bitter principle of quassia. Also **Qua·ssite.**

Quat (kwǫt). *Obs.* exc. *dial.* 1579. [Origin obsc.] **1.** A pustule; a small boil; a stye. †**2.** *transf.* Applied contemptuously to a (young) person -1623.

‖**Quatenus** (kwēⁱ·tĭnŏs), *adv.* 1652. [L. = how far, f. *qua* where + *tenus* up to.] In so far as; in the quality or capacity of; QUA.

Qua·ter-cente·nary (kwætəɹ). 1883. [f. L. *quater* four times.] A 400th anniversary.

Quaternary (kwǫ̆tə̄·ɹnări), *a.* and *sb.* late ME. [ad. L. *quaternarius*, f. *quaterni* four together, by fours.] **A.** *adj.* **1.** Consisting of four things or parts; characterized by the number four. Now chiefly *Chem.* in *q. compound*, a combination of four elements or radicals. 1605. **2.** *Geol.* Used, with the sense of 'fourth in order', as an epithet of the period following on the Tertiary, and of the deposits, animals, etc., belonging to it 1843. **B.** *sb.* A set of four (things); the number four. late ME.

A. 1. *Q. number*, usually = 4, but sometimes taken as = 10 (see B). **B.** *Q. of numbers*, the Pythagorean τετρακτός, or 1+2+3+4 = 10.

Quaternate (kwǫ̆tə̄·ɹnĕt), *a.* 1753. [f. as prec. + -ATE [2].] Arranged in or forming a set or sets of four; composed of four parts.

Quaternion (kwǫ̆tə̄·ɹniən). late ME. [ad. late L. *quaternio, -ionem*, f. *quaterni* four together.] **1.** A group or set of four persons or things. **2.** Of paper or parchment: **a.** A quire of four sheets folded in two. †**b.** A sheet folded twice. 1625. **3.** The number 4 or 10 (cf. QUATERNARY) 1637. **4.** *Math.* **a.** The quotient of two vectors, or the operator which changes one vector into another, so called as depending on four geometrical elements, and capable of being expressed by the quadrinomial formula $w + xi + yj + zk$, in which w, x, y, z are scalars, and i, j, k are mutually perpendicular vectors whose squares are -1. **b.** *pl.* That form of the calculus of vectors in which this operator is employed. 1843. **5.** *attrib.* or as *adj.* Consisting of four persons, things, or parts 1814.

1. This..Elementary Q. of Earth, Air, Water, and Fire 1695. Hence †**Quate·rnioned** *a.* arranged in quaternions.

Quaternity (kwǫ̆tə̄·ɹnĭti). 1529. [ad. late L. *quaternitas*, f. *quaterni* four together; see -TY.] A set of four persons (*esp.* in the Godhead, in contrast to the Trinity) or of four things. Hence **Quaternita·rian** (*rare*), one who believes that there are four persons in the Godhead.

Quatorzain (kæ·tǫɹzēⁱn). 1583. [a. F. *quatorzaine* a set of fourteen, f. *quatorze*; see next.] A piece of verse consisting of fourteen lines; a sonnet. Now *spec.* a poem of fourteen lines resembling a sonnet, but without strict adherence to sonnet-rules.

‖**Quatorze** (kătǭ·ɹz). 1701. [F. :—L. *quatuordecim* fourteen.] In piquet, a set of four similar cards (either aces, kings, queens, knaves, or tens) held by one player, which count as 14.

Quatrain (kwǫ·trēⁱn). 1585. [a. F., f. *quatre* four.] A stanza of four lines, usu. with alternate rimes; four lines of verse.

‖**Quatre** (kā·təɹ, Fr. katr). 1550. [F. = four.] The number four; the four in dice.

Quatrefoil (kæ·təɹfoil). 1494. [a. OF. **quatrefoil*, f. *quatre* four + *foil* leaf. Cf. CINQUEFOIL.] A compound leaf or flower consisting of four leaflets or petals radiating from a common centre; also, a representation or conventional imitation of this, *esp.* as a charge in Heraldry. **b.** *Arch.* An opening or ornament, having its outline so divided by cusps as to give it the appearance of four radiating leaflets or petals.

‖**Quattrocento** (kwattroˌtʃe·nto). 1875. [It. prop. 'four hundred', but used for 'fourteen hundred'; cf. CINQUECENTO.] The fifteenth century as a period of Italian art, architecture, etc. Hence **Quattroce·ntist**, an Italian artist, author, etc. of the 15th c.; also *attrib.* or as *adj.*

Quaver (kwēⁱ·vəɹ), *sb.* 1570. [f. next.] **1.** *Mus.* A note, equal in length to half a crotchet or one-eighth of a semibreve. **2.** *Mus.* A shake or trill in singing, or (*rarely*) in instrumental music 1611. **3.** A shake or tremble in the voice; a tremulous voice or cry 1748. **4.** A quivering or tremulous movement 1736.

Quaver (kwēⁱ·vəɹ), *v.* late ME. [f. *quave*, early ME. *cwavier* to shake + -ER [1].] **1.** *intr.* To vibrate, tremble, quiver. Now *rare.* **b.** Of the voice: To shake, tremble 1741. **2.** To use trills or shakes in singing 1538. **3.** *trans.* To sing (a note, song, etc.) with trills or quavers. Also with *forth, out.* 1570.

2. In Singing also the Italians Bleat, the Spaniards Whine, the Germans Howl, and the French Q. 1684. **3.** The Larke..Quaver'd her cleare Notes in the quiet Ayre DRAYTON. Hence **Qua·verer. Qua·very** *a.* apt to q.; somewhat quavering.

Quay (kī), *sb.* 1696. [Later spelling of *kay*, KEY *sb.*[2], after F. *quai.*] An artificial bank or landing-place, built of stone or other solid material, lying along or projecting into a navigable water for convenience of loading and unloading vessels.

But now arrives the dismal day, She must return to Ormond-q. SWIFT. Hence **Quay** *v.*[1] *trans.* to provide with a q. **Quayage** (kī·ĕdʒ), dues levied on goods landed or shipped at a q., or on vessels using the q.; q.-room.

†**Quay**, *v.*[2] [perh. alteration of QUAIL *v.*] *trans.* To depress, subdue, daunt SPENSER.

Queach (kwītʃ). *Obs.* exc. *dial.* 1450. [Origin obsc.] A dense growth of bushes; a thicket.

Queachy (kwī·tʃi), *a. Obs.* exc. *dial.* 1565. [f. prec. + -Y [1].] †**1.** Forming a dense growth or thicket -1586. **2.** Of ground: Swampy, boggy 1593. **3.** *dial.* Feeble, weak, small 1859.

2. The dampes that rise from out the quechy plots PEELE. **3.** They're poor queechy things, gells is G. ELIOT.

Quean (kwīn). [OE. *cwene* wk. fem. :—OTeut. **kwenōn-*, f. the stem which appears in Gr. γυνή woman, repr. a common Aryan type **gʷenā*; cf. QUEEN.] **1.** A woman, a female; hence, in disparagement: A bold or ill-behaved woman; a jade; and *spec.* a harlot, strumpet (esp. in 16–17th c.). **2.** *Sc.* A young woman, or girl; a (healthy and robust) lass 1470.

2. I see her yet, the sonsie q. BURNS.

Queasy (kwī·zi), *a.* 1459. [Earlier *coisy*, perh. conn. w. OF. *coisier* to hurt, wound.] †**1.** Of the times, etc.: Unsettled, troublous, ticklish -1611. †**b.** Of a matter: Uncertain, hazardous -1605. **2.** Of food: Causing sickness or nausea. Now *rare.* 1496. **3.** Of the stomach: Easily upset; unable to digest strong food. Hence of the body, heart, health, etc. 1545. †**b.** Of the mind, feelings, etc.: Fastidious, nice -1659. **c.** Of conscience, etc.: Tender, scrupulous 1579. **4.** Of pains, etc.: Of the nature of sickness; uneasy, uncomfortable 1589. **5.** Of persons: Having a queasy stomach; liable to turn sick; subject to, or affected with, nausea 1606.

1. The times being queasie, the King wisely forbare to take any seuere reuenge 1611. **b.** A queazie question SHAKS. **5.** *Ant. & Cl.* III. vi. 20. Hence **Quea·si-ly** *adv.*, **-ness.**

‖**Quebracho** (kebrā·tʃo). 1881. [Sp., f. *quebrar* to break + *hacha* axe.] Any of several Amer. trees, having extremely hard timber and medicinal bark; esp. the white q. of S. America (*Aspidosperma Q.*) and the red q. of Mexico (*Schinopsis Lorentzii*). Also *attrib.* as *q. bark, gum.* **b.** = The bark itself.

Queen (kwīn), *sb.* [OE. *cwén* :—OTeut. **kwǣniz* ablaut-var. of the stem repr. by OE. *cwene* QUEAN.] **1.** A (king's) wife or consort; a lady who is wife *to* a king. **2. a.** The wife or consort of a king. **b.** A woman who is the chief ruler of a state, having the same rank and position as a king. OE. **3.** As a title, placed immed. before or †after a personal name; also *the q.*, before or after the name (now *arch.*) OE. **4.** With specification of the people, country, etc. ruled over by a queen or by the king her consort, as *Q. of Scots*, etc. OE. **5.** *transf.* A female whose rank or pre-eminence is comparable to that of a queen; applied e.g. to the Virgin Mary, to the goddesses of ancient religions or mythologies, or to a woman as a term of endearment and honour OE. **6.** Applied to things personified OE. **7.** The perfect female of bees, wasps, or ants 1609. **8.** In games. **a.** *Chess.* The piece which has greatest freedom of movement, and hence is most effective for defending the king. Also, the position on the board attained by a pawn when it is queened. 1440. **b.** *Cards.* A playing-card bearing the figure of a queen, of which there are four in each pack 1575.

1. Hermione, Queene to the worthy Leontes, King of Sicilia SHAKS. **2. b.** My memorial which was given to the q. SWIFT. The q. of England is either q. regent, q. consort, or q. dowager BLACKSTONE. **5.** Poor q. of love, in thine own law forlorn SHAKS. Mooned Ashtaroth, Heav'n's Q. and Mother both MILT. *Q. of hearts* (cf. 8 b). *Q. of the May*: see MAY *sb.*[2] 2. *Q. of glory, grace, heaven, paradise, women*, etc., the Virgin Mary. **6.** May, of myrthfull monethis quene DUNBAR. Venice..the Q. of the Adriatic 1840. *Q. of heaven, the night, the tides*, the moon. *Q. of the meadow(s*, MEADOW-SWEET.

Comb.: †**q.-apple**, an early variety of apple; **-bee** (see 7); **-cake**, a small currant-cake; **-conch**, a large marine shell, *Strombus gigas*; †**-gold**, a former revenue of the king's consort, consisting of one-tenth on certain fines paid to the king; **-wasp** (see 7).

b. *Comb.* with **queen's. 1.** In titles or appellations, with the sense of 'belonging to, in the service of, the queen', 'royal', as *Queen's bench, counsel, English, evidence, messenger*, etc.: see these words. **2. queen's colours**, one of the pair of colours carried by a regiment, the royal colours; **queen's metal**, an alloy of tin, antimony, bismuth, and lead; **queen's pigeon**, a large and beautiful crested pigeon of the Papuan region, *Gaura Victoriæ*; **queen's pipe**, a furnace formerly used for destroying smuggled or damaged tobacco; **queen's shilling**, a shilling formerly given to a recruit on enlisting; **queen's ware**, (*a*) a cream-coloured kind of Wedgwood ware; (*b*) a kind of stone-ware; **queen's yellow**, turpeth mineral, used as a yellow pigment. **3.** In names of plants, as †**queen's balm**, alyssum; **queen's cushion**, cut-leaved saxifrage; **queen's delight**, an American euphorbiaceous plant, *Stillingia sylvatica*; **queen's pincushion**, the flowers of the guelder rose; etc. Hence **Quee·ndom. Quee·nhood. Quee·nless** *a.* **Quee·nlike** *a.*

Queen (kwīn), *v.* 1611. [f. prec.] **1.** *To q. it*: to be a queen; to act or rule as a queen; to have pre-eminence like a queen. **2.** *trans.* To make (a woman) a queen. Also *fig.* 1843. **3.** *Chess.* To advance (a pawn) to the opponent's end of the board, where it acquires the power of, and is replaced by, a queen or such other piece as the player may choose. Also *absol.* 1789.

Queen Anne. The Queen of Great Britain and Ireland who reigned from 1702 to 1714. **b.** *attrib.* as an epithet of the style of furniture, buildings, etc., characteristic of Queen Anne's reign, or of things made in this style. Also *absol.* 1881.

Queen Anne is dead, a phr. implying stale news. *Queen Anne's bounty*: see BOUNTY 5.

Queening (kwī·niŋ). late ME. [perh. f. QUEEN *sb.* + -ING [3].] A variety of apple.

Queenly (kwī·nli), *a.* 1540. [f. QUEEN *sb.* + -LY [1].] **1.** Belonging or appropriate to a queen. **2.** Resembling a queen; queenlike 1824.

1. A Q. manner CROMWELL. Hence **Quee·nliness.** So **Quee·nly** *adv.* in the manner of a queen.

Queen-mo·ther. 1577. **1.** A queen dowager who is the mother of the reigning sovereign. **2.** A queen who is a mother. Also applied to a queen-bee, and *fig.* 1602.

Quee·n-post. 1823. [Cf. KING-POST.] One of two upright timbers in a roof-truss, which are framed above into the rafters and below into the tie-beam, at points equidistant from its middle or ends.

Queenship (kwī·nʃip). 1536. [-SHIP.] **1.** The dignity or office of a queen. **2.** The personality of a queen; (her) majesty 1603.

Queer (kwīᵊɹ), *a.*[1] 1508. [Origin obsc.] **1.** Strange, odd, peculiar, eccentric, in appearance or character. **2.** Not in a normal condition; out of sorts; giddy, faint, or ill; *esp.* in phr. *to feel* (or *look*) *q.* Also *slang*: Drunk. 1800. **3.** *Q. Street*: an imaginary street where people in difficulties reside; hence, any difficulty, fix, or trouble, bad circumstances, debt, illness, etc. 1837.

1. Let me be known all at once for a q. Fellow, and avoided STEELE. 3. Q. Street is full of lodgers just at present DICKENS. Hence **Queeˑrish** *a.* **Queeˑr-ly** *adv.*, **-ness.**

Queer (kwīᵊɹ), *a.*[2] 1561. [Origin obsc.] *Thieves' cant.* Bad; worthless.

Queer (kwīᵊɹ), *v. slang.* 1790. [f. QUEER *a.*[1] or [2].] **1.** *trans.* **a.** To quiz or ridicule; to puzzle. **b.** To impose upon; to cheat. **2.** To spoil, put out of order 1812. **3.** To put (one) out; to make (one) feel queer 1845.

2. All they dared do they did to 'q.' her Scene 1884. Phr. *To q. the pitch*: to upset the 'game', put obstacles in the way.

Queerity (kwīˑrĭti). 1711. [f. QUEER *a.*[1] + -ITY.] Queerness, oddity.

Queest (kwīst). *Obs.* exc. *dial.* [late ME. *quisht*, perh. for **cusht*, var. of CUSHAT.] The ring-dove, wood-pigeon.

Quelch (kwelᵗʃ), *v. rare.* 1659. [Related to SQUELCH as *quash* to *squash*, etc.] *trans.* and *intr.* To squelch.

Quell (kwel), *sb. rare.* late ME. [f. next.] Slaying, slaughter; power or means to quell.

Quell (kwel), *v.* [OE. *cwęllan*:—OTeut. **kwaljan*, causative from the root *kwal-*.] **1.** *trans.* To kill, slay, destroy (a person or animal). Now *rare* or *Obs.* **2.** To destroy, put an end to, suppress, extinguish, etc. (a thing or state of things, a feeling, disposition, etc.) late ME. **3.** To crush or overcome (a person or thing); to subdue, vanquish, reduce to subjection or submission 1570. **†4.** *intr.* = QUAIL *v.* I. 2. -1616.

1. Yet him the dart Quell'd not COWPER. 2. The captain quelled this mutiny DE FOE. We soon succeeded in quelling their fears 1832. 3. The energy of William had thus thoroughly quelled all his foes FREEMAN. 4. Winters wrath beginnes to q. SPENSER. Hence **Queˑller**, one that quells.

Quench, *sb. rare.* 1529. [f. the vb.] The act of quenching; the state or fact of being quenched.

Quench (kwenʃ), *v.* [Early ME. *cwenken*, *quenchen*:—OE. *cwęncan*:—**kwaŋkjan*, causative form corresp. to the strong vb. *cwincan* to go out, be extinguished.] **I.** *trans.* **1.** To put out, extinguish (fire, flame, or light, *lit.* or *fig.*). Now *rhet.* **b.** To put out the fire or flame of (something that burns or gives light, *lit.* or *fig.*). Now *rhet.* late ME. **c.** To destroy the sight or light of (the eye) 1667. **2.** To extinguish (heat or warmth, *lit.* or *fig.*) by cooling. late ME. **b.** To cool (a heated object) by means of cold water or other liquid. late ME. **3.** *transf.* To put an end to, stifle, suppress (a feeling, act, condition, quality, etc.) ME. **b.** To slake (thirst) completely; †rarely, to satisfy (hunger). late ME. **4.** To destroy, kill (a person); to oppress or crush. Now *rare.* ME. **b.** To put down (in a dispute); to squash 1840.

1. Q. thou his light, Destruction dark SCOTT. **b.** As she turned..To q. the lamp MORRIS. **c.** These eyes..So thick a drop serene hath quencht thir Orbs MILT. 2. **b.** Hot Bricks, somewhat quenched with water 1612. 3. How mercifully dyd God q. the fury of the peple 1545. 4. I, Tyme,..quenche out the ungodly, their memory and fame 1567.

†II. *intr.* **a.** Of fire, a burning thing, etc.: To be extinguished, to go out, to cease to burn or shine -1623. Also *transf.* **b.** Of a person: To cool down SHAKS.

b. *Cymb.* I. v. 47. Hence **Queˑnchable** *a.* **Queˑncher,** one who, or that which, quenches; *colloq.* a drink. **Queˑnchless** *a.* unquenchable, inextinguishable; **-ly** *adv.*, **-ness.**

‖**Quenelle** (kəneˑl). 1846. [F., origin obsc.] A seasoned ball, of which the chief ingredient, usu. meat or fish, has been reduced to a paste.

Quercetin (kwɔ̄ˑɹsĭtin). 1857. [Arbitrarily f. L. *quercus* oak + -IN [1].] *Chem.* A yellow crystalline substance widely distributed in the vegetable kingdom, but now obtained by decomposition of quercitrin.

Quercitannin (kwɔ̄ɹsitæˑnin). 1845. [f. L. *querci-* oak- + TANNIN.] *Chem.* A form of tannin obtained from oak-bark. So **Quercitaˑnnic** *a.* in *quercitannic acid.*

Quercite (kwɔ̄ˑɹsəit). 1857. [f. L. *quercus* oak + -ITE [1] 4.] *Chem.* A sweet crystalline alcohol obtained from acorns.

Quercitron (kwɔ̄ˑɹsitrən). 1794. [Abbrev. f. *querci-citron*, f. L. *quercus* oak + CITRON.] The black or dyer's oak of N. America (*Quercus tinctoria*); also called *q. oak.* **b.** The inner bark of this, used as a yellow dye and in tanning; also *q. bark.* Hence **Queˑrcitrin,** the yellow crystalline colouring matter of q. bark.

Querent (kwīᵊˑrĕnt). 1598. [ad. L. *quærentem*, *quærere*.] One who asks or inquires; *spec.* one who consults an astrologer.

Querimonious (kwerimōᵘˑniəs) *a.* 1604. [ad. late L. *querimoniosus*; see next and -OUS.] Full of, addicted to, complaining. Hence **Querimoˑnious-ly** *adv.*, **-ness.**

Querimony (kweˑrimŏni). 1529. [ad. L. *querimonia*, f. *queri* to complain.] Complaint, complaining.

Querist (kwīᵊˑrist). 1633. [f. L. *quærere* + -IST.] One who inquires; a questioner.

Querl (kwɔ̄ɹl). *U.S.* 1880. [perh. a. Ger. *querl*, *quirl* from MHG. *twirl* TWIRL.] A curl, twist, twirl. So **Querl** *v.* to twirl, coil, etc.

Quern (kwɔ̄ɹn). [OE. *cweorn*, *cwiorn*, *cweorne*, f. (ult.) a pre-Teut. stem **gʷern-*.] An apparatus for grinding corn, usu. consisting of two circular stones, the upper of which is turned by hand; also, a small hand-mill for grinding pepper, mustard, etc.

Comb. **q.-stone,** one of the two stones forming a q.; a millstone.

†Querulaˑtion. 1614. [f. med.L. *querulari*, f. *querulus*; see next.] Complaint, complaining. So **Queruleˑntal, -leˑntial** *a.* querulous. **Queruˑlity, Queruloˑsity,** habit or spirit of complaining.

Querulous (kweˑrŭləs), *a.* 1450. [ad. late L. *querulosus*, f. *querulus*, f. *queri.*] **1.** Of persons: Complaining, given to complaining, peevish. **b.** Of animals or things: Uttering or producing sounds expressive or suggestive of complaint 1635. **2.** Of the nature of, characterized by, complaining 1540.

1. The q. are seldom received with great ardour of kindness JOHNSON. **b.** One q. rook, unable to sleep, protested now and then DICKENS. 2. The q. comments of old ladies 1874. Hence **Queˑrulous-ly** *adv.*, **-ness.**

Query (kwīᵊˑri), *sb.* 1635. [Anglicizing of *quere*, QUÆRE.] **1.** Introducing a question: = QUÆRE A. (Now usu. expressed by the abbreviations *qy.*, *qr.*, *qu.* or the sign ?) 1667. **2.** A question: = QUÆRE B. 1635. **3.** A mark of interrogation (?), or the abbrev. *qy.*, etc., used to indicate a doubt as to the correctness of a statement, phrase, letter, etc. 1836.

1. Q. if purchase money was ever paid 1888. 2. What News, is the Quæry 1719.

Query (kwīᵊˑri), *v.* 1639. [f. prec. Cf. QUÆRE *v.*] **†1.** *trans.* To put as a question -1755. **b.** To ask (*whether, if, what,* etc.) 1639. **c.** *absol.* To ask a question or questions 1681. **2.** To question, interrogate (a person). *rare.* 1654. **3.** To call (a thing) in question; to mark as doubtful. Also with *if*, etc. 1772.

1. I do..entreat you to answer all that I have queried on that head BERKELEY. 3. The returning officer..had queried 76 [votes] 1772.

Quesited (kwĭsəiˑtĕd), *a.* and *sb.* 1647. [f. med.L. *quesit-*, L. *quæsit-*, *quærere* + -ED [1].] **†A.** *adj.* Sought for, asked about, etc. -1674. **B.** *sb. Astrol.* The thing or person inquired about 1647. So **Queˑsitive** *a.* interrogative.

Quest (kwest), *sb.* ME. [a. OF. *queste* (F. *quête*):—pop.L. **questa*, pa. pple. of *querere*, L. *quærere* to seek, inquire.] **I. 1.** = INQUEST *sb.* 1. *Obs.* exc. *dial.* **2.** = INQUEST *sb.* 2. Now *rare.* ME. **3.** Any inquiry or investigation made in order to discover some fact; also, the object of such inquiry 1598.

2. One q. of gentlemen, another of yeomen passed upon him FULLER.

II. 1. Search or pursuit, made in order to find or obtain something. Const. *of, for.* ME. **†b.** A person (or set of persons) employed in searching SHAKS. **2.** In mediæval romance: An expedition or adventure undertaken by a knight to procure some thing or achieve some exploit; the knights engaged in such an enterprise. Also *transf.* late ME. **3. a.** The search for game made by hounds. **b.** The baying of hounds in pursuit of game; a peculiar barking uttered by dogs when in sight of game. *Obs.* exc. *dial.* late ME. **4.** *R. C. Ch.* The collection of alms or donations for religious purposes 1528.

1. Whose desire Was to be glorious; 'twas a foolish q. BYRON. Phr. *In q. of* (†*after*, or inf.); The ghost rides forth..in nightly q. of his head W. IRVING. **b.** *Oth.* I. ii. 46. 2. The q. of the Sancgreal MALORY. 3. *transf.* Gad not abroad at ev'ry q. and call Of an untrained hope or passion G. HERBERT.

Quest (kwest), *v.* ME. [a. OF. *quester* (F. *quêter*), f. *queste* QUEST *sb.*] **1.** *intr.* Of hunting dogs, etc.: To search for game. Also with *about.* **b.** Of animals: To search *about* for food 1796. **2.** Of hunting dogs: To break out into a peculiar bark at the sight of game; to give tongue; to bark or yelp. *Obs.* exc. *dial.* late ME. **3.** Of persons: To go about in search of something. Also with *about*, and const. *after, for.* (Chiefly *transf.* from sense 1.) 1624. **b.** *R.C. Ch.* To ask for alms or donations 1748. **4.** *trans.* To search for, pursue, seek *out* 1751.

1. Bevis, questing about, found the body SCOTT. 4. Flush found a hare, and quested it for two miles MISS MITFORD. Hence **Queˑster,** one who quests. So **†Queˑstant,** quester SHAKS.

Question (kweˑstyən, kweˑstʃən), *sb.* ME. [a. AF. *questiun*, OF. *question*, ad. L. *quæstionem*, f. *quærere* to ask, inquire; cf. QUERY.] **I.** The action of inquiring or asking. **1.** The stating or investigation of a problem; inquiry into a matter; discussion of some doubtful point. **2.** The action of questioning, interrogating, or examining a person, or the fact of being questioned, etc.; hence, †talk, discourse. late ME. **b.** *spec.* The application of torture as part of a judicial examination 1583.

1. The..vnquiet time Did push it out of farther q. SHAKS. Phr. *Beyond (all) q.*, *out of, past, without q.*, unquestionably. *In q.*, under consideration, forming the subject of discourse. *To come into q.*, to be thought of as possible. Phr. *To call in* (†or *into*) *q.*, (*a*) to examine judicially, bring to trial; to take to task; (*b*) to question the validity or status of; to raise objections to. †*In q.*, on trial; He that was in q. for the robbery SHAKS. 2. Others abide our q. Thou art free. M. ARNOLD.

II. What is asked or inquired (about). **1.** The interrogative statement of some point to be investigated or discussed; a problem; hence, a matter forming, or capable of forming, the basis of a problem; a subject involving more or less difficulty or uncertainty ME. **b.** *spec.* A subject or proposal for discussion in a meeting or deliberative assembly, esp. in Parliament; †the putting of this proposal to the vote 1658. **2.** A subject of discussion, debate, or strife *between* parties, or of one party *with* another. late ME. **3.** An interrogation, query, inquiry ME.

1. Phr. *The q.*, the precise matter receiving or requiring deliberation or discussion; But that is not the q.: the q. is concerning your marriage SHAKS. *To beg the q.*: see BEG *v.* 4. **b.** *Question!*, used (*a*) to recall a speaker to the subject under discussion, †(*b*) to demand that the vote be taken. *Previous q.*, see PREVIOUS *a.* *It is a q. of*, what is required or involved is, etc.; It was a q. of time FREEMAN. *Out of the q.*, foreign to the subject; hence, not to be considered or thought of; Retreat was out of the q. 1878. 2. A q. arose between the heir at law and the younger children, whether it passed by the will CRUISE. Phr. *It is no* (or *not a*) *q.*, *there is no q.*, or simply †*no q.*: There is no room for dispute or doubt (*but, that*). *To make no q.*, to raise or entertain no doubt (*of* or *about* a thing, *but* or inf.). †*No q.* (used parenthetically), no doubt, without q.; This no q. is his meaning CLARENDON. 3. Ask me no questions and I'll tell you no fibs GOLDSM. If you do not give a plain answer to a plain q., you will be committed 1776.

Comb.: **q.-mark, -stop,** a mark of interrogation.

Question (kweˑstyən, -tʃən), *v.* 1470. [a. OF. *questionner*, f. *question* QUESTION *sb.*] **1.** *trans.* To ask a question or questions of (a person or *fig.* a thing); to interrogate 1490. **b.** To examine judicially; hence, to call to account, challenge, accuse (*of*). Now *rare.* 1637. **†2.** *intr. To q. with*: To ask questions of; to dispute with -1772. **3.** To ask or put questions 1584. **b.** *trans.* With clause stating the question 1592. **4.** To raise the question (*whether, if,* etc.); hence, to doubt, hold as uncertain 1533. **5. a.** To call in question, dispute, oppose 1632. **†b.** To state as a question SIR T. BROWNE. **†6.** To investigate (a thing) -1655.

1. Her Father..Still question'd me the Storie of my life SHAKS. 3. Goe wee..to the man that tooke him To q. of his apprehension SHAKS. **b.** They never questioned what crime he had done HOBBES. 4. Whether the request..can be complied with..may be questioned 1883. Phr. *I do not q.* (*but*, etc.), I have no doubt, I am sure (that); also pass. *it cannot be questioned*, it is certain. 5. **a.** Wee q. the truth of your informacion 1632. 6. *Hen. V*, II. iv. 142.

Questionable (kweˑstyənăb'l, -tʃən-), *a.*

1590. [f. prec. + -ABLE.] †1. **a.** Of a person: That may be interrogated. **b.** Of a question: That may be asked or put. **c.** Of a place: Where questions may easily be asked (*rare*) –1607. †2. Of persons or acts: Liable to be called to account or dealt with judicially –1685. **3.** Of things, facts, etc.: That may be questioned or called in question (rarely const. *by*); doubtful, uncertain. Freq. in phr. *it is q.* (*whether*, *if*, etc.). 1607. **b.** Of qualities, properties, etc.: About the existence or presence of which there may be question 1796. **c.** In depreciatory sense: Of doubtful or dubious character or quality 1806.

1. **a.** Thou com'st in such a q. shape, That I will speake to thee SHAKS. **3.** Whatever rendered property q., ambiguous, and insecure BURKE. **b.** The q. privilege of having as many wives as he could support 1856. **c.** Stick not even at q. means SHELLEY. Hence **Questionabi·lity, Que·stionableness,** the state of being q. **Que·stionably** *adv.*

†**Que·stionary,** *sb. rare.* late ME. [ad. med.L. *questionarius*; see QUESTION and -ARY[1].] 1. = QUESTIONIST –1787. **2.** = QUESTOR 1. SCOTT.

Questionary (kwe·styənări), *a.* 1653. [ad. late L. *quæst-*, *questionarius*; see QUESTION and -ARY[1].] 1. Having the form of a question; consisting of questions; conducted by means of questioning. **2.** That asks questions STEELE.

Questioner (kwe·styənəɪ, -tʃən-). 1551. [f. QUESTION *v.* + -ER[1].] One who questions; an interrogator, inquirer.

The curious q., the foolishe answerer CRANMER.

Questionist (kwe·styənist, -tʃən-). 1523. [f. QUESTION *v.* + -IST.] 1. A habitual or professed questioner, *spec.* in theological matters. **2.** Formerly, at Cambridge and Harvard: An undergraduate in his last term before proceeding to the degree of B.A. 1549.

Questionless (kwe·styənlės, -tʃən-), *a.* and *adv.* late ME. [f. QUESTION *sb.* + -LESS.] **A.** *adj.* Not admitting of question; unquestionable, indubitable 1532. **B.** *adv.* Without question; unquestionably; undoubtedly.

B. The first man who came into the world was, q., the most perfect 1760. Hence **Que·stionlessly** *adv.* = B; also, without asking questions.

‖**Questionnaire** (kestyǭnē·ɪ). 1908. [F.] A formal list of questions, esp. as used in an official inquiry.

Que·stman. 1454. [f. QUEST *sb.* + MAN *sb.*] A member of a 'quest'; one appointed to make official inquiry into any matter; *spec.* †**a.** a parish or ward official elected annually –1761. **b.** *Eccl.* A churchwarden's assistant; a sidesman. Now *Hist.* 1454.

†**Que·stmonger.** late ME. [f. QUEST *sb.* + MONGER.] One who made a business of conducting inquests –1776.

Questor (kwe·stǫɪ, -əɪ). late ME. [a. med.L. *questor*, f. *querere* = *quærere* to ask. (Cf. QUÆSTOR.)] 1. *R.C. Ch.* An official appointed by the Pope or by a bishop to grant indulgences on the gift of alms to the Church; a pardoner. **2. a.** In France, one of the treasurers of the National Assembly 1848. **b.** In Italy, a commissary of police 1865.

†**Que·strist.** [f. QUESTER + -IST.] One who goes in quest of another SHAKS.

Quetch, quitch, *v. Obs.* exc. *dial.* [OE. *cwęccan*, causative from the root **cwac-*; see QUAKE.] †1. *trans.* and *intr.* To shake. (OE. and early ME.) **2.** *intr.* To stir; in later use *esp.* to shrink, wince, twitch, as with pain ME. **b.** To utter a sound 1530.

Queue (kiū), *sb.* 1592. [a. F. *queue*, OF. *coue*, *cue*, *coe*:—L. *cauda* tail; see CUE *sb.*[3]] 1. *Her.* The tail of a beast. **2.** A long plait of hair worn hanging down behind; a pig-tail 1724. **3.** A number of persons ranged in a line, awaiting their turn to proceed, as at a ticket-office; also, a line of carriages, etc. 1837. **4.** A support for the butt of a lance 1855.

Queue (kiū), *v.* 1777. [f. prec.] **1.** *trans.* To put up (the hair) in a queue. **2.** *intr.* To take one's place in a queue; to form a queue; to form *up* in a queue 1893.

Quibble (kwi·b'l), *sb.* 1611. [perh. dim. of *quib* (1550–1656), ad. L. *quibus*, dat. or abl. pl. of *qui* who, which, as a word much used in legal documents.] 1. A play upon words, a pun. **2.** An equivocation, evasion of the point at issue; an argument depending on some likeness or difference between words or their meanings, or on some purely trivial circumstance 1670. **b.** The use of quibbles, quibbling 1710.

2. To a plain understanding his objections seem to be mere quibbles MACAULAY.

Quibble (kwi·b'l), *v.* 1629. [f. prec.] †1. *intr.* To pun, to play on words –1751. **2.** To argue in a purely verbal way; to evade the real point by a quibble 1656. **3.** *trans.* With advs.: To cheat or bring *out of*, waste or explain *away*, by quibbling 1713.

1. Nothing is more usual than to see a Hero weeping and quibbling for a dozen Lines together ADDISON. **2.** Quibbling about the meaning of words 1864. Hence **Qui·bbler. Qui·bblingly** *adv.*

Quick (kwik), *a.*, *sb.*, and *adv.* [Com.Teut.: OE. *cwicu*, *c(w)ucu*, and *cwic*, *c(w)uc-*:—OTeut. **kwikwoz.*] **A.** *adj.* I. Characterized by the presence of life. 1. Living; endowed with life; animate. Now *dial.* or *arch.* †**b.** Of possessions or property: Consisting of animals; (live) stock –1745. **c.** *transf.* or *fig.* OE. **2.** Of persons and animals: In a live state, living, alive. Now *dial.* or *arch.* OE. †**b.** Of the flesh or parts of the body –1649. **c.** *transf.* and *fig.* of qualities, feelings, etc. ME. **3.** Of plants or their parts: Alive, growing OE. **b.** Composed of living plants, esp. hawthorn, as *q. fence*, *hedge*, etc. 1467. **4.** Const. *with.* **a.** *Q. with child*, said of a female in the stage of pregnancy at which the motion of the fœtus is felt. Now *rare* or *Obs.* †Also *absol.* 1450. **b.** Alive, instinct *with* (life, soul, feeling, etc.) 1837.

1. They could see no quicke things left but onely Owles 1611. **2.** There was a gray Frier burning quicke at S. Markes pillar 1632. Not the q. but dead worthies properly pertain to my pen FULLER. **c.** Strike dead our feare..Rather then keepe it q. CHAPMAN. **3. b.** On the top a palisade and q. hedge 1894. **4.** *L. L. L.* v. ii. 687. **b.** That languid form q. with excitement DISRAELI.

II. Of things: Having some specific quality characteristic or suggestive of a living thing. †1. Of the complexion: Having the freshness of life (*rare*) –1693. **2. a.** *Mining.* Of veins, etc.: Containing ore, productive 1676. **b.** Of stock, capital, etc.: Productive of interest or profit 1701. **3.** Of wells, streams, etc.: Running, flowing. Now *rare.* OE. **4.** Of soil, etc.: Mobile, shifting, readily yielding to pressure. Now *rare.* ME. **5.** †**a.** Of coals: Live, burning –1764. **b.** Of fire or flames: Burning strongly. Also of an oven: Exposed to a brisk fire. late ME. †**6.** Of speech, writings, etc.: Lively, full of vigour or acute reasoning –1625. †**7.** Of places or times: Full of activity; busy. Of trade: Brisk. –1746. †**8.** Of sulphur: Readily inflammable, fiery –1661. †**9.** Of wine and other liquors: Brisk, effervescent –1746. **10.** Of colour: Vivid, bright, dazzling (*rare*) 1664. **11.** Of feelings: Lively, vivid, keen, strongly felt 1449. **12.** †**a.** Of a taste or smell: Sharp, pungent; brisk –1797. †**b.** Of speech or writing: Sharp, caustic –1748. **c.** Of air or light: Sharp, piercing (*rare*) 1608.

2. b. The q. assets..amounted on August 31 last to 5,928,338 dols. 1891. **3.** Many quicke and running springs HOLLAND. **4.** The Solway sands,..as the tide makes,..become q. in different places SMOLLETT. **5. b.** Bake it in a q. oven three hours 1769. **10.** Slain are the poppies that shot their random scarlet Q. amid the wheatears G. MEREDITH. **12. c.** The air is q. there, And it pierces and sharpens the stomach SHAKS.

III. 1. Of persons (or animals): Full of vigour, energy, or activity (now *rare*); prompt or ready to act; acting with speed or rapidity. late ME. **b.** Of qualities, things, etc. late ME. **2.** Of the eye, ear, etc.: Keen or rapid in its function; capable of ready or swift perception. late ME. **b.** So of the senses, perception, feeling, etc. 1548. **3.** Mentally active or vigorous; of ready apprehension, wit, or invention; so of the mind, operations of the mind, etc. OE. **4.** Hasty, impatient, hot-tempered. Now chiefly in comb. *q.-tempered*; so of temper, disposition, etc. 1549. **5.** Moving, or able to move, with speed 1450. **6.** Of movement or succession: Rapid, swift ME. **7.** Of an action, occurrence, process, etc.: That is done, happens, or takes place, rapidly or with speed; *esp.* that is over within a short space of time; that is soon finished or completed 1548. **8.** Of a curve, turn, etc.: Sharp 1725. **9.** With various constructions, viz. *to* and inf., *in*, *of*, *at*, *for*, *unto* ME.

1. In all thy workes bee quicke *Ecclus.* xxxi. 22. **b.** O true Apothecary: Thy drugs are quicke SHAKS. He was a good patriot, of a q. and clear spirit FULLER. **3.** The quicke Comedians Extemporally will stage vs SHAKS. A man of q. observation and lively fancy 1804. **4.** The Byshop was some what quicke wyth theym, and signified that he was muche offended LATIMER. **5.** Q., cross lightning SHAKS. **6.** Incite them to quicke motion SHAKS. **7.** Give me a q. dispatch one way or other MARVELL. **9. a.** Quicke is mine eare to heare of good towards him SHAKS. **b.** Q. in temper 1837. **c.** Q. of foot DICKENS. **d.** Your hands then mine, are quicker for a fray SHAKS.

B. Ellipt. or absol. uses passing into sb. 1. **a.** *pl.* (Without article or *-s.*) Living persons OE. **b.** *The q.*, the living. Usu. *pl.* and in conjunction with *the dead.* OE. **2.** With *a* and *pl.* A living thing. *rare* (now *dial.*). OE. **3.** *collect.* Living plants, *spec.* of white hawthorn, set to form a hedge 1456. **b.** with *a* and *pl.* = QUICKSET 1 b. 1507. **4.** *The q.*: the tender or sensitive flesh in any part of the body, as that under the nails; also, the tender part of a sore or wound. Usu. in phr. *to the q.* 1523. **b.** *fig.* with ref. to persons, as *touched*, *galled*, *stung*, etc. *to the q.* 1526. **c.** *transf.* of things (esp. immaterial things): The central, vital, or most important part 1567. **d.** With *a* and *pl.*: A tender, sensitive, or vital part (*rare*) 1550. **5.** *The q.*: the life (see LIFE *sb.* I. 7.). Chiefly in phr. *to the q.* 1563. *Obs.* or *arch.*

1. **a.** The Iudge of quicke and dead *Acts* x. 42. **b.** He ascended into Heaven..From thence he shall come to judge the q. and the dead *Bk. Com. Prayer.* **3.** The workes..are curiously hedg'd with q. EVELYN. **4.** He was in the habit of biting his nails to the q. 1862. **b.** Tigranes..was galled to the q., and hit at the heart NORTH. A Tory to the q. TENNYSON. **c.** The point touched the q. of his experience GEO. ELIOT. **5.** To draw to the q. (or to the life) 1727.

C. *adv.* 1. = QUICKLY ME. **2.** Used imperatively (partly ellipt. for *be quick*) 1596.

1. I am told that you speak very q. CHESTERF. Phr. *As q. as lightning, thought, wink*, etc. **2.** Quicke, quicke, feare nothing; Ile be at thy Elbow SHAKS.

Combs.: **q.-beam** = QUICKEN *sb.*[1]; **-change,** *attrib.* as epithet of an actor, etc. who quickly changes costume or appearance in order to play a different part; also *transf.* and as vb.; **-fire,** *attrib.* of a type of gun which can fire shots in rapid succession; **-firer,** a quick-firing gun; †**-thorn,** thorn used for hedging.

Quick (kwik), *v. arch.* [OE. *cwician*, f. *cwic* QUICK *a.*] *intr.* = QUICKEN *v.* 1, 2, 3, 6.

Quicken (kwi·k'n), *sb.*[1] late ME. [app. f. QUICK *a.*] **a.** The mountain-ash or rowan-tree (*Pyrus aucuparia*). **b.** The service-tree (*Pyrus domestica*). †**c.** The juniper.

Quicken (kwi·k'n), *sb.*[2] *Sc.* and *n. dial.* 1684. [f. *quick*, northern f. QUITCH.] Couch-grass; also *pl.* the underground stems of this and other grasses.

Quicken (kwi·k'n), *v.* ME. [f. QUICK *a.* + -EN[5].] 1. *trans.* To give or restore life to; to animate (as the soul the body). **2.** To give, add, or restore vigour to (a person or thing); to stimulate, excite, inspire. late ME. **3.** To kindle (a fire); to cause or help to burn up ME. †**4.** To make (liquor or medicine) more sharp or stimulant –1799. **5.** To hasten, accelerate, give speed to 1626. **b.** To make (a curve) sharper (*rare*) 1711. **6.** *intr.* To receive life, become living; †also, to revive. late ME. **b.** Of a female: To reach the state of pregnancy at which the child shows signs of life 1530. **7.** *fig.* To come into a state comparable to life. Const. *to*, *into*. ME. **b.** To grow bright 1712. **8.** To become faster 1805.

1. A medicine..able to..Q. a rocke SHAKS. *fig.* It is the spirit that quykeneth, the fleysch profiteth nothing WYCLIF *John* vi. 64. **2.** Loue quickened hym day and night LD. BERNERS. This quickened my resolution DE FOE. *absol.* To consider of education and learning, what is good and quickneth 1581. **5.** It had induced him to q. his departure 1838. **6.** As Sommer Flyes..That q. euen with blowing SHAKS. **7.** The hopes that q...Are flowers that wither SHELLEY. **b.** Sees..keener lightnings q. in her eyes POPE. **8.** Tess's breath quickened T. HARDY. Hence **Qui·ckener,** one who or that which quickens.

Quickhatch (kwi·khætʃ). 1743. [Adaptation of the Cree (Indian) name.] The wolverene.

Qui·cklime. late ME. [f. QUICK *a.* + LIME, after L. *calx viva*, F. *chaux vive.*] Lime which has been burned and not yet slaked with water; calcium oxide, CaO.

Quickly (kwi·kli), *adv.* OE. [f. QUICK *a.* + -LY [2].] †1. In a living or lively manner; with animation or vigour; also, sensitively –1800. 2. Rapidly, with haste or speed ME.

1. We may fele our pulses bete quickly and continually 1526. This q. heals even cut Veins and Sinews WESLEY. Retaliation..q. followed 1847.

Quick march. 1752. [In 1, f. QUICK *a.* and MARCH *sb.* In 2, f. QUICK *adv.* and MARCH *v.*] *Mil.* 1. A march in QUICK TIME. 2. Used as a command to soldiers to march in quick time 1802.

Quickness (kwi·knės). ME. [f. QUICK *a.* + -NESS.] 1. Life, vitality, vital principle. Now *rare.* †2. Animation, briskness, vigour, freshness, etc. –1656. 3. Liveliness, readiness, or acuteness of feeling, perception, or apprehension. late ME. 4. Speed, rapidity (of action, motion, etc.); hastiness (of temper) 1548. †5. Sharpness; pungency or acidity of taste; sharpness of speech –1748.

1. The lyfe and quycknesse of the grayne 1545. 3. Q. of parts FULLER. Q. of sight 1841. 4. A q. of temper..marred the perfection of his character 1863.

Quicksand (kwi·ksænd). late ME. [f. QUICK *a.* II. 4.] 1. A bed of extremely loose wet sand, easily yielding to pressure and thus readily swallowing up any heavy object, as a man, a ship, etc. resting upon it. b. *fig.* Applied to things (more rarely to persons) of an absorbent, yielding, or treacherous character 1593. 2. Without article: Loose yielding sand 1838.

1. Conscious that there lay..quicksands in his way COWPER. b. He once more tried the quicksands of the Court 1879.

Quickset (kwi·kset), *sb.* and *a.* 1484. [f. QUICK *a.* I. 3 + SET *ppl. a.* and *sb.*] 1. a. *collect.* Live slips or cuttings of plants, set in the ground to grow, *esp.* those of whitethorn or other shrub of which hedges are made. b. With *a* and *pl.* One such slip or cutting 1519. 2. A quickset hedge or thicket 1573. B. *adj.* (or *attrib.*) Of a hedge: Formed of living plants. So also with *fence, row,* etc. Also *transf.* and *fig.* 1535. Hence †**Quickset** *v. trans.* to furnish (plant, enclose, etc.) with a q. hedge.

Quick-sighted, *a.* 1552. [f. *quick sight* + -ED [2].] Having quick sight. **Quicksi·ghtedness.**

Quicksilver (kwi·ksi:lvəɹ), *sb.* [OE. *cwic seolfor*, after L. *argentum vivum*; see QUICK *a.* and SILVER.] 1. The metal mercury, so called from its liquid mobile form at ordinary temperatures. 2. Used allus. with ref. to the quick motion of which the metal is capable 1562.

2. Thou hast q. in the veins of thee to a certainty SCOTT. Hence **Qui·cksi:lver** *v. trans.* to treat, imbue, or mix with q.; *esp.* to coat (the back of glass) with an amalgam of tin in order to give a reflecting power.

Quick step, qui·ckstep. 1802. 1. *Mil.* The step used in marching in quick time. Also quasi-*adv.*, at a quick step. 2. *Mus.* A march in military quick time 1811. 3. A fast fox-trot (*recent*).

Quick time. 1802. *Mil.* A rate of marching which in the British army now consists of 128 paces of 33 inches each (= 118 yards) in a minute, or four miles an hour.

Quick-witted, *a.* (Stress variable.) 1530. [f. *quick wit* + -ED [2].] Having a quick or ready wit; mentally acute, sharp, clever.

How likes Gremio these quicke-witted folkes? SHAKS. Hence **Quickwi·ttedness.**

‖**Quicumque vult** (kwaikʊ·mkwĭ vʊlt). 1450. [L. = whosoever will (be saved, *salvus esse*).] The Athanasian Creed, of which these are the opening words.

‖**Quid** (kwid), *sb.*[1] 1606. [L., neut. sing. of *quis.*] 1. That which a thing is. 2. *U.S.* (abbrev. of *tertium quid.*) A name given to a section of the Republican party in 1805–11.

Quid (kwid), *sb.*[2] *slang.* 1688. [Origin obsc.] A sovereign; †a guinea. (*Pl.* usu. without *-s*, as *two q. a week.*)

Quid (kwid), *sb.*[3] 1727. [var. of CUD *sb.*] A piece of something (usu. of tobacco), suitable to be held in the mouth and chewed.

Quid (kwid), *v.* 1775. [f. prec.] 1. *intr.* To chew tobacco; to chew the cud. 2. *trans.* Of horses: To let (food) drop from the mouth when half chewed 1831.

‖**Quidam** (kwəɪ·dæm). *rare.* 1579. [L., f. *qui* who.] Somebody; a certain person.

Qui·ddative, *a. rare.* 1642. Shortened from QUIDDITATIVE.

Quiddit (kwi·dit). Now *arch.* 1592. = QUIDDITY 2.

†**Qui·dditative,** *a.* 1600. [f. next + -ATIVE.] 1. Pertaining to the quiddity or essence of a thing –1656. 2. Full of equivocations –1637.

Quiddity (kwi·dĭti). 1539. [ad. schol.L. *quidditas*; see QUID *sb.*[1] and -ITY.] 1. The real nature or essence of a thing; that which makes a thing what it is 1569. 2. A captious nicety in argument; a quirk, quibble. (Alluding to scholastic arguments on the 'quiddity' of things.) 1539. b. Subtlety (of wit) 1600.

1. The q...of poetry as distinguished from prose DE QUINCEY.

Quiddle (kwi·d'l), *v.* Now chiefly *dial.* and *U.S.* 1567. [prob. f. prec. (sense 2), after *fiddle, piddle,* or *twiddle.*] *intr.* a. To discourse in a trifling way. b. To trifle, waste time (*with*) 1832. Hence **Qui·ddle** *sb.* a fastidious person. **Qui·ddler.**

Quidnunc (kwi·dnʊŋk). 1709. [f. L. *quid* what + *nunc* now.] One who is constantly asking: 'What now?' 'What's the news?'; hence an inquisitive person; a gossip.

Some wretched intrigue which had puzzled two generations of quidnuncs 1874.

‖**Quid pro quo** (kwid prōᵘ kwōᵘ), *sb.* 1565. [L., 'something for something'.] 1. One thing in place of another; *orig.* and *esp.* one medicinal substance used for another, either intentionally, fraudulently, or by mistake. b. The action or fact of using one thing for another; the result of this; a mistake or blunder consisting in such a substitution 1679. 2. One thing (or action) in return for another; tit for tat 1591.

1. b. A laughable *quid pro quo*..occurred to him in a conversation THACKERAY. 2. I shall be able..to bestow What you will find a *quid pro quo* 1820.

Quiesce (kwəi,e·s), *v.* 1828. [ad. L. *quiescere*, f. *quies.*] 1. *intr.* To become quiescent; to subside *into* 1833. 2. Of a letter: To become silent: said of the feeble consonants in Hebrew when their sound is absorbed in that of a preceding vowel 1828.

Quiescence (kwəi,e·sĕns). 1631. [ad. late L. *quiescentia*; see next and -ENCE.] The state of being quiescent; quietness; an instance of this. b. *spec.* in Heb. grammar; see prec. 2. 1828.

That there is no such thing in the World as an absolute q. 1664. So **Quie·scency.**

Quiescent (kwəi,e·sĕnt), *a.* and *sb.* 1609. [a. ppl. stem of L. *quiescere* to QUIESCE.] A. *adj.* 1. Motionless, inactive, at rest 1646. 2. Of a letter: Not sounded; silent; *spec.* in Heb. grammar (see QUIESCE *v.* 2) 1609. b. Of a person: Silent BOSWELL.

1. The q. and death-like condition of the pupa 1874. 2. The E silent or q., which yieldeth no sound 1609.

B. *sb.* 1. A quiescent letter 1727. 2. A quiescent verb in Heb. grammar 1831. Hence **Quie·scently** *adv.*

Quiet (kwəi·ət), *sb.* ME. [ad. L. *quiet-*, stem of *quies.*] 1. Absence of disturbance or tumult; social or political tranquillity. b. Absence of noise or (rapid) motion; calmness, stillness. late ME. 2. Freedom from external disturbance, molestation, or noise; †freedom from occupation; rest, repose ME. b. Freedom from mental agitation; calm or peace of mind 1628. 3. The condition of remaining quiet 1559.

1. Join with thee calm Peace, and Q. MILT. To whom the care of the Publique q. is committed HOBBES. 2. An arrant vixen of a wife soured his domestic q. FIELDING.

Quiet (kwəi·ət), *a.* late ME. [a. OF. *quiet(e* or ad. L. *quietus*, pa. pple. of *quiescere*, f. root of *quies* QUIET *sb.*] I. 1. Of persons (or animals): Making no stir, or noise; causing no disturbance; remaining at rest. b. (Also of nature or disposition.) Habitually or naturally peaceful or averse to making stir, noise, etc. Of an animal: Gentle. late ME. 2. Of things: Not active; not moving or stirring; also, making no noise; still 1599. b. Free from excess; moderate, gentle; *esp.* of colour, dress, style, etc.: Not obtrusive, glaring or showy 1560.

1. I wish you would be q., you have more tricks than a dancing bear SWIFT. As q. as mice 1843. *Q.!* an injunction to be silent. b. A q. horse 1811. 2. An eye made q. by the power Of harmony WORDSW. b. A q. ebb, or a tempestuous flow DRYDEN.

II. 1. Free from disturbance; not interfered or meddled with; left in peace. late ME. 2. Characterized by the absence of all strife, bustle, stir, or commotion; also, free from noise or uproar, silent, still 1514. b. Partaken of, or enjoyed, in q. 1837. 3. Of the mind, conscience, etc.: Not troubled; free from agitation or excitement. So also of persons in respect of the mind, etc. 1535.

1. A quyete slepe is right necessary and delycious 1532. Anything for a q. life 1626. The grantor may covenant..for the grantee's q. enjoyment BLACKSTONE. 2. I could be well content To entertaine the Laggeend of my life With q. houres SHAKS. b. A q. cup of tea DICKENS. 3. Truth hath a q. breast SHAKS.

III. Quasi- *sb.*, in phr. *On the q.*, privately, in secret. (For the abbrev. *q. t.* see Q.) *slang* or *colloq.* 1873. Hence **Qui·et-ly** *adv.*, **-ness.**

Quiet (kwəi·ət), *v.* 1440. [ad. med.L. *quietare*, f. L. *quietus* QUIET *a.*] †1. *trans.* To quit, acquit (oneself or another) –1473. 2. To make quiet (in various senses); to reduce to quietness 1526. 3. To settle or establish in quiet. Chiefly *Law.* 1586. 4. *intr.* To become quiet. Also *to q. down.* 1791.

2. Q. thy Cudgell, thou dost see I eate SHAKS. Those savage nations whom he had quieted HOLLAND. This quieted our apprehensions 1748. Measures which may q. the unhappy divisions of the country BURKE. 3. The Plaintiffs are entitled..to be quieted in the possession they have had for so many years 1884. 4. By and by she quieted, and..fell asleep 1865. Hence **Qui·eter,** one who or that which makes quiet.

Quieten (kwəi·ət'n), *v.* 1828. [f. QUIET *a.* + -EN [5].] *trans.* and *intr.* To make or become quiet.

Quietism (kwəi·ətiz'm). 1687. [ad. It. *quietismo*; see QUIET *a.* and -ISM.] 1. A form of religious mysticism (originated by Molinos, a Spanish priest), consisting in passive devotional contemplation, with extinction of the will and withdrawal from all things of the senses; also, any similar form of mysticism. 2. A state of calmness and passivity of mind or body; repose, quietness, tranquillity 1772.

Quietist (kwəi·ətist). 1685. [ad. It. *quietista*; cf. prec. and -IST.] 1. One who believes in or practises Quietism, or any similar form of mysticism. 2. One whose attitude towards political or social movements is analogous to Quietism in religion 1798.

2. He was not..a political q. from indifference SOUTHEY. Hence **Quieti·stic** *a.* belonging to, or characteristic of quietists.

Quietude (kwəi·ətiūd, -ĕtiūd). 1597. [a. F. *quiétude*, f. (ult.) L. *quietus* QUIET *a.*] Quietness; rest, calm, tranquillity.

‖**Quietus** (kwəi,ī·tʊ̆s). 1540. [Short for (med.)L. *quietus est* he is quit.] 1. An acquittance given on payment of sums due, or clearing of accounts; a receipt. †2. A discharge from office or duty –1788. 3. Discharge or release from life; death, or that which brings death 1602. b. Final extinction 1806. 4. (By assoc. with *quiet.*) Something which quiets or represses 1824.

3. When he himselfe might his q. make With a bare bodkin SHAKS. 4. The nurse ran to give its accustomed q. to the little screaming infant THACKERAY.

Quiff (kwif). 1902. [Origin unkn.] A lock or flat curl of hair coming low on the forehead and sometimes oiled.

‖**Qui-hy** (kwəi,həi). Also **-hi.** 1816. [Urdū (Hindī) *koī hai* 'is any one there?' a call used in India to summon a servant.] An Anglo-Indian, *esp.* one belonging to the Bengal Presidency.

Quill (kwil), *sb.*[1] late ME. [Origin obsc. Cf. LG. *quiele*, G. *kiel* quill (of a feather).] †1. A hollow stem or stalk, as that of a reed –1688. b. A piece of reed or other hollow stem on which yarn is wound; hence, a bobbin, spool, or pirn of any material. late ME. c. A musical pipe, made of a hollow stem 1567. d. A piece of cinnamon or cinchona bark curled up in the form of a tube 1797. †2. A small pipe or tube; *esp.* a small water-pipe –1712. 3. The tube or barrel of a feather, the part by which it is attached to the skin. Sometimes used loosely in the sense of 'feather' (*esp.* one of the strong wing- or tail-feathers) and *poet.* for 'wing'. 1555. b. The feather of a goose, etc., formed into a pen by pointing and slitting the lower end of the barrel 1552. c. A plectrum formed of the quill of a feather, used for plucking the strings of a musical instrument 1552. d. The float of a fishing line, made of a quill 1606. e. A toothpick made of a quill 1784. 4. One of the hollow sharp spines of a porcupine 1602.

1. c. Who now shall teach to change my oaten q. For trumpet 'larms P. FLETCHER. 3. b. A q. worn to the pith in the service of the State SWIFT. e. He picks clean teeth, and, busy as he seems With an old tavern q., is hungry yet COWPER. 4. Make..each particular haire to stand an end, Like Quilles upon the fretfull Porpentine SHAKS..

attrib. and *Comb.*, as **q.-bark,** cinchona bark in the form of quills; **-bit,** a boring-tool for a brace, having a hollow barrel; **-coverts,** the feathers which cover the base of the quill-feathers; **-driver,** one who works with a q. or pen; a clerk or author; **-feather,** one of the stiff, comparatively large, feathers arranged in two rows along the edge of a bird's wing; also, one of the similar feathers of the tail.

†**Quill,** *sb.*² *rare.* 1593. [perh. a. OF. **quille* = F. *cueille* gathering, harvest.] *In the* (or *a*) *q.*: in a body; in concert. *To jump in q.*, to act simultaneously or in harmony. -1690.

2 *Hen. VI*, I. iii. 4.

Quill (kwil), *v.* 1710. [f. QUILL *sb.*¹] 1. *trans.* To form into cylindrical pleats or folds resembling a quill; to goffer 1712. 2. To cut the quills off (a wing) SWIFT. 3. To cover with, or as with, quills 1783. 4. *intr.* To wind thread or yarn on a quill; to fill spools 1640.

1. His cravat seemed quilled into a ruff GOLDSM. Hence **Qui·lling** *vbl. sb.* the action of the vb.; a ribbon, strip of lace, etc. pleated into small cylindrical folds resembling a row of quills.

‖**Quillaia** (kwilē·yă). 1848. [mod.L., f. Chilian *quillai*, f. *quillcan* to wash.] a. A genus of S. Amer. rosaceous trees, the bark of which possesses soap-like properties. b. The soap-bark tree of Chili (*Quillaia saponaria*) or its bark (also *q.-bark*).

Quilled (kwild), *a.* and *ppl. a.* 1727. [f. QUILL *sb.*¹ and *v.* + -ED².] 1. Having the form of a quill or quills. 2. Having, or fitted with, a quill or quills, *spec.* of a suture: Having the thread secured to pieces of quill on each side of the wound 1767.

Quillet (kwi·lėt). 1588. [perh. abbrev. of obs. *quillity*, app. an alteration of QUIDDITY.] A verbal nicety or subtle distinction; a quirk.

Some tricks, some quillets, how to cheat the diuell SHAKS.

Quilt (kwilt), *sb.* ME. [a. OF. *cuilte, coilte* :—L. *culcita* a stuffed sack, mattress, etc.] 1. An article of bed-furniture, consisting essentially of two large pieces of woven material having a layer of wool, flock, down, or the like, placed between them; orig. used for lying on; now, a coverlet of similar make, *esp.* one in which the lining is kept in place by lines of stitching passing through the whole; hence, any thick outer bed-covering, a counterpane. b. *transf.* A thick covering. †Also applied joc. to a fat person. 1596. 2. A piece of padded material used to defend the body, as a substitute or lining for armour 1592. †3. A pad smeared or stuffed with a medicinal substance, and applied to some part of the body -1684.

1. Let his Bed be hard, and rather Quilts than Feathers LOCKE. b. How now blowne Jack? how now Q.? SHAKS.

Quilt (kwilt), *v.*¹ 1555. [f. prec.] 1. *trans.* To pad, line, or cover (a thing) with some material, after the method employed in making a quilt. b. To cover with interlaced cord 1611. 2. To fasten together (two pieces or thicknesses of woven material) by stitches or lines of stitching so as to hold in position a layer of some soft substance placed between them. Also, to sew (several thicknesses) together. 1555. b. *fig.* To compile (a literary work) by putting together scraps from various sources 1605. 3. To sew up (some object or material) between two pieces of stuff, as in making a quilt 1562. 4. *intr.* To make a quilt or quilts. *U.S.* 1861.

1. His black velvet bonnet was lined with steel, quilted between the metal and his head SCOTT. 2. b. Manuals, and Handmaids of Devotion,..clapt together and quilted out of Scripture phrases MILT. Hence **Qui·lter.**

Quilt (kwilt), *v.*² *dial.* and *U.S.* [perh. transf. use of prec.] *trans.* To beat, thrash, flog. Hence **Qui·lting** *vbl. sb.*² a flogging.

Quilting (kwi·ltiŋ), *vbl. sb.*¹ 1611. [f. QUILT *v.*¹] 1. The action of QUILT *v.*¹ 2. a. Quilted material; quilted work. b. Material for making a quilt. c. A kind of cloth with a diagonal pattern like that of a quilt. 1710. 3. *dial.* and *U.S.* A quilting-party 1819.

Comb.: **q.-bee, -feast, -frolic, -party** (*U.S.*), a gathering of women held for the purpose of making a quilt, and serving as an occasion for enjoyment.

Quin (kwin). 1840. [Etym. obsc.] A variety of pecten (*Pecten opercularis*).

Quina (kī·nă, kwəi·nă). 1830. [Sp. spelling of Quichua *kina* bark.] a. The bark of several species of *Cinchona* that yield quinine. b. *Chem.* = QUININE.

Quinary (kwəi·nări), *a.* and *sb.* 1603. [ad. L. *quinarius*, f. *quini* five each.] A. *adj.* Pertaining to, characterized by, the number five; consisting of five (things or parts).

Q. system, a principle of division in zoology, now discarded.

B. *sb.* A set of five; a compound consisting of five things. Now *rare.* 1651.

Quinate (kwi·n-, kwəi·nēt), *sb.* 1836. [f. QUINA + -ATE 1 c.] *Chem.* A salt of quinic acid.

Quinate (kwəi·nēt), *a.* 1806. [f. L. *quini* five each, after *binate.*] *Bot.* Of a leaf: Composed of five leaflets; quinquefoliolate.

Quince (kwins). ME. [prop. pl. of *quine*, COYN, used first as collective and then as sing.] 1. The hard, acid, yellowish, pear-shaped fruit of *Pyrus Cydonia*, used as a preserve or to flavour other fruits; the seeds are also employed in medicine and the arts. Also, the tree. 2. Applied to other fruits or trees resembling the quince 1876.

2. *Native Q.*, the Australian bitter-bark, emu-apple, or quinine-tree. *Wild Q.*, the Australian black ash.

Quincentenary (kwinsentī·nări), *a.* and *sb.* 1879. [irreg. f. L. *quin(que)* five + CENTENARY. Cf. QUINGENTENARY.] A. *adj.* Pertaining to or connected with a five-hundredth year. B. *sb.* A five-hundredth anniversary, or the celebration of this. So **Quincente·nnial.**

Quincuncial (kwinkv·nʃăl), *a.* 1601. [ad. L. *quincuncialis*; see next.] Arranged in the form of a quincunx or quincunxes; involving or characterized by this arrangement. b. *Bot.* Of æstivation: Having five leaves so disposed that two are exterior and two interior, while the fifth is partly exterior and partly interior. Hence **Quincu·ncially** *adv.* in a q. manner; in the form of a quincunx.

Quincunx (kwi·nkvŋks). 1647. [a. L., f. *quinque* five + *uncia* a twelfth, an OUNCE.] 1. *Astrol.* An aspect of planets in which these are at a distance of 5 signs or 150 degrees from each other (*rare*). 2. A disposition of five objects so placed that four occupy the corners, and the fifth the centre of a square or rectangle; a set of five things arranged in this manner 1658. b. *spec.* as a basis of arrangement in planting trees; a group of five trees so planted 1664. c. *Bot.* Quincuncial æstivation 1832. Hence **Quincu·nxial** *a.* (*rare*).

Quindecagon (kwinde·kăgǫn). 1570. [irreg. f. L. *quindecim*, after *decagon*, etc.; see -GON.] *Geom.* A plane figure having fifteen angles.

Quindecemvir (kwindǐse·mvəɹ). 1601. [L., f. *quindecim* fifteen + *vir* man.] *Rom. Antiq.* A member of a body, commission, etc., of fifteen men; *esp.* one of the priests who had charge of the Sybilline books.

Quindecim (kwi·ndǐsim). 1445. [Alteration of AF. *quinzisme* QUINZIÈME after L. *quindecim.*] †1. A tax or duty of a fifteenth part -1647. 2. *Eccl. Antiq.* = next 1445.

Quindene (kwi·ndīn). 1494. [ad. med.L. *quindena*, f. L. *quindeni* fifteen each.] *Eccl. Antiq.* The fifteenth (in mod. reckoning, fourteenth) day after a church-festival.

Quingentenary (kwindʒentī·nări), *a.* and *sb.* 1884. [f. L. *quingenti* five hundred, after *centenary*, etc.] = QUINCENTENARY.

Quinhydrone (kwinhəi·drōun). 1865. [f. QUINA + HYDRONE.] *Chem.* A green crystalline substance formed by direct union of quinol and quinone.

Quinia (kwi·niă). 1826. [mod.L., f. QUINA; see -IA¹.] *Chem.* (*Med.*) = QUININE.

Quinic (kwi·nik), **kinic** (ki·nik), *a.* 1814. [f. QUINA + -IC.] *Chem.* Derived from quina. *Q. acid*: a vegetable acid found chiefly in cinchona barks. Hence **Qui·nicine,** an alkaloid, isomeric with quinine and quinidine, from which it is obtained by heating with glycerol.

Quinidine (kwi·nidəin). 1836. [f. QUINA + *-id-* + -INE⁵.] *Chem.* An alkaloid found in some cinchona barks along with quinine, with which it is isomeric.

Quinine (kwinī·n, -əi·n, *U.S.* kwəi·nəin). 1826. [f. QUINA + -INE⁵.] An alkaloid ($C_{20}H_{24}N_2O_2$) found in the bark of species of cinchona and remigia, and used as a febrifuge, tonic, and antiperiodic, chiefly in the form of the salt, sulphate of quinine, which is popularly termed quinine. Hence **Quini·nic** *a.* pertaining to, derived from, q. **Qui·nism** = next.

Quinism (kwəi·nizm). 1880. [f. QUINA + -ISM.] *Path.* The physical state (giddiness, deafness, loss of sight, etc.) produced by the excessive use of quinine; cinchonism.

Quinnat (kwi·năt). 1829. [N.Amer. Indian.] The king-salmon; the Californian, Columbian, or Chinook salmon (*Oncorhyncus chouicha* or *quinnat*) of the N. Pacific coast.

Quinoa (kī·no,ă, kwinōu·ă). Also **quinua.** 1625. [Sp. spelling of Quichuan *kinua, kinoa.*] An annual plant (*Chenopodium Quinoa*) found on the Pacific slopes of the Andes, cultivated in Chili and Peru for its edible farinaceous seeds. Also *attrib.*

Quinoidine (kwinoi·dəin). Also **-ina.** 1836. [f. QUINA + -OID + -INE⁵.] *Chem.* A brownish-black resinous substance, consisting of amorphous alkaloids, obtained as a by-product in preparing salts of quinia.

Quinol (kwi·nǫl). 1881. [f. QUINA + -OL.] *Chem.* = HYDROQUINONE.

Quinoline (kwi·nŏləin). 1845. [f. as prec. + -INE⁵.] *Chem.* = CHINOLINE.

Quinologist (kwinǫ·lŏdʒist). 1869. [f. QUINA + -(O)LOGIST.] One who is versed in the scientific study of quinine. So **Quino·logy,** the scientific study of quinine.

Quinone (kwi·nōun, kwinōu·n). 1853. [f. QUINA + -ONE.] *Chem.* a. *spec.* A crystalline compound (benzoquinone, $C_6H_4O_2$), the simplest type of the class of quinones. b. Any one of a series of aromatic compounds derived from the benzene series of hydrocarbons when two hydrogen atoms are replaced by two of oxygen.

Quinovic (kwinōu·vik), **kino·vic,** *a.* 1838. [f. *quinova-*, shortened form of L. *quina nova* false cinchona bark + -IC.] *Chem. Q. acid*, an acid found in false cinchona bark. So **Quino·vin, kino·vin,** an amorphous bitter compound found in (false and other) cinchona-barks.

Quinquagenarian (kwi:nkwădʒinē·riăn), *sb.* and *a.* 1569. [ad. L. *quinquagenarius*, f. *quinquageni* distrib. of *quinquaginta* fifty + -AN.] A. *sb.* †1. A captain of fifty men (*rare*) -1609. 2. A person aged fifty; or between fifty and sixty 1843. B. *adj.* †1. Commanding fifty men (*rare*) -1629. 2. Of fifty years of age; characteristic of one of that age 1822. So **Quinquagenary** (*rare*). late ME.

‖**Quinquagesima** (kwinkwădʒe·simă). late ME. [med.L., fem. (sc. *dies*) of L. *quinquagesimus* fiftieth. So called after QUADRAGESIMA.] †a. The period beginning with the Sunday immediately preceding Lent and ending on Easter Sunday. †b. The first week of this period. c. (Also *Q. Sunday.*) The Sunday before Lent; Shrove Sunday. So **Quinquage·simal** *a.* belonging to a set of fifty; containing fifty days.

†**Qui·nquangle.** 1668. [ad. late L. *quinquangulus, -um*, f. *quinque* + *angulus.*] A pentagon -1788. Hence **Quinqua·ngular** *a.* having five angles or corners; pentagonal.

Quinquarticular (kwinkwaɹti·kiŭlăɹ), *a.* 1659. [ad. mod.L. *quinquarticularis*, f. *quinque* five + *articulus* ARTICLE.] Relating to the five articles or points of Arminian doctrine condemned by the Calvinists at the Synod of Dort in 1618.

Quinque- (kwi·nkwǐ), comb. form of L. *quinque* five, with the sense 'having, consisting of, etc. five (things specified)', in some words adopted from classical and later L., and in others, chiefly terms of *Bot.* and *Zool.*, of English formation.

Quinquepa·rtite [L. *partitus* divided], *a.* divided into, consisting of, five parts. **Qui·nquesect**, *v. trans.* to cut into five (equal) parts. **Quinque·virate**, an association, board, etc. consisting of five men. **Qui·nquifid**, *a. Bot.* cleft in five.

Quinquenniad (kwinkwe·niăd). 1842. [f. as next + -AD, after *decad*.] = QUINQUENNIUM.

Quinquennial (kwinkwe·niăl), *a.* and *sb.* 1460. [f. L. *quinquennis* + -AL; cf. *biennial*, etc.] **A.** *adj.* **1.** Lasting, continuing, holding office, etc. for five years. **2.** Occurring every fifth year 1610. **B.** *sb.* **1.** A period of five years 1890. **2.** A magistrate holding office for five years 1895. Hence **Quinque·nnially** *adv.*

‖ **Quinquennium** (kwinkwe·niŏm). *Pl.* **-ia.** 1621. [L., f. *quinque* five + *annus* year.] A period of five years.

Quinquereme (kwi·nkwĭrīm), *a.* and *sb.* 1553. [ad. L. *quinqueremis*, f. *quinque* five + *remus* oar.] **A.** *adj.* Of ancient ships: Having five banks of oars 1654. **B.** *sb.* A ship having five banks of oars 1553.

Quinquina (kinkī·nă, kwinkwəi·nă). 1656. [Sp. spelling of Quichuan *kinkina* or *kina-kina*, redupl. of *kina* bark, QUINA.] **a.** Peruvian or Jesuits' bark; the bark of several species of cinchona, yielding quinine and other febrifugal alkaloids. **b.** One or other of the trees producing cinchona-bark.

Quinquivalent (kwinkwi·vălent), *a.* 1877. [f. L. *quinqui-* five + *valent*, as in *equivalent*, etc.] = PENTAVALENT.

Quinsy (kwi·nzi). ME. [ad. med.L. *quinancia*, f. Gr. κυνάγχη CYNANCHE.] Inflammation of the throat or parts of the throat; suppuration of the tonsils; tonsillitis.

Quint (kwint), *sb.*[1] 1526. [a. F. *quint* or *quinte*:—L. *quintus, -a, -um*, ordinal to *quinque* five.] **1.** A tax of one-fifth. **2.** *Mus.* An interval of a fifth 1806. **b.** (In full *quint-stop*.) An organ-stop giving tones a fifth higher than the normal 1855.

Quint (kint, kwint), *sb.*[2] 1659. [a. F. *quinte* f.; see prec.] **1.** In piquet: A sequence of five cards of the same suit, counting as fifteen. †**2.** *transf.* A set of five persons BUTLER.

1. *Q. major*, the ace, king, queen, knave, and ten of a suit. *Q. minor*, the five cards from the knave to the seven.

Quint-, erron. used in combs. in place of QUINQU(E, as *quintangular*, etc.

Quintain (kwi·ntėn). *Obs.* exc. *Hist.* late ME. [a. OF. *quintaine*, usu. identified with L. *quintana* the market and business-place of a camp, as a place where military exercises may have been practised.] A stout post or plank, or some object mounted on such a support, set up as a mark to be tilted at with lances or poles, or thrown at with darts, as an exercise of skill for horsemen or footmen; also, the exercise or sport of tilting, etc. at such a mark.

fig. That which here stands vp Is but a quintine, a meere liuelesse blocke SHAKS.

Quintal (kwi·ntăl), **ki·ntal, ke·ntle.** 1470. [a. OF. *quintal*, pl. *quintaus*, ad. Arab. *qintar*.] **a.** A weight of one hundred pounds; a hundredweight (112 pounds). **b.** In the metric system: A weight of 100 kilograms.

Quintan (kwi·ntăn), *a.* and *sb.* 1657. [ad. L. *quintana* (sc. *febris*), fem. of *quintanus*, f. *quintus* fifth. Cf. QUARTAN.] **A.** *adj.* Of a fever or ague: Having a paroxysm every fifth (= fourth) day. **B.** *sb.* A fever or ague of this kind.

‖ **Quinte** (kæ̃nt). 1707. [F.; see QUINT *sb.*[1]] The fifth thrust or parry of the eight taught in fencing-schools.

Quintessence (kwinte·sĕns), *sb.* late ME. [a. F., or ad. med.L. *quinta essentia* fifth essence.] **1.** The 'fifth essence' of ancient and mediæval philosophy, supposed to be the substance of which the heavenly bodies were composed, and to be actually latent in all things. **2.** The most essential part of any substance; a highly refined essence or extract; *spec.* in older chemistry, an alcoholic tincture obtained by digestion at a gentle heat 1576. **b.** The purest or most perfect form or manifestation of some quality 1570. **c.** The most perfect embodiment of the typical qualities of a certain class of persons, etc. 1590.

2. b. The Law of England, which Lawyers say is the q. of reason MILT. **c.** The q. of bores SCOTT. Hence **Quinte·ssence** *v. trans.* (now *rare*), to extract the q. of; to take *out of* (something) as a q. **Quintesse·ntial** *a.* of the nature of a q.; the purest or most refined of its kind. **Quintessentia·lity. Quintesse·ntially** *adv.*

Quintet(te (kwinte·t). 1811. [a. F. *quintette*, ad. It. *quintetto*, f. *quinto* fifth.] **1.** *Mus.* A composition for five voices or instruments. **2. a.** *Mus.* A set of five singers or players. **b.** A set of five persons or things. 1882.

Quinti-, prop. a comb. form of L. *quintus* fifth, but sometimes incorrectly used in place of QUINQUE-.

Quintic (kwi·ntik), *a.* and *sb.* 1853. [f. L. *quintus* + -IC.] **A.** *adj.* Of the fifth order or degree. **B.** *sb.* A quantic or surface of the fifth degree 1856.

Quintile (kwi·ntil), *a.* and *sb.* 1610. [f. L. *quintus* fifth + -ILE.] *Q.* (*aspect*): a planetary aspect in which the planets are one-fifth of a circle, or 72 degrees, distant from each other.

Quintillion (kwinti·lyən). 1674. [f. L. *quintus* fifth + (*m*)*illion*; see BILLION.] **a.** In Great Britain: The fifth power of a million (1 followed by thirty ciphers). **b.** In U.S. (as in France): The cube of a million (1 followed by 18 ciphers).

Quintole (kwi·ntoul). 1884. [Obscurely f. It. *quinto* or L. *quintus* fifth.] *Mus.* A group of five notes to be played in the time of four.

Quintuple (kwi·ntiup'l), *a.* and *sb.* 1570. [a. F., f. L. *quintus*, after *quadruple*.] **A.** *adj.* Fivefold; multiplied by five; consisting of five things or parts. **B.** *sb.* A fivefold amount; a group of five (*rare*) 1684.

A. *Q. time, Mus.* having five crotchets in a bar.

Quintuple (kwi·ntiup'l), *v.* 1639. [f. prec.] **1.** *trans.* To multiply by five; to make five times as much or as great. **b.** To produce five times as much as 1824. **2.** *intr.* To become five times as many or as great 1816.

Quintuplet (kwi·ntiuplet). 1873. [f. QUINTUPLE *a.*] **1.** A set of five things; *Mus.* = QUINTOLE. **2.** *pl.* Five children born at a birth 1889.

Quinzaine (kwi·nzeⁱn, F. kæ̃nzęn). *rare.* 1863. [a. F., f. *quinze*; see next.] *Hist.* = QUINDENE.

Quinze (kwinz, F. kæ̃nz). 1716. [a. F.:—L. *quindecim*.] A card-game depending on chance, in which the winner is that player who obtains fifteen points, or comes nearest to that number without exceeding it.

Quinzième (F. kæ̃nzyęm). *Obs.* exc. *Hist.* late ME. [a. AF. *quinzisme, -zieme*, ordinal f. *quinze* fifteen.] A tax or duty of a fifteenth.

Quip (kwip), *sb.* 1532. [Short f. *quippy* (1519–1569), perh. a. L. *quippe* indeed, forsooth.] **1.** A sharp or sarcastic remark directed against a person; a clever gird or hit. Later, A clever, smart, or witty saying; a verbal conceit. **b.** A verbal equivocation; a quibble 1590. **2. a.** A curious, odd, or fantastic action or feature 1820. **b.** A knick-knack 1820.

1. Quips and Cranks, and wanton Wiles MILT. **b.** Tricks of controversy and quips of law JOWETT.

Quip (kwip), *v.* Now *rare.* 1579. [f. prec.] **1.** *trans.* To assail with a quip or quips 1584. **2.** *intr.* To use a quip or quips; to be wittily sarcastic. Const. *at.*

‖ **Quipu** (kī·pu, kwi·pu). 1604. [Quichuan.] A device of the ancient Peruvians for recording events, keeping accounts, sending messages, etc., consisting of cords or threads of various colours, knotted in various ways.

When they go to confession these quipoes serve them to remember their sins 1704.

Quire (kwəiᵊɹ), *sb.*[1] ME. [a. OF. *quaer, quaier* (mod. *cahier*) a quire of six sheets, etc.:—pop. L. **quaternum*, f. L. *quaterni* a set of four, f. *quattuor*.] **1.** A set of four sheets of paper or parchment doubled so as to form eight leaves; hence, any collection or gathering of leaves, one within the other, in a manuscript or printed book. Also twenty-four (sometimes twenty-five) sheets of writing-paper. 1450. **b.** *In quires*: unbound, in sheets 1480. †**2.** A small pamphlet or book, consisting of a single quire; a short poem, treatise, etc., which is or might be contained in a quire –1570.

Quire, *sb.*[2], *v.*[2]: see CHOIR *sb.* and *v.*

Quire (kwəiᵊɹ), *v.*[1] 1683. [f. QUIRE *sb.*[1]] *trans.* To arrange in quires.

Quirinal (kwi·rinăl). 1838. [ad. L. *Quirinalis* (sc. *collis* hill), one of the seven hills of Rome, f. *Quirinus* a name of Romulus.] The name of the palace in Rome occupied by the king of Italy; hence, the Italian court or government, or its policy (esp. as contrasted with *Vatican*).

Quiritary (kwi·ritări), *a.* 1865. [ad. late L. *quiritarius*, f. *Quirites* Roman citizens.] That is in accordance with Roman civil law; legal, as opp. to equitable (see BONITARIAN). Also of property: Held by legal right or under Roman law. So **Quirita·rian** *a.*

Quirk (kwɔ̄ɹk). 1547. [Origin obsc.] **1.** A verbal trick, subtlety, shift, or evasion; a quibble 1565. **b.** Quibbling 1674. **2.** A clever turn or conceit; a quip 1599. **3.** *Mus.* A sudden turn; a fantastic phrase (*rare*) 1579. **4.** A trick in action or behaviour; †a knack, a fad 1601. **5.** A start, sudden stroke SHAKS. **6.** A sudden twist, turn, or curve; *esp.* in drawing or writing: A flourish 1605. **7.** *techn.* or *dial.* **a.** In a stocking = CLOCK *sb.*[2] 1547. **b.** A piece added to, or taken from, a regular figure, or cut out of a certain surface 1679. **c.** *Arch.* An acute hollow between the convex part of certain mouldings and the soffit or fillet 1816.

1. Not with Syllogisms or Quirks of Wit; but with plain and weighty Reason 1678. **b.** Shiftiness, q., attorney-cunning..fancies itself..to be talent CARLYLE. **2.** I may chance haue some odde quirkes and remnants of witte broken on mee SHAKS. **4.** His manner was full of quirks HAWTHORNE. **5.** I haue felt so many quirkes of ioy and greefe SHAKS. Hence **Quirk** *v. trans.* to assail with quirks; *intr.* to use quirks. **Quirked** (kwɔ̄ɹkt) *ppl. a.* (*Arch.*) furnished with a q. **Qui·rkish** *a.* of the nature of a q.

Quirky (kwɔ̄·ɹki), *a.* *Sc.* 1806. [f. prec. + -Y.[1]] **1.** Full of quirks; tricky. **2.** Full of twists, turns, or flourishes 1885.

1. A quirkie bodie, capable o' making law no law at a' GALT. Hence **Qui·rkiness.**

Quirt (kwɔ̄ɹt), *sb.* *U.S.* 1851. [perh. ad. Sp. *corto* short, CURT, or *cuerda* CORD.] A riding-whip, having a short handle and a braided leather lash about two feet long. Hence **Quirt** *v. trans.*, to strike with a q.

Quit (kwit), *sb.* 1847. [Origin unkn.] Pop. name of many small Jamaican birds.

Quit (kwit). *predic. a.* [(1) ME. *quite* (surviving until 17th c.), a. OF. *quite*, ad. L. *quietus* quiet; (2) ME. *quitte*, a. OF. *quitte*, later f. *quite* (cf. med.L. *quittus*), prob. infl. by pa. pple. of next.] **1.** Free, clear. **b.** Free, clear, rid *of* (a thing or person) ME. **c.** Const. *from.* Now *rare.* 1471. †**2.** Destitute, deprived *of* (*from*) –1596. †**3.** = QUITS 2. –1757.

1. The judgment shall be against him only..and the other shall go q. 1817. *To be q. for*, to get off with, suffer nothing more than. **b.** To be q. of the trouble and expense 1840. **3.** To be full q. of those my Banishers Stand I before thee heere SHAKS. *Double or q.*: see DOUBLE *adv.*

Quit (kwit), *v.* Pa. t. and pple. **quitted;** quit (now *dial.* and *U.S. colloq.*) [(1) ME. *quiten*, a. OF. *quiter* = med.L. *quitare*, ad. med.L. *quietare*, f. *quietus* QUIET; (2) ME. *quitten*, a. later OF. *quitter* = med.L. *quittare*.] **I.** †**1.** *trans.* To set free, release, redeem (usu. a person; also *absol.*). Const. *from, out of*, and occas. with *out* adv. –1652. †**b.** To free, clear, rid of –1798. †**2.** To clear (a suspected or accused person) *from* a charge; to prove (one) innocent *of*. Chiefly *refl.* –1715. †**b.** To absolve, acquit (*of, from*) –1755. **3.** *refl.* To do one's part, behave, bear oneself (usu. in a specified way). Now *arch.* late ME. †**b.** To play (one's part) –1603. †**4.** To remit (a debt, etc.). *rare.* –1693. **5.** To give up, let go, renounce, etc.; to cease to have, use, enjoy, be engaged in or occupied with 1440. **b.** To give up, yield, hand over *to* another. Now *rare* or *Obs.* 1450. **c.** To let go (something held or grasped) 1633. **6.** To cease, stop (doing something). Now *U.S.* 1754. **b.** *absol.* 1641. **7.** To leave, go away or depart from (a place or person); to part or separate from (a thing) 1603. **b.** *absol.* To leave the premises which one occupies as a tenant 1768. **c.** *absol.* To go away. *dial.* and *U.S.* 1839. **8.** *trans.* To remove; to put, take, or send away (also with dat. of person); to dismiss. Now *rare.* 1575.

1. b. She..made me resolve to q. my hands of this office PEPYS. **3.** Q. your selues like men, and fight 1 *Sam.* iv. 9. **b.** *Meas. for M.* II. iv. 28. **4.** To q. the fine for one halfe of his goods, I am content

SHAKS. 5. There are very few men who know how to q. any great office 1851. 6. b. The good old maxim for speech-makers, 'Q. when you've done' 1868. 7. It is a serious matter to q. country and family and friends 1833. b. Giving reasonable notice to q. CRUISE. c. He rose at once, and said..he reckoned he would q. STEVENSON.

II. 1. To repay, reward, requite (a person *with* some return *for* something done). *Obs.* exc. *n. dial.* ME. †2. To make a return to (a person) for (something done, a benefit or injury received, etc.) -1548. b. To repay (something done to or for one) ME. †c. To be a return for, to balance; esp. in phr. *to q. the cost* -1787.

1. We han well deserued hyt, Therfore is ryght that we ben quyt CHAUCER. b. On this manner was the Duke of Orleance death quitted 1632.

III. To pay, clear off (a debt, etc.) ME.

A thousand markes..To q. the penalty, and to ransome him SHAKS.

‖**Qui tam** (kwəi· tæm). 1755. [L.; *qui tam* (*pro domino rege quam pro se ipso sequitur*) who as well (for the lord the king as for himself sues).] *Law.* An action brought on a penal statute by an informer, who sues for the penalty both on his own behalf and on that of the crown.

Quitch (kwitʃ). [OE. *cwice*; said to be related to *cwic* QUICK *a.*, in ref. to its vitality.] A species of grass = COUCH *sb.*[2] Also **q.-grass.**

Quitclaim (kwi·tklēⁱm), *sb.* 1450. [a. AF. *quiteclame*, sb. f. *quiteclamer*; see next.] †a. A formal discharge or release. b. A formal renunciation of a claim.

Quitclaim (kwi·tklēⁱm), *v.* ME. [a. AF. and OF. *quiteclamer, -claimer*, f. *quite* QUIT, + *clamer* to proclaim; assoc. later with QUIT *v.* and CLAIM *sb.*] †1. *trans.* To declare (a person) free; to release, acquit, discharge, etc. -1609. 2. To renounce, resign, give up (a possession, right, claim, etc.). late ME. b. With *quit* taken as vb. Const. *to.* 1706.

2. b. Having..remitted and quitted claim to the king for all..debts 1886.

Quite (kwəit), *adv.* ME. [f. *quite* QUIT *a.*] 1. Completely, wholly, altogether, entirely; to the fullest extent or degree. 2. Actually, really, truly, positively (implying that the case or circumstances are such as to justify the use of the word or phrase thus qualified) 1586. b. colloq. *Quite so* (or simply *quite*), used like F. *parfaitement*, to express assent. (Cf. *exactly*.) 1896.

1. It speaks a q. other language 1661. My distemper is almost q. gone 1785. Q. by myself 1816. For q. another reason 1845. I spent that day q. alone upon the Mer de Glace TYNDALL. 2. She was q. ill and restless 1805. That must have been q. a scene 1806. Up to q. a recent period MILL. I q. too awfully near put my foot in it! 1882. It was q. the thing to be in love 1888. You can't q. believe there is a God at all G. MACDONALD. Q. at hand LANDOR. b. 'Of course, he's an absolute scoundrel'. 'Oh, quite.' (*mod.*)

Quit-rent (kwi·trent). 1454. [f. QUIT *a.* + RENT.] 1. A rent, usu. of small amount, paid by a freeholder or copyholder in lieu of services which might be required of him 1460. †2. A charge upon an estate for some special purpose -1712.

1. *attrib.* The courtly laureate pays His quitrent ode, his peppercorn of praise COWPER.

Quits (kwits), *a.* and *sb.* 1478. [Cf. QUIT *a.*, but the *-s* is obsc.] A. *adj.* †1. Clear, discharged (of a liability) -1590. 2. Even or equal (*with* another) by means of repayment or retaliation 1663. B. *sb.* a. An equivalent, a recompense. b. Reprisal, retaliation. *rare.* 1806.

A. 2. I will be quits with him 1675. I shall be content to be q. with fortune for a very moderate portion W. IRVING. Phr. *To cry q.* (cf. QUITTANCE 4). *Double or q.*: see DOUBLE *adv.*

†**Qui·ttal, qui·tal.** 1530. [f. QUIT *v.* + -AL.] a. Requital. b. Acquittal. -1633.

Quittance (kwi·tăns), *sb.* ME. [a. OF. *quitance* (later *quittance*), f. *quiter* to QUIT.] 1. The act of freeing or clearing; release; †acquittal. 2. A release or discharge from a debt or obligation; a document certifying such discharge; a receipt ME. 3. Recompense or requital; repayment; reprisal 1590. †4. *To cry q.*, to declare oneself clear or even *with* another; hence, to make full repayment or retaliation -1679.

2. Hauing paid the custome, it behoueth to haue a q. HAKLUYT. *Prov.* That's all one: omittance is no q. SHAKS. Hence †**Qui·ttance** *v. trans.* to repay, requite (a person, service, injury, etc.) -1624.

Quitter, quittor (kwi·tər), *sb.*[1] ME. [perh. a. OF. *quiture, cuiture* cooking, etc.] †1. Pus; a purulent discharge from a wound or sore -1689. 2. *Farriery.* (Also †*q.-bone.*) An ulcer on the coronet of a horse's hoof 1703.

Quitter (kwi·tər), *sb.*[2] *U.S.* 1881. [f. QUIT *v.* + -ER[1].] One who, or that which, 'quits', goes away, shirks, etc.

Quiver (kwi·vər), *sb.*[1] ME. [a. AF. *quiveir*, OF. *quivre, coivre*, app. a. the Teut. word repr. by COCKER *sb.*[1]] 1. A case for holding arrows (sometimes also the bow). b. *transf.* and *fig.* late ME. †c. A quiverful -1623.

1. His arrowes..he wore in a Woolues skinne at his backe for his Q. 1624. b. Like as the arowes in the honde of the giaunte, euen so are the yonge children. Happie is the man, yᵗ hath his quyuer full of them. COVERDALE *Ps.* cxxvi[i]. 5.

Quiver (kwi·vər), *a.* *Obs.* exc. *dial.* [OE. **cwifer* (in *cwiferlice*), prob. onomatopœic.] Active, nimble; quick, rapid.

A little quiuer fellow SHAKS.

Quiver (kwi·vər), *v.* 1490. [prob. onomatopœic; cf. prec. and QUAVER.] 1. *intr.* To shake, tremble, or vibrate, with a slight but rapid agitation. 2. *trans.* To cause to vibrate or tremble 1599.

1. Upon the stream the moonbeams q. WORDSW. His hand trembled and his flesh quivered 1869. Hence **Qui·ver** *sb.*[2] an act of quivering, a tremble; *ellipt.* a trembling of the voice. **Qui·veringly** *adv.*

Quivered (kwi·vərd), *a.* and *ppl. a.* 1634. [f. QUIVER *sb.*[1] + -ED[2].] 1. Provided with a quiver. 2. Placed or kept in, or as in, a quiver 1651.

1. Like a quiver'd Nymph with Arrows keen MILT. 2. The lifted bow he bore, And quiver'd deaths POPE.

Quiverful (kwi·vəɹful). 1861. [f. QUIVER *sb.*[1] + -FUL.] As much as a quiver can hold. Usu. *fig.* with ref. to Ps. cxxvii. 5 (see QUIVER *sb.*[1] 1 b).

‖**Qui vive** (kī vīv). 1726. [F., lit. '(long) live who?', a sentinel's challenge, intended to discover to which side the party challenged belongs.] *On the q.*, on the alert or look-out.

Quixote (kwi·ksǫt). 1648. [Name of the hero of Cervantes' romance = Sp. *quixote*, now *quijote* a cuisse.] An enthusiastic visionary like Don Quixote, inspired by lofty and chivalrous but unrealizable ideals. b. *attrib.* = next 1708.

Quixotic (kwiksǫ·tik), *a.* 1791. [f. prec.] 1. Of persons: Resembling Don Quixote; hence, striving with lofty enthusiasm for visionary ideals. 2. Of actions, etc.: Characteristic of, appropriate to, Don Quixote 1851.

2. A q. mission to the Indians of Georgia 1874. Hence **Quixo·tical** *a.* **-ly** *adv.*

Quixotism (kwi·ksǫtiz'm). 1688. [f. as prec. + -ISM.] Quixotic principles, character, or practice; a quixotic action or idea. So **Qui·xotry.**

Quiz (kwiz), *sb.*[1] 1782. [Origin obsc.] 1. An odd or eccentric person, in character or appearance. Now *rare*. b. An odd-looking thing JANE AUSTEN. 2. One who quizzes 1797. 3. A practical joke; a hoax, a piece of banter or ridicule; a jest or witticism 1807. b. The act or practice of quizzing 1819.

1. He's a droll q., and I rather like him MAD. D'ARBLAY. 2. A true Q. is imperturbable 1836.

Quiz (kwiz), *sb.*[2] *U.S.* 1891. [f. QUIZ *v.*[2]] An act of quizzing or questioning; *spec.* an oral examination of a student or class by a teacher.

Quiz (kwiz), *v.*[1] 1796. [Cf. QUIZ *sb.*[1]] *trans.* To make fun of (a person or thing); *occas.*, to regard with an air of mockery. Hence **Qui·zzer,** one who or that which quizzes. **Qui·zzery,** the practice of quizzing; an instance of this.

Quiz (kwiz), *v.*[2] *dial.* and *U.S.* 1886. [prob. transf. use of prec.] *trans.* a. To question, interrogate (a person); *U.S.* to examine (a student or class) orally. Also *absol.* b. To find *out* (a thing) by questioning.

Quizzical (kwi·zikăl), *a.* 1789. [f. QUIZ *sb.*[1] and *v.*[1]] 1. Of the nature of a quiz or oddity; comical. 2. Given to quizzing; pertaining to, or characterized by, quizzing 1801. Hence **Qui·zzically** *adv.*

Qui·zzing-glass. *Hist.* 1802. A monocle.

Quo', abbrev. of QUOTH.

‖**Quoad** (kwōᵘ·æd). 1601. [L., 'so far as', 'as much as', 'as to', f. *quo* where, whither + *ad* to.] To the extent of, as regards, with respect to 1742. b. **Quoad hoc,** to this extent, as far as this, with respect to this 1601.

Quod (kwǫd), *sb. slang.* Also **quad.** 1700. [Origin unkn.] Prison. Hence **Quod** *v. trans.* to put in prison.

‖**Quodlibet** (kwǫ·dlibet). late ME. [a. L. *quodlibet*, f. *quod* what + *libet* it pleases.] 1. Any question in philosophy or theology proposed as an exercise in disputation; hence, a scholastic debate, thesis, or exercise on a question of this kind (chiefly *pl.* in Univ. use). Now *Hist.* 2. *Mus.* A fantasia, medley 1845. Hence **Quodlibeta·rian,** †one who does as he pleases; one who discusses quodlibets. **Quodlibe·tic, -al** *a.* of the nature of, connected or concerned with, a q. or quodlibets; **-ly** *adv.*

Quoin (koin), *sb.* 1532. [var. spelling of COIN.] 1. *Building.* a. An external angle of a wall or building; also, one of the stones or bricks serving to form the angle; a corner-stone. b. An internal angle or corner, as of a room 1825. 2. A wedge, or wedge-shaped block, used variously, as: a. *Printing.* to lock up a form 1570; b. *Gunnery.* to raise or lower, or fix the breech of, a gun 1627; c. *Naut.* to prevent casks from rolling 1711; d. *Building.* The key-stone, or any one of the voussoirs of an arch (*rare*). 1730. 3. An angle, or angular object (*rare*). 1838.

1. b. *Hollow q.*, a recess in the walls at each end of a canal lock, to receive the heel-post of the gate.

Comb. **q.-post,** the heel-post of a lock-gate. Hence **Quoi·ning,** the stone or brick-work forming the q. of a wall, or the manner in which this is placed.

Quoin (koin), *v.* 1683. [See prec. and COIN *v.*[2]] 1. *trans.* To secure or raise with a quoin or wedge. Also with *up*. 2. To provide with quoins or corners 1834.

Quoit (koit, kwoit), *sb.* late ME. [prob. of French origin.] 1. Orig. (now only with ref. to the Greek and Roman discus), a flat disc of stone or metal, thrown as an exercise of strength or skill; *spec.* in mod. use, a heavy flattish ring of iron, with an edge capable of cutting into the ground when it falls. Also, the ring of rope used in *deck-quoits* (see 2). 1440. 2. *pl.* (rarely *sing.*) The sport of throwing the quoit or of playing with quoits; in the mod. form of this the quoit is aimed at a pin stuck in the ground, and is intended to encircle the pin, or to cut into the ground as near to it as possible. *Deck-quoits*, an imitation of this game, played on shipboard with rings of rope. late ME. 3. *transf.* The flat covering stone of a cromlech or cist; also, by extension, a cromlech or cist as a whole 1753.

Quoit (koit, kwoit), *v.* 1440. [f. prec.] 1. *intr.* To play at quoits (*rare*). 2. *trans.* To throw like a quoit 1597.

1. To Q., to Run, and Steeds and Chariots drive DRYDEN.

‖**Quomodo** (kwōᵘ·mǫdo), **quo modo** (kwōᵘ mōᵘ·do). 1671. [L., 'in what way?'] *The q.*, the manner, way, means.

Quondam (kwǫ·ndæm), *adv., sb.*, and *a.* 1535. [L., 'formerly'.] A. *adv.* At one time, formerly, heretofore (*rare*). 1537. †B. *sb.* The former holder of some office or position -1583. C. *adj.* That formerly was or existed 1586.

B. Let him be..Jacke out of office, make him a Q. 1583. C. My q. friends RUSKIN.

Quop (kwǫp), *v.* *Obs.* exc. *dial.* 1658. [var. of QUAP *v.*] To beat, throb, palpitate.

Quorum (kwōᵊ·rǒm). 1455. [L., lit. 'of whom', from the wording of commissions in which persons were designated as members of a body by the words *quorum vos... unum* (*duos*, etc.) *esse volumus* of whom we will that you... be one (two, etc.).] 1. Orig., certain justices of the peace, usu. of special qualifications, whose presence was necessary to constitute a bench; later applied loosely to all justices. b. *transf.* Applied to similarly distinguished members of other bodies; hence, a select company 1602. 2. A fixed number of members of any body, society, etc., whose presence is necessary for the valid transaction of business 1616.

1. Old Sir John Wellborn, Justice of Peace and Q. MASSINGER. b. A Q. of Surgeons..should be ordered to..examine them 1747. 2. It was order'd that 5 should be a q. for a Council EVELYN.

Quota (kwōᵘ·tă), *sb.* 1668. [med.L. *quota*

(sc. *pars* 'how great a part'), fem. of *quotus*, f. *quot* how many.] **1.** The part or share which is, or ought to be, contributed by one to a total sum or amount. **2.** The part or share of a total which belongs, is given, or is due, to one 1700.

Comb. **q.-bill**, a Parliamentary bill passed in March 1795, under which each county and (by a supplementary bill passed in April) each port had to supply its q. of men to the navy. Hence **Quo·ta** *v.* to impose in quotas.

Quotable (kwōu·tăb'l), *a.* 1821. [f. QUOTE *v.* + -ABLE.] Capable of being quoted; suitable for quoting.

Passages of a..q. nature 1821. Hence **Quotabi·lity. Quo·tably** *adv.*

Quotation (kwŏtē¹·ʃən). 1532. [ad. med.L. *quotationem*, f. *quotare*.] †**1.** A (marginal) reference to a passage in a book; see QUOTE *v.* 2. -1683. **b.** *Typog.* (ellipt. for *q.-quadrat*.) A large (usu. hollow) quadrat used for filling up blanks (orig. the blanks between marginal references) 1683. **2.** The action or practice of quoting 1646. **b.** A passage quoted 1690. **3.** The amount stated as the price of stocks or any commodity for sale 1812.

2. Classical q. is the *parole* of literary men all over the world JOHNSON.

Comb. **q.-marks**, signs used in writing or printing to mark the beginning and end of a q.; in Eng. the inverted comma and apostrophe are employed. Hence **Quota·tionist**, one who (habitually) quotes.

Quote (kwōut), *sb.* 1600. [f. next] †**1.** A (marginal) reference; a note -1611. **2.** A quotation 1885. **b.** A quotation mark 1888.

Quote (kwōut), *v.* late ME. [ad. med.L. *quotare* to mark the number of, f. *quot* how many, or *quota* QUOTA.] **I.** †**1.** *trans.* To mark (a book) with numbers (as of chapters, etc.), or with (marginal) references (*rare*) -1596. †**2.** To give the reference to (a passage in a book) -1651. **3.** †**a.** To cite (a book, author, etc.) for a particular statement or passage. **b.** To copy out or repeat a passage or passages from. 1589. **4.** To copy out or repeat (a passage, statement, etc.) from a book, document, speech, etc., with some indication that one is giving the words of another 1680. **b.** *absol.* To make quotations 1663.

3. He shall q. and recite one Author against another STEELE. **4.** He quotes verses without mercy 1771. **b.** He..quotes largely from state documents GREEN.

II. †**1.** To write down; to make a note of in writing -1635. †**b.** To take mental note of; to notice -1640. **2.** †**a.** To take, note, *as* or *for* something; to mention *for* having done something -1722. **b.** To cite *as* an instance of or *as* being something 1806. **3.** To state the price of (a commodity) 1866.

1. *fig.* A fellow by the hand of Nature mark'd, Quoted, and sign'd to do a deede of shame SHAKS. **b.** *Rom. & Jul.* I. iv. 31. **2. a.** He's quoted for a most perfidious slaue SHAKS. **b.** This has,..been quoted as an excuse 1858. **3.** No shingles are quoted 1866. Hence **Quo·ter.**

Quoth (kwōuþ), *v.* (*pa. t.*) Now *arch.* or *dial.* ME. [pa. t. of obs. *quethe* vb., to say.] Said. **1.** Used with sbs., or pronouns of the first and third persons, to indicate that the words of a speaker are being repeated. †**2.** Used interrog. with a pronoun of the second person, with the same force as QUOTHA -1681.

1. Q. Mrs. Gilpin, 'That's well said COWPER.

Quotha (kwōu·þă), *interj.* Now *arch.* 1519. [For *quoth he* (see A *pron.*).] The phr. 'said he', used with contemptuous or sarcastic force in repeating a word or phrase used by another; hence = indeed! forsooth!

Learning, q.! a mere composition of tricks and mischief GOLDSM. The 'fickle moon', q.! I wish my friends were half as constant 1835.

Quotidian (kwŏti·diăn), *a.* and *sb.* ME. [a. OF. *cotidien*, *-ian*, or ad. L. *cot-*, *quotidianus*, f. *quotidie* every day, daily.] **A.** *adj.* **1.** Of things, acts, etc.: Of or pertaining to every day; daily. late ME. **b.** *spec.* of an intermittent fever or ague, recurring every day ME. **2.** Of persons: Performing some act, or sustaining some character, daily (*rare*) 1456. **3.** Of an everyday character; ordinary, trivial 1461.

3. Common and q. thoughts are beneath the grace of a Verse 1665.

B. *sb.* **1.** A quotidian fever or ague. late ME. **2.** A daily allowance or portion (*rare*) 1828. Hence **Quoti·dianly** *adv.* daily.

Quotient (kwōu·ʃĕnt). late ME. [f. L. *quotiens* how many times (f. *quot* how many), erron. taken as a ppl. form in *-ens*, *-ent-*.] *Math.* The result obtained by dividing one quantity by another; the number of times one quantity is contained by another as ascertained by division.

Quotiety (kwotəi·ĕti). 1862. [f. L. *quot*, after words in *-iety*.] Condition in respect of number; relative frequency.

‖**Quotum** (kwōu·tŏm). 1660. [L., neut. sing. of *quotus*; see QUOTA.] A number or quantity considered in its proportional relationship to a larger number or quantity; a quota.

‖**Quo warranto** (kwōu wŏræ·nto). 1535. [med.L., 'by what warrant'.] A King's Bench writ formerly in use, by which a person or persons were called upon to show by what warrant he or they held, claimed, or exercised an office or franchise.

Qy., abbrev. of QUERY.

R

R (ā.ɹ), the eighteenth letter of the modern and seventeenth of the ancient Roman alphabet, is derived through early Greek Ρ, Ρ from the Phoenician ᑫ. In general the character denotes an open voiced consonant, in the formation of which the point of the tongue approaches the palate a little way behind the teeth; in many languages this is accompanied by a 'trill' or vibration of the tongue. This trill is almost absent in the *r* of modern standard English, which moreover retains its consonantal value only when it precedes a vowel; in other positions it has been vocalized to an ə-sound, here denoted by (ɹ), and even this is entirely lost after certain vowels. By southern speakers *r* is frequently introduced in hiatus, as in *the idea(r) of, Asia(r) and Africa.*

I. 1. *The 'r' months*: those months with an *r* in their name (Sept. to April), during which oysters are in season. **2.** Used to denote serial order, as 'R Battery', 'MS. R', etc., or as a symbol of some thing or person, a point in a diagram, etc.

II. *Abbreviations.* **1.** Of Latin words and phrases. **a.** R. = *rex* king, *regina* queen. In medical prescriptions: R, ℞ = *recipe* take. **b.** R.I.P. = *requiescat (-ant) in pace* may he or she (they) rest in peace. **2.** Of English words and phrases: **a.** R. = Rabbi, radius, Railway, Reaumur, right, River, Royal, rupee; also various proper names, as Richard, Robert, etc.; r (*Naut.* in log-book) = rain; *r* = radius vector. R.A. = Rear-Admiral, Royal Academy or Academician, (*Astron.*) right ascension; R.A.M.C. = Royal Army Medical Corps; R.A.S.C. = Royal Army Service Corps; R.C. = Roman Catholic; R.E. = Royal Engineers; R.H. = Royal Highness; R.M. = Resident Magistrate; R.M.A. = Royal Marine Artillery; R.N. = Royal Navy; R.N.A.S. = Royal Naval Air Service; R.N.R. = Royal Naval Reserve; R.S. = Royal Society; R.T.O. = Railway Transport Officer; R.V. = Revised Version (of the Bible); R.W. = Right Worthy or Worshipful. **b.** *The three R's*: Reading, (W)riting, (A)rithmetic. **3.** R.S.V.P., abbrev. of the French phrase *répondez, s'il vous plaît*, 'reply, if you please'; commonly placed in one of the corners of invitation-cards. R.D. = Refer to drawer.

Rab (ræb). 1825. [ad. F. *rabot* in same sense.] A wooden beater, formed like a crutch, used for mixing the ingredients of mortar.

Rabatine. [app. f. F. *rabat* REBATO + -INE.] A low collar SCOTT.

Rabbet (ræ·bĕt), *sb.* late ME. [a. OF. *rabat*, *rabbat*, f. *rabattre* to beat back or down; see REBATE *v.*[1]] **I. 1. a.** A channel, groove, or slot cut along the edge or face of a piece (or surface) of wood, stone, etc., and intended to receive the edge or end of another piece or pieces, or a tongue to fit the groove. **b.** A rectangular recess made along a projecting angle or arris. **2.** †**a.** A tongue to fit into a groove. **b.** One of the sides of a rabbet made in an arris; a shoulder, a ledge. 1678. **II.** An elastic beam fixed so as to give a rebound to a large fixed hammer; a spring-pole 1825.

Rabbet (ræ·bĕt), *v.* 1565. [app. f. prec., but found earlier in vbl. sb. *rabityng* (Wyclif).] **1.** *trans.* To join or fix by means of a rabbet or rabbets. Also with *in*. **2.** To form a rabbet in; to cut *away* or *down* as in making a rabbet 1572. **3.** *intr.* To join *on* or lap *over* by means of a rabbet 1850. Hence **Ra·bbeting** *vbl. sb.* the process of cutting rabbets, or of fitting rabbeted boards together; the groove or rabbeted portion of such boards. late ME.

Rabbi (ræ·bəi, ræ·bi). OE. [a. (orig. through L. *rabbi*, Gr. ῥαββί) Heb. *rabbī* 'my master', f. *rabh* master, with pronominal suffix.] **1.** A title of respect (in use since the first century B.C.) given by the Jews to doctors of the law. **2.** A Jewish doctor of the law. In mod. Jewish use applied only to one who is authorized by ordination to deal with questions of law and ritual, and to perform certain functions. 1484. †**b.** *transf.* One whose learning, authority, or office is comparable to that of a Jewish rabbi. (Freq. contempt.) -1855.

1. Raby Moyses says alle þis HAMPOLE. Ye shall not suffre youre selves to be called Rabi TINDALE *Matt.* xxiii. 8. **2.** The gowned Rabbies..were of opinion that hee was a friend of Beelzebub MILT. *The rabbis* = *the rabbins* (see next).

Rabbin (ræ·bin). 1531. [a. F. *rabbin* or med.L. *rabbinus*.] = RABBI 2 (but mainly used in *pl.* to designate the chief Jewish authorities on matters of law and doctrine, most of whom flourished between the 2nd and the 13th centuries of the Christian era) 1579. †**b.** = RABBI 2 b -1632. **c.** Used as *pl.* 1826. Hence **Ra·bbinate**, the office or dignity of a rabbi; the period during which some one is a rabbi; *collect.* rabbis as a class. Hence **Ra·bbinite** = RABBINIST.

Rabbinic (răbi·nik), *a.* and *sb.* 1612. [f. prec. + -IC.] **A.** *adj.* = next. **B.** *sb.* Rabbinical Hebrew 1832.

Rabbinical (răbi·nikăl), *a.* 1622. [f. as prec. + -AL.] **1.** Of things: Pertaining to, or characteristic of, the rabbins, their learning, writings, etc. **b.** *spec.* of the later form of the Hebrew language or character used by the rabbins 1727. **2.** Of persons: Belonging to the class of rabbis or rabbins; resembling a rabbi; occupied with or skilled in r. literature 1642.

1. A R. opinion concerning Manna 1779. **2.** The Masoreths and Rabbinicall Scholiasts MILT. Hence **Rabbi·nically** *adv.*

Rabbinism (ræ·biniz'm). 1652. [f. RABBIN + -ISM.] **1.** The teaching or doctrine of the rabbins. **2.** A rabbinical expression; a peculiarity of the language of the rabbins 1832.

Rabbinist (ræ·binist). 1599. [f. as prec. + -IST.] An adherent or follower of the rabbins; *esp.* among the Jews, one who accepts the teaching of the Talmud and the rabbins, in contrast to the Karaites, who reject tradition. Hence **Rabbini·stic, -al** *a.*

Rabbit (ræ·bit), *sb.* late ME. [app. of Northern French origin; cf. Walloon *robett*, Flem. *robbe*. Ult. etym. unkn.] **1.** A common burrowing rodent of the hare family (*Leporidæ*), esp. the common European species, *Lepus Cuniculus*, which is naturally brownish-grey, but in domestication also white, black, or pied. †Orig. applied only to the young animal, the full-grown one being called a CONY. **2.** *transf.* Applied contempt. to a person, *spec.* to one who plays games (esp. cricket or tennis) badly 1597.

1. Rabbets will breed seven times a year PENNANT. **2.** Away, you horson, upright Rabbet, away SHAKS.

attrib. and *Comb.* as *r.-burrow*, *-hole*, *-hutch*, *-warren*, etc.; *r.-breeder*, *-fancier*, *-trapper*, etc.; **r.-fish**, a name for fishes having points of resemblance to a rabbit, as (*a*) the British fishes *Chimæra monstrosa* and the striped rock-gurnard, (*b*) an American fish of the genus *Lagocephalus* with teeth resembling a rabbit's incisors; **-foot** (clover) = HARE'S-FOOT 1. Hence **Ra·bbitry**, a place in which rabbits are kept; a collection of rabbits. **Ra·bbity** *a.* abounding in rabbits; resembling a r.

Rabbit (ræ·bit), *v.*[1] 1852. [f. prec.] **1.** *intr.* To hunt for or catch rabbits. Chiefly in *pres. pple.* **2.** To crowd *together* like rabbits 1892. Hence **Ra·bbitter**, a man or a dog that hunts rabbits.

Rabbit (ræ·bit), *v.*[2] *vulgar.* 1742. [prob. an alteration of *rat*, in *od rat*, *drat*.] A meaningless word used as an imprecation. Also *drabbit*, *od(d) rabbit*.

Rabble (ræ·b'l), *sb.*[1] (and *a.*). late ME. [perh. conn. w. RABBLE *v.*[1]] **A.** †**1.** A pack, string, swarm (of animals) -1634. **2.** A disorderly crowd of people, a mob. late ME. **b.** Applied contempt. to a class or body of persons imagined as a mob 1529. **c.** Without article: Persons of the lowest class 1687. **3.** A disorderly collection, a confused medley (of things) 1514. †**4.** A long string *of* words, etc., having little meaning or value -1656. **b.** A rigmarole. Now *dial.* 1592.

2. At last the r. broke up and so I away PEPYS. Rather a confused r. than a regular army BERKELEY. Phr. *The r.*, the common, low, or disorderly part of the populace; the mob. **c.** You live in Dublin among a parcel of r. 1734. **3.** A r. of books of all ages, sizes [etc.] 1803. A seditious r. of doubts 1847.

B. *attrib.* or *adj.* **1.** Of persons: Forming a rabble; of or belonging to the rabble 1549. **2.** Of things, actions, etc.: Characteristic of, appropriate to, the rabble 1603.

2. To burn the jails..was a good r. trick JOHNSON.

Rabble (ræ·b'l), *sb.*² 1664. [a. F. *râble* :—med.L. *rotabulum*, L. *rutabulum* fire-shovel, f. *ruere* to rake up.] †**1.** A kind of shovel used by charcoal-burners for taking off the covering from the burned pile EVELYN. **2.** An iron bar sharply bent at the end, used for stirring and skimming molten metal in puddling; also, a steam-pipe used for the same purpose 1861.

Rabble (ræ·b'l), *v.*¹ *Obs.* exc. *dial.* late ME. [= Du. *rabbelen* to speak indistinctly.] **1. a.** *trans.* To utter (words or speech) in a rapid confused manner. Also with *forth, off, out, over*. **b.** *intr.* To speak or read in this fashion; to gabble. **2.** To work in a hurried slovenly manner (*dial.*). **b.** *trans.* To rattle *up*. 1862.

Rabble (ræ·b'l), *v.*² 1644. [f. RABBLE *sb.*¹ 2.] **1.** *trans.* To attack or assail (a person or his property) as, along with, or by means of, a rabble; to mob. **2.** *intr.* To become a rabble 1813.

1. Some..were..active in rabbling the Clergy 1690.

Rabble (ræ·b'l), *v.*³ 1860. [f. RABBLE *sb.*²] To stir, skim, or rake with a rabble. Hence **Ra·bbler**, one who uses a rabble; an instrument for rabbling.

Rabblement (ræ·b'lměnt). 1545. [f. RABBLE *sb.*¹ + -MENT.] **a.** = RABBLE *sb.*¹ in various senses. **b.** Tumult or disturbance like that of a rabble; riotous conduct (*rare*) 1590.

a. As hee refus'd it, the r. howted SHAKS. A r. at the heels of Rosinante LAMB. **b.** The raskall many.. Heaped together in rude rablement SPENSER.

Rabble rout (ræ·b'lraut). 1599. [f. RABBLE *sb.*¹ + ROUT *sb.*] = RABBLE 2, 2 b.

Rabelaisian (ræbělē·ziăn), *a.* (and *sb.*) 1817. [f. name of François *Rabelais* (*c* 1490-1553) + -IAN.] **A.** *adj.* Pertaining to, characteristic of, or resembling Rabelais or his writings, which are distinguished by exuberance of imagination and language, combined with extravagance and coarseness of humour and satire. **B.** *sb.* A student or admirer of Rabelais 1893. Hence **Rabelai·sianism**, the characteristic style or attitude of Rabelais.

Rabid (ræ·bid), *a.* 1611. [ad. L. *rabidus*, f. *rabere* to be mad.] **1.** Furious, raging; madly violent in nature or behaviour. Also *transf.* of things or parts of the body. **2.** *spec.* Of beasts (rarely of human beings): Affected with rabies; mad 1804. **b.** Pertaining to, of the nature of, rabies 1806.

1. All the rabide flight Of winds that ruine ships CHAPMAN. R. Hunger DRYDEN. A r. pedant LAMB. **2.** Bites of r. animals 1880. **b.** An accompaniment of the r. virus 1887. Hence **Rabi·dity. Ra·bid-ly** *adv.*, **-ness.**

Rabies (rē·bi,īz). 1661. [a. L., f. *rabere* to rage, rave.] Canine madness; hydrophobia.

Ra·binet. *Obs.* exc. *Hist.* 1587. [app. later f. ROBINET.] A small variety of cannon.

†**Raccommo·de**, *v.* 1673. [ad. F. *raccommoder*, f. *re-* + *accommoder* to ACCOMMODATE.] *trans.* To restore to good relations (*with* a person); to set right -1756.

Raccoon, var. of **Racoon.**

Race (rēs), *sb.*¹ ME. [a. ON. *rás* = OE. *rǽs* running, race, rush (of water), etc.] **I. 1.** The act of running; a run. Now *Sc.* **b.** *fig.* The course of life or some portion of it 1513. †**2.** The act of riding rapidly on horseback; a course in a tournament -1600. †**b.** A journey or voyage -1557.

1. b. My r. of glory run, and r. of shame MILT.

II. †**1.** Onward movement, e.g. of the heavenly bodies, a vehicle, etc.; running or rush of water -1670. **b.** *esp.* The daily (or annual) course of the sun through the heavens. Similarly of the moon. 1590. **c.** The course of time 1595. †**d.** The course of events, or of a narrative -1626. **2.** A strong current in the sea or in a river. late ME.

1. b. The Sun..ere half his r. be run 1662. **c.** Fly envious Time, till thou run out thy r. MILT. **2.** A short cockling Sea, as if it had been a R. or place where two Tides meet DAMPIER. The R. (or Ras) of Alderney 1862.

III. As a portion of time or space. **1.** A piece of ground suitable for running or racing (*rare*) 1612. †**2.** The course, line, or path taken by a person or a moving body -1585. **b.** The channel or bed (of a stream); *esp.* an artificial channel, as in a mill or mining claim. Now chiefly *U.S.* See also HEAD-, MILL-, TAIL-RACE. 1565. **c.** *Weaving.* The channel along which the shuttle moves in crossing the web 1855. **d.** *Mech.* The space in which a drum or wheel revolves 1883. **3. a.** *Mining.* 'A small thread of spar or ore' (Raymond) 1580. **b.** A row or series. *dial.* and *techn.* 1877.

1. Nor yet the level South can shew a smoother r. DRAYTON.

IV. The act of running, riding, sailing, etc. in competition with one or more rivals; a contest of speed; in *pl.* usu. denoting a series of horse-races held at a fixed time on a regular course 1513.

To indite Warrs..or to describe Races and Games MILT. We're going on to the races DICKENS.

attrib. and *Comb.* as *r.-meeting, -week*, etc.; **r.-ball**, a ball held in connexion with a race-meeting; **-card**, a printed card giving information about races; **-day**, the day on which a race or set of races is held; **-glass**, a field-glass for use at races; **-way**, *U.S.* a passage or channel for water; the bed of a canal, etc.

Race (rēs), *sb.*² 1500. [a. F. *race*, a. It. *razza* = Sp. *raza*, of obsc. origin.] **I.** A group of persons, animals, or plants, connected by common descent or origin. **1.** The offspring or posterity *of* a person; a set of children or descendants. Chiefly *poet.* Also *transf.* and *fig.* 1570. †**b.** Breeding, the production of offspring -1667. †**c.** A generation (*rare*) -1741. **2.** A limited group of persons descended from a common ancestor; a house, family, kindred 1581. **b.** A tribe, nation, or people, regarded as of common stock 1600. **c.** A group of several tribes or peoples, forming a distinct ethnical stock 1842. **d.** One of the great divisions of mankind, having certain physical peculiarities in common 1774. **3.** A breed or stock of animals; a particular variety of a species 1580. †**b.** A stud or herd (of horses) -1667. **c.** A genus, species, kind of animals 1605. **4.** A genus, species, or variety of plants 1596. **5.** One of the great divisions of living creatures: **a.** Mankind. In early use always *the human race, the race of men* or *mankind*, etc. 1580. **b.** A class or kind of beings other than men or animals 1667. **c.** One of the chief classes of animals (as beasts, birds, fishes, etc.) 1726. **6.** Without article: **a.** Denoting the stock, family, class, etc. to which a person, animal, or plant belongs, chiefly in phr. *of* (*noble*, etc.) *r.* 1559. **b.** The fact or condition of belonging to a particular people or ethnical stock; the qualities, etc. resulting from this 1849. †**7.** Natural or inherited disposition SHAKS.

1. I will take some savage woman, she shall rear my dusky r. TENNYSON. **b.** Male he created thee, but thy consort Femal for R. MILT. **2.** The Bourbon is by no means a cruel r. STERNE. **b.** That Pigmean Race Beyond the Indian Mount MILT. **d.** The second great variety in the human species seems to be that of the Tartar r. GOLDSM. **3.** The plains.. bred a generous r. of horses GIBBON. **b.** *Merch. V.* v. i. 72. **c.** I wish the r. of cows were perished SHELLEY. **5.** That every tribe..Might feel themselves allied to all the r. COWPER. **b.** A R. of Demi-Gods DRYDEN. **6.** Two Coursers of ethereal r. GRAY. **b.** R. in the negro is of appalling importance EMERSON. **7.** I giue my sensuall r., the reine SHAKS.

II. A group or class of persons, animals, or things, having some common feature or features. **1.** A set or class of persons 1500. **b.** One of the sexes (*poet.*) 1590. **2.** A set, class, or kind of animals, plants, or things. Chiefly *poet.* 1590. †**b.** One of the three 'kingdoms' of nature (*rare*) -1707. **3.** A particular class of wine, or the characteristic flavour of this, due to the soil 1520. **b.** *fig.* Of speech, writing, etc.: A peculiar and characteristic style or manner, *esp.* liveliness, piquancy 1680.

1. The r. of learned men, Still at their books THOMSON. **2.** I hope [her disease] is not of the cephalick r. JOHNSON. **3.** A pipe Of rich Canary..Is it of the right r.? MASSINGER. **b.** His conversation had a r. and flavour peculiarly its own 1875.

Comb.: **r. suicide**, term for voluntary restriction of child-birth 1901.

Race (rēs), *sb.*³ 1450. [ad. OF. *rais, raiz* :—L. *radicem*; see RADISH, RADIX.] A root (of ginger).

Race (rēs), *v.*¹ 1672. [f. RACE *sb.*¹] **1.** *intr.* To run a race (*with*), to compete (*with*) in speed. **b.** To practise or engage in horse-racing 1827. **2.** To run, ride, sail, etc. swiftly 1757. **b.** Of inanimate things 1808. **c.** Of a steam engine, screw propeller, wheel, etc.: To run or revolve with uncontrolled speed, when resistance is diminished while the driving power continues the same 1862. **3.** *trans.* To race with 1809. **4.** To cause to move swiftly; to cause to run a race or races 1860. **5.** To suspend (a wheel, grindstone, etc.) in the proper position for running 1870.

1. I who..would r. With my own steed from Araby KEATS. **b.** I have been racing now getting on fifty years 1881. **2.** Run, Pheidippides, run and r., reach Sparta for aid! BROWNING. **b.** Like streamlet..racing forth SCOTT. **3.** Fought cocks, and raced their neighbours' horses W. IRVING.

Race (rēs), *v.*² 1440. [var. of RASE *v.*¹, now only techn. in sense 1.] **1.** *trans.* To scratch or tear with something sharp; to cut or slash. †**2.** To scrape *out*, erase. (Now written RASE or RAZE.) -1705. †**3.** To level with the ground; to RAZE -1679.

2. *fig.* To massacre them all, And r. their faction, and their familie SHAKS.

Ra·ce-course. 1764. [f. RACE *sb.*¹ + COURSE.] **1.** A piece of ground laid out with a track for racing. **2.** A water-way, mill-race 1841.

Ra·ce-horse. 1626. [f. RACE *sb.*¹ + HORSE.] **1.** A horse bred or kept for racing. **2.** A logger-head or steamer duck 1773.

Racemate (ræ·sǐmět). 1838. [f. RACEMIC + -ATE¹ 1 c.] *Chem.* A salt of racemic acid.

Raceme (răsī·m). 1785. [ad. L. *racemus* a cluster of grapes.] *Bot.* A simple inflorescence in which the flowers are arranged on short, nearly equal, pedicels, at equal distances on an elongated axis.

Compound r., one having the lower pedicels developed into secondary racemes. Hence **Race·med** *a.* disposed in racemes. So **Racemi·ferous** *a.* bearing racemes or clusters. **Race·miform** *a.* having the form of a r.

Racemic (răse·mik, răsī·mik), *a.* 1835. [f. prec. + -IC.] *Chem.* Derived from grapes or grape-juice.

Racemo- (răsī·mo), comb. form of L. *racemus* RACEME, with sense 'containing a proportion of racemic acid', as *r.-carbonate, r.-carbonic* adj., etc.

Racemose (ræ·sǐmōus), *a.* 1698. [ad. L. *racemosus*, f. *racemus*; see -OSE.] **1.** *Bot.* **a.** Of flowers: Arranged in racemes. **b.** Of an inflorescence or vegetable growth: Having the form of a raceme. **2.** *Anat.* Having the form of, arranged as, a cluster (esp. as an epithet of compound glands) 1835. So **Ra·cemous** *a.* (*rare*) = 1.

Racemule (ræ·sǐmiul). 1882. [dim. of L. *racemus*; see -ULE.] *Bot.* A small raceme. So **Race·mulose** *a.* resembling a r.; somewhat racemose 1864.

Racer (rē·sǝɹ). 1649. [f. RACE *v.*¹ + -ER¹.] **1.** One who races or takes part in a race. **2.** A race-horse 1670. **b.** Any animal having great speed; *spec.* as the name of species of American snakes, of a sand-crab, etc. 1699. **3.** Anything used for racing, as a bicycle, yacht, etc.; anything capable of great speed 1793. **4.** *Gunnery.* A rail, forming a horizontal arc, on which the carriage or traversing-platform of a gun is moved 1861.

2. As much difference..as..between a r. and a cart-horse 1833.

Rache, ratch (rætʃ). *Obs.* exc. *arch.* [OE. *ræcc*, related to ON. *rakki* dog.] A hunting-dog which pursues its prey by scent.

Rachi- (rē·ki), **rachio-** (rē·kio), comb. forms of RACHIS, used in some terms of *Anat.* and *Path.* relating to the spine or vertebral column. (Also occas. written with *rh-*.) **Rachia·lgia** [Gr. -αλγία pain], pain in or due to the spine; painter's colic; hence **Rachia·lgic** *a.* **Ra·chiodont** [Gr. ὀδοντ- tooth] *a.*, of a genus of serpents (*Rachiodon*): having vertebral processes which penetrate the gullet and serve as teeth. **Ra·chiotome** [Gr. -τόμος cutting], a dissecting instrument for cutting open the spinal canal. **Rachio·tomy** [Gr. -τομία], the operation of cutting into the spinal canal.

Rachidian (räki·diăn), *a.* Also **rha-**. 1848. [f. *r(h)achid-*, assumed stem of Gr. ῥάχις RACHIS + -IAN.] Of or pertaining to a rachis.

‖**Rachis** (rē̆ⁱ·kis). Also **rha-**. *Pl.* **rachides** (rē̆ⁱ·kidīz). 1693. [mod.L., a. Gr. ῥάχις spine, ridge, rib (of a leaf), etc. The pl. *rachides* is erroneous, as the stem is ῥαχι-.] **1.** *Anat.* The vertebral column, or the cord from which it develops. **b.** The median part of the odontophore of a mollusc, resembling a series of vertebrae 1851. **c.** A cord of protoplasmic matter in the ovary of nematoid worms, round which ova are developed 1877. **2.** *Bot.* **a.** The axis of an inflorescence in which flower-stalks occur at short intervals from each other, as in grasses 1785. **b.** The axis of a pinnately compound leaf or frond, corresponding to the midrib of a simple leaf 1832. **3.** *Ornith.* The stem or shaft of a feather, esp. the part bearing the vexillum 1874.

‖**Rachitis** (rækəi·tis). 1655. [mod.L., a. Gr. ῥαχῖτις (f. ῥάχις + -ιτις -ITIS), prop. meaning 'inflammation of the spine'.] = RICKETS. Hence **Rachitic** (ræki·tik) *a.* affected with rickets; connected with, or pertaining to, rickets.

Racial (rēⁱ·ʃăl), *a.* 1862. [f. RACE *sb.*² + -IAL.] Belonging to, or characteristic of, race. Hence **Ra·cialism**. **Ra·cially** *adv.*

Racing (rēⁱ·siŋ), *vbl. sb.* 1680. [f. RACE *sb.*¹ or *v.*¹ + -ING¹.] The action of RACE *v.*¹

attrib. and *Comb.* as *r.-boat*, etc.; **R. Calendar**, a yearly publication giving particulars of races run or to be run; **r.-tail**, the tail of natural length worn by race-horses.

Rack (ræk), *sb.*¹ ME. [Cf. Norw. and Sw. *rak* wreck, wreckage, rubbish, etc., f. *reka* to drive.] †**1.** A rush, shock, collision. Also, a noise as of a shock; a crash. –1513. **2.** Clouds, or a mass of cloud, driven before the wind in the upper air ME. †**b.** Driving mist or fog –1610.

2. The Windes in the Vpper Region (which moue the Clouds aboue which we call the Racke) BACON. **b.** *Ant. & Cl.* IV. xiv. 10. *fig.* The great Globe it selfe..shall dissolue, And..Leaue not a racke behinde SHAKS.

Rack (ræk), *sb.*² ME. [app. a. MDu. *rec*, *reck-* (Du. *rek*, †*rak*) prob. f. *recken* to reach, stretch.] **1.** app. An iron bar to which prisoners were secured –1590. **2.** A bar (usu. in *pl.*) or set of bars used to support a spit or other cooking utensil. *Obs.* exc. *dial.* late ME. **3.** A frame made with upright bars of wood or metal to hold fodder for horses or cattle, either fixed in a stable or movable ME. **4.** A framework in or on which articles are placed or suspended. Freq. differentiated, as *bottle-*, *case-*, *hat-*, *plate-r.*, etc. 1537. **5.** *spec.* or *techn.*: **a.** *Naut.* = FIDDLE 3 a. 1769. **b.** An inclined frame or table on which tin-ore is washed 1839. †**c.** An openwork side for a cart or wagon –1687. **d.** In organ-building = PIPE-*rack*. **6.** *Mech.* A bar having teeth or indentations on the side or edge, which gear into those of a wheel, pinion, or worm, or serve to hold something in a desired (and easily alterable) position. Often coupled with *pinion*. 1797.

3. Phr. *At r. and manger*, in the midst of abundance or plenty, wanting for nothing. Hence *R. and manger*, want of proper management, waste and destruction (now *dial.*).

Comb.: **r.-calipers**, calipers fitted with a r. and pinion; so **-compass**, **-easel**; **-rail**, a cogged rail, into which a cogged wheel on a locomotive works; **r. railway**, a railway having a r.-rail laid between or beside the bearing-rails; **r. saw**, a saw with wide-set teeth; **-wheel**, a cog-wheel; **-work**, mechanism of the nature of, or containing, a r.

Rack (ræk), *sb.*³ 1460. [Related to RACK *v.*³, and perh. formed from it in Eng.] **1.** An instrument of torture formerly in use, consisting (usu.) of a frame having a roller at each end; the victim was fastened to these by the wrists and ankles, and had the joints of his limbs stretched by their rotation. **b.** *transf.* and *fig.* That which (*rarely* one who) causes acute suffering, physical or mental; also, the result of this; intense pain or suffering 1591. **2.** A frame on which cloth is stretched. *Obs.* exc. *dial.* 1519. †**3.** A windlass or winch for bending a cross-bow –1687. **4.** = RACK-RENT. Now *rare* or *Obs.* 1605. **5.** That which racks or strains; stress of weather; a storm 1806.

1. The r. seldom stood idle in the Tower for all the latter part of Elizabeth's reign HALLAM. **b.** The r. of publicke censure DEKKER. Phr. *On the r.*, in a state of acute physical or mental suffering; in keen suspense. *To put* or *set* (faculties, †words, etc.) *on the r.*, to strain to the utmost. So *to be on the r.*, to be at full stretch or strain. **5.** A strong voice, unworn by age and the r. of various seas 1891.

Rack (ræk), *sb.*⁴ 1599. [var. of WRACK, WRECK.] Destruction; chiefly in phr. *to go to r. and ruin.* †**b.** A crash as of something breaking MILT.

Rack (ræk), *sb.*⁵ 1580. [Related to RACK *v.*⁴] A horse's gait in which the two feet on each side are lifted almost simultaneously, and all four feet are off the ground together at certain moments.

Rack (ræk), *sb.*⁶ 1602. Aphetic f. ARRACK. Also *attrib.*, as *r.-punch*, etc.

Rack (ræk), *v.*¹ 1590. [f. RACK *sb.*¹ 2.] *intr.* Of clouds: To drive before the wind.

Rack (ræk), *v.*² 1577. [f. RACK *sb.*²] †**1.** *trans.* To fit up (a stable) with racks (*rare*) –1583. **2.** *To r. up.* **a.** *intr.* To fill a stable-rack with hay or straw before leaving the horse or horses for the night 1778. **b.** *trans.* To fill the rack for (a horse) 1798. **c** To fasten (a horse) to the rack 1856. **3.** To place (a thing) in or on a rack 1855. **b.** *Mining.* To wash on the rack (RACK *sb.*¹ 5 b) 1891. **4.** *trans.* and *intr.* To move, or be moved, by means of a rack and pinion 1867.

Rack (ræk), *v.*³ late ME. [prob. a. MDu. *recken* (Du. *rekken*) or MLG. *recken* to stretch, draw out = OE. *reccan.*] **1.** *trans.* To stretch the joints of (a person) by tugging or pulling, *esp.* by means of a rack (see RACK *sb.*³). **b.** To affect with pain similar to that caused by the use of the rack. (Said esp. of diseases.) 1588. **c.** To torture, distract, lacerate (the mind, soul, etc.) 1576. †**2.** To stretch, pull out, increase the length of (a thing, period of time, etc.) –1642. **b.** To pull apart, to separate by force, to break up. *Obs.* exc. *dial.* 1549. **c.** To shake (a thing) violently; to strain 1840. **d.** *intr.* To undergo stretching, strain, or dislocation. Chiefly *Sc.* 1508. †**3.** To strain the meaning of (words, etc.); to give a forced interpretation to –1711. **b.** To strain, task severely (the mind, brain, etc.) 1583. †**c.** To stretch or raise beyond the normal –1618. **4.** To raise (rent) above a fair or normal amount. Cf. RACK-RENT. 1553. †**b.** To charge an excessive rent for (land) –1766. **c.** To oppress (a person) by extortions or exactions, *esp.* of excessive rent; to bear hard upon (one's purse, etc.) 1584. †**d.** To extort (money, etc.). Also *absol.* –1680. **e.** To exhaust (tenants, land, etc.) by exactions or excessive use. Also with *out.* 1778.

1. Some drowned,..some racked, some hanged on a gybet 1526. **b.** Ile racke thee with old Crampes, Fill all thy bones with Aches SHAKS. **c.** How must she be racked with Jealousy STEELE. **2. c.** A dreadful cough, which seemed to r. his whole shattered system 1840. **3.** Grant that I may never r. a Scripture simile beyond the true intent thereof FULLER. **b.** Racking his wits to contrive exquisite compliments 1880. **4.** They racke their rents vnto a treble rate 1598. **c.** Here are no hard Landlords to racke vs with high rents 1624.

Rack (ræk), *v.*⁴ 1530. [Origin obsc. Cf. RACK *sb.*⁵] *intr.* Of animals, *esp.* horses: To move with the gait called a rack. Hence **Ra·cker**, a racking horse.

Rack (ræk), *v.*⁵ 1460. [ad. Prov. (Gascon) *arracar*, f. *raca* the stem and husks of grapes, thick dregs.] **1.** *trans.* To draw off (wine, cider, etc.) from the lees. Also with *off.* †**2.** To empty (a cask) by racking. *rare.* –1703.

Rack, *v.*⁶ 1769. [?] *Naut.* To bind two ropes together with cross-turns. Hence **Ra·cking** *vbl. sb.*, spun yarn, etc. used for this 1711.

Racket (ræ·kėt), *sb.*¹ 1500. [a. F. *raquette*; origin unkn.] **1.** A bat used in rackets, tennis, etc., consisting of a network of cord, catgut, or steel wire stretched across a somewhat elliptical frame formed of a bent strip of wood or steel, to the base of which a handle is attached. **b.** A game of ball for two or four persons, played with rackets in a plain four-walled court. Now always *pl.* 1529. **2.** A snow-shoe made after the fashion of a racket, as used in Northern America 1613. **b.** A broad wooden shoe for man or horse to enable them to walk over marshy ground 1864.

1. The main object of modern lawn tennis is to meet the ball with a full r. 1890.

attrib. and *Comb.*, as *r.-court*, etc.; **r.-press**, a contrivance to keep a r. from warping.

Racket (ræ·kėt), *sb.*² 1565. [prob. onomatopœic.] **1.** Disturbance, loud noise, uproar, din. **b.** With *a* and *pl.* An instance of this 1622. **c.** Clamour, outcry; excitement or fuss (*about* something, or *with* a person) 1652. **2.** The whirl of society; excessive social excitement or dissipation 1784. **b.** A large or noisy social gathering 1745. **3.** *slang.* A trick, dodge, scheme, game, line of business or action 1812. Now usually, any scheme for obtaining money, or effecting some other object, by illegal, and often violent, means (*U.S. colloq.*) 1928. **4.** A trying experience; an ordeal 1823.

1. A quiet country life—no r. except the roosters in the morning 1877. **4.** Phr. *To stand the r.*, (*a*) to hold out against strain or wear and tear; (*b*) to face the consequences of an action.

†**Ra·cket**, *v.*¹ 1603. [f. RACKET *sb.*¹] *trans.* To strike with, or as with, a racket; to toss or bandy about. Chiefly *fig.* –1705.

Racket (ræ·kėt), *v.*² 1753. [f. RACKET *sb.*²] **1.** *intr.* To live a gay life, to take part in social excitement. Also with *about.* 1760. **2.** To make a noise or racket; to move about in a noisy way 1827. **3.** *trans.* To keep lively, to disturb, destroy by racketing 1753.

Racketeer (rækėtīə·ɹ), *sb. U.S.* 1927. [f. RACKET *sb.*² 3 + -EER.] One of an organized gang who blackmail traders by intimidation and violence. Hence **Racketee·r** *v.*, **-ee·ring** *vbl. sb.*

Ra·cket-tail. 1851. [f. RACKET *sb.*¹] A (bird's) tail shaped like a tennis-racket; hence, a name for various humming birds and motmots having such tails. So **Ra·cket-tailed** *a.* having a r.

Ra·ckety, *a.* 1773. [f. RACKET *sb.*² + -Y¹.] **1.** Addicted to making a racket. **2.** Characterized by noise, excitement, etc. 1827.

Ra·ck-rent, *sb.* 1591. [f. RACK *v.*³ + RENT.] A very high, excessive, or extortionate rent; a rent equal (or nearly equal) to the full annual value of the land. Also *transf.* and *fig.* Hence **Ra·ck-rent** *v. trans.* to subject (a person) to the payment of r. **Ra·ck-re·nter**, one who pays, or one who exacts, r.

Ra·ck-stick. 1859. [f. RACK *v.*³] A stick used for tightening a rope placed round anything. So **Ra·ck-pin.**

‖**Raconteur** (rakoṅtör). 1829. [F., f. *raconter* to relate; see RECOUNT *v.*¹] One skilled in relating anecdotes or stories. So **Raconteuse** (-tȫz), a female r.

Racoon, raccoon (răkū·n, rækū·n). 1608. [Powhatan (Virginia) dialect of Algonquin.] An American nocturnal carnivore of the genus *Procyon*. The common N. Amer. species is *P. lotor*, a grayish-brown furry animal with bushy tail and sharp snout.

Racovian (răkōᵘ·viăn), *a.* and *sb.* 1652. [f. mod.L. *Racovia*, f. *Rakow*, a town in Poland + -IAN.] **A.** *adj.* Of or pertaining to Rakow, or to the Unitarians (Socinians) who made it their chief centre in the 17th c. **B.** *sb.* An adherent of the doctrines taught at Rakow.

Racquet, -ette, var. ff. RACKET *sb.*, RAQUETTE.

Racy (rēⁱ·si), *a.* 1650. [f. RACE *sb.*² II. 3 + -Y¹.] **1.** Of wine, fruits, etc.: Having a characteristically excellent taste, flavour, or quality. So of taste, flavour, etc. Also *fig.* **2. a.** Of persons: Having a distinctive quality or vigour of character or intellect; lively, full of 'go'. So of actions, qualities, etc. 1668. **b.** Of animals or their parts: Showing high breeding or good blood 1841. **3.** Of speech, writing, etc.: Having a characteristic sprightliness, liveliness, or piquancy 1667. **b.** *U.S.* Salacious. **4.** Of pleasure, etc.: Peculiarly agreeable 1690.

1. The r. flavour and strong body of this wine 1756. 2. a. Yorkshire has such families here and there.. peculiar, r., vigorous C. BRONTE. 3. Brisk r. Verses, in which we The Soil from whence they came, tast, smell, and see COWLEY. Phr. *R. of the soil*, characteristic of a certain country or people (usu. with ref. to Ireland). Hence **Ra·cily** *adv.* **Ra·ciness.**

Rad (ræd). 1831. Abbrev. of RADICAL.

Raddle (ræ·d'l), *sb.*1 *Obs.* exc. *dial.* 1577. [a. AF. *reidele*, OF. *reddalle* stout stick or pole.] 1. *n. dial.* and *U.S.* A wooden bar with upright pegs, used to keep the threads of the warp in place while it is being wound upon the beam 1848. 2. A slender rod, wattle, or lath, fastened to or twisted between upright stakes or posts to form a fence, partition, or wall 1577. 3. A piece of wattled work; a hurdle, door, etc. made with intertwined raddles 1886.

Raddle (ræ·d'l), *sb.*2 1523. [var. of RUDDLE.] Red ochre, RUDDLE.

Raddle (ræ·d'l), *v.*1 1671. [f. RADDLE *sb.*1] *trans.* To weave or twist together (like raddles), to intertwine, interlace.

Raddle (ræ·d'l), *v.*2 1631. [f. RADDLE *sb.*2] *trans.* To paint or mark with raddle; to colour coarsely with red or rouge.

‖**Radeau** (rado). 1759. [F., a. Prov. *radel* :—L. **ratellus*, dim. of *ratis* raft.] A raft; *spec.* a floating battery.

Radial (rēi·diăl), *a.* and *sb.* 1570. [a. late L. *radialis*, or f. RADIUS + -AL.] **A.** *adj.* 1. Of light, beams, etc.: Proceeding or issuing as rays from a common centre; also, of or pertaining to light in the form of rays. Now *rare*. 2. Arranged like rays or the radii of a circle; having the position or direction of a radius 1750. 3. Having spokes, bars, lines, etc., extending from a centre; *spec.* applied to apparatus or machines having a part or parts thus arranged, as *r. drill, plane*, etc. 1762. 4. Of immaterial things: Characterized by the divergence of lines or parts from a centre; taking the direction of such lines 1833. 5. *Anat.* Pertaining to the radius or chief bone of the forearm, esp. in *r. artery, nerve, vein* 1741.

2. *R. axle*, an axle (of a railway carriage, tramway car, etc.) which on a curve of the track assumes the position of a radius to that curve; so *r. axle box*. 4. Another form of symmetry which is entirely absent in Man is r. symmetry MIVART. Hence **Ra·dially** *adv.*

B. *sb. Anat.* 1. A radiating segment of a crinoid, between the stem and the brachials 1872. 2. A radial nerve or artery 1871.

‖**Radiale** (rēidi,ēi·li). *Pl.* **-alia.** 1877. [L., neut. sing. of *radialis*; see prec.] 1. = prec. B 1. 2. The carpal bone or element which lies on the radial side of the carpus 1888.

Radian (rēi·diăn). 1879. [f. RADIUS + -AN.] *Trig.* An angle which subtends, at the centre of a circle, an arc whose length is equal to the radius.

Radiance (rēi·diăns). 1601. [ad. late or med.L. *radiantia* brightness; see RADIATE *v.* and -ANCE.] 1. Light shining with diverging rays; hence, brilliant light, vivid brightness, splendour. b. Brightness of the eye or look 1748. 2. = RADIATION 1800.

1. The Son..with r. crown'd Of majesty divine MILT. b. Sweet love their looks a gentle r. lends THOMSON. So **Ra·diancy.**

Radiant (rēi·diănt), *a.* and *sb.* 1450. [ad. L. *radiantem*, *radiare* to emit rays; see RADIUS.] **A.** *adj.* 1. Sending out rays of light; shining brightly. b. Represented as sending out rays of light, or having radial projections resembling this. In *Her.* = RAYONNÉ. 1610. c. Of the eyes or looks: Bright, beaming with joy or hope 1794. 2. Issuing or appearing in the form of rays (of light); hence, bright, shining, splendid. Also *transf.* of beauty, etc. 1509. 3. Moving or operating in a radial manner 1800. 4. (Chiefly *Bot.*) Extending in a radial manner; having parts so extending 1828. 5. Characterized by radiation 1825. 6. *R. point*: a. Any point forming a centre from which rays or radii proceed 1726. b. *Astron.* The apparent focal point of a meteoric shower. So *r. region*. 1864.

1. On his right The r. image of his Glory sat, His onely Son MILT. 2. With scintillations, or r. Halo's about their heads SIR T. BROWNE. 3. *R. heat*: see HEAT *sb.* 2.

B. *sb.* 1. *Physics.* A point or object from which light or heat radiates 1727. 2. *Geom.* 'A straight line proceeding from a given point or fixed pole about which it is conceived to revolve' (Brande) 1842. 3. *Astron.* A radiant point 1864. Hence **Ra·diantly** adv.

Radiary (rēi·diări). 1835. [ad. F. *radiaire* or mod.L. *Radiaria* (pl.), f. *radius* ray.] *Zool.* An animal of the class *Radiaria* (comprising certain Invertebrates).

‖**Radiata** (rēidi,ēi·tă), *sb. pl.* 1828. [neut. pl. of L. *radiatus*, *radiare* to furnish with rays.] *Zool.* One of the great divisions of the animal kingdom according to Cuvier (now discarded), consisting of animals with radial structure, as sea urchins, sea anemones and polyps.

Radiate (rēi·diĕt), *a.* (*sb.*) 1668. [ad. L. *radiatus*; cf. next.] 1. Having rays proceeding from a centre, or having parts arranged in this manner. 2. Arranged like rays, diverging from a centre 1822. 3. = RADIAL *a.* 4. 1859. †**B.** *sb.* A radiate animal; one of the Radiata -1863.

1. *R. crown*; see RADIATED *ppl. a.* 1. *R. flower*, a composite flower-head having radial (usu. ligulate) florets.

Radiate (rēi·di,eit), *v.* 1619. [f. L. *radiat-*, *radiare* to furnish with rays, to emit rays, f. *radius*.] 1. *intr.* To emit rays (of light or heat); to shine brightly 1649. b. *spec.* To transmit electro-magnetic waves 1927. 2. Of light or heat: To issue in rays 1704. 3. To spread or move in all directions from a centre; to diverge from a central point 1619. b. To converge to or towards a centre (*rare*) 1835. 4. *trans.* To emit (light or heat) in rays 1794. b. To spread as from a centre 1821. c. To transmit by wireless. 5. To irradiate (*rare*) 1658.

3. The..valleys that r. from the uplands 1856.

Radiated (rēi·di,eitėd), *ppl. a.* 1658. [f. prec.] 1. Furnished with rays; made or depicted with rays issuing from it, esp. *r. crown*. 2. Having or consisting of parts arranged like rays or radii 1731. b. *spec.* in *Ornith.* of the plumage or markings of birds 1781. 3. = RADIATE *a.* 2. 1748. 4. = RADIAL *a.* 4. 1798.

Radiation (rēidi,ēi·ʃən). 1570. [ad. L. *radiationem*.] 1. The action or condition of sending out rays of light. Now *rare*. 1626. b. A ray or quantity of light emitted by a radiant body. Usu. *pl.* 1570. 2. The manner in which the energy of a vibrating body is transmitted in all directions by a surrounding medium; the emission and diffusion of heat-rays; the process by which heat passes from a heated body 1812. b. The emission of Röntgen or X rays, or the rays characteristic of radio-active substances 1896. 3. Divergence from a central point; radial arrangement or structure 1658. b. One of a set of radiating things or parts 1843.

Comb.: **r.-fog**, a fog caused by r. of heat on low grounds; **-thermometer**, a thermometer specially adapted for measuring the effects of r.

Radiative (rēi·diĕtiv), *a.* 1837. [f. as RADIATE *v.* + -IVE.] Pertaining to, or connected with, radiation; having the quality of radiating.

Radiato- (rēi·di,ēito), comb. form of RADIATE *a.*, with the meaning 'in a radial direction, in the manner of rays', as *r.-striate*, etc.

Radiator (rēi·di,eitəɹ). 1836. [f. RADIATE *v.*] One who or that which radiates; *esp.* anything which radiates light or heat. b. A small chamber or compartment heated by means of steam or hot air, and radiating warmth into a room, etc. 1875. c. In a motor-car: A device for keeping the engine cool, consisting of tubes having a large radiating surface, through which water circulates 1902.

Radical (ræ·dikăl), *a.* and *sb.* late ME. [ad. late L. *radicalis*, f. *radic-* RADIX.] **A.** *adj.* Of or pertaining to a root or to roots. 1. *R. humour, moisture*: In mediæval philosophy, the moisture naturally inherent in all plants and animals, its presence being a necessary condition of their vitality. b. Of qualities: Inherent in the nature or essence of a thing or person; fundamental 1562. 2. Forming the root, basis, or foundation; original, primary 1560. 3. Going to the root or origin; thorough; esp. *r. change, cure* 1651. 4. *Math.* a. Pertaining to or forming the root of a number or quantity 1557. b. *Geom.* Used in several terms relating to the intersection of circles and planes, esp. *r. axis, centre*, etc. 1848. 5. *Philol.* Of or belonging to the roots of words; connected with, based on, roots 1577. b. *R. letter*: (*a*) an original unchanged letter (so also *r. sound*) 1645; (*b*) a letter belonging to the root of a word 1653. 6. *Mus.* Belonging to the root of a chord 1753. 7. *Bot.* Of or belonging to the root of a plant; *esp.* of leaves or stalks: Springing directly from the root-stock or the stem close to the root 1753.

1. b. The r. diversity of these rival maladies 1806. The r. rottenness of human nature 1871. 2. The r. articles of the French creed of the eighteenth century MORLEY. 3. *R. reform*, a thorough reform; *esp.* as a phr. of English politics. So *R. reformer* = sense B. 5. 4. a. *R. sign*, the sign √ used to indicate a root of the number to which it is prefixed. 5. *R. word*, a simple uncompounded word having the form of, or directly based on, a root. 6. By the root of a chord, or its R. Bass, is meant its Bass-note in its original, uninverted form 1873.

B. *sb.* 1. *Philol.* A root; a word or part of a word which cannot be further analysed 1641. b. A radical letter 1652. 2. A basis, a fundamental thing or principle 1657. b. A root or radicle 1850. 3. *Math.* a. A quantity forming or expressed as a root of another quantity 1738. b. The radical sign 1780. 4. *Chem.* An element or atom (*simple r.*), or a group of these (*compound r.*), forming the base of a compound and remaining unaltered during the ordinary chemical reactions to which this is liable 1816. 5. *Politics.* An advocate of 'radical reform'; one who holds the most advanced views of political reform on democratic lines, and thus belongs to the extreme section of the Liberal party 1802.

1. The Welsh, the Cornish and the Armoric dialects, whose radicals are so much alike 1797. 5. It is manifest to the Tory that the R. does not see the benefit there is in that which he wishes to destroy H. SPENCER. Hence **Ra·dicalism**, the political views characteristic of Radicals; *transf.* thoroughness of method. **Radica·lity**, r. state or condition; the fact of being r. **Ra·dicalize** *v. trans.* and *intr.* to make or become R. in politics. **Ra·dical-ly** *adv.*, **-ness.**

Radicant (ræ·dikănt), *a. rare.* 1753. [a. L. *radicant-*, *radicare* RADICATE.] *Bot.* Producing roots; usu. said of parts of a plant which produce adventitious roots.

Radicate (ræ·dikeit), *v.* Now *rare*. 1448. [ad. L. *radicat-*, *radicare* or *radicari* to take root, f. *radic-* RADIX.] 1. *trans.* To cause to take root; to plant or establish firmly. Usu. *fig.* with ref. to qualities. †2. *intr.* To take root, become established -1681.

1. My regard for you is so radicated and fixed, that it is become part of my mind JOHNSON. Hence **Ra·dicated** *ppl. a.* rooted, established; *esp.* of qualities. **Radica·tion**, the process of taking root; the fact of being rooted, established, etc.; an arrangement or system of roots.

Radicel (ræ·disel). 1819. [ad. mod.L. *radicella*, dim. of RADIX.] *Bot.* A rootlet.

Radici-, comb. f. L. *radix*, *radicem* RADIX, as in **Ra:diciflo·rous** *a.*, flowering from the root. **Radi·ciform** *a.*, having the form of a root.

Radicle (ræ·dik'l). 1671. [ad. L. *radicula* RADICULE.] 1. *Bot.* a. That part of the embryo of a plant which develops into the primary root. b. A rootlet 1829. 2. *Anat.* One of the branching subdivisions of veins, nerves, etc. resembling a part of a root 1830. 3. *Chem.* = RADICAL *sb.* 4. 1857.

Radicular (rădi·kiŭlăɹ), *a.* 1819. [f. L. *radicula* + -AR.] 1. *Bot.* Belonging to the radicle. 2. a. *Path.* Affecting the roots (of a tooth, nerve, etc.) 1878. b. *Anat.* Belonging to the roots of an artery, nerve, etc. 1897.

Radicule (ræ·dikiul). 1814. [ad. L. *radicula*, dim. of RADIX.] *Bot.* = RADICLE. Hence **Radi·culose** *a.* having radicles.

Radio (rēi·diou), *sb.* orig. *U.S.* 1915. [Short for *radio-telegraphy*, etc. (see next 2).] Wireless telegraphy or telephony; a message transmitted by these; wireless broadcasting; a wireless receiving-set. Also *attrib.*, as *r. announcer*, etc. Hence **Ra·dio** *v. trans.* and *intr.* to broadcast by wireless telephony; to send (a message etc.) by wireless telegraphy.

Radio- (rēi·dio), comb. form of RADIUS. 1. *Anat.* Belonging to the radius in conjunction with some other part, as **Ra:dio-ca·rpal, -mu·scular, -u·lnar** *adjs.* 2. *Physics.* Connected with rays or radiation, as **Ra:dio-condu·ctor**, part of the receiver of a wireless telegraphy apparatus (usu. a tube containing iron filings), which is converted into a conductor by the impact of the electric waves on the collecting wire; a 'coherer'. **Ra:dio-tele·graphy, -tele·phony,** wireless telegraphy or telephony; so **Ra:dio-te·legram,** etc.

Ra:dio-a·ctive, *a.* 1900. [f. prec. + ACTIVE.] Capable (as radium) of emitting spontaneously rays consisting of material particles travelling at high velocities; so **Ra:dio-acti·vity.**

Radiogram (rē¹·diogræm). 1896. [f. prec. + -GRAM.] 1. = next 2. 2. A message transmitted by wireless telegraphy 1907.

Radiograph (rē¹·diograf), *sb.* 1881. [f. as prec. + -GRAPH.] 1. An instrument for measuring and recording the duration and intensity of sunshine. 2. An impression or image of an object produced on a sensitive plate by means of the Röntgen rays 1896. So **Ra·diograph** *v. trans.* to make a r. of (a thing). **Ra:diogra·phic, -al** *adjs.* relating to radiography; of or connected with wireless telegraphy; **-ly** *adv.* **Radio·graphy,** the production of images on sensitized plates by means of the Röntgen rays.

‖**Radiolaria** (rē¹:diǫlē·riă), *sb. pl.* 1872. [mod.L., f. *radiolus*, dim. of RADIUS.] *Zool.* A class of rhizopods. Hence **Ra:diola·rian** *a.* of or pertaining to the R.; *sb.* one of the R.

Radiolite (rē¹·diǝlait). 1842. [f. RADIO- + -LITE.] *Palæont.* A cretaceous fossil bivalve of the family *Rudista*.

Radiology (rē¹diǫ·lŏdʒi). 1905. [f. RADIO- + -LOGY.] The theory of radio-activity; the method of curing disease, etc. by means of Röntgen rays. So **Radiolo·gical** *a.* **Radio·logist,** one who operates a Röntgen-ray apparatus.

Radiometer (rē¹di,ǫ·mĭtǝɹ). 1727. [f. RADIO- + METER.] †1. An instrument formerly used for measuring angles; a cross-staff, fore-staff –1802. 2. An instrument designed to illustrate the transformation of radiant energy into mechanical force 1875. So **Ra:diomicro·meter,** an instrument for measuring minute degrees of radiation.

Radiophone (rē¹·diofōun). 1881. [f. RADIO- + -PHONE.] An instrument for the production of sound by intermittent radiant energy, such as light or heat; the photophone is a special form. So **Radio·phony,** the theory or method of producing sound by radiant light or heat.

Radioscopy (rē¹di,ǫ·skǫpi). 1898. [f. as prec. + -SCOPY.] The examination of objects by means of the Röntgen rays.

†**Ra·dious,** *a.* 1500. [ad. F. *radieux*, or L. *radiosus*, f. *radius* ray.] Radiant, bright –1692. b. Forming rays of light. BERKELEY.

Radish (ræ·diʃ). [OE. *rædic, redic*, ad L. *radicem*; subseq. readopted from F. *radis*, a. Pr. *raditz* or It. *radice* :–L. *radicem*; see RADIX and RACE *sb.*³] a. The fleshy, slightly pungent, root of a cruciferous plant (*Raphanus sativus*), commonly eaten raw as a relish or in salads. b. The plant of which this is the root.

Wild r., a field-weed (*R. Raphanistrum*), also called *jointed charlock*.

Comb. **r.-fly** (U. S.), a small dipterous insect, *Anthomyia raphani*, whose larvæ burrow in radishes.

Radium (rē¹·diǫm). 1900. [f. L. *radius* ray, RADIUS + -IUM.] A highly radio-active metallic element found in minute quantities in combination in pitchblende: its chemical symbol is Ra and atomic weight 226·4.

Radius (rē¹·diǫs). *Pl.* **radii** (rē¹·di,ǝi). 1597. [a. L.] 1. A staff, rod, bar, or other straight object. †a. The staff of a cross –1742. b. *Anat.* The thicker and shorter of the two bones of the forearm in man; also, the corresponding bone of the foreleg in quadrupeds, and of the wing in birds 1615. 2. A rod, bar, etc., forming one of a set extending in several directions from one point; a wheel-spoke, a radiating part or filament, etc. 1726. b. *Bot.* (*a*) The ray or outer whorl of ligulate florets surrounding the disk in a composite flower-head; the border of enlarged petals on a partial umbel; (*b*) a peduncle supporting a partial umbel; (*c*) a medullary ray 1775. c. *Ornith.* One of the processes on the barb of a feather, a barbule 1893. 3. *Math.* A straight line drawn to the circumference of a circle or the surface of a sphere from the centre, all lines so drawn being equal in length 1656. b. A radial line of a curve, drawn from a certain point such as the focus to any point on the curve 1836. c. Any line in an arrangement of straight lines diverging from a point, and resembling the radii of a circle 1774. d. *R. vector*, a variable line drawn to a curve from a fixed point as origin; in astronomy usu. from the sun or a planet round which a satellite revolves 1753. 4. A circular area of which the extent is measured by the length of the radius of the circle which bounds it 1853. b. *spec.* in London, a circle of four miles in all directions from Charing Cross 1889.

Comb.: **r.-bar,** a bar pivoted at one end so that it can move in a circle or arc of a circle, used esp. in the parallel motion of a steam engine.

Radix (rē¹·diks). Pl. **radices** (rē¹·disīz), radixes. 1571. [a. L.] = ROOT. 1. *Math.* †a. A root of a number –1719. b. A number or quantity, etc. which is made the basis of a scale of numeration 1798. 2. The source or origin; that in which anything originates 1607. †3. *Philol.* = ROOT *sb.* III. 2 b. –1771. 4. *Bot.* The root of a plant 1727.

Radon (rē¹·dǫn). 1925. [f. RADIUM, and the termination of ARGON, NEON, XENON.] *Chem.* A gaseous radio-active element arising from the disintegration of radium, discovered in 1900. Symbol Rn.

‖**Radula** (ræ·diŭlă). 1877. [L., 'scraper,' f. *radere*; see RASE *v.*¹] *Zool.* = ODONTOPHORE. **Ra·dular** *a.* **Ra·duliform** *a.* rasp-like.

Raff¹ (ræf). ME. [See RIFF-RAFF.] 1. *Sc.* and *north.* Abundance, plenty; a large number or collection. 2. Worthless material, trash, rubbish, refuse. Now only *dial.* late ME. 3. *collect.* The common run (of people); the lowest class 1673. 4. A low worthless fellow 1785.

Raff² (ræf). 1440. [perh. a. G. *raf, raff(e*, obs. or dial. ff. *rafe* rafter, beam.] Foreign timber, usu. in the form of deals.

Raffaelesque, var. of **Raphaelesque.**

Raffia (ræ·fiă). Also **rafia.** 1882. [var. of RAPHIA.] 1. A palm of the genus *Raphia*. 2. The soft fibre from the leaves of *Raphia Ruffia* and *R. tædigera*, used for tying up plants, cut flowers, etc., embroidering, and plaiting or weaving into baskets, etc. 1882. Also *attrib.*

Raffinose (ræ·finōus). 1881. [f. F. *raffiner* to refine + -OSE.] *Chem.* A colourless crystalline compound with a sweetish taste found in various substances, as the sugar-beet, etc.

Raffish (ræ·fiʃ), *a.* 1801. [f. RAFF¹ + -ISH.] Disreputable, low. **Ra·ffish-ly** *adv.*, **-ness.**

Raffle (ræ·f'l), *sb.*¹ late ME. [a. F. *rafle*; origin unkn.] 1. A game of chance played with three dice, in which the winner was the one who threw the three all alike, or, if none did so, the one who threw the highest pair; also, the throwing of a doublet or triplet in this game. *Obs.* exc. *dial.* 2. A form of lottery in which an article is assigned by drawing of lots (prop. by casting of dice) to one person of a number who have each paid a certain part of its value 1766.

Raffle (ræ·f'l), *sb.*² 1470. [perh. a. OF. *rafle* in phr. *rifle ou rafle* anything whatsoever.] †1. A rabble; riff-raff –1670. 2. Rubbish, refuse 1848. b. *Naut.* Lumber, débris, a confused tangle of ropes, canvas, broken spars, etc. 1881.

2. *transf.* The r. of conversation that a man picks up as he passes KIPLING.

Raffle (ræ·f'l), *v.*¹ 1680. [a. F. *rafler* in same sense.] 1. *intr.* To cast dice, draw lots, etc. *for* something; to take part in a raffle. 2. *trans.* To dispose of by means of a raffle 1851.

1. Will you please to r. for a tea pot 1689.

Ra·ffle, *v.*² *rare.* 1712. [perh. var. of RUFFLE *v.*] *trans.* a. To indent, serrate (a leaf). b. To crumple 1728. c. *dial.* To ruffle 1868.

a. The best examples have all some trifling difference, principally in the raffling of the leaves 1817.

Rafflesia (ræflī·ʒiă, -ī·ziă). 1820. [mod.L., f. name of Sir T. Stamford *Raffles* (1781–1826), British governor in Sumatra.] *Bot.* A stemless, leafless plant of the order *Cytinaceæ*, found in Java and Sumatra growing as a parasite on the stems of various species of grape-vine, and remarkable for the size of its flowers.

Raft (raft), *sb.*¹ late ME. [a. ON. *raptr* rafter.] 1. A beam, spar, rafter. Now only *arch.* 2. A collection of logs, planks, casks, etc., fastened together in the water for transportation by floating 1497. 3. A flat structure of logs, inflated skins, etc., for the conveyance or support of persons or things on water 1590. b. *Mil.* A floating bridge 1802. 4. (Chiefly *U.S.*) A large floating mass or accumulation of fallen trees, logs, vegetation, ice, etc. Also, a dense flock of swimming birds. 1718.

attrib. and *Comb.*: **r.-bridge,** a bridge made of a r., or supported by rafts; **-duck,** *U.S.* the scaup or blackhead duck, so called from its flocking closely on the water; **-port,** a square hole cut in the sides of some ships for loading or unloading planks or pieces of timber.

Raft, *sb.*², var. of **Raff**².

Raft (raft), *v.* 1706. [f. RAFT *sb.*¹] 1. *trans.* To transport by water: a. in the form of a raft; b. on, or by means of, a raft 1766. 2. To form into a raft or rafts 1745. 3. To go upon or cross (a river) by means of a raft 1765. 4. *intr.* To work on or direct a raft 1741.

1. Phr. *To r. off*, to float off (water-casks, or the water in them) from the shore to a ship.

Rafter (ra·ftǝɹ), *sb.*¹ [OE. *ræfter*, related to ON. *raptr* RAFT *sb.*¹] One of the beams which give slope and form to a roof, and bear the outer covering of slates, tiles, thatch, etc. †b. A large beam such as is used for a rafter –1697.

Principal r., a strong beam in a truss, lying under the *common* or *ordinary rafters*.

Rafter (ra·ftǝɹ), *sb.*² 1809. [f. RAFT *sb.*¹ or *v.* + -ER ¹.] One who is employed in rafting timber.

Rafter (ra·ftǝɹ), *v.* 1538. [f. RAFTER *sb.*¹] 1. *trans.* To build or furnish with rafters. 2. *Agric.* To plough (land), leaving a space between the furrows 1733. 3. To form into rafters 1846.

Raftsman (ra·ftsmæ̆n). 1776. [f. RAFT + -s- + MAN.] One who works on a raft.

Rag (ræg), *sb.*¹ [ME. *ragge*, perh. repr. an OE. *ragg-, ad. ON. *rǫgg* tuft or strip of fur.] 1. A small worthless fragment or strip of some woven material; *esp.* one of the irregular scraps into which a piece of such material is reduced by wear and tear. b. *pl.* Ragged or tattered garments or clothes; freq. in phr. *in rags* ME. c. In neg. phrases, etc., the smallest scrap of cloth or clothing 1590. d. Similarly, the smallest scrap *of* sail 1653. e. In *sing.* without article, as a material 1808. 2. *transf.* A fragment, scrap, bit, remnant; a torn or irregularly shaped piece 1440. †b. of money. Hence in *Cant*, a farthing. –1700. 3. Applied contempt. to things, e.g. a torn or scanty garment, a flag, handkerchief, newspaper, etc. 1549. b. Similarly applied to persons 1566. 4. A sharp or ragged projection (*rare*) 1664.

1. Cowles, Hoods and Habits..tost And flutterd into Raggs MILT. b. Going in rags through the winter RUSKIN. *fig.* I begin, In virtue cloathed, to cast the rags of sin DRYDEN. c. Won't leave him a r. to his back, nor a penny in his pocket 1792. d. With every r. of sail set 1804. 2. Volumes and flying rags of cloud 1873. They have no r. of evidence to uphold them 1893. b. *Com. Err.* IV. iv. 89. 3. Every rubbishy r. now contains the 'news' 1889. b. You Witch, you Ragge, you Baggage SHAKS. 4. File off the rags left by the saw 1872.

attrib. and *Comb.*, as *r.-basket; r.-carpet, -doll, -paper*, etc.; *r.-made* adj.; *r.-picker, -seller*, etc.; also, **r.-engine,** a machine for reducing rags to pulp, used in paper-making; **-merchant,** a dealer in rags; **-money** (contempt.), paper-money; **-shop,** a shop for rags and old clothes; **-wool,** wool obtained by tearing rags to pieces.

Rag (ræg), *sb.*² ME. [Origin obsc.] 1. A piece (mass or bed) of hard, coarse or rough stone. *Obs.* exc. *dial.* b. A large coarse roofing-slate 1825. 2. A name for certain kinds of stone, chiefly of a hard coarse texture, and breaking up in flat pieces several inches thick ME.

Rag (ræg), *sb.*³ *Univ. slang.* 1892. [f. RAG *v.*²] An act of ragging; *esp.* an extensive display of noisy disorderly conduct, carried on in defiance of authority or discipline.

Rag (ræg), *v.*¹ 1440. [f. RAG *sb.*¹] 1. *trans.* †a. To tear in pieces. b. To make ragged. †2. *intr.* To become ragged (*rare*) –1683.

Rag (ræg), *v.*² *dial.* and *slang.* 1796. [Origin obsc.; cf. BULLYRAG.] 1. *trans.* a. To scold, rate, talk severely to. b. To annoy, tease, torment; *spec.* in *Univ. slang*, to assail in a rough or noisy fashion; to create wild disorder in (a room). Also *absol.* 1808. **2.** *intr.* To wrangle *over* a subject 1889.

Rag (ræg), *v.*³ 1875. [Origin obsc.] *trans.* To break up (ore) with a hammer, preparatory to sorting.

Ragabash (ræ·găbæʃ), *sb.* and *a.* *Sc.* and *n dial.* 1609. [app. f. RAG *sb.*¹, with fanciful ending.] **1.** An idle worthless fellow; a ragamuffin. **2.** *collect.* Rabble, riff-raff 1824. **B.** *adj.* Beggarly 1818.

Ragamuffin (ræ·gămɒfin), *sb.* and *a.* late ME. [prob. f. RAG *sb.*¹, with fanciful ending.] †**1.** The name of a demon. LANGLAND. **2.** A ragged, dirty, disreputable man or boy 1581. **b.** *attrib.* or as *adj.* Rough, beggarly, good-for-nothing, disorderly 1602.

Ra·g-bag. 1861. A bag in which rags or scraps of cloth are collected or stored. **b.** *transf.* and *fig.* A motley collection 1864.

b. The Convention was a r. of dissent LOWELL.

Ra·g-bolt. 1627. [perh. f. RAG *sb.*¹ 4.] A bolt having barbs directed towards the head, so that it cannot be easily withdrawn after it is driven in; a jag-bolt or barb-bolt.

Rage (rēⁱdʒ), *sb.* ME. [a. F. *raige, rage* :—*rabia*, late L. f. *rabies* RABIES.] **1.** Madness; insanity; a fit or access of mania. *Obs.* exc. *poet.* **2.** Violent anger, furious passion; a fit or access of such anger; †angry disposition ME. **3.** *transf.* Violent operation or action, 'fury' (of wind, the sea, fire, etc.) ME. **b.** A flood, high tide, sudden rising of the sea. late ME. **4.** A violent feeling, passion, or appetite. Also, violence (*of* a feeling, etc.). late ME. †**b.** Violent desire; sexual passion; heat –1697. **5.** A vehement passion *for*, desire *of*, a thing. Also const. *infin.* and *absol.* 1593. **6.** Poetic or prophetic inspiration; musical excitement 1600. **7.** Martial or high spirit, ardour, fervour, manly enthusiasm or indignation 1591. **8.** Excitement or violence *of* an action, operation, etc.; also, the acutest point or heat of this 1593.

1. *Com. Err.* IV. iii. 88. 2. [The horse] swalloweth the ground with fiercenesse and r. *Job* xxxix. 24 His green Eyes, that sparkled with his R. DRYDEN. 3. Bodies..exposed to the Sunnes fiery r. 1634. 4. The present r. of your sorrow 1691. In the R. of the Distemper STEELE. b. *Haml.* III. iii. 89. 5. The earth-consuming r. Of gold and blood SHELLEY. Phr. (*All*) *the r.*, said of the object of a widespread and usu. temporary enthusiasm. 7. The soldiers shout around with generous r. DRYDEN. 8. Great carnage did..ever attend the first r. of conquest BURKE.

Rage (rēⁱdʒ), *v.* ME. [ad. F. *rager*, f. *rage* RAGE *sb.*] †**1.** *intr.* To go mad; to be mad; to act madly or foolishly –1567. **2.** To show signs of madness or frenzy; to rave; to act or speak wildly or furiously; to storm; *Sc.* to scold. Also, to be full of anger. ME. †**3.** To behave wantonly or riotously; to take one's pleasure. Const. *with* (a person), *in* (an action, practice, etc.). –1645. **4.** *transf.* of things (e.g. wind, the sea, etc.): To be violent and boisterous; to move or rush furiously 1535. **b.** Of passions, feelings, etc.: To have or reach a high degree of intensity 1583. **c.** Of a storm, battle, etc.: To have course without check or with fatal effect; to be at the height 1667. **d.** Of a disease or pain: To be violent. Also *transf.* 1602. **5.** To be widely prevalent, or to spread widely, in a violent or virulent form 1563. **6.** To act with fury, ardour, or vehemence; to move furiously *over* (a place), or *about* 1593. †**7.** To be violently bent *upon*, to be furiously eager *to* (with inf.), to be impatient *for*. *rare.* –1671. **8.** *trans.* (in *pa. pple.*) To enrage. SHAKS.

2. Whereat hee inlie rag'd MILT. I raged against the public liar TENNYSON. 4. Come vp ye horses, and r. yee charets *Jer.* xlvi. 9. R. on, ye elements! WORDSW. b. The passion for play raged in him without measure MACAULAY. c. The gale..raged above our heads 1871. d. Some fever rages in thy blood 1611. 5. Sickness..raged throughout the camp 1893. 6. Why stand we..heere, Wayling our losses, while the Foe doth R. SHAKS.

Rageful (rēⁱ·dʒfŭl), *a.* 1580. [f. RAGE *sb.* + -FUL.] †**1.** Mad, frantic, frenzied –1635. **2.** Full of furious anger 1580. **3.** *transf.* of things: Full of furious activity 1597.

1. With ragefull eyes shee bad him defend himselfe SIDNEY. 3. Ragefull windes 1619. Hence **Ra·gefully** *adv.*

Rag-fair. 1722. [f. RAG *sb.*¹ + FAIR *sb.*¹] A market for the sale of old clothes, held at Houndsditch in London. Also *attrib.*

Ragged (ræ·gėd), *a.* ME. [f. RAG *sb.*¹ + -ED.] **I. 1.** Of animals, their fur, etc.: Rough, shaggy, hanging in tufts. **2.** Of a rough, irregular, or straggling form; having a broken jagged outline or surface; full of rough or sharp projections. late ME. **3.** *transf.* of immaterial things: **a.** Faulty, imperfect, irregular 1500. **b.** Of sounds: Harsh, discordant, rough 1600.

1. What Shepherd owns those r. Sheep? DRYDEN. 2. Herne the Hunter..with great rag'd-hornes SHAKS. Yon r. cliff COLLINS. A r. thorn COWPER. The thick r. skirts Of the victorious darkness SHELLEY. 3. a. My r. rhimes QUARLES. b. My voice is r.; I know I cannot please you SHAKS.

II. 1. Of cloth, garments, etc.: Rent, torn, frayed, in rags ME. **2.** Of persons: Wearing ragged clothes; dressed in rags. Hence of appearance, etc. late ME.

1. He draws back the r. curtain DICKENS. 2. A swarm of dirty and r. plebeians GIBBON.

Comb.: **r. hip**, in a horse: a hip standing away from the backbone; **R. Robert**, *Geranium Robertianum*; **r. school**, a free school for children of the poorest class. Hence **Ra·gged-ly** *adv.*, **-ness.**

Ragged Robin. 1741. [See ROBIN.] A pop. name of a well-known English flower, *Lychnis Floscuculi*. Also *attrib.*

Ragged staff. 1449. [RAGGED *a.* I. 2.] A staff with projecting stumps or knobs; chiefly in ref. to the badge or crest of the Earls of Warwick.

Old Neuils Crest, The rampant Beare chain'd to the ragged staffe SHAKS.

Raggle-taggle, *a.* Extended form of RAG-TAG, used *attrib.*

Raggy (ræ·gi), *a.* [Late OE., f. RAG *sb.*¹] = RAGGED *a.*

Raglan (ræ·glăn). 1864. [f. name of Lord Raglan, the British commander in the Crimean war.] An overcoat without shoulder seams, the sleeve going right up to the neck. Also *attrib.*

Ragman¹ (ræ·gmæ̆n). late ME. [f. RAG *sb.*¹ + MAN.] †**1.** A name given to the Devil, or one of the devils –1600. **2.** A rag-gatherer, rag-dealer 1586.

†**Ragman².** ME. [Origin obsc.] **1.** The name given to a statute of 4 Edw. 1, and to certain articles of inquisition associated with proceedings of *Quo warranto* under this statute. **2.** A roll, list, catalogue –1460. **3.** A document (contract, agreement, indenture, etc.) with seals attached –1470.

Ragman('s) roll. *Obs.* exc. *Hist.* 1523 [f. prec. + ROLL.] †**1.** RAGMAN 2. –1610. **2.** A set of rolls, now in the Public Record Office, in which are recorded the instruments of homage made to Edw. I by the Scottish King (Balliol), nobles, etc., in 1296. 1710.

Ragout (rægū·), *sb.* 1664. [F. *ragoût*, f. *ragoûter* to revive the taste of, f. GOÛT.] **1.** A dish of meat cut in small pieces, stewed with vegetables and highly seasoned. **b.** *transf.* or *fig.* 1672. †**2.** A sauce or relish –1750.

Ragout (rægū·), *v.* 1710. [f. prec.] **1.** *trans.* To make a ragout of, to stew with highly flavoured seasoning. †**2.** *transf.* To give piquancy or variety to –1753.

1. To r. a Leg of Mutton 1756.

Ra·gstone. ME. [f. RAG *sb.*²] = RAG *sb.*² 1, 2.

Rag-tag (ræ·g,tæg). 1820. [f. RAG *sb.*¹ + TAG.] **1. a.** *collect.* The raff or rabble of the community. **b.** One of the individuals forming this class. 1879. **2.** *Rag-tag* (or *rag, tag*) *and bob-tail* = 1 a. Also *transf.*; sometimes = 'the whole lot'. 1820.

Ra·g-time. Orig. *U.S.* 1901. Music in which there is frequent syncopation, as in many negro melodies. Also *attrib.*

Raguly (ræ·giŭli), *a.* 1658. [perh. based on *rag, ragged*, or *raggy*.] *Her.* Of a cross or other bearing Having short oblique projections resembling the stumps of branches cut off close to the stem. Hence of a division between parts of the field: Having alternate projections and depressions like a battlement, but set obliquely.

Ra·gweed. 1658. [Cf. RAGWORT.] **1.** = RAGWORT. **2.** *U.S.* A plant belonging to the genus *Ambrosia*, esp. *A. trifida* and *A. artemisiæfolia* 1866.

Ra·g-wheel. 1829. [f. RAG *sb.*¹] **1.** A wheel having projections which catch into the links of a chain passing over it, as in a chain-pump; a sprocket-wheel. **2.** A polishing wheel composed of rags 1884.

Ra·gwork. 1840. [f. RAG *sb.*²] Masonry composed of flattish pieces of ragstone, having an undressed surface.

Ra·gworm. 1865. [f. RAG *sb.*¹] A sand-worm (*Nephthys cæca*) of the British coasts, also called *white-rag worm* and *lurg*.

Ra·gwort. 1450. [prob. f. RAG *sb.*¹, in ref. to the ragged form of the leaves.] The pop. name of several species of the genus *Senecio*, esp. the Common Ragwort, *S. Jacobæa*.

‖**Raia** (rēⁱ·ă). Also **raja.** 1633. [L. *raia* (pl. *raiæ*).] *Zool.* = RAY *sb.*²

Raid (rēⁱd), *sb.* late ME. [Sc. f. OE. *rād* ROAD, revived by Scott, and subseq. extended in meaning.] **1.** A military expedition on horseback; a predatory excursion, prop. of mounted men; a foray, INROAD. **2.** *transf.* and *fig.* **a.** An invading troop, as of raiders 1826. **b.** A rush 1861. **c.** A sudden or vigorous descent, onset, or attack *upon* something to be seized, suppressed, or destroyed 1873. †**3.** A roadstead for ships –1636.

1. The Scottis maid dywerse incurtiouns and raidis in Ingland 1578. 2. b. A rapid r. into some of the nearest shops, for things remembered at the last moment 1877. c. A general r. upon Protestant literature all over France 1873.

Raid (rēⁱd), *v.* 1824. [f. prec.] **1.** *intr.* To go upon, or take part in a raid. **b.** *Stock Exchange*, etc. To act so as to depress prices or create uncertainty as to values 1889. **2.** *trans.* To make a raid on (a place, person, cattle, etc.) 1880.

2. Phr. *To r. the market*: see 1 b. Hence **Rai·der**, one who raids.

†**Rail,** *sb.*¹ [OE. *hrægl, hrægel*; etym. unkn.] **1.** A garment, dress –1552. **2.** A neckerchief formerly worn by women. See also NIGHT-RAIL. –1710.

Rail (rēⁱl), *sb.*² ME. [a. OF. *reille* :—L. *regula* straight stick, bar, etc. (see RULE).] **1.** A bar of wood, fixed in a horizontal position for hanging things on, etc., as *hat-, towel-r.* **b.** Used to support vines or other plants. late ME. **c.** Forming part of the sides of a cart 1530. **2.** A horizontal bar of wood or metal, fixed upon upright supports (posts) as part of a fence. (In *pl.* freq. = b.) 1464. **b.** A continuous series of bars forming the horizontal part of a fence; hence, a fence or railing, whether constructed of posts and rails, or of some other form 1541. **c.** The HAND-RAIL of a stair 1453. **d.** An altar-rail 1641. **e.** *Naut.* (*pl.*) Narrow pieces of wood nailed for ornament on parts of a ship's upper works 1750. **3.** *Carpentry.* One of the horizontal pieces in a door or other framework 1678. **4.** A bar or continuous line of bars (now usu. of iron or steel) laid on or near the ground (commonly in pairs) to bear and guide the wheels of a vehicle, and enable them to run more easily 1598. **5.** = RAILWAY, now chiefly in phr. *by r.* 1610. **b.** On the Stock Exchange in *pl.* = railway shares 1893.

4. Phr. *Off the rails* (freq. *fig.* = out of the proper or normal condition; morally or mentally astray).

attrib. and *Comb.* **a.** In senses 1 and 2, as *r.-fence* (U.S.), *-post, -splitter* (U.S.), etc.; **r.-bird**, the American spotted cuckoo. **b.** In sense 4, in many recent compounds, as *r.-chair, -joint, -layer, -mill*, etc. **c.** In sense 5, as *r.-head, track*, etc. **r.-motor** *a.* pertaining to motor vehicles running on a railway.

Rail (rēⁱl), *sb.*³ 1450. [a. F. *râle*, OF. *raale*; origin unkn.] A bird of the family *Rallidæ* and esp. of the genus *Rallus*: see LANDRAIL, WATER-RAIL.

Rail (rēⁱl), *sb.*⁴ *rare.* 1529. [f. RAIL *v.*⁴] An act of railing or reviling.

Rail (rēⁱl), *v.*¹ *Obs.* exc. *Sc.* ME. [a. OF. *reiller* :—L. *regulare*, f. *regula* RAIL *sb.*²] †**1.** *trans.* To set in order or array; to arrange; to regulate -1530. †b. To tie or fasten in a string or row (*rare*) -1634. **2.** To array, adorn, set (*with* something) ME.

1. b. Whiche rebelles were brought..to London railed in ropes like horses drawyng in a carte 1548.

Rail (rēl), *v.*[2] late ME. [f. RAIL *sb.*[2]] **1.** *trans.* To furnish or enclose (a place) with rails. **2.** To provide (a hedge, bench, etc.) with a rail or rails. Also with *about, in. rare.* 1577. **3.** To lay with rails 1888. **4.** To convey by rail 1865. **5.** *intr.* To travel by rail 1842.

1. *To r. in,* to enclose (a space or thing) with rails; A space was railed in for the reception of the..jurors 1802. *To r. off,* to separate by a railing.

†Rail, *v.*[3] ME. [Origin obsc.] *intr.* To flow, gush (*down*) -1600.

A tempest railed downe her cheekes amaine 1600.

Rail (rēl), *v.*[4] 1460. [a. F. *railler*; origin obsc.] **1.** *intr.* To utter abusive language. **†2.** To jest, to rally. Also const. *with.* -1685. **3.** *trans.* To bring (a person) *into* a certain condition by railing. Also rarely with a thing as obj. in other constructions. 1596.

1. To see you r. and rage at the rate you do BERKELEY. Don't r. against the women MISS BRADDON. **3.** I shal sooner rayle thee into wit and holinesse SHAKS.

Railing (rē·liŋ), *vbl. sb.* 1471. [f. RAIL *v.*[2]] **1.** The action of making fences or enclosing ground with rails. Also *railing-in.* 1543. **b.** *concr.* (also in *pl.*) A fence or barrier made of rails or in some other fashion 1471. **c.** Material for railings 1812. **2.** The laying of rails; a set or line of rails 1624.

Railing (rē·liŋ), *ppl. a.* 1526. [f. RAIL *v.*[4] + -ING [2].] That rails; characterized by railing.

The r. Eloquence of Cicero in his Philipics DRYDEN. Hence **Rai·lingly** *adv.* in a r. manner.

Raillery (rē·ləri). 1653. [a. F. *raillerie,* f. *railler* to rally. The older pronunc. (ræ·ləri) is still used by some (esp. *U.S.*) speakers.] Good-humoured ridicule, banter. **b.** With *a* and *pl.* An instance of this 1654.

By saying this of others, I expose my self to some R. COWLEY. **b.** There is a shocking familiarity both in his railleries and civilities ADDISON.

†‖Railleur (rayör). 1667. [F., f. *railler* to rally.] One who practises raillery -1751.

Railroad (rē·lrōud). (Now chiefly *U.S.*) 1775. [f. RAIL *sb.*[2] 4.] = next. Hence **Rai·lroad** *v. trans.* (*U.S.*) to rush (a person or thing) *to* or *into* a place, *through* a process 1884. **Rai·lroading** *vbl. sb.* travelling by rail; the business of making or working railroads.

Railway (rē·lwēi), *sb.* 1756. [f. RAIL *sb.*[2] 4 + WAY.] **1.** A way or road laid with rails (orig. of wood, subseq. of iron or steel), on which the wheels of wagons containing heavy goods are made to run for ease of transport; also the way composed of rails thus laid. **2.** *spec.* A line or track consisting of iron or steel rails, on which carriages or wagons conveying passengers or goods are moved by a locomotive engine. Hence also, the whole organization necessary for the working of this, and the company of persons owning or managing it. 1832.

attrib. and *Comb.,* as *r. accident, engine, man, station, train,* etc.; **r. novel,** a light novel, suitable for reading on a r. journey; **r. rug,** a rug used for warmth on a r. journey; **-spine,** an affection of the spine produced by concussion in a r. accident. Hence **Rai·lway** *v. intr.* to make railways; to travel by rail; *trans.* to supply with railways.

Raiment (rē·mĕnt). 1440. [aphet. f. ARRAYMENT; cf. RAY *v.*[2]] Clothing, clothes, dress, apparel. Now *rhet.* †b. With *a* and *pl.* A garment, a dress -1665.

The white r. destined to the saints CARY.

Rain (rēn), *sb.* [Com. Teut.: OE. *regn, rēn.*] **1.** The condensed vapour of the atmosphere, falling in drops large enough to attain a sensible velocity; the fall of such drops. **2.** *pl.* Showers of rain; rainfalls OE. **b.** In India, the rainy season 1616. **c.** *Naut.* A part of the Atlantic ocean, in which rain is frequent 1727. **3.** With indef. article: †a. A shower of rain -1597. **b.** A (specified) kind of rain (or shower) 1699. **4.** *transf.* The descent of liquid or solid particles or bodies falling in the manner of rain; the collective particles or bodies thus falling. Also *fig.* late ME. **b.** *spec.* A composition used in rockets, producing a shower of bright-coloured sparks 1749.

1. We may fairly expect the formation of rain to be preceded by that of cloud HUXLEY. **2. b.** One rains he died 1895. **3. b.** Set off in a mizzling r. 1853.

Comb.: **r.-band,** a dark band in the solar spectrum, caused by the presence of water-vapour in the atmosphere; **-cap, -coat,** etc. worn as a protection against rain; **-gauge,** an instrument measuring the amount of the rainfall; **-glass,** a barometer; **-goose,** the red-throated diver (*Colymbus septentrionalis*); **-map,** a map showing the distribution of the rainfall over a certain area; **-mark, -pit,** an indentation made in the ground by a raindrop; **-quail,** the Indian and African quail (*Coturnix coromandelicus*), abundant in some parts of India during the rainy season; **-wash,** the effect of rain in washing away earth, etc.; also, the matter thus washed away; **-worm,** the common earthworm. Hence **Rai·nless** *a.* destitute of rain.

Rain (rēn), *v.* [OE. *regnian* (rare), f. *regn* RAIN *sb.*] **I.** *intr.* **1.** *It rains*: Rain falls ME. **2.** Of the Deity, the sky, clouds, etc.: To send or pour down rain OE. **3.** Of rain: To fall ME. **b.** Of tears, immaterial things, etc.: To descend, fall, come, etc. like rain. late ME. **4.** *It rains in*: Rain enters or penetrates. Also *transf.* with other subjects. 1596.

1. It rained very hard DAMPIER. *Prov.* It never rains but it pours. **2.** Heavily the low sky raining Over tower'd Camelot TENNYSON. *fig.* To raine vpon Remembrance with mine Eyes, That it may grow SHAKS. **3.** The raine it raineth every day SHAKS. **b.** Manna also y[t] in desert reynyde 1450. As from a giant's flail, The large blows rain'd TENNYSON.

II. *trans.* **1.** *It rains*: There is a shower of (something falling from above) ME. **2.** To pour down (something falling through the air like rain) ME. **b.** To shed (tears) copiously 1588. **c.** *fig.* To pour down ME. **3.** To bring into a specified condition by raining ME.

1. It rayned fyre and brymstone from heauen COVERDALE *Luke* xvii. 29. *fig. Ant. & Cl.* III. xiii. 85. *To r. cats and dogs* (colloq.): to r. very heavily. **2.** He rained shells and redhot bullets on the city MACAULAY. **b.** His eyes r. tears JOWETT. **c.** Ladies, whose bright eies R. influence MILT.

Ra·in-bird. 1555. [f. RAIN *sb.* + BIRD.] **1.** The green woodpecker, *Gecinus viridis.* **2.** A Jamaican cuckoo 1725.

Rainbow (rē·nbou), *sb.* [OE. *regnboga.*] **1.** A bow or arch exhibiting the prismatic colours in their order, formed in the sky opposite the sun by the reflection, double refraction, and dispersion of the sun's rays in falling drops of rain. Also, a similar arch formed in the spray of cataracts, etc. **2.** *transf.* A brightly coloured arch, ring, etc., resembling a rainbow 1715. **3.** Short for *r.-trout* 1897.

1. I was beaten..into all the colours of the Rainebow SHAKS. *fig.* (cf. *Gen.* ix. 13-16) A new r. of hope 1876. *Lunar r.,* one formed by the moon's rays, rarely seen. *Marine* or *sea r.,* one formed on sea spray. *Secondary* or *supernumerary r.,* a fainter one formed inside or outside the primary by double reflection and double refraction, and exhibiting the spectrum colours in the opposite order to that of the primary. **2.** The peacock sends his heavenly dyes, His rainbows and his starry eyes COWPER.

Comb.: **r. trout,** a Californian species of trout, *Salmo irideus*; **r. wrasse,** a brilliantly coloured labroid fish (*Julis vulgaris* or *Coris Julis*). Hence **Rai·nbow** *v. trans.* to brighten or span with, or as with, a rainbow; to produce like a rainbow.

Rai·ndrop, ra·in-drop. [OE. *regndropa*; see RAIN *sb.* and DROP *sb.*] **1.** A single drop of rain. **2.** The dropping of rain or rain-water. *rare.* late ME.

Rai·nfall. 1848. [f. RAIN *sb.* + FALL *sb.*] **1.** A fall or shower of rain. **2.** The quantity of rain falling in a certain time within a given area, usu. estimated by inches (in depth) per annum 1854.

2. There is one arid region, with a normal r. of less than fifteen inches 1880.

†Rai·n-fowl. 1440. **1. a.** = RAIN-BIRD 1. -1769. **b.** The Mistletoe Thrush -1817. **2.** = RAIN-BIRD 2. -1694.

Rai·n-wa·ter. [OE. *regn-, rēnwæter*; see RAIN and WATER.] Water that falls from the clouds as rain. Also *attrib.*

Rainy (rē·ni), *a.* OE. [f. RAIN *sb.* + -Y [1].] **1.** Of weather or climate: Characterized by rain. **2.** Of periods of time: During or within which rain is falling, or usually falls OE. **b.** fig. *A r. day*: a time of need 1580. **3.** Of places: In which it rains or is raining; subject to rain. late ME. **b.** Of an action: Done in the rain. SHAKS. **4.** Of clouds, mist, etc.: Bringing rain; laden with rain; of the nature of or connected with rain. late ME. **b.** *fig.* Of the eyes: Tearful 1563.

2. The r. season came on DE FOE. **b.** In the Time of Plenty, they lay up for a Rainy-day 1677. Hence **Rai·nily** *adv.* **Rai·niness.**

Raisable (rē·zăb'l), *a.* Also **-eable.** 1644. [f. RAISE *v.* + -ABLE.] Capable of being raised.

Raise (rēz), *sb.*[1] 1538. [f. RAISE *v.*] †1. The act of raising; elevation -1626. **2.** A rising passage or road 1877. **3.** An increase in amount 1891.

Raise (rēz), *sb.*[2] *n. dial.* 1695. [a. ON. *hreysi* cairn.] A pile of stones, a cairn. (Freq. in place-names.)

Raise (rēz), *v.* ME. [a. ON. *reisa* = OE. *rǣran,* causative f. **rais-* ablaut-var. of **rīs-* to RISE.] **I.** To set upright; to make to stand up. **1.** *trans.* To set (a thing) on end; to restore (a fallen thing) to its usual position. Also *fig.* **b.** *spec.* To set up (paste, crust) without the support of a dish 1594. **2.** To lift (a person or animal) and place in a standing posture; to assist (one) to rise from the ground, etc. ME. **b.** *refl.* To rise, get up ME. **3.** *trans.* To restore (a dead person or animal) to life ME. **4.** To cause (a person or animal) to rise or stand up: †a. To make (one) waken or get out of bed ME. **b.** To rouse (a beast or bird) from a lair, retreat, or covert. late ME. **c.** To cause or compel (a person) to rise from a seat 1460. **5.** To rouse (a number of persons, a district, etc.) for the purpose of common action, esp. for attack or defence. late ME. **b.** To stir up, incite, instigate (one or more persons) *to* do something or *to* some feeling 1581. **6.** To rouse up, to give vigour to (the mind, spirit, etc.); to animate, stimulate. late ME. †b. To inspire (a person) *with* courage, hope, etc. -1697. **7.** *To r. the wind*: To cause the wind to blow ME.; hence *fig.* (with ref. to wind as a motive power), to procure money or necessary means 1789.

1. Stones of power By Druids raised in magic hour SCOTT. **b.** Miss Liddy can dance a Jig, r. Paste STEELE. **2.** If you fall you shall nat be reysed for me 1530. **3.** God was able to r. him from the dead 1770. **4. a.** Raising the people at midnight 1781. **b.** This being effected, they r. the Bear 1607. **5.** Danvers undertook to r. the City MACAULAY. **b.** That fixt mind And high disdain..That with the mightiest rais'd me to contend MILT. **6.** His spirits being a little raised with the dram I had given him, he was very cheerful DE FOE.

II. To build up, construct, create, produce, etc. **1.** To lift up and put in position the parts of (a structure); to construct by piling up, building, or fitting together; *spec.* in *U.S.,* to set up the wooden framework of (a house or other building) ME. †b. To found, build up (a scheme, plan, description, etc.) -1802. **c.** To form (a small projection or elevation), to cause (a blister, etc.) to rise or form 1551. **2.** To bring into existence, to produce, beget (offspring). Now *rare.* ME. **b.** To produce a supply of (persons of a certain class); to breed (animals) 1601. **3.** To foster, rear, bring up (a person). Now chiefly *U.S.* 1744. **b.** To rear or bring up (animals) 1767. **c.** To promote the growth of (plants), to grow (fruit, vegetables, flowers, etc.) 1669. **4.** To cause (a person of specified character) to come into existence or appear. late ME. **5.** To produce, bring into existence or action (various natural phenomena or forces; also *fig.*) late ME. **6.** To utter (a cry, etc.) with loud voice; to produce (a loud noise) by shouting or otherwise ME. **b.** Hence simply, to utter or produce (a sound) 1590. **c.** To sing; also, to strike up 1653. **7.** To cause, originate, give rise to, bring about, set going ME. **8. a.** *Law.* To draw up (a letter, summons, etc.), institute (an action or suit), establish (a use) 1632. **b.** To bring up (a question, point, etc.); to bring forward (a difficulty, objection, etc.); to advance (a claim) 1647.

1. Of Parian Stone a Temple will I r. DRYDEN. **2.** God..from him will r. A mightie Nation MILT. **b.** From this one, this single ewe, Full fifty comely sheep I raised WORDSW. **3.** I was raised..among the mountains of the north 1817. **4.** Thi Lord God schal reise a prophete of thi folk WYCLIF *Deut.* xviii. 15. Her gentleness had never raised her an enemy H. WALPOLE. **5.** To r. a storm in a tea-cup 1884. **6. b.** He rais'd a sigh SHAKS. **c.** An old negro..who raised a hymn 1856. **7.** A groundless Report that has been raised, to a Gentleman's Disadvantage ADDISON. Liberty.. Shall r. no feuds for armies to suppress

Cowper. Such manures as r. a fermentation 1765. 8. A use could not be raised without a sufficient consideration Blackstone.

III. To remove to a higher position. 1. To lift as a whole, to put or take higher, to elevate. Also, to hoist (sail, etc.) ME. b. *spec.* To draw or bring up (water, minerals, etc.) to the surface of the ground 1745. c. To turn (the eyes or look) upwards. late ME. 2. *fig.* To promote or advance (a person, people, etc.) to a higher rank, office, or position; to exalt in dignity or power ME. b. To exalt (one's name, state, etc.). *rare.* late ME. c. To extol, laud (*rare*) 1631. 3. *fig.* To elevate (persons) to a higher moral or mental condition ME. b. To elevate (the thoughts, mind, etc.) ME. c. To elevate (a subject, style, diction) 1668. 4. To cause (a spirit) to appear, esp. by means of incantations ME. 5. To make (the voice) heard. late ME. 6. To cause (dust, vapour, smoke, water, etc.) to ascend or rise; to send or force up, to stir up. late ME. 7. *Naut.* a. To come in sight of (another ship, land, a whale, etc.) 1556. b. To give a higher appearance to (a ship, etc.) by coming nearer 1574. 8. To levy (a tax, etc.); to collect (rents or other charges); hence, to bring together, obtain, procure by means of collecting or in any other way ME. b. *transf.* To obtain, procure (advantage, pleasure, praise, etc.) 1633. c. To succeed in producing 1841. 9. To levy, collect, gather, bring together (an army, troops, etc.). late ME. 10. To put an end to (a siege or blockade) by withdrawing the investing forces. late ME. b. To remove, rescind (a prohibition, etc.) 1887. 11. To end (a siege, etc.) by compelling the investing forces to desist or remove 1489. 12. To set in motion (an army or camp) 1470.

1. Then will I r. aloft the Milke-white-Rose Shaks. c. I reiside myn ȝen to the hillis Wyclif *Ps.* cxx. 1. 2. c. Fame that her high worth to r. Seem'd erst so lavish Milt. 3. b. What in me is dark Illumine, what is low r. and support Milt. 4. Phr. *To r. the Devil, Cain, the mischief*, to create trouble, uproar, or confusion. 5. Not a voice was raised in opposition 1868. 6. They doe nothing else but r. a dust 1581. 7. a. The last of June we raised the Antarticke Pole Sir T. Herbert. b. In going to the North, you doe rayse the Pole, and lay the Equinoctiall 1574. 8. The difficulty of raising Mony, for the necessary uses of the Common-wealth Hobbes. 11. He is besieg'd, the Siege that came to r. Drayton.

IV. 1. To increase in height or bulk; to cause to rise up or swell; to give a higher level to 1450. 2. *techn.* a. To bring up (the nap of cloth) by carding with teazles, etc.; to make a nap on (cloth) 1481. b. To cause (dough, bread) to expand and become light, as by the use of yeast. Also *absol.* late ME. c. To give (metal), a rounded form 1846. 3. To increase the amount of, to heighten (rent, taxes, prices, etc.) 1500. b. To increase, add to (one's reputation, interest, credit, etc.) 1654. c. *Math.* To increase (a number or quantity) by multiplication into itself 1706. 4. To increase the value, price, or rate of 1535. 5. To increase the degree, intensity, or force of (the voice, sensations, colours, the pulse, etc.) 1638.

3. This making of Christians will r. the price of Hogs Shaks. 4. *To raise the market*, to charge a higher price.

†V. *intr.* To rise, in various senses -1761.

Raised (rēⁱzd), *ppl. a.* 1582. In various senses of Raise *v.*

R. pie, a pie having a 'raised' crust (see prec. I. 1 b). *R. beach*, a former beach, now situated above sea-level. *R. upon* (*Naut.*), having a framework added to increase the height of the sides.

Raisin (rēⁱ·z'n). ME. [a. OF. *raiz-, razin*, etc. (F. *raisin*) :—L. *racemum* Raceme.] †1. A cluster of grapes; a grape -1669. 2. A grape partially dried, either in the sun or artificially. (Chiefly *pl.*) ME. b. *Raisins of the sun*, sun-dried grapes 1544.

Raising (rēⁱ·ziŋ), *vbl. sb.* ME. [-ing [1].] 1. The action of Raise *v.*; *spec.* in *Curling*, driving a partner's stone into one of the circles round the tee. b. With *a* and *pl.* An instance of this; *spec.* in *U.S.*, a house-raising. late ME. 2. Anything that is raised; a raised place 1572. 3. A crop raised 1869.

Comb.: r.-bee (*U.S.*), a gathering of neighbours to give assistance in raising the framework of a house, etc.; -hammer, a hammer used in giving metal a rounded form; -room, a room where cloth is raised.

Rai·sing-piece. 1548. [f. Rasen, assoc. with prec.] A wall-plate. So **Rai·sing-plate.**

‖ **Raison d'être** (rēzoṅ dētr). 1867. [F.] Rational ground for existence.

‖ **Raisonné** (rēzone), *a.* 1777. [F., pa. pple. of *raisonner* to reason, f. *raison* Reason.] Reasoned out, logical or systematical.

Catalogue r., a catalogue (of books, pictures, etc.) arranged according to subjects, and giving information beyond mere names or titles.

‖ **Raj** (rādʒ). 1800. [Hindī *rāj*; cf. next.] Sovereignty, rule; kingdom.

‖ **Raja, rajah** (rā·dʒā). 1555. [Hindī *rājā*, Skr. *rāja-* king, f. *rāj* to reign, rule; cogn. w. L. *rex, regis*, OIr. *rī, rīg* king.] Orig. the title given in India to a king or prince; later extended to petty chiefs or dignitaries (as Zemindars) or conferred as a title of nobility on Hindus, and adopted as the usual designation of Malay and Javanese rulers or chiefs. Hence **Ra·jahship**, the territory, rank, or power of a r.; also as a title.

‖ **Rajpoot, rajput** (rā·dʒpūt). 1598. [Hindī *rājpūt*, f. Skr. *rāja-* king + *putrá* son.] A member of a Hindu tribe or class, claiming descent from the original Kshatriyas and distinguished by its military spirit.

Rake (rēⁱk), *sb.*[1] [OE. *raca* m., *racu* fem., f. root **rek-* to gather, heap up.] 1. An implement, consisting of a bar fixed across a long handle and fitted with teeth pointing downwards, used for drawing together hay, grass, or the like, or for breaking up, levelling, or smoothing the surface of the ground (a *hand-rake*). Also, a large implement of the same character, mounted on wheels and drawn by a horse (a *horse-rake*), or one of the bars with teeth in a tedding-machine. b. *transf.* A very lean person 1582. 2. A similar implement, used for various purposes, sometimes having a flat blade in place of the bar with teeth 1530. b. A kind of rasp or scraper 1727.

1. Phr. *As lean* (also *thin*, †*rank*) *as a r.* b. Let vs reuenge this with our Pikes, ere we become Rakes Shaks.

Rake (rēⁱk), *sb.*[2] *Sc.* and *n. dial.* late ME. [a. ON. *rák* stripe, streak, f. ablaut-var. of *rek-* to drive.] 1. A way, path. 2. Course or path, *esp.* of cattle in pasturing; hence, pasture-ground, right of pasture 1640. 3. A leading vein of ore, having a more or less perpendicular lie. Also *r.-vein.* 1556. 4. A rut, groove 1691.

Rake (rēⁱk), *sb.*[3] 1626. [perh. f. Rake *v.*[3]] 1. *Naut.* a. The projection of the upper part of a ship's hull at stem and stern beyond the corresponding extremities of the keel (dist. as *forerake* and *sternrake*). b. The deviation (usu. towards the stern) of a ship's masts from a perpendicular to the keel 1815. 2. *transf.* The inclination of any object from the perpendicular or to the horizontal; slope 1802.

2. The arrangement of the plants follows the r. of the roof 1881.

Rake (rēⁱk), *sb.*[4] 1653. [abbrev. of Rake-hell.] A man of loose habits and immoral character; an idle dissipated man of fashion. b. A woman of like character 1712.

An old r. who has survived himself is the most pitiable object in creation 1836.

Rake (rēⁱk), *v.*[1] ME. [a. ON. *raka* to scrape, shave, etc., f. root **rak-*; see Rake *sb.*[1]] I. 1. To draw together, collect, gather (scattered objects) with, or as with, a rake. b. So with *together* 1550. 2. To draw or drag in a specified direction with, or as with, a rake. late ME. b. With *up*. Used *esp.* of searching for and bringing forward all that can be said against a person 1581.

1. Her exceeding greedines in raking mony 1598. 2. All the bad things..which Prynne could pick and r. out of Histories 1691. To see that your fire was safely raked out at night 1853. b. The old charges.. were again raked up against him Freeman.

II. †1. To cover with, or bury under, something brought together with, or as with, a rake -1786. 2. *spec.* To cover (a fire) with ashes or small coal in order to keep it in without active burning. Also with *up*. Now *dial.* late ME.

2. To work by Night, and r. the Winter Fire Dryden.

III. 1. To go over with a rake, so as to make clean, smooth, etc., or to find something. Also with *up, over.* 1523. b. *transf.* To search, etc., as with a rake 1618. 2. To scratch or scrape. Also *intr.* or *absol.* 1609. 3. *Farriery.* To clean (a costive horse or its fundament) from ordure by scraping with the hand 1575. 4. *Mil.* and *Naut.* To sweep or traverse with shot; to enfilade; *spec.* to send shot along (a ship) from stem to stern (in full *to r. fore and aft*) 1630. b. To command, overlook 1842. c. To sweep with the eyes; to look all over 1848. d. *Hawking.* Of a hawk: To strike (the game) in the air. Also *to r. off.* 1773. 5. *Dyeing.* To stir or mix (liquor) with a rake 1816.

1. R. the surface perfectly level 1856. b. The statesman rakes the town to find a plot Swift. Phr. †*To r. hell*; Suche a feloe as a manne should r. helle for Udall. 2. Sand raked his sores from heel to pate M. Arnold. *absol.* Thou..rakest like a Wolfe Burton. 4. Captain Peard..lay across his hawse, and raked him with several broadsides Nelson. *transf.* [Pictures hung] with their sides to the light, so that it 'rakes' them Ruskin. c. George took the glass again and raked the vessel Thackeray.

IV. *intr.* or *absol.* 1. To use a rake; to scrape with the fingers or similar means; to make search with, or as with, a rake 1440. b. *fig.* To make search; to poke *into* 1637. 2. To move *on* or *over* like, or with the effect of, a rake; to scrape *against* 1598. 3. To come *up* when raked (*rare*) 1778.

1. The Cock..raked in golden barley Tennyson. b. To r. into the histories of former ages Burke.

Rake (rēⁱk), *v.*[2] [OE. *racian*, perh. = Sw. *raka* to run, rush, slip.] 1. *intr.* To proceed, make one's way; to walk, stroll, wander. Now *dial.* 2. *spec.* a. Of hawks: To fly along after the game; also = *to r. out* (*off, away*), to fly wide of (or away from) the game; sometimes said of the game itself 1575. b. Of hunting dogs: To run with their noses close to the ground 1819.

Rake (rēⁱk), *v.*[3] 1627. [Origin obsc.] 1. *intr.* a. Of a ship, its hull, timbers, etc.: To have a rake at stem or stern. b. Of masts or funnels: To incline from the perpendicular 1691. 2. *trans.* To cause to incline. In *pa. pple.* 1842.

1. Two lines of masts, one raking one way, the other the other 1883.

Rake (rēⁱk), *v.*[4] 1700. [f. Rake *sb.*[4]] *intr.* To be a rake; to live a dissipated life.

Rake-hell (rēⁱ·khel). Now *arch.* 1547. [See Rake *v.*[1] III. 1. b.] 1. A thorough scoundrel or rascal; an utterly immoral or dissolute person; a vile debauchee or rake 1554. 2. *attrib.* or as *adj.* = Rakehelly *a.*

1. Al the rake-hels and loose vagabonds in a countrey 1603.

Rakehelly (rēⁱ·khe:li), *a.* and *sb.* 1579. [f. prec. + -y [1].] 1. Of persons. Of the nature of, or resembling, a rakehell or rakehells. 2. Characteristic of rakehells 1594. B. *sb.* = prec. 1. 1762.

Raker [1] (rēⁱ·kəɹ). late ME. [f. Rake *v.*[1]] 1. One who rakes. Also with *after, up.* 1563. 2. *spec.* A scavenger, street-cleaner. Now *arch.* late ME. 3. An implement for raking. b. *spec.* A gill-raker (see Gill *sb.*[1]). 1727.

Raker [2] (rēⁱ·kəɹ). *colloq.* 1876. [f. Rake *v.*[2]] An extremely fast pace.

Rakery (rēⁱ·kəri). Now *rare.* 1728. [f. Rake *sb.*[4] + -ery.] Rakish conduct; debauchery, dissoluteness; social excitement.

He..instructed his Lordship in all the r. and intrigues of the lewd town North.

Rakeshame (rēⁱ·k,ʃēⁱm). Now *rare.* 1599. [f. Rake *v.*[1] + Shame *sb.* Cf. Rakehell.] One who covers himself with shame; an ill-behaved, disorderly, or dissolute fellow.

Rakish (rēⁱ·kiʃ), *a.*[1] 1706. [f. Rake *sb.*[4] + -ish.] 1. Having the character, appearance, or manners, of a rake. 2. Characteristic of, appropriate to, a rake 1706.

1. A..r. youngster wild from school Byron. 2. R. talk 1722. The r. swagger..of the coxcombs Kingsley. Hence **Ra·kish-ly** *adv.*, -ness.

Rakish (rēⁱ·kiʃ), *a.*[2] 1824. [Origin obsc.] 1. *Naut.* Of a ship: Having an appearance indicative of smartness and fast sailing, freq. with suggestion of piratical character. 2. Of a hawk's wings: Smart-looking 1855.

‖ **Râle** (rāl). 1829. [F., vbl. sb. f. *râler*; etym. unkn.] *Path.* An abnormal sound additional to that of respiration, heard on auscultation of the lungs when these are not perfectly healthy.

||**Rallentando** (rælěntæ·ndo͡u). 1800. [It., pres. pple. of *rallentare*.] *Mus.* A direction indicating that a passage is to be played or sung in a time growing gradually slower.

Ralli-car, -cart. 1890. A form of light two-wheeled driving-trap for four persons, named after the first purchaser.

Ralline (ræ·ləin), *a.* 1885. [f. mod.L. *rallus* RAIL *sb.*³ + -INE ¹.] *Ornith.* Pertaining to, related to, or resembling the rail, or the family *Rallidæ*.

Rally (ræ·li), *sb.*¹ 1651. [f. RALLY *v.*¹] 1. A rapid reunion for concentrated effort, *esp.* of an army after repulse or disorganization. b. *Mil.* The signal for rallying 1897. 2. A quick recovery from a state of exhaustion, a renewal of energy, *esp.* a (temporary) recovery of strength during illness 1826. 3. a. *Theatr.* A general mêlée, scramble, or chase, of the characters in a pantomime 1870. b. *U.S. colloq.* A political mass-meeting 1878. 4. a. *Boxing.* A separate bout 1825. b. *Lawn Tennis.* The series of strokes made by both players between the service and failure to return the ball 1887.

1. They yielded at last..with frequent rallies, and sullen submission JOHNSON. 2. I made a r. to-day and wrote four pages SCOTT.

Rally (ræ·li), *sb.*² 1832. [f. RALLY *v.*²] A piece of rallying or banter.

Rally (ræ·li), *v.*¹ 1603. [ad. F. *rallier*, f. *re-* + *allier* to ALLY. See also RELY.] I. *trans.* 1. To reassemble, bring together again (an army or company which has been, or is, scattered) 1604. 2. To collect (persons) to one's assistance, or for concentrated action 1603. 3. To concentrate or revive (a faculty, etc.) by a strong effort of the will 1667. b. To pull together, revive, rouse, stimulate (a person or animal) 1624.

1. Their troops, being rallied by the dexterity of their generals, came on again to the charge DE FOE. 2. Even this blow failed to r. the Country round the Queen 1874. 3. She rallied her drooping spirits 1791.

II. *intr.* 1. To come together again, to reassemble, *esp.* in order to renew the conflict; to return in a body to the fray or contest 1655. b. Of a single person: To return and renew the attack; *spec.* in *Boxing* 1813. 2. Of persons: To come together in a body; to unite for a common purpose, *esp.* to assist or support some one. Usu. const. *round.* 1818. b. Const. *to.* (Also said of a single person.) 1879. 3. To revive, recover, acquire or assume fresh vigour or energy 1840. b. To recover in part from an illness 1853.

1. The battalions rallied and came boldly on to charge a second time DE FOE. 2. b. Mr. Gladstone ..rallied to the support of the Government 1879. 3. At last his flagging powers rallied 1871. Hence **Ra·llying** *vbl. sb.*, often *attrib.*, as *rallying cry, point*, etc.

Rally (ræ·li), *v.*² 1665. [ad. F. *railler*; origin obsc.] 1. *trans.* To treat or assail with banter, pleasantry, or good-humoured ridicule; to make fun or game of. †2. *absol.* or *intr.* To employ banter or pleasantry against one. Also const. *at, with* (a person), *upon* (a thing). -1792.

1. They rally'd next Vanessa's dress SWIFT. He rallied Simonides for his absurdity 1770. 2. I see Madam you are disposed to r. 1676.

Ralstonite (rǭ·lstənəit). 1875. [f. name of J. G. *Ralston* its discoverer; see -ITE.] *Min.* A hydrated aluminium fluoride containing traces of sodium and calcium.

Ram (ræm), *sb.*¹ [OE. *ram(m*, perh. related to ON. *rammr* strong.] 1. A male sheep; in domestication, one kept for breeding purposes, a tup. 2. *Astron.* (with cap.) The zodiacal sign ARIES OE. 3. = BATTERING-RAM OE. b. *Naut.* A solid point or beak projecting from the bows of a war-vessel, and enabling it to ram and batter in the sides of an opponent 1865. c. *Naut.* A battleship fitted with a ram 1862. 4. The weight of a pile-driving machine; a monkey 1440. b. A steam-hammer used in setting-up a bloom of metal 1875. c. A paviour's RAMMER 1885. 5. a. An automatic water-raising machine, in which the raising power is supplied by the concussion of a descending body of water in a pipe 1808. b. The piston of the large cylinder of a hydrostatic press 1816. c. A hydraulic lifting-machine 1861. d. The plunger of a force-pump 1883. 3. *fig.* The iron and rock, Which tryes, and counterstands the shock, And ramme of time HERRICK.

Ram, *sb.*² 1723. [Cf. RAM-LINE.] *Naut.* Length 'over all' of a boat.

Ram (ræm), *v.* [ME. *rammen*, perh. f. RAM *sb.*¹] 1. *absol.* To beat down earth with a heavy implement, so as to make it hard and firm. b. *trans.* To beat down (earth) thus 1596. c. To fix or make (a thing) firm by ramming the surrounding soil 1565. 2. To force or drive *down* or *in* by heavy blows; to drive (piles, etc.) *into* the soil in this way 1519. b. To force (a charge) into a fire-arm by means of a ramrod 1598. c. To cram, stuff, thrust (a person or thing) *into* something 1582. d. To push firmly *down*; to pen *up* closely 1602. 3. To force in or compress the charge or contents of (a gun, etc.) by ramming 1581. b. To cram or stuff hard *with* something 1590. 4. To stop, stuff, or block *up* 1548. 5. To dash violently against, to strike with great force; esp. *Naut.* to strike (a ship) with the ram 1864. 6. To dash, force, or drive (one thing *on, at,* or *into* another) 1715.

2. We r. some concrete between the piles 1840. d. He rams his old hat down on his head 1887. 5. The Tennessee was rammed by the Hartford 1864. 6. Ramming his horse well at it, he gets through 1858.

||**Ramadan** (ræmădā·n), **ramazan** (-zā·n). 1599. [a. Arab. *ramaḍān* (hence Turk. and Pers. *ramazān*), f. *ramaḍa* to be heated or hot.] The ninth month of the Mohammedan year, rigidly observed as a thirty days' fast, during the hours of daylight, by all Mohammedans.

Ramage (ræ·mědʒ), *sb. arch.* 1616. [a. F., :—late L. **ramaticum*, f. *ramus* RAMUS; see -AGE.] 1. The collective branches of trees 1656. †2. The song or cry of birds -1693.

†**Ra·mage**, *a.* ME. [a. OF., :—late L. **ramaticus*; see prec.] 1. Of hawks: Having left the nest, and begun to fly from branch to branch; hence, wild, untamed, shy. Also *transf.* of persons. -1773. 2. Of animals: Wild, untamed, unruly, violent -1639.

Ramal (rēⁱ·măl), *a.* 1856. [f. L. *ramus* branch.] 1. *Bot.* Of or belonging to a branch; growing on or out of a branch. 2. *Anat.* and *Zool.* Pertaining to, or of the character of, a ramus 1891.

Ramble (ræ·mb'l), *sb.*¹ 1654. [f. the vb.] 1. An act of rambling; a walk (†excursion or journey) without definite route, for pleasure or recreation. 2. Rambling, incoherence 1716.

Ra·mble, *sb.*² 1851. [Cf. Sw. *ramla* to fall down.] *Coal-mining.* A thin bed of shale lying above a coal-seam, which falls down as the coal is taken out, and requires to be separated from it.

Ramble (ræ·mb'l), *v.* 1620. [Origin unkn.] 1. *intr.* To wander, travel (now usu. to walk) about from place to place without definite aim or direction. b. *fig.* with ref. to mental pursuits or studies 1650. 2. To wander in discourse; to write or talk incoherently or without natural sequence of ideas 1640.

1. I go tomorrow towards Italy, where I will r. for two or three months 1672. The stream..As through the glen it rambles WORDSW. 2. He rambled on in a childish sort of way COBBETT. Hence **Ra·mbler**, one who rambles; *spec.* a rose which straggles or climbs freely, esp. the *Crimson R.*

Rambling (ræ·mbliŋ), *ppl. a.* 1623. [f. prec. + -ING ².] That rambles, in various senses. 1. Wandering, moving about, straying from place to place. b. Of life, etc.: Characterized by wandering 1699. 2. Of the thoughts, mind, speech, etc.: Straying from one subject to another, unsettled 1635. b. Of persons: Given to wandering in thought or discourse 1693. 3. Of plants: Straggling, spreading or climbing freely and irregularly 1728. 4. Having a straggling irregular form or plan 1849.

1. A kind of r. rheumatism 1741. b. Life's r. journey COWPER. 2. A long r. ghost story 1837. 3. The r. briar CRABBE. 4. [The house] was antique, r., and incommodious C. BRONTË. Hence **Ra·mblingly** *adv.*, **-ness.**

Rambunctious (ræmbʋ·ŋkʃəs), *a. U.S. slang.* 1854. Wild or unruly of behaviour.

Rambutan, -bootan (ræmbū·tăn). 1707. [a. Malay *rambūtan*, f. *rambut* hair, in allusion to its villose covering.] The fruit of *Nephelium lappaceum*, a tree of the Malay archipelago, having a reddish coat, covered with soft spines or hairs, and pulp of a subacid flavour.

Ra·m-cat. Now *dial.* 1672. [f. RAM *sb.*¹] A male cat.

Rame (rēⁱm). *rare.* 1578. [a. F. :—L. *ramus* branch.] A branch of a tree or shrub; also *transf.* of a nerve, etc.

Rameal (rēⁱ·mĭăl), *a. rare.* 1852. [a. F. *raméal*, f. *rame* branch.] *Bot.* = RAMAL.

Ramean (rēⁱ·mĭăn), *a.* and *sb.* 1710. [f. *Ramus* (see RAMIST) + -(E)AN.] A. *adj.* Belonging to, connected with, Ramus. B. *sb.* A Ramist.

Ramekin, ramequin (ræ·mĕkin). 1706. [ad. F. *ramequin*; etym. obsc.] A small quantity of cheese, with bread-crumbs, eggs, etc., usu. baked and served in a special mould. Chiefly *pl.*

Ramentaceous (ræmĕntēⁱ·ʃəs), *a.* 1816. [f. RAMENTUM + -ACEOUS.] *Bot.* 1. Covered with ramenta. 2. Resembling ramenta 1861.

||**Ramentum** (rămе·ntŏm). Chiefly in pl. ramenta. 1662. [L., f. *radere*; see RASE *v.*¹] 1. A fragment scraped off; †an atom, mote. 2. *Bot.* A thin membraneous scale formed on the surface of leaves and stalks 1819.

Rameous (rēⁱ·mĭəs), *a.* 1760. [f. L. *ramus* branch + -EOUS.] *Bot.* Of or belonging to branches.

Ramessid (ræ·mĕsid), **-ide** (-əid). 1854. [ad. Gr. *Ῥαμεσσίδης, f. *Ῥαμέσσης Rameses + -ίδης, patronymic suffix.] A member of the Egyptian royal family during the 19th and 20th dynasties. Also *attrib.* or as *adj.*

Ramie (ræ·mi). Also **ramee.** 1888. [Malay *rāmī*.] a. A Chinese and East Indian plant of the nettle family, *Bœhmeria nivea*, called also *Rhea* and *grass-cloth plant.* b. The fine fibre of this plant, extensively employed in weaving.

Ramiferous (rămi·ferəs), *a. rare.* 1819. [f. L. *ram-us* + -(I)FEROUS.] Bearing branches.

Ramification (ræ:mifikēⁱ·ʃən). 1677. [f. med.L. *ramificare* RAMIFY, perh. after F.] 1. The action or process of ramifying 1760. b. The branches of a tree collectively 1821. 2. A subdivision or single part of a complex structure analogous to the branches of a tree, *esp.* of veins, arteries, and other parts in animals and plants, and of rivers 1677. b. *transf.* Of immaterial things 1755.

2. b. One of the ramifications of the Whig plot MACAULAY.

Ramiform (ræ·mifǭɹm), *a.* 1822. [f. L. *ramus* branch + -FORM.] Branch-like; ramified.

Ramify (ræ·mifəi), *v.* 1541. [ad. F. *ramifier*, ad. med.L. *ramificare*, f. *ramus* branch; see -FY.] 1. *intr.* Of trees and plants or their parts: To form branches, to branch out, extend in the form of branches 1576. 2. To extend or spread in a number of subdivisions or offshoots analogous to branches; esp. *Anat.* of veins, nerves, etc. 1578. 3. To break up, divide, into branches or analogous parts 1541. 4. *trans.* To cause to shoot out, spread, or extend after the manner of branches 1565. 5. To separate into branches or analogous divisions. Also *absol.* 1800.

1. When they [asparagus plants] are older, and begin to r., they lose this Quality 1735. 2. Dissent had grown and spread and ramified throughout the land 1861. 3. The road..soon began to r. 1856. 4. Railways..may be ramified over a whole country 1825.

Ramillie (ræ·mili). *Obs.* exc. *Hist.* 1740. [From *Ramillies* in Belgium, the scene of Marlborough's victory in 1706.] 1. *attrib.* Applied a. to a wig having a long plait behind tied with a bow at top and bottom (so also with *tail*); b. to a method of cocking the hat. 2. *absol.* A Ramillie wig or tail 1752.

2. A head of fine flaxen hair..braided into a r. 1752.

Ramism (rēⁱ·miz'm). 1710. [f. *Ramus* (see next).] The logical system of Ramus.

Ramist (rēⁱ·mist), *sb.* (and *a.*). 1605. [f. the name of *Ramus* (Pierre de la Ramée, 1515–1572) + -IST.] A. *sb.* A follower of Ramus, as the author of a system of logic opposed in various respects to the Aristotelian. B. *attrib.*

or as *adj.* Of, pertaining to, characteristic of, Ramists or Ramism 1863.

Ra·m-ja·m, *adv. dial.* and *slang.* 1879. [f. RAM *v.* + JAM *v.*] *R. full,* crammed full.

Ram-line. 1664. [Cf. RAM *sb.*[2]] *Naut.* A line used to gain a straight middle-line upon a tree or mast.

Rammer (ræ·məɹ). 1497. [f. RAM *v.*] **1.** An instrument consisting of a heavy piece of wood held upright, for ramming or beating down earth, or forcing stones into the ground. **b.** A similar implement used for other purposes; a pestle or stamp 1643. **2.** A cylindrical block of wood fixed at the end of a staff, used to drive home the charge of a cannon; †the ramrod of a fire-arm 1497. **b.** A ramming instrument used in chemical experiments, or in blasting operations 1660. **3.** A pile-driver, or similar device 1688. **4.** One engaged in ramming earth 1876.

Rammish (ræ·miʃ), *a.* Now *dial.* late ME [app. f. RAM *sb.*[1]] Rank, strong; having a rank smell or taste.

Hir sauour is so rammyssh and so hoot CHAUCER. Hence **Ra·mmish-ly** *adv.*, **-ness.**

Rammy (ræ·mi), *a.* Now chiefly *n. dial.* 1607. [f. RAM *sb.*[1] + -Y [1].] Characteristic of, resembling (that of) a ram; *esp.* = prec.

Ramoon (rămū·n). Also **ramon.** 1756. [Sp. *ramon,* f. *ramo* branch.] The tops and leaves of a W. Indian and Central Amer. tree (*Trophis Americana*), used as fodder for cattle. Chiefly in comb. *r.-tree.*

Ramose (rămōu·s), *a.* 1689. [ad. L. *ramosus*; see RAMUS and -OSE.] = next **1.** Hence **Ramo·sely** *adv.*

Ramous (rē¹·məs), *a.* Now *rare.* 1562. [ad. L. *ramosus*; see prec.] **1.** Branching, as plants or plant-like forms. **b.** Applied (after ancient physics) to the particles of viscous or rigid bodies 1674. **2.** Belonging to, characteristic of, branches 1813.

†**Ramp,** *sb.*[1] 1440. [perh. f. RAMP *v.*[1] 5.] A bold, vulgar, ill-behaved woman or girl –1728.

Ramp (ræmp), *sb.*[2] 1671. [f. RAMP *v.*[1]] The act of ramping.

The bold Ascalonite Fled from his Lion r. MILT.

Ramp, *sb.*[3] *slang.* 1888. [f. RAMP *v.*[2] 2.] A swindle, esp. one depending upon an artificial boom in prices 1922.

A Christmas ramp in food prices 1922.

Ramp (ræmp), *sb.*[4] 1725. [a. F. *rampe,* f. *ramper* RAMP *v.*[1]] **1.** A slope; an inclined plane connecting two different levels, *esp.* in fortifications, or at the end of a railway station platform 1779. **2.** The difference in level between the abutments of a rampant arch 1725. **3. a.** Part of the handrail of a stair, having a concave or upward bend (freq. continued in a knee or convex bend), as at a landing 1778. **b.** A slanting (straight or curved) shoulder connecting two levels of the coping of a wall. Also, the sloping part of a stair parapet. 1842.

Ramp (ræmp), *v.*[1] ME. [a. OF. *ramper* to creep, crawl, climb; origin unkn.] †**1.** *intr.* To creep or crawl on the ground (*rare*) –1594. **2.** To climb, scramble. Now *dial.* 1523. **b.** Of plants: To climb (*up* or *upon* some support). Now chiefly *dial.* 1597. **c.** Of non-climbing plants: To grow rankly, to shoot up rapidly. Now *dial.* 1607. **3.** Of beasts (esp. in *Her.*): To rear or stand on the hind legs, as if in the act of climbing; to raise the fore-paws in the air; hence, to assume, or to be in, a threatening posture. (Chiefly said of lions.) Also of persons: To raise, or gesticulate with, the arms; †to clutch wildly *at.* ME. **4.** Of persons: To storm or rage with violent gestures; to act in a furious or threatening manner. Also *transf.* late ME. †**5.** To go about in a loose, immodest way –1611. **b.** = ROMP *v.* Now *dial.* 1657. **6.** To bound, rush, or range about in a wild or excited manner 1627. **b.** To sail swiftly, to scud 1872. **7.** *Arch.* Of a wall: To ascend or descend from one level to another 1855. **8.** *trans. Mil.* and *Arch.* To furnish with a ramp, to build with ramps 1848.

2. b. Ramping upon Trees, Shrubs, Hedges or Poles, they mount up to a great height RAY. **3.** Their bridles they would champ, And trampling the fine element would fiercely r. SPENSER. **4.** By this time the long dormant Usurer ramps for the payment of his money FULLER.

Ramp (ræmp), *v.*[2] 1567. [Origin obsc.] †**1.** *trans.* To snatch, tear, pluck –1633. **2.** *slang.* To rob or swindle; *spec.* to force (one) to pay a pretended bet 1812.

Rampage (ræmpē¹·dʒ), *sb.* 1861. [f. next.] A state of excitement or violent passion; the act of behaving or rushing about in a reckless or riotous fashion; esp. in phr. *on the r.*

Rampage (ræmpē¹·dʒ), *v.* 1715. [Orig. Sc., of obsc. origin.] **1.** *intr.* To behave violently or furiously; to storm, rage wildly. **2.** To go about in an excited, furious, or violent manner; to rush wildly hither and thither 1808.

Rampageous (ræmpē¹·dʒəs), *a.* 1822. Also occas. **-acious.** [f. RAMPAGE *sb.* + -OUS.] **1.** Violent; unruly; boisterous. **2.** *transf.* Glaring, outrageous 1889.

1. The primitive ages of a r. antiquity GALT. Hence **Rampa·geous-ly** *adv.*, **-ness.**

†**Rampa·llion.** 1593. [perh. based on RAMP *v.*[1] Cf. *rapscallion.*] A ruffian, villain, scoundrel; occas. of a woman –1822.

Rampancy (ræ·mpănsi). 1664. [f. next; see -ANCY.] The fact or condition of being rampant.

Rampant (ræ·mpănt), *a.* late ME. [a. F. *rampant,* pres. pple. of *ramper* RAMP *v.*[1]] **1.** Of beasts, esp. lions: Rearing or standing with the fore-paws in the air. **b.** *spec.* in *Her.* 'Standing on the Sinister hind-leg, with both forelegs elevated, the Dexter above the Sinister, and the head in profile' (Cussans). late ME. **c.** Given to ramping; of a fierce disposition. late ME. **d.** Exhibiting fierceness or high spirits by ramping or similar movements. Also const. *with.* 1529. **2.** *transf.* **a.** Of persons: Violent and extravagant in action, opinion, etc. 1628. **b.** Of things: Unchecked, unrestrained, aggressive, etc. 1619. †**3.** Lustful; vicious –1812. **4.** Of plants or their growth: Rank, luxurious 1733. **5.** *Arch.* Of an arch or vault: Having the abutments or springing lines on different levels 1725.

1. The Tawnie Lion..R. shakes his Brinded main MILT. **b.** Lillies, and Lions R., and Spread Eagles in Fields d'Or COWLEY. **2. a.** The Whiggs are r., and thinke to carry all before them 1709. **b.** It grieved him to see ignorance and impiety so r. FULLER. Hence **Ra·mpantly** *adv.*

Rampart (ræ·mpaɹt), *sb.* 1583. [ad. F. *rempart, rampart,* f. *remparer* RAMPIRE *v.*] *Fortif.* A mound of earth raised for the defence of a place, capable of resisting cannon-shot, wide enough on the top for the passage of troops, guns, etc., and usu. surmounted by a stone parapet.

This daie was begunne a R., at Northe newe Gate 1583. *transf.* That had the waters round about it, whose r. was the sea *Nahum* iii. 8. So **Ra·mpart** *v. trans.* to fortify or surround (as) with a r. 1557.

Rampion (ræ·mpiən). 1573. [Cf. F. *raiponce,* It. *rap-, ramponzolo.*] **1.** A species of bellflower, *Campanula rapunculus,* of which the white tuberous roots are sometimes used as a salad. **2.** A plant of the genus *Phyteuma* 1760. †**3.** The Lobelia –1760.

Rampire, -pier (ræ·mpəiəɹ), *sb.* Now *arch.* 1548. [a. obs. F. *rampar,* var. †*rempart* RAMPART.] **1.** = RAMPART. †**b.** A dam, barrier –1764. **2.** *transf.* and *fig.* A thing or person resembling or comparable to a rampart 1567.

1. Buttress, and rampire's circling bound SCOTT. **2.** The son of Thetis, r. of our hosts DRYDEN.

Rampire, -pier (ræ·mpəiəɹ), *v.* Now *arch.* 1550. [a. F. *remparer* to fortify, etc., f. *re-* RE- + *emparer* to take possession of, f. L. *ante* + *parare.*] †**1.** *trans.* To strengthen (a bulwark, gate, etc.) against attack; to block *up* (a gate) for this purpose, *esp.* by piling earth behind it; to close *up* (an opening) –1709. **2.** To fortify, strengthen, or protect (a place), *esp.* by a rampart 1550.

2. R. with abundant power Long Alba 1855.

Ram-rod (ræ·mrǫd). 1797. [f. RAM *v.* + ROD.] A rod used for ramming down the charge of a muzzle-loading fire-arm.

Ramshackle (ræ·mʃæk'l), *a.* 1830. [Later var. of next.] **1.** Loose and shaky; rickety, crazy, tumble-down. **2.** Of persons, actions, etc.: Unsteady, irregular, disorderly, rude. (Chiefly *dial.*) 1855.

1. A huddle of r. lath-and-plaster houses 1865. Hence **Ra·mshackle** *v. trans.* to 'rattle up'.

Ramshackled (ræ·mʃæk'ld), *ppl. a.* 1675. [perh. f. obs. *ram-, ranshackle* to RANSACK, as if = 'wrecked or destroyed by plundering'.] = prec. **1.**

Ram's-horn. ME. [f. RAM *sb.*[1]] **1.** The horn of a ram; the material of this. †**2.** An ammonite or nautilus (*Nautilus spirula*) –1798. **3.** A vessel in which fish are washed 1809.

Ramson (ræ·msən). [OE. *hramsan,* pl. of *hramsa, -se* wild garlic, but in later use a sing., with pl. *ramsons.*] The broad-leaved garlic, *Allium ursinum*; the bulbous root of this plant, used as a relish. Chiefly in *pl.*

Ramulose (ræ·miŭlōᵘs), *a.* 1753. [ad. L. *ramulosus*; see next and -OSE.] *Bot.* and *Zool.* Characterized by ramuli. So **Ra·mulous** *a.*

‖**Ramulus** (ræ·miŭlŏs). Pl. **-li** (-ləi). 1783. [L., dim. of *ramus.*] *Bot.* and *Anat.* A small branch or ramus.

‖**Ramus** (rē¹·mŏs). Pl. **-mi** (-məi). 1803. [L., = branch] **1.** *Anat.* A process of a bone, *esp.* of the ischium and pubes, and of the jawbone. **2.** *Ornith.* = BARB *sb.*[1] 6. 1882.

Ramuscule (rămʊ·skiŭl). 1831. [ad. late L. *ramusculus,* dim. of *ramus* RAMUS; see -CULE.] *Biol.* A small branch.

Ran (ræn). 1794. [Origin unkn.] A certain length of twine.

Ran, pa. t. and obs. pa. pple. of RUN *v.*

Rance (rɑns), *sb.*[1] 1598. [prob. of F. origin.] A kind of marble, of a red colour varied with veins and spots of blue and white.

Rance, ranse (ræns), *sb.*[2] Chiefly *Sc.* 1808. [perh. a. F. *ranche* pole, bar, etc.] A bar or baton; a prop or support.

Ranch (rɑntʃ, rɑnʃ), *sb. U.S.* 1808. [Anglicized f. RANCHO.] **1.** A hut or house in the country. **2.** A cattle-breeding establishment, farm, or estate. Also, the people employed or living on this. 1872. Hence **Ranch** *v.*[1] *intr.* to conduct a r. (whence **Ra·ncher,** a ranchman; **Ra·nching,** stock-raising or cattle-breeding on a r.). **Ra·nchman,** the owner of a r.; a man employed on a r.

Ranch (rɑnʃ), *v.*[2] *Obs.* exc. *dial.* late ME. [Nasalized f. RACE *v.*[2]] *trans.* To tear, cut, scratch, etc.

‖**Ranchero** (rantʃē·ro). 1840. [Sp., f. *rancho* RANCHO.] One employed on a ranch as herdsman or overseer; the owner of a ranch; a ranchman.

‖**Rancho** (rɑ·ntʃo). 1648. [Sp., = a mess, a company of persons who eat together.] **1.** In Spanish America: A rudely-built house, a hut or hovel; also, a collection of huts, a hamlet or village 1845. **b.** *spec.* A hut or shed, or a collection of these, put up for the accommodation of travellers 1648. **2.** In Western U. S., a cattle-farm, a ranch 1840.

Rancid (ræ·nsid), *a.* 1646. [ad. L. *rancidus.*] Having the rank unpleasant taste or smell of oils and fats when no longer fresh. Hence of tastes or smells.

The black wet bread, with r. butter spread 1813. Hence **Ra·ncid-ly** *adv.*, **-ness.** **Ranci·dity,** r. state or quality.

Rancorous (ræ·ŋkŏrəs), *a.* 1590. [f. next + -OUS.] **1.** Of feelings: Having, or partaking of, the nature of rancour. Also *transf.* **2.** Of actions, etc.: Proceeding from, or characterized by, rancour 1590. **3.** Of persons, the mind, heart, etc.: Feeling or displaying rancour 1592.

1. So flam'd his eyne with rage and r. yre SPENSER. **3.** In that age of harsh and r. tempers M. ARNOLD. Hence **Ra·ncorous-ly** *adv.*, **-ness.**

Rancour (ræ·ŋkəɹ). ME. [a. OF. *rancour* :—L. *rancorem* rancidity, rankness, etc.] **1.** Inveterate and bitter ill-feeling, grudge, or animosity; malignant hatred or spitefulness. **b.** *transf.* and *fig.* of things 1582. †**2.** Rancid smell; rancidity; rankness (*rare*) –1567.

1. Peace in their mouthes, and all rancor and vengeaunce in their hartes 1547. **b.** Through the rancor of the poyson, the wound was iudged incurable CAMDEN.

Rand (rænd), *sb.* [OE. *rand* = OHG. *rant.*] **1.** A border, margin, or brink (*esp.* of land). *Obs.* exc. *dial.* **2.** A strip or long slice: **a.** of meat. Now *dial.* late ME. **b.** of fish (esp. sturgeon).

Now *rare.* 1572. **3. a.** A strip of leather placed under the quarters of a boot or shoe, to make this level before the lifts of the heel are attached 1598. **b.** A strip of iron 1831.

†**Rand,** *v. rare.* 1601. [a. obs. Flem. *randen*, var. *ranten* to RANT.] **1.** *intr.* To rave, to rant –1607. **2.** *trans.* (with *out*). To utter in a furious manner –1609.

Randan (ræ·n,dæn), *sb.*[1] 1662. [perh. var. of *randon* RANDOM.] **1.** Riotous or disorderly behaviour; a spree. **2.** A riotous person (*rare*) 1809.

1. Phr. *On the r.*; They were a' on the ran-dan last night! STEVENSON.

Randan (ræn,dæ·n), *adv.*, *sb.*[2] (and *a.*). 1828. [Origin obsc.] **A.** *adv.* Applied to a style of rowing in which the middle one of three rowers pulls a pair of sculls, stroke and bow an oar each. **B.** *sb.* A boat for rowing in this fashion 1885. **C.** *attrib.* or *adj.* 1884.

Randing (ræ·ndiŋ). 1834. [perh. f. RAND *sb.*] *Mil.* A kind of basket-work used in fortifications in making gabions.

Random (ræ·ndəm), *sb.*, *a.*, and *adv.* ME. [a. OF. *randon*, f. *randir* to run fast, gallop.] **A.** *sb.* **I.** †**1.** Impetuosity, great speed, force, or violence (in riding, running, striking, etc.). Also with *a*, an impetuous rush, a rapid headlong course. –1611. **2.** Phr. *At r.*, orig. at great speed, without consideration, care, or control; hence **a.** At haphazard; without aim, purpose, or fixed principle; heedlessly, carelessly 1565. **b.** So with sbs. (*rare.*) 1653. **c.** (*To leave*) in a neglected or untended condition. Now *rare.* 1582. **c.** A random course. Now *rare.* 1561.

1. The frenchmen..came on them with great randon, their speares in their restes 1523. 2. **a.** He talkes at randon: sure the man is mad SHAKS. **b.** Thy words at r., as before, Argue thy inexperience MILT.

II. *techn.* †**1.** *Gunnery.* The range of a piece of ordnance; properly, long or full range obtained by elevating the muzzle of the piece; hence, the degree of elevation given to a gun, and *spec.* that which gives the utmost range –1803. **2.** *Mining.* The direction (*of* a rake vein, etc.) 1653.

1. Phr. †*At r.*, at any range other than point-blank.

B. *adj.* (from phr. *at r.*). **1.** Not sent or guided in a special direction; having no definite aim or purpose; made, done, occurring, etc. at haphazard 1655. **2.** Of persons: Living irregularly (*rare*) 1825. **3.** *techn.* Said of masonry, in which the stones are of irregular sizes and shapes 1823. **4.** *R. shot*, a shot fired at random (orig. in sense A II. 1, but now taken as sense B. 1) 1693.

1. Leaving the poor to be supported by r. charity 1764. 2. Men who were r. grow steady when they have children to provide for H. SPENCER. 4. *fig.* The r. shot of..self-created guides in matters of taste 1809.

C. *adv.* †**1.** = At random (*rare*) –1619. **2.** *Comb.*, as *r.-cast*, *-wise*, *-jointed.* Hence **Ra·ndom·ly** *adv.*, **-ness.**

‖**Ranee** (rā·nī). 1698. [Hindī *rānī* = Skr. *rājnī*, fem. of *rāja-* RAJAH.] A Hindu queen; a rajah's wife.

Rang, see RING *v.*[1] and [2].

Range (rēⁱndʒ), *sb.*[1] ME. [a. OF. *range* row, rank, file, f. *ranger* RANGE *v.*] **I. 1.** A row, line, file or rank of persons or animals. Now *rare.* **2.** A row, line, or series of things; *esp.* of mountains 1511. **b.** *spec. U.S.* A series of townships six miles in width 1843. **c.** *Math.* A set of points on a straight line 1858. **3.** Rank, class, order (*rare*) 1625. **4.** Line, direction, lie 1677.

2. The New-Street is a double R. of Palaces from one end to the other ADDISON. A magnificent r. of cliffs 1859. 3. The cohesion of the nation was greatest in the lowest ranges 1874. 4. Keeping the two Buoys in r. with the Lighthouse 1858.

II. 1. The act of ranging or moving about. Now *rare* in literal sense. 1470. **b.** Opportunity or scope for ranging; liberty to range 1793. **2.** An area, space, or stretch of ground, over which ranging takes place or is possible; *spec.* in *U.S.*, an extensive stretch of grazing or hunting ground 1470. **b.** *U.S.* Without article: Grazing ground 1766. **3.** *Bot.* and *Zool.* The geographical area over which a plant or animal is distributed. Also, the period of time during which it has existed on the earth; the limits of depth between which a marine animal is found. 1856. **b.** The area or period over or during which the occurrence of something is possible 1830. **4.** The area or extent covered by, or included in, some thing or concept 1661. **b.** A series, number, or aggregate 1847. **5.** Sphere or scope of operation or action; the extent to which energy may be exerted, a function discharged, etc. **a.** of immaterial things 1666. **b.** of instruments; *esp.* of musical instruments (and so of the voice); compass, register 1825. **c.** of persons, in respect of knowledge, ability, etc. 1847. **6.** The limits between which a thing may vary in amount or degree 1818. **b.** A series or scale (of sounds, temperatures, prices, etc.) extending between certain limits 1812. **7.** The distance to which a gun, rifle, etc. is capable of sending a ball or bullet. Also, the distance of the object aimed at. 1591. **b.** The position of a gun in firing 1669. **c.** A place fitted with targets, etc., used for practice in shooting 1873.

1. *fig.* This blest exchange Of modest truth for wit's eccentric r. COWPER. 4. Far as Creation's ample r. extends, The scale of sensual, mental pow'rs ascends POPE. **b.** The English derive their pedigree from such a r. of nationalities EMERSON. 5. **a.** He would not suffer them to fall without the r. of Mercy BUNYAN. **b.** Her..voice, a lyre of widest r. TENNYSON. 7. The enemy have got the r. of our camp 1860.

III. 1. A form of fire-grate, fire-place, or cooking apparatus. Now *spec.* a fire-place having one or more ovens at the sides, and closed on the top with iron plates having openings for carrying on several cooking operations at once. 1446. **2.** *Naut.* (*pl.*) Pieces of timber for fastening ropes to 1644. **3.** A length or stretch of something, e.g. of glass, of leather, cable, etc. 1537. **4.** *Shoemaking.* The lie or line of the upper edge of the counter in a top-boot, corresponding to (and continued in) that of the vamp 1840.

attrib. and *Comb.*, as *r.-finder*, etc.; **r.-heads** *Naut.*, the windlass bitts; **r. work,** (*a*) work having a straight face; (*b*) masonry laid in level courses.

Range (rēⁱndʒ), *sb.*[2] *Obs.* exc. *dial.* 1615. [Cf. RANGE *v.*[2]] A kind of sieve or strainer.

Range (rēⁱndʒ), *v.*[1] late ME. [a. F. *ranger*, f. *rang* var. *ranc* RANK *sb.*] **I.** *trans.* **1.** To place, set, or station (persons, rarely animals) in a row, line, or rank; to draw up, arrange (an army, etc.) in ranks. Chiefly *pass.* and *refl.* **b.** To place (a person or persons) in a specified position, situation, or company. Chiefly in *pass.* and *refl.*, and commonly *fig.* 1598. †**c.** To bring *under* obedience, or *to* something –1659. **2.** To set or dispose (things) in a line or lines; hence, to arrange, put in order. late ME. **b.** *Naut.* To lay out (a cable) so that the anchor may descend without check 1833. **3.** To place (persons or things) *in* a certain class or category; to divide *into* classes; to classify, arrange, etc. 1601. **4.** *refl.* (ad. F. *se ranger.*) To adopt a more regular mode of life 1855.

1. A double file of men..ranged themselves along the ropes 1877. **b.** To r. myself on the side of the Duke of Bedford BURKE. 2. Her Books..were ranged together in a very beautiful Order ADDISON. 3. To r. the faculties In scale and order WORDSW.

II. *intr.* **1.** Of buildings, large natural objects, etc.: To stretch out or run in a line, to extend 1607. **b.** To extend or lie in the same line or plane (*with*); esp. in *Printing*, of type, lines, or pages 1599. **2.** To take up or occupy a place or position. Also, of a number of persons: To draw up in rank or order (*rare*) 1596. **b.** *Naut.* of ships 1709.

1. **b.** Whatsoeuer comes athwart his affection, ranges euenly with mine SHAKS. 2. When all the full-faced presence of the Gods Ranged in the halls of Peleus TENNYSON. **b.** The Excellent ranged up within two feet of the San Nicholas NELSON.

III. 1. To move hither and thither over a comparatively large area; to rove, roam, wander, stray 1547. **b.** *Gunnery.* Of projectiles: To traverse, go (a specified distance) 1644. **2.** To change from one attachment to another; to be inconstant 1596. **3.** *Bot.* and *Zool.* Of plants and animals: To extend (i.e. to occur, be found) over a certain area or throughout a certain period of time 1859. **4.** To vary within certain limits 1835.

1. Brave beasts..In the wilde forrest raunging fresh and free SPENSER. As far as the eye can r. 1872. 2. My Mind is fixt, I will not r., I like my Choice too well to change 1706. 4. The thermometer..ranged from 42° to 52° 1857.

IV. *trans.* **1.** To traverse, to go over or through (a place or area) in all directions 1533. **b.** *Naut.* To sail along or about (a country, the coast, etc.) 1603. **2. a.** To pasture (cattle) on a range 1857. **b.** To place (a telescope) in position 1860. **c.** To throw (a projectile) a specified distance 1858. **d.** *absol.* To give a gun a certain range 1892.

1. To traverse seas, r. kingdoms COWPER.

Range (rēⁱndʒ), *v.*[2] *Obs.* exc. *dial.* 1538. [Origin unkn.] *trans.* To sift (meal).

Ranger (rēⁱ·ndʒəɹ). late ME. [f. RANGE *v.*[1] + -ER [1].] One who or that which ranges. **1.** A rover, wanderer; †a rake 1593. **b.** Applied *spec.* to certain animals 1686. **2.** A forest officer, a gamekeeper. Now only *arch.*, and as the official title of the keepers of the royal parks. late ME. **3.** *pl.* A body of mounted troops, or other armed men, employed in ranging over a tract of country. Chiefly *U.S.* 1742. **4.** One who sets in order (*rare*) 1611.

1. **b.** I had two horses; one was an old..'Texian R.' 1855. 3. The 'Sarawak Rangers'..are recruited from Malays and Dyaks 1882. Hence **Ra·ngership,** the office of r. of a forest or park.

Rangy (rēⁱ·ndʒi), *a.* Chiefly *U.S.* 1880. [f. RANGE *sb.*[1] or *v.*[1] + -Y.[1]] **1.** Of animals: **a.** Adapted for or capable of ranging 1891. **b.** Of a long slender form 1886. **2.** Of places. Giving scope for ranging; spacious 1880. **3.** *Austral.* Mountainous 1880.

Rani, var. of RANEE.

Raniform (rēⁱ·nifǭɹm), *a.* 1852. [f. *rani-* comb. f. L. *rana* frog + -FORM.] Frog-shaped.

Ranine (rēⁱ·nəin), *a.* 1819. [ad. mod.L. *raninus*, f. *rana* frog; see -INE [1].] **1.** *Anat.* Belonging to the under side of the tip of the tongue (the part liable to be affected by RANULA); in *r. artery* (the terminal branch of the lingual artery), *r. vein.* **2.** Pertaining to a frog; frog-like (*rare*) 1840.

Rank (ræŋk), *sb.* 1547. [a. obs. F. *ranc* (mod. *rang*), var. *renc*, supposed to be a. OHG. *hrinc*, *hring* RING.] **1.** A row, line, or series of things. **2.** A row or line of persons. Now *rare.* 1571. †**b.** Movement in line or file SHAKS. **3.** *Mil.* A number of soldiers drawn up in line abreast; *pl.* (with *the*) = forces, battalion, army. 1574. **b.** *pl.* (with *the*) The body of private soldiers; the rank and file 1809. **c.** *Chess.* One of the lines of squares stretching across the board from side to side 1597. **d.** *fig.* of things 1593. **4.** Without article: Line, order, array 1572. **5.** *R. and file*: see quot. and FILE *sb.*[2] II. 1. Chiefly *pl.* or without article in phr. *in r. and file.* 1598. **b.** *collect.* (The) common soldiers; (the) privates and non-commissioned officers 1796. †**6.** One of several rows of things placed at different levels –1734. **7.** A number of persons forming a distinct class in the social scale, or in any organized body; a grade of station or dignity, an order; hence, (a person's) social position or standing 1596. **b.** High station in society, etc.; social distinction. Also *concr.* persons of high position. 1742. **8.** A class (of persons, animals, or things) in a scale of comparison; hence, relative position or status, place 1605.

1. A r. of cabs (*mod.*). Also, the place where these stand; a cab-rank or -stand 1903. 2. **b.** *A. Y. L.* III. ii. 103. 3. **b.** Phr. *To rise from the ranks.* **d.** Simois..Whose waves to imitate the battle sought ..and their ranks began To break upon the galled shore SHAKS. 4. Phr. *In* (*into*) *r.*, *out of r.*, *to keep* or *break r.* 5. *Ranks and files*, are the horizontal and vertical lines of soldiers when drawn up for service 1802. **b.** Unless the R. and File are interested in their work, there will be no enthusiasm 1894. 6. Ranks of oars in the modern galleys 1734. 7. Reasonable and well-educated men of all ranks BERKELEY. **b.** The r. and fashion of the.. country 1883. 8. The Convertine, a Ship of the second R., that carried seventy Guns CLARENDON.

Rank (ræŋk), *a.* and *adv.* [OE. *ranc* = ON. *rakkr* bold.] **A.** *adj.* **I.** †**1.** Proud, high-minded, haughty; froward, rebellious –1560. **2.** Stout and strong. *Obs.* exc. *dial.* OE. **3.** Having great speed or force; swift; impetuous; violent. Also const. *of.* ME.

3. †*R. rider*, a rapid, headlong, or reckless rider; a moss-trooper, highwayman.

II. Full, large or gross in size, quantity, etc. †**1.** Full-grown; mature (*rare*) –1536. **2.** Vigorous or luxuriant in growth. In later use: Growing too luxuriantly; large and coarse.

Hence of growth, etc. ME. †3. Excessively great or large; *esp.* swollen, puffed up, grossly fat, too highly fed -1631. b. High or excessive in amount. *Obs.* exc. *Law.* 1602. †4. Abundant, copious -1632. 5. a. In close array, crowded together; thick, dense. *Obs.* exc. *n. dial.* late ME. b. Numerous, frequent. *Obs.* exc. *n. dial.* 1545. 6. *techn.* Projecting, standing out 1678.

2. The woods are choked with its r. luxuriance 1777. The male lion is adorned with a long, r., shaggy mane 1850. 3. b. The *modus* must not be too large, which in law is called a *r. modus* BLACKSTONE. 5. a. Where the sheep are 'r.' on the fell sides 1864. 6. When a ship has a deep keel, she is said to have a r. keel 1727.

III. Of a luxuriant, gross, or coarse quality. 1. Covered or filled with a luxuriant (and coarse) growth of grass or plants. late ME. 2. Grossly rich, heavy, or fertile; liable to produce rank vegetation. late ME. 3. Having an offensively strong smell; rancid 1529. b. Of smell: Offensively strong 1570. †4. Lustful, licentious; in heat -1765. 5. Gross, highly offensive or loathsome; in later use *esp.* coarse or indecent ME. b. Corrupt, foul; festering 1579. 6. Of a strongly marked, violent, or virulent type; absolute, downright, gross. (Used as an intensive of the bad qualities implied by the qualified sb.) 1513. b. Grossly apparent (*rare*) 1624.

1. The patch..now r. with weeds 1890. 2. A r. clay that requires the labour of years to make it mellow G. WHITE. 3. Our men made some butter..but it grew r. DE FOE. *fig.* Oh my offence is ranke, it smels to heauen SHAKS. 4. *Cymb.* II. v. 24. 5. The r. vocabulary of malice and hate MORLEY. 6. 'Tis a most r. untruth MIDDLETON. The rankest Idiot MARVELL. R. treason against the royalty of Virtue 1766.

B. *adv.* †1. In a rank manner SPENSER. 2. With adjs.: Completely, extremely 1607.

2. He's irrecoverable; mad, ranke madde MARSTON. Hence **Ra·nk-ly** *adv.*, **-ness.**

Rank (ræŋk), *v.* 1573. [f. RANK *sb.*] 1. *trans.* To arrange or draw up (persons, *esp.* soldiers) in a rank or in ranks. 2. To arrange (things) in a row or rows; to set in line; to put in order 1590. †b. To divide or form *into* ranks or classes -1690. †c. In *pa. pple.*, of a place: Surrounded or bounded with rows or ranks -1698. 3. To place, locate; to give a certain position or station to; to class or classify. Also *refl.* 1592. 4. *U.S.* To take precedence of 1865. 5. *intr.* To form a rank or ranks; to stand in rank; to take up a position in a rank 1582. b. To take or have a place in a certain rank or class; to have rank or place 1599. c. *Law.* Of creditors or claims: To have a place on the list of claims, or of those having claims, on a bankrupt estate 1883. 6. To move or march in rank; chiefly *Mil.* 1832.

1. In view Stood rankt of Seraphim another row MILT. 2. He knew to r. his Elms in even Rows DRYDEN. c. *Timon* I. i. 65. 3. Those who r. Lucan rather among historians in verse than epic poets DRYDEN. 5. b. Also (*U.S.*), to have the highest rank; to be supremely eminent.

Ranker (ræ·ŋkəɹ). 1832. [f. RANK *sb.* and *v.* + -ER [1].] 1. One who arranges in ranks. 2. One (esp. a soldier) in the ranks 1890. 3. An officer who has risen from the ranks 1878.

Rankle (ræ·ŋk'l), *v.* ME. [a. OF. *rancler, raoncler*, var. of *draoncler*, f. (ult.) med.L. *dranculus, dracunculus* a fester, ulcer.] I. *intr.* 1. To fester, esp. to a degree that causes pain. †2. To inflict a festering wound; to cause a painful festering -1698. 3. a. Of persons: To fret or chafe angrily (*rare*) 1582. b. Of a bitter or malignant feeling: To have course, or continue in operation, like a festering sore 1508. c. Of experiences, events, etc.: To continue to cause painful, bitter, or venomous feelings 1735. 4. To change *to* or *into*, by or as by festering 1741.

1. Therewithal their knees would r. MARLOWE. The wound..is but skinned over, and rankles still at the bottom 1741. 3. b. A bitter feeling rankled in his heart 1874. c. The sight of the palace of the English King..rankled in his soul FREEMAN. 4. Discontent will r. into disaffection 1831.

II. *trans.* To cause (flesh, wounds, etc.) to fester; to make painful 1530. b. To embitter, envenom (feelings); to cause painful irritation in (a person) 1606.

b. A fierce reformer once, now ranckl'd with a contrary heat MILT. Hence **Ra·nkle** *sb.* (*rare*).

Ranny (ræ·ni). *Obs.* exc. *dial.* 1559. [app. ad.L. *araneus mus.*] The shrew mouse or field mouse.

Ransack (ræ·nsæk), *v.* ME. [a. ON. *rannsaka*, f. *rann* house + *-saka*, ablaut-var. of *sœkja* to seek.] †1. *trans.* To search (a person) for something stolen or missing -1493. 2. To make thorough search in or throughout (a place, receptacle, collection of things, etc.) *for* something (in early use, something stolen) ME. b. *absol.* To make thorough search. Now *rare.* late ME. 3. To examine thoroughly; to overhaul and investigate in detail ME. 4. To search (a place, person, etc.) with intent to rob; hence, to rob, plunder, pillage (*of*). late ME. b. To search for and take (*away*) or carry off as plunder. Now *rare.* late ME.

2. I am ransacking my memory for..scraps of theatrical history CIBBER. 3. She ransacked her conscience..and took herself to task..for a thousand imaginary faults HAWTHORNE. 4. The palaces were ransacked of their valuables and then ruthlessly set on fire 1878. Hence **Ra·nsack** *sb.* 1589, **Ra·nsacker,** a pillager.

Ransom (ræ·nsəm), *sb.* ME. [a. OF. *rançon, raençon*:—L. *redemptionem* REDEMPTION.] 1. The action of procuring the release of a prisoner or captive by paying a price, or of obtaining one's own freedom in this way; the fact or possibility of being set free on this condition; the paying of money to this end. 2. The sum or price paid or demanded for the release of a prisoner or the restoration of captured property ME. b. *fig.* in religious use, of Christ or His blood ME. †3. The action or means of freeing oneself from a penalty; a sum of money paid to obtain pardon for an offence; a fine, mulct -1769.

1. Phr. *To hold to r.*; Gwesklen, taken prisoner by Chandos, was held by him to r. 1859. 2. *A king's r.*, a large sum; I'll not speak another word for a King's r. MARLOWE. b. Sending thee..his Mediator..Both R. and Redeemer voluntarie MILT. 3. This is the reason why fines in the king's court are frequently denominated ransoms BLACKSTONE.

Comb. **r.-bill, -bond,** an engagement to redeem or pay r., in later use esp. for a vessel captured by the enemy. Hence **Ra·nsomless** *a.* without r.

Ransom (ræ·nsəm), *v.* ME. [a. OF. *ransonner, -çonner*, f. *rançon*; see prec.] 1. *trans.* To redeem (from captivity or punishment); to procure the release of (a person) or restoration of (a thing) by payment of the sum or price demanded. late ME. b. To redeem, deliver, in religious sense ME. c. To purchase (life or liberty) by a ransom 1630. d. To atone or pay for, to expiate; †to procure respite of (time); to bring *into* by ransoming ME. 2. a. To permit to be ransomed; to admit to ransom; to set free on payment of a sum of money. late ME. b. To demand ransom from or for; to exact payment from; †thence, to oppress with exactions. Also *absol.* late ME. 3. To pay ransom to (a person). *rare.* 1722.

1. They were obliged to r. not only their prisoners but their dead THIRLWALL. b. His Brethren, ransomd with his own dear life MILT. d. Those tears are..rich and r. all ill deeds SHAKS. 2. b. These gentlemen contend that unfortified towns will never be bombarded or ransomed 1888. Hence **Ra·nsomable** *a.* **Ra·nsomer,** one who ransoms; a redeemer; (with cap.) a member of the R. C. Guild of Our Lady of Ransom which works for the conversion of England.

Rant (rænt), *sb.* 1649. [f. the vb.] 1. A high-flown, extravagant, or bombastic speech or utterance; a piece of turgid declamation; a tirade. †b. A violent scolding (*rare*) -1725. c. A ranting state or condition 1722. 2. Extravagant or bombastic language or sentiments; empty declamation 1708. b. A declamatory way of speaking. JOHNSON. 3. *n. dial.* and *Sc.* A noisy merrymaking; a spree 1675.

1. A R. Against the Envious, and the Ignorant DRYDEN. 2. The following passages are pure r. 1762. b. The players, Sir, have got a kind of r., with which they run on, without any regard either to accent or emphasis 1742.

Rant (rænt), *v.* 1598. [a. obs. Du. *randten, ranten* to talk foolishly, to rave.] 1. *intr.* (†or with *it*). To talk or declaim in an extravagant high-flown manner; to use bombastic language 1602. †b. To storm or scold violently. Const. *at, against.* -1710. 2. To be jovial, boisterous, uproariously gay or merry; also, to sing loudly 1598. 3. *trans.* To utter in a declamatory and bombastic manner; to mouth. Also with *out.* 1650.

1. Nay, and thou'lt mouth, Ile r. as well as thou SHAKS. b. They say you're angry, and r. mightily COWLEY. 3. Ranting Carlyle and Emerson by the volume MORLEY. Hence **Ra·ntingly** *adv.* †**Ra·ntism** (*rare*), the practice of ranting; *spec.* = RANTERISM.

Ranter (ræ·ntəɹ), *sb.* 1649. [f. RANT *v.* + -ER [1].] 1. One who rants, esp. in preaching. †2. A noisy, riotous, dissipated fellow; a rake -1828. 3. *spec.* (chiefly *pl.*) a. A member of a sect of Antinomians which arose *c* 1645. Now only *Hist.* 1651. b. A member of the Primitive Methodist body, which originated in 1807–10. 1823.

1. There went also, with this party, Sir Thomas Armstrong, Colonel Trevor, and most of their great ranters CROMWELL. Hence **Ra·nterism,** the practices or doctrines of Ranters.

Rantipole (ræ·ntipōul), *sb.* (and *a.*) Now *rare.* 1700. [Origin obsc.] 1. A romp; a wild, ill-behaved or reckless person; a scold, termagant. 2. *attrib.* or as *adj.* Wild, disorderly, rakish 1700.

Rantipole (ræ·ntipōul), *v.* 1712. [f. prec.] *intr.* To go *about*, or behave, in a romping, rude or noisy fashion.

She used to R. about the House, pinch the Children, kick the Servants 1712.

‖**Ranula** (ræ·niŭlă). 1657. [L. *ranula* a little frog, a little swelling on the tongue of cattle (Vegetius), dim. of *rana* frog.] *Path.* A cystic tumour under the tongue, caused by the obstruction of the salivary ducts or glands. Hence **Ra·nular** *a.*

Ranunculaceous (rănʊŋkiŭlēi·ʃəs), *a.* 1833. [f. next + -ACEOUS.] *Bot.* Belonging to the *Ranunculaceæ*, of which Ranunculus is the typical genus.

‖**Ranunculus** (rănʊ·ŋkiŭləs). *Pl.* **-culuses, -culi.** 1578. [L., a little frog, tadpole; also a medicinal plant; dim. of *rana* frog.] *Bot.* A genus of plants (also called CROWFOOT); the common species with yellow flowers are popularly called BUTTERCUPS; the usual cultivated species is *R. asiaticus.* b. A plant belonging to this genus.

‖**Ranz-des-vaches** (rañ(s) də vaʃ). 1801. [Swiss dial. of Fribourg.] One of the melodies peculiar to Swiss herdsmen, usu. played on an Alpine horn, and consisting of irregular phrases made up of the harmonic notes of the horn.

Rap (ræp), *sb.*[1] ME. [prob. echoic.] A blow or stroke, esp. one inflicted on a person. Now restricted to a sharp or smart stroke with a stick or the like, not causing serious hurt. b. A sharp knock such as is produced by striking on a wooden surface with something hard; esp. a knock at a door, or (in recent use) one supposed to be made by a spirit 1637.

Rap (ræp), *sb.*[2] 1724. [Origin obsc.] A counterfeit coin, worth about half a farthing, which passed current for a halfpenny in Ireland in the 18th c., owing to the scarcity of genuine money. Now *Hist.* b. Taken as a type of the smallest coin 1823. c. *fig.* An atom, the least bit. Chiefly in neg. phrases, and esp. *not to care a r.* 1834.

Rap (ræp), *v.*[1] late ME. [Related to RAP *sb.*[1]] 1. *trans.* To strike, smite (*esp.* a person); now, to strike smartly without causing serious hurt. 2. To drive, dash, knock, etc. with a rap. Chiefly *Sc.* late ME. 3. Usu. with *out.* To utter (*esp.* an oath) sharply, vigorously, or suddenly 1541. †b. *slang.* To swear (a thing) *against* a person. Also *intr.* To swear; to perjure oneself. -1818. 4. *intr.* To knock sharply (*esp.* at a door) 1440. b. *trans.* To strike with a rap; to rap at or on 1712. c. *To r. out*, to knock out; also (*esp.* of spirits) to declare by means of raps 1841.

1. Phr. *To r.* (a person's) *fingers* or *knuckles*, to check or punish him smartly. b. *U.S.* To criticize adversely; to reprove 1906. 3. Out he rapped Such a round of oaths BROWNING.

Rap (ræp), *v.*[2] Now *rare.* 1528. [In sense 1 perh. related to MLG. *rappen* to seize, snatch; in 2 app. a back-formation from RAPT *pa. pple.*] †1. *trans.* To seize or snatch for oneself; to take or get by snatching or stealing -1754. 2. To take up and carry off, to transport, remove 1599. b. To affect with rapture; to transport, ravish (with joy, etc.) 1599.

1. Phr. *To r. and rend* (common in 16–17th c.; now *arch.* or *dial.*); From foe and from friend He'd 'r. and he'd rend' BARHAM. 2. b. Is't a prognostication raps him so? B. JONS.

Rapacious (răpē¹·ʃəs), *a.* 1651. [f. L. *rapaci-*, *rapax* grasping (f. *rapere*) + -OUS.] 1. Given to grasping or taking for oneself; inordinately greedy. Also const. *of* and *inf.* 2. Of animals: Subsisting by the capture of living prey; raptorial 1661.

1. Who more r. in robbing, who more profuse in giving? COWLEY. Deliver me from this r. deep KEATS. The r. domination of the Fanariotes 1847. 2. Of R. Birds in General GOLDSM. Hence **Rapa·cious-ly** *adv.*, **-ness.**

Rapacity (răpæ·sĭti). 1543. [ad. L. *rapacitatem*, f. *rapax*.] The quality or fact of being rapacious; the exercise of rapacious tendencies.

The rapacite of wolues 1543. An act of wanton r. FREEMAN.

Rape (rē¹p), *sb.*¹ late ME. [a. AF. *rap(e*, prob. a back-formation from L. *rapere*; see RAPE *v.*] †1. The act of taking anything by force; violent seizure (of goods), robbery. Also with *a*: A case or instance of this. –1712. 2. The act of carrying away a person (*esp.* a woman) by force. late ME. 3. Violation or ravishing of a woman 1481. b. With *a* and *pl.* An instance of this 1577. †4. *concr.* One who is raped –1683.

1. The R. of the Lock (*title*) POPE. 2. The r. of the Sabines SCOTT. 3. Marrying or prostituting, as befell, R. or Adulterie MILT. b. An assault, with intent to commit a r. 1834. *fig.* A r. Vpon the maiden vertue of the Crowne SHAKS.

Rape (rē¹p), *sb.*² OE. [Etym. unkn.; first found in Domesday Book.] One of the six administrative districts into which Sussex is divided, each comprising several hundreds.

Rape (rē¹p), *sb.*³ late ME. [ad. L. *rapum* neut., *rapa* fem., turnip.] †1. (With *a* or in *pl.*) a. A turnip (? or radish). b. A plant of rape. –1714. 2. As a plant-name. †a. The common turnip. b. The plant *Brassica napus*, usu. grown as food for sheep. c. The plant *Brassica campestris oleifera*, from the seed of which oil is made; coleseed. late ME. 3. *Wild r.*, Charlock or Field-Mustard 1551.

Comb.: **r.-cake**, a flat cake made of rapeseed after the oil has been extracted from it; **-oil**, a thick brownish-yellow oil expressed from rapeseed, used for lubricating, etc.; **-seed**, (*a*) the seed of the r. (esp. *Brassica campestris oleifera*); (*b*) as a name for the plant (now *rare*).

Rape (rē¹p), *sb.*⁴ 1600. [In branch I a. F. *râpe*. In II prop. *rapé*, a. F. *râpé*, f. *râpe*.] I. 1. The stalks of grape-clusters, or refuse of grapes from which wine has been expressed, used in making vinegar. Also *pl.* in same sense. 1657. 2. A vessel used in the manufacture of vinegar 1805. †II. (In full *R. wine* = F. *vin râpé*.) Wine made either from the rape (sense 1 above) by addition of water, or from fresh grapes and light wine placed together in a cask –1733.

Rape (rē¹p), *v.* late ME. [prob. ad. L. *rapere*.] 1. *trans.* To take (a thing) by force. Also *absol.* b. To rob, strip, plunder (a place). *rare.* 1721. †2. To carry off (a person, *esp.* a woman) by force –1720. 3. To ravish, commit rape on 1577. 4. To transport, ravish, delight. Now *rare.* 1613.

Raphaelesque (ræ:fĕ,ēle·sk), *a.* Also **raffaell-**. 1830. [f. name of *Raphael* (It. *Raffaello*) the painter (1483–1520) + -ESQUE.] After the style of Raphael. Hence **Ra·phaelism**, the principles of art introduced by Raphael; his style or method. **Ra·phaelite**, one who adopts the principles or follows the style of Raphael.

‖**Raphanus** (ræ·fănŏs). 1730. [L., a. Gr. ῥάφανος = ῥαφανίς radish.] *Bot.* A genus of cruciferous plants, of which the common radish (*R. sativus*) is the most important species.

‖**Raphe** (rē¹·fī). 1706. [mod.L., a. Gr. ῥαφή seam, suture (of the skull, a wound, etc.).] 1. *Anat.* A line of union between the two halves of an organ or part of the body, having the appearance of a seam. 2. *Bot.* a. In certain ovules, a cord connecting the hilum with the chalaza, and usu. appearing as a ridge. b. In the Umbelliferæ, the line of junction or suture between the carpels. c. A median line or rib on the valves of diatoms. 1830. 3. *Ornith.* The groove along the under-side of the rachis of a feather 1859.

Raphia (rē¹·fiă). 1866. [Malagasy.] *Bot.* A palm of the genus so named, having short stems and long pinnate leaves.

attrib.: *R. grass* = RAFFIA.

Raphide (rē¹·fəid). 1884. [a. F. *raphide*, f. stem of Gr. ῥαφίς.] *Bot.* = next.

‖**Raphis** (rē¹·fis). Also **rha-**. *Pl.* **raphides** (ræ·fidīz). 1842. [Gr. ῥαφίς, ῥαφιδ- needle.] *Bot.* One of the minute crystals, usu. of acicular form, found in the cells of many plants.

Rapid (ræ·pid), *a.* (*adv.*), and *sb.* 1634. [ad. L. *rapidus*, f. *rapere*; see -ID¹.] A. *adj.* 1. Moving, or capable of moving, with great speed; swift, very quick. 2. Of movement: Characterized by speed 1697. 3. Quick in action, discourse, etc. 1791. b. *techn.* Said of photographic lenses, plates, or subjects, requiring only a short exposure 1878. 4. Taking place with speed; coming quickly into existence or to completion 1780. b. Of a slope: Descending quickly 1890. 5. quasi-*adv.* Rapidly 1791.

1. Part..shun the Goal With r. wheels MILT. On r. feet COWPER. 2. Fancy's r. flight 1730. I heard my name among those r. words BROWNING. 3. Homer is eminently r. M. ARNOLD. 4. The r. victories of these Eastern conquerors 1780.

B. *sb.* A part of a river where the bed forms a steep descent, causing a swift current. (Orig. *U.S.*, and usu. in *pl.*). 1776.

Mortal boat In such a shallow r. could not float SHELLEY. Hence **Rapi·dity**, the quality of being r. **Ra·pid-ly** *adv.*, **-ness** (now *rare*).

Rapier (rē¹·piəɹ). 1547. [a. F. *rapière*; origin unkn.] Orig., a long, pointed, two-edged sword adapted either for cutting or thrusting, but chiefly used for the latter. Later, a light, sharp-pointed sword designed only for thrusting; a small sword. Hence **Ra·piered** *a.* wearing or furnished with a r.; sharp-pointed.

‖**Rapilli** (rapī·llī). 1809. [It., pl. of *rapillo*.] Small fragments of pumice-stone.

Rapine (ræ·pəin), *sb.* late ME. [a. F., or ad. L. *rapina*, f. *rapere* to seize; see RAPE *v.* and -INE⁴.] The act or practice of seizing and taking away by force the property of others; plunder, pillage, robbery. b. *pl.* Acts of violent robbery or pillage (now *rare*) 1494. c. *Beast* (etc.) *of r.*: Beast of prey 1612.

The lawless r. of banditti 1769. Hence †**Ra·pine** *v. intr.* to commit r.; *trans.* to plunder, or carry away, by r. †**Ra·pinous** *a.* given to r.; rapacious.

Rapparee (ræpărī·). 1690. [a. Ir. *rapaire* short pike.] †1. A half-pike (*rare*). 2. *Hist.* An Irish pikeman or irregular soldier, of the kind prominent during the war of 1688–92; hence, an Irish bandit, robber, or freebooter 1690.

Rappee (ræpī·). 1740. [ad. F. (*tabac*) *râpé*, pa. pple. of *râper* to RASP.] A coarse kind of snuff made from the darker and ranker tobacco leaves, and orig. obtained by rasping a piece of tobacco.

‖**Rappel** (rapĕl). 1848. [F., f. *rappeler* to recall.] The roll or beat of a drum to summon soldiers to arms.

Rapper (ræ·pəɹ). 1611. [f. RAP *v.*¹ + -ER¹.] 1. One who raps or knocks; a spirit-rapper 1755. 2. Anything used for rapping; *spec.* †a door-knocker 1640. 3. a. An arrant lie. Now *dial.* 1611. b. A great oath. Now *dial.* 1678. †4. Something remarkably good or large –1672.

Rapport (ræpōᵊ·ɹt, F. rapōr). 1455. [F., f. *rapporter*; see RE- and APPORT *v.*] †1. Report, talk –1539. 2. Reference, relationship; connexion, correspondence 1661. b. *spec.* A state in which mesmeric action can be exercised by one person on another 1848. 3. In Fr. phr. *en rapport*, in connexion, etc. 1818.

2. Between whose Languages there is no more r., then the English hath to the Greek and Arabian 1662.

‖**Rapprochement** (raproʃmaṅ). 1809. [F., f. *rapprocher* (f. *re-* + *approcher* APPROACH) + -MENT.] A coming or bringing together, an establishment of harmonious relations.

Rapscallion (ræpskæ·liən). 1699. [Later f. RASCALLION.] A rascal, rogue, vagabond, scamp. Also *attrib.* or as *adj.*

Rapt (ræpt), *sb.* Now *rare.* 1440. [ad. L. *raptus*, f. *rapere* to seize.] †1. *Sc.* = RAPE *sb.*¹ 3. –1693. †2. A trance, ecstasy, rapture –1826. †3. The act or power of carrying forcibly away; sweep; force, current –1682.

Rapt (ræpt), *pa. pple.* (and *pa. t.*). late ME. [ad. L. *raptus*, pa. pple. of *rapere* to seize, RAPE *v.*] I. As *pa. pple.* passive. 1. (Also with *up*.) Taken and carried up *to* or *into* heaven (either in literal or mystical sense). 2. Carried away *in spirit*, without bodily removal 1470. 3. Transported with some emotion, ravished, enraptured. Also const. *with* or *by*. 1539. 4. Deeply engaged or buried *in* (a feeling, subject of thought, etc.); intent *upon* 1509. 5. Of a woman: Carried away by force; raped. late ME. 6. Carried away from one place, position, or situation to another. (Chiefly said of persons). 1552. b. Taken *away* by death 1820.

1. They are..r., perhaps, like Elijah, alive into Heaven 1760. 2. St. Paul when he was r. in the spirit into Paradise 1878. 3. Nor r., nor craving, but in settled peace WORDSW. 4. For a woman r. in love so marveylously 1509.

II. As *pa. pple.* active (*rare*) 1509.

What accident Hath r. him from us? MILT.

III. As *pa. t.* Chiefly *poet.*; now *rare.* 1594.

Sorrow and fear So struck, so roused, so r. Urania SHELLEY.

Rapt (ræpt), *ppl. a.* 1555. [See prec.] 1. Entranced, ravished, enraptured. 2. Indicating, proceeding from, characterized by, a state of rapture 1797.

1. Thy r. soul sitting in thine eyes MILT. 2. He listened..with a r. attention 1797.

†**Rapt**, *v.* 1577. [f. RAPT *pa. pple.*] 1. *trans.* To carry away by force –1619. 2. To transport, enrapture –1619. Hence †**Ra·pter**, a ravisher DRAYTON.

Raptor (ræ·ptǭɹ). 1609. [a. L., f. *rapere*.] 1. A ravisher. †2. A plunderer, robber –1720. 3. *Ornith.* One of the *Raptores* (see 4) 1873. 4. In L. pl. **raptores** (ræptōᵊ·rīz), as the name of an order of birds of prey, including the eagle, hawk, buzzard, owl, etc. 1823.

Raptorial (ræptōᵊ·riăl), *a.* 1825. [See prec. and -AL¹.] 1. Given to seizing prey, predatory; esp. *r. birds* = prec. 4. 2. Pertaining to, or characteristic of, predatory birds or animals; adapted for seizing prey 1839. So **Rapto·rious** *a.*

Rapture (ræ·ptiŭr, -tʃəɹ), *sb.* 1600. [f. RAPT *pa. pple.* + -URE. Cf. *capture*.] †1. The act of seizing and carrying off as prey or plunder –1639. 2. The act of carrying, or state of being carried, onwards; force of movement. Now *rare.* 1615. †3. The act of carrying off a woman –1728. †b. = RAPE *sb.*¹ 3. –1649. 4. The act of conveying a person from one place to another, *esp.* to heaven; the fact of being so conveyed 1647. 5. Transport of mind, ecstasy; now *esp.* ecstatic delight or joy 1629. b. With *a* and *pl.* An instance of this 1605. c. A state of passionate excitement; a paroxysm, fit. *rare.* (now *dial.*). 1607. d. A strong fit *of* (some emotion or mental state) 1795. 6. The expression of ecstatic feeling in words or music; a rhapsody 1620.

1. *Per.* II. i. 161. 2. Our Ship..'gainst a Rocke, or Flat, her Keele did dash, With headlong r. CHAPMAN. 3. The r. of Proserpine by a Centaure 1662. 5. Such musick sweet..As all their souls in blisfull r. took MILT. b. Phr. *To be in*, or *to go into raptures*; A place that strangers fell into raptures with 1862. c. *Cor.* II. i. 223. d. A r. of forgetfulness WORDSW. Hence **Ra·pture** *v. trans.* to enrapture (now *rare*). **Ra·ptured** *ppl. a.* ecstatic, enraptured.

†**Ra·pturist.** *rare.* 1663. [f. prec. + IST.] An enthusiast –1783.

Rapturize (ræ·ptiŭrəiz), *v.* 1882. [f. RAPTURE *sb.* + -IZE³.] *intr.* To fall into ecstasies.

Rapturous (ræ·ptiŭrəs, -tʃərəs), *a.* 1678. [f. as prec. + -OUS.] 1. Characterized by, expressive or partaking of, rapture. 2. Feeling or exhibiting rapture 1754.

1. A shout of r. applause 1853. 2. A r. imaginative girl 1851. Hence **Ra·pturous-ly** *adv.*, **-ness.**

‖**Raquette,** 1861. = RACKET *sb.*¹

‖**Rara avis** (rēᵊ·ră ē¹·vis). 1654. [L., = 'rare bird'.] A remarkable person; a paragon.

Rare (rēᵊɹ), *a.*¹ late ME. [ad. L. *rarus* or a. F. *rare.*] 1. Having the constituent particles not closely packed together. (Opp. to *dense.*) In later use chiefly of the air or gases. †2. a. Having the component parts widely set; of open construction; in open order (*rare*) –1647. b. Thinly attended or populated (*rare*) –1789. †3. Placed or stationed at wide intervals; standing or keeping far apart -1667. 4. (With pl. sbs.) Few in number and widely separated from each other (in space or time); forming a small and scattered class 1555. 5. Of a kind, class, or description seldom found, met with, or occurring; unusual, uncommon, exceptional 1542. 6. Unusual in respect of some good quality; remarkably good or fine 1483. b. *colloq.* Splendid, excellent, fine 1596. †c. Interjectionally in *O rare!* -1786. d. *colloq.* as an intensive, with sbs. and adjs. (also *r. and* with adjs.) 1833.

1. All pure and r. bodies ascend, as the Fire more than the Air 1669. 3. Among the trees in pairs they rose, they walk'd; Those r. and solitarie, these in flocks MILT. 4. I never saw but one Grey-ey'd, and therefore I suppose them r. 1698. 5. Gathering r. shells, delighted children stray 1812. Phr. *It is r. that..* (cf. F. *il est rare que..*). 6. A boat of r. device, which had no sail SHELLEY. b. He's a r. Fellow for giving a bad Captain a good Word 1706. c. 1 *Hen. IV*, I. ii. 72. Hence **Ra·re-ly** *adv.*, **-ness.**

Rare (rēᵊɹ), *a.*[2] 1655. [Later f. REAR *a.*[2]] †a. Of eggs: Left soft in cooking. b. Of meat: Underdone 1784.

b. The same flesh, rotten-roasted or r., on the Tuesdays LAMB.

Rare (rēᵊɹ), *a.*[3] and *adv.* *Obs.* exc. *dial.* 1574. [var. of RATHE *a.*] Early.

Rude mechanicals, that r. and late Work in the market-place CHAPMAN.

Rarebit: see **Welsh rabbit.**

Raree-show (rēᵊ·rīʃōᵘ). 1681. [app. the Savoyard showmen's pronunciation of *rare show.*] A show contained or carried about in a box; a peep-show; *transf.* a show or spectacle of any kind.

Rarefaction (rēᵊrǐfæ·kʃən). 1603. [f. L. *rarefacere* to RAREFY.] The action of rarefying or process of being rarefied; diminution of density. (Now chiefly of the air or gases, or *Path.* of bones.)

There is..thickening or r. of skull bones 1898.

Rarefa·ctive, *a.* 1656. [f. L. *rarefacere* to RAREFY.] Having the quality of rarefying; characterized by rarefaction. (In recent use only *Path.* of diseases of bones.)

Rarefy (rēᵊ·rǐfəi), *v.* late ME. [a. F. *raréfier*, or ad. L. *rarefacere*, f. *rarus* RARE *a.*[1] + *facere* to make.] 1. *trans.* To make rare or thin, esp. by expansion; to lessen the density or solidity of (a substance, now usu. air, or, in *Path.*, bone). 2. *fig.* To make less gross or material, to refine, to purify 1599. b. To make (an idea) subtle 1699. †3. To thin (a wood). FULLER. 4. *intr.* To become less dense; to be thinned (*rare*) 1658.

1. Water rarified becomes Ayre againe 1477. The hot wire rarefied the air in contact with it TYNDALL. 4. Like the mist sometimes rarefying into sunny gauze 1847. Hence †**Rarefiable** *a.* (*rare*). **Rarefica·tion** (*rare*) = RAREFACTION.

Ra·re-ripe, *a.* and *sb.* *dial.* and *U.S.* 1799. [f. RARE *a.*[3] + RIPE.] A. *adj.* Rathe-ripe. B. *sb.* An early fruit or vegetable. b. *attrib.* Of the colour of a peach called the *rare-ripe.*

Rarity (rēᵊ·rǐti). 1560. [ad. L. *raritas*, f. *rarus* RARE *a.*[1]; see -ITY.] 1. Of substances (now chiefly of air): Thinness of composition or texture. (Opp. to *density.*) 1644. 2. Relative fewness in number; the fact of occurring seldom or in few instances 1560. 3. Unusual or exceptional character, esp. in respect of excellence 1601. 4. A rare or uncommon thing or occurrence 1592.

4. It was a fine day, which is a r. with us SWIFT.

Rasant (rē̆·zănt), *a.* Now *rare* or *Obs.* 1696. [a. OF. *rasant*, pres. pple. of *raser* RASE *v.*[1]] *Mil.* In fortification: Sweeping, grazing.

Rascal (rɑ·skăl), *sb.* and *a.* ME. [a. OF. *rascaille*; origin unkn.] A. *sb.* †1. *collect.* The rabble of an army or of the populace; persons of the lowest class. *Obs.* exc. *arch.* †b. A rabble or mob (*rare*) -1532. †2. One belonging to the rabble; a man of low birth or station -1674. 3. A rogue, knave, scamp 1586. b. Used playfully, or as a mild term of reproof 1610. †4. *collect.* The young, lean, or inferior deer of a herd, dist. from the full-grown antlered bucks or stags -1607. b. Similarly applied to other animals 1530.

3. The Whip..is a Punishment inflicted upon all Vagabonds, Wandering Beggars and Idle Rascals 1688. b. You are a lucky r., and I wish..I were in your shoes 1899.

B. *adj.* 1. Belonging to, or forming, the rabble. Also *rarely*, rascally, knavish. late ME. †b. Common, private (soldiers) -1581. c. Pertaining or appropriate to (†the rabble, or) rascals 1566. †2. Wretched, miserable, mean -1748. †3. Of deer, etc.: see A. 4. -1664.

1. The R. Rabble DRYDEN. c. The Rascall humours of the vaine And giddy multitude 1618. 2. On what r. foundations were built up all the pretences to virtue which were set up in opposition to him H. WALPOLE. Hence **Ra·scaldom,** the world or body of rascals; rascally conduct, a rascally act. †**Ra·scaless** (*nonce-wd.*), a female r.

Rascality (rɑskæ·lǐti). 1577. [f. RASCAL *sb.* + -ITY.] 1. = prec. A. 1. 2. Rascally character or conduct; a rascally act or practice 1592.

1. The Chief Heads of their Clans, with all the several Rascalities depending on them 1652.

Rascallion (rɑskæ·liən). 1649. [perh. f. RASCAL with fanciful ending.] A low mean wretch or rascal.

Rascally (rɑ·skăli), *a.* 1596. [f. RASCAL *sb.* + -LY[1].] †1. = RASCAL *a.* 1. -1687. 2. Low, mean, or unprincipled in character or conduct; knavish 1598. 3. = RASCAL *a.* 1 c. 1596. 4. = RASCAL *a.* 2. 1606.

1. There was none of any quality, but poor and r. people PEPYS. 2. Our common soldiers are such a low r. set of people HUME. 3. Vile..r. verses B. JONS. 4. A whorson r. tisicke SHAKS. So **Ra·scally** *adv.*

†**Rase,** *sb.* 1530. [f. next.] 1. The act of scraping or scratching; the fact of being scratched or cut -1628. 2. A scratch, cut, slit -1677.

Rase (rē̆ⁱz), *v.*[1] late ME. [a. F. *raser* :— pop. L. **rasare*, f. *ras-*, ppl. stem of *radere* to scrape, etc.] †1. *trans.* To scratch or tear with something sharp; to cut, slit, or slash (esp. the skin or clothing) -1714. †b. *intr.* To slash; to make way or penetrate; to make an incised mark -1677. c. *trans.* To incise (a mark or line) 1815. 2. To remove by scraping or rasping. Somewhat *rare* in literal sense. late ME. b. *esp.* To erase (something written). late ME. 3. (Without const.) To erase, obliterate (writing), orig. by scraping with a knife. Now *rare* or *Obs.* late ME. †4. To scrape (a thing) so as to remove something from its surface; also, to scrape down into small particles -1743. †b. To alter (a writing) by erasure -1703. 5. To level with the ground; to RAZE. Now *rare.* 1537. †6. To graze -1786.

2. b. Unlesse you can r. these words..out of the Statute 1658. 3. To r. all records in their journals of that matter MARVELL. 4. b. Counterfeiting Rasing or Falsifying any Cocquet Certificate 1697. 5. They ..rased the noblest Structures in the Land, to sell the Materials 1680. 6. Sometimes his feet rased the surface of the water 1786.

†**Rase,** *v.*[2] late ME. [var. f. *race*, aphet. f. ARACE.] *trans.* To pull or pluck -1594.

He dreamt, the Bore had rased off his Helme SHAKS.

†**Ra·sen.** [OE. *ræsn*; origin obsc.] = RAISING-PIECE -1703.

Rash (ræʃ), *sb.*[1] Now *Hist.* 1578. [ad. F. *ras* = Sp., It. *raso* silk, satin, or fine serge, sb. use of adj. corresp. to L. *rasus* scraped, shaven, smooth; see RASE *v.*[1]] A smooth textile fabric made of silk (*silk r.*), or worsted (*cloth r.*).

Rash (ræʃ), *sb.*[2] 1709. [perh. a. OF. *rache*, *rasche* scurf, eruptive sores.] A superficial eruption or efflorescence of the skin in red spots or patches, as in measles, scarlet fever, etc.

Rash (ræʃ), *sb.*[3] 1668. [Echoic.] A rustling noise. DRYDEN.

Rash (ræʃ), *a.* and *adv.* ME. [= (M)Du. *rasch*, OHG. *rasc* (G. *rasch*) active, vigorous, healthy, quick, etc.] A. *adj.* 1. *Sc.* and *n. dial.* Active, fresh, vigorous; brisk, nimble, quick; eager. 2. Hasty, impetuous, reckless, acting without due consideration or regard for consequences 1509. †b. Of things: Operating quickly and strongly. SHAKS. 3. Of speech, actions, qualities, etc.: Characterized by, or proceeding from, undue haste and want of consideration 1558. †b. Urgent. SHAKS.

2. I was a fool, too r., and quite mistaken MILT. b. Though it doe worke as strong As Aconitum, or r. Gun-powder SHAKS. 3. R. aduentures speed not always best HOLLAND. b. I scarce haue leisure to salute you, My matter is so r. SHAKS. Hence **Ra·shly** *adv.*, **-ness.**

†B. *adv.* = RASHLY -1777.

Why do you speake so startingly and r.? SHAKS.

Rash (ræʃ), *v.*[1] Chiefly *Sc.* Now *rare* or *Obs.* late ME. [prob. onomatopœic.] 1. *intr.* To dash or rush hastily or violently. †2. *trans.* To dash (things *together*, or one thing *against*, *in*, or *through* another) -1666. †3. *To r. up*: To put together hurriedly; to rush or run up -1650.

†**Rash,** *v.*[2] 1500. [Alteration of RASE *v.*[1], perh. after prec. or next.] 1. *trans.* To cut, slash -1599. 2. To scrape out, erase -1650.

1. They..shields did share, and mailes did r., and helmes did hew SPENSER.

†**Rash,** *v.*[3] 1523. [Aphetic f. *arrache* = RASE *v.*[2]] *trans.* To pull, drag (*down*, *off*, *out*, etc.), to tear *away* -1697.

Rasher (ræ·ʃəɹ). 1592. [Origin obsc.] A thin slice of bacon or ham, cooked (or intended to be cooked) by broiling or frying.

‖**Raskolnik** (ræskǫ·lnik). 1799. [Russ.] A dissenter from the Orthodox Church of Russia.

Rasp (rɑsp), *sb.*[1] 1541. [a. OF. *raspe* (F. *râpe*), f. *rasper* RASP *v.*[1]] 1. A coarse kind of file, having separate teeth raised on its surface by means of a pointed punch; also, any similar tool or implement used for scraping or rubbing down. 2. *transf.* a. A rough surface like that of a rasp 1869. b. *Zool.* The radula of a mollusc, or one of the teeth on this 1826. 3. A rough sound as of a rasp 1851.

Comb. **r.-palm,** a Brazilian palm (*Iriartea exorhiza*), having exposed roots which are used by the natives as rasps; **-punch,** a punch for raising the teeth of rasps.

Rasp (rɑsp), *sb.*[2] 1555. [perh. a back-formation from RASPIS.] = RASPBERRY 1, 2.

Rasp (rɑsp), *v.*[1] ME. [app. a. OF. *rasper* (F. *râper*), perh. of Teut. origin.] 1. *trans.* To scrape or abrade with a rasp or the like. b. To scrape or rub in a rough manner 1715. c. *fig.* To grate upon, to irritate 1810. 2. To scrape *off* or *away* 1789. 3. *intr.* or *absol.* a. To scrape or grate, *esp.* on a stringed instrument 1842. b. To make a grating sound 1868.

1. The fuze must be rasped if necessary 1859. c. Her hard, metallic voice had rasped the invalid's nerves 1887. 2. I began to r. off the bark 1789. 3. a. Sorrily rasping on an execrable fiddle 1870. b. A loud, harsh, sharp tone, that rasps like a file 1868.

Rasp (rɑsp), *v.*[2] Now *dial.* 1626. [Origin unkn.] *intr.* and *trans.* To belch.

Raspatory (rɑ·spătəri). 1562. [ad. med. L. *raspatorium*, f. *raspare* RASP *v.*[1]] A form of rasp used in surgery.

Raspberry (rɑ·zbĕri). 1623. [f. RASP *sb.*[2] + BERRY.] 1. The fruit of several plants of the genus *Rubus*, esp. *R. idæus*, consisting of many small juicy grains or drupes of a subacid flavour arranged on a conical receptacle, from which the ripe fruit, usu. of a red colour, but also white or yellow, is easily detached. 2. The plant which produces the raspberry, or other similar plants of the genus *Rubus*. Also **r. cane.** 1733. 3. Raspberry wine 1768. 4. *slang.* A sound or manifestation of dislike or contempt; disapproval; dismissal 1915.

Rasper (rɑ·spəɹ). 1725. [f. RASP *v.*[1] + -ER[1].] 1. One who or that which rasps; a rasping-machine for beetroot, etc. 2. *Hunting.* A high difficult fence 1812. 3. *slang.* A person or thing that rasps or irritates; also, anything extraordinary in its own way 1839.

3. He's what you may a-call a r. DICKENS.

†**Ra·spis.** 1532. [Origin obsc.] 1. a. *collect.* Raspberries -1688. b. (With pl. in *-es.*) A raspberry -1678. 2. The raspberry plant -1682.

Raspy (rɑ·spi), *a.* 1838. [f. RASP *v.*[1] + -Y[1].] 1. Of a rasping nature; harsh, grating. 2. Irritable 1877.

Rasse (ræ·sě, ræs). 1817. [Javanese *rase.*] A kind of civet-cat (*Viverricula malaccensis*) found in India, the Malay Peninsula, Java, China, etc., and frequently kept in captivity for the sake of the perfume obtained from it.

Rasure (rē̆ⁱ·ziŭɹ, -ʒəɹ). Now *rare.* late ME. [a. F. *rasure*, or ad.L. *rasura*; see RASE *v.*[1] and -URE.] †1. The act of scraping or shaving; a scratch, mark, cut, slit -1721. †b. A particle, or the particles, scraped off -1669. †2. The act of shaving (the head, hair, etc.); tonsure -1737. 3. The act of scraping out something written; an erasure 1508. b. *transf.* Obliteration, effacement; cancelling 1603.

3. A specimen of his continual corrections and critical rasures D'ISRAELI. b. A forted residence 'gainst the tooth of time And razure of obliuion SHAKS.

Rat (ræt), *sb.* [OE. *ræt*; ult. origin unkn. Cf. RATTON.] 1. Any rodent of certain of the larger species of the genus *Mus*, esp. *M. rattus*, the black rat (now almost extinct), and *M. decumanus*, the common grey, brown, or Norway rat. (See also LAND-, MUSK-, WATER-RAT.) b. *transf.* Applied to animals of other species resembling the rat 1598. 2. With ref. to the alleged killing or expulsion of Irish rats by riming 1600. b. *slang.* Used ironically in *pl.* to express incredulity: 'humbug', 'nonsense' 1816. 3. As an opprobrious or familiar epithet 1594. 4. *spec.* †a. A pirate -1673. b. In politics, one who deserts his party 1788. c. A workman who refuses to strike along with others, or takes a striker's place; also, one who works for lower wages than the ordinary (or trade-union) rate 1881. 5. [f. RAT *v.*[1]] The act of ratting or changing one's side 1838.

1. It is the Wisedome of Rats, that will be sure to leaue a House, somewhat before it fall BACON. Phr. *To smell a r.*, to suspect something. *Like* (or *as wet as*) *a drowned r.* b. *Marsupial r.*, the opossum. *Pharaoh's r.*, the ichneumon. 2. I was neuer so berim'd since..I was an Irish R. SHAKS. 3. *Rich. III*, v. iii. 331.

Comb.: **r.-firm**, a firm which employs 'rats' or non-union workmen; **-fish**, a chimæra of the Pacific coast of America; **-kangaroo** = KANGAROO-RAT; **-mole** = MOLE-*rat*; **-pit**, a pit in which rats are confined to be worried by dogs; **-poison**, poison for destroying rats; **-snake**, a snake which kills rats, *esp.* a species found in Ceylon, frequently kept in domestication for this purpose.

Rat (ræt), *v.*[1] 1815. [f. prec.] 1. *intr.* (chiefly *pres. pple.*) To catch or hunt rats 1864. 2. a. To desert one's party, side, or cause, *esp.* in politics; to go *over* as a deserter 1812. b. To act as a 'rat' (sense 4 c) 1847.

2. a. If you have a mind to r., r. *sans phrase* 1817.

Rat (ræt), *v.*[2] *vulgar.* 1696. [Minced pronunciation of ROT *v.*; cf. DRAT.] A form of imprecation, = DRAT.

Rata (rā·tă). 1835. [Maori.] A large and handsome forest-tree of New Zealand, bearing crimson flowers and yielding a hard red wood.

Ratable, etc.: see RATEABLE, etc.

Ratafia (rætăfī·ă). 1699. [a. F., of unkn. origin.] 1. A cordial or liqueur flavoured with almonds or peach-, apricot-, or cherry-kernels. 2. A kind of cake or biscuit having the flavour of ratafia, or made to be eaten along with it 1845. 3. A variety of cherry 1835.

Ratal (rēⁱ·tăl). 1859. [f. RATE *sb.*[1] + -AL[2], prob. after *rental.*] The amount on which rates are assessed. Also *attrib.* or as *adj.*

Rataplan (rætăplæ·n). 1847. [a. F.; echoic.] A drumming or beating noise; a tattoo, rub-a-dub.

Ra·t-a-ta·t. 1681. [Echoic.] = RAT-TAT.

Ra·t-ca·tcher. 1592. [f. RAT *sb.*] One whose business it is to catch rats. b. Unconventional hunting dress 1930.

Ratch (rætʃ), *sb.* 1620. [var. of RATCHET.] †1. *Sc.* = FIRELOCK 1 (*rare*) -1657. 2. A ratchet 1721. 3. A ratchet-wheel 1696.

Ratch (rætʃ), *v.* 1777. [f. prec.] *Mech. trans.* To cut into teeth like those of a ratch; to turn *round* in the process of doing this.

Ratchel (ræ·tʃėl). *techn.* or *dial.* 1747. [Etym. obsc.] Fragments of loose shivery stone lying above the firm rock.

Ratchet (ræ·tʃėt), *sb.* 1659. [a. F. *rochet* a blunt form of lance-head, spool, ratchet, etc.]. 1. A set of angular or saw-like teeth on the edge of a bar or rim of a wheel, into which a cog, tooth, click, or the like may catch, usu. for the purpose of preventing reversed motion; also, a bar or wheel (*r.-wheel*) provided with such teeth. b. *pl.* in same sense (*rare*) 1721. 2. A click or detent, catching into the teeth of a ratchet-wheel 1846. Hence **Ra·tchet** *v. intr.* to move by means of a r.

Rate (rēⁱt), *sb.*[1] late ME. [a. OF. *rate*, ad. med.L. *rata* (from L. *pro rata parte* or *portione*, also *pro rata*, q.v. s.v. PRO[1]), pa. pple. fem. of *reri* to think, judge.] I. †1. The (total) estimated quantity, amount, or sum *of* anything, usu. as forming a basis for calculating other quantities or sums -1597. †b. A fixed portion or quantity (*rare*) -1611. 2. Estimated value or worth (of individual things or persons). late ME. †b. Estimation, consideration -1727. 3. Price, the sum paid or asked for a single thing 1590.

2. The low r. at which you seem to value my understanding *Junius Lett.* b. *Temp.* II. i. 109. 3. To purchase heaven for repenting, Is no hard r. G. HERBERT. Phr. †*At the r. of*, at the cost of. *At an easy r.*, without great expense; also *transf.* without great loss or suffering.

II. 1. The amount or number of one thing which corresponds or has relation to a certain amount or number of some other thing. Chiefly in phr. *at the r. of* 1497. 2. Value (of money, goods, etc.) as applicable to each individual piece or equal quantity 1488. b. The basis of equivalence on which one form of currency is exchanged for another 1727. 3. The amount *of* a charge or payment (such as interest, discount, wages, etc.) having relation to some other amount or basis of calculation 1540. b. A fixed charge applicable to each individual instance; *esp.* the (*or* an) amount paid or demanded for a certain quantity of a commodity, material, work, etc. 1526. †c. Relative cost or expense (of living) -1646. d. (Usu. *pl.*) Amount of assessment on property for local purposes. (Cf. POOR-RATE, etc.) 1712. 4. Degree of speed in moving from one place to another; the ratio between the distance covered and the time taken to traverse it. Chiefly in phr. (*to go*, etc.) *at a .. rate.* Also const. *of* (travelling, etc.). 1652. b. Relative speed of working, acting, etc. 1751. c. Of time-pieces: Amount of gain or loss on the correct time during twenty-four hours 1833. 5. Relative amount of variation, increase, decrease, etc. 1816.

1. [Interest] after the r. of six pounds per cent 1660. Although we were going at the r. of nine knots, the ship made no noise 1860. 2. The legal r. of an ounce of either of these metals in coin is called the mint price 1758. 3. It is not on this that the r. of wages depends 1833. b. The high rates of the railway companies prevented the cheaper kinds of fish from being sent to the markets 1883. d. Rates have increased in towns with great rapidity GLADSTONE. 4. The motion..swiftly augmented to the r. of an avalanche TYNDALL. 5. Three millions of paupers..increasing at a frightful r. per day CARLYLE.

III. †1. Standard or measure in respect of quality or condition; hence, class, kind, sort -1815. b. *Naut.* Class of vessels, *esp.* war-vessels, according to their size or strength 1649. c. Class or sub-class of buildings, in respect of purpose or size 1774. †2. Standard of conduct or action; hence, manner, style. Chiefly with *after.* -1792. 3. Degree or extent of action, feeling, etc. Chiefly in phr. *at a .. rate.* 1523.

1. He was very learned, according to the r. of that age FULLER. 2. They behaved themselves after another r. in private 1702. 3. I swore and curst at that most fearful R., that she was made to tremble to hear me BUNYAN.

Phrases. **At any r.** †a. On any terms. †b. (With negatives.) On any account. c. Under any circumstances; in any or either case. d. At all events; at least. †e. By any means. **At all rates.** †a. At any cost or by any means. b. At all events. **At that** (or **this**) **r.**, in that case, things being so, under these circumstances.

Rate (rēⁱt), *sb.*[2] 1575. [f. RATE *v.*[2]] *Hunting.* A reproof to a dog.

Rate (rēⁱt), *v.*[1] 1477. [f. RATE *sb.*[1]] †1. *trans.* To fix, assign, settle the amount of (a payment, fine, etc.) -1623. †b. To divide proportionally; to allot or apportion (*between* or *to* persons) as an amount or sum to be received or paid; also, to give or assign (one) his share -1661. 2. To reckon, estimate the amount or sum of. Now *rare.* 1597. 3. To estimate the (†nature) worth or value of; to appraise, value, †price 1599. b. To value *at* a certain sum 1570. c. To assign a certain value to (coin or metals) as, or in relation to, monetary standards. (Chiefly in *pass.*; also const. *to.*) 1758. 4. To reckon, esteem, consider, count 1565. 5. In *pass.* To be subjected or liable to payment of a certain rate; to be valued for purposes of assessment, taxation, etc. 1498. b. Const. *to* (the payment required) 1642. 6. Chiefly *Naut.* To place in a certain class or rank; to give rating to 1706. b. *intr.* To be rated *as* 1809. 7. *trans.* a. To calculate or fix at a certain rate 1845. b. To ascertain the variation of (a chronometer) from true time 1853.

1. b. *Ant. & Cl.* III. vi. 25. 2. To r. What millions died—that Cæsar might be great! CAMPBELL. 3. Instead of rating the man by his performance, we r. too frequently the performance by the man JOHNSON. b. You r. yourself too humbly 1884. c. Copper is rated very much above its real value ADAM SMITH. 4. Surely I may r. myself among their benefactors JOHNSON. 6. On board that ship I was rated as surgeon 1887. b. To r. as a full journeyman 1854. 7. b. The watch used in rating chronometers, should..be carried in a box 1875.

Rate (rēⁱt), *v.*[2] late ME. [Origin obsc.] 1. *trans.* To chide, scold, reprove vehemently or angrily. Const. *for*, †*of.* †2. To drive *away*, *back*, *from*, or *off*, by rating -1702. 3. *intr.* To utter strong or angry reproofs. Chiefly const. *at.* 1593.

1. The Bishop being angrie, rated the fellow roughly CAMDEN. When hounds are rated and do not answer the rate, they should be coupled up immediately 1781. 2. He..Rated my Vnckle from the Councell-Boord SHAKS. 3. Such a one As all day long hath rated at her child TENNYSON. Hence **Ra·ter**[2], one who rates or scolds. **Ra·ting** *vbl. sb.*[2] the action of reproving; an instance of this.

Rateable (rēⁱ·tăb'l), *a.* Also **ratable.** 1503. [f. RATE *v.*[1] + -ABLE.] 1. Capable of being rated, estimated, or calculated, esp. in accordance with some scale; proportional. 2. Liable to payment of rates 1760.

1. A r. distribution being made of their estates to the Kings well-deseruing friends 1611. 2. The r. property of the citizen 1846. Hence **Rateabi·lity**, the quality of being r. **Ra·teably** *adv.* proportionately 1490.

Ratel (rēⁱ·tĕl). 1777. [a. Cape Du. *ratel*; origin unkn.] A carnivorous quadruped of S. Africa, *Mellivora capensis*, of the family *Mustelidæ*; the honey-badger or honey-ratel. Also, the Indian species, *M. indica.*

Rater[1] (rēⁱ·təɹ). 1611. [f. RATE *v.*[1] + -ER[1].] 1. One who (or a thing which) rates, estimates, measures, etc. Now *rare.* 2. A vessel, etc. of a specified rate. (In recent use with ref. to the tonnage of racing vessels.) 1806.

Rath (rɑþ). 1596. [Ir. *rath*, now pronounced (rā).] *Irish Antiq.* An enclosure (usu. circular) made by a strong earthen wall, and serving as a fort and place of residence for the chief of a tribe; a hill-fort. (Often erron. ascribed to the Danes.)

Rathe (rēⁱð), **rath** (rɑþ), *a.* *poet.* and *dial.* late ME. [f. RATHE *adv.*] 1. Quick in action, speedy, prompt; eager, earnest, vehement. 2. Done, occurring, etc. before the natural time. (Orig. with *too.*) late ME. b. esp. of fruits, flowers, etc., which bloom or ripen early in the year 1572. 3. Early in the day; belonging to the morning 1596. 4. Belonging to the first part of some period of time 1850.

2. A r. December blights my lagging May 1833. b. The r. Primrose that forsaken dies MILT. 3. The r. Morning newly but awake DRAYTON. Hence †**Ra·thely** *adv.* = next 1.

Rathe (rēⁱð), *adv.* *poet.* and *dial.* [OE. *hraðe*, *raðe*, the adv. corresp. to OE. *hræd.*] †1. Quickly, rapidly, swiftly; *esp.* without delay, promptly, soon -1649. †b. With *too*: Too quickly, too soon; hence, too early; before the fitting or natural time -1541. 2. Early (in the morning or day). late ME.

2. I am the hunte, which r. and earely ryse 1575.

†**Ra·ther**, *a.* ME. [f. RATHER *adv.*] 1. Earlier -1620. b. Antecedent, prior; of greater importance (*rare*) -1668. 2. The earlier (of two persons or things); the former -1484.

1. The r. Lambes bene starved with cold SPENSER.

Rather (rā·ðəɹ), *adv.* OE. [Compar. of RATHE *adv.* A pronunciation with short sound (ræ·ðəɹ, rɑ·ðəɹ) is common in Scotland and U.S.; (rēⁱ·ðəɹ) is now only dial.] I. Denoting precedence in time. †1. (*The*) *r.*, (all) the more quickly, (all) the sooner -1605. 2. Earlier, sooner; at an earlier time, season, day, hour, etc. Now *dial.* OE. 3. Previously, formerly. Now *dial.* ME.

1. When Duncan is asleepe (Whereto the r. shall his dayes hard Iourney Soundly inuite him) SHAKS.

II. Denoting priority in nature or reason. 1. *The r.*, the more readily; (all) the more OE. 2. More truly or correctly; more properly speaking. late ME. 3. More (so) than not; more than anything else; hence, in a certain degree or measure; somewhat, slightly 1597.

4. *colloq.* Used as a strong affirmative in answer to a question: = 'I should rather think so'; very much so; very decidedly 1836.

1. A Case..which I the r. mention, because both Sexes are concerned in it 1710. 2. The Inhabitants..build their dwellings, rather like stoves then houses 1657. Say r., that he loves all the world GOLDSM. Last night, or r. very early this morning 1875. 3. His Appearance at the Baronet's must have been r. a silly one 1778. I r. think that you know him JOWETT. 4. 'Do you know the young lady?' 'Rather!' 1856.

III. Denoting prior eligibility or choice. 1. Sooner (as a matter of fitness, expediency, etc.); with better reason or ground; more properly or justly. With *than.* ME. 2. Sooner (as a matter of individual choice); more readily or willingly; with or in preference ME. b. Without *than*, in contrast to a preceding statement. Also rarely *the r.* ME. c. (One) *had r.* = (one) would rather. (See HAVE *v.* A. III.) 1450. †d. (One) *would r.* = (one) would rather have or choose -1675.

1. Therefore I r. deserve death than he 1573. 2. They would r. have died than refused MME D'ARBLAY. Painting cheeks with health r. than rouge RUSKIN. b. Ye..wol not applie you..unto the said marriage.. but r. induce yor said doghter to the contrarye 1480.

Ra·therest, *adv.* (and *a.*) late ME. [f. prec. + -EST.] 1. Most of all, most particularly. Now *dial.* 2. *Rather of the r.*, just a little too much or too little 1787.

'1. His..vntrained, or rather vnlettered, or r. vnconfirmed fashion SHAKS.

Rathe-ripe, rath-ripe (rēⁱ·ð-, rɑ·þ-), *a.* and *sb.* Now *poet.* and *dial.* 1578. [f. RATHE *a.* + RIPE *a.* With ref. to grain usu. spelt *rath-*.] A. *adj.* 1. Of fruits, grain, etc.: Coming early to maturity; ripening early in the year. 2. *fig.* Precocious. Now *dial.* 1617. B. *sb.* Applied to early peas, apples, etc. 1677.

A. 1. Fruits like the fig-tree's, r., rotten-rich BROWNING.

‖**Rathskeller** (rā·tskeləɹ). *U.S.* 1900. [Ger., town-hall cellar.] A beer-saloon or restaurant, usu. in a basement.

Ratification (rætifikēⁱ·ʃən). 1450. [a. F., or ad. med.L. *ratificatio.*] The action of ratifying or confirming; sanction, confirmation.

Ratify (ræ·tifəi), *v.* ME. [a. F. *ratifier*, ad. med.L. *ratificare*; see -FY.] 1. *trans.* To confirm or make valid (an act, compact, promise, etc.) by giving consent, approval, or formal sanction (esp. to what has been done or arranged for by another). †b. To confirm, to guarantee the fulfilment of (a purpose, hope, etc.) -1649. †c. To confirm the possession of -1611. 2. To declare or confirm the truth or correctness of (a statement, etc.). Now *rare* or *Obs.* late ME. †3. To bring to fulfilment or completion (*rare*) -1720.

1. To ratifie..the auncient friendship with a new peace 1579. b. God..onely can ratifie all our pious resolutions 1649. 2. The prophesie..thus ratified by the euent 1631. Hence **Ra·tifier,** one who or that which ratifies.

Ratihabition (rætihăbi·ʃən). 1561. [ad. late L. *ratihabitio*, f. *ratum* confirmed + *habere* to have, hold.] *Law.* Approval, sanction.

Rating (rēⁱ·tiŋ), *vbl. sb.*[1] 1534. [f. RATE *v.*[1] + -ING[1].] 1. The action of RATE *v.*[1] b. The (*or* an) amount fixed as a rate 1887. 2. *Naut.* 'The station a person holds on the ship's books' (Smyth); also *transf.*, position, class, etc., in general 1702. b. *Naut.* in *pl.* Men of a certain rating 1893.

Ratio (rēⁱ·ʃio). 1636. [L., f. *rat-*, ppl. stem of *reri* to think.; see also RATION, REASON.] †1. Reason, rationale (*rare*) -1752. 2. *Math.* The relation between two similar magnitudes in respect of quantity, determined by the number of times one contains the other (integrally or fractionally) 1660. b. The corresponding relationship between things not precisely measurable 1808. 3. *spec.* In monetary science, the quantitative relation in which one metal stands to another in respect of their value as money or legal tender 1879. †4. = RATION *sb.* 3. -1824.

2. The r...is exactly one to a hundred *Junius Lett.* b. Executorships..which excited his spleen or soothed his vanity in equal ratios LAMB. 4. A cow..eat up two ratios and half of dried grass STERNE.

Ratiocinate (rætiǫ·sineⁱt), *v.* 1643. [f. L. *ratiocinat-*, *ratiocinari* to calculate, etc., f. *ratio* RATIO.] *intr.* To reason, to carry on a process of reasoning. (Now *rare* in serious use.)

Ratiocination (ræ:tiǫsinēⁱ·ʃən). 1530. [ad. L. *ratiocinationem.*] 1. The process of reasoning. 2. With *a* and *pl.* An instance of this; also, a conclusion arrived at by reasoning 1620. 3. Power or habit of reasoning (*rare*) 1647.

Ratiocinative (rætiǫ·sinētiv), *a.* 1620. [ad. L. *ratiocinativus.*] Characterized by, given to, or expressive of, ratiocination. So **Ratio·cinatory** *a.*

Ration (ræ·ʃən, *U.S.* rēⁱ·ʃən), *sb.* 1550. [a. F. *ration*, or ad. L. *rationem* RATIO.] †1. Reasoning 1550. †2. = RATIO 2, 3. -1815. 3. A fixed allowance or share of provisions; *spec.* in the army and navy, the daily amount of certain articles of food allotted to each officer and man. (Sometimes, esp. *pl.*, simply = provisions, food.) 1702. b. *Mil.* The daily allowance of forage or provender assigned to each horse or other animal 1727. c. An allowance, share, portion *of* provisions or other supplies 1727.

3. A 'ration' in the literal military sense of the word means 1 lb. of bread and ¾ lb. of meat 1885.

Ration (ræ·ʃən, *U.S.* rēⁱ·ʃən), *v.* 1859. [f. prec.] 1. *trans.* To supply (persons) with rations; to provision; to put on a fixed allowance. 2. To divide (food, etc.) into rations; to serve *out* in fixed quantities 1870. 3. *intr.* (for *refl.*) To obtain a supply of food 1859.

Rational (ræ·ʃənăl), *a.* and *sb.*[1] late ME. [ad. L. *rationalis*; see RATIO, RATION, and -AL.] A. *adj.* 1. Having the faculty of reasoning; endowed with reason. b. Exercising one's reason in a proper manner; having sound judgement; sensible, sane 1632. 2. Of, pertaining or relating to, reason 1601. 3. Based on, derived from, reason or reasoning 1531. 4. Agreeable to reason; reasonable, sensible; not foolish, absurd, or extravagant 1601. 5. *Math.* Applied to quantities or ratios which can be expressed without the use of radical signs 1570.

1. We are r.: but we are animal too COWPER. b. R. and experienced men tolerably well know,..how to distinguish between true and false liberty BURKE. 2. *R. faculty, nature, power*, etc.: Our r. faculty is the gift of God 1788. 4. *R. dress*, a form of dress for women, proposed as more sensible than that in general use; usu. the use of knickerbockers in place of a skirt, esp. for cycling. 5. *R. horizon*: see HORIZON 3.

B. *sb.*[1] The adj. used absol. 1. a. A rational being. Chiefly in *pl.* = human beings, men. Now *Obs.* or *rare.* 1606. b. An advocate of something 'rational' 1756. †2. *Math.* A rational quantity (*rare*) -1797. 3. *pl.* 'Rational' dress; knickerbockers for women 1889. Hence **Ra·tional-ly** *adv.*, **-ness** (now *rare*).

Rational (ræ·ʃənăl), *sb.*[2] late ME. [ad. L. *rationale*, neut. of *rationalis* adj.; used in the Vulg. to translate Hebrew *ḥōshen*, after the LXX. λογεῖον oracle, oracular instrument.] †1. The breastplate worn by the Jewish high-priest -1674. b. An ornament formerly worn on the breast by bishops during the celebration of mass 1849. †2. = next 2. -1676.

1. The twelve stones in the Rationall or breast-plate of Aaron SIR T. BROWNE.

‖**Rationale** (ræʃiŏnēⁱ·li). 1657. [L., neut. of *rationalis.*] 1. A reasoned exposition of principles; a statement of reasons. 2. The fundamental reason, the logical or rational basis (*of* anything) 1688.

Rationalism (ræ·ʃənăliz'm). 1827. [f. RATIONAL *a.* + -ISM.] 1. *Theol.* a. The practice of explaining in a manner agreeable to reason whatever is apparently supernatural in the records of sacred history. b. The principle of regarding reason as the chief or only guide in matters of religion. 2. *Metaph.* A theory (opp. to *empiricism* or *sensationalism*) which regards reason, rather than sense, as the foundation of certainty in knowledge 1857.

Rationalist (ræ·ʃənălist), *sb.* and *a.* 1626. [f. as prec. + -IST.] 1. One who forms his opinions by pure or *a priori* reasoning. 2. *Theol.* One who rationalizes in matters of religion or sacred history; an adherent of rationalism 1640. b. *attrib.* or as *adj.* = next 1828.

Rationalistic (ræ:ʃənăli·stik), *a.* 1830. [f. prec.] Characterized by rationalism, given or inclined to rationalism. Hence **Rational·i·stical**, *a.*, **-ly** *adv.*

Rationality (ræʃənæ·līti). 1570. [ad. late L. *rationalitas*; see RATIONAL and -ITY.] 1. The quality of possessing reason; the power of being able to exercise one's reason 1628. 2. The fact of being based on, or agreeable to, reason 1651. b. A rational or reasonable view, practice, etc. 1660. 3. The tendency to regard everything from a purely rational point of view 1791. †4. *Math.* The quality of being rational 1570. †5. = RATIONALE 2. 1646.

1. Some kind of brute Force within, prevails over the Principle of R. 1726. 5. Many well directed intentions, whose rationalities will never beare a rigid examination SIR T. BROWNE.

Rationalization (ræ·ʃənăləizēⁱ·ʃən). 1846. [-ATION.] 1. The act of making rational or intelligible, or the result of this. 2. *Math.* The process of clearing from irrational quantities 1853. 3. *Econ.* The scientific organization of industry to ensure the minimum waste of labour, the standardization of production, and the consequent maintenance of prices at a constant level 1928.

Rationalize (ræ·ʃənăləiz), *v.* 1816. [f. RATIONAL *a.*] 1. *trans.* To render conformable to reason; to explain on a rational basis 1817. 2. *Math.* To clear from irrational quantities 1816. 3. *intr.* To employ reason or rationalism; to think rationally or in a rationalistic manner 1835. 4. *trans.* To organize (industry) in the manner defined in prec. 3. 1928.

3. When we ask for reasons when we should not, we rationalise J. H. NEWMAN.

Ratite (ræ·təit), *a.* 1877. [f. L. *ratis* raft + -ITE [2].] *Ornith.* Of or belonging to the *Ratitæ*, a class of birds having a keelless sternum, as the ostrich, emu, cassowary, etc. (opp. to *carinate.*)

Ratlin(e, ratling (ræ·tlin, -liŋ). 1481. [Origin obsc.] 1. Thin line or rope such as is used for the ratlines (see 2). 2. (Chiefly *pl.*) One of the small lines fastened horizontally on the shrouds of a vessel, and serving as steps to go up and down the rigging 1611.

Ratoon (rătū·n), *sb.* Also **ratt-**. 1777. [ad. Sp. *retoño* a fresh shoot or sprout.] A new shoot or sprout springing up from the root of the sugar-cane after it has been cropped. Hence **Ratoo·n** *v. intr.* (of the sugar-cane, etc.) to send up new shoots after being cut down or cropped.

Ratsbane (ræ·tsbēⁱn). 1523. [f. RAT *sb.* + BANE.] 1. Rat-poison; †*spec.* arsenic. (Now only *literary.*) 2. Applied to certain plants 1846. Hence **Ra·tsbaned** *ppl. a.* poisoned with r.

Ra·t's-tail. 1580. [f. RAT *sb.*] 1. *pl.* in *Farriery*: †a. Chaps or cracks on the back of a horse's hind legs. b. Warty or suppurating excrescences on the same part. 2. Applied to various things resembling a rat's tail in shape; e.g. the tapering end of a rope; a lank lock of hair, etc. 1869. 3. A rat-tail file 1827.

Ra·t-tail. 1705. [f. as prec.] 1. *pl.* = RAT'S-TAIL 1. 1753. 2. A tail resembling that of a rat; *esp.* a horse's tail with little or no hair; also, a horse having a hairless tail, or the diseased condition which causes the hair of the tail to fall off 1705. 3. A fish of the genus *Macrurus*, esp. *M. fabricii* 1882.

attrib.: *r. file*, a fine round file used for enlarging holes in metal, etc.

Ra·t-tailed, *a.* 1684. [f. RAT *sb.*] 1. Having a tail like that of a rat; *esp.* of horses, having a rat-tail. b. Of the larva of a drone-fly (*Eristalis*) having a long slender tail 1753. c. *spec.* in the names of certain animals 1846. 2. Of a spoon: Having a tail-like prolongation of the handle along the back of the bowl 1881.

1. c. *R. serpent*, an American viper. *R. shrew*, the Musk-rat. *R. snake*, the fer-de-lance.

Rattan, ratan (rătæ·n). 1660. [a. (ult.) Malay *rōtan*, app. for *rautan*, f. *raut* to pare, trim, strip.] 1. One of several species of the genus *Calamus*, climbing palms growing chiefly in the East Indies, and to a small extent in Africa and Australia, and notable for their long thin jointed and pliable stems; also, a plant belonging to one of these species 1681. 2. A portion of the stem of a rattan, used as a switch or stick, or for other purposes 1660. **3.** Without article, as a material 1748.

Rat-tat (ræ·tˌtæ·t). 1774. [Echoic.] A sharp rapping sound, *esp.* of a knock at a door. So **Rat-tat-tat**, etc. (cf. RAT-A-TAT).

Ratteen (rătī·n). 1685. [ad. F. *ratine*; origin unkn.] A thick twilled woollen cloth, usu. friezed or with a curled nap, but sometimes dressed; a frieze or drugget. Now *Hist.* **b.** A piece of ratteen 1706.

Ratten (ræ·t'n), *v.* 1867. [Back-formation from next.] **a.** *trans.* To molest (a workman or employer) by rattening. **b.** *intr.* To practise rattening. Hence **Ra·ttener.**

Ra·ttening, *vbl. sb.* 1843. [Origin obsc.] The act or practice of abstracting tools, destroying machinery, etc., as a means of enforcing compliance with the rules of a trade union, or of venting spite. Also *transf.*

Ratter (ræ·təɹ). 1834. [f. RAT *sb.* and *v.*[1] + -ER [1].] **1.** A ratcatcher; a dog or other animal which hunts rats 1858. **2.** One who 'rats': **a.** One who deserts his party. **b.** A workman who refuses to join a strike, etc. 1834.

Ratting (ræ·tiŋ), *vbl. sb.* 1816. [f. RAT *v.*[1] + -ING [1].] **1.** Desertion of one's party or principles. Also with *over.* **2.** The catching or killing of rats 1828.

Rattle (ræ·t'l), *sb.* 1500. [f. next.] **I. 1.** An instrument used to make a rattling noise; *esp.* a child's toy; also, one formerly used by watchmen to give an alarm 1519. **2.** A set of horny, loosely-connected rings forming the termination of the tail in the rattlesnake, by shaking which it produces a rattling noise. Also *pl.* 1624. **3.** Applied to certain plants having seeds which rattle in their cases when ripe: **a.** Yellow rattle, *Rhinanthus Crista-galli* = COCK'S-COMB 5; **b.** Red rattle, *Pedicularis sylvatica* 1578.

1. I wyll bye a rattell to styll my baby for cryenge 1519. *transf.* Such rattles as drums and trumpets H. WALPOLE.

II. 1. A rapid succession of short sharp sounds, caused by the concussion of hard bodies 1500. **b.** *transf.* Racket, uproar, noisy gaiety, stir 1691. **c.** A rattling sound in the throat, caused by partial obstruction; see RÂLE, and DEATH-*rattle.* Also in *pl.* (spec. as a pop. name for croup). 1752. **†2.** A sharp reproof -1711. **3. a.** A noisy flow of words 1627. **b.** Without article: Lively talk or chatter of a trivial kind 1780. **4.** A constant chatterer; one who talks incessantly in a lively or thoughtless fashion 1742.

1. Sent bounding down the slope with peal and r. TYNDALL. **b.** She cannot bear a place without some cheerfulness and r. JOHNSON. 4. My companion turned out to be a lively amusing r. 1859.

attrib. and *Comb.*: **r.-bag,** a r. in the form of a bag; also as *adj.*, rattling, reckless; **-box,** (*a*) a r. in the form of a box or case; (*b*) = RATTLE I. 3; (*c*) a species of rattlewort (*Crotalaria sagittalis*); **-brain,** an empty-headed noisy fellow; so **-brained** *a.*; **-weed,** (*a*) *U.S.* loco-weed; (*b*) *dial.* Bladder Campion; **-wort,** the genus *Crotalaria.*

Rattle (ræ·t'l), *v.*[1] [ME. *ratelen* = LG. *ratelen*, G. *rasseln*, prob. of echoic origin.] **I.** *intr.* **1.** Of things: To give out a rapid succession of short sharp sounds, usu. in consequence of rapid agitation and of striking against each other or against some hard dry body. **b.** Of sounds having this character 1587. **c.** Of places: To resound, be filled, with a noise of this kind 1622. **d.** Of an agent: To produce a succession of sharp sounds by striking or knocking on something, or by causing hard bodies to strike against each other 1676. **2.** To produce an involuntary sound of this kind, *esp.* in the throat. late ME. **3.** To talk rapidly in a thoughtless, noisy, or lively manner (esp. with *on, along,* etc.); to chatter 1594. **4.** To move, fall, etc. rapidly and with a rattling noise. Usu. with advs., as *along, by, in, out,* or advb. phr. 1555. **b.** To drive in a rapid rattling fashion 1838.

1. The stones did r. underneath COWPER. **b.** Rowling Thunder rattl'd o'er his Head DRYDEN. **d.** The storm that blows Without, and rattles on his humble roof THOMSON. 3. **b.** A resolution to break the ice, and r. away at any rate GOLDSM. 4. The car rattling o'er the stony street BYRON. **b.** All..entered the coach, and rattled off THACKERAY.

II. *trans.* **1.** To make (a thing or things) rattle 1560. **†b.** To assail with a rattling noise SHAKS. **2.** To say or utter in a rapid or lively manner. late ME. **b.** To play (music) in a rattling fashion on a piano 1848. **†3.** To scold, rate, or rail at, volubly -1736. **†b.** So with *up* or *off*, or complement -1722. **4.** *Sporting.* To beat up or chase vigorously 1829. **5.** To impel, drive, drag, bring, etc., in a rapid rattling manner 1825. **6.** orig. *U.S.* To shake or agitate (a person) by fear or consternation 1887.

1. To r. his chains by way of lullaby CARLYLE. 2. **b.** She rattled away a triumphant voluntary on the keys THACKERAY. 4. A fox well rattled, up to the first check,..is as good as half killed 1860. 5. The anchor was rattled up in a minute 1867.

Rattle (ræ·t'l), *v.*[2] 1729. [Back-formation from *rattling* RATLIN(E, taken as a vbl. sb.] *trans.* To furnish with ratlines. Usu. with *down.*

†Ra·ttle-head. 1641. **1.** An empty-headed noisy fellow -1788. **2.** *spec.* A Cavalier (in contrast to a ROUNDHEAD) -1649. So **Ra·ttle-headed** *a.*

Ra·ttle-pate. 1643. = RATTLE-HEAD 1. So **Ra·ttle-pated** *a.* 1633.

Rattler (ræ·tləɹ). 1449. [f. RATTLE *v.*[1] + -ER [1].] **1.** = RATTLE *sb.* II. 4. **2.** A thing which rattles 1594. **b.** *U.S.* A rattlesnake 1827. **3.** A sharp or severe blow, fall, storm, etc. 1812.

Rattlesnake (ræ·t'lˌsnēⁱk). 1630. [f. RATTLE *sb.* or *v.*[1] + SNAKE.] A venomous American snake, having a series of horny rings at the end of the tail which make a rattling noise when the tail is vibrated. Also *attrib.*

Comb., in names of American plants, as **r.-fern,** a species of moonwort or grape-fern, *Botrychium virginianum*; **-grass,** a kind of quaking-grass, *Glyceria canadensis*; **-herb,** the Bane-berry, *Actæa rubra* or *alba*, and some other plants; **rattlesnake('s) master,** the Button-snakeroot, *Liatris scariosa* or *squarrosa*, and other plants; **r. plantain,** one of three species of *Goodyera*, esp. *G. pubescens*; **-root,** (*a*) the root of a species of milkwort, *Polygala Senega* (see SENEGA); (*b*) one of several species of *Prenanthes*, esp. *P. serpentaria*; **r. weed,** (*a*) a species of *Eryngium*; (*b*) a species of hawk-weed, *Hieracium venosum*; **-wort** = *r.-root* (a).

Ra·ttletrap, *sb.* and *a.* 1766. [f. RATTLE *sb.* or *v.*[1] + TRAP.] **A.** *sb.* **1.** *pl.* Knick-knacks, trifles, odds and ends, curiosities, or the like. Also *sing.*, one such article. **2.** A rattling rickety coach or other vehicle 1822. **3.** Any rickety or shaky thing 1833. **4.** *slang.* The mouth 1824. **B.** *adj.* Rickety, shaky 1834.

Rattling (ræ·tliŋ), *ppl. a.* late ME. [RATTLE *v.*[1]] **1.** That rattles or makes a rattle. **2.** Of persons: Extremely lively 1727. **3.** Remarkably good, fine, fast, etc. 1690. **b.** advb. with adjs.: Remarkably, extremely 1829.

Rattling, var. of RATLIN(E.

Ratton (ræ·t'n). Now *Sc.* and *n. dial.* ME. [a. OF. *raton*, f. *rat* RAT.] A rat.

†Rattoon. 1656. var. of RACOON -1755.

Ra·t-trap. 1469. [f. RAT *sb.* + TRAP.] **1.** A trap for catching rats. **2.** Applied to a cycle pedal consisting of two parallel iron plates with teeth cut in them 1885.

Ratty (ræ·ti), *a.* 1865. [f. RAT *sb.* + -Y [1].] **1. a.** Characteristic of a rat or rats 1888. **b.** Infested with rats 1865. **2.** *slang.* Wretched, mean, miserable. **b.** Angry, irritated. 1885.

Rau·cid, *a.* [f. L. *raucus* + -ID [1].] Raucous LAMB.

Raucity (rǭ·sĭti). *rare.* 1607. [ad. L. *raucitas*, f. *raucus* RAUCOUS + -ITY.] Harshness, roughness, hoarseness.

Raucous (rǭ·kəs), *a.* 1769. [f. L. *raucus* hoarse + -OUS.] Hoarse, rough, harsh-sounding. Hence **Rau·cous-ly** *adv.*, **-ness.**

Raughty, variant of RORTY.

Ravage (ræ·vėdʒ), *sb.* 1611. [a. F. *ravage*, f. *ravir* to RAVISH; see -AGE.] The act or practice of ravaging, or the result of this; destruction, devastation, extensive damage, done by men or beasts. **b.** *pl.* Extensive depredations 1697. **c.** *transf.* 1704.

Noise of r. wrought by beast and man TENNYSON. **c.** If Mrs. Evergreen does take some pains to repair the ravages of time SHERIDAN. The ravages of the pestilence 1838. The r. of four years J. H. NEWMAN.

Ravage (ræ·vėdʒ), *v.* 1611. [ad. F. *ravager*, f. *ravage*; see prec.] **1.** *trans.* To devastate, lay waste, despoil, plunder (a country). Also *transf.* and *fig.* **2.** *intr.* To commit ravages; to make havoc or destruction 1627.

1. The barbarians who ravag'd Greece and Italy 1704. That sweet face so sadly ravaged by grief and despair THACKERAY. Hence **Ra·vager,** one who or that which ravages.

Rave (rēⁱv), *sb.*[1] 1530. [Origin obsc.] A rail of a cart; esp. *pl.* a framework of rails or boards (permanent or removable) added to the sides of a cart to enable a greater load to be carried. **b.** *U.S.* One of the vertical side-pieces in the body of a wagon or sleigh.

Rave (rēⁱv), *sb.*[2] 1598. [f. next.] The (*or* an) act of raving; frenzy, great excitement.

Rave (rēⁱv), *v.* late ME. [perh. a. OF. *raver*, app. a var. of *rêver* to dream, be delirious; origin obsc.] **1.** *intr.* †To be mad, to show signs of madness or delirium; hence, to talk or declaim wildly or furiously in consequence of madness or some other violent passion. Occas. (now *dial.*) to shout or bawl. **2.** *transf.* Of the sea, storms, etc.: To rage; to dash, rush, roar, etc., in a furious manner 1559. **3.** To talk or declaim with enthusiasm or poetic rapture 1704. **4.** *trans.* To utter in a frenzied or enthusiastic manner 1602. **5.** quasi-*trans.* with complement: To bring (into a specified state) by raving 1812.

1. She talks like one who raves in fever 1871. The *Times* is already raving about our having reached 'a crisis' 1884. 2. The milde Ocean, Who now hath quite forgot to r. MILT. When the pibroch bids the battle r. SCOTT. 3. Solitude, however some may r., Seeming a sanctuary, proves a grave COWPER. How people can r. about Italy, I can't think 1838. 4. For he now raved enormous folly SHELLEY. Hence **Ra·ver,** one who raves, a madman; an extravagant speaker. **Ra·ving** *vbl. sb.* the action of the verb; wild or delirious talk or declamation; an utterance of this kind.

Ravel (ræ·v'l), *sb.* 1634. [f. next.] **1.** A tangle, complication, entanglement. **2.** A broken thread, a loose end. Also *fig.* 1832.

Ravel (ræ·v'l), *v.* 1582. [app. a. Du. *rav-, rafelen* to tangle, to fray out, unweave.] **I.** *intr.* **1.** To become entangled or confused. *rare* exc. *dial.* 1585. **2.** Of a fabric: To fray *out*, to suffer disintegration 1611. **3.** Of a clue or thread: To unwind; to come off the clue, reel, etc. *rare.* (now *dial.*). 1649. **†4.** To examine or inquire *into* a thing -1710.

1. By thir own perplexities involv'd They r. more MILT. 2. The hem of a garment is that which binds it round, and prevents it from ravelling out 1860. 4. The malicious..r. into the conduct of a man of honour in the dark 1710.

II. *trans.* **1.** To entangle, confuse, perplex 1598. **2.** To unwind or unweave; to unravel 1607. **b.** *fig.* To take to pieces; to disentangle 1582. **3.** *To r. out*: To draw or pull out by unwinding or unweaving 1623. **†b.** To destroy, spoil, or waste, as by pulling a fabric into threads -1708. **c.** To disentangle, make plain or clear 1593.

1. It ravels and complicates the meaning of the prophecies 1845. 2. The night still ravell'd, what the day renew'd POPE. 3. A stitch in a man's stocking not taken up in time, ravels out all the rest 1623. **c.** Must I rauell out My weau'd-vp follyes? SHAKS. Hence **Ra·veller,** one who ravels.

Ravelin (ræ·vlin). 1589. [a. F., a. It. *rav-, revellino*, now *rivellino.*] *Fortif.* An outwork consisting of two faces which form a salient angle, constructed beyond the main ditch and in front of the curtain.

Ravelling (ræ·v'liŋ), *vbl. sb.* 1658. [f. RAVEL *v.*] **1.** The action of RAVEL *v.* 1673. **2.** *concr.* A thread from a woven fabric which is frayed or unravelled 1658.

Raven (rēⁱ·v'n), *sb.*[1] (*a.*) [Com. Teut.: OE. *hræfn.*] **1.** A widely distributed corvine bird (*Corvus corax*) of Europe and Asia, of large size, with black lustrous plumage and raucous voice, which feeds chiefly on carrion or other flesh. Applied also to birds belonging to other species of *Corvus*, esp. the American raven (*Corvus carnivorus*). **b.** *fig.* A croaker 1814. **2.** The figure of a raven on the flag of the Danish vikings; also, the flag itself or the warlike power typified by this OE. **†3.** *Astron.* The southern constellation Corvus (*rare*) -1551. **4.** *attrib.* or *adj.* Of the colour of a raven; glossy black; intensely dark or gloomy 1601.

1. The sad-presaging r., that tolls The sick man's

passport in her hollow beak MARLOWE. 4. Smoothing the R. doune Of darknes MILT.

Comb.: **r.-duck** [ad. G. *rabentuch*], a kind of canvas (also **raven's duck**); **r. standard**: cf. sense 2; **-stone** [ad. G. *rabenstein*], the place of execution, the gallows or gibbet.

Raven (ræ·v'n), *v.* 1494. [ad. OF. *raviner* :—L. **rapinare*, f. *rapina*; see RAPINE, RAVIN.] †1. *trans.* To take (goods) away by force; to seize or divide as spoil –1593. b. *absol.* or *intr.* To plunder; to seek *after*, to go *about*, with intent to plunder 1603. 2. To devour voraciously 1560. b. So with *up*, *down*, *in*. Now *rare*. 1598. 3. *intr.* or *absol.* To eat voraciously; to prey *on* or *upon* 1530. b. To have a ravenous appetite or desire *for* 1667. c. To have an intense longing for food 1858. 4. *intr.* To prowl ravenously; to go about in search of food 1560.

1. b. His Croats and loose hordes went openly ravening about CARLYLE. 2. Like a roaring lion rauening the pray BIBLE (Geneva) *Ezek.* xxii. 25. 3. For Greedy Cormorants to r. upon 1575. b. The more they fed, they ravened still for more DRYDEN. c. You must have been ravening hours ago 1881. 4. Beniamin shall rauine (as) a wolfe BIBLE (Geneva) *Gen.* xlix. 27. *fig.* The unclean pestilence ravins in your streets RUSKIN. Hence **Ra·vener.**

Ravening (ræ·v'niŋ), *ppl. a.* 1526. [f. prec.] That ravens, in the senses of the vb. (In early use esp. of wolves.) †2. Rabid, mad –1696. Hence **Ra·veningly** *adv.*

Ravenous (ræ·v'nəs), *a.* late ME. [a. OF. *ravineux* :—pop. L. **rapinosus*; see RAPINE, RAVIN, and -OUS.] 1. Addicted to plundering or taking by force; extremely rapacious. 2. Of animals: Given to seizing in order to devour; voracious, gluttonous. Hence of appetite, hunger, etc. late ME. 3. Excessively hungry 1719.

1. Nations who were r...treacherous and fierce DE FOE. 2. *transf.* Thy desires Are Woluish, bloody, steru'd, and rauenous SHAKS. 3. I got up r. DE FOE. Hence **Ra·venous-ly** *adv.*, **-ness.**

Ravin (ræ·vin), **raven**[2] (ræ·v'n). ME. [a. F. *ravine* :—L. *rapina* RAPINE.] 1. Robbery, rapine. †b. With *a* and *pl.*: An act of rapine –1593. 2. The act or practice of seizing and devouring prey or food; hence, voracity, gluttony. late ME. 3. *concr.* That which is taken or seized; plunder; prey (of men or beasts) ME. 4. *attrib.* as *adj.* = prec. late ME.

1. Blood, and ravin, and robbery are their characteristics RAWLINSON. 2. *Beast* (etc.) *of r.*: Beast of prey. 4. I met the rauine Lyon SHAKS.

Ravine (răvī·n), *sb.* 1450. [a. F. *ravine* a violent rush (now only of water), a ravine; identical with *ravine* RAVIN.] †1. Impetus, violence, force –1450. 2. A deep narrow hollow or gorge, a mountain cleft, prop. one worn by a torrent 1802. Hence **Ravi·ne** *v. trans.* to score with ravines; to hollow *out*.

Raving (rē¹·viŋ), *ppl. a.* 1475. [-ING [2].] Delirious, frenzied; raging. b. quasi-*adv.* with adjs., esp. *mad* 1786. Hence **Ra·vingly** *adv.*

Ravish (ræ·viʃ), *v.* ME. [a. F. *raviss-*, lengthened stem of *ravir*:—pop. L. **rapīre* for L. *rapere*.] 1. *trans.* To seize and carry off (a person); to take by violence; to tear or drag away *from* (a place or person). Now *rare*. †2. To carry away (a woman) by force. (Sometimes implying subsequent violation). –1665. b. To commit rape upon (a woman), to violate. late ME. †c. To spoil, corrupt SHAKS. 3. To carry away or remove from earth (esp. to heaven) or from sight. Now *rare*. ME. b. To transport *in spirit* without bodily removal ME. c. To transport with the strength of some feeling; to carry away with rapture; to entrance ME. 4. To seize and take away as plunder or spoil; to seize upon (a thing) by force or violence; to make a prey of. late ME. †b. To remove by force –1698. †5. To ravage, despoil, plunder –1619. †b. To despoil (a person) *of* something –1803.

2. c. O hateful, vaporous, and foggy Night..With rotten damps r. the morning air SHAKS. 3. c. She had suche ioye that of a great spase she coude speke no word, she was so rauysshyd LD. BERNERS. 4. I.. am not..obliged to r. my bread out of the mouths of others DE FOE. The Free-booters had used to r. away their lives and their cattle 1731. b. These are the ways of all soch as be covetous, that one wolde rauysh anothers life COVERDALE *Prov.* i. 12. Hence **Ra·visher. Ra·vishingly** *adv.*

Ravishment (ræ·viʃmĕnt). 1477. [ad. OF. *ravissement*; see prec. and -MENT.] †1. The act of carrying off a person; in *r. of ward* or *de gard*, the taking away of a ward; also, the writ issued in consequence of this –1700. 2. Forcible abduction or violation of a woman 1529. b. With *a* and *pl.* An instance of this 1576. 3. Transport, rapture, ecstasy. Also with *a* and *pl.* 1477.

3. A melody That, indistinctly heard, with r. Possess'd me CARY.

Ra·vissant, *a.* ME. [a. F., pple. of *ravir*; see RAVISH.] †1. Of beasts: Ravening (*rare*) –1549. 2. Ravishing, delightful 1653.

Raw (rǭ), *a.* (*sb.*). [Com. Teut.: OE. *hrēaw* :—OTeut. **hrawoz*, pre-Teut. **krouos*, related to L. *cruor*, Gr. κρέας, Skr. *kravíš* raw flesh.] A. *adj.* 1. Uncooked, not prepared for use as food by the action of fire or heat. b. Unburnt, unbaked; not hardened or fused by fire 1634. 2. In a natural or unwrought state; not yet subjected to any process of dressing or manufacture: a. of the materials of textile fabrics; esp. *r. silk*, silk simply drawn from the cocoons by reeling ME. b. of cloth: Unfulled. late ME. c. of leather or hides: Untanned, undressed. Also *rawhide*, a rope or whip of undressed hide. 1489. d. of other substances (or their qualities), e.g. undiluted (spirits), unrefined (oil), unmalted (grain); etc. 1567. e. with general terms, as *r. material*, *produce*, etc. 1738. 3. Crude, not brought to perfect composition, form or finish. (In mod. use chiefly of colouring). late ME. b. Uncultivated, uncivilized, brutal (*rare*) 1577. †4. Unripe, immature –1652. 5. Of persons: Inexperienced, unskilled, untrained; quite new or fresh to anything 1561. b. *esp.* of soldiers without training or experience in fighting 1577. c. of things, qualities, actions, etc. (*rare*) 1602. 6. Having the skin removed, so that the flesh is exposed; excoriated. late ME. b. Painful, as when the raw flesh is exposed 1590. c. †Showing through the skin; raw-boned 1596. †d. Affected with indigestion –1621. 7. Of the weather, etc.: Damp and chilly 1546.

1. b. R. glazes are employed for the common pottery 1825. 2. c. The r. materials, or necessary instruments of all manufactures 1796. 3. b. The man..R. from the prime, and crushing down his mate TENNYSON. 5. A r., innocent, young Creature, who thinks all the World as sincere as herself STEELE. b. With a r. and inexperienced army he engaged legions in perfect discipline FROUDE. 6. They were both flogged till their backs were r. 1788. 7. You shan't venture out this r. evening GOLDSM.

B. ellipt. or absol. uses passing into sb. 1. a. *The r.*, the exposed flesh. Chiefly in phr. *to touch* (a person) *on the r.* (usu. *fig.*) 1823. b. A raw place in the skin, a sore or sensitive spot 1825. 2. *The r.*, applied to any raw article (esp. raw spirits), or quality 1844. 3. A raw person, article, product, etc.; *spec.* in *pl.* raw sugars, or raw oysters 1868. Hence **Raw** *v. trans.* to make r. **Raw·ly** *adv.*, **-ness.**

†**Raw·-bone,** *a.* and *sb.* 1593. [f. RAW *a.* 6 c.] A. *adj.* = next –1772. B. *sb.* A very lean or gaunt person, a mere skeleton; *pl.* Death –1784.

Raw·-boned, *a.* 1591. [f. as prec.] Having projecting bones, barely covered with flesh; excessively lean or gaunt.

Raw·-head. 1550. [f. RAW *a.* 6 + HEAD *sb.*] The name of a nursery bug-bear, usu. coupled with BLOODY-BONES.

Rawhide: see RAW *a.* 2 c.

Rawish (rǭ·iʃ), *a.* 1602. [-ISH [1].] Somewhat raw.

Ray (rē¹), *sb.*[1] ME. [a. OF. acc. *rai* (nom. *rais*, *raiz*, mod. F. *rais*) :—L. *radium*, acc. of RADIUS.] I. 1. A single line or narrow beam of light; in mod. scientific use, the straight line in which the radiant energy capable of producing the sensation of light is propagated to any given point. b. A representation of a ray (esp. *Her.*); a brilliant stretch (of something) 1729. c. *fig.* of mental and moral influences, etc., comparable to light 1634. d. A trace of anything. (Chiefly with negs.) 1773. 2. (Chiefly *poet.*) Light, radiance; (freq. also implying heat) 1592. 3. a. (Chiefly *poet.*) A beam or glance of the eye; †also, sight 1531. b. A line of sight 1700. 4. Used in ref. to the emission or transmission of non-luminous physical energies propagated in radiating straight lines after the manner of light 1664.

1. 'Tis as conceivable as how the Rays of Light should come in a direct line to the eye GLANVILL. The rays of the moon stole through the leafless branches 1849. *Röntgen* (rö·ntyĕn) *rays*, a form of radiation discovered by Prof. Röntgen, having the power of penetrating many substances impervious to the rays of ordinary light. Also called *X-rays*. c. Only one r. of hope broke the gloom of her prospects 1838. d. Isn't it enough that you were seven boys before, without a r. of gal DICKENS. 2. Lamps, that shed at Ev'n a cheerful r. GRAY. 3. a. The Aire, No where so cleer, sharp'nd his visual r. To objects distant farr MILT. All eyes direct their rays On him POPE. 4. There are rays transmitted from the sun which do not illuminate SIR H. DAVY.

II. 1. *Math.* a. = RADIUS 3. Now *rare*. 1690. b. Any one of the lines forming a pencil or set of straight lines passing through a point 1879. 2. One of any system of lines, parts, or things radially disposed 1668. 3. *Bot.* a. The marginal portion of a composite flower, consisting of ligulate florets arranged radially 1766. b. A pedicel or branch of an umbel 1785. 4. *Zool.* a. = *fin-ray*, FIN *sb.* 1668. b. One of the radial divisions of a star-fish 1753.

Comb.: **r.-filter,** a means of separating the obscure from the luminous rays of electric light; **-fungus,** a fungus (*Actinomyces*) which enters the body and produces the disease *actinomycosis*.

Ray (rē¹), *sb.*[2] ME. [a. F. *raie* :—L. *raia* RAIA.] A selachian fish of the family *Raiidæ*, having a broad flat body and inferior gill-openings; *esp.* a skate. b. Dist. as *eagle-*, *rock-*, *shark-*, *sting-*, *whip-r.*; see these words.

†**Ray,** *sb.*[3] ME. [Aphetic form of ARRAY *sb.*] 1. Order, array, *esp.* of soldiers –1632. 2. A line or rank –1587. 3. Dress –1760.

3. *transf.* As a ship, whom cruell tempest drives Upon a rocke.., spoyling all her..goodly r. SPENSER.

Ray (rē¹), *sb.*[4] (and *a.*). *Obs.* exc. *Hist.* ME. [a. OF. **raié*, f. *raie* stripe, streak.] 1. A kind of striped cloth. So *cloth of r.* (cf. F. *étoffe de raies*). 2. *attrib.* or as *adj.* Striped; made of striped cloth. late ME.

Ray (rē¹), *v.*[1] 1598. [f. RAY *sb.*[1], or ad. F. *rayer*, OF. *raier* :—L. *radiare*, f. RADIUS.] 1. *intr.* Of light: To issue from some point in the form of rays. 2. Of luminous bodies or points: To emit light in rays 1647. 3. To radiate, extend in the form of radii 1659. 4. *trans.* To send *out* or *forth*, to emit (light) in rays 1789. 5. a. To furnish *with* rays or radiating lines. b. To irradiate. 1750.

Ray (rē¹), *v.*[2] *Obs.* exc. *dial.* late ME. [Aphetic ARRAY *v.*] †1. *trans.* To put (men) in order or array –1600. †2. To arrange, dispose, or deal with, in any fashion –1509. 3. To dress (oneself or another). Also *absol.* late ME. †4. To BERAY –1663.

‖**Rayah** (rai·ă). 1813. [a. Arab. *raᶜyah* flock or herd, subjects, peasants, f. *raᶜā* to pasture.] A non-Mohammedan subject of the Sultan of Turkey, subject to payment of the poll-tax.

Ray·-grass. 1677. = RYE-GRASS (now the usual form).

Rayless (rē¹·lės), *a.* 1742. [f. RAY *sb.*[1] + -LESS.] 1. Devoid of, not illumined by, any ray of light; dark, gloomy. 2. That sends out no rays; dull 1832. 3. Excluding, dispensing with, rays of light 1896. 4. Having no rays or ray-like parts 1769.

Rayon[1] (rē¹·ŏn, F. rĕyoṅ). 1591. [a. F., f. *rai* RAY *sb.*[1]] 1. A ray of light (*rare*). ‖2. = RADIUS 4. 1878.

Rayon[2] (rē¹·ǫn). 1924. [Arbitrary; with suggestion of *ray*, beam.] Trade name for artificial silk.

‖**Rayonné** (rĕyone), *a.* 1780. [F., pa. pple. of *rayonner*, f. *rayon* RAYON [1].] *Her.* Of a division between parts of the field: Having alternate pointed projections and depressions, whose sides are formed by wavy lines.

Raze (rē¹z), *v.* 1547. [var. RASE *v.*[1]] 1. = RASE *v.*[1], in various senses. b. *esp.* To cut or wound slightly, to graze 1586. †2. *spec.* To erase or obliterate (writing, etc.) by scraping or otherwise –1709. †3. To alter by erasure –1724. 4. a. To sweep away, efface, or destroy (a building, town, etc.) completely. In later use esp. to *r. to the ground*. 1547. b.

To take away, remove (*from* a place), in a thorough manner 1580.

2. The clause formerly razed..is agreed to be kept in the bill 1709. **4.** The fortifications were razed to the ground GIBBON. Hence †**Raze** *sb.* a slash, scratch, slit -1766.

Razee (răzī·), *sb.* 1803. [ad. F. *rasé(e*, pa. pple. of *raser* RASE *v.*[1]; see -EE.] *Naut.* A warship or other vessel reduced in height by the removal of her upper deck or decks.

Razee (răzī·), *v.* 1837. [f. prec.] **1.** *trans.* To cut down (a ship) to a lower size by reducing the number of decks 1842. **2.** *fig.* To abridge, prune, dock 1837.

1. The Merrimac..has been razeed and iron-plated 1862.

Razor (rē^i·zəɹ), *sb.* ME. [a. OF. *rasor*, *-our*, f. *raser* to RASE *v.*[1]] **1.** A sharp-edged instrument, specially used for shaving the beard or hair. **2.** = RAZOR-FISH, RAZOR-SHELL 1610.

1. His little weezen face as sharp as a r. 1765. *fig.* Phr. *On the razor's edge* (after Gk. ἐπὶ ξυροῦ ἀκμῆς), in a precarious position; Now on the eager razors edge, for life or death we stand CHAPMAN. *Occam's razor*, the leading principle of the nominalism of William of Occam, that for the purposes of explanation things not known to exist should not, unless it is absolutely necessary, be postulated as existing.

Comb.: **r.-bridge**, the bridge believed by Mohammedans to lead over hell; **-edge**, a keen edge, *fig.* a narrow foothold, a critical situation; **-grass**, a W. Indian sedge (*Scleria scindens*) with sharp-edged leaves and stems; **-paper**, paper specially made for sharpening razors on; **-paste**, a paste of emery- or crocus-powder for improving razor-strops. Hence **Ra·zor** *v. trans.* to shave as with a r.; to cut *down*. †**Ra·zorable** *a.* capable of, or fit for, being shaved SHAKS.

Ra·zor-back, *sb.* (and *a.*). 1823. [f. prec.] **A.** *sb.* **1.** A sharply-ridged back, like a razor 1844. **2.** The Razor-back whale or Rorqual 1823. **3.** A pig having a sharp ridge-like back 1849. **B.** *adj.* Having a very sharp back or ridge 1836. So **Ra·zor-backed** *a.*

Ra·zor-bill. 1674. [f. RAZOR *sb.* + BILL *sb.*[2]] **a.** A species of Auk (*Alca torda*). **b.** *U.S.* The Cut-water or Skimmer 1794. **c.** The red-breasted Merganser, *Mergus serrator* 1883. So **Ra·zor-billed** *a.* having a bill resembling a razor.

Ra·zor-fish. 1602. [f. RAZOR *sb.*] Any bivalve mollusc of the genus *Solen* or family *Solenidæ*, having a long narrow shell like the handle of a razor; esp. the European species *Solen ensis* or *siliqua*, common on sandy shores.

Ra·zor-gri·nder. 1825. [f. RAZOR *sb.*] **1.** One who grinds or sharpens razors 1833. **2.** A name of various birds: **a.** The Australian Dishwasher or Restless Fly-catcher (*Seisura inquieta*) 1825. **b.** *dial.* The Night-jar 1895. **c.** *dial.* The Grasshopper Warbler 1895.

Ra·zor-shell. 1752. [f. RAZOR *sb.*] The shell of a Razor-fish, or the mollusc together with its shell.

‖**Razzia** (ræ·ziă). 1845. [a. F., ad. Algerian Arab. *ghāzīah*, var. Arab. *ghazwah*, *ghazāh* war, raid against infidels.] A hostile incursion, foray or raid, for purposes of conquest, plunder, capture of slaves, etc., as practised by the Mohammedan peoples in Africa; also *transf.* of similar raids by other nations.

Ra·zzle-da·zzle. *slang*, orig. *U.S.* 1890. A rhyming formation on DAZZLE denoting bewilderment or confusion, rapid stir and bustle, riotous jollity or intoxication, etc. Also abbrev. *razzle*, esp. in phr. *on the razzle*.

Re (rē^i), *sb.* ME. [See UT.] **a.** The second note of Guido's hexachords, and of the octave in modern solmization. **b.** (As in F. and It.) The note D, the second of the natural scale of C major (*rare*). Hence †**Re** *v.* (nonce-use) SHAKS.

‖**Re** (rē), *prep.* 1707. [abl. of L. *res* thing, affair.] In the matter of, with reference to.

The L. phr. *in re* is similarly used.

Re-, *prefix*, of L. origin, with the general sense of 'back', or 'again', occurring in a large number of words adopted from L., or of later Rom. origin, and on the model of these freely employed in English.

In earlier L. *re-* was used bef. consonants, and *red-* bef. vowels or *h-*, as in *redire*, *redhibere* (rarely in other cases, as in *reddere*). In later L. *re-* was employed bef. vowels as well as consonants, as in *reagere*, etc. **2.** The original sense of *re-* in Latin is that of 'back' or backwards', but in use the prefix acquires various shades of meaning. **a.** 'Back from a point reached', 'back to or towards the starting-point', as in *recedere*, *revocare*, etc. **b.** 'Back to the original place or position', as in *reponere*, *restituere*, etc.; freq. implying 'back to one's hands or possession', as in *recipere*, *resumere*, etc. **c.** 'Again', 'anew', as in *recreare*, *regenerare*, etc. **d.** In some cases *re-* has the same force as Eng. *un-*, as in *recingere* to ungird, *recludere* to unclose, *revelare* to unveil. In *reprobare* to disapprove of, it expresses direct negation. **e.** 'Back in a place', i.e. 'from going forward', with verbs of keeping or holding, as *retinere*, etc.; or 'without going on or forward', with verbs of rest, as *remanere*, *residere*, etc. **3.** Words formed with the prefix *re-* first make their appearance in English about the year 1200. Towards the end of the 16th c. *re-* begins to rank as an ordinary English prefix, chiefly employed with words of Latin origin, but also freely prefixed to native verbs. Since 1600 the use of the prefix has been very extensive. **4.** In English formations, whether on native or Latin bases, *re-* is almost exclusively employed in the sense of 'again'. In all words of this type the prefix is pronounced with a clear *e* (rī), and frequently with a certain degree of stress, whereas in words of L. or Rom. origin the vowel is usu. obscured or shortened, as in *repair* (rĭpē^ə·ɹ), *reparation* (repărē^i·ʃən). In this way double forms arise, with difference of meaning, which in writing are usually distinguished by hyphening the prefix, as *recoil* and *re-coil*, *recover* and *re-cover*, etc. The hyphen is also freq. employed, when stress is laid on the idea of repetition, esp. when the simple word precedes the compound, as in *make and re-make*, *state and re-state*; also, when the main element begins with a vowel; before *e* it is usual to insert the hyphen, as *re-enter*, etc. **b.** *Re-* is occas. doubled or even trebled (usu. with hyphens inserted) to express further repetition, but not in serious writing. **5.** The number of forms resulting from the use of this prefix in English during the 19th c. is infinite, but they nearly all belong to one or other of three classes. **a.** Prefixed to ordinary verbs of action (chiefly trans.) and to derivatives from these, sometimes denoting that the action itself is performed a second time, and sometimes that its result is to reverse a previous action or process, or to restore a previous state of things; as *reaccept, reaccuse, reacknowledge, reacquire, readapt, readjourn, readminister, readopt, readorn, readvance, readvise, reaffirm, reafforest, re-allot, re-apply, re-appoint, re-approach, re-arrange, rebind, re-celebrate, re-clasp, recoin, recombine, recommission, reconduct, reconfirm, reconquer, reconsecrate, reconstitute, recross, recrystallize, redeliver, redemand, redescend, redirect, rediscover, redispose, redistil, re-edit, re-elect, re-embark, re-embody, re-emerge, re-enact re-endow, re-engage, re-engrave, re-enjoy, re-enlist, re-erect, reface, refashion, refasten, refind, refix, refloat, reflower, refold, reforge, refortify, reframe, refurbish, refurnish, regild, regrow, reheat, reillume, reillumine, reimpose, reimpress, reimprison, reincur, reinduce, reinfect, reinhabit, reinspire, reinstruct, reinterpret, reinterrogate, reintroduce, reinvigorate, reissue, rejudge, re-lay, re-let, relocate* (U.S.), *remake, re-mark, remelt, remix, remodel, remould, rename, renumber,* †*renumerate, reoccupy, reopen, reordain, reorder, reorganize, repack, repaint, reperuse, replate, repleat, repolish, repopulate, re-present, repurchase, re-rate, re-resolve, reseat, resell, reshape, reship, re-sign, re-sound, resow, respell, restock, restrengthen, resubject, resummon, resupply, resurvey, retell, re-trace, retransform, retranslate, retransmit, retype, revaccinate, revalue, revictual, revisit, rewake, rewaken, rewire, reword, rewrite,* etc. vbs.; *reaccess, readvancement, re-application, reconquest, redelivery, re-election, re-enactment, refoundation, regenesis, re-hire, reissue, replantation, representation, re-presentment, repurchase, resale, resolution, resurvey, retransmission, retrial, revaluation,* etc. sbs.; *re-eligible, reincarnate, remade, re-orient, re-soluble,* etc. adjs. **b.** Prefixed to vbs. and sbs. which denote 'making (of a certain kind or quality)', 'turning or converting into —', esp. those formed on adjs. by means of the suffix *-ize*, as *rebarbarize* vb., etc. **c.** Prefixed to vbs. and sbs. which denote fitting, furnishing, supplying, or treating with something, as *re-type*, etc. (Freq. in recent technical use.)

Reabso·rb, *v.* 1768. [RE- 5 a.] *trans.* To absorb anew or again; to take in again by absorption. So **Reabso·rption**, *spec.* in *Path.* = RESORPTION.

Reach (rītʃ), *sb.* 1526. [f. next.] **I.** An act of reaching. **1.** An (*or* the) act of reaching out with the arm, or with something held in the hand 1570. **b.** With indication of, or ref. to the space or distance covered in the act of reaching 1607. †**2.** *fig.* An attempt to attain or achieve something; a device, scheme, plan, contrivance -1785. **3.** A single stretch or spell of movement, travel, flight, etc. 1652. **b.** *Naut.* A run on one tack; a board 1830.

1. b. You needn't take quite such long reaches with your rake T. HARDY. **2.** In India this is a r. of deep policy BURKE.

II. Power of, or capacity for, reaching. **1.** The extent to which a person can stretch out the arm or hand, *esp.* so as to touch or grasp something; the distance to which an animal can extend a limb or other part, or to which any limb can be extended 1579. **b.** In prep. phrases, esp. *within*, *above*, or *out of* (one's) *r.* 1548. **c.** *transf.* of things 1586. **2.** Capacity or power to achieve some action, attain to some state or condition, etc. 1576. †**b.** Of the voice: Range, compass -1680. **3.** Capacity or power of comprehension; extent of knowledge or of the ability to acquire it; range of mind or thought 1542. **4.** Of the mind or mental powers: Range of efficiency in speculation, acquisition of knowledge, penetration, etc. 1580. **5.** Range, scope; extent of application, effect, influence, etc. 1546. **6.** Range (of carrying or traversing): **a.** of a gun, or shot 1591; **b.** of the eye or sight 1623; **c.** of the voice 1797. **7.** Power or possibility of getting to (or as far as) some place, person, or object; distance or limit from which some point may be reached 1784.

1. High from ground the branches would require Thy utmost r. MILT. **b.** The Tigre seeing them out of his r...falls a Roaring 1698. **c.** No lawful meanes can carrie me Out of his enuies r. SHAKS. **2.** His Learning was above ye common R. 1711. The highest r. of science is, one may say, an inventive power M. ARNOLD. **3.** Nothing beyond the r. of any man of good parts MACAULAY. **4.** The 'Utopia' of Sir Thomas More..shows a r. of thought far beyond his contemporaries JOWETT. **5.** My simple wit Can never found a judgment of such r. HEYWOOD. **6. b.** Above the r. of mortall ey MILT. **7.** Within r. of markets 1833. All the people within r. had suspended their business DICKENS.

III. That which reaches or stretches. **1.** A continuous stretch, course, or extent 1609. **2.** *spec.* **a.** That portion of a river, channel, or lake which lies between two bends; as much as can be seen in one view. Also, the portion of a canal between two locks. 1536. †**b.** A bay -1736. **c.** A headland or promontory. *Obs.* exc. *U.S.* (local). 1562.

1. Darksome night..dimming the spacious r. of heaven 1638. **2. a.** The king..examined every r. and turning of the river DE FOE.

Reach (rītʃ), *v.*[1] Pa. t. **reached**, †**raught.** [OE. *rǣcan*, *rǣhte* :—OTeut. **raikjan*.] **I.** *trans.* **1.** To stretch out, extend, hold *out* or *forth* (one's hand, arm, etc.). **b.** Of a tree: To extend (its branches) 1613. **2.** To hold out (a thing) and give (it) *to*, to hand *to* a person OE. **3.** To deal or strike (a blow). *rare* or *Obs.* late ME. **4.** To succeed in touching or grasping with the outstretched hand (or with something held in it) or by any similar exertion OE. †**b.** To obtain by seizure or otherwise -1612. †**c.** To take or lay hold of; to carry off -1667. **5. a.** To take or snatch *from* a person or thing; to take *away*, *hence*, *out*, *up*. Now *arch.* late ME. **b.** To draw or bring towards oneself (esp. to take down) *from* a certain place or position; to lift *up*, take *down*, etc. 1450. **6.** To succeed in touching with a weapon or with the hand in delivering a blow OE. **b.** To succeed in affecting or influencing by some means; to impress, convince, win over, etc. 1667. **7. a.** Of things (or of persons in respect of some part of the body): To come into contact with, to touch; to extend so far as to touch ME. **b.** Of immaterial things, *esp.* to succeed in affecting or influencing. late ME. **8.** To come to (a person, place, object, or point in space), to get up to or as far as ME. **b.** Of sounds: To come to (the ear, a person or place) 1649. **c.** Of the eye, a gun, etc.: To carry to (a point) 1667. **9.** To arrive at, to attain or come to (a point in time, a condition, quality, etc.) 1590. **10. a.** To succeed in understanding or comprehending. *Obs.* or *poet.* 1605. **b.** To succeed in acquiring or obtaining 1638. **11.** To stretch; to draw or pull *out* †or *in*. *Obs.* exc. *dial.* OE.

1. He raught out his right foot and dubbed me in the necke CAXTON. **b.** Where any row Of fruit-trees ..reachd too far Thir pamperd boughes MILT. **2.** I..bade one reche me a booke CHAUCER. **4.** Wilt thou r. stars, because they shine on thee? SHAKS. **c.** The hand of death hath raught him SHAKS. **6. b.** Men's opinions must be reached by reason, not by force 1851. **7. a.** His stature reacht the Skie MILT.

b. Liberty should r. every Individual of a People ADDISON. **8.** You may easily r. Harwich in a Day STEELE. **b.** My name, perhaps, hath reach'd your ear GAY. **9.** Till ryper yeares he raught SPENSER. This little work reached a second edition 1888. **10. a.** The words are twisted in some double sense That I r. not SHELLEY.

II. *intr.* **1.** To make a stretch *with* the arm or hand; to extend the arm, hold out the hand. Also of the arm or hand: To stretch out. OE. **b.** To grasp or clutch *at* 1562. **c.** *fig.* of mental striving 1646. **2.** To succeed in stretching one's arm, etc., so far ME. **3.** To stretch out (continuously), to extend; to project a certain distance (*above, beyond*, etc.) OE. **b.** Of a period of time, or with ref. to duration of time ME. †**c.** To suffice, be adequate or sufficient *to* (also with *infin.*). Chiefly of money. –1733. **d.** To amount *to* 1596. **4.** *Naut.* To sail on a reach 1832. **5.** To attain or succeed in coming *to* a place, point, person, etc. 1632. **b.** Of the eye, a gun, etc.: To carry 1632. **6.** To attain *to* an achievement, condition, etc. Now *rare* or *Obs.* ME. †**b.** To attain *to* (knowledge of) –1653.

1. What hinders then To r., and feed at once both Bodie and Mind? MILT. **b.** Put forth thy hand, r. at the glorious Gold SHAKS. **2.** By reaching beyond his reach, he reacheth nothing at all 1581. This woman hath herein reached beyond your conceit 1633. **3.** These vast domains, reaching from the Ebro to the Carpathian mountains BRYCE. **b.** The wyne haruest shal reache vnto the sowynge tyme COVERDALE *Lev.* xxvi. 5. **d.** 1 *Hen. IV*, IV. i. 129. **5. b.** As far as the eye could r. in either direction 1885. Hence **Rea·chable** *a.* that may be reached. **Rea·cher,** one who or that which reaches; †an exaggerated statement.

Reach (rītʃ), *v.*² Now *dial.* [OE. *hrǣcan*, f. *hrāca* spittle.] †**1. a.** *intr.* To spit; also, to hawk –1565. †**b.** *trans.* To spit or bring *up* (blood or phlegm) –1606. **2.** *intr.* To make efforts to vomit; to RETCH 1575.

Reachless (rī·tʃlės), *a.* 1599. [f. REACH *v.*¹ + -LESS.] That cannot be reached.

Rea·ch-me-dow·n, *a.* and *sb.* 1862. [f. REACH *v.*¹ I. 5 b.] **A.** *adj.* Of clothes: Ready-made; also, second-hand. **B.** *sb.* Chiefly *pl.* **1.** A ready-made or second-hand garment. 1862. **2.** orig. *U.S.* Trousers 1905.

React (riˌæ·kt), *v.*¹ 1644. [See RE- 2 a and ACT *v.*] **1.** *intr.* To act in return, or in turn, *upon* some agent or influence. **b.** *spec.* in *Chem.* of the action of reagents 1797. **2.** To act, or display some form of energy, in response to a stimulus; to undergo a change under some influence. Const. *to* (in recent use). 1656. **3.** To act in opposition to some force 1861. **4.** To move or tend in a reverse direction; to return towards a previous condition 1875.

Re-act (riˌæ·kt), *v.*² 1648. [f. RE- 5 a + ACT *v.*] *trans.* To act, do, or perform again.

Reactance (riˌæ·ktǎns). 1896. [f. REACT *v.*¹ + -ANCE.] *Electr.* That part of the impedance of an alternating-current circuit which is due to capacitance or inductance or both.

Reaction (riˌæ·kʃən). 1643. [f. RE- + ACTION.] **1.** Repulsion or resistance exerted by a body in opposition to the impact or pressure of another body. **2.** The influence which a thing, acted upon or affected by another, exercises in return upon the agent, or in turn upon something else 1771. **b.** *Chem.* The action of one chemical agent upon another, or the result of such action 1836. **3.** *Phys.* and *Path.* **a.** The supervention of an opposite physical condition, as the return of heat after cold, or of vitality after shock 1805. **b.** The response made by the system or an organ to an external stimulus 1896. **c.** *Wireless.* Method by which weak signals are strengthened 1923. **4.** A movement towards the reversal of an existing tendency or state of things, esp. in politics, a return, or desire to return, to a previous condition of affairs; a revulsion of feeling 1801.

1. The r. of the sides of the vessel against the fluid 1800. *fig.* It is the method of Charity to suffer without r. SIR T. BROWNE. **2.** Action and r. have thus gone on from prehistoric ages to the present time TYNDALL. **3. a.** The cold bath, when not followed by a healthy r., is anything but a tonic 1875. **b.** The r. to light was lost in both eyes 1899. **4.** In the ancient as well as the modern world there were reactions from theory to experience JOWETT.

attrib. and *Comb.*, as (sense 3) *r. period, stage, time*; **r. engine** or **machine,** a small apparatus in which the motive power is derived from the r. exerted by escaping steam; **r. wheel,** a water-wheel impelled by the r. of escaping water.

Reactionary (riˌæ·kʃənări), *a.* and *sb.* 1847. [f. prec. + -ARY¹.] **A.** *adj.* **1.** Of, pertaining to, or characterized by, reaction. **2.** Inclined or favourable to reaction 1858. **B.** *sb.* One who favours or is inclined to reaction 1858.

Rea·ctionist, *sb.* and *a.* 1858. [+ -IST.] **A.** *sb.* A professed reactionary 1862. **B.** as *adj.* So **Rea·ctionism.**

Reactive (riˌæ·ktiv), *a.* and *sb.* 1790. [f. REACT *v.*¹ + -IVE.] **A.** *adj.* **1.** Active or operative in return 1794. **2.** *Path.* **a.** Supervening on a previous opposite state; due to reaction 1822. **b.** Recuperative; responsive (*to* a stimulus) 1822. **3.** Characterized by reaction (sense 4) 1868. **4.** Possessing electrical reactance 1902. **B.** *sb.* *Chem.* [ad. F. *réactif.*] A reagent (*rare*) 1790. Hence **Rea·ctive-ly** *adv.*, **-ness.**

Reactor (riˌæ·ktəɪ). 1926. [f. as prec. + -OR.] **1.** *Electr.* An apparatus possessing electrical reactance. **2.** *Med.* An animal or patient reacting positively to a foreign substance 1928.

Read (rīd), *sb.* 1838. [f. next.] An act of perusal; a spell of reading.

Read (rīd), *v.* Pa. t. and pple. **read** (red). [Com. Teut.: OE. *rǣdan*:—OTeut. **rǣðan*, prob. related to Skr. *rādh-* to succeed, accomplish, etc.] **I.** *trans.* **To consider, interpret, discern*, etc. †**1. a.** To have an idea; to think or suppose *that*, etc. (*rare*) –1768. †**b.** To guess *what, who, why*, etc. –1590. **2.** To make out the meaning of (a dream, riddle, etc.); to declare or expound this to another OE. **b.** To foresee, foretell, predict. Chiefly in *to r. one's fortune.* 1591. †**3.** To see, discern. SPENSER.

***To peruse, without uttering in speech.* **4.** To inspect and interpret in thought (any signs which represent words or discourse); to look over or scan (something written, printed, etc.) with understanding of what is meant by the letters or signs; to peruse (a document, book, author, etc.). Also with advs., as *through, over* OE. **b.** To peruse books, etc. written in (a certain language); *esp.* to have such knowledge of (a language) as to be able to understand works written in it 1530. **c.** *transf.* and *fig.*; *gen.* of interpretation of signs or marks; *esp.* to make out the character or nature of (a person, the heart, etc.) by scrutiny or interpretation of outward signs 1611. **d.** To peruse (printer's proofs), comparing them with the copy; to examine as a proof-reader 1808. **e.** *To r. off*: to note in definite form (the result of inspection, esp. of a graduated instrument) 1812. **5.** To take in a particular way (what is read) 1624. **b.** *transf.* To regard (a person, thing, event, etc.) in a certain light 1847. **6.** Const. with preps. **a.** *refl.* To bring oneself *into* or *to* (a certain state) by reading 1676. **b.** To introduce (an additional idea or element) *into* what is being read or considered. (Freq. implying that the insertion is unwarranted or erroneous.) 1879. **7.** To adopt, give, or exhibit as a reading in a particular passage 1538.

4. Auld storys that men redys, Representis to thaim the dedys of stalwart folk BARBOUR. **b.** He read all the languages which are considered either as learned or polite JOHNSON. **c.** He reads the skies COWPER. One of the greatest of all difficulties in reading the hand 1867. This they call..reading men and manners SWIFT. You read us like books 1902. **e.** Before the height of the mercury is read off 1816. **5.** R. it how you will, it is not to purpose 1624. **6. b.** Men r. back developed ideas into undeveloped minds H. SPENCER. **7.** For *Lovaine* some copies of Wace r. *Alemaigne* 1847.

****To learn by perusal.* **8.** To see or find (a statement) in a written or otherwise recorded form; to learn by perusal of a book or other document OE. **b.** To discern or discover (something) *in* (or *on*) the face, look, etc. of a person 1590.

8. I haue read the cause of his effects in Galen SHAKS. *transf.* Her quick eye seemed to r. my thoughts DICKENS. **b.** Muffle your false loue..Let not my sister r. it in your eye SHAKS.

*****To peruse and utter in speech.* **9.** To utter aloud; to render in speech (the words of written or printed matter). Often, *to r. aloud.* Also *reading* = being read. **b.** Used of submitting a proposed measure to a legislative assembly by reading the whole or some part of it 1459. †**10.** To teach or impart (some art or branch of knowledge) *to* another by (or as by) reading aloud –1662. **11. a.** *To r. oneself in*: to enter upon office as incumbent of a benefice in the Church of England, by reading publicly the Thirty-nine Articles and making the Declaration of Assent 1857. **b.** *To r. out of*: to expel from (a body, party, etc.), properly by reading out the sentence of expulsion. Chiefly in *pass.* 1865. †**12.** To declare, as by reading aloud; to relate, tell, say –1591. †**b.** To speak of or mention; to describe; to name or call –1617.

9. R. the Will; wee'l heare it Antony SHAKS. The clerk and sexton read out the askings for the marriage 1890. Phr. *To r. a lesson* or *lecture*, freq. *fig.* to teach (a person) something, to administer a reprimand or check (to a preson).

II. *intr.* or *absol.* **1.** To apprehend mentally the meaning of written or other characters; to be engaged in doing this; to be occupied in perusing a book, etc. OE. **b.** Coupled with *write*, usu. with ref. to rudimentary education 1490. **c.** To study, esp. with a view to examination. Also *to r. up*, to collect information by reading. 1826. **2.** To find mention or record *of* something by, or in the course of, reading ME. **3. a.** To bear reading; to be readable 1668. **b.** To turn out (well or ill), or have a specified character, when read; to produce a certain impression on the reader 1731. **c.** To admit of interpretation 1866. **4.** To render in speech the words one is reading (in sense I. 4) OE. **b.** *To r. in* = I. 11 a. 1828. †**5.** To give instruction by means of reading aloud; to lecture or discourse *upon* a subject –1700.

1. Who reads Incessantly,..Uncertain and unsettl'd still remains MILT. *fig.* Phr. *To r. between the lines*: see LINE *sb.*² III. 5 a. **c.** [He] was reading for honours 1859. **2.** I have read of Caligula's Horse, that was made Consul 1645. **3. b.** Whose productions..r. better than they act 1789. **4.** Then he went up to his study to be read to till six 1879. **b.** I read in—i. e. read the Thirty-nine Articles J. H. NEWMAN.

Read (red), *ppl. a.* 1586. [f. prec.] **1.** That is read, *esp.* that is read out 1590. **2.** In pred. use: Experienced, versed, or informed *in* a subject by reading 1586. **3.** (Chiefly pred.) Informed by reading, acquainted with books or literature, learned. (Now only with advs., esp. WELL-READ.) 1588.

1. The trouble of attending the meeting to hear a r. speech 1901. **2.** An Oxford Man, extreamly r. in Greek PRIOR.

Readable (rī·dăb'l), *a.* 1570. [f. READ *v.*] **1.** Capable of being read, legible. **2.** Capable of being read with pleasure or interest. Usu. of literary work: Agreeable or attractive in style. 1826. Hence **Readabi·lity, Rea·dableness.**

Readdre·ss, *v.* 1611. [RE- 5 a.] **1.** *refl.* To address (oneself) anew. **2.** *trans.* To put a new address on (a letter, etc.) 1884.

1. Didymus..readdressed himself to her BOYLE.

Reader (rī·dəɪ). OE. [f. READ *v.* + -ER¹.] †**1.** An interpreter (of dreams) –1440. **2.** One who reads or peruses OE. **b.** A proof-reader employed by a printer 1808. **c.** One employed by a publisher to read works offered for publication and to report on their merits 1871. **3.** One who reads aloud; *spec.* one who reads parts of the service in a place of worship OE. **4.** One who reads (and expounds) to pupils or students; a teacher, instructor; *spec.* in some Universities, as the title of certain instructors 1519. **b.** In the Inns of Court, a lecturer on law 1517. **5.** A title for books containing passages for instruction or exercise in reading 1799. Hence **Rea·dership,** the office of a r.

3. *Lay reader*: see LAY *a.*

Readily (re·dili), *adv.* ME. [f. READY *a.* + -LY².] In a ready manner. **1.** Promptly, in respect of the voluntariness of the action; hence, willingly, cheerfully. **2.** Quickly, without delay; also, without difficulty, with ease or facility. late ME.

2. Her gratitude may be more r. imagined than described GOLDSM.

Readiness (re·dinės). late ME. [f. as prec. + -NESS.] **1.** Promptness in voluntary action; prompt compliance, willingness, etc. **2.** The quality of being prompt or quick in action, performance, expression, etc. late ME. **b.** The quickness or facility with which something is done 1585. **3.** A state of preparation, in phr. *in r.* 1541. **4.** The condition or fact of being ready or fully prepared (*rare*) 1548.

1. The r. of all the country to take arms was very singular SCOTT. 2. His r. in the French tongue GEO. ELIOT.

Reading (rī·diŋ), *vbl. sb.* OE. [f. READ *v.* + -ING[1].] **1.** The action of perusing written or printed matter; the practice of occupying oneself in this way. Also with *up, off.* **b.** The extent to which one reads or has read; literary knowledge, scholarship 1593. **c.** Ability to read; the art of reading 1599. **d.** A single or separate act or course of perusal 1757. **2.** The action of uttering aloud the words of written or printed matter OE. **b.** The delivery in this manner of a specified portion of matter; a single act or spell of this; also, the portion so read at one time OE. **c.** The formal recital of a bill before a legislative assembly 1647. **d.** A social or public entertainment at which the audience listens to a reader 1858. **†3.** The act of lecturing or commenting upon some subject, *esp.* a law text; also, the matter of such lecture or comment, a commentary or gloss -1741. **4.** The form in which a given passage appears in any copy or edition of a text; the actual word or words used in a particular passage 1557. **5.** Matter for reading, esp. with ref. to its quality or kind 1706. **6.** That which presents itself to be read; *spec.* the indication of a graduated instrument. So *r. off.* 1808. **7.** The interpretation or meaning one attaches to anything, or the view one takes of it; in recent use *esp.* the rendering given to a play or a character, a piece of music, etc. 1792.

1. R. is to the Mind, what Exercise is to the Body STEELE. **b.** A man of some r. 1797. 2. It was genuine r., not dramatic recitation 1878. **b.** They had their weekly Readings of the Law of Moses 1673. 4. *Various readings*: see VARIOUS. 7. She gave him her r. of the matter 1860.

attrib. and *Comb.*, as **r.-book**, a book containing passages for instruction in reading; **-desk**, a desk for supporting a book while it is being read, *spec.* a lectern; **-glass**, a large magnifying glass for use in reading; **r. room**, a room devoted to reading, *esp.* one in the premises of a club or library, or intended for public use; also, the proof-readers' room in a printing-office.

Reading (rī·diŋ), *ppl. a.* 1673. [f. READ *v.* + -ING[2].] **1. a.** *R. clerk*, the designation of one of the clerks to the House of Lords 1788. **b.** *R. boy*, a boy who reads copy aloud to the corrector of the press 1808. **2.** Given to reading; studious 1673.

2. *R. man*, applied *spec.* to a university student who makes reading his chief occupation.

Readju·st, *v.* 1611. [RE- 5 a.] *trans.* To adjust again or afresh; to put in order again. Hence **Readju·stment**.

Readju·ster. 1862. [f. prec.] One who readjusts. **b.** *U.S.* A member of a political party (formed in 1877–8) in Virginia, which advocated a legislative readjustment of the State debt 1879.

Readmission (rīˌædmi·ʃən). 1655. [RE- 5 a.] The action of admitting again.

Readmit (rīˌædmi·t), *v.* 1611. [RE- 5 a.] *trans.* To admit again. So **Readmi·ttance**.

Ready (re·di), *a.*, *adv.*, and *sb.* [Early ME. *rædi(ȝ), re(a)di*, app. f. OE. *rǽde* + *-iȝ*, -Y[1], from the Teut. stem **raið-* to put in order, prepare.] **A.** *adj.* **I. 1.** In a state of preparation for performing (or becoming the object of) such action as is implied or expressed in the context. **b.** *spec.* Properly dressed or attired; having finished one's toilet. late ME. **†c.** Used in replying to a call or summons SHAKS. **d.** *Mil.* and *Naut.* As a word of command 1802. **2.** Prepared, or having all preparations made, *to* do something ME. **b.** Willing; feeling or exhibiting no reluctance ME. **c.** Easily inclined or disposed 1596. **d.** Sufficiently angry to be on the point of (doing something violent) 1535. **3. a.** That has passed, or has been brought, into such a condition as to be immediately likely or liable (*to* do something). late ME. **b.** Likely, liable, 'fit' 1596. **4.** Const. with preps.: **†a.** With *to* or *unto* (rarely *into*): Prepared, inclined, or willing to do, give, suffer, etc. (what is indicated by the sb.) -1591. **b.** Prepared *for* (an event, action, state, etc.) 1591. **5.** Prompt, quick, expert, dexterous ME. **6. a.** Of the mind or mental powers: Quick to devise, plan, comprehend, observe, etc. ME. **b.** Of persons, etc.: Prompt or quick in speech, discourse, or writing ME. **c.** Proceeding from, delivered with, promptness of thought or expression 1583. **7.** Of action, etc.: Characterized by promptness or quickness. late ME. **b.** Characterized by alacrity or willingness in some respect 1548. **c.** Taking place easily or quickly 1596.

1. Some one be readie with a costly suite SHAKS. **b.** Whan thou arte vp and redy, than first swepe thy house 1523. **c.** *Mids. N.* III. i. 165. 2. My nephew was r. to sail DE FOE. **b.** Thou Lord art the God most mild Readiest thy grace to shew MILT. **c.** You are too r. to speak evil of men JOWETT. **d.** They are almost r. to stone me COVERDALE *Exod.* xvii. 4. 3. Cordials to take when r. to faint 1748. **b.** Winds..r. to cut you through 1698. 4. **b.** *Meas. for M.* III. i. 107. 5. My tonge is yᵉ penne of a r. writer COVERDALE *Ps.* xliv. 1. R. in gybes, quicke-answered, sawcie SHAKS. How r. he is at all these sort of things SHERIDAN. 6. **b.** Reading maketh a full man, conference a readye man BACON. 7. A r., tho' unwilling Obedience 1754. **b.** Open speech, and r. hand BYRON. **c.** That when at Market they may find a readier sale 1730.

II. 1. In the condition of having been prepared or put in order for some purpose ME. **2.** Close at hand; handy, convenient for use ME. **3.** Immediately available as currency; having the form of coin or money ME. **4.** Of a way, path, etc.: Lying directly before one; straight, direct, near. *Obs.* exc. *dial.* ME. **b.** Hence with *way* in the sense of 'method', 'means', etc.; and so *r. means* 1542. **†5.** Of payment or pay: Made or given promptly; not delayed or deferred. -1697.

1. A servant came to tell us the tea was r. BERKELEY. 2. The slightest, easiest, readiest recompence MILT. Phr. *R. to* (one's) *hand(s)*, *r. to hand.* 3. What advantage might be made of the r. Cash I had STEELE. 4. **b.** Teaching covetousness..a r. way to assault them FULLER.

Phr. **To make ready. a.** *refl.* To prepare (oneself); †*spec.* to array, attire or dress (oneself). **b.** *trans.* To prepare or put in order (a thing or things); †to dress (a person). (Cf. MAKE-READY.) **c.** *absol.* To make preparations.

Comb. Prefixed to pa. pples. to emphasize the completion of the process expressed by these, as *r.-cooked*, *-dressed*, *-prepared*, etc. **b.** *r.-for-service*, *-to-eat.*

B. *adv.* = READILY. (Now only in compar. and superl.) ME.

There was not..A child who..answered readier through his Catechism SOUTHEY.

C. *sb.* **1.** (usu. with *the.*) Ready money, cash. (*slang* or *colloq.*) 1688. **2.** (Usu. with *the.*) The position of a fire-arm when the person holding or carrying it is ready to raise it to the shoulder and aim or fire 1837.

1. He was not flush in r., either to go to law, or clear old debts ARBUTHNOT. 2. I..found the guard with his musket at the 'r.' 1837.

Ready (re·di), *v.* ME. [f. READY *a.*] **1.** *refl.* To make (oneself) ready in any way. **2.** *trans.* To make (a thing) ready; to prepare; put in order. Now *dial.* ME. **3.** *slang. Racing.* To prevent (one's horse) from winning, in order to secure a handicap in another race 1887.

Ready-made (stress var.), *ppl. phr.*, *a.*, and *sb.* late ME. [f. READY *a.* + MADE.] **†1.** Made ready, prepared -1588. **2.** Of made and manufactured articles: In a finished state, immediately ready for use; now *spec.* of articles which are offered for sale in this state 1535. **3.** Hence applied to any thing or person which exists in a finished or complete form; freq. used with depreciatory force, in allusion to the inferiority of 'ready-made' goods 1738. **b.** In *attrib.* use 1797. **4.** Pertaining to, dealing in, ready-made articles 1809. **B.** *sb.* A ready-made article; *esp.* a ready-made garment, etc. 1882.

3. A good Wife must be bespoke, for there is none ready made SWIFT. **b.** Some ready-made face Of hypocritical assent SHELLEY.

Rea·dy mo·ney. late ME. [READY *a.* II. 3.] **1.** Coined money, cash, as being immediately available for use; also, immediate payment in coin for anything bought. Hence **2.** *attrib. phr.* Characterized by immediate payment in money for articles bought 1712. **3.** Paying ready money 1796.

2. The landlord carried on a ready-money business 1808.

Rea·dy re·ckoner. 1757. [READY *a.*] A table, or tables, showing at a glance the results of such arithmetical calculations as are most frequently required in business, etc.

Ready-to-wear. Also **-for-.** 1905. = READY-MADE *a.* 2, *sb.*

Ready-witted, *a.* 1581. Of a ready wit or intelligence; quick of apprehension.

Reagency (rīˌē̆i·dʒĕnsi). 1842. [RE- 2 a.] Reactive power or operation.

Reagent (rīˌē̆i·dʒĕnt). 1797. [RE- 2 a; cf. REACT *v.*[1]] **1.** *Chem.* A substance employed as a test to determine the presence of some other substance by means of the *reaction* which is produced. **2.** A reactive substance, force, etc. 1856.

2. Mind is a r. against society 1865.

Re:aggrava·tion. 1611. [ad. med.L. *reaggravatio.* See AGGRAVATION 3.] *Eccl.* The second warning given to a person before final excommunication.

†Reaks, *sb. pl.* 1575. [Origin obsc.; cf. FREAK.] Pranks -1818.

Real (rī·äl, rē·äl), *sb.*[1] 1588. [Sp., sb. use of *real* adj., royal:—L. *regalem.*] **1.** A small silver coin and money of account in use in Spain and Spanish-speaking countries. **†2.** *R. of eight* = *piece of eight* (EIGHT A.) -1818.

†Real, *a.*[1] ME. [a. OF., :—L. *regalem* REGAL.] Royal, regal, kingly -1602. Hence **†Re·ally** *adv.*[1] royally -1578.

Real (rī·al), *a.*[2], *adv.*, and *sb.*[2] 1448. [a. OF. *real, reel*, or ad. late L. *realis*, f. *res* thing, etc. + -AL.] **A.** *adj.* **I. 1.** Having an objective existence; actually existing as a thing 1601. **b.** In *Philosophy* applied to whatever is regarded as having an existence in fact and not merely in appearance, thought, or language, or as having an absolute and necessary, in contrast to a merely contingent, existence 1701. **c.** *Math.* Of quantities. (Opp. to IMAGINARY, or IMPOSSIBLE.) 1727. **d.** *Optics* (see quot.) 1859. **2.** Actually existing or present as a state or quality of things; having a foundation in fact; actually occurring or happening 1597. **3.** That is actually and truly such as its name implies; possessing the essential qualities denoted by its name; hence, genuine, undoubted 1559. **b.** Natural, as opp. to artificial or depicted 1718. **4. a.** That is actually present or involved, as opp. to *apparent, ostensible*, etc. 1716. **b.** The actual (thing or person); that properly bears the name 1631. **5. †a.** Sincere, straightforward, honest -1709. **b.** Free from nonsense or affectation; 'genuine' 1847.

1. Whereat I wak'd, and found Before mine Eyes all r., as the dream Had lively shadowd MILT. **d.** If an image consist of points through which the light actually passes it is called r.; —in other cases virtual 1859. 2. He can imagin'd pleasures find, To combat against r. cares PRIOR. *R. presence*, the actual presence of Christ's body and blood in the sacrament of the Eucharist. 3. It was evidently r. and not affected doubt 1866. 4. **a.** There lurks the r. reason at the bottom of the ostensible one BENTHAM. Phr. *The r. thing*, the thing itself, as contrasted with imitations or counterfeits; hence *slang*, the 'genuine article'. 5. **b.** She had been so near r. people 1880.

II. 1. *Law.* (Opp. to PERSONAL.) **a.** Of actions, causes, etc.: Relating to things, or *spec.* to real property 1448. **b.** Connected in some way with things or real property 1467. **c.** Consisting of immovable property, as lands and houses; esp. *r. estate* 1641. **d.** *Chattels r.*: see CHATTEL 2. **2. a.** Relating to, concerned with, things 1593. **†b.** Of written characters: Representing things instead of sounds -1741. **c.** Corresponding to actuality; true 1657. **3.** Attached or pertaining to scholastic Realism 1528.

B. *adv.* (usu. with adjs.) Really, genuinely. Also (chiefly *Sc.* and *U.S.*): Very, extremely. 1658.

C. *absol.* or as *sb.* **†1.** = REALIST 1. -1684. **2.** A real thing; a thing having a real existence, either in the ordinary or in a metaphysical sense 1626. **3.** *The r.*: that which actually exists, contrasted (*a*) with a copy, counterfeit, etc., (*b*) with what is abstract or notional 1818. Hence **Re·alness**, the fact or quality of being r.; reality, truth.

Realgar (rīˌæ·lgăr). late ME. [a. med.L., ult. from Arab. *rehj al-ghār* 'powder of the cave'.] The native or factitious disulphide of arsenic, also called *red* (*sulphide* or *sulphuret of*) *arsenic* and *red orpiment*, used as a pigment and in pyrotechnics.

Realism (rī·ăliz'm). 1817. [f. REAL *a.*[2] + -ISM 2 b.] **1.** *Philos.* **a.** The scholastic doctrine of the objective or absolute existence of universals, of which Thomas Aquinas was the chief exponent. (Opp. to NOMINALISM and CONCEPTUALISM.) Also in later use: The attribution of objective existence to a subjective conception. 1838. **b.** Belief in the real existence of matter as the object of perception (*natural r.*); also, the view that the physical world has independent reality, and is not ultimately reducible to universal mind or spirit. (Opp. to IDEALISM 1.) 1836. **2.** Inclination or attachment to what is real; tendency to regard things as they really are; any view or system contrasted with IDEALISM 2. 1817. **3.** Close resemblance to what is real; fidelity of representation, rendering the precise details of the real thing or scene: in ref. to art and literature, often with implication that the details are of an unpleasant or sordid character 1856.

Realist (rī·ălist), *sb.* (and *a.*) 1605. [f. REAL *a.*[2] + -IST.] †**1.** One who occupies himself with things rather than words (*rare*) –1623. **2.** *Philos.* An adherent or advocate of Realism (as opp. either to NOMINALIST or to IDEALIST) 1695. **3. a.** One devoted to what is real, as opp. to what is fictitious or imaginary 1847. **b.** An artist or writer addicted to realism 1870. **4.** *attrib.* or as *adj.* Pertaining to, characteristic of, realists 1845.

3. b. [Fielding] is..as hearty a r. as Hogarth 1874.

Realistic (rīăli·stik), *a.* 1856. [f. prec. + -IC.] **1.** Characterized by artistic or literary realism; representing things as they really are. **2.** Concerned with, or characterized by, a practical view of life 1862. **3.** Of or pertaining to realists in philosophy; of the nature of philosophical realism 1874.

3. The r. tendency—the disposition to mistake words for things—is a vice inherent in all ordinary thinking 1874. Hence **Reali·stically** *adv.*

Reality (rīæ·lĭti). 1550. [ad. med.L. *realitas*, or F. *réalité*; see REAL *a.*[2] and -ITY.] **1.** The quality of being real or having an actual existence. †**b.** Correspondence to fact; truth –1793. **c.** Suggestion of, resemblance to, what is real 1856. †**2.** Sincere devotion or loyalty *to* a person; sincerity or honesty of character or purpose –1761. **3.** Real existence; what is real; the aggregate of real things or existences; that which underlies and is the truth of appearances or phenomena 1647. **4.** A real thing, fact, or state of things 1646. **5.** The real nature or constitution *of* something; also without const., the real thing or state of things 1690. **b.** That which constitutes the actual thing, as dist. from what is merely apparent or external 1840. †**6.** *Law.* = REALTY[2] 3. –1706.

1. Lucretius..makes no doubt of the R. of Apparitions ADDISON. 2. We..wait a time, to express our reallity to the Emperour FULLER. 3. To carry it on from Discourse and Design to R. and Effect COWLEY. Phr. *In r.*, really, actually, in fact. 5. b. A formal grant of the powers of which he already possessed the r. MACAULAY.

Realization (rīăləizē¹·ʃən). 1611. [f. next + -ATION.] The action or result of realizing. **1.** The action of making real; the process of becoming real; conversion into real fact. **b.** A case or instance of this 1837. **2.** The action of forming a clear and distinct concept, or the concept thus formed 1828. **3. a.** The action of converting (paper money, property, etc.) into a more available form; in later use chiefly applied to the sale of stock, or of a bankrupt's estate, in order to obtain the money value. **b.** The action of obtaining or acquiring (a sum of money, a fortune, etc.). 1796.

Realize (rī·ăləiz), *v.* 1611. [f. REAL *a.*[2] + -IZE, after F. *réaliser.*] **1.** *trans.* To make real, give reality to (something merely imagined, planned, etc.); to convert into reality. **b.** To make realistic or apparently real 1779. **2.** To make real as an object of thought; to present as real; to bring vividly or clearly before the mind 1646. **3.** To conceive, or think of, as real; to understand or grasp clearly 1775. **b.** *U.S.* To have actual experience of 1776. **4.** To convert (securities, paper money, etc.) into cash, or (property of any kind) into money 1727. **b.** *absol.* To realize one's property; to sell out 1781. **5.** To obtain or amass (a sum of money, a fortune, etc.) by sale, trade, or similar means; to acquire for oneself or by one's own exertions; to make (so much) out of something 1753. **b.** Of property or capital: To bring (a specified amount of money or interest) when sold or invested; to fetch (so much) as a price or return 1836.

1. Ideals are none the worse because they cannot be realized in fact JOWETT. 2. An Act of the Imagination, that realises the Event however fictitious, or approximates it however remote JOHNSON. 3. She cannot r. the change we must undergo W. IRVING. 4. Substantial securities..to be realised and converted into cash 1768. b. He realised with great prudence while this mine was still at its full vogue THACKERAY. 5. You, sir, who have realized a fortune 1775. b. His duty was to see that the property realised its full value 1885. Hence **Re·alizable** *a.* that may be realized. **Re·alizabi·lity.** **Re·alizer,** one who or that which realizes. **Re·alizingly** *adv.*

†**Re-ally·**, *v.* 1456. [a. obs. F. *real(l)ier*, var. *ral(l)ier* RALLY *v.*[1]; see RE- 2 and ALLY *v.*] **1.** *trans.* and *refl.* **a.** = RALLY *v.*[1] 1. Also with *up*. –1645. **b.** To connect, unite (again) *to* or *with* –1653. **2.** *intr.* (for *refl.*) = RALLY *v.*[1] II. 1. –1647. **3.** *trans.* To form (plans) again SPENSER.

Really (rī·ăli), *adv.*[2] late ME. [f. REAL *a.*[2] + -LY[2].] **1.** In a real manner; in reality; in point of fact; actually. **b.** Used to emphasize the truth or correctness of an epithet or statement; hence, positively, indeed 1610. **2.** In isolated position: **a.** As a term of asseveration or protest 1602. **b.** Interrogatively 1815.

1. The Account of such things as have r. happened ADDISON. b. This last Bill was r. frightful DE FOE. The king is r. and truly a Catholic MACAULAY. 2. Why r., I said, the truth is that I do not know JOWETT. b. She exclaimed, 'R.? It is r. true?' 1893.

Realm (relm). ME. [a. OF. *realme, reaume* :—pop. L. **regalimen*, f. L. *regalis* REGAL.] **1.** A kingdom. Now chiefly *rhet.*, and in such phrases as 'Statutes of the R.'. **2.** *transf.* and *fig.* **a.** The kingdom of heaven, or of God ME. **b.** Any sphere or region. (Occas. with suggestion of a ruling power.) late ME. **c.** The sphere, domain, or province *of* some quality, state, or other abstract conception 1667. **d.** A primary zoogeographical division of the earth's surface 1876.

1. The Duke of Argyle is to be created a Peer of this Realme 1705. 2. a. The avenging God! Who.. sits High in heaven's r. SHELLEY. b. The realms of Hell are gleaming fiery bright 1816. c. Thir legions ..Scout farr and wide into the R. of night MILT. Hence **Rea·lmless** *a.* destitute of a r.

Realtor (rī·ăltǫɹ). *U.S.* 1916. [f. REALTY[2] + -OR.] A dealer in real estate.

†**Re·alty**[1]. ME. [a. OF. *realté, reauté* :—med.L. *regalitatem* REGALITY.] Royalty; royal state, dignity, or power –late ME.

Realty[2] (rī·ălti). 1440. [f. REAL *a.*[2] + -TY.] †**1.** Reality –1644. †**2.** Sincerity, honesty –1667. **3.** *Law.* Real property or estate 1544.

Ream (rīm), *sb.*[1] *Obs.* exc. *dial.* [OE. *rēam* :—OTeut. **raumoz.*] **1.** = CREAM *sb.*[2] 1. **2.** *transf.* A scum or froth upon any liquid 1460.

Ream (rīm), *sb.*[2] [Late ME. *rēm* and *rīm* = Du. *riem*, OF. *rayme, reyme*, ad. Arab. *rizmah* bale or bundle (of clothes, paper, etc.).] A quantity of paper, properly 20 quires or 480 sheets, but frequently 500 or more, to allow for waste; of paper for printing, 21½ quires or 516 sheets (a *printer's r.*). **b.** A large quantity of paper, without ref. to the precise number of sheets 1597.

b. More fire than warms whole reams of modern plays SCOTT.

Ream, *v.*[1] *Obs.* exc. *dial.* [ME. *ræmien*; origin obsc.] **1.** *intr.* To stretch oneself after sleep or on rising. **b.** To reach after ME. **2.** *trans.* To draw out, stretch. late ME.

Ream (rīm), *v.*[2] Chiefly *Sc.* 1440. [f. REAM *sb.*[1]] **1.** *intr.* To froth or foam. Also const. *over*. **2.** *trans.* To take the cream off; to skim. Also *intr.*, to be skimmed. 1768.

Ream (rīm), *v.*[3] *techn.* Also **reem.** 1815. [Origin obsc.] **1.** *trans.* To enlarge or widen (a hole) with an instrument. **2.** To enlarge the bore of (a gun) by the use of a special tool. Chiefly with *out*. 1867. **3.** With *out*: To remove (a defect) by reaming 1861. Hence **Rea·mer** an instrument used to enlarge a hole or boring.

Reanimate (rīæ·nimeɪt), *v.* 1611. [RE- 5 a.] **1.** *trans.* To animate with new life, to make alive again, to restore to life or consciousness. **2. a.** To give fresh heart or courage to (a person); to stimulate anew 1706. **b.** To impart fresh vigour, energy, or activity to (a thing) 1762. **3.** *intr.* To recover life or spirit 1645.

1. Fame that will scarce re-animate their clay BYRON. 2. a. His late Majesty could not re-animate the Dutch with the love of liberty 1792. b. He reanimated the textile manufactures 1872. Hence **Re·anima·tion,** the action of restoring to life (also *fig.*); the fact or process of returning to life; renewal of vigour or liveliness.

†**Rea·nswer,** *v.* 1523. [f. RE- + ANSWER *v.*] *trans.* **a.** To answer –1599. **b.** To meet, be sufficient for, or equivalent to –1630.

b. *Hen. V*, III. vi. 136.

Reap (rīp), *sb.* [OE. *reopa, rypa*, related to *rīpan* REAP *v.*] A bundle or handful of grain or any similar crop; a sheaf, or the quantity sufficient to make a sheaf.

Reap (rīp), *v.* [OE. *rīpan, reopan*; not represented in cogn. langs.] **1.** *intr.* and *trans.* To perform the action of cutting grain (or any similar crop) with the hook or sickle, esp. in harvest; hence, to gather or obtain as a crop (usu. of grain) by this or some other process OE. **b.** *transf.* To cut (plants, flowers, etc.) after the fashion of reaping 1721. **2.** *fig.* To get in return; to obtain (esp. some profit or advantage) for oneself; to gain, acquire ME. **3.** *trans.* To cut down or harvest the crop or produce of (a field, etc.). late ME.

1. They dyd sowe, & we do repe 1526. Labouring the soile, and reaping plenteous crop MILT. *fig.* To r. the fullest fruits of a victory 1853. See also *Matt.* xxv. 24, *Luke* xix. 21, *Hosea* viii. 7. b. Compared with which The laurels that a Cæsar reaps are weeds COWPER. 2. Why do I..suing For peace, r. nothing but repulse and hate? MILT. 3. *transf.* His Chin new reapt, Shew'd like a stubble Land at Haruest home SHAKS. Hence **Reaped** *ppl. a.* **Rea·ping** *vbl. sb.*, often *attrib.*, as *reaping-hook, -machine*, etc.

Reaper (rī·pəɹ). OE. [f. prec.] **1.** One who reaps. **2.** A mechanical device for cutting grain without manual labour 1862.

1. A Reper and Carter..iij d. by the day 1495.

Reappear (rīăpīᵊ·ɹ), *v.* 1611. [RE- 5 a.] *intr.* To appear again. So **Reappea·rance,** the act of appearing again; a second or fresh appearance.

Rear (rīᵊɹ), *sb.* (and *a.*[1]) 1600. [Aphetic f. ARREAR *sb.*] **1.** *Mil.* (and *Naval*). The hindmost portion of an army (or fleet); that division of a force which is placed, or moves, last in order 1606. **2.** The back (as opp. to the front) of an army, camp, or person; also the space behind or at the back; the position at or towards the back 1600. **3.** *gen.* The back, back part 1641. **4.** *slang.* A latrine, W.C. 1900.

1. When the fierce Foe hung on our brok'n R. Insulting MILT. *fig.* While the Cock..Scatters the r. of darkness MILT.

Phrases. *In the r.* (less freq. *in r.*), in the hindmost part (of an army, etc.); hence, at or from the back, behind. *In* (or *on*) *one's r.*, behind one. *In the r. of*, at the back of, behind. *To bring up* (or *close*) *the r.*, to come last in order. *To hang on one's r.*, to follow closely, in order to attack or harass. *Front and r.*, used advb. = in front and behind.

B. *attrib.* passing into adj. **1.** Placed or situated at the back; hindmost, last 1600. **2.** With adverbial force: **a.** Towards the rear. **b.** From the rear. 1855.

Comb.: **r.-driver,** a cycle driven by means of the r. wheel; **-steerer,** a tricycle steered from the back.

Rear (rīᵊɹ), *a.*[2] [OE. *hrēr*, of unkn. origin.] Slightly or imperfectly cooked, underdone. In early use only of eggs.

Rear (rīᵊɹ), *v.* [OE. *ræran* :—OTeut. **raizjan.*] **I.** To set up on end; to make to stand up. **1.** *trans.* = RAISE *v.* I. 1. **b.** *spec.* of setting up the crust of a pie. Now *dial.* late ME. **2.** To lift (a person or animal) to or towards an erect or standing posture; usu., to set (one) on one's feet, assist to rise. Now chiefly *dial.* 1590. **b.** *refl.* To get up on one's feet, to rise up (*rare*); also of animals, to rise on the hind feet 1580. **c.** So with body, etc. as obj. 1588. **3.** To cause to rise: **a.** To rouse from bed or sleep. *Obs.* exc. *dial.* OE. †**b.** =

RAISE I. 4 b. -1846. **4.** = RAISE I. 5 *Obs.* exc. *dial.* late ME. †**5.** = RAISE I. 6. -1647.

1. The May-pole was reared on the green W. IRVING. **2.** Till gently reard By th' Angel, on thy feet thou stood'st at last MILT. **c.** Upright he rears from off the Pool His mighty Stature MILT.

II. To build up, create, bring into existence. **1.** To construct by building up OE. †**b.** To bring into existence -1591. †**2.** = RAISE II. 5, 7. -1590. **b.** To make (a noise) by shouting; to utter (a cry). *rare.* ME. **3.** To bring (animals) to maturity or to a certain stage of growth by giving proper nourishment and attention; *esp.* to raise (cattle, etc.) as an occupation. late ME. **b.** To bring up (a person), to foster, nourish, educate 1590. **c.** To attend to, promote, or cause the growth of (plants); to grow (grain, etc.) 1581.

1. A tower..rered by great crafte HALL. **b.** From their ashes shall be reard A Phœnix SHAKS. **3.** It is a common saying, the worst housewife will r. the best pigs 1759. **b.** The gentle hand That reared us COWPER. **c.** *transf.* Delightful task! to r. the tender thought, To teach the young idea how to shoot THOMSON.

III. 1. To lift up or upwards as a whole OE. **b.** To have, hold, or sustain (some part) in an elevated or lofty position. Also quasi-*refl.* 1667. **c.** *refl.* To rise up to a height, to tower 1774. **2.** To lift up, raise, elevate, exalt, in various fig. applications. Now *rare* or *Obs.* late ME. **3.** To turn or direct (*esp.* the eyes) upwards 1596. **4.** To cause to rise: **a.** *Naut.* = RAISE *v.* III. 7 a. late ME. †**b.** To make (the voice) heard -1818. †**5.** To levy, raise, gather, collect (fines, rents, etc.) -1599.

1. High in his hands he rear'd the golden bowl POPE. **b.** Sublime their starry fronts they r. GRAY. **3.** Up to a hill anon his steps he rear'd MILT. **4. b.** His voice then did the stranger r. SHELLEY.

IV. *intr.* To rise up; to rise high, to tower ME. **b.** Of a quadruped, *esp.* a horse: To rise on the hind feet. late ME.

b. Sometimes he trots,..Anon he reres vpright, curuets, and leaps SHAKS.

†**Rear,** *adv.* = RARE *adv.* GAY.

Rear-, comb. form, partly of OF. or AF. origin, as in *rearward*, etc. (and hence by analogy in *rear-admiral*, etc.), partly ad. F. *arrière-*, as in *rear-vassal*, etc., and partly attrib. use of REAR *sb.* In recent use occas. spelt RERE-, esp. in archaic or architectural terms (see REAR-ARCH, etc.).

Rea·r-a·dmiral. 1587. **1.** A flag-officer in the navy, the next in rank below a vice-admiral 1589. †**2.** A ship carrying a rear-admiral's flag -1690.

Rear-arch. Also **rere-.** 1849. *Arch.* The inner arch of a window- or door-opening, when differing in size or form from the external arch.

Rearer (rīᵊ·rəɹ). late ME. [f. REAR *v.*[1] + -ER [1].] One who rears; *spec.* a horse that rears, or has a habit of rearing.

Rear-guard (rīᵊ·ɹgāɹd). 1481. [a. OF. *rereguarde*, AF. *reregard*; see ARREAR-GUARD.] *Mil.* †**1.** = REAR *sb.* 1. -1636. **2.** A body of troops detached from the main force to bring up and protect the rear 1659.

2. *attrib.* The worst of all battles to fight—a rear-guard action 1898.

Reargue (rĭ,ā·ɹgiu), *v.* 1776. [RE- 5 a.] *trans.* To argue (*spec.* a case in law) a second time; to debate over again. So **Rea·rgument.**

Rea·r-horse. 1884. [f. REAR *v.* IV. b.] *Entom.* A mantis.

†**Rea·rly,** *adv. rare.* 1612. [f. REAR *a.*[2] + -LY [2].] Early -1714.

Rearm (rĭ,ā·ɹm), *v.* 1871. [RE- 5 a.] *Mil. trans.* To arm again; *esp.* to arm afresh with more modern weapons. So **Rea·rmament.**

Rearmost (rīᵊ·ɹmōust), *a.* 1718. [f. REAR *a.*[1] + -MOST.] Farthest in the rear, coming last.

Rearmouse, reremouse (rīᵊ·ɹmaus). Now *arch.* or *dial.* [OE. *hreremūs*, f. *mūs* MOUSE. The first element may represent the stem of OE. *hrēran* to move.] = BAT *sb.*[1]

Rear-vassal. Also **rere-.** 1728. [f. REAR- + VASSAL, after F. *arrière-vassal.*] *Hist.* A sub-vassal; one who does not hold directly of the sovereign.

Rear-vault. Also **rere-.** 1844. [f. REAR-, after F. *arrière voussure.*] *Arch.* The vaulted space connecting an arched window- or door-head with the arch in the inner face of the wall.

Rearward (rīᵊ·ɹwǭɹd), *sb.* ME. [a. AF. *rerewarde.*] **1.** *Mil.* (and *Naval*). That part of an army (or fleet) which is stationed behind the main body; the third division in a force drawn up for battle. *Obs.* exc. *arch.* **2.** *transf.* The hinder parts, posteriors. late ME.

1. *In* (or *at*) *the r.*, in the rear. *In the r. of*, in the rear of; Hee was the very Genius of Famine: he came euer in the rere-ward of the Fashion SHAKS.

Rearward (rīᵊ·ɹwǭɹd), *a.* 1598. [f. REAR- + -WARD.] **1.** Situated in the rear. **2.** Directed towards the rear; backward 1861.

Rearward (rīᵊ·ɹwǭɹd), *adv.* 1625. [f. as prec.] Towards the rear; backward. **b.** At the back *of* 1880. So **Rea·rwards** *adv.*

Reascend (rī,ăse·nd), *v.* 1450. [RE- 5 a.] *trans.* and *intr.* To ascend again.

To re-ascend that glorious height we fell from MASSINGER. So **Reasce·nsion. Reasce·nt,** the act of reascending; the way by which one reascends; the distance to which one reascends.

Reason (rī·z'n), *sb.* ME. [a. OF. *re(i)sun*, *-on*, (mod.F. *raison*) :—L. *rationem*, vbl. sb. f. *rat-*, ppl. stem of *reri* to think, reckon; see RATIO and RATION.] **I. 1.** A statement of some fact (real or alleged) employed as an argument to justify or condemn some act, prove or disprove some assertion, idea, or belief. (Since 1600 somewhat *rare.*) **b.** *Logic.* One of the premises in an argument; *esp.* the minor premise when placed after the conclusion 1826. †**2.** A statement, narrative, or speech; a saying, observation, or remark; an account or explanation *of*, or answer *to*, something. Also, without article, talk or discourse. -1635. †**3.** A sentence -1530. †**b.** A motto, posy -1548.

1. Strengthning their reasons with many examples 1600. Phr. *A woman's r.*; I haue no other but a woman's r.: I thinke him so, because I thinke him so SHAKS. *To give, yield,* or *render* (*a*) *r.*, to give an account (of one's acts or conduct). **2.** *L. L. L.* v. i. 2.

II. 1. A fact or circumstance forming, or alleged as forming, a ground or motive leading, or sufficient to lead, a person to adopt or reject some course of action or procedure, belief, etc. Const. *why, wherefore, that*; *of, for*; *to* with inf. ME. **2.** A ground or cause of, or for, something: **a.** of a fact, procedure, or state of things in some way dependent upon human action or feeling ME. **b.** of a fact, event, or thing not dependent on human agency. late ME. †**3.** Rationale, fundamental principle, basis -1678.

1. He made a Voyage to Grand Cairo for no other R., but to take the Measure of a Pyramid ADDISON. Phr. *R. of state*, a purely political ground of action on the part of a ruler or government, esp. as involving some departure from strict justice, honesty, or open dealing 1600. **2. a.** Custom it self, without a r. for it, is an argument only to fools 1698. **b.** There is not a hair or a line, not a spot or a color, for which there is not a r. 1879.

Phrases. *By r. of*, on account of. *By r.* (*that*), for the reason that, because (now *rare*). *There is* (*good*, etc.) *r.*; also with omission of vb. *To have r. for*, or *to* do, something; also *ellipt.*, without construction. *To see r.* (*to* do something). *With* or *without r.*

III. 1. That intellectual power or faculty (usu. regarded as characteristic of mankind, but sometimes also attributed in a certain degree to the lower animals) which is ordinarily employed in adapting thought or action to some end; the guiding principle of the human mind in the process of thinking ME. **b.** So (†*good* or) *right r.* Now *rare.* ME. **c.** In the Kantian philosophy: The power (*Vernunft*) by which first principles are grasped *a priori*, as dist. from UNDERSTANDING (*Verstand*) 1809. **2.** The ordinary thinking faculty of the human mind in a sound condition; sanity. late ME. **b.** A reasonable or sensible view of a matter; chiefly in phr. *to bring to r.* ME. **3.** In verbal phrases denoting the conformity of something to the dictates of reason: †**a.** *R. will* or *would* -1597. **b.** *It stands to r.* 1632. **4.** In prep. phrases, denoting agreement with, or opposition to, what reason directs or indicates (see quots.) ME. **5.** A matter, act, proceeding, etc., agreeable to reason. Now *rare.* ME. †**6.** That treatment which may with reason be expected by, or required from, a person; justice; satisfaction; chiefly in phr. *to do* (one) *r.* (tr. F. *faire raison*) -1662. **b.** With ref. to drinking. Now only *arch.* 1594. †**7.** A reasonable quantity, amount, or degree -1675. †**8.** *To have r.* (tr. Fr. *avoir raison*): to be right (esp. in making a statement) -1771. **9.** The fact or quality of being agreeable to the reason; such a (†procedure or) view of things as the reason can approve of 1470.

1. Of all the faculties of the human mind, it will, I presume, be admitted that R. stands at the summit DARWIN. **2.** So now my r. was restored to me SHELLEY. **4.** †*By r.* (= OF. *par raison*). *In r.*; If you want a cheque for yourself..you can name any figure you like—in r. G. B. SHAW. Also *in all r.*; in the opposite sense, *out of all r.* **5.** Phr. *It is r.* or *r. is* (also with *good, great*), *it is no* (or *not*) *r.*; It is, however, but r. that I should rejoice 1864. †*And r.*, placed after a statement. So †*and good r.* **6.** *Tit. A.* I. i. 278. **b.** I pray you..to do me r. in a cup of wine SCOTT. **7.** *Much Ado* V. iv. 74. **8.** The Objectors have R., and their Assertions may be allowed SWIFT. **9.** There is r. in what you say BERKELEY. Phr. *To hear, listen to, speak r.*; Your wife will listen to r. T. HARDY.

†**IV. 1.** The act of reasoning or argumentation -1647. **2.** Consideration, regard, respect -1533. **3.** Way, manner, method *spec.* the method of a science -1643. **b.** Possibility of action or occurrence. Const. *but. rare.* -1596. **4.** *Math.* = RATIO 2. -1713.

3. b. When I looke on her perfections, There is no r., but I shall be blinde SHAKS.

Reason (rī·z'n), *v.* ME. [ad. OF. *raisoner* (F. *raisonner*) :—late L. *rationare* to discourse, f. *rationem*; see prec.] †**1.** *trans.* To question (a person); to call (one) to account (*rare*) -1578. †**2.** *intr.* To hold argument, discussion, discourse, or talk *with* another -1671. †**b.** To argue, discourse, converse, talk -1667. **c.** To employ reasoning or argument *with* a person in order to influence his conduct or opinions 1847. **3.** To think in a connected, sensible, or logical manner; to employ the faculty of reason in forming conclusions 1593. **4.** With object-clause: **a.** To question, discuss *what, why*, etc. 1529. **b.** To argue, conclude, infer *that*, etc. 1527. **5.** *trans.* **a.** To discuss or argue (a matter). Now *rare.* 1526. **b.** To explain, support, infer, deal with, by (or as by) reasoning 1605. **6. a.** To bring (a person) *into, out of* (a state of mind, etc.) by reasoning 1599. **b.** To put *down* by reasoning 1686. **7.** To think *out*, to arrange the thought of in a logical manner 1736.

2. Now therefore stand still, that I may r. with you before the Lord *1 Sam.* xii. 7. **b.** And they reasoned among themselves, saying, It is because we haue taken no bread *Matt.* xvi. 7. Others..reason'd high Of Providence, Foreknowledge, Will, and Fate MILT. **c.** All he could do was..to r. with him 1847. **3.** Reasoning at every step he treads, Man yet mistakes his way COWPER. Whilst we enjoy, he reasons of enjoyment SHELLEY. Reasoning from experience of the past abuses..they anticipated a like result from the present 1844. **5. b.** *Lear* I. ii. 114. **6. a.** David tried to r. him out of his fears 1893. **b.** Love is not to be reason'd down ADDISON. Hence **Rea·soner,** one who reasons.

Reasonable (rī·z'năb'l), *a., adv.,* and *sb.* ME. [a. OF. *raison(n)able*, (mod.F. *raisonnable*), f. *raison* REASON, after L. *rationabilis.*] **A.** *adj.* **1.** Endowed with reason. Now *rare.* **2.** Having sound judgement; sensible, sane. Also, not asking for too much. ME. **b.** Requiring the use of reason (*nonce- use*). SHAKS. **3.** Agreeable to reason; not irrational, absurd or ridiculous ME. **4.** Not going beyond the limit assigned by reason; not extravagant or excessive; moderate ME. **b.** Moderate in price; inexpensive 1667. **5.** Of such an amount, size, number, etc., as is judged to be appropriate or suitable to the circumstances or purpose. late ME. †**b.** Of a fair, average, or considerable amount, size, etc. -1726.

1. For man is by nature r. BURKE. **2.** If mankind were r. they would want no government 1802. **3.** The conviction would be r., for it would be based upon universal experience 1877. **4.** The r. wishes of the whole people 1832. Doing a great service on r. terms to the Church of which he was a member MACAULAY. **5.** All..forage.. is to be taken for the use of the army and a r. price paid for the same 1755.

B. *adv.* Reasonably 1470.

The minister..made a r. long exhortation 1583.

†**C.** *absol.* as *sb.* A reasonable being -1633. Hence **Rea·sonableness,** the fact or quality of being r. **Rea·sonably** *adv.* in a r. manner; sufficiently, fairly.

Reasoning (rī·z'niŋ), *vbl. sb.* late ME. [f. REASON *v.* + -ING [1].] The action of REASON *v.*, *esp.* the process by which one judgement is deduced from another or others which are given. **b.** With *a* and *pl.* An instance of this 1552. **c.** *attrib.*, as *r. power*, etc. 1728.

There is no reazoning against those which denie the Principles 1587. **b.** Socrates is a man, and therefore a living creature, is a right r., and that most evident HOBBES.

Reasonless (rī·z'nlės), *a.* late ME. [f. REASON *sb.* + -LESS.] **1.** Not endowed with, acting without the aid of, reason; irrational. **2.** Devoid of ordinary reason; senseless. late ME. **3.** Not grounded upon reason or reasons; not supported by any reason 1553.

1. Reasonlesse creatures 1581. A purely r. concourse of atoms 1895. **3.** This proffer is absurd, and reasonlesse SHAKS. Hence **Rea·sonless-ly** *adv.*, **-ness.**

Reasse·mblage. 1744. [RE- 5 a.] A collecting, meeting, or gathering together again. So **Reasse·mbly.**

Reassemble (rīăse·mb'l), *v.* 1494. [RE- 5 a.] *trans.* and *intr.* To bring, or come, together again.

Reassert (rīăsə̄·ɹt), *v.* 1665. [RE- 5 a.] **1.** *trans.* To assert (a statement, claim, etc.) again. **2.** To claim (a thing) again (*rare*) 1725.

1. You replied with abuse, and reasserted your charge *Junius Lett.* So **Reasse·rtion,** a repeated assertion, a reaffirmation.

Reassume (rīăsiū·m), *v.* 1494. [f. RE- 5 a + ASSUME *v.*] **1.** *trans.* To take, or take up, again (a material thing laid down or handed to another). **b.** To revoke, take back (a grant, gift, etc.) 1609. **2.** †**a.** To take back (a person) into close relationship with oneself -1667. **b.** To take back (a thing) as a constituent part 1692. **3.** To take again upon oneself 1624. **4.** To take, resume (one's place) again 1640. **5.** To recommence, take up again, resume 1608. †**b.** *intr.* To resume, continue speaking, after a pause -1796.

2. a. Into his blissful bosom reassum'd In glory as of old MILT. **3.** At last, reason reassumed her empire 1774. He had re-assumed his hereditary name LYTTON. **5. b.** I own it is necessary, re-assumed the master of the hotel, that [etc.] STERNE. So **Reassu·mption.**

Reassurance (rīăʃūᵊ·răns). 1611. [RE- 5 a.] **1.** Renewed or repeated assurance. **2.** Renewed or restored confidence 1875. **3.** Reinsurance 1745.

Reassure (rīăʃūᵊ·ɹ), *v.* 1598. [RE- 5 a.] †**1.** *trans.* To re-establish, confirm (a thing). Also const. *to* (a person). **b.** To confirm (one) again in (an honour). -1764. **2.** To restore (a person, the mind, etc.) to confidence 1598. **b.** To confirm again in an opinion or impression. Const. *of.* 1811. **3.** To reinsure 1826.

2. This was a sort of explanation more likely to alarm than to r. the public 1879. **b.** And long he paused to r. his eyes BYRON. Hence **Reassu·rer. Reassu·ring** *ppl a.*, **-ly** *adv.*

Reasty (rī·sti), *a.* Now *techn.* 1573. [Later form of RESTY *a.*[2]] Rancid.

Reata: see RIATA.

Reattach (rīătæ·tʃ), *v.* 1607. [RE- 5 a.] †**1.** *trans. Law.* To seize (a person) by authority of a writ of reattachment. **2.** To attach again. Const. *to.* Also *refl.* 1813. So **Reatta·chment,** a fresh attachment, esp. in *Law.* 1574.

‖ **Réaumur** (rē·ǝmür). 1782. The name of a French physicist (1683–1757), used *ellipt.* to denote the thermometer or thermometric scale introduced by him, in which the freezing point of water is 0° and the boiling point 80°.

Reave (rīv), *v.*[1] Pa. t. and pa. pple. **reft.** Now only *arch.* or *poet.* [Com. Teut.; OE. *rēafian* :—OTeut. **raubōjan*, f. pre-Teut. **reup-*, *roup-*, *rup-*; the original sense is app. that of breaking.] **1.** *intr.* To commit spoliation or robbery; to plunder, pillage. Const. *from.* (In later use chiefly *Sc.*, often written *reive*, *rieve.*) †**2.** *trans.* To spoil, rob, or plunder -1567. **3.** To despoil, rob, or forcibly deprive (usu. a person) *of* something. (In mod. use chiefly in pa. pple. *reft.*) ME. †**4.** To take (a thing or person) from (one) by, or as by, robbery or violence; to deprive (one) of (a possession, quality, etc.) -1594. **5.** To take forcible possession of (something belonging to another); to take away from another for oneself OE. **b.** To take away (life, rest, sight, etc.) ME. **6.** To take or carry away (a person) *from* another, *from* earth, *to* heaven, etc.; also *ellipt.* to carry off to heaven; to take *away* from earth or this life ME.

1. Thor the strong could r. and steal LOWELL. **3.** Reft of a crown, he yet may share the feast GRAY. **5.** Lands reft from Canterbury 1884. **b.** Sith that false traytour did my honour r. SPENSER. **6.** Who hath reft (quoth he) my dearest pledge? MILT. Hence **Rea·ver, rei·ver,** a robber, plunderer: †a pirate, sea-robber.

Reave, *v.*[2] Pa. t. and pa. pple. **reft.** Now *dial.* or *arch.* ME. [app. a confusion of prec. with RIVE *v.*] *trans.* To tear; to split, cleave.

The patriot's burning thought..Of England's roses reft and torn SCOTT.

Rebaptism (rībæ·ptiz'm). 1795. [RE- 5 a.] A second baptism; rebaptizing. So †**Reba·ptist,** *spec.* = ANABAPTIST.

Rebaptize (rībæptəi·z), *v.* 1460. [a. late L. *rebaptizare.*] **1.** *trans.* To baptize again or anew. **2.** To give a new name to 1596. So †**Rebaptiza·tion,** the act or practice of baptizing again. **Rebapti·zer,** one who rebaptizes.

Rebarbative (rībā·ɹbătiv), *a. rare.* 1892. [a. F. *rébarbatif, -ive*, f. *barbe* beard.] Crabbed, unattractive, repellent.

Rebate (rī·beⁱt, rībēⁱ·t), *sb.*[1] 1656. [ad. F. *rabat*, f. *rabattre* REBATE *v.*[1]] A reduction from a sum of money to be paid, a discount; also, a repayment.

Rebate (rībēⁱ·t), *sb.*[2] 1674. [Respelling of RABBET *sb.*, after prec. In techn. use pronounced as if written *rabbet.*] A rabbet. Also *attrib.*, as *r.-plane.*

Rebate (rībēⁱ·t), *v.*[1] late ME. [ad. OF. *rabattre*, f. *re-* RE- + *abattre* ABATE *v.*[1]] †**1.** *trans.* **a.** To deduct (a certain amount from a sum); to subtract (one quantity or number from another) -1675. †**b.** To reduce or diminish (a sum or amount) -1677. †**c.** To give or allow a reduction to (a person) -1670. **2.** To reduce, lessen, diminish (a condition, quality, feeling, activity, etc.). Now *rare.* 1450. **b.** To reduce the effect or force of (a blow, stroke, etc.). Now *rare.* 1579. †**c.** To lessen the vigour or activity of (the mind, etc.); to repress, stop (a person or action) -1788. **3.** To make dull, to blunt 1467. **4.** *Her.* To diminish (a charge) by removal of a portion, esp. a point or projection. **b.** To remove (a point, etc.) from a charge. 1562.

2. To pacify her, or, at least, to r. her first violence RICHARDSON. **3.** Takes he his weapon? thou the edge rebatest C'TESS PEMBROKE. This shirt of mail worn near my skin Rebated their sharp steel 1625. *fig.* Compassion so rebated the edge of Choler SIDNEY. Hence **Reba·ter.**

Rebate, *v.*[2] 1475. [Later spelling of RABBET *v.*, after prec. For pronunc. see REBATE *sb.*[2]] **1.** *trans.* To make a rebate or rabbet in. **2.** To join *together* with a rebate 1838.

†**Reba·tement.** 1542. [a. OF. *rebatement*; see REBATE *v.*[1] and -MENT.] **1.** A sum to be deducted from another; a discount -1727. **2.** Diminution in amount, force, etc. -1701. **3.** *Her.* = ABATEMENT 3. -1727.

†**Reba·to.** 1591. [f. F. *rabat* collar, etc., after It. words in *-ato.*] A kind of stiff collar worn by both sexes -1630. **b.** A collar of this kind used to support a ruff, or a frame of wire serving the same purpose -1634.

Rebeck (rī·bek). Now only *Hist.* or *poet.* 1509. [a. F. *rebec*, app. var. of OF. *rubebe*, *rebebe*, ad. Arab. *rebāb.* Cf. RIBIBE.] A mediæval musical instrument, having three strings and played with a bow; an early form of the fiddle.

When..the jocond rebecks sound MILT.

Rebel (re·bĕl), *a.* and *sb.*[1] ME. [a. F. *rebelle*, ad. L. *rebellis* rebellious, f. *re-* RE- + *bellum* war.] **A.** *adj.* (Now only attrib.) **1.** Refusing obedience or allegiance, or offering armed opposition, to the rightful or actual ruler or ruling power of the country. **b.** Consisting of, belonging or falling to, in command of, rebels 1682. **2.** Disobedient to a superior or to some higher power; contumacious, refractory ME. **3.** Characterized by rebelliousness; characteristic of a rebel or rebels. late ME.

1. Amaze..and terrour seis'd the r. Host MILT. The R. States LOWELL. **b.** The r. ranks were broken GIBBON. **2.** To speak in thunder to the r. world SHELLEY. *transf.* From a pure heart commaund thy rebell will SHAKS.

B *sb.*[1] **1.** One who resists, or rises in arms against, the established governing power; one who refuses or renounces allegiance or obedience to his sovereign or the government of his country. late ME. **b.** *Law* (now only *Sc. Law*). One who resists or disobeys a legal command or summons 1592. **2.** One who, or that which, resists authority or control of any kind ME.

1. For such sentiments I am called a r. 1778. **2.** Our Wills controul; Subdue the R. in our Soul WESLEY.

†**Rebel,** *sb.*[2] late ME. [f. next.] Rebellion -1618.

Rebel (rībe·l), *v.* ME. [ad. F. *rebeller*, ad. L. *rebellare* to make war again, to revolt, f. *re-* RE- 2 c + *bellare* to make war, f. *bellum.*] *intr.* To rise in opposition or armed resistance against the rightful or established ruler or government of one's country. Const. *against*, †*from*, †*to.* late ME. **b.** To resist, oppose, or be disobedient to, some one having authority or rule ME. **c.** *transf.* or *fig.* To offer resistance, exhibit opposition, to feel or manifest repugnance, etc. late ME.

It is astonishing..the People should ever rebell for Slavery 1718. **b.** Rebellyng agaynst theyr prelates & curates 1526. **c.** Thus Conscience pleads her cause ..Though long rebelled against, not yet suppressed COWPER. Hence †**Rebe·lled** *ppl. a.* in active sense. MILT.

Rebeldom (re·bĕldǝm). 1859. [f. REBEL *sb.*[1] + -DOM.] **1.** The domain of rebels. (Chiefly applied by their opponents to the Confederate States during the American Civil War.) 1862. **2.** Rebellious behaviour 1859.

Rebe·ller. Now *rare.* late ME. [f. REBEL *v.* + -ER [1].] A rebel, one who rebels.

Rebellion (rībe·lyǝn). ME. [a. F. *rébellion*, ad. L. *rebellionem*, f. *rebellis* REBEL *a.*] **1.** Organized armed resistance to the ruler or government of one's country; insurrection, revolt 1440. **b.** With *a* and *pl.* An instance of this. late ME. **c.** *Law* (now only *Sc. Law*). Disobedience to a legal summons or command; also *ellipt.*, the fact of being regarded as a rebel on account of such disobedience 1550. **2.** Open or determined defiance of, or resistance to, any authority or controlling power ME.

1. There can be no doubt that r. is the last remedy against tyranny BUCKLE. **b.** *The Great R.*, the civil war of 1642–9 and the Commonwealth Government of 1649–60. **2.** Contempt of God, and r. against your parents DE FOE.

Rebellious (rībe·lyǝs), *a.* late ME. [f. L. *rebellis* or *rebellio.*] **1.** Insubordinate, defying lawful authority; belonging to a party of rebels. **2.** Of actions, etc.: Characteristic of a rebel or of rebels; marked by rebellion 1492. **3.** Of things: Offering resistance to treatment; refractory 1578.

1. My weak heart..Will beat, r. to its own resolves SOUTHEY. *absol.* Let not the r. exalt themselues *Ps.* lxvi. 7. *transf.* Hot and r. liquors SHAKS. A r. spear SCOTT. **3.** Very good against..r. old sores 1578. Hence **Rebe·llious-ly** *adv.*, **-ness.**

Rebellow (rībe·lōu), *v.* 1590. [f. RE- + BELLOW *v.*, after L. *reboare.*] **1.** *intr.* Of cattle: To bellow in reply or in turn 1596. **b.** Of places or material objects, sounds, etc.: To re-echo loudly 1590. **2.** *trans.* To return or repeat (a sound) in a bellowing tone 1765.

1. b. The earth Rebellow'd to the feet of steeds and men COWPER.

Rebirth (rībə̄·ɹþ). 1837. [RE- 5 a.] A second birth (physical or spiritual); also *fig.* of things.

Rebite (rībəi·t), *v.* 1816. [RE- 5 a.] *trans.* To bite again (in sense 9 of the vb.).

Reboant (re·bōuănt), *a.* Chiefly *poet.* 1830. [a. L. *reboant-*, *reboare*, f. *re-* RE- 2 a + *boare* to bellow.] Rebellowing, re-echoing loudly. So **Reboa·ntic** *a.*

†**Reboi·l,** *v.*[1] 1444. [a. OF. *rebouillir* :— L. *rebullire* to bubble up; see BOIL *v.*] **1.** *intr.* Of wine: To ferment a second time -1601. **2.** To boil up or over -1601.

2. Some of his companyons therat reboyleth ELYOT.

Reboil (rīboi·l), *v.*[2] 1615. [RE- 5 a.] *trans.* To boil again.

Reboisement (rīboi·zmĕnt). 1882. [a. F., f. *reboiser*, f. *re-* RE- + *bois* wood.] Reafforestation.

Re-book, *v.* 1864. [RE- 5 a.] *trans.* and *intr.* To book again (BOOK *v.* 4 b).

Reborn (rībǭ·ɹn), *pa. pple.* and *ppl. a.* 1598. [RE- 5 a.] Born again (physically or spiritually). Also *transf.* of things.

Rebound (rĭbau·nd, rī·baund), *sb.* 1530. [f. next.] The act of bounding back after striking; resilience, return, recoil. Also *transf.* and *fig.*

His head..made three rebounds upon the scaffold 1732. Phr. *To take, catch,* etc. *on the r.*

Rebound (rĭbau·nd), *v.* late ME. [ad. OF. *rebonder, -bondir,* to resound, bound back; see RE- and BOUND *v.*[2]] 1. *intr.* To spring back from force of impact, to bound back. Also *transf.* or *fig.* of immaterial things. 2. To re-echo, reverberate, resound. Now *rare* or *Obs.* 1440. 3. a. To bound or leap, esp. in return or response to some force or stimulus. Now *rare* or *Obs.* late ME. b. To bound back (without impact) 1513. 4. *trans.* To cause to bound back; to cast or throw back, to return. Now *rare.* 1560. 5. To re-echo, return (a sound). Now *rare.* 1555.

1. An evil example, that would r. back on themselves BURKE. When shell and ball Rebounding idly on her strength did light BYRON. 2. With hoarse allarms the hollow Camp rebounds DRYDEN. 3. At once with joy and fear his heart rebounds MILT. 5. The hollow hills..Were wont redoubled Echoes to r. SPENSER.

Reboundant (rĭbau·ndănt), *a.* 1688. [f. prec. + -ANT[1].] *Her.* = REVERBERANT *a.* 1.

Rebuff (rĭbʋ·f), *sb.* 1611. [a. obs. F. *rebuffe,* ad. It. *ribuffo,* f. *ri-* RE- + *buffo* puff.] 1. A peremptory check given to one who makes an advance of any kind; a blunt refusal of a request or offer; a snub. b. A check to further action or progress, due to circumstances 1672. 2. A repelling puff or blast (*rare*) 1667.

1. The..insolent rebuffs Of knaves in office COWPER. 2. The strong r. of som tumultuous cloud Instinct with Fire and Nitre MILT.

Rebuff (rĭbʋ·f), *v.* 1586. [ad. obs. F. *rebuffer,* ad. It. *rebuffare,* f. *ribuffo*; see prec.] 1. *trans.* To repel bluntly or ungraciously; to give a rude check or repulse to. 2. To blow or drive back (*rare*) 1747.

Rebuild (rībi·ld), *v.* 1490. [RE- 5 a.] *trans.* To build again; to reconstruct. Also *absol.* b. *Rebuilding* = being rebuilt 1668.

b. That most stately and magnificent structure now re-building 1668. Hence **Rebui·lder.**

Rebuke (rĭbiū·k), *sb.* late ME. [f. next.] †1. A shameful or disgraceful check; a shame or disgrace –1485. †b. Without *a* or *pl.*: Shame, disgrace, reproach –1590. 2. Reproof, reprimand. late ME. b. With *a* and *pl.* A reproof, a reprimand 1514.

1. b. For great r. it is love to despise SPENSER. 2. A wise sonne heareth his fathers instruction: but a scorner heareth not r. *Prov.* xiii. 1. b. Shee's a Lady So tender of rebukes, that words are stroke[s] SHAKS.

Rebuke (rĭbiū·k), *v.* ME. [a. AF. and ONF. *rebuker* = OF. *rebuch(i)er,* f. *re-* RE- + *bucher* to beat, strike.] †1. *trans.* To beat down or force back; to repress or check; to repulse –1605. 2. To reprove, reprimand, chide severely ME. b. To express blame or reprehension of (a quality, action, etc.) by reproof or reprimand addressed to persons. Also *transf.* and *fig.* 1529.

1. Wee could haue rebuk'd him at Harflewe SHAKS. 2. He rebuked them for their cowardice and want of faith 1883. b. The Palmer..much rebukt those wandring eyes of his SPENSER. Hence **Rebu·keable** *a.* (now *rare*) that may be rebuked; deserving of rebuke. **Rebu·ker. Rebu·kingly** *adv.*

Rebukeful (rĭbiū·kfŭl), *a.* 1523. [f. REBUKE *sb.*] 1. Of words: Of a rebuking character. b. Of persons: Full of, given to, rebuke 1868. †2. Deserving of rebuke; disgraceful, shameful –1570. Hence **Rebu·kefully** *adv.*, **-ness.**

Rebus (rī·bŏs), *sb.* 1605. [a. L. *rebus,* abl. pl. of *res* thing. Explained as denoting 'by things', from the representation being *non verbis sed rebus.* See also N.E.D.] An enigmatical representation of a name, word, or phrase by figures, pictures, arrangement of letters, etc., which suggest the syllables of which it is made up. b. In later use, a puzzle in which a punning application of each syllable of a word is given, without pictorial representation. Hence **Re·bus** *v. trans.* to mark or inscribe with a r. or rebuses.

Rebut (rĭbʋ·t), *v.* ME. [a. AF. *reboter,* OF. *reboter, rebuter,* f. *re-* RE- + *boter, buter* BUTT *v.*[1]] †1. *trans.* To assail (a person) with violent language; to revile, rebuke, reproach –1470. †2. To repel, repulse, drive back (a person, or an attack) –1590. b. *transf.* 1536. 3. To force or turn back (a thing, now usu. something abstract); to give a check to 1490. 4. *Law.* To repel by counter-proof, refute (evidence, a charge, etc.). Hence *gen.* To refute, disprove (any statement, theory, etc.). 1817. †5. *intr.* or *absol.* a. To draw back, retire, retreat, recoil –1624. b. *Law.* To bring forward a rebutter –1768.

2. But he..Their sharp assault right boldly did r. SPENSER. 3. Their points rebutted backe againe Are duld SPENSER. 5. b. The plaintiff may answer the rejoinder by a sur-rejoinder; upon which the defendent may r. BLACKSTONE. So **Rebu·tment** = REBUTTAL. **Rebu·ttable** *a.* that may be rebutted.

Rebuttal (rĭbʋ·tăl). 1830. [f. prec. + -AL.] Refutation, contradiction; *spec.* in *Law* (cf. prec. 4).

Rebutter (rĭbʋ·təɹ). 1540. [In sense 1, a. AF. *rebuter*; in 2, partly f. REBUT *v.* + -ER[1].] 1. *Law.* An answer made by a defendant to a plaintiff's surrejoinder. 2. That which rebuts, repels, refutes, etc.; a refutation 1794.

‖**Recado** (rekā·do). 1615. [a. Sp. or Pg. *recado* message, gift, etc.; origin unkn.] †1. A present; a message of compliment –1698. 2. A S. Amer. saddle 1826.

Recalcitrance (rĭkæ·lsitrăns). 1856. [See next and -ANCE.] Recalcitrant temper or conduct.

Recalcitrant (rĭkæ·lsitrănt), *a.* and *sb.* 1843. [a. F., f. L. *recalcitrare.*] A. *adj.* 1. 'Kicking' against constraint or restriction; obstinately disobedient or refractory. Also const. *to.* 2. Characterized by refractoriness 1865. B. *sb.* A recalcitrant person 1865.

Recalcitrate (rĭkæ·lsitreit), *v.* 1623. [f. ppl. stem of L. *recalcitrare* to kick out; see RE- and CALCITRATE *v.*] 1. *intr.* To kick out, kick backwards (*rare*). b. To 'kick out' *against* or *at* a thing; to show strong objection or repugnance; to be obstinately disobedient or refractory 1767. 2. *trans.* To kick back (*rare*) 1832.

1. b. Those who..r. at their caresses, they threaten with Tartarus LANDOR. 2. The more heartily did one disdain his disdain, and r. his tricks DE QUINCEY. Hence **Recalcitra·tion.**

Recalesce (rīkăle·s), *v.* 1887. [ad. L. *recalescere.*] *intr.* To grow hot again. So **Recale·scence.**

Recall (rĭkǭ·l), *sb.* 1611. [f. RE- + CALL *sb.*, after the vb.] 1. The act of calling back; *spec.* the calling back of an actor, etc. to the stage or platform; an encore. b. *Naut.* A signal flag used to call back a boat to a ship, or a vessel to a squadron 1832. c. Any sound made as a signal to return; esp. *Mil.* a signal sounded on a musical instrument to call soldiers back to rank or camp 1855. 2. The act or possibility of recalling, revoking, or annulling something done or past 1667.

1. The admiral..gave the signal of recal 1806. 2. Phr. *Beyond, past r.*; 'Tis done, and since 'tis done, 'tis past r. DRYDEN.

Recall (rĭkǭ·l), *v.* 1575. [f. RE- + CALL *v.*] 1. *trans.* To call back, to summon (a person, or *fig.* a thing) to return to or from a place 1591. b. To bring back by (or as by) calling upon 1582. c. To bring back (the attention, mind, etc.) *to* a subject. Also without const. 1667. 2. To call or bring back *to* (or *from*) a certain state, occupation, etc. 1575. 3. To call or bring back (a circumstance, person, etc.) *to* the mind, memory, thoughts, etc. 1611. b. To bring back to the mind; to cause one to remember 1651. c. To recollect, remember 1690. 4. To bring back, restore, revive, resuscitate (a feeling, quality, or state) 1593. 5. To revoke, undo, annul (a deed, sentence, decree, etc.) 1588. b. To revoke, take back (a gift) 1608.

1. Let them be recall'd from their Exile SHAKS. b. But past who can r., or don undoe? MILT. 2. If Henry were recall'd to life againe SHAKS. 3. The name does not r. any one to me 1875. 4. Once gone, You cannot now r. your sister's peace SHELLEY. 5. b. The Gods themselves cannot r. their gifts TENNYSON. Hence **Reca·llable** *a.* that can be recalled. **Reca·llment** = RECALL *sb.*

Recant (rĭkæ·nt), *v.* 1535. [ad. L. *recantare* to recall, revoke, f. *re-* RE- 2 d + *cantare* to sing; cf. Gr. παλινῳδεῖν.] 1. *trans.* To withdraw, retract, or renounce (a statement, opinion, belief, etc.) as erroneous, and *esp.* with formal or public confession of error in matters of religion. †b. To renounce (a course of life or conduct) as wrong or mistaken –1701. 2. a. To withdraw, retract (a promise, vow, etc.). Now *rare.* 1596. b. To renounce, give up (a design or purpose) 1652. 3. *intr.* To retract, renounce, or disavow a former opinion or belief; *esp.* to make a formal or public confession of error 1553.

1. He was content to r. his opinions at Paules crosse 1601. 2. a. He shall doe this, or else I doe r. The pardon that I late pronounced heere SHAKS. 3. Here I r., and of those words repent me 1633. Hence **Recanta·tion,** the action of recanting; an instance of this. **Reca·nter.**

Recapa·citate, *v. rare.* 1702. [RE- 5 a.] *trans.* and *refl.* To make (legally) capable again.

Recapitulate (rīkăpi·tiŭleit), *v.* 1570. [See RE- and CAPITULATE *v.*] 1. *trans.* To go over or repeat again, properly in a more concise manner; to summarize, restate briefly. Also *absol.* b. *transf.* in *Biol.* of young animals: see next b. Also *absol.* 1879. 2. To bring together again; to sum up or unite in one (*rare*) 1607. Hence **Recapi·tulator. Recapi·tulatory** *a.* of the nature of, characterized by, recapitulation.

Recapitulation (rīkăpitiŭlē·ʃən). late ME. [a. OF. *recapitulacion,* or ad. L. *recapitulationem.*] The action of recapitulating; a summing up or brief repetition. b. *Biol.* The repetition of evolutionary stages in the growth of a young animal. Also *attrib.* 1875. Hence **Recapitula·tionist,** an adherent of the doctrine of r. in Biology.

Recaption (rĭ-, rīkæ·pʃən). 1607. [f. RE- + CAPTION.] 1. *Law.* a. A second distraint. b. (Also *writ of r.*) A writ issued in favour of one who has been distrained twice 1607. 2. *Law.* The peaceful seizure without legal process of one's own property wrongfully taken or withheld 1768.

Recaptor (rīkæ·ptǭɹ). 1752. [f. RE- + CAPTOR.] 1. One who retakes by capture; *esp.* one who makes a recapture at sea. 2. *Law.* One who takes goods by a recaption or second distraint 1841.

Recapture (rīkæ·ptiŭɹ, -tʃəɹ), *sb.* 1752. [f. RE- + CAPTURE.] 1. The fact of taking, or being taken, a second time; recovery or retaking by capture. 2. That which is captured again 1861.

Recapture (rīkæ·ptiŭɹ), *v.* 1799. [RE- 5 a.] *trans.* To capture again; to recover by capture.

Recarriage (rīkæ·ridʒ). 1541. [f. RE- + CARRIAGE.] The act of carrying or conveying back again, *esp.* conveyance back of merchandise; also, the fact of being carried back.

Recast (rīkɑ·st), *sb.* 1840. [RE- 5 a.] An act or instance of recasting; the new thing or form produced by recasting.

Recast (rīkɑ·st), *v.* 1603. [RE- 5 a.] 1. *trans.* To cast or throw again. *rare.* 2. To cast or found (metal) again. Also *fig.* 1768. b. To refashion, remodel, reconstruct (a thing, *esp.* a literary work, a sentence, etc.); to invest with new form or character 1790. 3. To supply new actors for (a play) 1911.

2. b. I have recast and rewritten the chapters MALTHUS. Buonaparte recast the art of war 1840.

Recaulescence (rīkǭle·sĕns). 1880. [RE- 5 a; see CAULESCENT *a.*] *Bot.* The adhesion throughout its whole length of a bract or leaf to its stem.

Recede (rĭsī·d), *v.*[1] late ME. [ad. L. *recedere,* f. *re-* RE- 2 a + *cedere* to go, CEDE.] 1. *intr.* To go back or further off; to retreat, retire. late ME. b. To become more distant; to lie further back or away; to slope backwards 1777. †2. To depart *from* some usual or natural state, an authority, standard, principle, etc. –1796. b. Of things: To depart, differ, or vary *from* something else. Now *rare* or *Obs.* 1576.

3. To draw back, withdraw *from* a bargain, promise, position, opinion, etc. 1648. **4.** To go away, depart, retire (*from* or *to* a place or scene). *rare.* 1440. **5. a.** To go back or away in time 1831. **b.** To decline in character or value 1828.

1. As the sun recedes, the moon and stars discouer themselues GLANVILL. **2.** Receding from custome when their interest requires it HOBBES. **3.** How could I r. from such an engagement? 1792. **5. b.** Foreign Government stocks receded fractionally 1883.

Recede (rĭsī·d), *v.*[2] 1771. [f. RE- 5 a + CEDE *v.*] *trans.* To cede again, give up to a former owner.

Receipt (rĭsī·t), *sb.* [Late ME. *receite, receit* :—(ult.) L. *recepta*, fem. pa. pple. of *recipere* to RECEIVE.] **I. 1.** A formula or prescription, a statement of the ingredients (and mode of procedure) necessary for the making of some preparation, esp. in *Med.* (now *rare*) and *Cookery*; a RECIPE. **b.** The formula or description of a remedy *for* a disease; also *absol.* a remedy, means of cure 1586. **c.** The means to be adopted *for* attaining some end 1621. **†2.** A drug or other mixture compounded in accordance with a receipt –1773.

1. *fig.* Some..Write dull receipts how poems may be made POPE. **b.** Euery defect of the mind may haue a speciall receit BACON. **c.** From the knowledge of simples shee had a r. to make white haire black SIR T. BROWNE.

II. That which is received; the amount, sum, or quantity received. late ME.

An excess of actual revenue over estimated receipts 1863.

III. 1. The act of receiving something given or handed to one; the fact of being received. late ME. **b.** A written acknowledgement of money or goods received into possession or custody 1602. **2.** The act of receiving or taking in; admittance (of things) to a place or receptacle. *Obs.* or *arch.* late ME. **†3.** The act of receiving or admitting (a person) to a place, shelter, accommodation, assistance, etc.; the fact of being so received; reception –1676. **†b.** The ordinary or habitual reception of strangers or travellers; esp. in *place of r.* –1650. **†4.** Acceptance of a person or thing (*rare*) –1621. **5.** The fact of receiving (a blow, wound). *Obs.* or *arch.* 1533.

1. The r. and expenditure of large sums of money 1848. **b.** Make a receit for the same on the backside of the said Bill 1651. **2.** Ample cisternes for the receit of raine 1615. **3. b.** The greatest place of r. in Samaria FULLER.

IV. 1. The chief place or office at which moneys are received on behalf of the Crown or government; the public revenue-office. Also, *R. of the (King's) Exchequer.* Now only *Hist.* 1442. **b.** The receiving-place *of* custom. Hence *fig.* 1539. **†2.** A place for the reception of things; a receptacle –1605. **†b.** *esp.* A basin or other part of a fountain; a reservoir –1646. **†3.** A place of refuge –1625. **†b.** A chamber, apartment (*rare*) –1615. **†4.** *Hunting.* A position taken up to await driven game with fresh hounds; a relay of men or dogs placed for this purpose –1688.

1. b. He sawe a man (named Mathew) syttyng at the receate of custome BIBLE (Great) *Matt.* ix. 9. **3. b.** Atrides, and his..spouse,..In a retired receit, together lay CHAPMAN.

V. †1. Capability of receiving, accommodating, or containing; capacity, size –1703. **†b.** Mental capacity –1628. **†2.** Accommodation or space provided –1627.

1. *fig.* His popular manner was of such r. that he had room to lodge all comers FULLER.

Comb.: **r.-book**, (*a*) a book of medical or cooking receipts; (*b*) a book containing printed forms for receipts for payments made.

†Recei·pt, *v.*[1] ME. [a. OF. *receiter*, var. *receter* RESET *v.*[1]] *trans.* To receive, harbour (a person, esp. a criminal) –1733. So **†Recei·pter**, one who receives or harbours criminals or stolen goods.

Receipt (rĭsī·t), *v.*[2] 1787. [f. RECEIPT *sb.*] **1.** *trans. U.S.* To acknowledge in writing the receipt of (a sum of money, etc.). **2.** To mark (an account) as paid 1844. **3.** *intr. U.S.* To give a receipt *for* (a sum of money, etc.) 1880. Hence **Recei·ptor** *U.S.* a person who receipts property attached by a sheriff; a bailee.

Receivable (rĭsī·văb'l), *a.* late ME. [orig. a. AF. *receivable*, var. OF. *recevable*; in later use f. RECEIVE *v.* + -ABLE.] **1.** Capable of being received. **b.** Of certificates, paper money, etc.: That is to be received as legal tender 1790. **2.** Capable of receiving (*rare*) 1530.

1. The general rule of English law is, that hearsay evidence is not r. 1880. Hence **Receivabi·lity. Recei·vableness.**

Receival (rĭsī·văl). Now *rare.* 1637. [f. RECEIVE *v.* + -AL.] Receipt, reception.

Receive (rĭsī·v), *v.* ME. [a. ONF. *receivre* = OF. *reçoivre* :—L. *recipere*; or a. OF. *receveir* :—pop.L. **recipēre.*] **I. 1.** *trans.* To take in one's hand, or into one's possession (something held out or offered by another); to take delivery of (a thing) from another, either for oneself or for a third party. **b.** Of God: To take (a soul) to himself ME. **c.** To take (stolen goods) into one's keeping 1583. **d.** To take from another by hearing; to attend or give heed to. late ME. **2.** To accept (something offered or presented) ME. **3.** To become the support of (something superimposed). late ME. **b.** To catch (a person or thing descending) in the arms or otherwise 1470. **c.** To catch or intercept (a missile, blow, etc.); to encounter the force or effect of 1560. **d.** To catch (a sound) by hearing. late ME. **4.** To permit oneself to be the object of (some action, etc.); to allow (something) to be done to, or (some quality, etc.) to be conferred on, oneself; to submit to ME. **b.** To admit (an impression, etc.) by yielding or by adaptation of surface. late ME. **c.** To allow (something) to be applied to, or placed on, oneself 1549. **d.** Of recording instruments: To be affected, or operated on, by (the thing transmitted) 1862. **5.** To take in; to admit as to a receptacle or containing space; to allow to enter or penetrate ME. **b.** Of a place or building: To admit (a person); to give accommodation or shelter to ME. **c.** To afford proper room or space to; to hold or contain conveniently 1440. **6.** To take in by the mouth; to swallow. *Obs.* or *arch.* late ME. **b.** To participate in, take (the sacrament or holy communion) ME. **7.** To take into the mind; to understand; to learn 1603.

1. He..Received it. and at one draught drank it off SHELLEY. **b.** Jesu, do Thou my soul r. KEBLE. **d.** A wyse man wil receaue warnynge COVERDALE *Prov.* x. 8. **2.** We cannot r. parole evidence of their contents 1776. **3.** Make broad thy shoulders to r. my weight TENNYSON. **c.** The son..received the first discharge of her fury SMOLLETT. **4. b.** His tendrer cheeke receiues her soft hands print SHAKS. **c.** Egypt has since Received his yoke, and the whole Nile is Cæsar's ADDISON. **d.** Also, of wireless receiving-sets or the operators of these. **5. b.** Innes ordeyned..to resceyve bothe Man and Hors MAUNDEVILLE.

II. 1. To admit (a person) into some relation with oneself, esp. to familiar or social intercourse; to treat in a friendly manner ME. **b.** In religious use ME. **2.** To meet (a person) with signs of welcome or salutation; to pay attention or respect to (one who comes to a place); to greet upon arrival or entrance ME. **3.** To meet, welcome, or greet (a person) in a specified manner ME. **b.** *Mil.* To meet with resistance (an enemy, his attack, etc.). late ME. **4.** To admit (a person) to a place; *esp.* to give accommodation or shelter to; to harbour. late ME. **5.** To admit (a person or thing) *to, into* a state, condition, privilege, occupation, etc. late ME. **b.** To admit to membership of a society or class or to partnership in work; to take in *among* other persons or things. late ME. **6.** To take or accept (a person) in some capacity. late ME. **b.** To admit (a person) to plead or give evidence 1607. **7.** To take, accept, regard, hear, etc. (anything offered or presented, or to which attention is given) in a specified manner or with a specified expression of feeling. late ME. **8.** To accept as an authority, rule, or practice; to admit the truth or validity of; to make use of. late ME. **b.** To give credit to; to believe. Also *absol.* late ME.

1. He is a Gentleman so Receiv'd, so Courted, and so Trusted STEELE. **b.** God accept him, Christ r. him TENNYSON. **2.** Preparations to r. the King CLARENDON. **4.** Take heede what Guests You receiue SHAKS. **5.** R. me, at my death, to everlasting happiness JOHNSON. **b.** Forty-five persons have been received by immersion into the church 1843. **7.** But how hath she receiu'd his Loue? SHAKS. **8.** An axiom universally received BERKELEY. **b.** They..speak in ears That hear not or r. not their report COWPER.

III. 1. To have (a thing) given or handed to oneself; to get from another or others ME. **b.** To get (a letter, etc.) brought to oneself. late ME. **c.** To get by communication from another; to learn, ascertain, etc., in this way 1526. **2. a.** To get (a person) into one's custody, control, vicinity, society, etc. Now *rare* or *Obs.* ME. **b.** To get, or come into possession of (a town, country, etc.). *rare.* 1568. **c.** To get or acquire (some feature) 1789. **3.** To have (some quality, attribute, or property) given, bestowed, conferred, or impressed ME. **4.** To be the object of (some action); to experience or meet with (some treatment, etc.) ME. **5.** To have (a blow, wound, mark, etc.) inflicted or made upon one or *in* some part; to get (a specified injury). late ME. **b.** To come in the way of and suffer from (a missile, gun, etc.) 1715. **6.** To have (a law, etc.) imposed or laid on one; to get as a charge. late ME.

1. His mother..residing in one of them..and receiving rent for the others 1818. **b.** I receyved but one letter from my father 1530. **c.** On Mr. Anson's receiving any other intelligence 1748. **3.** Such collections of stony fragments..r. the name of Moraines 1813. **4.** The affronts she had received DICKENS. The proposal..deserves more attention than it is likely..to r. 1891. **5.** I stood like one that had received a blow TENNYSON. **b.** His bended arm received the falling stone POPE.

IV. Absol. uses. **1.** To take, accept, or get, in various senses; to be or become a recipient. late ME. **2.** To take the sacrament or holy communion; to communicate 1560. **3.** To hold receptions 1854.

Hence **Recei·ving** *vbl. sb.* (also *attrib.* as *r.-office, -room*, etc.; *r.-set* in Wireless) and *ppl. a.*

Receiver (rĭsī·vəɹ). ME. [orig. a. AF. *receivour*, f. *receivre, recevoir* to RECEIVE. In later use f. the vb. + -ER[1].] **1.** One who receives (see the vb.). **2.** One who receives on behalf of others: **a.** An official, officer, or servant appointed to receive money due; a treasurer, collector. Also *†general r.*: see RECEIVER-GENERAL. Now chiefly *Hist.* ME. **b.** A person appointed by a court to administer the property of a bankrupt, or property which is the subject of litigation, pending the suit. In recent use also *official r.* 1793. **3.** One who knowingly receives stolen goods or harbours offenders; a resetter ME. **4.** That which receives; a receptacle. late ME. **b.** A tank or reservoir; a vessel to hold anything 1538. **c.** A mould to receive molten metal 1846. **5.** As the name of certain parts of apparatus or machinery intended to receive and contain something; e.g. *Chem.* a vessel for receiving and condensing the product of distillation; the receptacle for mercury in a barometer 1576. **6. a.** A device or instrument which receives an electric current or a telegraphic message 1873. **b.** An apparatus which receives and reproduces sounds from another part of an electric circuit; that part of a telephone which is applied to the ear 1877. **c.** An apparatus for transforming broadcast waves into sound or light; a wireless receiving-set 1890. **Recei·vership** (sense 2).

Recei·ver-ge·neral. 1439. A chief receiver, esp. of public revenues. (See RECEIVER 2 a).

In Great Britain now only as the title of an official of the Duchy of Lancaster.

Recency (rī·sĕnsi). 1612. [f. RECENT; see -ENCY.] The state or quality of being recent.

Recense (rĭse·ns), *v.* 1597. [ad. L. *recensere* (f. *re-* RE- + *censere*) or F. *recenser.*] *trans.* To survey, review, revise (now *spec.* a text).

Recension (rĭse·nʃən). 1638. [ad. L. *recensionem*; see prec.] **1.** An enumeration, survey, review. Now *rare.* **b.** A review (of a book). GEO. ELIOT. **2.** The revision of a text, esp. in a careful or critical manner; a particular version of a text resulting from such revision 1818. **b.** *transf.* A revised or distinct form of anything 1835. Hence **Rece·nsionist**, one who makes a r.

Recent (rī·sĕnt), *a.* 1533. [ad. L. *recent-, recens*, or a. F. *récente.*] **1.** Lately done or made; that has lately happened or taken place, etc. **2.** Lately formed, created, originated, or begun; †new-born 1676. **b.** Fresh; not yet affected by decay, decomposition, or loss of moisture 1558. **c.** *poet.* Lately or freshly come or arrived *from* a place 1715. **3.** Belonging to a (past) period of time comparatively near to the present. (Opp. to *ancient* †or *antique.*) 1622. **b.** *Geol.* Of or pertaining to the present geological epoch 1830. **4.** Of a point or period of time: Not long past 1823. **b.** *Geol.* Applied to the later portion of the Quaternary or Post-Pliocene period 1833.

1. R. translations I have seen of it in French 1661. The bright drops of a r. shower 1837. **2.** Lorraine and Arles, two r. and transitory kingdoms GIBBON. **c.** R. from the roar of foreign foam SWINBURNE. **3.** Though it be an action of so r. memorie BACON. **b.** An intermixture of extinct and r. species of quadrupeds 1833. **4.** Up to a very r. period 1823. Hence **Re·cently** *adv.* at a r. date; lately, newly 1533. **Re·centness.**

Receptacle (rĭse·ptăk'l). late ME. [ad. L. *receptaculum*, f. ppl. stem of *recipere* to RECEIVE.] **1.** That which receives and holds a thing; a containing vessel, place, or space; a repository. **2.** Any place into which persons (ships, animals, etc.) are received or retire, esp. for shelter or security. late ME. **3.** *spec.* in scientific use. **a.** *Anat.* and *Bot.* An organ or space which receives a secretion, esp. *r. of chyle* (the dilated lower portion of the thoracic duct), *of secretion* (in plants) 1543. **b.** *Bot.* The common base which supports the floral organs, the torus or thalamus (*floral r.*). Also, the axis or rachis of a head, spike, or other cluster (*r. of inflorescence*). 1753. **c.** *Bot.* In Ferns, Mosses, Algæ, and Fungi, the support of the fructification or reproductive organs; an apothecium, pycnidium, sporophore, etc. 1842.

1. *fig.* The soule of man is the r. of Christ's presence HOOKER. **2.** Holy-wells, rocks and caves, which have been the reputed cells and receptacles of men reputed saints 1672. So **Recepta·cular** *a. Bot.* pertaining to the r. of a flower; also, of the nature of, or serving as, a r.

†**Rece·ptary,** *sb.* and *a.* *rare.* 1611. [f. L. *recept-*, *recipere* + -ARY [1].] **A.** *sb.* **1.** A book or collection of receipts –1656. **2.** An accepted notion or belief. **B.** *adj.* Merely accepted as true, without proof. –1646.

Receptible (rĭse·ptib'l), *a.* Now *rare.* 1574. [ad. late L. *receptibilis*; see -IBLE.] **1.** That may be received, receivable. **2.** Capable of receiving. Const. *of.* 1656. So **Rece:ptibi·lity,** the quality or state of being r.

Reception (rĭse·pʃən). late ME. [a. F., or ad. L. *receptionem.*] **1.** The action or fact of receiving or getting 1489. **2. a.** *Astrol.* The fact of each of two planets being received into the other's house, exaltation, or other dignity. late ME. **b.** The action of receiving (esp. persons), or fact of being received, into a place, company, state, etc. 1650. **c.** The action of receiving, or fact of being received, in a formal or ceremonious manner 1662. **d.** An occasion of ceremonious receiving; an assemblage of persons for this purpose 1882. **3.** The action of receiving, or taking in, physically or spatially. late ME. **4.** The action of accepting or admitting; acceptance, admittance, approbation 1660. †**b.** An idea accepted without evidence of its truth –1691. **5.** The action of receiving, or fact of being received, in a certain manner; kind or manner of reception 1647. **6.** The action of receiving or taking 1863. †**7.** Capacity for receiving –1698. †**8.** A receptacle –1696. †**9.** Recovery, recapture. BACON.

1. The prospect of the wealth which awaits man's r. 1834. **2. b.** All hope is lost Of my r. into grace MILT. **c.** The r. of a deputation 1886. **3.** Towers for the r. of the bells 1868. **4.** To persuade us into a R. of Divine Truth ATTERBURY. **5.** *spec.* The receiving of wireless signals, or the efficiency with which they are received 1907.

Comb.: **r.-order,** an order authorizing the r. and detention of a person in a lunatic asylum. Hence **Rece·ptionist,** (*a*) *Theol.* applied attrib. to a view of the Eucharist which makes the presence of Christ depend on the disposition of the communicant. (*b*) a person employed by a photographer, dentist, etc. to receive clients.

Receptive (rĭse·ptiv), *a.* 1547. [ad. med. L. *receptivus*; see RECEIPT and -IVE.] **1.** Having the quality of, or capacity for, receiving; able to receive; pertaining to, of the nature of, reception. **2.** *spec. R. spot,* the spot in an oosphere at which the male gamete is admitted 1875.

1. The passive r. work of the mind 1875. I should wish the citizens to be as r. of virtue as possible 1875. Hence **Rece·ptive-ly** *adv.*, **-ness.** **Receptivity** (rĭsepti·vĭti), ability or readiness to receive or take in.

‖ **Recercelé** (rĭsə̄·ɹsəli). 1766. [a. OF., pa. pple. of *recerceler*, f. *re-* RE- + *cercel* circle.] *Her.* Of a cross: Having the ends of the arms curling into divergent spirals.

Recess (rĭse·s), *sb.* 1531. [ad. L. *recessus*, f. *recedere* to RECEDE.] †**1.** The act of retiring, withdrawing, or departing; withdrawal, departure. (Freq. in phr. *access and r.*) –1692. †**2.** The (*or* an) act of retirement from public life or into privacy; the fact of living retired; a period of retirement –1762. **3.** The act of retiring for a time from some occupation; a period of cessation from usual work or employment 1642. †**b.** Cessation from work; relaxation –1781. †**4.** Delay, respite (*rare*) –1706. **5.** A place of retirement, a remote, secret, or private place 1636. **6.** The act of receding, of going back or away, from a certain point. (Used chiefly of the motion of things, and *esp.* of water, the sea, or the heavenly bodies.). 1607. **7.** A retired or inner place or part; one of the remotest or innermost parts or corners of anything 1616. **8.** A receding part or indentation in the line of some natural feature or object, as a coast, range of hills, etc. 1697. **b.** *spec.* A niche or alcove 1774. **c.** Any small depression or indentation; also *Anat.* a sinus or fold in an organ or part 1839. **9.** *Hist.* A resolution, decree, or act of the Imperial Diet of Germany or of the Diet of the Hanseatic League. [After med.L. *recessus.*] 1706.

3. In this r. of action, we had several treaties about prisoners 1671. In the r.,..or interval of suspended studies in the middle of the forenoon 1860. We are in a Parliamentary r. 1881. *The r.*: spec. the interval between two sessions of parliament. **5.** The last retreat, and r., of his every-day waning grandeur LAMB. **6.** An alternate r. and advance of the apsides 1834. *transf.* Painting the access and r. of his thought 1843. **7.** The gloomy recesses of the cloister 1801. *fig.* Deep in the close recesses of my soul POPE. **8.** His dwelling a r. in some rude rock COWPER.

Recess (rĭse·s), *v.* 1809. [f. prec.] **1.** *trans.* To place in a recess or in retirement; to set back or away. **b.** *spec.* To set (part of a wall or other structure) in a recess 1845. **2.** To make a recess or recesses in; to cut away, so as to form a recess 1876. **3.** *intr. U.S.* To take a recess or interval 1893.

1. **b.** The arches,..one recessed within the other 1845. Hence **Rece·ssed** *ppl. a.* set in a recess; as *recessed arch,* an arch set within another arch.

Recession (rĭse·ʃən). 1652. [ad. L. *recessionem.*] **1.** The action of receding; withdrawal, retirement. **b.** A setting or going back in time (*rare*) 1646. **2.** The action of receding, retiring or departing, in various *transf.* or *fig.* senses. Const. *from.* 1647.

Recessional (rĭse·ʃənăl), *a.* and *sb.* 1867. [f. prec. + -AL.] **A.** *adj.* **1.** Of or belonging to the recession or retirement of the clergy and choir from the chancel to the vestry at the close of a service; esp. *r. hymn,* a hymn sung while this retirement is taking place. **2.** Belonging to a recess (of Parliament) 1895. **B.** *sb.* A recessional hymn 1867.

Recessive (rĭse·siv), *a.* (and *sb.*) 1672. [f. L. *recess-*, *recedere* + -IVE.] Tending to recede; *spec.*, in the Mendelian theory of heredity, opp. to *dominant.* As *sb.* = a recessive character.

Rechabite (re·kăbəit). late ME. [ad. biblical L. *Rechabita*, used in pl. to render Heb. *Rēkābīm*, f. the personal name *Rēkāb*; see *Jer.* xxxv. 2–19.] One of a Jewish family descended from Jonadab, son of Rechab, which refused to drink wine or live in houses. Hence (*a*) one who abstains from intoxicating liquors; now *spec.* a member of the Independent Order of Rechabites, a benefit society founded in 1835; (*b*) a dweller in tents. Hence **Re·chabitism.**

Rechange (rītʃē·ndʒ). 1487. [f. RE- 5 a + CHANGE *sb.*] †**1.** The RE-EXCHANGE on a bill –1682. †**2.** The act of re-exchanging (money or goods) –1625. **3.** The act of changing or altering again 1550.

Recharge (rītʃā·ɹdʒ), *sb.* 1603. [f. RE- + CHARGE *sb.*] **1.** A fresh charge or load 1611. **2.** A renewed or return charge in battle 1603.

Recharge (rītʃā·ɹdʒ), *v.* late ME. [f. RE- + CHARGE *v.*] **1.** *trans.* †**a.** To reload (a vessel). Also *absol.* –1615. **b.** To put a fresh charge in; to refill, reload 1839. **2.** †**a.** To charge or accuse in return –1697. **b.** To make a new charge against 1895. **3.** To lay or impose again as a charge (*rare*) 1611. **4.** *intr.* To charge (in battle) again or in return 1598.

2. **b.** The magistrate..then directed that she should be re-charged for the assault on the..gaoler 1895.

Recha·se, *v.* *Obs.* exc. *dial.* late ME. [a. F. *rechasser*; see RE- and CHASE *v.*] †**1.** *trans.* To chase or drive back; to chase in turn –1614. **2.** †**a.** *Hunting.* To chase (a deer) back into the forest –1741. **b.** To drive back (cattle or sheep) from one pasture to another 1618.

‖ **Réchauffé** (reʃofe). 1805. [F., pa. pple. of *réchauffer*, f. *re-* RE- + *échauffer*; see CHAFE *v.*] A warmed-up dish; hence *fig.* something old served up again, esp. a rehash of literary matter.

It is really wasting time to confute this *r.* of a theory 1805.

Recheat (rĭtʃī·t), *sb.* *Obs.* exc. *arch.* 1470. [prob. ad. OF. *rachat, vbl. sb. f. *rachater* RECHEAT *v.*] †**a.** The act of calling together the hounds to begin or continue the chase of a stag, or at the close of the hunt (*rare*). **b.** The series of notes sounded on a horn for one or other of these purposes. So †**Recheat** *v. intr.* to blow a r. –1612.

‖ **Recherché** (rəʃerʃe), *a.* 1722. [F., pa. pple. of *rechercher*, f. *re-* RE- + *chercher* to seek.] Carefully sought out; hence, extremely choice or rare.

†**Recidivate,** *pa. pple.* and *v.* *rare.* 1528. [f. ppl. stem of med.L. *recidivare*, f. *recidivus* RECIDIVE.] **A.** *pa. pple.* Fallen back. **B.** *v. intr.* To fall back, relapse. –1677.

†**Recidivation.** late ME. [a. F. *récidivation*; see prec.] **1.** Relapse into sin, error, crime, etc.; backsliding, apostasy –1693. **2.** A relapse in a sickness or disease –1706.

Recidive (re·sidiv), *a.* and *sb.* *rare.* 1537. [ad. L. *recidivus*, f. *recidere.*] †**A.** *adj.* Falling back, relapsing –1659. **B.** *sb.* †**a.** = RECIDIVATION 2. –1600. **b.** = next 1854.

Recidivist (rĭsi·divist). 1880. [ad. mod. F. *récidiviste*, f. *récidiver*; see prec. and -IST.] One who relapses; *esp.* one who habitually relapses into crime. So **Reci·divism,** the habit of relapsing into crime.

Recidivous (rĭsi·divəs), *a.* 1658. [f. L. *recidivus* RECIDIVE + -OUS.] Liable to fall back or relapse.

Recipe (re·sipī), *v. imper.* and *sb.* late ME. [L. *recipe* take, used by physicians (abbrev. R, ℞) at the head of prescriptions, and hence applied to these and similar formulæ.] †**A.** *v. imper.* = Take –1652. **B.** *sb.* **1.** *Med.* A formula for a medical prescription; a prescription, or the remedy prepared in accordance with this 1584. **2.** A statement of the ingredients and procedure necessary for the making or compounding of some preparation, esp. of a dish in cookery; a receipt 1743. **3.** *transf.* A means (actual or suggested) for attaining or effecting some end 1643.

Recipience (rĭsi·piĕns). *rare.* 1882. [f. as next; see -ENCE.] The act or process of receiving.

Recipiency (rĭsi·piĕnsi). 1822. [f. next; see -ENCY.] Receptivity; reception.

Recipient (rĭsi·piĕnt), *a.* and *b.* 1558. [ad. L. *recipientem*, *recipere.*] **A.** *adj.* That receives or is capable of receiving; receptive 1610. **B.** *sb.* **1.** One who or that which receives 1615. †**2. a.** *Chem.* A receiver; a (glass) vessel for receiving or holding a liquid –1794. **b.** The receiver of an air-pump –1815. **3.** A re-entrant angle 1811.

Reciprocal (rĭsi·prŏkăl), *a.* and *sb.* 1570. [f. L. *reciprocus* (cf. RECIPROQUE) + -AL.] **A.** *adj.* †**1.** Having, or of the nature of, an alternate backward and forward motion. (Said *esp.* of tides.) –1726. †**b.** Of actions: Alternating –1758. **2.** Of the nature of or pertaining to a return made for something; given, felt, shown, etc., in return 1596. **b.** Existing on both sides; felt or shared by both parties; mutual 1579. **3.** Inversely correspondent or related; correlative, complementary; †opposed. Now chiefly *Math.* 1570. **b.** *Math.* Based upon an inverse relationship 1823. **4.** Corresponding or answering to each other, as being either similar or complementary 1570. †**5.** Convertible, synonymous -1733. **6.** *Gram.* Of pronouns and verbs, or their signification: Reflexive; now, more usu. expressing mutual action or relationship 1611.

2. He had a right to expect from them a r. demonstration of firmness *Junius' Lett.* **b.** Kindness is generally r. JOHNSON. Phr. *R. defence*, in *Fortif.*, a form of flanking defence. **3. b.** *R. equation*, one of those which contain several pairs of roots, which are the r. of each other.. *R. proportion* is when the reciprocals of the two last terms have the same ratio as the quantities of the first terms.. *R. ratio* is the ratio of the reciprocals of two quantities. 1823. **4.** Reciprocall figures are those, when the termes of proportion are both antecedentes and consequentes in either figure 1570. Let our reciprocall vowes be remembred SHAKS. Allegiance and Protection are r. in all Countries 1718. R., in mathematics, is applied to quantities which multiplied together produce unity 1797. **6.** A Pronoun or a Verb r. 1727. *One another, each other*, are sometimes called r. pronouns 1872.

B. *sb.* †**1.** One who is sent back. CHAPMAN. **2.** A thing corresponding in some way or other; a return, equivalent, counterpart, etc. 1570. †**3.** *Gram.* A reflexive verb -1766. **4.** *Math.* A function or expression so related to another that their product is unity; the inverse 1685.

2. Corruption is a Reciprocall to Generation BACON. Hence **Reciproca·lity**, †**Reci·procalness**, reciprocity.

Reciprocally (rĭsi·prǫkăli), *adv.* 1570. [-LY [2].] In a reciprocal manner; with reciprocity.

As the mind affects the body, the body r. affects the mind 1756. The existence of our kind is continuous, and its ages are r. dependent 1876. You must vnderstand it r., the battel is not alwayes to the strong, therefore it is sometimes to the weake 1628.

Reciprocate (rĭsi·prǫkeit), *v.* 1611. [f. L. *reciprocat-*, *reciprocare*, f. *reciprocus.*] **1.** *intr.* †**a.** To go back, return; to have a backward direction -1661. **b.** To move backwards and forwards (now *Mech.*); †to go up and down, to vary 1678. **c.** *trans.* To alternate the direction of; to cause to move backwards and forwards 1653. **2. a.** To give and receive in return or mutually; to interchange 1611. **b.** To return, requite; to do, feel, etc., in or by way of return 1820. **3.** *intr.* To make a return or interchange *with* (another or others). Now *rare* or *Obs.* 1626. **b.** *spec.* To make a return or exchange of good wishes 1779. †**4. a.** *trans.* To make correspondent or convertible *with*; to convert -1788. **b.** *intr.* To be correspondent or in agreement (*with* something); to be equivalent or convertible 1683. **5.** *Math.* **a.** *trans.* To find the reciprocal to (a curve) 1861. **b.** *intr.* To pass *into* by reciprocation 1861.

1. c. Vainly reciprocating the saw of endless contention 1677. **2. a.** The waters reciprocating their tides with the neighbouring sea EVELYN. **3. b.** Then when the two glasses of water were brought,..he said, 'Madam, let us r.' JOHNSON. Hence **Reci·procating** *ppl. a.* that reciprocates; *spec.* in *Mech.* (of machines, etc.) having a reciprocating part or parts. **Reci·procator**, one who, or that which, reciprocates.

Reciprocation (rĭsiprǫkē·ʃən). 1530. [ad. L. *reciprocationem.*] †**1.** Reflexive action; a reflexive mode of expression -1631. **2.** Motion backwards and forwards. Now *Mech.* 1646. **b.** Alternate action or operation (*rare*) 1656. †**c.** Alternation; vicissitude -1794. **3.** The action of making a return, or doing something in return; *esp.* a mutual return or exchange of acts, feelings, etc. 1561. **4.** The state of being in a reciprocal or harmonious relation; correspondence 1605. †**b.** *Logic.* The conversion of terms or propositions, or the relation involved by this -1677.

3. With a sincere r. of all your kindly feeling DICKENS.

Reciprocity (resiprǫ·sĭti). 1766. [ad. F. *réciprocité*, f. (ult.) L. *reciprocus.*] **1.** The state or condition of being reciprocal; a state or relationship in which there is mutual action, influence, giving and taking, correspondence, etc., between two parties or things. **2.** *spec.* **a.** Mutual or correspondent concession of advantages or privileges, as forming a basis for the commercial relations between two countries 1782. **b.** In the Kantian philosophy: Mutual action and reaction 1883.

2. a. New arrangements of trade, on the footing of r. and mutual convenience 1783.

†**Reciproque**, *a.* and *sb.* 1532. [a. F. *réciproque*, f. (ult.) L. *re-* back and *pro* forward.] **A.** *adj.* = RECIPROCAL *a.* -1619. **B.** *sb.* A return or equivalent. Also with *the*: The natural return, the like. -1648.

B. It is a true rule that loue is euer rewarded either with the r. or with an inward..contempt BACON.

Recision (rĭsi·ʒən). Now *rare.* 1611. [ad. L. *recisionem*, f. *recidere* to cut back.] **a.** The action of cutting back or pruning. †**b.** The action of rescinding -1706.

Recital (rĭsəi·tăl). 1512. [f. RECITE *v.* + -AL [2].] **1.** A rehearsal, account, or description *of* some thing, fact, or incident; also (esp. in early use), a relation of the particulars or details *of* something 1550. **b.** A discourse, account, relation, narrative 1565. **2.** *spec.* The rehearsal or statement in a formal or legal document of some fact or facts closely connected with the matter or purpose of the document itself; the part containing this statement 1512. **3.** An (*or* the) act of (†reading or) reciting 1612. **b.** *Mus.* A musical performance given by one person; a concert consisting of selections from one composer 1811.

2. The particular r. prefixed, by way of preamble, to this very clause BENTHAM. **3. b.** M. Liszt will also give a r. of one of his great fantasias 1840. *Opera r.*, a performance of the music and words of an opera without appropriate costume or acting. Hence **Reci·talist**, one who gives musical recitals.

Recitation (resitē·ʃən). 1484. [ad. L. *recitationem*, f. *recitare* to RECITE.] **1.** The action of rehearsing, detailing, †or enumerating; recital. **b.** An instance of this; an account, narrative 1641. **2.** The action of reciting (†or reading aloud); the repetition of something got by heart 1623. **b.** An instance of this; an act of reciting; also, a piece to be recited 1841. **3.** *U.S.* The repetition of a prepared lesson or exercise; an examination on something previously learned or explained 1824.

Recitative (re:sităti·v), *a.*[1] and *sb.* 1645. [ad. It. *recitativo* RECITATIVO.] *Mus.* **A.** *adj.* **1.** Of the nature of, in the style of, recitative. †**2.** Employing a recitative style -1660. **B.** *sb.* **1.** A style of musical declamation, intermediate between singing and ordinary speech, commonly employed in the dialogue and narrative parts of operas and oratorios 1656. †**b.** The tone or rhythm peculiar to any language -1791. **2.** Words or passages intended to be delivered in recitative 1716. **3. a.** A part rendered in recitative, or a piece of music intended for such a part 1754. **b.** A performance in r. 1873.

1. b. Some gentlemen of Ireland, to whom a slight proportion of the accent and r. of that country is an advantage BOSWELL. Hence †**Recitatively** *adv.*

Recitative (re·siteitiv, rĭsi·tătiv), *a.*[2] *rare.* 1860. [f. RECITE *v.* + -ATIVE.] Of the nature of a recital or repetition.

Recitativo (re:sităti·vo). 1645. [It., f. ppl. stem of *recitare* to RECITE + *-ivo* -IVE.] = RECITATIVE *sb.* 1.

†**Recite** (rĭsəi·t), *sb. rare.* 1685. [f. next.] A recital.

Recite (rĭsəi·t), *v.* late ME. [a. F. *réciter*, or ad. L. *recitare*, f. *re-* RE- + *citare* to CITE.] **1.** *trans.* To repeat or utter aloud (something previously composed, heard, or learned by heart); now *spec.* to repeat to an audience (a piece of verse, etc.) from memory and in an appropriate manner. Also, to read out or aloud (now *rare*). 1481. **2.** To relate, rehearse, narrate, tell, declare; to give an account of; to describe in detail. *Obs.* or *arch.* 1483. **b.** *Law.* To rehearse or state in a deed or other document (some fact bearing closely upon the matter in hand). late ME. †**3.** To compose; to write *down* (*rare*) -1654. **4.** To go through or over in detail; to enumerate, give a list of. Now *rare.* 1533. †**5.** To cite, quote -1793. †**b.** To cite or mention, to quote from (a book) -1807. **6.** *intr.* To repeat something from memory; *U.S.* to repeat a lesson, or be examined on one 1735.

1. I recited some Heroick Lines of my own STEELE. **2. b.** John Ivy, reciting that he had made a former will in the life of his wife 1818. **3.** Such as found out musical tunes, and recited verses in writing *Ecclus.* xliv. 5. **4.** By reciting the sins of their neighbours, men indulge their own foolish..desires WESLEY. Hence **Reci·ter**, one who recites; also used as the title of books containing passages for recitation.

Reck (rek), *sb. Obs.* exc. *poet.* 1568. [f. next.] Care, heed, consideration, regard.

Reck (rek), *v.* Now chiefly *rhet.* or *poet.* [Com. Teut.: OE. *reccan* :—OTeut. **rōkjan*. This is normally represented in ME. by *retche.* The surviving form with *ck* is due partly to ME. 2nd and 3rd pers. pres. ind. *rekst, rekþ*, partly to north. *rēke* :—ON. *rœkja.*] **1.** *intr.* **a.** To take care, heed, or thought *of* some thing (or person), with desire or favour towards it, interest in it, or the like; to set store or account *by*; to care *for.* Also with *inf.* **b.** To take heed or have a care *of* some thing (or person), so as to be alarmed or troubled thereby, or to modify one's conduct or purpose on that account. Also with *inf.* or dependent clause. OE. **c.** To know, be aware, or think *of* 1813. **2.** Without const. (usu. *ellipt.*): To care, heed, mind, etc. OE. **3.** *trans.* To heed, regard, care for, etc. ME. **4.** In impers. use: To concern or trouble (a person); to interest ME. **b.** *absol.* To matter; to be of importance or interest ME.

1. My master..little wreakes, to finde the way to heauen By doing deeds of hospitalitie SHAKS. Little recked he of flowers—save cauliflowers BARHAM. **b.** Then it was, old Father Care, Little reck'd I of thy frown SHERIDAN. **c.** Little recked Mr. Podsnap of the traps and toils besetting his Young Person DICKENS. **2.** I wreake not, though thou end my life to day SHAKS. Revenge..back on itself recoiles; Let it; I r. not MILT. **3.** Himself..reaks not his owne reade SHAKS. **4.** Of night, or loneliness it recks me not MILT.

Reckless (re·klės), *a.* [OE. *reccelēas*, *rēcelēas*, f. OE. **recce*, **rēce* (related to RECK *v.*) + *-lēas* -LESS. For the current form with *ck* see prec., etym. note. *Retchless*, the normal representative of the OE. form, continued till the 17th c.] **1.** Of persons: Careless of the consequences of one's actions; heedless (*of* something); lacking in prudence or caution. **2.** Of actions, conduct, things, etc. Characterized or distinguished by (†carelessness or) heedless rashness ME. **3.** Quasi-*adv.* Recklessly. late ME.

1. R. of life GROTE. A rough and r. soldier, caring for nothing but a fight 1879. **2.** A r. increase of population 1863. Hence **Re·ckless·ly** *adv.*, **-ness.**

Reckling (re·kliŋ). Also **wreck-.** 1611. [Origin unkn.] The smallest and weakest animal of a litter; the youngest or smallest child in a family.

Reckon (re·k'n), *v.* [OE. (*ge*)*recenian* :— OTeut. **rekenōjan*, perh. ult. from the root *rek-*, found in OE. *reccan* to relate.] **I.** *trans.* †**1.** To enumerate serially or separately; to go over or through (a series) in this manner ME. **b.** So with *up*, rarely *over* ME. †**c.** To recount, relate, narrate, tell -1586. †**d.** To mention -1596. **2.** To count, so as to ascertain the number or amount of; to ascertain (a number, quantity, etc.) by counting or calculating; to compute. Also with *out.* ME. **b.** To calculate or keep count of, in relation to some starting-point 1540. †**c.** To count out, to pay -1713. **d.** To count *up*; also, to sum *up*, to estimate the character of (a person) 1836. **3.** To include in a (*or* the) reckoning; hence, to place or class. late ME. **b.** To accept or state as a total 1563. †**4. a.** To estimate, value -1667. **b.** To take into consideration (*rare*) -1686. **5.** To consider, judge, or estimate by, or as the result of, calculation 1555. **b.** To set down or consider as being of a specified character, importance or value, or (rarely) as being in a certain condition ME. **c.** With *inf.* To regard as doing something 1513. **6.** To consider, think, suppose, be of opinion *that* 1513. **b.** *I reckon*, used parenthetically or finally. (Now *dial.* and Southern *U.S.*) 1603. †**7.** To account, assign, or attribute *to* (a person or thing) -1719.

1. b. I shall r. up only such authors whose records.. are lost and gone 1638. **2.** I am ill at these Numbers; I haue not Art to r. my grones SHAKS. **3.** In this class we may r. the Georgians, Circassians, and Mingrelians GOLDSM. **5.** They r. that this..Work will be finish'd in about fifty Years 1745. **6.** I r., said Socrates, that no one..could accuse me of idle talking JOWETT.

II. *intr.* †**1.** *To r. right*: to judge correctly -1667. **2.** To count, to make a calculation; to cast up an account or sum ME. **3.** To go over or settle accounts *with* one, or *together*

ME. b. *To r. with*: to take into consideration; to be prepared for 1885. 4. To calculate, design, or expect *to* do something. Now *dial.* 1550. b. To look *for* something 1848. 5. To account or think (much, etc.) *of*; to take account *of*, think highly or approve *of*. Now *rare* exc. *dial.* 1594. 6. To count, depend, or rely *on* or *upon* 1632. 7. To count, have a place or value 1879.

1. This to attain, whether Heav'n move or Earth, Imports not, if thou reck'n right MILT. 2. Phr. *To r. without one's host*: see HOST *sb.*[2] 2. 3. God..Will r. with us roundly for the abuse COWPER. b. A contingency to be reckoned with 1885. 4. You may have more to bear than you r. for J. H. NEWMAN. 6. He could r. on no support within England itself GREEN. Hence **Re·ckoner**, one who reckons; an aid to reckoning (see READY RECKONER).

Reckoning (re·k'niŋ), *vbl. sb.* ME. [f. prec. + -ING[1].] 1. The action of RECKON *v.*; enumeration, calculation, computation. b. Manner of computing or numbering. late ME. 2. An enumeration, calculation, or account. Also with *up*. ME. b. The process or result of (one's) counting. Freq. in phrases, as *to be out, in* or *of, to leave out of, to lose, one's r.* 1585. c. *spec.* The calculated period of pregnancy 1638. d. *Naut.* The estimate made of a ship's position by calculation from the log, the course steered, observation of the sun, etc. See also DEAD RECKONING. 1577. 3. A computation or account of the sum owing by, or due to, a person; a bill, *esp.* at an inn or tavern. late ME. b. *Dutch r.*: see quot. 4. The action of rendering an account of property entrusted to one's charge, etc.; an account so rendered ME. b. *spec.* With ref. to rendering an account of one's life or conduct to God at death or judgement ME. 5. The settlement of accounts or differences between parties 1470. 6. The action of calculating chances or contingencies; (an) anticipation or expectation 1568. †7. a. Mode of regarding a matter -1649. b. *To be*, or *come to, one r.*: to be equivalent -1674. †8. Estimation, consideration, distinction -1653.

1. b. The r. by Olympiads was not yet in use NEWTON. 2. b. I should lose my r. of time DE FOE. 3. They liked the wine, but not the r. which was to be paid for it FULLER. b. A Dutch r., wherein if you dispute the..exorbitance of the bill, the land lord shall bring it up every time with new additions SWIFT. 4. Howbeit, there was no r. made with them, of the money that was deliuered into their hand *2 Kings* xxii. 7. There will be a day of r. sooner or later DICKENS. 5. A firm bargain and a right r. make long friends 1776.

Reclaim (rĭklē·m), *sb.* Now *rare.* ME. [a. OF. *reclaim*, f. *reclaimer, reclamer*, to RECLAIM.] †1. The act of recalling a hawk -1486. †b. The recall or bringing back of a person -1590. 2. The act of recalling, or state of being recalled, to right conduct ME. b. The reclamation of land 1799. Hence **Reclai·mless** *a.* (*rare*) that cannot be reclaimed.

Reclaim (rĭklē·m), *v.* ME. [ad. OF. *reclamer*, †*reclaimer* :—L. *reclamare* to cry out against, etc.; see RE- and CLAIM *v.*] I. *trans.* †1. a. *Falconry.* To call back (a hawk which has been let fly) -1741. Also *transf.* b. To call back; to recall -1741. c. To restrain, check, hold back -1700. d. To withdraw (a statement); to revoke (*rare*) -1741. 2. To recall, bring back (a person or animal) *from* a wrong course of action, etc., *to* a proper state. late ME. b. To call back from wrong-doing or error; to reform 1577. c. To win back, win over (again). Also with *inf.* (*rare*) 1587. d. To put right, to remedy, correct, amend (an error, fault, etc.). *rare.* 1596. 3. To reduce to obedience, tame, subdue (*esp.* a hawk, also rarely a person). late ME. †b. To keep the growth of (wood or trees) within bounds -1697. c. To remove (rude qualities) by means of instruction or culture; to bring (savage people) to a state of civilization 1760. d. To bring (waste land, etc.) under, or into a fit state for, cultivation 1764. 4. To claim the restoration of, to demand or take back (a person or thing) 1450. †5. To cry out against (a thing or person); to gainsay -1650.

2. Henrietta had reclaimed him from a life of vice MACAULAY. c. Once alienated, [I doubt] whether he were ever to be reclaimed C. BRONTE. d. In reclaiming vulgar errors BACON. 3. c. A fair field,.. with no aborigines to be protected or reclaimed 1865. 5. Herod..in stead of reclaiming what they exclaimed, ..hug'd their praises as proper to himself FULLER.

II. *intr.* 1. To exclaim, protest. Now *rare.* 1440. b. With obj. clause. To declare or say in protest. 1449. c. *Sc. Law.* To appeal 1578. †2. To call out, cry loudly (*rare*) -1700. †3. a. To draw back; to recant (*rare*) -1604. b. To reform -1757.

1. The whole Context in Dionysius reclaims against this Emendation BENTLEY. 2. One whisper'd soft, and one aloud reclaim'd DRYDEN. Hence **Reclai·mable** *a.* **Reclai·mant, Reclai·mer,** one who reclaims.

Reclamation (reklămē̆·ʃən). 1533. [a. F., or ad. L. *reclamationem.*] 1. The action of protesting; a protest. 2. The action of calling or bringing back from wrong-doing, reformation 1633. b. The action of reclaiming *from* barbarism 1868. c. The making (of land) fit for cultivation 1861. 3. The action of claiming the return of something taken away; a claim *for* something 1787.

1. An act..done against the r. of the Law of Nature 1650.

‖**Réclame** (reklam). 1883. [Fr., f. *réclamer.*] The attainment of notoriety by 'puff' or advertisement.

Reclinant (rĭkləi·nănt), *a.* 1850. [a. F. *réclinant*, f. *récliner* to RECLINE.] *Her.* Bending or bowed.

Reclinate (re·klineᵗt), *a.* 1753. [ad. L. *reclinatus, reclinare.*] Bending downward; esp. *Bot.* of stems, branches, leaves, etc.

Reclination (reklinē̆·ʃən). 1578. [ad. late L. *reclinationem.*] 1. The action, posture, or practice of reclining. Now *rare.* †2. *Dialling.* The angle made by the plane of the dial with a vertical point intersecting it -1797. 3. *Surg.* An operation formerly used for cataract 1820.

3. 'R.' disposes of the cataract by tilting it backwards 1875.

Recline (rĭkləi·n), *sb. rare.* 1753. [f. the vb.] A recumbent or reclining posture.

†**Recli·ne**, *a.* 1667. [ad. L. *reclinis.*] Recumbent, reclining. MILT.

Recline (rĭkləi·n), *v.* late ME. [ad. L. *reclinare*, f. *re-* RE- + *-clinare*; see DECLINE *v.*] 1. *trans.* To lay down, or make to lie down (properly on the back); to cause to incline (backwards); to rest (the head, etc.) in this way. †2. *intr.* Of a dial: To have a backward inclination, to lie away back from the vertical -1797. 3. To rest in a recumbent or inclined position, lean or repose *on* or *upon* something 1697. b. *Mil.* Of one extremity of an army: To rest *upon* a place (*rare*) 1850. †4. To fall backwards or down. GOLDSM.

1. The sonne of man haþe not wer he may reclyne.. his hede 1440. Thus oft, reclined at ease, I lose an hour At evening COWPER. 3. The wood-crowned cliffs that o'er the lake r. WORDSW. Hence **Recli·ned** *ppl. a.* placed in a reclining position; characterized by recumbency. **Recli·ner**, one who or that which reclines; *spec.* a reclining dial or plane.

Reclining (rĭkləi·niŋ), *ppl. a.* 1668. [f. prec. + -ING[2].] That reclines.

Dials..are called inclining or r. dials, according as their planes make acute or obtuse angles with the horizon 1797.

†**Reclu·de**, *v.* late ME. [ad. L. *recludere* to open; later, to shut up; see RE- and CLOSE *v.*] 1. *trans.* To open (a gate, etc.) -1665. 2. To shut up (a thing or person); to close -1843. b. To shut (a person) off *from* a thing -1657.

Recluse (rĭklū·s), *a.* and *sb.* ME. [ad. F. *reclus, recluse*, pa. pple. of *reclure* :—L. *recludere* to shut up.] A. *adj.* 1. Of persons: Shut up, secluded from society, esp. as a religious discipline. 2. Of life, condition, etc.: Characterized by seclusion or close retirement 1645. 3. Of places: Secluded, solitary. Now *rare.* 1652. †b. Of things, actions, etc.: Hidden, private -1783.

1. I have lived r. in rural shades COWPER. The example of r. philosophers 1865. 2. His private habits were sober and r. GROTE. 3. The most r. retreats 1782.

B. *sb.* 1. a. A person shut up from the world for the purpose of religious meditation; a monk, anchorite or anchoress, *spec.* one who remains perpetually shut up in a cell under a vow of strict seclusion. b. One who mixes little with society. ME. †2. A place of seclusion -1772.

†**Reclu·se**, *v.* late ME. [f. L. *reclus-, recludere*; see RECLUDE *v.*] *trans.* To shut up, seclude -1713.

Reclusion (rĭklū·ʒən). late ME. [ad. L. *reclusionem.*] 1. The action of shutting up, or fact of being shut up, in seclusion; a state of retirement. b. The fact of being shut up as a prisoner, esp. in solitary confinement 1872. 2. A place of religious retreat 1797.

Reclusive (rĭklū·siv), *a.* 1599. [f. as RECLUSE *v.* + -IVE.] Marked by reclusion or retirement.

In some reclusiue and religious life, Out of all eyes SHAKS.

Reclusory (rĭklū·səri). 1821. [ad. med.L. *reclusorium*, f. *recludere.*] The cell of a recluse.

Recoct (rĭkǫ·kt), *v.* 1562. [f. L. *recoct-, recoquere*; see RE- and COOK *v.*] *trans.* To boil or cook a second time; also *fig.* to vamp or furbish up anew. So **Reco·ction.**

Recognition (rekǫ̆gni·ʃən). 1450. [ad. L. *recognitionem*, f. *recognit-, recognoscere.*] The act of recognizing. †1. Payment on the conclusion of a bargain. †2. *Sc. Law.* The resumption of lands by a feudal superior -1765. †3. Revision, recension -1862. b. *Hist.* The form of inquest by jury in use in England under the early Norman kings 1609. 4. The action of acknowledging as true, valid, or entitled to consideration; formal acknowledgement as conveying approval or sanction of something; hence, notice or attention accorded to a thing or person 1597. b. The formal acknowledgement by subjects of (the title of) a sovereign or other ruler; *spec.* as the name of a part of the Coronation ceremony 1558. 5. The acknowledgement or admission of a kindness, service, obligation, or merit, or the expression of this in some way. Now chiefly in phr. *in r. of.* 1570. 6. The action or fact of perceiving that some thing, person, etc., is the same as one previously known; the mental process of identifying what has been known before; the fact of being thus known or identified 1798. b. The action or fact of apprehending a thing as having a certain character or belonging to a certain class 1881.

4. A fourth kind of publick reading, whereby the lives of such saints had..solemn r. in the church of God HOOKER. 6. I could not escape r. 1866. b. The r. that certain things were not true 1881.

Recognitor (rĭkǫ·gnitǫ̆ɹ). Now *Hist.* 1574. [a. med.L. *recognitor*, f. *recognit-, recognoscere* to RECOGNOSCE.] A member of a jury impanelled on an assize or inquest.

Recognitory (rĭkǫ·gnitəri), *a.* 1822. [See prec. and -ORY[2].] Of or pertaining to recognition or acknowledgement.

Recognizable, -isable (re·kǫ̆gnəizăb'l), *a.* 1799. [f. RECOGNIZE *v.* + -ABLE.] Capable of being recognized; that admits of recognition. Hence **Recognizabi·lity**, r. quality. **Re·cognizably** *adv.*

Recognizance, -isance (rĭkǫ·nizăns, rĭkǫ·gn-). late ME. [a. OF. *recon(u)issance, recognussance*, (mod.F. *reconnaissance*), f. *recon(o)issant*, pr. pple. of *reconoistre* + -ANCE; see next.] 1. *Law.* A bond or obligation, entered into and recorded before a court or magistrate, by which a person engages himself to perform some act or observe some condition (as to appear when called on, to pay a debt, or to keep the peace); also, a sum of money pledged as a surety for such performance, and rendered forfeit by neglect of it. Usually *pl.* 2. Recognition or acknowledgement (of a person as holding a certain position, of a fact, duty, right, service, etc.). Now *rare.* late ME. b. Recognition (of a person) as the same, or as having a known character. Now *rare.* 1489. 3. A token, badge, emblem; a cognizance. Now *arch.* 1477.

3. That R. and pledge of Loue Which I first gaue her SHAKS.

Recognize, -ise (re·kǫ̆gnəiz), *v.* 1531. [a. OF. *reconuiss-, recognoiss-*, etc., pres. stem of *reconoistre* (mod.F. *reconnaître*) :—L. *recognoscere* to RECOGNOSCE. Cf. COGNIZE.] †1. *trans.* To look over again; to revise, correct, amend -1715. †b. To reconnoitre. Also *absol.* (*rare*) -1814. †2. To acknowledge by admission, confession, etc.; to admit (to oneself or another) -1641. 3. To acknowledge by special notice, approval or sanction; to treat as valid, as having existence or as entitled to consideration; to take notice of (a thing or person) in some way 1548. 4. To know again; to perceive to be identical with something previously known 1533. b. To know by means of some distinctive feature; to identify from knowledge of appearance or character 1725. c. To perceive clearly, realize 1865. 5. *Law.* (rĭkǫ·gnəiz) a. *U.S. refl.* and *intr.* To enter into a recognizance 1699. †b. *trans.* To bind over by a recognizance -1809.

3. The only army which the law recognized was the militia MACAULAY. 4. b. Without being able to express accurately all we mean by love, we r. it when we meet it 1876. c. Linnell has made us r. a new beauty in the heather 1865. Hence **Re·cognizer.**

Recognizee (rĭkǫg-, rĭkǫnizī·) 1544. [f. RECOGNIZE *v.* + -EE [1].] *Law.* The person to whom one is bound in a recognizance.

Recognizor (rĭkǫg-, rĭkǫnizǭ·ɪ). 1531. [f. as prec. + -OR 2 a.] *Law.* One who enters into a recognizance.

†Recognosce, *v.* 1533. [ad. L. *recognoscere*; see RE- and COGNOSCE.] *trans.* To recognize or acknowledge -1671.

Recoil (rĭkoi·l), *sb.* ME. [f. next.] **1.** The act of retreating, retiring, or going back. Now *rare.* **2.** The act of bounding or springing back, esp. through impact or elasticity; resilience 1613. b. *fig.* of feelings; *esp.* with ref. to shrinking *from* something 1643. **3.** *spec.* The rebound or 'kick' of a gun or firearm when discharged 1575.

2. We strain a bow and let its r. propel the arrow H. SPENCER. b. Indignant r. from ugliness RUSKIN. *Comb.*: **r. escapement,** an escapement in clocks and watches, in which the teeth of the crown- or balance-wheel act on the pallets by r.; **r. pallet,** a pallet in a r. escapement; **r. wave,** a dicrotic wave.

Recoil (rĭkoi·l), *v.* ME. [ad. OF. *reculer*, f. *re-* RE- + *cul* CUL :—L. *culus* the posteriors.] **†1.** *trans.* To beat, drive, or force back; to cause to retreat or retire -1713. †b. To return or retort (a thing) *upon* a person -1662. **2.** *intr.* To retreat, retire, go or draw *back* (or *aback*) before an enemy or opposing force. late ME. b. To stagger back (from a blow) 1533. †3. To go back (or backwards); to recede, retire, retreat, return -1651. †b. To fall back or away (from some state or condition), to degenerate (*rare*) -1611. †c. To go back in memory or in a narrative (*rare*) -1655. †4. To retire, withdraw oneself *to* a place -1627. †b. *fig.* To draw back *from* an act or course of action, a promise, etc. -1761. **5.** To start or spring back in fear, horror, disgust, or the like 1513. **6. a.** To rebound, to spring or fly back through force of impact 1581. b. Of firearms or artillery: To spring back by the force of the discharge 1530. **7.** To rebound, spring *back*, or return, to the starting-point or source. Chiefly *fig.* (now with *on*). 1599.

2. Skilfull darters who by recoyling are wont to gaine the day 1637. b. Ten paces huge He back recoild MILT. 3. c. *Wint. T.* I. ii. 154. 4. A whyle I read you rest, and to your bowres recoyle SPENSER. 5. Back they recoild affraid At first, and call'd me Sin MILT. *fig.* The age..recoiled from the cool cynicism of his crimes 1874. 7. The good or evil we confer on others, very often..recoils on ourselves FIELDING. Hence **Recoi·ler. Recoi·lingly** *adv.* **†Recoi·lment,** dismissal; the act of recoiling or springing back.

Recollect (re·kǫlekt), *sb.* 1626. [ad. L. *recollectus* or F. *récollet.*] A member of an Observantine branch of the Franciscan order, which originated in Spain in the end of the 15th c., and was so named 'from the detachment from creatures and recollection in God which the founders aimed at' (*Catholic Dict.*).

Recollect (rĭkǫle·kt), *v.*[1] 1513. [orig. ad. L. *recollect-*, *recolligere*, f. *re-* RE- + *colligere*, but later sometimes written *re-collect*, as if f. RE- 5 a + COLLECT.] **†1.** *trans.* To collect, gather -1670. †b. To collect *again* -1693. **2.** To collect, gather, or bring together (things or persons) again 1615. b. *intr.* To come together again (*rare*) 1631. **3.** *trans.* To collect (one's spirits, thoughts, mind, etc.) 1614. **4.** To gather or summon up (strength, courage, etc.); to rally; to recover by an effort 1655. †5. To bring back again *to* or *from* some position or state; to withdraw (oneself) *from* -1655.

2. How dust scattered and blown up and down should be recollected 1655. 3. He was timorous and bashful; but, when the talk became regular, he recollected his powers JOHNSON. 4. Then soon Fierce hate he recollects, and all his thoughts Of mischief.. thus excites MILT.

Recollect (rekǫle·kt), *v.*[2] 1559. [f. as prec., but now differentiated by the pronunciation.] **1.** *trans.* To call or bring back (something) to one's mind; to recall the knowledge of (a thing, person, etc.). †2. To reflect *with* (oneself) -1719. **3.** To concentrate or absorb (the mind, oneself, etc.) in contemplation; *spec.* in mystical religious use 1671. **4.** *refl.* To bring (oneself) back to a state of composure; to recover (oneself). Also const. *from.* Now *rare.* 1639.

1. Recollecting still that he is man, We trust him not too far COWPER. *absol.* To remember and to r. are different things JOHNSON. 'I can't remember.' 'But try and recollect' (*mod.*). 4. His heart beat violently, and he..stopped, to r. himself MAR. EDGEWORTH. Hence **Recolle·ctable** *a.*

Recollection[1] (rĭkǫle·kʃən). 1598. [a. F. *récollection* or ad. med.L. *recollectionem.* Now taken as f. RE- 5 a + COLLECTION.] **1.** A gathering together again. **2.** A recapitulation -1659.

Recollection[2] (rekǫle·kʃən). 1642. [Same wd. as prec. in special senses]. **1.** Religious or serious concentration of thought; †conduct regulated by this. **2.** Composure, calmness of mind, self-possession 1757. **3.** The act of recalling to the memory; the mental operation by which objects or ideas are revived in the mind; also, an instance of this 1683. b. The power of recalling to the mind; the sphere or period over which such power extends; the memory 1732. **4.** A thing or fact recalled to the mind; the memory *of* something 1781. **5.** *pl.* A message expressing recollection of, or a desire to be recollected by, another 1816.

3. The power of r. seems to depend on the intensity or largeness of the perception JOWETT. b. The scene of the preceding night ran in his r. SCOTT. 4. A r. or a fresh tradition 1883.

Recollective (rekǫle·ktiv), *a.* 1789. [f. RECOLLECT *v.*[2] + -IVE.] **1.** Relating to, characterized by, concerned with, recollection. **2.** Given to, distinguished by (the power of), occupied with, recollection 1813.

‖ **Recollet** (rekole). 1695. [F. *récollet*, ad. L. *recollectus*; cf. RECOLLECTION [2] 1.] = RECOLLECT *sb.*

†Reco·mfort, *sb.* late ME. [ad. F. *reconfort*; see RE- and COMFORT *sb.*] Comfort, support, consolation -1605. Hence **†Reco·mfortless** *a.* without comfort.

Recomfort (rīkɒ·mfəɹt), *v.* *Obs.* exc. *arch.* late ME. [ad. F. *reconforter*; see RE- and COMFORT *v.*] **1.** *trans.* †a. To strengthen or inspire with fresh courage -1667. b. To soothe, console, or relieve in distress or trouble. Now *rare.* late ME. †c. *refl.* and *absol.* To take courage or heart again -1654. **2.** *trans.* (Usu. of things): To strengthen or invigorate physically; to refresh. Also *absol.* Now *rare.* late ME.

1. a. As one from sad dismay Recomforted MILT. 2. My weary frame After short pause recomforted, again I journey'd CARY. Hence **†Reco·mforture,** consolation, comfort SHAKS.

Recommence (rīkǫme·ns), *v.* 1481. [ad. F. *recommencer*; see RE- and COMMENCE *v.*] **1.** *intr.* To begin again. b. With complement 1778. **2.** *trans.* To cause to begin again; to renew 1494.

2. The two brothers r. their exhortation to virtue JOWETT. So **Recomme·ncement,** a second commencement.

Recommend (rekǫme·nd), *v.* late ME. [ad. med.L. *recommendare*, f. *re-* RE- + *commendare* to COMMEND.] **1.** To commend or commit (oneself or another, one's soul or spirit) *to* God, his keeping, etc. Also (rarely) without const. b. (Chiefly *refl.*) To commit (oneself or another) *to* a person (or thing), or *to* some one's care, prayers, etc. late ME. †c. To give in charge, consign, commit, submit (a thing) *to* a person or thing -1601. †d. To communicate (a thing) *to* a person. Also without const., to mention. -1641. †e. To inform (a person). SHAKS. †2. *refl.* and *absol.* To commend (oneself) to the kindly remembrance of another -1572. †b. To speak of (a person) to another, with a view to exciting kindly remembrance -1773. †3. To praise, commend -1738. **4. a.** To name or speak of (a person) as fit or worthy to hold some position or employment 1641. b. To present or bring forward (a person) as worthy of notice, favour, care, etc. Const. *to* (a person, etc.) *for* (the thing desired). 1647 **5.** To mention or introduce (a thing) with approbation or commendation (*to* a person), in order to induce acceptance or trial 1581. **6.** To make (a person or thing) acceptable. (Chiefly of qualities, circumstances, or things.) Also *refl.* 1605. **7.** To counsel, advise 1733.

1. When I lay me down to Sleep, I r. myself to his Care ADDISON. c. *Twel. N.* v. i. 94. 2. b. R. me to the poor dear lady JOHNSON. 4. b. The trouble I gave in recommending a gentleman to your protection SWIFT. 5. Allow me..to r. this dish SHELLEY. We will conclude by recommending his work to our readers 1863. 6. That man has little enough to r. him whom women dislike 1863. 7. He recommended, that the whole disposition of the camp should be changed 1829. Hence **Recomme·ndable** *a.* that may be recommended. **Recomme·ndableness. Recomme·ndably** *adv.* **Recomme·nder.**

Recommendation (re:kǫmendē¹·ʃən). 1450. [a. OF., or ad. med.L. *recommendationem*, f. *recommendare* to RECOMMEND.] **†1.** The action of recommending oneself to another's remembrance; a message of this nature -1634. **†2.** Commendation, favour, repute, esteem -1585. **3.** The action of recommending a person or thing as worthy or desirable 1578. b. A letter or certificate of recommendation 1645. **4.** That which procures a favourable reception or acceptance 1647. **5.** Exhortation, advice 1585.

3. Buying at his Shop upon my R. STEELE. *Letter of r.*, a letter recommending a person; in later use, a letter of introduction. 4. Upon no other..r., than of the Beauty..of his Person CLARENDON.

†Recomme·ndative, *a.* and *sb.* *rare.* 1611. [f. RECOMMEND *v.* + -ATIVE.] **A.** *adj.* That recommends. **B.** *sb.* That which recommends. -1727.

Recommendatory (rekǫme·ndătəri), *a.* 1611. [f. RECOMMEND *v.*, after COMMENDATORY *a.*] **1.** Having the attribute of recommending; expressing or conveying a recommendation. **2.** Of a quality, feature, etc.: That recommends its possessor 1709. **3.** Of a resolution, appointment, etc.: In the form of a recommendation, without binding force 1690.

1. *R. letter*, a letter of recommendation.

Recommit (rĭkǫmi·t), *v.* 1621. [RE- 5 a.] **1.** *trans.* To send or refer (a bill, etc.) back to a committee. b. To entrust (a person or thing) again *to* a person 1783. **2.** To commit (a person) again (*to* a court, prison, etc.) 1647. **3.** To commit or do (an action) again 1647.

1. Ordered, That the said Act be re-committed for several Amendments 1729. So **Recommi·tment, Recommi·ttal,** a renewed commitment or committal.

Recompensation (rī:kǫmpĕnsē¹·ʃən). late ME. [a. OF. *recompensacion* :—late L. *recompensationem.*] †1. = next -1715. **2.** *Sc. Law.* In actions for debt, a counter-plea of compensation raised by a pursuer to meet the defendant's plea of compensation 1681.

Recompense (re·kǫmpens), *sb.* Also -pence. late ME. [a. OF., f. *recompenser* to RECOMPENSE.] **1.** Reparation or restitution made to another for some wrong done to him; atonement or satisfaction for some misdeed or offence. **2.** Compensation (received or desired) for some loss or injury sustained 1508. **3.** Return or repayment for something given or received 1473. **4.** Compensation or return for trouble, exertion, services or merit 1500. **5.** Retribution for some injury or offence 1538.

1. Sin cannot be taken away by recompence HOBBES. 2. Have you secured no r. for such a waste of honour? *Junius Lett.* 4. His lovely words her seem'd due r. Of all her passed paines SPENSER. 5. Such is the tyrant's r.: 'tis just: He who is evil can receive no good SHELLEY.

Recompense (re·kǫmpens), *v.* Also -pence. late ME. [ad. OF. *recompenser*, ad. late L. *recompensare*, f. *re-* RE- + *compensare* to COMPENSATE.] **1.** *trans.* To reward, requite, repay (a person) for something done or given. b. To compensate (a person) *for* some loss or injury sustained 1477. **2. a.** To make up for (some loss, injury, defect, etc.); †to take the place of. late ME. b. To make compensation or atonement for (a misdeed, wrong, etc.) 1450. c. To make a return or requital for (something done or given) 1530. †3. To mete out in requital –1535. 4. *intr.* To make repayment, return, or amends. late ME.

1. *absol.* Be his To r., who sees and can reward thee CARY. 2. a. The length of the journey will be recompensed by the goodness of the way FULLER. b. In some part to r. My rash but more unfortunate misdeed MILT. 3. Recompence to no man evyll for evyll TINDALE *Rom.* xii. 17. Hence **Re·compenser** (*rare*), one who or that which recompenses. **Re·compensive** *a.* (*rare*) that recompenses.

Recompose (rīkǫmpōu·z), *v.* 1611. [RE- 5 a. Cf. F. *récomposer.*] 1. *trans.* To put together again; to form again by composition. Chiefly in antithesis to *decompose.* 2. To put together in a new form or manner; to rearrange 1816. 3. To restore to composure. Also *refl.* 1649. 4. To restore to harmony 1856.

1. Whatever is decomposed may be recomposed by the being who first composed it PRIESTLEY. 3. I shall never r. my features to receive Sir Rowland CONGREVE. Our spirits, when disordered, are not to be recomposed in a moment FIELDING. 4. To r. the quarrels in the church 1856. Hence **Recompo·ser** (*rare*). **Recomposition** (rī:kǫmpǒzi·ʃən), the action or process of recomposing.

Reconcilable (re·kǫnsəilăb'l), *a.* Also **-cileable.** 1612. [f. next + -ABLE.] 1. Of statements, opinions, facts, etc.: Capable of being mutually reconciled. 2. Capable of being reconciled *with* something 1640. Also const. *to* (now *rare*), and †*ellipt.* without const. 3. Of persons, their natures, etc.: Easily conciliated or reconciled. Now *rare.* 1621. 4. Admitting of reconciliation MILT.

1. The opposite yet reconcileable vices of rapaciousness and prodigality GIBBON. 3. A peaceable and r. inclination 1621. Hence **Re·concilableness. Re·concilably** *adv.*

Reconcile (re·kǫnsəil), *v.* ME. [ad. F. *réconcilier*, or L. *reconciliare*, f. *re-* RE- + *conciliare* to CONCILIATE.] I. 1. *trans.* To bring (a person) again into friendly relations *to* or *with* (oneself or another) after an estrangement. †b. To recommend, make agreeable CLARENDON. 2. To win over (a person) again to friendship with oneself or another. late ME. 3. To set (estranged persons or parties) at one again; to bring back into concord, to reunite (persons or things) in harmony. late ME. †4. To bring (a person) back *to*, *into* peace, favour, etc. Also *refl.* –1594. †5. To bring back, restore, or re-admit to the Church, *spec.* the Church of Rome –1715. b. *pass.* and *refl.* To become united *to* a church 1639. 6. *Eccl.* To purify (a church, etc.) by a special service after profanation. late ME. †7. To conciliate, recover (a person's favour, etc.); to gain (credit) –1665. 8. To bring into a state of acquiescence (†*with*) or submission *to* a thing. Also *refl.* and with *inf.* 1606.

1. *refl.* Thou mightst..r. thyself with thine own heart And with thy God SHELLEY. b. His courtesy and affability..marvellously reconciled [him] to all men 1647. 2. The Gods are hard to r. TENNYSON. 3. Let it be mine honour..That I haue reconcil'd your friends and you SHAKS. 8. Trials often r. us to that, which..we looked on with aversion LOCKE.

II. 1. To adjust, settle, bring to agreement (a controversy, quarrel, etc.). late ME. 2. To make (discordant facts, statements, etc.) consistent, accordant, or compatible with each other 1560. 3. To make (an action, condition, quality, etc.) compatible or consistent in fact or in one's mind *with* another; to regard as consistent *with.* Also const. *to.* 1624. b. To make (a theory, statement, author, etc.) agree *with* another or with a fact; to show to be in agreement *with.* Const. *to.* 1613. 4. To make even or smooth, or fit together so as to present a uniform surface 1687.

1. The quarrel was..reconciled FIELDING. 2. Such welcome, and vnwelcom things at once, 'Tis hard to r. SHAKS. 3. A soul..That reconciled the sword unto the pen, Using both well 1624. b. A plain matter of fact, which men cannot r. with the general account they think fit to give of things BUTLER. Hence **Re·concilement,** reconciliation. **Re·conciler,** one who or that which reconciles; *spec.* applied to Christ.

Reconciliation (re:kǫnsili,ē¹·ʃən). ME. [a. F., or ad. L. *reconciliationem.*] 1. The action of reconciling persons or the result of this; the fact of being reconciled. late ME. b. *spec.* in religious use, of God and man ME. 2. Reunion of a person to a church 1625. 3. The purification, or restoration to sacred uses, of a church, etc., after desecration or pollution 1533. 4. The action of bringing to agreement, concord, or harmony 1560.

1. And so kissed me as a mark of r. RICHARDSON. 4. The absence of any appearance of r. between the theory and practice of life EMERSON.

Reconciliatory (rekǫnsi·liătəri), *a.* 1586. [ad. L. type *reconciliatorius*; see -ORY[1].] Of words, actions, etc.: Tending to reconciliation.

Recondite (re·kǫndəit, rīkǫ·ndəit), *a.* 1649. [ad. L. *reconditus*, *recondere* to put away, f. *re-* RE- + *condere.*] 1. Of things: Removed or hidden from view; kept out of sight. Now *rare.* 2. Removed from ordinary apprehension, understanding, or knowledge; deep, profound, abstruse 1652. b. Of learning, investigation, discussion, etc.: Consisting in, relating to, uncommon or profound knowledge 1654. c. Of writers, sources, etc.: Obscure, little known 1817. 3. Of persons: Writing in an obscure fashion 1788.

2. The r. principles of philosophy 1772. c. The traditional edition of a r. classical author 1865. Hence **Re·condite·ly** *adv.*, **-ness.**

†**Reco·nditory.** 1633. [ad. late L. *reconditorium.*] A store-house, repository –1685.

Reconnaissance (rīkǫ·nĕsăns). 1810. [F., f. *reconnaiss-*, *reconnaître* to RECONNOITRE.] 1. *Mil.* An examination or survey of a tract of country, made with a view to ascertain the position or strength of an enemy, or to discover the nature of the ground or resources of a district before making an advance. Also *Naval*, a survey of a coast, etc. made for similar purposes. b. A body of troops sent to reconnoitre 1811. 2. *transf.* A survey of a district made for practical or scientific purposes 1838. 3. Without article: Reconnoitring, surveying 1887.

1. *R. in force*, an advance made with a considerable body of troops to discover the position of the enemy.

Reconnoissance (rīkǫ·nisăns). 1672. Older spelling (now disused) of prec., used in senses of RECOGNIZANCE and RECONNAISSANCE.

Reconnoi·tre, *sb.* 1799. [f. next.] An act of reconnoitring; a reconnaissance.

Reconnoitre (rekǫnoi·təɹ), *v.* 1707. [a. F. *reconnoître* (now *reconnaître*) :—L. *recognoscere* to look over, inspect.] 1. *trans. Mil.* (and *Naval*). To make an inspection or take observations of (an enemy, his strength, position, etc.). Also *transf.* 2. *Mil.* To inspect, examine, or survey (a district or tract of ground) in order to discover the presence or position of an enemy, or to find out the resources or military features of the country. Also *transf.* 1726. 3. *absol.* or *intr.* To make a reconnaissance 1712. †4. *trans.* To recollect, remember, recognize –1787.

4. Whether, if the dead of past ages could revive, they would be able to r. the events of their own times, as transmitted to us H. WALPOLE.

Reconsider (rīkǫnsi·dəɹ), *v.* 1571. [RE- 5 a.] 1. *trans.* To consider (a matter or thing) again. b. To consider (a decision, etc.) a second time with a view to changing or amending it; to rescind, alter 1849. 2. *refl.* To reflect on one's conduct, with a view to repentance or amendment (*rare*) 1855. **Reconsidera·tion.**

Reconstitution (rī:kǫnstitiū·ʃən). 1853. [RE- 5 a.] A fresh constitution. b. In French criminal procedure, the action of going over the supposed details of a crime at the place where it was committed 1897.

Reconstruct (rīkǫnstrʊ·kt), *v.* 1768. [RE- 5 a.] 1. *trans.* To construct anew. 2. To construct anew in the mind; to restore (something past) mentally 1862. 3. *U.S.* To win over or reconcile to the Federal system of government 1904.

Reconstruction (rīkǫnstrʊ·kʃən). 1791. [RE- 5 a.] 1. The action or process of reconstructing. b. *U.S. Hist.* The process by which after the Civil War the States which had seceded were restored to the rights and privileges of the Union 1865. 2. An instance or example of reconstructing; a thing reconstructed 1795.

Reconstructive (rī:kǫnstrʊ·ktiv), *a.* and *sb.* 1862. [RE- 5 a.] A. *adj.* Related to, concerned with, reconstruction. B. *sb.* That which reconstructs, a reconstituent 1890.

†**Reconti·nuance.** 1540. [RE- 5 a; cf. next.] The act of recontinuing; resumption –1631.

Reconti·nue, *v. rare.* late ME. [ad. obs. F. *recontinuer*; see RE- 5 a and CONTINUE *v.*] *trans.* To go on again with (an action, occupation, state, etc., which has been discontinued).

Reconvention (rīkǫnve·nʃən). 1449. [a. F. See RE- and CONVENTION.] †1. An agreement made in return PECOCK. 2. *Law.* A counter-charge; a counter-action brought against the plaintiff by the defendant in a suit 1538. †3. The reassembling (of Parliament, etc.) –1664.

Reconvert (rīkǫnvə̄·ɹt), *v.* 1611. [RE- 5 a.] 1. *trans.* To convert back to a previous state. 2. *Logic.* To transpose again the subject and predicate of (a proposition) 1864. 3. *Law.* To change back again into something of equivalent value 1884.

1. I myself having known many Papists..reconverted WESLEY. The air was re-converted into water 1783. So **Reconve·rsion. Reconve·rtible** *a.* capable of being reconverted.

Reconvey (rīkǫnvē¹·), *v.* 1506. [RE- 5 a.] 1. *trans.* To convey (†or escort) back to a previous place or position; to convey in a reverse direction. Now *rare.* 2. *Law.* To make over again or restore to a former owner 1665.

1. The water..would be reconveyed to the sea at ebb tide 1846. So **Reconvey·ance,** the act of reconveying; *spec.* in *Law*, restoration to a former owner.

Record (re·kǭɹd), *sb.* ME. [a. OF., f. *recorder* to RECORD.] I. 1. *Law.* The fact or attribute of being, or of having been, committed to writing as authentic evidence of a matter having legal importance, *spec.* as evidence of the proceedings or verdict of a court of justice; evidence which is thus preserved, and may be appealed to in case of dispute. 2. The fact or condition of being preserved as knowledge, *esp.* by being put into writing; knowledge or information preserved or handed down in this way. Freq. in phrases (†*of*,) *on* or *upon r.* late ME. †3. Attestation or testimony of a fact; witness, evidence, proof –1646. †b. A witness –1768.

1. These Estates are created by word, by writing, or by r. BACON. Phr. *Matter* (*thing*, *debt*, etc.) *of r. Court of r.*, a court whose proceedings are formally enrolled and valid as evidence of fact, being also a court of the sovereign, and having authority to fine or imprison. So †*Judge of r.* 2. Having beaten the highest break on r. 1884. 3. *To bear r.*, to bear witness; Iohn bare r., saying [etc.] *John* i. 32. *To take* or *call to r.*, to call to witness. b. God is my r.,..that I do not speak it vauntingly STERNE.

II. 1. *Law.* An authentic or official report of the proceedings in any cause coming before a court of record, together with the judgement given thereon, entered upon the rolls of court and affording indisputable evidence of the matter in question 1455. b. A copy of the material points, pleadings, and issue between defendant and plaintiff on a matter of law, constituting the case to be decided by the court; hence, a case so constituted or presented 1627. 2. An account of some fact or event preserved in writing or other permanent form; a document, monument, etc., on which such an account is inscribed; also *transf.* any thing or person serving to indicate or give evidence of, or preserve the memory of, a fact or event; a memorial. Freq. in *pl.* a collection of such accounts, etc. Also, in recent use, a tracing or series of marks, made by a recording instrument. 1611. b. In full *gramophone r.*, the disk of wax, etc., bearing the record of the sounds to be reproduced by the gramophone 1896. c. The leading facts in the life or career of a person, *esp.* of a public man; the sum of what one has done or achieved (orig. *U.S.*) 1856. d. A performance or occurrence going beyond others of the same kind; *spec.* the best recorded achievement in any competitive sport. Freq. in phr. *to beat* or *break the r.*: to surpass all previous performances. 1883.

1. Phr. *To travel out of the r.*, to take notice of any thing that does not appear in it. Also *transf.*, to go off the subject. So *to keep to the r.* 2. *Ezra* vi. 2. e. Phr. (Chiefly *U.S.*) *To put* (oneself) *on r.*, to give (oneself) a place among recorded things; to express one's opinion; also *to go on r.*

†III. 1. Reputation, repute, account –1470. 2. Memory, remembrance, recollection –1601.

2. O that r. is liuely in my soule SHAKS.

IV. *Comb.* as *r.-breaker, -breaking, -maker, -making.* **b.** passing into *adj.* = largest, best, etc. recorded or on record 1893.

Record (rĭkǭ·ɹd), *v.* ME. [ad. OF. *recorder* :—L. *recordare* (classical *recordari*), f. *re-* RE- + *cord-*, *cor* heart.] **I.** †**1.** *trans.* **a.** To get by heart, to go over in one's mind. **b.** To say over as a lesson, to recite. -1656. **2.** To practise (a song, tune, etc.). In later use only of birds. late ME. †**b.** To sing of or about (something); to render in song -1597. **3.** *intr.* Of birds (rarely of persons): To practise or sing a tune in an undertone; to go over it quietly or silently. Now *techn.* 1510. †**b.** To sing or warble -1616.

2. b. Here can I..to the Nightingales complaining Notes Tune my distresses, and r. my woes SHAKS. 3. The young males continue practising, or, as the bird-catchers say, recording, for ten or eleven months DARWIN.

†**II. 1.** *trans.* To call to mind, to recall, remember -1460. **2.** To meditate, ponder (something) *with* oneself -1586. **3.** To think or meditate *on* a thing or person -1604.

3. Recorde on..Parys the fayre citee LYDG.

III. †**1.** *trans.* To relate in words; to tell or narrate orally -1738. **2.** To relate in writing; to put or set down in writing; to put on record. Also, in recent use, of telegraphic and other instruments: To set down (a message, etc.) in some permanent form; also *absol.*, of an instrument, etc., to be recorded thus for reproduction by a gramophone. ME. **b.** To have properly recorded; to give (a verdict or vote) 1596. †**3.** To bear witness to (a fact, etc.); to attest, confirm. Also *absol.*, To testify. -1607. †**b.** To call to witness. MARLOWE.

2. The last words of his that are recorded, are worthy the greatness of his soul W. IRVING. b. There is only one verdict which those who disapprove of it can r. 1884. 3. *Timon* IV. ii. 4. Hence **Reco·rdable** *a.* capable of being recorded.

†**Reco·rdance.** *rare.* 1450. [a. OF., = It. *ricordanza.*] Recording, setting on record; remembrance -1630.

Recordation (rekǫrdēⁱ·ʃən). late ME. [ad. L. *recordationem*, f. *recordari.*] †**1.** The faculty of remembering or recollecting -1666. †**2.** Remembrance or recollection *of* something -1748. †**3.** An act of commemorating or making mention; a commemorative account -1670. **4.** The action or process of recording or committing to writing 1802.

Recordative (rĭkǭ·ɹdǎtiv), *a.* 1551. [ad. late L. *recordativus*; see -IVE.] Commemorative.

Recorder[1] (rĭkǭ·ɹdəɹ). late ME. [orig. a. AF. *recordour*; later, partly f. RECORD *v.* + -ER [1].] **1.** A certain magistrate or judge having criminal and civil jurisdiction in a city or borough.

The Recorder was orig. a person with legal knowledge appointed by the mayor and aldermen to 'record' or keep in mind the proceedings of their courts and the customs of the city, his oral statement of these being taken as the highest evidence of fact. The Recorder of London is still appointed by the court of aldermen; in other cities and boroughs the appointment is made by the crown.

†**b.** The chief justice of an East Indian settlement -1800. **2.** One who records or sets down in writing 1537. **3.** A recording apparatus; *esp.* a device in a telegraphic instrument for recording the signals received 1873. Hence **Reco·rdership,** the office, or term of office, of a r. 1484.

Reco·rder[2]. *Obs.* exc. *Hist.* late ME. [app. f. RECORD *v.* (I. 2, 3) + -ER [1].] A wind instrument of the flute or flageolet kind. †**b.** One of the pipes of an organ -1650.

One of them plaied on a Lute;..another made a maruellous sweet countertenour vpon a R. 1598.

Recording (rĭkǭ·ɹdiŋ), *ppl. a.* 1761. [-ING [2].] That records, now *esp.* in phr. *r. angel.*

Recount (rīˑkaunt, rīˑkaunt), *sb.* 1884. [RE- 5 a.] A new count; a second or subsequent enumeration (*esp.* of votes in an election). So **Re:cou·nt** *v.*[2] *trans.* to count or reckon over again 1764.

Recount (rĭkau·nt), *v.*[1] 1456. [a. ONF. and AF. *reconter*, f. *re-* RE- + *conter* to COUNT. Cf. F. *raconter.*] **1.** *trans.* To relate or narrate; to give a full or detailed account of (some fact, event, etc.). **b.** (With pl. obj.) To relate in order; to enumerate by particulars 1483. †**2.** To regard, consider, or account (a person or thing) as possessing a certain character or quality -1661. †**3.** *intr.* and *trans.* To reckon, count *up* -1647.

1. b. To r. Almightie works What words or tongue of Seraph can suffice? MILT. Hence †**Recou·ntment,** relation, recital SHAKS.

Recoup (rĭkū·p), *v.* late ME. [ad. F. *recouper* to cut back, etc., f. *re-* RE- + *couper* to cut.] †**1.** *trans.* To cut short, interrupt -late ME. **2.** *Law.* To deduct; to take off or keep back. Also *absol.* to make a deduction. 1628. **3.** (With double obj.) To recompense (a person) for (some loss or outlay); to make up or make good (loss, etc.) to (a person) 1664. **b.** To recompense, repay (a person). Freq. *refl.* to recover what one has expended or lost. 1862. **4.** To make up for, make good 1860. **b.** To yield in return 1868.

2. The defendant might r. damages for a breach of warranty for the thing sold 1869. 4. How to r. the loss occasioned to the State revenue by the abolition of the salt tax 1880. Hence **Recou·pment,** the act of recouping or recompensing; the fact of being recouped for loss or expense.

Recourse (rĭkōᵊ·ɹs), *sb.* late ME. [a. F. *recours* :—L. *recursum*, f. *re-* RE- + *currere* to run; see COURSE *sb.*] †**1.** A running, coming, or flowing back, a return, refluence; also, opportunity or passage to return -1694. †**b.** A periodical recurrence -1677. †**2.** Course, movement, or flow in some direction; a course, passage, or path *to* or *into* something -1653. †**b.** The ebb and flow of the tide -1622. **3.** Resort *to* some person or thing for assistance, help, or safety. late ME. **4.** The thing, means, or person applied or resorted to for help, etc. 1440. **b.** *Law* (chiefly *Sc.*). The right to demand pecuniary compensation from some one; *esp.* the right which the holder of a bill of exchange has to come back upon the drawer and endorsers if the acceptor fails to meet it 1747. †**5.** Usual or habitual going or resorting to a particular place -1705. †**b.** Gathering or concourse (of people) at a particular time -1656. †**6.** Opportunity of resorting *to* a person; access, admission -1594.

1. The r. of the Blood into the Heart is hindred 1668. 3. *To have (a) r. to*, to apply to (a person, etc.) for help, advice, or information; If threats..proved ineffectual, he had often r. to violence GIBBON. 4. This is their usual r., when they are hard pressed by inconsistencies 1774. 5. They had their place of r. or rendevouz 1658. 6. I, but the doores be lockt,.. That no man hath r. to her by night SHAKS. Hence †**Recou·rseful** *a.* flowing back; ebbing and flowing.

Recourse (rĭkōᵊ·ɹs), *v.* 1500. [f. prec.] †**1.** *intr.* To run back, return (*to* a place) -1632. **2.** Const. *to.* To have recourse to, to fall back on. Now *rare* or *Obs.* 1586.

1. The flame departyng and recoursing thrise ere the woode tooke strength..to consume him FOXE.

Recover (rĭkʊ·vəɹ), *sb.* ME. [orig. a. OF. *recovre*, f. *recovrer* RECOVER *v.*[1]; later, f. the vb.] †**1.** Recovery, or means of recovery -1631. **2.** The act of bringing or coming back to a former position 1819. †**b.** *Mil.* (chiefly in phr. *at, on,* or *to the r.*). A position of the fire-arm forming part of the manual exercise -1847.

Recover (rĭkʊ·vəɹ), *v.*[1] ME. [ad. AF. *recoverer* :—L. *recuperare* to RECUPERATE.] **I.** *trans.* **1.** To get (†occas., to take) back again into one's hands or possession; to regain possession of (something lost or taken away). late ME. **b.** To regain (country, territory, etc.) by conquest or main force; to win back (ground lost in fighting). late ME. **c.** To find again, come upon a second time 1611. **d.** To reclaim (land) *from* the sea 1793. **2.** To regain, acquire again, resume, return to (health, strength, one's feet, etc.) ME. **3.** To bring, draw, or win back (a person) to friendship or willing obedience; to reconcile 1576. †**4.** To get in place of, or in return for, something else -1525. **5.** *Law.* To get back or gain by judgement in a court of law; to obtain possession of, or a right to, by legal process. late ME. **b.** To have (a judgement or verdict) given in one's favour 1768. †**6.** To get or obtain; to get hold of -1661. **b.** To get (the wind of one). *Obs.* exc. *arch.* 1602. **7.** To get to, reach, arrive at, gain (some place or point). Now *rare.* ME. **8.** To get back for another; to bring back, restore. Const. *to* or *unto* a person, country, etc. 1484. **9.** To restore or bring back (usu. a person) to life or consciousness. late ME. **b.** To restore (a person or animal) to health or strength; to cure, heal 1579. **c.** In passive, *To be recovered,* to be well again ME. †**10.** To restore (a person or thing) to a good or proper estate or condition; to set or make right again -1731. **11.** To rescue or reclaim (a person) *from* or *out of* a state, etc. 1614. **12. a.** To bring back (a weapon) to a certain position 1594. **b.** To pull back (a horse) on to its feet again 1646. **13.** To get over, get better from (a sickness, misfortune, or affliction) ME. **b.** To annul the effect of (a slip, stumble, etc.) 1748. **14.** To retrieve, make good, make up for (loss, damage, etc. to oneself). late ME. **15.** To put right, remedy (something wrong, a fault, etc.). Now *rare.* late ME.

1. For tyme y-lost..Be no way may recoverd be CHAUCER. Humanity had lost its title-deeds, and he had recovered them MORLEY. 2. The Lead..will not of it self r. its Sphæricity BOYLE. They stopped to r. their wind MARRYAT. I had by this time recovered my usual health 1849. 3. Harold's way of recovering rebels differed widely from William's FREEMAN. 4. For every wo ye shall r. a blisse CHAUCER. 5. This Law..enabled the Clergy to..r. Tithes 1710. An action to r. damages for false imprisonment 1891. b. A defendant, against whom judgment is recovered BLACKSTONE. 7. Without a pocket-compass..I should never have recovered the Fair Isle, for which we run SCOTT. 8. So had the glory of Prowess been recover'd To Palestine MILT. 9. From Death to Life, thou mights't him yet r. DRAYTON. The squire suddenly recovered her by calling for..a bucket of water 1841. 11. So men will be well guarded, or recovered from false Religions LOCKE. 12. *To r. arms*, a position of the firelock when the piece is held with the lock equal to the left shoulder, and the sling to the front 1802. 13. b. To r. so terrible a stumble 1768. 14. Many..losses.. which he was not able to r. 1682. 15. To r. the mischief he had done..was difficult 1869.

II. *refl.* **1. a.** To regain one's natural position or balance. late ME. **b.** To return to life or consciousness 1597 **c.** To get over a loss or misfortune; to recoup oneself (*rare*) 1645. **d.** To get over fatigue or illness. †Also const. *of.* 1745. **2.** †**a.** To retreat, retire *into* a place; to fall back *on* one as an authority -1655. **b.** To withdraw or escape *from* or *out of*, to return *to*, a position, state, or condition. Now *rare.* 1611.

1. a. We daily see..rope-dauncers..handsomly r. themselves after a perillous staggering and reeling 1638. 2. b. That they mav recouer themselues out of the snare of the deuill 2 *Tim.* ii. 26.

III. *intr.* or *absol.* **1.** To regain health after a wound or sickness; to get well again ME. **2.** To regain life, consciousness, or composure. Also const. *of, from, out of.* ME. †**3.** To rally, to return; to make one's way; to succeed in coming or passing (again) -1680. **4.** To regain one's footing, position, or balance; also, to make a return *from*, †to get the better *of*, a slip, etc. 1494. **b.** *Fencing.* To return to a position of guard after a thrust 1705. **c.** To rise again after bowing or curtseying 1711. **5.** *Law.* To obtain, by legal process, possession or restoration of the thing claimed; to succeed in a claim or suit of recovery. late ME.

1. If hee be sicke with Ioy, Hee'le recouer without Physicke SHAKS. The man recovered of the bite, The dog it was that died GOLDSM. 2. I soon r. from these needless frights COWPER. 5. The plaintiff shall r. according to the verdict 1817.

Recover (rīˑkʊ·vəɹ), *v.*[2] Also **re-cover.** late ME. [RE- 5 a.] *trans.* To cover again.

Recoverable (rĭkʊ·věrǎb'l), *a.* 1470. [f. RECOVER *v.*[1] + -ABLE.] **1.** Capable of being recovered or regained. **b.** Capable of being legally recovered or obtained 1590. **2.** Capable of being restored to a sound, healthy, or normal condition 1596. **b.** That may be amended; curable 1616. **c.** Capable of being retrieved or made good 1797. †**3.** Capable of being retraced. SHAKS.

1. b. That mere debts should not be r. by law JOWETT. 2. Having nowe both sowle and bodye greatly diseased, yet both r. SPENSER. 3. A Prodigall course Is like the Sunnes, but not like his recouerable SHAKS. Hence **Reco·verableness.**

Recoverance (rĭkʊ·věrǎns). Now *arch.* late ME. [a. OF. *recoverance*; see RECOVER *v.*[1] and -ANCE.] Recovery.

Recoveree (rĭkʊvərī·). Now *rare* or *Obs.*

1531. [f. RECOVER v.[1] + -EE [1].] *Law.* The person from whom some property is recovered; *spec.* the defendant in an action of common recovery.

Recoverer (rĭkʊ·vərəɹ). late ME. [f. as prec. + -ER [1].] One who recovers, regains, restores, etc.

Recoveror (rĭkʊ·vərər). Also **-er** (-ER [4]). 1628. [f. as prec. + -OR 2.] *Law.* The demandant who recovers a judgement, esp. in an action of common recovery.

Recovery (rĭkʊ·vəri). late ME. [a. AF. *recoverie, -ery,* f. pa. pple. of *recoverir* or *recov(e)rer*; see RECOVER v.[1] and -Y [3].] **I.** †**1.** Possibility or means of recovering, or of being restored to, a normal state; remedy -1686. **2.** The act of recovering oneself from a mishap, mistake, fall, etc. 1525. **b.** The act of regaining the natural position after curtseying 1712. **c.** *Rowing.* The act of returning to the proper position for making a fresh stroke 1856. **3.** Restoration or return to health from sickness 1599.

1. On purpose to ruine past r. a country that..subsists by making of silk 1686. 3. Phr. †*On the r.*, recovering.

II. 1. *Law.* The fact or procedure of gaining possession of some property or right by a verdict or judgement of court; *spec.* the process, based on a legal fiction, by which entailed estate was commonly transferred from one party to another (also called *common r.*) 1472. **2.** The recovering *of* something lost or taken away; the possibility of recovering such a thing 1538. **3.** The restoration or bringing back *of* a person (or thing) to a healthy or normal condition or to consciousness 1590. **4.** Restoration to a higher or better state: **a.** of persons 1593; **b.** of land (*rare*) 1853. **5.** The action of bringing back (an oar) to the original position 1856.

1. *Single r.*, a suit of r. in which a single vouchee was called (so *double, treble r.*). 3. What? doth shee swowne? vse meanes for her recouerie SHAKS.

Recreance [1] (re·krĭăns). 1475. [ad. L. type **recreantia*, f. *recreare*; see RECREATE v.[1]] Recreation, refreshment.

Re·creance [2]. 1879. [f. RECREANT *a.*] = next.

Recreancy (re·krĭănsi). 1602. [f. RECREANT *a.*; see -ANCY.] The quality of being recreant; mean-spiritedness, apostasy.

Recreant (re·krĭănt), *a.* and *sb.* Now *poet.* and *rhet.* ME. [a. OF. *recreant* adj. and sb., (one) who yields or gives up his cause, pr. pple. of *recroire* = med.L. *recredere*, f. *re-* RE- + *credere* to entrust.] **A.** *adj.* **1.** Confessing oneself to be overcome or vanquished; surrendering, or giving way, to an opponent; hence, cowardly, faint-hearted, craven, afraid. **2.** Unfaithful to duty; false, apostate 1643.

1. The loud r. wretch who boasts and flies BYRON. 2. Who..Turn'd r. to God, ingrate and false MILT. To rebuke the r. American 1863.

B. *sb.* **1.** One who yields in combat; a cowardly or faint-hearted person. late ME. **2.** One who breaks allegiance or faith; an apostate, deserter, villain 1570.

1. Hold! recreants! cowards! What, fear ye death, and fear not shame? SHERIDAN. Hence **Re·creantly** *adv.*, **-ness.**

Recreate (re·krĭeit), *v.*[1] 1470. [ad. L. *recreat-, recreare,* f. *re-* RE- + *creare* to CREATE.] **1.** To invest with fresh vigour or strength; to refresh, reinvigorate (nature, strength, a person or thing) 1535. †**2.** To refresh (a sense or its organ) by means of some agreeable object or impression -1710. †**b.** To refresh or enliven (the spirits, mind, a person) by some sensuous or purely physical influence; to affect agreeably in this way -1778. **3.** To refresh or cheer (a person) by giving comfort, consolation or encouragement. Now *rare.* 1470. **4.** To refresh or enliven (the mind, the spirits, a person) by some pastime, amusement, occupation, agreeable news, etc. Also *refl.* 1530. †**b.** To enliven or gratify (a feeling) -1686. **5.** *intr.* To take recreation 1587. †**6.** *trans.* To relieve (an occupation, state, etc.) by means of something of a contrary nature -1653.

1. Each living being requires a certain portion of air to r. itself with 1862. 2. Speckled with little red spots that r. the Sight EVELYN. 4. No busy faces to r. the idle man who contemplates them ever passing by LAMB. **b.** The other Attribute wherewith I r. my devotion, is His Wisdom SIR T. BROWNE.

Recreate (rĭkrĭ,ē·t), *v.*[2] Also **re-create.** 1587. [RE- 5 a.] *trans.* To create anew. Hence **Recrea·tion** [2] (rĭkrĭ,ē·ʃən), the action of creating anew; a new creation.

Recreation [1] (rekrĭ,ē·ʃən). late ME. [ad. L. *recreationem.*] †**1.** Refreshment by partaking of food; a refection; nourishment -1600. **2.** The action of recreating (oneself or another), or fact of being recreated, by some pleasant occupation, pastime or amusement. late ME. **b.** An instance of this; a pleasurable exercise or employment. late ME. **c.** One who or that which supplies recreation 1601.

2. **c.** If I do not gull him into an ayword, and make him a common r. [etc.] SHAKS.

attrib.: **r. ground,** a public ground with facilities for games, etc.

Recreative (re·krĭ,eitiv), *a.*[1] and *sb.* 1549. [f. RECREATE v.[1] and -IVE.] **A.** *adj.* Tending to recreate or refresh in a pleasurable manner; amusing, diverting. †**B.** *absol.* as *sb.* A recreative thing or pursuit -1620.

A. The r. literature of the day 1887. Hence **Re·creatively** *adv.*, **-ness** [1].

Recreative (rĭkrĭ,ē·tiv), *a.*[2] 1861. [RE- 5 a.] That creates anew. Hence **Recrea·tiveness** [2].

Recrement (re·krĭmĕnt). 1599. Now *rare.* [a. F. *récrément*, or ad. L. *recrementum* refuse, dross, etc., f. *re-* RE- + *cernere* to separate.] **1.** The superfluous or useless portion of any substance; refuse, dross, scum, off-scouring. **2.** *spec.* **a.** A waste product or excretion of an animal or vegetable body; also *Phys.*, a fluid which is separated from the blood and again absorbed into it, as the saliva or bile (opp. to *excrement*) 1615. **b.** The dross or scoria of metallic substances 1611.

1. *fig.* A r. of ancient tradition 1882. 2. **b.** Slag.. is the R. of Iron 1678. Hence †**Recreme·ntal** *a.* **Recrementi·tious** *a.* of the nature of r.

Recriminate (rĭkri·mineit). 1603. [f. L. *recriminat-, recriminari*; see RE- 2 and CRIMINATE *v.*] **1.** *intr.* To retort an accusation; to bring a charge or charges in turn against one's accuser 1611. **2.** *trans.* **a.** To accuse (a person) in return; to make a counter-charge against (the accuser). Now *rare.* 1621. †**b.** To return or retort (a charge or accusation) *against, upon* a person -1653.

1. To criminate and r. never yet was the road to reconciliation, in any difference amongst men BURKE. To re-criminate on my base accuser 1786. Hence **Recri·minative, Recri·minatory** *adjs.* involving, of the nature of, recrimination. **Recri·minator.**

Recrimination (rĭkriminē·ʃən). 1611. [a. F. *récrimination*, or ad. med.L. *recriminationem.*] **1.** The action of bringing a counter-accusation against a person. **2.** A counter-accusation; an accusation brought in turn by the accused against the accuser 1621.

Recru·dency. 1603. [f. L. *recrudescere* + -ENCY.] = RECRUDESCENCE (*rare*).

Recrudesce (rī-, rekrude·s), *v.* 1884. [ad. L. *recrudescere* to break out again, f. *re-* RE- + *crudescere* to become raw, f. *crudus*; see CRUDE *a.*] To break out again (*lit.* and *fig.*).

Recrudescence (rī-, rekrude·sens). 1721. [ad. L. **recrudescentia*, f. *recrudescere*; see prec. and -ENCE.] The state or fact of breaking out afresh. **a.** *fig.* Of a quality or state of things (usu. one regarded as bad), a disease, epidemic, etc. **b.** Of a wound or sore 1865.

a. The fears of a r. of the epidemic 1884. So **Recrude·scency.**

Recrudescent (rī-, rekrude·sĕnt), *a.* 1727. [See RECRUDESCE and -ENT.] Breaking out again.

Recruit (rĭkrū·t), *sb.* 1643. [a. obs. F. *recrute* = F. *recrue*, f. *recrû* pa. pple. of *recroître* to increase again.] **I.** †**1.** *Mil.* A fresh or auxiliary body of troops, added as a reinforcement to an army, regiment, garrison, etc., either to increase or to maintain its strength -1728. **b.** *pl.* †Fresh or auxiliary troops, reinforcements; the men composing such forces. Hence (in later use) also in *sing.*: One of a newly-raised body of troops; one newly or recently enlisted for service in the army. 1645. †**2.** A fresh supply or number of persons (or animals), either as additional to the previous number, or to make up for a decrease -1769. **3.** A fresh or additional supply of something. Now *rare.* 1650.

1. **b.** A r. remains a r. from the date of his enlistment until he has passed his drill 1876. *transf.* Recruits from our schools of art 1885. 3. This r. to my finances was not a matter of indifference to me SCOTT.

II. †**1.** *Mil.* Increase or reinforcement (of an army) by the addition or accession of fresh men -1724. **2.** Renewal or repair of something worn out 1691. **3.** Renewal of strength or vigour; restoration to a normal state or condition; recovery 1643. **4.** A means of recruital. Now *rare.* 1655.

4. Little quarrels often prove To be but new recruits of love BUTLER.

Recruit (rĭkrū·t), *v.* 1635. [ad. F. *recruter*, f. *recrute* RECRUIT *sb.*] **I.** *trans.* **1.** *Mil.* To strengthen or reinforce (an army, etc.) with fresh men or troops 1643. **b.** To add to or keep up the number of (a class or body of persons or things) 1770. **2.** To furnish *with* a fresh supply of something; to replenish. Now *rare.* 1661. **3.** To replenish the substance of (a thing) by addition of fresh material 1661. **b.** To increase or maintain (a quality) by fresh influence or operation 1678. **4.** To increase or restore the vigour or health of (a person or animal); to refresh, re-invigorate (one's spirits, etc.). Also occas. with inanimate object. 1676. **5.** To renew, or add to, one's supply of (a thing) 1748. **6.** *Mil.* (and *Naval*). To raise (men) as recruits; to enlist as soldiers (or sailors); to raise (a regiment, etc.) in this way 1814.

1. Public and private distress recruited the armies of the state GIBBON. 2. The contributions offered by the English Catholics did little to r. the Exchequer GREEN. 3. **b.** Since the Crimean War..Russia has been carefully engaged in recruiting her strength 1870. 4. Thy Rains from Heav'n parch'd Hills r. WESLEY. Our guide recruited himself with a large dish of thick sour milk 1856.

II. *intr.* **1. a.** *Mil.* To enlist new soldiers; to get or seek for fresh supplies of men for the army 1655. †**b.** To take fresh stores on board ship. DE FOE. **2.** To recover vigour or health; to employ means for recovering from exhaustion, etc. 1635. †**3.** To recover what one has expended in trade -1727.

2. Leaving four of my party to r. at this station KANE. Hence **Recrui·tal,** †a new or fresh supply; restoration to health. **Recrui·ter,** one who or that which recruits; *esp.* one who seeks to enlist recruits. **Recrui·tment,** a reinforcement; also, the act or process of recruiting.

Rectal (re·ktăl), *a.* 1872. [f. RECTUM + -AL 1.] *Anat.* and *Med.* Of or belonging to the rectum.

Rectangle (re·ktæŋg'l). 1571. [ad. late L. *rectiangulum* a right-angled triangle, neut. of *rectiangulus* adj.] **1.** *Geom.* A plane rectilineal four-sided figure having all its angles right angles, and therefore its opposite sides equal and parallel. †**b.** The product of two quantities -1763. †**2.** A right angle -1795. Hence **Re·ctangled** *a.* (now *rare*) right-angled.

Rectangular (rektæ·ŋgiŭlăɹ), *a.* 1624. [See RECTANGLE *sb.* and -AR [1] 1.] **1.** Shaped like a rectangle; having four sides and four right angles. **b.** Of a solid body: Having the sides, base, or section in the form of a rectangle, or with right-angled corners 1624. †**2.** Of a triangle: Right-angled -1678. **3.** Placed or lying at right angles. (Said also of the relative position of two things.). 1646. **4.** Having parts, lines, etc. at right angles to each other; characterized or distinguished by some arrangement of this kind 1727. **Rectangula·rity,** the quality or state of being r. **Recta·ngularly** *adv.*

Rectifiable (re·ktifəiăb'l), *a.* 1646. [f. RECTIFY *v.* + -ABLE.] Capable of being rectified; *spec.* in *Math.* (see RECTIFY *v.* 7 b).

Rectification (rektifikē·ʃən). 1460. [a. F., or ad. late L. *rectificationem.*] The action of rectifying. **1.** The correction of error; a setting straight or right; amendment, improvement, correction. **2.** *Chem.* The purification or refinement of any substance by renewed distillation or other means 1605. **3.** *Geom.* The finding of a straight line equal in length to a given curve 1685. **4.** *Electr.* (cf. RECTIFY *v.* 7 c) 1903.

1. They haue done more cures in this kind by r. of

Diet, then all other Physick BURTON. **2.** The Oil of Sugar that remains after R. 1712.

Rectifier (re·ktifəiəɹ). 1611. [f. RECTIFY *v.* + -ER [1].] **1.** One who, or that which, rectifies. **2.** †**a.** An instrument for ascertaining the variation of the compass -1704. **b.** A device for converting an alternating electric current into a direct or continuous one 1898. **3.** One who, or an apparatus which, rectifies spirit 1727.

Rectify (re·ktifəi), *v.* late ME. [ad. F. *rectifier*, ad. late L. *rectificare*, f. *rectus* right + *-ficare*; see -FY.] **1.** *trans.* To put or set right, to remedy (a bad or faulty condition or state of things); to correct, amend, make good (an error, omission, etc.) 1659. **2.** †**a.** To restore (an organ) to a sound or healthy condition -1694. **b.** To put or set (a person or thing) right 1529. **3.** *Chem.* To purify or refine (any substance) by a renewed or repeated distillation, or by some chemical process; to raise *to* a required strength in this way; also, to flavour (a liquor) with some substance during rectification 1450. **4.** To correct or reform (a person, one's nature, mind, etc.) from vice or moral defect 1450. †**b.** To correct (one who is mistaken or in error); to set right -1711. **5.** To correct by removal of errors or mistakes; to amend or improve in this way 1494. **b.** To correct or emend (a text). *rare.* 1730. **6.** To put right by calculation or adjustment 1559. **b.** To set right, adjust (an instrument or apparatus) 1669. **c.** *spec.* To adjust (a globe) for the solution of a problem. Also *absol.* 1646. †**7.** To make straight, straighten out (anything crooked, etc.); to bring into line -1793. **b.** *Geom.* To equate (a curve) with a straight line 1673. **c.** To transform (an electric current) from an alternating to a continuous 1893. †**8.** To guide or direct aright (*rare*) -1618.

1. Payne is good, for by it god rectifyeth synne 1526. The slight omission was rectified DICKENS. **2. b.** Rectifying his position 1882. **3.** *transf.* The Sunne, which rectifieth the aire 1620. **4.** Rectifie a noþer if that ye may,..And rectifie youre selfe first euery day 1460. **5.** Some Oracle Must rectifie our knowledge SHAKS. **7.** O Conscience,..Check me, and r. my devious Lines KEN. Hence **Re·ctified** *ppl. a.* esp. of spirit: purified or refined by renewed distillation; redistilled.

Rectilineal (rektili·nĭ͵ăl), *a.* 1646. [f. as next; see -AL 1.] = next *a.*

Rectilinear (rektili·nĭ͵ăɹ), *a.* and *sb.* 1659. [f. late L. *rectilineus* + -AR [1] 1.] **A.** *adj.* **1.** Of motion, course, or direction: Taking or having the course of a straight line; tending always to the same point. **2.** Lying in, or forming, a straight line 1704. **3.** Of a figure or angle: Bounded or formed by straight lines 1728. **4.** Characterized by straight lines 1727. **b.** Of a lens: see quot. 1874.

4. b. *Rectilinear*, a term applied to lenses which have been corrected for aberration as much as possible, so that in photographing architectural subjects the lines appear perfectly straight in the image 1890.

B. *sb. Photogr.* A rectilinear lens 1890. Hence **Rectilinea·rity,** the quality of being r.

Rection (re·kʃən). *rare.* 1637. [ad. L. *rectionem*, f. *regere*.] *Gram.* Syntactical government; regimen.

Rectiserial (rektisīᵊ·riăl), *a.* 1861. [f. L. *recti-*, *rectus* + SERIAL.] *Bot.* (See quot.)

The leaves..in strict vertical ranks, or..r. 1880.

Rectitude (re·ktitiŭd). late ME. [a. F., ad. late L. *rectitudo*, f. *rectus*; see -TUDE.] **1.** The quality or fact of being straight; straightness. Now *rare* or *Obs.* **b.** Straight line; direction in a straight line 1578. **2.** Moral straightness or uprightness; goodness, integrity; virtue, righteousness 1533. **3.** Correctness of the judgement, or of its conclusions 1651. **4.** Correctness of nature, procedure, or application. Also with *pl.*, an instance of this. 1656.

2. A man of singular piety, r., and virtue BURKE.

Recto (re·ktō), *sb.* and *adv.* (Abbrev. r°.) 1824. [a. L. *recto* (sc. *folio*), abl. of *rectus* right.] **A.** *sb.* In *Printing*, the right-hand page of the open book; hence, the front of a leaf as opp. to the back or VERSO. **B.** *adv.* On or to the right-hand side 1888.

Recto-, used as comb. form of RECTUM in terms of *Anat.* and *Path.*, with the sense 'relating to the rectum in conjunction with some other part of the body', as **r.-ure·thral, -vagi·nal, -ve·sical,** etc.

Rector (re·ktəɹ). late ME. [a. L., agent-n. f. *regere* to guide, lead straight, rule, govern.] †**1.** The ruler or governor of a country, city, state, or people -1685. †**b.** Applied to God as the ruler of the world, of mankind, etc. -1741. **2.** One who, or that which, has or exercises supreme or directive control in any sphere. Now *rare.* 1482. **3.** A parson or incumbent of a parish whose tithes are not impropriate. (Cf. VICAR.) In Roman Catholic use, the head priest of a parish. late ME. **4.** In scholastic use: **a.** The permanent head or master of a university, college, school, or religious institution (esp. a Jesuit college or seminary). In Eng. use now applied only to the heads of Exeter and Lincoln Colleges, Oxford. 1464. **b.** In Scottish universities: The holder of one of the higher offices 1522. **c.** The acting head, and president of the administrative body, in continental universities 1548.

3. *Lay r.*, a layman receiving the rectorial tithes, or in whom the rectory is vested. **b.** *U.S.* A Protestant Episcopal clergyman in charge of a parish. **Re·ctoral** *a.* of or pertaining to a r. or ruler. (Said only of God.) **Re·ctorate,** the office or position of a r.; the period during which the office is held. **Re·ctoress,** †a female ruler; *colloq.* the wife of the r. of a parish. **Re·ctorship,** the office of ruler or governor; government, rule (now *rare*); the office of r.

Rectorial (rektō°·riăl), *a.* (*sb.*) 1611. [f. RECTOR + -IAL.] **1.** Of or pertaining to a university rector. **2.** Of or belonging to the rector of a parish (esp. *r. tithes*); held by a rector 1769. **3.** Of or pertaining to a ruler or governor 1679. **B.** as *sb.* In Scottish and other universities: A rectorial election 1920.

Rectory (re·ktŏri). 1594. [ad. med.L. *rectoria*; see RECTOR and -Y [3].] **1.** A benefice held by a rector. **b.** The residence appertaining to a rector 1849. †**2.** Rectorship; administration -1675.

Rectress (re·ktrės). 1603. [See RECTOR and -ESS [1].] †**1.** A female ruler or governor -1656. **2.** The female head of a school or institution 1843. **3.** The wife of a rector 1906.

Rectrix (re·ktriks). 1611. [a. L.] **1.** = RECTRESS 1 (*rare*). **2.** *Ornith.* in *pl.* **rectrices** (rektrəi·sīz). The strong feathers of the tail in birds, by which their flight is directed 1768.

‖**Rectum** (re·ktŏm). 1541. [a. L. *rectum* (sc. *intestinum*), neut. of *rectus* straight.] *Anat.* and *Med.* The final section of the large intestine (so called from its form in some animals), extending in man from the sigmoid flexure of the colon to the anus.

‖**Rectus** (re·ktŏs). *Pl.* **recti** (re·ktəi). 1704. [a. L. *rectus* (sc. *musculus*).] *Anat.* The name of various muscles, esp. of the abdomen, thigh, neck, and eye, so called from the straightness of their fibres. So *r. muscle.*

†**Recuba·tion.** [f. L. *recubare* to recline, f. *re-* RE- + *cubare*; see -ATION.] The action of reclining, recumbency. SIR T. BROWNE.

Recueil (rəkö̈y), *sb.* 1474. [a. F., f. *recueillir*; see next.] **1.** A literary compilation or collection. (Now only as Fr.) †**2.** Reception, welcome; reset -1588.

†**Recueil,** *v.* 1474. [a. F. *recueillir* :—L. *recolligere* to collect, gather up, f. *re-* RE- + *colligere* CULL *v.*[1]] **1.** *trans.* To gather together -1566. **2.** To receive hospitably, entertain. CAXTON. **3.** To receive, catch. CAXTON.

†**Recu·mb,** *v.* 1677. [ad. L. *recumbere*; see RECUMBENT *a.*] *intr.* To lean, recline.

Recumbence (rĭkɒ·mběns). Now *rare.* 1676. [f. as next + -ENCE.] = RECUMBENCY.

Recumbency (rĭkɒ·mběnsi). 1642. [ad. L. **recumbentia*, f. *recumbere*; see RECUMBENT *a.*] **1.** The state of lying or reclining; a recumbent posture 1646. **b.** *fig.* Repose 1653. **2.** *fig.* Reliance *on* or *upon* a person or thing. Chiefly in religious use. Now *rare.* 1646. **b.** Without const. Also *pl.* 1642.

1. The Tricliniums, or places of festivall R. SIR T. BROWNE.

Recumbent (rĭkɒ·mběnt), *a.* 1705. [ad. L. *recumbentem*, *recumbere*, f. *re-* RE- + *-cumbere* to lie.] **1.** Of persons or animals: Lying down, reclining, reposing 1774. **2.** Of posture: Reclining, leaning or lying 1705. Hence **Recu·mbently** *adv.*

Recuperate (rĭkiŭ·pĕreit), *v.* 1542. [f. L. *recuperat-*, *recuperare*; see RECOVER *v.*[1]] †**1.** *trans.* To recover (a thing) -1661. **2.** To restore (a person) to health or vigour 1864. **3.** *intr.* To recover from exhaustion, ill-health, pecuniary loss, etc. 1864. So †**Recu·perable** *a.* recoverable.

Recuperation (rĭkiŭpĕrē¹·ʃən). 1481. [ad. L. *recuperationem*; see prec.] †**1.** The recovery or regaining *of* a thing -1685. **2.** Restoration to health, vigour, etc. 1865.

Recuperative (rĭkiŭ·pĕrătiv), *a.* (and *sb.*). 1623. [ad. late L. *recuperativus*; see RECUPERATE and -IVE.] †**1.** Recoverable. †**2.** Belonging to, concerned with, the recovery of something lost -1858. **3.** Having the power of restoring (a person or thing) to a proper state 1861. **b.** Of or belonging to recovery of health, vigour, etc. 1860. **B.** *sb.* A substance which restores land to fertility 1883.

Recuperator (rĭkiŭ·pĕreitəɹ). 1706. [a. L.; see -OR 2.] **1.** *Rom. Law.* A member of a commission for trying certain cases. **2.** *Mech.* The regenerator of a hot-air engine, gas-burning furnace, etc. 1884.

Recu·peratory, *a. rare.* 1656. [ad. L. *recuperatorius*; see -ORY [2].] Of or belonging to recovery or recuperators.

Recur (rĭkɒ̄·ɹ), *v.* 1468. [ad. L. *recurrere*, f. *re-* RE- + *currere* to run.] †**1.** *intr.* To move or run back, recede (*rare*) -1788. **b.** To return *into* or *to* a place (*rare*) 1468. **2.** To return, go back, in thought, memory, or discourse. Usu. const. *to.* 1620. **3.** To go back, resort *to* a thing (rarely a person), for assistance or argument 1529. **4.** Of something known, an idea, thought, etc.: To come back or return (†*into*, *in* or) *to* one's thoughts, mind or memory 1704. **b.** Without const.: To return to the mind 1711. **c.** Of questions, difficulties, etc.: To come up again for consideration; to present themselves, or confront one, again 1651. **5.** To occur, happen, take place, appear, again 1673. **b.** *Math.* Of a figure or figures in a decimal fraction: To return or come again (in the same order), to repeat 1801.

2. I know it is painful to her to r. to that terrible time 1833. **3.** If to avoid Succession in eternal Existence, they r. to the *Punctum Stans* of the Schools LOCKE. **4. b.** Wherever I have heard A kindred melody, the scene recurs COWPER. **c.** But still, the question recurs, whether man be free? BERKELEY. **5.** In some..the disease has appeared to r. 1851.

†**Recu·re,** *sb.* late ME. [f. next.] Recovery; remedy, succour; cure -1626.

Phr. *But*, *past*, or *without r.*, past or without hope or possibility of recovery.

†**Recu·re,** *v.* late ME. [ad. L. *recurare*, f. *re-* RE- + *curare* CURE *v.*[1]] **1.** *trans.* To cure (a person) *of* or *from* a disease, wound, trouble, etc.; to restore to health. Also *absol.* -1647. **b.** To restore after loss, damage, exhaustion, etc. Also const. *to* (a better state). -1667. **2.** To cure (a disease, sickness, etc.); to heal, make whole (a wound or sore) -1667. **b.** To remedy (a wrong, defect, etc.) -1631. **3.** *intr.* Of persons: To become whole; to regain health or a former state -1547. **4.** *trans.* To recover (something lost); to get, obtain, win -1746.

1. b. No Physick can r. my weaken'd State COWLEY. **4.** So hard was this lost Isle, so hard to be recur'd P. FLETCHER. Hence †**Recu·reless** *a.* incurable.

Recurrence (rĭkɒ·rěns). 1646. [See next and -ENCE.] **1.** Return (of a thing, state, event, etc.); renewed, frequent, or periodical occurrence. Also, with *a* and *pl.*, an instance of this. **2.** Resort, recourse, reference *to* something. Also without const. 1667. **3.** The action of going back mentally or in discourse *to* something. Also with *a* and *pl.*, an instance of this. 1751. **4.** Return or reversion *to* a state occupation, etc. 1812.

1. The r. of the same follies 1877. Atavism,..the name given to the r. of ancestral traits H. SPENCER. **2.** Such an alliance will occasion frequent r. to arms 1804. **3.** The announcement..effectually put a stop to any r. to the subject 1862. So †**Recu·rrency** (in sense 1).

Recurrent (rĭkɒ·rěnt), *a.* and *sb.* 1597. [ad. L. *recurrentem*, *recurrere.*] **A.** *adj.* **1.**

Anat. and *Bot.* Of a nerve, vein, artery, branch, etc.: Turned back so as to run or lie in a direction opposite to the former one 1611. **b.** *Path. R. sensibility*, the sensibility manifested by the anterior roots of the spinal cord owing to the recurrent course of the sensory fibres from the corresponding posterior roots 1873. **2.** Occurring or coming again (esp. frequently or periodically); reappearing 1666.

1. *R. nerves*, the laryngeal and meningeal branches of the pneumogastric nerve.

B. *sb.* A recurrent artery or nerve; *esp.* the right or left recurrent laryngeal nerve 1597. Hence **Recu·rrently** *adv.*

Recursant (rĭkʊ̄·ɹsănt), *a.* 1828. [ad. L. *recursantem*, *recursare* to hasten back, f. *recurs-*, ppl. stem of *recurrere*.] *Her.* Of an eagle: Having the back towards the spectator.

Recursion (rĭkʊ̄·ɹʃən). Now *rare* or *Obs.* 1616. [ad. L. *recursionem*, f. *recurrere*.] A backward movement, return.

Recurvate (rĭkʊ̄·ɹvĕt), *a.* 1776. [ad. L. *recurvatus*, *recurvare*.] Recurved.

Recurvate (rĭkʊ̄·ɹveⁱt), *v.* Now *rare.* 1597. [See prec. and RECURVE *v.*] **1.** *trans.* To bend (a thing) back (*rare*). **b.** In pa. pple. Bent backwards 1597. **2.** *intr.* Of a thing: To bend back; to recurve 1822.

Recurvation (rīkɒɹvēⁱ·ʃən). Now *rare.* 1597. [ad. L. **recurvationem*.] The fact of being bent or curved back; a backward bend or curve. So **Recu·rvature.**

Recurve (rĭkʊ̄·ɹv), *v.* 1597. [ad. L. *recurvare*, f. *re-* RE- + *curvare* to CURVE.] **1.** *trans.* To bend (a thing) back or backwards. **2.** *intr.* (Chiefly of a wind or current): To turn back in a curve upon its previous direction 1850. Hence **Recu·rved** *ppl. a.* bent back; having a backward curve.

†**Recu·rvity.** 1668. [f. L. *recurvus*; see -ITY.] The fact of being recurved. SIR T. BROWNE.

Recurvo-, used in *Bot.* as comb. form of L. *recurvus*, as **recu·rvo-pa·tent**, bent back and spreading, etc.

Recurvous (rĭkʊ̄·ɹvəs), *a. rare.* 1713. [f. L. *recurvus* + -OUS.] Recurved, bent back.

Recusance (re·kiuzăns, rĭkiū·zăns). 1597. [f. as next; see -ANCE.] = next.

Recusancy (re·kiuzănsi, rĭkiū·zănsi). 1563. [ad. L. **recusantia*; see next and -ANCY.] **1.** *Hist.* Refusal, esp. on the part of Roman Catholics, to attend the services of the Church of England 1600. **2.** Refusal to obey some authority or command 1563.

Recusant (re·kiuzănt, rĭkiū·zănt), *sb.* and *a.* 1552. **A.** *sb.* **1.** *Hist.* One, esp. a Roman Catholic (*Popish r.*), who refused to attend the services of the Church of England. **b.** Applied to other religious dissentients 1777. **2.** One who refuses to submit to some authority, comply with some regulation or request, etc. 1584.

1. It appears that this remote county was full of Popish recusants SCOTT. 2. Dealing with the dominions of the r. as being a forfeited fief FREEMAN.

B. *adj.* **1.** Refusing to attend the parish church; dissenting 1611. **2.** Refusing to acknowledge authority or to do something commanded or desired 1659.

1. The R. Lords 1647. 2. Those R. Jews MILT.

Recusation (rekiuzēⁱ·ʃən). Now *rare.* 1529. [a. F. *récusation*, or ad. L. *recusationem*.] *Civil* and *Canon Law.* The interposition of an objection or appeal; *esp.* an appeal grounded on the judge's relationship or personal enmity to one of the parties.

†**Recu·sative,** *a. rare.* [ad. late L. *recusativus*; see next and -IVE.] That tends to refuse or prohibit. JER. TAYLOR.

Recuse (rĭkiū·z), *v.* Now *rare.* late ME. [ad. F. *récuser*, ad. L. *recusare* to refuse, make an objection, f. *re-* RE- + *causa* CAUSE.] **1.** To reject, renounce (a person, his authority, etc.); to object to (a judge) as prejudiced. †**2.** To refuse *to* do something –1542.

Recussion (rĭkɒ·ʃən). *rare.* 1854. [ad. L. **recussionem*, f. *recutere* to strike back.] The action of striking by return or recoil.

Red (red), *a.* and *sb.* [Com. Teut.; OE. *rēad* :—OTeut. **rauðoz*, pre-Teut. **roudhos*. Cf. L. *rufus*, *ruber*, Gr. ἐρυθρός, Skr. *rudhirá-* red.] **A.** *adj.* **I. 1.** Having, or characterized by, the colour which appears at the lower or least refracted end of the visible spectrum, and is familiar as that of blood, fire, the poppy, the rose, and ripe fruits. (The shades of colour to which the name is applied vary from bright scarlet or crimson to reddish yellow or brown.) **2.** As an epithet (chiefly *poet.*) of blood ME. **b.** In pregnant uses, implying superior quality or value 1596. **3.** As a conventional (chiefly *poet.*) epithet of gold. Now only *arch.* OE. **b.** Golden, made of gold. Now only *thieves' slang.* late ME. **c.** *U.S.* As an epithet of the cent (formerly made of copper), usu. in negative expressions 1852. **4.** Of cloth, clothing, etc.: Dyed with red OE. **b.** *R. flag*, as a sign of battle, etc. 1602. **5.** Of persons: Having red hair; †of a red or ruddy complexion OE. **b.** Of animals: Having red or reddish hair; tawny, chestnut, or bay. late ME. **c.** Of certain peoples, esp. the N. American Indians: Having (or regarded as having) a reddish skin. See also RED MAN, RED SKIN. 1587. **6.** Wearing red clothing (uniform, livery) or armour. Now *rare.* late ME. **7.** Of the face, or of persons in respect of it: Temporarily suffused with blood, esp. as the result of some sudden feeling or emotion; flushed or blushing *with* (anger, shame, etc.) ME. **b.** Exceptionally high in colour. late ME. **8.** Stained or covered with blood ME. **b.** Of meat: Full of, coloured with, blood 1837. **c.** Consisting of blood 1816. **9.** Marked or characterized by blood or fire, or by violence suggestive of these ME. **b.** Extremely radical or revolutionary, *esp.* communistic 1854. **10.** Red-hot, glowing ME. **11.** Of eyes: (*a*) Naturally of a red colour. (*b*) Bloodshot. (*c*) Inflamed as with weeping. late ME.

1 Like a r. morne that euer yet betokend Wracke to the sea man SHAKS. The Thunder, Wing'd with r. Lightning MILT. Women with big black Eyes, and r. Cheeks 1687. One with a r. beard KINGSLEY. Phr. *R. as blood, fire, a rose, cherry, fiery r.*, etc. *To paint the town r.*, to behave riotously or uproariously; to go 'on the spree'. 2. I have..Seen through r. blood the war-horse dashing SCOTT. b. *Merch. V.* II. i. 7. 3. c. I don't care a r. cent what you say 1889. 4. The r. shirt of Garibaldi's troops 1868. *R. hat* (of cardinals): see HAT *sb.* 2. 5. The R. O'Donnell and others 1849. b. Master had the r. setter with him this morning 1882. 7. Mine enemies shall..then grow r. with shame MILT. b. As R. in the Gills as a Turkey-cock 1689. 8. Sad Philippi, r. with Roman Gore GRAY. b. Avoid altogether r. meat 1898. 9. Ye shal be deed by myghty Mars the rede CHAUCER. b. *Red flag*, a symbol of revolution, communism, etc. (see also sense 4 b above); the title of a revolutionary song. 10. A waking dream of houses, towers..expressed In the r. cinders COWPER.

II. In special applications. **a.** As a distinctive epithet of things in which the colour forms a natural or obvious mark of kind or class OE. **b.** Applied to various diseases marked by evacuation of blood or cutaneous eruptions. late ME. **c.** *R. squadron*, one of the three squadrons into which the Royal Navy was formerly divided 1702.

Comb. and collocations. **a.** used with the names of beasts, birds, fishes, plants, and minerals, as **r. ant,** any ant of this colour, esp. (*a*) a common small British ant *Formica* (*Myrmica*) *rubra*; (*b*) the hill- or horse-ant, *F. rufa* (*c*) the American house-ant, *Monomorium pharaonis*; **r. antimony** (ore) = KERMESITE; **r. ash,** (*a*) a N. Amer. ash, *Fraxinus pubescens*; (*b*) an Australian tree, *Alphitonia excelsa*; (*c*) the silky oak of Australia, *Orites excelsa*; **r. bass,** *U.S.* the red-drum or red-fish, *Sciæna ocellata*; **r. bay,** *U.S.* a lauraceous tree, *Persea carolinensis*; **r. birch,** an American birch, *Betula nigra*; **r. bird,** any of various small American birds with red plumage, esp. the scarlet tanager (*Piranga rubra*), Baltimore oriole, and cardinal grosbeak; **r. bug,** *U.S.* (*a*) the cotton-stainer, *Dysdercus suturellus*; (*b*) one of several red harvest-ticks; **r. chalk,** (*a*) ruddle; (*b*) *Geol.* a bed of chalk of a red colour, occurring in Norfolk and elsewhere; **r. cock,** the grouse; **r. copper ore,** CUPRITE; **r. coral** (see CORAL 1 a); **r. fir,** (*a*) *Picea Morinda*; (*b*) a N. Amer. fir, *Abies nobilis*; (*c*) the Oregon Pine, *Pseudotsuga Douglasii*; **r. fox,** (*a*) the common European fox, *Vulpes vulgaris*; the common N. Amer. fox, *V. fulvus*; (*c*) the kit-fox of N. America; **r. grouse** (see GROUSE 1 b); **r. kite,** the common kite; **r. lead ore,** CROCOITE; **r. maggot** (see MAGGOT 1); **r. manganese** (ore), DIALOGITE; **r. maple,** a species of maple, *Acer rubrum*, with crimson flowers; **r. pepper,** capsicum; **r. perch,** the rose-fish, *Sebastes marinus*; **r. ptarmigan,** the grouse; **r. robin,** (*a*) the redbreast; (*b*) the scarlet tanager; **r. spider,** a small red spider-like mite (*Tetranychus* or *Acarus telarius*) infesting plants, esp. in hothouses; **r. squirrel,** the chickaree; **r. viper,** (*a*) a species of British viper; (*b*) *U.S.* the copper-head; **r. weed,** (*a*) an Amer. plant or plants; now applied to a species of *Phytolacca*; (*b*) the corn-poppy; **r. wheat,** a variety of the common wheat, of a reddish colour; **r. worm,** (*a*) a variety of earth-worm much used as bait in angling; (*b*) a worm or grub attacking grain; **r. zinc** (ore), zincite.

b. prefixed to the name of a part (or some distinctive feature) used to denote the whole; (*a*) of persons, as **r.-hat,** a cardinal; **-shirt,** a revolutionary, an anarchist; (*b*) *spec.* forming the names of certain birds, fishes, plants, etc., as **r.-back,** *U.S.* the American dunlin or red-backed sandpiper, *Tringa americana*; **-belly,** (*a*) a species of lake-trout; (*b*) the Welsh char; (*c*) *U.S.* the red-bellied perch or sunfish; **-bud,** a tree belonging to any Amer. species of *Cercis*, esp. *C. Canadensis*; the Judas-tree; **-eye,** (*a*) the rudd, *Leuciscus erythrophthalmus*; (*b*) one of several American fishes, as the rock-bass, the red-fish; **-fin,** *U.S.* the shiner and various other American fishes; **-root,** *U.S.* (*a*) New Jersey tea, *Ceanothus americanus*; (*b*) the blood-root, *Sanguinaria canadensis*; (*c*) the stone-weed, *Lithospermum arvense*; (*d*) a plant of the blood-wort family, *Lacnanthes tinctoria*; **-tail,** (*a*) = REDSTART 1; (*b*) *U.S.* the red-tailed buzzard, *Buteo borealis*; **r. throat,** an Australian singing bird, *Pyrrholæmus brunneus*; **-underwing,** a species of moth, *Catocala nupta*.

c. with miscellaneous sbs., as **r. admiral,** a butterfly, *Vanessa Atalanta*; see also ADMIRAL 6; **r. ash,** *U.S.* a coal producing a red ash (also *attrib.*); **r. bark,** a variety of cinchona-bark; **r. body,** in fishes, an aggregation of capillaries on the inside of the swimming-bladder; **r. box,** a box (covered with red leather) used by ministers of state for holding official documents; **R. Crescent,** the Turkish ambulance society answering to the RED CROSS; **r. fire,** a pyrotechnic effect, or the mixture ignited to produce it; **r. fog,** a sea-haze due to the presence of sand or dust in the air; **r. game,** the red grouse *Lagopus scoticus*; **r. lac,** a species of sumach (*Rhus succedanea*, also called *red lac sumach*), from the fruit of which Japan wax is obtained; **r. lamp,** a lamp having red glass, used as a doctor's sign; in the war of 1914–18, the sign of a licensed brothel; **r. lane,** *colloq.* the throat; **r. lattice** (now *arch.*), a lattice painted red as the sign of an alehouse; hence *transf.* an alehouse, inn; **r. light (district),** *U.S.* quarters of licensed prostitutes; phr. *to see the r. light*, to suspect danger; **r. liquor,** a mordant used in calico-printing; **r. mass** [after F. *messe rouge*], a mass (usu. one of the Holy Ghost) at which red vestments are worn by the priest; **r. metal,** a name given to various alloys of copper having a reddish colour; **r. precipitate,** red oxide of mercury, prepared by solution (and repeated distillation) with nitric acid; **r. ribbon,** †(*a*) the crimson ribbon worn by Knights of the Order of the Bath, hence, membership of this Order, or the Order itself; (*b*) the band-fish; **r. sanders,** red sandalwood; the wood of an E. Indian tree, *Pterocarpus santalinus*, used in dyeing, and formerly as an astringent and tonic; **r. scale,** a scale-insect, *Aonidia aurantii*, infesting orange trees; **r. softening,** a variety of acute softening of the brain, marked by extravasation of blood in the tissue; **r. stuff,** an iron oxide, as crocus or rouge, used in grinding or polishing; **r. triangle,** a form of danger sign; **r. twig,** red root (*Ceanothus*); **r. water,** (*a*) a disease in cattle and sheep characterized by the presence of free hæmoglobin in the urine; (*b*) the poisonous red juice of the sassy-tree of W. Africa.

d. with adjs., as **r.-blind,** colour-blind in respect of red; **-ripe,** fully ripe, as indicated by the red colour.

e. parasynthetic (chiefly in the names of animals, birds, fishes, etc.), as *r.-blooded* (also *fig.* = strong, vigorous, virile), *-eyed, -legged, -necked, -nosed, -tailed, -throated*, etc.

B. *sb.* **1.** Red colour (dye, stain, etc.); redness. Often with defining terms prefixed, as *alizarin, cherry*, etc. ME. **b.** The red colour in roulette or rouge-et-noir 1849. **c.** The red ball in billiards 1866. **2. a.** Stuff, cloth, or the like, of a red colour (usu. as the material of a dress). late ME. **b.** Ruddle (now *dial.*); †rouge. late ME. **3.** Red wine. late ME. **4.** = *Red Squadron* (cf. A. II. c.) 1690. **5.** *pl.* (rarely *sing.* with *a*). **a.** Shades or tints of red 1633. **b.** Red kinds or varieties of cloth, wine, wheat, etc.; red cattle, ants, herrings, etc. 1566. **6. a.** *pl.* Red men; North American Indians 1804. **b.** An extreme radical or revolutionary; latterly *esp.* a communist 1864.

1. MILT. *Nativity* 230. *Red, white, and blue*, (the three colours of) the Union Jack. *To see red* (colloq.), to be overcome with rage, to lose control of one's temper or actions. *To come* (or *be*) *out of the r.* (U.S.), to (begin to) show a profit; to be on the credit side; so *to be in the r.*, to show a loss. (From the practice of recording debit balances in red ink.) Hence **Re·d-ly** *adv.*, **-ness.**

†**Red,** *v.* [OE. *rēadian*, f. *rēad* RED *a.*] **1.**

intr. a. To be red. b. To become or grow red; to blush. late ME. 2. *trans.* To make red -1736.

-red, *suffix*, repr. OE. *rǣden* condition. In ME. the full form *-ræden, -reden, -raden*, was by the general dropping of final *-n* reduced to *-rede*, and this was subseq. shortened to *-red*. See GOSSIPRED, HATRED, KINDRED.

Redact (rĭdæ·kt), *v.* late ME. [f. L. *redact-, redigere* to bring back, etc., f. *re(d)-* RE- + *agere* to drive; see ACT *v.* Revived in the 19th c.] †1. *trans.* To bring (matter of reasoning or discourse) *into* or *to* a certain form; to put *together* in writing -1639. †2. To bring together *into* one body -1550. †3. To reduce (a person or thing) *to, into* a certain state, condition, or action -1731. 4. a. To draw up, frame (a statement, decree, etc.) 1837. b. To put (matter) into proper literary form; to work up, arrange, or edit 1851.

4. a. The House of Commons..was busy redacting a 'Protestation' CARLYLE. So **Reda·ctor**, one who redacts; an editor 1816.

‖ **Rédacteur** (redaktör). 1804. [F.] = REDACTOR (see above).

Redaction (rĭdæ·kʃən). 1621. [In sense 1, ad. late L. *redactionem, redigere*; in sense 2, a. F. *rédaction.*] †1. The action of driving back, resistance, reaction -1659. 2. The action or process of preparing for publication; reduction to literary form; revision, rearrangement 1803. b. The result of such a process; a new edition 1810.

Redan (rĭdæ·n). 1684. [a. F. *redan* for *redent* 'a double notching or iagging, as in the teeth of a saw' (Cotgr.), f. *re-* RE- + *dent* tooth.] *Fortif.* A simple form of field-work, having two faces which form a salient angle. Also *attrib.*

Redargue (redā·giu), *v.* Now *Sc.* late ME. [ad. F. *rédarguer*, or L. *redarguere* to disprove, etc., f. *re(d)-* RE- + *arguere* to ARGUE.] †1. *trans.* To blame, reprove (a person or persons, an action, etc.). Also const. *of, for.* -1677. 2. To confute (a person) by argument. late ME. 3. To refute or disprove (an argument, statement, etc. Since *c* 1700 only *Sc.*, chiefly *Law.*) 1627. 4. *absol.* or *intr.* To reprove or refute; to employ argument for the purpose of refuting 1641.

1. Basil..severely redargues Origen's allegoric mode of Theologising 1677. 3. I may..r. your claim and statements, as the result of a mistake HAMILTON. Hence †**Reda·rgutory** *a.* (*rare*) pertaining to refutation or reproof.

Redargution (redaɪgiū·ʃən). 1483. [ult. ad. L. *redargutionem*; see prec.] †1. Reproof, reprehension (of a person, an action, etc.) -1690. 2. Confutation (of a person); refutation, disproof (of a statement, etc.). Now *rare.* 1529.

Red-backed, *a.* 1768. Having a red back; chiefly of birds, *esp.* the red-backed butcher-bird or shrike (*Lanius collurio*), and the red-backed sandpiper (*Tringa americana*).

Re·d book, re·d-book. 1479. A book bound in red. 1. As the name of individual books of an official character, or otherwise important. †b. A book containing the names of all persons holding office under the State or receiving pensions from it -1820. 2. A popular name for the 'Royal Kalendar, or Complete.. Annual Register' (published from 1767 to 1893); also, the title of a similar work of later date 1788.

1. *Red Book of the Exchequer*, a miscellaneous volume, containing copies of charters, statutes, surveys, etc.; orig. compiled in the 13th c. *Red book of Hergest*, a Welsh MS. of the 14-15th c., containing the tales known as the Mabinogion and other pieces.

Re·dbreast. late ME. The robin. b. Applied to other red-breasted birds, esp. *U.S.* to the migratory thrush (also called *robin*) 1775.

Re·dcap, red-cap, red cap. 1539. 1. Applied to one who wears a red cap 1550. b. *spec.* as the name of a sprite or goblin 1802. c. *slang.* A military policeman. †2. A red-hat, a cardinal -1609. 3. The goldfinch 1785.

Red cedar. 1717. a. An American evergreen tree, *Juniperus virginianus*, the wood of which is widely used for pencils. b. The toon-tree or Moulmein cedar, *Cedrela toona.* c. An Australian timber-tree, *Flindersia australis.*

Re·dcoat, red-coat, red coat. 1520. One who wears a red coat; *spec.* a soldier in the British army.

Red cross, red-cross. late ME. 1. A cross of a red colour; *esp.* a. as the national emblem of England; St. George's Cross. b. as the mark made on the doors of infected houses during the London plagues of the 17th c. 1636. c. as the badge of an ambulance service; the Geneva cross 1863. 2. *transf.* a. The Christian side in the Crusades 1801. b. An ambulance or hospital service organized in accordance with the Geneva convention of 1864, and distinguished by a cross (see 1 c); a person attached to an ambulance or hospital of this kind 1877. 3. *attrib.*, as (sense 1) *red cross knight*, etc., (sense 1 c or 2 b) *Red Cross hospital, Society*, etc. 1590.

Red currant. 1629. The fruit of the *Ribes rubrum* (see CURRANT 2) or the shrub itself. Also *attrib.*, as *red currant jelly, wine.*

Redd (red), *v.* *Sc.* and *n. dial.* late ME. [= MLG. *redden.*] *trans.* To clear, put in order; to clean *up* (also *U.S.*).

Red deer. 1470. a. A species of deer, *Cervus elaphus*, so named from its reddish-brown colour, still existing in a wild state in the Highlands of Scotland and some other parts of Great Britain. b. The Virginia deer, *Cariacus virginianus*, the common deer of N. America. c. The Caspian or Persian deer, *Cervus maral.*

Redden (re·d'n), *v.* 1611. [f. RED *a.* + -EN [5] 1.] *trans.* and *intr.* To make or become red. b. *intr.* To become red (in the face) *with* shame, rage, etc.; to flush, blush 1648.

Bright leaves, reddening ere they fall KEBLE. b. He would r. with Rage 1701.

‖ **Reddendum** (rĕde·ndŏm). 1607. [L., neut. sing. of *reddendus, reddere* to give in return, RENDER.] *Law.* A reserving clause in a deed.

Reddish (re·diʃ), *a.* late ME. [f. RED *a.* -ISH [1].] 1. Somewhat red, red-tinted. Hence **Re·ddishness.**

†**Reddi·tion.** 1449. [a. F., or ad. L. *redditionem*, f. *reddere* to give back.] 1. Restoration of something taken or received; also, surrender of a thing, a town, army, etc. -1794. 2. The application of a comparison, or the clause containing the application -1786. 3. Rendering, translation -1685.

2. We know that al Parables consiste of two parts, the proposition and R. or moral 1678.

†**Re·dditive,** *a.* and *sb.* 1590. [ad. L. *redditivus*; see prec. and -IVE.] A. *adj.* That answers to something already said; corresponding, correlative -1659. B. *sb. Gram.* A correlative word -1668.

Reddle (re·d'l), *sb.* 1668. [var. of RUDDLE.] Red ochre, ruddle. Hence **Re·ddle** *v. trans.* to paint or wash over with r. **Re·ddleman,** a dealer in r.

Rede (rīd), *sb.* Now *arch.* or *poet.* and *dial.* [Com. Teut.: OE. *rǣd* :—OTeut. **rǣđoz*, f. the stem of the vb. **rǣđan* to REDE.] 1. Counsel or advice given by one person to another. 2. Counsel, decision, or resolve taken by one or more persons; a plan, design, or scheme devised or adopted OE. 3. Tale, narrative, story; †a saying, proverb. late ME. †b. Speech. SPENSER. c. Interpretation. BROWNING.

2. Therefore swift r. I take with all things here MORRIS. 3. A final note..to bid the gentles speed Who long have listened to my r. SCOTT.

Rede (rīd), *v.* Now *arch.* or *poet.* and *dial.* OE. [Same word as READ *v.*, the common ME. spelling being retained for the archaic senses of the word.] I. †1. *intr.* To take counsel together or *with* another, to deliberate. Also of one person: To take counsel *for* others. -1494. †2. *trans.* To agree upon, resolve, decide, after consultation or deliberation -1559. II. 1. To advise or counsel (a person) OE. †2. To advise (a thing); to give as advice or counsel -1650. †3. *intr.* To give advice -1591. 4. *Sc.* To think, imagine, guess 1768. 5. To interpret, explain 1725. 6. To relate, tell 1840.

1. I can mine selue In this case nat r. CHAUCER. 2. Now read..What course ye weene is best for us to take SPENSER. 5. The secret of Man's being is still.. a riddle that he cannot r. CARLYLE. 6. I'll r. ye a lay of Grammerye BARHAM.

Redeem (rĭdī·m), *v.* late ME. [ad. F. *rédimer*, or L. *redimere* to buy back, etc., f. *re(d)-* RE- + *emere* to buy.] 1. *trans.* To buy back (a thing formerly possessed); to make payment for (a thing held or claimed by another). Also *absol.* b. To regain, recover (an immaterial thing) 1526. c. To regain or recover by force 1666. 2. a. To free (mortgaged property), to recover (a person or thing put in pledge), by payment of the amount due, or by fulfilling some obligation 1470. b. To buy off, compound for (a charge or obligation) by payment or some other way 1494. c. To fulfil, perform (a pledge, promise, etc.) 1840. 3. To ransom, liberate, free (a person) from bondage, captivity, or punishment; to save (a person's life) by paying a ransom. late ME. 4. To rescue, save, deliver 1470. b. To reclaim (land) 1721. 5. To free from a charge or claim 1494. 6. Of God or Christ: To deliver from sin and its consequences 1500. †7. To obtain by purchase, to buy -1645. 8. To save (time) from being lost 1526. 9. Of persons: To make amends or atonement for, to compensate (an error, fault, etc.) 1526. †b. To repay (some wrong sustained). SHAKS. c. To make good (a loss). *rare.* 1629. 10. Of qualities, actions, etc.: To make up for, compensate for, counterbalance (some defect or fault) 1586. b. To save (a person or thing) *from* some defect or blot 1601. 11. To restore, set right again (*rare*) 1575. †12. To gain, reach (a place). HERRICK.

1. That precious Time, which no sum..can either purchase or r. BOYLE. b. To r. his Honour DRYDEN. c. The Gael..Shall with strong hand r. his share SCOTT. 2. a. *fig.* My Honor is at pawne, And but my going, nothing can redeeme it SHAKS. b. To r. incumbrances 1818. 3. Wanting gilders to redeeme their liues SHAKS. 4. Redeeme Israel, O God, out of all his Troubles *Ps.* xxv. 22. *absol.* Is my hande shortened at all, that it cannot redeeme? *Isa.* l. 2. 6. Subiecte your selues whollye to God: for he hath redemed you 1558. 7. 1 *Hen. VI*, II. v. 108. 8. Walke wysely to them that are with out, and redeme the tyme TINDALE *Col.* iv. 5. 9. Which of ye will be mortal to r. Man's mortal crime? MILT. c. The Babe..That on the bitter cross Must r. our loss MILT. 10. His bravery had redeemed much of his earlier ill-fame GREEN. 11. With his barb'd horse..Stout Cromwell has redeem'd the day SCOTT. Hence **Redee·mless** *a.* irrecoverable; admitting of no redemption.

Redeemable (rĭdī·măb'l), *a.* and *sb.* 1611. [f. prec. + -ABLE.] A. *adj.* Capable of being redeemed. b. *spec.* Of property sold or mortgaged, bonds, stock, annuities, etc.: Capable or admitting of being repurchased or bought in again 1646.

b. The same is hereby created to the amount of £600,000 as a r. stock 1882.

B. *sb. pl.* Redeemable property, stocks, annuities, etc. Now *rare.* 1720. Hence **Redeemabi·lity** (*rare*). **Redee·mableness,** capability of being redeemed. **Redee·mably** *adv.*

Redeemer (rĭdī·məɹ). ME. [f. REDEEM *v.* + -ER [1].] 1. One who redeems, in religious sense; God or Christ regarded as saving man from sin or its effects. 2. One who redeems, in other senses of the vb. 1552.

1. Mans Friend, his Mediator, his design'd Both Ransom and R. voluntarie MILT.

Redeless (rī·dlės), *a.* *Obs.* exc. *arch.* [OE. *rǣdléas*; see REDE *sb.* and -LESS.] Devoid or destitute of counsel; *esp.* of persons, having no resource in a difficulty or emergency, not knowing what to do.

Redemise (rīdĭməi·z), *sb.* 1797. [RE-.] *Law.* The retransfer of land to one who has demised it. So **Redemi·se** *v. trans.* to demise (land) back again.

Redemption (rĭde·mᵖʃən). ME. [a. F., or ad. L. *redemptionem, redimere.*] 1. Deliverance from sin and its consequences by the atonement of Jesus Christ. 2. The action of freeing a prisoner, captive, or slave by payment; ransom. late ME. b. *Jewish Law.* The ceremony of redeeming the eldest son by an offering (Numb. xviii. 15). late ME. 3. The action of freeing, delivering, or restoring in some way 1470. b. That which redeems; a redeeming feature 1860. 4. The action of redeeming oneself from punishment; way or means of doing this; atonement 1468. †b. A recompense. BACON. 5. The fact of obtaining a privileged status, or admission to a society, by means of purchase 1500. 6. The action of clearing off a recurring liability or charge by payment of a single sum 1494. 7. The action of redeeming or buying back from another, in various applications 1548.

1. Proclaiming Life to all who shall believe In his r. MILT. *Year of Redemption* = ANNO DOMINI. 2. The r. of captives..is esteemed an act of piety MILMAN. 3. Phr. *Without* or *past r.*, without or beyond the possibility of deliverance, recovery, or restoration. 6. R. of the tolls 1867. 7. An Act for the more easy R. and Foreclosure of Mortgages 1734. *Equity of r.*: see EQUITY 5. Hence **Rede·mptional** *a.* of or belonging to r. †**Rede·mptionary**, one who enters a society by purchase. **Rede·mptionist**, †(*a*) a redeemer; (*b*) = RANSOMER 2 a. **Rede·mptionless** *a.* incapable of r.

Redemptioner (rǐde·mᵖʃənəɹ). 1617. [-ER¹.] †1. = REDEMPTIONARY. 2. *U.S.* An emigrant who received his passage to America on the condition that his services there should be disposed of by the master or owners of the vessel, until the passage-money and other expenses were repaid out of his earnings 1775. 3. One who clears off a charge by redemption 1897.

Redemptive (rǐde·mᵖtiv), *a.* 1647. [ad. L. *redemptivus; see -IVE.] Tending to redeem, redeeming.

Redemptor (rǐde·mᵖtǫɹ). Now *rare.* late ME. [a. or ad. F. *rédempteur*, or L. *redemptor*, f. *redimere.*] †1. = REDEEMER 1 -1634. 2. A redeemer, in other senses of the word (*rare*) 1880.

1. I wote ryght well that myn redemptour Lyueth yet 1400.

Redemptorist (rǐde·mᵖtŏrist). 1835. [ad. F. *rédemptoriste*; see prec. and -IST.] 1. A member of the Roman Catholic Congregation of the Most Holy Redeemer, founded at Naples in 1732 by St. Alphonsus Liguori, and devoted chiefly to work among the poor. 2. *attrib.* or *adj.* Belonging to this Order 1863.

Redemptory (rǐde·mᵖtŏri), *a.* Now *rare.* 1598. [ad. L. type *redemptorius; see -ORY².] Of or pertaining to redemption; redemptive.

†**Redevable**, *a.* (and *sb.*). 1502. [ad. F., f. *redevoir* + -ABLE.] Beholden, indebted. Also as *sb.*, a debtor. -1711.

Red fish, re·d-fish. late ME. 1. A male salmon in the spawning season, when it assumes a red colour. b. The salmon, in contrast to 'white' fish 1851. 2. a. The red gurnard, *Trigla cuculus* 1611. b. Any of various American fishes, *esp.* the blue-backed salmon (*Oncorhyncus nerka*) and the red perch or rose-fish 1876.

Re·d gum, re·d-gum¹. 1597. [Alteration of earlier *radegounde*, *red-gown(d*, *-gown*, the second element of which is OE. *gund* pus.] 1. A papular eruption or rash (*Strophulus intertinctus*) incident to young children, esp. during dentition, consisting of red pimples and patches irregularly disposed on the skin. *Rank red gum*, a virulent form of this (*Strophulus confertus*). 2. A form of rust in grain 1807.

Re·d gum, re·d-gum². 1738. 1. A reddish resinous substance exuded from the bark of various tropical or semi-tropical trees and shrubs, esp. that obtained from various Australian species of Eucalyptus. 2. A tree of one or other of the Australian species yielding a red gum; also, the wood of these trees 1802.

Red hand, red-hand, *a.* and *sb.* late ME. A. *adj.* 1. *Sc.* (orig. *Law*). = next 1. 2. = next 1 c. 1894. B. *sb.* 1. In phr. *with (the) red hand* = A. 1. Now *rare.* 1577. 2. *Her.* (See quot.) 1856.

2. The open red hand..,the noted *Lamh derg Eirin*, or red hand of Ulster 1863.

Red-handed, *a.* 1805. 1. In the very act of crime, having the evidences of guilt still upon the person, esp. in phr. *to take*, or *be taken*, *red-handed* 1819. b. Having the hands red with blood 1861. c. That sheds or has shed blood; bloody, sanguinary, violent 1879. 2. Having red hands 1805.

Re·d-head, re·dhead. ME. 1. *attrib.* Having a red head or hair 1664. 2. One who has a red head or hair ME. 3. Applied to various birds, *esp.* the American pochard and red-headed woodpecker 1814. So **Red-headed** (stress var.) *a.* having red hair; having a red head, esp. in names of birds, as **red-headed woodpecker**, *Melanerpes erythrocephalus.*

Red heat, red-heat. 1686. The state or condition of being red-hot; the degree of heat present when a substance is red-hot.

Red herring. late ME. *collect.* Herring to which a red colour is imparted in the process of curing them by smoke. b. A single herring cured in this way 1460.

Phr. *Neither fish, (nor) flesh, nor good red herring*, etc.: see FISH *sb.*¹ 3. *To draw a red h. across the track*, to attempt to divert attention from the real question; hence *red-herring*, a subject intended to have this effect.

Red-hot (stress var.), *a* (and *sb.*). late ME. 1. Heated to redness. b. *absol.* as *sb.* Red-hot metal 1832. 2. *fig.* a. Of persons: Highly inflamed or excited; fiery; violently enthusiastic, extreme (in some view or principle). Also as *sb.* 1608. b. Of things, actions, etc.: Burning, scorching, urgent, violent, furious, etc. 1647. c. Very warm (as the favourite for a race) 1882. 3. *Red-hot poker*, the flame-flower (*Tritoma*) 1897.

1. Showers of r. ashes 1878. 2. A r. Predestinarian WESLEY. b. A r. flirtation 1879.

‖**Redia** (rī·diă). *Pl.* **rediæ** (rī·dīī). 1877. [mod.L., f. *Redi*, name of an Italian naturalist.] *Zool.* An asexual stage in some trematodes, as the liver-fluke (*Distomum hepaticum*), hatched from eggs formed within the sporocyst, and in turn developing into a cercaria.

Redingote (re·dingōᵘt). 1835. [a. F., corruption of Eng. *riding-coat.*] a. In France: A double-breasted outer coat for men, with long plain skirts not cut away in the front. b. A similar garment worn by women, sometimes cut away in front.

†**Redintegrate,** *pa. pple.* 1501. [ad. L. *redintegratus*; see next.] Restored to a perfect state, renewed -1819.

Redintegrate (redi·ntǐgreᵉit), *v.* late ME. [f. L. *redintegrat-*, *redintegrare*, f. *red-* RE- + *integrare* to INTEGRATE.] 1. *trans.* To restore to a state of wholeness, completeness or unity; to renew, re-establish, in a united or perfect state. †2. To re-establish (a person) *in* a place (*rare*) -1649. b. To re-establish (a person) *in* (†*into*) a position, condition, etc. Chiefly *pass.* Now *rare.* 1622.

1. To r. the Honour and Credit of that exploded Faction 1734. 2. b. I..had to pay the..taxes..before I could be redintegrated in my own property THACKERAY.

Redintegration (redintǐgrēⁱ·ʃən). 1471. [ad. L. *redintegrationem*; see prec.] 1. The action of redintegrating; restoration, re-establishment, reconstruction, renewal 1501. 2. *spec.* †a. *Chem.* The restoration of any body or matter to its former state -1802. b. *Psychol.* (See quot.) 1836. †3. The restoration of a person to a previous condition -1741. †4. Reconciliation -1667.

1. A r. of love THACKERAY. 2. b. The law of R. or Totality..Those thoughts suggest each other which had previously constituted parts of the same entire or total act of cognition SIR W. HAMILTON.

Redire·ct, *a.* 1891. [RE- 5 a.] *U.S. Law.* The term applied to the further examination of a witness by the party calling him, after cross-examination by the opposing party.

Redisseisin (rīdisī·zin). 1535. [a. AF. *redisseisine*; see RE- and DISSEISIN.] *Law.* Repeated disseisin.

Redistri·bute, *v.* 1611. [RE- 5 a.] *trans.* To distribute anew. So **Redistribu·tion**, a fresh distribution, esp. of Parliamentary seats.

Redi·strict, *v.* *U.S.* 1850. [RE- 5 a.] *trans.* To divide or apportion anew into districts.

†**Redi·tion.** *rare.* 1595. [ad. L. *reditionem*, *redire*, f. *re(d)-* RE- + *ire* to go.] The action of going or coming back; return -1656.

Red lead, red-lead (-led). 1450. A red oxide of lead, largely used as a pigment.

Re·d-legs, re·d-leg. 1802. 1. *Ornith.* Any of various birds with red legs; *esp.* the redshank (*Totanus calidris*), the red-legged partridge (*Caccabis rufa*), and (*U.S.*) the turnstone (*Strepsilas interpres*). 2. The plant bistort (*Polygonum bistorta*) 1820.

Red letter. late ME. 1. (Chiefly *pl.*) A letter made with red ink, or with some red pigment, esp. as used in eccl. calendars to indicate saints' days and church festivals. 2. *attrib.* as *red-letter almanac*, etc.; †**red-letter man**, a Roman Catholic 1677. b. **Red-letter day**, a saint's day or church festival indicated in the calendar by red letters; hence, any memorable, fortunate, or specially happy day 1776.

Re·d man, red-man. 1610. †1. *Alchemy.* Red sulphide of mercury. B. JONS. 2. A N. American Indian; a redskin 1744.

Re-do·, redo, *v.* 1597. 1. *trans.* To do over again or afresh. b. To redecorate (a room) 1864. †2. To do back or in return -1650.

Red ochre. 1572. A variety of ochre commonly used for colouring with; reddle or ruddle. Also *attrib.* Hence **Red-ochre** *v. trans.*

Redolence (re·dŏlĕns). late ME. [a. OF., f. *redolent*; see -ENCE.] Sweet smell, fragrance, perfume. Also *fig.* So †**Re·dolency.**

Redolent (re·dŏlent), *a.* late ME. [a. OF., or L. *redolentem*, *redolere*, f. *re(d)-* RE- + *olere* to emit a smell.] 1. Having or diffusing a pleasant odour; sweet-smelling, fragrant, odorous. Now *rare.* 2. Of smell, odour, etc.: Pleasant, sweet, fragrant 1450. 3. Odorous or smelling *of* or *with* something; full of the scent or smell *of* 1700.

1. The r. breath Of the warm seawind TENNYSON. 2. All manner of r. Odors 1629. 3. The gales..seem.., r. of joy and youth, To breathe a second spring GRAY. *fig.* On every side Oxford is r. of age and authority EMERSON.

Redouble (rǐdɒ·b'l), *v.*¹ 1477. [a. F. *redoubler* (f. *re-* RE- + *doubler* to DOUBLE).] 1. *trans.* To double (a thing); to make twice as great or as much. b. *intr.* To be doubled. Also, to become doubly strong *in* some respect. 1490. 2. *trans.* To repeat; to do, say, etc., a second time 1581. b. *esp.* To repeat (a blow, etc.) 1593. †3. To repeat (a sound); to return, reproduce, re-echo -1679. b. *intr.* To re-echo, resound 1725. 4. *trans.* To duplicate by reflection 1827.

1. This made our people r. their efforts 1748. 2. b. Let thy blowes doubly redoubled, Fall like amazing thunder SHAKS. 3. Their moans The Vales redoubl'd to the Hills, and they To Heav'n MILT.

Redouble (rīdɒ·b'l), *v.*² 1530. [RE- 5 a.] To double again (esp. in *Bridge*).

Redoubt (rǐdau·t), *sb.* †Also **redout(e.** 1608. [ad. F. *redoute*, *ridotte*, ad. It. *ridotto* :—med.L. *reductus* a secret place, a refuge, f. L. *reductus* retired, pa. pple. of *reducere* to REDUCE.] 1. *Fortif.* †a. A small work made in a bastion or ravelin of a permanent fortification, or (*detached r.*) at some distance beyond the glacis, but within musket-shot from the covert-way. b. A species of out-work or field-work, usu. of a square or polygonal shape, and with little or no means of flanking defence. 2. *Fortif.* = REDUIT 1802.

1. b. *fig.* Conservatism, entrenched in its immense redoubts EMERSON.

Redoubt (rǐdau·t), *v.* Now *rhet.* late ME. [ad. F. *redouter*, †*redoubter*, f. *re-* RE- + *douter* to DOUBT.] *trans.* To dread, fear, stand in awe or apprehension of. Hence **Redou·bted** *ppl. a.* feared or dreaded; reverenced; noted, distinguished.

Redoubtable (rǐdau·tăb'l), *a.* (and *sb.*) late ME. [a. F. *redoutable*, †*redoubt-*; see prec.] To be feared or dreaded; formidable. †Also, of persons: Commanding respect.

That you marry this r. couple together—Righteousness and Peace CROMWELL. That spear, r. in war BURNS.

Redound (rǐdau·nd), *v.* late ME. [ad. F. *rédonder* :—L. *redundare*, f. *re(d)-* RE- + *undare* to surge, f. *unda.*] I. *intr.* †1. Of water, waves, etc.: To swell or surge up, to overflow -1725. †b. *transf.* To be in excess or superfluous -1667. †2. To be plentiful, abound -1581. †3. To flow, come, or go back; to return (*to* a place or person); to come again -1596. †4. To resound, reverberate, re-echo -1632. 5. To result in contributing or turning *to* some advantage or disadvantage for a person or thing. late ME. b. To turn *to* one's honour, disgrace, etc. 1474. 6. Of advantage, damage, praise, etc.: To result, attach, accrue *to*, *unto* (a person) 1500. **7.** Of honour or disgrace, advantage, etc.: To recoil or come back, to fall, *upon* a person 1589. †**8.** To proceed, issue, arise *from* or *out of* something –1796.

1. Round the descending nymph the waves redounding roar POPE. 5. Which could not but mightily r. to the good of the Nation MILT. b. Affyrming that it would redounde to the perpetuall shame of Germany 1560. 6. The clear gain redounding to the Commonwealth SWIFT. 8. The anxietie of spirit which redoundeth from knowledge BACON.

†**II.** *trans.* **1.** To reflect (honour, blame, etc.) *in, to, upon* a person –1712. **2.** To add, yield, cause to accrue –1690.

1. For fear they should r. Dishonour upon the Innocent STEELE. Hence **Redou·nd** *sb.* (*rare*) reverberation, echo; a resounding cry; also, the fact of redounding.

||**Redowa** (re·dŏvä). Also **redowak.** 1860. [a. F. or G. *redowa*, ad. Boh. *reydovák*, f. *reydovati* to turn or whirl round.] A slow waltz, of Bohemian origin, resembling the mazurka; also, the music for such a dance.

Re·dpoll[1], **-pole.** 1738. [f. RED *a.* + *pole* POLL.] **1.** Any of several species of the family *Fringillidæ* characterized by bright red feathers on the crest. **a.** The greater r., the male of the common linnet in summer plumage. **b.** The lesser or common r., a common British cage-bird, *Linota rufescens* or *Ægiothus linaria*. **c.** The mealy or stone r., *Ægiothus canescens*. Also the allied American species (*Æ. exilipes*). **2.** *Yellow r.*, an American warbler, *Dendræca palmarum*; the palm-warbler 1758. So **Re·dpolled** *a.* red-headed.

Re·dpoll[2], **-polled.** 1895. *pl.* Red-haired polled cattle.

Redraft (rīdrɑ·ft), *sb.* 1682. [RE- 5 a.] **1.** A bill of re-exchange. **2.** A second or new draft 1847.

Redraft (rīdrɑ·ft), *v.* 1798. [RE- 5 a.] *trans.* To draft again (a writing or document).

Red rag, red-rag. 1700. **1.** *slang.* The tongue. **2.** A variety of rust in grain 1851. **3.** (From the phr. *like a red rag to a bull.*) A source of extreme provocation or annoyance 1885.

Redraw (rīdrǭ·), *v.* 1692. [RE- 5 a.] **1.** *intr.* To draw a fresh bill of exchange to cover a former one. **2.** *trans.* To draw or take out again 1805. **3.** To draw (a picture, etc.) again 1830. Hence **Redraw·er.**

Redress (rīdre·s), *sb.* late ME. [a. AF. *redresse*, *-dresce*, f. *redresser* to REDRESS.] **1.** Reparation of, satisfaction or compensation for, a wrong sustained or the loss resulting from this. †**2.** Remedy for, or relief from, some trouble; assistance, aid, help –1759. †**b.** Correction, amendment, or reformation of something wrong –1764. †**3.** With *a* and *pl.* A means or way of redress; an act or arrangement whereby a person or thing is redressed; an amendment, improvement –1728. †**b.** One who, or that which, affords redress –1697. **4.** The act of redressing; correction or amendment *of* a thing, state, etc. 1538.

1. He who gives credit, and is cheated, will have no r. 1875. 2. My griefs..finding no r., ferment and rage MILT. Phr. †*Beyond, past, without r.*, beyond the possibility of remedy, aid, or amendment. 3. b. Fair majesty, the refuge and r. Of those whom fate pursues and wants oppress DRYDEN. 4. The great principle that r. of wrongs precedes a grant to the Crown GREEN.

Redress (rīdre·s), *v.*[1] late ME. [ad. F. *redresser*; see RE- and DRESS *v.*] †**1.** *trans.* To set (a person or thing) upright again; to raise again to an erect position –1711. †**2.** *fig.* To bring back to the right course; to correct or direct aright –1689. †**b.** To direct or amend (one's acts or ways) –1635. †**3.** To put (things) in order; to arrange –1585. †**4.** To put right, or in good order, again; to mend, repair; to reform, amend –1764. **b.** To correct, emend (*rare*) 1710. **c.** To adjust again. (Chiefly with *balance.*) 1847. †**5.** To restore (a person) to happiness or prosperity; to save, deliver *from* misery, death, etc. –1583. **6.** To set (a person) right, by obtaining, or (occas.) giving, satisfaction or compensation for the wrong or loss sustained. late ME. **7.** To remedy or remove (trouble or distress of any kind). late ME. **8.** To set right, repair, rectify (a wrong, injury, grievance, etc.). late ME. **9.** To correct, amend, reform or do away with (a bad or faulty state of things, now *esp.* an abuse). late ME. †**10.** To repair (an action); to atone for (a misdeed or offence) –1597.

1. To..r. a leaning Wall SHAFTESB. 2. b. Wherewith shal a yong man redresse his waie? BIBLE (Genev.) *Ps.* cxix. 9. 4. Rise God, judge thou the earth in might, This wicked earth r. MILT. b. The material estimate of worth should be redressed by a moral standard 1868. 6. 'Tis thine, O King, the afflicted to r. DRYDEN. 7. Such carbuncles..As no Hungarian water can r. 1687. You will..r. a Misfortune 1714. 8. To r. grievances HUME. To prevent or r. the threatened outrage 1863. 9. In a vigorous campaign he pacified Ireland while redressing the abuses of its government GREEN. Hence **Redre·ssable** *a.* **Redre·ssal**, redress. **Redre·sser**, one who redresses (*esp.* a wrong). **Redre·ssive** *a.* (*rare*) seeking to redress; bringing redress. **Redre·ssment**, the act of redressing; redress.

Redress (rīdre·s), *v.*[2] 1739. [RE- 5 a.] *trans.* and *intr.* To dress again.

Redre·ssor. 1884. [f. REDRESS *v.*[1] + -OR [1].] One who, or that which, redresses; *spec.* in *Surg.* (see quot.).

Redressor, a replacing instrument, e. g. the uterine r. 1884.

Red-sha·nk(s, re·dshank. 1500. **1.** One who has red legs; *spec.* (chiefly in *pl.*) one of the Celtic inhabitants of the Scottish Highlands and of Ireland. Now *Hist.* 1542. **2.** *Ornith.* A wading bird (*Totanus calidris*) of the snipe family (*Scolopacidæ*), so called from the colour of its legs 1500. **b.** Applied also, with defining word, to *Tetanus fuscus*, the Black, Dusky, or Spotted R. 1776.

attrib.: **red-shank gull**, the black-headed gull, *Larus ridibundus*.

†**Re·dshire, -share,** *a.* 1665. [ad. Sw. *rödskör*; see next.] *Metall.* = next –1794.

Re·d-short, *a.* 1730. [ad. Sw. *rödskört* (sc. *jern* iron), neut. of *rödskör*, f. *röd* red + *skör* brittle; cf. COLD-SHORT.] *Metall.* Of iron: Brittle while in a red-hot condition, owing to excess of sulphur in the metal. Hence **Re·d-shortness**, the quality or state of being r.

Re·dskin. 1699. [See RED A. 5 c.] A North American Indian.

Red snow. 1678. **1.** Snow reddened by a kind of alga (*Protococcus nivalis*), common in Arctic and Alpine regions. **2.** *transf.* The alga which gives a red colouring to snow 1825.

Redstart (re·dstɑɹt). 1570. [f. RED *a.* + START *sb.*[1]] *Ornith.* **1.** A common European singing-bird (*Ruticilla phœnicurus*), so named from its red tail, which it has a habit of moving quickly from side to side. **b.** *Black r.*, a related species, *Ruticilla titys*, occurring in southern England and common on the European continent 1836. **2.** An American fly-catching warbler, *Setophaga ruticilla*, outwardly resembling the common European redstart but generically distinct from it 1796.

Re·d-streak. Also †**-strake.** 1664. **1.** A red-streaked apple formerly highly esteemed for making cider. **b.** The cider made from this 1671. **2.** *transf.* A girl with red cheeks 1771.

Red-tape, red tape. 1696. **a.** Tape of a pinkish-red colour such as is commonly used in securing legal and other documents. Hence **b.** Excessive formality or attention to routine; rigid or mechanical adherence to rules and regulations. Also *attrib.*

His brain was little better than red tape and parchment W. IRVING. Hence **Red-ta·pism, -ta·peism**, the system or spirit of red-tape. **Red-ta·pist, -ta·peist**, one who adheres strictly or mechanically to official routine.

Re·d-top. 1800. **1.** *attrib.* Having a red top; red-topped. **2.** *U.S.* A kind of bent-grass, *Agrostis vulgaris*, highly valued for pasture. *Tall red-top*, a tall reddish grass, *Triodea cuprea*. 1819. **3.** A variety of turnip 1830.

†**Redu·b,** *v.* 1522. [ad. AF. *redubber*, f. *re-* RE- + *dubber* DUB *v.*[1]] *trans.* To repair or restore; to put right, remedy, improve, amend, redress –1568.

Reduce (rīdiū·s), *v.* late ME. [ad. L. *reducere* to bring back, f. *re-* RE- + *ducere* to lead, bring.] **I.** *trans.* †**1.** To bring back, recall (a thing or person) *to* the memory, mind, etc. –1624. †**b.** To bring back, recall (the mind, thoughts, etc.) *from* or *to* a subject –1706. †**2.** To lead or bring back *to, into, from*, etc. a place or way, or *to* a person –1731. †**3.** To take back, refer (a thing) *to* its origin or author –1660. **4.** To bring back, restore (a condition, state of things, time, etc.). Now *rare.* 1477. **5.** *Surg.* To restore (a dislocated, fractured, or ruptured part) to the proper position 1541. **b.** To adjust, set (a dislocation or fracture) 1836.

4. Abate the edge of Traitors..That would r. these bloudy dayes againe SHAKS.

II. †**1.** To lead or bring back from error in action, conduct, or belief; to restore to the truth or the right faith –1788. †**2.** To bring back or restore (a person, etc.) *from* or *to* a state or condition –1741. †**b.** To bring back (a thing, institution, etc.) *to* a former state. Also without const. –1765. †**3.** To bring (a person or thing) *to* or *into* a certain state or condition or *to* do something –1719. **b.** To bring (a theory, etc.) *to* (or *into*) practice or action 1625. †**4.** To adapt (a thing) *to* a purpose. *rare.* –1609. **b.** *Astron.* To adapt (an observation) *to* a particular place or point 1633. †**5. a.** To bring *into* another language; to render, translate –1581. **b.** To set down or record in writing; to put down or draw in a map –1603. **6.** To bring (†*into* or) *to* a certain order or arrangement 1570. **b.** To bring *to* (†*into* or *under*) a specified number of classes or heads; also, to assign or refer *to* a certain class 1526. **7.** To bring (†*into* or) *to* a certain form or character 1592. **b.** To put *into*, commit *to*, writing 1659. **8. a.** *Arith.* To change (a number or quantity) from one denomination *into* or *to* another 1579. **b.** To change (a quantity, figure, etc.) *into* or *to* a different form. Also *absol.* 1579. **c.** To resolve by analysis. Const. *to.* 1860. **9.** To turn *to*, convert *into*, a different physical state or form; esp. to break down, grind, or crush *to* powder, etc. 1605. **b.** *Metall.* To convert (ore) into metal; to smelt 1758. **c.** *Chem.* To remove oxygen from (a compound); also to diminish the valency of (an atom, an element) towards electro-negative radicals 1741. **d.** To break up (soil) into fine particles 1763. **10.** *Logic.* To bring a syllogism (†or proposition) into a different but equivalent form, *spec.* to one of the moods of the first figure 1727.

6. The infinite would be no longer infinite, if limited or reduced to measure JOWETT. b. Those who set up for Criticks in Poetry..may be reduced to two Classes STEELE. 7. A second Word,..reducing it to the English Orthography may be spelt thus, Houyhnhnm SWIFT. 8. b. To R. an Integer to the Form of a Fraction 1797. 9. b. Several attempts had been made to r. iron ore with coaked coal 1839.

III. 1. To bring *to* (or *into*) order, obedience, reason, etc., by constraint or compulsion 1490. †**b.** To make subject *to* a person; to cause to give obedience or adherence *to*; to bring *into* or *under* a person's power, *within* bounds, etc. –1833. **c.** *Law.* To bring (a thing or right) *into* (†*to*) possession 1766. **2.** To bring (a place) into subjection, to subdue, conquer; *spec.* to capture (a town, fortress, etc.); to compel to submit or surrender 1612. **b.** To subdue, conquer (a person) 1598. **c.** To constrain, compel, force (a person) *to* do something 1622. †**d.** To subdue, repress, moderate (a desire, temper, etc.) –1725. **3.** To bring down *to* a bad or disagreeable condition 1572. **b.** In *pass.*, with *inf.* To be compelled by want *to* do something; also, to be hard put to it 1693. **c.** To weaken physically 1734. **d.** To diminish the strength of (spirit) 1880. **4.** To bring down *to* a lower rank or position, dignity, etc. 1641. †**5.** *Mil.* To break up, disband (an army or regiment) –1802. **b.** To break up (a square, etc.) and restore the component parts to line or column 1672.

1. The clergy could not be allowed to r. Crown and barons into entire submission to their own pleasure FROUDE. 2. Chester was reduced by famine DE FOE. c. A blow..reduced him to measure his length on the ground FIELDING. 3. Reduced almost to penury 1820. b. Poor creature! he was reduced..to borrow five guineas of Sir Francis Dashwood H. WALPOLE. 4. Phr. *To r. to the ranks* (*Mil.*), to degrade (a non-commissioned officer) to the rank of private.

IV. 1. To bring or draw together. (In later

use only as implying diminution of bulk.) late ME. 2. To bring down, diminish *to* a smaller number, amount, extent, etc., or *to* a single thing 1560. b. To lower, diminish, lessen 1787. c. *intr.* To become lessened or limited 1811.

1. Tom reduced himself into the least possible space DICKENS. 2. Thus incorporeal Spirits to smallest forms Reduc'd thir shapes immense MILT. Reduced to half-price 1762. Hence †**Redu·ceable** *a.* = REDUCIBLE. †**Redu·cement**, reduction. **Redu·cer**, one who, or that which, reduces.

Reducent (rĭdiū·sĕnt), *a.* (and *sb.*). 1805. [ad. L. *reducentem.*] A. *adj.* 1. *Bot.* and *Zool.* Of a vein, channel, etc.: That carries something back from a certain part. (Opp. to *adducent.*) 2. *Med.* Lowering 1822. B. *sb.* That which reduces 1847.

Reducible (rĭdiū·sĭb'l), *a.* 1450. [ad. L. **reducibilis*; see REDUCE *v.* and -IBLE.] That may be reduced. Hence **Reducibi·lity**. **Redu·cibleness**. **Redu·cibly** *adv.*

Reducing (rĭdiū·siŋ), *vbl. sb.* 1488. [-ING¹.] The action of REDUCE *v.*; reduction.

Comb.: r. **compasses**, compasses adapted for copying figures on a smaller scale; r. **coupling** or **piece**, a pipe-coupling with ends of different diameters, used in joining pipes of different sizes; r. **valve**, a valve serving to reduce the pressure in a steam-engine; r. **works**, a place at which metallic ore is reduced.

†**Redu·ct**, *v.* 1558. [f. ppl. stem of L. *reducere.*] 1. *trans.* To bring, lead, lead back –1816. 2. To deduct (a sum) –1738.

‖**Reductio ad absurdum** (rĭdʊ·kʃio æd æbsɔ̄·ɹdɒ̆m): see REDUCTION II. 4.

Reduction (rĭdʊ·kʃən). 1474. [a. F., or ad. L. *reductionem.*] I. †1. The action of bringing (back) *to* or *from* a state, condition, belief, etc. –1677. †2. The action of bringing back (a person, thing, institution, etc.) to a place previously occupied; restoration –1741. 3. *Surg.* The restoration of a dislocated part to its normal position; the action of reducing a displacement, etc. 1656.

2. The whole History of their R. out of Egypt WARBURTON.

II. 1. Conquest or subjugation *of* a place, esp. a town or fortress 1474. b. The action of reducing *into* possession. Also without const. 1647. c. [ad. Sp. *reduccion.*] A settlement or colony of S. Amer. Indians converted and governed by the Jesuits 1712. 2. a. *Arith.* (*a*) The process of changing an amount from one denomination to another. (*b*) The process of bringing down a fraction to its lowest terms. 1542. b. *Alg.* (See quot.) 1702. c. *Astron.* The correction of observations by allowance for modifying circumstances, as parallax, refraction, etc. 1812. 3. *Logic.* The process of reducing a syllogism (†or proposition) to another, esp. to a simpler or clearer, form; *spec.* by expressing it in one of the moods of the first figure (*direct* or *ostensive r.*). Also, the process of establishing the validity of a syllogism by showing that the contradictory of its conclusion is inconsistent with its premisses (*indirect* or *apagogical r.*). 1551. 4. Conversion *into* or *to* a certain state, form, etc. 1605. 5. The action or process of reducing (a substance) to another (usu. a simpler) form, *esp.* by some chemical process 1650. b. The conversion of ore into metal; smelting 1797. 6. Diminution, lessening, cutting down 1676. b. The action or process of making a copy on a smaller scale; also, a copy of this kind 1727.

1. The r. of Syracuse THIRLWALL. 2. b. *R. of equations*..is the reducing them into a fit and proper Order or Disposition for a Solution 1702. 4. Phr. *R. to the absurd* or *to absurdity* (= L. *reductio ad absurdum*), a method of proving the falsity of a premiss, principle, etc., by showing that the conclusion or consequence is absurd; also, loosely, the pushing of anything to an absurd extreme. 6. Not one shilling towards the r. of our debt BURKE.

Comb.: r. **compasses**, reducing compasses; **-works**, works for the reduction of metallic ore.

Reductive (rĭdʊ·ktiv), *a.* and *sb.* Now *rare.* 1633. [f. as REDUCT *v.* + -IVE.] 1. That leads or brings back. Also with *of.* 1655. 2. That reduces, or serves to reduce; connected with, of the nature of, reduction. Also with *of.* 1633. †3. That may be referred to or derived from something else; reducible –1691. 4. *absol.* as *sb.* That which tends to reduce 1676. Hence **Redu·ctively** *adv.* (now *rare*), by reduction; by consequence or inference 1624.

‖**Reduit** (redwi). 1604. [F. *réduit* :—L. *reductus.* Cf. REDOUBT.] *Fortif.* A keep or stronghold into which a garrison may retire when the outworks are taken.

Redundance (rĭdʊ·ndăns). 1596. [ad. L. *redundantia*; see REDUNDANT and -ANCE.] = next.

Redundancy (rĭdʊ·ndănsi). 1601. [See prec. and -ANCY.] The state or quality of being redundant; superabundance, superfluity. Also with *a* and *pl.*, an instance of this. b. A redundant thing or part 1631. c. That which is redundant; the surplus 1733.

c. It is not the whole of the people..It is only the r. that we have to take care of. 1832.

Redundant (rĭdʊ·ndănt), *a.* and *sb.* 1596. [ad. L. *redundantem*; see REDOUND.] 1. Superabundant, superfluous, excessive. b. Characterized by superfluity or excess in some respect. Also const. *in.* 1638. 2. Abounding to excess or fullness; plentiful, copious, exuberant 1671. b. Characterized by copiousness, fullness, or abundance. Also const. *of*, *with.* 1653. †3. a. Flowing or swelling, wave-like –1726. †b. Swelling up, overflowing –1774. †B. *sb.* Something redundant –1797.

1. The employment of r. capital MACAULAY. b. Milton frequently uses..the hypermetrical or r. line of eleven syllables JOHNSON. 2. These r. locks Robustious to no purpose clustring down MILT. 3. a. The vest unbound Floats in bright waves r. o'er the ground POPE. b. R. Nile, Broke from its channel, overswells the pass 1719. Hence **Redu·ndantly** *adv.*

Reduplicate (rĭdiū·plikĕt), *a.* and *sb.* 1647. [ad. late L. *reduplicatus*; see RE- and DUPLICATE *a.*] A. *adj.* 1. Doubled, repeated. b. *Gram.* Reduplicated; connected with or involving reduplication 1841. 2. *Bot.* Valvate, with the edges reflexed 1856. B. *sb.* A double (one), a duplicate 1657.

Reduplicate (rĭdiū·plikeɪt), *v.* 1570. [f. ppl. stem of med.L. *reduplicare*, f. *re-* RE- + *duplicare* to DUPLICATE.] 1. *trans.* To make double; to repeat, redouble. b. *Gram.* To repeat (a letter or syllable); to form (a tense) by reduplication 1832. 2. *intr.* To become double or doubled (*rare*) 1709.

Reduplication (rĭdiūplikēɪ·ʃən). 1589. [ad. late L. *reduplicationem*; see prec. and -ATION.] †1. The action of doubling or folding. PUTTENHAM. b. A double or fold (*rare*) 1698. 2. The action of making or becoming double or two-fold; repetition; also, a double or counterpart 1649. b. Repetition of a word (or phrase) 1619. †3. *Logic.* The repetition of a term with a limiting or defining force; the addition of some limiting term to one already used, or the sense of a term as thus limited –1741. 4. *Gram.* Repetition of a syllable or letter, *esp.* in the perfect tense of verbs in Greek and other Indo-European languages 1650. b. A word-form produced by repetition of a syllable 1862.

4. *Attic r.*, the form exemplified in Gr. ἀκήκοα from ἀκούω, ἤγαγον from ἄγω.

Reduplicative (rĭdiū·plikĕtiv), *a.* 1605. [f. L. *reduplicat-*, *reduplicare* + -IVE.] 1. Of the nature of, pertaining or relating to, expressing or implying, reduplication of terms. (See prec. 3.) Now *rare.* b. Of propositions: Having a limiting repetition of the subject expressed 1704. 2. Formed by reduplication 1833. 3. *Bot.* = REDUPLICATE *a.* 2. 1866.

1. b. *R. Propositions*, are such wherein the Subject is repeated: Thus, Men, as Men, are Rational 1704. Hence **Redu·plicatively** *adv.*

Re·dwing, re·d-wing. 1645. *Ornith.* a. A common variety of thrush (*Turdus iliacus*), characterized by its red wings. b. The red-winged blackbird (*Agelæus phœniceus*) of N. America 1831. So **Red-winged** *a.* having red wings, as *red-winged blackbird* = b.

Re·dwood, *sb.* Also **red wood, red-wood.** 1633. 1. Wood of a red colour, obtained from many tropical trees; formerly applied esp. to such as were used for dyeing. 2. Any of various trees having a red wood, *esp.* a tall Californian timber-tree, *Sequoia sempervirens* 1716.

Ree (rī), *sb.* 1550. [Var. of REEVE *sb.*²] The female of the ruff.

Ree (rī), **rye** (rəi), *v. dial.* late ME. [Origin obsc.] *trans.* To clean or sift (winnowed grain, peas, etc.), *spec.* by giving a circular motion to the contents of the sieve, so that the chaff, etc. collects in the centre.

‖**Reebok** (rē·bɒk). 1775. [Du., = ROEBUCK.] A small S. African antelope, *Pelea capreola*, with sharp horns.

Re-e·cho, *v.* 1590. [f. RE- + ECHO *v.*] 1. *intr.* To echo (again), resound. 2. *trans.* a. To echo back; to return (a sound), reverberate, multiply by repetition 1595. b. To repeat like an echo 1636.

1. The thunder of the avalanche Re-echoes far behind SOUTHEY. 2. a. Severn shall reecho with affright The shrieks of death GRAY. b. Those who still r. Ricardo and Malthus 1875. So **Re-e·cho** *sb.* an echo; also, a second or repeated echo.

Reechy (rī·tʃi), *a. Obs.* exc. *dial.* 1460. [f. *reech*, REEK *sb.* + -Y¹.] Smoky; squalid, dirty; rancid.

Reed (rīd), *sb.* [Com. WGer.; OE. *hrēod* :—OTeut. **hreuđom*.] I. 1. One of the tall straight stalks or stems formed by plants of the genera *Phragmites* and *Arundo*; †also, a cane. 2. *collect.* Reeds (as plants); a growth or bed of reeds OE. b. Reeds employed for firing or thatching, or for plastering upon 1494. c. *transf.* Wheat-straw prepared for thatching. late ME. 3. Without article, as a material ME. 4. With *the*, as the distinctive name of the class of plants forming the genera *Phragmites* and *Arundo*, having a firm stem and growing in water or marshy ground; *esp.* the common species *Phragmites communis*, abundant in Britain and on the Continent; †also, the sugar-cane. late ME.

4. Up stood the cornie Reed Embattell'd in her field MILT.

II. 1. a. A reed used as a dart or arrow; hence *poet.* an arrow. late ME. b. In biblical use: A reed employed as a measuring-rod; hence, a Jewish measure of length (also called *Ezekiel's r.*), equal to six cubits. late ME. 2. A reed made into a rustic musical pipe. Also *transf.*, esp. in *oaten r.* late ME. b. *fig.* as the symbol of rustic or pastoral poetry 1582. 3. A part of various musical instruments. a. In the oboe and bassoon: A part of the mouth-piece, consisting of two slightly concave wedge-shaped pieces of reed or cane fixed face to face on the end of a metal tube. Also, a similar device fixed in the chanter of a bagpipe. (Now freq. called a *double r.*) 1530. b. In the organ: A small metal tube fixed at the lower end of a pipe, having a longitudinal opening covered or closed by a metal tongue, which is made to vibrate by the air entering the tube 1727. c. (*a*) A metal tongue used to produce sound by vibration, *esp.* that used in an organ-pipe; (*b*) a slip of cane used for the same purpose, as in the clarinet. (Sometimes called *single r.*; cf. a.) 1811. 4. *Mining.* A tube containing the powder-train for igniting the charge in blasting 1875. 5. A weaver's instrument for separating the threads of the warp and beating up the weft, formerly made of thin strips of reed or cane, but now of metal wires, fastened by the ends into two parallel bars of wood 1611. 6. *Arch.* One of a set of small semicylindrical mouldings 1745.

1. b. He measured the East side with the measuring reede, fiue hundreth reedes *Ezek.* xlii. 16. 2. The.. sound of pastoral r. with oaten stops MILT. 3. c. *Beating* or *striking r.*, one which strikes against its seat; in the organ, against the edges of the opening in the tube. *Free r.*, one which produces sound by vibration only, esp. one which vibrates in the opening of a tube without touching the edges, as in instruments of the reed-organ type.

Comb.: r.-**babbler** = REED-WARBLER; **-bird**, a bird which frequents reeds; *spec.* a N. Amer. bobolink, *Dolichonyx oryzivorus*; **-buck**, the rietbok, or other antelope frequenting reeds; **-bunting**, the r.-sparrow, *Emberiza schœniclus*; **-grass**, any of various reed-like grasses, as the bur-r., bent, etc.; **-organ**, a musical instrument of the organ type in which the sounds are produced by means of reeds; **-pipe**, (*a*) a musical pipe made of r.; (*b*) an organ-pipe fitted with a r.; **-sparrow**, (*a*) a common British bird, *Emberiza schœniclus*, frequenting reedy places; (*b*) the sedge-warbler; **-stop**, an organ-stop composed of r.-pipes; **-wren**, the r.-warbler; also, any of various allied American birds.

Reed (rīd), *v.* 1440. [f. prec.] 1. *trans.* To thatch with reed. Chiefly *pass.* 2. To make (straw) into reed 1817. 3. To fashion into, or decorate with, reeds; to furnish with a reed-moulding 1823.

Reeded (rī·dėd), *ppl. a.* 1819. [f. REED *v.* and *sb.*] 1. Overgrown with reeds 1876. 2. Thatched with reed 1819. 3. Ornamented with reed-moulding 1833.

Reeden (rī·d'n), *a.* Now *rare.* late ME. [f. REED *sb.* + -EN[4].] Made or consisting of reed; reed-like.

Re:-edifica·tion. 1473. [a. OF., or med.L. *reædificationem.*] The action of rebuilding or state of being rebuilt. Now *rare* or *Obs.*

Re-edify (rī,e·difəi), *v.* late ME. [ad. OF. *reedifier* :—late L. *reædificare*, f. *re-* RE- + *ædificare* to EDIFY.] 1. *trans.* To rebuild (a house or other building, a wall, city, etc.). 2. *fig.* To rebuild, restore, re-establish 1540. 3. *transf.* To build up again physically 1897.

Reeding (rī·diŋ), *vbl. sb.* 1440. [f. REED *v.* + -ING[1].] 1. The action of REED *v.* 2. a. A small semicylindrical moulding; ornamentation of this form 1815. b. The milling on the edge of coins 1875.

Comb.: **r.-plane,** a plane used for making reeds in wood.

Reedling (rī·dliŋ). 1840. [f. REED *sb.* + -LING.] The bearded titmouse, *Panurus biarmicus*. Also called *bearded r.*

Reed-mace. 1548. [REED *sb.*] **a.** An aquatic plant, *Typha latifolia*, common on the margins of ponds and lakes, having long ensiform leaves and tall stems, the latter terminated by dense cylindrical spikes of small brownish flowers. (Also called *cat's-tail, cat-tail*, and *bulrush.*) **b.** The smaller species, *T. angustifolia.*

Reed-warbler. 1802. [REED *sb.*] **a.** A common British sylvioid bird, *Acrocephalus streperus*, frequenting reed-beds. **b.** A related species, *A. arundinaceus* (also called *reed-thrush* and *great reed-warbler*), occas. seen in Britain.

Reedy (rī·di), *a.* late ME. [f. REED *sb.* + -Y[1].] 1. Abounding with, full of, or characterized by the presence of reeds. 2. Made or consisting of reed or reeds; reeden 1763. 3. Resembling a reed or reeds 1628. 4. Having a tone resembling that produced by a musical reed 1811. b. Having a reedy voice 1855.

1. To Simois reedie bankes the red bloud ran SHAKS. 3. The leek with crown globose and r. stem CRABBE. R. coarse grass 1863. Hence **Ree·diness.**

Reef (rīf), *sb.*[1] *Pl.* **reefs, †reeves.** [ME. *riff, refe*, from (ult.) ON. *rif* in the same sense.] 1. *Naut.* One of the horizontal portions of a sail which may be successively rolled or folded up in order to reduce the extent of canvas exposed to the wind. Freq. in phr. *to take in a r.* (also in fig. context). 2. A mode of reefing 1829.

1. He is wasting away, and is obliged to take in reefs in his waistcoat 1885. 2. We tried a Spanish r., that is, let the yards come down on the cap MARRYAT.

Comb.: **r.-band,** a long piece of canvas sewn across the sail, for strengthening it in the place where the reef-holes are made; **-knot,** (*a*) a knot made in tying the reef-points; (*b*) a certain form of knot used for this and other purposes; hence **r.-knot** *v. trans.*, to tie with a reef-knot; **-point,** one of a set of short ropes fixed in a line along a reef-band to secure the sail when reefed.

Reef (rīf), *sb.*[2] 1584. [= Du. *rif*, MLG. *rif, ref* from (ult.) ON. *rif* in same sense (prob. a transf. use of *rif* rib).] 1. A narrow ridge or chain of rocks, shingle, or sand, lying at or near the surface of the water. 2. *Gold-mining* (orig. *Austral.*). a. A lode or vein of auriferous quartz 1858. b. The bed-rock 1869. 3. Short for *r.-sponge* 1883.

1. CORAL R., BARRIER-*r.*, etc.: see these words.

Comb.: **r.-builder,** a coral insect which builds reefs; **-heron,** an Australian heron of the genus *Demiegretta*, as *D. jugularis* or *D. sacra*; **-sponge,** a kind of sponge obtained in the W. Indies. Hence **Reef** *v.*[2] *intr.* to work at a (mining) reef. **Ree·fy** *a.* full of reefs.

Reef (rīf), *v.*[1] 1667. [f. REEF *sb.*[1]] 1. *trans.* To reduce the extent of (a sail) by taking in or rolling up a part and securing it. Also *absol.* 2. a. To shorten (a topmast) by lowering, or (a bowsprit) by sliding inboard 1704. b. To alter (a paddle) by moving the floatboards nearer to the centre of the wheel, in order to diminish the dip when the vessel is deep 1838. Hence **Reefed** (rīft) *ppl. a.*

Reefer (rī·fəɹ). 1829. [f. REEF *v.*[1] + -ER[1].] 1. One who reefs; *spec.* a slang name given to midshipmen 'because they have to attend in the tops during the operation of taking in reefs' (Smyth). 2. A reefing jacket 1883.

Reefing (rī·fiŋ), *vbl. sb.* 1750. [f. REEF *v.*[1] + -ING[1].] *Naut.* The action of REEF *v.*[1] b. *attrib.*, as *r. breeze, point*, etc.; **r.-jacket,** a particular form of close-fitting jacket made of stout heavy cloth 1856.

Reek (rīk), *sb.* [(Also w. dial. *reech.*); OE. *rēc*:—OTeut. **raukiz*, from a stem *reuk-, rouk-*, app. not found outside Teut.] 1. Smoke from burning matter. (Now *Sc.* and *n. dial.* In standard Eng. only in literary use, and chiefly applied to dense or unctuous smoke.) 2. Vapour or steam arising from, or given off by, something in a moist or heated state, as wet or marshy ground, wet clothes, boiling water, etc. late ME. b. *spec.* The vapour given off by hops in drying 1846. 3. An exhalation; a fume emanating from some body or substance; in mod. use, a strong and disagreeable fume or smell 1659. b. Impure, fetid atmosphere 1873.

3. A r. of gin and powder filled the chamber 1871.

Reek (rīk), *v.* [OE. *rēocan* (Northumb. *rēca*) intr., *rēcan* trans.: see prec.] 1. *intr.* To emit smoke. 2. To emit hot vapour or steam; to smoke with heat; to exhale vapour (or fog). *dial.* OE. 3. To emit an unwholesome or disagreeable vapour or fume; hence, to smell strongly or unpleasantly; to stink 1679. †4. Of smoke, vapour, perfume, etc.: To be emitted or exhaled; to rise, emanate, etc. –1599. 5. *trans.* To expose to smoke; to dry or taint with smoke; to fumigate. Also *techn.*, to coat (moulds for steel) with soot. OE. 6. To emit (smoke, steam, etc.) 1598.

1. The kilne began to reeke 1500. While temples crash, and towers in ashes r. KEBLE. 2. The Violence of Action hath made you r. as a Sacrifice SHAKS. 3. She literally reeked of garlic 1881. 4. *fig.* I heard your guilty Rimes..Saw sighes reeke from you SHAKS.

Reeky (rī·ki), *a.* late ME. [f. REEK *sb.* + -Y[1].] 1. a. That emits vapour; steamy; full of rank moisture. b. Emitting smoke, smoky 1604. 2. Consisting of or resembling smoke 1513. 3. Full of smoke 1576. b. Blackened with smoke 1859.

1. b. A reekie cole JAS. I.

Reel (rīl), *sb.*[1] [OE. *hrēol*; not in cogn. langs.] 1. A rotatory instrument on which thread is wound after it is spun, or silk as it is drawn from the cocoons. b. A similar framework on which other materials are wound at some stage in the process of manufacture, as the separate spun-yarns in rope-making, paper as it comes from the machine, etc. 1797. 2. An apparatus by which a cord, line, etc., may be wound up and unwound as required 1727. b. A device of this kind attached to a fishing-rod, on which the line is wound up 1726. c. *Off the r.*, in an uninterrupted course or succession 1837. 3. A small cylinder, usu. of wood, with a rim or wider part at each end, on which thread is commonly wound for ordinary use; a quantity of thread made up in this way 1784. b. A small cylinder on which any flexible substance is wound 1839. *spec.* A quantity of positive cinematographic film rolled on one reel 1926. 4. A rotatory apparatus in various machines; *esp.* in a reaping-machine, an arrangement of radial arms with horizontal bars at their extremities, which by its rotation presses the grain against the knives 1839.

Reel (rīl), *sb.*[2] 1572. [f. REEL *v.*[1]] A whirl or whirling movement; an act of reeling; a roll or stagger. †b. *pl.* Revels, revelry (*rare*).

The drunken r. Of vice and folly round him BROWNING. b. Drinke thou: encrease the Reeles SHAKS.

Reel (rīl), *sb.*[3] 1585. [perh. same word as prec.] 1. A lively dance, chiefly associated with Scotland, usu. danced by two couples facing each other, and describing a series of figures of eight. b. *transf.* (perh. sometimes assoc. w. prec. sb.) 1768. 2. The music for such a dance 1591.

1. *Virginia r.*, an American country-dance supposed to be derived from the English *Sir Roger de Coverley*. b. About, about, in r. and rout The death-fires danced at night COLERIDGE.

Reel (rīl), *v.*[1] late ME. [Possibly related to REEL *sb.*[1]] 1. *intr.* To whirl round or about; to go with a whirling motion. 2. Of the eyes: To whirl, with dizziness or excitement 1513. b. Of the mind, head, etc.: To be in a whirl, to be or become giddy or confused 1796. c. To have, or seem to have, a rapid quivering motion 1847. 3. Of an army, rank, line of battle, etc.: To waver, become unsteady, give way. late ME. b. Of persons (or animals): To sway or stagger as the result of a blow or encounter. Often with *back, backward.* late ME. 4. Of persons (or animals): To sway unsteadily from side to side, as if about to fall; to swing about with the whole body in trying to walk or stand, as the result of intoxication, faintness, etc. 1477. b. *transf.* of parts of the body, etc. 1590. 5. Of things: To shake, rock, or swing violently; to totter, tremble 1495. b. *fig.* Of kingdoms or institutions 1577. c. To fall or roll hurriedly (*rare*) 1593. 6. To walk with the body swinging violently from side to side; to make one's way in a swaying or staggering manner, esp. under the effects of intoxication 1607. b. To move, fly, or dash, rapidly and unsteadily 1727. 7. *trans.* To cause to roll, whirl, or stagger; to impel violently. Now *rare.* late ME. 8. To reel through or along (a street) SHAKS.

1. Thus the World doth, and evermore shall Reele DRAYTON. 2. b. My head reels, doctor 1881. 3. b. Cossack and Russian Reel'd from the sabre-stroke Shatter'd and sunder'd TENNYSON. 4. b. Knees which r. as marches quicken KINGSLEY. 5. So quick the run, We felt the good ship shake and r. TENNYSON. 6. To r. drunk about the streets 1849.

Reel (rīl), *v.*[2] late ME. [f. REEL *sb.*[1]] 1. *trans.* To wind (thread, silk, etc.) on a reel. Also *absol.* b. *Angling.* To wind (the line) on the reel. Also with *up*, and *absol.* 1854. 2. To take *off* by reeling 1530. b. *transf.* To rattle *off* (a story, song, etc.) without pause or effort 1837. 3. To draw *out*, as with a reel; to draw *through* (something), or cause to move, by means of a reel 1855. b. *Angling.* To draw in (a fish, etc.) by reeling up the line 1881.

2. b. General Butler..can r. off nautical stories by the yard 1885.

Reel (rīl), *v.*[3] 1768. [f. REEL *sb.*[3]] *intr.* and *trans.* To dance a reel.

Reeler (rī·ləɹ). 1598. [f. REEL *v.*[2] + -ER[1].] 1. One who reels or winds yarn, cord, etc., upon a reel; also, one who employs such workers. b. The grasshopper-warbler, *Locustella nævia* 1871. †2. An instrument for reeling (*rare*) –1629.

‖**Reem** (rīm). 1719. [a. Heb. *rᵉ'ēm*, rendered in the Vulgate by *rhinoceros* and *unicornis*.] An animal mentioned in the O.T., now identified with the wild ox.

Re-enfo·rce, *v.* 1586. [f. RE- + ENFORCE *v.* Now rare in English, but common in American use.] 1. *trans.* To strengthen, give fresh or additional strength to. 2. = REINFORCE 1. 1596. †b. To reassemble –1599. †3. *intr.* To renew one's efforts; to insist –1642.

1. Thou, Jehova,..With strength my weaknesse r. 1586. 2. b. The French haue re-enforc'd their scatter'd men SHAKS. So **Re-enfo·rcement,** the act of re-enforcing, or the state of being re-enforced; that which re-enforces; a fresh supply.

Re-enter (rī,e·ntəɹ), *v.* 1442. [RE- 5 a + ENTER *v.*] 1. *intr.* To enter again. Const. †*in, into, upon.* 1483. b. *Law.* To enter again upon possession of lands or tenements 1461. 2. *trans.* To enter (a place, etc.) again 1442. 3. To enter again in a book or register 1839. 4. *techn.* a. In hand calico-printing: To apply (the secondary colours), to ground in 1839. b. In engraving: To cut (imperfect or worn lines) deeper in the plate 1854.

Re-e·ntering, *ppl. a.* 1696. [f. prec. + -ING[2].] 1. = next adj. 2. Returning into a place 1850.

Re-e·ntrant, *a.* (and *sb.*). 1781. [f. RE- + ENTRANT.] A. *adj. R. angle*, an angle pointing inward. B. *sb.* A re-entrant angle in a fortification 1900.

Re-entry (rī,e·ntri). 1450. [RE- 5 a.] 1. *Law.* The act of re-entering upon possession of lands, tenements, etc., previously granted or let to another 1461. 2. The act of re-entering or coming back into a place, etc.; a second or new entry 1450. 3. The act of setting down or recording again; the fact of being so set down; the entry thus made 1839.

2. *Card of re-entry*, in whist and bridge, a card which by winning a trick gives the lead to a player at an advanced stage of the hand.

Re-establish (rī͵estæ·bliʃ), *v.* 1483. [RE- 5 a.] *trans.* To establish again. 1. To establish (a person or thing) again *in* a former place, position, or state; to restore to a previous place or position. b. To fix or set up again (*rare*) 1669. 2. To set up again in a status or condition similar to the former one; to restore 1559. 3. To restore (one's health or strength) to the usual state. Usu. in *pass.* 1697. b. To restore to a proper condition 1812. 4. To reassure. DE FOE.

1. He could now deliuer them..and r. them in their former peace 1606. 2. America was..re-establishing a metallic currency 1866. 3. The jeweller..felt his strength re-established 1850. Hence **Re-esta·b-lisher. Re-esta·blishment,** the act of re-establishing; the fact or condition of being re-established.

Reeve (rīv), *sb.*[1] Now chiefly *Hist.* [OE. *gerēfa*; etym. unkn.] 1. *Hist.* An Old English official of high rank having a local jurisdiction under the king; the chief magistrate of a town or district. 2. †a. A bailiff, steward, or overseer; a minor officer appointed by a landowner to superintend his estates, tenants, or workmen. b. A local official of minor rank; an overseer of a parish, a churchwarden, or the like. ME. c. In Canada, the president of a village- or town-council 1890.

Reeve (rīv), *sb.*[2] 1634. [Origin obsc.] The female of the ruff, *Tringa pugnax*.

Reeve (rīv), *v.* Chiefly *Naut.* 1627. [Origin obsc.] 1. *trans.* To pass (a rope) through a hole, ring, or block. Also const. *through*. b. *transf.* To thrust or pass (a rod, etc.) *through* any aperture or opening 1681. c. *intr.* Of a rope: To pass *through* a block, etc. 1860. 2. *trans.* To place *in*, *on*, or *round*, to fix *to* something by reeving 1667. 3. To fit (a block) with a rope by reeving; to attach in this way; to tie 1639. b. Of a rope: To pass through (a block) 1775. c. *transf.* Of a ship: To thread (shoals or ice-pack) 1860.

Re-exa·mine, *v.* 1594. [RE- 5 a.] *trans.* To examine again; *spec.* in legal use, of a counsel, to examine (a witness) again, after cross-examination by the opposing counsel. So **Re-exa·minable** *a.* **Re:-examina·tion.**

Re-excha·nge. 1480. [RE- 5 a.] 1. *Comm.* (See quot.) 2. A second or fresh exchange 1856.

1. R. means the damages incurred by non-acceptance and non-payment, and they consist of protest charges on the amount of the bill, commission, bill brokerage, interest, stamps, and postages 1809.

Re-e·xport, *sb.* 1761. [RE- 5 a.] *Comm.* 1. A commodity re-exported. Also (chiefly in *pl.*), the amount (*of* something) re-exported. 2. = RE-EXPORTATION 1792.

Re-expo·rt, *v.* 1690. [RE- 5 a.] *Comm. trans.* To export (imported goods) again. So **Re-exporta·tion,** the exportation of imported goods.

†**Refa·ction.** 1640. [a. F. *réfaction*; see RE- and FACTION.] Recompense, satisfaction –1755.

†**Refe·ct,** *pa. pple.* late ME. [ad. L. *refectus*; see next.] Refreshed, restored –1456.

Refect (rĭfe·kt), *v.* Now *rare* or *Obs.* 1470. [orig. f. L. *refect-*, *reficere*, f. *re-* RE- + *facere* to make; in later use a back-formation from next.] *trans.* To refresh, esp. with food or drink; to restore after fatigue. Often *refl.*

Refection (rĭfe·kʃən). ME. [a. F. *réfection*, ad. L. *refectionem*; see prec.] 1. Recreation or refreshment received through some spiritual or intellectual influence. 2. The action of refreshing or partaking of refreshment; the fact of being refreshed, or of refreshing oneself, with food or drink after hunger or fatigue. Also, an instance or case of this. late ME. b. Entertainment with food and drink; the right of demanding, or duty of supplying, such entertainment. Now *Hist.* 1601. 3. An occasion of partaking of food; a meal. late ME. b. A portion of food or drink; a slight repast 1482.

1. The only sight of God is the true food and r. of our minds 1630. 2. She..toke only for her r. brede and water CAXTON. 3. b. A miserable r. of weak tea and tough toast MRS. CARLYLE. Hence **Refe·ctioner,** in a monastery or convent, the person having charge of the refectory and supplies of food.

†**Refective** (rĭfe·ktiv), *a.* and *sb.* 1611. [f. as REFECT *v.* + -IVE.] A. *adj.* Refreshing, restoring, nourishing –1665. B. *sb.* A medicine that restores the strength –1706.

Refectory (rĭfe·ktəri), *sb.* 1483. [ad. med. L. *refectorium*; see REFECT *v.* and -ORY [1].] A room for refreshment; *esp.* in religious houses and colleges, the hall or chamber in which the meals take place.

†**Refe·l,** *v.* 1451. [ad. L. *refellere* to disprove, refute, f. *re-* RE- + *fallere* to deceive, etc.] 1. *trans.* To refute, confute, disprove. Also *absol.* –1734. 2. To reject (a request, a thing offered, etc.) –1603. 3. To repel, force or drive back, repress –1652.

Refer (rĭfə̄·ɹ), *v.* late ME. [ad. OF. *referer* (mod.F. *référer*), or L. *referre*, f. *re-* RE- + *ferre* to bear, carry, etc.] I. *trans.* 1. To trace (back), assign, attribute, impute (something) *to* a person or thing as the ultimate cause, origin, author, or source. 2. To assign *to* a thing, or class of things, as being properly included or comprehended in this; to regard as naturally belonging, pertaining, or having relation *to*; to attach or attribute *to*. late ME. b. To assign *to* a particular place or date 1604. 3. *refl.* To betake, commit, commend, entrust (oneself) *to* some person or thing for assistance, advice, etc., or in a spirit of submission, acquiescence, or confidence. Now *rare* or *Obs.* 1450. 4. To commit, submit, hand over (a question, cause, or matter) *to* some special or ultimate authority for consideration, decision, execution, etc. Also rarely without const. 1456. †5. To defer, postpone, put off (something) –1751. b. To reserve (a subject, etc.) for later treatment. Also const. *to* and with *inf.* Now *rare*. 1559. 6. To send or direct (a person) *to* a person, a book or its author for information 1601. b. To direct (a person) *to* a fact, event, or thing, by drawing attention to it or pointing it out 1605. 7. To relate, recount, report, record. Now *rare*. 1568. †8. To hand over, give, transfer –1705.

1. Thanne folweth it that owre vices ben referred to the makere of alle good CHAUCER. 2. Thys law ys the ground and end of the other, to the wych hyt must euer be referryd 1538. 3. I doe referre me to the Oracle: Apollo be my Iudge SHAKS. 4. The King referred the matter to the council 1769. Bankers' phr. *Refer to drawer*. 5. b. My Account of this Voyage must be referred to the Second Part of my Travels SWIFT. 6. My wife..referred her to all the neighbours for a character GOLDSM. 8. *Cymb.* I. i. 6.

II. *intr.* 1. To have reference or relation *to* a thing; *esp.* to have allusion, to apply, *to*. late ME. b. To make reference or allusion, to give a reference, direct the attention, *to* something 1691. †2. To suggest, or leave, *to* a person to do something (*rare*) –1645. 3. To have recourse, make application, *to* a thing; to turn or appeal *to* for some purpose 1595.

1. My measurements r. to the ice at and near the surface TYNDALL. b. He refers to passages of his personal history JOWETT. 3. He is to r. to and obey all orders of the army referrible to the mode of treating the Spanish Colonel WELLINGTON. Hence **Re·ferable** (re·fĕrăb'l) *a.* capable of being referred or assigned *to* (some person or thing); assignable, ascribable.

Referee (refĕrī·), *sb.* 1621. [f. REFER *v.* + -EE [1].] †1. One appointed by Parliament to examine and report on applications for monopolies or letters patent –1663. b. One to whom the management or superintendence of something is entrusted 1705. c. A member of certain committees and courts appointed by the House of Commons to deal with private bills 1865. 2. *Law.* A person to whom (either alone or with others) a dispute between parties is referred by mutual consent; an arbitrator 1565. 3. One to whom any matter or question in dispute is referred for decision; an umpire 1670. b. In games or sports 1860.

3. Clear-sighted, unprejudiced, sagacious;..he was the universal r. DISRAELI. Hence **Referee·** *v. trans.* to preside over (a match) as r.

Reference (re·fĕrĕns), *sb.* 1589. [f. REFER *v.* + -ENCE.] 1. The act or expedient of referring or submitting a matter, esp. a dispute or controversy, to some person or authority for consideration, decision, or settlement (in legal use *spec.* to the Masters in Ordinary of the Court of Chancery). Also, the scope allowed to persons conducting an inquiry, of any kind. †2. Assignment. SHAKS. 3. Relation, relationship, respect, regard *to* some thing or person 1593. 4. An allusion or directing of attention *to* some thing or person 1613. 5. A direction to a book, passage, etc., where certain information may be found. Also without article. 1612. b. A mark or sign referring the reader to another part of a page or book (*esp.* from the text to a note), or serving to indicate the part of a figure or diagram referred to 1678. 6. The act of referring one person to another for information or an explanation 1815. b. The name of a person given as one prepared to vouch for the character of a person seeking employment or of goods offered for sale, etc.; the person himself, or (loosely) the testimonial given 1865. 7. *Book*, etc. *of r.*, one intended to be, or suitable for being, referred to or consulted 1836.

1. If the arbitrator refuses or ceases to act, the r. is at an end 1834. 2. *Oth.* I. iii. 238. 3. The world is a..system, whose parts have a mutual r. to each other 1736. *In* or *with r. to*, with respect or regard to; †with a view to, according to. *Without r. to*, without regard to, without consideration of or for. 4. No r. had been made to the former conversation 1865. 5. See also CROSS-REFERENCE. *Legislation by r.* (= by reference to previous statutes instead of by restatement). 6. I don't ask you to trust me, without offering a respectable r. DICKENS. 7. Books of r. such as..Encyclopædias, Lexicons, Dictionaries, etc. 1859. *For r.*, for the purpose of consulting or being consulted.

attrib.: **r. bible,** a bible furnished with marginal cross-references to parallel passages; **r. library,** a library where books may be consulted without being removed from it; **r. mark,** a mark or sign (as * † ¶ or superior numbers) used to refer the reader to notes.

Reference (re·fĕrĕns), *v.* 1621. [f. prec.] †1. *trans.* To refer, assign *to* a thing (*rare*) –1627. 2. To provide with references; to give a reference to (a passage); to find by reference 1891. 3. *intr.* To make out a return of the number of people to be displaced by proposed railway extension. Also *trans.* to schedule (property) for this purpose. 1884. Hence **Re·ferencer.**

Referendary (refĕre·ndări). 1528. [ad. med.L. *referendarius*; see REFERENDUM and -ARY [1].] 1. One to whom a matter in dispute is referred for decision; a referee. Now *rare*. 1546. 2. *spec.* A title given at various times to certain officials in the papal, imperial, and some royal courts, charged with the duty of examining and reporting on petitions, requests, use of the seal, and similar matters 1528. †3. One who, or that which, furnishes news or information; a reporter –1636.

3. Sir, when these places afford anything worth your knowledge, I shall be your r. DONNE.

‖**Referendum** (refĕre·ndʊ̆m). 1882. [L., f. *referre*.] 1. The act, practice, or principle (chiefly associated with the Swiss constitution) of submitting the direct decision of a question at issue to the whole body of voters. 2. A note from a diplomatic agent to his government, requesting instructions on a particular matter 1891.

Referent (re·fĕrĕnt), *sb.* and *a.* *rare.* 1844. [ad. L. *referentem*, *referre*.] A. *sb.* 1. One who is referred to or consulted. 2. A word referring to another 1899. B. *adj.* Referring, containing a reference 1899.

Referential (refĕre·nʃăl), *a.* 1660. [f. REFERENCE, after *inferential*, etc.] Having reference (*to* something); belonging to, or of the nature of, (a) reference; containing a reference or references.

The r. mark..referring to the note annexed 1806. Hence **Refere·ntially** *adv.*

†**Refe·rment.** 1558. [f. REFER *v.* + -MENT.] Reference –1655.

Referrer (rĭfə̄·rəɹ). 1683. [f. REFER *v.* + -ER [1].] One who refers.

Referrible (rĭfə̄·rib'l), *a.* 1596. [f. REFER *v.* + -IBLE.] = REFERABLE.

Refigure (rīfi·gər, -iŭɹ), *v.* late ME. [ad. late L. *refigurare*.] 1. *trans.* To figure again; to represent anew. 2. *spec.* To restore (a metallic speculum) to the original parabolic figure 1888.

Refill (rī·fi·l, rī·fil), *sb.* 1886. [RE- 5 a.]

That which serves to refill anything; a fresh fill for a memorandum or pencil case, etc.

Refi·ll, *v.* 1687. [RE- 5 a.] *trans.* and *intr.* To fill again.

Refine (rǐfəi·n), *v.* 1582. [f. RE- + FINE *v.*³, after Sp. *refinar*, F. *raffiner*, It. *raffinare.*] **1.** *trans.* To purify or separate (metals) from dross, alloy, or other extraneous matter; in iron-working, to convert grey pig-iron into white or plate metal by partial decarburization. **2.** To free from impurities; to purify or cleanse 1601. **b.** *spec.* To purify or clarify (a substance or product) by means of some special process; to make purer or of a finer quality; *esp.* to subject (raw sugar) to the processes of clarifying, condensing, and crystallizing 1613. †**3. a.** To clear (the spirits, mind, etc.) from dullness; to make clearer or more subtle –1728. **b.** To free or cleanse from moral imperfection; to raise to a higher spiritual state –1711. **4.** To free from imperfections or defects; to bring to a more perfect or purer state 1670. **b.** To polish or improve (a language, composition, etc.); to make more elegant or cultured 1617. **5.** To free from rudeness, coarseness, or vulgarity; to imbue with culture or polish, delicate feelings or instincts, etc. 1667. **6.** *intr.* To become pure; to grow clear or free from impurities 1604. **7.** To improve in polish, elegance, or delicacy 1620. **8.** To employ or affect a subtlety of thought or language 1713. **9.** To improve *on* or *upon* something, by introducing refinements 1662.

1. So doth the Fire the drossy Gold r. 1592. 2. To ..raise From the conflagrant mass, purg'd and refin'd, New Heav'ns, new Earth MILT. b. The Table was furnished with fat things, and with Wine that was well refined BUNYAN. 3. b. Tri'd in sharp tribulation, and refin'd By Faith and faithful works MILT. 4. They may as well r. the speech as the sentiments of their personages JOHNSON. 5. Love refines The thoughts, and heart enlarges MILT. 6. The pure stream..Works it self clear, and, as it runs, refines ADDISON. 7. Let a Lord once own the happy lines, How the wit brightens! how the style refines! POPE. 8. Who, too deep for his hearers, still went on refining, And thought of convincing, while they thought of dining GOLDSM. Hence **Refi·nable** *a.*

Refined (rǐfəi·nd), *ppl. a.* 1574. [f. prec. + -ED¹.] **1.** Purified; freed from impurities or extraneous matter 1595. **2.** Characterized or distinguished by the possession of refinement in manners, action, or feeling 1588. **b.** Free from rude, gross, or vulgar elements 1650. **c.** Of language, speech, etc.: Cultivated, polished, elegant 1611. **3.** †**a.** Having or affecting a subtlety of mind or judgement –1714. **b.** Raised to a high degree of subtlety, nicety, precision, etc. 1668.

1. To gilde r. Gold, to paint the Lilly..Is wastefull, and ridiculous excesse SHAKS. 2. Modern taste Is so r. and delicate and chaste COWPER. c. She spoke with a r. accent GEO. ELIOT. 3. Nothing subtle or r. should enter into the views of a Christian missionary 1812. Hence **Refi·nedly** (-ėdli) *adv.*

Refinement (rǐfəi·nmĕnt). 1611. [f. REFINE *v.* after F. *raffinement*, etc.] **1.** The act or process of refining; the result of refining, or the state of being refined. **2.** Fineness of feeling, taste, or thought; elegance of manners; culture, polish 1710. **b.** An instance of this 1708. **3.** The act or practice of refining in thought, reasoning, or discourse; an instance of this 1712. **b.** A piece of subtle reasoning; a subtlety 1694. **4.** An instance of improvement or advance towards something more refined or perfect; the state or thing thus arrived at or obtained 1710.

1. The renovation and r. of the present world by the last fire BOYLE. 2. That sensibility of pain with which R. is endued COWPER. b. The refinements of highly cultivated society W. IRVING. 4. For Emulation..is..but a r. upon envy LAW.

Refiner (rǐfəi·nəɹ). 1586. [f. REFINE *v.* + -ER¹.] One who or that which refines; *spec.* one who makes a business of refining (metal, sugar, etc.).

Refinery (rǐfəi·nəri). 1727. [f. as prec. + -ERY, after F. *raffinerie.*] A place, building, or establishment, where refining (of sugar, oil, metal, etc.) is carried on. **b.** A furnace for the conversion of cast into malleable iron 1825.

Refit (rǐfi·t), *v.* 1666. [RE- 5 a.] **1.** *Naut.* **a.** *trans.* To fit out (a ship, fleet, etc.) again; to restore to a serviceable condition by renewals and repairs. **b.** *intr.* To get refitted 1669. **2. a.** *trans.* To fit up or fit out afresh 1676. **b.** *intr.* To renew supplies or equipment 1802.

1. b. The Portland has come in to r., having lost her masts 1669. So **Refit** (stress var.) *sb.* an act or instance of refitting (*esp.* of a ship). **Refi·tment**, the act of refitting; a refit.

Reflation (rǐflēi·ʃən). 1932. [Badly f. RE- + IN(FLATION.] Inflation undertaken after deflation to restore the previous position.

Refle·ct, *sb.* 1596. [f. next.] Reflection –1829.

Reflect (rǐfle·kt), *v.* late ME. [a. OF. *reflecter*, or L. *reflectere*, f. *re-* RE- + *flectere* to bend.] **I.** *trans.* **1.** To turn or direct in a certain course, to divert; to turn away or aside, to deflect. **2.** To bend, turn, or fold back; to give a backward bend or curve to (a thing); to recurve. (Chiefly in *pa. pple.*, denoting the position of parts.) 1578. †**3.** To turn (back), cast (the eye or thought) *on* or *upon* something –1677. **4.** To throw or cast back again; to cause to return or rebound 1611. **b.** *spec.* Of bodies or surfaces: To cast or send back (heat, cold, or sound) after impact 1718. **5.** Of (smooth or polished) bodies or surfaces: To turn, throw, or cast back (beams, rays, or light) 1573. **6.** Of mirrors or other polished surfaces: To give back or exhibit an image of (a person or thing); to mirror. Also *absol.* 1592. **7.** To throw or cast (blame, dishonour, etc.) *on* or *upon* a person or thing 1670.

2. The bill is..not quite strait, but a little reflected upwards PENNANT. 3. Let me minde the Reader to r. his eye on our Quotations FULLER. 4. b. A cloud.. reflects or throws back upon the earth the heat HUXLEY. 5. The Light of the Moon reflected from frozen Snow BENTLEY. 6. The glass..Reflected now a perfect fright GOLDSM. *fig.* The law..reflects the plain sentiments of the better order of average men FROUDE. 7. This..reflects the greatest dishonour on his reputation ROBERTSON.

II. *intr.* †**1.** Of beams or rays of light: To return, turn back, after striking or falling upon a surface –1703. †**b.** To shine, cast a light –1653. †**2.** To return; to turn, come, or go back –1717. †**3.** To cast a look or glance *upon* a thing; to have a bearing *upon*, etc. –1662. †**b.** To bestow attention or regard *upon* a person or thing; to set a value *on* (*rare*) –1661. **4.** To turn one's thoughts (back) *on*, to fix the mind or attention *on* or *upon* a subject; to ponder, meditate *on* 1605. **b.** Without const.: To employ reflection 1704. **5.** To cast a slight or imputation, reproach or blame, *on* or *upon* a person or thing; to pass a censure *on* 1631. **6.** Of actions, circumstances, etc.: To cast or bring reproach or discredit *on* a person or thing 1647. **b.** To cast a certain light or character *on* 1856.

1. b. *Tit. A.* I. ii. 226. 3. b. *Cymb.* I. vi. 24. 4. We are..constituted such sort of creatures as to r. upon our own nature 1726. b. It is necessary..that we think and r. before we act PRIESTLEY. 5. I would not be thought to r. upon this very eminent physician's practice 1756. 6. Ill Language, and brutal Manners, reflected only on those who were guilty of 'em STEELE. Hence **Refle·cted** *ppl. a.*, **-ly** *adv.* **Refle·ctible** *a.* that may be reflected.

Reflecting (rǐfle·ktiŋ), *ppl. a.* 1590. [-ING².] **1.** That reflects, or casts back, light or images of things. **b.** Provided or fitted with some arrangement or apparatus serving to reflect light or images; esp. *r. telescope* 1704. **2.** Casting reflections on a person or thing 1687. **3.** Having or exercising reflection or thought; characterized by reflection 1711.

1. †*R. glass*, a mirror. 3. Grave and r. men MACAULAY. Hence **Refle·ctingly** *adv.*

Reflection, reflexion (rǐfle·kʃən). late ME. [a. F. *réflexion*, or ad. late L. *reflexionem* (med.L. also *reflectionem*). Except in scientific use, the form with *ct* is the prevailing one.] **1.** The action, on the part of surfaces, of throwing back light or heat (rays, beams, etc.) falling upon them; the fact or phenomenon of light and heat being thrown back in this way. **b.** Reflected light or heat 1555. **2.** The action of a mirror or other polished surface in exhibiting or reproducing the image of an object; the fact or phenomenon of an image being produced in this way. late ME. **b.** An image or counterpart thus produced 1587. **c.** The fact of colour being thrown by one thing upon another; a colour, hue, or tint received in this way; also *Zool.* an iridescence 1614. **3.** The action of bending, turning, or folding back; recurvation 1553. †**b.** The action of turning back from some point –1662. **4.** The action of throwing back, or fact of being thrown or driven back, after impact. late ME. **b.** *Phys.* Reflex action 1836. **5.** Animadversion, blame, censure, reproof 1651. **b.** A remark or statement reflecting on a person 1647. **c.** An imputation; a fact or procedure casting an imputation or discredit *on* one 1663. **6.** The action of turning (back) or fixing the thoughts on some subject; meditation, deep or serious consideration 1674. †**b.** Recollection or remembrance *of* a thing. Also without const. –1704. **c.** *Philos.* The mode, operation, or faculty by which the mind has knowledge of itself and its operations, or by which it deals with the ideas received from sensation and perception 1690. **7.** A thought or idea occurring to, or occupying, the mind 1647. **b.** A thought expressed in words; a remark made after reflection on a subject 1659.

1. Phr. *Angle of r.*, the angle which the reflected ray makes with a perpendicular to the surface (†or with the surface itself). b. *fig.* Shee 's a good signe, but I haue seene small r. of her wit SHAKS. 2. The eye sees not it selfe but by r., By some other things SHAKS. c. Feathers..golden-green, with grey edges, and all are glossed with brilliant metallic reflections 1840. 3. b. *Macb.* I. ii. 25. 5. For in English, to say Satire, is to mean R., as we use that Word in the worst sence DRYDEN. b. May no r. shed Its poisonous venom on the royal dead PRIOR. 6. Mankind act more from habit than r. PALEY. b. Though it made you a little uneasy for the present, yet the r. of it must needs be entertaining CONGREVE. c. R..., that notice which the Mind takes of its own Operations, and the manner of them LOCKE. 7. These reflections draw after them others that are too melancholy 1716.

Reflective (rǐfle·ktiv), *a.* 1627. [f. REFLECT *v.* + -IVE.] **1. a.** That gives back an image or reflection of an object; that mirrors or reproduces. **b.** That throws back something striking or falling on the surface; *esp.* that reflects light 1742. **c.** *Gram.* = REFLEXIVE 5. 1843. **2.** Of light: Produced by reflection, reflected, borrowed 1666. †**3.** That makes or contains reflections or censures *on* or *upon* a person –1677. **4.** Of mental faculties: Of or pertaining to reflection (on what is presented to the mind) 1678. **b.** Meditative thoughtful 1820.

1. The polished floor..as r. as a mahogany table RUSKIN. 3. Little said r. on me, though W. Pen and J. Minnes do mean me in one or two places PEPYS. 4. b. Elegy is the form of poetry natural to the r. mind COLERIDGE. Hence **Refle·ctive-ly** *adv.*, **-ness.**

Reflector (rǐfle·ktǫɹ). 1665. [f. REFLECT *v.* + -OR².] †**1.** One who reflects or meditates BOYLE. †**2.** One who casts reflections; a censor, critic –1748. **3.** A reflecting telescope, microscope, etc. 1767. **4.** A body or surface which reflects (rays of) light, heat, sound, etc. 1800. **b.** *spec.* A specially prepared surface of metal or glass (usu. of a curved or concave form), for the purpose of reflecting rays of light, heat or sound in a required direction 1797. **5.** A polished surface exhibiting images of objects 1831. **b.** *spec.* The speculum of a reflecting telescope 1815. **6.** That which reflects, in other senses 1840.

‖**Reflex** (rī·fleks), *sb.* 1508. [ad. late L. *reflexus* a bending back, f. ppl. stem of *reflectere* to REFLECT.] **1.** Reflection of light (or heat); reflected light; light or colour resulting from reflection. Now *rare*. **b.** *spec.* in *Art* and *Arch.* The light reflected, or supposed to be reflected, from a surface in light to one in shade 1695. **2.** The reflection or image of an object, as seen in a mirror or surface acting as such 1638. **b.** *fig.* An image, reproduction; something which reproduces certain essential features or qualities of another thing 1683. †**3.** The act of bending or turning the mind (back) *upon* a subject; reflection –1658. †**4.** A glance or side look (*lit.* and *fig.*); indirect reference or allusion –1650. †**5.** Return, rebound; indirect action or operation –1683. **6.** *Phys.* A reflex action 1877. **7.** *Wireless.* Ellipt. for *reflex set* (see next 7).

1. The r. from the window..lit his face C. BRONTE. b. Gradations of middle tint, local colour, and reflexes 1807. 2. To cut across the r. of a star That..gleamed Upon the glassy plain WORDSW. 5. Let us abstain from raillery least it return by r. upon our selves 1683.

Reflex (rī·fleks), *a.* 1649. [ad. L. *reflexus*, *reflectere.*] **1.** Bent or turned back; recurved

1658. **2.** Of light, rays, etc.: Reflected 1681. **3.** Of acts of thought: Directed or turned back upon the mind itself or its operations. Chiefly in *r. act.* 1649. **b.** Derived from, consisting in, the conversion of the mind or thought upon itself 1652. **4.** Coming by way of return or reflection 1822. **5.** *Phys.* **a.** *R. action*, involuntary action of a muscle, gland, or other organ, caused by the excitation of a sensory nerve being transmitted to a nerve-centre, and thence 'reflected' along an efferent nerve to the organ in question 1833. **b.** Of the nature of, characterized by, or connected with, such action 1833. **6.** *Gram.* Reflexive 1873. **7.** *Wireless. R. circuit*: a circuit in which the same valve gives high-frequency and low-frequency amplification; *r. receiver, set*, one acting by means of a r. circuit 1924.

3. Which I call the r. act of the Soul, or the turning of the intellectual eye inward upon its own actions HALE. b. This r. knowledge whereby we know what it is to know 1652. 5. a. Coughing and sneezing are familiar instances of r. actions DARWIN. Hence **Refle·xly** *adv.*

Reflex (rĭfle·ks), *v.* late ME. [f. L. *reflex-*, *reflectere*.] **1.** *trans.* = REFLECT *v.* I. 2. Chiefly *Her.* and *Bot.*, and only in pa. pple. 1572. **†2.** To reflect (light, an object, etc.) –1658.

1. The petals are reflexed, and turn over 1861. 2. For neither rain can fall upon the earth, Nor sun r. his virtuous beams thereon MARLOWE. Hence **Reflexed** (rĭfle·kst) *ppl. a.* in the senses of the vb.; also, †directed backwards.

Reflexible (rĭfle·ksĭb'l), *a.* 1706. [f. prec.] Capable of being reflected.

The Light of the Sun consists of Rays that are differently R. and Refrangible 1706. Hence **Reflexibi·lity.**

Reflexive (rĭfle·ksiv), *a.* and *sb.* 1588. [ad. L. **reflexivus*; see REFLEX *v.* and -IVE.] **A.** *adj.* **1.** Capable of bending or turning back (*rare*). **†2.** Of mental operations: Turned or directed back upon the mind itself –1708. **†b.** Reflective –1752. **†3.** Reciprocal, correspondent –1681. **†4.** Reflecting on a person –1716. **5.** *Gram.* Of pronouns, verbs, and their signification: Characterized by, or denoting, a reflex action on the subject of the clause or sentence 1837. **6.** Of a reflex character 1871.

2. Being not capable of a r. act, they know it not BEVERIDGE. 4. I would fain know what man..there is that does not resent an ugly r. word 1716.

B. *sb.* A reflexive verb or pronoun 1866. Hence **Refle·xive-ly** *adv.*, **-ness.**

†Refloa·t. *rare.* 1594. [ad. obs. F. *reflot*; see RE- 2 a and FLOAT *sb.* I. 2.] A flowing back; reflux, ebb (of the tide) –1626.

Reflow·, *sb.* 1610. [RE- 2 a.] A reflux, refluence, ebb of the tide.

Reflow·, *v.* Now *rare.* late ME. [RE- 2 a.] *intr.* To flow back; *esp.* of the tide, to ebb. Freq. in phr. *flow and r.*

Refluence (re·flŭĕns). 1592. [See next and -ENCE.] A flowing back; a reflux. So **†Re·fluency** (*rare*).

Refluent (re·flŭĕnt), *a.* late ME. [ad. L. *refluentem*, *refluere*, f. *re-* RE- 2 a + *fluere* to flow.] **1.** Flowing back, reflowing. **2.** Characterized by refluence, *esp.* tidal 1741. **†3.** Directed backwards. SHENSTONE.

1. *transf.* The once triumphant Peninsular hosts, r. through the passes of the Pyrenees 1842. 2. A phantom colony smoulder'd on the r. estuary TENNYSON.

Reflux (rī·flɒks). late ME. [f. RE- 2 a + FLUX.] A flowing back, return, refluence.

Ill-contrived sewers permitting a large r. of air into the houses 1869. Phr. *Flux and r.*

Refo·cillate, *v.* Now *rare.* 1611. [ad. late L. *refocillare* to revive.] *trans.* To revive, refresh, reanimate. So **Refocilla·tion**, refreshment, reanimation, reinvigoration 1576.

Reform (rĭfǭ·ɹm), *sb.* 1663. [f. next, or ad. F. *réforme.*] **1.** The amendment of some faulty state of things, *esp.* of a corrupt or oppressive political institution or practice; the removal of some abuse or wrong. **b.** An instance of this; a change for the better 1781. **2.** Amendment of conduct; reformation of persons or character 1784. **3.** Improvement or rectifying of something faulty or inexact 1856. **4.** A religious order created by the reduction of another to stricter observances 1727.

1. He said when any change was brewing, R. was a fine name for ruin 1786. b. The public..calling for sweeping reforms 1883. 2. Remorse begets r. COWPER. 3. The r. of the calendar EMERSON.

attrib.: **R. Act** or **Bill,** an act or bill to amend the system of parliamentary representation, esp. those brought in and passed in 1831–2.

Reform (rĭfǭ·ɹm), *v.*[1] ME. [ad. OF. *reformer* or L. *reformare*, f. *re-* RE- + *formare* to form.] **†1.** *trans.* To renew, restore, re-establish (peace) –1556. **†2.** To convert, bring back, or restore (a thing or person) to the original form or state, or to a previous condition –1579. **†3.** To rebuild, repair (a building) –1667. **4.** To convert into another and better form; to free from previous faults or imperfections. Now *rare.* late ME. **†b.** To correct, emend (a book, writing, chart, etc.); to recast –1779. **c.** *Law.* To allow an instrument to be corrected or construed according to the original intention, when an error has been committed in it 1586. **5.** To amend or improve (an arrangement, state of things, institution, etc.) by removal of faults or abuses. late ME. **6.** To put a stop or end to (an abuse, disorder, malpractice, etc.) by enforcing or introducing a better procedure or conduct. late ME. **†b.** To correct, put right (an error or mistake) –1784. **7.** To bring, lead, or force (a person) to abandon a wrong or evil course of life, conduct, etc., and adopt a right one; to bring about a thorough amendment in (a person, his conduct, oneself, etc.). late ME. **†8.** To cut down or back to a desired length; to trim, prune –1697. **†9.** *Mil.* [After F. *réformer.*] To form into a new regiment or company; to break up, partially or completely, for this purpose; hence also, to disband, dismiss from the service –1768. **10.** *intr.* (for *refl.*) To abandon wrong-doing or error; to free oneself from misconduct or fault 1582.

4. Romulus's calendar was reformed by Numa, who added two more months 1727. 5. To r. the administration of justice 1845. 7. A man is never thoroughly reformed till a new principle governs his thoughts BURNET. 8. Shall we doubt..To sow, to set, and to r. their growth? DRYDEN. 9. If you must r. two of them, be sure let him command the troop that is left PEPYS. 10. It is possible the young man may, in time, grow wiser and r. *Junius Lett.* Hence **Refo·rmable** *a.* capable of being reformed; admitting or susceptible of reformation.

Re-form, reform (rīfǭ·ɹm), *v.*[2] ME. [orig. same as prec., but in later use f. RE- 5 a and FORM *v.*] *trans.* and *intr.* To form a second time, form over again.

Reformado (refǭɹmē·do). Also **†-ade.** 1616. [a. Sp. *reformado*, ad. L. *reformatus*, *reformare* to REFORM.] **1.** *Mil.* Now *Hist.* **a.** An officer left without a command (owing to the 'reforming' or disbanding of his company) but retaining his rank and seniority, and receiving full or half pay. **b.** A volunteer serving in the army (or navy) without a commission, but with the rank of an officer. **2.** One who is (or has) reformed in some respect; also, one who favours reform; a reformer 1632.

Reformation (refǭɹmē·ʃən). late ME. [ad. L. *reformationem*; cf. F. *réformation.*] **1.** Improvement in form or quality; alteration to a better form; correction or removal of faults or errors; †rebuilding. **b.** Improvement in health. JOHNSON. **2.** Improvement of (or in) an existing state of things, institution, practice, etc.; a radical change for the better effected in political, religious, or social affairs 1460. **b.** *spec.* (with capital). The great religious movement of the 16th century, having for its object the reform of the doctrines and practices of the Church of Rome, and ending in the establishment of the various Reformed or Protestant Churches of central and north-western Europe 1563. **3.** The action of reforming (one's own or another's) conduct or morals; improvement or amendment in this respect; correction 1509. **†4.** Phr. *Under* (or *saving*) *your r.*: subject to your amendment or correction –1617. **†5.** A disbanding, dismissal (of troops); the removal of an officer from the active list –1670.

1. The late r. of the gold coin of Great Britain ADAM SMITH. 2. The r. of the church and that of learning began together BERKELEY. 3. My trouble came tumbling upon me again, and that over the neck of all my Reformations BUNYAN. *House of r.*, a reformatory.

Re-formation (rīfǭɹmē·ʃən). late ME. [orig. same word as prec.; in later use f. RE- 5 a + FORMATION.] The action of forming again; a second or new formation.

Reformative (rĭfǭ·ɹmătiv), *a.* 1593. [f. L. *reformat-*, *reformare* + -IVE.] Inclined to reform; that tends to, or makes for, reform.

Reformatory (rĭfǭ·ɹmătəri), *a.* and *sb.* 1589. [f. L. *reformat-* + -ORY.] **A.** *adj.* Having a desire or tendency to reform (a person or thing); designed for reforming. **B.** *sb.* An institution to which juvenile incorrigibles or offenders against the law are sent with a view to their reformation 1837.

attrib. The average r. population [in the United States] is about 15,000. 1885.

Reformed (rĭfǭ·ɹmd), *ppl. a.* and *sb.* 1563. [f. REFORM *v.*[1] + -ED[1].] **A.** *ppl. a.* **1. a.** Of religion, churches, etc.: Brought to a better or purer state by the removal of errors or abuses, esp. those imputed to the Church of Rome. Also *transf.* of persons, times, etc. **b.** Of parliament, *spec.* of that which met after the Reform Act of 1832. 1822. **2.** Improved in character, conduct or morals 1579. **3.** Altered in form or content; *esp.* put into a better form, corrected, amended 1584. **†4.** *Mil.* Of officers: Left without a command (see REFORMADO 1) 1629. **†B.** *sb.* **a.** as *pl.* Adherents of the Reformed religion; Protestants. **b.** *sing.* A Protestant (*rare*) –1772.

A. 1. The name of *R. Church(es)* sometimes includes all the Protestant churches, and sometimes is specifically restricted to the Calvinistic bodies as contrasted with the Lutheran. N.E.D.

Reformer (rĭfǭ·ɹməɹ). 1526. [f. as prec. + -ER[1].] **1.** One who reforms another (*rare*). **2.** One who reforms, or effects a reform in, a state of things, practice, etc. 1548. **3.** *spec.* **a.** One of the leaders in the reformation of religion in the 16th c. 1561. **b.** An advocate or supporter of political or parliamentary reform; *esp.* one who took part in the reform movement of 1831–2. 1785. **4.** A reviser, corrector, improver (*rare*) 1656.

2. Ambroise Paré was a great R. of Surgery 1767.

Reformist (rĭfǭ·ɹmist). 1589. [f. REFORM *v.*[1] + -IST.] **1.** One who advocates reform. **†2.** A member of a reformed religious order –1706. So **Refo·rmism.**

Refound (rīfau·nd), *v.*[1] 1500. [f. RE- 5 a + FOUND *v.*[1] Cf. F. *refonder.*] *trans.* To found (a town, etc.) again; to re-establish. Hence **Refou·nder,** one who refounds.

Refound (rīfau·nd), *v.*[2] 1649. [f. RE- 5 a + FOUND *v.*[2] Cf. F. *refondre.*] *trans.* To cast (objects of metal) again; to recast.

Refract (rĭfræ·kt), *v.* 1612. [f. L. *refract-*, *refringere*, f. *re-* RE- + *frangere* to break.] **1.** *trans.* *Physics.* Of substances: To break the course of (light, etc.) and turn (it) out of the direct line; *esp.* to deflect at a certain angle at the point of passage from one medium into another of different density. **b.** To produce by refraction (*rare*) 1728. **†2.** To throw back; to reflect –1694. **†3.** To break up; to impair (*rare*) –1676. **b.** *Chem.* To analyse (nitre) in order to discover the percentage of impurities 1842.

1. Glass refracts light more strongly than water does HUXLEY. Hence **Refra·ctable** *a.* refrangible. **Refra·cted** *ppl. a.* bent aside, deflected, connected with or produced by refraction.

†Refra·ctary, *a.* and *sb.* 1599. [ad. L. *refractarius*; see REFRACT *v.* and -ARY[1].] **A.** *adj.* = REFRACTORY –1694. **B.** *sb.* A refractory person –1657. Hence **†Refra·ctariness.**

Refractile (rĭfræ·ktil, -təil), *a.* 1847. [f. REFRACT *v.* + -ILE.] Capable of producing refraction.

Refracting (rĭfræ·ktiŋ), *ppl. a.* 1704. [-ING[2].] Causing refraction; refractive. **b.** Provided with some apparatus or arrangement for refracting light; esp. *r. telescope*, a telescope in which the rays of light are converged to a focus by an object glass 1764. **c.** *R. angle*, the angle between two faces of a prism or lens 1796.

Refraction (rĭfræ·kʃən). 1578. [ad. late L. *refractionem*; see REFRACT *v.*] **†1. a.** The action of breaking open or breaking up (*rare*) –1661. **†b.** Rebound, recoil (*rare*) –1661. **2.** The fact or phenomenon of a ray of light, heat, (†the sight,) etc., being diverted or deflected from its previous course in passing obliquely out of one medium into another of different density, or in traversing a medium not of uniform density 1603. Also with *a* and *pl.*, an instance of this. †b. Refracted beams –1649. **3. a.** *Astron.* The deflection of the beams or light from heavenly bodies when not in the zenith, due to the refracting power of the atmosphere, which increases their apparent elevation. (Spec. called *atmospheric* and *astronomical r.*) 1603. **b.** The effect of the atmosphere in making terrestrial objects appear higher than they are. (Spec. called *terrestrial r.*) 1698. **4.** The action *of* a medium in refracting light; refractive power or effect 1664. **5.** The ascertainment of the percentage of impurities contained in a sample of nitre; the sum of the impurities as thus ascertained 1842.

2. Phr. *Angle of r.*, the angle between the refracted ray and the perpendicular to the surface of the refracting medium at the point of incidence (†or that between the refracted ray and a continuation of the incident ray). *Double r.*, the fact of a ray of light being split up by certain minerals into two divergent, unequally refracted rays. *Index of r.*: see INDEX *sb.* 9.

Comb.: **r.-circle**, one of two or more graduated circles attached to a refracting telescope in order to adjust its direction.

Refractive (rǐfræ·ktiv), *a.* 1673. [ad. late L. *refractivus*, or f. REFRACT *v.* + -IVE.] **1.** That refracts light, etc.; possessed of, characterized by, the power of refracting. **2. a.** Due to, caused by, refraction 1717. **b.** Refrangible 1890. **3.** Relating to refraction 1727.

1. Tourmaline is a doubly r. substance 1854. Phr. *R. power*, the power which a transparent body has of refracting the light passing through it. *R. index* (see INDEX *sb.* 9). 2. a. R. aberration 1879. Hence **Refra·ctiveness, Refracti·vity.**

Refractometer (rǐfræktǫ·mǐtəɪ). 1876. [f. as REFRACT *v.* + -OMETER.] An instrument for measuring the indices of refraction of various substances.

Refractor (rǐfræ·ktǝɪ). 1769. [f. REFRACT *v.* + -OR.] A medium which refracts light; a refracting lens 1836. **b.** A refracting telescope 1769.

Refractory (rǐfræ·ktəri), *a.* and *sb.* 1599. [var. of REFRACTARY, after adjs. in -ORY[2].] **A.** *adj.* **1.** Stubborn, obstinate, perverse; unmanageable, rebellious 1606. †**2.** Strongly opposed, refusing compliance, *to* something –1723. **3.** *Med.* Of wounds, diseases, and the like: Obstinate, not yielding *to* treatment 1663. **b.** Able to offer resistance *to* a disease; not susceptible to morbid agencies 1884. **4.** Resisting the action of heat; difficult to fuse (or to work in any way) 1758.

A. 1. They were a parcel of r., ungovernable villains DE FOE. The r. proceedings of the crew 1748. 2. A People..so r. to all Culture 1723. 3. The wound was at first r. 1836. Hence **Refra·ctori·ly** *adv.*, **-ness.**

†**B.** *sb.* **1.** A refractory person –1633. **2.** A piece of refractory ware employed in the process of glazing pottery 1839.

†**Refragate,** *v.* 1593. [f. L. *refragat-*, *refragari* to resist.] *intr.* To oppose, controvert –1661.

Refrain (rǐfrē·n), *sb.* late ME. [a. OF. *refrein, refrain*, ult. f. pop. L. **refrangere* to break back, break again.] A phrase or verse recurring at intervals, esp. at the end of each stanza of a poem or song; a burden, chorus.

Refrain (rǐfrē·n), *v.* late ME. [ad. OF. *refrener* (mod.F. *refréner*), ad. L. *refrenare*, f. *re-* RE- + *frenum, frænum* bridle.] **I.** *trans.* †**1.** To restrain, hold back, check (a person or thing) –1645. **b.** *refl.* To restrain, put restraint upon (oneself); to repress any manifestation of emotion, impatience, etc. Now *arch.* late ME. **2.** To hold back, restrain (a person or thing) *from* something, esp. some act or course of action. Now *rare.* late ME. †**3.** To restrain, curb, check, stay (an action, proceeding, feeling, quality, etc.) –1683. **4.** To put a restraint or check upon (one's own desires, feelings, actions, etc.). late ME. †**5.** To keep from (an action), desist from, give up –1725. †**6.** To abstain from (a habit or practice); to give up, avoid, eschew –1751. †**7.** To avoid, shun, eschew (a person's company) –1716. †**b.** To avoid, keep away from (a place); also, to go away from, to leave –1748.

1. b. And thou, O human heart of mine, Be still, r. thyself, and wait CLOUGH. 2. Nor from the Holie One of Heav'n Refrein'd his tongue blasphemous MILT. 4. When we heard that, we were ashamed, and refrained our tears JOWETT.

II. *intr.* **1.** To abstain, forbear. late ME. **2.** To abstain, keep oneself, *from* some act or feeling, †using or partaking of something, interference with a person, etc. 1538.

1. Who could refraine, That had a heart to loue? SHAKS. 2. And now I say vnto you, refraine from these men, and let them alone *Acts* v. 38. Hence †**Refrai·ner** (*rare*), one who restrains. **Refrai·nment** (*rare*), refraining, abstinence.

Refrangent (rǐfræ·ndʒĕnt), *a. rare.* 1880. [f. pres. pple. of L. **refrangere* (for *refringere*); see REFRACT *v.*] Refracting; breaking up again.

Refrangible (rǐfræ·ndʒib'l), *a.* 1673. [ad. L. **refrangibilis*, f. **refrangere* (for *refringere*); see REFRACT *v.*] Capable of being refracted; admitting of, susceptible to, refraction. Hence **Refrangibi·lity, Refra·ngibleness.**

†**Refrenation.** 1450. [ad. L. *refrenationem*; see REFRAIN *v.* and -ATION.] **1.** The action of refraining or restraining –1652. **2.** *Astrol.* The prevention of a conjunction by the retrogression of one of the planets –1706.

Refresh (rǐfre·ʃ), *sb.* Now *colloq.* 1592. [f. next.] †**1.** The act of refreshing; refreshment; renewal of supplies –1648. **2.** A refreshment (esp. of liquor) taken by a person; a refresher 1884.

Refresh (rǐfre·ʃ), *v.* late ME. [a. OF. *refrescher*, f. *re-* RE- + *fresche* FRESH *a.*] **1.** *trans.* Of physical agents (esp. water): To impart freshness to (a place or thing, the air, etc.) by means of cooling or wetting. **2.** To make (a person) feel fresher than before; to reanimate, reinvigorate physically, mentally, or spiritually; to provide with refreshment. late ME. **b.** *refl.* (of persons): To make (oneself) fresher, by partaking of food or drink, by resting, etc. late ME. †**c.** To relieve *of* –1760. **3.** To freshen up (the memory), to make clear or distinct again 1542. †**4.** To restore, renovate (a building). *rare.* –1548. **5.** To restore to, or keep at, a certain level or condition by furnishing a fresh supply of something 1450. **6.** †**a.** To restore (a thing) to a fresh or bright condition; to brighten or freshen up –1818. **b.** To make (a surface) fresh, esp. by cutting 1658. **7.** *intr.* (for *refl.*) To refresh oneself; to take refreshment in some way; now *spec.* to partake of some refreshing liquor 1650. **b.** To lay in fresh supplies 1685.

1. Pearly Rains Descend in silence to r. the Plains DRYDEN. 2. We rose with the sun, refreshed and strong TYNDALL. 5. They went into the hut, and they refreshed the fire 1895. 6. a. The rest r. the scaly Snakes, that fold The Shield of Pallas, and renew their Gold DRYDEN. 7. b. It was not the most eligible place for a ship to r. at 1748.

Refresher (rǐfre·ʃəɪ). late ME. [f. REFRESH *v.* + -ER[1].] **1.** One who or that which refreshes. **b.** A refreshment; *colloq.* a drink 1822. **2.** A reminder 1837. **3.** In legal use: An extra fee paid to counsel in prolonged or frequently adjourned cases. Also *attrib.* 1850.

3. Daily refreshers should be abolished, as being one of the principal causes of the undue lengthening of trials 1881.

attrib.: **r. course,** a course of instruction for officers or men during intervals between fighting.

Refreshful (rǐfre·ʃfŭl), *a.* 1637. [f. REFRESH *v.* + -FUL.] Full of refreshment, refreshing. Hence **Refre·shfully** *adv.*

Refreshment (rǐfre·ʃmĕnt). late ME. [a. OF. *refreschement*, f. *refrescher* to REFRESH + -MENT.] **1.** The act of refreshing, or fact of being refreshed. Also, that which refreshes; the means of restoring strength or vigour, mental or physical. Freq. in phr. *to take r.* **2.** With *a* and *pl.* late ME. **b.** Applied to food and drink; now, of a light repast, and often *spec.* of drink. 1665. †**3.** *pl.* Fresh supplies of men or provisions –1803.

1. With singleness of heart to His glory, and the r. of His people CROMWELL. 2. b. To..allow of no refreshments but such as are consistent with the strictest rules of Christian Sobriety LAW. 4. *attrib.*, as *r. car, house, stall*, etc.; **R. Sunday,** mid-Lent Sunday.

†**Re·fricate,** *v. rare.* 1570. [f. L. *refricat-*, *refricare*, f. *re-* RE- + *fricare* to rub.] *trans.* To open up again, renew (a wound or grief); to stimulate (the memory) afresh –1657. Hence †**Refrica·tion.**

Refrigerant (rǐfri·dʒĕrănt), *a.* and *sb.* 1599. [a. F. *réfrigérant*, or ad. L. *refrigerantem*, *refrigerare*; see next.] **A.** *adj.* **1.** Of medicinal agents or appliances: Cooling the body or part; allaying heat or fever. Also with *property*, etc. †**b.** Refreshing, otherwise than by cooling. BACON. **2.** *gen.* Cooling, producing coolness 1766. **B.** *sb.* **1. a.** A medicinal agent or appliance employed to reduce abnormal heat, as in inflammation or fever; a cooling medicine 1676. **b.** *transf.* or *gen.* A means of cooling, *esp.* a cooling or refreshing drink 1826. †**2.** In distillation, a cooling vessel or apparatus at the head of a still –1727. **3.** A freezing agent 1885.

1. *fig.* This..never fails to prove a r. to passion 1783.

Refrigerate (rǐfri·dʒĕreɪt), *v.* 1534. [ad. L. *refrigerat-*, *refrigerare*, f. *re-* RE- + *frigerare.*] **1.** *trans.* To cause to become cold, to make or keep cool. Also *absol.* **b.** To expose to extreme cold for the purpose of freezing or preserving 1875. **2.** *intr.* To grow cold 1563.

2. I will make a fire, and leave them to r. as much longer as they please LOWELL.

Refrigeration (rǐfridʒĕrē·ʃən). 1471. [ad. L. *refrigerationem*; see prec.] **1.** The action of refrigerating, cooling, or freezing; the process of becoming cold. **b.** *Geol.* The gradual cooling of the earth from natural causes 1794. **c.** The freezing of provisions for the purpose of preserving them 1881. **2.** Reduction of heat in the body (now only *Med.*); †cooling and refreshing of the blood or spirits 1502.

Refrigerative (rǐfri·dʒĕrătiv), *a.* and *sb.* 1558. [See REFRIGERATE *v.* and -IVE.] **A.** *adj.* Tending to cool, refrigerant. **B.** *sb.* A cooling medicine (*rare*) 1706.

Refrigerator (rǐfri·dʒĕreɪtəɪ). 1611. [f. REFRIGERATE *v.* + -OR.] **1.** That which refrigerates or cools. **2.** An apparatus, vessel, or chamber for producing or maintaining a low degree of temperature; *esp.* **a.** any vessel, chamber, or apparatus in which the contents are preserved by maintaining a temperature, near, at, or below freezing-point, esp. in the cold storage of food; **b.** = next **1.** 1824.

Refrigeratory (rǐfri·dʒĕrătəri), *sb.* 1605. [See next and -ORY[1].] **1.** A vessel at the head of a still filled with cold water through which the worm passes, for condensing alcoholic and other vapours; any vessel or apparatus employed for a similar purpose. **2.** Any appliance, vessel or chamber by or in which the process of cooling or freezing is effected 1653.

Refrigeratory (rǐfri·dʒĕrătəri), *a.* 1721. [ad. L. *refrigeratorius*; see REFRIGERATE *v.* and -ORY[2].] Tending to cool or make cold; cooling.

†**Refrige·rium.** 1645. [a. late L.] A respite granted to the souls of the damned; also *transf.* hymns or prayers for such a respite –1667.

Refringency (rǐfri·ndʒĕnsi). 1882. [f. L. *refringere*; see -ENCY.] = REFRACTIVITY.

Refringent (rǐfri·ndʒĕnt), *a.* 1778. [ad. L. *refringent-*, *refringere* to REFRACT.] = REFRACTIVE.

Reft (reft), *ppl. a.* 1847. [See REAVE *v.*[1]] Robbed, bereft of something.

Refuge (re·fiūdʒ), *sb.* late ME. [a. F., ad. L. *refugium*, f. *re-* RE- back + *fugere* to flee.] **1.** Shelter or protection from danger or trouble; succour sought by, or rendered to, a person. **2.** One who, or that which, serves to give shelter, protection, aid, comfort, etc. late ME. **3.** A place of safety or security; a shelter, asylum, stronghold. late ME. **b.** A portion of the roadway marked off at busy crossings, for securing the safety of foot passengers 1881. **4.** †**a.** A resource; recourse *to* a practice –1734. **b.** A plea, pretext, excuse, or answer, in which one takes refuge 1549.

1. So violence Proceeded..Through all the Plain, and r. none was found MILT. Phr. *Of r.*, adapted or intended for shelter or protection, as in *city, country, harbour, place, port of r.*; also *house of r.*, an institution for sheltering the homeless or destitute. *To take r.*, to seek safety or shelter *in* (or *at*) a place; also *transf.* (const. *in*), to have recourse to (something) as a means of escape, consolation, etc. 2. Books—the

r. of the destitute KIPLING. 3. And like a dowve fle to his r. 1450. 4. b. 1 *Hen. VI*, v. iv. 69.

Refuge (re·fiūdʒ), *v.* Now *rare.* 1594. [f. prec., or ad. F. *réfugier.*] 1. *trans.* To afford a refuge, asylum, or retreat to (a person); to shelter, protect. †b. *refl.* To take refuge; to flee for refuge *to* a place –1748. 2. *intr.* To take refuge; to seek shelter or protection 1638.

Refugee (refiudʒī), *sb.* 1685. [ad. F. *réfugié*, pa. pple. of *refugier.*] 1. a. One who, owing to religious persecution or political troubles, seeks refuge in a foreign country; orig. applied to the French Huguenots who came to England after the revocation of the Edict of Nantes in 1685. b. A runaway; a fugitive from justice, etc. (*rare*) 1760. 2. *U.S.* A name given, esp. in New York State, to parties of marauders in the American revolutionary war who claimed British protection. *Obs.* exc. *Hist.* 1780.

Refulgence (rǐfv·ldʒĕns). 1634. [ad. L. *refulgentia*; see -ENCE.] The quality of being refulgent, splendour, brightness, radiance. So †**Refu·lgency** –1796.

Refulgent (rǐfv·ldʒĕnt), *a.* 1509. [ad. L. *refulgentem, refulgere*, f. *re-* RE- + *fulgere* to shine.] Shining with, or reflecting, a brilliant light; radiant, resplendent, gleaming.

There will be no clouds or fogs; but one bright r. day WESLEY. A most r. smile DICKENS. Hence **Refu·lgent-ly** *adv.*, **-ness.**

Refund (rǐfv·nd), *v.*[1] late ME. [ad. OF. *refunder* or L. *refundere*, f. *re-* RE- + *fundere* to pour.] 1. *trans.* To pour back, pour in or out again. Now *rare* or *Obs.* b. To give back, restore. Also *absol.* late ME. 2. To make return or restitution of (a sum received or taken); to hand back, repay, restore 1553. 3. To reimburse, repay (a person) 1736. 4. *absol.* To make repayment 1655.

1. One may as easily perswade the thirsty earth to r. the water she has suckt into her veins 1674. 2. Whatever charges you are at in copying I shall willingly r. 1723. Hence **Refu·nd** *sb.* repayment. **Refu·nder,** one who refunds. **Refu·ndment,** the act of refunding.

Refu·nd (rī-), *v.*[2] 1860. [RE- 5 a.] *trans.* To fund again or anew.

Refusable (rǐfiū·zăb'l), *a.* Now *rare.* 1570. [f. REFUSE *v.* + -ABLE.] That may be refused.

Refusal (rǐfiū·zăl). 1474. [f. REFUSE *v.* + -AL 2.] 1. The act of refusing; a denial or rejection of something demanded or offered. b. *spec.* in the game of écarté, the action of the dealer in refusing to allow a discard. Hence *r. hand*, a hand on which the dealer should so refuse. 1877. c. Of a horse: The action of stopping short (at a hedge, water, etc.) instead of leaping 1856. 2. The chance of refusing some thing, office, or the like before it is offered to others; the privilege or right of having it placed at one's disposal for acceptance; *esp.* in phr. *to have the r. of* 1563. 3. That which has been refused or rejected 1618.

1. Do they not seek occasion of new quarrels, On my r., to distress me more? MILT. 2. They had the first r. of any concessions he might obtain 1887.

†**Refu·se,** *sb.*[1] late ME. [a. OF. *refus*, f. *refuser* to REFUSE.] = prec. 1 and 2. –1753.

Refuse (re·fiūs), *a.* and *sb.*[2] ME. [app. ad. OF. *refuse* (= mod.F. *refusé*), pa. pple. of *refuser* to REFUSE.] A. *adj.* †1. Refused or rejected (*rare*) –1508. 2. Rejected or thrown aside as worthless or of little value 1464. B. *sb.* That which is cast aside as worthless; rubbish or worthless matter of any kind; the rejected or rubbishy part of anything 1440. b. The scum, off-scourings, dregs, etc. *of* some class of persons 1603. c. The leavings *of* something 1665.

A. 2. Certain trades pour their r. water into rivers 1869. B. The stones and r. on the shore DICKENS. c. Some Carcass half devour'd, the R. of gorg'd Wolves SWIFT.

Comb.: **r. consumer, destructor,** a furnace in which r. of various kinds is burned.

Refuse (rǐfiū·z), *v.* ME. [ad. F. *refuser* :—pop. L. **refusare*, f. *refusum, refundere* REFUND *v.*[1]] I. †1. To avoid, keep clear of or free from (sin, vice, etc.) –1691. 2. To decline to take or accept (something offered or presented); to reject the offer of (a thing) ME. b. To reject (a thing or person) in making a choice or selection. Now *rare.* 1526. 3. To decline to accept or submit to (a command, rule, instruction, etc.) or to undergo (pain or penalty). late ME. b. Of a horse: To stop short at (a hedge, water, etc.) instead of leaping 1840. 4. †a. To reject (a person); to decline to admit to a certain position, or to some relationship with oneself –1683. b. To reject, decline to have, as a wife or (now usu.) a husband. late ME. †c. To decline to meet (an opponent) –1606.

2. Lord Halifax began a health to me to-day;.. which I refused SWIFT. b. That hee may know to r. the euill, and choose the good *Isa.* vii. 15. 4. a. This Moses whom they refused, saying, Who made thee a ruler and a Iudge? *Acts* vii. 35.

†II. 1. To renounce –1684. 2. To renounce (God or Christ); to cast off (a person); to divorce (a wife) –1599. 3. To put or drive away, get rid of (*rare*) –1483. 4. To deny (a charge or allegation). *rare.* –1753.

1. Denie thy Father and r. thy name SHAKS. They still R. this World, to do their Father's will BUNYAN.

III. 1. With *inf.* To decline positively, to express or show a determination not *to* do something. Also *transf.* of things. late ME. 2. To decline to give or grant; to deny (something asked) *to* a person (or thing) 1585. b. *Mil.* To decline to oppose (troops) to the enemy; to withdraw or move back from the regular alignment 1796. 3. With double acc.: To decline to give, deny (something) to (a person or thing) 1621. b. With personal object only 1784. †4. To refuse (one) leave *to* do something; to prohibit or keep back *from* something –1688.

1. Seeing kindly sleep r. to doe His office SPENSER. Eliot refused to move from his constitutional ground GREEN. 2. He could not r. his tears to the unhappy fate of Carthage 1734. b. The French during the whole of the action..refused their right wing 1802. 3. I feel already that I can r. you nothing MISS BURNEY. b. Soon I could not have refused her SHELLEY.

IV. *intr.* To make refusal; to decline acceptance or compliance; to withhold permission; *spec.* in écarté (see REFUSAL 1 b). late ME. b. Of a horse: (see I. 3 b above) 1525.

But he refused, and sayde, I wil not eate COVERDALE 1 *Sam.* xxviii. 23. Hence **Refu·ser,** one who refuses; *esp.* a recusant.

†**Refu·sion.** *rare.* 1656. [a. F. *réfusion*, ad. late L. *refusionem*, f. *refundere.*] The action of pouring back; re-infusion (of the soul) –1741.

Refutable (re·fiŭtăb'l, rǐfiū·tăb'l), *a.* 1560. [ad. late L. *refutabilis*, f. *refutare.*] That may be (†rejected,) refuted, or disproved. Hence **Refutabi·lity** (*rare*), capability of being refuted. **Refu·tably** *adv.*

Refutal (rǐfiū·tăl). 1605. [f. REFUTE *v.* + -AL 2.] = next.

Refutation (refiutēⁱ·ʃən). 1548. [ad. L. *refutationem.*] The action of refuting or disproving a statement, charge, etc.; confutation.

An effectual r. of his own Principles BENTLEY.

Refutative (re·fiŭtēⁱtiv, rǐfiū·tătiv), *a. rare.* 1652. [f. L. *refutat-*, *refutare* + -IVE.] That tends to refute; belonging to refutation. So **Refuta·tory** *a.*

Refute (rǐfiū·t), *v.* 1545. [ad. L. *refutare* to repel, repress, rebut.] 1. *trans.* To prove (a person) to be in error, to confute. 2. To disprove, overthrow by argument, prove to be false 1597. 3. *absol.* To demonstrate error 1742.

2. An errour so gross..that it needs not the Microscope to r. it 1664. The surest way to r. such calumnies THIRLWALL. Would you not seek everywhere for proofs to r. the accusation? MANNING. Hence †**Refute** *sb.* refutation. **Refu·ter,** one who refutes.

Regain (rǐgēⁱ·n, rī-), *v.* 1548. [ad. F. *regagner*; see RE- and GAIN *v.*] 1. *trans.* To gain or get anew; to recover possession of (something). Also *absol.* †2. To win or bring back *to* a state or condition –1679. 3. To get back to, succeed in reaching (a place) again; to rejoin (a person) 1634. b. To recover (one's feet) 1814.

1. I began by degrees to r. confidence JOWETT. Hence **Regai·nment.**

Regal (rī·găl), *a.* and *sb.*[1] ME. [a. OF. *regal, -ale*, or L. *regalis*, f. *reg-*, *rex* king; see -AL.] A. *adj.* 1. Of or belonging to a king; royal. †2. Ruling, governing (*rare*) –1656. 3. Befitting, or resembling, a king; kingly; hence, splendid, magnificent, stately, etc. 1799.

1. When they see all R. Power Giv'n me to quell thir pride MILT. The r. title GIBBON.

†B. *sb.* 1. Royalty, sovereignty, royal authority –1460. 2. A prince, ruler (*rare*) –1821. 3. The chalice used for the communion at the coronation of British sovereigns –1662. †4. *pl* = REGALIA[1] 2. –1604. Hence **Re·gally** *adv.*

Regal (rī·găl), *sb.*[2] 1541. [a. F. *régale*, perh. f. *régal* REGAL *a.*] 1. Chiefly *pl.* A small portable organ, having one, or sometimes two, sets of reed-pipes played with keys by the right hand, while a small bellows was worked by the left hand. Now chiefly *Hist.* 2. One of certain reed-stops (*esp.* the *vox humana*) in organs 1799.

‖ **Regale** (rǐgēⁱ·li, F. regal), *sb.*[1] 1611. [a. F. *régale* (ad. L. *regalia*), or L. *regale.*] 1. *Eccl. Hist.* The right, on the part of the kings of France, of enjoying the revenues of vacant bishoprics or abbacies, and of presenting to benefices dependent on these. †2. A privilege or prerogative of royalty –1797.

Regale (rǐgēⁱ·l), *sb.*[2] 1670. [a. obs. F. *régale*, ad. It. *regalo* REGALO.] 1. A choice repast, feast, or banquet; †an entertainment or fête. Also *transf.* or *fig.* 2. A choice article of food or form of refreshment; a dainty 1673. 3. Refreshment 1753. †4. A complimentary present (*rare*) –1744.

2. I may therefore hope..to see the tables adorned with the r. of Devonshire cream 1791. 4. I had been threatened with a r. of hams and Florence wine H. WALPOLE.

Regale (rǐgēⁱ·l), *v.* 1656. [ad. F. *régaler*, It. *regalare*; etym. obsc.] 1. *trans.* To entertain or feast (a person, etc.) in a choice manner. b. Of things: To furnish (one) with a choice feast or refreshment 1721. 2. To gratify or delight (the mind) by some pleasing influence or occupation; to entertain (a person) in a highly agreeable manner 1671. b. To affect with a pleasurable sensation 1703. 3. To gratify, please, delight, by a gift, deference, etc. (*rare*) 1671. 4. *refl.* To entertain or recreate (oneself) with food, drink, or amusement 1719. 5. *intr.* To feast; const. *on, upon, with* 1678.

1. Regaling each other in the best style their respective camps afforded W. IRVING. 2. b. The peach's vernal bud regal'd his eye SHENSTONE. Hence **Rega·lement,** the act of regaling; a dainty.

‖ **Regalia**[1] (rǐgēⁱ·liă). 1540. [L., pl. of *regale* REGALE *sb.*[1]] 1. Rights appertaining to a king; royal powers or privileges. 2. The emblems or insignia of royalty; the crown, sceptre, and other distinctive ornaments of a king or queen which are used at coronations 1626. 3. The decorations or insignia of an order 1676.

Regalia[2] (rǐgēⁱ·liă). 1819. [a. Sp. *regalia* royal privilege.] A Cuban or other large cigar of superior quality.

Regalian (rǐgēⁱ·liăn), *a.* 1818. [a. F. *régalien*; see REGAL *a.* and -IAN.] Pertaining to a sovereign; regal.

Regalism (rī·găliz'm). 1869. [f. REGAL *a.* + -ISM.] The doctrine or practice of the supremacy of the sovereign in ecclesiastical matters. So **Re·galist,** a supporter of r.

Regality (rǐgæ·lĭti). late ME. [a. AF. (and OF.) *regalité*, or ad. med.L. *regalitatem*; see REGAL *a.* and -ITY.] 1. Royalty, kingship, sovereign rule or jurisdiction. 2. *Sc.* Territorial jurisdiction of a royal nature granted by the king. Now *Hist.* late ME. 3. *Sc.* A particular territory or area subject to a lord of regality. late ME. 4. A country or district subject to royal authority, a kingdom; a monarchical state 1486. 5. A right or privilege pertaining or appropriate to a king. Chiefly *pl.* 1523.

1. When raging Passion with fierce tyranny Robs Reason of her dew regalitie SPENSER. 2. *Lord of r.*, the person to whom r. was granted. 5. Before Ile be halfe a king, and contrould In any r., ile hazard all 1592.

‖ **Regalo** (rega·lo). Now *rare.* 1622. [ad. It. (also Sp. and Pg.) *regalo* a gift, related to *regalare* to REGALE.] A present, esp. of choice food or drink; a choice or elegant repast or entertainment, etc. (see REGALE *sb.*[2]).

†**Re·galty.** ME. [prob. a. AF. *regalté, regauté.] = REGALITY -1703.

Regard (rĭgā·ɹd), *sb.* late ME. [a. F. *regard*, f. *regarder* REGARD *v.*] I. 1. †Aspect, appearance; look (of persons); habit or manner of looking; air. 2. A look, glance, or gaze 1477. †b. An object of sight (*rare*) -1604. 3. The official inspection of a forest in order to discover whether any trespasses have been committed in it; the right of such inspection, or the office of one appointed to make it. *Obs.* exc. *Hist.* 1502. b. The district within the jurisdiction of the official regarders 1594. 4. †a. Reference *to* a person or thing. Chiefly in phr. *to have* (*a*) *r. to*. -1677. b. Respect, point, particular 1602. †c. ? Intention, purpose, design. SHAKS.

1. To whom with stern r. thus Gabriel spake MILT. 2. He..bites his lip with a politique r. SHAKS. b. To throw-out our eyes for braue Othello, Euen till we make the Maine,..An indistinct r. SHAKS. 4. b. I will pay every possible attention to your instructions in this r. SHELLEY. c. *Jul. C.* III. i. 224.

II. †1. Repute, account, or estimation, in which anything is held -1785. 2. Observant attention or heed bestowed upon or given *to* a matter. †Also *pl.* 1456. b. Care in doing something; close attention *to* some principle or method 1575. 3. Care or concern *for* something 1836. 4. Attention, heed, or consideration, given to a thing or person, as having an effect or influence on one's actions or conduct; respect or deference paid *to*, or entertained *for*, some authority, principle, etc. Orig. in phr. *to have* (†*make* or *take*) *r. to*; in later use also const. *of, for.* 1477. 5. A thing or circumstance looked to, or taken into account, in determining action; a consideration, a motive 1579. †b. A looking *to* another in order to direct one's actions or conduct (*rare*) -1732. 6. Esteem, affection, kindly feeling 1591. b. *pl.* in epistolary expressions of good-will 1775.

1. What things there are Most abiect in r., and deare in vse SHAKS. †*Of..r.*, of (small, great, etc.) account, estimation, or value. †*In* (one's) *r.*, in one's opinion, estimation, or judgement (*rare*). 2. The conduct pursued by the Governor-General is the next object of r. 1818. 3. R. for the safety of the hostages FREEMAN. 4. A religious r. was paid to fire BERKELEY. *Without r.* (†*of* or) *to*, without giving consideration or weight *to* a thing; without reference *to*. 5. A benevolence which shall lose all particular regards in its general light EMERSON. 6. There is no guide ..for whom I have a stronger r. TYNDALL.

Phrases. *In r. of*, in comparison with (now *arch.*) *In r. of* or *to*, *with r. to*, in respect of, with respect or reference to. *In one's r.*, with regard, respect, or reference to one. †*In r. of* or *to*, out of consideration for. †*In r.* (*that*), since, because, inasmuch as, considering that.

Regard (rĭgā·ɹd), *v.* late ME. [ad. F. *regarder*, f. *re-* RE- + *garder* to GUARD.] I. *trans.* 1. To look at, gaze upon, observe 1523. †b. Of places, etc.: To look or face toward -1750. 2. To take notice of, bestow attention or notice upon; to take or show an interest in; to give heed to; †to take care of. late ME. †3. To look to, have a care of or for (oneself, one's own interest, health, etc.) -1671. b. To look to, consider, take into account 1591. †4. To take notice of (a thing) as being of special value, excellence, or merit; to value or set store by -1656. b. To hold (a person) in great esteem; to have a regard for (a person) 1513. 5. To heed, or take into account, in regulating one's actions or conduct 1512. b. To have respect for or dread of (a person) 1526. c. To pay heed or attention to (one speaking or something said) 1535. d. To show consideration for (a thing or person) 1513. 6. To consider, look on, *as* being something 1607. b. To look upon *with* some feeling 1615. 7. To concern, have relation or respect to 1603. b. In *pres. pple.* Concerning, relating to 1793. c. *As regards*, so far as relates to 1819.

1. Your neece regards me with an eye of fauour SHAKS. 2. R. the weak and fatherless MILT. 3. b. *Two Gent.* III. i. 256. 4. b. I have in vain done all I can to make her r. me STEELE. 5. They that r. not the Law are a dishonourable seed *Ecclus.* x. 19. b. Here 's Beauford, that regards not God nor King SHAKS. c. Hee talk'd very wisely, but I regarded him not SHAKS. d. We may be led to think that the rights of England were..strictly regarded FREEMAN. 6. He regarded his submission as the end of the dispute FROUDE. b. The stamp of artless piety..The youth..Regards with scorn COWPER. 7. Morals and criticism r. our tastes and sentiments HUME.

II. 1. *absol.* or *intr.* a. To look, gaze (*rare*) 1523. b. To pay attention, give heed; to bestow attention *on* a thing 1611. †2. To look *to*; to refer *to* -1659. 3. To look, appear. SHELLEY.

1. a. We with blind surmise Regarding, while she read TENNYSON. b. I haue stretched out my hand, and no man regarded *Prov.* i. 24. 3. The hills and woods..R. like shapes in an enchanter's glass 1819.

Rega·rdable, *a.* Now *rare.* 1591. [f. prec. + -ABLE.] Worthy of being regarded, noticeable.

Regardant (rĭgā·ɹdănt), *a.* and *sb.* 1443. [a. F. *regardant*, pres. pple. of *regarder* to REGARD.] A. *adj.* 1. *Law.* (now *Hist.*) Attached to a manor. 2. *Her.* Looking backward 1500. 3. Observant, watchful, contemplative 1588. †B. *sb.* A villein regardant, a serf -1795.

A. 3. The look..was rather cogitative than r. SOUTHEY.

Regarder (rĭgā·ɹdəɹ). 1502. [f. REGARD *v.* + -ER[1].] 1. An officer charged with the supervision of a forest. Now *local* and *Hist.* 2. One who or that which regards 1525.

Regardful (rĭgā·ɹdfŭl), *a.* 1586. [f. REGARD *sb.*] 1. Heedful, attentive, observant. 2. Respectful; indicative of regard or esteem 1607. †3. Worthy of regard or attention -1650.

1. They ar more r. of their worldly gain..then they ar of a good conscience 1653. Hence **Rega·rdful-ly** *adv.*, **-ness.**

Regardless (rĭgā·ɹdlės), *a.* 1591. [f. REGARD *sb.*] 1. Heedless, indifferent, careless; without regard *of.* 2. Unregarded, slighted; unworthy of regard 1591. 3. advb. in *r. of*, without regard to; also *ellipt.* (orig. *U.S.*) 1872.

1. R. of the Bliss wherein hee sat MILT. Treading the May-flowers with r. feet WHITTIER. Hence **Re·ga·rdless-ly** *adv.*, **-ness.**

Regatta (rĭgæ·tă). 1652. [It. (Venetian) *regatta* 'a strife or contention or struggling for the maistrie' (Florio).] 1. The name given at Venice to certain boat-races held on the Grand Canal. 2. A boat- or yacht-race, or (usu.) an organized series of such races, forming a more or less sporting and social event 1775.

Regelate (rīdʒĕlēt), *v.* 1860. [f. RE- 5 a + ppl. stem of L. *gelare* to freeze.] *intr.* (and *refl.*) To freeze together again.

Regelation (rīdʒĕlē·ʃən). 1857. [See prec. and GELATION.] The action of freezing together again; *spec.* the fusion of two pieces of ice, having moist surfaces, at a temperature above freezing-point.

†**Re·gence.** *rare.* 1457. [a. F. *régence*; see next and -ENCE.] = next -1678.

Regency (rī·dʒĕnsi). late ME. [ad. med. L. *regentia*, or f. REGENT; see -ENCY.] 1. The position or office of ruler; exercise of rule or authority; government, dominion, control. Now *rare* or *Obs.* 1485. 2. The office and jurisdiction of a regent or vice-regent; government by a regent or by a body exercising similar authority. late ME. 3. †a. The governing body of certain (chiefly European) towns and Mohammedan states -1796. b. A body of men appointed to carry on the government during the absence, minority, or incapacity of the sovereign or hereditary ruler; a Government so constituted 1721. 4. A district under the control of a regent or regency 1667. 5. The period during which a regent governs *spec.* the period during which George, Prince of Wales (the Prince Regent, 1810–20) acted as regent 1727. 6. The office or function of a university regent 1639.

3. b. We expect some chagrin on the new R. at the head of which is to be the Duke H. WALPOLE.

Regeneracy (rĭdʒe·nĕrăsi). 1626. [f. next + -ACY.] The state of being regenerate.

Regenerate (rĭdʒe·nĕrĕt), *ppl. a.* and *sb.* 1471. [ad. L. *regeneratus*, *regenerare*; see next.] A. *ppl. a.* †1. Re-born; brought again into existence; formed anew -1610. 2. In religious use: Spiritually re-born 1526. b. Restored to a better state, reformed 1647. c. Of nations: Restored or raised again from a sunk or base condition 1811. †3. Degenerate, renegade (*rare*) -1607. †B. *sb.* A regenerate person -1652.

A. 1. The earthy author of my blood, Whose youthfull spirit in me r., Doth with a two-fold rigor lift mee vp SHAKS.

Regenerate (rĭdʒe·nĕreɪt), *v.* 1541. [ad. ppl. stem of L. *regenerare*; see RE- and GENERATE *v.*] 1. *trans.* In religious use: To cause to be born again in a spiritual sense; to invest with a new and higher spiritual nature 1557. b. To reform completely (a person or state of things, etc.) 1849. 2. *Path.* To reproduce, form afresh (some part of the body). Chiefly in *pass.* 1597. 3. To reproduce, re-create; to form or bring into existence again 1608. 4. To reconstitute on a higher plane; to place on a new basis 1789. 5. *intr.* a. To form again. Chiefly *Path.* 1541. b. To reform, become regenerate 1786. 6. *Electr.* To increase the amplification of (an electron current) by causing a part of the power in the output circuit to act upon the input circuit.

Regeneration (rīdʒenĕrē·ʃən). ME. [ad. F. *régénération* or L. *regenerationem*; see prec. and -ATION.] 1. The action of regenerating; the process or fact of being regenerated; re-creation, re-formation, etc. b. *fig.* Revival; renascence, re-constitution on a higher level 1627. 2. In religious use: The process or fact of being born again spiritually; the state resulting from this. late ME. 3. *Path.* The formation of new animal tissue; the reproduction of lost parts or organs. late ME. 4. *Electr.* (cf. prec. 6).

1. b. All great regenerations are the universal movement of the mass LYTTON. 2. Spiritual r. begins naturally among the poor and the humble FROUDE. 3. The local death of some tissues is followed by their r. HUXLEY.

Regenerative (rĭdʒe·nĕrĕtiv), *a.* late ME. [ad. F. *régénératif*, *-ive*, or med.L. *regenerativus*; see REGENERATE *v.* and -IVE.] 1. Tending to or characterized by regeneration. 2. *Mech.* Constructed on, or employing the principle of the REGENERATOR 1861.

1. The great r. work which he undertook 1871. *spec.* (*Electr.*) cf. REGENERATE *v.* 6, REGENERATION 4. 2. Mr. Siemens, the inventor of the so-called r. furnaces 1864. Hence **Rege·neratively** *adv.*

Regenerator (rĭdʒe·nĕreɪtəɹ). 1740. [f. REGENERATE *v.* + -OR. Cf. F. *régénérateur.*] 1. One who or that which regenerates. 2. *Mech.* A fuel-saving device attached to a furnace, consisting of layers of fire-brick which, becoming heated by the hot air and gases from the furnace, impart the heat to an incoming current of cold air or combustible gas acting alternately with the outgoing current 1835.

Regeneratory (rĭdʒe·nĕrătəri), *a.* 1803. [f. as REGENERATE *v.* + -ORY[2].] Of the nature of regeneration; regenerative.

Regent (rī·dʒĕnt), *sb.* late ME. [Subst. use of next.] 1. a. That which rules, governs, or has supremacy; a ruling power or principle. Now *rare.* b. One who rules or governs; a ruler, governor, director. Now *rare* or *Obs.* 1480. 2. a. One who is invested with royal authority by, or on behalf of, another; *esp.* one appointed to administer a kingdom during the minority, absence, or incapacity of the sovereign. late ME. b. The name given to the municipal authorities of some continental cities (*obs.*), and to the native chiefs in Java 1724. 3. In the Universities: a. At Oxford and Cambridge, a Master of Arts ruling or presiding over disputations in the Schools, a duty orig. discharged for one, and afterwards for five, years after graduation; hence, in later use, a Master of not more than five years standing. Now *Hist.* late ME. b. In France, the title usu. given to those who taught the more elementary classes; an instructor in arts or science 1611. c. *U.S.* A member of the governing board of a State University (and of the Smithsonian Institute, Washington) 1817. †4. The head master of a school -1796.

attrib.: R. **bird** or **oriole**, an Australian bird, *Sericulus melinus*, named in compliment to the Prince Regent, afterwards George IV. R. (**congregation** or) **house**, the upper of the two houses into which the Senate of Cambridge University was formerly divided. Hence **Re·gentess**, a female regent. **Re·gentship**, the office or position of a regent.

Regent (rī·dʒĕnt), *a.* ME. [a. F. *régent* or L. *regentem*, *regere*.] 1. In spec. senses (usu. placed after the sb.). a. Holding the position of a University regent. Now *Hist.* b. Acting as, having the position of, regent of a country, esp. *Queen r.* 1555. **2.** Ruling, governing, controlling. Now *rare.* 1613.

2. The r. helm her motion still commands 1762.

Regent (rī·dʒĕnt), *v.* Now *rare.* 1623. [f. REGENT *sb.*] **1. a.** *trans.* To superintend or teach (a college, class, etc.), as a regent. **b.** *intr.* To act as a University regent 1631. **2.** *trans.* To control (a person) as a regent 1797.

†**Rege·st,** *sb. rare.* 1670. [ad. late L. *regesta* (pl.) a list, f. *regerere.*] A register. MILT.

†**Re·gian.** 1653. [f. L. *regius* + -AN I.] An upholder of regal authority; a royalist –1670.

Regicidal (re·dʒisəidăl), *a.* 1779. [f. REGICIDE [2] + -AL I.] Pertaining to, characterized by, inclined to, regicide.

Regicide [1] (re·dʒisəid). 1548. [f. L. *regi-, rex* king + -CIDE I.] **1.** One who kills a king, esp. his own king; one who commits the crime of regicide. **2.** *spec.* **a.** *Eng. Hist.* One of those who took part in the trial and execution of Charles I. 1654. **b.** *Fr. Hist.* One of those Revolutionists concerned in the execution of Louis XVI 1796. **3.** *attrib.* or *adj.* 1645.

Regicide [2] (re·dʒisəid). 1602. [f. as prec. + -CIDE 2.] The killing or murder of a king. Hence **Re·gicidism,** the practice or principle of r.

‖**Régie** (reʒī). 1883. [F., fem. pa. pple. of *régir* to rule.] The revenue department established in some European countries for the entire control of the importation and manufacture of tobacco, salt, etc.

Regifuge (re·dʒifiūdʒ). 1654. [ad. L. *regifugium,* f. *regi-, rex* + *fuga* flight.] *Rom. Hist.* The flight or expulsion of the kings from Rome.

‖**Régime, regime** (reʒī·m). 1776. [F., ad. L. *regimen.*] **1.** = next 2. **2.** A manner, method, or system of rule or government; a system or institution having widespread influence or prevalence 1792.

1. Regime is better than physic 1776. **2.** Phr. *The ancient,* or *old, r.* (tr. F. *l'ancien régime*), the system of government in France before the Revolution of 1789. Also *transf.,* the old system or style of things.

Regimen (re·dʒimen). late ME. [a. L. *regimen,* f. *regere.*] **1.** The act of governing; government, rule 1456. **b.** A particular form or kind of government; a regime; a prevailing system 1734. **2.** *Med.* The regulation of such matters as have an influence on the preservation or restoration of health; a particular course of diet, exercise, or mode of living, prescribed or adopted for this end. late ME. **3.** *Gram.* The government of one word by another; the relation which one word in a sentence has to another depending on it 1600.

1. b. Nothing is so apt to follow as sedition from a popular r. HALLAM. **2.** Things..Very behoofull to the R. Of health 1646. Hence **Regi·menal** *a.* = REGIMINAL.

Regiment (re·dʒmĕnt, re·dʒimĕnt), *sb.* late ME. [ad. late L. *regimentum,* f. as prec.; see -MENT.] **1.** Rule or government over a person, people, or country; *esp.* royal or magisterial authority. Now *rare.* †**b.** Manner, method, or system of ruling or governing; a form of polity, a regime –1676. †**2. a.** The office or function of a ruler –1630. **b.** The time or period during which one rules; a reign –1630. †**3.** Government or control over oneself, one's feelings or actions –1679. †**b.** Control or influence exercised by one thing over another, or over a person –1674. †**4.** The ruling or governing *of* a person, people or place –1702. †**b.** The management, guidance, or control *of* a thing or affair (*rare*) –1741. †**5.** = REGIMEN 2. –1768. †**6.** A place or country under a particular rule; a kingdom, province, domain, district –1662. **7.** *Mil.* A considerable body of troops, more or less permanently organized under the command of a superior officer, and forming a definite unit of an army or military force; since the 17th c. the specific name of the largest permanent unit of the cavalry, infantry, and foot-guards of the British Army 1579. **b.** *transf.* and *fig.*: *esp.* a large array or number (of anything) 1605. †**c.** A class or kind –1656. †**8.** *pl.* Regimentals. H. WALPOLE.

3. The R. & gouernment of euery man, over himselfe BACON. **4. b.** The greatest Lords thought the R. of Sea-affairs worthy of the best of their Rank 1651. **6.** *transf.* Men who never saw the sea, yet desire to behold that r. of waters 1623. **7.** The..strength of a r. of infantry of a single battalion is 750. 1853.

Regiment (re·dʒmĕnt, re·dʒimĕnt), *v.* 1617. [f. prec.] **1.** *trans. Mil.* To form into a regiment or regiments. (Chiefly in *pass.*) **b.** To form (persons, now esp. workers) into a definitely organized body or group 1718. **c.** To bring or put (things) *into* some definite order or system; to organize, systematize 1698. **2.** To assign to a regiment or group 1774. Hence **Re·gimenta·tion,** the action or process of regimenting or organizing.

Regimental (redʒme·ntăl, redʒime·ntăl), *a.* and *sb.* 1702. [f. REGIMENT *sb.* + -AL.] **A.** *adj.* Of or belonging to, associated with, a regiment, or with some particular regiment. **B.** *sb. pl.* The dress proper to or characteristic of any particular regiment; military uniform 1708.

A. R. hospitals are of the greatest importance 1753. Hence **Regime·ntally** *adv.*

Regiminal (rĭdʒi·minăl), *a.* 1832. [f. REGIMEN, after L. types, as *criminal.*] *Med.* Of or pertaining to, of the nature of, regimen.

Reginal (rĭdʒəi·năl), *a.* 1568. [ad. med. L. *reginalis,* f. L. *regina* + -AL I.] **a.** Queenly, queenlike. **b.** Taking the side of the queen.

Region (rī·dʒən). ME. [a. AF. *regiun,* ad. L. *regionem* direction, district, etc., f. *regere* to direct.] **1.** †**a.** A realm or kingdom. **b.** A large tract of land; a country; a more or less defined portion of the earth's surface, now esp. as distinguished by certain natural features, climatic conditions, a special fauna or flora, or the like. **c.** An area, space, or place, of more or less definite extent or character 1726. **2.** A separate part or division of the world or universe, as the air, heaven, etc. ME. **b.** *fig.* A place, state or condition, having a certain character or subject to certain influences; the sphere or realm *of* something 1526. **3.** One of the successive portions into which the air or atmosphere is theoretically divided according to height. Also similarly of the sea according to depth. 1563. **4.** An administrative division of a city or district 1593. **5.** A part or division of the body or its parts. late ME. **6.** A space occupied by a thing 1664. **7.** *attrib.* 1600.

1. b. Nauigatours haue discouered few or no Regions wanting inhabitants 1625. **2.** Anon the dreadfull Thunder Doth rend the R. SHAKS. **b.** That he escaping the..paynes of eternall derkenes May euer dwel in the r. of lighte *Bk. Com. Prayer.* **3.** Regions of the Air, are distinguished into Upper, Middle, and Lower 1704. *fig.* He is of too high a R., he knows too much SHAKS. **5.** Let it fall rather, though the fork invade The r. of my heart SHAKS. **7.** The r. cloude hath mask'd him from me now SHAKS. Hence **Re·gional** *a.* of or pertaining to a particular r. or district; pertaining to a special part of the body.

Regionalism (rī·dʒənăliz'm). 1881. [f. REGIONAL + -ISM.] Tendency to, or practice of, regional systems or methods; localism on a regional basis. So **Re·gionalist. Regionali·stic** *a.* **Re·gionalize** *v.* to organize on a regional basis; **Re:gionaliza·tion.**

Regionary (rī·dʒənări), *a.* and *sb.* 1657. [ad. late L. *regionarius*; see REGION and -ARY [1].] **A.** *adj.* Of or pertaining to a region. **B.** *sb.* An account or description of the regions of Rome 1818.

A. *R. bishop,* a bishop without any particular diocese.

Register (re·dʒistəɹ), *sb.*[1] late ME. [a. F. *registre,* or med.L. *registrum, regestrum,* for *regestum,* from late L. *regesta* (pl.) matters recorded, f. *regerere,* f. *re-* RE- + *gerere* to carry.] **I. 1.** A book in which regular entry is made of details of any kind sufficiently important to be exactly recorded; a written record thus formed; †a list, catalogue. †**2.** As the title of a compilation containing the forms of writs of the Common Law, cited by English lawyers of the 16–17th c. –1628. **3.** As the name of certain official or authoritative records or books of record: e.g. **a.** of the baptisms, marriages, and burials in a parish, kept by the clergyman; or (in later use) of births, marriages, and deaths, kept by an official (a REGISTRAR) appointed for the purpose 1538. **b.** of seamen in the British mercantile marine 1695. **c.** of shipping, containing particulars of construction, materials, size, ownership, etc.; also, a certificate issued by the registering official, esp. as evidence of the nationality of the vessel 1825. **d.** of those entitled to vote in Parliamentary or municipal elections 1832. **4.** An entry in a register (esp. in sense 3 a) 1535. **5.** Registration, registry 1653.

1. He kept a r. of all the King's promises BURNET. *fig.* As you haue one eye vpon my follies,..turne another into the R. of your owne SHAKS. **4.** There being no R. of his Christening ARBUTHNOT.

II. 1. a. An index; a table of contents (*rare*) 1585. **b.** The series of signatures in a printed book; the list of these at the end of early printed books 1885. **2.** *Mus.* A slider in an organ; a set of pipes controlled by a slider, a stop; also, a stop-knob 1585. **b.** The compass of a voice or instrument; now *spec.* the particular range of tones which can be produced in the same way and with the same quality 1811. **3.** A contrivance, usu. consisting of a metal plate or plates by which an opening may be wholly or partially closed, used for regulating the passage of air, heat, or smoke 1610. **4.** A registering device; a mechanical contrivance or apparatus by which data of some kind are automatically recorded; an indicator 1830. **5.** *Printing.* †**a.** An inner part of a type-mould –1738. **b.** Precise adjustment of the type or printing; *esp.* exact correspondence of the printed matter on the two sides of a leaf 1683. **c.** *Photogr.* In a camera, proper correspondence between the focussing screen and the sensitive plate or film 1890.

2. b. The 'soprano register', the 'tenor register', denote that part of the scale which forms the usual compass of those voices; the 'head register' means the notes which are sung with the head voice; the 'chest register' those which are sung from the chest GROVE. **3.** Looke well to the r., And let your heat, still, lessen by degrees B. JONS.

Comb.: **r. book** = sense I. 1; **r.-ship,** a Spanish ship having a registered licence to trade with the Spanish possessions in America (now *Hist.*).

Register (re·dʒistəɹ), *sb.*[2] Now *rare* exc. in U.S. 1531. [prob. for REGISTRER.] The keeper of a register; a REGISTRAR. Hence †**Re·gistership,** the office of registrar.

Register (re·dʒistəɹ), *v.* late ME. [ad. F. *registrer,* or med.L. *registrare,* f. *registrum* REGISTER *sb.*[1]] **1.** *trans.* To set down (facts, names, etc.) formally in writing; to enter or record in a precise manner. †**b.** To set (a person) down *for,* or as, something –1611. **2.** *spec.* To make formal entry of (a document, fact, name, etc.) in a particular register; also, to get (a document, etc.) entered in the register by the person entitled to do so 1463. **3.** Of instruments: To record by some automatic device; to indicate 1797. **b.** Of a cinema actor or actress: To express (an emotion) by facial expression, etc. Also *transf.* 1901. **4.** *intr.* To coincide or correspond exactly 1839. **b.** *trans.* To adjust with precision, so as to secure the exact correspondence of parts 1839. **5.** *intr.* To manipulate the registers of an organ 1891.

1. Such follow him, as shall be registerd Part good part bad, of bad the longer scrowle MILT. **2. b.** *intr.* (U.S.) To have one's name entered on the list of qualified voters; also, to enter one's name in the register of an hotel or lodging-house 1850.

Re·gister o·ffice. 1760. An office at which a register of any kind is kept, or where registration is made; a registry.

Registrar (redʒistrā·ɹ, re·dʒistrāɹ). 1675. [f. REGISTER *v.* + -AR [2].] One whose business it is to keep an official register.

R.-General, the chief officer of the General Register Office, Somerset House.

Registrary (re·dʒistrări). 1541. Retained only at Cambridge. [ad. med.L. *registrarius*; see REGISTER *sb.*[1] and -ARY [1].] A registrar.

†**Re·gistrate,** *v.* Chiefly *Sc.* 1570. [f. med.L. *registrat-, registrare.*] *trans.* To register –1776.

Registration (redʒistrē̆ⁱ·ʃən). 1566. [ad. med.L. *registrationem.*] **1.** The act of registering or recording. **b.** With *a* and *pl.* An instance of this; an entry made in a register 1611. **c.** *attrib.*, as *r. act, fee,* etc. 1843. **2.** *Printing.* Adjustment 1890.

Re·gistrer. Now *rare.* late ME. [orig. a. AF. *registrere; later f. REGISTER *v.* + -ER [1].] †**a.** A registrar. **b.** = REGISTER *sb.*[1] II. 4.

Registry (re·dʒistri). 1589. [f. REGIST(ER) *v.* + -RY.] **1.** The act of registering, registration. **2.** A place where registers are kept; now often used (*a*) colloq. = district register office, where marriages take place, (*b*) short for *servants registry*, an office where the names of domestic servants seeking employment are registered 1603. **3.** A register, a book of record; also, an entry in a register 1622. **4.** *attrib.*, as *r. fee* (U.S.), *office*, etc. 1721.

Regius (rī·dʒiǒs). [L. = royal.] The designation of certain university professors of royal foundation and (for the most part) appointed by royal mandate.

†**Regle, reigle,** *v.* 1591. [ad. F. *régler*, †*reigler*, ad.L. *regulare.*] *trans.* To rule, regulate –1670.

‖**Re·glement** (rēgləmaṅ), †**reiglement.** 1598. [a. F. *règlement*, f. *régler*; see prec.] †**1.** The act of regulating or controlling –1734. **2.** A regulation. (Now only as Fr.) 1625.

1. The Reformation and Reiglement of Vsury BACON.

Regleme·ntary, *a. rare.* 1870. [ad. F. *réglementaire*; see prec. and -ARY [1].] Regular, according to regulations.

Reglet (re·glėt), †**riglet.** 1576. [a. F. *réglet*, f. *règle*, ad. L. *regula* + -ET.] †**1.** A narrow division of a page of a book; a column –1576. **2.** *Arch.* A narrow flat band used to separate mouldings or other parts from each other 1664. †**3.** A thin, flat piece or strip of wood used in carpentry or frame-making (*rare*) –1683. **b.** *Printing.* A thin, narrow strip of wood or metal, used to make wide blanks between lines of type 1683. **c.** Collectively, or as a material. Also *attrib.*, as *r. plane.* 1846.

‖**Regma** (re·gmă). *Pl.* **re·gmata.** 1839. [a. Gr. ῥῆγμα a fracture.] *Bot.* In Mirbel's classification, a dry fruit formed of three or more cells which break open when ripe.

Regnal (re·gnăl), *a.* 1612. [ad. med.L. *regnalis*, f. *regnum.*] **1. a.** *R. year*, any year of a sovereign's reign, reckoned from the date of his accession. **b.** *R. day*, the anniversary of a sovereign's accession 1877. **2.** Of or pertaining to a reign, kingdom, or king 1643.

Regnant (re·gnănt), *ppl. a.* 1600. [ad.L. *regnant-*, *regnare.*] **1.** Reigning, ruling. **2.** Of things, qualities, etc.: Ruling, exercising sway or influence, predominant, dominating 1621. **b.** Prevalent, wide-spread 1625.

1. Queens r. WOTTON. The r. house 1856. **2. b.** The belief in witchcraft and diabolical contracts which was r. in his day M. ARNOLD.

Regorge (rīgǭ·ɹdʒ), *v.* 1605. [ad. F. *regorger*, or f. RE- + GORGE *v.*] **1.** *trans.* To disgorge or cast up again; to throw or cast back (*lit.* and *fig.*). **b.** *intr.* To gush or flow back again 1654. **2.** *trans.* To engorge or swallow again (*rare*) 1700.

2. And tides at highest mark r. the flood DRYDEN.

Regrate (rīgrē¹·t), *v. Obs.* exc. *Hist.* 1467. [a. OF. *regrater*, mod.F. *regratter.*] **1.** *trans.* To buy up (market commodities, esp. victuals) in order to sell again at a profit in the same or a neighbouring market. **2.** To sell again (articles so bought), to retail 1582. Hence **Regra·ter, Regra·tor,** one who regrates victuals, etc.; a retailer; a middleman. †**Regra·tery,** the practice of regrating.

Regrede (rīgrī·d), *v.* 1865. [ad. L. *regredi*, f. *re-* RE- + *gradi* to go.] *intr.* To retrograde, go back. So †**Regre·dience,** return.

†**Regree·t,** *sb.* 1595. [f. next.] A (return of a) greeting –1665. **b.** *pl.* Greetings –1639.

Regree·t, *v.* Now *rare.* 1586. [f. RE- + GREET *v.*[1]] **1.** *trans.* To greet again or anew. **2.** To greet (a person) in return; also simply, to greet, give salutation to 1593.

Regress (rī·gres), *sb.* late ME. [ad. L. *regressus*, f. *regredi*; see REGREDE *v.*] **1.** The act of going or coming back; a return or withdrawal; re-entry *to* or *into* the place of issue or origin. Freq. in the phrases (orig. legal) *egress*, or *ingress, and r.* **2.** *Law.* †**a.** Return to possession; re-entry (*rare*) –1628. **b.** *Canon Law.* 'Right of returning to a benefice vacated in case of death, &c., of the actual incumbent' 1710. **3.** The fact of going back from, or in respect of, a state or condition 1590. **4.** The act of working back in thought from one thing to another, *spec.* from an effect to a cause 1620. **5.** *Astr.* = RETROGRADATION 1. 1642.

1. *fig.* The standing is slipery, and the regresse is either a downefall, or..an Eclipse BACON.

Regress (rīgre·s), *v.* 1552. [ad. L. *regress-*, *regredi*; see REGREDE *v.*] **1.** *intr.* To recede *from*; to return *to* a subject or place, or *into* a former state. **2.** To move in a backward direction. Chiefly *Astron.* 1823.

Regression (rīgre·ʃən). 1520. [ad. L. *regressionem*; see prec.] †**1.** Return to a subject –1620. **2.** The action of returning to or towards a place or point of departure 1597. **b.** *Geom.* Return of a curve 1727. **3.** Return *to* or *into* a state or condition; relapse; reversion to a less developed form 1646. **4.** = REGRESS *sb.* 4. 1637. **5.** *Astr.* = RETROGRADATION 1. 1823.

Regressive (rīgre·siv), *a.* 1634. [f. REGRESS *v.*] **1.** Retrogressive; returning, passing back. **b.** Acting in a backward direction; retroactive 1888. **2.** *Philos.* Proceeding from effect to cause, or from particular to universal 1836. **3.** *Med.* Tending towards, of the nature of, degeneration or decomposition 1865.

1. **b.** *R. assimilation*, assimilation of a sound to one following it, as in *comp-* from *conp-*. Hence **Regre·ssive·ly** *adv.* **-ness.**

Regret (rīgre·t), *sb.* 1533. [a. F., f. *regretter* REGRET *v.*] †**1.** Complaint, lament –1547. **2.** Sorrow or disappointment due to some external circumstance or event 1590. **b.** (*pl.*) An intimation of regret for inability to do something, *esp.* to accept an invitation 1859. **3.** Sorrow or pain due to reflection on something one has done or left undone 1641. **4.** Sorrow at, or *for*, some loss or deprivation or a lost thing or person. Also const. *of.* 1647.

2. The protestants beheld with r. the Earl of Argyll ..still adhering to the queen 1759. **3.** Pining regrets, and vain repentances SHELLEY. **4.** When for a friend long lost wakes some unhappy r. 1871.

Regret (rīgre·t), *v.* late ME. [ad. F. *regretter*; origin unkn.] **1.** *trans.* To remember, think of (something lost), with distress or longing; to feel (†or express) sorrow for the loss of (a person or thing). **2.** To grieve at, feel distress on account of (some event, fact, action, etc.) 1553.

1. He died at length regretted of all men DRYDEN. **2.** Poets, of all men, ever least r. Increasing taxes and the nation's debt COWPER. So **Regre·ttable** *a.* deserving of, calling for, regret. **Regre·ttably** *adv.*

Regretful (rīgre·tfŭl), *a.* 1647. [f. REGRET *sb.* + -FUL.] Full of sorrow or regret. Hence **Regre·tfully** *adv.*

Regue·rdon, *v. rare.* late ME. [ad. OF. *reguerdoner*; see RE- and GUERDON *v.*] *trans.* To reward. So †**Regue·rdon** *sb.* (*rare*) recompense, reward –1591.

‖**Regula** (re·giŭlă). 1563. [L., f. *regere* to make or lead straight.] *Arch.* A fillet or reglet; *spec.* a short band, with guttæ on the lower side, placed below the tænia in Doric Architecture.

Regulable (re·giŭlăb'l), *a.* 1660. [f. L. *regulare* to direct; see REGULATE *v.* and -ABLE.] Capable of being regulated.

Regular (re·giŭlăɹ), *a.*, *adv.*, and *sb.* late ME. [orig. a. OF. *reguler*, ad. L. *regularis*, f. *regula* RULE; later, f. L.] **A.** *adj.* **1.** *Eccl.* Subject to, or bound by, a religious rule; belonging to a religious or monastic order. (Opp. to *secular.*) **2.** Having a form, structure, or arrangement which follows, or is reducible to, some rule or principle; characterized by harmony or proper correspondence between the various parts or elements; symmetrical 1584. **b.** *Geom.* Of plane figures: Equilateral and equiangular; of solids; of which all the faces are equal in size and shape 1665. **c.** *Bot.* Having all the parts or organs of the same kind normally alike in form and size 1785. **3.** Characterized by the presence or operation of a definite principle; marked by steadiness or uniformity of action, procedure, or occurrence 1594. **b.** Recurring or repeated at fixed times or uniform intervals 1756. **c.** Habitually or customarily used, received, observed, etc.; habitual, constant 1797. **4.** Pursuing a definite course, or observing some uniform principle, of action or conduct; adhering to rule; now *esp.* observing fixed times for, or never failing in, the performance of certain actions or duties 1602. **b.** Orderly, well-ordered, well-behaved, steady 1705. **c.** Acting at the proper intervals 1783. **5.** Conformable to some accepted or adopted rule or standard; recognized as formally correct 1647. **b.** *Gram.* Of parts of speech, esp. verbs: Following some usual and uniform mode of inflexion or conjugation 1611. **6.** Properly constituted; normal 1638. **b.** Of persons: Properly qualified or trained 1712. **c.** *colloq.* Thorough, complete, absolute, perfect 1821. **7.** *Mil.* Of forces or troops: Properly and permanently organized; constituting the standing army 1706.

2. I cannot, however, tell you that her features are r. 1716. A r. and appropriate nomenclature 1815. Small r. teeth 1863. **b.** R. Figures are those where the Angles and Lines or Superficies are equal 1679. *R. Curves*, are such Curves as the Perimeters of the Conick Sections, which are always curved after the same R. Geometrical Manner 1704. **3.** He supposes the philosopher to proceed by r. steps, until he arrives at the idea of good JOWETT. **b.** How r. his meals, how sound he sleeps! COWPER. Her r. pulses SHELLEY. **c.** It 's past my r. time for going to bed DICKENS. **4.** The Herr Doctor was a r. man, and always appeared at his window at the same hour 1883. **b.** He grew first r., and then pious JOHNSON. **5.** Making acquaintances..without r. introductions 1831. **6. b.** A r. doctor JOHNSON. **c.** On Wednesday we had a r. flood, and it has been raining..ever since 1846. **7.** His Majesty's r. forces 1756.

B. *adv.* Regularly, steadily; thoroughly 1710.

C. *sb.* **1.** *Eccl.* A member of a religious order observing a RULE; one of the regular clergy 1563. **2.** A soldier belonging to the standing army; a member of the regular forces. Usu. *pl.* 1756. Hence **Re·gular·ly** *adv.*, **-ness.**

Regularity (regiŭlæ·rĭti). 1603. [f. prec. + -ITY.] The state or character of being regular.

Regularize (re·giŭlărəiz), *v.* 1780. [f. as prec. + -IZE 2.] *trans.* To make regular. Hence **Re·gularizа·tion.**

†**Re·gulate,** *ppl. a.* 1577. [ad. late L. *regulatus*; see next.] Regulated; regular –1644.

Regulate (re·giŭlēit), *v.* 1630. [f. late L. *regulat-*, *regulare*, f. *regula* RULE.] **1.** *trans.* To control, govern, or direct by rule or regulations; to subject to guidance or restrictions; to adapt to circumstances or surroundings. †**b.** To bring or reduce (a person or body of persons) to order –1839. †**c.** To correct by control –1682. **2.** To adjust, in respect of time, quantity, etc., with reference to some standard or purpose; *esp.* to adjust (a clock, etc.) so that the working may be accurate 1662.

1. Can freedom be regulated without being..in some part destroyed? 1792. **c.** To r. the Errors of the Mind 1680. **2.** Clocks ought to be regulated by the mean solar time 1812.

Regulation (regiŭlēi·ʃən). 1672. [f. prec.] **1.** The act of regulating, or the state of being regulated. Also, an instance of this. **2.** A rule prescribed for the management of some matter, or the regulating of conduct; a governing precept or direction; a standing rule 1715. **3.** *attrib.* That is prescribed by, or in accordance with, a regulation or regulations; hence, regular, ordinary 1836.

1. The advancement and r. of manufactures and commerce BLACKSTONE. **2.** It 's against regulations for me to call at night DICKENS. **3.** He can't afford more than his r. chargers THACKERAY.

Regulative (re·giŭlētiv), *a.* 1599. [f. REGULATE *v.* + -IVE.] Tending to regulate. Chiefly *Philos.*

Logic is not useless; it has a r., not a creative virtue 1874. Hence **Re·gulatively** *adv.*

Regulator (re·giŭlēitəɹ). 1655. [Agent-n. f. L. *regulare* to REGULATE.] **1.** One who regulates. **b.** *Eng. Hist.* A member of a commission appointed in 1687 to investigate and revise the constitution of various boroughs, for the purpose of influencing the election of members of parliament 1688. **c.** *U.S.* A member of one of the bands formed at various times in wild parts of the country, with the professed object of supplying the want of the regular administration of justice 1767. **2.** *techn.* A device for controlling machinery in motion, or for regulating the passage of air, electricity, gas, steam, water, etc. 1702. **b.** A device for adjusting the balance of a clock or watch, in order to regulate its speed 1696. **3.** A clock or watch keeping accurate time, by which other timepieces may be regulated 1758. **4.** Something which regulates; a regulating principle or power 1766.

1. c. The lynchers, or 'regulators' as they are often called, soon find that their foes organize also 1847.

Reguline (re·giŭləin), *a.* 1669. [f. REGULUS + -INE [1].] *Chem.* Of, or pertaining to, of the nature of, regulus.

Re·gulize, *v. rare.* 1778. [f. as prec. + -IZE.] *trans.* To reduce to regulus.

‖**Regulus** (re·giŭlŏs). *Pl.* **-li** (-ləi). 1559. [L., dim. of *reg-*, *rex* king.] **1.** *Astron.* A bright star (*α* Leonis) in the constellation Leo, called also *Cor Leonis.* **2.** *Chem.* †**a.** The metallic form of antimony, so called by early chemists, app. on account of its ready combination with gold. **b.** The purer or metallic part of a mineral, which sinks to the bottom of a crucible or furnace and is thus separated from the remaining matter. **c.** A product of the smelting of various ores, as copper, lead, and silver, consisting of metal in a still impure state. 1594. **3.** A petty king or ruler 1682. **4.** The golden-crested (and fire-crested) wren 1824.

Regurgitant (rĭgɔ̄·ɹdʒitănt), *ppl. a.* 1866. [See next and -ANT [1].] *Path.* Regurgitating; characterized by regurgitation.

Regurgitate (rĭgɔ̄·ɹdʒitēⁱt), *v.* 1653. [ad. med.L. *regurgitare*, f. *re-* RE- + late L. *gurgitare.*] **1.** *intr.* Of fluids, air, or gases: To gush, rush, or pour back (again). **b.** *transf.* of the containing vessel. BOYLE. **2.** *trans.* To pour or cast out again from a receptacle, *esp.* from the stomach 1753.

2. *absol.* The Whale that swallowed Jonah found him hard meat, and..was forced to r. 1657.

Regurgitation (rĭgɔ̄ɹdʒitēⁱ·ʃən). 1601. [ad. med.L. *regurgitationem.*] The act of pouring or gushing back; the fact of reissuing or being ejected again from a receptacle. Chiefly *Med.* with ref. either to the blood or to food.

Rehabilitate (rĭhăbi·litēⁱt), *v.* 1580. [f. ppl. stem of med.L. *rehabilitare*; see RE- and HABILITATE *v.*] **1.** *trans.* To restore by formal act or declaration (a person degraded or attainted) to former privileges, rank, and possessions; to re-establish (a person's good name or memory) by authoritative pronouncement. **b.** To re-establish the character or reputation of (a person or thing) 1847. **2.** To restore to a previous condition; to set up again in proper condition 1845.

1. The king alone can r. an officer noted, condemned, and degraded; or a gentleman who has derogated from his rank 1727. 2. The unwearied Lord Lieutenant..has been rehabilitating Courts of Justice in Dublin CARLYLE. Hence **Re·habilita·tion**, the action of rehabilitating, or state of being rehabilitated.

Rehash (rĭhæ·ʃ), *sb.* 1849. [f. RE- 5 a + HASH *sb.* 2.] A mere restatement in different words of opinions previously expressed; something served up afresh under a different form or name.

Reha·sh, *v.* 1822. [RE- 5 a.] *trans.* To restate (old ideas or opinions) in new language. All they did was to r. the old..arguments 1884.

Rehearsal (rĭhɔ̄·ɹsăl). late ME. [f. next + -AL 2.] **1.** The act of rehearsing; a recounting or recital; a repetition of words or statements; recitation. **2.** The practising of a play or musical composition preparatory to performing it in public; a private meeting of actors or performers held for this purpose 1579.

1. Many..made it a pretext for r. of old grievances 1842. 2. The second part of the *Beggar's Opera*..was almost ready for r. GAY. *Dress r.*, a final r. in full costume. *In r.*, in process of being rehearsed.

Rehearse (rĭhɔ̄·ɹs), *v.* ME. [a. OF. *rehercer, -cier*, app. f. *re-* RE- + *hercer, herser* to harrow; see HERSE.] **1.** *trans.* To recite or repeat aloud in a formal manner; to say over, or read aloud, from beginning to end. **b.** To repeat, say over again (something previously said or heard) ME. †**c.** To say, utter, speak –1567. **2.** To give an account of; to relate, narrate, recount, describe at length. Now *rare.* ME. **3.** To recount in order; to name or mention one after another; to enumerate, reckon up, †number. late ME. †**b.** To mention, make mention of; to cite, quote –1562. **4.** To go through or practise (a play, scene, part, etc.) in private, in preparation for a more formal or public performance 1579. **b.** To exercise, train, or make proficient by rehearsal 1768. **5.** To perform, practise, as in rehearsing (*rare*) 1700. **6.** *intr.* To recite; to engage in rehearsal 1693.

1. Words learned by rote a parrot may r. COWPER. b. The critic brings thee praise, which all r. 1822. 2. First of all we shall r...The Nativity of our Lord LONGF. 3. I will r. the captains and their fleets COWPER. 4. Sit downe..and r. your parts SHAKS. 6. We got together, in order to r. GOLDSM. Hence **Rehea·rser.**

Rei, assumed sing. of REIS [1].

‖**Reich** (raiχ). 1924. [G., kingdom.] The German state or commonwealth.

Reif (rīf). Chiefly *Sc.* [Com. WGer.: OE. *réaf* :—OTeut. **raubom*; see REAVE *v.*] †**1.** Spoil, plunder –1557. **2.** The act or practice of robbery; spoliation. *Obs.* exc. *arch.* ME.

Reify (rī·ifəi), *v.* 1854. [f. L. *res* a thing + -IFY.] *trans.* To convert mentally into a thing; to materialize. Hence **Reifica·tion.**

Reign (rēⁱn), *sb.* ME. [a. OF. *regne, reigne*, ad. L. *regnum*, f. *regere.*] **1.** Royal power or rule; kingdom, sovereignty; also *transf.* power or rule comparable to that of a king. Now *rare.* **b.** *transf.* Influence, dominion, sway (of something immaterial). late ME. †**2.** A kingdom or realm; a territory ruled over by a king –1725. †**b.** The kingdom of heaven or of God –1594. **c.** *poet.* A place or sphere under the rule of some specified person or thing, or having a specified character. Now *rare.* late ME. †**d.** = KINGDOM 5. (*rare*) –1781. **3.** The period of a sovereign's rule ME.

1. Under the r. of Queen Victoria THACKERAY. b. The owlet Night resumes her r. SHELLEY. 2. c. A shout that..Frighted the R. of Chaos and old Night MILT. d. The vegetable and the mineral reigns THOMSON. 3. After a r. of seventy years, he died 1841. Phr. *R. of Terror*: see TERROR.

Reign (rēⁱn), *v.* ME. [a. OF. *regner* (mod. F. *régner*), ad.L. *regnare*, f. *regnum*; see prec.] **1.** *intr.* To hold or exercise the sovereign power or authority in a state; to rule or govern as king or queen. Also *transf.* or *fig.* **2.** Of persons: To exercise authority of any kind; to hold sway; to rule ME. **3.** Of things: To have power, sway, or predominance; to prevail or be prevalent ME.

1. During the time Edward the third did raigne SHAKS. Who reigned'st in thy heaven, yet felt'st our hell 1633. While..Reigns in pomp the perfect moon 1871. 2. Yet he who reigns within himself, and rules Passions, Desires, and Fears, is more a King MILT. 3. Lord, Lord: to see what folly raignes in vs SHAKS. In thy heart eternal winter reigns POPE. Famine has long reigned CARLYLE. Hence †**Rei·gner**, a ruler.

‖**Reim** (rīm). *S. Afr.* 1865. [a. Du. *riem.*] A strip of ox-hide, a thong, strap.

Reimburse (rī,imbɔ̄·ɹs), *v.* 1611. [RE- 5 a.] **1.** *trans.* To repay or make up to a person (a sum expended). **2.** To repay, recompense (a person) 1637. **3.** With double object 1624.

1. The tardy sale of so voluminous a work could not have reimbursed the cost HALLAM. 2. I will see you fully and thankfully reimbursed for what charges shall attend the same PEPYS. 3. To r. him the costs of his trial 1841. Hence **Reimbu·rsable** *a.* that is to be reimbursed, repayable. **Reimbu·rsement**, the act of reimbursing, repayment. **Reimbu·rser.**

Reim-kennar (rəi·m,ke:naɹ). *pseudo-arch.* 1821. [app. formed by Scott on G. *reim* rhyme + *kenner* knower.] One skilled in magic rhymes.

Rein (rēⁱn), *sb.*[1] ME. [a. OF. *rene* (mod. F. *rêne*), earlier *resne*, usu. regarded as repr. a Com. Rom. **retina*, f. L. *retinere* to RETAIN; but this is doubtful.] **1.** A long narrow strap or thong of leather, attached to the bridle or bit on each side of the head, by which a horse, etc., is controlled and guided by the rider or driver; any similar device used for the same purpose. (The *pl.* has freq. the same sense as the *sing.*) **2.** *fig.* Any means of guiding, controlling, or governing; a curb, check, or restraint of any kind. late ME.

1. His horse in his hond held by the reyne 1400. In this Country they never use reins to their Oxen 1785. *Bearing-, bridle-, coupling-, gag-r.*, etc.: see the first element. Phr. *To give* (a horse) *the rein(s)*, to allow (it) free motion. *To draw r.*, to bring one's horse to a stand. 2. The council of state assumed the reins of government 1777. Phr. *To give the rein(s) to*, to allow full course or scope to.

Comb. **r.-orchis**, an orchis of the genus *Habenaria* the Fringed Orchis.

Rein (rēⁱn), *sb.*[2] 1555. [ad. Da. or Sw. *ren*, Norw. *rein* :—ON. *hreinn.*] The reindeer.

Rein (rēⁱn), *v.* ME. [f. REIN *sb.*[1]] †**1.** *trans.* To tie (a horse or its head) *to* something by the rein; to tie up in this way –1592. **2.** To fit or furnish with a rein or reins 1483. **3.** To check or stop, by pulling at the rein 1530. **b.** *fig.* To put a check or restraint upon (something); to restrain *from* something 1588. **4.** To govern, control, manage, or direct, by means of reins. Now *rare.* 1590. **b.** *fig.* To rule, guide, or govern 1581. **5.** To pull *up* or *back*, to check and hold *in*, by means of the reins 1552. **6.** *U.S.* To preserve or keep enclosed *from* stock. Also with *up.* 1799. **7.** *intr.* Of a horse: **a.** To bear, or submit to (the rein) in a specified manner 1565. **b.** To move *back*, etc. under the rein 1627. Also *fig.*

3. Sudden his steed the leader rein'd SCOTT. b. My tongue within my lips I r. GAY. 4. b. Lawes and statutes..Wherby good subjects easily are rain'd 1614. 5. *absol.* We reined in at last to a walk 1888. 7. a. Hee will beare you easily, and raines well SHAKS.

Reinca·rnate, *v.* 1858. [RE- 5 a.] *trans.* To incarnate anew. So **Re·incarna·tion** 1858.

Reindeer (rēⁱ·ndīəɹ). late ME. [Ult. repr. ON. *hreindýri*, f. *hreinn* (cf. REIN *sb.*[2]) + *dýr* DEER.] An animal of the deer kind, *Rangifer tarandus*, having large branching or palmated antlers, now confined to sub-arctic regions, where it is used for drawing sledges, and is kept in large herds for the sake of the milk, flesh, and hides.

Comb.: **r. lichen, moss**, a species of lichen, *Cladonia rangiferina*, which constitutes the winter food of the r.; **r. period, epoch**, a name sometimes given to the more recent stage of the Palæolithic period.

‖**Reinette** (rēne·t). 1583. [F.; see RENNET *sb.*[2]] A variety of apple, the rennet.

Reinforce (rī,infōᵊ·ɹs), *sb.* 1648. [f. next.] †**1.** *Mil.* A reinforcement of troops. EVELYN. **2.** A part (or one of two parts) of a gun next the breech, made stronger than the rest in order to resist the explosive force of the powder 1769. **3.** Any thing or part added to an object to strengthen it 1869.

attrib. (sense 2): **r. band, ring**, a flat ring or moulding round a gun at the points where the reinforces meet or terminate.

Reinforce (rī,infōᵊ·ɹs), *v.* 1600. [f. RE- + *inforce* ENFORCE *v.*] **I. 1.** *trans.* To strengthen (a military or naval force) by means of additional men. **b.** To increase the number or amount of 1839. **2.** To strengthen, make stronger; to furnish with additional support 1635. **b.** To strengthen (some material thing) by additional support, added thickness, etc. 1692. **3.** To make more forcible or cogent 1629. **b.** To increase by giving fresh force to; also simply, to increase 1659. **4.** *intr.* To obtain reinforcements (*rare*) 1611.

1. Fresh troops continually came up to r. those who were exhausted with fatigue 1849. 3. It is said, he reinforced the proposal by promising a liberal share of the proceeds of it 1843. 4. *Cymb.* v. ii. 18.

†**II. 1.** To renew or repeat with fresh force –1662. **2.** To enforce, or put in force, again –1720.

2. [To] attend his Majesty, desiring him to r...the laws against Conventicles MARVELL. Hence **Re·inforced** *ppl. a.*, *spec.* in **reinforced cement, concrete**, cement or concrete with metal bars, gratings, or wire embedded in it.

Reinforcement (rī,infōᵊ·ɹsmĕnt). 1607. [f. prec. + -MENT.] †**1.** A renewal of force; a fresh assault. SHAKS. **2.** The act of reinforcing with fresh troops 1617. **b.** A fresh supply of men to assist or strengthen a military or naval force 1646. **3.** Augmentation of strength or force; the act of strengthening or increasing in any way 1651. **4.** The act of enforcing anew. Now *rare.* 1641.

1. *Cor.* II. ii. 117. 3. What r. we may gain from Hope MILT.

†**Reinfu·nd**, *v.* [RE- 5 a.] *intr.* To pour in again. SWIFT.

Reinless (rēⁱ·nlĕs), *a.* 1559. [f. REIN *sb.*[1] + -LESS.] **1.** Without a rein or reins. **2.** *transf.* and *fig.* Unchecked, unrestrained 1566.

1. The r. steed SOUTHEY. The r. rider 1892. 2. R. speed SHELLEY.

Reins (rēⁱnz), *sb. pl.* Now *arch.* late ME. [a. OF. *reins*, ad. L. *renes* pl.] **1.** The kidneys. **2.** The region of the kidneys; the loins. late

ME. **b.** *Arch.* (See quot.) 1727. **3.** In or after Biblical use: The seat of the feelings or affections. late ME.

2. b. R., or fillings up of a Vault, are the sides which sustain it 1727. 3. I am nere to theyr mouthes, but I am ferre from theyr raynes 1526. Yea my reines shall reioyce, when thy lippes speake right things *Prov.* xxiii. 16.

Reinstate (rīˌinstēⁱ·t), *v.* 1599. [RE- 5 a.] **1.** *trans.* To reinstall or re-establish (a person or thing *in* a place, station, condition, etc.) **2.** To restore to its proper or original state; to instate afresh 1793.

1. The said archbishop is now reinstated in his majesty's favour 1628. The senators could not r. him by force 1878. 2. To r. the streets..so opened by them 1833. So **Reinsta·tement, Reinsta·tion,** the action of reinstating; re-establishment.

Reinsu·rance. 1755. [RE- 5 a.] A renewed or second insurance; *spec.* one in which an insurer or underwriter secures himself (wholly or in part) against the risk he has undertaken.

Reinsu·re, *v.* 1828. [RE- 5 a.] *trans.* To insure again; *spec.* to devolve the risk of an insurance on another insurer. So **Reinsu·rer.**

Reintegrate (rīˌi·ntĭgrēⁱt), *v.* 1581. [ad. med.L. *reintegrat-*; see REDINTEGRATE *v.*] †**1.** *refl.* To reinstate (oneself) –1648. **2.** *trans.* = REDINTEGRATE *v.* 2 b. Now *rare.* 1605. **3.** = REDINTEGRATE *v.* 1. 1626.

3. The atmosphere alone will r. a soil rested in due season 1798. So **Reintegra·tion.**

Reinvest (rīˌinve·st), *v.* 1611. [RE- 5 a.] **1.** *trans.* To invest again with or as with a garment. **b.** To re-endow *with* a possession, power, etc. 1648. **2.** To replace, re-establish. Const. *in.* 1617. **3.** To invest (money) again 1848.

3. The proceeds of sale have been..reinvested in land 1885. So **Reinve·stment,** a fresh investment.

‖**Reis**¹ (rēⁱs), *sb. pl.* 1555. [a. Pg. *reis* pl.; the correct sing. is *real* (see REAL *sb.*¹).] A Pg. money of account equal to about one-twentieth of a penny in Portugal and one-fortieth in Brazil.

‖**Reis**², **rais** (rəis, rais). 1585. [a. Arab. *raʾis*, f. *rās* head.] **1.** The captain of a boat or vessel. **2.** A chief or governor 1678.

2. *R. Effendi*, the title of a former officer of state in the Turkish empire, who acted as chancellor and minister of foreign affairs.

Reisner (rəi·snəɪ). 1833. [f. name of a German artist in wood, of the time of Louis XIV.] *R.-work* (also simply *R.*), a method of inlaying in wood of different colours.

†**Reit.** 1538. [Origin obsc.] Chiefly *pl.* Sea-weed –1661.

Reiter (rəi·təɪ). Now *Hist.* 1584. [a. G. *reiter* rider, f. *reiten* to RIDE.] A German cavalry soldier, *esp.* one of those employed in the wars of the 16th and 17th c.

Reiterant (rīˌi·tĕrănt), *a.* 1610. [ad.L. *reiterantem*; see REITERATE *v.*] Reiterating, repeating. So **Rei·terance,** repetition.

Reiterate (rīˌi·tĕrĕt), *pa. pple.* and *ppl. a.* 1471. [ad.L. *reiteratus*; see next.] Reiterated.

Reiterate (rīˌi·tĕrēⁱt), *v.* 1526. [f. L. *reiterat-*, *reiterare*, f. *re-* RE- + *iterare* to ITERATE.] **1.** *trans.* To repeat (an action); to do over again. **2.** To repeat (a request, statement, word, etc.); to give renewed expression to (a feeling) 1560. †**3.** To walk over (a place) again. HERRICK.

1. Which Sentence was barbarously executed, and afterwards reiterated upon others CLARENDON. 2. My father..reiterated his orders, that no one should presume to fire until he gave the word SCOTT. Hence **Rei·teratedly** *adv.*

Reiteration (rīˌitĕrēⁱ·ʃən). 1560. [ad. L. *reiterationem.*] The (or an) act of reiterating.

Reiterative (rīˌi·tĕrĕtiv), *a.* and *sb.* 1813. [f. as REITERATE *v.* + -IVE.] **A.** *adj.* Characterized by reiteration. **B.** *sb.* A word expressing reiteration. So **Rei·teratively** *adv.* 1619.

Reive(r, var. of REAVE(R.

Reject (rī·dʒekt, rĭdʒe·kt), *sb.* 1555. [f. next.] One who, a thing which, is rejected.

Reject (rĭdʒe·kt), *v.* 1494. [f. L. *reject-*, *reicere* (*rejicere*) to throw back, f. *re-* RE- + *jacere* to throw.] **1.** *trans.* To refuse to recognize, acquiesce in, submit to, or adopt (a rule, command, practice, etc.); to refuse credit to (a statement). **2.** To refuse to have or take for some purpose; to set aside or throw away as useless or worthless 1531. **3.** To refuse (something offered); to decline to receive or accept 1671. **4.** To expel from the mouth or stomach 1667. **5.** To repel or rebuff (one who makes advances); to refuse to accept, listen to, admit, etc. 1561. **b.** Of a woman: To refuse (a man) as lover or husband 1581. **6.** To refuse to grant, entertain, or agree to (a request, proposal, etc.) 1602. †**7.** To cast (a fault, etc.) back *upon* a person –1678. **8.** To throw or cast back 1603.

1. Nor perhaps ought we to r. the farther account.. as a groundless fiction THIRLWALL. 2. The stone which the builders reiected, the same is become the head of the corner *Matt.* xxi. 42. 3. Good counsel rejected, returns to enrich the giver's bosom GOLDSM. 5. Not to r. The penitent, but..to forgive MILT. 6. I could not r. his proposal SWIFT. Hence **Reje·ctable** *a.* that may, or ought to be rejected. **Reje·cter.**

‖**Rejectamenta** (rĭdʒektăme·ntă). 1816. [mod.L., pl. of *rejectamentum*; see REJECT *v.* and -MENT.] **1.** Things rejected as useless or worthless; refuse. **2.** Wrack or rubbish cast up by the sea 1819. **3.** *Phys.* Excremental matter 1879.

†**Rejecta·neous,** *a.* 1657. [ad. L. *rejectaneus*, f. *rejicere* to REJECT.] Deserving rejection, rejectable –1734.

Rejection (rĭdʒe·kʃən). 1552. [a. F. *réjection*, or ad. L. *rejectionem.*] The action of rejecting or the state of being rejected. **b.** *concr.* That which is rejected; excrement 1605.

Rejectment (rĭdʒe·ktmĕnt). 1677. [f. REJECT *v.* + -MENT.] †**1.** Rejection (*rare*) –1690. **2.** *concr.* Rejected matter, excrement. Also *pl.* 1828.

†**Rejoi·ce,** *sb.* 1445. [f. next.] Joy, rejoicing; a cause of joy –1682.

Rejoice (rĭdʒoi·s), *v.* ME. [a. OF. *rejoiss-*, *resjoiss-*, lengthened stem of *rejoir*, f. *re-* RE- + *joir* JOY *v.*] †**1.** *trans.* To enjoy by possessing; to have full possession and use of (a thing) –1577. **2.** To gladden, make joyful, exhilarate (a person, his spirits, etc.). late ME. **3.** *refl.* To make (oneself) glad or joyful; hence = sense 5. Now *rare.* late ME. †**4.** To feel joy on account of (an event) –1611. **5.** *intr.* To be full of joy; to be glad or greatly delighted; to exult. late ME.

2. I love to r. their poor Hearts at this season ADDISON. The King was rejoiced at seeing him 1841. 3. R. myself with a glance at the volutes of the Erectheium RUSKIN. 4. Nere Mother Reioyc'd deliuerance more SHAKS. 5. O reioyce Beyond a common ioy SHAKS. Rejoicing at that answer to his prayer TENNYSON. Hence **Rejoi·cement,** joy, exultation, rejoicing. **Rejoi·cer,** one who rejoices; one who or that which causes rejoicing. **Rejoi·cingly** *adv.*

Rejoicing (rĭdʒoi·siŋ), *vbl. sb.* late ME. [-ING¹.] **1.** The action of REJOICE *v.*; the feeling and expression of joy. **b.** With *a* and *pl.*: An instance, occasion, or expression of rejoicing; a festival 1540. †**2.** A cause or source of rejoicing or gladness –1611. **3.** *attrib.*, as *r.-fire*, etc. 1611.

1. My reioycing At nothing can be more SHAKS. b. The rejoycings upon this occasion were of short continuance 1707. 2. Thy word was unto me, the ioy and reioycing of my heart *Jer.* xv. 16.

Rejoin (rĭdʒoi·n), *v.*¹ 1456. [ad. F. *rejoign-*, *rejoindre*, f. *re-* RE- + *joindre* to JOIN.] **1.** *intr. Law.* To reply to a charge or pleading; *spec.* to answer the plaintiff's replication. †**2.** To answer a reply; also more loosely, to reply. Const. *to*, *with.* –1665. **3.** *trans.* To say in answer 1637.

2. Vnto whom..wee shall not contentiously rejoyne 1646.

Rejoin (rī-, rĭdʒoi·n), *v.*² 1541. [ad. F. *rejoign-* (see prec.), or f. RE- 5 a + JOIN *v.*] **1.** *intr.* Of things: To come together, or unite again. **2.** *trans.* To join again, reunite (persons or things, *to* or *with* another) 1570. **3.** To join (a person, company, etc.) again 1611.

2. As tin-soder doth knit and rejoyne a crackt peece of brasse 1603.

Rejoinder (rĭdʒoi·ndəɪ). 1450. [a. F. *rejoindre*, inf. used as sb. See REJOIN *v.*¹] **1.** *Law.* The defendant's answer to the plaintiff's replication. **2.** An answer to a reply; also simply, a reply 1566. **b.** Without article, in phr. *in r.* 1556.

†**Rejoi·ndure.** [prob. ad. F. *rejoindre* (see prec.), assim. to -URE.] Reunion. SHAKS.

†**Rejou·rn,** *v.* 1513. [f. RE- + (*ad*)*journ.*] **1.** *trans.* To adjourn, postpone, put off –1647 **2.** To refer (a person) *to* something. BURTON. So †**Rejou·rnment,** adjournment.

Rejuvenate (rĭdʒū·vĭnēⁱt), *v.* 1807. [irreg. f. RE- + L. *juvenis* young.] *trans.* To restore to youth; to make young or fresh again. Also *absol.* Hence **Rejuvena·tion.**

Rejuvenesce (rĭdʒūvĭne·s), *v.* 1879. [ad. late L. *rejuvenescere*, f. *re-* RE- + *juvenis* young.] a. *intr.* To become young again; *spec.* in *Biol.* of cells: To acquire renewed vitality. **b.** *trans.* To impart fresh vitality to (a cell).

Rejuvenescence (rĭdʒūvĭne·sĕns). 1631. [f. as prec. + -ENCE.] A renewal of youth, physical, mental, or spiritual. **b.** *spec.* in *Biol.* and *Bot.* The process by which a vegetative cell transforms itself into a new one 1855. So †**Rejuvene·scency.**

Rejuvenescent (rĭdʒūvĭne·sĕnt), *a.* 1763. [f. as prec. + -ENT.] **1.** Becoming young again 1807. **b.** *spec.* in scientific use 1859. **2.** Rejuvenating 1763.

1. The Crawley House in Great Gaunt Street was quite r. THACKERAY.

Rejuvenize (rĭdʒū·vĭnəiz), *v.* 1816. [Cf. REJUVENATE and -IZE.] *trans.* To rejuvenate, make young again.

Rekindle (rīki·nd'l), *v.* 1593. [RE- 5 a.] **1.** *trans.* To kindle again, set fire to afresh. **b.** *fig.* To inflame afresh, rouse anew 1652. **2.** *intr.* To take fire again 1597.

-rel, -erel (also formerly *-ral*, *-ril*), a diminutive and depreciatory suffix, repr. OF. *-erel* (mod.F. *-ereau*) or *-erelle*, in derivation from F.; hence suffixed to various native stems, and in other formations of uncertain origin, as *cockerel*, *mackerel*, *doggerel*, *mongrel*, *scoundrel.*

Relapse (rĭlæ·ps), *sb.*¹ 1533. [f. the vb.] **1.** A falling back into error, heresy, or wrongdoing; back-sliding. **2.** The fact of falling back again into an illness after a partial recovery; return of a disease or illness during the period of convalescence 1584. **3.** The act of falling or sinking back again 1876.

1. Which would but lead me to a worse r., And heavier fall MILT.

Relapse (rĭlæ·ps), *sb.*² Now *rare.* 1546. [ad. L. *relapsus*, pa. pple. of *relabi.*] A relapsed person; one who has fallen again into error or heresy.

Relapse (rĭlæ·ps), *v.* 1548. [f. L. *relaps-*, *relabi* to slip back; see RE- and LAPSE *v.*] **1.** *intr.* To fall back into wrong-doing or error; to backslide; *spec.* to fall again into heresy after recantation 1570. **2.** To fall back into an illness after partial recovery or from a convalescent state 1548. **b.** Of stock: To fall again in value 1896. **3.** To fall back or sink again *into* any state, practice, etc. 1593. †**b.** To fall away *from* a person –1687. †**4.** *trans.* To cause to fall back –1773.

1. The Children of Israel..relapsed into the Idolatry of the Egyptians HOBBES. 2. *transf.* The red fire.. Rallies, relapses, dwindles, deathward sinks! BROWNING. 3. He relapsed into a musing mood 1864. Hence **Rela·pser,** one who relapses, esp. into error or sin. **Rela·psing** *ppl. a.* that relapses; *r. fever*, a fever characterized by relapses.

Relate (rĭlēⁱ·t), *sb.* 1633. [ad. L. *relatus*, pa. pple. of *referre*, used subst.] †**1.** A relation, relative –1656. **2.** *Logic.* One of two objects of thought between which a relation subsists 1633.

Relate (rĭlēⁱ·t), *v.* 1530. [f. L. *relat-*, *referre* to REFER.] **I.** *trans.* **1.** To recount, narrate, tell, give an account of. †**2.** To bring back, restore. SPENSER. †**3.** To refer (a person) *to* a book, etc. –1657. **4.** To bring (a thing or person) into relation *to* another 1697. **b.** To connect, establish a relation between 1771.

1. Letters..wherein hee related..what hee had seene in the Indias 1582. What thought can measure thee or tongue R. thee? MILT. 4. b. Volta..first enabled us definitely to r. the forces of chemistry and electricity 1846.

II. *intr.* **1.** *Law.* To refer *back*, to have application *to* an earlier date 1596. **2.** To have reference *to* 1606. †3. Of persons: To make reference *to* -1655. 4. To be related, have relation, stand in some relation, *to* another thing (†person or place) 1646. †5. To discourse; to give an account -1747.

2. Old persons are quick to see and hear all that relates to them JOWETT. 4. The critic Eye..examines bit by bit: How parts r. to parts, or they to whole POPE. 5. Adam relating, she sole Auditress MILT. Hence **Rela·ter**, one who relates; a narrator, historian.

Related (rǐlēⁱ·tėd), *ppl. a.* 1604. [f. prec. + -ED [1].] 1. Narrated, recited; †referred to (*rare*). 2. a. Having relation *to*, or relationship *with*, something else. Also *attrib.* without const. 1662. b. Having mutual relation or connexion 1671. 3. Of persons: Connected by blood or marriage (*to* another, or with each other) 1702.

2. a. Saw Twelfth-Night acted well, though it be but a silly play, and not related at all to the name or day PEPYS. b. Whenever two things are said to be r. there is some fact or series of facts into which they both enter 1843. 3. A Persian of the highest rank, related to the royal family 1837. Hence **Rela·tedness**, the state or condition of being r.

Relation (rǐlēⁱ·ʃən). late ME. [a. F., or ad. L. *relationem*; see prec. and -ION.] 1. The action of relating in words; narration, recital, account; report. b. *Law.* The action of a relator. (Cf. INFORMATION 5 b.) 1632. 2. A particular instance of relating or narrating; a (or one's) narrative, account, statement 1500. 3. That feature or attribute of things which is involved in considering them in comparison or contrast with each other; the particular way in which one thing is thought of in connexion with another; any connexion, correspondence, or association, which can be conceived as naturally existing between things. late ME. 4. a. *To have* or *make r.*: to have or make reference or allusion *to* something. late ME. b. *Law* (in phr. *to have r.*). Reference or application *to* an earlier date 1491. †c. A fiction of law by which two times or other things are identified, and, for legal purposes, regarded as one and the same -1749. 5. Connexion between persons arising out of the natural ties of blood or marriage; kinship 1660. b. A person related to one by blood or marriage; a kinsman or kinswoman; a relative. Also freq. in *pl.*, kinsfolk, relatives. 1502. 6. The position which one person holds with respect to another on account of some social or other connexion between them; the particular mode in which persons are mutually connected by circumstances 1650. b. *pl.* The aggregate of the connexions, or modes of connexion, by which one person is brought into touch with another or with society in general 1687. c. *pl.* The various modes in which one country, state, etc., is brought into contact with another by political or commercial interests 1797.

1. I like no R. so well, as what mine eye telleth me 1601. 2. A r. of the great and Golden Citie of Manoa RALEIGH. 3. The Nature of R. consists in the referring or comparing two things one to another LOCKE. Phr. *In* or *with r. to.* 5. The r. is as real as that of husband and wife 1758. b. Their Friends attend the Herse, the next Relations mourn DRYDEN. 6. The r. of ruler and subject MACAULAY. The r. of every man to his lord FREEMAN. b. Our relations to each other are various and infinite GIBBON. c. Our commercial relations with the Baltic cities 1861.

Relational (rǐlēⁱ·ʃənăl), *a.* 1662. [f. as prec. + -AL 1.] 1. Of or belonging to human relationship. 2. Of, belonging to, or characterized by relation in general 1840.

Rela·tionism. 1858. [f. RELATION *sb.* + -ISM.] *Philos.* a. The doctrine of the relativity of knowledge; relativism. b. The doctrine that relations have a real existence. So **Rela·tionist**, one who maintains a theory based on a relation between ideas.

Relationship (rǐlēⁱ·ʃənʃip). 1744. [-SHIP.] The state of being related; a condition or character based upon this; kinship.

Relatival (relătəi·văl), *a.* 1869. [f. next + -AL 1.] Of or pertaining to a relative or relation. Chiefly *Gram.*

Relative (re·lătiv), *a.* and *sb.* late ME. [ad. F. *relatif, -ive*, or L. *relativus*; see RELATE *v.* and -IVE.] A. *adj.* 1. *Gram.* Relating or referring to an antecedent term; applied to a class of words (pronouns, adjectives, adverbs) having the function of introducing adjectival clauses 1530. 2. Having mutual relationship; related to, or connected with, each other 1594. b. Corresponding 1849. c. *Mus.* Of a minor key in relation to a major key: Having the same key-signature 1818. 3. Having relation to the question or matter in hand; pertinent, relevant 1602. 4. Arising from, depending on, or determined by, relation to something else or to each other; comparative 1611. b. Constituted, or existing, only by relation to something else; not absolute or independent 1704. 5. Of worship: Offered indirectly by means of or through an image 1624. 6. Of terms, etc.: Involving or implying relation; depending for meaning or significance upon some relationship of things or persons 1678. 7. Having, or standing in, a relation *to* something else; correspondent or proportionate *to* 1660. b. In proportion *to* something 1789. 8. Having application or reference *to* a thing 1765. b. Relating *to* a matter of fact, event, person, etc.; with reference *to* 1763.

1. The r. pronouns are *who, which, that, as* 1872. 3. Ile haue grounds More Relatiue then this SHAKS. 4. They were..so marked, that..they could..be restored to the same r. position SMEATON. b. Certainty is positive, evidence r. COLERIDGE. 6. A name is r. when, being the name of one thing, its signification cannot be explained but by mentioning another MILL. 7. b. Naples, the most populous of cities, r. to its size GIBBON. 8. Things r. to immediate Want 1765. b. I write to the Admiralty r. to my health NELSON.

B. *sb.* 1. *Gram.* A relative word; *esp.* a relative pronoun. late ME. 2. A thing (†or person) standing in some relation to another. late ME. b. A relative term. (See A. 6.) 1551. c. *Mus.* A relative major or minor key (see A 2 c) 1811. 3. One who is connected with another or others by blood or affinity; a kinsman 1657. †4. A relationship -1675. 5. *The r.*, that which is relative (in sense A. 4 b) 1856.

2. b. Some Terms which seem Absolute are Relatives 1697. 3. He had received intelligence of the death of a near r. TYNDALL. Hence **Re·lative·ly** *adv.*, -ness.

Relativism (re·lătiviz'm). 1885. [f. prec. + -ISM.] *Philos.* The doctrine that knowledge is only of relations. So **Re·lativist**, one who holds this doctrine.

Relativity (relăti·vĭti). 1834. [f. as prec. + -ITY.] The fact or condition of being relative, relativeness. b. Applied to various theories which assert the dependence of individuals or the reciprocal dependence of the individual and society 1890. c. The theory of the universe propounded by Albert Einstein, that all motion is relative. 1919.

R. of knowledge: (*a*) *Philos.* the doctrine that human knowledge is only relatively true or certain; (*b*) *Psychol.* the doctrine that sensations are significant only in relation to other sensations.

Relator (rǐlēⁱ·tǫɹ). 1591. [a. L.; see RELATE *v.*] 1. A relater, narrator. †b. (One's) informant -1610. 2. *Law.* An informer; *spec.* one who supplies the materials for an information by the Attorney General 1603.

†**Rela·x**, *sb.* 1627. [f. the vb.] Relaxation· an instance of this -1773.

Rela·x, *a. rare.* 1609. [f. next, after LAX *a.*] 1. Lax, wanting in strictness. †2. Relaxed, slack. BACON.

Relax (rǐlæ·ks), *v.* late ME. [ad. L. *relaxare*, f. *re-* RE- + *laxus* LAX *a.*] I. *trans.* †1. To make (a thing) less compact or dense; to loosen or open up by separation of parts -1676. b. *spec.* To render (a part of the body) less firm or rigid; to make loose or slack; to enfeeble or enervate. Also *absol.* 1620. c. To diminish the force or tension of; *esp.* to loosen (one's hold or grasp) 1781. 2. To make less strict, severe, or rigid; to mitigate, tone down, modify 1662. b. To slacken, abate, diminish (an effort, etc.) 1774. c. To cause to abate in zeal or force (*rare*) 1660. 3. Of the Inquisition: To hand over (heretics) to the secular power for execution 1838.

1. To r. thir serried files MILT. b. The heat relaxed my muscles TYNDALL. c. Charity may r. the miser's fist COWPER. 2. The old woman seemed somewhat to r. her tone of severity SCOTT.

II. *intr.* 1. To become loose or slack; to grow less tense or firm 1720. b. Of the features: To become less rigid or stern 1797. 2. To abate in degree or force 1701. 3. To become less severe, strict, or exacting; to grow milder 1749. b. Of persons To become less stiff or distant; to assume a friendlier manner 1837. 4. To slacken in zeal or application; to seek or take relaxation *from* work or occupation 1760.

1. Tired by the tides, his knees r. with toil POPE. b. His features would r. into a look of fondness DICKENS. 3. It was hoped..the Court would r. in its opposition 1789. 4. He did not however r. in his perseverance 1833. Hence †**Rela·xable** *a.* admitting of remission.

Relaxant (rǐlæ·ksănt), *a.* and *sb.* 1771. [ad. L. *relaxantem.*] *Med.* A. *adj.* Causing, or distinguished by, relaxation. B. *sb.* A practice or drug serving to produce relaxation 1832.

Relaxation (rīlæksēⁱ·ʃən). 1526. [ad. L. *relaxationem.*] 1. Partial (†or complete) remission *of* some penalty, burden, duty, etc.; †also, the document granting such remission. b. The action of RELAX *v.* I. 3. 1826. 2. The action of unbending the mind from severe application; release from ordinary occupations or cares; recreation 1548. 3. *Path.* A loosening or slackening of the fibres, nerves, joints, etc., of the body 1626. 4. Diminution of, release or freedom from, strictness or severity 1626. 5. Abatement of intensity, vigour, or energy 1695.

2. To thy bent mind some r. give, And steal one day out of thy life to live COWLEY. 3. Bathing or Anointing give a R. or Emollition BACON. 4. These are not times to admit of any r. in the little discipline we have left *Junius Lett.*

Relaxative (rǐlæ·ksătiv), *a.* and *sb.* 1611. [f. RELAX *v.*, after LAXATIVE.] A. *adj.* Tending to relax; of the nature of relaxation (*rare*). †B. *sb.* A means of relaxing; *esp.* a relaxing medicine -1671.

Relay (rǐlēⁱ·), *sb.* late ME. [ad. OF. *relais* hounds or (in later use) horses held in reserve, f. *relayer* to RELAY.] 1. A set of fresh hounds (and horses) posted to take up the chase of a deer in place of those already tired out; †also, the place where these are posted. *Obs.* exc. *arch.* 2. A set of fresh horses obtained, or kept ready, at various stages along a route to expedite travel 1659. b. The place where a fresh relay is obtained 1706. 3. A set of persons appointed to relieve others in the performance of certain duties; a relief-gang 1808. 4. An apparatus used in long-distance telegraphy, wireless telephony, etc. to enable an electric current which is too weak to influence recording instruments, or to transmit a message, etc., to the required distance, to do so indirectly by means of a local battery brought into connexion with it 1860.

2. A traveller may have relays of horses to carry him day and night at the rate of ten miles an hour 1879.

Comb.: **r.-race**, a team-race, in which the second and succeeding members of every team take up the race as the preceding members finish, each member at the end of his lap handing on to the next an object which has to be carried throughout the race.

Relay (rǐlēⁱ·), *v.* late ME. [ad. F. *relayer*, of unkn. origin.] †1. *trans.* Of a hunter: To let go (the fresh hounds) upon the track of the deer. late ME. only. 2. To place in relays; to provide with, or replace by, fresh relays 1788. 3. In wireless broadcasting, etc.: To retransmit (a programme, message, etc.) by means of a relay (sense 4) 1923. 4. *intr.* To get a fresh relay 1829.

Release (rǐlī·s), *sb.* ME. [a. OF. *reles*, *relais*, vbl. sb. f. *relesser*, *relaisser*; see RELEASE *v.*] 1. Deliverance or liberation from trouble, pain, sorrow or the like. 2. The act of freeing, or fact of being freed, from some obligation, duty, or demand; remission; discharge ME. b. A written discharge, acquittance, or receipt 1440. 3. *Law.* The act of conveying or making over an estate or right to another, or disposing of it in some legal fashion; a deed or document made for this purpose. late ME. 4. The action of setting free, or the fact of being set free, from restraint or confinement; permission to go free; also, a document giving formal discharge from custody 1586. b. The act of letting go something fixed or held in a certain position, or confined in some way; also, any device by which this is effected 1871. 5. The action of 'releasing' a cinema film, etc.; the fact of being so released; an article so released 1907.

1. Nowthir frende nor foo Shulde fynde reles in helle 1440. 3. *Lease and r.*, 'a conveyance of the fee-simple, right, or interest in lands or tenements.. giving first the possession, and afterwards the interest in the estate conveyed'. 4. All prisoners.. They cannot boudge, till your r. SHAKS.

Release (rĭlī·s), *v.* ME. [ad. OF. *relesser, relaiss(i)er*:—L. *relaxare* to RELAX.] I. †1. *trans.* To withdraw, recall, revoke, cancel (a sentence, punishment, condition, etc.) –1671. †2. To relieve, alleviate, or remove (labour, pain, etc.) –1597. 3. To remit; to grant remission or discharge of or for (something); *esp.* a debt, tax, tribute, etc. Now *Law.* late ME. 4. To give up, resign, relinquish, surrender (*esp.* a right or claim in favour of another person). late ME. b. *spec.* To surrender, make over, transfer (land, etc.) to another. Chiefly *Law.* late ME. †5. To relax, mitigate –1677.

3. Sire, I releesse thee thy thousand pound...I wol nat take a peny of thee CHAUCER. 4. That we should at once r. our claims JOHNSON. b. 2 *Hen. VI*, I. i. 51.

II. To set or make free; to liberate, deliver, *of* (now *rare*) or *from* pain, bondage, obligation, etc. Also without const. ME. b. To unfix, free (a thing) from some fastening 1833. c. To permit the public performance, exhibition, publication, or sale of (a play, cinema film, book, or the like) for the first time 1904.

The Duke of Buckingham and Marquesse of Dorchester are again releast from the Tow'r MARVELL. A mind released From anxious thoughts COWPER. *absol.* He that can bind, can r. HOBBES. Hence **Relea·see·** (*Law*), one to whom an estate is released. **Relea·ser**, one who or that which, releases or sets free. **Relea·sor** (*Law*), one who releases a claim or estate in favour of another.

Releasement (rĭlī·sment). 1548. [f. prec. + -MENT.] 1. The act of releasing, or the fact of being released, from prison, obligation, debt, trouble, etc. †2. Relaxation, remission, or removal *of* a thing –1647.

Relegate (re·lĭgeit), *v.* 1599. [f. ppl. stem of L. *relegare*, f. *re-* RE- + *legare* to send.] 1. *trans.* To send (a person) into exile; to banish *to* a particular place. 2. To consign *to* a place or position, esp. one of inferiority 1790. b. To consign (a subject) *to* some province, sphere, domain, etc. 1866. c. To assign or refer (a thing) *to* a class or kind 1870. 3. To refer (a matter) *to* some authority for decision 1846. b. To commit, hand over (a thing), *to* another to carry out or deal with 1864.

2. b. If occasionally we come across difficulties.. we r. some of them to the sphere of mystery JOWETT.

Relegation (relĭgē·ʃən). 1586. [ad. L. *relegationem*; see prec.] 1. The action of banishing; the state of temporary exile or banishment. In *Rom. Antiq.* banishment to a certain place, or to a specified distance from Rome, for a limited time and without loss of civil rights. b. Banishment or consignment *to* a place or position 1829. 2. The action of referring, consigning, etc., a thing *to* others for some purpose 1844.

†**Rele·nt**, *sb. rare.* 1590. [f. the vb.] 1. Slackening of speed. SPENSER. 2. Relenting, giving way –1686.

Relent (rĭle·nt), *v.* late ME. [ult. f. L. *re-* RE- + *lentus* tough, sticky, viscous, slow; but the immediate source is not clear.] †1. *intr.* To melt under the influence of heat; to assume a liquid form; to dissolve into water. Also *fig.* –1784. †b. To become soft or moist –1620. 2. To soften in temper; to grow more gentle or forgiving 1526. †b. To yield, give way; to give up a previous determination or obstinacy –1667. †3. *trans.* To dissolve, melt, soften –1661. †b. To soften (one's heart, mind, etc.); to cause (a person) to relent –1787. †4. To lessen, abate; to slacken –1667. †b. To relinquish, abandon, give over –1684. †5. To repent (an action, etc.). SPENSER.

1. All nature mourns, the Skies r. in show'rs POPE. 2. Perhaps God will r., and quit thee all his debt MILT. 3. b. Yet pitty often did the gods r. SPENSER. 4. Nothing might r. her hasty flight SPENSER. Hence **Rele·ntment** (now *rare*), the act of relenting; softening of rigour.

Relentless (rĭle·ntlės), *a.* 1592. [f. prec. + -LESS.] Incapable of relenting; pitiless.

Onely in destroying I finde ease To my r. thoughts MILT. Hence **Rele·ntless-ly** *adv.*, **-ness.**

Relessee·. *rare.* 1766. [f. RE- + LESSEE after *release.*] *Law.* One to whom a release is executed. So **Rele·sso·r**, one who executes a release.

Re·levance. 1733. [See next and -ANCE.] Relevancy.

Relevancy (re·lĭvănsi). 1561. [ad. L. type *relevantia; see next and -ANCY.] The quality or fact of being relevant.

His answer..would thus come with more r. and effect 1826.

Relevant (re·lĭvănt), *a.* 1560. [ad. med.L. *relevantem*, pres. pple. of L. *relevare* to raise up.] 1. Bearing upon, connected with, pertinent *to*, the matter in hand. 2. *Sc. Law.* Legally pertinent or sufficient 1561. †3. Relieving, remedial (*rare*) –1762.

1. Many things in a controversy might seem r., if we knew to what they were intended to refer JOWETT. Hence **Re·levantly** *adv.*

†**Releva·tion.** late ME. [a. OF. *relevacion*, or ad. L. *relevationem.*] The action of raising, lifting up, supporting, relieving, etc. –1658.

Reliability (rĭləiăbi·lĭti). 1816. [f. next + -ITY.] The quality of being reliable, reliableness.

Comb., as *r. test, trial*, etc.

Reliable (rĭləi·ăb'l), *a.* 1569. [f. RELY *v.* + -ABLE.] That may be relied upon; in which reliance or confidence may be put; trustworthy, safe, sure.

A very r. medicine 1792. Macaulay may not have been a r. guide in the regions of high art 1876. Hence **Reli·ableness. Reli·ably** *adv.*

Reliance (rĭləi·ăns). 1607. [f. RELY *v.* + -ANCE.] 1. The (†*or* an) act of relying; the condition or character of being reliant; dependence, confidence. 2. That on which one relies or depends 1798.

1. Little r. can be placed on statements unconfirmed by writing 1877. 2. The dogs, the indispensable r. of the party, were in bad working trim KANE.

Reliant (rĭləi·ănt), *a.* 1856. [f. as prec. + -ANT.] Having reliance or confidence; confident, trustful.

Relic (re·lik). ME. [a. F. *relique*, orig. pl. *relikes*, ad. L. RELIQUIÆ, q.v.] 1. In Christian use: An object (as a part of the body or clothing, an article of personal use, or the like) which remains as a memorial of a departed saint, martyr, or other holy person, and as such is carefully preserved and venerated. †b. Applied tot he sacred objects of the ancient Jewish and pagan religions –1606. †c. A precious or valuable thing (*rare*) –1470. d. Something kept as a remembrance or souvenir; a memento 1601. 2. *pl.* The remains of a person; the body, or part of the body, of one deceased. (Sometimes implying sense 1.) ME. b. *sing.* in the same sense (*rare*) 1635. 3. *pl.* That which remains or is left behind, in later use esp. after destruction or wasting away; the remains or remaining fragments (of a thing); the remnant, residue (of a nation or people). Also occas. in *sing.* of a single thing or person. ME. 4. A surviving trace *of* some practice, fact, idea, quality, etc. In early use chiefly *pl.* 1586. b. A surviving memorial *of* some occurrence, people, period, etc. 1695. 5. An object invested with interest by reason of its antiquity or associations with the past 1596.

1. The Friars keepe for a holy relike the Thorne wherewith Christ was crowned 1617. d. Luther's.. apartment..contains his portrait, bible, and other relics 1838. 2. Men took a lasting adieu of their interred Friends,..having no old experience of the duration of their Reliques SIR T. BROWNE. 3. The relikes of a Church 1615. Treat the poor, as our Saviour did the Multitude, to the reliques of some baskets SIR T. BROWNE. After a bloody conflict of eight years.., the relics of the nation submitted GIBBON. 4. A Relique of a certain Pagan Worship 1712. b. Curious relics of ancient times 1832.

Relict (re·likt), *sb.* 1450. [ad. L. *relictus*, pa. pple. of *relinquere* to RELINQUISH; in sense 2 ad. med.L. *relicta.*] 1. = RELIC 1, 1 d, and 5. Now *rare* or *Obs.* 1535. 2. The widow *of* a man 1450. 3. *pl.* Remains, remnants, residue. Also *sing.* a surviving part; †a survivor. 1598. b. A surviving trace, survival 1646. c. *pl.* The remains of one deceased (*rare*) 1649. †4. Leavings; refuse (*rare*) –1748.

2. He married the Earl of March's R. 1610. To the great prejudice of a poor r. and her helpless child 1776.

†**Reli·ct**, *a.* 1649. [f. as prec.; cf. DERELICT.] 1. Left by death, surviving –1661. 2. Of lands: a. Left by the recess of the sea. b. Abandoned, deserted. –1687.

1. His R. Lady..lived long in Westminster FULLER.

Relief[1] (rĭlī·f). ME. [a. OF. *relief*, f. *relever* to RELIEVE.] 1. A payment, varying in value and kind according to rank and tenure, made to the overlord by the heir of a feudal tenant on taking up possession of the vacant estate. Now *Hist.* exc. in *Sc. Law.* b. *Hist.* Formal acknowledgement of feudal tenure made by a vassal to his lord (*rare*) ME. 2. Ease or alleviation given to or received by a person through the removal or lessening of some cause of distress or anxiety; deliverance from what is burdensome or exhausting to the mind; mental relaxation. late ME. b. Ease from, or lessening of, physical pain or discomfort 1691. c. An agreeable change of object, esp. to the sense of sight 1712. d. A gradual widening in the bore of a gun-barrel towards the muzzle 1824. 3. Aid, help, or assistance given to a person or persons in a state of poverty or want; now *spec.* assistance in money or necessary articles given to the indigent from funds administered under the Poor Law or from parish doles. late ME. †b. Sustenance –1613. †c. A fresh supply or supplies of some article of food or drink –1725. 4. Assistance in time of danger, need, or difficulty; aid, help, or succour 1500. b. Aid or succour rendered to persons or places endangered by war; in later use *esp.* deliverance *of* a besieged town, etc. from the attacking force 1548. †c. A body of men coming to the relief of a person or place (*rare*) –1670. 5. Release from some occupation or post of duty; in later use *spec.* of the replacing of a sentinel or watch by a fresh man or body of men 1513. b. One who relieves another on duty 1822. 6. Deliverance (esp. in *Law*) from some hardship, burden, or grievance; remedy, redress 1616. 7. Alleviation *of* some pain, burden, etc.; remission *of* a tax (*rare*) 1526. †8. *Hunting.* Of the hare or hart: The act of seeking food; feeding or pasturing –1668. 9. *R. Church*, a Scottish sect founded in 1761 in assertion of the right of congregations to elect their ministers; in 1847 amalgamated with the United Secession to form the United Presbyterian Church.

2. It is a r. to turn from so painful a subject BUCKLE. c. A clump of beeches..were a r. to the eye 1833. 3. In their idea of r., there is always included something of punishment BURKE. 4. At night Boats and Pilots went off to her R. 1698. *R. works*, public works undertaken for the r. of unemployment b. Stilicho..advanced..to the r. of the faithful city GIBBON. 5. For this releefe much thankes SHAKS. Hence **Relie·f-ful** *a.*, **-less** *a.*

Relief[2] (rĭlī·f). 1606. [orig. ad. It. *relievo* RELIEVO, f. *rilevare* to raise; subseq. a. F. *relief.*] 1. In the plastic arts, the elevation or projection of a design, or parts of a design, from a plane surface in order to give a natural and solid appearance; also, the degree of such projection; the part which so projects. b. A composition or design executed in relief 1682. 2. The appearance of solidity or detachment given to a design or composition on a plane surface by the arrangement and disposition of the lines, colours or gradations of colour of which it is composed; hence, distinctness of outline due to contrast of colour 1789. b. *fig.* Vividness, distinctness, or prominence due to contrast or artistic presentation 1781. 3. a. *Fortif.* The height to which works are raised above the bottom of the ditch 1834. b. *Phys. Geog.* The contour of some part of the surface of the earth considered with ref. to variations in its elevation 1865.

1. *High* (†or *great*), *low*, and *middle r.*: see ALTO-, BASSO-, MEZZO-RELIEVO, and BAS-RELIEF. 2. A church with its dark spire in strong r. against the clear cold sky W. IRVING.

attrib.: r. map, a map in which the conformation of an area of the earth's surface is shown by elevations and depressions or by suitable colouring.

Relier (rĭləi·əɹ). *rare.* 1593. [f. RELY *v.* + -ER[1].] One who relies (*on* a person or thing).

Relievable (rǐlī·văb'l), *a.* 1670. [f. RELIEVE *v.*] **a.** Capable of receiving, admitting of, legal relief; also const. *against.* **b.** That may be relieved or assisted 1707.

Relieve (rǐlī·v), *v.* late ME. [ad. OF. *relever*, ad. L. *relevare* to raise again, assist, f. *re-* RE- + *levare*, f. *levis* light.] **I.** *trans.* **1.** To raise (a person) out of some trouble, difficulty, or danger; to rescue, succour, aid or assist in straits; to deliver *from* something troublesome or oppressive. Now somewhat *rare.* **b.** To bring assistance to (a besieged town); to free from siege 1586. **c.** *Law.* To free or clear (a person) from an obligation; to give (a person) legal relief. Also *absol.* 1562. **2.** To assist (the needy) by gifts of money or necessary articles; to help in poverty or necessity. late ME. **3.** To ease or free (a person, the mind, etc.) from sorrow, fear, doubt, or the like. late ME. **b.** To give (a person, part of the body, etc.) ease or relief from physical pain or discomfort. late ME. **c.** To widen or open up; to ease (some mechanical device) by making slacker or wider 1824. **4.** To ease or mitigate (what is painful or oppressive); to render less grievous or burdensome. late ME. **b.** To make less tedious, monotonous, or disagreeable by the introduction of variety or of something striking or pleasing 1771. **5.** *spec.* To release (a person) from guard, watch, or other duty by becoming or providing a substitute 1601. **b.** To set (a person) free *from*, to ease (a person) *of*, any task or burden 1671; *joc.* to rob *of* a thing (e.g. *He was relieved of his watch*).

1. b. Soon after Prince Rupert came to r. the Town We raised the siege LD. FAIRFAX. 2. To r. the Confederate prisoners in the Northern prisons 1864. 3. Proofs which should r. my mind of all doubt upon the subject TYNDALL. b. *To r. nature*: to evacuate urine or fæces. 4. The final cause of compassion is much more to r. misery 1729. b. No great work relieved the barrenness of the time 1869.

†**II. 1.** To lift or raise up again –1533. **2.** *intr.* **a.** To rise again –1533. **b.** To return or rally in battle –1513. **3.** *trans.* To take up or hold (a feudal estate) from the superior –1525. **III.** †**1.** To bring (a matter) into prominence; to make clear or evident (*rare*) –176.. **2.** To make (a thing) stand out; to render prominent or distinct; to bring into relief 1778. **b.** *intr.* To stand out in relief 1812.

2. To Ariadne is given (say the critics) a red scarf, to r. the figure from the sea which is behind her SIR J. REYNOLDS. Hence **Relie·ver**, one who or that which relieves.

†**Relie·vement.** 1443. [a. OF. *releve-*, *relievement*, f. *relever* to RELIEVE.] The act of relieving; relief –1631.

Relieving (rǐlī·viŋ), *ppl. a.* 1681. [f. RELIEVE *v.* + -ING [2].] That relieves or gives relief.

R. officer, an officer appointed by a parish or union to administer relief to the poor. *R. tackle*, one of two strong tackles used to prevent a ship from overturning on the careen; also, one of those which are occasionally hooked to the tiller in bad weather, or in action, when the wheel or tiller-rope is broken or shot away. *R. arch* (Arch.), an arch formed in the substance of a wall to relieve the pressure or weight upon the wall. Hence **Relie·vingly** *adv.*

Relievo (rǐlī·vo). 1625. [ad. It., see RELIEF [2].] = RELIEF [2] 1, 1 b, 2. *In r.*, in relief.

Religate (re·ligeit), *v.* *rare.* 1651. [f. L. *religat-*, *religare* to bind up or back; see RE- and LIGATE *v.*] *trans.* To bind together or unite. So **Religa·tion**, the action of tying or binding up.

‖**Religieuse** (rəlizyöz). 1796. [F., fem. of next.] A woman bound by religious vows, or devoted to a religious life; a nun.

‖**Religieux** (rəlizyö). Now *rare* or *Obs.* 1654. [F., ad. L. *religiosus* RELIGIOUS.] A man vowed to a religious life; a monk.

Religio-, mod. comb. form of RELIGION or RELIGIOUS, as in *r.-educational*, *-magical*, etc.

Religion (rǐli·dʒən). ME. [a. AF. *religiun*, F. *religion*, or ad. L. *religionem*; etym. obsc.] **1.** A state of life bound by monastic vows; the condition of one who is a member of a religious order; the religious life. **2.** A particular monastic or religious order or rule; †a religious house. Now *rare.* ME. **3.** Action or conduct indicating a belief in, reverence for, and desire to please, a divine ruling power; the exercise or practice of rites or observances implying this. Also *pl.*, religious rites. Now *rare*, exc. as implied in 5. ME. **4.** A particular system of faith and worship ME. †**b.** *The R.* [after F.]: the Reformed Religion, Protestantism –1674. **5.** Recognition on the part of man of some higher unseen power as having control of his destiny, and as being entitled to obedience, reverence, and worship; the general mental and moral attitude resulting from this belief, with ref. to its effect upon the individual or the community; personal or general acceptance of this feeling as a standard of spiritual and practical life 1535. †**6.** *transf.* Devotion to some principle; strict fidelity or faithfulness; conscientiousness; pious affection or attachment –1691. †**7.** The religious sanction or obligation *of* an oath, etc. –1704.

1. My father..was retired into r. in the Kingdom of Naples H. WALPOLE. †*Man of r.*, one bound by monastic vows or in holy orders. †*House*, etc. *of r.*, a religious house, a monastery or nunnery. 2. Some ships of the r. of Malta 1769. 3. The public r. of the Catholics was uniformly simple and spiritual GIBBON. 4. I wonder what r. he is of B. JONS. All important religions have sprung up in the East 1862. *transf.* We hear men speak of a r. of art, of a r. of work, of a r. of civilization 1872. 5. There are no signes..of R., but in Man onely HOBBES. Therfore on thy firme hand r. leanes In peace, & reck'ns thee her eldest son MILT. Phr. *To get r.*: see GET *v.* I. 10. 6. *Rom. & Jul.* I. ii. 93. Phr. *To make (a) r. of* or *to make (it) r. to*, to make a point of, to be scrupulously careful (†not) to do something. Hence **Reli·gionless** *a.* destitute of r.

Religionary (rǐli·dʒənări), *a.* and *sb.* 1663. [f. prec. + -ARY, or ad. F. *religionnaire* Protestant, Calvinist.] **A.** *adj.* Relating to religion; religious. Now *rare.* 1691. †**B.** *sb.* **a.** A person 'in religion'. **b.** A Protestant. –1760.

Religioner (rǐli·dʒənəɹ). 1812. [f. as prec. + -ER [1].] **a.** A person 'in religion'. **b.** = RELIGIONIST.

Religionism (rǐli·dʒeniz'm). 1791. [f. RELIGION + -ISM.] Marked or excessive inclination to religion; exaggerated or affected religious zeal.

Religionist (rǐli·dʒənist). 1653. [f. as prec. + -IST.] One addicted or attached to religion; one imbued with, or zealous for, religion. Occas., a religious zealot or pretender.

These pretended religionists are really a kind of superstitious atheists HUME. A dispassionate, placid, and mild r. 1812.

Religionize (rǐli·dʒənəiz), *v.* 1716. [f. as prec. + -IZE.] **a.** *trans.* To imbue with religion, to render religious. **b.** *intr.* To be addicted to, to affect, religion.

Religiose (rǐlidʒiōu·s), *a.* 1853. [f. as RELIGIOUS + -OSE [1].] Religious to excess; unduly occupied with religion; morbidly or sentimentally religious.

Religiosity (rǐlidʒiǫ·sĭti). late ME. [ad. late L. *religiositas*; see RELIGIOUS and -ITY.] Religiousness, religious feeling or sentiment. **b.** Affected or excessive religiousness 1799.

Religious (rǐli·dʒəs), *a.* and *sb.* ME. [a. AF. *religius*, OF. *religious*, or ad. L. *religiosus*, see -OUS.] **A.** *adj.* **1.** Imbued with religion; exhibiting the spiritual or practical effects of religion; pious, godly. **2.** Of persons: Bound by monastic vows; belonging to a religious order ME. **b.** Of things, places, etc.: Of, belonging to, or connected with, a monastic order ME. **3.** Of the nature of, pertaining or appropriate to, concerned or connected with, religion 1538. **b.** (Chiefly *poet.*) Regarded as sacred 1618. **4.** *transf.* Scrupulous, exact, strict, conscientious 1599.

1. That sober Race of Men, whose lives R. titl'd them the Sons of God MILT. Phr. *Most r.*, used as an epithet of royalty. 2. Houses of r. women 1745. b. Those r. places that are neare Oxford WOOD. 3. Storied Windows richly dight, Casting a dimm r. light MILT. Prayer is the most directly r. of all our duties J. H. NEWMAN. b. Thy Shrine in some r. wood COLLINS. 4. A Coward, a most deuout Coward, r. in it SHAKS. His library is preserved with the most r. neatness GOLDSM.

B. *sb.* **1.** As *pl.* Persons bound by monastic vows or devoted to the religious life according to the rules of an order or congregation in a Christian church ME. **b.** With ref. to non-Christian religions 1585. **2.** *sing.* A person devoted to the religious life, as a monk or nun ME. Hence **Reli·gious-ly** *adv.*, **-ness.**

Reli·ne (rī-), *v.*[1] 1851. [f. RE- 4 + LINE *v.*[1]] *trans.* To provide with a new lining.

Reli·ne (rī-), *v.*[2] 1875. [f. RE- 4 + LINE *v.*[2]] *trans.* To renew the lines of.

Relinquent (rǐli·ŋkwĕnt), *a.* and *sb.* *rare.* 1847. [ad. L. *relinquentem.*] **A.** *adj.* Relinquishing; vanquishing. **B.** *sb.* One who relinquishes.

Relinquish (rǐli·ŋkwiʃ), *v.* 1472. [ad. OF. *relinquiss-*, *relinquir*, ad. L. *relinquere*, f. *re-* RE- + *linquere* to leave.] †**1.** *trans.* To withdraw from, desert, abandon (a person). *rare.* –1552. †**b.** To give up as incurable. SHAKS. **2.** To give up or give over, to abandon, desist from (an idea, action, practice, etc.); to cease to hold, adhere to, or prosecute 1497. †**b.** To desist from putting forward for office. H. WALPOLE. **3.** To give up, resign, surrender (a possession, right, etc.). Also const. *to.* 1560. **b.** To let go (something held) 1850. †**4.** To leave behind (*rare*) –1679. †**5.** *intr.* To disappear, pass away. B. JONS.

1. I..shall vtterlye renounce, refuse, r., & forsake the bishop of Rome *Bk. Com. Prayer.* 2. Alarmed by this intelligence, he hastily relinquished the siege GIBBON. 3. They know my disinclination to r. the command WELLINGTON. Hence **Reli·nquishment**, the act of relinquishing; abandonment, giving up, surrender.

‖**Reliquaire** (re·likwēᵊɹ). 1769. [F.] = next.

Reliquary (re·likwări), *sb.* 1656. [ad. F. *reliquaire*; see RELIC and -ARY [1].] A small box, casket, shrine, etc., in which a relic or relics are kept.

Re·liquary, *a.* *rare.* 1826. [See prec. and -ARY [1].] Belonging to a relic or relics.

‖**Reliquiæ** (rǐli·kwiˌī), *pl.* 1835. [L. fem. sb. pl., f. *reliquus* remaining, f. *re-* RE- + *liq-*, *linquere* to leave.] **1.** Remains of any kind; *spec.* in *Geol.* remains of early animals or plants 1840. **2.** *Bot.* 'The withered remains of leaves, which, not being articulated with the stem, cannot fall off, but decay upon it' 1835.

Relish (re·liʃ), *sb.*[1] 1530. [Later f. †*reles*, a. OF. *reles*, var. of *relais* remainder, with assimilation of the ending to -ISH [2].] **1.** A taste or flavour; the distinctive taste *of* anything. **b.** *transf.* A trace or tinge *of* some quality; a suggestion; a sample or specimen; a small quantity 1597. †**2.** An individual taste or liking –1758. **3.** An appetizing or pleasing flavour; a savoury or piquant taste 1665. **b.** A savoury addition to a meal; an appetiser 1798. **4.** Enjoyment of the taste or flavour of something; liking, zest 1649. †**5.** Sense of taste; power of relishing. GOLDSM.

1. A Laplander or Negro has no notion of the r. of wine HUME. b. Your Lordship..hath yet some smack of age in you; some rellish of the saltnesse of Time SHAKS. 3. The tired glutton..finds no r. in the sweetest meat POPE. b. A r. they shall have—salt and olives and cheese JOWETT. 4. Cranmer.. seems to have done this with great r. 1882. A moral r. for veritable proofs of honesty MORLEY.

†**Re·lish**, *sb.*[2] 1561. [perh. ult. the same as prec.] *Mus.* A grace, ornament, or embellishment –1668.

Relish (re·liʃ), *sb.*[3] *rare.* 1611. [ad. OF. *relais.*] A projection; now *spec.* in *Joinery*, the projection of the shoulder of a tenon.

Relish (re·liʃ), *v.*[1] 1586. [f. RELISH *sb.*[1]] **1.** *trans.* **a.** To give or impart a relish to (a thing); to make pleasant to the taste. †**b.** To have a taste, tinge, or trace of (some quality or thing), to partake of –1702. †**c.** To provide with something relishing; to please, gratify, delight –1794. †**2.** To taste, take a taste of; to distinguish by tasting (*rare*) –1633. †**b.** To feel. SHAKS. **3.** To enjoy, take pleasure or delight in 1599. **b.** To like, have a liking for; to care for, be pleased or satisfied with; to approve of 1594. **c.** To take or receive in a particular manner. Now *rare.* 1600. †**d.** To appreciate, understand (*rare*) –1611. **4.** *intr.* To have a (or the) taste *of* something; to savour or smack *of*, have a touch or trace *of* 1602. **5.** To taste in a particular way; to have a specified taste or relish. Now *dial.* and *U.S.* 1600. †**6.** *fig.* To be agreeable or pleasant; to find acceptance or favour (*with* a person) –1740.

1. I have also a novel.., to r. my wine MACAULAY. c. They send her many dainty dishes..to rellish her palate 1626. 3. I once more smell the dew and rain, And r. versing G. HERBERT. b. They do not r. the prospect before them 1885. 4. To be thus affected, would r. too much of a Cynical Humour 1703. 5. Afflictions r. sour and bitter even to the palates of the best saints FULLER. 6. Indeed, if a Man sets up for a Sceptick, I don't expect the Argument should R. 1697. Hence **Re·lishable** *a.* **Re·lisher.**

†**Re·lish,** *v.*[2] 1591. [app. f. RELISH *sb.*[2]] *trans.* To sing, warble –1608.

Relish (re·liʃ), *v.*[3] *rare.* 1611. [Cf. RELISH *sb.*[3]] †1. *intr.* To project, jut out. COTGR. 2. *trans.* To make shoulders on (wood) in shaping tenons 1884.

Relive (rīli·v), *v.* 1548. [f. RE- 5 a + LIVE *v.*, in early use after *revive.*] †1. *trans.* To raise or restore again to life; to resuscitate –1592. 2. *intr.* To come to life again; to live anew 1548. 3. *trans.* To live (a period of time) over again 1711.

2. Will you deliuer how this dead Queene relives? SHAKS.

†**Reli·ver,** *v. rare.* 1456. [ad. OF. *relivrer.*] *trans.* To give up again, restore –1603.

Reloa·d (rī-), *v.* 1778. [RE- 5 a.] 1. *trans.* To make up again as a load; to furnish with a fresh load. 2. a. *absol.* To put in a fresh gun-charge 1784. b. To load (a fire-arm or cartridge) again 1853.

Relocation (relokēⁱ·ʃən, rī-). 1575. [In sense 1, f. late L. *relocare* to relet; in 2, f. RE- 5 a + LOCATION.] 1. *Sc. Law. Tacit r.*, the implied renewal of a lease when the landlord allows a tenant to continue without a fresh agreement, after the original lease has expired. 2. The action of locating afresh; a new allocation 1877.

Relucent (rīliū·sĕnt), *a.* Now *rare.* 1507. [ad. L. *relucentem, relucere* to shine back.] Casting back light; shining, gleaming, bright, refulgent.

In brighter mazes the r. stream Plays o'er the mead THOMSON. So **Relu·cence, -ency.**

Reluct (rīlʌ·kt), *v.* 1526. [ad. L. *reluctari*, f. *re-* RE- + *luctari* to struggle.] †1. *intr.* To strive or struggle *to* do something –1633. 2. To struggle, strive, or rebel *against*, to show dislike, to revolt *at*, to offer opposition *to*, a thing 1547. b. Without prep.: To offer opposition; to manifest or express reluctance; to object 1648.

2. I..r. at the inevitable course of destiny LAMB.

Reluctance (rīlʌ·ktăns). 1641. [f. RELUCTANT; see -ANCE.] 1. The act of struggling *against* something; resistance, opposition. Now *rare.* b. *Electr.* The property, in a magnetic circuit, of opposing to a certain extent the passage of the magnetic lines of force 1888. 2. Unwillingness, disinclination. Freq. in phr. *with* (or *without*) *r.* 1667. †3. A struggle or qualm of conscience. PEPYS.

1. Untam'd r., and revenge MILT. 2. There is nothing which we receive with so much R. as Advice ADDISON. Your r. to put the vanity of an author out of countenance CIBBER.

Reluctancy (rīlʌ·ktănsi). Now *rare.* 1621. [See next and -ANCY, and cf. prec.] †1. An internal or mutual struggle or contest –1662. †2. Resistance or opposition of one thing *to* another –1665. †b. Resistance or opposition on the part of persons *against* or *to* something. Also *pl.* –1679. 3. = RELUCTANCE 2. 1634.

3. The slowness and r. with which errors yield to conviction 1826.

Reluctant (rīlʌ·ktănt), *a.* 1667. [ad. L. *reluctantem, reluctari* to struggle against, f. *re-* RE- + *luctari.*] 1. Struggling; writhing (*rare*). b. Offering resistance or opposition *to* something (*rare*) 1726. 2. Unwilling, averse, disinclined 1706. b. *transf.* of things 1667. 3. Characterized by unwillingness, disinclination, or distaste 1725.

1. Down he fell A monstrous Serpent on his Belly prone, R., but in vaine MILT. 2. Edward was still r. to begin the war GREEN. b. R. on its rusty hinge Revolved an iron door SCOTT. 3. R. consent BURKE. Hence **Relu·ctantly** *adv.*

Reluctate (rīlʌ·kteⁱt), *v.* 1643. [ad. L. *reluctat-, reluctari*; see prec.] 1. *intr.* To offer resistance; to strive or struggle *against* something; to show reluctance. 2. *trans.* To strive against, refuse, reject (*rare*) 1681.

1. Having..something within him, which reluctated against those superstitions FULLER. So **Relucta·tion,** struggle, resistance, opposition; †reluctance, unwillingness.

Reluctivity (relʌkti·vĭti). 1888. [f. as RELUCT *v.* + -IVE + -ITY.] *Electr.* Degree of magnetic reluctance.

Relume (rīliū·m), *v.* 1604. [f. RE- + *-lume* (see ILLUME *v.*).] 1. *trans.* To relight, rekindle; to cause to burn afresh. 2. To make clear or bright again 1746. 3. To light up again; to re-illuminate; to shine upon anew 1786.

1. I know not where is that Promethean heate That can thy Light re-Lume SHAKS. 3. And Shakspeare's sun relumes the clouded stage 1786.

Relu·mine, *v. rare.* 16.. [ad. late L. *reluminare*; see RE- and ILLUMINE.] *trans.* = prec.

Rely (rīləi·), *v.* ME. [ad. OF. *relier* to bind together:—L. *religare*, f. *re-* RE- + *ligare* to bind.] †1. *trans.* To gather (soldiers, followers, etc.) together; to assemble, to rally –1608. 2. *intr.* To depend *on* a person or thing with full trust or confidence; to rest *upon* with assurance 1574. b. With ref. to facts or statements 1809. †c. To rest *upon* a support –1683. 3. To put trust or confidence *in* a person or thing. Somewhat *rare.* 1606. †4. *refl.* and *trans.* To repose (oneself, one's soul, faith, etc.) *on, upon,* or *in* some person or thing –1641.

2. Go in thy native innocence, relie On what thou hast of vertue MILT. Can I r. upon your secrecy? DICKENS. 3. Asdrubal placed his Gauls (in whom he least rely'd) in the Left Wing 1654.

Remain (rīmēⁱ·n), *sb.*[1] 1456. [a. OF. *remain*, f. *remaindre* REMAIN *v.* Now chiefly *pl.*] I. †1. Those left, surviving, or remaining out of a number of persons; the remainder or rest –1671. 2. That which remains or is left (unused, undestroyed, etc.) of some thing or quantity of things; also, that which remains to be done. Now *rare.* 1529. †b. (Also *pl.*) The balance or unpaid remainder of a sum of money –1669. 3. A remaining or surviving part or fragment of something. Now *rare.* 1570. 4. (With *pl.*) a. A survival; a relic *of* some obsolete custom or practice; a surviving trait or characteristic. Now *rare.* 1641. b. A material relic (*of* antiquity, etc.); an ancient monument, building, or other structure; an object which has come down from past times 1687. †c. A literary relic –1738.

1. I believe the number of these sent will be about a hundred; the r. also being forty or fifty CROMWELL. 2. *Cymb.* III. i. 87. 3. When this r. of horror has entirely subsided BURKE. Every yet inedited r. of Anglosaxon 1843. 4. b. The supposition..that Low Hill is a Druidical r. 1864.

II. *pl.* 1. Surviving members of a company, family, or other body of persons. Also rarely of a single person. 1456. 2. The remaining parts *of* some thing or things; all that is left of something; articles remaining from a store or stock 1500. b. Const. *of* the destroying force (*rare*) 1715. c. Const. as *sing.* 1801. 3. a. The literary works (*esp.* the unpublished ones) left by an author; also, the fragments of an ancient writer 1652. b. That which is left of a person when life is extinct; the (dead) body, corpse 1700. c. Substances of organic origin preserved in the earth in a fossilized condition 1799.

2. The wretched remains of a ruined reputation *Junius Lett.* c. This short remains of happiness 1801. 3. a. The remains of Clement and Polycarp 1873. b. I saw..her poor remains laid at rest in the convent garden 1797.

†**Remai·n,** *sb.*[2] *rare.* 1470. [f. the vb.] Stay –1605.

A..worke..Which often since my heere remaine in England, I haue seene him do SHAKS.

Remain (rīmēⁱ·n), *v.* late ME. [a. AF. *remeyn-, remayn-*, stressed stem of OF. *remanoir*:—L. *remanere*, f. *re-* RE- + *manere* to stay.] 1. *intr.* To be left after the removal or appropriation of some part, number, or quantity. 2. To be left over and above what has already been done or dealt with in some way. late ME. †3. To continue to belong *to* one –1605. 4. To continue in the same place (or with the same person); to abide, stay 1439. †b. To dwell –1611. 5. With complement: To continue to be 1509. b. To continue in the same state; to lie untouched or undisturbed 1839. 6. To continue to exist; to have permanence; to be still existing or extant. late ME. †b. To stick in the mind. Const. *with.* SHAKS. c. To continue with (a person). MILT. 7. To await, be left for (a person). *rare.* 1579.

1. There is not Sap enough remaining to nourish the Leaves 1707. 2. Nothing remaines, but that I kindle the boy thither SHAKS. What remains to tell TENNYSON. 3. *Lear* I. i. 82. 4. Charles remained six days in Paris ROBERTSON. b. But for my Mistris, I nothing know where she remaines SHAKS. 5. I formed them free, and free they must r. MILT. *I r.*, as the concluding formula of a letter; I r., my dear friend, Affectionately yours, W. C. 1793. 6. A little Verse my All that shall r. GRAY. 7. If thence he scape.., what remains him less Then unknown dangers and as hard escape MILT.

Remainder (rīmēⁱ·ndəɪ), *sb.*[1] late ME. [a. AF., subst. use of OF. *remaindre* inf.,:—pop. L. **remanēre*; see prec. and -ER [4].] 1. *Law.* The residual or further interest remaining over from an estate, coming into effect when this has determined, and created by the same conveyance by which the estate was granted. b. So *r. over.* Sometimes = a further remainder. 1544. c. *transf.* The right to succeed to a title or position on the death of the holder; *esp.* the right of succession to a peerage expressly assigned to a certain person or line of descent in default of male issue in the direct line 1809. 2. a. Those still left out of a number of persons; the rest 1547. b. That which is left when part has been taken away, used, dealt with, etc.; the residue 1560. 3. †a. A single person, or a few persons, remaining out of a number –1697. b. A remaining (†or still existing) part or fragment; chiefly *pl.* = remains, *esp.* of ancient buildings 1604. c. A remaining trace *of* some practice, quality, feeling, etc. Now *rare.* 1641. 4. a. *Arith.* The number which remains after subtraction of a lesser from a greater; the excess after a process of division 1571. b. = REMAIN *sb.*[1] I. 2 b. SHAKS. 5. In the book-trade: A number of copies remaining unsold out of an edition (esp. after the demand for it has fallen off or ceased), and frequently disposed of at a reduced price 1791. 6. *attrib.* or *adj.* Remaining, left over; reserve 1567.

1. *Cross remainders*, estates in r. arising where lands are devised to two or more persons in tail, with r. to either upon failure of the other's issue. *R. man*, the person to whom a r. is devised. 2. a. We drove the R. headlong off the Deck 1737. b. He should be permitted to pass the r. of his life in..exile GIBBON. 3. c. If you have any remainders of modesty or truth cry God mercy MILT. 6. His braine..is as drie as the r. bisket After a voyage SHAKS. Hence **Remai·nder** *v. trans.* to sell (a number of books, etc.) as remainders. **Remai·ndership** (*Law*) the possession of a r.; the fact of there being a r.

†**Remai·nder,** *sb.*[2] *rare.* 1594. [f. as prec.] Stay; time of staying or remaining –1646.

†**Remai·ndment.** 1596. [irreg. f. REMAINDER *sb.*[1]] *Law.* A remainder. BACON.

Remand (rīmɑ·nd), *sb.* 1771. [f. the vb.] 1. The act of remanding, or the fact of being remanded; now *spec.* recommittal of an accused person to custody. 2. A remanded prisoner 1888.

Remand (rīmɑ·nd), *v.* late ME. [ad. F. *remander*, or late L. *remandare* to send back word, to repeat a command; see RE- and MANDATE.] 1. *trans.* To send (a thing) back again *to* a place; to reconsign; also, to remit, consign. 2. To send back (a person); to command or order to go back *to* a place 1588. b. Of a court or magistrate: To send back (a prisoner) into custody, now *spec.* in order that further evidence on the charge may be obtained 1643. 3. To call or summon back, to recall. Now *rare* or *Obs.* 1525. †4. To demand back from another –1677.

1. Both dissuaded me from suffering it to be represented on the stage; and accordingly it was remanded back to my shelf FIELDING. 2. b. The said A. is remanded into custody 1794. 3. He remanded his own [men] from the pursuit 1656.

Remanence (re·mănĕns). 1666. [See REMANENT *a.* and -ENCE.] 1. That which remains; residuum (*rare*). 2. The fact of remaining; permanence. COLERIDGE. So †**Re·manency.**

†**Re·manent,** *sb.* late ME. [See next.] 1. The remainder, the remaining part, the rest –1651. 2. A remaining part or amount; a

remnant; *pl.* remains -1632. **3.** *Arith.* A remainder -1559.

Remanent (re·mănĕnt), *a.* Now *rare.* late ME. [ad. L. *remanentem*, *remanere* to REMAIN.] †**1.** In predicative use: Remaining, staying, abiding; continuing to exist -1649. **2.** Left behind, remaining, when the rest is removed, used, done, etc. Now *rare.* late ME. **3.** *Law.* = next 2 a. 1808.

1. There is no effect r. upon the body JER. TAYLOR.

Remanet (re·mănet). 1511. [L., 3rd sing. pres. indic. of *remanere* to REMAIN.] **1.** A remainder. **2. a.** *Law.* A cause or suit of which the hearing is postponed to another day or term 1734. **b.** A parliamentary bill left over till another session 1870.

Remark (rĭmā·ɹk), *sb.*[1] 1654. [ad. F. *remarque*, f. *remarquer* to REMARK.] †**1.** The fact or quality of being worthy of notice or comment -1702. **2.** Observation, notice; comment 1680. **b.** Air of observation; look. THOMSON. **3. a.** An act of observing or noticing; an observation. Now *rare.* 1660. **b.** A verbal or written observation; a comment; a brief expression of opinion or criticism 1673. †**4.** A sign, mark, indication -1709.

1. In which there were three Women, but of no great r. 1702. 2. Lord R. Churchill's latest escapade ..is the theme of general r. 1885. 3. b. He could not bear to hear Mr. Barker's chaffing remarks 1883.

Remark (rĭmā·ɹk), *sb.*[2] Also **re-mark.** 1880. Anglicized f. REMARQUE.

Remark (rĭmā·ɹk), *v.* 1633. [ad. F. *remarquer*; see RE- and MARK *v.*] †**1.** *trans.* To mark out, distinguish -1671. †**b.** To point out, indicate -1742. **2.** To observe, take notice of, perceive 1675. **3.** To say, utter, or set down, as an observation or comment 1704. **b.** *intr.* To make a remark *on* a thing 1859.

1. His manacles r. him, there he sits MILT. 2. Has not your highness remarked it? H. WALPOLE. b. The singular fact remarked on by several observers DARWIN.

Remarkable (rĭmā·ɹkăb'l), *a.* and *sb.* 1604. [ad. F. *remarquable*; see prec. and -ABLE.] **A.** *adj.* **1.** Worthy of remark, notice, or observation; hence, extraordinary, unusual, singular. †**2.** Perceptible; admitting of being observed or noted -1766. †**b.** Conspicuous, noticeable -1801.

1. The oddes is gone, And there is nothing left remarkeable Beneath the visiting Moone SHAKS. 2. A demure look, and some other r. signs of grace 1704.

B. *sb.* A noteworthy thing or circumstance; something extraordinary or exceptional. Chiefly in *pl.* Now *arch.* 1639.

After lunch to-day we..set forth to see the remarkables of Oxford HAWTHORNE. Hence **Remarkabi·lity, Rema·rkableness,** the fact or character of being r. **Rema·rkably** *adv.* in a r. manner.

Remarker (rĭmā·ɹkəɹ). Now *rare.* 1684. [f. REMARK *v.* + -ER[1].] †**1.** One who makes or publishes remarks on a literary work; a reviewer or critic; also, an author of 'Remarks' on some subject -1795. **2.** One who makes observations; an observer, commenter 1684.

‖**Remarque** (rəmark). 1882. [F.] *Engraving.* A distinguishing feature indicating a certain state of the plate, usu. consisting in the insertion of a slight sketch in the margin. Also *attrib.* in *r.-proof.*

‖ **Remblai** (raṅblẹ). Also in pl. form **remblais.** 1794. [F., f. *remblayer* to embank, f. *re-* RE- + *emblayer* to heap up.] **1.** *Fortif.* The earth used to form a rampart, or embankment. **2.** *Mining.* Material used to fill up the excavations made in a thick seam of coal 1867.

Rembrandtesque (rembrante·sk), *a.* 1879. [f. name of *Rembrandt*, the Du. painter and etcher (1608–1669), + -ESQUE.] Resembling the manner or style of Rembrandt. So **Re·mbrandtish** *a.* 1860.

Remeant (rī·miănt), *a. rare.* 1848. [ad. L. *remeantem*, *remeare*, f. *re-* RE- + *meare* to pass.] Returning.

Remede, remeid (rĭmī·d). Now *arch.* late ME. [a. OF. *remede*, ad. L. *remedium* REMEDY.] Remedy, redress.

Remediable (rĭmī·diăb'l), *a.* 1491. [a. F. *remédiable*, or ad. L. *remediabilis*; see REMEDY and -ABLE.] †**1.** Capable of remedying; remedial -1596. **2.** Capable of being remedied or redressed 1570. Hence **Reme·diableness. Reme·diably** *adv.*

Remedial (rĭmī·diăl), *a.* 1651. [ad. L. *remedialis*, f. *remedium* REMEDY; see -AL 1.] Affording a remedy, tending to relieve or redress.

Every good political institution must have a preventive operation as well as a r. BURKE. Suffering is a medicine, r. though bitter 1862. Hence **Reme·dially** *adv.*

Remediless (re·mĭdilės), *a.* late ME. [f. next + -LESS; orig. stressed *remē·diless.*] **1.** Of persons, etc.: Destitute of remedy; having no prospect of aid or rescue. Now *rare* or *Obs.* **2.** Of trouble, disease, etc.: Not admitting of remedy; incapable of being remedied, cured, or redressed 1513.

1. I'll rear up Malta, now r. MARLOWE. 2. Grief—deep r. grief SHELLEY. Hence **Re·mediless-ly** *adv.*, **-ness.**

Remedy (re·mĭdi), *sb.* ME. [a. AF. *remedie*, ad. L. *remedium*, f. *re-* RE- + *med-*, *mederi* to heal.] **1.** A cure for a disease or other disorder of body or mind; any medicine or treatment which alleviates pain and promotes restoration to health. **2.** A means of counteracting or removing an outward evil of any kind; reparation, redress, relief ME. **3.** Legal redress 1450. **4.** *Coining.* The small margin within which coins as minted are allowed to vary from the standard fineness and weight. Also called *tolerance.* late ME. **5.** At various schools (as still at St. Paul's and Winchester): A time specially granted for recreation; a half-holiday 1518.

1. The only R. is to lay the Bone open 1702. *fig.* Withdraw thy Action, and depart in Peace; The R. is worse than the Disease DRYDEN. The only r. for superstition is knowledge 1862. 2. A r. against those optical deceptions 1837. Phr. *There is no r.* (= way out of it, help for it, alternative) *but*, etc. †*No r.*, unavoidably. 3. Left to the remedie, which the Law of the place alloweth them HOBBES.

Remedy (re·mĭdi), *v.* late ME. [a. OF. *remedier*, or ad. L. *remediare*, f. *remedium* REMEDY *sb.*] **1.** *trans.* †**a.** To grant (a person) legal remedy; to right (a person) in respect of a wrong suffered -1662. **b.** To bring remedy to (a person, diseased part, etc.); to heal, cure, make whole again. Now *rare.* 1470. **2.** To cure (a disease, etc.); to put right, reform (a state of things); to rectify, make good. late ME.

1. b. Into the woods..shee went, To seeke for hearbes that mote him r. SPENSER. 2. They tooke up Armes to remedie their wrong DRAYTON. A great deal has been done to r. the deficiency 1853.

Remember (rĭme·mbəɹ), *v.* ME. [ad. OF. *remembrer*:—late L. *rememorari*, f. *re-* RE- + *memor* mindful.] **I. 1.** *trans.* To retain in, or recall to, the memory; to bear in mind. **b.** With *inf.* To bear in mind, not to forget, *to* do something. late ME. **2.** To think of, recall the memory of (a person) with some kind of feeling or intention. late ME. **b.** To bear (a person) in mind as entitled to a gift, recompense, or fee, or in making one's will; hence, to fee, reward, 'tip' 1470. †**3.** To record, mention, make mention of (a thing, person, etc.) -1749. †**b.** To commemorate -1658. **c.** To have mind *of* and mention (a person, his condition, etc.) in prayer 1602. **4.** *absol.* or *intr.* To have or bear in mind; to recall to the mind; also, to exercise or possess the faculty of memory. late ME. **5.** *refl.* To bethink or recollect, †to think or reflect upon (oneself). Now *rare.* late ME. **6. a.** *impers.* (*It*) *remembers me* [after OF. (*il*) *me remembre*], I remember. Now *arch.* late ME. **b.** *To be remembered*, to remember; also const. *of.* *Obs.* exc. *dial.* 1440.

1. I was..left by my father, whom I cannot r., to the care of an uncle JOHNSON. Phr. †*R. your courtesy*, be covered. b. You will also r. to take bonds for the money BERKELEY. 2. Remembre thy maker in thy youth, or euer the dayes of aduersite come COVERDALE *Eccl.* xii. 1. b. Anon, anon, I pray you r. the Porter SHAKS. 3. b. *Temp.* I. ii. 405. c. Nimph, in thy Orisons Be all my sins remembered SHAKS. 4. That shallow vassall..which as I r., hight Costard SHAKS. b. To have mind, memory, or recollection of something (now *rare* exc. in U.S.) CHAUCER. 5. *Lear* IV. vi. 233. 6. a. Whan that it remembreth me Up-on my yowthe CHAUCER.

II. 1. To remind (a person); esp. to put (one) in mind *of* a thing or person. Now *arch.* or *dial.* late ME. †**2.** To recall (a thing or person) *to* a person. Also with double obj., obj. clause, and without const. -1672. **b.** To mention (a person) *to* another as sending a friendly greeting. Also without const. 1560.

1. Emanuel..remember'd Azem of his Promises 1745. 2. By onely remembring them the truth of what they themselves know to be heer missaffirmed MILT. b. R. me In all humilitie vnto his Highnesse SHAKS. Katty Tatham desires to be remembered to you all 1872. Hence **Reme·mberable** *a.* capable or worthy of being remembered. **Reme·mberably** *adv.* **Reme·mberer,** one who, or that which, remembers (†or reminds).

Remembrance (rĭme·mbrăns). ME. [a. F.; see prec. and -ANCE.] **1.** Memory or recollection in relation to a particular thing. **2.** That operation of the mind which is involved in recalling a thing or fact; recollection. Freq. personified, or in fig. context. late ME. †**b.** Faculty or power of remembering or calling to mind -1631. **3.** With possess. pron. (A person's) memory or recollection; also, in later use, (a person's) power of remembering (cf. prec.). late ME. **b.** The point at which one's memory of events begins, or the period over which it extends 1565. **4.** The memory (†or thought) which one has *of* a thing or person. late ME. **b.** With *a* and *pl.* A recollection, reminiscence 1601. **c.** The surviving memory of a person 1579. **d.** *pl.* Greetings expressive of remembrance 1789. †**5.** Mention, notice -1631. †**b.** A memorial inscription -1599. †**6.** The act of reminding or putting in mind -1659. †**7.** A memorandum -1676. †**b.** A reminder; a remark intended to remind -1638. **8.** A keepsake, souvenir; a token. late ME. **b.** A memorial or record of some fact, person, etc. Now *rare.* 1470.

1. This ever grateful in r. bear POPE. R. rises faint and dim Of sorrows suffer'd long ago 1816. Phr. *To have in r.*, *to call to r.* 2. Not for thy life, lest fierce r. wake My sudden rage MILT. b. This Lord of weake r. SHAKS. 3. But now is my r. weak with eld 1864. b. Thee I have heard relating what was don Ere my r. MILT. 4. The dear r. of his native coast POPE. b. How sharpe the point of this r. is SHAKS. 5. b. *Hen. V*, I. ii. 229. 7. b. 2 *Hen. IV*, v. ii. 115. 8. b. On his brest a bloodie Crosse he bore, The deare r. of his dying Lord SPENSER.

Remembrancer (rĭme·mbrănsəɹ). 1455. [a. AF.; see prec. and -ER[1].] **1.** The name of certain officials of the Court of Exchequer. **b.** An official of the Corporation of the City of London, whose chief duty now is to represent that body before parliamentary committees and at Council and Treasury Boards 1710. **2.** One who reminds another; in former use, *esp.* one engaged or appointed for that purpose 1523. **3.** *fig.* of things; also, a thing serving to remind one; a reminder; a memento, souvenir 1589. **b.** A memorandum-book. THACKERAY. †**4.** One who sends remembrances to another. PEPYS.

1. The *King's* (or *Queen's*) *R.*, an officer responsible for the collection of debts due to the Sovereign; now an officer of the Supreme Court. 3. Premature consolation is but the r. of sorrow GOLDSM.

†**Reme·morate,** *v.* 1460. [ad. ppl. stem of late L. *rememorari.*] **a.** *trans.* To remind, put in mind (of). Also *absol.* **b.** *intr.* To remember 1606. So **Rememora·tion** (now *rare*), the action of remembering (†or reminding); an instance of this.

†**Reme·morative,** *a.* and *sb.* 1449. [f. as prec. + -IVE.] **A.** *adj.* Serving to remind -1641. **B.** *sb.* A reminder -1676.

†**Re·menant.** ME. [a. OF., pres. pple. of *remenoir* to REMAIN. See also REMNANT.] **1.** The rest or remainder. Also *pl.* -1573. **2.** A remaining thing or part; a remnant -1433.

†**Reme·rcy,** *v.* 1477. [ad. F. *remercier*, f. *re-* RE- + *merci* MERCY.] To thank -1592.

She him remercied as the Patrone of her life SPENSER. So †**Reme·rcy** *sb.* thanks -1606.

‖**Remex** (rī·meks). *Pl.* **remiges** (re·midʒīz). 1767. [L., f. *remus* oar.] *Ornith.* One of the principal feathers of a bird's wing, by which it is sustained and carried forward in flight; a wing-quill. Chiefly *pl.* Hence **Remi·gial** *a.* (*rare*) serving to propel; of or pertaining to the remiges.

Remiform (re·mifǭɹm), *a. rare.* 1860. [f. L. *remus* oar.] Shaped like an oar.

Remigrate (re·migreɪt, rĭməi·greɪt), *v.* 1601. [orig. f. L. *remigrat-*, *remigrare*; later, f. RE-

5 a + MIGRATE *v.*] †1. *intr.* To change back again -1680. 2. To migrate again or back 1623. So **Remigra·tion**, the action of remigrating; return.

Remind (rǐmai·nd), *v.* 1645. [f. RE- 5 a + MIND *v.*] 1. *trans.* To recall (a thing) to one's own mind; to remember, recollect. Now *rare* or *Obs.* †b. To recall to another's mind (*rare*) -1669. 2. To put (a person) in mind *of* something, *to do* something, etc. 1660.

2. The time of year reminds me how the months have gone DICKENS.

Reminder (rǐmai·ndəɹ). 1653. [f. prec. + -ER [1].] Something which reminds one; mention made for the purpose of reminding. b. *Path.* in *pl.* Secondary syphilitic symptoms 1897.

Remi·ndful, *a.* 1810. [f. as prec. + -FUL.] 1. Mindful, retaining the memory, *of*. 2. Reminiscent, reviving the memory, *of* 1864.

Reminisce (remini·s), *v. colloq.* or *joc.* 1829. [Back-formation from next.] 1. *trans.* and *intr.* To recollect, remember. 2. *intr.* To indulge in reminiscences 1882.

Reminiscence (remini·sĕns). 1589. [a. F. *réminiscence*, or ad. late L. *reminiscentia*, f. *reminisci* to remember, f. *re-* RE- + *men- (see MIND *sb.*).] 1. The act, process, or fact of remembering or recollecting; sometimes *spec.* the act of recovering knowledge by mental effort. 2. (Chiefly *pl.*) a. A recollection or remembrance, as a mental fact 1813. b. A recollection or remembrance of some past fact or experience related to others; freq. (in *pl.*), the collective memories or experiences of a person put into literary form 1811. 3. A feature, fact, etc., which recalls something else 1860.

1. The other part of memory, called R.: which is the Retreiving of a thing, at present forgot, or but confusely remembred 1692. 2. b. As he listened to these reminiscences of the sailors PRESCOTT.

†**Remini·scency.** 1655. [See prec. and -ENCY.] The faculty of reminiscence -1732.

Reminiscent (remini·sĕnt), *sb.* 1822. [f. as next.] A relater or writer of reminiscences.

Reminiscent (remini·sĕnt), *a.* 1765. [f. L. *reminiscentem, reminisci*; see REMINISCENCE.] 1. Pertaining to, characterized by, reminiscence. b. Having reminiscence *of* something 1830. 2. Of the nature of reminiscence or reminiscences 1863. 3. Evoking a reminiscence *of* a person or thing 1880.

1. b. Some other state of existence, of which we have been previously conscious and are now r. 1836. Hence **Remini·scently** *adv.*

Reminiscential (re:minise·nʃăl), *a.* 1646. [f. REMINISCENCE; cf. *essential.*] Of the nature of, pertaining to, reminiscence; of a reminiscent character.

Remiped (re·miped), *sb.* and *a.* 1826. [ad. F. *rémipède*, f. L. *remus* oar + *ped-*, *pes* foot.] *Zool.* A. *sb.* One of an order of coleopterous insects having tarsi adapted for swimming; also, a crustacean of the genus *Remipes*. B. *adj.* Having feet that are oar-shaped, or used as oars 1864.

†**Remi·se**, *sb.*[1] 1473. [a. F., vbl. sb. f. *remettre* to remit.] 1. *Law.* A transfer of property -1766. 2. A remission or cessation of sickness. FLORIO. 3. The act of remitting money; a remittance -1689.

‖**Remise** (rəmī·z), *sb.*[2] 1698. [F.; see prec.] 1. A coach-house. b. (Ellipt. for *voiture de remise*.) A carriage hired from a livery stable, of a better class than the ordinary hackney-carriage 1698. 2. *Fencing.* A second thrust made after the first has missed and while still upon the lunge; the act of making a thrust of this kind 1823. 3. A wired-in space planted to attract game-birds 1905.

Remise (rǐmai·z), *v.*[1] 1481. [f. F. *remis(e*, *remettre*:—L. *remittere* to REMIT.] †1. *trans.* To put back again *in* or *into* a place or state; to replace; to convert again *into*; to send back *to* a place -1623. 2. *Law.* To give up, surrender, make over to another, release (any right, property, etc.) 1487.

Remi·se, *v.*[2] 1889. [f. REMISE *sb.*[2] 2.] *Fencing. intr.* To make a remise.

Remiss (rǐmi·s), *a.* late ME. [ad. L. *remissus*; see REMIT.] †1. *Med.* Weakened; dilute -1625. 2. Of persons: Slack in the discharge of a task or duty; careless, negligent 1450. b. Of conduct, actions, etc.: Characterized by carelessness, negligence, or inattention 1502. †3. Characterized by a lack of strictness or proper restraint; lax, loose -1751. †b. Lenient -1651. 4. Free from vehemence or violence; also, lacking in force or energy 1550. †b. Not intense or strong; moderate, mild (esp. of heat and cold) -1686. †5. Diminished in tension; loose, relaxed -1667.

2. R. in the duties..of Religion BENTLEY. A very r. correspondent 1893. b. What had been r. in the conduct of his predecessor 1817. 3. A r. discipline JER. TAYLOR. 4. The passion must neither be too violent nor too r. HUME. 5. Pain Which..makes r. the hands of Mightiest MILT. Hence **Remi·ss-ly** *adv.*, **-ness.**

Remiss (rǐmi·s), *v. rare.* 1500. [f. L. *remiss-*, *remittere*; cf. REMISE *v.*[1]] †1. *trans.* To remit; to resolve or dissolve; to mitigate; to let go, pass over -1656. 2. *Law.* = REMISE *v.*[1] 2. 1809.

Remi·ssful, *a. rare.* 1603. [f. REMISS *v.* or *a.*] †1. Full of remission; merciful. DRAYTON. 2. Full of remissness; negligent 1836.

Remissible (rǐmi·sĭb'l), *a.* 1577. [a. F. *rémissible*, or ad. L. *remissibilis*.] Capable or admitting of remission; that may be remitted. Hence **Remissibi·lity, Remi·ssibleness**, r. state or condition.

Remission (rǐmi·ʃən). ME. [a. OF., ad. L. *remissionem*, f. *remittere*.] 1. Forgiveness or pardon *of* sins or other offences. 2. Forgiveness or pardon granted for sins or offences against divine law; the cancelling of, or deliverance from, the guilt and penalties of sin ME. b. Pardon for a political, legal, or other offence. Now *Hist.* late ME. †3. a. Release from a debt or payment -1608. b. Liberation from captivity, etc.; respite -1761. 4. The action of remitting or giving up partially or wholly (a debt, tax, penalty, etc.). late ME. †5. Relaxation; lessening of tension; slackening of energy or application -1741. 6. Diminution of force or effect; lowering or decrease of a condition or quality, esp. of heat or cold 1603. b. *Path.* A decrease or subsidence (esp. a temporary one) in the violence of a disease or pain; also *transf.* of violent emotions 1685. 7. The action of remitting or sending (back); a remittal (*rare*) 1724.

1. In..Scripture, R. of Sinne, and Salvation from Death and Misery, is the same thing HOBBES. 2. He gives repentance and r. DE FOE. b. *Two Gent.* I. ii. 65. 6. The r. of the cold did not continue long enough to afford me much relief JOHNSON. 7. The r. of a million every year to England SWIFT.

Remissive (rǐmi·siv), *a.* 1514. [ad. med. L. *remissivus*; see REMISS *v.* and -IVE.] †1. Careless, remiss (*rare*) -1640. 2. Inclined to, of the nature of, productive of, remission or pardon. Now *rare.* 1611. †3. Producing or allowing decrease *of* something -1718. 4. Characterized by remission or abatement 1686.

2. No contrition alone is r. of sins JER. TAYLOR.

Remissory (rǐmi·səri), *a. rare.* 1548. [f. as REMISS *v.* + -ORY [2].] Tending to, of the nature of, remission.

Remit (rǐmi·t), *v.* late ME. [ad. L. *remittere*, f. *re-* RE- + *mittere* to send.] I. *trans.* 1. To forgive or pardon (a sin, offence, †a person, etc.). †2. To give up, resign, surrender (a right or possession) -1670. 3. To abstain from exacting (a payment or service of any kind); to allow to remain unpaid (or unperformed) 1463. b. To refrain from inflicting (a punishment) or carrying out (a sentence); to withdraw, cancel; to grant remission of (suffering) 1483. †4. To discharge, set free, release, liberate (a person) -1647.

1. Whose synnes soeuer ye remytte they are remytted vnto them COVERDALE *John* xx. 23. 2. Th' Ægyptian Crown I to your hands r. DRYDEN. 3. She remitted the Arrears that were owing 1701. b. The queen remitted the quartering of his body 1693.

II. 1. To give up, lay aside (anger, etc.) entirely or in part. late ME. b. To give up or over, abandon, desist from (a pursuit, occupation, etc.) 1587. 2. To allow (one's diligence, attention, etc.) to slacken or abate 1510. †b. To mitigate, diminish, or abate. -1750. †3. To relax, relieve from tension -1711.

1. Our Supream Foe in time may much r. His anger MILT. b. Engaged..in a siege which they could not r. KINGLAKE. 2. Do not r. your care JOHNSON.

III. 1. To refer (a matter) for consideration, decision, performance, etc., *to* a person or body of persons, now usu. to one specially empowered or appointed to deal with it; also *spec.* in *Law*, to send back (a case) to an inferior court. late ME. b. To send (a person) from one tribunal *to* another for trial or hearing (*rare*) 1538. †c. To commit (a person) *to* the charge or control of another. Also *refl.* -1741. 2. To refer (a person) *to* a book, another person, etc., for information. late ME. 3. a. To send (a person) back to prison, or to other custody; to recommit. Now *rare.* late ME. †b. To emit or send out again. DRYDEN. 4. †a. *Law.* To restore to a former and more valid title; see REMITTER [2] 1. -1768. b. To put back *into*, to admit or consign again *to* a previous position, state, or condition 1591. 5. To postpone, put off or defer 1635. 6. To refer, assign, or make over *to* a thing or person 1641. †b. To enter or insert *in* (or *into*) a book -1716. 7. To send or transmit (money or articles of value) *to* a person or place. Also *absol.* 1640.

1. Wheche mater I remytte..to youre ryght wyse discrecion 1455. 2. Let us hear Du Cange, to whom Robertson remits us 1835. 4. b. You propose to r. to slavery three millions of negroes BRIGHT. 7. We parted; and he remitted me a small annuity JOHNSON.

IV. *intr.* 1. To abate, diminish, slacken 1629. 2. To relax *from* labour; to give over 1760.

1. How often have I blest the coming day, When toil remitting lent its turn to play GOLDSM. 2. Their enemies will not r.; rust, mould, vermin..all seize their own EMERSON. Hence **Remi·tment**, †remission, pardon; remitting of money. **Remi·ttal**, remission *for* sin, or *of* a debt, penalty, etc.; *Law*, the act of referring a case from one court to another. **Remittee·**, one to whom a remittance is made or sent. **Remi·tter** [1], one who forgives or pardons (*rare*); one who sends a remittance.

Remittance (rǐmi·tăns). 1705. [f. REMIT *v.* + -ANCE.] A sum of money sent from one place or person to another; a quantity of some article sent in this way; also, the act of sending money, etc., to another place.

R.-man, an emigrant who is supported or assisted by remittances from home.

Remittent (rǐmi·tĕnt), *a.* and *sb.* 1693. [ad. L. *remittentem*, *remittere*.] A. *adj.* That remits or abates for a time; *spec.* in *Path.* of a type of fever, the symptoms of which abate at intervals (without disappearing entirely as in the *intermittent* type). B. *sb.* 1. *Path.* A remittent fever 1693. 2. One who remits money 1855.

Remitter [2] (rǐmi·təɹ). 1445. [See REMIT *v.* and -ER [4].] 1. *Law.* a. A principle or operation by which one having two titles to an estate, and entering on it by the later or more defective of these, is adjudged to hold it by the earlier or more valid one. b. The act of remitting a case to another court for decision 1726. 2. Restoration to rights or privileges, or to a previous state (*rare*) 1623.

Remnant (re·mnănt), *sb.* and *a.* ME. [Contr. f. REMENANT.] A. *sb.* 1. With *the.* That which remains after the removal of a portion; the remainder, rest, residue. Now applied only to a small remaining number or part. 2. With *a* and *pl.* A (small) remaining number, part, or quantity 1611. b. Of a single person: A survivor (*rare*) 1594. 3. A remaining trace or survival *of* some quality, belief, condition, or state of things 1560. 4. A fragment, a small portion, a scrap. late ME. b. *spec.* among drapers and clothiers: An end of a piece of goods, left over after the main portion has been used or sold. late ME. †c. A scrap or tag of quotation. B. JONS.

1. The remnaunt of the captiuyte COVERDALE *Neh.* i. 3. The r. of my tale is of a length To tire your patience DRYDEN. 2. The remnants of their provisions on the voyage 1888. b. *Rich. III*, I. ii. 7.

B. *adj.* Remaining 1550.

Act through thy r. life the decent part PRIOR.

‖**Remolade** (reməlad). 1702. [a. F. *rémolade*, *rémoulade*, ad. It. *remolata*.] 1. An unguent used in farriery. 2. A piquant salad-dressing resembling mayonnaise 18..

Remonetize (rǐmɒ·nǐtəiz), *v.* 1878. [RE- 5 a.] *trans.* To restore (a metal or other substance) to its former use as full legal tender. So **Remonetiza·tion.**

Remonstrance (rǐmǫ·nstrǎns). 1477. [a. OF., = med.L. *remonstrantia*; see REMONSTRATE and -ANCE.] †1. An appeal, request -1490. †2. Demonstration, proof, evidence, manifestation of some fact, quality, etc.; also, a ground *of* some belief -1774. 3. †a. A (written or spoken) demonstration, statement, account, or representation. Usu. const. *of* (the matter declared or brought forward). -1772. b. A formal statement of grievances or similar matters of public importance, *esp.* the *Grand R.* presented by the House of Commons to the Crown in 1641. Now *Hist.* 1626. c. *Eccl. Hist.* A document presented in 1610 to the States of Holland by the Dutch Arminians, relative to the points of difference between themselves and the strict Calvinists 1662. 4. The action of remonstrating; expostulation 1603. b. With *a* and *pl.* An instance of this 1729. 5. A monstrance 1656. *Obs.* or *rare.*

2. The externall and visible remonstrances of religion JER. TAYLOR. 4. b. The remonstrances of the people were disregarded 1774.

Remonstrant (rǐmǫ·nstrǎnt), *a.* and *sb.* 1618. [ad. med.L. *remonstrantem*, *remonstrare.*] A. *adj.* 1. *Eccl. Hist.* Of or belonging to the Arminian party in the Dutch Reformed Church. 2. That remonstrates or expostulates 1641. B. *sb.* 1. *Eccl. Hist.* A member of the Arminian party in the Dutch Reformed Church (see REMONSTRANCE 3 c.) 1618. 2. One who remonstrates; †the author, or a supporter, of a remonstrance (in senses 3 a, b) 1641. Hence **Remo·nstrantly** *adv.* in a r. manner.

Remonstrate (rǐmǫ·nstreⁱt, re·mǫnstreⁱt), *v.* 1599. [ad. med.L. *remonstrat-*, *remonstrare* to demonstrate, f. *re-* RE- + *monstrare* to show.] †1. *trans.* To make plain or manifest, demonstrate, exhibit, show -1742. †2. To point out (a fault, etc.) to another by way of reproof, disapprobation, or complaint; to protest against (a wrong) -1751. †b. To point out, state, or represent (a grievance, etc.) to some authority. Also const. *to*. -1741. †3. *intr.* To raise an objection *to* a thing; to address a remonstrance *to* a person -1792. 4. To urge strong reasons *against* a course of action, to protest *against*; to expostulate *with* a person, *on* or *upon* an action. Also *absol.* 1695. 5. *trans.* To say, assert, or plead in remonstrance 1758.

1. Mr. Edw. Wood was the spokes-man: remonstrated that they were Oxon. scholars 1680. 2. b. The Parliament sent but six or seven, to r. their complaints 1647. 4. Corporal Trim, by being in the service, had learned to obey,—and not to r. STERNE. 5. 'I am a mortal', Scrooge remonstrated, 'and liable to fall' DICKENS. Hence **Remonstra·tion**, the action of remonstrating, expostulation; an instance of this. **Remo·nstrative** *a.* of or characterized by remonstrance. **Remo·nstrator**, one who remonstrates, a remonstrant. **Remo·nstratory** *a.* expostulatory.

Remontant (rǐmǫ·ntǎnt), *a.* and *sb.* 1883. [a. F., f. *remonter* to REMOUNT.] A. *adj.* Of roses: Blooming a second time or oftener in a season. B. *sb.* A hybrid perpetual rose blooming more than once in a season 1883.

‖**Remontoir** (rəmoṅtwār). 1801. [F., f. *remonter* to REMOUNT.] *Clock-making.* A device by which an exactly uniform impulse is given to the pendulum or balance. Also *attrib.*

Remora (re·mŏrǎ). 1567. [a. L., f. *re-* RE- + *mora* delay.] 1. The sucking-fish (*Echeneis remora*), believed by the ancients to have the power of staying the course of any ship to which it attached itself. 2. An obstacle, hindrance, impediment, obstruction 1604. 3. *Surg.* An instrument used to retain bones or other parts in place (*rare*) 1688.

1. Like the r., of which mariners tell marvels, it counteracts, as it were, both oar and sail LANDOR. 2. These numerous demands are likely to operate as a *r.*, and to keep us fixed at home COWPER.

†**Re·morate,** *v. rare.* 1638. [ad. L. *remorat-*, *remorari* to hinder, delay, f. *re-* RE- + *morari.*] *trans.* To detain, delay, obstruct -1657.

Remo·rd, *v. Obs.* (exc. as *nonce-wd.*). late ME. [ad. F. *remordre* :—L. *remordere*, f. *re-* RE- + *mordere* to bite, sting.] 1. *trans.* To visit with affliction. CHAUCER. 2. To afflict (a person, the mind, etc.) with remorse or painful feelings. late ME. b. To afflict (oneself) with remorseful thoughts; also, to unburden with contrition; to examine in a penitent spirit 1450. 3. To recall to mind with remorse or regret. late ME. 4. *intr.* To feel remorse 1440. 5. *trans.* To blame, rebuke 1523.

2. b. Others thought he must..have pillaged a church;..and now was committing the mistake of remording himself about it READE.

Remorse (rǐmǭ·ɹs), *sb.* late ME. [a. OF. *remors* (mod.F. *remords*), ad. late L. *remorsus.*] 1. *R. of conscience* (or *mind*) = 2. Now somewhat *rare* and *arch.* 2. A feeling of compunction, or of deep regret and repentance, for a sin or wrong committed. late ME. b. With *a* and *pl.* A fit of remorse -1761. †3. Sorrow, pity, compassion; also *pl.* signs of tender feeling -1700. †4. Regretful or remorseful remembrance or recollection *of* a thing -1695. †b. A solemn obligation. SHAKS. 5. Biting or cutting force. SPENSER.

1. One of these Lieutenants, having a R. of Conscience, discovered the..Mater 1704. 2. The fruit of our own ill-doing is r. HOOKER. 3. Curse on th' unpard'ning Prince, whom Tears can draw To no R. DRYDEN.

†**Remo·rse,** *v.* 1483. [f. L. *remors-*, *remordere*; see REMORD *v.*] *trans.* and *intr.* To affect with, or feel, remorse -1690.

Remorseful (rǐmǭ·ɹsfŭl), *a.* 1591. [f. REMORSE *sb.*] 1. Affected with or characterized by remorse; impressed with a sense of, and penitent for, guilt 1592. †2. Compassionate, full of pity -1611. †3. Pitiable. CHAPMAN.

1. Many a bitter hour and year of r. sorrow CARLYLE. 2. *Two Gent.* IV. iii. 13. Hence **Remo·rseful·ly** *adv.*, **-ness.**

Remorseless (rǐmǭ·ɹslės), *a.* 1593. [f. as prec. + -LESS.] Devoid of remorse; pitiless, cruel. b. quasi- *adv.* Without remorse 1593.

Remorsles cruelty MILT. A r. foe 1853. Hence **Remo·rseless·ly** *adv.*, **-ness.**

Remote (rǐmōᵘ·t), *a.* late ME. [ad. L. *remotus*, *removere* to REMOVE.] 1. Placed or situated at a distance or interval from each other; far apart. 2. Far away, far off, distant *from* some place, thing, or person; removed, set apart 1586. 3. Far-off, far-distant 1533. b. Out-of-the-way, retired, secluded 1611. c. In quasi-*adv.* use: At a distance, far off 1667. d. Distant in (past or future) time 1712. 4. Far off, or distant, in various *transf.* uses: *esp.* not immediately or closely related to, connected with, bearing upon, or affecting something else 1599. †b. Far-fetched; unusual (*rare*) -1781. c. Not closely related by blood or kinship 1760. †5. Antecedent; ultimate (*rare*) -1697. 6. Slight, faint. In later use, esp. *not the remotest*, not the slightest, not the least (idea, etc.) 1711.

1. Hearts r., yet not asunder SHAKS. 2. Some.. Hermitage, R. from all the pleasures of the world SHAKS. 3. To grace the Gentry of a Land r. SHAKS. b. Places r. enough are in Bohemia, There..leaue it crying SHAKS. c. The sound Of Thunder heard r. MILT. 4. Their nimble nonsense..gains r. conclusions at a jump COWPER. They had not foreseen how the remoter consequences would affect their own safety THIRLWALL. b. Words too familiar or too r., defeat the purpose of a poet JOHNSON. 6. It had a bearing—r. indeed, but real—on what is being done now 1861. Hence **Remo·te·ly** *adv.*, **-ness.**

†**Remoted,** *a.* 1580. [f. as prec. + -ED[1] 2.] Remote, distant; removed -1683.

Remotion (rǐmōᵘ·ʃən). Now *rare.* late ME. [ad. L. *remotionem*, f. *removere* to REMOVE.] 1. Remoteness. Now *rare.* 2. The action of removing; removal; putting or taking away 1449. †b. The process of arriving at some conception (*spec.* that of God) by removal of everything which is known not to be included in it -1677. †3. The action of removing or departing -1692.

1. Its utter solitude and r. from men or cities DE QUINCEY. 3. *Lear* II. iv. 115.

Remo·tive, *a. rare.* 1819. [f. L. *remot-*, *removere* + -IVE.] †1. *Bot.* Characterized by removal of the episperm from the sheath of the cotyledon. LINDLEY. 2. That may be removed 1834.

Remount (rī-, rǐmau·nt), *sb.* 1802. [f. the vb.] *Mil.* 1. a. A supply of fresh horses for a cavalry regiment. b. A horse used to replace another which is worn out or killed 1829. 2. *attrib.*, as *r. depot*, etc. 1812.

Remount (rī-, rǐmau·nt), *v.* late ME. [ad. OF. *remonter*, f. *re-* RE- + *monter* to MOUNT. Also partly f. RE- 5 a + MOUNT *v.*] I. *trans.* †1. To raise or lift up again -1577. b. To set up in place again; *esp.* to mount (a gun) again 1627. c. To mount, put together, again 1888. 2. a. To replace, to assist or enable (a person) to mount again, on horseback. late ME. b. To provide (cavalry) with fresh horses 1688. 3. a. To ascend or go up (a place or thing) again 1621. b. To mount (a horse, etc.) again 1788.

3. a. To r. the stream to its ancient source 1884.

II. *intr.* 1. To mount, rise, or move upwards again 1490. 2. To get on horseback again 1500. 3. To go back, in the course of an investigation or study, *to* a certain point, period, etc. 1738. b. To go back in time *to* a certain date 1831. c. To go back *to* a source 1839.

3. We soon r. to facts which lie beyond our powers of analysis and observation 1837. b. A practice which remounts to the first ages of Christianity 1844.

Removable (rǐmū·văb'l), *a.* and *sb.* 1534. [f. REMOVE *v.* + -ABLE.] 1. Subject to removal. 2. Capable of being removed (from one place to another, or entirely) 1564. B. *sb.* A removable resident magistrate in Ireland 1888. Hence **Remo:vabi·lity. Remo·vableness.**

Removal (rǐmū·văl). 1597. [f. REMOVE *v.* + -AL 2.] 1. The act of taking away entirely. 2. Dismissal from an office or post; also, transference to another office, etc. 1647. 3. The act of conveying or shifting to another place; the fact of being so transferred 1639. 4. The act of changing one's ground, place, or position; *esp.* change of habitation 1642.

2. The appointment and r. of magistrates 1863.

Remove (rǐmū·v), *sb.* 1553. [f. the vb.] †1. Removal of a person from a position or office; dismissal -1799. †b. The act of removing a person by death; murder -1653. 2. †a. The act of taking away, or doing away with, a thing -1676. b. *Farriery.* The act of taking off a horse's shoe in order to dress the hoof and replace the shoe on the same or another foot; hence, an old shoe used over again. Now *dial.* 1549. c. The act of taking away a dish or dishes at a meal in order to put others in their place; hence, a dish thus removed, or brought on 1773. 3. The act of removing a thing from one place to another 1582. †4. The act of transferring a person from one office or post to another; the fact of being so transferred -1751. b. Promotion, at school, to a higher class or division 1662. c. At some schools: An intermediate form or class 1718. 5. The (*or* an) act of changing one's place, *esp.* one's place of residence; departure to another place. Now *rare.* 1586. †b. A period of absence from a place. SHAKS. 6. Distance, in time, place, condition, etc. 1628. b. A step or stage in gradation of any kind; esp. in phr. *but one* (or *a*) *r. from* 1633. c. A degree in descent or consanguinity 1766.

1. b. He most violent Author Of his owne iust remoue SHAKS. 3. An Elephant for the r. of our baggage and commodities 1660. 4. b. Surprising I didn't get my r. this term 1894. c. Some unhappy wight in the r. DISRAELI. 5. Three removes are as bad as a fire FRANKLIN. 6. b. Yet nascent feudality was but one r. from anarchy BRYCE.

Remove (rǐmū·v), *v.* ME. [a. OF. *remeuv-* (whence ME. *remeve*), *remouv-*, *remouvoir* :—L. *removere*, f. *re-* RE- + *movere* to MOVE.] I. *trans.* 1. To move from or out of the place occupied; to lift or push aside, lift up and take away, take off, withdraw. b. To put (a person) out of the way; to assassinate, murder 1653. c. *pass.* Of dishes: To be replaced or followed *by*, after removal 1840. 2. To move, shift, or convey from one place to another; to change the place or situation of ME. †b. *Law.* To transfer (a cause or person) for trial from one court of law to another -1744. 3. To send or put (a person) away; to compel (a person) to go from, or quit, a place. late ME. b. To depose, dismiss from a position or office. late ME. 4. To take away (*from* a person), to relieve or free one from, some feeling, quality, condition, etc., esp. one of a bad or detrimental kind; †to do away with (a practice). late ME. †b. To put away (a feeling, etc.) *from* oneself -1703. †5. To move or persuade (a person) *out of* or *from* a purpose or resolve -1654.

1. God to r. his wayes from human sense, Plac'd

Heav'n from Earth so farr MILT. *To r. mountains*: to perform miracles: after Matt. xvii. 20, etc. **c.** Boiled haddock, removed by hashed mutton THACKERAY. **2.** Elizabeth was now removed to Canterbury 1839. **3.** To r. him I decree, And send him from the Garden MILT. **b.** None of the sheriffs now removed were employed again STUBBS. **4.** The death of Norfolk..removed the dread of..war 1874.

II. *intr.* **1.** To go away or depart from a place; to move off to somewhere else ME. **b.** *spec.* To change one's place of residence; also of a tenant, to quit a house or holding. late ME. †**c.** To shift one's place or position -1656. **2.** Of things: To change place; to move off or away; to disappear, etc. late ME. †**3.** To move, stir; to be in motion -1601.

1. He said, he'd r. into another room GLANVILL. **b.** One who, having liv'd in Long-Acre..had removed for fear of the Distemper DE FOE. **2.** The mountaynes shall remoue, & the hilles shal fall downe COVERDALE *Isa.* liv. 10.

Removed (rǐmū·vd), *ppl. a.* 1548. [f. prec. + -ED [1].] **1.** Distant in relationship by a certain degree in descent or consanguinity. **2.** †**a.** Remote; retired, secluded -1632. †**b.** Separated by time or space (*rare*) -1628. **c.** Lifted or taken away 1625. **3.** *predic.* Remote, separated, or distant *from* something 1617.

1. He is a cousin, several times r. DICKENS. **2. a.** Som still r. place MILT. **b.** *Twel. N.* v. i. 92. Hence **Remo·vedness.**

Remover (rǐmū·vəɹ). 1594. [f. REMOVE *v.* + -ER [1].] **1.** One who or that which removes or takes away; *spec.* a furniture-remover. **2.** One who changes his place (*rare*) 1600.

2. Loue is not loue Which..bends with the remouer to remoue SHAKS.

†**Remuable,** *a. rare.* late ME. [a. OF.] Changeable, unstable; mobile. late ME only.

†**Remue·,** *v.* ME. [a. OF. *remuer*, f. *re-* RE- + *muer*:—L. *mutare* to change.] **1.** *trans.* To remove or transfer to another place -1600. **2.** *intr.* To move off or away, depart -1482.

Remu·nerable, *a. rare.* 1593. [See next and -ABLE.] That may be rewarded; deserving of reward. Hence **Remunerabi·lity** (*rare*).

Remunerate (rǐmiū·nĕrēit), *v.* 1523. [f. L. *remunerat-*, *remunerari* to reward, f. *re-* RE- + *munus* a gift.] **1.** *trans.* To repay, requite, make some return for (services, etc.). **2.** To reward (a person); to pay (a person) for services rendered or work done 1588. **b.** Of things: To recompense or repay (a person) 1849.

2. b. The principle that our exclusive trade with the colonies remunerates us for the expense of colonial establishments COBDEN. Hence **Remunera·tion,** reward, recompense, repayment; payment, pay. **Remu·nerator** (*rare*), one who remunerates. **Remu·neratory** *a.* serving to r.; affording remuneration.

Remunerative (rǐmiū·nĕrĕtiv), *a.* 1626. [f. as prec. + -IVE.] †**1.** Inclined to remunerate (*rare*) -1626. **2.** That remunerates or rewards 1677. **3.** That brings remuneration; profitable 1853.

2. R. justice 1677. **3.** The scheme did not prove r. 1865. Hence **Remu·nerative-ly** *adv.*, **-ness.**

Remurmur (rǐmʊ̄·ɹmǝ̄ɹ), *v.* Chiefly *poet.* 1697. [ad. L. *remurmurare*; see RE- and MURMUR *v.*] **1.** *intr.* **a.** To give back or give forth a murmuring sound; to resound with murmurs. **b.** To answer with murmurs *to* a sound 1697. **c.** Of sounds: To echo in murmurs 1717. **2.** *trans.* To repeat in murmurs 1704.

1. b. Eurota's banks remurmur'd to the noise POPE. **2.** The trembling trees..Her fate r. to the..flood POPE.

Ren, obs. f. RUN *v.*

Renable (re·năb'l), *a. Obs.* exc. *dial.* ME. [a. OF. *re(s)nable*:—L. *rationabilem* reasonable.] **a.** Of persons: Ready of speech, eloquent; †esp. in phr. *r. of tongue.* **b.** Of speech: Ready, fluent, plain. late ME.

Renaissance (rǐnē·săns, F. rǝnesans). 1840. [F. (in full (*r. des lettres*), f. *renaître* to be born again; cf. RENASCENCE.] **1.** The revival of art and letters, under the influence of classical models, which began in Italy in the 14th c.; the period during which this movement was in progress 1845. **b.** *ellipt.* The style of art or architecture developed in, and characteristic of, this period 1840. **2.** Any revival in art, literature, etc. 1872.

2. Voltairism may stand for the name of the R. of the eighteenth century 1872.

Renaissant (rǐnē·sănt), *a. rare.* 1864. [a. F.; cf. RENASCENT.] Of or belonging to, characteristic of, the Renaissance.

Renal (rī·năl), *a.* 1656. [a. F. *rénal*, or ad. late L. *renalis*, f. *ren* kidney; see REINS.] Of or pertaining to the reins or kidneys.

Re·nardine, *a. rare.* 1866. [f. *Renard*, var. REYNARD.] Pertaining to Reynard the Fox.

Renascence (rǐnæ·sĕns). 1727. [See next and -ENCE.] **1.** The process or fact of being born anew; re-birth, renewal, revival. **2.** = RENAISSANCE 1. 1869. So **Rena·scency** = sense 1. 1664.

Renascent (rǐnæ·sĕnt), *a.* 1727. [ad. L. *renascentem*, pres. pple. of *renasci*, f. *re-* RE- + *nasci* to be born.] That is being born again, reviving, springing up afresh.

†**Rena·te,** *ppl. a. rare.* 1570. [ad. L. *renatus*, *renasci*.] Reborn, reincarnate -1660.

†**Renay·, reny·,** *v.* ME. [a. OF. *reneier*, *renier*:—pop. L. *renegare*.] **1.** *trans.* To renounce, abjure (one's faith, God, lord, etc.). **2.** To deny, disown -1512. **3.** To refuse *to* do something. SKELTON.

Rencontre (renkǫ·ntəɹ, F. rankontr'). 1619. [a. F., f. *rencontrer*.] = next 1, 1 b, 1 c, 3.

Rencounter (renkau·ntəɹ), *sb.* 1523. [ad. F. *rencontre*; see prec.] **1.** An encounter or engagement between two opposing forces; a battle, skirmish, conflict. **b.** A hostile meeting between two adversaries; a duel 1590. **c.** An encounter or contest of any kind; in early use, esp. a contest in wit or argument 1632. †**2.** An unpleasant experience -1682. **3.** A chance meeting of two persons, or of a person with a thing 1632. **b.** A meeting of two things or bodies; an impact, collision. Now *rare* or *Obs.* 1662.

1. Three little rencounters have happened with the enemy 1781. **3. b.** My nose and this very Post should have a R. SWIFT.

Rencounter (renkau·ntəɹ), *v.* Now *rare.* 1463. [ad. F. *rencontrer*.] **1.** *trans.* To meet or encounter (an army, person, etc.) in hostile fashion; to engage (a person) in fight. **2.** To meet or fall in with (a person) 1549. †**b.** *intr.* Const. *with.* -1676. †**3.** *trans.* To come into contact or collision with -1695. **b.** *intr.* To come together, collide 1712.

Rend (rend), *v. Pa. t.* and *pple.* **rent.** [OE. *rendan* = OFris. *renda*, *randa*, not found in other Teut. langs.] **1.** *trans.* To tear, to pull violently or by main force, *off, out of,* or *from* a thing or place; to tear *off* or *away.* **2.** To tear, wrench, drag *up* or *down* ME. **3.** To tear apart (*asunder*) or in pieces OE. **b.** To wear *out* (clothes) by tearing. SHAKS. **c.** *techn.* To make (laths) by cleaving wood along the grain into thin strips; also, to strip (trees) of bark 1688. **4.** To tear apart or in pieces, in later use, esp. to split into parties or factions. late ME. **5.** *absol.* To tear; to act by tearing ME. **6.** *intr.* To burst, break, or tear ME.

1. The Rocks are from their old Foundations rent DRYDEN. Phr. *To rap* (or *rive*) *and r.*: see RAP *v.*[2] 1 and RIVE *v.* **2.** God rent them up by the roots in the days of Pekah FULLER. **3.** A banner that was many a time rent but was never out of the field MORLEY. Lo, they will weep, and r. their hair 1839. **4.** Anon the dreadfull Thunder Doth r. the region SHAKS. The Commons live, by no Divisions rent DRYDEN. Her heart was rent by contending emotions 1891. **5.** Whose Rage doth r. Like interrupted Waters SHAKS. **6.** He laid hold vpon the skirt of his mantle, and it rent 1 *Sam.* xv. 27. Hence †**Rend** *sb.* a rent, split, division -1674. **Re·nder** *sb.*[1] one who rends.

Render (re·ndəɹ), *sb.*[2] ME. [f. next.] †**1.** A lesson, repetition. ME. only. †**2.** The act of rendering up, or making over to another; surrender (of a person or place) -1670. **3.** *Law.* **a.** (Usu. *grant and r.*) A return made by the cognizee to the cognizor in a fine; a conveyance of this nature 1594. **b.** A return in money or kind, or in some service, made by a tenant to the superior 1647. †**4.** The act of rendering an account, statement, etc.; an account of expenses -1768. **5.** The first coat of plaster or the like applied to a brick or stone surface 1833.

3. b. Payments in money and renders in kind 1897. **4.** *Cymb.* IV. iv. 11.

Render (re·ndəɹ), *v.* ME. [a. AF. *render* = OF. *rendre*:—pop. L. **rendere*, for L. *reddere* to give back, f. *red-* RE- + *dare* to give. The retention of the inf. ending is unusual. Cf. TENDER *v.*[1]] **I.** †**1.** *trans.* To repeat (something learned); to say over, recite -1565. **2.** To give in return, to make return of. Now somewhat *rare.* 1477. **b.** To return (thanks) 1484. †**3.** To give (†or hand) back, to restore. Also with *again* or *back.* 1513. **b.** *Law.* (usu. *grant and r.*) Of a cognizee: To make over as a return to the cognizor in a fine 1594. **c.** To give back, return (a sound, image, etc.) by reflection or repercussion. Also with *back.* 1600. **4.** To reproduce or represent, esp. by artistic means; to depict 1599. **b.** To play or perform (music) 1676. †**5.** To give or make (a person) out to be of a certain character or in a certain state -1726. **6.** To reproduce or express in another language, to translate 1610.

2. Receiving benefits and rendering none COWPER. **b.** To rendre thankes for the greate benefytes that we haue receyued at his handes *Bk. Com. Prayer.* **3.** I r. agayne to you all your londes LD. BERNERS. **c.** Who..like a gate of steele, Fronting the sunne, receiues and renders backe His figure, and his heate SHAKS. **4.** A fearefull Battaile rendred you in Musique SHAKS. **5.** *A. Y. L.* IV. iii. 123. **6.** The word has been rendered in different places either Temperance or Wisdom JOWETT.

II. 1. To hand over, deliver, commend, or commit, to another; to give, in various senses. late ME. **2.** To give *up*, surrender, resign, relinquish. late ME. †**3.** To give out, emit, discharge -1730. **4.** To give (an account, reason, answer, etc.); to submit to, or lay before, another for consideration or approval; also, in mod. use, to send in (an account) to a customer or purchaser 1481. †**b.** To declare, state. SHAKS. **5.** To pay as a rent, tax, tribute, or other acknowledgement of dependence 1526. **6.** To give, pay, exhibit, or show (obedience, honour, attention, etc.); to do (a service) 1588. **7.** *refl.* To present (oneself), take steps to be *at* (†or *in*) a certain place 1619.

1. Of all the treasure in this field atcheiued..We r. you the Tenth SHAKS. **2.** I r. my cause, as the swordmen would have it 1673. In the city rendered by compact, and not taken by storm 1865. **4.** By this hand, Claudio shall r. me a deere account SHAKS. *Account rendered*: entry describing the sum of an account that has been previously sent in. **b.** *Cymb.* V. v. 135. **5.** R. to Cesar the things that are Cesars *Mark* xii. 17. **6.** There were personal attentions to be rendered C. BRONTE.

III. 1. †To bring (a person) *into* a state or condition; to cause to be *in* a certain state (*rare*) 1490. †**b.** To present or expose *to*, to bring *under*, something -1661. **2.** To make, cause to be or become, of a certain nature, quality, etc. †Const. with *as* or *to be* 1560.

2. O ye Gods! R. me worthy of this Noble Wife SHAKS.

IV. *techn.* **a.** To melt (fat, etc.); to obtain or extract by melting; to clarify. late ME. **b.** *Plastering.* To cover (stone or brickwork) with a first coating of plaster 1750. **c.** *Naut.* (See next 3 b.) 1841. Hence **Re·nderable** *a.* (*rare*) capable of being rendered. **Re·nderer.**

Rendering (re·ndəriŋ), *vbl. sb.* 1440. [-ING [1].] **1.** The action of restoring, surrendering, yielding, etc.; also, that which is yielded or given. **2. a.** Translation, interpretation 1641. **b.** Reproduction, representation, performance 1862. **3.** *techn.* **a.** *Plastering.* The action of plastering with a first coat; the work so done; the plaster thus applied 1659. **b.** Yielding, slipping, or running out of tackle or lines 1769. **c.** Extracting or melting of fat, etc. 1865.

2. b. The painter has shown himself extremely skilful in his r. of curious effects of light 1893.

Rendezvous (re·ndĕvū, F. randevu), *sb. Pl.* **rendezvous.** 1591. [F., subst. use of *rendez vous* 'present or betake yourselves'.] **1.** *Mil.* A place appointed for the assembling of troops or armed forces. **b.** A place or port fixed upon, or suitable, for the assembling of a fleet or number of ships; also, instructions concerning a rendezvous 1600. **2.** *gen.* An appointed place of meeting or gathering; a place of common resort 1594. †**3.** A retreat, refuge -1645. †**b.** A last resort. SHAKS. **4.** A meeting or assembly held by appointment or arrangement 1600. †**b.** The assembling, or an assemblage, of things -1680. **5.** Without article, in *place* (*point, port,* etc.) *of r.* 1600.

1. He proclaimed the Rendez-vous at Sora, for his Soldiers there to meete HOLLAND. **2.** A tauerne is the Randeuous, the Exchange, the staple for good fellowes LYLY. Phr. †*To make* or *keep* (one's) *r.*, to meet, or be in the habit of meeting, in or at a place.

Rendezvous (re·ndévū, -vūz, F. randevu), *v.* 1645. [f. prec.] **1.** *intr.* To assemble at a place previously appointed; also, gen., to assemble, come together, meet. †**2.** Of a commander: To assemble his troops or fleet –1745. **3.** *trans.* To bring together (troops or ships) at a fixed place. Now *U.S.* 1654. †**b.** To bring together, collect, assemble (persons or things) –1719.

Rendition (rendi·ʃən). 1601. [a. obs. F., f. *rendre* to RENDER.] **1.** The surrender of a place, garrison, possession, etc. **b.** The surrender of a person 1649. **2.** Translation, rendering. Now *U.S.* 1659. **3.** orig. *U.S.* The action of rendering, giving out or forth, acting, performing, etc. 1858. **4.** *U.S.* The amount produced or rendered 1889.

1. The r. of Oxford to the Parliament forces 1691. b. His r. afterward to the Scotch Army MILT. 2. Calverley's complete r. of Theocritus 1875.

Rendrock (re·ndrǫk). 1880. [f. REND *v.* + ROCK *sb.*] A kind of explosive.

Renegade (re·nǐgeid), *sb.* (and *a.*) 1583. [Anglicized f. RENEGADO; see -ADE 3.] **1.** An apostate from any form of religious faith, *esp.* a Christian who becomes a Mohammedan. **2.** One who deserts a party, person, or principle, in favour of another; a turn-coat 1665. **3.** *attrib.*, passing into adj. 1705.

1. Like all renegades, he was a bitter and furious persecutor 1873. Hence **Re·negade** *v. intr.* to turn r.; to go over *from* a religion, party, etc.

Renegado (renǐgē¹·do), *sb.* (and *a.*) 1599. [a. Sp., ad. med.L. *renegatus* (see RENEGUE).] = prec. Hence **Renega·do** *v. intr.* to turn r.

Renegate (re·nǐgět), *sb.* (and *a.*) *Obs.* exc. *dial.* late ME. [ad. med.L. *renegatus*, *renegare*.] **1.** A renegade, deserter. **2.** *attrib.* or as adj. 1485.

Renegation (renǐgē¹·ʃən). 1615. [f. L. *renegare*.] The action of renouncing or renegading.

Renegue (rǐnī·g), *v.* 1548. Also *U.S.* **renig.** [ad. med.L. *renegare*, f. *re-* RE- + *negare* to deny.] **1.** *trans.* To deny, renounce, abandon, desert (a person, faith, etc.). Now *arch.* †**2.** *intr.* or *absol.* To make denial –1689. **3.** To refuse, decline (*rare*) 1582. **4.** *Card-playing.* To refuse or fail to follow suit; to revoke. Now *local* and *U.S.* 1680.

1. Those of this reformed Religion, who will not reneague it 1657. 2. *Lear* II. ii. 84.

Renew (rǐniū·), *v.* late ME. [f. RE- + NEW *a.*, after L. *renovare* to RENOVATE.] **1.** To make new, or as new, again; to restore to the same condition as when new, young, or fresh. **b.** To make spiritually new; to regenerate. late ME. **c.** To assume anew, to recover (one's original strength, youth, etc.) 1481. **2.** To restore, re-establish, set up again, bring back into use or existence. late ME. **3.** To take up again or afresh; to resume; to begin again, recommence. late ME. **b.** To say in resumption 1687. **4.** To go, or do, over again, repeat. late ME. **5.** To replace by some new or fresh thing of the same kind; to restore by means of substitution or a fresh supply; to fill (a vessel) again 1439. **6.** To revive, reawaken, resuscitate 1484. **7.** To grant anew, *esp.* to grant or give (a lease, bill, etc.) for a fresh period; also, to take afresh, to obtain an extension of 1617. **8.** *intr.* To grow afresh, become new again. late ME. †**9.** To begin a fresh attack, to return or come back, *upon* one; to renew the fight –1656. **10.** To begin again, recommence 1523.

1. In such a night Medea gathered the inchanted hearbs That did r. old Eson SHAKS. b. Graunt that we..maye dailye be renued by thy holy spirite *Bk. Com. Prayer.* c. Heav'n his wonted face renewed MILT. 2. We..In pleasing dreams the blissful age r. JOHNSON. 3. Socrates renews the attack from another side JOWETT. 4. The Lady renewed her Excuses STEELE. 5. The earth doth like a snake r. Her winter weeds outworn SHELLEY. 6. My fayre Frend, renewe not my sorowe CAXTON. 7. The lease expired..and she did not care to r. it RUSKIN. *absol.* 'Won't the party r.? THACKERAY. 8. R. I could not like the Moone SHAKS. 9. *Tr. & Cr.* V. v. 6. 10. Whereupon the combat renewed with more cruelty than before 1640. Hence **Renewabi·lity. Rene·wable** *a.* **Renew·al**, the act of renewing, or the state of being renewed; an instance of this. **Renew·ed·ly** *adv.*, **-ness. Renew·er. Renew·ment** (now *rare* or *Obs.*) renewal.

†**Renfo·rce**, *v.* 1525. [ad. F. *renforcer*; see RE- and ENFORCE *v.*] **1.** *trans.* To reinforce, strengthen –1652. **2.** To compel (a person) *to* do a thing again. SPENSER.

Reni-, comb. form of L. *ren* kidney (see REINS), used in some scientific terms, as *renicapsular.*

Reniform (rī·nifǫ̈m), *a.* 1753. [ad. mod. L. *reniformis*; see REINS and -FORM.] Having the form of a kidney; kidney-shaped.

†**Renitence.** 1652. [a. F. *rénitence*; see RENITENT and -ENCE.] = next –1743.

Renitency (rǐnai·tĕnsi, re·nitĕnsi). Now *rare.* 1613. [See prec. and -ENCY.] †**1.** Physical resistance, *esp.* the resistance of a body to pressure –1704. **2.** Resistance to constraint; opposition, reluctance 1626.

2. Nature has form'd the mind of man with the same..backwardness and r. against conviction STERNE.

Renitent (rǐnai·tĕnt, re·nitĕnt), *a.* Now *rare.* 1701. [a. F. *rénitent*, or ad.L. *renitentem*, *reniti*, f. *re-* RE- + *niti* to struggle.] **1.** That offers physical resistance; hard. **2.** Recalcitrant 1847.

Rennet (re·nĕt), *sb.*[1] late ME. [f. *renne*, obs. f. RUN *v.*] **1.** A mass of curdled milk found in the stomach of an unweaned calf or other animal, used for curdling milk in making cheese, etc.; also, a preparation of the inner membrane of the stomach, used for this or other purposes. **2.** Anything used to curdle milk, *esp.* the plant *Galium verum*, Lady's Bedstraw 1577.

attrib.: **r.-bag**, the stomach of a calf used as r.; **r. stomach**, the fourth stomach of a ruminant; **r. wort**, the plant *Galium aparine.*

Rennet (re·nĕt), *sb.*[2] 1568. [ad. F. *reinette* (see REINETTE), app. f. *reine* queen, but sometimes written *rainette*, as if f. *raine* frog, in allusion to the spots on some varieties.] One of a large class of dessert apples of French origin; †formerly applied to a pippin grafted on a pippin-stock.

†**Re·nnet**, *v. rare.* 1624. [f. RENNET *sb.*[1]] *trans.* To curdle (milk) with rennet; to supply with rennet –1648.

Men,..like Cheese o're-rennetted HERRICK.

Renounce (rǐnau·ns), *sb.* 1747. [ad. F. *renonce*, f. *renoncer* to RENOUNCE.] *Card-playing.* An act or instance of renouncing (cf. next 5). **b.** A chance of renouncing, by having no cards of a particular suit 1830.

Renounce (rǐnau·ns), *v.* late ME. [ad. F. *renoncer* :—L. *renuntiare* to announce, proclaim, disclaim, protest against, f. *re-* RE- + *nuntiare* to make known.] **1.** *trans.* To give up, resign, or surrender (†*to* another); *esp.* to give up in a complete and formal manner. **b.** To abandon, cast off, repudiate; to decline to recognize, hold, observe, etc. 1533. **2.** To abandon, give up (a practice, habit, intention, etc.) 1484. **b.** To abandon or give up (a belief or opinion) by open profession or recantation 1535. **3.** To cast off, disclaim or disown obedience, allegiance, or relationship to (a person) 1502. **4.** *intr.* or *absol.* †**a.** To make renunciation. Const. *to* (the thing renounced). –1728. **b.** *Law.* To make formal resignation of some right or trust, esp. of one's position as heir or executor 1604. **5.** *Card-playing.* To fail to follow suit; orig. implying the possession of, but now usu. the want of, a proper card. In the former case REVOKE is the current term. 1579.

1. I should require them..to r. in writing all claims upon myself 1856. Phr. *To r. the world*, to withdraw from worldly interests in order to lead a spiritual life. b. Napoleon renounced, once for all, sentiments and affections EMERSON. 2. He was compelled to r. the attempt GROTE. b. All others must..submit and r. their errors BLACKSTONE. 3. Your kindred r. you DICKENS. 4. a. He of my sons who fails to make it good, By one rebellious act renounces to my blood DRYDEN. b. Where there is a Will and the Executor renounces 1695. Hence **Renou·nceable** *a.* that may be renounced. **Renou·ncement**, the act of renouncing; a renunciation. **Renou·ncer.**

Renovate (re·nǒveit), *v.* 1535. [f. L. *renovat-*, *renovare*, f. *re-* RE- + *novare* to make new, f. *novus.*] †**1.** *trans.* To renew, resume (an action or purpose) –1796. **2.** To renew materially; to repair; to restore by replacing lost or damaged parts; to create anew 1552. **b.** To restore to vigour; to refresh 1671. **c.** To regenerate 1800.

2. Ethelwolde..did clerely r. and augmentid this Abbay LELAND. So **Re·novate** *pa. pple.* and *ppl. a.* renewed 1520. **Re·novator.**

Renovation (renǒvē¹·ʃən). late ME. [a. F. *rénovation*, or ad. L. *renovationem*; see prec.] **1.** The action of renovating, or the condition of having been renovated; renewal; restoration; an instance of this, a change effected by renewal. †**b.** Renewal of the body at the resurrection –1667. **2.** *Theol.* Renewal wrought by the Holy Ghost; the creation of a new spirit within one 1543. †**3.** The renewal or resumption of an action, agreement, condition, etc. –1798.

1. The regular return of genial months, And r. of a faded world COWPER.

†**Reno·vel**, *v.* ME. [ad. OF. *renoveler*, f. L. *re-* RE- + *novellus* NOVEL *a.*] To renew –1537.

Renown (rǐnau·n), *sb.* ME. [a. AF. *renoun*, *renun* = OF. *renon*, f. *renomer* to make famous, f. L. *re-* RE- + *nominare* to name.] **1.** *Of r.*, of fame or distinction; widely known or celebrated; esp. *of great* (*high*, etc.) *r.* **2.** The fact or condition of being widely celebrated or held in high repute; celebrity, fame, honourable distinction ME. **b.** The fame or reputation attaching to a particular person, place, etc. late ME. †**3.** Report, rumour (sometimes implying sense 2.) –1610. †**b.** Reputation of a specified kind (*rare*) –1608. †**c.** Good name, reputation. SHAKS.

1. Mightie men, which in olde time were men of renoume BIBLE (Genev.) *Gen.* vi. 4. 2. The inheritors of unfulfilled r. Rose from their thrones SHELLEY. b. The r. of the Spanish infantry had been growing GREEN. 3. b. A young Gentlewoman..of a most chaste r. SHAKS. c. *Cymb.* V. v. 202. Hence **Renow·nful, Renow·nless** *adjs.* (*rare*).

Renown (rǐnau·n), *v.* Now *rare.* 1530. [ad. OF. *renoumer*, var. *renomer*; the form *renown* has been assim. to the sb.] *trans.* To make famous, spread the fame of; to celebrate.

The Bard whom pilfer'd Pastorals r. POPE. Hence **Renow·ner**, one who celebrates or makes famous.

Renowned (rǐnau·nd), *ppl. a.* late ME. [f. as prec. after earlier *renomed* (F. *renommé*).] Full of or covered with renown.

Peace hath her victories No less renownd then warr MILT. Hence **Renow·ned·ly** *adv.*, **-ness.**

Rensselaerite (rensĕlē°·rait, re·nsĕlĕrait). 1846. [f. name of Gov. Stephen van *Rensselaer*; see -ITE 2 b.] *Min.* A variety of talc found in parts of New York State and Canada, capable of being worked on a lathe and manufactured into various articles.

Rent (rent), *sb.*[1] ME. [a. OF. *rente* :— pop. L. **rendita* (= L. *reddita*), f. **rendere*; see RENDER *v.*] †**1.** (In *pl.*) A source or item of revenue or income (e.g. a piece of property) –1611. †**b.** Revenue, income –1783. †**2.** A tribute, tax, or similar charge, levied by or paid to a person –1703. **3.** The return or payment made (in money or in kind) by a tenant to the owner or landlord, at certain specified or customary times, for the use of lands or houses ME. Called spec. *commercial r.* See also GROUND-RENT. **b.** The sum paid for the use of machinery, etc., for a certain time. **4.** A piece of property for which an annual rent is received or charged; esp. *pl.* a number of tenements or houses let out to others. Now *U.S. colloq.* (except in surviving proper names of such properties). 1466.

1. What are thy Rents? what are thy Commings in? SHAKS. b. To allow each of them such a r., as.. would make them easy SWIFT. 3. Some of them pay more r. yerely than theyr Fermes be worth 1560. *Economic* (*Ricardian*, *true*) *r.*: the annual value of the powers of production which are inherent in the soil; the difference between the return from a given piece of land and from land of equal area which is on the margin of cultivation; also, more widely, the differential advantage for production due to the preeminent qualities of a person, factory, etc.

Rent (rent), *sb.*[2] 1535. [f. RENT *v.*[2]] **1.** The result of rending; a separation of parts produced by tearing or the like; *esp.* a large tear in a garment or piece of woven stuff. **2.** A breach, split, schism, or dissension in a society or party or between persons (*rare*) 1608. **3.** A cleft, fissure, breach 1705. **b.** *Coal-mining.* A plane of cleavage running across a seam 1883. **4.** The act of rending or fact of being rent 1836.

1. See what a r. the enuious Casca made SHAKS. 2. It occasions..Rents, Confusions and Divisions in Families 1679.

Rent (rent), *v.*[1] late ME. [ad. OF. *renter*, f. *rente*; or f. RENT *sb.*[1]] †1. *trans.* To provide with revenues; to endow –1485. 2. To pay rent for (land, houses, etc.); to take, hold, occupy or use, by payment of rent 1530. 3. To let (*out*) for rent or payment; to hire out 1546. 4. *intr.* To let *at* a certain rent 1538. 5. *trans.* To charge (a person) with rent; to impose a certain rent on 1881.

2. If I can r. rooms in town to lodge in 1763. b. *intr.* (U.S.) To secure the use of a house in return for rent 1911. 4. Arable land rents at £3 and £4, or even £6 an acre 1815. 5. The power..to r. a man upon his own improvements 1894. Hence **Re·ntable** *a.* liable to pay rent; that may be rented, or let out for hire.

Rent (rent), *v.*[2] *Obs.* exc. *dial.* late ME. [var. of REND *v.*, after the pa. t. and pa. pple. *rent.*] 1. *trans.* To rend, tear, pull asunder or in pieces. 2. *intr.* To tear; to give way or separate by tearing or splitting 1526.

1. Rente youre clothes, and gyrd sack cloth aboute you COVERDALE 2 *Sam.* iii. 31. Rente your hertes, & not youre clothes COVERDALE *Joel* ii. 12.

Rent (rent), *ppl. a.* late ME. [pa. pple. of REND *v.*] Torn, in various senses.

Rentage (re·ntėdʒ). 1633. [f. RENT *sb.*[1] + -AGE.] Rent, rental, or renting; also, that which is held for rent.

Rental (re·ntăl). late ME. [a. AF.; see RENT *sb.*[1] and -AL 2.] 1. A rent-roll. Now *rare.* b. An income arising from rents received. late ME. 2. The amount paid or received as rent 1637. b. *U.S.* Returns from the lending of books; *Comb.* r. library 1928.

1. b. Emily's..r. offered a mark to his ambition 1801.

Re·nt-charge. Also **rent charge.** 1443. [f. RENT *sb.*[1] + CHARGE *sb.*] *Law.* A rent forming a charge upon lands, etc., granted or reserved by deed to one who is not the owner, with a clause of distress in case of arrears. Hence **Re·nt-cha:rger**, one in receipt of, or who benefits by, a rent-charge.

Renter (re·ntəɹ), *sb.* late ME. [f. RENT *v.*[1] + -ER [1].] 1. One who owns or lets lands, tenements, etc. (now *U.S.*). †2. A collecter of rents, taxes, or tribute –1762. 3. A farmer of tolls or taxes (*rare*) 1598. 4. A holder of lands, houses, or other property, by payment of rent 1655. †b. *spec.* A tenant-farmer –1792.

Rent-free, *a.* 1631. [RENT *sb.*[1]] Exempt from payment of rent.

‖**Rentier** (rañtye). 1881. [Fr., f. *rente* RENT *sb.*[1]] One whose income is derived from investments.

Re·nt-roll. 1534. [RENT *sb.*[1]] A roll or register of rents; a list of lands and tenements belonging to a person, together with the rents paid on them; hence, the sum of a person's income as shown by such a list.

Rent-seck. 1472. [a. AF. *rente secque* lit. dry rent.] *Law.* A rent reserved by deed in favour of some person, without a clause of distress in case of arrears (abolished in 1731).

Re·nt-se:rvice. 1477. [RENT *sb.*[1]] Personal service by which lands or tenements are held in addition to, or in lieu of, money payment; tenure of this kind.

Renule (re·niul), *sb.* 1847. [f. L. *ren* kidney + -ULE.] *Anat.* One of the separate lobules of which the kidneys in some animals are composed.

Renunciate (rǐnʊ·nsi,eit), *v.* 1656. [f. L. *renunciat-*, *renunciare.*] †1. *trans.* To proclaim or declare openly. BLOUNT. 2. To renounce, give up (*rare*) 1814.

Renunciation (rǐnʊnsi,ēⁱ·ʃən). late ME. [ad. L. *renunciationem*, f. *renunciare* to RENOUNCE.] 1. The action of renouncing, giving up, or surrendering (a possession, right, title, etc.); an instance of this; a document expressing this. b. The action of giving up something naturally attractive 1526. 2. The action of rejecting, disowning, or disclaiming; repudiation, formal rejection. late ME.

1. The queen's r. of her right of succession HALLAM. b. A r. of my old and more favourite pursuits TYNDALL.

Renunciative (rǐnʊ·nsi,ėtiv), *a.* late ME. [f. prec. + -IVE.] †1. Serving to announce or enunciate –1622. 2. Characterized by renunciation 1850. So **Renu·nciatory** *a.*

†**Renve·rse,** *v.* 1590. [ad. F. *renverser*, f. *re-* RE- + *enverser* to overturn.] 1. *trans.* To reverse; to turn upside down, turn the wrong way, turn back –1681. 2. To overturn or overthrow; to bring to confusion –1728.

1. Whose shield he beares renverst, the more to heap disdayn SPENSER. Hence †**Renve·rsement**, the act of reversing; the result of this.

Renversé (rañverse), *a.* 1725. [F., pa. pple. of *renverser*; see prec.] *Her.* Inverted; reversed.

†**Renvoy,** *sb.* 1600. [a. F. *renvoi*, f. *renvoyer*; see next.] The act of sending back; discharge, dismissal –1654.

†**Renvoy,** *v. rare.* 1477. [ad. F. *renvoyer*, f. *re-* RE- + *envoyer*; see ENVOY *sb.*[1]] *trans.* To send back –1622.

I doo Renvoye the..palmer thither agayn CROMWELL.

Reo·pen (rī-), *v.* 1733. [RE- 5 a.] 1. *trans.* To open again. b. To open up again, to renew 1848. 2. *intr.* To open again 1830.

Reordai·n (rī-), *v.* 1611. [RE- 5 a.] *trans.* To ordain again. So **Reordina·tion** 1597.

Reorganiza·tion (rī-). 1813. [RE- 5 a.] The action or process of reorganizing; a fresh organization.

A re-organization of the cavalry WELLINGTON.

Reo·rganize (rī-), *v.* 1681. [RE- 5 a.] *trans.* To organize anew.

Rep[1]. 1705. Now *U.S.* Abbrev. of REPUTATION.

Rep[2] (rep). Now *rare.* 1747. [Origin obsc.; perh. abbrev. of REPROBATE *sb.*] 1. A man (†or woman) of loose character. 2. An inferior article 1786.

Rep[3] (rep). Also **repp.** 1860. [ad. F. *reps*, of unkn. origin.] A textile fabric (of wool, silk, or cotton) having a corded surface.

Repair (rǐpēᵊ·ɹ), *sb.*[1] ME. [a. OF. *repeire, repaire* return, f. *repeirer, repairer* REPAIR *v.*[1]] 1. (Chiefly in phr. *to make* or *have r.*) Resort, frequent or habitual going, *to* a place. Now *arch.* or *Obs.* 2. The place to which one repairs; *esp.* a haunt, usual abode or dwelling-place. late ME. †b. So *place, house,* etc. *of r.* –1611. 3. Concourse or confluence of people in or at a place; common or extensive resort of persons *to* a place. Now *rare* or *Obs.* ME. †b. Following, retinue, company (*rare*) –1548. †4. The act of (†returning) going or making one's way *to* a place –1698.

1. Peter Heylin..was furnished with Books..by his r. to Bodlies Library WOOD. 2. b. Jehova is my fort, My place of safe repaire 1586. 4. At my..repayre thither it pleased his highnes to call for me 1531. Phr. *To make* (one's) *r. to* (a place or person). Now *arch.*

Repair (rǐpēᵊ·ɹ), *sb.*[2] 1595. [f. REPAIR *v.*[2]] 1. The act of restoring to a sound or unimpaired condition; the process by which this is accomplished; the result attained. b. *spec.* Restoration of some material thing or structure by the renewal of decayed or worn out parts, by refixing what has become loose or detached; the result of this. Also *pl.* 1661. 2. Relative state or condition of something admitting or susceptible of restoration in the event of damage or decay; chiefly in phr. *in good* (or *bad*) *r.* 1600.

1. I,..Dazl'd and spent, sunk down, and sought r. Of sleep MILT. 2. A Country-House in no very good R. SWIFT. Phr. *In r.*, in good or proper condition. *Out of r.*, in bad condition, requiring repairs.

Repair (rǐpēᵊ·ɹ), *v.*[1] ME. [a. OF. *repeirer, repairer*:—late L. *repatriare* to return to one's country, f. *re-* RE- + *patria.*] 1. *intr.* To go, betake oneself, make one's way. b. To resort to a place or person; to go commonly, frequently, or in numbers. late ME. †2. To return (*again*), to come or go back (*to* or *from* a place, person) etc. Also without const. –1633. †3. To be present, temporarily or habitually; to have one's resort; to dwell, reside –1560. †4. *trans.* To draw *back*, to recover. SPENSER.

1. To those Places straight r. Where your respective Dwellings are 1663. b. The people of Calais r. hither for their evening dance 1809. 2. *Mids. N.* IV. i. 72. If I might beseech you Gentlemen, to repayre some other houre SHAKS.

Repair (rǐpēᵊ·ɹ), *v.*[2] late ME. [a. OF. *reparer*, or ad. L. *reparare*, f. *re-* RE- + *parare* to put in order.] 1. *trans.* To restore (a composite thing, structure, etc.) to good condition by renewal or replacement of decayed or damaged parts, or by refixing what has given way; to mend. b. To heal or cure (a wound). Also *intr.* of a wound: To mend, heal up. 1590. 2. *trans.* To renew, renovate (some thing or part); to restore to a fresh or sound condition by making up in some way for previous loss, waste, decay, or exhaustion. late ME. †b. To revive, recreate (a person). SHAKS. †3. To restore (a person) to a previous state; to reinstate, re-establish, rehabilitate –1738. 4. To remedy, make up (loss, damage, etc.); to set right again 1533. b. To make good, make amends for (harm done, etc.) 1562.

1. He repared his navie and returned to Constantinople 1560. b. The wound was not repairing 1881. 2. So sinks the day-star in the Ocean bed, And yet anon repairs his drooping head MILT. The fair..Repairs her smiles, awakens ev'ry grace POPE. b. *Two Gent.* V. iv. 11. 4. Unskilful either in improving their victories, or repairing their defeats BURKE. The loss of such a man could not be easily repaired MACAULAY. b. The emperor seemed impatient to r. his injustice GIBBON. Hence **Repai·rable** *a.* capable of being repaired; that is to be repaired. **Repai·rer,** one who or that which restores or mends.

Repand (rǐpæ·nd), *a.* 1760. [ad. L. *repandus* bent backwards, turned up, f. *re-* RE- + *pandus* bent.] *Bot.* and *Zool.* Having an undulating margin, wavy.

Reparable (re·părăb'l), *a.* 1570. [a. F., ad. L. *reparabilis*; see REPAIR *v.*[2] and -ABLE.] 1. Capable of being repaired, mended, or set right again. 2. Liable to be repaired *by* some one 1864.

1. Twenty r...spare wheels 1809. Only slight and r. injuries 1884. 2. New streets..r. by the local authorities 1864. Hence **Re:parabi·lity. Re·parably** *adv.*

Reparation (repărēⁱ·ʃən). late ME. [a. OF. *reparacion*, ad. L. *reparationem.*] 1. The action of restoring to a proper state; restoration or renewal (*of* a thing or part). †b. Spiritual restoration, salvation; an instance of this –1725. 2. The action of repairing or mending, or the fact of being repaired. (Now more usu. expressed by REPAIR *sb.*[2] 1 b.) ME. 3. *pl.* Repairs. Now *rare.* 1439. 4. The action of making amends for a wrong done; amends; compensation. Now usu. *pl.* late ME.

2. The original charter records the r. of the Church FREEMAN. 4. Willing to make reasonable r. 1877.

Reparative (rǐpæ·rătiv), *a.* 1656. [See prec. and -ATIVE.] 1. Capable of effecting, or tending to effect, repair; relating to repair. 2. Pertaining to the making of amends, or the remedying of some wrong 1695.

†**Repa·rel,** *v.* ME. [ad. OF. *repareiller*, f. *re-* RE- + *apareiller* to APPAREL.] 1. *trans.* To repair (a thing or structure) –1560. 2. To restore *to* some state or condition, set right again; to recover (*rare*) –late ME. 3. To fit up, array, apparel (*rare*) –1579. So †**Repa·rel** *sb.* furniture, apparel.

†**Repa·rt,** *v.* 1574. [ad. F. *répartir*, f. *re-* RE- + *partir* to PART.] *trans.* To divide or distribute, esp. *among* a number of persons –1755.

Repartee (repaɹtī·), *sb.* 1645. [ad. F. *repartie*, f. *repartir* to start or set out again, f. *re-* RE- + *partir.*] 1. A ready, witty, or smart reply; a quick and clever retort. 2. Sharpness or wit in sudden reply; such replies collectively; the practice or faculty of uttering them 1668.

1. The Grave abound in Pleasantries, the Dull in Repartees and Points of Wit ADDISON. 2. Skill'd in no other arts..But dressing, patching and r. GOLDSM.

Repartee (repaɹtī·), *v.* 1668. [f. prec., or ad. F. *repartir.*] 1. *intr.* To make witty or smart replies. Now *rare.* †2. *trans.* To say by way of repartee or retort –1686. †3. To answer (a person or something said) with a repartee or retort (*rare*) –1743.

Repartition (repaɹti·ʃən, rī-). 1555. [See RE- and PARTITION *v.*] 1. Partition, distribution, allotment (in former use *esp.* of troops or military quarters). With *a* and *pl.* An instance of this. 2. A fresh distribution or allotment 1835.

1. No fair r. of burthens upon all the orders could possibly restore them BURKE.

Repass (rǐpa·s), *v.* 1456. [ad. F. *repasser*; see RE- and PASS *v.*] 1. *intr.* To pass again in the contrary direction; to return. Chiefly in *pass and r.* **2.** *trans.* To cross (the sea, a river, etc.) again in the contrary direction 1500. **b.** To pass again over, through, or by (a way, gate, place, etc.); to go past again 1618. **3.** To cause to pass again; to put *through* again 1565. **b.** To pass (a bill, resolution) again 1796.

1. A lawn terminated by water, with objects passing and repassing upon it 1785. *Hey pass, r.*, a conjurer's formula. 2. In repassing the mountains, great numbers of soldiers perished GIBBON. b. I..passed and repassed the spot many times 1898. So **Repassage** (rīpæ·sĕdʒ), [a. F. *repassage*] the act of repassing; passage back; liberty or right to repass. late ME.

Repassant (rĭpæ·sănt), *a.* 1828. [See RE- and PASSANT.] *Her.* Passant in opposite directions; counterpassant.

Repast (rĭpɑ·st), *sb.* ME. [a. OF., f. *repaistre*:—late L. *repascere*, f. *re-* RE- + *pascere* to feed.] **1.** A quantity of food and drink forming, or intended for, a meal or feast. †**2.** Food, supply of food or victuals –1732. **3.** The action or fact of taking food; the refreshment of food. Now *arch.* 1588. **b.** An occasion of taking or partaking of food; a meal or feast in this sense 1639. †**4.** Refreshment; repose –1615.

1. What neat r. shall feast us, light and choice,.. with Wine? MILT. 2. A Buck was then a week's r. POPE. 3. If (before r.) it shall please you to gratifie the table with a Grace SHAKS.

Repast (rĭpɑ·st), *v.* Now *rare.* 1470. [ad. L. *repast-*, *repascere* or f. prec.] †**1.** *refl.* To refresh (oneself) with food –1617. †**2.** *trans.* To feed, supply with food –1669. **3.** *intr.* To feed, feast 1520.

2. *Haml.* IV. v. 147. Hence †**Repa·ster**, one who takes a repast.

†**Repa·sture.** *rare.* 1588. [See REPAST *sb.* and PASTURE *sb.*] Food; a repast –1614.

Foode for his rage, r. for his den SHAKS.

Repatriate (rĭpæ·trieit, -pē·t-), *v.* 1611. [f. late L. *repatriat-*, *repatriare* to return to one's country, f. *re-* RE- + *patria*.] **1.** *trans.* To restore (a person) to his own country. **2.** *intr.* To return to one's own country (*rare*) 1656. Hence **Repatria·tion**, return or restoration to one's own country.

Repay (rĭpē·), *v.* 1530. [ad. OF. *repaier*, *rapaier*, f. *re-* RE- + *payer*.] **1.** *trans.* To refund, pay back (a sum of money, etc.). Also with double obj. **b.** To return (a blow, visit, salutation, etc.) 1593. **c.** To give (a thing) in return or recompense (*for* something) 1560. **2.** To make repayment or return to (a person); to pay (a person) back in some way 1542. **3.** To requite (an action, etc.) 1596. **4.** *intr.* To make repayment or return 1557.

1. What so ever you lay out it shalbe repayed you 1530. b. 3 *Hen. VI*, II. iii. 3. c. Euill pursueth sinners: but to the righteous, good shall be repayd *Prov.* xiii. 21. 2. Let me now you pray,.. Ye will me now with like good turne r. SPENSER. 4. Vengeance is mine: I wil repaye, saith the Lord N.T. (Genev.) *Rom.* xii. 19. Hence **Repay·able** *a.* that may be, or is to be, repaid.

Repayment (rĭpē·mĕnt, rī-). 1435. [f. prec. + -MENT.] **1.** The (*or* an) act of repaying; payment back (of money lent, etc.). **2.** Requital, return (of services, etc.) 1574.

Repeal (rĭpī·l), *sb.* 1483. [a. AF. *repel* = OF. *rapel* a recall, f. *repeler*, *rapeler*; see next.] †**1.** Recall, as from banishment –1658. **2.** The (*or* an) act of repealing (a law, resolution, sentence, etc.); abrogation 1503. **b.** *spec.* The cancelling of the Union between Great Britain and Ireland as an Irish political demand. Now *Hist.* 1831. **3.** Means or possibility of release (*from* punishment). *rare.* 1594.

1. The decree of repeale was authorized by the people, and the banished men returned to Syracvsa 1612. 3. That deep gulf without r. BYRON.

Repeal (rĭpī·l), *v.* ME. [ad. AF. *repel(l)er* = OF. *rapeler*, f. *re-* RE- + *appeler* to APPEAL.] **1.** *trans.* To revoke, rescind, annul (a resolution, law, sentence, etc.). †**b.** To recall, withdraw (a privilege, grant, etc.) –1598. †**2.** To withdraw or retract (a statement); to give up, abandon (a thought, feeling, etc.) –1667. †**3.** **a.** To recall (a person) from exile –1662. **b.** To call or summon back –1727.

1. The Soveraign..having power to make, and repeale Lawes HOBBES. 2. Adam soon repeal'd The doubts that in his heart arose MILT. 3. a. The banish'd Bullingbrooke repeales himselfe, And..is.. arriu'd At Rauenspurg SHAKS. b. His scar'd Senses returning to their proper Seat, and his stray'd Reason repeal'd 1727. Hence **Repea·lable** *a.* that may be repealed or revoked. **Repealabi·lity. Repea·lableness.** †**Repea·lment**, recall from banishment.

Repealer (rĭpī·lər). 1765. [f. prec. + -ER[1].] One who repeals or advocates repeal. **b.** *spec.* An advocate of the repeal of the Union between Great Britain and Ireland. Now *Hist.* 1831.

Repeat (rĭpī·t), *sb.* 1450. [f. the vb.] **1.** The (*or* an) act of repeating, repetition 1556. **b.** A repetition of a musical piece or performance, or of some part of these 1853. **2.** *Mus.* **a.** A passage repeated or performed twice; the repetition of a passage 1450. **b.** A sign directing that a passage is to be performed twice 1667. **3.** A duplicate of something 1842. **b.** A device or pattern on cloth, paper, etc., which is repeated uniformly over the surface 1845. **c.** *Comm.* A second or fresh supply of goods similar to one already received; also, an order for such a supply 1885.

3. c. We can tell how trade is going by the 'repeats' we get 1895. *attrib.* R. orders are coming in 1891.

Repeat (rĭpī·t), *v.* late ME. [ad. F. *répéter*, ad. L. *repetere*, f. *re-* RE- + *petere* to attack, make for, demand, seek, etc.] **I. 1.** *trans.* To say or utter over again, to reiterate. **2.** To say over, recite; also, to say or enunciate in a formal manner or in due order; to relate, recount. Also *absol.* 1559. †**b.** To celebrate, speak of (as). *rare.* –1671. **3.** To say or utter again after another or others 1595.

1. His still refuted quirks he still repeats COWPER. 2. R. me these verses again, slowly and deliberately SCOTT. b. Reserv'd alive to be repeated The subject of their cruelty, or scorn MILT. 3. I do but r. what has been said a thousand times STEELE.

II. †**1.** To seek again, return to, encounter, or undergo again –1697. **2.** To do, make, perform, or execute over again 1560. **b.** To cause to appear, to bring up or present again. Also freq. in *pass.*, denoting recurrence. 1714. **c.** *intr.* To recur 1714. **3.** *spec.* **a.** Of clocks and watches: To strike (the last hour or quarter) again. Also *absol.* 1727. **b.** *Naut.* To reproduce (signals made by the admiral). Also *absol.* 1769. **c.** *absol.* Of food: To rise in the gullet, so as to be tasted again 1879. **4.** *refl.* **a.** To reproduce or present (oneself) again; to reappear in the same form 1850. **b.** To say again what one has already said 1864.

2. There is scarce a painter but has repeated some one of his works 1706. 4. b. He spoke more than an hour without a note—never repeating himself FROUDE.

†**III.** Chiefly *Sc. Law.* To ask back, to demand the restitution of (money or goods); to claim, require –1649. Hence **Repea·tedly** *adv.* more than once, frequently.

Repeater (rĭpī·tər). 1577. [f. prec. + -ER[1].] †**1.** A rehearser, trainer. HOLINSHED. **2.** One who repeats something heard or learned; a relater, reciter 1598. **3.** **a.** A repeating watch or clock 1760. **b.** *Naut.* A repeating ship 1829. **c.** A repeating fire-arm 1868. **d.** *Telegraphy.* A device for automatically retransmitting signals from one circuit to another 1860. **4.** *Arith.* A recurring decimal 1773. **5.** *U.S.* **a.** One who votes, or attempts to vote, more than once at an election 1884. **b.** One who is frequently committed to prison 1884.

Repea·ting, *ppl. a.* 1688. [f. as prec. + -ING[2].] That repeats. **1.** **a.** Of watches and clocks, or parts of these. **b.** Of ships (see REPEAT *v.* II. 3 b) 1802. **c.** *R. circle*, an instrument for measuring angles, in which accuracy is obtained by repeated measurements on a graduated circle. So *r. instrument*, etc. 1815. **d.** Of fire-arms: Capable of firing a number of shots in succession without reloading 1824. **2.** *Arith.* Of decimals: Recurring 1773. **3.** That repeats a sound 1709.

Repel (rĭpe·l), *v.* late ME. [ad. L. *repellere*, f. *re-* RE- + *pellere* to drive.] †**1.** *trans.* To drive or put away; to remove, extinguish, quench –1586. **2.** To drive or force back (an assailant or invader, an attack, etc.); to repulse 1450. **b.** To resist, repress (a feeling, incentive, etc.) 1586. **c.** *Med.* To force back into the blood or system; to repress (a morbid humour, swelling, eruption, etc.). Now *rare* or *Obs.* 1719. †**3.** To reject or debar (a person *from* an office, right, etc.) –1766. †**b.** To stop, hinder, or restrain (a person) *from* an action or manner of acting –1617. **4.** To turn back, ward off (a weapon, blow, or wound) 1526. **b.** To ward off, resist (some outward evil) 1600. **5.** To drive or force back, esp. by physical resistance 1605. **b.** To force away by the operation of natural laws of matter 1710. **c.** To refuse to mix with (one another), or to admit (moisture) 1744. **6.** To refuse to accept or receive; *esp.* to reject (a statement, plea, etc.) as unfounded or invalid 1561. **7.** To drive away or repulse with harsh words or treatment, or by denial; to reject (a suit) 1571. **b.** To affect (a person) with distaste or aversion. Also *absol.* 1817.

2. So turn'd stern Ajax, by whole hosts repell'd POPE. 5. As the Rocks r. the greatest waves 1657. c. Why oil and water, mercury and iron, r...each other BERKELEY. 7. Like suitors that will not be repelled TYNDALL. b. A study which repels you is invaluable 1878.

Repellant (rĭpe·lănt), *a.* and *sb.* 1689. [f. REPEL *v.*] **A.** *adj.* = next A. 2, 3. 1768. **B.** *sb.* = next B. So **Repe·llance, -ancy**, the act of repelling; a repellent feature or trait.

Repellent (rĭpe·lĕnt), *a.* and *sb.* 1643. [ad. L. *repellentem*, *repellere*.] **A.** *adj.* **1.** Of medicines: Having the effect of repelling morbid humours, etc. Now *rare.* **2.** Having the power of repelling other bodies; characterized by repulsion 1744. **3.** Repelling by coldness of demeanour, or by some disagreeable feature; affecting one with distaste or aversion 1797.

1. All those means are said to be r., which check the Growth of the Tumour 1719.

B. *sb.* **1.** *Med.* An application serving to repel humours, etc. Now *rare.* 1661. **2.** A repelling power or influence 1802. Hence **Repe·llence, -ency**, the quality of being r.; repelling power. **Repe·llently** *adv.*

Repe·ller. 1611. [f. REPEL *v.* + -ER[1].] **1.** One who repels. †**2.** = prec. B. 1. –1753.

†**Repe·nt**, *sb.* 1590. [f. the vb.] Repentance; an act of repentance –1611.

Repent (rī·pĕnt), *a.* 1669. [ad. L. *repent-*, *repere* to creep.] **1.** **a.** *Bot.* Creeping; *esp.* growing along the ground, or just under the surface, and sending out roots at intervals. **b.** *Zool.* Creeping, crawling, reptant 1836. †**2.** *fig.* Unable to rise to high ideas. EVELYN.

Repent (rĭpe·nt), *v.* ME. [ad. F. *repentir*, f. *re-* RE- + Rom. **penitire*:—L. *poenitere*.] **1.** *refl.* To be affected with contrition or regret for something done. Now *arch.* **2.** *impers.* To cause (a person) to feel regret, etc. ME. **3.** *intr.* To feel contrition, compunction, sorrow, or regret for something one has done or left undone; to change one's mind with regard to past action or conduct through dissatisfaction with it or its results ME. †**b.** To be sad, to mourn (for an event). SPENSER. **4.** *trans.* To view or think of (any action, etc.) with dissatisfaction and regret; to be sorry for ME. **b.** *esp.* To feel regret, sorrow, or contrition for (some fault, misconduct, sin, or other offence). late ME. †**5.** To live *out* in repentance. SHAKS.

1. I r. me that the Duke is slaine SHAKS. 2. It salle r. vs..sore and we ryde forthire! late ME. 3. If your purpose is evil, pause a moment, and r. MRS. RADCLIFFE. Nor do I now r. of the manner of my defence JOWETT. 4. I do r. The tedious minutes I with her haue spent SHAKS. b. For a few minutes I repented my temerity SOUTHEY. Hence **Repe·nter**, one who repents. **Repe·ntingly** *adv.*

Repentance (rĭpe·ntăns). ME. [a. F.; see prec. and -ANCE.] The act of repenting or the state of being penitent; sorrow, regret, or contrition for past action or conduct; an instance of this.

R. is never too late, but it is a true saying, r. is never too soon 1591. Phr. *Stool of r.*, *r.-stool*, a stool formerly placed in a conspicuous position in Scottish churches for the use of offenders (esp. against chastity) making public repentance; also called CUTTY-STOOL.

Repentant (rĭpe·ntănt), *a.* and *sb.* ME. [a. F., pres. pple. of *repentir*; see REPENT *v.* and -ANT[1].] **A.** *adj.* **1.** Experiencing repentance; sorrowful for past sins, penitent. **2.** Expressing or indicating repentance 1594. †**B.** *sb.* One who repents, a penitent –1814.

A. 1. Thus they in lowliest plight r. stood MILT. 2. R. sighs POPE. Hence **Repe·ntantly** *adv.*

Repercuss (rĭpəɹkʊ·s), *v.* *Obs.* or *rare.* 1501. [f. L. *repercuss-*, *repercutere*, f. *re-* RE- + *percutere* to PERCUSS.] *trans.* †**a.** To beat or drive back (air, fluids, etc.) –1773. †**b.** To reflect (beams or rays of light) -1686. **c.** To return, reverberate (a sound). *rare.* 1585.

c. Whether a Man shall heare better, if he stand aside the Body Repercussing BACON.

Repercussion (rīpəɪkʌ·ʃən). late ME. [a. F. *répercussion*, or ad. L. *repercussionem*, f. *repercutere*; see prec.] **1.** The action of a thing in forcing or driving back an impinging or advancing body; also, the power of doing this. Now *rare.* 1536. †**2.** *Med.* The action of forcing back or driving away by the application of remedies; the operation of repelling (humours, swellings, etc.) from a particular part of the body; also, a medicine or application used for this purpose -1727. **3.** Repulse or recoil of a thing after impact; the fact of being forced or driven back by a resisting body 1553. **b.** *Med.* A method of diagnosing pregnancy in which, upon a sudden push with the finger upon the uterine wall, the fœtus is felt to move away and return again 1860. **4.** The return or reverberation of a sound; echo, echoing noise 1595. **b.** *Mus.* (*a*) Repetition of a chord or note; (*b*) the reappearance of the subject of a fugue after the exposition 1872. **5.** The action of a substance in reflecting light; †colour resulting from such reflection 1601. **b.** Reflection *of* beams, rays, etc. 1601. **6.** A blow or stroke given in return; also *fig.* a return of any kind of action, a responsive act 1603. †**7.** A repeated attack *of* pain. BURNS.

3. The waters are violently carried against the rocks: and in their r., form dangerous whirlpools 1760. 4. Like the echo which is a r. of the original voice J. H. NEWMAN.

Repercussive (rīpəɪkʌ·siv), *a.* and *sb.* late ME. [ad. F. *répercussif, -ive*, f. L. *repercuss-*, *repercutere* + -IVE.] **A.** *adj.* †**1.** Of medicines or medical applications: Serving to repel humours or reduce swellings -1694. **2. a.** Of sounds: Reverberating or reverberated; echoing, resounding; repeated 1598. **b.** Of things or places: Returning a sound 1695. †**3.** Of light: Reflected -1639.

1. Besides this, it is very drying, r., and anodyn 1694. 2. a. Amid Carnarvon's mountains rages loud The r. roar THOMSON. b. Ye noisie Waves Strike with Applause the r. Caves 1712.

†**B.** *sb. Med.* A repellent -1725.

Hence **Repercu·ssive·ly** *adv.*, **-ness.**

‖**Repertoire** (re·pəɹtwāɪ, F. repertwar). Also ré-. 1847. [F. *répertoire*, ad. L. *repertorium* REPERTORY.] A stock of dramatic or musical pieces which a company or player is accustomed or prepared to perform; one's stock of parts, tunes, songs, etc. *R. theatre* = REPERTORY *t.*

‖**Repertorium** (repəɪtōə·riŏm). 1667. [L., f. *repert-*, *reperire* to find.] †**a.** A catalogue. **b.** A storehouse, repository.

Repertory (re·pəɹtəri). 1552. [See prec. and -ORY¹.] †**1.** An index, list, catalogue or calendar -1761. **2.** A storehouse, magazine, or repository, where something may be found 1593. **3.** = REPERTOIRE 1845.

attrib. (sense 3) as *r. company, players*, etc.; **r. theatre,** a theatre to which is attached a permanent company of actors who perform plays belonging to a certain repertory or of the same class as these.

Repetend (re·pĭtend, repĭte·nd). 1714. [ad. L. *repetendum* '(that) which is to be repeated', f. *repetere.*] **1.** *Arith.* The recurring figure or figures in an interminate decimal fraction. **2.** A recurring note, word, or phrase; a refrain 1874.

Repetition (repĭti·ʃən). 1526. [a. OF. *repeticion*, or ad. L. *repetitionem.*] **1.** The action of repeating or saying over again; reiteration; an instance of this. **b.** *Rhet.* The use of repeated words or phrases 1553. **2.** The action of saying over something in order to retain it in the memory; †the rehearsal of a play 1581. **b.** The action of reciting in a formal manner, *esp.* recitation of something learned by heart; a piece set to be learned and recited 1597. **3.** Recital, narration, mention 1594. **4.** The action or fact of doing something again; renewal or recurrence of an action or event; repeated use, application, or appearance 1597. **b.** *Mus.* The action or fact of repeating; the rapid reiteration of a note 1597. **c.** The comparative ability of a musical instrument to repeat the same note in quick succession 1881. **5.** A copy or replica of a thing 1853.

1. When ye pray, vse no vaine repetitions as the heathen BIBLE (Genev.) *Matt.* vi. 7. 2. It is now in r. at the French comedy FOOTE. 3. A name Whose r. will be dogg'd with Curses SHAKS. Hence **Repeti·tional, Repeti·tionary** *adjs.* characterized by, of the nature of, r.

Repetitious (repĭti·ʃəs), *a.* 1675. [f. L. *repetit-*, *repetere* to REPEAT + -IOUS.] Abounding in, or characterized by, repetition, esp. of a tedious kind; tiresomely iterative. Hence **Repeti·tious·ly** *adv.*, **-ness.**

Repetitive (rĭpe·titiv), *a.* 1839. [f. as prec. + -IVE.] Characterized by, of the nature of, repetition; repetitious.

†**Repi·ne,** *sb.* 1592. [f. the vb.] The (*or* an) act of repining; discontent, grudge -1615.

Repine (rĭpəi·n), *v.* 1530. [app. f. RE- + PINE *v.*] **1.** *intr.* To feel or manifest discontent or dissatisfaction; to fret, murmur, or complain. **b.** To long discontentedly *for* something (*rare*) 1742. †**2.** *trans.* To regard with discontent or dissatisfaction; to fret or murmur at -1793.

1. Through the long and weary day he repines at his unhappy lot W. IRVING. b. These Ears, alas, for other Notes r. GRAY. 2. In signe Of servile yoke That nobler harts r. SPENSER. Hence **Repi·ner,** one who repines; a grumbler. **Repi·ningly** *adv.*

Repique (rĭpī·k), *sb.* 1668. [ad. F. *repic*; see RE- and PIQUE *sb.*[2]] In *Piquet*, the winning of thirty points on cards alone before beginning to play (and before the adversary begins to count), entitling the player to begin his score at ninety.

Repique (rĭpī·k), *v.* 1659. [f. prec.] **1.** *trans.* In *Piquet*, to score a repique against (the opposing player). **2.** *intr.* To score a repique 1719.

Replace (rĭplē·s), *v.* 1595. [f. RE- 5 a + PLACE *v.*] **1.** *trans.* To restore to a previous place or position; to put back again *in* a place. **2.** To take the place of, become a substitute for (a person or thing) 1753. **3.** To fill the place of (a person or thing) *with* or *by* a substitute 1765. **b.** To provide or procure a substitute or equivalent in place of (a person or thing) 1796.

1. To chaste th' vsurper and r. their king 1595. 2. Sir Edward Hawke, and Captain Saunders..went to r. Admirals Byng and West 1756. The paper [money] would be seasonably replaced by a metallic currency 1823. 3. b. The loss of such a treasure as he will not easily r. 1802. Hence **Repla·ceable** *a.* **Repla·ced** *ppl. a.* spec. applied to a crystal that has each of its edges or angles replaced by one or more planes. **Repla·cement,** the act or process of replacing; the fact of being replaced.

Replant (rīplɑ·nt), *v.* 1575. [RE- 5 a.] **1.** *trans.* To plant (a tree, plant, etc.) again. **2.** To plant (ground, etc.) again; to furnish with new plants (or inhabitants) 1652. **3.** *intr.* To provide and set fresh plants 1712.

1. *transf.* I will..r. Henry in his former state SHAKS. Hence **Repla·ntable** *a.*

Replay· (rī-), *v.* 1884. [RE- 5 a.] *trans.* To play (a match, etc.) again. Hence **Re·play** *sb.* a replayed match.

Replea·der. 1607. [RE- 5 a; see -ER⁴.] *Law.* The action of, right to, a second pleading.

Replenish (rĭple·niʃ), *v.* ME. [f. OF. *repleniss-*, *replenir*; see RE- and PLENISH.] **I.** *pass.* (*Obs.* exc. as direct pass. of II.) **1.** To be fully or abundantly stocked *with.* **b.** To be provided or furnished *with* 1533. †**2.** To be filled, or fully imbued *with* some quality or condition -1702. **3.** To be physically or materially filled *with* 1490.

1. b. His intellect is not replenished, hee is onely an animall SHAKS. 3. Generally all the earth is replenished with Brimstone 1612.

II. †**1.** *trans.* To make full *of*, to fill, stock or store abundantly *with*, persons or animals -1596. †**2.** To occupy (a place) as inhabitants or settlers, to inhabit, people -1788. **b.** To occupy the whole of (a space or thing). Now *rare.* 1563. †**3.** To fill with food; to satiate -1665. †**4.** To fill (a place or space) *with* something -1615. **5.** To fill up again; to restore to the former amount or condition 1612. **6.** *intr.* To become filled; to attain to fullness; to increase (*rare*) 1579.

2. The vacant habitations were replenished by a new colony GIBBON. 5. Full of wants of money and much stores to buy, for to r. the stores, and no money to do it with PEPYS. 6. Her Coffers began to r., Her Subjects were rich 1673. Hence **Reple·nisher,** one who or that which replenishes; *spec.* in *Elect.* a device for increasing or maintaining a charge in certain apparatus. **Reple·nishment,** the act of replenishing; that which replenishes; a fresh supply.

Replete (rĭplī·t), *a.* late ME. [a. F. *replet, replète*, or ad. L. *repletus, replere.*] **1.** Filled *with* (†or full *of*) some thing or substance. **b.** Filled to satisfaction *with*, full *of*, food or drink; sated, gorged. late ME. †**c.** Plethoric, fat -1758. **2.** Filled *with* (†full *of*), abundantly supplied or provided *with*, in various uses. late ME. **3.** Full, entire, perfect, complete 1601.

1. Sweet Gardens, repleat with fragrant flowres 1634. b. Herodes,..Whan he of wyn was repleet at his feeste CHAUCER. c. Of a strong and r. Habit of Body 1758. 2. Proceedings..r. with irregularity and injustice 1817. Hence **Reple·teness.**

Repletion (rĭplī·ʃən). late ME. [a. OF. *repletion*, ad. late L. *repletionem.*] **1.** The action of eating or drinking to excess; the condition of body arising from this. **2.** The fact or condition of being filled up, stuffed full, or crowded. late ME. **3.** The action of filling up; the filling *of* a cavity or receptacle 1646. **4.** The satisfaction of a desire or want 1654.

1. Repleccion ne made hire neuere sik, Attempree diete was al hir phisik CHAUCER. *fig.* Your malady, in this respect, is a disorder of r. BURKE. 2. The body of the house was filled to r. by adults 1870.

†**Reple·tive,** *a.* 1611. [ad. late L. *repletivus*; see REPLETE *a.* and -IVE.] Causing repletion, replenishing -1733. So †**Reple·tively** *adv.* 1601.

†**Reple·ve,** *v.* 1592. [ad. OF. *replevir* to REPLEVY.] *Law. trans.* To replevy; to bail out -1644.

Repleviable (rĭple·viăb'l), *a.* 1755. [f. REPLEVY *v.* + -ABLE.] *Law.* Replevisable.

Replevin (rĭple·vin), *sb.* 1461. [a. AF. *replevin(e*, f. OF. *replevir* to REPLEVY.] *Law.* **1.** The restoration to, or recovery by, a person of goods or chattels distrained or taken from him, upon his giving security to have the matter tried in a court of justice and to return the goods if the case is decided against him. †**b.** The bailing of, or bail for, a person -1651. **2.** A writ empowering a person to recover his goods by replevin 1465. **3.** An action arising out of a case in which goods have been distrained or taken and replevied 1515.

Replevin (rĭple·vin), *v.* 1659. [f. prec.] *Law.* †**1.** *trans.* = REPLEVY *v.* 1, 2 b -1720. **2.** = REPLEVY *v.* 2. Now *U.S.* 1678.

Replevisable (rĭple·visăb'l), *a.* 1532. [a. AF. *replevis(s)able.*] *Law.* That may be replevied.

Replevy (rĭple·vi), *sb.* Now *rare.* 1451. [f. next.] = REPLEVIN *sb.* 1, 1 b, 2.

Replevy (rĭple·vi), *v.* 1554. [ad. OF. *replevir*, f. *re-* RE- + *plevir* of doubtful origin.] *Law.* **1.** *trans.* To bail (a person), or admit to bail. **2.** To recover (cattle or goods) by replevin 1596. †**b.** Of the sheriff or bailiff: To recover for, or restore to, the owner by replevin -1683. **3.** *intr.* or *absol.* To carry out the act of replevin 1607.

Replica (re·plikă). 1824. [a. It., f. *replicare.*] A copy, duplicate, or reproduction of a work of art; prop., one made by the original artist. **b.** *transf.* A copy, reproduction, facsimile 1865.

†**Re·plicant.** 1631. [ad. L. *replicantem, replicare*; see REPLY *v.*] One who replies -1755.

Replicate (re·plikĕt), *sb.* 1730. [f. as next.] *Mus.* A tone one or more octaves above or below a given tone.

Replicate (re·plikĕt), *a.* 1832. [ad. L. *replicatus, replicare*; see REPLY *v.*] **1.** *Bot.* Of a leaf, etc.: Folded back upon itself; also, folded so as to form a groove or channel. **2.** *Entom.* Of the wings of certain insects: Provided with a joint by means of which the outer part folds back on the base 1891.

Replicate (re·plikeɪt), *v.* 1535. [f. L. *replicat-*, *replicare*; see REPLY *v.*] **1.** To answer, say in reply (*rare*). **2. a.** To repeat, reproduce (an action) *rare.* 1607. **b.** To make a replica of (a picture) 1882. **3.** To fold or bend back 1777.

Replication (replikē·ʃən). late ME. [a. OF., ad. L. *replicationem*, f. *replicare*; see

REPLY *v.*] **1.** The action of folding up or back; a fold (*rare*). **2.** Reply, answer, rejoinder. Also with *a* and *pl.* late ME. **3.** *spec.* A reply to an answer 1440. **b.** *Law.* The reply of the plaintiff to the plea or answer of the defendant, being the third step in common pleadings. (Superseded since the Judicature Act of 1875 by *reply.*) 1453. †**4.** Repetition –1683. **5.** Return of a sound; reverberation, echo 1601. **6.** A copy, reproduction. Also, the action of reproducing. 1692.

2. Your Discrete answers and replicacions made in that behalf 1535. Phr. †*Without* (*any*) *r.*, without reply being allowed; without protest or opposition. 5. Tyber trembled vnderneath her bankes To heare the r. of your sounds SHAKS.

Replier (rǐplai·əɹ). 1549. [f. REPLY *v.* + -ER [1].] One who replies or answers.

‖**Replum** (re·plŏm, rī·plŏm). *Pl.* **repla.** 1830. [L. *replum* 'a bolt for covering the commissure of the folding-door'.] *Bot.* The central frame or placenta left in certain fruits when the valves fall away by dehiscence.

Reply (rǐplai·), *sb.* 1560. [f. the vb.] **1.** An answer or response made in words or writing; *transf.*, a response made by an act, gesture, etc. **b.** *Law.* (*a*) The final speech of counsel in a trial; (*b*) a pleading delivered by the plaintiff after the delivery of the defence 1875. **c.** *Mus.* The answer or response in a fugue 1597. **d.** *attrib.*, as *r.-paid* adj., etc. 1884. **2.** A counter-answer, a replication 1702.

1. How pregnant..his Replies are! SHAKS.

Reply (rǐplai·), *v.* late ME. [ad. OF. *replier* :—L. *replicare* to fold back, reflect on, reply, f. *re-* RE- + *plicare* to fold.] **1.** *intr.* To answer or respond in words or writing. **b.** To respond by some gesture, act, or performance; *esp.* to return gun-fire 1818. **2.** To return a sound; to echo. late ME. **3.** To make counter-answer; *spec.* in *Law*, to answer a defendant's plea; to make a replication; also, to make the final speech in a trial 1453. **4.** *trans.* To return as an answer; to say in reply. late ME. **b.** To return, re-echo (a cry) 1650.

1. R. not to me, with a Foole-borne Iest SHAKS. b. The besieged replied..sharply 1829. 2. Blow, let us hear the purple glens replying TENNYSON. 4. Lords, vouchsafe To giue me hearing what I shall r. SHAKS. b. With his last Voice, Eurydice, he cry'd, Eurydice, the Rocks and River-banks reply'd. DRYDEN.

Repone (rǐpōu·n), *v. Sc.* 1525. [ad. L. *reponere*; see REPOSE *v.*] **1.** *trans. Law.* To restore a person to a position or office previously held; in later use *spec.* to restore to the ministry or a ministerial charge. **b.** To restore to a certain legal status, to rehabilitate (a person), esp. *against* a decree or sentence, so that the case may be tried afresh 1574. †**2.** To put (a person or thing) back in a place (*rare*) –1640.

Report (rǐpōə·ɹt), *sb.* late ME. [a. OF. *report*, *raport*, f. *reporter*, *rapporter* REPORT *v.*] **1.** Rumour, common talk. Now *rare.* **b.** With *a* and *pl.* A rumour; a statement generally made or believed. late ME. **c.** Repute, fame, reputation. (Now only with *good*, etc., as an echo of Biblical passages.) 1514. **2.** An account brought by one person to another, esp. of some matter specially investigated. late ME. **b.** Without article, in phr. *to make r.* 1534. **c.** A formal statement of the results of an investigation, or of any matter on which definite information is required, made by some person or body instructed or required to do so 1661. **d.** In Parliamentary practice, the account of a bill, etc., given to the House by the Committee appointed to consider it 1628. **3.** A statement made by a person; an account, more or less formal, *of* some person or thing. late ME. †**b.** Testimony *to*, or commendation of, a person or quality. SHAKS. **c.** *Law.* A formal account of a case argued and determined in any court, giving the important points in the pleadings, evidence, etc. Freq. in *pl.* 1617. **d.** An account, more or less complete, of the statements made by a speaker or speakers (as in a debate, lecture, etc.), of the proceedings at a meeting, or of any occurrence or event, *esp.* with a view to publication in a special form, or in the newspaper press 1812. †**4.** Relation, reference, bearing, connexion (*rare*) –1738. †**5.** *Mus.* A response; a note or part answering to or repeating another; loosely, a note, a musical sound –1662. **6.** A resounding noise, *esp.* that caused by the discharge of fire-arms or explosives 1590.

1. As that dishonest victory..Kil'd with r. that Old man eloquent MILT. b. He will..perhaps Ruine himself..by spreading Reports BOYLE. 2. c. The rest of the Committee did not think fit to sign the r. BURNET. d. Report—that is, the intermediate stage between the second and third reading 1886. 3. b. *L. L. L.* II. i. 64. c. The reports are extant in a regular series from the reign of king Edward the second inclusive BLACKSTONE. 4. The kitchen and stables are ill-placed..having no r. to the wings they joyne to EVELYN. 6. They..exploded with a very loud r. in the air TYNDALL.

Report (rǐpōə·ɹt), *v.* late ME. [a. OF. and AF. *reporter* :—L. *reportare*, f. *re-* RE- + *portare* to carry.] **I.** *trans.* **1.** To relate, narrate (a fact, event, etc.). Now *rare.* **2.** To carry, convey, or repeat (something said, a message, etc.) *to* another. late ME. **b.** To repeat (something heard); to relate as having been spoken by another. late ME. **c.** *spec.* To take down (a law-case, speech, discussion, etc.) in writing, now esp. for publication in a newspaper; to prepare a written account of (any meeting, event, etc.) 1600. **3.** To make a formal report on (some matter or thing); to state (something) in such a report 1580. **b.** To relate, state, or notify (something) as the result of special observation or investigation; to bring in a report of (something observed) 1631. **c.** To name (a person) to a superior authority as having offended in some way 1885. **d.** *refl.* To make known to some authority that one has arrived or is present at a certain place 1802.

1. He..found Already known what he for news had thought To have reported MILT. Phr. *It is reported*, it is commonly said or stated; On the Alpes, It is reported thou did'st eate strange flesh SHAKS. 2. I wyll reporte this tale unto Duke Maurice 1560. You would aske mee newes, in a time, when reporting it is dangerous 1638. 3. All goods not duly reported.. shall be forfeited 1833. b. If the Herald r. him a Gentleman 1631. d. Every officer on his arrival.. must r. himself to the governor 1802.

II. *intr.* or *absol.* **1. a.** To make a report *of*, to speak or talk in a certain way *of*, a person or thing 1432. **b.** To act as a (newspaper) reporter 1850. **2.** To make report (*on* a person or thing) 1450. **b.** To make or draw up, to give in or submit, a formal report 1628. **c.** To report oneself (see I. 3 d.) 1864.

1. *All's Well* III. v. 60. 2. This Pitch (as ancient Writers doe r.) doth defile SHAKS. b. The committee will r. at twelve o'clock 1828. c. I reported for duty at Jefferson Barracks 1885.

†**III.** *trans.* **1. a.** *refl.* To betake (oneself) for support, to appeal *to* a person or thing –1639. **b.** To refer *to*, esp. for information –1639. **2.** To bring or convey; to carry (news) –1590. **3.** To cause to re-echo or resound –1673. **b.** To send back, re-echo (a sound). *rare.* –1626. Hence **Repo·rtable** *a.* capable or worthy of being reported. **Repo·rtage**, †report, gossip. †**Repo·rtingly** *adv.* by hearsay.

Reporter (rǐpōə·ɹtəɹ). late ME. [orig. a. AF. **reportour* = OF. *reporteur.* In later use f. the vb. + -ER [1].] **1.** One who reports or relates; a narrator. Now *rare.* **b.** One specially appointed to make or draw up a report, or to give information of something 1625. **2. a.** One who takes down reports of law-cases 1617. **b.** One who reports debates, meetings, speeches, etc., esp. for a newspaper; a person specially employed for this purpose 1813. †**3.** A pistol –1865.

1. Ther-of was I noon Auctour; I was..but a reportour Of folkes tales HOCCLEVE. 2. b. His father ..was..seeking employment as a r. 1882.

Reportorial (repoɹtōə·riăl), *a.* Chiefly *U.S.* 1860. [irreg. f. REPORTER; see -ORIAL.] Consisting of, pertaining to, or characteristic of, reporters.

Reposal (rǐpōu·zăl). 1605. [f. REPOSE *v.*[1] and *v.*[2]] **1.** The act of reposing (trust, confidence, etc.); †trust or reliance *in* something (*rare*). †**2.** The fact or state of reposing or resting –1642. †**b.** That on which one reposes. BURTON.

Repose (rǐpōu·z), *sb.* 1509. [a. F. *repos*; see REPOSE *v.*[2]] **1.** Temporary rest or cessation from activity; *esp.* the rest given by sleep. **b.** *Eccl.* Death, decease (of a saint) 1869. **2.** Relief or respite from exertion, toil, trouble, or excitement 1529. †**3. a.** A place of rest –1671. **b.** *Painting.* A large mass of shadow –1738. **4.** A state of quiet or peaceful inaction or of freedom from disturbing influences 1651. †**b.** Peace of mind (*rare*) –1718. **5.** Quiet, calm or calmness, tranquillity 1717. **b.** *Painting.* Harmonious arrangement of figures or colours, having a restful effect on the eye 1695. **c.** Composure, quiet, ease of manner 1833. **6.** Absence of activity (in things); cessation of natural forces; quiescence 1757. **b.** Undisturbed or unagitated condition 1855. **c.** The fact of being left undisturbed 1844. **7.** Trust, confidence 1629.

1. So forth she rode, without r. or rest, Searching all lands SPENSER. Phr. *Altar of R.*, the altar on which the reserved sacrament rests after the mass of Maundy Thursday. *To take, seek, r.* 2. The state had need of some r. BYRON. 4. The Felicity of this life, consisteth not in the r. of a mind satisfied HOBBES. 5. b. The piece wants r. SIR J. REYNOLDS. c. That r. Which stamps the caste of Vere de Vere TENNYSON. 6. Vesuvius was virtually in r. RUSKIN. In Engineering, *angle of r.*, the greatest angle between two planes which is consistent with stability.

Repose (rǐpōu·z), *v.*[1] late ME. [f. L. *repos-*, *reponere*, after *dispose*, etc.] †**1.** *trans.* To replace, put back into the same place –1660. **2.** To place or put; *esp.* to deposit or lay up *in* a place. Now *rare.* 1548. **3.** To set or place (confidence, trust, etc.) *in* a thing or person 1560. **b.** To place or leave (something) *in* the control or management of another 1589. †**c.** To regard as existing *in* something –1614.

2. The brass cannon and mortars..were reposed for some days in Hyde Park H. WALPOLE. 3. Herein mainly should we r. our hopes DISRAELI.

Repose (rǐpōu·z), *v.*[2] 1470. [ad. F. *reposer* :—late L. *repausare*; see RE- and PAUSE *v.*] **1.** *refl.* To rest oneself; to lay oneself to rest. †**b.** *fig.* To settle oneself with confidence *on* something –1770. **2.** *trans.* To lay to rest or repose *on* or *in* something. In later use only *fig.* 1535. **b.** In pa. pple.: Rested, reclining, lying 1674. **3.** To give or afford rest to (a person), to refresh by rest 1549. **4.** *intr.* To take rest; to cease from exertion or travel; to enjoy freedom from disturbance 1548. **b.** To take rest by sitting or lying down; to lie down to rest; *transf.* to rest in death 1535. **c.** To remain still; to lie in quiet 1817. †**5.** To confide or place one's trust *in*, to rely *on*, a thing or person –1781. **6.** To rest *on* or *upon*, in various senses 1611.

1. Now may I r. me: Custance is mine owne UDALL. b. I can r. myself very confidently upon your prudence JOHNSON. 3. Have ye chos'n this place After the toyl of Battel to r. Your wearied vertue..? MILT. 4. c. When the centuries behind me like a fruitful land reposed TENNYSON. 6. Almost every glacier reposes upon an inclined bed TYNDALL.

Reposed (rǐpōu·zd), *ppl. a.* 1533. [f. prec. + -ED [1].] Settled, free from agitation or movement. Hence **Repo·sed·ly** *adv.* (*rare*), **-ness.**

Reposeful (rǐpōu·zfŭl), *a.* 1852. [f. REPOSE *sb.*] Full of repose; having an air of repose; quiet. Hence **Repo·seful·ly** *adv.*, **-ness.**

Reposit (rǐpǫ·zit), *v.* 1641. [f. L. *reposit-*, *reponere* to REPONE.] **1.** *trans.* To put or deposit (a thing) *in* a place; to lay up, store. **2.** To replace (*rare*) 1884.

Some reposite their Eggs or Young in the Earth 1713.

Reposition (rīpŏzi·ʃən). 1588. [ad. late L. *repositionem*, f. *reponere*; see prec. and -ION.] **1.** *Surg.* The operation of restoring to the normal position; replacement. **b.** Replacement (of a thing), in other senses 1874. **2.** The action of repositing, laying up or aside 1617.

Repositor (rǐpǫ·zitǫɹ). 1875. [f. REPOSIT *v.*] A replacing instrument.

Repository (rǐpǫ·zitəri), *sb.* 1485. [ad. obs. F. *repositoire* or L. *repositorium*; see REPOSIT *v.* and -ORY [1].] **1.** A vessel, receptacle, chamber, etc., in which things are, or may be placed, deposited, or stored. **b.** A place, room, or building, in which specimens, curiosities, or works of art are collected; a museum. Now *rare.* 1658. **c.** A place where things are kept or offered for sale; a warehouse, store, shop, mart 1785. **2.** A vault or sepulchre 1663. **3.** A place or thing within which something immaterial is thought of as deposited or contained 1645. **4.** A part or place in which something is accumulated or exists in quantities 1672. **5.**

A person to whom some matter is entrusted or confided 1697.

1. c. The Fine Art R. THACKERAY. 4. Cornwall is..an immense subterranean r. of copper and tin 1855. 5. Make me the r. of your sorrows SHELLEY.

Reposse·ss (rī-), *v.* 1494. [RE- 5 a.] 1. *trans.* To recover possession of (a place, etc.); to reoccupy. 2. To put (a person) in possession *of* something again 1591. b. *refl.* To regain possession *of* something 1670.

1. Earth repossesses Part of what she gave YOUNG. 2. b. When..the Hamburg banker wishes to r. himself of his money 1861. So **Reposse·ssion**, recovery; renewed possession.

‖ **Repoussé** (rəpuse), *a.* (and *sb.*) 1851. [F., pa. pple. of *repousser*, f. *re-* RE- + *pousser* PUSH *v.*] A. *adj.* Of metal work: Raised or beaten into relief, ornamented in relief, by means of hammering from the reverse side. B. *ellipt.* as *sb.* Metal-work of this kind; the process of hammering into relief 1875.

Reprehend (reprĭhe·nd), *v.* ME. [ad. L. *reprehendere*, f. *re-* RE- + *prehendere* to seize.] 1. *trans.* To reprove, reprimand, rebuke, censure, find fault with. Also *absol.* †2. To refute. BACON. ¶3. Misused by ignorant speakers for 'represent' and 'apprehend' 1588.

1. He reprehended me afore al the companye 1530. I nor advise, nor r. the Choice 1708. 3. *L. L. L.* I. i. 184. Hence **Reprehe·nder.**

Reprehensible (reprĭhe·nsĭb'l), *a.* late ME. [ad. late L. *reprehensibilis*, f. *reprehens-*, *reprehendere*; see prec. and -IBLE.] Deserving of reprehension, censure, or rebuke; reprovable; blameworthy.

In a meane man prodigalitie and pride are faultes more r. then in Princes PUTTENHAM. Hence **Reprehe·nsibleness. Reprehe·nsibly** *adv.*

Reprehension (reprĭhe·nʃən). late ME. [ad. L. *reprehensionem.*] 1. The action of reprehending; censure, reproof, rebuke, reprimand. b. With *a* and *pl.* An instance of this 1574. †2. Refutation; proof of fallacy –1620.

1. If they are corrupt, they merit..blame and r. BURKE.

Reprehensive (reprĭhe·nsiv), *a.* 1589. [f. REPREHEND *v.*; cf. *comprehensive*, etc.] Of the nature of reprehension; containing reproof. Now *rare.* Hence **Reprehe·nsively** *adv.* So **Reprehe·nsory** *a.* (now *rare*).

Represent (reprĭze·nt), *v.* late ME. [ad. OF. *représenter* or L. *repræsentare*, f. *re-* RE- + *præsentare* to PRESENT.] †1. *trans.* To bring into presence; *esp.* to present (oneself or another) *to* or *before* a person –1649. 2. To bring clearly and distinctly before the mind, esp. by description or by an act of imagination. late ME. b. To place (a fact) clearly before another; to state or point out explicitly or seriously *to* one, with a view to influencing action or conduct, freq. by way of expostulation or remonstrance 1582. c. *absol.* To protest *against* something. Now *rare.* 1717. 3. To describe as having a specified character or quality; to give out, assert, or declare to be of a certain kind 1513. 4. To show, exhibit, or display to the eye; to make visible or manifest. Now *rare.* late ME. b. *spec.* To exhibit by means of painting, sculpture, etc.; to portray, depict, delineate. late ME. c. Of pictures, etc.: To exhibit by artificial resemblance or delineation. late ME. 5. To exhibit or reproduce in action or show; to perform or produce (a play, etc.) upon the stage 1460. b. To exhibit or personate (a character) on the stage; to act the part of (some one) 1662. 6. To symbolize, serve as an embodiment of (some quality, fact, or other abstract concept). late ME. b. Of quantities: To indicate or imply (another quantity) 1860. 7. Of things: To stand for or in place of (a person or thing); to be the figure or image of (something). late ME. b. To be the equivalent of, to correspond to, to replace (*esp.* another animal or plant in a given region) 1855. 8. To take or fill the place of (another) in some respect or for some purpose; to be a substitute in some capacity for (a person or body); to act for (another) by a deputed right 1509. b. *spec.* To be accredited deputy or substitute for (a number of persons) in a legislative or deliberative assembly; to be member of Parliament for (a certain constituency); hence in *pass.*, to be acted for in this respect *by* some one; to have a representative or representatives 1655. 9. To serve as a specimen or example of (a class or kind of things); hence, in *pass.*, to be exemplified (*by* something) 1858.

2. Of all external things, Which the five watchful Senses r., She forms Imaginations MILT. b. It would have been useless to r. these things to James MACAULAY. 3. Sunderland they represented as the chief conspirator MACAULAY. 4. b. My wife desired to be represented as Venus GOLDSM. c. Two allegorical pieces by..Holbein, representing the Triumph of Riches and the Triumph of Poverty respectively 1861. 5. b. Persons who r. Heroes in a Tragedy STEELE. 6. No sovereign has ever represented the majesty of a great state with more dignity and grace MACAULAY. b. I knew the immense amount of mechanical force represented by four ounces of bread and ham TYNDALL. 8. Men who are in absolute liberty may..give Authority to One man to r. them every one HOBBES. b. I do not wish to r. Bristol, or to r. any place, but upon terms that shall be honourable BURKE. 9. A soup in which twenty kinds of vegetables were represented HAWTHORNE. Hence **Represe·ntable** *a.* capable of being represented.

Representant (reprĭze·ntănt). 1651. [= F. *représentant*; see prec. and -ANT [1].] 1. A person representing another or others; a representative (*rare*). 2. An equivalent 1863.

Representation (reprĭzentē·ʃən). late ME. [a. F., or ad. L. *repræsentationem*; see REPRESENT and -ATION.] †1. a. Presence, bearing, air –1640. b. Appearance –1664. 2. An image, likeness, or reproduction in some manner *of* a thing. late ME. b. A material image or figure; in later use *esp.* a drawing or painting (*of* a person or thing) 1477. c. The action or fact of exhibiting in some visible image or form 1483. 3. The exhibition of character and action upon the stage; the (*or* a) performance of a play 1589. 4. The action of placing a fact, etc., before another or others by means of discourse; a statement or account, *esp.* one intended to influence opinion or action 1553. b. *Insurance.* A special statement of facts relating to the risk involved, made by the insuring party to the insurer or underwriter before the subscription of the policy 1838. 5. A formal and serious statement of facts, reasons, or arguments, made with a view to effecting some change, preventing some action, etc.; hence, a remonstrance, protest, expostulation 1679. 6. The action of presenting to the mind or imagination; an image thus presented; a clearly-conceived idea or concept 1647. b. The act or process by which the mind forms an image or concept; the faculty of doing this; the product of such an act 1836. 7. The fact of standing for, or in place of, some other thing or person, esp. with a right or authority to act on their account; substitution of one thing or person for another 1624. b. *Law.* The assumption by an heir of the position, rights, and obligations of his predecessor 1693. 8. The fact of representing or being represented in a legislative or deliberative assembly, *spec.* in Parliament; the position, principle, or system implied by this 1769. b. The aggregate of those who thus represent the elective body 1789.

1. a. This yoong man of a noble birth, of a manly r. 1598. 2. The Play-House is a R. of the World in nothing so much as in this Particular STEELE. c. Fidelity of r. being..adhered to 1830. 3. Never having been before at a theatrical r. THACKERAY. 4. Drawing up a r. of the state of my victualling-business PEPYS. 5. Ferdinand..instructed his ambassador to make the strongest representations to the Pope 1841. 6. The word r...I have restricted to denote..the immediate object or product of Imagination 1838. 7. So cannot these Members be formed into a body but by the King, either by his Royal presence or r. 1660. b. *Right of r.*, the right whereby the son of an elder son deceased succeeds to his grandfather in preference to the latter's immediate issue. 8. We ought not to be quite so ready with our taxes, until we can secure the desired r. in parliament BURKE. Hence **Representa·tional** *a.* pertaining to, or of the nature of, r.; also, holding the doctrine of representationism. **Representa·tionary** *a.* (*rare*) representative.

Representationism (re:prĭzentē·ʃəniz'm). 1842. [f. prec. + -ISM.] The doctrine that the immediate object of the mind in perception is only a representation of the real object in the external world. So **Representa·tionist**, an adherent of this doctrine.

Representative (reprĭze·ntătiv), *a.* and *sb.* late ME. [ad. F. *représentatif*, or med.L. *repræsentativus*; see REPRESENT *v.* and -ATIVE.] A. *adj.* 1. Serving to represent, figure, portray, or symbolize. b. Presenting, or capable of presenting, ideas of things to the mind 1753. c. Relating to mental representation 1847. 2. Standing for, or in place of, another or others, *esp.* in a prominent or comprehensive manner 1624. b. *spec.* Holding the place of, and acting for, a larger body of persons (*esp.* the whole people) in the work of governing or legislating; pertaining to, or based upon, a system by which the people is thus represented 1628. c. Connected with, or based upon, the fact of one person representing another 1766. 3. Typical of a class; conveying an adequate idea of others of the kind 1788. 4. Taking the place of, replacing, other forms or species 1845.

1. b. The distinction between perception as a presentative, and Memory,..as a r., cognition 1842. 2. A king or queen, as r. persons in a nation 1861. b. The two Houses of Parliament being the R. Body of the Kingdome 1643. 3. This experiment is r., and it illustrates a general principle TYNDALL. 4. Many of these were 'r. forms' (species or races which take the place of other allied species or races) of others found on the opposite banks 1863.

B. *sb.* 1. A person (or thing) representing a number or class of persons (or things); hence, a sample or specimen 1647. b. A typical embodiment *of* some quality or abstract concept 1715. 2. One who (†that which) represents a number of persons in some special capacity; *spec.* one who represents a section of the community as member of a legislative body; a member of Parliament or (*U.S.*) of the House of Representatives 1658. †3. A representative body or assembly –1761. 4. One who represents another as agent, delegate, substitute, successor, or heir; also *spec.* a person appointed to represent his sovereign or government in a foreign court or country 1691. b. One who or that which in some respect represents another person or thing 1691.

1. Noah and his sons..were..the..representatives of all mankind 1676. b. An ideot..who was the r. of Credulity ADDISON. 2. The English nation declare they are grossly injured by their representatives *Junius Lett.* *House of Representatives*, the lower or popular house of the United States Congress or of a State legislature. 4. Lord lieutenants began to be introduced, as standing representatives of the crown BLACKSTONE. b. Money is only a commodious r. of the commodities which may be purchased with it 1788. Hence **Repre·se·ntative·ly** *adv.*, **-ness.**

Representer (reprĭze·ntəɹ). 1570. [f. as prec. + -ER [1].] 1. One who represents by acting; †an exhibitor; †an actor. 2. One who makes a representation, or states a matter in a certain light. Now *rare* or *Obs.* 1847. †3. A representative of a thing or person –1691. †b. *spec.* = REPRESENTATIVE B. 2. –1726.

Representment (reprĭze·ntmĕnt). 1594. [-MENT.] 1. The act of representing in some form or figure; the fact of being so represented, or the result of such representation. Now *rare.* †2. Representation by discourse or argument –1680.

Repress (rĭpre·s), *v.* late ME. [f. L. *repress-*, *reprimere*; see RE- and PRESS *v.*] 1. *trans.* To check, restrain, put down or keep under (something bad or objectionable). b. To check by some special treatment; to cure, stanch 1493. 2. To check or withstand (some passion, feeling, etc.) in another by opposition or control. late ME. b. To keep or hold back, to restrain or check (a person) from action or advance 1638. 3. To keep down, suppress (one's desires, feelings, etc.); to restrain, refrain from (an action); *spec.* in *Psychol.*, to suppress (a painful or otherwise undesirable memory, desire, etc.). late ME. 4. To reduce (troublesome persons) to subjection or quietness; to put down by force, suppress. late ME. b. To put down (a rebellion, riot, etc.) 1475. 5. To keep under, check, curb 1557. †6. To force or drive back –1662.

1. Authorised by law to r. spiritual abuses MACAULAY. b. When now the rage of hunger was represt POPE. 2. To r. the self-seeking tendencies in the mercantile classes FROUDE. 3. Desire of wine..Thou couldst r. MILT. 4. b. The duty of repressing riots..in England lay with the nobility in their several districts FROUDE. Hence **Repre·sser. Repre·ssive** *a.* having the nature of, or tending to, repression; **-ly** *adv.*, **-ness.**

Repression (rĭpre·ʃən). late ME. [ad. L. **repressionem*, f. *reprimere*; see REPRESS *v.*[1]] †1. Power of repressing. CHAUCER. 2. The action of repressing; an instance of this 1533.

2. The r. and punishment of Malefactors 1553.

Reprieval (rĭprī·văl). 1586. [f. REPRIEVE *v.* + -AL 2.] = next. Now *rare*.

Reprieve (rĭprī·v), *sb.* 1598. [f. the vb.] 1. The act of reprieving; the fact of being reprieved 1607. b. An instance of this; a formal suspension of the execution of a sentence; a remission or commutation of a capital sentence 1598. †c. The time during which one is reprieved. SHAKS. 2. A warrant granting or authorizing the suspension or remission of a capital sentence 1602. 3. *transf.* Respite from a natural or violent death 1633. b. A respite, or temporary escape, from some trouble, calamity, etc. 1635.

1. Without R. adjudg'd to death MILT. b. Like the felon, that feels there is no chance of a r. 1843. 2. A r. was brought to Newgate for Dr. Hensey, respiting his sentence for a fortnight 1758. 3. The sense of r. from approaching and apparently inevitable death had its usual effect SCOTT.

Reprieve (rĭprī·v), *v.* 1494. [First in pa. pple. *repryed*, app. ad. AF. *repris*, pa. pple. of *reprendre*; cf. REPRISE *v.*] †1. *trans.* To take or send back *to* prison; to remand; to detain on remand –1588. †2. To postpone, delay, put off (*rare*) –1664. 3. To respite or rescue (a person) from impending punishment; *spec.* to suspend or delay the execution of (a condemned person) 1596.

3. He who escapes from death is not pardoned, he is only reprieved, and reprieved to a short day FIELDING. Hence †**Reprie·vement**, the action of reprieving; a reprieve –1647.

Reprimand (re·primɑnd), *sb.* 1636. [ad. F. *réprimande*, f. *réprimer* to repress, reprove.] A sharp rebuke, reproof, or censure, esp. one given by a person or body having authority, or by a judge or magistrate to an offender.

Reprimand (reprimɑ·nd), *v.* 1681. [ad. F. *réprimander*, f. *réprimande*; see prec.] *trans.* To rebuke, reprove, or censure (a person) sharply or severely.

The Captain..reprimanded the sentinel for deserting his post W. IRVING. Hence **Reprima·nder**.

Re·print (rī-), *sb.* 1611. [f. the vb.] 1. A reproduction in print of any matter already printed; a new impression of a work previously printed; without alteration of the matter. 2. *Typog.* Printed matter used as copy to be set up and printed again; also *r. copy* 1824.

1. An uniform r. of the Novels LOCKHART.

Repri·nt (rī-), *v.* 1551. [RE- 5 a.] 1. *trans.* To print (a work) again in a new edition; to print (matter) a second time. b. To print again in a different form 1693. 2. To impress or stamp again 1662. Hence **Repri·nter**, one who reprints or who publishes a reprint.

Reprisal (rĭprəi·zăl). 1447. [a. OF. *reprisaille*; see REPRISE *v.* and -AL 2.] I. 1. (Without article or plural.) The act or practice of seizing by force the property (or persons) of subjects of another nation, in retaliation for loss or injury suffered from these or their countrymen. Now *Hist.* 2. An act or instance of seizing property or persons belonging to another state by way of indemnity or recompense for loss sustained 1611. †3. a. The taking *of* a thing as a prize –1596. b. A prize (*rare*) –1611. †c. Regaining, recapture –1867. 4. An act of retaliation for some injury or attack; *spec.* in warfare, the infliction of similar or severer injury or punishment on the enemy, e.g. by the execution of prisoners taken from them 1710.

1. *Letters* (or *Commission*) *of r.*, an official warrant authorizing an aggrieved subject to exact forcible reparation from the subjects of another state. 2. And indeed this custom of reprisals seems dictated by nature herself BLACKSTONE. *transf.* In the winter, when the sea is making reprisals on the delta 1849.

II. 1. (Chiefly *pl.*) A return or compensation; a sum or amount paid or received as compensation. Now *rare*. 1668. †2. = REPRISE *sb.* 3. H. WALPOLE.

Reprise (rĭprəi·z), *sb.* late ME. [a. F. *reprise*, f. *repris*, *reprendre* to take back, resume, etc. (see next).] 1. A deduction, charge, or payment falling to be made yearly out of a manor or estate. Chiefly *pl.* †b. A charge, duty, or tax. EVELYN. †2. a. A return or compensation received or paid –1736. b. Reprisal –1700. 3. A resumption or renewal of an action; a separate occasion of doing something. Chiefly in phr. *at* or *in* .. *reprises*. Somewhat *rare*. 1685. II. 1. *Arch.* A return (RETURN *sb.* II. 1) in an internal angle 1501. 2. *Mus.* †a. A refrain –1702. †b. A cadence –1811. c. The recurrence of the first theme or subject of a movement after the development 1879.

Repri·se, *v.* *Obs.* exc. *arch.* 1481. [f. F. *repris*, pa. pple. of *reprendre*, f. *re-* RE- + *prendre* to take.] †1. *trans.* To begin again, resume –1603. †b. To take anew. SPENSER. 2. To take back again, esp. by force; to recapture (a thing or person), to recover 1481. 3. To take or hold back out of a sum 1559. 4. To compensate (a person) 1662.

Reproach (rĭprō^u·tʃ), *sb.* late ME. [a. F. *reproche*, f. *reprocher* (see next).] 1. A source or cause of disgrace or shame (*to* a person, etc.). b. A thing, animal, or person forming a source of disgrace or discredit 1712. 2. Shame, disgrace, opprobrium, or blame, incurred by or falling upon a person or thing 1484. 3. Blame or censure directed against a person (in mod. use, often applied to mild upbraiding or rebuke) 1477. 4. An expression of disapproval, censure, reproof, or upbraiding; †a verbal insult 1548. b. *pl.* [tr. eccl. L. *improperia*, n. pl.] A series of antiphons and responses, in which Christ is represented as reproaching his people, sung in the Western Church on Good Friday 1884.

1. I pray'd for Children, and thought barrenness In wedlock a r. MILT. 2. Many good knyghtes and squyers..hadde rather a dyed, than to haue had any reproche 1523. And shee..bare a sonne, and said; God hath taken away my reproch *Gen.* xxx. 23. 3. I was sorry to see this way of r. taken against us PEPYS. *Term*, etc. *of r.*, one expressing strong censure or condemnation. 4. Thrice she assay'd with.. amorous reproaches to win from me My capital secret MILT. Hence **Reproa·chless** *a.* irreproachable 1826.

Reproach (rĭprō^u·tʃ), *v.* 1489. [ad. F. *reprocher*, perh. f. Rom. **repropriare* from L. *re-* + *proprius* own. Earlier ME. forms for sb. and vb. were *reproce*, *repruce*.] 1. *trans.* To object or cast up (a thing) *to*, or bring (up) *against*, a person as a reproach or fault. Now *rare*. 2. To upbraid, reprove, or rebuke (a person) 1513. b. To upbraid (a person) *with* something 1725. c. To censure or reprove (a thing, act, etc.) 1660. 3. To bring (a thing) into reproach or discredit; to be a reproach to (a person) 1593.

1. He failed not to r. unto the Pope his assisting of Francis 1648. 2. He reproached Fitzurse for ingratitude for past kindness FROUDE. b. The Duke.. reproached him in plain terms with his duplicity *Junius Lett.* c. His last sighs r. the faith of Kings JOHNSON. 3. Imputation, for that he knew you, might r. your life SHAKS. Hence **Reproa·chable** *a.* (now *rare*) deserving of, or liable to, reproach; †reproachful; **-ness**. **Reproa·chably** *adv.* (*rare*). **Reproa·cher**.

Reproachful (rĭprō^u·tʃfŭl), *a.* 1548. [-FUL.] †1. Full of reproach or shame; shameful, disgraceful. Also, deserving of reproach or censure; blameworthy. –1796. 2. Full of reproach, reproof, or censure; upbraiding, †abusive 1548. †3. Derogatory *to* a person, etc. (*rare*) –1645.

1. To be Ignorant, and to be deceived, we look upon as a wretched, and a r. thing 1681. 2. Not I, till I haue..Thrust these reprochfull speeches downe his throat SHAKS. Hence **Reproa·chful-ly** *adv.*, **-ness**.

Re·probacy. 1594. [f. REPROBATE *a.*; see -ACY.] The state or condition of being reprobate. So †**Re·probance**. SHAKS.

Reprobate (re·prŏbĕt, -eit), *sb.* 1545. [ad. L. *reprobatus*; see REPROBATE *v.*] 1. One rejected by God; one lost in sin. 2. An abandoned or unprincipled person; a scamp 1592.

2. Come from him, hee 's a r. HEYWOOD.

Reprobate (re·prŏbĕt), *a.* 1545. [ad. late L. *reprobatus*, *reprobare*; see next.] 1. Rejected or condemned as worthless, inferior, or impure. Now *rare*. †2. Depraved, morally corrupt –1671. 3. Rejected by God; lost or hardened in sin 1561. b. Of abandoned character; lost to all sense of religious or moral obligation; unprincipled 1660. 4. *absol.* Those who are rejected by God, and thus excluded from participation in eternal life with Him. (Opp. to *the elect.*) 1563. †5. Deserving or worthy of condemnation or reproof; appropriate to reprobates –1771.

1. Thei shal call them r. siluer, because the Lord hathe reiected them BIBLE (Genev.) *Jer.* vi. 30. 2. *L. L. L.* I. ii. 64. 3. Thir..Strength and Art are easily outdone By spirits r. MILT. 4. Can the predestinate be lost, or the r. saved? 1833. Hence **Re·probateness**.

Reprobate (re·prŏbeit), *v.* late ME. [f. L. *reprobat-*, *reprobare*, f. *re-* RE- 2 d + *probare* to PROVE.] 1. *trans.* To disapprove of, censure, condemn. 2. Of God: To reject or cast off from Himself; to exclude from participation in future bliss 1451. 3. To reject, refuse, put away, set aside 1609. b. *Law.* To reject (an instrument or deed) as not binding on one. (Chiefly in *Sc. Law.*) Also *absol.* 1726. c. To repudiate, cast off. *Obs.* or *arch.* 1748.

1. His neighbours reprobated his method of proceeding 1787. 2. For theyr synne they be reprobate & forsaken of god 1526. 3. Reprobated and rejected Was this Stone 1850. b. You cannot approbate and r. the same instrument 1836. Hence **Re·probater** (*rare*), one who reprobates.

Reprobation (reprŏbēi·ʃən). late ME. [ad. late L. *reprobationem*; see prec. and -ATION.] †1. Reproof, shame. late ME. only. 2. The action of raising objections or exceptions (*against* a thing or person); a legal objection or exception (*rare*) 1485. 3. *Theol.* Rejection by God; the state of being so rejected or cast off, and thus ordained to eternal misery. (Opp. to *election.*) 1532. 4. Rejection of a person or thing; condemnation as worthless or spurious 1582. b. Disapproval, censure, reproof 1727.

3. Austine doth call r. predestination to destruction 1651. 4. You are empowered to..set a brand of r. on clipt poetry, and false coin DRYDEN. b. The fear of public r. 1883. Hence †**Reproba·tioner**, a believer in the doctrine of r.

Reprobative (re·prŏbeitiv), *a.* 1835. [f. REPROBATE *v.* + -IVE.] Conveying or expressing disapproval or reprobation.

Reprobator (re·prŏbeitə̆ɹ). 1666. [ad. med.L. (*actio*) **reprobatoria*; see REPROBATE *v.* and -ORY[2].] *Sc. Law.* An action for the purpose of proving a witness to be liable to valid objections or to a charge of perjury.

Re·proba·tory, *a.* 1823. [f. as REPROBATE *v.* + -ORY[2].] Reprobative, condemnatory.

Reproduce (rīprŏdiū·s), *v.* 1611. [RE- 5 a.] 1. *trans.* To bring again into existence; to create or form anew; *spec.* in *Biol.* to form (a lost limb or organ) afresh; to generate (new individuals). b. *absol.* To multiply by generation 1894. 2. To produce again by means of combination or change 1666. 3. To bring about again; to effect, exhibit, or present anew; to repeat in some fashion 1688. b. To repeat in a more or less exact copy; to produce a copy of (a work of art, etc.), now *esp.* by means of engraving, photography, or similar processes 1850. c. *intr.* To turn out (well, etc.) in a copy 1891. 4. To present again in writing or print 1860. 5. To create again by a mental effort; to represent clearly to the mind 1869.

1. Man..reproduces his kind; and he vanishes into darkness 1800. b. It reproduces at the rate of hundreds per day 1894. 2. When the vapour of water is condensed it reproduces pure water HUXLEY. 3. b. The rude art of English masons strove to r. the campaniles of Northern Italy FREEMAN. 5. The novels of the eighteenth century enable us to r. the parson of the time with ease 1870. Hence **Reprodu·ceable** *a.* reproducible. **Reprodu·cer**. **Reprodu·cible** *a.* that may be reproduced.

Reproduction (rīprŏdv·kʃən). 1659. [f. prec., after *production.*] 1. The action or process of forming, creating or bringing into existence again. b. The process, on the part of certain animals, of reproducing parts of the organism which have been destroyed or removed. (Now freq. called *regeneration.*) 1727. c. The process of producing new individuals of the same species by some form of generation; the generative production of new animal or vegetable organisms by or from existing ones; also, power of reproducing in this way 1785. d. The action or process of bringing again before the mind in the same form 1800. e. The action or process of repeating in a copy 1883. 2. A copy or counterpart; in recent use *esp.* a copy of a picture or other work of art by means of engraving or some other process 1807.

b. A representation in some form or by some means of the essential features of a thing 1844.

Reproductive (rīprǫ̆dʊ·ktiv), *a.* 1753. [f. REPRODUCE, after *productive.*] **1.** Of the nature of, pertaining to, or effecting, reproduction. **2.** *spec.* in *Biol.* Connected with or effecting generative reproduction in animals or plants 1836. Hence **Reprodu·ctive·ly** *adv.*, **-ness. Reproducti·vity.**

Reproof (rĭprū·f). Also †**repref(e, -preve.** ME. [a. OF. *reprove, -prouve*, f. *reprover* to REPROVE.] †**1.** Shame, disgrace, ignominy, or reproach, adhering or resulting to a person in consequence or by reason of some fact, event, conduct, etc. (Occas. with *a* and *pl.*) –1631. †**2.** Insulting or opprobrious language or action used against a person; insult, contumely, scorn –1596. †**b.** With *a* and *pl.* An instance of this –1597. †**c.** An object of scorn or contempt –1535. **3.** Censure, rebuke, reprimand, reprehension ME. **b.** With *a* and *pl.* An instance of this 1513. **4.** Disproof, refutation. Now *rare* or *Obs.* 1529.

3. A foole despiseth his fathers instruction: but hee that regardeth reproofe, is prudent *Prov.* xv. 5. Those best can bear r., who merit praise POPE. **b.** How have I deserved these reproofs? 1794.

Reprovable (rĭprū·văb'l), *a.* ME. [f. as REPROVE *v.* + -ABLE.] Deserving of reproof or censure; blameworthy, reprehensible.

Reproval (rĭprū·văl). 1846. [f. next. + -AL 2.] The act of reproving; reproof.

Reprove (rĭprū·v), *v.* Also †**repreve, reprieve.** ME. [ad. OF. *reprover* :—L. *reprobare*; see REPROBATE *v.*] †**1.** *trans.* To reject –1604. **2.** To express disapproval of (conduct, actions, beliefs, etc.); to censure, condemn. Now *rare.* ME. **3.** To reprehend, rebuke, blame, chide, or find fault with (a person) ME. **4.** *absol.* To employ reprehension or rebuke ME. †**5.** To disprove; to prove (an idea, statement, etc.) to be false or erroneous –1691. †**b.** To refute or confute (a person) –1601.

2. Envy loves That humor best, which bitterly reproves All states 1615. 3. What if thy Son Prove disobedient, and reprov'd, retort, Wherefore didst thou beget me? MILT. 5. 2 *Hen. VI*, III. i. 40. **b.** Deceived they are, and may be reproved by the instance of fig-trees HOLLAND. Hence **Repro·ver. Repro·vingly** *adv.*

Reps (reps), var. of REP 3. 1867.

Reptant (re·ptănt), *a.* 1657. [ad. L. *reptant-, reptare* to creep.] Creeping, crawling.

Reptation (reptēi·ʃən). 1842. [ad. L. *reptationem.*] The action of creeping or crawling.

Reptile (re·ptəil), *sb.* late ME. [ad. late L., neut. of *reptilis*; see next.] **1.** A creeping or crawling animal; *spec.* an animal belonging to the class REPTILIA. **2.** *transf.* A person of a low, mean, grovelling, or repulsive character 1749.

1. *collect.* God said, let the Waters generate Reptil with Spawn abundant MILT. 2. These reptiles publish..a newspaper COBBETT. Hence **Reptili·ferous** *a.* containing fossil reptiles.

Reptile (re·ptəil), *a.* 1607. [ad. late L. *reptilis*, f. *rept-, repere* to creep + *-ilis* -ILE.] **1. a.** Of animals: Creeping, crawling; reptant. †**b.** Of plants: Repent (*rare*) –1738. **2.** Of the nature of, characterized by, pertaining to, the action of creeping or crawling 1727. **3.** *transf.* Grovelling, mean, low, malignant 1654.

‖**Reptilia** (repti·liă), *sb. pl.* 1627. [L., pl. of *reptile* REPTILE *sb.*] *Zool.* Those animals which creep or crawl; *spec.* in mod. use, that class of vertebrate animals which includes the snakes, lizards, crocodiles, turtles and tortoises.

Reptilian (repti·liăn), *a.* and *sb.* 1846. [See prec. and -AN I. 1.] **A.** *adj.* **1.** Resembling a reptile; having the characteristics of the Reptilia. **b.** Consisting or composed of reptiles 1851. **2.** Of or pertaining to, characteristic of, a reptile or the Reptilia 1849. **3.** *transf.* Mean, malignant, underhand 1859. **B.** *sb.* A member of the class Reptilia 1847.

Republic (rĭpʊ·blik), *sb.* (and *a.*) 1603. [ad. F. *république* or L. *respublica* (abl. *republica*), f. *res* thing, affair + *publicus* PUBLIC.] †**1.** The state, the common weal –1684. **2.** A state in which the supreme power rests in the people and their elected representatives or officers, as opp. to one governed by a king or the like; a commonwealth 1604. **b.** Applied to particular states having this form of constitution 1631. **3.** *transf.* and *fig.* Any community of persons, animals, etc., in which there is a certain equality among the members 1651. **4.** *attrib.* or as *adj.* Of the nature of, characteristic of or pertaining to, a republic or republics; republican. Now *rare* or *Obs.* 1638.

2. The Army..would depose the King, change the Government, and settle a Republick by their own Rules 1674. 3. *The r. of letters*, the collective body of those engaged in literary pursuits; the field of literature itself.

Republican (rĭpʊ·blikăn), *a.* and *sb.* 1659. [f. prec. + -AN I. 1.] **A.** *adj.* **1.** Of or belonging to a republic; having the form or constitution of a republic; characteristic of a republic or republics. **b.** Of persons or parties: Favouring, supporting, or advocating the form of state or government called a republic 1683. **2.** *U.S. politics* (with capital): **a.** Orig. applied to the *Anti-Federal* party, later to the *Democratic-R.* (see DEMOCRATIC 2). **b.** The name of a party opposed to the *Democratic*, formed in 1854 to resist the extension of slave territory, and favouring a liberal interpretation of the constitution, extension of the central power, and a protective tariff. 1806. **3.** *Ornith.* Living, nesting, or breeding, in large flocks or communities, applied esp. to the N. Amer. *r. swallow*, and the S. African *r. grosbeak* or *weaver-bird* 1829.

1. I would have the manners of the people purely and strictly r. *Junius Lett.* *R. calendar*, the calendar adopted for a short time by the French Republic; so *r. era*, dating from 22 Sept. 1792.

B. *sb.* **1.** One who believes in, supports, or prefers a republican form of government 1659. **2.** *U.S. politics.* A member of the Republican party 1782. **3.** *Ornith.* A republican weaver-bird or swallow 1801.

1. *Red r.*, one bent on maintaining extreme r. doctrines, even at the expense of blood 1864.

Republicanism (rĭpʊ·blikăniz'm). 1689. [f. prec. + -ISM.] Republican spirit; attachment to republican principles; republican government or institutions, etc.

Republicanize (rĭpʊ·blikănəiz), *v.* 1797. [ad. F. *républicaniser*; see REPUBLICAN and -IZE.] **1.** *trans.* To render republican in principles or character, convert into republican form. **2.** *intr.* To show republican tendencies 1834.

1. Agents commissioned..to republicanise the country 1871. *transf.* To r. our orthography and our syntax 1858. Hence **Repu·blicaniza·tion.**

Republication (rīpʊblikēi·ʃən). 1730. [RE- 5 a.] **1.** A fresh promulgation *of* a religion or law. **2.** A fresh publication *of* a will 1743. **3.** The action of republishing (a work), or the fact of being republished 1783. **b.** A work published again 1796.

2. The r. of a former will revokes one of a later date BLACKSTONE. **b.** Much of the correspondence would bear r. in a permanent form 1868.

Republish (rīpʊ·bliʃ), *v.* 1625. [RE- 5 a.] *trans.* To publish again.

No after-purchased lands will pass under such devise, unless..the devisor republishes his will BLACKSTONE. Hence **Repu·blisher**, one who republishes.

Repu·diable, *a. rare.* 1611. [See REPUDIATE *v.* and -ABLE.] That may be repudiated.

Repudiate (rĭpiū·diēⁱt), *v.* 1545. [f. L. *repudiat-, repudiare* to divorce, reject, etc., f. *repudium.*] **1.** *trans.* **a.** Of a husband: To put away or cast off (his wife); to divorce, dismiss. **b.** To cast off, disown (a person or thing) 1699. **2.** To reject; to refuse to accept or entertain (a thing), or to have dealings with (a person) 1548. **b.** To reject (opinions, conduct, etc.) with condemnation or abhorrence 1824. **c.** To reject (a charge, etc.) with denial, as being quite unfounded or inapplicable 1865. **3.** To reject as unauthorized or as having no binding force on one 1646. **b.** To refuse to discharge or acknowledge (a debt or other obligation). Chiefly of states disowning a public debt, and freq. *absol.* 1837.

1. **a.** His separation from Terentia, whom he repudiated not long afterward 1716. **b.** To r. and denounce his father DICKENS. 2. If they repudiated the empire placed within their reach, some other power would certainly seize it 1862. **b.** I r. the dreams of Pantheism 1865. 3. He hath obtained with some to r. the books of Moses SIR T. BROWNE. Hence **Repu·diator**, one who repudiates.

Repudiation (rĭpiūdiēⁱ·ʃən). 1545. [ad. L. *repudiationem*; see prec. and -ATION.] The action of repudiating or fact of being repudiated. **1.** Divorce (of a wife). **2.** The action of rejecting, disowning, disavowing, etc. 1848. **b.** *spec.* of a debt 1843. Hence **Repudia·tionist** *U.S.*, one who advocates the r. of a public debt.

Repugn (rĭpiū·n), *v.* late ME. [ad. L. *repugnare*, f. *re-* RE- + *pugnare* to fight.] †**1.** *intr.* To be contradictory or inconsistent; to be contrary *to*, to stand *against* something –1673. **2.** To offer opposition or resistance; to resist; to be recalcitrant; to object. Now *rare.* late ME. **3.** *trans.* To oppose, resist, or contend against (a thing or †person). Now *rare.* late ME. †**4.** To be contrary or opposed to (a thing) –1681. **5.** To affect (a person) with repugnance or aversion. Also *absol.* 1868.

2. To r...against a domineering Ritterdom CARLYLE. 3. The very nature of his Subject..repugns any such Suspicion 1731. Hence †**Repu·gnable** *a.* capable of being repugned; contrary, opposed. **Repu·gner.**

Repugnance (rĭpʊ·gnăns). late ME. [a. F. *répugnance*, or ad. L. *repugnantia*; see prec. and -ANCE.] **1.** Contradiction, inconsistency; contradictory opposition or disagreement of ideas or statements. Also with *a* and *pl.* †**2.** Resistance –1547. †**b.** Opposition or contrariety between or of things –1654. **3.** Strong dislike, distaste, antipathy, or aversion (*to* or *against* a thing). Also *pl.* 1592.

1. In it there is more than the usual r. between the title and the purport 1824. 3. Those national repugnances do not touch me SIR T. BROWNE. A deep r. against ecclesiastical tyranny 1854. So **Repu·gnancy**, in senses 1, 3.

Repugnant (rĭpʊ·gnănt), *a.* late ME. [a. F., or ad. L. *repugnantem, repugnare.*] **1.** Contrary or contradictory (*to*), inconsistent or incompatible (*with*). **2.** Making or offering resistance (*to* a person or thing); opposing, resisting, hostile, antagonistic, refractory 1460. **3.** Distasteful or objectionable *to* one 1777.

1. A condition either impossible, illegal, or r. 1766. The clause was void, because it was r. to the body of the act 1818. 3. Characters in comedy..which involve some notion r. to the moral sense LAMB. Hence **Repu·gnant·ly** *adv.*, **-ness.**

Repullulate (rĭpʊ·liŭlēⁱt), *v.* 1623. [f. ppl. stem of L. *repullulare.*] **1.** *intr.* To bud or sprout again. **2.** *Path.* Of a disease: To start afresh; to recur 1762.

1. Whose branches I fear are withered, never to r. again 1822. Hence **Repullula·tion.**

Repulse (rĭpʊ·ls), *sb.* 1533. [ad. L. *repulsus* or *repulsa*, f. *repuls-, repellere* to REPEL.] **1.** The act of repelling an assailant or hostile force; the fact of being driven back in an engagement or assault 1540. **2.** Refusal (of a request, suit, etc.); denial, rejection, rebuff 1533. **3.** The act of forcing or driving back; the fact of being forced back. Now *rare* or *Obs.* 1578.

1. The r. of the Turks before the City of Zenta 1879. 2. Applications for Places, with their respective Successes or Repulses ADDISON.

Repulse (rĭpʊ·ls), *v.* 1533. [f. L. *repuls-, repellere* to REPEL.] **1.** *trans.* To drive or beat back (an assailant); to repel by force of arms. †**b.** To repel or ward off (an injury) –1606. †**c.** To force back (a thing) –1664. **2.** To repel with denial; to reject, refuse, rebuff 1533. †**3.** To shut out, exclude *from* something –1602. **4.** To affect with repulsion (*rare*) 1845.

1. His valour withstood and repulsed the superior numbers of the Christians GIBBON. 2. Eve Not so repulst..at his feet Fell humble MILT.

Repulsion (rĭpʊ·lʃən). late ME. [ad. late L. *repulsionem.*] †**1.** Repudiation, divorce –1450. **2.** The action of forcing or driving back or away 1547. **b.** *Med.* The action of repelling humours, eruptions, etc., from the affected parts; †a means of effecting this 1725. **3.** *Physics.* The action of one body in repelling another; tendency of bodies to increase their mutual distance. (Opp. to ATTRACTION 5.) 1725. **b.** *transf.* Tendency to separate or put further apart, to introduce division or difference, etc. 1843. **4.** Influence tending to repel one from a person or thing; dislike, aversion 1751.

3. The production of motion by the mutual attractions and repulsions of distant or contiguous masses HERSCHEL. *Capillary r.*, the apparent r. of a liquid caused by capillarity. 4. There are many natures which..seem to start back from each other by some invincible r. JOHNSON.

Repulsive (rĭpʊ·lsiv), *a.* 1611. [f. REPULSE *v.* + -IVE.] **1.** Having the character of repelling; driving or forcing back; returning a sound; resisting moisture, etc. 2. *Physics.* Of the nature of, characterized by, repulsion. (Opp. to ATTRACTIVE.) 1704. 3. Intended or tending to repel by denial, coldness of manner, etc.; repellent 1598. 4. Repellent to the mind; disgusting 1816.

1. R. of his might the weapon stood POPE. The desolation of the spot was r. to his wishes 1791. 3. Mary was not so r. and unsisterly as Elizabeth JANE AUSTEN. 4. There was something so r. about the woman 1866. Hence **Repu·lsive·ly** *adv.*, **-ness.**

†**Repu·re,** *v. rare.* 1606. [RE- 5 a.] *trans.* To purify again -1635.

Reputable (re·piūtăb'l), *a.* 1611. [f. REPUTE *v.* + -ABLE.] †1. Capable of being regarded or taken into account. 2. Having a good reputation; of good repute; estimable, honourable, respectable 1674.

2. His Employment, as a Bookseller, I think a very r. one BENTLEY. The jury were men of fair and r. characters HUME. So **Re·putabi·lity. Re·putableness. Re·putably** *adv.*

Reputation (repiutē·ʃən). late ME. [ad. L. *reputationem* computation, consideration.] 1. The common or general estimate of a person with respect to character or other qualities; the relative estimation or esteem in which a person is held. 2. The condition, quality, or fact, of being highly regarded or esteemed; also, respectability, good report. late ME. b. With *a* and *pl.* Also, †a source of honour and credit; a person of note or distinction. 1653. 3. The honour or credit *of* a particular person or thing; one's good name, good report, or fame in general 1553. b. With *a* and *pl.* Some one's good name, etc. 1712. 4. The estimation, credit, or ascription *of* being or possessing something 1570.

1. Phrases. †*In* (*or of*) *r.*; in later use applied to titles given by courtesy. *To be, have, hold in no, great,* etc., *r.* (now *rare*). *Of no, great, small,* etc. *r.*; Other men, of slender r. SHAKS. 2. But in the company of women of r. I never saw such an idiot GOLDSM. Thus r. is a spur to wit COWPER. b. A great r. for learning THACKERAY. 3. The r. of the state was the first consideration BUCKLE. b. At ev'ry word a r. dies POPE. 4. The r. of Wisedome HOBBES. This very old Woman had the R. of a Witch all over the Country ADDISON.

Reputative (rĭpiū·tătiv), *a.* 1656. [See REPUTE *v.* and -IVE.] Considered or regarded as such; putative. Hence **Repu·tatively** *adv.* by repute.

Repute (rĭpiū·t), *sb.* 1551. [f. the vb.] †1. Opinion, estimate (*rare*) -1711. 2. Reputation of a specified kind 1551. †b. The reputation *of* (having or being) something -1699. †3. Relative estimation; rank or position -1700. 4. Reputation, distinction, honour, credit 1615. 5. The reputation of a particular person. Freq. in phr. *by r.* 1662.

2. Let them be men of good r. and carriage SHAKS. 4. Ceremony which giueth r. vnto things in themselues but triuiall 1615. 5. Omitting nothing that rage can invent to black his r. 1683. I know him well, by r. 1838. Hence †**Repu·teless** *a.* devoid of r.; inglorious. SHAKS.

Repute (rĭpiū·t), *v.* late ME. [ad. F. *réputer*, or L. *reputare*, f. *re-* RE- + *putare* to reckon, think.] 1. *trans.* To consider, think, esteem, reckon (a person or thing) to be, or as being, something 1460. †2. a. To take *for* something; to reckon, account *as* something -1670. b. To consider to be *in* a person or thing -1533. †3. To assign, attribute, impute, or reckon *to* a person -1659. †4. To have or hold (a person) in repute or esteem; to think (well, etc.) of; to value -1665. †5. *intr.* To think (highly, etc.) *of* a thing or person -1698.

1. To thende that they may be reputed and holden sage and wyse CAXTON. Ingratitude, which Rome reputes to be a hainous sinne SHAKS. 2. a. He..is content to r. me for Pious 1670. 3. It was reputed to him for righteousness 1659. Hence **Repu·tedly** *adv.* by repute or common estimation.

Request (rĭkwe·st), *sb.* ME. [a. OF. *requeste* (mod.F. *requête*); see QUEST *sb.* and REQUIRE *v.*] 1. The act, on the part of a specified person, of asking for some favour, service, etc.; the expression of one's desire or wish directly addressed to the person or persons able to gratify it. 2. An act or instance of asking for something; a petition or expressed desire; a writing or document of this nature; also, that which is asked for. late ME. 3. Without article. †a. *To make r.*, to ask or beg -1700. b. The act of asking or fact of being asked (to do something). Now esp. in *by r.*, in response to an expressed wish. 1460. 4. The state, fact, or condition of being asked for or sought after; demand; †vogue, fashion. Chiefly in phr. *in* or *into r.* 1586.

1. At my r...they let her go a drift 1687. Consider, 'tis my first r. POPE. 2. The r. made in the foregoing letter was conceded 1838. 3. a. Then yᵉ king said.., For what doest thou make r.? *Neh.* ii. 4. b. Where one is bound to levy a Fine upon R. 1683. 4. Idiots are still in R. in most of the Courts of Germany ADDISON.

Phr. *Courts of Request(s)*: †a. a former court of record, technically forming part of the king's council, held by the Lord Privy Seal and the Masters of Requests for the relief of persons petitioning the king; also, in later use, the hall at Westminster in which the court was held; b. a local court for the recovery of small debts. †*Master of* (*the*) *Request(s)*, one of the leading officers of the Court of Requests.

Request (rĭkwe·st), *v.* 1533. [ad. OF. *requester*, f. *requeste*; see prec.] 1. With *infin.* To express a wish or desire *to* have, etc.; to beg the favour or permission to be allowed *to do* something 1565. 2. *trans.* To ask, or ask for (something) 1594. 3. To ask (a person) *to do* something 1533. †b. *ellipt.* To ask (a person) to act *against* another, to come or go *to* a place, etc. (*rare*) -1613.

1. He requested to heare Erasmus judgement concerning Luther 1641. 2. To tell the ladies That I r. their presence SHELLEY. 3. Butler requested them to open the gate SCOTT. b. I was requested to supper last night B. JONS. Hence **Reque·ster.**

Requiem (re·kwiĕm). ME. [L., acc. of *requies* 'rest', from the Introit in the Mass for the Dead, 'Requiem eternam dona eis, Domine'.] 1. A special mass for the repose of the souls of the dead. Also *Mass of R.* b. A musical setting of a mass for the dead 1789. 2 Any dirge or solemn chant for the repose of the dead. Chiefly *poet.* 1611. †3. An invitation to rest or repose -1684. 4. Rest, repose, peace, quiet 1616.

1. Behind, four priests, in sable stole, Sung r. for the warrior's soul SCOTT. 4. Repose denies her r. to his name BYRON.

‖ **Requiescat** (rekwiˌe·skæt). 1824. [L., the first word of *requiescat in pace* 'may he rest in peace'.] A prayer for the repose of the dead.

Requiescence (rekwiˌe·sĕns). 1654. [f. L. *requiescere*, after QUIESCENCE.] A state of quiescence, rest, repose.

†**Requi·rable,** *a.* late ME. [orig. a. OF. *requerable*; later, f. REQUIRE *v.* + -ABLE.] Capable of being required; that may properly be asked for -1676.

Require (rĭkwəi·ɹ), *v.* late ME. [a. OF. *requer-*, *requier-*, stem of *requerre* :—L. *requirere*, f. *re-* RE- + *quærere* to ask, seek.] I. †1. *trans.* To ask (a person) a question; to inquire of (a person) *why, if,* etc. (*rare*) -1579. †2. To ask or request (a person) for something -1583. †3. To ask, request, or desire (a person) to do something -1641. 4. To demand of (any one) *to do* something 1751.

3. Defend vs mighty Lord wee thee r. 1584. 4. The government required each county to find its quota of ships FREEMAN.

II. 1. a. To ask for (some thing or person) authoritatively or imperatively, or as a right; to demand, claim, insist on having. late ME. b. To ask for (something) as a favour; to beg, entreat, or request. Now *rare.* late ME. c. *intr.* To make request or demand. late ME. 2. *trans.* To demand as necessary or essential on general principles, or in order to comply with some regulation. late ME. b. To call for or demand as appropriate or suitable in the particular case; to need for some end or purpose. late ME. c. To demand as a necessary help or aid; hence, to stand in need of; to need, want. late ME. d. *It requires*, there is need of 1820. 3. *intr.* To be requisite or necessary. Now *rare.* 1500. 4. To feel, or be under, a necessity *to* do something 1805. b. To fall necessarily, to need, *to be* done, etc. 1842.

1. Oliver Cromwell..requir'd, both of the Soldiers and others, the Oath of Fidelity 1720. b. They go commission'd to r. a Peace DRYDEN. 2. b. An acre of ground will r. ten pound of seed 1759. c. Light labour..Just gave what life required, but gave no more GOLDSM. 4. b. The wicked are miserable because they r. to be punished JOWETT.

†III. *trans.* To seek after, search for; to inquire after; to call upon, summon -1797.

A different Object do these Eyes r. GRAY. Hence **Requi·rer** (now *rare*), one who requires.

Requirement (rĭkwəi·ɹmĕnt). 1530. [-MENT.] †1. The act of requiring; a requisition, request. 2. That which is required; a want, need 1662. b. That which is called for or demanded; a condition which must be complied with 1841.

2. £15,000 would have amply met the requirements of the county 1878. b. The other professors are under more stringent requirements to teach 1868.

Requisite (re·kwizit), *a.* and *sb.* 1470. [ad. L. *requisitus, requirere.*] A. *adj.* Required by circumstances or the nature of things B. *sb.* Something that is requisite 1602.

A. There are..two poyntes r. vnto saluacion MORE. B. The two requisites of efficacy and economy 1880. Hence †**Re·quisite·ly** *adv.*, **-ness.**

Requisition (rekwizi·ʃən), *sb.* 1503. [a. F. *réquisition*, or ad. L. *requisitionem.*] 1. a. The action of requiring; a demand made by a person. b. A requirement, necessary condition 1836. 2. The (*or* an) action of formally requiring one to perform some action, discharge some duty, etc.; †the fact of being so called upon. Also, a written demand of this nature. 1553. 3. The action of requiring a certain amount or number of anything to be furnished; a demand or order of this nature, *esp.* one made upon a town, district, etc., to furnish or supply anything required for military purposes 1776. 4. The state or condition of being called or pressed into service or use 1796.

1. a. I obey your r., and inquire the purpose of it 1797. 2. There can be no ballot except on a r. signed by nine proprietors 1840. 3. After the battle of Jena.. the r. upon humbled Prussia was more than a hundred millions of francs 1860. 4. Phr. *To put* (*place, call*) *in* (or *into*) *r.* (*To be*) *in* (constant, etc.) *r.*; The guillotine was..in constant r. 1817. Hence **Requisi·tionist,** one who makes a r.

Requisition (rekwizi·ʃən), *v.* 1837. [f. prec.] 1. *trans.* a. To require (anything) to be furnished for military purposes; to put in requisition. b. To make demands upon (a town, etc.) 1870. 2. To make requisition for; to demand, call for, request to have or get 1874. b. To call in for some purpose 1887.

1. a. To r. such horses as might be needed 1870. b. When it is intended to r. a village or town, all the outlets should be guarded 1897. 2. b. The military had to be requisitioned 1887.

Requisitor (rĭkwi·zitǫɹ). *rare.* 1790. [f. L. *requisit-*, *requirere* + -OR 2 c.] One who makes a requisition or requisitions.

Requisitory (rĭkwi·zitəri), *sb. rare.* 1824. [ad. F. *réquisitoire*; cf. next.] In French legal practice, the demand made by a public prosecutor for the punishment of the accused on the charges stated.

Requisitory (rĭkwi·zitəri), *a. rare.* 1447. [ad. med.L. *requisitorius* (see REQUISITE and -ORY [2]).] a. Of the nature of, expressing or conveying, a request or requisition. b. Capable of making a requisition 1825.

Requitable (rĭkwəi·tăb'l), *a.* Now *rare* or *Obs.* 1610. [f. REQUITE *v.* + -ABLE.] Capable of being requited.

Requital (rĭkwəi·tăl). 1579. [f. REQUITE *v.* + -AL 2.] 1. Return for some service, kindness, etc.; recompense or reward for action or exertion. b. With *a* and *pl.* A return or repayment (*for* or *of* something) 1591. 2. Return of an injury, etc.; retaliation, revenge 1582.

1. Whose bold perseverance at length reap'd r. 1815. Phr. *In* (rarely †*for*) *r.* (*of*); In r. whereof, henceforth, carry your letters your selfe SHAKS. 2. In r. of that shameful act of perfidy 1885.

Requite (rĭkwəi·t), *v.* 1529. [f. RE- + *quite*, var. of QUIT *v.*] 1. *trans.* To repay, make return for, reward (a kindness, service, etc.). b. To make retaliation or return for, to avenge (a wrong, injury, etc.) 1555. 2. To repay (a person) for some service, etc. 1560. b. To pay back, make retaliation on (a person) for some injury, etc. 1590. †3. To repay with the like; to return (a visit) -1648. 4. To make return of; to give or do in return *for* something 1547. †5. To take the place of, make up for, to counterbalance or compensate -1697.

1. Requiting years of care with contumely SHELLEY. b. *absol.* The Lord God of recompenses shall surely r. *Jer.* li. 56. 2. I am so poore to r. you, you must looke for nothing but thankes of me 1611. b. Hee payes vs shot for shot; Well, wee shall r. him 1627.

4. In case of *talio*, or requiting like for like 1631. Hence **Requi·tement**, requital, revenge. **Requi·ter.**

Rere-, comb. form; see REAR-.

Re·re-brace. *Obs.* exc. *Hist.* ME. [a. AF. **rerebras*, f. *rere-* back + *bras* arm.] Armour for the upper arm from the shoulder to the elbow (orig. a plate protecting the back of the arm only).

Re·re-do:rter. *rare.* 1450. [RERE-.] A privy situated at the back of the dormitory in a convent or monastery.

Reredos (rīə·ɹdǫs). late ME. [a. AF. **reredos*, f. *rere-* RERE- + *dos* back.] 1. *Eccl.* a. An ornamental facing or screen of stone or wood covering the wall at the back of an altar. b. A choir-screen 1446. †2. A hanging of velvet or silk for covering the wall at the back of an altar –1552. 3. The brick or stone back of a fire-place or open hearth; an iron plate forming a fire-back. *Obs.* exc. *arch.* late ME.

Re·re-su:pper. *Obs.* exc. *arch.* ME. [a. AF. *rere-super*; see RERE- and SUPPER.] A supper (usu. of a sumptuous nature) following upon the usual evening meal, and thus coming very late at night.

Guilty of the enormity of rere-suppers SCOTT.

†**Resa·lgar.** late ME. [ad. Arab. *rahj al-ghār* (see REALGAR).] Realgar, disulphide of arsenic –1610.

Resalute (rīsălʼū·t), *v.* Now *rare.* 1493. [ad. L. *resalutare*, or (in sense 2) f. RE- 5 a + SALUTE *v.*] 1. *trans.* To salute in return. 2. To salute again or anew 1586.

Resa·rcelée, Resa·rcelled, *a. Her.* 1586. [ad. F. *recercelé*, f. *re-* + *cercelé* SARCELLY.] Applied to a cross surcharged with another of a different colour.

Rescind (rīsi·nd), *v.* 1637. [ad. L. *rescindere*, f. *re-* RE- + *scindere* to split, divide.] 1. *trans.* To cut off, take away, remove. Chiefly *fig.* †2. To cut through, sever. JER. TAYLOR. 3. To abrogate, annul, repeal 1637.

1. His unnecessary expences are rescinded, his superfluous cut off PRYNNE. 3. It required a particular Act of Parliament to r. this bye-law 1776. The vendor shall have the power of rescinding the contract 1846. Hence **Resci·ndable** *a.* **Resci·ndment.**

Rescission (rīsi·ʒən). 1611. [ad. late L. *rescissionem*, f. *rescindere* to RESCIND.] †1. The action of cutting off (*rare*) –1626. 2. The action of annulling or abrogating 1651.

2. A thing's being found damaged, or sold at above double the just value, is a good cause of r. 1727.

Rescissory (rīsi·səri), *a.* 1605. [ad. late L. *rescissorius*, f. *resciss-*, *rescindere.*] Of the nature of, or having the effect of, rescinding or revoking; connected with, or characterized by, rescission.

Next they fell upon forming an Act R., whereby former Acts..should be nulled 1654.

†**Rescou·nter**, *sb.* 1543. [ad. It. *riscontro* comparison, balancing, f. *ri-* RE- + *scontro* encounter.] 1. Encounter, hostile meeting (*rare*). 2. Balancing of contra-accounts; settlement or payment of differences on accounts, in later use *spec.* on the Stock Exchange –1796. 3. An engagement to pay the sum due on a balance of accounts –1682. So †**Rescou·nter** *v. intr.* to encounter *with* an enemy; *trans.* to balance or settle in the way of business.

†**Rescous**, *sb.* ME. [a. OF. *rescous(s)e*, f. *rescourre* to RESCUE.] 1. Rescue, assistance, aid –1602. 2. *Law.* = RESCUE *sb.* 2. –1768. So **Rescous** *v. trans.* to rescue –1625.

Rescribe (rīskrəi·b), *v.* 1462. [ad. L. *rescribere*, f. *re-* RE- + *scribere* to write.] †1. To write back, write in reply –1726. 2. To write again or anew; to rewrite. Now *rare.* 1565.

Rescript (rī·skript). 1528. [ad. L. *rescriptum*, *rescribere* to RESCRIBE.] 1. a. A decretal epistle from the Pope in reply to some question or difficulty referred to him; also, any Papal decision, decree, or edict. b. The reply sent by a Roman emperor to a magistrate or other person consulting him on a doubtful point of law or as to the action to be taken in particular circumstances 1589. 2. Any edict, decree, order, or formal announcement made by a ruler or governing body, or having an official character 1545. 3. Something written over again; a re-writing 1820. b. *U.S. Law.* A duplicate or counterpart 1843. 4. A palimpsest writing 1817.

1. The summes of money which the Pope receiveth for first fruits,..Indulgences, Bulls,..Rescrips,..cannot be counted 1635. 3. I wrote it three times..subduing the phrases at every r. C. BRONTË.

†**Rescri·ption.** 1588. [a. F., or ad. late L. *rescriptionem.*] 1. A rewriting, writing over again –1697. 2. The action of replying in writing; a written reply –1657. 3. A promissory note issued by a Government –1798.

Re·scuable, *a. rare.* 1611. [f. RESCUE *v.* + -ABLE.] Capable of being rescued.

Rescue (re·skiu), *sb.* late ME. [f. the vb., superseding RESCOUS.] 1. The (*or* an) act of rescuing (esp. persons) from enemies, saving from danger or destruction, etc.; succour, deliverance. 2. *Law.* The forcible taking of a person or goods out of legal custody; forcible recovery (by the owner) of goods distrained 1450. b. A person rescued from custody 1888.

1. R. would be out of the question, should the climber go over the edge TYNDALL. 2. Precautions.. justifiable..from the apprehensions so generally entertained of an expected r. SCOTT.

attrib. esp. in sense 'directed to, aiming at, the raising of falling or degraded women', as *r. home, work, worker.* **R.-bid** (Bridge), a bid made to get one's partner out of a difficult situation.

Rescue (re·skiu), *v.* ME. [a. OF. *rescou-*, stem of *rescourre*, *-corre* (F. *recourre*):—Rom. **re-excutere*; see RE- and EXCUSS *v.*] 1. *trans.* To deliver (a person) from the attack of, or out of the hands of, assailants or enemies. b. To liberate by unlawful force from legal custody 1600. 2. To deliver (a castle, town, etc.) from siege ME. b. To recover, take back by force 1450. 3. To deliver or save (a person or thing) *from* some evil or harm ME. 4. *refl.* To save oneself in some respect ME. 5. *absol.* To afford deliverance or safety (*rare*). late ME.

1. He took..many horse and arms, and rescued all their prisoners 1643. 2. Rescu'd is Orleance from the English Wolves SHAKS. 3. To r. Mankind from Tyranny and Oppression 1718. Hence **Re·scuer.**

Re·scusser. *rare.* 1632. [f. RESCOUS *v.* + -ER 1.] *Law.* One who makes a rescue.

Research (rīsɔ̄·ɹtʃ), *sb.* 1577. [ad. obs. F. *recerche* (mod.F. *recherche*); see RE- and SEARCH *sb.*] 1. The act of searching (closely or carefully) *for* or *after* a specified thing or person. 2. An investigation directed to the discovery of some fact by careful study of a subject; a course of critical or scientific inquiry. Freq. in *pl.* 1639. b. Without article: Investigation, inquiry into things. Also, habitude of carrying out such investigation. 1694.

1. Researches after gold and other precious metals 1889. 2. Cuvier was usually engaged for seven hours daily in his scientific researches 1850. b. A writer of painstaking r. 1861. *attrib.*, as *r. degree, student, work.* Hence **Resea·rchful** *a.* devoted to, characterized by, replete with, r.

Research (rīsɔ̄·ɹtʃ), *v.* 1593. [ad. obs. F. *recercher* (mod.F. *rechercher*); see RE- and SEARCH *v.*] a. *trans.* To search into (a matter or subject); to investigate or study closely. Now *rare* or *Obs.* b. *intr.* To make researches; to pursue a course of research 1801.

b. On these three subjects he is directed to read and r.—corn-laws, finance, tythes SOUTHEY.

Researcher (rīsɔ̄·ɹtʃəɹ). 1615. [f. prec. + -ER 1.] One who researches; an investigator, inquirer. b. One who devotes himself to scientific or literary research 1883. c. *Psychical R.*, a member of the Society for Psychical Research; one who investigates psychical phenomena.

Resect (rīse·kt), *v.* 1653. [f. L. *resect-*, *resecare* to cut off, f. *re-* RE- + *secare* to cut.] †1. *trans.* To cut off or away; to remove –1686. 2. *Surg.* To cut or pare down; to remove a portion of (bone, cartilage, nerve, etc.) in this way; to cut out (in part) 1846.

Resection (rīse·kʃən). 1611. [ad. L. *resectionem*; see prec.] †1. The action of cutting off or away –1662. 2. *Surg.* The operation of cutting or paring away a portion of bone, etc., esp. the articular ends of bones 1775.

2. Compound fracture about the elbow-joint, which rendered primary r. of the articulation necessary.

‖**Reseda.** 1753. [L., acc. to Pliny f. the imper. of *resedare* to assuage, allay (the words *reseda morbis* having been used as a charm when applying the plant to the reduction of tumours).] 1. (rīsī·dă) *Bot.* An extensive genus of herbaceous plants (typical of the *Resedaceæ*); including Mignonette (*R. odorata*) and Dyer's Weed (*R. luteola*). 2. (re·zĕdă, or as F. *rezeda*) A pale green colour similar to that of mignonette 1883.

Reseize (rīsī·z), *v.* late ME. [ad. OF. *resaisir*; see RE- and SEIZE *v.*] †1. *trans.* To invest or endow (a person) again *with*, put again in possession *of*, something; to replace *in*, or restore to, a former position or dignity –1647. 2. To seize, take hold or possession of (some thing or person) again 1567. Hence **Resei·zer.** So †**Resei·zure**, the act of seizing or taking back again –1683.

†**Rese·mblable**, *a.* late ME. [a. OF.; see RESEMBLE *v.* and -ABLE.] Capable of being compared or likened; comparable, similar (*to* some person or thing); like –1665.

Resemblance (rīze·mblăns). late ME. [a. AF.; see RESEMBLE *v.* and -ANCE.] 1. The quality of being like or similar; likeness or similarity in any respect; the fact of some likeness existing or being present. 2. The external appearance, or characteristic features, peculiar to an individual or a class of persons or things. late ME. †3. A symbol or figure *of* something –1669. †b. A simile or comparison; a thing compared to another –1694. 4. A likeness, image, representation or reproduction of some person or thing. late ME. †b. An appearance or show *of* some quality; a likelihood or probability –1603.

1. A vague comparison between two things which have little or no r. to each other *Junius Lett.* 2. His r. being not like the Duke SHAKS. A garden.. which..had the r. of a vast mosaic DISRAELI. 4. Fairest r. of thy Maker faire MILT.

Resemblant (rīze·mblănt), *a.* Now *rare.* late ME. [a. OF., pres. pple. of *resembler.*] 1. Similar, having resemblance or likeness, *to* something. 2. Characterized by resemblance or similarity; similar, like 1581. 3. Aiming at the production of resemblances 1870.

3. The object of the great R. Arts is..to resemble as closely as possible RUSKIN.

Resemble (rīze·mb'l), *v.*[1] ME. [ad. OF. *resembler*, f. *re-* RE- + *sembler*:—L. *similare*, *simulare*, f. *similis* like.] 1. *trans.* To be like, to have likeness or similarity to, to have some feature or property in common with (another person or thing). 2. To compare or liken (a person or thing) *to* another. Now *arch.* late ME. †b. To compare together, or *with* another thing –1673. †3. To represent, depict, make an image or likeness of (a person or thing); to figure, typify –1705. 4. To make like *to* some person or thing. Also in *pa. pple.*, made like, similar. Now *rare.* 1460. †5. *intr.* To seem, appear –1510. 6. To be like in some respect *to* another person or thing. Now *rare.* late ME. b. To have mutual likeness; to be like or similar to each other 1751.

1. Cunning resembles Prudence, as an Ape resembles a Man 1718. 2. Thus Solomon resembles the Nose of his Beloved to the Tower of Libanon ADDISON. 4. I hope we are resembled, Vowing our loves to equal death and life MARLOWE. 6. b. In one feature or two, nations r., which are placed at stages considerably remote 1817. Hence **Rese·mbler.** †**Rese·mblingly** *adv.*

†**Rese·mble**, *v.*[2] 1450. [f. RE- + *semble*, aphet. var. of ASSEMBLE *v.*] 1. *intr.* To assemble, collect, come together –1596. 2. *trans.* To bring together or collect –1494.

Resent (rīze·nt), *v.* 1605. [ad. F. *ressentir*, f. L. *re-* RE- + *sentire* to feel.] †I. 1. *refl.* [= F. *se ressentir.*] To have a feeling *of* pain; to feel pain or distress; to regret, repent –1654. 2. *trans.* To feel (something) as a cause of depression or sorrow; to feel deeply or sharply –1728. b. To repent, regret (an action) –1676. 3. To feel or experience (joy, sorrow, pain, etc.) –1734. 4. *fig.* To smell out, perceive –1665. II. †1. *refl.* To express one's resentment; to avenge oneself –1656. 2. *trans.* To feel injured or insulted by (some act or conduct on the part of another); to show displeasure or anger at (some wrong, injury, etc. sustained) 1628. †3. To take or receive in a certain way or with certain feelings; to take *well* or *ill* –1734. †4. To appreciate, be sensible of, feel grateful for (a kindness, favour, etc.); to remember with gratitude –1765.

2. It is best to be plain at once—r. my refusal as

you will SCOTT. 3. It was mighty well resented and approved of PEPYS. 4. If she gratefully resented that small thing for the sake of the hand it came from 1702.

†III. 1. To give forth, exhale (a perfume), to have an odour or suggestion of, to show traces of (some quality, etc.) *rare* –1633. 2. To savour *of*, have a touch or taste *of* (a person or thing) –1826.

2. Some works resent too much of their authour FULLER. Hence **Rese·nter**, †one who has a feeling or appreciation of something; one who feels or shows resentment (*rare*).

Rese·ntful, *a.* 1656. [f. prec. + -FUL.] Full of, inspired by, resentment 1656.

A look of r. mortification 1782. Hence **Rese·ntful-ly** *adv.*, **-ness.**

†Rese·ntiment. *rare.* 1595. [a. obs. F., f. *resentir* RESENT *v.*] = RESENTMENT –1661.

†Rese·ntive, *a.* 1662. [f. RESENT *v.* + -IVE.] Apt or inclined to resent –1735.

Resentment (rĭze·ntmĕnt). 1619. [ad. F. *ressentiment*, f. *ressentir* RESENT *v.*] 1. An indignant sense *of* injury or insult received, or *of* wrong or affront done to some person or thing to which one is attached. Now *rare.* 2. A strong feeling of ill-will or anger against the author or authors of a wrong or affront; the manifestation of such feeling against the cause of it. Also in *pl.* 1634. †3. A feeling or sense *of* some trouble, or loss; *of* something enjoyed, etc. –1698. †4. A feeling or emotion of any kind. Also without article. –1748. †5. Feeling or sensation; susceptibility to sensuous or mental impressions –1704. †6. An appreciation or understanding *of* something –1678. †b. Interest in a thing; regard *for*, care *of*, something (*rare*) –1751. †7. Grateful appreciation or acknowledgement (*of* a service, kindness, etc.); a feeling or expression of gratitude –1849. †8. A particular idea, opinion, or view *of* or *upon* something (*rare*) –1748.

2. The shocked conscience of mankind..was already kindling into r. FROUDE. 3. Hearts being ever tender in the ressentment of calamities 1632. 4. Deep impressions, and ravishing refreshing resentments 1658.

†Reserate, *v.* 1597. [f. L. *reserat-*, *reserare* to unbar, f. *re-* RE- 2 d + *sera* bar, bolt.] *trans.* To open up –1710. So **†Resera·tion,** the action of opening; that which opens up.

Reservation (rezəɹvēⁱ·ʃən). late ME. [a. OF., or ad. L. *reservationem*, f. *reservare.*] I. 1. *Eccl.* a. The action of reserving as a tithe. b. The action, on the part of the Pope, of reserving to himself the right of nomination to a vacant benefice, or the fact of this being reserved to him by some rule or constitution of the Church. late ME. 2. *Law.* The action or fact of reserving or retaining for oneself some right or interest in property which is being conveyed to another; an instance of this; a right or interest so retained; the clause or part of a deed by which something is thus reserved 1487. 3. The action or fact of reserving (for oneself or another) some right, power, privilege, etc.; a right, etc., thus reserved 1605. b. *U.S.* A tract of land set apart by Government for some special purpose, or for the exclusive use of certain persons, esp. of a native tribe 1789. 4. An expressed or tacit limitation or exception made with regard to something; the action of making an exception of this kind 1614. †5. The action of keeping back or concealing from others; something thus kept back or concealed; a secret; a deceptive answer or excuse –1645. †b. The fact or habit of being reticent; reservedness (*rare*) –1674.

2. The *reddendum* or r., whereby the grantor doth create or reserve some new thing to himself out of what he had before granted BLACKSTONE. 3. *Lear* II. iv. 255. c. The action or fact of engaging seats, rooms, places, etc. in advance; a seat or room reserved thus (*U.S.*) 1907. 4. Phr. *Mental r.*, a qualification tacitly introduced in making a statement, taking an oath, etc., when it is thought inexpedient or unnecessary to speak or dissent openly; also, the fact or practice of making such qualifications; This looks very much like lying, but..it is speaking the truth under a..mental r. 1888. 5. To make some reseruation of your wrongs *All's Well* II. iii. 260.

II. 1. *Eccl.* The action or practice of retaining or preserving for some purpose a portion of the eucharistic elements (esp. the bread) after the celebration of the sacrament; †also, a part of the elements thus reserved 1551. †2. The action or fact of keeping back a matter for further action or later decision –1659. †b. The action or fact of keeping back something from others or for one's own use –1634.

†Rese·rvatory. 1662. [ad. med.L. *reservatorium* store-house, f. *reservat-*, *reservare*; see RESERVE *v.* and -ORY[1].] 1. A receptacle for food; a cupboard; a store-room or store-house –1807. 2. A vessel for liquids (*rare*) –1720. 3. A reservoir for water, etc. –1790. b. A receptacle for fluids in animals or plants –1731.

Reserve (rĭzɔ̄·ɹv), *sb.* 1644. [a. F. *réserve*, f. *réserver* to RESERVE.] I. 1. Something stored up, kept back, or relied upon, for future use or advantage; a store or stock; an extra quantity 1658. b. The amount of capital kept on hand by a banker, insurance company, etc., in order to meet ordinary or probable demands. Also *pl.* 1866. 2. *Mil.* a. *pl.* Those troops or portions of an army which are withheld from action in order to serve as a reinforcement, or, in case of retreat, as cover to the main body. Also *sing.* in same sense. 1648. b. That portion of the military or naval forces of a state which is maintained as a further means of defence in addition to the regular army and navy, and is liable to be called out in time of war or emergency; also, in recent use, a member of this force, a reservist 1866. †3. a. A certain amount *of* some quality, feeling, etc., still retained or remaining (*rare*) –1714. b. A place or thing in which something is preserved or stored –1659. c. A thing or means to which one may have recourse; a refuge (*rare*) –1715.

1. There are three reserves of ammunition 1876. b. The banker does not lend all he receives. The difference is called his r. 1880. 3. a. A r. of Puerility we have not shaken off from School SIR T. BROWNE.

Phr. *In r.*, kept or remaining unutilized; still available. *Of r.* (after F. *armée* or *corps de réserve*), acting as, or destined for, a support or recourse; chiefly *Mil.* in *army, body*, or *corps of r.*

II. 1. Something reserved or set apart for some reason or purpose 1649. b. A district or place set apart for some particular use, or assigned to certain persons 1853. c. A distinction given to an exhibit at a show, indicating that it will receive a prize in the event of another being disqualified 1867. 2. An expressed limitation, exception, or restriction made concerning something. Now *rare.* 1654. b. A mental limitation or qualification of the adherence given to some principle, article of belief, etc. 1679. 3. *techn.* a. A preparation used to prevent or modify the action of colouring matter upon textile fabrics; a resist 1836. b. A preparation used for similar purposes in electroplating 1873.

1. A r. of Corn rent paid to Secular Priests, or to the Religious 1695. c. The Duke of York had a r. for a red-polled cow 1895. 2. How many reserves must be made in praising either his poetry, or his criticism! M. ARNOLD. Phr. *Without r.*, without limitation or restriction of any kind (in mod. use chiefly with ref. to sales by auction.)

III. 1. Self-restraint; self-control; imposition of some limit to one's action 1665. b. Reticence; also *spec.* in casuistry, an intentional suppression of truth in cases where it might lead to inconvenience 1704. c. Avoidance of too great familiarity; want of cordiality or open friendliness 1721. †2. An instance of keeping some knowledge from another person; a fact or item of information kept back or disguised; a secret –1805.

1. b. A furious critic, whose age, rank, or fortune gives him confidence to speak without r. JOHNSON. c. This frigid r. somewhat disgusted me JOHNSON. 2. Consult Mr. Grattan, with whom I have no reserves, and I wish you to have none BURKE.

IV. *attrib.* or as *adj.* Kept in reserve, constituting a reserve 1719.

The r. ammunition of a regiment 1876. *R. price*, the price set upon an object to be sold, which is the lowest that will be accepted by the seller.

Reserve (rĭzɔ̄·ɹv), *v.* ME. [ad. OF. *reserver*, ad. L. *reservare*, f. *re-* RE- + *servare* to keep, save.] 1. *trans.* To keep for future use or enjoyment; to store up *for* some time or occasion; to refrain from using or enjoying at once. b. To keep back or hold over to a later time or place or for further treatment; to postpone the discussion, decision, or declaration of (a matter). late ME. c. *refl.* To keep (oneself) in reserve *for* some occasion, etc. 1605. 2. To retain as one's own; to keep *to* or *for* oneself. late ME. †b. To keep (a matter) from the knowledge of others –1738. 3. To set apart, keep (†*to* or) *for* another. late ME. 4. *Eccl.* To set apart, keep back (cases for absolution) to be dealt with by a superior authority. late ME. 5. a. To retain or secure (some right or profit) for oneself or another by formal stipulation; †to provide or stipulate *that.* (Chiefly in legal use.) late ME. b. To set apart (a portion of rent) for payment *in* corn, etc. 1575. 6. To set (a thing) apart for some purpose or with some end in view; to keep *for* some use. late ME. b. To set (a person) apart *for* some fate, destiny, end, etc. Now *rare.* late ME. †c. To make an exception of (a thing or person); to exempt (a person) *from* something –1806. 7. To retain or preserve alive; to exempt from slaughter; to save *from* death. Now *rare.* late ME. †8. To keep or maintain (a person or thing) in a certain state or condition –1633. †9. To keep in store; to lay up as a store or stock; to deposit for preservation –1692. †b. To keep, preserve (things liable to decay or destruction) –1750. †10. a. To keep in one's possession –1604. b. To keep, preserve (antiquities, relics, etc.) –1708. 11. *Eccl.* To retain or preserve (a portion of the consecrated species) for certain purposes 1548. †12. To retain or preserve, to continue to have, possess, or show (a characteristic, quality, mark, etc.) –1726.

1. I shall r. the rest of my threatnings till further provocation SWIFT. b. Take each mans censure; but reserue thy iudgement SHAKS. 2. Man over men He made not Lord; such title to himself Reserving MILT. 3. The Fader..for the thirde, Cordeilla, reserued no thynge 1494. This discovery was reserved to our times BERKELEY. 6. Euery Printer shall reserue one Book..and shall..deliuer it to the Officer.. to be sent to the Librarie at Oxford 1637. b. We are decreed, Reserv'd and destin'd to Eternal woe MILT. 7. *M. for M.* v. i. 472. 10. a. *Sonn.* xxxii.

Reserved (rĭzɔ̄·ɹvd), *ppl. a.* 1474. [f. RESERVE *v.*] †1. Excepted. Chiefly in prep. use: With the exception of, except, save. –1591. 2. Averse to showing familiarity or to open expression of thought or feeling; cold or distant; reticent, uncommunicative 1601. 3. Restrained or restricted in some way 1654. 4. Set or kept apart; specially retained for some person or purpose 1616.

2. All her deseruing Is a reserued honestie SHAKS. As a statesman he was r., seldom showing his own thoughts FROUDE. 4. *R. sacrament*: see 11 above and RESERVATION II. 1. *R. seats*, those seats at a public entertainment or meeting which may be specially engaged beforehand. *R. list*, a list of naval officers removed from active service but liable to be called out in the event of their being required. So *r. officer, pay*, etc. Hence **Rese·rved·ly** *adv.*, **-ness.**

Reservist (rĭzɔ̄·ɹvist). 1876. [f. RESERVE *sb.* + -IST; cf. F. *réserviste.*] One who belongs to or serves in the reserve forces.

Reservoir (re·zəɹvwāɹ), *sb.* 1690. [a. F. *réservoir*, f. *réserver* to RESERVE + *-oir*; see -ORY[1].] 1. A receptacle (of earthwork, masonry, etc.) specially constructed to contain and store a large supply of water for ordinary uses 1705. b. A place or area in which water naturally collects in large quantities 1730. c. *fig.* A place where something is collected or tends to collect 1690. 2. A part of an animal or plant in which some fluid or secretion is collected or retained 1727. b. A part of some apparatus in which a fluid or liquid is contained 1784. 3. Any receptacle for fluids (or vapours) 1774. †b. A receptacle or repository for things or articles –1836. c. A store or collection, a reserve supply, *of* something 1784.

1. c. Rome—the r., as Tacitus says, into which all things infamous and shameful flowed 1882. 3. c. The labours of others have raised for us an immense r. of important facts DICKENS. Hence **Re·servoir** *v. trans.* to store up, keep in or as in a r.

Reset (rĭse·t), *sb.*[1] ME. [a. OF. *recet* :— L. *receptum.*] †1. The opportunity, advantage, privilege, etc., of being received or sheltered in a place; refuge, shelter, succour –1685. †b. A place of reception, refuge, or accommodation; an abode, haunt, usual retreat –1582. 2. *Sc. Law.* a. Reception or shelter given to another, *spec.* to a thief, criminal, or proscribed person; the act or practice of receiving or harbouring such persons. Now *arch.* 1456. b. The act or practice of receiving stolen goods 1768.

Reset (rī·set, rīse·t), *sb.*[2] 1847. [f. RESET

v.[2]] The act of resetting; matter set up again in type.

Reset (rĭse·t), *v.*[1] ME. [ad. OF. *receter, recetter* :—L. *receptare*, f. *recept-, recipere.*] 1. *trans.* To harbour (a person, *esp.* an offender against the law). Now *arch.* (in later use *Sc.*). 2. *Sc. Law.* To receive (stolen goods) from a thief with intent to cover or profit by the theft 1609.

1. You knew, that,..you were prohibited to r., supply, or intercommune with this..traitor SCOTT.

Reset (rīse·t), *v.*[2] 1655. [RE- 5 a.] *trans.* To set again; esp. *Typog.* to set up, compose (type) again.

Resetter (rĭse·təɹ). late ME. [a. OF. *recetour, -eur*; see RESET *v.*[1] and -ER.[1]] †a. A harbourer of criminals, thieves, etc. –1632. b. A receiver of stolen goods. Now *Sc.* 1440.

†**Re·siance.** 1577. [ad. obs. F. *reseance*; see next and -ANCE.] Abode, residence –1632. So †Re·siancy –1673.

Resiant (re·ziănt), *a.* and *sb.* late ME. [a. OF. *reseant*, pr. pple. of *reseoir* :—L. *residere*; see next]. A. *adj.* †1. *predic.*, or placed after the sb. Resident; abiding –1752. †2. a. Of residence or stay. b. = RESIDENT *a.* 2. (*rare*) –1600. B. *sb.* A resident. Now *rare.* late ME.

A. 1. A King..that hath the Spirit of the liuing God r. in him 1624.

Reside (rĭzəi·d), *v.*[1] 1456. [ad. F. *résider* or L. *residere* to remain behind, rest, f. *re-* RE- + *sedere* to sit.] †1. *intr.* To settle; to take up one's abode or station (*rare*) –1657. 2. To dwell permanently or for a considerable time, to have one's settled or usual abode, to live, *in* or *at* a particular place 1578. b. To live (at a place) for the discharge of official duties; to be 'in residence' 1456. 3. a. Of power, rights: To rest or be vested *in* a person 1607. b. Of qualities, attributes, etc.: To be present or inherent *in* a person or thing 1611. c. To be physically present *in* a thing. Now *rare.* 1620. †4. Of things: To lie, be placed, somewhere (*rare*) –1742.

2. There at the moated-Grange recides this deiected Mariana SHAKS. 3. a. Power—physical power—resides in the people BERKELEY. b. Cogitation Resides not in that man, that do's not thinke SHAKS. Hence **Resi·der**, a resident.

†**Resi·de**, *v.*[2] 1586. [ad. L. *residere*, f. *re-* RE- + *sidere* to sink.] *intr.* To sink down; to settle down as a deposit –1702.

Residence[1] (re·zidĕns). late ME. [a. F. *résidence*, ad. L. *residentia*; see RESIDE *v.*[1] and -ENCE.] 1. a. *To have* (†*hold, keep, make*) *one's r.*, to have one's usual dwelling-place or abode; to reside. *To take up one's r.*, to establish oneself; to settle. b. The circumstance or fact of having one's permanent or usual abode in or at a certain place; the fact of residing or being resident 1480. 2. The fact of living or staying regularly at or in some place for the discharge of special duties, or to comply with some regulation; also, the period during which such stay is required of a person. Now freq. in phr. *in r.* late ME. 3. The place where a person resides; his dwelling-place; the abode *of* a person (esp. one of some rank or distinction) 1595. b. A dwelling, *esp.* one of a superior kind; a mansion 1603. 4. *fig.* The (*or* a) seat *of* power, liberty, etc. 1642. 5. The time during which a person resides in or at a place 1683. b. A period of residing; a stay 1686.

1. The arts and sciences took up their r...at Rome 1788. b. *Haml.* II. ii. 343. 2. The Canon in R...gave orders that the Rolls..should be thrown into the fire 1892. At Oxford r. will not be resumed until the end of next week 1896. 3. Not many furlongs thence Is your Fathers r. MILT. b. A r. was assigned him at Bithur 1844. 4. The r. of the supreme authority,..the..Junta SCOTT.

†**Residence.**[2] 1541. [f. L. *residere* RESIDE *v.*[2]; see -ENCE.] That which settles as a deposit; the residuum or deposit left after any chemical process –1685.

Residency (re·zidĕnsi). 1579. [f. as RESIDENCE[1]; see -ENCY.] †1. = RESIDENCE[1] –1670. 2. The official residence of a representative of the Governor-general (formerly of the East India Company) at an Indian native court 1800. 3. An administrative division in the Dutch East Indies 1814.

Resident (re·zidĕnt), *a.* and *sb.*[1] late ME. [ad. L. *residentem, residere* RESIDE *v.*[1]] A. *adj.* 1. Resting, dwelling, or having an abode in a place. b. Of animals or birds: Non-migratory 1828. 2. Staying in or at a place in discharge of some duty or in compliance with some regulation. late ME. 3. Of qualities, etc.: Abiding, inherent, prevalent, established 1525. †4. Of things: Situated, lying –1695. †b. Remaining still; firm, abiding –1653.

1. He considered r. country gentlemen the greatest blessing of this country 1817. 2. Mr. Wachsell, the r. surgeon 1803. 4. b. The watry pavement is not stable and r. like a rock JER. TAYLOR.

B. *sb.* 1. One who resides permanently in a place; sometimes *spec.* applied to inhabitants of the better class 1487. b. A resident incumbent 1812. 2. A diplomatic representative, inferior in rank to an ambassador, residing at a foreign court. Now *Hist.* 1650. b A representative of the (†East India Company or) Governor-general of India residing at a (†commercial station or) native court 1786. c. The governor of a residency in the Dutch East Indies 1814. Hence **Re·sidentship,** the office or post of a R.

†**Resident,** *sb.*[2] *rare.* 1625. [ad. L. *resident-, residere* RESIDE *v.*[2]] Deposit or sediment –1666.

Residenter (re·zidentəɹ, *Sc.* rezide·ntəɹ). 1446. [f. RESIDENT *a.*] †1. *Eccl.* A residentiary –1719. 2. *Sc.* and *U.S.* A resident, inhabitant 1678.

Residential (rezide·nʃăl), *a.* 1654. [See RESIDENCE[1] and -AL 1.] †1. Serving or used as a residence; in which one resides –1740. b. Adapted or suitable for the residence of those belonging to the better class; characterized by houses of a superior kind 1878. 2. Connected with, pertaining or relating to, residence or residences 1856. 3. Of or belonging to a Resident (*rare*) 1885.

1. b. A considerable r. estate 1878. 2. The r. qualification of voters 1881.

Residentiary (rezide·nʃări), *sb.* and *a.* 1525. [ad. med.L. *residentiarius*; see RESIDENCE[1] and -ARY[1].] A. *sb.* 1. An ecclesiastic who is bound to official residence, *esp.* a canon of a cathedral or collegiate church. 2. One who or that which is resident 1615.

2. The r., or the frequent visitor of the favoured spot COLERIDGE.

B. *adj.* 1. *Canon r.*, a canon of whom residence is required 1632. b. Involving, relating or pertaining to, official residence 1662. 2. Residing or resident in a place 1640. b. Connected with residence 1871. Hence **Reside·ntiaryship,** the office of a (canon) r.

Residual (rĭzi·diu̦ăl), *sb.* 1557. [See next.] 1. *Math.* a. A residual quantity. b. Either of two systems of points which together make up all the intersections of any given curve with a plane cubic curve 1867. 2. A remainder; an amount remaining after the main part is subtracted or accounted for 1860. 3. A substance or product of the nature of a residuum 1885.

Residual (rĭzi·diu̦ăl), *a.* 1570. [ad. med. or mod.L. **residualis*, f. *residuum.*] 1. *Math.* Resulting from, formed by, the subtraction of one quantity from another. 2. Remaining; still left; left over 1609. b. In the physical sciences: Left as a residuum, *esp.* at the end of some process 1757. c. Left unexplained or uncorrected 1830.

1. *R. analysis*, a calculus proposed by the inventor, Mr. Landen, as a substitute for the method of fluxions 1801. *R. calculus*, the calculus of residuals or residues 1890. 2. b. The heat referred to is mainly..the r. heat of a cooling globe 1896. c. The r. error in our observations 1871.

Residuary (rĭzi·diu̦ări), *a.* and *sb.* 1726. [See RESIDUUM and -ARY[1].] A. *adj.* 1. *Law.* Of the nature of the residue of an estate. 2. Of the nature of a residuum or remainder of any kind; *esp.* with ref. to chemical processes, scientific observations, etc. 1793.

1. *R. legatee* or *devisee*, one to whom the residue of an estate is left. *R. clause*, a clause by which a residue is devised. 2. We celebrated it by an extra dinner..and a couple of our r. bottles of wine 1853.

B. *sb.* A residuary legatee (*rare*) 1817.

Residue (re·zidiu). late ME. [ad. F. *résidu*, ad. L. *residuum* RESIDUUM.] 1. The remainder, rest; that which is left. 2. *Law.* That which remains of an estate after all charges, debts, and bequests have been paid. late ME. 3. *Math.* = REMAINDER *sb.*[1] 4 a. *Obs.* exc. as in *quadratic r.*, the remainder left on dividing the square of a number by a given number; so *cubic r.*, etc. late ME. 4. = RESIDUUM 3. 1807. 5. *Chem.* The atom or group of atoms remaining after part of a molecule has been removed 1873.

1. *Method of Residues*: see Mill *Logic* (1843) III. viii. § 5. The resydew of our lyues LD. BERNERS. The R. of the conquer'd People fled to their Canoes DE FOE. †*In, for the r.*, as to the remainder.

Residuous (rĭzi·diu̦əs), *a.* Now *rare.* 1626. [ad. L. *residuus*; see next and -OUS.] Remaining.

Residuum (rĭzi·diu̦ɒ̆m). *Pl.* **residua** (rĭzi·diu̦ă). 1672. [a. L., neut. of *residuus* remaining, f. *residere* RESIDE *v.*[1]] 1. That which remains; a residue. (Chiefly of immaterial things.) b. Applied to persons of the lowest class 1867. 2. *Law.* = RESIDUE 2. 1743. 3. *spec.* That which remains after a process of combustion, evaporation, etc.; a deposit or sediment; a waste or residual product 1756.

1. b. The r., which there is in every constituency, of almost hopeless poverty and dependence BRIGHT.

Resign (rĭzəi·n), *v.* late ME. [ad. OF. *resigner*, ad. L. *resignare*, f. *re-* RE- 2 d + *signare* to SIGN.] I. *trans.* 1. To relinquish, surrender, give up, or hand over (something); *esp.* an office, position, right, claim, etc. Also with *up* (now *rare*). 2. To give up, make over, abandon, consign *to* a person, thing, or condition. late ME. b. To yield up (oneself, etc.) with confidence *to* another for care or guidance. late ME. c. To make surrender of (one's will, reason, etc.) in reliance upon another 1585. d. To give (oneself, one's mind, etc.) up *to* some emotion, condition, or state 1718. †3. To give over, desist or refrain from –1590.

1. Upon his resigning the great seal 1818. The commonwealth was required..to r...its foreign possessions 1839. 2. b. He..vows to r. himself to her direction 1869. d. I will r. myself to rest COWPER.

II. *intr.* 1. To give up an office or position; to retire; †to abdicate 1450. 2. To submit or yield, *to* a person or thing. Now *rare.* 1450. 3. To make surrender or relinquishment 1738.

1. If my Lord bishop wants to r. 1860. Hence †**Resignee·**, one to whom anything is resigned. **Resi·gner,** one who resigns. **Resi·gnment,** the act of resigning; resignation (now *rare*).

Resignation (rezignēⁱ·ʃən). late ME. [a. F. *résignation* or ad. med.L. *resignationem*; see RESIGN *v.* and -ATION] 1. The (*or* an) action of resigning an office, etc.; also, the document conveying this. 2. A giving up *of* oneself (to God) 1450. 3. The fact of resigning oneself or of being resigned; acquiescence, submission, compliance 1647.

1. Archbishopricks and bishopricks may become void..by r. BLACKSTONE. They..gave in their r. 1848. 3. Proba supported, with Christian r., the loss of immense riches GIBBON.

Resigned (rĭzəi·nd), *ppl. a.* 1654. [f. RESIGN *v.* + -ED[1].] †1. Given *up*, abandoned, surrendered –1666. 2. Full of resignation; submissive, acquiescent; characterized by resignation 1699. 3. That has retired from a position 1896.

2. Sufficiently philosophical to be r., he was yet too ambitious to be contented 1894. Hence **Resi·gned-ly** *adv.*, **-ness.**

Resile (rĭzəi·l), *v.* 1529. [ad. L. *resilire* to jump back, recoil, f. *re-* RE- + *salire.*] 1. *intr.* To draw back *from* an agreement, contract, statement, etc.; to shrink, retreat, *from* something with aversion or non-acceptance. 2. Of material things: To recoil or rebound after contact. b. Of elastic bodies: To return to their original position after being stretched or compressed 1709. 3. a. To turn back from a point reached 1887. b. To return to one's original position 1889. Hence **Resi·lement.**

Resilience (rĭzi·liĕns). 1626. [See RESILIENT and -ENCE.] 1. The (*or* an) act of rebounding or springing back; rebound, recoil. 2. Elasticity; the power of resuming the original shape or position after compression, bending, etc. 1824.

1. Whether there be any such R. in Eccho's BACON.

Resiliency (rĭzi·liĕnsi). 1668. [See RESILIENT and -ENCY.] 1. Tendency to rebound or recoil. 2. = RESILIENCE 2. 1835. 3. Buoyancy, power of recovery 1857.

Resilient (rĭzi·liĕnt), *a.* 1644. [ad. L. *resilientem*, pres. pple. of *resilire* to RESILE.] 1. Returning to the original position; springing back, recoiling, etc. 2. Resuming the original shape or position after being bent, compressed, or stretched 1674. 3. *fig.* Of persons, etc.: Rising readily again after being depressed; hence, cheerful, buoyant, exuberant 1830.

3. The r. spirit of roving Englishmen 1859.

†**Resili·tion.** 1658. [f. RESILE *v.* + -ITION.] The (*or* an) act of springing back; recoil, rebound, resilience -1738.

Resin (re·zin), *sb.* late ME. [ad. F. *résine*, ad. L. *resina*, cogn. with Gr. ῥητίνη. See also ROSIN.] 1. A vegetable product, formed by secretion in special canals in almost all trees and plants, from many of which (as the fir and pine) it exudes naturally, or can be readily obtained by incision; extensively used in making varnishes, etc., and in pharmacy. b. With *a* and *pl.* A particular kind of resin 1801. 2. A resinous precipitate obtained by special treatment of certain vegetable products; a similar substance obtained from bile 1681.

Comb.: **r.-bush**, a South African shrub, *Euryops speciosissimus*, so named because of a gummy exudation often seen on the stem and leaves; **-weed**, = ROSIN-WEED. Hence **Re·sin** *v.* to rub or treat with r. **Resina·ceous** *a.* (*rare*) that yields r. **Resi·nic** *a.* of, belonging to, or derived from r. **Resini·ferous** *a.* yielding or containing r. **Re·siniform** *a.* having the character of r. **Re·siny** *a.* resinous.

Resinate (re·zinĕt). 1838. [f. prec. + -ATE[1] 1 c.] *Chem.* A salt formed by the action of a resinous acid on a base.

Resinify (re·zinifəi), *v.* 1816. [ad. F. *résinifier*; see RESIN *sb.* and -FY.] 1. *trans.* To change into resin. 2. *intr.* To become resinous 1856. So **Re:sinifica·tion** [F. *résinification*] 1800.

Resino-, comb. form of RESIN *sb.*, as in **r.-electric** *a.*, containing or exhibiting resinous or negative electricity.

Resinoid (re·zinoid), *a.* and *sb.* 1830. [f. RESIN *sb.* + -OID.] A. *adj.* Resembling resin. B. *sb.* A resinous substance 1880.

Resinol (re·zinǫl). 1893. [f. RESIN *sb.* + -OL[1].] 1. *Chem.* Any of various alcohols found in resin. 2. = RETINOL 1893.

Resinous (re·zinəs), *a.* 1646. [ad. L. *resinosus*; see RESIN *sb.* + -OUS.] 1. Of the nature of resin. 2. Of plants or their parts: Containing resin 1656. 3. Of properties, etc.: Properly belonging to, or characteristic of, resin 1811. 4. Made or compounded of resin; affected or produced by the burning of resin 1808. 5. *Electr.* = NEGATIVE *a.* II. 3. 1797.

4. I can smell the heavy r. incense as I pass the church DICKENS. Hence **Re·sinous-ly** *adv.*, **-ness.**

Resipiscence (resipi·sĕns). 1570. [a. F., or ad. L. *resipiscentia*, f. *resipiscere* to come to oneself again, f. *re-* RE- + *sapere*.] Repentance for misconduct; recognition of errors committed; return to a better mind or opinion. So †**Resipi·scency.** **Resipi·scent** *a.* returning to a sound state of mind.

Resist (rĭzi·st), *sb.* 1535. [f. the vb.] †1. Resistance -1630. 2. In calico-printing, a preparation applied to those parts of the fabric which are not to be coloured, in order to prevent the dye from affecting them 1836. 3. Any composition applied to a surface to protect it from the effects of an agent employed on it for some purpose. Also *r.-varnish*. 1839.

Resist (rĭzi·st), *v.* late ME. [ad. F. *résister*, or L. *resistere*, f. *re-* RE- + *sistere*, redupl. f. *stare* to stand.] 1. *trans.* Of things: To stop or hinder (a moving body); to succeed in standing against; to prevent (a weapon, etc.) from piercing or penetrating. b. To withstand the action or effect of, fail to be affected by (a natural force, physical agency, etc.) 1567. 2. Of persons: To withstand, strive against, oppose. late ME. †3. To affect with distaste. SHAKS. 4. *intr.* †a. To stand *against*, make opposition *to*, a person or thing -1651. b. To offer resistance 1547.

1. Spiritual Armour, able to r. Satans assaults MILT. b. Able to r. fire 1567. *To r. a joke* (with neg.): to help making, or fail to be amused by, it. 2. Fleshly weaknesse, which no creature may Long time r. SPENSER. That mortal dint, Save he who reigns above, none can r. MILT. O King of Glory! thou alone hast power! Who can r. thy will? SHELLEY. 4. b. *Oth.* I. ii. 80.

Resistance (rĭzi·stăns). late ME. [a. F. *résistance*; see prec. and -ANCE.] 1. The act, on the part of persons, of resisting, opposing, or withstanding. 2. Power or capacity of resisting 1590. 3. Opposition of one material thing to another material thing, force, etc. 1625. b. *esp.* in the physical sciences, the opposition offered by one body to the pressure or movement of another 1656. 4. Non-conductivity in respect of electricity, magnetism, or heat 1860. b. A part of an electrical apparatus used to offer a definite resistance to a current 1878. 5. *Piece of r.*, = F. *pièce de résistance*: see PIÈCE b. 1797.

1. There is yet a spirit of r. in this country, which will not submit to be oppressed *Junius Lett.* Phr. *Passive r.*, simple refusal to comply with some demand, without active opposition; *spec.* refusal to pay voluntarily the education rate imposed by the Education Act of 1902. 3. The Heauens in their motion find no r. 1625. b. All the Bodies in the World, pressing a drop of Water on all sides, will never be able to overcome the R. it will make LOCKE. Phr. *Line of r.* 5. The good girl liked a piece of r., a solid tome 1858.

attrib. and *Comb.*, as **r.-box** (*Electr.*) a box containing one or more r. coils also *transf.*; **r. coil**, a coil introduced into an electric circuit, so as to increase the r.

Resistant (rĭzi·stănt), *a.* and *sb.* 1600. [a. F. *résistant*, pres. pple. of *résister* to RESIST.] A. *adj.* That makes resistance or opposition 1610. B. *sb.* One who or that which resists; a resister. Now *rare*. 1600. b. In calico-printing, = RESIST *sb.* 2. 1879.

†**Resi·stence.** late ME. [a. OF., ad. late L. *resistentia*, f. *resistere* to RESIST; see -ENCE.] = RESISTANCE -1738. So †**Resi·stency.**

Resistent (rĭzi·stĕnt), *a.* and *sb.* 1600. [ad. L. *resistentem*.] A. *adj.* = RESISTANT *a.* 1640. †B. *sb.* = RESISTANT *sb.* -1644.

Resister (rĭzi·stəɹ). late ME. [f. RESIST *v.* + -ER[1].] One who, or that which, resists.

Passive r.: see RESISTANCE 1.

Resi·stful, *a.* 1614. [f. as prec. + -FUL 1.] Capable of, or inclined to, resistance.

Resistibility (rĭzistibi·lĭti). 1617. [f. as next + -ITY.] 1. The quality of being resistible. 2. Power of offering resistance 1646.

Resistible (rĭzi·stĭb'l), *a.* 1643. [f. RESIST *v.* + -IBLE.] Capable of being resisted.

Earthquakes themselves, the least r. of natural violence JOHNSON. Hence **Resi·stibleness.** **Resi·stibly** *adv.*

Resi·sting, *ppl. a.* 1593. [-ING[2].] That resists or offers resistance. Hence **Resi·stingly** *adv.*

Resistive (rĭzi·stiv). 1603. [f. RESIST *v.* + -IVE.] Capable of or inclined to resistance. Hence **Resi·stive-ly** *adv.*, **-ness.** **Resisti·vity** (*Electr.*) the specific resistance of a substance.

Resistless (rĭzi·stlĕs), *a.* 1586. [f. RESIST *v.* + -LESS.] 1. That cannot be resisted; irresistible. 2. Powerless to resist 1591.

1. Try to Imprison the r. Wind 1693. Hence **Resi·stless-ly** *adv.*, **-ness.**

Resoluble (re·zǫliŭb'l), *a.* 1602. [ad. late L. *resolubilis*; see RE- and SOLUBLE. Cf. F. *résoluble*.] Capable of being resolved; resolvable. Hence **Resolubi·lity, Re·solubleness.**

†**Re·solute,** *sb. rare.* 1534. [See next.] 1. A payment -1610. 2. A resolute or determined person -1800.

2. A List of Landlesse Resolutes SHAKS.

Resolute (re·zǒl'ut), *a.* (and *pa. pple.*). late ME. [ad. L. *resolutus*, *resolvere* to RESOLVE.] †1. Dissolved. late ME. only. †2. Of rents: Paid, rendered -1670. †3. Determinate, decided, positive, absolute, final; esp. *r. answer* -1656. 4. Of persons, their minds, etc.: Determined, having a fixed resolve, constant, firm 1533. 5. Of actions: Characterized by determination or firmness of purpose 1603.

4. I am determined to continue r. in well doing 1634. They were few, but r. SHELLEY. R. for peace GREEN. 5. He..leads Invincibly a life of r. good SHELLEY. Hence **Re·solute-ly** *adv.*, **-ness.**

Resolute (re·zǒl'ut), *v.* Now *U.S.* 1548. [orig. f. L. *resolut-*, *resolvere*, but in mod. use a back-formation from next.] †1. *refl.* To resolve, decide (oneself) *upon* a person -1548. †2. *trans.* To resolve, dissolve *into* something -1727. 3. *U.S. intr.* To draw up or pass resolutions 1860.

Resolution (rezǒl'ū·ʃən). late ME. [a. OF., or ad. L. *resolutionem*.] I. †1. = Dissolution, death -1582. 2. The process by which a material thing is reduced or separated into its component parts or elements; a result of this. late ME. b. Const. *to, into*. Also, conversion *into* something else, or *into* a different form. 1519. c. The effect of an optical instrument in making the separate parts of an object (*esp.* the stars of a nebula) distinguishable by the eye 1860. 3. *Med.* †a. Dissolution or dispersion of humours or of morbid matter in the body -1778. b. Disappearance of inflammation without coming to suppuration 1783. †4. Conversion to a fluid state -1686. 5. Relaxation or weakening of some part of the body. Now *rare*. 1547.

1. The tyme of my resolucioun..is nyȝ WYCLIF 2 *Tim.* iv. 6.

II. 1. The process of resolving or reducing a non-material thing into simpler forms, or of converting it into some other thing or form. late ME. b. In prosody, the substitution of two short syllables for a long one 1884. †2. *Math.* and *Logic.* = ANALYSIS 7, 8. -1738. 3. *Mus.* The process by which a discord is made to pass into a concord 1727. 4. *Mech.* The substitution for a single force of two or more forces, to which it is mechanically equivalent, or of which it is the resultant 1798. III. 1. The answering *of* a question; the solving *of* a doubt or difficulty. Now *rare*. 1548. b. The solution *of* an arithmetical or mathematical problem. Now *rare* or *Obs.* 1579. 2. A statement upon some matter; a decision or verdict on some point. Now *rare* or *Obs.* 1581. b. A formal decision, determination, or expression of opinion, on the part of a deliberative body or other meeting; a proposal of this nature submitted to an assembly or meeting 1604. †3. An explanatory account *of* something -1658.

1. Of this question..we must be content to live without the r. JOHNSON. b. Of the R. of Equations 1797. 2. b. The passing by the House of Commons of such a r. as this FREEMAN.

IV. †1. a. The removal of a doubt on some point from a person's mind (*rare*) -1644. b. Confidence; conviction, certainty, positive knowledge (*rare*) -1637. 2. The (*or* an) act of resolving or determining; anything resolved upon; a fixed determination 1590. 3. Determination; firmness or steadiness of purpose; unyielding temper 1588.

1. b. *Lear* I. ii. 108. 2. To be praised then every man resolves; but resolutions will not execute themselves JOHNSON. 3. He comes, and settl'd in his face I see Sad r. and secure MILT. Hence **Resolu·tionist,** one who makes, or joins in, a r.

Resolutioner (rezǒl'ū·ʃənəɹ). 1693. [f. RESOLUTION + -ER.[1]] 1. *Hist.* A member of that party in Scotland which accepted the resolutions passed in 1650 for rehabilitating those persons who had not taken part in the struggle against Cromwell. 2. One who joins in or subscribes to a resolution. Now *Obs.* or *rare*. 1816.

Resolutive (re·zǒl'utiv), *a.* and *sb.* late ME. [ad. med.L. **resolutivus* (see RESOLUTE *v.* and -IVE).] A. *adj.* 1. a. Having the power to dissolve. b. *Path.* Terminating by resolution 1861. 2. *Law. R. condition*, a condition by the happening of which a contract or obligation is terminated 1623. †3. *Logic.* Analytical -1656. B. *sb.* A medical application or drug which serves to resolve or disperse morbid matter. late ME.

Resolutory (re·zǒl'utəri), *a. rare.* 1609. [ad. late L. *resolutorius* (cf. prec. and -ORY[2]).] †1. Explanatory, enlightening -1669. 2. *Law.* = RESOLUTIVE *a.* 2. 1818.

Resolvable (rĭzǫ·lvăb'l), *a.* 1646. [f. RESOLVE *v.* + -ABLE.] Capable of being resolved.

R. nebula, a nebula which admits of resolution by a powerful telescope. Hence **Resolvabi·lity.** **Reso·lvableness,** the capability of being resolved into parts.

Resolve (rĭzǫ·lv), *sb.* 1591. [f. the vb.] 1. A determination or resolution 1592. 2. Firmness or steadfastness of purpose 1591. 3. A determination of a deliberative body; a formal resolution. Now *U.S.* 1656. †4. Answer, solution –1670.

1. She made up her mind never to marry again, and she kept her r. 1889. 2. We must be stiffe and steddie in r. MARSTON. 3. Cæsar's approach has summon'd us together, And Rome attends her fate from our resolves ADDISON.

Resolve (rĭzǫ·lv), *v.* late ME. [ad. L. *resolvere*, f. *re-* RE- + *solvere* to loosen, dissolve.] I. †1. *trans.* To melt, dissolve, reduce to a liquid or fluid state –1732. 2. To disintegrate; to break up or separate into constituent or elementary parts. Now *rare* or *Obs.* late ME. †b. *Math.* To solve (an equation) –1798. c. To analyse (a force or velocity) into its components 1825. d. Of optical instruments (or persons using them): To separate, break up (an object) into distinguishable parts 1785. 3. *Med.* To soften (a hard tumour); to disperse or dissipate (humours, swellings, etc.). Now *rare* or *Obs.* late ME. b. To remove (inflammation) by resolution 1732. †4. To slacken, relax (the limbs, etc.); to weaken –1715. †b. To render lax in feeling or conduct –1611. 5. *Mus.* To cause (a discord) to pass into a concord 1727.

2. A mellow ground that is fat, and will soone be resolved 1577. 2. d. When he resolves one nebula into stars, he discovers ten new ones which he cannot r. HERSCHEL.

II. 1. To separate (a thing) *into* its component parts or elements; to dissolve *into* some other physical form. late ME. b. To convert, transform, alter (a thing) *into* some other thing or form 1570. 2. To reduce by mental analysis *into* more elementary forms, principles, or relations. late ME. 3. *refl.* Of things: To pass, by dissolution, separation, or change, *into* another form or *into* simpler forms 1602. b. Of a deliberative body: To convert (itself) *into* a committee 1710. 4. To reduce, transform, or change (a thing) *to* something else. Also *refl.* Now *rare.* 1538.

1. To r. the German Empire back again into its elements 1891. b. That the House be resolved into a Committee 1641. 2. Why may we not..r. Christianity into a system of practical Morality? 1841. 3. The argument..resolves itself into four parts 1814.

III. †1. To untie, loosen –1609. 2. To answer (a question, argument, etc.); to solve (a problem of any kind) 1577. b. To explain; to make clear 1585. 3. To remove, clear away, dispel (a doubt, difficulty, or obscurity) 1571. 4. To decide, determine, settle (a doubtful point) 1586. †b. To conclude, settle (a thing) in one's mind –1702. 5. To determine or decide upon (a course of action, etc.); often with obj. clause 1523. b. To adopt or pass as a resolution 1590. †6. To free (a person) from doubt or perplexity; to bring to certainty or clear understanding; to convince or assure *of* something –1767. †7. To inform, tell (a person) *of* a thing; to advise as to a decision; also with obj. clause –1697. b. To determine (a person) *on* a course of action 1836. 8. *refl.* †To make up one's mind, †free oneself *of* a doubt; to satisfy or convince oneself (*arch.*) 1528.

2. After a great part of life spent in enquiries which can never be resolved JOHNSON. 3. Myself can shew a catalogue of Doubts which are not resolved at the first hearing SIR T. BROWNE. 4. Happiness, it was resolved by all, must be some one uniform end 1719. 5. Warr Open or understood must be resolv'd MILT. b. Resolved unanimously, that this meeting [etc.] 1806. 6. Yet you are amaz'd, but this shall absolutely resolue you SHAKS. 1 *Hen. VI*, III. iv. 20. 7. My Letter will resolue him of my minde SHAKS. 8. He must r. himself on the question 1869.

IV. *intr.* †1. To melt, dissolve, become fluid –1759. 2. To undergo dissolution or separation into elements; to pass *into*, return or change *to*, some form or state. late ME. b. *Path.* To undergo resolution 1822. c. *Mus.* To change from discord to harmony 1889. 3. To come to a determination; to make up one's mind. Now usu. const. inf. or (*up*)*on*. 1570. †b. To decide to make *for* a place –1760. †4. To be satisfied or convinced –1659. †b. To consult, take counsel –1719.

1. Euen as a forme of waxe Resolueth from his figure 'gainst the fire SHAKS. 2. The phantom..Resolves to air POPE. It would r. into an equitable claim SCOTT. 3. He had resolved..to give way 1856. b. I will resolue for Scotland SHAKS.

Resolved (rĭzǫ·lvd), *ppl. a.* 1497. [f. prec. + -ED[1] 1.] In the senses of the vb. *esp.* 1. Of persons: Determined, decided, settled in purpose 1520. 2. Of actions, states of mind, etc.: Deliberate 1595. 3. Of persons, the mind, etc.: Characterized by determination or firmness of purpose; resolute 1586.

1. I am resolued what to doe *Luke* xvi. 4. 2. A resolu'd and honourable warre SHAKS. 3. The hat pulled over his r. brows SCOTT. Hence **Reso·lved·ly** *adv.*, **-ness**.

Resolvend (rĭzǫ·lvĕnd), *sb.* 1673. [ad. L. *resolvendum*, f. *resolvere* to RESOLVE.] *Arith.* The number formed by extending the remainder after subtraction in the process of extracting the square or cube root.

Resolvent (rĭzǫ·lvĕnt), *a.* and *sb.* 1676. [ad. L. *resolventem.*] A. *adj.* 1. Chiefly *Med.* Having the power to resolve; causing solution. 2. Of a proposition: That merely asserts what is already included in the conception of the subject 1856. B. *sb.* 1. *Med.* A medicine or application to cause the resolution of a swelling; a discutient 1676. 2. Something capable of resolving; a solvent 1706. 3. A means of removing difficulties, settling problems, etc. 1851.

Resolver (rĭzǫ·lvəɹ). late ME. [f. RESOLVE *v.* + -ER[1].] †1. A resolvent substance –1756. 2. One who, or that which, answers a question or solves a doubt or difficulty 1609. 3. One who makes a resolve; one who supports a resolution 1749.

Resonance (re·zŏnăns). 1491. [a. OF., ad. L. *resonantia* echo, f. *resonare* to resound; see -ANCE.] 1. The reinforcement or prolongation of sound by reflection, or *spec.* by synchronous vibration. b. *Path.* The sound heard in auscultation of the chest while the person is speaking, or that elicited by percussion of parts of the body 1822. c. *Electr.* The effect produced by an oscillatory current upon one of equal period 1889. 2. The quality of reinforcing or prolonging a sound by vibration 1669.

Resonant (re·zŏnănt), *a.* and *sb.* 1592. [ad. L. *resonant-* *resonare* to resound.] A. *adj.* 1. Of sounds: Re-echoing, resounding; continuing to sound or ring. 2. Of bodies: Causing reinforcement or prolongation of sound, esp. by vibration 1685. 3. Of places: Echoing or resounding *with* something 1813.

3. Fertile valleys, r. with bliss SHELLEY.

B. *sb.* A nasal consonant 1875. Hence **Re·sonantly** *adv.*

Resonate (re·zŏneit), *v.* 1873. [f. L. *resonare*; see -ATE[3].] *intr.* To produce or exhibit resonance.

Resonator (re·zŏnē¹təɹ). 1869. [f. L. *resonare.*] 1. An instrument responding to one single note, and used for its detection when combined with other sounds. 2. An appliance for increasing sound by resonance; a body or object which produces resonance 1871. 3. *Electr.* An apparatus used for the detection of Hertzian waves 1893.

Resorb (rĭsǭ·ɹb), *v.* 1640. [ad. L. *resorbere*, f. *re-* RE- + *sorbere* to drink in.] To absorb again.

The extravasated blood was resorbed 1902. So **Reso·rbence**, reabsorption. **Reso·rbent** *a.*

Resorcin (rezǭ·ɹsin). Also **-ine**. 1866. [f. RES(IN + ORCIN.] *Chem.* A colourless crystalline compound, formerly produced by the action of potash upon galbanum or other resins, now usu. prepared synthetically. It is used as a dye-stuff, and in medicine and photography. Hence **Reso·rcinol**, a form of r.; a compound of r. with other substances. **Resorcylic** (rezǫɹsi·lik) *a.* pertaining to, derived from, r.

Resorption (rĭsǭ·ɹpʃən). 1818. [f. L. *resorbere* RESORB *v.*] The fact or process of reabsorption, *spec.* of an organ, tissue, or excretion.

Resort (rĭzǭ·ɹt), *sb.* late ME. [a. OF., f. *resortir*; see next.] I. 1. That to which one has recourse for aid or assistance, or in order to accomplish some end. 2. Recourse *to* some person, thing, or expedient, for aid or assistance, for the settlement of some difficulty, or the attainment of some end 1474. 3. General or habitual repair of persons to some place or person. late ME. †4. Concourse or assemblage of people –1700. b. An assemblage, gathering, throng, crowd 1550. 5. A place to which people repair, as for holiday-making, restoration of health, etc. (*health, seaside r.*, etc.) 1754.

1. A fit one [*sc.* sledge] was not to be found, and a carriage was..the only r. TYNDALL. 2. It will be impossible to close the Committee to-night without r. to a sitting of unusual length 1884. Phr. *In the last r.* [after F. *en dernier ressort*], orig. as a judge or court from which there is no appeal; hence, as a last expedient, in the end, ultimately. *Without r.*, without appeal (*rare*). 3. To build Houses, Temples, and Places of Publick R. 1683. 6. This intellectual cloud, which hangs, like a fog, over every gay r. of our moral invalids 1754.

†II. A mechanical spring –1714.

Resort (rĭzǭ·ɹt), *v.* late ME. [ad. OF. *resortir* to rebound, retire, f. *re-* RE- + *sortir* to issue, go, of obscure etym.] †1. *intr.* To issue, come out, again –1480. †2. a. To return *to* oneself; to revert *to* a former condition or custom –1589. b. To return *to* a subject or matter; also, to go back in a discourse or in time –1749. c. To revert or fall *to* a person's lot or share –1676. †3. To turn, direct one's attention, *to* a subject –1581. 4. To betake oneself, repair or go, *to* a person for aid 1460. b. To have recourse *to* something for assistance or furtherance of an object 1647. 5. To repair, make one's way, come or go, esp. habitually or frequently *to* a person or place; to respond to a summons 1447. 6. To proceed or go *to* (or *towards*) a place 1450. 7. To have one's or its abode, stay 1453. †8. *trans.* To frequent or (a place) –1756.

4. b. At length we r. to actual experiment TYNDALL. 5. Crowes will to carrion still, Like euer vnto like r. 1607. The chop-house here, To which I most r. TENNYSON. 6. The Sons of Light Hasted, resorting to the Summons high, And took thir Seats MILT. 7. 'Tis pitty that thou liu'st To walke where any honest men r. SHAKS. Hence **Reso·rter**, a frequenter or visitor.

†**Resou·nd**, *sb.* 1586. [f. the vb.] A returned or re-echoed sound; a resonance –1701.

Resound (rĭzau·nd), *v.* late ME. [f. RE- + *soun*(*e* SOUND *v.*, after F. *resonner*, or L. *resonare.*] I. *intr.* 1. Of places: To ring, re-echo (*with* or †*of* some sound). 2. Of things: To make or produce an echoing sound 1530. 3. Of sounds: To echo, ring 1547. b. To be mentioned or repeated; to be celebrated or renowned 1578.

1. Together rush'd Both Battels maine..all Heav'n Resounded MILT. The dome resounded with the acclamations of the people GIBBON. 2. His arms resounded as the boaster fell POPE. 3. And echoing praises..r. at your return COWPER. b. Milton, a name to r. for ages TENNYSON.

II. *trans.* 1. To proclaim, repeat loudly (a person's praises, etc.); to celebrate (a person or thing) 1561. 2. To repeat or utter (words, etc.) in a loud or echoing manner. Now *rare.* 1594. 3. Of places: To re-echo 1579.

1. Let us..in our Mother Tongue r. his Praise DRYDEN. 3. Hell..sigh'd From all her Caves, and back resounded 'Death!' MILT. Cliffs, woods and caves, her viewless steps r. WORDSW.

Resource (rĭsōᵊ·ɹs). 1611. [ad. F. *ressource*, f. OF. *re*(*s*)*sourdre* to rise again, f. *re-* RE- + *sourdre* :—L. *surgere.*] 1. A means of supplying some want or deficiency; a stock or reserve upon which one can draw when necessary. Now usu. *pl.* b. *pl.* The collective means possessed by any country for its own support or defence 1779. 2. Possibility of aid or assistance. (Chiefly in phr. *without r.*) 1697. 3. An action or procedure to which one may have recourse in a difficulty or emergency; an expedient, device, shift 1697. 4. A means of relaxation or amusement 1776. 5. Capability in adapting means to ends, or in meeting difficulties 1853.

1. *sing.* The treasure of the Hotel de Ville presented an immediate r. 1849. *pl.* It was limited with respect to pecuniary Resources 1800. 2. Vanquish'd without r.; Laid flat by fate DRYDEN. 3. Us'd threatnings, mix'd with pray'rs, his last r. DRYDEN. 4. Reading had been her chief r. DISRAELI. 5. R. in difficulties is the distinction of great generals FROUDE. Hence **Resou·rceful** *a.* full of r.; abounding in resources; **Resou·rcefulness**. **Resou·rceless** *a.* without r.; destitute of resources; **Resou·rcelessness**.

Respect (rĭspe·kt), *sb.* late ME. [ad. L. *respectus*, f. ppl. stem of *respicere*; see next.] I. 1. †a. An aspect of a thing; a relative property or quality; a relationship –1753. b. A particular, point, detail. Only in phrases with *in*, as *in all, many*, or *some respects*, 1581. 2. A relationship of one person or thing *to* another; a reference *to* some thing or person

1551. †3. Relationship, reference -1662. †b. Bearings, results. DRYDEN.

1. a. Doth Relation to us alter the Case, and that R. alone impart Worth? 1748. b. I should like to know in what r. the argument is not sufficient 1875. 2. A worldly morality which has no r. to God 1850.

II. †1. A view; a backward survey (*rare*) -1661. 2. Regard, consideration. Const. *of* or *to*. 1530. b. Discrimination, partiality, or favour in regard *of* persons or things 1535. †c. Heed, care, attention -1647. †d. *pl.* Attention or consideration given to more than one point or matter -1656. 3. A consideration; a fact or motive which assists in, or leads to, the formation of a decision; an end or aim 1549.

1. Taking a prospect (or r. rather) of the Country they have passed FULLER. 2. R. and reason, wait on wrinkled age! SHAKS. b. Is there no r. of place, persons, nor time in you? SHAKS. c. When men shall carry a r. not to descend into any course that is corrupt BACON. 3. These Respects gave the first Rise to a Treaty of Peace 1673.

III. 1. Deferential regard or esteem felt or shown towards a person or thing 1586. b. The condition or state of being esteemed or honoured 1597. †c. Rank, standing, station in life -1652. 2. *pl.* †a. Deferential or courteous attentions; actions expressive of respect for a person; politenesses, courtesies -1707. †b. Deferential salutations. CLARENDON. c. In complimentary formulæ, usu. conveying a message expressive of regard or esteem 1645. d. *To pay one's respects*, to show polite attention *to* a person by presenting oneself or by making a call 1668.

1. Zeale to promote the common good..deserueth certainly much r. and esteeme 1611. b. Youth without honour, age without r. BYRON. c. *Jul. C.* I. ii. 59. 2. c. Pray give my respects to him Miss BURNEY. d. He expressed great eagerness to pay his respects to his master SMOLLETT.

Phrases. *To have r. to*: a. To have regard or relation *to*, or connexion with, something. b. To have reference, to refer, to something. †c. To have an eye *to*, to give heed *to*, by looking at. d. To give heed, attention, or consideration to something; to have regard *to*; to take into account. Also const. ellipt. with *that*. e. To have in view; to allude *to*. †*In r. of*, in comparison with. †*In r.*, in comparison. *In r. (of)*: a. With reference to; as relates to or regards. †b. In view of, by reason or because of. c. Considering, seeing, since (*that*). *Without r.*: †a. Without discrimination or consideration. b. Without consideration *of*, or regard *to*, something. *With r.*, with reference or regard *to* something.

Respect (rĭspe·kt), *v.* 1542. [f. L. *respect-*, *respicere* to look (back) at, regard; or ad. *respectare*.] †1. *trans.* To respite; to put off, neglect -1620. †2. To regard, consider, take into account -1668. †b. To pay attention to; to observe carefully -1662. †c. To regard as being of a certain kind, etc. (*rare*) -1602. 3. To be directed to; to refer or relate to; to deal or be concerned with 1563. b. In *pres. pple.* used as *prep.* With reference or regard to 1732. 4. To treat or regard with deference, esteem, or honour; to feel or show respect for 1560. †b. To esteem, prize, or value (a thing) -1638. c. To treat with consideration; to refrain from interfering with; to spare 1621. †5. To expect, anticipate, look (for). *rare.* -1623. 6. a. *Her.* Of charges: To look at, face (*esp.* each other) 1562. †b. To regard; to look upon -1620. †c. To look towards; to face -1734. d. *intr.* To face or look *to* or *towards* (*rare*) 1585.

2. c. To whom my father gave this name of Gasper, And as his own respected him B. JONS. 3. The greatest wits want perspicacity in things that r. their own interest 1663. *As respects*, with reference or regard to, concerning. b. He could not agree with him respecting the price 1802. 4. I always loved and respected him very much SWIFT. b. *Two Gent.* I. ii. 134. c. Lewis had,..repeatedly promised to r. the privileges of his Protestant subjects MACAULAY. 6. b. Wise men will not view such persons but with scorn, nor r. them but with disesteem 1620. c. The latter stands on a sharp cliff respecting the north 1734.

Respectability (rĭspektăbi·lĭti). 1785. [f. RESPECTABLE *a.* + -ITY.] 1. The state, quality, or condition of being respectable in point of character or social standing. b. *concr.* Those who are respectable 1808. 2. a. A person of respectable character 1840. b. *pl.* Those features of life and conduct which are regarded as respectable 1843. †3. Importance (*rare*) 1824.

1. A model of elderly English r. C. BRONTË. 2. b. Out of a regard to the respectabilities of life JOWETT.

Respectable (rĭspe·ktăb'l), *a.* and *sb.* 1586. [f. RESPECT *sb.* + -ABLE.] A. *adj.* †1. Worthy of notice, observation, or consideration (*rare*) -1605. 2. Worthy or deserving of respect by reason of some inherent quality or qualities 1599. b. Considerable in number, size, quantity, etc. 1755. c. Of comparative excellence; tolerable, fair 1775. d. Of writers, in respect of authority or literary merit 1781. 3. Of persons: Worthy of respect by reason of moral excellence 1755. 4. Of persons: Of good or fair social standing, and having the moral qualities naturally appropriate to this. Hence, in later use, honest and decent in character or conduct, without ref. to social position. Similarly of appearance, character, etc. 1758. b. Of decent or presentable appearance 1775. †c. Creditable; of a good or superior kind -1800.

2. Your studies, the r. remains of antiquity CHESTERF. c. Very r. literary talents 1799. d. The more r. English essayists 1866. 4. The r. middle classes, who had no sympathy with revolutionists FROUDE.

B. *sb.* A respectable person 1814. Hence **Respe·ctableness. Respe·ctably** *adv.*

Respectant (rĭspektănt), *a.* *rare.* 1688. [-ANT [1].] 1. *Her.* Of animals: Facing each other. 2. Looking backward 1830.

Respe·cter. 1611. [f. RESPECT *v.* + ER [1].] One who respects.

R. of persons: (after *Acts* x. 34), one who pays undue regard to wealth or exalted position.

Respectful (rĭspe·ktfŭl), *a.* 1598. [f. RESPECT *sb.*] †1. Mindful, heedful, careful (*of* something) -1663. †2. Worthy of, or commanding, respect -1702. 3. Full of, exhibiting, or marked by respect 1687.

3. The r. attention shown to him by Socrates JOWETT. A moderate man, r. of tradition 1892. Hence **Respe·ctful·ly** *adv.*, **-ness.**

†Respe·ction. late ME. [ad. late L. *respectionem*, f. *respicere*.] Sight; aspect; regard; respect (of persons) -1527.

Respective (rĭspe·ktiv), *a.* 1525. [ad. late L. *respectivus*; see RESPECT *v.* and -IVE.] †1. Of persons: Regardful, attentive, considerate, careful -1643. b. Careful or regardful *of* something. Now *rare.* 1599. 2. Of conduct, etc.: Marked by regardful care or attention; heedful. Now *rare.* 1598. †b. Discriminating; partial -1643. †3. Respectful, courteous (*to* or *towards* a person) -1785. †4. Worthy of respect or deference; respectable -1633. †5. Having relationship or reference *to* something; correspondent; also *absol.* relative -1865. 6. Properly pertaining to, or connected with, each individual, group, etc., of those in question 1646.

1. b. All such as are respectiue of their health 1620. 2. b. *Rom. & Jul.* III. i. 128. 4. What should it be that he respects in her, But I can make respectiue in my selfe? SHAKS. 6. To those places straight repair Where your r. dwellings are 1663. We cannot fix the r. amounts of truth and falsehood FREEMAN. Hence **Respe·ctiveness** (now *rare* or *Obs.*).

Respectively (rĭspe·ktivli), *adv.* 1556. [f. prec. + -LY [2].] †1. Carefully, attentively -1620. †2. Respectfully; with becoming respect, deference, or courtesy -1720. †3. Relatively; comparatively -1664. 4. Relatively to each of several persons or things; individually, singly, separately; each to each, severally 1626.

4. Of the three defendants..two were r. president and secretary of the..Society 1891.

Respectless (rĭspe·ktlės), *a.* 1542. [f. RESPECT *sb.* + -LESS.] †1. Regardless; heedless, reckless; unheeding, careless -1639. 2. Devoid of respect or deference; discourteous, disrespectful. Now *rare.* 1591. †3. Impartial, unbiassed (*rare*) -1612.

2. This fellow being in drinke, gave us manie insolent r. speeches 1617. Hence **†Respe·ctless·ly** *adv.*, **†-ness.**

†Respe·ctuous, *a.* 1603. [f. RESPECT *sb.* + -(U)OUS after F. *respectueux*.] 1. Worthy of respect -1686. 2. Respectful, deferent -1683.

Respirable (re·spirăb'l), *a.* 1779. [a. F., or ad. late L. *respirabilis*; see RESPIRE and -ABLE.] 1. Capable of, or fit for, being respired. 2. Capable of respiring 1822. Hence **Respirabi·lity, Re·spirableness,** the quality of being r.

Respiration (respirē¹·ʃən). late ME. [ad. L. *respirationem*, f. *respirare*.] 1. The action of breathing (†out); the inspiration and expiration of air. b. *Bot.* The process by which a plant absorbs oxygen from the air, and gives out carbon dioxide 1831. 2. A single act of breathing 1611. †3. Opportunity for breathing again; a breathing-space; a respite -1752.

1. *transf.* The r. of the sea, The soft caresses of the air LONGF. 2. Measuring the Number of Pulses by the Number of Respirations 1707. 3. A short r. from the fatigues of war JOHNSON. Hence **Respira·tional** *a.* relating to r.

Respirato-, used as comb. form with the sense 'respiratory as well as'.

Respirator (re·spirē¹tər). 1792. [Agent-n. in L. form, f. L. *respirare*.] †1. *Chem.* An apparatus used for testing the composition of exhaled air -1792. 2. A device of gauze or wire, covering the mouth, or mouth and nose, and serving to warm the inhaled air; in *Mil.* use, a chemical filtering apparatus to prevent the inhalation of dust, poisonous gases, etc. 1836.

Respiratory (rĭspəi°·rătəri, re·spirē¹təri), *a.* 1790. [ad. mod. L. *respiratorius*.] Of, pertaining to, or serving for respiration.

Respire (rĭspəi°·ɹ), *v.* late ME. [ad. F. *respirer*, or L. *respirare*, f. *re-* RE- + *spirare* to breathe.] I. *intr.* †1. To come up to the surface to breathe. T. USK. 2. To breathe; to inhale and exhale air 1599. †b. To draw breath, to live. DRAYTON. 3. *fig.* To breathe again, after distress, trouble, etc.; to recover hope, courage, or strength. late ME. 4. To take breath; to rest or enjoy relief from toil or exertion 1590. †5. Of wind: To blow (*rare*) -1762.

2. The ordinary Air in which we live and r. BENTLEY. b. Yet the braue Barons, whilst they do r., With Courage charge 1619. 3. Then shall the Britons.. From their long vassalage gin to r. SPENSER. 4. But let our weary Muse a while r. P. FLETCHER.

II. *trans.* 1. To breathe; to inhale and exhale (air, etc.) 1548. 2. To breathe or give out, to exhale (an odour, etc.). Chiefly *fig.* 1577. 3. To breathe (a thing) *into* a person's ear 1846.

1. *fig.* I seemed to r. hope and comfort with the free air W. IRVING. 2. The ayre respires the pure elyzian sweets, In which she breathes B. JONS.

Respite (re·spit, -əit), *sb.* ME. [a. OF. *respit* :—L. *respectus* RESPECT *sb.*] 1. Delay, or extension of time, asked or granted for some reason (orig. for further consideration of a matter). b. Delay specially granted in the carrying out of a capital sentence; a reprieve 1722. 2. Temporary cessation of labour, suffering, war, etc.; (an) interval of rest ME. †3. Delay in action; stay -1591. †4. Leisure; opportunity for doing something -1611. †5. Time granted to one until the coming *of* a certain date. MILT.

1. Give me some Respight, I'll discharge the Debt DRYDEN. Phr. *To put in r.*, to delay, postpone. b. *transf.* The annihilation of those hordes had given Rome a passing r. FROUDE. 2. Frequent respites from toil are the..safety-valves of professional men 1873. Hence **Re·spiteless** *a.* without r. or relief.

Respite (re·spit), *v.* late ME. [a. OF. *respiter* :—L. *respectare* to RESPECT.] I. 1. *trans.* To grant a respite to (a person); *esp.* from death or execution. †b. To save or prolong (a person's life) -1603. †2. To relieve by an interval of rest -1670.

1. Forty days longer we do r. you SHAKS. b. *Meas. for M.* II. iii. 41. 2. From the heat of Noon retir'd, To respit his day-labour with repast MILT.

II. 1. To grant delay or postponement of (a sentence, punishment, obligation, etc.). late ME. 2. To delay, postpone, put off. late ME. 3. †To cease from, give up; to suspend. late ME. 4. *Mil.* a. To suspend (a person) from pay 1705. b. To keep back, withhold (pay) 1802. †5. To rest; to recover *from* something -1769.

2. If you please..to respit your other Business,..I will relate some Passages that will not be unpleasant 1707. 5. For I and mine will r. here a space 1575.

Resplend (rĭsple·nd), *v.* 1492. [ad. L. *resplendere*, f. *re-* RE- + *splendere* to shine.] *intr.* To be resplendent or radiant; to shine brightly.

Resplendence (rĭsple·ndėns). late ME. [ad. late L. *resplendentia*; see prec. and -ENCE.] Brightness, brilliance, lustre, splendour.

The r...of the sonne 1561. The r. of those evident Truths MARVELL. So **Resple·ndency.**

Resplendent (rĭsple·ndėnt), *a.* 1448. [ad. L. *resplendentem*.] Shining, brilliant, splendid.

A temple..r...in colours and gold 1883. Hence **Resple·ndently** *adv.*

†Resple·ndish, *v.* 1475. [ad. F. *resplendiss-*, *resplendir* to RESPLEND.] *intr.* To be resplendent -1549.

Respond (rĭspǫ·nd), *sb.* late ME. [a. OF. f. *respondre*; cf. next and RESPONSE *sb.*] 1.

Eccl. a. = RESPONSORY *sb.* b. A response to a versicle 1555. 2. An answer, a response. Now *rare.* 1600. 3. *Arch.* A half-pillar or half-pier attached to a wall to support an arch 1448.

Respond (rǐspǫ·nd), *v.* 1600. [ad. L. *respondere*, f. *re-* RE- + *spondere* to pledge.] 1. *trans.* To answer or correspond to (something); to reciprocate. Now *rare* or *Obs.* b. *U.S.* To answer, satisfy 1890. 2. *intr.* a. To correspond *to* something (*rare*) 1591. b. To make answer or give a reply, in words 1719. c. To answer by some responsive act; to act in response *to* some influence 1726. d. *U.S.* To give satisfaction 1890.

2. b. I remember him in the divinity school responding and disputing with a perspicuous energy 1734. c. To every Theme responds thy various Lay 1726. d. The defendant is held to r. in damages 1890.

Respondence (rǐspǫ·ndĕns). 1590. [a. obs. F.; see RESPOND *v.* and -ENCE.] †1. Answer, response, to a sound –1600. 2. Correspondence, agreement, concord 1598. b. Response *to* some stimulus 1867.

1. Th' Angelicall soft trembling voyces made To th' instruments divine r. meet SPENSER. So **Respo·ndency**, correspondence, congruence.

Respondent (rǐspǫ·ndĕnt), *sb.* 1528. [f. as next.] 1. One who answers; *spec.* one who defends a thesis against one or more opponents. 2. A defendant in a lawsuit; now *spec.* in a divorce case 1562.

Respondent (rǐspǫ·ndĕnt), *a.* 1533. [ad. L. *respondent-*, *respondere* to RESPOND.] †1. Correspondent (*to* something else) –1726. 2. Answering; making reply. Also, having the position of defendant in an action. 1726. 3. Responsive *to* some influence 1766.

2. To hear the King's Speech, and the r. Address read H. WALPOLE.

‖**Respondentia** (respǫnde·nʃiă). 1727. [mod. L.] A loan upon the cargo of a vessel, to be repaid (with maritime interest) only if the goods arrive safe at their destination. (Cf. BOTTOMRY.)

†**Respo·nsal**, *sb.* late ME. [ad. med.L. *responsalis*, used as sb.] 1. A response –1652. b. A liturgical response or respond –1753. 2. The respondent in a disputation –1574. 3. One appointed by a prelate to give or send replies to questions; an apocrisiary –1610.

†**Respo·nsal**, *a.* late ME. [ad. late L. *responsalis*, f. *responsare* to reply.] 1. Answerable, responsible –1797. 2. Responsive; of the nature of responses –1738.

Response (rǐspǫ·ns). ME. [orig. a. OF. *respons* or *response*. Later, ad. L. *responsum*, f. *respondere*.] 1. An answer, a reply. b. *transf.* and *fig.* An action or feeling which answers to some stimulus or influence 1815. 2. *Eccl.* a. = RESPONSORY *sb.* 1450. b. A part of the liturgy said or sung by the congregation in reply to the priest. (Correl. to VERSICLE.) 3. An oracular answer 1513. 4. *Mus.* In contrapuntal music, the repetition by one part of a theme given by another part 1797.

3. The ancient oracle..from which..the Greeks of his time used to seek responses 1869. Hence **Respo·nseless** *a.* giving no r. or reply.

Responsibility (rǐspǫnsĭbi·lĭti). 1787. [See next and -ITY.] 1. The state or fact of being responsible. 2. With *a* and *pl.* A charge, trust, or duty, for which one is responsible 1796. b. A person or thing for which one is responsible 1832.

2. Anxious to be relieved of a r. that was becoming irksome C. BRONTE.

Responsible (rǐspǫ·nsĭb'l), *a.* 1599. [a. obs. F., f. L. *respons-*, *respondere* to RESPOND.] †1. Correspondent or answering *to* something –1698. 2. Answerable, accountable (*to* another *for* something); liable to be called to account 1643. b. Morally accountable for one's actions; capable of rational conduct 1836. 3. *U.S.* Answerable to a charge 1650. 4. Capable of fulfilling an obligation or trust; reliable, trustworthy; of good credit and repute 1691. b. Of respectable appearance 1780. 5. Involving responsibility or obligation 1855.

1. The Mouth large, but not r. to so large a Body 1698. 2. Being r. to the King for what might happen to us 1662. b. The great God has treated us as r. beings 1836. 4. Very r. tenants 1817. b. He is wrapped in a r. dressing-gown DICKENS. 5. High and r. positions 1880. Hence **Respo·nsibleness. Respo·nsibly** *adv.*

Responsion (rǐspǫ·nʃən). 1470. [a. F., or ad. L. *responsionem*, f. *respondere*.] 1. An answer or reply; a response. Now *rare.* 1502. †2. A sum due to be paid; *esp.* an annual payment which was required from knights of the military orders –1738. 3. *pl.* The first of the three examinations which candidates for the B.A. degree at Oxford are required to pass 1813. 4. A public university disputation 1841.

Responsive (rǐspǫ·nsiv), *a.* 1529. [a. F. *responsif, -ive*, or ad. late L. *responsivus*; see RESPOND *v.* and -IVE.] 1. Answering, responding; making answer or reply. 2. Correspondent or corresponding (*rare*) 1602. 3. Responding readily to some influence 1762. 4. Characterized by the use of responses 1778. †5. Responsible, answerable. JER. TAYLOR.

1. Celestial voices..Sole, or r. each to others note MILT. 3. Thus, and so quick, the helm r. flew 1762. Hence **Respo·nsive-ly** *adv.*, **-ness.**

Responsorial (respǫnsōᵊ·riăl), *a.* 1820. [See next and -AL 1.] 1. Making answer or reply; responsive. 2. Pertaining to, of the nature of, responses 1832.

Responsory (rǐspǫ·nsəri), *sb.* ME. [ad. late L. *responsoria* pl., f. *respons-*, *respondere*; see -ORY [1].] *Eccl.* An anthem said or sung after a lesson by a soloist and choir alternately.

†**Respo·nsory**, *a.* 1586. [ad. med.L. *responsorius*; see prec.] Of the nature of an answer or reply; relating or pertaining to answering –1737.

‖**Ressalah** (rĕsā·lă). 1758. [ad. Urdū (Arab.) *risālah*, f. Arab. *arsala* he sent.] In India, a squadron of native cavalry. Also **Ressaldar** (resăldā·ɹ), [Urdū *risāladār*], a native captain in an Indian cavalry regiment.

Rest, *sb.*[1] [OE. *ræst(e*, *rest(e*. The stem is Com. Teut. in various forms.] I. 1. The natural repose or relief from daily activity which is obtained by sleep. 2. Intermission of labour or exertion of any kind; repose obtained by ceasing to exert oneself. Also, later, with *a* and *pl.* OE. 3. Freedom from or absence of labour, exertion, or activity of any kind OE. b. The freedom from toil or care associated with the future life OE. c. Freedom from distress, molestation, or aggression OE. d. Spiritual or mental peace OE. e. Quietness, peacefulness, or tranquillity in nature 1820. 4. Place of resting or abiding; residence, abode. †Also, abiding, stay. OE. b. An establishment providing shelter or lodging for certain classes of persons during their spare time, or when unemployed 1892. 5. The repose of death or of the grave. Chiefly in phrases, as *to go, be laid, to r.* late ME. 6. a. *Mus.* An interval of silence occurring in one or more parts during a movement, frequently of all the parts together; a pause; also, the character or sign by which this is denoted 1579. b. A pause in speaking or reading 1612. 7. Absence, privation, or cessation of motion; continuance in the same position or place 1475. 8. *At r.* In a state of (physical or mental) repose, quiescence, or inactivity. Also, dead. late ME. b. *To set at r.*, to satisfy, assure; to settle, decide finally. *At r.*, settled 1590.

1. Mans ore-labor'd sense Repaires it selfe by rest SHAKS. Phr. *To go to* (one's) *r.*, to betake oneself to repose for the night; This floure gan close, and goon to r. CHAUCER. *To take* (one's) *r.* 2. Vnto hys chambre was he led anon, To take hys ease, and for to haue hys r. CHAUCER. After several rests, we got to the top 1687. Phr. *At r.* temporarily withdrawn from active warfare to r. and recuperate. *Day of r.* = SABBATH 1 a, b. 3. *transf.* The gale had sigh'd itself to r. SCOTT. b. There remaineth therefore a r. to the people of God *Heb.* iv. 9. c. And the land had r. from warre *Josh.* xiv. 15. d. The truth wherein r. is For every mind CARY. 4. Till we end In dust, our final r. and native home MILT. 7. The common Centre of Gravity..does not change its state of Motion or Rest 1715.

II. 1. a. A support for a fire-arm, employed in steadying the barrel to ensure accuracy of aim 1590. b. A support for a cue in billiards 1868. 2. A thing upon which something else rests; *esp.* that part of a lathe on which the cutting-tool is supported in the operation of turning 1609. 3. Something upon which one rests (*rare*) 1641. b. A projection for the foot to rest on 1869.

2. Seasoned board of oak layd uppon sufficient rests of oake tymber for the grounde floare 1617.

attrib.: **r. camp**, a camp to which an army retires to recuperate after fighting; **r. cure**, a medical cure of which complete rest from all activity is the chief feature; **r. gown**, a loose-fitting garment worn by women on informal occasions; **r. house**, a dawk bungalow; a boarding-house for persons requiring rest.

Rest, *sb.*[2] late ME. [a. F. *reste*, f. *rester* REST *v.*[2]] †1. That which remains over; a remainder or remnant –1693. b. *pl.* Remains, remnants, relics. Now *rare.* 1467. 2. a. The reserve or surplus fund of a bank, esp. of the Bank of England 1844. b. *Comm.* The striking of a balance in an account; the amount of a balance 1825. 3. The remainder or remaining part(s) *of* something 1530. b. The remainder *of* a number of persons, animals, or things 1535. 4. The remainder of something specified or implied in the context 1530. b. The remaining persons or things; the others 1535. 5. In tennis and battledore, a spell of quick and continuous returning of the ball or shuttlecock maintained by the players 1600.

1. Thou hast too, yet, I hope, a R. of Reputation 1693. 3. When England, in common with the r. of Europe, was Catholic 1861. b. The r. of us went to church BERKELEY. 4. In her tone and look he read the r. KEATS. b. The Duchess would drive over.. The r. were to ride DISRAELI. Phrases. (*As*) *for the r.*, as regards, with regard to, what remains. *As to the r.*, in other respects, otherwise. †*Above the r.*, especially. †*To set up one's r.* a. To venture one's final stake or reserve; from the old game of cards called primero, in which the loss of the 'rest', i.e. the stakes kept in reserve, and agreed upon at the beginning, terminated the game. b. *fig.* To stake, hazard, or venture one's all. c. To have or take a resolution; to be resolved. d. To fix or settle *upon* something. e. To take up one's (permanent) abode. †*To set down one's r.*, to stop, make an end; to take up one's residence.

Rest, *sb.*[3] late ME. [Aphetic f. *arest* ARREST *sb.*[1]] †1. Arrest of persons or goods –1587. 2. In mediæval armour, a contrivance fixed to the right side of the cuirass to receive the butt-end of the lance when couched for the charge, and to prevent it from being driven back upon impact. late ME. b. *Her.* A charge supposed to represent the above 1661.

2. A knight..who laid his lance In r., and made as if to fall upon him TENNYSON.

Rest, *v.*[1] [OE. *ræstan*, *restan* = OFris. *resta*, OHG. *restan*, etc.] I. *intr.* 1. To take repose by lying down, and *esp.* by going to sleep; to lie still or in slumber. b. To lie in death or in the grave OE. 2. To take repose by intermission of labour or exertion of any kind; to desist from effort or activity; to become or remain inactive. Also, in recent use, with *up.* OE. b. Of things OE. c. To cease *from*, to have intermission or cessation †*of*, something. late ME. 3. To be at ease or in quiet; also (of persons or things), to continue without change or removal; to stay, remain, lie, have place or station OE. b. To stop or cease at a certain point and remain otherwise inoperative or inactive 1577. c. To be at peace; to have quiet of mind 1782. 4. To have place or position, to settle, lie, be diffused, etc., *on* or *upon* some person or thing OE. b. Of the eyes in relation to the object looked at 1813. c. Of a wing or division of an army 1844. d. To lie as a charge or stigma *on* a person 1678. 5. To lie or lean *on*, *upon*, or *against* a person or thing to obtain repose or support. late ME. b. To rely *on* or *upon*, to trust *to*, some thing or person. late ME. c. To depend *upon*, to be based or founded *on*, something 1530. d. To decide *on* (a person). DRYDEN. 6. a. To remain confident or hopeful, to put trust, *in* something. late ME. b. To lie *in* or remain *with* one, as something to be accomplished or determined 1593.

1. Now good my Lord, lye heere, and r. awhile SHAKS. b. Thus rested Salomon with his fathers COVERDALE *Ecclus.* xlvii. 23. 2. I have often heard of the Pyramids, and shall not r. till I have seen them JOHNSON. Our men..had orders not to let the enemy r. 1896. b. The land was allowed 'to r.'—i.e. to remain unploughed for a period of years 1831. c. And he rested on the seuenth day from all his worke *Gen.* ii. 2. 3. This way the King will come..Here let vs r. SHAKS. Phr. *R. you merry, happy, fair.* b. The matter could not r. here 1782. *To let..rest*, to pursue or prosecute no further. 4. His indignation resteth vpon sinners *Ecclus.* v. 6. The roof..rested upon four concentric arches SCOTT. b. Her eyes resting on a lace cap she had been making 1813. c. Their left resting on the hills 1844. 5. c. Science rests on phenomena observed by the senses 1884. 6. a. Nor

did he doubt her more, But rested in her fealty TENNYSON. b. It rested in your Grace To vnloose this tyde-vp Iustice SHAKS.

II. 1. *refl.* To give oneself rest or repose OE. 2. *trans.* To give (a person) rest; to relieve or refresh by rest; to lay to rest ME. b. To allow (a thing) to rest; to permit to remain undisturbed or quiescent 1580. c. To hold (a weapon) in an easy position 1682. d. *Law.* To cease voluntarily from presenting evidence on (a case) 3. To lay (the head, etc.) *on* or *upon* something for support ME. b. To place (a thing) *upon* something to support it or keep it in position. late ME. c. To throw (some weight) *on* a thing 1809. d. To make or allow to depend, to base *on* something 1732. 4. To place or settle *in* something. late ME.

1. I was very glad to stay there a day to r. myself 1716. 2. He rests me in greene pasture SIDNEY. Phr. (*God* or *heaven*) *r. his soul, him*, etc. Now *arch.* †*God rest you merry.* 3. I vpon this banke will r. my head SHAKS. b. Its ground-sill was rested upon a bed of lead SMEATON. d. The plaintiff..rested her case on equitable grounds 1885. 4. 1 *Hen. VI*, I. i. 44.

Rest, *v.*[2] 1463. [ad. F. *rester* :—L. *restare*, f. *re-* RE- + *stare* to stand.] *intr.* 1. †a. Chiefly *Sc.* To remain due or unpaid -1781. †b. To remain after subtraction, diminution, etc. -1700. c. To be left still undestroyed or unremoved. Now *rare.* 1495. 2. With complement. To remain or be left in a specified condition 1472. b. In valedictory formulæ. Now *arch.* 1580. †3. a. To remain to be done -1667. b. To remain to be dealt with -1636.

1. c. What rested of a goodly face 1867. 2. R. equal happy both DRYDEN. Phr. *To r. assured, satisfied*, etc.; That I may r. assur'd Whether yond Troopes, are Friend or Enemy SHAKS. b. I r. thy affectionate brother, Walter Shandy STERNE.

Rest, *v.*[3] Now *dial.* late ME. [Aphetic f. *arest* ARREST *v.*] †1. *trans.* To stop, check, arrest (*rare*) -1471. 2. To arrest or apprehend (a person). late ME. 3. To arrest or seize (goods). Chiefly *Sc.* 1565.

2. *Com. Err.* IV. iv. 3.

†**Resta·gnate**, *v.* 1655. [f. ppl. stem of L. *restagnare* to overflow.] *intr.* To stagnate; to become or remain stagnant -1676. Hence †**Restagna·tion**, an overflow; stagnation -1706.

Restant (re·stănt), *a.* 1828. [a. F., or ad. L. *restant-*, *restare.*] *Bot.* Persistent.

Restaurant (re·stǫrănt, F. rĕstoraṅ). 1827. [a. F., sb. use of pres. pple. of *restaurer* to RESTORE.] An establishment where refreshments or meals may be obtained.

‖**Restaurateur** (rĕstoratōr). 1796. [F., f. *restaurer.*] 1. A keeper of a restaurant. 2. A restaurant 1804.

Restauration (restǫrē¹·ʃən). Now *rare.* late ME. [a. F., or ad. L. *restaurationem.*] †1. The restoration of a person to a former status or position, as of man to the divine favour or a state of innocence -1718. 2. The restoration of a thing, institution, etc. to its proper or pristine condition. late ME. 3. A restaurant [So G. *restauration.*] 1862.

Rest-balk (re·st₁bǫk), *sb.* 1523. [f. REST *sb.*[1] or *v.*[1] + BALK *sb.* 3.] A ridge left unploughed between two furrows, *esp.* in the process of raftering or ribbing. Hence **Re·st-balk** *v. trans.* to plough (land) with rest-balks.

Re·stful, *a.* ME. [f. REST *sb.*[1]] 1. Characterized by, of the nature of, productive of, rest or repose; free from strife or disturbance. 2. Quiet; peaceful; taking or enjoying rest. late ME.

1. Tyr'd with all these for restfull death I cry SHAKS. Hence **Re·stful-ly** *adv.*, **-ness.**

Re·st-harrow. 1550. [f. REST *sb.*[3] or *v.*[3] + HARROW.] A field-shrub (*Ononis arvensis*), with tough roots, also called CAMMOCK.

Restiff (re·stif), *a.* late ME. [a. OF. *restif* :—pop. L. **restivum*, f. *restare* REST *v.*[2]] = RESTIVE *a.*

Restiform (re·stifǭm), *a.* 1831. [a. mod. L. *restiformis*, f. *restis* a cord.] Cord-like; in *r. body*, one or other of two rounded bundles of fibrous matter lying on each side of the medulla oblongata and connecting it with the cerebellum. So *r. column, tract.*

†**Re·stiness.** 1540. [f. RESTY *a.*[1] + -NESS.] The quality of being restive; restiveness -1708.

Re·sting, *ppl. a.* late ME. [f. REST *v.*[1] + -ING[2].] 1. That rests or is taking a rest. b. *Bot.* in *r. spore, cell*, etc. 1857. 2. Remaining stationary. SHAKS.

1. b. Seeds and resting-spores..are organized in a manner especially adapted to preserve the latent vitality from injury by external influences 1857.

Restitute (re·stitiūt), *v.* 1500. [f. L. *restitut-*, *restituere*, f. *re-* RE- + *statuere* to set up.] 1. *trans.* To restore to a position or status; to reinstate, rehabilitate. Now *rare.* 2. To restore, refund. Also *absol.* To make restitution. 1727. So **Re·stitutor**, a restorer (*rare*). **Resti·tutory** *a.* of or relating to restitution.

Restitution (restitiū·ʃən). ME. [a. OF., or ad. L. *restitutionem*, f. *restituere*; see prec.] 1. The action of restoring or giving back something to its proper owner, or of making reparation to a person for loss or injury inflicted. 2. With *a* and *pl.* A restoration of something taken from another 1440. 3. The action of restoring a person or persons to a previous status or position; the fact of being restored or reinstated; a document authorizing such restoration. Now *rare.* late ME. 4. The action of restoring a thing or institution to its original state or form. (In later use only in echoes of, or with ref. to, Acts iii. 21). late ME. 5. †a. Reposition, replacement (*rare*) -1658. b. Tendency to return to a previous position by virtue of elasticity or resilience 1656.

1. Euer the Frenche Ambassadours promised restitucion of euery thyng, but none was restored 1548. Phr. *To make r.*; They had wronged her.., therefore they ought to make her r. 1720. 2. David passes sentence..that there should be a fourfold r. made 1729. 3. After the R. of King Charles the Second DE FOE. Phr. *R. in blood*, readmission to the privileges of birth and rank of one under sentence of corruption of blood (see CORRUPTION 2), or of his heirs. 4. The R. of all Things to their first State of Perfection 1781.

Restive (re·stiv), *a.* 1599. [later f. RESTIFF, assim. to adjs. in -IVE.] †1. Inclined to rest or remain still; inactive, inert -1833. †2. Persistent, obstinate, settled or fixed *in* an opinion or course of action -1826. 3. Of horses: Refusing to go forward; stubbornly standing still; obstinately moving backwards or to the side when being driven or ridden; hence, intractable, refractory 1656. b. *transf.* Of persons or things 1687. 4. Of actions: Characterized by unwillingness or resistance to control 1806.

1. What great imployment with stirring and mettald spirits, what perpetuall quiet with heavie and r. bodies 1599. 2. Every one being r. in his opinion, there can nothing..be concluded 1660. 3. The beasts..became r. and went back MACAULAY. b. He turned r. at the least attempt at coercion 1863. 4. The outward man yielded a reluctant and r. compliance SCOTT. Hence **Re·stive-ly** *adv.*, **-ness.**

Restless (re·stlės), *a.* OE. [f. REST *sb.*[1] + -LESS.] 1. Deprived of rest; finding no rest; *esp.* uneasy in mind or spirit. b. Marked by unrest; affording no rest 1605. 2. Constantly stirring or active, or desirous to be so; averse to being quiet or settled 1475. †b. Const. *to* (with inf.) or *of*: Impatient -1725. c. *spec.* in names of animals, as *r. cavy, thrush*, etc. 1771. 3. Of conditions: Unceasing, continuous. late ME. b. Of things: Never ceasing or pausing 1596. 4. quasi-*adv.* Restlessly. late ME.

1. R. he passed the remnants of the night DRYDEN. b. R. was the chair; the back erect Distress'd the weary loins COWPER. 2. Cities, humming with a r. crowd COWPER. All the reason..For so much rambling, was, a r. mind CRABBE. 3. A world of restlesse Cares SHAKS. b. That Goddesse blind, that stands vpon the rolling restlesse Stone SHAKS. Hence **Re·stless-ly** *adv.*, **-ness.**

Restorable (rĭstōᵊ·răb'l), *a.* 1611. [f. RESTORE *v.* + -ABLE.] That can be restored or brought back to a former condition.

Restoral (rĭstōᵊ·răl). 1611. [f. RESTORE *v.* + -AL 2.] Restoration, restitution.

Restoration (restǫrē¹·ʃən). 1660. [Later f. RESTAURATION, after RESTORE *v.*] 1. The action of restoring to a former state or position; the fact of being restored or reinstated. b. *Theol.* = RESTITUTION 4. 1781. 2. *Hist.* a. The re-establishment of the monarchy in England with the return of Charles II in 1660; also, the period marked by this event 1718. b. The reinstatement, in 1814, of the Bourbons in the sovereignty of France 1839. 3. The action of restoring a person to health or consciousness; recovery of physical strength 1605. 4. The action or process of restoring something to an unimpaired or perfect condition 1801. b. *Arch.* The process of carrying out alterations and repairs with the idea of restoring a building to something like its original form; a general renovation 1824. c. A representation of the original form of a ruined building, extinct animal, etc. 1836. 5. The action of restoring something to one who has been previously deprived of it 1788.

1. The happy R. of his Majesty to his People and Kingdoms 1660. That period which has been distinguished as the r. of letters 1841. 4. The r. of disfigured and decayed works of art 1835. The passages which defy r. 1874. b. Under the name of 'r.' the ruin of the noblest architecture..is constant throughout Europe RUSKIN. c. Fig. 81 represents a r. of this extinct elephant 1878. 5. The r. of estates that his predecessors had alienated 1877. Hence **Restora·tioner**, = RESTORATIONIST.

Restora·tionism. 1834. [f. prec. + -ISM.] The doctrine that all men will ultimately be restored to a state of happiness in the future life. So **Restora·tionist**, a believer in r.

Restorative (rĭstōᵊ·rătiv, -ǭ·rătiv), *a.* and *sb.* late ME. [a. OF. **restoratif*, var. of *restauratif.*] A. *adj.* Pertaining to restoration (of strength or health); capable of restoring or renewing.

To try if there was any r. quality in the more genial air of that climate 1807.

B. *sb.* A food, cordial, or medicine, which has the effect of restoring health or strength. late ME. b. A means of restoring one to consciousness 1852. Hence **Resto·ratively** *adv.*

†**Resto·re**, *sb.* 1450. [f. next.] Restoration -1646.

Restore (rĭstōᵊ·ɹ), *v.* ME. [a. OF. *restorer* :—L. *restaurare.*] 1. *trans.* To give back, to make return or restitution of (anything previously taken away or lost). 2. To make amends for; to compensate, make good (loss or damage). Now *rare* or *Obs.* ME. b. To set right, repair (decay, etc.). *rare.* 1567. 3. To build up again; to re-erect or reconstruct. Now *spec.* to repair and alter (a building) so as to bring it as nearly as possible to its original form ME. b. To bring back to the original state; to improve, repair, or retouch (a thing) so as to bring it back to its original condition 1679. c. To reproduce or represent (an extinct animal, etc.) in its original form 1771. 4. a. To replace (mankind) in a state of grace; to free from the effects of sin ME. b. To reinstate or replace (a person) in a former office, dignity, or estate 1450. c. To bring (a person or part of the body) back to a healthy or vigorous state. late ME. d. To bring back to mental calm. Now *rare.* 1582. 5. To renew; to set up or bring into existence again; to re-establish, bring back into use, etc. ME. b. To replace or insert (words or letters which are missing or illegible in a text) 1855. 6. To bring back (a person or thing) *to* a previous, original, or normal condition ME. b. To grant to or obtain for (a person) reinstatement *to* former rank, office, or possessions 1533. c. To take or put back *into*, to convey or hand back *to*, a place 1450.

1. Your helthe shall be restored to yow CAXTON. 2. Time may r. some losses FULLER. 3. At Winchester, where they are restoring the cathedral 1820. 4. a. R. thou them that be penitent *Bk. Com. Prayer.* b. *To r. in blood*: see BLOOD *sb.* III. 5. c. The quiet place, the pure air..will r. you in a few days DICKENS. 5. It was with great difficulty that the..man in the cocked hat restored order 1820. 6. The application of faradic electricity quickly restored the patient to consciousness 1882. b. The innocent were restored to their rank and fortunes GIBBON. Hence **Resto·rement**, the act of restoring; restoration, restitution. **Resto·rer**, one who restores.

Restrain (rĭstrē¹·n), *v.* ME. [a. OF. *restrai(g)n-*, stem of *restraindre* :—L. *restringere.*] 1. *trans.* To check, hold back, or prevent (a person or thing) *from* some course of action. b. Without const. To keep (a person) in check or under control. Freq. *refl.* late ME. c. To place under arrest or in confinement; to deprive of personal liberty or freedom of action; also, to shut in by material barriers 1494. d. To deprive (a person) *of* liberty by restraint 1530. 2. To check, to put a check or stop upon, to repress, keep down (a desire, feeling, activity, physical agent, force, etc.) ME. 3. To restrict, limit, confine ME. †4. To withhold, keep back, *from* a person –1594. †5. To forbid or prohibit (a person) *to* do something; to keep back *from* something desired –1791. †6. a. To draw tightly (*rare*) –1596. b. To compel or constrain (*rare*) –1655. 7. *intr.* To refrain (*from* something; †also with infin.). Now *rare.* 1594.

1. This faculty tends to r. men from doing mischief to each other 1729. b. If I want skill or force to r. the Beast that I ride upon COWLEY. 2. I could hardly r. my feelings 1839. The necessity of restraining population MILL. 6. a. *Tam. Shr.* III. ii. 59. b. By antient custome no Vestal Virgin or Flamen of Jupiter was restrained to swear FULLER. Hence **Restrai·nable** *a.* capable of being restrained. **Restrai·nedly** *adv.* with restraint. **Restrai·ner.** **Restrai·ningly** *adv.* †**Restrai·nment,** restraint –1688.

Restraint (rĭstrē¹·nt), *sb.* late ME. [a. OF. *restrainte*, f. *restraindre* to RESTRAIN.] 1. The action of restraining or checking a thing, operation, etc.; an instance of this, a stoppage. 2. A means of restraining or checking persons from a course of action, or of keeping them under control; any force or influence which has a restraining effect; an instance of restraining or of being restrained. late ME. b. Without article. Restraining action or influence, as applied to persons 1567. c. The state or condition of being restrained; *esp.* abridgement of liberty, confinement 1547. 3. †a. A prohibition –1594. b. An embargo. Usu. *r. of princes.* 1475. 4. Constraint; reserve 1601. †5. Restriction or limitation –1746.

1. A bill for the r. of the Press 1863. *Without r.*, freely, copiously. 2. All Government is a R. upon Liberty 1672. b. R. she will not brook MILT. c. 'Tis not R. or Liberty That makes Men prisoners or free BUTLER. 4. She..did angle for mee, Madding my eagernesse with her r. SHAKS. 5. This r. of Easter to a certaine number of dayes HOOKER.

Restrict (rĭstri·kt), *v.* 1535. [f. L. *restrict-*, *restringere* to RESTRINGE.] *trans.* To confine (some person or thing) *to* or *within* certain limits; to limit or bound. b. To restrain by prohibition 1835.

The power of preaching was restricted by the issue of licences only to the friends of the Primate 1874. b. The act..which restricted the Bank from making payments in gold 1835. Hence **Restri·cted-ly** *adv.*

Restriction (rĭstri·kʃən). late ME. [a. F., or ad. late L. *restrictionem*, f. *restringere* to RESTRINGE.] 1. A limitation imposed upon a person or thing; a condition or regulation of this nature. b. The action or fact of limiting or restricting 1629. 2. *Logic.* Limitation or qualification of a term 1551. 3. Constriction (*rare*) 1758.

1. The restrictions under which our first parents were laid 1772. b. Yet this must be understood with some r. BLACKSTONE. 3. Severe r. of the waist 1871. Hence **Restri·ctionary** *a.* imposing restrictions.

Restri·ctionist. 1849. [f. prec. + -IST.] One who advocates the restriction of some practice, institution, etc., such as the liquor-trade.

Restrictive (rĭstri·ktiv), *a.* and *sb.* late ME. [a. F. *restrictif, -ive*, ad. late L. *restrictivus*; see RESTRICT *v.* and -IVE.] A. *adj.* †1. = RESTRINGENT *a.* 1. –1727. 2. Of terms, expressions, etc.: Implying, conveying, or expressing restriction or limitation 1579. 3. Restricting; limitative *of* the power or scope of some thing or person 1652.

1. This Plaister being r. 1607. 2. In order to restrain the devise..it was necessary to shew r. words 1827. 3. The r. negative power of conscience CLARENDON.

B. *sb.* A term or expression having the force of, or implying, a restriction or qualification 1671.

The indeterminate character of the restrictives, *alone* and *only* BENTHAM. Hence **Restri·ctive-ly** *adv.*, **-ness** (*rare*).

Restringe (rĭstri·ndʒ), *v.* 1597. [ad. L. *restringere* to bind fast, confine, f. *re-* RE- + *stringere* to draw tight.] †1. *trans.* To affect (a person) with costiveness; to have an astringent effect upon (a part of the body) –1758. 2. To confine, limit, restrict. Now *rare.* 1604.

2. Of Passions..some..dilate, and some compresse and r. the heart 1604.

†**Restri·ngent,** *a.* and *sb.* 1578. [ad. L. *restringentem*; see prec. and -ENT.] A. *adj.* 1. Having astringent or binding properties; *esp.* tending to restrain the action of the bowels –1799. b. Of outward applications: Styptic –1834. 2. Constipated, costive (*rare*) –1635. B. *sb.* 1. A word which has a limitative or restricting force –1671. 2. A medicine or application which possesses astringent or styptic properties –1792. So †**Restri·ngency,** the quality or property of being r.

Resty (re·sti), *a.*[1] *Obs.* exc. *dial.* 1515. [Var. of RESTIFF *a.*; cf. *hasty, tardy.*] 1. = RESTIVE *a.* 3. †2. Disinclined for action or exertion; sluggish, indolent, lazy –1711. †3. Of land: Fallow, untilled (*rare*) –1649.

2. Some great household..where the Maister is too restie or too rich to say his own prayers MILT. Hence **Re·stily** *adv.* stubbornly.

†**Re·sty,** *a.*[2] ME. [a. OF. *resté* left over.] Rancid, REASTY –1671.

Result (rĭzɒ·lt), *sb.* 1626. [f. the vb.] †1. The action of springing back again *to* a former position or place. BACON. 2. A decision or resolution; the outcome of the deliberations of a council or assembly. Now *U.S.* 1647. b. The effect, issue, or outcome of some action, process, design, etc. 1651. c. The quantity, formula, etc., obtained by calculation in arithmetic or algebra 1771.

1. The sound being produced betweene the String and the Aire..by the Returne or the R. of the String 1626. 2. If our proposals once again were heard We should compel them to a quick r. MILT. b. The whole proceedings of the said resident were the natural r. of the treaty of Chunar BURKE. c. If you substitute 2 for *x*, the r. will be 24. 1771. Hence **Resu·ltful, Resu·ltless** *adjs.*

Result (rĭzɒ·lt), *v.* late ME. [ad. L. *resultare* to spring back, f. *re-* RE- + *saltare* to leap.] 1. *intr.* To arise as a consequence, effect, or conclusion *from* some action, process, etc.; to end or conclude *in* a specified manner. †2. To recoil; to rebound or spring back –1784. 3. a. *Law.* To revert *to* a person 1768. †b. To appertain or fall *to* a person –1793.

1. Crevasses..r. from the motion of the glacier TYNDALL. 2. The huge round stone resulting with a bound Thunders impetuous down POPE.

Resultance (rĭzɒ·ltăns). Now *rare.* 1440. [See RESULT *v.* and -ANCE.] †1. Origin, beginning. CAPGRAVE. †2. The sum or gist *of* something –1640. 3. †a. Something which issues, proceeds, or emanates from another thing –1680. †b. A reflection (of light) –1652. c. A result, effect, or outcome. Now *rare.* 1635. †4. The fact of issuing or resulting (*from* something); esp. *by r.*, derivatively –1680. So †**Resu·ltancy** –1701.

Resultant (rĭzɒ·ltănt), *sb.* late ME. [See next.] †1. *Arith.* The total or sum. late ME. only. 2. *Mech.* That force which is the equivalent of two or more forces acting from different directions at one point; *gen.* the composite or final effect of any two or more physical forces. Also *transf.* of other than physical forces. 1815. b. The product or outcome *of* something 1847. 3. *Math.* = ELIMINANT B. 1856.

2. b. Collective social action is the mere r. of many individual actions 1871.

Resultant (rĭzɒ·ltănt), *a.* 1615. [ad. L. *resultantem*; see RESULT *v.* and -ANT[1].] †1. Issuing or shining by reflection –1661. 2. That results, resulting; consequent 1639. Hence **Resu·ltantly** *adv.*

Resumable (rĭziū·măb'l), *a.* 1644. [f. RESUME *v.* + -ABLE.] Capable of being resumed.

Resume (rĭziū·m), *v.* late ME. [ad. OF. *resumer*, or L. *resumere*, f. *re-* RE- + *sumere* to take.] I. *trans.* 1. To assume, put on, or take to oneself anew (something previously lost, given up, or discarded). b. To take again, reoccupy (a place or seat) 1633. 2. To take up or begin again, recommence (some interrupted practice or occupation) 1440. b. *esp.* To go on again with (a discourse, discussion, remark) 1600. 3. To take back to oneself (something previously given or granted) 1450. 4. a. To take back (a person) to, or into some relation with, oneself 1494. b. To take or pick up (a thing) again; to return to the use of 1596. 5. To recapitulate or summarize (facts) 1676.

1. Ile r. the shape which thou dost thinke I haue cast off for euer SHAKS. Thus they out of their plaints new hope r. MILT. Could I see your natural good sense r. its influence over passion 1791. b. Reason resum'd her place, and passion fled DRYDEN. 2. I resumed some work I had dropped C. BRONTË. b. The Senate resumed the consideration of the Treaty 1795. 3. Gods..R. not, what themselves have giv'n SWIFT. 4. a. R. thy spirit from this world of thrall VAUGHAN. b. He was content to r. his pipe and listen 1873. 5. A philosophy which should r. all his views upon nature, man, and society 1878.

II. *absol.* 1. To reassume possession 1565. 2. To give a résumé 1770. 3. a. To begin to speak again 1802. b. To recommence work or business 1817. c. To continue; to begin again 1815.

1. *Cymb.* III. i. 15. 3. a. When he could again be heard.., he resumed, as follows 1802. b. The House then resumed 1817.

‖**Résumé** (rezüme). 1804. [Fr., pa. pple. of *resumer* to RESUME.] A summary, epitome.

Resu·mmons (rī-). Now *Hist.* 1495. [a. AF. *resomons.*] *Law.* A second or renewed summons.

Resumption (rĭzɒ·mᵖʃən). 1449. [a. F. *résumption*, or ad. L. *resumptionem*, f. *resumere* to RESUME.] 1. *Law.* The action, on the part of the Crown or other authority, of reassuming possession of lands, rights, etc., which have been bestowed on others; a case or instance of this. b. *gen.* The action of taking back or recovering something 1702. 2. The action of resuming, taking up, or beginning again 1589. b. *Banking.* A return to specie payments 1866. 3. Recapitulation, résumé (*rare*) 1727.

1. b. Resumptions are as ordinary with this lady [fortune] as with a House of Commons 1702. 2. The hour's past..For the r. of his trial BYRON. 3. A theory, in fact, which is the r. and complement of them all 1836.

Resumptive (rĭzɒ·mᵖtiv), *a.* late ME. [orig. ad. L. *resumptivus* restorative. In later use a new formation.] †1. *Med.* Restorative (*rare*) –1657. 2. That repeats, or summarizes 1854.

2. The statement is r. 1884. Hence **Resu·mptively** *adv.*

Resupinate (rĭsiū·pinēˡt), *a.* 1776. [ad. L. *resupinat-*, *resupinare* to bend back.] Chiefly *Bot.* Turned or twisted upwards. So **Resu·pinated** *ppl. a.* 1661.

Resupination (rĭsiūpinē¹·ʃən). 1624. [See prec. and -ATION.] †1. a. The effect of height upon the proportions of a standing figure (*rare*) –1638. b. The fact of lying on, or the action of turning upon, the back –1661. 2. *Bot.* Inversion of parts 1760.

Resupine (rĭsiupəi·n), *a.* 1628. [ad. L. *resupinus*; see RE- and SUPINE *a.*] †1. Listless, apathetic –1643. 2. Lying on the back; inclined backwards 1669.

2. One, r., Upcast it high toward the dusky clouds COWPER.

Resurge (rĭsɒ̄·ɹdʒ), *v.* 1575. [ad. L. *resurgere*, f. *re-* RE- + *surgere* to rise.] *intr.* To rise or come back again.

Resurgence (rĭsɒ̄·ɹdʒĕns). 1834. [See RESURGENT and -ENCE.] The act of rising again.

Resurgent (rĭsɒ̄·ɹdʒĕnt), *sb.* and *a.* 1768. [ad. L. *resurgentem, resurgere* to RESURGE.] A. *sb.* One who has risen again. B. *adj.* That rises, or tends to rise, again 1808.

R. Poland, he says, means r. Hungary, and even r. Italy 1854.

Resurrect (rezɒre·kt), *v.* 1772. [Back-formation from RESURRECTION.] 1. *trans.* To raise (a person) from the dead or from the grave; to restore to life or to view again. 2. *intr.* To rise again from the dead 1823.

1. *fig.* Slavery is already dead, and cannot be resurrected 1863.

Resurrection (rezɒre·kʃən). ME. [a. OF., or ad. late L. *resurrectionem*, f. *resurgere* to RESURGE.] 1. (Now with cap.) The rising again of Christ after his death and burial. 2. The rising again of men at the Last Day ME. 3. The action or fact of rising again from sleep, disuse, etc.; revival; restoration to previous status or vogue. late ME. 4. A resurrected thing (*rare*) 1771.

1. Forty dayes after his resurreccyon that blessed lorde ascended 1526. 2. So shalt thou ioyefully abide the general resurection. late ME. 3. See we not a yearly R. of grasse, herbs, grain,..every Spring tide? 1657. 4. His horse was..a r. of dry bones SMOLLETT.

attrib. and *Comb.*, as **r. flower** = *r. plant* b; **-man,** one who made a trade of exhuming bodies in order to sell them to anatomists; **r. pie,** a pie made out of remains from previous meals; **r. plant,** (*a*) a Californian plant, *Selaginella lepidophylla*, the dried fronds of which unfold again when moistened; (*b*) the Rose of Jericho, an Eastern plant having similar properties. Hence **Resurre·ctional** *a.* relating to, or concerned with, r. **Resurre·ctionary** *a.* restoratory; concerned or connected with the disinterment of bodies for anatomical purposes. **Resurre·ctionize**, *v. trans.* to resurrect.

Resurre·ctionist. 1776. [f. prec. + -IST.] 1. An exhumer and stealer of corpses; a resurrection-man. 2. One who revives or brings to light again. (Chiefly *transf.* from prec.) 1834.

†Resu·scitate, *pa. pple.* 1520. [ad. L. *resuscitatus, resuscitare*; see next.] Revived, restored to life –1680.

Resuscitate (rɪ̆sʊ·siteɪt), *v.* 1532. [f. ppl. stem of L. *resuscitare*, f. *re-* RE- + *suscitare* to raise.] 1. *trans.* To restore (a person) to life (physical or spiritual) or to consciousness. 2. To revive, renew, restore (a thing) 1532. 3. *intr.* To revive, come to life again 1652.

1. Her mother..took means to r. her child 1839. 2. No one discovery resuscitates the world 1851. 3. Every plant will earlier or later r. 1787. So **Resu·scitable** *a.* capable of being resuscitated. **Resu·scitative** *a.* revivifying, reviving. **Resu·scitator,** one who resuscitates or revives.

Resuscitation (rɪ̆sʊsitēɪ·ʃən). 1526. [ad. late L. *resuscitationem.*] 1. Restoration to life. b. *spec.* Restoration of life or consciousness in one almost or apparently drowned or dead 1788. 2. Revival, renewal, restoration (of something) 1663.

1. b. Efforts at r. should be kept up for at least two hours 1875. 2. The r. of their national life 1874.

Ret, *v.* 1440. [History obsc.; the mod. form corresponds to Du. *reten.*] 1. *trans.* To soak (esp. flax or hemp) in water, or expose to moisture, in order to soften or season. 2. Of hay, etc. *pass.*: To be spoiled by exposure to wet 1641. 3. *trans.* and *intr.* To rot 1846.

Retable (rɪ̄·teɪb'l). 1823. [a. F. *rétable, retable*; cf. med.L. *retrotabulum* 'rear table'.] *Eccl.* A shelf or ledge (on which ornaments may be placed), or a frame enclosing decorated panels, above the back of an altar. So ‖ **Reta·blo,** ‖ **Reta·bulum.**

Retail (rɪ̄·teɪl), *sb.* late ME. [a. OF., masc. or *retaille* fem., a piece cut off, f. *retaillier*, f. *re-* RE- + *taillier* to cut; see TAIL *v.*] 1. The sale of commodities in small quantities. (Often in adv. phrases, with *by*, *at*, or used advb. without prep.) †2. Detail (of a matter) –1678. 3. A retailer 1884. 4. *attrib.* or as *adj.* Of or pertaining to, connected with, engaged in, the sale of commodities in small quantities 1601.

1. What barbarous parents,..to oblige a person of my figure to deal out tea and sugar r.! 1784.

Retail (rɪ̆tēɪ·l), *v.* late ME. [See prec.] 1. *trans.* To sell (goods, etc.) in small quantities. b. *intr.* To be sold by retail 1881. 2. To recount or tell over again; to relate in detail; to repeat to others 1594.

1. He is Wits Pedler and retailes his Wares, At Wakes, and Wassels SHAKS. b. Turbot, brill, and halibut r. at 9*d.* per lb. 1897. 2. The licensed fool retail'd his jest SCOTT. Hence **Retai·ler,** one who retails goods, a small dealer or trader; one who repeats or relates. **Retai·lment,** the act of retailing.

Retain (rɪ̆tēɪ·n), *v.* late ME. [ad. OF. *retenir* (= L. *retinere*), f. *re-* RE- + *tenir* to hold.] I. *trans.* †1. To restrain; to hold back, check, or stop; to prevent or hinder –1737. b. To keep in custody or under control; to prevent from departing, issuing, or separating; to hold fixed in some place or position 1533. 2. †a. To entertain (*rare*) –1585. b. To keep attached to one's person or engaged in one's service 1450. c. To engage (a barrister) by the payment of a preliminary fee, in order to secure his services for one's own cause if necessary 1548. 3. To keep hold or possession of; to continue to have or keep, in various senses 1450. b. To continue to use, practise, etc. 1548. c. To continue to have or possess (some attribute, quality, etc.) 1582. d. To allow to remain, in place of discarding or removing; to preserve 1802. 4. To keep or bear in mind; to remember 1474.

1. b. Two Mils to retaine the water when the Sea ebs 1617. 2. b. A great number of knights were retained in his service HUME. c. *Cliens*..is also he whiche hath retayned a lawyer to susteyne his matter ELYOT. 3. His Power..he seem'd Above the rest still to r. MILT. He still aimed at retaining the most lucrative of his benefices FROUDE. c. A kind of Stone that long retains its whiteness 1687. 4. It requires a..good memory to r. these distinctions 1782.

II. *intr.* †1. To refrain *from* something –1602. 2. To adhere, belong, be attached, or be a retainer *to* one –1711. 3. To continue, remain. DONNE.

2. Most of the Members..thought it an honour to r. to some great Lord, and to wear his blew Coat 1681. Hence **Retai·nable** *a.* capable of being retained; whence **Retainabi·lity, Retai·nableness. Retai·nal,** retention. **Retai·nment,** the (*or* an) act of retaining; retention; †maintenance.

Retainer [1] (rɪ̆tēɪ·nəɹ). 1453. [f. RETAIN *v.* + -ER [4].] †1. The act or fact of retaining, withholding, or keeping for oneself; an authorization to do this. Now *rare.* 2. a. The fact of being retained in some capacity 1775. b. An authorization given to an attorney to act in a case. Chiefly *U.S.* 1816. 3. A fee paid to a barrister to secure his services; engagement by a retaining-fee 1818. b. A sum paid to secure special services if required 1859.

3. b. Half-pay to the disbanded officers..was meant to be a r. as well as a reward MACAULAY.

Retainer (rɪ̆tēɪ·nəɹ). 1540. [f. RETAIN *v.* + -ER [1].] 1. One who or that which retains or holds; a maintainer, preserver 1548. 2. A dependent or follower of some person of rank or position; one attached to a house or owing it service. Now *Hist.* or *arch.* 1540. b. *U.S.* A person irregularly attached to an army; a sutler, camp-follower 1890.

2. A swarm of armed retainers whom the lord could not control, and whom he conceived himself bound to protect STUBBS. *transf. Hen. VIII*, II. iv. 113. Hence **Retai·nership.**

Retaining (rɪ̆tēɪ·niŋ), *ppl. a.* 1611. [-ING.[2]] That retains; serving to retain or hold by physical force or resistance.

R. fee = RETAINER [1] 3. *R. wall*, a wall built to support a mass of earth or water.

Retaliate (rɪ̆tæ·lieɪt), *v.* 1611. [f. late L. *retaliat-, retaliare*, f. *re-* RE- + *talis.*] 1. *trans.* To requite, repay in kind, make return for: a. kindness, etc. Now *rare.* b. injury, ill-treatment, etc. 1631. c. Const. *upon* (a person). Also, to inflict in return, to cast back, *upon* (a person). 1676. 2. *intr.* To make return or requital (now only of injury, insult, etc.) 1658.

1. a. Our Ambassador sent word..to the Dukes son, his visit should be retaliated 1638. c. Thus did the Lord..r. upon him the innocent blood which he had shed 1676. So **Reta·liative** *a.* tending to, or of the nature of, retaliation; revengeful. **Reta·liatory** *a.* pertaining to, of the nature of, retaliation.

Retaliation (rɪ̆tæli,ēɪ·ʃən). 1581. [See prec. and -ATION.] 1. The action of retaliating; the return of like for like; repayment in kind; requital, reprisal. 2. An instance of this; a return or requital, *esp.* of injuries 1645.

1. Contentiousness and Cruelty seldom fail of R. BENTLEY. 2. This sanguinary r. on the Turks 1847.

‖**Retama** (retā·mă). 1852. [Sp. *retama*, ad. Arab. *retām*, pl. of *retem.*] A class of shrubby plants, chiefly found in the Mediterranean region, related to the broom, and usu. referred to the genus *Genista.* Hence **Reta·mine** (*Chem.*), an alkaloid extracted from *Retama sphærocarpa.*

Retard (rɪ̆tā·ɹd), *sb.* 1788. [a. F., f. *retarder*; see next.] 1. Retardation, delay. 2. *R. of the tide* or *of high water*, the interval between the moon's transit and the high water following upon this 1833.

1. *In r.*, retarded, delayed; in the rear *of*; I was far in r. of them in real knowledge RUSKIN.

Retard (rɪ̆tā·ɹd), *v.* 1489. [ad. F. *retarder*, or L. *retardare*, f. *re-* RE- + *tardus* slow.] 1. *trans.* To keep back, delay, hinder, impede (a person or thing in respect of progress, movement, action, or accomplishment). 2. To delay the progress or accomplishment of, to impede the course, of (an action, movement, etc.) 1572. b. To defer, put off (*rare*) 1735. 3. *intr.* To be delayed; to come, appear, or happen later; to undergo retardation 1646.

1. This fleet..was extremely retarded by the winds 1732. 2. They would r. instead of accelerating the further increase ADAM SMITH. b. To advance or r. the hour of refection SCOTT. 3. Putrefaction..shall r. or accelerate according to the subject and season of the year SIR T. BROWNE. So **†Reta·rdate** *v.* **Reta·rdative** *a.* tending or having power to r. **Reta·rdatory** *a.* having a retarding effect or influence. **Reta·rder,** one who or that which checks or delays. **Reta·rdment,** retardation; delay, check.

Retardation (rɪ̆taɹdēɪ·ʃən). late ME. [a. F., or ad. L. *retardationem*, f. *retardare.*] 1. The action of retarding in respect of action or movement, or making later in happening; an instance of this. 2. In the physical sciences: a. of motion or moving bodies. (Opp. to *acceleration.*) 1642. b. of the tides: (*a*) The excess of periods of high water above the solar day. (*b*) = RETARD *sb.* 2. 1797. c. of celestial bodies 1812. d. of rays or waves of light, heat, etc. 1831. 3. *Mus.* a. Delay in the progression of a part or note 1818. b. A slackening of the tempo 1853.

1. Causing a r. of reading, and some sloth or relaxation of memory BACON. This r. or decreased rate of growth 1891. 2. a. In an elliptical orbit there is now acceleration and now r. 1862. 3. a. When an interval of a melody (or of an inner part) is kept back in ascending, it is called a r. 1868.

Retch (retʃ, rɪ̄tʃ), *v.* 1548. [Var. of REACH *v.*[2]] †1. *intr.* To hawk, bring *up* phlegm –1623. 2. a. To make efforts to vomit 1850. b. *trans.* To throw up in vomiting 1888.

†Retchless, var. of RECKLESS *a.* q.v.

‖ **Rete** (rɪ̄·ti). *Pl.* **retia** (rɪ̄·tiă, rɪ̄·ʃiă). late ME. [L., = net.] †1. a. An open-work metal plate, affixed to an astrolabe, and serving to indicate the positions of the principal fixed stars –1613. b. A graduated scale affixed to an astronomical telescope –1677. 2. *Anat.* a. *R. mirabile*, an elaborate network or plexus of blood-vessels 1541. b. The under portion of the epidermis, in which the pigment-cells are situated. Usu. in full, *r. mucosum*, or *r. Malpighii.* 1797.

Retene (retɪ̄·n). 1867. [f. Gr. ῥητίνη resin; see -ENE.] *Chem.* A hydrocarbon, polymeric with benzene, obtained from resinous (esp. fossil) pine-wood.

Retention (rɪ̆te·nʃən). late ME. [a. OF. *retencion*:—L. *retentionem*, f. *retinere* to keep back.] 1. *Med.* The fact of retaining within the body one of the secretions (esp. the urine) which are normally evacuated; a case or instance of this. 2. a. The fact of retaining things in the mind; the power or ability to do this; memory 1483. b. The fact of maintaining, keeping up, or continuing to use something 1625. 3. The action or fact of keeping to oneself or in one's own hands, under one's power or authority 1540. 4. †a. Detention of persons by forcible or other means –1615. b. The action or fact of holding fast or keeping fixed in a place or position; the fact or property of being kept, or remaining, in place 1597. †c. Restraint –1633. 5. Power to retain; capacity for holding or keeping something 1601.

3. *Twel. N.* v. i. 84. 5. No womans heart So bigge, to hold so much, they lacke r. SHAKS.

†Rete·ntive, *sb.* late ME. [a. OF., or from the adj.] 1. Recollection, memory –1454. 2. A restraining force; a means of restraint –1650. 3. *pl.* The organs by which the natural excretions of the body are regulated –1717.

Retentive (rɪ̆te·ntiv), *a.*[1] late ME. [a. OF. *retentif, -ive*, repr. L. **retentivus*, f. ppl. stem of *retinere.*] 1. Of the mind or memory: Tenacious; good at remembering. b. Of persons: Possessed of a good memory 1758. †2. *The r. virtue* or *faculty*, the ability to retain the physical secretions, or to keep food within the stomach –1683. †3. Sparing, niggardly –1678. 4. Having the property of, tending or inclined to, the retention or keeping *of* something 1582. 5. Holding or confining; keeping firm hold 1601. b. *Surg.* Serving to keep (a dressing, organ, etc.) in the proper place 1597. c. Apt to retain or hold moisture 1730. †6. Restrained, cautious, reticent –1626.

1. The memory of the peple is not retentyf CAXTON. 3. Never was King more frugal, never King more r. in his largesses 1654. 5. *Jul. C.* I. iii. 95. Hence **Rete·ntive·ly** *adv.*, **-ness.**

†Rete·ntive, *a.*[2] [f. F. *retentir* + -IVE.] That reverberates or resounds. POPE.

Retenti·vity. 1881. [f. RETENTIVE *a.*[1] + -ITY.] *Electr.* The capacity for retaining magnetism after the action of the magnetizing force has ceased; also = coercive force (see COERCIVE *a.*).

‖ **Retenue** (rətənü). 1748. [F., pa. pple. fem. of *retenir* to restrain, used subst.] Reserve, restraint, caution, self-control.

Retepore (re·tɪ̆pōəɹ). 1878. [ad. mod.L. *Retepora*, f. L. *rete* net + *porus* PORE *sb.*] An ectoproctous polyzoan of the genus *Retepora.*

‖**Retiarius** (rīti,ē·riɒ̆s, rīʃ-). 1647. [L., f. *rete* a net.] A Roman gladiator who carried a net with which to entangle his adversary.

Retiary (rī·ʃiări), *a.* 1646. [f. as prec.] 1. Pertaining or relating to the making of webs, nets, or the like 1658. 2. Fighting with a net; using a net like a retiarius 1658. 3. *R. spider*, a spider which constructs a web; a geometrical spider. Also *ellipt.* as *sb.* 1646.

1. This kinde of Work in Retiarie and hanging tectures SIR T. BROWNE. 2. His scholastic r. versatility of logic COLERIDGE.

Reticence (re·tisĕns), *sb.* 1603. [a. F., or ad. L. *reticentia*, f. *reticere* to keep silence; see -ENCE.] Maintenance of silence; avoidance of speaking freely; disposition to say little. b. *pl.* Instances of silence or reserve 1814.

A man so known for impenetrable r. as Teufelsdröckh CARLYLE. Surprised at her unusual r. of epithets 1856. So **Re·ticency.**

Reticent (re·tisĕnt), *a.* 1834. [ad. L. *reticentem, reticere*, f. *re-* RE- + *tacere* to be silent.] Reserved; disinclined to speak freely; given to silence or concealment. Hence **Re·ticently** *adv.*

Reticle (re·tik'l). 1656. [ad. L. *reticulum*, dim. of *rete* net; cf. RETICULE.] †1. A little net, a structure resembling a net –1790. 2. A set of parallel wires, threads, etc., with others intersecting them at right angles, or of lines similarly ruled upon a sheet of glass, placed in the object-glass of a telescope, in order to facilitate accurate observations 1731.

Reticular (rīti·kiŭlăɪ), *a.* 1597. [ad. mod. L. *reticularis*, f. *reticulum*; see prec.] 1. Resembling a net in appearance or construction; net-like. 2. *Arch.* Of masonry: Constructed of lozenge-shaped stones, bricks, etc., or of square pieces set diagonally 1797. 3. Resembling a net in effect or operation; intricate, entangled 1818.

1. The r. covering of a coco-nut 1769. A delicate r. membrane 1805. Hence **Reti·cularly** *adv.*

Reticulate (rīti·kiŭlĕt), *a.* 1658. [ad. L. *reticulatus*, f. *reticulum*; see RETICULE.] Reticulated. Hence **Reti·culately** *adv.*

Reticulate (rīti·kiŭleɪt), *v.* 1787. [Back-formation from next.] 1. *trans.* To divide or mark in such a way as to resemble network. 2. *intr.* To divide so as to form a network, or something having that appearance 1862.

Reticulated (rīti·kiŭleɪtĕd), *a.* 1728. [f. as RETICULATE *a.* + -ED[1] 2.] 1. Constructed or arranged like a net; made or marked so as to resemble a net or network. 2. *Arch.* a. = RETICULAR *a.* 2. 1823. b. Of tracery: Formed by the repetition of the same foliated opening 1847. 3. Divided into small squares 1867.

1. *Network*, any thing r. or decussated, at equal distances, with interstices between the intersections JOHNSON. The r. rivers in the central valley LIVINGSTONE. Bodies..with the surface r. 1877.

Reticulation (rītikiŭlē·ʃən). 1671. [See RETICULATE *a.* and -ATION.] A network; an arrangement of lines, etc., resembling a net; reticulated structure or appearance.

fig. The minute reticulations of tyranny which he had begun..to spin about a whole people 1855.

Reti·culato-, comb. form of RETICULATE *a.*, as in *r.-ramose*, etc.

Reticule (re·tikiŭl). 1727. [a. F. *réticule*, ad. L. *reticulum*; see -CULE.] 1. = RETICLE 2. 2. A small bag, usu. made of some woven material, for carrying on the arm or in the hand, used by ladies as a pocket or workbag 1824. 3. *Astr.* One of the southern constellations, situated near Hydra 1868.

2. *R.-basket*, a small basket resembling, or serving the purpose of, a r.

Reti·culo-, comb. form of L. *reticulum*, as in *r.-ramose*, etc.

Reticulose (rīti·kiŭlōus), *a.* 1826. [f. L. *reticulum* + -OSE.] Of the nature of, resembling, network.

‖**Reticulum** (rīti·kiŭlɒ̆m). 1658. [L., dim. of *rete* net.] 1. *Anat.* a. The second stomach of a ruminant. †b. The omentum or mesentery –1738. 2. a. *Arch.* Reticulated work (*rare*) 1797. b. *Bot.* The fibrous sheath at the base of the leaves in palms 1835. c. A net-like structure; a membrane, etc., having a reticulated form or appearance 1858. 3. *Astr.* = RETICULE 3. 1841.

Retiform (rī·tifǭɹm), *a.* 1636. [ad. mod. L. *retiformis*, f. L. *rete* net; see -FORM.] Having the form of a net.

Retina (re·tină). late ME. [ad. med.L., (perh. f. L. *rete* net).] The innermost layer or coating at the back of the eyeball (esp. of vertebrates), which is sensitive to light, and in which the optic nerve terminates. Hence **Re·tinal** *a.* pertaining or relating to the r. **Retini·tis** (*Path.*), acute inflammation of the r.

‖**Retinaculum** (retinæ·kiŭlɒ̆m). *Pl.* **-ula.** 1825. [L., f. *retinere* to hold back.] *Ent.* and *Bot.* Anything serving to keep something in position; in various *spec.* uses. Hence **Retina·cular** *a.* relating to, of the nature of, a r.

Retinalite (re·tinăləit). 1836. [f. Gr. ῥητίνη resin + -LITE.] *Min.* A variety of serpentine which has a resinous lustre.

Retinasphalt (retinæ·sfælt). Also **-asphaltum.** 1804. [f. as prec. + L. *asphaltum* ASPHALT.] A fossil resin found with lignite.

Retinic (rĕti·nik), *a.* 1844. [f. as prec.] *Chem.* In *r. acid*, an acid found in retinasphalt.

Retinite (re·tinəit). Also **-it.** 1821. [a. F. *rétinite*, f. Gr. ῥητίνη resin + -ITE.] *Min.* a. Retinasphalt. b. A mineral resin derived from brown coal. c. Pitchstone.

Retino-, used as comb. form of RETINA, as in *r.-cerebral*, etc.

Retinol (re·tinǫl). Also **-ole.** 1838. [f. Gr. ῥητίνη resin + -OL.] *Chem.* A hydrocarbon, obtained from resins.

Retinoscopy (retinǫ·skŏpi). 1884. [f. RETINA + -SCOPY.] The method of examining the eye, for refraction, by the observation of the movement of a shadow on the retina, caused by the rotation of the mirror of the ophthalmoscope. Hence **Retinosco·pic** *a.* of or pertaining to, performed by, r. **Retinosco·pically** *adv.*

Retinue (re·tiniū), *sb.* late ME. [a. OF. *retenu(e*, pa. pple. of *retenir* to RETAIN.] †1. The fact of being retained in the service of another; a relationship of service or dependency –1607. 2. A number or company of persons retained in the service of, or attached to and following some one, esp. a sovereign, noble, or person in authority; a train or suite. late ME. b. Collectively, without article or pronoun 1665.

2. So many Nymphs, which she doth hold In her retinew SPENSER. An enormous r. of officers and servants 1878. b. Worth is not to be judg'd by Success, and R. GLANVILL. Hence **Re·tinue** *v. trans.* to furnish with a r.; to accompany as a r. 1827.

Retinula (reti·niŭlă). *Pl.* **-ulæ.** 1878. [Dim., on L. types, of RETINA.] *Biol.* One of the pigmented cells from which, in certain compound eyes of Arthropods, the rhabdom arises. Hence **Reti·nular, Reti·nulate** *adjs.*

Retiracy (rītəi·răsi). *U.S.* 1842. [f. RETIRE *v.*] 1. Retirement, seclusion, privacy. 2. A sufficient fortune to retire upon 1859.

1. I enjoy a considerable portion of r. 1842.

Retiral (rītəi·răl). 1611. [f. RETIRE *v.* + -AL 2.] 1. The act of retreating or withdrawing (*rare*). 2. The act or fact of withdrawing from, or of giving up an office, position, or vocation 1879.

Retire (rītəi·ɹ), *sb.* 1540. [f. the verb.] 1. Retirement; withdrawal from the world or the society of others. Now *rare.* †2. The act of retiring or withdrawing to or from a place or position –1676. †3. The act of drawing back or yielding ground in warfare –1606. 4. A place of retirement; a retreat. Now *rare.* 1595.

1. Eve..with audible lament Discover'd soon the place of her r. MILT. 3. Phr. *To sound a* (or *the*) *r.* (In mod. use the imper. of the vb. used subst.) 4. What r. or retreat could he find in any place? 1620.

Retire (rītəi·ɹ), *v.* 1533. [ad. F. *retirer* to withdraw, f. *re-* RE- + *tirer* to draw.] I. *intr.* 1. To withdraw *to* or *into* a place (or way of life) for seclusion, shelter, or security 1538. b. To withdraw *to* one's usual place of abode, or some customary occupation 1584. c. To withdraw from company and betake oneself *to* rest or bed. Also *ellipt.* in same sense. 1670. d. To withdraw from office or an official position; to give up one's business or occupation in order to enjoy more leisure or freedom (esp. after having made a competence or earned a pension) 1667. e. *Cricket.* To go out 1884. 2. Of an army, commander, etc.: To withdraw, fall back, or retreat, esp. in the face of opposition or superior force 1533. b. *Fencing.* To give ground before one's adversary; to take one or more steps backward 1594. 3. To withdraw, go away, remove oneself (*from* a place, etc.) 1585. b. To move back or away; to recede, or have the appearance of doing this 1585. c. To disappear *from* sight; to vanish 1697. †4. To return; to come back –1613. 5. In *pa. pple.* having retired 1610.

1. Shakspeare..retired to his native place before he was old L. HUNT. b. I'll r. to my own chamber, and think of what you have said CONGREVE. c. At their usual time the old couple r. to bed 1775. When most of the..people had 'retired', or, in vulgar language, 'gone to bed' 1860. d. He felt as a trader feels when he retires from business 1863. e. G. B. Studd retiring for six 1884. 2. The task of a rear guard retiring before a victorious enemy..is one of the most delicate of operations 1888. 3. When the ladies retired from the dinner table LOCKHART. 5. All things now retir'd to rest Mind us of like repose MILT.

II. *refl.* To withdraw or remove (oneself); to betake (oneself) away. Now *rare.* 1539. III. *trans.* 1. To withdraw, lead back (troops, etc.), esp. before a superior force 1550. †2. To put away; to withdraw, remove, lead away (a person or thing) –1719. †b. To withdraw the mind, thoughts, etc., *from* some object or sphere –1699. c. To withdraw (a thing) from notice; to hide away, put into obscurity 1605. 3. To draw or pull (a thing) back (again) 1593. 4. To withdraw from operation or currency; to take up or pay (*esp.* a bill) 1681. 5. To remove (an officer) from active service 1870. b. To remove from the usual sphere of activity; to take off 1883.

1. The French were soon seen to r. their heavy guns LEVER. 4. Two of his notes for £100..which he thinks nae mair of retiring than he does of paying the national debt SCOTT. 5. Admiral..Hamilton..was retired from the active list under the age clause 1894. Hence **Reti·rer**, one who retires or retreats. **Reti·ring·ly** *adv.*, **-ness.**

Retired (rītəi·ɹd), *ppl. a.* 1590. [f. prec. + -ED[1].] 1. Withdrawn into seclusion or away from contact with the world. 2. Secluded, sequestered; removed from places frequented by people 1593. 3. Withdrawn into oneself; reserved 1611. 4. a. That has receded or subsided. SHAKS. b. *R. flank*, in fortification, one bent back towards the rear of the work 1696. 5. Withdrawn from, no longer occupied with, business or official duties 1824.

1. The r. and solitary Student 1691. 2. An obscure, little, r. street WYCHERLEY. 5. *R. list*, a list of r. officers. *R. allowance* or *pay*, the pension given to a r. officer or official. Hence **Reti·red·ly** *adv.*, **-ness.**

Retirement (rītəi·ɹmĕnt). 1596. [a. F.; see RETIRE *v.* and -MENT.] 1. The act of falling back, retreating, or receding from a place or position. (In mod. use chiefly *Mil.*) 2. The act of withdrawing into seclusion or privacy; withdrawal *from* something 1599. b. Withdrawal from occupation or business activity 1648. 3. The state or condition of being withdrawn from society or publicity; seclusion, privacy 1603. b. A time or occasion of seclusion or privacy 1632. 4. A place or abode characterized by seclusion or privacy; a retreat 1652. 5. The act of withdrawing from circulation 1865.

1. On the r. of the Lacedæmonian force, the Samian exiles were left destitute GROTE. 2. For solitude ..is best societie, And short r. urges sweet returne MILT. b. R. is as necessary to me as it will be welcome WASHINGTON. 3. As the Duchess lived in close r. SCOTT. b. Dearly did he enjoy these retirements 1852. 4. Exmouth; where he has, as they say, a sweet country r. WILKES. 5. The r. of all paper currency of a lower denomination than ten dollars 1897.

Retorsion (rītǭ·ɹʃən). Now *rare.* 1657. [a. F., or ad. med.L. *retorsionem*, var. of *retortionem* RETORTION.] Retortion (of an argument, etc.).

Retort (rītǭ·ɹt), *sb.*[1] 1600. [f. RETORT *v.*[1]] 1. A sharp or incisive reply, esp. one by which the first speaker's statement or argument is in some way turned against himself, or is met by a counter-charge. 2. The act or practice of replying in a sharp or incisive manner 1791.

1. *A. Y. L.* v. iv. 76. 2. Johnson's dexterity in r... was very remarkable BOSWELL. Nothing is so easy.. as the r. of abuse and sarcasm W. IRVING.

Retort (rītǭ·ɹt), *sb.*[2] 1605. [a. F. *retorte*,

ad. med.L. *retorta*, fem. of L. *retortus*, f. *retorquere*; see next.] 1. A vessel usu. made of glass, and provided with a long neck, bent downwards, in which liquids, etc., subjected to distillation are heated. 2. A vessel in which mercury is separated from amalgam or impurity by volatilization 1683. 3. A clay or iron receptacle, forming a cylinder or segment of one, in which coal is heated for the production of gas 1808. 4. A furnace in which iron is heated with carbon, in order to produce steel 1868.

attrib.: r. carbon, carbon which remains as a residue in the retort when gas has been extracted from coal.

Retort (rĭtǭ·ɹt), *v.*[1] 1557. [f. L. *retort-*, *retorquere*, f. *re-* RE- + *torquere* to twist, turn.] I. 1. *trans.* To make return of (something done to one, *esp.* an injury); to repay or pay back; to requite by retaliation. b. To cast back, cause to return, *upon* or *against* the offending party 1559. 2. To cast or hurl back (a charge, epithet, etc.) 1596. 3. To reply in kind to (a jest, sarcasm, etc.); to answer with the like 1602. b. To say or utter by way of (sharp or aggressive) reply 1625. c. *intr.* To make a retort or retorts 1838. 4. To meet or answer (an argument, etc.) by a similar argument to the contrary; to turn or direct (his own statement) *against* an opponent 1610.

1. It was now his time to r. the humiliation 1817. b. They..r. upon the Aggressour the Injury, which they parry from themselves 1718. 2. He asserted that I was heterodox; I retorted the charge GOLDSM. 3. R. their raillery with raillery, always tempered with good breeding CHATHAM. c. He must smile and r., and look perfectly at his ease GEO. ELIOT. 4. Not a single voice was raised in either House..to r. the argument 1852.

†II. 1. To throw or hurl back (a weapon); to turn back (a blow) upon the striker -1771. 2. To reflect (heat or light); to return or re-echo (a sound); to drive back, etc. -1662. †3. To reject or refuse (an appeal). SHAKS. 4. To turn back or backwards; to bend or twist back -1718. 5. *intr.* To spring or fly back; to rebound, recoil; to twist -1710.

2. As when his vertues shining vpon others, Heate them, and they r. that heate againe To the first giuer SHAKS. Hence **Reto·rter** (*rare*), one who retorts.

Retort (rĭtǭ·ɹt), *v.*[2] 1879. [f. RETORT *sb.*[2]] *trans.* To purify (an amalgam, mercury, etc.) by subjecting to heat in a retort.

Retorted (rĭtǭ·ɹtĕd), *ppl. a.* 1599. [f. RETORT *v.*[1]] 1. Recurved; twisted or bent backwards. 2. Thrown or cast back; returned 1621. 3. Reverted; turned in a backward direction 1720.

Retortion (rĭtǭ·ɹʃən). 1591. [ad. med.L. *retortionem*, f. *retort-*, *retorquere* to twist back.] 1. The action or fact of bending or turning backwards; an instance of this. †2. a. A reply of the nature of a retort -1682. b. An answer made to an argument by converting it against the person using it -1741. c. The method or device of meeting an argument, etc., by retorting it -1732. 3. Return for something done; retaliation. Now *spec.* in international law. 1654.

Retortive (rĭtǭ·ɹtiv), *a. rare.* 1807. [f. L. *retort-*, *retorquere* + -IVE.] 1. Turned backwards. 2. Of the nature of a retort 1826.

Retouch (rĭtʊ·tʃ), *sb.* 1703. [prob. ad. F. *retouche*; cf. next.] A second or further touch given to some part of a picture, composition, etc., with a view to improving it.

Retouch (rĭtʊ·tʃ), *v.* 1650. [prob. ad. F. *retoucher*; see RE- and TOUCH *v.*] 1. *trans.* To touch again with a view to improving; to amend or improve by fresh touches; to touch up. Also *absol.* 2. To touch upon, to speak of, to introduce or bring in, again (*rare*) 1701. Hence **Retou·cher**, one who retouches, *esp.* one whose occupation is to retouch photographs.

Retrace (rĭtrē·s), *v.* 1697. [ad. F. *retracer*; see RE- and TRACE *v.*] 1. *trans.* To trace back to an origin or source; to track through preceding stages. 2. To trace again with the eyes; to look over again with care or close attention 1726. b. To trace again in memory; to recall 1748. 3. To go back upon (one's steps, way, etc.) 1794.

1. Then if the Line of Turnus you r.; He springs from Inachus of Argive Race DRYDEN. 2. The chief divine Gaz'd o'er his sire, retracing ev'ry line POPE. 3. With purpose to r. my steps, I turned CARY.

†**Retra·ct**, *sb.* 1553. [f. the vb.] 1. Retractation (of errors, statements, etc.) -1656. 2. Retreat on the part of an army or force -1614.

Retract (rĭtræ·kt), *v.*[1] late ME. [f. L. *retract-*, *retrahere*, f. *re-* RE- + *trahere* to draw.] I. *trans.* 1. To draw or pull (something) back. b. To draw back or in (some part of the body) 1664. †2. To restrain; to hold back or prevent *from* some course. Also *absol.* -1670. †3. To withdraw, remove, or take away (a person or thing) -1728.

1. b. Birds which have sharp claws..r. them when they hope to prevent their being blunted 1835.

II. *intr.* To undergo or exhibit retraction; to admit of being drawn back 1784.

In non-military rifles, the foresight..retracts within a strong sheath 1862.

Retract (rĭtræ·kt), *v.*[2] 1545. [ad. L. *retractare*, f. *re-* RE- + *tractare* to draw, pull.] 1. *trans.* a. To withdraw, recall, revoke, rescind (a decree, declaration, promise, etc.). b. To withdraw (a statement, etc.) as being erroneous or unjustified 1560. 2. *intr.* a. To make withdrawal or disavowal 1645. b. To draw back (from a promise, resolve, etc.) 1700. c. *Card-playing.* To draw back, change one's mind, after having agreed or declined to play with a certain hand 1830.

1. The permission..has been given, and cannot be retracted JOWETT. b. He had nothing, he said, to r. 1879. 2. a. The affront once given,..they fight first and r. afterwards 1833. b. She grants, denies, Consents, retracts, advances, and then flies 1735.

Retractable (rĭtræ·ktăb'l), *a.* 1620. [f. RETRACT *v.*[1] and *v.*[2] + -ABLE.] 1. That may be retracted or disavowed. 2. Retractile 1769.

Retractation (rĭtræktē·ʃən). 1451. [ad. L. *retractationem*.] 1. *pl.* The title of a book written by St. Augustine containing further treatment and corrections of matters treated in his former writings. 2. a. Withdrawal or recantation of an opinion, statement, etc., with admission of error 1548. b. Withdrawal from an engagement, promise, etc. 1654.

Retra·cted, *ppl. a.* 1643. [f. RETRACT *v.*[1] + -ED[1].] Drawn or pulled back; drawn or turned inwards. b. Of accent: Thrown back towards the beginning of a word 1888. c. *Phonetics.* Of a vowel sound: Pronounced with the tongue drawn back 1902.

Men not of r. Looks, but who carry their Hearts in their Faces SIR T. BROWNE.

Retractile (rĭtræ·ktəil), *a.* 1777. [a. F. *rétractile*; see RETRACT *v.*[1] and -ILE.] Admitting of retraction; capable of being drawn in or back; exhibiting the function or power of retraction.

The tongue..is attached by a very elastic r. membrane to the base of the right nostril 1808. Hence **Retracti·lity**, the fact of being r.

Retraction (rĭtræ·kʃən). late ME. [ad. late L. *retractionem*, f. *retract-*, *retrahere*; see RETRACT *v.*[1]] 1. = RETRACTATION 2 a, b. †2. *pl.* = RETRACTATION 1. -1734. 3. Withdrawal, revocation or recall, *of* something decreed, determined, advanced, etc. 1583. 4. The action of drawing or pulling back or in; the fact or condition of being drawn in or contracted; retractile power 1550. b. The placing of the accent as far from the end of a word as possible 1888. c. *Phonetics.* The drawing back of the tongue in the utterance of a sound; the modification (of a vowel) by means of this 1890.

3. He thought the r. of an error a deviation from honour 1756. 4. *fig.* There is a spirit of r. of one to his native country FULLER.

Retractive (rĭtræ·ktiv), *a.* and *sb.* late ME. [a. OF. *retractif*; see RETRACT *v.*[1] and -IVE.] A. *adj.* 1. Serving to retract or pull back. 2. Inclined to draw back; †backsliding (*rare*) 1509. †B. *sb.* A dissuasive -1644.

Retractor (rĭtræ·ktəɹ). 1837. [See RETRACT *v.*[1] and -OR 2 a.] 1. *Surg.* A bandage or other appliance, used, in various operations, to hold back parts that would impede the operator 1846. 2. *Anat.* A muscle that serves to retract a limb or member. So *r. muscle.* 1837.

Retrad (rī·træd). 1891. [f. L. *retro* + -AD II.; cf. *dextrad*.] To or towards the rear.

†**Retraict.** 1570. [a. F. *retraict(e*, obs. vars. of *retrait(e*; see next.] 1. The act of retreating, in various senses -1640. b. Possibility of retreat 1622. 2. A place of retreat 1596.

†**Retrai·t**, *sb.*[1] 1481. [a. F. *retrait* masc., or *retraite* fem., f. *retraire*:—L. *retrahere*; see RETRACT *v.*[1]] 1. A place of retreat or refuge -1626. 2. *Mil.* The signal for retiring -1648. 3. Retirement, retreat -1658.

†**Retrai·t**, *sb.*[2] *rare.* 1590. [ad. It. *ritratto*, on analogy of prec. or of *portrait*.] Portraiture.

†**Retrai·t**, *v.* 1548. [f. ppl. stem of F. *retraire*.] 1. *trans.* To withdraw, take away, remove -1614. 2. *intr.* To retreat, retire -1624. b. To have recourse *to* something. FULLER.

Retral (rī·trăl), *a.* 1875. [f. L. *retro* + -AL 1.] 1. Posterior; directed backwards. 2. Taking a backward direction 1885. **Re·trally** *adv.*

†**Retra·xit.** 1579. [L., 3rd pers. sing. perf. ind. of *retrahere* RETRACT *v.*] *Law.* The formal withdrawal of his suit by a plaintiff -1768.

Retrea·d (rī-), *v.*[1] 1598. [RE- 5 a.] To tread again.

Re-trea·d, *v.*[2] 1908. [f. RE- 5 c + TREAD *sb.* II. 5.] To furnish (a tire) with a new tread.

Retreat (rĭtrī·t), *sb.* late ME. [a. OF. *retret(e*, var. of *retrait(e* RETRAIT *sb.*[1]] 1. *Mil.* a. The signal to retire. Chiefly in phr. *to blow* or *sound the* (or *a*) *r.* †b. The recall of a pursuing force. SHAKS. c. A signal given by sounding a bugle, drum, etc., at sunset 1753. 2. The act of retiring or withdrawing in the face of opposition, difficulty, or danger. late ME. b. *esp.* of an army or armed force after defeat or to avoid an engagement 1579. c. Recession, retrogression (*rare*) 1781. 3. The act of retiring or withdrawing into privacy, or into some place of safety. Also in *place*, etc., *of r.* 1475. b. Retirement, seclusion 1646. c. *Eccl.* A period of seclusion or retirement from one's ordinary occupations devoted to religious exercises 1756. 4. A place of seclusion or privacy; a retired place or residence. late ME. b. A place of refuge or resort 1662. c. A hiding-place; a lair or den 1774. d. An establishment to which insane persons or habitual inebriates are admitted in order that they may be under proper supervision or control 1797. 5. *Arch.* Recessed work; a recess or recessed part in a wall, etc. 1687.

2. b. The famous R. of Xenophon..at the Head of ten thousand Greeks 1690. 3. I saw the great towns.. famous for the r. of the imperial court when Vienna was besieged 1716. 4. I am promised a retreate three miles from Bloys 1638. b. The building..should be a r. for seamen disabled in the service of their country MACAULAY. Hence †**Retrea·tful** *a.* (*rare*) serving as a r. CHAPMAN.

Retreat (rĭtrī·t), *v.* late ME. [ad. OF. *retraiter*, with vowel accommodated to the sb.] 1. *intr.* To withdraw, retire, draw back. b. Of an army or a combatant: To retire before superior force or after a defeat 1596. c. In *pa. pple.* with *is*, *was*, etc. 1648. d. To recede 1863. 2. *trans.* To draw or lead back; to remove, take away. Now chiefly in *Chess*, to move (a piece) back from a forward or threatened position. 1523. †b. To diminish, reduce. LOCKE.

1. You have now carried things too far to r. *Junius Lett.* c. Others..Retreated in a silent valley, sing.. Thir own Heroic deeds and hapless Fall MILT. d. The forehead..retreats somewhat HAWTHORNE. 2. He had no choice but to r. the bishop 1886.

Retreatant (rĭtrī·tănt). 1880. [f. prec. + -ANT[1].] One who takes part in a religious retreat.

Retrench (rĭtre·nʃ), *v.*[1] 1607. [ad. F. *retrencher*, obs. var. of *retrancher*; see RE- and TRENCH *v.*] †1. *trans.* To cut short, check, repress -1688. †2. To cut off, bar (a way or passage) -1618. 3. To cut down, reduce, diminish; *esp.* to curtail (one's expenses) by the exercise of economy 1625. †4. To cut short, reduce in size -1784. 5. To cut off, remove, take away 1650. b. To do away with (an item of expense) 1647. c. To cut out, omit, delete (some portion of a book or document) 1645. 6. *intr.* To reduce expenditure 1663. b. To make excisions or diminutions (*rare*) 1700.

3. Forced to r. my expensive Way of Living 1709. To r. the Evils of Life by the Reasonings of Philosophy ADDISON. 4. The very Lowness of your Subject has retrenched your Wings COWLEY. 5. To r. what is Superfluous 1718. b. To r. one Dish at my Table 1714. 6. If rich, they go to enjoy; if poor, to r. ROGERS. Hence **Retre·ncher**.

Retrench (rĭtre·nʃ), *v.*[2] 1598. [f. as prec.] *trans.* and *refl.* To protect by, to furnish with, a retrenchment. Also *absol.*

They perceived how the Turks were retrenched within 1600.

Retrenchment[1] (rĭtre·nʃmĕnt). 1600. [a. F. *retrenchement*, obs. var. of *retranchement*; see RETRENCH *v.*[1] and -MENT.] **1.** The act of cutting down, off, or out; curtailment, limitation, reduction. **b.** The act of excising, deleting, or omitting; an instance of this 1691. **2.** The act of economizing or cutting down expenditure; an instance of this 1667.

1. It was not a r. of superfluities DRYDEN. **b.** This one r. of the text 1867. **2.** Reform has gone too far in the way of r. 1868.

Retrenchment[2] (rĭtre·nʃmĕnt). 1589. [f. as prec.] *Mil.* A work, usu. consisting of a trench and parapet, constructed for the defence of a position; *esp.* an inner line of defence within a large work.

Retribute (re·trĭbiut), *v.* Now *rare.* 1575. [f. L. *retribut-*, *retribuere*, f. *re-* RE- + *tribuere* to give, assign.] **1.** *trans.* To give in return; to make return of; to retaliate (something) *on a* person. **2.** To make return for; to repay 1612. **3.** *intr.* To make a return or requital 1612.

1. To whom in particular were retributed no small rewardes 1579. **3.** A just God who will r. to every one according to the deeds done in the body DE FOE. So **Re·tributor**, one who makes retribution; a repaver.

Retribution (retribiū·ʃən). late ME. [a. OF. *retribucion*, *-ution*, or ad. L. *retributionem*, f. *retribuere*; see prec.] **1.** Repayment, recompense, return, for some service, merit, etc. Now *rare.* **2.** *Day of r.*, the day on which divine reward or punishment will be assigned to men (now usu. assoc. w. sense 3); also generally any day of punishment or nemesis 1526. **b.** Recompense, in another life, for one's good or bad deeds in this world 1633. **3.** A recompense for, or requital of, evil done; return *of* evil, etc. 1570.

1. Never did a charitable act go away without the r. of a blessing 1612. **2.** I..am led to believe that even in this world the day of r. rarely fails to come at last 1856. **b.** All who have thir reward on Earth.. here find Fit r., emptie as thir deeds MILT. **3.** In Revenges (that is, r. of Evil for Evil) HOBBES.

Retributive (rĭtri·biŭtiv), *a.* 1678. [f. as RETRIBUTE *v.* + -IVE.] Characterized by, of the nature of, retribution. Freq. with *justice.* Hence **Retri·butively** *adv.*

Retributory (rĭtri·biŭtəri), *a.* 1612. [f. as RETRIBUTE *v.* + -ORY[2].] Involving, producing, or characterized by retribution or recompense.

That sect, which in their prosperity shewed no mercy, now met with r. vengeance 1771.

Retrievable (rĭtrī·văb'l), *a.* 1711. [f. RETRIEVE *v.* + -ABLE.] Capable or admitting of being retrieved.

Retrieval (rĭtrī·văl). 1643. [f. RETRIEVE *v.* + -AL 2.] **1.** The act of retrieving or recovering; an instance of this. **2.** = next 2. 1707.

2. Matrimony clenches ruin beyond r. FIELDING.

Retrieve (rĭtrī·v), *sb.* 1575. [f. the vb.] †**1.** The second discovery and flight of a bird (esp. a partridge) which has already been sprung –1673. **2.** Possibility of recovery. With *beyond*, *past*, †*without*. 1697. **b.** The act of recovering. Now *rare.* 1701.

2. We're ruin'd and undone, past all r. 1700.

Retrieve (rĭtrī·v), *v.* [Late ME. *retreve*, ad. OF. *retroev-*, stressed stem of *retrover*, *retrouver*, f. *re-* RE- + *trouver* to find.] **I.** *trans.* **1.** Of dogs: **a.** To find or discover again (game which has been temporarily lost); *esp.* to flush or set up (partridges) a second time. **b.** To find and bring in (a bird, etc.) that has been wounded or killed 1856. **2.** To recover by study or investigation, esp. of the past; to restore to knowledge. Now *rare.* 1567. **b.** To recover by an effort of memory; to recall to mind 1644. †**c.** To find again –1660. **3.** To recover, get or take possession of (a thing, etc.) again 1589. †**4.** To bring back; to cause to turn back or return –1662. **b.** To rescue or save *from* or *out of* a place or state 1611. **c.** To save (time) from other occupations 1687. **5.** To restore, revive; to bring back to the original state or to a flourishing condition (*esp.* one's fortunes, honour, credit, etc.) 1676. **6.** To make good, repair, set right again (a loss, disaster, error, etc.) 1688.

1. *fig.* Popes vse Potentates but to retriue their Game 1592. **2.** An ancient word..grown so obsolete that the original purport could not be retrieved 1774. **3.** A warrant..to search for and r. the fugitive SMOLLETT. **5.** The spirit of the country was broken, and nothing could r. it 1861. No courage..could now r. the fortunes of the field 1880. **6.** He endeavoured to r. the error he had committed by the most solemn assurances 1844.

II. *intr.* **1.** Of dogs: †**a.** To find and set up game again (*rare*) –1635. **b.** To find and bring in wounded or dead game 1856. **2.** To recuperate; to recover 1675.

1. **b.** A little rough terrier, expressly broken to r. 1856. Hence **Retrie·vement**, (*rare*) retrieval.

Retriever (rĭtrī·vəɹ). 1486. [f. RETRIEVE *v.* + -ER[1].] **1.** A dog used for the purpose of retrieving; *esp.* one of a breed specially adapted for finding and bringing in dead or wounded game. **2.** One who retrieves or recovers 1658.

‖**Retro** (rī·tro), *adv.* *rare.* 1768. [L.; see next.] Backwards; into past time.

It is of the nature of all confirmations to operate *r.* 1768.

Retro- (rī·tro, re·tro), *prefix*, repr. the L. adverb *retro* backwards, back, which in post-cl. Latin appears in comb. with various vbs. and verbal nouns, as *retroagere*, etc. and rarely in adjectival forms, as *retrogradus*. From the 19th c., esp. the latter part of it, *retro-* has been very freely used as a prefix, chiefly in scientific terms. In most words the pronunciation of the prefix may be either (rītro) or (retro); recent dictionaries usu. prefer (rītro), exc. in *retrograde* and *retrospect*.

a. Miscellaneous terms, as **Retrocogni·tion**, knowledge of the past supernaturally acquired; so **Retroco·gnitive** *a.* **Retroco·pulant** *a.* (*rare*) that copulates backwards. **Retrocopula·tion**, the action or fact of copulating backwards. **Re·trofracted** *a.* (*Bot.*), sharply bent back, as if broken. **Retroge·nerative** *a.* retrocopulant. **Retromi·ngent** *a.*, that urinates backwards; also as *sb.*, an animal which does this; so †**Retromi·ngency.** **Retro-o·perative** *a.*, having a retrospective effect. **Retropu·lsion** (*Path.*), transference of an external disease to some internal part or organ. **Retropu·lsive** *a.* (*rare*) causing backward or reverse movement. **Retrovaccina·tion**, inoculation of cows with vaccine lymph from a human being.

b. Terms of *Anat.* and *Path.*, in which *retro-* is combined with an adj. denoting some part of the body, and has the sense 'situated behind' (the part in question), as *r.-mastoid*, *-ocular*, *-uterine*, etc.

Retroa·ct, *v.* 1795. [ad. L. *retroact*, *retroagere*; see RETRO- and ACT *v.*] *intr.* To react; also, to operate in a backward direction or towards the past.

Retroa·ction. 1727. [ad. L. **retroactio*; see prec. and ACTION.] **1.** A retrospective action. **2.** Return action; reaction 1829.

Retroa·ctive, *a.* 1611. [Cf. prec. and ACTIVE.] **1.** Of enactments, etc.: Extending in scope or effect to matters which have occurred in the past; retrospective. **b.** Directed backwards in time 1822. **2.** Operating in a backward direction (*rare*) 1611. †**3.** Reactive (*rare*) –1802.

1. The r. clause in the..Bill will be either cancelled or amended 1897. Hence **Retroa·ctively** *adv.* So **Retroacti·vity**, the condition or fact of being r.

Re·trocede, *v.*[1] 1654. [ad. L. *retrocedere*, f. *retro-* RETRO- + *cedere* to yield, go back.] **1.** *intr.* To go back, retire, recede. **2.** *Med.* Of gout: To strike inwardly 1866.

Retroce·de, *v.*[2] 1818. [ad. F. *rétrocéder*; see RETRO- and CEDE *v.*] *trans.* To cede (territory) back again *to* a country, etc. So **Retroce·ssion**[2], the action or fact of ceding territory back.

Retrocedent (-sī·dĕnt), *a.* 1583. [ad. L. *retrocedentem*, *retrocedere* RETROCEDE *v.*[1]] **1.** *Astr.* = RETROGRADE *a.* **1.** (*rare*). **2.** *Med.* **a.** Of gout: Striking inward 1776. **b.** Of tubercle: Retrograding or caseating 1898. So **Retroce·dence**, retrogression; retrocession.

Retrocession (-se·ʃən)[1]. 1646. [ad. late L. *retrocessio*, *retrocedere* RETROCEDE *v.*[1]] **1.** The action or fact of moving backward, retiring, or receding; retrogression. †**2.** *Astr.* = PRECESSION –1738. **3.** *Path.* The action or fact, on the part of a disease, of striking inwards, so as to affect the internal organs; the 'going in' of an eruption 1771.

Retrochoir (rī·troˌkwəiəɹ). 1802. [ad. med.L. *retrochorus*; see RETRO- and CHOIR.] *Eccl.* That part of a cathedral or large church which lies behind the high altar.

Re·troflex, *a.* 1776. [ad. mod. or med.L. *retroflexus*, *retroflectere.*] Bent or turned backwards; retorted. Chiefly *techn.* So **Re·troflexed** *a.*

Retrofle·xion. 1845. [ad. mod.L. *retroflexio.*] The fact or state of being turned back or retorted. Chiefly *Path.*, retroversion.

Retrogradation (rī·tro-, re·trogrădē̆·ʃən). 1554. [ad. L. *retrogradatio*, f. *retrogradare*; RETROGRADE *v.*] **1.** *Astr.* The apparent backward motion of a planet in the zodiac; motion of a heavenly body from east to west; a case or instance of this. **b.** The backward movement of the lunar nodes on the ecliptic 1727. **2.** The action or process of going back towards some point in investigation or reasoning 1577. **3.** The action or fact of moving or drawing back or backwards; retirement, retreat 1644. **4.** The action, fact, or condition of falling back in development; retrogression, decline 1748.

Retrograde (re·trogreid), *a.* and *sb.* late ME. [ad. L. *retrogradus*, f. *retro-* RETRO- + *gradus* step; cf. next.] **A.** *adj.* **1.** *Astr.* Of the planets: Apparently moving in a direction contrary to the order of the signs, or from east to west. **2.** Of movement: **a.** *Astr.* Apparently or actually contrary to the order of the signs; directed from east to west. late ME. **b.** Directed backwards; in a direction contrary to the previous motion; retiring, retreating 1622. **3.** Tending or inclined to go back or to revert; moving or leading backwards, *esp.* towards an inferior or less flourishing condition 1530. **4.** Moving backwards (in literal sense); returning upon the previous course 1564. **b.** Of order in enumeration, etc.: Inverse, reversed 1664. †**5.** Opposed, contrary, or repugnant *to* something –1797. **6.** As quasi-*adv.* In a backward or reverse direction 1619.

1. I would have sworn some r. planet was hanging over this unfortunate house of mine STERNE. **2. b.** A r. movement is always bad in this country WELLINGTON. **3.** The capital of a country may be stationary, progressive, or r. 1868. **5.** For your intent In going backe to Schoole in Wittenberg, It is most r. to our desire SHAKS. **6.** The reformation begun to go r. in Q. Elizabeth's time 1709.

B. *sb.* **1.** One who falls away or degenerates 1593. **2.** A backward movement or tendency (*rare*) 1613.

Retrograde (re·trogrēid), *v.* 1582. [ad. L. *retrogradi* or *retrogradare*, f. *retro-* RETRO- + *gradus* step.] **1.** *trans.* To turn back, reverse, revert; to make, or cause to become, retrograde. Now *rare.* **2.** *intr.* *Astr.* Of the planets, etc.: To go backward (in apparent motion) in the zodiac; to seem to travel from east to west 1601. **3.** To move backwards, to take a backward course; to retire, recede 1598. **4.** To fall back or revert towards a lower or less flourishing condition 1613.

1. We see, now, events forced on, which seem to retard or r. the civility of ages EMERSON. **4.** All that is human must r. if it do not advance GIBBON.

Re·trogress, *sb.* *rare.* 1814. [ad. L. *retrogressus*; see next.] A retrogression.

Retrogre·ss, *v.* 1819. [f. L. *retrogress-*, *retrogradi* to RETROGRADE.] *intr.* To move backwards; to go back.

Retrogression (-gre·ʃən). 1646. [ad. L. **retrogressio*, f. as prec.] **1.** *Astr.* = RETROGRADATION 1. **2.** Movement in a backward or reverse direction. In early use *Math.* 1704. **3.** The action or fact of going back in respect of development or condition; return to a less advanced state or stage; a case or instance of this 1768. **b.** *Path.* The disappearance of an eruption 1899.

3. We find at best a very slow progress and on the whole a r. MACAULAY.

Retrogre·ssive, *a.* and *sb.* 1802. [f. as RETROGRESS *v.* + -IVE.] **A.** *adj.* **1.** Working back in investigation or reasoning 1817. **2.** Moving or directed backwards 1830. **3.** Retrograde; tending to return to an inferior state; going back to a worse condition 1802. **b.** *spec.* in *Path.* or *Anat.* of changes in tissues or organs 1871. **B.** *sb.* One who has retrograde tendencies 1892. Hence **Retrogre·ssively** *adv.*

Retrorse (rĭtrǭ·ɹs), *a. rare.* 1825. [ad. L. *retrorsus*, contr. f. *retroversus*; see RETROVERSE *a.*] Turned backwards; reverted.

Retrospect (re·trospekt, rī·tro-), *sb.* 1602. [ad. L. **retrospectus*, f. *retrospect-*, *retrospicere* to look back.] **1. a.** A regard or reference *to* some fact, authority, precedent, etc. **b.** Application to past time 1727. **2.** A backward look or view (*rare*) 1675. **b.** A view or survey of past time, *esp.* with ref. to one's own life or experiences 1678. **c.** A survey or review of some past course of events, acts, etc.; *esp.* in a particular sphere or line of things 1663. **3.** *attrib.* or as *adj.* Retrospective 1709.

1. **b.** The deed given in 1762..becomes good..by r. 1792. 2. **b.** The most auspicious moment..for indulging in a r. 1807. **c.** A short r. is now necessary to view what Congress determined upon 1865.

Re·trospect, *v.* 1659. [f. prec.] **1.** *intr.* To indulge in retrospection. **b.** To look or refer back *to*; to reflect *on* 1689. **2.** *trans.* To consider, regard, or think of (some person or thing) retrospectively 1734.

1. **b.** To give a correct idea of the circumstances.., it may be useful to r. to an early period 1804.

Retrospection (retrǒspe·kʃən, rītrǒ-). 1633. [ad. L. **retrospectionem*, f. *retrospicere*; cf. RETROSPECT *sb.*] **1.** The action of looking back (*rare*). **2.** The action of looking back or referring *to* something; reference or allusion to past events 1674. **3.** The action or fact of looking back upon, or surveying, past time 1729. **b.** An instance of this; *esp.* a survey of past life or experiences 1697. **c.** A review of past events or of some matter 1753. **4.** A retrogressive course of thought 1870.

4. The long r. lodges us at length at..first principles J. H. NEWMAN.

Retrospe·ctive, *a.* 1664. [See RETROSPECT *sb.* and -IVE.] **1.** Directed to, contemplative of, past time. **2.** Of statutes, etc.: Operative with regard to past time; retroactive 1768. **3.** Backward; lying to the rear 1796.

1. The Sage, with r. eye POPE. R. researches 1873. 2. Sentencing a man to death by r. law MACAULAY. 3. R. views of Ambleside 1872. Hence **Retrospe·ctively** *adv.*

‖**Retroussé** (rətruse), *a.* 1837. [F., pa. pple. of *retrousser*, f. *re-* RE- + *trousser* to TRUSS.] Turned up. (Chiefly of the nose.)

Re·troverse, *a. rare.* 1849. [ad. L. *retroversus*, f. *retro-* RETRO- + *versus* turned.] Turned or directed backwards; reversed.

Retroversion (-vɔ̄·ɹʃən). 1776. [ad. L. L. **retroversio*; see RETRO- and REVERSION.] **1.** *Path.* The fact of (the uterus) becoming retroverted. **2.** The action of turning or looking back 1820. **3.** Retranslation into the original language 1888.

Retrove·rt, *v. rare.* 1639. [ad. late L. *retrovertere*, f. *retro-* RETRO- + *vertere* to turn.] *intr.* and *trans.* To turn back; to revert. Hence **Re·troverted** *ppl. a.* turned backwards, reverted; *spec.* in *Path.*, of the uterus.

†**Retru·se,** *a.* 1635. [ad. L. *retrusus*, *retrudere.*] Concealed, recondite –1697.

Retrusion (rĭtrū·ʒən). *rare.* 1657. [ad. L. **retrusio*, f. *retrudere.*] The action of putting away or back.

Rettery (re·təri). 1853. [f. RET *v.* + -ERY 2.] A place where flax is retted.

Re·tting, *vbl. sb.* 1727. [f. RET *v.* + -ING[1].] The preparation of flax, etc., by steeping or watering. Also *attrib.*

Retund (rĭtʌ·nd), *v.* Now *rare* or *Obs.* 1634. [ad. L. *retundere*, f. *re-* RE- + *tundere* to beat.] **1.** *trans.* To weaken (some physical quality or agent); to diminish the strength or effect of. **2.** To beat back, repress (malice, etc.) 1642. **b.** To put down or refute 1653. **3.** To dull or blunt (the edge of a weapon) 1691. **4.** To drive or force back 1654.

3. *fig.* None of all these things could r. the edge of his expectations to find the wreck 1702.

Return (rĭtɔ̄·ɹn), *sb.* late ME. [a. AF. *retorn*, *retourn*, f. *retorner*; see next.] **I. 1.** The act of coming back to or from a place, person, or condition. **b.** *ellipt.* A return-ticket 1868. **c.** *ellipt. Mining.* A passage through which the ventilating air returns to the upcast shaft 1883. **2.** The fact of (a certain time or thing) recurring or coming round again; †a spell of some action 1589. **3.** The recurrence or renewal of some condition; *esp.* of illness or indisposition 1648.

1. Uppon the King's returne from his recreations att Newmarkett 1670. Phr. *By* (†*the*) *r.*, *by r. of post*: see POST *sb.*[2] III. 2. At the returne of the yeere, the king of Syria will come vp against thee 1 *Kings* xx. 22. Phr. *To wish* (one) *many* (*happy*) *returns* (*of the day*). 3. The King had yesterday some returns of his ague 1694.

II. 1. A side or part which falls away, usu. at right angles, from the front or direct line of any work or structure. **a.** In cornices, pilasters, windows, etc. 1450. **b.** In appendages to, or minor parts of, buildings, walls, or other structures 1463. **c.** A wing or side of a building; †a side-street 1625. **2.** A bend or turn (in a line, etc.); a portion extending between two bends 1655. †**b.** A bend, turn, or winding in a stream, trench, gallery, etc. –1802. **3.** A consignment or cargo, an aggregate or class of commodities, which comes back (to a person) in exchange for merchandise sent out as a trading venture; the value or profits represented by this. (Now merged in b.) 1543. **b.** Pecuniary value resulting to a person from the exercise of some trade or occupation; gain, profit, or income, in relation to the means by which it is produced; also (in *pl.*), proceeds, results 1691. **c.** The fact of bringing value in exchange 1753.

2. We then put up a Line that was 666 Feet in Length, by eight Returns 1731. 3. He had also six rich Returnes from the East India 1614. **b.** If the Merchant's R. be more than his Vse, (which 'tis certain it is, or else he will not Trade) LOCKE. **c.** What maketh rich, is a small profit and a quick r. 1753.

III. 1. The act, on the part of a sheriff, of sending back a writ to the court from which it issued, together with a statement of how far he has been able to carry out its instructions; hence, the report of a sheriff upon any writ directed to him. late ME. **b.** *ellipt.* for RETURN-DAY 1577. **2.** The official report made by a returning officer (orig. the sheriff) as to the election of a member or members of Parliament; hence, the fact of being elected to sit in Parliament 1459. †**b.** A response to a demand; a reply to a letter or dispatch –1655. **c.** A report of a formal or official character giving information as to the numbers, amounts, etc., of the subjects of inquiry; a set of statistics compiled by order of some authority 1756. **3.** Restoration *of* something to a person; *spec.* in *Law* 1641. **4.** The act of giving, or (more usu.) that which is given or received, by way of recompense, acknowledgement, or reciprocity 1542. **b.** The yield of some productive thing considered in relation to the original amount or expenditure 1626. **5.** A reply, answer, or retort. Now *rare* or *Obs.* 1599. **b.** A thrust, stroke, volley, etc., given in reply to one from an opponent or enemy 1705. **c.** *gen.* The act of sending back 1841. **d.** The act of returning a ball to an opponent or to another player; skill in doing this 1886. **6.** The act of bringing a thing back to a former position 1638. **7.** *pl.* †Refuse-tobacco. Later, a mild light-coloured tobacco for smoking 1789. **8.** A thing or person sent back. Chiefly *pl.* 1875.

2. **c.** A r. of the stores at this place is enclosed WASHINGTON. 4. A grateful r. is due to the author of a benefit GIBBON. Phr. *In r.*; As rich men deale Guifts, Expecting in returne twenty for one SHAKS. *In r. for*; A present is usually given in r. for the hospitality 1857. **b.** In the course of a year they give two returns,—the lamb, and the fleece 1886. 5. *Hen. V*, II. iv. 127. 8. Any cheques or bill refused payment are called 'returns' 1875.

attrib. and *Comb.*, as *r. angle*, *cargo*, *current*, *journey*, *match*, etc.; **r. bend,** a U-shaped coupling for uniting the ends of pipes; **r. pipe,** a pipe through which water of condensation from a heater or radiator returns to the boiler; **-ticket,** a railway (or other) ticket available for the journey back from, as well as to, the place specified upon it. Hence **Retu·rnless** *a.* devoid of, not admitting of, a r.; that is without r.

Return (rĭtɔ̄·ɹn), *v.* ME. [ad. OF. *retorner*, *retourner*; see RE- and TURN *v.*] **I.** *intr.* **1.** To come or go back to a place or person. **b.** *transf.* Of immaterial things, as time, etc. late ME. **2.** To go back in discourse; to revert *to* or resume a topic or subject. late ME. **3.** To revert, go back again, *to* (or *into*) a previous condition or state; to come back *to* oneself 1484. **b.** To revert *to* some practice, opinion, etc. 1534. **4.** To go back or revert *to* a previous owner 1460.

1. He returned, and I went on alone TYNDALL. Aristotle..returned to Athens after the death of Plato JOWETT. **b.** Till many years over thy head r.: So maist thou live MILT. 2. I r. to the Story DE FOE. 3. Dust thou art, and vnto dust shalt thou returne *Gen.* iii. 19. **b.** They..retourned..to their errours agayne 1534.

II. 1. *trans.* To take or lead back upon the former direction; to turn at an angle to the previous course 1613. **2.** To turn or direct (one's eyes, sight, mind) back, or towards something 1509. **3.** To bring or convey back to a place or person. late ME. **b.** To bring back or restore (something) *to* or *into* a former position or state; to restore to a normal state 1462. **4.** To bring back in exchange; to yield in return. Now *rare.* 1596. †**b.** To turn over in business (*rare*) –1761. **5.** To put back *in* or *into* something; to restore *to* some receptacle 1611. **b.** *Mil.* To replace (arms, etc.) in the usual receptacle 1696.

1. I propose that the upper row of stalls should be returned at the west end of the chancel 1874. 2. The King..then returns his thoughts for France 1647. 3. Thou shalt my people returne from farre exyle 1538. **b.** Of a man turned into an asse, and returned againe into a man by one of Bodins witches 1584. 5. Arbaces and Salemenes r. their swords to the scabbards BYRON.

III. 1. To send (a person or thing) back again 1459. **b.** To send back or reflect (sound or light) 1693. **2.** To report in answer to a writ or to some official demand for information; to state by way of a report or verdict. late ME. **b.** Of a sheriff: To report (certain persons) as having been appointed to serve on a jury or to sit in Parliament. Hence, in later use, of constituencies: To elect as a member of Parliament or some other administrative body. late ME. **3.** To send or turn back, to visit (something) *upon* a person. Now *rare.* 1547. †**b.** To retort (a charge, argument, etc.) *to* or *upon* a person –1719. **c.** *absol.* To retort or reply (*to* or *upon* a person) 1652.

1. **b.** And lake and fell Three times return'd the martial yell SCOTT. 2. To be returned upon the surgeon's list as unfit for duty 1802. **b.** Hyde..was returned both by Shaftesbury and Wootton Basset 1845. 3. The Lord shall returne his blood vpon his owne head 1 *Kings* ii. 32.

IV. 1. To give or render back (*to* a person) 1607. **b.** To give or send in return; to reply with 1599. **2.** To give or send (an answer) 1591. **b.** To say or state by way of reply or answer 1593. **3.** To give or render (thanks) 1591. **4.** To repay or pay back in some way, esp. with something similar 1599. **b.** To repay, or respond to, by a similar courtesy, compliment, etc. 1674. **c.** In games: To respond to (the play of one's partner or opponent) 1742.

1. Weight is returned for weight, to any person who carries their gold and silver to the Tower 1771. **b.** When Tierce is thrusted, r. Tierce or Sagoone 1705. 2. Answer was return'd, that he will come SHAKS. **b.** He returned, that learning was beneath the greatness of a prince FULLER. 4. He returns my Envy with Pity STEELE. Herbert did not r. the blow SCOTT. **b.** To r. a visit GOLDSM. **c.** He returns his Partner's Lead 1742.

Returnable (rĭtɔ̄·ɹnăb'l), *a.* late ME. [a. AF. *retornable*, OF. *retournable*; see RETURN *v.* and -ABLE.] **1.** Of writs, etc.: Appointed to be returned (to the issuing court). **b.** That is (or are) to be returned 1658. **2.** Capable of being returned 1542. **3.** Able to return (*rare*) 1654. **4.** Admitting of return 1853.

1. **b.** The said letter..being..indorsed, r. to the pay-office 1758. 4. Return tickets at one fare..r. by the 7.30, 8.20 and 8.55 a.m. trains only 1856.

Retu·rn-day. 1651. [Cf. RETURN *sb.* III. 1.] *Law.* The day on which a writ is appointed to be returned.

Retu·rned, *ppl. a.* late ME. [-ED[1].] **1.** Bent or turned back in some way; *esp.* made with a return. **2.** That has come back 1600. **3.** Sent or brought back 1722.

3. *R. empty*, an empty cask, case, etc., returned to the sender; *transf.* a colonial clergyman who has come back to England.

Retu·rner. 1611. [-ER[1].] **1.** One who, or that which comes back or returns. **2.** One who or that which gives or brings back 1691.

Retuse (rĭtiū·s), *a.* 1753. [ad. L. *retusus*, *retundere* RETUND *v.*] *Bot.* and *Ent.* Terminating in a broad or rounded end with a depression in the centre.

Reunion (rīyū·niən). 1610. [= F. *réunion*; see RE- 5 a and UNION.] 1. The action of reuniting or coming together again; the state of being reunited. 2. The fact of (persons) meeting again after separation 1703. 3. A meeting or social gathering of persons acquainted with each other, or having some previous link of connexion. Often in F. form. 1820.

1. The re-union to the state, of all the Catholicks of that country BURKE. 2. His r. with his disciples 1843. Hence **Reu·nionist,** one who desires reunion; esp. of the Anglican with the Roman Catholic Church.

Reunite (rīyunəi·t), *v.* 1591. [f. med.L. *reunit- reunire*; see RE- and UNITE *v.*] 1. *trans.* To unite or bring together again; to join together after separation. 2. *intr.* To come together again and unite 1660. Hence **Reuni·table** *a.* **Reuni·tedly** *adv.*

Rev., abbrev. f. REVEREND.

Rev. (rev), abbrev. f. REVOLUTION 4 c. Hence **Rev** *v. trans.* to work *up* (an engine), to a high number of revolutions per minute; also *intr.* of the engine. 1901.

Revalenta (revăle·ntă). 1850. [Arbitrary alteration of *ervalenta*, f. *ervum lens* LENTIL.] A preparation of lentil and barley flour.

Revalorization (rīvæ:lŏrəizē·ʃən). 1926. [a. F.; cf. RE- and VALORIZATION.] Establishing a fresh price or value of a commodity, etc.; *esp.* restoration of currency to its former or normal value. So **Reva·lorize** *v. trans.*

Reveal (rĭvī·l), *sb.*[1] *rare.* 1629. [f. REVEAL *v.*] A revealing, revelation, disclosure.

Reveal (rĭvī·l), *sb.*[2] 1688. [f. late ME. *revale* to lower, bring down.] A side of an opening or recess which is at right angles to the face of the work; *esp.* the vertical side of a doorway or window-opening between the door- or window-frame and the arris.

Reveal (rĭvī·l), *v.* late ME. [ad. OF. *reveler* or L. *revelare*, f. *re-* RE- 2 d + *velum* VEIL.] 1. *trans.* To disclose, make known (*to* a person) in a supernatural manner. 2. To disclose, divulge, make known (*to* a person) by discourse or communication. late ME. †b. To betray -1657. 3. To display, show, make clear or visible, exhibit 1494.

1. A matter revealed and prefigured unto Domitian in a dream BACON. 2. Did not she..r. The secret wrested from me? MILT. 3. In compleat Glory shee reueal'd her selfe SHAKS. Our inward loue, let outward deedes reueale it 1605. Hence **Revealabi·lity. Revea·lable** *a.* capable of being revealed, **-ness. Revea·ler,** one who or that which reveals. **Revea·lment,** the act of revealing; revelation.

Revealed (rĭvī·ld), *ppl. a.* 1562. [f. prec.] Brought to light, disclosed; *esp.* made known by divine or supernatural agency, as *r. religion.*

Reveille (rĭvæ·li, rĭve·li). Also †**reveillez.** 1644. [ad. F. *réveillez*, imper. pl. of *réveiller* to awaken, f. *re-* RE- + *veiller*:—L. *vigilare* to keep watch.] A morning signal given to soldiers, usu. by beat of drum or by bugle, to waken them and notify that it is time to rise.

Sound a R., Sound, Sound, The Warrior God is come DRYDEN. While our slumbrous spells assail ye, Dream not..Bugles here shall sound reveillé SCOTT. vars. **Reveil, réveil** (*rare*). So **Reveillez.**

Revel (re·vĕl), *sb.* ME. [a. OF., vbl. sb. f. *reveler* REVEL *v.*[1]] 1. Riotous or noisy mirth or merry-making. late ME. 2. An occasion or course of merry-making or noisy festivity, with dancing, games, masking, acting, or other forms of lively entertainment ME. b. *spec.* In the south-western counties, a parish festival or feast; a fair 1478.

1. The brief night goes In babble and r. and wine TENNYSON. 2. Faerie Elves, Whose midnight Revels ..some belated Peasant sees MILT. Phr. *Master of the Revels*, a person (permanently or temporarily) appointed to organize or lead revels, esp. in the Royal Household or the Inns of Court.

Revel (re·vĕl), *v.*[1] ME. [a. OF. *reveler* :—L. *rebellare* to REBEL.] 1. *intr.* To make merry; to indulge in pastime or festivities; to take part in a revel. b. To enjoy oneself greatly, to take intense pleasure or delight, *in* something 1754. 2. *trans.* a. To spend or waste (time) in revelry 1628. b. To squander (money) in revelling 1813.

1. Antony that Reuels long a-nights SHAKS. Thou must..leave duty..to r. it gaily with the wild and with the wicked SCOTT. b. Maggots r. in putrefaction PALEY. Hence **Re·velment,** the act of revelling; revelry.

†**Reve·l,** *v.*[2] 1597. [ad. L. *revellere*, f. *re-* RE- + *vellere* to pull.] *trans.* To draw back (humours or blood) from some part of the system -1752.

Revelation (revĕl-, revĕlē·ʃən). ME. [a. OF. *revelaciun, -tion*, or ad. L. *revelationem*, f. *revelare.*] 1. The disclosure of knowledge to man by a divine or supernatural agency. 2. Something disclosed or made known by divine or supernatural means. late ME. b. A striking disclosure of something previously unknown or not realized 1862. 3. *The R.* (*of St. John*), the last book of the New Testament; the Apocalypse. So in pl. (*the*) *Revelations.* late ME. 4. Disclosure of facts made by a person; exposure of something previously disguised or concealed 1475.

1. He sayd, how he had all thinges shewed him by r. 1560. 2. b. We have a veritable r. in Science H. SPENCER. 4. This astounding r. excited alarm and anger 1880. Hence **Revela·tionist,** one who makes a r., *esp.* the author of the Apocalypse; one who believes in r. **Revela·tor,** one who or that which makes a r. **Re·velatory** *a.* serving to reveal.

Reve·llent, *a.* (*sb.*) *rare.* 1661. [ad. L. *revellent-, revellere.*] A. *adj.* Revulsive 1822. B. as *sb.* A revulsive agent.

Reveller (re·vĕlər). late ME. [f. REVEL *v.*[1] + -ER[1].] One who takes part in a revel; one who is given to revelling, or leads a disorderly life.

The barbarous dissonance Of Bacchus and his Revellers MILT.

Re·velous, *a. rare.* late ME. [a. OF.; see REVEL *sb.* and -OUS.] Given to or marked by revelling.

Re·vel-rout. *arch.* or *Obs.* 1553. [f. REVEL *sb.* + ROUT *sb.*] 1. Uproarious revelry; boisterous merriment. b. An occasion of revelling; a revel 1652. 2. A crowd or party of revellers (*rare*) 1655.

1. Then made they revell route and goodly glee SPENSER.

Revelry (re·vĕlri). late ME. [f. REVEL *sb.* + -RY.] The act of revelling, merry-making; boisterous gaiety or mirth.

Mean while welcom Joy, and Feast, Midnight shout, and R. MILT. There was a sound of r. by night BYRON.

‖**Revenant** (rəvnaṅ). 1828. [F., pres. pple. of *revenir* to return.] 1. One who returns from the dead; a ghost. 2. One who returns to a place 1886.

Revendication (rīvendikē·ʃən). 1760. [a. F.] The action of claiming back or recovering by a formal claim.

Revenge (rĭve·ndʒ), *sb.* 1547. [f. the vb.] 1. The act of doing hurt or harm to another in return for wrong or injury suffered; satisfaction obtained by repayment of injuries 1566. b. A desire to repay injuries by inflicting hurt in return 1586. 2. With possess. pron. a. One's desire to be revenged, or the gratification of this 1547. †b. The avenging of a person (*rare*) -1653. 3. A particular act of repaying injuries or wrongs 1582. 4. Repayment *of* some wrong, injury, etc., by the infliction of hurt or harm 1615. †5. Punishment; chastisement -1697. 6. An opportunity of retaliation or retrieval; *spec.* in cards, chess, etc., a return game, esp. in phr. *to give one* (*his*) *r.* 1672.

1. Reuenge now goes To lay a complot to betray thy Foes SHAKS. A desire of r. upon the plunderers of his country GOLDSM. b. Fury in his eyes and reuenge in his heart SIDNEY. 2. I..vowed to have my r. 1887. b. 1 *Hen. VI*, I. v. 35. 4. The Reuenge of that wrong, putteth the Law out of Office BACON. 6. I'll give you R. whenever you please SWIFT. Hence **Reve·ngeful** *a.* vindictive; **-ly** *adv.* **Reve·ngeless** *a.* unrevenging; unavenged.

Revenge (rĭve·ndʒ), *v.* late ME. [a. obs. F. *revenger* (var. of *revencher*, mod.F. *revancher*), f. *re-* RE- + *venger* to VENGE.] 1. *refl.* To avenge oneself; to take revenge *on* a person *for* a wrong, injury, insult, etc., received or resented. Also in *pass.* 2. *trans.* To inflict punishment or exact retribution for (an injury, harm, wrong, etc., done to oneself or another) 1456. b. To maintain, uphold, or vindicate (one's cause, etc.) by some act of retribution or punishment 1526. 3. To avenge (a person, etc.) 1470. †4. To punish, exact punishment for (a wrong, crime, or sin) -1713. 5. *absol.* To take vengeance or revenge 1456.

1. Methinks I should r. me of my wrongs MARLOWE. b. Now Ile doo 't, and so he goes to Heauen, And so am I reueng'd SHAKS. 2. When my Betters give me a Kick I am apt to r. it with six upon my Footman SWIFT. Her brother..was slain, and she revenged his death 1727. 3. The brother..immediately took up arms to r. him 1841. 4. The Lord will surely reuenge thy pride *Ecclus.* v. 3. 5. The Lord reuengeth, and is furious *Nahum* i. 2. Hence **Reve·ngeable** *a.* †revengeful; worthy or capable of being revenged. †**Reve·ngeance,** revenge, vengeance. **Reve·ngement,** revenge, retribution; †punishment. **Reve·nger. Reve·ngingly** *adv.*

Revengeful (rĭve·ndʒful), *a.* 1586. [f. REVENGE *sb.* + -FUL 1.] Full of revenge; vindictive. Hence **Reve·ngeful-ly** *adv.*, **-ness.**

Revenue (re·vĕniu). late ME. [a. OF. *revenu* masc. or *revenue* fem., pa. pple. of *revenir* used subst. The stressing *reve·nue* is old-fashioned.] †1. Return to a place (*rare*) -1532. †2. The return, yield, or profit *of* any lands, property, or other important source of income. Also *pl.* in same sense. -1654. 3. That which comes in to one as a return from property or possessions, esp. of an extensive kind; income from any source (but esp. when large and not directly earned). late ME. 4. *pl.* The collective items or amounts which constitute an income, *esp.* that of a person having extensive landed possessions, a ruler, city, state, etc. late ME. 5. An income; an amount of money regularly accruing to a person 1614. b. A separate source or item of (private or public) income 1624. 6. The annual income of a government or state, from all sources, out of which the public expenses are defrayed 1690. b. The department of the civil service which deals with the collection of the national funds 1700.

2. *Rich. II*, I. iv. 46. 3. I haue a Widdow Aunt, a dowager, Of great reuennew SHAKS. 4. They took Care of the Church's Revenues 1704. 5. b. This.. supplied a r. to the crown 1879. 6. *Inland r.*: see INLAND *a.* 2. b. When I was employ'd in the R. SWIFT. *attrib.* and *Comb.*, as *r. act, officer*, etc.; *r.-earning, -producing.* Hence **Re·venued** *a.* having (large or rich) revenues.

Reverb (rĭvō·ɹb), *v.* 1605. [irreg. ad. L. *reverberare*; in modern use, after Shakespeare.] *trans.* and *intr.* To reverberate, re-echo.

Reverberant (rĭvō·ɹbĕrănt), *a.* 1572. [a. F. *réverbérant*, or ad. L. *reverberantem.*] 1. *Her.* Of a lion's tail: Turned up like the letter S, with the end outwards. 2. Reverberating; resonant 1807.

Reve·rberate, *pa. pple.* and *ppl. a.* 1589. [ad. L. *reverberatus, reverberare*; see next.] 1. Reverberated. †2. Reverberating -1605.

2. Hallow your name to the reuerberate hilles SHAKS.

Reverberate (rĭvō·ɹbere^i^t), *v.* 1547. [f. L. *reverberat-, reverberare*, f. *re-* RE- + *verberare* to strike, beat.] I. *trans.* 1. To beat, drive, or force back; to repel, repulse. Now *rare* or *Obs.* b. To send back, return, re-echo (a sound or noise) 1591. c. To cast back, reflect (light, heat, etc.) 1638. d. *absol.* To cause reverberation 1763. 2. *trans.* To subject to the heat of a reverberatory furnace. Also *absol.* 1610.

1. b. The hilles, to heav'n, r. their voyce FLORIO. c. On which the Sun shining.., its Rays were reverberated as from another Sun 1745. 2. Steel corroded with Vinegar,..and after reverberated by fire 1646.

II. *intr.* 1. †a. To turn or bend back (*rare*) -1608. b. To recoil *upon*, to have a respondent effect *on*, to appeal responsively *to*, something (*rare*) 1713. c. Of material objects: To rebound 1837. 2. To shine or reflect *from* a surface, etc. 1598. †b. To shine or glow *on* (something) with reflected beams -1650. 3. Of sound: To resound, re-echo 1613. 4. Of flames, etc.: To strike *upon*, to pass *over* or *into*, as the result of being forced back 1704.

1. c. Our rifle-balls reverberated from their hides like cork pellets from a pop-gun target 1856. 3. The shock, the shout, the groan of war, R. along that vale BYRON.

Reverberation (rĭvōɹbĕrē·ʃən). late ME. [a. OF., or ad. late L. *reverberationem.*] 1. a. The fact, on the part *of* a thing, of being driven or forced back, esp. after impact (*rare*). b. Reflection *of* light or heat 1460. c. Return or re-echoing *of* sounds 1626. †2. a. The action *of* something in reflecting light or heat -1686. †b. The action *of* a thing in returning a sound, or the result of this -1657. 3. The action of driving or sending back, reflecting light, returning a sound, etc.; the fact of being reflected, returned, etc.; an instance of this 1597. b. The fact or process of subjecting to heat in a reverberatory furnace 1460. 4. a. A re-echoing sound 1845. b. A reflection of light or colour 1860.

1 a. The sound made by r. of the aire, which men call Eccho HOLLAND. b. Like the several Reverberations of the same Image from two opposite Looking-Glasses ADDISON.

Reverberative (rĭvə̄·ɹbĕrẽⁱtiv), *a.* 1716. [f. REVERBERATE *v.* + -IVE.] Inclined to reverberate; having the nature of a reverberation.

Reverberator (rĭvə̄·ɹbĕrẽⁱtəɹ). 1794. [-OR 2.] 1. A reflector; a reflecting lamp. 2. One who reverberates 1803.

Reverberatory (rĭvə̄·ɹbĕrătəri), *sb.* 1651. [See next.] A reverberatory furnace or kiln.

Reverberatory (rĭvə̄·ɹbĕrătəri), *a.* 1605. [See REVERBERATE *v.* and -ORY.] 1. Of fire: Forced or driven back by some contrivance upon the substance which is subjected to its operation. b. Of heat: Produced by reverberation 1799. 2. Of a furnace, kiln, etc.: So constructed that the flame is forced back upon the substance exposed to it 1672.

†**Reverdure,** *v.* 1525. [a. OF. *reverdurer.*] *trans.* To clothe again with verdure.

Revere (rĭvīə·ɹ), *v.* 1611. [ad. F. *révérer* or L. *revereri*, f. *re-* RE- + *vereri* to fear.] *trans.* To hold in, or regard with, deep respect or veneration. Also *absol.*

For all..revered the name of Cæsar BRYCE. Hence **Reve·rable** *a.* (*rare*). **Reve·rer,** a reverent admirer.

Reverence (re·vĕrĕns), *sb.* ME. [a. OF., or ad. L. *reverentia*; see REVERENT *a.* and -ENCE.] 1. Deep or due respect felt or shown towards a person on account of his or her position or relationship; deference. Now *rare* or *Obs.* b. Deep respect and veneration for some thing, place, or person regarded as having a sacred or exalted character ME. 2. A gesture indicative of respect; an obeisance; a bow or curtsy. late ME. 3. The condition or state of being respected or venerated. late ME. 4. *Your r.*, A respectful form of address, now only used by the lower classes, esp. in Ireland, in speaking to a clergyman ME. b. *His r.*, as the designation of a clergyman 1762.

1. In speakynge of my Princes I must use a due r. and regarde 1572. b. I hold the church in holy r. LYTTON. Women are notably deficient in real r. for authority 1897. Phr. *To do r. to*, to show respect or veneration for (a person or thing) by some action. 2. [He] had never seen his friend offer so low a r. 1833. 3. Two reigns..passed in external glory and domestic r. HALLAM. Phr. †*Save* (a person's) *r.*, an apologetic phrase introducing a criticism, contradiction, etc., that might offend the hearer; so †*saving* (a person's) *r.*

Reverence (re·vĕrĕns), *v.* ME. [f. prec.] †1. *trans.* To salute (a person) with deep respect; to show respect for (a person) by bowing, kneeling, etc.; to make obeisance to -1686. †b. To treat with respect or deference -1592. 2. To regard with reverence or veneration as having a divine or sacred character; †to worship in some manner ME. b. To hold in high respect; to venerate 1548.

2. Ye shall keepe my Sabbaths, and reuerence my Sanctuary *Lev.* xix. 30. b. So prone To rev'rence what is ancient COWPER. Hence **Re·verencer,** one who reverences; a respecter *of* some thing or person.

Reverend (re·vĕrĕnd), *a.* (and *sb.*). 1449. [a. OF., or ad. L. *reverendus*, gerundive of *revereri* to REVERE.] 1. Of persons: Worthy of deep respect or reverence on account of (†rank), age, or character; †commanding respect by personal ability or great learning. b. As a courteous or respectful form of address 1486. 2. As a respectful epithet applied to members of the clergy. Also *Very R.* (of deans), *Right R.* (of bishops), and *Most R.* (of archbishops). 1485. b. Prefixed to the name (and designation) of the person, and frequently abbreviated as *Rev.* 1642. c. *sb.* A clergyman; a cleric or divine. Also *Right R.*, a bishop. Now *illiterate.* 1608. 3. Of things, places, etc.: Worthy of, or inspiring, reverence 1586. 4. Connected with, characteristic of, belonging to, the clergy 1645. 5. = REVERENT *a.* 2. Now somewhat *rare.* 15..

1. Next Camus, r. Sire, went footing slow MILT. b. Yet Reuerend Madame, but forget what 's past HEYWOOD. 2. c. We are not so meddlesome as you reverends are 1894. 3. The big tears..straying down his r. cheeks RICHARDSON. 4. A r. ignorance in fear to be convicted MILT. Hence **Re·verendly** *adv.* reverently; in a way, to a degree, that inspires reverence.

Reverent (re·vĕrĕnt), *a.* late ME. [In sense 1, a. OF. *reverent* for *reverend.* In sense 2, ad. L. *reverentem, revereri* to REVERE.] 1. = REVEREND *a.* Now *illiterate.* 2. Characterized by, exhibiting or feeling, reverence; deeply respectful 1486.

1. No harm is intended to the r. sage of the mountain 1796. 2. Lowly r. Towards either Throne they bow MILT. Hence **Re·verent-ly** *adv.*, **-ness** (*rare*).

Reverential (revĕre·nʃăl), *a.* 1555. [ad. med.L. **reverentialis*, f. L. *reverentia*; see -AL 1.] 1. Of the nature of, inspired or characterized by, reverence; reverent. 2. Inspiring reverence; venerable, reverend (*rare*) 1654.

1. He did it for a r. fear he had of his father 1555. 2. [A] fatherly, prolixe, and reverentiall beard 1656. Hence **Revere·ntial-ly** *adv.*, **-ness.**

Reverie (re·vĕri), *sb.* late ME. [In early use a. OF. *reverie* rejoicing, f. *rever* to revel, etc. In 17th c. readopted from F. *resverie, rêverie.*] †1. A state of delight. CHAUCER. †2. Violent or rude language. late ME. only. 3. A fantastic, fanciful, unpractical, or purely theoretical idea or notion 1653. 4. A fit of abstracted musing; a 'brown study' or day-dream 1657. b. *Mus.* An instrumental composition suggestive of a dreamy or musing state 1880. 5. The fact, state, or condition of being lost in thought or engaged in musing 1690.

3. I indeed desire Men to look upon [this] rather as a Dream or Resvery than a rational Proposition 1687. 4. Walking about in a sad r.,..unconscious of the world around her W. IRVING. 5. His fits of r. were.. frequent 1762.

‖**Revers** (rĭvīə·ɹz, rĭ·vəɹz, F. rəvẹ̄r). 1838. [F., REVERSE *sb.*] A part of a coat, vest, bodice, etc., of which the edge is turned back so as to exhibit the under surface; the material covering this reversed edge. (Freq. used as a *pl.*)

Reversal (rĭvə̄·ɹsăl), *sb.* 1488. [f. REVERSE *v.* + -AL 2.] 1. *Law.* The act of reversing or annulling a decree, sentence, punishment, etc.; the fact of being reversed or annulled. 2. The act or process of reversing; an instance of this 1698. 3. Reversion *to* some practice, etc. (*rare*) 1862.

1. The effect of the r. of an outlawry in a civil action 1797. 2. The effects of the r. of the poles of magnets, as caused by lightning 1794.

†**Reve·rsal,** *a. rare.* 1656. [a. F. *réversal* or ad. med.L. *reversalis.*] Revocatory -1715.

Reverse (rĭvə̄·ɹs), *sb.* late ME. [a. OF. *revers* masc., or *reverse* fem., f. L. *revers-, revertere* to REVERT.] I. 1. The opposite or contrary of something. 2. The opposite or contrary *of* or *to* something specified. late ME. b. Used with general terms or with adjs. to express more than a mere negation 1783. 3. That side of a coin, medal, or seal which does not bear the main device or inscription; the back. (Opp. to OBVERSE B 1.) 1625. b. The design, etc., on the reverse side 1623. c. The back or verso of a leaf (in a book) 1824. d. In general use as the correlative of *obverse* 1831. 4. The back of a mountain, mound, etc. 1777. 5. *In r.* a. *Mil.* In the rear 1781. b. Contrary to the usual manner; of a motor-car, etc.: On the reverse gear 1875.

1. The r. also happens; and very plausible schemes ..have often shameful and lamentable conclusions BURKE. 2. b. Remarks which are the r. of complimentary 1860. 5. a. To take the enemy in r., and intercept their retreat 1781.

II. †1. A back-handed stroke or cut -1656. 2. An adverse change of fortune; a disaster; esp. in mod. use, a defeat in battle 1526. 3. = REVERSAL *sb.* Now *rare* or *Obs.* 1589. 4. The act of reversing in dancing 1888.

2. Some reverses which happened in the beginning of that war BURKE. Hence **Reve·rseless** *a.* (*rare*) incapable of being reversed.

Reverse (rĭvə̄·ɹs), *a.* and *adv.* ME. [a. OF. *revers*, or ad. L. *reversus, revertere.*] A. *adj.* 1. Opposite or contrary (*to* something else, or to each other) in character, order, succession, etc. b. Lying behind or to the back 1851. †2. Of blows, etc.: Back-handed -1667. 3. *Mil.* Connected with, commanding, or facing towards the rear 1702. 4. Acting in a way contrary or opposite to that which is customary 1860.

1. The..story is the contrary to truth, and happened in the very r. manner BURKE. 3. The flank at the other extremity from the pivot of a division is termed the r. flank 1867.

B. *adv.* In a reverse way; reversely. late ME.

The edg of their own Proverb falls r. upon themselves MILT. Hence **Reve·rsely** *adv.*

Reverse (rĭvə̄·ɹs), *v.* ME. [a.F. *reverser*, f. L. *re-* RE- + *versare* freq. of *vertere* to turn; cf. REVERT *v.*] I. *trans.* †1. a. To bring back *to* or *into* a state or condition, a place, the mind, etc. -1590. b. To remove or put away; to divert or turn away (*rare*) -1639. †2. To overthrow, overturn, upset, or throw down (a person or thing) -1587. †b. To confute -1581. 3. To turn or place upside down; to invert. late ME. b. To hold or carry (a weapon) in the position contrary to that in which it is ready for use 1650. †4. To turn back or trim (a garment) *with* some other material -1523. 5. To revoke, abrogate, annul (a decree, act, measure, etc.), *esp.* in legal use. late ME. b. To undo (work) 1725. 6. To turn the other way, in respect of position or aspect; to transpose, turn inside out. late ME. 7. To convert into something of an opposite character or tendency; to turn the contrary way; to alter or change completely 1500. b. To employ, perform, in a way opposite to the former or usual method 1728. 8. To turn in the opposite direction; to send on a course contrary to the previous one 1509. b. To cause (an engine) to work or revolve in the contrary direction. Also *absol.* 1860.

1. The knight..to his..remembraunce did r. The ugly vew of his deformed crimes SPENSER. b. That old Dame said many an idle verse, Out of her daughters hart fond fancies to r. SPENSER. 3. Without his rod revers't,..We cannot free the Lady MILT. 5. It was hoped..to get my Lord Chancellor to r. a decree of his PEPYS. As she could not r. the curse..she did what she could to mitigate it 1869. b. The work she plied; but, studious of delay, By night reversed the labours of the day POPE. 7. I like not this charitie reversed, when it begins farre off and neglects those at home FULLER. 8. The ingenious mode of consuming smoke by reversing the flame 1824. b. The engines..were stopped and reversed full speed 1883.

II. *intr.* 1. To draw back or away; to move backwards (*rare*). late ME. b. In dancing, *esp.* waltzing: To move or turn in a contrary direction 1884. †2. To fall over, fall down -1530. †3. To return *back* or *home* -1647. So **Reve·rsement,** the act of reversing, or fact of being reversed. **Reve·rser** (*spec.* in *Electr.*).

Reversed (rĭvə̄·ɹst), *ppl. a.* late ME. [f. REVERSE *v.* + -ED [1].] Turned backwards, or placed the contrary way; inverted. b. In various special uses 1682.

b. When the spire of a shell turns in a direction opposite to what is normal, it is said to be 'r.' 1888. Hence **Reve·rsedly** *adv.*

Reversible (rĭvə̄·ɹsĭb'l), *a.* and *sb.* 1648. [f. REVERSE *v.* + -IBLE.] A. *adj.* Admitting of being reversed; capable of reversing. B. *sb.* A cloth which is faced on both sides to allow of its being turned 1860. Hence **Reversibi·lity.**

Reve·rsing, *ppl. a.* 1864. [f. REVERSE *v.* + -ING [2].] 1. That reverses or causes reversal. 2. Of the nature of, characterized by, reversal (of an action, process, etc.) 1878.

1. *R. layer* or *stratum*, a stratum of the solar atmosphere, reversing the dark lines of the ordinary solar spectrum.

Reversion (rĭvə̄·ɹʃən). late ME. [a. OF. *reversion, -cioun* :—L. *reversionem*, f. *revers-, revertere* to REVERT.] I. 1. *Law.* That part of an estate which remains undisposed of after the determination of the particular estate, and falls into the possession of the original grantor or his representative. late ME. 2. *Sc. Law.* The power to redeem an estate that is security for a debt or a judgement 1469. 3. *transf.* The right of succeeding to the possession *of* something after another is done with it, or simply of obtaining it at some future time; a thing or possession which one expects to obtain 1530. b. The right of succession to an office or place of emolument, after the death or retirement of the holder 1623. 4. A deferred or reversionary annuity 1771.

1. A r. of the best lease 1587. 3. Is there no

bright r. in the sky, For those who greatly think, or bravely die? POPE.

Phr. **In r.**: (*a*) conditional upon the expiry of a grant or the death of a grantee; (*b*) destined to come into a person's possession or to be realized in the future. Were our England in reuersion his, And he our subjects next degree in hope SHAKS. The prospect of too good a fortune in r. when I married her JOHNSON. An annuity is said to be in r., when the purchaser.. does not immediately enter upon possession 1771. The whole capital which Nicholas found himself entitled to either in possession, r., remainder, or expectancy DICKENS.

II. †**1.** The residue or remainder *of* something; also, a remnant, a small number –1824. †**2.** The action or fact of returning to or from a place –1741. **b.** The action or fact of returning to a certain condition, practice, or belief; an instance of this 1582. **c.** *Biol.* The fact or action of reverting to a primitive or ancestral type or condition; an instance of this 1859. **3.** The act of turning something or fact of being turned the reverse way 1677. **b.** *Math.* (See quot.) 1698.

3. b. R. of series is the method of finding the value of the quantity whose several powers are involved in a series, in terms of the quantity which is equal to the given series 1797.

Reve·rsional, *a.* 1675. [f. prec. + -AL 1.] = next 2.

Reversionary (rĭvɔ̄·ɹʃənări), *a.* and *sb.* 1651. [f. as prec. + -ARY.] **1.** Entitled to the reversion of something (*rare*). **2.** Of the nature of, connected with, a reversion 1720. **3.** *Biol.* Relating to reversion to type; tending to revert; atavistic 1873.

2. A r. grant of the Mastership of the Rolls 1845. **3.** What may be termed r. degeneration 1896.

B. *sb.* A reversioner (*rare*) 1660.

Reversioner (rĭvɔ̄·ɹʃənəɹ). 1614. [f. REVERSION + -ER 1.] One who possesses the reversion to an estate, office, etc.; an heir in reversion.

‖**Reversis.** Now *Hist.* 1814. [a. F., var. of *reversi.*] An obsolete card game in which the object was to avoid winning the tricks.

Revert (rĭvɔ̄·ɹt, rī·vəɹt), *sb.* 1655. [f. next.] **1.** A return *to* some means, etc. 1895. **2.** One who returns to his previous faith 1655.

Revert (rĭvɔ̄·ɹt), *v.* ME. [a. OF. *revertir*, ad. L. *revertere*, f. *re-* RE- + *vertere* to turn.] **I.** *intr.* †**1.** To recover consciousness; to come to oneself again –1560. **2.** To return, to come or go back, to or from a place or position. Now *rare.* late ME. **3.** *Law.* To return to the former possessor or his heirs 1447. **4.** To return *to* a custom, practice, idea, etc. 1612. **5.** To go back, recur, *to* a former subject of discourse 1587. **b.** To return *to* a subject of thought 1822. **6.** To return *to* a former condition 1638. **b.** To return *to* an earlier or primitive form; to reproduce the characteristics of an ancestral type 1859. **c.** To fall back into a wild state 1884.

4. The Christians..had reverted to the habit of wearing the white turban 1836. **5. b.** His ideas.. naturally reverted to his neighbour SCOTT. **6. b.** That our domestic varieties, when run wild, gradually ..r. in character to their aboriginal stocks DARWIN.

II. *trans.* †**1.** To cause to return, *esp.* to bring back or restore, to a person, place, etc. –1651. **2.** To turn (one's eyes or steps) back; to direct backwards 1632. **3.** To turn the other way; to reverse, invert, turn up. Now *rare* or *Obs.* late ME. **b.** *Math. To r. a series*, to determine the value of a quantity whose several powers are involved in a series, in terms of the quantity which is the sum of the series 1737. †**4.** To reverse, revoke, recall, annul –1639.

2. But I my steps toward the ancient bard Reverting, ruminated on the words CARY. **3.** I apply my Finger..upon the Top of the Tube, and then invert it;..then I r. the Tube, or turn it up again 1755. Hence **Reve·rter** 2, one who or that which reverts. **Reve·rtible** *a.* capable of reverting; admitting of reversion.

Reverted (rĭvɔ̄·ɹtĕd), *ppl. a.* 1590. [f. prec.] **1.** Turned backwards or the wrong way; bent back; reversed. **2.** Of the eyes, steps, etc.: Directed backwards 1741.

Reverter 1 (rĭvɔ̄·ɹtəɹ). 1491. [f. REVERT *v.* + -ER 4.] *Law.* Reversion (of lands, etc.).

†**Reve·st,** *v.*1 ME. [a. OF. *revestir* (mod. F. *revêtir*):—late L. *revestire*, f. *re-* RE- + *vestire* to clothe.] **1.** *trans.* **a.** In *pa. pple.* Of priests, etc.: Arrayed in ecclesiastical vestments, esp. for the purpose of performing mass or other office –1609. **b.** *gen.* To clothe, apparel, attire –1664. **2.** *refl.* To dress or apparel (oneself), esp. in ecclesiastical vestments –1652. **3.** *trans.* To put on (attire) again –1867.

3. R. (yee States) your Robes of dignitie SYLVESTER. So †**Reve·sture** (*rare*), vesture, vestments –1621.

Revest (rīve·st), *v.*2 1561. [f. RE- 5 a + VEST *v.*] **1.** *trans.* To reinvest (a person) with power, ownership, or office; to reinstate. **2.** To vest (something) again *in* a person, etc. 1697. **3.** *intr.* To become reinvested (*in* a person) 1651.

2. A Bill to r. in the Universities the monopoly in Almanacks 1799. So **Reve·stment.**

Revestry (rĭve·stri). late ME. [ad. OF. *revestiaire*, after *vestry.*] The vestry of a church (†or temple). So **Reve·stiary,** in same sense.

Revet (rĭve·t), *v.* 1812. Also in pseudo-F. form **revête.** [ad. F. *revêtir*, OF. *revestir* REVEST *v.*1] *trans.* To face (an embankment or wall) with masonry or other material, *esp.* in fortification.

Revetment (rĭve·tmĕnt). 1779. Also in F. or quasi-F. form (1771). [ad. F. *revêtement*, f. *revêtir*: see prec.] **1.** *Fortif.* A retaining-wall (of masonry, etc.) supporting the face of an earthen rampart or the side of a ditch. **2.** *Civil Eng.* A facing of masonry, concrete, sods, etc., supporting or protecting a bank or embankment 1838. **3.** *Arch.* A facing of stone or other hard material over a less durable substance 1891.

†**Revie·,** *sb.* 1588. [a. F. *renvi*, f. *renvier* REVIE *v.*] In card-playing, a higher stake ventured by a player against that proposed by an opponent –1680.

†**Revie·,** *v.* late ME. [ad. F. *renvier*:—late L. *reinvitare*, f. L. *re-* RE- + *invitare* to invite.] **1.** *trans.* To return (an invitation). late ME. only. **2.** In card-playing: To meet by venturing a larger stake than that proposed by an opponent –1673. **3.** *intr.* To make a revie or revies –1680. **b.** To retort or retaliate –1734.

Review (rĭviū·), *sb.* 1565. [a. obs. F. *reveue* (mod.F. *revue*), f. *revoir*, f. *re-* RE- + *voir* :—L. *videre* to see.] **I. 1.** The act of looking over something (again), with a view to correction or improvement; a revision (of a book, etc.). Now *rare.* **2.** *Law.* Revision of a sentence, etc., by some other court or authority 1654. **3.** A formal inspection of military or naval forces by the sovereign or other high personage, or by the general or admiral in command 1683. **4.** An inspection, examination 1611. **5.** A general survey or reconsideration 1604. **b.** Without article, esp. *in* or *under r.* 1729. **6.** A retrospective survey of past actions, etc. 1673. **7. a.** A general account or criticism of a literary work (esp. a new or recent one), usu. published as an article in a periodical or newspaper 1649. **b.** A periodical publication consisting mainly of articles in which current events or questions, or literary works, are discussed or criticized 1705.

1. Some things having passed therein, which..in the r...I wished might be altered 1638. **2.** A Bill of R., which is brought to examine and reverse a decree made upon a former Bill, which has been duly enrolled, and thereby become a record of the Court 1838. **3.** Phr. *To march* or *pass in r.* **4.** *In r.*, under examination. **5.** He has taken a r. of the effects of all the schemes which have been successively adopted BURKE. **6.** I have lived a life of which I do not like the r. JOHNSON. **7. a.** Critical R. of Fox's Book of Martyrs 1824.

II. (rī·viu) A second or repeated view 1665.

Review (rĭviū·), *v.* 1576. [f. RE- and VIEW *v.*, after F. *revoir.*] †**1.** *trans.* To see or behold again –1796. **2.** (rī·viū). To view, inspect, or examine a second time or again 1576. †**3. a.** To revise (a book, etc.) –1715. **b.** To re-examine; to reconsider (*rare*) –1672. **4.** *Law.* To submit (a decree, act, etc.) to examination or revision 1621. **5.** To survey; to take a survey of 1600. **b.** To look back upon; to regard or survey in retrospection 1751. **6.** To hold a review of (troops, etc.) 1712. **7.** To write an appreciation or criticism of (a new literary work); also *absol.*, to write reviews; to follow the occupation of a reviewer 1781.

1. Anxious to r. his native shore 1762. **2.** How they viewed and reviewed us as we passed over the rivulet! STERNE. **4.** The order may be reviewed or may be appealed from 1858. **5. b.** The past he calmly hath reviewed WORDSW. **7.** I would never r. the work of an anonymous authour JOHNSON. Hence **Review·able** *a.* that may be reviewed. **Review·al,** the or an act of reviewing; a review.

Reviewer (rĭviū·əɹ). 1611. [f. REVIEW *v.* + -ER 1.] †**1.** One who revises –1720. **2.** One who criticizes new publications; a writer of reviews. In early use, the author of a special pamphlet criticizing another work 1651.

†**Revification,** erron. f. REVIVIFICATION.

†**Revi·le,** *sb.* 1579. [f. the vb.] **1.** A reviling speech or remark –1645. **2.** Revilement, reviling –1684.

2. Render them not reviling for r. BUNYAN.

Revile (rĭvəi·l), *v.* ME. [a. OF. *reviler*, f. *re-* RE- + *vil* VILE *a.*] †**1.** *trans.* To degrade, abase. ME. only. **2.** To subject to contumely or abuse; to assail with opprobrious or abusive language ME. **3.** *intr.* To use opprobrious language; to rail *at* a person or thing 1526.

2. The man..with reproachfull tearmes gan them r. SPENSER. **3.** When he was reviled, reviled not agayne TINDALE 1 *Pet.* ii. 23. Hence **Revi·ler.**

Revilement (rĭvəi·lmĕnt). 1590. [f. REVILE *v.*] **1.** The act, fact, or practice of reviling. **2.** An instance of this; a reviling speech 1637.

Revi·ling, *vbl. sb.* 1535. [f. as prec. + -ING 1.] The action of the vb.; a reviling remark or speech.

Their reuilings are grieuous to the eare *Ecclus.* xxvii. 15.

†**Revi·nce,** *v.* 1529. [ad. L. *revincere*, f. *re-* RE- + *vincere.*] *trans.* To refute, disprove –1686.

Revirescence (rīvire·sĕns). *rare.* 1741. [See next and -ENCE.] Return to a youthful or flourishing condition.

Revirescent (rīvire·sĕnt), *a.* *rare.* 1644. [ad. L. *revirescentem*, *revirescere.*] Flourishing anew.

Revisal (rĭvəi·zăl). 1612. [f. next + -AL 2.] The act of revising; a revision, re-examination.

He had not submitted his dispatch to official r. 1873.

Revise (rĭvəi·z), *sb.* 1591. [f. the vb.] **1.** The act of revising or reviewing; a revision, a looking over or examining again. **b.** A revised version or form 1894. **2.** *Typog.* A revised or corrected form of proof-sheet; a further proof submitted by the printer after having made the required corrections or additions 1612.

Revise (rĭvəi·z), *v.* 1567. [a. F. *reviser*, f. *re-* RE- + *viser* to look at, aim:—pop. L. **visare.*] †**1.** *intr.* To look again or repeatedly *at*, to look back or meditate *on*, something –1640. †**2.** *trans.* To see or behold, look at, again –1772. **3.** To look or read carefully over, with a view to improving or correcting 1611. **b.** To go over again, re-examine, in order to improve or amend; †to condense by revision 1596.

3. Neither did we disdaine to reuise that which we had done 1611. **b.** To r. the sentence of the court of delegates BLACKSTONE. Hence **Revi·sable** *a.* capable of being revised, liable to revision.

Revision (rĭvi·ʒən). 1611. [ad. late L. *revisionem*; see prec.] **1.** The action of revising; esp. critical or careful examination or perusal with a view to correcting or improving. **b.** A product of this; a revised version 1845. **2.** The fact of seeing some person or thing again 1796.

1. A very great work, the r. of my Dictionary JOHNSON. Hence **Revi·sional, Revi·sionary** *adjs.*

Revisionist (rĭvi·ʒənist). 1865. [f. prec. + -IST.] **1.** One who advocates revision. **2.** *pl.* The revisers of the Bible 1881.

Revisor (rĭvəi·zǭɹ). 1598. [See REVISE *v.* and -OR 2 a.] One who revises; a reviser.

Revisory (rĭvəi·zəri), *a.* 1846. [f. REVISE *v.* + -ORY 2.] Having power to revise; engaged in, of the nature of, revision.

Revivable (rĭvəi·văb'l), *a.* 1810. [f. REVIVE *v.* + -ABLE.] Capable of being revived. So **Revivabi·lity.**

Revival (rĭvəi·văl). 1651. [f. REVIVE *v.* + -AL 2.] **1.** The act of reviving after decline or discontinuance; restoration to general use acceptance, etc.; an instance or result of this. **b.** The act of restoring an old play to the stage, or of republishing an old literary work 1664. **c.** *Arch.* The reintroduction of Gothic architecture, towards the middle of the 19th c. 1850. **2. a.** Restoration to vigour or activity 1752. **b.** Restoration or return to life or consciousness 1788. **c.** *Chem.* Revivification 1788. **d.** The fact of renewing or raising again 1885. **3.** A general reawakening *of* or *in* religion in a community, or some part of one 1702. **b.** *ellipt.* freq. in depreciatory use 1818.

1. The happy R. of Masquerading among us SWIFT. *R. of learning, letters,* or *literature*, the Renaissance in its literary aspect. 2. d. The withdrawal and r. of objections 1885. 3. b. In the Methodist chapel.. where they are in the thick of a r. 1849.

Revivalism (rĭvəi·văliz'm). 1815. [f. prec. + -ISM.] **1.** The state or form of religion characteristic of revivals. **2.** Tendency or desire to revive what has gone out of use or belongs to the past 1874.

Revivalist (rĭvəi·vălist). 1820. [f. as prec. + -IST.] **1.** One who promotes, produces, or takes part in, a religious revival. **2.** One who revives former conditions, methods, etc. 1856.

1. The Irish Shouters, the Welsh Jumpers, and the Cornish Revivalists 1820. Hence **Revi·valistic** *a.*

†**Revi·ve,** *sb. rare.* 1589. [f. the vb.] **a.** Revival, restoration to life. GREENE. **b.** A revival (of a play) on the stage. PEPYS.

Revive (rĭvəi·v), *v.* late ME. [ad. F. *revivre,* = post-class. L. *revivere,* f. *re-* RE- + *vivere* to live.] **I.** *intr.* **1.** To return to consciousness; to recover from a swoon or faint. **2.** To return to life; to regain vital activity, after being dead; to live again 1526. **b.** *Chem.* To return to the metallic state 1825. **3.** To assume fresh life or vigour after nearly dying or becoming extinct 1526. **b.** To resume courage or strength; to recover from depression 1530. **4.** Of feelings, dispositions, etc.: To become active or operative again 1494. **b.** To return to a flourishing state; to assume fresh life or vigour after decline or decay; also in *Law,* to become valid again 1565. **c.** To return, come back again, after a period of abeyance 1759.

1. When he had drunke, his spirit came againe, and he reuiued *Judg.* xv. 19. 2. Henry is dead, and neuer shall reuiue SHAKS. 3. Even as a dying coal revives with wind SHAKS. b. I r. At this last sight, assur'd that Man shall live MILT. 4. Ambitious hopes which had seemed to be extinguished, had revived in his bosom MACAULAY. b. The abuses which he had suppressed began to r. MACAULAY. c. But the old time is dead also, never, never to r. STEVENSON.

II. *trans.* **1.** To restore to consciousness; to bring back from a swoon or faint, or from a state of suspended animation. late ME. **2.** To restore to life; to resuscitate or reanimate; to bring back *from* death or the grave 1470. **3.** To restore from a languid, depressed, or morbid state; to infuse fresh life or vigour into 1547. **b.** To renew; to restore again from or after decline or decay 1631. **4.** To set going, make active or operative, again 1494. **b.** To re-enact (a law, etc.); to renew or re-validate; to re-open (an election) 1548. **c.** To reawaken (a desire, etc.) 1590. **5.** To bring into existence or use, set up, again 1495. **b.** To bring back into knowledge, notice, or currency 1509. **c.** To put (an old play) upon the stage again 1823. **6.** To bring again before the mind; to renew the memory of (a person or thing); to recall 1638. **b.** To renew or freshen up, to bring back to a person (the memory *of* some person or thing) 1592. **7.** *Chem.* To convert, restore, or reduce (a metal, esp. mercury) to or into its natural condition or form; to restore *from* a mixed to a natural state; to revivify 1677. **8.** To treat (faded clothing, etc.) with a reviver; to renovate (*rare*) 1836. **b.** To restore to clearness 1861.

1. This Water reviv'd his Father more than all the Rum or Spirits I had given him DE FOE. 2. He Lazarus reuiued from the graue 1603. 3. He..with sweete delight Of Musicks skill revives his toyled spright SPENSER. b. Two poets in an age are not sufficient to r. the splendour of decaying genius GOLDSM. 4. To R. an old grudge 1696. b. You may wish to r. your will after you have revoked it 1858. c. Would'st thou r. the deep Despair GRAY. 5. The great danger..of reviving Jewish ceremonies 1653. To r. the ancient monarchy 1866. b. Prevailed upon to r. that ridiculous old story MISS BURNEY. 6. The surrounding scene revived..all the impressions of my boyhood TYNDALL. 8. b. Attempts have been made to r. the faded characters 1875. Hence **Revi·vement** (now *rare*), the (*or* an) act of reviving; a reviving influence.

Reviver (rĭvəi·vəɹ). 1592. [f. prec. + -ER 1.] **1.** That which revives, restores, or invigorates; also *slang,* a stimulating drink. **b.** A preparation for restoring a faded colour, polish, or lustre 1836. **2.** One who revives or restores that which has lapsed, become obsolete, or fallen into disuse 1607.

†**Revivi·ction.** *rare.* 1646. [irreg. f. L. *reviviscere.*] Reviviscence -1652.

Revivification (rĭvi:vifikē¹·ʃən). 1638. [See prec.] **1.** Restoration or return from death to life. **b.** *Nat. Hist.* Recovery or awakening from a state of torpidity 1801. **2.** *Chem.* Reduction or restoration of a metal, etc., after combination, to its original state 1643. **3.** Revival, restoration; renewal of vigour or activity 1756.

Revivify (rĭvi·vifəi), *v.* 1675. [ad. F. *revivifier* :—late L. *revivificare.*] **1.** *trans.* To restore to animation or activity; to revive or reinvigorate; to put new life into. **2.** To restore to life, make alive again 1744. **3.** *Chem.* **a.** = REVIVE *v.* II. 7. 1727. **b.** *intr.* = REVIVE *v.* I. 2 b. 1727.

1. *transf.* I have..endeavoured to r. the bygone times and people THACKERAY. 2. A germ to be revivified LAMB.

Revi·ving, *ppl. a.* 1592. [f. REVIVE *v.* + -ING 2.] **1.** That revives, or regains strength or consciousness. **2.** That refreshes, stimulates, or infuses fresh life 1601. **b.** Renewing an enactment 1769. Hence **Revi·vingly** *adv.*

Reviviscence (revivi·sĕns). 1626. [ad. L. **reviviscentia,* f. pres. pple. of *reviviscere* to revive.] **1.** Return to life or animation. **2.** Revival; restoration to a flourishing or vigorous condition 1711. So **Revivi·scency.**

Reviviscent (revivi·sĕnt), *a.* 1778. [ad. L. *reviviscent-, reviviscere.*] **1.** Returning to life or animation; reviving. **2.** Causing renewed life 1886.

Revivor (rĭvəi·vǭɹ). 1602. [f. REVIVE *v.* + -OR 2 a.] †**1.** Renewal, revival (*rare*) -1741. **2.** A proceeding for the revival of a suit or action abated by the death of one of the parties, or by some other circumstance. Chiefly in phr. *bill of r.* 1623.

Revocable (re·vŏkab'l), *a.* 1471. [a. OF., or ad. L. *revocabilis*; see REVOKE *v.* and -ABLE.] Capable of being revoked or recalled.

Your rash, and I hope r. resolution RICHARDSON. Acts..not r. by any subsequent authority BURKE. Hence **Re:vocabi·lity, Re·vocableness. Re·vocably** *adv.*

†**Re·vocate,** *v.* 1540. [ad. L. *revocat-, revocare* to REVOKE.] **1.** *trans.* To recall, call back -1548. **2.** To revoke, rescind -1595.

Revocation (revŏkē¹·ʃən). late ME. [a. OF., or ad. L. *revocatio,* f. *revocare.*] **1.** The action of recalling; recall (of persons); a call or summons to return. Now *rare* or *Obs.* **b.** *transf.* with ref. to things 1649. **2.** The action of revoking, rescinding, or annulling; withdrawal (of a grant, etc.). late ME. †**3.** Recantation; withdrawal (of statements) -1684.

1. The Envoy delivered his Letters of R., and is preparing to leave..Court 1710. 2. The r. of the edict of Nantz 1788. A general r. of all..grants 1861.

Revocatory (re·vŏkătəri), *a.* late ME. [ad. late L. *revocatorius*; see REVOCATE *v.*] Tending or pertaining to, expressive of, revocation; esp. *r. letters,* after med. L. *litteræ revocatoriæ.*

Revok(e)able (rĭvōᵘ·kăb'l), *a.* 1584. = REVOCABLE *a.*

Revoke (rĭvōᵘ·k), *sb.* 1709. [f. the vb.] **1.** *Cards,* esp. *Whist.* An act of revoking; a failure to follow suit when a card of that suit is held. **2.** Revocation, recall 1882.

Revoke (rĭvōᵘ·k), *v.* late ME. [ad. OF. *revoquer,* or L. *revocare,* f. *re-* RE- + *vocare* to call.] **I.** *trans.* †**1.** To recall, bring back *to* a (right) belief, etc., or *from* some belief or practice -1687. †**b.** To restrain or prevent *from* something -1616. †**c.** Without const. To check, restrain (*rare*) -1637. **2.** †**a.** To bring back *into* or *unto* life; to restore to consciousness -1664. **b.** To call back to memory. Now *rare.* 1565. †**c.** To bring back into use; to revive -1644. **3.** To recall; to call or summon back 1521. **4.** To annul, repeal, rescind, cancel. late ME. †**5.** To retract, withdraw, recant -1671. †**6.** To take back to oneself -1600. †**b.** To draw back, withdraw (*rare*) -1644.

2. b. Reuoking to minde the former talke betweene the captaine and him 1565. 3. Now the English forces were revoked from the marches of Scotland 1709. How readily we wish time spent revok'd COWPER. 4. Her only son, who stood by, implored her to r. the malediction LOCKHART.

II. *intr.* **1.** To make revocation 1500. **2.** *Cards,* esp. *Whist.* To fail or neglect to follow suit when a card of the required suit is held 1592. Hence †**Revo·kement** (*rare*), revocation. **Revo·ker** (*rare*). **Revo·king** *ppl. a.* (*Cards*) that revokes; so **Revo·kingly** *adv.* by way of revocation.

Revolt (rĭvōᵘ·lt, rĭvǫ·lt), *sb.*[1] 1560. [a. F. *révolte,* f. *révolter*; see REVOLT *v.*] **1.** An instance, on the part of subjects or subordinates, of casting off allegiance or obedience to their rulers or superiors; an insurrection. **b.** An act of this nature on the part of an individual; a movement of strong protest against, or refusal to submit to, some condition, practice, etc. 1599. **c.** An emphatic withdrawal *from* a party, etc. 1596. **2.** The act of revolting; also, language tending to this 1586. **b.** *In r.,* in a state of rebellion 1602. †**c.** Revulsion of appetite. SHAKS.

1. Who first seduc'd them to that fowl r.? Th' infernal Serpent MILT. 2. They fixed upon the 20th of May as the day of r. 1801.

†**Revo·lt,** *sb.*[2] 1585. [perh. ad. F. *révolté,* pa. pple. of *révolter.*] A revolter, or rebel -1627.

Revolt (rĭvōᵘ·lt, rĭvǫ·lt), *v.* 1548. [ad. F. *révolter* :—L. **revolutare,* f. *re-* RE- + *volutare* to roll, revolve.] **I.** *intr.* **1.** To cast off (†or change) allegiance; to rise against rulers or constituted authority. **b.** To fall away *from* a ruler, obedience, etc.; to rise *against* a person or authority 1560. **c.** To go over *to* a rival power 1560. †**2. a.** To go over *to* another religion; to become a pervert (*from* some faith) -1686. **b.** To draw back *from* a course of action, etc.; to return to one's allegiance -1610. **3.** To feel revulsion or disgust *at* something 1760. **b.** To rise in repugnance *against* something 1775. **c.** To turn in loathing *from* something 1782.

1. The youth revolted, and refused to receive their own fathers JOWETT. b. [I] shall soon..rid heav'n of these rebell'd..That from thy just obedience could r. MILT. 3. Errors, at the grossness of which common sense..revolts 1802. c. He knew well that her mind revolted from that means of escape 1863.

II. *trans.* †**1.** To turn back. SPENSER. **2.** To affect with disgust or repugnance; to nauseate 1751. **b.** *absol.* To cause revulsion 1898.

2. Grave churchmen..who were revolted by these achievements in an ecclesiastic 1855. Hence **Revo·lter.**

Revo·lting, *ppl. a.* 1593. [-ING 2.] **1.** Rebelling. **2.** Repulsive 1806. Hence **Revo·ltingly** *adv.*

Revoluble, *a. rare.* 1598. [ad. L. *revolubilis.*] Revolving; rolling. So **Revolubi·lity.**

Revolute (re·vŏliut), *a.* 1753. [ad. L. *revolutus, revolvere.*] In scientific use (chiefly *Bot.*): Rolled backwards, downwards, or outwards.

Revolution (revŏlⁱū·ʃən). late ME. [a. OF., or ad. late L. *revolutionem,* f. *revolvere* to REVOLVE.] **I. 1.** *Astr.* The action or fact, on the part of celestial bodies, of moving round in an orbit or circular course; the apparent movement of the sun, stars, etc., round the earth. **b.** The time in which a planet, etc., completes a full circuit or course. late ME. **2.** The return or recurrence of a point or period of time; the lapse of a certain time. late ME. †**b.** A cycle, or recurrent period of time; an epoch -1706. †**c.** The recurrence or repetition *of* a day, event, occupation, etc. -1784. †**3.** A turn or twist; a bend or winding -1737. **4.** The action, on the part of a thing or person, of turning or whirling round, or of moving round some point 1664. **b.** *esp.* Movement round an axis or centre; rotation 1710. **c.** A single act of rotation round a centre 1706.

2. They recur..at long intervals; they depend on the slow revolutions of ages 1842. 4. That fear Comes thundring back with dreadful r. On my defensless head MILT. c. The pinion will make 10 revolutions while the wheel performs one 1825.

†**II.** The action of turning over in the mind; consideration, reflection -1792.

Answerable to any hourely..change in his mistris reuolution B. JONS.

III. 1. Alteration, change, mutation (*rare*). late ME. **b.** An instance of a great change in affairs or in some particular thing 1450. **2.** A complete overthrow of the established government in any country or state by those who were previously subject to it; a forcible substitution of a new ruler or form of government. Also without article. 1600. 3. *Eng. Hist.* †a. The overthrow of the Rump Parliament in 1660, which resulted in the restoration of the monarchy -1725. b. The expulsion, in 1688, of the Stuart dynasty under James II, and the transfer of sovereignty to William and Mary 1688. 4. *French Hist.* The overthrow of the monarchy, and establishment of republican government, in 1789-95. 1790. 5. *Amer. Hist.* The overthrow of British supremacy by the War of Independence in 1775-81. 1789.

1. Heere 's fine Reuolution, if wee had the tricke to see't SHAKS. b. A complete r. in our national industry 1870. 2. Rebellion is the subversion of the laws, and R. is that of tyrants 1796. Hence **Revolu·tionism**, advocacy or spread of revolutionary principles. **Revolu·tionist**, a revolutionary.

Revolutionary (revǒlⁱū·ʃənări), *a.* and *sb.* 1774. [f. REVOLUTION + -ARY.] A. *adj.* 1. Pertaining to or connected with, characterized by, of the nature of, revolution. 2. Revolving; marked by rotation 1832.

1. A..r. government 1827. The R. war 1838.

B. *sb.* One who instigates or favours revolution; one who takes part in a revolution 1850.

What manner of men they are who become revolutionaries KINGSLEY. Hence **Revolu·tionariness.**

Revolu·tioner. 1695. [f. as prec. + -ER [1].] 1. A supporter or approver of the Revolution of 1688. Now *Hist.* 2. A revolutionary 1803.

Revolutionize (revǒlⁱū·ʃənəiz), *v.* 1797. [f. REVOLUTION + -IZE 3.] 1. *trans.* To bring (a country or state) under a revolutionary form of government. 2. To convert into revolutionary forms; to infect with revolutionary principles or ideas 1797. 3. To change (a thing) completely or fundamentally 1799.

1. To r. Bulgaria 1868. 2 They have not revolutionized..diplomatic forms and ceremonies 1797. 3. The opening of the Indies..revolutionized the channels and the direction of commerce 1861.

Revo·lvable, *a.* 1889. [f. REVOLVE *v.* + -ABLE.] Capable of being revolved.

Revolve (rĭvǫ·lv), *sb.* 1595. [f. the vb.] †1. Meditation, determination. 2. Revolution; rotation 1641.

Revolve (rĭvǫ·lv), *v.* late ME. [ad. L. *revolvere*, f. *re-* RE- + *volvere* to roll, turn.] I. *trans.* †1. To turn (the eyes or sight) back or round -1695. †2. To restore; to turn, bring, or roll back (*into* a place or state, or *upon* a person) -1665. 3. To turn over (something) *in* the mind, thoughts, etc. 1460. b. To consider, think over, meditate upon (something). late ME. 4. To turn over, search through, study, or read (a book, etc.). Now *rare.* 1480. 5. To cause (something) to travel in an orbit around a central point; to rotate (something) upon an axis 1667.

3. Revolving in his mind some subtle feat Of thievish craft SHELLEY. b. While I revolved the case of these unfortunate young ladies 1756. 4. This having heard, strait I again revolv'd The Law and Prophets MILT. 5. Then in the East her turn she shines, Revolvd on Heavns great Axle MILT.

II. *intr.* †1. To return *to* a person or place -1755. †2. To deliberate or consider; to meditate *upon* something -1785. 3. To perform a circular motion; to move in a regular orbit *about* or *round* a fixed point 1713. b. To rotate or move upon an axis or centre 1727. 4. To come round again, to move round, in various senses 1769.

2. If this fall into thy hand, reuolue SHAKS. 3. Those bodies that r. round the sun BERKELEY. b. It was made to r. upon hinges 1849. 4. The year revolves CRABBE. Hence **Revo·lvency,** tendency to r.; capacity for revolution. **Revo·lvingly** *adv.*

Revolver (rĭvǫ·lvəɹ). 1835. [f. prec. + -ER [1].] 1. A pistol provided with mechanism by which a set of loaded barrels, or (more usu.) of cartridge-chambers, is revolved and presented successively before the hammer, so as to admit of the rapid discharge of several shots without reloading. 2. A revolving furnace 1879.

Revue (rĭviū·). 1913. [a. F.] A theatrical entertainment purporting to give a review (often satirical) of current fashions, events, plays, etc.; often, an elaborate musical entertainment consisting of numerous unrelated scenes or episodes.

Revu·lsant. 1875. [ad. F. *révulsant*, or L. **revulsantem*.] *Med.* A revulsive.

†**Revu·lse,** *v. rare.* 1669. [f. L. *revuls-*, *revellere*; see REVEL *v.*[2]] *trans.* To drag, draw, or pull back; to tear away -1690.

Revulsion (rĭvʊ·lʃən). 1541. [a. F., or ad. L. *revulsio*, f. *revellere*; see REVEL *v.*[2]] 1. *Med.* The action or practice of diminishing a morbid condition in one part of the body by operating upon another. (Cf. DERIVATION 1 c.) 2. The action of drawing, or the fact of being drawn, back or away 1609. 3. A sudden violent change of feeling; a strong reaction in sentiment or taste 1816. 4. A sudden reaction or reverse tendency in trade, fortune, etc. 1812.

2. Thrown out of employment by the r. of capital from other trades ADAM SMITH. 3. A natural r. from the baldness and puerility into which Wordsworth too often fell 1853.

Revulsive (rĭvʊ·lsiv), *a.* and *sb.* 1616. [See REVULSE *v.* and -IVE.] *Med.* A. *adj.* Capable of producing revulsion; tending to revulsion. B. *sb.* An application used to produce revulsion 1661.

Rew. *Obs.* exc. *dial.* [OE. *rǣw*, var. of *rāw* ROW *sb.*] †1. In advb. phrases: a. *By r.*, in order, successively. Also *in r.* -1591. b. *On* or *in a r.*, in a row or line -1615. †2. A row or line of persons or things; a rank or series -1664. b. *dial.* A hedgerow OE.

Reward (rĭwǫ·rd), *sb.* ME. [a. ONF., = OF. *reg(u)ard* REGARD *sb.*] †I. Regard, consideration, heed -1475. II. 1. A return or recompense made to, or received by, a person for some service or merit, or for hardship endured. late ME. †b. Remuneration (regular or extra) -1776. c. A sum of money offered for the capture or detection of a malefactor, discovery of a missing person, recovery of lost or stolen property, etc. 1593. 2. Recompense or retribution for evil-doing; requital, punishment. late ME.

1. The most recent r. for military merit is the Victoria Cross 1876. c. Whoever shall discover the said Daniel De Foe..shall have a r. of fifty pounds 1702. 2. Hanging was the r. of treason and desertion 1874. Hence **Rewa·rdful** *a.* yielding or producing r. **Rewa·rdless** *a.* devoid of r.

Reward (rĭwǭ·ɹd), *v.* ME. [a. ONF. *rewarder*, = OF. *reg(u)arder* to REGARD.] †I. *trans.* To regard, heed, consider; to look at or observe -1475. II. †1. *trans.* To assign or give (to a person) as a reward or recompense -1650. 2. To repay, requite, recompense (a person) for some service, merit, etc. ME. 3. To requite, make a return for (a service, merit, exertion, etc.) 1533. 4. a. To requite or repay (a person) for evildoing; to punish, chastise 1484. b. To pay back (injury or wrong) to a person; to visit *upon* a person (*rare*). late ME. 5. *absol.* To make recompense. late ME.

1. Thou hast rewarded mee good, whereas I haue rewarded thee euill 1 *Sam.* xxiv. 17. 2. Then I will r. those that were faithful to me 1685. A magnificent view rewards the traveller 1872. 3. The discovery, when made, would not at all r. the labour expended in the search 1836. 4. The Lord shall r. the doer of euill, according to his wickednesse 2 *Sam.* iii. 39. Hence **Rewa·rdable** *a.*, **-ness.** **Rewa·rdably** *adv.* **Rewa·rder.**

†**Rex** [1]. 1566. [Origin obsc.; see REAKS. In sense 2 assoc. w. L. *rex.*] 1. = REAKS -1642. 2. *To play r.*, to act as lord or master; to domineer -1692.

‖**Rex** [2]. *rare.* 1617. [L.] A king.

Rexine (re·ksīn). 1911. Trade name of a variety of artificial leather used in upholstery.

Reynard (re·năɹd). ME. [a. OF. *Renart*, *Renard*, the name of the fox in the *Roman de Renart*, repr. the OHG. personal name *Reginhart.*] A quasi-proper name given to the fox; also occas. used as a common noun.

Rh, a consonantal digraph used in Latin, and hence in English, French, etc., to represent Gr. initial ῥ (with spiritus asper); in English it has the same phonetic value as the simple *r.*

†**Rha.** 1578. [Late L., a Gr. ῥᾶ, from Ῥᾶ, ancient name of the Volga.] Rhubarb -1597.

†**Rha·barb.** 1646. Var. f. RHUBARB -1698.

Rhabarbarate (răbā·ɹbărĕt), *a.* and *sb.* 1696. [f. med.L. *Rhabarbarum* + -ATE.] †A. *adj.* Tinctured with rhubarb (*rare*). B. *sb.* A salt of rhabarbaric acid 1840.

Rhabarbaric (ræbaɹbæ·rik), *a.* 1839. [f. med.L. *rhabarbarum* (see next) + -IC 1 b.] *Chem.* = CHRYSOPHANIC. So **Rhaba·rbarin** [-IN [1]], chrysophanic acid.

‖**Rhabarbarum** (răbā·ɹbărǒm). 1597. [med. L., = *rha barbarum* 'foreign RHA' (cf. RHAPONTIC).] Rhubarb-root.

Rhabdite (ræ·bdəit). 1881. [f. Gr. ῥάβδος + -ITE [1].] 1. *Zool.* One of the homogeneous rod-like bodies found in the integument of turbellarian worms 1885. 2. *Ent.* One of the three pairs of organs forming the ovipositor of some insects 1890. 3. *Min.* A phosphide of iron and nickel 1881.

Rhabdo- (ræ·bdo, ræbdǫ·), comb. form of Gr. ῥάβδος rod, occurring in a few technical terms (chiefly zoological): **Rha·bdocœl(e** [Gr. κοῖλος hollow] *a.* having a straight digestive cavity, as turbellarian worms; *sb.* a worm of this kind; one of the *Rhabdocœla*. **Rhabdocœ·lian, -cœ·lous** *adjs.* = prec. *a.* **Rha·bdolith** [Gr. λίθος stone], one of the rod-like bodies forming the armature of a rhabdosphere. **Rha·bdomere** [Gr. μέρος], one of the rod-like constituents of a rhabdom. **Rha·bdomyo·ma,** a myoma involving the striated muscular fibres. **Rha·bdosphere,** a name given to certain spherical bodies found in abundance on the surface of the waters in warm seas.

Rhabdoid (ræ·bdoid), *a.* and *sb.* Also **ra-.** 1858. [ad. mod.L. *rhabdoides*, a. Gr. ῥαβδοειδής, f. ῥάβδος rod; see -OID.] A. *adj.* Resembling a rod; rod-like. B. *sb.* A rod-shaped body 1900. So **Rhabdoi·dal** *a.*

Rhabdology (ræbdǫ·lŏdʒi). Also **rabdo-.** 1667. [ad. mod.L. *r(h)abdologia*, f. Gr. ῥάβδος rod + -λογία -LOGY.] The act or art of computing by NAPIER'S BONES (or rods). Now *Hist.*

Rhabdom (ræ·bdǒm). Also **-ome.** 1878. [ad. late Gr. ῥάβδωμα, f. ῥάβδος rod.] *Ent.* One of the rods supporting the crystalline lenses in a faceted eye.

Rhabdomancy (ræ·bdomænsi). Also **ra-.** 1646. [ad. late L. *rhabdomantia*, a. Gr. ῥαβδομαντεία, f. ῥάβδος + μαντεία (see -MANCY).] Divination by means of a rod or wand; *spec.* the art of discovering ores, springs of water, etc., in the earth by means of a divining-rod. So **Rha·bdomancer,** a dowser.

Rhachi(o)-, etc.: see RACHI-, etc.

Rhadamanthus (rædămæ·nþǒs). 1582. [L., a. Gr. Ῥαδάμανθος.] In Greek mythology, one of the judges in the lower world, a son of Zeus and Europa. Hence allusively: an inflexible judge; a rigorous or severe master. Hence **Rhadama·nthine** *a.* resembling or characteristic of R.

Rhætian (rī·ʃăn), *a.* and *sb.* Also **Rhe-.** 1779. [f. *Rhætia* (see next) + -IAN.] = RHÆTO-ROMANIC.

Rhætic (rī·tik), *a.* and *sb.* Also **Rhe-.** 1861. [ad. L. *Rhæticus*, adj. of *Rhætia*, ancient name of a district of the Alps.] A. *adj. Geol.* Applied to strata, extensively developed in the Rhætian Alps, regarded as passage beds between the lias and trias; belonging to or characteristic of these. B. *sb.* The R. formation; *pl.* R. series of strata.

Rhætizite (rī·tizəit). Also **rhe-;** *erron.* **rhœ-.** 1816. [ad. G. *rhätizit*, f. *Rhætia*; see prec. and -ITE [1] 2 b.] *Min.* A white variety of cyanite.

Rhæ·to-Roma·nic, *a.* and *sb.* Also **Rhe-.** 1867. [f. *Rhæto-*, comb. f. L. *Rhætus* Rhætian + ROMANIC.] *Philology.* Applied to those dialects of the Romance family which are spoken in south-eastern Switzerland and the Tyrol; sometimes particularly to the Rumansch of the Grisons or the Ladin of the Engadine. Also **Rhæ·to-Roma·nce.**

‖**Rhagades** (ræ·gădīz), *sb. pl.* 1601. [late L., a. Gr. ῥαγάδες, pl. of ῥαγάς rent, chink.] *Path.* Chaps or fissures of the skin.

Rhamn (ræm). ME. [ad. late L. RHAMNUS.] The buckthorn; the buckthorn berry.

‖ **Rhamnus** (ræ·mnǒs). 1562. [late L., a Gr. ῥάμνος.] Formerly the buckthorn (*R. cathartica*) or Christ's thorn (*Paliurus aculeatus*); now, a genus of shrubs typical of the family *Rhamnaceæ* and comprising the buckthorns. Also *attrib.*

Rhapontic (răpǫ·ntik). 1548. [ad. mod.L. (1) *rhaponticum* = *rha Ponticum* (see RHA and PONTIC *a.*[1]); (2) *r(e)uponticum* (altered form corresp. to *reubarbarum* RHUBARB).] †1. Greater Centaury, *Centaurea Rhapontica* –1617. 2. A species of rhubarb, *Rheum Rhaponticum*, or its root. Also applied to other species. Also *attrib.* 1578. Hence **Rhaponticin** (răpǫ·ntisin) [-IN[1]], *Chem.*, a yellow principle extracted from the root of *Rheum Rhaponticum*.

Rhapsode (ræ·psǫud). 1834. [ad. Gr. ῥαψῳδός, f. ῥάπτειν to stitch + ᾠδή song, ODE.] = RHAPSODIST 2. So †**Rhapsoder** = RHAPSODIST 1. (*rare*) –1711.

Rhapsodic (ræpsǫ·dik), *a.* 1782. [ad. Gr. ῥαψῳδικός, f. ῥαψῳδός or ῥαψῳδία.] 1. = next 2. 2. Consisting of the recitation of rhapsodies 1846.

Rhapsodical (ræpsǫ·dikăl), *a.* 1659. [f. as prec. + -AL 1.] †1. Of a literary work: Consisting of a medley of narratives, etc.; fragmentary or disconnected in style –1759. 2. Characteristic of or of the nature of rhapsody (sense 3); exaggeratedly enthusiastic or ecstatic in language or manner 1783. 3. Of the rhapsodists. SHELLEY. Hence **Rhapso·dically** *adv.*

Rhapsodist (ræ·psǒdist). 1646. [f. Gr. ῥαψῳδός RHAPSODE + -IST.] †1. A collector of literary pieces –1671. 2. *Antiq.* In Ancient Greece, a reciter of epic poems, *esp.* one of a school of persons whose occupation it was to recite the Homeric poems 1656. b. *transf.* and *gen.* A reciter of poems 1765. 3. One who rhapsodizes or uses rhapsodical language; in early use, with implication of want of argument or fact 1741.

2. b. The same populace sit for hours.., listening to rhapsodists who recite Ariosto CARLYLE.

Rhapsodize (ræ·psǒdəiz), *v.* 1607. [f. RHAPSODY + -IZE.] †1. *trans.* To piece (miscellaneous narratives, etc.) together; to relate disconnectedly –1765. 2. To recite in rhapsodies. Also *absol.* 1822. 3. *intr.* To utter rhapsody; to talk rhapsodically 1806.

1. To r. them, as I once intended, into the body of the work STERNE.

Rhapsody (ræ·psǒdi), *sb.* 1542. [ad. L. *rhapsodia*, a. Gr. ῥαψῳδία, related to ῥαψῳδός RHAPSODE.] 1. An epic poem or part of one, suitable for recitation at one time. †2. A miscellaneous collection; a medley or confused mass (*of* things); a 'string' (*of* words, sentences, tales, etc.) –1837. †b. A literary work consisting of miscellaneous or disconnected pieces; a written composition having no fixed form or plan –1764. †c. A collection (*of* persons, nations) –1701. 3. An exalted expression of sentiment or feeling; an effusion (e.g. a speech, letter, poem) marked by extravagance of idea and expression, but without connected thought or sound argument. Also without article. 1639. 4. *Mus.* An instrumental composition enthusiastic in character but of indefinite form 1880.

1. Those [verses] of Homer, which..were at length, by Pisistratus's order, digested into books, called rhapsodies CHAMBERS. 2. Such a deed, As..sweete Religion makes A rapsidie of words SHAKS. b. I have lately got A. Wood's R. [sc. *Athenæ Oxonienses*] 1710. c. A cento and a r. of uncircumcised nations 1647. 3. This looks like mere r. GLADSTONE. Hence **Rha·psody** *v. intr.* to rhapsodize.

Rhatany (ræ·tăni). Also **ra(t)any, ratanhy.** 1808. [ad. mod.L. *rhatania.*] The S. American shrub *Krameria triandra*; the astringent extract of its root, used in adulterating port-wine, and medicinally.

Rhea[1] (rī·ă). 1801. [mod.L. generic name, a use of the mythological name L. *Rhea*, Gr. Ῥέα.] The South American or three-toed ostrich; the genus to which this bird belongs.

Rhea[2] (rī·ă). Also **rheea.** 1853. [Assamese.] = RAMIE.

Rheic (rī·ik), *a.* 1847. [f. RHEUM[2] + -IC 1 b, after F. *rhéique.*] *Chem. R. acid*: = next.

Rhein (rī·in). 1838. [f. RHEUM[2] + -IN[1], after F. *rhéine.*] *Chem.* An orange-coloured principle obtained from rhubarb; rheic acid.

†**Rhein-berry.** 1578. [ad. MDu *rijnbesie*, f. *Rijn* RHINE[3] + *besie* berry.] The buckthorn berry –1706.

Rhematic (rimæ·tik), *a.* and *sb. rare.* 1830. [ad. Gr. ῥηματικός, f. ῥηματ-, ῥῆμα word, verb.] A. *adj.* a. Pertaining to the formation of words 1856. b. Formed on verbs 1877.

a. This period, during which expressions were coined for the most necessary ideas,..forms the first in the history of man,..and we call it the R. Period 1856.

B. *sb.* The science of sentences or propositions 1830.

Rhemish (rī·miʃ), *a.* 1589. [f. *Rhemes*, former Eng. spelling of *Rheims* + -ISH.] Of or pertaining to Rheims in the north-east of France: the specific designation of an English translation of the New Testament by Roman Catholics of the English college at Rheims, published in 1582. So **Rhe·mist**, one of the authors of the R. translation of and commentary on the New Testament.

Rhenish (re·niʃ), *a.* and *sb.* late ME. [orig. partly a. or ad. OF. *rinois*, etc.:—med.L. **Rhenensis*, f. *Rhenus*; partly ad. continental Germanic forms; see -ISH. The mod. spelling is due to L. *Rhenus.*] A. *adj.* 1. Of or belonging to the river Rhine, or the regions bordering upon it 1545. †b. Applied to the gulden formerly current in Germany and the Netherlands –1787. 2. *R. wine*: wine produced in the Rhine region. late ME. B. *sb.* Rhenish wine. Now *rare.* 1602.

As he dreines his draughts of Renish downe SHAKS.

Rheo- (rī·ǒ, riǫ·), combining form of Gr. ῥέος stream, current, used chiefly in names of electrical apparatus.

Rhe·ochord, -cord, a wire used in measuring the resistance or reducing the strength of an electric current. **Rhe·ograph, Rheo·meter,** instruments for measuring the force of electric and other currents; so **Rheome·tric** *a.* **Rheo·metry,** the measurement of electric currents. **Rhe·omotor,** an apparatus by which an electric current is generated. **Rhe·ophore** [Gr. -φορος bearing], (*a*) Ampère's name for the connecting wire of a voltaic cell; (*b*) one of the poles of a voltaic battery; an electrode; hence **Rheopho·ric** *a.* **Rhe·oscope,** an instrument for ascertaining the existence of an electric current; so **Rheosco·pic** *a.* applied to preparations of certain nerves of a frog for showing the variation of electric currents; so *rheoscopic frog, muscle.* **Rhe·ostat** [Gr. στατός], an instrument used to regulate the circuit so that any constant degree of force may be obtained; so **Rheosta·tic** *a.* **Rhe·otome** [Gr. -τομος cutting], a device for interrupting an electric current; = INTERRUPTER b. **Rhe·otrope** [Gr. -τροπος turning], an instrument for reversing an electric current.

‖ **Rhesis** (rī·sis). 1871. [a. Gr. ῥῆσις word, speech.] A set speech or discourse.

‖ **Rhesus** (rī·sǒs). 1839. [mod.L., arbitrary use of L. *Rhesus*, Gr. Ῥῆσος, a mythical king of Thrace.] In full, *R. monkey*: one of the macaques, *Macacus r.*, an Indian monkey.

Rhetor (rī·tǫɹ). late ME. [a. L., a. Gr. ῥήτωρ.] 1. A teacher or professor of rhetoric; a rhetorician. 2. An orator, esp. a professional one. Occas. in depreciatory use: a mere rhetorician. 1588. So **Rheto·ric** *a.* (*rare*) rhetorical; †eloquent.

Rhetoric (re·tǒrik), *sb.* ME. [a. OF. *rethorique* (mod.F. *rhétorique*), or ad. L. *rhetorica*, *-ice*, a. Gr. ῥητορική (*sc.* τέχνη), fem. of ῥητορικός RHETORIC *a.*] 1. The art of using language so as to persuade or influence others; the body of rules to be observed by a speaker or writer in order that he may express himself with eloquence. b. A treatise on, or 'body' of, rhetoric 1565. 2. †a. Elegance or eloquence of language; eloquent speech or writing. b. Speech or writing expressed in terms calculated to persuade; hence, language characterized by artificial or ostentatious expression. Often *ironical* or *joc.* late ME. †c. *pl.* Elegant expressions; rhetorical flourishes. Also rhetorical terms –1628. d. *transf.* and *fig.*, esp. of the persuasiveness of looks or acts 1569. †3. Skill in or faculty of using eloquent and persuasive language –1750.

1. The therde of the vii sciences is called Rethoryque CAXTON. *personified.* Some condemn Rhetorick as the mother of lies 1642. 2. And the perswasive R. That sleek't his tongue MILT. d. The heauenly Rhetoricke of thine eye SHAKS.

Rhetorical (ritǫ·rikăl), *a.* 1476. [See prec. and -ICAL.] 1. †a. Eloquent, eloquently expressed. b. Expressed in terms calculated to persuade; hence, of the nature of mere rhetoric (as opp. to sober statement or argument). 2. Of, belonging to, concerned with, or comprised in, the art of rhetoric 1530. 3. Of persons: Given to the use of rhetoric 1651.

1. The facts..were rather r. than logical 1869. *R. question*, one that does not require an answer, but is only put in the form of a question to produce a more striking effect. Hence **Rheto·rically** *adv.*, **-ness.**

Rhetorician (retǒri·ʃăn). late ME. [a. OF. *rethoricien*, f. L. *rhetoricus* or *rhetorica*; see -ICIAN.] 1. A professor or teacher of the art of rhetoric (esp. in Ancient Greece and Rome); a professional rhetor or orator. 2. †a. An eloquent or elegant writer. b. One who uses rhetorical language or expression; *esp.* (often in depreciatory use) a public speaker who indulges in rhetoric. late ME.

1. Isocrates was a R. by profession: the framing of sentences, and turning of periods, was the great business of his long life 1838.

Rhe·torize, *v.* Now *rare* or *Obs.* 1608. [ad. late L. *rhetorizare*, a. Gr. ῥητορίζειν, f. ῥητορ-, ῥήτωρ RHETOR; see -IZE.] *intr.* To use rhetorical language. Hence †**Rhe·torized** *ppl. a.* addressed rhetorically. MILT.

Rheum[1] (rūm). Now *arch.* late ME. [a. OF. *reume*, mod.F. *rhume*, ad. L. *rheuma*, a. Gr. ῥεῦμα flow, stream, f. root ῥευ- to flow.] 1. Watery matter secreted by the mucous glands or membranes, such as collects in or drops from the nose, eyes, and mouth, etc.; hence, an excessive or morbid 'defluxion' of any kind. b. *poet.* Used for: Tears 1593. †c. *transf.* and *fig.* Applied to pernicious moisture or humour, or something resembling it –1650. 2. *spec.* A mucous discharge caused by taking cold; hence, a cold in the head or lungs; catarrh. Chiefly *pl.* (occas. used = Rheumatic pains). late ME.

1. b. The Northeast wind..Awak'd the sleepie rhewme, and so by chance Did grace our hollow parting with a teare SHAKS. Hence **Rheumed** *ppl. a.* full of watery mucous.

‖ **Rheum**[2] (rī·ǒm). 1753. [mod.L., ad. Gr. ῥῆον.] *Bot.* The generic name for the Rhubarbs.

Rheumatic (rumæ·tik), *a.* and *sb.* late ME. [a. OF. *reumatique*, or ad. late L. *rheumaticus*, a. Gr. ῥευματικός, f. ῥευματ-, ῥεῦμα RHEUM[1].] A. *adj.* †1. Consisting of or of the nature of a watery discharge –1696. †2. Full of or dropping with watery mucus –1630. 3. Of persons, their bodies: †a. Suffering from a 'defluxion of rheum' or catarrh –1661. b. Affected with, suffering from, or subject to rheumatism or rheumatic pain 1727. 4. Of a disease, symptom: †a. Characterized by rheumy or catarrhal 'defluxion'. b. Of the nature of or characteristic of rheumatism. *R. fever*, an acute non-infectious febrile disease marked by inflammation and pain of the joints. 1563. 5. Of weather, places: Inducing or having a tendency to produce rheumatism 1565.

5. India is a very r. country 1879.

B. *sb.* 1. *pl.* Rheumatic pains, rheumatism. *colloq.* 1789. 2. A rheumatic patient (*rare*) 1884. So **Rheuma·tical** *a.*, **Rheuma·tically** *adv.* by or with rheumatism.

Rheumatism (rū·mătiz'm). 1601. [ad. late L. *rheumatismus*, a. Gr. ῥευματισμός, f. ῥευματίζειν.] †1. A 'defluxion of rheum'. 2. A disease of which inflammation and pain of the joints are prominent features. In early use commonly with *a* and *pl.*, an attack of this disease. 1688. 3. *attrib.* 1798.

2. *Acute* (*articular*) *r.*, rheumatic fever. *Muscular r.*, myalgia. 3. *r. root*, the root of (1) some species of *Jeffersonia*, (2) *Dioscorea villosa*; the plants themselves. Hence **Rheumati·smal** *a.* rheumatic. **Rheumati·smoid** *a.* resembling r. So **Rheu·matiz** (*dial.* and *vulgar*), rheumatism.

Rheu·mato-, comb. form of Gr. ῥεύματος, ῥεῦμα RHEUM[1], used in the sense of 'rheumatic', or 'rheumatic and..'.

Rheumatoid (rū·mătoid), *a.* 1859. [f. Gr. ῥευματ-, ῥεῦμα RHEUM[1] + -OID.] Having the characters of rheumatism. Also, suffering from rheumatism.

Chiefly in *r. arthritis*, a chronic disease of the joints characterized by changes in the synovial membranes, etc., and resulting in deformity and immobility. So **Rheumatoi·dal** *a.*, **-ly** *adv.*

Rheumy (rū·mi), *a.* 1591. [f. RHEUM¹ + -Y¹.] **1.** = RHEUMATIC *a.* **1, 2.** **2.** Moist, damp, wet; *esp.* of the air 1601.

1. The r. soberness of extreme age CARLYLE. 2. *Jul. C.* ii. i. 266.

Rhinal (rəi·năl), *a.* 1864. [f. Gr. ῥιν-, ῥίς + -AL 1.] Belonging to or connected with the nose.

Rhine¹ (rīn). *s.-w. dial.* 1698. [app. repr. OE. *ryne.*] A large open ditch or drain.

Rhine² (rəin). 1641. [orig. *rine hemp*, ad. G. *reinhanf*, lit. 'clean hemp'.] A fine quality of Russian hemp. Usu. *Riga r.* (*hemp*).

Rhine³ (rəin). 1843. Name of the chief river of Germany, used *attrib.* to designate wines made from grapes grown in the Rhine valley. So **Rhi·neland,** the country around the river Rhine; also *attrib.* as *Rhineland foot, perch*, etc. **Rhi·nestone,** (*a*) a variety of rock crystal; (*b*) an artificial gem of paste or strass, cut to imitate a diamond.

Rhi·negrave. 1548. [a. MDu. *Rijngrave* (mod. *-graaf*), G. *Rheingraf.*] A count whose domain borders on the river Rhine.

‖ **Rhinencephalon** (rəinense·fălǫn). 1851. [f. Gr. ῥιν-, ῥίς nose + ENCEPHALON.] *Anat.* The olfactory lobe of the brain. Hence **Rhinencepha·lic** *a.* pertaining to or consisting of the r.

Rhino¹ (rəi·nǫ). *slang.* 1688. [Origin unkn.] Money; often *ready r.*

Rhino² (rəi·nǫ). 1884. Colloq. abbrev. of RHINOCEROS.

Rhino- (rəi·nǫ, rəinǫ·), comb. form of Gr. ῥινο-, ῥίς nose. **Rhi·nolith,** a nasal calculus. **Rhinolo·gical** *a.* pertaining to rhinology. **Rhino·logist,** a student of rhinology. **Rhino·logy,** the study of the nose, as a part of pathology. **Rhi·nophor(e,** an external olfactory organ; *spec.* in certain molluscs, the hinder pair of tentacles, which appear to have this function. **Rhinopla·stic** [see PLASTIC *a.*], *a. Surg.* pertaining to the plastic surgery of the nose; connected with rhinoplasty; so **Rhi·noplasty,** the rhinoplastic operation. ‖ **Rhi·noscleroma,** a rare disease, characterized by a circumscribed, irregularly shaped, flattened, tubercular growth, having its seat about the region of the nose. **Rhi·noscope,** an instrument for examining the nasal cavity; so **Rhinosco·pic** *a.* pertaining to rhinoscopy; performed by means of the rhinoscope. **Rhino·scopy,** examination of the nasal cavity; use of the rhinoscope.

†**Rhinoce·rical,** *a.* 1688. [f. RHINOCEROS + -ICAL; in sense 2 with ref. to RHINO¹.] **1.** Of a nose: Like a rhinoceros' horn; retroussé –1710. **2.** *slang.* Having plenty of 'the rhino'; rich –1796.

Rhinoceros (rəinǫ·sĕrǫs). ME. [a. late L., a. Gr. ῥινόκερως, f. ῥινο-, ῥίς nose + κέρας horn.] A large, unwieldy quadruped of a genus now found only in Africa and Southern Asia, having a horn (or, in some species, two horns) on the nose, and a very thick skin disposed in plates and folds. **b.** *transf.* A large unwieldy person 1885.

attrib. and *Comb.*: **r. auk,** the bird *Ceratorrhina monocerata*, having a horn at the base of its beak; **r. beetle,** a kind of beetle having a horn; **r. bird,** †(*a*) the Indian bird *Buceros rhinoceros*; (*b*) the African Beef-eater or Ox-pecker, genus *Buphaga*, which rids the rhinoceros' skin of ticks; †**r. nose,** = L. *nasus rhinocerotis*, used as descriptive of a sneer. So **Rhino·cerot,** (now *rare*) rhinoceros. **Rhinocero·tic** *a.* of, belonging to, characteristic of, or resembling the r.

Rhizanth (rəi·zænþ). 1840. [ad. mod.L. *Rhizantheæ*, f. Gr. ῥίζα root + ἄνθος flower.] *Bot.* A plant of the class *Rhizantheæ*, producing (apparently) only a root and flowers. So **Rhiza·nthous** *a.* flowering (apparently) from the root.

Rhizo- (rəi·zo, rəizǫ·), comb. form of Gr. ῥίζα root, used in the formation of botanical and other terms. **Rhi·zocarp** [Gr. καρπός fruit], a plant of the group *Rhizocarpeæ* (= *Marsiliaceæ*). **Rhizoca·rpous** *a.* having a perennial root but perishing stems. ‖ **Rhizoce·phala** [Gr. κεφαλή head], an order of parasitic hermaphrodite crustaceans closely related to the cirripedes; also *sing.* ‖ **Rhizoce·phalon,** one of these. **Rhi·zodont** [Gr. ὀδοντ-, ὀδούς tooth] *a.* having teeth with branching fangs anchylosing with the jaw, as a crocodile; *sb.* a rhizodont reptile. **Rhi·zogen,** a plant parasitic on the roots of another plant. **Rhizo·phagous** *a.* feeding on roots. ‖ **Rhizo·stoma** [Gr. στόμα mouth], a genus of discomedusan hydrozoans having root-like oval arms; an animal of this genus (also **Rhi·zostome**). ‖ **Rhizota·xis, Rhi·zotaxy,** arrangement or disposition of roots.

Rhizoid (rəi·zoid). 1858. [f. Gr. ῥίζα + -OID.] **A.** *adj.* Resembling a root. **B.** *sb.* A root-hair or filament 1875.

‖ **Rhizoma** (rəizōu·mă). Pl. **rhizo·mata.** 1830. [mod.L., a. Gr. ῥίζωμα, f. ῥιζοῦσθαι to take root, f. ῥίζα root.] *Bot.* A prostrate or subterranean root-like stem emitting roots and usu. producing leaves at its apex; a rootstock. Hence **Rhizo·matous** *a.* consisting of or of the nature of a r.; having rhizomata. So **Rhi·zome,** anglicized and more usual form of r.

‖ **Rhizophora** (rəizǫ·fŏră). 1832. [mod.L. (sc. *planta*), f. Gr. ῥίζα + -φορος -bearing; see -A 2.] *Bot.* A genus typical of the family *Rhizophoraceæ*; a tree of this genus; a mangrove. So **Rhizo·phorous** *a.* root-bearing.

Rhizopod¹ (rəi·zǒpǫd). 1851. [ad. mod. L. RHIZOPODA.] *Zool.* An animalcule of the class *Rhizopoda.*

Rhizopod² (rəi·zǒpǫd). Also **-pode,** and in L. form. 1858. [ad. mod.L. *rhizopodium*, f. Gr. ῥίζα root + ποδ-, πούς foot.] *Bot.* The mycelium of fungi.

‖ **Rhizopoda** (rəizǫ·pŏdă), *sb. pl.* 1859. [mod.L., f. as prec.; see -A 4.] *Zool.* The lowest class of Protozoa comprising animalcules having pseudopodia. Hence **Rhizo·podal, Rhizopo·dic, Rhizo·podous** *adjs.* belonging to or characteristic of the R.

Rhodanate (rōu·dănĕt). 1867. [irreg. f. Gr. ῥόδον rose + -AN + -ATE².] *Chem.* = SULPHOCYANATE. **Rhodanic** (rodæ·nik) *a.* = SULPHOCYANIC *a.*

Rhodeoretin (rōudĭ,ǫ·rĭtin). 1845. [ad. G., f. Gr. ῥόδεος roseate + ῥητίνη resin.] *Chem.* = CONVOLVULIN.

Rhodes scholar (rōu·dz skǫ·lər), the holder of any of the scholarships founded at Oxford in 1902 by Cecil Rhodes and tenable by members of the British Dominions, the United States, and the German Empire.

Rhodian (rōu·diăn), *a.* and *sb.* 1550. [f. L. *Rhodius*, f. *Rhodos, -us*, = Gr. Ῥόδος Rhodes; see -IAN.] **A.** *adj.* **a.** Of or belonging to the order of the Knights of Rhodes or Hospitallers 1592. **b.** Belonging to or inhabiting the island of Rhodes in the Ægean Sea off the south-west coast of Asia Minor 1697.

b. *R. Law* is the earliest system of marine law known to history, said to be compiled.., about 900 years before the Christian era 1866.

B. *sb.* **a.** A Knight of Rhodes; a Hospitaller 1550. **b.** An inhabitant or native of Rhodes 1593.

Rhodium¹ (rōu·diǒm). 1661. [mod.L. (sc. *lignum* wood), neut. of *rhodius* rose-like (f. Gr. ῥόδον rose).] **1.** *R.-wood*, the sweet-scented wood of two species of Convolvulus, *C. floridus* and *C. scoparius*, of the Canary Islands. **2.** *Oil of r.* [= mod.L. *oleum rhodii*]: oil obtained from rose-wood; rosewood oil 1678.

Rhodium² (rōu·diǒm). 1804. [f. Gr. ῥόδον rose + -IUM.] *Chem.* A very hard white metal of the platinum group, discovered by Wollaston; so named from the rose-colour of a dilute solution of the salts containing it. Symbol Rh, formerly Ro.

attrib., as *r. salt*; **r. gold, ingot,** native gold containing r.; **r. pen,** a steel pen tipped with r. Hence **Rho·dic** *a.* containing r. in smaller proportions, relatively to oxygen, than the rhodous compounds. **Rho·dous** *a.* containing r. in larger proportions than the rhodic compounds.

Rhodizonic (rōudizǫ·nik), *a.* 1839. [f. Gr. ῥοδίζειν to be red, f. ῥόδον rose.] *Chem.* The name of two acids (so named because their salts are red) obtained from carboxide of potassium. Hence **Rhodizo·nate,** a salt of r. acid.

Rhodo- (rōu·dǒ), comb. form of Gr. ῥόδον rose, used chiefly in names of mineral and chemical substances. **Rhodochro·site** [Gr. ῥοδόχρως], carbonate of manganese occurring in rose-red crystals. **Rhodocri·nite,** a rose-like encrinite. **Rhodo·psin** [Gr. ὄψις sight], visual purple. **Rho·dosperm** [Gr. σπέρμα seed], a seaweed of the class *Rhodospermeæ* characterized by rose-coloured spores.

‖ **Rhododendron** (rōudǒde·ndrǫn). *Pl.* **Rhododendrons, -dendra.** 1601. [late L., a. Gr. ῥοδόδενδρον, f. ῥόδον rose + δένδρον tree.] †**1.** The rose-bay or oleander –1607. **2.** A genus of showy ericaceous shrubs or low trees, akin to the azaleas, much cultivated for their evergreen foliage and profusion of large beautiful flowers; a plant or flower belonging to this genus 1664.

Rhodonite (rōu·dǒnəit). 1823. [ad. G. *rhodonit*, f. Gr. ῥόδον; see -ITE¹ 2 b.] *Min.* Silicate of manganese, of a rose-pink colour when pure; manganese-spar, rose manganese.

Rhomb (rǫmb, rǫm). 1578. [ad. L. *rhombus* RHOMBUS.] **1.** *Geom.* A plane figure having four equal sides and the opposite angles equal (two being acute and two obtuse). Also, a lozenge-shaped object or formation; *Nat. Hist.*, etc., a part, disposition of parts, marking, etc. of this shape. **2.** *Cryst.* A solid figure bounded by six equal and similar rhombic planes; a rhombohedron 1800. †**3.** A circle; a magic circle (*rare*) –1697.

1. See how in warlike muster they appear, In Rhombs and wedges, and half moons, and wings MILT.

attrib. and *Comb.*: **r.-ovate** *a.*, partly rhomboid and partly ovate; **-porphyry,** a porphyry enclosing crystals of orthoclase of a rhombic outline; **-spar,** applied to certain specimens of dolomite.

Rhombic (rǫ·mbik), *a.* 1670. [f. RHOMB + -IC.] **1.** Of the form of a rhomb 1701. **b.** *Zool.* Lozenge- or diamond-shaped, often with the corners somewhat rounded 1815. **c.** *Bot.* Oval, but angular at the sides 1857. **2.** Of solid figures: Having a rhomb for its base or section plane; also, bounded by equal and similar rhombs; *Cryst.* = ORTHORHOMBIC 1670.

Rho·mbo-, comb. form of Gr. ῥόμβος RHOMBUS, used to denote (1) rhombic, as in *r.-dodecahedron*; (2) forming a rhombus (and another figure), as in *r.-quadratic*, etc.

Rhombohedron (rǫmbǒhī·drǫn). *Pl.* **-hedra.** Also **rhomboedron.** 1836. [f. Gr. ῥόμβος RHOMBUS + ἕδρα base.] *Cryst.* A solid figure bounded by six equal rhombs; a crystal of this form. So **Rhombohe·dral** (rǫmbǒhī·drăl) *a.* pertaining to or having the form of a r.; *Cryst.* denoting a system in which all the forms are derivable from the r.; also, belonging to this system. **Rhombohe·dric** *a.*

Rhomboid (rǫ·mboid), *a.* and *sb.* 1570. [(1) ad. F. *rhomboïde* or late L. *rhomboides* RHOMBOIDES; (2) ad. mod.L. RHOMBOIDEUS.] **A.** *adj.* **1.** Having the form of a rhomb; *spec.* in *Bot.*, oval, a little angular at the sides 1693. **2.** *Cryst.* = ORTHORHOMBIC. Now *rare.* 1670. **3.** *Anat.* **a.** *R. muscle* = RHOMBOIDEUS 1834. **b.** *R. ligament*: the costo-clavicular ligament. 1848. **B.** *sb.* **1.** A quadrilateral figure having only its opposite sides and angles equal 1570. **2.** *Cryst.* A solid bounded by six equal and similar rhombic faces parallel two and two 1800. **3.** *Anat.* = *R. muscle* 1835. Hence **Rho·mboidly** *adv.* (*rare*) with a r. form.

Rhomboi·dal, *a.* 1658. [ad. mod.L. *rhomboidalis.*] **1.** = prec. A. **1.** **2.** *Cryst.* = ORTHORHOMBIC 1729. Hence **Rhomboi·dally** *adv.* in the form of, or so as to form, a rhomboid.

‖ **Rhomboides** (rǫmboi·dīz). Now *rare* or *Obs.* 1570. [In sense 1, late L. *rhomboides*, a. Gr. ῥομβοειδές (sc. σχῆμα), neut. of ῥομβοειδής, f. ῥόμβος; in sense 2, *rhomboides* masc. (sc. *musculus*).] **1.** *Geom.* = RHOMBOID B. **1.** **2.** *Anat.* = RHOMBOIDEUS 1693.

‖ **Rhomboideus** (rǫmboi·dĭ,ǒs). *Pl.* **-ei** (ĭ,əi). 1835. [mod.L. (sc. *musculus*), f. *rhomboides*; see prec.] Used *attrib.* (with *muscle*) or *absol.*: Either of two muscles connecting the spinous process of the last cervical and first dorsal vertebræ with the scapula.

‖ **Rhombus** (rǫ·mbǒs). *Pl.* **rhombuses;** †**rhombi.** 1567. [L., a. Gr. ῥόμβος.] **1.** *Geom.*

= RHOMB 1. 2. A rhomb-shaped instrument, pattern, etc. 1614. 3. A genus of flat fishes comprising the turbot and the brill; a fish of this genus 1753. 4. *Conch.* A shell of the genus *Oliva* 1776.

‖ **Rhonchus** (rǫ·ŋkɒ̆s). Also **ronchus.** *Pl.* **rhonchi** (rǫ·ŋkəi). 1829. [L., a. Gr. *ῥόγχος, var. ῥέγχος snoring.] A dry sound heard by auscultation in the bronchial tubes; usu. identified with RÂLE. Hence **Rho·nchal,** also **ronchal,** *a.* pertaining to or characterized by snoring or (*spec.* in *Path.*) r.

Rhopalic (rǫᵘpæ·lik), *a.* 1682. [ad. late L. *rhopalicus*, Gr. ῥοπαλικός, f. ῥόπαλος a cudgel thicker towards one end.] *Pros.* Applied to verses in which each word contains one syllable more than the one immediately preceding it.

Rhopalocerous (rōᵘpălǫ·sĕrəs), *a.* 1882. [f. mod.L. *Rhopalocera*, n. pl. (f. Gr. ῥόπαλος club + κέρας horn) + -OUS.] *Ent.* Belonging to the sub-order *Rhopalocera*; lepidopterous insects having clubbed antennæ (i.e. butterflies).

Rhotacism (rōᵘ·tăsiz'm). Also **rotacism.** 1834. [ad. mod.L. *rhotacismus*, a. Gr. *ῥωτακισμός, f. ῥωτακίζειν.] 1. Excessive use or peculiar pronunciation of *r*; *spec.* the use of the burr or *r grasseyé*. 2. *Philol.* Conversion of another sound (esp. *s*) into *r* 1844.

Rho·tacize, *v.* [ad. Gr. ῥωτακίζειν, f. ῥῶ the letter R; see -IZE.] *intr.* To be characterized or marked by rhotacism.

Rhubarb (rū·baɹb). late ME. [a. OF. *reu-, reo-, rubarbe*, mod.F. *rhubarbe* :—L. *r(h)eubarbum*, shortened f. med.L. *r(h)eubarbarum*, altered by association with *rheum* (see RHEUM [2]) from RHABARBARUM.] 1. The medicinal rootstock, purgative and subsequently astringent, of one or more species of *Rheum* grown in China and Tibet and formerly imported into Europe through Russia and the Levant; usu. (*e.g.* in pharmaceutical and domestic use) called *Turkey* or *Russian r.*, but now known commercially as *East Indian* or *Chinese r.* b. *fig.* as a type of bitterness or sourness 1526. 2. Any plant of the genus *Rheum*. late ME. b. *English* or *French R.*: any of various species cultivated in England or France. *Common* or *Garden R.*: any of the species having heart-shaped, smooth, deep-green leaves growing on thick fleshy stalks; also the leaf-stalks themselves, which are much used in the spring as a substitute for fruit 1650. 3. *attrib.* or *adj.*: †a. *fig.* Bitter, tart 1586. b. Of the colour of medicinal rhubarb, yellowish-brown 1802. Hence **Rhu·barby** *a.* resembling r.

Rhumb (rʋm, rʋmb). 1578. [ad. F. *rumb* or Sp. *rumbo*, Pg. *rumbo, rumo*, ad. L. *rhombus* RHOMBUS.] †1. a. The line followed by a vessel sailing on one course or a wind blowing continuously in one direction. b. Any one of the set of lines drawn through a point on a map or chart and indicating the course of an object moving always in the same direction. *Obs.* exc. *Hist.* c. One of the principal points of the compass 1594. 2. The angular distance, = 11° 15', between two successive points of the compass 1625.

attrib.: **r.-line** = 1 a, b. **-sailing,** sailing on a r.-line.

‖ **Rhus** (rʋs). 1611. [late L., a. Gr. ῥοῦς.] A genus of shrubs and trees, mostly poisonous, especially abundant at the Cape of Good Hope; a plant of this genus, a sumach. b. A drug obtained from the sumach 1878.

Rhyme (rəim), *sb.* 1610. [Graphic var. of RIME *sb.*[1], which arose through etymological association with the ultimate source, L. *rhythmus.*] 1. A piece of poetry or metrical composition in which the consonance of terminal sounds (see 3) is observed; usu. *pl.*, verses, poetry. 2. Verse marked by consonance of the terminal sounds (see 3) 1652. 3. *Pros.* Agreement in the terminal sounds of two or more words or metrical lines, such that (in English prosody) the last stressed vowel and any sounds following it are the same, while the sound or sounds preceding it are different 1663.

Examples: *which, rich*; *peace, increase*; *descended, extended.* (See FEMALE, FEMININE, MALE, MASCULINE, RICH, TAILED.)

Imperfect rhymes are tolerated to a large extent in English, e.g. *phase, race*; *did, seed*; among these some rhyme only to the eye, as *loved, proved*; etc. The term is sometimes extended to include assonance and even alliteration (*initial* or *head rime*).

b. Coupled with *reason.* Chiefly in neg. phrases used to express lack of good sense or reasonableness. 1664. c. An instance of rhyme; a rhyme-word 1656.

1. He knew Himself to sing, and build the lofty r. MILT. 2. Things unattempted yet in Prose or Rhime MILT. To make old prose in modern r. more sweet KEATS. *R. royal*, that form of verse which consists of stanzas of seven five-stress lines rhyming *ababbcc.* (This name succeeded to the older designation *ballade royal.*) 3. b. This won't do. There's neither r. nor reason about it. 1888. c. *Single, double, triple* (or *treble*) *r.*, one involving one, two, or three syllables respectively.

Rhyme (rəim), *v.* 1660. [Graphic var. of RIME *v.*[1]; cf. prec.] 1. *intr.* To make rhymes or verses; to versify 1697. 2. *trans.* With obj. and compl.; esp. in *to r. to death*, (*a*) orig. with ref. to the alleged destruction of rats in Ireland by incantation; (*b*) to destroy the reputation of (a person) by writing verses upon him; also, to pester with rhymes 1660. 3. a. To put (one's thoughts) into rhyming form. b. To compose (rhymed verses). 1848. 4. *intr.* a. Of words or metrical lines: To terminate in sounds that form a rhyme. b. Of a word: To be a rhyme *to* (another word). Also const. *with.* 1672. 5. To use rhyme; to find or furnish a rhyme *to* (a word) 1690. 6. To cause (words) to rhyme; to use as rhymes 1824.

1. I am going to Ashestiel for eight days, to fish and r. SCOTT. 2. Ratts Rhimed to Death, Or, the Rump-Parliament Hang'd up in the Shambles 1660. 3. a. I r. my thoughts without an aim 1848. 4. b. The Couplet where a-Stick rhimes to Ecclesiastick STEELE. 6. *fig.* Nature never rhymes her children, nor makes two men alike EMERSON. Hence **Rhy·mer, Rhy·mester,** one who makes (poor) rhymes or verses; a mere versifier. **Rhy·mist,** a writer of rhymes or verses; one who uses (good or bad) rhymes.

Rhynchocephalian (riŋkosĭfē·liăn), *a.* (and *sb.*) 1867. [f. mod.L. *Rhynchocephala* (f. Gr. ῥύγχος snout + κεφαλή head) + -IAN.] Belonging to the order *Rhynchocephala* of reptiles (including *Hatteria*). As *sb.* A rhynchocephalian reptile.

Rhynchocœle (ri·ŋkosīl), *a.* and *sb.* 1877. [ad. mod.L. *Rhynchocœla*, f. Gr. ῥύγχος snout + κοῖλος hollow.] *Zool.* A. *adj.* Belonging to the *Rhynchocœla*, a group of turbellarians comprising the Nemerteans. B. *sb.* A rhynchocœle turbellarian. Hence **Rhynchocœ·lous** *a.*

Rhyncholite (ri·ŋkǒləit). 1836. [f. Gr. ῥύγχος beak + λίθος stone, -LITE.] *Geol.* A fossilized beak of a tetrabranchiate cephalopod.

Rhynchophore (ri·ŋkofoᵊɹ). 1826. [ad. mod.L. *Rhynchophora*, neut. pl. of *rhynchophorus*, f. Gr. ῥύγχος snout + -φορος -bearing; see -A. 4.] *Ent.* A beetle of the group *Rhynchophora*, having the head prolonged into a beak or snout; a weevil. So **Rhyncho·phorous** (riŋkǫ·fŏrəs) *a.* belonging to the *Rhynchophore.*

Rhynchotous (riŋkōᵘ·təs), *a.* 1890. [f. mod.L. *Rhynchota* (f. Gr. ῥύγχος snout) + -OUS.] *Ent.* Belonging to the order *Rhynchota* (= *Hemiptera*) of insects.

Rhyolite (rəi·ǒləit). 1872. [ad. G. *rhyolit*, irreg. f. Gr. ῥύαξ stream (of lava) + λίθος stone; see -LITE.] *Geol.* A variety of trachyte found in Hungary, containing quartz; later, a general name for volcanic rocks exhibiting a fluidal texture. Hence **Rhyoli·tic** *a.*

Rhyparographer (ripărǫ·grăfəɹ). 1656. [f. late L. *rhyparographos* = Gr. ῥυπαρογράφος, f. ῥυπαρός filthy; see -GRAPHER.] A painter of mean or sordid subjects. So **Rhyparo·graphist. Rhyparogra·phic** *a.* characteristic of a r. **Rhyparo·graphy,** the painting of mean and sordid subjects; *spec.* still-life or genre painting.

Rhysimeter (rəisi·mĭtəɹ). 1871. [f. Gr. ῥύσις flowing, stream + -METER.] An instrument for measuring the velocity of fluids or the speed of ships.

Rhythm (ri·ð'm, ri·þ'm). 1557. [In branch I, a graphic var. of RIME *sb.*[1] (cf. RHYME *sb.*), assim. to L. *rhythmus* or F. *rhythme.* The rhyme-words *time, crime*, etc. attest the pron. (rəim). In branch II, directly ad. L. *rhythmus.*] I. †1. Rhyming or rhymed verse; a form or variety of this –1695. †2. A piece of rhyming verse –1677. †3. The fact of lines ending in the same sound; an instance of this –1680.

2. When ye these rythmes doo read, and vew the rest SPENSER. And..build a lofty Rhythm, that shall outlast the insolence of time 1677.

II. 1. *Pros.* The measured recurrence of arsis and thesis determined by vowel-quantity or stress, or both combined; kind of metrical movement, as determined by the relation of long and short, or stressed and unstressed, syllables in a foot or line 1560. b. Rhythmical or metrical form 1656. c. The measured flow of words or phrases 1832. 2. *Mus.* a. That feature of musical composition which depends on the systematic grouping of notes according to their duration. b. Kind of structure as determined by the arrangement of such groups. 1776. 3. *Art.* Due correlation and interdependence of parts, producing a harmonious whole 1776. 4. *gen.* Movement marked by the regulated succession of strong and weak elements, or of opposite or different conditions 1855. b. *Phys.* and *Path.* of functional movements as the heart, respiration, etc. 1722.

1. All Metre is therefore R., but not all R. Metre 1737. b. One began and sang in r., the rest..hearing with silence 1657. c. In every sentence, however uttered, there is a r. 1863. 3. The r. and symmetry of a stately Italian palace 1867. 4. So do flux and reflux—the r. of change—alternate and persist in everything under the sky T. HARDY. c. The 'r.' of cell-division 1890. Hence **Rhy·thmist,** one versed in r. **Rhy·thmless** *a.*

Rhythmed (ri·ðmd, ri·þmd), *a.* 1695. [f. prec.] †1. Rhymed. 2. Marked by rhythm; rhythmical 1863.

Rhythmic (ri·ðmik, ri·þmik), *a.* and *sb.* 1603. [ad. F. *rhythmique* or L. *rhythmicus*, a. Gr. ῥυθμικός, f. ῥυθμός RHYTHM.] A. *adj.* 1. = next 3, 4.

1. Much of it, too,..is r.; a kind of wild chanting song CARLYLE. The r. rattling of the train 1873.

B. *sb.* The science or theory of rhythm 1603. Also **Rhy·thmics** 1864.

Rhythmical (ri·ðmikăl, ri·þmikăl), *a.* 1567. [f. as prec.; see -ICAL.] †1. Composing verse; rhyming. †2. Written in rhyming verse –1706. 3. a. Of language, verse: Marked by or composed in rhythm; often, having a good, smooth, or flowing rhythm 1589. b. *gen.* Of motion, etc. 1619. c. *Phys.* and *Path.* 1840. d. *Art.* 1880. 4. Relating to, concerning, or involving rhythm 1619.

3. The rhapsode recited..a species of musical and r. declamation 1846. b. The r. cadence of the oars 1889. c. R. actions, such as that of the respiration 1883. 4. Less through rythmical skill than a musical ear POE. Hence **Rhy·thmically** *adv.*

Rhythmo·meter. 1812. [f. Gr. ῥυθμός RHYTHMUS; see -METER.] A kind of metronome.

‖ **Rhythmus** (ri·ðmɒ̆s, ri·þmɒ̆s). *Pl.* **-mi** (-məi). 1531. [L., a. Gr. ῥυθμός, related to ῥεῖν to flow.] 1. *Pros.* = RHYTHM *sb.* II. 1, 1 b. 2. *Mus.* = RHYTHM *sb.* II. 2. 1734.

‖ **Rhytina** (ritəi·nă). Also **Rytina.** 1835. [mod.L., f. Gr. ῥυτίς wrinkle; see -INA [1].] A genus of *Sirenia*, represented by one species, *R. stelleri*, now extinct; an animal of this genus; the Arctic Sea-cow.

Rial (rəi·ăl), *sb.* Now *Hist.* late ME. [f. RIAL *a.*, after F. and (later) Sp. models.] †1. A royal person –1475. †2. The second branch of a stag's horn, lying immediately above the brow-antler –1486. 3. A gold coin formerly current in England, orig. worth ten shillings, first issued by Edward IV in 1465. Now *Hist.* 1473. †4. A Spanish coin; = REAL *sb.*[1] 1. –1809. †b. *R. of plate* (Sp. *real de plata*), an eighth of a dollar or $6\frac{1}{2}d.$ –1748. †c. *R. of eight*, = REAL *sb.*[1] 2. –1738.

†**Ri·al,** *a.* ME. [a. OF., var. of *real, roial*; see REAL *a.*[1], ROYAL *a.*] Royal, regal –1584.

‖ **Ria·lto.** 1879. [Name of the quarter in Venice in which the Exchange is situated.] An exchange or mart.

Riant (rəi·ănt, F. riaṅ), *a.* Also occas. **riante** (riaṅt). 1567. [a. F. *riant* masc., *riante* fem., pres. pple. of *rire* :—L. *ridere* to laugh.] Smiling, mirthful, cheerful, gay.

A..r. landskip 1792. He was jovial, r., jocose rather than serious 1867. Hence **Ri·antly** *adv.*

‖ **Riata** (riˌā·tă). 1869. [Sp. *reata*, f. *reatar*

to tie again, f. *re-* RE- + *atar* :—L. *aptare.*] = LARIAT.

Rib, *sb.* [Com. Teut.: OE. *rib, ribb* neut.; OS. *ribba* fem.] I. 1. One of the curved bones articulated in pairs to the spine in men and animals and enclosing or tending to enclose the thoracic or body cavity, whose chief organs they protect. b. *Zool.* One of the meridional plates characteristic of the *Ctenophora*; a ctenophore 1890. 2. One of these bones taken from the carcase of an ox, pig, etc., with the meat adhering to it, as used for food. late ME. 3. With allusion to the creation of Eve (*Gen.* ii. 21): A (person's) wife; a woman 1589. †b. So *r. of man(kind), lost r.* –1647.

1. *Asternal, floating ribs*: see those adjs. *False r.* = asternal rib. *Sternal* or *true ribs*, those attached to the breast-bone or sternum. *To smite* (a person) *under the fifth r.*, to strike to the heart. 2. Dined well on some good ribbs of beef roasted and mince pies PEPYS. 3. b. Surely if feasting ever be in season it is at the recovery of the lost r. [i. e. marriage] 1647.

II. 1. The central or principal nerve or vein of a leaf, extending from the petiole to the apex = MIDRIB 2; also, one of the smaller or secondary nerves. Now *Bot.* late ME. b. The shaft or quill of a feather 1545. c. *Ent.* A nervure in an insect's wing 1843. d. *Bot.* A more dense or firm part extending along or through an organ or structure 1847. 2. A hard or rocky portion of a mountain, etc., esp. when in the form of a projecting ridge 1586. b. A vein of ore, or the solid part of one; a stratum or dyke of stone or rock. Now esp. *Geol.* 1667. c. *Mining.* A wall of coal left standing to support the roof of the workings 1839. 3. a. A narrow strip of land, as that between furrows; also *dial.*, a furrow. b. A narrow ridge separating a roadway from the ditch. 1670. 4. In techn. use, an artificial ridge raised upon some object: a. *Mech.* A raised band or flange, esp. one made upon a metal plate in order to stiffen it 1793. b. *Gunmaking.* A bar or ridge of metal made on each barrel of a double-barrelled gun, and serving to connect the two 1815. c. A raised ridge in a knitted stocking, cloth, or the like 1829. d. *Bookbinding.* One of the raised bands upon the back of a book, serving as a covering for the cords and as an ornament 1875. 5. *Conch.* A salient ridge upon a shell 1711.

2. b. Soon had his crew Op'nd into the Hill a spacious wound And dig'd out ribs of Gold MILT.

III. 1. *Naut.* One of the curved frame-timbers of a ship, extending from the keel to the top of the hull, upon which the planking of the side is nailed; also, in later use, a piece of strong ironwork serving the same purpose 1553. 2. *Building.* a. A piece of timber forming part of the framework or roof of a house; in mod. *dial.*, a purlin. late ME. b. An arch supporting a vault; one or other of the transverse or oblique arches by which a compound vault is sustained; the edge or groin of two intersecting arches in a vault. Also, in later use, a projecting band or moulding on a groin or ceiling (whether vaulted or flat), or on some other architectural feature. 1726. c. One of a set of arched wooden trusses used for the centring of a bridge; one of a set of parallel timbers or iron beams (whether arched or flat) serving to carry a bridge 1735. d. One of the curved pieces of stone-, timber-, or ironwork which form the framework of a dome 1766. 3. A bar or rod (of wood or iron) serving to strengthen or support a structure 1547. b. A bar of a grate or the like. Now *Sc.* and *n. dial.* 1651. c. One of the two horizontal bars of a printing-press upon which or in the grooves of which the carriage supporting the bed slides on its way towards the platen 1683. 4. a. One of the curved pieces of wood forming the body of a lute or the sides of a violin 1676. b. One of the strips of whalebone or stout metal wires composing the framework of an umbrella or sunshade 1716. c. One of the hoops which serve to form the folds in organ-bellows 1881.

1. Vailing her high top lower then her ribs SHAKS. *Ribs and Trucks*, used figuratively for fragments 1867. Hence **Ri·bless** *a.* **Ri·blet**, a small r.

Rib, *v.* 1547. [f. RIB *sb.*] 1. To furnish or strengthen with ribs; to enclose as with ribs. †b. To form the ribs of (a ship). COWPER. 2. To mark with rib-like ridges; to form or shape into ridges 1548. b. *Agric.* To plough (land), leaving a space between the furrows; to rafter or half-plough 1735.

1. Your Isle, which stands As Neptunes Parke, ribb'd, and pal'd in With Oakes vnskaleable SHAKS. Hence **Ri·bbing**, the action of the vb.; ribs collectively.

Ribald (ri·băld), *sb.* and *a.* ME. [a. OF. *ribau(l)t, -au(l)d*, mod.F. *ribaud*; origin unkn.] A. *sb.* †1. One of an irregular class of retainers who performed the lowest offices in royal or baronial households, and were employed in warfare as irregular troops; hence, a menial or dependent of low birth –1647. †2. A low, base, worthless, or good-for-nothing fellow; a varlet, knave, rascal, vagabond –1641. †3. A wicked, dissolute, or licentious person –1590. 4. One who uses offensive, scurrilous, or impious language; one who jests or jeers in an irreverent or blasphemous manner. late ME.

4. What eylythe the, rebawde, on me to raue? 1529.

B. *adj.* Offensively abusive, scurrilous, wantonly irreverent or impious 1500.

The ribbald invectives which occupy the place of argument BURKE. The r. crowd SHELLEY. A r. cuckoo 1890. Hence †**Ri·baldish** *a.* (*rare*) ribald-like. **Ri·baldrous** *a.* of ribald character; ribald (now *Obs.* or *arch.*).

Ribaldry (ri·băldri). ME. [a. OF. *re-, ribau(l)derie.* See prec. and -RY.] †1. Debauchery; lasciviousness, vice –1645. 2. Obscenity or coarseness of language; †a coarse tale; in later use, scurrilous or irreverent jesting ME.

Riband (ri·bănd), *sb.* Now *arch.* late ME. Also **ribband.** [a. OF. *riban, ruban*; perh. of Teut. origin.] 1. = RIBBON *sb.* 1. b. = RIBBON *sb.* 2. 1766. 2. *Her.* = RIBBON *sb.* 3. 1562. 3. *pl.* Reins 1840. 4. a. A narrow strip *of* something; an object resembling a ribbon in form 1801. b. *pl.* Torn strips; shreds, tatters 1818.

Comb.: **r. jasper,** a variety of jasper having the colours in broad stripes. So **Ri·band** *v. trans.* (now *arch.*) to adorn with ribands. **Ri·banding,** ribbons; ribbon-work.

Ribband (ri·bănd). 1711. [Taken as f. RIB *sb.* + BAND, but perh. transf. use of *ribband*, var. of RIBAND *sb.*] 1. *Shipbuilding*, one of a number of long narrow flexible pieces of timber which are nailed or bolted externally to the ribs of a ship from stem to stern, to keep them temporarily in position. 2. In launching vessels, a square timber fastened on the outer side of the bilge-ways, to prevent the cradle from slipping outwards 1779. 3. *Mil.* A wood scantling used in the construction of a gun or mortar platform 1859. 4. A light spar used in the construction of a pontoon-bridge 1899.

Ribbed (ribd), *ppl. a.* 1523. [f. RIB *sb.* or *v.*] 1. Having ribs of a specified kind or number, or arranged in a certain way; as *five-r., close-r.*, etc. 2. Having ribs or ridges; marked with ribs 1742. 3. Furnished with ribs 1814.

2. A waistcoat of r. black satin DICKENS. *R. grass* = RIB-GRASS. **R.-nose baboon,** the mandrill. 3. Some horses are what is called r. home; there is but little space between the last rib and the hip-bone 1831.

Ribble-rabble (ri·b'l ræ·b'l), *adv.* and *sb.* 1460. [Redupl. of RABBLE *sb.*[1]] A. *adv.* In great confusion (*rare*). B. *sb.* 1. Confused meaningless language; rigmarole, gibble-gabble. *arch.* 1601. 2. = RABBLE *sb.*[1] 2. 1635.

Ribbon (ri·bən), *sb.* 1527. [Later f. *riban* RIBAND.] 1. A narrow woven band of some fine material, as silk or satin, used to ornament clothing or headgear, or for other purposes. a. Without article, as a material. b. With *a* and *pl.*: A piece or length of this. Also, a particular kind or make of it. 1611. 2. The badge of an order of knighthood; also *transf.*, high distinction in anything 1651. 3. *Her.* A sub-ordinary, in width one eighth of the bend, and one half of the cost, usu. borne couped 1704. 4. *pl.* Reins 1813. 5. A long narrow strip of anything, e.g. of metal, sky, etc. 1763. 6. a. *Anat.* and *Zool.* A tissue or structure having the form of a ribbon. *Lingual r.*, = ODONTOPHORE 1803. b. *Bot.* A leaf, branch, or other structure, resembling a ribbon 1855. 7. *pl.* Torn strips of anything; tatters, shreds 1820. 8. A ribband; a wale or strip of wood 1711.

1. a. From her lifted hand Dangled a length of r. TENNYSON. 2. There were one or two stars and ribbons 1879. 7. The sails hung in ribbons from the yards 1883.

attrib. and *Comb.* 1. In sense 1, as *r.-weaver, factory*, etc.; **R. Society,** a Roman Catholic secret society formed in the north and north-west of Ireland early in the 19th c. to counteract the Protestant influence, and associated with agrarian disorders; so *R. association, pass-word, system, work.* 2. In sense 'resembling a r. or ribbons, 'forming a long narrow strip or strips', as *r. border, lightning*, etc.; **r. building,** the erection of houses, etc. along main roads. b. Marked with bands or stripes, as *r. agate, jasper, onyx.* c. In names of plants, as **r. fern,** etc. d. In names of animals, fishes, etc., as **r. gurnard** (*Lepidosomatida*), **worm.** Hence **Ri·bboner,** a member of the R. Society. **Ri·bbonism,** the principles or policy of the R. Society.

Ribbon (ri·bən), *v.* 1716. [f. the sb.] 1. *trans.* To adorn with ribbon or ribbons; to mark or stripe in a way resembling ribbons. Usu. in *pa. pple.* b. To separate into thin narrow strips 1856. 2. *intr.* Of melted soap, wax, etc.: To form into 'ribbons' 1895.

Ri·bbon-fish. 1793. *Zool.* A fish having a very long, slender, flattened body, as those of the genera *Cepola* and *Regalecus.*

Ri·bbon-grass. 1786. A grass having long slender leaves, esp. a variegated variety of *Phalaris.*

Ribbony (ri·bəni), *a.* 1839. [f. RIBBON *sb.* + -Y [1].] Abounding in, decked with, ribbons; resembling a ribbon or ribbons.

R. gum, a name in N. S. Wales for *Eucalyptus viminalis.*

‖ **Ribes** (rəi·bīz). 1562. [a. med.L., ad. Arab. *rībās* sorrel.] †1. As *pl.* (Red, Black, or White) Currants –1657. 2. *Bot.* A genus of plants comprising the currants and gooseberry 1731.

Rib-grass (ri·bgrɑs). 1538. [f. RIB *sb.* + GRASS.] 1. = RIBWORT. 2. The Native Plantain (*Plantago varia*) of Australia and Tasmania 1898.

†**Ribibe.** late ME. [ad. OF. *rebebe*, ad. Arab. *rebāb.*] 1. = REBECK –1450. 2. An opprobrious or abusive term for an old woman –1616.

Ri·b-roast, *v.* Now *arch.* 1570. [f. RIB *sb.* + ROAST *v.*] *trans.* To belabour with a cudgel; to beat severely; to thrash.

Ribston (ri·bstən). Also **Ribstone.** 1769. [f. *Ribston* Park, between Knaresborough and Weatherby in Yorks.] 1. *R. pippin*, a choice variety of dessert apple. 2. *ellipt.* The (*or* a) R. pippin 1844.

Ribwort (ri·bwɒ̄ɹt). late ME. [f. RIB *sb.* + WORT.] The Narrow-leaved Plantain (*Plantago lanceolata*); ribgrass; so *R. Plantain.* b. A plant belonging to the *Plantaginaceæ* 1846.

Ricardian (rĭkā·ɹdiăn), *a.* and *sb.* 1863. [f. the name *Ricardo.*] A. *adj.* Of, pertaining to, or accepting the doctrines of the political economist David Ricardo (1772–1823). B. *sb.* A follower of Ricardo 1886.

Rice (rəis). [ME. *rys, ris*, a. OF. *ris* (F. *riz*), ad. It. *riso*, repr. L. **orizum*, var. of *oriza, oryza*, a. Gr. ὄρυζα, prob. of Oriental origin.] 1. The seeds of the plant *Oryza sativa*, forming one of the important food-grains of the world. 2. The rice-plant, *Oryza sativa* 1562. 3. With *pl.* A kind or variety of rice 1681. 4. *Wild r.*, = Canada or Indian Rice 1814.

1. Wot you forsooth why R. is so generally eaten and so valuable? 1638.

attrib. and *Comb.* as *r.-arrack, -bread, -field*, etc.; **r.-bunting,** the r.-bird or bobolink; **-grains,** *Astr.*, granular markings observed on the surface of the sun; **-rat,** an American rodent feeding upon r.; **-troopial,** = *r.-bunting*; **-weevil,** a small beetle, *Calandra Oryzæ*, which is very injurious to r.

Ri·ce-bird. 1704. †1. An E. Indian bird which lives among the rice. 2. The Paddy bird or Java sparrow 1743. 3. The reed-bird or bobolink 1747.

Ri·ce-paper. 1822. A Chinese paper consisting of thin slices of the pith of *Aralia papyrifera*, a tree of Formosa; so *r. plant* or *tree*, the shrub *Aralia* or *Fatsia papyrifera.*

Ri·ce-water. 1797. 1. A liquid for drinking or other purposes, prepared from rice boiled in water. 2. Used *attrib.* to describe the evacuations of cholera-patients 1866.

Rich (ritʃ), *a., adv.*, and *sb.* [Com. Teut.: OE. *rīce*, = Goth. *reiks*, prob. repr. an early Teut. adoption of Celtic **rix* = L. *rex* king.]

A. *adj.* †1. Of persons: Powerful, mighty, exalted, noble, great –1535. 2. Having large possessions or abundant means; wealthy, opulent OE. b. Of places, countries, etc.: Abounding in wealth or natural resources ME. 3. With preps: Wealthy *in*, amply provided *with*, some form of property or valuable possessions ME. 4. Valuable; of great worth ME. 5. Of dress, etc.: Splendid, costly; of expensive or superior material or make ME. b. Of buildings, furniture, etc.: Made of, or adorned with, valuable materials; also, elaborately ornamented or wrought ME. †c. *gen.* Fine, splendid, magnificent –1578. d. Of feasts: Sumptuous, luxurious ME. 6. Of choice or superior quality; esp. of articles of food or drink; also, composed of choice ingredients; containing plenty of fat, butter, eggs, sugar, fruit, etc. ME. b. Of colour: Strong, deep, warm ME. c. Of musical sounds: Full and mellow in tone 1592. d. Of odours: Full of fragrance 1599. 7. Plentiful, abundant 1450. b. Of a full, ample, or unstinted nature; highly developed or cultivated 1561. c. Of rhyme (after F. *rime riche*): Characterized by exact identity between the syllables involved 1656. d. Highly entertaining or amusing; also, preposterous, outrageous 1760. 8. Of mines or ores: Yielding a large quantity or proportion of the precious metals 1555. b. Of soil, lands, etc.: Abounding in the qualities necessary to produce good vegetation or crops 1577.

2. R. sons forget they ever had poor fathers MASSINGER. He was..passing r. with forty pounds a year GOLDSM. b. New Spain is by far the richest mineral country in the world 1802. 3. How r. with regal spoils! DRYDEN. Mines..r. in gold and silver 1802. *fig.* Her ample page, R. with the spoils of time GRAY. 4. With ribanes of red golde and of riche stones LANGL. 5. Silks..so r., they'd stand alone CRABBE. b. An ancient..knocker..of r. Venetian sculpture 1864. d. A r. repast COWPER. 6. As leanest land supplies the richest wine COWPER. b. Red as the Roses, richest of coloure late ME. c. Instruments of a soft and r. tone 1836. d. The moist r. smell of the rotting leaves TENNYSON. 7. A r. theme for scandal 1867. d. O Garrick! what a r. scene of this would thy..powers make! STERNE. 8. b. The r. grass-fen 1865.

B. *adv.* with pa. and pres. pples., as *rich-laden* ME. **C.** *absol.* or as *sb.* 1. Those who are rich; rich persons as a class OE. 2. One who is rich; a rich person ME.

1. The pore schul be made domysmen Apon the ryche at domysday. late ME. Ring out the feud of r. and poor TENNYSON. 2. The r. hath many friends *Prov.* xiv. 20. Hence **Ri·chen** *v. trans.* to make richer or more intense; *intr.* to become richer. **Ri·ch·ly** *adv.* in a r., sumptuous, or splendid manner; so as to be r.; amply, thoroughly; intensely; **-ness.**

Riches (ri·tʃéz). ME. [var. of next, assuming the form of a pl., and finally construed as such.] 1. Abundance of means or of valuable possessions; wealth. Also, the possession of wealth, the condition of being rich. †a. Construed as a sing. Also, a particular form of wealth. –1667. b. Construed as a pl. late ME.

1. Here is not forbidden to haue r. TINDALE. *transf.* People are the R. of a Country SWIFT. 2. *transf.* For that ritches where is my deseruing? SHAKS. 3. As Salomon saith; R. are as a strong hold BACON.

†Richesse. ME. [a. OF. *richeise, -esse*, f. *riche* RICH; see -ESS [2].] Wealth; opulence –1687. b. In pl. form –1677.

2. All the beauties and richesses of the Vniuers 1601.

Rich-weed. *U.S.* 1788. [f. RICH *a.*] **a.** A species of Baneberry (*Actæa racemosa*). **b.** Horse-balm or Stone-root (*Collinsonia canadensis*). **c.** Clearweed (*Pilea pumila*).

‖ **Ricinus** (ri·sinŏs). 1694. [L.] *Bot.* A genus of plants, of which the castor-oil plant (*Ricinus communis*) is the type.

Rick (rik), *sb.*[1] [OE. *hréac*. Cf. dial. *ship* for *sheep* (OE. *scéap*).] A stack of hay, corn, peas, etc., esp. one regularly built and thatched; a mow. b. *transf.* A heap or pile 1606.

Rick (rik), *sb.*[2] 1854. [Related to RICK *v.*[2]] A sprain or overstrain, *esp.* in the back.

Rick (rik), *v.*[1] 1623. [f. RICK *sb.*[1]] *trans.* To form (hay, corn, etc.) into a rick; to stack.

Rick (rik), *v.*[2] 1798. [prob. a variant spelling of WRICK *v.*] 1. *trans.* To sprain, twist, or wrench (any limb or joint). 2. *Coursing.* To cause (a hare) to 'wrench' or turn less than quite about. Also *intr.* of a hare: To 'wrench'. 1839.

Ricker (ri·kəɹ). 1820. [perh. ad. G. *rick* (pl. *ricke(n)* pole.] *Naut.* A spar or pole made out of the stem of a young tree.

Ri·cket, sing. f. RICKETS, used attrib. or in comb.

Rickets (ri·kėts). 1645. [Origin doubtful; taken by Whistler (1645) as a corruption of Gr. ῥαχίτης or ῥαχῖτις, the latter of which he adopted as the scientific name.] 1. A disease particularly incident to children, characterized by softening of the bones, esp. of the spine, and consequent distortion, bow-legs, and emaciation. Technically known as RACHITIS. †2. A form of blight in corn –1759.

Rickety (ri·kėti), *a.* Also **ricketty.** 1685. [f. RICKET + -Y.[1]] 1. Affected with, suffering from, rickets; subject to rickets. †b. *transf.* Of grain: Weakly, unhealthy –1759. 2. Weakly, feeble, shaky, tottering; lacking in strength or firmness 1738. 3. Of the nature of rickets; pertaining to rickets 1801.

1. Bones..not unlike those of ricketty children 1720. *fig.* This benevolence, the ricketty offspring of weakness BURKE. 2. Crude and r. Notions 1738. An old-fashioned and r. stair 1842. A r. canter 1898. 3. Ricketty curvature of legs 1879. Hence **Ri·cketily** *adv.*

Rickshaw, ricksha (ri·kʃǭ, ri·kʃă). 1887. Abbrev. of JINRICKSHA.

Ri·ck-yard. 1712. [f. RICK *sb.*[1]] A farm-yard or enclosure containing ricks; a stack-yard.

Ricochet (ri·kǒʃē, ri·kǒʃet), *sb.* 1769. [a. F., the skipping of a shot, etc.] *Mil.* **a.** A method of firing by which the projectile is made to glance or skip along a surface with a rebound or series of rebounds; also, the skipping of a cannon-ball or bullet, intentional or accidental. *By r.* (F. *à ricochet*), at a rebound. **b.** The subjection *of* a place to this kind of firing 1828.

a. The shot..buried itself in the soft sand. We had no r. to fear. STEVENSON.

Ricochet (ri·kǒʃē, ri·kǒʃet), *v.* 1828. [f. the sb. The suppression of the *t* in pronunciation is also extended to the forms *ricochetted, ricochetting* (cf. *crochetted*, etc.). Stressing on the third syllable is common.] 1. *intr.* Of a projectile or the like: To glance or skip with a rebound or series of rebounds. 2. *trans.* To subject to ricochet firing 1841.

‖**Rictus** (ri·ktŏs). 1760. [L., open mouth or jaws, f. ppl. stem of *ringi* to open the mouth wide.] 1. *Bot.* The orifice or throat of a bilabiate corolla. 2. Of persons: The expanse or gape of the mouth. Similarly of birds and fishes. 1827. Hence **Ri·ctal** *a.* of or pertaining to the r.

Rid (rid), *v.* *Pa. t.* **rid, ridded.** *Pa. pple.* **rid, ridded;** *Sc.* **ridden.** ME. [a. ON. *ryðja*.] **I.** 1. *trans.* To clear (a way or space), *esp.* to clear (land) of trees, undergrowth, etc.; to stub. b. To free from rubbish or encumbrances; to clean or clear out. Also formerly with *up*. late ME. c. To clear (a table); to clear *up* (a room, etc.). Now *dial.* 1599. 2. To deliver, set free, rescue, save (*from, out of, of*, etc.). Now *rare*. ME. 3. To make (a person or place) free *of* (or *from*) something; to disencumber *of* 1569.

1. If the Spring be forward, cleanse and r. the Coppices 1669. c. When you r. up the Parlour Hearth in a Morning SWIFT. 2. She..bid me deuise some meanes To r. her from this second Marriage SHAKS. 3. I am ridding you of a troublesome companion SWIFT. Phr. *To be rid of*, to be freed from (a troublesome or useless thing or person). So *to get rid of*.

II. 1. To remove, to take or clear away. Also const. *from, out of*, etc. 1475. †b. To remove by violence; to kill, destroy –1639. 2. To dispatch, accomplish, get through, clear *off* or *away* (work of any kind). Now *dial.* 1530. †3. *To r. ground* (or *space*), to cover ground, to move ahead, to make progress –1785.

1. I shal sone ryd his soule out of his body 1533. b. 2 *Hen. VI*, III. i. 233. 3. We..Will thither straight, for willingnesse rids way SHAKS. Ridding away all the business that you can WESLEY. Hence **Ri·dder,** one who rids.

Riddance (ri·dăns). 1535. [f. RID *v.* + -ANCE.] 1. Removal, clearance; an instance of this; a clearing out, scouring. †2. Progress or dispatch in work –1763. †b. Progress in moving –1647. 3. Deliverance *from* something 1591. 4. A deliverance which consists in getting rid of something. Freq. with *good, happy*, etc. Also *transf.*, something of which one gets rid. 1596.

1. Phr. *To make* (*clean*, etc.) *r*. 2. The nether milstone is heauie, slow, and of small r. 1608. 3. R. from the wicked 1886. 4. The loss of so many captives was treated as a happy r. 1844. A good r. of bad rubbish 1863.

Riddle (ri·d'l), *sb.*[1] [OE. *rǽdels, rǽdelse* counsel, opinion, conjecture, riddle; f. *rǽdan* to READ, REDE; see -ELS.] 1. A question or statement intentionally worded in a dark or puzzling manner, and propounded in order that it may be guessed or answered, esp. as a form of pastime; an enigma; a dark saying. 2. *transf.* Something which puzzles or perplexes; a difficult or insoluble problem; a mystery. late ME. 3. *concr.* A person or being whose nature or conduct is enigmatical 1663.

1. As that Theban Monster that propos'd Her r., and him, who solv'd it not, devour'd MILT. 2. The r. of life is unsolved 1859. Judaism is said to have been a dark r. which tormented Hegel all his life 1879. 3. I am still a r. they know not what to make of SWIFT.

Riddle (ri·d'l), *sb.*[2] [Late OE. *hriddel*, earlier *hrider, hridder*, f. *hrid-* to shake.] 1. A coarse-meshed sieve, used for separating chaff from corn, sand from gravel, ashes from cinders, etc. 2. A board or metal plate set with pins, used in straightening wire 1843.

1. Phr. *A r. of claret*, thirteen bottles; so named because the wine was brought in on a r. *To make a r. of*, to pierce with holes; I was to be made a r. of, if I attempted to escape 1842.

Riddle (ri·d'l), *v.*[1] 1571. [f. RIDDLE *sb.*[1]] 1. *intr.* To speak in riddles, or enigmatically; to propound riddles. 2. *trans.* To interpret or solve (a riddle or question) 1588. †3. To be a riddle to (a person); to puzzle. SCOTT.

1. Madam, you r. strangely 1660. 2. Were I as wise a warlock as Michael Scott, I could scarce r. the dream you read me SCOTT. Phr. *R. me a* (or *my*) *riddle*; *r. me this, that, why*, etc.

Riddle (ri·d'l), *v.*[2] ME. [f. RIDDLE *sb.*[2]] 1. *trans.* To pass (corn, gravel, etc.) through a riddle; to separate with a riddle; to sift. 2. To pierce with holes like those of a riddle; to perforate (*with* bullets or the like); to shatter by missiles 1849. b. *esp.* in pa. pple. *riddled* (*with* holes, etc.) 1817.

1. As ridiculous as..a Duchess ridling cinders! 1784. 2. Worms will r. the wood-work of a ship 1886. b. *fig.* They are as poor as Job and riddled with debts 1897. Hence **Ri·ddler. Ri·ddlingly** *adv.*

Ri ddlemeree·, ri·ddle-me-ree·. 1710. 1. A fanciful variant of the phrases *riddle me a riddle, riddle my riddle*, etc. 2. Rigmarole, nonsense 1736.

Ride (rəid), *sb.* 1779. [f. RIDE *v.*] **I. a.** An excursion or journey in a conveyance, now esp. a public one; †a drive. **b.** A turn or spell of riding 1815. **c.** One of the divisions into which a country is divided for purposes of excise. *R.-officer*, an exciseman 1858. **2. a.** A road or way for riding on horseback, esp. through a wood 1805. **b.** *spec.* The riding-course in Hyde Park, London 1814. **3.** A batch of mounted recruits 1833. **4.** A saddle-horse 1787.

1. b. A few hours' bicycle r. in the country 1898. 2. b. We..reach'd the r. Where gaily flows the human tide M. ARNOLD.

Ride (rəid), *v.* *Pa.t.* **rode** (rōud), *arch.* **rid.** *Pa. pple.* **ridden,** *arch.* **rid.** [Com. Teut.: OE. *rídan* (*rád, riden*).] **I.** *intr.* 1. To sit upon, and be carried by, a horse or other animal; to move about or journey upon horseback (or on a cycle). b. To serve in a cavalry regiment 1711. c. Of persons: To weigh when mounted 1836. d. To sit on and manage a horse properly 1881. 2. *spec.* To go on horseback upon a warlike expedition; to take part in a raid or foray. *arch.* ME. 3. To mount the female; to copulate. (Now low and indecent.) ME. 4. To be conveyed, travel, or journey *in* a wheeled or other vehicle ME. b. To be carried or drawn about (*on* or †*in* a cart, hurdle, etc.) as a punishment 1556. 5. To sit or be carried *on* or *upon* something after the manner of one on horseback; †to hang *on* the gallows, *in* a rope, etc. OE. 6. a. Of horses: To admit of being ridden; to carry a rider 1470. b. Of land: To be of a specified character for riding upon 1864.

1. We..rode over the place of burial of the Turks

1617. *fig.* A young guardsman who had just rode into her heart 1803. Phrases. *To r. whip and spur*: see WHIP *sb.* *To r. for a fall*, to ride recklessly so as to be liable to a fall; usu. *fig.* *To r. off* (e.g. on a side issue). *To r. to hounds*, to hunt. **c.** He rode little under fourteen stone 1857. **d.** He can stick in his saddle somehow,..but he can't r. 1881. **2.** As if a tenant could have helped riding with the Laird SCOTT. **4.** I rid with my sword drawn in the coach PEPYS. **b.** Ah! many a wretch has rid on a hurdle who has done less mischief SHERIDAN. **5.** I saw him beate the surges vnder him, And r. vpon their backes SHAKS. *fig.* Death rides upon the sulphury Siroc BYRON. **6. a.** Commonly Rides with her Tongue out of her Mouth 1714. **b.** Rain..made the ground r. soft 1889.

II. 1. Of vessels: To lie *at* (or †*on*) anchor; freq. *to* (or †*at*) *an anchor*. Also ellipt. OE. **2.** To float or move upon the water; to sail, esp. in a buoyant manner OE. **3.** Of things: To move in any way, to be carried or supported, after the manner of one riding 1586. **b.** Of the heavenly bodies: To appear to float in space 1632. **4.** To rest or turn *on* or *upon* something of the nature of a pivot, axle, or protuberance 1597. **b.** To extend or project *over* something 1601. **c.** *ellipt.* in previous senses 1683. **5.** Of a dress, etc.: To work *up* so as to form folds or creases; to ruck 1854.

1. *fig.* This..snug little road-stead, where I thought to r. at anchor for life SCOTT. **2.** It has been prosperous, and you are riding into port THACKERAY. **3.** *fig.* On whose foolish honestie My practises r. easie SHAKS. **b.** When the Sun with Taurus rides MILT. **4.** Strong as the Axletree In which the Heauens r. SHAKS.

III. *trans.* **1.** To traverse on horseback; to ride over, along, or through ME. **2.** To pursue, proceed upon (one's way, etc.) on horseback ME. **3.** *To r. out.* Of a ship: To sustain (a gale or storm) without great damage or dragging anchor 1529. **b.** *fig.* To endure or sustain successfully, to last to the end of, †to spend, pass 1529.

1. The Lord High Admiral, Riding the streets, was traitorously shot MARLOWE. They could not r. the water, it being great 1670. Phr. *To r. a race, course, circuit, match*, etc. **3.** The ship Lagoda..rode out the gale in safety 1840. **b.** That our faith may r. out every storm of doubt 1877.

IV. *trans.* **1.** To sit or be carried on, to go or travel upon (a horse, etc.); to manage or control while seated on ME. **b.** *Racing.* To urge (a horse) to excessive speed; to 'squeeze' 1863. **c.** To bring into a certain condition by riding, e.g. *to ride to death* 1440. **2.** To mount or cover (the female) 1500. **3. a.** Of the nightmare, witches, etc.: To sit upon, use as a horse 1597. **b.** To have the mastery of (a person); to manage at will; to oppress or harass; to tyrannize over; to dominate completely 1583. **4.** To sit upon, be carried or borne along upon (something) 1597. **b.** Of things: To rest upon, esp. by projecting or overlapping 1713. **5.** *To r. down*: To exhaust (a horse) by excessive riding; to overtake by pursuit on horseback; to charge, or collide with, so as to overthrow 1670. **6.** To cut (an animal) *off* or *out* from the herd by skilful riding 1843. **7.** To cause (a person) to ride 1711. **b.** To convey in a cart or other vehicle. Chiefly *U.S.* 1687. **c.** To keep (a ship) moored; to secure or maintain at anchor 1726.

1. Grimes rode the donkey in front KINGSLEY. *fig.* There is a set of Bishops..Will r. the Devill off his legs, and break his wind 1647. **3. a.** The Men they commonly laid asleep at the place, whereto they rode them 1693. **b.** The tradesman..is ridden by the routine of his craft EMERSON. **4.** The boys will 'r.' a log down the current 1890. **b.** Of spectacles that rode his nose 1801. **7.** To..r. him on a rail for body-snatching 1876. **c.** Bays to r. our Fleets in NELSON.

Phr. **R. and tie.** Of two (or three) persons: To travel with one horse by alternately riding and walking, each one riding ahead for some distance and tying up the horse for the one who comes behind; also as *sb.* or *adv.* (sometimes hyphened.) Hence **Ri·dden** *ppl. a.* **Ri·deable, ri·dable,** *a.* capable of being ridden through, over, etc.; capable of being ridden or used for riding.

Rider (rəi·dəɹ). [Late OE. *ridere*; see RIDE *v.* and -ER[1].] **I.** †**1. a.** A knight; a mounted warrior –1596. **b.** A mounted reaver or raider, a moss-trooper. Now *arch.* 1549. **2.** One who rides a horse or other animal (also, a cycle); a mounted person. See also ROUGH-RIDER. ME. **3.** A gold coin, having a figure of a horseman on the obverse, formerly current in Flanders and Holland; also, a gold coin current in Scotland during the 15–16th centuries. (After Du. and Flem. *rijder.*) 1479. †**4.** A riding-master; a horse-trainer –1678. †**5.** A commercial traveller, a bagman –1837. **6.** *Curling.* A stone driven so as to dislodge other stones blocking the tee 1891.

1. b. The Border riders who had subsisted by depredation SCOTT. **2.** A hard r. across country 1881.

II. 1. *Naut.* **a.** *pl.* An additional set of timbers or iron plates used to strengthen the frame of a ship internally or externally 1627. **b.** *pl.* A second or upper tier of casks in a hold 1846. **c.** A rope, or turn of one, overlying another 1841. **2.** *Mining.* **a.** A contrivance of wood and rope on which the miner rides down and up the shafts 1653. **b.** A thin seam of coal or deposit of ore overlying a principal seam or lode 1875. **3.** An additional clause tacked on to a document after its first drafting; *esp.* a supplementary and amending clause attached to a legislative Bill at its final reading 1669. **b.** A corollary or addition supplementing, or naturally arising from, something said or written 1813. **c.** *Math.* A problem arising either directly or indirectly out of the proposition to which it is appended 1851. **d.** A clause added as a corollary to a verdict 1884. **4.** An object bestriding or surmounting another (in various techn. uses) 1793.

3. Colonel B—h..carried a R. as it is called, being a Clause to be added at the last Reading 1734. **d.** The jury..added a r. condemning the use of paraffin lamps..in the Hospital 1886. Hence **Ri·derless** *a.*

Ridge (ridʒ), *sb.* [Com. Teut.; OE. *hrycg*:—Teut. **hrugjoz.*] †**1.** The back or spine in man or animals –1678. **2.** The top, upper part, or crest *of* anything, esp. when long and narrow OE. **3.** The horizontal edge or line in which the two sloping sides of a roof meet at the top; the uppermost part or coping of a roof OE. **b.** *Fortif.* The highest part of the glacis 1853. **4.** A long and narrow stretch of elevated ground; a range or chain of hills or mountains OE. **b.** A line or reef of rocks 1695. **5.** *Agric.* A raised or rounded strip of arable land, usu. one of a series (with intermediate open furrows) into which a field is divided by ploughing in a special manner. late ME. **b.** Used as a measure of land OE. **c.** *Hort.* A raised hot-bed on which cucumbers or melons are planted 1725. **6.** A narrow elevation running along or across a surface 1523. **b.** A raised line, bank, bed, or strip *of* something 1763.

2. Dancing upon the r. of dreadful waves 1665. The line that forms the r. of the nose JOHNSON. **5.** *transf.* Each Warriour..expert, When to..close The ridges of grim Warr MILT.

attrib. and *Comb.*: **r.-band** (now *dial.*) = BACK-BAND; **-piece,** a beam at the apex of a roof, upon which the upper ends of the rafters rest; **-pole,** (*a*) the horizontal pole of a tent; (*b*) = *r.-piece*; **-rope,** the centre rope of an awning; any of the ropes along the rigging to which it is stretched; a life-line; **-tree,** = *r.-piece*. Hence **Ri·dgelet,** a small r. **Ri·dgy** *a.* rising in ridges or after the manner of a r.

Ridge (ridʒ), *v.* 1445. [f. RIDGE *sb.*] **1.** *trans.* To provide (a building) with a ridge, or a proper covering for this; to make or renew the ridge of (a house, etc.). **2.** To break or throw up (land, a field, etc.) into ridges. Freq. with *up*. 1523. **3.** To mark with or as with ridges; to raise ridges or ripples upon (a surface) 1671. **4.** To plant (*out*) in ridges or hot-beds 1731. **5.** *intr.* To form ridges; to rise (*up*) in ridges 1864.

3. Bristles..like those that r. the back Of chaf't wild Boars MILT. **5.** The Biscay, roughly ridging eastward, shook..her TENNYSON. Hence **Ridged** *ppl. a.* rising in or marked by a ridge or ridges.

Ri·dge-bone. [OE. *hrycgbán.*] The spine or back-bone. Now *rare* or *Obs.*

Ridgel (ri·dʒĕl). Now *dial.* 1597. [App. f. RIDGE *sb.* 1, the testicle being supposed to remain near the animal's back.] An animal which has been imperfectly castrated, or whose genital organs are not properly developed; *esp.* a male animal (ram, bull, or horse) with only one testicle. So **Ri·dgeling** (now *rare*).

Ri·dge-tile. Also **ridge tile.** 1496. [RIDGE *sb.*] A tile used for roofing the ridge of a building.

Ri·dgeway. [OE. *hrycgweg*; see RIDGE *sb.* 4 and WAY *sb.*] A way or road along a ridge, esp. one following the ridge of downs or low hill-ranges.

Ridicule (ri·dikiūl), *sb.*[1] 1673. [a. F., or ad. L. *ridiculum*, neut. of *ridiculus*; see RIDICULE *a.*] **1.** A ridiculous or absurd thing, feature, characteristic, or habit; an absurdity. Now *rare*. 1677. †**b.** A laughing-stock –1694. **2.** Ridiculous nature or character (*of* something) 1711. **b.** That which is ridiculous 1712. **3.** The act or practice of making persons or things the object of jest or sport; language intended to raise laughter against an object 1690. †**4.** A piece of derisive mirth or light mockery –1774.

1. He marked every fault of taste, every weakness, every r. MACAULAY. **2.** The r. of such a supposition 1824. **3.** Such a proposal is just one of those things which admits of great r. 1875. Phr. *To turn* (*in*) *to r.*, to make ridiculous.

Ri·dicule, *sb.*[2] *Obs.* exc. *dial.* 1805. [a. F. perversion of *réticule.*] = RETICULE 2.

†**Ri·dicule,** *a.* 1672. [a. F., ad. L. *ridiculus*, f. *ridere* to laugh.] = RIDICULOUS *a.* 1. –1683.

Ri·dicule, *v.* 1684. [f. prec. or RIDICULE *sb.*[1]] †**1.** To render ridiculous (*rare*) –1735. **2.** To treat with ridicule or mockery; to make fun of, deride, laugh at 1700.

1. When he..Preaches, Cants, and ridicules himself 1684. **2.** Humanity and compassion are ridiculed as the fruits of superstition and ignorance BURKE. Hence **Ri·diculer.**

Ridiculous (ridi·kiūləs), *a.* 1550. [ad. L. *ridiculus* (see RIDICULE *a.*) or *ridiculosus.*] **1.** Exciting ridicule or derisive laughter; absurd, preposterous, comical, laughable. **b.** Outrageous. *dial.* and *U.S.* 1839. **2.** *absol.* with *the*: That which is ridiculous 1742.

1. Gazelles..with r. magnitude of horns 1848. **2.** One step above the sublime, makes the r. 1795. Hence **Ridi·culous-ly** *adv.*, **-ness.**

Riding (rəi·diŋ), *sb.* [Late OE. **þriðing* or **þriding*, ad. ON. *þriðjungr* third part, f. *þriði* third; the suffix is -ING[3]. The preceding *t* or *th* of *east*, *west*, *north* subsequently coalesced with the initial consonant.] **1.** One of the three administrative districts into which Yorkshire is divided (East, West, North). **2.** A similar division of other counties or districts in the United Kingdom or its Colonies 1675.

Riding (rəi·diŋ), *vbl. sb.* ME. [f. RIDE *v.* + -ING[1].] **1.** In the senses of RIDE *v.* **2.** A way or road specially intended for persons riding; *esp.* a green track or lane cut through (or skirting) a wood or covert; a ride ME.

attrib. and *Comb.*: **r.-master,** a teacher of horsemanship; esp. *Mil.*, an officer having charge of the instruction of troopers in a cavalry regiment; **-officer,** a mounted revenue officer; **-school,** a school for instruction in horsemanship.

Riding (rəi·diŋ), *ppl. a.* OE. [-ING[2].] **1.** That rides (see RIDE *v.*); mounted. †**2.** *R. knot*, a running knot, a slip-knot –1650. **3.** That 'rides' upon, surmounts, or projects over an object or part of an object 1677.

Ri·ding-coat. 1507. [RIDING *vbl. sb.*] A coat worn in riding, *esp.* an overcoat to protect the rider from wet.

Ri·ding-habit. 1666. [RIDING *vbl. sb.*] A dress or costume used for riding; *spec.* a riding-dress worn by ladies, consisting of a cloth skirt worn with a double-breasted tight-fitting jacket.

Ri·ding-hood. 1459. [RIDING *vbl. sb.*] A large hood originally worn while riding, but in later use forming an article of outdoor costume for women and children. (Now chiefly familiar from the tale of *Little Red Riding Hood.*)

Ri·ding rhyme. 1575. [RIDING *vbl. sb.* or *ppl. a.*] The form of verse (the heroic couplet) used by Chaucer in his Canterbury Tales, and, after him, by Lydgate and others.

Spenser thought he was imitating what wiseacres used to call the riding-rhyme of Chaucer 1875.

‖ **Ridotto** (ridǫ·to), *sb.* *Obs.* exc. *Hist.* 1722. [It., = F. *réduit*, med.L. *reductus*, *reducere* to REDUCE.] An entertainment or social assembly consisting of music and dancing.

‖ **Riem** (rīm). *S. Afr.* 1849. [Du., = OE. *réoma*; see RIM *sb.*[2]] A long strip or thong of undressed leather.

‖ **Rifacimento** (rifatʃime·nto). 1773. [It., f. *rifac-*, stem of *rifare* to remake.] A new-modelling or recasting of a literary work.

Rife (rəif), *a.* and *adv.* [Late OE. *rýfe* = **rífe.*] **A.** *adj.* **1.** Of common or frequent occurrence; prevalent; widespread; in later use *esp.* of infectious diseases or epidemics.

2. a. Of rumours, reports, etc.: Common; generally current in popular knowledge or talk ME. **b.** Of words or phrases: Commonly or frequently heard. Now *rare.* 1513. **3.** Abundant, plentiful, ample; large in quantity or number ME. **4.** Characterized by plenty *of*, rich *in*, something. Now *rare.* ME. **b.** Amply provided *with* something 1787. **5.** Disposed or inclined; ready, prompt; quick. Const. *for*, †*of*, †*to*. Now *dial.* late ME.

1. It is r. and catching 1705. The activity and noise of city day were r. in the street DICKENS. 2. a. A rumour of the queen's arrest was r. in London 1856. 3. Direfull comets never rifer were 1627. Where the foliage was rifest LYTTON. 4. b. Language r. With rugged maxims hewn from life TENNYSON.

B. *adv.* **1.** Abundantly, copiously, largely; manifoldly ME. †**2.** Frequently, often –1618. †**3.** Promptly, speedily, readily –1525. Hence †**Ri·fe·ly** *adv.*, †**-ness** (*rare*).

Riffle (ri·f'l), *sb. U.S.* 1796. [Cf. RIFFLE *v.*] **1.** A rocky obstruction in the bed of a river; a piece of broken water produced by this; a rapid. **2.** In gold-washing: A slat, bar, cleat, or block, placed across the bottom of a cradle or sluice in order to break the current and detain the gold 1862. **b.** A groove or channel across the bottom of a cradle or sluice, or the space between two bars, etc., serving to catch the gold; a mercury-bath in a washing-table 1875. **c.** *attrib.*, as *r.-bed*, *-sluice* 1862.

Riffle (ri·f'l), *v. rare.* 1754. [perh. partly a var. of RUFFLE *v.*, and partly ad. F. *riffler*, obs. var. of *rifler*.] **1.** *intr.* To form a riffle or rapid. *U.S.* **2.** *trans.* To handle in a hesitating manner, so as to produce a slight rattle 1852. **3.** In card-sharping: To bend up (cards) at the corners in shuffling; to shuffle in this manner 1894.

Ri·ffler. 1797. [ad. F. *rifloir*, f. *rifler* to scrape, file.] A tool with a curved file-surface at each end, used by sculptors, metal-workers, and wood-carvers.

Riff-raff, riffraff (ri·f,ræf). 1470. [f. ME. *riff and raff*, a. OF. *rif et raf* one and all.] **1.** Persons of a disreputable character or belonging to the lowest class of a community. **b.** The scum *of* a community, class, etc.; the rabble 1545. **c.** One belonging to the rabble (*rare*) 1602. **2.** Worthless stuff; odds and ends; trash, rubbish. Now chiefly *dial.* 1526. **3.** *attrib.* or as *adj.* **a.** Of persons: Low or disreputable; belonging to the rabble 1612. **b.** Of things: Worthless, trashy 1608.

1. A mere parcel of r.! petty traders and shop-keepers 1811. b. All the boys and r. of the towns 1851. 3. b. The large 4to ed. of Sallust full of r. Notes 1711.

Rifle (rəi·f'l), *sb.*[1] Now *dial.* and *U.S.* 1459. [a. OF. *riffle* a stick, billet of wood.] **1.** A piece of wood used by mowers for sharpening their scythes. **2.** A bent stick attached to the butt of a scythe for laying the corn in rows 1573.

Rifle (rəi·f'l), *sb.*[2] 1751. [f. RIFLE *v.*[3]] **1.** One of a set of spiral grooves cut on the interior surface of a gun-barrel with the object of giving to the projectile a rotatory movement on its own axis. **2.** A fire-arm, *esp.* a musket or carbine, having a spirally grooved bore 1775. **b.** *pl.* Troops armed with rifles; riflemen 1853.

2. Rifles for sporting purposes differ from military pieces in being double-barrelled 1880.

attrib. and *Comb.*, as *r.-ball*, *-barrel*, *team*, etc.; **r. brigade**, the title of certain regiments of the British army; **-grenade**, a small explosive shell shot from a r.-barrel; **-green** *a.* of the colour of a rifleman's uniform; *sb.* this shade of green **-pit**, an excavation made to give cover to a rifleman in firing at an enemy.

Rifle (rəi·f'l), *v.*[1] ME. [a. OF. *rifler*, *riffler* to graze, scratch, strip, plunder; of obscure origin.] **1.** *trans.* To despoil, plunder, or rob (a person) in a thorough fashion, *esp.* by searching his pockets or clothes; to search (a person) thoroughly with intent to rob. **b.** To plunder or pillage (a receptacle, place, etc.); to ransack, *esp.* in order to take what is valuable. late ME. **c.** To despoil or strip bare *of* something 1495. **2.** *absol.* To engage in pillage or plunder, or in searching with a view to this. late ME. **3.** *trans.* To carry off as booty; to plunder, steal. late ME. †**4.** To affect strongly or injuriously; to break or strip off –1770.

1. The Gyant was rifling of him, with a purpose after that to pick his Bones BUNYAN. b. Is it well done to riffell my cofer whyle I am absent? 1530. c. Pure Chastity is rifled of her store SHAKS. 2. Rob, then, r. if ye will LYTTON. 3. Shall he r. all thy sweets, at will? SMOLLETT. 4. That lightning which harms not the skin, and rifles the entrals MILT. Hence **Ri·fler** (now *arch.*), a robber, plunderer, spoiler.

Ri·fle, *v.*[2] *Obs.* exc. *dial.* 1590. [ad. Du. *rijfelen*, obscurely related to F. *rafler* RAFFLE *v.*[1]] **1.** *intr.* To play at dice; to gamble or raffle (*for* a stake). **2.** *trans.* To dispose of by raffling; to gamble *away* 1607.

Rifle (rəi·f'l), *v.*[3] 1635. [In sense 1 ult. repr. F. *rifler* to scratch, scrape. In sense 2 f. RIFLE *sb.*[2] 2.] **1.** *trans.* To form spiral grooves in (the barrel of a gun or the bore of a cannon). **2.** To shoot with a rifle. Also *intr.* with *at*. 1821. Hence **Ri·fled** *ppl. a.* (*a*) of firearms: having a spirally grooved bore; (*b*) of balls, shells, etc.: grooved; having projecting studs or ribs which fit into the grooves in the bore. **Ri·fling** *vbl. sb.* the operation of making grooves in the bore of a fire-arm; the grooving itself, or the nature of this.

Ri·fle-bird. 1831. [f. RIFLE *sb.*[2]] An Australian bird of the genus *Ptilorrhis*.

Rifleite (rəi·f'l,əit). 1891. [f. RIFLE *sb.*[2] 2 + -ITE.] A special slow-burning powder used in certain kinds of rifles.

Rifleman (rəi·f'lmæn). 1775. [f. RIFLE *sb.*[2] 2.] **1.** A soldier armed with a rifle; one who shoots with a rifle; as a prefixed designation = private of a rifle regiment. **2.** *Ornith.* = RIFLE-BIRD 1826.

Ri·fle-range. 1850. [f. RIFLE *sb.*[2] 2 + RANGE *sb.*[1]] **1.** The distance that a rifle-ball will carry. **2.** A place for practising rifle-shooting 1885.

Ri·fle-shot, ri·fleshot. 1840. [f. RIFLE *sb.*[2] 2.] **1.** Such a distance as may be covered by a shot from a rifle. **2.** One skilled in shooting with a rifle 1850. **3.** A shot fired with a rifle 1875.

Rift, *sb.*[1] ME. [Of Scand. origin. The stem is that of the vb. RIVE, to split.] †**1.** An act of tearing or rending; a splitting, riving –1440. **2.** A cleft or chasm in the earth, a rock, etc. ME. **b.** An opening or break in clouds or mist. late ME. **c.** A split, crack, rent, or chink in any object or article. Now somewhat *rare.* late ME. †**d.** A chap or crack in the skin –1614.

2. b. The Clouds From many a horrid r. abortive pour'd Fierce rain with lightning mixt MILT. c. The little r. within the lute TENNYSON. (The phr. has become proverbial and allusive = incipient dissension or malady.) Hence **Ri·ftless** *a.*

Rift, *sb.*[2] *U.S.* 1755. [Of obscure etym.] **1.** A rapid, a cataract. **2.** The wash of the surf on a shore 1869.

Rift, *v.*[1] ME. [Of Scand. origin; cf. ON. *ripta* to break (a bargain, etc.).] †**1.** *intr.* To form fissures or clefts; to gape open, split –1664. **2.** *trans.* To rend apart or asunder, split, cleave 1566. **b.** To form or force by cleaving 1849.

1. *Wint. T.* v. i. 66. 2. At sight of him the people with a shout Rifted the Air MILT.

Rift, *v.*[2] Now *Sc.* and *n. dial.* ME. [a. ON. *rypta*, f. a stem **rup-*.] **1.** *trans.* To belch out (wind, etc.). **2.** *intr.* To break wind upwards from the stomach; to belch ME.

Rig, *sb.*[1] ME. [North. and Sc. form of RIDGE *sb.*] = RIDGE *sb.*

Rig, *sb.*[2] Now *dial.* ME. [perh. a. ON. *hregg* storm.] A storm, tempest, strong wind.

Rig, *sb.*[3] *slang* or *colloq.* 1725. [Origin obsc.] **1.** Sport, banter, ridicule. Chiefly in phr. *to run* (one's) *rig(s) upon* (another), to make sport or game of. Now *dial.* **2.** A trick, scheme, or dodge; a method of cheating or swindling 1775. **b.** = CORNER *sb.* 8. 1877. **3.** A frolic or prank; an act of a mischievous or wanton kind; a 'game' 1811.

2. (Thimble-riggers) The r. is practised at fairs, at races, or on public roads 1830. Phr. *R. sale*, a sale by auction under false pretences. 3. Phr. *To run a* (or *the*) *r.*, *to run* (one's) *r.*, to play pranks, to run riot; He little dreamt, when he set out, Of running such a r.! COWPER.

Rig, *sb.*[4] 1822. [f. RIG *v.*[1]] **1.** *Naut.* The arrangement of masts, sails, etc., on a vessel. **2.** *colloq.* Costume, outfit, style of dress. Also *rig-up* and RIG-OUT. 1857. **3.** *U.S.* **a.** Apparatus for well-sinking 1875. **b.** An equipage; a horse vehicle 1885.

1. The r. suited to very small river boats 1856. 2. You'll do very well as to r., all but that cap HUGHES.

Rig, *v.*[1] 1489. [Origin unkn. Norw. and Sw. *rigga*, Da. *rigge*, in naut. use, are prob. from English.] **1.** *trans.* To make (a ship) ready for the sea; to fit out with the necessary tackle. **b.** In passive sense: To be rigged; to get rigged (afresh) 1614. **c.** To assemble and adjust the parts of (an aircraft). **2.** To dress, clothe, fit out or provide with clothes. Now *colloq.* or *slang.* 1534. **3.** To furnish or provide, to fit or fix *up*, *with* something. Also, rarely, without const. 1594. **b.** To fit *out* in some way 1679. **4.** To adjust or fix. Chiefly *Naut.* 1627. **b.** *Naut.* To run *out*, draw *in*, a boom or stay. Also *intr.* 1769. **5.** To fit up, esp. as an expedient or makeshift 1823.

1. *fig.* That fatall and perfidious Bark Built in th' eclipse, and rigg'd with curses dark MILT. b. Eight of the king's ships are rigging and making ready for sea 1614. 2. Once in seven years came up Madam in the stage coach, to..r. out herself and her family FIELDING. 4. We must r. the pumps 1836.

Rig, *v.*[2] Now *dial.* 1570. [Origin unkn.] *intr.* To play the wanton; to romp or climb about. So **Rig** *sb.*[5], a wanton girl or woman. **Ri·ggish** *a.* wanton, licentious.

Rig, *v.*[3] *slang* or *colloq.* 1823. [f. RIG *sb.*[3]] **1.** *trans.* To hoax, play tricks on, befool. **2.** To manage or manipulate in some underhand or fraudulent manner 1851.

2. Phr. *To r. the market*, to cause an artificial rise (or fall) of prices with a view to personal profit; to send *up* prices artificially. Hence **Ri·gger**[2], a thimble-rigger, one who rigs the market, etc.

Riga (rəi·gă, rī·gă). 1765. Name of a seaport of Livonia, used attrib. in names of products exported from there, as *R. deal*, *fir*, *hemp*, *oak*, etc. *R. balsam*, an essential oil (also called *Carpathian balsam*) obtained by distillation from *Pinus Cembra*.

Rigadoon (rigădū·n), *sb.* 1691. [a. F. *rigaudon*, *rigodon*, of doubtful origin. Perh. f. *Rigaud*, name of its inventor.] **1.** A lively and somewhat complicated dance for two persons, formerly in vogue. **2.** The music for such a dance 1731.

1. He..gained a great Reputation, by his Performance in a R. ADDISON. Hence **Rigadoo·n** *v. intr.* to dance a r.

Rigel (rəi·dʒĕl, rəi·gĕl). 1592. [a. Arab. *rijl* foot.] The star β in the constellation Orion.

Rigescent (ridʒe·sĕnt), *a.* 1873. [ad. pres. pple. of L. *rigescere*.] *Bot.* Tending to be rigid or stiff. So **Rige·scence**, stiffening 1768.

Rigger[1] (ri·gəɹ). 1611. [f. RIG *v.*[1]] **1.** *Naut.* One who rigs ships. **2.** *Mech.* A band-wheel 1797. **3.** A long pointed sable brush, used by marine painters to delineate the cordage of ships 1883. **4.** A vessel with a specified rig 1897. **5.** Colloq. abbrev. of OUTRIGGER 3. **6.** One who attends to the rigging of aircraft 1921.

Ri·gging, *vbl. sb.* 1486. [f. RIG *v.*[1]] **1.** *Naut.* The action of equipping a vessel with the necessary shrouds, stays, braces, etc. **2.** The ropes or chains employed to support the masts (*standing r.*), and to work or set the yards, sails, etc. (*running r.*) 1594. **3.** *transf.* Clothing, dress 1662. **4.** Equipment, outfit 1849.

4. This claim has a splendid hydraulic r. 1877.

Right (rəit), *sb.*[1] [OE. *riht*, related to RIGHT *a.*] **I.** †**1.** The standard of permitted and forbidden action within a certain sphere; law; a rule or canon –1610. **2.** That which is consonant with equity or the light of nature; that which is morally just or due. (Often contrasted with *might* or *wrong*.) OE. **b.** The fact or position of being in the right. Chiefly in phr. *to have r.* Now *rare.* late ME. **c.** Consonance with fact; correctness 1796. **3.** Just or equitable treatment; fairness in decision; justice. Freq. in phr. *to do* (a person) *r.* OE. †**b.** With ref. to drinking, in phr. *to do* (one) *r.* –1624. **4.** In prep. phrases, †*with*, *by* (in mod. use, *by rights*), or †*of r.*, = rightfully; with reason or justice OE. **5.** *The r.*: that which is right; righteousness, justice, truth; *esp.* the cause of truth or justice OE.

2. You must acknowledge a Distinction betwixt R. and Wrong, founded in Nature..by which Actions may be call'd just or unjust 1737. 3. King Charles, and who'll do him r. now? BROWNING. b. 2 *Hen. IV*,

v. iii. 76. 4. I should haue beene a woman by r. SHAKS. 5. Too fond of the r. to pursue the expedient GOLDSM. Phr. *To be in the r.*, to have justice, reason, or fact upon one's side; Your Sex Was never in the r., y're always false, Or silly OTWAY.

II. 1. Justifiable claim, on legal or moral grounds, to have or obtain something, or to act in a certain way OE. 2. In prep. phrases, *with, of, by* (*good*) *r.*, also now *by rights*, denoting justifiable title or claim to something OE. 3. A legal, equitable, or moral title or claim to the possession of property or authority, the enjoyment of privileges or immunities, etc. OE. 4. With possessive pron. or genitive: The title or claim to something properly possessed by one or more persons OE. 5. That which justly accrues or falls to any one; what one may properly claim; one's due OE. †b. A territory, estate, dominion -1596. †c. (Usu. *pl.*) The last sacrament of the Church -1509. d. *pl.* A stag's full complement of antlers, consisting of the brow, bay, and tray. late ME.

1. Nor doth it follow that he hath the best in r., who hath the best in fight 1642. Phr. *In r. of* (a person or thing): so *by r. of*. 2. May I with r. and conscience make this claim? SHAKS. Estates, which of r. belonged to the poorer classes COBBETT. Any little matters which ought to be ours by rights DICKENS. 3. *Civil, natural*, etc., *rights*: see the adjs. *Declaration* or *Bill of Rights*, 'a Bill declaring the Rights and Liberties of England, and the Succession to the Crown', passed in 1689. *To have a* or *no r. to* (do something); in dial. use also employed with ref. to obligation; I have no r. to maintain idle vagrants SMOLLETT. 4. Human nature at last asserted its rights MACAULAY. Phr. *In r. of, in one's* (*own*) *r.*; She has a little money in her own r. DICKENS. 5. *fig.* Grief claim'd his r., and tears their course SCOTT.

III. 1. *To rights*: a. †In a proper manner; to or into a proper condition or order. In later use chiefly with *bring, put*, or *set*. ME. b. At once, straightway (now *U.S.*); †completely, altogether. Formerly freq. in phr. †*to sink to rights*. 1663. 2. (Now *pl.*) The true account or interpretation *of* a matter. 1749.

1. a. In my chamber, setting things and papers to rights PEPYS. b. The Hulk.., by Reason of many Breaches.., sunk to Rights SWIFT. 2. I have never heard the rights of that story 1846.

IV. 1. a. = RIGHT HAND 2. ME. b. The right wing of an army, etc.; the right-hand extremity of a line of men 1707. c. *Politics*. In Continental legislative chambers, the party or parties of conservative principles 1887. 2. a. A boot or shoe for the right foot; a glove for the right hand 1825. b. A blow given with the right hand 1898. †3. The direct road or way (*rare*) -1595.

1. a. Far to the r., where Apennine ascends GOLDSM. b. The Chief occupied the centre of the middle rank, instead of being on the extreme r. SCOTT. 2. b. Sharkey put over a straight r. on Corbett's nose 1898. 3. *John* I. i. 170. Hence **Ri·ghtless** *a.* †wrongful, lawless; devoid or deprived of rights.

Right, *sb.*[2] 1590. Erron. spelling for RITE.

No doubt they rose vp early, to obserue The r. of May SHAKS.

Right (rəit), *a.* [Com. Teut.; OE. *reht, riht*, related to L. *rectus*, f. root *reg-* to make or lead straight.] I. †1. Straight; not bent, curved, or crooked. Also *r. with*, in a line with. -1704. 2. *R. line*, a straight line 1551. 3. Formed by or with reference to a right line or plane perpendicular to another right line or plane ME. b. Of solid figures: Having the ends or base at right angles with the axis 1674.

2. The r. lines and measured regularity of an American city 1898. 3. *R. sphere*, is that where the Equator cuts the horizon at R. angles 1795. *R. circle*, a circle drawn at right angles with the plane of projection 1846. *R. sailing*, running a course on one of the four cardinal points, so as to alter only a ship's latitude, or longitude 1867. *R. horizon*, the celestial horizon of a place on the equator the plane of which is perpendicular to that of the equinoctial. *R. ascension*: see ASCENSION 3.

II. 1. Of persons or disposition: Disposed to do what is just or good; upright, righteous. Now *rare*. OE. 2. Of actions, conduct, etc.: In accordance with what is just or good; equitable; morally fitting. In later use chiefly predicative. OE. 3. Agreeing with some standard or principle; correct, proper. Also, agreeing with facts; true. OE. b. Of belief: Orthodox, true; that ought to be accepted or followed OE. c. With agent-nouns: Correct, exact 1568. d. Leading in the proper direction or towards the place one wishes to reach 1814. 4. Fitting, proper, appropriate; exactly answering to what is required or suitable OE. 5. *R. way*. a. The way of moral rightness or spiritual salvation OE. b. The correct method, or that most conducive to the end in view 1561. c. As *adv.* In the proper direction 1704. 6. *R. side*: a. That side of anything which is regarded as the principal, or is naturally turned towards one; the face or upper side 1511. b. The party or principle of which one approves 1649. c. (With *on*.) The better aspect of anything 1713. d. The safe, advantageous, appropriate, desirable side *of* anything 1700. 7. Properly pertaining or attached to a person or thing ME. 8. Of the mind or mental faculties: Normal, natural, sound, whole. Chiefly in phr. *to be in one's r. mind* or *senses*. ME. 9. Of persons: a. Mentally normal or sound sane. Chiefly with negs. 1662. b. In good health and spirits; sound, well, comfortable 1837. 10. Of persons: Correct in opinion, judgement, or procedure 1597. 11. In a satisfactory or proper state; in good order 1662.

1. According to the rule of a r. conscience 1576. He is a r. man BURKE. 2. With some regard to what is just and r. [they] Shall lead thir lives MILT. Phr. *It is r. to* or *that*. 3. A r. description of our sport, my Lord SHAKS. d. The change..was in the r. direction 1861. 4. God knows if his heart lay in the r. place 1809. Phr. *Mr. R., Miss R.*, the destined husband or wife. 5. b. [He] took the r. way to be depos'd MILT. 6. c. At all events,..it 's a fault on the r. side 1855. d. A widow on the r. side of thirty 1809. 7. Thou hast frighted the word out of his r. sence SHAKS. 8. So also Harry Monmouth being in his r. wittes,.. turn'd away the fat Knight SHAKS. 9. a. Phr. *Not r. in the head*. b. Phrases. *To set* or *put* (a person) *r.*, to correct or direct; also, to justify (oneself). *R. as my glove, as ninepence, as a trivet*, etc. 10. A fool must now and then be r., by chance COWPER. Phr. *Right!* = You are r.; you say well; also *R. you are*. 11. Phr. *To get..r.*, to set in order. *To make it r.*, to square or settle matters. *To come* (*all*) *r. All r.*, used to express acquiescence or assent. *R.-ho! R.-o!* (slang), used as an expression of agreement or assent: Very well 1902.

III. 1. Having due title or right; rightful, legitimate, lawful. Now *arch.* OE. 2. Justly entitled to the name; having the true character of; true; real, genuine, not counterfeit or spurious OE.

1. To the r. heyres of the same Elizabeth 1492. 2. Behold a r. hisrahelite, in whom is no guile TINDALE *John* i. 47. Half an Ounce of r. Virginia Tobacco STEELE. *R. whale* A whale-bone whale, esp. of the genus *Balæna*.

IV. 1. The distinctive epithet of the hand (see RIGHT HAND) normally the stronger; by extension also of that side of the body, its limbs, their clothing, etc.; hence *transf.* of corresponding parts of other objects. *R. bank* (of a river), that on the right of a person facing down the stream. 2. *R. side*. a. The right-hand side; the right-hand quarter or region ME. b. *To rise*, or *get out of bed, on the* (†*one's*) *r. side*, used with allusion to the supposed luckiness of the practice, or its effect on one's temper 1562.

1. The Virgin Mary crowned, with her Babe in her r. arm 1797. 2. a. The king..layd him downe on his r. side MORE. *attrib.* The r. side tool..is thus named because it cuts from the r. hand towards the left 1846. Hence **Ri·ghten** *v. trans.* to put or set r. in various senses. **Right-si·ded** *a.* (*Path.*) situated in or affecting the r. side of the body; having a tendency to use the limbs on the r. side of the body. **Right-ward, -wards** *adv.*

Right (rəit), *v.* [Com. Teut.; OE. *rihtan*, f. *riht* RIGHT *a.*] †I. *trans.* 1. To make straight (a path, way, etc.); to straighten -ME. 2. To guide, direct (movements, etc.) -1440. 3. To guide as ruler; to govern, rule, judge -1512. II. 1. †To set up, establish, to raise, rear, erect, set upright. Now *dial.* OE. 2. a. *Naut. To r the helm*, to bring it into line with the keel 1627. b. To bring (a ship) back into a vertical position 1748. c. *intr.* Of a ship, etc.: To recover or reassume a vertical position 1745. d. *refl.* To recover one's balance or equilibrium; to recover one's footing; to correct a false step 1805. e. To restore to the proper position after a fall, overturn, breakdown, etc. 1823. 3. To do justice or make reparation to (a person); to redress the injuries of; to avenge OE. b. To vindicate, set right, justify. Chiefly *refl.* late ME. 4. To avenge or redress (an injustice or injury). late ME.

2. b. They were forced to cut away the masts to r. her 1834. c. The lab'ring ship may bend, ne'er more to r. 1762. e. We soon righted the carriage 1841. 3. He thinks that when he is wronged, it is the business of the ruler..to r. him at once 1891. *refl.* *L. L. L.* v. ii. 734.

III. 1. To bring into accordance with truth; to correct or render exact (accounts, etc.); to set right or inform (a person) correctly. Also with *up*. OE. 2. To set in order, to adjust, to set or put right. Now *rare*. OE. 3. *refl.* To return to a proper or normal condition 1833.

1. He said he was righting his accounts 1690. 2. After righting all matters to our satisfaction 1793. 3. Slowly all things r. themselves 1838. Hence **Ri·ghtable** *a.* capable of being righted. **Ri·ghter**, one who settles or sets right.

Right (rəit), *adv.* [OE. *rehte, rihte*, f. *reht, riht* RIGHT *a.*] I. 1. Of motion or position: Straight; in a direct course or line. b. In the proper course ME. c. *R. up*, straight up, upright. Now *dial.* 1440. 2. In a straight or direct course leading quite up *to* a place, person, or thing; hence, all the way *to, into, round, through*, etc.; also with advs. OE. b. Quite or completely *off, out, round*, etc. late ME. 3. a. Immediately *after* some event ME. b. †*R. forth*, at once. So *r. off, r. away*, immediately, without delay (orig. *U.S.*). 1440. c. *U.S.* Straight (with temporal connotation) 1849. 4. *R. out*, = OUTRIGHT *adv.* 3, 4; also *dial.*, completely 1610.

1. We had a constant gale blowing r. upon our stern 1748. b. He..directed them that went r. *Ecclus.* xlix. 9. 2. The broad verandah which runs r. round the house 1865. 3. b. I saw now that 'R. away' and 'Directly' were one and the same thing DICKENS. 4. *Temp.* IV. i. 101.

II. 1. Precisely, exactly, just, quite, altogether, to the full. Now *dial.* or *arch.* 2. Qualifying advs. (or advb. phrases) of time, esp. *r. now*, †*then*, etc. Now *arch.* OE. 3. With preps. or advs. of place, as *r. at, in, on*, etc. OE. b. With *here, there*. Now *U.S.* ME. 4. Qualifying *as* or *so* in various constructions. Now *arch.* OE. 5. With intensive force: Very. Now *arch.* ME. b. In titles or forms of address. late ME. †6. With negs.: At all; whatever -1571.

2. Haue you forgotten what you said r. now? 1624. 3. The Wind is r. in our teeth 1669. 5. I know r. well how tedious I haue beene 1600. *R. honourable*: see HONOURABLE *a.* 2 b.

III. 1. Righteously, uprightly; in harmony with the moral standard of actions OE. 2. In a proper or fitting manner; in the required or necessary way; properly; duly, aright OE. b. In due or proper order ME. 3. In accordance with facts or the truth of the case; accurately; correctly OE. 4. On or towards the right side (*of*). See also RIGHT AND LEFT. ME.

1. Thou satest in the throne judging r. *Ps.* ix. 4. 2. The first thing should be taught him is to hold his Pen r. LOCKE. Phr. *All r., r. enough*. b. When once our grace we haue forgot Nothing goes r. SHAKS. 3. Yes, you guess r. 1878. 4. 'Tention eyes r.!' 1816.

-right, *suffix*, repr. OE. *riht* adj. and *rihte* adv., which are employed as suffixes in OE. *forðriht, -rihte* FORTHRIGHT, and *upriht, -rihte* UPRIGHT. See also OUTRIGHT.

Right about, *sb., adv.* (and *a.*) Also **right-about, rightabout.** 1700. [f. RIGHT *sb.*[1] IV. 1 a + ABOUT *adv.* II. 2; orig. as two separate words.] A. *sb. Mil.* In phr. *To the right about*, a command to turn towards the right so far as to face the opposite way (now simply *right about*). Hence with vbs., as *turn, face*, etc. Also *gen.*

Their fox took the opportunity to swing to the rightabout 1883. Phr. **To send to the r. a.** To cause (troops) to turn and retreat or flee. b. To send packing; to dismiss or turn away unceremoniously.

B. 1. *adv.* = A. 1; usu. as a command with additional word, as *wheel, face, turn* 1796. b. Hence *right about face* as a compound vb. or adv. 1815. 2. *attrib.* or as *adj.* with *face* or *turn*. Also in fig. use, denoting a complete change of front; an entire reversal of principles or policy 1862.

1. b. Southey,..True turn-coat, can right about face, pliant lad 1815. 2. The Tory right-about-face 1891.

Right and left, right-and-left, *adv.* (*v.*), *a.*, and *sb.* ME. A. *adv.* On or towards the right and the left; on both sides, in both directions. b. *transf.* On all hands 1893.

b. He is being robbed right and left 1893.

B. *adj.* Of or pertaining to the right and the left hand side, etc.; turning to the right and the left; fitting the right and left hand or foot respectively 1854.

An excellent right-and-left shot 1863. *Right-and-left screw*, one having the threads at the two ends running opposite ways.

C. *sb.* A right-and-left shot 1856.

Ri·ght a·ngle. ME. [f. RIGHT *a.* I. 3 + ANGLE *sb.*²] *Math.* An angle of 90°.

At right angles, perpendicularly (*to* another line, etc.); so as to form an angle of 90°.

Ri·ght-angled, *a.* 1571. [f. as prec. + ANGLED *a.*] 1. Containing or forming a right angle or right angles; rectangular. 2. Characterized by right angles 1833.

Right boys. An irregular association formed in S.W. Ireland in 1785-6, and connected with political or agrarian disorders; named after one of their leaders, Captain Right.

Ri·ght-down, *adv.* and *a.* Also **right down, rightdown.** 1623. [f. RIGHT *adv.* + DOWN *adv.*] A. *adv.* †1. With verbs: Positively; without any limitation; right out -1709. 2. With pples. or adjs.: Thoroughly; out and out 1648. B. *adj.* Positive; thorough 1623.

Such fellows..become r. scamps 1875.

Righteous (rəi·tyəs, rəi·tʃəs), *a.* (*sb.*) and *adv.* [OE. *rihtwīs*, f. *riht* RIGHT *a.* + *-wīs* WISE *sb.* The spelling *righteous* appears in the first half of the 16th c.] 1. Of persons: Just, upright, virtuous; guiltless, sinless; acting rightly or justly. (See also RIGHTEOUSNESS.) Also used *absol.* (in sing. or pl.) with *the*. †b. As *sb.* A righteous person -1667. 2. Of actions, etc.: Characterized by justice or uprightness; morally right or justifiable OE. †3. As *adv.* Righteously; rightfully -1470.

1. Let me be recorded by the r. Gods, I am as poore as you SHAKS. In his dayes shall the r. flourish *Ps.* lxxii. 7. b. The onely r. in a World perverse MILT. 2. Instructing men in the way of r. living HOBBES. Hence †**Ri·ghteous** *v. trans.* to set right; to justify; to do justice to: to make r.

Ri·ghteously, *adv.* [OE. *rihtwīslīce*; see -LY.²] In a righteous manner.

Ri·ghteousness. [OE. *rihtwīsnisse.*] 1. The quality or condition of being righteous; conformity of life or conduct to the requirements of the divine or moral law; *spec.* in *Theol.* applied e.g. to the perfection of the Divine Being, and to the justification of man through the Atonement. †2. *pl.* Righteous deeds -1611.

2. All our righteousnesses are as filthy ragges *Isa.* lxiv. 6.

Rightful (rəi·tfŭl), *a.* [Late OE. *rihtful*, f. *riht* RIGHT *sb.*¹ + -FUL 1.] 1. Of persons: Disposed to do right; upright, just. Now *rare* or *Obs.* 2. Of actions, etc.: In conformity with what is right or just; equitable, thoroughly fair ME. 3. Legal, lawful, legitimate ME. 4. Proper, fitting, correct. Now *rare.* late ME.

1. *Merch. V.* IV. i. 301. 2. For we by rightfull doom remediles Were lost in death MILT. 3. Her vndoubted and rightfull successor CAMDEN. 4. Danube scarce retains his r. course PRIOR. Hence **Ri·ghtful·ly** *adv.*, **-ness.**

Right hand. Also **right-hand, right-hand.** OE. [f. RIGHT *a.* IV. 1.] 1. That hand which is normally the stronger of the two. (Opp. to LEFT HAND.) b. *transf.* (*a*) as a symbol of friendship or alliance (rendering L. *dextræ*); (*b*) a person of usefulness or importance; an efficient or indispensable helper or aid 1528. 2. a. The right side. b. The direction towards the right. ME. †c. The position of honour. *To take the right hand of*, to take or assume precedence of. -1704. †d. Of errors: *On the right hand*, on the right side, in the right direction -1785.

1. To horse!..or by this good right hand..I smite you COWPER. *attrib.* Two right-hand gloves 1884. b. For Mrs. Jane is the Right-hand of her Mother STEELE. 2. b. Turne vpon your right hand at the next turning SHAKS.

attrib. and *Comb.* **right-hand lock,** one enabling a door to swing to the right; **right-hand man,** †a soldier holding a position of responsibility on the right of a troop of horse; an efficient and reliable helper or aid; **right-hand rope,** a rope twisted towards the right; **right-hand screw,** one with the thread turning to the right. Hence **Right-ha·nder,** a blow struck with the r.; a right-handed person.

Right-handed, *a.* (*adv.*). late ME. [f. prec. + -ED¹.] 1. Having the right hand or arm stronger or more useful than the left; using the right hand by preference. 2. On the right side; of the right kind 1656. 3. a. Pertaining or belonging to the right hand. b. Of a blow: Delivered with the right hand. c. Of implements, etc.: Fashioned for the right hand. 1700. 4. *Conchol.* = DEXTRAL *a.* 2. 1838. 5. Characterized by rotation or direction towards the right. Also as *adv.* b. Of rotatory polarization (see quots.) 1827. c. Producing right-handed polarization 1827. 6. In the direction of the right; also as *adv.*, to the right 1900.

1. Some are..ambidexterous or right handed on both sides SIR T. BROWNE. 5. b. I shall..designate the polarization right-handed or left-handed, according as we have to turn the analyzing prism to the right or to the left 1854. Hence **Right-ha·nded·ly** *adv.*, **-ness.**

Ri·ght-ho, right-o, see RIGHT *a.* II. 11.

Right-lined, *a.* 1551. [f. RIGHT *a.* I. 2 + LINE *sb.*²] = RECTILINEAR *a.*

Rightly (rəi·tli), *adv.* [OE. *rihtlīce*; see RIGHT *a.* and -LY².] 1. In accordance with equity or moral rectitude. 2. In the right or proper manner OE. 3. Correctly, accurately, †precisely OE. †4. Directly, straight -1635.

3. He cannot see r. and shoots..with help of an opera-glass CARLYLE. 4. *Rich. II*, II. ii. 18.

Right-minded, *a.* 1585. [f. RIGHT *a.* + MIND *sb.*] 1. Having a mind naturally disposed towards what is right. 2. *colloq.* Of sound mind 1877. Hence **Right-mi·ndedness.**

Rightness (rəi·tnės). [OE. *rehtnisse, rihtnesse*; see RIGHT *a.* and -NESS.] 1. Uprightness, integrity, moral rectitude. †2. Straightness; the fact of being straight -1626. 3. Correctness, accuracy; fitness 1561. b. An instance of this 1872.

1. A r. which..hath had everlasting residence in the character of the Godhead 1834. 3. You are answerable, not for the r., but uprightness of the decision 1787.

Right of way (rəitəvwē¹·). Also **right-of-way.** 1768. 1. The legal right, established by usage, of a person or persons to pass and repass through grounds or property belonging to another. 2. A path or thoroughfare which one may lawfully make use of, *esp.* one traversing the property of another 1855. 3. *U.S.* = PERMANENT *way*.

-rights, *suffix*, ME. var. of -RIGHT.

Rigid (ri·dʒid), *a.* 1538. [ad. L. *rigidus*, f. *rigere* to be stiff.] 1. Stiff, unyielding; not pliant or flexible; firm, hard. 2. Of cold, etc.: Severe, hard, rigorous (*rare*) 1611. 3. Of conduct, persons, etc.: Harsh, severe, inflexible, strict 1624. 4. Strict in opinion or observance; scrupulously precise in respect of these 1598. 5. Exact, precise in procedure; admitting of no deviation from strict accuracy 1646.

1. With upright beams innumerable Of r. Spears MILT. *fig.* The..r. forms of antiquity HAZLITT. b. *spec.* Of an airship: Having the gas containers enclosed within compartments of a framework, as of metal, which carries the cabins, motors, etc.; also as *sb.* a r. airship 1909. 3. O r. gods! 1752. R. justice, untempered by mercy, easily changes into oppression 1868. 4. R. looks of Chast austerity MILT. R. parsimony 1861. R. Catholics 1874. 5. True, in the most r. sense 1729. Hence **Ri·gid·ly** *adv.*, **-ness.**

Rigi·dity. 1624. [ad. L. *rigiditas.*] 1. The state of being rigid: stiffness, hardness. 2. Strictness, harshness, inflexibility 1653.

Rigmarole (ri·gmărōᵘl), *sb.* (and *a.*). 1736. [app. a colloq. survival and alteration of RAGMAN ROLL (sense 2).] 1. A succession of incoherent statements; a rambling discourse; a long-winded harangue of little meaning or importance. b. Without article: Language of this kind 1809. 2. *attrib.* or *adj.* Incoherent; having no proper sequence of ideas 1753.

1. That's better than a long r. about nothing 1779. Hence **Ri·gmarolish** *a.*, **-ly** *adv.*

Ri·gol, *sb.* *Obs.* exc. *dial.* 1593. [ad. F. *rigole* water-course, gutter, groove.] †1. A ring or circle -1597. 2. A small channel, gutter or groove 1879.

‖**Rigor** (rəi·gǭɹ, ri·gǭɹ). late ME. [L., related to *rigidus* RIGID *a.*] *Path.* 1. A sudden chill, *esp.* one accompanied with fits of shivering which immediately precedes certain fevers and inflammations. 2. *R. mortis*, the stiffening of the body following upon death 1839.

Rigorism (ri·gŏriz'm). Also **rigourism.** 1704. [f. L. *rigor* RIGOUR + -ISM.] 1. The principles and practice of a rigorist; austerity, stringency; extreme strictness. 2. *R. C. Theol.* The doctrine of the rigorist school of moral theology 1882.

Rigorist (ri·gŏrist). Also **rigourist.** 1714. [f. as prec. + -IST.] 1. One who favours or insists upon the severest or strictest interpretation or enforcement of a law, precept, principle, or standard of any kind. 2. *R. C. Theol.* One who holds that in doubtful cases of conscience the stricter course is always to be followed 1715.

Rigorous (ri·gŏrəs), *a.* late ME. [a. OF. *rigorous* (mod.F. *rigoureux*); see RIGOUR and -OUS *a.*] 1. Characterized by rigour; rigidly severe or unbending; austere, harsh, stern; extremely strict. 2. Of the weather, etc.: Severe; bitterly cold. 3. Scrupulous, unswerving, strict (*rare*) 1641. 4. Severely exact, rigidly accurate 1651.

1. I..hope she will not be too r. with the young ones JOHNSON. The r. conditions of peace and pardon GIBBON. 3. A life of..r. abstinence 1847. 4. We have need of a more r. scholastic rule 1838. Hence **Ri·gorous·ly** *adv.*, **-ness.**

Rigour (ri·gəɹ). Also formerly (now U.S.) **rigor.** late ME. [a. OF. *rigor, rigour* (mod.F. *rigueur*), ad. L. *rigor* RIGOR.] I. 1. Severity in dealing with a person or persons; extreme strictness; harshness. b. An instance of this 1548. 2. The strict terms, application, or enforcement *of* some law, rule, etc. late ME. 3. Of weather or climate: Severity; extremity or excess of cold; †violence (of storms) 1548. b. Extreme distress or hardship 1769. 4. Strictness of discipline, etc.; austerity of life; an instance of this 1440. b. Puritanic strictness; rigorism; †an instance of this 1597. 5. Strict accuracy, severe exactitude 1565.

1. If..they haue tempered r. with lenitie HOOKER. 2. A clear fire, a clean hearth, and the r. of the game LAMB. Phr. *The* (..) *r. of the law.* 3. From regions of Arctic r. 1878. b. The utmost r. of famine 1769. 4. The r. of the monastic discipline 1833. b. R. makes it difficult for sliding virtue to recover RICHARDSON. 5. The term philosophy..when employed in propriety and r. 1836.

II. 1. = RIGOR 1. 1541. †2. Of material objects: Stiffness, hardness -1700.

2. The Stones..Did first the r. of their kind expel, And suppled into softness as they fell DRYDEN.

Ri·g-out. *colloq.* 1823. [f. RIG *v.*²] An outfit; a suit of clothes; a costume.

Rig-veda (rig,vē¹·dă). 1776. [Skr. *rigveda*, f. *ṛic* praise + *veda* knowledge; see VEDA.] The principal of the Vedas or sacred books of the Hindus.

Rile (rəil), *v.* Chiefly *U.S.* and *colloq.* 1825. [Later form of ROIL *v.*²] 1. *trans.* To make (a liquid) thick or turbid by stirring up the sediment; to make muddy 1838. 2. To excite, disturb; to vex, annoy, make angry 1825. b. *absol.* with *up.* To get angry 1844.

2. b. The little fellow riled up at this 1863. Hence **Riled** *ppl. a.*

Rill (ril), *sb.* 1538. [cf. mod.Du. *ril*, G. *rille.*] 1. A small stream; a brook, runnel, rivulet. 2. A small narrow trench; a drill. Now *dial.* 1658. 3. *Astr.* = RILLE 1888.

1. Shallow rills run trickling through the grass ADDISON. *fig.* Rills of oily eloquence..lubricate the course they take COWPER.

Rill (ril), *v.* 1610. [f. prec.] 1. *intr.* To flow in a small stream. 2. *trans.* a. To form by flowing. b. To utter in liquid notes. 1845. †3. To make drills in a garden bed. EVELYN.

1. Time's sand-dry streamlet through its glassy strait Rilled restless 1855.

Rille (ril). 1868. [a. G.; see RILL *sb.*] *Astr.* One of the long narrow trenches or valleys observed on the surface of the moon.

Rillet (ri·lėt). 1538. [f. RILL *sb.* + -ET or -LET. Recoined or revived by Tennyson.] A small rill or rivulet; a brooklet.

Those rillets that attend proud Tamer and her state DRAYTON.

Rim, *sb.*¹ [OE. *rima* (chiefly in compounds) = ON. *rime, rimi* a raised strip of land, a ridge.] 1. The peripheral portion or outer ring of a wheel, connected with the nave or boss by spokes or by a web. late ME. b. The hoop-shaped piece of wood which forms the outer frame of a sieve, etc. Also *dial.* a hoop. 1660. c. A circular mark or object 1860. 2. *Naut.* The surface *of* the water 1602. 3. The edge, border, or margin *of* an object, *esp.* one which has a more or less circular form 1603. **b.** The verge *of* the horizon, sea, hills, etc. Chiefly *poet.* 1842. **4.** An edge, margin, or border; *esp.* a raised or projecting one upon something having a circular form 1669. **b.** A verge or margin of land, sea, etc.; a narrow strip 1781.

1. **b.** A wheat-riddle of wood..with an oak r. 1844. **3.** The moon lifting her silver r. Above a cloud KEATS. **b.** The steel-blue r. of the ocean 1858. **4.** One little boy complained..that there was no r. to his plate 1832. **b.** The ragged rims of thunder brooding low TENNYSON.

Comb.: **r.-fire** *a.* of a cartridge, having the detonating substance disposed round the edge (opp. to *centre-fire*); hence, of a gun, adapted for such cartridges; **-lock**, a lock having a metal case which stands out from the face of the door. Hence **Rim** *v. trans.* to furnish with a r.; to border or encircle in some way. **Ri·mmed** *a.* having a r. of a specified form, colour, etc.; having or furnished with a r.

Rim, *sb.*[2] Now *dial.* [OE. *reoma* (*reama*), = MDu. *rieme* (Du. *riem*) RIEM.] †1. A membrane, pellicle, caul -1601. **2.** *R. of the belly* (*womb, paunch*, etc.), the peritoneum. Now *dial.* Also *ellipt.* 1565.

2. I will fetch thy rymme out at thy Throat, in droppes of Crimson blood SHAKS.

‖**Rima** (rəi·mă). 1835. [L., chink.] *Physiol.* Short for *rima glottidis*, the passage in the glottis between the vocal chords and the arytenoid cartilages. So †**Rime** *sb.*[2] -1657.

Rime (rəim), *sb.*[1] ME. [a. OF. *rime* fem., for earlier *ridme*, **ritme*, L. *rithmus, rythmus*, a. Gr. ῥυθμός RHYTHM.

In med.L. *rithmi* and *rithmici versus* were used to denote accentual in contrast to quantitative verse (*metra*). As similarity of the terminal sounds was a common feature of accentual verse, *rithmus* naturally came to have the sense of 'rime'.

About 1560 *rime* (*ryme*) was altered on classical models to *rithme, rythme, rhythm(e*. Soon after 1600, prob. from a desire to distinguish between 'rime' and 'rhythm', the intermediate forms *rhime, rhyme* came into use, and *rhyme* finally became the standard form (see RHYME *sb.*). From about 1870 the use of *rime* has been considerably revived.]

1. = RHYME *sb.* †**2.** = RHYTHM *sb.* 1, 4. -1677.

1. *Much Ado* v. ii. 37. Beautie making beautifull old r., In praise of Ladies dead, and louely Knights SHAKS. The Anglosaxon poets..generally used measures without r. 1774. The R. of the Ancyent Marinere COLERIDGE.

Comb.: **r.-letter**, the distinctive initial letter in a line of alliterative verse. Hence **Ri·meless** *a.* **Ri·mester**, a poetaster.

Rime (rəim), *sb.*[2] [OE. *hrīm*. Cf. OF. *rime, rimée*, which are of Teut. origin.] Hoar-frost; frozen mist. Also *dial.* a chill mist or fog.

Moonlight splendour of intensest r., With which frost paints the pines in winter time SHELLEY. *fig.* Tales that have the r. of age LONGF. Hence **Ri·me** *v.*[2] *trans.* to cover with hoar-frost. **Ri·my** *a.*

Rime (rəim), *v.*[1] ME. [ad. OF. *rimer*, f. *rime* RIME *sb.*[1] In the 17th c. the usual spelling became RHYME; see RIME *sb.*[1]] **1.** *intr.* To make rimes or verses; to compose riming verse; to versify *on, upon*. Cf. RHYME *v.* 1. **2.** *trans.* To recount or celebrate in verse or rime; to turn into, or compose in, riming verse ME. **b.** To cause (a word) to rime *with* (another); to use as a rime 1887. **3.** To bring by riming 1584. **4.** *intr.* To form a rime. Also *fig.*, to agree. 1450. **b.** To have riming endings 1660. **5.** To use rime 1602.

1. How vildely doth this Cynicke r.! SHAKS. **2.** He rimed history, ballads and legends 1887. **3.** These fellowes..that can ryme themselues into Ladyes fauours SHAKS. **5.** *Haml.* III. ii. 296. Hence **Ri·mer** *sb.*[1]

†**Ri·me-frost.** ME. = RIME *sb.*[2] -1626.

Rimer (rəi·məɹ), *sb.*[2] 1815. = REAMER.

Rimose (rəi·mǝus, rəimōu·s), *a.* 1726. [ad. L. *rimosus*, f. *rima*.] Full of, or having, fissures or chinks. Chiefly *Bot.* So **Ri·mous** *a.* 1709.

Rimple (ri·mp'l), *sb.* 1440. Now *dial.* [Corresp. in sense to (M)Du. and (M)LG. *rimpel*. See also RUMPLE *sb.*] **1.** A wrinkle. **2.** A ripple 1877. Hence **Ri·mple** *v. trans.* to wrinkle, pucker; to ripple. **Ri·mpled** *a.* (now *dial.* or *U.S.*), wrinkled, puckered; rippled.

Rind (rəind), *sb.*[1] [OE. *rind* = MDu. *rinde, rende, runde*, OS. *rinda*, OHG. *rinda, rinta*.] **1.** The bark of a tree or plant; sometimes, inner as contrasted with outer bark. Also with *a* and in pl. (now *rare*). **b.** *Bot.* False, as contrasted with true, bark 1857. †**2.** Coupled with *root* -1530. **3.** The peel or skin of fruits and vegetables. late ME. **4.** The outer crust, skin, or integument (esp. now of cheese, bacon) OE. †**b.** The verge or rim *of* something; the border *of* a country -1608. **5.** The skin of a person or animal. Now *dial.* 1513. †**b.** A membrane or pellicle; *esp.* the pia mater or the peritoneum -1693. **6.** *fig.* (chiefly from sense 1). The surface or external aspect *of* something OE.

3. Take three or four seville oranges.., and boil the rinds 1764. **5.** The Pilot..With fixed Anchor in his skaly r. Moors by his side MILT. **6.** To inspect beyond the Surface and the R. of Things SWIFT. Hence **Rind** *v. trans.* to strip the r. or bark from (a tree, etc.). **Ri·ndless** *a.* (*rare*), without r. or bark. **Ri·ndy** *a.* having a r. or hard skin.

Rind (rəind), *sb.*[2] [ME. *rynd*; cf. MDu. *rijn, rine*, MLG. *rîn, ryn*.] An iron fitting serving to support an upper millstone on the spindle.

Rinderpest (ri·ndəɹpest). 1865. [G., f. *rinder*, pl. of *rind* ox.] A virulent, infectious disease affecting ruminant animals, *esp.* oxen, characterized by fever, dysentery, and inflammation of the mucous membranes; cattle-plague.

Rindle (ri·nd'l). [OE. *rinnelle, rynele* fem., *rynel* masc., f. stem *rin-, run-*; see RUN *v.*] A small watercourse or stream; a runnel.

Ring (riŋ), *sb.*[1] [Com. Teut.: OE. *hring*:—pre-Teut. **krengho-*.] **I. 1.** A small circlet of (real or simulated) precious metal, frequently set with precious stones, or imitations of these, for wearing upon the finger either as an ornament or as a token (*esp.* of betrothal, marriage, or investiture), and sometimes for use as a seal. **b.** A metal circlet worn elsewhere than on the finger as an ornament OE. **2.** = MAIL *sb.*[1] 1. OE. **3.** A circle of metal, etc., of any dimension, employed as a means of attachment, suspension, compression, etc. OE. **b.** A circular knocker upon a door. Now *rare*. late ME. **c.** [a. LG. *ring*.] A measure of boards (= 240) or staves for casks (= 4 shocks) 1674. **4.** A circlet of metal suspended from a post which each of a number of riders endeavoured to carry off on the point of his lance 1513. **5. a.** One of the raised bands passing round the body of cannon as formerly made. Chiefly in combs., as *cornice-, reinforce-, trunnion-r.* 1610. **b.** A kind of gas-check used in a cannon. In full *Broadwell's ring.* 1868.

1. The manne shall geue vnto the womanne a r. *Bk. Com. Prayer.* As if they had King Gyges his enchanted R., they walk invisible 1679. **b.** They wore rings in their ears 1660. **4.** Phr. *To run* or *ride at the r.*

II. 1. The border, rim, or outer part of some circular object, *esp.* of a coin or a wheel OE. **2.** An object having the form of a circle; a circular fold, coin, or bend; a piece or part (of something) forming a circle. late ME. **b.** *Anat.* A structure of circular form; *esp.* one of the annular joints of the bodies of caterpillars and insects, or one of the cartilages of the trachea 1580. **c.** One of the concentric circular bands of wood constituting the yearly growth of a tree 1671. **d.** One of the raised circular marks at the base of the horns of oxen or cows, varying in number according to the animal's age 1725. **e.** *Bot.* = ANNULUS 3. 1796. **3. a.** A circular mark; also = FAIRY-RING 1626. **b.** A circle, or circular band, of light or colour 1648. **c.** One of the expanding circular ripples caused by something falling or being cast into still water 1821.

III. 1. A circle or circular group of persons OE. **b.** A number of things arranged in a circle 1587. **2.** A combination of interested persons to monopolize and control a particular trade or market for their private advantage. Chiefly *U.S.* 1869. **b.** An organization which endeavours to control politics or local affairs in its own interest 1872.

2. The 'r.' is being succeeded by a more elaborate organization, known as the 'trust' G. B. SHAW. **b.** The war was the creation of the Whig 'r.' 1882.

IV. 1. An enclosed circular space within which some sport, performance, or exhibition (*esp.* of riding or racing) takes place ME. †**b.** A circular course in Hyde Park, used for riding and driving -1848. **2. a.** A space, originally defined by a circle of bystanders, for a prize-fight or a wrestling-match; often in phr. *to make a r.* Hence *the r.*, pugilism as an institution or profession; also *collect.* those interested in boxing. 1700. **b.** An enclosed space in a racing-ground frequented by bookmakers; also *collect.* the bookmaking profession 1859. **c.** An enclosed or clear space in an auction-mart, used for the display of live-stock, etc. 1890. **3.** A circular or spiral orbit or course 1589.

1. The sawdust r. of a bankrupt circus 1883. **3.** First, wide around,..in airy rings they rove THOMSON.

Comb.: **r.-armour**, armour composed of metal rings, r.-mail; **-bolt** *Naut.*, a bolt with an eye at one end to which a r. is attached; **-boot**, a rubber ring placed on a horse's fetlock to prevent interfering; **-bored** *a.* of a gun-barrel, bored roughly, so as to leave the metal in rings; **-canal**, a circular canal forming part of the structure of cœlenterates and of echinoderms; †**-carrier**, a go-between; **-cartilage**, the cricoid cartilage; **-craft**, skill in pugilism; **r. dropper**, a sharper who pretends to have found a dropped r. and offers to sell it; **-farm**, a farm enclosed by a r.-fence; **-joint**, a pipe-joint formed of circular flanges; **-mail** (see MAIL *sb.*[1] 2); **-master**, the manager of a circus performance; **-road**, a road encircling a town which acts as a by-pass road for traffic; **-shell, -shot**, a projectile in which the body is made of iron rings; a segment-shell; **-stopper** = *cathead-stopper*; **-time**, a time of giving or exchanging rings (*nonce-use*); **-wall**, a wall completely surrounding a certain area; *techn.* the inner lining of a furnace; **-work**, (*a*) a circular entrenchment; (*b*) work executed with rings; (*c*) performance in the boxing-r.

b. In names of birds, reptiles, fishes, etc., as **r.-bill**, the ring-necked duck or moon-bill; **-bird**, the reed-bunting (*local*); **r. blackbird, -ouzel**, a bird (*Turdus torquatus*, closely allied to the blackbird) having a white r. or bar on the breast; **-snake**, (*a*) the common European grass- or ringed snake (*Tropidonotus natrix*); (*b*) *U.S.*, a snake of the genus *Diadophis*, esp. *D. punctatus*; **-thrush** = *r.-ouzel*.

Ring (riŋ), *sb.*[2] 1549. [f. RING *v.*[2]] **1.** A set or peal *of* (church) bells. **2.** A ringing sound or noise 1622. **b.** A ringing tone or quality in the voice, or in a (recited) composition 1859. **c.** The resonance of a coin or glass vessel by which its genuineness or wholeness is tested 1855. **3.** An act of ringing; a pull *at* a bell; the sound thus produced 1727.

1. Here is also a very fine r. of six bells, and they mighty tuneable PEPYS. **2.** He must come to the R. of the Midnight Bell 1706. **b.** There was a r. of scorn in the last words GEO. ELIOT. **c.** *transf.* There does not seem always the right r. about him 1886.

Ring (riŋ), *v.*[1] Pa. t. and pple. **ringed.** late ME. [f. RING *sb.*[1] Cf. OE. *ymbhringan*, to surround.] **I. 1.** *intr.* To make a circle or ring; to gather in a ring *about* or *round* (a person). Now *rare*. **b.** Of a hawk, etc.: To rise spirally in flight 1879. **c.** Of a stag, fox, or hare: To take a circular course when hunted 1882. **2.** *trans.* To surround, encompass, encircle. Also with *round, about*. 1590. **b.** To hem in (cattle or game) by riding or beating in a circle round them; to beat or stalk round (a stretch of country) for game 1835. **c.** To hem or shut *in* 1871. **3.** To place or fasten round something in the form of a ring 1799.

2. A girdle of mist will r. the slopes 1884. Ringed about with cannon smoke and thunder STEVENSON.

II. 1. To adorn (the fingers or nose) with a ring or rings (*rare*) 1552. **2.** To put a ring in the nose of (swine or cattle) to restrain them from rooting or violence; also, to place a ring round the leg of (fowls, pigeons, etc.) as a means of identification 1519. **3.** To deprive (trees) of a ring of bark, in order to check too luxuriant growth and bring into bearing, or to kill them 1800. **4.** To cut into annular slices or rounds 1839.

1. I will..r. these fingers with thy houshold wormes SHAKS. **4.** The onions, being cut in slices and ringed, are put into the frying-pan 1839.

Ring (riŋ), *v.*[2] Pa. t. **rang, rung.** Pa. pple. **rung.** [OE. *hringan*, perh. imitative.] **I.** *intr.* **1.** To give out the clear or resonant sound characteristic of certain hard metals when struck with, or striking upon, something hard. Also of a trumpet, etc.: To sound loudly. **b.** *fig.* To impress one as having a certain (genuine or false) character 1611. **2.** Of bells: To give forth a clear metallic note under the impact of the hammer or clapper ME. **b.** To convey a summons *to* service, prayers, church, etc. 1509. **3.** Of places: To resound, re-echo, with some sound or noise ME. **b.** To be filled with talk or report *of*, to resound *with* the report or fame of, a thing, event, or person. Also with *that* and clause. 1608. **4.** Of a sound: To be loud or resonant; to resound, re-echo. Also with *out*. late ME. **5.** Of the ears: To be affected by a sensation similar to that produced by the sound of bells, etc.; to tingle, hum, or be filled *with* a sound. late ME.

1. The harp..Which to the whistling wild responsive rung 1768. **b.** But Crassus, and this Caesar here r. hollow B. JONS. 2. The great bell rung out for Earle of C. C. Coll., fellow WOOD. **b.** Though the day be never so longe, At last the belles ringeth to evensonge 1509. 3. The arched cloister..Rang to the warrior's clanking stride SCOTT. **b.** The world should r. of him TENNYSON. 4. *fig.* Fairfax, whose name in armes through Europe rings MILT. Phr. *To r. in one's ears, fancy, heart*, to haunt the memory. 5. The ears r. with unusual sounds 1822.

II. *trans.* 1. To cause (a bell) to give forth sound. Also *absol.* OE. 2. To summon *to* (divine service, church, etc.) by means of a bell. late ME. 3. With cogn. obj.: To sound forth (a peal, knell, etc.); to perform upon bells ME. 4. To announce or proclaim (an hour, time, etc.) by sound of bells OE. 5. To usher *in* or *out* with the sound of bells; to bring or convey in this manner 1554. **b.** To summon (a person) by ringing a bell. Also with *down, in, up*, etc. **c.** To direct (a theatre-curtain) to be drawn *up* or let *down* by causing a bell to ring. Also *absol.* 1836. **d.** *To r. off*, to give signal by a bell for the severance of communication upon a telephone 1888. 6. To cause to give out a ringing sound; to make to resound. late ME. **b.** To test (coin, etc.) by making it ring 1702. 7. To utter sonorously; to proclaim aloud; to re-echo. Also with *out.* late ME. **b.** To cause to resound, din, *in* one's ears 1657.

1. *fig.* Fooles can not holde hir tunge; A fooles belle is sone runge CHAUCER. The ringers rang with a will TENNYSON. *To r. up*, to raise (a bell) directly over the beam and r. it in that position. 2. Phr. *To r. (all) in*, to give the final peal before the service begins. 3. Sea-Nimphs hourly r. his knell SHAKS. Phr. *To r. the changes*: see CHANGE *sb.* 7 b. 4. *transf.* Ere the first Cock his Mattin rings MILT. 5. **b.** *To r. up*, to communicate with (a person) by telephone; also *absol.* **c.** The curtain had to be rung down before the play was ended 1887. 6. **b.** Debating about the genuineness of a coin without ringing it RUSKIN. 7. **b.** Persecution was every day rung in our Ears SWIFT. Hence **Ri·nging** *vbl. sb.* the action of the vb.; *ringing engine*, a form of pile-driver, worked by men pulling at ropes after the manner of bell-ringers. **Ri·nging-ly** *adv.*, **-ness.**

Ri·ng-bark, *v.* 1887. [f. RING *v.*[1] II. 3.] **a.** *intr.* To remove rings of bark from trees, in order to kill them. **b.** *trans.* To bark (trees) in this way.

Ri·ng-bone. Also **ringbone, ring bone.** 1523. [f. RING *sb.*[1]] 1. A deposit of bony matter on the pastern-bones of a horse. 2. The growth of such bony matter, as a specific disease of horses 1594. Hence **Ri·ng-boned** *a.*

Ri·ng-dove. 1538. [f. RING *sb.*[1]] 1. The wood-pigeon, cushat, or queest (*Columba palumbus*); also called *ring-pigeon.* 2. The Collared Turtle, *Columba risonia* 1841.

Ringed (riŋd), *ppl. a.* OE. [f. RING *sb.*[1] or *v.*[1]] 1. Of armour: made of rings (*rare*). 2. Of persons: Wearing a ring or rings; also, wedded with a ring. late ME. **b.** Of the fingers, etc.: Provided or adorned with a ring or rings 1599. 3. Marked or encircled by a ring or rings; surrounded by a circular band or bands, etc. 1513. **b.** Deprived of a ring of bark 1820. 4. Having, put into, the form of a ring 1593. **b.** *Zool.* Composed of rings; annulated 1840.

2. I was born of a true man and a ring'd wife TENNYSON. 3. **R. seal**, *Phoca hispida*; **R. snake** = *ring snake* (see RING *sb.*[1]).

Ringent (ri·ndʒěnt), *a.* 1760. [ad. L. *ringent-, ringere* to gape, grin.] Gaping or grinning; esp. *Bot.* applied to a labiate corolla having the lips widely opened.

Ringer[1] (ri·ŋəɹ). 1858. [f. RING *sb.*[1] or *v.*[1] + -ER.[1]] 1. *Quoits.* A quoit so thrown that it encloses the pin; a throw of this kind 1863. 2. *Mining.* A crow-bar 1858. 3. An animal which runs in a ring when hunted 1891.

Ringer[2] (ri·ŋəɹ). ME. [f. RING *v.*[2] + -ER[1].] One who rings; *esp.* a bell- or change-ringer.

Ri·ng-fence, *sb.* 1769. [f. RING *sb.*[1]] A fence completely enclosing an estate, farm, or piece of ground. Often in fig. phr. Hence **Ri·ng-fence** *v. trans.* to enclose with a ring-fence.

Ri·ng-fi·nger. OE. [RING *sb.*[1]] The third finger of the hand, *esp.* of the left hand.

Ri·nglea·der. 1503. [f. obs. phr. *to lead the ring* to be foremost or first.] 1. One who takes a leading part among a number of persons whose character or conduct is reprehensible; *esp.* a chief instigator or organizer of a mutiny, tumult, etc. †2. In good or neutral sense: A leader or head –1668.

1. He had been the r. in everything wicked for years 1867.

Ringlet (ri·ŋlět). 1555. [f. RING *sb.*[1] + -LET.] 1. A small ring. 2. A circular dance or course; a circle of dancers; a fairy-ring 1590. **b.** An annular appearance, marking, formation, part, or piece 1755. 3. A curled lock or tress of hair 1667. 4. *Entom.* One of the satyrid butterflies, *Hyparchia hyperanthus* 1812.

2. Through the mystic ringlets of the vale We flash our faery feet in gamesome prank COLERIDGE. 3. Shee..Her unadorned golden tresses wore Disheveld, but in wanton ringlets wav'd MILT. Hence **Ri·nglet(t)ed** *a.* (of the hair) curled; wearing the hair in ringlets. **Ri·nglet(t)y** *a.* tending to curl in ringlets.

Ri·ng-man. 1483. [f. RING *sb.*[1]] 1. The ring-finger. Now *dial.* 2. A bookmaker 1857.

Ri·ng-neck. 1817. **A.** *adj.* = next. **B.** *sb.* A ring-necked plover or duck 1876.

Ri·ng-necked, *a.* 1852. [RING *sb.*[1]] Having the neck ringed or marked with a band or bands of colour. In various names of birds and animals, as *r. barnacle, duck, loon, pheasant*, etc.

Ri·ngster. *U.S.* 1881. A member of a RING (*sb.*[1] III. 2, b).

Ri·ng-straked, *a.* 1611. [f. RING *sb.*[1]] Having bands of colour round the body.

Ri·ngtail, ri·ng-tail, *sb.* and *a.* 1538. [f. RING *sb.*[1]] **A.** *sb.* 1. **a.** The female of the hen-harrier. (Formerly regarded by many as a distinct species.) **b.** The golden eagle before its third year. Usu. *ring-tail eagle* 1776. 2. *Naut.* 'A small sail shaped like a jib, set occasionally in light winds; it is hoisted on the outer end of the main or spanker gaff' (Young). Freq. *attrib.* with *boom, sail*, etc. 1769. **B.** as *adj.* = next 2, 3. Also *absol.* 1771.

Ri·ng-tailed, *a.* 1725. [Cf. prec.] 1. *R. harrier* = prec. 1 a. *R. eagle* = prec. 1 b. 2. Having the tail ringed with alternating colours 1729. 3. Having the tail curled at the end, *spec.* applied to certain phalangers 1835.

Ringworm (ri·ŋwɒɹm). late ME. [f. RING *sb.*[1]] A skin-disease usu. manifesting itself in circular patches, and frequently affecting the scalp in childhood; tinea.

Tinea sycosis, or r. affecting the beard, and *tinea circinata*, or r. affecting the body 1887. *fig.* I have not inke enough to cure all the..Ring-wormes of the State 1647.

Rink (riŋk), *sb.* late ME. [app. a. OF. *renc* row, rank.] †1. The space of ground within which a combat, joust, or race takes place; a course marked out for riding or running in –1637. 2. A stretch of ice measured off or marked out for the game of curling 1787. **b.** One of the sets of players into which the sides in a curling, quoiting, or bowls match are divided 1823. 3. A sheet of ice for skating, sometimes under cover; also, a smooth floor, usu. of asphalt or wood, for roller-skating 1867. Hence **Rink** *v. intr.* to skate on a r.; **ri·nking** *vbl. sb.* the act or practice of skating on a r.

Rinse (rins), *sb.* Also **rinze, rince.** 1837. [f. RINSE *v.*] A rinsing; a final application of water to remove impurities; *colloq.* a wash. **b.** A wash to cleanse the mouth 1898.

Rinse (rins), *v.* Also **rince.** ME. [a. F. *rincer*, of unkn. origin.] 1. *trans.* To wash out (a cup, etc.) by pouring in water or other liquid and emptying it out again (usu. after swilling or stirring it about). **b.** To clean (the mouth, teeth, etc.) by taking a mouthful of water and emitting it again 1565. 2. To dip (a thing) into, agitate in, or drench with water in order to remove impurities. late ME. **b.** To treat (clothes or textile fabrics) in this way; *spec.* to put through clean water in order to remove the soap used in washing 1440. 3. To remove, take *away*, clear *out*, by rinsing 1565.

1. Leave the Dregs of..Liquors in the Bottle: To rince them is but Loss of Time SWIFT. 3. That whole flood could not wash or rinch away that one spot of his atheisme 1607. Hence **Ri·nser** (*rare*). **Ri·nsing** *vbl. sb.* the action of the vb.; *pl.* the liquid or liquor with which anything has been rinsed out.

Riot (rəi·ət), *sb.* ME. [a. OF. *riote, riot* debate, dispute, quarrel; origin obscure.] 1. Wanton, loose, or wasteful living; debauchery, dissipation, extravagance. Now *rare.* **b.** Unrestrained revelry, mirth, or noise 1728. 2. An instance or course of loose living; a noisy feast or wanton revel; a disturbance arising from this ME. **b.** A vivid display *of* (colour) 1894. 3. *Hunting.* The action, on the part of a hound, of following the scent of some animal other than that which he is intended to hunt. Also in phr. *to hunt* or *run r.* late ME. 4. Violence, strife, disorder, tumult, *esp.* on the part of the populace. late ME. **b.** A violent disturbance of the peace by an assembly or body of persons; an outbreak of active lawlessness or disorder among the populace. late ME.

1. All now was turn'd to jollitie and game, to luxurie and r., feast and dance MILT. 3. *To run r.* (in fig. use), to act without restraint or control; to disregard all limitations; to grow luxuriantly or wildly, etc. 4. Every species of r. and disorder *Junius Lett.*

Riot Act, the Act (1 Geo. I, st. 2, c. 5) providing that if twelve or more persons unlawfully or riotously assemble and refuse to disperse within an hour after the reading of a specified portion of it by a competent authority, they shall be considered as felons; also *jocular* in phr. *to read the Riot Act*; **r. call** *U.S.* a message for means to deal with a riot.

Riot (rəi·ət), *v.* late ME. [a. OF. *rioter*, related to *riote* RIOT *sb.*] I. 1. *intr.* To live in a wanton, dissipated, or unrestrained manner; to revel; to indulge to excess *in* something. **b.** To take great delight or pleasure *in* something 1741. 2. *trans.* To spend or waste (money, etc.) in riotous living; to pass (time) in riot or luxury. Const. *away* or *out.* 1597.

1. *Ant. & Cl.* II. ii. 72. 2. Whilst wee..Ryot away, for nought, whole Prouinces DANIEL.

II. 1. †**a.** To force (a person) by persistence or importunity; *to* do some action so, to prevent (a person) *from* doing something –1781. **b.** Of rioters: To attack (persons or property) 1886. 2. *intr.* To make a disturbance; to storm 1787.

1. This rattle..Mrs. Thrale most kindly kept up, by way of rioting me from thinking 1781. Hence **Ri·otry**, rioting, riotousness; also riotous persons.

Rioter (rəi·ətəɹ). late ME. [a. AF. *riotour* (see RIOT *v.* and -OUR), with later change of suffix.] 1. A dissolute person; a reveller. Now *arch.* 2. One who takes part in a riot or rising against constituted authority 1460.

Riotous (rəi·ətəs), *a.* late ME. [a. OF., f. *riot(e* RIOT *sb.*] 1. Of persons: Given to wantonness, revelry, or dissolute life; prodigal, extravagant. Now *rare.* 2. Of life, conduct, etc.: Wanton, dissolute, extravagant; marked by excessive revelry. late ME. **b.** Noisy, tumultuous, unrestrained 1508. 3. Marked by rioting or disturbance of the peace; taking part in or inciting to a riot or tumult; turbulent. late ME.

1. Drunkards and riotus persons they [Persians] hate 1613. 2. Dancing is always the last act of r. banquets 1755. 3. Such a r. act; to wit when hee came to dragg the five Members out of the House MILT. Hence **Ri·otous-ly** *adv.*, **-ness.**

Rip, *sb.*[1] *dial.* ME. [a. ON. *hrip.*] A wicker basket or pannier, esp. for holding fish.

Rip, *sb.*[2] 1711. [f. RIP *v.*] 1. A rent made by ripping; a laceration, tear. 2. *ellipt.* A rip-saw 1846.

Rip, *sb.*[3] 1775. [app. related to RIP *v.*] 1. A disturbed state of the sea, resembling breakers; an overfall. 2. A stretch of broken water in a river 1857.

Rip, *sb.*[4] 1778. [perh. a later form of REP[2].] 1. An inferior, worthless, or worn-out horse. 2. A worthless, dissolute fellow; a rake 1797. **b.** Applied to a woman (*rare*) 1791. 3. A person or thing of little or no value 1815.

Rip (rip), *v.* 1477. [Origin obsc.] I. 1. *trans.* To cut, pull, or tear (anything) away from something else in a vigorous manner. 2. To cut or tear apart in a rough or slashing fashion. Also with compl. as *asunder, open.* 1530. **b.** To split or cleave (timber); to saw in the direction of the grain 1532. **c.** To take out or cut away by quarrying, etc.; to divest or clear of surface-soil 1807. 3. To slash *up* with a sharp instrument; to tear or open *up* with violence; to open *up* (wounds or sores) again in a harsh manner 1565. 4. *fig.* **a.** To open up, lay bare, disclose, make known; now chiefly, to open *up*, rake *up*, bring *up* again into notice or discussion (esp. something unpleasant or discreditable) 1549.

1. Macduffe was from his Mothers womb Vntimely ript SHAKS. 2. Sails ript, seams op'ning wide, and compass lost COWPER. 3. He..ripp'd up his Wastcoat to feel if he was not wounded DE FOE. It 's little my part to r. up old sores 1830. 4. To r. up old grievances HAZLITT.

II. 1. *intr.* To split, tear, part asunder 1840. 2. *dial.* To use strong language; to swear 1772. b. To break *out* angrily 1856. c. *trans.* with *out.* To utter with violence 1828. 3. To rush along recklessly. Chiefly in phr. *let her r.* Orig. *U.S.* 1859.

2. c. He ripped out a horrid blasphemous curse 1889. 3. Let him r.,..we can turn him out when his time is up 1877.

Riparial (rəipē·riăl), *a.* 1870. [f. L. *riparius* (f. *ripa*) + -AL 1.] 1. = next A. 2. *Zool.* Living upon, or frequenting, the banks of streams, ponds, etc. 1891. So **Ripa·rious** *a.* (*rare*) growing or living on the borders of rivers, etc. 1656.

Riparian (rəipē·riăn), *a.* and *sb.* 1849. [f. as prec.] A. *adj.* Of, pertaining to, or situated on, the banks of a river; riverine. B. *sb.* A riparian proprietor 1884.

Ripe (rəip), *sb.* Now *rare.* 1470. [ad. L. *ripa* bank.] The bank of a river; the seashore.

Ripe (rəip), *a.* [OE. *rīpe* = OS. *rīpi*, OHG. *rīfi, rīfe* (G. *reif*); perh. related to REAP *v.*] 1. Of grain, fruits, etc.: Ready for reaping or gathering; ready for eating or for use as seed. b. Resembling ripe fruit; red and full 1590. 2. Of birds and animals: Fully fledged or developed; *esp.* come to a fit condition for being killed and used as food ME. b. Of persons: Fully developed in body or mind; mature, †marriageable. Now *rare.* late ME. c. Ready for birth (*rare*) 1565. d. Of fish, etc.: Ready to lay eggs or spawn 1861. 3. a. Of liquor: Ready for use; fully matured, mellow. late ME. b. Of suppurations, etc.: Ready to lance or break; fit for curative treatment. late ME. c. Of natural products, etc.: Arrived at a mature or perfect state 1635. 4. Of persons: Of mature judgement or knowledge; fully informed; thoroughly qualified by study and thought. So of the mind, judgement, etc. ME. 5. Properly considered or deliberated; matured by reflection or study ME. 6. Of age: a. Characterized by full development of the physical or mental powers. late ME. b. Well advanced in years. late ME. 7. Fully prepared, ready, or able, *to* do or undergo something. late ME. b. Ready or fit *for* some end or purpose 1592. c. Quite prepared *for* action of some kind, *esp.* mischief, revolt, etc. 1599. 8. Ready for action, execution, or use; arrived at the fitting stage or time for some purpose 1601. b. Of time: Sufficiently advanced 1596.

1. I gathered the ears a little before they were r. 1676. *Provb.* All the glorie of man..is as the flower of the fielde, soone r., soone rotten 1569. b. How r. in show, Thy lips those kissing cherries, tempting grow! SHAKS. 2. b. R. men, or blooming in life's spring,..Stood by their Sire WORDSW. 3. c. With riper beams when Phœbus warms the day POPE. 4. He was a Scholler, and a r., and good one SHAKS. As sound in judgement as r. in experience 1615. 5. So wise and rype wordes hadde she CHAUCER. 6. Some man of rype yeares and counsell 1560. b. The r. age of eighty-five 1873. 7. The cause is then r. to be set down for hearing 1768. c. The mob were only too r. for a tumult 1879. 8. A lie R. at their fingers' ends 1789. Hence **Ri·pe·ly** *adv.*, **-ness.**

Ripe (rəip), *v.* [OE. *rīpian*, f. *rīpe* RIPE *a.* Now usu. RIPEN.] 1. *intr.* To grow or become ripe. 2. *trans.* To make ripe. late ME. †3. *Med.* To bring to a head; to mature -1614.

Ripen (rəi·p'n), *v.* 1561. [f. RIPE *a.* + -EN [5].] 1. *intr.* To grow ripe; to come to maturity. b. *fig.* To develop *into* (or *towards*) something 1606. 2. *Med.* To come to a head; to maturate 1704. 3. Of natural products, etc.: To reach the proper condition or stage for being utilized 1756. 4. *trans.* To make ripe; to bring to maturity or to the proper condition for being used 1565. 5. To develop to a mature state or condition; to bring to perfection 1570. 6. *Med.* To bring to a head 1599.

1. All its allotted length of days, The flower ripens in its place TENNYSON. b. The acquaintance had ripened into friendship 1833. 4. The pleached bower, Where hony-suckles ripened by the sunne, Forbid the sunne to enter SHAKS. 5. Prosperity ripened the principle of decay GIBBON. Hence **Ri·pener,** one who, or that which, causes ripening; one who, or that which, comes to ripeness.

Ripidolite (rəipi·dǫləit). 1850. [f. Gr. ῥιπιδο-, ῥιπίς fan + -LITE.] *Min.* A green mineral resembling chlorite but crystallizing on the monoclinic system.

‖**Ripieno** (rĭpyē·no), *a.* and *sb.* 1724. [It., f. *ri-* RE- + *pieno* full.] *Mus.* 1. Supplementary, re-enforcing. b. *sb.* A supplementary player or instrument 1753. 2. *transf.* Serving to fill up; supernumerary 1811.

1. Handel's scores contain few bassoon parts, and those..mostly of a r. character 1879. Hence **Ripie·nist,** a performer who assists in the r. parts.

‖**Riposte** (ripōu·st), *sb.* Also **ripost.** 1707. [F., ad. It. *risposta* response, reply.] 1. *Fencing.* A quick thrust given after parrying a lunge; a return thrust. 2. *transf.* A counterstroke; an effective reply by word or act 1865.

‖**Riposte** (ripōu·st), *v.* Also **ripost.** 1707. [ad. F. *riposter*; see prec.] 1. *Fencing. intr.* To make a riposte. Also *trans.* with personal obj. 2. *transf.* To reply or retaliate 1851.

2. The Cardinal riposted by an interdict LANG.

Ripper (ri·pəɹ). 1611. [f. RIP *v.* + -ER 1.] 1. One who rips. Chiefly in techn. uses. 2. That which rips; esp. (*a*) a tool used in removing old slates; (*b*) a rip-saw 1793. 3. *slang.* A 'ripping' person or thing 1851.

Rippier (ri·piəɹ). Now *Hist.* Also **ripier.** late ME. [f. RIP *sb.*[1] + -(I)ER. In old statutes latinized *riparius*, as if f. *ripa.*] One who carries fish inland to sell.

Ri·pping, *ppl. a.* 1714. [f. RIP *v.* + -ING [2].] 1. That rips or tears; *fig.*, cutting. 2. *slang.* Excellent, splendid; rattling 1826. Hence **Ri·ppingly** *adv.* splendidly.

Ripple (ri·p'l), *sb.*[1] 1660. [= Fris. *ripel*, Du. *repel*, G. *riffel.*] An implement toothed like a comb, used in cleaning flax or hemp from the seeds. Also *attrib.*

Ripple (ri·p'l), *sb.*[2] 1755. [f. RIPPLE *v.*[3]] 1. a. *U.S.* A piece of shallow water in a river where rocks or sand-bars cause an obstruction; a shoal. 2. A light ruffling of the surface of water, such as is caused by a slight breeze; a wavelet 1798. b. *transf.* A mark, appearance, or movement resembling or suggestive of a ripple on water 1843. c. *ellipt.* A ripple-mark 1852. 3. A sound as of rippling water 1859. 4. = RIFFLE *sb.* 2. 1857.

2. If water be rippled, the side of every r. next to us reflects a piece of the sky RUSKIN. b. Her black hair waved..with a natural r. THACKERAY.

attrib. and *Comb.*: **r.-cloth,** a soft woollen material with a rippled surface used for making dressing-gowns, etc.; **-mark** (chiefly *Geol.*), a wavy surface, line, or ridge on sand, mud, or rock formed by the action of waves or the wind or both; so **r.-marked** *a.* Hence **Ri·pplet,** a small r.; a wavelet. **Ri·pply** *a.* marked or characterized by ripples.

Ripple (ri·p'l), *v.*[1] [ME. *ripelen*, to scratch, Du. *repelen*, G. *riffeln.*] 1. *trans.* To draw (flax or hemp) through a kind of comb in order to remove the seeds; to clean from seeds in this manner. 2. To remove or take *off* (the seeds) by this process 1480. Hence **Ri·ppler,** one who ripples flax; also, an instrument for rippling.

Ri·pple, *v.*[2] Now *n. dial.* late ME. [Cf. Norw. *ripla* to scratch.] 1. *trans.* To scratch slightly; to graze or ruffle. 2. To break up (ground) slightly 1764.

Ri·pple, *v.*[3] 1670. [Origin obsc.] I. *intr.* To have or present a ruffled surface; to form ripples. b. To flow in ripples 1769. c. Of sound: To flow in a sprightly manner 1879. 2. *trans.* To form little waves upon (the surface of water); to agitate lightly 1786. b. To mark with or as with ripples; to cause to undulate slightly 1860.

1. b. *transf.* Stone walls..fragrant with..violets that r. down their sides 1873. Hence **Ri·pplingly** *adv.*

Ri·pple-grass. *Sc.* and *U.S.* 1824. [f. RIPPLE *sb.*[2]] Rib-leaved plantain.

Rip-rap (ri·pˌræp), *sb.* 1580. [f. RAP *sb.*[1] or *v.*[1]] †1. An imitation of the sound caused by a succession of blows; hence, a sharp blow. 2. *U.S.* Loose stone thrown down in water or on a soft bottom to form a foundation for a breakwater or other work 1847. So **Ri·p-ra·p** *v. trans.* to found upon, or cover with, a deposit of loose stone.

Ri·p-saw, *sb.* 1846. [f. RIP *v.*] A saw used for cutting wood in the direction of the grain. Hence **Ri·p-saw** *v. trans.* to cut with a r.

Ripstone, erron. form of RIBSTONE.

Ripuarian (ripiuˌē·riăn), *a.* and *sb.* 1781. [f. med.L. *Ripuarius* (also *Ribuarius*); derivation from L. *ripa* is doubtful.] A. *adj* 1. The distinctive epithet of the ancient Franks living on the Rhine between the Moselle and Meuse 1839. 2. The distinctive epithet of the code of law observed by the Ripuarian Franks 1781. B. *sb. pl.* The Ripuarian Franks 1781. So **Ri·puary** *a.* = A 2.

Rise (rəiz), *sb.* late ME. [f. the vb.] I. †1. The act, on the part of a hare, of finally rising to return to its form. †2. a. A spring or bound upwards; *esp.* one made with the help of a run -1681. b. A start or aid towards rising in a leap; a place from which to rise or soar -1728. 3. The coming of the sun (moon, or planets) above the horizon; hence also, the region of sunrise, the east. (Now usu. *rising.*) 1599. 4. Upward movement; ascent; transference to a higher level 1573. b. Capacity for rising 1716. 5. Elevation in fortune or rank 1632. An occasion or means of rising (in fortune or rank) 1680. b. Upward course 1721. 6. *Angling.* The movement of a fish to the surface of the water to take a fly or bait; an instance of this 1651. 7. The act of rising from the dead, or *from* some condition 1738.

3. She..Lookt left and right to r. and set of day R. BRIDGES. *fig.* So spake our Morning Star then in his r. MILT. 4. Beyond Gosforth a steep r. is made 1872. 5. It was considered a r. in life 1866. b. The r. and fall of the Whig party 1888. 6. Phr. *To get, have,* or *take a r. out of* (a person), to raise a laugh at, by some form of pretence or dissimulation.

II. 1. A piece of rising ground; a hill 1639. 2. An upward slope or direction, *esp.* of strata, coal-beds, veins of ore, etc. 1698. b. *Mining.* An excavation or working on the up side of a shaft 1839. 3. The vertical height of a step, an arch, an inclined surface or object, etc., measured from the base or springing-line to the highest point 1663. 4. a. A flight *of* steps 1710. b. = RISER II. 1. 1711.

1. Distant cumuli,..hanging on the rises of the moorland RUSKIN. 4. b. The flat surface of a stair is called the tread, and the upright face is termed the r. 1879.

III. 1. An increase in height of the sea, streams, or water, by tides, floods, etc., or of a liquid in a vessel; the amount of this increase 1626. 2. *Mus.* An increase of pitch in a tone or voice 1626. 3. An increase in amount 1699. b. *colloq.* An advance in wages or salary 1836. 4. An increase in the value or price *of* a thing 1691.

1. *transf.* The r. And long roll of the Hexameter TENNYSON. 3. A small r. in the annual payment 1817. 4. Phr. *On the r.*, becoming more valuable or dearer.

IV. 1. An origin or source; a beginning; a start. Freq. in phr. *to have* or *take one's r.* 1630. †2. An occasion; a ground or basis -1820. b. *To give r. to*, to occasion, bring about, cause 1705. 3. The act of coming into existence or notice 1656.

1. Nor Plague of unknown R. that kills In Darkness WESLEY. 3. The r. of a poet in their tribe 1777.

Rise (rəiz), *v.* Pa. t. **rose**; pa. pple. **risen.** [Com. Teut.; OE. *rīsan.*] I. *intr.* To get up from sitting, lying, or repose. 1. To get up from a sitting, kneeling, or lying posture; to get upon one's feet ME. b. Of animals, esp. game: To get up, issue, from lair or covert. late ME. c. Of a horse, etc.: To assume an erect position *on* the hind legs 1658. d. Of hair, etc.: To become erect or stiff. Also of things which have been bent: To resume an upright position. 1500. 2. To get up, or regain one's feet, after a fall ME. b. *fig.* To recover from a spiritual fall, or a state of sin ME. 3. To get up from sleep or rest ME. 4. To return to life; to come back from death or out of the grave. Also with *up.* ME. 5. To fall or set *upon*, to take hostile steps or measures *against* OE. b. To take up arms, make insurrection *against* (†*on, upon*); to rebel or revolt OE. 6. a. *Mil.* To break up camp; to retire or draw off *from* (a siege) 1557. b. Of a deliberative assembly, etc.: To adjourn, *esp.* for a vacation or recess 1663. †7. *To r. up to*, to show deference to (some authority, etc.) -1699.

1. Then shall the Priest r., the people still reuerently knelyng *Bk. Com. Prayer.* 2. Pride falls unpitied, never more to r. COWPER. 3. *Prov.* He that would thrive—must r. by five SCOTT. 4. Others were raised but He onely rose DONNE. *fig. Haml.* I. ii. 257. 5. O God the proud against me r. MILT. b. How vain Against th'Omnipotent to r. in Arms MILT. 6. b. There is an idea that Congress will r. about the middle of July 1790.

II. To ascend, mount up. 1. Of the heavenly bodies: To come above the horizon. Also *transf.* of daylight, darkness, ships, etc. ME. 2. a. Of smoke, vapour, or the like: To ascend into the air ME. b. Of trees, etc.: To grow, in respect of height 1601. 3. Of the sea, rivers, or water: To increase in height, esp. through the tides or floods; to swell ME. b. To attain to a greater height or size; to swell up; to puff out. late ME. c. Of dough or paste: To 'work' or swell under leaven; to expand under heat 1548. d. Of fluids: To reach a higher level in a containing vessel. Hence of a thermometer or barometer in respect of the mercury in the tube. 1658. e. Of liquids: To boil up 1839. 4. Of the heart or emotions: a. To be elated with joy or hope; to become more cheerful. late ME. b. To be stirred by excitement, *esp.* by indignation or passion ME. c. Of the stomach: To nauseate or keck (*at* something) 1508. 5. To extend directly upwards or away from the ground; to exhibit successive superposition of parts; to form an elevation from the level ME. b. To have an upward slant or curve; to slope or incline upwards 1634. 6. To move or be carried upwards; to ascend. late ME. b. Of birds: To take wing and ascend from the ground 1528. c. Of a horse in leaping 1839. 7. To come up to the surface of the ground or water. Also with *out.* 1530. b. Of a fish: To come to the surface of the water to take a fly, bait, etc. 1653.

1. The Moon Rising in clouded Majestie MILT. *fig.* Kings are like stars—they r. and set SHELLEY. 2. a. As Ev'ning Mist Ris'n from a River o're the marish glides MILT. 3. The sun was obscured.., and the sea was rising fast 1836. 4. a. His spirits rising as his toils increase COWPER. b. When I cease..to feel my soul r. against oppression, I shall think myself unworthy to be your son MACAULAY. 5. Along the lawn, where scattered hamlets rose GOLDSM. 6. 'Tis he, I ken the manner of his gate, He rises on the toe SHAKS. *fig.* Whose Fortunes shall r. higher, Cæsars or mine? SHAKS. b. Again their ravening eagle rose In anger TENNYSON. 7. A large alligator rose within three feet of the boat 1862.

III. To attain to a higher stage or degree. 1. To ascend to a higher level of action, feeling, thought, or expression; to become more elevated, striking, impressive, or intense. Also const. *to* action of some kind ME. 2. To advance in consequence, rank, influence, fortune, or social position; to attain *to* distinction or power; to come *into* estimation ME. 3. To increase in amount, number, or degree; to amount or reach *to* ME. b. To become dearer or more valuable; to increase *in* price, value, etc. 1513. 4. a. Of the wind: To increase in force; to become more vehement 1620. b. Of the voice, etc.: To increase in pitch or volume; to ascend in the musical scale 1548. c. To become more intense or strong; to increase in strength *to* a certain point 1593.

1. Thoughts and expressions in which he [Plato] rises to the highest level 1875. We do not r. to philanthropy all at once 1850. 2. Some r. by sinne, and some by vertue fall SHAKS. 3. His expenses, with his income, r. 1746. b. Sugar is ris', my boy THACKERAY. 4. a. The winds r., and the winter comes on POPE. b. His voice rising with his reasoning, so that it was very loud at last DICKENS. c. In the presence of danger the courage of the man rose to its full height 1874.

IV. To spring up, come into existence. 1. Of persons: To come upon the scene; to appear; to be born; to spring or issue *of* or *from* a person or family. Also with *up.* ME. 2. a. Of plants or trees: To spring up; to grow ME. b. Of blisters, etc.: To become prominent on the skin or surface. late ME. 3. To originate; to result or issue. Const. *of, from, out of.* ME. 4. To come to pass, come about, occur, happen, take place ME. 5. Of wind, etc.: To begin to blow or rage ME. b. Of sounds: To strike upon the ear, esp. in a loud manner ME. c. Of reports, rumours, etc.: To come into circulation ME. 6. Of a river: To have its spring or source. late ME. 7. To be built or reared 1570. 8. To come into being by growth or creation 1601. b. To come before the eye or mind 1712.

1. A holy Prophetesse, new risen vp SHAKS. 2. a. Sweet Plants that r. naturally ADDISON. 3. From study will no comforts r.? CRABBE. 4. Then rose a little feud betwixt the two TENNYSON. 5. a. The winds begin to r. And roar from yonder dropping day TENNYSON. 7. Beside the eternal Nile, The Pyramids have risen SHELLEY.

V. *trans.* 1. To raise (the dead) to life (*rare*) 1440. 2. To rouse or stir up; to start; to put up or flush (birds); to cause to rise 1500. b. *Angling.* To cause or induce (a fish) to come to the surface of the water 1850. 3. To increase; to make higher or dearer. Now *rare* exc. *dial.* 1605. 4. *Naut.* = RAISE *v.* III. 7 b. 1669. b. To raise; to lift up; to cause to ascend or mount up 1706. c. To promote (a person) in dignity or salary 1801. 5. To surmount, gain the top of (a hill or slope); to ascend. Chiefly *U.S.* 1808. 6. *colloq.* To raise or grow; to rear, bring up 1844.

2. b. I killed three salmon and rose many more 1867. 4. Since she had tacked, she had risen her hull out of the water 1842. 5. [We] discovered two horsemen rising the summit of a hill 1808. Hence **Ri·sen** (ri·z'n) *ppl. a.* that has risen, in the senses of the vb.

Riser (rəi·zəɹ). late ME. [f. RISE *v.* + -ER [1].] **I.** 1. One who rises up, *esp.* from bed 1440. †2. One who rises in revolt -1655. 3. A fish that rises to an angler's fly or bait 1867. **II.** 1. The upright part of a step; the vertical piece connecting two treads in a stair 1771. 2. *Mining.* An upthrow fault 1846. 3. *Founding.* An opening through a mould, into which metal rises as the mould fills 1875. 4. An electrical conductor or water-pipe passing from one floor of a building to another 1909.

Risible (ri·zĭb'l), *a.* and *sb.* 1557. [ad. late L. *risibilis*, f. *ris-, ridere*; see -IBLE.] **A.** *adj.* 1. Having the faculty or power of laughing; inclined or given to laughter. 2. Pertaining to, or used in, laughter 1747. 3. Capable of exciting laughter; laughable, ludicrous 1727.

1. He is the most r. misanthrope I ever met with SMOLLETT. 2. The Dutch negroes at Communipaw.. are famous for their r. powers 1809. 3. The jokes.. are extremely queer and r. 1789.

B *sb. pl.* The risible faculties or muscles. Chiefly *U.S.* 1785. Hence **Risibi·lity**, the faculty of laughing; laughter; a disposition to laugh; *pl.* the r. faculties (*U.S.*). **Ri·sibly** *adv.*

Rising (rəi·ziŋ), *vbl. sb.* ME. [f. RISE *v.*] In the senses of RISE *v.*; *esp.* 1. Resurrection. More fully *r. again, r. from the dead.* 2. The act of taking up arms or engaging in some hostile action; an insurrection or revolt. late ME.

Rising (rəi·ziŋ), *ppl. a.* 1548. [f. RISE *v.*] 1. Having an upward slope or lie; elevated above the surrounding or adjacent level. 2. That ascends or rises; mounting 1596. b. Of tides or water: Mounting, increasing in height 1697. 3. Of the heavenly bodies: Appearing or emergent above the horizon 1610. 4. Increasing in degree, force, or intensity 1603. b. Advancing in fortune, influence, or dignity 1631. c. Increasing in pitch 1674. 5. Coming into existence; developing, growing 1667.

2. A gradually r. glass foretells improving weather if the thermometer falls 1860. b. *fig.* He would stem the r. tide of revolution 1875. 4. Riseing winds the face of Ocean sweep GRAY. b. He was looked on at court as a r. man HUME. 5. The hopes of the r. generation JOHNSON.

Comb.: **r. diphthong**, one in which the stress falls on the second element; so *r. stress*; **r. front** (*Photogr.*), a camera front which can be elevated so as to reduce the foreground in a view; **r. main**, the vertical pipe of a pump; **r. rod**, part of the mechanism of a Cornish steam-engine.

Rising (rəi·ziŋ), *pr. pple.* 1610. [f. RISE *v.*] 1. *Her.* Preparing for flight; taking wing. 2. Of horses, and *transf.* of persons: Approaching (a given age) 1760. 3. *U.S.* a. In excess *of*, upwards *of* 1817. b. Fully as much as; rather more than 1848.

Risk, *sb.* 1661. [a. F. *risque*, ad. It *risco, rischio.*] 1. Hazard, danger; exposure to mischance or peril. Freq. const. *of.* 2. The chance or hazard of commercial loss, *spec.* in the case of insured property or goods 1719. 3. *Risk-money*, an allowance made to a cashier to cover accidental deficits 1849.

1. To cut my Elder Brother's Throat, without the Risque of being hanged for him 1696. Phr. *To run a* or *the r.* 2. An Insurance made on Risks in Foreign Ships 1755. Hence **Ri·skful** *a.* hazardous, uncertain.

Risk, *v.* Also †**risque.** 1687. [ad. F. *risquer*, ad. obs. It. *riscare, rischiare*, f. *risco* RISK *sb.*] 1. *trans.* To hazard, endanger; to expose to the chance of injury or loss. 2. To venture upon, take the chances of 1705.

1. To risque the certainty of little for the chance of much JOHNSON. 2. Nor had Emana Christos forces enough to r. a battle 1790. Hence **Ri·sker**, one who risks something.

Risky (ri·ski), *a.* 1826. [f. RISK *sb.* + -Y [1].] 1. Dangerous, hazardous, fraught with risk. 2. [After F. *risqué.*] Involving suggestions of or verging upon what is improper or indelicate 1881.

1. 'Twill be a r. job 1827. 2. 'R.' situation and indelicate suggestion W. S. GILBERT. Hence **Ri·skily** *adv.*, **-ness.**

‖**Risotto** (rīsǫ·to). 1884. [It.] A stew or broth made with rice, chicken, onions, etc.

‖**Risqué** (rĭske), *a.* 1883. [F., pa. pple. of *risquer* to RISK.] = RISKY *a.* 2.

Rissole (ri·sǒul). 1706. [a. F. *rissole*, OF. *ruissole*, perh. repr. pop. L. *russeola*, fem. of L. *russeolus* reddish.] An entrée made of meat or fish, chopped up and mixed with breadcrumbs, egg, etc., rolled into a ball or small thick cake and fried.

‖**Risus** (rəi·sǒs). 1693. [L., f. *ridere.*] *Path. R. sardonicus*, an involuntary or spasmodic grin consequent on some morbid condition.

Rite (rəit). ME. [ad. L. *ritus* ceremony.] 1. A formal procedure or act in a religious or other solemn observance. b. A custom or practice of a formal kind 1581. 2. The general or usual custom, habit, or practice of a country, people, class of persons, etc.; now *spec.* in religion or worship, e.g. *the Roman r.* late ME.

1. The rytes and sacramentes and the articles of our faith 1529. b. The rites of hospitality 1865. *transf.* Time goes on crutches, till Loue haue all his rites SHAKS. 2. The English observe the R. of the Church of England, prescribed in the Book of Common Prayer 1728. Hence **Ri·teless** *a.* destitute of r. or ceremony. †**Ri·tely** *adv.* in due form -1675.

‖**Ritornello** (ritǫɹne·lo). 1675. [It., dim. of *ritorno* RETURN *sb.*] *Mus.* An instrumental refrain, interlude, or prelude in a vocal work.

A Returnello by Martial Instruments 1675. Also in anglicized form **Ritorne·l.**

†‖**Ritra·tto.** 1722. [It.] A picture, portrait -1771.

‖**Ritter** (ri·təɹ). 1824. [G., var. of *reiter.*] A mounted warrior; a knight.

Ri·ttmaster. *rare.* 1648. [ad. G. *rittmeister*, f. *ritt* riding.] The captain of a troop of horse.

Ritual (ri·tiuăl), *a.* and *sb.* 1570. [ad. L. *ritualis*, neut. *rituale* (as. sb.), f. *ritus* RITE.] **A.** *adj.* 1. Pertaining or relating to, connected with, rites. 2. Of the nature of, forming, a rite or rites 1631.

1. The r. laws restrained the Jews from conversing familiarly with the heathens 1740. Phr. *R. choir*, that part of the church in which the choir-offices are performed. 2. R.-murder as a practice has been learnedly and thoroughly disproved 1896.

B. *sb.* 1. A prescribed order of performing religious or other devotional service 1649. b. A book containing the order, forms, or ceremonies, to be observed in the celebration of religious or other solemn service 1656. 2. *pl.* Ritual acts or observances 1656. 3. The performance of ritual acts 1867.

1. There was a..dignity in the Jewish r. 1772. 3. *attrib.* The appointment of the R. Commission 1882. **Ri·tualize** *v. intr.* to practice ritualism; *trans.* to convert into a r.; to bring over to ritualism. **Ri·tually** *adv.*

Ritualism (ri·tiuăliz'm). 1843. [f. RITUAL + -ISM.] The observance, practice, or study of religious rites; ritual observance (cf. next 2).

Ritualist (ri·tiuălist). 1657. [f. prec. + -IST.] 1. One versed in ritual; a student of liturgical rites and ceremonies. 2. One who advocates or practises the observance of religious rites. (In the 19th century applied *spec.* to the extreme High Church party in the Church of England.) 1677.

2. *attrib.* The whole extreme R. party is practically infallibilist PUSEY. Hence **Rituali·stic** *a.* of or per-

taining to, characteristic of, ritualists or ritualism; devoted to, or fond of ritual; -ally *adv.*

Rivage (rəi·vēdʒ). ME. [a. F., f. *rive*:—L. *ripa* bank.] 1. A coast, shore, or bank. Now *poet.* †2. Shore or river dues -1706.

1. The River full of Ships,..the r. full of sea-faring men 1658.

Rival (rəi·văl), *sb.* and *a.* 1577. [ad. L. *rivalis*, orig. one living on the opposite bank of a stream from another, f. *rivus* stream.] A. *sb.* 1. One who is in pursuit of the same object as another; one who strives to equal or outdo another in any respect. 2. One who, or that which, disputes distinction or renown with some other person or thing 1646.

1. The medical name for a r. is 'colleague' 1899. 2. The Spanish generals stood without rivals in their military skill 1874.

B. *adj.* Holding the position of a rival or rivals 1590.

The R. Chariots in the Race shall strive DRYDEN. Hence **Ri·valess**, a female r. or competitor. **Ri·valless** *a.* without a r.

Rival (rəi·văl), *v.* 1605. [f. RIVAL *sb.*] 1. *trans.* To enter into competition with; to strive to equal or excel (another) 1609. 2. *intr.* To act as a rival, be a competitor 1605.

1. These Beauties R. each other on all Occasions STEELE. *transf.* A crash which rivalled thunder 1860. 2. *Lear* I. i. 194.

Rivality (rəivæ·lĭti). 1582. [ad. L. *rivalitas*; see RIVAL *sb.* and -ITY.] = RIVALRY.

Rivalry (rəi·vălri). 1598. [f. RIVAL *sb.* + -RY.] The act of rivalling; competition, emulation.

Jealousies, rivalries, envy, intervene to separate others from our side SCOTT.

Rivalship (rəi·vălʃip). 1632. [f. RIVAL *sb.* + -SHIP.] The state or character of a rival; emulation, competition, rivalry.

Rive (rəiv), *v.* Pa. t. **rived**; pa. pple. **rived, riven.** ME. [a. ON. (Icel.) *rífa*, = OFris. *rīva.*] I. *trans.* 1. To tear apart or in pieces by pulling or tugging; to rend or lacerate with the hands, claws, etc.; to pull asunder. Also with various advs. and preps. 2. To sever, cleave, or divide, by means of a knife or weapon; †to pierce or thrust. late ME. 3. To rend or split by means of shock, violent impact, or pressure, etc.; to strike asunder ME. b. To split or cleave (wood, stone, etc.) by appropriate means. Also with *up*, *off*. 1440. 4. To rend (the heart, soul, etc.) with painful thoughts or feelings ME.

1. Thy loved one from thee riven BYRON. It went through the land,..riving sects 1863. I would r. the heart out of my breast 1873. 2. She rofe hir selfe to the herte CHAUCER. 3. Yonder blasted boughs by lightening riven 1768. 4. All thoughts to r. the heart are here, and all are vain HOUSMAN.

II. *absol.* 1. To commit spoliation or robbery; to take away *from*. Now *dial.* 1489. 2. To tear voraciously; to tug *at* something 1552.

2. Standing..roared and riven at by the wind DICKENS.

III. *intr.* 1. To part asunder; to cleave, split, crack, open up ME. b. Of wood or stone: To admit of splitting or cleaving 1699. 2. *fig.* a. Of the heart: To break or burst with sorrow. late ME. b. Denoting the effect of repletion, excessive laughter, etc. 1586.

1. b. The body of the willow tree rives into pales 1772. Hence **Rive** *sb.* a pull, tug, tear, crack.

Rivel (ri·v'l), *v.* Now *rare.* ME. [Cf. next.] 1. *intr.* To become wrinkled or shrivelled; to form wrinkles or small folds. 2. *trans.* To cause (the skin) to wrinkle or pucker; to shrivel *up* 1583.

2. A man with a sour rivell'd Face ADDISON. So †**Ri·vel** *sb.* a wrinkle or fold upon the skin (*esp.* of the face) or on the rind of a fruit.

Rivelled (ri·v'ld), *a.* Now *dial.* or *arch.* [OE. *rifelede*; etym. obsc.] 1. Wrinkled; full of wrinkles or small folds; corrugated, furrowed. 2. Shrunken, shrivelled, esp. by heat 1629. 3. Twisted, coiled (*rare*) 1594.

Riven (riv'n), *ppl. a.* ME. [Pa. pple. of RIVE *v.*] 1. Split, cloven, rent, torn asunder. †2. Ornamentally slashed (*rare*) -1548.

River (ri·vəɹ), *sb.*[1] ME. [a. OF. *rivere*, *riviere* (mod.F. *rivière*):—pop. L. **riparia*, f. *ripa* bank.] 1. A copious stream of water flowing in a channel towards the sea, a lake, or another stream. b. *transf.* A copious stream or flow *of* (something). late ME. c. Used euphemistically for the boundary between life and death 1790. †2. A stream, or the banks of a stream, as a place frequented for hawking. Hence, the sport of hawking. -1625. †3. The coast or littoral (of Genoa) -1693.

1. 'Tis like a rolling r., That murm'ring flows, and flows for ever! GAY. *fig.* The fruitfull Riuer in the Eye SHAKS. b. A Crimson riuer of warme blood SHAKS. c. And hast thou crost that unknown r., Life's dreary bound? BURNS.

attrib. and *Comb.* as *r.-bar*, *-basin*, *-channel*, etc.; *r.-boy*, *-rat*, etc.; **r.-bank**, the raised or sloping edge of a r.; the ground adjacent to a r.; **-bed**, the channel in which a r. flows; **-craft**, boats or vessels used in r. traffic. b. With the names of fishes and other animals (freq. contrasted with *sea-*), as **r. bass** (*U.S.*), the black bass, *Micropterus*; **r. chub** (*U.S.*), the horny-head or jerker, *Ceratichthys biguttatus*; **r. crab**, any crab which inhabits rivers, freshwater pools, or swamps; also, a crayfish; †**r. dragon**, the crocodile (with allusion to Pharaoh of Egypt); **r. duck**, any duck belonging to the *Anatinæ*; **r. eel**, the common freshwater eel; **r. herring** (*U.S.*), = ALEWIFE[2]; **r. hog**, (*a*) the capybara or water-hog; (*b*) a S. African hog of the genus *Potamochærus*; **r. jack (viper)**, a West African viper having a flat head and a somewhat long horn on either side of the snout; **r. limpet**, a pulmonate gasteropod of the genus *Ancylus*, found in rivers; **r. wolf**, †(*a*) the pike; (*b*) a kind of otter (*Lutra Brasiliensis*) found in South America. Hence †**Ri·ver** *v. trans.* to wash (wool or sheep) in a r. **Rivered** (ri·vəɹd) *ppl. a.* watered by rivers; furnished with a r. or rivers. **Ri·verling**, a small r., or stream. **Ri·very** *a.* (*rare*). †resembling a r.; abounding in streams or rivers; pertaining to a r.

River (rəi·vəɹ), *sb.*[2] 1483. [f. RIVE *v.* + -ER[1].] 1. One who rives, rends, or cleaves. †2. One who robs; a reaver -1568.

Riverain (ri·vərein), *a.* and *sb.* 1858. [a. F. *riverain*, f. *rivière* RIVER *sb.*[1]] A. *adj.* 1. Pertaining to a river or its vicinity. 2. = RIVERINE *a.* 1. B. *sb.* One who dwells on the banks or in the vicinity of a river 1867.

Ri·ver-drift. 1839. [f. RIVER *sb.*[1] + DRIFT *sb.*] *Geol.* Ancient alluvia of rivers in which early palæolithic remains are found.

Riveret (ri·veret). Now *rare* or *Obs.* 1538. [ad. OF. *riverete* (F. *rivièrette*); see RIVER *sb.*[1] and -ET.] 1. A small river or stream; a rivulet or brook. 2. *transf.* A surface vein 1603.

Ri·ver-fish. late ME. Any fish whose habitat is in a river or stream; a freshwater fish.

Ri·ver-god. 1661. [f. RIVER *sb.*[1] + GOD *sb.* 1.] *Mythol.* A tutelary deity supposed to dwell in and to preside over a river.

Ri·ver-horse. 1601. [f. RIVER *sb.*[1] + HORSE *sb.*] 1. The hippopotamus. 2. The water-kelpie; see KELPIE 1851.

Riverine (ri·vərəin), *a.* and *sb.* 1860. [f. RIVER *sb.*[1]] A. *adj.* 1. Situated or dwelling on the banks of a river; riparian. 2. Of or pertaining to a river 1871. B. *sb.* The banks or vicinity of a river 1895.

Ri·verside. Also **river-side.** ME. [f. RIVER *sb.*[1] + SIDE *sb.*] The side or bank of a river; the ground adjacent to, or stretching along, a river. Also *attrib.*, as *r. inn*, etc.

Ri·ver-wa:ter. Also **river water.** late ME. [f. RIVER *sb.*[1] + WATER *sb.*] Water in, forming, or obtained from, a river or stream.

Rivet (ri·vĕt), *sb.*[1] late ME. [a. OF., f. *river* to fix, clinch.] A short nail or bolt for fastening together metal plates or the like, the headless end of which is beaten out after insertion. b. A burr or clinch upon a nail (*rare*) 1634.

The Armourers accomplishing the Knights, With busie Hammers closing Riuets vp SHAKS.

Rivet (ri·vĕt), *sb.*[2] 1580. [Origin obsc.] Bearded or cone wheat. Also in pl. form *rivets*. Also used *attrib.* with *wheat*.

Rivet (ri·vĕt), *v.* late ME. [f. RIVET *sb.*[1]] 1. *trans.* To secure (a nail or bolt) by hammering or beating out the projecting end of the shank into a head or knob; to clinch. Also with *down*. 2. To secure or fasten with or as with rivets. Also with *down, in, together*. late ME. 3. *transf.* To fix, fasten, or secure firmly 1629. 4. To fix intently (the eye or the mind); to command or engross (the attention) 1602. b. To engross the attention of (a person) 1762.

2. Seize him,..R. him to the rock MRS. BROWNING. 3. I am wholly ignorant in what manner..his first attachment may have riveted his affections 1788. Things become riveted in the memory 1849. 4. Giue him needfull note, For I mine eyes will riuet to his Face SHAKS. Hence **Ri·veter**, one who rivets; a machine which rivets.

‖**Rivière** (rivyę̄r). 1880. [F.; see RIVER *sb.*[1]] A necklace of diamonds or other gems, esp. one consisting of more than one string.

†‖**Ri·vo.** 1592. [app. of Sp. origin.] An exclam. used at revels or drinking-bouts -1607.

Rivose (rəi·vōᵘs, ri-), *a.* 1826. [ad. late L. *rivosus*, f. *rivus* stream.] *Entom.* Applied to somewhat sinuate furrows which do not run in a parallel direction.

Rivulet (ri·viŭlĕt). 1587. [perh. ad. It. *rivoletto*, dim. of *rivolo*, dim. of *rivo*:—L. *rivus* stream; see -ET.] A small stream or river; a streamlet.

By Fountain or by shadie R. He sought them both MILT. *transf.* The rivulets of intelligence which are continually trickling among us JOHNSON.

Rix-dollar (ri·ksdǫləɹ). Now *Hist.* 1598. [ad. older Du. *rijcksdaler* = Sw. *riksdaler*, G. *reichsthaler*.] A silver coin and money of account, current *c* 1600–1850 in various European countries and in their commerce with the East; the value varied from about 4*s.* 6*d.* to 2*s.* 3*d.*

Ri·zzar, *v. Sc.* 1818. [ad. obs. F. *ressorer*, f. *re-* RE- + *sorer* to dry, or make red; see SORE *a.*] *trans.* To dry or parch (esp. haddocks) in the sun. So **Ri·zzared** *ppl. a.*

Roach (rōᵘtʃ), *sb.*[1] ME. [a. OF. *roche*, *roce*, also *roque*, *rocque*; origin unkn.] A small freshwater fish (*Leuciscus rutilus*) of the Carp family, common in the rivers of northern Europe. *Blue r.* = AZURINE. In *U.S.*, also applied to various small fishes resembling, or mistaken for, the roach. Also *attrib.*, as *r.-backed*, etc.

Phr. *As sound as a r.* = F. *sain comme un gardon.*

Roach (rōᵘtʃ), *sb.*[2] 1794. [Origin unkn.] *Naut.* 'An upward curve cut in the foot of a square sail'.

Roach, *sb.*[3] 1836. Abbrev. of COCKROACH.

Roach (rōᵘtʃ), *v.* 1848. [f. ROACH *sb.*[2]] 1. *trans.* To cut (a sail) with a roach 1851. 2. *U.S.* To clip or trim (a person's hair or horse's mane) so that it stands on end 1833.

Road (rōᵘd), *sb.* [OE. *rád*, f. pret. stem of *rídan* to ride.] †1. The act of riding on horseback; also, a spell of riding; a journey on horseback -1613. †2. *spec.* A hostile incursion by mounted men; a foray, raid -1665. 3. A sheltered piece of water near the shore where vessels may lie at anchor in safety; a roadstead. Usually *pl.* ME. 4. An ordinary line of communication between different places, used by horses, travellers on foot, or vehicles 1596. b. *U.S.* A railroad or railway 1837. 5. Any path, way, or (material) course 1602. b. *fig.* A way or course, esp. *to* some end 1599. 6. A way or direction taken or pursued by a person or thing; a course followed in a journey 1612. 7. The usual course, way, or practice. In phr. *out of the r. of.* 1608.

1. *Hen. VIII*, IV. ii. 17. 2. Borderers, whan they make rodes into Scotlande 1523. 3. The Towne Gravesend is a knowne Roade 1617. Phr. †*At r.*, riding at anchor. 4. The most villanous house in al London rode SHAKS. Phr. *On, upon, the r.*, travelling, journeying, upon or during a journey, etc.; on tour. *To take the r.*, to set out. *The r.*, the highway; *to go upon, take to, the r.*, to become a highwayman; *gentleman, knight of the r.*, a highwayman (now *arch.*). *To give* (a person) *the r.*, to allow one to pass. *To take the r. of*, to take precedence of. *The rule of the r.*, the fixed custom which regulates the side to be taken by vehicles, etc. (or *transf.* by vessels) in progressing or passing each other. b. A prominent station on the Central Pacific r. 1872. 5. Where Silver Swans sail down the Wat'ry Rode DRYDEN. b. Precipitating themselves in the r. to ruin 1783. Phr. *Royal r.*, a smooth or easy way. 6. Phr. *Out of the* (or *one's*) *r.*, out of the way, in various senses (chiefly *Sc.* and *n. dial.*). *In one's* (or *the*) *r.*, in one's way, so as to cause obstruction or inconvenience.

attrib. and *Comb.*: **r.-agent** (*U.S.*), a highway robber; **R.-Board**, the authority entrusted with the business of making and improving roads, and having the administration of a *r. fund*; **-book**, also **r. book**, a book exhibiting or describing the roads of a district or country; **r. hog**, one who rides or drives recklessly and dangerously on the r. without regard to the comfort of others; esp. a reckless cyclist or motorist; **-metal**, broken stone used in making roads; hence *r.-metalling*; **r. post**, (*a*) a signpost; (*b*) a military post stationed or situated on a r.; **-runner** (*U.S.*), the paisano or chaparral cock; **-sense**, the faculty of perceiving instinctively and promptly the best method of dealing with all kinds of emergencies on the r. Hence **Roa·dless** *a.* destitute of or having no roads.

Road (rōᵘd), *v.* 1856. [Origin obsc.] *trans.* Of a dog: To follow up (a game-bird) by the scent. Also with *up*, and *absol.*

Roa·d-maker. 1799. [f. ROAD *sb.*] One who makes roads.

Roa·dside. Also **road-side.** 1712. [ROAD *sb.* 4.] †1. The side next to the road. STEELE. 2. The side, or border, of the road; wayside 1744.

Roadstead (rōᵘ·dsted). 1556. [f. ROAD *sb.* 3.] A place where ships may conveniently or safely lie at anchor near the shore.

Roadster (rōᵘ·dstəɹ). 1744. [f. ROAD *sb.* 3 and 4.] 1. *Naut.* A vessel lying, or able to lie, at anchor in a roadstead; one which lies at anchor in a roadstead when tide or wind is unfavourable. 2. A horse for riding (or driving) on the road 1818. b. A cycle or car for use on the road 1883. 3. One who is accustomed to the road; a coach-driver or traveller 1841. 4. *Hunting.* One who keeps to the road 1858.

Roa·dway. 1597. [ROAD *sb.* 4.] 1. A way used as a road; †a highway. 2. The main or central portion of a road, *esp.* that used by vehicular traffic, in contrast to the side-paths 1807. 3. That portion of a bridge, railway, etc., on which traffic is conducted 1834.

Roa·dworthy, *a.* 1819. [ROAD *sb.* 4.] Fit for the road; in a suitable condition for using on the road. Hence **Roa·dworthiness.**

Roam (rōᵘm), *v.* ME. [Origin obsc.] 1. *intr.* To wander, rove, or ramble; to walk about aimlessly, esp. over a wide area. 2. *trans.* To wander over or through (a place) 1603.

1. Shaggy forms o'er ice-built mountains r. GRAY. 2. False titl'd Sons of God, roaming the Earth MILT. Hence **Roam** *sb.* the act of wandering or roaming; a ramble. **Roa·mer,** one who roams; a wanderer.

Roan (rōᵘn), *a.* and *sb.*[1] 1530. [a. OF. *roan, rouen,* F. *rouan,* of unkn. origin.] A. *adj.* Of animals: Having a coat in which the prevailing colour is thickly interspersed with some other; *esp.* bay, sorrel, or chestnut mixed with white or grey. Also *absol.* as the name of a colour. (In the case of horses, the prevailing colour is freq. expressed, as *black, blue, red, silver, strawberry r.*) B. *sb.* A roan horse, cow, antelope, etc. 1580.

Roan (rōᵘn), *sb.*[2] late ME. [perh. *Roan,* an old form of the place-name *Rouen.*] †1. *R. skin,* some kind of skin or leather -1583. 2. A soft flexible leather made of sheepskin, used in bookbinding as a substitute for morocco 1818.

Roan-tree, var. of ROWAN-TREE.

Roar (rōᵊɹ), *sb.*[1] late ME. [f. the stem of OE. *rārian,* ME. *roren* to ROAR. Later, perh. re-formed from the vb.] 1. A full, deep, prolonged cry uttered by a lion or other large beast; a loud and deep sound uttered by one or more persons, esp. as an expression of pain or anger. b. A boisterous outburst *of* laughter; also *ellipt.* for this 1778. 2. *transf.* The loud sound of cannon, thunder, a storm, the sea, or other inanimate agents 1548.

1. Sure it was the roare Of a whole heard of Lyons SHAKS. A r. of hired applause KINGSLEY. b. A r. of laughter interrupted him KIPLING. 2. Arm! arm! it is..the cannon's opening r.! BYRON.

†**Roar,** *sb.*[2] late ME. [a. MDu. *roer* = OS. *hrōra,* OHG. *ruora* (MHG. *ruore,* G. *ruhr*).] Confusion, tumult, disturbance -1610. b. A wild outburst of mirth. (In mod. use assoc. w. prec.)

By your Art..you haue Put the wild waters in this Rore SHAKS. b. *Ham.* v. i. 211.

Roar (rōᵊɹ), *v.* [OE. *rārian* = MDu. *reeren, reren* (still in dial. use); prob. imitative.] 1. *intr.* Of persons: To utter a very loud and deep or hoarse cry (or cries), *esp.* under the influence of rage, pain, or great excitement; to vociferate, shout, yell. †b. To shout in revelry; to behave in a noisy, riotous manner -1763. 2. Of animals (*esp.* of lions): To utter a loud deep cry. Also with *out.* ME. b. Of horses: To make a loud sound in breathing 1880. 3. Of cannon, thunder, wind, the sea, etc.: To make a loud noise or din ME. b. Of a place: To resound or echo with noise. late ME. 4. *trans.* To utter or proclaim loudly; to shout (*out*). late ME. b. With compl.: To force, call, bring, render, etc., by roaring 1607.

1. You..roared for mercy, and still ranne and roar'd SHAKS. 2. Whereat his horse did snort, as he Had heard a lion r. COWPER. b. The tendency to r. is not a matter of heredity 1889. 3. The faggot blazed and crackled, and roared up the chimney 1861. 4. The songs those young fellows were roaring THACKERAY. b. We'll r. the rusty rascal out of his tobacco 1617.

Roarer (rōᵊ·rəɹ). late ME. [f. ROAR *v.* + -ER[1].] 1. One who or that which roars. †b. A noisy, riotous bully or reveller -1709. 2. A horse affected with roaring 1811. 3. *U.S. slang.* Something superlatively good 1852.

1. What cares these roarers for the name of King? SHAKS.

Roaring (rōᵊ·riŋ), *vbl. sb.* OE. [f. ROAR *v.* + -ING[1].] 1. The utterance of a loud deep cry. †2. Bullying, boisterous, or riotous conduct -1642. 3. A disease of horses, causing them to make a loud noise when breathing under exertion; the act of making this noise 1823.

Roa·ring, *ppl. a.* late ME. [f. as prec. + -ING[2].] 1. That roars or bellows; *spec.* of horses (see prec. 3). 2. Behaving or living in a noisy, riotous manner. Now *arch.* 1611. 3. Of voice, sound, etc.: Extremely loud 1548. 4. Characterized by riotous or noisy revelry; full of din or noise 1715. b. *The r. forties*: see FORTY *sb.* 5. Of trade: very brisk, highly successful 1796.

1. They gaped vpon me..as a rauening and a r. Lyon *Ps.* xxii. 13. 4. We'll have a r. Night 1759. *The r. game* (or *play*), the game of curling. *R. drunk,* excessively drunk and noisy. Hence **Roa·ringly** *adv.*

Roast (rōᵘst), *sb.* ME. [In sense 1, a. OF. *rost* masc. (mod.F. *rôt*) or *roste* fem., roasting, roast meat, f. *rostir.* In sense 2, a subst. use of the pa. pple. of ROAST *v.* In other senses mainly from the verbal stem.] 1. A piece of roast meat, or anything that is roasted for food; a part of an animal prepared or intended for roasting. 2. Roast meat; roast beef. late ME. 3. An operation of roasting (metal, coffee, etc.), or the result of this 1582. 4. The process of bantering unmercifully 1740.

1. I love no rost, but a nut browne toste And a crab layde in the fyre 1575. Phr. *To rule the r.,* to be master; The ladies always rule the r. in this part of the world 1778. 2. He eateth flesh: he rosteth rost, and is satisfied *Isa.* xliv. 16.

Roast (rōᵘst), *v.* ME. [ad. OF. *rostir* (mod. F. *rôtir*), of Teut. origin; cf. OHG. *rōsten,* f. *rōst* masc., *rōste* fem., gridiron, grill.] 1. *trans.* To make (flesh or other food) ready for eating by prolonged exposure to heat at or before a fire. Also freq. in mod. use, to cook (meat) in an oven (= *bake*). b. *techn.* To expose (metallic ores, etc.) to protracted heat in a furnace; to calcine 1582. c. To expose (coffee beans) to heat in order to prepare for grinding 1724. 2. To torture by exposure to flame or heat ME. 3. To ridicule, banter, jest at, quiz (a person) in a severe or merciless fashion 1726. 4. *absol.* To perform, carry on, the process of roasting. late ME. 5. *intr.* To undergo the process of being cooked, tortured, or calcined by exposure to fire or heat ME.

1. That day of an auncient custome there is roosted a whole Oxe 1560. 2. Blow me about in windes, r. me in Sulphure, Wash me in steepe-downe gulfes of Liquid fire SHAKS. 4. I have had no difficulty in teaching men how to r. 1877. 5. Cast thereon smale salt as he rosteth 1450.

Roast (rōᵘst), *ppl. a.* ME. [Old pa. pple. of ROAST *v.*] Roasted.

Roast beef. 1635. [ROAST *ppl. a.* Hence F. *rosbif.*] Beef roasted for eating.

Roaster (rōᵘ·stəɹ). 1440. [f. ROAST *v.* + -ER.[1]] 1. One who roasts. 2. *Min.* A furnace in which metallic ores are calcined 1778. b. A kind of oven in which meat, etc., can be cooked by roasting 1799. c. An apparatus for roasting coffee-beans 1837. 3. A pig, or other article of food, fit for roasting 1690.

Roasting (rōᵘ·stiŋ), *vbl. sb.* late ME. [f. ROAST *v.*] The action of the vb. b. *attrib.,* as *r.-ear* (of maize), one suitable for roasting; *r.-jack,* a contrivance for turning meat, etc., while it is being roasted.

Roast meat. Also **roast-meat.** 1530. [f. ROAST *ppl. a.*] Meat cooked by roasting.

Phr. †*To make roast meat of,* to burn (a person); to destroy or finish off. †*To cry roast meat,* to be foolish enough to announce to others a piece of private good luck or good fortune.

Rob (rǫb), *sb.* Now *rare.* 1578. [a. mod.L. or F. *rob,* f. (ult.) Arab. *robb, rubb* or Pers. *rob, rub* fruit-syrup.] The juice of a fruit, reduced by boiling to the consistency of a syrup and preserved with sugar; a conserve of fruit.

Rob (rǫb), *v.* ME. [ad. OF. *robber, rober,* of Teut. origin; cf. REAVE *v.*] 1. *trans.* To deprive (a person) of something by unlawful force or the exercise of superior power; to despoil by violence. 2. To plunder or strip (a person) feloniously *of* (something belonging to him); to deprive (a person) *of* (something due) ME. 3. To plunder, pillage (a place, house, etc.). Freq. const. *of* that which is taken. ME. 4. *absol.* To commit depredations; to plunder; to take away property by force ME. 5. To carry off as plunder; to steal. Now *rare.* ME. 6. *Card-playing.* To exchange the trump-card, if an ace, for any other card in the pack 1611.

1. Se yᵗ thou robbe not yᵉ poore because he is weake COVERDALE *Prov.* xxii. 22. Phr. *To r. Peter to pay (clothe) Paul*: see PETER *sb.* 1. 2. For who would r. a Hermit of his Weeds MILT.? 3. One that is like to be executed for robbing a Church SHAKS. 4. I am accurst to r. in that Theefe company SHAKS. 5. The descendants of the Negroes who were robbed from Africa 1887.

Roband (rōᵘ·bæ̆nd). ME. [Later var. of †*raband,* f. obs. Sc. *ra* sailyard + BAND *sb.*[1] Sometimes improved into *rope-band.*] *Naut.* A piece of small rope passed through an eyelet-hole in the head of a sail and used to secure it to the yard above.

Robber (rǫ·bəɹ). ME. [a. AF. and OF. *robbere, robere,* f. *robber* to ROB.] One who practises or commits robbery; a depredator, plunderer, despoiler.

Then Theeues and Robbers raunge abroad vnseene SHAKS.

attrib. and *Comb.*: *r.-gold, -inn, r. lair,* etc.; **r.-council** or **-synod,** the ecclesiastical council held at Ephesus in 449, the decrees of which were subsequently rescinded; **-crab,** a large tropical crab which feeds on coco-nuts; **-fly,** a fly of the family *Asilidæ,* given to preying upon other insects.

Robbery (rǫ·bəri). ME. [a. OF. *roberie,* f. *rober* to ROB; see -ERY.] 1. The action or practice of robbing; spoliation, depredation. b. An instance of this; a depredation ME. †2. *concr.* Plunder, booty -1535.

1. R. is committed by Force, or Terror, of which neither is in Theft; for Theft is a secret Act HOBBES. 2. They gather together euell gotten goodes, and laye vp r. in their houses COVERDALE *Amos* iii. 10.

Ro·bbin. Now *rare* or *Obs.* 1497. [var. of ROBAND.] *Naut.* = ROBAND.

Robe (rōᵘb), *sb.* ME. [a. OF., = Catal. and It. *roba*; the stem is that of the verb ROB, the original sense being 'spoil, booty', as in OF.] 1. A long loose outer garment reaching to the feet or the ankles, worn by both sexes in the Middle Ages, and still by men of some of the Eastern nations; a gown. Now *rare,* exc. as in 2. b. A trade name for a special form of lady's dress; a piece of material, partly shaped for a gown 1878. 2. A long outer garment of a special form and material worn in virtue of, and betokening, a particular rank, calling, condition, or office. Also *pl.* with the same connotation ME. 3. *pl.* Outer garments or clothes in general 1575. b. *fig.* A covering or vesture compared to a long enveloping garment 1623. 4. *U.S.* and *Canada.* The dressed skin of a buffalo, musk-ox, etc. used as a garment or rug 1836.

1. Turbans and flowing robes are adapted to hot countries 1796. 2. *The long r.,* (the dress of) the legal or clerical profession; *the short r.,* (that of) 'all that profess arms, or usually wear swords' (Cotgr.); so *both robes, either r.* *The R.,* the legal profession. Phr. *Coronation, parliament robes,* etc. *Master, Mistress, Yeoman, of the Robes*: see these words. 3. b. Another [cottage] wore A close-set r. of jasmine TENNYSON.

Robe (rōᵘb), *v.* ME. [f. the sb.] 1. *trans.* To clothe or invest in a robe or robes; to apparel; to dress. 2. *intr.* To put on robes or vestments 1626.

1. Ulysses rob'd him in the cloak and vest POPE. *fig.* Love robed her in a blush 1850. 2. Only to Roab, and Feast, and performe Rites BACON.

‖**Robe de chambre** (rob də ʃaṅbr). 1731. [F.; see ROBE *sb.* and CHAMBER *sb.*] A dressing-gown or négligé.

Robert (rǫ·bəɹt). ME. [a. F., ult. Teut.] †1. = ROBIN (REDBREAST). -late ME. 2. = HERB

ROBERT. Also *robert's bill.* 1847. **3.** A policeman. (Cf. BOBBY 2.) 1870. **4.** A waiter. (From articles in *Punch*, 1881–2, professedly written by a waiter named Robert.) 1886.

Robin[1] (rǫ·bin). late ME. [a. OF., dim. or familiar form of ROBERT.] **I.** The personal name.

Iakke þe iogeloure..And Robyn þe Rybaudoure *Piers Plowman.*

II. 1. = ROBIN REDBREAST 1 a. 1549. **b.** Any bird of the genus *Erithacus* 1855. **2.** *U.S.* The red-breasted thrush, *Turdus migratorius* 1798. **3.** The name given to various colonial birds, as in New Zealand to those of the genus *Miro*, in Australia to species of *Petroica* and other genera, etc. 1880. **b.** Used attrib. or appositively in names of various birds 1555.

1. On the nigh-naked tree the r. piped Disconsolate TENNYSON. 2. In America I shoot robins and find them thrushes 1888. 3. *Blue r.*, the bluebird. *Golden r.*, the Baltimore oriole. **b. R. breast,** = *r. snipe*; **R. dipper** (*U.S.*), the buffle-headed duck; **R. snipe,** (*a*) = KNOT *sb.*[2]; (*b*) the red-breasted snipe.

III. A name given locally or dialectally to various plants, as red campion, ragged robin, herb Robert, etc. 1694. **b.** In genitive combs., as **robin's eye(s, flower,** herb Robert, rose campion, etc.; **robin's plantain** (*U.S.*), a species of fleabane (*Erigeron belledifolium*) 1846. **IV.** The name of various fishes: **a.** *dial.* A small or inferior codfish 1618. **b.** *U.S. Decapterus punctatus*; also, the sea-robin 1876.

†**Robin**[2]. 1748 = ROBING *vbl. sb.* 2 –1789.

Robinet (rǫ·binet). late ME. [a. OF., dim. of *Robin* ROBIN[1].] †**1.** Some form of hoisting-tackle –1512. †**2.** A kind of small cannon –1611. **3.** = ROBIN[1] II. 1. Now *n. dial.* late ME. **4.** A cock or faucet of a pipe 1867.

Ro·bing, *vbl. sb.* 1470. [f. ROBE *v.* + -ING[1].] **1.** Apparel, array; a costume or gown. **2.** A trimming in the form of bands or stripes upon a gown or robe 1727. **3.** The action of putting on robes 1838.

attrib.: **r.-room,** a room specially appropriated to the putting on of official robes.

Robin Goodfellow (rǫ·bin gu·dfelō^u). 1531. [See ROBIN[1] and GOODFELLOW.] A sportive and capricious elf or goblin believed to haunt the English countryside in the 16–17th centuries; also called Hobgoblin or Puck. †**b.** *gen.* A fairy or goblin of this kind–1635.

When Hobgoblin and Robin good Fellow made country wenches keepe their houses cleane ouernight 1622.

Robin Hood (rǫ·bin hu·d). late ME. [A personal name, perh. fictitious.] **1.** The name of a popular English outlaw traditionally famous from at least the 14th c.; hence allusively, an outlaw or bandit, or a leader of such persons. †**2.** One who acted the part of Robin Hood in a mummer's play or yearly festival; the play or festival itself. Hence *Robin Hood's days, men.* –1616.

1. †*A tale* (or *gest*) *of Robin Hood*, an extravagant story.

‖ **Robinia** (robi·niă). 1759. [mod.L. (Linn.), f. *Robin*, name of the royal gardener at Paris, who introduced these trees to Europe in 1635.] *Bot.* A genus of N. Amer. trees and shrubs of the bean family, chiefly represented by the locust-tree.

Ro·bin re·dbreast. 1450. [Cf. ROBIN[1] and REDBREAST.] **1. a.** The European redbreast or robin (*Erithacus rubecula*), usu. as a proper name, but also with *a* and pl. **b.** *dial.* The red campion, *Lychnis diurna* 1886. **2.** *slang.* A Bow Street runner 1841.

Roborant (rō^u·b-, rǫ·bŏrănt), *sb.* and *a.* 1661. [ad. L. *roborant-*, *roborare*; see next.] **A.** *sb.* An invigorating or strengthening medicine. **B.** *adj.* Strengthening; restorative 1836.

†**Ro·borate,** *v.* late ME. [ad. L. *roborat-*, *roborare* to strengthen, f. *robor-*, *robur* strength.] **1.** *trans.* To ratify, confirm (a charter, league, etc.) –1655. **2.** To strengthen, invigorate; to fortify –1710. So †**Robora·tion** 1657.

Robot (rō^u·bǫt). 1923. [Czech *robot-*, stem of *robotiti* to work, drudge = Russ. *rabótat'* to work, f. *rabóta* work. (The orig. Slavonic stem is related to G. *arbeit* work.)] One of the mechanical men and women in the play *R.U.R.* (*Rossum's Universal Robots*) by Karel Capek; hence, a living being that acts automatically (without volition). **b.** A machine devised to function in place of a living agent; one which acts automatically or with a minimum of external impulse 1925.

Robots..persons all of whose activities were imposed upon them and who were not allowed 'even the luxury of original sin' G. B. SHAW. Hence **Robote·sque, Robo·tian,** *adjs.* **Ro·botism. Ro·botize** *v. trans.* to mechanicalize. **Ro·botry.**

Rob Roy (rǫb₍roi·). 1866. [Name (meaning 'Red Robert') of a Highland freebooter (1671–1734) given by John Macgregor (1825–1892) to a canoe.] *Rob Roy canoe*, a light canoe for a single person propelled by alternate strokes of a double-bladed paddle.

‖ **Robur** (rō^u·bǭı). *rare.* 1601. [L.] A very hard-wooded variety of oak. Also *robur-oak.*

Roburite (rō^u·bərəit). 1887. [f. L. *robur* strength + -ITE[1] 4.] A flameless explosive of very high power.

R...consists of chlorinated dinitrobenzene mixed with sufficient ammonium nitrate to completely oxidize it 1891.

Robust (robɒ·st), *a.* 1549. [ad. L. *robustus*, f. *robur* strength.] **1.** Of persons: Strong and hardy in body or constitution; strongly and stoutly built; of a full and healthy habit. **b.** Similarly of the body or the constitution; of plants, animal structures, etc. 1625. **2. a.** Coarse, rough, rude. Now *rare.* 1560. **b.** Pertaining to, or requiring, bodily strength or hardiness; vigorous 1683. **3.** *fig.* Strong, vigorous, healthy 1788. **b.** Vigorous in mind, voice, etc. 1852.

1. Stronge & robuste persons 1563. **b.** Your r. nervous system 1860. 2. **a.** He..began a r. flirtation with one of them 1872. **b.** R. exercises 1801. 3. English is a r. language 1888. **b.** A most r. thinker 1852. Hence **Robu·st-ly** *adv.*, **-ness.**

Robustious (robɒ·stiəs), *a.* *arch.* 1548. [f. ROBUST + -IOUS.] **1.** Of persons, the body, etc.: Robust; stout and strong or healthy-looking. **b.** Of things: Big and strong; massive 1548. **2.** Violent, boisterous, noisy, strongly self-assertive 1548. **b.** Of storms or climate: Violent, severe 1612.

1. This Gunner was a r. Vulcan 1654. 2. You are so r., you are like to put out my Eye SWIFT. Hence **Robu·stious-ly** *adv.*, **-ness** (now *rare*).

Roc (rǫk). 1579. [ad. Arab. *rokh*, *rukh*(*kh.*)] A mythical bird of Eastern legend, imagined as being of enormous size and strength.

Rocambole (rǫ·kămbō^ul). 1698. [a. F.; origin obsc.] **1.** A species of leek (*Allium Scorodoprasum*) indigenous to Northern Europe, used as a seasoning for dishes; Spanish garlic, sand-leek. **2.** A plant of this, or the edible portion of one 1707.

Roccellic (rǫkse·lik), *a.* 1838. [a. F. *roccellique*, f. *roccelle* orchil, = It. *roccella*, f. *rocca* rock.] *Chem.* In *r. acid*, an acid forming white, rectangular crystals, $C_{17}H_{32}O_4$. Hence **Rocce·llate,** a salt formed by the action of r. acid upon a base.

Roccellin (rǫkse·lin). 1852. [f. as prec. + -IN[1].] *Chem.* A coal-tar colour used in dyeing, derived from the orchil lichen.

Roche (rō^utʃ), *sb.* Now *dial.* ME. [a. OF., var. of *rocque*, *roke* ROCK *sb.*[1]] A rock or cliff; a rocky height.

Roche (rō^utʃ), *v.* 1631. [f. prec.] †**a.** *intr.* To form crystals –1673. **b.** *trans.* To recrystallize (alum) in lead-lined casks after previous dissolution by water or steam 1678.

Roche alum (rō^utʃ,æ·ləm). ME. [f. ROCHE *sb.* + ALUM, after F. *alun de roche.*] = Rock alum.

Roche lime. 1756. [f. ROCHE *sb.*] Unslaked lime; lime shells.

Rochelle (roʃe·l). late ME. [Place-name (*La*) *Rochelle*, a seaport of western France.] †**1.** Used *attrib.* or *absol.* to designate the wine exported from this place –1731. **2.** *R. salt*, sodium potassium tartrate. †*R. powder* = Seidlitz powder. 1753.

2. *R. Salt*..is prepared by not quite neutralizing hot solution of carbonate of soda with powdered cream of tartar 1888.

Rochet[1] (rǫ·tʃĕt). late ME. [a. OF., = It. *rocchetto*, a dim. of the Germ. word which appears as G. *rock*, OS. *hroc*, OE. *rocc.*] **1.** An outer garment of the nature of a smock-frock, cloak, or mantle. Now *dial.* **2.** *Eccl.* A vestment of linen, of the surplice type, usu. worn by bishops and abbots. late ME. **b.** *transf.* One who wears a rochet; a bishop 1581.

2. The r. is only a modification of the surplice 1849.

Rochet[2] (rǫ·tʃĕt). Now *local.* late ME. [a. OF. *rouget*, f. *rouge* red.] The Red Gurnard.

Roching (rō^u·tʃiŋ), *vbl. sb.* 1631. [f. ROCHE *v.* + -ING[1].] The action of recrystallizing (alum); chiefly *attrib.* in *r. cask, pan.*

Rock (rǫk), *sb.*[1] late ME. [a. OF. *roke*, F. *roc.*] **1.** A large rugged mass of stone forming a cliff, crag, or natural prominence on land or in the sea. **b.** A boulder; also *U.S.* and *Austral.*, a stone of any size 1709. **2. a.** Without article, or in generalized use: Hard and massive stone 1590. **b.** *Agric.* The base on which the sub-soil immediately lies 1765. **c.** *Geol.* One of the stratified or igneous mineral constituents of which the earth's crust is composed, including sands, clays, etc. 1789. **3.** *transf.* A hard confection of candied sugar, variously flavoured; *dial.* sweetstuff 1736. **4. a.** = ROCK-FISH 1. 1698. **b.** The rock-dove or rock-pigeon (*Columba livia*). Usu. *blue r.* 1863.

1. A ragged, fearefull, hanging Rocke SHAKS. *fig.* If it dasheth against the rocke of sinne, it is in great ieopardie 1606. Be thou my r., though I poore changeling rove 1633. He that was a r. to all assaults of might and violence 1667. Phr. *Of the old*, or *new r.*, said of precious stones. *On the rocks*, quite destitute of means. *To pile up the rocks* (U.S. slang), to make money.

Comb.: **r. apostle,** St. Peter (Matt. xvi. 18); **r.-bed,** a floor or under-stratum of r.; **r.-butter,** (*a*) a soft yellowish mixture of alum and iron which exudes from certain aluminiferous rocks; (*b*) a sauce made by beating butter with about twice its weight of sugar and flavouring; **-cake,** a small cake or bun with a rugged surface; **r. cork,** a light variety of asbestos; pilolite; **-drill,** a r.-boring instrument or machine; **r. English,** the mixed English of Gibraltar; **-flint,** impure flint; chert; **-garden,** a garden consisting of rocks and r.-plants; **-hammer,** a hammer used for r.-breaking; **-meal,** a white cotton-like variety of carbonate of lime, occurring as an efflorescence, which falls into powder when touched; **-oil,** native naphtha; †**-ruby,** a species of garnet or amethyst; **-scorpion,** a nickname applied to a person born at Gibraltar; **r. silk,** a silky variety of asbestos; **-soap,** a kind of bole; mountain soap; **r. tar,** petroleum.

b. In names of beasts, as **r. barnacle,** a cirriped of the genus *Balanus*; **r. cavy,** a Brazilian species of cavy (*Cavia rupestris*); **r. crab,** a crab frequenting rocky coasts, *esp.* the American *Cancer irroratus*; **r. goat,** the ibex; **r. kangaroo** = *r. wallaby*; **r. lobster,** a crustacean of the family *Palinuridæ*, to which the crayfish belongs; **r. rabbit,** a rodent of the genus *Hyrax*, esp. the Syrian and South African species; **r. seal,** the common seal (*Phoca vitulina*); **r. serpent,** (*a*) = *r. snake*; (*b*) a poisonous Indian snake of the genus *Bungarus*; **r. snake,** a python, esp. *P. reticulatus* or *molurus*; **r. wallaby,** a kangaroo of the genus *Petrogale.*

c. In names of birds: **r.-bird,** a bird that haunts rocks; *esp.* a puffin; **-dove,** = ROCK-PIGEON; **r. duck,** the harlequin duck; **-hawk,** the merlin; **-hopper (penguin),** a species of crested penguin (*Eudyptes chrysocome*); **-ouzel,** the ring-ouzel; **r. parakeet,** an Australian grass parakeet (*Euphema petrophila*); **r. partridge,** (*a*) the white grouse or ptarmigan; (*b*) the Greek or Barbary partridge; **r. pipit,** the sea-lark (*Anthus obscurus*) of the British Islands; **r. plover** (*local U.S.*), the purple sand-piper; **r. ptarmigan,** the Amer. species, *Lagopus rupestris*; **r. sparrow,** a bird of the genus *Petronia*; **-thrush,** a thrush of the genus *Monticola*; **r. warbler,** *Origma Rubricata*, also called Cataract Bird; **r. wren,** a brownish gray Amer. bird, speckled with black and white dots.

d. In names of fishes: **r. bass,** any of several Amer. fishes, as the red-eye or goggle-eye (*Amboplites rupestris*), the striped bass, and black sea-bass; **r. codling,** a N. Amer. species of cod; **r. cook,** a species of wrasse; †**r. ray,** the thorn-back; **r. salmon,** (*a*) the coalfish; (*b*) an Amer. fish of the genus *Seriola*; **r. trout,** (*a*) a New Zealand fish, *Galaxias alepidotus*; (*b*) a N. Amer. fish, *Chirus constellatus.*

e. In names of plants: **r. cress,** (*a*) a plant of the genus *Arabis*; †(*b*) samphire; **r. moss,** (*a*) the orchil lichen; (*b*) cudbear; **r. tripe,** name in N. America for several species of lichens belonging to *Gyrophora* and *Umbilicaria.* Hence **Ro·ckless** *a.* devoid of rocks.

Rock (rǫk), *sb.*[2] ME. [Cf. MDu. *rocke*, OHG. *rocco*, ON. *rokkr.* Possibly a native English word.] **1.** A distaff. Now *arch.* or *Hist.* **2.** A distaff together with the wool or flax attached to it; the quantity of wool or flax placed on a distaff for spinning 1550.

1. The three Parcæ,..the one holding the r., the other the spindle, and the third the sheeres B. JONS.

Rock (rǫk), *v.* [Late OE. *roccian*, app. f. Teut. stem *rukk-*; cf. MDu., MLG. *rocken*, *rucken*, G. *rücken.*] **1.** *trans.* To move (a child) gently to and fro in a cradle, in order to soothe or send it to sleep. **b.** *transf.* and *fig.* of the wind, sea, earth, sleep, etc. 1597. **2.** To bring into a state of slumber, rest, or peace by gentle motion to and fro. Const. *to, into,* or *asleep.* late ME. **b.** To maintain *in* a lulling state of security, plenty, hope, etc. 1581. **3.** To move or sway (a person) to and fro, esp. in a gentle or soothing manner. late ME. **4.** To make (a cradle) swing to and fro, in order to put a child to sleep. late ME. **b.** *transf.* In gold-washing (see CRADLE *v.* 7.). Hence *absol.*, to use a rocker in gold-digging. Also *trans.*, to work *out* with a rocker. 1849. **5.** To cause to sway to and fro or from side to side; to move backwards and forwards. Also *refl.* ME. **6.** *intr.* To sway to and fro under some impact or stress; to oscillate. Also *dial.*, to stagger or reel in walking. late ME. **b.** Of vessels under the effect of waves 1513. **c.** To swing oneself to and fro, esp. while sitting in a rocking-chair 1795.

1. That 's not my native place, where I was rockt MARSTON. b. Sleepe rocke thy Braine SHAKS. 2. As the working of a sea Before a calm, that rocks itself to rest COWPER. 4. All the Graces rockt her cradle being borne SPENSER. 5. The god whose earthquakes r. the solid ground POPE. 6. The earth rocked beneath his feet 1797.

Comb.: **r.-staff**, part of the apparatus for working a smith's bellows. Hence **Rock** *sb.*[3] the action of the vb. **Ro·cky** *a.*[2] unsteady, tottering; in early use, tipsy.

Rockaway (rǫ·kăwēɪ). *U.S.* 1846. [prob. f. prec.] A four-wheeled carriage, open at the sides, with two or three seats and a standing top.

Ro·ck-ba·sin. 1754. [ROCK *sb.*[1]] A basin-shaped hollow in a rock, esp. one of natural origin; *spec.* in *Geol.* a large depression in a rocky area, attributed to the action of ice-masses.

Ro·ck-bed. 1839. [ROCK *sb.*[1]] A floor or base of rock; a rocky bottom or under-stratum.

Ro·ck-bo·ttom, *sb.* and *a.* 1884. *colloq.* orig. *U.S.* [f. ROCK *sb.*[1] + BOTTOM *sb.*] **A.** *sb.* The very bottom. **B.** *attrib.* or as *adj.* The lowest possible.

Tools at absolutely r. prices 1922.

Ro·ck cod. 1634. [ROCK *sb.*[1]] **1.** A cod found on rocky sea-bottoms or ledges. Chiefly *Sc.* and *north.* **2.** Applied to various fishes of other genera, as the Californian yellow-tailed rock-fish, the red garrupa, the rock-trout of Puget Sound, etc. 1796. So **Ro·ck co·dfish.**

Ro·ck cry·stal. 1666. [ROCK *sb.*[1]] **1.** Pure silica or quartz in a transparent and colourless form, most usu. occurring in hexagonal prisms with hexagonal pyramid ends. **2.** A piece of this 1839.

Rocker (rǫ·kəɹ). late ME. [f. ROCK *v.* + -ER[1].] **1.** A nurse or attendant charged with the duty of rocking a child in the cradle. Now *arch.* or *Obs.* Also *gen.*, one who rocks a cradle. **2.** One of the pieces of wood with a convex under-surface fixed to each end of a cradle, to the legs of a chair, or to any other thing, in order to enable it to rock 1787. **3.** Something which rocks or is rocked after the manner of a cradle: **a.** A rocking-horse 1846. **b.** *U.S.* A rocking-chair 1857. **c.** A gold-miner's cradle 1858. **d.** A scientific instrument illustrating the effect of heat in producing vibration 1863. **e.** *Engraving* = CRADLE *sb.* 12. 1875. **4.** Chiefly *U.S.* A skate with a curving sole 1869. **b.** = *rocking-turn* 1893.

2. Phr. *Off one's r.*, crazy; distracted; demented (*vulg. slang*). Hence **Ro·ckered** *a.* curved like a r.

Rockery (rǫ·kəri). 1845. [f. ROCK *sb.*[1] + -ERY.] **1.** A heap or pile of rough stones and soil used for the ornamental growing of ferns and other plants. **2.** Natural rockwork 1856.

Rocket (rǫ·kėt), *sb.*[1] 1530. [a. F. *roquette*, ad. It. *ruchetta*, dim. of *ruca* :—L. *eruca* a kind of cabbage.] **1.** A cruciferous annual (*Eruca sativa*) having purple-veined white flowers and acrid leaves, used in Southern Europe as a salad. Also, †wild rocket. **b.** With specific epithets, esp. *Garden r.*, *Roman r.*, and *R. gentle* 1548. **2.** A cruciferous plant of the genus *Hesperis*, esp. *H. matronalis*, a garden-flower which is sweet-scented after dark 1629.

Base r., the wild mignonette (*Reseda luteola*). **Blue r.**, (*a*) one of several kinds of wolf's-bane or aconite; (*b*) applied to several kinds of larkspur (*Delphinium*); (*c*) the blue-bell (*Scilla nutans*). **Wild r.**, hedge mustard. **Yellow r.**, the winter-cress.

Rocket (rǫ·kėt), *sb.*[2] 1611. [a. F. *roquet*, or ad. It. *rocchetta*, app. a dim. of It. *rocca* ROCK *sb.*[2], with ref. to the form of the rocket.] An apparatus consisting of a cylindrical case of paper or metal containing an inflammable composition, by the ignition of which it may be projected to a height or distance. Also *attrib.*, as *r. apparatus, brigade*, etc.

Congreve r.: see CONGREVE 1.

Rocket (rǫ·kėt), *v.* 1803. [f. ROCKET *sb.*[2]] **1.** *trans.* To discharge rockets at; to bombard with rockets. **2.** *intr.* **a.** Of a horse or rider: To spring or bound up like a rocket; to dart like a rocket 1883. **b.** Of game-birds: To fly up almost vertically when flushed; to fly fast and high overhead 1860.

2. b. Nothing was shot, though some pheasants 'rocketed' over our guns 1860. Hence **Ro·cketer, Ro·cketter,** a game-bird that rockets.

Ro·ck-fish. 1611. [ROCK *sb.*[1]] A fish frequenting rocks or rocky bottoms, *spec.* as the name of many unrelated fishes, such as the black goby or sea-gudgeon, the striped bass, the wrasse, etc. Also, with defining words, applied to a number of Amer. fishes, chiefly of the genera *Sebastichthys* and *Sebastomus.*

Rocking (rǫ·kiŋ), *ppl. a.* late ME. [ROCK *v.*] That rocks; swaying, oscillating; also, causing to rock. **2.** In technical terms, as *r. shaft*, etc. 1805.

attrib. and *Comb.*: **r.-chair**, a chair mounted on rockers; also, a chair having a rocking seat attached to the base by springs; **r.-horse**, a wooden horse mounted on rockers for children to ride upon with a rocking motion; **r.-stone**, a large stone or boulder so poised on a limited base so as to be easily swayed to and fro; a logan-stone; **r. turn** *Skating*, a turn in which one edge of the skate only is used, the body being revolved in the same direction as in the corresponding three turns.

Rockling (rǫ·kliŋ). 1602. [f. ROCK *sb.*[1] + -LING.] A small gadoid fish of the genera *Onos* or *Rhinonemus* (formerly *Motella*), esp. the sea-loach or whistle-fish (*R. cimbrius*).

Ro·ck-pi·geon. 1611. [ROCK *sb.*[1]] **1.** A species of dove (*Columba livia*) inhabiting rocks and believed to be the source of the domestic pigeon; the rock-dove. **2.** *Anglo-Ind.* A sand-grouse 1885.

Ro·ck-plant. 1691. [ROCK *sb.*[1]] †**1.** A petrified plant -1753. **2.** A plant that grows upon or among rocks 1694.

Ro·ck-rose. 1731. [ROCK *sb.*[1]] A plant of the genus *Helianthemum* or *Cistus* (formerly united in the Linnæan genus *Cistus*), esp. *H. vulgare.*

Ro·ck-salt. 1707. [ROCK *sb.*[1]] Salt found in a free state disposed in strata, and capable of being extracted in large lumps.

Ro·ck-shaft. 1875. [ROCK *v.*] A shaft which merely rocks or oscillates about its axis in place of making complete revolutions; *esp.* one working the levers connected with certain valves in some forms of engines.

Ro·ck-weed. 1626. [ROCK *sb.*[1]] A seaweed, esp. one of the genera *Fucus* and *Sargassum*, growing on tide-washed rocks.

Ro·ck-work. 1706. [ROCK *sb.*[1]] **1.** A natural mass or group of rocks or stones. **2.** Stones piled together with soil interspersed for growing Alpine and other plants in a garden; also, grotto-work, rough stone-work resembling or imitating natural rocks 1790. **3.** *Arch.* Masonry very roughly or rudely faced. 1842. **4.** Skill in climbing rocks; rock-craft 1898.

Rocky (rǫ·ki), *a.*[1] late ME. [f. ROCK *sb.*[1] + -Y[1].] **1.** Full of, abounding in, rocks; consisting or formed of rock; having the character of rock. **2.** *fig.* **a.** Of the heart or disposition: Flinty, stony, unfeeling 1586. **b.** Firm as a rock; unflinching, steadfast 1622. †**3.** *R. bone*, the petrosal portion of the temporal bone -1683. **4.** Growing upon or among rocks (*rare*) 1640.

1. England.., Whose r. shore beates backe the enuious siedge Of watery Neptune SHAKS. *R. Mountains*, the great mountain-range lying towards the western coast of N. America; called also *The Rockies* (quasi-*sb.*). Hence **Ro·ckiness.**

Rococo (rokōᵘ·ko), *a.* and *sb.* 1836. [a. F., perh. a fanciful formation on the stem of *rocaille* pebble-work.] **A.** *adj.* **1.** Old-fashioned, antiquated. **2.** Of furniture or architecture: Having the characteristics of Louis Quatorze or Louis Quinze workmanship, such as conventional shell-and scroll-work and meaningless decoration; tastelessly florid or ornate 1844.

2. That *r.* seventeenth-century French imitation of the true Renaissance PATER.

B. *sb.* The style of architecture, art, etc., having rococo characteristics 1840.

Rod (rǫd), *sb.* [OE. *rodd*; prob. related to ON. *rudda* 'club'.] **I. 1.** A straight, slender shoot or wand, growing upon or cut from a tree, bush, etc. **b.** *fig.* An offshoot, a scion; a tribe. (*Biblical.*) 1460. **2.** An instrument of punishment, either one straight stick, or a bundle of twigs bound together OE. **b.** *fig.* A means or instrument of punishment; also, punishment, chastisement. late ME. **3.** A wand or stick carried in the hand, such as a walking-stick, shepherd's or herdsman's stick, enchanter's wand, etc. ME. **b.** A stick or switch carried in the hand when riding. late ME. **c.** A divining-rod 1617. **4.** A wand or staff (of wood, ivory, or metal) carried as a symbol of office, authority, or dignity. (See also BLACK ROD.) 1440. **b.** As a symbol of power or tyrannical sway 1526. **5.** An angling-rod; a fishing-rod 1450. **b.** *transf.* An angler 1867.

2. Phr. *To spare the r.*, etc.: see SPARE *v.* **b.** *To make a r. for one's own back. To kiss the r.*: see KISS *v.* 6: *A r. in pickle*, usu. *fig.* a punishment in store. 4. The sergeantes smote him with their rods of office 1557. b. Hands that the r. of empire might have sway'd GRAY.

II. 1. A stick used for measuring with. Also *measuring r.* 1495. **2. a.** A measure of length, equal to $5\frac{1}{2}$ yards or $16\frac{1}{2}$ feet; a PERCH or POLE 1450. **b.** A measure of area: A square perch or pole 1477. **c.** A measure of brickwork 1663. **III. a.** A straight slender bar of metal; a connecting part or shaft which is slender in proportion to its length. See also *connecting-, lightning-, piston-rod.* 1728. **b.** In scientific use: An animal or vegetable structure having an elongated slender form 1864. **c.** Something resembling a rod in shape 1860. **IV.** *attrib.* in sense 'having the form of a rod', as *r.-bolt, -iron, -lead*; *r.-body, -cell* 1690.

Rode (rōᵘd) *v.* 1768. [Origin obsc.] **1.** *intr.* Of wild-fowl: To fly landward in the evening. **2.** Of woodcock: To perform a regular evening flight during the breeding season 1865.

Rodent (rōᵘ·dĕnt), *a.* and *sb.* 1833. [ad. L. *rodent-, rodere.*] **A.** *adj.* **1.** *Zool.* Gnawing; belonging to the order *Rodentia.* **2.** *Path* Of an ulcer or cancer 1853. **B.** *sb. Zool.* An animal of the order *Rodentia*, characterized by having no canine teeth and strong incisors 1835. Hence **Rode·ntial** *a.* of or pertaining to the *Rodentia* or r. animals.

‖**Rodeo** (rodē·o). *U.S.* 1834. [Sp. *rodeo* a going round, f. *rodear* to go round.] **1.** A driving together of cattle in order to separate, count, inspect, or mark them; a round-up. **2.** A place or enclosure where cattle are brought together for any purpose 1847. **3.** An exhibition of skill in rounding up cattle, riding unbroken horses, etc.; *transf.* an exhibition of 'stunting' in the riding of motor-cycles, etc. 19..

3. There will be a..motor-cycle r. in the afternoon 1928.

Rodomont (rǫ·dǫmǫnt). *arch.* 1598. [a. F., or It. *rodomonte*, from the name of the boastful Saracen leader in Ariosto's *Orlando Furioso.*] A great bragger or boaster.

Rodomontade (rǫdǫ̆mǫntēɪ·d), *sb.* and *a.* †Also rhod-. 1612. [a. F.; see prec. and -ADE.] **A.** *sb.* **1. a.** A vainglorious brag or boast; an extravagantly boastful or arrogant saying or speech; †an arrogant act. **b.** Extravagant boasting or bragging 1648. †**2.** *transf.* = RODOMONT -1697.

1. Challengers cartells, full of Rodomontades DONNE. b. We could discern its meaning through a cloud of r. MACAULAY.

B. *adj.* Bragging; boastful; ranting 1754. So **R(h)odomonta·de** *v. intr.* to boast, brag. **R(h)odomonta·der.** †**R(h)odomonta·do** *sb.* and *a.* rodomontade.

Roe[1] (rōᵘ). [Com. Teut.; OE. *rāha, rā*; etym. unkn.] A small species of deer (*Capreolus capræa*, formerly *Cervus capreolus*) inhabiting various parts of Europe and Asia; a deer belonging to this species.

Roe[2] (rō͡u). [ME. *roȝ(e, row(e.*] The mass of eggs contained in the ovarian membrane of a fish.

Hard r., the spawn of a female fish; *soft r.*, the milt or sperm of a male fish.

Roebuck (rō͡u·bɒk). late ME. [f. ROE[1] + BUCK.] The buck or male of the roe-deer.

Roed (rō͡ud), *a.* 1611. [f. ROE[2].] Having roe; full of spawn; as *hard-, soft-r.*

Roe·-deer. OE. [f. ROE[1] + DEER.] Deer, or a deer, of the roe kind; a roe.

Roentgen, etc.: see RÖNTGEN, etc.

Roe·stone. 1804. [f. ROE[2].] = OOLITE.

Rogation (rogē͡i·ʃən). late ME. [ad. L. *rogatio, -ionis* (f. *rogare* to ask).] **1.** *Eccl.* (usu. *pl.*) Solemn supplications consisting of the litany of the saints, chanted during procession on the three days before Ascension Day; hence freq. the days on which this is done, the Rogation days **2.** *Rom. Antiq.* The act, on the part of a consul or tribune, of submitting a proposed law to the people for their acceptance; also, a law so submitted and accepted. late ME. †**3.** A formal request –1680.

1. *R. days*, the Monday, Tuesday, and Wednesday preceding Ascension Day. *R. week*, the week in which Ascension Day falls. *R. Sunday*, the fifth Sunday after Easter, being the Sunday before Ascension Day. *R. flower*, the milkwort (*Polygala vulgaris*), formerly made into garlands and carried in processions on Rogation days.

Roger (rǫ·dʒəɹ). 1631. [A personal name of men, a. OF. *Roger, Rogier*, of Teut. origin.] **1.** Used as a generic or special name for persons. **2.** *The Jolly R.*, the pirate's flag 1785.

Roger de Coverley (rǫ·dʒəɹ dĭ kɒ·vəɹli). 1685. [In early use *Roger of Coverly*; the later form is due to Addison's use of it in the *Spectator.*] An English country-dance (and tune). Also used with the prefix *Sir*, and abbreviated as *Sir Roger.*

Rogue (rō͡ug), *sb.* 1561. [One of the canting words introduced about the middle of the 16th c.] **1.** One belonging to a class of idle vagrants or vagabonds. Now *arch.* as a legal term. **2.** A dishonest, unprincipled person; a rascal 1578. †**b.** Applied abusively to servants –1781. **3.** One who is of a mischievous disposition 1597. **4.** *Hort.* An inferior plant among seedlings 1859. **5.** [tr. Cingalese *hora, sora* = Skr. *chōra* thief] An elephant, etc., driven away, or living apart, from the herd, and of a savage or destructive disposition 1859. **6.** A horse which is inclined to shirk its work on the racecourse or in the hunting-field 1881.

2. He who is carried by horses must deal with rogues 1858. b. My Lord, your R. has me safe here STEELE. 3. That sly r. Cupid has pierced your heart 1784.

Comb. with genitive: **rogue's gallery**, a collection of the portraits of criminals; **rogue's Latin**, thieves Latin or cant; **rogue's march**, one played by the trumpeters or fifers of a regiment in drumming out a man from a camp or garrison; **rogue's yarn**, 'a thread of worsted in the strands of rope manufactured for the Royal Navy, introduced for the purpose of detecting theft or embezzlement;..it serves also to trace any bad rope to the precise yard where it was made'. Hence **Ro·gueship**, the state of being a r.; used as a mock-title in *your rogueship*, etc.

Rogue (rō͡ug), *v.* 1570. [f. ROGUE *sb.*] **I.** *intr.* To wander idly about after the manner of rogues; to live like a rogue or vagrant; later, to play the rogue or rascal. †**2.** *trans.* To call (a person) a rogue; to accuse of roguery –1683. †**b.** To cast discredit on (something) –1685. **3.** To swindle 1841. **4.** To free from inferior plants or seedlings 1766.

Roguery (rō͡u·gəri). 1596. [f. ROGUE *sb.* + -ERY.] **1.** Conduct or practices characteristic of rogues; knavishness, rascality; †idle vagrancy. **2.** A knavish or rascally act 1620. **3.** Playful mischief; waggishness; fun 1664.

1. The unrighteous man..had far better not yield to the illusion that his r. is clever 1875.

Roguish (rō͡u·giʃ), *a.* 1572. [f. ROGUE *sb.* + -ISH[1] 2.] **1.** Pertaining or appropriate to, characteristic of, rogues (†or vagrants); disreputable. **2.** Acting (†or wandering) like rogues; knavish or rascally in conduct 1596. **3.** Playfully mischievous; arch, waggish 1681. **4.** Of plants: Inferior 1762.

1. Bought an idle rogueish French book PEPYS. 3. She has twa sparkling rogueish e'en BURNS. So **Ro·guish-ly** *adv.*, **-ness.** †**Ro·guy** *a.* (in senses 1–3).

Roil, *v.*[1] *Obs.* exc. *dial.* ME. [Origin obsc.] †**1.** To roam or rove about; to gad about, wander –1619. **2.** To play or frolic; to romp, rampage 1788.

Roil, *v.*[2] Now *U.S.* and *dial.* 1590. [Origin obsc.] **1.** *trans.* To render (water or any liquid) turbid or muddy by stirring up the sediment. **2.** To disturb in temper; to vex, irritate, make angry 1734. Hence **Roil** *sb.* agitation or stirring up (of water).

†**Roin,** *sb.* late ME. [a. OF. *roigne*, F. *rogne*, of unkn. origin.] A scab, scurf. CHAUCER. Hence †**Roi·nish** *a.* covered with scale or scurf; scabby, coarse, mean, paltry, base.

Roister (roi·stəɹ), *sb.* Now *arch.* 1551. [ad. F. *rustre* (†*ruistre*), var., with excrescent *r*, of *ruste* :—L. *rusticum* RUSTIC *a.*] A swaggering or blustering bully; a riotous fellow; a rude or noisy reveller. (Now usu. ROISTERER.) **b.** *dial.* A romp 1790. Hence **Roi·ster** *v. intr.* to play the r.; also with *it*. **Roi·sterer**, a swaggering or noisy reveller. **Roi·sterous** *a.* given to noisy revelling; uproarious.

Roke (rō͡uk), *sb.* Now *dial.* ME. [Prob. of Scand. origin. Cf. REEK *sb.*[1]] Smoke, steam; vapour, mist, fog; drizzling rain. Hence **Roke** *v. intr.* to give off steam or vapour; to steam; to smoke; to be foggy or misty (now *dial.*). **Ro·ky** *a.* misty; foggy; drizzly (chiefly *dial.*).

Roland (rō͡u·lănd). ME. [OF. *Roland.*] The legendary nephew of Charlemagne, celebrated in the *Chanson de Roland* (frequently together with his comrade Oliver); hence, one comparable to Roland in respect of courage, warlike deeds, or friendship; one who is a full match for another.

England all Oliuers and Rowlands bred, During the time Edward the third did raigne SHAKS. Phr. (*To give*) *a R. for an Oliver*, (to give) as good as one gets, a quid pro quo or tit for tat.

‖**Rôle** (rō͡ul). Also †**roll.** 1606. [Fr., prop. the roll containing the actor's part.] The part or character which one undertakes, assumes, or has to play. Chiefly *fig.* with ref. to the part played by a person in society or life.

Roll (rō͡ul), *sb.*[1] ME. [a. OF. *rolle, role* (mod.F. *rôle* RÔLE) :—L. *rotulus.*] **I. 1.** A piece of parchment, paper, or the like, which is written upon or intended to contain writing, etc., and is rolled up for convenience of handling or carrying; a scroll. **2.** *spec.* Such a piece of parchment, paper, etc., inscribed with some formal or official record; a document or instrument in this form. late ME. **3.** A register, list, or catalogue (of names, deeds, etc.). late ME. **b.** The official list of those qualified to act as solicitors (†or attorneys). Commonly pl. 1840. **4.** A list of names used to ascertain whether each one of a set of persons is present; esp. *Mil.* (= MUSTER-ROLL) or in scholastic use 1597.

1. Atlas bearing Heauen with a roule inscribed in Italian CAMDEN. A r. of music 1888. 2. *Rolls of Chancery, Court, Parliament*; COURT-, RENT-ROLL, etc. *Master* (also †*Clerk* or *Keeper*) *of the Rolls*, one of the four ex-officio judges of the Court of Appeal and a member of the Judicial Committee, who has charge of the rolls, patents, and grants that pass the great seal, and of all records of the Court of Chancery. *The Rolls*, the former buildings in Chancery Lane in which the records in the custody of the Master of the Rolls were preserved (now represented by the Public Record Office). Also = *Rolls Court*. *attrib.*, as *Rolls-Chapel, -Court*. Also **Rolls Series**, a series of 'chronicles and memorials of Great Britain and Ireland published under the direction of the Master of the Rolls'; so *Rolls edition*. 3. *R. of fame*; Happy King, whose name The brightest shines in all the rolls of fame! POPE. *R. of honour*, a list of those who died for their country in war. b. Phr. *To be struck off the rolls*, to be debarred from practising as a solicitor in consequence of some delinquency. 4. Where 's the R.?..let them appeare as I call SHAKS.

II. 1. A quantity of material (*esp.* cloth) rolled or wound up in a cylindrical form, sometimes forming a definite measure. Also, a number of papers, etc., rolled together. late ME. **b.** A quantity (usu. small) of some soft substance formed into a cylindrical mass 1547. **c.** A quantity of tobacco leaves rolled up into a cylindrical mass; tobacco in this form 1633. **2.** A small quantity of cloth, wool, straw, etc., rolled up into the form of a band or fillet. Now *spec.* a carding of this form. 1548. **3.** †**a.** A round cushion or pad of hair or other material, forming part of a woman's head-dress –1777. **b.** An annular pad for placing on the head in order to facilitate or ease the carrying of heavy articles on it. Now *dial.* 1681. **4.** A small loaf of bread, properly one which has been rolled or doubled over before baking 1581. **5. a.** *Arch.* A spiral scroll used in Corinthian and Ionic capitals; a cylindrical moulding; a curl, volute 1611. **b.** *Building.* A strip of wood, rounded on the top and fastened on the ridge or the lateral joints of a roof, to raise the edges of sheet-lead or zinc and so prevent the entrance of rain-water 1833. **6.** A part which is rolled or turned over 1671.

3. b. Those rolls our prudent milk-maids make use of to fix their pails upon 1716. 4. I have sat at home all day, and eaten only a mess of broth and a r. SWIFT. 5. a. *R. and fillet*, 'a round moulding with a small square fillet on the face of it'.

III. 1. A cylindrical piece of wood or metal used to facilitate the moving of something; a windlass. late ME. **b.** *Bookbinding.* A revolving patterned tool used in impressing and gilding; the pattern produced by this 1656. **2. a.** A roller used for levelling soil or crushing clods 1634. **b.** A roller used to crush, flatten, or draw out something, esp. in metal-working 1656.

Roll, *sb.*[2] 1688. [f. ROLL *v.*] **1.** The act of rolling; the fact of moving in this manner. Also with *a* and *pl.* **b.** A rolling gait or motion; a swagger 1836. **2.** *Mil.* Of a drum: A rapid, uniform beating, produced by alternate strokes of the sticks, and falling upon the ears as a continuous sound 1688. **3.** Of thunder, etc.: A loud, reverberating peal; a continuous reverberation; a prolonged shout 1818. **4.** A rich sonorous or rhythmical flow of words in verse or prose 1730. **5.** An undulation or swell on the surface of land 1874.

1. The r. of the Atlantic was full, but not violent 1871. *fig.* I hear the r. of the ages TENNYSON. 2. *Long r.*, a beat of drum by which troops are assembled at any particular spot or rendezvous or parade 1802. 4. The r. of Ciceronian prose 1870.

Roll (rō͡ul), *v.* late ME. [ad. OF. *roler* :—pop. L. **rotulare*, f. *rotula*, dim. of *rota* wheel.] **I.** *trans.* **1.** To move or impel forward (an object) on a surface by making it turn over and over; to shift about, to send down to a lower level, etc., in this manner. Also with *up* or *down, away*, etc. **b.** To drive or draw on wheels; to wheel (a cycle); to move by means of rollers 1513. **c.** To convey in a wheeled vehicle 1778. **2.** To form into a mass by turning over and over; to pile up in this manner 1547. **3.** To drive or cause to flow onward with a rolling or sweeping motion. Also with *down*. 1667. **b.** To cause (smoke, etc.) to ascend in rolls 1743. **4.** *transf.* **a.** To utter, give forth (words, etc.) with a full, rolling sound or tone. Chiefly with *out*. 1561. **b.** To pronounce or sound with a trill 1846. **5.** To turn round on or as on an axis; to cause to revolve or rotate; to turn over and over *in* something or between the hands; also, to carry *round* in revolving. late ME. **b.** *Naut.* Of vessels: To cast (masts, etc.) overboard, to submerge (tackle, etc.) by rolling 1633. **c.** To cause to swing or sway from side to side 1804. **d.** To cause to fall and turn *over* by means of a blow, shot, etc.; to bowl *over* 1850. **6.** *fig.* To revolve, turn over (a matter) *in* the mind; †to consider, meditate upon (something). late ME. **7.** To turn (the eyes) in different directions with a kind of circular motion 1513. **8.** To coil round and round upon itself or about an axis; to form into a roll or ball; to wind, fold, or curl up. Also with *up*. 1526. **9.** To wrap, envelop, or enfold *in* something; to wrap *about* with something. Also with *up*. late ME. **10.** To spread out (paste) with a rolling-pin; to level or smooth (ground) with a roller; to render compact, smooth, or flat by means of pressure with a cylinder. Also with *out*. late ME. **b.** To reduce (stone or rock) to a smooth, rounded form by propulsion in flowing water and consequent attrition 1811.

1. An Egg that fell from Heaven into Euphrates, and [was] by Fishes rolled on Land 1665. Phr. *R. up* (*Mil.*) to drive the flank of the enemy line back and round so that the line is shortened and surrounded. 2. Down they fell By thousands, Angel on Arch-Angel rowl'd MILT. 3. Where..fringed with roses, Tenglio rolls his stream THOMSON. *fig.* Hearing the

holy organ rolling waves Of sound on roof and floor TENNYSON. 5. He hath..rolled me in the dust COVERDALE *Lam.* iii. 16. 6. I came home rolling resentments in my mind and framing schemes of revenge SWIFT. 8. *fig.* Housemaid, butler, and footman rolled into one 1887. 9. Their Kings, whose bodies are.. lapped in white skinnes and rowled in mats PURCHAS. 10. The gold bars are rolled cold to the thickness of the coin 1866.

II. *intr.* 1. To move by revolving or rotating on (or as on) an axis; to move forward on a surface by turning over and over. Also with advs. late ME. b. To advance with an easy, soft, or undulating motion. late ME. c. Of vehicles: To move or run on wheels 1721. 2. a. To wander, roam, travel or move about. late ME. b. *To r. up* (slang), to congregate, gather, assemble (orig. *Austral.*) 1887. 3. To ride or travel in a carriage 1513. b. To be carried, or move, upon flowing water 1672. 4. Of times or seasons: To elapse; to move *on* or *round*; to pass *over* or *away* 1513. 5. Of the heavenly bodies: To perform a periodical revolution 1604. b. With compl. To traverse in revolving 1667. 6. Of seas, rivers, etc.: To flow with an undulating motion; to move in a full, swelling, or impetuous manner 1565. b. To move or sweep along or up with a wave-like motion; to ascend or descend in rolls or curls 1626. c. Of land: To undulate; to extend in gentle falls and rises 1847. 7. Of thunder, etc: To reverberate; to form a deep continuous sound like the roll of a drum 1598. b. Of language, talk, etc.: To flow; to run *on* 1743. c. Of sound: To flow in deep or mellow tones 1819. 8. To turn over (and over). late ME. b. Of the eyes: To move or turn round in the sockets; to rotate partially. late ME. c. To turn upon an axis 1646. d. †To hinge or depend *on* something; to turn or centre *on* a subject 1707. 9. To turn oneself over and over *in* something; hence *fig.* to luxuriate or abound *in* riches, luxury, etc. 1535. 10. Of thoughts, etc.: To revolve in the mind 1547. 11. Of a ship: To sway to and fro; to swing from side to side. (Opp. to *pitch.*) Also of masts. 1600. b. To sail with a rolling motion 1796. c. To walk with a rolling gait; to swagger 1843. 12. To form into a roll; to shrink or fold *together*; to curl *up* 1613.

1. The ball..rolled between his legs DICKENS. b. The poor distressed panther rowled after him in humble manner 1607. c. The carriages of the nobility and guests r. back to the West THACKERAY. 2. b. The miners all rolled up to see the fun 1887. 4. Generations and ages might r. away in silent oblivion GIBBON. 5. A stone by nature is inclined to descend, and the Sunne to rowle about the world 1604. b. Thrice hath Hyperion roll'd his annual race GRAY. 6. Through midst thereof a little river rold SPENSER. *fig.* Deep woes r. forward like a gentle flood SHAKS. b. The fog rolleds lowly upward 1858. c. Before them rolled the sweep of upland 1894. 7. The organ rumbled and rolled as if the Church had got the colic DICKENS. 8. b. Eyes which rowle towards all, weep not but sweat DONNE. d. Our conversation rolled chiefly on literary and political subjects BORROW. 9. Rolling in wealth which you do not want 1782. 11. The Sloop.. rolled and pitched..violently 1748. Hence **Ro·llable** *a.* capable of being rolled. **Ro·llway** *U.S.*, a natural slope on the bank of a river, or an inclined shoot for expediting the descent of logs, etc., to the surface of water or ice; *transf.* the pile of logs on a river-bank awaiting transportation.

Roll-call (rōᵘ·lˌkǭl). 1802. [f. ROLL *sb.*[1] + CALL *sb.*] 1. The act of calling over a list of the names of persons forming a military or other body, in order to ascertain who are present; the marking of such a list at a particular time. 2. *Mil.* The signal summoning men to be present at the calling of the roll 1890.

Ro·ll-co:llar. 1836. [ROLL *sb.*[1]] A turned-over collar on a garment.

Rolled (rōᵘld), *ppl. a.* 1467. [f. ROLL *v.*] In the senses of ROLL *v.*

R. gold, orig., a thin coating of gold applied to a baser metal by rolling; now, a kind of filled gold rolled or drawn out so that the gold becomes very thin.

Roller (rōᵘ·lər), *sb.*[1] late ME. [f. ROLL *v.*] I. 1. A rolling-pin. Now *dial.* 2. A cylinder of wood or metal, revolving on pivots or a fixed axis, for lessening the friction of anything passed over it; also, a rounded piece of wood over which an endless towel is passed. late ME. b. The revolvable drum, barrel, or axis of a winch or windlass 1659. 3. One of a number of cylinders of wood, etc., either attached or free, for diminishing friction when rolling or moving a heavy body 1565. 4. A heavy cylinder of wood, stone, or (now usu.) metal, fitted in a frame with shafts or a handle, for crushing clods, etc., and smoothing the ground by compression 1530. b. A rotating cylinder or roll for pressing, stamping, crushing, or rolling; one of a set of rolls for forming metal, etc., into bars or sheets; also, the revolving cylinder of a printing-machine for impressing the paper upon the printing-matter 1728. c. *Printing.* A cylinder or roll of thick, elastic composition, mounted on a metal or wooden axis, for inking a form of letter, etc., before printing; also, a metal cylinder for distributing ink upon this 1790. 5. A cylindrical piece of wood, etc.; esp. one on which cloth or other material is rolled up 1567. 6. *Organ-building.* A rounded slip of wood or piece of metal tube, turning, by the action of the key, on pins inserted into its ends, and having two or more arms at right angles to its length 1632. b. The toothed or studded revolvable barrel of a musical box 1875. 7. A small wheel rotating on an axle or axis; a short cylinder serving as a wheel 1802. 8. A roller-chain for a cycle (i.e. one in which flexibility is attained by the use of small rollers in each link) 1897. II. A long bandage, formed in a roll, for winding firmly round a limb, etc. Now more freq. *r.-bandage.* 1534. b. A broad, padded girth for a horse 1688. III. 1. *Zool.* A variety of tumbler-pigeon 1867. 2. A long swelling wave, moving with a steady sweep or roll; a heavy billow 1829. IV. One who rolls up or forms into a roll or coil; one who compresses or shapes metal by passing it between cylinders or rolls 1591. 2. A butterfly or moth which causes leaves to roll up 1832.

attrib. and *Comb.*: **r.-bandage**, = sense II; **board**, the board carrying the rollers in an organ; **-bolt**, part of the splinter-bar of a carriage, serving also as a step; **-gin**, a cotton-gin in which the cleaning is effected by rollers; **-mill**, a mill in which the grinding is done by rollers; **-shop**, the part of an iron-works where the metal is rolled; **-towel**, a towel running on a r.

Roller (rōᵘ·lər), *sb.*[2] 1678. [a. G., f. *rollen* to roll.] 1. An insessorial coracoid bird (usu. the common r., *Coracias garrulus*), having the form of a crow, and brilliant plumage. b. Applied to other birds, as *Eurystomus Australis*, *E. azureus*, etc. 1752. 2. A variety of canary, remarkable for rolling or trilling in song 1884.

Ro·ller-skate. 1874. orig. *U.S.* [ROLLER *sb.*[1] I. 7.] A skate mounted on small wheels or rollers, usually two pairs, for use in skating on smooth flooring, etc. Hence **Ro·ller-skate** *v. intr.* to use or to perform on roller-skates.

Rolley (rǫ·li). Also **rolly.** 1825. [perh. conn. w. ROLL *v.*] 1. *Mining.* A kind of truck without sides, formerly much in use for carrying corves along underground horse-roads or upon rails to the shaft. 2. A lorry 1886.

Rollick (rǫ·lik), *v.* 1826. [Origin unkn.] *intr.* To frolic, sport, or romp, in a joyous, careless fashion; to go off, move along, enter, etc., in this manner. Freq. *transf.* of things or animals.

'Q.' appears as a rollicking humourist. He rollicks ..a little too laboriously. 1888. Hence **Ro·llick** *sb.* exuberant gaiety or joviality; a sportive frolic or escapade. **Ro·llicker.** **Ro·llicking** *ppl. a.* extremely jovial or gay; boisterously sportive.

Rolling (rōᵘ·liŋ), *ppl. a.* ME. [f. ROLL *v.*] 1. That turns over and over, esp. so as to move forward on a surface or down a slope 1500. b. That moves or runs upon wheels 1565. c. Of a person, his opinions: Changeable, shifting, variable, inconstant. Now *rare* or *Obs.* 1561. d. Of time or seasons: Steadily moving onwards; also, moving round, recurring 1695. 2. Revolving, rotating; turning on, or as on, an axis; moving round a centre 1591. b. Of the eyes: Moving to and fro or up and down in the sockets 1576. c. Turning round, turned over, in a coil or fold. late ME. d. Swinging, swaying; as a *r. gait* 1755. 3. Heaving, surging, swelling, flowing steadily and strongly onwards 1633. b. Ascending or moving in curls or rolls 1664. 4. Producing a continuous swelling sound; reverberating, resounding 1652. b. Continuously sounded or trilled 1863. 5. Of prairie-land, etc.: Having a succession of gentle undulations. Also *transf.* Orig. *U.S.* 1819.

1. His thoughts are like a r. axeltree *Ecclus.* xxxiii. 5. b. A R. wagon 1648. d. Oft as the r. Years return PRIOR. 2. The r. world 1848. c. The r. scrolls, borrowed from the Romans 1883. 3. *fig.* Fix'd in the r. flood of endless years COWPER. b. A tremulous.. Agitation of rowling fumes 1664. 4. A r. organ-harmony Swells up TENNYSON. 5. A r., rugged down, flecked with patches of..heath 1890.

attrib. **r.-stock**, the locomotives, wagons, carriages, etc. used on a railway. **Ro·llingly** *adv.*

Ro·lling-mill. 1787. [f. *rolling vbl. sb.* or *ppl. a.*] A mill or powerful machine in or by which metal, etc., is rolled out or flattened.

Ro·lling-pin. 1589. [f. as prec.] A cylindrical piece of wood or other material for rolling out dough, paste, or, formerly, leather.

Ro·lling-press. 1625. [f. as prec.] 1. A copperplate-printers' press in which the plate passes in a bed under a revolving cylinder. 2. A press which flattens, smooths, etc., by means of cylinders or rollers; a rolling-machine 1833.

Rolling stone, ro·lling-stone. 1546. [f. as prec.] 1. In the provb. *A rolling stone gathers no moss*, or variants of this; see MOSS *sb.* II. 1. 2. A rambler, wanderer; a good-for-nothing 1611. 3. A cylindrical stone used for crushing, flattening, etc. 1611.

Ro·ll-top. 1890. [f. ROLL *v.*] The sliding cover of a writing desk, made of parallel slats fastened to a flexible backing; also, = *roll-top desk.*

Roly-poly (rōᵘ·liˌpōᵘ·li), *sb.* and *a.* Also rolypoly. 1601. [app. a fanciful formation on ROLL *v.*] A. *sb.* †1. A worthless fellow; a rascal –1609. 2. The name of various games, in most of which the rolling of a ball is the chief feature 1713. 3. A pudding, consisting of a sheet of paste covered with jam or preserves, formed into a roll and boiled or steamed 1848. B. *adj.* Short and stout; podgy, dumpy, plump. Chiefly of children. 1820.

‖**Rom** (rǫm). Also *pl.* **Roma(s).** 1841. [Gipsy (Romany) *rom* man, husband; pl. *romá.*] A male Gipsy, a Romany.

Romaic (romēⁱ·ik), *a.* and *sb.* 1809. [ad. Gr. Ῥωμαϊκός Roman (f. Ῥώμη Rome), used spec. of the Eastern empire.] A. *a.* 1. Forming, composed in, pertaining to, the vernacular language of modern Greece. 2. *R. dance* = next 2. 1830. B. *sb.* The vernacular language of modern Greece or a dialect of it 1810.

Romaika (romēⁱ·ikă). 1625. [ad. mod. Gr. ῥωμαϊκή; see prec.] †1. = prec. B. PURCHAS. 2. A modern Greek dance 1811.

‖**Romal, rumal** (ro-, rumā·l). 1683. [Urdū (Pers.) *rūmāl*, f. *rū* face + *māl* wiping.] 1. A silk or cotton square or handkerchief; a thin silk or cotton fabric with a handkerchief pattern. 2. The handkerchief or bandage used by Indian Thugs to strangle their victims 1836.

Roman (rōᵘ·măn), *sb.* OE. [ad. L. *Romanus*, f. *Roma* Rome.] I. 1. An inhabitant or native of ancient Rome; a Roman citizen or soldier; one belonging to the Roman state or empire. b. An inhabitant or native of mediæval or modern Rome 1547. 2. *pl.* Those inhabitants of ancient Rome who had accepted the Christian faith. late ME. b. *ellipt.* St. Paul's Epistle to the Romans: abbrev. *Rom.* late ME. 3. *Printing.* The style of letters distinguished by this name (see ROMAN *a.* 5.); also *pl.* letters of a Roman fount 1598.

1. *King*, or *Emperor, of the Romans*, the sovereign head of the Holy Roman Empire. 2. Paul commendeth his calling to the Romanes *Rom.* i.

II. A member or adherent of the Roman Catholic Church; a Roman Catholic. Now *colloq.* 1547.

Roman (rōᵘ·măn), *a.* ME. [orig. a. OF. *Romain*, subseq. ad. L. *Romanus*; see prec.] I. 1. Of persons: Inhabiting, belonging to, or originating from the ancient city of Rome or its territory; holding the position of a citizen or member of the ancient republic or empire of Rome. 2. Of things: Of or pertaining to, connected with, ancient Rome, its inhabitants or dominion; practised or used by, current or usual among, the Romans, etc. ME. b. Of language, etc. = LATIN *a.* 2. ME. 3. Of antiquities, etc.: Belonging to, surviving from, the time of the Romans 1548. 4. Of a type or kind characteristic of, or exemplified by, the Romans; Roman-like, esp. in respect of honesty, strictness, courage, or frugality 1577. **b.** Of a nose: Having a prominent upper part or bridge 1624. **5.** Of letters: Belonging to the modern type which most directly represents that used in ancient Roman inscriptions and manuscripts, esp. in contrast to *Gothic* (or *black letter*) and *Italic* 1519. **b.** Of handwriting: Round and bold 1601. **6. a.** Of the alphabet or its characters: Employed by the Romans, and (with modifications) by all the modern nations of Western Europe and their colonies 1728. **b.** Of numeral letters: The letters I, V, X, L, C, D, M. (Opp. to *Arabic.*) 1728. **7.** *Arch.* = COMPOSITE *a.* 2. 1624. **8.** Engaged in the study of Roman law, antiquities, history, etc. 1845.

1. The R. Emperors residing in the East 1660. 2. The northern nations who established themselves upon the ruins of the R. Empire 1776. Tin, used in the R. coinage 1819. *R. Law*, the system or code of law developed by the ancient Romans, and still accepted in principle by many countries. 3. Ride by the side of the R. road 1774. 4. He was dispos'd to mirth, but..A Romane thought hath strooke him SHAKS. 5. b. I thinke we doe know the sweet Romane hand SHAKS. 8. To the R. lawyer the study of R. antiquities is essential 1845.

II. 1. Pertaining to Rome in its ecclesiastical aspect; belonging to, connected with, the Church of Rome; = ROMAN CATHOLIC *a.* 1535. **2.** (*Holy*) *R. Empire*: the Romano-Germanic Empire which originated with Charlemagne in 800, and continued to exist down to 1806. So *R. Emperor*. 1610. †**3.** = ROMANCE I b. -1804.

1. *R. collar*, a special form of collar worn by Roman Catholic, and some Anglican, clerics.

III. Of or pertaining to mediæval or modern Rome or its inhabitants; printed at Rome, etc. 1608.

R. school, the school of painting of which Raphael is the leading representative. *R. fever*, a form of malarial fever prevalent in Rome.

Special collocations: **R. alum**, a reddish alum found in Italy, or a manufactured imitation of this; **R. balance, beam**, the ordinary form of steelyard; **R. candle**, a cylindrical firework which throws out a succession of stars; **R. cement**, a cement or hydraulic mortar made by the addition of calcareous or argillaceous matter to lime, sand, and water; also as vb.; **R. mosaic**, a mosaic 'formed of short and slender sticks of coloured glass'; **R. steelyard** = *R. balance*.

Ro·man Ca·tholic, *sb.* and *a.* 1605. [Representing the full official designation 'Ecclesia *Romana Catholica* et Apostolica' (see ROMAN *a.* II. 1. and CATHOLIC *a.* II. 2); app. orig. used as a conciliatory term, in place of *Roman*, *Romanist*, or *Romish*, early in the 17th c. Now the recognized legal and official designation, though in ordinary use *Catholic* alone is common.] = ROMAN *sb.* II, *a.* II. 1. Hence **Ro·man-Catho·lically, -Ca·tholicly** *advs.* **Ro·man Catho·licism.**

Romance (romæ·ns), *sb.* (and *a.*). [ME., a. OF. *romanz, romans* :—pop. L. **Romanice* adv., f. L. *Romanicus*; see ROMANIC.] **I. a.** *orig.* The vernacular language of France, as opp. to Latin. In later use also extended to related forms of speech, as Provençal and Spanish, and now a generic or collective name for the whole group of languages derived from Latin. **b.** *attrib.* or as *adj.* Derived from or representing the old Roman tongue; descended from Latin. Also composed in, using, etc., a vernacular tongue of Latin origin. late ME.

II. 1. A tale in verse, embodying the life and adventures of some hero of chivalry, and belonging in matter and form to the ages of knighthood; also, in later use, a prose tale of a similar character ME. **2.** A fictitious narrative in prose of which the scene and incidents are very remote from those of ordinary life; *esp.* one of the class prevalent in the 16th and 17th centuries, with long disquisitions and digressions. Also occas., a long poem of a similar type. 1638. **b.** A romantic novel or narrative 1831. **3.** A Spanish historical ballad or short poem of a certain form 1605. **b.** *Mus.* A short vocal or instrumental piece of a simple or informal character 1797. **4.** That class of literature which consists of romances; romantic fiction 1667. **b.** Romantic or imaginative character or quality; suggestion of or association with the adventurous and chivalrous 1801. **5.** An extravagant fiction, invention, or story; a wild or wanton exaggeration; a picturesque falsehood. Also without article. 1497. **6.** *attrib.*, as *r.-novel*; also as *adj.* with the sense: Having the character or attributes associated with romance; chivalrous, romantic 1653.

1. The first metrical r...is the famous *chanson de Roland* 1802. 2. In the Romance you lent me none of the great Heroes were ever false in love GAY. b. The r. of the Pirate SCOTT. *transf.* The last romance of Science..is the Story of the Ascent of Man 1894. 4. And what resounds In Fable or R. of Uthers Son MILT. *fig.* Lady of the Mere, Sole-sitting by the shores of old r. WORDSW. b. R. goes out of a man's head when the hair gets grey 1873. 5. This is r.—I'll not believe a word on't 1667. 6. The poetical or r. accounts of these last Gaulish invasions 1842. Hence **Roma·nceless** *a.* unromantic. †**Roma·ncial** *a.* (*rare*) 1653. **Roma·ncical** *a.* (*rare*) of the nature of r., composing or inventing romances 1656. †**Roma·ncy** *a.* romantic 1654-82.

Romance (romæ·ns), *v.* 1671. [f. the sb., or ad. F. *romancer.*] **a.** *intr.* To exaggerate or invent after the fashion of romances; to talk hyperbolically. **b.** To have romantic ideas; to use romantic language 1849.

a. Now, when, for the first time, they told the truth, they were supposed to be romancing MACAULAY.

Romancer (romæ·nsəɹ). ME. [f. ROMANCE *v.* + -ER.] **1.** The author of a romance; a writer of romances or romantic fiction. **2.** One who deals in extravagant fictions; an inventor of false history; a fantastic liar 1663.

Romancist (romæ·nsist). 1656. [ad. Sp. (and Pg.) *romancista*, f. *romance* ROMANCE *sb.*] A composer of romances; a romantic novelist.

Romanesque (rōᵘmăne·sk), *a.* (and *sb.*). 1715. [a. F., f. *roman* romance: see -ESQUE.] **1.** = ROMANCE *sb.* I. b. **2.** *Arch.* Prevalent in, or distinctive of, the buildings erected in Romanized Europe between the close of the classical period and the rise of Gothic architecture 1819. **b.** Built in the Romanesque style 1830. **c.** Characterized by the use or prevalence of the Romanesque style 1850. **d.** *absol.* as *sb.* The Romanesque style of art or architecture 1830.

2. b. The three great R. cathedrals 1830. c. The later R. period 1850.

Romanic (romæ·nik), *a.* (and *sb.*). 1708. [ad. L. *Romanicus*, f. *Romanus* ROMAN *sb.*] **1.** Of languages: Descended from Latin; Romance. **b.** *absol.* as *sb.* = ROMANCE *sb.* I. a. 1708. **2.** Derived or descended from the Romans; belonging to the Romance peoples 1847.

Romanish (rōᵘ·măniʃ), *a.* and *sb.* OE. [f. L. *Romanus* + -ISH[1] 1.] †**1.** = ROMAN *a.* I. 1. -ME. **2.** = ROMISH *a.* 1. 1591. **3.** *absol.* as *sb.* = ROMANSH 1689.

Romanism (rōᵘ·măniz'm). 1674. [f. ROMAN *a.*] **1.** The Roman Catholic religion or doctrines, Roman Catholicism. **2.** A feature of Roman architecture 1827. **3.** Roman institutions; the prevailing spirit of the Roman world; Roman sway or influence 1877.

Romanist (rōᵘ·mănist), *sb.* (and *a.*). 1523. [ad. mod.L. *Romanista* (Luther); see ROMAN *a.* and -IST.] **1.** A member or adherent of the Church of Rome; a Roman Catholic. **b.** *attrib.* or as *adj.* Belonging or adhering to the Church of Rome 1635. **2.** One who is versed in or practises Roman Law; a lawyer of the Roman school 1647. **3.** A student of Roman antiquities 1858. **4.** One who makes a special study of Romance languages or philology 1886.

Romanize (rōᵘ·mănəiz), *v.* 1607. [f. ROMAN *a.* + -IZE.] **1.** *trans.* To render Roman in character; to bring under the influence or authority of Rome. **2.** *intr.* To follow Roman custom or practice; to accept the principles of Roman law 1629. **b.** To follow, tend towards, or go over to, the Church of Rome; to become Roman Catholic 1637.

2. b. So apishly Romanizing, that the word of command still was set downe in Latine MILT. Hence **Ro·maniza·tion. Ro·manizer.**

Romano- (romē·no), used as comb. form of ROMAN *a.*, as *Romano-Celtic*, etc.

Romansh (roma·nʃ), *sb.* and *a.* 1663. [a. the native name *Rum-, Roman(t)sch, -on(t)sch*, etc. :—pop. L. **Romanice* adv.; see ROMANCE *sb.*] The language, of Latin origin, spoken in the Grisons or eastern district of Switzerland. Also *attrib.* or as *adj.*

Romantic (romæ·ntik), *a.* and *sb.* 1659. [f. *romant*, ROMAUNT (mod.L. *romantia*) or ad. mod.L. *romanticus*; hence G. *romantisch*, F. *romantique.*] **A.** *adj.* **1.** Of the nature of or having the qualities of romance in respect of form or content. **b.** *Mus.* Characterized by the subordination of form to theme, and by imagination and passion 1885. **2.** Of a fabulous or fictitious character; having no foundation in fact 1667. †**b.** Imaginary; purely ideal -1711. **3.** Of projects, etc.: Fantastic, extravagant, quixotic; going beyond what is rational or practical 1671. **4.** Having a tendency towards romance; readily influenced by the imagination 1690. **b.** Tending towards or characterized by romance as a basis or principle of literature or art. (Opp. to *classical.*) 1754. **5.** Marked by or invested with romance or imaginative appeal 1666.

1. It was a step in my advance towards r. composition SCOTT. 2. These things are almost romantique, and yet true PEPYS. 3. The r. and visionary scheme of building a bridge over the river at Putney 1671. 4. I am not r.;—I have not the least design of doing good to either of you 1778. b. *R. movement*, the movement in literature (and art) originating in a revolt against the formalities and conventions of classicism, and characterized in the 19th c. by conscious preoccupation with the subjective and imaginative aspects of nature and life. 5. You feel that armour is r., because it is a beautiful dress, and you are not used to it RUSKIN. The grandest and most r. character that Israel ever produced, Elijah the Tishbite 1856. Hence **Roma·ntical** *a.* 1678, **-ly** *adv.* 1668. **Roma·nticize** *v. trans.* to render r. in character; *intr.* to indulge in romance. **Roma·ntic·ly** *adv.* 1681, **-ness.**

B. *sb.* **1.** A feature, characteristic, idea, etc., belonging to, or suggestive of, romance 1679. **2.** A romantic person; *esp.* an adherent of romanticism in literature 1865.

Romanticism (romæ·ntisiz'm). 1803. [f. ROMANTIC *a.*] **1.** A romantic fancy or idea. **2.** Tendency towards romance or romantic views 1840. **3.** The distinctive qualities or spirit of the romantic school in art, literature, and music 1844.

3. Stein belonged to the class of society which naturally furnished recruits to R. 1878. So **Roma·nticist**, an adherent of r. (sense 3).

Romany (rǫ·măni), *sb.* and *a.* Also **Rommany**, etc. 1812. [Gipsy *Romani*, fem. and pl. of *Romano* adj., f. *Rom* gipsy; see ROM.] **1.** A gipsy; also *collect.* the gipsies. **2.** The language of the gipsies 1812. **3.** *attrib.* or as *adj.* = GIPSY 4. 1841.

Romaunt (romǭ·nt), *sb.* and *a. arch.* 1530. [a. OF. *romant* (later *roman*), an analogical var. of *romanz, romans* ROMANCE.] **1.** A romance; a romantic tale or poem. **2.** A Romance form of speech; also *attrib.*, Romance, Romanic, in respect of language 1530.

1. The Romante of the Rose PALSGR. There are the minstrels, with their romaunts and ballads SCOTT.

Rombowline (rvmbōᵘ·lin). Also **r(h)um-**. 1841. [Orig. unkn.] *Naut.* Condemned canvas, rope, etc. used for temporary purposes not requiring strength.

Rome (rōᵘm), *sb.* Also †**Roome.** OE. [a. L. *Roma* and OF. *Rome*. Pronounced (rūm) by some as late as the 19th c.] **1.** The city or state of Rome; the Roman empire. Freq. personified. **2.** The city of Rome as the original capital of Western Christendom, and the seat of the Pope; hence, the Roman Catholic Church, its influence or institutions, etc. late ME.

1. Theym that founded roome CAXTON. R.. has been the source of law and government 1841. 2. King Iohn hath reconcil'd Himselfe to R. SHAKS.

Romeine (rōᵘ·məin). 1849. [Named after the crystallographer *Romé de L'Isle.*] *Min.* A native antimoniate of calcium occurring in yellow crystals. Also **Ro·meite.**

Ro·me-penny. Now *Hist.* OE. [f. ROME *sb.* 2 + PENNY.] = PETER('S)-PENNY.

Ro·me-scot. Now *Hist.* OE. [See ROME *sb.* 2 and SCOT *sb.*] = ROME-PENNY.

Romeward (rōᵘ·mwǭɹd), *adv.* and *a.* ME. [-WARD.] **1.** Towards or in the direction of Rome. **2.** Towards the Roman Catholic Church or Roman Catholicism 1864. **3.** as *adj.* Directed to or tending towards the Roman Catholic Church 1851.

3. His distinct repudiation of R. doctrine 1887. So **Ro·mewards** *adv.*

Romic (rōᵘ·mik), *a.* and *sb.* 1877. [f. ROMAN *a.* + -IC.] The name of a system of phonetic notation devised by Dr. Henry Sweet.

This system, which I call 'Romic' (because based on the original Roman value of the letters) SWEET.

Romish (rōu·miʃ), *a.* 1531. [f. ROME *sb.* + -ISH[1] 1.] 1. Belonging, pertaining, or adhering to Rome in respect of religion; Roman Catholic. (Chiefly *hostile.*) †2. = ROMAN *a.* 1. -1797.

1. Upon promise of the Duke to become R. MILT. Hence **Ro·mish-ly** *adv.*, **-ness.**

Romp (rǫmp), *sb.* 1706. [perh. var. of RAMP *sb.*[1]] 1. One who romps; *esp.* a play-loving, lively, merry girl (or woman). 2. A piece of lively, boisterous play; a merry frolic. Freq. in *pl.* 1734.

2. My little rogue soon engaged him in a r. 1797. Hence **Ro·mpish** *a.* inclined to romp.

Romp (rǫmp), *v.* 1709. [perh. a var. of RAMP *v.*[1]] 1. *intr.* To play, sport, or frolic in a very lively, merry, or boisterous manner. 2. Chiefly *Racing slang*: a. To move, cover the ground, easily and rapidly 1891. b. To get *in* (or *home*), to win a race, prize or contest with the greatest ease 1888.

2. b. Eclipse..romped in, the easiest of winners 1888.

†**Rompee.** 1610. [Alteration of F. *rompu* (pa. pple. of *rompre*) after heraldic terms in *-ee.*] *Her.* Broken -1728.

Romper (rǫmpəɹ). 1922. [f. ROMP *v.* + -ER[1].] Chiefly *pl.* A washable overall worn by small children to protect their clothes.

Ro·mping, *ppl. a.* 1711. [f. ROMP *v.* + -ING.[2]] 1. Of persons: That romps; engaged in, or given to, romping. 2. Of actions etc.: Having the character of a romp or romps 1802. Hence **Ro·mpingly** *adv.*

‖**Roncador** (rǫŋkădōəɹ). *U.S.* 1882. [Sp., agent-n. f. *roncar* to snore, snort.] One or other of several sciænoid fishes of the Pacific coast of N. America.

‖**Rondache** (rǫndæ·ʃ, F. rondaʃ). 1604. [F., f. *rond* round.] 1. A small circular shield or buckler. †2. *transf.* A foot-soldier -1646.

Ronde (rǫnd). 1838. [a. F. *ronde*, adj. fem.] *Typog.* A form of type imitating handwriting.

‖**Rondeau** (rǫ·ndo, F. rondo). 1525. [F., later form of *rondel*; see next.] 1. A short poem, consisting of ten, or in stricter sense of thirteen, lines, having only two rimes throughout, and with the opening words used twice as a refrain; *transf.* a refrain. 2. *Mus.* = RONDO 1773.

Rondel (rǫ·ndĕl). ME. [a. older F. *rondel* masc. (later *rondeau*; see prec.), or *rondelle* fem., f. *rond* ROUND *a.* Cf. ROUNDEL.] 1. A circle; a circular object. Now *arch.* †b. *Fortif.* A round tower -1704. 2. A rondeau, or a special form of this. late ME.

2. With Charles d'Orléans, the r. took the distinct shape..of fourteen lines on two rhymes 1887.

‖**Rondeletia** (rǫndĕlī·ʃiă). 1771. [mod.L., after the French naturalist *Rondelet.*] 1. A tropical American genus of *Cinchonaceæ*; a plant or shrub of this genus. 2. A perfume resembling that which is characteristic of this genus of plants 1840.

‖**Rondo** (rǫ·ndo). 1797. [It. *rondo*, a. F. *rondeau.*] *Mus.* 1. A piece of music having one principal subject, to which a return is twice made after the introduction of other matter. 2. = ROUND *sb.*[1] IV. 1 b.

Rondure (rǫ·ndiŭɹ). 1600. [ad. F. *rondeur.*] A circle or round object; roundness.

All things rare, That heauens ayre in this huge r. hems SHAKS.

Röntgen (rö·ntyĕn). 1896. Name of a German scientist (Prof. Conrad W. *Röntgen*), used attrib. in *R. rays* (see RAY *sb.*[1] 1.) Hence **Rö·ntgenism,** morbid condition induced by R. rays. **Rö·ntgenize** *v. trans.* to discharge electricity through gases by means of R. rays. **Rö·ntgenogram,** a photograph taken by R. rays. **Röntgeno·graphy,** photography by R. rays. **Röntgeno·logy,** the study of R. rays. **Röntgeno·scopy,** observation by means of R. rays. **Rö·ntgenothe·rapy,** healing by means of R. rays.

Rood (rūd), *sb.* [OE. *rōd.*] I. †1. = CROSS *sb.* 1. -late ME. 2. The cross upon which Christ suffered; the cross as the symbol of the Christian faith. Now *arch.* OE. b. In asseverations, *by the r.!* etc. Now *arch.* ME. 3. A crucifix, *esp.* one stationed above the middle of a rood-screen; also *rarely*, a figure of the cross in wood or metal, as a religious object OE.

2. Good hope I have Of help from Him that died upon the r. MORRIS. b. By the r.! they are wise enough 1896. See also HOLY ROOD (DAY).

attrib. and *Comb.*: **r.-beam,** a transverse beam supporting the r., usu. forming the head of a r.-screen; **-cloth,** a cloth used to cover the crucifix over the r.-screen during Lent; **-loft,** a loft or gallery forming the head of a r.-screen; **-screen,** a screen, properly surmounted by a r. crossing the nave of a church beneath the chancel-arch and separating the nave from the choir; **-steeple, -tower,** the tower or steeple built over the intersection of the body and cross-aisles of a church; †**-tree.** = sense 2.

II. 1. As a linear measure: A rod, pole, or perch. Now only *local*, and varying from 6 to 8 yards. OE. 2. A superficial measure of land, properly containing 40 square poles or perches, but varying locally; a plot of land of this size OE. b. A measure (of land, paving, building, etc.) corresponding to a square pole or perch, but with local and other variations 1464.

Roo·d day. *Hist.* ME. [ROOD *sb.* 2.] The Exaltation of the Cross (14 Sept.), or the Invention of the Cross (3 May).

Roof (rūf), *sb.* [OE. *hrōf* = OFris. *rhoof*, MDu. *roof.*] 1. The outside upper covering of a house or other building; also, the ceiling of a room or other covered part of a house, building, etc. b. Used by extension to denote a house or chamber. Chiefly *poet.* 1591. 2. *fig.* a. The highest point or summit of something; that which completes or covers in OE. b. Something which in form or function is comparable to the covering of a house 1611. c. *Mining.* The stratum lying immediately over a bed of coal; the top of a working or gallery 1686. 3. *The roof of the mouth*, the palate. Also *ellipt.* So of other parts of the body, etc. OE. 4. The top of a carriage, coach, etc. 1706.

1. Among the ancients, in those countries where it seldom rained, roofs were made quite flat 1815. For about two years they lived..under the r. of their father's youngest sister 1888. b. *A. Y. L.* II. iii. 17. 2. This most excellent Canopy the Ayre..this Maiesticall Roofe SHAKS. Why should we only toil, the r. and crown of things? TENNYSON 4. The r. of a crazy coach 1806.

attrib. and *Comb.*: **r.-cat,** an Indian species of cat; **-garden,** a garden or collection of plants in large pots, etc., on the (flat) r. of a house or other building; **-mask,** an outer r. which protects the inner r. from the weather; **-swell,** a variety of organ swell. Hence **Roo·fage,** the material of a r.; roofing. **Roo·fless** *a.* **Roo·fy** *a.* furnished with a r.; abounding in roofs.

Roof (rūf), *v.* 1475. [f. prec.] 1. *trans.* To provide or cover with a roof. Also with *in*, *over*. 2. To be or form, to lie as, a roof over (something). Also with *in*. 1615. b. To shelter, house 1820.

1. Ancient Roman buildings..roofed with either vaults or arches ADDISON. 2. As thunder-clouds that ..Roof'd the world with doubt and fear TENNYSON. Hence **Roo·fer,** (*a*) one who constructs or repairs roofs; (*b*) a letter of thanks for entertainment sent by a departed visitor.

Roofed (rūft), *ppl. a.* 1500. [f. ROOF *v.* + -ED[1].] 1. Having a roof; covered with or as with a roof also with *in, over.* 2. In combs. denoting a particular kind of roof 1600.

1. Here had we now our Countries Honor, roof'd, Were the grac'd person of our Banquo present SHAKS. 2. Their houses are flat-roofed HAKLUYT.

Roo·fing, (*vbl.*) *sb.* 1440. [f. ROOF *sb.* or *v.* + -ING[1].] 1. The act of covering with a roof; material used or suitable for roofs; that which forms a roof or roofs. 2. *Mining.* The wedging of the top of the loaded skip against the top of an underground passage 1747.

1. The hovel was of mud-walls, without any r. 1760.

Roo·f-tree. 1440. [f. ROOF *sb.*] The main beam or ridge-pole of a roof.

Ye have riven the thack off seven cottar houses—look if your ain r.-tree stand the faster SCOTT.

‖**Rooinek** (rōu·inek). 1898. [Afrikaans (= Du. *rood-e* red + *nek* neck).] A British or European immigrant in S. Africa; in the Boer War, a British soldier.

Rook (ruk), *sb.*[1] [OE. *hrōc*; perh. orig. imitative.] 1. A black raucous-voiced European and Asiatic bird (*Corvus frugilegus*), nesting in colonies; in the north of Britain usu. called a *crow*. 2. Applied to persons as an abusive or disparaging term 1508. b. A cheat, swindler, or sharper, *spec.* in gaming 1577. †c. A gull, a simpleton -1637.

1. A blackening train Of clamorous rooks thick urge their weary flight THOMSON. 2. Rakish rooks like Rob Mossgiel BURNS.

Comb.: **r.-pie,** a pie made with (young) rooks; **-rifle,** a rifle of small bore for shooting rooks. Hence **Roo·ky** *a.* full of, abounding in, consisting of, rooks.

Rook (ruk), *sb.*[2] ME. [a. OF. *roc(k*, f. (ult.) Pers. *rukh.*] *Chess.* One of four pieces which at the beginning of the game are set in the corner squares, and have the power of moving in a right line backwards, forwards, or laterally over any number of unoccupied squares; a castle. Hence **Rook** *v.*[2] *intr.* to castle.

Rook (ruk), *v.*[1] 1590. [f. ROOK *sb.*[1] 2 b.] 1. *trans.* To cheat; to defraud by cheating, *esp.* in gaming; to charge extortionately. Chiefly *slang* or *colloq.* †2. To take by cheating -1695. †3. *intr.* To practise cheating -1693.

1. Drawn in by guinea-droppers, and rook'd of forty guineas and a watch 1710.

Rookery (ru·kəri). 1725. [f. ROOK *sb.*[1] + -ERY.] 1. A collection of rooks' nests in a clump of trees; a colony of rooks. 2. A breeding-place, common resort, or large colony (of sea-birds, *esp.* penguins, also of seals or other marine mammals) 1838. 3. A cluster of mean tenements densely populated by people of the lowest class 1829.

1. The many-winter'd crow that leads the clanging r. home TENNYSON. 3. Market Street,..a well-known r. of prostitutes 1851.

Room (rūm, rum), *sb.* [Com. Teut.: OE. *rūm* = MDu. *ruum*, OHG. *rūm* (G. *raum*).] I. 1. Space; dimensional extent. 2. Sufficient space; accommodation. Also const. *for*, or *to* with infin. OE. 3. *To make r.*: †a. To clear a space for oneself -1535. b. To make way, yield place, draw back or retire, so as to allow a person to enter, etc. So *to give r.*, and with imperative suppressed. late ME. c. To provide or obtain space or place for something by the removal of other things 1666. 4. *transf.* and *fig.* Opportunity or scope *to* do something OE. b. Opportunity or scope *for* something, by which it is rendered possible 1692.

1. Both Labour and R. was saved by their repeated Contractions 1699. 2. Syt nye together, yt I maye haue rowme COVERDALE *Isa.* xlix. 20. Phrases. *No r. to turn in, no r. to swing a cat*, implying extremely restricted space. b. Is there roome in thy fathers house for vs to lodge in? *Gen.* xxiv. 23. b. Make roome and let him stand before our face SHAKS. Roome for Antony, most Noble Antony SHAKS. 4. R. to deny ourselves KEBLE. b. As to most of the provisions there was little r. for dispute MACAULAY. Phr. *R. for improvement*, implying a state of affairs not entirely satisfactory.

II. 1. A particular portion of space; a certain space or area ME. †2. A particular place or spot, without ref. to its area -1674. 3. An interior portion of a building divided off by walls or partitions; *esp.* a chamber or apartment in a dwelling-house 1457. b. *pl.* Lodgings 1837. c. The persons assembled in a room; the company 1712. 4. In various techn. applications; *esp.* one of the passages or spaces for working left between the pillars of a coal-mine. Chiefly in phr. *pillar and r.* 1789.

1. A journal of the weather..which exhibits in a little r., a great train of different observations JOHNSON. *R. and space* (Shipbuilding) is the distance from the edge of one timber to the corresponding edge of the timber next to it; *space* being the distance between the two timbers and *R.* the width of a timber 1846 3. The rooms of the cottage were low 1891. b. I trust I shall have the pleasure of seeing you and your friend at my rooms DICKENS.

III. 1. †a. A particular place assigned or appropriated to a person or thing -1721. b. Contrasted with *company* 1577. †2. An office, function, appointment; a post, situation, employment -1644. 3. An office or post considered as pertaining to a particular person; *esp.* by right or by inheritance. *Obs.* exc. in phrases. 1450.

1. b. I'd rather have his r. than his company 1880. 2. He..forsooke a right worshipfull roome when it was offered him CAMDEN 3. *In one's r.*, in one's place, denoting substitution of one person or thing for another. *In the r. of*, in the place (†or office) *of*, in lieu *of*, instead *of*. Hence **Roo·mage** *U.S.*, space; internal capacity; accommodation. **Roo·mful,** as much or as many as a r. will hold. **Roo·mful** *a.* capacious, roomy. **Roo·mless** *a.* (*rare*).

†**Room,** *a. Obs.* exc. *Sc.* [Com. Teut.: OE. *rūm.*] Spacious, large; wide, extensive -1635.

Ther was no rommer herberwe in the place CHAUCER. Hence †**Roo·msome** *a.* ample, capacious, roomy.

Room (rūm, rum), *v. U.S.* 1828. [f. Room *sb.*] **a.** *intr.* To occupy rooms as a lodger; to share a room or rooms *with* another. **b.** *trans.* To accommodate or lodge (guests) 1864.

a. She rooms with me, and is very interesting and agreeable 1828. Hence **Roo·mer** *U.S.*, a lodger who occupies a room or rooms without board.

Roomed (rūmd), *a.* 1548. [f. Room *sb.* + -ed[2].] With defining word prefixed: Having rooms of a specified number or kind, as *one-*, *double-r.*; also *wide-r.*, †spacious.

Roo·m-mate. *U.S.* 1838. One who occupies the same room or rooms with another.

Roomth (rūmþ). Now *dial.* 1504. [f. Room *a.* + -th.] **1.** Space; *esp.* ample or unconfined space 1540. †**2.** An office, function, or dignity –1604. †**b.** *In the r. of*, in the place *of*, instead *of*. Also with possessives. –1625. Hence **Roo·mthy** *a.* (now *dial.*), roomy.

Roomy (rū·mi), *a.* 1627. [f. Room *sb.* + -y[1].] **1.** Of ample dimensions; capacious, large; wide. **2.** Of female animals: Of large proportions internally 1796.

1. This makes a Ship more r. 1627. Hence **Roo·mily** *adv.* **Roo·miness.**

Roop (rūp). 1674. [var. of Roup *sb.*[3]] Hoarseness; a hoarse note or sound. Hence **Roo·py** *a.* (chiefly *dial.*), hoarse.

Roorback (rūə·ɹbæk). *U.S.* Also **-bach.** 1864. [A fictitious personal name.] A false report or slander invented for political purposes.

Roosa, rusa (rū·sā). 1853. [Hindī *rūsā*.] *R. grass*, an Indian grass (*Andropogon Schœnanthus* or *Cymbopogon martini*), from which *r. oil* is distilled.

Roost (rūst), *sb.*[1] [OE. *hrōst* = MDu., Flem. *roest*, and prob. OS. *hrōst* spars of a roof.] A perch for domestic fowls; also *gen.* a perching- or resting-place of a bird. **b.** A hen-house, or that part of one in which the fowls perch at night 1580. **c.** A collection or number *of* fowls, etc., such as may occupy a roost 1827. **d.** *fig.* A resting-place; a lodging, bed 1858.

Sooner than the matin-bell was rung, He clapp'd his wings upon his r., and sung Dryden. Phrases. *To go*, etc., *to r.*; also *fig.* of persons: to retire to rest. *At r.*, roosting, perched. *To take r.*, to perch. *To come home to r.*, to recoil upon the originator.

attrib.: **r.-cock** (now *rare*), a domestic cock. Hence **Roo·ster** (chiefly *U.S.* and *dial.*), a cock; also *transf.* of persons.

Roost (rūst), *sb.*[2] 1654. [a. ON. *rǫst*.] A tumultuous tidal race formed by the meeting of conflicting currents off various parts of the Orkney and Shetland Islands.

Roost (rūst), *v.* 1530. [f. Roost *sb.*[1]] **I.** Of birds: To settle on a perch or the like for sleep or rest; to settle for sleep, go to rest. **b.** Of persons: To seat oneself, to perch. *colloq.* 1816. **2.** To lodge, harbour. In mod. use: To pass the night. 1593. **3.** *trans.* To afford a resting-place to (a person) 1854.

1. On the cliff-side the pigeons R. deep in the rocks M. Arnold. 2. Stopped to r. at Terracina 1855.

Root (rūt), *sb.* [Late OE. *rōt*, a. ON. *rót*. The original stem **wrot-* is connected with L. *radix* and with OE. *wyrt* Wort[1].] **I. 1.** That part of a plant or tree which is normally below the earth's surface; in *Bot.*, the descending axis of a plant, tree, or shoot, developed from the radicle, and serving to attach the plant to and convey nourishment from the soil, with or without subsidiary rootlets or fibres; also applied to the corresponding organ of an epiphyte, and to the rootlets attaching ivy to its support. **2.** The permanent underground stock of a plant from which the stems or leaves are periodically produced; also, by extension, a plant, herb ME. **3.** The underground part of a plant used for eating or in medicine; now *spec.* in *Agric.*, one of a fleshy nature, as the turnip or carrot, and, by extension, any plant of this kind OE. **4. a.** The imbedded or basal portion of the hair, tongue, teeth, fingers, nails, etc. ME. **b.** The more or less 'muddy' base of a crystal or gem, esp. of an emerald 1695. **c.** That part of anything by which it is united to something else 1632. **5.** The bottom or base *of* something material; *esp.* the foot of a hill. late ME.

1. Phr. *By the root(s*, denoting the complete pulling up of a plant or tree. *To take r.*, to settle properly in the ground. 3. Very few turnips are with us this season; this r. having generally failed 1801.

II. 1. The source or origin *of* some quality, condition, tendency, etc. Also occas. without const. ME. **2.** A source of some quality, etc.; *esp.* a virtue or vice giving rise to some condition or action ME. **3.** A person or family forming the source of a lineage, kindred, or line of descendants ME. **b.** A scion, offshoot. (Chiefly Biblical.) ME. **4.** That upon or by which a person or thing is established or supported; the basis upon which anything rests ME. **5.** The bottom or real basis, the inner or essential part, of anything. late ME. **6.** *To take, strike r.*, to obtain a permanent footing or hold; to settle down *in* a place, etc. 1535.

1. The r. of all this ill is prelacy Shelley. 2. Faith, the r. whence only can arise The graces of a life that wins the skies Cowper. 3. It was saide..that my selfe should be the Roote, and Father Of many Kings Shaks. b. In that day there shall bee a roote of Iesse, which shall stand for an ensigne of the people *Isa.* xi. 10. 4. A high wind under a cloudless sky..seems to have no r. in the constitution of things Stevenson. 5. His resolute desire to get at the r. of things Swinburne. *The r. of the matter*, a literal rendering of Heb. *shōresh dābār* in Job xix. 28. 6. The idea struck r. 1899. Phr. *Root and branch*: see Branch *sb.*; in advb. use: Completely, utterly; also in attrib. use of persons and things.

III. 1. *Math.* **a.** A number, quantity, or dimension, which, when multiplied by itself a requisite number of times, produces a given expression. *Cube* (or *third*) *r.*: see Cube *sb.* 2 *Square* (or *second*) *r.*: see Square *a.* I. 1. **b.** The value or each of the values of an unknown quantity which will satisfy a given equation 1728. **2.** *Philol.* One of those ultimate elements of a language that cannot be further analysed, and form the base of its vocabulary. †**b.** A primary word or form from which others are derived. 1530. **3.** *Mus.* The fundamental note of a chord; the note on which the harmonics are based, and which gives its name to the chord 1811.

2. Sharon, a name of the same r. as that used to designate the table-lands beyond the Jordan Stanley. b. It is a fault only in the declension and the roots of the words continue untouch'd Sterne.

attrib. and *Comb.*: **r.-beer** *U.S.*, a beverage prepared from roots; **-climber**, a plant which climbs by the aid of rootlets developed on the stem; **-form**, (*a*) a basal or primitive form (of something); (*b*) an insect form which infests roots; **-house**, (*a*) an ornamental building made principally of tree-roots, esp. in a garden; (*b*) a house or barn for storing roots; **-leaf**, a radical leaf; **-position** *Mus.*, that position of a chord in which the r. is the lowest note; **-run**, the space over which the roots of a plant extend. Hence **Roo·tery**, a pile formed of tree-roots with interspersed soil for the ornamental growing of garden-plants; cf. Rockery. **Roo·tless** *a.* without roots; destitute of roots. **Roo·tling** = Rootlet 1.

Root (rūt), *v.*[1] ME. [f. Root *sb.*] **I. 1.** *trans.* To furnish with roots; to fix or establish firmly; to implant deeply, attach strongly. Const. *in*, *into*, *to*, etc. **2.** *intr.* Of plants: To take or strike root 1440. **b.** *fig.* To take root; to settle, establish oneself. Freq. with *in*. ME. **c.** To have a basis *in* something 1882.

1. Amazement roots me to the ground Dryden. 2. A tender plant, that will scarce r. in stiff or rocky ground 1673. b. The small continuous vices, which r. under ground and honeycomb the soul 1869.

II. 1. *trans.* To pull, tear, drag, or dig *up* by the roots; to uproot. late ME. **2.** To pull, dig, or take *out* by the roots; hence *fig.*, to extirpate, exterminate, destroy 1450. **3. a.** To clear *away* completely. late ME. **b.** To drag, tear, remove by force, *from* a place 1567. **c.** Without const. To uproot, outroot 1582. **4.** To lop the roots or rootlets from 1844.

1. The Lord..shall r. vp Israel out of this good land, which hee gaue to their fathers 1 *Kings* xiv. 15. 2. To r. out popular Errors Addison. 3. b. To see thy brother's seede Ruin'd, and rent, and rooted from the earth 1624.

Root (rūt), *v.*[2] 1538. [Later form of *wroot* vb. (OE. *wrōtan*). Cf. Rout *v*[4].] **1.** *intr.* Of swine: To turn up the soil by grubbing with the snout; to dig with the snout in search of food. Also *transf.* of certain fishes, worms, etc. **b.** *dial.* To poke about, rummage; to pry or poke *into* a thing, to lounge or idle about 1831. **c.** *U.S. slang.* To be active *for* another by giving support, encouragement, or applause 1895. **2.** *trans.* To turn over, dig up, with the snout. Also *fig.*, to search *out*, hunt *up*. 1592. Hence **Roo·ter**[2] (*rare*).

1. **d.** *Root, hog, or die* (U.S.), used of or addressed to persons, implying the necessity of labour or exertion to maintain life or prosperity 1834.

Rooted (rū·tėd), *ppl. a.* late ME. [f. Root *v.*[1] and *sb.*] **1.** Having roots; furnished with roots 1557. **2.** Planted in the ground; attached or fixed by roots; firmly implanted; having taken root. late ME. **b.** *transf.* Of habits, opinions, etc. 1526. **c.** Of maladies: Deep-seated, chronic 1744. **3.** Torn *up* by the roots 1797.

2. There was nevere r. tre, That stod so faste Gower. b. Can'st thou not..Plucke from the Memory a r. Sorrow? Shaks. A..r. dislike to the society of women 1883. Hence **Roo·ted-ly** *adv.*, **-ness.**

Rooter[1] (rū·təɹ). 1560. [f. Root *v.*[1] or *sb.*] **1.** An extirpator, eradicator, uprooter (*of* something). Usu. const. *out*, *up*. **2.** *spec.* A 'root-and-branch' man. Now *Hist.* 1642.

Rootlet. (rū·tlėt). 1793. [f. Root *sb.* + -let.] **1.** A branch of the root of a plant; a subsidiary root. **2.** *Malting.* The radicle of a steeped grain. Also *collect.* 1830. **3.** *Anat.* A slender branch or fibre of some structure, such as a vein or nerve 1875.

Roo·t-stock. 1832. [f. Root *sb.*] **1.** *Bot.* A rhizome; a stem that grows entirely underground; a creeping stem. **2.** A source from which offshoots have arisen; a primitive form 1877.

Rooty (rū·ti), *a.* 1483. [f. Root *sb.* + -y[1].] Abounding in, full of, or consisting of roots. Hence **Roo·tiness.**

Rope (rōup), *sb.*[1] [Com. Teut.; OE. *rāp*, = MDu. and Du. *reep*, OHG., G. *reif*.] **I. 1.** A length of strong and stout line or cordage, usu. made of twisted strands of hemp, flax, or other fibrous material, but also of strips of hide, pliant twigs, metal wire, etc. **b.** Without article, as a material 1769. **2.** In special uses: **a.** A stout line used for measuring; a sounding line; hence, in later use, a certain measure of length, esp. for walling or hedging. Now *local.* Also *r.-length.* OE. **b.** = Tight-rope 1620. **c.** *pl.* The cords marking off a prize-ring or other enclosed space 1854. **3.** A cord for hanging a person; a halter; the hangman's cord ME. †**b.** As an allusive or derisive cry –1663.

1. b. The strength of Manilla r. is less than that of hemp r. 1876. 3. b. 1 *Hen. VI*, I. iii. 53.

Phrases. *To give a person r.* (*enough*, or *plenty of r.*), to allow him free scope or action, esp. in order that he may commit himself. *To come to the end of one's r.*, to be finally checked in wrong-doing. *To know the ropes*, to understand the way to do something; to know all the dodges; so *to learn, put one up to, the ropes.* *On the high ropes*: see High *a.* II. Phrases. *On the r.* (of mountaineers) roped together.

II. 1. A rope-like structure; a thing having the elongated form of a rope or cord. late ME. **2.** A number *of* onions, etc., strung or plaited together 1469. **b.** A (thick) string *of* pearls. Also *ellipt.* 1630. **3.** A viscid or gelatinous stringy formation in beer, etc. 1747.

1. Phr. *A r. of sand*, something having no coherence or binding power; Like ropes of sand..doe these things hang together 1624. 2. b. Rubies, sapphires, And ropes of orient pearl Massinger.

attrib. and *Comb.*: **r.-drill,** a form of military drill in which a stretched r. is used to represent part of a company; **-ferry,** a ferry worked by a r.; **r. ladder,** a ladder made of two long pieces of r. connected at intervals by pieces of r., wood, or metal; **-pump,** a pump consisting of a r. rapidly revolving over two pulleys, one of which is at the top and the other in the water of the well; **-walk,** a stretch of ground appropriated to the making of ropes; **-walker,** a r.-dancer. Hence **Ro·pish** *a.* somewhat ropy; tending to ropiness.

Rope (rōup), *sb.*[2] Now *dial.* [OE. *rop* (*hrop*), = MDu. *rop*, of uncertain relationship.] A gut, entrail, intestine. Freq. in *pl.*

Rope (rōup), *v.* ME. [f. Rope *sb.*[1]] **1.** *trans.* To tie, bind, fasten, or secure with a rope. Also with *up*. **b.** In mountaineering, to attach (persons) to each other by means of a rope for greater safety 1862. **c.** To assist with ropes 1890. **2.** To enclose or mark off (a certain space) with a rope. Usu. const. *in*, *off*, *out*, *round*. 1738. **3.** *Naut.* To sew a bolt-rope round the edges of (a sail) 1846. **4. a.** *U.S.* and *Austral.* To catch with a rope; to lasso 1848. **b.** *To r. in*, to draw into some enterprise, to ensnare, lure, or decoy. Orig. *U.S.* 1848.

5. *Racing.* To pull back or check (a horse) so as to prevent it from winning in a race 1857. b. *absol.* To lose a race intentionally by holding back 1887. 6. *intr.* To be drawn out into a filament or thread; to become viscid or ropy 1565. b. *trans.* To pull, draw out, or twist into the shape of a rope 1843.

1. The slain deer roped on to the pony 1873. 2. The ground is roped out 1866. 4. b. I won't be roped into this kind of business again 1899.

Ro·pe-band. 1769. Etymologizing form of ROBAND.

Ro·pe-da·ncer. 1648. [ROPE *sb.*[1] I. 2 b.] One who 'dances' or balances on a rope suspended at some height above the ground; a funambulist. So **Ro·pe-da·ncing** *vbl. sb.*

Roper (rōu·pəɹ). ME. [f. ROPE *sb.*[1] + -ER[1].] 1. One who makes ropes; a rope-maker. 2. One who secures bales, etc., with a rope 1850. 3. *Racing.* A jockey who prevents a horse from winning by holding it in; one who intentionally loses any race by similar methods 1870. 4. *U.S.* One who uses a lasso 1808. 5. A gambling-house decoy 1859.

Ropery (rōu·pəri). late ME. [f. ROPE *sb.*[1] + -ERY 1.] 1. A place where ropes are made; a rope-walk. 2. Trickery, knavery, roguery. Now *arch.* 1530.

2. What sawcie Merchant was this that was so full of his roperie? SHAKS.

Rope's end, *sb.* 1460. [ROPE *sb.*[1]] 1. The end of a rope; *esp.* a piece from the end of a rope used as an instrument of punishment. 2. A halter; a hangman's noose 1821.

1. I beat him, and then went up in to fetch my rope's end PEPYS. Hence **Rope's-end** *v. trans.* to flog with a rope's end.

Ro·pe-work. 1797. [ROPE *sb.*[1]] 1. A place where ropes are made. 2. An arrangement of ropes 1816.

Ro·pe-yarn. Chiefly *Naut.* 1623. [ROPE *sb.*[1]] 1. A single yarn forming part of a strand in a rope; a piece of yarn obtained by unpicking an old rope. b. Used to denote a small or trifling thing 1801. 2. Yarn obtained by untwisting an old rope, or such as is used for making ropes 1626.

1. b. If you touch a r. of this ship, I shall board instantly 1879.

Ropy (rōu·pi), *a.* 1480. [f. ROPE *sb.*[1] + -Y[1].] 1. Forming or developing viscid, glutinous, or slimy threads; sticky and stringy. Also *transf.* of the air. 2. Having the form or tenacity of a rope; suggestive of a rope 1765.

1. Like Snakes engendring were platted her Tresses, Or like to slimy streaks of R. Ale 1651. b. My lungs.. have been irritated..by the thick r. air 1788. Hence **Ro·pily** *adv.* **Ro·piness.**

‖**Roquefort** (rokfor). 1837. A kind of cheese made with a mixture of goats' and ewes' milk at Roquefort in the S. W. of France.

Roquelaure (rǫ·kĕlōᵊɹ). Now *Hist.* 1716. [a. F., named after the Duke of *Roquelaure* (1656–1738).] A cloak reaching to the knee worn by men during the eighteenth and the early part of the nineteenth centuries.

Roquet (rōu·ke), *v.* 1862. [app. an arbitrary variation of CROQUET.] *trans.* In croquet: †a. = CROQUET *v.*; also *absol.* b. Of a ball: To strike (another ball). c. To strike (another player's ball) with one's own; also *absol.* Hence **Rou·quet,** the act of hitting another player's ball with one's own. **Roqueted** (rōu·ked) *ppl. a.* **Roqueting** (rōu·ketiŋ), *vbl. sb.* and *ppl. a.*

Roral (rōᵊ·răl), *a. rare.* 1656. [f. L. *ror-, ros* dew.] Dewy, roscid. So **Rori·ferous** *a.* bringing or bearing dew.

†**Ro·rid,** *a.* 1602. [ad. L. *roridus,* f. *ror-, ros* dew.] Dewy; of the nature of dew –1715. So †**Ro·ry** *a.* (*rare*) dewy –1621.

Rorqual (rǭ·ɹkwǫl). 1827. [a. F., ad. Norw. *røyrkval,* repr. OIcel. *reyðarhvalr,* f. *reyðr* the specific name + *hvalr* whale.] A whale of the genus *Balænoptera*; the finner.

Rorty (rǭ·ɹti), *a. slang.* Also **raughty.** 1864. [?] Fine, splendid, jolly.

Rosace (rōu·zeɪs, F. rozas). 1849. [a. F., f. *rose* ROSE *sb.*] 1. A rose-window. 2. A design resembling a rose; a rosette 1873.

Rosaceous (rozēɪ·ʃəs), *a.* 1731. [ad. L. *rosaceus,* f. *rosa* ROSE *sb.*] 1. *Bot.* Belonging to or characteristic of the family *Rosaceæ,* of which the rose is the type. 2. Resembling a rose in form or colour; rose-like 1783. So **Rosa·cean** *Bot.,* a plant of the family *Rosaceæ,* a rosaceous plant.

Ro·sal, *a. rare.* 1566. [f. ROSE *sb.* + -AL 1.] †1. Rosy, roseate, ruddy –1641. 2. *Bot.* Rosaceous (*rare*) 1846.

†**Rosalger.** late ME. [var. of RESALGAR.] Realgar, disulphide of arsenic –1662.

Rosaniline (rōuzæ·niləin). 1862. [f. ROSE *sb.* + ANILINE.] *Chem.* A powerful organic base, derived from aniline by treatment with a reagent, yielding crystalline salts much used in dyeing; a dye-colour obtained from this.

Rosarian (rozēᵊ·riăn). 1864. [f. L. *rosarium* (see ROSARY) + -AN I. 1.] 1. One who cultivates roses; *esp.* an amateur rose-grower. 2. *R. C. Ch.* A member of a Confraternity of the Rosary 1867.

‖**Rosarium** (rozēᵊ·riɒ̆m). 1841. [L.; see ROSARY.] A rose-garden.

Rosary (rōu·zări). late ME. [ad. L. *rosarium* rose-garden, f. *rosa* ROSE *sb.*] 1. *Hist.* A base or counterfeit coin, of foreign origin, of the value of one penny, declared illegal in England by Edward I. late ME. 2. A piece of ground set apart for the cultivation of roses; a rose-garden; a ROSERY 1440. †3. Used as the title of a book of devotion –1583. 4. (More fully *R. of Our Lady.*) A form of prayer or set of devotions consisting in the recitation of fifteen decades of Aves, each decade being preceded by a Paternoster and followed by a Gloria; Our Lady's Psalter; a book containing this 1547. 5. A string of a hundred and sixty-five beads divided into fifteen sets (each having ten small and one large bead), used to assist the memory in the recitation of the Rosary; also, a similar set of fifty-five beads (*the lesser r.*). The small beads represent Aves and the large ones Paternosters and Glorias. 1597. 6. Any similar devotion or aid thereto 1651.

2. Alas, the Rosaries, how are they broken down! 1657. 6. Every day propound to your selfe a R. or Chaplet of good Works, to present to God at night 1667.

†‖**Rosa solis** (rōu·ză sōu·lis). Also **rosa-solis.** 1563. [mod.L., lit. 'rose of the sun' (f. *rosa,* and *solis,* gen. of *sol* sun).] 1. The plant sundew, *Drosera rotundifolia* –1796. 2. A cordial orig. made from or flavoured with the juice of the plant sundew, but subseq. composed of spirits (esp. brandy) with various essences or spices, sugar, etc. –1818.

Roscian (rǫ·ʃiăn), *a.* 1636. [f. Quintus *Roscius* Gallus, a famous Roman actor.] Characteristic of Roscius as an actor; eminent in respect of acting.

Roscid (rǫ·sid), *a.* Now *rare.* 1626. [ad. L. *roscidus* dewy, f. *ros* dew.] Dewy, moist, dank; resembling or falling like dew.

Rose (rōuz), *sb.* and quasi-*adj.* [OE. *rose* or *rōse,* ad. L. *rosa,* prob. an adoption of Gr. *ῥοδέα.*] A. *sb.* I. The flower or plant. 1. A beautiful and usu. fragrant flower which grows upon a shrub of the genus *Rosa,* usu. of a red, white, or yellow colour. 2. A rose-plant, rose-bush, or rose-tree. late ME. 3. With defining term prefixed (denoting either one of the numerous varieties of the common rose, or some other plant), as *Banksian, blush-, brier-, cabbage-, Christmas-r.,* etc. 1797. b. With defining term (genitive phrase) added 1598.

1. As soon Seek roses in December—ice in June BYRON. *Oil of roses,* r.-oil. 2. I have a green R., evidently a climber 1882. 3. Eglantine r., or sweet briar 1786. The single Macartney R. 1837. b. *R. of Jerusalem,* a species of Amomum. *R. of the Virgin,* the rose of Jericho. Also ROSE OF JERICHO, ROSE OF SHARON.

II. In allusive, emblematic, or fig. uses. 1. a. The flower as distinguished by its beauty, fragrance, or rich red colour OE. b. With ref. to the prickles (commonly called *thorns*) of the rose-bush OE. c. In miscellaneous uses. late ME. 2. *transf.* A peerless or matchless person; a paragon; *esp.* a woman of great beauty, excellence, or virtue. Also const. *of.* late ME. 3. *Eng. Hist.* The flower, white or red, which was respectively the badge, emblem, or symbol of the rival houses of York and Lancaster. Also *transf.,* the parties thus symbolized. 1509. b. As the emblem of England 1629.

1. a. Sweet as a r. her breath and lips GAY. Red as a r. is she COLERIDGE. b. As the r. amonge the thornes, so is my loue amonge the daughters COVERDALE *Song Sol.* ii. 1. c. The Saints are virgins; They love the white r. of virginity TENNYSON. Phr. *Bed of roses,* (*fig.*) a delightful resting place, a position of ease and comfort. 2. Mystical R., Pray for us 1720. A Saxon heiress..a r. of loveliness SCOTT. 3. Whose marriages conioyn'd the White-rose and the Red DRAYTON. *Wars of the Roses,* the civil wars in the fifteenth century, between the Yorkists and Lancastrians.

Phr. *Under the r.,* privately, in secret, in strict confidence; SUB ROSA.

III. As a designation of colour. 1. A delicate red or light crimson colour 1530. 2. Chiefly *pl.* The fresh pink or ruddy hue of the complexion, esp. in young women 1590. 3. *The r.,* a popular term for erysipelas or St. Anthony's fire 1599. 4. A rose-coloured or reddish variety of apple, pear, potato, etc. 1676.

1. One great mountain that soaked up all the r. of sunset 1864. 2. How now my love? Why is your cheek so pale? How chance the Roses there do fade so fast? SHAKS.

IV. A figure or representation of the flower. 1. a. *Her.* A conventional design or figure representing this flower, usu. consisting of five lobes or petals ME. b. As an emblem of the houses of York and Lancaster, or of England 147... 2. A rose-shaped design of metal or other material; an imitation of a rose in metal-work, etc. 1459. b. †The card of a mariner's compass, or of a barometer 1527. c. A knot or ornamental device inserted in the sound-hole or the table of certain stringed instruments of the guitar type 1676. d. *Arch.* = ROSETTE 2. 1728. 3. An ornamental knot of ribbon, etc., worn upon a shoe-front 1602. b. A rosette worn on a cap or hat, *spec.* that of a clergyman 1779. 4. A perforated metal cap or nozzle attached to the spout of a watering-pot, etc., to distribute water in fine sprays 1706. 5. *ellipt.* a. = ROSE DIAMOND 1678. b. A rose-window 1823. c. = ROSE-NAIL 1851.

2. *Golden r.,* an ornament of wrought gold, blessed by the pope on the fourth Sunday in Lent, and usu. sent as a mark of favour to some notable Roman Catholic person, city, or church. 3. Two Prouinciall Roses on my rac'd Shooes SHAKS.

V. *attrib.* and *Comb.* 1. attrib.: a. *gen.,* as *r.-amateur, -bloom,* etc. ME. b. In the sense of 'used for cultivating roses', 'overgrown, overspread with roses', 'bordered with roses', as *r.-arbour, -garden, -walk,* etc. OE. c. In sense 'made of roses', as *r.-garland, -wreath* late ME. d. In sense 'made from roses', as *r. camphor, -oil, -powder,* etc. 1552. e. In sense 'designed or made in the form of a rose', as *r.-knot,* etc. 1510. 2. attrib., in sense 'having the colour of a rose'; passing into *adj.,* rosy, roseate, rose-coloured 1816.

2. She was ordinarily pale, with a faint r. tinge in her cheeks THACKERAY. The lights, r., amber, emerald blue TENNYSON.

Comb.: **r.-burner,** a form of gas-burner in which the gas issues from a circle of holes; **-catarrh, -cold, -fever,** *U.S.,* a kind of fever resembling hay-fever; **-nozzle** = sense IV. 4; **-point,** point lace exhibiting the raised pattern of a conventional r.; **-pump,** one having a r. at the shaft-end; **-rash** *Path.,* = ROSEOLA; **-spot** *Path.,* a red spot characteristic of certain fevers; **-sprinkler** = sense IV. 4; **-vinegar,** a preparation made by steeping r. petals in vinegar, and used as a perfume. b. In names of plants, flowers, etc.: **r. acacia,** a tree (*Robinia hispida*) having r.-coloured flowers; the Amer. moss-locust; **r. briar,** a r.-tree; **r. geranium,** a r.-scented species of geranium, *Pelargonium capitatum*; **r. laurel,** the oleander; **r. mallow,** (*a*) the hollyhock, *Althæa* (or *Malva*) *rosea*; (*b*) the genus *Hibiscus* of the family *Malvaceæ*; a plant of this genus; **r. vine** *U.S.,* a climbing r., c. *Entom.* In the names of insects which frequent and feed upon the r.: **r.-aphis,** the plant-louse *Aphis* (or *Siphonophora*) *rosea*; **-beetle, -bug, -fly,** the ROSE-CHAFER; **r. gall-fly,** an insect which produces galls on r.-leaves; **-grub, -maggot,** a grub or maggot of a r.-infesting insect. d. Special collocations in sense V. 2: **r.-aniline,** = ROSANILINE; **-comb,** a flesh-coloured caruncle lying flat upon the head of certain fowls, as in the Sebright cock; also, a Sebright cock; **-ear,** a dog's ear so hanging as to expose the flesh-coloured inner side; **-fish,** a scorpænoid fish, *esp.* the Norway haddock, *Sebastes marinus,* or the red-fish; **-garnet** *Min.,* a r.-red variety of garnet found in Mexico; **r. manganese** *Min.,* rhodonite; **r. quartz** *Min.,* a translucent variety of quartz, of a r.-red colour.

Rose (rōuz), *v.* 1610. [f. ROSE *sb.* In sense 3 after F. *roser.*] 1. *trans.* To colour like a rose; to make rosy. Usu. in *pa. pple.* **2.** To perfume with rose-scent 1875. **3.** To treat (wool, etc.) with a chemical mixture in order to impart a rosy tint 1839.

1. Ros'd all in lively crimsin ar thy cheeks 1610.

Roseal (rōᵘ·ziăl), *a.* Now *arch.* 1531. [f. L. *roseus* + -AL.[1]] = ROSEATE *a.* 1–3.

Rose-apple. 1626. [f. ROSE *sb.* + APPLE.] †1. A kind of apple having rose-coloured flesh –1693. **2. a.** A small tree of the genus *Eugenia* (esp. *E. Jambos*), extensively grown in the tropics for its foliage and fruit. **b.** The edible, sweet-scented fruit of this tree, used for making preserves, etc. 1812.

Roseate (rōᵘ·ziĕt), *a.* 1589. [f. L. *roseus* + -ATE[2].] 1. Rose-coloured, rose-red, rosy. **2.** Formed of, consisting of, roses 1607. †**3.** Rose-scented (*rare*) –1720. **4.** *fig.* Rosy; happy, 1873. **b.** Rose-coloured, optimistic 1868.

1. The r. whiteness of ridged snow on Alps 1874. 2. Devise sweet roseat coronets 1607. 4. b. A. .person who could depict the merits of his scheme with r. but delusive eloquence 1881. Hence Ro·seately *adv.*

Ro·se-bay. 1548. [f. ROSE *sb.* + BAY *sb.*[1]] 1. The oleander or rose-laurel, *Nerium Oleander.* Also *rose-bay tree.* **2. a.** The rhododendron and azalea. **b.** A tree or plant of either of these 1760. **3.** The willow-herb, *Epilobium angustifolium* 1671.

Ro·sebud. Also **rose-bud.** 1611. [f. ROSE *sb.*] 1. The flower of a rose before it opens. **2.** *transf.* A pretty maiden; a girl in the first bloom of womanhood 1790. **b.** *U.S.* A young débutante 1885.

1. Gather ye Rose-buds while ye may HERRICK.

Ro·se-bush. 1587. [f. ROSE *sb.* + BUSH *sb.*[1]] A bush of the rose kind.

Rose-campion. 1530. [f. ROSE *sb.* + CAMPION[2].] A pretty garden-plant of the genus *Lychnis* or *Agrostemma*, having rose-coloured flowers; esp. *L.* or *A. coronaria*; mullein-pink.

Ro·se-cha·fer. 1704. [f. ROSE *sb.* + CHAFER[1].] *Entom.* A beetle of the genus *Cetonia* (esp. *C. aurata*), of a burnished green or copper colour, frequenting roses and in the grub-state very destructive to vegetation; the rose-fly.

Ro·se-co·lour. ME. [f. ROSE *sb.* or *a.*] 1. The colour of a rose; rosy or crimson tint or hue. **2.** *fig.* A pleasant experience or outlook. (Cf. COULEUR DE ROSE.) 1883.

2. Even a fashionable painter's life is not all r. 1883.

Ro·se-co·loured, *a.* 1526. [f. ROSE *sb.*] 1. Having the pink or light crimson colour of a rose; roseate, rosy. **2.** *fig.* Characterized by cheerful optimism, or tendency to regard matters in a highly favourable light 1861.

2. He continued. .to behold towers, and quadrangles, and chapels,. .through r. spectacles 1861.

Ro·se-cut, *a.* and *sb.* Also **rose cut.** 1842. [ROSE *sb.* IV. 5.] Cut as a rose-diamond; as *sb.* = next and ROSE IV. 5 a.

The rose cut consists of triangular facets arranged upon and around a central hexagon 1850.

Rose-diamond. 1698. [f. ROSE *sb.* IV. 5.] A nearly hemispherical flat-bottomed diamond, having the upper surface cut into many triangular facets or planes, a rose-cut diamond.

Ro·se-drop. 1719. [f. ROSE *sb.* + DROP *sb.*] 1. A hyperæmic form of acne, *acne rosacea*, which marks the skin with red blotches. **2.** A lozenge flavoured with essence of rose 1858.

Ro·se-engine. 1839. [f. ROSE *sb.*] An appendage to a turning-lathe by means of which curvilinear or intricate patterns can be engraved.

Ro·se-leaf. late ME. [f. ROSE *sb.* + LEAF *sb.*] The leaf of a rose; usu., a rose-petal.

Phr. *Crumpled r.*, a slight vexation disturbing general happiness or comfort (with ref. to the fairy story of the princess and the rose-leaf).

Rose-lipped, *a.* Also **-lipt.** 1604. [f. ROSE *sb.* + *lipped* ppl. a.] Having lips of a rosy hue.

Roselite (rōᵘ·zĕləit). 1830. [f. Prof. G. *Rose*, a German mineralogist + -LITE.] *Min.* A rare hydrous arsenate of cobalt and calcium, of vitreous lustre, found in rose-red crystals at Schneeberg in Saxony.

Rose·lla[1]. 1847. [app. for *Rose-hiller*, f. *Rose-hill*, Parramatta, near Sydney.] The rose parakeet of Australia, *Platycercus eximius.*

Rose·lla[2], **rose·lle.** Also **rozelle.** 1857. [perh. corrupt. f. F. *l'oseille* (sorrel) *de Guinée.*] The red or Indian sorrel, *Hibiscus sabdariffa.*

Rosemary (rōᵘ·zmări). 1440. [An alteration of ROSMARINE, ad. L. *ros marinus* or late L. *rosmarinum* 'sea-dew'. In Eng. altered after ROSE *sb.* and perh. the name of the Virgin.] 1. An evergreen shrub (*Rosmarinus officinalis*), of the family *Labiatæ*, native to the south of Europe, the leaves of which have an agreeable fragrance, and are used in perfumery and cookery, and to some extent in medicine. **b.** With *pl.* A plant or species of rosemary 1866. **2.** Used as an emblem, or on particular occasions (as funerals and weddings), or for decoration, etc. 1584. **3.** Applied to other plants, usu. with qualifying word prefixed, as *golden, Spanish, wild r.* 1597.

2. Rosemarie is for remembrance 1584. My body to the earth without any ceremony then R. and wine 1682. As trim as a Brides r. 1601.

Ro·se-nail. 1640. [f. ROSE *sb.*] A wrought nail having a round head made with, or cut into, triangular facets.

Rose noble. Now *Hist.* 1473. [f. ROSE *sb.* + NOBLE B. 2.] A gold coin current in the 15th and 16th centuries, having a rose stamped upon it, and of varying value at different times and places.

Ro·seo-, comb. form, repr. L. *roseus* in the sense 'rose-coloured', in names of salts, alkalis, etc., as *r.-chrome, -cobalt, -cobaltia, -rhodium.*

Rose of Jericho. late ME. [Cf. *Ecclus.* xxiv. 14.] A small annual cruciferous plant (*Anastatica hierochuntina*), native to the arid deserts of South-west Asia and North-east Africa, the dried fronds of which unfold under the influence of moisture; the resurrection plant, Mary's flower, or rose of the Virgin.

Rose of Sharon (ʃēᵊ·rǫ̆n). 1611. [Heb. *Shārōn*, name of a fertile level tract of Palestine between Joppa and Mount Carmel.] An Eastern flower variously identified with the crocus, polyanthus, narcissus, and cistus.

fig. I am the rose of Sharon, and the lillie of the valleys *Song Sol.* ii. 1.

Roseola (rozī·ŏlă). 1818. [mod.L., f. *roseus* + dim. suffix *-ola.*] *Path.* A rash of rosy spots or eruptions occurring in measles, etc.; also, false or German measles. Hence **Rose·olar, Rose·olous** *adjs.* of or pertaining to, of the nature of, r.

Rose-pink, *sb.* and *a.* 1735. [f. ROSE *sb.* + PINK *sb.*[5]] **A.** *sb.* 1. A pigment of a pinkish hue, produced by colouring whiting or chalk with a decoction of Brazil-wood, etc. **2.** A pink tint or hue like that of roses 1864. **B.** *adj.* 1. Of a pinkish colour resembling that of the rose; rosy pink, roseate 1843. **2.** *fig.* = ROSE-COLOURED *a.* 2. 1837.

2. That rosepink vapour of Sentimentalism CARLYLE.

Rose-red, *a.* and *sb.* ME. **A.** *adj.* Red like a rose; rose-coloured. **B.** *sb.* A red like that of a rose. late ME.

Rose rial. *Obs.* exc. *Hist.* 1617. [f. ROSE *sb.* + RIAL *sb.* 3.] A gold coin of the value of thirty shillings, coined by James I, and having the figure of a rose upon one side.

Ro·se-root. 1597. *Bot.* One of certain related herbaceous plants, esp. *Sedum rhodiola* or *Rhodiola rosea*, growing in rocky districts or on cliffs, the root of which emits a rose-like fragrance when bruised or dried.

Rosery (rōᵘ·zəri). 1864. [f. ROSE *sb.* + -ERY.] A portion of a garden set apart for growing roses; a rosarium; a plantation of rose-bushes.

Roset (roze·t). 1485. [Based upon ROSE *sb.*] †1. A rose-coloured pigment, or the colour produced by this –1688. **2.** = ROSETTE 1807.

Ro·se-tree. Also **rose tree.** ME. [f. ROSE *sb.* + TREE *sb.*] A rose-bush.

Rose·tta-wood. 1843. An East Indian wood, of an orange-red colour.

Rosette (roze·t). 1797. [a. F., dim. of ROSE *sb.*; see -ETTE.] 1. A bunch or knot of ribbons, leather strips, worsted or the like, concentrically disposed so as to resemble a rose, and worn as an ornament or badge 1802. **b.** *spec.* as a decoration of harness 1858. **2.** *Arch.* An ornament resembling a rose in form, painted, sculptured, or moulded upon, attached to, or incised in a wall or other surface 1806. **b.** A rounded ornamental perforation; a rosace or rose-window 1836. **3.** *Metall.* One of the disk-like plates formed by successive sprinklings of water upon the molten copper in a crucible 1797. **4.** *Biol.* A cluster of organs or parts, a marking or group of markings, resembling a rose in form or arrangement 1834. **5. a.** A circular rose-like pattern; also, one of the pattern-disks of a rose-engine 1843. **b.** Any object, or arrangement of parts, resembling a rose in form 1856.

Comb.: **r. copper** (see sense 3). Hence **Rose·tted** *a.*

Rose-water (rōᵘ·z,wǭ:təɪ). late ME. [f. ROSE *sb.* + WATER *sb.*] 1. Water distilled from roses, or impregnated with essence of roses, and used as a perfume, etc. Also with *a* and *pl.* (*rare*). **2.** *attrib.* in fig. uses: **a.** Mild, sentimental 1837. **b.** Elegant, superfine 1840.

1. We may yet find a r. that will wash the negro white EMERSON. 2. a. It is not a Revolt, it is a Revolution; and truly no r. one! CARLYLE. b. Not dandy, poetical, r. thieves, but real downright scoundrels THACKERAY.

Rose-window. 1773. [f. ROSE *sb.* + WINDOW *sb.*] *Eccl. Arch.* A circular window, *esp.* one divided into compartments by mullions radiating from a centre, or filled with tracery suggestive of the form of a rose; a Catherine or marigold window.

Rosewood (rōᵘ·zwud). 1660. [f. ROSE *sb.* + WOOD *sb.*] 1. One of several kinds of valuable, fragrant, close-grained cabinet-wood, chiefly that yielded by tropical leguminous trees of the genera *Dalbergia* (esp. *D. nigra*) and *Machærium*; also, a tree yielding this wood. **2.** The fragrant wood of certain species of Convolvulus, as *C. floridus* and *C. scoparius*, and of the allied genus *Rhodorrhiza*, natives of the Canary Islands 1671. **3** The West Indian candlewood, *Amyris balsamifera*; also *A. montana* 1756. **4.** Applied to several Australasian trees, esp. *Trichilia glandulosa*, of New South Wales 1779. **5.** With defining terms 1866.

5. **African r.**, the West African tree *Pterocarpus erinaceus*; also, the wood of this. **Jamaica r.**, the sweet-smelling wood of *Amyris balsamifera*, or of *Linociera ligustrina.*

Rosewort (rōᵘ·zwɒɪt). 1578. [f. ROSE *sb.* + WORT *sb.* With sense 1 cf. G. *rosenwurz.*] 1. = ROSEROOT. Now *rare.* †**2.** = ORPINE 2. –1758. **3.** *pl.* Lindley's name for the *Rosaceæ* 1845.

Rosicrucian (rōᵘzikrū·ʃiăn), *sb.* and *a.* 1624. [f. mod.L. *rosa crucis* (Du Cange) or *crux*, as tr. G. *Rosenkreuz*; cf. F. *rose-croix*, etc.] **A.** *sb.* A member of a supposed society or order, reputedly founded by one Christian Rosenkreuz in 1484, but first mentioned in 1614, whose members were said to claim various forms of secret and magic knowledge, as the transmutation of metals, the prolongation of life, and power over the elements. **B.** *adj.* Belonging or pertaining to, connected with, or characteristic of this Society 1662.

Ro·sier. *Obs.* exc. *poet.* 1523. [a. F., :—L. *rosarium*, f. *rosa* ROSE *sb.*] A rose-tree, rose-bush.

Rosin (rǫ·zin), *sb.* ME. [Alteration of RESIN *sb.*] 1. = RESIN *sb.*; *spec.*, this substance in a solid state obtained as a residue after the distillation of oil of turpentine from crude turpentine. **b.** With *a* and *pl.* A particular kind of rosin 1604.

Comb.: **r.-oil**, an oil obtained from the resin of the pine-tree, used by painters for lubricating machinery, etc.; **-weed** *U.S.*, the compass plant (*Silphium laciniatum*).

Rosin (rǫ·zin), *v.* 1497. [f. prec.] 1. *trans.* To smear over, or seal up, with rosin; to rub (*esp.* a violin bow or string) with rosin. Also *absol.* **2.** *fig.* To supply with liquor; to make drunk; also *intr.*, to indulge in drink. Now *dial.* 1729.

1. Those, who make musick with so harsh an instrument, need to have their bow well rosend before 1642.

Rosinante (rǫzinæ·ntĭ). 1759. [ad. Sp. *Rocinante* (f. *rocin* horse, jade), the name of the horse ridden by Don Quixote.] A poor, worn-out, or ill-conditioned horse; a hack, jade.

†**Rosmarine.** OE. [Earlier form of ROSEMARY.] 1. Rosemary –1742. **2.** Sea-dew. B. JONS.

2. That purer brine, And wholsome dew called Rosmarine 1616.

Rosolic (rozǫ·lik), *a.* 1835. [f. L. *rosa* + -OL + -IC 1 b.] *Chem.* In *R. acid* = AURIN.

Rosolio (rozōu·lio). 1819. [a. It. var. of *rosoli*; see ROS SOLIS.] A sweet cordial made in Italy and Southern Europe from spirits, raisins, sugar, etc.

Ross (rǫs), *sb.*[1] 1475. The name of a county in the north of Scotland, used *attrib.* in *Ross herald*, one of the six Scottish heralds.

Ross (rǫs), *sb.*[2] 1577. [app. of Scand. origin, corresp. to Norw. dial. *ros* (*rus*) scrapings.] †1. Rubbish, refuse, dregs -1630. 2. The scaly outer portion of the bark of trees. Chiefly *U.S.* 1778.

Ross, *v. U.S.* 1864. [f. prec.] *trans.* To remove the ross from; to divest a tree of (bark).

† ‖ **Ros solis.** 1578. [L. *ros* dew + *solis*, gen. of *sol* sun.] = ROSA SOLIS -1757.

Rostel (rǫ·stĕl). 1793. [Anglicized f. ROSTELLUM.] *Bot.* The radicle of a seed.

‖**Rostellum** (rǫste·lŏm). 1760. [a. L., dim. of ROSTRUM.] †1. *Bot.* a. A radicle -1832. b. The short beak-shaped process on the stigma of many violets and orchids 1841. 2. *Zool.* a. The tubule and enclosed siphuncle of the various species of louse, replacing the usual mouth apparatus of insects 1826. b. The protruding fore-part of the head of tapeworms, armed with hooklets or spines 1849. Hence **Roste·llar, Roste·llate, Roste·lliform,** *adjs.*

Roster (rōu·stəɹ). †Also **rolster, rollster.** 1727. [ad. Du. *rooster* table, list, transf. use of *rooster* gridiron (f. *roosten* to roast), in allusion to the parallel lines drawn on the paper.] 1. *Mil.* A list or plan exhibiting the order of rotation, or turns of duties and service, of officers, men, and bodies of troops. 2. *transf.* A list or table exhibiting the names of a set of persons, esp. as taking turns of duty 1858.

Rostral (rǫ·străl), *a.* (and *sb.*) late ME. [ad. late L. *rostralis*, f. L. *rostrum* beak; see -AL.] †1. *R. bone*, the coracoid process. Also *absol.* as *sb.* -1541. 2. Of columns, pillars, etc.: Adorned with the beaks of galleys or with representations of these 1709. 3. *Zool.* Of or pertaining to, situated in or upon, the rostrum 1826.

2. *R. crown*, a golden crown, adorned with figures of ships' beaks, awarded to the person who first boarded an enemy's ship.

Rostrate (rǫ·strĕt), *a.* 1601. [ad. L. *rostratus*, f. *rostrum* beak; see -ATE[2].] †1. = prec. 2. -1674. 2. *Bot., Zool.*, etc. Having, or furnished with, a rostrum; terminating in a rostrum. 1819. So **Ro·strated** *a.* in sense 2.

Rostri·ferous, *a.* 1852. [f. *rostri-*, as comb. form of L. *rostrum* + -FEROUS.] Having a rostrum (esp. as dist. from a proboscis).

‖**Rostrum** (rǫ·strŏm). Pl. **rostra,** *rarely* **rostrums.** 1579. [a. L., a beak.] 1. *Rom. Antiq.* The platform or stand for public speakers in the Forum of ancient Rome, adorned with the beaks of ships taken from the Antiates in 338 B.C.; also, that part of the Forum in which this was situated. a. In *pl.* 1579. b. In *sing.*; also applied to the orators' stand in the Athenian Assembly 1713. 2. *transf.* A platform, stage, stand, etc., adapted for public speaking 1766. b. *spec.* A pulpit 1771. 3. *Rom. Antiq.* = BEAK 7. 1674. †4. a. The beak or nose of an alembic or still -1684. b. A pair of forceps of a beak-like form -1722. 5. *Zool., Bot.*, etc. A beak or snout; an oral apparatus of an elongated form 1753.

2. Mr. Tappertit mounted on an empty cask which stood by way of r. in the room DICKENS.

Rosulate (rǫ·ziulĕt), *a.* 1832. [f. late L. *rosula*, dim. of *rosa* rose + -ATE[2].] *Bot.* Arranged like the petals of a rose, or in the form of a rosette.

Rosy (rōu·zi), *a.* late ME. [f. ROSE *sb.* + -Y[1].] 1. Having the crimson or pink colour of a rose; rose-red. b. Said of persons, their features, etc., esp. as betokening good health 1593. c. Blushing 1611. d. *ellipt.* as a slang term for 'wine'. DICKENS 2. Resembling a rose; *esp.* sweet-smelling as a rose, rose-scented 1586. 3. Abounding in, decorated with, roses; composed of roses 1508. 4. Of times, circumstances, etc.: Bringing happiness; bright; promising, hopeful 1775.

1. For see the Morn..begins Her rosie progress smiling MILT. b. That sweet Rosie Lad SHAKS. 3. His rosie Wreath was dropt not long before DRYDEN.

Comb. as *r.-bosomed, -cheeked*, etc.; also, **r. cross,** the supposed emblem of the Rosicrucians (also *attrib.*); **r. drop** [tr. medical L. *gutta rosacea*], an inflamed condition of the face of hard drinkers, etc. Hence **Rosy** *v.* (*rare*) *trans.* and *intr.* to make or become r. or rose-red.

Rosy-fingered, *a.* 1590. Having rosy fingers. Chiefly after Homeric ῥοδοδάκτυλος (ἠώς).

The rosy fingred Morning faire SPENSER.

Rot (rǫt), *sb.* ME. [app. of Scand. origin; cf. Icel., Faroese, Norw. *rot.*] 1. The process of rotting or state of being rotten; decay, putrefaction; also, rotten or decayed matter. 2. A virulent disease affecting the liver of sheep which are fed on moist pasture-lands; inflammation of the liver caused by the fluke-worm, liver-rot. Usu. with *the*. late ME. b. A particular form, instance, or epidemic, of this disease 1538. 3. A putrescent or wasting disease in people. late ME. 4. Decay in timber or other vegetable products, stone, etc. See also DRY-ROT. 1830. 5. *slang.* Nonsensical rubbish; trash, bosh 1848. 6. *Cricket.* A rapid break-down or fall of wickets during an innings 1884.

2. His cattel must of R. and Murren die MILT. *White r.*, the plant *Hydrocotyle vulgaris*, belonging to the order *Umbelliferæ*; marsh pennywort, sheep-rot; also, rot-grass. b. *fig.* Among the muses there 's a general r. 1667. 5. You are just the sort of woman to believe in that kind of r. 1882.

Rot (rǫt), *v.* [Com. Teut.; OE. *rotian.*] 1. *intr.* Of animal substances: To undergo natural decomposition; to decay, putrefy, through disease, mortification, or death. Also of timber, fruit, vegetable matter, etc. 2. *fig.* in various contexts, chiefly denoting decay of a moral or abstract kind ME. 3. Of persons: To become affected with some putrescent or wasting disease, esp. as the result of confinement in jail ME. b. Of sheep: To become affected with the rot 1523. 4. *trans.* To affect with decomposition, putrescence, or decay; to make rotten. late ME. 5. To affect (sheep) with the rot. Also *absol.* late ME. 6. Used in imprecations 1588. 7. *slang.* To chaff severely. Also *absol.*, to talk nonsense. 1890.

1. Corne not reaped, but suffered to rotte 1581. Dead men rotting to nothing MORRIS. 3. b. The hungry Sheep..R. inwardly, and foul contagion spread MILT. 4. *fig.* Better that we had rotted out our lives in exile 1848. 6. The South-Fog r. him SHAKS.

Rota (rōu·tă). 1660. [a. L. *rota* wheel.] 1. A political club, founded in 1659 by J. Harrington, which advocated rotation in the offices of Government; also, a society of this type. 2. A rotation (of persons, etc.); a round or routine (of duties, etc.); †a rote 1673. b. A list of persons acting in rotation; a roster 1856. 3. *R. C. Ch.* (with cap.) The supreme court for ecclesiastical and secular causes 1679.

2. According to a r. to be agreed on between each other 1868. 3. The *R.* consists of twelve Doctors, chosen out of the four Nations of Italy, France, Spain, and Germany 1728.

Rotal (rōu·tăl), *a.* 1656. [ad. late L. *rotalis* wheeled, or f. *rota* + -AL 1.] 1. Pertaining to a wheel or wheels. 2. Pertaining to rotation or circular motion 1855. 3. *R. C. Ch.* Connected with the Rota 1907.

Rotalian (rotē̆·liăn), *sb.* and *a.* 1862. [f. mod.L. *Rotalia*, neut. pl. of late L. *rotalis*; see prec.] A. *sb.* A foraminifer of the genus *Rotalia* 1869. B. *adj.* Of, belonging to this genus 1862.

Rotarian (rotēᵊ·riăn), *a.* and *sb.* 1912. Of or pertaining to, a member of, a Rotary club.

Rotary (rōu·tări), *a.* and *sb.* 1731. [ad. late L. *rotarius*, f. *rota* wheel; see -ARY.] A. *adj.* 1. Of motion: Circular: taking place round a centre or axis. 2. Operating by means of rotation; rotative 1799. 3. (With initial cap.) Epithet of a world-wide society, with many branches, of representatives of trades, businesses, or professions, organized for the purpose of international service to humanity; orig. named from the fact that the first club (formed at Chicago in 1905) met at the premises of each member in turn. B. *sb.* A rotary machine or apparatus 1888.

A. 2. All our general storms are cyclonic in their character, that is, r. and progressive 1884.

Rotate (rōu·tĕt), *a.* 1875. [f. L. *rota* wheel + -ATE[2].] *Bot.* Wheel-shaped; *esp.* of a monopetalous corolla with a short tube and spreading limb.

Rotate (rotē̆·t), *v.* 1808. [f. L. *rotat-, rotare* to turn or swing round, revolve, f. *rota* wheel.] 1. *intr.* To move round a centre or axis; to perform one or more revolutions. 2. *trans.* To cause (a thing) to turn round or revolve on a centre or axis 1831. 3. To change, or take, in rotation 1879.

3. She could mow a field,..and r. its crops 1879.

Rotation (rotē̆·ʃən). 1555. [ad. L. *rotationem*; see ROTATE *v.* and -ATION.] 1. The action of moving round a centre, or of turning round (and round) on an axis; also, the action of producing a motion of this kind. 2. The fact of coming round again in succession; return or recurrence; a recurring series or period 1610. b. Regular and recurring succession in office, duties, etc., of a number of persons. Freq. in phr. *by* or *in r.* 1656. c. *Agric.* A change or succession of crops in a certain order on a given piece of ground, in order to avoid the exhaustion of the soil 1778.

1. *fig.* The perpetuall R. of fortune 1647. 2. Medicines..suffer a r. of fashions like our cloaths 1756. b. In America..the tendency is towards 'rotation' in office 1888. c. A regular r. of Crops and Fallow 1778. Hence **Rota·tional** *a.* acting in r.; of or belonging to r.

Rotative (rōu·tătiv), *a.* 1778. [f. L. *rotat-, rotare*; see ROTATE *v.*] 1. Rotating, turning round like a wheel; acting or operating by circular motion. b. Produced by rotation; producing, connected with or of the nature of rotation 1823. 2. Acting or coming in rotation; recurrent 1813.

1. A r. or wheel engine 1778. b. The Earth's r. movement 1868. 2. Cotton was cultivated..as a r...crop 1864.

Rotativist (rotē̆·tivist), *sb.* and *a.* 1909. [f. prec. + -IST.] One who supports an autocratic system of government whereby persons and parties pass in and out of office by mutual arrangement, without reference to the interests or desires of the public. Also freq. *attrib.* or as *adj.*

The collapse of the Portuguese colonial empire must come with the continuance of the struggle between r. Royalism and revolutionary Republicanism 1917. So **Rota·tivism.**

Rotator (rotē̆·təɹ). 1676. [a. L., f. *rotare.*] 1. *Anat.* A muscle by which a limb or part can be moved circularly. 2. A thing, apparatus or part which has a rotary motion or action 1772. 3. One of the *Rotatoria*; a rotifer 1876.

Rotatory (rōu·tătəri), *a.* and *sb.* 1755. [See ROTATE *v.* and -ORY.] A. *adj.* 1. a. Of the nature of rotation; connected with rotation. b. Rotating; working by means of rotation 1812. c. Causing rotation 1828. 2. Going round, or coming, in rotation 1824.

1. A r. movement at the hip-joint 1845. b. The track of five..r. storms 1850. 2. I become..wearied with the repetition of r. acts 1831.

B. *sb.* A rotifer 1835.

Rotche (rǫtʃ). Also **rotch, roach; rotchie.** 1809. [Later form of Du., Fris. *rotge* (Martens, 1675), of obsc. origin.] The little auk.

Rote (rōut), *sb.*[1] ME. [a. OF. *rote*, prob. ult. :—Teut. **hrotta*, ad. Celtic *chrotta*; see CROWD *sb.*[1]] A mediæval musical instrument, probably of the violin class. Now *Hist.*

Rote (rōut), *sb.*[2] ME. [Origin unkn.] †1. a. Custom, habit, practice -1440. b. Mechanical practice or performance; regular procedure; mere routine -1768. 2. *By r.*, in a mechanical manner, by routine, *esp.* by the mere exercise of memory without proper understanding of, or reflection upon, the matter in question; also, †with precision, by heart. late ME.

2. Hee tels you lyes by r. EARLE. To learn to play by r. or ear without Book 1662. Words learn'd by r. a parrot may rehearse COWPER.

Rote (rōut), *sb.*[3] Now *U.S.* 1610. [Origin obsc.] The roaring of the sea or surf.

While the seas r. doth ring their dolefull knell 1610.

Rote (rōut), *v.* 1593. [f. ROTE *sb.*[2]] 1. *trans.* To repeat, run *over*, rattle *off*, from memory. Also *absol.* †2. To learn or fix by rote (*rare*) -1775.

2. Words That are but roated in your Tongue SHAKS.

Ro·t-gut, ro·tgut. 1633. [f. ROT *v.* + GUT *sb.*] 1. An adulterated or unwholesome liquor; *spec.* bad small beer, or (in *U.S.*) inferior whiskey. 2. *attrib.* or as *adj.* Of liquor: Unwholesome, injurious to the system 1706.

Rother (rǫ·ðəɹ). Now *dial.* [OE. *hriðer, hrȳðer*, a deriv. from the stem *hrið-* (found in *hriðfald*, etc.).] An ox; an animal of the ox kind; *pl.* oxen. So †**R.-beast** -1698.

Rother, obs. f. RUDDER.

Rothesay (rǫ·þsē). late ME. Name of an ancient castle in Scotland, used *attrib.* in *R. herald*, one of the six Scottish heralds. Also *ellipt.*

‖**Rotifera** (roti·fĕră). 1830. [mod.L., neut. pl. of *rotifer(us)*, f. L. *rota* wheel + *-fer* bearing.] A class of minute (usu. microscopic) animalcules, having rotatory organs which are used in swimming. So **Ro·tifer** (rōᵘ·tifəɹ), an animalcule belonging to this class 1793.

Rotograph (rōᵘ·tŏgraf). 1898. [f. L. *rota* wheel + -GRAPH.] A photographic print made by exposing the object through a lens and prism, so that its reversed image is thrown upon part of a roll of sensitive paper.

‖**Roto·nda.** Now *rare.* 1670. [It., fem. of *rotondo* round.] 1. *spec.* The Pantheon. †2. A round or circular object. ADDISON. 3. A rounded part of a coach 1874.

Rotor (rōᵘ·təɹ). 1903. [Irreg. for ROTATOR.] 1. The rotating part of a dynamo or motor. 2. A vertical rotating metal cylinder used as a means of obtaining greater power from wind 1924.

Rottan (rǫ·t'n). 1500. Var. of RATTON.

Rotten (rǫ·t'n), *a.* ME. [a. ON. *rotinn*; cf. ROT *v.* and RET *v.*] I. 1. Of animal matter: In a state of decomposition or putrefaction; decomposed, putrid. 2. Of vegetable substances, etc.: In a state of thorough decay ME. †3. Of air, water: Putrid, corrupted, tainted, foul -1802. 4. Of ground, soil, etc.: Extremely soft, yielding, or friable by reason of decay 1440. b. Of rocks: Partly decomposed 1805. 5. Of sheep: Affected with the rot 1460. 6. *local.* Damp, wet, rainy 1599.

1. The sweet War-man is dead and r. SHAKS. 2. In the r. Trunks of hollow Trees DRYDEN. *fig.* You'l be r. ere you bee halfe ripe SHAKS. 3. †*R. fever*, putrid fever. 4. The ice [was] very dangerous, being r. 1806. 6. A raw r. fog after frost 1844.

II. 1. Morally, socially, or politically corrupt. late ME. b. *R. borough*: see BOROUGH 3. 2. Weak, unsound 1607. b. *slang.* In a very poor state, of a very bad quality, quite worthless. Also as a mere expletive. 1881.

1. Root up the r. race of the ungodly 1555. He is R. at the Core, and his Soul is dishonest 1718. 2. Nor sleepe, nor sanctuary..shall lift vp Their r. Priuiledge..'gainst My hate to Martius SHAKS. b. You may imagine how r. I have been feeling STEVENSON. Just like you. Forgot the r. centrebit. 1892. Hence **Ro·tten-ly** *adv.*, **-ness.**

Rotten-hearted, *a.* ME. Of a thoroughly corrupt nature or character.

Þis roten hertid synne of Accidie CHAUCER.

Ro·tten Row·. 1799. [app. f. ROTTEN *a.* + ROW *sb.*[1] Reason for the name unkn.] A road in Hyde Park, extending from Apsley Gate to Kensington Gardens, much used as a fashionable resort for horse or carriage exercise. Now usu. called *The Row.*

Ro·tten-stone, ro·ttenstone. 1677. [f. ROTTEN *a.* + STONE *sb.*] A decomposed siliceous limestone chiefly used as a powder for polishing metals. Hence **Ro·tten-stone** *v.trans.* to polish with r.

Rotter (rǫ·təɹ). *slang.* 1894. [f. ROT *v.*] In vaguely depreciative use: One who is objectionable on moral or other grounds.

‖**Rotula** (rǫ·tiŭlă). Pl. usu. **-læ** (lī). late ME. [L., dim. of *rota* wheel.] 1. *Anat.* a. The knee-cap, patella. b. The point of the elbow 1760. 2. One of five radial pieces forming part of the oral skeleton of sea-urchins 1877. Hence **Ro·tular** *a.*

Rotund (rotʊ·nd), *a.* 1705. [ad. L. *rotundus*, f. *rota* wheel; cf. ROUND *a.*] 1. Round, circular, orbicular. Now *rare* exc. in scientific use. 2. Of the mouth: Rounded in the act of utterance. Hence *transf.*, sonorous, full-toned. (After L. *ore rotundo.*) 1830. 3. Of the physique: Rounded 1834.

2. A most r. and glowing negative DICKENS. Hence **Rotund** *sb.* (*rare*), a round object or expanse. **Rotu·nd·ly** *adv.*, **-ness** (*rare*).

‖**Rotunda** (rotʊ·ndă). 1687. [var. of ROTONDA, after L. *rotunda* adj. fem. See also ROTUNDO.] 1. A building round in shape both inside and outside, *esp.* one with a dome 1700. b. As the name of the Pantheon at Rome and other buildings of this form 1687. 2. A circular hall or room within a building 1828.

2. The Reading Room of the British Museum.. that immense r. 1901.

Rotundate (rotʊ·ndĕt), *a.* 1776. [ad. L. *rotundatus, rotundare*, f. *rotundus.*] *Bot.* and *Zool.* Rounded off.

Rotu·ndi-, comb. form of L. *rotundus* round, used in **rotundifo·liate, -fo·lious** *adjs.*, having round leaves; etc.

Rotundity (rotʊ·nditi). 1589. [ad. L. *rotunditas*, f. *rotundus* round see -ITY.] 1. The condition of being round or spherical; roundness, sphericity 1597. b. *concr.* A round or spherical mass; a round building, etc. 1744. 2. Rounded fullness, *esp.* of language 1589. 3. Roundness of the body or its parts; fullness of habit. Also *concr.* 1786.

1. They believe the r. of the earth 1660. 2. He began..with true legal r. of verbiage 1879. 3. The faultless rotundities of a lusty country girl HARDY.

Rotu·ndo. Now *rare* or *Obs.* 1625. [Alteration of ROTUNDA.] †1. A circular form or figure -1632. 2. A circular building, chamber, or space 1632. 3. = ROTONDA 3. 1867.

Rotu·ndo-, used as comb. form of L. *rotundus*, as in **r.-ovate** *a.*, oval but roundish.

‖**Roture** (rotūr). 1682. [F., app.:—L. *ruptura* breaking, rupture.] 1. Plebeian tenure. 2. Plebeian rank 1795.

‖**Roturier** (rotürye), *sb.* and *a.* Also fem. **-iere** (-yēr). 1586. [F.; see prec. and -IER.] A. *sb.* 1. A plebeian; a person of low rank. 2. In Canada, one who holds real estate subject to an annual rent 1861. B. *adj.* Plebeian 1614.

His manners, though courteous.., are *r.* and vulgar 1835.

Rouble (rū·b'l). 1554. [a. Russ. *rubli*, app. prop. piece cut off, f. *rubiti* to cut.] 1. The Russian monetary unit, in early times a money of account equal in value to an English mark, or 13*s.* 4*d.*, now a silver coin worth (since 1897) 2*s.* $1\frac{1}{4}$*d.* 2. A paper money of less value than the silver rouble 1811.

Roucou (rūkū·), *sb.* 1666. [a. F., ad. Tupi *urucú.*] 1. A dye-yielding tree, *Bixa orellana*, of the West Indies and S. America. Also *r.-tree.* 2. The dye or dye-stuff obtained from this tree, also called *anatta* or *arnatto* 1666.

‖**Roué** (ruˑe). 1800. [F., pa. pple. of *rouer* to break on the wheel.] One who is given to, or leads, a life of pleasure and sensuality; a debauchee, a rake.

Rouen (ruˑañ). 1728. Name of a city in Northern France, used *attrib.* in *R. bushel, duck* (a common domestic variety), *lilac.*

Rouge (rūʒ), *a.* and *sb.*[1] 1485. [a. F.:—L. *rubeum*, acc. of *rubeus*, related to *ruber* and *rufus*, and (ult.) to RED *a.*] A. *adj.* 1. *R. Croix* (or †*Cross*), *R. Dragon*, the titles of two of the Pursuivants of the English College of Arms, so called from their badges. 2. *R. royal*, a Belgian marble of a reddish colour 1858. B. *sb.* 1. A fine red powder prepared from safflower, and used as a cosmetic to give an artificial colour to the cheeks or lips 1753. 2. A red preparation of oxide of iron, used as a plate powder 1839. 3. A 'red', republican, etc. 1821. 4. The red colour in the game of *rouge et noir* 1827.

‖**R. et noir** (rūʒ e nwār), a card game, so called because the table at which it is played has two red and two black diamond-shaped marks, upon which the players place their stakes according to the colour which they favour.

Rouge (rūdʒ), *sb.*[2] 1863. [Eton College term; origin obsc.] a. A scrimmage. b. A point in the wall-game, three of which make a goal.

Rouge (rūʒ), *v.* 1777. [f. ROUGE *sb*[1].] *trans.* To colour with rouge. Also *absol.* b. *fig.* To cause to colour or blush 1815.

Rough (rʊf), *sb.* 1480. [f. next.] **I. 1. a.** Rough or broken ground. b. A stretch of rough ground; *esp.* a steep bank or slope covered with undergrowth or trees; a coppice. Now *local.* 1600. c. The rough ground at the edge of, or between the greens on, a golf-course 1901. 2. A spike inserted in each heel of a horseshoe in 'roughing' horses to prevent slipping 1884.

1. a. The fiend..through strait, r., dense, or rare,.. pursues his way MILT. c. Thanks to Vardon having pulled into the r. the Scotsman secured the sixteenth [hole] 1901.

II. 1. The rough disagreeable part, side, or aspect of anything; that which is harsh or unpleasant; rough treatment, hardship 1642. 2. A rowdy 1837. III. 1. Rough or refuse matter in the working of minerals 1677. 2. The rough state or material of anything 1799.

Phr. *In the r.*, (*a*) in a rough, imperfect, or unfinished state; in a preliminary sketch or design; (*b*) in disorder; without preparation.

Rough (rʊf), *a.* [OE. *rúh*; cf. Du. *ruig*, G. *rauh.*] I. 1. Having a surface diversified with small projections, points, bristles, etc.; not even or smooth. b. Of cloth: Coarse OE. 2. Having the skin covered with hair; hairy, shaggy. In later use *spec.* unclipped, unshorn; having a rough coat of hair. OE. 3. Of ground: Difficult to traverse; uneven, broken; uncultivated, wild OE.

1. The tongue is r., and beset with prickles GOLDSM. 2. Till new-borne chinnes Be r., and Razor-able SHAKS. 3. These high wilde hilles, and r. vneeuen waies, Drawes out our miles SHAKS.

II. 1. a. Of the sea, weather, wind, etc.: Stormy, violent ME. b. Of a voyage or journey: Attended with, performed in, rough weather 1854. 2. Of actions, etc.: Violent; marked by violence towards, or harsh treatment of, others ME. 3. Of persons, their actions, language, appearance, etc.: Inclined to be harsh, violent, rude, or ungentle. late ME. †b. Of horses: Not properly broken in (*rare*) -1797. †4. Of remedies, medicines, etc.: Violent in effect; strong, powerful -1705. 5. *colloq.* a. Bearing or falling hardly *on* a person 1870. b. Severe *on*, 'down' *on*, a person 1870.

1. a. *fig.* A quiet ebb will follow this r. tide 1596. Time, and the Houre, runs through the roughest Day SHAKS. Nor is the wind less r. that blows a good man's barge M. ARNOLD. 2. R. deeds of Rage, and sterne Impatience SHAKS. Things promised a r. time for the Church at Ephesus 1891. 3. The..r. frowne of Warre SHAKS. [He] called him..Lyar, Dog, and other r. Appellatives STEELE. White Winter, that r. nurse, Rocks the death-cold Year today SHELLEY. Phr. *To cut up r.*: see CUT *v.* *The rougher sex*, the male sex. 5. a. Phr. *R. luck*, *r. luck on* (a person), worse luck than he deserves. b. They're mighty r. on strangers 1870.

III. 1. Of sounds: Discordant, harsh. late ME. b. *Gram.* Aspirated 1736. 2. Sharp or harsh to the taste, *esp.* of wine or cider 1545. 3. Of persons, diction, style, etc.: Wanting grace or refinement; unpolished, rugged 1535. 4. Of occupations or exercises: Requiring or associated with rude energy or strength 1717.

1. The r. and woeful music that we have SHAKS. b. H still remained as the r. breathing 1880. 3. A plain, r., honest Man, and wise, tho' not learned ADDISON. A sort of r. eloquence SCOTT. A r. and hearty welcome 1873. 4. The softness and warmth of the climate forbid..all r. exercises 1717.

IV. 1. Of materials: In a natural or crude state; undressed, unwrought; not brought by working into a finished condition or form. late ME. 2. Made in a general way without detailed minuteness; having an approximate accuracy or adequacy; rudely sufficient; also, in a preliminary form 1607. 3. Not very good or perfect 1812. b. Lacking in comfort or refinement 1859. 4. Comprising or requiring only the ruder degrees or processes of workmanship or skill 1680. b. Ignoring, or incapable of, fine distinctions; not entering into minutiæ or details 1819.

1. A chair or pulpit of r. timber GIBBON. 2. The r. Draught of the Marriage Settlement STEELE. I add a r. drawing of the arms SCOTT. The supposed deeds were only r. copies 1888. 4. We know..their Pharmacy was R. and Barbarous 1704. b. In this r. justice of the world there is a natural distribution of rewards 1873.

Special collocations: **r. coat,** the first coat of plaster on lath; **r. coating,** = ROUGH-CAST *sb.* 2; **r. diamond,** see DIAMOND *sb.*; **r. file,** a file with a deep-cut face; **r. house** *U.S.*, a disturbance, row; hence as *vb.* (*trans.* and *intr.*); **mast,** a spar fit for making a mast; **r. neck** *U.S.*, a rough, 'tough'; **r. rice,** unhusked rice, paddy; **-scuff** *U.S.*, = *r. neck*; **r. strings,** the framed timbers which support the steps of a staircase; **r. stuff,** (*a*) the bottom stuff for boots and shoes; (*b*) coarse paint used before the final coat; **r.-waller,** a builder of rough-stone walls. Hence **Rou·gh·ly** *adv.*, **-ness.**

Rough (rʋf), *adv.* 1560. [f. prec.] In a rough manner; roughly, rudely without special care or accuracy.

Phr. *To lie* (or *sleep*) *r.*, to sleep at night in one's clothes without bedding, esp. out of doors.

Comb.: **r.-spoken** *a.* blunt or rough in speech; **-wrought** *a.* roughly worked, shaped, or prepared.

Rough (rʋf), *v.* 1483. [f. the adj.] **I. 1.** *trans.* †**a.** To raise a nap on (cloth). **b.** To turn, pull, scrape or rub *up*, so as to make rough 1763. **c.** To make rough; to ruffle 1844. **d.** *spec.* To put large-headed nails into a horse's shoes in order to prevent the horse from slipping 1825. **2. a.** To use rough language to (a person); to ruffle 1861. **b.** To deal roughly with, ill-use 1868. **3.** *intr.* To bristle or ruffle *up* 1904.

1. **b.** If the hurricane roughs up the straw on all the ricks 1879. **2. a.** [He] lost no chance of roughing him in his replies HUGHES.

II. 1. *To r. it*, to do without ordinary conveniences or luxuries; to live in a rough way 1768. **2.** *trans.* **a.** To break in (a horse) 1802. **b.** To expose (an animal) to rough weather and hard or scanty fare 1858.

1. We were obliged to ruff it the whole passage 1768.

III. 1. With various advs. **a.** To trim or work *off* in a rough fashion 1789. **b.** To shape or cut *out* roughly; to plan or sketch *out* roughly 1793. **c.** To fill or work *in*, to sketch *in*, roughly 1864. **2.** To work or shape in a rough preliminary fashion 1815. **b.** To heckle (flax) roughly 1882.

Roughage (rʋ·fėdʒ). 1883. [f. ROUGH *a.* + -AGE.] The rough or refuse part of grain or crops; in dietetics, the bran of cereals or vegetable fibre, which stimulates the movements of the alimentary canal.

Rough-and-ready, *a.* 1810. **1.** Of things: Not elaborately ordered, contrived, or finished; just good enough to serve the purpose. **2.** Of persons: Ready to take things as they come; not finical or particular; working in a rough but prompt and effective manner 1849. **3.** Of manner, etc.: Roughly efficient or effective, without entering into minutiæ or observing a regular procedure 1860.

3. The rough and ready style which belongs to a people of sailors..farmers and mechanics 1860.

Rough-and-tumble, *a.*, *sb.*, and *adv.* 1810. [orig. boxing slang.] **A.** *adj.* **1.** Having the character of a scuffle or scramble 1832. **2.** Of persons: Practising irregular methods of boxing; inclined to be rough or violent 1848. **3.** *transf.* Riotous, disorderly, forming a confused mass or group 1858.

1. That circle of r. political life where the fine-fibred men are at a discount 1872.

B. *sb.* **1.** Haphazard or random fighting, struggling, or adventure; scuffle, scramble 1810. **2.** With *a*. A random or free fight or set-to 1821. **C.** *adv.* In a rough, informal manner 1818.

Rough-cast, roughcast (rʋ·fkɑst), *ppl. a.* and *sb.* 1519. [f. ROUGH *adv.* and *a.* See CAST *v.* and *sb.*] **A.** *ppl. a.* **1.** Of walls, etc.: Roughly coated with a mixture of lime and gravel. **2.** Roughly or rudely contrived, designed, or made; of a rough, imperfect type 1591. **B.** *sb.* **1.** A composition of lime and gravel, used as a plastering for the outside of walls 1590. **b.** *attrib.* Consisting of rough-cast 1599. †**2.** A rough sketch or outline. (Prop. in two words.) –1644.

A. **2.** A half-true and roughcast opinion 1880.

Rough-cast (rʋ·fkɑst), *v.* 1565. [f. ROUGH *adv.* + CAST *v.*] **1.** *trans.* To coat, cover, or fill in, with rough-cast. **2.** To mould or shape roughly; to prepare in a rough form 1586.

2. I have commenced, and have rough-cast several of the chapters W. IRVING. Hence **Rou·gh-ca·ster,** a workman who puts on rough-cast.

†**Rou·gh-draw,** *v.* 1672. [ROUGH *adv.*] *trans.* To draw, draft, or design roughly –1779.

Rou·gh-dry, *v.* 1837. [ROUGH *adv.*] *trans.* To dry (clothes) without smoothing or ironing. So **Rou·gh-dry** *a.*

Roughen (rʋ·f'n), *v.* 1582. [f. ROUGH *a.* + -EN [5].] **1.** *trans.* To render or make rough; to bring into a rough state. Also with *up*. **b.** To rough (a horse) 1864. **c.** *fig.* To irritate, ruffle 1859. **2.** *intr.* To become rough 1730.

2. The wind was rising and the sea roughening 1865.

Rou·gh-footed, *a.* 1495. [ROUGH *a.*] **1.** Having feathered feet, as *r. dove, eagle*, etc. **2.** Wearing shoes of undressed hide with the hair on. Now *Hist.* 1529.

Rou·gh-grind, *v.* 1660. [ROUGH *adv.*] *trans.* To grind roughly or so as to leave an unsmoothed or uneven surface.

Rough-hew (rʋ·fhiū), *v.* 1530. [ROUGH *adv.*] *trans.* To hew (timber) roughly; to shape out roughly; to work or execute in the rough.

fig. There's a Diuinity that shapes our ends, R. them how we will SHAKS. Hence **Rou·gh-hewer.**

Rough-hewn (rʋ·fhiūn), *ppl. a.* 1530. [ROUGH *adv.* Cf. prec.] **1.** Roughly hewn or shaped out, roughly wrought. **2.** Of persons: Lacking in refinement; uncultivated, plain, blunt; †rough-natured, cruel 1600.

2. The r. native of the north SCOTT.

Roughing (rʋ·fiŋ), *vbl. sb.* 1755. [f. ROUGH *v.*] **1.** The action of making rough. **2.** The action or operation of preparing roughly or treating in a preliminary manner. Also with advs., as *down, in, up*. 1825. **3.** The fact of undergoing hardships, or living under hard conditions 1841.

2. Bastard stucco is of three coats, the first is r. in or rendering 1873.

Roughings (rʋ·fiŋz). *dial.* 1674. [app. a var. of ROWEN, infl. by ROUGH *a.* through the var. ROW *a.*] Aftermath.

Roughish (rʋ·fiʃ), *a.* 1764. [f. ROUGH *a.* + -ISH.] Somewhat rough.

Rough leaf. 1733. [ROUGH *a.*] **1.** The first true leaf of a (garden or field) plant, as dist. from the cotyledons; a foliage leaf 1754. **2.** The stage of growth when the true leaves have appeared 1733.

Rough-legged, *a.* 1611. [ROUGH *a.*] Having hairy or feathered legs; *esp.* of birds: having the tarsi feathered.

Rough-rider (rʋ·fˌrəi:dəɹ). 1791. [ROUGH *a.*] **1.** A horse-breaker. **b.** *Mil.* A non-commissioned officer who assists the riding-master 1802. **2.** A horseman of a rough type; one engaged in rough work or who can ride an unbroken horse 1828. **b.** *Mil.* An irregular cavalryman 1884.

Roughshod (rʋ·fʃǫd), *a.* and *pa. pple.* 1688. **A.** *adj.* Of horses: Having shoes with the nail-heads projecting; chiefly *fig.* in phr. *to ride r. over*, to domineer or tyrannize over, to treat without any consideration. **B.** *pa. pple.* Provided with shoes which are roughed to prevent slipping 1826.

Rought, obs. pa. t. of REACH, RECK.

Rough-tree. 1629. [In earlier use a var. of RUFF-TREE and ROOF-TREE 2; later also f. ROUGH *a.*] *Naut.* A mast, yard, or boom, serving as a rail or fence above the ship's side, from the quarter-deck to the forecastle; any unfinished mast or spar.

‖**Roulade** (rulad). 1706. [F., f. *rouler* to roll.] *Mus.* A quick succession of notes, prop. as sung to one syllable.

‖**Rouleau** (rulō·). *Pl.* **-eaus, -eaux.** 1693. [F., repr. OF. *rolel*, f. *role* ROLL.] **1.** A number of gold coins made up into a cylindrical packet. **b.** *transf.*, esp. of blood-corpuscles 1858. **2.** A roll, coil 1795. **3.** A trimming of a rolled form 1827.

‖**Roulette** (rule·t). 1734. [F., dim. of *rouelle* wheel.] †**1.** A small wheel. NORTH. **2.** A game of chance played on a table with a revolving centre, on which a ball is set in motion, which finally drops into one of a set of numbered compartments 1745. **b.** The centre part of a roulette table 1850. **3.** *Geom.* The curve traced by any point in the plane of a given curve when the latter rolls without sliding over another fixed curve. 1867. **4.** A device to keep the hair in curl 1860. **5.** *Engraving.* A small instrument used to produce a series of dotted lines on a plate 1854. **6.** A revolving toothed wheel for perforating postage stamps 1867. Hence **Roule·tted** *pa. pple.* of postage stamps: perforated by means of a r.

Rouman (rū·măn), *sb.* and *a.* 1856. [ad. F. *Roumain*, ad. native name *Român*:—L. *Romanus.*] = next.

Roumanian, Rum-, (rumēi·niăn), *a.* and *sb.* 1865. [See prec. and -IAN.] **A.** *adj.* Of, or belonging to, Roumania. **B.** *sb.* A native of Roumania; the language of Roumania 1878.

Roumeliote, Rum- (rumī·liǒut). 1838. [ad. mod. Gr. Ῥουμελιότης; see -OTE.] A native of Roumelia. Also *attrib.* or as *adj.*

Rounce (rɑuns). 1683. [ad. Du. *ronse*; perh. a deriv. of *rond* round.] *Typog.* **1.** The handle of the winch by which the spit and wheel are turned so as to run the carriage of a hand-press in and out. **2.** The spit and wheel (or girth-barrel) of a printing-press 1683.

Rouncival (rɑu·nsivăl). 1573. [perh. f. the place-name *Roncesvalles* (*Roncevaux*).] In full *R. pea*, a large variety of garden or field pea.

Rouncy (rɑu·nsi). Now *arch.* ME. [a. OF. *ronci, roncin, runcin* (mod. F. *roussin*); origin unkn.] A horse, *esp.* a riding-horse.

Round (rɑund), *sb.*[1] ME. [Partly a. F. *rond* masc. or *ronde* fem., and partly absol. uses of ROUND *a.*] **I. 1.** A spherical or globular body; a sphere, globe, planet. Somewhat *rare*. **b.** The vault of heaven 1590. **2.** An object of a circular form 1500. **b.** A large round piece *of* beef, usually one cut from the haunch 1821. **c.** *Brewing.* A large vessel or cask employed in the final process of fermenting beer 1806. **3.** A rung or rundle of a ladder 1548. **b.** A tooth or stave of a trundle 1731. **c.** A round cross-bar connecting the stilts of a plough, or the legs of a chair; a stretcher 1875. **4.** †**a.** A piece of sculpture or statuary executed in the round –1700. **b.** *Arch.* A rounded moulding 1673. **c.** A plane with a convex bottom and iron, for working hollows or grooves 1846. **5.** *The r.*: **a.** That form of sculpture in which the figure stands clear of any ground, as dist. from *relief* 1811. **b.** A rounded or convex form 1797. **c.** The natural form of timber, without being squared in any way 1813.

1. *This* (*earthly*, etc.) *r.*, the earth; To the uttermost convex Of this great R. MILT. **b.** Nature that heard such sound Beneath the hollow r. Of Cynthia's seat MILT. **3.** A Ladder of Ten Rounds 1709. *fig.* I may consider myself on the first r. of the ladder 1875. **4. a.** A r. is better to draw by..than any flat or painting whatsoever 1622. **5. a.** Many early pieces, modelled in high relief and in the r., are probably of this origin 1873.

II. 1. The circumference or outer bounds *of* some circular object; the complete circle *of* something (with or without implication of the included area). late ME. **2.** A circle, ring, or coil; an annular enclosing line or device. late ME. **b.** A single turn of yarn, etc., when wound as on a reel 1753. **3.** A structure, or part of one, a building, enclosing wall, etc., having a circular form 1578. **b.** A circular part, form, or arrangement of natural origin 1602. **c.** A curve or bend, as of a river, bay, etc. 1616. **4.** A circular group, knot, or assemblage of persons. Freq. in phr. *in a r.*, in a ring. 1590. **b.** A circular group of things; a number of things set or arranged in a ring 1598.

1. The wide r. of earth..holds nothing that I would call a recompense SCOTT. **2.** What is this, that.. weares vpon his Baby-brow, the r. And top of Soueraignty? SHAKS. **4. b.** *fig.* Repeating again and again the same small r. of memories GEO. ELIOT.

III. 1. A dance in which the performers move in a circle or ring, or around a room, etc. 1513. **2.** Movement in a circle, or about an axis; motion round a certain course or track 1604. **b.** A roundabout way or course; one which turns round in a circle 1590. **3.** A recurring or revolving course *of* time 1710. **b.** A recurring or continuous succession or series *of* events, occupations, duties, etc. 1655. **4.** *Mil.* The walk or circuit performed by the watch among the sentinels of a garrison, camp, etc., esp. during the night. Chiefly in phr. *to go, pace,* or *walk the r.* 1598. **b.** A watch under the command of an officer, which goes round a camp, the ramparts of a fortress, etc., to see that the sentinels are vigilant, or which parades the streets of a town to preserve good order; a military patrol 1581. **5.** A customary circuit, walk, or course; the beat or course traversed by a watchman, constable, vendor, etc. Freq.

in phr. *to walk, take, go*, etc., *one's round(s)*. 1607. **6.** A turn, walk, or drive round a place or to a series of places, for the purpose of recreation, sight-seeing, purchasing, etc. 1611. **b.** A series *of* visits or calls 1772. **c.** *Golf.* A spell of play in which the player goes right round the course 1879. **7.** The circuit *of* a place, etc. 1609. **b.** *To go the r.*, of communications, news, etc., to be passed or handed on round a whole set of persons. Also const. *of*. 1669. **c.** *pl.* Cf. ROUNDSMAN 1. 1795.

1. *fig.* Where rivulets dance their wayward r. WORDSW. **2.** His kill-joy visage will never again stop the bottle in its r. SCOTT. **b.** Ile leade you about a R...through bush, through brake, through bryer SHAKS. **3.** Shall Error in the r. of time Still father Truth? TENNYSON. **b.** This is the r. of my day JOHNSON. **5.** The watchful Bellman march'd his R. STEELE. **6. c.** A 'round', as it is termed, of the links is very nearly four miles 1879. **7.** You have danc d the R. of all the Courts ARBUTHNOT. **b.** The following anecdote, that is now going the r. of the papers THACKERAY. **c.** Most labourers are, (as it is termed,) on the Rounds; that is, they go to work from one house to another round the parish 1795.

IV. 1. *Mus.* †**a.** A song sung by two or more persons, each taking up the strain in turn -1683. **b.** A species of canon, for three or more equal voices, in which one voice sings a short complete melody, which is then sung by a second voice, the first voice proceeding to another accompanying melody 1776. **2.** A quantity of liquor served round a company, or drunk off at one time by each person present 1633. **b.** A piece *of* toast, made from a slice cut right across the loaf 1840. **3.** A single discharge of each piece of artillery or firearm; each of the shots fired by a single piece 1725. **b.** A single charge of ammunition for a firearm 1747. **4. a.** *Card-playing.* A single turn of play by all the players 1735. **b.** *Pugilism.* A single bout in a fight or boxing-match 1812. **c.** *Sport.* A spell of play forming a definite stage in a competition or match 1902. **5. a.** A separate or distinct outburst *of* applause, cheers, etc. 1815. **b.** A single stroke in succession from each bell of a set or peal 1826.

2. Serve out a r. of brandy to all hands 1883. **3.** The great Guns..fired several Rounds 1725. **b.** Wolfe's regiment carried into the field 24 rounds a man 1747. **4. b.** The r. lasted three minutes 1812. **5. a.** The roars of welcome and the rounds of cheers DICKENS.

Round (raund), *sb.*² 1769. [f. ROUND *v.*¹] The act of rounding. Chiefly *Naut.* with *aft, down*.

Round (raund), *a.* ME. [a. OF. *rund-, rond-, round-* (mod.F. *rond, ronde*) :—L. *rotundus* ROTUND *a.*] **I. 1.** Having all parts of the surface equidistant from the centre; spherical, globular; resembling a ball. **2.** Cylindrical; circular in respect of section ME. **b.** Of the shoulders: Having a forward bend from the line of the back 1709. **3.** Of persons (or animals): Plump, free from angularity; also, stout, corpulent ME. **b.** Of limbs: Plump, full; well-shaped. late ME. **c.** Of garments: Made so as to envelop the body or limbs in a circular manner; cut circularly at the bottom, so as to have no train or skirts. late ME. **4.** Having all parts of the circumference equidistant from the centre; circular, formed like a circle; also, annular, spiral ME. **b.** Exhibiting a curvilinear form or outline; curved; forming a segment of a circle 1662. **c.** Of vowels: Produced by contracting the lips towards a circular form 1867. **5.** Going round in, tracing out, a circle. *R. dance*, one danced by people in couples and including whirling or revolving steps 1530. **6.** *Boxing.* Of blows: Delivered with a swing of the arm 1808.

1. *R. shot*, spherical balls of cast-iron or steel for firing from smooth-bore cannon. **2.** Hollow Engins long and r. Thick-rammd MILT. **b.** The Butler..was noted for r. Shoulders, and a Roman Nose 1709. **3.** A little, r., fat, oily man of God THOMSON. **c.** A r. cloth jacket for winter wear 1882. **4. b.** *R. chisel*, an engraver's tool having a rounded belly. *R. plane*, a plane with a round sole for making rounded work. 1875. **c.** R. or Labialised Vowels 1867. **6.** The left elbow must be raised outwards until in a line with the shoulder...The blow is a r. one. 1901.

II. 1. Of numbers: Full, complete, entire; esp. *r. dozen*. Also *transf.* expressed roundly. ME. **b.** Of computation, etc.: Approximately exact; roughly correct (*rare*) 1631. **2.** Of a sum of money: Large, considerable in amount 1579. **3.** Brought to a perfect finish or completeness; neatly turned or finished off 1568. †**b.** Thoroughly accomplished (*rare*) -1665. **c.** Of the voice, sounds, etc.: Full and mellow; sonorous, full-sounding 1832.

1. A r. half dozen of pretty girls HAWTHORNE. Phr. *R. number*, a number which is only approximately correct, usu. one expressed in tens, hundreds, etc., without precise enumeration of units; so *r. figures*. **b.** I may form a r. guess SCOTT. **2.** A good r. somme of money 1579. **3.** All his sentences be rownd and trimlie framed ASCHAM.

III. †**1.** Of blows, etc.: Heavy, hard, severe, swingeing -1772. †**b.** Of fighting: Vigorous; general -1654. †**c.** Of measures, etc.: Summary, vigorous; severe, harsh -1715. **2.** Of movement: Quick, brisk, smart. Chiefly in phr. *a (good) r. pace*. 1548. **3.** Plain, honest, straightforward 1516. **4.** Of persons: Plain-spoken, uncompromising, severe in speech (†or dealings) *with* another 1524. **b.** Of speech, esp. reproof or chiding. late ME. **5.** Of lies or oaths: Bold, arrant, downright; not toned down in any way 1645. **b.** Of assertions, etc.: Positive, unqualified 1737.

1. **c.** A good r. Whipping ARBUTHNOT. **2.** He..proceeded on his way at a r. trot PEACOCK. **3.** I will a r. vn-varnish'd Tale deliuer SHAKS. **4.** He will not heare, till feele: I must be r. with him SHAKS. **b.** Your reproofe is something too r. SHAKS. **5.** To swear a few r. oaths DICKENS.

Special collocations: **r.-back**, a person having a rounded back; **r. coal**, coal from which the small has been separated; large or lumpy coal; **r. game**, any game, esp. at cards, in which each of a number of persons plays on his own account; **r. meal**, coarse oatmeal; **round O**, (*a*) a 'round' lie; (*b*) a circle or number of persons; **r. text**, large r.-hand; **r. tool**, a r.-nosed chisel for making concave mouldings; **-top** *Naut.*, a platform (formerly circular) about a masthead; **r. towel**, one which has the two ends sewed together; **r. tower** *Archæol.*, one of a number of high circular towers, somewhat tapering from the base to a conical roof-crowned top, which are found in Ireland, etc.; **r. trip**, (*U.S.*) a circular tour or trip; an outward and return journey; **r. turn**, one complete turn of a rope round anything. **b.** In names of fishes, etc., as **r. fish**, fish of a rounded (as opp. to flat) form; **r.-fish**: (*a*) the pilot-fish, *Coregonus quadrilateralis*; (*b*) the common carp.

Comb. **r.-nosed** *a.* having a r. nose; chiefly of tools; **-winged** *a.* (*Ent.*) in the names of moths as *r. winged muslin*, etc.

Round (raund), *adv.* and *prep.* ME. [f. ROUND *a.* or *sb.*¹ In early use perh. for *around*.] **A.** *adv.* **I. 1.** Of motion: With a circular course, so as to return again to the point of departure. Also *transf.* of time. **b.** To each in turn of an assembled company (orig. as seated at table); hence, with (successive) inclusion of all those belonging to a company, body of persons, etc. 1613. †**c.** From all sides; all over (*rare*) -1766. **d.** Throughout; from beginning to end. Chiefly in phr. *all the year r.* (also used *attrib.*). 1753. **e.** So as to include or visit in succession a number of places or persons 1821. **2.** In a ring or circle; so as to encompass, encircle, or enclose something; on each wall or side (of a room, etc.) ME. **3.** In every direction from a centre; on all sides; all about 1440. **b.** By measurement in all directions from a given centre 1656. **c.** In the neighbourhood or vicinity; round about 1785. **4.** By a circuitous, roundabout, or indirect way or course 1668. **b.** Denoting arrival or presence at some point or place reached by an indirect route 1698. **5.** *Cricket.* **a.** In the direction lying behind the batsman; 'to leg' 1857. **b.** = ROUNDARM 1. 1859.

1. Once more the slow dumb years Bring their avenging cycle r. 1863. **b.** A health Gentlemen, Let it goe r. SHAKS. **e.** Employing a number of young men to go r. with samples 1884. **2.** Twice five miles of fertile ground With walls and towers were girdled r. COLERIDGE. **3.** All r. the forest sweeps off, black in shade M. ARNOLD. **b.** All the sheep..for a mile r. 1833. **4.** The horse-way..was five miles r., though the foot-way was but two GOLDSM.

II. 1. With a rotatory or whirling movement 1500. **2.** In a curve, spirally 1611. **3.** In the opposite direction; to or towards the opposite quarter 1765. **b.** To the opposite view; to a different opinion, frame of mind, etc. 1825.

1. He that is giddie thinks the world turns r. SHAKS. **3.** If his horse has stopt and turned r. five thousand times with him 1787. **b.** He had talked him pretty well r. 1855.

†**III. 1.** Roundly; with a full or round utterance; in round terms -1780. **2.** With a free or easy motion; with celerity or freedom -1597. **b.** Openly, straightforwardly (*rare*) -1650.

2. **b.** I went r. to worke, And (my yong Mistris) thus I did bespeake SHAKS.

B. *prep.* **1.** Of motion: So as to encircle, or make the complete circuit of; so as to go around 1602. **b.** So as to include, traverse, visit, etc., in turn or successively; also, all about (a certain area) 1605. **c.** Throughout, all through; from beginning to end of (a period of time) 1715. **2.** Around; about; on the circuit or outer bounds of; so as to surround or envelop 1662. **b.** Having (some person or thing) as the central figure or subject 1898. **3.** In all (or various) directions from; on all sides of 1729. **4.** So as to revolve about (a centre or axis) 1728. **5.** So as to make a turn or partial circuit about, or reach the other side of 1743.

1. The God, dove-footed, glided silently R. bush and tree KEATS. **b.** R. the Streets the reeling Actors ran DRYDEN. **c.** Verdant olives flourish r. the year POPE. **2.** We sate..r. a temperate repast GOLDSM. **3.** When r. me silent Nature speaks of death 1816. **5.** They..drove him r. the bay 1894. Phr. *To come r.*: see COME *v.* *To get r.* (a person), to cajole, wheedle; to circumvent, get the advantage of.

Round (raund), *v.*¹ late ME. [f. ROUND *a.*, in early use perh. after OF. *rondir*.] **I.** *trans.* **1.** To make round; to invest with a circular or spherical form. Also *refl.*, to contract into a circle or ball. **b.** To draw together, or expand, into a rounded form. Also *refl.* 1867. **c.** To labialize (a vowel) 1867. **2.** †**a.** To deface (coin) by cutting or paring -1625. †**b.** To cut (the hair) short round the head; to trim, crop (the head, a person) in this way -1781. **c.** To crop (the ears of dogs) 1781. **3.** To make convex or curving in outline; to raise to a relief; to form into a cylinder 1677. **b.** To develop or fill out to a rounded form 1839. **4.** To finish off, bring to completeness or to a perfect form 1610. **b.** To frame or turn (a sentence, etc.) neatly or gracefully; to finish or end (a sentence) *with* something 1732.

1. What rounded the sun and planets? TYNDALL. **2. b.** Ye shall not r. the corners of your heads *Lev.* xix. 27. **3.** Getting one [block of wood] as big as I had Strength to stir, I rounded it DE FOE. **4.** We are such stuffe As dreames are made on; and our little life Is rounded with a sleepe SHAKS.

With advs. **R. down** (*Naut.*) = OVERHAUL *v.* 1. **R. in. a.** (*Naut.*) To haul in. **b.** = *R. up* c. **R. off. a.** To make round, convex, or curved by trimming off edges or angles; to cut off (points, etc.) so as to make round. **b.** To finish off, complete (an estate, etc.) by addition of adjacent lands. **c.** To finish or complete appropriately; to end neatly or elegantly. **R. over**, to turn over so as to close at the end. **R. up. a.** To gather up in a round mass or ball. **b.** (*Naut.*) To shorten a tackle. **c.** (orig. *U.S.* and *Austral.*) To collect (cattle, etc.) by riding round the scattered herd and driving it together; also *transf.*

II. 1. To make the complete circuit of, to pass or travel round (the world, a place, etc.) 1592. †**b.** To walk round, make the rounds of (a place, etc.) -1736. **2.** To pass round so as to get to the opposite side of (a place) 1743. **3.** To surround or encircle; to encompass *with* something 1593. **4.** To cause to turn round, or move in a circle; to bring round. Also with *off*. 1728.

1. The low Sun..in thir sight Had rounded stil th' Horizon MILT. **2.** The daring adventurer..rounded the Cape of Good Hope 1874. **3.** The hollow Crowne That rounds the mortall Temples of a King SHAKS. **4.** The day..slowly rounded to the east The one black shadow from the wall TENNYSON.

III. *intr.* **1.** To walk or go about; *spec.* of a guard, to go the rounds 1532. **b.** To take a circular or winding course; to make a turn, curve, or sweep; to turn round 1674. **d.** *Naut. R. to*, to come to the wind and heave to 1830. **e.** *slang.* To become an informer, peach *on* 1859. **f.** To turn *on* (a person) with reproach or rebuke 1877. **2.** To become round, circular, or spherical; to grow or develop to a full round form 1611. **b.** To have or assume a curved or rounded form; to curve or inflect. Also with *away* or *up*. 1670. **c.** Of a whale: To prepare or make ready to dive by arching the back 1889. **d.** *To r. up*, to collect in a body 1890.

1. **b.** We tore clear from her, and rounding to the wind shot a-head MARRYAT. **d.** She rounded-to and let go her anchor 1840. **2.** *Wint. T.* II. i. 16. Hence **Rou·nded** *ppl. a.* (*Phonetics*) of a vowel: affected by labialization.

Round (raund), *v.*² Now *arch.* [OE. *rú-*

nian. The *d* is excrescent; cf. SOUND *sb.* and BOUND *ppl. a.*[1] 1. *intr.* To whisper; †also occas., to mutter or murmur. 2. *trans.* To whisper (something) OE. 3. To address (a person) in a whisper; in later use *esp.* to take privately to task. late ME. b. To whisper (something) to (a person) 1579.

2. What rowne ye with oure mayde? CHAUCER. Ill Margraf rounded things into the Crown-Prince's ear, in an unmannerly way CARLYLE. 3. b. He slily rounded the first lady in the ear, that an action might lie against the Crown LAMB.

Round about, *adv.* and *prep.* ME. [See ROUND *adv.* and ABOUT.] A. *adv.* 1. In a ring or circle; all round; on all sides or in all directions. 2. With a circular or encircling movement; so as to pass or turn right round 1500. 3. To the opposite direction 1582. 4. By a circuitous route 1870. 5. Approximately 1926.

1. From Jerusalem and the costes rounde aboute TINDALE *Rom.* xv. 19.

B. *prep.* 1. So as to move or pass round; so as to encircle by moving round 1484. 2. In a ring or circle about; on all sides of; in all directions from 1535.

1. Round about the Caldron go SHAKS. 2. Round about the prow she wrote 'The Lady of Shalott' TENNYSON.

Roundabout (rau·ndăbaut), *sb.* and *a.* Also **round-about.** 1535. [f. prec.] A. *sb.* 1. A circle; a circular course or object; a circular encampment, a surrounding hedge, etc. b. A one-way circular system of traffic 1927. 2. *U.S.* a. A short jacket 1818. b. An armchair with a rounded back 1864. 3. A circuitous or indirect way; a detour 1755. b. An indirect utterance; a circumlocution 1616. 4. †a. A kind of round dance –1815. b. A merry-go-round 1763.

4. b. Phr. *To make up on the swings what one loses on the roundabouts*, (with allusion to two prominent features of fairs), to make 'things' balance.

B. *adj.* 1. Not following a straight course; not straightforward; circuitous, indirect 1608. 2. Taking a complete survey (*rare*) 1704. 3. Of garments: Cut circularly round the bottom; without a train or tails; going right round 1710. 4. Of persons: Plump in figure 1806. 5. That surrounds or encircles 1860.

1. I would.. prepare him by some r. insinuation SMOLLETT. A rogue is a r. fool COLERIDGE. 2. Large, sound, round about Sense LOCKE.

Rou·nd-arch. 1840. [ROUND *a.*] *Arch. attrib.* Characterized by arches of a semicircular or rounded form, as in the Romanesque style.

Rou·nd-arm, *a.* (and *adv.*). 1850. [ROUND *a.*] 1. *Cricket.* Of bowling: Performed with an outward swing of the arm; also *ellipt.* 2. Of blows: Dealt with a circular sweep of the arm. Also as *adv.* 1886.

Round-eared, *a.* 1704. [ROUND *a.*] Having round ears, or ear-like appendages.

The round-ear'd shining Willow 1704. A gentle, quiet, old-fashioned looking girl, in a white apron and r. cap 1847.

Roundel (rau·ndĕl). ME. [ad. OF. *rondel* masc. or *rondelle* fem., f. *rond* ROUND *a.* See RONDEL.] I. 1. A circle drawn, marked out, or formed in any way. Now *dial.* b. Something forming a ring or circle. Now *rare.* 1486. 2. A circular wooden trencher 1797. 3. A small round shield. Now *Hist.* 1538. 4. A small circular object; a little disk or rounded piece 1542. 5. a. *Her.* = ROUNDLE 1 b. 1562. b. A decorative panel, plate, medallion, etc., of a round form 1859. c. A small round pane or window 1865. 6. †a. A sphere or globe –1601. b. A ball or bead-moulding 1535. 7. *Fortif.* A circular bastion 1853. II. 1. A rondeau or rondel. late ME. 2. A round dance 1590.

1. He rode.. Humming a r. with a smile MORRIS. 2. Rousing the mole-cricket with their midnight roundels upon the pearly grass 1863.

Roundelay (rau·ndĕlē). 1573. [ad. F. *rondelet* ROUNDLET, f. *rondel* ROUNDEL, with the ending assim. to LAY *sb.*[2]] 1. A short simple song with a refrain. b. *transf.* A bird's song or carol 1641. 2. The music of a song of this type 1593. 3. A kind of round dance 1589.

1. b. The Cuckoe and the Nightingale.. with their pleasant roundelayes bid welcome in the Spring WALTON. 2. The breath of Winter.. plays a r. Of death among the bushes and the leaves KEATS.

Rounder (rau·ndəɹ). 1624. [f. ROUND *sb.*[1] and *v.*[1]] I. 1. One who goes round, in special senses: †a. One who goes the round of a watch or sentinels; esp. *Mil.* an officer or soldier of the round –1770. b. *U.S.* One who makes the round of prisons, workhouses, drinking saloons, etc.; a habitual criminal, loafer, or drunkard 1884. 2. *pl.* A game played usu. with bat and ball between two sides, in which each player endeavours to hit and send the ball as far away as he can, and to run to a base or right round the course without being struck by the fielded ball 1856. b. A complete run at this game 1856.

2. Rounders and marbles were our principal amusements 1894.

II. 1. *slang.* One who rounds on others 1884. 2. One who rounds any kind of work; *esp.* in shoemaking 1881. 3. a. A kind of boring-tool 1839. b. A tool by which a rounded form is given to something 1846. 4. *Phonetics.* A sign used to indicate the rounding of a vowel 1888.

Rou·nd-hand. 1682. [f. ROUND *a.* + HAND *sb.*] 1. A style of handwriting in which the letters are round, bold, and full. 2. *attrib.* Of bowling: Performed with a horizontal swing of the hand or arm; round-arm 1851.

Roundhead, round-head (rau·ndhed). *sb.* (and *a.*). 1641. [ROUND *a.*] 1. *Eng. Hist.* A member or adherent of the Parliamentary party in the Civil War of the 17th c., so called from their custom of wearing the hair close cut. (In this sense now usu. with capital and as one word.) †2. A kind of weapon –1645. 3. a. A siluroid fish of S. America. b. The weakfish of N. America. 1842. 4. *attrib.* or as *adj.* Round-headed 1840.

1. A R. is a man whose braine's compact, Whose Verilies and Trulies are an Act Infallible 1642.

Round-headed, *a.* 1598. [ROUND *a.*] Having a round head, in various senses; *esp.* 1. Of persons: Wearing the hair closely cut; *spec.* belonging to the Roundhead party. 2. Of arches, windows, etc., or buildings characterized by these 1758.

Rou·nd-house. 1589. [In sense 1 app. f. ROUND *sb.*[1] III. 4 b; in 2, 3, f. ROUND *a.*] 1. A lock-up; a place of detention for arrested persons Now *Hist.* 2. *Naut.* A cabin or set of cabins on the after-part of the quarter-deck 1626. 3. *U.S.* A circular shed for locomotives, with a turn-table in the centre 1875.

Rou·nding, *vbl. sb.* 1551. [f. ROUND *v.*[1] + -ING[1].] 1. The action of ROUND *v.*[1], in various senses. 2. A rounded edge or surface; a curvature; a curved part or outline 1551. 3. *Naut.* A service of small rope or cordage, wound round a cable, spar, etc., to prevent chafing 1748. 4. *pl.* Clippings, parings 1883.

Rou·ndish, *a.* 1545. [-ISH[1] 3.] Somewhat round.

Roundle (rau·nd'l). 1544. [var. of ROUNDEL.] 1. A ring or circle; an object of circular form; a disk, round plate, etc. Now *rare.* 1559. b. *Her.* One of various circular charges distinguished by their tincture 1610. †2. A sphere or globe –1674. †3. A round of a ladder –1663. †4. = ROUNDEL II. 1. –1579.

4. Sike a r. never heard I none SPENSER.

Rou·ndlet. late ME. [ad. OF. *rondelet*, dim. of *rondel* ROUNDEL.] †1. A short roundel –1589. 2. A small circle or circular object. late ME. b. *Her.* = ROUNDLE 1 b. 1688. †3. A small cask; a runlet –1730.

Roundly (rau·ndli), *adv.* 1450. [f. ROUND *a.* + -LY[2].] 1. To the full; completely, thoroughly; in a thoroughgoing manner. 2. Plainly, outspokenly, bluntly 1528. b. Frankly, openly 1593. 3. Without circumlocution, straight 1534. b. Without qualification; absolutely 1596. 4. Sharply, severely; unsparingly 1570. †5. Fluently, glibly; readily –1696. 6. Rapidly, smartly, briskly, promptly 1548. 7. In a circular manner; in a circle; rotundly 1565.

1. We are able to produce the most perfectly and r. illdone things that ever came from human hands RUSKIN. 2. Tell him r. of his faults 1682. 4. He takes them vp.. very r., calleth them a generation of vipers 1607. 5. *Rich. II*, II. i. 122. 6. I.. enforced my commands with a blow, which he returned as r. SCOTT.

Roundness (rau·ndnės). late ME. [f. ROUND *a.*] 1. The quality of being round; rotundity. 2. Compass; circumference. Now *rare* or *Obs.* late ME. 3. A round object or formation; a rounded projection. late ME. 4. Fullness or careful finish of language or style 1557. 5. Plainness or severity (of speech) 1610.

1. Righte as the Perl of his owne kynde takethe Roundnesse, righte so the Dyamand.. takethe squarenesse MAUNDEV. 4. The r. of periods charms the ear, and affects the mind 1727.

Round Ro·bin. 1546. †1. A blasphemous name for the Sacrament –1555. †2. Applied to persons –1671. 3. A document (esp. one embodying a complaint, remonstrance, or request) having the names of the subscribers arranged in a circle so as to disguise the order in which they have signed 1731. 4. *U.S.* The fish *Decapterus punctatus* 1876.

1. There were at Paules.. fixed railing bils against the Sacrament, terming it Jacke of ye boxe, the sacrament of the halter, round Robin, with lyke unseemely termes RIDLEY. 3. [He] so tormented his crew that they signed a round robin, and sent it to the Admiralty 1870.

Round-shouldered, *a.* 1586. [ROUND *a.*] Having round shoulders; round-backed.

Ro·undsman. 1795. [f. ROUND *sb.*[1]] 1. A labourer in need of parochial relief, who was sent round from one farmer to another for employment, partly at the expense of the farmer, and partly at the cost of the parish. 2. One who makes rounds of inspection; esp. *U.S.*, a police-officer in charge of a patrol 1883. 3. A person employed by a tradesman to go the round of his customers for orders and the delivery of goods 1884.

Round Table. Also **Table Round.** ME. [a. OF. *table ronde.*] 1. a. The table, celebrated in mediæval legend, round which Arthur and his chosen knights were supposed to have sat, and which was made round so that there might be no pre-eminence or rivalry. b. The body of knights of the order of the Round Table ME. †c. A meeting of Arthur's knights and nobles –1470. 2. An imitation of Arthur's Round Table as an institution; an assembly of knights for the purpose of holding a tournament and festival. late ME. 3. A name applied locally to various natural or artificial antiquities, freq. reputed to have associations with King Arthur. late ME. 4. Used generally (alone or as *attrib.* phrase) to denote a number of persons seated round a circular table, or imagined as forming a gathering of this kind; *esp.* in *round-table conference* 1826.

1. For I shalle gyue hym the table round, the whiche Vtherpendragon gaue me MALORY. In dyuers places of Englond many remembraunces ben yet of hym.. At wynchester the rounde table CAXTON. 4. The snug round-table dinner-party 1852. The 'New Round Table' is a symposium on Home Rule 1889.

Rou·nd-up. 1769. [See ROUND *sb.*[2] and *v.*[1]] 1. *Ship-building.* The upward curvature or convexity to which the transoms and beams of a ship are shaped. 2. (orig. *U.S.* and *Austral.*). The driving of cattle, etc., together or into an enclosure, usu. for the purpose of registering ownership or counting. 1878. Also *transf.*

Roundure (rau·ndiŭɹ). 1600. [f. ROUND *a.*] Roundness; rounded form or space.

Rou·ndwise, *adv.* and *a.* 1577. [f. ROUND *a.* + -WISE.] A. *adv.* In a circular form, disposition, or arrangement; circularly. †B. *adj.* Circular, round. P. FLETCHER.

Round-worm, round worm. 1565. A parasitic worm of a rounded form infesting the human intestines: a. A worm of the genus *Lumbricus* or *Ascaris.* b. A nemathelminth or a nematode worm 1836.

Roup (raup), *sb.*[1] *Sc.* and *north.* 1693. [f. ROUP *v.* 2.] An auction; the act of selling or letting by auction.

Roup (rūp), *sb.*[2] 1551. [Origin unkn.] A disease in poultry characterized by morbid swellings on the rump.

Roup (rūp), *sb.*[3] 1585. [prob. imitative.] 1. *Sc.* and *north.* Hoarseness, huskiness. 2. A form of purulent catarrh affecting domestic poultry 1808.

Roup (raup), *v.* *Sc.* and *north.* ME. [Of Scand. origin; cf. Icel. *raupa* to boast, brag.] 1. *intr.* To cry, shout, roar; to croak. Now *arch.* †b. *trans.* To proclaim with a loud voice –1572. 2. To sell or let by auction 1568. b. To sell up (a person) 1817. Hence **Rou·per.**

Rousant (rau·zănt), *a.* 1688. [f. ROUSE *v.* + -ANT [1].] *Her.* Applied to a bird rising, as if preparing to take wing.

Rouse (rauz), *sb.*[1] 1589. [f. ROUSE *v.*] †1. A shake (of the feathers, etc.) -1672. 2. *Mil.* The signal for arousing; the réveille 1802. 3. A violent stir 1824.

2. The first notes of the r. are dismal 1863.

Rouse (rauz), *sb.*[2] Now *arch.* 1602. [prob. aphet. f. *carouse*, due to wrong division of the phr. *to drink carouse.*] 1. A full draught of liquor; a bumper. 2. A carousal or bout of drinking 1602.

2. She has heard..Your rowses and your wenches 1619. Phr. *To take one's r., have, give a r.*

Rouse (rauz), *v.* 1486. [orig. a techn. term in hawking and hunting, and so prob. of AF. origin.] I. †1. *refl.* Of a hawk: To shake the feathers (*rare*) -1825. 2. *trans.* To cause (game) to rise or issue from cover or lair 1531. †3. a. To raise or set up, to ruffle -1604. b. To raise or lift up -1650. 4. To cause to start up from slumber or repose; to awaken from sleep, meditation, etc. Also with *up, out.* 1593. †b. To disturb, chase away (sleep). MILT. 5. *fig.* a. To awaken or startle from a state of ease or security 1594. b. To stir up, provoke to activity 1586. 6. To stir up, agitate, put into motion, bring into an active state 1582. 7. *Naut.* To haul *in, out, up*, with force 1625.

2. Thou mayst..Rouze from their Desart Dens, the bristled Rage Of Boars DRYDEN. 3. a. An Eagle, seeing pray appeare, His aery plumes doth rouze SPENSER. b. 2 *Hen. IV*, IV. i. 118. 4. Rouz'd vp with boystrous vntun'd drummes SHAKS. Sweete, r. your selfe SHAKS. 5. a. I mean to r., to alarm the whole nation PITT. b. Emetics .. might r. the liver from its state of torpor 1808. 6. He began.. to rowze vp his furie 1589. Blustring winds, which all night long Had rous'd the Sea MILT.

II. *intr.* †1. Of hawks or other birds and animals: To shake the feathers or body -1678. 2. Of game: To rise from cover (*rare*) 1575. †3. To rise up, stand on end. SHAKS. 4. To get up from sleep or repose; to waken up 1589. b. Of qualities or feelings 1671.

2. A red buck roused, then crossed in view 1826. 4. Whiles Nights black Agents to their Prey's doe rowse SHAKS. *fig.* Be it ours to r. at once To action COWPER. b. His fierie vertue rouz'd From under ashes into sudden flame MILT.

Rouser (rau·zəɹ). 1611. [f. ROUSE *v.* + -ER [1].] 1. One who or that which rouses or stirs up. b. An implement or apparatus used for stirring (*esp.* beer in brewing) 1830. 2. One who, or that which, is remarkable in some respect; *esp.* an outrageous lie 1825. 3. A loud noise; a noisy person, song, etc. 1731.

Rousing (rau·ziŋ), *ppl. a.* 1641. [f. ROUSE *v.*] 1. That rouses, awakens, or stirs up. 2. a. Of a lie: Outrageous 1664. b. Of a fire: Roaring 1682. c. Of trade, etc.: Brisk, lively 1767. 3. Of the nature of, connected with, awakening or rising 1671.

3. Now lapdogs give themselves the rowsing shake POPE. Hence **Rou·singly** *adv.*

‖**Roussette** (ruset). 1774. [F., a deriv. of OF. *rous* (F. *roux*) red.] 1. The frugivorous bat, *Pteropus vulgaris.* 2. A shark of the family *Scylliidæ* 1882.

‖**Roussillon** (rusiʹyoṅ). 1768. [See def.] A red wine made in the old province of Roussillon in the south of France.

Roust (raust), *sb.* Now *Sc.* ME. [a. ON. *raust.*] Voice, cry; shout, roar. Hence **Roust** *v.*[1] *intr.* to shout, bellow, make a loud noise.

Roust (raust), *v.*[2] *dial.* and *U.S.* 1658. [perh. alteration of ROUSE *v.*] *trans.* To rout *out.*

Roustabout (rau·stăbaut). 1868. [f. ROUST *v.*[2]] 1. *U.S.* A wharf labourer or deck hand. 2. *Austral.* A handy man 1883.

Rout (raut), *sb.*[1] [ME. *rute*, a. AF. *rute*, OF. *route*:—L. *rupta*, fem. of *ruptus* broken, the orig. sense being 'division, detachment'.] I. 1. A company, assemblage, band, or troop of persons. Now chiefly *poet.* b. A number of animals going together; a pack, flock, herd. Now *rare.* ME. c. A large number or collection of things. late ME. 2. An attendant company; a suite, retinue, train ME.

1. The r. of rurall folk come thronging in B. JONS. Phr. *In* (*ton*) *a r.*, in a troop, body, etc.

II. 1. A disorderly, tumultuous, or disreputable crowd of persons ME. b. *Law.* An assemblage of three or more persons proceeding to commit an unlawful act. late ME. 2. The whole number of persons constituting a certain (disreputable) class. late ME. †3. *The* (*common, vulgar*) *r.*, the common herd, the rabble -1730. 4. Riot, disturbance, stir, uproar. Now *poet.* or *arch.* late ME. b. Fuss, clamour, noise. Now *dial.* 1684. 5. A fashionable gathering or assembly, a large evening party or reception, much in vogue in the 18th and early 19th centuries 1742.

1. A hireling r. scraped together from the dregs of the people MILT. 3. Did ever God or Man's Lawe preferre the feete before the head, the rowt before the ruler 1593. 4. Then made they revell route and goodly glee SPENSER. b. Phr. *To make a r. about* (something). 5. One rarely heard..of her going to a theatre, or a r., or a cricket-match RUSKIN.

Rout (raut), *sb.*[2] 1598. [ad. obs. F. *route* (cf. F. *déroute*):—L. *rupta*; see prec.] 1. Disorderly retreat on the part of a defeated army, body of troops, etc. 2. An instance of this; a complete overthrow and flight 1611. 3. A defeated and fleeing band or army 1621.

1. Men once disordered..commonly fall to r. 1598. Phr. *To put to* (*the*) *r.*; The Dragon, put to second r., Came furious down MILT. 2. Then beganne..A Rowt, confusion thicke: forthwith they flye SHAKS.

Rout (raut), *v.*[1] Now *dial.* [OE. *hrūtan*, prob. echoic.] *intr.* To snore.

Rout (raut, *Sc.* rut), *v.*[2] Now *rare.* Chiefly *north.* and *Sc.* ME. [prob. of Scand. origin; cf. Norw. *ruta* in same sense.] *intr.* Of the sea, winds, thunder, etc.: To roar, make a loud noise. Hence **Rout** *sb.*[3] a loud shout or noise.

†**Rout,** *v.*[3] ME. [a. OF. *router*, f. *route* ROUT *sb.*[1] and ROUTE *sb.*] 1. *intr.* To assemble; to gather or herd *together* -1622. 2. To stir, move; to make a movement -1553. 3. To be riotous, behave riotously -1591.

Rout (raut), *v.*[4] 1547. [irreg. var. of ROOT *v.*[2]] 1. *intr.* Of swine: To turn up the soil with the snout in search of food. Now chiefly *dial.* b. To poke about, rummage 1711. 2. *trans.* To turn over, or dig *up*, with the snout 1571. b. *transf.* To tear *up*, scoop *out* 1726. 3. To fetch or turn (a person) out of bed; to cause to get up. Also with *out.* 1787. b. To search out, bring to light 1805. 4. To toss or drive about 1845.

Rout (raut), *v.*[5] 1600. [f. ROUT *sb.*[2]] 1. *trans.* To put (an army, etc.) to rout; to compel to flee in disorder. †2. *intr.* To break into rout; to flee in disorder. Also *refl.* in same sense. -1680.

1. Stand,..The lane is guarded: Nothing rowts vs, but The villany of our feares SHAKS.

Route (rūt), *sb.* Also †**rout.** ME. [a. F. *route* (OF. also *rute*):—L. *rupta* (sc. *via*), fem. of *ruptus* broken. In military use and in U.S. still pronounced (raut).] 1. A way, road, or course; a certain direction taken in travelling from one place to another; a regular line of travel or passage. 2. Routine, regular course (*rare*) 1725. 3. *Mil.* The order to march 1784. ‖4. See EN ROUTE 1779.

1. They had gone by separate routes to separate ports FROUDE. 3. Phr. *To get, give, the r.*, to receive, or issue, marching orders. *Column of r.*, the formation assumed by troops when on the march. *R. march*, march of a battalion, etc. for training purposes. 4. They changed horses twice en route 1872. Hence **Route** *v. trans.* to mark as available, to send or forward, to direct to be sent, by a certain route.

†**Rou·ter,** *sb.*[1] late ME. [a. AF. *routour*, OF. *routeur*: cf. RUTTER.] 1. A lawless person; a robber, ruffian -1536. 2. A swaggering soldier or bully 1557–76.

Router (rau·təɹ), *sb.*[2] 1846. [f. ROUT *v.*[4] 2 b.] 1. A kind of plane used in moulding. 2. One who routs *out* or draws forth 1890. Hence **Rou·ter** *v. trans.* to cut out with a r.

Routine (rutī·n). 1676. [a. F., f. *route* ROUTE *sb.*] 1. A regular course of procedure; a more or less mechanical or unvarying performance of certain acts or duties 1680. b. A set form (of speech); a regular set or series (of phrases, etc.) 1676. 2. Without article: Regular, unvarying, or mechanical procedure or discharge of duties 1789. Hence **Routi·nary** *a.* (*rare*) according to r. **Routinee·r, Routi·nist,** one who acts by, or adheres to, r. **Routi·nism,** prevalence or domination of r.

Routous (rau·təs), *a.* Now *arch.* 1632. [f. ROUT *sb.*[1]] *Law.* Of the nature of, concerned in, constituting, a rout. Hence **Rou·tously** *adv.* in a r. manner (now *arch.*).

Rove (rōᵘv), *sb.*[1] 1440. [a. ON. *rō*, in the same sense. The *v* is excrescent.] A small metal plate or ring on which the point of a nail or rivet is clinched or beaten down in the building of boats or small ships; a burr.

†*R. and clinch* (*nails*), nails provided with roves for clinching.

Rove (rōᵘv), *sb.*[2] 1702. [f. ROVE *v.*[1]] 1. A ramble or wandering 1742. 2. *dial.* A method of light ploughing 1702.

Rove (rōᵘv), *sb.*[3] 1789. [Related to ROVE *v.*[3]] 1. A sliver of any fibrous material (esp. cotton or wool) drawn out and very slightly twisted. 2. *collect.* Textile material in this form 1901.

Rove (rōᵘv), *v.*[1] 1474. [Origin obsc.] I. †1. *intr.* To shoot with arrows *at* a mark selected at pleasure or at random, and not of any fixed distance. Also without const. -1674. †2. To shoot away *from* a mark; hence, to wander *from* the point; to diverge, or digress -1648. †3. To shoot (an arrow, etc.) without fixed aim. Hence, to utter at random. -1607. 4. *intr. Angling.* To troll with live bait 1661.

2. But from that mark how far they roave we see MILT.

II. 1. *intr.* To wander about with no fixed destination; to move hither and thither at random or in a leisurely fashion; to stray, roam, ramble 1536. b. Of the eyes: To look in various directions; to wander 1656. 2. *trans.* To wander over, traverse 1634.

1. On Sea we rou'd three dayes as darke as night 1627. *fig.* Then roved his spirit to the inland wood CRABBE. b. A Boer searchlight..roved like an angry eye from end to end of our line of march 1902. 2. Roving the trackless realms of Lyonnesse TENNYSON.

†**Rove,** *v.*[2] 1548. [ad. MDu. or MLG. *roven* to rob.] *intr.* To practise piracy; to sail as pirates -1698. Hence †**Ro·ving** *vbl. sb.*[2]

Rove (rōᵘv), *v.*[3] 1789. [Origin obsc.] *trans.* To form (slivers of wool or cotton) into roves or rovings. So **Ro·ver**[3] one who makes cotton etc., into roves; an attendant at a roving-frame.

Ro·ve-beetle. 1781. [perh. f. ROVE *v.*[1]] A beetle of the family *Staphylinidæ.*

Rover[1] (rōᵘ·vəɹ). 1468. [f. ROVE *v.*[1]] 1. *Archery.* A mark selected at will or at random, and not of any fixed distance from the archer. Also, later, a mark for long-distance shooting (contrasted with *butt*). Usu. in phr. (*to shoot*) *at rovers.* †2. *At rovers* (rarely *at r.*), without definite aim or object; at random, haphazard -1725. 3. One who roves or wanders, *esp.* to a great distance; a roving person or animal 1611. †b. An inconstant lover; a male flirt -1721. 4. *Croquet.* a. A ball that has gone through all its hoops and is ready to peg out 1863. b. A player whose ball is a rover 1874.

1. The god nine days the Greeks at rovers kill'd DRYDEN. *fig.* But Nature shoots not at Rovers 1661. 2. Phr. *To run, talk, live*, etc., *at rover*(*s*). 3. c. A boy scout over seventeen years of age.

Rover[2] (rōᵘ·vəɹ). late ME. [a. MDu. or MLG., f. *roven* to rob.] 1. A sea-robber, pirate. †b. A pirate-ship; a privateer -1726. †2. A marauder, robber -1707.

1. Algier hauing beene of olde, and still continuing a receptacle of Turkish Rouers PURCHAS.

Roving (rōᵘ·viŋ), *vbl. sb.*[1] 1479. [f. ROVE *v.*[1]] 1. *Archery.* The action or practice of shooting at a random mark. 2. The action of wandering or roaming 1611. So **Ro·ving** *ppl. a.* Hence **Ro·vingly** *adv.* †without fixed mark or aim; in a wandering fashion.

Ro·ving, *vbl. sb.*[2]: see ROVE *v.*[2]

Roving (rōᵘ·viŋ), *vbl. sb.*[3] 1795. [f. ROVE *v.*[3]] 1. The process of converting cotton, wool, etc., into roves 1825. 2. *concr.* A rove; roves collectively 1802. 3. *attrib.*, as *r.-box, -frame*, etc.; *r.-department, -waste* 1795.

Row (rōᵘ), *sb.*[1] ME. [perh. OE. *rāw*, var. of *rǣw* REW *sb.*] 1. A number of persons or things arranged in a straight line. b. A number of persons or things arranged in a circle (*rare*) 1576. c. *transf.* A string or series *of* something 1510. 2. An array of persons (or things) of a certain kind; a class or category. Now *rare.* ME. †3. A (written or printed) line -1598. **4.** A number of houses standing in a line; a street (esp. a narrow one) formed by two continuous lines of houses. Chiefly *Sc.* and *north.* 1450. **b.** In Yarmouth, one of a number of narrow lanes connecting the main streets 1599. **c.** In Chester, one of several raised and covered galleries running along the sides of the four main streets 1610. **5.** A line of seats in a theatre, etc. 1710. **6.** A line of plants in a field or garden 1733.

1. He knew to rank his Elms in even Rows DRYDEN. **2.** She has an only daughter..who is..approaching the old-maid's r. 1787. **3.** He most rede many a Rowe On Virgile or on Claudian CHAUCER. **4.** *The R.*, used *ellipt.* for Goldsmiths' Row (?), Paternoster Row, and Rotten Row, in London. **6.** Phr. *To have a hard* (*long*, etc.) *r. to hoe*, to have a difficult task to perform. *To hoe one's own r.*, to do one's own work; to mind one's own business. (Both *U.S.*) Hence **Rowed** *a.* having (a specified number of) rows.

Row (rau), *sb.*[2] *Slang* or *colloq.* 1787. [Origin unkn.] **1.** A violent disturbance or commotion; a noisy dispute or quarrel. **2.** Noise, din, clamour 1845.

1. Phrases. *To make, kick up, a r. What's the r.?* What is all the noise about? What is the matter? *To get into a r.*, to be severely reprimanded or rated. **2.** Never was there heard..such a noise, r., hubbub, babel, shindy, hullabaloo KINGSLEY.

Row (rōu), *sb.*[3] 1847. [f. ROW *v.*[1]] A spell of rowing; a journey on the water in a rowing-boat.

Row (rau), *a.* Now *dial.* or *arch.* OE. [Inflexional var. of ROUGH *a.*] = ROUGH *a.* Hence †**Row** *adv.* roughly; angrily, fiercely -1500.

Row (rōu), *v.*[1] [OE. *rówan*. The root *rō-* is also the base of OE. *rōðor* RUDDER; cf. L. *remus*, Gr. *ἐρετμόν, ἐρέτης*.] **I. 1.** *intr.* Of persons: To use oars, sweeps, etc., for the purpose of propelling a boat or other vessel. **b.** With complement denoting the place of the rower in the boat 1856. **2.** Of a boat or other vessel: To move along the surface of water by means of oars. late ME. **b.** *trans.* To be fitted or rowed with, to carry (so many oars) 1769. **3.** Of †persons, waterfowl, fish: To swim, paddle 1631.

1. They pray as they r., backwards 1706. Phr. *To r. over*, to go over the course without a competitor, thus winning a race or heat; in bumping races, to complete the course without bumping or being bumped. *To r. against the flood, stream, wind and tide*, etc., freq. in fig. use, to undertake a difficult or arduous task; to work in adverse circumstances or in the face of opposition. *To r. in the same* or *in one boat*, to be embarked in the same scheme; to be of similar principles. **b.** A companion who will not mind a few splashes..should be put in to 'r. stroke' 1856. **2. b.** A light little yawl..that rowed four oars 1854. **3.** In the pond The finely-checker'd duck before her train Rows garrulous THOMSON.

II. 1. *trans.* To propel (a boat, etc.) by means of oars ME. **b.** To make (a stroke), use (an oar), in the course or exercise of rowing 1866. **c.** With *race, heat*, etc., as compl. 1888. **2.** To convey (a person) on the water in a boat propelled by oars. Also *refl.* late ME. **3.** *transf.* To convey, transport, propel, move in a manner or with a movement similar to rowing 1667. **4.** *U.S. slang.* **a.** *To r.* (a person) *up Salt River*, to rout or defeat in politics; also = b. 1835. **b.** *To r.* (a person) *up*, to treat him to a severe verbal castigation 1845. **5. a.** To have, make use of, in a rowing-match 1888. **b.** To row against (another person or crew) 1888. **c.** *To r. down*, to overtake by rowing 1869.

1. Alone he row'd his boat CRABBE. **c.** This is the only dead heat ever rowed in this race 1888. **2.** This Mayer..was rowed thyther by water 1513. **3.** The Swan..Rowes Her state with Oarie feet MILT. **5. a.** Corpus..rowed an untrained man 1900. **b.** Beach..rowed Wallace Ross for the championship 1888. Hence **Row·able** *a.* (*rare*) capable of being rowed or rowed upon. **Row·ing** *vbl. sb.*[1] also *attrib.* as *r.-boat* a boat propelled by oars.

Row (rau), *v.*[2] *slang* or *colloq.* 1790. [f. ROW *sb.*[2]] †**1.** *trans.* To assail (a person) in a rough manner; to rag (a man or his rooms) -1863. **2.** To rate or scold (a person) angrily or severely; to take sharply to task 1809. **3.** *intr.* To make a row or disturbance 1797.

2. She rowed me for writing to Lord Palmerston about her accident GLADSTONE. Hence **Row·ing** *vbl. sb.*[2] a rating, scolding, or severe talking to.

Rowan (rōu·ăn), *Sc.* rau·ăn). *north.* and *Sc.* 1804. [Of Scand. origin, perh. corresp. to Norw. *raun* (*roun*, Sw. *rön*.)] **1.** = next. **2.** The berry of the mountain ash. Also *r.-berry* 1814.

Row·an-tree. *north.* and *Sc.* 1548. [See prec.] The mountain ash, *Pyrus aucuparia*.

Row-boat (rōu·bōut). 1538. [f. ROW *v.*[1]] A boat propelled by oars; a rowing-boat.

Row-de-dow (raudidau·). 1848. [Echoic.] Noise or din, uproar, disturbance.

Row-dow-dow (raudau,dau·). 1814. [Echoic.] An imitation of the sound of a drum. Cf. *tow-row-row*.

Rowdy (rau·di), *sb.*[1] and *a.* 1819. [Of American origin.] **A.** *sb.* Orig., a backwoodsman of a rough and lawless type; hence, a rough, disorderly person. **B.** *adj.* **1.** Belonging to the class of rowdies; of a rough, disorderly type 1819. **b.** *transf.* Of animals: Refractory; inclined to give trouble 1872. **2.** Characteristic of rowdies; *esp.* marked by disorderly roughness or noise 1852. Hence **Row·diness. Row·dyish** *a.* **Row·dyism**, r. conduct.

Rowdy-dowdy *a. slang.* 1882. [Reduplicated f. prec.] Characterized by rowdiness.

Rowel (rau·ĕl), *sb.* late ME. [ad. OF. *roel*, *rouel*, dim. of *roe, roue* :—L. *rota* wheel.] **1.** A small stellar wheel or disk with sharp radial points and capable of rotation, forming the extremity of a spur; also *attrib.*, as *r.-deep* adv., *-head*, etc. **b.** The rowel-head 1844. †**2.** A knob on a horse's bit -1607. **3.** *Farriery.* A circular piece of leather or other material, with a hole in the centre, inserted between the flesh and skin of a horse or other animal to cause discharge of humours; also, any kind of insertion used for this purpose 1580.

1. With sounding whip, and rowels dyed in blood COWPER. **2.** The yron rowels into frothy fome he bitt SPENSER.

Rowel (rau·ĕl), *v.* 1580. [f. prec.] **1.** *trans.* To insert a rowel in (a horse or other animal). **2.** *intr.* To use the spur-rowels 1599.

Rowen (rau·ĕn). Now chiefly *dial.* and *U.S.* ME. [a. ONF. **rewain*, = OF. (and mod.F.) *regain*; see GAIN *v.*[2]] **1.** The second growth or crop of grass or hay in a season; aftermath, eddish. Cf. ROUGHINGS. Also *pl.* **2.** *attrib.*, as *r. crop, hay*, etc.; also †**r. (-tailed) partridge**, a partridge frequenting a field of r. grass or hay.

Rower (rōu·əɹ). ME. [f. ROW *v.*[1]] One who rows; an oarsman.

Rowlock (rɒ·lǭk). 1750. [prob. an alteration of OARLOCK.] A device, usu. consisting of a notch, two thole-pins, or a rounded fork, on the gunwale of a boat, forming a fulcrum for the oar in rowing.

Row·-port. 1769. [f. ROW *v.*[1] + PORT *sb.*[3] 2.] *Naut.* An opening cut through the sides of a small sailing-vessel so that sweeps may be used during calm weather.

Roxburghe (rǫ·ksbɔ̆rə). 1877. [Named after the 3rd Duke of *Roxburghe* (1740–1804).] A style of bookbinding consisting of plain leather backs with gilt lettering, cloth or paper sides, and leaves with untrimmed edges.

Royal (roi·ăl), *a.* and *sb.* late ME. [a. OF. *roial* (mod.F. *royal*) :—L. *regalem* REGAL *a.*] **A.** *adj.* **I. 1.** Of blood, etc.: Originating from, connected with, a king or a line of kings. **b.** Of persons: Having the rank of king or queen; belonging to the royal family 1513. **c.** Of parts of the body 1598. **2.** Of rank, etc.: Of or pertaining to a sovereign, or the dignity or office of a sovereign. late ME. **b.** So of insignia or emblems of royalty. late ME. **c.** Of persons: In the service of the king or sovereign. Also *transf.* of pawns in chess. 1648. **3.** Belonging to, occupied or used by, a king or kings. late ME. **4.** Pertaining to the king (or queen) as civil or military head or representative of the state 1593. **5.** *R. Burgh*, a Scottish burgh which derives its charter directly from the Crown 1648. **6.** Founded or established by, under the patronage of, a sovereign or royal person 1509. **7.** Proceeding from, performed by, a (or the) sovereign 1611. **b.** Of the king or sovereign 1821.

1. Of the R. Stock Of David..shall rise A Son MILT. **b.** *R. Highness*: see HIGHNESS 2. **c.** The power of the r. hand that heals in touching RUSKIN. **2.** On a Throne of R. State MILT. **b.** This royall Throne of Kings, this sceptred Isle,.. this England SHAKS. **c.** The chief art in the Tacticks of Chess consists in the nice conduct of the r. pawns 1763. **3.** The..town which contained the r. mansion 1835. Phr. *R. fish*, fish in which the crown has special rights: The term 'r. fish' includes the..sturgeon, whale, and porpoise 1883. **4.** *R. Artillery, Engineers, Marines, Naval Reserve*, etc. **6.** *R. Society*, a Society incorporated by Charles II in 1662 for the pursuit and advancement of the physical sciences. *R. Academy*: see ACADEMY 5. **7.** Besides that which Solomon gaue her of his royall bountie 1 *Kings* x. 13. **b.** His innocence ..could not save him from the r. vengeance 1845.

II. 1. Befitting, appropriate to, a sovereign; *esp.* stately, magnificent, splendid. late ME. **b.** Finely arrayed; resplendent; grand or imposing. late ME. **c.** Having rank comparable to that of a king. late ME. **d.** *colloq.* Noble, splendid, first-rate 1583. **2.** Of persons: Having the character proper to a king; noble, majestic; generous, munificent; also applied to animals. late ME. **b.** Of character, feelings, etc. 1565. **3.** In various military and related uses, denoting something on a grand scale, or of great size or strength, esp. *battle r.* 1489. **4.** *R. paper*, †*paper r.*, paper of a size measuring 24 by 19 inches as used for writing and 25 by 20 for printing 1497. **5. a.** In names of birds, reptiles, animals, etc., as *r. eagle, r. leopard, r. python, r. stag* (see B 3 c) 1575. **b.** In plant-names, as *r. bay*, the plant *Laurus Indicus*; *r. fern*, osmund royal; *r. palm*, the palm *Oreodoxa regia* found in the West Indies and Florida 1849.

1. Rich, Royall food! Bountyfull Bread! CRASHAW. **b.** A Royall Traine beleeue me SHAKS. **2.** Hee..can ..recount, what a royall housekeeper his great grandfather was 1616. **b.** Pitt's bearing, in this grand juncture and crisis, is r. CARLYLE. **4.** *R. folio, quarto, octavo.*

Special collocations: **r. antler** (see B. 3 b); **r. arch**, one of the degrees of freemasonry; **r. evil** = KING'S EVIL; **r. flush** *Poker*, the ace, king, queen, knave, and ten of the same suit; **r. mast** (*Naut.*), a smaller mast at the head of the topgallant mast; **-sail** (*Naut.*), a small sail hoisted above the topgallant sail; **r. tine** = B 3 a.

b. With names of colours, as **r. blue**, a deep bright blue; *r. purple, red.*

B. *sb.* **1.** *colloq.* A member of the royal family; a royal personage 1788. †**2. a.** = RIAL *sb.* 3. -1688. **b.** = REAL *sb.*[1] 1. -1755. **c.** = REAL *sb.*[1] 2. -1634. **3.** †**a.** The second branch or tine of a stag's horn, lying above the brow-antler -1623. †**b.** The antler next above the bez-antler -1627. **c.** A stag having a head of twelve points or more 1857. **4.** *Naut.* A royal sail 1769. **b.** *attrib.* (also for *r. mast*) 1840. **5.** A kind of small mortar 1790. **6.** *pl.* A name for the First Regiment of Foot, also called *Royal Scots* 1762.

2. a. *Rose r.* = ROSE-NOBLE.

Royalet (roi·ălet). Now *rare.* 1650. [f. ROYAL *sb.* + -ET, perh. after F. *roitelet*.] A petty king or chieftain; a kinglet, princelet.

Royalist (roi·ălist). 1643. [f. ROYAL *a.* + -IST.] A supporter of the sovereign or the sovereign's rights, esp. in times of civil war, rebellion, or secession; a king's man; a monarchist. So **Ro·yalism**, attachment to the monarchy or to the principle of monarchical government. **Royali·stic, -al** *adjs.*

Royalize (roi·ăləiz), *v.* 1586. [f. ROYAL *a.* + -IZE 2.] **1.** *trans.* To render royal; to invest with a royal character or standing 1590. **b.** To render famous, celebrate 1586. **2.** *intr.* To bear rule as a monarch; to play the king. Also with *it.* 1606. Hence **Royaliza·tion.**

Royally (roi·ăli), *a.* [f. ROYAL *a.* + -LY [2].] In a royal manner; *colloq.* gloriously, splendidly.

Royal oak. 1771. **1.** A sprig of oak worn to commemorate the restoration of Charles II in 1660. Hence *Royal Oak Day*, the 29th of May, Oak Apple Day. (Now *local.*) **2.** The species *Quercus regia* 1841.

Royalty (roi·ălti). late ME. [a. OF. *roialté*; see ROYAL *a.*] **1.** The office or position of a sovereign; royal dignity; royal power, sovereignty. †**b.** The personality of a sovereign; (his or her) majesty -1611. †**c.** The sovereignty or sovereign rule *of* (a state) -1594. †**2.** Magnificence, pomp, splendour -1642. **3.** Kinglike or majestic character or quality; greatness, lordliness; munificence, generosity 1548. **4.** Royal persons collectively or individually

1480. b. *pl.* Royal persons; members of the royal family 1813. 5. *pl.* Prerogatives, rights, or privileges pertaining to, or enjoyed by, the sovereign. Also rarely in *sing.* late ME. †b. *pl.* Emblems or insignia of sovereignty -1769. 6. A royal prerogative or right, esp. in respect of jurisdiction, granted by the sovereign to an individual or corporation. Also *pl.* (In later use, denoting chiefly rights over minerals.) 1483. b. A payment made to the landowner by the lessee of a mine in return for the privilege of working it 1839. c. A sum paid to the proprietor of a patented invention for the use of it 1864. d. A payment made to an author, editor, or composer for each copy of a book, piece of music, etc., sold by the publisher, or for the representation of a play 1880. †7. A domain, manor, etc., in possession of royal rights or privileges -1710. 8. A royal domain; a kingdom, realm; a monarchical state 1638. b. Monarchical government 1878.

1. Heare our English King, For thus his Royaltie doth speake in me SHAKS. *fig.* His striped blanket that hung like r. upon his stately form KINGLAKE. b. *Wint. T.* I. ii. 15. c. *Rich. III*, III. iv. 42. 3. Profane thy inborn r. of mind GRAY. 4. To the succeeding R. he leaues The healing Benediction SHAKS. 5. Wherefore do I assume These Royalties, and not refuse to Reign? MILT. 6. The lordship of Man was accounted as a r. and conveyed within the island itself certain sovereign rights STUBBS. 7. I have bought that little Hovel which borders upon his Royalty STEELE. So †**Roya·lity** (*rare*).

Royston crow (roi·stən). 1611. [f. the place-name *Royston*.] The hooded or grey crow.

Rub (rɒb), *sb.*[1] 1586. [f. RUB *v.*[1]] 1. An act or spell of rubbing 1615. 2. a. *Bowls.* An impediment by which a bowl is hindered in, or diverted from, its proper course; also, the fact of a bowl meeting with such impediment 1586. †b. *gen.* Any physical obstacle or impediment to movement -1821. 3. An obstacle, impediment, hindrance, or difficulty, of a non-material nature. Now *rare* or *Obs.* 1590. †4. A roughness; an unevenness or inequality -1747. 5. a. An intentional wound or chafe given to the feelings of another; in later use *esp.* a slight reproof or teasing 1642. b. An encounter with something annoying or disagreeable 1645. 6. *dial.* A mower's whetstone 1823.

1. The feathers all came off with a r. 1891. 2. a. It is impossible to play at bowls without meeting with rubs 1757. *R. of* (or *on*) *the green*, in golf, an accidental interference with the course or position of a ball. 3. I have no sense to sorrow for his death, whose life was the only r. to my affection 1607. Phr. *There's* (or *Here lies*) *the r.*; To sleepe, perchance to Dreame; I, there's the r. SHAKS. 4. To leaue no Rubs nor Botches in the Worke SHAKS. 5. a. Each felt the r., And in Spain not a Sub..can stomach a snub 1841. b. Let not the rubs of earth Disturb thy peace QUARLES.

Rub (rɒb), *sb.*[2] 1830. Abbrev. of RUBBER *sb.*[2]

Rub (rɒb), *v.*[1] [ME. *rubben* = LG. *rubben*; etym. unkn.] I. *trans.* 1. To subject (a surface or substance) to the action of something (as the hand, a cloth, etc.) moving over it, or backwards and forwards upon it, with a certain amount of pressure and friction. late ME. b. To make (one's hands) move over and press upon each other, as a sign of satisfaction 1778. c. *spec.* (See quot.) 1856 (implied in *brass-rubber*). 2. To subject to pressure and friction in order to clean, polish, make smooth, or sharpen. Also const. *with.* late ME. b. *fig.* To revive, stir up, in respect of memory or recollection. More freq. with *up.* 1580. 3. a. To affect painfully or disagreeably; to annoy, irritate 1523. b. To chafe, abrade, make rough or ragged 1805. 4. To treat (a surface) *with* some substance applied by means of friction and pressure 1535. 5. To bring into contact with another body or surface by means of friction accompanied with pressure. Const. *against, on, over,* and *together.* late ME. b. To bring (a part of the body) into reciprocal contact; hence *to r. shoulders* (etc.) *with*, to come into contact, to associate, *with* others 1645. 6. a. To remove, take or clear away, *from, off,* or *out of,* by rubbing 1508. b. To reduce *to* powder by rubbing 1726. c. To force *into* or *through*, spread *over*, a surface by rubbing 1778.

1. The king awoke,..And yawn'd, and rubb'd his face TENNYSON. b. [He] rubbed his hands, and was scarce able to contain the fullness of his glee MISS BURNEY. c. These brasses are capable of being 'rubbed', that is, of having an impression taken of them..by covering them with paper, and rubbing with some fitting substance upon the paper 1861. 2. I rubbe thynges with a cloute to make them cleane 1530. 3. You r. the sore, When you should bring the plaister SHAKS. 4. A rubs himselfe with Ciuit SHAKS. 5. He rubs his Sides against a Tree DRYDEN. b. She had rubbed shoulders with the great THACKERAY. Phr. *To r. noses*, of some savages, to greet each other. With advbs. **R. away,** to remove by rubbing. **R. down.** a. To clean (a horse) from dust and sweat by rubbing. b. To make smooth, reduce, grind down, etc.; by rubbing. **R. in.** a. To apply (dry colours) by rubbing; to draw or sketch in this way. b. To apply (an ointment, etc.) by continued rubbing. c. *slang.* To emphasize or reiterate (*esp.* something disagreeable). **R. off,** to remove by rubbing. **R. out.** a. To efface, erase, obliterate by rubbing. Also *fig.* (chiefly *U.S.*), to wipe out, kill. b. To extract (corn) from the ear by rubbing. **R. over,** to go over (with the hand, a tool, etc.) in the process of rubbing. **R. up.** a. To revive, recall to mind (some recollection, incident, etc.). b. To refresh (one's memory, etc.); to make clearer or stronger. c. To brush up, revive one's knowledge of (a subject). d. To prepare or mix by rubbing. e. With *the wrong way* (cf. I. 3 a).

II. *intr.* 1. To exert friction accompanied by pressure; to move and at the same time press *upon* or *against* something ME. b. Of a bowl: To encounter some impediment which retards or diverts its course 1588. 2. *fig.* To continue in a certain course with more or less difficulty or restraint; to contrive to get *on, through, along*, live or last *out*, pass or go *off* 1469. 3. To go, run, make *off.* Now *rare* or *Obs.* 1540. 4. To admit of being rubbed (*off, out* 1683.

1. Where the fish lye so thick, the ship brushes, and rubbes upon them 1660. b. So, so, r. on, and kisse the mistresse SHAKS. 2. I hope we shall always manage to r. on somehow 1880.

†**Rub,** *v.*[2] 1597. [var. of ROB *v.* 6.] *intr.* At cards: To take all the cards of one suit -1642.

Rub-a-dub (rɒ·bădɒ:b), *sb.* 1787. [Echoic.] The sound of a drum; a drumming sound. So **Rub-a-dub** *v. intr.* **Rub-a-dub-dub.**

‖**Rubato** (rubā·to). 1887. Ellipt. for *tempo rubato* (lit. 'robbed time'): see TEMPO.

Rubber (rɒ·bəɹ), *sb.*[1] 1536. [f. RUB *v.*[1] + -ER [1].] I. 1. A hard brush, a cloth, or the like, used for rubbing in order to make clean. †b. A strigil -1623. c. A towel used for rubbing the body after a bath 1577. 2. A whetstone, RUBSTONE. Now *dial.* 1566. 3. An implement of metal or stone used for rubbing, esp. in order to smooth or flatten a surface 1664. b. A pad or roll used for rubbing and polishing 1837. 4. A large coarse file. Also *r.-file.* 1677. 5. A part of some apparatus which operates by rubbing; a machine which acts by rubbing 1771. II. 1. A masseur or masseuse 1610. b. An attendant who rubs the bathers at a Turkish bath 1680. 2. One who rubs in any way 1611. b. One who takes rubbings of brasses, etc. 1861. 3. *fig.* A rebuke or irritating remark; a source of annoyance 1706. III. Ellipt. for INDIA-RUBBER. 1. Caoutchouc. Also *colloq.* A piece of this for erasing pencil marks. 1788. b. *pl.* Overshoes made of rubber. *U.S.* 1859. 2. *attrib.*, as *r. tire, r. plant, r. tree,* etc. 1866.

Hence **Ru·bber** *v.* (*U.S. slang*) = r.-neck. *Comb.* **rubber-neck** (orig. *U.S. slang*), one who cranes his neck or gapes in curiosity; *attrib.*, as *r.-n. car*, etc., for tourists to see the sights of a place; also as vb.

Rubber (rɒ·bəɹ), *sb.*[2] 1599. [Origin unkn.] In various games of skill or chance, e. g. bowls, whist, cribbage, backgammon, a set of (usu.) three games, the last of which is played to decide between the parties when each has gained one; hence, two games out of three won by the same side. Also, a set of five games, or the winning of three of these by one side.

Ru·bbing, *vbl. sb.* [-ING.[1]] The action of RUB *v.*[1]; *concr.* a copy made by rubbing (1845).

Ru·bbing-stone. 1648. [f. RUB *v.*[1]] A stone used for rubbing.

Rubbish (rɒ·biʃ), *sb.* (and *a.*). [ME. *robows, robeux*; perh. pl. of an old form *robel, = mod. Eng. *rubble* (Skeat).] 1. Waste or refuse material, in early use, esp. such as results from the decay or repair of buildings; debris, litter; rejected and useless matter of any kind. †Also, a heap of rubbish. 2. *fig.* Worthless stuff; trash 1601. b. Worthless, ridiculous, nonsensical ideas, discourse, or writing 1612. c. In interjectional use 1863. 3. *attrib.* or †as *adj.* 1594.

1. We perceiving from the Walls several Arms and Legs in the Air, mingled with the Smoke and Rubbidge 1684. The r. of mortar from houses 1813. 2. The body is but meer r. to the soul 1656. b. From hence to the end of your Book, I find nothing but R. and Trifles 1692. The jumbled r. of a dream TENNYSON. c. 'Oh, r.,..How can a skeleton sit and air himself?' 1888.

Comb.: **r.-price,** a paltry price, such as might properly be paid for r.; **r. pulley,** 'a simple form of tackle-block used with a rope in hoisting materials from a foundation or excavation'. Hence **Ru·bbishy** *a.* abounding in, covered with, r. or litter; paltry, contemptible, worthless.

Rubble (rɒ·b'l). late ME. [app. related in some way to prec.] 1. Waste fragments of stone, esp. from decayed or demolished buildings; †also, rubbish in general. 2. Pieces of undressed stone used in the construction of walls, esp. as a filling-in. Also *r.-stone.* 1565. b. *ellipt.* Rubble-work 1815. 3. *Geol.* Loose angular stones or fragments of broken material forming the upper covering of some rocks, and found beneath alluvium or overlying soil; also, water-worn stones. Also *r.-stone.* 1796. b. Small coal; slack 1883. 4. *local.* The bran of wheat, before it is sorted into pollard, bran, sharps, etc. 1858.

2. They were equally at home in the use of brick, or flint, or r. 1878. Hence **Ru·bbly** *a.* abounding in, consisting of, r.; having the nature or form of r.

Ru·bble-work, ru·bblework, ru·bble work. 1823. [f. prec.] Masonry composed of rubble or unwrought stones; also, fragments of stone mixed with mortar and used as a filling-in.

Rubefacient (rūbĭfē¹·ʃĕnt), *a.* and *sb.* 1804. [ad. pres. pple. of L. *rubefacere*; see RUBIFY *v.*] *Med.* A. *adj.* Producing redness or slight inflammation; *spec.* of counter-irritants. B. *sb.* An application producing redness of the skin; *esp.* a counter-irritant having this effect 1805.

Rubefaction (rūbĭfæ·kʃən). 1658. [See RUBIFY and -FACTION.] 1. *Med.* The action of making (the skin) red; redness of the skin, esp. as produced by some application. 2. The production of a red colour in water 1860.

‖**Rubella** (rube·lă). 1883. [mod.L., neut. pl. of *rubellus* reddish.] *Path.* German measles.

Rubellite (rū·bĕlait). 1796. [f. L. *rubellus* reddish + -ITE [1] 2 b.] *Min.* A variety of tourmaline.

‖**Rubeola** (rubī·ŏlă). 1676. [mod.L., neut. pl. of *rubeolus, dim. form of L. *rubeus* reddish.] *Path.* †1. Small red spots, usu. incident to smallpox or measles -1693. 2. Measles. Now *rare* or *Obs.* 1803. 3. German measles; rubella 1858.

Ruberythric (rūbĕri·þrik), *a.* 1857. [f. L. *rubia* madder + ERYTHRIC *a.*] *Chem. R. acid*, a yellow crystalline compound contained in madder-root.

Rubescent (rube·sĕnt), *a.* 1731. [ad. pres. pple. of L. *rubescere*, f. *ruber* red.] Tending to redness; reddening, blushing. Hence **Rube·scence** (*rare*), the fact of becoming red.

Rubiaceous (rūbi,ē¹·ʃəs), *a.* 1832. [f. mod. L. *Rubiaceæ*, f. *Rubia* (L. *rubia*) the genus madder.] *Bot.* Pertaining to or characteristic of a family of plants of which madder (*Rubia*) is the typical genus.

Rubiacin (rū·biăsin). 1848. [f. L. *rubia* + -(*c*)*in*.] *Chem.* A yellow colouring matter obtained from madder-root. So **Rubia·cic** *a.*

Rubian (rū·biăn). 1851. [f. L. *rubia* + -AN[1] 1.] *Chem.* The bitter principle of madder-root. Hence **Rubia·nic** *a.* applied to an acid produced by the oxidation of r. in contact with alkalis.

Rubicelle (rū·bisel). 1671. [a. F., app. a dim. of *rubis* ruby.] A variety of spinel, of a yellow or orange-red colour.

Rubicon (rū·bikŏn). 1626. [Ancient name of a small stream which formed part of the boundary between Italy and Cisalpine Gaul; the crossing of it by Cæsar marked the beginning of the war with Pompey.] 1. *To cross* or *pass the R.*, to take a decisive or final step, *esp.* at the outset of some undertaking or enterprise. 2. A boundary, bounding line, or limit.

lit. or *fig.* 1690. **3.** *attrib.* Applied to a variety of bezique 1887.

1. The die being cast and R. crossed 1643. 2. The bancks of the Boyn.., the ould R. of the Pale 1711.

Rubicund (rū·bikʊnd), *a.* 1503. [a. F. *rubicond*, or ad. L. *rubicundus*, f. *rubere* to be red.] †1. Of things: Inclined to redness; red –1671. **2.** Of the face, etc.: Reddish, flushed, highly coloured, esp. as the result of good living 1696. **b.** Of persons: Red-faced (with good living) 1827.

2. A sleepy eye, a r. face, and carbuncled nose SMOLLETT. Hence **Rubicu·ndity**, the state of being r.; redness.

Rubidine (rū·bidəin). 1868. [f. L. *rubidus* red + -INE 5.] *Chem.* A compound belonging to the pyridine series.

‖**Rubidium** (rubi·diŏm). 1862. [f. L. *rubidus* red, with ref. to the two red lines in its spectrum.] A soft, silvery-coloured metal belonging to the group which includes cæsium, lithium, potassium, and sodium.

†**Rubifica·tion.** 1592. [f. mod.L. **rubificat-*, *rubificare*; see -ATION.] The process of heating to redness –1645.

Rubify (rū·bifəi), *v.* late ME. [a. OF. *rubifier*, *rubefier* (mod.F. *rubéfier*) = med.L. *rubificare*, a Rom. form repl. L. *rubefacere*, f. *rubeus* red; see -FY.] *trans.* To make red; to redden. Now *rare.*

Rubiginous (rubi·dʒinəs), *a.* 1656. [f. L. *rubigin-*, *rubigo* rust, blight + -OUS.] **1.** Rusty, rust-coloured, ferruginous 1671. †**2.** Of plants: Affected by rust or blight. BLOUNT. So **Rubi·ginose** *a.* (*Bot.*) applied to a surface whose peculiar colour is due to glandular hairs.

†**Ru·bin(e.** 1511. [var. of RUBY, corresp. to OF. and Sp. *rubin*, med. L. *rubinus.*] A ruby –1691.

‖**Rubor** (rū·bǫ̈ɪ). 1656. [L., related to *ruber* red.] Redness, ruddiness.

Rubric (rū·brik), *sb.* and *a.* late ME. [ad. F. *rubrique* or L. *rubrica.*] **A.** *sb.* **1.** Red earth, red ochre, ruddle. Now *arch.* **2.** A heading of a chapter, section, etc., of a book, written or printed in red, or otherwise distinguished in lettering; a particular passage or sentence so marked 1450. **b.** *transf.* A descriptive heading or title; a designation or category (*rare*) 1831. **3.** A direction for the conduct of divine service inserted in liturgical books, and properly written or printed in red. late ME. **4.** A red-letter entry (of a saint's name) in the Church calendar; hence, a calendar of saints 1611. **5.** The title or heading of a statute or section of a legal code (orig. written in red) 1604.

2. The event is so unusual that it deserves to be printed as a r. in the official report 1885. 3. As a Minister, I teach her Doctrines. I use her Offices. I conform to her Rubricks. WESLEY. 5. It is neither mentioned in the title nor the r. of the Act of Parliament SCOTT.

B. *attrib.* passing into *adj.* **1.** Written or printed in red 1475. †**b.** Inscribed with the titles of books –1755. **2.** Red, ruddy, rubicund. Now *arch.* 1659. **b.** Applied to certain lake-colours 1835.

1. What tho' my Name stood r. on the walls POPE. b. Curl's chaste press, and Lintot's r. post POPE. 2. A rubrick nose, and a canonical belly 1694. Hence **Ru·bric** *v. trans.* to rubricate.

Rubrical (rū·brikăl), *a.* 1641. [f. RUBRIC *sb.* + -AL 1.] †**1.** Pertaining to the colour red. MILT. **2.** Marked by red letters (*rare*) 1666. **3.** Of or pertaining to liturgical rubrics; conforming to, enjoined by, the rubrics 1754.

3. A lifeless r. piety WARBURTON. Hence **Ru·brically** *adv.*

Rubricate (rū·brikeᵗt), *v.* 1570. [f. L. *rubricat-*, *rubricare*, f. *rubrica* RUBRIC *sb.*] **1.** *trans.* To mark or colour with red; to write, print, or mark in red letters. **b.** To place in the calendar as a red-letter saint 1570. **c.** To furnish with red-letter headings; to regulate by rubrics 1846. **2.** *intr.* To sign by mark instead of name 1846.

1. c. A formal..religion, according to which the thoughts of men were to be clast and rubricated for ever after 1846. So †**Ru·bricate** *ppl. a.* rubricated. **Rubrica·tion,** the action or result of rubricating. **Ru·bricator,** one charged with the execution of the rubrics in manuscripts, etc.

Rubrician (rubri·ʃăn). 1849. [f. RUBRIC *sb.* + -IAN.] One who studies or adheres to liturgical rubrics. So **Ru·bricist.**

Rubricity (rubri·sĭti). 1800. [f. as prec. + -ITY. **1.** Assumption of a red colour. **2.** Adherence to liturgical rubrics 1876.

1. The periodical..r. of the Nile GEDDES.

Rubstone (rʊ·bstōᵘn). late ME. [f. RUB *v.*¹ + STONE *sb.*] A stone used for rubbing or sharpening; *esp.* a kind of whetstone.

Ruby (rū·bi), *sb.* and *a.* ME. [a. OF. *rubi*, more usu. *rubis*, repr. the Rom. stem *rubin-* (see RUBIN(E), obscurely related to L. *rubeus*, *ruber* red.] **1.** A very rare and valuable precious stone (the *true* or *oriental r.*), of a colour varying from deep crimson or purple to pale rose-red; now classed as a variety of corundum. Also, a less valuable stone (an aluminate of magnesium) dist. as the *spinel* ruby, or a rose-pink variety of this, the *balas* ruby. **b.** The jewel of a watch (in the finest work usu. a variety of ruby) 1875. **2.** A red pimple on the face 1558. **3.** The colour of the ruby; a glowing purple-tinged red. Also †*Her.* = GULES. 1572. **4.** *transf.* Applied to: **a.** *pl.* The lips 1592. **b.** Red wine 1671. **c.** *Pugilistic slang.* The blood 1860. **5.** (See quots.) 1696. **6.** *Printing.* A size of type, intermediate between nonpareil and pearl. (Cf. AGATE *sb.* 4.) 1778. In U.S. = BRILLIANT *sb.* 4.

This line is printed in Ruby type.

7. as *adj.* Having the colour of the ruby 1508.

1. At thee the R. lights its deep'ning glow THOMSON. Phr. *Above rubies*, of inestimable value. 3. The swinging spider's silver line, The r. of the drop of wine EMERSON. 4. b. Still the Vine her ancient R. yields FITZGERALD. 5. What is called r. of arsenic or of sulphur is the realgar; the r. of zinc is the red blende; and the r. of silver is the red silver ore 1797. 7. *Jul. C.* III. i. 2 60.

Special collocations: **r. blende,** red silver, proustite; **r. glass,** glass coloured by the oxides of copper, iron, lead, tin, etc.; **r. silver,** proustite; **r. spinel** = *spinel r.*; **r. tail** *a.* having a r.-red hinder part; applied to hymenopterous insects of the genus *Chrysis*, esp. the golden wasp; *sb.* the golden wasp; so also **r.-tailed** *a.*; **r.-throat,** a r.-throated humming-bird or warbler; **r.-throated** *a.* having a r.-red gorget; **r. wood,** 'an E. Indian wood, the produce of *Pterocarpus santalinus*'; **r. zinc,** sphalerite or zincite of a deep-red colour. Hence **Ru·bied** *a.* coloured like a r.; r.-tinged. **Ru·bious** *a.* r.-coloured. **Ru·by** *v. trans.* to dye or tinge with the colour of the r.

Rucervine (rusɜ̄·ɪvəin), *a.* 1881. [f. mod. L. *Rucervus*; see RUSA and CERVINE *a.*] *Zool.* Of or belonging to a genus (*Rucervus*) of East Indian deer.

‖**Ruche** (ruʃ, F. rüʃ), *sb.* 1827. [F. *ruche* (†*rouche*, *rusche*) bee-hive, and (in allusion to the plaits of a straw hive) frill.] A frill or quilling of ribbon, gauze, lace, or the like, used to ornament some part of a garment or headdress. Hence **Ruche** *v. trans.* to trim with a r. **Ruching,** a trimming consisting of ruches.

Ruck (rʊk), *sb.*¹ ME. [app. of Scand. origin, corresp. to Norw. *ruka* with the same meanings.] **1.** A heap or stack of fuel or combustible material. **2.** A rick or stack of hay, corn, etc.; †a shock or stook. *Sc.* and *n. dial.* 1546. **3.** A heap or pile of any material. Freq. in phr. *in a r.* Now *dial.* 1601. **b.** *transf.* A large number or quantity; a multitude, crowd, throng 1581. **4.** *The r.*: **a.** *Racing.* Those horses which are left behind in a body by the fastest goers. **b.** The undistinguished crowd or general run (of persons or things). 1846.

3. b. Finishing with a r. of figures all at once 1847. 4. a. Who headed the R.? 'I', said Lord George 1846. b. Far more honest,..than the r. of their sect 1859.

Ruck (rʊk), *sb.*² 1787. [a. ON. *hrukka.*] A crease, fold, or wrinkle; a ridge.

Ruck (rʊk), *v.*¹ Now *dial.* ME. [perh. of Scand. origin; cf. Norw. dial. *ruka* to crouch.] *intr.* To squat, crouch, cower, huddle together.

Ruck (rʊk), *v.*² 1812. [f. RUCK *sb.*²] **1.** *intr.* To slip *up* or work into creases or ridges; to become creased or wrinkled. **2.** *trans.* To crease; to wrinkle or cause to work *up* into ridges 1828. **b.** To draw or gather into small folds 1896.

2. Mr. Sawyer..rucked his plaid trousers up to his knees 1860.

Ruckle (rʊ·k'l), *v.*¹ 1839. [f. RUCK *v.*² + -LE 3.] **1.** *intr.* To work (*up*) into folds or wrinkles. **2.** *trans.* To form, draw together, into folds 1889.

Ruckle (rʊ·k'l), *v.*² 1530. [Of Scand. origin.] *intr.* To make a rattling or gurgling sound; to rattle in the throat.

Rucksack (rʊ·ksæk). 1895. [ad. G. *rucksack*, f. *rucken*, dial. var. of *rücken* back + *sack* SACK *sb.*¹] A kind of knapsack worn by tourists.

Ruction (rʊ·kʃən). *dial.* or *colloq.* 1825. [Origin unkn.] Usu. *pl.* A disturbance, riot, tumult, row.

Rud (rʊd), *sb.* Now *dial.* and *arch.* [OE. *rudu*, related by ablaut to *réad* RED *a.*] **1.** Red or ruddy colour; redness, ruddiness. **2.** Complexion (of those parts of the face which are naturally reddish) OE. **3.** Chiefly *dial.* Ruddle; †a red cosmetic OE.

Rud, *v.* Now *dial.* ME. [Related to prec. and RUDDY *a.*] †**1.** *trans.* To make red or ruddy –1700. **2.** *dial.* To mark or colour with ruddle 1680.

Rudas (rū·dăs). *sb.* and *a.* *Sc.* 1725. [Origin obsc.] **A.** *sb.* A coarse, unmannerly (old) woman; a termagant, virago, hag. **B.** As *adj.* Hag-like; coarse, unmannerly 1802.

Rudd (rʊd). 1606. [app. f. RUD *sb.*] A freshwater cyprinoid fish (*Leuciscus erythrophthalmus*) resembling the roach; the red-eye.

Rudder (rʊ·dəɪ). [OE. *róðer* :—Teut. **roþra-*, from the stem of ROW *v.*] †**1.** A paddle or oar used for steering or propelling a vessel –1602. **2.** A broad, flat piece or framework of wood or metal, attached vertically to the sternpost of a boat or ship (later, also to an aeroplane or airship) in such a way that it can be employed in steering it ME. **b.** *fig.* One who or that which guides, directs, or controls. late ME. **3.** *Brewing.* A kind of paddle used in stirring malt in the mash-tub 1440. **4.** *Ornith.* = RECTRIX 2. 1884.

2. The Barke abandoned of her Rother, ranne whither the wind carried her 1632. b. Rhime the Rudder is of Verses 1663.

attrib. and *Comb.*, as *r.-chain*, etc.; also in specific names of birds and fishes, as **r.-bird, -duck,** a name for *Erismatura rubida*, one of the Spiny-tailed Ducks; **-perch** = next (*a*). Hence **Ru·dderless** *a.* having no r.; *fig.* without guidance or control.

Ru·dder-fish. 1734. [RUDDER *sb.*] The name of several species of fish which follow or accompany vessels; *esp.* (*a*) the rudder-perch, a W. Indian sea-fish; (*b*) the pilot-fish, *Naucrates ductor*; (*c*) the log- or barrel-fish (*Lirus* or *Palinurus perciformis*) of America; (*d*) a bluish fish (*Seriola zonata*), native to the Western Atlantic.

Ruddle (rʊ·d'l), *sb.*¹ 1538. [Related to RUD *sb.* and *v.* Cf. RADDLE *sb.*², REDDLE *sb.*] A red variety of ochre used for marking sheep and for colouring.

Ru·ddle, *sb.*² 1582. Var. of RIDDLE *sb.*² 1.

Ruddle (rʊ·d'l), *v.* 1718. [f. RUDDLE *sb.*¹] *trans.* To mark, smear, or paint with ruddle.

A woman..was ruddling her doorstep 1859.

Ruddock (rʊ·dək). [OE. *rudduc*, related to RUD *sb.*, RUDDY *a.*; see -OCK.] **1.** The redbreast or robin, *Erithacus rubecula.* Now chiefly *dial.* †**2.** *Cant.* A gold coin; hence *pl.*, gold, money –1628. †**3.** A species of toad –1749.

1. The tame rodok & the coward kyte CHAUCER. 2. If..he haue golden ruddocks in his bagges, he must be wise and honourable LYLY.

Ruddy (rʊ·di), *a.* (*sb.*). [OE. *rudig*, f. the same stem as RUD *sb.* and *v.*] **1.** Of the face, complexion, etc.: Freshly or healthily red. **b.** Of persons: Having a fresh red complexion ME. **c.** Characterized by, or associated with, healthy redness of feature 1820. **2.** *gen.* Red or reddish. late ME. †**b.** Causing redness in vegetation –1719. **3.** *slang.* Euphemism for BLOODY *a.* 8. 1914. **B.** *absol.* or as *sb.* Ruddy colour. late ME.

1. R. his lips, and fresh and fair his hue DRYDEN. b. The Inhabitants comely and tall, rather ruddie then blacke 1613. c. A figure..instinct with r. vigorous life 1860. 2. Faire and whiteish ruddie cloudes sparkeling aboute the skie 1554. As deere to me, as are the r. droppes That visit my sad heart SHAKS. R. duck..with the neck all round and the upper parts brownish-red 1872. R. plover..head, neck and upper parts varied with black, ashy and bright reddish 1872. B. The r. of youth had fled his cheek 1823. Hence **Ru·ddily** *adv.* **Ru·ddiness.**

Ruddy (rʊ·di), *v.* 1689. [f. prec.] **1.** *trans.* To render ruddy in hue; to redden. **2.** *intr.*

To blush (*rare*) 1845. Hence **Ru·ddied** *ppl. a.* rendered r., reddened.

Rude (rūd), *a.* and *adv.* ME. [a. OF. *ruide, rude* (F. *rude*), or ad. L. *rudis* unformed, inexperienced.] **A.** *adj.* **I. 1.** Uneducated, unlearned; ignorant. late ME. **b.** *absol.* as *pl.* The unlearned or ignorant. late ME. †**c.** Of animals: Irrational. -late ME. **2.** Inexperienced, inexpert, unskilled. Now *arch.* and *rare.* late ME. **b.** Inexact, superficial 1691. **3.** Uncultured, unrefined. late ME. **b.** Uncivilized, barbarous 1483. **4.** Unmannerly, uncivil, impolite; offensively or deliberately discourteous. late ME. **5.** Ungentle, violent, harsh, rugged; marked by unkind or severe treatment of persons, etc. late ME. **b.** Involving hardships or discomfort 1734. **c.** Of persons: Acting in a rough or harsh manner; violent in action 1800. **6.** Turbulent, violent, boisterous, rough. Chiefly of the sea, winds, etc. late ME. **b.** Of health: Robust, vigorous 1792. **7.** Of sounds: Discordant, harsh, unmusical ME.

1. They shall leave their cure not to a r. and unlerned person but to a good, lerned, & experte curate CROMWELL. **c.** The r. asse and the ox also. late ME. **2.** Here the r. chisel's rougher strokes I traced 1746. He was altogether r. in the art of controversy MACAULAY. **b.** He has been but a r. observer of them 1691. **3.** The r. Porter that no manners had Did shut the gate against him in his face SPENSER. The r. state of manners and general ignorance of the clergy 1827. **b.** The r. people he framed to a civilitie HOOKER. **4.** We have done with civility. We are to be as r. as we please. JOHNSON. The profound respect..was..changed into r. familarity GIBBON. **5.** Let goe that r. unciuill touch SHAKS. Hands more r. than wintry sky BYRON. **b.** Such is our r. mortal lot SHELLEY. **c.** The exasperated r. Titan rives and smites these Girondins CARLYLE. **6.** In Cradle of the r. imperious Surge SHAKS. R. thunders rake the crags 1807. **7.** Peace you vngracious, Clamors peace r. sounds SHAKS. This man's r. and clamorous grief SCOTT.

II. 1. Of language, composition, etc.: Lacking in elegance or polish; deficient in literary merit ME. **b.** Of drawings, etc.: Rough; not very accurate or finished 1679. **c.** Roughly correct 1854. **2.** Coarse, inelegant, rough (*rare*). late ME. **3.** Of natural scenery or objects: Rugged, rough; uncultivated, wild. late ME. **4.** Imperfect, unfinished. Now *rare* or *Obs.* late ME. **b.** Of natural products: Unwrought; unmanufactured, raw 1555. **c.** Left in a natural rough state; undressed 1800. **5.** Of a rough, inelegant, or rugged form; in early use, big and coarse; strong but ill-shaped. late ME. **b.** Roughly made or formed; imperfect 1612. **6.** Of an imperfect, undeveloped, or primitive character 1600.

1. A r. version of the Old Testament 1861. **b.** Some r. design In crayons or in charcoal 1746. A r. school-boy hand 1890. **3.** An open, r. common 1756. The r. rock remains uncovered 1867. **4. b.** Either the r. or manufactured produce ADAM SMITH. The cotton..in its r. state DISRAELI. **c.** Three pillars of r. stone WORDSW. **5.** The Heav'n-born-childe, All meanly wrapt in the r. manger lies MILT. **b.** It is easy to descend into it by a r. path SCOTT. **6.** In the r. idolatry of the Arabs GIBBON.

B. *adv.* In a rude manner; rudely (*rare*) 1475. Hence **Ru·de·ly** *adv.*, **-ness. Ru·dish** *a.* somewhat r.

Rudesby (rū·dzbi). Now *arch.* 1566. [f. RUDE *a.*; see -BY 2.] An insolent, unmannerly, or disorderly fellow.

Rudesheimer (rū·dəshəimər). 1797. [ad. G. *Rüdesheimer* (sc. *wein*).] A fine white wine produced at Rüdesheim on the Rhine.

Rudiment (rū·diměnt), *sb.* 1548. [ad. L. *rudimentum* beginning, f. *rudis* imperfect, RUDE.] **1.** *pl.* The first principles or elements of a subject; those points which are first taught to, or acquired by, the beginner; also const. *of* (the thing to be learned). **b.** *sing.* A first principle; an initial step or stage 1548. **2.** *pl.* The imperfect beginnings of some (material or immaterial) thing, which are the foundation of later growth or development 1566. **b.** *sing.* A beginning; an initial or imperfect form or stage 1626.

1. From these first Rudiments he grew To nobler Feats 1680. The rudiments of Arithmetick 1638. **2.** Rudiments, however, may occur in one sex, of parts normally present in the other sex DARWIN. *Rudiments of the world*; We, as longe as we were children, were in bondage vnder the rudiments of the worlde N.T. (Genev.) *Gal.* iv. 3. **b.** Several species have been found..with a r. of a thumb 1880. Hence **Rudime·ntal, Rudime·ntary** *adjs.* pertaining to, connected with, the rudiments of knowledge; of the nature of a r.; undeveloped, immature, imperfect.

Rudolphine (rudǫ·lfəin), *a.* 1656. [f. the name *Rudolph* (see def.) + -INE [1].] *R. tables, numbers*, a series of astronomical calculations published by Kepler in 1627 and named after the Emperor Rudolph II.

Rue (rū), *sb.*[1] Now *dial.* or *arch.* [OE. *hrēow*, related to *hrēowan* RUE *v.*] **1.** Sorrow, distress; repentance; regret. **2.** Pity, compassion ME.

1. With r. my heart is laden For golden friends I had HOUSMAN.

Rue (rū), *sb.*[2] late ME. [a. F. *rue*, for earlier *rude*:—L. *ruta*, ad. Gr. ῥυτή, orig. a Peloponnesian word.] **1.** A perennial evergreen shrub of the genus *Ruta*, esp. *R. graveolens*, having bitter, strong-scented leaves formerly much used in medicine. **2.** With qualifying word prefixed applied to various plants 1731. **b.** With *pl.* A species of rue 1731.

Then purg'd with Euphrasie and R. The visual Nerve, for he had much to see MILT. *fig.* For one shall..drink life's r., and one its wine 1862. **2. Goat's r.** (see GOAT).

Rue (rū), *v.* [OE. *hrēowan* = (M)Du. *rouwen*, OHG. *(h)riuwan* (G. *reuen*), etc.] †**I.** *trans.* With dat. (or acc.) of the person, and usu. with impersonal subject. **1.** To affect a person with penitence (for sins or offences committed). -late ME. **2.** To affect with regret (for some act); to make (one) wish one had acted otherwise -1440. **3.** To affect with sorrow; to distress or grieve -1548. **4.** To affect with pity or compassion -1590.

2. Me rewith sore I am unto hir teyd CHAUCER. **4.** Deare dame, your suddein overthrow Much rueth me SPENSER.

II. *trans.* With personal subject. **1.** To repent of (wrongdoing); to feel penitence (for sin) ME. **2.** To repent of (some act or course of action); to regret and wish undone or altered, on account of the consequences ME. **3.** To regard or think of (an event, fact, etc.) with sorrow or regret; to wish that (something) had never taken place or existed ME. †**4.** To regard with pity or compassion; to feel sorry for (a person, etc.) -1611.

1. Ruing the spoile done by his fatall hand DRAYTON. **2.** Rome has had to r. many a too hasty step 1874. Phr. *To r. it, the day, hour*, etc.; Ye shall r. the day ye took it 1782. **3.** The world will have cause to r. this iniquitous measure BURKE. Take him away, before I r. the day I saw him 1887. **4.** Die is my dew; yet rew my wretched state SPENSER.

III. *intr.* **1.** To be penitent or contrite; to feel repentance or remorse ME. **2.** To be repentant, or full of regret and dissatisfaction, in respect of some act (in mod. *Sc.* use *esp.* of a bargain or promise). late ME. **3.** To feel sorrow or grief, *esp.* by reason of suffering from some fact or event; to lament ME. †**b.** To be sorry, feel reluctant, *to* do something -1630. **4.** To have, take, or feel pity or compassion. With †*of, on* or *upon* (arch.); †also without const. ME.

1. Hereafter..honour awakes, causeth a wretch to r. 1871. **2.** Avoid green gooseberries, or you will have cause to r. 1830. **4.** R. on this realme, whoes ruine is at hand SURREY.

Rueful (rū·fŭl), *a.* ME. [f. RUE *sb.*[1] + -FUL 1.] **1.** Exciting sorrow or compassion; pitiable; doleful, dismal; expressive of sorrow. †**2.** Full of pity or compassion -1440.

1. [The cat] maketh a rufull noise, and a gastefull, when one profereth to fighte with another 1572. *Knight of the R. Countenance*: Don Quixote. Hence **Rue·ful·ly** *adv.*, **-ness.**

‖**Ruelle** (rü͜el). late ME. [F., dim. of *rue* street.] **1.** The space between a bed and the wall; the part of a bed next the wall. **2.** A bedroom, where ladies of fashion, in the seventeenth and eighteenth centuries, esp. in France, held a morning reception of persons of distinction; hence, a reception of this kind 1676.

Rufescent (rufe·sěnt), *a.* and *sb.* 1815. [ad. L. *rufescent-, rufescens, rufescere*, f. *rufus* reddish.] Of a colour tending to reddish; somewhat rufous. Hence **Rufe·scence**, r. tendency.

Ruff (rɒf), *sb.*[1] late ME. [perh. f. ROUGH *a.*] †**1.** A sea-bream or other sparoid fish -1668. **2.** A small freshwater fish (*Acerina cernua*) of the perch family, of olive-brown colour with brown and black spots, and having rough prickly scales 1450.

Ruff (rɒf), *sb.*[2] 1523. [perh. subst. use of ROUGH *a.*] †**1.** A circular outstanding frill on the sleeve of a garment; a ruffle -1647. **2.** An article of neckwear, usu. consisting of starched linen or muslin arranged in flutings, and standing out all round the neck, worn esp. in the reigns of Elizabeth and James I. 1555. **3.** A collar of projecting or distinctively coloured feathers or hair round the neck of various animals 1698. **b.** An artificial variety of the domestic pigeon resembling the jacobin 1735. **4.** A circular object resembling a ruff 1693.

2. That heath'nish Ruffe of thine, that perks Upon thy stiffe-neckt coller QUARLES. **3.** The grouse..wears A sable r. around his mottled neck 1856. **4.** Soft on the paper r. its leaves I spread POPE.

Ruff (rɒf), *sb.*[3] 1589. [ad. OF. *roffle, rouffle*, earlier *romfle, ronfle*, = It. *ronfa*.] †**1.** A former card-game. Also *r. and honours.* -1688. **2.** The act of trumping at cards, esp. in whist 1856. So **Ruff** *v.*[2] *trans.* to trump 1598.

Ruff (rɒf), *sb.*[4] 1634. [perh. f. RUFF *sb.*[2] 3.] The male of a bird of the sandpiper family (*Tringa* or *Machetes pugnax*), distinguished during the breeding season by a ruff and ear-tufts.

Ruff (rɒf), *sb.*[5] 1688. [perh. imitative.] = RUFFLE *sb.*[3]

†**Ruff**, *sb.*[6] 1548. [Cf. Sw. *ruff* spirit, 'go'.] **1.** The highest pitch or fullest degree *of* some exalted or excited condition -1692. **2.** An exalted or elated state; elation, pride; vain-glory -1690. **3.** *Her.* Of a ship: *In her r.*, in full course -1688. **4.** Excitement, passion, fury; freq. *in a r.* -1641. Hence †**Ruff** *v.*[4] *intr.* to swagger, bluster, domineer.

Ruff (rɒf), *v.*[1] Now *rare.* 1548. [perh. f. RUFF *sb.*[2]] **1.** *trans.* To form into a ruff or ruffs; to provide with a ruff or ruffs. Also with *up.* †**2.** Of a bird: To ruffle (the feathers) -1597. †**3.** *Falconry.* Of a hawk: To strike (the quarry) without securing it -1646.

Ruff (rɒf), *v.*[3] *Sc.* 1826. [f. RUFF *sb.*[5]] **1.** *trans.* To beat a ruff or ruffle upon (a drum). Also *intr.* of a drum: To be thus beaten. 1827. **2.** *trans.* and *intr.* To applaud by making a noise with the feet 1826.

†**Ru·ff-coat.** 1653. [prob. f. *ruff*, obs. var. of ROUGH *a.*] The caddis-worm -1833.

Ruffed (rɒft), *ppl. a.* 1586. [f. RUFF *sb.*[2] or *v.*[1]] **1.** Ruffled 1591. **2.** Wearing a ruff; provided with ruffs 1586. **b.** In names of animals: Having a ruff-like collar or markings, as *r. grouse, pigeon*; *r. lemur*, etc. 1783.

Ruffian (rɒ·fiăn), *sb.* and *a.* 1531. [a. OF. *rufien, ruffian* (mod.F. *rufien, rufian*); ult. origin obsc.] **1.** A man of a low and brutal character; one habitually given to acts of violence or crime; a cut-throat villain. †**2.** One distinguished as a swaggering bully or dissolute person by his dress or appearance -1675. †**3.** A confederate or protector of prostitutes. Cf. BULLY *sb.*[1] 4. 1618. **4.** *attrib.* or as *adj.* **a.** Characteristic of or appropriate to ruffians 1553. **b.** Having the manners, behaviour, or appearance of ruffians 1597.

1. Stab me yourself, nor give me to the knife Of midnight ruffians 1752. **3.** The Common sorte lodge with Baudes called Ruffians, to whome in Venice they pay of their gayne the fifth parte 1618. **4. a.** Some fought from r. thirst of blood SCOTT. Hence **Ruffian** *v. intr.* to play the r.; *esp.* of wind, etc., to rage, bluster. **Ru·ffianage**, ruffianism; ruffians collectively. **Ru·ffianish** *a.* (*rare*) ruffianly. **Ru·ffianism,** conduct or manners befitting a r.; violence, brutality; ruffians collectively. †**Ru·ffianous** *a.* ruffianly.

Ru·ffian-like, *a.* and *adv.* 1580. [f. RUFFIAN *sb.*] **A.** *adj.* Befitting, appropriate to, a ruffian; resembling, having the qualities or manners of, a ruffian. **B.** *adv.* In the manner of a ruffian (*rare*) 1600.

Ruffianly (rɒ·fiănli), *a.* 1570. [f. RUFFIAN *sb.* + -LY [1].] **1.** Having the character, appearance, or demeanour of a ruffian. **2.** Characteristic of or appropriate to ruffians 1579.

2. Two common soldiers of r. aspect 1874.

†**Ru·ffin.** ME. [Origin unkn.] **1.** The name of a fiend -1500. **2.** *Cant.* The Devil -1641.

Ruffle (rɒ·f'l), *sb.*[1] 1533. [f. RUFFLE *v.*[1]] **I.** †**1.** Disorder, confusion -1712. **2.** A disturbed state (of the mind); perturbation, excitement 1704. b. A disturbing or annoying experience or encounter; annoyance, vexation 1718. 3. A break or alteration in the evenness or placidity of some surface 1713. 4. The act of ruffling cards 1872.

1. An administration..calm and without r. 1767. 3. A r. of sourness shot over the features of the earl MEREDITH. Never..a r. on the gently heaving water 1894.

II. †1. The loose turned-over portion or flap of a top-boot. B. JONS. 2. A strip of lace, etc., gathered on one edge and used as an ornamental frill on a garment, esp. at the wrist, breast, or neck 1707. b. An object resembling a ruffle; *esp.* the ruff of a bird 1862.

Ru·ffle, *sb.*[2] 1534. [f. RUFFLE *v.*[2]] 1. A riotous disturbance or tumult; a hostile encounter or skirmish; a contention or dispute. †2. a. *Sc.* A check or defeat –1721. b. A disturbing cause or event; a commotion –1716. †3. Ostentatious bustle or display –1694. †4. = RUFF *sb.*[6] –1688.

1. In the r. between two pretenders, the right owner often finds the possession 1710.

Ru·ffle, *sb.*[3] 1802. [Cf. RUFF *sb.*[5]] *Mil.* A vibrating drum-beat, which is less loud than a roll. So **Ruffle** *v.*[3] *intr.* of a drum: to beat a r.

Ru·ffle, *v.*[1] ME. [Origin obsc.] I. 1. *trans.* To destroy the smoothness or evenness of, to spoil the regular or neat arrangement of (cloth, the skin, etc.). b. To roughen, raise, or abrade (the skin, etc.) as by rubbing or grazing upon 1615. c. To draw together in a ruffle or ruffles; to trim with ruffles. (Usu. in pa. pple.) 1653. 2. To disorder, disarrange (hair or feathers); to cause to stick up or out irregularly 1490. b. Of a bird: To set *up*, stiffen (the feathers), esp. as a sign of anger 1643. 3. *gen.* To disorder, render uneven or irregular, in some manner. Also *refl.* 1528. 4. †a. To stir *up* to indignation. SHAKS. b. To annoy, irritate, vex, discompose (a person, the mind, etc.) 1658. c. To trouble, disturb (a state of mind, etc.) 1701. 5. To turn over (the leaves of a book) hurriedly; to slip (cards) rapidly through the fingers 1621. 6. *intr.* To rise unevenly or irregularly; to form small folds or bends; to flutter in this manner 1577. b. To stir with anger or impatience 1719.

1. Pray thee looke the gowne be not rufled 1607. A brow..too apt to be ruffled 1833. c. The legs ruffled with black riband like a pigeon's leg PEPYS. 2. Not a hair Ruffled upon the scarfskin TENNYSON. b. A swan ruffling up its feathers at the presence of an eagle 1870. 3. A hurricane blew..ruffling the lake 1883. 4. a. *Jul. C.* III. ii. 232. b. He is sensible of every Passion, but ruffled by none STEELE. 6. [The sea] ruffles to the breeze and swells into the storm 1887.

†II. 1. *trans.* To put into disarray or confusion; to tangle, ravel –1638. b. To involve in obscurity or perplexity; to bewilder (a person) –1679. 2. To fold, wrap, heap, rattle *up*, in a rough or careless manner –1658. Hence **Ru·ffler**[1], an attachment to a sewing-machine for making ruffles.

Ruffle (rʊ·f'l), *v.*[2] 1440. [Origin obsc.] 1. *intr.* To contend or struggle *with*, to do battle *for*, a person or thing. Now *arch.* 2. To make a great stir or display; to hector, swagger, bear oneself proudly or arrogantly. Now *arch.* Also const. with *it* and *out* 1484. 3. Of winds, etc.: To be turbulent, rage, bluster 1579. †4. *trans.* To handle roughly; to set upon with violence; to bully –1721. †b. To handle (a woman) with rude familiarity –1720. †5. To take or snatch rudely –1715.

1. Men of activity that could..r. with the several rude persons in the country 1660. 2. [He] gets drunk, ruffles, and roysters KINGSLEY. b. I..would willingly r. it out once more in the King's cause SCOTT. 5. *Lear* III. vii. 41.

Ruffler[2] (rʊ·flər). Now *arch.* 1535. [f. RUFFLE *v.*[2]] †1. One of a class of vagabonds prevalent in the 16th c. –1818. 2. A proud, swaggering, or arrogant fellow 1536.

†**Ruff-tree**: see ROOF-TREE and ROUGH-TREE.

Rufi- (rū·fi), comb. form of L. *rufus* red, as in *ruficarpous* having red fruit, *ruficaudate* red-tailed, *rufigallic*, etc.

Rufo- (rū·fo), comb. form (on Gr. types) of L. *rufus* red, in some adjs. denoting colour with the sense 'rufous', as *rufo-fulvous*, etc.

Rufous (rū·fəs), *a.* (*sb.*). 1782. [f. L. *rufus*; see -OUS.] 1. Of a brownish-red colour; reddish; ferruginous. 2. *ellipt.* as *sb.* a. A brownish-red colour 1783. b. A r.-coloured moth 1832.

Ru·fter-hood. 1575. [Origin obsc.] A form of hood used for a newly-taken hawk.

Rug (rʊg), *sb.* 1551. [perh. of Scand. origin; cf. Norw. *rugga*, *rogga* coarse coverlet, etc.] †1. A rough woollen material, a sort of coarse frieze, in common use in the 16–17th century –1711. †b. With *pl.* A kind of frieze; also, a frieze cloak or mantle –1680. 2. A large piece of thick woollen stuff (freq. of various colours) used as a coverlet or as a wrap in driving, railway-travelling, etc. 1591. 3. A square or oblong mat for the floor, usu. of thick or shaggy stuff 1810.

1. December must be..clad in Irish rugge, or coorse freeze 1622. 2. Mighty hot weather; I lying this night..with only a rugg and a sheet upon me PEPYS. *attrib.*: r.-headed *a.* shock-headed.

†**Rug**, *a.* 1700. [Gaming slang; origin unkn.] Safe, secure –1797.

Fear nothing, Sir; Rug 's the Word, all 's safe ROWE.

Rug (rʊg), *v.* *Sc.* and *n. dial.* ME. [prob. of Scand. origin; cf. Norw. *rugga*, obs. Da. *rugge*, to rock (a cradle), to sway.] 1. *trans.* To pull forcibly, violently, or roughly; to tear, tug. 2. *intr.* To pull, tear, or tug (*at* something) ME. †b. *R. and reave*, to practise robbery –1596.

‖**Ruga** (rū·gă). Pl. **rugæ** (rū·dʒī). 1775. [L.] *Bot.*, *Zool.*, etc. A wrinkle, fold, or ridge. So **Ru·gate** *a.* having rugæ; wrinkled.

Rugby (rʊ·gbi). Name of the public school at Rugby in Warwickshire, used *attrib.* or *absol.* to designate one of the two leading forms of the game of football. Hence **Rugbeian** (-bī·ăn), a former or present pupil of Rugby school.

Rugged (rʊ·gėd), *a.* (and *adv.*). ME. [prob. of Scand. origin; cf. RUG *sb.*, and Sw. *rugga* to roughen.] A. †1. Rough with hair; hirsute, shaggy; also of horses, rough-coated –1726. †b. Of cloth: Hairy, coarse, rough –1826. 2. Having small rough projections; broken into irregular prominences; rough, uneven 1548. b. Of ground: Broken, uneven; full of stones, rocks, abrupt rises or declivities, etc. 1656. 3. Of features: Wrinkled, furrowed; irregular; strongly marked 1596. b. Wrinkled with care or displeasure; frowning 1605. 4. Of weather, etc.: Rough, stormy, tempestuous. Now *rare.* 1549. b. Involving hardships or severe toil 1730. 5. Rough to the ear; harsh; unpolished 1590. 6. Austere, harsh, severe, ungentle 1597. 7. Lacking in culture and refinement; rude, uncultivated; also, rough and hardy 1625. 8. Of a rough but strong or sturdy character 1827. 9. *U.S.* Strong, robust, vigorous 1848. B. As *adv.* Ruggedly 1661.

1. Approach thou like the r. Russian Beare SHAKS. 2. Beneath those r. elms GRAY. b. The road very r. with stones BERKELEY. 3. You have a good face now, but 'twill grow r. 1617. b. Sleeke o're your r. Lookes, Be bright and Iouiall SHAKS. 4. He..question'd every gust of r. wings That blows from off each beaked Promontory MILT. b. R. hours and fruitless toil KEATS. 5. But ah! my rymes too rude and r. arre SPENSER. 6. We..dislike those r. pastors who will make no allowance for the follies of the age 1817. 7. Force is a r. Way of making Love 1680. Hence **Ru·gged-ly** *adv.*, **-ness.** So **Ru·ggy** *a.* (now *dial.*) rugged: rough; †shaggy; †wild; stormy.

Rugger (rʊ·gəɪ). orig. *University slang.* 1893. RUGBY football.

†**Rug gown.** 1558. [f. RUG *sb.*] 1. A gown made of rug –1657. 2. One wearing a rug gown; *spec.* a watchman –1646.

Rugose (rū·gōᵘs), *a.* 1703. [ad. L. *rugosus*, f. *ruga.*] Marked by rugæ or wrinkles; wrinkled, corrugated, ridgy.

R. leaf, that whose veins are sunk deep, and between which the membranous and fleshy part of the leaf rises in irregular forms 1753. Hence **Rugo·sely** *adv.* So **Ru·gous** *a.* 1615.

Rugosity (rugǫ·sĭti). 1599. [ad. L. *rugositas* or F. *rugosité*; see prec. and -ITY.] 1. The state of being rugose or wrinkled. 2. With *a* and *pl.* A corrugation or wrinkle; a slight roughness or inequality 1664.

2. *fig.* History is apt to smooth out these rugosities 1900.

Rugulose (rūgiulōᵘs), *a.* 1819. [f. **rugula*, dim. of L. *ruga* + -OSE[1].] *Entom.*, *Bot.*, etc. Having small wrinkles; slightly rugose.

Ruin (rū·in), *sb.* [Late ME. *ruyne*, *ruine* a. (O)F. *ruine*, ad. L. *ruina*, f. *ruere* to fall.] I. 1. The act, on the part of some building or structure, of giving way and falling down. Now *rare.* 2. A ruinous condition. late ME. b. That which remains after decay and fall; ruins (*rare*) 1460. 3. *pl.* The remains of a decayed and fallen building or town. Freq. *fig.* of persons, features, institutions, states, etc. 1454. c. *transf.* Of material things 1597. 4. A ruined or ruinous building, town, etc. 1592. 5. *pl.* Damage, injury, done to anything 1592.

1. The death of the Duke of Britaine, slaine by the ruine of a wall 1632. 2. The old towne fals to r. 1582. Whilst here the Vine o'er hills of ruine climbs ADDISON. 3. Palestine is a land of ruins 1856. 4. *fig.* The Noble ruine of her Magicke, Anthony,..Leauing the Fight in heighth SHAKS. 5. Vain endeavours to repair by Art and Dress the Ruins of time SWIFT.

II. 1. The downfall or decay of a person or society; utter loss of means, position, or rank. late ME. b. Dishonour of a woman; degradation resulting from this 1624. c. Complete destruction *of* anything 1673. 2. The condition of being ruined or reduced to an abject or hopeless state. late ME. 3. That which causes destruction or downfall. late ME. 4. *gen.* Destruction, complete overthrow or devastation 1586. 5. *slang.* Gin of a poor quality. Usu. *blue r.* (see BLUE *a.*) 1817.

1. To perfecte their Ruine, there hapned another fatal Mischance to them 1665. 2. Princely counsel in his face yet shon, Majestick though in r. MILT. Phr. *Rack and r.*: see RACK *sb.*[4] 3. They were the ruine of him, and of all Israel 2 *Chron.* xxviii. 23. 4. R. seize thee, Ruthless King! GRAY.

attrib.: r. agate, jasper, marble (so called from the markings they exhibit).

Ruin (rū·in), *v.* 1581. [ad. F. *ruiner*, or med.L. *ruinare*, f. *ruina* RUIN *sb.*] I. *trans.* 1. To reduce (a place, etc.) to ruins 1585. b. *fig.* To overthrow, destroy (a kingdom, etc.) 1585. †2. To destroy, extirpate, eradicate; to do away with by a destructive process –1725. 3. To inflict or bring great and irretrievable disaster upon (a person or community) 1613. b. To bring to financial ruin; to reduce to a state of poverty 1660. c. To dishonour (a woman) 1679. d. To demoralize completely 1832. 4. To spoil, damage, injure, in a completely destructive manner 1656. b. To involve in disaster or failure; to make entirely abortive 1596. c. To invalidate entirely 1665.

1. The wall, which was of tough mud, was imperfectly ruined 1849. b. What ruins Kingdoms, and lays Cities flat MILT. 3. Marke but my Fall, and that that Ruin'd me SHAKS. b. Many gentlemen and ladies are ruined by play BERKELEY. d. It was universally agreed that college had ruined me DISRAELI. 4. He rides..till the thorns have ruined his silken surcoat 1889. b. People r. their fortunes by extravagance 1736. c. It ruines his hypothesis 1693.

II. *intr.* 1. To fall into ruins; to fall headlong; to go down with a crash. Also with *in.* 1604. 2. To come to ruin; to be brought to poverty; to be overwhelmed by failure 1596.

1. Hell saw Heav'n ruining from Heav'n MILT. Hence **Ru·inable** *a.* that may be ruined; perishable. **Ru·iner**, one who or that which ruins.

Ruinate (rū·ineᶦt), *ppl. a.* 1538. [ad. med. L. *ruinatus*, *ruinare*; see RUIN *v.*] 1. Of buildings, etc.: Ruined, ruinous. Now somewhat *rare.* 2. Involved in ruin or disaster. Now *rare.* 1591.

1. A famous Citie now r. MILT.

Ruinate (rū·ineᶦt), *v.* 1548. [f. ppl. stem of med.L. *ruinare*; see prec.] 1. *trans.* To reduce to ruins. 2. To bring destruction upon, to overthrow (a kingdom, state, etc.) 1574. 3. To ruin or impoverish (a person) 1577. †4. To demolish or destroy; to lay waste –1740. †5. To overthrow, overturn, subvert utterly –1695. 6. *intr.* To go or fall to ruin 1560.

1. *fig.* You r. the whole tower of Faith 1670. 5. T' attempt to r. So glorious a Design DANIEL. Hence **Ru·inated** *ppl. a.* **Ruina·tion**, the action of ruining; the fact or state of being ruined.

Ruinous (rū·inəs), *a.* late ME. [ad. F. *ruineux*, *-euse*, or L. *ruinosus*; see RUIN *sb.* and -OUS.] 1. Falling or fallen into ruin; decayed, dilapidated, broken down. 2. Brought to, sunk into, ruin or decay (*rare*) 1587. 3. Bringing or tending to bring ruin; disastrous, destructive, pernicious 1526. †4. Pertaining to a fall or crash. MILT.

1. The Town..is very r., nothing left entire 1660. 2. Is yon'd despis'd and r. man my Lord? SHAKS. 3. Any attempts to raise its price..would be r. to the wool trade 1842. Hence **Ru·inous·ly** *adv.*, **-ness.**

Rulable (rū·lăb'l), *a.* Also **ruleable.** 1449. [f. RULE *v.* and *sb.* + -ABLE.] †1. Capable of being ruled; governable –1680. 2. *U.S. colloq.* Allowable by rule; permissible 1888.

Rule (rūl), *sb.* [ME. *riule*, a. OF. *riule*, *rule* :—L. *regula* straight stick, ruler, pattern.] I. 1. A principle, regulation, or maxim governing individual conduct. b. *transf.* Applied to a person or thing. late ME. 2. The code of discipline or body of regulations observed by a religious order or congregation; hence *occas.*, the order or congregation itself ME. 3. A principle regulating practice or procedure; a fixed and dominating custom or habit. late ME. b. A regulation determining the methods or course of a game or the like 1697. c. Without article: Rigid system or routine. *Out of r.*, contrary to custom. 1796. 4. *Law.* a. An order made by a judge or court, the application of which is limited to the case in connexion with which it is granted. Also called a *particular r.* or *r. of court.* 1447. b. A formal order or regulation governing the procedure or decisions of a court of law; an enunciation or doctrine forming part of the common law, or having the force of law. Also called a (*standing*) *r. of court.* 1530. 5. A regulation framed or adopted by a corporate body, public or private, for governing its conduct and that of its members 1558. 6. *The rules*, a defined area in the neighbourhood of certain prisons, *esp.* those of the Fleet and King's Bench, within which certain prisoners, esp. debtors, were permitted to live on giving proper security 1662. b. The freedom of these bounds or 'rules' 1766.

1. All endeavour to deduce rules of action from balance of expediency is in vain RUSKIN. 2. There are foure rules, or religious Orders 1631. Their r...obliges them to..a total abstinence from flesh 1738. 3. Phr. *R. of the road*: see ROAD *sb.* 4. So *Rule(s) of the sea.* b. The Rules of fair battle will be punctually observed SCOTT. 4. a. Phr. *R. absolute*, an order following a rule nisi and changing a conditional direction into a peremptory command. *R. nisi*: see NISI. 5. *Joint r.*, one observed by both branches of a legislature of two houses. *Standing r.*, a permanent regulation of a corporate body governing its ordinary procedure. 6. b. *On r.*, allowed to live in the rules; Her lodgers used commonly to be prisoners on r. from that place [*sc.* the Fleet] THACKERAY.

II. 1. A principle regulating the procedure or method necessary to be observed in the pursuit or study of some art or science. (See also RULE OF THUMB.). late ME. b. *Grammar.* A general principle formulated concerning the form or position of words in a sentence 1495. 2. *Math.* A prescribed method or process for finding unknown numbers or values, or solving problems 1542. 3. Without article in preceding senses, esp. in phr. *by r.* late ME.

1. [This] May prove, though much beside the rules of art, Best for the public COWPER. 2. *R. of alligation, practice*, etc.: see those words. *R. of three*, a method of finding a fourth number from three given numbers, of which the first is in the same proportion to the second as the third is to the unknown fourth. Also called the *golden r.* (see GOLDEN *a.* 5), *r. of proportion.* 3. A certain skill in quarrelling by r. 1859.

III. 1. A standard of discrimination or estimation; a criterion, test, canon. late ME. 2. A fact, or the statement of one, that holds generally good; that which is normally the case ME.

1. There can be no hard and fast r. by which to construe..commercial agreements 1884. 2. The possession of the gift throughout the Christian community was the r. and not the exception 1862. Phr. *As a* (or *the*) *r.*, normally, usually. (*The*) *exception proves the rule*: see EXCEPTION 1.

IV. †1. *Good* (or *right*) *r.*, good order and discipline. So without adj. –1605. †2. Conduct, behaviour, manner of acting –1601. †b. Misrule, disorder, stir, riot –1703. 3. Control, government, sway, dominion. late ME. 4. The control or government *of* (= exercised by) a person or thing ME. 5. The control, management, government, etc. *of* (= exercised over or in) something. late ME.

1. *Macb.* v. ii. 16. 3. The woman's power is for r., not for battle RUSKIN. 4. Lead forth the Years for Peace and Plenty fam'd, From Saturn's R., and better Metal nam'd PRIOR. 5. Neptune..Took in by lot..Imperial r. of all the Sea-girt Iles MILT.

V. 1. A graduated strip of metal or wood (marked with feet, inches, etc.) used for measuring length, esp. by carpenters and masons ME. 2. *poet.* A shaft or beam *of* light 1634. †3. A straight line drawn on paper, *esp.* for the writing of music –1662. 3. = RULER 3 b. 1703. 4. *Typog.* A thin slip of metal (usu. brass) used for separating headings, columns of type, articles, etc., and in ornamental work; also a dash, short or long, in type-metal, thus – (en rule) or thus — (em rule), used in punctuation, etc. 1683. b. Without article (*brass r.*), as a material 1771. c. A composing- or setting-rule 1683.

1. Phr. *To run the r. over* (colloq.), to go thoroughly over (a person as in medical examination), to estimate (his qualifications, etc.) or to go through (his pockets as a pickpocket, etc.). 2. Som gentle taper..visit us With thy long levell'd r. of streaming light MILT.

Rule (rūl), *v.* ME. [ad. OF. *riuler*, *ruler* :—L. *regulare* to regulate.] I. 1. *trans.* To control, guide, direct, exercise sway or influence over (a person, his actions, life, etc.). 2. To moderate, restrain, curb (one's appetites, etc.) by the exercise of self-control. late ME. 3. To direct, guide, manage (a thing); to have under one's control. late ME. 4. To govern, exercise sovereign power over, to control with authority. late ME. 5. *absol.* To exercise sovereignty, to govern; to hold supreme command or sway 1509. 6. *Comm.* Of prices: To be at a certain rate; to be current or prevalent 1629. b. Of commodities or trade: To bear a (specified) current price or value; to maintain a (given) average or quality 1690. c. To go in a certain way; to have a certain character, place, or quality 1676.

1. My blood begins my safer Guides to r. SHAKS. Phr. *To be ruled*, to submit to counsel, guidance, or authority; to listen to reason. 2. He that ruleth his spirit [is better] then he that taketh a citie *Prov.* xvi. 32. 4. She, who ne'er answers till a Husband cools, Or, if she rules him, never shews she rules POPE. The star that ruled his doom was far too fair SHELLEY. 5. What madnesse rules in braine-sicke men SHAKS. A prince that rules by example, more than sway B. JONS. 6. Sales dragged somewhat, prices ruling about the same as on Monday last 1889. b. Trade ruled dull at barely late rates 1881.

II. *trans.* To lay down judicially or authoritatively; to decide, determine, declare formally. In later use const. *that*, or with *out of*. late ME. b. To decide, settle; to decree 1843. c. To shut or put *out* by formal decision 1890.

Public opinion..rules that every conclusion is absurd ..except such as it recognizes itself NEWMAN. c. Four instructions were ruled out..as capable of being dealt with in Committee 1893.

III. 1. To mark (paper, etc.) with parallel straight lines drawn with a ruler or by a machine 1440. 2. To form or mark out (a line) with or as with a ruler 1599.

Rule-joint. 1782. A movable joint such as is used for measuring-rules.

Ruleless (rū·l,lės), *a.* 1443. [f. RULE *sb.* + -LESS.] 1. Ungoverned; lawless, unrestrained; not subject to rule or order. 2. Devoid of rules, irregular 1867.

Rule of thumb. Also hyphened. 1692. [RULE *sb.*] A method or procedure derived entirely from practice or experience, without any basis in scientific knowledge; a roughly practical method.

The English..have in all their changes proceeded, to use a familiar expression, by the rule of thumb M. ARNOLD. *attrib.* Beyond this rule of thumb calculation, no experience could bring him to penetrate his mystery 1837.

Ruler (rū·ləɹ). late ME. [f. RULE *v.* + -ER[1].] 1. One who, or that which, exercises rule, *esp.* of a supreme or sovereign kind. 2. One who has control, management, or headship within some limited sphere. Now *Obs.* or *arch.* late ME. 3. †a. = RULE *sb.* V. 1. b. A straight-edged strip or cylinder, usu. of wood or ivory, used for guiding a pen, pencil, etc. in forming straight lines upon paper, etc. late ME. 4. A workman who rules straight lines in account-books, etc. 1858.

1. Stern r. of the sky! Whose sport is man, and human misery 1757. 3. *Parallel ruler(s)*: see PARALLEL *a.* 1 b. Hence **Ru·lership.**

Ruling (rū·liŋ), *vbl. sb.* ME. [f. RULE *v.*] 1. The action of governing; exercise of authority. 2. A judicial decision; also *gen.* an authoritative pronouncement 1560. 3. The action of using a ruler. Also *attrib.* as *r.-machine*, *-pen*, etc. 1611. b. *concr.* A ruled line or lines 1890.

Ruling (rū·liŋ), *ppl. a.* 1593. [f. RULE *v.*] 1. Exercising rule or authority; governing, reigning 1648. b. *R. Elder*, among Presbyterians, a lay elder. 1593. 2. Predominating, dominant, prevalent 1732. 3. Of prices, etc.: Current, general; average 1861.

1. He belonged half to the r. and half to the subject caste MACAULAY. 2. The r. Passion conquers Reason still POPE. Hence **Ru·lingly** *adv.*

Ruly (rū·li), *a.* late ME. [orig. f. RULE *sb.* + -Y[1].] Observing or amenable to rule or good order; law-abiding, disciplined, orderly. Opp. to UNRULY.

Rum (rʊm), *sb.*[1] 1654. [perh. an abbrev. of RUMBULLION or RUMBUSTION.] 1. A spirit distilled from various products of the sugar-cane (esp. molasses and dunder), and prepared chiefly in the West Indies and Guiana. b. *U.S.* Used generically as a hostile name for intoxicating liquors 1858.

Comb.: **r.-bud**, redness casued by excessive drinking, appearing first on the nose, and extending over the face; also, an excessive drinker; **r. punch, shrub, toddy,** beverages in which r. is the principal ingredient.

†**Rum**, *sb.*[2] *slang.* 1720. [Partly f. RUM *a.*] 1. A poor country clergyman in Ireland. SWIFT. 2. Ellipt. for *rum customer* –1845.

Rum (rʊm), *a. slang.* 1774. [perh. var. of ROM gipsy, in collocations like *rum cove.*] Odd, strange, queer.

There 's rummer things than women in this world though, mind you DICKENS. This was the rummest go he ever saw THACKERAY. Phr. *R. start*, (slang.) surprising occurrence. *R. customer*, a person or animal that is dangerous to meddle with. Hence **Ru·mly** *adv.*, **-ness.**

Rumal, var. of ROMAL.

Rumbelow (rʊ·mbĕlōᵘ). Now *rare.* ME. [See sense 1.] 1. A meaningless combination of syllables serving as a refrain, orig. sung by sailors when rowing. (Cf. HEAVE-HO.) 2. A kind of carriage 1881.

1. Heue and how rombelow, row the bote, Norman, rowe SKELTON.

Rumble (rʊ·mb'l), *sb.* late ME. [f. RUMBLE *v.*[1]] 1. A low, continuous, murmuring, grumbling, or growling sound, as that of thunder, distant cannon, heavy vehicles, etc. b. Applied to language or utterance 1680. †2. Commotion, bustle, tumult, uproar –1682. 3. The hind part of a carriage when so arranged as to provide sitting accommodation, or to carry luggage 1808.

1. The r. of a distant Drum FITZGERALD. 2. A stormy peple..Delitynge euere in rumbul that is newe CHAUCER. 3. Miss D. and Isabella go in the r., as it is called, behind 1808. Hence **Ru·mbly** *a.* of a rumbling character.

Rumble (rʊ·mb'l), *v.*[1] [ME. *romblen*, *rumblen*, of onomatopœic origin.] 1. *intr.* To make a low, heavy, continuous sound. 2. To move or travel with a continuous murmuring, or low, rolling sound. late ME. b. *transf.* Of persons: To be conveyed in a rumbling vehicle 1832. 3. To produce a rumbling noise by agitating or moving something (*rare*). late ME. 4. *trans.* To utter, run *over*, drone *out*, give *forth*, send *down*, with a rumbling sound 15..

1. Romble, romble goe the waters DEKKER. The wind-shaken ropes r. and rustle 1638. 2. A Spring of water mildely romblyng downe SPENSER. 4. They rumbled and roared..prayers with a zeal that shook the window-panes 1892. Hence **Ru·mbler,** one who or that which rumbles. **Ru·mbling** *vbl. sb.* and *ppl. a.* **Ru·mblingly** *adv.*

Rumble, *v.*[2] *slang.* 1898. [Origin unkn.] *trans.* To discover, detect, fathom.

Ru·mble-tu·mble. 1801. [f. RUMBLE *v.* + TUMBLE *v.*] †1. = RUMBLE *sb.* 3. –1858. 2. A rumbling coach, carriage, or cart 1806. 3. A rough or tumbling motion. BROWNING.

Rumbo (rʊ·mbo). Now *arch.* 1751. [app. f. RUM *sb.*[1]] A variety of strong punch, made chiefly of rum.

Rumbow·ling. *Naut. slang.* 1874. [perh. var. of ROMBOWLINE.] Grog.

†**Rumbu·llion.** 1651. [Origin unkn.] Rum –1672.

†**Rumbu·stion.** 1652. [Origin unkn.] Rum.

Rumen (rū·men). 1728. [a. L., the throat.] The first stomach of a ruminant animal.

‖**Rumex** (rū·meks). 1771. [L., sorrel.] *Bot.* A genus of plants which includes the sorrel and dock; a plant of this genus.

Rumicin (rū·misin). Also **-ine.** 1864. [f. L. *rumic-, rumex* sorrel.] *Chem.* An acid obtained from the root of *Rumex Hydrolapathum*; chrysophanic acid.

Ruminant (rū·minănt), *sb.* and *a.* 1661. [ad. L. *ruminant-, ruminari* or *ruminare* to RUMINATE.] **A.** *sb.* An animal that chews the cud; one of the *Ruminantia*. **B.** *adj.* **1.** Chewing the cud, ruminating 1691. **2.** Contemplative, meditative 1849.

‖**Ruminantia** (rūminæ·nʃiă). 1830. [L. neut. pl. of pr. pple. of *ruminari* or *ruminare.*] The class of ruminant animals.

Ruminate (rū·minēⁱt), *v.* 1533. [f. L. *ruminat-, ruminari* or *ruminare,* f. *rumen* RUMEN.] **1.** *trans.* To revolve, turn over and over in the mind; to meditate deeply upon. **b.** To meditate, consider (a design, etc.) with a view to subsequent action 1588. **2.** To chew or turn over in the mouth again 1609. **3.** *intr.* To chew the cud 1547. **4.** To muse, meditate, ponder 1575.

1. Conduct me, where from company, I may reuolue and r. my greefe SHAKS. **b.** Ruminating wrath, he scorns repose POPE. 3. He made various sounds with his mouth; sometimes as if ruminating, or what is called chewing the cud BOSWELL. 4. My head But ruminates on necromantic skill MARLOWE. The blossom of an idea..came out into full blow as I ruminated upon my pillow MME D'ARBLAY. Hence **Ru·minated** *ppl. a.* meditated, considered, digested. **Ru·minative** *a.* contemplative, meditative. **Ru·minator,** one who ruminates.

Rumination (rūminē¹·ʃən). 1600. [ad. L. *ruminatio*; see prec. and -ATION.] **1.** Contemplation, meditation. **b.** *pl.* Meditations, reflections 1638. **2.** The action of chewing the cud 1658.

1. In which my often r. wraps me in a most humorous sadnesse SHAKS. 2. The Voluntary Motion of the Stomach, is that only which accompanies R. 1676.

Ru·mkin¹. Now *arch.* 1636. [app. of LG. origin.] A variety of drinking-vessel.

Ru·mkin². 1672. [app. f. RUMP *sb.* + -KIN.] The Persian rumpless or tailless cock or hen.

Rummage (rɒ·mėdʒ), *sb.* 1526. [orig. aphetic a. older F. (also Sp.) *arrumage* (mod. *arrimage*), f. *arrumer* (mod. *arrimer*), of unkn. origin.] **1.** †**a.** *Naut.* The arranging of casks, etc., in the hold of a vessel –1688. **b.** Miscellaneous articles, lumber; rubbish 1598. †**c.** Place of storage; storage capacity –1639. **2.** Bustle, commotion, turmoil. *Obs.* exc. *Sc.* 1575. **3.** An overhauling search 1753. **b.** *spec.* A thorough search of a vessel by a Customs examining officer 1867.

2. *Haml.* I. i. 107. 3. I shall have a r. for it among the old music-book shops 1873.

Comb.: **r. goods,** goods out of date in warehouse; **r. sale,** (*a*) a clearance sale of unclaimed goods at the docks, or of odds and ends left in a warehouse; (*b*) a kind of charity bazaar.

Rummage (rɒ·mėdʒ), *v.* 1544. [f. prec.] **I.** *trans.* †**1.** *Naut.* **a.** To arrange, or re-arrange (goods) in the hold of a ship. Also *gen.* –1725. †**b.** To set in order, put straight (a ship, the hold) by re-arranging the cargo –1625. **2.** *Naut.* **a.** To search thoroughly, ransack (the hold of a vessel, etc.) 1628. **b.** *spec.* of Customs officers 1763. **3.** To make a search in or among; to overhaul in order to find something 1616. **4.** To scrutinize, examine minutely, investigate 1704. **5.** To disarrange or disorder; to knock, stir, or drive about; to force or rout out by searching or making a stir. Somewhat *rare.* 1591. **b.** To bring *out* by searching; to fish *out* or *up* 1715.

2. **a.** We rummaged our Prize, and found a few Boxes of Marmalade 1697. 3. We rummaged our pockets in vain for the required passport 1833. 4. Upon this, they fell again to rummage the Will SWIFT. 5. **b.** She has also rummaged up a coop that will hold six chickens COWPER.

II. *intr.* **1.** *Naut.* To make search (†arrange or re-arrange cargo, etc.) in a vessel 1595. **2.** To engage in a search, make an investigation, of any kind 1666.

1. Their Business is to r. in the Hold on all Occasions 1728. 2. He pulled out a pocket-book, and rummaged some time, but to no purpose 1789. A jolly ghost, that..tapt at doors, and rummaged like a rat TENNYSON. Hence **Ru·mmager,** †one who arranges cargo in a ship; one who makes a search or overhaul.

Rummer (rɒ·məɹ). 1654. [repr. WFlem. *rummer, rommer,* or Du. *romer, roemer*; the orig. meaning is perh. 'Roman glass'.] A large drinking-glass.

Rummy (rɒ·mi), *sb.* 1919. A card-game, played with two packs, in which the players aim at making sequences of the same suit and sets of the same denomination, each player in turn taking either an exposed or a revealed card, and in exchange discarding a card from his hand.

Rummy (rɒ·mi), *a. slang* or *colloq.* 1828. [f. RUM *a.* + -Y¹.] Odd, queer, singular. Hence **Ru·mmily** *adv.* **Ru·mminess.**

Rumorous (rū·mŏrəs), *a.* 1550. [f. RUMOUR *sb.* + -OUS.] **1.** Making a loud confused sound; resounding. Now *arch.* **2.** Of the nature of rumour; rumoured (*rare*) 1605. **3.** Full of rumours or reports (*rare*) 1641.

Rumour (rū·məɹ), *sb.* Also (chiefly *U.S.*) **rumor.** late ME. [a. OF. *rumour* (mod.F. *rumeur*):—L. *rumorem,* accus. of *rumor* voice.] **1.** †**a.** A (widespread) report of a favourable or laudatory nature. late ME. only. **b.** Talk or report *of* a person or thing in some way noted or distinguished. Now *arch.* 1440. †**c.** The fact of being generally talked about; reputation, renown. MILT. **2.** General talk, report, or hearsay, not based upon definite knowledge. late ME. **3.** A statement or report circulating in a community, of the truth of which there is no clear evidence. late ME. †**4.** Loud expression of disapproval or protest –1568. **5.** Clamour, outcry; noise, din. Now *arch.* 1440. †**6.** Uproar, tumult, disturbance –1639.

1. **b.** Great is the r. of this dreadfull Knight SHAKS. **c.** Fame..Nor in the glistering foil Set off to th' world, nor in broad r. lies MILT. 2. You seem..Too..companionable a man To act the deeds that r. pins on you SHELLEY. 3. Does the Rumor hold for true That hee's so full of Gold? SHAKS. 5. The r. of the wind among the garden trees 1885.

Rumour (rū·məɹ), *v.* Also *U.S.* **rumor.** late ME. [f. prec.] **1.** *intr.* †**a.** To resound with disapproval. late ME. only. **b.** To invent or circulate rumours 1858. **2.** *trans.* To circulate by way of rumour 1594. **3.** *intr.* To make a murmuring noise 1900.

2. This haue I rumour'd through the peasant-Townes SHAKS. 3. The sea that rumoured light and soothingly round the rock of Doom 1900. Hence **Ru·mourer** (*rare*), one who disseminates rumours.

Rump (rɒmp). [ME. *rumpe,* prob. of Scand. origin.] **1.** That part of the body (of an animal or bird) from which the tail springs; †the tail; hence, the hind-quarters, posteriors, buttocks. **2.** This part of an animal or fowl as cut off and used for food 1486. **3.** *fig.* A small, unimportant, or contemptible remnant or remainder of a body of persons (esp. of a Parliament) 1649. **b.** *Hist.* The remnant of the Long Parliament (restored in May, 1659) which was dissolved by Monk in 1660; also (esp. in later use) the earlier remnant of the same Parliament from the time of Pride's Purge (Dec. 1648) to its dissolution by Cromwell in April, 1653. 1659. **c.** So *R. Parliament* 1670.

3. **b.** The R. was universally detested and despised MACAULAY.

Comb.: **r.-band,** a leather band passing over the r. of a horse to support the trace-chains; **-bone,** the coccyx (now *rare*); **-fed** *a.* fed on the best joints, pampered; **-strap** = *r.-band.* Hence **Ru·mper,** (*Hist.*) a member or supporter of the R. parliament. **Ru·mpless** *a.* having no r. or tail; tailless.

Rumple (rɒ·mp'l), *sb.* Now *rare.* 1500. [ad. MDu. (also Du.) *rompel,* f. MDu. *rompe* wrinkle.] A wrinkle, fold, crease. Hence **Ru·mply** *a.* full of rumples (*rare*).

Rumple (rɒ·mp'l), *v.* 1603. [f. prec., or ad. MDu. *rompelen.*] **1.** *trans.* To wrinkle, crease, draw into wrinkles, render uneven or irregular. **2.** To touzle, disorder, crumple. Also with *up.* 1650. †**3.** To squeeze together, distort –1687.

1. Beds of bogbean foliage, rumpling the green floating carpet of lily-leaves 1893. 2. Girls like to be.. rumpled a little..sometimes GOLDSM. Hence **Ru·mpled** *ppl. a.* wrinkled, crumpled, creased; touzled.

Rumpus (rɒ·mpŏs), *sb. colloq.* 1764. [prob. fanciful.] A riot, uproar, disturbance, row. Hence **Ru·mpus** *v. intr.* to make a disturbance.

Run (rɒn), *sb.* 1450. [f. RUN *v.*] **I. 1.** A single spell or act of running. **b.** A distance covered, or taking a certain time to cover, by running 1596. **2. a.** *Cricket.* An act of running successfully from one popping-crease to the other by both batsmen, counting as an addition of one to the score 1746. **b.** *Baseball.* A unit of scoring obtained by running the round of the bases 1875. **3. a.** A spell of riding after hounds or in a race 1812. **b.** A round of running at hare-and-hounds. Also, the course taken by the harriers. 1857. **4. a.** A spell of sailing, esp. between two ports 1712. **b.** An excursion, trip; a rapid journey accompanied by a short stay at a place 1854. **c.** A single journey made by a locomotive engine; the distance thus traversed 1870. **5.** A landing of smuggled goods 1832. **6.** A rapid course; esp. *with a r.,* rapidly, with a rapid fall 1822. **7.** *Golf.* A stroke in which the ball is made to run along the ground; usu. *r.-up* 1901. **8.** With advs., as **run-in**; *spec.* in Rugby football, an act of running over the touch-line of the opposite side with the ball; also, the home stretch in a run at hare and hounds, or in a race; **run-out,** an instance of a batsman being put out while trying to make a run.

1. Phr. *To have a r. for one's money,* to have some kind of return or satisfaction for one's expenditure or exertions. (Orig. racing slang.) 2. **a.** We had made our 80 runs in less than two hours 1859. 3. **a.** A real Lincolnshire r. at a good hunting pace 1812.

II. 1. A small stream, brook, rivulet, or watercourse; a channel or overflow. Chiefly *U.S.* and *n. dial.* **b.** A strong rush or sweep of the tide, etc. 1814. **c.** A flow of sand; a slip, slide, sudden fall of earth. Chiefly *Mining.* 1854. **2.** *Mus.* A roulade 1835. **III. 1.** A continuous stretch *of* something 1674. **b.** A continued course or spell *of* some condition or state of things 1714. **c.** A course or spell of (good or ill) fortune, *esp.* in games of chance 1697. **d.** *Mining.* and *Geol.* A continuous vein of rock or ore 1747. **2.** A continuous series or succession 1709. **b.** A shoal of fish in motion, *esp.* ascending a river from the sea for spawning 1820. **c.** A pair of millstones. *U.S.* 1828. **3.** A series or rush of sudden and pressing demands made upon a bank or treasury for immediate payment 1692. **b.** An extensive or well-sustained demand for something. Const. *on.* 1818. **c.** *Gaming.* A continued spell of chance falling *on* a particular colour, etc. 1826. **d.** A concourse or resort of customers, etc. 1844. †**4.** A persistent set *against,* or attack *upon,* some thing or person –1779. **5.** A success with the public, so as to be extensively bought or run after 1719. **6.** A continuous period of being represented on the stage 1714. **7.** A spell of making or allowing something liquid to run; the amount run off at one time 1710. **b.** A spell of making or allowing machinery to run or continue to work 1875. **8.** *Common, general,* or *ordinary r.,* the usual, or average type or class; the generality or great majority. Also without adj. 1712. **b.** A line or class of goods 1883.

1. A very promising r. of trout and grayling water 1867. **b.** Wicked men have..a continu'd r. of success 1714. **c.** The dice took a r. against him STERNE. 2. A r. of wet seasons 1774. 3. When a r. comes upon them, they..endeavour to gain time by paying in sixpences 1776. 5. It is impossible for detached papers to have a general r...if not diversified with humour ADDISON. 6. This comedy..had a lengthened r. 1857. 7. **b.** An experimental r. to test the machinery 1882. 8. In the common R. of Mankind, for one that is Wise and Good you find ten of a contrary Character ADDISON. **b.** Makers of the ordinary runs of cloth 1883.

IV. 1. A regular track made by certain animals 1821. **b.** An enclosure for domestic animals or fowls to range or take exercise in 1856. **2.** An extensive range of pasture- or grazing-land. Chiefly *Austral.* 1826. **3.** A slope, track, or support along or on which something may run or move 1834. **4.** A pipe or trough along or down which water may run 1833.

1. Hares have their regular highways or 'runs' 1878. 2. It is, generally speaking, a good sheep r.

1826. 3. b. *U.S.* A rent or ladder in a garment 1922.

V. 1. *Naut.* That part of a ship's bottom which rises from the keel and bilge, and narrows toward the stern (†or bows) 1618. 2. a. The time during which a dramatic work holds the stage continuously 1705. b. The progress or prevalence *of* a disease 1717. 3. The act of running, esp. in rapid retreat or flight. Chiefly in phr. *to* or *on the r.* 1660. b. A running pace 1840. c. Capacity for, or power of, running 1857. 4. The rush, flow, or onward movement *of* water, air, etc. 1626. b. The flow or melody *of* verse 1725. c. *By the r.* = with a run 1800. 5. The course, direction, or tendency *of* something immaterial 1730. 6. a. The direction, line, or lie *of* anything 1748. b. *Mining.* 'The horizontal distance to which a drift may be carried' 1864. 7. a. The freedom or range *of* a house, etc.; the privilege of free resort, access, or use 1755. b. *The r. of one's teeth*: free board, usu. in return for work done; maintenance, support 1841. c. The pasture of an animal for a certain period 1854.

1. A rakish..craft,..with a deep keel and sharp r. 1831. 2. a. The usage was to engage stars for the r. of the piece 1885. 3. b. We started at a r., men and dogs, for the solid ice 1856. 5. The r. of luck is against us 1809. 7. a. I have the r. of two good houses 1809.

Run (rɒn), *v.* [OE. has (1) *rinnan, ran, *runnon, gerunnen*, strong intr. verb, subject to metathesis, of which very few examples occur in OE. texts. (2) A weak trans. verb, of which the orig. form was **rannjan*, appears in OE. only in the metathetic form *ærnan, earnan* (usu. in the sense of 'to ride'). ME. *rinne(n* and *renne(n* are probably due to the influence of ON. *rinna* and *renna.*]

I. Intransitive senses. (Occas. conjugated in compound tenses with *be* instead of *have* to the end of the 18th c.) **Of persons and animals.* 1. To move the legs quickly (the one foot being lifted before the other is set down) so as to go at a faster pace than walking; to cover the ground rapidly in this manner. b. Used to denote (hurried) travelling or going about, esp. to distant places ME. 2. To go about freely, without being restrained or checked in any way. Freq. with *about*; also with predicative adjs., as *wild.* OE. 3. To hasten *to* some end or object, or *to* do something; to make haste, be active OE. b. To go or resort *to* a person, etc., *esp.* for help or guidance ME. 4. To retire or retreat rapidly; to take to flight; to abscond or desert. Also const. *from* a place, person, etc. ME. b. So *to r. for it* 1642. 5. To rush *at, on,* or *upon* a person with hostile intention; to make an attack *on* ME. †6. To ride on horseback at a quick pace; *spec.* to ride in a tournament, to tilt or joust -1652. 7. To compete, or take part, in a race (*for* a prize). Occas. with compl. denoting final position in the race. ME. b. To compete, stand as a candidate, *for* a position, seat, etc. Orig. *U.S.* 1861. 8. *transf.* Of fish: To swim rapidly 1520. b. *spec.* To pass to or from the sea; to migrate 1887.

1. She is run upstairs,..this very instant STERNE. The young ones r. about as soon as they are out of the shell GOLDSM. Phr. *That he who runs may read*, an alteration of *Habakkuk* ii. 2, 'That he may r. that readeth it'. b. I have sometimes been obliged to r. half over London, in order to fix a date correctly BOSWELL. 2. This meane whyle ranne sir Tristram naked in the forest MALORY. R. about and divert yourself 1782. 3. The people..r. almost from all places to assist his cause 1654. b. That day first I did seem to glimpse why folk in trouble r. to drink so READE. 4. He..had been forced to cut and r. 1893. 5. He ran at me and kicked me 1889. 6. 1 *Hen. IV*, II. iv. 377. Phr. *To r. (full) tilt at* or *against*: see TILT *sb.* 7. A Plate of 40 *l.* Value was to be run for 1713. Gossoon..had run second to her for the Champagne Stakes 1891. Phr. *Also ran*, said of a horse which is not 'placed' in a race; hence as *sb.*, and *fig.* a failure. b. If he..ran for President 1870. 8. The pike made a splendid fight, often running to weed 1867. b. The season when the eels are 'running' 1892.

***Of inanimate things in rapid motion.* 9. Of things, esp. the heavenly bodies: To move rapidly through space OE. b. Of vehicles, etc.: To move easily or rapidly by reason of being set on wheels ME. 10. Of a vessel (or those on board): To sail swiftly or easily OE. b. To sail or be driven *on* or *upon* the shore, rocks, etc.; to come *aground* or *ashore* ME. c. *To r. foul of*, to collide or become entangled with (another vessel, etc.); to foul 1698. 11. a. To take a (hurried) journey for the purpose of making a short stay at or visit to a place. Chiefly with *down, over, up.* 1798. b. Of a conveyance, vessel, etc.: To ply between (two) places 1825. 12. a. To spread, pass, or move quickly from point to point: usu. with advb. phrases OE. b. Of sounds: To spread or pass rapidly *along, down, through* a place, company, etc.; to be caught up or repeated in quick succession. late ME. c. Of statements, reports, etc.: To spread abroad rapidly; to be or become widely current. late ME. d. Of plants: To creep or climb 1565. 13. a. Of thoughts: To come suddenly *into*, to course or pass *through*, the mind ME. b. Of the eye: To glance, look quickly. Also of persons, to give a rapid glance (*with* the eye). 1611. c. To go *back* in retrospect 1702. 14. Of a weapon, etc.: To pass easily and quickly *through* something, *to* a certain point, etc. ME. 15. To slip, slide, or move easily or freely: freq. with preps. or advs. ME. b. Of the tongue: To wag freely 1553. c. Of bark: To peel off easily from a tree 1784. d. To unravel, come undone 1878. e. To slip, diverge, go awry 1846. 16. Of a ball, etc.: To roll forward on a surface. Said also of dice when thrown. late ME. b. *transf.* Of a player at billiards: To make the ball roll 1875. 17. To revolve on or as on an axis ME. b. Of machinery or mechanical devices: To go; to continue operating 1562. 18. Of thoughts, etc.: To revolve *in* the mind; to return persistently to the memory 1601. b. To form, be present as, an impression 1798.

9. Far ran the naked moon across The..ocean's heaving field TENNYSON. b. *fig.* Your tongue so runs on wheels HOBBES. 10. We were obliged to r. away afore the wind DE FOE. b. They had no escape but to r. aground 1877. Phr. *To r. aboard, on board (of)*: see BOARD *sb.* V. 1. 11. a. I wish you could have run over for a week 1831. b. Steam-boats r. between London Bridge and Chelsea on weekdays 1886. 12. a. Squalls Ran black o'er the sea's face M. ARNOLD. c. There r. reports that made me shudder CARLYLE. 13. a. The extravagant analogies which then ran through my brain TYNDALL. 14. Looke, in this place ran Cassius Dagger through SHAKS. 15. *fig.* Life ran smoothly in its ordinary grooves 1889. b. Though your teeth be gone..Yet your tongue can renne on patins UDALL. 16. He who blows upon a ball when running makes the stroke foul 1850. 18. This Thought run long in my Head DE FOE.

*** *Of liquids, sand, etc.* (*or vessels containing these*). 19. Of milk, etc.: To coagulate, curdle, form a curd. Now *dial.* late ME. b. To unite, combine (*into one*), esp. in a moist or melted state 1715. 20. Of liquids: To flow. OE. 21. Of the sea, tides, etc.: To course or flow, esp. in an impetuous manner. Also with compl., esp. *to r. high* (see HIGH *adv.*), or *mountain(s high* (see MOUNTAIN I. 1.) ME. 22. a. To flow as the result of melting; to melt and flow. late ME. b. To spread on being applied to, or poured upon, a surface 1612. c. Of colours: To spread in a fabric when immersed in water or exposed to moisture 1711. 23. a. Of the sands of an hour-glass: To pass from one compartment into the other 1557. b. Of loose earth: To slip or fall in 1799. 24. To flow, stream, be wet *with* a liquid. Also with adjs., as *r. red.* ME. 25. a. To discharge (or carry off) a liquid ME. b. Of a vessel: To overflow; to leak ME. c. Of an hour-glass: To allow the sand to pass from one compartment to the other. 1500.

19. b. The Church party and the Dissenters were now run into one 1715. 20. He thrashed his naked back, until the blood ran 1862. *fig.* His Verses r. like the Tap EARLE. 21. What a devilish Sea there runs? 1694. Evil and good r. strong in me 1887. c. Beg her not to wash them too hard, or they may r. 1867. 23. a. Now our sands are almost run SHAKS. 24. Her veins r. with water, not blood 1884. 25. a. Syn that my tappe of lif bigan to renne CHAUCER. c. Look on thy glass, see how it runs 1650.

**** *Of time, money, practices, or other things having course, continuance, or extension.* 26. Of a period of time: To come to an end, be complete, expire. Only in pa. pple. OE. 27. Of time: To pass or go by; to elapse; also, to be passing or current ME. b. To continue, go on, last; to remain existent or operative ME. c. Of a play: To be played continuously (for a specified time) 1808. 28. a. Of money: To have currency; to be in circulation; to pass current ME. b. Of a writ, proclamation, etc.: To issue; to have legal course or effect; to operate. late ME. c. Of payments, practices, etc.: To be current or generally prevalent. late ME. 29. To have course or continuance; to go on; to go, proceed, etc., in various fig. uses ME. b. Of qualities, etc.: To be persistent or common *in* a family 1777. 30. To extend or stretch; to form a continuous line or boundary. late ME. b. *Law.* Of memory, recollection, etc.: To extend or go back in time 1447.

26. The night was almost run DE FOE. 27. b. Leases r. in general for nineteen years 1843. c. The piece..will r. the season 1828. 28. b. Countrees where the Kynges Writt renneth noght 1436. 29. The covenant will not r., that is, it will not bind the assignee, nor pass to him 1837. b. Learning that had r. in the family like an heir-loom SHERIDAN. 30. Tartaria..runneth along without controll by the high looking walls of China 1630. *fig.* His patriotism very often runs far. into the region of prejudice 1890. b. The memory of man runneth not to the contrary 1765.

***** *Of things passing into, assuming, or maintaining a certain condition or quality.* 31. To pass into or out of a certain state. late ME. b. With adj. or other compl.: To become, end in being, turn, grow, fall, etc. 1449. 32. a. To have a given tenor or purport; to be worded or expressed in a specified manner 1586. b. To be constituted or conditioned 1724. 33. To have a specified character, quality, arrangement, form, etc. Const. with preps. and adjs. 1658. b. To be of a specified (average or maximum) size, price, etc. 1762. c. To be in the (average) proportion of 1849.

31. Many one there be, that renne out of their wyttes..for their wyues sakes COVERDALE 1 *Esdras* iv. 26. b. *To r. amuck* (see AMUCK 2), *mad* (see MAD *a.* 1), *riot* (see RIOT *sb.* 3). *To r. dry*, to cease to yield water or milk; hence *fig.*, to become exhausted or spent. *To r. low*, to be nearly exhausted, to become scanty. *To r. short*: see SHORT *a.* 32. a. So runs the Fable POPE. b. We must take things rough and smooth as they r. 1764. 33. German traditions of obedience r. on different lines entirely 1890. b. The trout r. to a good size in Portugal 1890. c. His oats run 44 lb. to the bushel 1892.

II. Transitive senses.

* *To traverse, accomplish, aim at or avoid, etc., by running.* 1. To pursue or follow (a certain way or course) in running, sailing, etc. OE. b. *Hunting.* To pursue, follow up (a scent) 1607. c. *transf.* Of immaterial things 1864. 2. To traverse or cover by running, sailing, etc. ME. b. To scour, run about in (a place) 1648. c. To slip or shoot down (a rope, river, etc.) 1883. 3. To perform or accomplish by running or riding 1494. 4. a. To go upon (an errand or message) 1500. b. *Billiards.* See COUP *sb.*[3] 3. 1850. d. *Croquet.* To play through (a hoop) or up to (a peg) 1874. 5. To flee or escape from (a place, country, etc.); to desert from (a ship) 1608. 6. †a. *To r. ...fortune(s)*, in various phrases denoting voluntary sharing of another's lot -1713. b. To expose oneself, or be exposed, to (a chance, danger, etc.) 1592. c. To incur, meet with, encounter 1624. 7. a. *To r. it*, or *a voyage*, to sail without convoy in time of war 1787. b. *To r. the* (or *a*) *blockade*: see BLOCKADE *sb.* 1. 1869. 8. To sew slightly and quickly, usu. by taking a number of stitches on the needle at a time 1708. 9. To pursue, chase, hunt (game, etc.) 1484. b. To contend with (a person, etc.) in a race 1786. c. To press *hard* or *close*, so as to inconvenience in some way. Also without adv. 1790. d. To press (a person or thing) *close* or *hard* in competition or rivalry 1806.

1. Our fox..did not r. the chain of woodlands, but held on southwards 1892. b. Hounds are running a high scent through a stiff country 1890. c. Affairs ran their fated course 1889. 2. We..run from forty to fifty leagues a day 1748. b. Many..would sooner let their children r. the streets 1861. 3. The doom has run its course, the hour is here 1854. The Derby has been run in a snowstorm 1873. Phr. *To r.* (a thing) *fine*, to leave a very slight margin (*esp.* of time). *To r. the gauntlet*: see GAUNTLET[2]. 5. Some..were..obliged to r. their Country 1727. 6. b. He who goes to Sea, or to War, runs a Venture 1675. *To r. a risk*: see RISK *sb.* 1. 8. b. To attach (a ribbon, etc.) to cloth by passing it through a series of holes.

** *To cause to run, move rapidly, or extend.* 10. To cause or force (a horse, etc.) to go rapidly, esp. when riding it OE. b. *Racing.* To enter (a horse, etc.) for a race; also *fig.* to pit (lives) against each other 1750. c. To allow to run or feed at large, to graze (cattle, sheep, etc.) 1812. 11. To bring into a certain state, affect in a certain way, by running. Chiefly *refl.* and in phrases. 1548. b. To bring, lead, drag, or force (one) *into* some state, action, etc. 1621. c. To force, drive (a person or thing) *out of*, or *off*, some place 1727. 12. To cause (a boat or ship) to move rapidly or easily forwards, esp. towards or against the land 1548. b. To bring, convey, transport, in a vessel, down a stream, along rails, etc. 1700. c. To land, smuggle (contraband goods) 1706. d. To sail (a vessel) in time of war without a convoy 1813. e. To get (something) hastily carried through 1891. 13. a. To drive or cause (one's head, etc.) to strike forcibly *against* (a person or thing) 1589. b. To thrust, *esp.* to dash or force (one's head, etc.) *into* or *through* something 1523. 14. a. To drive (a vehicle, etc.) *into*, *against*, or *through* something 1663. 15. To thrust or force (a weapon or the like) *through* or *into* a person, etc. 1480. b. To pierce or stab (a person). Usu. with *through* (a specified part). 1533. 16. a. To cause to roll quickly; *spec.* in *Bowling*, to drive away (the jack) 1593. b. To cast or pass (the eye, hand, etc.) rapidly *along*, *down*, *over* (etc.) something 1728. c. To allow (bills or accounts) to accumulate for some time before paying 1861. 17. To cause to move, slide, pass, etc., in a quick or easy manner. Usu. with advs. or preps. denoting direction. 1683. b. To carry, pass, or suspend (a line or rope) between two points 1769. 18. To cause (a conveyance, vessel, etc.) to ply from place to place, or between two places 1764. b. To keep (a mechanical contrivance, etc.) moving or working 1849. c. To direct, conduct, carry on (a business, etc.). Orig. *U.S.* 1864. d. To introduce or push (a person) in society 1897. 19. a. To put or set up as a candidate. Orig. *U.S.* 1862. b. *U.S.* and *Austral.* To tease, nag, or vex 1879. c. To prosecute (a person); to bring (a person) in *for* damages 1891. 20. a. To cut (a mark), draw or trace (a line), on a surface 1641. b. To trace or pursue (a parallel, resemblance, etc.); to draw (a distinction) 1716. c. To lead, take, extend, carry (a thing) in a certain direction, or to a certain length 1713. d. *Plastering.* To form (a cornice, etc.); also, to cover (a space) with plaster 1825.

10. As they that r. their horses for a wager, spur hardest at the races end 1647. b. An owner runs his horse ostensibly to win 1892. 11. He had almost run himself to a standstill 1892. b. These wild woods.. Will r. me mad FLETCHER. c. Arresting a free negro, with a view to r. him out of the State 1822. 12. Our Palinurus now ran us ashore 1816. c. It was a smuggler running a cargo 1887. 13. a. If we r. our heads against walls we're safe to hurt ourselves 1887. 14. a. He..pretty nearly ran us into a cart 1872. 15. If you had run a poniard into him SCOTT. b. Ile r. him vp to the hilts, as I am a soldier SHAKS. 16. a. *Rich. II*, II. i. 123. c. At Oxford I ran what accounts with the tradesmen I liked RUSKIN. 17. R. a red-hot fire-shovel over it, to brown it MRS. GLASSE. 18. b. The hands we can't employ, the mills we can't r. C. BRONTE. c. *transf.* It is often said of the President that he is ruled, or as the Americans express it, 'run' by his secretary 1888. Phr. (*slang*) *To r. the show*, to 'manage' an undertaking. 20. a. *To r. the line(s*, to determine or mark off a boundary-line (*U.S.*). b. One might r. the parallel much farther STERNE.

*** *To cause to flow or come together.* 21. To give forth, to flow with (a specified kind of liquid) ME. 22. a. To cause to coagulate, or to unite in a viscid mass. late ME. b. To unite or combine 1781. c. To convert *into* a certain form 1700. 23. a. To smelt (metal); to form into sheets, bars, etc., by allowing to flow into moulds 1663. b. = CAST *v.* IX. 1690. c. To cause (a liquid) to flow *into* a vessel, *through* a strainer, etc. 1728. 24. To fill up or fasten *together* with molten metal, etc. 1657. 25. To let water escape through or from (a sluice, pool, etc.); esp. *r. dry*. 1839.

21. Rivers are said to r. blood after an engagement 1835. 22. b. The events of two days have been run into one 1868. 23. a. It should be first run into ingots, then melted 1873. 25. The sluices have been run to night 1839.

Specialized uses, with preps. **Run across—**, to meet or fall in with. **R. after—.** a. To endeavour to gain the companionship or society of; to pursue with admiration or attentions. b. To follow or take up with, eagerly. **R. against—.** a. To act, operate, take effect, or be directed, against (one). b. To dash rapidly and forcibly against (a person or thing); to encounter suddenly or casually. **R. in—,** to lapse or fall into arrears of (payment, debt, etc.). **R. into—.** a. To incur (blame, displeasure, loss, etc.); to involve oneself in (debt, expenses, etc.); b. To rush headlong, fall into (some practice). c. To go on, advance, into (something); to mount up or amount to. d. To pass by change or transformation, to develop, into (something). e. To merge into; to blend or coalesce with. f. To fall into; to tend towards; to be displayed in. g. To dash into or collide with, esp. by accident. Also of dogs, to close with (an animal). **R. on—.** a. To discourse on; to refer or relate to. b. Of the mind: To be engrossed or occupied with (a subject). c. To show a marked demand or preference for (some particular thing). **R. out of—,** to come to the end of, to exhaust, one's supply of (something). **R. over—.** a. To take a mental review of; to think over. b. To glance over; to survey, scan, peruse, or read, rapidly. c. To repeat or recite quickly; to tell over again. d. To treat, perform, enjoy, etc., in a slight or hasty manner. e. To go over with the hand; to go through (a piece of music) rapidly. f. Of a vehicle, rider, or driver: To pass over (a person, etc., knocked down or lying in the way). **R. through—.** a. To examine, inspect, peruse, treat of or deal with, rapidly. b. To pass or go through, in the way of trial or experience. c. To wear out, consume, spend, waste, in a rapid or reckless manner. d. To be or continue present in; to pervade. **R. to—.** a. To come, amount in numbers, extend in size or depth, to (a specified quantity). (*b*) To be able for (*esp.* capable of purchasing). (*c*) To cover the expense of, be sufficient for. b. To lapse or fall to (waste, ruin, etc.). c. Of land: To produce naturally. d. Of plants: To tend to the (undesirable) development of (seed, straw, etc.). e. To pass or develop into (some excess). **R. upon—.** a. To have a tendency to, or a favour or fancy for, to seek much after (something). b. To dwell upon, be occupied with (a subject) in thought or discourse. c. To incur, bring on oneself, fall into. d. To make a sudden demand upon (a bank) for the purpose of withdrawing deposits, etc. e. To come upon suddenly. **R. with—.** a. To go along with; to accompany; to march with. b. To concur, accord, or agree with.

With advs. **R. away.** a. To make off, retreat hurriedly, flee, in the face of danger or opposition. b. To abscond; to depart surreptitiously *from* or *to* a person; to elope *with* some one. c. *To r. away with*: (*a*) To depart surreptitiously with, to carry off (something). (*b*) To take up with, accept, believe (an idea, etc.) hurriedly, without due reflection. (*c*) To carry off, gain. (*d*) To consume or exhaust. d. Of a horse, etc.: To rush off ungovernably, to bolt (*with* a person). e. To get away *from*, to outdistance completely, in running or racing. **R. down.** a. *intr.* Of a clock, etc.: To become completely unwound; to cease to go. b. To decline, fall off, in vigour or health. c. To diminish or decrease. d. To deteriorate. e. *trans.* To knock down or overthrow (a person); to dash into, collide with, sink (a vessel). f. To pursue (game) until caught or killed; to hunt down. g. To put down, overwhelm (a person) by superior force, argument, talk, etc. h. To disparage or vilify. **R. in.** a. *intr.* To rush in, close with, in attacking or assailing. b. *Rugby football.* To run with the ball and touch it down behind the adversary's goal-line. c. To pay a short or passing visit *to* a person. d. *trans.* To fix, fill in, *with* (melted lead, etc.). e. To arrest and take (a person) into custody f. To insert, slip in. g. To enter and secure the election of (a person). **R. off.** a. *intr.* To take to flight; to abscond or elope (*with* a person or thing). b. Of water, etc.: To flow off or away. c. To diminish. d. To go off, digress, in talk. e. *trans.* To dash or rattle off; to write or recite rapidly. f. To allow to flow out; to draw or drain off (a liquid). g. *Sport.* To decide (a race) finally. **R. on.** a. *intr.* To continue running or going on. b. To continue in operation, effect, etc. Also const. *to* (a certain point). c. Of time: To pass or elapse. d. To continue speaking; to speak volubly; also, to chatter. e. To expand or develop *into*. f. *Printing.* To make (two paragraphs, etc.) into one; so in phr. *r. on chapters*, an intimation that the beginning of chapters in a work is not necessarily to start on a fresh page. g. *trans.* To continue to narrate (a story). **R. out.** a. *intr.* Of a period of time, etc.: To expire, terminate, come to an end. b. Of water, etc.: To escape from the containing vessel, part, etc. (*b*) Of vessels, etc.: To leak. c. (*a*) To come to the end of one's resources or stock. (*b*) To become expended or exhausted; to come to an end. d. *Cricket.* To move out rapidly from the block to hit the ball. e. Of a rope; To pass out in continuous length. f. To extend or project; to protrude, jut out. g. To shoot out (*into* excrescences, etc.); to go on *to* something. h. To come out of (a contest) in a specified manner or position. i. *trans.* To finish or complete (a race, or period of time). (*b*) *Sport.* To bring (a race, etc.) to a conclusive result; to decide. †j. To go through, spend, squander (money or property). (*b*) *Agric.* To impoverish, exhaust (land). k. (*a*) To advance (a gun) so that the muzzle projects from the port-hole (or embrasure). (*b*) To expand, extend, or fill out. (*c*) To allow or cause (a line) to be drawn or carried out. l. *Cricket.* To put out (a batsman) while he is running between the popping-creases. m. *refl.* To exhaust (oneself) by running; to come to an end, exhaust one's means, etc. **R. over.** a. *intr.* Of a vessel, etc.: To overflow. b. Of liquid or grain: To flow over the side of a vessel. c. (*passing into*) *trans.* To recount, relate, or repeat rapidly or succinctly. d. To review rapidly. Usu. *in* the mind, etc. e. To glance over, read hurriedly. f. To retouch slightly or quickly. **R. through.** a. To pierce or stab through the body with a weapon, etc. b. To read over rapidly. c. To draw a line through (words). **R. together.** a. To combine, coalesce, unite, *esp.* in a moist or melted state. †b. To join in combat, engage in fight; *esp.* to tilt or joust. **R. up.** a. *intr.* To shoot up; to grow rapidly. (*b*) To increase, mount up. b. To go back in time or memory. c. To rise *to* a high price or value. (*b*) To amount *to* a large sum. (*c*) To attain *to* a certain weight, size, etc. d. Of cloth, etc.: To shrink or contract after wetting. e. *Sporting.* To be runner-up in a race, etc. f. *trans.* (*a*) To make up (a sum or number); to augment (one's fortune). (*b*) To accumulate (a bill, debt, etc.) against oneself or another. (*c*) To bid against (a person) at an auction in order to compel him to pay more. (*d*) To cause (prices) to rise; to force (a thing) up to a higher price. g. To trace or follow up in some way. h. (*a*) To build, erect, set up (a wall, etc.). (*b*) To bring (a gun) up to the firing position. i. (*a*) To build or construct rapidly or hurriedly (and unsubstantially). (*b*) To add up (a column of figures, etc.) rapidly. (*c*) To sew quickly (and loosely).

Run (rɒn), *ppl. a.* 1669. [f. RUN *v.*] I. 1. Of liquor That has run out or leaked. 2. *Naut.* That has deserted. *R. man*, a deserter. 1702. *Obs.* or *arch.* 3. Of a fish: That has made a migration up a freshwater stream from the sea 1828. 4. a. *Mining.* Of coal: Soft, bituminous 1730. b. *dial.* Of milk: Coagulated, clotted 1866. II. 1. Of goods: Illicitly landed or imported; smuggled 1714. 2. Poured in or out in a melted state; caused to flow out. *R. butter*: see BUTTER *sb.*[1] 1806. b. *R. metal*, *steel*, a form of cast iron 1833. 3. Carried on, continuous, running 1811. 4. *R. stitch*, a running stitch. Also as *vb.* 1880.

Ru·n-about, runabout. 1549. 1. One who runs about from place to place; *dial.* a pedlar. b. *attrib.* Given to wandering or roving 1788. 2. *Austral. pl.* Cattle left to graze at will 1890. 3. A small light horse-vehicle or motor-car. Also *attrib.* with *car*. 1890.

Runagate (rɒ·năgeᵉit), *sb.* (and *a.*). Now *arch.* 1530. [Alteration of *renna-*, RENEGATE, by association with *ren(ne*, RUN *v.* + AGATE *adv.*] †1. An apostate -1692. 2. A deserter, fugitive, runaway 1548. 3. A vagabond, wanderer; a run-about 1547. 4. *attrib.* or as *adj.* 1563.

2. Crews of these desperadoes,..the runagates of every country and every clime W. IRVING. 3. A crew of wild thieves and runnagates 1677. 4. A r. rogue without property..or influence 1851.

Runaway (rɒ·năweᵉi), *sb.* (and *a.*). 1547. [f. RUN *v.* + AWAY *adv.*] A. *sb.* 1. One who runs away; a fugitive, a deserter. †b. An apostate, a renegade -1647. c. A horse which bolts while being ridden or driven 1607. 2. An act of running away; *spec.* an elopement, a runaway match 1724.

1. A general Defection ensu'd upon this Run-aways Example 1712. 2. Many of the young people made.. a 'r.' 1830.

B. *attrib.* or as *adj.* 1. Of persons: Having run away; given to running away; fugitive 1548. b. Pertaining to, connected with, accompanied by, running away or elopement 1748. 2. Of horses, etc.: Escaped, or given to escaping, from the control of the rider or driver 1607. 3. *Sporting.* Easily won; one-sided 1895.

1. Rather more than half were r. rebels and murderers DARWIN. b. All the dinners and duels..and run-away matches, were..discussed 1871. *R. knock, ring*, one given at a door as a trick or joke, and followed by the rapid flight of the giver.

Runch (rɒnʃ). *Sc.* and *north.* 1552. [Origin unkn.] a. Charlock or wild mustard, *Brassica Sinapistrum*. b. Wild radish, *Raphanus Raphanistrum*.

Runcinate (rɒ·nsinĕt), *a.* 1776. [f. L. *runcina* a plane (formerly taken to mean a saw).] *Bot.*, etc. Irregularly saw-toothed, with the lobes or teeth curved toward the base. So **Ru·ncinated** *a.* Also **Ru·ncinato-**, comb. form.

Rundale (rɒ·ndēl). 1545. [f. RUN *v.* + DALE[2] 1.] 1. A form of joint occupation of land, each joint holder occupying and cultivating several small strips or patches not contiguous to each other. **2.** Land occupied in this manner, or a share in such land 1819.

Rundle (rv·nd'l). ME. [var. of ROUNDLE.] †**1.** A circle; a circular or annular form, appearance, or arrangement; a round –1843. †**2.** An object of a circular or spherical form –1680. **b.** A circular enclosure or field. Now *dial.* 1577. **3.** *Her.* = ROUNDEL 5 b. 1562. †**4.** *Bot.* A whorl, verticil, umbel –1807. **5. a.** A cylinder or roller of wood; *spec.* one of the bars in a lantern-wheel 1565. **b.** A solid wheel or barrel 1611.

Run-down, *ppl. a.* 1683. [RUN *v.*] †**1.** Downtrodden, oppressed (*rare*). **2.** Of watch-plates: Faced with only one coat of enamel 1834. **3.** Completely unwound 1894. **4.** In a low state of health 1901.

Rune (rūn). 1690. [a. ON. and Icel. *rún*, cogn. w. OE. *rún* whisper, secret counsel, mystery, etc. In sense 2 a. Finnish *runo*, a. ON. *rún*.] **1.** A letter or character of the earliest Teut. alphabet, which was most extensively used by the Scandinavians and Anglo-Saxons. Also, a similar character or mark having mysterious or magical powers attributed to it. **2.** †**a.** An incantation or charm denoted by magic signs (*rare*) –1796. **b.** A Finnish poem or division of a poem, *esp.* one of the separate songs of the Kalevala. Also incorrectly applied to old Scandinavian poems. 1854. **c.** *transf.* Any song, poem, or verse 1847. **3.** *attrib.*, in sense 'inscribed with runes', as *r.-stone*, etc. 1151.

2. c. My heart would sit and sing Shrillest runes of wintry cold 1860.

Rune-staff. 1705. [a. Sw. *runstaf*, f. *run* RUNE + *staf* STAFF.] **a.** A magic wand inscribed with runes. **b.** A runic calendar or clog-almanack.

Rune-stave. Now only *arch.* [OE. *rún-stæf*, f. *rún* RUNE + *stæf* STAFF, STAVE.] A runic letter or symbol.

Rung (rvŋ), *sb.* [OE. *hrung*; not traceable outside of Teut.] **1.** A stout stick of a rounded form, *esp.* one used as a rail (in a cart, etc.), cross-bar, or spoke. **2.** A round or stave of a ladder ME. **3.** *Shipbuilding.* A floor-timber. Now *rare.* 1625.

2. *fig.* One of the lowest rungs of Memory's ladder 1883. Hence **Runged** *ppl. a.* **Ru·ngless** *a.*

Rung, *ppl. a.* 1630. [f. RING *v.*[1]] **a.** Having a ring inserted in the nose. **b.** Ring-barked.

Runic (rū·nik), *a.* and *sb.* 1662. [ad. mod.L. *runicus*, f. ON. *rún* RUNE.] **A.** *adj.* **1.** Consisting of runes. **b.** Carved or written in runes; expressed by means of runes 1685. **c.** Inscribed with runes 1728. **2.** Of poetry, etc.: Such as might be written in runes; belonging to the peoples or the age which made use of runes; *esp.* ancient Scandinavian or Icelandic. Now *rare.* 1690. **b.** *transf.* Applied to ancient Scottish poetry or poets 1759. **3.** Belonging to ancient Scandinavia or the ancient North 1665. **b.** Of ornament: Of the interlacing type (orig. Celtic) which is characteristic of rune-bearing monuments, metal-work, etc. 1838.

1. Lyons, bears,..&c. wrought on the hardest rocks, together with R. characters EVELYN. b. Odin invented Poetry; the music of human speech, as well as that miraculous r. marking of it CARLYLE. 3. Time, Which settles all things, Roman, Greek, or R. BYRON.

B. *sb.* †**1.** The ancient Scandinavian tongue –1690. **2.** A runic inscription 1866. **3.** *Typog.* A style of display lettering (in the Roman alphabet) having a thickened face, and often of a condensed form 1873.

Runlet[1] (rv·nlėt). Now only *arch.* or *Hist.* late ME. [a. OF. *rondelet*, dim. of *rondelle*, f. *ronde* ROUND *a.*] A cask or vessel of varying capacity; the quantity of liquor contained in this.

Large runlets appear usu. to have varied between 12 and 18½ gallons, small ones between a pint or quart and 3 or 4 gallons.

Runlet[2] (rv·nlėt). 1755. [f. RUN *sb.* + -LET.] A little run or stream †a channel.

Runlets that brattle down the green hills 1853.

Runnel (rv·n'l). 1577. [Later form of OE. *rynel*, f. the stem *rin-*, *run-*; see RUN *v.*] **1.** A small stream of water; a brooklet, rivulet, rill, or trickle. **2.** A small watercourse or channel; a gutter 1669.

1. A little runnell tumbled neere the place 1600. Herons stand in the little runnels which trickle over the flats 1883.

Runner (rv·nəɹ). [ME. *urnare*, *rennere*, etc.; f. RUN *v.* + -ER[1]; anticipated by OE. *fore-iornere* fore-runner.] **I. 1.** One who runs; a racer. †**2.** A fugitive, deserter –1624. **3.** One who carries messages on foot or horseback; a messenger, courier, errand-bearer; a scout ME. †**b.** One employed as spy to a gambling-den, band of thieves, etc. –1776. **c.** One employed or acting as a collector, agent, or intelligencer for a bank, broker, †government, †newspaper, book-maker, etc. 1768. **d.** A police-officer. Also *Bow-street r.* (see BOW-STREET) and *police-r.* (see POLICE *sb.*). Now *Hist.* 1771. **e.** One who solicits custom for a hotel, tradesman, etc. Orig. *U.S.* 1840. **4.** A horse capable of running well; a good roadster or racer; a horse taking part in a race 1582. **5. a.** The water-rail, *Rallus aquaticus*; also *dial.* the land-rail 1668. **b.** A bird belonging to the order *Cursores* 1870. **c.** *U.S.* A name given to several fishes 1876. **6.** A fast-sailing ship; †*esp.* one for the carrying of dispatches without convoy in time of war 1700. **7. a.** One engaged in running contraband goods; a smuggler; also, a smuggling vessel. Now *dial.* 1721. **b.** A blockade-runner 1867. **8.** A strip of cloth, usu. embroidered, used as a decoration for tables, pianos, etc. **II. 1.** *Founding.* A channel along which molten metal runs from the furnace to the mould 1843. **2. a.** A horizontal millstone capable of revolution, being usu. the upper one of a pair 1533. **b.** A vertical millstone, or a disk of stone, metal, etc., employed in the same manner 1707. **c.** A slab of stone or (rarely) iron, used in polishing stone surfaces 1850. **3.** *Naut.* A stout rope rove through a single block, with one end passed round a tackle-block and the other having a hook attached to it. Often coupled with *tackle.* Also *attrib.*, as *r.-block*, etc. 1625. **4.** A naked creeping stem thrown out from the base of the main stem of the strawberry and certain other plants, and itself taking root 1664. **b.** One of several varieties of beans which twine round stakes for support, esp. the scarlet runner (see SCARLET *a.*). 1786. **5.** A ring or other device capable of sliding along a strap, rod, etc., or through which something may readily be passed or drawn 1688. **6.** A long piece of wood or metal, curved at the ends, supporting the body of a sledge, toboggan, or the like 1765. **b.** The blade of a skate; a skate with a blade curving up at the toe 1860. **7.** A support or groove, along, on, or in which anything slides; a roller 1833. **8.** A wagon or trolley 1853.

Ru:nner-u·p. 1842. **1.** *Coursing.* A dog that takes the second prize, losing only the final course to the winner. **b.** *gen.* A competitor or competing team that comes in second, or takes second place 1886. **2.** One who 'runs up' bids at an auction 1905.

Running (rv·niŋ), *vbl. sb.* OE. [f. RUN *v.* + -ING[1].] **1.** The action of RUN *v.*, in various senses. *esp.* **2.** The action, on the part of a horse, of going at (great) speed, *esp.* in a race; racing; †a race OE. **3.** Capacity for or power of running or racing 1842. **4.** The flowing or discharge of blood or humours from the body: a sore which discharges matter OE. **5.** The flow of liquor during the process of wine-making, brewing, or distillation; the liquor obtained at a specified stage of process 1601.

2. Phr. *To make* (*strong*, etc.) *r.* *To make the r.*, to set the pace. *To take up the r.*, to take the lead. *Out of the r.*, having no place among the leading competitors in a race. 3. He had plenty of r. still in him 1842. 5. *fig.* From the Dregs of Life, think to receive What the first sprightly r. could not give DRYDEN.

Comb.: **r. board,** orig. *U.S.*, a footboard along the side of a locomotive, motor-car, or the roof of a freight-car; **r. powers,** permission granted to a railway company to run trains over the lines of another company.

Running (rv·niŋ), *ppl. a.* ME. [f. RUN *v.* + -ING[2].] **I. 1.** Of water, streams, etc.: Flowing. **2. a.** Fluid, liquid; melting readily. late ME. **b.** Of sand or soil: Having no coherence 1833. **3.** Of sores, etc.: Discharging matter; suppurating 1535.

1. *R. water*, water taken straight from a running stream; river-water. 3. Ne can my r. sore find remedie SPENSER.

II. 1. Passing rapidly from place to place. late ME. **b.** Of diseases, etc.: Passing from one part of the body to another; *esp.* spreading over the skin. late ME. **2.** Employed to run as a messenger, etc. 1604. **b.** Moving rapidly about, esp. in the course of one's business or profession 1611. **3.** Of plants: Creeping, climbing, or spreading rapidly; sending out many runners 1548. **4.** Of metre, music, etc.: Of a smooth, easy, or rapid character 1589. **5.** Of a ship: Sailing in time of war without a convoy 1816.

2. b. He might be a 'R. Lecturer', not tied to one locality CARLYLE.

III. 1. Performed with, or accompanied by, a run; rapid, hasty ME. †**b.** Of a banquet, collation, etc.: Taken hurriedly; slight –1728. **2.** *R. hand*, a cursive form of script 1648.

1. *R. fire*, a rapid successive discharge of firearms by each of the men forming a rank or ranks; a rapid and continuous fire. *R. fight*, a naval engagement carried on during a retreat or flight. b. A r. collation to stay his stomach—no set meal to satisfy his hunger FULLER.

IV. 1. Carried on or extending continuously. Used *esp.* of architectural or decorative ornament. late ME. **b.** Of measurements: Linear 1663. **2.** Continuous, sustained; going on, carried on, right through or continuously 1492. **b.** Of accounts, etc.: Allowed to run on for a certain (specified or indefinite) time 1742. **3.** (Placed after the sb.) Following each other; successive, in succession 1719.

1. *R. title, head(line)*, a short title or headline placed at the top of the page. 2. His face is the r. comment on his acting HAZLITT. *R. commentary* spec., a broadcast report by an eye-witness of a ceremony, sporting event, etc.

V. 1. Current, prevalent, general 1449. **2.** That is in progress, going on, or existing, at the present time 1584. †**b.** Of cash: Available for use –1727. **3.** Temporary 1632.

2. My r. quarter's salary 1861. b. The r. Cash of the Nation,..must daily diminish SWIFT.

VI. 1. Moving easily or rapidly by mechanical means or as a piece of mechanism; easily moved, slid along, shifted, etc. late ME. **2.** Of ropes, etc.: Capable of moving when pulled or hauled; *esp.* moving or passing through a block, ring, etc. Chiefly *Naut.* 1625. **3.** Of knots, nooses, etc. Slipping or sliding easily, esp. so as to catch something tightly 1648. **4.** *R. stitch*, a loose open stitch 1850.

1. The r.-gear of a good waggon 1876. 2. A r. bow-line passed around the fish's tail 1885. *R. rigging*: see RIGGING *sb.* 2. 3. Every man speaks under correction of the yard-arm and a r. noose SCOTT. Hence **Ru·nningly** *adv.* †concurrently *with* something; rapidly, readily.

†**Ru·nnion.** An abusive term applied to a woman SHAKS.

Runo-, comb. form of mod.L. *runa* RUNE, used in **Runo·logist,** one who studies or is skilled in runes 1866; **Runo·logy,** the study or science of runes.

Runrig (rv·nrig). *Sc.* 1437. [f. RUN *v.* + RIG *sb.*[1] 3.] **1.** A ridge of land lying among others held by joint tenure. **2.** = RUNDALE 1. 1583. **3.** As *adv.* In separate ridges cultivated by different occupiers 1695. **4.** *attrib.* Held or characterized by this mode of tenure 1751.

Runt (rvnt). 1501. [Origin unkn.] **1.** An old or decayed stump of a tree. Now *dial.* **2.** An ox or cow of a small breed or size 1549. **b.** A small or inferior horse 1725. **c.** A small pig, esp. the smallest in a litter. *dial.* and *U.S.* 1841. **3.** *transf.* **a.** An ignorant, uncouth, or uncultivated person 1614. **b.** An old woman; a hag. Now *Sc.* or *dial.* 1652. **c.** A stunted or undersized person; a dwarf 1700. **d.** A dwarfish or diminutive object 1845. **4.** A domestic pigeon of a breed characterized by size and stoutness of build 1661.

1. Neither yong poles nor old runts are fit for durable building HOLLAND. 3. a. A pretty pass, when a set of beggarly Welsh runts use threats to their betters 1830. Hence **Ru·ntish** *a.* of animals, stunted, dwarfish. **Ru·nty** *a.* dwarfish, undersized; small and ill-made; of low, thick-set build.

Run-up. 1834. [f. RUN *v.*] The act of running up to a certain point; esp. **a.** *Coursing.* The race between two greyhounds up to the first turn or wrench of the hare. **b.** The act of taking or sending a ball up to the goal or into a position for final play 1897.

b. Vardon, after being short in his run up, missed the hole for a 3. 1901.

Runway (rv·nwē). Chiefly *U.S.* 1873. [f. RUN *v.*] **1.** The customary track or run of an animal (*esp.* of deer) or a fish. **2.** Any artificial (sloping or horizontal) track or gangway made for convenience of passage or carriage 1888. **3.** A groove in which anything slides 1890.

Rupee (rupī·). 1612. [ad. Urdū *rūpiyah*, = Skr. *rūpya* wrought silver.] The monetary unit of India, represented by a silver coin now valued at 1*s.* 6*d.*

Rupert's drop, metal: see DROP *sb.* I. 8. and PRINCE *sb.*

‖**Rupia** (rū·piă). 1815. [mod.L., f. Gr. ῥύπος filth, dirt.] *Path.* A skin disease characterized by an eruption of broad, flattish, scattered vesicles, succeeded by thick ulcerating scabs. Hence **Ru·pial** *a.* pertaining to, of the nature of, affected with, r.

Ruption (rɒ·pʃən). Now *rare.* 1483. [ad. obs. F. *ruption*, or late L. *ruptio*, f. *rumpere*.] **1.** Breach of the peace; disturbance (*rare*). **2.** Breaking or rupture of some membrane or tissue of the animal body 1541.

Rupture (rɒ·ptiŭı, -tʃəı), *sb.* 1481. [a. F., or ad. L. *ruptura*, f. *rupt-*, *rumpere*; see -URE.] **1.** †**a.** Breach *of* a covenant, intercourse, or the peace -1645. **b.** A breach of harmony or friendly relations between two persons or parties 1583. **2.** *Path.* Abdominal hernia; a case of this 1539. **3.** †**a.** A break in a surface or substance, such as the skin, flesh, etc. -1674. **b.** A break in the surface of the earth; a ravine, chasm, gorge, rift 1555. **4.** The act of breaking or bursting; the fact of being broken or burst 1642.

1. The r. of the Treaties with Spain 1645. **b.** The r. between Church and State was now complete 1862. **4.** The Egg that soon Bursting with kindly r. forth disclos'd Thir callow young MILT.

Rupture (rɒ·ptiŭı, -tʃəı), *v.* 1739. [f. prec.] **1.** *trans.* **a.** To break, burst (a vessel, membrane, etc.). **b.** To cause a breach of; to sever 1854. **c.** To affect (a person) with hernia 1818. **2.** *intr.* To suffer a break or rupture 1863.

Ru·pturewort. 1597. [f. RUPTURE *sb.* 2.] **1.** A plant of the genus *Herniaria*, esp. *H. glabra*, formerly supposed to cure rupture or hernia. **2.** A West Indian plant, *Alternanthera polygonoides* 1864.

Rural (rūə·răl), *a.* and *sb.* late ME. [a. F., or ad. L. *ruralis*, f. *rur-*, *rus* country; cf. RUSTIC *a.*] **A.** *adj.* **1.** Of persons: Living in the country; having the standing, qualities, or manners of country-folk; agricultural or pastoral. **2. a.** *R. dean, deanery*: see DEAN[1] 5. 1450. **b.** Employed or stationed in country districts 1840. **3.** Of or pertaining to, characteristic of, country-folk; rustic 1513. **4.** Of poetry, music, etc.: Natural or appropriate to the country or to country-people; unpolished, simple 1470. **5.** Of, pertaining to, or characteristic of the country or country life as opp. to the town 1590. **6.** Of a rustic form or make (*rare*) 1624.

1. To keep company—odious phrase—with some r. swain 1876. **3.** I see the r. virtues leave the land GOLDSM. **4.** It was a kind of rurall harpe 1610. **5.** On to thir mornings r. work they haste Among sweet dewes and flours MILT.

B. *sb.* An inhabitant of the country; a countryman, rustic. Now *rare.* 1513.

Every r. began to be busie in the fields 1657. Hence **Ru·ralism,** r. quality or character; country life. **Ru·ralist,** a countryman, peasant; one who leaves the town for the country. **Rura·lity,** r. quality or character, rusticity; country life, manners, or scenery; also with *a* and *pl.* **Ru·rally** *adv.*

Ruralize (rūə·rələiz), *v.* 1805. [f. RURAL *a.* + -IZE 2.] **1.** *trans.* To render rural or rustic in character. **2.** *intr.* To go into the country; to rusticate 1822.

Ruridecanal (rūəridĭkē·năl, -de·kănăl), *a.* 1861. [f. L. *ruri-*, *comb.* f. *rus* country + DECANAL *a.*] Of or pertaining to a rural dean or deanery.

Rusa (rū·să). 1827. [mod.L., a. Malay.] **a.** A genus of large East Indian deer, including the sambur and rusa proper. **b.** A deer of this genus, esp. the Javanese *R. hippelaphus.* Hence **Ru·sine** *a. Zool.* of or belonging to, characteristic, of the genus *R.*

Ruse (rū·z). late ME. [a. F., f. *ruser*; see next.] †**1.** *Hunting.* A detour; a doubling or turning of a hunted animal to elude the dogs. late ME. only. **2.** A trick, stratagem, artifice, 'dodge' 1625. **b.** Without article 1815.

2. b. Seizing by r. the game that evaded other snares 1863.

Rush (rɒʃ), *sb.*[1] [OE. *risc* (*rix*) and *risce* (*rixe*), ME. *risch*(*e*, *rusche*, possibly connected ultimately with G. *rusch* adj.] **1.** A plant of the order *Juncaceæ*, having straight naked stems or stalks (properly leaves) and growing in marshy ground, or on the borders of rivers or ponds; a single stem or stalk of this. **b.** Used for burning; also *ellipt.*, a rush-light. late ME. †**c.** Used for making a finger-ring -1601. †**d.** In reference or with allusion to the practice of strewing fresh rushes for visitors -1738. **e.** Without article 1728. **2.** As a type of something of no value or importance, esp. in neg. phrases as *not to care a r.*, *not worth a r.* ME. **3.** With specific epithets. **a.** Denoting various species of *Juncus* 1753. **b.** Applied to many plants of different genera, more or less resembling the rush, as *bog-*, *sweet*, *wood-r.*, etc.

1. The Queene..sate alone alowe on the rushes all desolate T. MORE. **b.** Without the glimmer of a farthing r.! HOOD. **c.** *All's Well* II. ii. 24. **d.** Rushes, Ladys, rushes, Rushes as green as Summer for this stranger FLETCHER. **2.** A figge for the whole world. A r. for thee. 1610.

attrib. and *Comb.*: **r.-grass,** a species of grass having a r.-like appearance; **-holder,** a device for holding a rushlight; **-toad,** the natter-jack; **-wheat,** a species of wild wheat (*Triticum junceum*) growing on sandy shores. Hence †**Rusher**[1], one who strews rushes on a floor -1630.

Rush (rɒʃ), *sb.*[2] late ME. [f. RUSH *v.*[2]] **1.** The act, or an act, of rushing; a sudden violent or tumultuous movement; a charge, an onslaught. **2. a.** *Football, etc.* An attempt by one or more players, *esp.* the forwards, to force the ball through the opponents' line and towards their goal. Also, a player who is skilled in this. 1857. **b.** *Croquet.* A roquet played with considerable force 1874. **c.** *Amer.* A scrimmage or struggle between first and second year students 1871. **3.** A sudden migration of numbers of people to a certain place, *esp.* to a new goldfield 1850. **b.** *transf.* The scene of such a migration 1855. **4.** An eager demand *for*, a strong run *on*, something 1856. **5.** Dysentery in cattle 1799.

1. Some mighty current, r., or eddy of the tide 1789. The ceaseless clangour, and the r. of men Inebriate with rage SHELLEY. *fig.* To this hour I have sudden vague rushes of terror DICKENS. **2. a.** The Dark Blues broke away, but the r. was well saved 1897. **4.** There was..a bit of a r. on American rails 1884. Phr. *With a r.*, with a sudden onset; in a rapid or sweeping manner 1859.

attrib. and *Comb.*: **r. hour,** the part of the day in which there is normally a r. on trains, shops, etc.: **r. order,** an order for goods required in a hurry.

Rush (rɒʃ), *v.*[1] late ME. [f. RUSH *sb.*[1]] **1.** *trans.* **a.** To strew with rushes. **b.** To tie up, work or make, with rushes 1848. **2.** *intr.* To gather rushes (*rare*) 1530.

2. Don't y' go a-rushing, maids, in May 1896. Hence **Ru·shed** *ppl. a.* overgrown or strewn with rushes.

Rush (rɒʃ), *v.*[2] late ME. [a. AF. *russher* = OF. *re*(*h*)*usser*; ult. origin obsc.] **I.** *trans.* †**1.** To force out of place or position by violent impact; to drive back, down, etc. late ME. only. **2.** To cause to move with great speed and force; to send or impel violently. Chiefly with preps. late ME. **3.** †**a.** *refl.* To move with speed and force; to impel (oneself) heedlessly, violently, or hurriedly *upon* or *on* something -1659. **b.** *trans.* To drag, force, or carry rapidly and violently *into*, *to*, *out of*, etc. 1577. **c.** *transf.* To get or bring *out*, carry *through*, push on, etc., in an unusually rapid manner 1830. **4.** To force at an unusual or excessive pace or speed. Also with *on*, *up*. 1850. **b.** To cheat, 'do'; to extort from; to charge (a person) so much (esp. an exorbitant price); also, *for* so much. *slang.* 1885. **5. a.** *Mil.* To overcome, take, capture, carry by means of a sudden rush 1865. **b.** To cross, penetrate, traverse, negotiate (or endeavour to do so) with a rush 1884. **c.** To occupy by a rush (of gold-miners) 1879. **d.** *Croquet.* To roquet (a ball) with considerable force 1874. **e.** *Football, etc.* To make a rush for (the opposite goal).

2. Into what a sea of misery have I now rushed saile! 1654. **3.** What, stab her, And r. her into blood? YOUNG. **c.** There is no disposition to r. business 1893. **4.** While the country boy is allowed to grow up, the city boy is rushed up 1887. **5. a.** The Arabs 'rushed the town, putting every man to the sword 1884. **c.** The locality was 'rushed' for gold 1879.

II. *intr.* **1.** Of persons or animals: To run, dash, or charge with violence or impetuous rapidity. Usu. const. with advs. or preps. late ME. **b.** *fig.* To make an attack or descent, *on* or *upon* a person 1535. **c.** *fig.*, denoting rash or precipitate action. Freq. const. *into*. 1560. **d.** To pass or travel rapidly 1852. **2.** Of things: To move, flow, fall, etc., with great speed or impetuosity. late ME. **b.** To come suddenly into view 1798.

1. Then the colt rushed by them..hard held 1862. **c.** So many foolish persons are rushing into print 1872. **2.** Nor slept the winds Within thir stony caves, but rush'd abroad MILT. *fig.* A dreadful rumour rushed through the University THACKERAY. **b.** The Sun's rim dips; the stars r. out COLERIDGE. Hence **Ru·sher**[2], one who or that which rushes; *colloq.* a 'go-ahead' person. **Ru·shingly** *adv.*

Ru·sh-bea:ring. 1617. [RUSH *sb.*[1]] An annual ceremony in northern districts of carrying rushes and garlands to the church and strewing the floor or decorating the walls with them.

Ru·sh-ca:ndle. 1591. [RUSH *sb.*[1]] A candle of feeble power made by dipping the pith of a rush in grease; a rushlight.

Rushen (rɒ·ʃn), *a.* [OE. *riscen*, f. *risc* RUSH *sb.*[1]] Made of rushes, or of a rush.

Ru·sh-grown, *a.* 1545. [RUSH *sb.*[1]] †**1.** Having the slender tapering form of a rush -1828. **2.** Overgrown with rushes 1777.

Ru·shlight. Also **rush-light.** 1710. [RUSH *sb.*[1]] **a.** = RUSH-CANDLE. **b.** Without article: The light of a rush-candle 1847.

Ru·sh-like, *a.* 1578. [RUSH *sb.*[1]] Resembling a rush or rushes.

Ru·sh-ring. 1579. [RUSH *sb.*[1]] A ring made of a rush or rushes. **b.** Used as a wedding-ring 1668.

b. I'l Crown thee with a Garland of straw then, and I'le Marry thee with a Rush ring DAVENANT.

Rushy (rɒ·ʃi), *a.* late ME. [f. RUSH *sb.*[1] + -Y[1].] **1.** Made or consisting of rushes; rushen. **2.** Producing, full of, covered with, rushes 1586. **3.** Resembling a rush or rushes; rush-like 1597.

1. Then turn tonight, and freely share..My r. couch and frugal fare GOLDSM.

Rusk (rɒsk). 1595. [a. Sp. or Pg. *rosca* twist, and spec. twisted roll of bread.] **1.** Bread in the form of small pieces which have been re-fired so as to render them hard and crisp; formerly much used on board ships. **2.** A piece of bread hardened or browned by re-firing and sometimes sweetened 1759.

Ruskin (rɒ·skin). The surname of John Ruskin (1819-1900), distinguished as a writer on art and social subjects, used *attrib.* in *R. linen*, a kind of hand-woven linen produced near Keswick in Cumberland; *R. ware*, a kind of pottery with leadless glaze produced at Birmingham. Hence **Ruski·nian** *a.*, characteristic of R.; *sb.* a follower of R. (so **Ru·skinite**).

Rusma (rɒ·zmă). 1615. [app. ad. Turk. *Khirisma*, ad. Gr. χρῖσμα ointment (see CHRISM).] A depilatory composed of lime and orpiment, now chiefly used in tanning.

Russ (rɒs), *sb.* and *a.* 1567. [ad. Russ. *Rusĭ*, native name of the people and country.] **A.** *sb.* **1.** A Russian. Now *rare.* †**b.** An adherent of the Russian Church -1635. **2.** The Russian language 1571. **B.** *adj.* Russian 1574. Hence **Ru·ssify** *v. trans.* to Russianize; hence **Ru·ssifica·tion.**

†**Russel.** 1488. [prob. Flem. *Rijsel* Lille.] A kind of woollen fabric -1703.

Russell (rɒ·sĕl). 1868. [?] A ribbed or corded fabric formerly in use. Also *R. cord.*

Russet (rɒ·sĕt), *sb.* and *a.* ME. [a. OF. *rousset*, dim. of *rous* (mod.F. *roux*) red.] **A.** *sb.* **1.** A coarse homespun woollen cloth of a reddish-brown, grey, or neutral colour, formerly used for the dress of peasants and country-folk; also with *a* and *pl.*, a kind or make of this. †**b** *pl.* Garments of such cloth -1645. **2.** A reddish-brown colour; a shade of this 1532. **3. a.** A variety of eating apple, of a reddish or yellowish brown colour, or marked with brownish spots, and having a rough skin; an apple of this kind 1708. †b. A variety of pear -1725.

1. I wore r, before I wore motley SCOTT.

B. *adj.* 1. Of a reddish-brown colour. late ME. b. Applied to varieties of apples (†and pears) 1664. 2. Of garments, etc.: Made of russet cloth 1440. 3. Clad in russet or home-spun cloth 1613. 4. Rustic, homely, simple 1588. 5. Of boots or shoes: Tan, brown 1667.

1. R. Lawns, and Fallows Gray, Where the nibling flocks do stray MILT. 2. The Morne in R. mantle clad SHAKS. 4. R. yeas, and honest kersie noes SHAKS. Hence **Ru·sset** *v.* to make or become r. in colour. **Ru·ssety** *a.* inclining to a r. colour.

Russet coat. 1552. 1. A coat of russet cloth or colour, typical of a humble or rustic condition. †2. A peasant, rustic -1597. 3. A russet apple 1602.

Russet-coated, *a.* 1596. [RUSSET *a.*] Wearing a russet coat; rustic, homely.

A plain russet-coated Captain who knows what he fights for CROMWELL.

Russeting (rɒ·sėtiŋ). 1588. [f. RUSSET *sb.* or *a.* + -ING [3].] †1. Russet clothing. †2. A peasant, rustic; a simple fellow -1632. 3. A russet apple 1607.

Russia (rɒ·ʃă). 1658. [med.L., f. *Russi* the Russians; see RUSS.] The name of the country in the east of Europe which is now the Union of Socialist Soviet Republics (U.S.S.R.); used attrib. in specific designations.

R. leather, a very durable leather made of skins impregnated with oil distilled from birch-bark, extensively used in bookbinding. Also simply *russia*. *R.-matting*, 'matting manufactured in Russia from the inner bark of the linden'. *R. sheet-iron*, 'sheet-iron made in Russia, and having a smooth, glossy surface of a purplish colour, sometimes mottled'.

Russian (rɒ·ʃăn), *sb.* and *a.* 1538. [ad. med.L. *Russianus*, f. *Russia*; see prec.] A. *sb.* 1. A native of Russia. 2. The language of Russia; also, a form or dialect of this 1716. 3. *ellipt.* for *R. hemp, iron, leather, wheat* 1862.

1. My grooms are Arabs;..my housemaids Russians 1776.

B. *adj.* 1. Of or pertaining to Russia or its people; inhabiting, native to, characteristic of, Russia 1588. 2. Of or pertaining to, concerned with, the Russian language or literature 1797. Hence **Ru·ssianize** *v. trans.* to render R. in character.

Russniak (rɒ·sniæk), *sb.* and *a.* 1829. [a. the native name *Rusnyák*.] Little Russian or Ruthenian.

Russo- (rɒ·so), comb. form (on Gr. analogies) of RUSS, as in *Russo-Turkish*, etc.; also in adjs. or sbs. denoting tendency to admire or favour Russia, Russian methods, policy, etc., as **Ru·ssophil(e, Russophilism** (-ǫ·filiz'm); or morbid dread of these, as **Ru·ssophobe, -pho·bia, -pho·bian, -pho·bism, -pho·bist.**

Rust (rɒst), *sb.* [OE. *rúst*:—pre-Teut. **rudhsto-*, f. stem of RED *a.*] 1. A red, orange, or tawny coating formed upon the surface of iron or steel by oxidation, esp. through the action of air or moisture; also, a similar coating formed upon any other metal by oxidation or corrosion. 2. Moral corrosion or canker; corruption OE. 3. Any deteriorating or impairing effect or influence upon character, abilities, etc., esp. as the result of inactivity OE. 4. A disease in plants marked by ferruginous spots and caused by uredinous fungi; also loosely, any plant-disease presenting a similar appearance ME. b. One or other of the uredinous fungi producing 'rust' in plants 1813. 5. A coating or stain resembling rust 1684. 6. The colour of rust 1716.

1. *fig.* Authors, like coins, grow dear as they grow old; It is the r. we value, not the gold POPE. 2. I hope to Rube A-waye the Ruste, with penaunce, frome my gostely syhte 1440. 3. Sunday clears away the R. of the whole Week ADDISON.

attrib. and *Comb.*: **r.-cement**, a composition for joints which oxidizes on exposure to the air; **-joint**, a joint made with r.-cement; **-mite**, a gall-mite producing r.-like excrescences on plants. Hence **Ru·stless** *a.* free from r.; not liable to be rusted.

Rust (rɒst), *v.* [ME. *rusten, rouste(n)*, f. prec.] I. *intr.* 1. Of iron or other metals: To contract rust, grow rusty; to undergo oxidation. †b. To form a rust. SHAKS. 2. To deteriorate, degenerate, spoil, *esp.* through inactivity or want of use. Also with *out*. ME. 3. To become rust-coloured 1541. 4. Of wheat, etc.: To become affected with rust or blight 1868.

1. Thy needles..Now r. disus'd, and shine no more COWPER. 2. Then must I r. in Ægypt, never more Appear in Arms? DRYDEN. 3. When the bracken rusted on their crags TENNYSON.

II. *trans.* 1. To affect with rust; to oxidize 1596. 2. To corrupt or corrode morally or physically 1697. 3. To affect (corn, etc.) with rust or blight 1759. 4. To waste *away* by idling 1853.

1. Keepe vp your bright Swords, for the dew will r. them SHAKS. 4. We must not r. away our lives here 1887.

Rustic (rɒ·stik), *a.* and *sb.* 1440. [ad. L. *rusticus*, f. *rus* country.] A. *adj.* 1. Of or pertaining to the country (as opp. to the town); found in the country. 2. Of persons: Living in the country as opp. to the town; following country occupations; of peasant or agricultural stock or condition 1601. 3. Of persons: Having the appearance or manners of country people; lacking in elegance, refinement, or education; *occas.*, clownish, boorish 1585. 4. Characteristic or typical of country-folk or peasants; *esp.* unmannerly, unrefined; rough 1589. b. Plain and simple; unsophisticated; having the charm of the country 1600. 5. Of rude or country workmanship; of a plain or simple form or structure; *spec.* constructed of roughly trimmed branches or roots of trees 1594. b. Of letters: Having a free or negligent form; applied *spec.* to one of the styles employed in early Latin manuscripts (in contrast to *square*) 1784. 6. *Arch.* Characterized by a surface artificially roughened or left rough-hewn, or by having the joints (esp. the horizontal ones) deeply sunk or chamfered; also, †of or pertaining to the Tuscan order 1563. b. *R. work*, masonry of this type 1715.

1. Of that kind Our rusticke Garden's barren SHAKS. 2. And many a holy text around she strews, That teach the r. moralist to die GRAY. 3. A Rustick Fellow, one..without cleanliness, and of a slovenly Speech 1688. 4. Unmannerly and rusticke behaviour 1637. b. The r. grace and sweetness of the *May Queen* 1855. 5. Three rustick arches, set off with ivy, moss, icicles and all the rocky appurtenances 1752.

B. *sb.* 1. A countryman, peasant 1550. b. A boorish person (*rare*) 1706. 2. *Arch.* Rustic work 1731. b. A stone (†or joint) of the kind employed in rustic work. Usu. in *pl.* 1728.

1. In how many countrey affairs must the scholar take the r. for his master? 1722. Hence **Ru·sticly** *adv.* in a r. manner; rustically.

Rustical (rɒ·stikăl), *a.* and *sb.* late ME. [ad. OF., or med.L. *rusticalis*; see prec. and -AL.] A. *adj.* 1. = RUSTIC *a.* 2. Now *arch.* 2. = RUSTIC *a.* 3. 1513. †b. Physically strong, robust -1693. 3. = RUSTIC *a.* 1. 1546. 4. = RUSTIC *a.* 4. 1550. 5. Of a kind, make, or fashion appropriate to the country; *esp.* plain or simple 1483.

2. b. The others..are more r. and hardy EVELYN.

B. *sb.* A countryman, peasant, rustic. Now *arch.* 1555.

If thou doe not kiss hir.., then thou shalt be taken for a rusticall 1579. Hence **Ru·stical·ly** *adv.*, **†-ness** -1661.

Rusticate (rɒ·stikeit), *v.* 1660. [f. L. *rusticat-*, *rusticari* to live in the country, f. *rusticus* RUSTIC *a.*] 1. *intr.* To go or retire into the country; to stay or sojourn in the country; to assume rural manners; to live a country life. 2. *trans.* a. To dismiss or 'send down' from a university for a specified time, as a punishment 1714. b. To remove or send into, settle (a person) in, the country. Also *refl.* 1733. 3. To imbue with rural manners; to countrify 1766. 4. To mark masonry by sunk joints or roughened surfaces 1715.

1. We went to..an old lonely Inn, where was the last place we rusticated 1698. 2. a. I was rusticated for..painting the college pump scarlet 1868.

Rustication (rɒstikēi·ʃən). 1623. [ad. L. *rusticatio*, f. *rusticari*; see prec.] 1. The action of rusticating; a spell of residence in the country; †a rural pursuit or occupation. b. The condition naturally attaching to life in the country 1771. 2. Temporary dismissal from a university; an instance or period of this 1734. 3. The action of banishing, or the state of being banished, into the country 1751. 4. *Arch.* The action or practice of rusticating masonry; the style of masonry produced by this 1815. b. A rustic feature or part 1839.

Rusticity (rɒsti·sĭti). 1531. [ad. F. *rusticité* or L. *rusticitas*; see RUSTIC *a.* and -ITY.] 1. Lack of breeding, culture, or refinement; clownishness. b. An instance of this 1803. 2. Lack of intellectual culture; ignorance 1583. 3. Of language, composition, etc.: Lack of polish or refinement; uncouthness, inelegance 1565. b. A rustic expression 1711. 4. Rustic or rural life, quality, or character 1638. b. A rural feature or characteristic; a rural thing or object 1662.

1. The wisedome of God receives small honour from those vulgar heads that rudely stare about, and with a grosse r. admire his workes SIR T. BROWNE.

Rustle (rɒ·s'l), *sb.* 1759. [f. the vb.] 1. A continuous succession of light crisp sounds produced by some kind of movement. 2. *U.S. colloq.* Bustle, hustle 1899.

1. Thou shalt hear..R. of the reaped corn KEATS.

Rustle (rɒ·s'l), *v.* late ME. [Imitative.] 1. *intr.* Of things: To give forth a continuous succession of light, rapid, crisp sounds, as the result of some kind of movement. b. Of persons or animals: To cause sounds of this nature to be produced 1560. 2. With advs. or preps.: To come, go, move, etc., with a rustling sound 1586. b. To go about, be finely dressed, *in* some material which rustles 1598. 3. *trans.* a. To cause to move in some way with a rustling sound 1648. b. To shake or stir with a rustling sound 1821. 4. *U.S. colloq.* a. *intr.* To bestir oneself or move about vigorously; to work with strenuous energy; to hustle 1872. b. *trans.* To shift, deal with, rapidly; to acquire or get together, by one's own exertions 1882.

1. The dry leaf rustles in the brake SHELLEY. b. Woman rustles, and bustles, and creaks, and fusses 1892. 2. Where the deer r. through the twining brake THOMSON. b. Rustling in unpayd-for Silke SHAKS. 3. a. Many sleeping Saints..Russled their Dust together, and gat up 1648.

Rustler (rɒ·slər). 1820. [f. RUSTLE *v.* + -ER [1].] 1. One who or that which rustles. 2. *U.S.* a. An energetic or bustling man 1872. b. A cattle-thief 1882.

Rusty (rɒ·sti), *a.*[1] [OE. *rústig*, f. *rúst* RUST *sb.*] I. 1. Covered or affected with rust or red oxide of iron; rusted. †2. Morally foul or corrupt -1586. 3. Of persons: Presenting an appearance suggesting something old and rusted. late ME. 4. a. Lacking in polish or refinement; rough, rude; surly, morose, churlish 1500. b. Hoarse, raucous, harsh, grating. Now *rare*. 1570. 5. a. Stiff through want of exercise or old age 1508. b. Of knowledge, accomplishments, etc.: Impaired by neglect; requiring to be polished up 1796. 6. Old, antiquated, obsolete 1551.

1. Bars and bolts Grew r. by disuse COWPER. 3. A little r., musty old fellow, always groping among ruins W. IRVING. 5. a. My body so lusty, Whiche for lacke of exercise is nowe almost rustye 1537. b. For the benefit of those whose Greek is rather r.., I have added a Latin version 1796. 6. That Prayer..has lain by till 'tis almost r. BUNYAN.

II. 1. Of plants: Affected with rust or mildew 1502. 2. Having the colour of rust; rubiginous, ferruginous; *spec.* in *Path.*, of sputa 1528. b. Of (dark) clothes: Showing signs of age or use; shabby, worn, or faded 1709. c. Of colours: Inclining towards, modified by, the colour of rust 1791.

1. The wheat was r. 1880. 2. b. His r. old suit of clothes was the cast-off of a waiter 1892.

Rusty (rɒ·sti), *a.*[2] Now chiefly *dial.* 1515. [var. of RESTY *a.*[2], perh. after prec.] Reasty, rancid.

Rusty (rɒ·sti), *a.*[3] 1562. [var. of RESTY *a.*[1], perh. infl. by RUSTY *a.*[1]] 1. Of horses: Restive. b. In phr. *to ride* or *run r.* Freq. of persons: To become intractable or obstinate; to be angry or annoyed; to take offence. 1709. 2. *colloq.* Ill-tempered, cross, nasty. Chiefly in phr. *to cut up r.*, *turn r.* 1815.

2. The people got r. about it SCOTT.

Rut (rɒt), *sb.*[1] late ME. [a. OF., var. of *ruit*:—pop. L. **rugitum* for L. accus. of *rugitus*, f. *rugire* to roar.] 1. The annually recurring sexual excitement of male deer; also, *transf.* of other animals. †2. The company of deer among which a stag goes to rut -1640. Hence **Rut** *v.*[1] *intr.* to be at rut.

Rut (rɒt), *sb.*[2] 1580. [Origin obsc.] 1. A (deep) furrow or track made in the ground, esp. in a soft road, by the passage of a wheeled vehicle or vehicles. **b.** *fig.* A settled habit or mode of procedure; a narrow, undeviating course of life or action; a groove 1839. **2.** A track or passage hollowed out, cut, or excavated in the ground (*rare*) 1611. **3.** *transf.* A deep mark or depression on the skin, some part of the body, etc. 1623.

1. b. Parliaments, lumbering along in their deep ruts of commonplace CARLYLE. 2. The soil lying hollow with the mole's ruts 1787. Hence **Ru·tty** *a.* marked by or full of ruts.

Rut (rɒt), *sb.*³ Now *U.S.* and *dial.* 1633. [Cf. ROTE *sb.*³] The roaring of the sea.

Rut (rɒt), *v.*² 1607. [f. RUT *sb.*²] *trans.* To mark (a road or the ground) with ruts; to furrow. (Chiefly in *pa. pple.*)

Rutaceous (rutēⁱ·ʃəs), *a.* 1830. [f. mod. L. *Rutaceæ* the rue family, f. L. *ruta* rue.] Of or belonging to the family *Rutaceæ*; resembling rue; rue-like.

Ruth (rūþ). Now *arch.* [Early ME. *reuðe*, f. *rewen* RUE *v.* Cf. OE. *hrēow* RUE *sb.*¹] **1.** The quality of being compassionate; pitifulness; compassion, pity. **2.** Contrition, repentance; remorse. Now *rare.* ME. **3.** Sorrow, grief, distress; †lamentation ME. †**4. a.** Matter or occasion of sorrow or regret –1626. **b.** Mischief; calamity; ruin –1647. †**5.** With *a* and *pl.* in senses 3, 4. –1589.

1. Look homeward Angel now, and melt with r. MILT. Phr. *To have r.*, usu. const. †*of, on* or *upon.* So *to take r.* 2. When our Teares doe testifie our r. 1603. 3. Here lies, to each her Parents r., Mary, the Daughter of their youth B. JONS.

Ruthenate (rū·þěnět). 1879. [f. RUTHENIUM + -ATE¹ 1 c.] *Chem.* A salt formed by the action of ruthenic acid. So **Ruthe·niate.**

Ruthene (ruþī·n), *sb.* and *a.* 1548. [ad. med.L. *Rut(h)eni* (pl.), related to *Ruzi, Russi* Russians; cf. RUSSIAN.] **1.** Of or pertaining to, a member of, the Little Russian race, inhabiting the south of Russia and portions of the north-west of Austria. **2.** The language of the Ruthenes 1891. So **Ruthe·nian** 1850.

Ruthenium (ruþī·niŏm). 1848. [f. med. L. *Ruthenia* Russia (having been first noticed in platinum ores from the Ural Mountains) + -IUM.] A metal of the platinum group, first isolated by Claus in 1845. Chem. symbol Ru. Hence **Ruthenic** (ruþe·nik) *a.* pertaining to or derived from r.; containing r. **Ruthe·nious** *a.*

Ruthful (rū·þfŭl), *a.* Now *arch.* ME. [f. RUTH.] **1.** Full of compassion or pity; compassionate. **2.** That excites compassion or pity; lamentable, piteous, rueful ME. **b.** Of sounds, actions, etc.: Expressive of grief or sorrow ME. **c.** Of persons or feelings: Sad, dejected, doleful 1513.

2. Or say a r. chance broke woof and warp BROWNING. Hence **Ru·thful-ly** *adv.*, **-ness.**

Ruthless (rū·plės), *a.* ME. [f. RUTH *sb.* + -LESS.] Devoid of pity or compassion; pitilessly merciless.

What a ruthlesse thing is this.., to take away the life of a man? SHAKS. Hence **Ru·thless-ly** *adv.*, **-ness.**

Rutic (rū·tik), *a.* 1857. [f. L. *ruta* rue + -IC 1 b.] *Chem. R. acid*, a colouring matter discovered in the common rue; capric acid.

Rutilant (rū·tilănt), *a.* Now *rare.* 1497. [ad. L. *rutilant-*, *rutilare*, f. *rutilus* reddish.] Glowing, shining, with either a ruddy or a golden light.

Rutile (rū·til). 1803. [a. F. or G. *rutil*, ad. L. *rutilus* red.] *Min.* An ore of titanium (a form of titanium dioxide). So **Ru·tilite.**

Ru·tin. 1857. [a. G., f. L *ruta* RUE *sb.*²; see -IN¹.] *Chem.* Rutic acid, capric acid.

Rutter (rɒ·təɹ). 1500. [a. MDu., var. of *ruter, ruyter* (Du. *ruiter*, whence G. *reuter*), ad. OF. *routier, routeur.*] A cavalry soldier (*esp.* a German one), of the kind employed in the wars of the 16th and 17th centuries. Now *arch.* Hence †**b.** A gay cavalier, a dashing gallant –1603.

You are a R. borne in Germanie 1592. Hence †**Ru·tterkin,** a swaggering gallant or bully –1581.

Ru·ttier. Now *arch.* 1500. [ad. F. *routier*, f. route ROUTE *sb.*] A set of instructions for finding one's course at sea; a marine guide to the routes, tides, etc.

†**Ru·ttish,** *a. rare.* 1601. [f. RUT *v.*¹ + -ISH¹ 3.] Lewd, lustful, lascivious –1602. Hence **Ru·ttishness** (*rare*).

Ruttle (rɒ·t'l), *v.* Now *dial.* late ME. [= MLG. *rutelen*, prob. echoic; cf. RATTLE *v.*] *intr.* To rattle; to make a rattling noise in the throat. Hence **Ru·ttle** *sb.* a noise of this kind.

Rutyl (rū·til). 1868. [f. as RUTIC *a.* + -YL.] *Chem.* = CAPRYL.

Rutylene (rū·tilīn). 1868. [f. prec. + -ENE.] *Chem.* A hydrocarbon polymeric with acetylene.

-ry, *suffix*, a reduced form of -ERY, occurring chiefly after an unstressed syllable ending in *d, t, l, n,* or *sh,* but also after stressed vowels or diphthongs. The older examples sometimes represent OF. forms in *-rie*, with variants in *-erie*, but the majority are comparatively late English formations. Examples are *ribaldry*; *harlotry, devilry*; *yeomanry*; *Irishry*; *avowry.*

Rye (rəi). [OE. *ryge* = ON. *rugr* :—**rugiz*, of which there are various Balto-Slavonic representatives. Prob. of Eastern European origin.] **1.** A food-grain obtained from the plant *Secale cereale*, extensively used in northern Europe. **2.** The plant itself. Also *collect.*, a number of growing plants of this kind (in a field). 1440. **b.** *Wild r.*: Any of various grasses of the genus *Elymus*; esp. *Elymus virginicus* or Lime Grass 1475.

Comb.: **r.-asthma,** hay-fever; **r.-brome grass,** a variety of brome with rye-like seeds, occurring as a weed in wheat-fields; **-flour,** flour made from r.; **-straw,** (*a*) the dried haulm of r.; (*b*) a single straw of this; *fig.* a weak insignificant person.

Rye-bread. 1579. Bread made from rye.

Rye-grass (rəi·gras). 1753. [In sense 1, an alteration of RAY-GRASS. In sense 2, perh. f. RYE.] **1.** One or other of several species of *Lolium*, esp. *L. perenne* (common r.) and *L. italicum* (Italian r.), extensively used as forage and fodder grasses. **2.** = *Wild rye* 1760.

Ryepeck (rəi·pek). Also **rypeck, ripeck.** 1857. [Origin unkn.] An iron-shod pole used for mooring a punt, or serving as a mark for competitors in aquatic sports.

Ryot (rəi·ət). 1625. [Urdū *raiyat*, ult. of Arabic origin; see RAYAH.] An Indian peasant, husbandman, or cultivating tenant.

‖**Ryotwar** (rəi·ətwār), *a.* 1827. [Urdū *raiyatwar*, f. *raiyat* RYOT + *-wār* pertaining to.] = next A.

‖**Ryotwary** (rəi·ətwāri), *a.* and *sb.* 1834. [Urdū *raiyatwāri*, f. *raiyatwār*; see prec.] **A.** *adj.* Of land-tenure in India: Characterized by direct settlement between the government and the cultivators, without the intervention of a zemindar or landlord. **B.** *sb.* The ryotwary system 1858.

‖**Rype** (rū·pə). *Pl.* **ryper.** 1743. [a. Norw.] The ptarmigan. (The sing. and pl. forms are often confused by English writers.)

S

S (es), the nineteenth letter of the English, and the eighteenth of the ancient Roman, alphabet, derives its form (through the ϟ, Σ, Ʒ of early Latin and Greek inscriptions) from the Phœnician W, which represented a voiceless sibilant: in some of the Semitic langs. (s), in others (ʃ). In ancient Greek and Latin the value of the letter is believed to have been always (s).

In mod. English the general rule is that *s* is pronounced (s) at the beginning of a word or of the second element of a compound, and when doubled or in contact with a voiceless consonant. Between vowels, and as an inflexional final element, a single *s* is mostly (z). But there are many anomalies and variations, especially in classical derivatives; cf., e.g., *absurd* (æbsɒ̄·ɹd), *observe* (ǒbz-); *dishonour* (dis-, diz-).

The phonetic combinations (sy), (zy), which arose from the collocation of (s), (z) with the first element of such diphthongs as (yu), (yə) have passed into (ʃ), (ʒ), which are consequently symbolized by *s* in combination with certain letters or groups of letters, as in *sure* (ʃūəɹ), *sugar* (ʃu·gəɹ), *censure* (se·nʃəɹ), *mission* (mi·ʃən), *Asia* (ēⁱ·ʃă), *treasure* (-ʒūɹ, -ʒəɹ), *evasion* (-ʒən).

S is silent in some words adopted from Old French, as in *aisle, isle*; in the Law French *mesne, demesne*, a silent *s* was inserted by false analogy.

1. The letter and its sound. 2. The shape of the letter; an object having this shape. **b.** *Collar of S, S's, SS.*, or *Esses*: see COLLAR *sb.* 2. **c.** *attrib.* and *Comb.*, as *S-shaped* adj.; *S-curve, -piece*, etc. **3.** Used to denote serial order, applied to the nineteenth (or more usu. eighteenth, either I or J being omitted) member of a series.

Abbreviations: **a.** S. = various proper names, as Samuel, Sarah, etc.; = Saint; so SS. = Saints; = Society (L. *societas*), as in F.R.S., Fellow of the Royal Society; F.S.A., Fellow of the Society of Antiquaries S.J., Society of Jesus; S.P.G., Society for the Propagation of the Gospel (in Foreign Parts); S.P.C.K., Society for the Promotion of Christian Knowledge; *Mus.* = Solo; *Chem.* = Sulphur; *Anat.* and *Zool.* = sacral (vertebra); *Her.* (also *l.c.*) = Sable; = snow (in ship's log-book). S.A. = (*a*) Salvation Army. (*b*) Sex Appeal. (*c*) small-arms. S.B. = smooth bore (gun); simultaneous broadcast. S.M. = Silver Medallist (in shooting competition); = short metre. S.P. = starting price (in betting). S.S. = steam ship. **b.** S. = South; also S.E., SE., South-east, etc. **c.** s. = L. *solidus* and so used for shilling(s); = second (of time). **d.** S.O.S: see SOS.

'S, a euphemistic shortening of *God's* in certain oaths; written continuously with the following word, as in 'SBLOOD, 'SDEATH. Cf. ZOUNDS.

's, repr. a shortened pronunc. of various monosyllables when unstressed. (Written continuously with the preceding word.) **1.** = *is*; see BE *v.* Now *colloq.* and *poet.* 1584. **2.** = *has*: see HAVE *v. colloq.* 1845. **3.** = US *pron.* Now *dial.* exc. in *let's* = let us (*colloq.*) 1588.

-s, *suffix*, forming advs.; orig. *-es*, identical with the suffix of the genitive sing. of many neut. and masc. sbs. and adjs. See also -WARDS, -WAYS.

Sabæan, Sabean (săbī·ăn), *a.* and *sb.* 1586. [f. L. *Sabæus*, Gr. Σαβαῖος (f. *Saba*, Σάβα, Arabic *Saba'*, ancient name of the people of Yemen, by Gr. and Roman writers imagined to be the name of the capital city) + -AN.] **A.** *adj.* Of or belonging to the ancient population of Yemen in Arabia. In poetic use, often with allusion to the ancient renown of the spices brought from Yemen. **B.** *sb.* One of the ancient inhabitants of Yemen 1607.

Sabaism (sēⁱ·bēⁱ,iz'm). Also **Sabeism, Tsabaism, Zabaism.** 1669. [f. Heb. *çābā* host + -ISM 2.] The worship of 'the host of heaven'; star-worship. Also sometimes used for SABIANISM. So **Sa·baist** 1662. **Sabai·stic** *a.*

‖**Sabaoth** (sæ·be,ǫþ). ME. [L., a. Gr. Σαβαώθ, a. Heb. *çᵉbāōth* pl. of *çābā* army.] A Heb. word (lit. 'armies', 'hosts') retained untranslated in the N.T. and the *Te Deum*, in the designation *The Lord* (*Lord God*) *of Sabaoth.* ¶ **b.** Confused with *sabbath.* SPENSER.

‖**Sabbat** (saba). 1652. [F.; a special application of *sabbat* SABBATH.] A 'witches' sabbath'; see SABBATH 3.

Sabbatarian (sæbătēᵊ·riăn), *a.* and *sb.* 1613. [a. L. *sabbatarius*, f. *sabbatum* SABBATH; see -ARIAN.] **A.** *adj.* †**a.** Of or pertaining to the Sabbath or its observance. **b.** Having relation to the tenets of the Sabbatarians. 1631. **B.** *sb.* **1.** A Jewish observer of the (Saturday) Sabbath 1613. **2.** A Christian who regards the Lord's Day as a Sabbath, deducing its obligation from the Fourth Commandment. Also, more usu., one whose observance of Sunday is excessively strict. 1620. **3.** A member of a Christian sect which maintained that the Sabbath should be observed on the seventh day of the week; a Seventh-day Baptist 1645.

2. I am not a S., I showed it by travelling on Sunday 1864. Hence **Sabbata·rianism,** S. principles or practice.

Sabbath (sæ·băþ). OE. [ad. L. *sabbatum*, Gr. σάββατον (partly through F. *sabbat*), ad. Heb. *shabbāth*, f. root *shābath* to rest. The initial cons. reflects the L. and Gr. forms, the final the Heb. Now often written with initial capital.] **1. a.** *orig.* The seventh day of the week (Saturday) considered as the day of religious rest enjoined on the Israelites by the fourth commandment of the Decalogue. b. Since the Reformation, often applied to 'the Lord's day', i.e. the first day of the week (Sunday) observed by Christians in commemoration of the resurrection of Christ 1509. c. *gen.* Applied occas. to the day of the week set apart for rest or worship by any religious body, e.g. to the Friday as observed by Mohammedans 1613. d. Applied to the sabbatical year of the Israelites. late ME. 2. *transf.* and *fig.* A time or period of rest; a cessation from labour, trouble, pain, and the like. late ME. 3. A midnight meeting (*witches' s.*) of demons, sorcerers and witches, presided over by the Devil, supposed in mediæval times to have been held annually as an orgy or festival. Also SABBAT. 1660.

1. a. The Primitive Church kept both the S. and the Lords day JER. TAYLOR. b. Severe and sunless remembrances of the Sabbaths of childhood HAWTHORNE. 2. Why will you break the S. of my days? POPE.

Comb.: **S.-school,** (*a*) = SUNDAY-SCHOOL; (*b*) a Jewish school held on the Saturday for giving religious instruction to children. Hence **Sa·bbathless** *a.* observing no S.

Sa·bbath-day·. ME. 1. = SABBATH 1 a. 2. = SABBATH 1 b. 1440. 3. *gen.* A Sabbath, a day of sacred rest 1755.

1. *Sabbath day's journey*, the distance (2,000 *ammōth* = 1,225 yards) which, according to Rabbinical prescription in the time of Christ, was the utmost limit of permitted travel on the Sabbath.

Sabbatian (sæbē·ʃiăn). 1708. [f. *Sabbatius* + -AN I.] A member of a sect founded by Sabbatius, who seceded from the Novatianists before 380 A.D.

Sabbatic (sæbæ·tik), *a.* 1649. [ad. F. *sabbatique*, ad. med.L. **sabbaticus*, a. Gr. σαββατικός, f. σάββατον SABBATH; see -IC 1.] Of or pertaining to the Sabbath; resembling or appropriate to the Sabbath.

Sabbatical (sæbæ·tikăl), *a.* 1599. [f. med.L. **sabbaticus* (see prec.) + -AL 1.] 1. Pertaining or appropriate to the Sabbath 1645. b. *S. river*: an imaginary river celebrated in Jewish legend, which was said to dry up on the Sabbath 1613. c. Of the nature of a Sabbath or period of rest 1836. 2. a. *S. year*: (*a*) the seventh year, prescribed by the Mosaic law to be observed as a 'Sabbath' in which the land was to remain untilled and all debtors and Israelitish slaves were to be released 1599; (*b*) in American universities, a year of absence from duty for the purposes of study and travel, granted to professors at certain intervals 1895. b. *S. millenary, millennium*: the last of the seven thousands of years which (on the analogy of the seven days of creation) were supposed to form the destined term of the world's existence 1646. Hence **Sabba·tical·ly** *adv.*, **-ness.**

Sabbatism (sæ·bătiz'm). *rare.* 1582. [ad. late L. *sabbatismus*, a. Gr. σαββατισμός, f. σαββατίζειν to keep the Sabbath, f. σάββατον.] 1. A sabbatical rest: in allusions to Heb. iv. 9. 2. The formal observance of the Sabbath 1611.

Sabbatize (sæ·bătəiz), *v.* late ME. [ad. L. *sabbatizare*, ad. Gr. σαββατίζειν, f. σάββατον; see -IZE 1 a.] 1. *intr.* To keep the Sabbath; to observe a specified day as a day of rest 1608. b. *fig.* To enjoy or undergo a period of rest analogous to a Sabbath. late ME. 2. *trans.* To observe or keep as a Sabbath; to assimilate to a Sabbath 1609. Hence **Sabbatiza·tion,** the action of sabbatizing.

‖**Sabella** (săbe·lă). 1851. [mod.L., perh. f. *sabulum* sand.] *Zool.* A tubicolous annelid of the family *Sabellidæ*.

Sabellian (săbe·liăn), *a.*[1] and *sb.*[1] late ME. [ad. eccl.L. *Sabellianus*, f. *Sabellius* (see B); see -AN.] *Theol.* A. *adj.* Pertaining to the Sabellians (see B) or their doctrine 1577. B. *sb.* One who accepts the view of Sabellius (an African heresiarch of the 3rd c.) that the Father, Son, and Holy Ghost are merely different aspects or modes of manifestation of one Divine person. late ME. Hence **Sabe·llianism,** belief in the S. doctrine of the Trinity.

Sabellian (săbe·liăn), *a.*[2] and *sb.*[2] 1601. [f. L. *Sabellus* + -IAN.] *Hist.* A. *adj.* Pertaining to a group of related peoples who inhabited certain parts of ancient Italy, comprising the Sabines, Samnites, and Campanians. B. *sb.* A person belonging to any of these peoples.

Sabian (sē·biăn), *sb.* and *a.* 1661. [f. Arab. *çâbi'* + -AN.] A. *sb.* 1. An adherent of a religious sect mentioned in three passages of the Koran (ii. 40, v. 73, xxii. 17), and by later Arabian writers. 2. In erroneous use: A worshipper of 'the host of heaven'; a star-worshipper 1716.

1. In the Koran the Sabians are classed with Moslems, Jews, and Christians, as believers in the true God. N.E.D.

B. *adj.* Pertaining to the Sabians (in both senses) 1796. Hence **Sa·bianism,** the religion of the Sabians; chiefly in erroneous use, worship of 'the host of heaven', star-worship.

Sabicu (sæbikū·). 1866. [Cuban Sp. *sabicú*.] A timber tree, *Lysiloma Sabicu*, native of Cuba, valued for the hardness and durability of its wood; the wood of this tree.

Sabine (sæ·bəin), *a.* and *sb.* late ME. [ad. L. *Sabinus*.] *Hist.* A. *adj.* Of or pertaining to the Sabines; see B. 1697. B. *sb.* One of a race of ancient Italy who inhabited the central region of the Apennines late ME.

Sable (sē·b'l), *sb.*[1] late ME. [a. OF., sable fur, also quasi-adj. in *martre sable* sable marten as the name of the animal and its fur. The OF. word is prob. from Slavonic.] 1. A small carnivorous quadruped, *Mustela zibellina*, nearly allied to the martens, and native of the arctic and sub-arctic regions of Europe and Asia. Also *Russian, Siberian s.* b. A pencil made of the sable's hair 1891. 2. The skin or fur of the sable. late ME. 3. A superior quality of Russian iron, so called from being orig. stamped with a sable 1815.

Comb.: **s.-mouse** [= G. *zobelmaus*] = LEMMING.

Sable (sē·b'l), *sb.*[2] and *a.* ME. [a. F., commonly identified with prec., although the fur of the sable is not black but brown.] A. *sb.* 1. *Her.* Black, as one of the heraldic colours; in engraving represented by horizontal and vertical lines crossing each other. Abbrev. *S, Sa.*, †*Sab.* 2. The colour black; black clothing, also, esp. as a symbol of mourning. *poet.* and *rhet.* late ME. †b. Blackness, darkness –1781. 3. *pl.* Mourning garments; a suit of black worn as an emblem of grief. *poet.* or *rhet.* 1602. 4. A book-name of several species of pyralid moths, esp. of the genera *Botys* and *Ennychia* 1832. 5. In full *s. antelope*: A large stout-horned antelope, *Hippotragus* (*Ægocerus*) *niger*, native of South and East Africa, the male of which is black in colour 1850.

2. Now haue ye cause to clothe yow in s. CHAUCER. 3. The sables she wore were not solely for the dead Earl OUIDA.

B. *adj.* 1. *Her.* Of a black colour; black 1470. 2. *gen.* Black. Chiefly *poet.* and *rhet.* Now, as applied to negroes, slightly *joc.* 1485. †3. Mournful –1780.

2. Was I deceiv'd, or did a s. cloud Turn forth her silver lining on the night? MILT. The ceremonies were performed by a s. archbishop 1815. Phr. *His s. Majesty*, the devil. 3. Such a s. state of mind as I labour under COWPER. Hence **Sa·ble** *v.* (chiefly *poet.*) *trans.* to blacken or darken; also, to clothe in sables.

‖**Sabot** (sabo). 1607. [F., prob. related to *savate*, Pr. *sabata* shoe.] 1. A shoe made of a single piece of wood shaped and hollowed out to fit the foot. 2. *Mil.* a. A wooden disk attached to a spherical projectile by means of a copper rivet for the purpose of keeping it evenly in place in the bore of the piece when discharged. b. A metal cup fixed by means of metal straps to a conical projectile, to cause it to 'take' the rifling of the gun. 1855. 3. *Mech.* A cutting armature at the end of a tubular boring-rod 1884. Hence **Saboted** (sæ·boud) *ppl. a.* shod with sabots.

Sabotage (sæ·botădʒ). 1910. [a. F., f. *saboter* to make a noise with sabots, execute badly, destroy wantonly, f. *sabot*; see prec. and -AGE.] The malicious damaging or destruction of an employer's property by workmen during a strike or the like; hence *gen.* any malicious or wanton destruction. Hence **Sa·botage** *v. trans.* to wreck or damage by s.; also *fig.*

Sabre (sē·bəɹ), *sb.* Also *U.S.* **saber.** 1680. [a. F., alteration of *sable*, a. G. *sabel* (now *säbel*). Perh. ult. of Oriental origin.] 1. A cavalry sword having a curved blade specially adapted for cutting. b. *fig.* Military force 1851. 2. A cavalry unit; a soldier armed with a sabre 1829.

Comb.: **s.-bill,** a S. Amer. dendrocolaptine bird of the genus *Xiphorhyncus*; **-rattler,** a reckless militarist; so **-rattling**; **-toothed** *a.* in *s.-toothed lion* or *tiger*, a large extinct feline mammal of the genus *Machairodus*, with long s.-shaped upper canines; also **s.-tooth** *a.* and *sb.* Hence **Sa·bre** *v. trans.* to cut, strike, or wound with a s.

Sabretache (sæ·brtaʃ). 1812. [a. F., ad. G. *säbeltasche*, f. *säbel* sabre + *tasche* pocket.] A leather satchel suspended on the left side by long straps from the sword-belt of a cavalry officer.

‖**Sabreur** (sabrör). 1845. [F.; f. *sabrer* to SABRE.] One who fights with a sabre; usu. applied to a cavalry soldier distinguished rather for bravery than for skill in war.

Sabulous (sæ·biŭləs), *a.* 1632. [ad. L. *sabulosus*, f. *sabulum* sand; see -OUS.] Sandy; consisting of or abounding in sand; arenaceous. b. *Med.* Applied to a granular secretion, esp. in the urinary organs 1670.

Sac[1]. [repr. OE. *saca*, accus. and gen. pl. of *sacu* SAKE.] *Old Eng. Law.* Properly only in *sac and soc* (or *soke*), a modernized form of the expression used in charters to denote certain rights of jurisdiction which by custom belonged to the lord of a manor, and which were specified (along with others) as included in the grant of a manor by the crown.

The priviledge called Sake is for a man to have the amerciaments of his tenants in his owne Court 1641.

Sac[2] (sæk). 1741. [a. F., or ad. L. *saccus* (see SACK *sb.*[1]) in mod.L. applications.] 1. *Biol.* Any natural bag-like cavity with its membranous covering, in an animal or vegetable organism. 2. *Path.* A pouch formed by the morbid dilatation of a part, the membranous envelope of a hernia, cyst, tumour, etc. 1802.

Saccate (sæ·keit), *a.* 1830. [ad. med.L. *saccatus*, f. *saccus* SAC[2]; see -ATE[2].] 1. *Bot.* Dilated into the form of a sac. 2. = ENCYSTED 1846.

Saccharate (sæ·kărēt), *sb.* 1815. [f. SACCHARIC + -ATE[1].] *Chem.* A salt of saccharic acid.

Saccharated (sæ·kăreitèd), *a.* 1784. [f. med.L. *saccharum* sugar + -ATE[3] + -ED[1].] Containing or made with sugar; sweetened.

Saccharic (săkæ·rik), *a.* 1800. [f. med. L. *saccharum* + -IC 1 b.] *Chem. S. acid*: (*a*) a dibasic acid formed by the action of nitric acid on dextrose; oxalhydric acid; (*b*) a monobasic acid forming crystalline salts prepared by the action of bases on glucoses. *S. ether*, an ether obtained from s. acid.

Sacchariferous (sækări·fĕrəs), *a.* 1757. [f. med.L. *saccharum* + *-fer* bearing + -OUS.] Yielding or containing sugar.

Saccharify (săkæ·rifəi, sæ·kărifəi), *v.* 1839. [f. as prec. + -(I)FY.] *trans.* To convert (starch) into sugar. Hence **Sa:ccharifica·tion,** the natural process by which starch and gum become converted into sugar.

Saccharimeter (sækări·mĭtəɹ). 1874. [a. F. *saccharimètre*, f. Gr. σάκχαρι (= σάκχαρον) sugar + μέτρον measure; see -METER.] A form of polariscope, an instrument for testing sugars by polarized light. So **Sacchari·metry** = SACCHAROMETRY. **Saccharime·tric, -al** *adjs.*

Saccharin (sæ·kărin). 1880. [f. med.L. *saccharum* or Gr. σάκχαρον + -IN[1].] *Chem.* 1. The anhydride of saccharic acid. 2. An intensely sweet substance obtained from coal-tar, used instead of sugar for sweetening food or drink. In non-techn. use commonly called **saccharine** (sæ·kărīn). 1885. Hence **Saccha·ri·nic** *a.* = SACCHARIC.

Saccharine (sæ·kărəin, -in), *a.* and *sb.* 1674. [f. as prec. + -INE.] A. *adj.* 1. Of, pertaining to, or of the nature of, sugar; characteristic of sugar; sugary. 2. Composed chiefly of sugar; of a plant, containing a large proportion of sugar; also, of urine, containing sugar in excess of what is normal 1710. 3. Resembling sugar. a. *Geol.* Of rocks: Granular in texture 1833. b. *Bot.* Covered with shining grains like those of sugar 1891.

1. *S. fermentation* = SACCHARIFICATION. 2. *S. dia-*

betes, diabetes characterized by excess of s. matter in the urine.

B. *sb.* Saccharine matter, sugar 1841.

Saccharo- (sæ·kǎrǫ), comb. form of Gr. σάκχαρον sugar, forming compounds with the sense 'partly saccharine and partly (something else)'; 'containing sugar and (something else)', as *saccharo-farinaceous*, etc.

Saccharoid (sæ·kǎroid), *a.* and *sb.* 1833. [f. Gr. σάκχαρον sugar + -OID.] **A.** *adj. Geol.* Having a granular texture resembling that of loaf-sugar. **B.** *sb. Chem.* A saccharine substance 1882. So **Saccharoi·dal** *a.* = A.

Saccharometer (sækărǫ·mǐtəɹ). 1784. [f. Gr. σάκχαρον sugar + -METER.] **1.** A form of hydrometer for estimating the amount of sugar in a solution by specific gravity. **2.** Used for SACCHARIMETER (*rare*) 1852. So **Saccharo·metry**, the process of determining the quantity of sugar in a solution.

‖**Saccharomyces** (sæ:kărǫməi·sīz). 1873. [mod.L., f. Gr. σάκχαρον sugar + μύκης mushroom.] A genus of ascomycetous fungi, including the yeast-fungi; a fungus of this genus, esp. the yeast-plant.

Saccharose (sæ·kărōus). 1876. [f. Gr. σάκχαρον sugar + -OSE.] *Chem.* Any one of the group of sugars having the formula $C_{12}H_{22}O_{11}$.

Saccharum (sæ·kărǒm). 1839. [med.L., a. Gr. σάκχαρον sugar.] An invert sugar prepared from cane sugar, used chiefly in brewing.

Sacchulmin (sækǒ·lmin). 1842. [f. med. L. *saccharum* sugar + ULMIN.] *Chem.* A brown substance obtained in the decomposition of sugar by dilute acids. So **Sacchu·lmic** *a.* in *s. acid*, an acid obtained by treating s. with alkaline solutions.

Sacciform (sæ·ksifǫ̆m), *a.* 1819. [ad. mod.L. *sacciformis*, f. *saccus* SAC[2]; see -FORM.] Having the form of a sac or pouch; sac-shaped.

Saccoon (săkū·n). *Obs.* exc. *Hist.* 1708. [Oral adoption of F. *seconde* (sǝkǭnd).] = SECONDE.

Saccular (sæ·kiŭlăɹ), *a.* 1861. [f. SACCULUS + -AR[1].] Of the nature of or resembling a sac.

Sacculated (sæ·kiŭleˑtĕd), *a.* 1835. [f. SACCULUS + -ATE[2] + -ED[1].] Composed of or divided into saccules. So **Sa·cculate** *a.* **Saccula·tion**.

Saccule (sæ·kiŭl). 1836. [Anglicized f. next.] A small sac, cyst, or bag; esp. the smaller of the two vesicles in the internal ear.

‖**Sacculus** (sæ·kiŭlǒs). *Pl.* **-li** (-ləi). 1621. [L., dim. of *saccus* SAC[2].] †**1.** A small bag containing medicaments -1693. **2.** *Anat.*, *Biol.* A small sac; a pouch-like dilatation 1728.

‖**Sacellum** (săse·lǒm). *Pl.* **sacella** (săse·lă). 1806. [L., dim. of *sacrum* shrine, neut. of *sacer* holy.] **1.** *Eccl. Arch.* A monumental chapel in a church; also, a small chapel in a village. **2.** *Rom. Antiq.* A small roofless temple consecrated to some deity 1832.

Sacerdocy (sæ·səɹdōusi). 1657. [ad. L. *sacerdotium* priestly office, f. *sacerdot-*, *sacerdos* priest; see SACERDOTAL *a.*] **a.** The sacerdotal character, spirit, or system. **b.** A priestly function or office.

Sacerdo·tage. *joc.* 1859. [f. L. *sacerdot-* (see next) with allusion to *dotage*.] **a.** The sacerdotal order, or the partisans of sacerdotalism. **b.** Sacerdotalism as characteristic of a religion in its 'dotage'.

Sacerdotal (sæsəɹdōu·tăl), *a.* late ME. [a. F., ad. L. *sacerdotalis*, f. *sacerdot-*, *sacerdos*, f. *sacri-*, *sacer* holy, sacred (neut. pl. *sacra* sacrifices) + *do-*, ablaut-var. of *da-* in *dare* to give.] **A.** *adj.* **1.** Of or belonging to the priests or priesthood; of or pertaining to a priest; befitting or characteristic of a priest; priestly. **b.** Holding the office of a priest 1681. **2.** Applied to doctrines that assert the existence in the Christian Church of an order of priests charged with sacrificial functions and invested with supernatural powers transmitted to them in ordination 1871.

1. That 's a s. thought, And not a soldier's BYRON. **2.** The sacramental and s. developments of Anglicanism 1871. Hence **Sacerdo·tally** *adv.*

Sacerdotalism (sæsəɹdōu·tăliz'm). 1847. [f. prec. + -ISM.] **1.** The sacerdotal spirit or system; the principles or practice of the priesthood. Chiefly dyslogistic: Undue assumption of authority on the part of the priesthood; pursuit of or excessive devotion to the interests of the priestly order. **2.** The assertion of the existence in the Christian church of a sacerdotal order (see prec. 2) 1856. So **Sacerdo·talist**, one who advocates or defends s. **Sacerdo·talize** *v. trans.* to make subservient to s.

Sachem (sēi·tʃĕm, sæ·tʃĕm). 1622. [a. Narragansett.] **1.** The supreme head or chief of some American Indian tribes. **2.** *U.S. Politics.* One of a body of twelve high officials in the Tammany Society of New York 1890.

Grand s., the head of the Tammany Society. Hence **Sa·chem-dom, -ship**, the position or 'realm' of a s.

Sachet (sæ·tʃet, F. saʃe). 1483. [F., dim. of *sac*:—L. *saccus* bag, SACK *sb.*[1]] †**1.** A small bag, a wallet (*rare*) -1487. **2.** A small perfumed bag or satchel 1838. **3.** A dry perfume made up into a packet for placing among articles of clothing, etc. 1855.

Sack (sæk), *sb.*[1] [OE. *sacc*, ad. L. *saccus* sack, sackcloth, a. Gr. σάκκος, ad. Heb. (perh. Phœnician) *saq*.] **I. 1.** A large bag oblong in shape and open at one end, usu. made of coarse flax or hemp, used for the storing and conveyance of corn, flour, fruit, wood, coal, etc. **2.** A sack with its contents; also, the amount usu. contained in a sack; hence as a unit of measure or weight for corn, flour, fruit, wool, coal, etc. ME. **3.** slang. *To give* (a person) *the s.*: to dismiss from employment or office; *transf.* to discard, turn off (a lover). So *to get the s.*: to receive one's dismissal. 1825

1. *The sack*, the punishment (awarded in ancient Rome to a parricide) of being sewn in a sack and drowned.

†**II.** Sackcloth, esp. as the material of penitential or mourning garments. Also, a piece or garment of sackcloth. -1620.

Comb. **s.-coal**, screened coal for delivery in sacks; **s. race**, a race in which each competitor is enveloped in a sack, the mouth of which he holds round his neck.

Sack (sæk), *sb.*[2] 1549. [a. F. *sac* (in phr. *mettre à sac*), ad. It. *sacco*, of doubtful origin.] The action of SACK *v.*[2]; sacking, plundering; esp. in phr. *to put to s.*

Those inhabitants who had favoured the insurrection expected s. and massacre MACAULAY.

Sack (sæk), *sb.*[3] *Obs.* exc. *Hist.* 1531. [Early 16th c. *wyne seck*, ad. F. *vin sec* 'dry wine'.] A general name for a class of white wines formerly imported from Spain and the Canaries. **b.** With qualifying word, as *Canary*, *Malaga*, *Sherris* or *Sherry s.* 1597.

If sacke and sugar be a fault, God helpe the wicked SHAKS.

Comb., in the names of beverages, etc., made with s., as **s.-cream, -mead, -posset, -whey.**

Sack (sæk), *sb.*[4] Also **sacque**. 1599. [Cf. G. *französischer sack*, Du. *zac*. Perh. transf. uses of SACK *sb.*[1]] **1.** †A loose kind of gown worn by ladies. Also, from the 18th c., an appendage of silk attached to the shoulders of such a dress, and forming a train. **2.** A loose-fitting coat the back of which is not shaped to the figure, but hangs more or less straight from the shoulders 1847.

1. My wife this day put on first her French gown, called a Sac PEPYS.

Sack (sæk), *v.*[1] late ME. [f. SACK *sb.*[1]] **1.** *trans.* To put into a sack; to pack or store (goods) in sacks. **b.** To put (a person) in a sack to be drowned. late ME. **2.** *colloq.* To 'pocket' 1807. **3.** *slang.* **a.** To 'give the sack' to, dismiss (a person) from, his employment or office. Chiefly *pass.* 1841. **b.** To beat in a contest 1820. **4.** *intr.* To bulge or 'bag' 1799.

1. It threshes, cleans, and finally sacks the grain 1845. **2.** To s. a reasonable profit 1830. **3. a.** The committee ought to be sacked 1890.

Sack (sæk), *v.*[2] 1547. [f. SACK *sb.*[2]] *trans.* To give over (a city, town, etc.) to plunder by the soldiery of a victorious army; to strip (a person or place) of possessions or goods; to plunder, despoil.

We sack't the City after nine Moneths siege 1634. Hence **Sa·cker**, one who sacks or plunders.

Sackage (sæ·kĕdʒ), *sb.* Now *rare*. 1577. [a. F. *saccage*, f. *sac* SACK *sb.*[2]] The action, or an act, of sacking (a city, etc.).

Sackbut (sæ·kbǒt). 1509. [a. F. *saquebute*, presumably identical with ONF. *saqueboute*, explained as a lance furnished with 'an iron hook for pulling men off their horses'. The first element is ONF. *saquier* to pull, draw.] An obsolete musical instrument; a bass trumpet with a slide like that of a trombone for altering the pitch. †**b.** A player on the sackbut -1647.

Sackcloth (sæ·kˌklǫþ). ME. [f. SACK *sb.*[1] + CLOTH.] A coarse textile fabric (now of flax or hemp) used chiefly in the making of bags or sacks and for the wrapping up of bales, etc.; sacking. late ME. **b.** As the material of mourning or penitential garb; also, as the coarsest possible clothing, indicative of extreme poverty or humility ME.

In s. and ashes (Bibl.), clothed in s. and having ashes sprinkled on the head as a sign of lamentation or abject penitence. Hence **Sa·ckclothed** *a.* clad in s.

Sackful (sæ·kful). 1484. [f. SACK *sb.*[1] + -FUL 2.] As much as would fill a sack; hence, a great quantity.

Sacking (sæ·kiŋ). 1707. [f. SACK *sb.*[1] + -ING[1].] A coarse woven material of flax, jute, hemp, etc., used chiefly in the making of sacks and bags. Also, a piece of such material.

Sackless (sæ·klĕs), *a.* [Late OE. *sacléas* (see SAC[1] and -LESS).] †**1.** Secure from accusation or from dispute; unchallenged, unmolested -1819. **2.** Not guilty, innocent. Now *arch.* OE. **b.** *Sc.* and *n. dial.* Innocent of wrong intent, guileless, simple; also, of a thing, harmless. Hence, feeble-minded; lacking energy, dispirited. 1600.

Sacque: see SACK *sb.*[4]

Sacral (sēi·krăl), *a.*[1] (*sb.*). 1767. [ad. mod. L. *sacralis*, f. SACRUM; see -AL.] *Anat.* Pertaining to the sacrum. **b.** Belonging to the lower part of the body 1803. **c.** *sb.* = *s. vertebra* 1854.

Sacral (sēi·krăl), *a.*[2] 1882. [f. L. *sacrum* sacred thing, rite, etc. (neut. sing. of *sacer*) + -AL 1.] *Anthropology.* Of or pertaining to sacred rites and observances.

Sacrament (sæ·krămĕnt), *sb.* ME. [a. F. *sacrement*, ad. L. *sacramentum*, f. *sacrare* to consecrate, f. *sacr-*, *sacer* SACRED. In Christian Latin the word was the accepted rendering of Gr. μυστήριον MYSTERY[1].] **1.** *Eccl.* Any one of certain rites of the Christian Church, of which Baptism and the Lord's Supper are held to be generally necessary to salvation.

Those who accept the number seven, and many of those who admit only two, hold that the sacraments differ from other rites in being channels by which supernatural grace is imparted. Others differentiate the two 'sacraments' from other observances by their paramount obligation as having been expressly commanded by Christ Himself, and by the special spiritual benefits arising from their faithful use.

2. *spec.* (with *the*). The Lord's Supper, Eucharist, or Holy Communion. Often called *the S. of the Altar, the Blessed S., the Holy S.* ME. **b.** The consecrated elements, esp. the bread or Host ME. **3.** In widened application: **a.** Something likened to the recognized sacraments, as having a sacred character or function; the pledge of a covenant between God and man ME. **b.** A type, token, sign, or symbol 1534. **c.** [After L. *sacramentum* as a rendering of μυστήριον.] A mystery; something secret or having a secret meaning. late ME. **4.** An oath or solemn engagement, esp. one which is ratified by a rite. (Chiefly as a Latinism.) late ME. **5.** *Rom. Law.* The *sacramentum* or pledge which each of the parties deposited or became bound for before beginning a suit 1880.

1. *Q.* What meanest thou by this word *S.*? *A.* I mean an outward and visible sign of an inward and spiritual grace given unto us [etc.] *Bk. Com. Prayer, Catechism.* **2.** Phr *To receive, take the s.*, to communicate. *To take* or *receive the s.* (*to do* something, or *upon* a matter), to receive Holy Communion as a confirmation of one's word. Ile take the S. on 't SHAKS. **3. b.** The Temple..was a figure, a S., or a signification of Christe 1563. **c.** This s., or hid trewthe WYCLIF *Dan.* ii. 30. **4.** Bound by no s. of military obedience to the state 1832.

attrib.: as **s.-money** the alms collected at Holy Communion, formerly used as a fund for poor-relief; **S. Sunday**, the Sunday on which the Lord's Supper is celebrated. So **Sa·crament** *v.* (*rare*) *trans.* to bind by an oath or solemn engagement; to make sacred, consecrate.

Sacramental (sækrăme·ntăl), *a.* and *sb.* late ME. [a. F. †*sacramental*, or ad. late L. *sacramentalis*; see prec. and -AL.] **A.** *adj.* **1.** Pertaining to, or of the nature of, a sacrament of the Church. **b.** *spec.* Pertaining to the sacrament of the Lord's Supper 1552. **c.** Of religious doctrine and the like: Based upon the sacraments 1871. **2.** Of the nature of, relating to, or expressed by, an outward sign or symbol 1534. **3.** Of an oath, obligation, etc.: Peculiarly sacred; ratified by a religious sanction 1460. **4.** *Rom. Law.* Belonging to an action in which a *sacramentum* or pledge was deposited by each of the parties beforehand 1861. **5.** *joc.* Of a form of speech: Sacred to the occasion; 'consecrated' 1896.

1. Afterwards it was brought so Sacramentall, that no adultery or desertion could dissolve it MILT. 3. A s. obligation 1863.

B. *sb. Eccl.* A rite, ceremony, or observance analogous to a sacrament, but not reckoned among the sacraments; e.g. the use of holy water and of holy oil, the sign of the cross 1450. Hence **Sacrame·ntalism** = SACRAMENTARIANISM. **Sacrame·ntalist** (*rare*) = SACRAMENTARIAN B. 1, 3. **Sa·cramenta·lity,** s. character. **Sacrame·ntally** *adv.* in a s. manner.

Sacramentarian (sækrămĕntē³·riăn), *a.* and *sb.* 1535. [f. eccl.L. *sacramentarius* SACRAMENTARY + -AN 1.] **A.** *adj.* **1.** *Hist.* Relating to the views held by the Sacramentarians concerning the Eucharist (see B. 1) 1640. **2.** *gen.* Relating to the sacraments (or to 'high' doctrine in regard to them) 1865. **B.** *sb.* **1.** *Hist.* A name given by Luther to those Protestant theologians (esp. Zwingli and Œcolampadius) who maintained that it is merely in a 'sacramental' or metaphorical sense that the bread and wine of the Eucharist are called the body and blood of Christ. Hence used in the 16th c. as a hostile name for all deniers of the Real Presence 1535. **2.** *Hist.* A nickname given to the early Methodists at Oxford 1733. **3.** One who holds 'high' doctrine as to the sacraments 1651. Hence **Sacramenta·rianism,** 'high' doctrine in regard to the sacraments.

Sacramentary (sækrăme·ntări), *a.* and *sb.* Now *rare.* 1538. [ad. med. and mod.L. *sacramentarius*; see SACRAMENT and -ARY[1] 1.] **A.** *adj.* = prec. A. 1. Of a person: Holding sacramentarian views. 1563. **B.** *sb.* **1.** *Hist.* = prec. B. 1. 1538. **2.** [med.L. *sacramentarium.*] An early form of office book in the Western Church, containing the rites and prayers belonging to the several sacraments 1624.

1. A few years later, a s. had ceased to be a criminal FROUDE. 2. The S. comprised the collects and the canon or prayers that never varied 1832.

‖**Sacrarium** (săkrē³·riŏm). *Pl.* **sacraria** (-riă). 1727. [L., f. *sacr-*, *sacer* holy; see -ARIUM.] **1.** *Rom. Antiq.* Any place in which sacred objects were deposited and kept; the adytum of a temple; also, a small apartment in a house where the images of the penates were kept 1746. **2.** *Eccl.* **a.** That part of a church immediately surrounding the altar or communion table; the sanctuary 1727. **b.** In R.C. use: = PISCINA 2. 1848. So †**Sacrary** = sense 1, 2 a -1727.

†**Sa·cre,** *v.* ME. [a. F. *sacrer*, ad. L. *sacrare*, f. *sacr-*, *sacer* sacred.] **1.** *trans.* To consecrate (the elements, or the body and blood of Christ) in the Mass -1485. **2.** To consecrate (a king or bishop) to office- 1648. **3.** To bless, sanctify, make holy -1677. **4.** To dedicate -1641.

Sacred (sē³·krĕd), *a.* and *sb.* ME. [f. prec. + -ED[1].] **A.** *adj.* **1. a.** Consecrated *to*; esteemed especially dear or acceptable *to* a deity. **b.** Dedicated, set apart, exclusively appropriated *to* some person or some special purpose 1667. **2.** Of things, places, persons and their offices, etc.: Set apart for or dedicated to some religious purpose; made holy by association with a god or other object of worship; consecrated, hallowed. late ME. **b.** Applied as a specific defining adj. to various animals and plants that are or have been considered sacred to certain deities 1783. **3.** *transf.* and *fig.* Regarded with or entitled to respect or reverence similar to that which attaches to holy things 1560. **b.** *esp.* as an epithet of royalty. Now chiefly *Hist.* or *arch.* 1590. **4.** Secured by religious sentiment, reverence, sense of justice, etc., against violation, infringement, or encroachment 1530. **b.** Of a person or his office: Sacrosanct, inviolable; protected by some sanction *from* injury or incursion 1565. **5.** [After L. *sacer.*] Accurst. Now *rare.* 1588.

1. The dove s. to Venus 1874. **b.** S. to the memory of Samuel Butler 1721. The papyrus, s. to literature 1811. 2. I trace the village, and the s. spire 1744. The s. boats of the dead 1857. *S. book, writing*, etc., one of those in which the laws and teachings of a religion are embodied. *S. concert*, a concert of s. music. *S. history*, the history contained in the Bible. *S. music*, music which accompanies religious words or which is intended for performance in a church, etc. *S. number*, a number (esp. seven) held peculiarly significant in religious symbolism. *S. poetry*, poetry concerned with religious themes. **b.** The S. Ibis (*I. religiosa*) 1840. The S. Monkey of the Hindoos (*Semnopithecus entellus*) 1870. 3. S. and sweet was all I saw in her SHAKS. To a feather-brained schoolgirl nothing is s. C. BRONTE. To obtain from Mr. Bentham's executors a s. bone of his great, dissected Master M. ARNOLD. 4. He assured them that their property would be held s. MACAULAY. **b.** The s. and vnuiolable power of the Tribunes 1565. S. from punishment 1845. 5. Our Empresse with her s. wit To villainie and vengance consecrate SHAKS.

Special collocations. **S. axe,** a mark on Chinese porcelain, supposed to designate warriors. **S. college:** see COLLEGE *sb.* 1. **S. fire** [L. *sacer ignis*], erysipelas. **S. malady** [L. *sacer morbus*], epilepsy. **S. War:** see WAR.

†**B.** *sb. pl.* [after L. *sacra* neut. pl.] Sacred rites or solemnities -1749. Hence **Sa·cred·ly** *adv.*, **-ness.**

†**Sacri·fical,** *a.* 1608. [ad. L. *sacrificalis*, f. *sacrificus*, f. *sacri-*, *sacer.*] Sacrificial.

Sacrificator (sæ·krifikē³tə̆ɹ). *rare.* 1548. [a. L.; see SACRIFY *v.*] One who sacrifices. So †**Sa·crificatory** *a.* belonging to sacrifice.

Sacrifice (sæ·krifəis), *sb.* ME. [a. F., ad. L. *sacrificium*, f. *sacrificus* SACRIFIC *a.*] **1.** Primarily, the slaughter of an animal as an offering to God or a deity. Hence, the surrender to God or a deity, for the purpose of propitiation or homage, of some object of possession. Also *fig.* the offering of prayer, thanksgiving, penitence, submission, etc. **2.** That which is offered in sacrifice; a victim immolated on the altar; anything offered to God or a deity as an act of propitiation or homage ME. **3.** *Theol.* The offering by Christ of himself to the Father as a propitiatory victim in his voluntary immolation upon the cross; the Crucifixion in its sacrificial character. late ME. **b.** Applied to the Eucharistic celebration regarded as a propitiatory offering of the body and blood of Christ in perpetual memory of the sacrifice offered by him in his crucifixion 1504. **4.** The destruction or surrender of something valued or desired for the sake of something having a higher or more pressing claim; the loss entailed by devotion to some other interest; also, the thing so devoted or surrendered 1592. **b.** A victim; one sacrificed to the will of another; also, a person or thing that falls into the power of an enemy or destructive agency. Now *rare.* 1697. **5.** A loss incurred in selling something below its value for the sake of getting rid of it 1844.

1. Divines divide Sacrifices into bloody, such as those of the old law; and bloodless, such as those of the new law 1727. 2. Make of your Prayers one sweet S. SHAKS. 3. **b.** He exhorteth the people to flee from the accustomed sacrifices of the masse 1560. 4. As rich shall Romeo by his Lady ly, Poore sacrifices to our enmity SHAKS. Phr. *The great, last,* or *supreme, s.*, death for one's country in war.

Sacrifice (sæ·krifəis), *v.* ME. [f. prec.] **1.** *trans.* To offer as a sacrifice; to make an offering or sacrifice of. **2.** *intr.* To offer up a sacrifice ME. **3.** *trans.* To give up (something) for the attainment of some higher advantage or dearer object 1706. **b.** To permit injury or ruin to the interests of (a person) for the sake of some desired object. Also *refl.* 1751.

1. The Picture of..Abraham sacrificing his son SIR T. BROWNE. 3. Henry..was never known to s. an inclination to the interest or happiness of another 1837. **b.** He is too much an artist to s. himself to his clothes 1873. Hence **Sa·crificer,** one who sacrifices; *spec.* a sacrificial priest.

Sacrificial (sækrifi·ʃăl), *a.* 1607. [f. L. *sacrificium* + -AL 1.] **1.** Pertaining to or connected with sacrifice. **2.** *Comm.* Involving 'sacrifice' or loss to the vendor 1895.

1. Raine Sacrificiall whisperings in his eare SHAKS. 2. Next week's s. sales 1895.

†**Sa·crify,** *v.* ME. [a. OF. *sacrifier*, ad. L. *sacrificare*, f. *sacrificus* SACRIFIC.] **1.** *trans.* To offer as a sacrifice -1590. **2.** *intr.* To offer sacrifice -1555.

Sacrilege (sæ·krilėdʒ). ME. [a. OF., ad.L. *sacrilegium*, f. *sacrilegus* one who steals sacred things or commits sacrilege, f. *sacri-*, *sacer* sacred + *-leg-*, *legere* to gather.] **1.** The crime or sin of stealing or misappropriating what is consecrated to God's service. In eccl. use, extended to include any kind of outrage on consecrated persons or things, and the violation of any sacred obligation. Also, an instance of this offence. **b.** *spec.* in pop. use as a name for robbery from a church, etc. 1820. **2.** *transf.* and *fig.* The profanation of anything held sacred. late ME.

1. After this adding s. to profanation he carried away the altar of incense 1734. 2. To kill a herald was, by the law of arms, s. FROUDE. Hence **Sa·crileger** (*arch.*), one who commits s. So **Sacrilegist** (sækrilī·dʒist).

Sacrilegious (sækrili·dʒəs, -ī·dʒəs), *a.* 1582. [f. L. *sacrilegium* SACRILEGE + -OUS.] **1.** Committing sacrilege; guilty of sacrilege. **2.** Involving sacrilege 1621.

1. The wicked sacrilegous, non-conformists 1696. Hence **Sacrile·gious·ly** *adv.*, **-ness.**

Sacring (sē³·kriŋ), *vbl. sb.* Now *literary.* ME. [f. SACRE *v.* + -ING[1].] **1.** The consecration of the eucharistic elements in the service of the Mass. **2.** The ordination and consecration of persons to certain offices, as those of bishop, king, queen ME.

Sa·cring-bell. late ME. [f. prec.] **1.** A small bell rung at the elevation of the Host. **2.** In post-Reformation times applied to a small bell rung to summon parishioners to morning service, or to mark the point in the Communion Service at which the people should go up to communicate 1598.

Sacrist (sē³·krist). 1577. [a. OF. *sacriste*, ad. med.L. *sacrista*, f. *sacer* sacred + *-ista*; see -IST.] An official charged with the custody of the sacred vessels, relics, vestments, etc., of a religious house or a church.

Sacristan (sæ·kristăn). late ME. [ad. med.L. *sacristanus*, f. *sacrista* SACRIST + -AN 1.] **a.** The sexton of a parish church. *Obs.* or *arch.* **b.** = SACRIST.

Sacristy (sæ·kristi). 1656. [a. F. *sacristie*, a. med.L. *sacristia*, f. *sacrista* SACRIST.] The repository in a church in which are kept the vestments, the sacred vessels, and other valuable property.

Sacro-[1] (sæ·kro, sē³·kro), assumed as comb. form of L. *sacer* sacred, as in **s.-pictorial** *a.*, relating to sacred portraiture; **-secular** *a.*, partly sacred and partly secular.

Sacro-[2] (sē³·kro), *Anat.*, used as comb. form of L. (*os*) *sacrum* SACRUM, forming compounds with the sense 'pertaining jointly to the sacrum and (some other part indicated by the second element)', as in *s.-coccygeal*, *-iliac* adjs.

Sacrosanct (sæ·krosæŋkt, sē³·kro-), *a.* 1601. [ad. L. *sacrosanctus*, prop. two words, *sacro* abl. of *sacrum* sacred rite, and *sanctus* pa. pple. of *sancire* to render holy or inviolable.] Of persons and things, esp. obligations, laws, etc.: Secured by a religious sanction from violation or encroachment; inviolable, sacred. Hence **Sa·crosa·nctity,** inviolability, sacredness.

Sacrum (sē³·krŏm). *Pl.* **sacrums, sacra.** 1753. [Subst. use of neut. sing. of *sacer* sacred, in *os sacrum.*] *Anat.* A composite, symmetrical, triangular bone which articulates laterally with the ilia, forming the dorsal wall of the pelvis and resulting from the ankylosis of two or more vertebræ between the lumbar and coccygeal regions of the spinal column.

Sad (sæd), *a.* and *adv.* [Com. Teut.: OE. *sæd*:—OTeut. **sado-* full, satiated :—Indo-Eur. **sətó-*; the word is a pa. pple. with suffix *-tó-* from the root **sā-* to satisfy.] **A.** *adj.* **I.** †**1.** Having had one's fill; sated, weary, or tired (of something) -1450. †**2.** Settled, firmly established, in purpose or condition; steadfast, firm, constant -1667. †**3.** Orderly and regular in life; of trustworthy character and judgement; grave, serious –1665. **b.** Of thought, consideration: Mature, serious. *Obs.* exc. *arch.* in phr. *in s. earnest.* 1485. **4.** Of persons, their feelings or dispositions: Sorrowful, mournful. late ME. **b.** Of looks, tones, gestures, costume, etc.: Expressive of sorrow. late ME. **c.** Of times, places, actions, etc.: Characterized by sorrow, sorrowful. late ME. †**d.** Morose, dismal-looking. SHAKS. **e.** Causing sorrow; distressing, calamitous, lamentable. late ME. **5.** Deplorably bad chiefly as an intensive. Often *joc.* 1694.

1. Yet of that Art they kan nat wexen sadde ffor vnto hem it is a bitter sweete CHAUCER. 2. Settl'd in his face I see S. resolution and secure MILT. 3. What woman nowe-a-dayes (that is sadde and wyse) will be knowne to haue skill of dauncing, &c.? 1579. 4. Th' Angelic Guards ascended, mute and s. For Man MILT. A sadder and a wiser man He rose the morrow morn COLERIDGE. I felt a little s. at the thought 1860. b. Where the love-lorn Nightingale Nightly to thee her s. Song mourneth well MILT. His s. enquiring eye 1792. c. A place.., s., noysom, dark MILT. 'Tis a s. life, for a woman to have no help from her husband in things that are good DE FOE. e. S. overthrow and foul defeat MILT. How s. is the condition of a Gentleman without Learning 1688. 5. *S. dog* cf. DOG *sb.* 3 b; *Sil.* You are an ignorant, ..impudent Coxcomb. *Braz.* Ay, ay, a s. Dog. 1706.

II. 1. Of material objects. †**a.** Solid, dense, compact; massive, heavy –1641. **b.** Of soil: Stiff, heavy. *Obs.* or *dial.* ME. **c.** Of bread, pastry, etc.: That has not risen properly; heavy; not thoroughly baked. Now *dial.* 1688. **2.** Of colour: Dark, deep. In later use: Not cheerful-looking; neutral-tinted, dull, sober. late ME. †**b.** Dark-coloured, sober-coloured –1711. †**3.** Of blows: Heavy –1578.

1. To those that..tell you..I am but as a feather, I shall be found sadder than lead STRAFFORD. 2. Colours lyght and s. 1578. She had always..been dressed in s. colours 1867. b. A Man..between 20 and 30 years of Age, pale Visage and s. Hair 1711.

B. *adv. Obs.* exc. *poet.* = SADLY.

Towards Eden..his grievd look he fixes s. MILT.

Sad (sæd), *v.* late ME. [f. SAD *a.*] **1.** *trans.* To make solid, firm, or stiff; to compress. Now *dial.* †**2.** To make sorrowful; to sadden –1810.

Sadden (sæ·d'n), *v.* 1600. [f. SAD *a.* + -EN[5].] **1.** *trans.* = SAD *v.* 1. Now *dial.* **2.** To render sad or sorrowful; to depress in spirits. Also, to give a sad appearance to. 1628. **b.** *intr.* To become sad or gloomy 1718. **3.** *Dyeing*, etc. To tone down (colours) by the application of certain chemicals 1791.

1. If Marle s. Land, or make it stiff or binding, you must dung it well 1707. 2. Her gloomy presence saddens all the scene POPE. b. Better be merry with the fruitful Grape Than s. after none, or bitter, Fruit FITZGERALD.

Saddle (sæ·d'l), *sb.* [Com. Teut.: OE. *sadol, -ul* :—OTeut. **saðuloz.*] **I. 1.** A seat for a rider, to be used on the back of a horse or other animal; esp. a concave seat of leather having side flaps and fitted with girths and stirrups. Also, an analogous kind of seat for use on a cycle. **2.** That part of the harness of a shaft-horse which takes the bearing of the shafts; a cart- or gig-saddle 1837.

1. *For the s.*, for riding purposes. *In the s.*, on horseback; *fig.* in office; also, in readiness for work. †(*I will*) *either win the s. or lose the horse* (or vice versa), said by one engaging in an adventure of which the issue will be either highly profitable or ruinous. *To lay, put*, or *set the s. upon the right horse*, to lay the blame on the right person.

II. Something resembling a saddle in shape or position. **1.** *Physical Geogr., Mining*, etc. **a.** A depression in a hill or line of hills. **b.** A long elevation of land with sloping sides; a ridge, esp. one connecting two hills; also, a similar formation of ice or snow. 1555. **2.** In mechanical uses, e.g. **a.** *Naut.* A block of wood, hollowed out above and below, fastened to a spar to take the bearing of another spar attached to it 1512. **b.** *Bridge-construction.* (*a*) A block on the top of a pier to carry the suspension cables. (*b*) A frame used in the construction of a pontoon-bridge. 1831. **c.** *Telegraphy.* A bracket to support the wire on the top of a pole or ridge 1867. **3.** *Cookery.* In full *s. of mutton*, etc. A joint of mutton, venison, etc., consisting of the two loins and conjoining vertebræ 1747.

attrib. and *Comb.*, as **s.-bar** *Glazing*, each of the small horizontal bars to which the lead panels are secured; **-gall**, a sore produced on the back of a horse by the chafing of the saddle; **-horse**, a horse used for riding; **-oyster**, any of certain anomioid bivalves, the shape of which resembles that of a saddle; **-pin**, the pin of a cycle saddle which fits into a socket on the cycle frame; **-roof**, a saddleback roof; **-room**, a room in which saddlery is kept; **-shaped** *a.* resembling a saddle in shape; *Geol.* anticlinal; **-shell** = *s.-oyster*; **-sore** *a.* chafed with the s.; **s. wire** *Telegr.*, the wire running along the tops of telegraph posts.

Saddle (sæ·d'l), *v.* [OE. *sadolian*, f. *sadol* SADDLE *sb.*] **1.** *trans.* To put a riding-saddle upon (a horse, etc.); freq. *to s. up.* Also *absol.* †**2.** *trans.* To ride, bestride (an animal) –1713. **3.** *intr.* To get into the saddle. In Colonial use, *to s. up.* 1835. **4.** *trans.* To charge or load *with* (a burden); now only *fig.* to load *with* (something) as a burden 1693. **5.** To put (a burden) *upon* (another's back) 1808. **6.** To bend downwards in the middle 1803.

1. He sadled vp his horse, and roade in post away 1587. Phr. *To s. and bridle* fig., to subject to control. 4. I'll s. him with this scrape SHERIDAN. 5. I found her only too eager to marry anyone upon whom she could s. her debts 1881. 6. Walls are cracked and roofs 'saddled' in every direction 1880.

Saddleback (sæ·d'lbæk), *sb.* and *a.* 1545. [f. SADDLE *sb.* + BACK *sb.*] **A.** *sb.* **1.** †**a.** *Archery.* A saddle-backed feather. **b.** A saddle-backed hill. **2.** *Arch.* A roof of a tower, having a gable at two opposite sides connected by a ridge-roof; a packsaddle roof 1849. **3.** Any of various birds and fishes; *esp.* **a.** The adult of either of the Black-backed Gulls, *Larus marinus* and *L. fuscus*; also *s. gull.* **b.** The male of the Greenland or Harp Seal (*Phoca grœnlandica*) when three years old; in full *s. seal.* **c.** A kind of oyster, considered unfit for human food. 1847. **4.** *Geol.* An anticlinal 1887. **B.** *adj.* **1.** = next 1677. **2.** *Geol.* Anticlinal 1854. **3.** Used for 'horse-back' 1899.

Saddle-backed (sæ·d'lbækt), *a.* 1545. **1.** Having the back, upper surface, or edge curved like a saddle; having a concavely curved outline. **2.** Of a horse: Having a considerable hollow behind the withers 1650. **3.** *Arch.* **a.** Of coping: Thicker in the middle than at the edges 1842. **b.** Of a tower: Having a saddleback 1870. **4.** Applied to birds having saddle-like markings on the back, as *s. crow*, the Grey Crow, *Corvus cornix* 1838.

Sa·ddle-bag. 1796. **1.** A bag carried at the saddle; esp. one of a pair laid across the back of a horse, behind the saddle. **2.** *attrib.* Applied to a fine quality of carpeting, made in sizes and designs imitating the saddle-bags carried in the East by camels 1882.

Sa·ddle-bow. Now *arch.* or *poet.* OE. [BOW *sb.*[1] Cf. G. *sattelbogen.*] The arched front of a saddle-tree or of a saddle.

Sa·ddle-cloth. 1481. A cloth placed on a horse's back beneath the saddle; †in early use, a foot-cloth, housing-cloth.

Saddled (sæ·d'ld), *ppl. a.* OE. [f. SADDLE *v.* + -ED[1].] **1.** Furnished with a saddle. **2.** Applied to fishes, insects, etc., having saddle-like markings 1803.

Saddler (sæ·dlər). late ME. [f. SADDLE *sb.* + -ER[1].] **1.** One who makes or deals in saddles or saddlery. **2.** *Mil.* An official who has charge of the saddlery in a cavalry regiment. Also *s. corporal, sergeant.* 1865. **3.** A saddle-horse. *colloq. U.S.* 1888. **4.** The saddleback seal; see SADDLEBACK 3 b. 1873.

Saddlery (sæ·dləri). 1449. [f. prec. + -Y[3].] **1.** The art or occupation of a saddler. **2.** *collect.* Articles made or sold by a saddler; saddles and other articles pertaining to the equipment of a horse 1796. **3.** A place where saddles, etc., are made or kept 1841.

Sa·ddle-tree. late ME. **1.** The framework which forms the foundation of a saddle. **2.** The N. Amer. tulip tree, *Liriodendron tulipifera* 1866.

Sadducaic (sædiŭkē·ik), *a.* 1840. [f. Gr. Σαδδουκαῖος (see SADDUCEE), after PHARISAIC.] Pertaining to or characteristic of the Sadducees.

Sadducean, -cæan (sædiŭsī·ăn), *a.* and *sb.* 1547. [f. late L. *Sadducæus* SADDUCEE + -AN 1.] **A.** *adj.* Of, belonging to, or resembling, the Sadducees. †**B.** *sb.* = next –1678.

Sadducee (sæ·diŭsī). OE. [ad. late L. *Sadducæus*, a. late Gr. Σαδδουκαῖος, f. late Heb. *Çaddūqī*, app. f. the personal name *Çaddūq* (English Bible Zadok).] **1.** A member of one of the three 'sects' (the others being the Pharisees and Essenes) into which the Jews were divided in the time of Christ. They denied the resurrection of the dead, the existence of angels and spirits, and the obligation of the unwritten law alleged by the Pharisees to have been handed down by tradition from Moses. **2.** A person of Sadducean disposition; a materialist, a denier of the resurrection. Also as *adj.* 1607. Hence **Sa·dduceeism**, the doctrine or tenets of the Sadducees; the character and spirit of the Sadducees; materialistic unbelief; denial of immortality.

Sade (sēⁱd), *v.* [OE. *sadian* :—W. Ger. **sadōjan*, f. **sado-* SAD *a.*] *intr.* and *trans.* To become or make weary.

Sa·d-iron. 1832. [f. SAD *a.* or *v.*] A smoothing iron, prop. a solid flat-iron, as dist. from a box-iron.

Sadism (sēⁱ·diz'm, sā·diz'm). 1888. [ad. F. *sadisme*, f. the name of the Count (usu. called 'Marquis') de *Sade* (1740–1814; infamous for his crimes and the character of his writings); see -ISM.] A form of sexual perversion marked by a love of cruelty. So **Sa·dist**, one affected with s. **Sadi·stic** *a.*

Sadly (sæ·dli), *adv.* ME. [f. SAD *a.* + -LY[2].] †**1.** Heavily –1633. †**2.** Firmly, tightly, closely –1485. †**3.** Steadfastly, firmly, fixedly, unchangingly –1622. †**4.** Seriously; in earnest; gravely, soberly –1777. **5.** Sorrowfully, mournfully ME. **6.** In a manner to cause sadness; lamentably, grievously, deplorably, badly 1658. **7.** *predic.*: In bad health, ill, poorly. Now *dial.* 1711.

1. An empty cart runs lightly away: but if it be soundly laden, it goes s. 1633. 4. This can be no tricke, the conference was s. borne SHAKS. 5. Musick to heare, why hear'st thou musick s.? SHAKS. 6. Authors..Are s. prone to quarrel COWPER. So **Sa·dness**, the condition or quality of being sad; †*in (sober) sadness*, in earnest, not joking.

‖**Safari** (săfā·ri). 1892. [Swahili, f. Arab. *safara* to journey, travel.] In East and Central Africa, a hunting expedition; the men, animals, and equipment of such an expedition; a caravan.

Safe (sēⁱf), *sb.* 1440. [orig. *save*, f. SAVE *v.*; later assim. to SAFE *a.*] A receptacle for the safe storage of articles; esp. **a.** A ventilated chest or cupboard for provisions; a meat-safe. **b.** A fire-proof and burglar-proof receptacle for valuables 1838.

Safe (sēⁱf), *a.* [ME. *sauf*, a. F. :—L. *salvus* uninjured, entire, healthy.] **I.** Free from hurt or damage. **1.** Unhurt, uninjured, unharmed; having escaped some real or apprehended danger. Now only with quasi-advb. force after verbs of coming, going, bringing, etc. ME. †**2.** In sound health, well, 'whole'; usu. healed, cured, restored to health –1526. †**3.** *Theol.* [After L. *salvus* in the Vulgate.] Delivered from sin or condemnation, saved; in a state of salvation, spiritually 'whole' –1562. †**4.** Mentally or morally sound or sane –1611.

1. The papers came s. to hand 1737. Phr. *S. and sound*, occas. *s. and sure.* *To be, arrive*, etc. *s.* (or *s. and sound*): a colloq. or epistolary formula for 'to be duly arrived'. 4. A Trade Sir, that I hope I may vse with a s. Conscience SHAKS. Are his wits s.? Is he not light of Braine? SHAKS.

II. Free from danger; secure. **1.** Not exposed to danger; not liable to be harmed or lost; secure. late ME. **2.** Of a place or thing: Affording security or immunity; not exposing to danger; not likely to cause harm or injury. late ME. **3.** *transf.* in S.-CONDUCT, SAFE-GUARD; hence with sbs. of similar meaning, as *s. convoy*, etc. 1536. **4.** Of an action, procedure, etc.: Free from risk, not involving danger or mishap, guaranteed against failure. Sometimes = free from risk of error, as in *it is s. to say..* 1568. **5.** Secured, kept in custody; unable to escape. Hence, not likely to come out, intervene, or do hurt; placed beyond the power of doing harm, not at present dangerous. 1600. **6. a.** Sure in procedure; not liable to fail, mislead, or disappoint expectation; trustworthy. **b.** Cautious, keeping to 'the safe side'. 1604. **7.** †**a.** With *of*: Sure to obtain –1846. **b.** *To be s.* followed by inf., is predicated of a person or thing to express the certainty of the fact or event involved in the predication. Hence used attrib. in colloq. phrases like 'He is a s. first' = he is s. to take a first class. 1790.

1. I greatly feare my monie is not s. SHAKS. Whil'st thou ly'st warme at home, secure and s. SHAKS. A person once infected with the small-pox is s. from having it a second time 1801. 2. A Station s. for Ships, when Tempests roar DRYDEN. That part of the world is at a s. distance DICKENS. 4. 'Tis never s. to despise an enemy DE FOE. *On the s. side*: with a margin of security against error. 5. *Provb.* S. binde, s. finde 1573. But Banquo's s.? *Mur.* I, my good Lord: s. in a ditch he bides. SHAKS. 6. b. My blood begins my safer Guides to rule SHAKS. 7. b. He'll win it, as s. as s.! 1860. Phr. *A s. catch.*

Special collocations. **S. deposit** (orig. *U.S.*), a place in which valuables are stored; also *attrib.* **S. edge,** a smooth edge of a file. **S. load,** a load which leaves a required margin of security against causing breakage or injury to a structure. Hence †**Safe** *v.* (*rare*) *trans.* to render s. or secure; to conduct safely *out of* -1611. **Sa·fe-ly** *adv.*, **-ness.**

Safe-conduct (sēⁱ·fkǭ·ndɒ̆kt), *sb.* ME. [a. F. *sauf-conduit*, f. *sauf* SAFE *a.* + *conduit* CONDUCT *sb.*] 1. The privilege, granted by a sovereign or other competent authority, of being protected from arrest or molestation while making a particular journey or travelling within a certain region. 2. A document by which this privilege is conveyed. late ME. 3. The action of conducting in safety; safe convoy ME.

1. *In, with s., under, upon (a) s.*; He had come over under a safe conduct, and he was not detained FROUDE. Hence †**Safe-conduct** *v. trans.* to lead convoy, or conduct safely -1639.

Safeguard (sēⁱ·fgaɹd), *sb.* [late ME. *save-garde*, a. F. *sauvegarde*, f. *sauve* fem. of *sauf* SAFE + *garde* GUARD *sb.*] 1. Protection, safety. Now *rare* or *Obs.* 2. Protection or security afforded by a specified person (or thing). Now *rare* or *Obs.* 1456. †3. = SAFE-CONDUCT 1. -1607. 4. = SAFE-CONDUCT 2. Also, a guard or escort granted for the same purpose. 1633. 5. A warrant granted by a military commander to protect a place from pillage. Also, a guard or detachment of soldiers sent to protect the place. 1706. 6. *gen.* Something that offers security from danger; a defence, protection; e.g. a legal proviso or a stipulation serving to prevent some encroachment; a course of action, a habit or sentiment, tending to protect the subject against some temptation 1471. †7. An outer skirt or petticoat worn by women to protect their dress when riding -1789.

2. Phr. *In, under (the) s. of.* 3. On safegard he came to me SHAKS. 4. Whosoever shall presume to violate a Save-gard, shall die without mercy 1642. 6. His owne valour was his s. 1634. The old reticence of the Bench was a grand s. of its dignity 1891.

Safeguard (sēⁱ·fgaɹd), *v.* 1494. [f. prec.] *trans.* To keep secure from danger or attack; to guard, protect, defend. Now chiefly with immaterial obj. (e.g. interests, rights); *spec.* = PROTECT *v.* 2. Hence **Sa·feguarding** *vbl. sb.* = PROTECTION 4.

Safe-hold. 1793. [f. HOLD *sb.*[1]; cf. STRONGHOLD.] A place of safety from attack.

Sa·fe-kee·ping, *vbl. sb.* late ME. The action of keeping safe; protection, custody.

Safety (sēⁱ·fti). [late ME. *sauvete*, a. F. *sauveté*, ad. med.L. *salvitatem*, f. *salvus* SAFE.] 1. The state of being safe; exemption from hurt or injury; freedom from danger. †b. Sometimes *pl.* = the safety of more than one person -1814. †2. Close custody or confinement -1595. †3. A means or instrument of safety; a protection, safeguard -1793. 4. The quality of being unlikely to cause hurt or injury; freedom from dangerousness; safeness 1717. 5. *Engineering. Factor* or *coefficient of s.*: the ratio between the strains put upon any material and the ultimate strength of the material 1858. 6. In full *s.-bolt.* A contrivance for locking the trigger of a gun, so as to prevent accidental discharge. Also, a gun fitted with this 1881. 7. In full *s. bicycle.* The type of bicycle now in use, differing from its predecessor in the lower position of the saddle, whereby greater safety is afforded to the rider 1877.

1. It is..his duty..not to hazard the s. of the Community *Junius Lett.* *Provb.* There is s. in numbers. Phr. *In s.*: safe(ly). *To play for s.* (Billiards): Of a player, to leave his opponent's ball in such a position as to make his next stroke a very difficult one; hence *gen.* (usu. with derogatory implication) to act with circumspection so as not to be exposed to danger or risk. 2. *Rom. & Jul.* v. iii. 183. 4. *S. first*: a maxim or slogan inculcating caution, esp. on the highway.

attrib. Used freely since *c* 1800 as a specific designation for contrivances for ensuring safety, or for implements, machines, etc., constructed with a view to safety in use; as **s. bicycle** (see sense 7); **s. bolt, catch** (see sense 6); **s. cage,** (*a*) the wire guard of a safety lamp; (*b*) a miner's cage fitted with apparatus to prevent its falling if the rope breaks; **s. curtain,** a fireproof curtain in a theatre cutting off the auditorium from the stage; **s. fuse,** a fuse which can be ignited at a safe distance from the charge; **s. lamp,** a miner's lamp the flame of which is so protected that it will not ignite fire-damp; **s. match,** one which ignites only when rubbed on a prepared surface; **-razor,** a razor provided with guards for the blade.

Sa·fety-pin. 1857. 1. A pin for fastening clothing, bent back on itself so as to form a spring, and with a guard or sheath to cover the point and prevent its accidental unfastening. 2. A pin used for fastening, locking, or securing some part of a machine 1878.

Sa·fety-valve. 1797. 1. A valve in a steam-boiler which automatically opens to permit steam to escape when the pressure is becoming dangerous. Also, a similar valve opening inwards, to admit air when a partial vacuum has been formed. 2. *fig.* An opening or channel for 'letting off steam', giving vent to excitement, or the like 1818. 3. Phr. *To sit on the s.*, to follow a policy of repression.

Safflower (sæ·flauəɹ). 1562. [a. Du. *saffloer(s*, a. OF. *saffleur*, a. early It. *saffiore.* Ult. origin obsc.] 1. The dried petals of the *Carthamus tinctorius*, also the red dye produced from these petals. 2. The thistle-like plant *Carthamus tinctorius*, extensively cultivated for the dye obtained from its flowers; the seeds yield an oil used for lamps 1682.

Saffron (sæ·frən), *sb.* and *a.* ME. [a. F. *safran*, f. (ult.) Arab. *za'farān*, of unkn. origin.] A. *sb.* 1. An orange-red product consisting of the dried stigmas of *Crocus sativus* (see 2). Now used chiefly for colouring confectionery, liquors, etc., and for flavouring. b. *Indian s.*: any plant of the genus *Curcuma* 1727. 2. The Autumnal Crocus, *Crocus sativus*, which produces saffron. late ME. b. Bastard S. = SAFFLOWER 2; called also American, Dyer's, †Mock S. Meadow or Wild S., *Colchicum autumnale.* 1548. 3. The orange-yellow colour of saffron (sense 1). late ME.

Comb.: **s. cake,** a cake flavoured with s.; **s. wood,** the timber of a S. African tree, *Elæodendron croceum.*

B. *adj.* Resembling saffron in colour 1567.

There let Hymen oft appear In S. robe MILT.

Collocations: **s. butterfly, moth,** collectors' names for certain lepidoptera having yellow wings; **s. plum,** a W. Indian sapotaceous tree (*Bumelia cuneata*) having a yellow fruit. Hence **Sa·ffron** *v.* (*rare*) *trans.* to season or dye with s.; to give a s.-yellow colour to. **Sa·ffroned** *a.* coloured with, or having the colour of, s.; flavoured with s. **Sa·ffrony** *a.* (*rare*) of a colour somewhat resembling s.

Safranin (sæ·frănin). 1868. [f. F. *safran* SAFFRON *sb.* + -IN [1].] *Chem.* a. The yellow colouring matter of saffron. b. A coal-tar colour which dyes yellowish-red.

Sag (sæg), *sb.* 1580. [f. next.] The action of sagging. 1. *Naut.* Movement or tendency to leeward. 2. In a rope, wire, etc. supported at two points: The dip below the horizontal line, due to its weight 1861. 3. A sinking or subsidence; quasi-*concr.* a place where the surface has subsided, a depression 1872. 4. *Comm.* A decline in price 1891.

Sag (sæg), *v.* Infl. **sagged, sagging.** late ME. [perh. conn. w. MDu. *zakken*, Norw. dial. *sakka* to subside, settle down.] 1. *intr.* To sink or subside gradually, by weight or pressure. b. Of a part of the body (occas. of a person): To droop; to sink or hang *down* loosely 1526. c. Of a garment: To hang unevenly, to slip out of position. Now chiefly *dial.* and *U.S.* 1592. d. To bend or curve downwards in the middle, from its own weight or superincumbent pressure. Said, e.g., of a rope supported at two points, of a beam, plank, etc. 1753. 2. To decline to a lower level, through lack of strength or effort. (Common in U.S.) 1508. b. *Comm.* To decline in price 1887. 3. To drag oneself along wearily or feebly 1573. 4. *Naut.* Of a ship or boat: To drift, be carried out of the intended course. Chiefly in the phr. *to s. to leeward.* 1633. 5. *trans.* To cause to bend downwards in the middle 1755.

1. The old pavements have sunk or sagged considerably DARWIN. b. The head slowly sagged down on to the cushions 1902. d. One..comes to wonder why the whole ceiling does not s. 1886. 2. The minde I sway by, and the heart I beare, Shall neuer sagge with doubt, nor shake with feare SHAKS. 4. We're sagging south on the Long Trail KIPLING. 5. Their bottoms were thus sagged down by the cargoes 1777.

‖**Saga** (sā·gă). 1709. [ON. and Icel. *saga* = OE. *sagu* SAW *sb.*[2]] 1. Any of the narrative compositions in prose that were written in Iceland or Norway during the Middle Ages; in Eng. use often applied *spec.* to those which embody the traditional history of Icelandic families or of the kings of Norway. Also *transf.*, a story of heroic achievement or marvellous adventure. ¶2. (Partly after G. *sage*). A mythical story, which has been handed down by oral tradition; historical or heroic legend 1864.

1. *transf.* Dick delivered himself of the s. of his own doings KIPLING. 2. The Sagas of Guy of Warwick and Bevis of Hampton 1883.

Comb. **s.-man** [= ON. *sǫgumaðr*], a writer of sagas.

Sagacious (săgēⁱ·ʃəs), *a.* 1607. [f. L. *sagacem, sagax*, f. the root **săg-* (= OTeut. **sōk-* SEEK *v.*) in *sagire* to discern acutely.] †1. Acute in perception, esp. by smell -1732. 2. Gifted with acuteness of mental discernment; of keen penetration and judgement; shrewd 1650. b. Characterized by sagacity 1831. 3. Of animals: Intelligent 1759.

2. True Charity is s., and will find out hints for beneficence SIR T. BROWNE. b. This s. conjecture 1857. Hence **Saga·cious-ly** *adv.*, **-ness.**

Sagacity (săgæ·siti). 1548. [ad. F. *sagacité*, ad. L. *sagacitatem*, f. *sagacem* SAGACIOUS *a.*; see -ITY.] The quality of being sagacious. †1. Acute sense of smell -1798. 2. Acuteness of mental discernment; keenness and soundness of judgement; penetration, shrewdness 1548. b. *pl.* Sagacious observations 1866. 3. Of animals: Exceptional intelligence 1555.

1. Some [animals] show that nice s. of smell COWPER. 2. Men of skill and s. do sometimes foretel futurities 1693. A man of great s. in money matters DICKENS. 3. The s. of the beaver in cutting down trees 1837.

Sagamore (sæ·gămōəɹ). 1613. [a. Penobscot *sagamo*; see SACHEM.] = SACHEM.

‖**Sagan** (sēⁱ·găn). 1625. [Late (Talmudic) use of Heb. *sāgān* or *segen*, a. Assyrian *shaknu* prefect (of conquered territory). In the Bible the word denotes a civil governor.] *Jewish Antiq.* The deputy of the Jewish high-priest; the second highest functionary of the Temple.

‖**Sagapenum** (sægăpī·nɒ̆m). 1579. [Late L., a. Gr. σαγάπηνον a plant, prob. *Ferula persica*; also its gum.] A gum-resin, the concrete juice of *Ferula persica*, formerly used as an anti-spasmodic and emmenagogue, or externally. Also *gum s.*

Sagathy (sæ·găþi). *Obs.* exc. *Hist.* 1707. [In Fr. *sagatis*, Sp. *sagati*; origin unkn.] A light-weight stuff made either of silk and wool or silk and cotton. b. *attrib.* or *adj.* Made of s. 1711.

Sage (sēⁱdʒ), *sb.*[1] [ME. *sauge*, a. F. :—L. *salvia.*] 1. A plant of the genus *Salvia*, of the *Labiatæ*; esp. *S. officinalis*, an aromatic culinary herb. Hence, the dried leaves of this plant used in cooking. 2. Cookery. *S. and onions*: a stuffing chiefly composed of those ingredients, used for goose, duck, pork, etc. Also *s.-and-onion stuffing.*

attrib. and *Comb.*, as *s. ale, bread, wine*, etc.; also **s.-brush, -bush,** a collective name applied to various species of *Artemisia*, esp. *A. tridentata*; **-cheese,** a kind of cheese which is flavoured and mottled by mixing a decoction of sage-leaves with the cheese-curd; **-green,** a dull greyish green resembling that of the foliage of the s.-plant *Salvia officinalis*; **s. tea,** an infusion of s.-leaves, used as a stomachic and slight stimulant; **-willow,** a dwarf grey American willow, *Salix tristis.*

b. In the names of animals, etc. found chiefly in the sage-brush districts of N. America, as **s.-cock, grouse,** the largest grouse found in America, *Centrocercus europhasianus*; **s. hare** = *s. rabbit*; **s. hen,** the female of the sage grouse; **s. rabbit,** a small hare, *Lepus artemisia*; **-sparrow,** a sparrow of the genus *Amphispiza*, esp. *A. belli*; **s. thrasher,** the mountain mocking bird, *Oreoscoptes montanus.* Hence **Sa·gey, sa·gy** *a.* (*rare*) of the nature of s.

Sage (sēⁱdʒ), *a.* and *sb.*[2] ME. [a. F. :—Com. Rom. *sabio* :—pop. L. **sapius*, f. *sapere* to be wise.] **A.** *adj.* Now *literary.* **1.** Of a person: Wise, discreet, judicious. In mod. use: Practically wise, rendered prudent or judicious by experience. **b.** Of advice, conduct, etc.: Characterized by profound wisdom; based on sound judgement 1531. **c.** Of the countenance, bearing, etc.: Exhibiting sageness or profound wisdom. Now usu. somewhat *ironical.* 1816. †**2.** Grave, dignified, solemn –1644.

1. S. graue men SHAKS. The wise reasoning of a certain s. magistrate BERKELEY. b. Little thought he of this s. caution MILT. 2. Great Bards beside In s. and solemn tunes have sung, Of Turneys MILT.

B. *sb.* A man of profound wisdom; *esp.* one of those persons of ancient history or legend who were traditionally famous as the wisest of mankind; hence, one entitled to a like degree of veneration with these. Occas. in weaker sense, a wise man. ME. **b.** Used playfully or ironically 1751.

A Starr.. proclaims him com, And guides the Eastern Sages, who enquire His place MILT. *The seven sages of Greece*: Thales, Solon, Periander, Cleobulus, Chilon, Bias, and Pittacus, to each of whom some wise maxim is attributed by ancient writers. b. The sages of the village 1822. Hence **Sa·ge·ly** *adv.*, **-ness.**

‖**Sagene**[1] (sa·ʒen). 1737. [Russ.] A measure of length used in Russia, equal to seven English feet.

Sagene[2] (sădʒī·n). *rare.* 1846. [ad. L. *sagena*, a. Gr. σαγήνη.] A fishing-net; *fig.* a network (of railways, etc.).

Sagenite (sădʒĭ·nəit). 1802. [f. Gr. σαγήνη + -ITE[1] 2 b.] *Min.* A variety of rutile in which slender crystals are interlaced, forming a network. Hence **Sageni·tic** *a.*

Saggar (sæ·găɹ), **seggar** (se·găɹ), *sb.* 1768. [Prob. a contr. of SAFEGUARD *sb.*] **1.** A protecting case of baked fire-proof clay in which the finer ceramic wares are enclosed while baking in the kiln. **2.** The clay of which saggars are made 1839.

Saginate (sæ·dʒineɪt), *v. rare.* 1623. [f. L. *saginat-*, *saginare*, f. *sagina* process or means of fattening.] *trans.* To fatten (animals). So **Sagina·tion** 1607.

‖**Sagitta** (sădʒi·tă). 1594. [L., lit. an arrow.] **1.** *Astr.* A northern constellation lying between *Hercules* and *Delphinus* 1704. **2.** *Geom.* The versed sine of an arc 1594. **3.** *Arch.* The keystone of an arch 1703. **4.** The middle horizontal stroke in the Greek letter ϵ 1864. **5.** *Anat.* The sagittal suture 1891. **6.** *Zool.* **a.** One of the otoliths of a fish's ear 1888. **b.** One of the components of certain sponge-spicules 1898.

Sagittal (sădʒi·tăl), *a.* 1541. [ad. mod.L. *sagittalis*, f. L. *sagitta* arrow; see -AL 1.] **1.** *Anat.* **a.** *S. suture*: the median suture between the parietal bones of the skull. **b.** Pertaining to the sagittal suture; pertaining to or lying in the median longitudinal antero-posterior plane of the body, or to any plane parallel with this 1831. **2.** Pertaining to an arrow; resembling an arrow or an arrow-head in shape (*rare*) 1656. Hence **Sagi·ttally** *adv. Anat.* 'in the direction of the s. plane'.

‖**Sagittarius** (sædʒitē·riŏs). late ME. [L., archer.] **1.** *Astr.* (With capital S.) The zodiacal constellation of the Archer; hence, the ninth sign of the zodiac, which the sun enters about 22 Nov. **b.** The mythical Centaur who was fabled to have been transformed into this constellation 1590. **2.** *Her.* A bearing representing a centaur with a drawn bow 1619.

Sagittary (sæ·dʒitări). late ME. [ad. L. *sagittarius* pertaining to arrows, as sb. an archer; f. *sagitta* arrow.] †**1.** *Astr.* = prec. 1. –1788. **2.** A centaur; *spec.* the centaur who according to mediæval romance fought in the Trojan army against the Greeks 1509. **3.** A representation of a centaur or of a mounted archer; *spec.* in *Her.* = prec. 2. 1610. **4.** An archer 1832.

Sagittate (sæ·dʒiteɪt), *a.* 1760. [ad. mod. L. *sagittatus*, f. L. *sagitta* arrow; see -ATE[2].] *Bot.* and *Zool.* Shaped like an arrow-head. So **Sa·gittated** *a.* 1752.

Sago (sē·go). 1555. [a. Malay *sāgū.*] **1.** The tree from which sago (see 2) is obtained. **2.** A species of starch prepared from the pith of the trunks of several palms and cycads, esp. *Metroxylon læve* and *M. Rumphii*, chiefly used as an article of food 1580.

2. *French s.*, common arrowroot. *Japan s.*, the s. prepared from various species of *Cycas*. *Pearl s.*: see PEARL.

attrib. and *Comb.*: **s.-palm (tree)** = sense 1; **-spleen,** amyloid degeneration of the Malpighian corpuscles of the spleen, resembling boiled sago.

Sagoin (săgoi·n). 1607. [a. F. *sagouin*, a. Pg. *saguim*, a. Guarani *sagui*, *çagui.*] A small S. Amer. monkey, *esp.* one of the genus *Callithrix.*

‖**Sagum** (sē·gŏm). *Pl.* **saga.** 1600. [L.; also *sagus*, = late Gr. σάγος; said to be of Gaulish origin.] *Rom. Antiq.* A Roman military cloak; also, a woollen cloak worn by the ancient Gauls, Germans, and Spaniards.

Sahara (săhā·ră). 1613. [a. Arab. *çaḥra* desert.] The great desert of Libya or northern Africa. (With capital S.) **b.** *transf.* and *fig.* A desert, wilderness 1862. Hence **Saha·ran, Saha·rian, Saha·ric** *adjs.*

‖**Sahib** (sā·hib). 1627. [Urdū use of Arab. *çāḥib*, orig. 'friend'.] A respectful title used by the natives of India in addressing an Englishman or European (= 'sir'); also, in native use, an Englishman or European. Also affixed as a title (= 'Mr.' prefixed) to the name or office of a European. (See also MEM-SAHIB.)

Sahidic (săhi·dik), *a.* 1825. [f. Arab. *ṣa'īd* (with article *aṣ-ṣa'īd*, lit. 'the Upper', a name for Upper Egypt) + -IC.] Belonging to the dialect of Coptic spoken in Thebes and Upper Egypt. Also quasi-*sb.*, the S. language, or the S. version of the Bible.

Sahlite (sā·ləit). 1807. [a. G. *sahlit*, f. *Sahla* (*Sala*) in Sweden; see -ITE[1] 2 b.] *Min.* A variety of pyroxene.

‖**Sai** (sā·i). 1774. [a. Brazilian *sahy*, *çahy.*] A S. Amer. monkey, *Simia capucina.*

‖**Saic** (seɪ·ĭk). 1667. [a. F. *saïque*, ad. Turkish *shāīqā.*] A kind of sailing vessel common in the Levant.

Said (sed), *ppl. a.* ME. [pa. pple. of SAY *v.*[1]] **1.** Named or mentioned before. (Also *abovesaid*, *aforesaid.*) †**2.** Spoken, uttered; in phr. *s. saw* –1659.

Saiga (sē·gă, sai·gă). 1801. [a. Russ.] A kind of antelope (*S. tartarica*) of the steppes of Russia. Also *s.-antelope.*

Sail (sē·l), *sb.*[1] [Com. Teut.: OE. *seg(e)l* :—OTeut. **seglom*. Ulterior origin obsc.] **1.** One of the shaped pieces of canvas or other textile material fastened to the masts, spars, or stays of a vessel, so as to catch the wind and cause the vessel to move through the water. Also occas. a similar apparatus for propelling a wind-driven carriage. **b.** *transf.* Applied to the wing of a bird (*poet*). Also *techn.* in Falconry, the wing of a hawk. 1590. **2.** Sails collectively. late ME. **3. a.** In collective sing. (also †in pl.) chiefly with numeral: (So many) sailing-vessels. late ME. **b.** A ship or other vessel, esp. as descried by its sails 1517. **4.** An apparatus (now usu. an arrangement of boards) attached to each of the arms of a windmill for the purpose of catching the wind. Also (windmill) sails collectively, surface presented by the sails. ME. **5.** *Zool.* **a.** The large dorsal fin of the sail-fish. **b.** One of the two large tentacles of the Nautilus, formerly believed to be used as sails. 1817. **6.** *S. Afr.* A tarpaulin or canvas sheet for covering a wagon 1850.

1. Thy tacklings are loosed..they could not spread the saile *Isa.* xxxiii. 23. *fig.* Where Tullie doth set vp his saile of eloquence ASCHAM. b. The mountain eagle..Spread her dark sails on the wind SCOTT. 2. The Admiral..carried all s. 1806. *Full s.*: a sail (or sails collectively) filled by the wind; the condition of a ship with sails so filled. *At*, †*with full sail(s* [= L. *pleno velo*, *plenis velis*, F. *à pleines voiles*], (sailing) with a strong favourable wind, at full speed; so also *full s.* as advb. phr. In mod. use, *in full s.* is applied to describe the condition of a ship with all sails set. *Under s.*, having the sails set. 3. The Royal navy comprised in all twenty-seven s. 1863. †*Sail of the line*; a squadron of the largest ships of the royal navy. b. A S., a S. Where? Fair by us. 1669.

Comb.: **s.-arm,** one of the beams of a windmill: = WHIP *sb.* III. 2; **-axle,** the axle on which the sails of a windmill revolve; **-boat** (*U.S.*), a sailing-boat; **-fish,** any of various fishes, as *Selachus maximus*, having a large dorsal fin; **-fluke,** the whiff, *Rhombus megastoma*; **-hook,** a small hook for holding the seams of a sail while it is being sewn; **-loft,** a place where sails are constructed; **-maker,** one whose business it is to make, repair, or alter sails; **-needle,** a large needle used in sewing canvas; **-room,** a room (in a ship) for storing sails; **-winged** *a. poet.* [after L. *velivolus*], (*a*) of ships, having sails that serve as wings. (*b*) *transf.* as an epithet of the sea; (*c*) having wings like sails. Hence **Sai·lless** *a.* having no sails or ships.

Sail (sē·l), *sb.*[2] 1602. [f. next.] **1.** An act of sailing; a voyage or excursion on a sailing-vessel 1604. **2.** Only in *nonce-uses.* A number sailing 1608. **3.** Sailing qualities; speed in sailing 1602.

1. Phr. *To take s.*, to embark. 2. Wee haue descryed.., a portlie saile of ships SHAKS.

Sail (sē·l), *v.* [OE. *siglan*, *segl(i)an* :—OTeut. type **segljan*, f. **seglom* SAIL *sb.*[1]] **I.** *intr.* **1.** Of persons: To travel on water in a vessel propelled by the action of wind upon sails; now often, to travel on water in a vessel propelled by any means other than oars; to navigate a vessel in a specified direction. **2.** Of a ship or other vessel: To move or travel on water by means of sails, or (in mod. use) by means of steam or any other mechanical agency ME. **3.** To begin a journey by water; to set sail. late ME. **4.** *transf.* To glide on the surface of water or through the air, either by the impulsion of wind or without any visible effort. late ME. **5.** Of persons, in *transf.* senses. **a.** To move or go in a stately or dignified manner, suggestive of the movement of a ship under sail. (Chiefly of women.) 1841. **b.** *To s. in* (slang): to proceed boldly to action 1889.

1. I loue nat to sayle by see, but when I can nat chose 1530. Phr. *To s. near* (or *close to*) *the wind*: (see WIND *sb.*[1] III. 3); *fig.* to come very near to transgression of a law or a received moral principle; to run the risk of disaster. 2. Light boates saile swift, though greater hulkes draw deepe SHAKS. Steamships s. from every shore 1886. 3. The fleet of the prince was already sailed GOLDSM. On the 13th,..I sailed from Plymouth Sound 1777. 4. Swans that s. along the Silver Flood DRYDEN. Where great whales come sailing by M. ARNOLD. 5. a. Then all the great people sailed in state from the room C. BRONTE.

II. *trans.* **1.** To sail over or upon, to navigate (the sea, a river, etc.). Now somewhat *arch.* late ME. **2.** With cognate obj.: *To s. through*, *out*: to continue (a sailing-match, race), to the end 1886. **b.** To sail or glide through (the air) 1725. **3.** To navigate (a ship or other vessel) 1566. **b.** To put (a toy boat) on the water and direct its course 1863.

1. A thousand Ships were man'd to s. the Sea DRYDEN. 2. The uninjured vessel shall s. out the race 1899. b. The buzzard..on broad wings..slowly sails the sky 1899. 3. He loved the sea; he liked to s. his own boat 1890. Hence **Sai·lable** *a.* (now *rare* or *Obs.*) of a ship: that is in a condition to sail; of the sea, etc.: that can be sailed on; navigable.

Sailcloth (sē·lklǫþ). ME. [f. SAIL *sb.*[1] + CLOTH *sb.*] †**1.** A piece of cloth forming or designed to form part of a sail of a vessel or a windmill –1598. **2.** Canvas or other textile material such as is used for sails 1615. **b.** A piece of this used as a covering 1778.

Sailer (sē·ləɹ). late ME. [f. SAIL *v.* + -ER[1].] **1.** One who sails. Now *rare.* **2.** A ship or vessel with ref. to her powers of sailing 1582. **b.** A sailing vessel 1871.

2. A very strong light ship, and a..good s. DE FOE.

Sailing (sē·liŋ), *vbl. sb.* OE. [f. SAIL *v.* + -ING[1].] **1.** The action of SAIL *v.* **2.** Progression, style or speed of progression, of a ship or other vessel (orig. of a sailing-vessel) 1687. **3.** Departure (of a ship) from port 1748.

Comb.: **s.-boat,** a (small) boat propelled by a sail; **-line,** the line on a vessel's hull which marks the level of the water when she is ballasted and rigged for sailing, but not laden or armed; **-master,** an officer charged with the navigation of a vessel (in British use chiefly with ref. to yachts; in the U.S. navy, a commissioned officer, usu. a lieutenant, appointed to direct the navigation of a ship of war); **s. orders,** the directions given to a captain of a vessel with regard to time of departure, destination, etc.

Sailor (sē·ləɹ). 1642. [Alteration of SAILER: see -OR 2 d.] **1.** One who is professionally occupied with navigation; a seaman, mariner. Also, a member of a ship's company below the rank of officer. †**2.** = SAILER 2. –1775. **3.** Short for *s. hat* 1898.

1. Phr. *To be a good s.* [= F. *être bon marin*]: to be exempt from sea-sickness.

attrib. and *Comb.*: **s.-fish** = *sail-fish*; **s. hat,** a hat such as is worn by sailors; hence, a form of hat (with flat brim of even breadth all round) formerly worn by women, and to a different form (with turned-up brim) worn by children; **-man**, in uneducated and joc. use = sense 1; also *occas.* an adult sailor. **b.** with possessive: **sailor's choice**, *U.S.*, a name given locally to various American fishes; **sailors' home**, a home built by subscription, for the accommodation of sailors on moderate terms; **sailor's knot**, any of the kinds of knot used by sailors; also, a kind of knot used in tying a neck-tie. Hence **Sai·lorless** *a.* without sailors. **Sai·lorly** *a.* befitting, or having the characteristics of, a s.

Sailyard (sē¹·lyāɹd). OE. [f. SAIL *sb.*[1] + YARD *sb.*] *Naut.* One of the yards or spars on which the sails are spread.

‖**Saimiri** (saimī³·ri). 1774. [Brazilian Pg. *saimirim*, a. Tupi *çahy miri* little monkey (f. *çahy* SAI + *miri* little).] A small S. Amer. squirrel-monkey of the genus *Chrysothrix*.

Sain (sē¹n), *v.* Now *arch.* and *dial.* [OE. *segnian*, ad. L. *signare* to sign (in eccl. use to sign with the cross), f. *signum* SIGN *sb.*] **1.** *trans.* To make the sign of the cross on (a thing or person) in token of consecration or blessing; or for the purpose of exorcizing a demon, warding off the evil influences of witches, poison, etc. **b.** *refl.* To cross (oneself) OE. **2.** *trans.* To bless ME. ¶**b.** Associated by some mod. writers with L. *sanare* to heal 1832. **3.** To secure by prayer or enchantment *from* evil influence 1670.

1. Patrick sained the earth and it swallowed up the wizard 1887. **2.** Mary, Mother, s. and save! 1839. **b.** There flowers no balm to s. him HOUSMAN.

Sainfoin (sē¹·nfoin). 1626. [a. F., app. f. *sain* health-giving + *foin* hay.] A perennial herb, *Onobrychis sativa*, much grown as a forage plant. Also, locally, lucerne (*Medicago sativa*).

Saint (sē¹nt; unstressed sĕnt, snt), *a.* and *sb.* ME. [a. OF., :—L. *sanctus*, prop. pa. pple. of *sancire* to consecrate.] **A.** *adj.* = HOLY, in special applications. **1.** Prefixed to the name of a canonized person (see B. 2), also to the names of the archangels; now felt to be the sb. used appositively. Abbrev. S. and St., *pl.* SS. and Sts. **2.** *transf.* †**a.** Of heathen deities, etc. –1588. **b.** allus. or iron. *Obs.* in general use. late ME. †**3.** Prefixed to various common nouns (in collocations taken over from Latin and French), esp. *Charity*, *Cross*, *Spirit*, *Trinity* –1710. **4.** Attributive and possessive collocations of proper names with the prefix 'Saint' ('St.') in sense 1. **a.** Many plants, animals, and other objects have been named after saints of the calendar. For these see the saints' names or the sbs. qualified by them. **b.** Many diseases have been named after saints that are supposed to ward off or relieve them. **c.** Many objects are called after a place-name or a surname beginning with 'Saint' ('St.'); see below.

1. The possessive of names preceded by 'Saint' is often used ellipt. in names of churches, as *St. Paul's*, *St. Peter's*. Hence various names of towns, villages, etc., as *St. Albans*, *St. Andrews*, *St. Bees*. **2. a.** Saint Cupid then, and Souldiers to the field SHAKS. **b.** *St. Monday*: see MONDAY. *St. Lubbock's day*, (joc.) any of the bank holidays instituted by Sir John Lubbock's Act, 1871. **3.** By gis, and by S. Charity SHAKS. **4. b.** *St. Anthony's fire*: see FIRE *sb.* 12. *St. Vitus' dance*: see DANCE *sb.* **c. St. Bernard** (dog), in full *Great St. Bernard dog*, a dog of a breed kept by the monks of the Hospice of the Great St. Bernard (a dangerous pass in the Alps between Switzerland and Italy) for the rescue of travellers in distress. **St. Germain pear**, a fine dessert pear. **St. Leger**, a horse-race for three-year-olds run at Doncaster; instituted by Colonel St. Leger in 1776. **St. Michael's**, the name of one of the Azores, which produced a fine quality of orange.

B. *sb.* A holy person. **1.** One of the blessed dead in Heaven. Usu. *pl.* ME. **2.** *Eccl.* One of those persons who are formally recognized by the Church as having by their exceptional holiness of life attained an exalted station in heaven, and as being entitled in an eminent degree to the veneration of the faithful; a canonized person ME. **b.** A representation or image of a saint 1563. **3.** In Biblical use, one of God's chosen people; in the N.T., one of the elect under the New Covenant; a member of the Christian church; a Christian. Hence used as their own designation by some puritanical sects in the 16–17 c., and by the Mormons. late ME. **b.** In Biblical use applied to angels. late ME. **4.** A person of extraordinary holiness of life. Sometimes *iron.*, A person making an outward profession of piety. 1563. **5.** A nickname for: **a.** A member of a religious association at Cambridge. Now *Hist.* 1793. **b.** One of the party which promoted the agitation in England against slavery. Now *Hist.* 1830.

1. She, half an angel in her own account, Doubts not hereafter with the saints to mount COWPER. **2.** In a cave To bidde, and rede on holy seyntes lyves CHAUCER. A considerable number of churches are called after the names of the primitive saints of our island 1847. *transf.* The graves of Moslem saints 1876. **3.** The fellowship of his Saincts in this present world HOOKER. **b.** Gabriel..lead forth my armied Saints MILT. **4.** For such an iniurie would vexe a very s. SHAKS.

Comb.: **saint's day**, a day set apart by the Church for observing the memory of a s. Hence **Sai·ntdom**, the condition of a s.; saints collectively. †**S.-errant** [after KNIGHT-ERRANT], a s. who travelled in quest of spiritual adventures (*ironical*). **Sai·ntess**, a female s. **Sai·ntish** *a.* s.-like (chiefly *contempt.*). **Sai·ntling**, a little or petty s.

Saint (sē¹nt), *v.* ME. [f. prec.] **1.** *pass.* To be or become a saint in Heaven. *Obs.* or *arch.* **2.** *trans.* To call (a person) a saint, give the name of 'saint' to; *spec.* to enrol among the number of saints formally recognized by the Church; to canonize. late ME. **3.** To cause to be regarded, or to appear, as a saint; to represent as a saint (*rare*) 1609. †**4.** To ascribe holy virtues or a sacred character to –1657. **5.** *intr.* To act or live as a saint; to play the saint. In later use chiefly with *it*. 1460.

1. I hold you as a thing en-skied, and sainted SHAKS. **2.** A Shooe-maker that has been Beatify'd, tho' never Sainted ADDISON. **3.** The Picture..would Martyr him and S. him to befoole the people MILT. **5.** Whether the Charmer sinner it or s. it POPE.

Sainted (sē¹·ntĕd), *ppl. a.* 1598. [f. prec. + -ED[1].] **1.** Enrolled among the saints; canonized; that is a saint in Heaven 1631. **2.** Of sanctified or holy life or character 1605. **3.** Such as belongs to or befits a saint; sacred 1598.

1. The s. Figures on the Casement painted LONGF. **2.** His virtuous and s. wife DISRAELI. **3.** The broad sun Hangs over s. Lebanon MOORE.

Sainthood (sē¹·nthud). 1550. [f. SAINT *sb.* + -HOOD.] The condition, status, or dignity of a saint; also, saints collectively.

Sai·ntlike, *a.* 1580. [f. as prec. + -LIKE.] Resembling a saint or that of a saint; of saintly life or character.

Saintly (sē¹·ntli), *a.* 1660. [f. SAINT *sb.* + -LY[1].] Of, belonging to, or befitting a saint or saints; of great holiness or sanctity; sainted.

The same weake silly lady as ever, asking such s. questions PEPYS. Hence **Sai·ntliness.**

Saintship (sē¹·nt,ʃip). 1606. [f. as prec. + -SHIP.] **1.** The condition or status of a canonized saint 1631. **2.** The condition of being a saint or saintly person; saintliness of life or character 1613. **3.** As a kind of title. Often *ironical.* 1606.

Saint-Simonian (sē¹nt-, sĕnt,simōᵘ·niăn), *a.* and *sb.* Also **St.-**. 1831. [f. *Saint-Simon* + -IAN.] **A.** *adj.* Belonging to or characteristic of the socialistic system propounded by the Comte de Saint-Simon (1760–1825), who advocated state control of all property and a distribution of the produce according to individual vocation and capacity. **B.** *sb.* An advocate of this system. Also **Saint-Simonist** (sɔi·mŏnist). Hence **Saint-Simo·nianism, -Si·monism**, advocacy of or adherence to this system.

Saithe (sē¹ð). *Sc.* 1632. [a. ON. *seiðr*, Icel. *seið* fry of codfish.] The coal-fish.

‖**Sajou** (saʒū·). 1774. [F., shortened from *sajouassu*, a. Tupi *saiuassu*, f. *sai* SAI + *-uassu* augm. suffix.] One of various small S. Amer. monkeys, varieties of Sapajous, and Capuchin monkeys.

Sake (sē¹k). [OE. *sacu* :—OTeut. **sakā*, related to the str. vb. **sak-*, represented by OE. *sacan* to quarrel, accuse.] †**I.** As an independent sb. **1.** Contention, strife, dispute; in OE. also, a lawsuit, cause, action –ME. **2.** A charge or accusation (of guilt); a ground of accusation –late ME. **3.** Guilt, sin; a fault, offence, crime –1450. †**4.** *nonce-use.* Regard or consideration for some one. SPENSER.

4. Tho mov'd with wrath, and shame, and Ladies s. SPENSER.

II. Phr. *For the s. of*; *for* (one's, a thing's) *s.* **1.** Out of consideration for; on account of one's interest in, or regard for (a person); on (a person's) account ME. **b.** When the preceding genitive is pl., the pl. *sakes* is often used 1530. **2.** Out of regard or consideration for (a thing); on account of, because of (something regarded as an end, aim, purpose, etc.); often = out of desire for, in order to attain. ME.

1. For my own s. as well as for yours, I will do my very best JOWETT. **b.** For both our sakes I would that word were true SHAKS. **2.** It is doing mischief for mischiefs s. 1770. Flattering of rich men for the s. of a dinner JOWETT. For sweet marriage-s. SWINBURNE. Phr. *For one's name('s) s.*, out of regard for one's name. *For God's s.*, *for goodness'*, *Heaven's*, *s.*; Hold on, for Heaven's s.! 1879. †*For any s.*, in any case, at all events. *For old sake's s.*, for the s. of old friendship. *Sakes alive*! and simply *Sakes*! : a vulgar exclam. of surprise (*dial.* and *U.S.*).

‖**Saké, saki** (sæ·ke). 1687. [Japanese.] A Japanese fermented liquor made of rice.

Saker (sē¹·kəɹ). late ME. [a. F. *sacre*, ad. Sp., Pg. *sacro*, It. *sagro*, prob. a. Arab. *çaqr*.] **1.** A large lanner falcon (*Falco sacer*), used in falconry, esp. the female. **2.** An old form of cannon smaller than a demi-culverin, formerly much employed in sieges and on ships. Now *Hist.* or *arch.* 1521.

Sakeret (sē¹·kərĕt). *Obs.* or *arch.* late ME. [a. F. *sacret*, dim. of *sacre* SAKER.] The male of the saker.

Saki (sāki). 1774. [a. F., app. incorrectly a. Tupi *çahy* SAI.] A S. Amer. monkey of the family *Cebidæ*, of either of the two genera *Pithecia* or *Brachyurus*.

‖**Sal**[1] (sæl). late ME. [L., = salt.] †**1.** *Chem.*, *Alch.*, and *Pharm.* = SALT *sb.*[1] –1674. **2.** With qualifying word: †*s. marine* [med.L. *sal marinus*], common salt; *s. mirabile* (*-is*) [mod.L., 'wonderful salt'], Glauber's salts, sulphate of soda; *s. soda* [med.L. *sal sodæ*], crystallized sodium carbonate. See also SAL-AMMONIAC, SAL VOLATILE. late ME.

Sal[2] (sāl). Also **saul.** 1789. [Hindī *sāl* = Skr. *sāla*.] A valuable timber tree of India, *Shorea robusta*, yielding the resin dammar.

‖**Sala** (sā·la). 1611. [It., Sp. = SALLE.] A hall or large apartment; *spec.* a dining-hall.

Salaam (sălā·m), *sb.* 1613. [Arab. *salām* = Heb. *shālōm* peace.] The Oriental salutation (*as*)*salām* (*ᵃalaikum*), Peace (be upon you). Hence applied to a ceremonious obeisance accompanying this salutation, consisting (in India) of a low bow with the palm of the right hand placed on the forehead. **b.** *transf.* Respectful compliments 1623.

1. The Moor rose instantly, with profound salaams, before her 1867.

Salaam (sălā·m), *v.* 1693. [f. prec.] **1.** *trans.* To make a salaam to; to salute with a salaam; to offer salutations to. **2.** *intr.* To make a salaam or obeisance 1698.

2. Putting their hands to their brow, and salaaming down to the ground 1852.

Salacious (sălē¹·ʃəs), *a.* 1645. [f. L. *salaci-*, *salax*, f. root of *salire* to leap; see -IOUS.] **1.** Lustful, lecherous; sexually wanton 1659. **2.** Tending to provoke lust (*rare*) 1645. Hence **Sala·cious·ly** *adv.*, **-ness.**

Salacity (sălæ·sĭti). 1605. [ad. L. *salacitatem*, f. *salac-*, *salax* (see prec.).] The quality or condition of being salacious; lustfulness, lecherousness, sexual wantonness.

Salad (sæ·lăd). Also (*dial.* or *arch.*) **sallet.** late ME. [a. OF. *salade*, a. Pr. *salada* :—pop. L. **salata*, f. **salare* to salt, f. L. *sal* salt.] **1.** A cold dish of herbs or vegetables (e.g. lettuce, endive), usu. uncooked, to which is often added sliced hard-boiled egg, cold meat, fish, etc., the whole being seasoned with salt, pepper, oil, and vinegar. Also (*fruit s.*) extended to a mixture of fruits served in their syrup. **b.** *fig.* and allus., as a type of something mixed (or †savoury) 1601. **2.** Any vegetable or herb used in a raw state as an article of food, esp. in the dish described in **1**; = *s.-herb* 1460.

1. The s. is the glory of every French dinner and the disgrace of most in England 1846. **b.** I remember one said, there was no Sallets in the lines, to make the matter sauoury SHAKS. Our Garrick's a s., for in him we see Oil, vinegar, sugar, and saltness agree GOLDSM.

attrib.: **s. burnet**, the common burnet, *Poterium sanguisorba*; **s. days**, days of youthful inexperience; **s. dressing** (see DRESSING *vbl. sb.* 4 a); †**s.-herb** = sense 2; **-oil**, olive oil of superior quality, such as is used in dressing salads. Hence **Sa·lading,** herbs and vegetables used for salad.

Salal (sæ·lăl). 1838. [Chinook Jargon *sallal.*] An evergreen shrub (*Gaultheria Shallon*) of California and Oregon, bearing sweet edible berries.

Salamander (sæ·lămændəɹ, sælămæ·ndəɹ). ME. [a. F. *salamandre,* ad. L. *salamandra,* a. Gr. *σαλαμάνδρα.*] **1. a.** A lizard-like animal supposed to live in, or to be able to endure, fire. Now *allusive.* **b.** Any tailed amphibian of the urodelous family *Salamandridæ,* or some closely allied family 1611. **c.** A figure of the mythical salamander used as an emblem 1688. **2.** *transf.* and *fig.,* applied to persons, etc. with ref. to sense 1 a. 1596. **b.** A spirit supposed to live in fire 1657. **3.** Applied to various articles used in fire or capable of withstanding great heat. †**a.** Asbestos -1700. **b.** An iron or poker used red-hot for lighting a pipe, igniting gunpowder, etc. 1698. **c.** *Cookery.* A circular iron plate which is heated and placed over a pudding, etc., to brown it 1769. **4.** *local U.S.* A pouched rat or gopher, esp. *Geomys pinetis* 1859. **5.** A German form of drinking a toast 1868.

1. a. Like the S., that is ever in the fire and never consumed 1591. **c.** *S.* (*Her.*), an emblem of constancy, is represented in flames 1823. **2.** I haue maintain'd that S. [= fiery-red face] of yours with fire, any time this two and thirtie yeeres SHAKS.

Comb.: **s.-cloth,** an incombustible cloth made from asbestos; **salamander's hair,** a kind of asbestos; †**s. stone** = AMIANTHUS; †**salamander's wool,** asbestos. Hence **Salama·ndrian** *a.* resembling (that of) a s.; *sb.* a salamandrian batrachian.

Salamandrine (sælămæ·ndrin), *a.* and *sb.* 1712. [f. L. *salamandra* SALAMANDER + -INE[1].] **A.** *adj.* **1.** Resembling or characteristic of the salamander in being able to resist fire, or live in it. **2.** *Zool.* Of or pertaining to the *Salamandrinæ* 1865. **B.** *sb.* A spirit supposed to live in fire; also = SALAMANDER 1 b. 1797.

Salamandroid (sælămæ·ndroid), *a.* and *sb.* 1854. [ad. mod.L. *salamandroides, -oideus,* f. *salamandra* SALAMANDER; see -OID.] **A.** *adj.* Resembling a salamander. **B.** *sb.* A urodele of the genus *Salamandra* or allied genera 1863.

‖**Salame** (sālā·me). *Pl.* **salami.** 1852. [It., repr. pop. L. *salamen, f. *salare* to salt.] A kind of sausage.

Sal-ammoniac (sælămōᵘ·niæk). ME. [See AMMONIAC A. 1.] Ammonium chloride.

Salamstone (sălæ·m,stōᵘn). 1816. [ad. G. *salamstein.*] *Min.* A blue variety of sapphire from Ceylon.

Salangane (sæ·lăngēⁱn). 1793. [a. F., or ad. mod.L. *salangana,* sc. *avis,* f. *salamga* name of the bird in Luzon.] *Zool.* One of the birds of the genus *Collocalia,* which make edible nests; an esculent swallow.

Salariat (sălēᵊ·riăt). 1918. [Fr., f. *salaire* salary, after *prolétariat.*] The body of people in an industry, trade, or department who receive a salary (as dist. from wage-earners).

Salaried (sæ·lărid), *ppl. a.* 1600. [f. SALARY *sb.* or *v.* + -ED.] **1.** Having or receiving a salary. **2.** Having a salary attached to it 1836.

1. Most of them are his s. schollers, or agents 1600. **2.** The poorly-s. Chair of Civil History 1872.

Salary (sæ·lări), *sb.* late ME. [a. AF. *salarie* = OF. *salaire,* ad. L. *salarium,* orig. money allowed to Roman soldiers for the purchase of salt, hence, their pay; sb. use of neut. sing. of *salarius* pertaining to salt, f. *sal* salt.] **1.** Fixed payment made periodically to a person as compensation for regular work; now usu. for non-manual or non-mechanical work (as opp. to *wages*). †**2.** Remuneration for services rendered; fee, honorarium -1643. †**b.** *gen.* Reward, recompense -1686.

1. Sir Humphry Winch, Baronet, hath from the Court 500*l.* per annum Sallery 1677. **2. b.** Felicitie, which is the salarie and reward of Vertue 1619.

Salary (sæ·lări), *v.* 1477. [Chiefly f. SALARY *sb.* In early use a. F. *salarier.*] *trans.* To recompense, reward; to pay for something done (*Obs.* or *arch.*); to pay a regular salary to.

The Chinese system—s. the doctor and stop his pay when you get ill 1893.

Salband (sā·lbænd). Also **sahlband.** 1811. [G., selvage, earlier *sahlband.*] *Geol.* A thin crust or coating of mineral, etc.

Sale (sēⁱl). *sb.* (and *a.*) [Late OE. *sala,* prob. a. ON. *sala,* f. root *sal-* of *saljan to SELL.] **1.** The action or an act of selling; the exchange of a commodity for money or other valuable consideration. Also: (Ready, slow, etc.) disposal of goods for money; opportunity of selling. **b.** *spec.* A putting up of goods to be sold publicly; a public auction 1673. **c.** A special disposal of shop goods at reduced prices in order to get rid of them rapidly, e.g. at the end of a 'season' 1886. **2.** *attrib.* or *adj.* That is made to be sold; that may be purchased (not being needed for home use); hence, ready-made; of inferior quality 1455.

1. b. He should pull down the bills advertising the s. of his effects TROLLOPE.

Phrases. *To s.* = 'for s.' Now only in *to put up to s. On s.* = 'for s.' †*Of s.,* that is to be sold; vendible, venal. *For s.*; used adjectively, = intended to be sold; used advb., = with a view to selling. *At s.*: among booksellers, at 30% discount off the published price. *S. and* (*or*) *return,* a contract, by which goods are delivered to a retailer, to be paid for at a certain rate, if sold by him; and if not sold, to be returned to the vendor. *S. of work,* a sale of articles made by members of a congregation or association on behalf of some charitable or religious object.

attrib. and *Comb.,* as *s.-price, -room,* etc.; **s. ring,** the ring of buyers formed round an auctioneer at a s. Also with pl., **sales-book,** a book or record of sales; **sales-room** = *s.-room.*

Saleable (sēⁱ·lăb'l), *a.* 1530. [f. prec. + -ABLE.] **1.** Capable of being sold; fit for sale; commanding a ready sale. **b.** Said of the price which an article will fetch 1778. **2.** Venal, mercenary. Now *rare* or *Obs.* 1579.

1. b. Goods to the s. value of 172*l.* 1778. Hence **Saleabi·lity. Sa·leableness. Sa·leably** *adv.*

Salempore (sæ·lĕmpōᵊɹ). 1598. [Hind. *Salampur* (a district of Nellore), f. Telugu *sāle* weaver + Skr. *pura* town.] A blue cotton cloth formerly made at Nellore (Madras) in India, and largely exported to the W. Indies.

Salep (sæ·lĕp). 1736. [= F., a. Turk. *sālep* a. Arab. *thaˢleb.*] A nutritive meal, starch, or jelly made from the dried tubers of various orchidaceous plants, chiefly those of the genus *Orchis*; formerly also used as a drug.

Saleratus (sælərēⁱ·tŏs). *U.S.* 1846. [a. mod.L. *sal aeratus* 'aerated salt'.] An impure bicarbonate of potash containing more carbon dioxide than pearl-ash does, much used as an ingredient in baking-powders. Now also applied to sodium bicarbonate similarly used.

Salesian (sălī·ʒiăn), *a.* and *sb.* 1884. [f. name of S. François de *Sales* + -IAN.] Of or pertaining to, a member of, an order (*a*) of nuns of the Visitation, founded by S. François de Sales, (*b*) of brothers founded by Dom Bosco for the care of poor and neglected children.

Salesman (sēⁱ·lzmăn). 1523. [f. *sale's,* genitive of SALE + MAN *sb.* Cf. *tradesman,* etc.] A man whose business it is to sell goods or conduct sales; *spec. U.S.,* a commercial traveller. So **Sa·leswo:man,** a woman who sells goods (e.g. in a shop).

Salian[1] (sēⁱ·liăn), *a.* and *sb.* 1653. [f. L. *Salius* (f. *salire* to leap) + -AN I. 1.] **A.** *adj.* Of or pertaining to the Salii or priests of Mars in ancient Rome. **B.** *sb.* One of the Salii.

Salian[2] (sēⁱ·liăn), *a.* and *sb.* 1614. [f. late L. *Salii* the Salian Franks + -AN I. 1.] **A.** *adj.* Of or belonging to a tribe of Franks who inhabited a region near the Zuyder Zee, and to whom the ancestors of the Merovingian dynasty belonged. (Cf. SALIC.) **B.** *sb.* A Salian Frank.

Salic (sæ·lik, sēⁱ·lik), *a.* 1548. [ad. F. *salique* or med.L. *Salicus,* f. *Salii* (see prec.).] **1.** *S. Law*: orig., the alleged fundamental law of the French monarchy, by which females were excluded from succession to the crown; hence *gen.,* a law excluding females from dynastic succession. In this sense often *Salique* (sălī·k). **2.** In the original sense of L. *Salicus*: Pertaining to the Salian Franks. Chiefly in *S. law* or *code* (L. *lex Salica*), a Frankish law-book, written in Latin, and extant in five successive enlarged recensions of Merovingian and Carolingian date. 1781.

Salicaceous (sælikēⁱ·ʃəs), *a.* 1846. [f. mod. L. *salicaceus,* f. L. *salic-, salix* willow; see -ACEOUS.] *Bot.* Belonging to the family *Salicaceæ,* which consists of two genera, *Salix* (willow) and *Populus* (poplar).

Salicin (sæ·lisin). 1830. [ad. F. *salicine* f. L. *salic-, salix* willow; see -IN[1].] A bitter crystalline principle obtained from willow-bark, and much used medicinally.

Salicional (săli·ʃənăl). 1843. [a. G. *saliz-, salicional,* f. L. *salic-, salix* willow, with obsc. suffix.] An organ stop of a soft reedy tone resembling that of a willow pipe. So **Sa·licet.**

Salicyl (sæ·lisil). 1839. [ad. F. *salicyle,* f. L. *salic-, salix* willow; see -YL.] *Chem.* The diatomic radical of salicylic acid. Hence **Sa·licylide,** the anhydride of salicylic acid. **Sa·licylite,** a salt formed by the action of salicylol on oxides and hydrates of metals. **Sa·licylol,** an oil intermediate in composition between salicylic acid and salicylic aldehyde.

Salicylate (săli·silĕt). 1842. [f. next + -ATE[1] 1 c.] *Chem.* A salt of salicylic acid.

Salicylic (sælisi·lik), *a.* 1840. [f. SALICYL + -IC 1 b.] **1.** *Chem.* Belonging to a group of benzene derivatives obtainable from salicin; esp. in *s. acid,* a white crystalline substance, and much used as an antiseptic and in the treatment of rheumatism. **2.** *Therapeutics.* Made from, impregnated with, or involving the use of, s. acid 1876. Hence **Sa·licylism,** a toxic condition produced by the administration of s. acid or salicylates. **Sa·licylize** *v. trans.* to treat with s. acid in order to prevent fermentation.

Salicylous (săli·siləs), *a.* 1840. [f. as prec. + -OUS c.] *Chem.* In *s. acid*: a liquid obtained by distillation of salicin with sulphuric acid and bichromate of potash; salicyl aldehyde.

Salience (sēⁱ·liĕns). 1836. [f. next; see -ENCE.] †**1.** The quality of leaping or springing up. L. HUNT. **2.** The fact, quality, or condition of projecting beyond the general outline 1849. **3.** A salient or projecting feature, part, or object 1837. So **Sa·liency** 1664.

Salient (sēⁱ·liĕnt), *a.* and *sb.* 1562. [ad. L. *salientem, salire* to leap.] **A.** *adj.* **1.** Leaping, jumping; *esp.* of animals, saltatorial 1646. **b.** Of water: Jetting forth; leaping upwards 1669. **2.** *Her.* Having the hind legs in the sinister base and the fore paws elevated near together in the dexter chief, as if in the act of leaping 1562. **3.** *S. point* [= F. *point saillant,* mod.L. *punctum saliens*]: in old medical use, the heart as it first appears in an embryo; hence, the first beginning of life or motion; the starting-point of anything. *Obs.* or *arch.* 1672. **4.** Of an angle: Pointing outward, as an ordinary angle of a polygon (opp. to *re-entrant*); chiefly in *Fortif.,* pointing away from the centre of the fortification. So *s. point,* etc. 1687. **5. a.** Of material things: Standing above or beyond the general surface or outline; jutting out; prominent among a number of objects 1789. **b.** Of immaterial things, qualities, etc.: Standing out from the rest; prominent, conspicuous. Often in phr. *s. point.* 1840.

1. b. *fig.* He had in himself a s., living spring, of generous and manly action BURKE. **3.** That was the s. point from which all the mischiefs..of the present reign took life *Junius Lett.* **5. a.** Large s. eyes 1854. **b.** The s. feature in the picture GROTE.

B. *sb.* A salient angle or part of a fortification or system of trenches 1828. Hence **Sa·liently** *adv.*

Saliferous (săli·fĕrəs), *a.* 1828. [f. L. *sal, sali-* salt + -FEROUS.] Containing a large proportion of salt; said chiefly of strata.

Salifiable (sæ·lifəi,ăb'l), *a.* 1790. [a. F. *salifiable,* f. *salifier* to SALIFY.] *Chem.* Capable of combining with an acid to form a salt.

Salification (sæ:lifikēⁱ·ʃən). 1684. [ad. mod.L. *salificationem,* f. *salificare* to SALIFY.] Conversion into a salt; the action or condition of being salified.

Salify (sæ·lifəi), *v.* Now *rare.* 1790. [ad. F. *salifier,* ad. mod.L. *salificare,* f. L. *sal, sali-* salt; see -FY.] *Chem. intr.* To form a salt.

Saligenin (sæli·dʒĕnin). 1852. [a. F. *saligénine,* f. *sali(cine)* SALICIN; see -GEN and -IN[1].] *Chem.* A substance obtained in the decomposition of salicin by dilute acid.

Saligot (sæ·ligǫt). 1578. [a. OF.] The water-chestnut, *Trapa natans.*

Salimeter (săli·mĭtəɹ). 1866. [f. L. *sal, sali-* salt + -METER.] An instrument for determining the amount of salt in a solution.

‖**Salina** (sălɔi·nă). 1589. [a. Sp., :—L. *salina*, only in pl. *salinæ* (sc. *fodinæ*).] A salt lake, spring, or marsh; a salt-pan, salt-works.

Saline (sē¹·lɔin, sălɔi·n), *a.* and *sb.* 1450. [ad. L. **salinus*, f. *sal* salt; see -INE [1].] **A.** *adj.* **1.** †Composed of salt; of the nature of salt; having salt as a preponderating constituent. **b.** Of springs, lakes, etc.: Impregnated with salt or salts 1805. **2.** Like that of salt; like salt; salty 1651. **3.** Of or pertaining to chemical salts; of the nature of a salt 1771. **4.** Of medicines: Consisting of or based upon salts of the alkaline metals or magnesium 1789. **5.** Of plants, †animals: Growing in or inhabiting salt plains or marshes 1802.

1. The s. contents of sea-water 1832. b. Medicinal springs, s. and sulphurous 1872. 2. The..s. taste of nitre 1857. 4. The use of s. purgatives 1802.

B. *sb.* **1.** = SALINA 1450. **2.** A s. purge (see A. 4) 1875. Hence **Sali·neness** (*rare*).

Salinity (săli·nĭti). 1658. [f. prec. + -ITY.] The quality of being saline; saltness.

Salino- (sălɔi·no), comb. form of SALINE, in the sense 'consisting of salt (and ...)', as *s.-sulphureous*, etc.

Salinometer (sælinǫ·mĭtəɪ). 1844. [f. SALINE + -(O)METER.] An apparatus for ascertaining the salinity of water, *esp.* one for indicating the density of brine in marine boilers.

Saliretin (sæliri·tin). 1840. [ad. F. *salirétine*, f. SALI(CIN) + Gr. ῥητίνη RESIN.] *Chem.* A resinous substance obtained by the action of dilute acids on saligenin.

Saliva (sălɔi·vă). late ME. [a. L.] Spittle; the mixed secretion of the salivary glands and of the mucous glands of the mouth, a colourless liquid, having normally an alkaline reaction, which mixes with the food in mastication. So **Sali·val** *a.* (*rare*) salivary. **Salivant** (sæ·livănt), *a.* promoting salivation; *sb.* a sialagogue.

Salivary (sæ·livări, sălɔi·vări), *a.* 1709. [ad. L. *salivarius*, f. *saliva* SALIVA; see -ARY [1] A.] **1.** Secreting or conveying saliva. **2.** Consisting of saliva 1841. **3.** Pertaining to or existing in the saliva or salivary glands 1807.

1. The s. glands in man are the parotid, submaxillary, and sublingual N.E.D.

Salivate (sæ·livē¹t), *v.* 1657. [f. L. *salivat-*, *salivare*, f. *saliva* SALIVA.] **1.** *trans.* To produce an unusual secretion of saliva in (a person), generally by the use of mercury; to produce ptyalism in. **2.** *intr.* **a.** To secrete or discharge saliva. **b.** To secrete saliva in excess under the influence of sialagogues. 1681. So **Saliva·tion**, secretion or discharge of saliva; *esp.* the production of an excessive flow of saliva by administering mercury 1598.

†**Sali·vous**, *a.* 1567. [ad. L. *salivosus*, f. *saliva*; see -OUS.] Pertaining to, of the nature of, saliva -1676.

‖**Salle** (sal). 1762. [Fr.; of Teut. origin.] **1.** A hall, room (*rare*) 1819. **b.** The sorting department of a paper factory. **2.** In Fr. combinations. **Salle-à-manger** (salamañʒe), a dining-hall, dining-room. **Salle d'attente** (saldatañt), a waiting-room (at a station).

Sallee-man (sæ·līmæn). 1637. [f. *Sallee*, a Moroccan seaport formerly of piratical repute.] **1.** A Moorish pirate-ship. *Obs.* exc. *Hist.* **2.** A marine hydrozoan, *Velella vulgaris* 1756.

Sallender (sæ·lĕndəɪ). Now only *pl.* 1523. [Origin obsc.] A dry scab affecting the hock of a horse.

Sallet (sæ·lĕt), **salade** (sălā·d). 1440. [a. F. *salade*, ad. Sp. *celada* or It. *celata*, believed to represent L. *cælata* (sc. *cassis* or *galea*) (a helmet) ornamented with engraving.] *Antiq.* In mediæval armour, a light globular headpiece, either with or without a vizor, and without a crest, the lower part curving outwards behind.

Many a time but for a Sallet, my braine-pan had bene cleft with a brown Bill SHAKS.

Sallet, arch. or dial. f. SALAD.

Sallow (sæ·lo[u]), *sb.* Also **sally.** [OE. *sealh* :—**salhoz*; cognates are L. *salic-*, *salix*, Gr. ἑλίκη.] **1.** A plant of the genus *Salix*, a willow; chiefly, as dist. from 'osier' and 'willow', applied to several species of *Salix* of a low-growing or shrubby habit. Also, one of the shoots of a willow. **2.** The wood of the sallow tree. late ME. **3.** Collector's name for certain moths the larvæ of which feed on the willow; esp. a moth of the genus *Xanthia* 1829.

Comb.: **sally-fly**, a kind of stone fly; **sallow thorn**, a plant of the genus *Hippophae*.

Sallow (sæ·lo[u]), *a.* [OE. *salo* :—OTeut. **salwo-*, whence F. *sale*, It. *salavo* dirty.] Of the skin or complexion: Having a sickly yellow or brownish yellow colour.

Ful salowe was waxen hir colour CHAUCER. *transf.* While s. Autumn fills thy lap with leaves COLLINS. Hence **Sa·llow** *v. trans.* to make s. **Sa·llowish** *a.* somewhat s. in hue. **Sa·llowness.**

Sallowy (sæ·loui), *a.* 1840. [f. SALLOW *sb.* + -Y.] Abounding in sallows or willows.

Sally (sæ·li), *sb.*[1] 1542. [a. F. *saillie*, f. *saillir* SALLY *v.*[1]] **1.** A sudden rush (*out*) from a besieged place upon the enemy; a sortie 1560. †**b.** A sally-port -1598. **2.** A going forth, setting out, excursion, expedition (of one or more persons) 1650. **3.** A sudden start into activity 1605. **4.** A breaking forth from restraint; an outburst or transport (*of* passion, delight, etc.); a flash (*of* wit) 1662. **5.** An escapade. Now *rare*. 1639. **6.** A sprightly or audacious utterance or literary composition; now usu., a brilliant remark, a witticism 1756. **7.** A leaping movement. *Obs.* exc. *Naut.* and *dial.* 1589. **8.** *Arch.* A deviation from the alignment of a surface; a projection 1665.

1. A garrison..which is able..to make successful sallies 1786. 2. I made my second s. into the world DE FOE. 3. Fretted by sallies of his mother's kisses WORDSW. 5. This excursion was esteemed but a S. of youth WOTTON.

Sally (sæ·li), *sb.*[2] 1668. [Perh. an application of prec. 7.] *Bell-ringing*. **1.** The first movement of a bell when 'set' for ringing; a 'handstroke', as dist. from the 'backstroke'; also, the position of a bell when 'set'. Now *local*. **2.** The woolly grip for the hands near the lower end of a bell-rope 1809.

Comb. **s.-hole**, a hole through which the bell-rope passes.

Sa·lly, *v.*[1] *rare*. 1440. [irreg. ad. F. *saillir*.] *intr.* To leap, bound, dance -1543.

Sally (sæ·li), *v.*[2] 1560. [f. SALLY *sb.*[1]] **1.** *intr.* Of a warlike force: To issue suddenly from a place of defence or retreat in order to make an attack; *spec.* of a besieged force, to make a sortie. **2.** Of a person or party of persons: To set out boldly, to go forth (from a place of abode); to set out on a journey or expedition 1590. **3.** Of things: To issue forth; *esp.* to issue suddenly, break out, burst or leap forth 1660.

1. And now, all girt in armes the Ports, set wide, They sallied forth CHAPMAN. 2. In the morning we all sallied forth to hunt DARWIN. 3. While yet his warm blood sallied from the wound COWPER.

Sally Lunn (sæ·li lv·n). 1798. [Said to be from the name of a young woman in Bath who first made them about 1797.] A kind of sweet light teacake, containing sultanas, currants, etc., and eaten with butter.

Sa·llyport. 1649. [f. SALLY *sb.*[1] + PORT *sb.*[3]] **1.** *Fortif.* An opening in a fortified place for the passage of troops when making a sally; sometimes used for 'postern'. **2.** A landing-place at Portsmouth set apart for the use of men-of-war's boats 1833.

Salmagundi (sælmăgv·ndi). 1674. [a. F. *salmigondis*, of unkn. origin.] *Cookery.* A dish composed of chopped meat, anchovies, eggs, and onions, with oil and condiments.

fig. His mind was a sort of s. 1797.

Salmi (sæ·lmi). 1759. [a. F., perh. short for prec.] A ragoût of partly roasted game, stewed with wine, bread, condiments, etc.

Salmiac (sæ·lmiæk). 1799. [a. G. *salmiak*, contr. of L. *sal ammoniacum*.] *Min.* Native sal-ammoniac.

Salmon (sæ·mən), *sb.* and *a.* ME. [a. AF. *sa(l)moun*, *saumoun*, etc. (mod.F. *saumon*) :—L. *salmonem*, *salmo*, prob. f. *salire* to leap.] **A.** *sb.* **1.** A large fish belonging to the genus *Salmo*, family *Salmonidæ*, esp. *Salmo salar*, which has red flesh and a silvery skin marked with large black and red spots, and is highly prized as an article of food. **b.** Applied to fishes belonging to other genera of the same family; e.g. a fish belonging to any of the species of the genus *Oncorhynchus*, called the *Pacific s.* 1884. **c.** Applied to fishes resembling a salmon, but not belonging to the *Salmonidæ*. In U.S., the SQUETEAGUE. In Australia and New Zealand, *Arripis salar*. 1798. **2.** Short for *s. colour* 1892.

Comb.: **s. berry** (*U.S.*), a name for certain species of *Rubus*, esp. *R. Nutkanus*, the white flowering raspberry; **-colour**, an orange shade of pink; **s. fishing**, (*a*) the catching of s.; (*b*) a salmon-fishery; **s. ladder**, a fish ladder for s.; **s. leap** (see LEAP *sb.*[2]); **s. pass** = *s. ladder*; **s. weir**, a weir for the taking of s.

B. *adj.* [The sb. used *attrib.*] Of the colour of the flesh of salmon; a kind of orange-pink 1786. Hence **Sa·lmonet**, a samlet. **Salmonoid** (sæ·lmŏnoid) *a.* and *sb.* (a fish) of the family *Salmonidæ*; resembling a fish of this family.

Sa·lmon-trou·t. late ME. **1.** A fish of the species *Salmo trutta*, resembling the salmon. **2.** In U.S. and N.S.W. applied to other fishes; *esp.* the Char, or Red-spotted Trout, and the Gray-spotted or Lake Trout 1882.

Salol (sæ·lǫl). 1887. [f. SAL(ICYL) + -OL.] *Chem.* A white, crystalline, aromatic powder, prepared from salicylic and carbolic acids, used as an anti-pyretic and antiseptic.

‖**Salon** (salon̄). 1715. [F.; see next.] **1. a.** A large and lofty reception-room in a palace or other great house. **b.** A drawing-room. (Now only with ref. to France or other continental countries.) **2.** *spec.* The reception-room of a Parisian lady of fashion; hence, a reunion of notabilities at the house of such a lady; also, a similar gathering in other capitals 1810. **3.** *The S.*: the annual exhibition at Paris of painting, sculpture, etc. by living artists 1875.

Saloon (sălū·n). 1728. [a. F. *salon*, ad. It. *salone*, augm. of *sala* hall.] **1.** = prec. 1 a. **b.** = prec. 1 b. Now *U.S.* **2.** = prec. 2. Now *rare*. 1810. **3.** A large room or hall, esp. in a hotel or other place of public resort, adapted for assemblies, entertainments, exhibitions, etc. 1747. **4. a.** A large cabin for first-class or for all passengers on a ship (also in a large aeroplane) 1842. **b.** In full *s. car* or *carriage*: A railway carriage without compartments furnished luxuriously as a drawing-room, or for a specific purpose, as *dining*, *sleeping s.* Later, also = *s. car*. 1855. **5.** A public apartment for a specified purpose, as *billiard*, *dancing*, *shaving s.*, etc. 1852. **6.** (orig. *U.S.*) A drinking bar; now, in Eng., a first-class bar in a public house or hotel (a *saloon bar*) 1872.

2. I find saloons and compliments too great bores SHELLEY. 5. In London..we went to places of entertainment, and low dancing saloons 1852.

Comb.: **s. car**, a coach-built covered-in motor-car; also see 4 b; **s. carriage** (see 4 b); **s. deck**, a deck for the use of s. passengers; **s.-keeper** *U.S.*, one who keeps a drinking s.; **s. pistol, rifle**, light firearms for firing at short range.

Saloop (sălū·p). 1712. [Altered f. SALEP.] **1.** = SALEP. **2.** A hot drink consisting of an infusion of powdered salep, or (later) of sassafras, with milk and sugar, formerly sold in the streets of London.

S. bush, an Australian shrub, *Rhagodia hastata*.

Salopian (sălō[u]·piăn), *a.* and *sb.* 1700. [f. *Salop*, a name of Shropshire (f. *Sloppesberie*, an AF. corruption of OE. *Scrobbesbyrig*, Shrewsbury) + -IAN.] **A.** *adj.* Of or belonging to Shropshire 1706. **B.** *sb.* **1.** A native or inhabitant of Shropshire 1700. **2.** A past or present member of Shrewsbury School 1866.

Salp (sælp). 1835. [a. F. *salpe*, ad. mod. L. *salpa*.] *Zool.* = next.

‖**Salpa** (sæ·lpă). *Pl.* **salpæ**; also **salpas.** 1852. [mod.L.] *Zool.* A genus of tunicates, the sole representative of the family *Salpidæ*; also, a tunicate of this genus. So **Sa·lpian**, an individual of the genus *S.* 1839.

†‖**Salpicon** (sæ·lpikǫn). 1726. [F., a Sp., f. *salpicar* to sprinkle, pickle, f. *sal* salt + *picar* to pick.] *Cookery.* A kind of stuffing for veal, beef, or mutton -1832.

‖**Salpiglossis** (sælpiglǫ·sis). 1833. [mod. L., irreg. f. Gr. σάλπιγξ trumpet + γλῶσσα tongue, from the shape of the corolla.] A genus of herbaceous plants of the family *Scrophulariaceæ*, natives of Chile, cultivated for their showy blossoms.

Salpingitis (salpindʒɔi·tis). 1861. [mod. L., f. Gr. σαλπιγγ- (see next) + -ITIS.] *Path.* Inflammation of the Fallopian or the Eustachian tubes.

Salpingo- (sælpi·ŋgo), comb. form of Gr. σαλπιγγ-, σάλπιγξ, lit. 'trumpet', but used in mod.L. to denote either the Fallopian or the Eustachian tubes.

‖**Salpinx** (sæ·lpiŋks). 1842. [Gr. σάλπιγξ.] 1. *Antiq.* An ancient Greek trumpet 1865. 2. **a.** The Eustachian tube. **b.** The Fallopian tube. 1842.

‖**Sal-prunella** (sæ:lprune·lă). 1677. [mod. L. *sal prunella* or *prunellæ*; see SAL and PRUNELLA [3].] Fused nitre cast into moulds.

Salse (sæls). 1832. [a. F., ad. It. *salsa*, orig. proper name of a mud volcano near Modena.] *Geol.* A mud volcano.

Salsify (sæ·lsifi). 1675. [a. F. *salsifis*, app. corruptly ad. It. *sassefrica*, of unkn. origin.] A biennial composite plant, the Purple Goat's-beard, *Tragopogon porrifolius*, producing an esculent root.

Black s., *Scorzonera hispanica.*

‖**Salsola** (sæ·lsŏlă). 1801. [mod.L., a. It. †*salsola*, dim. of *salso* salt.] A genus of herbaceous plants belonging to the family *Chenopodiaceæ*; esp. *S. soda*, a species yielding soda. Also, a plant of this genus. Hence **Salsola·ceous** *a.* belonging to or resembling the genus *S.*

Salsuginous (sælsiū·dʒinəs), *a.* 1657. [f. L. *salsuginem* saltness + -OUS.] †Impregnated with salt; brackish. **b.** Of plants: Growing in salt-impregnated soil.

Salt (sǭlt), *sb.*[1] [Com. Teut.: OE. *sealt* (*salt*):—OTeut. *saltom*, cogn. w. Gr. ἅλς, L. *sal*, etc.] 1. A substance, sodium chloride (NaCl), extensively prepared for use as a condiment, a preservative of animal food, and in various industrial processes. Freq. called *common s.* 2. Taken as a type of a necessary adjunct of food, and hence as a symbol of hospitality. late ME. **b.** With ref. to the bitter saline taste of tears 1595. **c.** With ref. to the saltness of the sea, in phrases denoting inclination for a seafaring life 1886. 3. *fig.* **a.** *The s. of the earth* (after Matt. v. 13): the excellent of the earth; in recent trivial use, the powerful, aristocratic, or wealthy OE. **b.** That which gives liveliness, freshness, or piquancy to a person's character, life, etc. 1579. **c.** Poignancy of expression; pungent wit; †point 1573. 4. †**a.** *Old Chem.* A solid soluble non-inflammable substance having a taste –1797. **b.** *Salt* (*salts*) *of lemon(s)*, binoxalate of potash, potash combined with oxalic acid 1815. **c.** *colloq. pl.* (*a*) Smelling salts 1767. (*b*) Short for *Epsom salts* (see EPSOM) 1772. 5. *Chem.* A compound formed by the union of an acid radical with a basic radical; an acid having the whole or part of its hydrogen replaced by a metal. (In wider theoretical use the term 'salt' includes acids, as salts of hydrogen.) 1790. 6. = SALT-CELLAR 1493. 7. *pl.* Salt marshes or saltings 1621. 8. *pl.* Salt water entering a river from the sea 1658. 9. *colloq.* A sailor, esp. one of much experience 1840.

1. They threw the s. over their shoulders,..in propitiation of evil powers, when they spilled it at table 1884. *White s.*, salt refined mainly for household use (as contrasted with rock-salt, which is brownish-red). *In s.*, sprinkled with s. or immersed in brine; in pickle. *To cast, drop a pinch of, put, s. on the tail of*, to capture, in allusion to the joc. advice given to children to catch birds by this means. *With a grain of s.* [= mod.L. *cum grano salis*], (to accept a statement) with some reserve. (*To be*) *worth one's s.*, efficient or capable. 2. Phr. *To eat s. with* (a person), *to eat* (a person's) *s.*, to enjoy his hospitality; also occas. to be dependent on him. **b.** The s. of most vnrighteous Teares SHAKS. 3. **b.** Wee haue some s. of our youth in vs SHAKS. **c.** Humour, the s. of well-bred conversation 1874. *Attic s.*: see ATTIC *a.* 2. 6. Under every s. there was a bill of fare PEPYS. Phr. *Above* (or *below, beneath, under*) *the s.*, at the upper (or lower) part of the table, *i.e.* among the more honoured (or less honoured) guests (with ref. to the formerly prevailing custom of placing a large s.-cellar in the middle of a dining-table). 9. If you want to hear about the sea, talk to an 'old s.' 1877.

Comb.: **s. bottom** *U.S.*, a 'bottom' (BOTTOM *sb.* 4) covered with saline efflorescence; **s. bush**, any of the plants of the genus *Atriplex*, which grow extensively on the interior plains of Australia; **cake,** (*a*) s. in the form of a cake; (*b*) crude sulphate of soda; **s. glaze,** a thin glaze of silicate of soda, produced on some stoneware by throwing common salt into the furnace while the ware is still glowing; **-lick,** a place where cattle collect to lick the earth impregnated with s.; **-looking** *a.* of sailor-like appearance; **-marsh,** marsh overflowed or flooded by the sea; **s. mine,** a mine yielding rock salt; **-pit,** a pit where s. is obtained; **-pond,** a pond into which sea-water is run in order to be evaporated; **-radical** *Chem.*, in the binary theory of salts, any body which forms a s. with a metal or its equivalent; **-stand,** a salt-cellar; **-tax** = GABELLE 1; **-well,** a salt spring or well; now, a bored well from which brine is obtained; **-works,** a s. manufactory. Hence **Sa·ltless** *a.* without s.; unsalted. **Sa·ltly** *adv.* with the taste or smell of s. **Sa·ltness,** the property or state of being s., or impregnated with s.

†**Salt,** *sb.*[2] 1519. [a. F. *saut* (lit. 'leap'):—L. *saltus, salire.*] Sexual desire or excitement (usu., of a bitch) –1648.

Salt (sǭlt), *a.*[1] [OE. *sealt*:—OTeut. **saltoz* :—pre-Teut. **sald-*; cf. L. *salsus*, f. **sald-* + *-tos.*] 1. Impregnated with or containing salt; hence, having a taste like that of salt; saline. 2. Cured, preserved, or seasoned with salt; salted OE. 3. †**a.** Of fishes: Living in the sea; opp. to *freshwater.* **b.** Of plants: Growing in the sea or on salt marshes. ME. 4. Of speech wit, etc.: Pungent, stinging. Now *rare.* 1600.

1. He seylith in the salte se CHAUCER. Salte teeres CHAUCER. Sea-mud, salt-sand,..and river-sludge 1838. The keen s. air 1873. 2 S. cod for Lent 1861 Phrases (*Naut. joc.*): **S. eel,** a rope's end. **S. horse:** salted beef. **S. junk:** see JUNK *sb.*[2] 3. **S. rising** (*U.S.*), salted batter used as a leaven for bread.

†**Salt,** *a.*[2] 1541. [Aphet. f. ASSAUT *adv.* in phr. *to go* or *be assaut.*] Of bitches: In heat –1737. **b.** *transf.* Of persons: Lecherous, salacious; hence (of desire), inordinate –1683.

b. Whose s. imagination yet hath wrong'd Your well defended honor SHAKS.

Salt (sǭlt), *v.* [(1) OE. *sealtan*, f. OTeut. **salto-* :—pre-Teut. **saldo-* SALT *sb*[1]. (2) OE. **sieltan, seltan* :—**saltjan*, f. OTeut. **salto-*.] 1. *trans.* To cure or preserve with salt, either in solid form or in the form of brine. Also with *down.* 2. **a.** In biblical use: To sprinkle salt upon (a sacrifice); to rub (a new-born child) with salt. **b.** To rub salt into (a wound). **c.** To sprinkle (snow) with salt in order to melt it. ME. 3. To season with salt OE. 4. To render salt or salty. Also *fig.*, to embitter. 1786. 5. *fig.* To season; to render poignant or piquant 1576. 6. *Photogr.* To impregnate (paper, etc.) with a solution of salt or a mixture of salts 1879. **b.** To treat with chemical salts 1904. 7. *Comm. slang. To s. an invoice, account*, etc.: to put down an extreme price for each article. *To s. books*: to make fictitious entries in books, so as to swell the apparent turn-over, when selling a business, etc 1882. 8. *Mining slang.* To make (a mine) appear to be a paying one by fraudulently introducing rich ore, sprinkling gold dust in it, etc. 1864.

1. In Ffraunce the peple salten but lytill mete, except thair bacon 1460. Snails she had salted down in a barrel 1875. Phr. *To s. down, away* (slang), to put by, store away (money, stock). 5. **b.** *To s. down* (U.S. colloq.), to 'dress' down 1904. 8. He purchased some valuable specimens of gold quartz, with which he salted the estate 1892.

Saltant (sæ·ltănt), *a.* 1601. [ad. L. *saltantem.*] †**a.** Leaping, dancing –1827. **b.** *Her.* Applied to small animals when salient 1850.

‖**Saltarello** (sæltăre·lo). 1724. [It. *salterello* cracker, squib; related to It. *saltare* to leap, dance.] An Italian and Spanish dance for one couple, in which there are frequent sudden skips or jumps. Also, the music for this.

Saltate (sæ·lteit), *v. rare.* 1623. [f. L. *saltat-, saltare* to dance, freq. of *salire.*] *intr.* To leap, jump, skip.

Saltation (sæltē·ʃən). 1623. [ad. L. *saltationem.*] 1. Leaping, bounding, or jumping; a leap 1646. **b.** *spec.* Dancing; a dance 1623. **c.** *fig.* An abrupt movement, change, or transition 1844. †2. *spec.* Pulsation or spurting forth of blood –1767.

1. Locusts..being ordained for s., their hinder legs doe far exceed the other SIR T. BROWNE. **c.** We greatly suspect..that she [*sc.* Nature] does make considerable jumps in the way of variation now and then, and that these saltations give rise to some of the gaps which appear to exist in the series of known forms HUXLEY.

Saltatorial (sæltătō·riăl), *a.* 1789. [f. L. *saltatorius* SALTATORY + -AL 1.] 1. Of, pertaining to, or characterized by leaping (or *spec.* dancing). 2. Adapted for leaping; *spec.* belonging to the group *Saltatoria* of insects 1842. So **Saltato·rious** *a.*

Saltatory (sæ·ltătəri), *a.* 1656. [ad. L. *saltatorius.*] Of, pertaining to, characterized by, or adapted for leaping or dancing; *spec.* = prec. 2. **b.** *fig.* Proceeding by abrupt movement 1844.

I soon began to avoid exhibiting my s. talents, and I seldom danced EDGEWORTH. The Frog is a small s. Reptile 1874. **b.** Nature hates calculators; her methods are s. and impulsive EMERSON.

Sa·lt-cat. ME. [Orig. northern; the second element is unexplained.] A mass of salt, or salt mixed with other matter; *esp.* a mixture of salt, gravel, old mortar or lime, cummin seed, and stale urine, used to attract pigeons and to keep them at home.

Sa·lt-ce·llar. late ME. [f. SALT *sb.*[1] + †*saler* salt-cellar, a. OF. *saliere* :—L. *salariam* pertaining to salt (assim. in spelling to CELLAR).] 1. A small vessel placed on the table for holding salt. 2. The depression above the collar-bone, when conspicuous, in a woman's neck, regarded as a disfigurement 1913.

Salted (sǭ·ltėd), *ppl. a.* ME. [f. SALT *sb.*[1] or *v.* + -ED[1] 1.] 1. Cured, preserved, or pickled with salt. 2. Containing or impregnated with salt 1526. **b.** Treated with salt 1824. 3. *fig.* 'Seasoned' with wit or good sense; sensible 1647. 4. *slang.* or *colloq.* Of horses, etc.: Seasoned; hence of persons: Experienced in some business or occupation 1879. 5. *slang.* Of a mine, business, etc.: Having its value fraudulently enhanced 1886.

4. A 's.' horse will always command a good price 1879. An old s. trader 1892. 5. Their bogus companies and their s. gold-mines 1889.

Salter (sǭ·ltəɹ). [OE. *sealtere*, f. *sealtan* SALT *v.*; see -ER [1].] 1. A manufacturer of or dealer in salt; also *spec.* = DRYSALTER. 2. A workman at a salt-works 1606. 3. One who salts meat or fish 1611.

Saltern (sǭ·ltəɹn). [OE. *sealtærn*, f. *sealt* + *ærn* dwelling.] A building in which salt is made by boiling or evaporation; a salt-works; a plot of land, laid out in pools and walks, in which sea-water is allowed to evaporate naturally.

Saltigrade (sæ·ltigrēid), *a.* and *sb.* 1840. [f. mod.L. *Saltigradæ* pl., f. *saltus* leap + *gradi* to advance.] *Zool.* **A.** *adj.* Belonging to the *Saltigradæ*, a group of vagabond spiders having legs adapted for leaping. **B.** *sb.* A spider of this group.

‖**Saltimbanco** (sæltimbæ·ŋko). 1646. [It., f. *saltare* to leap + *in* on + *banco* bench.] A mountebank; a quack.

Saltimbancoes, Quacksalvers, and Charlatans 1646.

Salting (sǭ·ltiŋ), *vbl. sb.* ME. [f. SALT *v.* + -ING [1].] The action of SALT *v.*; *spec.* 1. The curing of meat, fish, etc., with salt. 2. Chiefly *pl.* Salt lands 1712.

Saltire (sæ·ltəiəɹ). late ME. [a. OF. *saut(e)oir, salteur.* :—L. *saltatorium.*] *Her.* An ordinary in the form of a St. Andrew's cross, formed by a bend and a bend sinister, crossing each other. Hence *In s.*: crossed like the limbs of a St. Andrew's cross. Hence **Sa·ltireways, -wise** *advs.* in s.

Saltish (sǭ·ltiʃ), *a.* 1477. [f. SALT *a.*[1] + -ISH [1].] †**a.** Salt, salty. **b.** Somewhat salt. Hence **Sa·ltish-ly** *adv.*, **-ness.**

Sa·lt-pan. 1493. [Cf. G. *salzpfanne.*] **a.** (Usu. *pl.*) A shallow depression near the sea, in which sea-water evaporates, leaving a deposit of salt; in Africa, applied (after Du. *zoutpan*) to dried-up salt lakes or marshes. **b.** A shallow vessel in which brine is evaporated in salt-making; *pl.* a salt-works.

Saltpetre (sǭltpī·təɹ). Also (now *U.S.*) -peter. 1501. [Altered f. *salpetre* (a. OF., ad. med.L. *salpetra*), after SALT *sb.*[1]] A crystalline substance, potassium nitrate, having a saline taste; the chief constituent of gunpowder.

Chili or *cubic s.*, sodium nitrate.

attrib. and *Comb.*: as **s. paper** = TOUCH PAPER; **s. rot,** white efflorescence which forms on new or damp walls, caused by s. working through to the surface. Hence **Saltpe·treing,** the formation of s. rot.

Salt rheum. 1590. [SALT *a.*[1]] †1. A running cold. SHAKS. 2. *U.S.* A popular name for various cutaneous eruptions, particularly for those of eczema 1828.

Salt water, *sb.* and *a.* OE. [SALT *a.*[1]]

A. *sb.* Water impregnated with salt; sea-water. **b.** Applied *joc.* to tears. late ME. **B.** *attrib.* as *adj.* Of, pertaining to, consisting of, or living in salt water 1528. **b.** In specific names of sea animals, as *salt-water louse*, etc. 1828.

Sa·ltwort. 1568. [prob. after Du. *zoutkruid.*] **1.** Any plant of the genus *Salsola*, spec. *S. Kali* (Common or Prickly S.). **2.** Black S., *Glaux maritima*. = MILKWORT 2. 1597. **3.** A plant of the genus *Salicornia*, esp. *S. herbacea*; = GLASSWORT a. 1597.

Salty (sǫ·lti), *a.* 1440. [f. SALT *sb.*[1] + -Y [1].] **1.** = SALT *a.*[1] 1. †**2.** Consisting of salt (*rare*) –1665. Hence **Sa·ltiness.**

Salubrious (săliū·briəs), *a.* 1547. [f. L. *salubris* (f. *salus* health) + -OUS.] Favourable or conducive to health.

A species of food so very palatable and s. as turtle 1748. In summer the air is remarkably s. 1774. Hence **Salu·brious-ly** *adv.*, **-ness.**

Salubrity (săliū·briti). late ME. [ad. L. *salubritas*, f. *salubris* SALUBRIOUS.] **1.** The quality of being salubrious. ¶**2.** Healthy condition, health 1654.

1. The s. of the air had a surprising effect in strengthening both the appetite and digestion 1767.

†**Salue·**, *v.* ME. [a. F. *saluer* :—L. *salutare* to SALUTE.] *trans.* = SALUTE *v.* –1606.

And he saleweth hire with glad entente CHAUCER.

Saluki (sălū·ki, sălū·gi). 1890. Also **sa-, selug(h)i.** [Arab.; of disputed origin.] The Arabian gazelle-hound.

Salutary (sæ·liŭtări), *a.* 1490. [ad. F. *salutaire*, or L. *salutaris*, f. *salutem*, *salus* health; see -ARY [2].] **1.** Conducive to health; usu., serving to promote recovery from disease, or to counteract a deleterious influence 1649. **2.** Conducive to well-being; beneficial. Often with fig. notion of sense 1. 1490.

1. Abana and Pharphar..were not so s. as the waters of Jordan to cure Naamans leprosie 1649. 2. The natives having a s. dread of the guns LIVINGSTONE.

Salutation (sæliŭtēⁱ·ʃən). late ME. [a. OF. *salutacion*, ad. L. *salutationem.*] **1.** The action, or an act, of saluting; a manner of saluting; an utterance, form of words, gesture, or movement, by which one person salutes another. **b.** *Naut.* The action of saluting by the firing of guns, lowering of flags, etc.; an instance of this. Now *rare.* 1585. **2.** Ellipt. for 'I offer salutation'. *arch.* 1535.

1. In all publick meetings, or private addresses..use those forms of s...which..[are] usual amongst the most sober persons JER. TAYLOR. He had bowed his head and taken off his hat in s. 1851. *The Angelical S.*, †*the s. of our Lady*, etc., the AVE MARY (see *Luke* i. 29); also, a representation of the Annunciation. 2. S. and greeting to you all SHAKS.

Salutatorian (săliŭtătōᵊ·riăn). *U.S.* 1847. [f. next + -AN [1] 1.] The student who delivers the 'salutatory' (see next A. b) oration at the annual commencement day exercises.

Salutatory (săliū·tătəri), *a.* and *sb.* 1641. [ad. L. *salutatorius*, f. *salutare* to SALUTE.] **A.** *adj.* Pertaining to, or of the nature of, a salutation 1895. **b.** *U.S.* Applied to the address of welcome (usu. in Latin), which introduces the exercises of commencement in American schools and colleges 1702. **B.** *sb.* †**1.** [= med. L. *salutatorium.*] A place of salutation –1656. **2.** *U.S.* The 'salutatory' oration (see A. b) 1851. Hence **Salu·tatorily** *adv.* (*rare*) by way of greeting.

Salute (săliū·t), *sb.* late ME. [a. F. *salut*; (1) vbl. sb. f. Com. Rom. (L.) *salutare* to SALUTE; (2) orig.:—L. *salutem*, *salus* health.] **1.** An utterance, gesture, or action of any kind by which one person salutes another; a salutation. **2.** A kiss, by way of salutation 1590. **3.** *Mil.* and *Naut.* **a.** A discharge of cannon or small arms, display of flags, dipping of sails, cheering of men, manning the yards, etc., as a mark of respect, or as military, naval, or official honour, for a person, nation, event, etc. 1698. **b.** A raising of the hand to the cap by an inferior when meeting or leaving, addressing, or addressed by a superior, both being in uniform 1832. **c.** The position of the sword, rifle, hand, etc., or the attitude assumed in saluting 1833. **4.** *Fencing.* A formal greeting of swordsmen when about to engage, consisting of a conventional series of guards, thrusts, etc. 1809.

1. O what avails me now..that s. Hale highly favour'd, among women blest MILT. 3. **c.** Phr. (*To stand*) *at* (*the*) *s.*

Salute (săliū·t), *v.* late ME. [ad. L. *salutare*, f. *salutem*, *salus* health.] **1.** *trans.* To accost or address with some customary formula, or with words expressing good wishes, respect, etc.; to greet in words. **b.** To hail or greet (as king, etc.) 1560. **c.** *poet.* Of birds, etc.: To greet (the sun, the dawn) with song 1682. **2.** To greet with some gesture or visible action conventionally expressive of respect or courteous recognition 1440. **b.** *absol.* and *intr.* To perform a salutation 1589. **c.** *spec.* in *Mil.* and *Naval* use. (*a*) *trans.* To pay respect to (a superior) by a prescribed bodily movement, the presenting of arms, or the like. (*b*) Of a ship, a body of troops, a commander: To honour or ceremoniously recognize by a discharge of artillery or small arms, by lowering of flags, or the like. (*c*) *absol.* and *intr.* To perform a salute. 1582. **d.** *Fencing.* To perform the salute used in fencing 1809. **e.** *trans.* To kiss, or greet with a kiss (*arch.*) 1716. †**3.** To pay one's respects to; to pay a complimentary visit to –1698. **4.** *transf.* and *fig.* Of inanimate things: To appear or come forth as if in welcome of; to approach, come into contact with; †(in Shaks.) to affect or act upon in any way 1440. **b.** Of a sight or sound: To strike (the eye or ear) 1586.

1. Being admitted to his presence they saluted him in the queen's name 1845. Phr. *I s. you*, used as itself a formula of salutation; I s. thee, Mantovano, I that loved thee since my day began TENNYSON. **b.** King Henrie..for the time was saluted Lord of Ireland 1617. 2. Deere Earth, I doe s. thee with my hand SHAKS. **e.** I had the honour of saluting the far famed Miss Flora Macdonald JOHNSON. 4. Would I had no being If this s. my blood a iot SHAKS. Hence **Salu·ter**, one who salutes.

Salutiferous (sæliuti·fĕrəs), *a.* 1540. [f. L. *salutifer* (f. *salut-* health + *-fer* bringing) + -OUS.] Conducive to health, well-being, safety, or salvation.

Safe, wholesome and s. Medecins 1604. The..s. streames of the waters of life 1629. Hence **Saluti·ferously** *adv.*

Salvability (sælvăbi·lĭti). 1654. [f. as next + -ITY.] *Theol.* Capability of being saved.

Salvable (sæ·lvăb'l), *a.* 1667. [ad. L. **salvabilis*, f. *salvare* to SAVE; see -ABLE.] **1.** *Theol.* Capable of being saved, admitting of salvation. **2.** Of a ship, cargo: That can be salvaged 1797.

1. He is not in a s. state WESLEY. Hence **Sa·lvableness.**

Salvage (sæ·lvėdʒ), *sb.* 1645. [ad. med. L. *salvagium*, f. L. *salvare* to save; see -AGE.] **1.** A compensation to which those persons are entitled who have by their voluntary efforts saved a ship or its cargo from impending peril or rescued it from actual loss; e.g. from shipwreck (*civil s.*) or from capture by the enemy (*military* or *hostile s.*). **2.** The action of saving a ship or its cargo from wreck, capture, etc. 1713. **b.** *gen.* The saving of property from fire or other danger 1878. **3.** Property salved or saved 1755.

2. S. of life is rewarded at a higher rate than s. of property 1886. Phr. *To make s. of.*

Comb.: **s. corps**, a body of men kept in some towns to save property from fire; a fire brigade; **s. money** = sense 1. Hence **Sa·lvage** *v. trans.* to make s. of; to save from shipwreck, fire, etc.

Salvarsan (sæ·lvăɹsæn). 1910. [a. G. (P. Ehrlich), f. L. *salv*(*are* to save + G. *ars*(*enik.*] *Chem.* Proprietary name of an arsenical compound, dihydrochloride of dioxy-diamino-arseno-benzene, $C_{12}H_{12}O_2N_2As_2(HCl)_2 2H_2O$, used in the treatment of syphilis; also called 606.

Largely superseded by a later invention of Ehrlich, *neo-salvarsan* or 914.

Salvation (sælvēⁱ·ʃən). ME. [a. OF. *salvatiun*, ad. late L. *salvationem*, f. *salvare* to SAVE.] **1.** The saving of the soul; the deliverance from sin, and admission to eternal bliss, wrought for man by the atonement of Christ. [eccl. L. *salvatio*, rendering Gr. σωτηρία.] **2.** *gen.* Preservation from destruction, loss, or calamity. (In mod. use chiefly with some allusion to sense 1.) late ME. **3.** A source, cause, means of salvation; a person or thing that saves. Now chiefly in phr. *to be the s. of.* late ME.

1. Euen so worke out your awne saluacion with feare and tremblynge COVERDALE *Phil.* ii. 12. 2. Shall Ionathan die, who hath wrought this great saluation in Israel? 1 *Sam.* xiv. 45. 3. Sleep is the s. of the nervous system 1878. Hence **Salva·tional** *a.* (*rare*). **Salva·tionalism** = SALVA·TIONISM b.

Salvation Army. 1878. An organization, on a quasi-military model, founded by the Rev. William Booth for the revival of religion among the masses.

Salva·tionism. 1883. [-ISM.] **a.** Religious teaching which lays prime stress on 'salvation', or the saving of the soul. **b.** The principles or methods of the Salvation Army. So **Salva·tionist**, a member of the Salvation Army.

Salvatory (sæ·lvătəri), *sb.* 1549. [ad. med.L. *salvatorium* place of preservation, f. *salvare* to SAVE.] †**1.** A box for holding ointment –1715. **2.** *gen.* A repository for safe storage (*rare*) 1677.

Salvatory (sæ·lvătəri), *a.* *rare.* 1830. [ad. L. **salvatorius*; see prec.] Saving, imparting safety or salvation (*to*).

Salve (sāv), *sb.*[1] [OE. *sealf* :—OTeut. **salbā* :—pre-Teut. **solpā*, perh. cogn. w. Gr. ὄλπη, ὄλπις oil-flask.] **1.** A healing ointment for application to wounds or sores. **b.** A mixture, usu. of tar and grease, for smearing sheep 1523. **2.** *fig.* **a.** A remedy (esp. for spiritual disease, sorrow, etc.) Now *rare.* ME. **b.** *esp.* Something which serves to soothe wounded feelings, honour, or a tender conscience 1736.

2. **b.** Let us hope that this little s. to self-esteem never lost its efficacy 1874.

†**Salve**, *sb.*[2] 1577. [a. F., ad. It. *salva*; see SALVO [2].] = SALVO [2] –1693.

†**Salve**, *sb.*[3] 1628. [f. SALVE *v.*[2]; cf. SALVO [1].] **a.** A solution of a difficulty; also, a sophistical excuse or evasion. **b.** A salvo or means of salving a person's honour, etc. –1665.

‖**Salve** (sæ·lvi), *sb.*[4] late ME. [L., = 'hail', 'good morning'; 2nd sing. imper. of *salvere* to be well.] **1.** The utterance of the word *s.* or its equivalent; a salutation on meeting 1583. **2.** (More fully *S. Regina.*) In the R. C. Ch., an antiphon, beginning 'Salve, Regina', now recited after the Divine Office from Trinity Sunday to Advent. A musical setting for this. late ME.

Salve (sāv), *v.*[1] [OE. *sealfian* :—OTeut. **salbōjan*, f. **salbā* SALVE *sb.*[1]] **1.** *trans.* To anoint (a wound, etc.) with salve or healing unguent. *Obs.* or *arch.* **b.** *trans.* To smear (sheep) with a mixture of tar and butter, or the like 1523. †**2.** In extended sense: To heal or remedy (a disease). Chiefly *fig.*, to heal (sin, sorrow, etc.). –1624. †**b.** To heal (a person) *of* (sickness, sin, etc.) –1596. †**3.** *fig.* To heal, remedy, make good, make up, smooth over (something amiss, a disgrace, offence, etc.) –1712. **4.** *fig.* (From sense 1.) To soothe (irritated feeling, an uneasy conscience, etc.) 1825.

1. Since plain speech salves the wound it seems to make BROWNING. 3. But Ebranck salved both their infamies with noble deedes SPENSER. 4. In the endeavour to s. their wounded pride 1878.

†**Salve**, *v.*[2] 1571. [app. ad. L. *salvare* to SAVE.] **1.** *Astr. To s.* (*the appearances*, *the phenomena*), to frame a hypothesis which will account for all the observed facts of the apparent motions of the heavenly bodies. Hence *gen.*, to account for by hypothesis. –1691. **2.** To clear up, account for (a difficulty, point in dispute, etc.); to overcome (a doubt, objection); to harmonize (a discrepancy) –1744. **3.** To render tenable (an opinion); to vindicate from incredibility (an alleged fact) –1720. **4.** To maintain unhurt (one's honour, credit, etc.). Hence, to make good (one's oath). –1814.

2. What may we do..to s. this seeming inconsistence? MILT. 4. An afterthought to s. decorum SOUTHEY.

Salve (sælv), *v.*[3] 1706. [Back-formation from SALVAGE.] *trans.* To save (a ship, its cargo) from loss at sea; to save (property) from destruction by fire; to make salvage of.

Salver (sæ·lvəɹ). 1661. [f. F. *salve* (with suffix *-er* after *platter*, etc.), ad. Sp. *salva*, primarily the 'assaying' of food or drink, and hence a tray on which the cup was placed when its contents were shown to be safe, f. *salvo* SAFE *a.*, or *salvar* to 'assay' food or drink.] A tray, used for handing refreshments, presenting letters, etc.

Comb.: **s.-shaped** *a.* (*Bot.*) = HYPOCRATERIFORM *a.*

‖**Salvia** (sæ·lviă). 1844. [L., SAGE *sb.*¹] *Bot.* A large genus of *Labiatæ*, including the common sage; a plant of this genus.

Salvo (sæ·lvo), *sb.*¹ 1642. [a. L., abl. neut. sing. of *salvus* SAFE *a.*, as occurring in med.L. law phrases like *salvo jure* 'without prejudice to the right of' (some specified person), etc.] **1.** A saving clause; a reservation. Const. *of* (a right, etc.). **2.** A dishonest mental reservation; a quibbling evasion; a consciously bad excuse 1665. †**3.** A solution (of a difficulty), an answer (to an objection) -1770. **4.** An expedient for saving (a person's reputation) or soothing (offended pride, conscience) 1754.

1. With an express s. of their right to liberty of conscience 1826. 2. Some new attempt on his part to find a s. for staying in office 1828. 4. This would be a s. for the disgrace of removing them 1855.

Salvo (sæ·lvo), *sb.*² 1591. [orig. *salva*, a. It. *salva*, perh. a. Com. Rom. formation on L. *salve* hail!] **1.** A salute consisting in the simultaneous discharge of artillery or other firearms 1719. **2.** A simultaneous discharge of artillery or other firearms, whether with hostile intent or otherwise 1591. **b.** *transf.* Chiefly used for a 'volley' of applause 1734.

2. The Russians..were firing salvoes by batteries of eight guns 1879. Hence **Sa·lvo** *v.* to salute (a vessel, etc.) by firing of a s.

Sal volatile (sæl vŏlæ·tĭlĭ). 1654. [mod. L., 'volatile salt'; see SAL and VOLATILE *a.*] Ammonium carbonate, *esp.* an aromatic solution of this used as a restorative in fainting fits.

Salvor (sæ·lvəɹ, sæ·lvǫɹ). 1678. [f. SALVE *v.* + -OR 2.] **1.** One who saves or helps to save vessels or cargo from loss at sea. **2.** A vessel used in salvage 1815.

Sam (sæm), *sb. slang.* 1823. [Origin obsc.] **1.** *To stand S.*: to pay expenses, esp. for refreshment or drink. **2.** *Upon my S.*: a jocular asseveration 1879.

†**Sam,** *adv.* ME. [Shortened f. OE. **samen*, *somen*, ME. *samen* together.] Together; mutually -1600.

For what concord han light and darke s.? SPENSER.

‖**Samara** (sæ·mără). 1577. [mod.L. use of L. *samara* seed of the elm.] *Bot.* The indehiscent winged fruit of the elm, ash, etc.

Samaritan (sămæ·rĭtăn), *sb.* and *a.* OE. [ad. late L. *Samaritanus*, f. Gr. Σαμαρείτης, f. Σαμάρεια Samaria.] **A.** *sb.* A native or inhabitant of Samaria, a district of Palestine; *esp.* one who adheres to the religious system which had its origin in Samaria. **b.** *fig.* with ref. to the 'good Samaritan'; see Luke x. 33. 1644. **B.** *adj.* Of or pertaining to Samaria or the Samaritans. late ME.

S. Pentateuch, a recension of the Hebrew Pentateuch used by the Samaritans. Hence **Sama·ritanism,** the S. religious system; also, imitation of the 'good S.'

Samarium (sămē·riŏm). 1883. [f. SAMAR(SKITE) + -IUM.] *Chem.* A metallic element (symbol Sm); the bands supposed to indicate it were first found in the spectrum of samarskite.

‖**Samarra** (sămæ·ră). 1688. [med.L.; see SIMARRE.] *Hist.* A garment, painted with flames, worn on the way to execution by persons condemned by the Inquisition to be burnt.

Samarskite (sămā·ɹskəit). 1849. [Named after Col. *Samarski*; see -ITE ¹ 2 b.] *Min.* A complex columbate of uranium and other bases.

Sambo (sæ·mbo). *Pl.* **-bos, -boes.** 1748. [a. Sp. *zambo*, perh. identical with *zambo* bandy-legged. See also ZAMBO.] **1.** Applied in America and Asia to persons of various degrees of mixed negro and Indian or European blood. **2.** (With capital S.) A nickname for a negro. [perh. a different word.] 1860.

1. A quadroon looks down upon a mulatto, while a mulatto looks down upon a s., that is, half mulatto half negro MARRYAT.

Sam Browne (sæm braun). 1915. In full *Sam Browne belt* (1898): an officers' field belt having a supporting strap over the right shoulder, invented by Gen. Sir *Sam*uel J. *Browne* (1824-1901).

‖**Sambuca** (sæmbiū·kă). late ME. [L., ad. Gr. σαμβύκη, prob. of Eastern origin.] **1.** *Ancient Music.* A triangular stringed instrument having a shrill tone. **2.** *Rom. Antiq.* A military engine for storming walls 1489.

Sambur (sæ·mbəɹ). 1698. [a. Hindī *sābar*, *sāmbar*.] The Indian elk, *Rusa aristotelis.*

Same (sēⁱm), *a.*, *pron.*, *adv.* [ME., a. ON.; a Com. Teut. wd., lost in OE.; = Skr. *samá* equal, same, Gr. ὁμός same:—Indo-Eur. **somo-*.] The ordinary adjectival and pronominal designation of identity. Normally preceded by *the*, exc. after a demonstrative; the omission of the article occurs only in dial. or vulgar speech and in certain specially elliptical varieties of diction (e.g. in commercial correspondence). **A.** *adj.* **I. 1.** Identical with what is indicated in the following context. Const. *as*, *with*, or relative clause. **2.** Identical with what has been indicated ME. **3.** Expressing the identity of an object designated by different names, standing in different relations, or related to different subjects or objects 1621. **b.** More explicitly, *one and the s.* 1551. **4.** Coupled for emphasis with a synonymous adj., as in *the very s.* ME. **5.** Appended redundantly to a demonstrative (*this, these, that, those, yon*). Usu. expressing some degree of irritation or contempt, sometimes playful familiarity. Now *arch.* ME.

1. The standard itself was blown down the s. night it had been set up CLARENDON. The Horse and Man on the Medal are in the s. Posture as they are on the Statue ADDISON. The Greeks and Macedonians.. looked on the Egyptian Ammon as the s. god with their own Zeus 1873. He defends it on the s. ground that he would defend the 'Lycidas' of Milton 1876. 2. Into poudre must I crepe, ffor of that s. kynde I am. late ME. 3. The s. Person is to be paid twice for the s. thing STEELE. All the planets travel round the Sun in the s. direction 1868. 5. This s. Truth, is a Naked, and Open day light BACON.

Phrases. *At the s. time*: see TIME *sb.* *By the s. token*: see TOKEN *sb.*

II. In modified senses. **1.** Exactly agreeing *in* (amount, quality, etc.). Of a person: Unchanged in character, condition of health, etc. Chiefly *predic.* 1611. **b.** Corresponding in relative position 1672. **2.** *predic.* Equally acceptable or the contrary; indifferent 1803.

1. What matter where, if I be still the s. MILT. She was always the s. to me DICKENS. His salary was the s. with that of the Lord Lieutenant MACAULAY. b. He and I were both shot in the s. leg at Talavera THACKERAY. 2. It's all the s. to me DICKENS.

B. *absol.* and as *pron.* **1.** The same person or persons ME. **2.** The same thing ME. †**3.** Pleonastically emphasizing a demonstrative, used absol. or with ellipsis of sb. -1611. **4.** *The s.*, †*that* (*this*) *s.*: the aforesaid person or thing. Often merely, he, she, it, they. Still common in legal documents; also (with ref. to things) in commercial language (where *the* is sometimes omitted). late ME. **b.** †As an answer when addressed by name; = 'I am he'; *colloq.* in confirming a conjecture as to the identity of a person mentioned by the speaker 1599.

2. Here that common Proverbe holds true, 'When two do the s. it is not the s.' 1677. 3. What Letter is this s.? SHAKS. 4. But he that shall endure vnto the end, the s. shall be saued *Matt.* xxiv. 13. b. *Ben.* Count Claudio. *Clau.* Yea, the s. SHAKS.

C. *adv.* **1.** *The s.*: **a.** in the same manner. Const. *as.* (Now rare in literary use.) Also occas. = 'all the same'. 1766. **2.** *All the s.*: nevertheless, notwithstanding 1803. **3.** *Just the s.*: **a.** Exactly in the same manner. Const. *as.* **b.** None the less. 1874.

1. a. *To think the s. of*, to have the same (good) opinion of (a person); You'll never think the s. of me again GEO. ELIOT. 2. What you say is well worth attention; but all the s. I feel we are on the eve of a..crisis DISRAELI. 3. And..Dillingham will continue his visits here just the s.? 1874.

Samel (sæ·mĕl), *a.* 1601. [Origin obsc.; perh. repr. an OE. **samǽled* half-burnt.] Of a brick or tile: Imperfectly burnt.

Samely (sēⁱ·mli), *a.* 1799. [f. SAME *a.* + -LY ¹.] Monotonous. Hence **Sa·meliness.**

Sameness (sēⁱ·mnės). 1581. [f. SAME *a.* + -NESS 1.] **1.** The quality of being the same. **2.** Uniformity, monotony; an instance of this 1743.

Samian (sēⁱ·miăn), *a.* and *sb.* 1580. [f. L. *Samius*, Gr. Σάμιος + -AN ¹ 1.] **A.** *adj.* Of or pertaining to Samos, an island in the Ægean Sea, the birthplace of Pythagoras.

S. letter, the letter Y, used by Pythagoras as an emblem of the different roads of virtue and vice. **S. ware,** a fine kind of pottery found extensively on Roman sites.

B. *sb.* A native or inhabitant of Samos 1580.

Samiel (sēⁱ·miĕl). 1687. [a. Turk. *samyel*, f. *sam*, a. Arab. *samm* (see SIMOOM) + *yel* WIND.] The simoom.

‖**Samisen** (sæ·misen). 1864. [Jap. f. Chinese *san-hsien* (*san* three, *hsien* string).] A Japanese guitar of three strings, played with a plectrum.

Samite (sæ·məit). *Obs.* exc. *Hist.* ME. [a. OF. *samit*, ad. med. Gr. ἑξάμιτον, f. Gr. ἑξα- comb. form of ἕξ six + μίτος thread.] A rich silk fabric worn in the Middle Ages, sometimes interwoven with gold. Also, †a garment or cushion of this.

In the myddes of the lake Arthur was ware of an arme clothed in whyte samyte MALORY.

Samlet (sæ·mlėt). 1655. [Contr. f. SALMON + -LET.] A young salmon.

Sammy (sæ·mi), *v.* 1891. [Extended form of *sam* vb., of obsc. origin.] *Leather-dressing. trans.* To dry (leather) partially. So **Sa·mmier,** a machine for expressing water from skins during tanning 1884.

Samnite (sæ·mnəit), *sb.* and *a.* late ME. [ad. L. *Samnites* pl. (sing. *Samnis*); perh. cogn. w. SABINE.] **A.** *sb.* One of a people of ancient Italy, believed to be an offshoot of the Sabines; their territory, Samnium, was adjacent to Latium. **B.** *adj.* Of or pertaining to the Samnites; in use among the Samnites 1696.

Samoan (sămōᵘ·ăn), *a.* and *sb.* 1846. [f. *Samoa*, an island in the Pacific, + -AN ¹ 1.] **A.** *adj.* Pertaining to Samoa, or the Samoans. **B.** *sb.* A native of Samoa; the Samoan language 1846.

Samosatenian (sæmosătī·niăn), *sb.* and *a.* 1597. [f. L. *Samosatenus*, Gr. Σαμοσατηνός (f. *Samosata*) + -AN ¹ 1.] Pertaining to, a follower of, Paul of Samosata.

Samothracian (sæmoþrēⁱ·ʃiăn), *sb.* and *a.* 1653. [f. L. *Samothrace*, Gr. Σαμοθράκη, an island in the Ægean Sea + -IAN.] **A.** *sb.* An inhabitant of Samothrace. **B.** *adj.* Of or pertaining to Samothrace; *esp.* with ref. to the Cabiric mysteries which originated there.

‖**Samovar** (sæmovā·ɹ). 1830. [Russ., f. *samo-* self, *varitĭ* to boil.] A Russian tea-urn.

Samoyed(e (sæmoye·d, -ī·d), *sb.* and *a.* 1556. [Russ.] **A.** *sb.* **1.** One of a Mongolian race inhabiting Siberia. **2.** (usu. *-ede*) A dog of a white Arctic breed 1889. **B.** *adj.* Of or pertaining to the Samoyeds. Also quasi-*sb.*, their language. 1667.

A. 2. Samoyede sledge dog 1889. B. From the North Of Norumbega, and the Samoed shoar MILT. Hence **Samoye·dic** *a.* of or pertaining to the Samoyeds; quasi-*sb.* their language.

Samp (sæmp). *U.S.* 1643. [a. Algonkin *nasamp*, lit. 'softened by water'.] Coarsely-ground Indian corn; a porridge made from it.

Sampan (sæ·mpæn). 1620. [a. Chinese *san-pan* boat (*san* three, *pan* board).] Applied by Europeans in the China seas to any small boat of Chinese pattern.

Samphire (sæ·mfəiəɹ). 1545. [orig. *sampere*, *-pire*, a. F. (*herbe de*) *Saint Pierre*, lit. 'St. Peter's herb'.] **1.** The plant *Crithmum maritimum* (growing on rocks by the sea), the aromatic, saline, fleshy leaves of which are used in pickles. Also called *Rock s.* **b.** As a name for other maritime plants, esp. the glasswort (*Salicornia*) 1703. **2.** *Cookery.* The leaves of samphire, used chiefly as a pickle 1624.

1. Halfe way downe Hangs one that gathers Sampire: dreadfull Trade SHAKS.

Sample (sɑ·mp'l), *sb.* [ME., aphet. f. *essample* EXAMPLE *sb.*] †**1.** A fact, incident, story, or suppositious case, which serves to illustrate, confirm, or render credible some proposition or statement -1529. **2.** A relatively small quantity of material, or an individual object, from which the quality of the mass, group, species, etc., which it represents may be inferred; a specimen; a pattern. Now chiefly *Comm.* late ME. †**3.** = EXAMPLE *sb.* 6. -1611. **4.** *attrib.* Serving as a sample 1820.

2. A s. of his Ingenuity 1706. The collection of samples of air for analysis 1882. 3. Liu'd in Court.., A s. to the yongest SHAKS. 4. That..s.-bottle of Hollands THACKERAY.

Comb. **s. card,** a piece of cardboard to which is fastened a s. of cloth, etc.; = *pattern-card.*

Sample (sɑ·mp'l), *v.* 1592. [f. prec.] †**1.** *trans.* To parallel; to intend as a match *for.* Also, to put in comparison *with.* -1689. †**2.**

To illustrate or explain by examples or analogies; to symbolize -1664. 3. To take a sample or samples of; to judge of the quality of (a thing) by a sample or specimen; to obtain a representative experience of 1767. b. To present samples or specimens of 1870.

3. I won't turn my back..on any man in the country at sampling wheat 1858.

Sampler[1] (sɑ·mplǝɹ). ME. [Aphetic f. OF. *essamplaire* EXAMPLAR.] †1. An example to be imitated; a model, pattern; an archetype -1680. 2. †a. A piece of embroidery serving as a pattern to be copied -1675. b. A piece of canvas embroidered by a beginner as a specimen of her skill, usu. containing the alphabet and some mottos, with various decorative devices 1523. 3. *Forestry.* A young tree left standing when the rest are cut down 1535.

2. b. [To] create upon a s. Beasts that Buffon never knew CALVERLEY. Hence **Sa·mplery,** the making of samplers; s. work.

Sampler[2] (sɑ·mplǝɹ). 1778. [f. SAMPLE *v.* + -ER[1].] One who samples goods.

‖**Samshoo** (sæ·mʃū). 1697. [Pidgin-English; of doubtful etym.] Chinese spirits distilled from rice or sorghum.

Samson (sæ·msǝn). Also †**Sampson.** 1565. [a. L. (Vulg.) *Sam(p)son*, Gr. Σαμψών, a. Heb.] The name of the Hebrew hero whose exploits are recorded in Judges xiii–xvi, applied allus. to persons, with ref. to his enormous strength, to his having been blinded, etc. Hence **Samso·nian** (sæmsōu·niăn) *a.* and *sb.* 1654.

Samson's post. 1577. [prob. named in allusion to Judges xvi. 29.] †1. A kind of mousetrap -1828. 2. *Naut.* A strong stanchion passing through the hold of a merchant-ship, or between the decks of a man-of-war.

‖**Samurai** (sæ·murai). 1874. [Japanese.] In feudal Japan, one of the class of military retainers of the daimios; sometimes more widely, a member of the military caste. Now applied to any Japanese army officer. (Unchanged in the pl.)

San. 1927. Colloq. abbrev. of SANATORIUM (3).

Sanative (sæ·nătiv), *a.* late ME. [a. OF. *sanatif* or med.L. *sanativus*, f. L. *sanare*, f. *sanus* healthy.] 1. Having the power to heal; conducive to health; curative, healing. 2. Of, pertaining to or concerned with healing 1695.

Sanatorium (sænătō·riǒm). *Pl.* **-ia.** Also *erron.* **-arium.** 1840. [a. mod.L., f. *sanare* to cure; see -ORY[1].] 1. An establishment for the treatment of invalids, esp. convalescents and consumptives. 2. A place with good climatic and other conditions, to which invalids resort; *spec.* a hill-station in a hot country, esp. in India, to which residents periodically resort to recuperate 1842. 3. A room in a school, etc. for the isolation of the sick 1860.

Sanatory (sæ·nătǝri), *a.* 1832. [As if ad. mod.L. *sanatorius*; see -ORY[2].] = SANATIVE.

2. The mechanical parts of the s. art 1870.

Sanbenito (sænbenī·to). 1560. [a. Sp. *San Benito* St. Benedict. (So called from its resemblance to the scapular introduced by St. Benedict.)] Under the Spanish Inquisition, a yellow penitential garment, resembling a scapular in shape, and having a red St. Andrew's cross before and behind, worn by a confessed and penitent heretic; also, a similar garment of a black colour ornamented with flames, devils, and other devices (occas. called a SAMARRA) worn by an impenitent confessed heretic at an auto-da-fé.

‖**Sancho** (sæ·ŋko). 1817. [Ashanti *osanku.*] A kind of simple guitar used by West African negroes.

Sanctification (sæŋktifikē·ʃǝn). 1526. [ad. eccl. L. *sanctificationem*, f. *sanctificare* to SANCTIFY.] 1. *Theol.* The action of the Holy Ghost in sanctifying or making holy the believer, by the implanting within him of the Christian graces and the destruction of sinful affections. Also, the condition or process of being so sanctified. 2. The action of consecrating or setting apart as holy or for a sacred use or purpose; hallowing 1550. 3. *Eccl.* Canonization as a saint 1855.

1. The only sign of S. is Holiness 1754. 2. The s. of dayes and times is a token of that thankfulnesse.. which we owe to God HOOKER.

Sanctified (sæ·ŋktifǝid), *ppl. a.* 1485. [f. SANCTIFY *v.* + -ED[1].] 1. Of a person: Made holy; *spec.* made holy by the divine grace of the Holy Spirit. 2. Affecting holiness; sanctimonious 1600. 3. Of things: Holy or consecrated; rendered spiritually profitable 1632. b. Of ground, etc.: Consecrated (*rare*) 1525.

2. I see not why we should give ourselves such s. airs 1860. 3. b. *All's Well* I. i. 152.

Sanctifier (sæ·ŋktifǝi,ǝɹ). 1548. [f. next + -ER[1].] 1. *Theol.* One who sanctifies or makes holy; *spec.* the Holy Ghost. 2. *occas.* Something that sanctifies 1753.

Sanctify (sæ·ŋktifǝi), *v.* [Late ME. *seintefie*, later (after L.) *sanctifie*, a. OF. *saintifier*, ad. eccl. L. *sanctificare*, f. L. *sanctus* holy; see -FY.] †1. *trans.* To set apart religiously for an office or function; to consecrate (a king, etc.) -1660. †2. To honour as holy; to ascribe holiness to -1601. b. To manifest (God, his might, etc.) as holy 1535. 3. To consecrate (a thing); to set apart as holy or sacred 1483. 4. To make (a person) holy; to cause to undergo sanctification 1526. b. Chiefly in O.T.: To free from ceremonial impurity 1500. 5. To render holy, impart sanctity to (a thing, quality, action or condition); to render legitimate or binding by a religious sanction. late ME. 6. *transf.* To impart real or apparent sacredness to; to give a colour of morality or innocence to; to justify, sanction. Now *rare* or *Obs.* 1606. 7. To make productive of or conducive to holiness or spiritual blessing 1597.

1. Thus God sanctified Aaron JER. TAYLOR. 3. And [God] blessed the seuenth daye, & sanctified it COVERDALE *Gen.* ii. 3. 5. That holy Man, amaz'd at what he saw, Made haste to sanctifie the Bliss by Law DRYDEN. 6. Custom, which sanctifies all absurdities BENTHAM. 7. Sanctifie, we beseech thee, this thy fatherly correction to him *Bk. Com. Prayer, Visit. Sick.* Hence **Sa·nctifyingly** *adv.*

Sanctimonious (sæŋktimōu·niǝs), *a.* 1603. [f. L. *sanctimonia* SANCTIMONY + -OUS.] †1. Possessing sanctity; sacred, holy, consecrated -1801. 2. Of pretended or assumed sanctity or piety, affecting the appearance of sanctity 1603.

2. *Meas. for M.* I. ii. 7. A set of s. humbugs and thieves 1871. Hence **Sanctimo·nious-ly** *adv.*, **-ness.**

Sanctimony (sæ·ŋktimǝni). 1540. [a. OF. *sanctimonie*, ad. L. *sanctimonia*, f. *sanctus* holy.] †1. Holiness of life and character; the profession of holiness; religiousness, sanctity -1725. †2. Sacredness -1683. 3. Pretended, affected or hypocritical holiness or saintliness; assumed or outward sanctity 1618.

1. *All's Well* IV. iii. 59.

Sanction (sæ·ŋkʃǝn), *sb.* 1563. [a. F., or ad. L. *sanctionem*, f. *sancire* to render sacred or inviolable.] 1. [So L. *sanctio.*] A law or decree; esp. an eccl. decree. Now *Hist.* 2. *Law.* The specific penalty enacted in order to enforce obedience to a law 1633. b. Hence, The provision of rewards for obedience, along with punishments for disobedience, to a law (*remuneratory* as dist. from *punitive s.*) 1692. c. [After L. *sanctio.*] The part or clause of a law which declares the penalty attached to infringement thereof 1651. 3. *Ethics.* A consideration which operates to enforce obedience to any law or rule of conduct; a recognized motive for conformity to moral or religious law 1681. 4. Binding force given to an oath; something which makes an oath or engagement binding; a solemn oath or engagement 1611. 5. The action of rendering legally authoritative or binding; solemn confirmation given to a law, enactment, etc., by a supreme authority 1658. 6. An express authoritative permission or recognition (e.g. of an action, custom, institution, etc.) 1720. b. *fig.* Now more loosely, countenance or encouragement given to an opinion or practice by custom, public sentiment, etc. 1738. 7. Something which serves to support, authorize, or confirm an action, procedure, etc. 1728. †b. A testimonial -1813.

1. *Pragmatic S.*, see PRAGMATIC A. 1. 2. The fear of death..is the most formidable s. which legislators have been able to devise MACAULAY. 3. With regard to any supposed moral standard—what is its s.? what are the motives to obey it? MILL. 4. We swear by thee! and to our oath do thou Give s. SHELLEY. 6. b. Follies that have the s. of antiquity PENNANT. 7. The wedded yoke that each had donned, Seeming a s., not a bond PATMORE. Hence **Sa·nctionary** *a.* relating to sanctions (sense 1). **Sa·nctionist** *a.* and *sb.* (sense 2 c). **Sa·nctionless** *a.* having no s. attached.

Sanction (sæ·ŋkʃǝn), *v.* 1778. [f. prec.] 1. *trans.* To ratify or confirm by sanction or solemn enactment; to authorize; to countenance. 2. To enforce (a law, etc.) by attaching a penalty to transgression 1825.

1. These statements are sanctioned by common sense 1836. A covenant sanctioned by all the solemnities of religion 1838. Hence **Sa·nctionative** *a.* (*Law*) pertaining to sanctioning.

Sanctitude (sæ·ŋktitiūd). 1450. [ad. L. *sanctitudo*, f. *sancti-*, *sanctus* holy; see -TUDE.] The quality of being holy or saint-like; holiness, sanctity. Now *rare.*

Sanctity (sæ·ŋktĭti). late ME. [a. OF. *saintelé*, ad. L. *sanctitas*, *-tatem*, f. *sancti-*, *sanctus* holy; see -ITY.] 1. Holiness of life, saintliness. 2. The quality of being sacred or hallowed; claim to religious reverence; inviolability 1601. b. *pl.* Sacred obligations, feelings, etc.; also quasi-*concr.*, objects possessing sanctity 1808.

1. For deep discernment prais'd And..fam'd For s. of manners undefil'd COWPER. 2. His affirmations have the s. of an oath LAMB. b. Woman completes her destiny by occupying herself with the industries and sanctities of the home 1894.

Sanctorian (sæŋktō·riăn), *a.* 1740. [f. mod.L. *Sanctorius* (It. *Santorio*), a Venetian physician (1561–1636); see -AN[1] 1.] Of or pertaining to Sanctorius, who made experiments and calculations on insensible perspiration.

S. perspiration, insensible perspiration, first discovered by Sanctorius.

Sanctuarize (sæ·ŋktiŭ,ărǝiz), *v.* *rare.* 1602. [f. next + -IZE.] *trans.* To afford sanctuary to; to shelter by means of sacred privileges.

Sanctuary (sæ·ŋktiu,ări). ME. [a. OF. *sain(c)tuarie*, mod.F. *sainctuaire*, semi-pop. ad. L. *sanctuarium*, app. irreg. f. *sanctus* holy.] I. A holy place. 1. *gen.* A building or place set apart for the worship of God or of one or more divinities; applied, e.g., to a Christian church, the Jewish temple, a heathen temple, etc.; also *fig.* to the church or body of believers. b. *fig.* Used for: The priestly office or order. late ME. c. Applied to Heaven. late ME. 2. A specially holy place within a temple or church. a. The HOLY PLACE, including the 'Holy of holies'; sometimes the latter only. late ME. b. *Eccl.* The sacrarium; also *occas.* the chancel. late ME. c. The most sacred part of any temple; the cella, adytum. late ME. 3. A piece of consecrated ground; the precincts of a church; a churchyard, cemetery. Now *dial.* late ME.

1. *transf.* The famous isle of Iona was once the seat and s. of western learning 1796. c. From santuary hy Let him come downe SIDNEY *Ps.* xx. ii.

II. 1. A church or other sacred place in which, by the law of the mediæval church, a fugitive from justice, or a debtor, was immune from arrest. Hence, any place in which by law or custom a similar immunity is secured to fugitives. late ME. b. A similar place of refuge in a non-Christian country. late ME. 2. Immunity from punishment and the ordinary operations of the law secured by taking refuge in a sanctuary; the right or privilege of affording such shelter; shelter, refuge, protection. late ME. 3. *Hunting.* The 'privilege of forest'; the close season 1603.

1. All the while he by his side her bore, She was as safe as in a S. SPENSER. *transf.* They have made.. London..a s. to refugees of every political and religious opinion EMERSON. 2. Phr. *Privilege of s.* *To violate* or *break s.*, to violate the privilege or right of a s. *To take s.*, to take refuge in a s.

‖**Sanctum** (sæ·ŋktǒm). 1577. [L., neut. of *sanctus* holy.] 1. The 'holy place' of the Jewish tabernacle and temple. Also, a sacred place or shrine in other temples and churches. 2. = next 2. 1819.

2. He found the banker in his private s. LYTTON.

‖**Sanctum Sanctorum** (sæ·ŋktǒm sæŋktō·rǒm). *Pl.* sancta sanctorum. ME. [L.; transl. Hebr. *qōdesh haqqŏdāshīm*, 'Holy of holies.'] 1. The Holy of holies of the Jewish temple and tabernacle. †In early use also pl. 2. A person's private retreat, where he is free from intrusion 1706.

‖ **Sanctus** (sæ·ŋktʊ̆s). late ME. [L., = 'Holy', the first word of the hymn.] **1.** The 'angelic hymn' (from Isa. vi. 3) beginning with the words *Sanctus, sanctus, sanctus* ('Holy, holy, holy') which forms the conclusion of the Eucharistic preface. Also called TERSANCTUS (thrice holy). Also the music for this. †**2** *Black s.*, a burlesque hymn; a discord of harsh sounds expressive of contempt -1861.

Sa·nctus bell. 1479. [f. prec. + BELL *sb.*¹] A bell rung at the Sanctus at Mass; in post-Reformation times often used to summon the people to Church.

Sand (sænd), *sb.* [Com. Teut.; OE. *sand, sǫnd*:—OTeut. *sando-, prob.:—earlier *samdo-, *samado-, corresp. to Gr. ἄμαθος.] **1.** A material consisting of comminuted fragments and water-worn particles of rocks (mainly siliceous) finer than those of gravel; often *spec.* as the material of a beach, desert, etc. **b.** With *a* and *pl.* A sand-bank, shoal 1495. **c.** A sandy soil. Chiefly *pl.* 1610. **d.** A grain of sand 1596. **e.** *Geol.* and *Mining.* A stratum of sand or soft sandstone 1851. **2.** Metaphorical and similative uses, with ref. to the innumerability of the grains of sand, to its instability as a foundation, etc., or in phrases implying the exercise of fruitless labour OE. **3.** *pl.* Tracts of sand: **a.** Along a shore, estuary, etc. or composing the bed of a river or sea 1450. **b.** Sandy or desert wastes 1547. **4.** As used for various purposes, e.g. as an adulterant, as an ingredient of mortar, to dry wet ink marks. late ME. **5.** The sand of a sand-glass or hour-glass; also, with *a* and *pl.*, a grain of this 1557. **6.** Chiefly *U.S. slang.* Firmness of purpose, pluck, stamina, 'grit' 1883. **7.** *Anat.* and *Path.* Applied to substances resembling sand, present either normally or as morbid products in certain animal organs or excretions 1577.

1. A shore of hard white s. Met the green herbage MORRIS. **b.** *Henry V*, IV. i. 100. **c.** On bad sands trefoile and ray grass are chosen 1794. **e.** *Oil s.*: see OIL *sb.* **2.** A heart As full of Sorrowes, as the Sea of sands SHAKS. That s. on which thy crumbling power is built SHELLEY. Phr. *Rope of s.*: see ROPE *sb.* II. 1. *To plough the sands*: see PLOUGH *v.* **3. a.** Come vnto these yellow sands SHAKS. **b.** Oceans unknown, inhospitable sands! GRAY. **4.** Everything..was..shining with soft soap and s. DICKENS. The tales we hear about the presence of s. in sugar 1857. His system, as Caius said of his style, was s. without lime 1862. **5.** The Sands are numbred, that makes vp my Life SHAKS. **7.** *Urinary s.*, a substance of finer particles than those of gravel.

Comb.: †**s. ball,** a kind of toilet soap, mixed with fine s.; **-bank,** a bank of s. formed in a river or sea by the action of tides and currents; also = SAND-HILL; **-bath** *Chem.*, a vessel of heated sand used as an equable heater for retorts, etc.; **-bar,** a bank of sand formed at the mouth of a river or harbour by the action of the water; **-bed,** a layer or stratum of s.; *Founding*, a bed of s. into which the iron from a blast-furnace is run; **s. belt,** an arid ridge of sand often extending many miles; **-blast,** a contrivance for depolishing or grinding glass, metal, etc. by means of a jet of s. impelled by compressed air or steam; **-boy,** perh. a boy who hawks s. for sale; in provb. phr. *as jolly as a sand-boy*; **-crack,** a disease incident to the hoofs of a horse; **-drift,** (an accumulation of) drifting sand; **-furnace** = *s.-bath*; **-hog** *U.S.* a man who works underground, as in a caisson; **-man,** one who digs s.; in nursery language, a personification of sleep or drowsiness; **-mould,** a mould for a casting, composed of s.; **-pillar** = *s.-spout*; **-pipe,** (*a*) *Geol.* a tubular cavity in chalk, filled with gravel and s.; (*b*) a pipe conducting s. to the rails from the sand-box of a locomotive; **-pit,** a pit from which sand is excavated; **-pump,** a pump for raising wet sand, detritus, etc., from a drill-hole, oil-well or caisson; **-rock,** a sandstone rock; **-shoes,** shoes for wearing on the sands or at the sea-side, *spec.* canvas shoes with gutta-percha or hemp soles; **-spout,** a pillar of s. raised by a whirlwind in a desert; **-storm,** a desert storm of wind accompanied with clouds of s.; **s. valve,** the valve by which the escape of s. from the sand-box of a locomotive is regulated.

b. In the names of animals, etc., as **s.-badger,** (*a*) a Javanese badger, *Meles ankuma*; (*b*) the Indian badger, *Arctonyx collaris*, also called **s. bear**; **s. bird,** a bird whose habitat is the sea-shore, esp. the SANDPIPER; **-bug,** (*a*) a member of the family *Galgulidæ*; (*b*) a burrowing crab, *Hippa talpoidea*; **-crab,** (*a*) a crab of the family *Ocypodidæ*; (*b*) the Lady Crab, *Platyonichus ocellatus*; **-cricket** *U.S.*, a cricket belonging to the genus *Stenopelmatus*, esp. *S. fasciatus*; **-eel,** (*a*) a fish of the genus *Ammodytes*, having a body like that of an eel; (*b*) a fish of the genus *Gonorhynchus*; **s. flea,** (*a*) = CHIGOE; (*b*) *U.S.*, a crustacean belonging to the genus *Orchestia*; (*c*) a brine shrimp, *Artemia salina*; **-fly,** a small fly or midge, esp. one belonging to the genus *Simulium*; **-grouse,** any bird of the genus *Pteroclomorphæ*, inhabiting sandy tracts of the old world; **-hopper,** a crustacean, *Talitrus locusta*; also, a s.-flea of the genus *Orchestia*; **-lizard,** a common European lizard, *Lacerta agilis*; **s. martin,** a variety of the martin, *Hirundo* or *Cotile riparia*, which nests in the sides of sand-pits; **-monitor,** the land-crocodile, *Monitor* or *Psammosaurus arenarius*; **-partridge,** a partridge of the genus *Ammoperdix*; **s. rat,** a N. Amer. rat of the genus *Thomomys*, esp. *T. talpoides*; **s. roller,** the trout perch; **s. runner,** a sand-plover or sandpiper; **-saucer,** the egg-mass of the *Nauticas*: **-shark,** (*a*) *U.S.*, a kind of shark *Odontaspis littoralis*; (*b*) *Australia*, a variety of ray-fish, *Rhinobatus granulatus*; **-snipe,** any species of sandpiper; **-sole,** *Solea lascaris*; **-sucker,** the flat-fish *Platessa limandoides*; **-swallow,** *Hirundo riparia* **-worm,** the lug-worm *Arenicola marina* or *piscatorum*.

c. In the names of plants: **s. elm,** a variety of elm, *Ulmus suberosa*; **s. grass,** any species of grass which grows in s. and serves as a s.-binder; **s. myrtle,** *Leiophyllum* or *Ledum buxifolium*; **-wort,** (*a*) the genus *Arenaria*; (*b*) any of various plants which grow in sandy places.

Sand (sænd), *v.* late ME. [f. prec.] **1.** *trans.* To run (a ship) on a sandbank; also *pass.* of a person, to be run aground 1560. **2.** To sprinkle with or as with sand. late ME. **3.** To overlay with sand, to bury under a sand drift 1624. **b.** To put sand upon (land) as a dressing 1721. **4.** To intermix sand with (sugar, wool, etc.) with fraudulent intent 1848.

4. To s. the sugar, and sloe-leave the tea KINGSLEY.

Sandal (sæ·ndăl), *sb.*¹ late ME. [ad. L. *sandalium*, ad. Gr. σανδάλιον, dim. of σάνδαλον.] **1.** A protective covering for the sole of the foot fastened by means of fillets or thongs of leather passed over the instep and round the ankle. **2.** A half-shoe of red leather, silk, etc., embroidered and fastened with straps and bands, forming part of the regalia of a sovereign or of the official dress of a bishop or abbot 1485. **b.** Applied to various kinds of low shoes, slippers, etc. 1794. **3.** A strap for fastening a low shoe or slipper, passed over the instep or round the ankle 1829.

1. While the still morn went out with Sandals gray MILT. **2. b.** Dancing sandals..made of pink satin 1900.

attrib.: **s. shoon** (*arch.*), sandals. Hence **Sa·ndaling,** elastic web woven in narrow strips for sandals.

Sandal (sæ·ndăl), *sb.*² late ME. [a. med. L. *sandalum*, f. (ult.) Skr. *candana* (Hindī *candan*).] = SANDALWOOD. †An ointment made of powdered sandalwood.

Sandal (sæ·ndăl), *v.* 1713. [f. SANDAL *sb.*¹] *trans.* To furnish with or as with sandals.

Sa·ndalwoo:d. 1511. [SANDAL *sb.*²] **1.** A scented wood obtained from several species of *Santalum*; also, an inodorous dye-wood, *Pterocarpus santalinus*, RED SANDERS. **2.** Applied to trees of other genera, which produce a wood often used as a substitute for the true sandalwood 1846.

1. *White s.* is obtained from *S. album*, a tree resembling the myrtle, found on the Malabar coast. *Citron* or *Yellow s.* is from *S. Freycinetianum*, found in the South Sea Islands. *Red s.* = RED SANDERS.

Sandarac (sæ·ndăræk). 1550. [ad. L. *sandarăca*, a. Gr. σανδαράκη, -άχη, prob. an Assyrian word.] **1.** = REALGAR. **2.** In full *gum s.* A resin which exudes from the tree *Callitris quadrivalvis*, native of N.W. Africa; it is used in the preparation of spirit varnish and pounce 1655.

Sa·nd-bag, sa·ndbag, *sb.* 1590. [SAND *sb.*] **1. a.** *Fortif.* A bag filled with sand or earth; used to make the parapet of a trench, etc. **b.** used as ballast; esp. for a boat or balloon 1831. **c.** as a weapon: In recent use (chiefly *U.S.*), a long, cylindrical bag (sometimes an eelskin) filled with sand, by which a heavy blow may be struck without leaving a mark 1594. **d.** A bag or cushion filled with fine sand, used in engraving, as a support for the plate 1658. **e.** A long narrow bag, usu. of flannel, containing fine sand, used to cover a crevice and exclude draught or light 1858. Hence **Sa·ndbag** *v. trans.* to furnish with sand-bags; to fell with a blow from a s. **Sa·nd-ba·gger** *U.S.*, one who uses a sand-bag as a weapon.

Sa·nd-blind. Now *arch.* and *dial.* late ME. [Prob. a perversion of OE. *samblind, f. *sam- half- + BLIND *a.*, after SAND *sb.*] Half-blind, dim-sighted, purblind.

Sa·nd-box. 1572. [f. SAND *sb.* + BOX *sb.*²] **1.** A box with a perforated top for sprinkling sand as a blotter upon wet ink. *Obs.* exc. *Hist.* **2. a.** A sand-mould. **b.** A box of sand on a locomotive for use when the wheels slip. **c.** *Golf.* A receptacle for the sand used to 'tee' the ball. 1688. **3.** The fruit of the W. Indian forest tree, *Hura crepitans*; the tree itself 1750.

Sanded (sæ·ndĕd), *ppl. a.* 1570. [f. SAND *sb.* and *v.*] †**1.** Of a sandy colour -1686. †**2.** Composed of or covered with sand -1746. **3.** Sprinkled with sand 1760. **4.** Adulterated with sand 1883.

Sandemanian (sændĭmēⁱ·niăn), *sb.* and *a.* 1792. [See sense 1.] **A.** *sb.* One of a religious sect developed by Robert *Sandeman* (1718–71) from the Glassites. **B.** *adj.* Of or belonging to the Sandemanians. Hence **Sandema·nianism.**

Sanderling (sæ·ndəɹliŋ). 1602. [perh. repr. OE. *sandyrðling, f. SAND *sb.* + *yrðling* ploughman, also the name of some bird.] A small wading bird, *Calidris arenaria.*

Sanders (sa·ndəɹz). ME. [a. OF. *sandre*, var. of *sandle* SANDAL ².] **1.** = SANDALWOOD. †**2.** The sandalwood tree; sandalwood trees -1783.

Sa·nd-glass. 1556. [f. SAND *sb.* + GLASS *sb.*] A contrivance for measuring time, consisting of two glass vessels connected by a narrow neck, and containing so much sand as will take a given time to pass from the receptacle placed uppermost into that placed below; an hour-glass, a minute-glass, an egg-boiler, etc.

Sa·nd-hill. OE. [SAND *sb.*] A hill or bank of sand; esp. a dune on the sea-shore. Hence **Sa·nd-hiller,** one of a class of 'poor whites' living in the pine-woods that cover the sandy hills of Georgia and S. Carolina.

Sandiver (sæ·ndivəɹ). late ME. [app. a. F. *suin de verre* (*suin*, now *suint*, exudation from wool, app. f. *suer* to sweat; *de* of; *verre* glass).] A liquid saline matter found floating over the glass after vitrification; glass-gall.

Sandling (sæ·ndliŋ). 1611. [f. SAND *sb.* + -LING.¹] A small flat-fish; a dab.

Sa·nd-pa·per, sa·ndpa:per, *sb.* 1812. [SAND *sb.*] Paper upon which a layer of sand has been fixed by means of an adhesive, used chiefly for smoothing or polishing woodwork. Hence **Sa·ndpa:per** *v. trans.* to smooth with or as with s.

Sandpiper (sæ·ndpəi:pəɹ). 1674. [f. SAND *sb.* + PIPER.] A small wading bird which runs along the sand and utters a piping note; esp. *Tringoides hypoleucus*, the Common S., and *Actitis macularia*, the N. Amer. S.

Sandstone (sæ·ndstōᵘn). 1668. A rock composed of consolidated sand.

Old and *New Red S.*, two series of British rocks lying respectively below and above the carboniferous.

Sandwich (sæ·ndwitʃ, -widʒ), *sb.* 1762. [Named after John Montagu, 4th Earl of *Sandwich* (1718–1792), who once spent twenty-four hours at the gaming-table without other food than beef sandwiches.] **1.** Two slices of bread with a layer of sliced meat, usu. beef or ham (or, later, any comestible) placed between; freq. specified as *ham, egg, watercress s.* Also, a confection of layers of sponge cake with jam or cream between. **2.** = *s.-man* 1864.

attrib.: **s.-board,** a board carried by a sandwich-man; **-boat,** the boat occupying the last position in a higher, and the first in a lower, division in bumping races at Oxford and Cambridge, and thus rowing twice in the same day; **s. box, case,** a box or case in which to carry sandwiches; **-man,** a man who carries two advertisement boards suspended from the shoulders, one in front and the other behind.

Sandwich (sæ·ndwitʃ, -widʒ), *v.* 1861. [f. prec.] *trans.* To put in or as in a sandwich; chiefly *fig.*, to insert (some person or thing) between two others, freq. of a widely different character; rarely, to enclose like a sandwich.

Sandy (sæ·ndi), *sb.* 1473. A shortened hypocristic form of Alexander, chiefly used in Scotland. Hence, a nickname for a Scotchman.

Sandy (sæ·ndi), *a.* [OE. *sandig*, f. SAND *sb.* and -Y.¹] **1.** Of the nature of sand; containing a large proportion of sand. **b.** Of or containing sand as used for measuring time (*poet.*) 1591. **2.** *fig.* Like sand in lacking cohesion or stability 1590. **3.** Having hair of a yellowish-red colour; of hair, yellowish-red 1523. **4.** Qualifying the names of colours 1819.

1. With s. Ballast Sailors trim the Boat DRYDEN. b. 1 *Hen. VI*, IV. ii. 36. 2. S. sentences without lime NASHE. 3. A florid young man..with s. hair MARRYAT. Hence **Sa·ndiness.**

‖**Sandyx** (sæ·ndiks). *Hist.* 1601. [L., a. Gr. σάνδυξ.] A red pigment, mentioned by ancient writers.

Sane (sēⁱn), *a.* 1628. [ad. L. *sanus* healthy.] **1.** Of the body, its organs or functions: Healthy, sound, not diseased (*rare*) 1755. **2.** Sound in mind; in one's senses; not mad. Also, of the mind: Not diseased. 1721. **3.** Sensible, rational; free from delusive prejudices or fancies 1843.

2. The activity of s. minds in healthful bodies COLERIDGE. *Of s. memory*: see MEMORY 2. Hence **Sa·ne·ly** *adv.*, **-ness.**

Sangaree (sæŋgărī·). 1736. [a. Sp. *sangria* (lit. bleeding), 'a drink composed of lemon water and red wine'.] A cold drink composed of wine diluted and spiced, used chiefly in tropical countries.

‖**Sang-de-bœuf** (sañdəböf). 1886. [Fr.; lit. 'bullock's blood'.] A deep red colour found in old Chinese porcelain.

‖**Sang-froid** (sañfrwa). 1712. [F., lit. 'cold blood'.] Coolness, indifference, absence of excitement or agitation.

†**Sa·nglier.** late ME. [a. OF. *sangl(i)er* :—L. *singularem* solitary, used subst. in late L. for a boar separated from the herd.] A full-grown wild boar -1725.

Sangrail (sæŋgrēⁱ·l). 1450. [a. OF. *Saint Graal* 'Holy Grail'] = GRAIL[2].

Sanguiferous (sæŋgwi·fĕrəs), *a.* 1682. [f. mod.L. **sanguifer*; see -FEROUS.] Bearing or conveying blood.

Sanguification (sæ·ŋgwifikēⁱ·ʃən). 1578. [ad. mod.L. *sanguificationem*, f. *sanguificare* SANGUIFY *v.*] The formation of blood; conversion into blood.

†**Sa·nguify,** *v.* 1620. [ad. mod.L. *sanguificare*, f. L. *sanguis*; see -FY.] **1.** *intr.* To produce blood -1677. **2.** *trans.* To convert into blood -1707.

‖**Sanguinaria** (sæŋgwinēᵊ·riă). 1842. [mod. L. use of L., adj. fem., pertaining to blood.] The blood-root, *Sanguinaria canadensis*; also the rhizome of this, used in medicine.

Sanguinary (sæ·ŋgwinări), *a.* (and *sb.*) 1550. [ad. L. *sanguinarius*, f. *sanguinem*, *sanguis* blood; see -ARY[1].] **1.** Attended by bloodshed; characterized by slaughter; bloody. Of laws: Imposing the death-penalty freely. 1625. **2.** Bloodthirsty; delighting in carnage 1623. †**b.** *absol.* as *sb.* A sanguinary person -1632. **3.** Of or pertaining to blood (*rare*) 1684. ¶**4.** Used joc. as a euphemism for BLOODY, in reports of vulgar speech.

1. We may not..propagate Religion, by Warrs, or by S. Persecutions, to force Consciences BACON. 2. A s. bishop in the reign of Queen Mary 1751. Hence **Sa·nguinarily** *adv.* **Sa·nguinariness.**

Sanguine (sæ·ŋgwin), *a.* and *sb.* late ME. [a. F. *sanguin*, ad. L. *sanguineus* SANGUINEOUS.] **A.** *adj.* **1.** Blood-red. Also *s. red* (sometimes hyphened). Now *literary*. **b.** *Nat. Hist.* Chiefly in names of animals and plants 1783. **2.** Of or pertaining to blood; consisting of or containing blood. Now *rare*. 1447. **b.** Causing or delighting in bloodshed; bloody, sanguinary. Now *poet.* or *rhet.* 1705. **3.** In mediæval physiology: Belonging to that one of the four 'complexions' in which the blood predominates over the other three humours, and which is indicated by a ruddy countenance and a courageous, hopeful, and amorous disposition. late ME. **b.** Red in the face 1684. **4.** Of persons, etc.: Having the mental attributes characteristic of the sanguine complexion (see sense 3); hopeful, confident 1509.

1. Like to that s. flower inscrib'd with woe MILT. 3. A prince of haut corage, young lusty and sanguyne of complexion 1548. 4. That s. temper which overlooks..the obstacles in its way 1855. It far surpassed our most s. expectations 1876.

B. *sb.* †**1.** A blood-red colour -1612. †**2.** The sanguine 'complexion' or temperament -1718. **3.** *Art.* A crayon coloured red with iron oxide; a drawing executed with red chalks 1854.

3. An interesting Greuze sketch in s. 1886. Hence **Sa·nguine·ly** *adv.*, **-ness.**

Sanguineous (sæŋgwi·nĭəs), *a.* 1520. [f. L. *sanguineus* (f. *sanguin-*, *sanguis* blood) + -OUS.] **1.** Of or pertaining to blood; of the nature of or containing blood 1646. †**b.** Of animals: Having blood -1667. **2.** Of the colour of blood 1520. **3.** Of or pertaining to bloodshed; giving rise to bloodshed; bloodthirsty, sanguinary. Now *rare*. 1612. **4.** Of persons, etc.: = SANGUINE *a.* 3, 4. In recent use, Full-blooded, plethoric. 1732.

2. His passion, cruel grown, took on a hue Fierce and s. KEATS. Hence **Sangui·neousness.**

Sanguinity (sæŋgwi·nĭti). 1470. [f. SANGUINE *a.* + -ITY.] †**1.** CONSANGUINITY 1. -1741. **2.** The quality of being sanguine (*rare*) 1737.

Sanguinivorous (sæŋgwini·vərəs), *a.* 1828. [f. L. *sanguin(i)-*, *sanguis*; see -VOROUS.] = SANGUIVOROUS.

Sanguinolent (sæŋgui·nŏlĕnt), *a.* 1577. [ad. L. *sanguinolentus*, f. *sanguin-*, *sanguis*.] **1.** Of or pertaining to blood; tinged, stained with or containing blood. Now chiefly *Path.* 1597. **2.** Bloodthirsty; cruel; merciless (*rare*) 1577.

Sanguivorous (sæŋgwi·vŏrəs), *a.* 1842. [f. L. *sanguis*; see -VOROUS.] Feeding on blood.

Sanhedrim, Sanhedrin (sæ·nĭdrim, -in). 1588. [a. late Heb. *sanhedrīn*, a. Gr. συνέδριον council, lit. 'sitting together', f. σύν together + ἕδρα seat.] *Jewish Antiq.* The highest court of justice and supreme council at Jerusalem; also applied to lower courts of justice. Hence **Sa·nhedrist,** a member of the S.

Sanicle (sæ·nik'l). ME. [a. OF., ad. med. L. *sanicula*, *-um*, prob. f. L. *sanus* healthy, with ref. to its healing powers.] **1.** The umbelliferous plant *Sanicula europæa* (more fully *wood s.*). Also, any plant of the genus *Sanicula*, as *S. marilandica*, the black snakeroot. **2.** Applied to various plants of other genera, as *Heuchera villosa*, American s. late ME.

Sanidine (sæ·nidīn). 1815. [a. G. *sanidin*, f. Gr. σανιδ-, σανίς board; see -INE[5].] *Min.* A variety of orthoclase, found in flat crystals.

‖**Sanies** (sēⁱ·ni,īz). 1562. [L.] **1.** *Path.* A thin fetid pus mixed with serum or blood, secreted by a wound or ulcer. †**2.** Any watery fluid of animal origin -1834. So **Sa·nious** *a.* of the nature of s.; consisting of, or containing s.; yielding a discharge of s.

Sanify (sæ·nifəi), *v.* 1836. [f. L. *sanus* SANE + -(I)FY.] **1.** *intr.* To become sane or reasonable. **2.** *trans.* To make healthy; improve the sanitary conditions of 1872.

Sanitarian (sænitēᵊ·riăn), *sb.* and *a.* 1859. [f. SANITARY *a.* + -AN[1] 1.] **A.** *sb.* One who studies sanitation or who favours sanitary reform. **B.** *adj.* Pertaining to sanitary matters; advocating sanitary reforms 1884. Hence **Sanita·rianism. Sa·nitari·ly** *adv.* **-ness.** So **Sa·nitarist.**

Sanitarium (sænitēᵊ·riŏm). Chiefly *U.S.* 1851. [quasi-L., f. *sanitas* health; see next and -ARIUM.] = SANATORIUM.

Sanitary (sæ·nitări), *a.* 1842. [ad. F. *sanitaire*, as if ad. mod.L. **sanitarius*, f. L. *sanitas* health; see SANITY and -ARY[2].] **1.** Of or pertaining to the conditions affecting health, esp. with ref. to cleanliness and precautions against infection, etc.; pertaining to or concerned with sanitation. Also *occas.* free from deleterious influences. **b.** Used as the distinctive epithet of appliances specially contrived with a view to sanitary requirements 1862. **2.** *U.S.* Intended or tending to promote health 1853.

1. *S. cordon*: see CORDON 4.

Sanitation (sænitēⁱ·ʃən). 1848. [irreg. f. prec. + -ATION.] The devising and application of means for the improvement of sanitary conditions. Hence **Sa·nitate** *v. trans.* to put in a sanitary condition; to provide with sanitary appliances. **Sanita·tionist,** one who is skilled in or advocates s.

Sanity (sæ·nĭti). late ME. [a. F. *sanité*, ad. L. *sanitas*, f. *sanus* healthy; see -ITY.] **1.** Healthy condition, health. *arch.* **2.** The condition of being sane; mental health 1602.

‖**Sanjak** (sæ·n,dʒæk). 1537. [Turk. *sanjāq*; lit. 'banner'.] **1.** In the Turkish Empire, one of the administrative districts into which an eyalet or vilayet is divided. †**2.** Misused for ‖**Sa·njakbeg, -bey,** the governor of a s.

Sannup (sæ·nŏp). 1630. [a. Narraganset *sannop*.] A married male member of the community; the husband of a squaw.

San(n)yasi, -asin, var. ff. SUNNYASEE.

Sans (sænz), *prep.* ME. [a. OF. *sen(s*, later *san(s*, *sanz* :—pop.L. **sene* (for class. L. *sine*) and **senes* (with analogical *s*).] Without. Now *arch.* (chiefly with reminiscence of Shakspere) and *Her.*

Second childishnesse, and meere obliuion, S. teeth, s. eyes, s. taste, s. euery thing SHAKS. ‖ Fr. phrases and combs. (not naturalized): **sans cérémonie, sans façon,** unceremoniously, without the usual polite form; **sans-gêne** [*gêne* constraint], disregard of the ordinary forms of civility or politeness; **sans peur,** fearless, often in the phr. applied to the Chevalier de Bayard, *s. peur et s. reproche*; **sans phrase** [after *la mort s. phrase*, the alleged words of Sieyes in voting for the death of Louis XVI], without more words, without circumlocution; **sans reproche,** blameless (see *s. peur* above) **sans souci,** lit. without care or concern; as *sb.*, unconcern.

‖**Sansculotte** (sænzkiulǫ·t, F. sañkülot). 1790. [F., f. *sans* without + *culotte* knee-breeches; origin obsc.] **1.** In the French Revolution, a republican of the poorer classes in Paris. Hence *gen.* an extreme republican or revolutionary. **2.** *transf.* A tatterdemalion; a ragamuffin 1812. Hence ‖**Sansculo·tterie,** the principles, spirit or behaviour characteristic of sansculottes; sansculottes collectively. **Sansculo·ttic** *a.* pertaining to the sansculottes or to sansculottism; revolutionary; unbreeched, hence, inadequately clothed. **Sansculo·ttism,** the principles or practice of sansculottes.

Sansculottid (sænskiulǫ·tid). 1813. [a. F. *sansculottide*, f. prec.] One of the five (in leap-years six) complementary days added at the end of the month Fructidor of the Republican Calendar; *pl.*, the festivities held during these days. Also *attrib.* in *S. days.*

Sanserif (sænse·rif). 1830. [app. f. SANS *prep.* + SERIF.] *Typog.* A form of type without serifs; called also *grotesque.*

Sanskrit, Sanscrit (sæ·nskrit), *sb.* and *a.* 1617. [ad. Skr. *saṃskṛta* put together, well-formed, perfected, f. *sam* together + *kṛ* to make, do, perform.] **A.** *sb.* The ancient and sacred language of India, the oldest known member of the Indo-European family, in which the Hindu literature from the Vedas downwards is composed. In a narrower sense, the classical Sanskrit (opp. to the Epic and Vedic), the grammar of which was fixed by Pāṇini. **B.** *adj.* Of, belonging to, or written in Sanskrit 1773. Hence **Sanskri·tic** *a.* relating to, derived from, based on, or resembling S.; using the S. language. **Sa·nskritist,** a person versed in the S. language or writings.

Santa Claus (sæ·ntă klǭ·z). 1828. [Orig. U.S., a. Du. dial. *Sante Klaas*, Saint Nicholas; see NICHOLAS.] A legendary character who fills stockings with presents for children during the night of Christmas Eve.

Santal (sæ·ntăl). 1672. [a. F., ad. med.L. *santalum*, a. Gr. σάνταλον SANDAL *sb.*[2]] **1.** Sandalwood. Also *s.-wood.* **2.** *Chem.* A substance ($C_8H_6O_3$) obtained from sandalwood 1894.

Santalaceous (sæntălēⁱ·ʃəs), *a.* 1845. [-ACEOUS.] Belonging to the family *Santalaceæ*, typified by the genus *Santalum* or sandalwood.

Santalic (sæntæ·lik), *a.* 1849. [f. as next + -IC 1 b.] *Chem.* In *s. acid*: = next.

Santalin (sæ·ntălin). 1833. [a. F. *santaline*, f. mod.L. *santalum* SANTAL.] *Chem.* The colouring principle of red sanders.

Santon (sæ·ntǫn). 1599. [a. F. or Sp., f. *santo* SAINT.] A European designation for a monk or hermit among the Mohammedans; a marabout; also, incorrectly, †a yogi, Hindoo ascetic. So ‖**Sa·nto.**

Santonate (sæ·ntŏnēⁱt). 1841. [f. next + -ATE[1] 1 c.] *Chem.* A salt of santonic acid.

Santonic (sæntǫ·nik), *a.* 1836. [ad. L. *Santonicus* pertaining to the Santones or Santoni, a people of Aquitania.] *Chem.* In *s. acid*: an acid derived from santonin.

Santonin (sæ·ntŏnin). 1838. [f. L. *Santonica* (sc. *herba*) a kind of wormwood; see prec.] *Chem.* A bitter principle obtained from the dried unexpanded flowers of species of *Artemisia*, and used as a powerful anthelmintic. Hence **Santoni·nic** *a.* in *s. acid*, an acid obtained from s., isomeric with santonic acid.

Sap (sæp), *sb.*[1] [Com. WGer.: OE. *sæp*, prob. repr. *sapo^m, *sappo^m:—pre-Teut. *sapnó-; perh. cogn. w. L. *sapere* to taste, *sapor* taste, savour.] **1.** The vital juice which circulates in plants. †**2.** Juice or fluid of any kind –1613. **3.** = SAP-WOOD 1483.

1. The s. is the life of the tree, as the bloud is to mans body 1615. The s. of youth shrinks from our veins 1832. **2.** *fig. Hen. VIII*, I. i. 148.

attrib. and *Comb.*, as **s.-ball**, a local name for certain fungi of the genus *Polyporus*; **-rot**, a disease of timber, dry-rot; **-sucker**, a name in N. Amer. for many of the smaller woodpeckers, esp. those of the genus *Sphyropicus*; **-tube**, a vessel that conveys s. Hence **Sa·pful** *a.* abounding in s.

Sap (sæp), *sb.*[2] 1591. [Late 16th c. *zappe*, *sappe*, ad. It. *zappe* and a. F. *sappe* spade, spadework, sap.] **1.** †The process of undermining a wall or defensive work; the process of constructing covered trenches in order to approach a besieged place. **b.** *fig.* Applied to stealthy or insidious methods of attacking or destroying anything 1748. **2.** A covered trench made for the purpose of approaching a besieged place under the fire of the garrison. In recent use, a narrow communicating trench. 1642.

1. b. Exempt forever from the s. of age COWPER.

Comb.: **s. battery**, a battery at the head of a s.; **-faggot**, a fascine used in sapping, to fill up the spaces between gabions; **-head**, the foremost end of a s.; **-roller**, a large gabion covering the sap-head.

Sap (sæp), *sb.*[3] *School slang.* 1798. [Cf. SAP *v.*[2]] One who studies hard or is absorbed in books.

Sap (sæp), *sb.*[4] 1815. [Short for SAPSKULL.] A simpleton, fool.

Sap (sæp), *v.*[1] 1598. [a. F. *saper* = It. *zappare*, f. *zappa*; see SAP *sb.*[2]] **1.** *intr.* To dig a sap; to approach a besieged place by means of a sap. **b.** *fig.* To make way in a stealthy or insidious manner. Also *trans.* in *to s. one's way*. 1732. **2.** *trans.* To dig under the foundations of (a wall, etc.); *transf.* of natural agencies: To undermine 1652. **3.** *fig.* To weaken or destroy insidiously (esp. health, strength, courage, etc.) 1755.

1. b. Lies, while they s. their way and hold their tongues, Are safe enough LANDOR. **2.** We have begun to sappe the Glacis 1689. Sap'd by floods, Their houses fell DRYDEN. *fig.* Not one who did not..s. the foundation of some old opinion 1857.

Sap (sæp), *v.*[2] *School slang.* 1830. [prob. fig. use of SAP *v.*[1] **1.** Cf. SAP *sb.*[3]] *intr.* To pore over books; to be studious.

Sapajou (sæ·pădʒū). 1698. [a. F., said to be a Cayenne word.] A S. Amer. monkey of the genus *Cebus*.

Sapan, sappan (sæ·păn). 1598. [a. Malay *sapaŋ* of South Indian origin.] A dye-wood yielding a red dye, obtained from trees belonging to the genus *Cæsalpinia*, indigenous to tropical Asia and the Indian Archipelago, esp. *C. sappan*. Now *s. wood*.

Sap-green, *sb.* (and *a.*). 1578. [f. SAP *sb.*[1] + GREEN.] A green pigment prepared from the juice of buckthorn berries; the colour of this pigment. Also *attrib.* and *adj.*

Sa·phead. 1828. [f. SAP *sb.*[1] (sense 3).] A fool, simpleton. So **Sap-headed** *a.* 1665.

‖**Saphena** (săfī·nă). late ME. [med.L., ad. Arab. *çāfin*.] *Anat.* The distinctive name of two veins in the leg: (1) the *long* or *internal s.*, which extends from near the ankle-joint along the inner surface of the leg, and ends in the femoral vein; (2) the *short*, *posterior*, or *external s.*, which extends from the foot along the calf of the leg, and finally joins the popliteal vein.

Saphenous (săfī·nəs), *a.* 1840. [f. prec. + -OUS.] Pertaining to or connected with the saphena.

S. vein, the saphena. *S. nerve* = saphena nerve.

Saphie (sæ·fi). *N. Africa.* 1799. [Mandingo *safaye*.] A charm.

Sapid (sæ·pid), *a.* 1634. [ad. L. *sapidus*, f. *sapere* to taste.] **1.** Of food, etc.: Having a decided taste or flavour, *esp.* a pleasant one, savoury, palatable 1646. **2.** In neutral sense: Having taste or flavour 1634. **3.** *fig.* Grateful to the mind or mental taste 1640.

1. Thus Camels to make the water sapide do raise the mud with their feet SIR T. BROWNE.

Sapidity (săpi·dĭti). 1646. [ad. L. **sapiditatem*, f. *sapidus*; see -ITY.] The quality of being sapid or having taste and flavour.

The body of that element [air] is ingustible, void of all s. SIR T. BROWNE.

Sapience (sēⁱ·piĕns). late ME. [a. OF., ad. L. *sapientia*, f. *sapientem* SAPIENT; see -ENCE.] **1.** Wisdom, understanding. (Now *rare* in serious use.) †**b.** Correct taste and judgement –1796. **2.** Used depreciatively or ironically: Would-be wisdom. late ME.

1. That Supreme Master of Politicall S. 1659. **2.** This is a piece of s. not worth the brain of a fruit-trencher MILT.

Sapient (sēⁱ·piĕnt), *a.* and *sb.* 1471. [a. OF., or ad. L. *sapientem*, pres. pple. of *sapere* to have a taste, to be wise.] **A.** *adj.* Wise. Now usu. *ironical*.

Where the S. King Held dalliance with his faire Egyptian Spouse MILT.

B. *sb.* [= L. *sapiens*.] A wise man, sage. In later use *joc.* 1549. Hence **Sa·piently** *adv.*

Sapiential (sēⁱpie·nʃiăl), *a.* 1485. [a. F., f. L. *sapientia* SAPIENCE.] **1.** Belonging to or characterized by wisdom; esp. belonging to the wisdom of God. **2.** Epithet of the 'wisdom' books of the Bible (Proverbs, Ecclesiastes, Canticles, Wisdom, Ecclesiasticus); also applied occas. to kindred writings outside the canon 1568. Hence **Sapie·ntially** *adv.*

Sapless (sæ·plĕs), *a.* 1591. [f. SAP *sb.*[1] + -LESS.] **1.** Destitute of sap; dry; withered. **b.** Of soil: Without moisture; barren 1655. **2.** *transf.* and *fig.* **a.** Of persons: Lacking energy or vigour; lacking in character, insipid 1598. **b.** Of immaterial things, ideas, etc.: Destitute of inner worth; insipid, pointless 1602.

2. a. Now s. on the verge of Death he stands DRYDEN. **b.** Old stories and s. anecdotes 1891. Hence **Sa·plessness.**

Sapling (sæ·pliŋ). late ME. [f. SAP *sb.*[1] + -LING[1] 2.] **1.** A young tree. **2.** *transf.* A young or inexperienced person 1588. **3.** A greyhound less than twelve months old 1832. **4.** *appositively* or as *adj.* That is a s. 1700.

Sapodilla (sæpǫdi·lă). 1697. [a. Sp. *zapotilla*, dim. of *zapote* SAPOTA.] **1.** A large evergreen tree, *Achras Sapota*, native of tropical America, having a durable wood and an edible fruit. Also called NASEBERRY. **2.** The fruit of this tree 1750.

attrib.: **s.-plum** = sense 2; **-tree** = sense 1.

Sapogenin (săpǫ·dʒĕnin). 1862. [f. SAPO(NIN + -GEN + -IN[1].] *Chem.* A crystalline compound obtained by treating saponin with dilute acids.

Saponaceous (sæpǫnēⁱ·ʃəs), *a.* 1710. [f. mod.L. *saponaceus*, f. L. *saponem* SOAP *sb.*; see -ACEOUS.] **1.** Of the nature of, resembling, consisting of, or containing soap; soapy. **2.** *joc.* Soapy, *lit.* and *fig.*; unctuous in manner; 'slippery', evasive 1824.

2. Among all his pecuniary, s., oleaginous parishioners SYD. SMITH. Hence **Saponacity** (*joc.*).

Saponification (săpǫ:nifikēⁱ·ʃən). 1821. [a. F., f. *saponifier* SAPONIFY *v.*; see -FICATION.] The process of saponifying; the conversion of a fat into soap by the addition of an alkali, the remaining constituent, glycerine, being thereby liberated.

Saponify (săpǫ·nifəi), *v.* 1821. [ad. F. *saponifier*, ad. mod.L. *saponificare*, f. *sapon-* SOAP; see -IFY.] **1.** *trans.* To convert (a fat or an oil) into soap by combination with an alkali. **2.** *intr.* To become converted into soap 1823. Hence **Sapo·nifiable,** *a.* **Sapo·nifier,** an alkali used in saponification.

Saponin (sæ·pŏnin). 1831. [a. F. *saponine*, f. L. *sapon-* SOAP; see -IN[1].] *Chem.* A glucoside obtained from *Saponaria officinalis*, *Quillaja saponaria*, and many other plants.

Saponite (sæ·pŏnəit). 1849. [f. L. *sapon-* SOAP + -ITE[1] 2 b.] *Min.* A hydrous silicate of aluminium and magnesium, occurring in soft, soapy, amorphous masses, filling veins in serpentine, and cavities in trap-rock.

Sapor, sapour (sēⁱ·pǫɹ, -pəɹ). 1477. [a. L. *sapor*, *saporem* taste, f. *sapere* to be sapid.] A quality such as is perceived by the sense of taste, as sweetness, etc.; a taste, savour; the taste or savour of a substance, esp. of an article of food and drink. Now chiefly in scientific use. **b.** In generalized sense: Quality in relation to the sense of taste 1650.

The exquisite sapor of their French dishes 1826.

Saporous (sēⁱ·pŏrəs), *a. rare.* 1670. [ad. mod.L. *saporosus*, f. *saporem* SAPOR; see -OUS.] Of or pertaining to taste; having flavour or taste; yielding some kind of taste. †Also, savoury. So **Saporo·sity,** that property of a body by which it imparts the sensation of taste.

‖**Sapota** (săpōᵘ·tă). 1560. [repr. Sp. and Pg. *zapote*, a Mexican *zapotl*, *çapotl*.] = SAPODILLA. As mod.L., a genus, the type of the *Sapotaceæ*, now referred to *Achras*. Also *attrib.*, as *s. plum*, *wood*, etc.

Sapotaceous (sæpotēⁱ·ʃəs), *a.* 1845. [f. mod.L. *Sapotaceæ* (f. prec.); see -ACEOUS.] *Bot.* Of, pertaining to, or characteristic of the *Sapotaceæ*, a family of gamopetalous plants typified by the *Achras* (formerly *Sapota*).

Sapper (sæ·pəɹ). 1626. [f. SAP *v.*[1] + -ER[1], after F. *sapeur*.] One who saps, *spec.* a soldier employed in working at saps, the building and repairing of fortifications, etc.; as a prefixed designation = private of the Royal Engineers.

(*Royal*) *Sappers and Miners*, former name of non-commissioned officers and privates of the Engineers, now called Royal Engineers.

Sapphic (sæ·fik), *a.* and *sb.* 1501. [a. F. *saphique*, †*sapphique*, ad. L. *Sapphicus*, a. Gr. Σαπφικός.] **A.** *adj.* Of or pertaining to Sappho (Σαπφώ), the poetess of Lesbos (*c* 600 B.C.); *spec.* epithet of the metres used by her. **B.** *sb.* A metre used by Sappho or named after her. Chiefly *pl.*, verses written in the Sapphic stanza. 1586.

Greater S., a logaœdic distich of which the first line is –⏑⏑–⏑–⏑̄ and the second (the Greater S. verse) is ⏓̄–⏑̄–⏑⏑–‖–⏑⏑–⏑–⏑̄. *Lesser S.*, a logaœdic hendecasyllable with a dactyl in the third place (–⏑–⏑̄–⏑⏑–⏑–⏑̄). The 'S. stanza' consists of three Lesser Sapphics followed by an Adonic (–⏑⏑–⏑̄).

Sapphire (sæ·fəiəɹ). [ME. *saphyr*, *safir*, a. OF. *safir*, ad. L. *sapphirus*, also *sapp(h)ir*, a. Gr. σάπφειρος, said to mean lapis lazuli; prob. a. some Semitic form. Cf. Heb. *sappīr*.] **1.** A precious stone of a beautiful transparent blue. It is a variety of native alumina akin to the ruby. **b.** *Min.* Used as a general name for all the precious transparent varieties of native crystalline alumina, including the ruby. A colourless variety is called *white* or *water s.* 1668. **c.** The deep blue colour of the sapphire 1686. **d.** *Her.* The tincture blue or azure, in blazoning by the names of precious stones 1562. **2.** A name for certain humming-birds 1843. **3.** quasi-*adj.* Sapphire-coloured. late ME.

1. Of Rubies, saphires, and of peerles white Were alle hise clothes brouded vp and down CHAUCER.

Comb. **s.-stone** = sense 1.

Sapphirine (sæ·firəin), *sb.* 1823. [f. prec. + -INE[5].] *Min.* **a.** A silicate of aluminium and magnesium found in pale blue grains. **b.** A blue variety of spinel.

Sapphirine (sæ·firəin), *a.* late ME. [ad. L. *sapphirinus*, a. Gr. σαπφείρινος, f. σάπφειρος SAPPHIRE.] Consisting of or like sapphire, having the qualities, esp. the colour, of sapphire.

The s. hue of the zenith in spring T. HARDY. *absol.* Thunder from the safe sky's s. BROWNING.

Sapphism (sæ·fiz'm). 1890. [f. the name of *Sappho* (see SAPPHIC), who was accused of this vice; see -ISM 2.] Unnatural sexual relations between women. So **Sa·pphist.**

Sappho (sæ·fo). 1843. [Applications of the name of the poetess (see SAPPHIC).] **1.** *Ornith.* The name of a genus of humming-birds. Hence, a bird of this genus; = COMET *sb.* 3; usu. *S. comet.* **2.** *Astr.* The name of the eightieth asteroid 1875.

Sappy (sæ·pi), *a.* OE. [f. SAP *sb.*[1] + -Y[1].] **1.** Of a plant, tree, etc.: Abounding in sap. **2.** *fig.* Full of vitality, 'goodness' or substance 1558. †**3.** Juicy, succulent –1825. **4.** Fat, plump. Now *dial.* 1694. **5.** Full of moisture; wet; sodden; rainy. Now *d al.* 1470. **b.** Of meat: Putrescent, tainted. *dial.* 1573. **6.** Consisting of or containing sap-wood 1466. **7.** Foolish 1670. Hence †**Sa·ppily** *adv.* -1724. **Sa·ppiness.**

‖**Sapræmia** (sæprī·miă). 1886. [mod.L., f. Gr. σαπρός putrid + αἷμα blood.] Poisoning by means of septic or putrefactive organisms. Hence **Sapræ·mic** *a.* of, pertaining to or affected with, s.

Saprogenic (sæprodʒe·nik), *a.* 1876. [f. Gr. σαπρός putrid + -GEN + -IC 1.] Causing, or produced by, putrefaction. So **Sapro·genous** *a.*

Saprophagous (sæprǫ·făgəs), *a.* 1819. [f. mod.L. *saprophagus* (f. Gr. σαπρός + -φάγος eating) + -OUS.] Living on decomposing matter. So **Sapro·phagan,** belonging to, an insect of, the tribe *Saprophaga.*

Saprophile (sæ·profəil), *sb.* and *a.* 1882. [f. Gr. σαπρός + -φίλος loving; see -PHILE.] **A.** *sb.* A bacterium inhabiting putrid matter. **B.** *adj.* Of bacteria: Found in putrid matter.

Saprophyte (sæ·profəit). 1875. [f. Gr. σαπρός + φυτόν plant; see -PHYTE.] Any vegetable organism that lives on decayed organic matter. Hence **Saprophytic** (-fi·tik) *a.* of or pertaining to saprophytes. **Sa·prophytism,** the state of living as a s.

Sapsago (sæpsē·go). *U.S.* 1846. [Corruptly a. G. *schabziger,* f. *schaben* to grate + *ziger* a kind of cheese.] A kind of hard cheese made in Switzerland, flavoured with melilot.

Sapskull (sæ·pskɒl). Now *dial.* 1735. [f. SAP *sb.*[1] (sense 3) + SKULL.] = SAP-HEAD.

‖**Sapucaia** (sapukā·ya). 1613. [Tupi.] **1. a.** A S. Amer. tree of the genus *Lecythis.* **b.** The fruit of the tree, a s.-nut. **2.** *attrib.,* as **s.-nut,** the edible fruit of *Lecythis Zabucajo* and *L. Ollaria.*

Sa·p-wood. 1791. [SAP *sb.*[1]] The softer and more recently formed wood between the bark and heart-wood in exogenous trees.

Sarabaite (særăbē·əit). late ME. [ad. eccl. L. *Sarabaita*; of unkn. origin.] One of a class of monks in the early Church who lived together in small bands without rule or superior.

Saraband (sæ·răbænd). 1616. [ad. F. *sarabande,* ad. Sp. *zarabanda,* prob. of Oriental origin.] **1.** A slow and stately Spanish dance in triple time. **2.** A piece of music for this dance or in its rhythm, in which the second note of the measure is usu. lengthened 1625.

1. I can dance..Jiggs and Sarabands 1675.

Saracen (sæ·răsĕn), *sb.* and *a.* [In OE. *Sarracene* pl., ad. L. *Saraceni* pl.; in ME., a. OF. *Sar(r)azin, -cin,* ad. late L. *Saracenus,* a. late Gr. Σαρακηνός.] **A.** *sb.* **1.** Among the later Greeks and Romans, a name for the nomadic peoples of the Syro-Arabian desert; hence, an Arab; by extension, a Mohammedan or Moslem, *esp.* with ref. to the Crusades. †**2.** A non-Christian; a heathen or pagan; an infidel -1552. **B.** *adj.* = next. (By Sir C. Wren erroneously applied to Pointed or 'Gothic' architecture.) ME.

Comb. †**Saracen's all-heal, consound,** *Senecio saracenicus,* used by the Saracens in healing wounds; **Saracen's head,** the head of a S., Arab, or Turk, used as a charge in heraldry, as an inn-sign, etc.

Saracenic (særăse·nik), *a.* 1638. [ad. med. L. *Saracenicus,* f. late L. *Saracenus* SARACEN; see -IC 1.] Of, pertaining to, or characteristic of the Saracens. **b.** Applied to Mohammedan architecture, or to any features in it 1768. So **Sarace·nical** *a.* 1613.

‖**Sarafan** (sæ·răfæn). 1799. [Russian.] A long mantle, veil, or sleeveless cloak, forming part of the national dress of Russian peasant women.

Saratoga (særătōu·gă). 1893. [prob. f. *Saratoga Springs,* a summer resort in New York State.] In full *S. trunk*: A large kind of trunk much used by ladies.

Sarcasm (sa·ɹkæz'm). Also †**sarcasmus.** 1579. [ad. late L. *sarcasmus,* a. late Gr. σαρκασμός, f. σαρκάζειν to tear flesh, speak bitterly, f. σαρκ-, σάρξ flesh.] A sharp, bitter, or cutting expression or remark; a bitter gibe or taunt. Now usu. *gen.*: Sarcastic language; sarcastic meaning. Hence †**Sarca·smous** *a.* sarcastic.

Sarcast (sā·ɹkæst). 1654. [ad. Gr. *σαρκαστής, f. σαρκάζειν (see prec.).] A sarcastic writer or speaker.

Sarcastic (saɹkæ·stik), *a.* 1695. [ad. Gr. *σαρκαστικός, f. σαρκάζειν; see SARCASM and -IC 1.] Characterized by or involving sarcasm; given to the use of sarcasm; bitterly cutting or caustic.

Their merriment bluntly sarcastick JOHNSON. So **Sarca·stical** *a.* 1641. **Sarca·stical-ly** *adv.*, **-ness.**

†**Sa·rcel.** 1496. [a. OF. *cercel*:—late L. *circellus,* dim. of *circus* circle.] A pinion feather of a hawk's wing -1688.

fig. Vnfledg'd Witt Imp't from that ragged Sarcill Chaucer drop't 1649.

Sarcelle (saɹse·l). late ME. [a. OF. *cercelle,* mod.F. *sarcelle*:—pop. L. **cercedula,* for class. L. *querquedula.*] A name for the teals and closely allied ducks (*e.g.* the garganey, the long-tailed duck).

Sarcelled (sā·ɹsĕld), *a.* 1688. [Anglicized f. *sarcelle* SARCELLY.] *Her.* = next 2, 3.

Sarcelly (sā·ɹsĕli), *a.* 1500. [a. AF. *sercelé, cercelé* ringleted, curled.] *Her.* **1.** Applied to a variety of the cross moline in which the points are recurved or curled back. **2.** Applied to a cross (esp. a cross moline) voided and open at the ends 1661. **3.** Cut through the middle 1864.

Sarcenet, var. SARSENET.

‖**Sarcina** (sā·ɹsină). *Pl.* **-næ** (nī). 1842. [L., = bundle, f. *sarcire* to patch, mend.] *Bot.* A genus of schizomycetous fungi or bacteria, forming masses of cells united in fixed numbers, which are found in various animal fluids.

Sarco- (sā·ɹko, saɹkǫ·), comb. form of Gr. σαρκ-, σάρξ flesh, as in:

‖**Sa·rcobasis** *Bot.,* a very fleshy gynobase. **Sa·rcoblast,** (*a*) one of the minute yellow bodies present in rhizopods (*b*) a germinal particle of protoplasm. **Sa·rcocarp** *Bot.,* the fleshy part of a drupaceous fruit lying between the epicarp and the endocarp; the part usu. eaten. **Sa·rcocele** (sā·ɹkosīl) *Path.,* hard fleshy enlargement of the testicle. **Sa·rcoderm,** ‖**Sarcode·rma** *Bot.,* the fleshy layer in some seeds, lying between the internal and external integuments. **Sarcola·ctic** *a. Chem.,* in *s. acid,* an acid, isomeric with lactic acid, obtained from muscular tissue. **Sarcole·mma** [LEMMA.[2]] *Anat.,* the transparent tubular sheath investing muscular fibre. **Sa·rcolite** *Min.,* a silicate of aluminium, sodium, and calcium found in flesh-coloured crystals. **Sarcopside** (saɹkǫ·psid) *Min.,* phosphate of iron and manganese exhibiting a flesh-red colour or fracture.

Sarcocol(l (sā·ɹkǒkǫl). Now *rare.* late ME. [ad. late L. *sarcocolla*; see next.] = next.

‖**Sarcocolla** (sāɹkǒkǫ·lă). 1599. [late L., a. Gr., f. σαρκο-, σάρξ flesh + κόλλα glue; so called because of its reputed property of agglutinating wounds.] A sub-viscid gum-resin brought from Arabia and Persia in light yellow or red grains.

Sarcode (sā·ɹkǒud), *sb.* and *a.* 1853. [a. F., f. Gr. σαρκ-, σάρξ flesh; see -ODE.] *Biol.* **A.** *sb.* The PROTOPLASM of animals. **B.** *adj.* Sarcodic; protoplasmic 1855. Hence **Sarcodic** (-ǫ·dik) *a.* of, pertaining to, of the nature of s.

Sarcoid (sā·ɹkoid), *a.* and *sb.* 1841. [f. Gr. σαρκ-, σάρξ + -OID.] **A.** *adj.* Resembling flesh; flesh-like; applied to sponges, plants, etc. **B.** *sb.* A sponge particle 1875.

Sarcology (saɹkǫ·lŏdʒi). 1728. [f. SARCO- + -LOGY.] That branch of anatomy which treats of the fleshy parts of the body. Hence **Sarcolo·gic, -al** *adjs.* **Sarco·logist.**

‖**Sarcoma** (saɹkōu·mă). *Pl.* **sarco·mata.** 1657. [mod.L., a. Gr. σάρκωμα, f. σαρκοῦν to become fleshy, f. σαρκ-, σάρξ.] **1.** *Path.* †**a.** A fleshy excrescence -1752. **b.** A tumour composed of embryonic connective tissue 1804. **2.** *Bot.* The fleshy disk surrounding the ovary 1832. So **Sarco·matous** *a.* pertaining or relating to, of the nature of, s.

‖**Sarcophagus** (saɹkǫ·făgǒs). *Pl.* **-phagi** (-fădʒəi). 1601. [L., a. Gr. σαρκοφάγος, orig. adj., f. σαρκο-, σάρξ flesh + -φάγος eating.] **1.** A kind of stone reputed among the Greeks to have the property of consuming the flesh of dead bodies deposited in it, and consequently used for coffins. Now *Antiq.* **2.** A stone coffin, often embellished with sculptures or bearing inscriptions, etc. 1619. **3.** A flesh-eating person or animal (*rare*) 1617.

2. A s. with ribbed work and mouldings H. WALPOLE.

Sarcophagy (saɹkǫ·fădʒi). *rare.* 1650. [ad. Gr. σαρκοφαγία, f. σαρκοφάγος; see prec. and -PHAGY.] The practice of eating flesh.

There was no Sarcophagie before the flood SIR T. BROWNE.

‖**Sarcoptes** (saɹkǫ·ptīz). 1874. [mod.L., irreg. f. Gr. σαρκ-, σάρξ flesh + κόπτειν to cut.] *Zool.* A genus of parasites comprising the itch-mite; a mite of this genus. Hence **Sarco·ptic** *a.* caused by itch-mites.

Sarcosin(e (sā·ɹkǒsin). 1848. [a. G. *sarkosin,* irreg. f. Gr. σαρκ-, σάρξ + -INE [5].] *Chem.* A nitrogenous substance, one of the constituents of creatine; methyl glycocoll.

Sarcous (sā·ɹkəs), *a.* 1840. [f. Gr. σαρκ-, σάρξ flesh + -OUS.] Consisting of flesh or muscular tissue.

Sard (sāɹd), *sb.*[1] late ME. [prob. a. F. *sarde,* ad. L. *sarda,* a synonym of *sardius* SARDIUS.] A variety of CORNELIAN [1], varying in colour from pale yellow to reddish orange.

Sard (sāɹd), *a.* and *sb.*[2] 1822. [ad. It. *Sardo,* L. *Sardus.*] = SARDINIAN *a.* and *sb.*

Sardanapalian (sāɹdănăpē·liăn), *a.* 1555. [f. L. *Sardanapalus,* Gr. Σαρδανάπαλος, name given to the last king of Nineveh, notorious for luxurious effeminacy.] Resembling Sardanapalus; luxuriously effeminate.

Sardelle (sāɹde·l). 1598. [ad. It. *sardella,* dim. of *sarda*:—L. *sarda,* a. Gr. σάρδη sardine.] A fish, *Clupea* or *Sardinella aurita,* resembling the sardine and prepared like it in certain Mediterranean ports.

Sardian (sā·ɹdiăn), *a.* and *sb.* 1551. [ad. L. *Sardianus,* a. Gr. Σαρδιανός, f. Σάρδεις pl., L. *Sardis, Sardes,* the ancient capital of Lydia.] **A.** *adj.* Of or pertaining to Sardis.

S. stone = SARD *sb.*[1]

B. *sb.* **1.** An inhabitant of Sardis 1598. **2.** = SARD *sb.*[1] 1741.

Sardine [1] (sā·ɹdəin). late ME. [ad. late L. *sardinus* occurring in the Vulgate of Rev. iv. 3.] A precious stone mentioned in Rev. iv. 3.

Sardine [2] (saɹdī·n). late ME. [a. F., ad. It. *sardina*:—L. *sardina*; perh. related to L. *Sardinia.*] A small fish of the herring family, *Clupea pilchardus,* abundant off the shores of Sardinia and Brittany, or a young Cornish pilchard, when cured, preserved in oil and packed in tins or glass for sale as a table delicacy. **b.** Any of various fishes resembling the sardine, or similarly preserved, e.g. *U.S.* the young of the herring or menhaden 1876.

Sardinian (saɹdi·niăn), *a.* and *sb.* 1598. [f. *Sardinia* (see below) + -AN [1] 1.] **A.** *adj.* **1.** Of or pertaining to either the island, or to the kingdom of Sardinia (1720–1859), which included Piedmont and adjacent territories as well as the island 1748. †**2. a.** Used for SARDONIAN, SARDONIC. **b.** tr. L. *sardonius,* as the epithet of the plant producing 'sardonic' laughter. -1752.

2. a. What the Latins call S. Laughter, a distortion of the face without gladness of heart JOHNSON.

B. *sb.* An inhabitant or native of Sardinia 1598; the language of the Sardinians 1841.

‖**Sardius** (sā·ɹdiǒs). late ME. [L., ad. Gr. σάρδιος, -ον, f. Σάρδεις Sardis.] A precious stone mentioned by ancient writers; see SARD *sb.*[1]

S., topacius, and iaspis WYCLIF *Ezek.* xxviii. 13.

†**Sardo·nian,** *a.* 1586. [f. L. *sardonius* + -AN I. 1.] = SARDONIC *a.* -1794.

And with S. smyle Laughing on her, his false intent to shade SPENSER.

Sardonic (saɹdǫ·nik), *a.* 1638. [a. F. *sardonique,* as if ad. L. **sardonicus,* an alteration of *sardonius,* ad. Gr. Σαρδόνιος Sardinian, which in late Gr. was substituted for σαρδάνιος as the epithet for bitter or scornful laughter.] Of laughter, a smile: Bitter, scornful, mocking. Hence of a person, etc.: Characterized by or exhibiting bitterness, scorn or mockery.

Then smil'd Ulysses a Sardanique smile HOBBES. The s. historian, whose rule it is to exhibit human nature always as an object of mockery 1833. Hence **Sardo·nical** *a.,* **-ly** *adv.*

Sardonyx (sā·ɹdǒniks). late ME. [a. L., a. Gr. σαρδόνυξ, app. f. σάρδιος SARDIUS +

ὄνυξ ONYX.] A variety of onyx or stratified chalcedony having white layers alternating with one or more strata of sard.

Our highly valued emeralds and sardonyxes 1875.

‖ **Saree, sari** (sā·rī). 1785. [Hindī *sāṛhī, sāṛī.*] A long wrapping garment of cloth or silk, worn by Hindu women; also, the material of this.

Sargasso (saɪgæ·so). 1598. [a. Pg. *sargaço.*] = GULF-WEED; a mass or species of this. **S. Sea,** a tract of the North Atlantic Ocean between the Azores, Canaries, and the Cape Verde Islands, where masses of s. are found.

Sargo (sā·ɪgo). 1880. [a. Sp., :—L. *sargus* SARGUS.] Any of many species of fishes, several of which occur in the Mediterranean and the neighbouring parts of the Atlantic.

‖ **Sargus** (sā·ɪgɒs). 1591. [L., = Gr. σάργος.] A fish of the genus *Sargus*, the type of the family *Sparidæ*, the sea-breams.

‖ **Sarigue** (sarī·g). 1683. [F., a. Pg. *sarigué*; used erron. for Brazilian *sarigueya*, a deriv. of *Sarigué*, name of a tribe of Indians.] A S. Amer. opossum, *Didelphys opossum.*

Sark (sāɪk), *sb. Sc.* and *north.* [OE. *serc* = ON. *serkr* :—OTeut. **sarkiz.*] A garment worn next the skin; a shirt or chemise; occas. a nightshirt; *transf.* a surplice. Hence **Sark** *v. trans.* to furnish with or clothe in a s.

Sarlac (sā·ɪlăk). 1781. [Calmuck *sarluk.*] = YAK.

Sarmatian (saɪmēⁱ·ʃăn), *a.* and *sb.* 1613. [f. L. *Sarmatia* the land of the *Sarmatæ* (Gr. Σαρμάται, also Σαυρομάται).] **A.** *adj.* Of or belonging to the ancient Sarmatia, now occupied approximately by the Russians and Poles. **B.** *sb.* One of a nomadic people formerly inhabiting this territory 1613. So **Sarma·tic** *a.* = A.

Sarment (sā·ɪmĕnt). Now *rare.* late ME [ad. L. *sarmentum*, chiefly in pl., twigs lopped off, f. *sarpere* to prune.] A twig, †a cutting of a tree. So **Sarmenta·ceous, Sarmento·se, Sarme·ntous** *adjs.* (of a stem) producing slender prostrate runners or branches.

‖ **Sarong** (sărǫ·ŋ). 1834. [Malay *sārung.*] The Malay national garment, a long strip of cloth, worn tucked round the waist like a skirt.

‖ **Saros** (sēᵊ·rǫs). 1613. [Gr. σάρος, σαρός, a. Assyro-Babylonian *šār(u).*] **1.** *Antiq.* The Babylonian name for the number 3600, and for a period of 3600 years. **2.** *Astr.* Adopted by modern astronomers as the name of the cycle of 18 years and 10⅝ days, in which solar and lunar eclipses repeat themselves 1812.

Sarpo (sā·ɪpo). 1753. [a. Sp. *sapo*, lit. 'large toad'.] The toad-fish, *Batrachus tau*, or *B. pardus.*

‖ **Sarracenia** (særăsī·niă). 1786. [mod.L.; orig. *Sarracena*, after Dr. D. *Sarrazin* of Quebec.] *Bot.* A genus of insectivorous plants, the type of the family *Sarraceniaceæ*, to which belong many of the pitcher-plants.

‖ **Sarrasin** (sæ·răzin). 1621. [a. F., for *blé sarrasin* Saracen wheat.] Buckwheat.

Sarsa (sā·ɪsă). 1625. Short for next.

Sarsaparilla (sāɪsăpări·lă). 1577. [a. Sp. *zarzaparrilla*, f. *zarza* bramble + **parrilla*, perh. dim. of *parra* vine.] **1.** A plant belonging to any of the species of the family *Smilaceæ*, indigenous to tropical America from Mexico to Peru; esp. *Smilax officinalis* the Jamaica sarsaparilla. **b.** The dried roots of plants of the various species of *Smilaceæ*; a preparation of the root of *S. officinalis* used as an alterative and tonic 1577. **2.** Applied to plants of other genera, resembling the true sarsaparilla or furnishing a root used as a substitute for it 1840.

Sarsen (sā·ɪs'n). 1644. [app. identical with *Sarsen*, var. of SARACEN.] (In full *s.-stone, boulder.*) One of the numerous large boulders or blocks of sandstone found scattered on the surface of the chalk downs, esp. in Wiltshire.

Sarsenet, sarcenet (sā·ɪsnĕt). late ME. [a. AF. *sarzinet*, prob. a dim. of *sarzin* SARACEN (see -ET).] **1.** A very fine and soft silk material now used chiefly for linings; a dress of this. **2.** *attrib.* or as *adj.* Composed of sarsenet 1521. †**b.** *fig.* Resembling s. in softness –1820.

2. Hange over the eye..a greene sarsenet cloth 1547. **b.** 1 *Hen. IV*, III. i. 256.

Sartor (sā·ɪtǫɪ). 1656. [a. L., f. *sarcire* (*sart-*) to botch, patch.] A tailor (*joc. pedantic*).

Sartorial (saɪtōᵊ·riăl), *a.* 1823. [f. L. *sartorius*, f. *sartor*; see prec. and -AL 1.] Of or belonging to a tailor or his art; characteristic of a tailor.

‖ **Sartorius** (saɪtōᵊ·riɒs). 1704. [mod.L. *sartorius* (*musculus*); see prec. So called as being used in the cross-legged position in which a tailor sits at work.] A long narrow muscle which crosses the thigh obliquely in front.

‖ **Sarum** (sēᵊ·rɒm). 1570. [med.L., prob. evolved from misunderstanding of the abbrev. *Sarȝ* for *Sarisburia*, Salisbury.] Eccl. name of Salisbury, used attrib. in *S. use*, the order of divine service used in Salisbury from the 11th c. to the Reformation; so *S. missal, rubric.*

Sash (sæʃ), *sb.*[1] 1590. [orig. *shash*, a. Arab. *shāsh* muslin, turban-sash.] †**1.** A band of a fine material worn twisted round the head as a turban by Orientals –1718. **2.** A scarf, worn by men, either over one shoulder or round the waist. Also, a similar article worn round the waist by women and children. 1681. Hence **Sash** *v.*[1] *trans.* to dress or adorn with a s.

Sash (sæʃ), *sb.*[2] late ME. [Corruption of CHASSIS, app. mistaken for a pl.] **1.** A frame, usu. of wood, rebated and fitted with one or more panes of glass forming a window or part of a window; *esp.* a sliding frame or each of the two sliding frames of a SASH-WINDOW. Also (now *U.S.*) applied to a casement. **b.** A glazed light of a glass-house or garden frame; a sash-light 1707. **2.** *U.S.* A rectangular frame in which a saw-blade is stretched to prevent its bending or buckling 1875.

Comb.: **s. cord,** a cord used for hanging window sashes; **s. frame,** (*a*) a frame fixed in the opening of a wall to receive the s. or sashes of a window; also, a s. or sash-light; (*b*) *U.S.* = sense 2; **s. pulley,** a pulley in a window frame over which the s. cord runs; **s. tool,** a glaziers' brush; also, a small brush for painting sashes; **s. weight,** a weight attached to each of the two cords of a s. to counterbalance it at any height. Hence **Sash** *v.*[2] *trans.* to furnish with s.-windows; to construct as a s.-window.

Sa·sh-wi·ndow. 1686. [f. prec.] A window consisting of a sash or glazed wooden frame; esp. one having a sash or pair of sashes made to slide up and down, as dist. from a casement.

Sasin (sæ·sin). Also **saisin.** 1834. [Nepalese.] The common Indian antelope, *Antilope bezoartica* or *cervicapra.*

Sasine (sēⁱ·sin). 1669. [Sc. var. of SEISIN, after Law Latin *sasina.*] *Sc. Law.* The act of giving possession of feudal property.

Saskatoon (sæskătū·n). 1875. [Contracted a. Cree *misāskwatomin*, f. *misāskwat* the amelanchier + *min* berry.] The shrub or small tree *Amelanchier canadensis*, and its fruit.

Sassaby (săsēⁱ·bi). 1820. [a. Sechwana *tsessébe, -ábi.*] A large S. African antelope, *Alcelaphus lunata*, sometimes called the Bastard Hartebeest.

Sassafras (sæ·săfræs). 1577. [a. Sp. *sasafras*; etym. dub.] **1.** A small tree, *Sassafras officinale*, with green apetalous flowers and dimorphous leaves, native to N. America. **2.** The dried bark of this tree, used as an alterative; also, an infusion of this 1577.

1. Australian or Tasmanian s. (*Atherosperma moschata*), Brazilian s. (*Nectandra Puchury*), Swamp s. (*Magnolia glauca*), trees of other genera having similar medicinal properties to the s.

Sassanian (sæsēⁱ·niăn), *a.* and *sb.* Also **Sasanian.** 1788. [f. *Sasan* (Pers. *Sāsān*) + -IAN.] **A.** *adj.* Of or pertaining to the family of Sasan, rulers of the Persian Empire A.D. 211–651. **B.** *sb.* A member of this family, esp. one of the Sassanian kings. So **Sassanid,** (sæ·sənid) *sb.* and *a.* 1776.

†**Sasse.** 1642. [a. Du. *sas*; origin unkn.] = LOCK *sb.*[2] II. 3. –1861.

Sassenach (sæ·sĕnăχ). 1771. [repr. Gael. *Sasunnach*, f. *Sasan-*, repr. the Teut. ethnic name SAXON.] The name given by the Gaelic inhabitants of Great Britain and Ireland to their 'Saxon' or English neighbours.

Sassoline (sæ·solīn). 1807. [a. G. *sassolin*, f. Lago del *Sasso* in Tuscany + -INE[5], with euphonic *l.*] *Min.* Native boracic acid, found as a crystalline deposit in the hot springs of Tuscany.

‖ **Sassy** (sæ·si). 1856. [W. African; believed to represent Eng. SAUCY *a.*] Used *attrib.* in *s.-tree*, the African tree *Erythrophlæum guineense*; also in *s.-bark, -wood*, the bark of this tree, a decoction of which is used in West Africa as an ordeal poison.

Satan (sēⁱ·tăn). OE. [a. L. *Satan* (Vulgate) = Gr. Σατάν or Σατᾶν, a. Heb. *sāṭān* adversary, f. *saṭan* to oppose, plot against.] **1.** The proper name of the supreme evil spirit, the Devil. (Now always with capital S.) †**2.** In wider sense: A devil –1688. **b.** Applied to a person or animal as a term of abhorrence. Now *rare.* 1596.

2. We in all likelihood are to possess the very places from which the Satans by transgression fell BUNYAN.

Satanas (sæ·tănæs). Now *arch.* OE. [a. L. (Vulgate) *Satanas*, a. Gr. Σατανᾶς, ad. Jewish Aramaic *sāṭānā*, emphatic form of *sāṭān* (a. Heb.); see prec.] = SATAN 1.

Satanic (sătæ·nik), *a.* 1667. [f. SATAN + -IC 1.] **1.** Of or pertaining to Satan. **2.** Characteristic of or befitting Satan; diabolical, devilish, infernal 1793. **3.** *S. school*: Southey's designation for Byron, Shelley, and their imitators; subsequently often applied to other writers accused of defiant impiety and delight in the portraiture of lawless passion 1821.

2. A criminal..who with s. wickedness had murdered his benefactor 1793. So **Sata·nical** *a.* 1548. **Sata·nical-ly** *adv.*, †**-ness.**

Satanism (sēⁱ·tăniz'm). 1565. [f. SATAN + -ISM 1 b.] **1.** A satanic or diabolical disposition, doctrine, spirit, or contrivance. **2.** The characteristics of the 'Satanic school' 1822. **3.** The worship of Satan; the principles and rites of the Satanists 1896. So **Sa·tanist,** one who is regarded as an adherent of Satan (now *rare*); one who worships Satan 1559.

Satanize (sēⁱ·tănəiz), *v. rare.* 1598. [f. SATAN + -IZE 5.] *trans.* To render like Satan; to make into, or like a devil.

Satanology (sēⁱtănǫ·lŏdʒi). 1862. [f. SATAN + -(O)LOGY.] That part of knowledge which relates to Satan.

Satanophany (sēⁱtănǫ·făni). 1864. [f. SATAN, after *theophany*; see -PHANY.] The appearing, or visible manifestation, of Satan.

Satchel (sæ·tʃĕl). ME. [a. OF. *sachel* :— L. *saccellus*, dim. of *saccus* SACK *sb.*[1]] A small bag; *esp.* a bag for carrying school-books, with or without a strap to hang over the shoulders.

Then, the whining Schoole-boy with his Satchell ..creeping..Vnwillingly to schoole SHAKS. Hence **Sa·tchelled** *a.* having or carrying a s.

Sate (sēⁱt), *v.* 1602. [app. altered from SADE *v.*, after L. *sat, satis* enough; cf. SATIATE *v.*] **1.** *trans.* To fill or satisfy to the full (with food); to gratify to the full any appetite or desire 1613. **b.** To surfeit or cloy by gratification of appetite or desire; to glut, satiate 1602. †**2.** To saturate –1759.

1. Wherefore did Nature powre her bounties forth, ..But all to please, and s. the curious taste? MILT. **2.** A spring strongly sated with a kind of salt 1759. Hence **Sa·teless** *a.* insatiable (chiefly *poet.*).

Sate: see SIT *v.*

Sateen (sătī·n). 1878. [Altered f. SATIN, after *velveteen.*] A cotton or woollen fabric with a glossy surface like that of satin.

Satellite (sæ·tĕləit). 1548. [a. F., ad. L. *satellitem, satelles* attendant, guard.] **1.** An attendant upon a person of importance, forming part of his retinue. Often with implication of subservience or unscrupulous service. **2.** A small or secondary planet which revolves round a larger one 1665. **3.** The name of (*a*) a moth; (*b*) a humming-bird 1832. **4.** *S. vein*: a vein that accompanies an artery (mod.L. *vena satelles, vena comes*) 1846.

1. Boswell was..made happy by an introduction to Johnson, of whom he became the obsequious s. 1850. **2. b.** *attrib.* passing into *adj.* Secondary, minor, satellitic 1923. Hence **Satelli·tic** *a.* of, pertaining to, of the nature of, a s. or lesser planet; also *transf.*

Satiable (sēⁱ·ʃiăb'l), *a.* 1570. [ad. L. **satiabilis*, f. *satiare.*] That can be satiated.

Satiate (sēⁱ·ʃiĕt), *pa. pple.* and *ppl. a.* Now *rare.* 1440. [ad. L. *satiatus, satiare*, f. *satis* enough.] †A. *pa. pple.* Satiated. B. *ppl. a.* Satiated, filled to repletion, glutted.

Satiate (sēi·ʃi̯ĕⁱt), *v.* 1532. [f. L. *satiat-*, *satiare*; see prec.] 1. *trans.* To fill, satisfy (with food). Hence *gen.*, to gratify to the full (a person or his desires). Now *rare.* 2. To gratify beyond one's natural desire; to weary or disgust by repletion; to glut, cloy, surfeit 1620. †3. To saturate –1791.

1. The idea that satiating the servants of the public with wealth is a secret for rendering them honest 1817. 2. Quite fatigued and satiated with this dull variety BURKE. Hence **Satia·tion,** the action of satiating or fact of being satiated.

Satiety (sătəi·ĕti). 1533. [ad. F. *satiété*, ad. L. *satietatem*, f. *satis* enough.] 1. The state of being satiated with food; the feeling of disgust or surfeit caused by excess of food. b. *gen.* The condition of having any appetite or desire gratified to excess; hence, weariness or dislike *of* (an object of desire) caused by gratification or attainment 1553. †c. The condition of being filled or fully gratified –1722. 2. A sufficiency or abundance (*rare*) 1635.

1. It is always a case of famine or s. LIVINGSTONE. b. Thy words with Grace Divine Imbu'd, bring to thir sweetness no satietie MILT. Phr. *To s.* [= L. *ad satietatem*], to an amount or degree which satisfies or gluts desire.

Satin (sæ·tin), *sb.* (and *a.*) late ME. [a. F., app. ad. It. †*setino*, f. L. *seta* silk.] 1. A silk fabric with a glossy surface on one side, produced by a method of weaving by which the threads of the warp are caught and looped by the weft only at certain intervals. b. Applied to fabrics resembling satin, but made of other materials than silk 1517. 2. The plant Honesty, *Lunaria biennis.* Also *white s.* 1597. 3. *slang.* Gin. Also *white s.* 1854. 4. Collector's name for a glossy white moth. Also *white s.* 1766. 5. *attrib.* or *adj.* Made of, resembling, s. 1521.

1. Cledde In fyne blak satyn de owter mere CHAUCER. b. ‖*Satin beauté*, a soft draping dress material of a fine weave, dull crêpe back, and satin face. 5. His high-crown'd hat and sattin-doublet GRAY.

Comb.: **s. cloth,** a woollen cloth woven like s., chiefly produced at Roubaix in France; **-finish,** a polish for silver produced by means of a metallic brush; also a satin-effect produced on materials; **-paper,** a fine writing paper; **s. sheeting,** a composite material of waste silk and cotton; **s. stitch,** a kind of stitch in embroidery and wool-work, imitating the appearance of s.; **-straw,** soft flexible straw used for hats. b. In names of insects, plants, minerals, etc., having a s.-like lustre or smoothness: **s. beauty,** a moth, *Boarmia abietaria*; **-carpet,** a moth, *Ceratopacha fluctuosa*; also = *s. beauty*; **-flower,** (*a*) Honesty; (*b*) the Greater Stitchwort; **s. gypsum,** a fibrous variety of gypsum; **-spar,** a fibrous variety of carbonate of lime; also = *s. gypsum*; **-white,** artificial sulphate of lime; **-wood,** the wood of the Indian tree *Chloroxylon Swietenia* and of several W. Indian trees. Hence **Sa·tin** *v. trans.* to give (to wall-paper) a glossy surface resembling that of s. **Sa·tiny** *a.* resembling s.

Satinette, satinet (sætine·t, sæ·tinĕt). 1703. [a. F. *satinet*; see prec. and -ET.] a. An imitation of satin woven in silk, or silk and cotton. b. A fabric woven with a cotton warp and woollen weft, with a satin-like surface 1837.

Satire (sæ·təiᵊɹ). 1509. [a. F., or ad. L. *satira*, later form of *satura*, a specific application of *satura* medley.] I. 1. A poem, now occas. a prose composition, in which prevailing vices or follies are held up to ridicule. Sometimes, less correctly, a lampoon. b. *fig.* A thing, fact, or circumstance that has the effect of making some person or thing ridiculous 1693. 2. a. Satirical composition 1589. b. The employment, in speaking or writing, of sarcasm, irony, ridicule, etc. in denouncing, exposing, or deriding vice, folly, abuses, or evils of any kind 1675.

1. The *Rape of he Lock*, is the best S. extant 1756. b. Their very names are a s. upon all government *Junius Lett.* 2. My verse is s. YOUNG. I have seen no specimen of Hindú s. 1841.

†II. A satirical person, a satirist –1709.

Misacmos is a S., a quipping fellow 1596.

Satiric (săti·rik), *a.* and *sb.* 1509. [ad. F. *satirique*, ad. late L. *satiricus* (*a.* and *sb.*), f. *satira* SATIRE.] A. *adj.* 1. Of, pertaining to, or of the nature of satire; consisting of, or containing satire; that writes or composes satires. †2. Addicted to satire, satirical –1763.

1. S. novels, poets bold and free CRABBE. 2. A lively and satyric People 1763.

B. *sb.* †1. A writer of satires; a satirist (*rare*) –1603. 2. *pl.* Satirical writings (*rare*) 1600.

Satirical (săti·rikăl), *a.* 1529. [f. late L. *satiricus*: see -ICAL.] 1. = prec. A. 1. 2. Given to, indulging in, or characterized by satire 1590. Hence **Sati·rical-ly** *adv.*, **-ness.**

†**Sa·tirism.** *rare.* 1593. [f. SATIRE + -ISM 1.] Indulgence in satire; satirical utterance –1716.

Satirist (sæ·tĭrist). 1589. [f. SATIRE + -IST.] A writer of satires; (const. *of*) one who satirizes some person or thing.

It is for the satyrist to expose the ridiculous BURKE.

Satirize (sæ·tĭrəiz), *v.* 1601. [ad. F. *satiriser*, f. *satire* SATIRE; see -IZE.] 1. *intr.* To write satires; to assail some one or something with satire. Now only as absol. use of 2. 2. *trans.* To assail with satire; to make the object of, or expose to, satire or censure; to describe or ridicule in a satirical manner 1630.

2. It is as hard to s. well a man of distinguished vices, as to praise well a man of distinguished virtues POPE. Hence **Sa·tirizer.**

Satisfaction (sætisfæ·kʃən). ME. [a. F., ad. L. *satisfactionem*, f. *satisfacere* to SATISFY.] The action of satisfying; the state or fact of being satisfied. I. With ref. to obligations. 1. The payment in full of a debt, or the fulfilment of an obligation or claim; the atoning *for* an injury, offence, or fault. Also quasi-*concr.*, the pecuniary or other gift or penalty, or the act, by which these are discharged, fulfilled, or atoned for. Now chiefly *Law.* late ME. b. An act of compensation or amends; an amount paid in compensation; a penalty. Now *rare.* 1440. 2. *Eccl.* The performance by a penitent of the penance enjoined by his confessor as payment of the temporal punishment due to his sin ME. 3. *Theol.* The atonement made by Christ for the sins of the world. So *doctrine of s.* late ME. 4. The opportunity of satisfying one's honour by a duel; the acceptance of a challenge to a duel from the person who deems himself injured. Chiefly in phr., *to give, demand s.* 1602.

1. Unless for him Som other able, and as willing, pay The rigid s., death for death MILT. Phrases. *To make* (or †*do*) *s.*; *in s.* (*of*). *To enter* (*up*) *s.* (Law), to place on the record of a court a statement that the payment ordered by it has been duly made; so *entry of s.* 4. It is called *Giving a Man S.*, to urge your Offence against him with your Sword STEELE.

II. With ref. to desires or feelings. 1. The action of gratifying (an appetite or desire) to the full, or of contenting (a person) by the fulfilment of a desire or the supply of a want; the fact of having been thus gratified or contented. late ME. b. Satisfied or contented state of mind; now usu., gratification or pleasure occasioned by some fact, event, or state of things 1477. c. A particular instance of satisfaction; something which occasions gratification 1687. 2. Release from suspense; removal of doubt or difficulty; conviction 1586.

1. My guide..did his duty entirely to my s. TYNDALL. b. The grettest richesse is satisfacion of the herte 1477. Jones expressed the utmost s. at the account FIELDING. c. A quick Relish of the Satisfactions of Life STEELE. 2. Phr. *to* (*a person's*) *s.* Hence **Satisfa·ctionist** (*rare*), one who holds that Christ suffered punishment as s. for the sins of man.

Satisfactive (sætisfæ·ktiv), *a. rare.* 1829. [f. L. *satisfact-*, *satisfacere*; see -IVE.] In Bentham's use: Consisting in or concerned with satisfaction or reparation.

Satisfactory (sætisfæ·ktəri), *a.* and *sb.* 1547. [ad. F. *satisfactoire* (14th c.), ad. med L. *satisfactorius*, f. L. *satisfacere* to SATISFY.] 1. *Eccl.* and *Theol.* Serving to make satisfaction or atonement for sin 1547. 2. Serving to satisfy a debt or obligation (*rare*) 1604. †3. Of an explanation or argument: Serving merely to satisfy the inquirer or objector; merely plausible. BACON. 4. a. Adequate for the needs of the case. Of an argument: Convincing. b. That justifies a feeling of satisfaction. 1640.

4. a. A s. reply MACAULAY. b. Went home with a triumphant light in his eyes after concluding a s. marriage for his son GEO. ELIOT. Hence **Satisfa·ctori-ly** *adv.*, **-ness.**

Satisfy (sæ·tisfəi), *v.* late ME. [a. OF. *satisfier*, irreg. ad. L. *satisfacere*, orig. two words, *satis* enough, *facere* to do.] I. With ref. to debt or obligation. 1. *trans.* To pay off or discharge fully (a debt, obligation); to comply with (a demand). Now *rare* exc. in legal use. b. To pay (a creditor). Now *rare* exc. in legal use. late ME. †c. To remunerate –1771. †2. To make compensation or reparation for (a wrong, injury); to atone for (an offence) –1715. b. To make atonement or reparation to (a person, his honour, etc.) 1602. 3. *intr.* To make satisfaction, full payment, reparation, or atonement. Now *Theol.* (said of Christ). 1450.

1. After all my dettes are satisfied 1578. 2. Thy death shall satisfie thy iniury, & my malice SIDNEY. 3. So Man..Shall satisfie for Man MILT.

II. With ref. to feelings or needs. 1. *trans.* To meet or fulfil the wish or desire or expectation of; to be accepted by (a person, his taste, judgement, etc.) as all that could be reasonably desired; to content. Also with obj. a desire, expectation, etc. 1489. b. In *pass.*, To be content (*with*); to find it sufficient, desire or demand no more than *to do* something. Also, to be well pleased (*with*, †*at*). 1533. 2. *absol.* and *intr.* To cause or give satisfaction or contentment 1600. 3. *trans.* To cause to have enough; to put an end to (an appetite, want) by fully supplying it 1500. 4. To furnish with sufficient proof or information; to set free from doubt or uncertainty; to convince 1520. 5. To answer sufficiently (an objection, question); to fulfil or comply with (a request); to solve (a doubt, difficulty) 1581. 6. To answer the requirements of (a state of things, hypothesis, etc.); to accord with (conditions) 1651. b. *Algebra.* Of a known quantity: To fulfil the conditions of, be an admissible solution of (an equation) 1826.

1. It is harde to satisfye all men 1530. I have it in my power to s. your curiosity 1717. Phr. *To s. the examiners*, in English Universities, to be entitled to a 'pass', but not to 'honours'. b. We were fain to rest satisfied then, with what we saw of that Monastery from the top of the Mount 1687. 3. Hee will not be satisfied with blood *Ecclus.* xii. 16. 4. Where I cannot s. my reason, I love to humour my fancy SIR T. BROWNE. No one can..be satisfied of the contrary 1736. 5. Revelation was not given us to s. doubts, but to make us better men 1834. Hence **Sa·tisfiable** *a.* †satisfactory; able to be or that may be satisfied. **Sa·tisfied-ly** *adv.*, **-ness. Sa·tisfier. Sa·tisfying-ly** *adv.*, **-ness.**

Satispassion (sætispæ·ʃən). 1614. [ad. med.L. **satispassionem*, f. phr. *satis pati* to suffer enough.] *Theol.* Atonement by an adequate degree of suffering.

†**Sa·tive,** *a.* 1599. [ad. L. *sativus*, f. *sa-*, root of *serere* to sow.] Sown or planted; cultivated, not wild –1725.

Satrap (sæ·træp). late ME. [ad. L. *satrapa*, *satrapes*, a. Gr. σατράπης, ad. OPers. *xšaθrapāvan-*, lit. protector of the country, f. *xšaθra-* country + *pā* to protect.] 1. A governor of a province under the ancient Persian monarchy. 2. *transf.* A subordinate ruler; often with imputation of tyranny or ostentation. late ME. Hence **Sa·trapal** *a.* of or pertaining to a s. or satraps. **Sa·trapess,** a female s. **Satra·pic, -al** *adjs.* pertaining to a s.; *fig.* cruel, tyrannical.

Satrapy (sæ·trăpi). 1603. [a. F. *satrapie*, ad. L. *satrapia*, *satrapea*, a. Gr. σατραπεία, f. σατράπης SATRAP.] 1. A province ruled over by a satrap. 2. The dignity of a satrap 1641. 3. The period of rule of a satrap 1846.

‖**Satsuma** (sæ·tsiŭmă). 1872. [A province in the island of Kiusiu, Japan.] In full *S. ware*, a kind of cream-coloured Japanese pottery.

Saturable (sæ·tiŭrăb'l, sæ·tʃə-), *a.* 1570. [ad. L. *saturabilis*, f. *saturare* to SATURATE; see -BLE.] Capable of saturation.

Saturate (sæ·tiŭrĕt, sæ·tʃə-), *a.* 1550. [ad. L. *saturatus*, *saturare*; see next.] †1. Satisfied, satiated –1604. 2. Soaked through, saturated with moisture. Chiefly *poet.* 1784. 3. Of colours: Intense, deep 1669.

2. The lark is gay, That dries his feathers, s. with dew, Beneath the rosy cloud COWPER. 3. It would yield a deep s. green tincture 1669.

Saturate (sæ·tiŭrĕⁱt, sæ·tʃə-), *v.* 1538. [f. L. *saturat-*, *saturare*, f. *satur* full, cogn. w. *satis* enough.] †1. *trans.* To satisfy, satiate –1816. 2. To soak thoroughly, imbue *with* 1756. 3. *Chem.* To cause (a substance) to combine with or dissolve the utmost possible quantity of another substance 1681. 4. *Physics.* a. To charge (air or vapour) with the utmost quantity of moisture that it can hold in suspension 1812. b. To magnetize (a piece of metal), charge (a body) with electricity, to the fullest extent of its capacity 1832.

2. Thatch that had got saturated with the smoke 1873. *fig.* A mind not thoroughly saturated with the tolerating maxims of the Gospel BURKE. Hence **Sa·turator**, one who or that which saturates, e.g. a device for supplying air saturated with water-vapour to a room, etc.

Saturated (sæ·tiŭrēⁱtėd, sæ·tʃə-), *ppl. a.* 1668. [f. prec. + -ED[1].] †1. Filled to repletion –1820. 2. Penetrated with moisture, soaked through 1728. 3. *Physics.* That has combined with or dissolved the largest possible proportion of some other substance 1788. 4. *Physics.* Charged to the full extent of its capacity 1848. 5. Of colours: Not diluted with white 1853. 6. *Phys. Chem.* That has equal and opposite quantities of electricity in each molecule or atom 1888.

2. And s. earth Awaits the morning beam THOMSON. 3. A s. solution of nitre 1788. 4. *S. steam,* steam charged with such an amount of heat that less would produce condensation, and more super heat.

Saturation (sætiŭrēⁱ·ʃən, sætʃə-). 1554. [ad. late L. *saturationem,* f. *saturare* to SATURATE.] †1. Satiation –1832. 2. The action of thoroughly soaking or the condition of being thoroughly soaked with fluid 1846. 3. The action of charging, or the state of being charged, up to the limit of capacity; *spec.* in *Chem.* the condition of a substance when combined with or holding in solution the largest proportion of another substance that it can take; in *Physics,* the condition of holding as much suspended matter, or being as fully charged with electricity, heat, etc. as possible 1659. 3. *Chromatics.* Degree of intensity (of a colour); relative freedom from admixture of white 1878.

2. Phr *Point of s.,* the degree of charge at which a substance becomes saturated.

Saturday (sæ·təɹdeⁱ, -di). [OE. *Sætern(es)-dæg,* a half-translated adoption of L. *Saturni dies,* day of (the planet) Saturn.] The seventh day of the week.

Hospital S.: see HOSPITAL *sb.* *Saturday-to-Monday* often *attrib.* with ref. to railway and other excursion tickets covering this period.

Saturn (sæ·tŏɹn). OE. [ad. L. *Saturnus,* perh. f. root *sa-* to SOW.] 1. *Mythol.* An Italic god, orig. the god of agriculture, but in classical times identified with the Greek Cronos, the father of Zeus (Jupiter). 2. *Astr.* A primary planet of the solar system, the most remote known to ancient astronomy OE. 3. *Alch.* The technical name for lead. late ME. 4. *Her.* The tincture sable, in blazoning by the names of heavenly bodies 1572.

2. Satourn disposith to malencolye LYDG. Saturne that dull and malevolent planet 1640.

Saturnal (sătŏ·ɹnăl), *a.* and *sb.* 1487. [ad. L. *Saturnalis*; see -AL.] †A. *adj.* Pertaining to Saturn or his astrological influence –1683. B. *sb. pl.* [a. F. *saturnales* pl.] = next. 1487.

‖**Saturnalia** (sætŏɹnēⁱ·liă), *sb. pl.* 1591. [L., neut. pl. of *Saturnalis* SATURNAL *a.*] 1. *Rom. Antiq.* (Now always with cap.) The festival of Saturn, held in December, observed as a time of general unrestrained merrymaking, extending even to the slaves. 2. *transf.* and *fig.* (Freq. with small initial.) A period of unrestrained licence and revelry. Occas. as *sing.* 1782.

2. Malignity at least will have its S. H. WALPOLE. Hence **Saturna·lian** *a.* pertaining to the S.; appropriate to S.

Saturnian (sătŏ·ɹniăn), *a.* and *sb.* 1557. [f. L. *Saturnius* (f. *Saturnus* SATURN) + -AN I. 1.] A. *adj.* 1. Pertaining to the god Saturn (chiefly with ref. to the 'golden age' under his reign). 2. Distinctive epithet of the metre (*versus Saturnius*) used in early Roman poetry, before the introduction of Greek metres 1693. 3. Of or pertaining to the planet Saturn; †due to the baleful influence of Saturn 1557.

1. Through the fortunate S. land, Into the darkness of the West SHELLEY.

B. *sb.* 1. One born under the influence of the planet Saturn; a person of saturnine temperament 1591. 2. An inhabitant of the planet Saturn 1738. 3. *pl.* Saturnian verses 1899.

Saturnic (sătŏ·ɹnik), *a.* 1879. [f. SATURN + -IC.] Affected with lead-poisoning.

Saturnicentric (sătŏɹnise·ntrik), *a.* 1790. [f. SATURN, after *geocentric.*] Calculated with reference to the centre of Saturn.

Saturnine (sæ·tŏɹnəin), *a.* late ME. [ad. med.L. **Saturninus,* f. *Saturnus* SATURN.] 1. a. *Astrol.* Born under or affected by the influence of the planet Saturn. b. Hence, sluggish, cold, and gloomy in temperament. 2. Of or pertaining to lead 1669. b. *Path.* Of disorders: Caused by absorption of lead. Of a patient: Suffering from lead-poisoning. 1823.

1. S. heauy headed blunderers NASHE.

Saturnism (sæ·tŏɹniz'm). 1855. [a. mod. L. *Saturnismus* (also used), f. L. *Saturnus* SATURN; see -ISM 1 b.] *Path.* Lead-poisoning.

Satyr (sæ·təɹ). late ME. [ad. L. *satyrus,* a. Gr. σάτυρος.] 1. *Myth.* One of a class of woodland gods or demons, in form partly human and partly bestial, supposed to be the companions of Bacchus; also *fig.,* as the type of lustfulness. 2. A kind of ape (so Gr. σάτυρος); in mod. use, the orang-utan, *Simia satyrus* (*rare*) late ME. 3. Any butterfly of the group *Satyridæ* 1871.

1. So excellent a King, that was to this Hiperion to a Satyre SHAKS.

‖**Satyriasis** (sætĭrəi·ăsis). 1657. [mod.L., a. Gr. σατυρίασις, f. σάτυρος SATYR; see -ASIS.] *Path.* Excessively great sexual desire in the male. Also = PRIAPISM 1.

Satyric (săti·rik), *a.* and *sb.* 1607. [ad. L. *satyricus,* Gr. σατυρικός, f. σάτυρος SATYR; see -IC.] A. *adj.* Pertaining to satyrs; *esp.* as the epithet of that species of drama in which the chorus was habited to represent satyrs. †B. *sb.* A satyric drama. DRYDEN. So **Saty·rical** *a.* 1590.

Satyrion (săti·riŏn). late ME. [a. L. *satyrion, -um,* a. Gr. σατύριον, f. σάτυρος SATYR, in allusion to the reputed aphrodisiac properties of the plant so named.] Any of various kinds of Orchis.

Sauba (sǭ·bă, ‖sau·ba). 1863. [Tupi.] The leaf-cutting ant (*Œcodoma cephalotes*) of tropical S. America.

Sauce (sǭs), *sb.* ME. [a. F., :—pop. L. *salsa,* fem. of *salsus* salted; see SALT *a.*[1]] 1. Any preparation, usu. liquid or soft, intended to be eaten with food as a relish. Often with qualifying word denoting the predominant ingredient, as *bread, egg, mint, parsley s.* 2. *fig.* Something which adds piquancy to a word, idea, thought or action 1500. 3. Chiefly *U.S.* Vegetables or fruit, fresh or preserved, taken as part of a meal, or as a relish. Often = SALAD. 1629. 4. A solution of salt and other ingredients used in some manufacturing processes 1839. 5. †a. *vocatively.* An impudent person, a saucebox –1697. b. Impertinence. *colloq.* and *dial.* 1835.

1. Of poynaunt s. hir neded neuer a deel CHAUCER. Prov. *What's s. for the goose is s. for the gander.* 2. What is enticing to other men, must, to interest them, have the piquant s. of extreme danger SCOTT. Phr. *To serve with the same s.,* to subject to the same kind of usage. 3. *Long s.* (U.S.) = beet, carrots, and parsnips; *short s.* = potatoes, turnips, onions, etc.

Sauce (sǭs), *v.* 1440. [f. SAUCE *sb.*] 1. *trans.* To season, dress, or prepare (food) with sauces or condiments. *arch.* 2. *fig.* a. To furnish a pleasing accompaniment to; to make pleasant or agreeable, reduce the asperity of 1514. †b. To qualify with a mixture of bitterness –1655. c. To 'season', make piquant 1555. 3. *joc.* or *colloq.* †a. To charge extortionate prices to. SHAKS. †b. To belabour, flog –1726. c. To rebuke smartly. Now *dial.* 1600. d. To speak impertinently to. *vulgar.* 1864.

2. a. This sad news I shall s. with a little that is more pleasant 1621. b. Joy sauced is with payne 1510. 3. c. Ile s. Her with bitter words SHAKS. d. They bully the slavey (but then the slavey sauces them, so perhaps it is only tit for tat) 1885.

Sauce-alone (sǭ·s,ălōᵘn). 1530. [app. f. SAUCE *sb.* + ALONE, implying that the plant is a sufficient sauce by itself.] The plant *Sisymbrium Alliaria,* a tall hedge-weed formerly used as a flavouring for sauces and salads.

Sauce-boat (sǭ·sbōᵘt). 1747. A small vessel with a lip, used for serving sauce.

Saucebox (sǭ·sbǫks). *colloq.* 1588. [f. SAUCE *sb.* 5 + BOX *sb.*[2]] A person addicted to making saucy remarks.

Saucepan (sǭ·s,păn). 1686. [f. SAUCE *sb.* + PAN *sb.*[1]] A vessel of metal, with a handle projecting from the side, and usu. with a lid; employed for boiling things in cookery.

Saucer (sǭ·səɹ). ME. [a. OF. *saussier* masc., *saussiere* fem., vessel for holding sauce, f. *sauce* SAUCE *sb.*] †1. A dish or deep plate in which salt or sauces were placed upon the table –1742. 2. Any small shallow dish or deep plate of circular shape 1607. 3. A small round shallow vessel, usu. with concave sides and flat at the bottom, used for supporting a cup, and catching any liquid that may be spilled from it 1753. 4. Something like a saucer; as *Bot.* any part of a plant resembling a saucer, as the involucre of the *Euphorbiaceæ,* and the tubercle of lichens 1578.

3. Don't pour your tea in your s.—that's vulgar! 1840. There sat the dog with eyes as big as saucers, glaring at him 1876.

Saucer eye. Usu. *pl.* 1664. An eye as large and round as a saucer, generally ascribed to spectres and ghosts. So **Saucer-eyed** *a.* having saucer eyes 1622.

†‖**Sauci·sse.** 1604. [F.] *Mil.* = next 3. –1795.

‖**Saucisson** (sosisoṅ). 1634. [F., augm. of *saucisse* SAUSAGE.] 1. A large thick sausage 1760. 2. A kind of firework, consisting of a tube of paper or canvas packed with gunpowder 1634. 3. *Mil.* a. A large fascine 1702. b. A long tube of waterproof canvas, etc., packed with gunpowder and used for firing a mine 1827.

Saucy (sǭ·si), *a.* 1508. [f. SAUCE *sb* + -Y[1].] †1. Flavoured with or pertaining to sauce; resembling sauce; savoury –1630. 2. Of persons, their dispositions, language, etc.: Insolent towards superiors; presumptuous. Now chiefly *colloq.* with milder sense: Impertinent, 'cheeky'. 1530. b. Occas. with the notion: Wanton, lascivious 1603. c. Applied to a ship or boat: †(*a*) Presumptuous, rashly-venturing. (*b*) Smart, stylish. 1600. 3. Scornful, disdainful. Now *dial.* 1716.

2. Sawcy Rascal, to disturb my Meditations DRYDEN. Alençon had a s. tongue 1879. b. *Cymb.* I. vi. 151. c. S. little crab boats 1873. 3. In sawcy State the griping Broker sits GAY. Hence **Sau·cily** *adv.* **Sau·ciness.**

‖**Sauerkraut, sourcrout** (sau·əɹ-, sauᵊ·ɹ-kraut). 1617. [G.; *sauer* sour + *kraut* cabbage.] Cabbage which has undergone an acid fermentation, an article of diet in Germany.

Sauger (sǭ·gəɹ). 1882. The smaller Amer. pike-perch, *Stizostedium canadense.*

Saulie (sǭ·li). *Sc.* Now *Hist.* 1621. [Origin obsc.] A hired mourner at a funeral.

†**Sault**[1]. ME. [a. F. *saut* :—L. *saltus,* f. *salire* to leap.] A jump; *spec.* of horses –1752.

‖**Sault**[2] (sō, commonly sū). *N. Amer.* 1600. [Colonial F., 17th c. spelling of *saut.*] A waterfall or rapid.

‖**Saumur** (somür). 1888. [Name of a town in the department of Maine-et-Loire in France.] A French white wine resembling champagne.

Saunter (sǭ·ntəɹ), *sb.* 1712. [f. next.] 1. The action or habit of sauntering 1728. 2. A leisurely careless gait 1712. 3. A leisurely loitering walk or ramble; a stroll 1828.

2. S. and swagger both united to stamp *prodigal* on the Bond Street Lounger LYTTON. 3. A quiet s. about a cathedral 1828.

Saunter (sǭ·ntəɹ), *v.* 1475. [Origin obsc.] †1. *intr.* app. To muse, be in a reverie –1589. 2. †a. To wander about aimlessly or unprofitably; to travel as a vagrant. b. To walk with a leisurely and careless gait; to stroll. 1667. †3. To loiter over one's work, to dawdle –1776.

2. Mr. Harrel sauntered into the breakfast room 1782. Hence **Sau·nterer. Sau·nteringly** *adv.*

Saurel (sore·l). 1882. [a. F.] A fish of the genus *Trachurus.*

‖**Sauria** (sǭ·riă), *sb. pl.* 1834. [mod.L., f. Gr. σαύρα, σαῦρος lizard.] *Zool.* An order of Reptiles, orig. including the Lizards and Crocodiles; subseq. restricted to the Lizards alone. Now commonly repl. by *Lacertilia.*

Saurian (sǭ·riăn), *a.* and *sb.* 1807. [f. prec. + -AN I. 1.] *Zool.* A. *adj.* 1. Belonging to the order *Sauria.* 2. Pertaining to or characteristic of a saurian 1826. B. *sb.* A reptile of the order *Sauria.* Now chiefly in pop. use, applied esp. to crocodiles, and to the ichthyosaurus, plesiosaurus, etc. 1807.

Sauro- (sǭ·ro), bef. a vowel **saur-**, comb. form of Gr. σαῦρος lizard; as in **Sauropterygian** (sǭ:rǫptĕri·dʒiăn) [Gr. πτερύγιον wing, fin.] *Palæont.*, *a.* of or pertaining to the *Sauropterygia* (usu. called *Plesiosauria*), an order of extinct marine reptiles in Owen's classification; *sb.* a reptile of this order; a plesiosaur.

Saurognathous (sǭrǫ gnăþəs), *a.* 1874. [f. mod.L. *Saurognathæ* pl., f. Gr. σαῦρος lizard + γνάθος jaw; see -OUS.] *Ornith.* Of, pertaining to, or characteristic of the *Saurognathæ* (the woodpeckers and their allies), characterized by an arrangement of the bones of the palate similar to that in lizards. So **Sauro·gnathism**, s. formation of the palate.

Sauroid (sǭ·roid), *a.* and *sb.* 1836. [a. F. *sauroïde*, ad. Gr. σαυροειδής, f. σαῦρος lizard + -ειδής; see -OID.] **A.** *adj.* **1.** Resembling a saurian or lizard; a distinctive epithet of an order of fishes (*Sauroidei*). **B.** *sb.* **1.** A sauroid fish 1836. **2.** An animal belonging to the *Sauroidea* (later SAUROPSIDA) 1863.

Sauropod (sǭ·rǫpǫd), *a.* and *sb.* 1891. [f. mod.L. *sauropoda*, f. Gr. σαῦρος + ποδ-, πούς foot.] **A.** *adj.* = SAUROPODOUS *a.* **B.** *sb.* A member of the order *Sauropoda* of gigantic herbivorous dinosaurs. So **Sauro·podous** *a.* of, pertaining to, or connected with the *Sauropoda*.

‖**Sauropsida** (sǭrǫ·psidă), *sb. pl.* 1864. [mod.L., f. Gr. σαύρα, σαῦρος lizard + ὄψις appearance.] *Zool.* The second of the three primary groups of *Vertebrata* in Huxley's classification, comprising reptiles, birds, etc. Hence **Sauro·psidan** *a.* of or pertaining to the *S.*; *sb.* a member of the *S.*

Saury (sǭ·ri). 1771. [app. irreg. ad. mod. L. *saurus*.] Any of various fishes, esp. the skipper or bill-fish, *Scomberesox saurus*; also *attrib* as *s. pike*, *salmon*.

Sausage (sǫ·sėdʒ). [ME. *sausige*, a. ONF. *saussiche* (mod.F. *saucisse*) :—late L. *salsicia*, f. *salsus* salted.] **1.** Orig., a quantity of finely chopped pork, beef, or other meat, spiced and flavoured, enclosed in a short length of the intestine of some animal so as to form a cylindrical roll; later also *gen.*, meat thus prepared. Now, in its widest use, a preparation of comminuted beef, pork, etc., or a mixture of these, either fresh, salted, pickled, smoked, or cured, with salt, spices, flour, etc. and stuffed into a container made from an intestine or other animal tissue. **2.** *Mil.* **a.** = SAUCISSON 3. 1645. **b.** An observation balloon 1916.

1. *Bologna s.*: see BOLOGNA. *German s.*: see GERMAN *a.*[2]

attrib. and *Comb.*, as in *s. factory*, *maker*; also in names of appliances for making sausages, as *s.-cutter*, *-machine*, etc.; **s. balloon** = 2 b; **-curl**, a curl resembling a s.; **-meat**, meat minced and spiced to be used in sausages or as a stuffing; **-roll**, a s., or a roll of s.-meat, enclosed in pastry, and cooked.

Saussurite (sǭ·siŭrəit). 1811. [Named after Prof. H. B. de *Saussure* (1740–99); see -ITE[1] 2 b.] *Min.* A very compact variety of zoisite. Hence **Saussuri·tic** *a.*

‖**Sauté** (sote), *a.* and *sb.* 1813. [F., pa. pple. of *sauter* to leap.] *Cookery.* **A.** *adj.* Of meat, vegetables, etc.: Fried in a pan with a little butter over a quick fire, while being tossed from time to time; (of potatoes) cut into finger-shaped pieces and fried in deep fat; 'chipped' 1869. **B.** *sb.* A dish cooked in this manner 1813. Hence **Sauté** *v. trans.* to cook thus.

‖**Sauterne** (sotǭ·ɹn). 1711. [Named from the district of *Sauterne* near Bordeaux.] A French white wine of the Bordeaux class.

‖**Sauve-qui-peut** (sovkipö). 1815. [F., sb. use of a phrase = 'Save (himself) who can'.] A general stampede or complete rout.

Savable, saveable (sēⁱ·văb'l), *a.* 1450. [f. SAVE *v.* + -ABLE.] Capable of being saved; orig. chiefly *Theol.*

Savage (sæ·vėdʒ), *a.* and *sb.* Also (now *arch.*) salvage. ME. [a. F. *sauvage* :—L. *silvaticus* (in pop. L. also *salvaticus*) woodland, wild, f. *silva* wood, forest.] **A.** *adj.* **I.** That is in a state of nature, wild. **1.** Of animals: Wild; undomesticated; untamed. (Now exclusively with implication of ferocity.) **2.** Of land, country, scenery: †Uncultivated. Hence, Horribly wild and rugged. ME. †**3.** Of a plant, tree, etc.: Uncultivated –1820. **4.** Of movements, noise, manners, etc.: Ungoverned; rude, unpolished. *arch.* late ME. **5.** Uncivilized; existing in the lowest stage of culture 1588. **b.** Pertaining to or characteristic of savages 1614. †**c.** Solitary –1680.

1. To binden leounes sauuage ME. 2. The moste part of the yle is hilly and sauage 1585. 4. The sauage strangenesse he puts on SHAKS. 5. I will take some s. woman, she shall rear my dusky race TENNYSON. *Salvage man* (Her.), the conventional representation of a savage; a human figure naked or enveloped in foliage (*arch.*). **c.** O might I here..live s. MILT.

II. With ref. to disposition or temper. †**1.** Rude, harsh, ungentle (also *transf.* of the sea, a river) –1655. **2.** Fierce, ferocious, cruel. late ME. **3.** Enraged, furiously angry; rough or unsparing in speech. (Chiefly *colloq.*) 1825.

2. A roaring voice of most sauage wilde beasts *Wisd.* xvii. 19. Musick has Charms to soothe a s. Breast CONGR. *transf.* Within the direfull grasp Of S. hunger MILT. 3. I think the Doctor was pretty s. with old Briggs 1899.

B. *sb.* †**1.** A wild beast –1831. **2.** An uncivilized, wild person 1588. **b.** *transf.* A cruel or fierce person. Also, one who is destitute of culture or ignorant or neglectful of the rules of good behaviour. 1606. **3.** = *Salvage man* 1780.

2. I am as free as Nature first made man,..When wild in woods the noble S. ran DRYDEN. Hence **Sa·vage-ly** *adv.*, **-ness.**

Savage (sæ·vėdʒ), *v.* 1563. [f. SAVAGE *a.*] †**1.** *intr.* To act the savage; to indulge in cruel or barbarous deeds (*rare*) –1646. **2.** *trans.* To render savage, barbarous, or fierce 1611. **3.** Of an animal, esp. a horse: To attack and bite or trample 1880. Also *fig.*

2. Its bloodhounds savaged by a cross of wolf SOUTHEY. 3. [The horse] galloped about.., savaging every horse or man it could reach 1896.

Savagedom (sæ·vėdʒdəm). 1845. [f. SAVAGE *a.* or *sb.* + -DOM.] The condition of being a savage; savage people collectively.

Savagery (sæ·vėdʒri, sæ·vėdʒəri). 1595. [f. SAVAGE *a.* + -RY.] **1.** The quality of being fierce or cruel; savage disposition, conduct, or actions; also with *a* and *pl.*, a cruel action or deed. **2.** The condition of being wild or uncivilized; the characteristics of savages; the savage state of human society 1825. **3.** Wildness, as of nature, scenery, etc. 1872. **4.** Wild creatures or savages collectively 1599.

1. This is the bloodiest shame, The wildest Sauagery ..That euer wall-ey'd wrath..Presented to the teares of soft remorse SHAKS. 2. The s. of the primeval Celt 1904. 4. *Hen. V*, v. ii. 47. So **Sa·vagism**, = sense 2.

Savannah (sǎvæ·nă). 1555. [In 16th c. *zavana*, a. Sp. *zavana*, *çavana*, perh. a Carib word.] A treeless plain; prop., one of those in parts of tropical America.

attrib.: **s. flower**, a W. Indian name for various species of *Echites*; **s. fox**, *Vulpes cancrivora*. **s. sparrow**, a sparrow of the genus *Passerculus*, esp. *P. savanna*, common throughout the greater part of N. America; **-wattle**, the W. Indian trees *Citharexylum quadrangulare* and *C. cinereum*.

‖**Savant** (savaṅ). 1719. [F.; sb. use of adj., orig. pr. pple. of *savoir* to know:—pop. L. *$sap\bar{e}re$ = cl. L. $sap\check{e}re$ to be wise.] A man of learning or science; esp. one professionally engaged in learned or scientific research. So ‖**Savante** (savaṅt), a learned (French) woman.

‖**Savate** (savat). 1862. [F.; lit. a kind of shoe.] A method of fighting (commonly used instead of or in conjunction with boxing) in which the feet are used.

Save (sēⁱv), *sb.* 1890. [f. SAVE *v.*] *Football, Hockey*, etc. An act of preventing the opposite side from scoring.

Save (sēⁱv), *v.* [ME. *salve*, *sauve*, a. OF. OF. *salver*, *sauver* :—late L. *salvare* to save, f. *salvus* SAFE.] **I.** To rescue or protect. **1.** *trans.* To deliver or rescue from peril or hurt; to make safe, put in safety; also *absol.* **2.** *Theol.* To deliver (a person, the soul) from sin and its consequences; to admit to eternal bliss ME. **b.** *transf.* To be the 'salvation' of 1894. **3.** Used in formulas of benediction, greeting, etc.; as *God s. you!* ME. †**4.** To spare instead of killing, allow to live, give (a person) his life –1642. **5.** To deliver *from* some evil which is likely to befall one; to ensure (a person) immunity from hurt or annoyance ME. **6.** To keep, protect, or guard (a thing) from damage, loss, or destruction late ME. **7.** To keep intact or unhurt (honour, credit, chastity, and the like) ME. **8.** With adj. complement: To keep or preserve *whole*, *unhurt*, etc. ME. †**9.** To store, preserve –1728. **10.** †**a.** Astr. *To s. the appearances, the phenomena* [tr. Gr. σῴζειν τὰ φαινόμενα]: said of a hypothesis which explains all the observed facts –1667. Hence **b.** *To s. appearances*: to contrive to keep up an appearance of propriety, solvency, or the like 1711. **11.** To prevent the loss of (a game, match, wager, etc.) 1611. **12.** To be in time for, manage to catch 1732.

1. One that I sau'd from drowning SHAKS. Cou'd Troy be sav'd by any single hand POPE. A great many lives were saved by the salutary practice of inoculation 1803. Eternal Father, strong to s. 1860. Phr. *To s. one's skin*, to escape unhurt. *To s. one's bacon*: see BACON. 2. We can not be saued wythout fayeth LATIMER. Phr. *As I hope to be saved*, †*so God* (or *Christ*) *s. me*, etc. 3. (*God*) *s. the mark*: see MARK *sb.*[1] III. 6. *God s. the king!* 5. S., s., oh! s. me from the candid friend! CANNING. 6. Phr *To s. one's pocket*, to avoid spending one's money. *To s. one's face*, to avoid being disgraced or humiliated (orig. in imitation of Chinese idioms). 7. The loan saved my credit, and made my fortune LYTTON. Phr. *To s. the situation*, to avert imminent disaster. 8. If they saue vs aliue, we shall liue 2 *Kings* vii. 4. 12. I have but a moment to s. the post CANNING.

II. To reserve, lay aside. **1.** To keep for a particular purpose or as likely to prove useful; to set apart, lay by, reserve. late ME. **2.** *spec.* To collect and keep (seed) in stock for sowing 1657. **b.** To dry (corn, hay, peat) by exposure to the air; to harvest, stack 1719. **3.** To store up or put by (money, goods, etc.) by dint of economy; also *absol.* and with *up.* late ME. **4.** To avoid spending, giving, or consuming (money, goods, etc.); to keep (a given amount) from being spent, consumed, or lost and so to retain it in one's possession. Also: To enable a person to avoid spending, giving, or losing. late ME. **b.** With immaterial obj., e.g. labour, time, distance to be travelled, etc. 1579. **5.** To use or consume sparingly 1600. **6.** To treat carefully, so as to obviate or reduce fatigue, wear and tear, etc. 1785.

1. I saved the Skins of all the Creatures that I kill'd DE FOE. 3. He was able to s. money for his son's education 1856. I set myself to s. up for my own old age 1884. 4. You have already saved several millions to the publick SWIFT. 5. Phrases. *To s. oneself*, to reduce the amount of one's exertions. *To s. one's breath*, to be silent, refrain from giving advice. *To s. one's pains, trouble*, to refrain from useless exertions.

III. To avoid for one's own part or enable another to avoid (some burden or inconvenience); *occas.* to avoid or obviate the necessity for 1606. †**b.** *To s.* (a woman's) *longing*, to anticipate and so to prevent it –1665. **c.** *Games.* To prevent the opposing side from gaining (a run, goal, etc.). Also *absol.* = to save a goal. 1816.

My letters lie there for me, as it saves their being sent down to Rosebank SCOTT. Hence **Sa·ver.**

Save (sēⁱv), quasi-*prep.* and *conj.* ME. [Developed from SAFE *a.*, after F. *sauf.*] **A.** quasi-*prep.* Except, with the exception of, but. **b.** = but for 1522. **B.** *conj.* **1.** Introducing a sentence which states an exception; now only *s. that* ME. **b.** = 'Were it not' 1600. **c.** = 'Unless', 'if...not'. late ME. **2.** = EXCEPT C. 3. ME. **b.** *S. for*: but for 1594.

A. Al thinges haue an ende at last by deth, saufe onely deathe LD. BERNERS. I do intreat you, not a man depart, Saue I alone SHAKS. But all saue thee I fell with Curses SHAKS. **b.** She seem'd a splendid angel, newly drest, S. wings, for heaven KEATS. **B. 1.** Naked from the waste vpwards, saue that their heads are couered 1634. **b.** From these would I be gone, Saue that to dye, I leaue my loue alone SHAKS. **2.** S. where the beetle wheels his droning flight GRAY. **b.** S. for the slumbering fire, all was dark within the house 1894.

Save-all (sēⁱ·vǭl). 1645. [f. SAVE *v.* + ALL.] **1.** A means for preventing loss or waste 1655. **2.** A contrivance for holding a candle-end in a candlestick while burning so that it may burn to the end 1645. **3.** A stingy miserly person. Now *dial.* 1785. **4.** *Naut.* A sail set under another sail or between two other sails 1794. **5.** A pinafore, overall. *dial.* 1864. **6.** *attrib.* or *adj.* Parsimonious, stingy 1812.

6. Still pursuing his s. theory of a pin a day is a groat a year 1856.

Saveloy (sæ·vėloi). 1837. [Corruption of

F. *cervelas* (sɛrvəla).] A highly seasoned cooked and dried sausage.

Savin, savine (sæ·vin). OE. [a. OF. *savine* :—L. (*herba*) *Sabina*, lit. 'Sabine herb'.] **1.** A small bushy evergreen shrub, *Juniperus sabina*, a native of Europe and Western Asia, with spreading branches covered with short imbricating leaves, and bearing a small, round, bluish-purple berry. Also applied to other trees and shrubs resembling this. **2.** The dried tops of this shrub, used as a drug OE.

Saving (sē̆ⁱ·viŋ), *vbl. sb.* ME. [f. SAVE *v.* + -ING [1].] **1.** The action of SAVE *v.*; an instance of this. **2.** *concr.* A sum of money saved; chiefly *pl.* sums of money saved from time to time and put by 1737. **3.** A reservation, saving clause. Now only in *Law.* 1477.

2. (*War*, 1916), (*national*, 1920) *savings certificate*, a certificate declaring that the holder has invested in a particular form of government funds.

Saving (sē̆ⁱ·viŋ), *ppl. a.* ME. [f. SAVE *v.* + -ING [2].] **1.** That delivers, rescues, or preserves 1535. **2.** *Theol.* That delivers from sin and eternal death by the power of God's grace ME. **3.** *gen.* That delivers from moral or intellectual error; of a quality, 'redeeming' 1599. **4.** Accustomed to save, hoard up, or economize; parsimonious, economical 1581. †**5.** Neither winning nor losing –1832. **6.** Making a reservation; furnishing a proviso 1700.

3. I am not..without a s. sense of humour 1902. 4. To be sauing in Apparell BACON. Mrs. Crawley was a s. woman and knew the price of port wine THACKERAY. Hence **Sa·ving·ly** *adv.*, **-ness** (*rare*).

Saving (sē̆ⁱ·viŋ), *prep.* and *conj.* late ME. [absol. use of the pr. pple. of SAVE *v.* Cf. *excepting*.] **A.** *prep.* **1.** = SAVE *prep.* 1. **2.** Without prejudice or offence to. late ME.

2. Sauing your tale Petruchio, I pray let vs that are poore petitioners speake too? SHAKS. *S.* (one's) *reverence*: see REVERENCE *sb.* 4. *S. correction* [= F. *sauf correction*], subject to correction.

B. *conj.* = EXCEPT, SAVE *conjs.* 1535.

S. in the country I seldom go out until after dark DICKENS. S. for her 'plentiful lack of inborn baby-worship SWINBURNE.

Sa·vings ba·nk. Orig. **saving bank**; also **savings' bank.** 1817. [f. *savings* pl. (see SAVING *vbl. sb.* 2) + BANK *sb.*[3]] An institution for encouraging thrift, by receiving small deposits at interest.

Saviour (sē̆ⁱ·vyəɹ). [ME. *sauveur, sauveour*, a. OF. *sauvëour* (mod.F. *sauveur*) :—late L. *salvatorem*, f. *salvare* to SAVE.] **1.** One who delivers or rescues from peril. **2.** He who saves mankind from sin and its consequences: as a title of God, and esp. of Christ. (Now always with cap. S.) ME.

2. That Season..Wherein our Sauiours Birth is celebrated SHAKS. Hence **Sa·viouress**, a female s.

‖**Savoir faire** (savwar fɛ̄r). 1815. [F.; lit. 'to know how to do'.] Tact, address; instinctive knowledge of the right course of action in any circumstances.

‖**Savoir vivre** (savwar vivr). 1755. [F.; lit. 'to know how to live'.] Ability in the conduct of life, knowledge of the world and of the usages of good society.

The use of red wine with oysters shews great want of sçavoir vivre 1806.

Savorous (sē̆ⁱ·vŏrəs), *a.* late ME. [a. OF. :—late L. *saporosus*, f. *sapor* SAPOR; see -OUS.] Of good savour, pleasant to the taste 1450. †**b.** *fig.* That is relished or enjoyed, delightful –1657. Hence **Sa·vorously** *adv.*

Savory (sē̆ⁱ·vəri), *sb.* late ME. [ult. from L. *satureia*.] Any plant of the labiate genus *Satureia*; esp. the annual herb *Satureia hortensis* (Garden, Summer S.), or the perennial, *S. montana* (Mountain or Winter S.), used as flavouring in cookery.

Savour, savor (sē̆ⁱ·vəɹ), *sb.* ME. [a. OF. *savur, savour* :—L. *saporem*, f. *sapere* to taste. The spelling with *-or* is regular in U.S.] **1.** Quality in relation to the sense of taste; a specific mode of this quality, as sweetness, bitterness; a taste. Now *rare*, exc. as denoting a 'smack'. **b.** Sapidity, tastiness 1440. **2.** A smell, perfume, aroma. *poet.* and *arch.* ME. **b.** *fig.* Repute, estimation. Now *poet.* 1535. **3.** Orig. *fig.* from sense 1: †**a.** Character, style, sort –1639. **b.** Essential virtue or property (with allusion to Matt. v. 13). Also, power to excite relish, interest. 1650. **c.** A 'smack', tinge, or admixture 1795.

1. Meats of noblest sort And s. MILT. **b.** I see auld fruit has little s. SCOTT. **2.** The sweet s. of the roasted meat SHELLEY. **b.** A name of evil s. in the land TENNYSON. **3. a.** This admiration Sir, is much o' th' s. Of other your new prankes SHAKS. **b.** All the s. of life is departed 1885. Hence **Sa·vourless** *a.* destitute of s.; tasteless or odourless.

Savour, savor (sē̆ⁱ·vəɹ), *v.* ME. [a. OF. *savourer*, late L. *saporare*, f. *sapor* SAVOUR *sb.*, q.v.] **I.** To have a savour. †**1.** *intr.* Of food and drink: To taste (well or ill); chiefly, to have an agreeable taste. Often with *dat.*; hence *trans.* to be agreeable to the taste of. –1686. **2.** *intr.* To give forth a (specified) scent or odour; to smell *of* something. *arch.* ME. **3.** *fig.* †**a.** To be agreeable or pleasing. **b.** With qualification: To be *well* or *ill* pleasing. *arch.* ME. **4.** *To s. of*: to show traces of the presence or influence of; to have the appearance of proceeding from. Also *trans.* 1548.

3. What is loathsome to the young Savours well to thee and me TENNYSON. 4. Wilful barrenness, That.. savours onely Rancor and pride MILT. I have written nothing which savours of Immorality DRYDEN.

II. To give a savour to. **1.** To season, flavour; to give tone or character to 1579. **2.** To impart a savour or scent to 1832. **III.** To perceive a savour. **1.** *trans.* To taste, perceive by the sense of taste. In mod. use, to taste with relish, to dwell on the taste of, *fig.*, to give oneself to the enjoyment or appreciation of. late ME. **2.** To be conscious or sensible of (an odour). *Obs.* or *arch.* late ME. **3.** To relish, like, care for. *Obs.* or *arch.* ME. †**4.** To perceive, apprehend; also, to discover traces of, experience 1659.

1. Savoring in advance the long list of dainties for the day 1889. **2.** What vaileth the flower To stand still and wither; If no man it s. It serves only for sight WYATT. **3.** He savoureth only the doctrine of this world BUNYAN. Hence **Sa·vourer. Sa·vouringly** *adv.*

†**Sa·vourly,** *adv.* late ME. [f. SAVOUR *sb.* + -LY [2].] **1.** With enjoyment; with relish; pleasantly; agreeably; keenly –1690. **b.** Of weeping: Passionately, bitterly –1722. **2.** With understanding; wisely; effectively –1664.

Savoury (sē̆ⁱ·vəri), *a.* and *sb.* [Early ME. *savure*, app. a. OF. *savouré* sapid, fragrant, pa. pple. of *savourer* SAVOUR *v.*] **A.** *adj.* **1.** Pleasing to the taste; appetizing; agreeable. late ME. **b.** Fragrant. (Now *rare* exc. in neg. context.) 1560. **2.** *fig.* **a.** Pleasant; acceptable ME. †**b.** In religious use. (*a*) Full of spiritual 'savour'; spiritually delightful. (*b*) Having the savour of holiness; of saintly repute or memory. –1855. **3.** Used, in contradistinction to *sweet*, as the epithet of articles of food having a stimulating taste or flavour 1661.

1. All..with keen gust the sav'ry viands share POPE. **2. a.** The..parable, savouriest of all Scripture to rogues RUSKIN. **b.** Practised by the savouriest of people called Quakers 1720. **3.** Omelette, a S. one 1806.

B. *sb.* A savoury dish; *spec.* one served at the beginning or end of dinner as a stimulant to appetite and digestion 1661. Hence **Sa·vouri·ly** *adv.*, **-ness.**

Savoy (săvoi·). 1578. [a. F. *Savoie*, a region of S.E. France.] **1.** In full, *S. cabbage* (*sprouts*). A rough-leaved hardy variety of the common cabbage, much grown for winter use. **2.** In full, *S. biscuit.* A kind of sponge biscuit, made of finger-shaped pieces of paste covered with sifted sugar which when baked are joined together in pairs; so also *S. drop, ring.* Similarly *S. cake*, a large sponge cake baked in a mould. 1764.

Savoyard (săvoi·aɹd, sæ·voi‚aɹd), *sb.* and *a.* 1687. [In A 1, B, a. F., f. *Savoie*; see prec. and -ARD. In A 2, 3, f. *Savoy* in London names.] **A.** *sb.* **1.** A native or inhabitant of Savoy. **2.** An inhabitant of the precinct of the Savoy Palace in London, which formerly possessed the right of sanctuary 1700. **3.** An actor in Gilbert and Sullivan Opera at the Savoy Theatre, London 1908. **B.** *adj.* Belonging to Savoy 1820.

Savvy, savey (sæ·vi), *sb. slang.* 1785. [f. next.] Practical sense, 'nous', gumption.

Savvy, savey (sæ·vi), *v. slang.* 1785. [orig. Negro-Eng. and Pidgin-Eng., after Sp. *sabe usted* you know.] *trans.* To know.

Saw (sǭ), *sb.*[1] [OE. **sagu* (in oblique cases *sagē*) :—OTeut. **sagā*; f. pre-Teut. root **sok-*: **sek-* to cut: cf. L. *secare* to cut.] **1.** A cutting tool consisting of a plate (or, in some forms, a band or a tube) of metal (usu. steel), one edge of which is formed into a continuous series of teeth. (Some saws for cutting stone are without teeth.) Freq. with defining words, indicating special varieties of form, structure, mode of operation, or purpose, as *circular s.*, *fretsaw*, *hand-s.*, *keyhole s.*, etc. **2.** *Zool.* A part or organ with teeth like those of a saw 1664. **3.** [Prop. a distinct word, f. SAW *v.*] **a.** A sawing movement. **b.** *Whist.* = SEE-SAW 1746.

1. *fig.* Faction, hatred, livor, emulation, which..are, *serræ animæ*, the sawes of the soule BURTON.

attrib. and *Comb.*: **s.-bar,** either of the two bars which hold the s. in a fretwork machine; **-belly** *U.S.*, the glut herring (*Clupea æstivalis*), or the alewife (*C. serrata*); **-bench,** a circular s. with a bench to support the material and advance it to the s.; **-buck** *U.S.* [a. Du. *zaagbok*], see BUCK *sb.*[6]; **-edge,** a serrated edge; **-file,** a file for sharpening the teeth of saws; **-frame,** (*a*) the frame in which a saw-blade is stretched; (*b*) the sash or gate of a mill s.; **-gate** = GATE *sb.*[1] 6 b; **-gin,** a form of cotton-gin in which the fibres are torn from the seed by revolving toothed disks or circular saws; **-grass** *U.S.*, a sedge of the genus *Cladium*; **-horse,** a saw-buck; **plate,** (*a*) the blade of a s.; (*b*) iron in plates of the thickness of the blade of a s.; **s. palmetto,** a palmetto, *Serenoa serratula*, with prickly leaf-stalks; **-set,** an instrument for setting the teeth of a s.; **-sharpener,** (*a*) one who sharpens saws; (*b*) the Great Titmouse, *Parus major*; **-whet** *U.S.*, a little owl, *Nyctala acadica*; **-whetter,** (*a*) = *s.-whet*; (*b*) the marsh titmouse, *Parus palustris*; **-wort,** any of various species of the genera *Serratula* (esp. *S. tinctoria*), *Saussurea*, and *Carduus arvensis.*

Saw (sǭ), *sb.*[2] [OE. *sagu* :—OTeut. **sagā*, **sagōn-*, f. root of **sagǣjan* SAY *v.*[1] Cf. SAGA.] †**1.** A saying; discourse; speech –1621. †**2.** A decree, command –1595. **3.** A sententious saying; a traditional maxim, a proverb ME.

1. His felawe That was so ny to herknen al his sawe CHAUCER. **2.** So love is Lord..And rules the creatures by his powrfull s. SPENSER. **3.** Full of wise sawes, and moderne instances SHAKS.

Saw (sǭ), *v.* Pa. t. **sawed**; pa. pple. **sawed, sawn.** ME. [f. SAW *sb.*[1]] **1.** *trans.* To cut with a saw. **b.** To form by cutting with a saw 1530. **c.** *absol.* To use a saw; to cut with a saw ME. **d.** *intr.* with passive force. To admit of being sawn 1726. **2.** *transf.* With ref. to the to-and-fro movement used in sawing. **a.** *trans. To s. the air*: to gesticulate with the hands as if sawing something 1602. **b.** To work (the bit) from side to side in a horse's mouth 1850.

1. *Heb.* xi. 37. Phr. *To s. wood* (fig.), to work while others deliberate (*U.S. slang*) 1909. **b.** This method of sawing out a pattern 1875. **d.** Beech..will s. into extreme thin Planks 1726. **2. a.** Do not s. the Ayre too much your hand thus, but vse all gently SHAKS.

Sawbill (sǭ·bil). 1843. [f. SAW *sb.*[1] + BILL *sb.*[2]] Any of various birds having serrated bills; *esp.* the merganser (also *s. diver, duck*). So **Saw·-billed** *a.* having a serrated bill.

Sawbones (sǭ·bōunz). *slang.* 1837. [f. SAW *v.* + BONE *sb.*] A surgeon.

Sawder (sǭ·dəɹ), *sb. colloq.* 1836. [A use of *sawder* SOLDER *sb.*] *Soft s.*: flattery, blarney. So **Saw·der** *v. trans.* to flatter, 'butter' 1834.

Sawdust (sǭ·dʊ̆st), *sb.* 1530. [f. SAW *sb.*[1] + DUST *sb.*] **1.** Wood in the state of small particles, produced in the process of sawing. Freq. *transf.* and *fig.* (Sometimes with ref. to the use of s. for stuffing dolls or puppets.). **2.** In wider sense: Dust of any material produced in the process of sawing 1672.

1. *fig.* **b.** I'll knock the saw-dust out of any two men in this hole of a place 1890. Hence **Sawdust** *v. trans.* to cover, sprinkle, or strew with s. **Saw·dusty** *a.* abounding in, savouring of, or resembling s.

Sawer (sǭ·əɹ). late ME. [f. SAW *v.* + -ER [1].] One who saws. Now *rare*; as a designation of employment repl. by SAWYER.

Sawfish (sǭ·fiʃ). 1664. [SAW *sb.*[1]] A fish of the genus *Pristis*, the snout of which ends in a long flat projection with teeth on each edge. Also applied to fishes of certain allied genera.

Saw·-fly. 1773. [SAW *sb.*[1]] An insect of the family *Tenthredinidæ*, distinguished by the saw-like construction of the ovipositor.

Sawmill (sǭ·mil). 1553. [f. SAW *sb.*[1] + MILL *sb.*] A factory in which wood is sawn into planks or boards by machinery (now usu. propelled by steam or electricity).

Sawney (sǭ·ni), *sb. colloq.* 1700. [repr. a Sc. local var. of SANDY, short for Alexander.] **1.** A derisive nickname for a Scotchman 1704. **2.** A simpleton 1700.

Sawney (sǭ·ni), *a.* 1805. [app. f. prec.] Foolish; foolishly sentimental. So **Saw·ney** *v. intr.* to wheedle, cant; to fool.

Saw·-pit. ME. [f. SAW *sb.*¹] A pit, over the mouth of which a framework is erected on which timber is placed to be sawn with a long two-handled saw by two men, the one standing in the pit and the other on a raised platform.

Sa·w tooth. 1601. [SAW *sb.*¹] **a.** A tooth of a saw. **b.** A tooth (of an animal or of a machine) shaped like a saw, or forming one of a serrated series.

Sawyer (sǭ·yəɹ). ME. [Altered f. SAWER.] **1.** A workman whose business it is to saw timber, esp. in a saw-pit. **2. a.** Any wood-boring insect larva, as that of the longicorn beetle of the genus *Monohammus*. **b.** A grasshopper, *Deinacrida megacephala*, native to New Zealand. 1789. **3.** *U.S.* A tree which has fallen into a stream and lies with its branches projecting above and swaying with the motion of the water 1797.

Sax (sæks). [OE. *seax* :—OTeut. *sahsom, f. root *sah-, sag- to cut; see SAW *sb.*¹] †**1.** A knife; a short sword or dagger -late ME. **2.** A chopping-tool used for trimming slates 1669.

Saxatile (sæ·ksătəil, -til), *a.* 1661. [a. F., or ad. L. *saxatilis*, f. *saxum* rock, stone.] *Zool.* and *Bot.* Living or growing among rocks.

Saxaul (sæ·ksǭl). 1874. A shrub, *Anabasis* (*Holoxylon*) *Ammodendron*, growing on the steppes of Asia.

Sa·xboard. 1857. *Boat-building.* [Cf. ON. *sax* prow.] The uppermost strake of a boat.

Saxe (sæks). 1864. [a. F. *Saxe* Saxony (G. *Sachsen*).] Used *attrib.* to designate articles which come from Saxony, as *S. china*; **S. blue** (also ellipt. **Saxe**) = SAXONY *blue*.

Sax-horn, saxhorn (sæ·kshǭɹn). 1845. [f. the name *Sax*.] One of a group of brass musical instruments of the trumpet kind, invented by a Belgian, Charles Joseph Sax (1791–1865), and improved by his son Antoine Joseph, known as Adolphe. Called also **sax-cornet.** So **Sax-tuba**, a brass instrument of this class.

‖**Saxicava** (sæksi·kăvă). *Pl.* **-æ.** 1826. [mod.L., fem. of *saxicavus*; see next.] A genus of boring bivalve molluscs; a member of this genus.

Saxicavous (sæksi·kăvəs), *a.* 1850. [f. mod.L. *saxicavus* (f. *saxum* rock + *cavare* to hollow) + -OUS.] *Zool.* Hollowing out rock or stone: epithet of certain molluscs.

Saxicoline (sæksi·kǒləin), *a.* 1899. [f. mod.L. *saxicolus* (f. *saxum* rock) + -INE.] *Zool.* and *Bot.* **a.** Living or growing among rocks. **b.** *spec.* Pertaining to the sub-family *Saxicolinæ* of passerine birds (the stone-chats).

Saxicolous (sæksi·kǒləs), *a.* 1856. [f. as prec. + -OUS.] *Bot.* Growing on rocks.

Saxifragaceous (sæksifrăgēi·ʃəs), *a.* 1845. [-ACEOUS.] *Bot.* Belonging to the family *Saxifragaceæ*.

Saxifrage (sæ·ksifrėdʒ). ME. [a. OF., ad. L. *saxifraga* (sc. *herba*), f. *saxum* + *frag-*, *frangere* to break.] Any plant of the genus *Saxifraga*, esp. *S. granulata* (White Meadow S.). The species are mostly dwarf herbs with tufted foliage and panicles of white, yellow, or red flowers; many root in the clefts of rocks. Also applied to related plants, as the genus *Chrysosplenium* (Golden S.), *Pimpinella Saxifraga* (Burnet or Rough S.), *Silaus pratensis* (Meadow or Pepper S.), the genus *Seseli* (Meadow S.). **b.** (with *pl.*) Any member of the genus *Saxifraga* or of the family *Saxifragaceæ* 1578.

Saxigenous (sæksi·dʒĭnəs), *a.* 1842. [f. late L. *saxigenus*, f. *saxum* rock + *-genus* begotten (erron. taken to mean 'producing') + -OUS.] That produces (coral) rocks or reefs.

Saxon (sæ·ksən), *sb.* and *a.* ME. [a. F., ad. L. *Saxonem*, a. WGer. *Saxon- (OE. *Seaxan*, *Seaxe* pl.).] **A.** *sb.* **1.** One of a Germanic people which dwelt in a region near the mouth of the Elbe, and of which one portion, dist. as *Anglo-Saxons*, conquered and occupied certain parts of South Britain in the 5th and 6th centuries, while the other, the *Old Saxons*, remained in Germany. **b.** In mod. use *spec.* An Englishman as dist. from a Welshman or Irishman, a Lowland Scot as dist. from a Highlander 1642. **2.** A native or inhabitant of Saxony in its modern German sense 1737. **B.** *adj.* **1.** Of or belonging to the Saxons (see A. 1). Formerly used (like *Anglo-Saxon*) as the distinctive epithet of the Old English language, and of the period of English history preceding the Norman Conquest. 1568. **b.** Applied to the element in the English tongue which is derived from Anglo-Saxon 1589. **c.** Used (primarily by Celtic speakers) for 'English' in contradistinction to Welsh, Irish, or Gaelic. Also, like *Anglo-Saxon*, applied to people of the English-speaking communities, chiefly in contradistinction to 'Latin'. 1787. **d.** *Arch.* Designating the variety of Romanesque architecture which preceded the Norman in England 1770. **2.** *absol.* (quasi-*sb.*) The language of the Saxons: **a.** = ANGLO-SAXON. Often used for Modern English speech of Saxon or Anglo-Saxon origin. late ME. **b.** *Old Saxon*: the language of the Old Saxons (see A. 1) 1841. **3.** Of or belonging to Saxony in its modern German sense 1634.

1. *Old S.*, pertaining to the Old Saxons or their language. **3.** *S. blue* = SAXONY *blue*. *S. green*, cobalt green. Hence **Sa·xondom** = ANGLO-SAXONDOM. **Sa·xonist**, a S. scholar; one learned in Anglo-Saxon. **Sa·xonize** *v. trans.* to make S. or Anglo-Saxon.

Saxonic (sæksǫ·nik), *a.* 1550. [ad. med.L. *Saxonicus*, f. L. *Saxon-* SAXON.] **1.** Of or belonging to Saxony 1645. **2.** Belonging to the Anglo-Saxons or their language 1550.

Saxonism (sæ·ksəniz'm). 1676. [f. SAXON + -ISM 3.] **1.** An Anglo-Saxon idiom or expression; Anglo-Saxon characteristics in speech. **2.** The characteristics of the Anglo-Saxon race; attachment to what is Anglo-Saxon 1884.

Saxony (sæ·ksəni). 1843. [ad. late L. *Saxonia*, the country of the Saxons, f. *Saxon-* SAXON.] The name of a kingdom in Germany (G. *Sachsen*, F. *Saxe*), used *attrib.* to designate products of the country: *esp.* **1.** A fine kind of wool, and cloth made from it. Also *absol.* = *S. cloth*. 1844. **2.** *S. blue*: a solution of indigo in concentrated sulphuric acid, much used as a dye. Also called *Saxe, Saxon, blue*. 1843.

Saxophone (sæ·ksǒfōun). 1851. [f. the name *Sax* (see SAXHORN) + Gr. -φωνος voiced.] A brass wind-instrument with a clarinet mouth-piece, invented by Adolphe Sax.

Say (sēⁱ), *sb.*¹ ME. [a. F. *saie* :—L. *saga*, pl. of *sagum* military cloak.] A cloth of fine texture resembling serge; formerly partly of silk, subseq. entirely of wool.

†**Say**, *sb.*² ME. Aphet. f. ASSAY *sb.* -1817.

Say (sēⁱ), *sb.*³ 1571. [f. SAY *v.*¹] **1.** What a person says; words as compared with action; also, a saying, dictum. Now *poet.* †**2.** A proverb, saw -1650. **3.** What one has planned to say; chiefly in phr. *to say* (*out*) *one's s.* 1692. **4.** A talk *to* or *with* a person. Now *dial.* 1786.

1. You hearken to the lover's s., And happy is the lover A. E. HOUSMAN. Phr. *To have a s.*, to have a 'voice' in a matter; to have the right to be consulted. *To have the s.* (U.S.), to be in command. **3.** *To have one's s.*, to avail oneself of an opportunity of expressing one's views.

Say (sēⁱ), *v.*¹ 3rd pers. sing. pres. indic. **says** (sez), (*arch.*) **saith** (seþ). Pr. pple. **saying** (sēⁱ·iŋ). Pa. t. and pple. **said** (sed). [OE. *sęcgan*, *sægde* :—OTeut. *sagjan, *sagǣjan :—pre-Teut. *sokēi-. The root is perh. WIndo-Eur. *soqᵘ-, found in Gr. ἔννεπε imper., ἐνισπεῖν aorist inf., to tell, say, L. *inquam* I say.] **1.** *trans.* To utter or pronounce (a specified word or words, or an articulate sound). Also used of an author or book, with quoted words as obj. **2.** To declare or state in words (a specified fact, thought, opinion, or intention) OE. †**b.** [After L. *dicere*, F. *dire*.] With compl.: To speak of, call (by a specified name or designation); chiefly *pass.* Also *pass.* with adj. or descriptive sb., = 'to be said to be', 'to be called'. -1690. **3.** Absol. uses of 1 and 2. OE. **b.** Used in parenthetic clause indicating the author of a quoted saying. Also in parenthetic expressions like 'shall I say?', 'let us say'. ME. ¶ In this use, the 3rd sing. pres. is often substituted colloq. for the pa. t. *said*. Hence, in vulgar speech, *says I*, *says you* = 'said I', 'said you'. 1682. **4.** †**a.** Of words: To mean, signify -1604. **b.** *That is to say* (orig. gerundial inf.): used to introduce a more explicit or intelligible re-statement of what immediately precedes, or a limiting clause necessary to make the statement correct ME. **5.** To declare or make known (*who, what, how, whether*, etc.) OE. **b.** To judge, decide; freq. in expressions like 'it is hard to say', 'I cannot say' 1709. **c.** *absol.* In the imperative, introducing a direct question. Now *poet.* ME. †**6.** To deliver (a speech, discourse); to relate (a story); to express, give (thanks); to tell, speak (truth, lies); to express (one's opinion) -1657. **7.** To recite or repeat (something that has a prescribed form); occas. to recite from memory, in contradistinction to reading ME. **8.** The imperative **say** is idiomatically used: **a.** to introduce a clause, with the sense 'supposing', 'on the assumption *that*'; **b.** parenthetically, to indicate that a preceding sentence expresses a supposition or a selected instance; **c.** prefixed to a designation of number, quantity, date, etc. to mark it as approximate or hypothetical. 1596.

1. Then said they vnto him, S. now, Shibboleth: and he said, Sibboleth *Judg.* xii. 6. **2.** What I have said I have said WYCHERLEY. What s. you to that? SWIFT. *It is* (*has been, will be*) *said* (with clause, expressed or understood, as real subject): in pres. tense now chiefly = 'it is commonly said', 'people say'. Phrases. *To have something* (*nothing*) *to s. to* (or *with*), *fig.* to have (no) dealings with; of things, to have (no) connexion with or bearing upon. *To have* (*something, nothing*, etc.) *to s. for oneself*, to be able to adduce (something, nothing) in defence or extenuation of one's conduct. Also (colloq.), *To have nothing to say for oneself*, to be habitually silent. **3.** Be persuaded by me, and do as I s. 1875. *You don't s. so!* colloq. expression of astonishment at some statement. **b.** Amen, to that faire prayer, say I SHAKS. Says Cary, says he,..I never heard of such a thing SWIFT. **4. b.** Three hours after, that's to s., about eleven a Clock 1687. **5.** How ferful trowly there is no tong can saye 1485. **c.** Say? How is that? SHAKS. **7.** *To s. grace, a lesson,* (*a*) *mass, a prayer,* (*one's prayers*). **8. c.** Early in the week, or s. Wednesday DICKENS. The wages of my people..average 11*s.* per week...Harvesting, s. £5 more. KINGSLEY.

Phrases, etc. **Not to s...**: used (*a*) to imply that the speaker is content with a more moderate statement than that which he might have made; (*b*) *colloq.* = 'not what one may call..', 'not.., properly speaking'. **I say**: **a.** introducing a word, phrase, or statement repeated from the preceding sentence (now somewhat *rare*); **b.** *colloq.* quasi-*int.* (In U.S. *say*.) used to call attention to what is about to be said; also as a mere exclam. *When all is said and done*, after all. **S. on.** In the imper. = 'say what you wish to say'. Now only *intr.* **S. out.** *trans.* (*a*) To say openly. †(*b*) To say to the end. **S. over.** *trans.* To repeat from memory. Hence **Say·able** *a.* capable of being said. **Say·er**¹, one who says.

†**Say**, *v.*² late ME. = ASSAY *v.* -1813. So †**Say·er**² -1835.

Saying (sēⁱ·iŋ), *vbl. sb.* ME. [f. SAY *v.*¹ + -ING¹.] **1.** The action of SAY *v.*¹; utterance, enunciation; recitation. **2.** Something that is said; a dictum; a proverb; *occas.* †a current form of speech ME.

1. Saying and doyng, are twoo thinges, we say HEYWOOD. **2.** I can see into a mill-stone as far as another (as the S. is) STEELE.

Say-so (sēⁱ·sōu), *sb.* Now *dial.* and *U.S.* 1637. [f. SAY *v.*¹ + So *adv.*] (A person's) mere word or dictum; an ipse dixit. Phr. *To have the s.*, to be the authority.

‖**Sayyid** (sēⁱ·yid). Also **seyd, syed.** 1615. [Arab.; lit. 'lord', 'prince'. Cf. SIDI.] In Mohammedan countries, a descendant of the Prophet, through his elder grandson Husain.

‖**Sbirro** (sbi·rro). *Pl.* **sbirri** (sbi·rri). 1668. [It.] An Italian police officer.

'Sblood (zblɒd). *Obs.* exc. *arch.* 1598. Euphemistic shortening of *God's blood*, used as an oath or asseveration.

'Sbo·dikins. *Obs.* exc. *arch.* 1676. Euphemistic shortening of *God's bodikins* (BODIKIN 2).

Sc., abbrev. of SCILICET.

Scab (skæb), *sb.* ME. [a. ON. *skabb-r, corresp. to OE. *sceabb*.] †**1.** Disease of the skin in which pustules or scales are formed; a general term for skin diseases, but sometimes *spec.* = itch or scabies, ringworm or tinea, syphilis; *wet s.*, eczema -1791. **2.** A cutaneous disease in animals, esp. sheep, resembling the itch and the mange. late ME. **b.** A disease of cultivated plants, causing a scab-like roughness 1750. **3.** The crust which forms over a wound or sore during cicatrization. late ME. **b.** *Iron-founding.* A blister on the surface of a casting 1881. **4.** *slang.* **a.** A mean, low, 'scurvy' fellow; a scoundrel 1590. **b.** (orig. *U.S.*) A workman who refuses to join an organized movement on behalf of his trade 1811.

Scab (skæb), *v.* 1683. [f. prec.] **I.** *intr.* and *pass.* To become encrusted with a scab or scabs. Also with *over.* **b.** *Iron-founding.* To form 'scabs' 1881. **3.** *slang.* To behave as a 'scab' or 'blackleg' 1905.

Scabbard (skæ·bǎɹd), *sb.*[1] ME. [a. AF. *escauberc, escauberge, app. a. some Teut. compound.] **1.** The case or sheath which protects the blade of a sword, dagger, or bayonet when not in use. †**2.** *transf.* Applied to various kinds of sheath or integument; a cocoon, etc. -1753.

1. Whiles the sworde of iustice, slept in his scaberd NASHE. *To throw away the s.* (fig.), to abandon all thought of making peace.

Comb.: **s.-fish,** *Lepidopus caudatus*, a fish of long, compressed s.-like form and silvery-white colour; **s. razor-shell,** a razor-shell, *Solen vagina.*

Scabbard (skæ·bǎɹd), *sb.*[2] 1635. [app. ad. MLG. *schalbort* thin board sawn off a length of timber in squaring it, f. *schale* shell, rind + *bort* BOARD.] Thin board used in making splints, scabbards of swords, veneer, etc., and by printers in making register (now called *scale-board*). **b. s.-plane** = SCALEBOARD-*plane* 1846.

Sca·bbard, *v.* 1579. [f. SCABBARD *sb.*[1]] *trans.* To furnish with a scabbard; to sheathe.

Scabbed (skæbd, skæ·bèd), *a.* Now *rare.* ME. [f. SCAB *sb.* + -ED [2].] **1.** Having the scab or a similar skin-disease; covered with scab or scabs. †**2.** 'Scurvy', mean, contemptible -1786. Hence †**Sca·bbed-ly** *adv.*, **-ness.**

Scabble (skæ·b'l), *v.* 1620. [Later var. of SCAPPLE.] **1.** *trans.* To rough-dress (stone). **2.** *Iron-manuf.* = CABBLE *v.* 1849.

Scabby (skæ·bi), *a.* 1526. [f. SCAB *sb.* + -Y [1].] **1.** = SCABBED *a.* 1. **2.** *fig.* Contemptible, mean, vile; stingy, shabby. Now *vulgar.* Hence **Sca·bbiness,** the condition or quality of being s.

‖**Scabies** (skēⁱ·bi,īz). late ME. [L., f. *scabere* to scratch, scrape.] *Path.* †**1.** A general term for skin-diseases characterized by scabby or scaly eruption -1742. **2.** A contagious skin-disease, due to a parasite, *Sarcoptes scabiei*; the itch 1814.

Scabious (skēⁱ·biəs), *sb.* late ME. [ad. med.L. *scabiosa* (sc. *herba*), fem. sing. of *scabiosus*; see next.] Any of the herbaceous plants of the dipsacaceous genus *Scabiosa*, formerly believed to be efficacious for the cure of certain skin-diseases. **b.** *U.S.* Applied to some species of *Erigeron* 1830.

Blue S., *S. succisa.* **Purple** or **Sweet S.,** *S. atropurpurea.* **Devil's bit S.:** see DEVIL'S BIT.

Scabious (skēⁱ·biəs), *a.* Now *rare.* 1603. [ad. F. *scabieux* or L. *scabiosus*, f. *scabies* SCABIES.] Of the nature of or pertaining to scabies or itch; in early use = SCABBED *a.* 1.

Scabrid (skēⁱ·brid), *a.* 1866. [ad. late L. *scabridus.*] *Bot.* Somewhat scabrous.

Scabrous (skēⁱ·brəs), *a.* 1549. [f. L. *scabr-*, *scaber* (related to *scabere* to scrape, scratch) + -OUS.] **1.** Rough with minute points or knobs, as dist. from unevenness of surface; esp. *Nat. Hist.* and *Phys.* **2.** Of an author, his style, etc.: Harsh, unmusical, unpolished 1585. **3.** Full of obstacles, difficult, 'thorny' 1646. **4.** Risky, bordering upon the indelicate 1881.

2. His verse is s., and hobbling DRYDEN. Hence **Sca·brous-ly** *adv.*, **-ness.**

Scad (skæd). Also **skad.** 1602. [Origin un'kn.; app. first used in Cornwall.] The fish *Caranx trachurus* (*Trachurus saurus*), found abundantly on the British coasts, and characterized by having its lateral line armed with bony plates; also applied to other fishes of the genus *Caranx* and related genera; the horse-mackerel.

Scaffold (skæ·fǒld), *sb.* ME. [a. NF. forms corresp. to Central OF. *shaffaut, eschafaut* formed w. prefix *es-* (:—L. *ex-* out) on the Com. Rom. word represented by OF. *chafau(l)t* :—pop. L. *catafalcum CATAFALQUE.] **1.** A temporary platform, usu. supported on poles, designed to hold the workmen and materials employed in the erection, repairing, or decoration of a building. Also *pl.*, but now usu. *sing.* = SCAFFOLDING. †**2.** A raised platform, seat, or stand, used for exhibiting persons or actions to the public view, making proclamations, or the like -1687. **3.** *spec.* A (temporary) platform or stage on which theatrical performance or exhibition takes place. Now *Hist.* late ME. †**4.** A raised platform or stand for holding the spectators of a tournament, play, etc. Also, a gallery in a theatre or church. -1770. **5.** An elevated platform on which a criminal is executed; *the s.*, execution, capital punishment 1557. **6.** A raised framework of wood used for other purposes; among the N. Amer. Indians, for the disposal of the dead 1534. **7.** *Iron-founding.* An obstruction in a blast furnace caused by an accumulation of unreduced materials adhering to the lining 1861.

1. The building 's set up, let the scaffolds be pulld down 1646. Every bricklayer who falls from a s. MACAULAY. **2.** An heraud on a s. made an ho CHAUCER. **4.** The other side was op'n, where the throng On banks and scaffolds under Skie might stand MILT. **5.** Phr. *To go to the s.*, to be executed. *To bring or send to the s.*, etc.; Paths which naturally conduct a minister to the s. *Junius Lett.*

Scaffold (skæ·fǒld), *v.* 1548. [f. prec. Cf. OF. *eschafauder.*] †**1.** *trans.* To furnish with a platform, stand, or gallery -1704. **2.** To put scaffolding up to (a building) 1662. **3.** To place (food) on a raised framework of wood, for the purpose of drying it or protecting it from animals; among N. Amer. Indians, to expose corpses on a scaffold 1775. **4.** *Iron-founding. intr.* To form a 'scaffold' 1880. Hence **Sca·ffoldage** (*rare*) = next 1.

Scaffolding (skæ·fǒldiŋ), *vbl. sb.* ME. [f. SCAFFOLD *sb.* + -ING [1].] **1.** The temporary framework of platforms and poles constructed to accommodate workmen and their materials during the erection, repairing, etc. of a building. **2.** The action of SCAFFOLD *v.* 1862.

1. *fig.* Sickness, contributing..to the shaking down this S. of the Body POPE.

‖**Scaglia** (skā·lyă). 1774. [It. = scale, chip of marble; see SCALE *sb.*[2]] *Geol.* A local name in the Italian Alps for limestone of various colours.

Scagliola (skælyōᵘ·lă). 1582. [a. It. *scagliuola*, dim. of *scaglia* (see prec.).] †**1.** = prec. -1774. **2.** Plaster-work of Italian origin, designed to imitate kinds of stone 1747.

Scalable (skēⁱ·lăb'l), *a.* 1579. [f. SCALE *v.*[3] + -ABLE.] Capable of being scaled or climbed.

Scalade (skălā·d). Now *rare* or *Obs.* 1591. [ad. It. *scalada*, f. *scalare* to scale, f. *scala* ladder.] **1.** = ESCALADE *sb.* **2.** A scaling ladder 1632. So †**Scala·do** -1847.

Scalar (skēⁱ·lăɹ), *a.* and *sb.* 1656. [ad. L. *scalaris*, f. *scala* ladder.] **A.** *adj.* **1.** Resembling a ladder; *Bot.* = SCALARIFORM. **2.** *Math.* Of the nature of a scalar 1853. **B.** *sb.* *Math.* In quaternions, a real number 1853.

Scalarian (skălēᵊ·riăn), *a.* and *sb.* 1841. [f. mod. L. *Scalaria*, f. *scala* ladder.] (A gasteropod) belonging to the genus *Scalaria.*

Scalariform (skălæ·rifǭɹm), *a.* 1836. [ad. mod. L. *scalariformis*, f. L. *scalaris* SCALAR; see -FORM.] *Bot.*, etc. Of the form of, resembling, a ladder; characterized by ladder-like formation, as cells or vessels of plants having the walls thickened so that they form transverse ridges.

Scalawag, variant of SCALLYWAG.

†**Scald,** *sb.*[1] 1561. [Altered f. SCALL *sb.*, after SCALD *a.*] = SCALL *sb.* -1693.

Scald (skǭld), *sb.*[2] 1601. [f. SCALD *v.*] **1.** An injury to the skin and flesh caused by hot fluid or steam. **b.** *transf.* Inflammation caused by heat; an inflamed part. Also, applied to diseases which produce a similar effect. 1882. **2.** The action or an act of scalding food, utensils, etc. 1661. **3.** A hot liquor or solution used for scalding 1684.

Scald, *sb.*[3]: see SKALD.

Scald (skǭld), *a.*[1] Now *arch.* and *dial.* 1500. [Later spelling of SCALLED.] **1.** Affected with the 'scall'; scabby 1529. **2.** *fig.* 'Scurvy', mean, paltry, contemptible 1500.

2. S. Rimers SHAKS. *Comb.* **s.-pate** = SCALD-HEAD.

Scald (skǭld), *a.*[2] 1791. [pa. pple. of SCALD *v.*] Scalded.

S. cream, clotted or clouted cream.

Scald (skǭld), *v.* ME. [a. ONF. *escalder*, *escauder* :—late L. *excaldare* to wash in hot water, f. *ex-* + *cal(i)dus* hot, warm.] **I.** 'To burn with hot liquor' (J.). **1.** *trans.* To affect painfully and injure with very hot liquid or steam. **b.** *absol.* or *intr.* To be scalding hot ME. **c.** *intr.* for *pass.* To become injured by hot liquid or steam 1590. **2.** *trans.* To produce an injurious effect upon (something) similar to that produced by boiling water ME. **3.** To wash and cleanse with boiling water ME. **4.** *Cookery.* **a.** To heat liquid to a point just short of boiling point. Also *intr.* for *pass.* 1483. **b.** To subject to the action of hot water; to pour hot liquid over. late ME.

1. They all drink it sipping, for fear of scalding themselves 1687. **c.** Now scalds his soul in the Tartarian streams MARLOWE. **2.** I am bound Vpon a wheele of fire, that mine owne teares Do scal'd, like molten Lead SHAKS. **3.** Gut and s. your Pig MRS. GLASSE. Preparing to s. out the frying-pan 1869.

II. To burn. **1.** *trans.* Of the sun, fire, etc.: To scorch, burn. Also said of certain soils. Now *dial.* ME. **b.** *intr.* for *pass.* 1513. †**2.** *trans.* Of desire, thoughts, etc.: To 'burn', inflame, irritate -1667.

2. I am scalded with my violent motion..to see your Maiesty SHAKS. Would not a secret..S. you to keep it? MASSINGER.

Sca·ld-fish. 1812. [app. f. SCALD *a.*[1]] The smooth sole, *Pleuronectes arnoglossus.*

Scald head, sca·ld-head. 1546. [SCALD *a.*[1]] **1.** A person's head diseased with ringworm, etc. **2.** A popular term for tinea or similar scalp affections 1675. So **Scald-headed** *a.*

Scalding hot, *a.* late ME. [f. *scalding*, vbl. sb. f. SCALD *v.* + HOT *a.*] Hot enough to scald.

Scale (skēⁱl), *sb.*[1] ME. [a. ON. *skál* bowl, *pl.* (weighing) scales :—OTeut. *skǣlā, ablaut-var. of *skalā, whence OE. *scealu* shell, husk.] †**I.** A drinking-bowl or cup -1800. **II.** Apparatus for weighing. **1.** The pan, or each of the pans, of a balance. late ME. **2.** *pl.* A weighing instrument; *esp.* one (often called *a pair of scales*) consisting of a beam which is pivoted at its middle and at either end of which a dish, pan, board, or slab is suspended 1480. **3.** *sing.* = sense 2. Often *fig.*, esp. in *to turn the s.*: said of an excess of weight on one side or the other. 1440. **4.** *Astr.* (*pl.* and †*sing.*) The sign of Libra. Chiefly *poet.* 1631.

1. Your vowes to her, and me, (put in two scales) Will euen weigh, and both as light as tales SHAKS. **2.** Their Scales were false, their Weights were light 1719. Phr. *To hold the scales even* or *equally*, to judge impartially. **3.** When the s. was trembling between life and death 1861. Phr. *Equal, even s.* (poet.), a just balance; a condition of equilibrium or indecision; Long time in eeven s. The Battel hung MILT. *Clerk of the Scales* (Racing), the official who weighs the jockeys. *To ride, go to s.*, (of a jockey) to go to the weighing-room before or after the race.

Scale (skēⁱl), *sb.*[2] ME. [Aphetic a. OF. *escale*, mod.F. *écale* husk, pod, chip of stone :—OTeut. *skalā (see prec.).] **1.** One of the small thin membranous or horny modifications of the skin in many fishes and reptiles, and some mammals, usu. overlapping, and forming a complete covering for the body; also *collect. sing.* **2.** One of the small laminæ of epidermis which become detached from the tissue beneath in certain diseases of the skin. late ME. **3.** A part (e.g. a husk) that may be peeled off or detached in flakes; a thin plate, lamina, or flake of any kind 1450. **b.** The tartar that collects on the teeth 1594. **c.** *Bot.* A flattened, membranous, more or less circular plate of cellular tissue, usu. a rudimentary or degenerate leaf, as the covering of leaf-buds of deciduous trees, the bracts of catkins, etc. 1578. **d.** The protective covering of insects of the family *Coccidæ*, which remains when they die and protects the eggs and afterwards the young beneath it; hence, = *scale-insect*; also, the diseased condition of plants caused thereby 1822. **4.** Taken (after *Acts* ix. 18) as a type of that which causes blindness (physical or moral) ME. **5.** Now usu. *collect. sing.* The film of oxide which forms on iron or other metal when heated and hammered or rolled 1526. **b.** *Salt-making.* An incrustation of dirt or lime on the pan bottoms. **c.** The hard deposit or 'fur' which gathers in boilers, etc. in which water is habitually heated (rarely *pl.*). 1848. **6.** Any of the thin pieces of metal composing scale-armour. Also *collect. sing.* 1809. **7.** *Cutlery.* **a.** Each of the two plates of bone, horn, ivory, or wood which form the outside of the handle of a knife or razor 1834. **b.** Each of the metal sides of the handle of a pocket-knife on which such plates are riveted 1834. **8.** [F. *écaille.*] A plate of metal worn instead of an epaulette by soldiers, sailors, and firemen 1846.

1. Leviathan..Turns to the stroke his adamantine scales COWPER. Fishes which were isles of living s. SHELLEY. **3. c.** The glandular scales of the Hop 1884. **4.** The skailes of darknesse which our eyes benight 1629. **6.** Armour of impenetrable s. SHELLEY.

attrib. and *Comb.*: **s.-armour,** armour consisting of small overlapping plates of metal, leather, or horn; **-beetle,** a tiger-beetle (family *Cicindelidæ*); **-blue,** the groundwork of royal blue with a s.-pattern characteristic of some Worcester china; **s. carp,** the common carp, *Cyprinus carpio*; **-fern** = CETERACH; **-insect,** any of the insects of the genus *Coccus* or family *Coccidæ*, having the appearance of scales, which infest and injure certain plants; **-pattern,** an imbricated pattern; **-wing,** a lepidopter; **-winged** *a.* lepidopterous **-work,** work of an imbricated pattern.

Scale (skēˈl), *sb.*³ late ME. [ad. It. *scala* or L. *scala* :—prehist. **scanslā* (*scand-* + *-tlā*), f. *scandere* to climb.] †**I. 1.** A ladder; in early use, a scaling-ladder –1682. **b.** *fig.* and *allus.*, freq. with ref. to Jacob's ladder (*Gen.* xxviii. 12) –1820. **2.** A rung or step of a ladder –1682. **3.** A flight (of stairs); a staircase –1705.

1. b. In th' ascending S. Of Heav'n the Starrs that usher Evening rose MILT.

II. 1. *Mus.* **a.** A definite series of sounds ascending or descending by fixed intervals, *esp.* such a series beginning on a certain note selected for the purposes of musical composition. **b.** Any of the graduated series of sounds into which the octave is divided, the sounds varying according to the system of graduation adopted. 1597. **c.** (chiefly *pl.*) Any scale taken as a subject of instruction or practice 1865. **2.** A succession or series of steps or degrees; a graduated series, succession, or progression 1605. **b.** A regular series of tones or shades of colour produced by mixing with different proportions of white or black 1854. **3.** *Math.* **a.** A number of terms included between two points in a progression or series 1695. **b.** *Arith.* Any system of notation based on a number chosen as 'radix' or constant multiplier 1797. **4.** A graduated table (of prices, charges, etc.) 1788.

1. CHROMATIC, DIATONIC, HARMONIC, MAJOR, MINOR, etc. *s.*: see those words. **c.** I do wish she would forget to play her scales some morning 1888. **2.** Plants low in the s. of organisation DARWIN. **3. b.** When the radix is 2, the s. is called Binary; when 3, Ternary; when 10, Denary or Decimal 1861. **4.** Reduction in S. of Charges for Advertisements 1865.

III. 1. A set or series of graduations (marked along a straight line or a curve) used for measuring distances, etc.; a graduated line, arc, etc.; *spec.* the equally divided line on a map, chart, or plan which indicates its scale, and is used for finding the distance between two points. late ME. **2.** A strip or blade of wood, ivory, metal, or cardboard having graduated and numbered spaces upon it, used for measuring or laying down distances 1607. **3.** The proportion which the representation of an object bears to the object itself; a system of representing or reproducing objects in a smaller or larger size proportionately in every part 1662. **4.** Relative or proportionate size or extent; degree, proportion 1607. **5.** *fig.* A standard of measurement, calculation, or estimation 1626.

2. *Diagonal, Gunter's, Marquois scales*: see the qualifying words. **3.** Phr. *To s.*, with exactly proportional representation of each part of the model. **5.** The Degrees of Crime are taken on divers Scales HOBBES. Phr. *On* or *upon a* (*large, small, liberal,* etc.) *s.*; Were education..Conducted on a manageable s. COWPER.

attrib. and *Comb.*, as *s. drawing, plan*; **s.-micrometer,** a graduated scale in the field of a telescope for measuring the distance between objects; **-paper,** paper having printed upon it divisions in eighths, tenths, etc. of an inch for drawing in proportion.

†**Scale** (skēˈl), *sb.*⁴ 1577. [f. SCALE *v.*³] = ESCALADE –1667.

Scale (skēˈl), *v.*¹ 1603. [f. SCALE *sb.*¹] **1.** *trans.* To weigh in scales, find the weight of 1691. †**2.** *fig.* To weigh as in scales; hence, to compare, estimate. SHAKS. **3.** To weigh (so much) 1862. **b.** *Racing.* intr. To be weighed 1859.

2. Skaling his present bearing with his past SHAKS. **3. b.** Phr. *To s. in,* to be weighed after the race.

Scale (skēˈl), *v.*² 1440. [f. SCALE *sb.*²] **1.** *trans.* To remove the scales from (fish). **b.** *techn.*, esp. (*a*) To clean the bore of (a gun or cannon) by firing off a charge of powder; (*b*) To remove tartar from (the teeth) 1784. **2.** To remove as scale; to take *off* or *away* in scales; to separate *into* layers 1552. **3.** *intr.* To come *off* (or *away*) in scales, flakes, or thin pieces; to flake or peel *off.* Of skin eruptions: To shed scales. 1529.

2. Phr. *To be scaled,* to have the surface removed in scales; The stones being..scaled by frost 1843.

Scale (skēˈl), *v.*³ late ME. [f. SCALE *sb.*³] **I. 1. a.** *trans.* To attack with scaling ladders; to take by escalade. **b.** To climb, get to or reach the top of (a wall, mountain, etc.) 1579. **2.** To 'mount' (the skies); to ascend or climb up into (heaven). late ME. **3.** *intr.* To climb (*over*), ascend, mount 1547. **b.** Of steps, etc.: To ascend, mount 1667.

1. b. How often have I scaled the craggie Oke, All to dislodge the Raven of her nest? SPENSER. **3. b.** The lower stair That scal'd by steps of Gold to Heav'n Gate MILT.

II. To measure or regulate by a scale. **1.** *trans.* To fix the exact amount of. *U. S.* 1798. **b.** With *down*: To reduce in amount according to a fixed scale or standard 1887. **2.** *Lumber-trade.* **a.** To measure (logs), or estimate the amount of (standing timber) 1867. **b.** Of timber: To produce or furnish (so much) 1853. **3.** To estimate the proportions of 1877.

Sca·le-board. 1771. [f. SCALE *sb.*² + BOARD *sb.*²] Thin board used for hat-boxes, silk hats, etc., and by printers for justifying.

S.-plane, a plane for cutting from a board thin pieces for use as s.

Scaled (skēˈld), *ppl. a.* late ME. [f. SCALE *sb.*² + -ED ².] **1.** Having, or furnished with scales, as a fish or a serpent; scaly. Now *rare* exc. in comb. and *Her.* **2. a.** Of armour 1555. **b.** = IMBRICATED 2, 3. 1776. **c.** Covered with tiles in imitation of scales 1862.

2. c. The earlier house and its little gables and grey s. roofs W. MORRIS.

Scaleless (skēˈ·l,lės), *a.* 1611. [f. SCALE *sb.*² + -LESS.] Having no scales.

Scalene (skeˈlīˈn), *a.* and *sb.* 1642. [ad. late L. *scalenus* SCALENUS.] **A.** *adj.* **1.** *Geom.* **a.** Of a triangle: Having three unequal sides 1734. **b.** *S. cone, cylinder*: one of which the axis is not perpendicular to the base 1684. **2.** *Anat. S. muscle* = SCALENUS 1827. **B.** *sb.* **1.** A scalene triangle 1642. **2.** *Anat.* = SCALENUS 1891.

Scalenohedron (skeˈlīno,hīˈdrǫn). 1854. [mod.L., f. Gr. σκαληνός SCALENE + ἕδρα seat, base.] *Cryst.* A hemihedral form of the rhombohedral system in which the faces are similar scalene triangles. So **Scalenohe·dral** *a.* pertaining to, having the form of, a s.

Scalenous (skeˈlīˈnəs), *a.* Now *rare.* 1656. [f. L. *scalenus* + -OUS.] = SCALENE A. 1 a, b.

‖ **Scalenus** (skeˈlīˈnǒs). *Pl.* **-i** (-əi). 1704. [mod.L. (sc. *musculus*), a. Gr. σκαληνός.] *Anat.* One of a set of muscles of triangular form situated in the lower lateral region of the neck.

Scaler (skēˈ·ləɹ). 1611. [f. SCALE *v.*² + -ER ¹.] **1.** One who removes scales or scale from fish, boilers, etc. **2.** An instrument for removing scales or scale 1881.

Scaliness (skēˈ·linės). 1611. [f. SCALY + -NESS 1.] The condition or character of being scaly.

Scaling (skēˈ·liŋ), *vbl. sb.*¹ 1591. [f. SCALE *v.*² or *sb.*² + -ING ¹.] **1.** The action of SCALE *v.*²; the removal or peeling off of scales or scale. **b.** *concr.* That which scales off; scale, scales 1651. **2.** Arrangement of scales 1721.

Scaling (skēˈ·liŋ), *vbl. sb.*² 1513. [f. SCALE *v.*³] **1.** Climbing, mounting; escalade. **2.** Measurement or estimation of quantities; the construction of a scale 1710.

Sca·ling-ladder. late ME. [f. prec.] A ladder used in the assault of fortified places. **b.** A fireman's ladder used for scaling buildings 1868.

Scall (skǭl), *sb.* and *a.* Now *Sc.* and *n. dial.* ME. [prob. a. ON. *skalle* a bald head, app. f. OTeut. **skal-*.] **A.** *sb.* A scaly or scabby disease of the skin, esp. of the scalp.

Dry s., psoriasis. *Humid* or *moist s.*, eczema.

B. *attrib.* or *adj.* = SCALD *a.* 1598.

Hence **Scalled** *a.* (now *rare*) = SCALD *a.*

Scallion (skæ·liən). ME. [a. AF. *scal(o)un* = OF. *eschalo(i)gne* :—pop. L. **escalonia*, for class. L. *Ascalonia* (sc. *cæpa* onion), f. *Ascalon*, a seaport of Palestine.] **a.** The shallot. Now *dial.* **b.** The Welsh onion or 'chibol'. **c.** An onion which fails to bulb but forms a long neck and strong blade; *pl.* shoots of old onions planted a second year.

Scallop, scollop (skǫ·ləp, skæ·ləp), *sb.* ME. [Aphetic a. OF. *escalope* ESCALLOP. Usu. pron. (skǫ·ləp), but spelt *scallop.*] **1.** A shell-fish of the genus *Pecten* 1440. **b.** A scallop-shell; a vessel resembling one, used in baptism, etc. late ME. **c.** A pilgrim's cockle-shell worn as a sign that he had visited the shrine of St. James at Compostella ME. **2.** Anything resembling a scallop-shell 1609. **b.** *esp.* One of a series of convex rounded projections forming the scalloped edge of a garment, etc. Also, a scalloped form, a scalloping. 1612. †**c.** A scalloped lace band or collar –1661.

Sca·llop, sco·llop, *v.* 1737. [f. prec.] **1.** *trans.* To shape or cut (*out*) in the form of a scallop-shell; to ornament or trim with scallops 1749. **2.** *Cookery.* To bake (oysters, etc.) in a scallop-shell or similar-shaped utensil with bread crumbs, cream, butter, etc. 1737.

Scalloped, scolloped (skǫ·ləpt, skæ·ləpt), *ppl. a.* 1682. [f. SCALLOP *sb.* or *v.* + -ED.] **1.** Having the border, edge, or outline cut into a series of segments of circles like a scallop-shell. **2.** *Cookery.* (See SCALLOP *v.* 2.) 1737.

Scalloper (skǫ·ləpəɹ). 1881. [f. SCALLOP *v.* and *sb.* + -ER ¹.] **a.** One who makes scalloped edging, etc. **b.** One who gathers scallops.

Sca·llop-shell. 1530. The shell of the scallop, or, more usu. one valve of it: freq. with ref. to its being a pilgrim's badge.

Scallywag, scallawag (skæ·liwæg, -ăwæg). *slang* or *colloq.* (orig. *U.S.*) 1848. [Origin obsc.] **1.** A disreputable fellow; a good-for-nothing, scapegrace, blackguard; formerly in *Trade Union slang*, a man who will not work. **2.** An imposter or intriguer, *esp.* in politics 1864. **3.** *U.S.* A name for undersized or ill-conditioned cattle 1854.

Scalp (skælp), *sb.*¹ [Northern ME. *scalp*; app. of Scand. origin.] **1.** The top or crown of the head; the skull, cranium. Now only *Sc.* and *n. dial.* **2.** The integument of the upper part of the head, usu. covered with hair and moving freely over the underlying bones 1616. **b.** *Her.* The skin of the head of an animal 1688. **3.** The scalp with the hair belonging to it cut or torn from a man's head; prized by Amer. Indians as a battle trophy 1601. **4.** A wig made to cover a part of the scalp 1801. **5.** Anything resembling a scalp; e.g. a bare piece of rock or stone, the cap of a mountain 1721.

attrib. and *Comb.*: **s.-dance,** a war-dance of N. Amer. Indians, in which scalps were carried in celebration of a victory; **-lock,** a lock of hair left on the head (the rest being shaved) by N. Amer. Indians as a challenge to their enemies; **-money,** money paid as a reward for 'bringing in' scalps of men or animals.

Scalp (skælp), *sb.*² Chiefly *Sc.* and *north.* 1521. [perh. specific use of prec.] A bank providing a bed for shellfish, *esp.* oysters and mussels; an oyster or mussel bed or colony.

†**Scalp,** *v.*¹ 1552. [ad. L. *scalpere.*] *trans.* To carve, engrave; to scrape, scratch –1802.

Scalp, *v.*² 1676. [f. SCALP *sb.*¹] **1.** *trans.* To cut off the scalp of (a person): chiefly said of the N. Amer. Indians. **2.** *dial.* To strip off (the turf or upper soil) 1806. **3.** *Milling.* To separate the 'hair' or 'fuzz' from (wheat, etc.), also, to separate the different sizes of grain from one another by attrition and screening 1883. **4.** *Stock Exch.*, etc. To buy at very low rates so as to be able to sell at less than official rates 1888.

Scalpel (skæ·lpəl), *sb.* 1742. [ad. L. *scalpellum, -us*, dim. of *scalper, scalprum.*] A small light knife used in surgical and anatomical operations.

Scalper [1], **scauper** (skæ·lpəɹ, skǭ·pəɹ). 1688. [f. SCALP *v.*[1] + -ER [1].] *Engraving.* A kind of graver used for hollowing out the bottom of sunken designs.

Scalper [2] (skæ·lpəɹ). 1795. [f. SCALP *v.*[2] + -ER [1].] 1. One (esp. an Amer. Indian) who removes scalps. 2. *U.S. slang.* One who buys and sells at a profit, but at a price lower than the official one, *esp.* unused portions of long-distance railway tickets 1882.

Sca·lping-knife. 1759. [f. *scalping*, vbl. sb. f. SCALP *v.*[2]] A knife such as is used by the N. Amer. Indians in scalping their enemies.

Scalpriform (skæ·lprifǭɹm), *a.* 1828. [f. L. *scalprum* (see next) + -FORM.] Chisel-shaped: applied to the incisors of rodents.

Scalprum (skæ·lprŏm). 1688. [L., f. *scalpere* SCALP *v.*[1]] 1. *Surg.* A rasping instrument; a raspatory. 2. *Anat.* The cutting edge of an incisor. Also, a scalpriform incisor. 1842.

Scaly (skē̆·li), *a.* 1528. [f. SCALE *sb.*[2] + -Y [1].] 1. Abounding in, covered with, or consisting of scales; having a surface that peels off in thin plates or layers 1538. 2. Of fishes, serpents, etc.; freq. in poetry = pertaining to or consisting of fish 1528. 3. Of plants and their parts: Covered with scales or consisting of scale-like elements 1597. 4. *slang.* Poor, shabby, despicable; *esp.* (of persons) mean, stingy; occas. 'seedy' 1793.

2. So hear the s. herd when Proteus blows DRYDEN. *S. ant-eater, lizard*, the pangolin. 4. They had proved themselves so very scaley, by forgetting to remember the waiter 1823.

Scamble (skæ·mb'l), *v.* 1539. [app. related to SHAMBLE and SCRAMBLE *vbs.*] †1. *intr.* = SCRAMBLE *v.* 2. -1687. 2. *trans.* To scatter (money, food) for a crowd to scramble for. Now *dial.* 1573. 3. *intr.* To make one's way as best one can; to stumble along. Now *dial.* 1571. 4. To throw out the limbs in a loose and awkward manner in walking; to shamble. Now *dial.* 1633. 5. *trans.* To 'scrape' *together, up.* Now *dial.* 1577. 6. To remove piecemeal 1707.

1. *John* IV. iii. 146. 2. A largesse of money skambled amongst the tribes HOLLAND. 5. We have scambled vp More wealth by farre then those that brag of faith MARLOWE.

Scammony (skæ·mŏni). OE. [ad. L. *scammonia, scammonium*, a. Gr. σκαμμωνία, -ώνιον.] 1. A gum-resin obtained from the tuberous roots of *Convolvulus Scammonia*, used in medicine as a strong purgative; also, the dried tuberous root from which the drug is prepared. 2. The plant *Convolvulus Scammonia*, native in Syria and Asia Minor, having a fleshy root which furnishes the scammony of commerce 1567.

Scamp (skæmp), *sb.* 1782. [f. SCAMP *v.*[1]] 1. A highway robber. *arch.* 2. A good-for-nothing, worthless person, a 'waster'; a rascal. Also *playfully* as a mild term of reproof 1808.

Scamp (skæmp), *v.*[1] 1753. [app. cogn. w. SCAMPER *v.*] *intr.* †a. *cant.* To rob on the highway. b. *Sc.* To wander *about* idly 1867.

Scamp (skæmp), *v.*[2] 1837. [prob. of dialectal origin.] 1. *trans.* To do (work, a task, etc.) negligently or hurriedly. 2. *U.S. intr.* To be stingy or excessively economical 1894.

‖**Scampavia** (skampavī·a). 1723. [It., f. *scampare* to run off, decamp + *via* way, away.] A swift sailing vessel used in the Mediterranean.

Scamper (skæ·mpəɹ), *sb.* 1697. [f. next.] The action of scampering; an instance of this.

Scamper (skæ·mpəɹ), *v.* 1687. [Origin obsc.; perh. from It. *scampare* to decamp, run away.] †1. *intr.* To run away, decamp, 'bolt' -1833. 2. To run or caper about nimbly; to go or journey hastily from place to place 1691.

2. Barefooted children were scampering up and down these stairs at play 1833. Hence **Sca·mperer.**

Scampish (skæ·mpiʃ), *a.* 1847. [-ISH [1].] Having the character or disposition of a scamp; characteristic of a scamp. Hence **Sca·mpishly** *adv.*, **-ness.**

Scan (skæn), *sb.* 1706. [f. next.] The action of scanning; close scrutiny; perception, discernment; a scanning look.

Scan (skæn), *v.* late ME. [ad. L. *scandere*, lit. to climb, in late L. to scan verses.] 1. *trans.* To analyse (verse) by determining the nature and number of the feet or the number and prosodic value of the syllables; to indicate the structure or test the correctness of (a verse) by reciting it with metrical emphasis and pauses, or by counting the feet on the fingers. Also *occas.* to describe prosodically (a word or sequence of words); to find (a particular kind of foot) in a given portion of a verse. Also *absol.* b. *intr.* (for *pass.*). To admit of being scanned, to be found metrically correct 1857. †2. *trans.* To criticize; to judge *by* a certain rule or standard -1817. †b. *intr.* To pass judgement *on, upon*; to form an opinion *of* -1610. 3. *trans.* To examine, consider, or discuss minutely 1550. †4. To interpret, assign a meaning to -1641. 5. To perceive, discern. Now *rare.* 1558. 6. To look searchingly at, examine with the eyes 1798. 7. *Television.* To resolve (a picture) into its elements of light and shade for purposes of transmission 1928.

1. *absol.* An eare that could measure a just cadence, and s. without articulating MILT. 2. Know then thyself, presume not God to s. POPE. 3. Careless their merits or their faults to s. GOLDSM. 4. Hence men came to s. the Scriptures by the Letter MILT.

Scandal (skæ·ndăl), *sb.* [Early ME. *scandle, scha(u)ndle*, a. ONF. *escandle*, semi-pop. ad. eccl. L. *scandalum* cause of offence or stumbling, ad. Gr. σκάνδαλον, perh. f. the Indo-Eur. **skand-* to spring, leap; cf. L. *scandere* to climb.] 1. In religious use. a. Discredit to religion occasioned by the conduct of a religious person. Also, perplexity of conscience occasioned by the conduct of one who is looked up to as an example. b. An occasion of unbelief or moral lapse; a stumbling-block 1582. 2. Damage to reputation; rumour or general comment injurious to reputation 1590. †b. A disgraceful imputation; in later use, a slander -1814. 3. A grossly discreditable circumstance, event, or condition of things 1591. b. *concr.* A person whose conduct is a gross disgrace to his class, country, position, etc. 1634. 4. Offence to moral feeling or sense of decency 1622. 5. The utterance of disgraceful imputations; defamatory talk. Now often in milder sense, malicious gossip. 1596. 6. *Law.* Any injurious report published concerning another which may be the foundation of legal action 1838. b. An irrelevancy or indecency introduced into a pleading to the derogation of the dignity of the court 1750.

1. Catholics..could not appear in Protestant assemblies without causing s. to the weaker brethren FROUDE. b. Heresies and Schismes, are of all others, the greatest Scandals BACON. 2. Get drunk like a Gentleman, with no S. 1706. 3. Fleet marriages.. one of the strangest scandals of English life 1878. 4. To the great s. of the county 1848. 5. No s. about Queen Elizabeth, I hope? SHERIDAN.

Scandal (skæ·ndăl), *v.* 1592. [f. prec.] †1. *trans.* To disgrace, bring into ill repute or obloquy -1684. 2. a. To spread scandal concerning (a person); to defame. Now *arch.* and *dial.* †b. To vituperate, revile. 1601. †3. To shock the feelings of; to scandalize -1701.

2. Charms and Sigils, for Defence Against ill Tongues that s. Innocence DRYDEN. Hence †**Sca·ndalled** *ppl. a.* shameful; slandered -1660.

Scandalize (skæ·ndăləiz), *v.*[1] 1489. [a. F. *scandaliser*, ad. eccl. L. *scandalizare*, ad. late Gr. σκανδαλίζειν, f. σκάνδαλον SCANDAL *sb.*; see -IZE 1.] †1. To make a public scandal of (a discreditable secret). CAXTON †2. To injure spiritually by one's example -1609. 3. To utter false or malicious reports of (a person's) conduct; to slander. Now *rare.* 1566. b. *absol.* and *intr.* To talk scandal 1745. 4. *trans.* To bring shame or discredit upon; to disgrace. Now *poet.* 1583. 5. To horrify or shock by some supposed violation of morality or propriety 1647.

Sca·ndalize, *v.*[2] 1862. [Alteration of †*scantelize* vb., to shorten.] *Naut. trans.* To reduce the area of (a sail) by lowering the peak and tricing up the tack.

Scandalous (skæ·ndăləs), *a.* 1592. [a. F. *scandaleux*, f. eccl. L. *scandalum* SCANDAL *sb.*; see -OUS.] †1. Of the nature of or causing an occasion of offence; also, bringing discredit on one's class or position -1670. 2. Of the nature of a scandal; grossly disgraceful. Also (now *rarely*) of a person: Infamous. 1595. 3. Of words and writing: Defamatory, libellous 1603. 4. Of a statement, etc.: Not pertinent to the case, irrelevant 1750.

1. The debate concerning..the punishing of s. Clergymen MARVELL. 2. The most s. Election that ever was in Oxford 1720. 3. The most s. tongues have never dared censure my reputation FIELDING. Hence **Sca·ndalous-ly** *adv.*, **-ness.**

‖**Sca·ndalum magna·tum.** *Pl.* **scandala magnatum.** Now *Hist.* 1607. [med.L., 'scandal of magnates'.] *Law.* The utterance or publication of a malicious report against any person holding a position of dignity. Also *transf.* in joc. use, something scandalous.

Scandent (skæ·ndĕnt), *a.* 1682. [ad. L. *scandentem, scandere.*] *Zool.* and *Bot.* Climbing; ascending.

Scandinavian (skæ:ndinē̆·viăn), *a.* 1765. [f. L. *Scandinavia* + -AN [1].] Of or pertaining to Scandinavia, a geographical term including the three countries Norway, Sweden, and Denmark. Also as *sb.*, one connected ethnographically with one of these three countries.

Scandium (skæ·ndiŏm). 1879. [f. L. *Scandia* (app. = Scandinavia) + -IUM.] *Chem.* A metal discovered by Nilson in the Scandinavian mineral euxenite.

Scanmag (skæ·nmæ·g). *slang.* 1779. Abbrev. (*scan. mag.*) of SCANDALUM MAGNATUM, used joc. as = 'scandal'.

Scansion (skæ·nʃən). 1671. [ad. L. *scansionem*, f. *scandere* to climb, SCAN.] *Pros.* The action or art of scanning verse; the division of verse into metrical feet; an instance of this. Hence **Scan·sionist,** one versed in the art of s.

‖**Scansores** (skænsǭ·rīz), *pl.* 1835. [mod. L., pl. of **scansor*, agent-n. f. *scandere* to climb.] *Ornith.* Illiger's first order of birds, comprising the climbers.

Scansorial (skænsǭ·riăl), *a.* 1806. [a. L. *scansorius*, used for climbing + -AL.] 1. Of or pertaining to climbing; *spec.* of the feet of birds and animals, adapted for climbing. 2. That climbs or is given to climbing; *spec.* of a bird, belonging to the Order SCANSORES 1835.

Scant (skænt), *sb. Obs.* exc. *dial.* ME. [a. ON. *skamt* (neut. adj. used *absol.*); see next.] Scanty supply; dearth, scarcity.

Scant (skænt), *a.* and *adv.* Now chiefly *literary.* late ME. [a. ON. *skamt*, neut. of *skammr* short.] A. *adj.* 1. Existing or available in inadequate or barely sufficient amount, quantity, or degree; stinted in measure, not abundant. b. Preceding a sb. without article or other qualifying word: Very little, less than enough 1852. 2. Of a quantity or amount of anything: Limited, stinted; not full, large, or copious 1556. b. Hardly reaching (a specified number or amount). Chiefly *U.S.* 1856. 3. Limited in extent; not wide or spacious 1533. 4. Poorly furnished. Const. *of.* 1577. 5. Deficient or lacking in quality; poor, meagre, not full or rich. Chiefly of immaterial things. Const. *in.* 1631. †6. Sparing, not liberal. Also in good sense: Chary, not lavish. Const. *of.* -1651. 7. *Naut.* Of wind: Too much ahead, so that the ship has to sail very close. (Opp. to *large* or *free.*) 1600.

1. In the country money is rather s. BORROW. b. You do s. justice to Dover DICKENS. 2. In such a s. allowance of Star-light MILT. b. A s. two day's allowance of meat 1856. 3. Though the realme of Italy was s., their hertes were grette 1533. 4. He's fat, and s. of breath SHAKS. 6. For this time, Daughter, Be somewhat scanter of your Maiden presence SHAKS.

B. *adv.* 1. Hardly, scarcely; barely. Now *dial.* 1450. †2. Scantily (*rare*) -1620.

1. Some who could s. brook the name of Bishop were content to give..him a good Report FULLER. Hence **Sca·nt-ly** *adv.*, **-ness.**

Scant (skænt), *v.* late ME. [f. SCANT *a.*] I. *intr.* †1. To become scant or scarce -1624. †2. *Naut.* Of the wind: To become unfavourable, to draw too much ahead. Const. *upon, with.* -1823. II. *trans.* †1. To furnish (a person) with an inadequate supply; to stint; to put or keep on short allowance. In *pass.*, to be straitened (*for*). -1719. b. To put or keep on short allowance *of*; to keep (a person) short *of*. In *pass.*, to be badly off for. Now *rare.* 1565. †c. To limit or restrict *in* (a supply, etc.) -1836. 2. To make scant or small; to reduce in size or amount, cut down. *obsol.*

1590. **3.** To stint the supply of; to refrain from giving, withhold; to be niggardly of. Now *rare*. 1573. †**4.** *gen.* To confine within narrow bounds; to limit, restrict, hedge in -1631. **5.** To treat slightingly or inadequately; to neglect, do less than justice to. Now *rare*. 1604.

1. He..scants vs with a single famisht kisse SHAKS. **b.** A man, whose fortune scants him of meanes to do you service 1597. **2.** S. not my Cups SHAKS. **3.** Doth like a Miser spoyle his Coat, with scanting A little Cloth SHAKS.

Sca·ntity. *rare.* late ME. [irreg. f. SCANT *a.* + -ITY, perh. after *quantity*.] Scantiness.

Sca·ntle, *sb.* 1596. [app. f. next.] **1.** A small piece or portion, a scantling. **2.** *Slate-making.* A gauge for measuring slates 1850.

1. 1 *Hen. IV*, III. i. 100 (1st Qo.).

†**Sca·ntle,** *v.* 1581. [perh. dim. of SCANT *v.*; see -LE 3.] **1.** *trans.* = SCANT *v.* II. 1. -1630. **2.** To make scant or small; to cut down, limit, restrict -1641. **3.** To make proportionate *to* -1711.

Scantling (skæ·ntliŋ), *sb.* 1476. [Alteration of earlier †*scantillon*, aphetic f. OF. *escantillon* (mod.F. *échantillon*).] †**1.** A builder's or carpenter's measuring-rod -1678. **2.** Measured or prescribed size, dimensions, or calibre; now *techn.* with ref. to the measurement of timber, stone, etc. 1526. †**3.** Limited measure, space, amount, etc.; a limit -1691. †**b.** *spec.* in *Archery*, applied to the distance from the mark, within which a shot was not regarded as a miss -1661. **4.** A portion, allotted quantity, allowance. *arch.* 1659. **5.** A small or scanty portion or amount, a modicum 1476. †**6.** A sample, pattern, specimen. Hence, a sketch, outline, rough draft. -1838. **7.** *concr.* in techn. use. **a.** A small beam or piece of wood; *spec.* one less than five inches square 1663. **b.** *collect. sing.* Timber in the form of scantlings 1794. **c.** A block or slice of stone of a fixed size; also *collect. sing.* stone cut into scantlings 1726.

2. A fine twin screw steamship, built of steel to the same scantlings as if of iron 1888. Phr. †*Of one* (or *a*) *s.*, of the same size; hence, much alike. †*To take a s. of*, to measure or estimate the size or amount of; hence, to judge of, estimate. **3.** Such as exceede not this s. to bee sollace to the Soueraigne and harmelesse to the people BACON. **5.** I am really ashamed to send this s. of paper by the post H. WALPOLE.

Scanty (skæ·nti), *a.* 1660. [f. SCANT *sb.* or *a.* + -Y[1].] **1.** Meagre, slender, not ample or copious. **2.** Deficient in extent, compass, or size 1701. **3.** Existing or present in small or insufficient quantity; not abundant 1674. †**4.** Parsimonious. Of soil: Yielding little. -1796.

1. Me, in no s. measure, thou excell'st COWPER. **2.** S. trousers..and a forward set of the hat 1874. **3.** My paper is s. and time more so 1705. **4.** With..daily toil Soliciting for food my s. soil COLERIDGE. Hence **Sca·nti-ly** *adv.*, **-ness.**

Scape (skēⁱp), *sb.*[1] ME. [Aphetic var. of ESCAPE *sb.*[1]] **1.** = ESCAPE *sb.*[1] 1. *arch.* (Often written *'scape*.) †**2.** A transgression due to thoughtlessness -1681.

1. *Oth.* I. iii. 136. **2.** Slight scapes are whipt, but damned deeds are praised MARSTON.

Comb.: **s.-spring,** a spring that is automatically liberated; **-wheel,** = *escape-wheel*.

Scape (skēⁱp), *sb.*[2] 1601. [ad. L. *scapus*, a. Gr. σκᾶπος, cogn. w. σκῆπτρον SCEPTRE.] **1.** *Arch.* The shaft of a column 1663. **2.** *Bot.* A long flower-stalk rising directly from the root or rhizome; †*gen.*, a stem or stalk 1601. **4.** *Ent.* The first joint of the antenna of an insect 1826. Hence **Sca·peless** *a.*[1] (*Bot.*)

Scape (skēⁱp), *sb.*[3] 1773. [Back-formation from LANDSCAPE.] A view of scenery of any kind. Also as the second element of combs., as SEA-SCAPE, *cloud-scape*, etc.

Scape (skēⁱp), *v.* ME. [Aphetic var. of ESCAPE *v.* Now *arch.* and *poet.*, and often written *'scape*.] = ESCAPE *v.*

Comb.: **s.-gallows,** one who has escaped the gallows though deserving of capital punishment.

Scape (skēⁱp), *int.* 1862. Conventional imitation of the cry of the snipe when flushed. Hence as *sb.* a nickname for the snipe.

Scapegoat (skēⁱ·pgōut). 1530. [f. SCAPE *sb.*[1] or *v.* + GOAT. App. invented by Tindale as tr. Heb. *'ăzāzel*, (Vulgate *caper emissarius*), represented in the R.V. by 'Azazel' (as a proper name), and 'dismissal' in the margin.] **1.** In the Mosaic ritual of the Day of Atonement (Lev. xvi), that one of two goats that was chosen by lot to be sent alive into the wilderness, the sins of the people having been symbolically laid upon it, while the other was sacrificed. **2.** One who is blamed or punished for the sins of others. (So F. *bouc émissaire*.) 1824.

Scapegrace (skēⁱ·pgrēⁱs), *sb.* and *a.* 1809. [f. SCAPE *v.* + GRACE *sb.*, as if 'one who escapes the grace of God'.] **A.** *sb.* A man or child of reckless and disorderly habits; an incorrigible scamp. Often used playfully. **B.** *adj.* That is a s.; characteristic of a s. 1830.

Scapeless (skēⁱ·plės), *a.*[2] 1850. [f. SCAPE *sb.*[1] or *v.* + -LESS.] Inevitable.

The s. net spread in thy sight around thee R. BRIDGES.

Scapement (skēⁱ·pmĕnt). 1755. Aphetic f. ESCAPEMENT.

Scaphander (skæfæ·ndəɹ). 1825. [ad. F. *scaphandre*, f. Gr. σκάφη boat + ἀνδρ-, ἀνήρ man.] A cork belt used as a support in swimming.

Scaphite (skæ·fəit). 1822. [ad. mod.L. *scaphites*, f. Gr. σκάφη boat; see -ITE.] *Palæont.* A cephalopod of the genus *Scaphites*.

Scapho- (skæ·fo, skăfǫ·), comb. form of Gr. σκάφη boat, as in **Scapho·cerite** [Gr. κέρας horn], the third section of the antenna of an insect. **Scapho·gnathite** [Gr. γνάθος jaw], a flat oval plate in the gill chamber of fishes, which by movement promotes a constant flow of water through the gill. **Scapholu·nar** *a.*, the epithet of a small bone in the carpus of some animals; also *ellipt.* as *sb.*

‖**Scaphocephalus** (skæ:fose·fălǝs). 1863. [mod.L., f. Gr. σκάφη boat + κεφαλή head; after *hydrocephalus*.] *Path.* 'Boat-shaped head'; a condition of the skull (caused by premature ossification of the sagittal suture preventing transverse development) in which the length greatly exceeds the breadth. Hence **Sca:phocepha·lic, Scaphoce·phalous** *adjs.* **Scaphoce·phalism, Scaphoce·phaly.**

Scaphoid (skæ·foid), *a.* and *sb.* 1741. [ad. mod.L. *scaphoides*, a. Gr. σκαφοειδής, f. σκάφη boat; see -OID.] **A.** *adj.* Shaped like a boat. Chiefly *Anat.* and *Zool.* *S. bone* = B. **B.** *sb.* [Short for *s. bone*.] The first proximal carpal bone in Mammalia, or the corresponding bone in the foot 1846.

Scapiform (skēⁱ·pifǭɹm), *a.* 1796. [f. L. *scapus* SCAPE *sb.*[2] + -FORM.] Having the form of a SCAPE.

Scapolite (skæ·pǒləit). 1802. [ad. G. *skapolith*, f. Gr. σκᾶπος rod + λίθος stone; see -LITE.] *Min.* One of a group of minerals (including dipyre, ekebergite, marialite, etc.) composed of silicates of aluminium, calcium, and sodium.

Scapple (skæ·p'l), *v.* 1443. [Aphetic a. OF. *escapeler, eschapeler* to dress timber.] *trans.* To reduce the faces of (a block of stone, †timber) to a plane surface without working them smooth.

‖**Scapula** (skæ·piŭlă). *Pl.* **-æ.** 1578. [L., in class. L. only pl. *scapulæ*.] **1.** *Anat.* The shoulder-blade, blade-bone, or omoplate (in man or other animals). **2.** *Ent.* Applied to various analogous parts of insects 1826.

Scapular (skæ·piŭlăɹ), *sb.* 1483. [ad. med. L. *scapulare*, f. *scapula* shoulder.] **1.** *Eccl.* **a.** A short cloak covering the shoulders; adopted by certain religious orders as a part of their ordinary costume. **b.** An article of devotion composed of two small squares of woollen cloth, fastened together by strings passing over the shoulders, and worn as a badge of affiliation to the religious order which presents it 1870. †**2.** *Surg.* A bandage passing over and around the shoulders to support other bandages, etc. -1758. **3.** *Ornith.* [Ellipt. for *scapular feather*.] Any feather which grows from the *pterylæ humerales* or scapular region 1688.

Scapular (skæ·piŭlăɹ), *a.* 1688. [ad. mod. L. *scapularis*, f. L. *scapula* SCAPULA; see -AR[1] 1.] **1.** Of or pertaining to the scapula 1713. **2.** *Ornith.* Applied to any feather which grows upon the *pterylæ humerales* 1688.

Scapulary (skæ·piŭlări), *sb.* ME. [ad. med.L. *scapularium*, var. of *scapulare* SCAPULAR *sb.*] **1.** *Eccl.* = SCAPULAR *sb.* 1 a, b. **2.** = SCAPULAR *sb.* 3. 1854.

Scapulary (skæ·piŭlări), *a.* 1548. [ad. F. *scapulaire* and mod.L. *scapularius*; see SCAPULA and -ARY[1].] †**1.** *S. mantle*: a cloak covering the shoulders. **2.** = SCAPULAR *a.* 1. 1785.

Scapulette (skæ·piŭlet). Also **scapulet.** 1887. [a. G.; see SCAPULA and -ETTE.] *Zool.* A leaf-like appendage of the manubrium of certain *Cnidaria*.

Scapulo- (skæ·piŭlo), comb. form of L. *scapula* SCAPULA, as in **S.-clavi·cular** *a.*, of or belonging to the scapula and the clavicle; also *sb.*, the scapulo-clavicular joint.

‖**Scapus** (skēⁱ·pǒs). *Pl.* **scapi** (skēⁱ·pəi). 1563. [L.; see SCAPE *sb.*[2]] †**1.** *Arch.* = SCAPE *sb.*[2] 1. -1728. **2.** *Ornith.* The shaft of a feather 1882.

Scar (skāɹ), *sb.*[1] ME. [App. a. ON. *sker* SKERRY.] †**1.** A rock, crag -1535. **2.** A lofty steep face of rock upon a mountain-side; a precipice, cliff 1673. **3.** A low or sunken rock in the sea; a rocky tract at the bottom of the sea 1712.

2. O sweet and far from cliff and s. The horns of Elfland faintly blowing! TENNYSON.

attrib.: **s.-limestone,** a carboniferous rock occurring in the Pennine Range.

Scar (skāɹ), *sb.*[2] late ME. [prob. aphetic a. OF. *escare*, ad. late L. *eschara* ESCHAR, a. Gr. ἐσχάρα lit. 'hearth'.] **1.** The trace of a healed wound, sore, or burn. **b.** *fig.* A fault or blemish remaining as a trace of some former condition or resulting from some particular cause 1583. **2.** *Nat. Hist.* A mark or trace indicating the point of attachment of some structure that has been removed; *Bot.* = CICATRIX 2. 1793.

1. A scarre nobly got, Or a noble scarre, is a good liu'rie of honor SHAKS. **b.** The leprous scars of callous Infamy SHELLEY.

Scar (skāɹ), *sb.*[3] 1748. [ad. L. *scarus*.] = SCARUS. Also *s.-fish*.

Scar (skāɹ), *v.* 1555. [f. SCAR *sb.*[2]] **1.** *trans.* To mark with a scar; to disfigure by inflicting a wound. **2. a.** *trans.* with *up*. To heal, cover with a scar. **b.** *intr.* with *over*. To heal; to become covered with a scar as a sign of healing. 1609.

1. Yet Ile not shed her blood, Nor scarre that whiter skin of hers then Snow SHAKS. *transf.* Durham has been scarred and blackened by..industrialism 1908.

Scarab (skæ·răb). 1579. [ad. F. *scarabée* SCARABEE, ad. L. *scarabæus* SCARABÆUS.] **1.** In early use, a beetle of any kind. Now *rare* exc. as applied to the scarabæid beetle, *Ateuchus sacer*, reverenced by the ancient Egyptians. **2.** *Antiq.* A gem (of cornelian, emerald, etc.) cut in the form of a beetle (*scarabæus*), having on the flat under-side a design in intaglio 1871.

Scarabæid (skæræbī·id), *a.* and *sb.* 1891. [f. mod.L. *scarabæidæ*, f. L. *scarabæus* SCARABÆUS; see -ID[3].] *Ent.* **A.** *adj.* Of or belonging to the *Scarabeidæ*, a large family of lamellicorn beetles, including cockchafers, stag-beetles, dung-beetles, etc. **B.** *sb.* A s. beetle.

‖**Scarabæus** (skæræbī·ǒs). *Pl.* **-bæi** (-bī·əi). 1664. [L.; cf. Gr. κάραβος.] **1.** *Ent.* A beetle of the genus *Scarabæus*, an Old World genus of lamellicorn beetles typical of the *Scarabæidæ*. **2.** *Antiq.* = SCARAB 2. 1775.

Scarabee (skæ·răbī). *arch.* 1591. [a. F. *scarabée*; see SCARAB.] = SCARAB 1.

Scaraboid (skæ·răboid), *sb.* and *a.* 1879. [f. SCARAB + -OID.] **A.** *sb.* **1.** *Antiq.* A scarab only vaguely resembling the insect in shape. **2.** A scarabæid 1891. **B.** *adj.* Resembling a scarab or scaraboid 1888.

Scaramouch (skæ·rămautʃ), *sb.* 1662. [ad. It. *Scaramuccia* (see sense 1); the name is a use of *scaramuccia* SKIRMISH *sb.*, in allusion to the character of the personage.] **1.** (As proper name, with capital S.) A stock character in Italian farce, a boastful poltroon, who is constantly being cudgelled by Harlequin. **b.** A puppet representing Scaramouch 1816. **2.** *transf.* and *fig.* A rascal, scamp 1676.

1. Stout Scaramoucha with Rush Lance rode in, And ran a Tilt at Centaure Arlequin DRYDEN. **2.** He swore no s. of an Italian robber would dare to meddle with an Englishman W. IRVING.

Scarborough (skā·ɹbɹə). 1546. The name of a town on the coast of Yorkshire, used *attrib.*, in **S. warning,** very short notice, or no notice at all; a surprise. **S. lily,** *Vallota purpurea*.

Scarce (skēᵊɹs), *a.* and *adv.* [ME. *scars*, a. ONF. *scars, escars* (mod.F. *échars*) :—pop. L. **scarsus*, prob. repr. an older **excarpsus*, pa. pple. of **excarpere* (= class. L. *excerpere* to EXCERPT), f. *ex* + *carpere* to pluck.] A. *adj.* †1. Restricted in quantity, size, or amount; scanty –1732. †2. Of persons, etc.: Stingy, sparing, parsimonious, penurious. Also with *of*. –1639. 3. Of food, etc.: Existing or accessible in deficient quantity. late ME. 4. Existing in limited number; rare. Said chiefly of things sought after by collectors. late ME. 5. *Scarce of*: poorly or scantily supplied with; deficient in; short of. Now *rare* or *Obs.* 1541.

2. They knewe him to be of nature scarse, and not liberal 1562. 3. In þat tyme money was skarse 1450. 4. A scarse Book 1710. Knowledge is s., wisdom is scarcer 1884. 5. We are s. of provisions MARRYAT.

Phr. *To make oneself s.*, (colloq.) to absent oneself.

B. *adv.* †1. Scantily, sparsely –1450. 2. Barely, only just; not quite. Now *literary*. late ME. †3. Seldom, rarely –1663. 4. Used (after L. *vix*) for: With difficulty (*rare*) 1667.

2. With worldly cares he was so toste, that scarse he tooke his reste 1577. There he her met, Scarse from the Tree returning MILT. A s. heard Whisper FITZGERALD. 4. Scarse from his mould Behemoth biggest born of Earth upheav'd His vastness MILT.

Scarcely (skēᵊ·ɹsli), *adv.* ME. [f. SCARCE *a.* + -LY [2].] †1. Scantily, in small quantities; inadequately, sparingly, parsimoniously –1669. 2. Orig. = 'barely', 'only just'; hence also, = 'barely, or not quite', 'only just, if at all'. In sentences relating to belief, expectation, etc., the word now serves as a restricted negative (= 'not quite'). Often, however, it qualifies the degree of the speaker's belief; thus 'You will s. maintain, etc.' = 'I cannot quite believe that you will maintain, etc.' ME. b. With ref. to time: Barely, only just. Chiefly with pluperfect tense, before a clause introduced by *when* or *before*. 1542.

1. It was verie s. inhabited PURCHAS. 2. The genius of Petrarch was s. of the first order MACAULAY. My partner..could s. believe his ears 1885. b. In old-fashioned days,..when you were s. born THACKERAY.

Scarcement (skēᵊ·ɹsmĕnt). *Sc.* and *north.* 1501. [app. f. †*scarce* vb. to become or make less (f. SCARCE *a.*) + -MENT.] a. *Building.* A flat set-off or rebate in a wall, or in a foundation or bank of earth. Also *transf.* a flat ledge projecting from the face of a rock. b. *Mining.* A ledge left projecting into a mine-shaft 1839.

Scarceness (skēᵊ·ɹsnės). Now *rare.* ME. [f. SCARCE *a.* + -NESS.] †1. Niggardliness, stinginess. Of soil: Infertility. –1678. 2. Deficient supply, scarcity; †*absol.* scarcity of food or provisions. late ME. †3. Want, poverty –1650. 4. Uncommonness, rarity 1672.

4. The folly of man rateth things by their s. 1744.

Scarcity (skēᵊ·ɹsiti). ME. [a. ONF. *escarceté*, f. *esc(h)ars* SCARCE *a.*; see -ITY.] †1. Frugality, parsimony; niggardliness, meanness –1531. 2. Insufficiency of supply ME. 3. *absol.* Insufficiency of supply, in a community, of the necessaries of life, dearth. Also, a period of scarcity, a dearth. 1450. †4. Deficiency, shortcoming –1450. †5. The condition of being slenderly or inadequately provided (const. *of*). Also *absol.*, penury, hardship. –1610.

2. A great s. of rain 1881. *attrib.*: **s. value**, an enhanced value due to s.; so *s. price, rent.* 3. After such a famine there followed a Scarsitie in South Wales 1584. 5. S. and want shall shun you SHAKS.

Scare (skēᵊɹ), *sb.*[1] late ME. [f. SCARE *v.*] †1. Fear, dread –1616. 2. An act of scaring or a state of being scared; *esp.* a state of general or public alarm occasioned by baseless or exaggerated rumours; *occas.* in generalized use, panic 1548. †3. Something that scares; *spec.* a scarecrow –1828.

2. He was seiz'd upon the S. of the Popish Plot HEARNE.

Comb.: **s.-head, heading**, a heading to a column of newspaper matter written in language so extravagant as to produce a scare; **-line**, a sensational announcement upon a newspaper poster.

Scare (skēᵊɹ), *sb.*[2] 1881. [orig. Sc. dial., a. ON. *skǫr*.] *Golf.* The part of a golf club where the head joins the shaft.

Scare (skēᵊɹ), *v.* Pa. t. and pple. **scared** (skēᵊɹd). [ME. *skerre*, a. ON. *skirra*, f. *skiarr* (:—**skerro-*) shy, timid, startled.] 1. *trans.* To frighten, terrify. b. To frighten away, drive off. Now chiefly with adv., except with ref. to keeping off birds from corn, etc. late ME. †2. *intr.* To take fright; to be scared (at) –1721.

1. Who scared me with that Gorgon face? 1839. *S. up, out* (U.S.), to frighten (game) out of cover; hence *fig.*, to bring to light, discover.

Scarecrow (skēᵊ·ɹkrōᵘ). 1553. [f. SCARE *v.* + CROW *sb.*[1]] 1. A person employed in scaring birds (*rare*). 2. A device for frightening birds away from growing crops, usu. a figure of a man dressed in old ragged clothes 1592. b. *fig.* Something (not really formidable) that frightens or is intended to frighten 1589. 3. One who resembles a scarecrow in his dress or whose appearance is ridiculous; †a gaunt figure 1590.

2. b. That idle s.,—the Bribery Act 1812. 3. Half a dozen scarecrows out at knees and elbows DICKENS.

†**Sca·re-fire.** 1572. [prob. corruption of SCATHEFIRE, after SCARE *sb.*[1]] A sudden conflagration –1684.

Scaremonger (skēᵊ·ɹmɒŋgəɹ). 1888. [f. SCARE *sb.*[1] + MONGER.] One who busies himself in spreading alarming reports.

Scarf (skāɹf), *sb.*[1] *Pl.* **scarfs, scarves.** 1555. [prob. a. ONF. *escarpe* (mod.F. *écharpe*).] 1. A broad band of silk or other material, worn (chiefly by soldiers or officials) either diagonally across the body from one shoulder to the opposite hip, or round the waist. 2. *Eccl.* A band of silk or other material worn round the neck with the two ends pendent from the shoulders in front, as a part of clerical costume. In the 18th c. *spec.* the scarf worn by a nobleman's chaplain; hence, a chaplaincy. 1555. 3. A broad strip of silk, gauze, etc., worn hung loosely over the shoulders or otherwise as an ornamental accessory to the costume 1562. b. *spec.* The scarf of black crape or silk worn over the shoulder by mourners at a funeral 1739. c. A band of warm and soft material worn round the neck in cold weather 1844. d. A necktie or cravat that more or less covers the bosom of the shirt 1865. †4. A sling for an ailing limb –1828. 5 *Her.* = SCARP *sb.*[1] 1688.

3. Trickt in skarffe and feather HEYWOOD.

Comb.: **s.-loom**, a loom for weaving figured fabrics of moderate breadth; **-pin**, a pin for fastening a s., or worn for ornament in a s.; **-ring**, a ring for holding a s. in position.

Scarf (skāɹf), *sb.*[2] 1497. [perh. f. (ult.) Sw. *skarf*, Norw. *skarv* piece added to lengthen a board or garment.] 1. *Carpentry* and *Shipbuilding.* A joint by which two timbers are connected longitudinally into a continuous piece the ends being halved, notched, or cut away so as to fit into each other with mutual overlapping. †b. *Shipbuilding.* The overlapping of adjacent timbers in a ship's frame, in order to secure continuity of strength at the joints –1850. 2. *Metal-working.* The chamfered edges of iron prepared for welding 1875.

Comb.: **s.-joint** = senses 1 and 2; hence **-jointing**, the process of joining timbers by means of a s.

Scarf (skāɹf), *sb.*[3] *Orkn.* and *Shetl. dial.* 1668. [a. ON. *skarfr*.] A cormorant or shag.

Scarf (skāɹf), *sb.*[4] 1851. [Cf. SCARF *v.*[3]] *Whaling.* A longitudinal cut made in a whale's body.

Scarf (skāɹf), *v.*[1] 1598. [f. SCARF *sb.*[1]] 1. *trans.* To cover or wrap with or as with a scarf or scarves; to invest with a scarf. 2. To wrap (a garment) *about* or *around* a person in the manner of a scarf (*rare*) 1602. †3. To bind up (wounds) with, or as with a scarf –1643.

1. *transf.* Come, seeling Night, Skarfe vp the tender Eye of pittifull Day SHAKS. 2. Vp from my cabin My sea-gowne scarft about me in the darke, Grop'd I to find out them SHAKS.

Scarf (skāɹf), *v.*[2] 1532. [f. SCARF *sb.*[2]] 1. *trans.* To join by a scarf-joint. 2. *Metal-working.* To bevel or flatten (the ends or edges of the pieces of metal to be welded) 1831. 3. *intr.* To be joined with a scarf 1794.

Scarf (skāɹf), *v.*[3] 1851. [Goes with SCARF *sb.*[4]] *Whaling. trans.* To make a 'scarf' in the blubber of (a whale). Also *absol.*

Sca·rf-skin. 1615. [SCARF *sb.*[1], in sense 'light outer covering'.] The outer layer of the skin; the epidermis, cuticle.

Not a hair Ruffled upon the s. TENNYSON.

Scarification (skærifikēⁱ·ʃən). late ME. [ad. late L. *scarificationem*, f. *scarificare* to SCARIFY.] 1. The action of scarifying; an instance of this. 2. *concr.* A slight incision or a number of these made by scarifying 1541.

Scarificator (skæ·rifikēⁱtəɹ). 1611. [a. mod.L., f. late L. *scarificare*.] *Surg.* An instrument used in scarification, for making several incisions simultaneously.

Scarifier (skæ·rifəiəɹ). 1566. [f. SCARIFY *v.* + -ER [1].] 1. One who or something which scarifies, *lit.* and *fig.* 2. = SCARIFICATOR 1611. 3. *Agric.* An implement for loosening the soil 1797. 4. *Road-making.* A machine used for breaking up a road 1892.

Scarify (skæ·rifəi), *v.* 1440. [a. F. *scarifier*, ad. late L. *scarificare*, altered f. *scarifare* to scarify, ad. Gr. σκαριφᾶσθαι to scratch an outline, etc., f. σκάριφος pencil, stilus.] 1. *trans.* (chiefly *Surg.*). To make a number of scratches or slight incisions in (a portion of the body, a wound). Hence *gen.* to cover with scratches. 1541. b. *fig.* To make sore, wound. Also, in mod. use, to subject to merciless criticism. 1582. c. *transf.* To cover with scars, to scar 1687. 2. To make incisions in the bark of (a tree) 1440. 3. *Agric.*, etc. To break up or loosen (ground, a road) with a scarifier 1805.

Scariose (skēᵊ·riōᵘs), *a.* 1785. [ad. mod. L. *scariosus*, of obsc. origin.] *Bot.* = next.

Scarious (skēᵊ·riəs), *a.* 1806. [ad. F. *scarieux*, ad. mod.L. *scariosus*.] 1. *Bot.* Having a dry and shrivelled appearance. 2. *Zool.* Dry, not fleshy 1861.

Scarlatina (skāɹlătī·nă). 1803. [a. mod. L., a. It. *scarlattina*, fem. of *scarlattino* adj., dim. of *scarlatto* SCARLET.] *Path.* = SCARLET FEVER. (Pop. often misapprehended as denoting a mild form of the disease.) Hence **Scarlati·nal** *a.* belonging to, resulting from, s. **Scarlati·nous** *a.* affected with s.

Scarless (skā·ɹlės), *a.* 1630. [f. SCAR *sb.*[1] + -LESS.] 1. Showing no scar; lacking blemish. 2. Leaving no scar 1823.

Scarlet (skā·ɹlėt), *sb.* and *a.* ME. [Aphetic a. OF. *escarlate* (mod.F. *écarlate*), supposed to be an alteration of Pers. *saqalāt* a kind of rich cloth.] A. *sb.* 1. †a. In early use, some rich cloth, often of a bright red colour. b. Later, cloth or clothing of the colour described in 2. 2. A brilliant vivid red colour, inclining to orange 1440. b. A pigment or dye of this colour. Now also *spec.*, any one of a certain group of coal-tar colouring matters used in scarlet pigments and dyes. 1653. 3. Official or ceremonial costume of scarlet; also, the scarlet coat worn in the hunting field. Hence *occas.* the rank, dignity, or office signified by a scarlet robe. 1496.

1. b. An Ambassador, whose robes are lined with a s. dyed in the blood of Judges BURKE. 2. His Friend demanding what S. was? the blind Man answered, It was like the sound of a Trumpet LOCKE. 3. After this he made little account of his S., or degree of Cardinal 1685.

B. *adj.* (Orig. the sb. used attrib.) 1. Having, or pertaining to, the colour scarlet. late ME. b. Clothed in scarlet, wearing a scarlet uniform, etc. 1591. c. Red with shame or indignation 1593. 2. *fig.* Of an offence (after Isa. i. 18): Heinous, deep-dyed 1603.

1. The poppies show their s. coats KEATS. c. She flushed s. 1881.

Special collocations: **s.-day**, an occasion in university or civic life marked by the public wearing of state or official robes of s.; **s. lady, whore, woman**, abusive epithets applied to the Church of Rome in allusion to Rev. xvii. 1–5. b. In names of birds, insects, etc.: **s. ibis**, *Eudocimus ruber*, a bird congeneric with the typical Ibis, native in tropical America; **s. mite**, *Trombidium holosericeum*; **s. tanager**, the RED BIRD, *Pyranga rubra*; **s. tiger (moth)**, *Hypercampa dominula*. c. In names of plants and fruits: **s.-bean** = *s. runner*; **s. geranium**, a pelargonium with s. blossoms, largely used as a bedding-plant; **s. maple**, *Acer rubrum*; **s. oak**, *Quercus coccinea*; also, †the Holm Oak, *Quercus Ilex*; **s. pimpernel**, *Anagallis arvensis*; **s. runner (bean)**, *Phaseolus multiflorus*. Hence †**Sca·rlet** *v. trans.* to clothe in s.; to colour s. –1688.

Sca·rlet fe·ver. 1676. A contagious febrile disease, distinguished by a scarlet efflorescence of the skin and of the mucous membrane of the mouth and pharynx. Cf. SCARLATINA. b. *joc. slang.* A passion for soldiers (red-coats) 1889.

Scarp (skāɹp), *sb.*[1] 1562. [a. ONF. *escarpe* (mod.F. *écharpe*), lit. sash; see SCARF *sb.*[1]]

Her. A diminutive of the bend sinister, one-half its width, crossing the shield diagonally from the sinister chief to the dexter base.

Scarp (skāɹp), *sb.*[2] 1589. [ad. It. *scarpa*, whence F. *escarpe* ESCARP.] **1.** *Fortif.* = ESCARP *sb.* **2.** The steep face of a hill 1802.

Scarp (skāɹp), *v.* 1596. [f. prec.] *trans.* = ESCARP *v.* Hence **Scarped** *ppl. a.* reduced to a steep face, laid bare, cut away, steep.

Scarred (skāɹd), *ppl. a.* 1440. [f. SCAR *v.* + -ED[1].] **1.** Of the body or its parts: Bearing scars or traces of wounds or sores. **2.** *transf.* Of inanimate objects: Bearing traces of injury, weathering, or the like. Often of rocks: Broken as by a convulsion of nature. 1600. **3.** *Bot.* Marked with cicatrices or traces of leaves that have fallen off 1793.

Scarry (skā·ɹi), *a.* late ME. [f. SCAR *sb.*[1] + -Y[1].] Precipitous, rocky.

‖**Scarus** (skēᵊ·rɒ̆s). *Pl.* **scari** (skēᵊ·rəi). 1601. [L., a. Gr. σκάρος.] A fish described by ancient writers; in mod. use, the typical genus of the family *Scaridæ*; a fish of this genus, a PARROT-FISH.

Scary (skēᵊ·ri), *a.* Also *vulgar* **skeery.** 1582. [f. SCARE *sb.*[2] + -Y[1].] **1.** Terrifying, frightful. **2.** Frightened, timorous 1827.

2. Women are skeery critters 1873.

Scat (skæt), *sb.* late ME. [a. ON. *skattr* tribute.] **a.** *gen.* A tax, tribute. Now *Hist.* **b.** In Orkney and Shetland, the land-tax paid to the Crown by a udal tenant 1577.

Scat (skæt), *int. colloq.* 1869. [Origin obsc.] Begone! Hence joc. used as verb (*intr.*).

Scathe (skēⁱð), *sb.* Now *arch.* and *dial.* OE. [a. ON. *skaði* = OE. *sc(e)aða* harm :— OTeut. *skaþon-, f. root *skaþ-; cf. Gr. ἀσκηθής unscathed.] †**1.** One who works harm; a malefactor –ME. **2.** Harm, damage OE. **b.** Something which works harm 1579. **3.** Matter for sorrow or regret. [Cf. G. *schade.*] ME.

2. To the great hurt and skaith of the king's lieges 1670. Phr. *To do s.*, to do harm; And wherein Rome hath done you any s., Let him make treble satisfaction SHAKS. Hence †**Sca·thefire,** a destructive fire or conflagration –1796.

Scathe (skēⁱð), *v.* ME. [a. ON. *skaða* impers., it hurts :—OTeut. *skaþōjan, f. *skaþon- SCATHE *sb.*] **1.** *trans.* To injure, hurt, damage. Now *arch.* and *Sc.* †**b.** *spec.* To subject to pecuniary loss –1602. **2.** To injure or destroy by fire, lightning, or the like; to blast, scorch, sear. *poet.* and *rhet.* 1667. **3.** *fig.* To 'wither' with fierce invective or satire 1852.

1. As when Heavens Fire Hath scath'd the Forrest Oaks,..With singed top their stately growth though bare Stands on the blasted Heath MILT. 3. His satire..scathing..his old enemies the monks 1867.

Scatheful (skēⁱ·ðfŭl), *a. arch.* OE. [f. SCATHE *sb.* + -FUL[1].] Harmful, injurious.

Scatheless (skēⁱ·ðlĕs), *a.* ME. [f. SCATHE *sb.* + -LESS.] Without scathe; unharmed. Hence **Sca·thelessly** *adv.*

Scathing (skēⁱ·ðiŋ), *ppl. a.* 1794. [-ING[2].] **1.** That scathes or blasts. **2.** Of invective, etc.: Very sharp and damaging; searing, 'withering', cutting 1865.

2. He launched from the pulpit the most s. invectives 1865. Hence **Sca·thingly** *adv.*

Scatology (skătǫ·lŏdʒi). 1876. [f. Gr. σκατ-, σκῶρ dung + -(O)LOGY.] **1.** That branch of medical science which deals with diagnosis by means of the fæces 1897. **2.** *Palæont.* The study of fossil excrement or coprolites 1889. **3.** Filthy literature (*rare*) 1876.

Scatophagous (skătǫ·făgəs), *a.* 1891. [f. mod.L. *scatophagus*, a. Gr. σκατοφάγος, f. σκατ(ο)-, σκῶρ dung.] Feeding upon dung.

Scatter (skæ·təɹ), *sb.* 1642. [f. next.] **1.** The action or an act of scattering; wide or irregular distribution. Now chiefly with ref. to shot. **2.** A scattering, sprinkling (*rare*) 1859.

Scatter (skæ·təɹ), *v.* [Early ME.; of obscure origin; formed with iterative suffix (see -ER[5]).] **1.** *trans.* To dissipate, squander (goods or possessions). *Obs.* or *arch.* **2.** To separate and drive in various directions; to disperse, dissipate; to dispel (clouds, mists) ME. **b.** *intr.* for *refl.* To separate and disperse; to go dispersedly or stragglingly. late ME. **3.** *trans.* To throw about in disorder in various places ME. **4.** To distribute to various positions; to place here and there at irregular intervals. late ME. **5.** To throw or send forth so that the particles are distributed or spread about; to sow or throw broadcast; to sprinkle; to diffuse (fragrance) 1450. **b.** *intr.* for *refl.* 1576. **c.** *trans.* Of a gun: To distribute (the shot). Chiefly *absol.* 1741. **d.** *Physics.* Of a surface, semi-opaque substance: To throw back (light) brokenly in all directions 1833. **6.** To sprinkle or strew *with* something 1590.

1. I leave the rest of all my goods to my first-born Edward, to be consum'd or scatterd (for I never hoped better) 1645. 2. Buckingham's Armie is dispers'd and scatter'd SHAKS. **b.** The fugitives scattered for miles 1909. 4. Many tributes to his memory are scattered over his friend's other works LOCKHART. 5. He..scatereth yᵉ horefrost like ashes COVERDALE *Ps.* cxlvii. 16. **b.** The small shot..scattered among them DE FOE. **c.** The gun scatters well 1823. 6. The ground was scattered with elephant's teeth DE FOE. Hence **Sca·tteredly, Sca·tteringly** *advs.* **Sca·tterer.**

Sca·tter-brain. 1790. [f. prec. + BRAIN *sb.*] One who is incapable of serious connected thought; a thoughtless, giddy person. So **Sca·tter-brained** *a.*

Scattergood (skæ·təɹgud). 1577. [f. SCATTER *v.* + GOOD *sb.*] One who squanders goods or possessions; a spendthrift.

Scattering (skæ·təriŋ), *vbl. sb.* ME. [-ING[1].] **1.** The action of SCATTER *v.*; an instance of this. late ME. **2.** *concr.* That which is scattered ME. **b.** A sparse number or amount; a small proportion interspersed 1628.

Scatterling (skæ·təɹliŋ). Now *arch.* 1590. [f. SCATTER *v.* + -LING[1].] A wandering or vagabond person; a vagrant.

Neighbour Scots, and forrein Scatterlings SPENSER.

Scattery (skæ·təri), *a.* 1816. [f. SCATTER *v.* + -Y[1].] Scattered; sparse; straggling.

Scaturient (skătiūᵊ·riĕnt), *a.* 1684. [ad. L. *scaturientem*, *scaturire*, f. *scatere* to flow out.] That flows out or gushes forth.

Scaup (skǭp). 1797. Short for next.

Scaup-duck (skǭ·pˌdɒk). 1672. [perh. f. *scaup* SCALP *sb.*[2]] A duck of the genus *Fuligula*, esp. *F. marila*, inhabiting the northern seas.

Scaur (skǭɹ). Var. (chiefly *Sc.*) of SCAR *sb.*[1]

Scavage (skæ·vėdʒ). 1474. [a. AF. *scawage*, *schawage* = North-Eastern OF. *escauwage*, f. *escauwer* to inspect, ad. Flem. *scauwen* = OE. *scéawian* SHOW *v.*] A toll formerly levied on merchant strangers by the mayors, sheriffs, or corporations of various towns, on goods offered for sale within their precincts. Now *Hist.* So †**Sca·vager** = SCAVENGER 1.

Scavenge (skæ·vėndʒ), *v.* 1644. [Back-formation from next.] **1.** *trans.* To clean *out* (dirt, etc.). **2.** To scrape dirt from (the streets); also, to cleanse (the surface of a river) 1851. **3.** *absol.* or *intr.* 1883. **4.** Of an internal-combustion engine: To expel exhaust gases, etc. from the cylinder 1894. Also as *sb.*

Scavenger (skæ·vėndʒəɹ), *sb.* 1503. [Altered f. SCAVAGER, with intrusive *n.*] **1.** An officer whose duty it was to take 'scavage', and, later, to keep the streets clean. Now *Hist.* **2.** A person whose employment is to clean streets, by scraping or sweeping together and removing dirt 1530. **b.** *transf.* One who or something which removes dirt or putrid matter. Applied to animals that feed on decaying matter, esp. the s. beetle. 1596. **c.** *fig.* One who collects filth; one who does 'dirty work'. Also, in favourable sense: One who labours for the removal of public evils. 1562. **3.** A child employed in a spinning-mill to collect loose cotton lying about the floor or machinery. Also, a roller used to collect the loose fibres or fluff; also called *s.-roll.* 1833.

Comb.: **s.-beetle,** a necrophagous beetle, esp. one of the family *Scaphidiidæ*; **-crab,** any crab which feeds on dead animal matter; **-vulture,** *Neophron percnopterus.* Hence **Sca·venger** *v. trans.* (*rare*) to remove dirt from, chiefly *fig.*; also, to make dirty with scavenging.

Scavenger's daughter. Also **Skevington's, Skeffington's daughter.** 1564. [From a joc. perversion of the name *Skevington.*] An instrument of torture (invented in the reign of Hen. VIII by Leonard Skevington, Lieutenant of the Tower), which (bringing the head to the knees) so compressed the body as to force the blood from the nose and ears.

Scavengery (skæ·vėndʒəri). 1656. [f. SCAVENGER *sb.* + -Y[3].] The municipal or state arrangements for cleaning and removing dirt, refuse, etc.; the action of collecting and removing dirt from the streets.

‖**Scazon** (skēⁱ·zǫn). *Pl.* **scazons,** also **scazontes** (skăzǫ·ntīz). 1651. [L., a. Gr. σκάζων, sb. use of pr. pple. of σκάζειν to limp, halt.] *Prosody.* = CHOLIAMB. Also *s. iambic.* Hence **Scazo·ntic** *a.* written in scazons; *sb.* = SCAZON.

Scelerate (se·lĕrĕt), *a.* and *sb.* 1513. [ad. L. *sceleratus*, *scelerare*, f. *sceler-*, *scelus* wickedness; see -ATE[2].] †**A.** *adj.* Atrociously wicked –1734. **B.** *sb.* An atrociously wicked person, a villain, wretch. *Obs.* exc. *arch.* 1715.

Scelidosaur (se·lidosǭɹ). 1861. [ad. mod. L. *scelidosaurus*, f. *scelido-* used for stem of (f. Gr. σκέλος leg) + Gr. σαύρα, σαῦρος lizard.] *Palæont.* A member of the genus *Scelidosaurus* of stegosaurian herbivorous dinosaurs.

‖**Scelidotherium** (se:lidoþīᵊ·riɒ̆m). 1840. [mod.L., f. *scelido-* (see prec.) + Gr. θηρίον wild animal.] *Palæont.* A genus of megatherioid edentate mammals.

‖**Scena** (ʃē·nă). 1819. [It., ad. L. *scena* SCENE.] **a.** A scene in an Italian opera; the words and music of the scene. **b.** A composition consisting largely of recitative of a dramatic and impassioned character, for one or more voices with accompaniment.

‖**Scenario** (ʃenā·rio). 1880. [It., f. *scena* SCENE.] **a.** A sketch of the plot of a play; giving particulars of the scenes, situations, etc. **b.** The detailed directions for a cinema film.

†**Sce·nary.** 1695. [ad. It. *scenario*; see prec. and -ARY[1] B. 2.] **1.** = prec. a. –1736. **2.** 'The representation of the place in which an action is performed' (J.) –1808. **3.** = SCENERY 3. –1808.

Scend, var. SEND *sb.* and *v.*[2]

Scene (sīn). 1540. [a. F. *scène*, ad. L. *scena*, *scæna* stage, scene, a. Gr. σκηνή tent or booth, stage, scene.] **I.** With ref. to the theatre. **1.** *Antiq.* The stage of a Greek or Roman theatre, including the platform on which the actors stood, and the structure which formed the background 1638. **2.** The stage or theatre as standing for either the dramatic art or the histrionic profession. Now *arch.* 1682. **3.** A stage performance; a play in representation. *Obs.* exc. in phr. 1592. **4.** The place in which the action of a play, or part of a play, is supposed to occur. Also, the setting of a dialogue, novel, etc 1592. **5.** A subdivision of an act of a play, or of a short play not divided into acts, marked by the entrance or departure of one or more actors (and often by a change of *local*). Hence, the action and dialogue comprised in any one of these subdivisions; a situation *between* certain actors. 1540. **6.** The painted hangings, slides, etc., set at the back and sides of the stage, and intended to give the illusion of a real view of the *local* in which the action of a play takes place, or to symbolize it; the view thus presented to the spectators. Also, any one of these painted hangings, slides, etc. 1540. **b.** *transf.* A curtain or veil; also, a decorative hanging on a wall 1638. **7.** *Behind the scenes*: amidst the actors and stage-machinery, where ordinary spectators are not admitted. Freq. *fig.* 1668.

2. Giddy with praise,..She quits the tragic s. CHURCHILL. 3. *The s. opens* or *is opened*, the action of a play (an act or scene) begins; S. opens, Muly Labas appears bound in Chains 1673. 4. Phr. *To lay the s.* (see LAY *v.* III. 4 b.); In faire Verona, where we lay our S. SHAKS. 5. Does not this poisoning s. The sacred right of Tragedy profane 1756. 6. Back fly the scenes, and enter foot and horse POPE. 7. *fig.* I, who have been behind the scenes, both of pleasure and business CHESTERF.

II. 1. The place where an action is carried on and people play their parts as in a drama 1594. **b.** The world in which man is an actor; the theatre of this life 1662. **2.** A view or picture presented to the eye (or to the mind) of a place, concourse, incident, series of actions or events, assemblage of objects, etc. 1653. **3.** An action, episode, complication of events, or situation, in real life 1679. **b.** An episode, situation, etc., forming a subject of narration or description

1630. **4.** An exhibition of excited or strong feeling between two or more persons; a stormy encounter or interview (cf. F. *faire une scène à quelqu'un*) 1761.

1. Phr. *To enter* or *appear on the s.*, *to quit the s.* *The s. of action*, the place where events are happening or business being done. **b.** This universal living s. of things is after all as little a logical world as it is a poetical J. H. NEWMAN. Phr. *To quit the s.*, to die. **2.** The smiling S. wide opens to the Sight POPE. **3.** You were not made for scenes of danger 1766. **b.** Scenes of Clerical Life GEO. ELIOT. **4.** The folly of making a s. 1831.

Comb.: **s.-painter**, one who paints scenes or scenery for the theatre; **-painting**, the art of painting scenes according to the rules of stage-perspective; **-shifter**, one who shifts and arranges the scenes during the performance of a play.

Scenery (sī·nĕri). 1748. [Alteration of SCENARY, as if f. SCENE + -ERY.] †**1.** Dramatic action; a moving exhibition of feeling –1808. **2.** The decoration of a theatre-stage, consisting of painted hangings, slides, etc., representing the scene of the action; theatre-scenes collectively 1770. **3.** The general appearance of a place and its natural features, regarded from the picturesque point of view; the aggregate of picturesque features in a landscape 1784. **4.** (With *a* and *pl.*) A landscape or view; a picturesque scene. Now *rare*. 1777.

3. A..passion for s. and natural beauty..has..gained an extraordinary power over people's minds 1871.

Scenic (sī·nik, se·nik), *a.* 1623. [a. F. *scénique*, ad. L. *scenicus*, *scænicus*, a. Gr. σκηνικός belonging to the stage, f. σκηνή SCENE.] **1.** Of or belonging to the stage, dramatic, theatrical. **b.** Represented on the stage 1747. **c.** Of or belonging to stage-scenery or stage effect 1868. **2.** *fig.* Dramatic or theatrical in style 1857. **3.** With ref. to painting or sculpture: Representing a 'scene' or incident in which several persons are concerned 1848.

Scenic railway, a miniature railway running through artificial picturesque scenery, forming an attraction at fairs. So **Sce·nical** *a.* scenic; theatrical; †fictitious, imaginary. late ME. **Sce·nically** *adv.* in a s. or scenical manner.

Scenograph (sī·nograf). 1842. [ad. Gr. σκηνογράφος, f. σκηνή SCENE + γράφειν to write, draw, paint.] = next.

Scenographer (sīnǫ·grăfəɹ). 1598. [f. as prec. + -ER [1].] A scene-painter; one who draws buildings, etc. in perspective.

Scenography (sīnǫ·grăfi). 1645. [a. F. *scénographie*, or ad. L. *scenographia*, a. Gr. σκηνογραφία, f. σκηνή SCENE; see -GRAPHY.] †**1.** The representation of a building or other object in perspective; a perspective elevation –1843. **2.** Scene-painting (in ancient Greece) 1738. So **Scenogra·phic, -al** *adjs.*; **-ally** *adv.*

Scent (sent), *sb.* [Late ME. *sent*, f. *sent* SCENT *v.* Orig. a term of hunting.] **1.** The faculty or sense of smell. Now only with ref. to animals (esp. dogs) which find their prey or recognize objects by this sense 1470. **2.** The odour of an animal or man as a means of pursuit by a hound; hence a track or trail as indicated by this odour. late ME. **3.** In wider sense: Distinctive odour. Now almost exclusively applied to agreeable odours, e.g. those of flowers. 1471. **4.** An odoriferous liquid prepared by distillation from flowers, etc.; a perfume 1750.

1. The perfect Hound, in S. and Speed Unrivall'd 1735. *fig.* A s. for heresy 1857. **2.** He [*sc.* a hound] ..twice to day pick'd out the dullest sent SHAKS. *fig.* Trim found he was upon a wrong s. STERNE. *transf.* To find s. (i.e. fragments of paper for scattering on the ground) for..Hare-and-Hounds HUGHES. *Cold s.*: see COLD *a.* II. 7. *Hot s.*: see HOT *a.* 7. *To lay*, *put* (hounds) *on* or *upon the s.*; hence fig. *to put* (a person) *on* or *off the s.*, also *on a false*, *wrong s.* *To lose*, *recover the s.*, lit. (of hounds) and fig.; also, *to lose the s.*, (of the game) to baffle the hounds by passing through water. *To carry a* (or *the*) *s.*, (of ground) to retain the scent of the game; also (of fox-hounds) to follow the scent. **3.** A spicy s. Of cinnamon and sandal blent LONGF. *fig.* Perhaps some s. of the coming danger reached him 1868.

Comb.: **s.-bag**, (*a*) a pouch, sac, or gland found in some animals, containing a secreted odoriferous substance; (*b*) a bag containing a strong-smelling substance, drawn over ground to make an artificial scent for hounds; (*c*) = SACHET 3; **-bottle**; **-gland**, a gland which secretes an odoriferous substance; **-organ** *Ent.* and *Zool.*, an organ that secretes scent, a scent-bag, scent-gland; **-spray**, an ornamental s.-bottle with apparatus for distributing the s. in a fine spray. Hence **Sce·ntful** *a.* full of s., fragrant.

Scent (sent), *v.* [Late ME. *sent*, a. F. *sentir*, to feel, perceive, spec. to smell:—L. *sentire* to feel, perceive.] **1.** *trans.* To find or track (game, prey, etc.) by the smell; also, *to s. out*. In later use: To become aware of by the sense of smell. **b.** *fig.* To perceive as if by smell; to find out instinctively; to detect 1553. **2.** *intr.* Of a hound or other animal: †**a.** To perceive the smell *of* (the quarry). **b.** To hunt by the sense of smell; also, to sniff the air for a scent. late ME. **3.** To exhale an odour; to smell. Now *rare* or *Obs.* late ME. **4.** *trans.* To impregnate with an odour; to perfume 1697.

1. But soft, me thinkes I sent the Mornings Ayre SHAKS. Like vultures scenting their prey afar 1878. **b.** Perhaps not senting the Design of the Clowns 1658. **2. b.** So sented the grim Feature, and upturn'd His Nostril wide into the mirky Air MILT. **3.** *fig.* The very air scents of knavery 1831. **4.** With Smoak of burning Cedar s. thy Walls DRYDEN.

Scented (se·ntĕd), *ppl. a.* 1579. [f. SCENT *v.* and *sb.*] †**1.** With prefixed adv.: Endowed with the power of tracking by sense of smell –1656. **2.** Impregnated with perfume 1740. **3.** That has a scent; exhaling a scent 1666.

2. *S. caper*: see CAPER *sb.*[1] 3. **3.** The scentless and the s. rose COWPER.

Scentless (se·ntlĕs), *a.* 1605. [f. SCENT *sb.* + -LESS.] †**1.** Without the faculty of smell. **2.** Without odour or perfume 1618.

Scepsis (ske·psis). 1876. [a. Gr. σκέψις inquiry, doubt, f. σκέπτεσθαι; see SCEPTIC.] Sceptical attitude in philosophy.

Sceptic, *U.S.* **skeptic** (ske·ptik), *a.* and *sb.* 1575. [ad. F. *sceptique*, or late L. *scepticus*, lit. inquiring, reflective, distinctive epithet of the disciples of Pyrrho; f. Gr. σκεπ- in σκέπτεσθαι to look out, consider, ablaut-var. of σκοπ- in σκοπεῖν, σκοπός; see SCOPE *sb.* The spelling with *sk-* is rare in Eng., usual in U.S. The pron. with (sk) is due to reversion to Gr.] **A.** *adj.* = SCEPTICAL *a.* Now *rare* exc. as the epithet of a school of philosophers. **B.** *sb.* **1.** *Philos.* One who, like Pyrrho and his followers, doubts the possibility of real knowledge of any kind; one who holds that there are no adequate grounds for certainty as to the truth of any proposition whatever. Also, less correctly, applied to those who deny the competence of reason outside the limits of experience. 1587. **2.** One who doubts the validity of what claims to be knowledge in some particular department of inquiry (e.g. metaphysics, theology, natural science, etc.); *pop.*, one who maintains a doubting attitude with reference to some particular question or statement. Also, a person of sceptical temper. 1615. **3.** *spec.* One who doubts, without absolutely denying, the truth of the Christian religion or important parts of it; often *loosely*, an unbeliever in Christianity 1638. **4.** occas., A seeker after truth; an inquirer who has not yet arrived at definite convictions 1618.

1. Hee is a Scepticke, and dare hardly giue credit to his senses 1608. **2.** The Sceptick will not take Pains to search Things to the Bottom, but when he sees Difficulties on both Sides resolves to believe neither of them WATTS. **3.** In listening to the arguments of a s. you are breathing a poisonous atmosphere 1863. **4.** The Sceptick doth neither affirm, neither denie any Position: but doubteth of it RALEIGH.

Sceptical, *U.S.* **skeptical** (ske·ptikăl), *a.* 1639. [f. prec. + -AL 1.] **a.** Of persons: Inclined to or imbued with scepticism; in mod. use often, dubious or incredulous. **b.** Of doctrines, opinions, etc.: Characteristic of a sceptic; of the nature of scepticism. Hence **Sce·ptically**, *U.S.* **ske·ptically** *adv.*

Scepticism, *U.S.* **skepticism** (ske·ptisiz m). 1646. [ad. mod.L. *scepticismus*, f. late L. *scepticus*; see SCEPTIC and -ISM.] **1.** *Philos.* The doctrine of the Sceptics; the opinion that real knowledge of any kind is unattainable 1661. **2.** Sceptical attitude in relation to some particular branch of science; doubt as to the truth of some assertion or supposed fact. Also, sceptical temper in general. 1646. **3.** Doubt of the Christian religion, unbelief 1800.

1. Consistent rationalism always in the end collapses into s. 1908. **2.** A state of s. and suspense may amuse a few inquisitive minds GIBBON.

Scepticize (ske·ptisəiz), *v.* 1698. [f. SCEPTIC + -IZE 3.] *intr.* To play the sceptic; to take up the position of a philosophical doubter.

He hath a great mind to S., and to maintain Paradoxes 1698.

Sceptre (se·ptəɹ), *sb.* [ME. *ceptre*, *septre*, *sceptre*, a. OF. *ceptre*, *sceptre* (mod.F. *sceptre*), ad. L. *sceptrum*, a. Gr. σκῆπτρον, f. root of σκήπτεσθαι to prop oneself.] **1.** An ornamental rod or wand (often of gold and jewelled) borne in the hand as a symbol of regal or imperial authority. **b.** *Her.* A representation of this 1610. **2.** *fig.* Taken as the power or authority symbolized by a sceptre; hence, royal or imperial dignity, sovereignty, supremacy. late ME. †**3.** A constellation in the southern hemisphere –1850.

1. His Scepter shewes the force of temporall power, The attribute to awe and Maiestie SHAKS. **2.** The septre fro Juda shal not be takun awey WYCLIF *Gen.* xlix. 10. Hence **Sce·ptral** *a.* pertaining to, serving as. a s. **Sce·ptreless** *a.* obeying no s.; wielding no s.

Sceptre (se·ptəɹ), *v.* late ME. [f. prec.] **1.** *trans.* To furnish with a sceptre. **2.** To touch (with a sceptre) as a sign of royal assent or ratification (bills passed by Parliament) 1851.

1. Crown'd with sharp Thorns, and scepter'd with a Reed 1711.

Sch. In mod. Eng. (sk) is the normal pronunciation of *sch* in words of classical derivation, where it represents L. *sch*, Gr. σχ. (The only exceptions are *schist*, etc. *schedule*, and *schism*, etc.) *Sch* is also pronounced (sk) in Italian words, e.g. *scherzo*. The only words in which *sch* represents (s) are *schism* and its derivatives, the pronunciation of the ME. form *cisme* (from OF. *cisme*) having survived although the spelling has been refashioned. The pronunciation of *sch* as (stʃ) occurs only medially in *escheat*, *eschew*, *discharge*, etc. where the *s* and the *ch* belong to different syllables. In a few alien words from German (e.g. *schnapps*), in *schist*, and in *schedule* *sch* has the value (ʃ).

‖**Schadenfreude** (ʃā·dənfroidə). 1922. [G., lit. = shame-joy.] Malicious joy in the misfortunes of others.

‖**Schanse, schanze, schantze** (skans). *S. Afr.* 1880. [Du. *schans* (Cape Du. *skans*) = G. *schanze*.] A heap or breastwork of stones used as a protection against rifle fire.

Schappe (ʃæp). 1885. [G., = 'silk-waste'.] A strong dull-surfaced silk fabric.

Schedule (ʃe·diūl, *U.S.* ske·diul), *sb.* [Late ME. *cedule*, *sedule*, a. OF. *cedule*, ad. late L. *scedula* (in med. and mod.L. also *schedula*), dim. of L. *sceda* (in med.L. also *scheda*).] †**1.** A slip or scroll of parchment or paper containing writing; a ticket, label, placard; a short note –1650. **2.** †**a.** Orig., an explanatory or supplementary paper or slip of parchment accompanying or appended to a document; in 16–17th c. occas. used for a codicil to a will. **b.** Hence, an appendix to an Act of Parliament or a legal instrument containing a statement of details. **c.** In wider sense, any tabular or classified statement, as, e.g. an insolvent's statement of assets and liabilities, a return of particulars liable to income-tax, etc. Occas. a blank form to be filled up by the insertion of particulars under the several headings. late ME. **3.** A time-table. Chiefly *U.S.* 1873.

3. *transf.* Halting was not in [his] s. for that afternoon 1873. *On s.* (*time*), to schedule time (orig. *U.S.*).

Schedule (ʃe·diūl, *U.S.* ske·diul), *v.* 1862. [f. prec.] **1.** *trans.* To enter in a schedule or list. In railway use: To enter (a train) in the time-table. Often in *ppl. a.* **2.** To affix as a schedule (*to* an Act of Parliament) 1885.

1. The train got in at the scheduled time (*mod.*).

Scheelite (ʃī·ləit). 1837. [f. name of K. W. *Scheele*, the discoverer of tungstic acid + -ITE [1] 2 b.] *Min.* Tungstate of calcium, found in brilliant crystals of various colours.

‖**Schelling** (ske·liŋ, Du. sχe·liŋ). *Obs.* exc. *Hist.* 1535. [Du. Cf. SKILLING [2].] A silver coin formerly current in the Low Countries, of the value of 6 stivers or from 5*d.* to 7½*d.* sterling.

‖**Schelm** (ʃelm). *arch.* 1584. [G.] A rascal.

Schema (skī·mă). *Pl.* **schemata** (skī·mătă). 1839. [a. Gr. σχῆμα SCHEME *sb.*[1]] *Philos.* In Kant: Any one of certain forms or rules of the 'productive imagination' through which the understanding is able to apply its 'categories' to the manifold of sense-perception in the process of realizing knowledge or experience.

Schematic (skimæ·tik), *a.* 1701. [ad. mod.L. *schematicus*, f. *schemat-*, SCHEMA, SCHEME *sb.*[1]] **1.** Pertaining to a scheme or schema; †corresponding (to something else) according to a scheme. **2.** Pertaining to logical 'figure' 1838. **3.** Suggested or modified by a preconceived system 1894. **4.** *Fine Art.* Following a conventional type 1868.

4. Their art symbolised these in grand s. forms 1868.

Schematism (skī·mătiz'm). 1617. [ad. mod.L. *schematismus*, a. Gr. σχηματισμός, f. σχηματίζειν SCHEMATIZE *v.*] †**1.** The use of a 'scheme' or rhetorical figure. COLLINS. **2.** Mode of arrangement of parts or particles; inner structure. Now *rare.* 1660. **3.** A schematic arrangement; a set form for classification or exposition. Also, the schematic method of presentation. 1701. **4.** *Philos.* 'Schematizing' action (of the intellect). In Kant: The application of the categories, by means of schemata, to the data of sense-perception. 1839.

Schematist (skī·mătist). 1693. [f. Gr. σχηματ-, σχῆμα + -IST.] **1.** The framer of a 'scheme' or system of doctrine. †**2.** One who expounds a scheme; a projector -1739.

Schematize (skī·mătəiz), *v.* 1828. [ad. Gr. σχηματίζειν, f. σχηματ-, σχῆμα.] **1.** *trans.* To reduce to a scheme or formula. **2.** *Kantian Philos.* To apply the categories, by means of schemata, to the data of sense-perception 1839.

Scheme (skīm), *sb.*[1] 1550. [a. med.L. *schema*, a. Gr. σχῆμα form, figure, f. root σχ-, connected w. Gr. ἔχειν to have, be in such or such a condition.] †**1.** *Rhet.* = FIGURE *sb.* V. 1. -1684. †**2.** A diagram showing the relative positions, either real or apparent, of the heavenly bodies; *esp.* in *Astrol.*, a horoscope -1824. †**3.** In wider sense: A diagram; a figure drawn to illustrate a mathematical proposition, etc.; a map or plan of a town; an architect's designs for a building; and the like -1826. **4.** An analytical or tabular statement. **a.** An epitome exhibiting the structure of a book, passage, argument, etc.; also, an outline draft of a projected literary work 1647. **b.** A table; a prearranged system of classification 1677. **5. a.** A plan, design; a programme of action 1647. **b.** Hence, A plan of action devised in order to attain some end; a project, enterprise. Often with unfavourable notion, a self-seeking or an underhand project, a plot, or a visionary or foolish project. 1718. **c.** An escapade of a humorous character, a 'spree'. Now *dial.* 1758. **6.** †**a.** A theory -1725. **b.** A body of related doctrines, a speculative system 1685. **7.** A system of correlated things, institutions, arrangements, etc.; the manner in which such a system is organized 1736. **b.** Painting. *S. of colour*: the system of selection and arrangement of colours characteristic of a particular painter or school, or adopted in a particular picture. Also *c. scheme*, often used gen. for any arrangement of colours. 1884. †**8.** Form, aspect, appearance -1743.

2. To make a small velvet bag, for the scheme of nativity SCOTT. 3. A s. of the city of Lepanto 1682. 4. a. I intend this but for a S. of a larger Design 1695. b. In Chapter ix. is given his S. of Sciences 1868. 5. a. That is the whole s. and intention of all marriage-articles GAY. b. But this deep-laid s. was in a moment disconcerted 1759. The great irrigation schemes of the North-West Provinces 1888. Phr. *To lay a s.* 6. b. His comprehensive s. of theology 1858. 7. Ah Love! could thou and I with Fate conspire To grasp this sorry S. of Things entire, Would not we shatter it to bits FITZGERALD. 8. For they had the s. of truth not the substance 1677.

Scheme (skīm), *sb.*[2] 1690 (**skeen**). [Origin obsc.] In full **s.-arch**: The arch of larger radius in the middle of a three-centre arch or elliptical arch. **b.** quasi-*adj.* Constructed with a 'scheme' 1703.

Scheme (skīm), *v.* 1716. [f. SCHEME *sb.*[1]] **1.** *trans.* To devise as a scheme; to lay schemes for; to effect by contrivance or intrigue 1767. **b.** *intr.* To use ingenuity, resort to contrivance; to devise plans, esp. underhand or with sinister motive 1842. **2.** *trans.* To reduce to a scheme or formula (*rare*) 1716.

1. To..s. a mode of escape 1868. Hence **Sche·mer**, one who devises or enters into schemes; one who plots. **Sche·mingly** *adv.*

Schemist (skī·mist). 1724. [f. SCHEME *sb.*[1] + -IST.] †**1.** An intriguing plotter -1825. **2.** One who forms a scheme; a projector 1753.

‖**Scherm** (skerm). *S. Afr.* 1861. [Du., = G. *schirm* screen.] A screen or barrier of brushwood or the like which serves as a protection for troops, as an ambuscade from which to shoot game, or to prevent cattle from straying.

‖**Scherzando** (skertsa·ndo), *adv.* 1811. [It., f. *scherzare* to play, f. *scherzo.*] *Mus.* A direction: Playfully, sportively. Also *attrib.* (quasi-*adj.*), and *ellipt.* as *sb.*, a s. movement.

‖**Scherzo** (ske·rtso). 1862. [It., lit. sport, jest.] *Mus.* A lively movement, occupying the second or third place in a symphony or sonata.

‖**Schiedam** (skī·dæm, skidæ·m). 1821. A variety of gin, so called from the town in Holland where it is distilled.

‖**Schiller** (ʃi·ləɹ). 1804. [G., play of colours, etc.] *Min.* **1.** In terms adapted from G., denoting minerals or rocks having a shining surface, as *s. asbestos, rock, -stone.* **2.** A peculiar lustre characteristic of certain minerals, as hypersthene. Also *attrib.* 1835.

Schillerize (ʃi·lərəiz), *v.* 1885. [f. prec. + -IZE.] *trans.* To subject (a crystal) to schillerization. Hence **Schi:lleriza·tion**, a process of change in crystals, giving rise to a 'schiller' appearing when the crystal is turned in various directions.

Schiller spar (ʃi·ləɹ,spāɹ). 1796. [ad. G. *schillerspath*; see SCHILLER 1 and SPAR *sb.*] *Min.* = BASTITE.

‖**Schilling** (ʃi·liŋ). 1693. [G.; see SHILLING.] A silver coin and money of account formerly in use in North Germany. **b.** A modern Austrian coin (par about 7*d.*), 100 groschen.

‖**Schindylesis** (skindilī·sis). 1830. [mod. L., a. Gr. σχινδύλησις.] *Anat.* An articulation formed by the reception of a thin plate of one bone into a fissure or groove in another.

‖**Schipperke** (ʃi·pəɹkĭ, ski·p-, Du. ‖sχi·pərkə). 1887. [Du. dial., lit. 'little boatman'.] A kind of lapdog.

Schism (siz'm). [Late ME. *scisme*, a. OF. ad. eccl. L. *schisma*, a. Gr. σχίσμα rent, cleft, f. σχιδ-, σχίζειν to split, rend. Refashioned in 16th c. after Gr.] **1.** In the versions of the N.T.: A (metaphorical) rent or cleft. **2.** *Eccl.* A breach of the unity of the visible Church; the division of the Church, or of some portion of it, into separate and mutually hostile organizations; the condition of being so divided, or an instance of this late ME. **b.** *spec.* A state of divided spiritual allegiance in Western Christendom caused by a disputed election to the Papacy; esp. *The Great (Western) S.* (1378-1417) 1460. **c.** The offence of causing or promoting divisions in the Church. late ME. **d.** A sect or body formed by division within the Church; a schismatic sect 1511. **3.** *gen.* In early use, a state of disunion, dissension, or mutual hostility. Now, a division into mutually opposing parties of a body of persons that have previously acted in concert. Also, in recent use, a discord, breach (between persons or things). late ME.

1. 1 *Cor.* xii. 25. 2. c. From all false doctrine, heresy, and s. *Bk. Com. Prayer, Litany.* 3. The eternal and inevitable s. between the Romanticists and the Classicists 1839.

Comb.: **S. Act,** the statute 13 Anne c. 7 (1714; repealed in 1719 by 5 Geo. I, c. 4), requiring all teachers to conform to the Established Church.

‖**Schisma** (ski·zmă). *Pl.* **schismata.** 1653. [late L. *schisma* 'dimidium commatis', spec. use of Gr. σχίσμα division.] *Acoustics.* †**a.** In ancient Gr. use, the half of a comma. **b.** The difference between a diaschisma and a syntonic comma, represented by the ratio 32.805 : 32.768.

Schismatic (sizmæ·tik), *a.* and *sb.* [Late ME. *cysmatyke*, *scismatik*, etc., a. OF. *cis-*, *scismatique*, ad. eccl. L. *schismaticus*, a. eccl. Gr. σχισματικός, f. σχισματ-, σχίσμα SCHISM.] **A.** *adj.* Of or pertaining to schism or schismatics; of the nature of schism; guilty of the offence of schism 1440.

Though the s. Swede, Gustavus, is Gone home BYRON.

B. *sb.* One who promotes or countenances schism in the Church; one who is guilty of the sin of schism; a member or adherent of a schismatical body. late ME. **b.** *spec.* In R.C. use, one of those Roman Catholics who in the reign of Elizabeth conformed by occasionally attending the services of the Church of England, in order to avoid the penalties denounced against recusants 1584. So **Schisma·tical** *a.*, **-ly** *adv.*, **-ness.**

Schismatize (si·zmătəiz), *v.* 1601. [a. OF. *scismatiser*, f. Gr. σχισματ-, σχίσμα SCHISM + -IZE 1.] **1.** *intr.* To behave as a schismatic; to favour or advocate schismatic principles; to lead or belong to a schismatic body. **2.** *trans.* **a.** To lead into schism. **b.** To divide into parties. *rare.* 1645.

Schist[1] (ʃist). 1793. [a. F. *schiste*, a. L. *schistos* fissile, a. Gr. σχιστός, f. σχιδ-, σχίζειν to split; see SCHISM.] *Geol.* A crystalline rock whose component minerals are arranged in a more or less parallel manner.

Schist[2] (skist). *rare.* 1875. [ad. Gr. σχιστόν, neut. of σχιστός; see prec.] *Acoustics.* An interval equal to one-eighth of a schisma. Hence **Schistic** (ski·stik) *a.*, based on an allowance for the difference of a 'schist'.

Schistose (ʃi·stōus), *a.* 1794. [f. SCHIST[1] + -OSE[1].] *Geol.* Laminated; having a formation resembling a schist. Hence **Schisto·sity** *Geol.*, the direction or line of cleavage in a rock of crystalline formation.

Schistous (ʃi·stəs), *a.* 1802. [f. SCHIST[1] + -OUS.] **1.** *Geol.* = prec. 1. **2.** Formed of schist 1829.

Schizanthus (skəizæ·nþŏs, ski-). 1829. [mod.L., f. SCHIZO- + Gr. ἄνθος flower.] Any plant of the solanaceous genus so-called, having finely divided leaves and showy flowers.

Schizo- (skəi·zo, skəizǫ·), comb. form irreg. repr. Gr. σχίζειν to split.

Schi·zocarp [Gr. καρπός fruit] *Bot.*, a term applied to dry fruits which break up into two or more one-seeded mericarps without dehiscing. **Schi·zocœle** (-sīl) [Gr. κοῖλον hollow] *Zool.*, a perivisceral cavity formed by a splitting of the mesoblast. ‖**Schizoge·nesis** *Biol.*, fissiparous generation. **Schizognathism** (-ǫ·gnăþiz'm) [Gr. γνάθος jaw] *Ornith.*, a condition in which the bony palate is cleft from the posterior nares to the end of the beak; hence **Schizo·gnathous** *a.* having a cleft palate. **Schizogony** (-ǫ·gŏnī) [Gr. -γονία reproduction] *Zool.*, = *schizogenesis*; hence **Schizogo·nic** *a.*, pertaining to schizogony; spec. *s. cycle*, the second of the two stages in the life-history of a Coccidian. ‖**Schizomycetes** (-məisī·tīz) *sb. pl.* [MYCETES], a group of microscopic, rod-like, unicellular organisms, multiplying by fission, variously known as *Bacteria*, *Microbes*, etc.; *rarely* in sing. **schizomycete.** **Schi·zophyte** (-fəit) (-PHYTE) *Biol.*, a microscopic organism multiplying by fission, akin to *Schizomycetes.* **Schi·zopod** (-pǫd) *Zool.*, a member of the ‖**Schizo·poda** *sb. pl.* [Gr. ποδ- foot], a sub-order of crustaceans, named from the apparent splitting of the thoracic limbs produced by the great development of the exopodites; hence **Schizo·podous** *a.* **Schizorhi·nal** *a.* [Gr. ῥίν-, ῥίς nose] *Ornith.* having each nasal bone deeply cleft or forked.

‖**Schloss** (ʃlǫs). 1838. [G.] A (German) castle.

‖**Schmelz** (ʃmelts), **Schmelze** (ʃme·ltsə). 1851. Also **schmelz glass.** [G. *schmelz(glas)*, f. *schmelz* enamel, fusion of colours.] Applied to various kinds of Bohemian glass prepared to receive colour.

‖**Schnapps** (ʃnæps). 1818. [G.] An ardent spirit resembling Hollands gin.

Schnebelite (ʃnē·bĕləit). 1893. [f. the name *Schnebelin* + -ITE[1] 4.] An explosive principally composed of specially treated chlorate of potash, invented by the brothers Schnebelin.

Schneiderian (ʃnəidī°·riăn), *a.* 1803. [f. name of C. V. *Schneider* of Würtemberg (1610-80).] *S. membrane*, the mucous membrane of the nose.

‖**Schnorrer** (ʃnǫ·rəɹ). *Jewish.* 1892. [Yiddish var. of G. *schnurrer*, f. *schnurren* (slang) to go begging.] A Jewish beggar.

Scholar (skǫ·lăɹ). [OE. *scolere*, *scoliere*, ad. late L. *scholaris* (f. *schola* SCHOOL). In ME. a. AF. *escoler*, OF. *escolier*, of the same origin.] **1.** One who is taught in a school; now *esp.* a boy or girl attending an elementary school. **b.** A pupil (*of* a particular master). Now *arch.* or *rhet.* OE. **c.** *transf.* One who acknowledges another as his master; a disciple 1577. **d.** With qualifying adj.: One who is quick (slow, etc.) at learning 1605. **2.** One who studies in the 'schools' at a university; a member of a university, esp. a junior or undergraduate member. Now *Hist.* and in official use. ME. **3.** A learned or erudite person; esp. one who is learned in the classical languages and their literature. late ME. **b.** In illiterate use, one whom the speaker regards as exceptionally learned. Often merely, one who is able to read and write. 1644. **4.** A student who receives emoluments, during a fixed period, from the funds of a school, college, or university, towards defraying the cost of his education or studies, and as a reward of merit 1511.

1. I am no breeching scholler in the schooles SHAKS. **c.** The Romans confessed themselves the scholars of the Greeks JOHNSON. 3. As becommed a Gentleman and a Scholer 1621. **b.** Nay, faith, sir, I am not so good a schollard to say much 1667.

Scholarch (skǭ·lɑɹk). 1863. [ad. Gr. σχολάρχης, f. σχολή school + -αρχης ruler.] *Hist.* The head of a school: *spec.* **a.** The head of an Athenian school of philosophy. **b.** In some Continental countries, an official formerly charged with the inspection of schools.

Scho·larism. Now *rare.* 1588. [f. SCHOLAR + -ISM 1 b.] The learning of the 'schools'; scholarship. Occas. used disparagingly.

†Schola·rity. *rare.* 1599. [ad. med.L. *scholaritatem*, f. *scholaris* SCHOLAR; see -ITY.] The status of a scholar –1895.

Scho·larlike, *a.* and *adv.* 1551. [-LIKE.] **A.** *adj.* †1. Pertaining to scholars or 'the schools'; scholastic –1592. **2.** Resembling or befitting a learned man; scholarly 1589. †**B.** *adv.* Like a scholar or learned man; in a manner befitting a scholar –1627.

A. 2. Truewit was a S. kind of man DRYDEN.

Scholarly (skǫ·lǎɹli), *a.* 1638. [f. SCHOLAR + -LY[1].] Pertaining to, or characterizing, a scholar; befitting, or natural to, a scholar; learned, erudite.

A slight s. stoop R. BRIDGES.

Scholarly (skǫ·lǎɹli), *adv. rare.* 1598. [f. SCHOLAR + -LY[2].] As befits a scholar.

Speake schollerly, and wisely SHAKS.

Scholarship (skǫ·lǎɹʃip). 1535. [-SHIP.] **1.** The attainments of a scholar; learning, erudition; esp. proficiency in the Greek and Latin languages and their literature. Also, the collective attainments of scholars; the sphere of polite learning. 1589. **b.** Applied, by unlearned speakers, etc., to more modest educational attainments 1620. **2.** The status or emoluments of a scholar (see SCHOLAR 4) at a school, college, or university 1535.

1. **b.** Then for my schollership a gentleman, Both reade and write, and cast a count I can 1620. 2. I'd sooner win two School-house matches running than get the Balliol scholarship any day HUGHES.

Scholastic (skǒlæ·stik), *a.* and *sb.* 1596. [ad. L. *scholasticus*, a. Gr. σχολαστικός, f. σχολάζειν to devote one's leisure (to learning), orig. to be at leisure, f. σχολή leisure; see SCHOOL *sb.*[1]] **A.** *adj.* †1. Of persons: Having the characteristics of the scholar or student. MILT. **2.** Of or pertaining to the teaching or methods of the Schoolmen 1596. **3.** Pertaining to schools or school education 1647. **4.** Following the methods of the 'schools'; befitting the school; in bad sense, 'pedantic, needlessly subtle' (J.) 1779.

2. The absurdities of s. philosophy GOLDSM. 3. It is too common for those who have been bred to the scholastick profession..to disregard every other qualification JOHNSON.

B. *sb.* **1.** A Schoolman or a disciple of the Schoolmen 1644. †**2.** A scholar, man of learning; *occas.* a mere scholar, as opp. to a man of the world –1748. **3.** *R. C. Ch.* A member of the third grade in the organization of the Society of Jesus 1853.

1. The shallow commenting of Scholasticks MILT. So †**Scholastical** *a.* 1531–1793; **-ly** *adv.* 1559.

Scholasticism (skǒlæ·stisiz'm). 1756. [f. prec. + -ISM.] **1.** The doctrines of the Schoolmen; the predominant theological and philosophical teaching of the period A.D. 1000–1500, based upon the authority of the Christian Fathers and of Aristotle and his commentators 1756. **2.** Servile adherence to the methods and teaching of the schools; narrow or unenlightened insistence on traditional doctrines and forms of exposition 1861.

Scholiast (skǭ·liæst). 1583. [ad. late L. *scholiasta*, a. late Gr. σχολιαστής, f. σχολιάζειν, f. σχόλιον SCHOLIUM.] One who writes explanatory notes upon an author; esp. an ancient commentator upon a classical writer. Hence **Scholia·stic** *a.* of or pertaining to a s.

‖**Scholion** (skǭ·liǫn). Now *rare.* 1579. [Gr.; see next.] = next 1.

A..Glosse, or s., for thexposition of old wordes 1579.

‖**Scholium** (skǭ·liǒm). *Pl.* **scholia** (skǭ·liǎ). 1535. [med.L., ad. Gr. σχόλιον, f. σχολή SCHOOL *sb.*[1]] An explanatory note or comment; *spec.* an ancient exegetical note or comment upon a passage in a Greek or Latin author. **b.** In certain mathematical works: A note added by the author illustrating or further developing some point treated in the text 1704. So †**Scho·ly** *sb.* scholium –1697; *v. trans.* to write scholia upon; *intr.* to comment –1641.

School (skūl), *sb.*[1] [OE. *scól*, a. L. *schola* school, a. Gr. σχολή, orig. leisure.] **I. 1.** An establishment in which boys or girls, or both, receive instruction. **b.** Used, without article, to mean: Instruction in, attendance at, a school OE. **c.** Used, without article, for: A session of school; the set time of attendance at school 1598. **d.** Those who are present in, or are attending, a school ME. **e.** Applied (as in *upper, lower s.*) to a division of a large school, comprising several forms or classes. Also, in Jesuit schools, a form or class. 1629. **f.** The building in which a school is carried on. At Rugby, a school-house; also, the large class-room of a school-house. 1843. **g. High School.** A designation applied to certain classes of schools for secondary education in the British Islands and the U.S. 1531. **2.** The place in which an ancient Greek or Roman philosopher taught his hearers. late ME. **3.** *gen.* An institution in which instruction of any kind is given (whether to children or adults). In recent use, after French example, employed as the official title of various institutions for superior technical or scientific instruction, e.g. *The S. of Mines, The S. of Economics*, etc. 1440. **b.** *spec.* = *riding-s.* 1850. **4.** *fig.* A place, environment, etc., where one gains instruction in virtue, accomplishments, or the like; a person or thing regarded as a source of instruction or training OE. **5.** The body of persons that are or have been taught by a particular master (in philosophy, science, art, etc.); hence, a body or succession of persons who are disciples of the same master, or who are united by a general similarity of principles and methods 1612; also, a type or brand of doctrine or practice 1892. **b.** *fig.* A set of persons who agree in certain opinions, etc. 1798.

1. BOARD-, CHARITY-, GRAMMAR-, INFANT-, PUBLIC, SUNDAY-SCHOOL: see those words; also *Free school* (FREE *a.* IV. 7). **b.** Phr. *To be at s., to go to s., to put, send to s.*; She was a vixen when she went to schoole SHAKS. *To go to s. (to)*, fig., to submit to be taught (by). *To put to s.*, fig., to subject to teaching; often, to presume to correct (one's superior). *To keep (a) s.*, to be the master or mistress of a s. *To tell tales out of s.*, said *lit.* of children (now *rare* or *obs.*); hence *fig.* to betray damaging secrets. **c.** How now Sir Hugh, no Schoole to day? SHAKS. Keeping me in after s. to study 1893. 3. *Dancing, music, riding s. fig.* The S. for Scandal SHERIDAN (*title*). 4. Empires, and Monarchs, and thir radiant Courts, Best s. of best experience MILT. 5. The Roman, the Florentine, the Bolognese schools..These are the three great schools of the world in the epick stile. SIR J. REYNOLDS. **b.** *Of the old s.*, old-fashioned.

II. Senses of mediæval academic origin. **1.** An organized body of teachers and scholars in one of the higher branches of study cultivated in the Middle Ages; *esp.* a faculty of a university. Now *Hist.* OE. **b.** *collect. pl.* (In later use always *the schools.*) The faculties composing a university; universities in general; the sphere or domain of academic discussion or traditional academic doctrines and methods. late ME. **2.** *The S., the Schools*: the Schoolmen, the scholastic philosophers and theologians collectively. Now *rare* or *Obs.* 1614. **3. a.** *sing.* The building or room set apart for the lectures or exercises of a particular 'school' (in a university). **b.** *pl.* A building belonging to a university, containing rooms orig. for lectures in the several faculties, later for the disputations and exercises for degrees, etc. Hence, in mod. Oxford use: The building in which most of the university examinations are held. 1590. **4.** In mod. Oxford use. **a.** *pl.* The periodical examinations for the degree of B.A. 1828. **b.** Each of the several courses of study, in any of which an 'honours' degree in Arts may be taken: corresponding to the Cambridge 'Tripos' 1873.

1. Siche doutes we shulden sende to þe scole of Oxenforde WYCLIF. **b.** This whole mystery of Genera and Species, which make such a noise in the Schools LOCKE. 3. **b.** There is no more characteristic spot in Oxford than the quadrangle of the schools HUGHES.

†**III.** A particular method or discipline taught –1529.

Frenssh she spak ful faire and fetisly, After the scole of Stratford atte Bowe CHAUCER.

IV. Repr. L. *schola*, Gr. σχολή, in late senses. †1. A public building, gallery, or the like– 1601. **2.** *Hist.* One of the cohorts or companies into which the Imperial guard was divided 1776.

Comb.: **s.-book,** a book of instruction used at s.; **-craft** (*arch.*), knowledge taught in schools; **-dame,** an old woman who keeps a small s. for young children; **-day,** (*a*) *pl.* the days or period (of one's life) in which one is at s.; (*b*) a day on which there is ordinary instruction in a day-s.; **-divine** = SCHOOLMAN 1; **-divinity,** the religious principles and doctrines taught in the mediæval 'Schools'; **-doctor,** †(*a*) = SCHOOLMAN 1; (*b*) the medical attendant of a s.; **-inspector** (cf. INSPECTOR 1); **-learning,** †(*a*) the learning of 'the schools'; (*b*) education at s.; **-ma'am, -marm,** a schoolmistress; **-mate,** a companion at s.; **-ship,** a ship used for training boys in practical seamanship; **-time,** (*a*) the time at which s. commences, or during which s. continues; (*b*) that period of life which is passed at s. Hence **Schoo·lery** (*rare*), that which is taught in a s., or as in a s.

School (skūl), *sb.*[2] late ME. [a. Du. *school* troop, multitude, 'school' of whales :—MDu. *schole*, OS. *scola* troop = OE. *scolu* :—OTeut. **skulā*, perh. orig. 'division', f. **skel-, skal-, skul-* to divide.] **1.** A shoal or large number of fish, porpoises, whales, etc. swimming together whilst feeding or migrating. **2.** *transf.* †**a.** A troop, crowd (of persons); a large number, mass (of inanimate things). **b.** A flock, company (of animals). 1555.

1. A Scool of Pilchards, came swimming..into the Harbour DE FOE.

School (skūl), *v.*[1] 1573. [f. SCHOOL *sb.*[1]] **1.** *trans.* To put or send to school; to educate at school 1577. **2.** 'To teach with superiority, to tutor' (J.) 1573. †**b.** To chastise –1628. **3.** To educate, train (a person, his mind, tastes, powers, etc.); to render wise, skilful, or tractable by training or discipline. Often *transf.*, said of God, the experiences of life, surrounding influences, etc. 1591. **b.** To discipline, bring under control, correct (oneself, one's thoughts, feelings, etc.) 1579. **c.** *pass.* To be educated *in* (certain beliefs, sentiments, habits). Also const. *inf.* 1841. **4.** To instruct (a person) how to act; to teach (a person) his part 1579. **5.** To train or exercise (a horse) in movements 1869. **b.** *intr.* To ride straight across country 1885.

1. Yet hee's gentle, neuer school'd, and yet learned SHAKS. 2. He schooleth and lessoneth the Pope plainly 1624. 3. They were too well schooled in the tricks of reservation 1856. **b.** I pray you schoole your selfe SHAKS. 4. Herodias schooled Salome in the part she was to play 1874.

School (skūl), *v.*[2] 1597. [f. SCHOOL *sb.*[2]] *intr.* To collect or swim together in 'schools'. *To s. up*: to collect at or near the surface of the water, said of fishes.

Schoo·l board. 1870. [BOARD *sb.* II. 4 b.] In England and Wales from 1870–1902, and in Scotland since 1872, a body of persons elected by the ratepayers of a 'school district' to provide sufficient accommodation in public elementary schools for all the children of the district.

Schoolboy (skū·lboi). 1588. [f. SCHOOL *sb.*[1] + BOY.] **1.** A boy attending or belonging to a school. **2.** *attrib.* or *adj.* 1687.

1. Every Schole-boy knows it JER. TAYLOR.

Schoolfellow (skū·lfe:lou). 1440. [f. SCHOOL *sb.*[1] + FELLOW *sb.*] One who is or formerly was at the same school at the same time with another.

Schoolgirl (skū·lgɜɹl). 1809. [f. SCHOOL *sb.*[1] + GIRL.] A girl attending school. Hence **Schoo·lgi:rlish** *a.*

Schoo·l-house. late ME. **1.** A building appropriated for the use of a school; also, the dwelling-house provided for the use of the schoolmaster or schoolmistress, usu. adjoining a school. **2.** At some public schools, the name given to the head master's house Also, the boys belonging to this house. 1857.

Schooling (skū·liŋ), *vbl. sb.* 1449. [f. SCHOOL *v.*[1] + -ING [1].] **1.** The action of teaching, or the state or fact of being taught, in a school; scholastic education. **b.** The maintenance of a child at school; cost of school education 1563. †**2.** Disciplinary correction, chastisement; admonition, reproof –1818. **3.** The exercising of horse and rider in the riding-school, or of horses in the hunting-field 1753.

2. I confess I thought the s. as severe as the case merited SCOTT.

Schoolman (skū·lmæ̆n). 1540. [SCHOOL *sb.*[1]] **1.** One of the writers, from about the 9th to the 14th c., who treat of logic, metaphysics, and theology as taught in the mediæval 'schools' or universities; a mediæval scholastic. †**2.** One who is versed in the learning of the 'schools', *esp.* one who is expert in formal logic or school-divinity –1732. **3.** One engaged in scholastic pursuits; a professional teacher or student 1712.

1. He would stand, like the Schoolman's Ass, irresolute. .betwixt equal Motives HUME.

Schoolmaster (skū·lmɑːstəɹ). ME. [f. SCHOOL *sb.*[1] + MASTER *sb.*[1]] **1.** The master of a school, or one of the masters in a school. †**b.** Applied to a private tutor –1654. **2.** Used as a name for certain species of fishes 1734.

1. *The s. is abroad*, a saying of Ld. Brougham, orig. expressing exulting confidence in the results of the spread of popular education, but later used chiefly in derision. **b.** *Tam. Shr.* I. i. 94. Hence **Schoo·lmaster** *v.* (*rare*) *trans.* to govern, regulate, or command in the manner of a s. **Schoo·lmastering** *vbl. sb.* the occupation or profession of a s.; also, an education in school. **Schoo·lmasterish** *a.*

Schoolmistress (skū·lmiːstrės). 1500. [f. SCHOOL *sb.*[1] + MISTRESS.] A woman who teaches in a school; the mistress of a school. †In early use, a female teacher, governess.

Schoolroom (skū·lrūm). 1775. [f. SCHOOL *sb.*[1] + ROOM *sb.*] A room in which a school is held. Also, a room in a private house, in which the children of the family receive instruction or prepare their lessons.

Schoolward (skū·lwǫ̈ɹd), *adv.* and *a.* 1801. [f. SCHOOL *sb.*[1] + -WARD.] **A.** *adv.* Towards, in the direction of, school. **B.** *adj.* Directed or going toward school 1888. So **Schoo·lwards** *adv.*

Schooner (skū·nəɹ), *sb.*[1] 1716. [Origin uncertain. Usu. derived from a supposed New England verb *scoon or *scun 'to skim along on the water'.] **1.** A small sea-going fore-and-aft rigged vessel, orig. with only two masts, but now often with three or four, and carrying one or more topsails. **2.** *Prairie s.*, a large wagon with a canvas hood, used esp. by settlers crossing the prairies. *U.S.* 1858.

Schooner (skū·nəɹ), *sb.*[2] 1886. [Origin obsc.] **a.** *U.S.* A tall beer-glass containing about double the quantity of an ordinary tumbler. **b.** Hence, in local British use, a retail measure of about 14 fluid ounces for beer.

Schorl (ʃǭɹl). 1779. [a. G. *schörl*; origin unkn.] *Min.* Tourmaline, esp. the black variety. Hence **Schorla·ceous** *a.*

‖**Schottische** (ʃǫtīʃ, ʃǫ·tiʃ), *sb.* 1859. [a. G. (*der*) *schottische* (*tanz*) the Scottish dance.] A dance of foreign origin resembling the polka, first introduced in England in 1848. Also, the music for this. Hence **Schotti·sche** *v. intr.* to dance a s.

Schout (skaut, Du. sχaut). *Hist.* 1481. [Du.] An administrative or municipal officer in the Low Countries and the Dutch Colonies.

Schreibersite (ʃrəi·bəɹzəit). 1846. [f. name of von *Schreibers*, of Vienna.] *Min.* A phosphide of iron and nickel occurring in meteoric iron.

‖**Schuit** (skoit, Du. sχöit). Also **schuyt.** 1617. [Du.; see SCOUT *sb.*[1]] A Dutch flat-bottomed river-boat.

Schultze (ʃu·ltsə). 1881. [Name of E. *Schultze*, the inventor, used attrib.] *S.* (also *Schultze's*) *gunpowder, powder*: an explosive having nitrolignin as its chief constituent; hence *S. cartridge*, one charged with this powder.

‖**Schwärmerei** (ʃvē·rmərai). 1886. [G., f. *schwärmen* to rave.] Enthusiastic devotion, esp. of an unwholesome kind.

Schwenkfeldian (ʃweŋkfe·ldiăn). *sb.* and *a.* Also †**Swen(c)k-.** 1562. [f. the name *Schwenkfeld* + -IAN.] **A.** *sb.* One of a sect founded by Caspar Schwenkfeld, a Silesian Protestant mystic (1490–1561). **B.** *adj.* Belonging to this sect.

Sciænoid (səi,ī·noid), *a.* and *sb.* 1840. [f. mod.L. *sciæna* (used for a fish of this genus), a. Gr. σκίαινα: see -OID.] **A.** *adj.* Belonging to, characteristic of, or resembling a sciænoid or the sciænoids. **B.** *sb.* A fish of the family *Sciænidæ* (type *Sciæna*).

Sciagraphic (səi,ăgræ·fik), *a.* 1815. [f. Gr. σκιαγράφος (f. σκιά shadow + -γράφος depicting) + -IC **1.**] Of or pertaining to sciagraphy. So **Sciagra·phical** *a.* 1690, **-ly** *adv.* 1727.

Sciagraphy (səiæ·grăfi). 1598. [a. F. *sciagraphie, sciographie*, ad. L. *scia-, sciographia*, a. Gr. σκια-, σκιογραφία; see prec.] **1.** That branch of perspective which deals with the projection of shadows; also, the delineation of an object in perspective with its gradations of light and shade. †**2.** A sciagraphic delineation or picture –1648. †**3.** An outline, draught, rough sketch. Chiefly *fig.* –1738. †**4.** The art or practice of finding the hour of the day or night by observation of the shadow of the sun, moon, or stars upon a dial –1721.

Sciamachy (səi,æ·măki), **skiamachy** (skəi-). 1623. [ad. Gr. σκιαμαχία, f. σκιά shadow + μαχ-, μάχεσθαι to fight.] A sham fight for exercise or practice; also, the action of fighting with a shadow.

Scian (səi·ăn), *a.* 1820. [f. *Scio*, It. name of *Chios*, reputed birthplace of Homer.] Chian.

†**Sciathe·rical,** *a.* 1614. [f. late Gr. σκιαθηρικός + -AL **1.**] Concerned with the recording of the shadows cast by the planets, esp. that of the sun as a means of finding out the hour of the day –1755. So †**Sciathe·ric** *a.* –1755.

Sciatic (səi,æ·tik), *a.* and *sb.* 1541. [a. F. *sciatique*, ad. med.L. *sciaticus*, corrupt f. L. *ischiadicus* ISCHIADIC.] **A.** *adj.* **1.** Affecting the hip or the sciatic nerves 1547. **2.** Of or belonging to the ischium or hip 1597.

1. S. pains GIBBON. *S. passion*, sciatica. **2.** *S. artery*, the larger of the two terminal branches of the internal iliac. *S. nerve*, each of the two divisions of the sacral plexus, esp. the *great s. nerve*, which is the largest nerve in the human body.

B. *sb.* †**1.** The ischium or hip –1565. †**2.** = SCIATICA –1801. **3.** Short for *s. nerve* 1541.

Sciatica (səi,æ·tikă). 1444. [a. med.L. *sciatica* (sc. *passio*), fem. of *sciaticus* SCIATIC *a.*] A disease characterized by pain in the great sciatic nerve and its branches 1450. **b.** An attack of this disease 1444. Hence **Scia·tical** *a.* (now *rare*) pertaining to or of the nature of s.; (of a person) affected with s.

Science (səi·ĕns). ME. [a. F., ad. L. *scientia* knowledge, f. *scientem, scire* to know.] **1.** The state or fact of knowing; knowledge or cognizance *of* something specified or implied; also, knowledge (more or less extensive) as a personal attribute. Now *Theol.*, and occas. *Philos.* **2.** Knowledge acquired by study; acquaintance with or mastery of any department of learning. late ME. **b.** Trained skill. Now *esp.* (somewhat joc.) with ref. to pugilism. 1785. **3.** A particular branch of knowledge or study; a recognized department of learning: often opp. to *art* (ART *sb.* II. 2) ME. †**b.** A craft, trade, or occupation requiring trained skill –1660. **4.** A branch of study which is concerned either with a connected body of demonstrated truths or with observed facts systematically classified and more or less colligated by being brought under general laws, and which includes trustworthy methods for the discovery of new truth within its own domain 1725. **5.** The kind of knowledge or intellectual activity of which the 'sciences' are examples. In early use, with ref. to sense 3: What is taught in the Schools, or may be learned by study. In mod. use chiefly: The sciences (in sense 4) as dist. from other departments of learning; scientific doctrine or investigation. late ME. **b.** In mod. use, often = 'Natural and Physical Science'. Also *attrib.*, as in *s.-master, -teaching*, etc. 1867. †**c.** *Oxford Univ.* Formerly applied to the portions of ancient and modern philosophy, logic, etc., included in the course of study for a degree in the School of Literæ Humaniores –1903.

1. Life is not the object of S.; we see a little, very little; and what is beyond we can only conjecture JOHNSON. **2.** Be love my youth's pursuit, and s. crown my Age GRAY. **b.** Phr. *The noble s.* (*of defence*), boxing or fencing (now *joc.*) **3.** In the Middle Ages, 'the seven (liberal) sciences' was often used synonymously with 'the seven liberal arts', for the group of studies comprised by the *Trivium* (Grammar, Logic, Rhetoric) and the *Quadrivium* (Arithmetic, Music, Geometry, Astronomy). N.E.D. **4.** Those truths which are the objects of particular sciences 1794. *Exact, experimental, natural, physical sciences*: see the adjs. **5.** This species is new to s. 1864. **c.** He had none of his brother's love for the Greek philosophy, then known as 'science' 1903.

Man of science. †**a.** A man who possesses knowledge in any department of learning, or trained skill in any art or craft. **b.** In mod. use, a man who has expert knowledge of some branch of science (usu., of physical or natural science), and devotes himself to its investigation.

Scient (səi·ĕnt), *a.* late ME. [ad. L. *scientem, scire* to know.] Having science, knowledge, or skill. Now *rare.*

‖**Scienter** (səi,e·ntəɹ), *adv.* 1824. [L., f. *scientem* SCIENT.] *Law.* Knowingly. Often as *sb.* in the phrase *to prove* (*a*) *s.*, etc., to prove that the act complained of was done knowingly; *law of s.*, the law with regard to the necessity of 'proving a s.' in order to obtain damages.

Sciential (səi,e·nʃăl), *a.* 1456. [ad. med. L. *scientialis*, f. L. *scientia* SCIENCE.] **1.** Of or pertaining to knowledge or science. **2.** Endowed with knowledge 1477.

Scientific (səi,ĕnti·fik), *a.* and *sb.* 1637. [ad. late L. *scientificus* (used orig. as transl. of Gr. ἐπιστημονικός making knowledge, Arist. *Ethics* VI. i. § 6), f. *scientem, scire* + *-ficus* making, f. *facere* to make.] **A.** *adj.* †**1.** Of a syllogism, a proof: Producing knowledge, demonstrative –1667. **2.** Of persons, books, institutions, etc.: Occupied in or concerned with science or the sciences 1815. **3.** Of or pertaining to science or the sciences; of the nature of science 1722. **4.** Of an art, practice, operation, or method: Based upon or regulated by science, as opp. to mere traditional rules or empirical dexterity. Of a worker or agent: Guided by a knowledge of science, acting according to scientific principles 1678. **b.** Devised on scientific principles 1794. **c.** Characterized by 'science' or trained skill 1862.

2. The opinion of the s. world 1815. S. periodicals 1888. **3.** Analogy confirmed by experiment becomes S. truth 1812. To study religions in a s. spirit 1902. **4.** The one is profitless taxation, the other s. taxation CHAMBERLAIN. **c.** A batsman. .steady and s. 1862.

B. *sb.* A man of science. *colloq.* 1830.

Scientifical (səi,ĕnti·fikăl), *a.* 1588. [f. late L. *scientificus*: see prec. and -AL **1.**] †**1.** = prec. *a.* **1.** –1732. †**2.** Designed for the furthering of knowledge –1642. **3.** Expert in science; occupied in or concerned with science. Now *rare.* 1645. **4.** Of or pertaining to science (*rare*) 1777. Hence **Scienti·fical·ly** *adv.*, **-ness.**

Scientist (səi·ĕntist). 1840. [irreg. f. *scient-* (in L. *scientia* SCIENCE and in SCIENTIFIC) + -IST.] A man of science.

‖**Scilicet** (səi·liset), *adv.* (*sb.*). late ME. [L., = *scire licet* 'it is permitted to know'.] **A.** *adv.* To wit; that is to say; namely. Abbrev. **scil.** or **sc.** **B.** as *sb.* The word 'scilicet' or its equivalent, introducing a specifying clause 1650.

‖**Scilla** (si·lă). 1824. [L., = Gr. σκίλλα.] **a.** *Bot.* A genus of liliaceous plants; a plant of this genus, a squill. **b.** *Pharmacy.* The bulb of *Urginea Scilla* (formerly *Scilla maritima*).

Scillitin (si·litin). 1819. [a. F. *scillitine*, f. *scillitique*, ad. L. *scilliticus*, a. Gr. σκιλλιτικός, f. σκίλλα SCILLA; see -ITE [1] and -IN **4.**] *Chem.* A bitter extract from the squill.

Scillonian (silōu·niăn), *a.* and *sb.* 1750. [f. *Scilly* + *-onian* (perh. after *Devonian*).] **A.** *adj.* Pertaining to the Scilly Isles or their inhabitants. **B.** *sb.* An inhabitant of these.

Scimitar (si·mitǟɹ). 1548. [Adopted in various forms from F. *cimeterre*, It. *scimitarra*, etc. Origin unkn.] A short, curved, single-edged sword, used among Orientals, esp. Turks and Persians.

Comb.: **s.-pod**, the legume of the tropical climber *Entada scandens*; **s. razor-shell**, the *Solen ensis*.

Scincoid (si·ŋkoid), *a.* and *sb.* 1790. [ad. mod.L. *scincoides*, f. *scincus* SKINK; see -OID.] **A.** *adj.* Resembling a skink; belonging to the group *Scincoidea* or the family *Scincidæ* of skink-like lizards. **B.** *sb.* A skink-like lizard. So **Scincoi·dian** *a.* and *sb.*

‖ **Scintilla** (sinti·lǎ). 1692. [L. = spark.] A minute particle, an atom.

Scintillant (si·ntilǎnt), *a.* 1610. [ad. L. *scintillantem*, *scintillare* to SCINTILLATE. Cf. F. *scintillant*.] Scintillating 1737. **b.** *Her.* Emitting sparks 1610.

Scintillate (si·ntileⁱt), *v.* 1623. [f. ppl. stem of L. *scintillare*, f. SCINTILLA.] **1.** *intr.* To send forth sparks or little flashes of light; to sparkle, twinkle. **2.** *trans.* To emit as a spark or sparks; to send forth (sparkles of light); to flash forth 1809. **3.** *pass.* To be ornamented with bright specks 1851.

1. *fig.* A work scintillating throughout with wit and humour 1864. **2.** Too much given to s. bitter epigram 1866. So **Scintilla·tion**, the action of scintillating; a flash, spark; a flash, a brilliant display (of wit, etc.); *occas.* misused for SCINTILLA.

Sciolism (səi·ŏliz'm). 1816. [f. next; see -ISM.] The character or qualities of a sciolist; pretentious superficiality of knowledge.

Sciolist (səi·ŏlist). 1615. [f. late L. *sciolus* (see next) + -IST.] A superficial pretender to knowledge; a conceited smatterer. So **Scioli·stic** *a.*

Sciolous (səi·ŏləs), *a.* Now *rare*. 1639. [f. late L. *sciolus* smatterer (dim. of *scius* knowing, f. *scire*) + -OUS.] Having a smattering of knowledge.

Sciomancy (səi·ŏmænsi). 1623. [ad. mod. L. *sciomantia*, f. Gr. σκιο-, σκιά shadow + μαντεία; see -MANCY.] Divination by communication with the shades of the dead.

Scion (səi·ən). ME. [a. OF. *cion*, *sion*, mod.F. *scion*, of obsc. origin.] **1. a.** *gen.* A shoot or twig; also, a sucker. Now only *fig.* **b.** *spec.* A slip for grafting, a graft. **2.** An heir, a descendant 1814.

1. a. *fig.* An humble and secular s. of that old stock of religious constancy LAMB. **2.** A s. of the imperial Hapsburg line 1871.

Scioptic (səi,ǫ·ptik), *a.* and *sb.* 1738. [f. Gr. σκιά shadow + ὀπτικός pertaining to vision; see OPTIC *a.*] = SCIOPTRIC.

Sciopticon (səi,ǫ·ptikǫn). 1876. [f. as prec. with Gr. neuter ending.] A magic lantern for the exhibition of photographed objects.

Scioptric (səi,ǫ·ptrik), *a.* and *sb.* Now *rare* or *Obs.* 1704. [f. Gr. σκιά shadow, after *catoptric*, etc.] **A.** *adj.* *S. ball*: a ball of wood with a hole made through it in which a lens is placed, used in the camera obscura 1764. **B.** *sb.* = *s. ball.* 1704.

‖ **Scire facias** (səi·ri fē¹·ʃiæs). 1445. [Law Latin phr. *scire facias* 'do (him) to wit' used subst.] *Law.* A judicial writ, requiring the sheriff to do the party concerned to wit that he should come before the Court to 'show cause' why execution should not be taken against him, or why letters patent, such as a charter, should not be revoked. Often abbrev. *sci. fa.*

Scirrhoid (si·roid, sk-), *a.* 1855. [f. SCIRRHUS + -OID.] Resembling scirrhus.

Scirrhosity (sirǫ·sīti, sk-). 1599. [ad. mod.L. *scirrhositas*, f. late L. *scirrhosus* SCIRRHOUS; see -ITY.] A morbid hardness or scirrhous condition of an organ or a part; the quality or state of being scirrhous.

Scirrhous (si·rəs, sk-), *a.* 1563. [ad. F. *scirr(h)eux* (now *squirreux*), ad. mod.L. *scirrhosus*, f. L. *scirrhus* SCIRRHUS; see -OUS.] Proceeding from, of the nature of, or resembling a scirrhus. **b.** *transf.* Indurated; covered with hard excrescences 1658.

S. cancer 1878. **b.** Shining, s. skin 1845.

‖ **Scirrhus** (si·rǒs, sk-). *Pl.* **scirrhi**, also **scirrhusses.** 1605. [mod.L., a. Gr. σκίρρος, prop. σκῖρος a hard coat or covering, a hardened swelling or tumour, related to σκιρός hard.] *Path.* **1.** A hard, firm, and almost painless swelling or tumour; now *spec.* a hard cancer 1615. **2.** The disease of having a scirrhus; an instance or attack of this disease 1605.

Scissel (si·sěl). 1622. [a. F. *cisaille*, f. *cisailler* to clip with shears.] Metal clippings; *spec.* the scrap metal from which coin blanks have been cut.

Scissile (si·səil, -il), *a.* 1621. [ad. L. *scissilis*, f. *scindere*.] Capable of being cut or divided; *spec.* in *Min.*, that splits into laminæ, esp. of alum.

Scission (si·ʃən). 1443. [a. F., ad. late L. *scissionem*, f. L. *scindere* (ppl. stem *sciss-*).] **1.** The action or an act of cutting or dividing, as with a sharp instrument 1676. **2.** *fig.* Division, separation; in early use = SCHISM 1443.

Scissiparity (sisipæ·rīti). 1877. [f. L. *sciss-* (see prec.) + *parere* to bring forth + -ITY.] *Biol.* Reproduction by fission, schizogenesis.

Scissor (si·zəɹ), *v.* 1612. [f. next.] **1.** *trans.* To cut with scissors, to cut *up*, *off*, or *into* pieces with scissors. **2.** To clip out (extracts) from newspapers or the like 1865.

Scissors (si·zəɹz), *sb. pl.* [Late ME. *sisours*, *cysowres*, a. OF. *cisoires*, ad. late L. **cisoria*, pl. of *cisorium* cutting instrument, f. *-cis-*, *-cidere*, the forms in prepositional compounds of *cæs-*, *cædere* to strike, beat, slay, cut. The spelling with *sc* is app. due to confusion with L. *scissor*, f. *scindere* to cut.] **1.** A cutting instrument consisting of a pair of handled blades, so pivoted on a pin in the centre that the instrument can be opened to a shape resembling that of the letter X, and the handles then brought together again so as to cause the edges of the blades to close on the object to be cut. **a.** in *pl.* form with pl. construction, either in sing. or pl. sense. When qualification by a numeral or an indef. article is required, *pair of s.* is used. late ME. ¶ **b.** in *pl.* form construed as *sing.* (*rare*) 1843. **2.** *Wrestling.* A grip with the wrists crossed like a pair of scissors 1904. Also in *Rugby Football* and *Swimming.*

1. The s. of Destiny CARLYLE. Phr. *S. and paste* (†*paste and s.*), referred to as the instruments used by the newspaper sub-editor or the mere compiler. **b.** Which is easily removed with a s. 1906.

attrib. and *Comb.* (chiefly in form *scissor-*), as **scissor-bill**, a skimmer or shearwater, esp. *Rhynchops nigra*; **scissor(s)-grinder**, (*a*) a man who grinds scissors; (*b*) *dial.* the nightjar, *Caprimulgus europæus*; **scissor-tail**, either of two American birds of the family *Tyrannidæ*, *Milvulus forficatus* and *M. tyrannus.*

Scissure (si·ʃŭɹ). Now *rare* or *Obs.* late ME. [a. F., ad. L. *scissura*, f. *scindere* to cut, divide; see SCISSION.] **1.** A longitudinal cleft or opening made by cutting or separation of parts; a rent, fissure 1511. **b.** *fig.* A split, division, schism 1643. **2.** *Anat.*, etc. A natural cleft or opening in an organ or part. late ME.

Sciurine (səi·iŭrəin, -in), *a.* and *sb.* 1842. [f. L. *sciurus*, ad. Gr. σκίουρος squirrel (f. σκιά shadow + οὐρά tail) + -INE.] **A.** *adj.* Of or pertaining to the genus *Sciurus* or subfamily *Sciurinæ* of squirrels. **B.** *sb.* A sciurine rodent; a squirrel. So **Sciuroid** (səi,iū·roid) *a.* *Zool.* of or pertaining to the *Sciuridæ*, or squirrel-family; *Bot.* bushy, like a squirrel's tail.

Sciuromorph (səi,iū·romǫɹf), *a.* 1882. [ad. mod.L. *Sciuromorpha*, f. Gr. σκίουρος (see prec.) + μορφή form.] A rodent of the super-family *Sciuromorpha*, comprising the *Sciuridæ*, *Anomaluridæ*, etc. Hence **Sciuromo·rphic**, **-mo·rphine** *adjs.*

Sclaff (sklæf), *v.* 1893. [A use of Sc. *sclaff* to shuffle along, etc. Prob. onomatopœic.] *Golf.* **a.** *intr.* To scrape the surface of the ground with the sole of the club before striking the ball. **b.** *trans.* To scrape (the ground) behind the ball in striking; also, to hit (a ball) after having scraped the ground with the club.

‖ **Sclera** (sklī·rǎ). 1888. [mod.L., f. Gr. σκληρός hard.] The sclerotic coat of the eyeball. Hence **Scle·ral** *a.* of or pertaining to the s. or sclerotic.

‖ **Sclerema** (skliˑrī·mǎ). 1858. [mod.L. form of F. *sclérème*, f. Gr. σκληρός hard, after *œdème* ŒDEMA.] A hardening of the cellular tissue.

Sclerenchyma (sklīˑre·ŋkimǎ). 1861. [mod.L., f. Gr. σκληρός hard + ἔγχυμα an infusion, after *parenchyma*.] **1.** *Zool.* The hard substance of the calcareous skeleton of sclerodermic corals. **2.** *Bot.* The tissue of cells with thickened or lignified walls 1875. Hence **Sclerenchy·matous** *a.*

‖ **Scleriasis** (skliˑrəi·ǎsis). 1684. [mod.L., f. Gr. σκληρός hard, after *elephantiasis*.] *Path.* A hard tumour or induration; a scirrhus.

Sclerite (sklīˑrəit). 1861. [f. Gr. σκληρός + -ITE [1].] *Zool.* In the anatomy of invertebrates, each of the definite component portions into which the hard portion of the substance of certain animals is divided. Hence **Scleri·tic** *a.*

Scleritis (sklīˑrəi·tis). 1861. [f. SCLERA + -ITIS.] Sclerotitis.

Sclero- (sklīˑro), occurring in scientific terms.

1. As comb. form of Gr. σκληρός hard: **Scle·robase** [Gr. βάσις BASE], *Zool.* the axis or stem of a compound actinozoan when forming a horny or calcareous skeleton; hence **Scleroba·sic** *a.* pertaining to or consisting of a sclerobase. **Scle·roblast** [-BLAST], *Bot.* a stone-cell; *Zool.* the tissue from which sponge-spicules are produced. **Scle·roderm** [Gr. δέρμα skin], (*a*) a fish of the group *Sclerodermi*, which have the skin covered with hard scales; (*b*) a polyp of the division *Sclerodermata.* ‖ **Sclerode·rma**, *Path.* a chronic hardened condition of the skin, resulting from hypertrophy of connective tissue; so **Sclerode·rmia. Sclerode·rmatous, Sclerode·rmic** *adjs.*, (*a*) *Zool.* belonging to the division *Sclerodermata* of zoantharian polyps; (*b*) *Path.* pertaining to the scleroderma. **Sclerode·rmite,** one of the hard bodies of which the skeleton of Crustacea is composed; also, one of the hard skeletal parts in certain Actinozoans. **Scle·rogen** [-GEN], *Bot.* the hard lignified matter on the sides of some cells, which gives hardness to wood, fruit-stones, etc. **Scleroge·nic** *a.*, *Phys.* and *Path.* tending to produce hardening (of animal tissues). **Sclero·genous** *a.*, (*a*) sclerogenic; (*b*) consisting of sclerogen. **Sclero·meter** [-METER], an instrument for measuring the hardness of crystals.

2. As comb. form of SCLERA: **Scle·ro-iri·tis**, inflammation of the sclerotic coat and the iris.

3. Used (after SCLEROTIUM, etc.) to form the names of a number of substances obtained from ergot, as **Scleromu·cin**, a gummy nitrogenous substance.

Scleroid (sklīˑroid), *a.* 1856. [f. Gr. σκληρός + -OID.] *Bot.* and *Zool.* Hard; having a hard texture.

‖ **Scleroma** (skliˑrōu·mǎ). 1684. [mod.L., a. Gr. σκλήρωμα, f. σκληροῦν to harden, f. σκληρός; see -OMA.] *Path.* = SCLERIASIS.

Sclerosed (skliˑrōu·st), *ppl. a.* 1878. [f. next + -ED [1].] **a.** *Path.* Affected with sclerosis; rendered abnormally hard. **b.** *Bot.* Hardened; lignified 1881.

Sclerosis (skliˑrōu·sis). late ME. [mod. L., a. Gr. σκλήρωσις, f. σκληροῦν to harden, f. σκληρός; see -OSIS.] **1.** *Path.* †**a.** A hard external tumour. **b.** A morbid hardening of any tissue or structure. **2.** *Bot.* Induration of a tissue or a cell-wall by lignification 1884.

Sclerotal (skliˑrōu·tǎl). 1854. [f. mod.L. *sclerotis* SCLEROTICA + -AL 2.] *Anat.* Any of the component plates of the bony ring which protects the sclerotic coat of the eyeball in certain birds and reptiles.

Sclerotic (skliˑrǫ·tik), *a.*[1] and *sb.* 1543. [a. med. and mod.L. *scleroticus*, a. late Gr. *σκληρωτικός, f. σκληροῦν to harden, f. σκληρός.] **A.** *adj.* **1.** *Anat.* In *s. coat*, *membrane*, *tunic* = B. 1. **b.** Of or pertaining to, connected with, the sclerotic coat of the eye 1822. **2.** Of medicines: Adapted to harden the tissues 1696. **3.** *Path.* Of or pertaining to sclerosis; affected with sclerosis 1543. **4.** *Bot.* Hardened, stony in texture 1884.

1. b. *S. bone*, *plate* = SCLEROTAL; *s. ring*, the ring formed by the s. bones of the eyeball. **4.** *S. cells*, grit-cells; *s. parenchyma*, stone-cells in pears, etc.

B. *sb.* **1.** The hard outer coat of the posterior portion of the eyeball, forming the white of the eye 1690. **2.** A medicine for hardening the flesh, etc. 1728.

Sclerotic (skliˑrǫ·tik), *a.*[2] 1876. [f. SCLEROTIUM + -IC 1 b.] *Chem.* In *s. acid*, one of the two most active constituents of ergot.

‖ **Sclerotica** (skliˑrǫ·tikǎ). 1541. [med.L.

a. Gr. *σκληρωτικός SCLEROTIC *a.*] = SCLEROTIC *sb.* 1.

‖**Sclerotitis** (sklīərotəi·tis). 1822. [mod.L.; see -ITIS.] *Path.* Inflammation of the sclerotica.

‖**Sclerotium** (skliərōu·tiŏm). *Pl.* **-tia.** 1790. [mod.L., f. Gr. σκληρός.] †1. A former genus of *Cryptogamia*, comprising hard black bodies producing smut in wheat and ergot in rye; now known to be a particular stage of growth of the mycelium of certain fungi –1845. 2. A tuberous body forming on the mycelium of a fungus, from which it becomes detached when its growth is complete 1871. 3. *Zool.* In *Mycetozoa*, a cyst-like growth enclosing a portion of the plasmodium in its dormant stage 1885.

Sclerotome (sklīə·rotōum). 1857. [f. Gr. σκληρός hard + τομή section, and -τόμος cutter; see -TOME.] *Anat.* 1. A sclerous element intervening between successive myotomes. 2. A knife used in incising the sclerotic 1885. So **Sclero·tomy**, incision into the sclera.

Sclerous (sklīə·rŏs), *a.* 1845. [f. Gr. σκληρός + -OUS.] a. *Phys.* Of animal tissues: Hard, bony. b. *Path.* Indurated, affected by sclerosis.

Scobiform (skōu·bifǭım), *a.* 1760. [f. L. *scobs* sawdust, filings + -(I)FORM.] *Bot.* Like sawdust or filings in appearance.

Scoff (skǫf), *sb.*[1] [ME. *scof*, *skof*, of obsc. origin. Cf. early mod. Da. *skuf*, *skof* jest, mockery.] 1. a. 'Contemptuous ridicule; expression of scorn; contumelious language' (J.); mockery. Now *rare* or *Obs.* b. A derisive jest; an expression of mockery 1573. 2. An object of contempt or scorn; a mark for derision or scoffing 1640.

1. b. The scoffs and sarcasms of Swift 1751. 2. Is not he the common s. of all beholders? 1660.

Scoff (skǫf), *sb.*[2] *S. Afr.* 1879. [Cape Du., repr. Du. *schoft* quarter of a day, hence each of the four meals of the day.] Food; a meal.

Scoff (skǫf), *v.*[1] late ME. [f. SCOFF *sb.*[1]] 1. *intr.* To speak derisively, mock, jeer. Chiefly implying unworthy derision, as of something deserving reverence or consideration. 2. *trans.* To scoff at, deride, ridicule irreverently. *Obs.* exc. *U.S.* 1579.

1. Harvey's grand discovery..was scoffed at for nearly a whole generation 1886. 2. I would not scoffe you, nor with taunts torment ye 1624. Hence **Sco·ffer**, one who scoffs; often *spec.* one who scoffs at religion or morality 1470. **Sco·ffingly** *adv.*

Scoff (skǫf), *v.*[2] *slang* and *dial.* 1849. [Orig. a variant of dial. *scaff*; latterly assoc. w. SCOFF *sb.*[2]] 1. *trans.* To eat voraciously, devour; also *gen.* to eat. b. *intr.* To eat or feed 1899. 2. *trans.* To seize, plunder 1893.

Scoinson (skoi·nsən). 1842. [Refashioned f. SCUNCHEON, after its source, OF. *escoinçon*.] *Arch.* Used *attrib.* in *s. arch* = REAR-ARCH.

Scoke (skōuk). *U.S.* 1794. [Origin obsc.] The poke-weed, *Phytolacca decandra.*

Scold (skōuld), *sb.* ME. [app. a. ON. *skáld* SKALD, orig. meaning a poet; in the sense-development 'lampooner' is prob. an intermediate stage.] 1. In early use, a person (esp. a woman) of ribald speech; later, a woman (rarely a man) addicted to abusive language. 2. [from the vb.] A scolding. *dial.* or *colloq.* 1706.

1. I know she is an irkesome brawling s. SHAKS. *Common s.*, a woman who disturbs the peace of the neighbourhood by her constant scolding.
Comb.: **scold's bit, bridle** = BRANKS 1.

Scold (skōuld), *v.* late ME. [f. prec.] 1. *intr.* †a. Orig., to behave as a scold; to quarrel noisily, brawl; to use unseemly language in vituperation: said chiefly of women. b. Now: To use undignified vehemence or persistence in reproof or fault-finding; *colloq.* freq. = to utter continuous reproof. 2. *trans.* To address (esp. an inferior or a child) with continuous and more or less angry reproach; to chide 1715.

1. Mark'd you not how hir sister Began to s., and raise vp such a storme, That mortal eares might hardly indure the din SHAKS. 2. She scolds the servants from morning till night THACKERAY. Hence **Sco·lder**[1], one who scolds; †a common scold.

Scolder[2] (skōu·ldəı). *Orkneys.* 1795. The oyster-catcher, *Hæmatopus ostrilegus.*

Scolecid (skolī·sid). 1864. [ad. mod.L. *Scolecida*, f. Gr. σκώληξ SCOLEX; see -ID[3].] An animal of the class *Scolecida* of *Annuloida.*

Scolecite (skǫ·lĭsəit). 1823. [f. Gr. σκωληκ-, σκώληξ SCOLEX + -ITE[1] 2 b.] 1. *Min.* Hydrous silicate of aluminium and calcium, found in needle-shaped crystals and fibrous or radiated masses. 2. *Bot.* The vermiform carpogonium of certain fungi 1875.

‖**Scolex** (skōu·leks). *Pl.* **scoleces** (skolī·sīz), also *erron.* **scolices** (skōu·lisīz). 1855. [mod. L., a. Gr. σκώληξ worm.] The larva or embryo produced directly from the egg in metagenesis; esp. the larva or head of a tapeworm or other parasitic worm.

Scolion (skǫ·liǒn). 1603. [Gr. σκόλιον.] *Gr. Antiq.* A song sung in turn by the guests at a banquet.

‖**Scoliosis** (skǫliōu·sis). 1706. [mod.L., a. Gr. σκολίωσις, f. σκολιός bent, curved; see -OSIS.] *Path.* Lateral curvature of the spine. Hence **Scolio·tic** *a.*

Scollop, *sb.* and *v.*: see SCALLOP.

Scolopaceous (skǫlopēⁱ·ʃəs), *a.* 1785. [f. mod.L. *scolopaceus*, f. *scolopax* snipe, a. Gr. σκολόπαξ; see -ACEOUS.] *Ornith.* Resembling a snipe; *spec.* used as an epithet of a species of courlan, *Aramus scolopaceus*. Also = next.

Scolopacine (skǫ·lopăsəin, -in), *a.* and *sb.* 1889. [ad. mod.L. *scolopacinus*, f. L. *scolopacem*, *scolopax*; see prec. and -INE.] A. *adj.* Belonging to the sub-family *Scolopacinæ* or the family *Scolopacidæ*, typified by the genus *Scolopax*, and including the woodcock, redshank, etc. B. *sb.* A scolopacine bird.

‖**Scolopendra** (skǫlǒpe·ndră). 1520. [L., a. Gr. σκολόπενδρα.] †1. A fabulous sea-fish –1635. 2. A centipede or millipede. Also, a Linnean genus of myriapods, including the largest and most formidable of the centipedes 1608. So **Scolope·nder** 1562. **Scolope·ndrine** *a.* resembling or related to the centipedes.

‖**Scolopendrium** (skǫlope·ndriŏm). Also †-ia. 1520. [mod.L. = L. *-ion*, ad. Gr. σκολοπένδριον, so called from a fancied resemblance to the scolopendra.] = HART'S-TONGUE.

Scolytid (skǫ·litid). 1899. [ad. mod.L. *Scolytidæ*, f. *Scolytus*; see -ID[3].] A member of the family *Scolytidæ* of small wood-boring beetles.

‖**Scomber** (skǫ·mbəı). *Pl.* **scombri** (skǫ·mbrəi). 1623. [L., ad. Gr. σκόμβρος tunny or mackerel.] A mackerel. In mod. use only as the L. name of the genus.

Scombroid (skǫ·mbroid), *a.* and *sb.* 1841. [f. Gr. σκόμβρος SCOMBER + -OID.] A. *adj.* Resembling the mackerel; belonging to the family *Scombridæ*. B. *sb.* A s. fish 1842.

†**Scomm.** 1619. [ad. L. *scomma*, a. Gr. σκῶμμα, f. σκώπτειν to jeer, scoff.] A flout or scoff –1711.

Sconce (skǫns), *sb.*[1] late ME. [Aphet. a. OF. *esconse* lantern (also hiding-place), ad. monastic L. *sconsa*, shortened f. *absconsa* pa. pple. fem. of *abscondere* to hide.] †1. A lantern or candlestick with a screen to protect the light from the wind, and a handle to carry it by –1747. b. A flat candlestick with a handle for carrying 1834. 2. A bracket-candlestick to fasten against a wall. Also, a candle-bracket for a piano, etc. 1450. 3. The tube in an ordinary candlestick in which the candle is inserted 1850.

2. Candles, arranged upon the walls on sconces 1881.

Sconce (skǫns), *sb.*[2] *arch.* 1567. [Origin obsc.; perh. slang use of prec.] Used *joc.* for: The head; esp. the crown or top of the head; hence, ability, sense, wit.

He had received a crack on the s. 1888.

Sconce (skǫns), *sb.*[3] 1571. [a. Du. *schans*, assim. in form to SCONCE *sb.*[1] and *sb.*[2]] 1. *Fortif.* A small fort or earthwork; esp. one built to defend a ford, pass, castle-gate, etc., or erected as a counter-fort. 2. *transf.* A protective screen or shelter (from fire or the elements) 1591. 3. *dial.* a. A screen, partition 1695. b. [perh. a different word.] A seat at one side of the fire-place in an open chimney 1781. 4. (Also *s.-piece.*) A low water-washed iceberg 1856.

1. *fig. Com. Err.* II. ii. 37. Phr. †*To build a S.*, to run a Score at an Ale-house, Tavern, &c. so as to be afraid to go there, for fear of being dunn'd BAILEY.

Sconce (skǫns), *sb.*[4] 1650. [f. SCONCE *v.*[2]] At Oxford: †a. A fine imposed for a breach of university or college discipline. b. A fine of a tankard of ale or the like, imposed by undergraduates on one of their number for some breach of customary rule when dining in hall.

†**Sconce**, *v.*[1] 1598. [f. SCONCE *sb.*[3]] 1. *trans.* To fortify, entrench; in later use, to shelter, protect –1746. 2. To hide, screen from view –1663.

Sconce (skǫns), *v.*[2] 1617. [Origin obsc.] *trans.* At Oxford: To fine, mulct; often with the penalty as second object. Now said only of undergraduates when dining in hall: To fine (one of their number) a tankard of ale or the like, as a penalty for breach of good manners or conventional usage.

Scone (skōun, skǫn). Orig. *Sc.* 1513. [perh. a shortened adoption of MDu. *schoonbrot*, MLG. *schonbrot* 'fine bread'.] A large round cake made of wheat or barley-meal baked on a griddle; one of the four quadrant-shaped pieces into which such a cake is often cut, or a cake of this shape separately baked.

Drop, dropped s., one made of a small portion of batter dropped on to a griddle or tin and baked.

Scoop (skūp), *sb.*[1] [ME. *scope*, (1) a. MDu. *schôpe*, *schoepe* (mod. Du. *schoep*) vessel for drawing or bailing out water, etc.:—WGer. **skōpōn-*, f. **skōp-*, **skap-*, root of **skappjan* to draw water; (2) MDu. *schoppe* (mod. Du. *schop*) = MLG. *schuppe* shovel:—OTeut. type **skuppōn-*.] 1. A utensil for bailing out, ladling, or skimming liquids; usu. in the form of a ladle or a concave shovel with a straight handle. Now chiefly *Naut.* and *dial.* b. The bucket of a water-wheel or of a dredging or draining machine 1591. 2. A kind of shovel used for dipping out or shovelling up and carrying materials of a loose nature; usu. an implement of iron, tin, etc. with a short handle and a broad, concave, or curved blade, the part of which next the handle is often covered over to form a receptacle for the material scooped up 1487. 3. An instrument with a spoon-shaped or gouge-shaped blade, used for cutting out a piece from some soft material, or for removing a core or an embedded substance 1739. b. Applied to certain tools used in excavation of soil; hence, the quantity taken up at once by a scoop 1706. 4. A variety of coal-box, somewhat resembling a flour-scoop in shape 1850.

Comb. **s.-wheel**, [cf. 1 b], a wheel driven by wind or steam for lifting water.

Scoop (skūp), *sb.*[2] 1742. [f. SCOOP *v.*] 1. The action or an act of scooping. 2. *concr.* A place scooped or hollowed out; also, a natural hollow resembling this; *rarely*, an artificial basin for water 1762. 3. *slang.* a. orig. *U.S.* An exclusive piece of information for a newspaper 1886. b. A lucky stroke of business, a 'haul' 1893.

3. b. Her engagement..at the Palace is a big 's.' 1909.

Scoop (skūp), *v.* ME. [f. SCOOP *sb.*[1]] 1. *trans.* To ladle or bail out (water) with or as with a scoop. Now *rare.* 2. To remove or detach (a portion of friable or soft material, etc.) with a scoop, so as to leave a rounded hollow; to rake in as with a scoop. Also, to take *out* (a core, etc.) with or as with a scoop. Also *absol.* 1622. 3. To hollow *out* with or as with a scoop; to form a concavity or depression in 1708. 4. To form by scooping or as by scooping. Also with *out.* 1730. 5. *slang.* a. To take or take up in large quantities; to appropriate (something) in advance of or to the exclusion of other competitors 1882. b. In journalistic use (orig. *U.S.*). To 'cut out' a rival reporter or editor, or his paper, by obtaining and publishing exclusive or earlier news 1884.

Hence **Scoo·per**, (*a*) one who or that which scoops; (*b*) the avocet, from the shape of its beak.

Scoo·p-net. 1792. [f. SCOOP *sb.*[1] or *v.*] A small long-handled net; a dip-net.

Scoot (skūt), *v. slang* or *colloq.* 1758. [Origin obsc.] *intr.* To go suddenly and swiftly, to dart; to go away hurriedly.

Scooter (skū·təı). 1825. [f. prec. + -ER[1].] 1. One who 'scoots' or goes hurriedly. 2. *U.S.* A boat, propelled by sails, capable of being used both on ice and in water 1903. b. A fast motor-boat, used in the war of 1914–18.

3. A child's toy consisting of a narrow flat piece of wood on low wheels, with a steering-handle, propelled by pushing with one foot on the ground; also, a similar machine propelled by a motor 1917.

Scop (skǫp). *Hist.* Often erron. **scóp, scôp.** [OE.] An Old English poet or minstrel.

‖ **Scopa** (skōᵘ·pă). 1802. [L., in class. use only in pl. *scopæ* twigs, shoots, a broom or brush.] *Ent.* A bundle or tuft of bristly hairs on the legs of bees, used for collecting pollen; a pollen-brush. Hence **Sco·pate,** having a s.

Scoparin (skōᵘ·părin). 1850. [f. next + -IN[1].] A diuretic principle found in the broom.

‖ **Scoparium** (skopēᵊ·riŏm), **Scoparius** (skopēᵊ·riŏs). 1871. [Use of mod.L. specific name.] Pharmacopœial names for the tops of the common broom, *Spartium scoparium* or *Cytisus* (*Sarothamnus*) *scoparius.*

Scope (skōᵘp). 1534. [ad. It. *scopo* aim, purpose, ad. Gr. σκοπός mark for shooting at, aim, f. σκοπ- ablaut-var. of σκεπ-, σκέπτεσθαι to look out.] †1. A mark for shooting or aiming at -1683. 2. Something aimed at or desired; an end in view; an object, purpose, aim. Now *rare.* 1555. †b. *To s.*: to the purpose. SHAKS. 3. The main purpose, intention, or drift of a writer, speaker, book, etc. Now *rare.* 1536. b. The intention or tendency of a law; the drift or meaning of a proposal 1647. 4. The range of a missile weapon 1548. 5. The distance to which the mind reaches in its workings or purpose; reach or range of mental activity; extent of view, outlook, or survey 1600. b. The sphere or area over which any activity operates or is effective; the field covered by a branch of knowledge, an inquiry, concept, etc. 1830. 6. Room for exercise, opportunity or liberty to act; free course or play 1534. †b. An instance of liberty or licence. SHAKS. 7. (With more ref. to *literal* space or motion.) Space or range for free movement or activity 1555. 8. Extent in space, spaciousness; a (large) space, extent, tract, or area 1590. 9. *Naut.* The length of cable at which a ship rides when at anchor. Also *riding-s.* 1697.

2. Alas, poor Dean! his only S. Was to be held a Misanthrope SWIFT. 3. This is the s. of all I say: That by this course the good become best, the bad prove worst 1617. 5. Desiring this mans art, and that mans skope SHAKS. b. Art, if it lost much in purity and propriety, gained in s. 1874. Phr. *Within, beyond* (one's) *s.* 6. Phr. *To give s.* (*to* a person or thing); *to have, take, s.*; I gave full s. to my imagination STERNE. 7. Publick virtue..requires abundant s. and room, and cannot spread and grow under confinement BURKE. 9. We'll..ride to a short s. 1893. Hence **Sco·peless** *a.* not affording s.

-scope, an ending repr. mod.L. *-scopium* (f. Gr. σκοπεῖν to look at, examine) in MICROSCOPE and TELESCOPE. Hence used to form words denoting scientific instruments or contrivances for enabling the eye to view or examine or make observations, as *baroscope, gyroscope, laryngoscope, stethoscope,* etc.

Scopelid (skǫ·pĭlid). 1882. [ad. mod.L. *Scopelidæ*, f. SCOPELUS; see -ID[3].] A fish of the family *Scopelidæ.*

Scopeloid (skǫ·pĭloid), *sb.* and *a.* 1880. [f. next + -OID.] *Zool.* A. *sb.* A fish of the family *Scopelidæ.* B. *adj.* Like or pertaining to the *Scopelidæ.*

‖ **Scopelus** (skǫ·pĭlŏs). 1840. [mod.L.; introduced by Cuvier, who gives the etymon as 'σκόπελος, Greek name of an unknown fish'.] *Zool.* The typical genus of the family *Scopelidæ.*

Scopiform (skōᵘ·pifǭɹm), *a.* 1794. [f. L. *scopa* SCOPA + -(I)FORM.] *Nat. Hist.* Arranged in bundles; broom-shaped, fascicular.

Scopol- (skopǫ·l), used *Chem.* and *Pharm.* to form names of certain extractive principles obtained from *Scopolia japonica* (Japanese belladonna), as *scopolamine.*

Scopoline (skǫ·pŏlīn). 1887. [f. prec. + -INE[5].] *Chem.* A base; $C_8H_{13}O_2N$, obtained from scopolamine and used as a mydriatic.

Scops (skǫps). 1706. [a. mod.L. *Scops* (generic name), a. Gr. σκώψ the little horned owl.] A genus of *Strigidæ* containing nearly forty species distinguished by plumicorns upon the head; now usu. *s. owl.* Also, a member of this genus, a horn-owl.

†**Sco·ptical,** *a.* 1611. [f. Gr. σκωπτικός + -AL 1.] Mocking, satirical -1684. Hence †**Sco·ptically** -1686.

‖ **Scopula** (skǫ·piŭlă). 1802. [Late L., dim. of *scopa* a broom.] *Ent.* A small brush-like group of hairs upon the tarsus of bees and spiders. Hence **Sco·pulate** *a.* furnished with or having a s. So **Sco·pulipede** *a.* (of certain bees) having the feet furnished with scopulæ.

Scorbutic (skǫɹbiū·tik), *a.* and *sb.* 1655. [ad. mod.L. *scorbuticus*, f. *scorbutus* :—F. *scorbut*, app. of LG. or Du. origin; see -IC.] *Path.* A. *adj.* 1. Of or pertaining to scurvy; symptomatic of or proceeding from scurvy; of the nature of scurvy. Of a patient: Affected with scurvy. †2. Of articles of diet, remedies, etc.: Good against scurvy, antiscorbutic -1789. B. *sb.* †1. An antiscorbutic -1774. 2. A person affected with scurvy 1855. Hence †**Scorbu·tical** *a.* -1753, †-**ly** *adv.* -1676.

‖ **Scorbutus** (skǫɹbiū·tŏs). 1866. [mod.L.; see prec.] *Path.* Scurvy.

Scorch (skǭɹtʃ), *sb.* 1611. [f. next.] 1. A mark or impression produced by scorching. 2. Scorching effect (of the sun or fire) 1646. 3. An act of 'scorching'; a rapid run on a cycle or motor-car 1885.

Scorch (skǭɹtʃ), *v.*[1] late ME. [Origin obsc.] 1. *trans.* To heat to such a degree as to shrivel, parch, or dry up, or to char or discolour the surface; to burn superficially. b. *transf.* To shrivel up as if by heat 1600. c. *intr.* for *pass.* To be parched, etc. with heat 1707. 2. *intr.* To cycle or motor at excessive speed. [Cf. F. *brûler le pavé.*] 1885.

1. Power was giuen vnto him to s. men with fire *Rev.* xvi. 8. Summer drouth, or singed air Never s. thy tresses fair MILT. Hence **Sco·rching** *ppl. a.* that scorches; -**ly** *adv.*

†**Scorch,** *v.*[2] 1550. [Altered f. SCORE *v.*] *trans.* To slash as with a knife -1656.

We have scorch'd the snake, not kill'd it SHAKS.

Scorched (skǭɹtʃt), *ppl. a.* 1593. [f. SCORCH *v.*[1] + -ED[1].] 1. Burnt and discoloured by heat, touched by fire 1595. 2. Parched by the sun 1593. 3. *Nat. Hist.* Having colouring resembling a scorch 1832.

2. Like to a Lyon of scortcht desart Affricke MARLOWE.

Scorcher (skǭ·ɹtʃəɹ). 1874. [f. as prec. + -ER[2].] One who or that which scorches; *esp.* (*colloq.* or *slang*) a very hot day, one who cycles or motors furiously, a scathing rebuke or attack.

‖ **Scordatura** (skordatū·ra). 1876. [It., f. *scordare* to be out of tune.] *Mus.* An alteration in the manner of tuning some stringed instruments in order to produce particular effects.

Score (skōᵊɹ), *sb.* [Late OE. *scoru*, a. ON. *skor* notch, tally, four hundred, in Icel. twenty :—OTeut. **skurā*, f. **skur-*, wk. grade of **sker-* to cut, SHEAR *v.*] I. A cut, notch, mark. 1. †A crack, crevice; a cut, notch, or scratch; a line drawn with a sharp instrument. late ME. b. *Naut.* and *Mech.* (*a*) The groove of a block or dead-eye round which the rope passes; (*b*) a notch or groove made in a piece of timber or metal to allow another piece to be neatly fitted into it 1794. 2. A line drawn; a stroke, mark; a line drawn as a boundary. Now *rare.* ME. 3. *spec.* The 'scratch' or line at which a marksman stands when shooting at a target, or on which the competitors stand before beginning a race 1513. 4. *Mus.* A written or printed piece of concerted music, in which all the vocal or instrumental parts are noted on a series of staves one under the other 1701. b. A musical composition with its distribution of parts 1881.

2. Draw a s. through the tops of your t's SCOTT. 3. Phr. *To go off* (*set off, start*) *at s.*, of a horse, etc., to make a sudden dash at full speed; *fig.* of a person, to break out suddenly into impetuous speech or action; so *to go off full s.*

II. Notch cut for record, tally, reckoning. †1. A notch cut in a stick or tally, used to mark numbers in keeping accounts; also the tally itself -1593. †b. *Games.* A mark made for the purpose of recording a point or the like -1801. 2. A record or account (of items of uniform amount to be charged or credited) kept by means of tallies, or (in later use) by means of marks made on a board (with chalk), on a slate, or the like. Hence occas. *transf.*, a customer's account for goods obtained on credit. late ME. 3. The sum recorded to a customer's debit in a 'score'; the amount of an innkeeper's bill or reckoning 1600. 4. [Orig. a fig. use of sense II. 2.] Account, reason, ground, sake, motive. In phrases *on, upon the s.* (*of*). 1651. †5. A list, enumeration; number as counted -1596. 6. *Games.* The record or register of points made by both sides during the progress of a game or match; also the number of points made by a side or individual 1742. 7. *colloq.* [from the vb.] a. *lit.* in games: An act of 'scoring' or gaining a point or points. b. *fig.* A successful 'hit' in debate or argument. 1844.

1. 2 *Hen. VI*, IV. vii. 38. 2. There shall bee no mony, all shall eate and drinke on my s. SHAKS. 3. After he scores, he neuer payes the s. SHAKS. Phr. *To clear, pay, quit a s.*, or *scores*, to requite an obligation; sometimes, to revenge an injury. 4. Men..began to be over-easie upon that S. DE FOE. 6. Phr. *To make a s. off one's own bat*, with ref. to a s. made by a player's own hits; *fig.* solely by his own exertions, by himself.

III. A group of twenty. [app. from the practice, in counting sheep, etc., of counting orally from 1 to 20, and making a 'score' or notch on a stick, before proceeding to count the next twenty.] 1. A group or set of twenty. Primarily a sb., const. *of* (in OE. *gen. pl.*), but often serving as a numeral adj. OE. 2. A weight of twenty or twenty-one pounds, esp. used in weighing pigs or oxen 1460. †3. A distance of twenty paces -1672.

1. Shee may perhaps call him halfe a s. knaues, or so SHAKS. There were a s. of generals now round Becky's chair THACKERAY. 3. As easie, as a Canon will shoot point-blanke twelue s. SHAKS.

attrib. and *Comb.*: **s.-board,** (*a*) a blackboard in a public-house, on which debts are chalked up; (*b*) in *Cricket*, a large board erected so as to be seen by the onlookers, on which the s. of the game is kept; **-book,** a book for preserving the scores of games; **-card,** a printed card with a blank form on which to enter the s. in a game of cricket, etc.; **-game** *Golf*, a game decided by strokes (opp. to *match-game*, which is decided by holes): also in *Lawn Tennis.*

Score (skōᵊɹ), *v.* late ME. [a. ON. *skora* to make an incision, count by tallies, f. *skor*; see prec.] I. To cut, mark with incisions. 1. *trans.* To cut superficially; to make scores or cuts in; to mark with incisions, notches, or abrasions of the skin. b. *spec.* in *Cookery.* To make long parallel cuts upon (meat, etc.) 1460. †c. To mark by cuts of a whip. Also *absol.* -1806. d. *Geol.* To mark with scratches or furrows; said esp. with ref. to glacial action 1862. 2. To produce (marks, figures, etc.) by cutting. Also, to record or express by cuts or notches. 1590. 3. *Naut.* To make a 'score' or groove in; to fix by means of a 'score' 1779. 4. *U.S.* To rate, scold severely 1891.

1. Trees..scored by the axe 1824. c. Let vs s. their backes SHAKS. d. All around the rocks are carved, and fluted, and polished, and scored TYNDALL.

II. 1. To mark with a line or lines. late ME. †b. To mark *out* (a path, boundary) -1712. 2. To draw a line through (writing, etc.) in order to cancel. Often with *out.* 1687. 3. *Mus.* a. To write down in score. b. To compose or arrange for orchestral performance. 1839.

1. Passages had been scored in his favourite books THACKERAY.

III. To record by scores. 1. To record (debts) by means of notches on a tally; hence, to write down as a debt. Also with *up.* late ME. †2. *intr.* To run up a score; to obtain drink, goods, etc. on credit -1779. b. *trans.* To add (an item) to one's score 1681. 3. To enter as a debtor. Also with *up.* 1592. †b. To placard as an offender -1596. 4. To record the number of (anything) by notches or marks; to count and set down the number of (e.g. sheep). Also with *up.* late ME. 5. In a game or contest: To set down in the score. Chiefly in *pass.* 1742. b. *absol.* or *intr.* To record the points in a game or contest, to act as scorer 1846. 6. *trans.* Of a player or competitor: To add (so many points) to one's score. Also said of an incident in the game: To count for (so many points) in a player's score. 1742. b. *intr.* To make points in a game or contest: said of a player or competitor; also, of a card or an incident in the game 1844. c. To be reckoned in a score 1885. 7. *transf.* and *fig.* (chiefly *colloq.*) a. *trans.* To gain, win (a success, etc.) 1883. b. *intr.* To achieve a success; to make a hit. *To s. off* (a person): to make a point at the expense of. 1882.

1. *fig.* Nor need I tallies thy dear love to s. SHAKS. 3. b. *Tam. Shr.* Induct. ii. 25. 5. b. Mr. Whittaker..accompanied Mr. Mynn, and scored for him 1846. 6. My first stroke scored three 1856. *To s. a miss*: see MISS *sb.*[1] III. 1. c. The hazard scores to the striker 1885. 7. She felt that she had scored the first success in the encounter 1883.

IV. *intr.* To 'go off at score' (see SCORE *sb.* I. 3) 1858.

Scorer (skōᵊ·rəɹ). late ME. [f. prec. + -ER[1].] One who or that which scores; *esp.* one who records the score in a game or contest.

‖**Scoria** (skōᵊ·riă). *Pl.* **scoriæ** (skōᵊ·ri,ī) and (occas.) **sco·rias.** late ME. [L., a. Gr. σκωρία, f. σκῶρ dung.] 1. The slag or dross remaining after the smelting out of a metal from its ore. 2. Rough clinker-like masses formed by the cooling of the surface of molten lava upon exposure to the air, and distended by the expansion of imprisoned gases 1792. Hence **Sco·riac, Scoria·ceous** *adjs.*

Scorification (skōᵊ:rifikēⁱ·ʃən). 1754. [f. SCORIFY; see -FICATION.] The process of reducing to scoria; formation of scoria or slag; *spec.* as a method of refining or assay.

Scorifier (skōᵊ·rifəiəɹ). 1758. [f. SCORIFY + -ER[1].] A vessel of fire-clay used in the process of purifying metals in assaying.

Scoriform (skōᵊ·rifǭɹm), *a.* 1794. [f. SCORIA + -FORM.] Having the form of, resembling, scoria.

Scorify (skōᵊ·rifəi), *v.* 1754. [f. SCORIA + -FY.] 1. *trans.* To reduce to scoria or slag. 2. To convert (lava) into scoria 1852.

Scoring (skōᵊ·riŋ), *vbl. sb.* 1546. [f. SCORE *v.* + -ING.[2]] 1. The action of SCORE *v.*; an instance of this. 2. *concr.* Lines or figures scored 1688.

attrib. **s.-board** = SCORE-*board* (*b*); **-book** = SCORE-*book*; etc.

Scorious (skōᵊ·riəs), *a.* 1646. [f. SCORIA + -OUS.] Of the nature of scoria; abounding in scoria.

Scorn (skǭ·ɹn), *sb.* [Early ME. *skarn, scharne*, aphetic a. OF. *escarn, escharn*; a Com. Rom. word of Teut. origin.] 1. Mockery, derision, contempt; in mod. use, indignant or passionate contempt. 2. A manifestation of contempt; a derisive utterance or gesture; a taunt, an insult. *arch.* ME. 3. †a. Matter for scorn, something contemptible. b. An object of mockery or contempt. ME.

1. Disdaine and Scorne ride sparkling in her eyes, Mis-prizing what they looke on SHAKS. A Briton's s. of arbitrary chains COWPER. 2. Do but..marke the Fleeres, the Gybes, and notable Scornes That dwell in euery Region of his face SHAKS. 3. Made of my enemies the s. and gaze MILT.

Phrases. *To laugh to s.*: see LAUGH *v.* 3. *To speak s. of*, to revile. *To think s. of*, to despise. *To think (it) s.* (now *arch.* and *literary*), to disdain (const. *that* or *inf.*)

Scorn (skǭɹn), *v.* [Early ME. *scarne, schorne*, aphetic a. OF. *escarnir, escharnir*:— Com. Rom. **skernire*, of Teut. origin.] †1. *intr.* To speak or behave contemptuously; to use derisive language, jeer -1816. †2. *trans.* To treat with ridicule, to show extreme contempt for, to mock, deride -1631. 3. To hold in disdain, to contemn, despise ME. 4. With *inf.* as obj. To feel it beneath one, disdain indignantly *to* do something 1605.

1. She gecked and scorned at my northern speech and habit SCOTT. 3. Heav'n has no Rage, like Love to Hatred turn'd, Nor Hell a Fury, like a Woman scorn'd CONGREVE. *fig.* Where lawns extend that s. Arcadian pride GOLDSM. 4. The congress scorned to receive them BURKE. Hence **Sco·rner**, one who scorns; esp. one who scoffs at religion; *seat (chair, stool) of the scorner*, the position of a mocker (cf. Ps. i. 1).

Scornful (skǭ·ɹnfŭl), *a.* late ME. [f. SCORN *sb.* + -FUL 1.] 1. Full of scorn, contemptuous, derisive. Also *absol.* †2. Regarded with scorn, contemptible -1624.

1. Blessed is ye man, y^t..sytteth not in ye seate of the scornefull COVERDALE *Ps.* i. 1. And dart not scornefull glances from those eies SHAKS. The English Muse..S. of Earth and Clouds, should reach the Skies PRIOR. 2. The scornefull marke of euerie open eye SHAKS. Hence **Sco·rnfully** *adv.*, **-ness.**

Scorodite (skǫ·rŏdəit). 1823. [ad. G. *skorodit*, f. Gr. σκόροδον garlic (so called from its odour when heated); see -ITE[1].] *Min.* Hydrous phosphate of iron, found in pale-green or brown crystals and crusts.

‖**Scorpæna** (skǫɹpī·nă). 1706. [L., ad. Gr. σκόρπαινα a kind of fish; app. irreg. fem. f. σκορπίος SCORPION.] In early use, applied vaguely to various prickly fishes, chiefly of the families *Scorpænidæ* and *Cottidæ*. Now only as the name of a genus of acanthopterygian fishes; the typical genus of the family *Scorpænidæ*. Hence **Scorpæ·nid**, a fish of the family *Scorpænidæ*. **Scorpæ·noid** *a.* of or pertaining to the *Scorpænidæ*; *sb.* a scorpænoid fish.

Scorpene (skǭ·ɹpīn). 1777. [Anglicized f. prec.] = prec.; now only *U.S.*, the species *Scorpæna guttata.*

Scorper (skǭ·ɹpəɹ). 1843. [A misspelling of *scauper*; see SCALPER[1].] *Wood-* and *Metal-work.* A gouging tool for working in a depression. Also = SCALPER[2] 2.

‖**Scorpio** (skǭ·ɹpio). late ME. [L.; see SCORPION.] *Astr.* A zodiacal constellation, the Scorpion. Also, the eighth sign of the zodiac, named from this; situated between Libra and Sagittarius, and entered by the sun about 23 October.

Scorpioid (skǭ·ɹpioid), *a.* and *sb.* 1839. [ad. Gr. σκορπιοειδής, f. σκορπίος SCORPION; see -OID.] A. *adj.* 1. *Bot. S. cyme*, a unilateral cyme the undeveloped portion of which is circinate. 2. *Zool.* a. Resembling a scorpion; belonging to the scorpion family. b. Resembling the tail of a scorpion. 1864. B. *sb.* 1. *Bot.* A circinate inflorescence 1855. 2. *Zool.* A scorpion or scorpion-like animal 1887. So **Scorpioi·dal** *a.* = SCORPIOID *a.* 1. 1835.

Scorpion (skǭ·ɹpiən). ME. [a. OF. :— L. *scorpionem (scorpio)*, extended f. *scorpius*, a. Gr. σκορπίος.] 1. An arachnid of any of the genera (*Scorpio, Buthus, Androctonus*, etc.) forming the group *Scorpionidæ*, having a pair of large nippers and a general resemblance to a miniature lobster; they inhabit tropical and warm temperate countries in both hemispheres. The intense pain caused by the sting of the scorpion (situated at the point of the tail) is proverbial. b. *Her.* A representation of a scorpion as an armorial bearing 1780. c. Applied to other animals resembling or popularly confounded with the scorpion; e.g. in the U.S., to tarantulas, centipedes, various lizards, etc. 1709. 2. *Astr.* The constellation and (now somewhat rarely) the zodiacal sign SCORPIO. late ME. 3. In Australia and America, the local name for certain species of *Scorpænidæ* 1874. 4. A kind of whip made of knotted cords, or armed with plummets of lead or steel spikes, so as to inflict excessive pain (cf. 1 Kings xii. 11 and 2 Chron. x. 11). late ME. b. Hence quasi-*Hist.* as the name of a supposed ancient instrument of torture. Also *Antiq.* as the name of a mediæval weapon. 1541. 5. (tr. Gr. σκορπίος, L. *scorpio, scorpius*.) An ancient military engine for hurling missiles, used chiefly in the defence of the walls of a town. late ME.

1. *fig.* O, full of Scorpions is my Minde SHAKS. 4. My fader beet ȝou with scourgis, I forsothe schal beten ȝou with scorpiouns WYCLIF 2 *Chron.* x. 11. Back to thy punishment, False fugitive, and to thy speed add wings, Least with a whip of Scorpions I pursue Thy lingring MILT.

attrib. and *Comb.*: **s.-bug** *U.S.*, the water-scorpion; **s. fish**, any spiny fish of the genus *Scorpæna* or family *Scorpænidæ*; **-fly**, an insect of the family *Panorpidæ*, the slender abdomen of which is armed with forceps, and curls like the tail of a s.: **s. senna**, the *Coronilla Emerus*, a common plant of Southern Europe, with bright-yellow flowers; **-shell**, a gastropod of the Indian seas and Pacific, of the genus *Pteroceras*, having a development of long tubular spines from the outer lip of the aperture; **-spider**, any arachnidan of the order *Pedipalpi*; **scorpion's tail**, any plant of the genus *Scorpiurus*; **scorpion('s thorn**, a plant of South-western Europe, *Genista scorpius*; **-wort**, (*a*) = SCORPION GRASS; (*b*) *Ornithopus scorpioides*, native of Southern Europe.

Scorpion grass. 1578. A plant of the genus *Myosotis* the forget-me-not or mouse-ear.

Scorpionid (skǭ·ɹpiənid), *a.* 1895. [f. mod. L. *Scorpionidæ* pl., f. L. *scorpionem*; see -ID[3].] Of or pertaining to the group *Scorpionidæ* of arachnidans, typified by the genus *Scorpio.*

Scorse (skǭɹs), *v.* Now *dial.* 1509. [Early 16th c. *scose, scorse*, related to COSS, CORSE *vbs.*] *trans.* and *intr.* To barter or exchange. Hence **Sco·rser.**

Scortation (skǫɹtēⁱ·ʃən). *rare.* 1556. [f. L. *scortari*, f. *scortum* harlot; see -ATION.] Fornication. So **Sco·rtatory** *a.* (*rare*).

Scorzonera (skǭɹzonīᵊ·ră). 1629. [a. It., prob. f. *scorzone* some kind of venomous snake.] A plant of the modern genus *Scorzonera*, esp. *S. hispanica* or black salsify, much cultivated in Europe for its root which somewhat resembles the parsnip.

Scot[1] (skǫt). [OE. **Scot*, pl. *Scottas*, ad. late L. *Scottus*; infl. by ON. *Skotar.*] 1. *Hist.* One of an ancient Gaelic-speaking people, first known to history as inhabitants of Ireland, who in the 6th century A. D. settled in the north-west of Great Britain, and from whom the northern part of the island ultimately received its name. 2. A native of Scotland, a Scotchman ME.

Scot[2] (skǫt). ME. [Differentiated form of OE. *sc(e)ot, ʒesc(e)ot* SHOT *sb.*] 1. A payment, contribution, 'reckoning'; esp. payment for entertainment; a or one's share of such payment; chiefly in the phr. *to pay (for) one's s. lit.* and *fig.* †2. A custom paid to the use of a sheriff or bailiff; a local or municipal tax -1646. 3. *spec.* A tax levied on the inhabitants of the marshes and levels of Kent and Sussex 1793.

Phr. *S. and lot* (earlier *lot and s.*), a tax levied by a municipal corporation in proportionate shares upon its members for the defraying of municipal expenses. *To pay* (a person *off*) *lot and s.*, (fig.) to pay out thoroughly, to settle with.

Sco·tale, sco·t-ale. *Obs.* exc. *Hist.* ME. [f. SCOT[2] + ALE.] An 'ale' or festival at which ale was drunk at the invitation of the lord of the manor or a forester or other bailiff, for which ale a forced contribution was levied.

Scotch (skǫtʃ), *sb.*[1] 1450. [Cogn. with SCOTCH *v.*[1]] 1. An incision, cut, score or gash. 2. *spec.* A line scored or marked upon the ground, in the game of HOPSCOTCH 1677.

Scotch (skǫtʃ), *sb.*[2] 1601. [Belongs to SCOTCH *v.*[2]; origin obsc.] A block placed under a wheel, a cask, or the like, to prevent moving or slipping.

Scotch (skǫtʃ), *a.* and *sb.*[3] 1591. [Contr. var. of SCOTTISH.] A. *adj.* 1. Of persons: Of, belonging to, or native to, Scotland 1606. b. Characteristic of Scotland or its people 1815. 2. Of things: Of or pertaining to Scotland or its inhabitants 1591. b. As the epithet of various weights and measures, etc. (differing from the English standard) used formerly in Scotland 1774. 3. As the designation of the variety of northern English which is vernacular in Scotland. Hence of words, idioms, etc., belonging to this, and of works composed in it. 1730.

1. He had no S. blood in him that I know of! 1894. *S. cousin*, a distant relative (in allusion to the practice in Scotland of tracing kinship to remote degrees). 2. b. *S. acre*, 6,084 square yards. *S. ell*, 37·0958 inches. 3. To secure the adherence of stout, able-bodied, and, as the S. phrase then went, *pretty* men SCOTT.

Special collocations. **S. bonnet** (see BONNET *sb.* 1); **S collops** (see COLLOP[1] 2); **S. fir** (see FIR 1) **S. marriage** (see MARRIAGE 2); **S. mist** (see MIST *sb.*[1] 1); **S. pebble** (see PEBBLE *sb.* 2 b) **S. spur** *Her.*, a bearing representing a prick spur; **S. terrier** (see TERRIER[2]). **S. woodcock** (see WOODCOCK 3 c). b. In names of plants: **S. broom**, *U.S.*, the common broom; **S. kale**, a variety of borecole with less wrinkled leaves, of a purplish colour; **S. pine** (see PINE *sb.*[2] 2); **S. thistle**, a species of thistle (*Onopordon acanthium*), regarded as the national emblem of the Scotch.

B. *sb.* [The adj. used ellipt.] 1. *The S.* (pl.): The inhabitants of Scotland or their immediate descendants in other countries 1781. 2. The Scotch language: see A. 3. 1700. 3. Often *ellipt.*, e.g. for *S. whisky*; also = a glass of S. whisky. Also formerly for *S. snuff*. 1823.

2. I can read French as well as I can English, but it is impossible for me to comprehend S. 1896. 3. Two bitters and a small S. 1893.

Scotch (skǫtʃ), *v.*[1] late ME. [Origin obsc.] †1. *trans.* To make an incision or incisions in; to cut, score, gash -1747. **2.** [From Theobald's emendation of *scorch'd* in Shaks. *Macb.* III. ii. 13.] To inflict such hurt upon (something regarded as dangerous) that it is rendered temporarily harmless 1798. **b.** To crush, stamp upon, stamp out (something dangerous) 1825.

1. S. with your knife the back of the Carp 1675. 2. The snake must be killed not scotched 1798. Hence **Scotched** *ppl. a.* cut, scarred; also in *scotched collops*, etymologizing perversion of SCOTCH *collops*.

Scotch (skǫtʃ), *v.*[2] 1601. [f. SCOTCH *sb.*[2]] **1.** *trans.* To block or wedge (a wheel, log, gate, etc.) so as to keep from moving or slipping 1642. **2.** *intr.* (Chiefly w. neg.) To hesitate, scruple, boggle, or stick *at*; to hesitate *to do* something. *Obs.* exc. *dial.* 1601.

1. *fig.* I scotched the project of retreat for this council, at any rate 1897.

Scotch cap. 1591. A man's head-dress made of thick firm woollen cloth, without a brim, and decorated with two tails or streamers.

Scotch-Irish, *a.* 1876. Belonging to that part of the population of northern Ireland which is descended from Scotch settlers. Also *absol.* in pl. sense.

Scotchman (skǫ·tʃmǣn). 1570. [f. SCOTCH *a.* + MAN.] **1.** A man of Scottish nationality. (The usual English form. Cf. SCOTSMAN.) **b.** (Also *Flying S.*, (*Flying*) *Scotsman.*) A familiar name for the Scotch express (London to Edinburgh) on the London and North Eastern Railway 1874. **2.** *Naut.* A piece of hide, wood, or iron, etc. placed over a rope to prevent its being chafed 1841. **3.** *S. Afr.* A florin 1879. So **Sco·tchwo:man,** a woman who is a native of Scotland or of Scotch descent.

Scoter (skōu·təɹ). 1674. [Origin obsc.] A duck of the genus *Œdemia*, esp. *Œ. nigra*, a native of the Arctic regions and common in the seas of northern Europe and America. Also *s.-duck*.

Scot-free, *a.* ME. [f. SCOT *sb.*[2] + FREE *a.*] Free from payment of 'scot', tavern score, fine, etc.; exempt from injury, punishment, etc.; scatheless. Almost always *predic.*

Oxford escaped scot fre of the plague WOOD.

||**Scotia** (skōu·ʃiă). 1563. [L., a. Gr. σκοτία, f. σκότος darkness (so called from the dark shadow within the cavity).] *Arch.* = CASEMENT 1.

Scotic (skǫ·tik), *a.* 1645. [ad. late L. *Scoticus*, f. *Scotus.*] †**1.** *absol.* The Scottish dialect. **2.** Pertaining to the ancient Scots 1796.

Scotist (skōu·tist), *sb.* and *a.* 1530. [ad. med.L. *Scotista*, f. *Scotus*, proper name.] *Eccl.* **A.** *sb.* A follower of John Duns Scotus (known as 'the Subtle Doctor'), a scholastic philosopher and theologian of the 13th c., whose system in many respects was opposed to that of Thomas Aquinas. **B.** *adj.* Belonging to the Scotists. So **Sco·tism,** the teaching of Scotus or the Scotists.

Scotland Yard (skǫ·tlănd yā·ɹd). Name of a short street off Whitehall, London, until 1890 the head-quarters of the Metropolitan Police Force, now at New Scotland Yard on the Thames Embankment; hence, the force itself, *esp.* the detective department.

Scoto- (skǫ·to, skōu·to), comb. form of late L. *Scotus* SCOT *sb.*[1], as in *S.-Britannic, -Irish, -Scandinavian*, adjs.

Scotography (skotǫ·grăfi). *rare.* 1896. [f. Gr. σκότος darkness; see -GRAPHY.] = RADIOGRAPHY. Hence **Scotogra·phic** *a.*

||**Scotoma** (skotōu·mă). *Pl.* **scotomata** (skotōu·mătă). 1543. [late L., a. Gr. σκότωμα dizziness, f. σκοτοῦν to darken, f. σκότος darkness.] *Path.* †**1.** Dizziness accompanied by dimness of sight -1829. **2.** An obscuration of part of the visual field, due to lesion of the retina or of the ophthalmic centres in the brain 1875. So †**Sco·tomy** = sense 1. -1710.

†**Sco·toscope.** 1664. [f. Gr. σκότος darkness + -SCOPE.] An instrument which enables the user to see in the dark -1670.

Scots (skǫts), *a.* (*sb.*) ME. [orig. *Scottis*, northern var. of SCOTTISH.] **1.** Of or belonging to Scotland or its inhabitants, Scottish, Scotch. **b.** Qualifying the name of a coin or money of account (in contradistinction to *sterling*), as *pound S., shilling S.* Also in names of weights and measures denoting a particular variation from the English standard. *arch.* or *Hist.* 1520. **c.** With ref. to law 1766. **d.** In the names of trees and plants (more commonly SCOTCH) 1710. **2.** Of language: The distinguishing epithet of the dialect of English spoken by the inhabitants of the Lowlands of Scotland. Also *absol.* as *sb.*, the Scottish dialect. 1542. **3.** *Mil.* In names of regiments in the British army, as *S. Fusiliers, S. Guards* 1637.

2. Kilted loons that dinna ken the name o' a single herb..in braid S., let abee in the Latin tongue SCOTT. 3. *S. Greys*: see GREY *sb.* 8.

Scotsman (skǫ·tsmǣn). late ME. [f. SCOTS *a.* + MAN *sb.*] = SCOTCHMAN. (The prevalent form used now by Scotch people.) So **Sco·tswoman** = SCOTCHWOMAN.

||**Scotticè, Scoticè** (skǫ·tisī), *adv.* 1818. [med.L.] In Scotch.

Scotticism, Scoticism (skǫ·tisiz'm). 1717. [f. late L. *Scoticus* (*Scotticus*) + -ISM 3.] **1.** An idiom or mode of expression characteristic of Scots; esp. as used by a writer of English. **2.** Scottish sympathies 1807.

2. He seems to me a remarkably good critic, where his Scoticism doesn't come in his way 1862.

Scotticize (skǫ·tisəiz), *v.* 1763. [f. as prec. + -IZE.] **1.** *trans.* To imbue with Scottish ideas or characteristics. **2.** To give a Scottish form to (a foreign word); to turn (a work) into Scottish dialect 1874.

Scottish (skǫ·tiʃ), *a.* and *sb.* [Late OE. *Scottisc*, f. *Scotta* SCOT *sb.*[1] + *-isc* -ISH[1].] **A.** *adj.* **1.** Of or belonging to Scotland or to the people of Scotland; of Scotch nationality, birth, or descent. **b.** With ref. to law 1726. †**2.** *transf.* Marked by Scottish characteristics -1620. **3.** Applied to the language (see SCOTS *a.* 2) 1718.

1. The King's Own S. Borderers 1888.

B. *sb.* (the adj. used absol.) **1.** The Scottish language 1708. **2.** *The S.* (with pl. sense): the Scots (*rare*) 1632.

Scoundrel (skau·ndrəl), *sb.* and *a.* 1589. [Origin unkn.] **A.** *sb.* 'A mean rascal, a low petty villain' (J.). Now usu., an audacious rascal, one destitute of all moral scruple. Also *attrib.* and *appositive.*

If your ancient, but ignoble blood Has crept thro' scoundrels ever since the flood POPE.

B. *adj.* Now *rare.* **1.** Of a person: That is a scoundrel; scoundrelly. Of a company: Composed of scoundrels. 1643. **2.** Pertaining to or characteristic of a scoundrel. Of conduct: Mean, unprincipled. 1681.

2. 'A penny savèd is a penny got'—Firm to this s. maxim keepeth he THOMSON. Hence **Scou·ndreldom,** the world of scoundrels, scoundrels collectively; also = *scoundrelism.* **Scou·ndrelism,** the character, conduct, or practices of a s.; also, a piece of scoundrelism. **Scou·ndrelly** *a.* having the character of a s.; of, belonging to, or characteristic of a s.; characterized by scoundrelism.

Scour (skauəɹ), *sb.* 1619. [f. SCOUR *v.*[2]] **1.** An apparatus for washing auriferous soil. **2.** The action of a current or flow of water in clearing away mud or other deposit; in *Civil Engineering*, an artificial current or flow produced for this purpose; also, an engineering work constructed for the purpose of producing such a current 1729. **3.** A place in a river where the bottom is scoured by the stream; a river-shallow with a gravel bottom 1681. **4.** A kind of diarrhœa in cattle 1764. **5.** An act of scouring, cleansing, or polishing 1825.

Scour (skauəɹ), *v.*[1] ME. [Origin obsc.] **1.** *intr.* To move *about* hastily or energetically; *esp.* to range about in search of something, or in movements against a foe. **b.** To move rapidly, go in haste, run ME. **2.** *trans.* To pass rapidly over or along (a tract of land or water); *esp.* to traverse in quest of something, or in order to capture or drive away a foe. late ME. †**3.** *spec.* in 17th-18th c. slang (cf. SCOURER[1] 2). **a.** *intr.* To roam about at night uproariously, breaking windows, beating the watch, and molesting wayfarers -1756. **b.** *trans.* To ill-treat or 'maul' (the watch, wayfarers, etc.) while roistering in the streets -1723.

1. Sirra go you and scoure about the hill HEYWOOD. b. I..scoured on my way with more speed than before BORROW. 2. Patrols..s. the streets, all that night CARLYLE. 3. b. Scowring the Watch grows out of fashion wit DRYDEN.

Scour (skauəɹ), *v.*[2] late ME. [prob. a. MDu. or MLG. *schūren*, app. a. OF. *escurer* :—pop. L. **excurare* to polish, scour, f. L. *ex* + *curare.*] **1.** *trans.* To cleanse or polish (metal, earthenware, wood, etc.) by hard rubbing with some detergent substance. Sometimes with compl. adj., as *bright, clean*, etc. Also const. *of, from* (rust, etc.). Also *absol.* or *intr.* **b.** To clean the inside of (a gun) after firing 1611. **2.** To remove grease or dirt from (cloth, wool, silk, etc.) by some detergent process. Also *absol.* 1467. **3.** To wash vigorously (the hands, face, teeth); to 'scrub'. Now only *joc.* 1589. **4.** To cleanse (a wound, ulcer, the entrails of an animal) by treating with some medicament. late ME. **5.** To clear out (a channel, ditch, drain, etc.) by removing dirt, weeds, etc. late ME. **6.** To clear out or cleanse by flushing with water 1587. **7.** To purge (an animal, a person, the body, etc.); to evacuate (the stomach or bowels). Also, to cleanse (worms, fish, etc.) by purging. late ME. **b.** *intr.* (for *refl.*) To be purged. Of cattle: To have diarrhœa. 1592. **8.** *fig.* To rid, clear (a place, the sea, etc.) *of* or *from* an enemy or other undesirable occupants ME. †**9.** *fig.* To beat, scourge. Hence, to punish, treat severely. -1730. **10.** To sweep or rake (a place, position, etc.) with gun-shot. Also, to command (a position) with one's guns. 1563. **11.** To remove, get rid of. Chiefly with advs., as *away, off, out.* late ME.

1. *absol.* Item, she can wash and scoure SHAKS. 2. *absol.* Warme Water scoureth better than Cold BACON. 4. Take your eel and s. it well with salt MRS. GLASSE. 5. Working hard to s. their moats DE FOE. 9. But I will pay the dog, I will s. him FIELDING. 11. The stains will not easily (if at all) be scoured off again 1631. The tide enters far up each channel, scouring out mud and sand 1849. Hence **Scoured** (skauəɹd) *ppl. a.* in various senses; also *sb.* (*Austral.*) = scoured wool.

Scourer[1] (skauə·rəɹ). late ME. [In sense 1 orig. aphetic f. DISCOVERER; afterwards as agent-n. f. SCOUR *v.*[1] + -ER[1].] †**1.** One sent out to reconnoitre; a scout or avant-courier -1826. **2.** In the 17th-18th c.: One who made a practice of roistering through the streets at night, beating the watch, breaking windows, etc. 1672.

Scourer[2] (skauə·rəɹ). late ME. [f. SCOUR *v.*[2] + -ER[1].] **1.** One who cleanses by rubbing; esp. as the designation of certain servants in the Royal Household 1576. **2.** A person or thing which cleans or scours; *spec.* †a contrivance for cleaning out the bore of a gun. late ME.

Scourge (skɔ̄ɹdʒ), *sb.* ME. [a. AF. *escorge, escurge*, related to OF. *escorgiee* (mod.F. *écourgée*) :—pop. L. **excoriata* scourge, lit. strip of hide, f. late L. *excoriare*, f. *ex-* EX- + *corium* hide.] **1.** A whip, lash. Now only *rhet.* **2.** *fig.* and in fig. context; chiefly, a thing or person that is an instrument of divine chastisement. late ME. **3. a.** A cause of (usu., widespread) calamity. **b.** One who 'lashes' vice or folly. 1535. †**4.** [After L. *flagellum.*] An offshoot of a vine or other tree, a sucker -1578.

1. Mortify Your flesh, like me, with scourges and with thorns TENNYSON. 2. *The S. of God* (= L. *flagellum Dei*); a title given by historians to Attila, the leader of the Huns in the 5th century. 3. a. Raleigh, the s. of Spain! THOMSON. b. Swift, that severe s. of the vices and follies of his time 1756.

Scourge (skɔ̄ɹdʒ), *v.* ME. [a. OF. *escorgier*, f. *escorge* SCOURGE *sb.*] **1.** *trans.* To beat with a scourge; to whip severely, flog. Now *rhet.* **b.** To drive or force by or as by blows of a whip 1667. **c.** In fig. context 1591. **2.** *fig.* To punish, chastise, correct (often said of God, with ref. to Heb. xii. 6); to 'lash' with satire or invective; to afflict, torment; to devastate (a country) with war or pestilence. late ME. **3.** *Sc.* To exhaust the fertility of (land) 1799.

1. Therfore Pilat took thanne Jhesu and scourgide WYCLIF *John* xix. 1. b. Scourged from the council with a storm of blows 1870. c. The waves..Scourged by the wind's invisible tyranny SHELLEY. 2. Forsoth he scourgith euery sone that he receyueth WYCLIF *Heb.* xii. 6. 3. Flax..is a crop which scourges the ground 1888. Hence **Scou·rger,** one who scourges or flogs (*lit.* and *fig.*).

Scouse (skaus). 1840. [Shortened f. LOBSCOUSE.] = LOBSCOUSE.

Scout (skaut), *sb.*[1] late ME. [a. MDu. *schûte* SCHUIT.] A flat-bottomed boat; 'a Dutch vessel, galliot rigged, used in the river trade of Holland'.

Scout (skaut), *sb.*[2] 1553. [a. F. *escoute* action of listening, listener, scout, f. *escouter* :—L. *auscultare*.] 1. The action of spying out or watching in order to gain information; chiefly in *on* or *in* (*the*) *s.*, *to the s.* 2. *Mil.* One sent out ahead of the main force in order to reconnoitre the position and movements of the enemy. Hence occas.: One sent out to obtain information. 1555. b. **Boy s.**: a member of an organization consisting of boys who meet periodically to practise exercises and to undergo training in the duties belonging to a scout 1908. †3. A body of men sent out to gain information –1775. 4. One who keeps watch upon the actions of another; a watchman. †Formerly often: A mean spy, a sneak. 1584. 5. A type of war-vessel adapted for the purposes of reconnoitring; also, an air-vessel similarly used 1706. †6. *Cricket.* = FIELDSMAN a. Also in *Baseball.* b. A boy who is employed to run after the balls at 'practice'. 1824.

1. I set my self upon the S. as often as possible DE FOE. 2. Scouts each Coast light-armed scoure, Each quarter, to descrie the distant foe MILT.

Scout (skaut), *sb.*[3] 1596. [Origin obsc.] A local name for various sea-birds native to Great Britain; as the Guillemot, Razor-bill, and Puffin.

Scout (skaut), *sb.*[4] 1708. [Origin unkn.] At Oxford (also at Yale and Harvard): A (male) college servant.

Scout (skaut), *v.*[1] late ME. [f. SCOUT *sb.*[2]] 1. *intr.* To act as a scout, to play the spy; to travel about (in search of information). 2. *trans.* To reconnoitre, to examine with a view to obtaining information 1704.

1. S. mee for him at the corner of the Orchard like a bum-Baylie SHAKS. 2. To s. the country 1900. Hence **Scou·ting** *vbl. sb.* the action of the vb.; the exercises practised by boy scouts'.

Scout (skaut), *v.*[2] 1605. [Of Scand. origin; cf. ON. *skúta, skúte* taunt.] †1. *trans.* To mock at, deride. Also *absol.* –1768. 2. To reject with scorn (a proposition); to treat as absurd (an idea); to dismiss scornfully the pretensions of (a person, a work, etc.) 1710.

1. Flout 'em, and cout 'em: and skowt 'em, and flout 'em SHAKS.

Scou·tmaster, scou·t-master. 1579. [f. SCOUT *sb.*[2] + MASTER *sb.*[1]] A leader or captain of a band of scouts. Now also, the officer who has charge of a 'troop' of boy scouts.

S. General (Hist.), the chief of the intelligence department of the Parliamentary army.

Scow (skau), *sb.* *U.S.*, *Scotland*, and *Ireland.* 1775. [a. Du. *schouw*, related to OS. *scaldan* to push (a boat) from the shore.] A large flat-bottomed lighter or punt. Hence **Scow** *v. intr.* to cross *over* (a river) by means of a s.; *trans.* to transport in a s.

Scowl (skaul), *sb.* 1500. [f. next.] A louring or malevolent look. b. *transf.* Of clouds, the elements, etc. 1648.

Received with scowls and curses 1909. b. Sky—what a s. of cloud BROWNING.

Scowl (skaul), *v.* ME. [prob. of Scand. origin.] 1. *intr.* To look with louring brows and a malignant or threatening expression; to look angry or sullen. Const. *at, on, upon.* b. To be exhibited or expressed frowningly or with a scowl. *poet.* or *rhet.* 1719. 2. *transf.* and *fig.* Of inanimate things (sometimes personified): To assume a gloomy, forbidding, or threatening aspect 1587. 3. *trans.* in *nonce-uses.* To send forth or express with a scowl 1667.

1. Myne enemy skouleth vpon me with his eyes COVERDALE *Job* xvi. 9. b. A menace scowled upon the brow W. IRVING. 2. When winter scowls COWPER. Hence **Scow·ler. Scow·lingly** *adv.*

Scr- may represent OE. *scr-* (variously in mod. dialects as ʃr-, ʃər-, sr-) or ON *skr-*, as in SCRAPE *v.*; cf. *shred* and *screed* from OE. *scréade*, and *shrew*, dial. *screw*, from OE. *scréawa.* 2. There are many instances of initial *scr-* varying with *cr-*, e.g. *scrag, crag; scrunch, crunch.*

Scrabble (skræ·b'l), *sb.* 1842. [f. next.] A scrawling character in writing; hence, a document composed of such characters. Also, a picture composed of or characterized by careless or hastily-executed line-work.

Scrabble (skræ·b'l), *v.* 1537. [a. Du. *schrabbelen*, freq. of *schrabben* to scratch, scrape.] 1. *intr.* To make marks at random; to scrawl, scribble. b. *trans.* To write or depict (something) in a scrawling manner; also, to scrawl upon (something) 1856. 2. *intr.* Of an animal: To scratch about hurriedly with the claws or paws; hence, of a person, to scratch or scrape about with the hands or feet 1600. 3. Of a person: To scramble on hands and feet; to stumble or struggle along; also *occas.* of an animal. Now somewhat *rare.* 1638.

1. And he..scrabled on the dores of the gate BIBLE (1537) 1 *Sam.* xxi. 13. 2. Gangs of the prying gull That shriek and s. on the river hatches KIPLING. 3. Little-faith came to himself, and getting up made shift to s. on his way BUNYAN.

Scrabe (skrēⁱb). *Sc.* and *n. dial.* 1676. [a. Da., ad. Færöese *skrápur.*] The Manx Shearwater, *Puffinus anglorum.*

Scraber (skrēⁱ·bəɹ). *Sc.* 1698. [Origin obsc.] A name for the Manx Shearwater, and the Black Guillemot, *Uria Grylle.*

Scrag (skræg), *sb.*[1] 1542. [prob. altered f. CRAG *sb.*[2]] 1. A lean person or animal. (In depreciatory use.) 2. The lean and inferior end of a neck of mutton (or veal). Also (earlier) *s.-end.* 1644. 3. *slang.* The neck (of a human being) 1756. 4. **S. whale**, a finner-whale of the sub-family *Agaphelinæ*, esp. *Agaphelus gibbosus*, common in the North Atlantic 1701.

2. Lady Mac-Screw..serves up a s.-of-mutton on silver THACKERAY. Hence **Scragged** (skrægd) *a.*[2] scraggy.

Scrag (skræg), *sb.*[2] Now chiefly *dial.* 1567. [Origin obsc.] 1. A stump of a tree; also, a rough projection (on a pole, trunk, or stump of a tree, rock, etc.). 2. Rough, rocky and barren ground 1858.

Scrag (skræg), *v.* *slang.* 1756. [f. SCRAG *sb.*[1]] *trans.* To hang (on the gallows). b. To wring the neck of; also, to garotte 1823. Hence **Scra·gger**, the hangman.

†**Scragged**, *a.*[1] 1519. [app. alteration of CRAGGED *a.*[1]] Rough and irregular in outline; of ground, rugged and barren –1725.

Scraggy (skræ·gi), *a.*[1] 1611. [f. SCRAG *sb.*[1] + -Y[1].] 1. Lean, thin, bony. (Chiefly *depreciatory.*) b. *transf.* and *fig.* Meagre, thin, scanty 1837. 2. Of meat: Lean 1725.

1. A bevy of dowagers, stout or s. THACKERAY. b. The scraggiest of prophetic discourses CARLYLE. Hence **Scra·ggily** *adv.*[1] **Scra·gginess**[1].

Scraggy (skræ·gi), *a.*[2] 1574. [f. SCRAG *sb.*[2] + -Y[1].] Rough, irregular or broken in outline or contour; esp. of rocks, rugged. Hence **Scra·ggily**, *adv.*[2] **Scra·gginess.**[2]

Scramble (skræ·mb'l), *sb.* 1674. [f. next.] 1. A struggle with others for something or a share of something; hence, an indecorous struggle, a confused or disorderly proceeding. 2. An act of scrambling; a scrambling journey 1755.

1. But the s. for new lands..will become less acute as there is less territory to be absorbed 1907. 2. A brisk s. to the top 1873.

Scramble (skræ·mb'l), *v.* 1586. [Origin obsc.] 1. *intr.* To raise oneself to an erect posture, to get through or into a place or position, by the struggling use of the hands and feet; hence, to make one's way by clambering, crawling, jumping, etc. over difficult ground or through obstructions. b. *trans.* To collect or gather *up* hastily or in disorder 1822. 2. *intr.* To strive or struggle with others for mastery; to contend with a crowd for a share of food, coin, wealth, etc. 1590. b. *trans.* To contend or struggle with others for (a share of something distributed) 1647. 3. To cook (eggs) in the manner called 'scrambled' 1850.

1. We..then scrambled up a very high and steep hill 1687. *fig.* I had not even scrambled into my clothes 1900. b. He hastily scrambled up the papers 1833. 2. Of other care they little reck'ning make, Then how to s. at the shearers feast, And shove away the worthy bidden guest MILT. Hence **Scra·mbler.**

Scrambled (skræ·mb'ld), *ppl. a.* 1609. [f. prec. + -ED[1].] In senses of the verb.

S. eggs, a dish of eggs broken into the pan and cooked with milk, butter, salt, and pepper.

Scrambling (skræ·mbliŋ), *ppl. a.* 1607. [f. as prec. + -ING[2].] 1. Of persons: That scramble or contend one with another. 2. Irregular or rambling in form or habit. Of a plant: Of straggling growth. 1688. b. Of a person: Shambling, uncouth 1765. 3. Irregular, unmethodical 1778.

2. A huge old s. bed-room SCOTT. Hence **Scra·mblingly** *adv.*

Scran (skræn). *slang* and *dial.* 1724. [Origin unkn.] †A reckoning at a tavern; eatables, provisions; broken victuals. *Bad s. to* (Irish): bad luck to.

Scranch (skrǭnʃ), *v.* *Obs.* exc. *dial.* 1620. [App. echoic.] *trans.* = CRUNCH *v.* 1, 2.

Scrannel (skræ·nĕl), *a.* 1637. [Cf. Norw. *skran* lean, shrivelled.] Thin, meagre. Now chiefly, after Milton: Harsh, unmelodious.

Their lean and flashy songs Grate on their s. Pipes of wretched straw MILT.

Scranny (skræ·ni), *a.*[1] Chiefly *dial.* 1820. [Cf. prec.] Lean, thin. Of diet: Poor, meagre.

Scranny (skræ·ni), *a.*[2] orig. *dial.* Crazy.

Scrap (skræp), *sb.*[1] late ME. [a. ON. *skrap* scraps, trifles, f. root of *skrapa* SCRAPE *v.*] 1. *pl.* The remains of a meal; fragments (of food); broken meat. *rare* in *sing.* 2. A remnant; a fragmentary portion 1583. b. A small picture, cutting, etc. to be put in a SCRAP-BOOK or used for ornamenting a screen, box, or the like 1880. 3. *pl.* The pieces of blubber, fish, etc. remaining after the oil has been extracted. Also *collect. sing.* 1631. 4. *Founding.* a. *pl.* Remnants of metal produced in cutting up or casting 1736. b. = SCRAP-IRON 1846. 5. *attrib.* quasi-*adj.* Consisting of scraps 1815.

1. 'Twas but for scraps he ask'd POPE. 2. Forced to get what Scraps of Learning I could by my own Industry STEELE. There is not a s. of evidence in support of it 1868. *S. of paper* (with allusion to an alleged reference (Aug. 1914) by the German Chancellor to the treaty securing the neutrality of Belgium), any agreement that can be lightly set aside or disregarded.

Scrap (skræp), *sb.*[2] *slang.* 1874. [Cf. next.] A struggle, scrimmage, tussle; a boxing-match. b. A row, quarrel, heated discussion 1889.

Scrap (skræp), *v.*[1] *slang.* 1874. [f. prec.] a. *intr.* To fight, box. Also, to scrimmage. b. *trans.* To box with (an opponent) 1893. c. *intr.* To quarrel, engage in angry dispute 1909.

Scrap (skræp), *v.*[2] 1891. [f. SCRAP *sb.*[1]] 1. *trans.* To break up into scrap-iron (machinery, etc.); to consign to the scrap-heap 1902. 2. To make scrap or refuse of (menhaden or blubber) 1891.

Scra·p-book. 1825. [f. SCRAP *sb.*[1]] A blank book in which pictures, newspaper cuttings, and the like are pasted for preservation.

Scrape (skrēⁱp), *sb.* 1440. [f. next.] I. 1. A scraper. 2. An act of scraping 1483. b. An awkward bow or salutation in which the foot is drawn backwards on the ground 1628. c. A drawing of the bow over the violin 1831. d. A sound of scraping 1886. 3. A place scraped bare on a hillside. *dial.* 1781. 4. A layer (of butter) scraped thin; chiefly in *bread and s.* (*colloq.*) 1847.

2. *S. of a pen* (Sc.), a hasty scribble, a small scrap of writing. b. I..made him abundance of bows and scrapes DE FOE.

II. An embarrassing or awkward predicament or situation, usu. one into which a person is brought by his own imprudence and thoughtlessness 1709.

I was generally the leader of the boys and sometimes led them into scrapes 1771.

Scrape (skrēⁱp), *v.* Pa. t. and pple. **scraped** (skrēⁱpt). [ME., perh. repr. OE. *scrapian*; perh. a. ON. *skrapa* to scrape, erase :—OTeut. type **skrapōjan*, f. root **skrap-*, ablaut-var. of **skrep-* in OE. *screpan* to scrape.] 1. *trans.* To remove (an outer layer, etc.) by drawing across the surface the edge of some instrument held nearly perpendicularly. Chiefly with advs. late ME. †b. *spec.* To erase (writing, etc.) with a knife –1688. 2. To deprive of an outer layer or to free from excrescent or adhering matter by drawing the edge of some instrument over the surface; to abrade, clean, or render smooth, or to obtain scrapings from, by this process. late ME. b. To inscribe or portray on stone by scraping away the surface 1532. c. To produce (a mezzotint engraving) by scraping the prepared copper plate 1747. †3. Of a beast or bird: To remove (soil, etc.) by scratching with the feet or claws; to make (a hole) thus -1662. b. *trans.* with adv. or phr. 1530. †4. To scratch with the finger-nails or claws; also *intr.* -1607. 5. (*fig.* of sense 3.) 'To gather by great efforts, or penurious or trifling diligence' (J.); to amass, collect, or bring together with difficulty. Now only with *together* or *up.* 1549. b. *To s.* (*an*) *acquaintance*: to get on terms of acquaintance *with* by careful effort and insinuation 1600. c. *absol.* and *intr.* To hoard up penuriously; to gather together money, etc. with labour and difficulty. Now chiefly *dial.* 1552. 6. Used disparagingly for: To play (a fiddle); occas. *to s. catgut*; to play (a tune, etc.) on the fiddle 1599. 7. To rub harshly on (a surface) in passing along or over it; to draw (something) roughly over a surface 1731. b. *intr.* To graze *against* or *on* 1774. c. To draw one's feet noisily over the floor 1561. 8. *intr.* To make obeisance, to bow awkwardly, drawing the foot back 1645.

1. Like dry colours scraped off a picture 1877. b. *Meas. for M.* I. ii. 9. 2. An ironclad's..bottom is always foul when she cannot be periodically docked and scraped 1884. b. The family arms were just new scraped in stone THACKERAY. 5. The first money he was able to s. together by strict frugality 1888. b. To slave..and s. to get a house over your head 1881. 7. c. Another [orator] was coughed and scraped down MACAULAY. 8. Bowing and scraping and rubbing his hands together TROLLOPE.

Phrases. *To s. along*, to manage or 'get along' with difficulty. *To s. through*, to get through a trial, an examination, so as just to escape failure.

Comb.: **s.-gut**, a fiddler; **†-penny**, a miser. Hence **Scra·ping** *ppl. a.* that scrapes; *esp.* money-grubbing, miserly.

Scraper (skrēⁱ·pəɹ). 1552. [f. SCRAPE *v.* + -ER¹.] I. One who scrapes. 1. One who 'scrapes together'; *esp.* a money-grubber. Now *rare.* 1561. 2. One who scrapes (something specified or implied); *esp.* a fiddler 1591. II. An instrument for scraping with. 1. A scraping instrument held in the hand. a. *gen.* 1552. b. = STRIGIL 1667. c. An instrument used for scraping off paint, tar, adhesive labels, etc. from wooden surfaces 1691. d. *Engraving.* A three-sided tool used to remove burrs left by the graver, etc., or to obliterate lines. Also the similar instrument used in 'scraping' mezzotint. 1747. 2. An appliance fixed outside the door of a house for persons to scrape off upon it the dirt from the soles of their boots or shoes before entering 1729. 3. A machine (or scoop) drawn by horses or oxen for excavating ditches, canals, etc., for levelling and making roads, or for raising and removing soil, dirt, weeds, etc. a short distance 1840. b. An instrument for scraping dirt, mud, etc. from roads, etc. Also *road-s.* 1831.

Scra·pe-tre·ncher. *Obs.* exc. *Hist.* 1603. [f. SCRAPE *v.* + TRENCHER.] A servant whose office was to scrape the trenchers after use.

Scra·p-heap, *sb.* 1838. [f. SCRAP *sb.*¹] A heap of SCRAP IRON. Hence *fig.* in phrases, as *to consign to the s.*, to cast aside as worn out or superseded. Hence **Scra·p-heap** *v. trans.* to consign to the s.

Scraping (skrēⁱ·piŋ), *vbl.sb.* 1440. [-ING¹.] 1. The action of SCRAPE *v.* b. The noise produced by drawing something roughly over a surface 1561. 2. *pl. concr.* That which is scraped off, up, or together. Rarely *sing.* 1511.

2. The dust and scrapings from roads 1790.

Scrap iron. 1823. [f. SCRAP *sb.*¹] Iron which has already been cast or wrought and broken up or cast aside for re-casting or reworking; broken pieces and small articles of old and disused ironwork. Also *attrib.*

Scrappy (skræ·pi), *a.* 1837. [f. SCRAP *sb.*¹ + -Y¹.] Consisting of scraps; made up of odds and ends; disjointed, unconnected.

A dreadfully s. dinner THACKERAY. Hence **Scra·ppily** *adv.* **Scra·ppiness.**

Scrat, *sb. Obs.* or *dial.* [OE. *scratta (app. miswritten *scritta*).] A hermaphrodite.

Scrat, *v. Obs.* exc. *dial.* [Early ME. *scratte*; etym. dub.] 1. *intr.* To use the nails or claws for attack; to scratch (*at* a person). 2. *trans.* and *intr.* = SCRATCH *v.* 1, 4, 5. ME.

Scratch (skrætʃ), *sb.*¹ 1586. [f. SCRATCH *v.*] I. Result of scratching. 1. A slight tearing or incision of the skin produced by a sharp instrument. (Sometimes applied slightingly to a trifling flesh-wound.) 2. *pl.* A disease of horses, in which the pastern appears as if scratched 1591. 3. A mark or furrow produced by the grinding contact of two substances; a shallow linear incision 1662. 4. A rough or irregular mark made by a pencil, paint-brush, etc.; hence, a slight sketch, a hasty scrawl 1646. 5. *Sporting.* A line or mark drawn as an indication of a boundary or starting-point; in *Pugilism*, the line drawn across the ring, to which boxers are brought for an encounter 1778. b. The starting-point in a handicap of a competitor who receives no odds 1867. 6. The sound produced by the friction of two more or less rough surfaces 1787; *spec.* during the reproduction of a sound film or record 1930.

1. A little s., rather then a wound SIDNEY. 4. Every s. of his pen was accounted a treasure COWPER. 5. Phr. (often fig.) *To come up to* (*the*) *s.*, *to bring to the s.*, *to toe the s.*

II. An act of scratching (*rare*) 1765. III. Ellipt. for *scratch periwig* 1755.

Comb.: (in sense 5b) as **s.-line**, **-player**; **s.-cat**, (joc.) a spiteful person; **-grass**, a dial. name for cleavers, and, in U.S., the arrow-leaved tear-thumb; **-periwig**, **-wig**, a small, short wig.

Scratch (skrætʃ), *sb.*² *colloq.* (now chiefly *dial.*). 1740. A name for the devil, usu. *Old S.*

Scratch (skrætʃ), *a.* 1853. [orig. SCRATCH *sb.*¹ used attrib.] 1. Hastily sketched. 2. Hastily assembled or put together 1859.

2. *S. vote, division, majority*, one which, owing to accident or stratagem, does not represent the actual state of opinion in a deliberative body, etc.

Scratch (skrætʃ), *v.* 1474. [app. produced by confusion of SCRAT and CRATCH *vbs.*] 1. *trans.* To wound superficially by dragging the claws or finger-nails over the skin. Also, in wider sense: To wound superficially with anything pointed and hard dragged over the skin or in contact with its moving surface, so as to produce a slight linear tearing or abrasion. b. With adv.: To tear *out* (e.g. the eyes) or to drag *off* (a portion of the skin, a pimple, etc.) with the claws or nails 1591. c. *absol.* or *intr.* To use the claws or nails as weapons of offence. Also occas. of inanimate things, to produce a scratch. 1589. 2. *trans.* To rub or scrape lightly (a part of the body) with the finger-nails or claws (e.g. to relieve itching). So *to s. one's head*, as a gesture indicating perplexity. Also *intr.* for *refl.* 1530. 3. To make slight linear abrasions on (a surface of any kind) 1669. b. *hyperbolically.* To furrow (the soil) very lightly for the purpose of cultivation 1697. c. To produce (marks) or portray (an object) by light incisions on a surface 1644. 4. *intr.* Of a bird or animal: To remove earth, etc. with the claws 1520. 5. *fig.* a. To struggle to make money, to 'scrape'. Also *trans.* to scrape up (money). Now *dial.* 1509. b. *intr.* with adv. To get *along, on, through* with difficulty 1838. †6. *trans.* To seize rapaciously, as a bird with its claws; to get possession of by effort or with difficulty -1680. 7. a. trans. *To s. out*: to erase (writing) with a penknife; also, to delete by crossing through with a pen 1711. b. To erase the name of (a person) from a list; hence, to expunge from a list of candidates or competitors; *Sporting*, to withdraw (a horse, etc.) from the list of entries for a race, etc. 1685. c. *U.S. Politics.* Of a voter: To erase the name of (a candidate) from the party ticket 1888. d. *intr.* for *refl.* To withdraw from a competition; *joc.* to withdraw one's acceptance of an invitation 1866. 8. To drag the nails or claws over a surface so as to make a faint grating noise. Also, of a pen, to move over the paper with a slight noise. 1703. b. *trans.* To rub gratingly on a rough surface 1864. 9. To scribble, write hurriedly or carelessly 1789.

1. He scracchid hym in the visage CAXTON. c. How the long brambles do s. HOOD. 2. If my haire do but tickle me, I must s. SHAKS. The homely adage, 'S. my back and I'll s. yours' 1885. 3. Marble is soft, and can be scratched with a knife 1794. *To s. the surface* (fig.), to be superficial. 4. Phr. *To s. out*, to extricate or disinter with the claws. *To s. up*, to heap up by scratching. 8. b. A match being scratched on a box 1875.

Comb.: **s.-back**, an instrument for scratching the back to allay itching, usu. in the form of a small hand of ivory or metal fixed to a long handle; formerly, a toy which produces a sound of tearing cloth when rubbed upon a person's back.

Scratch-brush (skræ·tʃ₁brɒʃ), *sb.* 1797. [f. SCRATCH *sb.* or *v.*] A brush of fine wire used in gilding, electroplating, etc. to polish or clean articles of metal. Hence **Scra·tch-brush** *v. trans.* to polish by means of a s.

Scratcher (skræ·tʃəɹ). 1517. [f. SCRATCH *v.* + -ER¹.] One who scratches. b. *Ornith.* Used in *pl.* to render mod.L. *Rasores* (Illiger), an order of birds that scratch for their food 1831. c. A tool used in plastering to roughen the surface of the preliminary coating 1812.

Scratchy (skræ·tʃi), *a.* 1817. [f. SCRATCH *sb.*¹ + -Y¹.] 1. Of work executed with the pen or brush: Composed of scratches, as opposed to bold, firm lines. 2. Apt to scratch 1866. 3. *Sporting.* Of action: Ill-sustained, uneven, 'ragged' 1881.

2. Written with a s. pen 1866.

Scraw (skrǭ). *dial.* (Anglo-Irish, Sc., Manx.) 1725. [a. Irish and Gael. *sgrath*, pronounced (skrā).] 1. A turf. †2. A thin covering of grass-grown soil formed upon the surface of a bog -1820.

Scrawl (skrǭl), *sb.*¹ 1693. [f. SCRAWL *v.*²] 1. Something scrawled; a hastily and badly written letter, a careless sketch. †b. *pl.* Scrawled or illegible characters -1807. 2. A careless illegible style of handwriting 1710.

1. A s. from his pencil brings an enormous price 1840. 2. Her hand-writing..a miserable s. 1775.

Scrawl (skrǭl), *sb.*² *dial.* 1847. [Cf. OF. *escrouelle* river-shrimp.] The young of the dog-crab (*Cancer caninus*).

Scrawl, *v.*¹ *Obs.* exc. *dial.* late ME. [App. altered f. CRAWL *v.*] †1. *intr.* To spread the limbs abroad in a sprawling manner; to gesticulate -1582. 2. = CRAWL *v.* 1. 1530.

Scrawl (skrǭl), *v.*² 1611. [perh. a use of prec.] 1. *trans.* To write or draw in a sprawling, untidy manner 1612. b. To cover (a surface) with scrawling inscriptions or marks. Also with *over.* 1647. 2. *intr.* To scribble, to write carelessly or awkwardly 1611.

1. b. The windows of all the inns are scrawled with doggrel rhimes SMOLLETT. Hence **Scraw·ler**, one who writes carelessly. **Scraw·ly** *a.* badly or untidily written; irregularly designed.

Scrawny (skrǭ·ni), *a.* *U.S.* 1833. [var. of SCRANNY.] Lean, scraggy.

Scray (skrēⁱ). 1668. [History obsc.] The common tern, *Sterna hirundo.*

Scraze (skrēⁱz), *v. dial.* 1662. [Blending of SCRATCH, GRAZE *vbs.*] *trans.* To graze.

Screak (skrīk), *v.* Now chiefly *dial.* 1500. [a. ON. *skrækja*, prob. echoic; cf. SCREECH, SHRIEK *vbs.*] *intr.* To utter a shrill harsh cry; to screech or scream. Also with *out.* b. Of an ungreased hinge or axle, etc.: To make a shrill grating sound 1565. Hence **Screak** *sb.* a shrill cry; a shrill grating sound.

Scream (skrīm), *sb.* 1513. [f. next.] A shrill piercing cry, usu. expressive of pain, alarm, mirth, or other sudden emotion. b. *slang.* Something which causes one to 'scream' with laughter; a supremely ridiculous person or thing. (Cf. the earlier SCREAMER 4 b.) 1915.

She dropped them with a s. of terror THACKERAY. *transf.* The eagles answer'd with their s. SCOTT.

Scream (skrīm), *v.* [Early ME. *scræmen*, *screamen*, perh. :—OE. *scrǽman.] 1. *intr.* To utter a shrill piercing cry, normally expressive of pain, alarm, mirth, or other sudden emotion. Also, to produce unpleasantly loud and shrill upper notes in singing. b. Of certain birds and beasts: To emit their characteristic shrill cry ME. c. To make a noise like a scream 1784. 2. *trans.* To utter with a scream 1710.

1. She screamed for help MACAULAY. quasi-*trans.* She would s. the house down 1862. b. I heard the Owle schreame, and the Crickets cry SHAKS. c. The fiddle screams Plaintive and piteous COWPER.

Screamer (skrī·məɹ). 1712. [f. prec. + -ER¹.] 1. One who screams; one who sings in shrill piercing tones. 2. An animal that utters a cry like a scream 1801. 3. *spec.* a. Any bird of the S. Amer. family *Palamedeidæ*; esp. the KAMICHI or Horned S., and *Chauna Chavaria*, the Crested S. 1773. b. The swift (*local*) 1813.

4. *slang.* **a.** A person, animal, or thing of exceptional size, attractiveness, etc.; a splendid specimen 1837. **b.** A composition of a startling or exaggerated character; e.g. a thrilling or funny story, a 'screaming' farce 1844.

4. a. I..lost one s. just up the back ditch there. He must have been a four-pounder. 1861.

Screaming (skrī·miŋ), *ppl. a.* 1602. [-ING².] **1.** That screams; sounding shrilly. **2.** *transf.* and *fig.* **a.** Tending to excite screams of laughter; said esp. of a farce 1854. **b.** Violent or startling in effect; glaring 1848. **c.** *slang.* First-rate, splendid 1864.

1. Like so many s. grasse-hoppers B. JONSON. 2. c. A s. success 1879. Hence **Screa·mingly** *adv.*

Scree (skrī). 1781. [a. ON. *skriða* landslip, cogn .w. *skriða* to slide, glide.] A mass of detritus, forming a precipitous, stony slope upon a mountain-side. Also, the material composing such a slope.

Screech (skrītʃ), *sb.* 1560. [f. next.] **1.** A loud shrill cry, usu. one expressive of violent and uncontrollable pain or alarm. **2.** *transf.* A harsh, squeaking sound made by some inanimate object 1832.

Comb.: in dial. names of birds with ref. to their harsh discordant cry, as **s.-bird, -thrush,** the Fieldfare (*Turdus pilaris*); **-hawk,** the Nightjar (*Caprimulgus Europæus*); **-thrush,** the Missel-thrush (*Turdus viscivorus*).

Screech (skrītʃ), *v.* 1577. [Echoic var. of SCRITCH *v.*] **1.** *intr.* To utter a sharp, piercing cry, as of pain or alarm; to call out shrilly; also occas. used *transf.* of inanimate things. **2.** *trans.* To utter (a word or sentence) with a loud, shrill, piercing sound 1844.

1. A draggled fishwife screeches at the gates 1888. Hence **Scree·cher,** one who screeches; *dial.* any of several birds having a harsh screaming cry, e. g. the Swift, the Gull-billed Tern, the Missel-thrush.

Scree·ch-owl. 1593. [f. SCREECH *v.*; altered f. SCRITCH-OWL.] **1.** The Barn Owl, from its discordant cry, supposed to be of evil omen. **2.** *transf.* Applied to a bearer of evil tidings, or one who presages misfortune 1606.

1. The time when Screech-owles cry, and Bandogs howle SHAKS. 2. *Tr. & Cr.* v. x. 16.

Screechy (skrī·tʃi), *a.* 1830. [f. SCREECH *sb.* + -Y¹.] Of a voice: Given to screech; loud, shrill, and discordant.

Screed (skrīd). ME. [var. of SHRED *sb.*, repr. OE. *scréade.*] **1.** A fragment cut, torn, or broken from a main piece; in later use, a torn strip of some textile material. *Obs.* exc. *dial.* **b.** A strip of land; a parcel of ground 1615. **2.** *fig.* A long roll or list; a lengthy discourse or harangue; a gossiping letter or piece of writing 1789. **3.** *Plastering.* An accurately levelled strip of plaster formed upon a wall or ceiling, as a guide in running a cornice or in obtaining a perfectly even surface in plastering; a strip of wood used for the same purpose 1812.

2. Richardson's reply is a s. of malevolence 1902.

Screen (skrīn), *sb.* [Late ME. *skre(e)ne*, perh. repr. some AF. var. or deriv. of F. *écran*, OF. *escran*, of corresponding sense.] **1.** A contrivance for warding off the heat of a fire or a draught of air. **a.** An upright board, or a frame hung with leather, canvas, etc., or two or more such boards or frames hinged together. **b.** A frame covered with paper or cloth, or a disk of thin wood, etc., with a handle by which a person may hold it between his face and the fire 1548. **c.** A wooden seat or settle with a high back to keep away draughts 1826. **d.** A flat vertical surface prepared for the reception of images from a magic lantern or the like; a contrivance in the form of a screen for affording an upright surface for the display of objects of exhibition 1815. **2.** *Arch.* A partition of wood or stone, pierced by one or more doors, dividing a room or building (e.g. a church) into two parts; *spec.* = *chancel-s.*, *rood-s.* 1460. **b.** A wall thrown out in front of a building and masking the façade 1842. **3.** *transf.* **a.** Applied to any object that affords shelter from heat or wind 1538. **b.** Something so interposed as to conceal from view 1605. **c.** *Mil.* A small body of men detached to cover the movements of an army 1892. **d.** A line or belt of trees planted to give protection from the wind 1644. **4.** *fig.* A means of securing from attack, punishment, or censure 1610. **5.** An apparatus used in the sifting of grain, coal, etc. 1573. **6.** Applied to various parts of optical, electrical, and other instruments, serving to intercept light, heat, electricity, etc. 1819. **b.** *Electr.* A device which protects an electrical apparatus from external electric or magnetic influences 1915. **c.** *Photog.* A transparent plate or sheet of glass, ruled with fine lines, used in photographing for half-tone reproduction 1897.

1. d. *Silver s.*, the s. on which cinematograph pictures are projected; hence, cinematography. **e.** *Cricket.* An erection of white canvas or wood placed near the boundary to enable a batsman to see the ball better 1895. 3. **b.** *Macb.* v. vi. 1. 4. There be so many Skreenes betweene him, and Envy BACON.

Comb.: **s.-craft,** the cinematographic art; **-struck** *a.* (after *stage-struck*); **-wiper,** a device for keeping the wind-screen of a motor vehicle clear.

Screen (skrīn), *v.* 1485. [f. prec.] **1.** *trans.* To shelter or protect with or as with a screen, *from* heat, wind, light, missiles, or the like 1632. **b.** To shut *off* by something interposed 1700. **2.** To hide from view as with a screen; to shelter from observation or recognition 1686. **b.** *Mil.* To employ a body of men to cover (an army's movements). Also *absol.* 1881. **3.** To shield or protect from hostility or impending danger; *esp.* to save (an offender) *from* punishment or exposure; to conceal (a person's offence) 1485. **4.** *trans.* To sift by passing through a 'screen' 1664. **5.** In the Inns of Court: To post upon a screen or notice-board 1870. **6.** To project (a lantern-slide, cinematograph picture, etc.) upon a screen; hence, to make a cinema film of 1915. Hence **Scree·ning** *vbl. sb.* (*concr.* cf. sense 4).

Screeve (skrīv), *v. slang.* 1851. [f. (ult.) L. *scribere.*] *intr.* To be a 'pavement artist'. Hence **Scree·ver,** a pavement artist.

Screw (skrū), *sb.* late ME. [app. a. OF. *escroue*, also *escro* female screw, nut; ultimate etym. unkn.] **I.** The general name for that kind of mechanical appliance of which the operative portion is a helical groove or ridge cut either on the exterior surface of a cylinder (*male s.*) or on the interior surface of a cylindrical cavity (*female s.*). **1.** A male screw (see above) with a correspondingly grooved or ridged socket; used for the purpose of converting a motion of rotation into a motion of translation bearing a fixed proportion to it. **a.** As an apparatus for raising weights or applying pressure or strain. **b.** Considered as one of the mechanical powers; in mechanical theory treated as a modification of the inclined plane 1570. **c.** Used for regulating or measuring longitudinal movement 1612. **2.** *fig.* A means of 'pressure' or coercion 1648. **3.** A metal pin or bolt (cylindrical or slightly tapering) with a spiral ridge upon its shank, used in joining articles of wood or metal, fastening fittings to woodwork, etc. (It is turned and driven in by means of a screwdriver or spanner.) 1622. **4.** Each of the component parts of a screw-fastening or screw-joint 1648. **5.** The worm or boring part of a gimlet 1577. **6.** An instrument terminating in a 'worm' for screwing into something in order to pull it out; esp. a corkscrew; also, the 'worm' itself 1657. **7.** A screw-propeller (see PROPELLER 3) 1838. **8.** A ship driven by a screw-propeller 1867. **9.** Something having a spiral course or form 1649. **b.** = *s.-stone* 1729.

1. *Bench s.*, a joiner's vice. *Double s.*, one with a pair of screws to carry the vice-cheek with a parallel motion. *Endless s.*, see ENDLESS *a.* *Perpetual s.* = *endless s.* *S. of Archimedes, water s.* = ARCHIMEDEAN screw. *The screws* (rarely *the s.*), an instrument of torture designed to compress the thumbs of a prisoner; *dial.* or *colloq.*, rheumatism. 2. Phr. *To put on, apply, turn the s.*, or *screws*, etc.: (*a*) to apply moral pressure; (*b*) to force the payment of a debt or loan; also *rarely*, to limit the giving of credit. 3. Phr. *A s. loose*, fig. something wrong in the condition of things; a dangerous weakness in some arrangement; *to have a s. loose*, to be 'dotty'. 6. *S. or kettle* = corkscrew (*i.e.* wine) or hot water (*i.e.* grog).

II. From SCREW *v.* **1.** An act of screwing up; a turn of the screw 1709. **b.** *Billiards.* A stroke by which a twist is given to the cue-ball by striking it below its centre; also, the twist resulting from this stroke, esp. in the phr. *to put on s.* 1849. **c.** *Cricket.* A twist imparted to the ball in its delivery 1867. **2.** The state of being twisted awry; a contortion 1708. **3.** A small portion (of a commodity) wrapped up in a twist or cornet of paper; esp. a penny packet (of tobacco); also, a wrapper of this kind 1836. **4.** One who forces down (prices) by haggling; a stingy, miserly person 1835.

3. A knife, some butter, a s. of salt DICKENS. 4. They both agreed in calling him an old s. THACKERAY.

III. Senses of obsc. origin. **1.** A horse not perfectly sound 1821. **2.** *slang.* Salary, wages 1864.

attrib. and *Comb.*: **s. battery,** a battery composed of s.-guns; **-blank,** the piece of metal on which a thread or worm is to be cut to form a s.; **-bolt,** a bolt with a thread or worm at the end to be secured by means of a s.-nut; hence **-bolt** *v. trans.*, to fasten with a s.-bolt; **-box,** a tool for cutting the thread on a wooden s.; **-dock** *U.S.*, a dock in which the cradle is raised by screws; **s. engine,** (*a*) a machine for raising water by means of a s., a water-s.; (*b*) a steam-engine adapted to drive a screw-propeller; **-gear,** gear consisting of an endless s. and a toothed wheel; **-joint** (*a*) *Mech.*, a joint formed by screwing together the ends of piping, etc. (*b*) *Anat.*, a joint in which there is a slight lateral sliding of one bone upon the other; **-key,** (*a*) = *s.-wrench*; (*b*) a key furnished with a thread or worm; **-machine,** (*a*) a machine operated by a s.; (*b*) a machine for making screws; **s. nut** (see NUT *sb.* II. 3); **-plate,** a hardened steel plate for cutting the threads of small screws by means of a series of drilled and tapped holes of various diameters; **-press,** a machine in which pressure is applied by means of a s.; **s. propeller** (see I. 7); **-pump,** an ARCHIMEDEAN s.; **s. spanner** = *s.-wrench*; **-stone,** a stone containing the hollow cast of an encrinite; **-thread,** the spiral ridge of a s.; also, one complete turn of its thread as a portion of a unit of length of the axis of the s.; **s. tool,** a lathe-tool for cutting screws; **-wheel,** the toothed wheel associated with the endless s. in s.-gearing; **-worm,** the larva of certain American flesh-flies; **-wrench,** a wrench or spanner adapted to fit over or grasp the heads of s.-bolts, nuts, etc., and turn them. **b.** In names of plants, as **s.-bean, -mezquit,** *Prosopis pubescens*, so called from the s.-like form of its pods; **-palm, -pine,** any of the plants belonging to the family *Pandanaceæ.*

Screw (skrū), *v.* 1599. [f. prec.] **I.** *trans.* To attach with an inserted screw or screws; hence *fig.*, to fix firmly 1611.

To s. down, up, to close and secure with screws; Think of being screwed down in a coffin, and put into the cold ground 1862.

II. 1. To press, strain, or force with or as with a screw; to compress or hold fast in or as in a vice 1612. **2.** To stretch tight by turning a screw; *esp.* to increase the tension or pitch (of a musical string) by winding *up* the screws or keys 1652. **b.** With immaterial obj.; *esp.* to stretch, strain the meaning of (words) 1628. **3.** To operate or adjust (an instrument) by turning its screw 1708. **4.** To extort by pressure 1622. **5.** To put compulsion upon, to constrain, oppress 1658. **b.** To examine rigorously. *Obs.* exc. in *U.S.* college slang. Also *absol.* 1626. **6.** To produce, attain, or elicit with an effort 1679. **7.** *intr.* To be parsimonious 1849.

1. Phr. *To s. up*, to tighten by turning a screw. *To s. in, up*, to compress the waist of (a person) by tight-lacing. 2. They break the strings by scruing them up too high 1656. *fig.* But. s. your courage to the sticking place, And wee 'le not fayle SHAKS. **b.** *To s. up*, to raise (a payment, rent, etc.) to an exacting or extortionate figure. 4. I screwed out of him these particulars SCOTT. The rate of taxation is simply the maximum that can be screwed out of the people 1882. 5. They are so screwed by taxes..that they never have a farthing in hand 1838. 7. I must s. and save in order to pay off the money THACKERAY.

III. To turn a screw. **1.** *trans.* To work (a screw or something fashioned as a screw) by turning 1635. **2.** To insert or fix one thing *in, into, on, to,* or *upon* another or two things *together* by a turning or twisting movement, one or both having the surface or part of it cut into a screw for the purpose 1611. **b.** *intr.* in passive sense. To be adapted for joining or taking apart by means of component screws 1680. **3.** *intr.* To penetrate as a screw; to penetrate with a winding course; *fig.* to worm one's way 1614.

2. *fig. To have one's head screwed on the right way* (colloq.), to be able to use one's brains to advantage, to 'know what one is about'. **b.** Rods..in three pieces..which screwed together 1776.

IV. To move in a twisting direction. **1.** *trans.* To twist round, esp. to twist with violence so as to alter the shape 1711. **2.** To twist awry, contort (the features, body, mouth); to twist (one's head, oneself) *round* in order to look at something 1599. **3.** To propel by a spiral movement; to force or squeeze (one's body) *into, through*, etc. (a comparatively small space) 1635. **4.** *Sporting.* **a.** *intr. Rowing.* To swing the body from one side to the other during the stroke 1875. **b.** *trans. Rugby Football.* To cause (the scrummage or one's opponents in a scrummage) to twist round by pushing in a body to the right or left. Also *absol.* 1887. **c.** *Cricket*, etc. To impart a screw or twist to (the ball); to cause to swerve. Also *absol.* 1839. **d.** *intr.* (for *refl.*) *Racing.* Of a horse: To force his way *through*. Also *trans.* To force (a horse) *over* (an obstacle); *to s. in*, to force to the front at the finish of a race. 1840. **5.** Of ice-floes: To ram together 1901.

1. Phr. *To s.* (a person's) *neck*, to kill by wringing the neck. *To s. up*, to twist (e.g. a piece of paper) into a spiral form. 2. *To s. up*, to contract the surrounding parts or (the mouth, eyes); Jo screws up his mouth into a whistle DICKENS.

V. 1. *trans.* To furnish with a helical groove or ridge; to furnish (a screw-blank, pin, etc.) with a thread or worm; to cut a screw-thread *upon* 1635. **2.** *intr.* To travel on the water by means of a screw-propeller; also *trans.* in *to s. its way* 1860.

Comb.: **s. back** *Billiards*, a rotary motion causing the ball to run backwards after striking another ball; **s. cannon** (also **screw-back cannon**) *Billiards*, a cannon made by striking the ball very low down and so causing it to recoil from the object ball; **s. kick, shot, stroke** (in various games), one that causes the ball to swerve. Hence **Screw·er. Screw·ing** *vbl. sb.* freq. in combs. in the sense 'cutting screw threads', as *screwing machine*.

Screwdriver (skrū·drəivəɹ). 1812. A tool for turning screws into or out of their places. It is shaped like a chisel, with a blunt end which fits into the nick in the head of the screw.

Screwed (skrūd), *ppl. a.* 1646. [f. SCREW *v.* + -ED [1].] **1.** In the senses of SCREW *v.* **2.** Partly intoxicated; 'tight' 1838.

Screw·-pin. 1614. [SCREW *sb.*] A pin with a screw cut upon it: **a.** the screw of a vice; **b.** an adjusting screw, finger screw; **c.** the pin which forms the foundation of a screw.

Screwy (skrū·i), *a.* 1820. [f. SCREW *sb.* and *v.* + -Y [1].] **1.** Slightly tipsy. **2.** Of a person: Given to screwing, mean, stingy 1851. **3.** Of a horse (see SCREW *sb.* III. 1). Unsound 1852.

Scribable (skrəi·băb'l), *a. Obs.* exc. *arch.* late ME. [irreg. f. L. *scribere*; see -ABLE.] Suitable for being written on.

Scribal (skrəi·b'l), *a.* 1857. [f. SCRIBE *sb.*[1] + -AL I.] **1.** Of, pertaining to, or characteristic of a scribe or copyist, or his work. **2.** Of or pertaining to the Jewish scribes 1863.

Scribble (skri·b'l), *sb.* 1577. [f. next.] **1.** Something hastily or carelessly written, esp. a depreciatory term for a letter (usu. one's own); also, a worthless or trivial composition. **2.** Hurried or negligent and irregular writing; an example of this. Also, a number of irregular and unmeaning marks made with a pen, pencil, or the like. 1709.

1. He made a shift to get a livelyhood by his mendicant scribbles WOOD. 2. The s. of men who think good writing a thing for clerks and shopmen 1881.

Scribble (skri·b'l), *v.*[1] 1465. [app. ad. late med.L. *scribillare*, dim. f. L. *scribere*.] **1.** *trans.* To write hastily or carelessly. **a.** To write in an irregular, slovenly, or illegible hand through haste or carelessness. **b.** To write hurriedly or thoughtlessly. **c.** To cover with scribblings. Chiefly with *over*. 1540. **2.** *intr.* To write something hastily or carelessly, either as to handwriting or composition; to produce abundance of worthless writing 1534.

1. **b.** Writers who s. bosh 1884. **c.** 2 *Hen. VI*, IV. ii. 88. 2. If a man scribbles for a Newspaper, or writes a magazine article 1880. Hence **Scri·bblement**, something scribbled. **Scri·bblingly** *adv.*

Scribble (skri·b'l), *v.*[2] 1682. [prob. from LG.; cf. SCRUB *v.*] *trans.* To card or tease (wool) coarsely, to pass through a 'scribbler'.

Scribbler [1] (skri·bləɹ). 1553. [f. SCRIBBLE *v.*[1] + -ER [1].] One who scribbles; hence 'a petty author, a writer without worth' (J.).

Scribbler [2]. 1682. [f. SCRIBBLE *v.*[2] + -ER [1].] **1.** A person who scribbles wool, or who tends a scribbling-machine. **2.** A machine for scribbling (wool) 1805.

Scribbling (skri·bliŋ), *vbl. sb.*[1] 1532. [f. SCRIBBLE *v.*[1] + -ING [1].] **1.** The action of SCRIBBLE *v.*[1] **2.** Something scribbled; a scrawl or scribble 1705.

attrib., as *s.-block*, *-book*, etc.; **s. itch**, tr. L. *cacoethes scribendi*.

Scri·bbling, *vbl. sb.*[2] 1682. [f. SCRIBBLE *v.*[2] + -ING [1].] The action of SCRIBBLE *v.*[2]; the first process in carding wool. Also *attrib.*, as *s.-machine*, *-mill*, etc.

Scribe (skrəib), *sb.*[1] late ME. [ad. L. *scriba* writer, etc., f. *scribere*.] A writer; one whose business is writing. **1.** *Jewish Hist.* A member of the class of professional interpreters of the Law after the return from the Captivity; in the Gospels often coupled with the Pharisees as upholders of ceremonial tradition. **2.** *Anc. Hist.* A general designation for any public official concerned with writing or the keeping of accounts; a secretary, clerk. late ME. †**3.** One who writes at another's dictation; an amanuensis -1838. **4.** A copyist or transcriber of manuscripts; now esp. the writer of a particular MS. copy of a classical or mediæval work 1535. **5.** A penman, one (more or less) skilled in penmanship. Now somewhat *arch.* 1588. **6.** One who writes or is in the habit of writing; an author; the writer (of a letter, etc.) 1585. **b.** Applied to a political pamphleteer or journalist; a party hack 1826.

1. And so may sarasenes be saued, scribes and iewes LANGL. 6. As I am often writing..he commonly calls me the s. MME D'ARBLAY.

Scribe (skrəib), *sb.*[2] 1812. [f. next.] A tool for scribing in *Carpentry, Building*, etc.

attrib. **s.-mark**, a mark made with a scribing-iron on a log, etc.

Scribe (skrəib), *v.* 1678. [History obsc.] **1.** In techn. uses. **a.** *trans.* Orig., in *Carpentry*, to mark the intended outline of (a piece of timber) with one point of a pair of compasses, moved parallel with the other point which is drawn along the edge of the piece to which the 'scribed' piece is to be fitted. Now more widely: To mark or score (wood, metal, bricks) with a pointed instrument in order to indicate the outline to which the piece is to be cut or shaped; to draw (a line, etc.) in this way. **b.** Hence, to shape the edge of (a piece of timber, metal, etc.) so that it will fit into the irregular edge of another piece or to an uneven surface 1679. **c.** To mark (timber, a cask, etc.) with a scribing-iron 1859. **2. a.** *intr.* To act as a scribe, to write. **b.** *trans.* To write down. *rare* exc. *dial.* 1742. Hence **Scri·bing** *vbl. sb.* the action of the vb.; *concr.* the identifying mark on a cask, etc.; *pl.* incised markings on stone, etc.; also *attrib.*, in *scribing-block*, *-iron*, etc.

Scriber (skrəi·bəɹ). 1834. [f. prec. + -ER [1].] A tool or appliance for scribing.

Scribism (skrəi·biz'm). 1657. [f. SCRIBE *sb.*[1] + -ISM 2 b.] The teaching and literature of the ancient Jewish scribes; also, their qualities.

Scriggle (skri·g'l), *v.* Chiefly *dial.* 1806. [Phonetically symbolic.] *intr.* To wriggle or struggle. Hence **Scri·ggle** *sb.* a wriggle; a scrawly piece of writing.

Scrim (skrim). 1792. [Origin obsc.] A kind of thin canvas used for lining in upholstery, etc. Also *attrib.*

Scrimmage (skri·midʒ), **scrummage** (skrʊ·midʒ), *sb.* 1470. [Altered f. *scrimish* SKIRMISH *sb.*] †**1.** = SKIRMISH *sb.* Also, a fencing bout -1643. **2.** *colloq.* A noisy contention or tussle; also, a confused struggle between persons, a scuffle 1780. **3.** *Rugby Football.* (Now usu. abbrev. SCRUM.) Orig., a confused struggle in which each side endeavours to force its opponents and the ball towards the opposite goal; now, an ordered formation in which the two sets of forwards pack themselves together with their heads down and endeavour by pushing to work their opponents off the ball and break away with it or heel it out 1857. **b.** A tussle for the ball among players (in various games) 1883.

3. Phr. *To carry the s.*, to gain ground in a s. *To hold the s.*, to prevent one's opponents from gaining ground.

Scri·mmage, scru·mmage, *v.* 1833. [f. prec.] **1.** To bustle about. **2.** *Rugby Football.* To put (the ball) in a scrummage as a means of re-starting the game when and where it has been temporarily stopped, as for some breach of the rules; also, to propel or take along in a scrimmage 1881.

Scrimp (skrimp), *a.* and *adv.* 1718. [Origin obsc.] **A.** *adj.* Scant, scanty, meagre. †**B.** *adv.* Scarcely, barely -1834.

Scrimp (skrimp), *v.* 1774. [See prec.] **1.** *trans.* To keep on short allowance, *esp.* of food. **2.** To cut short in amount, be sparing of 1834. **3.** *intr.* To economize, be niggardly 1848.

3. While we are saving and scrimping at the spigot, the government is drawing off at the bung 1848.

Scrimpy (skri·mpi), *a.* 1825. [f. SCRIMP *a.* + -Y [1].] Of meagre dimensions, scanty. Hence **Scri·mpiness.**

Scrimshank (skri·mʃæŋk), *v.* 1890. [Origin obsc.] *Mil. slang. intr.* To shirk duty. Hence **Scri·mshanker**, a shirker.

Scrimshaw (skri·mʃǭ), *sb.* 1851. [Origin obsc.; cf. the surname *Scrimshaw*.] *Naut.* A general name (also *s. work*) for the handicrafts practised by sailors by way of pastime during long whaling and other voyages, and for the products of these, as carvings on bone, ivory, shells, and the like. Also **Scri·mshaw** *v. trans.* to decorate or produce as s. work; *absol.* to employ oneself in s. work.

Scringe, *v. Obs.* exc. *dial.* 1608. [Altered f. CRINGE.] **1.** *trans.* To screw up (one's face); to shrug (the back or shoulders) from cold. **2.** *intr.* To flinch, cower 1825.

Scriniary (skri·niări). 1866. [ad. late L. *scriniarius*, f. *scrinium*.] A keeper of archives.

Scrip (skrip), *sb.*[1] ME. [prob. a. OF. *escrep(p)e* wallet, etc.] A small bag, wallet, or satchel; *esp.* one carried by a pilgrim, shepherd, or beggar.

A staffe and scryppe of Seynt James 1524.

Scrip (skrip), *sb.*[2] *Obs.* exc. *dial.* 1617. [app. an alteration of SCRAP *sb.*, prob. assoc. w. SCRIPT.] **1.** A small piece or scrap (of paper, etc.). **2.** *S.* (*of a pen*): a small scrap of writing 1710. **3.** *U.S.* Fractional paper currency 1889.

Scrip (skrip), *sb.*[3] 1762. [Short for SUBSCRIPTION.] **1.** (Short for †*subscription receipt*.) Orig., a receipt for a portion of a loan subscribed. Now, a provisional document entitling the holder to a share or shares in a joint-stock undertaking, and exchangeable for a formal certificate when the necessary payments have been completed; often *collect. sing.* Hence, loosely, share certificates in general. Also *attrib.* **2.** *Book-selling.* (Short for *subscription price*.) A trade price 25 per cent. below the published price 1884.

Scripee (skripī·). *U.S.* 1909. [See -EE.] One to whom land is allotted by scrip.

Scrippage (skri·pėdʒ). 1600. [f. SCRIP *sb.*[1] + -AGE.] In Shakespearian phr. *scrip and s.*, modelled on *bag and baggage*; rarely used independently.

Script (skript). late ME. [ad. L. *scriptum*, neut. pa. pple. of *scribere*, used subst.] **1.** Something written; a piece of writing. Now *rare.* **2.** Handwriting; the characters used in handwriting. Also *attrib.*, as in *s. hand, letter.* 1860. **b.** *Typog.* (In full *s. type*.) Type resembling handwriting 1838.

This line is in Script type.

c. Used *attrib.* of systems of shorthand which resemble longhand in general appearance and in the movements of the hand that are required 1888. **3.** A kind of writing, a system of written characters 1883. **4.** *Law.* The original or principal instrument, where there is also a counterpart 1856. **5.** *Theatr.* Short (*'script*) for MANUSCRIPT 1897.

Scription (skri·pʃən). 1597. [ad. L. *scriptionem*.] †**1.** A writing, document, inscription -1693. **2.** Handwriting; a kind of handwriting (*rare*) 1846.

‖ **Scriptorium** (skriptōə·riŏm). *Pl.* **-ia**, **-iums.** 1774. [med.L., f. L. *script-*, *scribere*; see -ORIUM.] A writing-room; *spec.* the room in a religious house set apart for the copying of manuscripts.

Scriptory (skri·ptəri), *a.* and *sb. rare.* 1483. [ad. L. *scriptorius*, f. *script-*, *scribere*;

see -ORY.] A. *adj.* 1. Pertaining to or used in writing 1682. 2. Expressed in writing, written 1704. B. *sb.* A scriptorium 1483.

A. 2. Of Wills, *duo sunt genera*, Nuncupatory and S. SWIFT.

Scriptural (skri·ptiŭrăl, -tʃər-), *a.* 1641. [ad. mod.L. *scripturalis*, f. L. *scriptura* SCRIPTURE.] 1. Based upon, derived from, or depending upon Holy Scripture. 2. Of or pertaining to writing 1802. Hence **Scri·ptural-ly** *adv.*, **-ness.**

Scripturalism (skri·ptiŭrăliz'm, -tʃər-). 1858. [f. prec. + -ISM.] Close adherence to or dependence upon the letter of Holy Scripture. So **Scri·pturalist**, an advocate of s. 1857.

Scripture (skri·ptiŭɹ,- tʃər). ME. [ad. L. *scriptura* writing, f. *script-*, *scribere*; see -URE.] 1. (Usu. with initial cap.) The sacred writings of the Old or New Testament, or (more usu.) of both together; Holy Writ; the Bible. Often with *holy* prefixed. b. A particular passage or text of the Bible. Now *rare* (after biblical use). late ME. c. *pl.* or (now rarely) *sing.* Sacred writings 1581. 2. The action or art of writing; handwriting, penmanship. Also *concr.* written characters. Now *rare*. late ME. 3. An inscription or superscription; a motto, legend, or posy. Also *gen.*, inscribed words. *Obs.* exc. *arch.* late ME. 4. A written record or composition; *pl.* writings. *Obs.* exc. *arch.* late ME. †b. Written composition –1595. 5. *attrib.* a. With the sense 'of or pertaining to Holy Scripture', as in *s.-lesson*, etc.; 'recorded in Holy Scripture', as in *s. history, miracle*, etc. 1627. b. With the sense 'used in or adopted from Holy Scripture', as in *s. expression*, etc.; 'derived from, prescribed by, or conformable to Holy Scripture, scriptural', as in *s. doctrine*, etc. 1594.

1. The diuell can cite S. for his purpose SHAKS. That there is a God; or, That the S. is his Word 1676. I would teach the knowledge of the scriptures only 1782. c. Most men do not know that any nation but the Hebrews have had a s. 1854. 2. The handwriting was of that form of s. which attracts; refined yet energetic; full of character DISRAELI. 4. What is heere, The Scriptures of the Loyall Leonatus, All turn'd to Heresie? SHAKS. Hence **Scriptu·rian** (*rare*), a scripturist. **Scri·pturism**, reliance on the Scriptures alone devotion to S.

Scripturist (skri·ptiŭrist, -tʃər-). 1624. [f. SCRIPTURE *sb.* + -IST.] 1. One who is versed in the Scriptures 1661. 2. One who bases his religious belief or opinions upon Scripture alone 1624.

Scritch (skritʃ), *sb. arch.* 1513. [See next.] A screech, shriek, loud cry.

Sudden scritches of the jay TENNYSON.

Scritch (skritʃ), *v. arch.* ME. [Echoic; cf. SHRIEK *v.*] *intr.* To utter a loud cry; to screech or shriek.

Scri·tch-owl. Now *arch.* 1530. [f. SCRITCH *sb.* + OWL.] = SCREECH-OWL.

Scrivener (skri·v'nəɹ). late ME. [f. †*scrivein*, aphetic a. OF. *escrivein* + -ER [1].] 1. A professional penman; a scribe, copyist; a clerk, secretary, amanuensis. 2. A notary 1477. 3. One who 'received money to place out at interest, and who supplied those who wanted to raise money on security' (Tomlins). Also *money s.* *Obs.* exc. *Hist.* 1607.

1. *Scrivener's cramp, palsy*, writer's cramp. 3. The Scrieueners and Broakers doe valew vnsound Men BACON.

Scrobicular (skrobi·kiŭlăɹ), *a.* 1888. [f. mod.L. *scrobicula* or late L. *scrobiculus* + -AR [1] 1.] Pertaining to or surrounded by scrobicules.

Scrobiculate (skrobi·kiŭlĕt), *a.* 1806. [formed as prec. + -ATE [2].] *Bot.* and *Zool.* Having many small depressions; furrowed or pitted; *Ent.* foveate. So **Scrobi·culated** *a.*

Scrobicule (skrōᵘ·bikiŭl). 1880. [ad. mod. L. *scrobicula* or late L. *scrobiculus*, dim. of *scrobs* trench.] *Biol.* A small pit or depression; *spec.* the smooth area around the tubercles of a sea-urchin.

Scrod (skrǫd). *U.S.* Also **scrode.** 1873. [perh. a. Du. †*schrood*, MDu. *schrode* piece cut off = OE. *scrēade* SHRED.] A young cod weighing less than three pounds, *esp.* one that is split and fried or boiled.

Scrofula (skrǫ·fiŭlă). late ME. [In early use pl. after late L. *scrofulæ* swelling of the glands, dim. of *scrofa* breeding sow (supposed to be subject to the disease). Later sing. after med.L. *scrofula*.] A constitutional disease characterized mainly by chronic enlargement and degeneration of the lymphatic glands. Also called KING'S EVIL and STRUMA. So **Scro·fulide** (skrǫ·fiŭlid) *Path.*, [F. *scrofulide*] a scrofulous or strumous skin-disease.

Scrofulous (skrǫ·fiŭləs), *a.* 1612. [f. prec. + -OUS. Cf. F. *scrofuleux*.] 1. Caused by, or of the nature of, scrofula. 2. Affected with, or suffering from, scrofula 1708. 3. *fig.* Of literature, etc.: Morally corrupt 1842.

1. He had inherited..a s. taint MACAULAY. 3. My s. French novel On grey paper with blunt type! BROWNING. Hence **Scro·fulous-ly** *adv.*, **-ness.**

Scrog (skrǫg), *sb.* Chiefly *Sc.* and *n. dial.* late ME. [app. related to SCRAG *sb.*[2]] A stunted bush; usu. *pl.*, brushwood, underwood. b. *Her.* A branch of a tree; a blazon sometimes used by Scottish heralds 1780. Hence **Scro·ggy** *a.* abounding in s. Also, of trees, stunted.

Scroll (skrōᵘl), *sb.* late ME. [In 15th c. *scrowle*, altered f. earlier SCROW.] 1. A roll of paper or parchment, usu. one with writing upon it. b. A roll or bundle of any material 1852. 2. A piece of writing, *esp.* a letter 1534. b. A list, roll, or schedule (of names) 1546. 3. A strip or ribbon-shaped slip of paper with a legend inscribed; a graphic or plastic representation of this 1600. b. *Her.* The ribbon-like appendage to a coat of arms, on which the motto is inscribed. Also *transf.*, the words inscribed upon the scroll. 1610. 4. An ornament resembling a scroll of paper partly unrolled. a. A convoluted or spiral ornament; *spec.* the volute of the Ionic and Corinthian capitals 1611. b. *Shipbuilding.* A curved piece of timber bolted to the knee of the head 1797. c. The curved head of instruments of the violin kind 1836. d. *U.S.* A flourish (or sometimes a circle) added to a person's signature to represent a seal, and having the same value 1856. 5. Applied variously in techn. use to scroll-shaped or spiral parts, figures, etc. 1868. b. *Geom.* A skew ruled surface 1862.

1. And heven vanysshed awaye as a s. when hit is rolled togedder TINDALE *Rev.* vi. 14. 2. Do not exceede The Prescript of this Scroule SHAKS. b. Now good Peter Quince, call forth your Actors by the scrowle SHAKS.

attrib. and *Comb.*, as **s.-bone**, a turbinal bone; **s. chuck**, a lathe-chuck with a spiral arrangement for operating the jaws· **-gear**, a spiral gear-wheel; **-head** = sense 4 b; **-saw**, a saw for cutting scrolls; **-wheel**, a wheel actuated by scroll-gear.

Scroll (skrōᵘl), *v.* 1606. [f. prec.] I. *trans.* To write down in a scroll (*rare*). 2. *intr.* for *refl.* To roll or curl up 1868.

Scrolled (skrōᵘld), *ppl. a.* 1603. [f. SCROLL *sb.* or *v.* + -ED.] 1. In the form of, or decorated with, scrolls; *transf.* curled. 2. Inscribed with mottoes 1875.

1. *transf.* An envoy with a s. mustache GEO ELIOT.

Scroop (skrūp), *v.* 1787. [Echoic.] *intr.* To make a strident, grating, or scraping sound; to grate, creak, squeak. So **Scroop** *sb.* a harsh, strident, or scraping noise.

‖ **Scrophularia** (skrǫfiŭlēᵊ·riă). 1663. [mod.L. (sc. *herba*), f. med.L. *scrophula* SCROFULA; cf. -ARY [1] B 3.] *Bot.* A genus of monopetalous plants (the fig-worts), typical of the family *Scrophulariaceæ*; a plant of this genus. Hence **Scrophularia·ceous** *a.* belonging to the family *Scrophulariaceæ*.

Scrotal (skrōᵘ·tăl), *a.* 1800. [ad. mod.L. *scrotalis*, f. SCROTUM.] Of or pertaining to the scrotum.

Scrotiform (skrōᵘ·tifǫɹm), *a.* 1775. [f. SCROTUM + (I)FORM.] *Bot.* and *Biol.* Pouch-shaped.

Scrotocele (skrōᵘ·tosīl). 1693. [f. *scroto-* comb. f. SCROTUM + CELE.] *Path.* A scrotal hernia.

‖ **Scrotum** (skrōᵘ·tŏm). 1597. [L.] *Anat.* The tegument enclosing the testicles.

Scrouge (skrūdʒ, skraudʒ), *v. colloq.* and *vulgar.* 1755. [app. an alteration of SCRUZE *v.*] *trans.* To incommode by pressing against (a person); to encroach on (a person's) space in sitting or standing; to crowd. Also *intr.*

Scrounge (skraundʒ), *v. slang.* 1919. [Origin obsc.: cf. dial. *scrunge* and *scringe* to squeeze, search carefully, pry into.] *trans.* To hunt about for; to take without permission, steal. Hence **Scrou·nger.**

Scrow (skrōᵘ), *sb.* ME. [Aphetic a. OF. *escrowe* ESCROW.] †1. = SCROLL *sb.* 1. –1615. †b. *pl.* Writings –1646. 2. *pl.* or *collect. sing.* Strips or clippings of hide or leather used for making glue ME.

†**Scroyle.** 1595. [?] A scoundrel –1821.

Scrub (skrʋb), *sb.*[1] late ME. [var. of SHRUB.] I. 1. A low stunted tree. 2. *collect.* Brushwood; also, a tract of country overgrown with this 1809.

1. *Mallee s.* (*Eucalyptus oleosa*), *Horizontal s.* (*Anodopetalum biglandulosum*), Australian trees, common in thickets and undergrowth.

II. 1. A breed of cattle distinguished by their small size 1555. 2. *transf.* A mean insignificant fellow 1589.

2. He is an arrant s., I assure you FIELDING.

attrib. and *Comb.*: as **s.-itch**, a skin-disease peculiar to the jungles of New Guinea; **-oak,** *Villaresia moorei* and *Casuarina cunninghamii.*

Scrub (skrʋb), *sb.*[2] 1621. [f. SCRUB *v.*] 1. The action or an act of scrubbing. 2. A broom or brush with short hard bristles 1687. 3. One who scrubs; a drudge 1709. b. *U.S.* A player not belonging to the regular team; a second or weaker team 1903.

attrib. **s.-race, -game,** *U.S.* an impromptu race or game between untrained competitors.

Scrub (skrʋb), *a.* 1710. [SCRUB *sb.*[1] used attrib.] Chiefly *U.S.* = SCRUBBY *a.* 3.

Scrub (skrʋb), *v.* 1595. [History obsc.; ad. or corresp. to MLG., MDu. *schrobben*, *shrubben*, perh. related to SCRAPE.] †1. *trans.* To scratch, rub (a part of one's body) –1725. 2. To clean (esp. a floor, wood, etc.) by rubbing with a hard brush and water 1595. 3. *techn.* To cleanse (coal-gas) by means of a scrubber 1885. 4. *Comb.*, as *s.-brush*, *-woman* (U.S.).

†**Scru·bbed,** *a.* 1596. [f. SCRUB *sb.*[1] + -ED [2].] Stunted, dwarfed –1835.

Scrubber (skrʋ·bəɹ). 1839. [f. SCRUB *v.* + -ER [1].] 1. One who or something which scrubs. 2. An apparatus for cleansing coal-gas from impurities 1853.

Scrubbing-brush (skrʋ·biŋbrʋʃ). 1681. A brush with hard bristles for scrubbing.

Scrubby (skrʋ·bi), *a.* 1591. [f. SCRUB *sb.*[1] + -Y [1].] 1. Stunted, under-developed. 2. Covered with brushwood 1676. 3. Insignificant, shabby, paltry, of poor appearance 1782.

1. S. lichens 1860. 2. S. Pasture 1676. 3. To be treated like a little s. apprentice? 1782.

Scruff (skrʋf), *sb.*[1] 1526. [Metathetic var. of SCURF *sb.*[1]] 1. SCURF *sb.*[1] 2. 2. A thin crust or coating 1591. 3. Refuse, litter; †*spec.* base money; also used (like 'muck') as a contemptuous term for money 1559. Hence **Scru·ffy** *a.* scaly, covered with scurf.

Scruff (skrʋf), *sb.*[2] 1790. [Corrupt f. SCUFF *sb.* assim. to prec.] The nape of the neck.

Scrum (skrʋm). 1888. [Abbrev. f. SCRUMMAGE.] = SCRIMMAGE *sb.* 3. Comb. **s.-half.**

Scrummage: see SCRIMMAGE *sb.* and *v.*

Scrumptious (skrʋ·mpʃəs), *a. colloq.* or *vulgar.* 1836. [prob. identical w. dial. *scrumptious*, stingy, close-fisted, f. (ult.) SCRIMP *v.*] 1. Fastidious, hard to please. ? *U.S.* only. 1845. 2. a. *U.S.* Stylish, handsome. b. First rate, 'glorious'. 1836. **Scru·mptious-ly** *adv.*, **-ness.**

Scrunch (skrʋnʃ), *sb.* 1854. [f. next.] The noise made by, or an act of, scrunching.

Scrunch (skrʋnʃ), *v.* 1825. [Cf. CRUNCH *v.*] 1. *trans.* = CRUNCH *v.* 1, 2. 2. *intr.* To produce a sound of being scrunched 1844. Hence **Scru·nchy** *a.*, that emits a crunching sound when crushed.

Scruple (skrū·p'l), *sb.*[1] 1564. [ad. L. *scrupulus*, more freq. *scrupulum*, regarded as identical with *scrupulus* SCRUPLE *sb.*[2]] 1. A unit of weight = 20 grains, $\frac{1}{3}$ drachm, $\frac{1}{24}$ oz. Apothecaries' weight Denoted by the character ℈. 2. One sixtieth of a degree; a minute of arc 1610. †3. As a unit of time. *S. of an hour*: the sixtieth part of an hour, a minute 1603. 4. *fig.* A very small quantity or amount; a very small part or portion 1574.

4. Look into Italy and Spain, whether those places be one s the better MILT.

Scruple (skrū·p'l), *sb.*[2] 1526. [ad. F. *scrupule*, ad. L. *scrupulus*, lit. a pebble, fig. a cause of uneasiness, dim. of *scrupus* rough or hard pebble.] **1.** A thought or circumstance that troubles the mind or conscience; a doubt, uncertainty, or hesitation in regard to right and wrong, duty, propriety, etc.; esp. one which is regarded as over-refined or over-nice. Also in generalized sense. †**2.** An intellectual difficulty, perplexity, or objection –1741. †**b.** Disbelief or doubt *of* –1672.

1. Some crauen s. Of thinking too precisely on th'euent SHAKS. Phr. *S. of conscience. Without s. To have scruples; to have little, no s.*, etc., *about* (a matter), *in* doing something). *To make s.* (also *a, no*, etc. *s.*) to entertain or raise a scruple or doubt; to hesitate, be reluctant, esp. on conscientious grounds. **2. b.** Phr. †*To have* or *make s. of*, to hesitate to believe or admit; Whereat, I..Made s. of his praise SHAKS.

Scruple (skrū·p'l), *v.* 1627. [f. prec.] †**1.** *trans.* To have or make scruples about; to demur to, take exception to; to hesitate or stick at (doing something) –1837. †**2.** To doubt, question, hesitate to believe (a fact, allegation, etc.) –1846. †**3.** To cause (a person) to feel scruples –1689. **4.** *intr.* To entertain or raise scruples; to hesitate, demur, †doubt. Chiefly *to s. at.* Now *rare.* 1639. **5.** Const. *inf.*: To hesitate or be reluctant (*to do* something), esp. on grounds of conscience or propriety 1660.

1. He scrupled no means to obtain his ends CHESTERF. **3.** The dangerous tentations of the devil..do mainly..s. the consciences of the weaker amongst us 1657. **4.** The sovereigns..who scrupled at no means for securing themselves on the throne SOUTHEY. **5.** He scrupl'd not to eat Against his better knowledge MILT. Hence **Scru·pler**, one who scruples, one who has scruples. So **Scru·pulist**, one who has scruples or raises difficulties.

Scrupulosity (skrūpiulǫ·siti). 1526. [a. F. *scrupulosité*, or ad. L. *scrupulositatem*, f. *scrupulosus* SCRUPULOUS; see -ITY.] **1.** The state or quality of being scrupulous; an instance of this; †a scruple. †**2.** *Astr.* Minute determination (of time) 1633.

1. Avoid a needless S. of Conscience, as a thing which keeps our Minds always uneasie 1690.

Scrupulous (skrū·piŭləs), *a.* 1450. [ad. F *scrupuleux* or L. *scrupulosus*, f. *scrupulus* SCRUPLE *sb.*[2]; see -OUS.] **1.** Troubled with doubts or scruples of conscience; over-nice or meticulous in matters of right and wrong. Also (of things, actions, etc.), characterized by such scruples. †**b.** Prone to hesitate or doubt; cautious or meticulous in acting, deciding, etc. Also (of actions, etc.), characterized by doubt or distrust; (of objections) cavilling. –1695. †**2.** Of a thing: Causing or raising scruples; liable to give offence; dubious, doubtful –1685. **3.** Careful to follow the dictates of conscience; strict in matters of right and wrong 1545. †**b.** With inf.: Careful (to do something) in obedience to one's conscience 1729. **4.** Of actions, etc.: Characterized by a strict and minute regard for what is right 1756. **5.** Minutely exact or careful (in non-moral matters); strictly attentive even to the smallest details 1638.

1. 3 *Hen. VI*, IV. vii. 61. **2.** As the Cause of a Warre ought to be Iust; so the Iustice of that Cause ought to be Euident; Not Obscure, not S. BACON. Phr. †*To make it s.*, to scruple, hesitate (*to do* something) **3. b.** We should be religiously s. and exact to say nothing..but what is true 1729. **4.** He gave to business the most s. attention 1779. **5.** Great men are seldom over s. in the arrangement of their attire DICKENS. Hence **Scru·pulous·ly** *adv.*, -**ness.**

Scrutable (skrū·tăb'l), *a.* 1600. [f. L. *scrutari*; see SCRUTATOR.] That can be understood by scrutiny.

Scrutation (skrutē̆·ʃən). 1593. [ad. L. *scrutationem*, f. *scrutari.*] Minute search or examination.

Scrutator (skrutē̆·tə.ɪ). 1580. [a. L., f. *scrutari* to examine, scrutinize, app. f. *scruta* pl., 'old or broken stuff, trash, frippery, trumpery'.] **1.** One who examines or investigates 1593. **2.** *spec.* One whose office it is to examine or investigate closely; *esp.* one who acts as an examiner of votes at an election 1680. **b.** As the title of a university official. Now *Hist.* 1580

Scrutineer (skrūtinīᵊ·ɪ). 1557. [f. SCRUTINY + -EER.] One whose duty it is to scrutinize or examine, esp. one who examines votes at an election, etc.

Scrutinize (skrū·tinəiz), *v.* 1671. [f. next + -IZE.] **1.** *trans.* To subject to scrutiny. **b.** *spec.* with ref. to votes 1750. †**2.** *intr.* To make scrutiny. Const. *into.* –1788.

1. She began..to s. her heart, with an uncommon degree of severity 1800. **b.** The Westminster election, which is still scrutinising, produced us a parliamentary event this week H. WALPOLE. Hence **Scru·tinizer.** So **Scru·tinous** *a.* [ad. F. †*scrutineux*] (now *rare*), closely examining; searching 1599; **Scru·tinously** *adv.* 1649.

Scrutiny (skrū·tini). 1450. [ad. late L. *scrutinium*, f. *scrutari*; see SCRUTATOR.] **1.** The formal taking of individual votes, as a method of electing to an office or dignity, or of deciding some question; an instance of this procedure. Now chiefly in *Canon Law.* **2.** Investigation, critical inquiry; an instance of this 1604. **b.** An official examination of the votes cast at an election, in order to eliminate any votes that are invalid, and to rectify or confirm the numbers stated in the return 1728. **3.** The action of looking searchingly at something; a searching gaze 1796.

1. We have at last a new Pope, after many scrutinies 1623. **2.** An accurate scrutinie of all my actions past EVELYN. **3.** A careful s. of her countenance DICKENS.

Scrutoire (skrutwā·ɪ, -twǭ·ɪ). 1626. [Aphet. ad. F. *escritoire.*] = ESCRITOIRE.

Scruze (skrūz), *v.* Now *dial.* 1590. [perh. suggested by SCREW and SQUEEZE *vbs.*] *trans.* To squeeze.

†**Scry**, *sb.* late ME. [Aphet. f. ASCRY *sb.*; cf. next.] **1.** Crying out, exclamation, clamour –1819. **2.** An attack; a reconnoitre –1587.

Scry (skrəi), *v.* 1528. [Aphet. f. DESCRY *v.*] **1.** *trans.* To descry, see, perceive. *Obs.* exc. *dial.* 1555. **2.** *intr.* To see images in a crystal, etc. which reveal the future or secrets of the past or present; to act as a crystal-gazer. (Revived recently as a techn. term.) 1528. Hence **Scry·er**, a crystal-gazer.

Scud (skʊd), *sb.* 1609. [f. next.] **1.** The action of scudding; hurried movement. **2. a.** Light clouds driven rapidly before the wind 1669. **b.** A driving shower (of rain or snow) 1687. **c.** A sudden gust of wind 1694. **d.** Ocean foam or spray driven by the wind 1850. **3.** *School slang.* A swift runner 1857.

2. a. The S. comes against the Wind, twill blow hard 1669. **d.** The air was drenched with spume and flying s. 1894.

Scud (skʊd), *v.* 1532. [Origin obsc.] **1.** *intr.* To run or move briskly or hurriedly; to dart nimbly from place to place. **b.** In the imper.: Be off! Make haste! 1602. **2.** To sail or move swiftly on the water. Now chiefly (in techn. nautical use), to run before a gale with little or no sail. 1582. **3.** Of clouds, foam, etc.: To be driven by the wind 1699. **4.** *trans.* To pass, travel, or sail quickly over 1632.

1. The Trout within the weeds did s. 1613. **2.** There was too much wind to s. 1884. **3.** Crisp foam-flakes s. along the level sand TENNYSON.

Scuddle (skʊ·d'l), *v.* Now *dial.* 1577. [Frequentative of prec.] *intr.* To run away hastily, to scuttle.

‖**Scudo** (skū·do). *Pl.* **scudi** (skū·di). 1644. [It. = OF. *escu* (mod.F. *écu*), Sp., Pg. *escudo* shield, hence the name of a coin bearing a shield:—L. *scutum* shield.] A silver coin and money of account formerly current in various Italian states, usu. worth about four shillings.

Scuff (skʊf), *sb.* 1787. [Origin obsc.] The nape of the neck (only in references to seizing by the 'scuff (of the neck)'.

Scuff (skʊf), *v.* 1768. [perh. partly echoic; perh. conn. w. SCURF *v.* With sense 3, cf. CUFF *v.*[1]] **1.** *trans.* To touch lightly in passing 1824. **b.** To scrape (the ground, boards, etc.) with the feet; to wear off by treading 1897. **2.** *intr.* To walk (through, dust, snow, etc.) so as to brush it aside or throw it up; hence *trans.*, to throw *up* (dust by this manner of walking) 1768. **b.** To shuffle with the feet 1847. **3.** *trans.* To buffet (a person) 1841.

Scuffle (skʊ·f'l), *sb.*[1] 1606. [f. SCUFFLE *v.*[1]] **1.** A scrambling fight; an encounter with much hustling and random exchange of blows; a tussle **2.** The action of scuffling; confused utterance (of speech); shuffling (of feet) 1899.

1. There had been a s. among them in which one of their canoes had been overset DE FOE. *transf.* A s. for places BURKE.

Scuffle (skʊ·f'l), *sb.*[2] 1798. [a. Du. *schoffel* weeding-hoe.] **1.** = SCUFFLER[2]. **2.** A gardener's thrust-hoe. *local* and *U.S.* 1841.

Scuffle (skʊ·f'l), *v.*[1] 1579. [Frequentative f. a base perh. of Scand. origin.] **1.** *intr.* To struggle confusedly *together* or *with* another; to fight at close quarters in a disorderly manner 1590. **2.** *trans.* To put *on, out, up*, etc. in a scrambling or confused manner 1579. **3.** *intr.* To struggle *through, on, along*; hence, to go hurriedly or superficially (*through* or *over* some operation) 1784. **4.** To go in hurried confusion; to move with much effort and fuss; also *trans.* (causatively) 1838. **5.** To move with a shuffling gait; also, to shuffle (with the feet) 1825.

1. I..haue seene in former dayes The best Knights of the world, and scuffled in some frayes DRAYTON. *transf.* Both at Sea and Land we Tug and S. for Dominion and Wealth 1678. Hence **Scu·ffler**[1], one who scuffles. **Scu·ffingly** *adv.*

Scuffle (skʊ·f'l), *v.*[2] 1766. [f. SCUFFLE *sb.*[2]] *trans.* To scarify or stir the surface of (land) with a thrust-hoe or horse-hoe; to hoe (a crop), cut up (weeds), turn in (seed) by means of a scuffle or scuffler. Hence **Scu·ffler**[2], an implement for scarifying and stirring the surface of the ground, esp. between the rows of crops; a horse-hoe.

Scull (skʊl), *sb.*[1] ME. [Origin obsc.] **1.** A kind of oar. **a.** An oar used to propel a boat by working it from side to side over the stern of the boat, reversing the blade at each turn. **b.** One of a pair of short and light oars, which can be operated at once by one person, who sits midway between the sides of the boat. †**2.** A sculling-boat –1661. †**3.** A sculler (*rare*) –1719. **4.** *pl.* A sculling-race 1878. **5.** An act of sculling 1886.

Scull (skʊl), *sb.*[2] 1813. A local name for various species of gulls.

Scull (skʊl), *v.* 1624. [f. SCULL *sb.*[1]] **1.** *intr.* or *absol.* To proceed by means of a boat propelled with a scull or a pair of sculls; to use a scull or a pair of sculls in propelling a boat. **b.** *trans.* To make (a particular stroke) in sculling 1875. **2.** To propel (a boat) by means of a scull or a pair of sculls 1665. **b.** *intr.* Of a boat: To admit of being sculled (well, easily, etc.) 1891. **3.** *trans.* To convey (a person) by water in a sculling-boat or by sculling 1827. Hence **Scu·ller**, one who sculls; a boat propelled by sculling, a sculling-boat.

Scullery (skʊ·ləri). 1440. [a. OF. *escuelerie*, f. *escuelier* maker or seller of dishes, f. *escuele*:—L. *scutella* flat dish, salver.] **1.** The department of a household concerned with the care of the plates, dishes, and kitchen utensils. Also the room or rooms devoted to this. *Obs.* exc. *Hist.* **2.** In mod. use: A small room attached to a kitchen, in which the washing of dishes and other dirty work is done 1753.

attrib., as *s. maid*, etc.

Scullion (skʊ·lyən). 1483. [perh. alteration of F. *souillon*, assim. to SCULLERY.] A domestic servant of the lowest rank in a household, who performed the menial offices of the kitchen; hence, a person of the lowest order, esp. as an abusive epithet. Now *arch.* **b.** quasi-*adj.* Base, mean 1658.

Haveloke..having been first a skullen in the King's Kitchin HOLLAND. Hence **Scu·llionship.**

†**Sculp**, *sb.* 1696. [f. next.] An engraving used as an illustration in a book –1706.

Sculp (skʊlp), *v.* 1535. [f. L. *sculpere* to carve.] †**1.** *trans.* To carve or engrave (upon something) –1695. **2.** To sculpture. Now chiefly *colloq.* or *joc.* Also *intr.* or *absol.* 1784.

2. Men who write, and paint, and s. KIPLING.

Sculpin (skʊ·lpin), *sb.* 1672. [perh. corruption of SCORPENE.] **1.** A name for various small worthless fish having a spiny appearance; **a.** A fish of the genus *Callionymus*, e.g. *C. draco*; **b.** A fish of the genus *Cottus*, e.g. *C. virginianus*; **c.** *Hemitripterus hispidus* or *americanus*; **d.** *Scorpæna guttata* (see SCORPENE). **2.** *transf.* A mean, worthless person or animal 1833.

Sculpt (skʊlpt), *v.* *rare* exc. *joc.* 1864. [ad. F. *sculpter*, f. L. *sculpt-*, *sculpere*, but apprehended as a jocular back-formation from

SCULPTOR.] *trans.* To sculpture; *absol.* to practise the art of sculpture.

†**Scu·lptile,** *a.* and *sb.* ME. [a. L. *sculptilis*, f. *sculpt-*, *sculpere.*] A. *adj.* Sculptured, graven -1842. B. *sb. pl.* Graven images -1609.

Sculptor (skɒ·lptəɹ). 1634. [a. L., f. *sculpere.*] 1. One who practises the art of sculpture; chiefly, an artist who produces works of statuary in marble or bronze. †2. An engraver -1658. So **Scu·lptress,** a female s.

Sculpture (skɒ·lptiŭɹ, -tʃəɹ), *sb.* late ME. [ad. L. *sculptura*, f. *sculpere* to carve.] 1. Orig., the process or art of carving or engraving a hard material so as to produce designs or figures in relief, in intaglio, or in the round. In mod. use, that branch of fine art which is concerned with producing figures in the round or in relief, either by carving, by fashioning some plastic substance, or by making a mould for casting in metal; the practice of this art. (Now chiefly used with ref. to work in stone or bronze, and to the production of figures of considerable size.) 2. *concr.* a. The product of the sculptor's art; sculptured figures in general. late ME. b. A work of sculpture; a sculptured figure or design 1616. †3. An engraving; engravings collectively -1781. 4. *Nat. Hist.* Marking of the skin, shell, or surface of any animal or plant resembling that produced by a carving tool 1826.

2. Some frail memorial still erected nigh, with uncouth rhimes and shapeless s. deck'd GRAY. 4. But in some of these plants the seeds also differ in shape and s. DARWIN. Hence **Scu·lptural** *a.* of or pertaining to s.; having the qualities of a piece of s.; -ly *adv.* **Sculpture·sque** *a.* like s., having the qualities of s.

Sculpture (skɒ·lptiŭɹ, -tʃəɹ), *v.* 1645. [f. prec.] 1. *trans.* To represent in sculpture, to carve (a design or figure) from the solid. 2. To decorate with sculpture. Also *pass.* (*Nat. Hist.*), to bear marks resembling sculpture. 1645.

1. They who sculptured loveliness in stone 1852. *transf.* The edges are soon sculptured off by the action of the sun TYNDALL.

Scum (skɒm), *sb.* ME. [a. MLG. *schûm*, MDu. *schûm(e* :—OTeut. **skūmo-*, f. Teut. and Indo-Eur. root **skeu-* to cover. The Teut. word was adopted in Rom. as OF. *escume* (mod.F. *écume*), Pr., Sp., Pg. *escuma*, etc.] †1. Foam, froth; *pl.* bubbles -1694. 2. †a. Dross which rises to the surface in the purifying of a metal; refuse, slag -1811. b. A film or layer of floating matter formed upon the surface of a liquid in a state of fermentation, ebullition, etc.; hence, a film formed upon stagnant or foul water 1440. 3. *transf.* Applied to persons: The offscourings of humanity; the lowest class of the population of a place or country 1586. †b. An assemblage or body of 'scum' -1829. †c. A worthless wretch -1818.

1. *fig.* The s. & froth of my letters 1637. 2. b. Spawn, weeds, and filth, a leprous s., Made the running rivulet thick and dumb SHELLEY. 3. Scoundrels! Dogs! the S. of the Earth! 1712. b. A s. of Brittaines, and base Lackey Pezants SHAKS. Hence **Scu·mmy** *a.* having the appearance of s.; abounding in s.

Scum (skɒm), *v.* late ME. [f. the sb.] †1. *trans.* To clear (the surface of a liquid) of impurities or floating matter; to SKIM. Also, to skim *off*. -1817. †2. To scour (the sea or land) -1690. 3. *intr.* †a. To rise to the surface as scum -1525. b. To throw up foul matter as a scum; to become covered with a scum 1661.

1. Some scumd the drosse that from the metall came SPENSER. 2. Without certain seat, they liv'd by scumming those Seas and shoars as Pyrats MILT.

Scu·mber, *sb.* *Obs.* exc. *dial.* 1647. [f. next.] The dung of a dog or fox. Hence *dial.*, filth, dirt.

Scu·mber, *v.* *Obs.* exc. *dial.* late ME. [app. aphet. a. OF. *descombrer* (mod.F. *décombrer*) to relieve of a load.] 1. *intr.* Of a dog or fox: To evacuate the fæces. Also *joc.* of a person. 2. *trans.* To void (ordure); *fig.* to produce (something foul) 1596.

Scumble (skɒ·mb'l), *sb.* 1834. [f. next.] A thin coat (of colour) put on by scumbling; a softened effect produced by scumbling.

Scumble (skɒ·mb'l), *v.* 1675. [perh. freq. f. SCUM *v.*] *trans.* In *Oil Painting.* To soften (the colours in a portion of a picture) by overlaying with a thin coat of opaque or semi-opaque colour; to spread or 'drive' (a colour) thinly over a portion of a picture in order to soften hard lines or blend the tints; to produce (an effect) by this process. Also *absol.* So in *Pencil, Chalk,* or *Monochrome drawing,* to soften the lines by rubbing with a stump, etc.

†**Scu·mmer.** ME. [f. SCUM *v.* + -ER [1].] 1. A shallow ladle or sieve for removing scum or floating matter from the surface of a liquid -1825. 2. One who scours the sea; a rover, pirate -1585.

Scumming (skɒ·miŋ), *vbl. sb.* 1530. [f. SCUM *v.* + -ING [1].] 1. The action of removing scum from the surface of a liquid 1611. 2. *concr.* in *sing.* and *pl.* The matter removed in the form of scum. †Also, the matter rising to the surface as scum. 1530.

Scuncheon (skɒ·nʃən). late ME. [a. OF. *escoinson* (mod.F. *écoinson*), app. f. *es-* Ex- + *coin* angle.] *Arch.* The bevelled inner edge of the side or jamb of a window, door, etc.

Scunner (skɒ·nəɹ), *sb.* *Sc.* and *n. dial.* 1500. [f. next.] A loathing disgust; esp. in the phr. *to take a s. at, against.*

Scunner (skɒ·nəɹ), *v.* *Sc.* and *n. dial.* late ME. [Origin obsc.] 1. *intr.* †a. To shrink back with fear, to flinch. b. To be affected with violent disgust, to feel sick. 2. *trans.* To disgust, sicken 1871.

Scup (skɒp). *U.S.* 1848. [Shortened a. Narragansett *mishcup* 'thick-scaled', f. *mishe* large + *cuppi* scale.] The fish *Pagrus argyrops.*

Scuppaug (skɒ·pǭg). *U.S.* 1873. [Shortened a. Narragansett *mischcuppâuog*, pl. of *mishcup*; see prec.] = prec.

Scupper (skɒ·pəɹ), *sb.* 1485. [Etym. obsc.] An opening in a ship's side on a level with the deck to allow water to run away.

Scupper (skɒ·pəɹ), *v.* *Mil. slang.* 1885. [perh. f. prec. sb.] *trans.* To annihilate, 'do for'. Often *pass.* to be 'done for', killed.

Scuppernong (skɒ·pəɹnǫŋ). *U.S.* 1854. [Name of a river in North Carolina.] *S.* (*grape*), a variety of the Fox-grape (*Vitis vulpina*) indigenous to the basin of the Scuppernong River.

Scurf (skɒɹf), *sb.*[1] [Late OE. *scurf*, later f. OE. *sceorf* (also *scruf* SCRUFF *sb.*[1]) :—OTeut. **skurbo-*, **skurfo-*, prob. from the root represented in OE. *sceorfan* to gnaw.] †1. A morbid condition of the skin, esp. of the head, characterized by the separation of branny scales, without inflammation -1661. †b. A similar condition in animals -1607. 2. The scales or small laminæ of epidermis that are continually being detached from the skin; esp. such scales detached in abnormally large quantity, as a consequence of disease, or forming accumulations at the roots of the hair. †Formerly also, a single scale or lamina of this kind. OE. b. *transf.* in *Bot.* Minute scales found on the leaves of certain plants 1839. 3. Any incrustation upon the surface of a body; rust, †a scab; a saline or sulphurous deposit, mould, or the like. Now *rare.* 1440. b. *spec.* A deposit of coke on the inner surface of a gas retort 1884. †4. A thin layer of turf -1726. 5. The 'scum' of the population (*rare*) 1688.

3. *fig.* By length of time The S. is worn away, of each committed Crime DRYDEN.

Scurf (skǭɹf), *sb.*[2] 1483. [perh. identical w. prec.] The Sea-trout, *Salmo eriox* or *S. trutta.*

Scurf (skǭɹf), *v.* 1599. [f. SCURF *sb.*[1]] †1. *trans.* To cover with a scurf or incrustation -1699. 2. To remove by scraping; to chip off (hard deposits) from the surface of a boiler or retort 1839.

Scurfy (skǭ·ɹfi), *a.* 1483. [f. SCURF *sb.*[1] + -Y [1].] 1. Covered with scurf; suffering from cutaneous disease. Also, of the nature of scurf. 2. *transf.* Covered as with scurf incrusted; like scurf 1731. Hence **Scu·rfi·ly** *adv.*, **-ness.**

Scurrile, scurril (skɒ·ril), *a.* Now somewhat *arch.* 1567. [a. F., or ad. L. *scurrilis*, f. *scurra* buffoon.] = SCURRILOUS.

That it containe not base, filthy or s. matter 1586.

Scurrility (skɒri·lĭti). 1508. [a. F. *scurrilité*, or ad. L. *scurrilitas*, f. *scurrilis*; see prec. and -ITY.] The quality of being scurrilous; buffoon-like jocularity; coarseness or indecency of language, esp. in invective and jesting. b. Something scurrilous 1589. †c. Buffoon-like behaviour -1624.

Your reasons..haue beene..pleasant without scurrillity SHAKS. b. Several dull and dead scurrilities in the..London Journals POPE.

Scurrilous (skɒ·riləs), *a.* 1576. [f. SCURRILE *a.* + -OUS.] 'Using such language as only the licence of a buffoon can warrant' (J.); characterized by coarseness of language, esp. in jesting and invective.

They are grown s. upon the Royal family ADDISON. Hence **Scu·rrilous·ly** *adv.*, **-ness.**

Scurry (skɒ·ri), *sb.* 1823. [f. next.] 1. The act of scurrying; a hurried movement, a rush; hurry, haste, bustle. 2. *Sporting.* A short quick run or race on horseback 1824. 3. A fluttering assemblage (e.g. of birds, snow, foam) moving or driven rapidly through the air. †Also, a confused tangle of material. 1839.

1. The s. and the scramble..of London life 1910.

Scurry (skɒ·ri), *v.* 1810. [perh. taken from HURRY-SCURRY, redupl. f. HURRY *v.*] 1. To go rapidly, move hurriedly. 2. *trans.* To cause to go hastily or move rapidly 1850.

1. They s. away like rabbits when they see her coming 1872.

Scurvy (skǭ·ɹvi), *sb.* 1565. [Subst. use of next; perh. suggested by F. *scorbut* SCORBUTUS.] A disease characterized by general debility of the body, extreme tenderness of the gums, foul breath, subcutaneous eruptions, and pains in the limbs, due to malnutrition arising from the lack of suitable food. †b. *pl.* Attacks of this disease -1764.

Comb.: **s.-grass,** a cruciferous plant, *Cochlearia officinalis*, believed to possess anti-scorbutic properties.

Scurvy (skǭ·ɹvi), *a.* 1515. [f. SCURF *sb.*[1] + -Y [1].] †1. Covered with scurf; suffering from, or of the nature of, skin disease; scurfy, scabby -1758. b. *transf.* Of vegetable growths: Resembling scurf, scurfy 1763. 2. *fig.* Sorry, worthless, contemptible. Of treatment, etc.: Shabby, discourteous. 1579.

1. Whether he be blynde,..or is gleyd, or is skyrvye or scaulde COVERDALE *Lev.* xxi. 20. *S. disease* = SCURVY *sb.* 2. Steele and I sat among some s. company over a bowl of punch SWIFT. Hence **Scu·rvi·ly** *adv.* (now *arch.*), †-**ness** -1727.

Scuse, 'scuse (skiūz), *v.* 1476. Aphetic f. EXCUSE *v.* Now careless or jocular *colloq.*

Scut (skɒt). 1440. [Origin obsc.] 1. A short erect tail, esp. that of a hare, rabbit, or deer 1530. 2. A hare. 3. A contemptible fellow (*colloq.* or *dial.*) 1895.

1. My Doe, with the blacke S.? SHAKS. 2. Masid as a marche hare, he ran lyke a s. SKELTON.

Scutage (skiū·tėdʒ). *Obs.* exc. *Hist.* 1460. [ad. med.L. *scutagium*, f. *scutum* shield, after OF. *escuage* ESCUAGE.] A tax levied on knight's fees: chiefly, such a tax paid in lieu of military service.

Scutal (skiū·tăl), *a.* 1857. [ad. mod.L. *scutalis*, f. L *scutum* SCUTUM.] 1. *Zool.* Of the nature of or pertaining to a scutum. 2. Of or pertaining to a (heraldic) shield. *Extra-scutal* adj., (*Her.*) placed outside the shield. 1868.

Scutate (skiū·tėɪt), *a.* 1826. [ad. L. *scutatus* provided with a shield, f. *scutum* SCUTUM.] 1. *Zool.* Covered with scuta or large flat scales. 2. *Bot.* Buckler-shaped 1836. Hence **Scu·tated** *a.* = sense 1. **Scuta·tion** *Zool.*, arrangement of scuta.

Scutch (skɒtʃ), *sb.*[1] 1688. [a. OF. *escouche* (mod.F. *écouche*).] = SCUTCHER 1. Also *s.-rod.*

Scutch (skɒtʃ), *sb.*[2] *dial.* 1685. [Var. of SQUITCH.] = QUITCH *sb.*

Scutch (skɒtʃ), *v.*[1] Now chiefly *dial.* 1611. [prob. echoic.] *trans.* To strike with a stick or whip, to slash, switch. Also *intr.* to strike *at.*

Scutch (skɒtʃ), *v.*[2] 1733. [a. OF. **escoucher*, *escousser* to shake :—pop. L. **excussare.*] 1. *trans.* To dress (fibrous material, flax, hemp, cotton, silk, wool) by beating. 2. To strike the grain from (ears of corn) 1844.

Comb.: **s.-mill,** a mill for preparing flax.

Scutcheon (skɒ·tʃən). Sometimes written **'scutcheon.** late ME. [Aphetic var. of ESCUTCHEON.] 1. = ESCUTCHEON 1, 2. †2. A badge -1598. 3. Anything shaped like an escutcheon; *esp.* a keyhole plate, name-plate, etc. 1483.

1. The burial..was a most vile thing..No plumes,..

ied horses, scutcheons, or open chariots. H. WALPOLE. *fig.* Carefully avoiding a sort of blot in their s. which they think would degrade them for ever BURKE. Hence **Scu·tcheoned** *ppl. a.* furnished or decorated with scutcheons.

Scutcher (skʊ·tʃəɹ). 1766. [f. SCUTCH *v.*[2] + -ER[1].] **1.** An implement or apparatus for scutching. **2.** The part of a thrashing machine which strikes off the grain 1797. **3.** A person employed in scutching 1847.

Scute (skiūt). late ME. [ad. L. *scutum*.] = ECU. *Obs.* exc. *Hist.* **b.** Used vaguely for a coin of small value 1594. **2.** *Zool.* A large scale or bony plate, forming part of the integument of certain animals, as the tortoise, armadillo, echinoderms, various fishes, etc. 1848.

Scutella (skiute·lă). *Pl.* **-æ.** 1771. [mod. L.; orig. a use of L. *scutella* platter, but mistaken for a dim. of L. *scutum* shield.] = SCUTELLUM.

Scutellate (skiū·telēit), *a.* 1785. [ad. mod.L. *scutellatus*, orig. f. L. *scutella* platter, but apprehended as if f. SCUTELLUM + -ATE[2].] **1.** Saucer- or platter-shaped; esp. *Bot.* **2.** *Zool.* Having a scutellum; covered with scutella 1826. So **Scu·tellated** *a.* 1729.

Scutellation (skiūtělēi·ʃən). 1872. [f. prec.; see -ATION.] *Zool.* **a.** Scutellate formation (of the feet of birds). **b.** Arrangement of scutes or scales (in lizards, serpents, etc.).

Scutelliform (skiute·lifǭɹm), *a.* 1826. [f. next + -FORM.] Having the form of a scutellum.

Scutellum (skiute·lɒ̆m). *Pl.* **-a.** 1760. [mod.L.; app. intended as a correction of SCUTELLA, as if a dim. of L. *scutum* shield.] **1.** *Bot.* **a.** An orbicular concave fructification. **b.** An anterior cotyledon in certain grasses 1832. **2.** *Zool.* **a.** *Ent.* The third of the four sclerites composing any segment of the tergum of an insect 1819. **b.** *Ornith.* One of the horny plates which cover the feet of certain birds 1840.

Scutibranchiate (skiūtibræ·ŋkiĕt), *a.* and *sb.* 1836. [f. mod.L. *Scutibranchiata*, f. *scutum* shield + *branchiæ* gills; see -ATE[2].] **A.** *adj.* Pertaining to the *Scutibranchiata*, a group of gasteropods comprising the sea-ears and limpets. **B.** *sb.* A member of this group. So, in the same senses, **Scutibra·nchian** *a.* and *sb.*; **Scutibranch** (skiū·tibræŋk) *a.* and *sb.*

Scutiform (skiū·tifǭɹm), *a.* 1656. [ad. mod.L. *scutiformis*, f. L. *scutum* shield; see -FORM.] Chiefly *Anat.* Shield-shaped.

‖**Scutiger** (skiū·tidʒəɹ). 1842. [Late L., f. *scutum* + *-ger*, *gerere* to bear.] *Zool.* A centipede of the genus *Scutigera*; any member of the family *Scutigeridæ*.

Scutter (skʊ·təɹ), *sb.* Chiefly *dial.* 1826. [f. next.] An act of 'scuttering'; a hasty, scrambling, noisy rush.

Scutter (skʊ·təɹ), *v. colloq.* and *dial.* 1781. [perh. alteration of SCUTTLE *v.*] *intr.* To go hastily with much fuss and bustle, as from excitement or timidity.

Scuttle (skʊ·t'l), *sb.*[1] [OE. *scutel* = ON. *skutill*, G. *schüssel*, ad. med.L. *scutila*, L. *scutella* dish, platter.] †**1.** A dish, trencher, platter –1701. **2. a.** A basket for sifting or winnowing corn; hence, a large shovel to cast grain in winnowing, a casting-shovel. Now *dial.* late ME. **b.** A large open basket wide at the mouth and narrow at the bottom, usu. of wicker-work, used for carrying corn, earth, vegetables, etc. late ME. **c.** More fully COAL-SCUTTLE: A scoop-shaped receptacle with a handle for holding coals for a fire 1849. **Scu·ttleful**, as much as will fill a s.

Scuttle (skʊ·t'l), *sb.*[2] 1497. [Origin obsc.; = F. *écoutille* hatchway.] **1.** *Naut.* A square or rectangular hole or opening in a ship's deck smaller than a hatchway, furnished with a movable cover or lid, used as a means of communication between deck and deck; also a similar hole in the deck or side of a ship for purposes of lighting, ventilation, etc. **b.** The lid of a scuttle-hole or hatchway 1688. **2.** An opening in the roof, floor, wall, etc. of a building closed with a shutter or lid; a trap-door; also the shutter of such an opening. Now *U.S.* 1707. **3.** The section of an automobile connecting the bonnet and body; the 'cowl' 1914.

Comb.: **s.-butt, -cask,** a butt or cask with a square hole cut in it, kept on deck to hold water ready for use; **-hole** = sense 1.

Scuttle (skʊ·t'l), *sb.*[3] 1530. Altered f. CUTTLE *sb.*[1] Also *s. fish.*

Scuttle (skʊ·t'l), *v.*[1] 1450. [Origin obsc.] *intr.* To run with quick hurried steps. Chiefly with *away*, *off*. **b.** *transf.* in *Political slang.* To withdraw in a precipitate and undignified manner from the occupation or control of a country 1883. Hence **Scu·ttle** *sb.*[4] the action or an act of scuttling.

Scuttle (skʊ·t'l), *v.*[2] 1642. [f. SCUTTLE *sb.*[2]] **1.** *trans.* To cut or bore a hole or holes in the sides or bottom of (a vessel, for the purpose of sinking her). **2.** To cut a hole in (the deck of a vessel), esp. for the purpose of salving the cargo 1789.

1. The mildest manner'd man That ever scuttled ship or cut a throat BYRON.

‖**Scutulum** (skiū·tiŭlɒ̆m). *Pl.* **-a.** 1888. [mod.L. use of L. dim. of *scutum* shield.] *Path.* A shield-shaped crust or disk developed in the skin-disease favus. **b.** *Zool.* A scutellum 1902.

‖**Scutum** (skiū·tɒ̆m). *Pl.* **scuta** (skiū·tă). 1771. [mod.L. use of L. *scutum* shield, f. Indo-Eur. root **skū-* (: **skeu-*) to cover.] **1.** *Bot.* 'The broad dilated stigma in some asclepiads' 1832. **2.** *Ent.* The second segment of each of the three divisions of the tergum in insects 1830. **3.** *Zool.* A shield-like dermal plate; a scute 1771.

‖**Scybalum** (si·bălɒ̆m). Usu. pl. **scybala.** 1684. [med.L., a. Gr. σκύβαλον.] *Path.* One of a collection of round masses of constipated fæces formed in the bowels in certain diseases.

Scye (səi). 1830. [A use of a Sc. and Ulster dial. word of obsc. etym.] *Tailors' term.* The opening in a coat into which a sleeve is inserted.

Scylla (si·lă). 1520. [L., a. Gr. Σκύλλα.] A rock upon the Italian side of the Straits of Messina facing CHARYBDIS (q.v. for phr. *between S. and Charybdis*, etc.); also personified as a dangerous sea-monster.

‖**Scypha** (səi·fă). 1832. [mod.L., a. Gr. σκύφη, var. of σκύφος drinking-cup.] *Bot.* = SCYPHUS.

Scyphi- (səifi), comb. form of L. *scyphus* SCYPHUS. **Scy·phiform** *a. Bot.*, cup-shaped; *Zool.*, boat-shaped, scaphoid. ‖**Scyphisto·ma** *Zool.*, = SCYPHOSTOMA.

Scypho- (səi·fo, səifǫ·), repr. Gr. σκυφο-, comb. form of σκύφος SCYPHUS. **Scy·phomancy** [-MANCY], divination by means of a cup. ‖**Scy:phomedu·sa** [mod.L.] *Zool.*, a group of Hydrozoa. **Scy·phophore** (-fōᵊɹ) [ad. mod.L. *scyphophorus*] *Zool.*, a member of the *Scyphophori*, an order of physostomous fishes. **Scypho·stoma** [Gr. στόμα mouth] *Zool.*, a non-sexual hydroid form of the Hydrozoan Acraspeda.

‖**Scyphus** (səi·fɒ̆s). *Pl.* **scyphi** (səi·fəi). 1777. [mod.L. use of L. *scyphus*, ad. Gr. σκύφος a large drinking vessel without a foot.] **a.** The corona of certain plants when forming a cup or funnel-shaped appendage. **b.** A dilatation of the podetium in lichens bearing shields on its margin.

Scythe (səið), *sb.* [OE. *sīðe*, earlier **sigði* :—OTeut. **segiþjoz*, f. root **seg-* to cut (cf. L. *secare*). Spelt with *sc* through erroneous association w. L. *scindere* to cut.] **1.** An implement for mowing grass or other crops, having a long thin curving blade fastened at an angle with the handle and wielded with both hands with a long sweeping stroke. **2.** *transf.* and *fig.*, esp. as the attribute of Time or Death. late ME. **3.** A weapon having a long curving blade resembling a reaping hook. *Obs.* exc. *Hist.* with ref. to scythed chariots. ME.

1. Thy valleys.., Where now the sharp-edg'd Sithe sheeres vp the spyring grasse DRAYTON. 2. And nothing gainst Times sieth can make defence SHAKS.

Comb.: **s.-stone,** a whetstone for scythes.

Scythe (səið), *v.* 1597. [f. prec.] *trans.* To cut or mow with a scythe.

Time had not sithed all that youth begun SHAKS.

Scythed (səiðd), *ppl. a.* late ME. [f. SCYTHE *sb.* and *v.* + -ED.] **1.** Furnished with a scythe; esp. *Hist.* (= Gr. δρεπανηφόρος, L. *falcatus*) of war-chariots provided with scythes fastened to a revolving shaft projecting from the axle-trees; attributed by classical writers to the Persians and the Britons. **2.** Cut down with a scythe 1865.

Scytheman (səi·ðmæn). 1577. [f. SCYTHE *sb.* + MAN *sb.*] **1.** One who uses a scythe. **2.** One of an irregular body of troops armed with a scythe as a weapon 1849. **2.** *fig.* Applied to Time and to Death 1818.

Scythian (si·ðiăn, si·þiăn), *a.* and *sb.* 1543. [f. L. *Scythia*, a. Gr. Σκυθία (f. Σκύθης) + -AN.] **A.** *adj.* Pertaining to Scythia, an ancient region extending over a large part of European and Asiatic Russia, or to the nomadic people who inhabited it 1567. **B.** *sb.* **1.** A person belonging to the race by which Scythia was inhabited 1543. **2.** The language of Scythia 1668. So **Scy·thic** *a.* Scythian.

'Sdeath (zdeþ), *int. Obs.* exc. *arch.* 1606. A euphemistic abbrev. of *God's death*, used in oaths and asseverations.

†**Sdeign**, *sb. rare.* 1590. [ad. It. *sdegno*, f. *sdegnare*.] Disdain –1819. So †**Sdeign**, *v.* 1590. [ad. It. *sdegnare*, aphet. for *disdegnare* to DISDAIN.] –1667.

As if he..sdeign'd the low degree SPENSER.

Se-, *prefix*, occurring only in L. derivs., represents the L. *se-*, = OLatin *se* (also *sed*) prep. and adv., without, apart, in *secede*, *seclude*, *secure* adj., *sedition*, etc.

Sea (sī). [Com. Teut.; OE. *sǽ* :—OTeut. **saiwiz*.] **1.** The continuous body of salt water that covers the greater part of the earth's surface. Often *poet.* with epithet as *broad*, *deep*, *salt*, etc. **b.** Often coupled with *land*, to express the idea of the whole surface of the earth OE. **c.** *pl.* Different parts or tracts of the ocean OE. **d.** In pregnant use, with ref. to naval operations, the shipping trade, etc. ME. **2.** A part of the general body of salt water, having certain land-limits or washing a particular coast, and having a proper name, as *Red*, *Black*, *Adriatic S.* OE. **3.** A large lake or landlocked sheet of water, whether salt or fresh. *Obs.* exc. in *inland s.* and in proper names, as the S. of Galilee, etc. OE. **4.** The volume of water in the sea considered in regard to the ebb and flow of the tide OE. **5.** With an epithet indicating the roughness or smoothness of the waves. Hence without qualification = a heavy swell, rough water. OE. **b.** The direction of the waves or swell 1769. **c.** A large heavy wave 1582. **6.** *fig.* With ref. to metaphorical sailing, drowning, waves, etc.; also, a copious or overwhelming mass (*of* something) ME. **7.** *transf.* **a.** A large level tract (*of* some material substance or aggregate of objects) 1585. **b.** Hyperbolically, a great quantity of liquid, esp. (in fig. context) of blood 1598. **8.** *Antiq.* The great brazen laver in the Jewish Temple. [Literalism from Heb.] late ME.

1. This precious stone, set in the siluer s. SHAKS. **b.** The light that never was, on sea or land WORDSW. **c.** Magic casements, opening on the foam of perilous seas KEATS. **d.** The Command of the Seas BACON. *To keep the sea*, to prevent the enemy from occupying it, to keep it clear for one's own ships and traffic. **High s.** (Now usu. *pl.*) The deep or open sea; the main sea or main. *spec.* in *Law.* (*sing.* and *pl.*): (*a*) The main sea, as far as it is regarded as being within the jurisdiction of the courts of admiralty; (*b*) The area of the sea not within the jurisdiction of any nation, but the free highway of all nations. 2. *The four seas*, the seas bounding Great Britain on the four sides. *Within the four seas* = in Great Britain. *The Severn S.* (arch.), the Bristol Channel. 4. †*Full s.*, high tide (also *fig.*). 5. It was pitch-dark, a good deal of s. on 1837. Phr. *Salt* or *bitter s.*, sea-water (*poet.*). **c.** A s. struck us on the weather side 1861. 6. To take Armes against a S. of troubles SHAKS. 7. So on this windie S. of Land, the Fiend Walk'd up and down alone MILT. **b.** These wars, which have spilled such seas of blood BURKE.

Phrases. **At sea. a.** Out on the sea, on shipboard; in employment as a sailor. **b.** *fig.* In a state of uncertainty or perplexity, at a loss. Also *all at s.* **Beyond (the) s.** or **seas.** Out of the country, abroad. **By s.** †**a.** At the sea-side. (Now *by the s.*) **b.** By way of the sea, on or over the sea (as a mode of transit or conveyance). **c.** In the region of the sea, at sea. †**By long s.** Short for *by long sea passage.* Also *by the long seas.* **On** or **upon the s. a.** On the sea's surface, afloat, at sea, on shipboard. **b.** Of a dwelling, etc.: At the sea's edge, on the sea-coast. **Over the s. a.** Of motion: Across the sea, to the other side of the sea. **b.** Of position: On the other side of the sea; abroad. **To s.** Out on the water, on a voyage, or on ship-board. *To go to s.*, to go on a voyage; to enter upon, or follow, the profession of a sailor. *To put, put off, put out, to s.*: see PUT *v.*[1] *To stand out to s.*: see STAND *v.* **To take the s.** To go on board ship, embark; to start on a sea-voyage, launch forth, put out to sea (said also of the ship). Cf. F. *prendre la mer.*

Comb.: **s.-anchor** = *drift-anchor* (see DRIFT *sb.*); **-bathing**, bathing in the s.; **-beach** = BEACH *sb.* 2; †**borderer**, one who inhabits the land adjacent to the sea; **-bordering**, *a.* (*rare*), bordering on the s.; **-bound**, *a.*[1] bound or confined by the s.; **-bound**, *a.*[2] bound for or on the way to the s.; **-change**, a change wrought by the sea; **-chest**, a seaman's chest or box for his own clothing, etc.; **-cloth**, a painted cloth spread over the stage and moved so as to represent waves; **-cook**, a cook on board ship; esp. in *son of a s.-cook*, used as a term of abuse; **-crust**, the incrustation formed on an iron ship during a s.-voyage; **-dike**, an embankment against the s., a s.-wall; **-fencible**, an old coast-guard; **-fire**, phosphorescence at sea; **-froth**, (*a*) s.-foam; (*b*) meerschaum; †**-ground**, the bottom of the s.; **-horizon**, the line where sky and sea seem to meet; in *Navigation*, 'the small circle which bounds the portion of the surface visible to a spectator in the open sea'; **-ivory**, ivory from the tusks and horns of marine mammalia; **-law**, a law relating to the duties and rights of persons on the seas; **-league**, three nautical miles; **-light**, a beacon, lighthouse, or harbour-light to guide ships at s.; **-log**, an official record of a ship's voyage; **-lord**, a naval lord (of the Admiralty); **-mile**, a geographical or nautical mile (see MILE *sb.*[1]); †**-ox**, the hippopotamus; **-pass**, a document carried in time of war by neutral merchant vessels to show their nationality; **-purple** = PURPLE *sb.* 3, also the dye derived from it; **-rim**, the s. horizon; **scout**, a maritime auxiliary of the Boy Scout; **-song**, a song such as is sung by sailors; **-speed**, the ordinary speed of a vessel when at sea, as dist. from *full speed*; **-thief**, a pirate, s.-rover; **-valve**, any one of several valves in the bottom or side of a steamship communicating with the sea below the water-line; **-view**, (*a*) a s.-scape; (*b*) a view or prospect of the s., or at s.

b. In names of marine mammalia, as **s.-bear**, the ursine or fur-seal, *Callorhinus ursinus*, of the N. Pacific; also applied to the smaller otaries of the southern seas; **-canary**, a sailor's name for the white whale, *Delphinapterus leucas*; **-leopard**, any one of various seals of the antarctic and southern seas, esp. of the genus *Ogmorhinus*; **-morse**, = MORSE *sb.*[2]; **-pig**, applied to the porpoise, the dolphin, the dugong, etc.

c. In names of birds: **s.-coot**, †(*a*) the cormorant; (*b*) the guillemot; (*c*) the American coot; **-crow**, local name for various birds as the cormorant, chough, razor-billed auk, etc.; **-dotterel**, the turnstone, *Strepsilas interpres*; also *local*, the ring-plover; **-drake**, a cormorant or s.-crow; also *U.S.*, the male eider-duck; **-duck**, any duck of the subfamily *Fuligulinæ*, as the common scoter, the eider-duck, etc.; **-goose** *U.S.*, a phalarope; **-hawk**, one of various gull-like birds, as one of the skuas, and the frigate-bird; **-lark**, local name for various small birds frequenting the seashore as the ringed plover, various sandpipers, etc.; **-mall**, **-maw** = SEA-MEW; **-pigeon**, local name for various birds, as the rock-dove, *Columba livia*, the black guillemot, grey kittiwake, etc.; **-quail** *U.S.*, the turnstone; **-turtle**[1], the black guillemot; **-widgeon**, (*a*) the pintail duck; (*b*) the scaup duck.

d. In names of fishes, jelly-fishes, molluscs, shells, etc., as **s.-acorn** = ACORN-SHELL; **-adder**, the pipe-fish; **-anemone**, (see ANEMONE 2); **-angel**, the angel-fish, *Squatina squatina*; **-bass**, *U.S.* (*a*) a serranoid fish, *Centropristis furvus* (black s.-bass); (*b*) a sciænoid fish, *Cynoscion nobilis* (white s.-bass); (*c*) *Sciæna ocellata*; **-bat**, (*a*) a flying-fish, esp. the flying gurnard, *Dactylopterus volitans*; (*b*) *Malthe vespertilio*; (*c*) a fish of the genus *Platax*; **-blubber** = BLUBBER *sb.* 3; **-bream**, any of several sparoid fishes, esp. *Pagellus centrodontus*; **-cat**, (*a*) the wolf-fish, *Anarrhichas lupus*; (*b*) the great weever, *Trachinus draco*; (*c*) a shark, *Scyllium catulus*; (*d*) *Chimæra monstrosa*; (*d*) any s.-catfish; **-catfish**, any of various marine siluroid fishes; **-crab**, a marine crab, as dist. from a river- or land-crab; **-ear**, a univalve mollusc of the genus *Haliotis*; **-eel**, a salt-water eel, a conger; **-egg**, a s.-urchin; **-fan**, an alcyonarian polyp of the sub-order *Gorgoniacea*, esp. *Rhipidogorgia flabellum*; **-feather**, a coral or polyp of the family *Pennatulidæ*; **-fox**, the thrasher-shark, *Alopias vulpes*; **-gherkin**, one of several holothurians, akin to the s.-cucumber; **-hare**, a mollusc, *Aplysia depilans* (and other species), having an oval body with four tentacles; **-hog**, the porpoise (now *rare*); **-hound**, a dog-fish; **-jelly**, a jelly-fish; **-lemon**, (*a*) a nudibranchiate gastropod of the family *Dorididæ*; (*b*) *Austral.*, a holothurian of the genus *Cuvieria*; **-lungs**, an acaleph of the *Ctenophora* (said to be so called from the alternate contraction and expansion, as if breathing); **-melon**, a holothurian of the family *Pentactidæ*; **-needle**, the garfish, *Belone vulgaris*; **-nettle**, any of certain radiate marine animals of the class *Acalephæ*, having the property of stinging when touched; **-orange**, a large holothurian (*Lophothuria fabricii*) of a globose shape and orange-coloured; **-orb**, a swell, globe, or orb-fish; **-owl**, the lump-fish, *Cyclopterus lumpus*; **-pad**, a star-fish; **-pear**, an ascidian or sea-squirt of the genus *Boltenia*; **-pen**, a polyp of the genus *Pennatula* or family *Pennatulidæ*; **-pheasant**, the turbot; **-porcupine**, the porcupine-fish, *Diodon hystrix*; **-scorpion**, (*a*) a scorpion-fish; (*b*) a sculpin, *Cottus scorpius*; **-sleeve**, a cuttle-fish or calamary; **-squirt**, any ascidian or tunicate; **-strawberry**, a polyp, *Alcyonium rubiforme*; **-sunflower**, a sea-anemone; **-toad**, (*a*) the fishing-frog, *Lophius piscatorius*; (*b*) *U.S.* the sculpin; (*c*) the toad-fish; **-turtle**[2], a turtle; **-unicorn**, the narwhal; **-wife**, a kind of wrasse, *Acantholabrus yarrelli*; **-wing**, a wing-shell.

e. In names of seaweeds: **s.-belt**, *Laminaria saccharina*; **-colander** U.S., *Agarum turneri*; **-girdle**, *Laminaria digitata*; **-lace**, *Chorda filum*; **-lentil**, the gulf-weed; **-lettuce**, *Ulva Lactuca* and *U. latissima*; **-moss** = CORALLINE *sb.*[1]; **-thong**, any of several cord-like seaweeds, as *Chorda filum*, etc.; **-trumpet**, a large seaweed, *Ecklonia buccinalis* (so called because the hollow upper stem is used as a trumpet at the Cape of Good Hope); **-turnip**, a seaweed of the genus *Nereocystis*.

f. In names of plants growing on the sea-shore: **s.-beet**, (*a*) a variety of the common beet, *Beta vulgaris*, often called *Beta maritima*; (*b*) = *s.-lavender*; **-bent**, *Psamma* or *Ammophila arenaria*; **-blite**, *Suæda fruticosa*; **-cabbage**, **-cole** = SEA-KALE; **s. campion**, *Silene maritima*; **-fennel**, samphire; **-gilliflower** = SEA-PINK; **-heath**, a 'heath' of the genus *Frankenia*; **-laurel**, the seaside laurel; **-lavender**, *Statice Limonium*; **s. matgrass, matweed**, *Psamma arenaria*; **-plantain**, *Plantago maritima*; **-radish**, a variety of the wild radish, sometimes regarded as a species (*Raphanus maritimus*); **-rush**, a species of *Juncus*; **-starwort**, *Aster tripolium*; **-thistle** = SEA-HOLLY; **-thrift** = SEA-PINK; **-willow**, the papyrus or paper-reed, BIBLUS.

Sea air. 1685. The air above or in the neighbourhood of the sea; air containing saline or gaseous matter derived from sea-water.

Sea-bank. ME. [BANK *sb.*[1]] **1.** †**a.** The sea-coast or sea-shore –1794. **b.** A dune or sand-hill 1848. **2.** An embankment built for protection against the sea, a sea-wall 1647.

Sea·-bean. 1607. †**1.** A small stone or pebble –1847. **2.** A name given to the seeds of the tropical leguminous plant *Entada scandens*, carried by sea to the British coasts, and often made into trinkets 1696. **3.** A small univalve shell of the family *Triviidæ*; also, the operculum of any shell of the family *Turbinidæ* 1885.

Sea·-beast. 1450. A beast living in the sea.

Sea·-bird. 1589. A bird frequenting the sea, or the land near the sea. Also *attrib.*

Seaboard (sī·bōᵊɹd), *sb.* and *a.* 1490. [f. SEA + BOARD *sb.*] **A.** *sb.* †**1.** With preps. *a*, *at*, *on*, *to s.*, on or to the seaward side (of a ship, etc.) –1635. †**2.** *By* (*be*) *s.*: by sea. *On s.*: at sea, on board ship. –1597. **3.** The line where land and sea meet, the coast-line; the sea-shore or the land near the sea 1825.

3. On the seabord of this wild land is a rim of grassy country, where cattle can subsist CARLYLE.

B. *adj.* Bordering on or adjoining the sea (*rare*) 1590.

Sea·-boat. OE. **1.** †**a.** A boat for the sea. **b.** A vessel considered in ref. to her behaviour at sea. **2.** A *Chiton* or coat-of-mail shell 1884.

Sea·-born, *a.* 1593. Born in or of the sea. **a.** Of persons, chiefly mythological, esp. of Venus. **b.** Produced by or having its origin in the sea 1646. **c.** Of an island, etc. rising from the sea 1726.

a. Like Neptune and his Sea-borne Neece 1645.

Sea·-borne, *a.* 1823. [BORNE *ppl. a.*] **1.** Conveyed by sea. (Said usu. of articles of commerce.) **2.** Of a ship, etc.: Carried or floating on the sea 1840. **3.** *ellipt.* quasi-*sb.* Sea-borne coal 1892.

Sea·-breeze. 1697. [BREEZE *sb.*[2]] A breeze blowing from the sea.

Sea·-calf. late ME. [CALF [1].] The seal, esp. the common seal, *Phoca vitulina*.

Sea·-captain. 1612. The captain or commander of a ship, usu. of a merchant vessel.

†**Sea·-card.** 1555. [CARD *sb.*[2]] **1.** A chart of the sea –1745. **2.** The card of the mariner's compass –1710.

Sea·-cliff. OE. A cliff on the sea-shore. In *Geol.* occas. a rock which is now inland, but was on the shore of a former sea.

Sea-coal (sī·kōᵘl). OE. †**1.** In OE.: Jet (which was washed up by the sea). **2. a.** Mineral coal (prob. so called locally because brought by sea). Now *Hist.* ME. **b.** Very small coal cast up by the sea 1645.

Sea-coast. ME. **1.** The land adjacent to the sea. **2.** *attrib.* or *adj.* 1622.

Sea·-cock. 1684. [COCK *sb.*[1]] **1.** *local.* Any of various birds, as the grey plover, *Squatarola helvetica*. **2.** A name for species of gurnard, *Trigla cuculus* and *T. hirax* 1704. **3.** *joc.* A bold sea-rover 1865. **4.** In a marine steam-engine: A cock on the pipe which runs from the boiler into the sea 1855.

Sea·-cow. 1613. [COW *sb.*[1]] **1.** The manatee; also the dugong and other sirenians. †**2.** The morse or walrus –1837. **3.** [S. Afr. Du. *zeekoe.*] The hippopotamus 1731.

Sea cucumber. 1601. [= F. *concombre de mer.*] Any holothurian; sometimes restricted to the *Psolidæ*.

Sea·-de:vil. 1594. **1.** A devil supposed to inhabit the sea. **2.** Any of various ugly fish, as the fishing-frog, various large rays, etc. 1611.

Sea·-dog. 1598. [Cf. Du. *zeehond*, G. *seehund.*] **1.** The common or harbour seal, *Calocephalus vitulinus*. †**2.** A dog-fish or small shark –1802. **3.** A privateer or pirate, esp. of the time of Queen Elizabeth 1659. **4.** A sailor, usually one long used to the sea, an 'old salt' 1840. **5.** A luminous appearance near the horizon, regarded by mariners as a prognostic of bad weather 1825.

Sea·-dra:gon. 1551. **1.** Various fishes, as the weever; the bullhead; a dragonet; a flying sea-horse, etc. **2.** A mythical marine monster resembling a dragon 1749.

Sea·-ea:gle. 1668. **1.** An eagle of the genus *Haliaëtus*, esp. the White-tailed Eagle, *H. albicilla*. Also, the frigate-bird and the skua-gull. **2.** The eagle ray 1722.

Sea·-e:lephant. 1601. The elephant seal, *Macrorhinus elephantinus* or *proboscideus*. Formerly applied to the morse or walrus.

Seafarer (sī·fēᵊrəɹ). 1513. [f. SEA + FARER. Cf. G. *seefahrer.*] A traveller by sea, esp. one whose life is spent in voyaging, a sailor.

Seafaring (sī·ˌfēᵊ:riŋ), *sb.* 1592. [f. SEA *sb.* + *faring* vbl. sb. f. FARE *v.*] Travelling by sea; the business or calling of a sailor.

Sea·-fa:ring, *a.* ME. [f. SEA + *faring*, ppl. a. of FARE *v.*] Travelling on the sea; following the sea as a calling.

Sea·-fern. 1688. **1.** Any alcyonarian polyp or coral resembling a fern. **2.** A fern, the sea-spleenwort 1855.

Sea·-fight. 1600. A naval battle.

Sea·-fish. OE. [Cf. ON. *sǽfiskr.*] A fish of the sea as dist. from a freshwater fish. So **Sea·-fishery, -fishing**, the business or occupation, etc. of catching fish in the sea.

Sea·-flower. 1805. A flower growing in or by the sea. Also, an actinia or sea-anemone.

Sea·-foam. ME. **1.** Foam of the sea. **2.** [tr. G. *meerschaum.*] = MEERSCHAUM 1837.

Sea·-food. *U.S.* 1836. Food obtained from the sea; fish or shell-fish, etc. used as food.

Sea·-fowl. ME. [Cf. OE. *sǽfugol* only as proper name.] A sea-bird.

Sea-front. 1879. **1.** That portion or side of a building, etc. which faces the sea. **2.** The land on the side of a town, etc. facing the sea.

Sea·-gate[1]. 1583. [GATE *sb.*[2]] A long rolling swell; also, the condition in which two vessels are when thrown aboard one another by such a swell.

Sea·-gate[2]. 1861. [GATE *sb.*[1]] **1.** A gate towards, or giving access to, the sea; or a convenient approach to the sea. **2.** A place of access to the sea 1883.

Sea·-girt, *a.* 1621. Girt or surrounded by the sea. (Sometimes said of a peninsula.)

Sea·-god. 1565. A god of the sea, a marine deity. So **Sea·-go:ddess**, a goddess of the sea.

Sea·-go:ing, *a.* 1829. **1.** Going on the sea, applied to a vessel which makes distant journeys, as opp. to a coasting, harbour, or river vessel. 2. Going to the sea, esp. of a fish, catadromous 1842. 3. Seafaring 1855.

Sea·-grape. 1578. 1. The glassworts, *Salicornea herbacea* and *Salsola Kali.* 2. In W. Indies, the grape-tree or seaside grape, *Coccoloba uvifera* 1806. 3. *pl.* The clustered egg-cases of the cuttle-fish and other cephalopods 1835. 4. The gulf-weed, which has large bladders in clusters resembling grapes 1825.

Sea·-grass. 1578. [Cf. G. *seegras, meergras.*] 1. A grass which grows by the sea. 2. One of various plants and seaweeds growing in the sea; *esp.* the eel-grass or grass-wrack, *Zostera marina* 1591.

Sea·-green, *a.* and *sb.* 1598. [Cf. F. *vert de mer.*] A. *adj.* Pale bluish-green 1603. B. *sb.* A sea-green colour 1598.

Sea·-gull. 1542. = GULL *sb.*[1]

‖ **Seah** (sī·ă). 1705. [Heb. *seāh*, in the Eng. Bible translated 'measure' (e.g. 2 Kings vii. 1).] A Hebrew dry measure = six times the cab, and one-third of the ephah.

Sea·-he:dgehog. 1602. 1. An echinus or sea-urchin. 2. The globe-fish or other diodont fish; so called from having erectile spines.

Sea·-hen. 1611. 1. The piper-gurnard, *Trigla lyra*, and the lump-fish, *Cyclopterus lumpus.* 2. A local name for the common guillemot and the great skua 1672.

Sea·-ho:lly. 1548. Eryngo.

Sea·-holm. 1550. [HOLM [2].] = prec.

Sea·-horse. 1475. [Cf. G. *seepferd.*] 1. The walrus. 2. A fabulous horse-like marine animal, represented as having the fore-parts of a horse and the tail of a fish 1587. 3. = HIPPOCAMPUS 2. 1589. †4. The hippopotamus -1759.

4. Sea-Horses floundring in the slimy mud DRYDEN.

Sea·-i:sland, *a.* 1807. Applied to a fine variety of cotton grown on the islands off the coast of Georgia and South Carolina, now also acclimatized in other countries. Also *absol.*

Sea·-kale. 1699. A cruciferous plant, *Crambe maritima*, found wild on the shores of western Europe, and often cultivated for its young shoots.

Sea·-king. 1582. [In sense 1, after ON. *sǽkonungr*; = OE. *sǽcyning.*] 1. One of the piratical Scandinavian chiefs, who in the ninth and succeeding centuries ravaged the coasts of Europe 1819. 2. Applied to the god of the sea 1582.

Seal (sīl), *sb.*[1] [OE. *sĭol-, sĕol-, seolh* :— OTeut. **selhoz.*] 1. A member of the family *Phocidæ*, sub-order *Pinnipedia*, of aquatic carnivorous mammals, with limbs developed into flippers and adapted for swimming, and having an elongated body covered with thick fur or bristles and terminated by a short tail; *spec.* the Common Seal, *Phoca vitulina.* Also with defining word. 2. Short for SEALSKIN 1886.

1. *Elephant, Fur, Hair*, etc. *s.* (see these words). **Bottle-nosed S.**, *Phoca leonina.* **Great S.**, *Phoca barbata.* **Marbled S.**, *Calocephalus discolor.*

Comb.: **s. calf**, the young of the seal; **-fur**, the skin of the hair-seal (*Otaria*) used as a material for garments; **-grain**, a preparation of seal-leather used in ornamental work; **-plush**, a fabric made to imitate sealskin.

Seal (sīl), *sb.*[2] ME. [a. OF. *seel* (mod.F. *sceau*) :—L. *sigillum* small picture, engraved figure, seal, dim. of *signum* SIGN *sb.*] 1. A device impressed on a piece of wax or other plastic material adhering or attached to a document as evidence of authenticity or attestation; also, the piece of wax, etc. bearing this impressed device. b. *fig.* A token or symbol of a covenant; something that authenticates or confirms; a final addition which completes and secures ME. c. The impression of one's signet placed upon an article as evidence of a claim to possession; *fig.* a mark of ownership 1782. d. *transf.* An impressed mark serving as visible evidence of something 1592. e. An impression left by the foot of an animal in soft ground or mud, esp. that of the otter 1686. 2. A piece of wax or some other plastic or adhesive substance fixed on a folded letter or document, or on a closed door or receptacle of any kind, in such a way that an opening cannot be effected without breaking it ME. b. *fig.* That which 'seals a person's lips'; an obligation to silence, a vow of secrecy; esp. *the s. of confession* or *the confessional.* Also (often with allusion to Rev. v and vi) that which prevents the understanding of Holy Scripture or some other book. ME. 3. An engraved stamp of metal or other hard material used to make an impression upon wax, etc. affixed as a 'seal' (in sense 1 or 2) ME. b. As a mark or sign of office. Chiefly *the seals*, as the symbol of the position of Lord Chancellor or of Secretary of State. 1480. c. A device or inscription engraved on a seal 1609. d. A trinket, containing either an engraved stone for sealing letters, or a flat stone, etc., simulating this, formerly often worn as an appendage to a watch-guard. Hence *pl.* applied to the bunch of such trinkets worn in this manner. 1837. 4. **Great Seal.** The seal (in sense 3) used for the authentication of documents of the highest importance issued in the name of the sovereign or (in the case of a republic) of the highest executive authority; also, the impression of this on wax. Formerly also BROAD SEAL. late ME. †b. *ellipt.* The custodian of the Great Seal, the Lord High Chancellor or Lord Keeper -1641. †5. An assembly for the purpose of witnessing the affixing of the Great Seal to documents; a sealing by the Chancellor or the Commissioners having the custody of the Great Seal -1705. 6. *techn.* (transf. use of 2.) a. = DIP-*pipe*. b. The quantity of water or tar left in the dip-pipe for preventing the escape of gas. c. A small quantity of water left in a trap to prevent the escape of foul air from a sewer or drain. 1853.

1. Till thou canst raile the seale from off my bond Thou but offend'st thy Lungs to speake so loud SHAKS. Phr. *To set one's s.*, to affix one's seal *to* a document; *fig.* to express one's assent *to. Under (one's) s.*, in a document attested by one's seal. b. *Mids. N.* III. ii. 144. c. The haughty..passions that..set their s. upon her brow DICKENS. d. But my kisses bring againe, bring againe, Seales of loue, but seal'd in vaine, seal'd in vaine SHAKS. 2. What Letter is this same?..Ile be so bold to breake the seale for once. SHAKS. 3. b. Sunderland..was suffered to retain his seals MACAULAY. c. The s. a sunflower; '*Elle vous suit partout*' BYRON.

attrib. and *Comb.* **s.-lock**, a lock fitted with a 'seal' (often a small square of glass) which must be broken before the lock can be opened; **-pipe** = DIP-*pipe*; **-ring**, a finger ring bearing a s.; **-top** *a.* (of a spoon) having the handle finished with a s. (also ellipt.)

Seal, *sb.*[3] Now *dial.* 1579. [Stem of inflected forms of OE. *sealh* SALLOW *sb.*] A willow. In Spenser: Willow twigs.

Seal (sīl), *v.*[1] ME. [a. OF. *seeler, seieler* (mod.F. *sceller*), f. *seel, seiel* SEAL *sb.*[2]] I. To attest by a seal. 1. *trans.* To place a seal upon (a document) as evidence of genuineness, or as a mark of authoritative ratification or approval. Also *absol.* b. *fig.* To authenticate or attest solemnly by some act compared to the affixing of a seal 1600. c. To conclude (an agreement, etc.) by affixing the seals of the parties to the instrument. Also *fig.*, to ratify or clinch (a bargain) by some ceremonial act. 1470. d. To grant (a charter) under one's seal; †also *fig.* 1625. e. To impose (an obligation, a penalty) *on* a person in a binding manner 1622. f. *fig.* Of a thing or act: To attest or ratify as a seal does; to be a 'seal' of 1648. g. To decide irrevocably (the fate of a person or thing); to complete and place beyond dispute or reversal (a victory, defeat, etc.) 1810. 2. To mark by a seal as reserved for a particular destination. Chiefly *fig.*: To designate, set apart, assign *to* another person or bind *together*, by an inviolable token or pledge. ME. b. In allusions to Rev. vii. 5-8. 1637. c. Among the Mormons: To set apart (a woman) *to* a man as one of his 'spiritual wives' 1857. 3. To impress a seal upon (weights or measures) to indicate that their correctness has been tested by lawful authority. Also, to place an official stamp on (merchandise) to certify that it is of standard measure or quality. 1467. †4. *intr.* To set one's seal (*to* a document). Also *spec.* to set one's seal to or execute a promissory note; to become security *for* a person. -1683.

1. Goe with me to a Notarie, seale me there Your single bond SHAKS. *Signed, sealed,* and *delivered*, a legal phrase indicating the complete execution of a deed. c. Peace was concluded, and sealed by a marriage 1836. f. Then with his sable Brow he gave the Nod, That seals his Word POPE. g. Tomorrow would s. his triumph DISRAELI. 2. Hath some wound,..seal'd him for The grave 1630. b. An Epistle, answering to one that asked to be Sealed of the Tribe of Ben B. JONS.

II. To fasten with or as with a seal. 1. *trans.* To fasten (a folded letter or other document) with melted wax or some other plastic material and impress a seal upon this, so that opening is impossible unless the seal is broken ME. b. To stamp the wax fastening (a letter) *with* something substituted for a seal 1718. c. To fasten up (a letter, parcel) with sealing-wax, a wafer, gum, or the like 1818. 2. To place a seal upon the opening of (a door, a chest, etc.) for security. Also with *up*. ME. 3. To close (a vessel, an aperture, etc.) securely by placing a coating of wax, cement, or lead, over the orifice, or by any kind of fastening that must be broken before access can be obtained. Also *absol.* 1661. b. *Surg.* To close up (a wound) with a covering that is not to be removed until healing has taken place 1862. 4. To fasten *on* or *down* with wax or cement 1665. b. *fig.* To fasten, fix immovably 1661. 5. *transf.* (*trans.*) To enclose, shut *up* within impenetrable barriers 1667.

1. I will s. my letter early SWIFT. c. This letter, sealed with a wafer 1848. 2. Phr. (fig.) *To s.* (a person's) *lips*, to bind to silence or secrecy. *To s.* (a person's) *eyes* or *ears*, to render blind or deaf, also to restrain from looking or listening. 4. b. But, ah, she gave me never a look, For her eyes were sealed to the holy book M. ARNOLD. 5. In case we should lose our vessels or become sealed up in permanent ice 1853.

Seal (sīl), *v.*[2] 1828. [f. SEAL *sb.*[1]] *intr.* To hunt for seals.

Sea·-law:yer. 1811. 1. A shark, the tiger-shark. Also the grey or mangrove snapper. 2. An argumentative sailor 1848.

Sealed (sīld), *ppl. a.* ME. [f. SEAL *v.*[1] + -ED [1].] 1. Bearing the impression of a signet in wax, etc., as evidence or guarantee of authenticity. b. *Nat. Hist.* In specific names: Bearing a mark resembling a seal 1803. 2. Fastened with a seal; so closed that access (to the contents) is impossible without breaking the fastening. Also *fig.* late ME.

1. **Sealed Book**: any of the printed copies of the authentic Book of Common Prayer of 1662 certified under the Great Seal and deposited as a standard in cathedrals and collegiate churches. **S. pattern,** in British military and naval use, a pattern (e.g. of a weapon, etc.) accepted by the War Office or the Admiralty. 2. *S. orders*, written directions given to the commander of a vessel concerning the destination of a voyage, which are not to be opened until the vessel has left port. *S. verdict*, a verdict delivered in a sealed packet in the absence of a judge. *A s. book*, often used predic. of something involved in obscurity, or beyond a person's comprehension.

Sea· legs, *pl. joc.* 1712. [Cf. F. *avoir le pied marin.*] In phrases, *To have* or *get one's sea legs* (*on*), *to find one's sea legs*, to have or acquire the power of walking steadily on the deck of a ship in motion.

Sealer (sī·ləɹ), *sb.*[1] late ME. [f. SEAL *v.*[1] + -ER [1].] 1. One who affixes a seal to a document. 2. †a. One who attaches the official mark or seal to leather or other material as evidence of quality, etc. b. An inspector of weights and measures. 1467.

Sealer (sī·ləɹ), *sb.*[2] 1820. [f. SEAL *v.*[2] + -ER [1].] 1. A vessel engaged in sealing. 2. One who hunts the seal 1842.

Sea·-le:vel. 1806. The mean level of the surface of the sea, the mean level between high and low tide.

Sea·-line. 1687. [LINE *sb.*[2]] 1. The coast-line or sea-board. 2. The horizon, the line where sea and sky appear to meet 1880. 3. A line used at sea: (*a*) a sounding-line; (*b*) a long line used in sea-fishing in deep water 1828.

Sea·ling-wax. ME. [f. *sealing*, vbl. sb. of SEAL *v.*[1]] In early use, beeswax or a composition containing this, later, a composition consisting of shellac, rosin, and turpentine, prepared for the purpose of receiving the impression of seals.

Sea·-lion. 1601. †1. A kind of lobster or crab. HOLLAND. 2. A fabulous animal 1661. 3. One of several large eared seals: (*a*) the largest otary of the North Pacific, *Otaria*

(*Eumetopias*) *stelleri*, Steller's or the Northern s.; (*b*) the Southern or Patagonian s., *Otaria jubata*; (*c*) the *Zalophus lobatus* of the Australian seas, also the distinct species *Z. californianus* of the North Pacific.

Sea·-louse. 1601. [= L. *pediculus marinus* (Pliny).] **1.** A parasitic isopod crustacean of *Cymothoa* and allied genera; a fish-louse. **2.** The Molucca crab, *Limulus moluccensis* 1681.

Sealskin (sī·lskin), *sb.* and *a.* ME. [f. SEAL *sb.*[1] + SKIN *sb.*] **A.** *sb.* **1.** The skin of any of the fur seals, prepared for use as a garment, for the covering of a box, etc. **b.** Applied to textile fabrics imitating the appearance of sealskin 1860. **2.** A garment made of sealskin 1873. **B.** *adj.* Made of sealskin 1769.

Sealyham (sī·liăm, sī·lihæm). 1894. [Name of the seat of the Edwardes family in Pembrokeshire.] A breed of wire-haired terrier.

Seam (sīm), *sb.*[1] [Com. Teut.; OE. *sēam* :—OTeut. **saumoz*, f. **sau-*, ablaut-var. of *su-* (cf. L. *suere* to sew).] **I.** Suture, junction. **1.** The junction made by sewing together the edges of two pieces of cloth, leather, etc.; the ridge or the furrow in the surface which indicates the course of such a junction; occas. the protruding edges of the joined pieces on the wrong side of the cloth. **b.** An embellished seaming used in joining costly fabrics; an ornamental strip of material inserted in or laid over a seam; also, material for this purpose. late ME. †**2.** *Anat.* A suture –1668. **3.** An interstice formed by the abutting edges of planks; a narrow crevice between the edges and ends of the planks or plates of a ship. Chiefly *pl.* OE. **4.** A line, groove, furrow, or the like, formed by the abutting edges of two parts of a thing; an indentation or mark resembling this; *esp.* the scar of a healed wound ME. **5.** *Geol.* A thin layer or stratum separating two strata of greater magnitude 1592. **6.** A joint used in uniting the edges of sheet metal; also, the line produced by this process 1825. **7.** *Knitting.* [transf. use of **1.**] A line of purled stitches down the leg of a stocking, simulating the appearance of a joining. Also = *s.-stitch* 1825.

1. *fig.* Chidynge and reproche..vnsowen the seemes of freendshipe in mannes herte CHAUCER. *French s.*, a seam formed by stitching once on the right side of the material, then paring close and turning, so as to re-seam on the wrong side. **3.** The ship ..let in the water at every s. 1748. **4.** A deep gash, now healed into an ugly s. DICKENS.

II. Sewing, needlework. *White s.*, plain needlework. *Obs.* exc. *dial.* late ME.

Comb.: **s.-lace**, lace used for insertion in or for covering and ornamenting seams; also *seaming-lace*; **s. set**, a set for smoothing or closing the seams (of boots and shoes, thin metals, etc.); **-stitch** (see I. 7 above) = *purl-stitch*.

Seam (sīm), *sb.*[2] [OE. *sēam*, OHG., MHG. *soum* (G. *saum*), a WGer. adoption of med.L. *sauma*, *salma*, *sagma* load (a. Gr. σάγμα pack-saddle, f. σαγ-, σάττειν to pack, load).] **1.** A pack-horse load. Now *dial.* **b.** The amount of a horse-load ME. **2.** A cart-load; esp. a definite amount of 3 cwt. (of hay or manure) or 2 cwt. (of straw). *w. dial.* 1726.

Seam (sīm), *sb.*[3] ME. [a. OF. *saim*, later *sain* (mod.F. only in *saindoux* lard) :—Com. Rom., pop. L. **sagimen*, related to cl. L. *sagina* fattening, fatness.] †**1.** Fat, grease –1697. **2.** Hogs' lard 1530.

1. Part scour the rusty Sheilds with S. DRYDEN.

Seam (sīm), *v.* 1582. [f. SEAM *sb.*[1]] **1.** *trans.* To sew the seam or seams of; to fasten or join *on*, *together*, *up* with a seam or seams. †**b.** To furnish or ornament with an inserted seam; also, of a material, to serve as a seam for –1740. **c.** *Knitting. trans.* and *intr.* To form a seam-stitch; to make a seam or seam-stitch in (a piece of knitting) 1842. **2.** *trans.* To mark (a surface) with lines or indentations; to furrow 1596. **3.** *trans.* To join (sheets of lead or metal) by means of a seam 1703.

2. A most beautifull and sweet countrey..seamed throughout with many goodly rivers SPENSER. Scars of Honour seam'd his manly Face 1695. Her..meagre face Seam'd with the shallow cares of fifty years TENNYSON.

Sea·-maid. *poet.* 1590. = MERMAID 1. Also, a goddess or nymph of the sea.

Certaine starres shot madly from their Spheares, To heare the Sea maids musicke SHAKS. So **Sea-maiden.**

Seaman (sī·mæn). *Pl.* **-men.** OE. **1. a.** *gen.* One whose occupation is on the sea; a sailor as opp. to a landsman. Now *poet.* or *rhet.* Also, with qualifying word: One skilled in navigation. **b.** *spec.* A sailor below the rank of officer. †**2.** = MERMAN –1753.

1. *Leading, able, ordinary s.*, the three grades (beginning with the highest) of seamen in the R. N. *Merchant s.*, a seaman in the merchant service.

Seamanlike (sī·mænləik), *a.* and *adv.* 1796. [f. prec. + -LIKE.] **A.** *adj.* Characteristic of or befitting a (good) seaman. **B.** *adv.* In a seamanlike manner. So **Sea·manly** *a.* and *adv.*

Seamanship (sī·mænʃip). 1766. [f. SEAMAN + -SHIP.] The art or practice of managing a ship at sea; the skill of a good seaman.

Sea·-mark. 1485. **1.** The boundary or limit of the flow of the sea. **2.** A conspicuous object distinguishable at sea which serves to guide or warn sailors in navigation 1566.

Seamew (sī·miū). late ME. [f. SEA *sb.* + MEW *sb.*[1]] The common gull, *Larus canus*.

Seaming (sī·miŋ), *vbl. sb.* 1450. [-ING[1].] The action of SEAM *v.*; *concr.* a seam or seams.

attrib., as **s. lace** = *seam-lace*; **s. machine,** a machine for forming the joints at the edges of sheet-metal plates.

Seamless (sī·mlės), *a.* 1483. [f. SEAM *sb.*[1] + -LESS.] Without a seam; of a garment, woven without a seam.

Sea·-monk. 1611. †**1.** The monk-fish –1666. **2.** The monk-seal 1891.

Sea·-monster. 1586. A monster of the sea. **1.** A huge fish, cetacean, or the like. **2.** A fabulous marine animal of terrifying proportions and shape 1596.

2. Dagon his Name, Sea Monster, upward Man And downward Fish MILT.

Sea·-mouse. 1520. **1.** A marine dorsibranchiate annelid of the family *Aphroditidæ*, esp. *Aphrodite aculeata*. **2.** *local.* The dunlin and other small shore-birds 1885.

Seamster, sempster (sī·mstəɹ, se·mᵖstəɹ). [OE. *sēamestre* fem., corresp. to *sēamere* tailor; see -STER.] One who sews; one whose occupation is sewing; a tailor, seamstress. (Now only applied to one of the male sex.)

Seamstress, sempstress (sī·mstrės, se·mᵖstrės). 1613. [See prec. and -ESS[1].] A woman who seams or sews; a needlewoman whose occupation is plain sewing.

Seamy (sī·mi), *a.* 1604. [f. SEAM *sb.*[1] + -Y[1].] **1.** Having a seam or suture, characterized by seams. **2.** Of the nature of or resembling, marked with, a seam or seams 1776.

1. *S. side*, lit. the under side of a garment, etc. on which the rough edges of the seams are visible; *fig.* (after Shaks.) the worst, most degraded, or roughest side (of life, etc.). **2.** A one-eyed woman, with a scarred and s. face 1857.

‖**Séance** (sē·ans). 1803. [F., = a sitting, f. OF. *seoir* (:—L. *sedere*) to sit.] **1.** *gen.* A sitting of a deliberative or other body or society, or of a number of persons assembled for discussion, instruction, etc. **2.** *spec.* A meeting for the study of spiritualistic phenomena 1845. **3.** A 'sitting' for medical treatment 1875.

Sea·-nymph. 1565. **1.** *Myth.* A nymph (NYMPH 1) supposed to inhabit the sea; a Nereid. **2.** An antarctic petrel, *Procellaria nereis* 1875.

Sea·-otter. 1664. A marine otter of the shores of the North Pacific, *Enhydris marina* or *lutris*.

Sea-otter's cabbage, the large seaweed *Nereocystis Lütkeana* of the North Pacific, the fronds of which are a favourite resort of sea-otters.

Sea·-parrot. 1664. **1.** The puffin. **2.** One of several fishes (see PARROT-FISH) 1666.

Sea·-pie[1]. 1531. [PIE *sb.*[1]] The oyster-catcher, *Hæmatopus ostralegus*.

Sea·-pie[2]. 1751. [PIE *sb.*[2]] A dish of meat and vegetables, etc. boiled together, with a crust of paste.

Sea·-piece. 1656. A picture representing a scene at sea.

Sea-pike. [PIKE *sb.*[4]] Any of several sea-fishes resembling the pike in their elongate form and voracity, as the garfish, hake, barracuda.

Sea·-pink. 1731. [PINK *sb.*[4]] The plant Thrift, *Armeria maritima*.

Sea-plane, seaplane (sī·plēin). 1913. [PLANE *sb.*[3] 1 e (*b*).] An aeroplane adapted for rising from and landing on water.

Seaport (sī·poəɹt). 1596. [PORT *sb.*[1]] = PORT *sb.*[1] 1 and 2. Also *attrib.*

Sea-purse. 1806. **1.** A zoophyte of the genus *Alcyonium*. **2.** The horny egg-case of a skate, ray, or shark; a mermaid's purse 1856. **3.** *U.S., Atlantic coast.* A swirl of the undertow or a double undertow formed by two waves meeting at an angle, making a small whirlpool on the surface of the water, dangerous to bathers 1891.

Sea·-quake, sea·quake. 1680. [After EARTHQUAKE.] A convulsion or sudden agitation of the sea from a submarine eruption or earthquake.

Sear (sīəɹ), *sb.* 1560. [History obsc.] The catch in a gun-lock which keeps the hammer at full or half-cock, and which is released (at full cock) by pressure upon the trigger.

Tickle or *light of the s.*, (fig.) easily made to 'go off'.

Comb. **s.-spring,** a spring which keeps the s. in position, also, in some gun-locks, a spring which throws the hammer back to half-cock after a discharge.

Sear (sīəɹ), *v.* [OE. *sēarian* :—OTeut. **saurējan*, f. **sauro-*, OE. *sēar* SERE *a.*] **1.** *intr.* To dry up, wither away; to become sere. Now *rare.* **2.** *trans.* To cause to wither, to blight. late ME. **3.** To burn or char (animal tissues) by the application of a hot iron; to cauterize (a wound, etc.) in order to destroy virus or prevent the flow of blood 1530. **b.** *fig.* Chiefly after 1 Tim. iv. 2, to render (the conscience) incapable of feeling 1582. **c.** *To s. up*, to close (a wound, vein, etc.) by actual cautery 1600. †**d.** To brand, stigmatize –1644. †**4.** To burn, scorch –1810.

2. When summer sears the plains COWPER. **3. b.** Sear'd in heart, and lone, and blighted BYRON. **d.** Calumnie will seare Vertue it selfe SHAKS.

Sea·-raven. 1611. **1.** The cormorant. **2.** A large N. Amer. fish, *Hemitripterus americanus* 1672.

†**Searce,** *sb.* [Late ME. *sa(a)rce*, a. OF. *saas* (mod.F. *sas*) :—pop. L. **sætaceus* (*pannus*), lit. (cloth) made of bristles, f. L. *sæta* bristle.] A sieve or strainer –1844.

†**Searce,** *v.* late ME. [f. prec.] *trans.* To sift through a searce –1831. Hence **Sea·rcer,** a searce or sieve.

Search (sɔ̄ɹtʃ), *sb.* late ME. [a. AF. *serche*, OF. *cerche* (mod.F. *cherche*), vbl. sb. f. *cerchier* SEARCH *v.*] **1.** The action or an act of searching; examination or scrutiny for the purpose of finding a person or thing. Const. *after*, *for*, †*of* (the object sought). †Also, effort to ascertain something. **2.** *spec.* **a.** An examination of a ship's cargo, etc. for the purpose of enforcing customs duties 1462. **b.** An examination of a register or of documents in public custody, for the discovery of information which is believed to be contained therein 1465. †**3.** Range to which search extends –1792. **4.** Searching effect (of cold or wind) 1609. **5.** *concr.* Applied to persons: †**a.** A searcher, examiner –1652. †**b.** A search-party. SHAKS.

1. Robin Oig absconded, and escaped all s. SCOTT. A s. after knowledge JOWETT. Phr. *In s. of*, in quest of, in order to find; also, *predic.*, occupied in searching for. *To make (a) s.*, to search (*for* some lost, concealed, or desired object). **2.** Phr. *Right of s.*, the right, recognized by the law of nations, by which a duly commissioned ship of war is empowered, outside neutral waters, to stop and examine a merchant vessel for contraband.

attrib. and *Comb.*: **s.-party,** a company of people organized to make search for a person, etc. **-room,** the room in the Public Record Office provided for members of the public who wish to search documents there preserved; **-warrant,** a warrant authorizing the searching of the dwelling of a person suspected of crime. Hence **Sea·rchful** *a.* diligent in search.

Search (sɔ̄ɹtʃ), *v.* ME. [a. OF. *cerchier* (mod.F. *chercher*) :—late L. *circare* to go round, f. *circus* circle.] **I.** To explore, examine thoroughly. **1.** *trans.* To go about (a country or place) in order to find, or to ascertain the presence or absence of, some person or thing; to explore in quest of some object. **2.** To look through (a building, an apartment, a receptacle) in quest of some object concealed or lost. late ME. **3.** To examine (a person) by handling, removal of garments, and the like, to ascertain whether any article (usu., something stolen or contraband) is concealed in his clothing. late ME. **4.** To look through, examine (writings, records) in order to discover whether certain things are contained there. late ME. **5.** With immaterial object: To investigate; to examine rigorously (one's own heart, thoughts, etc.); to examine, penetrate the secrets of (another's mind or thoughts). Also with *out*. late ME. **b.** Of an impersonal agency: To test, reveal the nature of 1586. **6.** To look scrutinizingly at 1811. **†7.** To probe (a wound) –1687. **8.** Of wind, cold, fire-arms, etc.: To penetrate, reach the weak places of. late ME.

1. Send thou men, that they may s. the lande of Canaan *Num.* xiii. 2. 2. Even now they s. the tower, and find the body SHELLEY. 4. I have been at the trouble to s. the Journals in the period between the two last wars BURKE. 5. O Lorde, thou searchest me out, and knowest me COVERDALE *Ps.* cxxxix. 1.

II. To look for or seek diligently; to try to find. Now only with *out* exc. (*rarely*) *poet.* ME. **†b.** To seek to discover. Also with *out*. –1644.

He hath bin search'd among the dead & liuing; But no trace of him SHAKS. His primary object is to s. out the truth 1887.

III. *absol.* and *intr.* **1.** To make a search. Const. *after*, *for*, *into* ME. **†2.** To devise means (*to do* something) –1567.

1. S. even as thou wilt, But thou shalt never find what I can hide SHELLEY. Hence **Sea·rchable** *a.* capable of being searched. **Sea·rchableness.**

Searcher (sǝ̄·ɹtʃǝɹ). late ME. [(1) a. AF. *cerchour*, OF. *cercheor*, f. *cerchier* SEARCH *v.*; (2) f. SEARCH *v.* + -ER [1].] **1.** One who searches. Also *s.-out*. **2.** One whose office is to search; *esp.* **a.** An officer of the custom-house appointed to search ships, baggage, or goods for dutiable or contraband articles. late ME. **†b.** One appointed to observe and report on any offences against discipline or good order in a religious house, a community, body of workmen, etc. –1845. **†c.** As the designation of various municipal and government officials; e.g. a sanitary inspector; an inspector of markets; an examiner of certain articles of manufacture; etc. –1835. **†d.** A person appointed to view dead bodies and to make report upon the cause of death –1759. **e.** An official appointed to search the clothing and person of any one arrested and detained by the police 1726. **3.** An instrument used in making a search. **a.** *Surg.* A probe or sound 1597. **†b.** An instrument for testing the soundness of cannon after discharge –1859. **c.** In microscopical work: An objective of low power used to obtain a general view of the object 1870.

Searching (sǝ̄·ɹtʃiŋ), *ppl. a.* 1580. [-ING [2].] That searches. **1.** Of observation or examination: Minute, rigorous. Of a look: Penetrating, keenly observant. **b.** Of liquids, wind, rain, etc., or of bodily diseases: That finds out weak points, keen, sharp, piercing 1593. **2.** Engaged in or given to searching 1626.

1. b. A maruellous s. Wine SHAKS. Hence **Sea·rching-ly** *adv.*, **-ness.**

†Sea·rchless, *a.* 1605. [f. SEARCH *sb.* + -LESS.] Inscrutable, impenetrable –1834.

Sea·rchlight. 1883. [f. SEARCH *sb.* + LIGHT *sb.*] An electric arc-lamp or acetylene light fitted with a reflector and suspended in a frame so that it may throw a beam of light in any desired direction; used in naval, military, and air defence and for signalling, etc. **b.** The beam of light thrown by such a lamp.

Searing (sīǝ·riŋ), *vbl. sb.* late ME. [f. SEAR *v.* + -ING [1].] The action of SEAR *v.*

Comb.: **s.-iron**, an iron used for cauterizing, branding, etc.

Sea·-ro·bin. 1844. [ROBIN [1].] **1.** *U.S.* A gurnard or trigloid fish, esp. of the genus *Prionotus*. **2.** *local.* **a.** *U.S.* The red-breasted merganser, *Mergus serrator* 1891. **b.** The spotted fly-catcher, *Muscicapa grisola* 1899.

Sea·-room. 1554. Space at sea free from obstruction in which a ship can be manœuvred easily. Esp. in phr. *to have, give, or take s.*

Sea·-ro·ver. 1579. [ROVER [2].] **1.** A pirate. (Now often apprehended as meaning one who 'roves' over the sea.) **2.** A pirate-ship 1828. Hence **Sea-roving** *vbl. sb.* and *ppl. a.*

Sea-salt, *sb.* 1601. Common salt obtained by the evaporation of sea-water. So **Sea·salt** *a.* (*rare*) salt like the sea; impregnated with or containing s.

Sea-sand. ME. **1.** Sand of the sea or seashore. **2.** *pl.* Tracts of sea-sand. late ME.

Sea-scape, seascape (sī·skeᵗp). 1799. [After LANDSCAPE; see SCAPE *sb.*[3]] **1.** A picture of the sea, a sea-piece; sea-pieces collectively. **2.** A picturesque view or prospect of the sea 1806.

Sea·-se·rpent. 1646. **1. a.** Any ophidian inhabiting the sea; esp. any of the venomous snakes of the order *Hydrophidæ*, inhabiting the tropical Indo-Pacific Ocean 1671. **b.** *The* (*great*) *s.*: a sea-monster of serpentine form and great length, frequently reported to have been seen at sea 1774. **2.** Applied to various fishes. **†a.** A kind of eel or muræna found in the Mediterranean. **†b.** = ELLOPS 2. **c.** The king of the herrings, *Regalecus glesne*. 1646.

Sea·-se·rvice. 1610. Service at sea; the condition or function of serving in the navy; naval as opp. to land service. Also, service or employment (of a person, ship, etc.) on the high seas, as dist. from shore or harbour duty.

Sea·-shell. OE. A marine shell, the shell of any salt-water mollusc. **b.** Material consisting of sea-shells 1837.

Sea-shore. 1526. The coast of the sea, or the land lying adjacent to the sea; also, the ground actually washed by the sea at high tides (usu. covered with sand or shingle).

Sea·-sick, *a.* 1566. **1.** Suffering from sea-sickness. Chiefly *predic.* **†2.** Weary of travelling by sea. SHAKS. So **Sea-sickness,** nausea and vomiting induced by the motion of a ship.

Sea-side, seaside. ME. **1.** (sī·sǝi·d) The margin or brink of the sea. Now *rare* or *Obs.* **2.** Now chiefly: The sea-coast as resorted to for health or pleasure 1797. **3.** (sī·sǝid) The side towards or facing the sea 1867. **4.** *attrib.* or quasi-*adj.* (sī·sǝid) Belonging to, situated or taking place at the sea-side 1784.

Sea·-slug. 1779. **1.** = TREPANG. **2.** Any marine gasteropod of the order *Opisthobranchiata* 1845.

Sea·-snail. OE. **1.** Any of various marine gasteropods. **2.** A fish of the family *Liparididæ*, esp. the *Liparis vulgaris*, or unctuous sucker 1672.

Sea·-snake. 1755. = SEA-SERPENT 1 a, b.

Sea·-snipe. 1767. **1.** A local name for the dunlin, the knot, and other sandpipers. **2. †a.** A kind of gar-fish. **b.** The trumpet-fish or snipe-fish, *Centriscus scolopax*, so called from its long tubular snout 1826.

Season (sī·z'n), *sb.* [ME. *seson*, a. OF. *seson*, *seison* (mod.F. *saison*):—L. *sationem* act of sowing (in vulgar L. seed-time), f. *sa-*, root of *serere* to sow.] **I.** A period of the year. **1.** Any one of the periods into which the year is naturally divided by the earth's changing position in regard to the sun, and which are marked by varying length of day and night, by particular conditions of temperature, weather, etc. More specifically, each of the four equal periods—Spring, Summer, Autumn, Winter—into which the year is divided by the passage of the sun from equinox to solstice and from solstice to equinox; also, each of the two periods—the rainy and the dry—into which the year is divided in tropical climates. **b.** A day or period of the year marked by some special festivity, as Christmas and New Year 1791. **c.** In reckoning time or age: A year (*rare* or *poet.*) 1827. **2.** A period or time of year mentioned with ref. to the conditions of weather, etc. that characterize it in a particular year. late ME. **3.** The time of year assigned to some particular operation of agriculture ME. **4.** The time of year when a plant flourishes, when it blooms or bears fruit, etc. ME. **5.** The time of year when an animal is in heat, pairs, breeds, migrates, is killed for food or hunted, etc. (Also *pairing, breeding, close, etc. s*). late ME. **6.** A period of time astronomically fixed or recurring 1535. **7.** The portion of a year regularly devoted to a particular business, sport, or amusement, or when the greatest activity prevails therein 1656. **8.** The period of the year during which a particular place is most frequented for business, fashion, or amusement; esp. the time (now May to July) when the fashionable world is assembled in London 1705. **9.** *transf.* (from 2). **†a.** A spell of (bad or inclement) weather –1667. **b.** *spec.* The 'rains' or spells of wet weather in tropical countries. In the southern U.S., a shower of rain or period of damp weather suitable for setting out tobacco plants, etc. 1707.

1. Now had the s. returned, when the nights grow colder and longer LONGF. b. The compliments of the s. to my worthy masters LAMB. 2. A most extraordinary wet and cold s. EVELYN. 4. Like a tre.., yᵗ bringeth forth his frute in due s. COVERDALE *Ps.* i. 3. 6. He in whose hand all times and seasons roul MILT. 7. *The fishing, hunting, publishing, racing, theatrical, holiday s. Dead, dull,* or *off s.*, the period when such pursuits are inactive. *Silly s.*: see SILLY *a.* 5 b. 8. You cannot figure a duller s.: the weather bitter, no party, little money H. WALPOLE. *Dead s.*, the period when 'society' has departed from a place of resort. 9. a. *Lear* III. iv. 32.

II. *gen.* A time, period, occasion. **1.** A particular time or period during which something happens, or which is defined by some characteristic feature or circumstance ME. **2.** A time at which, or an occasion when, something happens. Now *rare*. ME. **3.** The right, proper, due or appointed time; a fit or favourable occasion, an opportunity ME.

1. Phr. *For a s.*, for an indefinite period, for some time; This..beautiful human soul; who walked with me for a s. in this world CARLYLE. 2. He knew the proper s. to shew the violence of his Revenge 1686. 3. When my s. comes to sit On David's Throne MILT.

†III. [f. the vb.] Seasoning, relish, flavour –1664. **IV.** Short for *s.-ticket* 1896.

Phrases. **In season. a.** At the right and proper time, opportunely. **b.** Of game, etc.: At the time for hunting, catching, etc. *To be in s.* (of a plant or animal) to flourish, be in the best condition for eating; also, (of an animal) to be in heat. So *to come in* or *into s.* **Out of s. a.** Unseasonably, inopportunely; *predic.* unseasonable, inopportune. **b.** Not in season; not at the time for hunting, catching, eating, etc. **c.** Not in fashion. **In s. and out of s.** At all times, without regard to what is considered opportune.

Comb.: **s.-ticket**, a ticket which admits the holder to travel on a boat or on a line of railway, to enter an exhibition, place of amusement, etc., an unlimited number of times during a season or specified period, at a reduced rate of payment; hence *s.-ticket holder*. Hence **Sea·sonless** *a.* having or knowing no change of s.

Season (sī·z'n), *v.* late ME. [a. OF. *saisonner*, f. *saison* SEASON *sb.*] **1.** *trans.* To render (a dish) more palatable by the addition of some savoury ingredient. **b.** *fig.* To mix, intersperse, or imbue with something that imparts relish; to adapt or accommodate *to* a particular taste 1520. **†c.** To moderate, alleviate, temper. SHAKS. **†2.** *transf.* To imbue with a taste or scent –1591. **†b.** To imbue (a person, his mind) *with* opinions, ideas, etc.; in later use only in a good sense –1791. **†3.** *trans.* To embalm –1638. **4.** To mature, ripen; to render fit for use by prolonged exposure, or by gradual subjection to conditions of the kind to be undergone in actual working; often, to dry and harden (timber) by keeping. Also *intr.* for *refl.* 1545. **b.** *trans.* To fortify (a person) by habit against conditions that might otherwise be deleterious; to acclimatize 1601. **†c.** To prepare or fit (a person); also, to discipline, train –1658. **†5.** To impregnate, to copulate with –1601.

1. All s. their food with a great quantity of spices 1769. b. You s. still with sports your serious hours DRYDEN. c. S. your admiration for a while With an attent eare SHAKS. 2. b. Garrick, who I can attest.. had his mind seasoned with pious reverence BOSWELL. 3. *Twel. N.* I. i. 30. 4. Knowledge and timber shouldn't be much used till they are seasoned O. W. HOLMES. b. In war well season'd, and with labours tann'd BYRON. c. Am I then reuveng'd, To take him in the purging of his Soule When he is fit and season'd for his passage? SHAKS.

Seasonable (sī·z'năb'l), *a.* late ME. [f. SEASON *v.* and *sb.* + -ABLE.] Opportune. **b.** Of weather, etc.: Suitable to the time of year. late ME. **c.** = SEASONAL *a.* 2. 1923.

His Caution was so s., and his Advice so good DE FOE. Hence **Sea·sonableness. Sea·sonably** *adv.*

Seasonal (sī·z'năl), *a.* 1838. [f. SEASON *sb.* + -AL 1.] **1.** Pertaining to or characteristic of the seasons of the year, or some one of them. b. *transf.* Pertaining to the seasons or periods of human life 1843. 2. Of certain trades: Dependent on the seasons. Of workers, servants: Employed only during a particular season. 1904. 3. Periodical, (regularly) recurrent 1880.

1. *S. dimorphism*, a variation in the appearance of different broods of the same insect according to the time of year at which they are produced. 2. The problem of the casual and s. worker 1904. Hence **Sea·sonally** *adv.*

Seasoner (sī·z'nəɹ). 1598. [f. SEASON *v.* + -ER [1].] One who or something which seasons.

Seasoning (sī·z'niŋ), *vbl. sb.* 1511. [-ING [1].] 1. The action of SEASON *v.* 2. *concr.* Something added to a dish which gives it a distinctive or appetizing flavour 1580.

2. *fig.* His favourite clown..whose jests..served for a sort of s. to his evening meal SCOTT.

Sea· spi·der. 1666. a. A spider-crab or maioid. b. A marine arthropod of the group *Pycnogonida* 1855. c. An octopus 1858.

Sea·-star. OE. †1. (*esp.* tr. L. *stella maris*, title of the B.V.M.) A star which guides mariners at sea –1817. 2. A starfish 1569.

Sea·-swa·llow. 1598. 1. = FLYING FISH. 2. a. Any one of the terns (from their general resemblance to swallows). b. The stormy petrel, *Procellaria pelagica.* 1647. 3. The trepang or bêche-de-mer (see SWALLO) 1802.

Seat (sīt), *sb.* ME. [a. ON. *sæti* :— OTeut. *(*ga*)*sætjom*, f. **sæt-*, ablaut-var. of **set-*; see SIT *v.*] I. Action or manner of sitting. †1. *gen.* The action of sitting –1420. 2. Manner of sitting (on horseback). Also *predic.*, one who has a (good, etc.) seat, a (good, etc.) horseman. 1577.

2. A firm and graceful S. on Horseback LOCKE.

II. Place or thing to sit upon. 1. The place on which a person is sitting, or is accustomed to sit; a place to seat one person at a table, in a conveyance, etc. ME. b. Hence, the use of, or right to use, a seat (in a church, theatre, conveyance, etc.) 1520. c. A right to sit as a member, or the position of being a member, of a deliberative or administrative body, *esp.* of Parliament or other legislative assembly; a place (whether occupied or temporarily vacant) in the membership of the House of Commons, Congress, or the like 1774. 2. Something adapted or used for sitting upon, as a chair, stool, sofa, etc. Also *spec.* a bench to seat one or more persons; a horizontal board or framework in a boat, etc. late ME. b. That part (of a chair, saddle, etc.) upon which its occupant sits 1778. 3. Contextually applied to the throne of a king or a bishop, or the like, the throne of God or of an angel. Hence *fig.* the authority or dignity symbolized by sitting in a particular chair or throne. ME. b. *spec.* The throne *of* a particular kingdom 1599. 4. The sitting part of the body; the posteriors. Also joc., *s. of honour*, etc. 1607. b. That part (of a garment) which covers the posteriors 1835. 5. The 'form' of a hare. *rare.* 1735. 6. *Boot-trade.* An engagement to work at making boots of a specified kind 1791.

1. She ordered me a s. at her right hand 1716. c. A s. in the cabinet 1849. By the..Reform Act of 1867.. twenty-six seats were taken from boroughs 1885. 2. They came To a stone s. beside a spring SHELLEY. b. Chairs without any seats 1809. 3. I, for myself, th' Imperial S. will gain DRYDEN. Phr. †*Apostolic s.*, *Holy s.*, *Peter's s.*, the papal chair, its occupant, or his office; = SEE *sb.* 2 c. b. We neuer valew'd this poore seate of England SHAKS.

III. Residence, abode, situation. 1. Applied *spec.* (after L. *sedes*) to: The abiding place or resting place (of departed souls); a position in this place. Now *arch.* or *poet.* ME. 2. A city in which a throne, court, government is established or set up; a capital. late ME. b. = SEE *sb.* 2 d. Now only *s. of a bishop.* late ME. 3. The thing (esp. the organ or part of the body) in which a particular power, faculty, function or quality 'resides'; the locality of a disease, sensation, or the like. late ME. b. Similarly, of the soul or its parts 1579. 4. A place where something takes place, or where some particular condition of things prevails 1560. b. A city or locality in which (a branch of trade, learning, etc.) is established 1585. 5. A place of habitation or settlement (of a tribe, people, etc.). Also *transf.* (of birds). 1535. b. = COUNTRY-*seat* 1607. †6. Local position or situation –1695. 7. Position as regards surroundings, climate, etc.; situation, site 1549. †8. A definite place (on a surface, in a body or organ, in a series) –1775.

1. Mount, mount my soule, thy seate is vp on high SHAKS. 2. Peking, the Royal S. of the Chinese Emperor DE FOE. 3. The heede is pryncypall place and seete of wyttes TREVISA. b. Sin has its s. in the soul 1847. 4. Phr. *S. of war* [= L. *sedes belli*], the region in which warfare is going on. b. Blackfriars was.. the s. of fashion 1865. 5. The s. of the old Irish..was the province of Ulster CLARENDON. 6. †*S. of living*, habitat (of an animal). 7. This Castle hath a pleasant s. SHAKS.

IV. Basis, foundation, support. †1. A place prepared for something to be erected or set up upon it; a building site –1662. 2. The part upon which a thing rests or appears to rest 1661. 3. *Mech.* A part or surface upon which the base of something rests 1805. 4. *Shoemaking.* A piece of leather pegged or sewn to the boot as a foundation for the heel 1882.

Phrases. *To hold, keep a* or *one's s.*, to remain seated, to keep from falling; also, to retain one's position as a Member of Parliament; so, *to lose one's s.* *To take a s.*, to sit down. *To take one's s.*, to take the sitting-place assigned to one; to assume one's official position, to be formally admitted to Parliament or Congress. *To take a* or *the back s.*, orig. *U.S.*, *fig.* to occupy a subordinate place.

Comb. **s.-bone** *Anat.*, the innominate bone or hip-bone; more strictly the ISCHIUM; **-stick**, a walking-stick which may be adapted to form a seat. Hence **Sea·tless** *a.* having no seat or seats.

Seat (sīt), *v.* 1577. [f. prec.] I. *trans.* To place on a seat or seats; to cause to sit down 1613. b. *refl.* To take one's seat, sit down 1589. †c. *intr.* for *refl.* To sit down. Of a hare: To sit in its form. –1772. d. *trans.* To cause or enable to sit *in* or *on* a throne, chair of state or office, etc. Hence, to establish (a person) in a position of authority or dignity. 1593. e. To put into a seat in a deliberative assembly 1797. f. To find seats for; to assign seats to. Of a building, room, etc.: To afford sitting accommodation for. 1828. 2. *pass.* To be sitting 1608. 3. *trans.* To settle or establish in a particular locality. Now *rare.* 1589. †b *refl.* To settle (in a place). Also *intr.* for *refl.* –1797. 4. *trans.* With a thing as object: To place in a 'seat' or situation. (*rare* exc. *pass.* as in 5.) 1603. 5. *pass.* To have its seat, be situated 1577. b. Of a disease: To have its seat *in* a certain part of the body. Also *to be deeply seated*: lit. to be situated far below the surface; hence (often *fig.*) to be beyond the reach of superficial remedies. 1619. †6. *trans.* To 'plant' with inhabitants, settle (a country) –1784. 7. To fix a seat on (a chair); to repair (trousers, a chair) by renewing or mending the seat 1762. 8. To furnish (a building, room, etc.) with seats 1818.

1. So now y'are fairely seated SHAKS. d. To inshrine Belus or Serapis thir Gods, or s. Thir Kings MILT. 2. While Shepherds watched their flocks by night All seated on the ground TATE. 5. *Merch. V.* I. ii. 8. The Garden, seated on the level Floor DRYDEN. 8. A portion of which was seated with pews, and used as a church SCOTT.

-seater (sī·təɹ). 1906. [f. SEAT *sb.* and *v.* + -ER [1].] Freq. in comb., as *two-s.*, *four-s.*, etc., a motor car, etc. having seats for two, four, etc. in the body.

Seating (sī·tiŋ), *vbl. sb.* 1596. [f. SEAT *sb.* and *v.* + -ING [1].] †1. The action of providing with a residence, or of settling in a country; quasi-*concr.* opportunity for settling, footing –1699. 2. The action of providing with seats; the manner in which a building, etc. is seated; *concr.* the seats with which a building, etc. is provided 1880. 3. Material for upholstering the seats of chairs, etc. 1833. 4. *Mech.* A fitted support for a part of a structure or machine, usu. *pl.* or *collect. sing.* 1844. 5. That part of a structure, etc. which rests on some other part 1805.

2. The s. of the church is but little altered 1880. *attrib.*, as *s. accommodation*, *capacity*.

Sea·-trout. 1745. 1. The *Salmo trutta* = SALMON-TROUT 1; also the bull or grey trout, *S. eriox.* 2. In U.S. and Australia applied to other fishes 1859.

Sea·-urchin. 1591. An animal of the genus *Echinus* or the order *Echinoidea*.

Seave (sīv). *north.* late ME. [a. ON. *sef.*] A rush; also, a rushlight. Hence **Sea·vy** *a.* containing or overgrown with rushes; composed of rushes.

Sea-wall. OE. 1. A wall or embankment to prevent the encroachment of the sea, etc. 2. The sea as a wall or barrier of defence (*rare*) 1879. So **Sea-walled** (wǭld) *a.* surrounded or protected by the sea as a wall of defence.

‖**Seawan(e, seawant** (sī·wǣn, -wǫnt). *Amer. Ind.* 1701. [Narragansett *seawohn* scattered, loose (in opposition to the strung beads, called *peag*).] Wampum.

Seaward (sī·wǭɹd), *adv.* (and quasi-*sb.*) and *a.* late ME. [f. SEA *sb.* + -WARD.] A. advb. phrases and *adv.* 1. Phrases. a. *To* (*the*) *s.*: towards, in the direction of, the sea; away from the land. *To the s. of*: to or at a place nearer the sea (or, at sea, farther from the land) than. b. *From* (*the*) *s.*: from the direction in which the sea lies 1719. 2. *adv.* Towards the sea or the open sea (away from the land) 1610. B. *adj.* 1. Going out to sea, going to seaward 1621. 2. Directed or looking towards the sea; situated on the side or portion (of a thing) which is nearest the sea 1725. b. Of a wind: Blowing from the sea 1810.

2. Your cannons moulder on the s. wall TENNYSON. Hence **Sea·wardly** *a.* habituated to looking s.; *adv.* towards the sea (*rare*).

Seawards (sī·wǭɹdz), *adv.* 1517. [f. SEA *sb.* + -WARDS.] = prec. adv.

Sea·-ware. [OE. *sǣwār*, f. *sǣ* SEA + *wār* 'alga'.] Seaweed; esp. coarse large seaweed thrown up on the shore by the sea, and used as manure, etc.

Sea·-wa·ter. OE. The water of the sea, or water taken from the sea.

Sea·-way, sea·way. OE. 1. A way over the sea; the sea as a means of communication; the open sea. 2. The progress of a ship through the sea 1787. 3. A rough sea 1840.

3. The coracle..was a very safe boat..both buoyant and clever in a s. STEVENSON.

Seaweed (sī·wīd). 1577. [f. SEA *sb.* + WEED *sb.*] 1. *collect.* Any marine plants of the class *Algæ* (see ALGA). 2. A particular marine alga 1700.

Sea·-wolf. ME. †1. A fabulous amphibious beast of prey –1607. 2. A voracious sea-fish; esp. the bass, *Labrax lupus*, and the wolf-fish, *Anarrhichas lupus.* late ME. †3. A seal; a sea-elephant or sea-lion –1839. 4. quasi-*arch.* A pirate, sea-robber; also, a privateer vessel 1849.

Seaworthy (sī·wɒ̄ɹði), *a.* 1807. [f. SEA *sb.* + WORTHY *a.*] Of a ship: In a fit condition to undergo a voyage, and to encounter stormy weather. Hence **Sea·wo·rthiness**, s. condition.

Sea·-wrack. 1548. †1. *pl.* Property cast ashore by the sea. 2. a. *collect.* Seaweed, esp. any of the large coarse kinds cast up on the shore, as *Fucus*, *Laminaria*, etc. 1551. b. A particular kind of seaweed 1611.

Sebaceous (sǐbēⁱ·ʃəs), *a.* 1728. [f. L. *sebaceus*, f. *sebum* tallow; see -ACEOUS.] 1. Pertaining to, of the nature of, or resembling tallow or fat; oily, greasy 1783. 2. *Phys.* a. Having the nature or characteristics of SEBUM; as *s. humour*, etc. 1747. b. Connected with the secretion of sebum; as *s. follicle, gland*, etc. 1728. 3. *Path.* Of a cyst, tumour: Formed upon a sebaceous gland 1872.

Sebacic (sǐbæ·sik), *a.* 1790. [f. L. *sebaceus* + -IC 1 b.] *Chem. S. acid*: an acid obtained by the distillation of oleic acid.

Sebastine (sǐbæ·stin). 1884. [Patented in Sweden in 1872.] An explosive composed of nitroglycerine, charcoal, and saltpetre.

‖**Sebat** (sī·bæt), **Shebat** (ʃī·bæt). late ME. [Heb. *sh'bāṭ.*] The eleventh month of the Jewish ecclesiastical and fifth of the civil year.

Sebate (sī·bēⁱt). 1794. [f. L. *sebum* tallow + -ATE [1].] *Chem.* A combination of sebacic acid with a base.

Sebesten (sǐbe·stĕn). late ME. [a. Arab. *sabastān*, a. Pers. *sapistān.*] *Bot.* The plum-like fruit of a tree of the genus *Cordia* (formerly *Sebestena*); a preparation of this used as a medicine. Also the tree itself.

Sebiparous (sǐbi·părəs), *a.* 1855. [f. SEBUM + -(I)PAROUS.] Producing sebum.

Seborrhœa (sebǝrīˑă). 1876. [f. *sebo-* as comb. form of SEBUM + Gr. ῥοία flow, flux.] *Path.* An excessive discharge from the sebaceous glands forming a greasy or scaly coating upon the skin.

‖**Sebum** (sīˑbǒm). 1876. [mod.L. use of L. *sebum* suet, grease.] *Phys.* The fatty secretion which lubricates the hair and the skin.

‖**Sec** (sɛk). 1889. [Fr.] Of wines = DRY *a.* 8.

Sec., abbreviation of SECANT, SECOND (for which it is used colloq. as a word, e.g. 'half a sec'), SECRETARY, SECTION.

Secant (sīˑkănt), *a.* and *sb.* 1593. [ad. L. *secantem*, *secare* to cut.] **A.** *adj. Geom.* Of a line or surface in relation to another line or surface: Cutting, intersecting. **B.** *sb.* (Ellipt. for *s. line.*) **a.** *Trig.* orig. The length of a straight line drawn from the centre of a circular arc through one end of the arc, and terminated by the tangent or line touching the arc at the other end; in mod. use, the ratio of this line to the radius, or (equivalently, as a function of an angle) the ratio of the hypotenuse of a right-angled triangle to that of one side, the given angle (or, if obtuse, its supplement) being that contained between them. (Abbrev. *sec*) 1593. **b.** *Geom.* A line that cuts another; esp. a straight line that cuts a curve in two or more parts 1684. Hence **Seˑcancy**, the fact of being s.

‖**Sécateur** (sekatǭr). 1881. [Fr., as if ad. L. **secator*, f. *secare.*] A kind of pruning shears with crossed blades. (Usu. *pl.*)

‖**Secco** (seˑkko), *a.* and *sb.* 1852. [It.:— L. *siccus* dry.] **A.** *adj. Mus.* Performed without accompaniment 1876. **B.** *sb. Painting.* Ellipt. for It. *fresco secco* 'dry fresco', a process of painting on dry plaster with colours mixed with water 1852.

Seccotine (seˑkǒtīn), *sb.* 1894. [app. arbitrarily f. It. *secco* dry.] Maker's name for a composition serving as a strong adhesive. Hence **Seˑccotine** *v. trans.* to cement with s.

Secede (sǐsīˑd), *v.* 1702. [ad. L. *secedere*, f. *se-* SE- + *cedere* to go.] †**1.** *intr.* To go away from one's companions, go into retirement. **2.** To withdraw formally from an alliance, an association, a federal union, a political or religious organization 1755. Hence **Seceˑder**, one who secedes; *spec.* a member of the Secession Church.

Secern (sǐsǭˑɹn), *v.* 1656. [ad. L. *secernere*, f. *se-* SE- + *cernere* to separate.] **1.** *trans.* To separate; now only, to separate in thought; to distinguish, discriminate. **2.** *Phys.* To separate from the blood; to SECRETE. Now *rare.* 1657.

1. Whereby the good from ill they might s. 1855. 2. An unusual proportion of bile is secerned 1822. Hence **Seceˑrnment**, the action of secreting.

Secernent (sǐsǭˑɹnĕnt), *a.* and *sb.* 1808. [ad. L. *secernentem*; see prec.] **A.** *adj.* That secretes 1822. **B.** *sb. Phys.* A secreting organ 1808.

†**Seceˑss.** 1563. [ad. L. *secessus*, f. *secedere.*] Withdrawing, retirement; a secession –1675.

Secession (sǐseˑʃǝn). 1533. [ad. L. *secessionem*, f. *secedere* SECEDE *v.*] †**1.** The action or an act of going away from one's accustomed neighbourhood, or of retiring from public view; the condition of being retired –1847. **2.** *Rom. Hist.* Used as tr. L. *secessio* (*plebis*), the temporary migration of the plebeians to a place outside the city, in order to compel the patricians to grant redress of their grievances 1533. **3.** The action of seceding or formally withdrawing from an alliance, a federation, a political or religious organization, etc. Hence, a body of seceders. 1600. **b.** *spec.* The separation from the Established Church of Scotland in 1733; the religious body (more fully *the S. Church*) which originated from this separation 1733.

3. *War of S.*, the American Civil War (1861–5), which arose out of the attempt of eleven of the Southern States to secede from the United States of North America.

attrib., as *S. church*, *movement*, etc.; also as *adj.* = secessionist. Hence **Seceˑssional** *a.* of or pertaining to s. **Seceˑssionism** *U. S. Hist.*, the principles of those in favour of s.; *Scottish Ch. Hist.*, the principles and doctrines of the S. Church. **Seceˑssionist**, one who favours s.; one who joins in a s.; *spec.* in *U.S. Hist.*; also *attrib.* or as *adj.*

Seckel (seˑkĕl). Also **Seckle.** 1817. [Name of originator.] A kind of pear. Also *S. pear.*

Seclude (sǐklūˑd), *v.* 1451. [ad. L. *secludere*, f. *se-* SE- + *claudere* to shut.] †**1.** To shut off (a thing) –1548. **2.** †**a.** To shut up apart –1746. **b.** To remove or guard from public view; to withdraw from opportunities of social intercourse. Often *refl.*, to live in retirement or solitude. 1628. **c.** To shut off or screen *from* some external influence 1601. †**3.** To shut or keep out *from* a place, society, etc.; to debar *from* a privilege, dignity, etc. –1775. †**4.** To exclude from consideration –1725. **5.** *Textual criticism.* To exclude as spurious 1893. †**6.** To separate, keep apart, select –1876.

2. a. The women were secluded from the men, being seated above in galleries EVELYN. b. Great Allowances should be given to a King who lives wholly secluded from the rest of the World SWIFT. 6. No plunder taken in war was used by the captor until the Druids determined what part they should s. for themselves GOLDSM.

Secluded (sǐklūˑdĕd), *ppl. a.* 1604. [f. prec. + -ED[1].] **1.** Shut up; withheld from view or from society. Now *rare.* **2.** Of localities: Remote from observation or access; seldom visited or seen on account of inaccessibility 1798.

Secluse (sǐklūˑz), *a.* Now *rare.* 1597. [ad. L. *seclusus*, *secludere* SECLUDE.] Secluded.

Seclusion (sǐkluˑʒǝn). 1623. [ad. med.L. *seclusionem*, f. L. *seclus-*, *secludere* SECLUDE *v.*] **1.** The action of secluding; †exclusion. **2.** The condition or state of being secluded; an instance of this 1784. **3.** A place or abode in which one is secluded 1791.

2. Oh, blest s. from a jarring world, Which he, thus occupied, enjoys! COWPER. *In s.*, apart from society. Hence **Secluˑsionist**, one who advocates s.; applied e.g. to a supporter of monasticism, and to a Chinese or Japanese who is averse to the admission of foreigners to his country.

Seclusive (sǐklūˑsiv), *a.* 1834. [f. L. *seclus-*, *secludere*; see SECLUDE *v.*] Serving or tending to seclude; affecting seclusion.

Second (seˑkǝnd), *sb.*[1] late ME. [a. F. *seconde*, ad. med.L. *secunda*, fem. of L. *secundus* SECOND *a.*, used ellipt. for *secunda minuta*, lit. 'second minute', i.e. the result of the second operation of sexagesimal division; the result of the first such operation (now called 'minute' simply), being the 'first' or 'prime minute' or 'prime' (see PRIME *sb.*[2] 2.).] *Math.* **1.** *Geom.* (*Astr.*, *Geog.*, etc.) A sixtieth part of a minute, $\frac{1}{3600}$th part of a degree. **2.** In measurement of time: The sixtieth part of a minute, $\frac{1}{3600}$th of an hour 1588. **b.** Used vaguely for an extremely short time, an 'instant' 1825.

2. The pendulum which vibrates seconds at London, has been commonly esteemed 39,2 English inches 1762. b. There was a second's panic in the crowd 1897.

attrib. and *Comb.*: **s.-** (**seconds-**) **hand**, a hand or pointer of a timepiece indicating seconds; **s.-** (**seconds-**) **mark** *Math.*, the character ″, denoting a second or seconds (either of angle or of time).

Second (seˑkǝnd), *a.* and *sb.*[2] ME. [a. F., ad. L. *secundus* following (hence favourable), next, second, f. root of *sequi* to follow.] **A.** *adj.* **1.** Coming next after the first: the ordinal corresponding to the cardinal two. Often with ellipsis of sb. understood from the context. **2.** Next in rank, quality, importance, or degree of any attribute, *to* (a person or thing regarded as first). Hence, in neg. and limiting contexts, Inferior (*to none*, *only to*...). late ME. **b.** In designations of office, denoting the lower of two, or the next to the highest of several persons holding the same office; e.g. *s. lieutenant* (in the army), *s. lord* (of the Admiralty), *s. master* (in a school), etc. 1702. **c.** *Mus.* Used to distinguish the next to the highest part in a piece of concerted music. Hence of a voice or instrument: Rendering such a part. 1724. **3.** Having the degree of quality, fineness, etc. next to the best; of the second grade or class. Now only *Comm.* in stereotyped uses. 1440. **4.** Other, another; additional to that which has already taken place, been mentioned, etc. late ME. **5.** quasi-*adv.* Secondly (*rare*); as the second in succession. late ME.

1. The secund day of Maii 1507. S. Nuptials DRYDEN. I liked her at first sight, and better at s. RICHARDSON. *The s.*, appended to a personal name to designate the second bearer of the name in a succession of persons (chiefly sovereigns); hence after the names of ships, horses, etc. 2. S. to none that liues heere in the Citie SHAKS. Phr. *S. in command* (Mil.), holding a position only subordinate to the chief commander of an army or one of its subdivisions; often *absol.* (quasi-*sb.*). c. Assuming the disguise of a S. Trombone, I joined the band W. S. GILBERT. 3. My coat..made of good s. cloth 1799. S. butter 1856. 4. Could any one bear the story of a s. city being taken by a wooden horse? SCOTT. *S. self* [after L. *alter idem*, Gr. ἄλλος or ἕτερος αὐτός], a friend who agrees absolutely with one's tastes and opinions, or for whose welfare one cares as much as for one's own. *S. nature* (in allusion to the Latin provb. *consuetudo est altera* (or *secunda*) *natura*).

Comb., as *s. childhood*, *cousin*, *fiddle*, *intention*, *order*, *thought(s*, *wind*, etc. (see these words); **s. Adam, Man** *Theol.*, titles given to Christ with ref. to 1 Cor. xv. 45, 47; **S. Advent** *Theol.*, the expected s. coming of Christ as judge; hence **S. Adventist,** one who believes that the S. Advent will precede the millennium; **s. ballot**, an electoral system whereby, if the winner on the first ballot has not polled more than half the votes cast, a second ballot is taken between him and the candidate with the next highest number of votes; **s. birth**, (*a.*) *Theol.* = REGENERATION 2; †(*b*) = SECUNDINE 1; †(*c*) the entrance upon a new life after death; **s. chamber**, in a bicameral legislature, the chamber which has chiefly the function of revising the measures prepared and passed by the other; **s. division** (*a*) *Civil Service*, the lower grade of government clerks; (*b*) prison treatment prescribed by the judge which is intermediate between hard-labour and first division; **s. floor**, the floor or story of a building next but one above the ground-floor; also *attrib.*; **S. Person (of the Trinity)** *Theol.*, the Son; **s. string**, a person or thing held in reserve as a resource if the one preferred should fail.

B. *sb.*[2] **I.** One who or something which is second. **1. a.** *Gram.* Used ellipt. for *second person* (usually before *singular* or *plural*) 1530. **b.** A place in the second class in an examination; one who takes such a place. Also, the competitor who comes next to the winner in a contest. 1852. **2.** One next to the first in rank, quality, etc. Also, †a second instance, a match *to* something. 1594. **b.** = *Second in command* 1604. **3.** *Mus.* **a.** A note one diatonic degree above or below any given note; the interval between two such notes; a tone (*major s.*) or diatonic semitone (*minor s.*); the harmonic combination of two such notes 1597. **b.** The next to the highest part in a piece of concerted music. Hence, a voice suitable to such a part. 1774. **4.** *pl. Comm.* A quality (of bricks, flour, stockings, etc.) second and inferior to the best 1600. **5.** In the duodecimal system of mensuration: The twelfth part of a 'prime' or inch 1703.

1. b. Miss Jones has a first-class and Miss Smith a s. 1907. 2. And see if Time..Can shew a S. to so pure a Love DRAYTON. 3. a. *Augmented s.*: the interval equivalent to three semitones, a minor third.

II. One who or something which renders aid or support to another. †**a.** *gen.* –1740. **b.** *spec.* One who acts as representative of a principal in a duel, carrying the challenge, loading weapons, etc. Similarly in a pugilistic contest. 1613. †**c.** Assistance. Also pl. *rare.* –1640.

a. He be thy S. SHAKS. b. It was usual to have more seconds even to the number of five or six SCOTT.

Second (seˑkǝnd), *v.*[1] 1586. [a. F. *seconder*, ad. L. *secundare*, f. *secundus* SECOND *a.*] **1.** *trans.* To support, back up, assist, encourage. †**b.** To follow, attend, accompany. In *pass.*, to be accompanied (*with*). –1632. **2.** *esp.* To support (a combatant, a body of troops) in attack or defence. Also, to act as second to (a pugilist). 1588. †**b.** To take the place of, succeed (a combatant who is *hors de combat*) –1614. **3.** To support (a speaker, or proposition) in a debate or conference by speaking in the same sense; *spec.* to rise to support (a mover or motion) as a necessary preliminary to further discussion or to the adoption of the motion 1597. †**b.** To support, back (a statement, opinion, a person *in* his opinion); to confirm (a report) –1741. **4.** To further, reinforce (a thing, activity, etc.) 1586. †**5.** To follow up or accompany *with* (or *by*) some second thing –1774. †**b.** To repeat (an action, esp. a blow) –1831. †**6.** To match with a second instance –1632.

1. His family had imbibed all his views, and seconded them DISRAELI. 2. Let him feele your Sword, Which we will s. SHAKS. b. 2 *Hen. IV*, IV. ii. 45, 46. 3. It is a good precept generally in seconding another: yet to adde somewhat of ones owne BACON. 4. Deeds must s. words 1858.

Second (sǐkǫˑnd), *v.*[2] 1802. [f. F. *second*

in the phr. *en second*.] *trans.* To remove (an officer) temporarily from his regiment or corps, for employment on the staff, or in some other extra-regimental appointment. Also *transf.*

Secondary (se·kəndări), *a.* and *sb.* late ME. [ad. L. *secundarius* of the second class or quality, f. *secundus* SECOND *a.*; see -ARY [1].] A. *adj.* 1. Belonging to the second class in respect of dignity or importance; entitled to consideration only in the second place. Also, and usu.: Not in the first class; of minor importance, subordinate. †b. Second best -1601. c. Of a lower kind. late ME. †d. Of an official: Second in rank or status. Of a judge: = PUISNE *a.* 1 b. -1630. e. Of persons: Second-rate (*rare*) 1827. f. Subsidiary, auxiliary 1751. 2. Derived from, based on, or dependent on something else which is primary; not original, derivative. late ME. b. Having only a derived authority; subordinate 1667. c. *Philos.* (*a*) Applied to those qualities of bodies that were supposed to be derived from the four 'primary' qualities recognized by Aristotle, hot, cold, wet, dry. *Obs.* exc. *Hist.* 1656. (*b*) Applied to those properties or qualities of matter (as colour, smell, taste, etc.) which are distinguished as not existing, like 'primary' qualities, in the bodies themselves independently of perception, but depending upon the action of the primary qualities on the percipient. Cf. PRIMARY *a.* 3. 1656. d. *Cryst.* Of crystalline forms: Derivative, not primitive 1805. e. *Electr.* Of a current: Induced. Hence of apparatus, etc.: Pertaining to an induced current. Also *s. battery*, a storage battery as dist. from one in which a current is produced. 1843. f. *Chem.* Applied to certain types of organic compounds which are formed from others by certain definite processes of replacement 1862. g. *Meteorology.* Said of a subsidiary depression taking place on the border of a primary cyclone 1876. 3. a. Belonging to the second order in a series of subdivisions or ramifications. Chiefly *Biol.* 1796. b. Belonging to the second stage in a process of compounding or combination; consisting of two primary elements 1807. 4. With ref. to temporal sequence: Pertaining to a second period or condition of things; adventitious, not primitive. Chiefly scientific and techn. a. *Geol.* = MESOZOIC 1813. b. *Biol.* Belonging to the second stage of development or growth 1857. c. *Surg.* Performed or occurring after a definite time or occurrence 1837. d. *Path.* Characteristic of or pertaining to the second stage or period of a disease, esp. of syphilis 1722. e. *S. education* or *instruction*: that between the primary or elementary education and the higher or university education. *S. school*, one in which such education is given. 1861. 5. Connected with what is second in local position 1768.

1. Things..purely Ornimental, are no more than of s. Consideration 1735. 2. A s. and derivative Virtue 1738. *S. cause*, a proximate or instrumental cause, a cause produced by a primary cause (also used in sense 1). *S. planet*, a satellite which revolves round a primary planet. *S. circle* (Geom. and Astr.), a great circle passing through the poles of another great circle perpendicular to its plane. *S. bow* or *rainbow*, an outer and fainter bow parallel with the primary bow. c. (*b*) Among the s. qualities [of matter] are classed heat and cold, colour and sound, taste and odour 1856. 3. b. *S. colours*: see COLOUR *sb.* I. 2. 4. c. *S. amputation*, amputation performed after suppuration has set in. 5. *S. feather*, *quill*, a feather growing from the second joint of a bird's wing. *S. wing*, one of the hind wings of an insect.

B. *sb.* [the adj. used ellipt. Mostly in *pl.*] 1. *gen.* One who acts in subordination to another; a delegate or deputy; also, a thing which comes second in importance. Now *rare.* 1595. b. A cathedral dignitary of second rank. late ME. c. An officer of the corporation of the City of London. †Also, an official in certain government offices and law courts. 1461. 2. Short for *s. planet* 1721. 3. Short for *s. circle* 1715. 4. *Path.* in *pl.* Secondary symptoms (of syphilis) 1843. 5. *Geol.* The secondary series of rocks, or any of the secondary formations 1890. 6. *Ornith.* Short for *s. feather* 1768. 7. *Electr.* Short for *s. coil* or *wire* 1869. 8. *Meteorology.* Short for *s. depression* 1887. Hence **Se·condarily** *adv.*, **-ness.**

Second best, second-best, *a.* late ME. 1. Next in quality to the first. 2. *absol.* Something inferior to the best 1708. 3. quasi-*adv.* In phr. *to come off second best*, to be defeated in a contest 1777.

Second-class, *a.* 1837. 1. Of or belonging to the class next to the first. b. *S. matter* (U.S.): postal matter consisting of periodicals sent from the office of publication 1883. 2 quasi-*adv.* By a second-class conveyance 1906.

‖ **Seconde** (səgō·nd). 1707. [F., fem. of *second* SECOND *a.*] The second of the eight parries recognized in sword-play.

Seconder (se·kəndəɹ). 1598. [f. SECOND *a.* and *v.* + -ER [1].] I. [f. the adj.] 1. One who comes second, or in the second rank. Now *local*, a second hand on a farm. 2. A student of the second grade in social rank at the Universities of Glasgow and St. Andrews. *Obs.* exc. *Hist.* 1655. II. [f. the vb.] a. One who supports (what is proposed by another); one who furthers the designs of another 1607. b. *spec.* One who seconds a motion; one who seconds a nomination or candidature 1678.

Second hand, second-hand. 1474. [Cf. F. *de seconde main.*] A. *phrase.* (*Second hand.*) †1. In sb. use: An intermediary, middleman -1727. 2. In advb. phrases 1474.

2. *At second hand*, (to buy, receive, learn, etc.) from another than the maker, or original vendor (of goods), or the primary source (of information, etc.). †*By second hand*, through another person as agent.

B. *adj.* (*Second-hand.*) 1. Not original or obtained from the original source; borrowed; imitative, derivative 1654. 2. Not new, having been previously worn or used by another, as *s. clothes*, *books*, etc. 1673. 3. quasi-*adv.* = at second hand 1849.

1. Even of this s. knowledge there was very little 1868. 2. The warehouse of some second hand Bookseller 1656. So **Second-ha·nded** *a.* (now *dial.*).

Secondly (se·kəndli), *adv.* late ME. [f. SECOND *a.* + -LY [2].] †1. For a second time -1771. 2. In the second place. late ME. 3. quasi-*sb.* The word *secondly* used in making subdivisions of a subject 1759.

2. Man, consider first the nature of the thing that thou intendest, and s. thine owne nature 1610.

Second-rate, *a.* and *sb.* 1669. A. *adj.* Of the second 'rate' (said of ships). Hence, Of the second class in quality or excellence; usu.: Not first-rate, of only moderate quality.

Any of the s. theatres in London 1748.

B. *sb.* 1. *Naut.* A war-vessel of the second 'rate' 1679. 2. *transf.* A person or thing of inferior class 1799. Hence **Second-rater.**

Second sight. 1616. 1. A supposed power by which occurrences in the future or things at a distance are perceived as though they were actually present. 2. The image or vision produced by this faculty 1763.

1. Their Faith and firm Belief In Second Sight, and Mother Shipton 1763. Hence **Second-sighted** *a.* having the gift of second sight.

Secrecy (sī·krĕsi). late ME. [Alteration of †*secretee*, *-tie*, app. f. †*secre* or SECRET *a.* + -TY or -Y [3].] 1. The quality of being secret or of not revealing secrets; the action, habit, or practice of keeping things secret. 2. The condition or fact of being secret or concealed 1563. †b. Retirement, seclusion -1667. 3. Something which is or has been kept secret; a secret; the secret nature or condition of something. Often *collect. sing.* or *pl.*, secret matters, mysteries. *Obs.* or *arch.* 1450. †4. Intimate acquaintance, confidence -1671.

1. Constant you are..and for secrecie, No Lady closer SHAKS. 2. *In s.*, secretly; The Lady Anne, Whom the King hath in secrecie long married SHAKS. 3. Leaving secrecies to conscience MILT.

Secret (sī·krĕt), *a.* and *sb.* late ME. [a. F., ad. L. *secretus* adj. (neut. *secretum* used sb., a secret), orig. pa. pple. of *secernere* to SECERN.] A. *adj.* 1. a. *predic.* Kept from public knowledge, or from the knowledge of persons specified. b. Of a place: Retired, remote, secluded; hence, affording privacy or seclusion. Chiefly *arch.* 1500. †c. Of a person, etc.: Secluded from observation -1667. d. Of actions, etc.: Done with the intention of being concealed; clandestine 1548. e. Of doctrines, ceremonies: Kept from the knowledge of the uninitiated 1526. f. Of feelings, thoughts: Not openly avowed or expressed; concealed, disguised 1500. †g. Abstruse, recondite -1775. h. Of a committee, etc.: Conducted with secrecy 1667. i. Hidden from sight; unseen, invisible 1559. j. Of a door, drawer, etc.: Designed to escape observation or detection 1591. k. Of an agent: That works in secret. Of a person: That is secretly (what is expressed by the sb.). 1600. l. quasi-*adv.* Apart; secretly, in secret 1539. 2. Of a person: †Reticent or reserved in conduct or conversation; not given to indiscreet talking or the revelation of secrets; uncommunicative, close. Also *fig.* of silence, night, etc. 1440. †3. That is a confidant; intimate *with* -1648.

1. a. The Renegados..kept his death s. 1600. b. Put them in s. holds SHAKS. c. In this Citty will I stay, And liue alone as s. as I may SHAKS. d. Hide me from the s. counsel of the wicked *Ps.* lxiv. 2. f. I haue vnclasp'd To thee the booke euen of my s. soule SHAKS. I had a s. joy at the news DE FOE. g. *Macb.* IV. i. 48. i. *S. parts*, *members*, the external organs of sex. j. *S. ink*, 'invisible' or 'sympathetic' ink. k. Others, who were my s. Enemies SWIFT. l. She had devised How she might s. to the forest hie KEATS. 2. I can be s. as a dumbe man SHAKS. 3. He was s. with y[e] Duke 1533.

Special collocations: **S. service**: services rendered to a government, the nature of which cannot be disclosed to the public, but which are paid for from a fund set apart for the purpose; also *attrib.*, as *s. service agent*, *fund*, etc. **S. society**, an organization formed to promote some cause by secret methods, its members being sworn to observe secrecy.

B. *sb.* Something kept secret. 1. Something unknown or unrevealed or that is known only by initiation or revelation; chiefly *pl.*, the hidden affairs or workings (of God, Nature, Science, etc.). late ME. 2. In Liturgical use: A prayer or prayers said by the celebrant in a low voice after the Offertory and before the Preface. See SECRETA [1]. late ME. 3. Some fact, affair, design, action, etc., known only to oneself or shared only with a limited number 1450. 4. A method or process (of an art, etc.) hidden from all except the initiated 1486. b. (Const. *of.*) That which accounts for something surprising or extraordinary; the essential thing to be observed in order to secure some end 1738. †5. A place of concealment or retreat -1635. †6. *pl.* = *s. parts* (see A. 1 i). Also *sing.* -1758. 7. *Antiq.* A coat of mail or piece of armour concealed under one's usual dress 1578.

1. Jealous Nature hath lock'd her secrets in a Cabinet DAVENANT. 3. Sir Thurio, giue vs leaue (I pray) a while, We haue some secrets to confer about SHAKS. Phr. *An open s.*, something which is ostensibly a s., but which requires little effort or penetration to discover. 4. A pretended s. of multiplying gold EVELYN. b. The..s. of success KINGSLEY.

Phrases. *In s.* [= L. *in secreto*, F. *en secret*], in private; secretly. *To be in the s.*, to be one of the participants in a s. *To let* (a person) *into the s.*, to confide to him the s. (*of* an affair, trade). *To make a s. of* (something), to make it a matter of concealment; to keep it to oneself. Hence †**Se·cret** *v. trans.* to keep s., conceal -1734. **Se·cret·ly** *adv.*, **-ness.**

‖ **Secreta** [1] (sĭkrī·tă). *Pl.* **-tæ.** 1740. [eccl. L. *secreta* (sc. *oratio*), fem. of L. *secretus.*] *Eccl.* = SECRET *sb.* 2.

‖ **Secre·ta** [2], *pl.* 1877. [L.; neut. pl. of pa. pple. of *secernere* SECRETE *v.* [1]] The products of secretion.

Secretage (sĭ·krĭtedʒ). 1791. [a. F. *secrétage*, f. *secréter* SECRETE *v.* [3] and -AGE.] A process of preparing furs for felting by the application of nitrate of mercury.

‖ **Secretaire** (sekrĭtēə·ɹ, F. səkretēr). 1818. [F.] A piece of furniture in which private papers can be kept, with a shelf for writing on, and drawers and pigeon-holes; a bureau.

Secretarial (sekrĭtēə·riăl), *a.* 1801. [f. med.L. *secretarius* SECRETARY; see -AL.] Of or pertaining to a secretary or secretaries. So †**Secreta·rian** *a.* (*rare*) 1734-1801.

Secretariat(e (sekrĭtēə·riăt, -ĕ̆t). 1811. [a. F. *secrétariat*, ad. med.L. *secretariatus*, f. *secretarius*; see -ATE [1].] The office of a secretary; the body or department of secretaries; the place where a secretary transacts business, preserves records, etc.

Secretary (se·krĭtări), *sb.* (and *a.*). late ME. [ad. med.L. *secretarius* secretary, etc., a title applied to various confidential officers, f. *secretum* SECRET *sb.*; see -ARY [1] B. 1.] A. *sb.* †1. A confidant; one privy *to* a secret. Also *fig.* of things personified. -1815. 2. One whose office it is to write for another; esp. one who is employed to conduct correspondence, to keep records, and (usu.) to transact other business, for another person or for a society, corporation, or public body. late ME. †b. In the titles of books on the art of letter-writing -1715. 3. In the official designations of certain ministers presiding over executive departments of state 1599. b. *Mr. Secretary*: used before the name of a secretary of state, or as a title instead of his name. Now only *official* and *Hist.* 1529. 4. Short for *s. hand, type* 1771. 5. A secretaire 1833. 6. The secretary-bird 1781.

1. Reueale it she durst not, as daring in such matters to make none her secretarie LODGE. *fig.* The night, sad s. to my mones KYD. 2. *Private s.*, a s. employed by a minister of state, etc. for the personal correspondence connected with his official position; also applied to a s. employed in purely personal service. *S. of embassy, legation*, an official ranking next to the ambassador or envoy, and empowered to some extent to supply his place in his absence. 3. In peace-time..the duties of the Colonial S., in his character as S. of War, were very slight KINGLAKE. b. A letter from Mr. S. Pitt 1760.

Comb.: **s.-bird**, a raptorial bird of South Africa, *Serpentarius secretarius*: so called from a tuft of feathers at the back of the head which have a fanciful resemblance to pens stuck behind the ear.

B. *adj.* As the distinctive epithet of a style of handwriting used chiefly in legal documents from the 15th to the 17th c. Hence applied to a kind of black-letter type imitating this. 1571. Hence **Se·cretaryship**, the office of a s.

Secrete (sǐkrī·t), *v.*[1] 1707. [f. L. *secret-, secernere*; see SECERN *v.*] 1. *trans.* To produce by means of secretion. 2. *intr.* To perform the act of secretion 1872.

Secrete (sǐkrī·t), *v.*[2] 1741. [Alteration of SECRET *v.*] 1. *trans.* To place in concealment, to keep secret. 2. To remove secretly, to appropriate (the possessions of another) in a secret manner 1749.

1. How had Sibyll dared to s. from him this hoard LYTTON. A..French lady..had secreted herself on board the vessel 1893. 2. The secreting of the 500 l. was a matter of very little hazard FIELDING.

Secre·te, *v.*[3] 1839. [a. F. *secréter*, f. *secret* SECRET *sb.* (in the sense of 'secret process').] *trans.* To subject to the process of SECRETAGE.

Secretin (sǐkrī·tin). 1902. [app. irreg. f. SECRETION + -IN[1].] *Chem.* A substance produced by the action of the acid of the gastric juice on the intestinal mucous membrane and acting as a stimulus to pancreatic secretion.

Secretion (sǐkrī·ʃən). 1646. [a. F. *sécrétion*, ad. L. *secretionem*, f. *secernere*; see SECERN *v.*] 1. *Phys.* In an animal or vegetable body, the action of a gland or some analogous organ in extracting certain matters from the blood or sap and elaborating from them a particular substance, either to fulfil some function within the body or to undergo excretion as waste. 2. *concr.* That which is produced by the action of a secreting organ 1732. †3. In etym. sense: a. Separation. b. *Philos.* (= Gr. ἀπόκρισις.) Giving off of particles. -1678.

Secretive (sǐkrī·tiv), *a.* 1853. [Back-formation from next; but apprehended as f. SECRETE *v.* + -IVE.] Addicted or inclined to secrecy; reticent; not frank or open. b. *transf.* of things. Also of looks, etc.: Indicating secretiveness. 1865.

She was a shy, s. maid 1884. b. A s. smile 1865.

Secretiveness (sǐkrī·tivnės). 1815. [Formed after F. *secrétivité*, f. *secret* SECRET; see -IVE and -NESS.] The quality of being secretive; disposition to secrecy.

Secretory (sǐkrī·təri), *a.* and *sb.* 1692. [f. L. *secret-* (see SECRETE *v.*) + -ORY.] A. *adj.* Having the function of secreting; pertaining to or concerned with secretion. B. *sb.* A secreting vessel or duct 1768.

‖**Secretum** (sǐkrī·tŏm). *Pl.* **-ta.** 1864. [L., neut. of *secretus* SECRET *a.*; in med.L. ellipt. for *sigillum secretum* secret seal.] *Antiq.* A private seal.

Sect (sekt). late ME. [a. F. *secte*, or ad. L. *secta* following, f. root of *sequi* to follow.] †1. A class or kind (of persons) -1628. †b. A religious order -1814. c. Sex. Now only in illiterate or joc. use. late ME. †2. Body of followers or adherents -1667. 3. A religious following; adherence to a particular religious teacher or faith. *esp.* a. A body of persons who unite in holding certain views differing from those of others who are accounted to be of the same religion; a party or school among the professors of a religion; sometimes applied *spec.* to parties that are regarded as heretical. late ME. b. In mod. use, commonly applied to a separately organized religious body having its distinctive name and its own places of worship; a 'denomination'. Also, less widely, one of the bodies separated from the Church. 1577. 4. The system or body of adherents of a particular school of philosophy. late ME. 5. *transf.* A school of opinion in politics, science, etc. 1605.

1. c. 'Tis the easiest Art and cunning for our s. to counterfeit sicke MIDDLETON. 3. Kynge Salamon louyd ouermoche..straunge wymen of other sectes CAXTON. a. *The Clapham S.*, a derisive name applied early in the 19th c. to a coterie of persons of Evangelical opinions and conspicuous philanthropic activity, some of whom lived at Clapham; among the chief members were Wilberforce, Zachary Macaulay, and Henry Thornton. b. *The sects*, applied by Anglicans to the various bodies of Dissenters, by Roman Catholics to all forms of Protestantism. 4. The S. Epicurean MILT. 5. Socialism is rather a s. than a party 1899.

Sectarial (sektē°·riăl), *a.* 1816. [f. SECTARY (or med.L. *sectarius*) + -AL.] Pertaining to or distinctive of sect. Chiefly with ref. to Indian religions.

Sectarian (sektē°·riăn), *a.* and *sb.* 1649. [f. next + -AN.] A. *adj.* 1. Pertaining to a sectary or sectaries; 'belonging to a schismatical sect' (Phillips). *Obs.* exc. *Hist.* 2. Pertaining to a sect or sects; confined to a particular sect; bigotedly attached to a particular sect. In recent use, often a pejorative synonym of *denominational*, esp. with ref. to education. 1796.

2. A Christian, and yet not s. University 1836.

B. *sb.* 1. Orig., an adherent of the 'sectarian party' (i.e. the Independents as designated by the Presbyterians); subsequently, a schismatic. Now chiefly *Hist.* 1654. 2. An adherent of a specified sect; a sectary of a particular teacher. Now *rare.* 1819. 3. A bigoted adherent of a sect; a person of sectarian views or sympathies 1827. Hence **Secta·rianism**, adherence or excessive attachment to a particular sect or party, esp. in religion; undue favouring of a particular denomination. **Secta·rianize** *v. intr.* to act in a s. manner; *trans.* to render s.

Sectary (se·ktări), *sb.* and *a.* 1556. [ad. F. *sectaire*, or med.L. *sectarius*, f. *secta* SECT.] A. *sb.* 1. A member of a sect; one who is zealous in the cause of a sect 1558. 2. An adherent of a schismatical or heretical sect. In the 17-18th c. commonly applied to the English Protestant Dissenters. Now chiefly *Hist.* 1556. 3. A follower *of* a particular leader, teacher, party, or school. Now *rare* (with mixture of sense 1). 1589.

1. It is not as religious sectaries they [school inspectors] have to discharge their duties, but as civil servants M. ARNOLD. 2. Many sectaries experienced much inhuman treatment 1860.

B. *adj.* Of or pertaining to a sect; sectarian 1590.

A kind of S. passion 1638. Hence **Se·ctarism**, sectarianism. †**Se·ctarist** = A. 1. -1833.

Sectator (sektē°·təɹ). Now *rare.* 1541. [a. L., f. *sectari*, freq. of *sequi* to follow.] A follower, disciple; one who follows a particular school, teacher, or leader; a partisan, sectary.

Sectile (se·ktil, -əil), *a.* 1716. [a. F., ad. L. *sectilem*, f. *sect-, secare* to cut.] Capable of or suited for being cut. Hence **Secti·lity.**

Section (se·kʃən), *sb.* 1559. [a. F., or ad. L. *sectionem*, f. *sect-, secare* to cut.] 1. The action, or an act, of cutting or dividing. Now *rare* exc. with ref. to surgery or anatomical operations. 2. A part separated or divided off from the remainder; one of the portions into which a thing is cut or divided. *esp.* a. A subdivision of a written or printed work, a statute, or the like. Often represented by the symbol § (preceding a numeral figure); also abbrev. *sect.* (rarely *sec.*). 1576. b. *Nat. Hist.* Used variously for a subdivision of a classificatory group, e.g. of a class, order, family, or genus. In *Bot.* now chiefly = *sub-genus*. 1720. c. A separable portion of any collection or aggregate of persons, e.g. of the population of a country; a group forming part of a political or religious party, etc. 1832. d. (*a*) *U.S.* An area of one square mile into which undeveloped lands are divided; (*b*) *Colonial.* A division of undeveloped land; (*c*) Chiefly *U.S.* A district or portion of a town or country exhibiting uniform characteristics or considered as divided from the rest on account of such characteristics 1816. e. *Mil.* A fourth part of a company (now of a platoon) 1805. f. *U.S. Railways.* (*a*) A portion of a sleeping-car containing two berths 1874; (*b*) The smallest administrative subdivision of a railway 1890. g. One of the component parts of something which is built up of a number of similar portions so as to admit of enlargement when necessary, or which is constructed to be taken to pieces for facility of transport 1875. 3. *Math.* †a. A segment of a circle -1715. b. The curve of intersection of two superficies 1704. c. The cutting of a solid by a plane; the plane figure resulting from such a cutting; the area of this. Hence, of a material object, the figure which would be produced by cutting through it in a certain plane. 1704. d. The action of dividing a line into parts 1820. 4. A drawing representing an object as it would appear if cut through in a plane at right angles to the line of sight 1669. b. *Geol.* A surface exposed by a cutting or by some natural agency, showing the succession of strata 1858. 5. A thin slice of a vegetable or animal structure, or of an inorganic body, cut off for microscopic examination 1870. 6. *Printing.* The sign §, orig. used to introduce the number of a 'section'; subseq. used also as a mark of reference to notes in the margin or at the foot of a page. Also called *s.-mark.* 1728.

2. a. In the printed editions..we see each statute divided into sections, and each s. numbered BENTHAM. c. The Church had at this time..sunk into a mere s. of the landed aristocracy 1874. g. There is always a steamer in sections in every story of a good expedition 1897.

Comb.: **s. line**, †(*a*) the boundary of a s.; (*b*) a line drawn to indicate the manner of making a s.; **-liner**, a device for ruling parallel lines; **-mark** (see sense 6). Hence **Se·ction** *v. trans.* to divide into sections. **Se·ctionary** *a.* †of or pertaining to a s. or sections (*rare*); *sb.* a member of a s. (of a party, etc.) opposed to the remainder.

Sectional (se·kʃənăl), *a.* 1816. [f. prec. + -AL.] 1. Pertaining to a section or division of a larger part, e.g. of a country, society, or population; sometimes (of interests, etc.) with implied opposition to *general.* 2. Of or pertaining to a section (sense 4), relating to the view of the structure of a body in section 1825. 3. Composed of several sections or parts fitting into one another 1875.

1. The further embitterment of s. and sectarian strife [in Ireland] 1886. Hence **Se·ctionalism**, confinement of interest to a narrow sphere, undue accentuation of minor local, political, or social distinctions. **Se·ctionalize** *v. trans.* to divide into sections. **Se·ctionally** *adv.* from a s. point of view.

Sectionize (se·kʃənəiz), *v.* 1828. [f. SECTION *sb.* + -IZE.] *trans.* a. To divide into sections or parts. b. To delineate in section 1876. c. To cut sections or thin slices from 1896.

Sectism (se·ktiz'm). 1864. [f. SECT + -ISM 2 b.] Devotion to a sect; sectarian spirit. So †**Se·ctist**, a sectary -1654.

Sector (se·ktəɹ), *sb.* 1570. [a. late L., as tr. Gr. τομεύς, lit. 'cutter,' but used in the senses I. 1 a, b.] I. 1. *Geom.* a. A plane figure contained by two radii and the arc of a circle, ellipse, or other central curve intercepted by them. b. *S. of a sphere*: a solid generated by the revolution of a plane sector about one of its radii 1656. c. *Mil.* A section of a front corresponding to the sector of a circle of which a headquarters is the centre 1916. 2. A body or figure having the shape of a sector 1715. II. 1. A mathematical instrument, invented by Thomas Hood and improved by Edmund Gunter, used for the mechanical solution of various problems. (In its present form it consists of two flat rules stiffly hinged together, inscribed with various kinds of scales.) 1598. 2. An astronomical instrument consisting of a telescope turning about the centre of a graduated arc. See DIP-*s.*, ZENITH-*s.* 1711. Hence **Se·ctor** *v. trans.* to divide into sectors; to provide with sectors.

Sectorial (sektō°·riăl), *a.*[1] 1803. [f. prec. + -IAL.] Of or pertaining to a sector.

Sectorial (sektōᵊ·riăl), *a.*² 1840. [f. mod. L. *sectorius* (f. L. *sector* cutter) + -AL 1.] Having the function of cutting; the distinctive epithet of the premolar teeth.

Secular (se·kiŭlăı), *a.* and *sb.* ME. [In branch I, a. OF. *seculer*, ad. L. *sæcularis*, f. *sæculum* generation, age, in Christian L. 'the world', esp. as opp. to the church. In branch II, directly ad. L. *sæcularis*.] **A.** *adj.* **I.** Of or pertaining to the world. **1.** *Eccl.* Of members of the clergy: Living 'in the world', and not subject to a religious rule: dist. from 'regular' and 'religious'. **b.** Of or pertaining to secular clergy 1570. **2.** Belonging to the world and its affairs as dist. from the church and religion; civil, lay, temporal. Chiefly as a neg. term, with the meaning non-ecclesiastical, non-religious, or non-sacred. ME. †**b.** *transf.* Of or belonging to the 'common' or 'unlearned' people -1629. **c.** Of literature, history, art (esp. music), hence of writers, artists: Not concerned with or devoted to the service of religion; not sacred; profane. Also of buildings, etc.: Not dedicated to religious uses. 1450. **d.** Of education, instruction: Relating to non-religious subjects. Of a school: That gives secular education. 1526. **3.** Of or belonging to the present or visible world; temporal, worldly 1597. **b.** Unspiritual (*rare*). late ME.

1. *S. abbot*, a person not a monk, who had the title and part of the revenues, but not the functions of an abbot. 2. *S. arm* (= med.L. *brachium seculare*, F. *le bras séculier*), the civil power as 'invoked' by the church to punish offenders; Truth never fears the encounter; she scorns the aid of the s. arm FRANKLIN. b. Hang him poore snip, a s. shop-wit! B. JONS. 3. I do not believe that s. motives are adequate either to propel or to restrain the children of our race GLADSTONE.

II. Of or belonging to an age or long period. **1.** Occurring or celebrated once in an age, century, or very long period 1599. **2.** Living or lasting for an age or ages. Also (of trees, etc., after F. *séculaire*), centuries old. 1629. **3.** In scientific use, of processes of change: Having a period of enormous length; continuing through long ages 1801.

1. *S. games, plays, shows* [L. *ludi sæculares*], in ancient Rome, games continuing three days and three nights, celebrated once in an 'age' or period of 120 years. *S. poem* [L. *carmen sæculare*], a hymn composed to be sung at the secular games. 2. The s. leisures of Methusaleh 1870. A forest of s. trees 1876. 3. The contraction of the globe due to s. cooling 1880.

B. *sb.* **1.** One of the secular clergy, as dist. from a 'regular' or monk ME. †**2.** One who is engaged in the affairs of the world as dist. from the church; a layman -1829. Hence **Se·cular-ly** *adv.*, **-ness**.

Secularism (se·kiŭlăriz'm). 1846. [f. SECULAR *a.* + -ISM 2 b.] **1.** The doctrine that morality should be based solely on regard to the well-being of mankind in the present life, to the exclusion of all considerations drawn from belief in God or in a future state. **2.** The view that national education should be purely secular 1872.

Secularist (se·kiŭlărist), *sb.* (and *a.*). 1851. [f. SECULAR + -IST.] **1.** An adherent of secularism. **2.** An advocate of exclusively secular education 1872. **3.** *attrib.* and *appos.* (quasi-*adj.*) 1890. Hence **Se:culari·stic** *a.* of or pertaining to secularism.

Secularity (sekiŭlæ·rĭti). late ME. [a. F. *sécularité*, or ad. med.L. *sæcularitas*, f. L. *sæcularis*; see -ITY.] †**1.** Secular jurisdiction or power -1535. **2.** The condition or quality of being secular; *esp.* occupation with secular affairs (on the part of clergymen); also occas., worldliness, absence of religious principle or feeling. late ME. **3.** A secular matter. Chiefly *pl.* Secular affairs; worldly possessions or pursuits. 1511. **4.** The character of having long periods 1844.

2. The s. of the clergy in complying with the..vanities..of the age 1711.

Secularization (se:kiŭlărəizēⁱ·ʃən). 1706. [ad. F. *sécularisation*; see next and -ATION.] **1.** The conversion of an ecclesiastical or religious institution or its property to secular possession and use; the conversion of an ecclesiastical state or sovereignty to a lay one. **2.** The giving of a secular or non-sacred character or direction to (art, studies, etc.); the placing (of morals) on a secular basis; the restricting (of education) to secular subjects 1863.

Secularize (se·kiŭlărəiz), *v.* 1611. [ad. F. *séculariser*, f. L. *sæcularis* SECULAR; see -IZE.] **1.** *trans.* To make secular; to convert from ecclesiastical to civil possession or use. **b.** To laicize 1846. **2.** To make (a monk or monastic order) secular 1683. **3.** To convert from religious or spiritual to material and temporal purposes; to turn (a person, his mind, etc.) from a spiritual state to worldliness 1711.

1. To surprize the possessions of the Church, and to S. her patrimony 1657.

Secund (sĭ·kʊ·nd), *a.* 1777. [ad. L. *secundus* following, SECOND.] *Bot.* and *Zool.* Arranged on or directed towards one side only; esp. *Bot.* of the flowers, leaves, or other organs of a plant.

Secundine (se·kʊndəin, -in). late ME. [ad. late L. *secundinæ* pl., f. *secundus* following; see SECOND *a.* and -INE ⁴.] **1.** *Obstetrics.* The placenta and other adjuncts of a fœtus extruded from the womb after the expulsion of the fœtus in parturition; the afterbirth. Freq. *pl.* **2.** *Bot.* The second of two coats or integuments of an ovule, orig. the inner one, later applied to the outer covering: see PRIMINE 1671.

Secu:ndoge·niture. 1855. [f. L. *secundo*, advb. form of *secundus* SECOND *a.*, after *primogeniture*.] The right of succession or inheritance belonging to a second son; the possession so inherited.

The kingdom of Naples..was constituted a s. of Spain 1876.

Secundum (sĭkʊ·ndʊ̆m). 1563. [L., 'according to'.] Used in various med.L. phrases, sometimes occurring in Eng. contexts.

S. artem: in accordance with the rules of the art (chiefly of medicine). *S. magis et minus*: 'according to more and less'; in a quantitative manner or respect; in various degrees. *S. naturam*: naturally. *S. quid*: 'according to something', in some particular respect only (opp. to *simpliciter*).

‖ **Secundus** (sĭkʊ·ndʊ̆s), *a.* 1826. [L. *secundus* SECOND *a.*] Added to a personal name: The second of that name.

Securance (sĭkiūᵊ·răns). *rare.* 1642. [f. SECURE *v.* + -ANCE.] The action or means of securing; assurance, security.

Secure (sĭkiūᵊ·ɹ), *sb.* 1802. [f. SECURE *v.*] The position in which a rifle or musket is held when it is 'secured'; see SECURE *v.* 2 c.

Secure (sĭkiūᵊ·ɹ), *a.* 1533. [ad. L. *securus*, f. *se-* SE- + *cura* care.] **I.** (Often in predic. use, esp. *poet.*) **1.** Without care, careless; free from care, apprehension, anxiety, or alarm; over-confident. Now *arch.* **b.** Said of times, places, actions: In which one is free from fear or anxiety 1602. †**2.** Free from doubt or distrust; feeling sure or certain -1794. †**b.** Confident in expectation -1732.

1. The way to be safe, is never to bee s. 1641. Lie still, dry dust, s. of change TENNYSON. b. Vpon my s. hower thy Vncle stole With iuyce of cursed Hebenon in a Violl SHAKS. 2. *John* IV. i. 130. b. S. to be as blest, as thou canst bear POPE.

II. 1. Rightly free from apprehension; protected from or not exposed to danger; safe 1582. **b.** Of actions or conditions: Involving no danger; safe 1617. **c.** Of an argument, means, agent, etc.: Not liable to fail, trustworthy, safe 1729. **d.** Of a material thing, a support or fastening: Not liable to be displaced or to yield under strain; firmly fixed, safe 1841. **2.** Of a place, also of means of protection or guardianship: Affording safety 1610. **3.** *predic.* In safe custody; safely in one's possession or power 1591. **4.** Free from risk as to the continued or future possession *of* something; having a safe prospect *of* some acquisition or desirable event 1664. **5.** Of a possession, acquisition, desirable event, etc.: That may be counted on with certainty; sure to continue or to be attained 1713.

1. Your grace may sit s., if none but wee Doe wot of your abode MARLOWE. The divell..would perswade him he might be s. if hee cast himselfe from the pinacle SIR T. BROWNE. From the contagion of the world's slow stain, He is s. SHELLEY. b. A seeming-secure and supine sleep 1643. 2. I could pity thee exil'd From this s. retreat COWPER. 3. In Iron Walls they deem'd me not s. SHAKS. 4. When they seemed most s. of victory SCOTT. 5. If the worst comes to the worst..my retreat is s. THACKERAY. Hence **Secu·re-ly** *adv.*, **-ness**.

Secure (sĭkiūᵊ·ɹ), *v.* 1593. [f. SECURE *a.*] †**1.** *trans.* To make free from care or apprehension; also, to make careless or over-confident (*rare*) -1655. †**b.** To satisfy, convince. Also, to make (a person) feel secure *of* or *against* some contingency. -1668. **2.** To make secure or safe. Also †*refl.* 1593. **b.** *Mil.* To render secure from attack or molestation by the enemy; to take defensive means for the safe execution of (a movement); to guard efficiently (a pass, a defile) 1617. **c.** *To s. arms*: 'to hold a rifle or musket with the muzzle down, and lock well up under the arm, the object being to guard the weapon from the wet' 1802. **3.** To make secure or certain; 'to place beyond hazard' (J.), to ensure 1610. **b.** To make (a creditor) certain of receiving payment, by means of a mortgage, bond, pledge or the like 1677. **c.** To make the payment of (a debt, pension, etc.) certain by a mortgage or charge *upon* certain property 1818. **4.** To seize and confine; to keep or hold in custody; to imprison. Now somewhat *rare*. 1645. **5.** To make fast or firm 1663. **b.** *Surg.* To close (a vein or artery) by ligature or otherwise, in order to prevent loss of blood 1662. **6.** To get hold or possession of (something desirable) as the result of effort or contrivance 1743.

1. *Oth.* I. iii. 10. 2. A pass..securing me through Brabant and Flanders EVELYN. The hedge-hog, so well secured against all assaults by his prickly hide BURKE. b. The out workes, which secured the suburbs 1645. 3. For he who sings thy Praise, secures his own DRYDEN. 4. Wilson and Robertson,..each secured betwixt two soldiers of the city guard SCOTT. 5. A girdle..secured by a large buckle of gold SCOTT. 6. We took Care to s. some Powder, Ball, and a little Bread 1743. Hence **Secu·rable** *a.* (*rare*) capable of being secured.

Securement (sĭkiūᵊ·ɹmĕnt). *rare.* 1622. [f. SECURE *v.* + -MENT.] The action or an act of securing; ensuring or making sure.

Securi- (sĭkiūᵊ·ri, se:kiŭri·), comb. form of L. *securis* axe, f. *secare* to cut, as in ‖ **Secu·rifer** [L.], *Ent.* one of the *Securifera* or phyllophagous hymenoptera.

Securiform (sĭkiūᵊ·rifǫ̈ɹm), *a.* 1760. [f. SECURI- + -FORM.] Axe-shaped, having the form of an axe or hatchet.

Security (sĭkiūᵊ·rĭti). late ME. [ad. L. *securitas*, f. *securus* SECURE *a.*; see -ITY.] **I.** The condition of being secure. **1.** The condition of being protected from or not exposed to danger; safety. **2.** Freedom from doubt. Now chiefly, well-founded confidence, certainty. 1597. **3.** Freedom from care, anxiety or apprehension; a feeling of safety. *arch.* Formerly often *spec.* culpable absence of anxiety, carelessness. 1555.

1. The emperor and his court enjoyed..the s. of the marshes and fortifications of Ravenna GIBBON. 2. She told Mr. Hall they might count on her with s. C. BRONTE. 3. S. Is Mortals cheefest Enemie SHAKS.

II. A means of being secure. **1.** Something which makes safe; a protection, guard, defence 1586. **2.** Ground for regarding something as secure, safe, or certain; an assurance, guarantee 1623. **3.** Property deposited or made over, or bonds, recognizances, or the like entered into, by or on behalf of a person in order to secure his fulfilment of an obligation, and forfeitable in the event of non-fulfilment 1450. **4.** One who pledges himself (or is pledged) for another, a surety 1597. **5.** A document held by a creditor as guarantee of his right to payment. Hence, any form of investment guaranteed by such documents. Chiefly *pl.* 1690.

1. Concealment was his only s. 1791. A good fire.. was always a perfect s. against..wild beasts 1832. 2. When love is an unerring light, And joy its own s. WORDSW. 3. Phr. *To enter* (*in* or *into*), *find, give* (*in*), *go*, †*put in, take s.*; Being this day summoned ..to give in s. for his good behaviour PEPYS. *transf.* The word of a Gracchus..was his bond; and a bond which was a first-rate s. 1878. 5. Liquid Securities, or in other words, those easily convertible into cash when necessity arises 1879.

Sedan (sĭdæ·n). 1635. [Origin obsc.] **a.** A closed vehicle to seat one person, borne on two poles by two bearers, one in front and one behind. **b.** *transf.* A litter, palanquin, or the like 1646. **c.** A motor car having a single compartment for four or more persons including the driver (*U.S.*) 1915.

Sedan chair. *Hist.* 1615. = prec. a, b.

Sedate (sǐdēⁱ·t), *a.* 1663. [ad. L. *sedatus*, *sedare* to settle, allay, f. root *sed-* as in L. *sedere*; see SIT *v.*] 1. Calm, quiet, composed; cool, sober, collected; undisturbed by passion or excitement. †2. Of physical objects: Quiet; motionless, or smooth and steady in motion –1728.

1. He was..of a s. look, something approaching to gravity STERNE. That s. and clerical bird, the rook DICKENS. Hence **Seda·te·ly**, *adv.*, **-ness.**

Sedation (sǐdēⁱ·ʃən). 1543. [a. F. *sédation*, or ad. L. *sedationem*, f. *sedare*; see prec.] The action of allaying, assuaging, or making calm.

Sedative (se·dătiv), *a.* and *sb.* late ME. [a. F. *sédatif*, or ad. med.L. *sedativus*, f. L. *sedare*; see SEDATE and -IVE.] *Med.* **A.** *adj.* That has the property of allaying, assuaging, or soothing. **B.** *sb.* A sedative medicine 1785.

‖**Se defendendo** (sī dǐfende·ndo). 1548. [Law Latin.] *Law.* 'In self-defence': a plea which if established is held to remove legal guilt from a homicide.

Sedent (sī·děnt), *a.* 1682. [ad. L. *sedentem*, *sedere* to sit.] Of a figure: Sitting.

Sedentary (se·děntări), *a.* and *sb.* 1598. [ad. F. *sédentaire*, ad. L. *sedentarius*, f. *sedentem* SEDENT; see -ARY[1].] **A.** *adj.* 1. Of habits, occupations, etc.: Requiring continuance in a sitting posture 1603. 2. Of persons: Accustomed or addicted to sitting still; engaged in sedentary pursuits; not in the habit of taking physical exercise 1662. †b. Slothful, inactive –1707. 3. Remaining in one place of abode; not migratory. Of a tribunal, assembly, judge, etc.: Established in one place; not ambulatory. Now *rare.* 1598. †b. Of a material thing: Motionless –1787. c. *Zool.* Inhabiting the same region through life; not migratory. Also of mollusca, etc.: Confined to one spot, not locomotory. Of spiders: see B. 1834. †4. Deliberate –1673.

1. If thy life be s., exercise thy body FULLER. 2. S. victims of unhealthy toil 1816. 3. b. While the sedentarie Earth,..attaines Her end without least motion MILT. 4. S. sinnes FULLER.

B. *sb. Zool.* One of a group of spiders (*Sedentariæ*) which take their prey by means of a web in or near which they remain watching 1815. Hence **Se·dentari·ly** *adv.*, **-ness.**

‖**Sederunt** (sǐdīə·rŏnt). *Sc.* 1628. [L., 'there were sitting' (*sc.* the following persons), 3rd pers. pl. perf. ind. of *sedere* to sit, used subst.] 1. A sitting of a deliberative or judicial body; now chiefly of an eccl. assembly. b. *transf.* A sitting for discussion or talk. Also, loosely, a sitting (of a person) at some occupation, over the bottle, or the like. 1825. 2. The list of persons present at a sitting 1701.

1. Phr. *Act of S.* (Sc. Law), an ordinance for regulating the forms of procedure before the Court of Session.

Sede vacante (sī·dǐ vǎkæ·ntǐ). 1535. [L., 'the seat being vacant'.] ‖ 1. *Eccl.* As advb. phr.: During the vacancy of an episcopal see. 2. As *sb.*: The vacancy of a see or seat 1589.

Sedge (sedʒ). [OE. *secg*:—OTeut. **sagjoz*, f. **sag-*; cf. SAW *sb.*[1]] 1. Any of various coarse grassy, rush-like or flag-like plants growing in wet places; also variously applied *spec.*, e. g. to the cyperaceous genera *Carex* and *Cladium*, to the Sweet Flag (*Acorus*) and the Wild Iris (*Iris Pseudacorus*). b. An individual plant or stalk of sedge (*rare*) 1450. c. *Bot.* Formerly, a plant of the genus *Carex*; now usu. in wider sense, a plant of the family *Cyperaceæ* 1785. 2. Short for *s.-fly*. Chiefly *silver s.* 1889.

attrib. and *Comb.*: **s.-fly**, a caddis or may-fly; also, an imitation of this used in fly-fishing; **-warbler**, a small bird, *Acrocephalus schœnobænus*, of the family *Sylviidæ*, common in marshy districts.

Sedged (sedʒd), *a.* 1610. [f. prec. + -ED[2].] †1. Woven with sedge. SHAKS. 2. *Agric.* Of oats: Affected with SEDGING 1844. 3. Bordered with sedge 1866.

3. And what s. brooks are Thames's tributaries M. ARNOLD.

Sedging (se·dʒiŋ). 1820. [f. SEDGE + -ING[1].] *Agric.* A disease incident to oats, characterized by a thickening of the stem near the ground, said to be caused by a grub.

Sedgy (se·dʒi), *a.* 1566. [f. SEDGE + -Y[1].] 1. Covered or bordered with sedge or sedges. 2. Having the nature or properties of sedge 1625. †3. Made of or thatched with sedge –1835.

1. On the gentle Seuernes siedgie banke SHAKS.

‖**Sedile** (sǐdəi·lǐ). *Pl.* **sedilia** (sǐdi·liă). 1793. [L., f. root of *sedere* to sit.] *pl.* A series of seats in a church, usu. three in number, either movable or recessed in the wall and crowned with canopies, pinnacles, etc., usu. placed on the south side of the choir near the altar for the use of the clergy. Rarely *sing.* one of the sedilia.

Sediment (se·dimĕnt), *sb.* 1547. [a. F. *sédiment*, ad. L. *sedimentum*, f. *sedere* to sit, settle.] 1. Matter composed of particles which fall by gravitation to the bottom of a liquid. 2. *spec.* (in *Geol.*, etc.). Earthy or detrital matter deposited by aqueous agency 1684.

2. The snow gradually wasted, but it left its s. behind TYNDALL. Hence **Se·diment** *v. trans.* to deposit as s. **Sedime·ntal** *a.* of the nature of s. (*rare*).

Sedimentary (sedime·ntări), *a.* and *sb.* 1830. [f. prec. + -ARY[1].] **A.** *adj.* 1. Of, pertaining to, or of the nature of sediment 1846. 2. *Geol.* Of rocks, etc.: Formed by the deposition of sediment 1830. **B.** *sb.* A s. formation or deposit 1878.

Sedimentation (se:dimĕntēⁱ·ʃən). 1874. [f. SEDIMENT *sb.* + -ATION.] Deposition of sediment; *spec.* in *Geol.* (see SEDIMENT *sb.* 2).

Sedition (sǐdi·ʃən). [a. OF., ad. L. *seditionem*, f. *sed-* (see SE-) + *itionem* a going, f. *ire* to go.] †1. Violent party strife; an instance of this –1628. 2. a. A concerted movement to overthrow an established government; a revolt, rebellion, mutiny. Now *rare.* 1585. b. Conduct or language inciting to rebellion against the constituted authority in a state 1838.

1. But there would be thoughts of s. in one towards another in the city HOBBES. 2. a. The matter of seditions is of two kindes, Much povertye and much discontent BACON. b. As for s. itself I do not think that any such offence is known to English law 1883. Hence **Sedi·tionary** *sb.* = SEDITIONIST (now *rare*); *adj.* seditious.

Seditionist (sǐdi·ʃənist). 1786. [f. prec. + -IST.] One who practises sedition or incites others to sedition.

Seditious (sǐdi·ʃəs), *a.* 1447. [ad. OF. *seditieux*, ad. L. *seditiosus*, f. *seditionem* SEDITION; see -OUS.] 1. Given to or guilty of sedition; in early use, factious, turbulent; now chiefly, engaged in promoting disaffection or inciting to revolt against constituted authority. b. *absol.* Seditious persons 1535. 2. Of, pertaining to, or of the nature of sedition; tending to incite to or provoke sedition 1455.

1. That sedicious and wicked cite COVERDALE 1 *Esdras* iv. 12. An illegal or possibly s. club 1908. 2. He had made sedicious sermons 1560. S. words, s. libels, and s. conspiracies 1883. Hence **Sedi·tious·ly** *adv.*, **-ness.**

Seduce (sǐdiū·s), *v.* 1477. [ad. L. *seducere* to lead aside or away, f. *se-* SE- + *ducere.*] 1. *trans.* To persuade (a vassal, servant, soldier, etc.) to desert his allegiance or service. 2. To lead (a person) astray in conduct or belief; to tempt, entice, or beguile *to do* something wrong, foolish, or unintended 1519. 3. To induce (a woman) to surrender her chastity 1560. 4. To decoy (*from* or *to* a place); to lead astray (*into*). *Obs.* exc. with notion of sense 2. 1668.

1. Suttle he needs must be, who could s. Angels MILT. 2. For me, the Gold of France did not s. SHAKS. He is seduced into a life of pleasure 1875. Hence **Sedu·ceable**, **Sedu·cible** *a.*

Seducement (sǐdiū·smĕnt). *Obs.* or *rare.* 1586. [f. prec. + -MENT.] 1. The action of seducing. 2. Something which seduces; an insidious temptation 1644. 3. The fact or condition of being seduced 1605.

Seducer (sǐdiū·səɹ). 1545. [f. as prec. + -ER[1].] One who or something which seduces; *esp.* one who seduces a woman.

He, whose firm faith no reason could remove, Will melt before that soft s., love DRYDEN.

Seducing (sǐdiū·siŋ), *ppl. a.* 1575. [f. SEDUCE *v.* + -ING[2].] That seduces. 1. Tempting to evil. 2. Alluring, attractive, 'bewitching'. (Cf. F. *séduisant.*) Now *rare.* 1748.

2. Well, it is very s. to be pitied, after all SCOTT. Hence **Sedu·cingly** *adv.*

Seduction (sǐdɒ·kʃən). 1526. [a. F. *séduction* or ad. L. *seductionem*, f. *seducere* SEDUCE *v.*] 1. The action or an act of seducing (a person) to err in conduct or belief. †b. The condition of being led astray –1653. 2. The action of inducing (a woman) to surrender her chastity 1785. 3. Something which seduces; a cause of error; an allurement 1554.

3. Surrounded by all the seductions most dazzling to youth 1838.

Seductive (sǐdɒ·ktiv), *a.* 1771. [f. L. *seduct-*, *seducere* SEDUCE *v.*; see -IVE.] †1. Tending to lead astray –1782. 2. Alluring, enticing, winning 1771.

2. The s. pleasures of opium-eating 1871. Hence **Sedu·ctive·ly** *adv.*, **-ness.**

Seductress (sǐdɒ·ktrĕs). 1803. [f. †*seductor* (a. OF., F. *séducteur*, ad. L. *seductor*) + -ESS[1].] A female seducer.

Sedulity (sǐdiū·lĭti). 1542. [ad. L. *sedulitas*, f. *sedulus* SEDULOUS; see -ITY.] The quality of being sedulous; painstaking attention to duty, diligent application, industry. †b. *pl.* Assiduities, attentions –1707.

I stood amazed at his s. and memory EVELYN.

Sedulous (se·diŭləs), *a.* 1540. [f. L. *sedulus* + -OUS.] 1. Diligent, active, constant in application to the matter in hand; assiduous, persistent 1593. 2. Of actions: Constant, persistent 1540.

1. He was s. in paying court to the people 1836. 2. He paid s. attention to the interests of his borough 1833. Hence **Se·dulous·ly** *adv.*, **-ness.**

‖**Sedum** (sī·dŏm). 1440. [L., houseleek.] †a. Any of certain crassulaceous plants, houseleek, stonecrop, orpine, etc. b. *Bot.* A genus of plants (family *Crassulaceæ*), the British species of which are known as stonecrop.

See (sī), *sb.* ME. [a. OF. *sé*, *sed*, var. of *sié*, *sied*:—pop. L. **sēdem*, altered f. cl. L. *sēdem* seat.] 1. A seat, place of sitting. †a. A seat of dignity or authority; esp. a royal seat, throne. Hence the rank or position symbolized by a throne. –1590. †b. *transf.* and *fig.* (One's) place of abode –1596. 2. a. The seat, chair, or throne of a bishop in his church. Now only *arch.* ME. b. The office or position indicated by sitting in a particular episcopal chair; the position of being bishop of a particular diocese 1450. c. *spec.* (Chiefly with defining word, e. g. *Apostolic*, *Holy*.) The office or position of Pope; the Papacy; the authority or jurisdiction belonging to the Pope; occas. the Pope in his official capacity ME. †d. A city in which the authority symbolized by the throne (of a bishop, etc.) is considered to reside –1757.

1. a. Ioue laught on Venus from his soueraigne s. SPENSER.

See (sī), *v.* Pa. t. **saw** (sǭ); pa. pple. **seen** (sīn). [Com. Teut. str. vb.; OE. *séon*, derived from pre-Teut. **seqᵘ-*, of disputed relationship.] 1. *trans.* To perceive (light, colour, external objects and their movements) with the eyes, or by the sense of which the eye is the specific organ. b. predicated of the eye ME. c. To behold (visual objects) in imagination, or in a dream or vision ME. d. With sb. or pron. and inf. or compl. as obj. OE. 2. *absol.* and *intr.* To perceive objects by sight. Formerly often, to have the faculty of sight, not to be blind. ME. 3. (*fig.*) *trans.* To perceive mentally; to apprehend by thought (a truth, etc.), to recognize the force of (a demonstration). Often with ref. to metaphorical light or eyes. ME. b. In literary use, expressions like 'we have seen', 'we shall s.', etc. are common with ref. to what has been or is to be narrated or proved in the book. late ME. c. *absol.* Often with virtual ellipsis of obj.-clause, esp. in parenthetic use, or preceded by *as* or *so* ME. d. *trans.* To perceive, apprehend, or appreciate in a particular manner. Also *absol.* esp. in *to s. with* = to agree in opinion with another person. 1586. 4. *trans.* With mixed literal and fig. sense: To perceive by visual tokens ME. b. To learn by reading. late ME. 5. To direct the sight (literal or metaphorical) intentionally to; to look at, contemplate, examine, inspect, or scrutinize; to visit (a place); to attend (a play, etc.) as a spectator ME. b. To look at, read (a book, document, etc.). Now chiefly in certain formulæ (see below). ME. c. The imper. *see* is used in books to refer to a passage elsewhere in which information will be found 1608. **d.** The imper. is often employed exclamatorily: = Behold! OE. **6.** With indirect question as obj.: To ascertain by inspection, inquiry, experiment, or consideration. Also *absol.* late ME. **b.** To make sure by inspection *that* certain conditions exist 1440. **7.** With adv. or phrase: To escort (a person) *home, to the door*, etc. 1607. **8.** To ensure by supervision or vigilance that something shall be done or not done ME. **b.** Coupled by *and* with another verb: To be careful to (do something) *colloq.* 1766. **9.** To view or regard as, to judge, deem ME. **10.** To know by observation (ocular and other), to witness; to meet with in the course of one's experience; to have personal knowledge of; to be living at (a certain period of time) OE. **b.** With clause, obj. and inf., or obj. and complement: To observe, find. Also (chiefly in the future tense), to find, to come to know in the course of events. Often *absol.* late ME. **c.** Willingness (or unwillingness) *to s.* an event is often predicated as equivalent to willingness (or unwillingness) that the event should occur. Hence, occas. = to allow (something to happen). late ME. **d.** *transf.* Of things, places, etc.: To be contemporary with and in the neighbourhood of, to be the scene of (an event); to be in existence during (a period of time). Also of a period of time: To be marked by (an event). 1739. **11.** To experience in one's own person; to undergo, enjoy, or suffer. Now *rare.* OE. **12.** To be in the company of, to meet and converse with (a person) ME. **b.** To obtain an interview with, call upon, or meet in order to consult or confer with, give directions to or receive directions from. In U.S. *colloq.* 'To interview or consult in order to influence, esp. improperly, as in order to bribe'. 1782. **c.** To receive as a visitor; to admit to an interview 1500. **†d.** absol. *To s.* (*together*): to meet one another –1613. **13.** *Gaming.* To meet (a bet), or meet the bet of (another player), by staking an equal sum. Now chiefly in *Poker.* 1599. **14.** *Mil.* Of a fortification, artillery, etc.: To command or dominate (a position) 1829.

1. The other Comet could be seen with the naked eye 1665. Phr. *To s. double*, to s. two objects where only one exists, esp. as a sign of drunkenness. *To s. the red light*, to see danger ahead; to take fright. *To s. the back of*, to be rid of (an unwelcome visitor, etc.); so *to s. the last of. To s. things* (colloq.), to have hallucinations. *To s. the light, red, one's way*: see the associated words. *To s. daylight* or *light*, to have a clear perception of things. **c.** Phr. *To s. a vision.* **d.** I saw the tears start from his eyes 1779. I say what I saw done SWINBURNE. **2.** I write and read till I can't s., and then I walk 1712. So drunk that he could not s. FIELDING. There are no ears to hear, or eyes to s. KEATS. **3.** She saw nothing before her but distress and misery 1825. I see that you are speaking your mind 1875. Why didn't you tell Geoffrey you didn't s. the good of sending so many? 1888. **b.** What..the English did will be seen later on KIPLING. **c.** Look'ee Serjeant, no Coaxing, no Wheedling, d'ye s. FARQUHAR. *I s.*, often used *colloq.* in assenting to an explanation or argument. *You s.*, sometimes appended parenthetically to a statement of a fact known to the hearer, which explains or excuses something that provokes surprise or blame. **d.** Thou..dost neuer s. me as I am SIDNEY. Phr. *To s. eye to eye*: see EYE *sb.*[2] I. 4. **4.** Don't you s. I am tired to death? 1765. She was never seen angry but twice or thrice in her life THACKERAY. **b.** Did you s. her death in the paper? THACKERAY. **5.** The finish was one worth going miles to s. 1878. We have trotted about,..and seen the sights 1881. **b.** No man would advance money upon an estate without seeing the title deeds 1818. *Seen and allowed, seen and approved*, etc., a formula used in certifying the official inspection of a document. **d.** But s., the evening star comes forth! WORDSW. **6.** I am just going to ride out to s. if air and exercise will get me a stomach 1766. *absol.* Ah, something terrible has happened! I must run and s.! HAWTHORNE. **7.** We saw the ladies into the brougham 1888. *To s.* (a person) *off*, to be present at (his) starting for a journey; used *imper.* to a dog to urge him to scare a person away. *To s.* (a book) *through the press.* **8.** It behoves us to s. that we are not outstripped by our rivals abroad 1884. **b.** If you get your letters ready.., I will s. and get them franked 1825. **9.** Others may doe as they s. good 1663. **10.** I never saw his equal for pluck and daring THACKERAY. Phr. *To s. life, the world*, to acquire experience of the activities or pleasures of human existence. *To have seen better days*, to have been formerly better off than now. *To have seen one's day, one's best days*, to be no longer in one's prime. **b.** At length he came to a resolution..to 'wait and s.' what would turn up for the best 1825. See also WAIT *v.* **c.** Phr. *I'll s. him hanged* (*damned, further*, etc.) *first* (colloq.). **d.** Eighteen rivers have seen their navigation improved 1849. **11.** Remember, my sonne, that shee saw many dangers for thee *Tobit* iv. 4. They s. A happy youth, and their old age Is beautiful and free WORDSW. *To have seen service*: see SERVICE[1] II. 6 b. **12.** Phr. *To go* or *come to* (or *and*) *s.*, to visit, call upon. *To s. much* or *little of* (a person), to be often or seldom in his society; He saw little of any Whigs MACAULAY. **b.** I want him to come and s. a physician about the illness of which he spoke to me 1875. **c.** My master is just going to dinner, and can't s. anybody now 1802. **d.** *Cymb.* I. i. 124.

Phr. *Let me s., let us s.*, indicating that the speaker is trying to recall something to memory, or finds it necessary to reflect before answering a question. (*Fair*, etc.) *to see*, in visible aspect.

Phraseological combs. *with preps. **See about —.** To attend to; to take steps with reference to; also, to see what can be done with regard to. *I'll s. about it*, often used *colloq.* to evade giving an immediate decision. **S. into —.** To perceive (by physical or mental sight) what is below the surface of. **†S. on, upon —.** To look on, look at. **S. through —.** To s. objects on the other side of (an aperture, or something transparent). Hence *fig.*, to penetrate (a disguise, fallacious appearance), to detect an imposture), to perceive the real character or aims of (a person). Phr. *To s. through a brick wall*, to have abnormal acuteness. **S. to —. a.** To attend to, do what is needful for; to provide for the wants of; to charge oneself with (a duty, a business). **b.** To take special care about (a matter). **with advs. **S. out. a.** To survive. **b.** In a drinking contest, to outlast. **c.** To go through with to the end. **S. through.** To continue to watch or take part in (a matter) until the end; to take care that (a person) comes successfully through his difficulties.

See-bright (sī·brəit). 1863. [f. SEE *v.* + BRIGHT *a.* A rendering of *clear-eye*, perversion of *clary*.] = CLARY *sb.*[2]

Seed (sīd), *sb.* [OE. *sǣd* :—OTeut. **sǣdi-, sǣdo-*, f. root **sǣ-* to SOW.] **1. a.** That which is or may be sown; the (ripe) ovules of a plant or plants, esp. as collected for the purpose of being sown. Also, *Agric.* and *Hort.*, applied to other parts of plants (e.g. tubers, bulbs) when preserved for the purpose of propagating a new crop. In *pl.*, kinds of seed. **b.** An individual grain of seed. In *Bot.*, restricted to the fertilized ovule of a phanerogam, but pop. applied also to the 'spore' of a cryptogam, etc. OE. **c.** *pl.* (*a*) Land sown with corn. (*b*) Clover and 'artificial' grasses raised from seed. 1794. **d.** *collect. sing.* and *pl.* Various kinds of grain suitable as the food of a cage-bird 1897. **2.** *fig.* The germ or latent beginning of some growth or development. Also, with ref. to the Parable of the Sower, applied to religious or other teaching, viewed with regard to its degree of fruitfulness. OE. **3.** = SEMEN. Now *rare.* ME. **4.** Offspring, progeny. Now *rare* exc. in Biblical phraseology. OE. **5. a.** *sing.* and *pl.* The ova of the lobster and of the silkworm moth 1620. **b.** Oyster-spat 1721.

1. Every herb bearing s. *Gen.* i. 29. Phr. *To run to s.* (see RUN *v.*[2]); also *†to grow to s., be in s.*; Oh fie, fie, 'tis an vnweeded Garden That growes to S. SHAKS. **b.** Like the dry remnant of a garden flower Whose seeds are shed WORDSW. **2.** Yet then likewise the wicked seede of vice Began to spring SPENSER. The seeds of knowledge may be planted in solitude, but must be cultivated in publick JOHNSON. **4.** His s. shal bycome faderles in straunge lond CAXTON.

attrib. and *Comb.*: **s.-bed**, a bed for sowing seeds; the seedlings growing there; **-box,** (*a*) the receptacle for the s. in a grain-sowing-machine; (*b*) *U.S.* a plant of the genus *Ludwigia* (from its cubical pod); **-bud,** *Bot.* the lower part of the pistil; the rudiment of the s.-vessel or the embryo fruit; **-coat,** *Bot.* = TESTA; **-cotton,** cotton in its native state, with the seed not separated; **-eater, -feeder,** any granivorous bird, *spec.* the Grass-quit, *Phonifara bicolor*; **-field,** a field where s. is sown; **-lac,** resin broken off the twigs of trees and triturated with water; **-leaf, -lobe,** = COTYLEDON 3; **-pan,** a pan of red earthenware used for the raising of plants from seed; **-plant,** (*a*) a plant grown from seed, a seedling; (*b*) a plant grown for its seed; **-plot** = *s.-bed* (now only *transf.* and *fig.*); **-snipe,** a bird of the S. Amer. genus *Thinocorys*; **-tick,** a mite of the family *Ixodidæ*; **-vessel** = PERICARP; **-weed,** a weed that propagates itself by seeding. Hence **See·dless** *a.* devoid of s. or seeds.

Seed (sīd), *v.* late ME. [f. prec.] **I.** *intr.* To produce seed; to run to seed. †Also occas. *pass.* **b.** To develop *into* something undesirable 1898.

First doe we bud, then blow; next s., last fall 1600.

II. *trans.* **1.** To sow (land) with seed 1440. **2.** To sow (a particular kind of seed) upon land 1560. **†3.** To sprinkle or cover a surface lightly with; so, to decorate the material of a garment with powdering of small ornament –1678. **4.** To remove the seeds from (fruit), to 'stone' 1904. **5.** *Lawn Tennis*, etc. To place the names of selected players in a tournament in certain places in an order of names otherwise decided by lot, so as to ensure that those players shall not meet in an early stage of the tournament (orig. *U.S.*) 1911.

1. He giues them also Wheat to s. their land 1598. Phr. *To s. down*, to sow grass or clover seeds amongst (a crop of oats, wheat, etc.). **3.** Theosophia,..all in white, a blue mantle seeded with starres B. JONS.

See·d-cake. 1573. A sweet cake flavoured with caraway seeds.

See·d-corn. 1592. Grain (*occas.* a grain of corn) for sowing in order to produce a new crop.

Seeder (sī·dəɹ). [OE. *sǣdere*, f. *sǣd* SEED *sb.*; see -ER[1].] **†1.** One who sows seed; a sower –1500. **2.** A mechanical contrivance for sowing seed 1875.

Seedling (sī·dliŋ), *sb.* and *a.* 1660. [f. SEED *sb.* + -LING[1].] **A.** *sb.* **1.** A young plant developed from a seed, esp. one raised from seed as dist. from a slip, cutting, etc. **2.** A small seed 1809.

2. Not so much as the shadow, hint, or merest s. of a kiss HARDY.

B. *adj.* **1.** Developed or raised from seed 1683. **2.** Of the nature of a small seed; existing in a rudimentary state 1886. **3.** Of oysters: Hatched from 'seed' 1862.

2. He saw that I..had some s. brains which would come up in time RUSKIN.

Seed-lip (sī·dlip). [OE. *sǣdlēap*; see SEED *sb.* and LEAP *sb.*[2]] A basket in which seed is carried in the process of sowing by hand.

†See·dness. 1440. [f. SEED *v.* + -NESS.] The action of sowing or state of being sown –1710.

Seed-pearl (sī·dpɔ̄ɹl). 1551. [f. SEED *sb.*] A minute pearl having the appearance of a seed, usu. drilled and fastened to some material to be worn as an ornament.

Bracelets of braided Hair, Pomander, and Seed-Pearl STEELE.

Seedsman (sī·dzmǣn). 1592. [f. genitive of SEED *sb.* + MAN *sb.*] **1.** A sower of seed. **2.** A dealer in seed 1691.

Seed-time (sī·d,təim). late ME. [f. SEED *sb.* + TIME *sb.*] The season of sowing seed.

While the earth remaineth, seed-time and haruest ..shall not cease *Gen.* viii. 22.

Seedy (sī·di), *a.* 1574. [f. SEED *sb.* + -Y[1].] **1.** Abounding in seed, full of seed. **2.** Shabby, ill-looking (like a flowering plant that has run to seed) 1739. **b.** Unwell, poorly, 'not up to the mark' 1858. **3.** *Glass-making.* Containing minute bubbles 1856.

2. A s. (poor) half-pay Captain 1739. **b.** This morning I was very dull and s. DICKENS.

Comb.: **s.-toe,** a diseased condition of a horse's foot. Hence **See·di·ly** *adv.*, **-ness.**

Seeing (sī·iŋ), quasi-*conj.* 1503. [orig. pres. pple. of SEE *v.*] *S.* (*that*): Considering the fact that; inasmuch as; since, because.

As towching the house of the Charterhouse I pray.. that it may be turned into a better use (s. it is in the face of the world) CRANMER.

Seek, *sb.* 1500. [f. next.] A series of notes upon a horn calling out hounds to begin a chase. Usu. *to blow a s.* –1826.

Seek (sīk), *v.* Pa. t. and pa. pple. **sought** (sǭt). [Com. Teut. wk. vb.; OE. *sēcan, sōhte*, f. OTeut. **sōk-* :—pre-Teut. **sāg-*; cf. L. *sagire* to perceive by scent, Gr. ἡγεῖσθαι to lead. The normal representative of OE. *sēcan* is dial. *seech* (cf. BESEECH).] **I.** *trans.* **1.** To go in search or quest of; to try to find, look for. **2.** To try to discover or find out. Also with *out, up.* Now *rare* or *Obs.* OE. **3.** To go to, visit, resort to (a place). *arch.* OE. **†4.** To come or go to (a person) in order to see or visit him; to resort to (for help, or the like) –1538. **b.** *spec.* To approach, draw near to (God), in prayer, etc. [A Hebraism.] OE. **†5.** To pursue with hostile intention; to go to attack, advance against; to persecute, harass, afflict –1606. **6.** To try to obtain; to try to bring about or effect. Also with *out.* OE. **7.** To ask for, demand, request (*from* a person); to inquire OE. **b.** *pass.* To be courted, to be 'in request' as a companion. Of a woman: To be wooed or asked in marriage. 1671. **8.** To search, explore (a place) in order to find something ME. †**b.** With immaterial obj.: To examine, investigate, scrutinize; to try, test -1611. **9.** To make it one's aim, to try or attempt *to* (do something) OE.

1. I will go seeke Some Ditch, wherein to dye SHAKS. Other persons should be sought who can do the necessary business with more skill BURKE. Phr. *To s. dead*, chiefly in the imper., as an order given to a dog to seek and retrieve killed game. 2. Now let vs on, my Lords,..And seeke how we may preiudice the Foe SHAKS. Its cause must be sought in the state..of the atmosphere 1803. 3. †*To. s. a saint*, etc., to visit his shrine; To Caunturbury they wende The hooly blisful martir for to seke CHAUCER. 4. b. O God..early wil I seke the COVERDALE *Ps.* lxii[i]. 5. *Ant. & Cl.* II. ii. 161. 6. She sought consolation in district visiting 1908. 7. I will seeke satisfaction of you SHAKS. b. His daughter, sought by many Prowest Knights MILT. 8. b. *Cymb.* IV. ii. 160. 9. He sought to drown his sorrow for the defeat in floods of beer THACKERAY.

II. *intr.* **1.** *absol.* To make search OE. **2.** To go, resort, pay a visit (*to, unto* a person, *to, into* a place). *Obs.* exc. *arch.* ME. **b.** To apply, have recourse *to* or *unto* (a person, *for* something); to pay court, make request or petition *to*. *Obs.* exc. *arch.* late ME. †**c.** To resort to (a remedy, means of help) -1819.

1. Yf ȝe wyll haue hym, goo, & syke, syke, syke! 1450. *To have far to s.*: cf. III. 1. 2. Wisdoms self Oft seeks to sweet retired Solitude MILT. b. You have been sought to by some of the first Families in the Nation, for your Alliance RICHARDSON. c. S. to prayer and penance SCOTT.

Phr. **S. after** —. To go in quest of, look for; to try to find, reach, or obtain. Now chiefly in passive: To be desired or in demand; to be courted, to have one's presence desired. **S. for** —. (= I. 1, 2, 5.) †**S. on, upon** —. a. To set on, attack, assail. b. To approach, (a person) in order to obtain something.

III. Uses of the infinitive *to seek*. **1.** Not to be found or not yet found, not at hand, absent, missing, lacking. *Far to s.*, far out of reach, a long way off. late ME. **b.** With neg.: Not hard to find, not absent or wanting. Also *not far to s.* late ME. **2.** Of a person, his faculties, etc.: **a.** At a loss or at fault; unable to act, understand, etc.; puzzled to know or decide. *Obs.* or *arch.* late ME. **b.** Wanting or deficient *in*; without skill or learning *in*. With *for*: At a loss for, unable to find. *arch.* 1522.

Comb.: **s.-no-farther, -further**, a kind of apple.

Seeker (sī·kəɹ). ME. [f. SEEK *v.* + -ER [1].] **1.** One who seeks. **b.** *Eccl. Hist.* (With capital S.) As the designation assumed by a class of sectaries in the 16-17th c., who professed to be seeking the true church, etc. 1645. **2.** An instrument used in seeking or searching 1658.

†**Seel**, *v.*[1] 1618. [Origin obsc.] *Naut. intr.* Of a ship: To make a sudden lurch to one side -1753. Hence †**Seel** *sb.* -1753.

Seel (sīl), *v.*[2] 1500. [Later f. *sile*, ad. OF. *ciller*, f. *cil* eyelash.] **1.** *trans.* To close the eyes of (a hawk or other bird) by stitching up the eyelids with a thread tied behind the head; chiefly used as part of the taming process in falconry. Also, to stitch *up* (the eyes of a bird). **2.** *transf.* To close (a person's eyes). Also *fig.* to make blind, hoodwink. 1591.

2. Shee that so young could giue out such a Seeming To seele her Fathers eyes vp SHAKS.

Seely (sī·li), *a.* *Obs.* exc. *dial.* [Com. WGer.; OE. *sǣliʒ:—OTeut. *sǣligo-, f. *sǣliz luck, happiness. See SILLY.] **1.** Happy, blissful; fortunate, lucky, well-omened, auspicious. **2.** Spiritually blessed; pious, holy, good ME. **3.** Innocent, harmless ME. **4.** Deserving of pity or sympathy; miserable; helpless, defenceless ME. **5.** Insignificant; mean, poor; feeble ME. **7.** Foolish, simple, silly 1529.

Seem (sīm), *v.* [ME. *seme*, a. ON. *sǿma*, f. *sǿmr* fitting, seemly.] †**I.** quasi-*trans.* with obj. orig. dative. To be suitable to, befit, beseem. Also *absol.* -1615.

For it seemeth much in a King, if..he can take hold of any superficiall Ornaments and shewes of learning BACON.

II. *intr.* To have a semblance or appearance. **As personal verb.* **1.** To appear to be, to be apparently (what is expressed by the complement) ME. **2.** With *inf.*: To appear *to be* or *to do* something ME. **b.** In mod. use, the combination of *seems* with an inf. often = the finite verb qualified by 'probably', 'if the evidence may be trusted' 1841. **c.** To appear to oneself; to imagine oneself, or think one perceives oneself, *to do* something 1638. **3.** To appear to exist or to be present. Chiefly in *there seems* (followed by the subject); otherwise *poet.* or *rhet.* Also, *there seems to be*. late ME.

1. As the mone lyght, Ageyn whom all the sterres semen But smale candels CHAUCER. A silly rogue, but one that would seem a gentleman PEPYS. 2. The Parian Marble, there, shall s. to move, In breathing Statues DRYDEN. Young women are not the angels they s. to be 1756. b. Sicily seems to contain no iron 1841. c. I s. again to share thy smile, I s. to hang upon thy tone SHELLEY. 3. There seemed a general consensus of opinion that inventors were a nuisance 1883.

***Impersonal uses.* **1.** *It seems.* **a.** It appears, it is apparently true (*that*); it is seen (*that*). Also followed by *as if, as though*. ME. **b.** Used parenthetically. Often = 'So I am informed', or 'As it appears from rumour or report'. late ME. **c.** *It should s., it would s.*: expressing more of hesitation or uncertainty than *it seems*. late ME. **2.** The *it* of the impersonal verb is sometimes omitted ME.

1. It seemes to mee, That yet we sleepe, we dreame SHAKS. It seems I must remit seeing you 1687. Phr. *It seems so, so it seems* = 'it seems that it is so'. b. There is still, however, it seems, a hope for mankind MACAULAY. c. From all this it would s. that he could not have been much under fifty when he was compelled to abjure 1902. 2. Her seemed she scarce had been a day One of God's choristers D. G. ROSSETTI. If he did so, as seems likely enough, it was excusable (*mod.*).

†**III.** *trans.* To think, deem. *To s. good* = to think good. -1627. **b.** To think fit -1610.

It was a Fairye, as al the peple semed CHAUCER. Hence **See·mer**, one who seems, or makes a pretence or show.

Seeming (sī·miŋ), *vbl. sb.* late ME. [-ING [1].] The action of SEEM *v.* **1.** The action or fact of appearing to be. **2.** The form in which a person or thing seems or appears; look, aspect. late ME. **3.** External appearance considered as deceptive, or as distinguished from reality; an illusion, a semblance 1576.

1. The events which are the most threatening in their s., speak to us of hope 1845. Phr. *In s., in all s.*, to all appearance. †*To (my) s.*, as (I) think. 2. Your behaviour is above your s. H. WALPOLE.

Seeming (sī·miŋ), *ppl. a.* ME. [-ING [2].] That seems. †**1.** Suitable, beseeming; according -1687. **2.** Apparent to the senses or to the mind, as distinct from what *is* ME. **3.** Used advb. (often hyphened) with other adjs. = next 2. 1590.

2. A s. Widow, and a secret Bride DRYDEN. 3. With chaunge of cheare the s. simple maid Let fall her eyen SPENSER. Hence **See·mingness**, unreal pretence, plausibility; s. existence or presence.

Seemingly (sī·miŋli), *adv.* 1483. [f. prec. + -LY [2].] **1.** Fittingly, becomingly. Now *rare*. **2.** To external appearance, apparently 1598. **3.** So far as it appears from the evidence; so far as one can judge from circumstances 1715. **b.** *parenthetically*. As it seems 1702.

2. Now the City-Dame was so well bred, as s. to take All in Good Part 1692.

See·mless, *a.* *Obs.* exc. *arch.* 1596. [f. SEEM *v.* (assumed to be the source of SEEMLY *a.*) + -LESS.] Unseemly; shameful; unfitting.

Seemly (sī·mli), *a.* [ME. a. ON. *sǿmiligr*, f. *sǿmr* becoming; see SEEM *v.* and -LY [1].] **1.** Of a pleasing or goodly appearance, fair, well-formed, handsome. *Obs.* exc. *dial.* **2.** Of things: Pleasant (*esp.* to the sight); handsome in appearance; of fine or stately proportion ME. **3.** Of conduct, speech, appearance: Conformable to propriety or good taste; becoming, decorous ME. †**4.** Appropriate -1634.

1. She is nothing so Fayre as she hathe bene reportyd, howbeit she is well and semelye CROMWELL. 2. Their gownes..white or of other seemlie colour 1585. 3. That our liues be honest and semely, not dissolute and lawlesse 1579. 4. Delight is not seemely for a foole *Prov.* xix. 10. Hence **See·mlihead**, (*arch.*) seemliness. †**See·mli·ly** *adv.*, **-ness**.

Seemly (sī·mli), *adv.* ME. [a. ON. *sǿmiliga*, f. *sǿmr*; see prec. and -LY [2].] **1.** In a pleasing manner; so as to present a fair, handsome, or stately appearance. Now *arch.* **2.** Fittingly, appropriately; becomingly ME.

1. A man before him stood, Not rustic as before, but seemlier clad MILT.

Seen (sīn), *ppl. a.* late ME. [pa. pple. of SEE *v.*] **1.** In senses of the verb. Now *rare* exc. in antithesis with *unseen*. **2.** *To be (well, ill*, etc.) *s.*: to be (well, ill, etc.) versed *in* some art or science. Now *arch.* 1528. (See also WELL-SEEN.)

2. A schoole-master Well seene in Musicke SHAKS. Men of mature yeares, and seene in the warres 1620.

Seep (sīp), *v.* *dial.* and *U.S.* 1790. [perh. repr. OE. *sipian*; see SIPE *v.*] *intr.* = SIPE *v.* So **Seep** *sb.* moisture that seeps out; a small spring; *U.S.* a place where petroleum oozes out slowly. **See·py** *a.* *U.S.* badly drained.

Seepage (sī·pėdʒ). *dial.* and *U.S.* 1825. [f. prec. + -AGE.] Percolation or oozing of water or fluid; leakage; also, that which oozes.

Seer [1] (sīᵊɹ, in sense 1 also sī·əɹ). late ME. [f. SEE *v.* + -ER [1].] **1.** *gen.* One who sees (*rare*). **2.** One to whom divine revelations are made in visions. In mod. use occas. *transf.*, one gifted with profound spiritual insight. late ME. **3.** A magician; one who has the power of second sight. Also a crystal-gazer, a scryer. 1661.

1. Strangers & seldome seers feel the beauty of them more than you who dwell with them JER. TAYLOR. Hence **See·ress**, a female s. **See·rship**, the office or function of a s.

‖ **Seer** [2] (sīᵊɹ). *Anglo-Ind.* *Pl.* **seer, seers.** 1618. [Hindī *ser*.] A denomination of weight varying in different parts of India from over 3 lb. to 8 ounces (usu. = 2 lb.). As a measure of capacity = a litre, or 1·76 pints.

Seer-fish: see SEIR-FISH.

Seersucker (sīᵊ·ɹsɒkəɹ). 1757. [E. Indian corruption of Pers. *shīr o shakkar* lit. 'milk and sugar', transf. 'a striped linen garment'.] A thin linen, occas. cotton, fabric of Indian manufacture, striped and having a crapy surface. Now chiefly applied to imitations made in the U.S.

See-saw, *int.*, *sb.*, and *a.* 1640. [A reduplicating formation symbolic of alternating movement.] **A.** *int.* (sī·sǭ·) Used as part of a rhythmical jingle, app. sung by sawyers, or by children imitating them at their work. Hence in nursery songs. **B.** *sb.* (sī·sǭ) **1.** The motion of going up one moment and down the next, or of swaying backwards and forwards. Also, a child's amusement in which children sit one or more at each end of a board or piece of timber balanced so that the ends move alternately up and down. 1704. **b.** *Whist.* = CROSS-RUFF 2. 1746. **2.** A plank arranged for playing see-saw 1824. **C.** *adj.* (sī·sǭ) Moving up and down, or backwards and forwards, in the manner of a see-saw. Also *fig.* 1735.

His wit all s., between *that* and *this*, Now high, now low, now master up, now miss POPE.

See-saw, *v.* 1712. [f. SEE-SAW *sb.*] **1.** *intr.* **a.** To move up and down, or backwards and forwards; to undergo a see-saw motion; also to play see-saw. **2.** *trans.* To cause to move in a see-saw motion 1801.

2. He ponders, he see-saws himself to and fro LYTTON.

Seethe (sīð), *v.* Pa. t. **seethed**, †**sod.** Pa. pple. **seethed**, †**sodden.** [Com. Teut. str. vb.; OE. *sēoðan*, f. OTeut. root **seuþ-*.] **1.** *trans.* To boil; to make or keep boiling hot; to subject to the action of boiling liquid; *esp.* to cook (food) by boiling or stewing; also, to make an infusion or decoction of (a substance) by boiling or stewing. *Obs.* or *arch.* **2.** *intr.* (for passive). To be boiled; to be subjected to boiling or stewing; to become boiling hot. ME. **3.** *trans.* To reduce to a condition resembling that of food which has lost its flavour or crispness by boiling or stewing; to soak or steep in a liquid; to dissipate the vitality or freshness of (the brain, blood, spirits, etc.) by excessive heat or by intoxicating liquor. Chiefly *pass.* 1599. **4.** *intr.* (transf. from 2). Of a liquid, vapour, etc: To rise, surge or foam up, as if boiling; to form bubbles or foam 1535. **5.** *fig.* To be in a state of inward agitation, turmoil, or 'ferment' 1606.

1. Cold meat, seethed, Italian fashion, in nauseous oil 1835. 2. The water begins to seeth 1801. 3. They drown their wits, seeth their brains in ale BURTON. 5. The city had all through the interval been seething with discontent 1874. Hence **Seethe** *sb.* seething, ebullition; intense commotion or heat. **See·thingly** *adv.*

Sefton (se·ftən). 1885. [From the title of the Earl of *Sefton*.] A form of landau.

Segment (se·gmĕnt), *sb.* 1570. [ad. L. *segmentum*, f. *sec-*, *secare* to cut; see -MENT.] **1.** A piece cut or broken off; a fragment (*rare*) 1586. **2.** *Geom.* A plane figure contained by a right line and a portion of the circumference of a circle. In full *s. of a circle*. 1570. **b.** A segmental portion of anything having a circular or spherical form 1646. **3.** *Geom.* The finite part of a line between two points; a division of a line 1617. **b.** *Acoustics.* Each of the portions into which the length of a vibrating string, wire, etc. is divided by the nodes 1863. **4.** Each of the parts into which a thing is or may be divided; a division, section 1762. **5.** *Bot.* Each of the portions into which a leaf or other plant-organ is divided by long clefts or incisions 1713. **6.** *Biol.* and *Embryol.* **a.** Each of the longitudinal divisions composing the body in some animals, esp. in the Articulata; a somite, metamere 1826. **b.** A cell formed by segmentation 1862. **7.** *Anat.* Each complete series of bones forming a vertebra of the spinal column; also, each of the three annular divisions of the cranium proper 1844. **b.** A division of the spinal cord and nerves 1855. **8.** = *s.* (or SEGMENTAL) *arch.* 1836.

2. *S. of a sphere*, a solid figure bounded by a portion of the surface of a sphere and an intersecting plane. **4.** Being unable to divide the orange into its segments, he ventures upon a great liquid bite 1847.

attrib. and *Comb.*, with the meaning SEGMENTAL (sense 1), esp. in the names of mechanical appliances, parts of machinery, etc., indicating the shape of the essential or working part, *s.-arch*, *-roof*, *vault*; *s.-gear*, *-valve*, *-wheel*, etc.

Segment (se·gmĕnt), *v.* 1859. [f. prec.] **1.** *trans.* To subject to the process of segmentation or division and multiplication of cells; to produce (new cells) by this process. **2.** *intr.* Of a cell or ovum: To divide or split up and give origin to one or more new cells by segmentation 1888. **3.** *trans.* To divide into segments 1872. Hence **Se·gmented** *ppl. a. Anat.*, *Bot.*, etc. consisting of, divided into, segments; divided or split up by segmentation into cells.

Segmental (segme·ntăl), *a.* 1816. [f. SEGMENT *sb.* + -AL.] **1.** Having the form of a segment (or, loosely, of an arc) of a circle; *esp. Arch.* of an arch, a pediment, window-head, etc. 1816. **2.** Of, pertaining to, or composed of segments or divisions 1854. **b.** *Path.* Characterized by segmentation or division into segments 1896. Hence **Segme·ntally** *adv.*

Segmentary (segme·ntări), *a.* 1853. [f. as prec. + -ARY. Cf. F. *segmentaire*.] **1.** Segmental. **2.** Pertaining to segments or divisions; composed of segments 1898.

Segmentation (se:gmĕntēⁱ·ʃən). 1851. [f. SEGMENT *v.* + -ATION.] The process of division into segments, chiefly in biological applications; *spec.* in *Embryol.*, the process by which, in the Metazoa, the germinal cell or protoplasmic mass is converted by division into a multitude of cells, which become metamorphosed into the tissues of the body.

attrib.: **s. cavity** = BLASTOCELE.

Segregate (se·grĭgĕt), *a.* and *sb.* late ME. [ad. L. *segregatus*, *-are* SEGREGATE *v.*] **A.** *adj.* **1.** Separated, set apart, isolated. Now *rare*. **2.** *spec.* (*Zool.*, *Bot.*, etc.) Separated (wholly or partially) from the parent or from one another; not aggregated 1793. **B.** *sb. Math.* One of a smallest select aggregate of products of irreducible covariants which suffices to provide by linear combination all covariants of every degree and order 1878.

Segregate (se·grĭgeⁱt), *v.* 1542. [f. L. *segregat-*, *segregare* to separate from the flock, etc., f. *se-* SE- + *greg-*, *grex* flock.] **1.** *trans.* To separate (a person, a body or class of persons) from the general body, or from some particular class; to set apart, isolate, seclude. **2.** To separate or isolate (one thing from others); *esp. Chem.*, *Geol.*, etc. (of natural agencies) to separate out and collect (certain particular constituents of a compound or mixture). In scientific classification: To remove (certain species) etc. from a group and place them apart. 1579. **3.** *intr.* for *refl.* To separate from a main body or mass and collect in one place 1863.

1. So the Anabaptistes in our time..segregated themselues from the companye of other men LATIMER.

Segregation (segrĭgēⁱ·ʃən). 1555. [ad. late L. *segregationem*, f. *segregare*; see prec.] **1.** The action of segregating 1615. **b.** The separation of a portion or portions of a collective or complex unity from the rest; the isolation of particular constituents of a compound or mixture 1612. **†c.** *spec.* Separation from a church or ecclesiastical organization –1683. **2.** The condition of being segregated 1668. **3.** *concr.* Something segregated 1563.

Segregative (se·grĭgeⁱtiv), *a.* 1588. [ad. med.L. *segregativus*, f. L. *segregare* SEGREGATE *v.*] **1.** Having the power or effect of separating. **†a.** *Gram.* and *Logic.* Applied to adversative and disjunctive conjunctions. Hence of a proposition, Consisting of members joined by a segregative conjunction. –1626. **b.** Having the property of separating the elements or constituent parts of matter 1674. **2.** Of persons: Given to separation or disunion. Of an individual: Unsociable. 1685.

Segregator (se·grĭgēⁱtəɹ). 1903. [f. SEGREGATE *v.* + -OR.] An instrument for obtaining the urine from each kidney separately.

‖**Seguidilla** (segĭdī·lʸa). 1763. [a. Sp., f. *seguida* following, sequence, f. *seguir* (:—L. *sequi*) to follow.] A Spanish dance in $\frac{3}{4}$ or $\frac{3}{8}$ time; also, the music for this.

‖**Seicento** (seiˌtʃe·ntǫ). 1866. [It.; short for *mil seicento* one thousand six hundred.] The 17th c. considered as a period of Italian art.

Seidlitz (se·dlits). 1784. Name of a village in Bohemia, where there is a spring impregnated with magnesium sulphate and carbonic acid. Used *attrib.* in **†S. salt,** magnesium sulphate; **†S. water,** an artificial aperient water of the same composition as the water of the S. spring. Hence in **S. powder** (arbitrarily named), a dose consisting of two powders, one of tartaric acid and the other of a mixture of potassium tartrate and sodium bicarbonate, which are mixed in water and drunk while effervescing.

‖**Seigneur** (sęnʸör). 1592. [F. :—L. *seniorem* SENIOR.] **a.** *Fr. Hist.*, A feudal lord; a noble taking his designation from the name of his estate. **b.** In Canada, the holder of a SEIGNEURY; one of the landed gentry.

Grand s., a person of high rank or whose deportment or behaviour suggests this.

Seigneurial (sēⁱniūᵊriăl), *a.* 1656. [a. F., f. *seigneur*.] Pertaining to a seigneur (in France or Canada). Also occas. = SEIGNORIAL.

Seigneury (sēⁱ·niŭri), ‖**Seigneurie** (sęnʸöri). 1620. [ad. F. *seigneurie*, later form of *seignorie*, assim. to *seigneur*.] **1. a.** *Fr. Hist.* A territory under the government of a seigneur. **b.** In Canada, a landed estate, held (until 1854) by feudal tenure. **2.** In Canada, the mansion of a seigneur 1895.

Seignior (sēⁱ·niŏɹ). ME. [a. AF. *segnour*, OF. *seignor*, *-eur* (mod.F. *seigneur*), a Com. Rom. word :—L. *seniorem* SENIOR.] **1.** Orig., synonymous with LORD; a person high in rank or authority, a ruler, a feudal superior; the lord of a manor. Now *rare*. **†2.** Used to represent It. SIGNOR or F. SEIGNEUR in designations of Italians or Frenchmen –1718.

Seigniorage, seignorage (sēⁱ·nyŏrėdʒ). 1444. [a. OF. *seignorage*, *-eurage*, f. *seigneur* SEIGNEUR.] **†1.** Lordship, dominion –1820. **2.** A duty levied on the coining of money for the purpose of covering the expenses of minting, and as a source of revenue to the crown, claimed by the sovereign by virtue of his prerogative 1444. **3.** A duty claimed by the over-lord upon the output of certain minerals, a royalty 1859.

3. The seignorage levied on tin in the Duchy of Cornwall MACAULAY.

Seigniory, seignory (sēⁱ·nyŏri). ME. [a. OF. *seignorie*, f. *seigneur*.] **†1.** Lordship, domination, sovereignty –1684. **2.** *spec.* Feudal lordship or dominion; the authority, rights, and privileges of a feudal lord 1464. **b.** A particular feudal lordship; in *Eng. Law* chiefly, the relation of the lord to the tenants of a manor 1466. **3.** The territory under the dominion of a lord; *esp.* a feudal domain. Sometimes used for SEIGNEURY with ref. to France or Canada. ME. **4.** A body of 'seigniors' or lords. Often with ref. to Italy, = SIGNORIA. 1485.

1. If hee would..do homage to him, he should accept his seniory 1638. **2. b.** A s. appendant passes with the grant of the manor; a s. in gross—that is a s. which has been severed from the demesne lands of the manor to which it was originally appendant—must be specially conveyed by deed of grant 1886.

Seignoral (sēⁱ·nyŏrăl), *a. Hist.* 1627. [f. SEIGN(I)OR + -AL.] = next.

Seignorial (sēⁱnyōᵊ·riăl), *a.* 1818. [f. *seignor* SEIGNIOR + -IAL.] Pertaining to a seignior or seigniors.

Seine (sēⁱn), *sb.* [OE. *segne* :—WGer. **sagina*, a. L. *sagena* (whence F. *seine*), a. Gr. σαγήνη.] A fishing net designed to hang vertically in the water, the ends being drawn together to enclose the fish.

To shoot a s. (or *s.-net*), to throw it out into position. *Comb.*: **s.-boat,** a boat adapted for carrying and throwing out a s.; **-net,** a s. Hence **Sei·ner,** a fisherman who uses a s., or one employed to haul in a s.; also, a s.-boat.

Seine (sēⁱn), *v.* 1836. [f. prec.] **a.** *intr.* To fish or catch fish with a seine. **b.** *trans.* To catch or fish with a seine.

Seir-fish, seer-fish (sīᵊ·ɹfiʃ). 1727. [The first element is a corruption of Pg. *serra* lit. 'saw'.] An East Indian scombroid fish, *Cybium guttatum*.

Seise, *v. Law.* The usual spelling of SEIZE *v.* in the sense: To put in possession, invest with the fee simple *of*.

Seisin (sī·zin). ME. [a. F. *saisine*, f. *saisir* SEIZE *v.*] **1.** In early use, Possession. Now only in *Law*, Possession as of freehold. **b.** In pop. language occas. applied loosely to the object (e.g. a turf, key, staff) handed over in 'livery of s.' (see LIVERY *sb.* 5 a) as a token of possession 1523. **2.** *Sc. Law.* The act of giving possession of feudal property by the delivery of symbols; also, the instrument by which such possession is proved. late ME.

1. Phrases. *To have, take s.* (*in*, *of*). ***Primer*** (also *premier*) *s.*: see PRIMER *a.* 3 b.

Seismic (səi·zmik), *a.* 1858. [f. Gr. σεισμός earthquake (f. σείειν to shake) + -IC.] Pertaining to, relating to, characteristic of, connected with, or produced by an earthquake, earthquakes, or earth-vibration. So **Sei·smical** *a.*, **-ly** *adv.* **Seismi·city,** the frequency per unit area of earthquakes of a particular country; the number representing this.

Seismism (səi·zmiz'm). 1902. [f. Gr. σεισμός + -ISM.] The phenomena of earthquake movements collectively.

Seismograph (səi·zmǫgraf). 1858. [f. *seismo-*, comb. form of Gr. σεισμός + -GRAPH.] An instrument for recording automatically the phenomena of earthquakes. Hence **Seismogra·phic, -al** *adjs.* connected with, furnished by, or relating to a s.; of or pertaining to seismography. **Seismo·graphy,** the descriptive science of earthquakes; also, the use of the s.

Seismology (səizmǫ·lŏdʒi). 1858. [f. *seismo-*, comb. form of Gr. σεισμός + -LOGY.] The science and study of earthquakes, and their causes, effects, and attendant phenomena. Hence **Seismolo·gic, -al** *adjs.* of or pertaining to s. **Seismo·logist,** an investigator of s.

Seismometer (səizmǫ·mĭtəɹ). 1841. [f. *seismo-* (see prec.) + -METER.] An instrument for measuring the intensity, direction, and duration of earthquakes. Hence **Seismome·tric, -al** *adjs.* of or pertaining to seismometry, or to a s. **Seismo·metry,** the scientific study, determination and recording of earthquake phenomena, esp. by means of the s.; the scientific study, theory, and application of the s.

Seismoscope (səi·zmoskōᵘp). 1851. [f. as prec. + -SCOPE.] A simple form of seismometer; a contrivance for detecting or indicating the occurrence of an earthquake shock.

Seity (sī·ĭti). *rare.* 1709. [ad. med.L. *seitas*, f. L. *se* oneself; see -ITY.] That which constitutes the self, selfhood.

Seizable (sī·zăb'l), *a.* 1461. [f. next + -ABLE.] Capable of being seized. Chiefly of property, that may lawfully be seized.

Seize (sīz), *v.* ME. [a. OF. *saisir*, *seisir*, :—Frankish L. *sacire*, app. ad. Teut. **satjan* to SET in the phr. *ad propriam sacire*.] **I.** To put in possession. **1.** *Law.* (In techn. use written **seise.**) *trans.* To put (a person) in legal possession *of* a feudal holding; to invest or endow *with* property; to establish *in* a holding or an office or dignity. **b.** *To be seised of* or *in*: to be the legal possessor of. late ME. **2.** *transf. To be seized* (*seised*) *of* or †*with*: to be in possession of. Now only *arch.* and with allusion to the legal use. 1477. †**3.** To settle, establish in a place; to place, seat, fix –1633. †**b.** Of a beast of prey: To fasten (its claws) upon. SPENSER.

1. b. Phr. *To be seised in fee, to be seised of* (a manor, etc.) *in his demesne as of fee*, to be the holder of the fee simple. **2.** If any that sell Goose Eggs do chance to be taken siesed with Hens eggs..they are presently punished with thirty lashes 1653.

II. To take possession. **1.** Of a feudal superior or a sovereign: To take possession of, confiscate (the property of a vassal or subject). Also, to annex (a country) to one's own dominions. ME. **b.** To take possession of (goods) in pursuance of a judicial order 1482. **2.** To take possession of by force; to capture (a city); to take as plunder ME. **b.** To take prisoner, to catch. late ME. **3.** To take hold of with the hands, claws, teeth, etc.; in mod. use, to take hold of suddenly or eagerly, to clutch ME. **b.** *To s. hold of*: to take hold of suddenly and roughly 1839. **4.** *fig.* **a.** With impersonal subject, e.g. death, calamity: To oppress or attack suddenly. Also of a fear, belief, etc.: To take sudden possession of (a person, his mind). late ME. **b.** Of an object of perception, a fact, etc., hence of a speaker, writer, or artist: To arrest (the attention), to impress irresistibly (the mind, etc.) 1772. **c.** To avail oneself eagerly or dexterously of, take advantage of (an opportunity) 1618. **d.** To grasp with the mind or perceptive faculties 1855. **5.** *intr.* **a.** *To s. on* or *upon* = to seize (in senses II. 2–4). late ME. †**b.** Of a weapon: To penetrate deeply *in* –1600.

1. Phr. *To s. into one's hands*; The said Citie..was seised into the saide King Edward's hondes 1447. **b.** Being quite moneyless, and in danger of having my goods seized for rent 1733. **2.** Robbers, who seized church goods without remorse 1883. **3.** Lothaire abruptly seized him by the arm 1797. **4.** Ruin s. thee, ruthless King! GRAY. The young prince..was seized by the small pox MACAULAY. **d.** A beauty which a foreigner cannot perfectly s. M. ARNOLD. **5. a.** A morbid melancholy seized upon the Irishman BORROW.

III. Techn. **1.** *trans.* (*Naut.*). †**a.** To reach, arrive at. Also with *in*. –1635. **b.** To fasten (two ropes or parts of a rope) together, or to attach (a rope) to something else, by binding with marline, yarn, or the like 1644. **2.** *intr.* Of a part of a machine, etc. To become stuck owing to excessive heat or pressure 1878.

b. *To s. up*, to fasten (a man) by the wrists to the shrouds, in preparation for a flogging. Hence **Sei·zer**, one who or that which seizes.

Seizing (sī·ziŋ), *vbl. sb.* ME. [f. SEIZE *v.* + -ING [1].] **1.** The action of SEIZE *v.* late ME. **2.** *concr. Naut.* †**a.** A rope for attaching a boat to a ship. **b.** A small cord for 'seizing' two ropes together, or a rope to something else **c.** Cordage or yarn used for 'seizing'. ME.

Seizure (sī·ʒiŭı). 1482. [f. SEIZE *v.* + -URE.] **1.** The action or an act of seizing, or the fact of being seized; confiscation or forcible taking possession (of land or goods); a sudden and forcible taking hold. †**b.** Grasp, hold; a fastening –1621. **c.** A sudden attack of illness, esp. a fit of apoplexy or epilepsy. Also, a sudden visitation (of calamity). 1779. †**2.** Possession, seisin –1658. **3.** The action of SEIZE *v.* III. 2. 1903.

1. The s. of the estates of the church BURKE. **c.** The s. was, I think, not apoplectical JOHNSON. **2.** When chillie age had seasure of this earth LODGE.

Sejant (sī·dʒănt), *a.* 1500. [prop. *seiant*, a. OF. **seiant*, var. of *seant*, pres. pple. of *seoir* to sit :—L. *sedere*.] *Her.* In a sitting posture; *esp.* of a quadruped: Sitting with the fore-legs upright.

Sejoin (sĭdʒoi·n), *v. rare.* 1568. [f. SE- + JOIN *v.*, after L. *sejungere*.] *trans.* To separate, disjoin. So **Seju·nction** 1530.

‖ **Séjour** (seʒūr). 1755. [F., f. *séjourner* to SOJOURN.] **1.** The act of staying or sojourning in a place (for a longer or shorter period). **2.** A place of sojourn or residence 1769.

Selachian (sĭlē·kiăn), *a.* and *sb.* 1835. [f. mod.L. *Selache* (a. Gr. σελάχη, pl. of σέλαχος shark) or *Selachii* + -IAN.] **A.** *adj.* Of or belonging to the genus *Selache* of sharks, or to the group *Selachii*, the sharks and their allies. **B.** *sb.* A shark or allied fish.

‖ **Seladang** (sĕlā·dæŋ). Also **saladang.** 1884. [Native name.] **1.** The large wild ox or gaur of the Malay countries. **2.** The Malayan tapir 1909.

‖ **Selaginella** (sĭleidʒ-, sĭlædʒine·lă). 1865. [mod.L., dim. of SELAGO.] *Bot.* A genus of cryptogams; (with *pl.*) a plant of this genus.

‖ **Selago** (sĭlēi·go). 1627. [L.] †**a.** The club-moss *Lycopodium Selago*. **b.** A Linnæan genus of S. African herbs or undershrubs.

‖ **Selah** (sī·lă). 1530. [Heb. *se·lāh*.] A Hebrew word, occurring frequently at the end of a verse in the Psalter, etc., by the LXX rendered διάψαλμα; supposed to be a musical or liturgical direction, perhaps indicating pause or rest. Hence *allus.*

†**Se·lcouth**, *a.* OE. [f. OE. *seldan* SELDOM + *cūð* COUTH *a.*] Unfamiliar, unusual; strange, marvellous, wonderful –1815.

†**Seld**, *adv.* and *a.* [Early ME. *selde*, formed as positive to (OE.) *seldor, seldost*, compar. and superl. of *seldan* SELDOM.] = next –1652.

Seldom (se·ldəm), *adv.* and *a.* [OE. *seldan*, f. OTeut. **seldo-* (prob. an adj.).] **A.** *adv.* On few occasions, in few cases or instances, not often; rarely, infrequently.

Listners seldome hear good of themselves 1678.

B. *adj.* Rare, infrequent. *Obs.* exc. occas. with agent-n. or noun of action. 1483.

Blunting the fine point of seldome pleasure SHAKS. Seldom-readers are slow readers LAMB. Hence †**Se·ldom·ly** *adv.* –1620, **-ness.**

†**Se·ldseen**, *a.* [OE. *seldsiene*.] Seldom to be seen or met with; rare –1616.

Select (sĭle·kt), *a.* (and *sb.*). 1565. [ad. L. *selectus, seligere*, f. *se-* SE- + *legere* to collect, etc.] **A.** *adj.* **1.** Selected, chosen out of a larger number, on account of excellence or fitness; picked. **2.** Choice; composed of or containing the best, choicest or most desirable; superior 1590. **b.** Of persons, company, etc. Now often: Unexceptionable with regard to social standing or estimation. 1602. **3.** Careful in selection. Hence, (of a society, etc.) exclusive; (of a place of resort) frequented only by persons of good social position. 1842.

1. To the smaller plot..only a few s. traitors were privy MACAULAY. *S. committee* (of the House of Commons, etc.), one consisting of a small number of members, selected to investigate a special matter. *S. meeting*, (amongst Quakers) a meeting of ministers and elders. **2.** Most s. Remedies for every Disease 1656. **b.** Company at first aristocratic and s. CARLYLE. **3.** Such a sweet, s. watering-place. All the best people go there. 1888.

†**B.** *sb.* **a.** A selected person or thing. **b.** A selected class or group, a selection. –1805. Hence **Sele·ct·ly** *adv.*, **-ness.**

Select (sĭle·kt), *v.* 1567. [f. L. *select-*, *seligere* (see prec.).] **1.** *trans.* To choose or pick out in preference to another or others. **2.** *intr.* To make a selection 1833.

1. You desire me to s...some Things from the first Volume of your Miscellanies POPE. Hence **Sele·ctor**, one who or that which selects; also, as a name for various appliances in metallurgy, telegraphy, etc.

Selection (sĭle·kʃən). 1646. [ad. L. *selectionem, seligere*; see prec.] **1.** The action of selecting or choosing out; also the fact of being selected or chosen. **2.** A particular choice; choice of a particular individual or individuals; *concr.* the (†person or) thing selected; a number of selected (†persons or) things 1805. **b.** *Sporting.* The horse or horses selected by a racing prophet as likely to win or obtain a place 1901. **3. a.** Applied *spec.* to the action of a breeder in selecting individuals from which to breed, in order to obtain some desired quality or characteristic in the descendants 1813. **b.** Hence *Biol.*, used to designate any process, whether artificial or natural, which brings about a particular modification of an animal or vegetable type by ensuring that in successive generations the individuals that reproduce their kind shall be those that have transmissible variations from the ancestral form in the direction of this modification 1857.

1. It should seem, then,..that the essence of right conduct lay in s. and rejection 1744. **2.** The English public..does not pretend to care for poetry except in 'selections' 1887. **3.** *Natural s.*, the operation of natural causes by which those individuals of a species that are best adapted to the environment tend to be preserved and to transmit their characters, while those less adapted die out, so that in the course of generations the degree of adaptation to the environment tends progressively to increase. *Sexual s.*, that kind of natural s. which arises through the preference by one sex of those individuals of the other sex that have some special characteristic, in consequence of which that characteristic tends to be transmitted, with progressive enhancement in succeeding generations.

Selective (sĭle·ktiv), *a.* 1625. [f. SELECT *v.* + -IVE.] Having the quality or faculty of selecting; characterized by choice or selection. **b.** *Wireless Telegr.* Having the power to select a particular wave-length or frequency and to exclude others 1903. Hence **Selecti·vity,** the quality of being s.

Sele·ctman. *U.S.* 1646. [f. SELECT *a.* + MAN *sb.*] One of a board of officers elected annually to manage various local concerns in a 'town' or 'township' in New England.

Selenate (se·lĭnēt). 1818. [f. SELENIUM, after SELENIC *a.*] *Chem.* A salt of selenic acid.

Selenic (sĭle·nik), *a.* 1818. [f. SELENIUM + -IC.] *Chem. S. acid*, a dibasic acid, H_2SeO_4, forming salts called *selenates*.

Selenide (se·lĭnəid). 1849. [f. as prec. + -IDE.] *Chem.* A combination of selenium with an electro-positive element or with a radical.

Seleniferous (selĭni·fĕrəs), *a.* 1823. [f. SELENIUM + -FEROUS.] Containing or yielding selenium.

Sele·nio-, sele·no-. 1831. Used as comb. forms of SELENIUM, as in *selenocyanide*, etc.

Selenious (sĭlī·niəs), *a.* 1834. [f. SELENIUM; see -OUS.] *Chem. S. acid*, a dibasic acid, H_2SeO_3, forming salts called *selenites*.

Selenite [1] (se·lĭnəit). 1567. [ad. L. *selenites* SELENITES.] **1.** A stone described by ancient writers; app. to be identified with the mineral now so called (see 2). **2.** *Min.* Sulphate of lime (gypsum) in a crystalline or foliated form. Also, a slip or film of this mineral used for the polarization of light. 1668. †**b.** *Chem.* Sulphate of lime without regard to structure –1823.

Selenite [2] (sĭlī·nəit). 1645. [f. Gr. σεληνίτης (pl. Σεληνῖται men in the moon), f. σελήνη moon.] A supposed inhabitant of the moon.

Selenite [3] (se·lĭnəit). 1831. [f. SELENIUM + -ITE [1] 4.] *Chem.* A salt of selenious acid.

†‖ **Selenites** (selĭnəi·tīz). late ME. [L., = Gr. σεληνίτης λίθος (lit. 'moonstone', because supposed to wax and wane with the moon), f. σελήνη; see -ITE [1].] = SELENITE [1] –1820.

Selenitic (selĭni·tik), *a.* 1756. [f. SELENITE [1] + -IC. Cf. F. *sélénitique*.] Of, pertaining to, resembling or containing selenite. †Of water: Impregnated with sulphate of lime. So †**Seleni·tical** *a.* 1755–1799.

Selenium (sĭlī·niŏm). 1818. [mod.L., f. Gr. σελήνη moon; see -IUM.] *Chem.* One of the rarer elements, closely resembling tellurium in properties, formerly classed among the metals, but now regarded as non-metallic. Symbol Se; atomic weight 79.

Selenocentric (sĭlīnose·ntrik), *a.* 1852. [f. Gr. σελήνη moon + CENTRIC *a.*] Having relation to the centre of the moon or to the moon as a centre; as seen or estimated from the centre of the moon.

Selenodont (sĭlī·nodŏnt), *a.* and *sb.* 1883. [f. Gr. σελήνη + ὀδοντ- tooth.] **A.** *adj.* Of molar teeth: Having crescentic ridges on the crowns. Also, having such teeth, of or pertaining to the *Selenodonta*. **B.** *sb.* A s. animal.

Selenograph (sĭlī·nograf). 1868. [f. as prec. + -GRAPH.] A map or chart of a part of the surface of the moon.

Selenography (selĭnǫ·grăfi). 1650. [ad. mod.L. *selenographia*, f. Gr. σελήνη moon; see -GRAPHY.] **a.** A description of the moon's surface. **b.** The description and delineation of the moon's surface; the descriptive science relating to the moon, 'lunar geography' 1784. Hence **Seleno·grapher**, one engaged in s. **Selenogra·phic, -al** (sĭlī·nogræ·fik, -ăl) *adjs.* belonging to s. **Seleno·graphist,** a selenographer.

Selenology (selĭnǫ·lŏdʒi). 1821. [f. Gr.

σελήνη + -OLOGY.] The science relating to the moon; chiefly, the science of the movements and astronomical relations of the moon (or, occas., the science of the formation of the moon's crust, lunar 'geology'), in contradistinction to *selenography*. Hence **Selenolo·gical** *a.*, **-ly** *adv.* **Seleno·logist,** one versed in s.

Selenotropic (sǐlīnotrǫ·pik), *a.* 1883. [f. Gr. σελήνη + -τροπος turning + -IC.] *Bot.* Bending or turning under the influence of moonlight. So **Seleno·tropism. Seleno·tropy.**

Self (self), *pron.*, *a.*, and *sb. Pl.* **selves.** [Com. Teut.; OE. *self, selfa*:—OTeut. **selƀo-, *selƀon-*; ult. etym. obscure.] **A.** *pron.* and *pronominal adj.* In the sense of the Latin *ipse.* In concord with a sb. or pron., to indicate emphatically that the reference is to the person or thing mentioned and not, or not merely, to some other. **1.** With sb. *Obs.* exc. *arch.*; superseded by the use of the 'emphatic pronouns', *himself, herself,* etc., or, after a def. art. or demonstrative, by (*the, this, that*) *very.* †**2.** With pers. pron. in the nominative (*rare* after OE.) -1633. **3.** Following a pron. in oblique case. *Obs.* exc. in HIMSELF, HERSELF, THEMSELVES. OE. †**b.** Used in 16-17th c. for: Own, peculiar -1654. †**4.** Used *absol.* as independent pron. (= he himself, I myself, etc.) -1616. **5.** In commercial use (hence *joc.* or *colloq.*) substituted for *myself*, or occas. for *himself* 1758.

1. Thys is the thing selfe that is in debate 1532. I confess to a satisfaction in the s. act of preaching LOWELL. 2. S. did I see a swain not long ago P. FLETCHER. 3. **b.** *Macb.* v. viii. 70. They Gormandize at their selfe pleasures 1632. 5. I am, dear Sirs, for s. and partners, Yours most faithfully, Samuel Jackson THACKERAY. S. and friend took train..for Leatherhead 1863.

B. *adj.* **I.** = SAME (and in derived senses). †**1.** = SAME *a.* I. 1-3. -1632. **2.** Of a colour: The same throughout, uniform. Often prefixed to adjs. denoting colour (sometimes hyphened), as *s.-black, s. russet.* 1601. **b.** Of a carnation: Self-coloured 1852. **3.** Of whiskey: Not blended 1904.

1. Two gentlemen, subiect to the selfe and same lawes 1606. I neuer saw any that selfe Nation, to begge bread 1632. Phr. †*One s.*, one and the same. 2. A peece of selfe russet cloth HOLLAND. **b.** A new variety of s. carnation 1902.

II. Senses related to the pronominal use. **1. a.** Of a portion of an instrument: Of one piece with the instrument itself 1888. **b.** Of a trimming: Of the same material as the garment itself 1904. **2.** Of a bow: Made all of one piece 1801. †**3.** *Mining.* Of a rock, etc.: Detached, of material different from its surroundings -1855.

C. *sb.* **I.** From the pronoun. **1.** (The pronominal notion expressed subst.) **a.** Preceded by a possessive pron., with which it forms a comb. serving as a reflexive or an emphatic personal pronoun. Often qualified by an adj., as *my own s., your dear s., our two selves,* etc. ME. **b.** Preceded by a sb. in the possessive = the sb. + *himself, herself, itself,* etc. ME. **2.** *transf.* in various uses, *esp.* a person whom one loves as oneself or who is a counterpart of oneself (*obs.* exc. in *other s., second s.*) 1605. **3.** Chiefly *Philos.* That which in a person is really and intrinsically *he* (in contradistinction to what is adventitious); the ego (often identified with the soul or mind as opp. to the body); a permanent subject of successive and varying states of consciousness 1674. **4. a.** What one is at a particular time or in a particular aspect or relation; one's nature, character, or (sometimes) physical constitution or appearance, considered as different at different times. Chiefly with qualifying adj., (*one's*) *old, former,* etc. *s.* 1697. **b.** An assemblage of characteristics and dispositions which may be conceived as constituting one of various conflicting personalities within a human being 1595. **5.** One's personal welfare and interests as an object of concern; chiefly in bad sense, self-interested motives, selfishness 1680.

1. **a.** Their hideous wives, their horrid selves and dresses BYRON. **b.** She..Delia's s...surpass'd MILT. 2. My dear heart and s. and son Charles H. WALPOLE. 3. A secret s. I had enclos'd within TRAHERNE. I, one and the same s., perceive both colours and sounds BERKELEY. 4. **a.** In vain he burns..And in himself his former s. requires DRYDEN. **b.** *Better s.*, the better part of one's nature. 5. S. is their god and Selfishness their religion 1906.

II. From the adj. **1.** A 'self-coloured' flower, esp. a carnation 1852. **2.** A self bow 1856.

D. -self in compound pronouns. **1.** *To be —self.* **a.** *colloq.* To be in (one's) normal condition of body or mind; to be in (its) accustomed state 1849. **b.** To act according to one's true character, without hypocrisy or constraint 1864. **2.** The refl. pron. assumes in certain contexts the sense: The normal condition (of the person or thing) 1450. **3.** *By —self*: alone, without society; unaided; separately OE.

1. *To feel like —self.* **b.** For..a girl to dare to be herself 1896. 2. Phr. *Out of —self* (now *rare*), *beside —self*, out of (one's) mind or senses, deranged. 3. Mr. C. dines all by himself at present, I merely looking on MRS. CARLYLE.

Self, *v.* 1910. [f. prec.] *pass.* To be fertilized by self-pollination.

Self-, the word SELF used as a prefix [OE. *self-, sylf-*] with refl. meaning = 'oneself', 'itself'.

The basis of compounds falling under headings 1 and 2 (below) is normally a reflexive verbal phrase; thus, from 'to accuse oneself', is formed a series of formally related words, *self-accusation, -accusatory, -accusing, -accused,* any of which may arise independently of the others.

1. Compounds in which *self-* is in the objective relation to the second element: **a.** With nouns of action; as *self-abandonment*, abandonment by oneself of oneself, one's power, rights, desires, or the like; *-accusation, -advancement, -criticism,* and many more. **b.** With vbl. sbs.; as *s.-abominating* = self-abomination, *-advertising, -schooling,* etc. **c.** With agent-nouns; as *s.-advertiser*, one who advertises himself, etc. **d.** With nouns of state or condition; as *s.-awareness*, the condition of being aware of oneself; *-mastery*, mastery of oneself, self-command; *-reverence*, etc. **e.** With adjs.; as *s.-adaptive*, capable of adapting oneself or itself, (hence, by extension) pertaining to, involving, or characterized by self-adaptation; *-communicative, -laudatory*, etc. **f.** With ppl. adjs. in *-ing*; as *s.-abandoning*, abandoning oneself, (hence, by extension), pertaining to, involving, or characterized by self-abandonment; *-betraying, -mastering,* etc. **g.** With †vbs. and pres. pples.; as *s.-blind, -vaunting,* etc. **h.** With advs. related to actual or possible formations in **e** and **f** (above); as *s.-consolingly, -vindicatingly,* etc.

2. Compounds with pa. pples. and ppl. adjs. in which *self-* denotes the agent or what is conceived as the agent; = by oneself or itself, by one's own (unaided) efforts or action, without help from others.

Such compounds may qualify the designation of: (*a*) a person or thing that is the subject and object of the action, as *s.-appointed censors* = censors appointed by themselves; (*b*) a thing that is operated upon, performed, produced, etc. by oneself, as *s.-appointed duties* = duties appointed by the person himself; (*c*) a thing conceived as operated upon by itself, as *s.-arched rocks* = rocks formed into arches of themselves without human or mechanical agency; *s.-balanced* = balanced without external support. **b.** Rarely, with adjs. in *-able*; as *s.-impairable* = liable to be impaired by one's own action.

3. Compounds in which *self-* is adverbial: **a.** With sbs., adjs., vbs., advs. = for, in, into, on or upon, to or towards, with oneself or itself, the prep. to be supplied being that required in the construction of the word which forms the second element; e.g. *s.-absorbed, -absorption* = absorbed, absorption in oneself; *s.-acquaintance* = acquaintance with oneself; *s.-addressed* = addressed to oneself; *s.-compassion* = compassion for oneself. **b.** With adjs. and related sbs., vbs., pples. = of or in oneself or itself, of or in one's or its own nature or power; e.g. *s.-apparent* = apparent of itself. **c.** With pples. = from or out of oneself or itself (as a source or point of origin); e.g. *s.-arising*, arising from or out of oneself.

4. In techn. use, forming compounds to designate machines, appliances, or processes, by or in which certain operations are performed without human or animal agency or special manipulation or adjustment for the purpose; usu. = automatic, automatically; as in *s.-adjusting, -feeding, -starter, -winding,* etc.

5. Compounds in which *self-* is in the adjective relation: †**a.** = relating to oneself, one's own, personal, individual, private, intimate; as *s.-affairs, -disgrace,* etc. **b.** = inherent in, depending upon, or proceeding from oneself (itself), one's nature, etc.; belonging to oneself (itself) as an independent creature; in 17th c. often *spec.*, dependent or relying upon one's own efforts or merits apart from the grace of God; as *s.-ability, -excellency, -insufficiency,* etc. *Obs.* or *arch.* **c.** = having an independent existence, position, or authority; †pristine, original; as *s.-agency, -sovereignty,* etc. **d.** = having self as the object or aim; as *s.-desire, -profit,* etc. **e.** = caused or brought about by oneself; e.g. *s.-captivity, -portrait,* rare.

Self-aba·sement. 1656. [SELF- 1 a.] Humiliation of oneself. So **Self-aba·sed** *ppl. a.*, **Self-aba·sing** *ppl. a.*

Self-abu·se. 1605. [SELF- 1 a.] †**1.** Self-deception. SHAKS. **2.** Abuse or revilement of oneself 1795. **3.** Self-pollution 1728.

Self-a·cting, *ppl. a.* 1740. [SELF- 3 b, 4.] **1.** Acting independently, without external impulse or influence. Also applied to motion characterized by such action. **2.** *Mech.* Acting automatically without the manipulation (or mechanism) which would otherwise be required. Also said of the operation. 1824. So **Self-a·ction,** action uninfluenced by external impulse. †**Self-a·ctive** *a.* acting of itself without external impulse 1642-92. **Self-a·ctor** *Mech.*, a s. mule in a spinning-machine.

Self-applau·se. 1678. [SELF- 1 a.] Approval or commendation of oneself. So **Self-applau·ding** *ppl. a.* given to s. 1654.

Self-asse·rtion. 1806. [SELF- 1 a.] The action of asserting one's individuality, or insisting upon one's claims or supremacy. So **Self-asse·rting, -asse·rtive** *adjs.* full of or characterized by s.

Self-assu·rance. 1594. [SELF- 1 d.] Feeling of security as to oneself; self-confidence. So **Self-assu·red** *a.* self-confident.

Self-bego·tten, *pa. pple.* and *ppl. a.* 1671. [SELF- 2.] Begotten of oneself by one's own power.

Self-bi·nder. orig. *U.S.* 1882. [SELF- 4.] A reaping-machine which has an apparatus for binding the corn into sheaves automatically. So **Self-bi·nding** *ppl. a.*

Self-born, *ppl. a.* 1587. [SELF- 3 b.] Born of or originating from oneself or itself.

From himself the Phœnix only springs: S. DRYDEN.

Self-ce·ntred, *ppl. a.* 1676. [SELF 3 a.] **1.** Fixed or stationary, as a centre round which other things move. **2.** Of persons, their activities, etc.: Centred in oneself (or itself); independent of external action or influence 1764. **b.** Engrossed in self, selfishly independent 1783.

1. There hangs the ball of Earth and Water mixt, Self-Center'd, and unmov'd DRYDEN. 2. **b.** That s. satisfaction which makes life tolerable 1884. So **Self-ce·ntring** *ppl. a.* †(*a*) = prec. 1; (*b*) *Mech.* applied to chucks, etc., which hold the object in a central position without the necessity of tentative adjustments.

Self-colle·cted, *ppl. a.* 1711. [SELF- 3 a.] = COLLECTED 2.

Self-co·lour 1665. [SELF B. 2.] **1.** One uniform colour; orig. used of flowers. Also, a colour belonging to the same series as another. **2.** The natural colour 1851. So **Self-co·loured** *ppl. a.* of one colour; of the natural colour.

Self-comma·nd. 1699. [SELF- 1 a.] Control of one's actions or feelings, self-control.

Self-compla·cence, -co·mplaisance. 1748. [SELF- 3 a.] = COMPLACENCE 1. So **Self-compla·cency** 1687. **Self-compla·cent** *a.* = COMPLACENT *a.* 2. 1763.

Self-concei·t. 1588. [SELF- 1 a.] One's opinion or estimate of oneself; *esp.* exaggerated opinion of oneself, one's talents, attainments, etc. So **Self-concei·ted** *ppl. a.* (now somewhat *rare*) full of or marked by s.; **-ly** *adv.*, **-ness.**

Self-co·nfidence. 1653. [SELF- 3 a.] Confidence in oneself; often, arrogant or impudent reliance on one's own powers.

Self-confidence is the first requisite to great undertakings JOHNSON. So **Self-co·nfident** *a.*, **-ly** *adv.*

Self-congratula·tion. 1712. [SELF- 1 a.] Congratulation of oneself.

Self-co·njugate, *a.* 1866. [SELF- 3 a.] *Math.* Applied to a figure each side of which is, relatively to some conic, the polar of the opposite vertex.

Self-co·nscious, *a.* 1697. [SELF- 1 e.] **1.** *Philos.* Having consciousness of one's identity, actions, sensations, etc.; reflectively aware of one's actions. Also said of action, thought, etc. †**b.** Of which one is conscious in oneself -1824. **2.** Marked by undue or morbid preoccupation with one's own personality; so far self-centred as to suppose one is the object of observation by others 1837.

1. **b.** My s. Worth DRYDEN. 2. S., conscious of a world looking on CARLYLE. Hence **Self-co·nsciously** *adv.*

Self-co·nsciousness. 1690. [SELF- 1 d.] **1.** *Philos.* Consciousness of one's own identity, acts, thoughts, etc. **2.** Internal knowledge or conviction *of* a thing 1751. **3.** The condition of being self-conscious (sense 2) 1851.

Self-co·nsequence. 1778. [SELF- 5 a.] Self-importance. So **Self-co·nsequent** *a.*

Self-consi·stency. 1692. [SELF- 3 a.] The quality of being self-consistent. So **Self-consi·stent** *a.* marked by consistency; constantly adhering to the same principles of thought or action.

Self-contai·ned, *ppl. a.* 1591. [SELF- 3 a.] Having all that one (it) needs in oneself (itself); independent of external means or relations; esp. (of persons) not dependent upon, or communicating oneself to, others; reserved or restrained in behaviour. **b.** Of a house, etc.: Of which the apartments and approaches are restricted to the use of one household 1827. **c.** Of a machine or device: Complete in itself 1828.

Se·lf-contradi·ction. 1658. [SELF- 1 a.] The act or fact of contradicting oneself (or itself); also, a statement which contains elements that contradict one another. So **Self-contradi·cting** *ppl. a.* 1655. **Self-contradi·ctory** *a.*

Self-contro·l. 1711. [SELF- 1 a.] Control of oneself, one's desires, etc.

Self-convi·cted, *ppl. a.* 1729. [SELF- 2.] Convicted by one's own words or action. So **Self-convi·ction** 1640.

Self-crea·ted, *ppl. a.* 1677. [SELF- 2.] Created, brought into existence, or constituted by oneself.

Self-cu·lture. 1847. [SELF- 1 a.] The cultivation or development by one's own efforts of one's mind, faculties, manners, etc.

Self-dece·ption. 1677. [SELF- 1 a.] The action or fact of deceiving oneself; self-delusion. So **Self-decei·t.** **Self-decei·ved** *ppl. a.* 1671.

Self-defe·nce. 1651. [SELF- 1 a.] The act of defending oneself, one's rights or position.

Homicide in s., or *se defendendo*, upon a sudden affray, is..excusable rather than justifiable, by the English law BLACKSTONE. Phr. *The (noble, manly) art of self-defence*, †(*a*) fencing; (*b*) pugilism, boxing. So **Self-defe·nsive** *a.* of, pertaining to, or involving the principle of, s.

Self-deli·very. 1864. [SELF- 4.] Automatic delivery: **a.** by a reaping-machine of the corn in swaths or sheaves; **b.** of a pattern from the mould in founding.

Self-delu·sion. 1634. [SELF- 1 a.] The act of deluding oneself; an instance of this. So **Self-delu·ded** *ppl. a.*

Self-deni·al. 1642. [SELF 1 a.] Abnegation of oneself; sacrifice of one's personal desires.

Self-deny·ing, *ppl. a.* 1632. [SELF- 1 e.] That denies himself; characterized by or involving self-denial.

Self-denying ordinance (Eng. Hist.), 'an Ordinance appointing, That no Member of either House, during the Time of this War, shall have or execute any Office or Command, Military or Civil' (Jrnl. Ho. Commons, Dec. 11, 1644); also *transf.* (*colloq.*) applied to any course of action by which a person deprives himself of some advantage or benefit. Hence **Self-deny·ingly** *adv.*

Self-depe·ndent, *a.* 1677. [SELF- 3 a.] Possessing or characterized by self-dependence. So **Self-depe·ndence, -depe·ndency,** dependence entirely upon oneself, one's own efforts, etc. **Self-depe·ndently** *adv.* **Self-depe·nding** *ppl. a.*

Self-destroy·er. 1654. [SELF- 1 c.] One who is the cause of his own destruction 1657. **b.** A suicide 1654. So **Self-destroy·ing** *vbl. sb.* and *ppl. a.* 1612.

Self-destru·ction. 1586. [SELF- 1 a.] Destruction of oneself, one's life; *esp.* self-murder, suicide. So **Self-destru·ctive** *a.* 1654.

Se·lf-determina·tion. 1683. [SELF- 1 a.] Determination of one's mind or will by oneself or itself. **b.** The independent determination by a state or community of its own polity 1911. So **Self-dete·rmining** *ppl. a.* determining one's own acts; possessing s. 1662.

Self-distru·st. 1789. [SELF- 1 d.] Distrust of oneself, one's powers, etc.

Selfdom (se·lfdəm). *rare.* 1863. [f. SELF *sb.* + -DOM.] The realm or domain of self.

Self-effa·cement. 1866. [SELF- 1 a.] The keeping of oneself out of sight or in the background.

Self-ele·cted, *a.* 1818. [SELF- 2.] Elected by oneself, (of a body) elected by its members; *transf.* of an office to which a person has appointed himself. So **Self-ele·ction,** election of oneself by oneself 1790. **Self-ele·ctive** *a.* having the right of electing oneself 1787.

Self-estee·m. 1657. [SELF- 1 a.] Favourable appreciation or opinion of oneself. **b.** *Phrenology.* One of the mental faculties to which a 'bump' is assigned; the 'bump' itself 1815.

Self-e·vidence. 1682. [SELF- 1 d.] **a.** Evidence of its own truth. **b.** The quality or condition of being self-evident.

Self-e·vident, *a.* 1690. [SELF- 3 b.] Evident of itself without proof; axiomatic. Hence **Self-e·vidently** *adv.*

Se·lf-examina·tion. 1647. [SELF- 1 a.] Examination of oneself with regard to one's conduct, motives, etc., esp. as a religious duty.

Self-exci·ting, *ppl. a.* 1884. [SELF- 1 f.] *Electr.* Designating a dynamo-electric machine that excites its own field. So **Self-excita·tion.**

Self-exi·stence. 1697. [SELF- 5 c.] Existence of a being by virtue of his inherent nature independently of any other being.

Self-exi·stent, *a.* 1701. [SELF- 3 b.] **1.** Having the property of self-existence; existing of or by oneself (itself). **2.** Having a primary or independent existence 1779.

Self-explai·ned, *ppl. a.* 1725. [SELF- 2.] Explained by itself, understood without specific explanation. So **Self-explai·ning** *ppl. a.*, **-expla·natory** *a.*

Self-expre·ssion. 1892. [SELF- 1.] The expression (often esp. artistic or literary) of one's personality.

Self-fee·ling. 1879. [SELF- 1 d, 5 d. Cf. G. *selbstgefühl.*] **1.** Feeling centred in oneself. **2.** The sense of one's individual identity 1908.

Self-fe·rtile, *a.* 1859. [SELF- 3 b.] *Bot.* Of a flower: Having the property of fertilizing itself by the action of its pollen on its pistil. Of a plant: Fertilized by the pollen of its own flowers alone. Also applied to hermaphrodite animals. So **Self-fertiliza·tion. Self-fe·rtilized** *ppl. a.*

Self-forge·tful, *a.* 1864. [SELF- 1 e.] Forgetful of one's self or one's own individuality; having or characterized by no thought of self. So **Self-forge·tfulness** 1832.

Self-glo·rious, *a.* 1599. [SELF- 3 a.] Marked by vain-glory or boasting.

Self-go·vernment. 1734. [SELF- 1 a.] **1.** Self-control, Now *rare.* **2.** Administration by a people or state of its own affairs without external direction or interference 1798.

2. The residuary rights are reserved to their (the American States) own s. JEFFERSON. So **Self-go·verned** *ppl. a.* acting or living according to one's own desires uninfluenced by others; marked by self-control; having s.

Self-heal (se·lfhīl). late ME. [f. SELF- 1 + HEAL *v.*] Any of various plants believed to have great healing properties, esp. *Prunella vulgaris* (Common S.), *Sanicula europæa*, and formerly *Pimpinella Saxifraga.*

Self-he·lp. 1831. [SELF- 1 a.] **1.** The action or faculty of providing for oneself without assistance from others. **2.** *Law.* Redress of one's wrongs by one's own action, without recourse to legal process 1875.

Selfhood (se·lfhud). 1649. [f. SELF *sb.* + -HOOD; orig. repr. G. *selbheit.*] **1.** The quality by virtue of which one is oneself; personal individuality; ipseity; that which constitutes one's own self or individuality; (one's) self. **2.** Oneself as the centre of one's life and action; hence, self-centredness; devotion to self, selfish life or conduct 1649. **3.** One's personality, one's personal interests or character 1854.

Self-ide·ntity. 1866. [SELF- 3 a.] The identity of a thing with itself. So **Self-ide·ntical** *a.*

Self-impo·rtance. 1775. [SELF- 5 a.] The sense of one's own importance; bearing or conduct arising from this. So **Self-impo·rtant** *a.* marked by self-importance, having an exaggerated opinion of one's own importance.

Self-impo·sed, *ppl. a.* 1781. [SELF- 2.] Imposed on one by oneself.

Self-indu·ction. 1873. [SELF- 3 b.] *Electr.* The production of an induced current in a circuit by means of a variation in the current of that circuit. So **Self-indu·ctance,** in same sense; also, the coefficient of s. **Self-indu·ced, -indu·ctive** (1834) *adjs.* produced by s.

Self-indu·lgence. 1753. [SELF- 1 a.] Indulgence of one's desires. So **Self-indu·lgent** *a.*

Self-infli·cted, *ppl. a.* 1784. [SELF- 2.] Inflicted by oneself or one's own hand.

Self-i·nterest. 1649. [SELF- 5 a.] **1.** One's personal profit, benefit, or advantage. Now *rare* or *Obs.* 1658. †**b.** A private or personal end -1867. **2.** Regard to, or pursuit of, one's own advantage or welfare, *esp.* to the exclusion of regard for others 1649. Hence **Self-i·nterested** *a.* actuated solely by regard for one's personal advantage or welfare.

Self-invo·lved, *ppl. a.* 1842. [SELF- 3 a.] Wrapped up in oneself or one's own thoughts. So **Self-involu·tion** 1817.

Selfish (se·lfiʃ), *a.* 1640. [f. SELF *sb.* + -ISH [1] 2.] Devoted to or concerned with one's own advantage or welfare to the exclusion of regard for others. **b.** Used (by adversaries) as a designation of those ethical theories which regard self-love as the real motive of all human action 1847.

Want makes almost every man s. JOHNSON. 'Well, but what's to become of me?' urged the s. man DICKENS. **b.** The Epicurean, or S., System 1868. Hence **Se·lfish-ly** *adv.*, **-ness.**

Selfism (se·lfiz'm). 1791. [f. SELF *sb.* + -ISM.] Devotion to or concentration upon one's own interests; self-centredness Also, the 'selfish theory' of morals.

Selfist (se·lfist). *rare.* 1649. [f. SELF *sb.* + -IST.] A self-centred or selfish person.

Self-ju·dgement. 1745. [SELF- 1 a.] Judgement passed upon oneself.

Self-ju·stified, *ppl. a.* 1897. [SELF- 2.] *Printing.* Arranged by means of automatic justifying mechanism. So **Self-ju·stifying** *ppl. a.* 1895.

Self-know·ing, *ppl. a.* 1667. [SELF- 1 f, 3 b.] **1.** Knowing oneself; having self-knowledge. **2.** Knowing of oneself, without help from another 1828.

Self-know·ledge. 1613. [SELF- 1 a, d.] Knowledge of oneself, one's character, capabilities, etc.

Selfless (se·lf,lės), *a.* 1825. [f. SELF *sb.* + -LESS.] Having no regard for or thought of self; not self-centred; unselfish. Hence **Se·lflessly** *adv.*, **-ness.**

Se·lf-life. 1613. **1.** [SELF- 5 c.] = SELF-EXISTENCE. **2.** [SELF- 5 d.] Life lived for oneself; life devoted to selfish ends 1848.

Self-lo·ve. 1563. [SELF- 1 a, d.] **1.** Love of oneself; in early use most freq. = AMOUR-PROPRE; later, usu. = regard for one's interests or well-being; chiefly *opprobrious*, self-centredness, selfishness. **2.** *Philos.* Regard for one's own well-being or happiness, considered as a natural and proper relation of a man to himself 1683.

2. That..sort of Benevolence which we call s. 1688.

Self-made, *ppl. a.* 1615. [SELF- 2.] Made by oneself, one's own action or efforts; of one's own making.

S. man, one who has risen from obscurity or poverty by his own exertions (orig. *U.S.*).

Se·lf-mate, *sb.* 1888. [SELF- 1 a.] *Chess.* Checkmate produced by the side that is mated. Also as *vb.*

Self-mo·tion. 1619. [SELF- 5 c.] Motion produced by inherent power apart from external impulse; voluntary or spontaneous motion.

Self-mu·rder. 1563. [SELF- 1 a.] The taking of one's own life; self-destruction; suicide. So **Self-mu·rderer.**

Se·lfness. 1586. [f. SELF *sb.* + -NESS.] **1.** Self-centredness; egoism; selfishness; †occas. *pl.* selfish acts or manifestations. Also, due regard for oneself (*rare*). †**2.** Individuality, essence (*rare*) -1651.

Self-opi·nion. Now *rare.* 1579. [SELF- 1 d.] High opinion of oneself, self-esteem; esp. self-conceit; obstinacy in one's own opinion. So **Self-opi·nioned** *ppl. a.* 1624.

Self-opi·nionated, *ppl. a.* 1671. [f. prec.] **1.** Having an exaggerated opinion of oneself; self-conceited. **2.** Obstinate in one's opinion 1770.

Self-pi·ty. 1621. [SELF- 1 d.] Pity or tender feeling for oneself.

Self-pollu·tion. 1626. [SELF- 1 a.] Masturbation, self-abuse.

Se·lf-portrait. 1840. [After G. *selbstbildnis.*] A portrait made by a person of himself.

Self-posse·ssed, *ppl. a.* 1838. [Formed after next; see SELF- 2.] Characterized by self-possession.

Self-posse·ssion. 1745. [SELF- 1 d.] Command of one's faculties or feelings; self-command, composure.

Self-prai·se. 1549. [SELF- 1 a.] Praise or commendation of oneself.
S. is no commendation 1826.

Se·lf-preserva·tion. 1614. [SELF- 1 a.] The preservation of one's existence; *esp.* applied to the natural law or instinct which impels living creatures to take measures to prolong life and avoid injury.
S. is the first of laws DRYDEN.

Self-pri·de. 1586. [SELF- 3 a.] Pride in oneself, one's achievements, one's position; personal pride.

Self-ra·ising, *ppl. a.* 1869. [SELF- 3 b.] Applied to a kind of flour which causes dough or paste to rise without the addition of baking-powder, etc.

Se·lf-realiza·tion. 1876. [SELF- 1 a.] The fulfilment by one's own efforts of the possibilities of development of the self.

Self-rega·rd. 1595. [SELF- 1 a, 3 a.] **1.** Regard of or consideration for oneself. **2.** = SELF-RESPECT 2. 1811.

Self-reli·ance. 1837. [SELF- 3 a.] Reliance upon oneself, one's own powers, etc. So **Self-reli·ant** *a.* **Self-rely·ing** *ppl. a.*

Self-repre·ssion. 1870. [SELF- 1 a.] Repression of oneself, one's desires or opinions.

Self-reproa·ch. 1779. [SELF- 1 a.] Reproach of oneself.

Self-repu·gnance. Now *rare.* 1649. [SELF- 1 d.] Self-contradictory quality or character. So **Self-repu·gnant** *a.* self-contradictory.

Self-respe·ct. 1613. [In 1, SELF- 5 a, d; in 2, SELF- 1 d.] †**1.** A private, personal, or selfish end. (Chiefly *pl.*) –1675. **2.** Proper regard for the dignity of one's person or one's position 1795.

Self-restrai·nt. 1775. [SELF- 1 a.] Restraint imposed by oneself upon one's actions, etc. So **Self-restrai·ned** *a.* marked by or involving self-restraint 1700.

Self-ri·ght, *v.* 1881. [Back-formation from SELF-RIGHTING.] *intr.* To right itself. So **Self-ri·ghter,** a self-righting boat.

Self-ri·ghteous, *a.* 1680. [SELF- 3 b.] Righteous in one's own esteem. So **Self-ri·ghteously** *adv.* **Self-ri·ghteousness,** the condition of being s. 1656.

Self-ri·ghting, *vbl. sb.* 1855. [SELF- 1 b.] Of a boat: The action of righting itself after being upset. So **Self-ri·ghting** *ppl. a.*

Self-sa·crifice. 1805. [SELF- 1 a.] Sacrifice of oneself; the giving up of one's own interests, happiness, and desires, for the sake of duty or the welfare of others. So **Self-sa·crificing** *ppl. a.*
Give unto me, made lowly wise, The spirit of s. WORDSW.

Selfsame (se·lfsēⁱm), *a.* (*sb.*) Now *literary.* late ME. [orig. two words (see SELF A. 1 b, B. 1 c, and SAME A. 4); later, written as a compound with a hyphen, now as one word.] **A.** *adj.* (The) very same, very identical. †**B.** *absol.* or *sb.* The selfsame person or thing; rarely as *sb. pl.* identical things –1701.
A. We were nurst upon the self-same hill MILT.

Se·lf-satisfa·ction. 1793. [After next.] The condition or quality of being self-satisfied.

Self-sa·tisfied, *ppl. a.* 1734. [SELF- 3 a.] Satisfied with oneself, one's achievements, etc.; marked by self-satisfaction. So **Self-sa·tisfying** *ppl. a.* that satisfies oneself; affording self-satisfaction 1671.
The s. smirk of flash Toby Crackit DICKENS.

Self-see·ker. 1632. [After next.] One who selfishly seeks his own welfare.

Self-see·king, *vbl. sb.* 1586. [SELF- 1 b.] The seeking after one's own welfare before that of others. So **Self-see·king** *ppl. a.*

Self-slau·ghter. 1602. = SELF-MURDER.

Self-sown, *ppl. a.* 1608. Sown by itself without human or animal agency.

Self-sta·rter. 1887. [SELF- 4.] A mechanism for starting an internal-combustion engine without the use of a crank-handle, etc. So **Self-starting** *ppl. a.*

†**Self-substa·ntial,** *a. rare.* [SELF- 3 b.] Derived from one's own substance. SHAKS.

Self-suffi·ciency. 1623. [f. next (see -ENCY), rendering Gr. αὐτάρκεια.] The quality or condition of being self-sufficient; *esp.* as an attribute of God. So **Self-suffi·cience.**

Self-suffi·cient, *a.* 1589. [SELF- 3 b; in 1, tr. Gr. αὐτάρκης.] **1.** Sufficient in or for oneself (itself) without external aid or support; able to supply one's needs oneself. Not now of persons. **2.** Having excessive confidence in oneself, one's powers, etc.; characterized by overweening behaviour 1734.
1. A compleat s. Country, where there is rather a Superfluity than Defect of anything 1645. **2.** A s. jackanapes 1842. So **Self-suffi·cing** *ppl. a.*

Self-sugge·stion. 1899. [SELF- 3 b.] Suggestion to oneself; the voluntary fixing in one's mind some idea in order that it may afterwards operate subconsciously or automatically. So **Self-sugge·stive** *a.* 1848.

Self-suppo·rt. 1774. [SELF- 1 a.] The act of supporting oneself (itself) without external assistance; the fact of being self-supporting. So **Self-suppo·rting** *ppl. a.*, supporting oneself (itself) without external aid, (of a physical object) not requiring the usual support, (of an enterprise) paying its way.

Self-surre·nder. 1702. [SELF- 1 a.] The surrender or giving up of oneself to an influence, emotion, or the like.

Self-taught, *ppl. a.* 1725. [SELF- 2.] Taught by oneself without direct aid from others; self-educated. **b.** Of what is learnt: Acquired by one's own unaided efforts 1774.

†**Self-vi·olence.** 1671. [SELF- 3 a.] The laying of violent hands upon oneself: a euphemism for SELF-MURDER –1787.

Self-wi·ll. [Com. Teut.; OE. *selfwill*; see SELF- and WILL *sb.*] †**1.** One's own will or desire –1456. **2.** Wilful or obstinate persistence in following one's own desires or opinions. late ME. So †**Self-wi·lly** *a.*, self-willed –1631.

Self-willed, *a.* 1470. [f. prec. + -ED [2].] Wilful or obstinate in the pursuit of one's own desires or opinions; characterized by self-will. Hence **Selfwi·lledness.**

Self-wise, *a.* 1561. [SELF- 3 b.] Wise in one's own conceit, relying on one's own wisdom. So **Self-wi·sdom,** the condition of being s.

Selion (se·liǒn). *Hist.* and *local.* 1450. [ad. Anglo-L. *selionem, seilonem,* AF. *seilon* = mod.F. *sillon* furrow.] A portion of land of indeterminate area comprising a ridge or narrow strip lying between two furrows formed in dividing an open field, a 'narrow-land'.

Seljuk (se·lʤuk), *a.* and *sb.* 1834. [f. Turk. *seljūq,* name of the reputed ancestor of the Seljuk dynasties.] **A.** *adj.* The distinctive epithet of certain Turkish dynasties which ruled over large parts of Asia from the 11th to the 13th c. **B.** *sb.* A member of the Seljuk tribe or dynasty 1841. So **Seljukian** (seldʒū·kiăn) *a.* (1603) and *sb.* (1638).

Sell (sel), *sb.*[1] Now *arch.* late ME. [a. F. *selle* :—L. *sella* :—**sedla,* f. *sed-, sedere* to sit.] †**1.** A seat, a low stool; a seat of dignity –1627. **2.** A saddle. late ME.

Sell (sel), *sb.*[2] 1838. [f. SELL *v.*] **1.** An act of betraying or giving up to justice. **2.** *slang.* A contrivance, fiction, etc., by which a person is 'sold'; a hoax, take-in. Also, something that utterly disappoints high expectations. 1853. **3.** *U.S.* **Sell-out.** An agreement or contract corruptly made by a public body, involving sacrifice of public to private interest 1890.

Sell (sel), *v.* Pa. t. and pple. **sold** (sōuld). [Com. Teut. wk. vb.; OE. *sellan* :—OTeut. **saljan,* f. **salā* gift, delivery, SALE *sb.*] †**1.** *trans.* To give, in various senses; esp. to hand over (something, esp. food, a gift) voluntarily or in response to a demand or request; to deliver up (a person, esp. a hostage) to the keeping of another; to grant (forgiveness, etc.) -ME. **2.** To give up (a person) treacherously to his enemies; to betray (a person, cause, country, etc.) OE. **3.** To give up or hand over (something) to another person for money (or something that is reckoned as money); esp. to dispose of (merchandise, possessions, etc.) to a buyer for a price; to vend. Also, in habitual sense, of a shopkeeper, etc.: To deal in, keep for sale (a particular commodity). OE. **b.** To dispose of (one's commission in the army) by sale under the purchase system. Now *Hist.* Also *absol.* 1713. **c.** *causatively.* To promote the sale of 1709. **d.** To hand over (a person, a people) into slavery or bondage for a sum of money. In Biblical use (after Heb.) often, To hand over to the dominion of another, to enslave. OE. **4.** *absol.* and *intr.* ME. **5.** *To s.* (gerundial inf. used predic.): on sale, offered for sale. Now *rare.* ME. **6.** *intr.* in passive sense. Of a commodity: To find purchasers. *To s. for, at* = to fetch (a price). 1606. **7.** *trans.* In various fig. uses. ME. **8.** *slang.* To cheat, trick, deceive, take in 1607.
2. Brougham, it is said, grossly, has sold the Queen 1820. **3.** Yet s. your face for fiue pence and 'tis deere SHAKS. **d.** 2 *Kings* xvii. 17. **e.** *U.S.* To advertise or publish the merits of (a book, etc.) to encourage sales 1925. **f.** *U.S.* To give (a person) information *on* the value of something; to inspire with desire to possess something 1926. **4.** *Merch. V.* I. iii. 36. **6.** Prior's *Journey* sells still SWIFT. **7.** 2 *Hen. VI*, IV. i. 41. [They] Have..sold my Reputation for a Song FITZGERALD. Phr. *To s. one's life dear, dearly,* etc., to destroy many of one's adversaries before giving up one's life in an encounter. *To s. oneself,* to dispose of one's services for money; to enslave oneself. *To s. a match, game,* to lose it for a bribe. *To sell the pass, a pup*: see PASS *sb.*[1] II. 1 b, PUP *sb.*[1]
With advs. **S. off.** *trans.* To dispose of by sale (esp. at reduced prices); to sell the whole of (one's stock, possessions, etc.). Also *absol.* **S. out. a.** *trans.* To distribute by sale. **b.** To dispose of (stocks, shares, etc.) by sale. Also *absol.* **c.** *intr.* To dispose of one's commission in the army by sale. Now *Hist.* **d.** *trans.* To dispose of the whole of (one's stock, property, etc.) by sale. Also *absol.* **S. up. a.** *trans.* To dispose of the whole of (a person's stock, goods, etc.) by sale. Also *absol.* **b.** To dispose of the whole or a portion of the goods of (an insolvent or bankrupt person) for the benefit of his creditors. Also with the goods as obj.

‖**Sella** (se·lă). 1693. [L., seat, saddle.] *Anat.* A saddle-shaped portion of the sphenoid, more fully *sella equina, sphenoidalis* or *turcica.*

Sellenger's round. 1567. [*Sellenger* represents the pronunciation of the surname *St. Leger.*] An old country dance; also, the music for this.

Seller (se·lər). ME. [f. SELL *v.* + -ER [1].] **1.** One who sells. **2.** A book, later, any article or type of article with a (wide, poor, etc.) sale; also, without qualification, a book, etc. that sells well 1900. Now esp. in *best-s.* (1912). **3.** *colloq.* = SELLING-*race* 1922.

Selling (se·liŋ), *vbl. sb.* ME. [f. SELL *v.* + -ING [1].] The action of SELL *v.*; an instance of this.
attrib. and *Comb.* **s. price,** the price at which an article is sold; **s. race,** a race for horses which are to be sold after the race; so *s. handicap, plate* (hence *s. plater*).

S'elp. Also **swelp.** ME. Contr. of 'So help', in the oath 'So help me God'. Now *vulgar.*

Seltzer (se·ltsər). 1741. [Alteration of G. *Selterser,* f. *Selters,* a village in Hesse-Nassau, Prussia.] (In full *s.-water.*) An effervescent mineral water obtained near Nieder-Selters, containing sodium chloride and small quantities of sodium, calcium, and magnesium carbonates. Also, an artificial mineral water of similar composition.

Seltzogene (se·ltsŏdʒīn). 1860. [a. F. *sel(t)zogène,* f. *seltz, selz* seltzer water + *-gène* -GEN.] An apparatus for the production of artificial seltzer and other mineral and aerated waters.

Selvage, selvedge (se·lvėdʒ), *sb.* 1460. [app. f. SELF + EDGE *sb.*, after early mod. Du. *selfegghe,* now *zelfegge.*] **1.** The edge of a piece of woven material finished in such a manner as to prevent the ravelling out of the weft. Also, a narrow strip or list at the edge of a web of cloth, which is intended to be cut off or covered by the seam when the material is made up. **b.** *transf.* A marginal tract, border, edge 1650. **2.** *Naut.* and *Mil.* = SELVAGEE 1711. **3.** *Mining.* A thin layer of clayey or earthy matter surrounding a metalliferous vein 1757.

Selvage, selvedge (se·lvėdʒ), *v.* 1611. [f. prec.] *trans.* To form a boundary or edging to.

Selvagee (se·lvădʒī). 1750. [app. f. SELVAGE *sb.* (sense 2).] A hank or skein of rope-yarn marled together, and used as a strap to fasten round a shroud or stay, or as slings, etc.

Semantic (sĭmæ·ntik), *a.* and *sb.* 1895. [ad. Gr. σημαντικός, significant, f. σημαίνειν to show.] **A.** *adj.* Relating to signification or meaning. **B.** *sb. pl.* = SEMASIOLOGY 1894.

Semaphore (se·măfōᵊɹ), *sb.* 1816. [f. Gr. σῆμα sign, signal + -PHORE.] An apparatus for making signals, consisting of an upright post with one or more arms moving in a vertical plane. **b.** *attrib.*, as *s. house, lamp.* Also, in recent use, applied to a special form of flag-signalling. 1821. Hence **Se·maphore** *v. trans.* and *intr.* to signal by s. **Semapho·ric, -al** *adjs.* relating to, of the nature of, a s.; **-ly** *adv.*

Semasiology (sĭmēˈsiˌǫ·lŏdʒi). 1877. [f. Gr. σημασία signification + -LOGY.] That branch of philology which deals with the meanings of words and their sense-development. Hence **Semasiolo·gical** *a.*, **-ly** *adv.*, **-o·logist.**

Sematic (sĭmæ·tik), *a.* 1890. [f. Gr. σηματ-, σῆμα sign + -IC.] *Biol.* Of mimetic colours: Serving for signal or warning.

Sematography (sĭmătǫ·grăfi). 1902. [f. as prec. + -GRAPHY.] The use of signs or symbols (instead of letters) in writing. So **Semato-gra·phic** *a.* of or pertaining to s.

Sematology (sī-, sematǫ·lŏdʒi). 1831. [f. as prec. + -LOGY.] **1.** The doctrine of the use of 'signs' (esp. words) in relation to thought and knowledge. **2.** = SEMASIOLOGY 1880.

Semblable (se·mblăb'l), *a.* (and *sb.*). late ME. [a. F., f. *sembler* to seem, appear; see -ABLE.] **A.** *adj.* †**1.** Like, similar. Const. *to.* –1840. †**b.** The like, such-like –1653. †**2.** Corresponding, proportional, suitable –1817. **3.** Apparent, seeming, not real. †Of treason: Presumptive, constructive (*rare*). 1627.

1. It is a wonderfull thing to see the s. Coherence of his mens spirits, and his SHAKS. **3.** What is gained..by supposing..the miracle was only s., not real? 1874.

†**B.** *sb.* **1.** *absol.* and quasi-*sb.* (occas. pl. *semblables*): Something that is like or similar –1627. **2.** With qualifying possessive: (One's) like, (one's) fellow –1607.

2. To make true dixion of him, his s. is his mirrour SHAKS. Hence †**Se·mblableness** (*rare*) –1638. **Se·mblably** *adv.*

Semblance (se·mblăns). late ME. [a. F., f. *semblant* SEMBLANT *a.*] **1.** The appearance or outward aspect of a person or thing. **b.** The form, likeness or image *of* a person or thing, considered in regard to another that is similar. late ME. **2.** A person's appearance or demeanour, expressive of his thoughts, feelings, etc., or feigned in order to hide them. late ME. **3.** An appearance or outward seeming *of* (something which is not actually there or of which the reality is different from its appearance) 1489. **4.** A person or thing that resembles another; an image or copy *of* 1513. **5.** The fact or quality of being like something 1576.

1. A timely-parted Ghost, Of ashy s. SHAKS. **b.** And now the lake narrowed to the s. of a tranquil river 1867. **2.** A dissembling friend with faire and false words and semblances draweth his neighbour into some dangerous inconvenience 1633. **3.** To reach down a well-bound s. of a volume LAMB. The fall of Strafford had put an end to all s. of rule 1874.

Phr. *In s.*, in seeming, in appearance (only). *To make s.*, to make an appearance or pretence.

†**Se·mblant,** *sb.* ME. [a. F., sb. use of pr. pple. of *sembler* SEMBLE *v.*¹] **1.** A person's outward aspect or appearance; esp. demeanour, look, expression –1651. **2.** Appearance, seeming, outward aspect; also, an appearance or show (whether true or false) *of* some quality, etc. Also, something that exists only in appearance or pretence. –1624. **3.** A likeness or resemblance, an image or portrait (*of*) –1617.

1. A minde which could cast a carelesse s. vppon the greatest conflictes of Fortune SIDNEY.

Phr. **To make s.** [= F. *faire semblant*]. **a.** To have or assume a (specified) expression, look, or demeanour. **b.** To make a show, appearance, or pretence *of*; to seem likely, threaten *to do.* **c.** With neg.: Not to let one's thoughts, feelings, etc., appear; to show no sign (*of*); not to seem (or not to seem likely) *to be* or *do* something.

Semblant (se·mblănt), *a.* 1485. [a. OF., pr. pple. of *sembler* SEMBLE *v.*¹] †**1.** Like, similar –1729. **2.** Seeming, counterfeit 1840.

†**Se·mble,** *v.*¹ ME. [a. F. *sembler* :—L. *similare, simulare,* f. *similis* like.] **1.** *trans.* To be like, resemble –1713. **2.** *intr.* To seem, appear –1526. **3.** *trans.* To simulate, feign; *absol.* to practise simulation –1590. **4.** To represent, picture –1706.

‖ **Semble** (se·mb'l), *v.*² *impers.* 1817. [F., 3rd pers. sing. pres. ind. of *sembler* to seem.] *Law.* = 'It seems'; used in judicial utterances to introduce the incidental statement of an opinion on a point which it is not necessary to decide authoritatively. Abbrev. *sem., semb.*

‖ **Semée** (se·mi, F. səme), *a.* 1562. [a. F., fem. of *semé*, pa. pple. of *semer* to sow.] *Her.* = POWDERED *ppl. a.* 2. Also **Se·méed** *a.*

Semeiology (sīməiˌǫ·lŏdʒi). 1694. [f. Gr. σημεῖον sign + -LOGY.] **1.** Sign language. **2.** The branch of medical science which is concerned with symptoms 1839. Hence **Semeio-lo·gic, -al** *adjs.* pertaining to s. **Semeio·logist,** one skilled in sign-language.

Semeiotic (sīməiˌǫ·tik), *a.* 1625. [a. Gr. σημειωτικός significant.] Relating to symptoms. So **Semeio·tical** *a.* 1588.

Semeiotics (sīməiˌǫ·tiks). 1670. [ad. Gr. σημειωτική (sc. τέχνη).] The branch of medical science relating to the interpretation of symptoms.

Semen (sī·men). late ME. [a. L., f. root *se- of *serere* to SOW.] The impregnating fluid of male animals; the seed or sperm.

Semester (sĭme·stəɹ). 1827. [a. G., ad. L. (*cursus*) *semestris* (period) of six months, f. *se-, sex* six + *mensis* month.] A period or term of six months, esp. in German universities and some U.S. colleges, the college half-year. So **Seme·strial, seme·stral** *a.* half-yearly; taking place every six months; lasting for six months, (of persons) holding office for six months; exercising office every six months.

Semi (se·mi). *Sc.* 1661. [app. short for *semi bejanus* (see BEJAN).] In some Scottish universities, a student in his second year; also called *s.-bachelor, s.-bejan.*

Semi- (se·mi), *prefix.* [repr. L. *semi-* = Skr. *sāmi-* Gr. ἡμι-, OHG. *sâmi-*, OS. *sâm-*, cogn. w. OE. *sam-* :—Indo-Eur. **sēmi-*.] = HALF-; cf. DEMI-, HEMI-.

I. In general use. **1.** Compounded with adjs. and pples., with the meaning 'half, partly, partially, to some extent'; as **s.-animate, -animous,** half-alive; **-attached,** partially or loosely attached; **-divine,** half-divine; that is a demigod; **-feral,** half-wild; **-formed,** half-formed; **-nude,** half-naked; **-occasional,** *U.S.*, occurring once in a while; **-opaque,** partly opaque; only partially transparent; **-perfect** (*rare*), imperfect, incomplete; **-skilled**; etc. **b.** Compounded with a sb. to form an adj. phrase, as **s.-state,** etc. **2.** Compounded with sbs.: **a.** with nouns of action or condition, as **s.-allegiance,** partial, imperfect, or incomplete allegiance; **-opacity,** the condition or quality of being s.-opaque; **b.** with descriptive sbs., as **s.-acquaintance,** one with whom one is partially acquainted; **-barbarian,** one who is half-barbarian; **-deity, -god,** a demigod; **-savage** = *s.-barbarian.* **3.** Compounded with vbs., as **s.-castrate,** to castrate partially; **-flex,** to bend into a position half-way between that of extension and that of complete flexure. **4.** With advs., as **s.-consciously,** half-consciously; **-occasionally** *U.S.*, every now and then.

II. In special and technical use. **1. a.** With designations of quantity, extent of space or time and the like, as *s.-arc, -century,* etc. **b.** With adjs., advbs., and sbs. expressing periodical recurrence or duration, *semi-* denotes that the period is halved (after SEMI-ANNUAL); **s.-centennial** *a.*, of or pertaining to a period of 50 years; **-daily** *a.* and *adv.*, (occurring) twice daily; **-horal** *a.*, half-hourly; **-mensual** *a.*, recurring twice a month; **-millenary** *a.*, lasting 500 years; **-monthly** *a.* and *adv.*, (occurring, issued, etc.) twice a month; also *sb.* a fortnightly periodical; so **-weekly.**

c. *Mus.* Designating a note, etc. of half the length, as SEMIBREVE, SEMIQUAVER.

d. *Astr.* †**s.-quadrate,** †**-quartile, -quintile, -sextile,** denoting aspects of planets when they are 45°, 36°, 30°, respectively, distant from one another; **-square** = *S.-quadrate.*

2. a. Designating a (geometrical) form derived from another by bisection (usu.) in a vertical or longitudinal direction, as *s.-canal, -cone, -cylinder, -dome, -ellipse, -globe, -hexagon; -hexagonal, -oval, -ovate, -rotund* adjs.; *-spheroid* adj., etc.

b. *Math.* Designating a bisected line, arc, area, segment, etc., or the half of a definite quantity, as *s.-angle, -circumference, -diameter, -segment,* etc.; (in conic sections) *-ordinate, -parameter, -transverse*; also, **s.-axis,** the half of the axis of an ellipse, etc.; **-difference,** half the difference between two quantities; **-infinite** *a.*, limited in one direction, and extending to infinity in the other; **-quadrantally** *adv.*, from 0° to 45°; **-sum,** half the sum of two or more quantities; **-tangent,** the tangent of half an arc.

c. *Nat. Hist.* With adjs. and sbs. descriptive of shape in the contour or marking of natural objects; **s.-annular,** of the form of a half-ring; **-collar, -coronet, -fascia, -ring,** a band, etc., roughly semicircular or extending half-way round a part or an organ; **-coronate(d** *a.*, having a semicircle of spikes, bristles, etc.; **-floret,** a floret having a ligulate corolla, as in the dandelion.

d. *Nat. Hist.* Denoting that a part has a certain form or character (*a*) for half the extent, or along half the length, etc. of an organ, 'half-way', as *s.-adherent, -bifid, -erect,* etc.; (*b*) on one side only, or so as to exhibit the half of a particular figure, as *s.-cordate(d, -lanceolate, -terete,* etc.

e. In *Building*, designating structural forms of half the full width, breadth, or girth, resulting from (usu.) vertical or longitudinal bisection, as *s.-arch, -column, -shaft,* etc.; **s.-beam** = CANTILEVER 2; **-engaged** *a.*, (of a column) attached to a wall so that half its diameter projects; etc.

f. *Cryst.* **s.-prismated,** applied to a crystal in which 'only half of the edges on the common basis are obliterated by lateral planes'; etc.

g. *Her.* = DEMI- B. 1; as *s.-chevron,* etc.

h. *Printing.* **s.-quotes** *colloq.*, single quotation-marks (' ').

3. = to the extent of (only) a half, imperfect(ly), incomplete(ly). **a.** With adjs. and sbs. expressing kinds or degrees of composition, consistency, texture, colour, as *s.-cartilaginous, -coagulated, -crystalline, -diaphanous, -pasty, -resinous, -solid, -transparent, -vitreous,* etc.

b. In designations of heresies, sects, and schools of thought, expressing partial adherence to the tenets or theories connoted by the second element of the compound, as *s.-Augustinian, -Darwinian, -infidel,* etc.

c. *Gram.*, as *s.-nasal* adj.; **s.-consonant** = SEMI-VOWEL; **-deponent,** a verb in Latin in which the tenses of the present group have active forms and those of the perfect group passive forms, as *gaudeo, gavisus sum*; etc.

d. *Nat. Hist.* = imperfectly, incompletely, partly (of a certain habit, form, texture, etc.), as *s.-aquatic, -articulate, -osseous, -palmate,* etc.

e. Designating an animal or vegetable form, class, species, etc., which has only some of the characteristics of that denoted by the second element, or is intermediate between that and another, as *s.-ape* (= HALF-APE, lemur), *-lichen, rapacious* adj.; **s.-nymph,** a nymph of such insects as undergo only a slight change in passing to the imago stage.

f. In *Anatomy*, chiefly in names of muscles (*a*) situated partly in a certain region, as *s.-spinalis*, or (*b*) being partly of a certain texture or shape, as *s.-membranosus, -orbicularis,* etc.; **s.-bulb,** the bulbous vestibuli, either of two vascular bodies on either side of the entrance of the vagina.

g. In *Pathology* and *Therapeutics*, as *s.-albinism, -coma, -prone,* etc.

h. In *Chemistry*, as *s.-acid, -oxygenated,* etc.; **s.-combined** *a.*, partially or loosely combined.

i. In *Geology, Mineralogy,* and *Geography*, as *s.-calcareous, -extinct, volcanic* adjs.

j. In names of articles or processes of manufacture; **s.-china, -porcelain,** ware resembling china, etc., but having an inferior glaze and finish; **-steel,** puddled steel.

k. Denoting styles of architecture having only some of the features connoted by the second element, as *s.-classic, -Gothic,* etc.

l. In names of mechanical contrivances, as **s.-automatic,** having only some of the movements automatic; **-rotary,** partly rotary; etc.

4. Miscellaneous: **s.-bull** *R. C. Ch.*, a bull issued by a pope before his coronation; **-final,** in football and other contests, the match or round immediately preceding the final one; **-precious** *a.*, (of stones) not of sufficient value to rank as gems; **-rigid** *a.*, (of an airship) having a stiffened keel attached to a flexible gas container.

Semi-a·nnual, *a.* (and *sb.*). 1794. [SEMI- II. 1 b.] **1.** Recurring every half-year; half-yearly. **2.** Lasting for half a year (only); esp. of plants. Also *sb.* = s. plant. 1882.

Semi-A·rian, *a.* and *sb.* 1616. [ad. eccl. L. *semiarianus*; see SEMI- II. 3 b and ARIAN.] **A.** *adj.* Partially Arian; used chiefly with ref.

to a sect which arose in the 4th c. A.D., holding that the Son is of like substance (ὁμοιούσιος) but not of the same substance (ὁμοούσιος) with the Father. **B.** *sb.* One who holds S. views.

Semibreve (se·mibrīv). 1591. [f. SEMI- II. 1 c + BREVE *sb.* 2, after obs. F. *semibreve.*] *Mus.* A note having half (†in 'perfect time', one third) the length of a breve; in mod. music the longest note in ordinary use. (Its figure is now an open oval ○.) Also *attrib.*, as *s. rest.*

Semi-cho·rus. 1797. [mod.L., tr. Gr. ἡμιχόριον.] **a.** One of two parts into which the main body of a chorus is divided; chiefly *Mus.* **b.** A piece of music to be performed by a company of singers selected from a chorus. Hence **Semi-cho·ric** *a.*

Semicircle (se·misɔ̄ık'l). 1526. [ad. L. *semicirculus*; see SEMI- II. 2 b and CIRCLE *sb.*] **1.** The half of a circle divided by a diameter, or the half of its circumference. **2.** A set of objects or an arrangement in the form of a half-circle 1597. **3.** = GRAPHOMETER 1712. Hence **Se·micircle** *v. trans.* to surround with a s.; *intr.* to form a s. **Se·micircled** *ppl. a.* (chiefly *poet.*) of the form of a s.; arranged in a s.

Semicircular (semisɔ̄·ıkiŭlăı), *a.* late ME. [ad. med.L. *semicircularis.*] Of the form of a semicircle. **b.** *Anat.* Designating †(*a*) the orbicular muscle of the eyelid; (*b*) the three canals of the internal ear 1706. Hence **Semici·rcularly** *adv.* in a s. form; in a half-circle.

Semicirque (se·misɛ̄ık). *poet.* 1795. [f. SEMI- II. 2 a + CIRQUE.] A semicircle.

Semicolon (semikōu·lǫn). 1644. [f. SEMI- + COLON².] A punctuation-mark consisting of a dot placed above a comma (;). In its present use it is the chief stop intermediate in value between the comma and the full stop.

Semi-cu·bical, *a.* 1677. [SEMI- II. 2 b.] *Math.* Applied to the curve of the third degree with a cusp referred to rectangular axes, the equation to which can always be reduced to the form $ay^2 = x^3$.

The exponent of the power of the abscissa which is proportional to the ordinate is 3/2, whence the name.

Semi-demi-. 1836. Used (1) = half-half, i.e. quarter, in **semidemisemiquaver,** a note the 64th part of a semibreve; (2) vaguely in a diminutive sense, as in *semi-demi-dinner.* Cf. DEMI-SEMI.

Se:mi-deta·ched, *a.* 1859. [SEMI- I. 1.] Partially detached. **b.** *spec.* Designating either of a pair of houses joined together and forming a block by themselves 1859.

Se:mi-diu·rnal, *a.* 1594. [SEMI- II. 1 a.] **1.** *Astr.* Pertaining to, consisting of, or performed in, half the time between the rising and setting of a celestial body. Chiefly in *s. arc.* **2.** Occurring every twelve hours. Chiefly of the tides. 1794. **3.** *Ent.* Partly diurnal, flying at twilight 1890.

Semi-dou·ble, *a.* (*sb.*) 1720. [SEMI- I. 1.] **1.** *Liturg.* Also *sb.* = s. feast, a feast of less solemnity than a double, only the first half of the antiphon being recited before the psalms. 1728. **2.** Of flowers: Having the innermost stamens perfect, while the outermost have become petaloid 1720.

1. Sundays and Days within an Octave are Semi-doubles 1850.

Semiflu·id, *a.* and *sb.* 1731. [SEMI- II. 3 a.] **A.** *adj.* Of a consistency midway between fluid and solid 1775. **B.** *sb.* A semi-fluid substance 1731.

Se·mi-form. 1836. [SEMI- I. 2, II. 2 f.] An imperfect form; *Cryst.*, a hemihedral form.

Semilunar (semil'ū·năı), *a.* (*sb.*) 1597. [ad. mod.L. *semilunaris*, f. **semiluna* half-moon; see SEMI- II. 2 a and LUNAR.] **A.** *adj.* Half-moon-shaped; crescentic; *spec.* in *Zool.*, *Bot.*, and *Anat.*

S. Valves..are little Valves or Membranes of a S. Figure, placed in the Orifice of the Pulmonary Artery, to prevent the Relapse of the Blood into the Heart at the time of its Dilatation 1728. In man..[the third eyelid] exists..as a mere rudiment, called the s. fold DARWIN.

B. *sb.* A semilunar bone, valve, etc. 1893. So **Semilu·nary** *a.* (now *rare* or *Obs.*) = A. **Semilu·nate** *a.* = LUNATE.

Se·mi-lune. 1858. [As if ad. L. **semiluna* half-moon; see SEMI- II. 2 a and LUNE³.] A semilunar or crescent-shaped form, structure, etc.; *Fortif.* = DEMI-LUNE 2.

Semi-me·tal. 1661. [ad. mod.L. *semimetallum*; see SEMI- I. 2, II. 3 i.] *Old Chem.* A non-malleable metal. Hence **Se:mi-meta·llic** *a.* partly metallic; *spec.* of the nature of a s.

Seminal (se·minăl), *a.* (and *sb.*) late ME. [a. F. *séminal*, ad. L. *seminalis*, f. *semin-*, *semen* SEMEN; see -AL.] **A.** *adj.* **1.** Of or pertaining to the seed or semen of men and animals; of the nature of semen. **2.** With ref. to plants: Pertaining to or of the nature of seed. *Bot.* Of organs or structures: Serving to contain the seed. 1658. †**b.** Produced from seed -1796. **3.** *gen.* Of or pertaining to the seed or reproductive elements existing in organic bodies, or attributed in pre-scientific belief to inorganic substances. Formerly often in *s. power*, *virtue*, the power of producing offspring. 1605. **4.** *fig.* Having the properties of seed; containing the possibility of future development 1639.

1. Animals, of spontaneous and s. generation 1673. 2. The s. spike of Mercurie weld SIR T. BROWNE. 4. It is pleasant to see great works in their s. state, pregnant with latent possibilities of excellence JOHNSON.

†**B.** *sb.* A seminal particle; a seed, germ -1682. Hence †**Semina·lity,** s. quality, principle, or condition; *pl.* s. properties; s. particles, germs. **Se·minally** *adv.* in a s. state or manner; as regards germination or reproduction.

‖ **Seminar** (se·minăı). 1889. [G., ad. L. *seminarium* SEMINARY *sb.*¹] In German universities (hence in certain British and American universities), a select group of advanced students associated for advanced study and original research under the guidance of a professor. Also *transf.*, a class that meets for systematic study under the direction of a teacher.

Seminarist (se·minărist). 1583. [f. next + -IST.] **1.** A Roman Catholic priest educated in a foreign seminary in the 16th and 17th c., esp. at Douay for the English mission. Now *Hist.* **2.** A student in a seminary; chiefly, one in a seminary for the training of Roman Catholic priests 1835. **b.** *pl.* The teaching staff in a seminary 1668. **3.** A member of a seminar 1865.

Seminary (se·minări), *sb.*¹ 1440. [ad. L. *seminarium* seed-plot, orig. neut. of *seminarius* SEMINARY *a.*] †**1.** A piece of ground in which plants are sown (or raised from cuttings, etc.) to be afterwards transplanted; a seed-plot -1829. †**2.** *transf.* A place where animals are bred; a region which supplies (some kind of animal). Also, a stock or breed (of animal). -1665. **3.** *fig.* **a.** A place or thing in which something (e.g. an art or science, a virtue or vice) is developed or cultivated 1592. **b.** A place, country, society, condition of things, or the like, in which some particular class of persons is produced or trained 1604. **4.** A place of education, a school, college, university, or the like (often with qualifying word, as *s. of science, theological s.*) 1585. **5.** *R. C. Ch.* A school or college for training persons for the priesthood. Also *attrib.*, as *s. priest.* 1581. **6.** = SEMINAR 1889. †**7.** Short for *s. priest* -1685.

1. Then taking your grafted trees out of the s., you shall transplant them into this nursery EVELYN. 3. **a.** The bloud of this noble Army of Martyrs became the fruitful s. thereof 1656. 4. Westminster School a most famous seminarie of learning FULLER. To place his daughter in a s. for female education SCOTT. Hence **Semina·rian,** †**a** seminary priest; a seminarist.

†**Se·minary,** *a.* and *sb.*² 1583. [ad. L. *seminarius*, f. *semin-* SEMEN.] **A.** *adj.* **1.** = SEMINAL *a.* -1742. **2.** Occupied in sowing seed. *fig.* with allusion to prec. 7. -1640. **B.** *sb.* **1. a.** A germ, embryo, seminal particle -1671. **b.** *spec.* The morbific matter or principle (of a disease); *pl.* germs (of infection) -1694. **2.** A sower of seed. -1680.

Seminate (se·mineit), *v.* Now *arch.* 1535. [f. L. *seminat-*, *seminare* to sow, f. *semin-* SEMEN; see -ATE³.] *trans.* To sow; chiefly *fig.* to disseminate. So **Se·minative** *a.* (*rare*) having the function of sowing or propagating. late ME.

Semination (seminēi·ʃən). 1531. [a. L. *seminationem*, f. *seminare*; see prec.] **1.** The action or process of sowing. Chiefly *fig.* **2.** The production of seed or semen 1658. **3.** The natural dispersion of seeds 1765.

Seminiferous (semini·fĕrəs), *a.* 1692. [f. L. *semin-*, *semen* SEMEN + -(I)FEROUS.] **1.** *Bot.* Bearing or producing seed. **2.** *Anat.* Containing or conveying the seminal fluid; bearing or producing semen 1831.

1. *S. scale*, in *Coniferæ* the scale above the bract-scale bearing the ovules, and ultimately the seeds.

‖ **Seminium** (sĭmi·niŏm). *rare.* *Pl.* **-ia.** 1676. [L., f. *semin-*, *semen* SEMEN.] The first principle (of anything), the germ, etc.

Se:mi-noctu·rnal, *a.* 1594. [SEMI- II. 1 b.] *Astr.* Pertaining to, or accomplished in, half a night.

Semi-o·pal. 1794. [tr. G. *halbopal.*] An inferior variety of opal harder and more opaque than common opal.

Se:mipara·bola. 1656. [SEMI- II. 2 b.] *Math.* **1.** Half of a parabola. **2.** 'A curve of such a nature that the powers of its ordinates are to each other as the next lower powers of its abscissas' 1728. Hence **Se:mi-parabo·lical** *a.* comprising half a parabola.

Se·mi-ped(e. 1756. [ad. L. *semiped-*, *-pes*, f. *semi-* SEMI- + *ped-*, *pes* foot.] *Pros.* A half-foot.

Se:mi-Pela·gian, *a.* and *sb.* 1600. [ad. eccl. L. *Semipelagianus*; see SEMI- II. 3 b and PELAGIAN.] **A.** *adj.* Pertaining to the semi-Pelagians or semi-Pelagianism 1626. **B.** *sb.* An adherent of semi-Pelagianism 1600. Hence **Se:mi-Pela·gianism,** a doctrine intermediate between Augustinianism and Pelagianism, taught by Cassian of Marseilles in the 5th c.

Semiquaver (se·mikwēivəı). 1576. [SEMI- II. 1 c.] *Mus.* A note half the length of a quaver, the sixteenth part of a semibreve. †**b.** *allus.* A very short space of time -1635.

Semi-Sa·xon, *a.* and *sb.* 1735. [SEMI- I. 1, 2.] **A.** *adj.* Intermediate between 'Saxon' and 'English'; formerly used by philologists to designate the first period of Middle English, from *c* 1100–50 to *c* 1250. **B.** *sb.* The 'Semi-Saxon' language; Early Middle English.

Se·misphere. Now *rare.* 1659. [f. SEMI- + SPHERE.] A hemisphere. Hence **Semisphe·ric, -al** *adjs.*

‖ **Semita** (se·mită). 1877. [mod.L. use of L., narrow path.] *Zool.* A band of minute close-set tubercles which bear ciliated clubbed spines, characteristic of the spatangoid sea-urchins.

Semite (sī·-, se·məit). 1875. [ad. mod.L. *Semita*, f. late L. *Sem*, Gr. Σήμ Shem; see -ITE¹.] A person belonging to the race of mankind which includes most of the peoples mentioned in Gen. x. as descended from Shem son of Noah, as the Hebrews, Arabs, Assyrians, and Aramæans. Also, a person speaking a Semitic language as his native tongue.

Semitertian (semitɔ̄·ıʃăn), *a.* (*sb.*) 1611. [ad. mod.L. *semitertiana* (*febris*), rendering Gr. ἡμιτριταία; see SEMI- and TERTIAN.] *Old Path.* Applied to an intermittent fever combining the symptoms of a quotidian and a tertian, consisting of a paroxysm occurring every day with a second stronger one every other day.

Semitic (sĭmi·tik), *a.* and *sb.* 1813. [ad. mod.L. *Semiticus*, f. *Semita* SEMITE.] **A.** *adj.* Of or pertaining to the Semites. (In recent use often *spec.* = Jewish.) 1826. **b.** The distinctive epithet of that family of languages of which Hebrew, Aramæan, Ethiopic, and ancient Assyrian, are the principal members. Hence, (in *S. scholar, studies*, etc.) concerned with the S. languages. 1813. **B.** *sb.* **a.** A Semite (*rare*). **b.** The Semitic family of languages; *occas.* the Semitic language of Babylon in opposition to Sumerian. **c.** *pl.* *U.S.* The scientific study of the language, religion, etc. of Semitic peoples. 1875.

Semitism (sī·-, se·mitiz'm). 1851. [f. SEMITE + -ISM 3.] **1.** The attributes characteristic of the Semitic peoples. Also, the fact of being Semitic. **b.** Jewish ideas or influence in politics and society 1885. **2.** A Semitic word or idiom 1886. So **Se·mitist,** a Semitic scholar. **Se·mitize** *v. trans.* to render Semitic in character, language or religion.

Semitone (se·mitoun). 1609. [f. SEMI-

+Tone *sb.* (Earlier forms were †*semitoyn* 1486, †*-tune* 1607). Senses 2 and 3 (usu. written *semi-tone*) are new formations distinct from 1.] 1. *Mus.* An interval approximately equal to half a tone, the smallest interval in the ordinary scales. 2. *Art.* An intermediate tone or tint in a picture; a half-tone 1782. 3. A soft or gentle tone of voice; an undertone 1837. Hence **Se·mitonal, Semito·nic** *adjs.* pertaining to or consisting of a s. or semitones; (of a scale) chromatic.

Semi-u·ncial, *a.* (*sb.*) 1734. [Semi- II. 1 a.] *Palæogr.* Applied to a style of writing intermediate between uncial and minuscule.

Semivowel (se·mivau|ěl). 1530. [f. Semi- II. 3 c+Vowel, after L. *semivocalis.*] A vocal sound that partakes of the nature of a vowel and of a consonant; a letter representing such a sound.

As a technical term the word now most commonly denotes only *w* and *y*, but sometimes it includes these together with the liquids and nasals, chiefly in their non-syllabic values.

Semmit (se·mit). *Sc.* An undershirt or vest.

Semolina (semǒlī·nă). 1797. [Altered f. It. *semolino*, dim. of *semola* bran.] An article of food consisting of those hard portions of 'flinty' wheat which resist the action of the millstones, and are collected in the form of rounded grains. Also *attrib.*, as *s. pudding.*

‖**Semper-** (se·mpəɹ), the L. adv. *semper* always, used in various combs., as **s.-green**, an evergreen; **sempervirent** (-vəi·rěnt) *a.* [L. *virentem, virere* to be green] evergreen.

‖**Sempervivum** (sempəɹvəi·vǒm). 1591. [L., 'ever-living'.] a. The houseleek. b. A genus of crassulaceous plants containing the houseleek, *S. tectorum*, and about 50 other species; a plant of this genus.

Sempitern (se·mpitǝɹn), *a. arch.* late ME. [a. OF. *sempiterne*, ad. L. *sempiternus*, f. *semper* always; see Eterne *a.*] = next.

Sempiternal (sempitǝ·ɹnăl), *a.* late ME. [a. F. *sempiternel*, or ad. late L. *sempiternalis*, f. L. *sempiternus*; see prec. and -al 1.] Enduring constantly and continually; everlasting, eternal. Hence **Sempite·rnally** *adv.*

Sempstress: see Seamstress.

‖**Semsem** (se·msem). 1841. [Arab.] = Sesame.

‖**Semuncia** (sǐmɒ·nʃiă). *Pl.* **-iæ** (-i|ī). 1656. [L., f. *semi-* Semi- + *-uncia* Ounce *sb.*[1]] *Rom. Antiq.* A half-ounce, the twenty-fourth part of an *as*. Hence **Semu·ncial** *a.*

‖**Sen** (sen). 1802. [Japanese.] A Japanese copper or bronze coin of small value. Usu. *collect.* as *pl.*

‖**Senarius** (sǐnēᵊ·riǒs). *Pl.* **-ii.** 1540. [L., adj., consisting of six each, f. *seni* six each, f. *sex* six; used subst. by ellipsis of *versus* verse.] *Prosody.* A (Greek or Latin) verse consisting of six feet, each of which is either an iambus or some foot which the law of the verse permits to be substituted; an iambic trimeter. (More fully *iambic s.*) So **Sena·rian** = s.

Senary (sī·nări, se·nări), *a.* 1661. [ad. L. Senarius.] Pertaining to the number six.

S. scale, the scale of arithmetical notation of which the radix is six. *S. division*, division into six parts.

Senate (se·năt). ME. [a. OF. *senat, senaz*, ad. L. *senatus*, lit. council of old men, f. *senem, senex* old; see -ate[1].] 1. An assembly or council of citizens charged with the highest deliberative functions in the government of a state. a. In ancient Rome: A legislative and administrative body, consisting orig. of representatives elected by the patricians, and later, partly of appointed members, and partly of the actual and former holders of certain high offices of state. b. Used as the equivalent of Gr. γερουσία (lit. 'body of elders') and βουλή (lit. 'council') 1586. c. *gen.* The governing or legislative assembly of a nation. Often applied to the British parliament. 1560. d. In the 18th and 19th c. adopted as the official name for the upper and smaller branch of the legislature in various countries, as the United States (and each of the separate states of the Union), France, Italy, etc. 1780. 2. In the Univ. of Cambridge, and in some other British universities, the official title of the governing body. (Cf. Senatus.) 1736. b. *U.S.* In some American colleges, a council composed of members of the faculty and elected students, having the control of the discipline, etc., of the students 1891.

1. a. The S. was..a body composed of men of any order who had secured the suffrages of the people Froude. c. He says there is no place in the bar or the s. that Georgy may not aspire to Thackeray.

Se·nate-house. 1550. [House *sb.*[1]] 1. A house or building in which a senate meets. 2. *spec.* The building which serves for the meetings of the senate of a university, esp. of Cambridge 1748.

attrib.: **S. examination**, examination for degrees in Cambridge University; so **S. examiner; S. problem**, a mathematical problem proposed in a S. examination.

Senator (se·nătəɹ). ME. [a. OF. *senateur*, ad. L. *senator*, f. *senem, senex* old, old man.] 1. A member of a senate. b. In vaguer sense: A counsellor, statesman; †a leader in Church or State. late ME. 2. In papal Rome, the title given at various periods from the 12th c. onwards to the civil head of the city government, appointed by the Pope ME. 3. *S. of the College of Justice*: in Scotland, the official designation of a Lord of Session 1540.

1. The Senators of Athens, greet thee Timon Shaks. b. *fig.* Those green-rob'd senators of mighty woods, Tall oaks Keats. Hence **Se·natorship**, the office or dignity of a s.

Senatorial (senătōᵊ·riăl), *a.* 1740. [f. L. *senatorius* (f. *senatorem* Senator) + -al 1.] 1. Of or pertaining to a senator or senators; characteristic of or befitting a senator; consisting of senators. 2. Of a Roman province under the Empire: Administered by the senate (not by the emperor) 1841. 3. *U.S.* Entitled to elect a Senator, as a s. district 1891.

1. *S. order*, the highest of the three ranks of citizens in the later Roman republic. Hence **Senato·rially** *adv.*

Senatorian (senătōᵊ·riăn), *a.* 1614. [f. as prec. + -an I. 1.] = prec. 1, 2.

Senatory (se·nătəri). 1804. [ad. F. *sénatorerie*, f. L. *senator*; see -ery.] *Fr. Hist.* The landed estate granted to a senator under the consulate and the First Empire.

‖**Senatus** (sǐnē·tǒs). 1835. [L.; see Senate.] The title given to the governing body in certain universities. More fully *s. academicus.*

‖**Sena·tus consu·ltum.** *Pl.* **consulta.** Also anglicized **senatus consult.** 1696. [L.] a. A decree of the ancient Roman senate. b. A decree of the 'senate' in certain modern states, e.g. France under Napoleon I and Napoleon III 1813.

Send (send), *sb.* Also **scend.** 1726. [Belongs to Send *v.*[2]] *Naut.* 1. The carrying or driving impulse of a sea or wave; more fully *s. of a* or *the sea.* 2. A sudden plunge (of a boat) *aft, forward*, etc. 1836.

Send. (send), *v.*[1] Pa. t. and pa. pple. **sent** (sent). [Com. Teut. wk. vb.: OE. *sęndan* :— OTeut. **sandjan*, f. **sanđ-*, ablaut-var. of the root found in OE. *sīð* journey.] I. To order or direct to go or be conveyed. 1. *trans.* To commission, order, or request (a person) to go *to* or *into* a place or *to* a person. Chiefly, to dispatch as a messenger or on an errand. b. With specified destination considered as a place of residence, or connoting a sphere of employment; e.g. *to s.* (one or more members) *to Parliament* (said of a constituency) 1531. c. To occasion or induce to go to a place or in a particular direction; to recommend or advise to go to a place or a person; *fig.* to refer (a reader) to some author or authority 1449. d. Without the notion of destination or errand: To cause or order to depart *from* one; to dismiss. Chiefly with *away, off.* 1533. 2. To compel or force to go; to drive, impel. Also *transf.* of a circumstance, impulse, etc. OE. b. To drive (a person) *into* some state or condition; to cause to go *to* sleep; also with adj. complement 1831. 3. To cause (a person) to be carried or conducted to a destination OE. 4. To cause (a thing) to be conveyed or transmitted by an intermediary to another person or place OE. b. To serve up (food, a course, meal); only with *in, up*, and in phr. *to s. to table* 1662. c. *transf.* and *fig.* Also with *up.* ME. 5. To dispatch (a boat, carriage, etc.) OE. 6. To dispatch (a message, letter, telegram, etc.), by messenger, post, etc. So *To s.* (*out*) *cards* (of invitation). OE. 7. Of God, fate, chance: 'To grant as from a distant place' (J.); to cause to happen or come into existence; to ordain as a blessing or a punishment OE. 8. *absol.* To send a message or messenger. Const. *after, to.* OE. 9. **S. for** —. a. To send a messenger or message for; to send (a person) to fetch ME. b. With adv. qualifying 'to come' or 'be brought' understood 1592. c. Of a sovereign: To command the attendance of; *esp.* to summon a prominent member of a political party, for the purpose of offering him the office of prime minister 1744.

1. If he was sent of an errand he would forget half of it De Foe. b. He was sent to sea to be got rid of Marryat. *To s. to school, college*, etc. (sometimes with the notion of defraying the expenses of the person's education). *To be sent* (*into the world*), said of a child as born for some divine purpose, or as a gift to the parents. d. And the rich hee hath sent emptie away *Luke* i. 53. *To s. flying, packing*: to dismiss summarily. 2. Such a volley of musketry as sent the rebel horse flying in all directions Macaulay. b. He..sent the Colonel to sleep, with a long, learned, and refreshing sermon Thackeray. 3. Thus was I.. sent to my account With all my imperfections on my head Shaks. Ere they could strangle him, he sent three of them to the Deuill 1634. Rascals; men fit to s. to the hulks Thackeray. 4. c. We from the West will send destruction Into this Cities bosome Shaks. 6. He s. to him to meet The Prince and me Kyd. *To s.* (a person) *word*, to transmit a message (to a person); to inform, notify. *To s.* (one's) *compliments, love, respects*, etc. 7. God s. him well Shaks. The Nymphs..have..sent a Plague among thy thriving Bees Dryden. Lord s. us safe to Old England, say I! 1776. 8. S. to me in the morning Shaks. I have sent every half hour to know how she does Richardson. 9. a. The guard..sent for drink Clarendon. b. S. for him up Swift. c. The King could do no better than to s. for Lord Grenville 1806.

II. To cause to go, by physical means or by direct volition. 1. *trans.* To discharge and direct (a missile); to throw or propel in a particular direction; occas. †to thrust (a dagger). Also said of a missile weapon. OE. b. To deliver (a blow) 1626. c. To drive (a ball) 1782. 2. To emit, give forth as a source OE. 3. To direct (a thought, look, glance). late ME. 4. To cause (sound, one's voice) to 'carry' or travel. Chiefly *poet.* 1593. 5. To drive by pulsation, impulse, etc. 1767. 6. Of a blow, etc., also of the agent, a weapon: To cause to go or fall violently. Also with *down.* 1822. 7. To cause (a thing, prices, one's spirits, etc.) to go *down, up*, etc. 1657. 8. To cause to move or travel; to cause to work 1864.

1. In his right hand Grasping ten thousand Thunders, which he sent Before him Milt. 2. Doth a fountayne sende forth at one place swete water and bytter also? Coverdale *Jas.* iii. 11. When ev'ry star..Sent forth a voice Cowper. It sends out several stems from the root 1812. 4. The cry of a gull sent seaward Henley. 6. In an instant it was sent flying to the other side of the road 1887. 7. Marriage sends a doctor's income up Doyle. 8. To s. the engines full speed astern 1885.

In idiomatic combination with advs. **S. along.** *trans.* To cause to travel rapidly; *fig.* to accelerate the progress or growth of. **S. down. a.** *trans.* To dispatch from the King or the Lords to the Commons, from the capital, a city, etc. into the country. **b.** To compel (an undergraduate) to leave the University (permanently or for a specified time) as a punishment. **S. in. a.** *trans.* To give (one's name), hand (one's card) to a servant when making a call. **b.** To cause (a thing) to be delivered at its destination; esp. to render (an account, a bill). **c.** *Cricket.* To s. (a batsman) into the field to bat. **S. round. a.** *trans.* To circulate. **b.** *To s. round the hat*: see Hat *sb.* **c.** *colloq.* To s. (something; also *absol.* to send a message) to some one in the neighbourhood. **S. up. a.** *trans.* Of things: To emit, give off, shoot out (something that rises or travels upwards). **b.** To cause (a person) to go or (a thing) to be taken 'upstairs'; esp. to serve up (a meal), to s. in (one's name or card as a visitor). **c.** *Public Schools.* To s. (a boy) to the headmaster (*a*) for reward, (*b*) for punishment. **d.** *slang.* To put in prison.

Send (send), *v.*[2] Pa. t. **sended.** Also **scend.** 1625. [perh. a use of Send *v.*[1]] *Naut. intr.* Of a ship: To pitch deeply with head or stern into the trough of a wave.

Sendal (se·ndăl). Now *Hist.* ME. [a. OF. *cendal*; a Com. Rom. word.] 1. A thin rich silken material; also, a covering or garment of this. †2. As tr. L. *sindon*: Fine linen, lawn; a piece of this- 1606.

1. There was pyght vp a pauilyon of crymasyn sendall, right noble and riche 1523.

Sender (se·ndəɹ). ME. [f. SEND *v.*[1] + -ER [1].] One who or something which sends. **b.** One who signals a message 1904. **c.** The transmitting instrument of a telephone or telegraphic apparatus = TRANSMITTER b. 1879.

Se·nd-off. *colloq.*, orig. *U.S.* 1872. A friendly demonstration on the occasion of a person's starting on a journey or undertaking.

Seneca (se·nĭkă). *U.S.* 1826. [app. identical with *Seneca*, the name given by white men to one of the 'Six Nations' of the Iroquois confederacy, living near Lake Seneca (N.Y.).] *attrib.* in **S. grass,** Northern holy-grass (*Hierochloa borealis*); †**S. oil,** crude petroleum.

Senectitude (sĭne·ktitiūd). 1796. [ad. med.L. *senectitudo*, irreg. f. *senectus*.] Old age. So **Sene·ctude** 1756.

Senega (se·nĭgă). 1738. [app. a variant form of SENECA.] The N. Amer. plant *Polygala Senega*. Also, a drug obtained from the root of this plant, formerly used as an antidote for snake-bite.

Senegal (se·nĭgǭl). 1781. The name of a French colony, and river, of western Africa used *attrib.* **a.** In many names of beasts, birds, and plants native to this district. **b.** *S. gum* = GUMS. 1887.

Senegin (se·nĭgin). 1830. [f. prec. + -IN.] An amorphous glucoside, consisting of sapogenin and sugar, obtained from senega.

Senescence (sĭne·sĕns). 1695. [f. next; see -ENCE.] The process or condition of growing old.

Senescent (sĭne·sĕnt), *a.* 1656. [ad. L. *senescentem*, *senescere* to grow old; see -ENT.] Growing old, elderly.

Seneschal (se·nĭʃăl). late ME. [a. OF.; a Com. Rom. word ad. OTeut. **seniskalkoz*, f. **seni-* old + **skalkoz* servant.] **1.** An official in the household of a sovereign or great noble, to whom the administration of justice and entire control of domestic arrangements were entrusted. In wider use: a steward, 'major-domo'. **2.** As the title of a governor of a city or province, and of various administrative or judicial officers. Now *Hist.* exc. with ref. to the Channel Islands. late ME.

1. Then marshal'd Feast Serv'd up in Hall with Sewers, and Seneshals MILT. Hence **Se·neschalship** *Hist.*, the office and functions of a s.

Sengreen (se·ngrīn). Now *dial.* [OE. *singréne*, sb. use of *singréne* adj. evergreen (OTeut. **sen-* always + **grônjo-* GREEN *a.*)] **1.** The houseleek, *Sempervivum tectorum*. **2.** Applied to other plants, *esp.* **a.** the sedums; **b.** varieties of saxifrage; **c.** the periwinkle, *Vinca minor*; **d.** **Water s.,** *Stratiotes aloides*. OE.

‖ **Senhor** (senʸō·r). 1795. [Pg.:—L. *seniorem*, *senior* SENIOR.] In Pg. use, or with ref. to Portuguese: A term of respect placed before the name of a man in addressing him or speaking of him = 'Mr.' Also used without the name as a form of address, = 'sir'. Hence, a Portuguese gentleman. So ‖**Senhora** (senʸō·ra), a term of respect applied to Portuguese ladies; hence, a Portuguese lady. ‖**Senhorita** (senʸorī·ta), applied to young Portuguese ladies.

Senile (sī·nəil), *a.* 1661. [ad. L. *senilis*, f. *senex*; see -ILE.] **1.** Belonging to, suited for, or incident to old age. Now only of diseases, etc.: Peculiar to the aged. **2.** Exhibiting the weakness of old age 1848. **3.** *Phys. Geog.* Approaching the end of a cycle of erosion 1902.

1. S. gangrene 1875. 2. S. anger 1848. Hence **Se·nilely** *adv.* **Senility** (sĭni·lĭti), the condition of being s.; old age or the infirmity due to old age 1628.

Senior (sī·niəɹ), *a.* and *sb.* late ME. [a. L., compar. of *senem*, *senex* old, cogn. w. Gr. ἕνος old, Skr. *sána* old.] **A.** *adj.* **1.** Older, elder; esp. used after a person's name to denote the elder of two bearing the same name in a family. Abbrev. *sen.* (U.S. *sr.*). **2.** That ranks before others in virtue of longer service or tenure of a position; superior *to* others in standing 1513. **b.** In school and college use. Applied in the U.S. to a student in his last year or term. 1651. **c.** In commercial use, applied to the partner in a firm who has precedence of the rest in the formal enumeration of the members 1864.

1. Tho. Crabb, Sen. and Tho. Crabb, Jun. of Malborrow 1708. 2. Phr. *The s. service*, the navy as dist. from the army. **b.** *S. student* (Christ Church, Oxford): see STUDENT 3 a. *S. fellow*, applied at Cambridge and Dublin to a select number of the fellows of longest standing in a college, in whom the greater part of its government was formerly vested.

Special collocations: **S. wrangler,** the head of the 'wranglers', i.e. of the first class of those who are successful in the Mathematical Tripos at Cambridge; similarly **S. classic, S. moralist,** the student who takes the first place in the Classical and the Moral Sciences Tripos respectively. (The status indicated by these titles has ceased to exist, the class-lists being now arranged alphabetically.) **S. optime,** one placed in the second class in the Mathematical Tripos.

B. *sb.* An elder person. **1.** One superior or worthy of deference by reason of age; one having pre-eminence in dignity by priority of election, appointment, etc. late ME. **2.** In school and college use: (*a*) one of the more advanced students; (*b*) one no longer a freshman; (*c*) a graduate, as dist. from a non-graduate, member of a college or university. In *U.S.* a student in his fourth year. 1612. **b.** A senior fellow of a college 1645.

1. His s. at the bar SCOTT. She was a year or two my s. 1862.

Seniority (sīniǫ·rĭti). 1450. [a. med.L. *senioritas*, f. L. *senior*: see -ITY.] **1.** The state or quality of being senior; priority by reason of birth, superior age 1533. **2.** Priority or precedence in office or service; esp. *Mil.* Superiority in standing to another of equal rank by reason of earlier entrance into the service or an earlier appointment 1450. **3.** The body of seniors or senior fellows of a college 1678.

Senna (se·nă). 1543. [mod.L. *senna*, *sena*, a. Arab. *sanā*.] **1.** *Bot.* A shrub of the genus *Cassia*, native in tropical regions, bearing yellow flowers and flat greenish pods. **b.** Applied to shrubs of other genera having similar medicinal properties; as **Bladder s.,** *Colutea arborescens*; **Wild s.,** *Poinciana pulcherrima* or *Globularia Alypum*. **2.** *Pharm.* The dried leaflets of various species of *Cassia*, used as a cathartic and emetic 1571.

attrib.: **s.-tea,** an infusion of the drug taken as a purgative.

Sennachie (se·năχi). 1534. [a. Gael. *seanachaidh*, f. *sean* old.] In Ireland and the Scottish Highlands, one professionally occupied in the study and transmission of traditional history, genealogy, and legend; now chiefly *Sc.* a Gaelic teller of legendary romances.

†**Se·nnet** [1]. 1590. [app. a var. of SIGNET, in the sense 'sign, token'.] A set of notes on the trumpet or cornet, ordered in the stage-directions of Elizabethan plays, apparently as the signal for the ceremonial entrance or exit of a body of players -1619.

Sennet [2] (se·nĕt). 1671. [perh. from some W.-Indian language.] *Nat. Hist.* A West-Indian fish; = BARRACUDA.

Sennight (se·nəit). *arch.* [orig. two words: OE. *seofon* SEVEN, *nihta*, pl. of *niht* NIGHT *sb.*] A week.

The bold Iago, Whose footing heere anticipates our thoughts, A Senights speed SHAKS. Newes.. That Waller was at Abingdon on Tuesday last was sevenight 1644.

Sennit (se·nit). 1625. [var. of SINNET.] *Naut.* **a.** = SINNET. **b.** Plaited grass, palm leaves, etc., used for making hats.

Senocular (sĭnǫ·kiŭlăɹ), *a.* 1713. [f. L. *seni* six each + *oculi* eyes + -AR [1] 1.] Having six eyes. So **Seno·culate** *a.*

Senonian (sĭnōᵘ·niăn), *a.* (*sb.*) 1850. [ad. F. *sénonien*, f. L. *Senones*, a people of central Gaul.] *Geol.* Designating a subdivision of the Cretaceous system in France and Belgium corresponding to the 'Upper Chalk with flints' of British geologists.

‖ **Señor** (senʸō·r). *Pl.* **señores** (senʸō·res). 1622. [Sp.:—L. *seniorem*.] In Spanish use or with ref. to a Spaniard: A title of respect placed before the name of a man, = 'Mr.' **b.** Used without the name as a form of address 1832. **c.** A Spanish gentleman 1868.

‖ **Señora** (senʸō·ra). 1579. [Sp., fem. of prec.] A title of respect prefixed to the name of a Spanish lady, or used without the name in addressing her; hence, a Spanish lady.

‖ **Señorita** (senʸorī·ta). 1845. [Sp., dim. of SEÑORA.] A Spanish title of respect prefixed to the name of a young lady, or used without the name in addressing her 1850. **b.** A young Spanish lady 1845.

Sensate (se·nsĕt), *a.* 1500. [ad. late L. *sensatus* gifted with sense, f. *sensus*; see -ATE [2] 2.] **1.** Endowed with physical sensation. **2.** Perceived by the senses 1847.

Sensate (sensē·t), *v.* 1652. [f. L. *sensus* SENSE *sb.* + -ATE [3], after SENSATION.] **1.** *trans.* To perceive by sense; to have a sensation of. †**2.** *intr.* To have sensation -1687.

Sensation (sensēⁱ·ʃən). 1615. [ad. med. L. *sensationem*, f. L. *sensus* SENSE *sb.*, after late L. *sensatus* SENSATE *a.*; see -ATION.] **1.** An operation of any of the senses; a psychical affection or state of consciousness consequent on and related to a particular condition of some portion of the bodily organism, or a particular impression received by one of the organs of sense. Now commonly, in more precise use, restricted to the subjective element in any operation of one of the senses, a physical 'feeling' considered apart from the resulting 'perception' of an object. **b.** In generalized use: The operation or function of the senses; 'perception by means of the senses' (J.). Now commonly the subjective element in the operation of the senses; physical 'feeling'. 1642. **c.** Faculty of perceiving by the senses, physical sensibility 1799. **2.** A mental feeling, an emotion. Now chiefly, the characteristic feeling arising in some particular circumstances. 1755. **b.** Mental apprehension, sense, or 'realization' *of* something 1639. **3.** An excited or violent feeling. **a.** An exciting experience; a strong emotion aroused by some particular occurrence or situation. Also, the production of violent emotion as an aim in works of literature or art. 1808. **b.** A condition of excited feeling produced in a community by some occurrence 1779. **c.** An event or a person that 'creates a sensation' 1864.

1. When I grasp an ivory ball in my hand, I feel a certain sensation of touch 1785. **b.** O sunken souls, slaves of s. 1642. 2. A s. of distress 1755. **b.** So to represent familiar objects as to awaken..freshness of s. COLERIDGE. 3. **a.** The cheap publications which supply s. for the million in penny and halfpenny numbers 1863. **b.** His death created a profound s. 1879. **c.** The greatest s. of the day: grand Incantation Scene from Der Freischütz 1864.

Comb. as *s.-monger*, *-seeking*.

Sensational (sensēⁱ·ʃənăl), *a.* 1840. [f. prec. + -AL 1.] **1.** Of, pertaining to, or dependent upon, sensation or the senses. **2.** Of philosophical theories: Regarding sensation as the sole source of knowledge 1855. **3.** Of works of literature or art, hence, of writers: Dealing in sensation (see SENSATION 3 a), aiming at violently exciting effects. Also of incidents: Calculated to produce a startling impression. 1863.

1. No experience of external things is purely s. 1840. Hence **Sensa·tionally** *adv.*

Sensationalism (sensēⁱ·ʃənăliz'm). 1865. [f. prec. + -ISM.] **1.** *Philos.* The theory that sensation is the only source of knowledge 1867. **2.** Addiction to what is sensational in literature or art 1865.

Sensationalist (sensēⁱ·ʃənălist). 1855. [f. as prec. + -IST.] **1.** *Philos.* One who regards the senses as the ultimate source of all knowledge. **2.** One whose aim is to make a sensation; a sensational writer 1868.

Sensationalize (sensēⁱ·ʃənăləiz), *v.* 1863. [f. as prec. + -IZE.] *trans.* **a.** To subject to the influence of 'sensation' or factitious emotion. **b.** To exaggerate in a sensational manner.

Sensationism (sensēⁱ·ʃəniz'm). 1863. [f. SENSATION + -ISM.] = SENSATIONALISM 2. So **Sensa·tionist,** one who deals in sensation; a sensational novelist, journalist, etc. 1861.

Sense (sens), *sb.* late ME. [a. F. *sens* or ad. L. *sensus* perception, feeling, faculty of perception, meaning, f. *sentire* to feel.] **I.** Faculty of perception or sensation. **1.** Each of the special faculties, connected with a bodily organ, by which man and other animals perceive external objects and changes in the condition of their own bodies. Usu. reckoned as five—sight, hearing, smell, taste, touch. Also called *outward* or *external s.* 1526. †**b.** Used for: An organ of sense -1604. **c.** *pl.* The faculties of physical perception or sensation as opp. to the higher faculties of intellect, spirit, etc. 1841.

d. Applied to similar faculties of perception, not scientifically delimited, or only conjectured to exist 1690. **2.** *transf.* An instinctive or acquired faculty of perception or accurate estimation. Now chiefly const. *of* (locality, distance, etc.). 1567. **3.** *gen.* The senses viewed as forming a single faculty in contradistinction to intellect, will, etc.; the exercise or function of this faculty, sensation 1538. **4.** *pl.* The faculties of corporeal sensation considered as channels for gratifying the desire for pleasure and the lusts of the flesh. Also *sing.*, any one of such faculties so regarded. 1597. **b.** *collect. sing.* 1586. †**5.** Capability of feeling, as a quality of the body and its parts; liability to feel pain, irritation, etc. –1771. **6.** *pl.* A general term for the faculties of perception (including the 'five senses'), which are in abeyance when their owner is asleep or otherwise unconscious. Also *sing.*, any one of these faculties. 1597. **b.** *collect. sing.* The perceptive faculty of a conscious animate being 1585. **7.** Applied to faculties of the mind or soul compared or contrasted with the bodily senses usu. with defining word, as *inner, interior, s.* 1566. **8.** Capacity for perception and appreciation *of* (beauty, humour, some quality, etc.) 1604. **9.** *pl.* The mental faculties in their normal condition of sanity; one's 'reason' or 'wits' 1568. †**b.** *sing.* (with the same meaning) –1694. **10.** Natural understanding, intelligence, esp. as bearing on action or behaviour; practical soundness of judgement 1684.

1. I must have the evidence of more senses than one to confirm me of its truth FARQUHAR. My s. of hearing is painfully acute BECKFORD. **b.** Mine Eyes, mine Eares, or any Sence SHAKS. **d.** *Muscular s.*: see MUSCULAR *a.* 1. *Sixth s.*, a faculty of perception supposed not to depend upon any 'outward sense'; instinct, intuition. **2.** Take from them now The sence of reckning SHAKS. **3.** Thus wee adore vertue, though to the eyes of s. shee bee invisible SIR T. BROWNE. **4. b.** This bastard Loue..vtterly subuerts the course of nature, in making reason giue place to s. SIDNEY. **7.** *Moral s.*: see MORAL *a.* 1 c. **8.** A strong s. of humour 1885. **9.** Phr. *In one's* (*right*) *senses*, in one's right mind. *To bring* (a person) *to his senses*, to cure of his folly (one who is behaving 'madly'). (*To frighten*, etc.) *out of one's* (*seven*) *senses*, out of one's wits. **b.** *Lear* IV. iv. 9. **10** You speak, ma'am, like a lady of s. MISS BURNEY. Phr. *To have the s.*, to be wise enough *to do* something. So *to have too much s. to, to have more s. than to* do something. **b.** Knowledge of how to act under given conditions; usu. with defining word, as *court s., road s., stage s.*

II. Actual perception or feeling. **1.** A feeling or perception *of* (something external) through the channels of touch, taste, etc.; the feeling or consciousness *of* some bodily affection as pain, fatigue, comfort, etc. 1586. **2.** A more or less vague perception or impression *of* (an outward object, as present or imagined) 1596. **3.** A more or less indefinite consciousness or impression *of* (a fact, state of things, etc.) as present or impending 1604. **4.** Mental apprehension, appreciation, or realization *of* (some truth, fact, state of things) 1540. **b.** The recognition *of* (a duty, virtue, etc.) as incumbent upon one, or as a motive or standard for one's own conduct 1604. **5.** Emotional consciousness of something; a glad or sorrowful, grateful or resentful recognition *of* (another person's conduct, an event, a fact or a condition of things) 1604. **6.** A consciousness or recognition *of* (some quality, condition, etc.) as attaching to oneself 1614. **7.** An opinion, view, or judgement held or formed †**a.** by an individual –1761. **b.** by an assemblage of persons (or by a majority of their number). Now *arch.* 1654.

1. An idle craving without s. of flavours GEO. ELIOT. **2.** And the darkening air Thrills with a s. of the triumphing night HENLEY. **3.** There was a general s. of security MACAULAY. **4.** He seemed visited by a s. of the vanity of all things J. H. NEWMAN. **b.** These fellows have no s. of gratitude DE FOE. **5.** No better way of showing our s. of his hospitality.. has occurred to us HAWTHORNE. **6.** To confess herself mistaken was..opposed to her s. of personal dignity 1908. **7. a.** Phr. †*To speak* or *give one's s.*, to express one's opinion. †*In one's s.*, in one's opinion. †*To abound in one's own s.*: see ABOUND *v.*[1] 4. **b.** Phr. *To take the s. of*, to ascertain the general feeling or opinion of.

III. Meaning, signification. **1.** The meaning or signification of a word or phrase; also, any one of the different meanings of a word 1530. **b.** A meaning recorded in a dictionary 1755. **2.** The meaning of words in connected or continuous speech; the meaning of a passage or context. Also, one of two or more meanings which the words naturally bear. 1513. †**b.** The meaning or interpretation of a dream, or of anything cryptic or symbolical –1650. **c.** The gist of words spoken or written 1596. **3.** Any of the various meanings or interpretations (*literal, mystic, moral*, etc.) of which a word or passage of Holy Scripture was considered to be susceptible. Hence *transf.* late ME. †**4.** The meaning of a speaker or writer –1735. **5.** The substance of a passage 1568. **6.** Discourse that has a satisfactory and intelligible meaning 1598. **7.** What is wise or reasonable 1600. **8.** [After F. *sens.*] A direction in which motion takes place (*rare*) 1797.

1. There bee some wordes that bee not of the same s. euery where 1611. **2.** He had barely enough Greek to make out the s. of the epigram GEO. ELIOT. **c.** This is the general s. of his remark 1777. **3.** These Greekes,..follow the literall s. of the Scriptures 1617. **4.** Let no Court Sycophant pervert my s. POPE. **6.** Phr. *To talk, speak, write* (*good*) *s.* *To make s. of* to find a meaning in. *To give, have, make s.*, to be intelligible. **7.** Phr. *There is not much s. in this.*

Phrases. *In a* (specified) *s.*, according to a particular acceptation or interpretation (of a word, phrase, etc.); often *in a s., in any s., in no s.* (which sometimes come to mean 'in some degree', 'in no respect', etc.).

Sense (sens), *v.* 1598. [f. the sb.] †**1.** *trans.* To perceive (an outward object) by the senses; also, to feel (pain) –1873. †**b.** To test, make trial of. BUNYAN. †**2.** To expound the sense or meaning of; to ascribe a meaning to; to take in a particular sense –1726. **3.** To perceive, become aware of, 'feel' (a fact, state of things, etc.) more or less vaguely or instinctively 1872. **4.** To comprehend, 'take in'. Chiefly *U.S.* and *dial.* 1860. **5.** *Philos.* To have a sense-perception of. Also *absol.*, to experience sensations. 1661.

3. He 'senses' the least coldness towards himself 1872. **5.** Is he sure, that objects are not otherwise sensed by others, then they are by him? 1661.

Senseful (se·nsfŭl), *a.* 1591. [f. SENSE *sb.* + -FUL 1.] **1.** Full of sense or meaning; significant. †**2.** Intelligent –1700.

1. Sensefull speach SPENSER. **2.** Men, otherwise s. and ingenious, quote such things..as would never pass in conversation 1700.

Senseless (se·nslės), *a.* 1557. [f. SENSE *sb.* + -LESS.] **1.** Destitute or deprived of sensation; physically insentient. **b.** That is in a state of unconsciousness 1585. **c.** Of things: Incapable of sensation or perception 1577. **2.** Destitute of mental sensibility, incapable of feeling or perception. Also const. *of*. Now *rare* or *Obs.* 1561. **3.** Of a person, etc.: Devoid of sense or intelligence, stupid, silly, foolish 1565. †**b.** quasi-*adv.* Unreasonably. SHAKS. **4.** Of actions, words, etc.: Proceeding from lack of sense or intelligence, foolish. Also, without sense or meaning; unmeaning, meaningless, purposeless. 1579.

1. I would I were senselesse sir, that I might not feele your blowes SHAKS. **b.** I was almost s. with terror MISS BURNEY. **c.** I stand, immoveable, like s. marble! 1720. **2.** I am senselesse of your Wrath SHAKS. **3.** An honest senselesse dolt, A good poore foole MARSTON. **4.** The horrid and s. Custom of Duels STEELE. Hence **Se·nseless-ly** *adv.*, **-ness.**

Sensibility (sensibi·lĭti). late ME. [ad. L. *sensibilitas* f. *sensibilis* SENSIBLE *a.*; see -ITY.] **1.** Power of sensation or perception; †the specific function of the organs of sense. Now often, the (greater or less) readiness of an organ or tissue to respond to sensory stimuli; sensitiveness. **b.** *Philos.* Power or faculty of feeling, capacity of sensation and emotion as dist. from cognition and will 1838. **2.** Emotional consciousness; glad or sorrowful, grateful or resentful, recognition of a person's conduct, or of a fact or a condition of things 1751. **3.** Quickness and acuteness of apprehension or feeling; sensitiveness. Also, with const., sensitiveness *to*, keen sense *of* something. 1711. **b.** *pl.* Emotional capacities 1634. **c.** *sing.* and *pl.* Liability to feel offended or hurt by unkindness, or lack of respect; susceptibilities 1769. **4.** In the 18th and early 19th c. (subseq. somewhat *rarely*): Capacity for refined emotion; delicate sensitiveness of taste; also, readiness to feel compassion for suffering, and to be moved by the pathetic in literature or art 1756. **5.** Of plants and their organs, also of instruments or other inorganic objects: Aptness to be affected by external influences; sensitiveness. Const. *to*, (rarely *of*). 1662.

1. S. resides in the nervous system 1834. Common sensation or tactile s. 1875. **b.** Even though these pleasures are much diminished by..decay of his passive sensibilities MILL. **2.** A s. of our own weakness 1790. **3.** A man's s. to pecuniary influence BENTHAM. A s. to colour..being very different from a s. to form RUSKIN. **b.** Doubtless this feeling was due to his unusually acute sensibilities—his keen sense of the beautiful 1892. **4.** Where Affectation holds her seat, And sickly S. BYRON.

Sensible (se·nsĭb'l), *a.* (and *sb.*). late ME. [a. F., ad. late L. *sensibilis*, f. *sens-*, *sentire* to perceive, feel; see -IBLE.] **A.** *adj.* **I. 1.** Perceptible by the senses. (In *Philos.*, opp. to INTELLIGIBLE 3; in this use, now *rare.*) †**b.** Of or pertaining to the senses or sensation –1793. **2.** Perceptible by the mind or the inward feelings 1597. **3.** Easy to perceive, evident 1586. **4.** Large enough to be perceived or to be worth considering; appreciable. Now only of immaterial things (as quantities, magnitudes, etc.). late ME. †**5.** Of discourse, etc.: Easily understood; striking, effective –1744. †**6.** Such as is acutely felt; markedly painful or pleasurable –1819.

1. Taste and other s. Qualities 1732. Phr. *S. horizon*: see HORIZON 1. *S. heat*: used in contradistinction to *latent heat* (HEAT *sb.* 2 c). *S. perspiration*, sweat, as dist. from the emission of vapour through the pores. **b.** *Haml.* I. i. 57. **2.** The visible and s. connexion of sacred and profane history 1734. **3.** A very s. odor of garlic 1816. **4.** We could discover no s. difference in weight SIR T. BROWNE. **6.** Scorpions..whose stinging is most s., and deadly 1655.

II. Capable of feeling or perceiving. **1.** Endowed with the faculty of sensation. late ME. †**2.** Having (more or less) acute power of sensation; sensitive –1831. †**b.** Sensitive *to* or *of* –1829. **3.** Capable of or liable to mental emotion; *esp.* sensitive *to* some specified emotional influence. Also const. *of*. Now *rare.* 1675. **4.** *transf.* Of material things or substances, esp. of instruments of measurement, as a balance, a thermometer: Readily affected by physical impressions or influences, sensitive. Now *rare.* 1661.

1. It is the Understanding that sets Man above the rest of s. Beings LOCKE. Outside of the s. skin 1850. **2.** These Gentlemen, who are of such s. and nimble Lungs, that they alwayes vse to laugh at nothing SHAKS. **b.** Albinoes..are painfully s. to light 1829. **3.** Johnson had, from his early youth, been s. to the influence of female charms BOSWELL. **4.** A very s. hygrometer LOCKE.

III. Actually perceiving or feeling. **1.** Cognizant, conscious, aware of something (often as a ground for pleasure or regret). Now somewhat *rare.* late ME. **2.** Emotionally conscious; having a pleasurable, painful, grateful, or resentful sense *of* something. Now usu., gratefully conscious *of* (kindness, etc.). 1634. **3.** Conscious, free from physical insensibility or delirium 1732.

1. Which shows how little we are s. of the weight of the business upon us PEPYS. Looking s. Of having play'd the fool BYRON. **2.** Lady Carlisle..is..very s. of your goodness to us all 1775.

IV. Endowed with good sense; intelligent, reasonable, judicious 1584. **b.** Of action, behaviour, discourse, etc.: Marked by, exhibiting, or proceeding from good sense 1653.

A moral, s., and well-bred man Will not affront me, and no other can COWPER. It was tame,..s., and not near so noisy or dirty as a Chimpanzee 1860. **b.** A s. and penetrating countenance MME. D'ARBLAY.

B. *absol.* and *sb.* **1.** That which produces sensation; that which is perceptible; an object of sense, or of any one of the senses 1589. †**2.** The element (in a spiritual being) that is capable of feeling. MILT.

1. A blind man conceives not colours, but under the notion of some other s. 1665. Hence **Se·nsibleness,** the quality or state of being s.

Sensibly (se·nsĭbli), *adv.* late ME. [f. SENSIBLE *a.* + -LY[2].] **1.** In a manner perceptible to the senses; so far as can be perceived; appreciably. †**2. a.** With self-consciousness, consciously. **b.** Of feeling: Acutely, intensely. –1806. †**3.** Clearly, strikingly –1700. **4.** With good sense, intelligently; judiciously, reasonably 1755.

1. The sea is said to be s. decreasing in size 1880. 2. a. As each thing to more perfection grows, It feels more s. both good and pain CARY. 3. He behaved s. under the circumstances (*mod.*).

Sensifacient (sensifē·ʃĕnt), *a.* 1879. [f. L. *sensus* SENSE + -(I)FACIENT.] Producing sensation.

Sensiferous (sensi·fĕrəs), *a.* 1656. [f. as prec. + -IFEROUS.] Conveying sensation.

Sensific (sensi·fik), *a.* 1822. [ad. late L. *sensificus*, f. L. *sensus*; see -IFIC.] Of nerves: Producing sensation.

Sensify (se·nsifəi), *v.* 1678. [ad. late L. *sensificare*, f. *sensus*; see -IFY.] *trans.* To transform (physical changes) into sensation.

Sensile (se·nsil, -əil), *a.* 1813. [ad. L. *sensilis*, f. *sens-*, *sentire* to feel; see -ILE.] Capable of perception, sentient.

Sensist (se·nsist). 1874. [f. SENSE *sb.* + -IST.] = SENSATIONALIST 1.

Sensitive (se·nsitiv), *a.* and *sb.* late ME. [a. F. *sensitif, -ive*, ad. med.L. *sensitivus*, irreg. f. L. *sens-*, *sentire* to feel.] **A.** *adj.* 1. Having the function of sensation or sensuous perception. **b.** Of life, knowledge, perception (also formerly †of desires, feelings): Connected with the senses, sensuous. †Of objects: Perceptible by the senses. 1530. 2. Of living beings: Endowed with the faculty of sensation. Formerly often: †'Having sense or perception, but not reason' (J.). 1509. 3. Of plants and their organs: Capable of responding to stimulation 1633. 4. That feels quickly and acutely. **a.** In physical sense, of a living being, an animal organ or tissue: Having quick or intense perception or sensation; readily and acutely affected with pain or pleasure by some particular influence 1849. **b.** With ref. to mental feelings: Impressionable; easily wounded by unkindness; *occas.*, ready to take offence, 'touchy' 1816. 5. *transf.* Readily altered or affected by some influence specified or implied 1828. **b.** *Photogr.* Of paper, chemical substances, etc.: Susceptible to actinic influence 1839. **c.** Of a scientific instrument: Indicating readily slight changes of condition, easily moved or affected 1857. **d.** Of market prices, stock, etc.: Having a tendency to fluctuate rapidly upon the publication of outside reports 1866. 6. Mus. *S. note*: the leading note of a scale 1867.

1. *S. soul* [med.L. *anima sensitiva*], in scholastic philosophy, that one of the three kinds of 'soul' or of constituent parts of the soul which is concerned with sensation, and which is characteristic of animals; dist. from the *vegetative soul*, which is common to animals and plants, and from the *intellective soul* which in rational animals (men) is superadded to the two others. Similarly *s. virtue* [*virtus sensitiva*], the faculty of sensation. **b.** Our s. perception of objects 1877. 3. **S. plant**, a shrub (*Mimosa pudica*, or *M. sensitiva*) possessing a high degree of irritability, causing the leaflets of the bipinnate leaves to fold together at the slightest touch; also applied with defining word to various plants having a similar quality; e.g. **American S. plant** (*Cassia nictitans*), also called *Wild S. plant* and *S. pea*. **S. Brier,** *Schrankia uncinata*. **S. Fern,** *Onoclea sensibilis*. 4. **a.** The tongue is one of the most sensitive of organs JOWETT. **b.** The scenes of blood which followed shocked his s. nature 1824. 5. Plants..s. of drought 1828. **b.** The paper is..very s. to all white light 1893. **c.** Balances are made s. to the fraction of a grain 1872.

B. *sb.* †1. A being that is capable of sensation –1727. †2. The faculty of sensation –1627. 3. The Sensitive plant 1707. 4. One sensitive to spiritualist or other occult influences, a medium 1850. 5. One in whom the sensitive faculty is highly developed. Also = SENSITIVIST. 1884. Hence **Se·nsitive·ly** *adv.*, **-ness.**

Sensitivist (se·nsitivist). 1891. [f. SENSITIVE *a.* + -IST.] One of a school of novelists in Holland, who aim at combining in their methods the valuable qualities of impressionism and realism.

Sensitivity (sensiti·vĭti). 1803. [f. as prec. + -ITY.] 1. The quality of being sensitive. 2. The experience of the senses 1889.

Sensitize (se·nsitəiz), *v.* 1856. [f. as prec. + -IZE.] 1. *trans.* (*Photogr.*) To render (a plate, film, or paper) sensitive to the influence of light. 2. To make (a person) sensitive 1880.

1. Nitrate of silver..is the salt usually employed to sensitise the paper 1865. Hence **Se·nsitiza·tion,** the act or process of sensitizing. **Se·nsitizer,** a substance or preparation used for sensitizing.

Sensitometer (sensitǫ·mǐtəɹ). 1880. [f. SENSITIVE *a.* + *-ometer*; see -METER.] *Photogr.* An instrument for ascertaining the degree of sensitiveness of photographic plates, films, etc.

†**Se·nsive,** *a.* 1553. [a. OF. *sensif*, ad. L. **sensivus*, f. *sens-*, *sentire* to feel; see -IVE.] Having the function of sensation or sensuous perception –1865.

Sensor (se·nsǫɹ), *a.* 1865. [irreg. shortened f. SENSORY, after *motor*.] = SENSORY *a.*

Sensori- (se·nsŏri), comb. form of SENSOR or SENSORY, chiefly in **sensori-motor** *a.*, applied to nerves which are both sensory and motor; also to reflex actions which arise from stimulation of the organs of sense. Similarly *s.-reflex*, *volitional* adjs., etc.

Sensorial (sensōᵊ·riăl), *a.* 1768. [f. SENSORIUM or SENSORY + -AL 1.] Of or relating to the sensorium. Also, relating to sensation or sensory impressions. †**b.** Pertaining to the brain as the centre of nervous energy; esp. in *s. power*, vital energy proceeding from the brain to the rest of the system –1833.

‖ **Sensorium** (sensōᵊ·riŏm). 1647. [Late L., f. *sens-*, *sentire* to feel; see -ORY [1].] The seat of sensation in the brain of man and other animals; the percipient centre to which sense-impressions are transmitted by the nerves. Also *common s.* (L. *sensorium commune*). Formerly used in a wider sense, for the brain as the organ of mind and the centre of nervous energy. **b.** Used playfully (sometimes for 'brain' or 'mind') 1759.

Sensory (se·nsŏri), *sb.* 1626. [ad. L. *sensorium*; see prec. and -ORY [1].] †1. An organ of sense –1714. 2. = prec. 1653.

Sensory (se·nsŏri), *a.* 1749. [ad. L. **sensorius*; see prec. and -ORY [2].] Belonging to sensation; carrying or transmitting sensation.

Sensual (se·nsiŭăl, -ʃŭăl), *a.* and *sb.* 1450. [ad. late L. *sensualis*, f. L. *sensus* SENSE *sb.*; see -AL.] **A.** *adj.* 1. Of or pertaining to the senses or physical sensation; sensory. Now *rare.* **b.** Perceptible by the senses (*rare*) 1529. †2. Endowed with the faculty of sensation (but not with reason) –1696. 3. Of appetites and pleasures: Connected with the gratification of the senses. **a.** In neutral use: Sensuous, physical. Now *rare.* 1542. **b.** In pejorative use, now often, lewd, unchaste 1477. 4. Of persons, their conduct, etc. **a.** Absorbed in the life of the senses; indifferent to intellectual and moral interests. In religious use: Destitute of spiritual life, worldly, irreligious. Now *rare* or *Obs.* 1557. **b.** Excessively inclined to the gratification of the senses, voluptuous; often *spec.*, lewd, unchaste. Of physiognomy, etc.: Indicative of a sensual disposition. 1530. 5. Of opinions or ideas: Materialistic 1656.

1. Ye soft pipes, play on; Not to the s. ear, but.. Pipe to the spirit ditties of no tone KEATS. 3. **a.** No gratification, however s., can, of itself, be esteemed vicious HUME. **b.** To roule with pleasure in a s. stie MILT. The s. pleasure of the glutton 1850. 4. **a.** These are they which segregate themselues, s., hauing not the Spirit *N.T.* (Rhem.) *Jude* 19. S. Men are not willing to believe any thing whereby they have not a sufficient Evidence, as they think, to their Sense 1676. **b.** By nature coarse and s. in his habits 1881. The full mouth, with the s. lips 1905. 5. The common s. idea of heaven 1871.

†**B.** *sb. pl.* 1. **a.** The sensual faculties and appetites. **b.** The objects of sense. –1676. 2. Beings capable only of sensation, brutes –1644. Hence **Se·nsually** *adv.*

Sensualism (se·nsiŭ-, -ʃŭăliz'm). 1803. [f. SENSUAL *a.* + -ISM.] 1. *Philos.* The doctrine that the senses are the sole source of knowledge; sensationalism. 2. Addiction to sensual indulgence 1813.

2. A face coarsened by s. 1906.

Sensualist (se·nsiŭ-, -ʃŭălist). 1662. [f. as prec. + -IST.] 1. One whose disposition and conduct are sensual; chiefly, one who is devoted to sensual pleasure, or given to vicious indulgence of the animal passions. 2. = SENSATIONALIST 1852. Hence **Se:nsualī·stic** *a.* pertaining to sensualism in philosophy or art.

Sensuality (sensiŭ-, -ʃŭæ·lĭti). ME. [a. F. *sensualité*, ad. late L. *sensualitas*, f. *sensualis* SENSUAL *a.*] †1. The part of the nature of man that is concerned with the senses; chiefly, the animal instincts and appetites; the lower nature as dist. from the reason; also *occas.* the faculty of sensation –1828. †2. The lower or animal nature regarded as a source of evil; the lusts of the flesh. Also *pl.* –1621. 3. Excessive fondness for, or vicious indulgence in, the pleasures of the senses 1450. 4. *spec.* Lasciviousness, unchastity 1463.

3. Those pampred animalls, That rage in sauage sensualitie SHAKS. *pl.* The pleasures and sensualities of a luxuriant table 1803. 4. Judging the s. of a nation by its statistics of illegitimate births 1869.

Sensualize (se·nsiŭ-, -ʃŭăləiz), *v.* 1612. [f. SENSUAL *a.* + -IZE.] 1. *trans.* To render sensual; to explain by reference to sensation; *esp.* to imbue with sensual habits or dispositions; to inure to vicious indulgence 1687. 2. *intr.* **a.** To live sensually 1612. **b.** To entertain sensual notions 1846.

1. Not to suffer ones self to be sensualiz'd by pleasures 1725. Locke sensualized the conception of the understanding 1877. Hence **Se·nsualiza·tion,** the action of sensualizing.

Sensuism (se·nsiŭ-, -ʃŭ͵iz'm). 1829. [f. L. *sensus* SENSE *sb.* + -ISM.] *Philos.* = SENSUALISM 1.

Sensuous (se·nsiŭ͵əs, -ʃŭ͵əs), *a.* 1641. [f. L. *sensus* SENSE *sb.* + -OUS. App. coined by MILTON.] 1. Of or pertaining to the senses; derived from, perceived by, or affecting the senses; concerned with sensation or sense-perception. **b.** Of words, etc.: Relating to sensible objects. Of opinions, etc.: Based on representations of sense, material. 1864. **c.** Of pleasure: Received through the senses 1856. 2. Readily affected by the senses; keenly alive to the pleasures of sensation. Also of physiognomy, etc., indicating a sensuous temperament. 1870.

1. To which Poetry would be made subsequent or indeed rather precedent, as being lesse suttle and fine, but more simple, s., and passionate MILT. **b.** Their religion..was of a s. character 1864. 2. Keats as a poet is abundantly and enchantingly s. M. ARNOLD. Hence **Se·nsuous·ly** *adv.*, **-ness.**

Sent (sent), *ppl. a.* 1483. [pa. pple. of SEND *v.*] In senses of the vb. *rare* exc. in comb. as *heaven-sent*.

Sent, obs. form of SCENT.

Sentence (se·ntĕns), *sb.* ME. [a. F., ad. L. *sententia* opinion, maxim, etc., irreg. (for **sentientia*) f. *sentire* to feel.] †1. Way of thinking, opinion –1609. †2. The opinion pronounced by a person on some particular question –1725. 3. An authoritative decision; a judgement pronounced by a tribunal. †**a.** *spec.* = s. of excommunication –1523. **b.** *gen.* The judgement or decision of a court in any civil or criminal cause. Now *rare* in pop. use; still techn. applied to the decisions of the eccl. and admiralty courts. late ME. **c.** The judicial determination of the punishment to be inflicted on a convicted criminal. Hence, the punishment to which a criminal is sentenced. ME. †4. A quoted saying of some eminent person, an apophthegm. Also, a pithy or pointed saying, an aphorism, maxim. –1823. †**b.** Aphoristic speech, sententiousness –1649. 5. An indefinite portion of a discourse or writing; a 'passage'. Now only, a short passage of Scripture in liturgical use. late ME. 6. A series of words in connected speech or writing, forming the grammatically complete expression of a single thought; in pop. use often, such a portion of a composition or utterance as extends from one full stop to another. In *Grammar*, the verbal expression of a proposition, question, command, or request, containing normally a subject and a predicate. 1447. **b.** *Mus.* A complete idea, usu. consisting of two or four phrases 1891. †7. Sense, substance, or gist –1561. †**b.** *gen.* Significance –1589.

1. Touching the s. of antiquitie in this cause HOOKER. 2. My s. is for open Warr MILT. *The four books* (or *the Book*) *of the Sentence(s*, the *Sententiarum libri quatuor*, a compilation of the opinions of the Fathers on questions of Christian doctrine, by Peter Lombard (12th c.), thence called *The Master of the Sentences*. 3. **b.** A S. of Judicial Separation 1857. **c.** When s. of death,..is pronounced BLACKSTONE. *fig.* We are all under a s. of death for the first Man's sin DE FOE. 4. Sentences have great weight in discourse for two reasons 1823. **b.** A discourse full of s. MILT. 5. After which he reads a short S. of Scrip-

ture 1753. **6.** I would not lose a s. that I could gain from lips so instructive RICHARDSON. English grammarians usually recognize three classes: simple sentences, complex sentences (which contain one or more subordinate clauses), and compound sentences (which have more than one subject or predicate). N.E.D. **7.** *Mulier est hominis confusio*: Madame, the s. of this latyn is, Womman is mannes Ioye and al his blis CHAUCER.

Sentence (se·ntĕns), *v.* late ME. [ad. F. *sentencier*, f. *sentence* SENTENCE *sb.*] †**1.** *intr.* To pass judgement –1710. †**2.** *trans.* To decree or order judicially; to decide judicially; to declare judicially or authoritatively –1681. †**3.** To pass judgement on (a person or his actions, the merit of anything) –1809. **4.** To pronounce sentence upon; to condemn *to* a punishment 1592.

3. After this cold considerance, s. me SHAKS. **4.** The offender was sentenc'd and repriev'd EVELYN. *transf.* The man sentenced to a living tomb 1895. Hence **Se·ntencer**, one who sentences.

Sentential (sente·nʃăl), *a.* Now *rare.* 1475. [ad. L. *sententialis* in the form of a sentence, f. *sententia* SENTENCE *sb.*; see -AL 1.] †**1.** Containing, or of the nature of 'sentences' or maxims –1645. **2.** Pertaining to a sentence or series of words in syntactical connexion 1646. †**3.** Of the nature of a 'sentence' or final judicial decision –1701. Hence **Sente·ntially** *adv.* (*Obs.* or *rare*) by way of (judicial) sentence.

Sententiary (sente·nʃări). *Hist.* 1603. [f. med.L. *sententiarius*, f. L. *sententia* SENTENCE *sb.*; see -ARY [1].] **a.** One who writes or utters sentences or aphorisms. **b.** A compiler of 'sentences' or opinions of doctors of the Church on theological questions. **c.** A commentator or lecturer on the Book of Sentences.

Sententiosity (sentenʃiǫ·sĭti). *rare.* 1646. [f. L. *sententiosus* SENTENTIOUS + -ITY.] Sententiousness; also, a sententious remark.

Sententious (sente·nʃəs), *a.* 1440. [f. L. *sententiosus*, f. *sententia* SENTENCE *sb.*; see -OUS.] †**1.** Full of meaning; of persons, full of intelligence or wisdom –1648. **2.** Of the nature of a 'sentence' or aphoristic saying 1542. **3.** Of discourse, style, etc.: Abounding in pointed maxims, aphoristic. Now often in bad sense, affectedly or pompously formal. 1509. **4.** Of persons: Given to the utterance of maxims or pointed sayings. Now often in bad sense, addicted to pompous moralizing. 1598.

1. Your reasons at dinner haue been sharpe & s. SHAKS. **2.** Brief s. precepts MILT. **3.** His grace..in speaking..was pleasant and yet graue:..s., and yet familiar 1579. A long s. letter, full of Latin quotations KINGSLEY. **4.** Sallust was a s. pedant BERKELEY. Hence **Sente·ntious-ly** *adv.*, **-ness.**

Sentience (se·nʃĭĕns). 1839. [f. SENTIENT *a.*; see -ENCE.] The condition or quality of being sentient, consciousness, susceptibility to sensation. So **Se·ntiency.**

Sentient (se·nʃĭĕnt), *a.* and *sb.* 1603. [ad. L. *sentientem*, *sentire* to feel.] **A.** *adj.* **1.** That feels or is capable of feeling; having the power or function of sensation or of perception by the senses 1632. **2.** *Phys.* Of organs or tissues: Responsive to sensory stimuli 1822. **3.** Characterized by the exercise of the senses 1906.

1. [The legend] ascribes to the ship s. powers GROTE. **3.** S. experience..is reality 1906.

B. *absol.* and *sb.* **a.** That which has sensation or feeling. **b.** One who or something which has sensation. 1603. Hence **Se·ntiently** *adv.*

Sentiment (se·ntimĕnt). late ME. [a. OF. *sentement*, or ad. med.L. *sentimentum*, f. L. *sentire* to feel.] †**1.** Personal experience, one's own feeling. late ME. only. †**2.** Sensation, physical feeling. In later use, a knowledge due to vague sensation. –1829. **3.** What one feels with regard to something; mental attitude (of approval or disapproval, etc.); an opinion or view of what is right or agreeable. Often *pl.* with collective sense. 1639. †**b.** In wider sense: An opinion, view (e.g. on a question of fact or scientific truth) –1838. **4.** A mental feeling, an emotion. Now chiefly applied to those feelings which involve an intellectual element or are concerned with ideal objects. 1652. **b.** *Phrenology.* In *pl.*, used as the name for the class of 'faculties' (including Veneration, Self-esteem, Wonder, etc.) which are concerned with emotion, and to which 'organs' are assigned at the top of the brain 1815. **5.** A thought coloured by or proceeding from emotion 1762. **b.** *esp.* An emotional thought expressed in literature or art 1709. **c.** An epigrammatical expression of some striking or agreeable thought or wish announced in the manner of a toast 1777. **6.** *gen.* **a.** Refined and tender emotion; emotional reflection or meditation; appeal to the tender emotions in literature or art. Now chiefly as conveying an imputation of insincerity or mawkishness. 1768. **b.** Emotional regard to ideal considerations, as a principle of action or judgement 1851.

2. She cold was and withouten sentement CHAUCER. **3.** In one s., indeed, you are pretty well agreed—that the Bible is to be discarded 1852. **4.** My uncle assured him he..spoke from a s. of friendly regard to his interest SMOLLETT. **5. b.** The sentiments and language are the poet's own COLERIDGE. **c.** Come, Mr. Premium, I'll give you a s.; here's *Success to usury!* SHERIDAN. **6. a.** The tear of elegant s. permanently in his eye STEVENSON. **b.** Family s. is not everything 1908.

Sentimental (sentime·ntăl), *a.* 1749. [f. prec. + -AL 1.] **1.** Characterized by sentiment. orig., Characterized by or exhibiting refined and elevated feeling. In later use: Addicted to indulgence in superficial emotion; apt to be swayed by sentiment. Also *absol.* (with *the*). **2.** Pertaining to sentiment. **a.** Arising from or determined by feeling rather than reason 1752. **b.** That is a matter of sentiment and not of material interest 1891. **3.** Of literary compositions, etc.: Appealing to sentiment; expressive of the tender emotions, esp. those of love 1762.

1. A soft s. whisper DISRAELI. You have no s. nonsense, no silly infatuation..to fear from me 1862. Hence **Sentime·ntalism,** the s. habit of mind; an idea or expression indicative of sentimentality. **Sentime·ntalist,** one who cultivates or affects sentimentality; one who holds s. doctrines. **Sentimenta·lity,** the quality of being s.; affectation of sensibility, exaggerated insistence upon the claims of sentiment; *pl.* s. notions. **Sentime·ntally** *adv.*

Sentimentalize (sentime·ntăləiz), *v.* 1764. [f. prec. + -IZE.] **1.** *intr.* To indulge in sentimental thoughts or expressions. **2.** *trans.* To make (a person, etc.) sentimental; to imbue (a person, work of art, etc.) with sentiment or sentimental qualities 1821.

1. Here the historian of the conspiracy sentimentalizes SOUTHEY. Hence **Sentime·ntalizer.**

Sentinel (se·ntinĕl), *sb.* 1579. [a. F. *sentinelle*, ad. It. *sentinella*; ult. etym. unkn.] **1.** = SENTRY *sb.*[1] 2. Also *transf.* and *fig.* One who or something which keeps guard like a military sentinel. †**2.** The occupation, duty, or service of a sentinel; chiefly in *to keep s.* –1703. †**3.** A military watch-tower for the defence of a camp or the walls of a city –1643. †**4.** (*Private*) *centinel*: a private soldier –1894.

1. They went all to sleep,..without so much as a centinel placed for their guard DE FOE. Phr. *To stand s.* The grim cliff on which the castle stands s. over the North Sea 1908.

attrib.: **s. crab,** a crab of the Indian Ocean, *Podophthalmus vigil.* Hence **Se·ntinelship.**

Sentinel (se·ntinĕl), *v.* 1593. [f. prec.] **1.** *trans.* To stand guard over, to watch as a sentinel. †**2.** *intr.* To act as sentinel, stand sentinel, keep guard (*rare*) –1610. **3.** *trans.* To furnish with or as with a sentinel or with sentinels 1656. **4.** To post as a sentinel 1827.

1. And mountains, that like giants stand, To s. enchanted land SCOTT. **4.** A statue of the builder sentinelled high up in an airy niche 1870.

Sentry (se·ntri), *sb.*[1] 1611. [perh. a shortening of or back-formation from *centrinel*, obs. var. of SENTINEL.] †**1.** = SENTINEL *sb.* 3. –1653. **2.** *Mil.* and *Naval.* An armed soldier or marine posted at a specified point to keep guard and to prevent the passing of an unauthorized person; spec. *Mil.*, each of the men of a military guard posted at regular intervals round an army in garrison or in the field to watch the enemy, prevent a surprise attack, and to challenge all comers 1632. **b.** *transf.* and *fig.* One who or something which keeps guard like a military sentry 1650. **3.** The occupation, duty, or service of a sentry; also, the watch kept by a sentry, esp. in *to keep s.* 1639. **4.** *Naut.* An apparatus in the form of an inverted kite (towed from the stern of a vessel at a set depth), which is automatically released from its slings on striking the bottom and thus gives warning of the shoaling of the water by sounding a gong on board the vessel 1894.

2. On the approach of any person, the S. will port Arms and call out, Halt! 1877. Phr. *To stand s.* **b.** Wild geese..when on the feed throw out sentries which keep a strict look out 1901. **3.** Here Toils, and Death, and Death's half-brother, Sleep, Forms terrible to view, their Centry keep DRYDEN.

Sentry (se·ntri), *sb.*[2] *Obs.* exc. *Comb.* in proper names. 1590. [Contr. form of *sentuarie*, var. of SANCTUARY infl. by F. *saintuaire.*] = SANCTUARY.

Sentry (se·ntri), *v.* *rare.* 1873. [f. SENTRY *sb.*[1]] **a.** *trans.* To guard as a sentry. **b.** *intr.* To perform the office of a sentry.

Se·ntry-box. 1728. [f. SENTRY *sb.*[1] + BOX *sb.*[2] III. 1.] A small wooden structure in which a sentry may stand at his post in bad weather.

Se·ntry-go. 1852. [orig. a phr. of command; SENTRY (used vocatively) + GO *v.* (imper.).] †**a.** An order to a new sentry to proceed to the relief of the previous one. **b.** The patrol of a sentry; also, the duties of a sentry.

Sepal (se·păl). 1829. [ad. F. *sépale*, mod. L. *sepalum*, originated and derived by H. J. de Necker (1790) from Gr. σκέπη covering.] *Bot.* Each of the divisions or leaves of the calyx of a flower. Hence **Se·pal(l)ed** *a.* only in comb., as *gamo-*, *two-sepalled*, etc. having united, two sepals, etc.

Sepaline (se·pălin), *a.* 1857. [ad. mod.L. *sepalinus*, f. *sepalum* SEPAL; see -INE [1].] Of or belonging to the sepal of a flower.

Sepalody (se·pălǫudi). 1887. [f. mod.L. *sepalum* + -ODE + -Y [3], after *phyllody*.] *Bot.* The reversion of the petals of a flower into sepals by inverse metamorphosis.

Sepaloid (se·păloid), *a.* 1830. [ad. mod.L. *sepaloideus*, f. *sepalum* SEPAL; see -OID.] *Bot.* Of the nature of or resembling a sepal.

Separable (se·părăb'l), *a.* late ME. [a. F. *séparable*, or ad. L. *separabilis*, f. *separare* SEPARATE *v.*; see -ABLE.] Capable of being separated.

That the Magistrate is s. from the man is evident 1643. *S. accident, quality*, one which can be separated from its subject. *S. prefix* (Gram.), a prefix which can be used as an independent word. Hence **Se·parabi·lity, Se·parableness. Se·parably** *adv.*

Separate (se·părĕt), *pa. pple.*, *a.*, and *sb.* late ME. [ad. L. *separatus*, *separare* SEPARATE *v.*] †**A.** *pa. pple.* Separated –1692. **B.** *adj.* **1.** Parted, divided, or withdrawn *from* others; disconnected, detached, set or kept apart 1667. **b.** Of persons, a dwelling, etc.: Withdrawn from society or intercourse; shut off from access 1600. **2.** Withdrawn or divided from something else so as to have independent existence by itself 1700. **b.** Belonging or peculiar to one, not common to or shared with the other or the others 1673. **c.** Considered or reckoned by itself; single, individual 1840.

1. He sought them both, but wish'd his hap might find Eve s. MILT. **b.** Phr. *S. confinement*, *s. system*, the system of confining prisoners in s. cells. **2.** An Essay on the s. existence of Matter 1861. Phr. *S. establishment*, often used to indicate that a married man maintains a paramour. **b.** A married woman, although having s. estate, and living apart from her husband 1858. *S. maintenance*: see MAINTENANCE 2.

C. *sb.* (the adj. used absol. or ellipt.) **1.** One who withdraws from the Church; a separatist 1612. **2.** *U.S.* An article or document issued separately; esp. a copy of an article reprinted from a magazine, volume of transactions, etc., for separate distribution 1886. Hence **Se·parate·ly** *adv.*, **-ness.**

Separate (se·părĕit), *v.* late ME. [f. L. *separat-*, *separare*, f. *se-* SE- + *parare* to make ready, prepare.] **I.** *trans.* **1.** To put apart, set asunder (two or more persons or things, or one *from* another); to disunite, disconnect, make a division between. **b.** To put asunder in thought; to distinguish, treat as distinct 1651. **2.** To remove from conjugal cohabitation, esp. by a judicial decree 1540. **3.** To keep apart or divide by an intervening space or barrier. Of the intervening medium: To part by lying between; to occupy the interval between. 1553. **4.** To segregate for a special purpose. Const. *for*, *to*, *unto*. (Chiefly in Biblical language.) 1526. **5.** To remove or part (a substance) *from* another with which it is combined or mixed. Also with *out*. 1617.

1. Life and these lips haue long bene seperated SHAKS. Being thus separated from my attendants, I lost my way 1839. b. Men had not yet learned to satisfy their consciences by separating the person from the office 1864. 3. The goulph of Ponthus..separateth Asia from Europe 1585. 4. Seperat me Barnabas and Saul for the worke where vnto I have called them TINDALE *Acts* xiii. 2. 5. It is in the furnace that the dross is separated 1850. Hence **Separated** *ppl. a.*, often *spec.* of married people living apart.

II. *intr.* 1. To go away, secede, or withdraw *from* (esp. a church) 1684. b. Of two or more persons: To quit each other's society or company; (of a company) to break up 1690. c. To withdraw from conjugal cohabitation 1686. 2. Of a thing: To part (*from* something else); to be disunited or disjoined, to become detached; to draw apart or asunder 1638. b. Of a mineral or chemical substance: To be parted or disengaged from a mass or compound; to be drawn *out* from a solution in the form of crystals or as a precipitate 1863.

2. The roof of the nave has separated in one place from the wall 1832.

Separation (sepărēⁱ·ʃən). late ME. [a. OF., ad. L. *separationem*, f. *separare* SEPARATE *v.*] 1. The action of separating; the state of being separated or parted. 2. The action of separating oneself, withdrawing, or parting company 1450. 3. Cessation of conjugal cohabitation, either by mutual consent of the parties or imposed by a judicial decree granted at the suit of one of them 1600. 4. The place where two or more objects separate or are divided from one another; a parting, line of division 1615. 5. Something that separates; an interval or break between two objects; a cause of separating (*rare*) 1715. †6. *Alchemy* and *Old Chem.* A process of analysis, extraction, or the like –1728. 7. *Med.* The process by which dead tissue becomes detached from the sound flesh 1612.

1. After the age of six years, the time has arrived for the separation of the sexes JOWETT. 3. The usual Causes of S. is assign'd as the Fault of the Wife 1700. *Judicial s.*, the name now given to the 'divorce *a mensa et thoro*'; see DIVORCE *sb.* 1.

attrib.: **s. allowance**, an allowance paid to the wife of a soldier in war-time; **-order**, an order of court for judicial separation.

Separatism (se·părătiz'm). 1628. [f. SEPARATE *a.* + -ISM.] The disposition to separate or to be separate; advocacy of separation (esp. in regard to Church or State); the principles and practices of separatists.

Separatist (se·părătist), *sb.* and *a.* 1608. [f. SEPARATE *a.* or *sb.* + -IST.] A. *sb.* 1. One who advocates ecclesiastical separation; one who belongs to a religious community separated from the Church or from a particular church. b. *gen.* A schismatic, sectarian; also, a member of a congregation not belonging to any recognized denomination 1641. 2. Often interpreted to mean: One who holds himself apart from others on the ground of superior piety. Hence as tr. *Pharisee*. 1620. 3. One who advocates political separation; applied, e.g. (by opponents) to the advocates of Home Rule for Ireland 1871.

1. They [*sc.* Wesleyan methodists] ought more properly, perhaps, to be called separatists than dissenters 1846. 2. The Separatists, or Sanctified, as they terme themselves 1620.

B. *attrib.* or as *adj.* That is a separatist; pertaining to, consisting of, or characteristic of separatists 1830. Hence **Se:paratistic** *a.* pertaining to or of the nature of separation.

Separative (se·părĕtiv), *a.* 1592. [a. F. *séparatif*, or ad. late L. *separativus*, f. L. *separare* SEPARATE *v.*; see -IVE.] 1. Tending to separate or to cause separation. 2. *Gram.* Of conjunctions: Alternative, disjunctive 1888. Hence **Se·parative·ly** *adv.*, **-ness**.

Separator (se·pĕrēⁱtəɹ). 1607. [a. late L., f. *separare*.] 1. One who or something which separates; *spec.* †one who separates from the Church, a separatist; a critic who ascribes the Iliad and Odyssey to different authors (tr. Gr. χωρίζων). 2. An instrument or appliance for separating, in various arts and crafts; often short for *cream-s.* 1830.

Se·paratory, *a.* 1715. [ad. mod.L. *separatorius*, f. L. *separare*; see -ORY ².] Having the function of separating.

‖ **Separatrix** (se·părēⁱtriks). 1660. [Late L. (sc. *linea*), f. L. *separare*.] †1. The mark (orig. L, later |), formerly used to separate the figures representing decimals from those representing integers; now superseded by the decimal point. 2. The slanting stroke used in proof correction to mark and separate alterations 1892. 3. The line separating light and shade on a partly illuminated surface 1891.

‖ **Sephardi** (sĭfā·ɹdi). *Pl.* **Sephardim** (-dim), **-din** (-din). 1851. [mod. Heb. *sᵉphardī*, f. *sᵉphārād*, the name of a country mentioned only *Obad.* 20, and identified by the Rabbins with Spain.] A Spanish or Portuguese Jew, a Jew of Spanish or Portuguese descent. Hence **Sepha·rdic** *a.* pertaining to the Sephardim.

Sephen (se·fen). 1854. [a. mod.L., a. Arab. *safan* shagreen.] A kind of sting-ray.

‖ **Sephiroth** (se·firoþ), *pl.* Rarely in *sing.* sephira. 1569. [Late Heb., f. *sāphar* to number.] In the philosophy of the Cabbala, the ten hypostatized attributes or emanations by means of which the Infinite enters into relation with the finite.

Sepia (sī·piă). 1569. [a. L., a. Gr. σηπία.] 1. The cuttle-fish; now *rare* exc. *Zool.* a cuttle of the genus *Sepia* or family *Sepiidæ*; also, the genus itself. 2. A pigment of a rich brown colour (used in monochrome water-colour painting) prepared from the inky secretion of the cuttle-fish; the colour of this pigment. Also called *Roman s.* Often *attrib.* as in *s. drawing, tone.* 1821. 3. In full *s. bone*: Cuttle-bone, *esp.* as used in pharmacy, etc. 1840. Hence **Se·pioid**, a cuttle-fish of the genus *S.*

Sepiacean (sīpiˌēⁱ·ʃăn), *a.* and *sb.* 1842. [f. mod.L. *Sepiaceus*, f. SEPIA; see -ACEAN.] *Zool.* Pertaining to, or a member of, the group *Sepiacea* of cuttle-fishes. So **Sepia·ceous** *a.*

‖ **Sepiola** (sīpəi·ŏlă). 1797. [L., dim. of SEPIA.] *Zool.* A cuttle-fish of the genus so named.

Sepiolite (sī·piŏləit). 1854. [ad. G. *sepiolith*, f. Gr. σήπιον SEPIUM; see -LITE.] *Geol.* Meerschaum.

Sepiostaire (sīpiŏstē·ɹ). 1836. [ad. F. *sépiostaire*, f. Gr. σηπία SEPIA + ὀστοῦν bone + *-aire* (cf. -ARY ¹).] *Zool.* Cuttle-bone.

‖ **Sepium** (sī·piŏm). 1835. [mod.L., a. Gr. σήπιον.] *Zool.* Cuttle-bone.

†**Sepo·se**, *v.* 1593. [f. L. *seposit-*, *seponere*, after POSE *v.*¹, etc.] 1. *trans.* To set aside –1664. 2. To set apart or reserve –1641. So †**Seposi·tion**, setting aside –1656.

Sepoy (sī·poi, sīpoi·), **sipahi** (sipā·i). *Anglo-Ind.* 1717. [ad. Urdu = Pers. *sipāhī* horseman, soldier, f. *sipāh* army; cf. SPAHI.] A native of India employed as a soldier under European, esp. British, discipline.

attrib.: **s.-crab**, a species of crab found in the Indian and Pacific Oceans; **S. Mutiny** or **Rebellion**, a revolt against British rule in India in 1857–8, commonly called *the Indian Mutiny*.

Seps (seps). 1562. [a. L., a. Gr. σήψ, f. σήπειν to make rotten.] 1. A very venomous serpent described by classical writers. 2. A lizard of the scincoid genus *Seps*, having a serpentlike body; a serpent-lizard 1802.

Sepsine (se·psin). 1880. [f. next + -INE ⁵.] a. A poisonous crystalline substance obtained from decomposing yeast. b. A ptomaine causing septic poison.

‖ **Sepsis** (se·psis). 1876. [mod.L., a. Gr. σῆψις, f. σήπειν to rot.] Septic poisoning.

Sept (sept), *sb.*¹ 1548. [ad.L. *septum* SEPTUM.] 1. An enclosure; an area marked off for a special purpose; a fold (*fig.*). 2. *Arch.* A dividing screen, railing, etc. 1821.

Sept (sept), *sb.*² 1517. [prob. a var. of SECT.] A division of a nation or tribe; a clan; orig. in ref. to Ireland. b. *transf.* A 'tribe' or class 1610.

ThErle of Desmonde, and the Geraldines of his kyn and septe 1536. Hence **Se·ptal** *a.*²

‖ **Septæmia** (septī·miă). Also *U.S.* **septemia**. 1887. [mod.L., f. Gr. σηπτός putrefying, putrefactive (f. σήπειν to rot) + αἷμα blood.] = SEPTICÆMIA.

Septal (se·ptăl), *a.*¹ 1839. [f. SEPTUM + -AL 1.] Pertaining to, consisting of, or forming a septum or septa.

†**Septangle**. 1551. [ad. late L. *septangulus*, f. *septem* + *angulus*.] A heptagon –1656.

Septangular (septæ·ŋgiŭlăɹ), *a.* 1656. [ad. mod.L. **septangularis*, f. *septangulus* (see prec.).] Having seven angles, heptagonal.

‖ **Septarium** (septē·riŏm). *Pl.* **-aria** (-ē·riă). 1785. [mod.L., f. L. *septum*; see SEPTUM and -ARIUM.] *Geol.* 1. A septal arrangement. 2. A nodule of argillaceous limestone, ironstone, or the like, of which the parts near the centre are cracked, the spaces between being filled with some mineral: formerly much used for cement 1791. Hence **Septa·rian** *a.* of the form or character of septaria.

Septate (se·ptēⁱt), *a.* 1846. [ad. mod.L. *septatus* (in late L. = surrounded); see SEPTUM and -ATE ².] *Nat. Hist.* Containing or divided by a septum or septa. So **Se·ptated** *a.* **Septa·tion**, division by a septum or septa.

Septem-, L. *septem* seven, = SEPTI-¹ (which is more frequent): as in **Septe·mfluous** [L. *septemfluus*] *a.* flowing in seven streams. **Septemfo·liate** *a. Bot.* having seven leaflets. **Septempa·rtite** *a. Bot.* divided nearly to the base into seven parts.

September (septe·mbəɹ). Abbrev. **Sep.**, **Sept.**, in 17th c. also 7ᵇʳ. OE. [a. L., f. *septem*, this month being the seventh of the old Roman year.] The ninth month of the year (according to the modern reckoning).

Septembrist (septe·mbrist). 1840. [f. prec. + -IST.] a. In Portugal, a supporter of the (successful) insurrection of September 1836 in favour of the restoration of the constitution of 1822. b. = SEPTEMBRIZER 1.

Septembrize (se·ptembrəiz), *v.* Also **-ber-**. 1793. [ad. F. *septembriser*, f. *septembre* SEPTEMBER; see -IZE.] *trans.* and *intr.* (orig. *Fr. Hist.*) To assassinate like the Septembrizers.

Septembrizer (se·ptembrəizəɹ). Also **-ber-**. 1794. [ad. F. *septembriseur*, f. *septembriser* (see prec.).] 1. *Fr. Hist.* One who took part in or advocated the massacre of the political prisoners in Paris on September 2nd–5th, 1792. Also *transf.*, a bloodthirsty revolutionary. 2. = SEPTEMBRIST a. 1840. 3. One who shoots partridges (in September): with allusion to sense 1. 1824.

Septemvir (septe·mvəɹ). *Pl.* **-viri** (-virəi). 1760. [L., sing. of *septemviri*, f. *septem* + *viri* men.] One of a body of seven men associated in an office or commission.

Septemvirate (septe·mvirĕt). 1640. [ad. L. *septemviratus*, f. *septemvir*; see -ATE ¹.] 1. The office or dignity of a septemvir, government by septemviri. 2. A group or set of seven men 1750.

‖ **Septenarius** (septĭnē·riŏs). *Pl.* **-arii** (-ē·riˌəi). 1819. [L., f. *septeni* seven each.] *Pros.* A line of seven feet, esp. the trochaic or iambic tetrameter catalectic.

Septenary (se·ptĭnări, septī·nări), *a.* and *sb.* 1577. [ad. L. *septenarius*, f. *septeni*; see prec. and -ARY.] A. *adj.* Pertaining or relating to the number seven; forming a group of seven 1601. b. With ref. to the division of time into periods based on the number seven, e.g. a week 1646.

S. number, the number seven. b. That s. notation of days which we call the week 1848.

B. *sb.* †1. The number seven –1690. 2. A group or set of seven 1594. 3. A period of seven years (*occas.* weeks, days) 1577. 4. *Mus.* The seven notes of the diatonic scale 1662. 5. *Pros.* = SEPTENARIUS 1887.

3. The dayes of men are usually cast up by septenaries SIR T. BROWNE.

Septenate (se·ptĭnĕt), *a.* 1830. [f. L. *septeni* seven each + -ATE ².] *Bot.* Growing in sevens, having seven divisions, heptamerous.

Septennary (septe·nări), *a.* 1644. [f. L. *septennis* (f. *septem* + *annus*) + -ARY ¹.] Septennial.

Septennate (septe·nĕt). 1874. [ad. F. *septennat*, f. L. *septennis* (see prec.) + *-at* -ATE ¹.] A period of seven years during which office is held, etc.

Septennial (septe·niăl), *a.* 1640. [f. L. *septennium* + -AL 1.] 1. Consisting of, or lasting, seven years 1656. 2. Recurring every seven years 1640.

1. A s. parliament 1772. 2. S. revaluations 1886. Hence **Septe·nnially** *adv.* every seven years.

‖ **Septennium** (septe·niŏm). 1855. [L., f. *septem* + *annus* year.] A period of seven years.

†**Septentrial**, *a.* 1549. [irreg. f. L. *septentrio* (see next) + -AL 1.] = SEPTENTRIONAL -1631.

Septentrion (septe·ntriŏn), *sb.* and *a.* *Obs.* exc. *arch.* late ME. [ad. L. *septentrio*, sing. of *septentriones*, orig. *septem triones*, the seven stars of the Great Bear, f. *septem* + *triones*, pl. of *trio* plough-ox.] A. *sb.* 1. *pl.* (chiefly as Latin.) The constellation of the Great Bear, *occas.* the Little Bear 1532. 2. The north; the northern region(s) of the earth or the heavens. late ME. 3. A northerner (*rare*) 1607. B. *adj.* Northern; = next 1632.

A. 2. Thou art as opposite to euery good, As..the South to the S. SHAKS. B. Cold S. blasts MILT.

Septentrional (septe·ntriŏnăl), *a.* Now *rare.* late ME. [ad. L. *septentrionalis*, f. *septentrio.*] Belonging to the north, northern; formerly (of learning, etc.), pertaining to northern countries.

Dr. Marshall the..reviver of S. Learning in the University of Oxford 1718.

Septet(t, -ette (septe·t). 1837. [a. G. *septet*, f. L. *septem*; see -ET, -ETTE.] *Mus.* A composition for seven voices or instruments. b. *transf.* A set of seven 1886.

Septfoil (se·tfoil). 1578. [ad. late L. *septifolium*, as if through OF.; see SEPTI-[1] and FOIL *sb.*[1]] 1. The plant tormentil. Now *rare.* 2. *Arch.* An ornament with seven cusps or points 1849.

Septi-[1], comb. form of L. *septem* seven, in Eng. forming adj. compounds for the most part adapted from or modelled on L. compounds.

Se·ptico·loured *a.* of seven colours. **Septifo·lious** [L. *folium* leaf], *a.* having seven leaves. **Se·ptiform** *a.*[1] sevenfold. **Septila·teral** *a.* seven-sided. **Se·ptipartite** *a.* = SEPTEMPARTITE. **Septi·valent** *a.* *Chem.* combining with seven atoms of hydrogen or other univalent element or radical.

Septi-[2], comb. form of SEPTUM, as in **Se·pticidal** [L. *-cidere*, comb. f. *cædere* to cut] *a.* *Bot.* applied to the form of dehiscence in which the pod splits through the dissepiments. **Septi·ferous**, *a.* having a septum or septa. **Se·ptiform**, *a.*[2] of the form or nature of a septum. **Septi·fragal** [L. *frag-*, *frangere* to break] *a.* *Bot.* applied to the form of dehiscence in which the septa are separated from the valves.

Septic (se·ptik), *a.* and *sb.* 1605. [ad. late L. *septicus*, a. Gr. σηπτικός, f. σήπειν to putrefy.] A. *adj.* Putrefactive, putrefying; in mod. use, of disease, caused by the absorption of the products of putrefaction. †B. *sb.* A septic or putrefactive substance -1771.

‖ **Septicæmia** (septisī·miă). Also *U.S.* **septicemia.** 1866. [mod.L., f. Gr. σηπτικός SEPTIC + αἷμα blood; see -IA[1].] Septic poisoning. Hence **Septicæ·mic** *a.*

Se·ptical, *a.* Now *rare* or *Obs.* 1646. [f. as SEPTIC; see -ICAL.] = SEPTIC *a.* Hence **Se·ptically** *adv.* so as to produce putrefaction.

Septicity (septi·sĭti). 1828. [f. SEPTIC + -ITY, after F. *septicité.*] The quality or condition of being septic.

Septillion (septi·lyən). 1690. [ad. F., f. *septem* seven, after *million.*] *Arith.* The seventh power of a million, denoted by 1 followed by 42 ciphers. In American (following the later Fr.) use, the eighth power of a thousand, denoted by 1 followed by 24 ciphers.

Septimal (se·ptimăl), *a.* 1855. [f. L. *septimus* + -AL 1.] 1. Of a numerical system: Based on the number 7. 2. *Mus.* Pertaining to a seventh 1867.

Septime (se·ptim). 1889. [ad. L. *septimus.*] *Fencing.* A parry.

Septimole (se·ptimōul). 1854. [Arbitrarily f. L. *septimus*; cf. QUINTOLE.] *Mus.* A group of seven notes to be played in the time of four or six.

Septinsular (septi·nsiŭlăı), *a.* (*sb.*) 1809. [f. L. *septem* + *insula* island.] *S. Republic*, etc.: the Ionian Islands. Also as *sb. pl.*, the people of the Ionian Islands.

Septo-[1], comb. form of Gr. σηπτός, vbl. adj. f. σήπειν to rot, as in **Septoge·nic**, *a.* producing sepsis; etc.

Septo-[2], used as comb. form of SEPTUM, as in **Se·pto-maxi·llary** *a.* applied to a small bone lying above the vomer in some birds and fishes.

Septuagenarian (se:ptiŭădʒĭnē·riăn), *a.* and *sb.* 1715. [f. L. *septuagenarius*, f. *septuageni* seventy each.] A. *adj.* 1. Pertaining to the number seventy (*rare*). 2. Seventy years old; characteristic of that age 1793. B. *sb.* A person seventy years old 1805.

Septuagenary (se:ptiŭădʒī·nări), *a.* and *sb.* Now *rare.* 1605. [f. as prec.] = prec.

Septuagesima (se:ptiŭădʒe·simă). late ME. [a. L. *septuagesima* (sc. *dies*), fem. of *septuagesimus* seventieth, f. *septuaginta* seventy.] 1. In full *S. Sunday*: the third Sunday before Lent. †2. The seventy days beginning with the third Sunday before Lent and ending with the Saturday in Easter week -1483.

Septuagint (se·ptiŭădʒint). 1577. [ad. L. *septuaginta* seventy, f. weakened form of *septem.*] †1. The 'seventy translators' of the Old Testament into Greek (see 2); = L. *septuaginta* (*interpretes*), Gr. οἱ Ο'. Also *pl.* in the same sense. -1684. 2. The Greek version of the Old Testament, which derives its name from the story that it was made by seventy-two Palestinian Jews at the request of Ptolemy Philadelphus (284–247 B.C.) and completed by them, in seclusion on the island of Pharos, in seventy-two days. (Denoted by LXX.) 1633. 3. A group of seventy 1864. Hence **Se:ptuagi·ntal** *a.* of or pertaining to the S.

‖ **Septulum** (se·ptiŭlŏm). 1826. [mod.L., dim. of next.] *Nat. Hist.* A small or thin septum. Hence **Se·ptulate** *a.* having a s.

‖ **Septum** (se·ptŏm). *Pl.* **septa** (se·ptă). 1720. [a. L. *septum*, *sæptum*, f. *sepire*, *sæpire* to enclose, f. *sepes*, *sæpes* hedge.] A partition; a dividing wall, membrane, layer, etc.; a dissepiment 1728. b. *Anat.* e.g. the partition between the nostrils (*septum nasi*), the membrane separating the ventricles of the heart (*septum cordis*) 1726. c. *Bot.* e.g. the division-wall of a cell, a partition in a compound ovary or spore 1720. d. *Zool.* e.g. one of the radiated plates of the cell of corals, one of the partitions of a chambered shell 1815.

Septuor (se·ptiŭŏı). 1850. [a. F., f. L. *septem*, after *quatuor* quartet.] *Mus.* = SEPTET.

Septuple (se·ptiup'l), *a.* and *sb.* 1692. [ad. late L. *septuplus*, f. *septem* seven.] A. *adj.* 1. Sevenfold 1834. 2. *Mus.* Having seven beats in a bar 1884. B. *sb.* The seventh multiple 1692. So **Se·ptuple** *v. trans.* to multiply by seven, increase seven times 1615.

Septuplet (se·ptiŭplet). 1891. [f. L. *septuplus* (see prec.) after *triplet*, etc.] *Mus.* = SEPTIMOLE.

Sepulchral (sĭpv·lkrăl), *a.* 1615. [ad. L. *sepulcralis*, f. *sepulcrum*; see -AL 1.] 1. Of or pertaining to burial or a place of burial. a. Pertaining to or serving as a sepulchre or tomb; forming part of a sepulchre, or its furniture; monumental 1631. b. Pertaining to burial rites and customs 1615. 2. *transf.* Appropriate to a tomb; dismal, gloomy, melancholy 1711.

1. a. Old s. urns COWPER. b. S. libations 1729. 2. A deep sepulcral sound the cave Return'd SOUTHEY. Hence **Sepu·lchrally** *adv.*

Sepulchre (se·pŏlkəı), *sb.* ME. [a. OF. *sepulcre*, ad. L. *sepulcrum* (less correctly *sepulchrum*), f. root of L. *sepultus*, *sepelire* to bury.] 1. A tomb or burial-place. Now only *rhet.* or *Hist.* Also *transf.* and *fig.* 2. *The Holy S.*: The cave in which Jesus Christ was buried outside the walls of Jerusalem; hence, the buildings erected over the traditional site of this cave. Also in the title of churches erected in memory of this. 3. *Antiq.* A permanent or temporary structure prepared in a church for the symbolic burial of the reserved Sacrament (sometimes also the Cross) on Maundy Thursday. late ME. b. The altar of repose (REPOSE *sb.* 1) 1753. 4. Interment, burial (*rare*). late ME.

1. *Whited* (†*painted*) *s.*, in biblical language, used for a hypocrite, or one whose fair outward semblance conceals inward corruption. *fig.* The whole earth is the s. of famous men JOWETT. 2. *Knight of the (Holy) S.*, a member of a secular confraternity of those knighted in the crusades, esp. at the Holy S. itself; since 1342, a religious organization, having the Latin Patriarch of Jerusalem as its Grand-master.

Sepulchre (se·pŏlkəı), *v.* 1591. [f. prec.] 1. *trans.* To place in a sepulchre; to bury. 2. To receive as in a sepulchre, to serve as a burial-place for 1605.

1. My bones s. not from thine apart COWPER. *fig.* Where merit is not sepulcher'd aliue B. JONS. 2. When Ocean shrouds and sepulchres our dead BYRON.

Sepulture (se·pŏltiŭı, -tʃəı), *sb.* ME. [a. OF., ad. L. *sepultura* burial, f. *sepult-*, *sepelire* to bury.] 1. Interment, burial. 2. A burial-place, grave, tomb. Now *arch.* late ME.

1. Even the honours of s. were long withheld from his remains MACAULAY. *fig.* For dronkenesse is verray s. Of mannes wit and his discrecion CHAUCER. Hence **Sepu·ltural** *a.* of or pertaining to s. **Se·pulture** *v. trans.* to bury, inter.

Seq. *Pl.* **seqq.** Also **sq.** *Pl.* **sqq.** 1726. Abbrev. forms in *sing.* of L. *sequens* the following, *sequente* and in what follows, *sequitur* it follows; in *pl.* of *sequentes*, *-tia* the following, *sequentibus* in the following places. Also, *et seq.*

Sequacious (sĭkwē·ʃəs), *a.* 1640. [f. L. *sequac-*, *sequax* that follows, a follower, f. *sequi* to follow.] 1. Given to following another or others, esp. a leader. †Const. *to*, *of*. 1643. b. Given to slavish or unreasoning following of others (esp. in matters of thought or opinion) 1653. †2. Of things: Readily yielding to traction; easily moulded; ductile, pliable, flexible -1752. 3. Of musical notes, metrical feet: Following one another with unvarying regularity of order 1795.

1. Trees unrooted left their Place, S. of the Lyre DRYDEN. 2. Of all Fire there is none so ductile, so s. and obsequious as this of Wrath 1640. 3. The long s. notes Over..surges sink and rise COLERIDGE. Hence **Sequa·cious-ly** *adv.*, **-ness.**

Sequacity (sĭkwæ·sĭti). 1626. [ad. late L. *sequacitas*, f. *sequac-* (see prec.) + -ITY.] †1. Ductility, pliability (of matter). BACON. 2. Disposition or readiness to follow; lack of independence 1654.

Sequel (sī·kwĕl), *sb.* late ME. [a OF. *sequelle*, ad. L. *sequela* (*sequella*), f. *sequi* to follow.] †1. A train of followers, following, suit; *rarely*, a follower. In *Feudal Law*, the offspring, retinue, chattels, and appurtenances of a villein. -1640. †2. Descendants, posterity; successors in inheritance -1572. 3. That which follows as a result of an event or course of action; an after-consequence 1477. †4. That which follows or is thought to follow as a logical consequence; an inference -1689. †5. Sequence, order of succession; also, a series -1771. 6. What happened or will happen afterwards; the ensuing course of affairs; issue, result, upshot 1524. b. An age or period as following and influenced by (a former period) 1837. 7. The ensuing narrative, discourse, etc.; the remaining part of a narrative, etc.; that which follows as a continuation; esp. a literary work that, although complete in itself, forms a continuation of a preceding one 1513.

3. That every phenomenon in the moral or material world was the s. of a natural cause 1883. 4. 'Tis a false s...to suppose That, 'cause it is now ill, 'twill ere be so LOVELACE. 5. Homer..wrote a s. of Songs and Rhapsodies BENTLEY. 6. O plague right well preuented! so will you say, when you haue seene the sequele SHAKS. The October-Club..proved in the S. to be the chief Support of those who suspected them SWIFT. 7. In *Love's Last Shift*, and in the S. of it, the *Relapse* CIBBER. We shall meet with it again..in the s. of this history 1884.

‖ **Sequela** (sĭkwī·lă). *Pl.* **-læ** (-lī). 1793. [L.; see prec.] *Path.* A morbid affection occurring as the result of a previous disease. Chiefly *pl.* b. *transf.* A consequence 1883.

Sequence (sī·kwĕns). late ME. [ad. late L. *sequentia*, f. *sequentem*, *sequi* to follow; see next and -ENCE.] 1. The fact of following after or succeeding; the following of one thing after another in succession; an instance of this 1593. 2. Order of succession 1586. b. *Gram.* Chiefly in *s. of tenses*, the manner in which the tense of a subordinate clause depends on that of the principal clause 1848. 3. A continuous or connected series 1575. b. *Mus.* The repetition of a melodic or harmonic progression at a different pitch 1752. 4. *Cards.* A group of three or more cards of the same suit following in numerical order; a 'run' 1575. 5. Something that follows. a. A logical consequence; also †an inference, conclusion 1613. b. A subsequent event; sometimes contextually, a consequent event, a result 1853. 6. The quality of being sequent; the fact of following as a logical inference or as a necessary result; continuity, consecutiveness 1828. 7. *Eccl.* A composition in rhythmical prose or accentual metre said or sung, in the Western Church, between the Gradual and the Gospel. Also called *prose*; see PROSE *sb.* 2. late ME.

1. For how art thou a King But by faire s. and succession? SHAKS. There are fixed in his..memory certain sequences as always occurring 1884. *Phr. In s.*, one after another. 2. Works..arranged in chronological s. 1862. 3. Then came a long s. of reflections SCOTT. 4. A S. of King, Queen, and Knave 1746. 5. b. Maritime commerce was the natural s. to that along the courses of rivers 1872. 6. In this remarkable Volume,..of true logical method and s. there is too little CARLYLE. So **Se·quency,** the quality of being sequent.

Sequent (sīˑkwĕnt), *a.* and *sb.* 1560. [a. OF., ad. L. *sequentem*, pres. pple. of *sequi.*] A. *adj.* 1. That follows or comes after. †a. That one is about to say or mention; (the) following –1821. b. That succeeds in time or serial order 1601. That follows another (*rare*) 1612. 2. That follows as a result or logical conclusion. Const. *to, on, upon.* 1601. 3. Following one another or in a series; successive 1604. b. Characterized by continuous succession; consecutive 1600.

1. b. The Rector..enjoyed his s. glass of port 1873. 2. Indeed your O Lord sir, is very s. to your whipping SHAKS. 3. The Gallies Haue sent a dozen s. Messengers..at one anothers heeles SHAKS.

B. *sb.* †1. A follower, attendant. SHAKS. †2. A unit of a sequence; esp. of playing-cards –1734. 3. That which follows in order 1833. 4. That which follows naturally as a result; the consequent of an antecedent 1838.

Sequential (sĭkweˑnʃăl), *a.* 1822. [f. late L. *sequentia* SEQUENCE; see -AL 1.] 1. That follows as a sequel or a sequela. 2. That is characterized by the regular sequence of its parts; continuous 1844. 3. *Mus.* Of the nature of a sequence 1889. Hence **Seque·ntially** *adv.*

†Seque·ster, *sb.*[1] ME. [a. L.] In *Civil Law*, a person with whom the parties in a suit deposit the thing contested until the case has been decided. Also, a mediator. –1633.

†Seque·ster, *sb.*[2] 1568. [a. F. *séquestre*, ad. L. *sequestrum*, orig. neut. of *sequester* adj.] 1. Sequestration, seclusion, isolation. SHAKS. 2. The office or court to which goods sequestered are taken 1568.

Sequester (sĭkweˑstəɹ), *v.* late ME. [ad. late L. *sequestrare* to place in safe keeping, etc., f. L. *sequestr-*, *sequester*; prob. f. **seques-*, **sequos* a position apart.] 1. *trans.* To set aside, separate; †to separate and reject. †b. *Eccl.* To excommunicate –1642. †c. To set apart, consecrate to a particular service –1697. †d. To remove from membership of a body, or from a public office or station –1827. e. To seclude (a person, thing, or place) from general access or intercourse. Now *rare* or *Obs.* exc. in SEQUESTERED *ppl. a.* late ME. 2. To confiscate, appropriate, take forcible possession of 1513. 3. *Law.* a. To remove (property, etc.) from the possession of the owner temporarily; to seize and hold the effects of a debtor until the claims of creditors be satisfied; *Eccl.* to divert the income of a benefice to the payment of debts due from the incumbent, or for the purpose of making good the dilapidations; to hold the income of a benefice during a vacancy for the benefit of the next incumbent 1530. b. To apply the process of sequestration to (a person); to sequestrate the estate or benefice of 1681. †4. *intr.* To withdraw into seclusion, to retire, keep apart –1838.

1. e. I had wholly sequestred my thoughts from ciuill affaires BACON. He sequestered himself from his subjects in the recesses of his palace DE QUINCEY. 2. He is in rebellion and his estate sequestered 1644. 4. To s. out of the world into Atlantick and Eutopian polities..will not mend our condition MILT.

Sequestered (sĭkweˑstəɹd), *ppl. a.* 1600. [f. prec. + -ED [1].] †1. Separated; cut off from congenial surroundings –1782. b. Under sentence of sequestration; esp. *Eccl. Hist.* of the dispossessed clergy under the Commonwealth: Deprived of a benefice 1661. 2. Sheltered, retired, secluded 1658. b. Of persons: Retired, living a secluded life or in a quiet, unfrequented place 1643.

1. *A.Y.L.* II. i. 33. b. He is a poor sequestred Parson 1673. 2. Along the cool sequester'd vale of life They kept the noiseless tenor of their way GRAY. b. Eremites, (the most s. of begging Fryers) FULLER.

†Seque·strable, *a.* 1652. [f. as prec. + -ABLE.] Capable of being sequestered, liable to sequestration –1807.

Sequestral (sĭkweˑstrăl), *a.* 1887. [f. SEQUESTRUM + -AL 1.] Of or pertaining to a sequestrum.

Sequestrate (sĭkweˑstrēit, sīˑkwĕstrēit), *v.* 1513. [f. late L. *sequestrat-*, *sequestrare* SEQUESTER *v.*; see -ATE [3].] 1. *trans.* To remove, put away; to seclude, keep away from general access or intercourse; to put in a place of concealment or confinement. Now *rare.* 2. *Law.* To divert the income of an estate or benefice, temporarily or permanently, from its owner into other hands (cf. SEQUESTER *v.* 3 a) 1609. b. *Sc. Law.* To place (lands) in the control of a judicial factor or trustee; now, to take the property of a bankrupt into judicial possession 1726. 3. *gen.* To confiscate 1640.

Sequestration (sīkwestrēˑʃən). late ME. [ad. late L. *sequestrationem*, f. L. *sequestrare* SEQUESTER *v.*] 1. An act or the action of sequestering, banishment, exile; esp. *Eccl.*, excommunication. b. *transf.* Separation, disjunction 1567. 2. A state of being sequestered, separation, seclusion, retirement 1565. 3. *Law.* a. The appropriation of the income of a property in order to satisfy claims against the owner; esp. *Eccl.*, the diversion of the income of a benefice to the advantage of the creditors of the incumbent; a writ for this 1565. b. An order of court appointing the goods of a deceased person whose executor or executors have renounced probate to be secured and administered; also, a writ of Chancery empowering commissioners or a sheriff to seize the property of the person against whom it is directed 1591. c. Seizure of the possessions of a subject by the state; esp. the act of a belligerent power in seizing debts owing from its own subjects to the opposing power 1568. d. *Sc. Law* (see prec. 2 b) 1765. 4. *gen.* Seizure, confiscation 1640.

2. It is no other, but a place of retyring, and s. from the World 1628. 3. c. His former delinquencies..were severely punished by fine and s. SCOTT.

Sequestrator (sīˑkwestrēitəɹ). 1644. [a. late L., f. L. *sequestrare.*] One who sequestrates; a trustee or bailiff having control of property upon which there are claims by creditors. Also, a person named in a writ of sequestration as authorized to collect and administer the income of a sequestrated estate. So **†Sequestree·**, sequestrator 1611–1845.

‖ **Sequestrum** (sĭkweˑstrŏm). *Pl.* **sequestra.** 1831. [mod.L. use of L. *sequestrum* something separated, neut. of *sequester* placed apart.] *Path.* A detached piece of bone lying within a cavity formed by necrosis. Also applied to a portion of skin separated by disease from the surrounding parts.

Sequin (sīˑkwin), *sb.* 1617. [a. F., ad. It. *zecchino*, f. *zecca* the mint, ad. Arab. *sikkah* die for coining.] 1. An Italian gold coin (orig. Venetian), worth about 9 shillings. Now *Hist.* 2. A small spangle used to ornament dresses, etc. 1882. Hence **Se·quin** *v. trans.* to ornament with sequins.

‖ **Sequitur** (seˑkwitŭɹ). 1836. [L., 'it follows'.] An inference or conclusion following from the premisses. Cf. NON SEQUITUR.

Sequoia (sĭkwoiˑă). 1866. [mod.L.; after *Sequoiah*, a Cherokee who invented a syllabary for writing his native language.] A genus of large American coniferous trees belonging to the *Abietinæ*; a tree of this genus. Pop. often called *Wellingtonia.*

Serac (sĕræˑk). 1860. [a. Swiss-Fr. *sérac*, orig. the name of a kind of white cheese.] An irregular-shaped pinnacle of ice on a glacier, formed by the intersection of crevasses.

Seraglio (sĕrāˑlyo, sĕ-). 1581. [a. It. *serraglio*:—pop. L. **serraculum* enclosure, place of confinement, f. **serrare* for *serare* to lock up, f. *sera* lock or bolt.] I. Enclosure, place of confinement. 1. The part of a Mohammedan dwelling-house (esp. of the palace of a sovereign or great noble) in which the women are secluded; the apartments reserved for wives and concubines; a harem. b. The inmates of the harem; a polygamous household 1634. †2. *gen.* An enclosure; a place of confinement –1700.

1. b. *transf.* Woman was his mistress; and the whole Sex his S. 1709. 2. The Jewes dwell as in a suburbe by themselues..I passed by the Piazza Judea, where their S. begins EVELYN.

II. = SERAI †1, 2. 1599.

‖ **Serai** (sərāiˑ). 1609. [a. Turk. (orig. Pers.) *serāī* lodging, residence, palace.] 1. In Eastern countries, A building for the accommodation of travellers; a caravanserai. 2. A Turkish palace; esp. the palace of the Sultan at Constantinople 1617.

Serail (sərēˑl). Now *rare.* 1585. [a. F. *sérail*, ad. It. *serraglio* SERAGLIO.] 1. = SERAGLIO I. 1. †2. = SERAI 2. –1782.

Seralbumen, -in (sīərælbiūˑmen, -in). 1835. [f. SERUM + ALBUMEN.] *Chem.* The albumen of the blood.

‖ **Serang** (səræˑŋ). *Anglo-Ind.* [Hind. and Hindī, vulgar form of (Pers.) *sarhang* commander.] A native boatswain or captain of a Lascar crew.

‖ **Serape** (serāˑpe). 1847. [Mexican Sp.] A shawl or plaid worn by Spanish-Americans.

Seraph (seˑrăf). 1667. [Back-formation from SERAPHIM, SERAPHIN (on the analogy of *cherubim, -in, cherub*).] One of the SERAPHIM. b. *fig.* A seraphic person, an 'angel' 1853.

Brightest S. tell In which of all these shining Orbes hath Man His fixed seat MILT.

Seraphic (sĕræˑfik), *a.* 1632. [a. eccl. L. *seraphicus*, f. *seraphim* SERAPHIM.] 1. Of or pertaining to the seraphim. 2. Of attributes: Resembling what pertains to the seraphim; worthy of a seraph; ecstatically adoring 1659. 3. Resembling a seraph; characterized by ecstatic fervour of devotion 1762. b. Of discourse, actions, appearance: Showing ecstasy of devout contemplation 1668.

1. S. choirs 1755. 2. Seraphick Ardour dwelling in each Vein KEN. On the thick Hyperborean, cherubic reasoning, s. eloquence were lost CARLYLE. 3. S. saints, and gorgeous scenes by Tintoret 1870.

Special collocations: **S. Doctor,** St. Bonaventura; **S. Father,** St. Francis; **S. friar,** a Franciscan, hence *s. habit, order*; **S. hymn,** the Sanctus (see Isa. vi. 3). So **Sera·phical** *a.* 1540, **-ly** *adv.*

Seraphim (seˑrăfim), **†seˑraphin.** OE. [a. late L. *seraphim* (Vulg.), in MSS. often *seraphin*, a. Heb. *serāphīm* (only in Isa. vi), pl. of **sārāph.*] 1. In Biblical use: The living creatures with six wings, hands and feet, and a (presumably) human voice, seen in Isaiah's vision as hovering above the throne of God. late ME. 2. By Christian interpreters the seraphim were from an early period supposed to be a class of angels, the highest of the nine orders. The presumed derivation of the word from a Heb. root *sāraph* to burn, led to the view that the seraphim are specially distinguished by fervour of love, and to the symbolic use of red as the colour appropriate to them in artistic representations. OE. 3. A Swedish order of knighthood 1784. 4. *Geol. sing.* and *collect.* A fossil crustacean of the genus *Pterygotus* 1839. 5. A moth of the genus *Lobophora* 1832.

2. Where the bright S. in burning row Their loud up-lifted Angel trumpets blow MILT.

Seraphine (seˑrăfīn). Also **seraphina.** 1839. [f. SERAPH + -INE [4].] A musical instrument of the reed kind.

‖ **Seraskier** (serǣskīəˑɹ). 1684. [repr. Turk. pronunciation of Pers. *serʿasker*, f. *ser* head + Arab. *ʿaskar* army.] The title of the Turkish minister of war, who is also commander in chief of the army. Hence ‖ **Seraskieˑrat(e,** the war office at Constantinople.

Serb (sɔ̄ɹb), *sb.* and *a.* 1813. [a. Serbian *Srb.*] A. *sb.* 1. †a. A Wend of Lusatia. b. A native of Serbia, a Serbian. 2. The Serbian language 1886. B. *adj.* Serbian 1876.

Serbian (sɔ̄ˑɹbiăn), *a.* and *sb.* Formerly SERVIAN. 1862. [f. prec. + -IAN.] A. *adj.* Of or pertaining to Serbia, a country of south-eastern Europe occupied by a Slavonic people and now, with Slavonia and Croatia, forming Yugoslavia 1876. **B.** *sb.* A native or inhabitant of Serbia; the language of Serbia 1862.

Serbo-, used as comb. form of SERBIAN.

Serbonian (səɹbōᵘ·niăn), *a.* 1667. [f. Gr. Σερβωνίς (λίμνη) + -AN I. 1.] *S. bog*: Milton's name for Lake Serbonis in Lower Egypt, a marshy tract (now dry) covered with shifting sand. Hence *allus.*

A gulf profound as that S. Bog,..where Armies whole have sunk MILT.

†**Sere,** *sb.* 1606. [a. OF. *serre*, f. *serrer* to hold fast :—pop. L. **serrare*, for late L. *serare*, f. *sera* bolt, bar.] A claw, talon -1864.

Sere, sear (sīᵊɹ), *a.* [OE. *sēar* :—OTeut. **sauzo-* :—Indo-Eur. **sausó-*, whence Gr. αὖος dry.] **1.** Dry, withered. Now *poet.* or *rhet.* †**2.** Of textile fabrics: Thin, worn -1798.

1. He is..crooked, old, and s. SHAKS. I haue liu'd long enough, my way of life Is falne into the Seare, the yellow Leafe SHAKS. 2. A roaring wind..shook the sails That were so thin and s. COLERIDGE.

‖**Serein** (sərǣn). 1870. [Fr.; see SERENE *sb.*[1]] *Meteorol.* A fine rain falling from a cloudless sky after sunset.

Serenade (serĭnēⁱ·d, serə-), *sb.* 1649. [a. F. *sérénade*, app. ad. It. *serenata* SERENATA.] **1.** A performance of vocal or instrumental music given at night in the open air, esp. such a performance given by a lover under the window of his lady. **2.** *Mus.* A piece of music suitable or specially composed for singing or playing in the open air as a complimentary performance 1728.

1. Serenate, which the starv'd Lover sings To his proud fair MILT.

Serenade (serĭnēⁱ·d, serə-), *v.* 1668. [f. the sb.] **1.** *trans.* To entertain (a person) with a serenade 1672. **2.** *intr.* (or *absol.*) To perform a serenade 1668. Hence **Serena·der.**

‖**Serenata** (serenā·ta). 1743. [a. It., an evening song, app. f. *sereno* the open air.] **1.** A song or form of cantata suitable for performance in the open air. **2.** A piece of instrumental music, developed from the orchestral suite, and usu. composed of a march, and a minuet interposed between two movements of another kind 1883.

Serendipity (serendi·pĭti). 1754. [f. *Serendip(-b)*, former name of Ceylon + -ITY; coined by Horace Walpole upon the title of the fairy-tale *The Three Princes of Serendip*, the heroes of which 'were always making discoveries, by accidents and sagacity, of things they were not in quest of'.] The faculty of making happy and unexpected discoveries by accident.

†**Serene,** *sb.*[1] 1591. [a. F. *serein* :—pop. L. **seranum*, f. *serum* evening, sb. use of neut. of L. *serus* late.] A light fall of moisture or fine rain after sunset in hot countries (see SEREIN), regarded as a noxious dew or mist -1682.

Serene (sĭrī·n, sĕ-), *a.* and *sb.*[2] 1508. [ad. L. *serenus* clear, fair, calm (of weather, etc.).] **A.** *adj.* **1.** Of the weather, air, sky: Clear, fine, and calm (without cloud or rain or wind). **b.** Of the heavenly bodies: Shining with a clear and tranquil light 1704. **c.** Hence *poet.* of colour: Pure, clear, bright. Also, quiet, sober. 1750. **2.** Of other natural phenomena (e.g. the sea): Calm, tranquil 1812. **3.** Of a person, his mind, etc.: Calm, tranquil, untroubled, unperturbed. Of the countenance: Expressive of inward calm, unruffled. 1635. **4.** An honorific epithet given to a reigning prince (esp. of Germany), formerly also to a royal house, etc. **5.** *Drop s.*: Milton's rendering of L. *gutta serena* amaurosis. Hence *allus.* 1667.

1. Regions milde of calm and s. Ayr MILT. **b.** The moon, s. in glory, mounts the sky POPE. **c.** Full many a gem of purest ray s. GRAY. 2. A brighter Hellas rears its mountains From waves serener far SHELLEY. 3. He who resigns the World..is in constant Possession of a s. Mind STEELE. *All s.* (slang), 'all's well', 'all right' 1856.

B. *sb.* (the adj. used absol.). Now *rare* or *Obs.* **a.** A condition of fine quiet weather 1644. **b.** The serene expanse of clear sky, air, or calm sea 1769. **c.** Calm brightness 1821. **d.** Serenity, tranquillity (of mind or conditions) 1742.

b. The bark that plows the deep s. COWPER. Yet did I never breathe its pure s. KEATS. **c.** With moonlight patches..Or fragments of the day's intense s. SHELLEY. Hence **Sere·ne-ly** *adv.*, **-ness.**

Serene (sĭrī·n, sĕ-), *v.* Now *rare* or *Obs.* 1613. [ad. L. *serenare*, f. *serenus* SERENE *a.*] *trans.* To make serene.

Hope, like a cordial,..Man's heart, at once, inspirits, and serenes YOUNG.

Serenity (sĭre·nĭti). 1450. [a. F. *sérénité*, ad. L. *serenitas*, f. *serenus*; see -ITY.] **1.** Clear, fair and calm weather; clearness and stillness of air and sky 1538. **2.** Tranquillity, peacefulness (of conditions, etc.) 1635. **3.** Cheerful tranquillity (of mind, temper, countenance, etc.) 1599. **4.** A title of honour given to reigning princes and other dignitaries 1450.

1. There is never no Rain, Dew, Hail, Snow, or Wind but still a clear s. 1669. 3. His countenance had recovered its usual s. 1794.

‖**Seres** (sīᵊ·rez), *pl.* late ME. [L. *Seres* (Gr. Σῆρες), whence *sericum* silk.] A people anciently inhabiting some part of Eastern Asia (prob. China), whose country was believed to be the original home of silk.

Serf (sɔ̄ɹf). 1483. [a. OF. :—L. *servum* slave.] †**1.** A slave, bondman -1484. **2.** A person in a condition of servitude or modified slavery, dist. from what is properly called 'slavery' in that the services due to the master, and his power of disposal of his 'serf', are more or less limited by law or custom 1611.

2. In most of the typical examples of serfdom, the serf was 'attached to the soil' (*adscriptus glebæ*), i.e. he could not be removed (except by manumission) from the lord's land, and was transferred with it when it passed to another owner. N.E.D. Hence **Se·rfage, Se·rfdom,** the state or condition of a s.; bondage. **Se·rfhood,** the collective body of serfs.

Serge (sɔ̄ɹdʒ). late ME. [a. OF. *serge, sarge* :—pop. L. **sarica* = class. L. *serica* (*lana*); see SERIC *a.* and SILK. Orig. app. a silken material, though there is no evidence for this.] **1.** A woollen fabric; now a very durable twilled cloth of worsted, or with the warp of worsted and the woof of wool, extensively used for clothing. **b.** A garment made of serge 1583. **2.** *Silk s.*: a silk fabric twilled in the manner of serge, used for linings of coats, and formerly for mantles *Hist.* 1844. **3.** *attrib.* or *adj.* Made of serge 1608.

Sergeancy, serjeancy (sā·ɹdʒənsi). *Hist.* ME. [a. AF. *sergeancie*, graphic var. of *sergeantie* SERGEANTY. In later use, f. SERGEANT + -CY.] †**1.** The body of sergeants in a country, the sergeant-class. ME. only. †**2.** = SERGEANTY 1. -1630. **3.** The office of a sergeant or serjeant in various senses; also the commission of sergeant in the army 1670.

Sergeant, serjeant (sā·ɹdʒənt). ME. [a. OF. *sergent, -jant* :—L. *servientem*, pr. pple. of *servire*. The spelling *serjeant* is now used in designating a member of the legal profession, while *sergeant* is the prevailing form in the other senses.] †**1.** A serving-man, attendant, servant -1450. †**b.** *transf.* A servant (of God, of Satan) -1570. †**2.** A common soldier -1490. †**3.** A tenant by military service under the rank of a knight; esp. one of this class attending on a knight in the field -1425. †**4.** An officer who is charged with the arrest of offenders or the summoning of persons to appear before the court -1680. **5. Sergeant (or Serjeant)-at-Arms.** †**a.** In early use *gen.*, an armed officer in the service of a lord; *spec.* one of a body of men of knightly rank, who were required to be in immediate attendance on the king's person, to arrest traitors and other offenders. **b.** An officer of each of the two Houses of Parliament, who is charged with the duty of enforcing the commands of the House, the arrest of offenders, etc. Hence, an officer having corresponding duties under the U.S. Senate and House of Representatives, etc. late ME. **6.** As a title borne by a lawyer. (Now always written **serjeant.**) **a.** A member of a superior order of barristers (abolished in 1880), from which, until 1873, the Common Law judges were always chosen (hence a serjeant was always called by a judge 'my brother So-and-so'). More explicitly **Serjeant at law** ME. **b.** *The King's* (or *Queen's*) *Serjeant*: a title given to a limited number of the serjeants at law, appointed by patent. late ME. **c.** *Prime serjeant*: the first in rank of the three (earlier two) serjeants at law in Ireland. (Since 1805 called *first s.*) 1666. **d. Common Serjeant (at law).** A judicial officer appointed by the Corporation of London as an assistant to the Recorder 1556. **7.** (Now usu. written **sergeant.**) In the titles of certain officers of the Royal Household. **a.** The head of a specified department, as *s. of the cellar*, etc. 1450. **b.** Prefixed to certain designations of office, as *s.-cater, -surgeon, -trumpeter*, etc. 1614. **8.** In the titles of certain inferior officers employed by the Corporation of the City of London, and by other municipal bodies. late ME. **9.** *Mil.* (Now always written **sergeant.**) In mod. use, a non-commissioned officer of the grade above that of corporal. See also COLOUR-*s.*, DRILL-*s.*, SERGEANT-MAJOR, etc. 1548. **b.** Prefixed to various designations of offices in which sergeants are employed, as *s. armourer, farrier, instructor*, etc. 1810. **10.** (Now always written **sergeant.**) A police-officer of higher rank than a simple constable; in Great Britain ranking next below an inspector 1839.

4. Saul sente sergeauntis that schulden rauysche Dauid WYCLIF 1 *Sam.* xix. 14. *fig.* Had I but time (as this fell Sergeant death Is strick'd in his arrest) oh I could tell you SHAKS. 9. Serjeants, Corporals, Drummers, and private Men 2d per diem each, besides Bread 1690. Hence **Se·rgeantship, Se·rjeantship,** the office of a s., in various senses.

Se·rgeant-ma·jor. 1573. [f. prec. + MAJOR *a.*] †**1.** In the 16–17th c.: **a.** A field officer, one in each regiment, next in rank to the lieutenant-colonel, and corresponding partly to the 'major', partly to the 'adjutant' of the modern army -1704. †**b.** A general officer, corresponding to the modern major-general -1647. **2.** A non-commissioned officer of the highest grade 1802. **3.** An Amer. fish, the cow-pilot 1876. **4.** *s.-m.'s tea slang*, tea with rum in it.

†**Se·rgeantry, se·rjeantry.** late ME. [a. OF. *sergenterie*, f. *sergent* SERGEANT; see -ERY.] = next -1830.

Sergeanty, serjeanty (sā·ɹdʒənti). 1449. [a. OF. *serjantie, sergentie*, f. *serjant, sergent* SERGEANT; see -Y[3]. Now usu. **serjeanty.**] *Hist.* A form of feudal tenure on condition of rendering some specified personal service to the king 1467. **b.** Dist. as *grand* and *petit* (or *petty*) *s.* 1449.

According to *Britton, grand s.* obliges the tenant to a service 'touching the defence of the country', such as acting as marshal, putting an army in the field,..while *petit s.* binds him to a service 'amounting to half a mark or less', such as carrying to the king a bag, a brooch, an arrow, or a bow without string, etc. N.E.D.

Serial (sīᵊ·riăl), *a.* and *sb.* 1841. [ad. mod. L. *serialis*, f. *series* SERIES; see -AL.] **A.** *adj.* Belonging to, forming part of, or consisting of a series; taking place in a regular succession 1854. **b.** *spec.* of the publication of a literary work, *esp.* a story, in successive instalments 1841. **c.** In scientific use; *esp.* applied to the disposition of the parts of an organism in a straight line or longitudinal succession 1855.

b. *S. rights*, rights attaching to the publication of a story in serial form. **c.** *S. temperatures*, temperatures taken at different successive depths between the bottom and the surface of water.

B. *sb.* A serial or periodical publication, *esp.* a novel published in serial (as opp. to *book*) form 1846. Hence **Seria·lity** (sīᵊriæ·lĭti), s. arrangement. **Se:rializa·tion,** publication in s. form. **Se·rialize** *v. trans.* to publish in s. form. **Se·rially** *adv.*

Seriate (sīᵊ·riĕt), *a.* 1846. [ad. mod.L. **seriatus*, f. SERIES.] Chiefly *Zool.* and *Bot.* Arranged or occurring in one or more series or rows. So **Se·riated** *a.* **Se·riately** *adv.*

Seriatim (sīᵊriēⁱ·tim), *adv.* (and *a.*) 1680. [med.L., f. L. *series*, after GRADATIM, etc.] One after another, one by one in succession.

Seriation (sīᵊriēⁱ·ʃən). 1658. [ad. mod.L. **seriationem*, f. L. *series* SERIES; see -ATION.] Serial succession; formation of or into a series.

Seric (se·rik), *a.* *rare.* 1842. [ad. L. *sericus* = Gr. σηρικός (neut. σηρικόν silk), f. Σῆρες SERES.] **1.** Chinese. **2.** Silken 1886.

Sericeous (sĭri·ʃiəs), *a.* 1777. [f. L. *sericus* SERIC; see -EOUS.] *Zool.* and *Bot.* Silky, covered with silky down.

Sericin (se·risin). 1841. [f. L. *sericum*

silk + -IN[1].] 1. = MYRISTIN. 2. The gelatinous constituent of silk 1868.

Sericite (se·risəit). 1854. [ad. G. *sericit*, f. L. *sericum* silk; see SERIC and -ITE[1] 2 b.] *Min.* A fibrous variety of muscovite. b. *attrib.* Sericitic 1879. Hence **Sericitic** (serisi·tik) *a.* containing or having the character of s.

‖**Sericterium** (seriktīə·riŏm). *Pl.* **-eria** (-īə·riă). 1826. [mod.L., irreg. f. Gr. σηρικόν silk (see SERIC) + -τηριον, after *sialisterium* (σιαλιστήριον) salivary gland of insects.] *Entom.* A glandular apparatus in silkworms for the production of silk; a silk or spinning gland.

Sericulture (se·rikɒltiŭɹ, -tʃəɹ). 1851. [Shortened ad. F. *séricicułture*, f. L. *sericum* + *cultura.*] The production of raw silk and the rearing of silkworms for the purpose. Hence **Sericu·ltural** *a.* **Sericu·lturist.**

Seriema (seri,ī·mă), **çariama, cariama** (sæ-, kæriā·mă). 1836. [mod.L. *seriema*, *cariama*, a. Tupi *siriema*, *sariama*, *çariama*, explained as = crested.] A large long-legged crested bird, *Cariama cristata*, inhabiting parts of Brazil; the crested screamer.

Series (sīə·rīz, -iz, sīə·ri,īz). *Pl.* **series.** 1611. [a. L., f. *serere* to join, connect.] I. General senses. 1. A number or set *of* material things of one kind ranged in a line, either contiguously or at more or less regular intervals. 2. A number *of* things of one kind (chiefly immaterial) following one another in temporal succession, or in the order of discourse or reasoning 1618. b. A number *of* persons in succession holding the same office or having some characteristic in common 1625. †3. A succession, sequence, or continued course (*of* action or conduct, *of* time, life, etc.) –1816. †4. The connected sequence (*of* discourse, writing, thought) –1712. †5. Order of succession; sequence –1779. 6. A number of magnitudes, degrees of some attribute, or the like, viewed as capable of being enumerated in a progressive order. Also, a set of objects of one kind, differing progressively in size, composition, etc., or having a recognized order of enumeration. 1786.

1. The s. of squares called Belgravia EMERSON. 2. That the repayment of the money to be borrowed should be spread over a s. of years 1886. 3. A more decent..and prudent s. of proceeding BURKE. 5. The s. of his works I am not able to deduce JOHNSON.

II. Technical senses. 1. *Math.* A set of terms in succession (finite or infinite in number) the value of each of which is determined by its ordinal position according to a definite rule known as the *law* of the series 1671. 2. A set of coins, medals, etc. belonging to a particular epoch, locality, dynasty, or government. Also, a set of postage stamps, bank notes, etc., of a particular issue. 1697. 3. A set of literary compositions having certain features in common, published successively or intended to be read in sequence; a succession of volumes or fascicules forming a set by itself. Also, in recent use, a succession of books issued by one publisher in a common form and having some similarity of subject or purpose. 1711. 4. *Nat. Sci.* A group of individuals exhibiting similar characteristics or a constant relation between successive members 1823. 5. *Geol.* A set of successive deposits or group of successive formations having certain common fossil or mineral features 1822. 6. *Electr.* and *Magn.* A number of cells or conductors so placed that the current passes through each in succession. (Such cells or conductors are said to be *in s.*) 1873. b. *attrib.* or as *adj.* = (*a*) arranged or connected in series; (*b*) Short for *s.-wound*, i.e. wound in series, or so that the coils on the field-magnets are placed in series with the outer circuit. 1884. 7. *Philol.* (tr. G. *reihe.*) In the Indo-European languages, a set of vowels, or of diphthongs and vowels or sonants, which are mutually related by ablaut 1888. 8. A parcel of rough diamonds 1909.

Serif (se·rif). Also †**ceriph,** †**seriph.** 1831. [Origin obsc.] *Typogr.* One of the fine cross-strokes at the top and bottom of a letter.

Serin[1] (se·rin). 1530. [a. F., = canary; of disputed origin.] 1. A bird of the genus *Serinus*. 2. In full, *S. finch*: the finch *S. serinus* (*S. hortulanus*), a native of central Europe 1672.

Serin[2] (se·rin). 1876. [f. SERUM + -IN.[1]] *Chem.* a. Serum albumin. b. Amido-glycerol.

Seringa (sĕri·ŋgă, sė-). 1740. [a. F., ad. L. SYRINGA.] 1. = SYRINGA. ‖2. The Pg. name for Brazilian plants of the genus *Hevea* (*Siphonia*), yielding india-rubber 1853.

Serio- (sīə·rio), used as comb. form (see -O-) of SERIOUS, = partly serious, and partly . . .

Se:rio-co·mic, *a.* (*sb.*) 1783. [f. SERIO- + COMIC *a.*] Partly serious and partly comic; (of an actor, vocalist, etc., or his performance) presenting a comic plot, situation, etc. under a serious form. b. as *sb.* A s. actor, vocalist, etc. 1907. So **Se:rio-co·mical** *a.* 1749, **-ly** *adv.*

Serious (sīə·riəs), *a.* 1440. [ad. F. *sérieux* or late L. *sēriosus*, f. L. *sērius.*] 1. Of persons, their actions, etc.: Having, involving, expressing, or arising from earnest purpose or thought; of grave or solemn disposition or intention; not light or superficial; now often, concerned with the grave and earnest sides of life. †b. Earnestly bent or applied; keen –1671. 2. Earnest about the things of religion; religious 1796. 3. Dealing with or regarding a matter on its grave side; not jesting, trifling, or playful; in earnest. Hence, of theatrical compositions or actors, not jocular or comic. 1590. 4. Requiring earnest thought, consideration, or application; performed with earnestness of purpose 1531. 5. Of grave demeanour or aspect 1613. 6. Weighty, important, grave; (of quantity or degree) considerable 1584. b. Attended with danger; giving cause for anxiety 1800.

1. He was too s. to smile; indeed, I cannot remember him ever smiling, except sadly 1882. b. All my mind was set S. to learn and know MILT. 2. Pleasant Place, Finsbury. Wages, twelve guineas. No tea, no sugar. S. family. DICKENS. 3. The gentlemen are not s., but are only playing with you 1875. 4. He makes Cards and Dice his s. Entertainment 1706. 5. A weighty and a s. brow SHAKS. 6. The damage is not thought to be s. 1884. b. It is feared that his condition is s. 1891. Hence **Se·rious-ly** *adv.*[2] in a s. manner; **-ness.**

†**Se·riously,** *adv.*[1] late ME. [tr. med.L. *seriose*, used as adv. of *series.*] From beginning to end; seriatim –1611.

Serjeant, etc.: see SERGEANT, etc.

†**Sermocina·tion.** 1514. [ad. L. *sermocinationem*, f. *sermocinari* to talk.] Talk; a discourse, sermon –1674. So †**Sermocinator.**

Sermon (sɔ̄·ɹmən), *sb.* ME. [a. AF. *sermun* = OF. *sermon*, ad. L. *sermonem*, *sermo* talk, discourse.] †1. Something that is said; talk, discourse –1594. †b. *pl.* The satires (*sermones*) of Horace –1671. 2. A discourse, usu. delivered from a pulpit and based upon a text of Scripture, for the purpose of religious instruction or exhortation ME. b. as a written or published work. late ME. c. Applied to the discourses of our Lord and the Apostles ME. 3. *transf.* and *fig.* a. A discourse (spoken or written) on a serious subject, and containing instruction or exhortation. Also *contempt.* a long or tedious discourse or harangue. 1596. b. Something that affords instruction or example 1600.

2. Which is worse, to stay from a S., or sleep at a S.? 1692. Phr. *At, after s.* = at, after church. b. And Sermons are less read than Tales PRIOR. *S. on the Mount*, the discourse recorded in Matt. v–vii and introduced by the words 'he went up into a mountain..and taught them, saying'. 3. a. Making a s. of continencie to her SHAKS. b. Bookes in the running brookes, Sermons in stones SHAKS.

attrib. and *Comb.*: **s. paper,** writing paper of foolscap 4to size. Hence **Sermone·tte,** a short sermon. **Sermo·nic** *a.* of the form or nature of a s.; resembling (that of) a s. (somewhat *depreciatory*). **Se·rmonish** *a.* sermonic.

Sermon (sɔ̄·ɹmən), *v.* Now *rare.* [ME. a. AF. *sarmuner* = OF. *sermouner*, f. *sermon* (see prec.). Now f. SERMON *sb.*] 1. *trans.* To preach to (a person). 2. To preach (*at* a person). KEATS. †3. *intr.* To speak (*of* a thing) –1606.

Sermoner (sɔ̄·ɹmənəɹ). *rare.* ME. [f. SERMON *sb.* + -ER[1]; in ME. after AF. *sarmuner.*] A preacher of sermons.

†**Se·rmoning,** *vbl. sb.* ME. [f. SERMON *v.*] 1. Preaching; also, a sermon –1657. 2. Talk, discourse, conversation –1535.

Sermonist (sɔ̄·ɹmənist). 1630. [f. SERMON *sb.* + -IST.] A preacher, sermonizer.

Sermonize (sɔ̄·ɹmənəiz), *v.* 1635. [f. as prec. + -IZE.] 1. *intr.* = PREACH *v.* 1. Chiefly *depreciatory.* b. To talk seriously. Also with *it.* 1753. 2. *trans.* To preach a sermon to (*rare*); to talk seriously or earnestly to, 'preach' to, 'lecture' 1802. 3. To bring into a specified condition by preaching 1768.

Sero- (sīə·ro), used as comb. form of SERUM in the senses: (*a*) of or pertaining to serum, as *serothe·rapy*, treatment of disease or infection by serums, serum-therapy; (*b*) pertaining to, consisting of, or involving serum (and something else), as *sero-pus*, serous pus; (*c*) characterized by serous effusion or infiltration, or involving a serous membrane, as *s.-dermatosis.*

Serolin (sīə·rŏlin). 1835. [ad. F. *séroline*, f. *sérum* SERUM, L. *oleum* oil + *-ine* -IN.] A fatty substance found in blood serum.

Serology (siərǫ·lŏdʒi). 1913. [f. SERO- + -LOGY.] The scientific study of serums and their action. Hence **Sero·logist.**

Seron (sīə·rǫ̆n, sĭrū·n). 1545. [ad. Sp. *seron* hamper, crate (f. *sera* large basket), partly through F. *serron.*] A bale or package (of exotic products, e.g. almonds, medicinal bark, cocoa) made up in an animal's hide.

Serosity (sĭrǫ·sĭti). 1601. [ad. F. *sérosité*, f. L. *serosus* SEROUS.] 1. Watery fluid in an animal body; the serous or watery part of blood or milk, serum; freq. *pl.* in 17–18th c. = watery humours. b. A yellowish alkaline liquid produced when serum is heated 1807. 2. The condition of being serous (*rare*) 1743.

Serotine (se·rŏtəin), *sb.* 1771. [ad. F. *sérotine*, ad. fem. of L. *serotinus*, f. *sero* late.] A small European bat flying late in the evening, *Vespertilio serotinus.*

Serotinous (sĭrǫ·tinəs), *a.* 1656. [f. L. *serotinus*; see prec.] Late in occurrence or development; chiefly of plants, late-flowering.

Serous (sīə·rəs), *a.* 1594. [ad. F. *séreux*, ad. L. *serosus*, f. *serum* SERUM.] 1. Of or pertaining to serum; consisting of or containing serum; of the nature of serum. b. *Path.* Involving or characterized by an effusion of serum 1779. 2. *Anat.* Secreting or moistened with serum, as a membrane 1732.

Serow (se·rou). Also **surow, saraw.** 1847. [Native name.] Any of the Asiatic antelopes of the genus *Nemorhædus*, esp. *N. thar* (*N. bubalinus*), the THAR.

Serpent (sɔ̄·ɹpĕnt), *sb.* ME. [a. OF., :—L. *serpentem*, *serpens* creeping thing, serpent, prop. pr. pple. of *serpere* to creep, cogn. w. Gr. ἕρπειν, Skr. *sṛp.*] 1. Any of the scaly limbless reptiles regarded as having the properties of hissing and 'stinging'; *Zool.* a reptile of the genus OPHIDIA; a snake; now applied chiefly to the larger and more venomous species. †b. A creeping thing or reptile, *esp.* one of a noxious kind –1691. c. Applied to serpent-like animals inhabiting the sea 1608. d. In proverbs, etc. referring to the serpent's guile, treachery, or malignancy. late ME. 2. The serpent that tempted Eve (Gen. iii. 1–5); the Tempter, the Devil, Satan. Also, *the Old S.* (after Rev. xii. 9). ME. 3. *fig.* as a symbol of envy, jealousy, malice, or wiliness. late ME. b. A treacherous, deceitful, or malicious person 1590. 4. A representation of a serpent, esp. as a symbol or an ornament ME. 5. *Astron.* The northern constellation *Serpens* 1565. 6. A kind of firework which burns with a serpentine motion or flame 1634. 7. An obsolete bass wind instrument of deep tone, about 8 feet long, made of wood covered with leather and formed with three U-shaped turns 1730. 8. *transf.* A candle of spiral form; a 'rope' of hair; the crank-shaft in a weaving-machine. *Pharaoh's s.*: see PHARAOH. 1802. 9. quasi-*adj.* Resembling a serpent or that of a serpent 1592.

1. The green s. from his dark abode,..At noon forth-issuing THOMSON. d. †*The serpent's tongue*, vulgarly supposed to be the 'sting'; *allus.* 'venomous speech'. 3. b. With doubler tongue Then thine (thou s.) neuer Adder stung SHAKS.

Comb.: **s.-bearer** = OPHIUCHUS; **s. cucumber,** a cucumber of the genus *Trichosanthes*, having long serpent-like fruit, esp. *T. colubrina*; **s. eagle,** a bird of prey of the genus *Spilornis*; **-eater,** (*a*) the secretary-bird; (*b*) the markhor; **-fish,** the red snake-fish, *Cepola rubescens*; **-star,** an ophiuran; **-wand,** the caduceus; **-withe,** *Aristolochia odoratissima.* b. with *serpent's*: **serpent's head, skull,** species of cowry; **serpent's tongue,** †(*a*) ADDER'S-TONGUE; (*b*) the fossil tooth of a shark.

Se·rpent, *v.* Now *rare.* 1606. [ad. F. *serpenter*, f. *serpent* SERPENT *sb.*] *intr.* To move in a serpentine manner; to follow a tortuous course; to wind.

‖**Serpentaria** (sɔ̄ɹpĕntē·riă). 1803. [Late L. (sc. *planta*), fem. of *serpentarius*, f. *serpent-*, *serpens* SERPENT *sb.*; see -ARY [1].] = SERPENTARY 2. **b.** *Chem.* An alkaloid obtained from serpentary 1831.

Serpentarius (sɔ̄ɹpĕntē·riɒ̆s). 1728. [mod. L. (see next).] *Astron.* = OPHIUCHUS.

Serpentary (sɔ̄·ɹpĕntări), *sb.* 1450. [ad. late and med.L. *serpentaria* (in 1, sc. *retorta*, in 2, sc. *planta*), fem. of *serpentarius*, f. *serpen-*, *-ens*; see -ARY [1].] †1. A kind of retort or still –1615. 2. Virginian Snake-root, *Aristolochia serpentaria*; its root, used medicinally 1658.

Serpentiform (səɹpe·ntifɔ̄ɹm). 1777. [ad. mod.L. *serpentiformis*; see -FORM.] Having the form of a serpent; serpentine in shape.

Serpentine (sɔ̄·ɹpĕntəin), *sb.* late ME. [a. OF. *serpentin* and *serpentine*, ad. med.L. *serpentinum* and *serpentina*, absol. uses of the neut. and fem. of *serpentinus*.] 1. A name for certain plants reputed to contain an antidote to the poison of serpents; e.g. dragonwort, fenugreek. 2. A kind of cannon. Now only *Hist.* 1450. 3. A rock or mineral, consisting mainly of hydrous magnesium silicate, of a dull green colour with markings resembling those of a serpent's skin. Also, an ornamental stone made of this. late ME. 4. The coiled pipe or worm of a distilling apparatus. *Obs.* exc. as repr. F. *serpentin.* 1519. 5. A winding path or line 1885.

Serpentine (sɔ̄·ɹpĕntəin), *a.* late ME. [a. F. *serpentin*, ad. L. *serpentinus*, f. *serpent-* SERPENT *sb.* + *-inus* -INE.[1]] 1. Of or pertaining to a serpent or serpents; of the form of or resembling a serpent, or that of a serpent. 2. Having the evil qualities of a serpent; pertaining to the Serpent as the tempter of mankind; diabolical, Satanic; devilishly wily or cunning. late ME. 3. Following a course resembling that of a serpent in motion; tortuous, winding 1615.

1. *S. verse*, a metrical line beginning and ending with the same word. 2. A s. generation,..made of fraud, of policies and practises 1599. 3. The branching and serpentin cours of the River Seine 1645. *S. temple* (Antiq.), one having the supposed symbolical form of a serpent. Hence **Se·rpentinely** *adv.*

Serpentine (sɔ̄·ɹpĕntəin), *v.* 1774. [f. prec.] 1. *intr.* To move in a serpentine manner; to pursue a serpentine or tortuous path; to wind. 2. *trans.* To cause to take a serpentine direction; to wind 1850.

Serpentine marble. 1601. [= med.L. *marmor serpentinum.*] The mineral serpentine in massive form.

Serpentinize (sə·ɹpĕntinəiz), *v.* 1791. [f. SERPENTINE *sb.* or *a.* + -IZE.] 1. *intr.* = SERPENTINE *v.* 1. 2. *trans.* (*Geol.*) To convert into serpentine 1889.

Serpentinous (sɔ̄·ɹpĕntəinəs), *a.* 1833. [f. SERPENTINE *sb.* or *a.* + -OUS.] 1. Of the nature of or consisting of serpentine. 2. Serpentine, winding 1882.

Serpentize (sɔ̄·ɹpĕntəiz), *v.* Now *rare.* 1629. [f. SERPENT *sb.* + -IZE.] 1. *intr.* = SERPENTINE *v.* 1. 2. *trans.* To cause to take a serpentine shape, motion, or course 1762.

1. The Euphrates serpentizes among wonderful plants 1718.

Serpentry (sɔ̄·ɹpĕntri). 1818. [f. SERPENT *sb.* + -RY.] 1. Serpents or serpentine creatures collectively. 2. A place where serpents are kept and reared 1846. 3. A winding like that of a serpent 1848.

Se·rpent-stone. 1681. 1. = AMMONITE 1. Now *Obs.* or *local.* 2. An artificial 'stone' used as a remedy for the poison of serpents. Also = BEZOAR 2 a. 1681.

‖**Serpigo** (səɹpei·go). *Pl.* **serpigines** (səɹpi·dʒinīz), **serpigoes.** late ME. [med.L., f. *serpere* to creep.] A general term for creeping or spreading skin diseases; *spec.* ringworm. Hence **Serpiginous** (səɹpi·dʒinəs) *a.*, **-ly** *adv.*

‖**Serpula** (sɔ̄·ɹpiŭlă). *Pl.* **-læ.** 1767. [mod. L. use of late L. *serpula* small serpent.] *Zool.* A marine annelid which inhabits a tortuous calcareous tube. Hence **Serpu·lean, Serpu·lidan,** an annelid belonging to a group or family of which *Serpula* is a typical genus. **Se·rpulite** *Geol.*, a fossil s.

‖**Serra** [1] (se·ră). *Pl.* **serræ.** 1450. [L., = saw, saw-fish.] 1. **a.** A fabulous marine monster. **b.** A saw-fish 1854. 2. Dentation resembling the teeth of a saw, as of the edge of a leaf, the sutures of the skull; *pl.* the 'teeth' of a serrated edge 1800.

‖**Serra** [2] (se·ra). 1830. [Pg. :—L. *serra* saw. Cf. SIERRA.] A ridge of mountains or hills (in Portuguese territory).

Serran (se·răn). 1803. [ad. mod.L. *serranus*, f. *serra*; see -AN.] *Ichth.* A fish of the genus *Serranus* or the family *Serranidæ*, which includes many food-fishes, as the black seabass. Hence **Se·rranoid** *a.* and *sb.* belonging to, a fish of, the family *Serranidæ*.

Serrate (se·rĕⁱt), *a.* 1668. [ad. L. *serratus*, f. *serra* saw; see -ATE [2].] Chiefly *Nat. Hist.* Having or forming a row of small projections resembling the teeth of a saw; jagged or notched like a saw.

Serrate (se·ɹeⁱt), *v.* 1750. [f. L. *serrat-*, *serrare*, f. *serra* saw.] *trans.* To make serrated or saw-toothed; to impress in a serrated form. So **Se·rrated** *a.* = prec. 1703.

Serration (seɹēⁱ·ʃən). 1842. [ad. mod.L. *serrationem*, f. *serrare*, f. *serra* saw.] The condition of being serrated; indentation like that of a saw; chiefly *concr.* and *pl.* saw-like indentations.

Serra·to-, comb. form (see -O-) of L. *serratus* SERRATE *a.*, in the senses 'serrate and ..', 'in a serrate manner, with serrate indentation', as *s.-dentate*, etc.

Serrature (se·ratiŭɹ, -tʃəɹ). 1541. [ad. L. *serratura*, f. *serratus* SERRATE *a.*; see -URE.] = SERRATION.

Serrefile (se·rəfəil). 1796. [ad. F., f. *serrer* + *file* FILE *sb.*[2]] *Mil. pl.* The line of supernumerary and non-commissioned officers placed in the rear of a squadron or troop; *sing.* one of these.

Serri-, comb. f. SERRA [1] with sense 'serrated', as in *se·rricorn, serriro·strate.*

Serried (se·rid), *ppl. a.* 1667. [app. f. SERRY *v.* + -ED [1].] Of files or ranks of armed men: Pressed close together, shoulder to shoulder, in close order.

transf. The dark ranks of the s. clouds 1834.

Serrulate (se·riŭlĕⁱt), *a.* 1793. [ad. mod. L. *serrulatus*, f. late L. *serrula*, dim. of L. *serra* saw.] *Nat. Hist.* Finely or minutely serrated; having small serrations. So **Se·rrulated** *a.* Hence **Serrula·tion,** the condition of being s.

Serry (se·ri), *v.* 1581. [As a 16th c. military term, app. f. F. *serré*, pa. pple. of *serrer* :—L. *serare*, f. *sera* lock, bolt. In recent use, back-formation from SERRIED.] 1. *intr.* To press close *together* in the ranks; to stand or move in close or serried order. 2. *trans.* To cause to stand in close order, to close up (the ranks) 1635.

‖**Sertularia** (sɔ̄ɹtiŭlē·riă). *Pl.* **-iæ, -ias.** 1767. [mod.L., f. L. *sertula*, dim. of *serta* garlands.] *Zool.* One of a genus of branching hydroids having small sessile hydrothecæ; the genus itself. Hence **Sertula·rian** *a.* of or belonging to the genus *S.* or the family *Sertularidæ* of hydroids; *sb.* a sertularian hydroid.

‖**Sertulum** (sɔ̄·ɹtiŭlɒ̆m). Also **se·rtule.** 1831. [mod.L., dim. of *sertum*, assumed sing. of *serta* n. pl., garlands.] *Bot.* A simple umbel.

Serum (sīᵊ·rɒ̆m). *Pl.* **sera** (sīᵊ·ră), **serums.** 1672. [L., = whey, watery fluid.] Watery animal fluid, normal or morbid; *spec.* blood-serum, the greenish yellow liquid which separates from the clot when blood coagulates. **b.** *Therapeutics.* The blood serum of an animal used as a therapeutic or diagnostic agent 1895.

Servable (sɔ̄·ɹvăb'l), *a.* 1855. [f. SERVE *v.* + -ABLE.] That may be served, worthy to be served.

Servage (sɔ̄·ɹvĕdʒ). ME. [a. OF., f. (ult.) L. *servus* slave, SERF; see -AGE.] †1. Servitude, bondage, slavery –1586. †2. A service, or its equivalent in money, due from a serf to his lord –1587. 3. Serfdom (*rare*) 1848.

Serval (sɔ̄·ɹvăl). 1771. [a. mod.L., a. Pg. (*lobo*) *cerval* lynx (cf. F. *loup-cervier.*] †**a.** Some Asiatic wild cat or lynx; also, an American animal resembling this. **b.** A carnivorous quadruped, *Felis s.*, native of S. Africa, having a tawny coat spotted with black, a short tail, and large ears. So **Se·rvaline** *a.* resembling the s.

Servant (sɔ̄·ɹvănt,) *sb.* ME. [a. F., sb. use of pr. pple. of *servir* SERVE *v.*] A person of either sex who is in the service of a master or mistress; one who is under obligation to work for the benefit of a superior, and to obey his (or her) commands. 1. A personal or domestic attendant. (Sometimes with defining word, as *domestic s.*). 2. One who is under the obligation to render certain services to, and to obey the orders of, a person or a body of persons, esp. in return for wages or salary. late ME. **b.** *fig.* Applied to things ME. **c.** Applied occas. to any state official, as expressing his relation to the sovereign. So *s. of the state, public s.*, etc. 1570. 3. In the N. Amer. colonies in the 17–18th c., and subseq. in U.S., *servant* was the usual designation for a slave 1643. 4. *transf.* †**a.** A professed lover; one who is devoted to the service of a lady. Also, a paramour, gallant. –1700. **b.** With religious signification ME. **c.** *Your* (*humble, obedient*) *s.*: one of the customary modes of subscribing a letter, or of addressing a patron in the dedication of a book. †(*Your*) *s.*: a mode of expressing submission to another's opinion; **a form of** greeting or leave-taking. 1474.

1. *Upper s.*, a domestic s. of superior grade of employment, as a butler or a housekeeper. *General s.*, *s. of all work*, a female servant who does all kinds of housework. *Servants' hall*, a room for use as a common room by the servants in a large house; The ethics of the kitchen and servants'-hall 1813. 2. **b.** Fire and water be good servants, but bad masters 1639. **c.** Public Servants voting at Elections 1845. 4. **a.** Pegg, and her s., Mr. Lowther PEPYS. **b.** *S. of the servants of God* tr. *servus servorum Dei*, a title assumed by the Popes (first by Gregory the Great).

attrib., as *s.-girl, -maid.* Hence **Se·rvantless** *a.* having no s. **Se·rvantry** (*rare*), servants collectively. **Se·rvantship,** the condition of being a s.

†**Se·rvant,** *v. rare.* 1607. [f. prec.] *trans.* To put in subjection *to.* SHAKS.

Serve (sɔ̄ɹv), *sb.* 1688. [f. next.] *Tennis.* An act of serving, a service.

Serve (sɔ̄ɹv), *v.* ME. [a. OF. (and F.) *servir* :—L. *servire* to be a servant or slave, to serve, f. *servus.*] I. 1. *intr.* To be a servant; to perform the duties of a servant. †**b.** To be a slave or bondman; to labour as a bondman. Also with cogn. obj. (A latinism.) –1671. 2. To go through a term of service under a master. Usu. with advb. accus. denoting the period, as *to s. one's time*, etc. 1553. **b.** *trans.* To go through, work out (a term of imprisonment, a penal sentence). Also ellipt. *to s. time* and simply *to s.* 1873. 3. To be a servant to; to work for (a master or mistress) ME. **b.** To work for (a body of persons, a company) as a paid servant 1844. 4. To attend upon (as a servant does); to wait upon, minister to the comfort of ME. 5. To assist (a priest) *at* mass as server. Also *absol.*, to act as server. Also *to s. mass* (= F. *servir la messe*). late ME. 6. (In the earliest use, with obj. in dative.) To be (officially) a servant of (God, a heathen deity); to take official part in the worship of ME. 7. †**a.** *trans.* To worship (God, a deity) with religious rites; to offer praise and prayer to, give divine honour to –1702. **b.** To render habitual obedience to (God, a heathen deity, Satan) ME. 8. To render obedience and service to, to fulfil one's duty to (a feudal superior, a sovereign) ME. **b.** To be the 'servant' or lover of (a lady). late ME. †9. To obey (a person's will); to execute (a command, etc.) –1822. **b.** To gratify (desire); to minister to, satisfy (one's need). late ME. 10. *To s. the time* [L. *tempori servire*]: to shape one's conduct in self-interested conformity to the views that are in favour at the time 1560. 11. To render active service to (a king or commander) as a soldier or sailor; to fight for, 'to obey in military actions' (J.) 1518. 12. *intr.* To take one's part in war under a sovereign or commander; to be a soldier or man-of-war's-man. Said also of a ship. 1518. 13. *trans.* To perform the duties of (an office, cure of souls, etc.). late ME. **b.** To work for, assist at, take part in (a function); to take part in the service of (an institution); esp. to minister in (a church) or at (an altar) 1477. **14.** *intr.* To perform official duties, hold office (e.g. as sheriff or M.P., or on a jury) 1477. **15.** *trans.* To render useful service to (a person); to work for or assist *in* any matter 1638. **b.** To labour for (a cause) 1847.

1. Better to reign in Hell, then s. in Heav'n MILT. **b.** The Egyptians made the children of Israel to serue with rigour *Exod.* i. 13. **3.** A young Fellow who had served my Aunt 1740. **4.** S. yourself, would you be well served, is an excellent adage LONGF. **6.** A priest who has forsworn the God he serves SHELLEY. **7.** The costome of the primitive Saints in serving God with Hymns EVELYN. **b.** Who best beare his milde yoak, they s. him best MILT. **8. b.** That gentle Lady, whom I loue and serue SPENSER. **10.** Who never sold the truth to s. the hour TENNYSON. **12.** The 84th Regiment, in which I formerly served 1869. **15.** In all his calamities, they never discovered the least inclination to s. him SMOLLETT.

II. 1. Of a thing: To be subordinate or subsidiary to (another) ME. **2.** To be useful or advantageous to; to answer the requirements of; to be used by. Const. inf. of purpose. With neg.: To avail or profit (a person) nothing. ME. **b.** To be used in common by (a number of persons). late ME. **c.** Of a bodily faculty or organ: To render its normal service to (the owner) ME. **d.** Of a thing: To supply the need or contribute to the working of (another thing) 1580. **3.** *intr.* To have a definite use or function, answer a purpose, effect or conduce to an end; to admit of being used for some end. With neg. = to be of no use, not to avail. ME. **b.** To be usable or available *for* 1528. **4.** *trans.* To help to fulfil or bring about (an end, purpose, etc.); to be a means to, conduce to 1568. **5.** *trans.* and *intr.* To discharge a specified function; to take the place of some specified agency. late ME. †**6.** *trans.* Of one s courage, conscience, inclination, etc.: To prompt (one) *to do* something; (with neg.) to permit, suffer. Also *intr.* –1597. **7.** *trans.* and *intr.* Of time, occasion, wind, weather, etc.: To be opportune or favourable (*to*); to afford (one) opportunity. late ME. **8.** *trans.* and *intr.* Of the memory: To assist or prompt its owner, be at his call 1634. **9.** *trans.* To suffice (a person) in regard to some need or requirement. Also, to last (a person) *for* a specified time. 1450. **b.** To furnish what is requisite for (a thing) 1566. **10.** *intr.* To meet the needs of the case; be adequate or sufficient. Also, to last for a given period. 1496. †**11.** To hold good; to be available *for*; to be satisfactory. Of coin: To pass current. –1726. **12.** *trans.* To suit, fit. (Chiefly of clothes.) *Obs.* exc. *Sc.* 1540.

2. That scuse serues many men to saue their gifts SHAKS. **c.** Her eyes serving her as well as ever EVELYN. **3.** This little Brand will s. to light your Fire DRYDEN. The manganese that has been once used..will s. again 1815. The nerve of vision..can never serve for hearing 1844. **4.** It would s. no useful purpose 1893. **5.** One turfe shall serue as pillow for vs both SHAKS. My Stomach serves me instead of a Clock SWIFT. **6.** *Merch. V.* II. ii. 1. **7.** If fortune serue me, Ile requite this kindnesse SHAKS. When opportunity serves 1879. **8.** Or perhaps your memory don't s. you as well as it did 1861. **9.** It will serue you to mend your shooes SHAKS. Phr. *To s. one's turn*, see TURN *sb.* V. 3. **10.** Tis not so deepe as a well, nor so wide as a Church doore, but 'tis inough, 'twill serue SHAKS. **12.** *Two Gent.* IV. iv. 167.

III. 1. To wait upon (a person) at table; hence, to set food before, help (a person) to food ME. **b.** To supply (a person) *with* food at a meal, to help (a person) to food ME. **2.** *absol.* To wait at table ME. **3.** *trans.* To set food on (the table), to spread *with* food. late ME. **4.** To set food before, feed (animals) 1523. **5.** To attend to the request of (a customer in a shop). Hence, to supply (a customer) *with* a commodity. late ME. **b.** *intr.* To attend to customers in a shop 1825. **6.** *trans.* To supply or furnish with something necessary or requisite. Also, to furnish (a person, town, etc.) with a regular or continuous supply. ME. **b.** To supply with means of transit and conveyance: esp. of railways 1866. †**7.** *refl.* To make use *of*, avail oneself *of*. Also const. *with*. [After F. *se servir de*.] –1846.

1. Let your Betters be serv'd before you SWIFT. **b.** S. him with ven'son, and he chooses fish COWPER. Prov. *First come, first served.* **2.** For whether is greater, he that sitteth at meate: or he that serveth? TINDALE *Luke* xxii. 27. **3.** *To s. tables* (cf. Acts vi. 2), now sometimes used with ref. to the secular functions of the clergy, viewed as encroaching on the time available for their more spiritual work. **5.** Phr. *To s. the shop*, to attend to customers. **6.** A Conduit of water which serves all the Towne 1617. A woman who..used to s. my family with butter 1726.

IV. 1. To set (meat or drink) on the table or before a person; to bring in or dish up (a meal). late ME. **b.** To dish up or send to the table in a specified manner. late ME. **2.** *To s. out*, to distribute or deal out (food, ammunition, etc.) in portions 1802. †**3.** To supply, furnish (a commodity); to yield a regular or continuous supply of –1700. **4.** †To play (a person) a *trick*; to do (a person) a *good* or *bad turn* 1591.

1. It was getting on for two before supper was served 1885. **b.** Boil these gently together and s. on toast 1864. **2.** I served out some kegs of gunpowder 1827. **3.** The pump..that serves water to his garden EVELYN.

V. 1. To treat in a specified (usu. unpleasant or unfair) manner. Now chiefly *colloq.* ME. **2.** *To s. out*: To punish, take revenge on; to retaliate on (a person) *for* something objectionable. *colloq.* (orig. pugilists' slang) 1817.

1. Phr. *To s.* (a person) *right*, to treat (an offender) as he deserves; now chiefly *it serves* (me you, etc.) *right*; also colloq. *serves* (you, etc.) *right*, (*and*) *s.* (you, etc.) *right*, an exclamation of satisfaction at seeing a person punished for his folly or wrong-doing.

VI. Techn. senses. **1.** *Law.* To make legal delivery of (a process or writ). Const. *on* or *upon* (a person). 1442. **b.** To present (a person) *with* a writ 1575. **2.** *Tennis* (and similar games). **a.** *intr.* To start play by striking the ball into the opposite court 1585. **b.** *trans.* To put (the ball) in play 1696. **c.** To strike the ball to (one's opponent) 1647. **3.** Of a male animal: To cover (the female); esp. of stallions, etc. kept and hired out for the purpose. Also *absol.* 1577. **4.** *Falconry* and *Coursing.* To provide quarry for 1576. **5.** Chiefly *Naut.* **a.** To bind (a rope, rod, etc.) with small cord or the like, so as to protect or strengthen 1627. **b.** To wrap (a rope, bandage) round an object 1586. **6.** *Mil.* To operate, keep in play or action (a gun, battery, etc.) 1706.

Serventism (serve·ntiz'm). 1833. [f. It. *servente* (in *cavaliere servente*; see CAVALIER *sb.*) + -ISM.] The system which countenances the devotion of a man to a married woman; cicisbeism.

Server (sɔ̄·ɹvəɹ). late ME. [f. SERVE *v.* + -ER [1].] **1.** One who serves, in various senses. **b.** *Eccl.* One who attends and assists a celebrant at the altar (cf. SERVE *v.* I. 5) 1853. **2.** Something which is used for serving. **a.** = SALVER [2] 1686. **b.** *pl.* A spoon and fork for serving salad or other foods 1884.

Servian (sɔ̄·ɹviăn), *a.* and *sb.* 1555. [f. mod.L. *Servia.*] Older form of SERBIAN.

Service [1] (sə̄·ɹvis). [Early ME. (or late OE.) *serfise*, *servise*, a. OF. *servise*, *-ice*, ad. L *servitium*, f. *servus* slave.] **I. 1.** The condition, status, or occupation of a servant. (In mod. use almost exclusively *spec.* = *domestic s.*) **2.** Const. *of* or possessive: The condition of being a servant of a particular master ME. **b.** The condition or fact of being a servant (of God); †the condition of being the 'servant' (of one's lady). late ME. **3.** †**a.** A place as servant. **b.** A particular employ; the serving of a certain master or household. 1469. **4.** The condition or employment of a public servant (of a sovereign or state) ME. **5.** A branch of public employment, or a body of public servants, concerned with some particular work or the supply of some particular need 1685. **b.** *The s.*: the Army, the Navy, or the Air Force (as implied in the context) considered as a sphere of duty or occupation, or as a profession. So *the* (*fighting*) *services*, the Army, the Navy, and the Air Force 1706.

1. *In, out of s.; to be in s.; to go, get, put into s.*; He had put two of his daughters into s. THACKERAY. **2.** To leaue a rich Iewes service SHAKS. **b.** O God ..whose seruice is perfect fredome *Bk. Com. Prayer, Morn. Prayer.* **4.** *In the British, French*, etc. *s.*: (chiefly of a soldier or sailor). *To take s.*, to join a fighting force. **5.** *The consular s., the diplomatic s., the* CIVIL SERVICE, etc. **b.** The S. is going to the dogs 1872. *The United Services*, the Army and the Navy. *The senior s.*, the Navy.

II. 1. Performance of the duties of a servant; attendance of servants; work done in obedience to and for the benefit of a master ME. **b.** An act of serving; a duty or piece of work done for a master or superior ME. **2.** In feudal use: †**a.** Feudal allegiance, fealty; homage –1595. **b.** A duty which a tenant is bound to render periodically to his lord ME. **3.** *transf.* In complimentary expressions: Respect, 'duty'. Now *rare* or *Obs.* 1601. †**b.** *pl.* in the same sense –1723. **c.** *At* (a person's) *s.*: ready to obey his commands 1554. **4.** The devotion or suit of a lover; professed love. *arch.* late ME. **5.** The serving the sovereign or the state in an official capacity; the duties or work of public servants. late ME. **6.** The duty of a soldier or sailor; the performance of this duty. Often, actual participation in warfare; more fully *active s.* 1590. **b.** A military or naval operation in which a soldier or a regiment serves (often *pl.*) 1590.

1. He was allowed the s. of a boy 1845. **b.** *Temp.* IV. i. 35. **2. a.** Vpon your oath of seruice to the Pope SHAKS. **3.** Phr. *My s. to you*, a phrase accompanying the drinking to a person. *Give my s. to* (in letters) = remember me respectfully to (a third person). **c.** †*At your s.* used *ellipt.* as a phr. of politeness. **5.** *On His* (or *Her*) *Majesty's S.*, a formula (often abbrev. O.H.M.S.) printed on the cover of a letter to indicate that it is official (and therefore exempt from postage). *Secret s.*: see SECRET *a.* **6.** Phr. *To see s.*, (of a soldier) to have experience of warfare; hence (in perfect tense) of a thing, to have been much used or worn.

III. In religious uses. **1.** The serving (God) by obedience, piety, and good works ME. **2.** Worship; esp. public worship according to form and order. Now *rare* or *Obs.* exc. in *divine s.* ME. **3.** A celebration of public worship. (Often without the article.) late ME. **4.** A ritual or series of words and ceremonies prescribed for public worship, or for some particular occasion or ministration. Often with defining word, as *baptismal, burial, communion, marriage s.* (The earliest recorded sense.) **b.** In full *divine s.* †(*a*) The daily office or hours of the breviary –1583; (*b*) Morning and Evening Prayer (Matins and Evensong) 1549. **5.** A musical setting of those portions of the church-offices which are sung; esp. the music for the canticles at Morning and Evening Prayer 1691. **6.** A service-book. Now only *Church S.*, a volume containing the Book of Common Prayer together with the daily lessons. 1700.

1. Our voluntarie s. he requires MILT. **2.** A drear and dying sound Affrights the Flamins at their s. quaint MILT. **3.** I looked into the church, where s. was going on 1859.

IV. 1. The action of serving, helping, or benefiting; conduct tending to the welfare or advantage of another. Chiefly in *to do, render s.* 1582. **b.** An act of helping or benefiting; an instance of beneficial or friendly action 1533. **c.** *collect. pl.* Friendly or professional assistance 1832. †**2.** With *of* or possessive: A person's interest or advantage –1774. **3.** The work which an animal or thing is made to do 1470. **4.** Supply of the needs *of* (persons, occas. of things) ME. **5.** Serviceableness, utility. Now *rare.* 1595. †**6.** *At one's s.*, at one's disposal, ready or available for one to use 1669.

1. He also rendered good s. to our old ally the Porte 1853. **c.** We..shall have no need of Mr. Bowls's kind services THACKERAY. **3.** Phr. *To do s.*; I passed the rod to X——, in whose hands it did better s. 1882. **4.** A great fountain for the common seruice of the house 1585. **5.** *Of s.* (predic.): of use or assistance; useful, helpful.

V. 1. The act of waiting at table or dishing up food; the manner in which this is done. late ME. **b.** That which is served up or placed on the table for a meal. Now *rare.* ME. †**c.** A course –1765. **2.** The furniture of the table. Often with defining word, as *dinner, dessert, breakfast, tea s.* 1468. **b.** A set of vessels for †the altar, the toilet, etc. 1700. **3.** The supply or laying-on of gas, water, etc., through pipes from a reservoir; the apparatus of pipes, etc., by which this is done 1879. **4.** Provision (of labour, material appliances, etc.) for the carrying out of some work for which there is a constant public demand 1853. **5.** Accommodation for conveyance or transit afforded by vehicles plying regularly on a route 1854.

1. Phr. *The s. of the table* (now *arch.*). c. His dinner—four services 1765. 4. [The hospital] has a s. of 710 beds 1886. b. Expert advice or assistance given to customers after sale by manufacturers or vendors 1925. 5. The ordinary s. of trains 1885.

VI. Action of serving, in technical senses. **1.** *Law.* The action or an act of serving (a writ, notice, etc.) upon a person. late ME. **b.** *Sc. Law.* The procedure for ascertaining and declaring the heir of a person deceased 1597. **2.** *Tennis*, etc. The act of 'serving' the ball; a particular player's manner of doing this; the ball served 1611. **3.** *Naut.* Small cord, or the like, wound about a rope to protect it 1729. **4.** The action of covering a female animal 1844.

1. Phr. *To accept s.* (of a writ): see ACCEPT *v.* 3
Comb.: **s.-book**, a book containing one or more forms of divine service, (in the 17th c. often applied to the Book of Common Prayer); **s. flat**, one of a number of flats having the cooking and serving of meals, cleaning, etc. performed by a common staff of servants; **s. measure, metre**, the 14-syllable line which is the equivalent of a couplet of common metre; also used = common metre (see COMMON *a.* 19); **-time**, the time of divine service.

Service[2] (sɔ̄·ɹvis). 1530. [orig. *serves*, pl. of †*serve*, OE. *syrfe*, a. pop. L. **sorbea*, f. *sorbus*.] **1.** A tree, *Pyrus* (*Sorbus*) *domestica*, bearing small pear-shaped or round fruit edible when in an over-ripe condition. **†2.** The fruit of this tree –1796. **3.** *Wild S.*: a bush or low tree (*Pyrus torminalis*) bearing bitter fruit 1741.

attrib. and *Comb.*: **s.-berry**, †(*a*) the fruit of the S.; (*b*) a N. Amer. shrub, *Amelanchier Canadensis*, the Shad-bush; (*c*) the fruit of the white-beam, *Pyrus Aria*; **-tree**, (*a*) = sense 1; (*b*) the wood of this tree; (*c*) *wild s.-tree* = sense 3; (*d*) = *s.-berry* b.

Serviceable (sɔ̄·ɹvisăb'l), *a.* ME. [a. OF. *serviçable, servisable*, f. *service* SERVICE[1]; see -ABLE.] **1.** Ready to do service; willing to be of service; active or diligent in service. Now *rare*. **†b.** Of actions or conditions: Involving or expressing readiness to serve –1629. **2. a.** Of persons: Profitable, useful 1660. **b.** Of things: Capable of being applied to an appropriate purpose, or to the performance of a proper function. late ME.

1. A seruiceable Villaine, As duteous to the vices of thy Mistris, As badnesse would desire SHAKS. b. And all about the Courtly Stable, Bright-harnest Angels sit in order s. MILT. 2. b. The barometer.. is also s. in measuring the heights of mountains GOLDSM. Hence **Se·rviceableness. Se·rviceably** *adv.*

Servient (sɔ̄·ɹviĕnt), *a.* 1615. [ad. L. *servientem, servire*.] **1.** Subordinate, subject to rule. †Also *absol.* **2.** Law. *S. land, tenement*: a land or tenement over which a servitude has been granted or acquired in favour of a dominant land or tenement. *S. proprietor*: the tenant of a servient land or tenement. 1681.

Serviette (sɔ̄ɹvie·t). Latterly considered *vulgar*. 1489. [a. F., of obsc. formation, conn. w. *servir* SERVE *v.*] A table-napkin.

Servile (sɔ̄·ɹvəil, *U.S.* -il), *a.* and *sb.* late ME. [ad. L. *servilis*, f. *servus* slave; see -ILE.] **A.** *adj.* **1.** Of, belonging to or proper to a slave or slaves 1450. **b.** Of arts, employments, labour: Befitting a slave; unworthy of a free man; hence, 'mechanical' as opp. to *liberal* 1514. **2.** Of a person: Subject as a slave or serf to a master or owner; living in servitude. Of a class, etc.: Composed of slaves or serfs. 1565. **†b.** Belonging to the serving class or to the lower orders –1727. **3.** Of a person: That behaves like a slave; meanly submissive, 'cringing, fawning' (J.); destitute of independence in thought and action 1605. **b.** Befitting, or characteristic of a slave or a state of servitude; slavish, ignoble 1526. **4.** Of a people, state, its condition, etc.: Politically enslaved; subject to despotic or oppressive government or to foreign dominion. Now *rare* or *Obs.* 1547. **†5.** Of immaterial things: Subject *to* the control of something else; not free –1805. **6.** Of imitation, translation, etc.: Unintelligently close to the exemplar or original; slavish. Hence of a person as agent. 1605. **7.** *Philol.* **a.** Of words: Expressing mere grammatical relations, auxiliary 1668. **b.** *Semitic Gram.* Of a letter: Not belonging to the root of the word in which it occurs; serving to express a derivative or flexional element. Opp. to *radical*. 1653.

1. This lad of s. birth PATER. †*S. habit*, formerly sometimes applied *transf.* to the dress of a labourer or a poor man. *S. war, insurrection*, one raised by slaves against their masters. b. Phr. *S. work* [after L. *opus servile*], in religious use applied *spec.* to laborious or mechanical work forbidden on the Sabbath and hence on the major festivals of the Church. 2. b. *Tit. A.* v. ii. 55. 3. Be courteous to all men, s. to none LYTTON. b. The..S. Fears usual in those of a mean depending Condition 1705. 4. His Subjects..shall s. be to Turks and Infidels 1661. 5. Reason thus with life..a breath thou art, Seruile to all the skyie-influences SHAKS.

B. *sb.* (the adj. used ellipt. or absol.) **1.** A servile person 1830. **2.** *Heb. Gram.* A servile letter 1738. Hence **Se·rvile-ly** *adv.*, **-ness.**

Servilism (sɔ̄·ɹviliz'm). 1831. [f. SERVILE *a.* + -ISM.] **1.** Systematic servility. **2.** The doctrine which advocates political 'slavery' (a hostile term for anti-Liberal opinions) 1831.

Servility (səɹvi·lĭti). 1573. [f. SERVILE *a.* + -ITY.] **†1.** Servile condition; the quality or status of being a slave –1667. **2.** Servile disposition or conduct; *esp.* mean submissiveness, cringing 1573.

2. This unhappy s. to custome 1674. The domestics ..had an air of s. and constraint 1797.

Serving (sɔ̄·ɹviŋ), *vbl. sb.* ME. [f. SERVE *v.* + -ING[1].] The action of SERVE *v.* in various senses; an instance of this. **b.** *concr.* A helping (of food, etc.) 1769.

Serving (sɔ̄·ɹviŋ), *ppl. a.* ME. [f. SERVE *v.* + -ING[2].] **1.** That serves, or does service to, another; that acts as a servant. Often hyphened, as in *serving-maid*, etc. **2.** Of a soldier, etc. That is on service 1570.

S.-man (now *arch.*), a man who serves; a male servant or attendant; so **s.-wo·man.**

Servite (sɔ̄·ɹvəit), *sb.* and *a.* 1550. [ad. med.L. *Servitæ* pl., f. L. *servus* servant (in *Servi Beatæ Mariæ*, the formal name of the order); see -ITE[1].] **A.** *sb.* A friar or nun of the order of 'Servants of Blessed Mary', founded in 1233. **B.** *adj.* Of or pertaining to this order 1756.

Servitor (sɔ̄·ɹvitəɹ). ME. [a. OF., a. late L., f. *servire* SERVE *v.*] **1.** A (male) personal or domestic attendant; a man-servant. Now *arch.* **b.** *gen.* A servant 1450. **†2.** Used in expressions of humility or politeness –1645. **3.** One who serves in war; *spec.* one of a class of persons to whom lands were assigned in Ulster under James I, as having served in a military or civil office in Ireland. *Obs.* exc. *Hist.* 1561. **4.** *Oxford Univ.* Formerly, in certain colleges, one of a class of undergraduate members who received their lodging and most of their board free, and were excused lecture fees. (Orig. the servitors acted as servants to the fellows.) 1642. **5.** *Glassmaking.* †A master workman's assistant; *spec.* the second man of a 'chair' 1662.

3. A valiant servitour in sundry wars beyond sea 1640. Hence **Se·rvitorship**, the position, state, or duties of a s. at an Oxford college (*Obs.* exc. *Hist.*).

Servitude (sɔ̄·ɹvitiūd). 1471. [a. F., ad. L. *servitudo*, f. *servus*; see -TUDE.] **1.** The condition of being a slave or serf; absence of personal freedom. Often, and now usu., with additional notion of subjection to the necessity of excessive labour. Also, a (more or less rigorous) state of slavery or serfdom. **b.** With ref. to animals: Subjection to mankind. Now *rare* or *Obs.* 1697. **c.** Subjection to a foreign power or to oppressive rule 1471. **d.** *transf.* and *fig.* A state of degrading or burdensome subjection 1474. **†e.** *concr.* Slaves or servants collectively. MILT. **2.** The condition of being a servant, service; esp. domestic service. Now *rare* or *Obs.* 1651. **†3.** Apprenticeship –1835. **4.** Compulsory labour as a punishment for criminals. Chiefly *penal s.* 1828. **5.** *Civil* (and *Scots*) *Law.* (= L. *servitus*). A subjection or subserviency of property either: (1) to some definite person other than its owner (*personal s.*), or (2) to some definite property other than that of its owner for the benefit of the dominant property (*prædial s.*) 1652.

1. The greatest part of the nation was gradually reduced into a state of s. GIBBON. c. A disturbed Liberty is better than a quiet s. ADDISON. d. This is s., To serve th' unwise MILT.

Servo- (sɔ̄·ɹvo), = SERBO-.

Servo-motor. 1889. [ad. F. *servo-moteur*, f. L. *servus* slave + F. *moteur* MOTOR.] An auxiliary motor, e.g. one used for directing the rudders of a Whitehead torpedo, or the reversing gear of a large marine engine.

Sesame, †sesam (se·sămi, †se·săm, sī·săm). 1440. [a. or ad. L. *sesamum, -ama* = Gr. σήσαμον, σησάμη, prob. of oriental origin. The mod. currency is due to translations of the 'Arabian Nights', and the present pron. to Gr. σησάμη.] A widely cultivated E. Indian plant, *Sesamum indicum*. Also the seeds of this plant from which an oil is expressed. **b.** = OPEN SESAME 1785.

attrib.: **s. grass** = GAMA GRASS.

Sesamoid (se·sămoid), *a.* and *sb.* 1696. [ad. L. *sesamoides*, a. Gr. σησαμοειδής, f. σήσαμον; see -OID.] **A.** *adj.* Shaped like a sesame-seed; applied in *Anat.* to certain small bones and cartilages formed in tendinous structures. **B.** *sb.* A sesamoid bone or cartilage 1854. So **Sesamoi·dal, Sesamoi·deal** *adjs.*

‖**Sesamum** (se·sămŏm). 1577. = SESAME.

Sesban (se·sbæn). 1860. [ad. F., ult. ad. Pers. *sīsabān*.] Any leguminous plant of the genus *Sesbania*, esp. *S. ægyptiaca* and *aculeata*.

Sescuple (se·skiup'l), *a.* Now *rare*. 1694. [ad. L. *sescuplus* or *sescuplex*, var. *sesquiplus* or *sesquiplex*, f. *sesqui-* SESQUI- + *-plus, -plex* -FOLD.] = SESQUIALTER *a.*

Sesqui- (se·skwi), a. L. prefix [*sesqui-*, contr. of **semis-que* a half in addition], expressing a superparticular ratio.

1. With designations of measure or amount, denoting one and a half times the unit; as **se·squipes**, a foot and a half (see SESQUIPEDALIAN); **†se·squitone** *Mus.*, an interval consisting of a tone and a semitone, a minor third. b. *Chem.* In the names of salts, expressing a proportion of 3 to 2 between the constituents, *viz.* a combination of 3 atoms or equivalents of the substance denoted by the word to which it is prefixed with 2 atoms of another element or radical; e.g. **sesquibro·mide**, a bromide containing 3 atoms of bromine for 2 of another substance; so **sesquio·xide; sesquiba·sic** [see BASIC *a.*], having 3 equivalents of the base for 2 of the acid. c. In *Astrol.*, **sesqui-qua·drate, -qua·rtile**, denoting an aspect of planets when 135° from one another; so **sesqui-squa·re.** †d. Prefixed to words descriptive of forms of religious belief, = extreme(ly), excessive(ly), ultra-; e.g. *ses-qui-conformist, -deist*.

2. With an ordinal numeral adjective, denoting the proportion $1 + \frac{1}{n} : 1$, *i.e.* n + 1 : n, where n is the corresponding cardinal number, as *sesquioctavus*, bearing the ratio of $1\frac{1}{8} : 1$, *i.e.* 9 : 8; so SESQUIALTER, -ALTERA, etc. b. *Mus.*, after SESQUIALTERA, etc.; **sesquiqua·rta, -qui·nta**, etc., applied (*a*) to harmonic intervals producible by sounding four-fifths, five-sixths, etc. of a given string; (*b*) to rhythmic combinations of four notes against five, five against six, etc.

‖**Sesquialter** (seskwiæ·ltəɹ), *a.* (*sb.*). 1570. [L., f. *sesqui-* SESQUI- + *alter* second.] **1.** Of a proportion: That is as $1\frac{1}{2}$ is to 1. Of an object: Proportionate *to* another object as $1\frac{1}{2}$ is to 1; that is such a multiple *of*. **2.** = next **2.** 1841.

‖**Sesquialtera** (seskwiæ·ltĕră), *a.* (*sb.*). 1501. [L., fem. (sc. *ratio*) of *sesquialter* (see prec.).] **†1.** = prec. Also as *sb.*, a sesquialteral proportion. –1650. **b.** *Mus.* (See quot.) Also, a perfect fifth. 1501. **2.** An organ stop, consisting of several ranks of pipes, of a brilliant tone. Usu. *absol.* as *sb.* 1688.

1. b. In rhythmic combinations, S. is used as the general symbol of Triple Time. The term S. is also applied to passages of three notes sung against two. 1883.

Sesquialteral (seskwi,æ·ltĕrăl), *a.* 1603. [f. L. *sesquialter.*] = SESQUIALTER **1.** So **Sesquia·lterate, -a·lterous** *adjs.*

Sesquiduple (se·skwidiū:p'l), *a.* 1850. [f. SESQUI- + DUPLE, to express the meaning 'two and a half' (on a false analogy), after *sesquialteral.*] Involving a ratio of $2\frac{1}{2}$ to 1. So **Sesquidu·plicate** *a.* 1775.

Sesquipedal (sĕskwi·pĭdăl, se·skwipedăl), *a.* 1611. [ad. L. *sesquipedalis*, f. SESQUI- + *ped-, pes* foot.] = next.

Sesquipedalian (se:skwipĭdē·liăn), *a.* and *sb.* 1615. [f. L. *sesquipedalis*; see prec. and -IAN.] **A.** *adj.* Of words, etc. (after Horace, *A.P.* 97): Of many syllables 1656. **b.** *transf.* Given to using long words 1853.

Finding one of his s. words hang fire BOSWELL.

B. *sb.* **1.** A person or thing that is a foot and a half in height or length 1615. **2.** A sesquipedalian word 1830. Hence **Se:squipeda·lian-**

ism, style characterized by the use of long words; lengthiness; so **Sesquipe·dalism**; **Sesquipeda·lity**, s. quality; *transf.* lengthiness.

Sesquiplicate (seskwi·plikĕt), *a.* 1714. [ad. mod.L. *sesquiplicatus*, f. SESQUI- + *plicatus* folded, PLICATE, to express 'subduplicate of the triplicate'. (L. *sesquiplex* = taken once and a half.)] Bearing or involving the ratio of the square roots of the cubes of the terms of a certain ratio.

Thus, *a* is to *a'* in the s. ratio of *b* to *b'*, when $a : a' :: \sqrt{b^3} : \sqrt{b'^3}$.

‖ **Sesquitertia** (seskwitɔ̄·ɹʃă). 1597. [L., fem. (sc. *ratio*) of *sesquitertius*, f. SESQUI- + *tertius* third.] Denoting a ratio of 1⅓ to 1, *i.e.* 4 to 3; chiefly *Mus.* denoting (*a*) an interval having this ratio, viz. the perfect fourth; (*b*) a rhythm of three notes against four. Hence †**Sesquite·rtial** *a.* -1696; †**Sesquite·rtian** *a.* -1774, expressing a ratio of 4:3.

†**Sess**, *v.* 1465. [Aphet. f. ASSESS *v.*] = CESS *v.*[1], 1, 2, 4. -1764.

†**Se·ssa**, *int.* [perh. var. of *sa-sa*.] An exclam. of uncertain meaning. SHAKS.

Sessile (se·səil, se·sil), *a.* 1753. [a. L. *sessilis* sitting down, dwarfed, stunted, f. *sess-*, *sedere* to sit; see -ILE.] 1. Having no footstalk. **a.** *Bot.* Of leaves, fruits, flowers, etc.: Immediately attached by the base; not having a peduncle, pedicel, or the like. **b.** *Zool.* Of limbs or organs: Having no connecting neck or footstalk. Also of certain animals. 1777. **c.** *Path.* Of morbid growths, warts, etc.: Adhering close to the surface 1725. **2.** Of certain animals: Sedentary, fixed to one spot; not ambulatory. Of cells: Immobile. 1860.

Session (se·ʃən). late ME. [a. F., ad. L. *sessionem*, f. *sedere* to sit.] 1. The action or an act of sitting; the state or posture of being seated; also a manner of sitting. Now *rare.* 1615. **b.** *spec.* The 'sitting' of Christ at the right hand of God 1557. **2.** The sitting together of a number of persons (esp. of a court, a legislative, administrative, or deliberative body) for conference or the transaction of business. Also (now somewhat *rarely*), a single continuous sitting of persons assembled for conference or business. 1444. **3.** A continuous series of sittings or meetings of a court, a legislative, administrative, or deliberative body, held daily or at short intervals; the period or term during which the sittings continue to be held; opp. to *recess* or *vacation* 1553. **b.** *spec.* The period between the opening of Parliament and its prorogation 1577. **c.** In some universities and colleges, an academical year 1775. **4.** A judicial sitting. **a.** *gen.* A sitting of a judge or judges to determine causes; a judicial trial or investigation. *sing.* and *collect. pl.* (often const. as *sing.*) *Obs.* exc. *arch.* late ME. **b.** **Sessions of the peace** (in ordinary language simply **sessions**): the periodical sittings of justices of the peace (or, in some instances, of a stipendiary magistrate or a recorder). Often const. as *sing.* late ME.

1. Vivien..Leapt from her s. on his lap TENNYSON. 2. A Prayer for the High Court of Parliament, to be read during their S. *Bk. Com. Prayer.* The British geologists..here in solemn annual s. assembled HUXLEY. 3. b. I doubt the s. will not be over till the end of April SWIFT. *Autumn s.*, the exceptional resumption of the sittings of the Houses, after an adjournment, in what is normally the autumn recess: a use condemned by parliamentary authorities as incorrect. c. Also of a school, and in U.S., the teaching period of a day. 4. b. *Petty* (†*petit*) *sessions*, a court held by two or more justices or a stipendiary magistrate, exercising summary jurisdiction in minor offences within a particular district. *Brewster* or *licensing sessions*, a periodical meeting of the justices of a division for the hearing of applications for licences to sell alcoholic drinks. *General* or *quarter sessions*, a court held four times a year (in a county, riding, etc. by the justices of the peace, and in certain boroughs by the recorder), having a limited civil and criminal jurisdiction and certain administrative functions. (*The sessions*, without qualification usu. = the quarter sessions.) Hence **Se·ssional** *a.* pertaining to a s. or sessions. **Se·ssionally** *adv.*

Sesterce (se·stəɹs). *Pl.* **sesterces** (se·stəɹsiz). 1598. [ad. L. *sestertius*, prop. adj. (sc. *nummus* coin) = that is two and a half, f. *semis* half + *tertius* third.] A Roman coin, orig. = 2½ asses, later 4 asses; the fourth part of a denarius.

‖ **Sestertium** (sestɔ̄·ɹʃiŏm). *Pl.* **sestertia** (-ʃiă). 1540. [L., usu. explained as the gen. pl. *sestertium* of *sestertius* SESTERCE (with ellipsis of *mille* a thousand), taken as neut. sing.] A sum of a thousand sesterces.

‖ **Sestertius** (sestɔ̄·ɹʃiŏs). *Pl.* **sestertii** (-ʃi,əi). 1567. [L.; see SESTERCE.] = SESTERCE.

Sestet(t, sestette (seste·t). 1801. [ad. It. *sestetto*; see next and -ET, -ETTE, and cf. SEXTET.] 1. *Mus.* A composition for six voices or instruments. **2.** *Pros.* The last six lines of a sonnet 1859.

‖ **Sestetto** (seste·to). 1801. [It., f. *sesto* sixth (:—L. *sextus*) + dim. suffix *-etto*.] = prec. 1.

‖ **Sestina** (sestī·nă). 1838. [It., f. *sesto* sixth.] *Pros.* A poem of six six-line stanzas (with an envoy) in which the line-endings of the first stanza are repeated, but in different order, in the other five. So **Sesti·ne** 1586.

Set (set), *sb.*[1] Also **sett** (now prevalent in many techn. senses). late ME. [f. SET *v.*, partly directly from the vb.-stem, and partly a sb. use of SET *ppl. a.*] **I.** The action of setting or condition of being set. 1. The act of setting (of a luminary); the apparent descent of the heavenly bodies towards the horizon at the close of their diurnal period. Now only *poet.* exc. in SUNSET. †**2.** The condition of being stopped or checked; a check -1768. **3.** The act of a dog in setting game 1727. **4.** = *dead set*, a, b. 1829. **5.** (Usu. *sett.*) A form of power used by shipwrights 1794. **6.** The action of setting or hardening, or the condition of being set 1837. **7.** **Dead set**, often in phr. *to make a dead s. at.* **a.** A pointed attack; a determined onslaught; const. *at*, *against*. Also, an attitude or position of hostility. 1835. **b.** Of a woman: A determined attempt to gain a man's affections. Also *occas.* conversely of a man. 1823. **c.** A complete check; phr. *at a dead s.* 1806. **d.** *Sporting.* An abrupt stop made by an animal with its muzzle in the direction of the prey; *esp.* the position taken up by a dog in pointing game 1819.

1. That will be ere the s. of Sunne SHAKS. *S. of day*, (*a*) the time at which the sun sets; (*b*) the west. 4. No one could say that Miss N. was making a s. at him 1887. 7. a. The disaffected sections of the Irish population made a dead s. against him 1885.

II. The manner or position in which a thing is set. 1. Tendency, inclination; determination in a certain direction; often = settled direction, fixed habit 1567. **2.** The direction in which a current flows or a wind blows; also, the action of the water, etc. in taking a particular direction 1719. **3.** *Weaving.* (Usu. *sett.*) The adjustment of the reeds (of a loom) necessary for the making of a fabric of a particular texture; hence, the make of a fabric as determined by this 1780. **b.** (Usu. *sett.*) Each or any of the squares in the pattern of a tartan; the pattern itself 1721. **4.** The form which a body assumes as the result of strain or pressure or in the process of solidification, etc.; *esp.* the permanent deflexion of a bar or plate of metal or wood 1812. **5.** The way in which an article of dress is arranged or 'hangs'; similarly of a ship's sails 1822. **6.** The position or attitude given to a limb or a part of the body 1855. **7. a.** The dip of the arm of an axle-tree; the elevation of a gun 1844. **b.** The slight lateral deflexion in opposite directions of the alternate teeth of a saw; the amount of this deflexion 1837. **c.** *Typogr.* The position of the letters with ref. to the amount of space between them 1892.

1. According to..the S. of the Time DANIEL. 2. A straw will prove the s. of a current 1876. 6. The s. of her head and neck GEO. ELIOT.

III. Something which is set. 1. (Usu. *sett.*) The area of ground worked by a particular mining company. Chiefly *Cornwall.* 1778. **2.** 'Any thing not sown, but put in a state of some growth into the ground' (J.); a twig, slip, or sucker, used for planting or grafting; also, a young plant, *esp.* a bedding-out plant 1513. **b.** A potato, or a portion of a potato, used as seed 1767. †**3.** The stake put down at dice, etc. -1611. †**4.** A game at dice or cards; hence, the number of points to be made in order to be 'up' -1687. †**b.** *fig.* Match, contest -1687. **5.** *Tennis.* (Occas. spelt *sett.*) A certain series of games: see quot. 1578. †**6.** One of the pleats of a ruff; also, the arrangement of a ruff in pleats -1651. **7.** (Usu. *sett.*) A squared stone (chiefly granite) used for paving 1871. **8. a.** *Plastering.* The finishing coat on walls prepared for painting 1823. **b.** A young oyster when first attached; the crop of young oysters in a locality 1881.

IV. A place where something is set. 1. A place where stationary fishing nets are fixed 1745. **2.** The earth or burrow of a badger 1898.

V. (Often *sett.*) A tool or device used for 'setting' in various techn. senses 1750.

5. Six Games make a S. of Tennis, but if what is called an Advantage S. is played, two successive Games above five Games must be won to decide; or, in Case it should be six Games all, two successive Games must still be won on one Side to conclude the S. 1769.

Set (set), *sb.*[2] Also **sett**. late ME. [orig. (in sense I. 1) a. OF. *sette* :—L. *secta* SECT *sb.* but later infl. by SET *v.* and taken as = 'number set together' (branch II, perh. in part due to MLG. *gesette*).] **I.** A number or group of persons. †1. A religious body, sect -1538. **2** A number, company, or group (*of* persons) associated by community of status, habits, occupations, or interests. Often *depreciatory*. Also *absol.* 1682. **3.** A group of persons in society having its own peculiar interests, fashions, and conventions; a social group of a select or exclusive character 1777. **4.** The number of couples required to perform a country dance or square dance 1766.

2. A s. of smugglers, gipsies, and other desperadoes SCOTT. 3. They will move in the first s. in Bath JANE AUSTEN.

II. A collection or number of things. 1. A collection of instruments, tools, or machines customarily used together in a particular operation; a complete apparatus employed for some specific purpose 1561. **2.** †**a.** A number *of* musical instruments arranged to play together; a band; also *s. of music.* **b.** A suite *of* bells to be rung together. 1561. †**3.** A 'pair' of beads -1634. **4.** A collection of volumes by one author, dealing with one subject, belonging to one department of literature, or issued in a series 1596. **b.** A number of musical compositions forming a whole, as a church 'service' 1590. **c.** A complete series of the parts of a periodical publication 1701. **d.** A series of prints by the same engraver 1768. **e.** A definite number of copies of a bill of lading or of exchange 1818. **5.** A number of things connected in temporal or spatial succession or by natural production or formation 1604. **b.** The complement *of* teeth (natural or artificial) with which a person (or animal) is furnished 1654. **6.** A number of things grouped together according to a system of classification or conceived as forming a whole 1690. **7.** The complete collection of the 'pieces' composing a suite of furniture, a service of china, a clothing outfit, etc. 1687. **8.** A series of buildings or apartments associated in use; *esp.* a suite of apartments let as lodgings 1722. **b.** *Mining.* In full *s. of timber(s*: A frame for supporting the side of a level or shaft, or the roof of a gallery 1830. **9.** A team of (usu. six) horses 1687. **10.** The series of movements or figures that make up a square dance or country dance, *esp.* the quadrille; the music adapted to this 1834.

1. A Sett of Mathematical Instruments 1773. b. *Wireless.* A receiving apparatus. 5. A new s. of words to the old tune of 'Over the Water to Charlie' SCOTT. 6. The s. of notions which he had acquired from his education 1802. 7. A s. of Irish diamonds and cairngorms THACKERAY. 8. First we went into lodgings,—into three sets in three weeks THACKERAY.

Set (set), *v.* Pa. t. and pple. **set.** [Com. Teut.; OE. *sęttan* = Goth. *satjan*; causal of **setjan* (*sitjan*) to SIT. The spelling **sett** is still occas. found in techn. senses.] **I.** To cause to sit, seat; to be seated, sit. 1. *trans.* To place in a sitting posture; to cause to occupy a seat; to seat. **b.** To put (a hen) to sit on eggs 1440. **2.** *pass.* To be seated ME. **b.** To be seated to partake of a meal (*to meat*, *at* or *to dinner*, etc.). *Obs.* or *arch.* ME. **3.** *intr.* To sit, be seated. Now *dial.* or *vulgar.* ME. **b.** Of a hen: To sit *upon* eggs 1586. **c.** To have a certain 'set'; to sit (well or ill, tightly or loosely, etc.) 1804. **4.** *trans.* To become, befit, suit. Chiefly *Sc.* (in mod. use often ironical). 1480.

1. Setting us upon Camels 1735. Provb. *To s. a*

beggar on horseback, to give an undeserving person an advantage he will misuse. **2.** Most of the party were set to cards THACKERAY. **3. c.** Sleeves lined with stiff or harsh linings never s. well 1887.

II. To sink, descend. Of the sun or other luminary: To go down; to make an apparent descent towards and below the horizon ME. **b.** Of the day: To come to its close. *poet.* 1604. **c.** *fig.* To decline, wane 1607.

The sun setting red SCOTT. **c.** The glory of Egypt seemed to have set 1892.

III. To put (more or less permanently) in a definite place. **1.** *trans.* To put (a shoot, young plant, tuber, or bulb) into the ground to grow; to plant (a tree, also by extension, a vineyard, a crop). Also, less usu., to plant (seed) by hand, as opp. to *sowing*. OE. **2.** †To deposit (a security); to put down as a stake; to stake, wager. *Obs.* or *arch.* OE. **b.** *absol.* or *intr.* To put down a stake, lay money *on* (or *at*). Also *fig.* to give a challenge *to*. *Obs.* or *arch.* 1553. **c.** *Dominoes.* To play first 1897. **3.** *trans.* To put (a thing) in a place allotted or adapted to receive it; (contextually) to fit, fix ME. †**b.** To fit or attach (one thing) to another –1595. **c.** To put (eggs) *under* a hen to be hatched 1726. **4.** *pass.* To have a certain position or arrangement by nature ME. **5.** *trans.* To put or place, cause to be, lie, rest, or stand, in a locality specified by an advb. expression OE. **b.** *pass.* To be situated, lie (in a certain locality); to be placed (at a certain height, interval, etc.) OE. **6.** *trans.* To place (a part of the body) upon a surface or an object OE. **7.** To put down in a record, catalogue, etc.; to mention or treat of in writing: now *s. down* ME. **8.** To put (one's signature), affix (a seal) *to* (†*on*) a document ME.

1. The seed is to be set by hand 1830. **2.** He is nettled, and sets me twenty: I win them too DRYDEN. **3.** While the Creator Great His constellations set MILT. **b.** *John* IV. ii. 174. **5.** S. him brest deepe in earth, and famish him SHAKS. Phr. *To s. before*, orig. = to place so as to be seen by; hence, to put before one for use, consideration, imitation, etc. **b.** Betwixt them and you will be a great gulf set 1650. **6.** *To s. (one's) hand to*, to lay hold of, take into one's hand; *fig.* to set about, engage upon. **7.** All his faults obseru'd, Set in a Note-Booke SHAKS. **8.** In witness whereof I have hereunto set my Hand and Seal 1736.

IV. To place or cause to be in a certain position (other than merely local), condition, relation, or connexion. **1.** *trans.* To place in a state or sphere specified by an advb. expression. (Now less freq. than *place* or *put.*) ME. **2.** To cause to be or become (so-and-so) OE. †**3.** To place (a person) in some sphere of activity or occupation; esp. *to s. to school* –1697. **b.** orig. *to s. upon the muzzle*: To muzzle (a horse) so as to prevent him feeding improperly 1834. **4.** To place (a person or thing) in one's possession or control, or in a condition to be used, dealt with, or occupied ME. **5.** To cause (a thing) to assume a certain physical position expressed by a complementary adj. or advb. phr.; chiefly *to s. open, s. on end, s. upright* ME. **6.** To place (a person, his body, or limbs) in a certain posture. Also *refl.* late ME. **7.** *To s. fire to* (†*in*): to kindle, ignite. late ME. **8.** To stake the welfare or existence of (something) *upon*; also *pass.* to be dependent for its destiny *upon* 1594. **9.** To put (one thing) in the balance *against* another; to compare (one thing) *by* or *to* another 1589. **10.** To place (one's hope or trust) *in* (†*on*); to cause (one's thoughts or affections) to dwell *upon* or be centred *in* something. Phr. *to s. one's heart on.* OE. **11.** To rest (one's eye, one's look) *upon* ME. **12.** To put (a mark, impression) *upon*; to place as a distinguishing mark, token, or imprint. Now *rhet.* OE. **13.** To lay or spread (a surface of a certain kind) *on* an object; hence, to put (a favourable or specious appearance) *upon* a thing 1540. **14.** To put (an edge or point) *on*, *to* 1600. **15.** To fix (a certain price) *upon* a thing; now chiefly in *to s. a price upon one's head*, and the like 1530. **b.** *fig.* To put (a certain value) *upon*, have (a certain estimate) *of* 1611. †**16.** To lay (something burdensome) *upon*; to impose or inflict (a penalty, etc.) *upon* –1761.

1. Everything remains in the course and order wherein it was set at the Creation 1662. **2.** Phr. *To s. at ease, at rest, to rest, at peace; to s. at odds, at one, at variance, at war, by the ears; to s. agog, astray; to s. aglow, afire, on fire, aflame, inflame(s*, etc.; *to s. in array, in order, in readiness, to rights; to s. at large, at leisure, at liberty; to s. on edge; to s. in or on a roar; to s. in action, motion, operation; to s. at bay, at fault; to s. at contempt, at defiance*; etc. **4.** Phr. *To s. in hand*: †(*a*) to take in hand, undertake; also *intr.* with *with*, in the same sense; (*b*) to put out to be done. *To s. to (for, on) sale*: see SALE *sb.* **6.** Phr. *To s. on one's feet, legs*: see FOOT *sb.*, LEG *sb.* I. 1 c. **8.** To s. Vpon one Battell all our Liberties SHAKS. **9.** Against his professed theory may be s. his actual practice SPENCER. **10.** He had set his heart on seeing his son a clergyman 1870. **11.** The first time I s. eyes on captain Wilkins ..I accost him 1765. **12.** In womens waxen hearts to s. their formes SHAKS. **13.** Phr. *To s. a good face upon*: cf. FACE *sb.* II. 3; Kick'd out, we set the best face on't we could DRYDEN. **14.** This did but s. an edge to her wanton appetite 1620.

V. To appoint, institute (a person); to prescribe, ordain, establish (a thing). **1.** To post or station (a person) in a certain place *to* perform certain duties OE. **2.** To place in a position of superiority or control *over* another (e.g. as a ruler, protector, guard) OE. **3.** To appoint (a boundary, limit) OE. **4.** To ordain or establish (a regulation); to lay down (a law); to prescribe (a form or order). *Obs.* or *arch.* OE. **5.** To fix or appoint (a time) for the transaction of an affair, or as the term of a period. Also, to fix a time for. OE. **6.** To present (an example or pattern) for others to follow; to introduce (a fashion) ME. **b.** To put before a person (a specimen of work) to be followed; to mark out (the lines) on which he is to work or proceed 1593. **7.** To allot or enjoin (a task) ME. **b.** *Mining.* To appoint the amount of (work to be done) 1742. **c.** To propound (a question or set of questions) to be solved or answered; to prescribe (a book) for an examination or a course of study 1711. **8.** To let on lease, lease, let. Now *local.* late ME. †**9.** *trans.* To establish by agreement or authority (a settled condition, an alliance, etc.) –1652.

1. Loke that ye set good watche at euery gate 1533. **2.** Us his prime Creatures,..Set over all his Works MILT. **3.** Ambitious fellows, who set no bounds to their desires SMOLLETT. **5.** The club's opening day ..is set for April 22. 1893. **6.** A fashion, as the phrase goes, has to be 'set' 1895. Phr. *To s. the pace*, to proceed at a rate of speed to be followed by another (freq. *fig.*); so *to s. the stroke* (in rowing). **b.** I could turn writing-master..and s. copies to children POPE. **7.** The Club were set 94 runs to win 1892.

VI. To put in position, arrange, fix, adjust. **1.** *trans.* To spread (a net) to catch animals, lay (a trap) OE. **2.** To put (a thing) in place; to fix up in the proper or required manner; in early use often = *s. up* i. late ME. **b.** = *s. going* 1500. **3.** To insert (a stitch). Phr. *to s. a stitch*, to sew. 1683. **4.** *Baking, Glass-making*, etc. To put into the oven or furnace 1483. **5.** To fix (a stone or gem) in a surface of metal as an ornament 1500. **b.** *transf.* and *fig.* To place (a thing) *in* a certain setting 1530. **c.** To fix (artificial teeth) on the plate 1844. **6.** To put (a sail) up in position to catch the wind. Also said of a ship carrying (so much canvas). ME. **b.** Phr. *To s. sail*: to start on a sea voyage 1513. **7.** To put (a movable part of an instrument or piece of mechanism) in a certain position. late ME. **8.** *Bell-ringing.* To ring (a bell) up till it stands still in an inverted position, either balanced or held by the stay and the slider. Also *intr.* of the bell. 1671. **9. a.** To put (liquid) in a vessel, at a certain temperature, strength, etc., ready to undergo a process; *spec.* in *Cheese-making* 1736. **b.** *Baking* and *Brewing.* To add barm or yeast to. *To s. the sponge*: to leaven a mass of flour. 1743. **10. a.** To make (a table) ready for a meal, spread (a table) *with* food, etc. **b.** To lay (a meal). late ME. **c.** To arrange the colours in the desired order on (a palette) 1847. **11.** *Printing.* To compose, set up (type); hence, to put (manuscript) into type 1530. **12.** To put (words) *to* music; to write (a musical composition) *for* certain voices or instruments 1502. **13.** *Theatr.* To make up (a scene) on the stage; to arrange (an item of the scenery) in a particular way. Also *to s. the stage.* 1779. **14.** To put an edge on (a cutting instrument, *esp.* a razor) 1461. **b.** fig. phr. *To be sharp* or *keen set*: to be hungry or keen 1540. **15.** To adjust (the teeth of a saw) by deflecting them alternately in opposite directions so as to produce a kerf of the required width. Also *to s. a saw.* 1678. **16.** To stretch (leather) 1884. **17.** To put (a broken or dislocated bone) in a position adapted to the restoration of the normal condition. Also *intr.* said of the bone. 1572. **18.** To adjust, settle (†the attire, the hair) ME. **19.** *Weaving.* To fix the texture of (a fabric) 1839. **20.** To give the requisite adjustment, alinement, or shape to (a mechanical contrivance, an instrument, etc.) 1879. **21.** To regulate, adjust *by* a standard; *esp.* to put (a clock, etc.) right. late ME. **22.** To fix the amount of (a fine or other payment), put down *at* a certain amount. *Obs.* or *arch.* late ME.

1. The snare was set..outside the field 1890. **5.** Vertue is like a rich stone, best plaine sett BACON. **d.** To fix (the hair) when damp so that it dries in waves 1926. **10. a.** She gan the hous to dighte, And tables for to sette CHAUCER. **18.** Combing his Peruke and setting his Cravat DRYDEN.

VII. To place mentally; to suppose, estimate. †**1.** *trans.* To posit, assume, suppose. Phr. *s. the case* = suppose, supposing. ME. **2.** To place mentally or conceptually in some category; †to regard as being (so-and-so); to consider (a thing) to reside *in* or to depend *on* another. late ME. **b.** To place (a person or thing) *before* or *after* another in estimation. Now *poet.* late ME. **3.** To fix the value of (a thing), to assess (a person), *at* so much. *Obs.* or *arch.* 1460. **b.** To estimate the amount of *at* so much 1863. **4.** To assess (a person) *at* so much. *Obs.* or *arch.* 1521. **5.** To have (a certain estimate) of a person or thing: in idiomatic phrases ME.

1. S. the case that there be two men who make a covenant BUNYAN. **2.** Tradition sets Wiklif's birth in the year 1324 ROGERS. **3.** *fig.* There shall no figure at that Rate be set, As that of true and faithful Juliet SHAKS. Phr. *To s. at naught* or *nought* (see NOUGHT *sb.* 2), *at little, at nothing; to s. at a pin's fee.* **b.** The yearly increase..is set at about 8*s.* per acre 1863. **5.** Phr. *To s. little, much, more*, etc. *by* (*Obs.* exc. *arch.* or *dial.*). *To s. (no, more*, etc.) *store by*; see STORE *sb.* *To s. a (great, little) price upon.*

VIII. To put or come into a settled or rigid position or state. **1.** *pass.* To be resolved or determined; to have a settled purpose. Now *dial.* ME. **2.** To have one's mind or will fixed *upon* something. late ME. **3.** trans. *To s. one's* or *the face (countenance)*: to give a fixed or settled expression to the countenance 1560. **b.** *pass.* and *intr.* (and *refl.*). Of the eyes, the features, the countenance: To have or assume a fixed look or expression 1601. **4.** *trans.* To press (the teeth, lips) together into a rigid position; to clench (the teeth), compress (the lips, mouth). Also *refl.* and *intr.* 1602. **b.** *pass.* and *intr.* Of muscles, or the like: To have or assume a rigid attitude or state 1851. **c.** *intr.* To become bent or twisted as a result of strain 1798. **5.** *Dyeing.* (*trans.*) To make (a colour) fast or permanent 1601. **6.** To cause to become firm, hard, or rigid in consistency; to curdle, coagulate (milk, etc.). Also *intr.* 1736. **b.** Of cream: To collect and settle on the top of the milk 1859. **7.** To cause (fruit) to form on a tree by the process of fertilization; to cause (a flower) to develop into fruit: said of bees, etc. and (also *absol.*) of the tree bearing the fruit 1693. **b.** *intr.* Of blossom or fruit: To develop as the result of fertilization. Also said of hemp fibre. 1718. **8.** *Plastering.* To put a finishing coat on 1693. **9. a.** *Sheep-breeding.* To settle or establish (a particular stock) 1782. **b.** *intr.* Of a period of time or weather: To become settled 1800. **c.** *Cricket.* (*pass.*) To have become accustomed to the bowling 1865. **10.** *trans* To check; to puzzle, nonplus, 'stump'; to tax the resources of. Now *n. dial.* 1586. **11.** *Dancing.* (*intr.*) To take up a position and perform a number of steps with one's face *to* one's partner or *to* the dancer on one's right or left. Chiefly in *s. to partners, to corners.* 1652.

2. When I perceiv'd all set on enmity MILT. **3.** *To s. one's face as a flint*, after Isa. l. 7. **b.** His face set and sulky 1898. **4.** The old woman set her lips firmly, and drew her dagger KINGSLEY. Phr. *To s. one's teeth*; see TOOTH. **10.** Learning was pos'd, Philosophie was set G. HERBERT.

IX. To put in the way of following a certain course, cause to take a particular direction. **1.** *intr.* To proceed in a specified direction; to begin to move, start off, put out, set out. Now only in *s. forth, forward, off, on*, etc. OE. **2.** Of a current, wind: To take or have a (certain) direction or course. late ME. **3.** *trans.* To cause to pass into a certain place or from one place to another; to convey, transport. Now *rare.* late ME. **b.** To accompany or escort (a person) for part or all of the way he has to go. Chiefly *n. dial.* 1737. **4.** Of a current, wind, etc.: To cause to move, carry along in a (certain) direction 1450. **5.** To propel (a boat or other craft) with a pole; to punt. Also *absol.*, to use a punt pole or setting pole; now *esp.* in punt-shooting, to move up *to* the fowl, to get within shooting distance 1566. **6.** To direct or point (one's face, foot, etc.) *to, towards, for* a place 1611. **b.** To put (a person) *on the way* leading to a destination 1678. **7.** To put (a person) *to* a piece of work or a task. Also const. inf. ME. **8.** To direct (one's mind, intention, or will) *to* the consideration or performance of something ME. **b.** *refl.* To apply oneself *to* a piece of work, a task, or employment. Now always const. inf. Also *intr.* in the same sense. ME. **9.** trans. *To s.* (a person) *upon*: to cause to be occupied with (something); often with implication of urging or impelling. Also const. gerund (esp. *to set (a-)going*). late ME. **10.** To cause to be busy *about.* Also *refl.* and *pass.* 1622. **11.** To incite (a dog or other animal, also a person) to make an attack or pursuit: chiefly with preps. *at, on* 1440. **b.** To encourage (an animal) to perform some evolution or feat; to pit (fighting cocks) 1586. **12.** To place in a position of hostility or opposition; to cause to be hostile or antagonistic; to pit (one) *against* (another). Also *refl.* and *pass.* ME. **b.** *intr.* To make an attack ME.

1. The King is set from London SHAKS. 2. The prevalent winds s. from the west 1890. *fig.* The public opinion..is setting against the practice 1885. 3. After being set across [the ferry].., we drove back to Melrose HAWTHORNE. 6. I, with my wife, &c. set our faces towards home EVELYN. b. Your host comes out with you to set you upon your way 1883. 7. We set the children to their regular lessons 1836. Provb. *S. a thief to catch a thief. transf.* By setting one evil thing to counteract another 1841. 8. All my mind was set Serious to learn and know MILT. b. She set herself to study it 1880. 9. Phr. *To set afoot* or *on foot*, to originate or start; to set going. This rude shock..set Usher upon a more careful examination 1879. 11. They set dogs on us as though we were rats 1889. b. She would s. her horse at anything 1890. 12. Will you s. your wit to a Fooles? SHAKS. Phr. *To s.* (a person) *against*, to cause him to have an antipathy for. *To s. one's face against*, to take up an attitude of determined hostility towards.

X. Senses which appear to have arisen by reversal of construction or by an ellipsis. **†1.** *trans.* To beset (a place) for the purpose of intercepting or capturing a person –1593. **2.** To plant (ground) *with* 'sets' or (young) trees. *To be s. with* = to have growing upon it. ME. **3.** To ornament (metal or other surface) by inlaying or encrusting it with stones or gems. late ME. **b.** To surround (a large stone) *with* a mount of small stones; to mount (an object) *in* a particular metal 1506. **4.** *pass.* To be studded, dotted, lined, etc. *with* a number of objects. *To be set about* (arch.) or *round with*, to be surrounded or encircled with, to have a circle of. late ME. **5.** *trans.* **†a.** To beset or besiege (a place or a person) –1530. **b.** *fig.* esp. in *to be hard set*, to be in great straits or hard put to it. late ME. **6.** Of a hunting dog: To mark the position of (game) by stopping dead and pointing the muzzle towards it. Also *intr.* 1621. **7.** *Naut.* To take the bearings of (an object) 1626. **8.** To mark down as prey, fix on as a victim; to watch for the purpose of apprehending or robbing. *slang.* 1670.

3. A superb watch, set with brilliants 1795. 4. How thick the City was set with Churches ADDISON. 5. b. They were ill set to liue 1673. 7. We set the Tower of Arabia near the port of Alexandria 1769.

Comb. **1.** With preps. in specialized senses (intr.). **S. about —. a.** To begin working at, take in hand, begin upon. **b.** To set upon, attack (*colloq.*). **S. against —. †a.** To make an attack upon, be hostile to. **b.** To move in a direction opposed to. **S. at —.** To assail, attack. **S. on —.** = *s. upon.* **S. upon —. a.** To attack, assail, fall violently upon. **b.** To urge strongly (*rare*). **†c.** = *s. about* a.

2. With advs. in specialized senses (trans. or intr.). **S. about.** To circulate (a statement, report). Chiefly *n. dial.* **S. abroach.** *arch.* **a.** To broach (a cask, liquor). **b.** To set on foot, give publicity to. **S. afloat.** *arch.* **a.** To launch, float. **b.** To bring to the surface (as the dregs of a liquid); hence *fig.* to set (*esp.* something bad) in motion, set agog, stir up, make active. **S. apart.** To separate for a special purpose; to devote to some use. **S. aside. a.** To put on one side. **†b.** To discontinue the performance or practice of. **c.** To dismiss from one's mind, abandon the consideration of. **d.** To reject or throw over as being of no value, cogency, or pertinence; to overrule. **e.** To discard or reject from use or service, in favour of another. **f.** To annul, quash, render void or nugatory. Chiefly *Law.* **g.** To separate out for a particular purpose. **S. back. a.** To hinder the progress of, give a check to. **b.** To put (a clock, its hands) to an earlier time. **c.** *intr.* To flow in the reverse direction. **S. by.** To lay up or lay by for future use. **S. down. a.** See simple trans. senses and DOWN *adv.* **b.** To place so as to rest upon a surface; to put down, as upon the ground. Also *absol.* (*b*) To cause or allow to alight from a vehicle; to 'drop' (a person at a place). Also *absol.* **c.** To put down in writing or in print; to put on paper; to enter in a catalogue or account; to write out, compose; to put on record; to relate. (*b*) To put down, as in a schedule or table, *to be* performed at a certain time; †to appoint a time for the performance of (something). **d.** To estimate, reckon; now only, to regard (a person) *as*, take (him) *for*, consider (him) *to be* (so-and-so). **e.** *refl.* To begin to devote oneself *to.* **†f.** *intr.* To be encamped; to 'sit down' *before* (a town) to besiege it. **S. forth. a.** To promulgate, publish, issue (a regulation, proclamation, etc.). **b.** To publish (a literary work). **c.** To express in words, give an account of, present a statement of, *esp.* in order, distinctly, or in detail; to declare, expand, relate, narrate, state, describe. **d.** To adorn, decorate. Now *rare.* **e.** *intr.* To set out *on* a journey, *against* an enemy, *in* pursuit, etc. **S. forward** (**†forwards**). **a.** To carry, send, or thrust forward. *To s. one's* (*best*) *foot forward*: see FOOT *sb.* **b.** To assist (a person) in the way of progress; to help on (a matter, plan, etc.); to advance, promote. **c.** To put forward, promulgate; to advance (an opinion). **d.** *intr.* To go forward, set out, start. **S. in. a.** See simple trans. senses and IN *adv.* **b.** *intr.* To set to work, begin (upon something); *esp.* followed by *to, for. Obs.* exc. *dial.* **c.** To begin, become prevalent: chiefly of the weather entering upon a particular state. **d.** Of a current or wind: To flow or blow towards the shore. **S. off. a.** See simple trans. senses and OFF *adv.* **b.** To start off, give (a person or thing) a start; to send off *into* a fit of laughter, etc. **c.** To apportion or assign to a particular purpose; to portion off. **d.** To mark or measure off (a certain distance) on a surface; to lay off (the lines of a ship). **e.** To set in relief, make prominent or conspicuous by contrast. **f.** To show to advantage, enhance, embellish. **g.** To give a flattering description of, commend, praise. **h.** To take into account by way of compensation or equivalent; to put in the balance (*against* something); *spec.* in *Law*, to allow or recognize as a counter-claim. Also *absol.* **i.** *intr.* To start on a journey or course; *transf.* to start (doing something). **j.** *Printing.* To soil the next leaf or sheet: said of the ink or of the printed page. **S. on. a.** See simple senses and ON *adv.* **†b.** To set on foot, instigate, promote. **c.** (*a*) To urge (an animal, *esp.* a dog) to attack. (*b*) To instigate, urge on (a person) *to do* something. **d.** To set in motion, set going. **e.** To start (a person) doing something. **f.** To set or appoint (a person) to do something. **g.** *intr.* To advance, go forward. **h.** To make an attack. Now *dial.* in *s. on at* or *to.* **S. out. a.** See simple senses and OUT *adv.* **†b.** To fit out (a ship, fleet) for a voyage; to equip for an expedition; to send out (forces), fit out (an expedition). **†c.** To issue, promulgate. **d.** To display (wares) for sale. **†e.** To extol, 'crack up'. **†f.** To embellish, adorn, deck out, trick out. **g.** To put down on paper in express or detailed form; to describe or enumerate expressly; to detail. **h.** To delimit, define, mark out. **i.** (*a*) To arrange (a table, a room, etc.) for a meal or other purpose; to spread (a table, etc.) *with* ornaments, etc.; to dress (a window). (*b*) To put out or arrange (things necessary for a meal, game, etc.), *esp.* on a table; to lay (a meal). (*c*) To arrange (objects) at proper intervals or with a due amount of display; *spec.* to plant out; to leave (plants) at a distance apart, by thinning. **j.** *intr.* To begin or start on a journey; to start on one's way. (*b*) const. *inf.* To begin one's career or start off with the object of doing something; to lay oneself out (*to do*). **k.** To start on a certain course; to begin or start *off* (*with* or *by doing* something). **S. over. †a.** To convey to the other side of (a piece of water). Also *absol.* or *intr.* **b.** To make over, transfer. **S. to. †a.** To affix (one's seal or signature). **b.** *intr.* To make a beginning; *esp.* to begin seriously or energetically. (*b*) *Pugilism.* To begin fighting (*with*). **S. up. a.** To place in a high or lofty position; to raise to an elevated situation. **†b.** To hoist (sail, a flag). **c.** To raise (a cry); to utter (vocal sound). **†d.** To put up for sale or auction. **e.** To post up (a paper or notice); to give notice of, advertise. **f.** *Naut.* To take in the 'slack' of (shrouds, stays), make taut. **g.** To place in an exalted, eminent, or superior position; to raise to power or authority; sometimes *spec.* to put on the throne. Also *absol.* (*b*) To appoint (an officer or functionary). (*c*) To appoint to or nominate for a position. **h.** To make (a person), elated, proud, or vain; *esp.* in *pass.* to be elated; to be 'stuck-up'. **i.** To place in an erect position; to set or stand upright; to erect (an image, statue); to raise (a standard). (*b*) *To s. up one's bristles*: to be irate. *To s. one's back up*: see BACK *sb.*[1] **j.** To erect and make ready for use; to pitch (a tent); †to erect (a building). **k.** To put together the parts of (a machine) and erect it in position. (*b*) To start (a piece of work) on a loom, etc. **l.** *Typogr.* To put (types) into the composing-stick; to arrange (type) in words or blocks of words; to put (a book, etc.) into type. Also *absol.* **m.** To place (the dead body of an animal stuffed or otherwise treated for preservation) in an erect or lifelike position. **n.** *To be well* (*straight*) *set up*: to have a stalwart, well-knit frame. **o.** To make erect and soldierly by drill. **p.** To put into operation; to bring into use or vogue; to establish a course or series of. Now *rare.* (*b*) To cause (a certain condition, *esp.* of disease) to arise. Often *pass.* **q.** To establish (a state of things, a custom, a form of government, a society, etc.). **r.** To set on foot, establish (a business, profession); to begin (housekeeping, life). (*b*) To begin the use or practice of; to adopt as part of one's establishment, etc. **s.** To provide (a person) with means; to place in a position of prosperity or in the way of retrieving one's fortune; to set 'on one's legs' *again.* **t.** To establish or start (a person) in a business or profession; *transf.* said of the money, stock, or outfit sufficient to equip a person. **u.** To bring to a proper state of health and strength; to restore to health. **v.** To put into an attitude of hostility or opposition; to incite, instigate. **w.** To put forward (a claim, defence, a case in law). **x.** To advance, propose, put forward (a theory, idea, plan). **y.** (orig. *absol.* of **r.**) To start in business, begin the exercise of a trade or profession. **z.** To **s. up for.** (*a*) *To s. up for oneself*, to start on a career on one's own account. (*b*) To lay claim to being (so-and-so). (*c*) To lay claim to (a quality, virtue, etc.). **aa.** (*absol.* of **w.**) To lay claim or pretend *to be.* **†bb.** To put up *at* an inn or other lodging. **cc.** To punt, esp. so as to get close *to* water-fowl to shoot them. **dd.** Of a soft-nosed bullet: To expand on impact.

Set (set), *ppl. a.* OE. [pa. pple. of SET *v.*] **1.** In various strictly ppl. uses, with ref. to the corresponding senses of the vb.; *esp.* **a.** Of a task, a subject of discourse or study: Imposed or prescribed. Now *rare* exc. in *s. book.* ME. **b.** Of the teeth: Clenched 1810. **c.** Of types: That have been 'set up' 1837. **2.** Appointed or prescribed beforehand. Hence, Fixed, definite, not subject to uncertainty or alteration. OE. **3.** Deliberate, intentional 1456. **4.** (In *s. battle, field*) = PITCHED *ppl. a.* 2. Now *rare.* late ME. **5.** Formal, ceremonious, regular 1513. **6.** That has assumed a permanent form or condition; immovable, persistent 1605. **7.** With prefixed adv.: Having a specified position, arrangement, build, adjustment, disposition, etc. ME.

1. When you are to talk on a S. Subject 1709. 2. Which a sett rent can no wise afoord 1587. The Indians have no s. time of eating 1769. No s. form of liturgy 1883. 3. *Of s. purpose. In good s. terms* (after Shaks.), 'roundly', with outspoken severity. 5. *S. speech*, public speech more or less elaborate; an oration, as dist. from extemporaneous or informal utterances. 6. Those even, s. tones, so common among readers 1760. He is very s. in his ways 1848. *S. fair*, (of weather) usu. marked on English barometers at the point indicating that the height of the mercury is 30½ inches.

Comb.: **s. changes** *Bellringing*, = *s. peal*; **s. dance**, a quadrille, country-dance, or the like; **s. iron** *Shipbuilding*, a bar of soft iron, admitting of being bent so as to be used for transferring curves from the scrive-board to the bending plate; **s. line**, a fishing-line with baited hooks, pegged or anchored; **s. net**, a fishing net fastened across a stream or channel, into which the fish are driven; **†s. peal** *Bellringing*, a ringing of a peal of bells in one position for a considerable length of time before a change is given; **s. piece**, (*a*) a painting or a sculptured group of figures; (*b*) a picture or design composed of fireworks; **s. scene**, an apparatus built up and placed in position upon a theatrical stage before the rise of the curtain; a collection of side scenes, 'skies', etc. depending upon one another for a particular effect; so *s. scenery*; **s. square**, (*a*) a plate of wood, metal, etc. in the form of a right-angled triangle, the acute angles being either 60° and 30° or both 45°, used by draughtsmen as a guide for drawing lines at one of these angles; (*b*) a form of T-square with an additional arm turning on a pivot, for drawing lines at fixed angles to the head; (*c*) a joiner's square.

Set-, the stem of SET *v.* in comb., chiefly in sbs. derived from phrases with advs.

s.-in, the beginning of a period of time, a spell of weather, or the like; **-up**, (*a*) an object set up or upright; (*b*) the manner or position in which a thing is set up; *U.S.*, personal bearing or carriage; also *fig.*

‖**Seta** (sī·tă). *Pl.* **setæ** (sī·tī). 1793. [L., bristle.] **1.** *Bot.* A stiff hair or bristle-like body. Also, the stalk which supports the theca or capsule of mosses. **2.** *Zool.* A bristle; a bristle-like appendage 1820.

Setaceous (sĭtē¹·ʃəs), *a.* 1664. [f. mod.L. *setaceus*, f. L. *seta* bristle; see -ACEOUS.] **1.** Having the form or character of a bristle. Chiefly in scientific use, of the nature of a seta or setæ. **2.** Bristly 1787. Hence **-ly** *adv.*

Se·t-back. 1674. [f. vbl. phr. *set back.*] **1.** *fig.* A check to progress, a retardation or retrograde movement, a relapse, reverse. **2.** *Arch.* A plain, flat set-off in a wall 1864. **3.** A setting back or backward 1900. **4.** *U.S.* = BACK-SET *sb.* 2. 1888.

Set-down. (Stress variable.) 1761. [f. vbl. phr. *set down.*] **1. a.** A single drive (ending where the passenger first alights) in a vehicle plying for hire; the distance covered by such a drive. **b.** A 'lift' 1792. **2.** An unexpected and humiliating rebuff. Also, a severe scolding. 1786.

Seti-, used as comb. form of L. *seta* SETA, as in: **Seti·ferous**, *a.* having setæ or bristles. **Se·tiform**, *a.* having the form of a seta or bristle; bristle-shaped. **Setiger** (sĭ·tidʒəɪ), a setigerous worm. **Seti·gerous** *a.* furnished with or having setæ. **Seti·parous** *a.* producing setæ.

Setness (se·tnės). 1642. [f. SET *ppl. a.* + -NESS.] The quality, state, or character of being set; also, an instance of this.

Se·t-off. *Pl.* **set-offs.** 1621. [f. vbl. phr. *set off.*] **1.** Something used to set off or adorn; an adornment, decoration, or ornament. **2.** The act of setting off on a journey, etc.; a start 1759. **3.** *Comm.* and *Law.* An act of 'setting off' one item of an account against another; an item or amount which is or should be set off against another in the settlement of accounts; a counter-claim, or a counterbalancing debt, pleaded by the defendant in an action to recover money due; also, this mode of defence 1766. **b.** More widely: A taking into account of something as a counterbalance to, or a partial compensation for, something else; a counterbalancing or compensating circumstance or consideration 1773. **4. a.** *Arch.* (Also *sett-off.*) = OFFSET *sb.* 6. 1717. **b.** A similar reduction in a metal bar, etc. 1830. **5.** *Printing*, etc. The transference of ink from one page to another 1842. **b.** An impression transferred 1839.

3. b. Something is required from you as a set off against the sin of your retirement 1799.

Seton (sī·tən), *sb.* late ME. [ad. med.L. *setonem*, app. f. L. *seta* bristle, in med.L., also silk. Cf. OF. *seton.*] *Surg.* **1.** A thread, piece of tape, etc. drawn through a fold of skin so as to maintain an issue or opening for discharges, or drawn through a sinus or cavity to keep this from healing up. **2.** The issue so formed 1597.

1. *S.-needle*, a needle used for passing a s. through the skin.

Setose (sī·tōus), *a.* 1661. [ad. L. *setosus*, f. *seta*; see -OSE[1].] **1.** *Anat.* and *Zool.* Set or covered with bristles or stiff hairs, bristly. Also, of a bristly nature. **2.** *Bot.* Having setæ or bristles 1760.

Set-out. (Stress variable.) Chiefly *colloq.* and *dial.* *Pl.* **set-outs.** 1806. [f. vbl. phr. *set out.*] **1.** A display, e. g. of plate, china, food, etc.; a 'turn-out', i. e. a carriage with its horses, etc.; a person's 'get-up'; a show or public performance. **2.** A beginning or start 1821. **3.** Outfit, equipment 1831.

Sett: see SET *sb.*[1] and [2].

Settee[1] (setī·). Now *Hist.* 1587. [a. It. *saettia*, commonly regarded as f. *saetta* arrow.] A decked vessel, with a long sharp prow, carrying two or three masts with a kind of lateen sails, in use in the Mediterranean.

Settee[2] (setī·). 1716. [perh. a fanciful variation of SETTLE *sb.*; see -EE[2].] A seat (for indoors) holding two or more persons, with a back and (usu.) arms.

Setter (se·təɪ). late ME. [f. SET *v.* + -ER[1].] **I.** One who or something which sets. **1.** *gen.* One who sets something specified or contextually implied. Often as the second element of a compound, as in BONE-SETTER, TYPE-SETTER, etc. **b.** With advb. extension or complement, as *s.-forth*, †*-on*, *-up*, etc. 1548. **2.** A workman employed to 'set' something, e. g. jewels, saws, razors, etc. late ME. **3.** In *Dice-play.* The player who stakes on the throw of the 'caster' 1726. **4.** In quarrying and mining work: The foreman by whom the contracts are made with the workmen 1884. **5. a.** A confederate of sharpers or swindlers, employed as a decoy 1592. **b.** A police spy or informer 1630. **6.** A dog trained to 'set' game; *esp.* as the name of a special breed 1576.

5. a. O 'tis our S., I know his voyce: Bardolfe, what newes? SHAKS. 6. Of the breed now so called, there are three varieties, the *English*, the *Irish*, and the *Gordon setters.* The name was formerly applied to a kind of spaniel. N.E.D.

II. An instrument or tool used in setting; *esp.* in *Gunnery*, a wooden instrument used, with the aid of a mallet, to set the fuse into a shell 1526.

Setterwort (se·təɪwɔ̄ɪt). 1551. [ad. MLG. *siterwort*; the first element is of unkn. origin.] The plant Bear's-foot or Fetid Hellebore, *Helleborus fœtidus*; also, the Green Hellebore, *H. viridis.*

Setting (se·tiŋ), *vbl. sb.* late ME. [f. SET *v.* + -ING[1].] **I. 1.** The action of SET *v.* in various trans. senses. Also, the fact of being set. **b.** *Sport.* (*a*) The action of a dog in indicating game 1621. (*b*) The sport of 'putting up' game with a setter 1661. **2.** The manner or position in which anything is set, fixed, or placed. late ME. **3.** The manner in which a jewel is 'set' or mounted; *concr.* the frame or bed (of precious metal or the like) in which a jewel is set 1815. **b.** *transf.* and *fig.* A person's or thing's environment; literary or historical background, or the like 1841. **4.** The manner in which a poem or form of words is set to music; a piece of music composed for a particular poem, etc. 1879. **5.** *Plastering.* The finishing coat of plaster, the *s. coat* 1823.

3. b. The s. of the piece is charming 1885.

II. Senses related to intr. uses of SET *v.* **1.** The sinking of a heavenly body towards and below the horizon; the quarter or direction in which a heavenly body sets. Also, the fall of night or darkness. late ME. **2.** The process or fact of becoming set, hard, or stiff; coagulation 1791. **3.** The flowing of a current in a particular direction; the direction of flow 1595.

1. *fig.* The Soul that rises with us, our life's Star, Hath had elsewhere its s. WORDSW. 3. *fig.* The powerful s. of the current of human motive and inclination 1875.

Comb.: **s. coat,** a finishing coat of fine plastering, **-pole,** a pole, esp. one used by wild-fowlers for propelling a boat or punt on mud-banks, securing wounded birds, etc.; **-rule,** a composing-rule.

†Setting dog. 1611. = SETTER I. 6. –1835.

Settle (se·t'l), *sb.* [OE. *setl* :—OTeut. **setlo-* :—pre-Teut. **sedlo-*, cogn. w. L. *sella* (:—**sedla*), f. Indo-European root **sed-*; see SIT *v.*] †**1.** Something to sit upon; a chair, bench, stool, etc. –1483. **2.** *spec.* A long wooden bench, usu. with arms and a high back, and having a locker or box under the seat 1553. **3.** A ledge, raised platform 1611.

Settle (se·t'l), *v.* [OE. *setlan*, f. *setl* seat, place of rest; see prec.] **I.** To seat, place. †**1.** *trans.* To seat; to put in a seat or place of rest; also, to cause to sit down –1692. **2.** To place (material things) in order, or in a convenient or desired position; to adjust (e.g. one's clothing) 1515. **3.** To place (a person) in an attitude of repose, so as to be undisturbed for a time. Chiefly *refl.* 1515. **b.** *pass.* To be installed in a residence, to have completed one's arrangements for residing 1643. **4.** To cause to take up one's residence in a place; *esp.* to establish (a body of persons) as residents in a town or country; to plant (a colony) 1573. **b.** To fix or establish permanently (one's abode, residence, etc.) 1562. **c.** To assign to (a person) a legal domicile in a particular parish. Chiefly *pass.* 1572. **d.** To furnish (a place) with inhabitants or settlers 1702. †**5.** To fix (something) *in* (a person's heart, mind, etc.) –1690. †**6.** To set firmly on a foundation; to fix (a foundation) securely –1666.

2. He adjusted the cock of his hat a-new, settled his sword-knot STEELE. 3. The man..settled her comfortably in the stern-sheets 1893. b. We were soon settled in barracks 1837. 4. Maryland..was first settled by Roman Catholics 1830. 6. Before the mountaines were setled.. was I begotten BIBLE (Geneva) *Prov.* viii. 25.

II. To come to rest after flight or wandering. **1.** *intr.* Of a bird, flying insect: To take up a position of rest *from* flight; to alight *on* something ME. **b.** Of things, esp. flying or floating objects, also *transf.* and *fig.* of darkness, silence, etc.: To come down and remain. late ME. **2.** To come together from dispersion or wandering; esp. *Hunting*, (of hounds) to keep steadily to the scent. late ME. **3.** Of things: To lodge, come to rest, in a definite place after wandering 1622. **b.** Of pain or disease: To establish itself *in* or *on* a definite part of the body 1594. **c.** Of the wind: To become 'set' *in* (*at*, *into*) a specified quarter 1626. **d.** Of affections, etc.: To come after wandering *to*, become fixed *on*, an object 1628. **4.** Of persons: To cease from migration and adopt a fixed abode; to establish a permanent residence, become domiciled. Also with *down*, *in.* 1627. **b.** Of a people: To take up its abode in a foreign country. Also, to establish a colony. 1682. **5.** = *to s. oneself* (sense I. 3). *To s. in*: (*a*) to dispose oneself for remaining indoors; (*b*) now, to establish oneself in new quarters. 1818.

1. The common blue fly which settles on meat 1875. b. A deep gloom settled on his spirits 1779. 3. b. A cough settled on her chest 1856. 4. My Father being a Foreigner of Bremen, who settled first at Hull DE FOE. 5. Like a clamour of the rooks..ere they s. for the night TENNYSON.

III. To descend, sink down; to lower. [From sense II. 1.] **1.** To sink down gradually by or as by its own weight. Of the ground: To subside. Of a structure: To sink downwards from its proper level. ME. **2.** *Naut.* **a.** Of a ship: To sink gradually; also with *down* 1819. **b.** *trans.* To diminish the height of, to reduce to a lower level (a deck, topsail) 1625. **3.** *intr.* Of soil, loosely compacted materials: To subside into a solid mass. Of new masonry or brickwork: To become consolidated by its own weight and drying of the mortar. 1560. **b.** *trans.* To cause to subside into a solid mass; to consolidate. Also with *down*, *home.* 1611.

1. The..Pier..was observed to s. 1751. 2. a. The ship was evidently settling now Fast by the head BYRON. 3. Roads s. in spring after frost and rain 1828. b. Then give the whole a good watering to s. the soil 1845.

IV. To come or bring to rest after agitation. **1.** *intr.* Of a liquid: To become still after agitation or fermentation, so that the suspended particles or impurities are separated as scum or sediment. late ME. **b.** *trans.* To cause (liquor) to deposit dregs or work off impurities; to clarify 1599. **2.** *intr.* Of suspended particles or impurities in a liquid: To come to rest after agitation or disturbance; now chiefly, to sink to the bottom as sediment. Also *to s. out.* late ME. **3.** To subside, calm down; to become composed 1578. **4.** *trans.* To quiet, tranquillize, compose (a person, his mind, nerves, etc.); to allay (passion) 1530. **b.** *To s. the stomach*: to check vomiting or nausea 1662. **5.** To quiet with a blow; to knock down dead or stunned; to 'do for' 1611. **6.** *intr.* To come to an end of a series of changes or fluctuations and assume a definite form or condition. Also *to s. down* (*to*). 1684. **b.** Of the weather: To become steadily fine. Also, *to s.* (*in*) *for*: to come gradually to a steady condition of (rain, frost, etc.). 1719.

3. Then till the fury of his Highnesse s. Come not before him SHAKS. Maurice Blake was too excited.. to s. at once to sleep 1896. 4. Hoping that sleep might s. his brains, with all haste they got him to bed BUNYAN. 5. There 's nothing will s. me but a Bullet SWIFT. Phr. *To s.* (a person's) *hash*: see HASH *sb.* 2. 6. This smile should not s. into a simper 1859.

V. To render or become stable or permanent; to fix or become fixed in a certain condition. **1.** *trans.* To ensure the stability or permanence of (a condition of things, a quality, power, etc.). late ME. **2.** To fix, make steadfast or constant (a wavering, irresolute or doubting person, heart, mind, etc.). late ME. **3.** *refl.* To fix one's attention *upon* an object; to make up one's mind *to do* something; to set oneself steadily *to* some employment. Now usu., to compose oneself after excitement or restlessness and apply oneself quietly to work. (Often with *down.*) Also *intr.* in the same senses. 1530. **4.** *trans.* To secure or confirm (a person) *in* a position of authority, an office; to establish *in* an office, an employment 1548. **b.** (Chiefly *Sc.* and *U.S.*) To appoint (a minister) to the charge of a parish; also, to appoint a minister to (a parish) 1719. **5.** To establish (a person) in the matrimonial state. Now chiefly *refl.* and *pass.* 1566. **b.** *intr.* 'To establish a domestic state' (J.) 1718. **6.** *trans.* To secure (payment, property, title) *to, on,* or *upon* (a person) by decree, ordinance, or enactment 1625. **b.** Of a private individual: To secure (property, succession) *to, on,* or *upon* (a person) by means of a deed of settlement 1661. **7.** To subject to permanent regulations, to set permanently in order, place on a permanent footing (institutions, government); to bring (a language) into a permanent form 1597. **b.** *To s. one's estate, one's affairs*: to arrange for the disposal of one's property, the payment of one's debts, etc., esp. with a view to one's death, retirement from business, etc. 1652.

1. 'Tis hard to s. order once again TENNYSON. 3. When I s. myself down to my pursuits 1833. She went down into the drawing-room, and could not s. to anything 1865. 5. Phr. *To s. in the world* or *in life*. b. Why don't you marry, and s.? SWIFT. 6. The statute settling the present title to the Crown 1863. b. I..have settled upon him a good Annuity for Life ADDISON. 7. To s. the Government on a Parliamentary basis 1874. Tyndale, Coverdale, and Cranmer had done so much to s. our language 1886. b. I..made my Will, settled my estate, and took leave of my friends STEELE.

VI. To fix (what is uncertain), to decide (a question). **1.** To appoint or fix definitely beforehand, to decide upon (a time, place, plan of action, price, conditions, etc.) 1596. **b.** To fix by mutual agreement 1620. **c.** *intr.* To come to a decision; to decide *to do* something; to decide *upon* (a plan of action, an object of choice) 1782. **2.** *trans.* To decide (a question, a matter of doubt or discussion); to bring to an end (a dispute) 1651. **b.** *Law.* To decide (a case) by arrangement between the contesting parties. More fully, *to s. out of court.* 1900. **c.** To put beyond dispute (a principle, fact) by authority or argument 1733. **3.** *intr.* To come to terms or agreement *with* a person 1527. **b.** To make an arrangement to compound *with* a creditor 1838. **4.** *trans.* To close (an account) by a money payment; to pay (an account, bill, score) 1687. **b.** *absol.* or *intr.* To settle accounts by payment. Chiefly const. *with.* 1788.

1. Then it 's as good as settled 1891. b. We have at last settled that Business 1687. c. But settling upon new clothes is so trying HARDY. 2. In settling the value of a copyhold fine 1883. The dispute at Llandulas quarries has been settled 1886. 4. b. The 'settling' days occur twice in each month, when the transactions of the preceding fortnight are settled for in cash 1873.

Settled (se·t'ld), *ppl. a.* 1556. [f. prec. + -ED¹.] In various senses of the vb.; firmly fixed, established, determined, etc.; **b.** *spec.* (Of weather of a specified kind.) Established and maintaining itself without change 1628; (of weather without specification) calm and fine 1717. Hence †**Se·ttledly** *adv.*, **-ness.**

Settlement (se·t'lměnt). 1626. [f. SETTLE *v.* + -MENT.] **I. 1.** The act of fixing (a person or thing) in a secure or steady position; the state of being so fixed. **b.** Establishment in life, in marriage, in an office or employment, in a permanent abode, (in Presbyterian churches) in a pastoral charge 1651. **c.** Legal residence or establishment in a particular parish, entitling a person to relief from the poor rates; the right to relief acquired by such residence 1662. **2.** The act of settling as colonists or new-comers; the act of peopling or colonizing a new country, or of planting a colony 1675.

1. b. Every Man..Applies himself..toward the Attaining of his End; whether it be Honour, Wealth, Power, or any other sort of Advantage, or S. in the World 1692.

II. 1. The act or process of regulating or putting on a permanent footing; the act of establishing (public affairs, etc.) in security or tranquillity; a settled arrangement, an established order of things 1645. **b.** Decision of a question, dispute, etc.; the establishing of an opinion, the text of a document, etc. 1777. **2.** *Law.* The act of settling property upon a person or persons; the particular terms of such an arrangement; the deed or instrument by which it is effected. Often *spec.* = *marriage s.* 1677. **b.** *U.S.* A sum of money or other property granted to a minister on his ordination, in addition to his salary 1828. **3.** The settling or payment of an account; the act of coming to terms (*with* a person) 1729. **b.** *spec.* The fortnightly (or, for government securities, monthly) settling of accounts on the Stock Exchange 1772. **4.** In India: The process of assessing the government land-tax over a specific area 1789.

1. The s. that should be made after the war 1900. 2. Your wife..may..claim a s. out of it for herself and her children 1858.

III. 1. The act of settling and clarifying after agitation or fermentation 1626. **2.** A sinking down or subsidence (of a structure, loose earth, etc.) 1793. **3.** The process of becoming calm or tranquil 1837.

IV. An assemblage of persons settled in a locality. **1.** A community of the subjects of a state settled in a new country; a tract of country so settled, a colony, esp. one in its earlier stages 1697. **2.** In the outlying districts of America and the Colonies: A small village or collection of houses. Also, the huts forming the living quarters of the slaves on a plantation. 1827. **3.** An establishment in the poorer quarters of a large city where educated men or women live in daily personal contact with the working class for co-operation in social reform 1884.

1. *Back s.*: see BACK *a.* 1. *Straits Settlements*, the British possessions in the Malay Peninsula.

Settler (se·tləɹ). 1598. [f. SETTLE *v.* + -ER¹.] **1.** One who or a thing which settles, fixes, decides, etc. **b.** *colloq.* Something that settles or 'does for' a person, a finisher; a crushing or finishing blow, shot, speech, etc. 1744. **2.** One who settles in a new country; a colonist 1695. **b.** *gen.* One who settles in a place as a resident 1815. **3.** *Law.* = SETTLOR 1800. **4.** A pan or vat into which a liquor is run off to 'settle' or deposit a sediment 1674.

1. b. This was a s.; I could make no answer to that HOGG. 2. The half-pay provincial officers are valuable settlers 1786.

Settling (se·tliŋ), *vbl. sb.* 1440. [-ING¹.] The action of SETTLE *v.* **1.** The action of fixing, establishing, arranging permanently, deciding, coming to rest, etc. 1553. **2.** The adjusting or liquidating of accounts; also *s. up* 1761. **b. Settling day,** a day appointed for settling accounts; *spec.* the fortnightly pay-day on the Stock Exchange 1806. **3.** The action of sinking down, subsiding, forming a deposit or sediment, etc.; also, the result of this 1440. **b.** *concr.* Sediment, lees, dregs. Chiefly *pl.* 1594.

Settlor (se·tlǫɹ). 1818. [Altered f. SETTLER; see -OR 2 d.] *Law.* One who makes a settlement of property.

Set-to (set,tū·). *Pl.* **set-tos** (-tū·z). 1743. [f. vbl. phr. *set to.*] **a.** orig. *Pugilism.* The action of 'setting to'; hence, a bout or round; a pugilistic encounter or boxing match. **b.** *gen.* and *fig.* A fight, contest (often, a verbal dispute, sharp argument) 1794. **c.** An attack or 'go' (*at*) 1801. **d.** *Racing.* The struggle at the end of a race between two horses that are nearly equal 1842.

Setule (sī·tiul, se·tiul). 1826. [ad. mod.L. *setula* (also used), dim. of *seta* SETA.] A small seta or bristle. Hence **Se·tulose, Se·tulous** *adjs.* covered with setules.

Setwall (se·twǫl). ME. [a. AF. *zedewale* = OF. *citoual, citual,* etc., ad. med.L. **zedoale*, var. *zedoarium*, ad. Arab. *zedwār*; see ZEDOARY.] †**1.** = ZEDOARY -1640. **2.** The plant valerian, *Valeriana pyrenaica* 1548.

‖**Sève** (sę̄v). 1742. [F., = sap.] The fineness and strength of flavour proper to a wine.

Seven (se·v'n), *a.* and *sb.* [Com. Teut.: OE. *seofon*:—OTeut. **sebun*, cogn.w. Skr. *saptá*, Gr. ἑπτά, L. *septem*, OSl. *sedmĭ*.] The cardinal number next after six, represented by the symbols 7, VII, vii. **A.** *adj.* **1.** In concord with a sb. expressed. **b.** Used predic. 1622. **c.** Used (*a*) symbolically, often denoting completion or perfection (esp. in echoes of the Bible), or (*b*) typically, in expressions of time, etc. for a large number or quantity OE. **2.** With ellipsis of sb. OE. **3. a.** Multiplying another numeral OE. **b.** Coupled with a higher (cardinal or ordinal) numeral, so as to form a compound (cardinal or ordinal) numeral OE. **c.** Forming fractional numerals 1726.

1. When s. girls succeed each other in one family 1865. *S. days.* a week; the period of the Creation; in England a common term of imprisonment. *S. months' child*, one born at the seventh month; a type of weakliness. b. The stars in her hair were s. ROSSETTI. c. Add thy Spear, A Weavers beam, and s.-times-folded shield MILT. †*This s. year(s*, etc. (= a long period). 2. Sure it is no sinne, Or of the deadly seuen it is the least SHAKS. *S.* (i.e. hours) *o'* (†*of the*, †*a*) *clock*; also simply *s.*; *half-past s., s. fifteen,* etc. *To be more than s.*, to 'know one's way about'. *The S.*, (*a*) the seven deacons of Acts vi. 5; †(*b*) The Seven Sages of Greece (see SAGE *sb.*² B); (*c*) the seven Argive heroes that made war against Thebes. 3. Tomorrow I may be Myself with Yesterday's Sev'n Thousand Years FITZGERALD. b. The seuen and sixtieth Chapter 1579. Slashed by s.-and-twenty wounds CARLYLE.

Special collocations: **S. bishops,** those who protested against James II's Declaration of Indulgence in 1688. **S. champions,** the national saints of England, Scotland, Wales, Ireland, France, Spain, and Italy, viz. George, Andrew, David, Patrick, Denys, James, and Anthony. **S. Seas,** the Arctic, Antarctic, North and South Pacific, North and South Atlantic, and Indian Oceans.

B. *sb.* **1.** The abstract number seven OE. **2.** A set of seven persons or things 1590. **b.** A playing card marked with seven pips 1656. †**3.** In the game of hazard, with ref. to the throwing of a main -1839. **4.** A person or thing numbered seven in a set or series, e.g. in an eight-oared boat, the rower occupying the seat behind stroke. Also *number s.* 1830.

1. *At sixes and sevens*: see SIX *sb.* 2. 2. Of euery cleane beast thou shalt take to thee by seuens *Gen.* vii. 2. b. With the s. and eight of diamonds 1783. 3. *Seven's the main*: see MAIN *sb.*²; A gambling-house, whence many a bout of seven's-the-main..has been had THACKERAY.

Comb.: **s.-bore**, a shot-gun with calibre seven; **-gills**, a shark of the genus *Heptanchus* or *Notidanus*.

Seven-day(s, -days', *attrib. phr.* 1797. **1.** Consisting of or extending over seven days or a week 1823. **2.** *Seven-day(s disease*, a form of tetanus 1797.

Sevenfold (se·v'nfōᵘld), *a.* and *adv.* [OE. *seofonfeald*; see SEVEN and -FOLD.] **A.** *adj.* **1.** Consisting of seven together or seven in one; having seven parts, divisions, elements, or units. **b.** *Theol.* [tr. eccl. L. *septiformis*.] Applied to seven gifts of the Holy Ghost enumerated in Isaiah xi. 2; see also Rev. i. 4. OE. **2.** Seven times as great or numerous; seven times increased or repeated. Hence, typically = very great, strong, etc. OE. **3.** Seven in number. *poet.* 1614.

1. From seuenfold Nilus to Taprobany GREENE. b. Thou the anointing Spirit art, Who dost thy s. gifts impart 1627. 2. A s. night of superstition and unbelief 1872. 3. Thebes of the gates s. MORRIS.

B. *adv.* In a sevenfold manner or degree; seven times. Hence, exceedingly, greatly. ME. The population..has multiplied s. MACAULAY.

Se·ven-hilled, *a.* 1608. Standing on seven hills; epithet of the city of Rome.

Se·ven-league(d, *a.* 1799. *Seven-league(d boots* [F. *bottes de sept lieues*], the boots in the fairy story of Hop o' my Thumb, which enabled the wearer to cover seven leagues at each step. Hence allus. = of enormous size or speed.

Sevenpence (se·v'npěns). 1671. [f. SEVEN + PENCE.] A sum equal to seven pennies.

Sevenpenny (se·v'npěni), *a.* late ME. [See PENNY *sb.*] Costing or valued at sevenpence; hence, †trifling, contemptible.

Seven sisters. ME. **1.** The Pleiades. **2.** *Hist.* Seven cannon, resembling each other in size and make, cast by Robert Borthwick and used at the battle of Flodden 1513.

Seven sleepers. OE. [tr. L. *septem dormientes*.] Seven youths of Ephesus said to have hidden in a cave during the Decian persecution and to have slept there for several hundred years. Also occas. *transf.* in *sing.*

†**Seven stars.** [OE. *seofon steorran*.] **a.** The Pleiades. **b.** The Great Bear. -1860.

Seventeen (sev'ntī·n, se·v'ntīn; see -TEEN), *a.* and *sb.* [OE. *seofontiene, -tēne, -týne*; see SEVEN and -TEEN.] The cardinal number next after sixteen, composed of ten and seven, represented by the symbols 17, XVII, xvii. **A.** *adj* **1.** In concord with a sb. expressed. Also, qualifying a higher numeral. **2.** With various ellipses, esp. of *years* ME.

1. There was an old woman toss'd in a blanket, S. times as high as the moon 17.. **2.** From seuentene to seuen and twentie (the most dangerous tyme of all a mans life) ASCHAM. *Sweet s.*, used typically for the most attractive period of a girl's life.

B. *sb.* The abstract number seventeen; the symbol representing this 1594.

Seventeenth (sev'ntī·nþ, se·v'ntīnþ), *a.* and *sb.* [OE. *seofontéoþa*; see prec. and -TEENTH.] **A.** *adj.* The ordinal number corresponding to the cardinal seventeen; qualifying a sb. expressed or implied. **B.** *sb.* **1.** A seventeenth part 1728. **2.** *Mus.* A note seventeen degrees above or below a given note (both notes being counted); the interval between, or consonance of, two notes seventeen degrees apart; a chord containing this interval 1597.

Seventh (se·v'nþ), *a.* and *sb.* [OE. (Anglian) *seo-, siofunda*, ME. *sevende* :—OTeut. **seƀunþo-*; also ME. *seventhe*, a new formation on SEVEN and -TH.] The ordinal number corresponding to the cardinal SEVEN. **A.** *adj.* **1.** In concord with a sb. expressed or understood. **b.** With various ellipses 1598. **2.** *S. heaven*: see HEAVEN *sb.* 1818. **3.** = SEVENTHLY (*rare*) 1576.

1. **b.** He ordered me to picket two squadrons of the s. 1841.

B. *sb.* **1.** = Seventh part 1557. **2.** *Mus.* **a.** A note seven degrees above or below a given note (both notes being counted); the note immediately below the octave in a scale = *leading note.* **b.** The interval between two notes seven degrees apart. **c.** (In full, *chord of the s.*) A chord consisting of a note together with its third, fifth, and seventh; denominated from that note of the scale which forms the root, as *dominant s.*, *tonic s.* 1591.

Se·venth-day. 1684. The seventh day of the week, Saturday; the (Jewish) Sabbath; *transf.* Sunday 1692. **b.** In the designations of bodies of Christians who observe the seventh day of the week (Saturday) as the principal day of rest and religious observance 1684.

b. *S. adventists*, a millenarian sect holding sabbatarian principles. *S. Baptist*: see SABBATARIAN *sb.* 3.

Seventhly (se·v'nþli), *adv.* 1532. [f. SEVENTH *a.* + -LY [2].] In the seventh place (in an enumeration). **b.** as *sb.* with ref. to the heads of a sermon 1815.

Seventieth (se·v'ntieþ), *a.* ME. [f. next + *-eth*, -TH.] The ordinal numeral corresponding to the cardinal SEVENTY.

Seventy (se·v'nti), *a.* and *sb.* [OE. (*hund*)-*seofontiȝ*; see SEVEN and -TY.] **A.** *adj.* **1.** The cardinal number equal to seven tens, represented by 70, LXX, or lxx: **a.** with sb. expressed or implied. **b.** With various ellipses. late ME. **2.** In comb. with numbers below ten (ordinal and cardinal), as *seventy-one, one and s., s. and one, seventy-first*; often with ellipsis (e.g. of *years*) ME.

1. A ship..that carried s. guns CLARENDON. **b.** My first friendship at sixteen, was contracted with a man of s. POPE. *The S.*, (*a*) the s. disciples of our Lord whose mission is recorded in Luke x. 1; (*b*) = SEPTUAGINT. **2.** *S.-five* (= F. *soixante-quinze*), a French rapid firing 75 mm. field gun. *S.-four*, a ship carrying s.-four guns (now *Hist.*). *S. twos, s.-twomo* [= 72mo], the size of the page of a book in which each leaf is one s.-second part of a whole sheet.

B. *sb.* **1.** A set of seventy persons or things 1590. **2.** *The seventies*: the decade 70 to 79 in a century or in a person's life 1865.

Seven year(s, -years', *attrib. phr.* 1593. Consisting of or lasting for seven years; having a period of seven years.

†*These* (*this*) *seven years day*, this long time. *Seven Years' War*, the third Silesian war (1756–63), in which Austria, France, Russia, Saxony, and Sweden were allied against Frederick II of Prussia.

Sever (se·vəɪ), *v.* late ME. [a. AF. *severer*, OF. *sevrer* to wean:—pop. L. **seperare*, L. *separare* to SEPARATE.] **I.** *trans.* **1.** To put apart, set asunder (two or more persons or things, or one *from* another). †**b.** To part or remove by some technical process (a substance) *from* another with which it is combined or mixed –1796. †**c.** (In Biblical language.) To set apart or segregate for a special purpose. Also with *out.* –1718. **2.** To separate in thought or idea; to distinguish, treat as distinct; to mark off *from.* late ME. **3.** To keep distinct or apart by an intervening barrier or space. Of the intervening medium: To occupy the space or interval between. late ME. **4.** To divide into (two or more) parts. Now *rare* or *Obs.* exc. as in 5. late ME. **5.** To part or divide suddenly or forcibly; to cut in two, cleave or rend asunder. late ME. **b.** To break up, scatter, disperse (an assemblage or company of individuals). Now *rare.* late ME. **6.** 'To part by violence from the rest' (J.); to separate suddenly and forcibly; to cut, tear, or pull off 1626. **7.** *Law.* **a.** To divide (a joint estate) into independent parts 1544. **b.** To detach (growing fruit or trees, minerals, fixtures, etc.) from the soil 1602. **c.** To separate and remove (one of the plaintiffs in a joint action, when he is nonsuited) 1602. **d.** To part (two or more defendants) in their trial 1660. **8.** *absol.* To make a separation or division (*between*). *rare.* 1611.

1. Least harm Befall thee sever'd from me MILT. Her lips are sever'd as to speak TENNYSON. A revolution which severed England from the papacy 1856. **2.** He is a poor Divine that cannot s. the good from the bad 1654. **3.** Immense The space that severed us! WORDSW. **5.** Thus it was that this great tie was severed 1861. **6.** I struck, and with a single blow The tangled root I severed WORDSW.

II. *intr.* **1.** Of a person: To go away, part, be sundered *from.* Of two or more: To be separated, quit each other, go asunder, part. late ME. **b.** Of things 1545. **c.** Of a whole or aggregate: To part, become divided, be separated into parts. late ME. **2.** *Law.* **a.** Of two or more defendants: To plead independently 1625. **b.** Of joint tenants: To divide their jointure 1895.

1. Ae fond kiss, and then we s. BURNS. **2. a.** The defendants had severed in their defence to the action 1884. Hence **Se·verable** *a.* capable of being severed.

Several (se·vĕrăl), *a.*, *adv.*, and *sb.* late ME. [a. AF., ad. med.L. *separalis*, f. L. *separ* separate, distinct.] **A.** *adj.* **I.** Existing apart, separate. †**1.** Having a position, existence, or status apart; separate, distinct –1707. **2.** Qualifying a pl. sb.: Individually separate, different 1445. **b.** In legal use: More than one 1531. **3.** Being one of a number of individuals of the same class 1543. **4.** As a vague numeral: Of an indefinite (but not large) number exceeding two or three; more than two or three but not very many. (The chief current sense.) 1661. †**b.** A good many –1753. **c.** *ellipt.* and *absol.*, esp. followed by *of* 1685. †**5.** Of diverse origin or composition –1674.

1. The Reeve, the Miller, and the Cook, are s. Men DRYDEN. **2.** It seems to have been built at s. times, and by different Persons 1710. Three s. pillars, each a rough-hewn stone WORDSW. Now combine These s. propositions 1866. **b.** S. counts on the same cause of action shall not be allowed 1853. **3.** *Every* or *each s.*: every or each individual or single; Ile kisse each seuerall paper, for amends SHAKS. **4.** Some of the men..remembered..to have seen s. strangers on the road STEVENSON. **c.** There are still s. of these Topicks that are far from being exhausted ADDISON.

II. Pertaining to an individual person or thing. **1.** Chiefly *Law.* (Opp. to *common.*) Private; privately owned or occupied. late ME. **2.** Belonging, attributed, or assigned distributively to certain individuals referred to; different for each respectively 1457. **3.** *Law.* (Opp. to *joint.*) Pertaining separately to each of the tenants of an estate, parties to a bond or suit, etc. Of inheritance, tail: By which land is conveyed or entailed to two persons separately by moieties. Of an obligation to which several are parties: Enforceable against each of the parties independently of the others 1532.

1. The commons..are inclosed, made seueral 1583. *S. fishery*, a right to fish derived through or on account of ownership of the soil. **2.** Bid each kinde their severall places fill P. FLETCHER. While each pursues his s. road WORDSW. **3.** The..rule of law is, that a contract of s. persons is joint and not s. 1863.

†**B.** *adv.* = SEVERALLY *adv.* –1777. **C.** *sb.* **1.** **In several** [AF. *en several*]: †**a.** Of land, pasture: As private property; in private hands, under separate ownership, not common –1707. **b.** Separately, individually; apart from others or the rest; as a separate member, unit, etc. Now *rare.* 1586. **2.** Land in private ownership or over which a person has a particular right; chiefly, a plot of such land; *esp.* enclosed pasture land, as opp. to common. *Obs.* exc. *dial.* 1460. †**b.** *gen.* Private property or possession –1642. **3.** *pl.* †**a.** Particular or individual points, parts, or qualities; particulars, details –1703. †**b.** Individual persons or things –1650. **c.** Several persons or things. *Sc.*, *Ir.*, and *U.S.* 1654.

1. **a.** Good store of Pasture, either in s. or common 1707. **b.** They all, will fight in seuerall then CHAPMAN. **3. a.** All our abilities, gifts, natures, shapes, Seuerals and generals of grace SHAKS. **b.** *Wint. T.* I. ii. 226.

Se·veral-fold, *a.*, *adv.*, and *sb. rare.* 1738. [f. SEVERAL *a.* + -FOLD.] Used like MANIFOLD, but with the implication of not very many.

Severality (sevĕræ·lĭti). *rare.* 1562. [f. as prec. + -ITY.] *pl.* Individual or particular points, matters, or objects.

Se·veralize, *v. rare.* 1645. [See -IZE.] *trans.* To separate or distinguish (*from*).

Severally (se·vĕrăli), *adv.* late ME. [-LY [2].] **1.** Separately, individually; each of a number of persons or things by himself or itself; each successively or in turn. **b.** In legal language, opp. to *jointly* 1447. **2.** Apart from others or from the rest; not together or in a company; independently. *arch.* 1530. **3.** Respectively 1585. †**4.** Differently, variously –1644.

1. He turned s. to each for their opinion GOLDSM. **2.** Abraham, Isaac, and Jacob..to whom the Promise of the Blessed Seed was s. made 1709. **3.** The parts which I and they have s. taken 1827.

Severalty (se·vĕrălti). 1449. [a. AF. *severalte, -aute*; see SEVERAL *a.* and -TY.] **1.** The condition of being separate or distinct; separateness, distinctness, independence. **2.** Land held by an individual not joined with other owners. The condition of land so held; a state of being owned by individuals. 1570.

2. Till land is placed in a state of s.,..inclosures are seldom erected in any country 1814.

Phr. **In severalty** [AF. *en severalte*]. **a.** *Law.* Of land: (Held) in a person's own right without being joined in interest with another (opp. to joint-tenancy, coparcenary, and tenancy-in-common); (held) as private enclosed property (opp. to common). **b.** Separately, apart from others, particularly. **c.** In or into several divisions or parts.

Severance (se·vĕrăns). late ME. [a. AF., OF. *sevrance*, f. *sevrer* SEVER *v.*; see -ANCE.] **1.** The act or fact of severing; the state of being severed; separation. **2.** *Law.* **a.** The division of a joint estate into independent parts; the destruction of the unity of interest in a joint estate 1539. **b.** The detaching of fruit, minerals, fixtures, etc. from the soil 1602. **c.** The separation of two or more parties joined in a writ 1607.

1. Our s. from the British empire 1787. To draw..lines of s. between truth and falsehood GLADSTONE.

Severe (sĭvī·ɹ), *a.* 1548. [a. F. *sévère* or ad. L. *severus.*] **I.** Rigorous in condemnation or punishment. **1.** Of persons, their disposition, etc.: Rigorous in one's treatment of, or attitude towards, offenders; unsparing in the exaction of penalty; not inclined to leniency. Also *absol.* **b.** Of a person's looks, demeanour, etc.: Betokening a severe mood or disposition 1565. **2.** Of law, judgement, punishment, discipline, and the like: Involving strict and rigorous treatment; carried out with rigour; not leaning to tenderness or laxity; unsparing 1562. **b.** Of a compact: Stringent. Of an account: Unsparingly exacted. 1591. **3.** Unsparing in censure, criticism, or reproof 1561.

1. His seuere wrath shall he sharpen for a sword *Wisd.* v. 20. Men of s. tempers 1715. Justice, to herself s. GRAY. **b.** The Iustice,..With eyes seuere, and beard of formall cut SHAKS. **2.** Severer penalties awaited drunkenness, dissipation, or dicing 1861. **b.** Strict and seuere Couenants SHAKS. **3.** Her very appearance was sufficient to silence the severest satirist of the sex GOLDSM. Phr. *To be s. on* (or *upon*): to pass harsh judgement upon, 'to be hard upon'.

II. Conforming to a rigorous standard. **1.** Extremely strict in matters of conduct or behaviour; austere with oneself 1565. **2.** Of intellectual operations, thought, etc.: Conforming to an exacting standard of mental effort; rigidly exact or accurate; not shrinking from what is toilsome or difficult 1605. **3.** Of style, etc.: Shunning redundance or unessential ornament; sober, restrained, austerely simple 1665.

1. Come, you are too seuere a Moraller SHAKS. The Spartan manners were rough, simple, and s. 1828. **2.** Truth s., by Fairy Fiction drest GRAY. *absol.* Happily to steer From grave to gay, from lively to s. POPE. **3.** Even Brummel..was marked by the severest simplicity in dress 1856.

III. Of impersonal agencies: Pressing hardly, rigorous. 1. Of the weather, etc.: Causing great discomfort or injury to living things; very cold, wet or stormy 1676. b. Of fire or light: Painfully or searchingly intense (*rare*) 1652. c. Of an attack of illness or disease: Attended with a maximum of pain or distress, violent 1725. 2. Of pain, suffering, loss, or the like: Grievous, extreme 1742. 3. Of events or circumstances, labour or exercise, a struggle, test, trial, etc.: Hard to sustain or endure; arduous 1774. 4. *colloq.* (chiefly *U.S.*) A vague epithet denoting superlative quality; very big or powerful; hard to beat 1834. 5. quasi-*adv.* Severely 1599.

1. This had been the severest winter that any man alive had known in England EVELYN. c. I finally caught a s. cold 1823. 2. The loss inflicted on the infantry was also s. 1838. 3. The pace was too s. 1867. 5. The Lord shall scoff them, then s. Speak to them in his wrath MILT. Hence **Seve·reness.**

Severely (sĭvīᵊ·ɹli), *adv.* [-LY [2].] In a severe manner, in various senses; phr. *to leave* or *let s. alone*, to avoid, ignore, or isolate deliberately or of set purpose.

Severity (sĭve·rĭti). 1481. [a. F. *sévérité*, ad. L. *severitas*, f. *severus* SEVERE *a.*; see -ITY.] 1. Strictness or sternness in dealing with others; stern or rigorous disposition or behaviour; rigour in treatment, discipline, punishment, or the like 1530. b. An act or instance of severity 1538. c. Harshness of judgement, criticism, or rebuke. Also *pl.*, severe rebukes or criticisms. 1660. d. Sternness of aspect or countenance; a severe look or expression 1711. 2. Strictness or austerity of life, morals, etc. 1481. 3. Strictness in matters of thought or intellect; rigid accuracy or exactness; undeviating conformity to truth or fact. Also *pl.* instances of this. 1638. 4. Austere purity or simplicity of style, taste, etc. 1709. 5. Rigour or inclemency (of weather or climate); esp. extremity of cold 1676. 6. Violence or acuteness (of illness) 1808. 7. Grievousness (of affliction, penalties, etc.) 1849.

1. Excessive s. in the laws HUME. c. Bacon has been judged with merciless s. 1884. 2. He affected the s. of the Stoic 1741. 3. The process of reasoning called *deductio ad absurdum*, which even the s. of geometry does not reject BURKE. 4. The s. of French taste GOLDSM. 7. The tax falls with excessive and undue s. upon one class 1893.

Severy (se·vĕri). late ME. [ad. OF. **civorie, civoire* :—L. *ciborium* CIBORIUM.] *Arch.* A bay or compartment of a vaulted roof. Also, a compartment or section of scaffolding.

Seville (se·vil), *a.* late ME. [Name (Sp. *Sevilla*) of a city and province of Andalusia, used attrib.] †1. *S. oil*: olive oil brought from S. -1618. 2. *S. orange*: the bitter orange, *Citrus Bigaradia*, used for making marmalade 1593.

‖**Sèvres** (sęvr), *a.* 1764 [Name of a town in France, near Paris.] The designation of a costly porcelain made at Sèvres. Also *absol.*

‖**Sevum** (sī·vŏm). 1440. [L.] Suet, as used in pharmacy.

Sew (sōᵘ), *v.*[1] Pa. t. **sewed** (sōᵘd). Pa. pple. **sewed, sewn** (sōᵘn). [Com. Teut. and Indo-European: OE. *siwan, siowan* :—OTeut. **siwjan*, cogn. w. L. *suere*, Gr. (κασ-)σύειν, Skr. *siv.*] 1. *trans.* To fasten, attach, or join (pieces of textile material, leather, etc.) by passing a thread in alternate directions through a series of punctures made either with a needle carrying the thread, or with an awl; to make the seams of (a garment, etc.). b. *Surgery.* = *s. up*: see 4 a 1502. c. *Bookbinding.* To fasten together the sheets of (a book) by passing a thread or wire backwards and forwards through the back fold of each sheet, so as to attach it to the bands: dist. from *stitch* 1637. 2. *absol.* and *intr.* To work with a needle and thread 1450. 3. *trans.* = *s. up*: see 4 b ME. 4. **S. up.** a. To close (an orifice, a wound, also anything that envelops) by stitching the edges together 1490. b. To enclose *in* a cover or receptacle and secure it by sewing 1611. c. *slang.* (*a*) To tire out (a horse) 1826. (*b*) To tire out, exhaust (a person); to nonplus, bring to a standstill; to put *hors de combat*; to outwit, cheat, swindle 1837. (*c*) To make hopelessly drunk 1829.

1. Shoes, That are wel sowed 1576. To S. on a Button 1855. 3. The diamonds were sewed into her habit THACKERAY. 4. c. (*b*) 'Busy!' replied Pell; 'I'm completely sewn up' DICKENS. Hence **Sewed** (sōᵘd) *ppl. a.* joined, etc. by stitching (esp. of books). **Sewer** (sōᵘ·əɹ) *sb.*[3] one who sews.

†**Sew**, *v.*[2] 1440. [Back-formation from SEWER *sb.*[2]] *trans.* To place (food) on the table as a sewer does; *intr.* to act as a sewer -1609.

Sew (siū), *v.*[3] 1513. [a. OF. **sewer*, aphet. f. *essewer, essever* :—pop. L. **exaquare*, f. L. *ex-* out + *aqua* water.] 1. *trans.* To drain, draw off the water from. Now *dial.* 2. *intr.* Of a liquid: To ooze out. (Said also of the containing vessel.) Now *dial.* 1565. 3. *Naut.* Of a ship: To be grounded or high and dry; to have its water-line (so much) above the water 1588.

3. If the water has left her two feet, she has sued two feet 1882.

Sewage (siū·ĕdʒ), *sb.* 1834. [Formed after SEWER *sb.*[1] by substitution of suffix; see -AGE.] 1. Refuse matter conveyed in sewers. 2. = SEWERAGE 1, 2. *rare.* 1834.

1. *fig.* The literary s. which is pouring forth from the Paris press 1884.

attrib. and *Comb.*: **s. farm,** a farm on which s. irrigation is practised; so **s. farming; s. grass,** grass grown on land fertilized by s.; **s. irrigation,** the system of disposing of liquid s. by turning it on to land. Hence **Sew·age** *v. trans.* to irrigate or fertilize with s.; to drain with sewers.

Sewellel (sĭwe·lĕl). 1814. [Columbia River Indian.] A small rodent, *Haplodon rufus*, of the Western coast of the U.S. Called also *mountain-beaver.*

Sewer (siū·əɹ), *sb.*[1] late ME. [a. AF. OF. (north-eastern) *se(u)wiere* channel to carry off overflow from a fishpond :—L. **exaquaria*, f. **exaquare* (L. *ex-* out + *aqua* water).] 1. An artificial watercourse for draining marshy land and carrying off surface water into a river or the sea. Also *water-s.* 2. An artificial channel or conduit, now usu. covered and underground, for carrying off and discharging waste water and the refuse from houses and towns 1606.

2. *Common s.*, a drain through which all or a large part of the sewage of a town passes, a main drain collecting and discharging the contents of auxiliary drains: *fig.* London! the needy villain's general home. The common s. of Paris, and of Rome JOHNSON.

Comb.: **s.-air, gas,** atmospheric air mixed with gas formed by the decomposition of sewage; **-rat,** the brown rat (*Mus decumanus*) common in sewers and drains. Hence **Sew·er** *v. trans.* to furnish (a town, road, etc.) with a system of sewers.

Sewer (siū·əɹ), *sb.*[2] Now *Hist.* late ME. [Aphetic a. AF. *asseour*, f. OF. *asseoir* to cause to sit, seat :—L. *assidere*, f. *ad* + *sedere* to sit.] An attendant at a meal who superintended the arrangement of the table, the seating of the guests, and the tasting and serving of the dishes. Formerly an officer of the Royal Household.

The s. with savoury meats Dish after dish, served them COWPER.

Sewerage (siū·ərĕdʒ). 1834. [f. SEWER *sb.*[1] + -AGE.] 1. Drainage by means of sewers; a system of draining by sewers. 2. *concr.* Sewers collectively; the system of sewers draining a particular locality 1834. 3. Sewage 1851.

Sewin (siū·in). 1532. [Origin obsc.] A fish of the salmon tribe (*Salmo cambricus* or *eriox*), the bull-trout, found in Welsh rivers.

Sewing (sōᵘ·iŋ), *vbl. sb.* ME. [f. SEW *v.*[1] + -ING [1].] 1. The action of SEW *v.*[1]; the use of a needle and thread; the uniting of pieces of material, etc. by this means. 2. *concr.* Work sewn; materials to be sewn; the stitches or seams of anything. late ME. 3. *pl.* Sewing thread or silk 1844.

attrib. and *Comb.* as *s.-class, -cotton, -maid*, etc.; **s.-machine,** a machine which performs the operation of sewing.

Sewn (sōᵘn), *ppl. a.* 1866. [pa. pple. of SEW *v.*[1]] Stitched, fastened by means of sewing. Chiefly with prefix, as *hand-s., machine-s.*

Sex (seks), *sb.* late ME. [ad. L. *sexus.*] 1. Either of the two divisions of organic beings distinguished as male and female respectively; the males or the females (esp. of the human race) viewed collectively. 2. Quality in respect of being male or female 1526. 3. The distinction between male and female in general. In recent use: The sum of those differences in the structure and function of the reproductive organs on the ground of which beings are distinguished as male and female, and of the other physiological differences consequent on these; the class of phenomena with which these differences are concerned 1631. ¶4. Used, by confusion, in senses of SECT 1575.

1. *The fair(er), gentle(r), soft(er), weak(er) s., the devout s., the second s.*, the female sex, women. *The sterner s.*, men. *The s.*, the female sex (now *rare*). Cf. F. *le (beau) sexe.* 3. *Organs of s.*, the reproductive organs in sexed animals or plants.

Comb. **s.-cell,** a reproductive cell, with either male or female function; a sperm-cell or an egg-cell. b. Characterized by excessive or morbid consciousness of sex; pertaining to the reactions of a member of one sex to a member of the other; as *sex appeal, instinct, urge.*

Sex (seks), *v.* 1884. [f. prec.] *trans.* To determine the sex of, by anatomical examination; to label as male or female.

Sex- (seks), repr. L. *sex* six in comb. (as in *sexennis* SEXENNIAL), occurs in many mod. formations, chiefly scientific or technical.

1. Forming parasynthetic compounds, as *sexlocular, sexradiate*, adjs.; **sexdi·gital, -di·gitate(d)** *adjs.*, having six digits (fingers or toes); **sexdi·gitism,** the condition of having six digits; **sexdi·gitist,** one who has six digits. b. *Chem.* In the name of classes of compounds, denoting the presence of six atoms, molecules, or combining proportions of the substance indicated by the second part of the compound, as *sexdecyl*, etc. Also in **sexva·lent** *a.*, having an equivalence of six, combining with or replacing six hydrogen atoms. 2. Combined with a numerical element: **sexde·cimo** = SEXTO-DECIMO; **sexmille·nary, -mille·nial** *adjs.*, of 6,000 years.

Sexagenarian (se:ksădʒĭnēᵊ·riăn), *a.* and *sb.* 1738. [f. L. *sexagenarius*; see next and -IAN.] A. *adj.* Of the age of sixty years. Also, characteristic of one sixty years old. 1862. B. *sb.* A person sixty years old 1738. Hence **Sexagena·rianism,** the state of being sixty years old.

Sexagenary (seksæ·dʒĭnări), *a.* and *sb.* 1594. [ad. L. *sexagenarius*, f. *sexageni* sixty each, distributive of *sexaginta* sixty.] A. *adj.* 1. *Math.* Of or belonging to the number 60; composed of or proceeding by sixties; pertaining to a scale of numbers of which the modulus is 60. 2. = prec. A. 1638.

1. *S. arithmetic* = SEXAGESIMAL *arithmetic. S. table*, a table of proportional parts which shows at sight the product or quotient of any two sexagenary numbers.

B. *sb.* †1. *Math., Astr.* = SEXAGESIMAL B. -1728. 2. = prec. B. Now *rare* or *Obs.* 1814.

Se·xagene. Also in L. form. 1570. [ad. mod.L. *sexagena*, fem. sing. f. L. pl. *sexageni, -æ, -a*; see prec.] *Math.* A quantity or number multiplied by sixty or a power of sixty; an arc of sixty degrees.

Sexagesima (seksădʒe·simă). late ME. [eccl. L., fem. (sc. *dies*) of L. *sexagesimus* sixtieth, f. *sexaginta* sixty.] In full *S. Sunday*: the second Sunday before Lent.

Sexagesimal (seksădʒe·simăl), *a.* and *sb.* 1685. [ad. med.L. *sexagesimalis*, f. L. *sexagesimus*, ordinal of *sexaginta.*] A. *adj.* Proceeding by sixties; *esp.* pertaining to, involving, or based upon division into sixty equal parts (as seconds and minutes). b. *S. fraction*: a fraction whose denomination is 60 or a power of 60 1685.

S. arithmetic, a method of computation based upon the number 60. *S. table* = SEXAGENARY *table.*

B. *sb. pl.* Sexagesimal fractions; also, the system of sexagesimal fractions 1685. Hence **Sexage·simally** *adv.* into sixtieths.

Sexcentenary (seks,se·ntĭnări), *a.* and *sb.* 1779. [In A. 1, f. L. *sexcenteni* 600 each; in A. 2 and B, f. SEX- + CENTENARY.] A. *adj.* 1. Pertaining to the number 600. 2. Relating to a period of 600 years 1864. B. *sb.* The six-hundredth anniversary (of an event) 1885.

Sexed (sekst), *a.* 1598. [f. SEX *sb.* + -ED [2].] 1. Pertaining to one or both of the sexes (specified by a prefixed word). 2. Of an animal or plant: Having sex; not neuter or asexual. 1891. Also with prefixed adv., as *highly s., over-s.*

Sexennial (sekse·niăl), *a.* 1646. [f. L. *sexennis* or *sexennium* + -AL 1.] Continuing for a period of six years; occurring every six years. Hence **Sexe·nnially** *adv.*

Sexfoil (se·ksfoil), *a.* and *sb.* 1688. [f. SEX-, after *trefoil*, etc.] A. *adj.* Having six foliations 1848. B. *sb. Arch.* and *Her.* = SIXFOIL 1688. So Se·xfoiled *a.* = A.

Sexi-, occas. used as comb. form of L. *sex* six: Se·xifid = *sexfid* (see SEX- 1). **Sexisylla·bic** *a.*, of six syllables; so **Sexisy·llable.**

Sexless (se·ksles), *a.* 1598. [f. SEX *sb.* + -LESS.] Without sex; lacking the characteristics of sex; asexual. b. *Nat. Hist.* = NEUTER *a.* 4. 1827. Hence **Se·xless·ly** *adv.*, **-ness.**

Sexpartite (sekspā·ɹtəit), *a.* 1760. [ad. mod.L. *sexpartitus*; see SEX- and PARTITE *a.*] Divided into or consisting of six parts.

Sext (sekst). late ME. [In 1, ad. L. *sexta* (sc. *hora* hour), fem. of *sextus* sixth. In 2, ad. L. *sextus* (sc. *liber* book). In 3, ad. L. *sexta* (sc. *pars* part).] 1. *Eccl.* The third of the lesser canonical hours; so called because belonging orig. to the sixth hour of the day (midday). Also *pl.* 2. *Eccl.* The sixth book added to the Decretals by Pope Boniface VIII. 1656. 3. *Mus.* a. An interval of a sixth. b. An organ stop of two ranks of pipes having an interval of a sixth between them 1876.

Sextan (se·kstăn), *a.* 1657. [ad. mod.L. *sextana* (sc. *febris* fever), f. L. *sextus* sixth; see -AN I. 1.] Designating a fever of which the paroxysms recur every fifth (according to old reckoning, every sixth) day.

Sextant (se·kstănt). 1596. [ad. L. *sextant-*, *sextans*, sixth part (of an as, acre, etc.), f. *sextus* sixth; see -ANT [1].] †1. The sixth part of the Roman as -1656. †2. The sixth part of a circle -1730. 3. An astronomical instrument resembling a quadrant, furnished with a graduated arc equal to a sixth part of a circle, used for measuring angular distances between objects, esp. for observing altitudes of celestial objects in ascertaining latitude at sea 1628. 4. *Bot.* Each of a group of six segment-cells 1875. 5. *Astr.* The constellation *Sextans* 1795.

Sextary (se·kstări). late ME. [ad. L. *sextarius* (also used), f. *sextus* sixth; see -ARY.] 1. An ancient Roman liquid measure containing the sixth part of a CONGIUS. 2. A dry measure containing the sixth part of a MODIUS. late ME.

Sextet (sekste·t). Also **-ett.** 1841. [Alteration of SESTET after L. *sex* six.] 1. *Mus.* = SESTET 1. 2. A stanza of six lines 1850. 3. A group or set of six persons or things 1873.

Sextic (se·kstik), *a.* and *sb.* 1853. [f. L. *sextus* + -IC.] *Math.* A. *adj.* Of the sixth degree or order. B. *sb.* A quantic, or equation, of the sixth degree; a curve of the sixth order 1872.

Sextile (se·kstəil, -il), *a.* and *sb.* 1557. [ad. L. *sextilis*, f. *sextus* sixth; see -ILE.] *Astrol.* A. *adj.* S. *aspect*, the aspect of two heavenly bodies which are 60° or one sixth part of the zodiac distant from each other. B. *sb.* A sextile aspect. Phr. *in* (*a*) *s.* 1592.

Sextillion (seksti·lyən). 1690. [ad. F. *sextillion*, f. L. *sex* six, after *septillion*, etc.] *Arith.* The sixth power of a million, denoted by 1 followed by 36 ciphers. In American (and later Fr.) use, the seventh power of a thousand, denoted by 1 followed by 21 ciphers.

Sexto (se·ksto). 1847. [a. L., abl. case of *sextus* sixth; cf. QUARTO, etc.] The designation of the size of a book, or of the page of a book, in which each leaf is one-sixth of a sheet.

Sexto-decimo (sekstoˌde·simo). 1688. [a. L., abl. of *sextus decimus* sixteenth.] = DECIMO-SEXTO, SIXTEENMO.

Sextole (se·kstoul). 1854. [a. G., arbitrarily f. L. *sextus.*] *Mus.* A group of six notes to be played in the time of four. So **Se·xtolet.**

Sexton (se·kstən). ME. [a. AF. *segerstaine* = OF. *segrestein*, *secrestein*, etc., semi-pop. ad. med.L. *sacristanus* SACRISTAN.] 1. A church officer having the care of the fabric of a church and its contents, and the duties of ringing the bells and digging graves. (In pop. use from the 16th c. usu. = bell-ringer and grave-digger.) 2. A sexton beetle 1885.

1. I haue bin sixeteene heere, man and Boy thirty yeares SHAKS.

Comb.: **s. beetle**, a beetle of the genus *Necrophorus*; a burying beetle. Hence **Se·xtoness**, a female s. (or sacristan). **Se·xtonship**, the office or position of a s.

Sextry (se·kstri). late ME. [perh. f. SEXTON after *vestry*, or an alteration of OF. *sacrestie.*] †1. = SACRISTY -1691. 2. The residence of a sacrist or sacristan 1585.

Sextuor (se·kstiuǫɹ). 1824. [a. F., irreg. f. L. *sex* six, after QUATUOR.] *Mus.* = SESTET 1.

Sextuple (se·kstiup'l), *a.* and *sb.* 1626. [ad. med L. **sextuplus*, irreg. f. L. *sex* six, after late L. *quintuplus* QUINTUPLE, etc.] A. *adj.* Sixfold; six times as great or numerous; consisting of six parts or things. B. *sb.* The number which is six times a specified number 1657. Hence **Se·xtuple** *v. trans.* to multiply by six; *intr.* to increase sixfold.

Sextuplet (se·kstiuplet). 1852. [f. SEXTUPLE *a.* after *triplet.*] A group, set, combination, etc. of six things; esp. *Mus.* = SEXTOLE.

Sextuplex (se·kstiupleks), *a.* 1668. [a. med.L., f. L. *sex* six, after *triplex*, etc.] Sixfold. b. *Electric Telegr.* Applied to a system by which six messages may be transmitted simultaneously by the same wire 1889.

Sexual (se·ksiuăl, -kʃu-), *a.* 1651. [a. late L. *sexualis*, f. L. *sexus* SEX.] 1. Of or pertaining to sex or the attribute of being either male or female; existing or predicated with regard to sex. 2. Pertaining to sex as concerned in generation or in the processes connected with this 1799. b. Of or pertaining to the organs of sex 1836. 3. Relative to the physical intercourse between the sexes or the gratification of sexual appetites, as *s. morality*, *excess*, etc. 1878. 4. Of animal and plants: Having sex; sexed; separated into two sexes; having sexual organs; producing offspring by means of sexual congress. (Opp. to *asexual.*) 1830. b. Of reproduction in animals or plants: Taking place by means of the congress of the two sexes. (Opp. to *asexual* or *agamic.*) 1872. 5. Characteristic of or peculiar to the one sex or the other 1815.

1. The stage of s. differentiation HUXLEY. 2. *S. intercourse*, copulation (of human beings). *S. organs*, the organs of s. generation in animals or plants *S. system* (or *method*), the Linnæan classification of plants, based on the differences in their s. organization. b. *S. diseases*, diseases of the s. organs 1898. 4. *S. cell*, a male or a female reproductive cell; a sperm-cell or an egg-cell. 5. *Secondary s. characters*, those marks of sex (e.g. the beard in man, the distinctive plumage in birds) which are not immediately connected with the reproductive structure. Hence **Se·xualist** (*rare*), one who attributes sexuality to certain organisms; an adherent of the 's. system' of botanical classification. **Se·xualize** *v. trans.* to make s., endow with sex, attribute sex to. **Se·xually** *adv.* in a s. manner; with respect to sex.

Sexuality (seksiuæ·lĭti, -kʃu-). 1800. [See SEXUAL *a.* and -ITY.] 1. The quality of being sexual or having sex. 2. Possession of sexual powers, or capability of sexual feelings 1879. 3. Recognition of or preoccupation with what is sexual 1848.

†'Sfoot, *int.* 1602. Short. f. *God's foot* -1662.

‖Sforzando (sfǫɹtsa·ndo). 1801. [It., gerund of *sforzare* to force.] *Mus.* A direction indicating that the note so marked is to be specially emphasized or rendered louder than the rest. Abbrev. *sf.*, *sfz.*

‖Sforzato (sfǫɹtsā·to). 1801. [It., pa. pple. of *sforzare.*] = prec.

‖Sgraffito (sgrafˌfī·to). *Pl.* **sgraffiti** (sgrafˌfī·tī). 1730. [It.; see GRAFFITO; the *s-* repr. L. *ex-* (see EX-).] = GRAFFITO.

Sh, a consonantal digraph representing the simple sound (ʃ). From the time of Caxton it has been the established notation for (ʃ) in all words except those in which (as *machine*, *schedule*, *Asia*, the derivs. in *-tion*, etc.) it is otherwise represented on etymological grounds.

Sh (ʃ), *int.* Also written **'sh** (as if an abbrev. of *hush*). 1847. = HUSH *int.*

†Sh. Abbrev. of SHILLING.

Shab (ʃæb), *sb.* [OE. *sceabb*, f. Teut. **skab* to scratch, SHAVE:—Indo-Eur. **skăbh-*, whence L. *scabies* itch, *scabere* to scratch.] 1. = SCAB *sb.* 1-3. Now *dial.*, a cutaneous disease in sheep. †2. *slang.* A low fellow -1851. Hence **Shabbed** *a.*, †scabby; shabby (*Obs.* exc. *dial.*)

Shab (ʃæb), *v.* *Obs.* exc. *dial.* 1677. [Origin obsc.] 1. *trans.* with *off*: a. To get rid of; get (a person) out of the way. b. To put (a person) off *with* (something unsatisfactory) 1840. 2. *intr.* with *off* or *away*: To slink away, sneak off 1700.

Shabby (ʃæ·bi), *a.* 1669. [f. SHAB *sb.* + -Y [1].] 1. That has lost its newness or freshness of appearance; dingy and faded from wear or exposure 1685. b. Of persons, their appearance, etc.: Poorly-dressed, 'seedy' 1669. c. *transf.* Discreditably inferior in quality, making a poor appearance 1820. 2. Of persons, their actions, etc.: Contemptibly mean, ungenerous, or dishonourable. Often applied to conduct which is less friendly or generous than one had hoped for. 1679. b. Of a gift or the like: Small or poor as estimated by the giver's means 1753.

1. A s. house DICKENS. An old book in a very s. binding 1866. A poacher In s. velveteen 1884. b. A s. old half-pay father 1882. c. My Lord Duke's entertainments were both seldom and s. THACKERAY. 2. A s. excuse THACKERAY. b. This s. present was an insult to us 1857. Hence **Sha·bbi·ly** *adv.*, **-ness.**

Sha:bby-gentee·l, *a.* 1754. Attempting to look genteel and to keep up appearances in spite of shabbiness.

‖Shabracque, shabrack (ʃæb·ræk). 1667. [a. G. *schabracke*, F. *schabraque*, from some lang. of Eastern Europe.] A saddle-cloth used in European armies.

†‖Shabunder (ʃābʊ·ndəɹ). 1599. [a. Pers. *shāh-bandar*, lit. 'king of the port'.] The title of an officer at native ports in the Indian seas, often also head of the customs -1797.

Shack (ʃæk), *sb.*[1] Now *dial.* 1536. [f. *shack*, dial. var. of SHAKE *v.*] 1. Grain fallen from the ear, and available for the feeding of pigs, poultry, etc., after the harvest; a supply of fallen grain for this purpose. Also, fallen beech-mast or acorns. 2. a. In phr. *to be*, *go*, *run at s.*, said of pigs, poultry, etc., when turned into the stubble to feed on the 'shack'. Hence b. The right of sending pigs or poultry to 'run at s.' on another's land after the harvest; also, the right of pasturing cattle in winter on another's land. 1629. 3. An animal or animals 'at s.' 1842.

Shack, *sb.*[2] *dial.* and *U.S.* 1682. [Origin obsc.] 1. An idle disreputable fellow, a vagabond. 2. A worthless horse (*U.S.*) 1911.

1. A fellow..having much the appearance of a town s. BORROW.

Shack, *sb.*[3] *U.S.* and *Canadian.* 1881. [Origin obsc.] A roughly built cabin or shanty of logs, mud, etc.

Shack (ʃæk), *v.*[1] *dial.* 1658. [f. SHACK *sb.*[1]] *trans.* To turn (pigs or poultry, etc.) into stubble-fields; also, of animals, to feed on (stubble). Also *intr.* to feed *upon* stubble.

Shack, *v.*[2] *dial.* 1787. [f. SHACK *sb.*[2]] *intr.* To idle away one's time; to loaf *about.*

Shackbolt (ʃæ·kbōult). 1610. [perh. shortened f. *shackle-bolt*; see next.] *Her.* A shackle or fetter used as a charge.

Shackle (ʃæ·k'l), *sb.* [OE. *sceacul*:— OTeut. **skakulo-*.] I. A kind of fetter. 1. A fetter for the ankle or wrist of a prisoner, usu. one of a pair connected together by a chain, which is fastened to a ring-bolt in the floor or wall of the cell. In OE., a ring or collar for the neck of a prisoner. †2. A fetter-like bond, esp. one used as an ornament, an armlet or anklet (*rare*) -1697. †3. A hobble for a horse -1814.

1. They resolved rather to dye fighting then to live in schackells 1641. *fig.* To knock off the Shackles of Ignorance and Prejudice 1738.

II. In techn. senses. 1. A ring, clevis, or similar device, used for attaching or coupling, so as to leave some degree of freedom of movement; often a U-shaped piece of iron, closed by a movable bar passing through holes in the ends; as, a fastening for a port-hole, a coupling for lengths of chain cable, the hinged and curved bar of a padlock which passes through the staple, etc. ME. 2. *Telegr.* A form of insulator used in overhead lines for supporting the wire where a sharp angle occurs 1855.

Comb.: **s.-bar**, (*a*) the swingle-tree of a coach, etc.; (*b*) *U.S.* the coupling between a locomotive and its tender; **-bolt**, the bolt which passes through the eyes of a s.; (*Her.*) this used as a bearing; **-bone** (*Sc.* and *dial.*) the wrist; **-joint**, (*a*) a joint in the form of a s. (sense II. 1), esp. one for adjusting the tension of rods, wires, etc.; (*b*) a peculiar kind of articulation in the vertebræ of some fishes.

Shackle (ʃæ·k'l), *v.* 1440. [f. prec.] **1.** *trans.* To confine with shackles; to put a shackle or shackles on. **2.** To join, couple, or fix by means of a shackle. Also *intr.* for *refl.* 1834. **3.** *Telegr.* To attach to or furnish with a shackle (SHACKLE *sb.* II. 2) 1852.

1. Edmond Mortimer..whome..Owen Glendor kepte in filthy prison shakeled with yrons 1548. *fig.* The views of Paul were..less shackled by associations 1879.

Shackly (ʃæ·kli), *a.* *U.S.* and *dial.* 1848. [f. *shackle*, freq. of SHAKE *v.*] Shaky, rickety; ramshackle.

Shad (ʃæd). [OE. *sceadd*; origin unkn.] **1.** Any clupeoid fish of the genus *Alosa*; the British species are the allice, *A. communis* or *vulgaris*, and the twaite (or herring-s.), *A. finta*; the common or white s. of America is *A. sapidissima*, and the Chinese s. is *A. reevesi*. **2.** *U.S.* Applied to other fishes, as **gizzard s.**, the genus *Dorosoma*; **green-tailed, hard-head(ed, yellow-tailed s.**, the menhaden; **Ohio s.**, *Pomolobus chrysochloris* 1884.

Comb. (U.S. names of plants which are in flower or fruit when the s. are found in the rivers, and of birds, insects, etc. that appear about that time) **s.-berry**, the s.-bush or its fruit; **-bush**, the genus *Amelanchier*, esp. *A. canadensis*, also called *June-berry* or *service-berry*; **-fly**, a fly which appears when s. are running; **-frog**, *Rana halecina* or *virescens*; **-trout**, the squeteague; **-waiter**, the Menomonee whitefish, *Coregonus quadrilateralis*.

Sha·d-be·lly. *U.S.* 1842. [f. prec. + BELLY *sb.*] In full, *s. coat*, a Quaker coat, so called from its shape; hence a Quaker.

Shaddock (ʃæ·dǫk). 1696. [After a Captain *Shaddock*.] The fruit of *Citrus decumana* (also called POMPELMOOSE) resembling an orange, but very much larger. In stricter use, applied to the large pear-shaped varieties of the species, the smaller and rounder varieties being called *grape-fruit*. **b.** The tree bearing this fruit 1785.

Shade (ʃēd), *sb.* [ME. *schade*, repr. OE. *sceadu*, *scead*. See also SHADOW *sb.*] **I.** Comparative darkness. **1.** Partial or comparative darkness; absence of complete illumination; esp. the comparative darkness caused by a more or less opaque object intercepting the direct rays of the sun or other luminary. **b.** *fig.* Comparative obscurity 1650. **c.** *transf.* A fleeting look of displeasure, a 'cloud' on a person's brow or countenance 1818. **2.** *pl.* **a.** *The shades* (*of night, of evening*, etc.): the darkness of night; the growing darkness after sunset 1582. **b.** *The shades*: the darkness of the nether world; the abode of the dead, Hades 1594. **3.** *Drawing* and *Painting*. Absence of complete illumination as represented pictorially; the part or parts of a picture representing this; the darker colour expressing absence of illumination. Often in *light and s.* 1662. **4.** Degree of darkness or depth of colour; hence, any of the slightly differing varieties of quality that may exist in what is broadly considered as one and the same colour 1690. **b.** *transf.* and *fig.* A minutely-differentiated degree or variety (of a quality, a condition, meaning, etc.). Often advb. with comparatives, *a s. better, less*, etc. 1749. **c.** A tinge, a minute qualifying infusion (of some quality); *colloq.*, a minute quantity or portion added or removed 1791.

1. The pensive s. of twilight was pleasing to her MRS. RADCLIFFE. **b.** Phr. *To be in the s.*, to be in retirement, to be little known. *To cast, throw into the s., put into the s.*, to obscure by contrast of superior brilliancy, to surpass so as to render insignificant. **c.** A s. of annoyance crosses his face 1879. **2. b.** Then let our swords..Dismiss him to the shades 1749. **3.** *fig.* The shades which were in his private conduct, are to be forgotten BOSWELL. *Light and s.*, in a literary work, a musical performance, or the like, the contrast necessary to artistic effect, of passages of lighter and graver tone, or of greater and less brilliancy. **4. b.** Men of all shades of opinion..combined against him 1888. **c.** There was now in his conduct a s. of lunacy SCOTT.

II. 1. A dark figure thrown upon a surface by a body intercepting light; a shadow. Now *dial.* and *poet.* OE. **b.** *fig.* An unsubstantial image of something real; something that has only a fleeting existence, or that has become reduced almost to nothing. Now *poet.* or *rhet.* ME. **2.** The visible but impalpable form of a dead person, a ghost. Also, a disembodied spirit, an inhabitant of Hades (= L. *umbra*). Often collect. pl., *the shades*: the world of disembodied spirits, Hades. 1616. †**b.** A spectre, phantom. SHAKS. **c.** In humorous invocation of the spirit of a deceased person, as likely to be horrified or amazed by some action or occurrence 1818. †**3.** = SILHOUETTE *sb.* 1. –1842.

1. After a few hours, we see the shades lengthen JOHNSON. **b.** They are but shades, not true things where we live SIDNEY. **2.** Where grateful Science still adores her Henry's holy S. GRAY.

III. Protection from glare and heat. **1.** Cover afforded by the interposition of some opaque or semi-opaque body between an object and light, heat, etc.; esp. the shelter from the sun afforded by trees; quasi-*concr.* (*sing.* and *pl.*) overshadowing foliage OE. **2.** A place sheltered from the sun; chiefly, a piece of ground overshadowed by trees. Now *rare* exc. in *collect. pl.*, with poetical colouring. OE. **b.** *transf.* A retired spot. Hence, a quiet habitation. Chiefly *pl.* Now *poet.* or *rhet.* 1605. **3.** Something which affords protection from light, heat, etc.; as a covering worn to protect the eye from light; a globe or cylinder of some semi-transparent substance placed over the flame of a candle, lamp, etc. to soften or diffuse the light; *U.S.* a window-blind; etc. 1624.

1. Vnder the s. of melancholly boughes SHAKS. Phr. *In the s.*, in a position screened from the direct action of the sun's rays; opp. to *in the sun*. **2. b.** In the depth of college shades..the poor student shrunk from observation LAMB. **3.** One shot broke the mirror over the chimney piece, another the s. of the clock KINGLAKE. The two customary candles were burning under their green shades HARDY. Hence **Sha·deful** *a.* (*rare*) abounding in s.; umbrageous.

Shade (ʃēd), *v.* late ME. [f. prec.] **1.** *trans.* To screen from light or heat, to protect from the glare or heat of the sun's rays. †**b.** *transf.* To overshadow protectingly; to protect –1701. **c.** To cover with a screen, to protect (a light) from draughts 1827. **2.** To conceal from view; to hide partially, as by a shadow; to veil, obscure; to disguise 1530. **3.** To cover with shadow, to darken 1599. **b.** To appear like a shadow upon 1704. **4.** *Painting* and *Drawing*. To represent the shade or shadow on (an object); to furnish (a picture) with the indications of shade. In black-and-white or monochrome work: To furnish (a drawing) with the gradated dark markings indicating shade and colour of the object. Hence *occas.* to darken (parts of a diagram, etc.) in a similar manner. 1786. **5. a.** *intr.* Of a colour, hence *gen.*: To pass by imperceptible degrees *to* or *into* something else; also with *away, off* 1819. **b.** *trans.* To change or make to pass by imperceptible degrees *into* something else; also with *away, off* 1818. **c.** To modify the pitch of (an organ pipe) 1890.

1. The overhanging rock That shades the pool SHELLEY. **b.** Now good Angels..s. thy person Vnder their blessed wings SHAKS. **2.** A Seraph wing'd: six wings he wore, to s. His lineaments Divine MILT. **5. d.** *Commerce.* To make a slight or gradual reduction in (prices) 1898.

Shadeless (ʃē·dlės), *a.* 1814. [f. SHADE *sb.* + -LESS.] **1.** Lacking shade, without shelter (from heat, etc.). **2.** Affording no shade 1890. **3.** Not marked by shadows, unrelieved by shade 1835. Hence **Sha·delessness.**

Shading (ʃē·diŋ), *vbl. sb.* 1611. [f. SHADE *v.* + -ING[1].] The action of SHADE *v.* **1.** Protection from light or heat. **2.** Delineation of shade; a marking or colouring resembling this 1663. **3.** A minute variation or difference (of a colour, hence of a quality, species, etc.) 1775. **b.** *S.-off*: decrease in the intensity of a colour, or its passage *into* some other, by imperceptible gradations; also *fig.* of a quality, species, or the like 1858.

Shadoof (ʃădū·f). 1836. [Egyptian Arabic *shādūf*.] A contrivance used in the East for raising water for irrigation purposes, consisting of a rod or pole working upon a pivot, at one end of which is fastened a bucket and at the other a weight to serve as a counterpoise.

Shadow (ʃæ·dou), *sb.* ME. [repr. OE. *scead(u)we*, oblique case of *sceadu*; the nom. sing. is represented by SHADE *sb.* The OTeut. form was prob. **skadwoz* masc. or **skadwā* fem. :—Indo-Eur. **skotwós, -wā*; cf. Gr. σκότος darkness.] **I. 1.** Comparative darkness, esp. that caused by interception of light; a tract of partial darkness produced by a body intercepting the direct rays of the sun or other luminary. **b.** *fig.* Gloom, unhappiness; a temporary interruption of friendship; something that obscures the lustre of a reputation; etc. 1855. **2.** *pl.* The darkness of night; the growing darkness after sunset. late ME. **3.** *Painting* and *Drawing*. = SHADE *sb.* I. 3 (now more usual) 1486.

1. The fronts of the ridges..remain in s. all the day TYNDALL. Phr. *S. of death*, a Biblical expression; in the O.T. = 'intense darkness'; and used chiefly to denote the gloom and horror of approaching dissolution. *The valley of the s. of death* (Ps. xxiii. 4), often applied to the experience of being brought by illness apparently near to the grave. **b.** There never was a s. between us until this accursed affair began 1894.

II. Image cast by a body intercepting light. **1.** The dark figure which a body 'casts' or 'throws' upon a surface by intercepting the direct rays of the sun or other luminary; the image which this figure presents of the form of the intercepting body ME. **b.** As a type of what is fleeting or ephemeral ME. **2.** A reflected image ME. **3.** *fig.* **a.** An unreal appearance; a delusive semblance or image; a vain and unsubstantial object of pursuit. Often contrasted with *substance*. ME. †**b.** Applied rhet. to a portrait as contrasted with the original –1679. **c.** An obscure indication; a symbol, type; a prefiguration, foreshadowing. late ME. **d.** Something of opposite character that necessarily accompanies or follows something else, as shadow does light 1830. **e.** An imitation, copy; a counterpart 1693. **f.** Used to designate a person extremely emaciated or feeble 1588. **g.** An attenuated remnant 1450. **h.** A slight or faint appearance, a trace 1586. **4.** A spectral form, phantom. late ME. **5.** One that constantly accompanies or follows another like a shadow. **a.** A parasite, toady; also (= L. *umbra*) a companion whom a guest brings without invitation 1579. **b.** A spy or detective who follows a person in order to keep watch upon his movements 1859.

1. *fig.* Coming events cast their shadows before CAMPBELL. Phr. *To be afraid of one's own s.*, to be unreasonably timorous. *May your s. never grow (be) less!* may you keep on increasing (in prosperity)! [A Persian phrase.] **b.** Man..passes away Als a shadu on the somers day HAMPOLE. **2.** Such Mirrors ..That you might see your s. SHAKS. **3.** What shadows we are, and what shadows we pursue BURKE. **b.** To your s., will I make true loue SHAKS. **c.** But all these were but fygures and shadowes of thynges to come 1526. **e.** The Roman Empire was the s. of the Popedom 1864. **f.** He appeared to wither into the s. of himself SCOTT. **g.** The prerogative of the Crown was reduced to a s. BROUGHAM. Phr. *S. of a name* = L. *nominis umbra*, a shadowy renown.

III. Shelter from light and heat. **1.** Protection from the sun; shade. Now *rare*. ME. **2.** Overshadowing (of wings, etc.) as affording security; protection or shelter from danger or observation ME. †**3. a.** A handscreen; also, a parasol, sunshade –1623. **b.** A woman's headdress, or a portion of a headdress, projecting forward, so as to shade the face –1641.

Comb.: **s.-boxing**, boxing against an imaginary opponent as a form of training; **s. cabinet**, a cabinet formed by Opposition leaders; **-land**, a place conceived as the abode of phantoms and ghosts, an imaginary land of spirits; **-photograph**, a picture taken by means of the Röntgen rays: hence **-photography**; **s.-test**, (*a*) a method of finding out by refraction whether an eye is myopic or hypermetropic; (*b*) a method of examining the outer side of an eye affected with cataract in its second stage. Hence **Sha·dowless** *a.* casting no s.; having no shadows on its surface; unsheltered from the sun.

Shadow (ʃæ·dou), *v.* [OE. *sceadwian*, f. *sceadu* SHADOW *sb.*] **1.** *trans.* To protect or shelter (a person or thing) from the sun; to shade. Now *rare* or *Obs.* **2.** = OVERSHADOW *v.* 2. Chiefly in Biblical use. *Obs.* exc. *poet.* with *over*. OE. †**3.** To screen, protect from attack; to be a security or protection to; to screen from blame or punishment, or from wrong –1704. **4.** To cast a shadow upon, to cover or obscure with a shadow. late ME. **b.** *intr.* To cast a shadow. Now *rare*. late ME. †**5.** *trans.* To screen from view or knowledge; to keep dark, conceal –1608. **6.** To represent by a shadow or imperfect image; to symbolize, typify, prefigure. Now chiefly with *forth, out.*

1575. †7. To paint the likeness of; to draw or paint (a picture) -1669. †8. To depict the shadows in (an object, a scene); to place the shadows in (a picture); to shade -1821. 9. *intr.* (Also *pass.*) To pass by degrees, shade off *to* or *into* a certain hue 1839. 10. To follow (a person) like a shadow; in mod. journalistic language said of a detective who dogs the steps of a person under surveillance 1602.

2. Let Thy dove S. me over, and my sins Be unremember'd TENNYSON. 3. This tree, So faire and great, that shadowed all the ground SPENSER. 5. *Macb.* v. iv. 5. 6. Augustus is still shadow'd in the Person of Æneas DRYDEN. 10. A Spanish Steamer shadowed by a British Cruiser 1899. Hence **Sha·dowed** *ppl. a.* furnished with or lying in shade; indicated obscurely, disguised. Hence **Sha·dower.**

Shadowgraph (ʃæ·dougraf), *sb.* 1888. [f. SHADOW *sb.* + -GRAPH.] 1. A picture formed by a shadow (usu., of the operator's hands) thrown upon a screen or other lighted surface. 2. A photograph taken by means of X-rays, a radiograph 1896. Hence **Shadowgraph** *v.*

Shadowing (ʃæ·douiŋ), *vbl. sb.* OE. [-ING [1].] The action of SHADOW *v.*: *esp.* 1. The position or distribution of shadow, in a visible object or scene; the placing of the shadows in a picture 1603. 2. An imperfect or obscure representation; a prefiguring or adumbration. Also with *forth.* 1642.

Shadowy (ʃæ·doui), *a.* late ME. [f. SHADOW *sb.* + -Y [1].] 1. Resembling or of the nature of a shadow; unsubstantial; fleeting; spectral; vague. †b. Symbolic, typical -1726. 2. a. Protected from the sun, shaded. late ME. b. Enveloped in shadow 1840. †c. Retired; hence, remote, inaccessible -1613. 3. Casting a shadow, affording shade 1607.

1. Thise shadewy transitorie dignitees CHAUCER. A silken robe of white, That s. in the moonlight shone COLERIDGE. A s. sail, silent and gray, Stole like a ghost across the bay HENLEY. b. Indeed the description is,..typicall and shadowie MILT. 2. a. S. lanes 1824. b. From the s. archway came a shining lantern 1876. 3. The s. palm 1796. Hence **Sha·dowi-ly** *adv.*, **-ness.**

Shady (ʃē·di), *a.* 1579. [f. SHADE *sb.* + -Y [1].] 1. Affording shade. 2. Shaded, protected by shade 1589. 3. †Opaque; also (now *poet.*), not luminous, dark 1605. 4. *colloq.* a. Of questionable merit or prospects of success; uncertain, unreliable 1848. b. Of a nature or character unable to bear the light; disreputable 1862.

1. The s. trees couer him with their shaddow *Job* xl. 22. 2. Her angels face..made a sunshine in the s. place SPENSER. Phr. (fig.) *On the s. side of*, older than (a specified age). 3. From dawning Day till s. Night 1746. 4. a. What looks very well one way may look very s. the other 1858. b. A rather s. attorney 1882. Hence **Sha·diness.**

Shafiite (ʃæ·fiˌəit). 1838. [f. Arab. *shāfiʿī* -ITE [1].] A member of one of the four sects or schools of the Sunnites or orthodox Mohammedans, named from the cognomen (*ash-Shāfiʿī*) of their founder, Abu Abdallah Muhammed ibn Idris, 767–819.

Shaft (ʃaft), *sb.*[1] [Com. Teut.; OE. *sceaft* :—OTeut.**skafto-*, **skaftiz*:—pre-Teut.**skapto-*, *-tis.*] 1. The long slender rod forming the body of a lance or spear, or of an arrow. Also of a staff, harpoon, etc. b. A spear or lance. Now *arch.* OE. 2. An arrow. *Cloth-yard s.*: see CLOTH-YARD. late ME. b. *loosely.* A missile. *rhet.* 1786. c. *transf.* A beam or ray (of light, etc.), a streak of lightning, etc. Chiefly *poet.* late ME. 3. A pole, flagstaff; *spec.* †a maypole. *rare.* OE. 4. A stem, a columnar or straight portion of something. a. The stem or trunk of a tree. Now *rare.* late ME. b. In scientific uses. (*a*) The main stem or scape of a feather 1748. (*b*) The part of a hair between the root and the point 1851. (*c*) *Anat.* The middle portion of a long bone 1835. (*d*) *Ent.* The scape of an antenna or of a halter. c. The part of a candlestick which supports the branches. late ME. d. The part of a chimney between the base and the cornice 1450. e. *Arch.* The body of a column or pillar between the base and the capital 1483. f. The upright part of a cross; *esp.* the part between the arms and the base 1781. g. The long straight handle of a tool, etc.; the shank of an anchor; the stem of a pipe; †the stalk or foot of a goblet or wine-glass 1530. 5. a. *Arch.* A slender column, *esp.* one of the small columns which are clustered round pillars, or used in the jambs of doors or windows, in arcades and the like 1835. b. *U.S.* An obelisk or column erected as a memorial 1847. 6. a. One of the long bars, between a pair of which a horse is harnessed to a vehicle; a thill 1613. b. Either of the two side-pieces of a ladder 1888. 7. *Mech.* A long cylindrical rotating rod upon which are fixed the parts for the transmission of motive power in a machine; also, a separable portion of a line of shafting 1688. 8. *Weaving.* Each of a pair of long laths between which the heddles are stretched; also applied to the pair taken together 1801.

1. b. Hyperion's march they spy, and glitt'ring shafts of war GRAY. 2. The air was darkened by the shafts from the hosts of English archers 1854. *fig.* Shafts Of gentle satire.., That harm'd not TENNYSON. 5. b. The gray s. that commemorated the Morristown dead of the last civil war 1873.

Shaft (ʃaft), *sb.*[2] late ME. [Corresponds in sense to MHG. *schaht*, app. a specific application of LG. *schacht* SHAFT *sb.*[1], the primitive notion being that of something cylindrical.] 1. A vertical or slightly inclined well-like excavation made in mining, tunnelling, etc., as a means of access to underground workings, for hoisting out materials, testing the subsoil, ventilation, etc. 2. *transf.* Applied to other well-like excavations, or passages 1820. Hence **Sha·fting** [2], the sinking of a s.; the shafts of a mine collectively.

Shaft (ʃaft), *v.* 1611. [f. SHAFT *sb.*[1]] 1. *trans.* To fit (an arrow-head, a weapon or tool) with a shaft. 2. To propel (a barge, etc.) with a pole 1869.

Shafted (ʃa·fted), *a.* 1586. [f. SHAFT *sb.*[1] + -ED [2].] Having or furnished with a shaft or shafts. a. *Her.* Of a spear, arrow, etc.: Having the shaft of a specified tincture. b. Furnished with a shaft or handle 1641. c. *Arch.* Ornamented with or resting upon shafts 1801.

c. Hence proceeded the pointed arches, the s. columns 1801.

Shafting [1] (ʃa·ftiŋ). 1825. [f. SHAFT *sb.*[1] + -ING [1].] 1. A system of connected shafts for communicating motion from the prime mover to the machinery. Also, material from which to cut lengths of shafts. 2. Shafts or ornamental columns 1868.

Sha·ftment. *Obs.* exc. *dial.* [OE. *sceaftmund*, f. *sceaft* SHAFT *sb.*[1] + *mund* hand, handbreadth.] The distance from the end of the extended thumb to the opposite side of the hand, used as a measure, = about 6 inches.

Shafty (ʃa·fti), *a.* 1891. [f. SHAFT *sb.*[1] (sense 8) + -Y [1].] Of wool: Having a long, close, strong staple.

Shag (ʃæg), *sb.*[1] [OE. *sceacga* :—**skaggon-*, cogn. w. ON. *skegg* beard (:—**skagjom*), OE. *sceaga* coppice, SHAW.] 1. Rough matted hair, wool, etc. *rare* or *arch.* b. A mass of matted hair; also shreds (of bark) 1607. c. The nap (esp. long and coarse) of cloth 1661. d. A (tangled) mass of shrubs, trees, foliage, etc. 1836. e. *fig.* Roughness, brutality of manner 1784. 2. A cloth having a velvet nap on one side, usu. of worsted, but sometimes of silk. Also, a kind or variety of this. 1592. †3. A garment, rug, or mat of shaggy material -1854. 4. (In full *s. tobacco.*) A strong tobacco cut into fine shreds 1789.

1. d. Dark shags of ling BLACKMORE. e. Ability to smooth The s. of savage nature COWPER.

Shag (ʃæg), *sb.*[2] 1566. [perh. a use of prec., with ref. to the 'shaggy' crest.] A cormorant, esp. the crested cormorant, *Phalacrocorax graculus*, which in the breeding season has a crest of long curly plumes.

Shag (ʃæg), *a.* Now *rare* or *arch.* 1592. [From attrib. use of SHAG *sb.*[1]] 1. Having shaggy hair. †2. Of hair, a mane, etc.: Long and rough, shaggy -1647.

1. Round hooft, short ioynted, fetlocks s., and long SHAKS. So **Shag-haired** *a.* (*arch.*) having shaggy hair 1577.

Shag (ʃæg), *v.* 1596. [f. SHAG *sb.*[1]] †1. *intr.* To be shaggy; to hang down in a shaggy manner (*rare*) -1801. 2. *trans.* To render rough or shaggy, *esp.* the surface of the earth, a rock, etc. (*with* a growth of trees, etc.) 1612.

2. Caverns shag'd with horrid shades MILT.

Shagbark (ʃæ·gbāɹk). *W. Ind.* and *U.S.* 1691. [f. SHAG *a.* + BARK *sb.*[1]] 1. *W. Ind.* A W. Indian tree *Pithecolobium micradenium.* 2. *U.S.* A variety of HICKORY; also the wood or the nut of this tree 1751.

Shagged (ʃægd, ʃæ·gėd), *a.* Now *rare.* [OE. *sceacgede*, f. *sceacga* SHAG *sb.*[1]; see -ED [2].] 1. Having or covered with shaggy hair; rough with hair. Chiefly said of animals. †2. Of textile fabrics, garments: Having a rough or long nap -1691. b. *transf.* Of a hill-side, etc.: Covered with scrub, trees, or some rough or shaggy growth 1820. c. Jagged; having a rough, uneven surface 1589. 3. Of hair, etc.: Long and rough; shaggy 1587.

Shaggy (ʃæ·gi), *a.* 1590. [f. SHAG *sb.*[1] + -Y [1].] 1. Covered with or having long coarse or bushy hair. Of persons: Unkempt. b. *Phys.*, *Path.*, etc. Bristling with hair-like processes 1799. c. *transf.* = prec. 2 b. 1591. d. Having a rough surface 1693. 2. Of hair, etc.: Rough, coarse, tangled 1638. b. *transf.* Of a wood, trees, etc.: Resembling a rough growth of hair 1789.

1. A mounted shepherd on his wild and s. horse 1882. 2. b. Land of brown heath and s. wood SCOTT. Hence **Sha·ggi-ly** *adv.*, **-ness.**

Sha·g-rag, *a.* and *sb.* 1590. [Jingling alteration of SHAKE-RAG.] A. *adj.* Ragged, rascally; shaggy, unkempt. B. *sb.* A ragged, disreputable person; a rascally fellow 1611.

Shagreen (ʃăgrī·n). 1677. [var. of CHAGRIN *sb.*] A species of untanned leather with a rough granular surface, prepared from the skin of the horse, ass, etc., or of the shark, seal, etc., and frequently dyed green. Also, an imitation of this. b. The skin of various sharks, rays, etc., which is covered with close-set calcified papillæ, forming a hard rough surface; used for polishing, etc. 1870. Hence **Sha·gree·ned** *a.* having a roughened surface or appearance like s.; covered with s.

Shah (ʃā). 1564. [a. Pers. *shāh*, shortened from OPers. *χšāyaþiya* king, prob. orig. an adj. = 'mighty', allied to Skr. *kšatra* dominion, Gr. κτᾶσθαι to acquire, get.] A Persian title equivalent to 'king'; in Europe the usual designation of the monarch of Persia, the PADISHAH.

‖**Shaheen** (ʃahī·n). 1839. [Urdū, a. Pers. *shāhīn*, lit. royal (bird), f. prec.] An Indian falcon, *Falco peregrinator* and other species.

‖**Shahi** (ʃā·i). 1566. [Pers. *shāhī* royal, f. SHAH.] Formerly a small silver, now a small copper, coin of Persia.

‖**Shahzadah** (ʃāzā·dă). 1662. [Pers., f. SHAH + *zādah* son.] The son of the Shah; a king's son.

‖**Shaitan** (ʃēitā·n). 1638. [Arab. *shaiṭān*, corruptly a. Heb. *sāṭān* SATAN.] 1. The Devil, Satan; an evil spirit. 2. *transf.* An evil-disposed or vicious person or animal 1834. 3. A dust-storm 1900.

Shake (ʃēik), *sb.* 1565. [f. next.] I. The action or an act of shaking. 1. An act of shaking a person or thing 1581. b. (Usu. in full *a s. of the hand.*) An act of shaking hands or a person's hand, a handshake 1712. c. *S. of the head*: see SHAKE *v.* III. 2. 1713. d. An act of shaking oneself 1712. e. *colloq.* or *slang.* As the type of instantaneous action, esp. in the phr. *in a s.*, *in a brace* or *couple of shakes* 1816. 2. Irregular vibratory or tremulous movement, esp. as the result of impact or disturbance of equilibrium; irregular lateral movement (of something revolving or moving in a line). *Naut.* A fluttering or shivering (of a sail). 1665. b. The shock of an earthquake. Now only *U.S.* 1622. 3. A shivering or trembling of the body or limbs; also, a state of tremor. *The shakes*, nervous agitation caused by fear or horror. 1624. b. An attack of a shaking disease 1782. c. A tremor (in the voice) 1859. 4. *Mus.* A regular and rapid alternation of a note with the note above 1659. 5. A concussion or blow which impairs the stability of something; often *fig.* a damaging blow (e. g. to an institution, a person's health); a shock (to the mind or nerves) 1565.

1. b. Our Salutations..consisting of many kind Shakes of the Hand ADDISON. e. He'll be up at the

church in a couple of shakes BARHAM. 3. b. The Dismal Swamp is a first-rate place for concealment, if you are not afraid of shakes and agues 1867. Phr. *To be no great shakes*, to be nothing extraordinary in ability or importance. *S. out* (Stock Exchange), a crisis in which the weaker speculators are driven out of the market. *S. up*, a rousing up to activity.

II. Something produced by shaking. **1.** A natural cleft or fissure produced during growth or formation 1651. **2.** *U.S.* pl. **a.** A set of barrel staves 1820. **b.** Pieces of split timber, a kind of shingles 1845. **3.** *Printing.* A slur 1888.

1. *Water s.*, a cleft in a rock into which a stream empties itself.

Shake (ʃēⁱk), *v.* Pa. t. **shook** (ʃuk); pa. pple. **shaken** (ʃēⁱ·k'n). [OE. *scacan, scōc, scacen* :—OTeut. **skakan.*] †**I.** *intr.* A poet. word for: To go, pass, move, journey; to flee, depart -1500.

II. To vibrate irregularly. **1.** Of things having freedom of movement: To move irregularly and quickly to and fro, up and down, or from side to side; to quiver, quake, vibrate, waver OE. **2.** Of a thing normally stable or still: To vibrate irregularly, tremble, either as a whole or in its parts, as the result of impact or disturbance of equilibrium. Hence, to totter, lose stability, become weakened. ME. **b.** Of a band of persons: To become unsteady, to reel, give way. late ME. **3.** Of a person, his body, limbs, etc.: To quake or tremble with physical infirmity or disease; to quiver with emotion; to shiver with cold, to quake with fear ME. **b.** To be convulsed with laughter 1728.

1. The mighty pine-forests which s. In the wind 1872. 2. We felt the good ship s. and reel TENNYSON. 3. Her small frame shook with weeping 1909. Phr. *To s. in one's shoes*, to tremble with fear.

III. To cause to vibrate, agitate. **1.** *trans.* To brandish or flourish threateningly (a weapon or something used as a weapon); †to wield. Also, to flourish, wave (something) in ostentation or triumph. OE. **2.** To move to and fro irregularly or tremulously, agitate (some part of the body); (of a bird) to flap, flutter (its wings) esp. as preparing to fly. Also said of a thing personified. late ME. **b.** *refl.* Of a person or animal: To give a shake to his or its body (e.g. in order to throw off wet, snow, dust, etc., or to remove the stiffness caused by repose); *fig.* to bestir oneself. late ME. **3.** *trans.* To cause to move irregularly to and fro by external force; to make to flutter or quiver; to agitate. *Naut.* To cause (a sail) to flutter in the wind. OE. **b.** With additional notion of a purpose of dislodging or discharging something adhering or contained. late ME. **4.** To grasp or seize and move (a person) roughly to and fro ME. **b.** Of an animal: To worry (its antagonist or prey) 1565. **5.** To clasp and move to and fro (another person's hand) as a customary salutation or an expression of friendly feeling 1535. **b.** *absol. To s.* = to shake hands. In mod. use *U.S. slang* (chiefly *imper.*). 1601. **6.** To put into a quaking, quivering, or vibrating motion (a thing normally firm or fixed); to cause (a structure) to totter; hence, to impair the stability of. *To s. down*, to cause to totter and fall. OE. **7.** Of physical infirmity, emotion, etc.: To cause (a person, his frame, etc.) to quiver or tremble; to agitate, convulse. late ME. **b.** To disturb, upset 1567. **c.** To cause (a person, his sides) to quiver with laughter or mirth. Also, *to s. one's sides*, to be convulsed with laughter. 1593. **8.** With adv. or phr.: To reduce by shaking to a specified condition. late ME. **9.** To dislodge or get rid of (something, a person's hold, etc.) by shaking one's body, limbs, clothes, etc. Const. *from, off*; also with adv. ME. **10.** To dislodge or eject by shaking the receptacle or support 1500. **11.** To distribute with a shake, to scatter, sprinkle. Also with *forth, down.* late ME. **b.** To cast (dice) usu. with a preliminary shake; also with personal object, to 'throw' against (a person) *for* whatever is staked 1570. **12. a.** *refl.* and *intr.* Of timber: To split or crack 1679. **b.** *trans.* To separate the staves of (a cask) 1867. **13.** *Mus.* To accompany or execute with a shake; also *absol.* or *intr.* to execute a shake 1611.

1. And over them triumphant Death his Dart Shook, but delaid to strike MILT. 2. Rattlesnakes..swiftly vibrating and shaking their tailes EVELYN. Shaking wide thy yellow hair SHELLEY. Phr. *To s. one's head*, to turn the head slightly to one side and the other in sorrow or scorn, or to express disapproval, dissent, or doubt. *To s. one's ears* (fig.), to bestir oneself; also, to show indifference or dislike, pleasure in freedom, mirth, etc. *To s. one's elbow*, to gamble with dice. *To s. a foot, leg, toe, one's bones*, etc. = to dance. b. Just s. yourself sober and listen, will you? GEO. ELIOT. 3. Went ye out to se a rede shaken with the wynde? TINDALE *Matt.* xi. 7. b. S. the table clothe or you laye it on agayne 1530. Ere our comming see thou s. the bags Of hoording Abbots SHAKS. 4. He hath also taken me by my necke, and shaken me to pieces *Job* xvi. 12. Though he s. thee something roughly by the shoulders, to awake thee SCOTT. 5. *To s. hands* (said of two persons mutually saluting thus); We shoke handes, and parted 1546. Now we have shaken hands on the bargain 1908. *To s. hands with* (another); I have long since shook hands with the world WESLEY. 6. Age shakes Athena's tower, but spares gray Marathon BYRON. *fig.* That no compunctious visitings of Nature S. my fell purpose SHAKS. Too much shaken in mind and body to compose a letter THACKERAY. An attempt was made to s. the dominion which he had established over Wessex 1871. 7. A sudden fit of ague shook him GRAY. 8. *To s. down*, to cause to settle or subside by shaking. *To s. together*, to shake so as to ensure intimate mixture or subsidence into smaller compass. *To s. down* (intr. for refl.), to find temporary accommodation, esp. with ref. to sleeping, to occupy a 'shakedown'. *To s. down into*, to settle *into*, to accommodate oneself to (circumstances, a condition, position, etc.). *To s. together*, (of a company of persons) to mix, get on friendly terms with each other. 9. Vile thing let loose, Or I will s. thee from me like a serpent SHAKS. Phr. *To s. the dust from* or *off one's feet*, lit. in Gospel passages; hence *allus.* to take one's departure from an uncongenial place. 10. Macbeth Is ripe for shaking SHAKS. 11. S. down plenty of straw in the great barn SCOTT.

With advs. **S. off. a.** To cast off or get rid of with a shake or an effort. **b.** To get rid of (a person); to draw away from (a competitor in a race). **c.** *Naut* To unfasten (a sail). **S. out. a.** To cast out or remove with a shake. **b.** To unfasten or unfurl and let out with a shake (a flag, sail); to straighten out by shaking (something crumpled or folded). **S. up. a.** To shake together for the purpose of combining or mixing; to shake (a liquid) so as to stir up the sediment. **b.** To rouse up with or as with a shake. **c.** To loosen (bedding, etc.) by shaking. †**d.** To rate soundly. Also, to harass, afflict. Also as *sb.*

Sha·ke-down. 1730. **1.** A bed made upon straw loosely disposed upon the floor; hence, any makeshift bed, esp. one on the floor. **2.** An act of shaking down 1878. **b.** *U.S.* A forced contribution; an exaction 1903.

Sha·kefork. Now *dial.* ME. [f. SHAKE *v.*] A wooden fork with two tines or prongs used by threshers to shake and remove the straw from the grain; also, a pitchfork.

Shaken (ʃēⁱ·k'n), *ppl. a.* 1523. [pa. pple. of SHAKE *v.*] **1.** Put into a quick or violent alternating motion; (of seed, etc.) sprinkled 1725. **2.** Moved abruptly or violently with a blow or shock; hence, weakened in structure 1614. **3.** Of a cask: Taken to pieces and bound up in a compact form for transport 1557. **4.** Of timber: Cracked or split defectively 1523.

2. *transf.* This our s. Monarchy, that now lies labouring under her throwes MILT.

Shaker (ʃēⁱ·kəɹ). 1440. [f. SHAKE *v.* + -ER [1].] **1.** One who or something which shakes. **2.** †**a.** In the 17th c. applied to various sectaries whose devotional exercises were accompanied by 'shaking' or convulsions; often used as = 'Quaker' -1694. **b.** One of an American religious sect (calling itself 'The Society of Believers in Christ's Second Appearing'), which exists in the form of mixed communities of men and women living in celibacy 1784. **3.** In full, *s. pigeon*: The fan-tail pigeon 1668. **4.** An implement, machine, etc. used for shaking 1791. Hence **Sha·keress**, a female S. **Sha·kerism**, the principles and practice of the Shakers.

Sha·ke-rag. 1571. [f. SHAKE *v.* + RAG *sb.*] A ragged disreputable person; also *attrib.* or *adj.*, beggarly.

Shakespearian (ʃēⁱkspīᵊ·riăn), *a.* (and *sb.*) Also **Shaksperian, -ean.** [f. *Shakespeare* + -IAN.] **A.** *adj.* Of or pertaining to, or having the characteristics of William Shakespeare (1564–1616) or his dramatic and poetical productions. **B.** *sb.* An authority on or student of the writings of Shakespeare; a Shakespearian scholar 1837.

Hence **Shakespea·rianism,** (*a*) a form of expression peculiar to or imitated from Shakespeare; (*b*) the imitation of Shakespeare or the effects of his influence.

Shaking (ʃēⁱ·kiŋ), *vbl. sb.* late ME. [-ING [1].] **1.** The action of SHAKE *v.* **2.** A disease in sheep and swine. Also the ague. Chiefly in *pl.* 1642. **3.** *concr.* That which is shaken off, out, down, etc.; esp. *Naut. pl.*, refuse of cordage, canvas, etc. late ME.

Shako (ʃæ·kou). 1815. [a. Magyar *csákó*, short for *csákó(s) süveg* peaked cap.] A military cap in the shape of a truncated cone, with a peak and either a plume or a ball or 'pompom'.

Shaky (ʃēⁱ·ki), *a.* Also **shakey.** 1703. [f. SHAKE *v.* or *sb.* + -Y [1].] **1.** Of timber: Fissured. **2.** Of a structure: Given to shaking by the looseness of its parts; liable to break down or give way; unsound. Of ground: Not firm or solid. 1850. **3.** Of a person or his limbs: Trembling with age, infirmity, apprehension, or fear 1850. **b.** Of writing: Tremulous 1848. **4.** In immaterial sense. **a.** Of a person's credit, position, securities, etc.: Insecure, unreliable 1841. **b.** Uncertain, not to be depended on 1860. **c.** Not completely sound in health 1844. **d.** Unsettled in allegiance or belief 1853.

1. Some of the pines..were s. 1868. 2. The bridge was so frail and s. 1860. 3. b. A s., clerk-like hand THACKERAY. 4. a. His seat in Parliament was s. 1908. b. He is s. in his spelling 1889. c. I am rather s. just now DICKENS. Hence **Sha·ki·ly** *adv.*, **-ness.**

Shale (ʃēⁱl), *sb.*[1] *Obs.* exc. *dial.* [OE. *sc(e)alu* :—OTeut. **skalō*, ablaut-var. of **skǣlō*, represented by ON. *skál* SCALE *sb.*[1]] †**1.** A shell, husk, esp. the shell of a nut -1668. **2.** A scale (of a fish, of metal, of a scaly disease, etc.). late ME.

Shale (ʃēⁱl), *sb.*[2] 1747. [perh. a use of prec.] An argillaceous fissile rock, the laminæ of which are usu. fragile and uneven, and mostly parallel to the bedding; often overlying a coal formation. **b.** A variety or specimen of this rock 1830.

Comb.: **s.-naptha, -oil,** naphtha and oil obtained by the destructive distillation of bituminous shale; **-tar,** tar derived from bituminous shale.

Shale (ʃēⁱl), *v.* *Obs.* exc. *dial.* late ME. [f. SHALE *sb.*[1]] †**1.** *trans.* To free from the shell or husk; to remove, take *off* (the shell or husk) from a nut, bean, fruit, etc.; to decorticate (hemp) -1693. **2.** *intr.* Of grain, seed, etc.: To drop out 1578.

Shall (ʃæl), *sb.* 1553. [f. next.] **1.** An utterance of the word 'shall'; a command, promise, or determination. **2.** The word 'shall' as idiomatically used in contradistinction to 'will' 1837.

1. The external *shalls* and *shall nots* of the law M. ARNOLD. 2. Perhaps no Scot ever yet mastered his 'shalls' and 'wills' 1891.

Shall (ʃæl, *unstressed* ʃəl, ʃl), *v.* Pa. t. **should** (ʃud, ʃəd). [A Com. Teut. preterite-present vb.: OE. *sceal, sculon, sc(e)olde* :—Teut. root (**skel-*:) **skal-*: **skul-* to owe. In Eng. the vb. has no inf. or pples.] †**I.** *trans.* To owe (money, allegiance). -late ME.

And by that feyth I shal to god and yow CHAUCER.

II. Followed by an infinitive (without *to*). **The present tense* **shall.** †**1.** In general statements of what is right or becoming: = 'ought' -1562. †**2.** In OE. and ME. = 'must', 'must needs'; later, in stating a necessary condition: = 'will have to', 'must' (if something else is to happen) -1818. †**3.** Indicating what is appointed or settled to take place = the mod. 'is to', 'am to', etc. -1625. **4.** In commands or instructions, equiv. to imper. OE. **5.** In the second and third persons, expressing the speaker's determination to bring about (or, with neg., to prevent) some action, event, or state of things in the future, or (occas.) to refrain from hindering what is otherwise certain to take place, or is intended by another person OE. **6.** In special interrogative uses related to the senses 4 and 5. **a.** In the first person, used in questions to which the expected answer is a command, direction, or counsel, or a resolve on the speaker's own part OE. **b.** Similarly in the third person, where the subject represents or includes the speaker 1610. **c.** In the second and third person, where the expected answer is a decision on the part of the speaker or of some person other than the subject ME. **d.** In indirect question OE. **7.** As a mere auxiliary, forming (with present infinitive) the future, and (with perfect infinitive) the future perfect tense. **a.** Used, in all persons, for prophetic or oracular announcements of the future, and for solemn assertions of the certainty of a future event OE. **b.** In the first person, used as the normal auxiliary for expressing mere futurity. (*a*) Of events conceived as independent of the speaker's volition. (To use *will* in these cases is now a mark of Scottish, Irish, provincial, or extra-British idiom.) ME. (*b*) Of voluntary action or its intended result. Here *I* (*we*) *shall* is always admissible exc. where the notion of a present (as dist. from a previous) decision or consent is to be expressed (in which case *will* must be used). Further, *I shall* often expresses a determination insisted on in spite of opposition, and *I shall not* (colloq. *I shan't*) a peremptory refusal. ME. **c.** In the second person, *shall* as a mere future auxiliary is normal only in categorical questions; e.g. '*Shall* you miss your train? I am afraid you will.' **d.** In the third person. *Obs.* (repl. by *will*) exc. when another's statement or expectation respecting himself is reported in the third person, e.g. 'He says he shall not have time to write' (though here also *will* is probably more frequent) ME. †**e.** In neg. (or virtually neg.) and interrog. use, *shall* often = 'will be able to' -1773. **f.** Used in statements of a result to be expected from some action or occurrence. Now usu. (exc. in the first person) repl. by *will*; but *shall* survives in literary use. ME. **g.** In clause expressing the object of a promise, or of an expectation accompanied by hope or fear. Now only where *shall* is the ordinary future auxiliary. 1475. **8.** In the idiomatic use of the future to denote what ordinarily or occasionally occurs under specified conditions, *shall* was formerly the usual auxiliary. In the second and third persons, ordinary language now substitutes *will* or *may*. OE. **9.** In hypothetical, relative, and temporal clauses denoting a future contingency, the future auxiliary is *shall* for all persons alike ME. **10.** In clauses expressing the purposed result of some action, or the object of a desire, intention, command, or request. (Often replaceable by *may*.) ME.

2. You s. seeke all day ere you finde them SHAKS. 3. Arte thou he that s. come? TINDALE *Luke* vii. 19. 4. Thow shalt not tak the name of the Lord thi God in veyn WYCLIF *Exod.* xx. 7. Your Grace s. pardon me, I will not backe SHAKS. Scandalous persons shal be kept from the Sacrament 1645. 5. And syker assuraunce and borowes ye shal haue MALORY. Verona s. not hold thee SHAKS. 6. a. O Cuckoo! s. I call thee Bird, Or but a wandering Voice? WORDSW. 'It's rather slow work', said he, 'down here; what s. we do?' THACKERAY. b. O where now s. a man trust? 1871. c. What s. he haue that kild the Deare? SHAKS. d. Let her say what shall be done with it 1865. 7. a. Now do I Prophesie..A Curse s. light vpon the limbes of men SHAKS. b. (*a*) When s. we three meet againe? SHAKS (*b*) I..s. let my wife and daughters know, that I will be master of my own house 1779. e. If I draw forward, and others draw backwards, what s. it avail? 1565. f. ȝif ony thing falle in to that Lake, it schalle nevere comen up aȝen MAUNDEV. g. I hope his visits shall not be intruded upon me FIELDING. 8. He was as handsome a man, as you s. see on a summer's day 1760. One man s. approve..the same thing that another man s. condemn 1793. 9. If you s fail to understand What England is ..On you will come the curse of all the land TENNYSON. We extend our sympathies..to the unborn generations which..s. follow us on this earth 1874. When War's loud shuttle shall have woven peace 1896. 10. I'll take you five children from London, who shall cuff five Highland children JOHNSON. Mr. Mill recommends that all males of mature age..s. have votes MACAULAY.

** *The past tense* **should** *with temporal function.* †**11.** Expressing a former obligation or necessity: = 'was bound to', 'had to' -late ME. †**12.** = 'was to', or (contextually) 'was about to' -1622. **13.** Used in indirect reported utterances, or other statements relating to past time, where *shall* would be used if the time referred to were present OE. **14.** Forming with the inf. a substitute for the pa. t. indic. (or, with perf. inf., for the pluperf.) in the oblique report of another's statement in order to imply that the speaker does not commit himself to the truth of the alleged fact. *Obs.* exc. *dial.* OE. **15.** In indirect question relating to a past matter of fact. (The pa. t. or perf. is now preferred.) *Obs.* exc. *arch.* ME. **16.** In questions introduced by *who, whom, what*, and followed by *but*, serving to express the unexpectedness of some past occurrence 1626.

13. 'Tis commanded I should do so SHAKS. I thought I never should have got out 1846. Clancarty was pardoned on condition that he should leave the kingdom MACAULAY. He had wished that the doctor should inquire into the cause of his trouble 1861. 15. The Assembly were wondering what should be the meaning of it 1704. 16. Just as he said this, what should hap At the chamber door but a gentle tap? BROWNING.

*** *The past tense* **should** *with modal function.* **17.** In statements of duty, obligation, or propriety (orig., as applicable to hypothetical conditions not regarded as real) OE. **b.** *Should be*: ought according to appearances to be, presumably is 1605. **c.** *You should hear, see* = I wish you could hear, etc. 1842. **18.** In the apodosis of a hypothetical proposition (expressed or implied), indicating that the supposition, and therefore its consequence, is unreal. **a.** Where *shall* (in senses II. 4, 5, 6, 7, or 8) would be used if the hypothesis were accepted OE. **b.** When the pres. tense of the principal verb would be used if the hypothesis were accepted. late ME. **c.** With vbs. of liking, preference, etc., *should* in the first person (and interrogatively in the second) is regarded as more correct than *would* 1779. **d.** The original conditional notion is obscured in the phr. *It should seem.* So *I should think*, (*suppose*, etc.) = 'I am inclined to think (suppose, etc.)'; also *colloq.* as a strong affirmation. late ME. **e.** *I should* (*do* so and so): orig. with expressed or understood protasis 'if I were you', but now often used loosely = 'I would advise you to (do, etc.)' 1908. **19.** In a hypothetical clause expressing a rejected supposition ME. **20.** In a hypothetical clause relating to the future, *should* takes the place of *shall*, or of the equivalent use of the present tense, when the supposition, though entertained as possible, is viewed as less likely or less welcome than some alternative. (With future, future perf., or imper. in the apodosis.) 1675. **21.** In a noun-clause (normally introduced by *that*). **a.** In dependence on expressions of will, desire, etc. ME. **b.** In statements relating to the necessity, propriety, etc. of something contemplated as future, or as an abstract supposition 1527. **c.** In expressions of surprise or its absence, approval or disapproval, of some present or past fact ME. **d.** In clause dependent on sentence expressing possibility, probability, or expectation 1600. **e.** In clause expressing the object of fear or precaution. late ME. **22.** In special interrogative uses. **a.** In questions introduced by *why* (or equivalent word), implying the speaker's inability to conceive any reason for something actual or contemplated, or any ground for believing something to be fact OE. **b.** In questions introduced by *how*, implying that the speaker regards something as impossible or inadmissible ME.

17. Some men should have been women, and he, I think, is one 1756. *Provb. phr.* That same Lord Stewkly is no better than he should be 1764. 18. a. I often think we should all be better without it THACKERAY. b. I shouldn't know how to begin 1882. c. I should like to have stayed longer at Noyon 1869. d. I should rather think he has a mind to finger its finances 1775. 19. Pope writing dialogue resembled a wolf, which, instead of biting, should take to kicking MACAULAY. Phr. *As who should say* [cf. F. *comme qui dirait*] = as much as to say (*arch.*). 20. Should any soluble salt remain it will be soda 1846. 21. a. Chantrey..wishes I should sit to Bartolini 1819. b. It is time..That old hysterical mock-disease should die TENNYSON. e. However, lest conversation should lag, I'll give it you BORROW. 22. a. Men have one common original, and why should relations quarrel? 1779. b. How *should* you understand what is so little intelligible? MISS BURNEY.

III. Elliptical and quasi-elliptical uses. **23.** = 'shall go'. *arch.* OE. **24.** With ellipsis of active infinitive to be supplied from the context OE. **25.** The place of the inf. is sometimes supplied by *that* or *so* placed at the beginning of the sentence ME. †**26.** With ellipsis of *be* or passive inf., or with *so* in place of this (where the preceding context has *is, was*, etc.) -1749.

23. If the bottome were as deepe as hell, I shold down SHAKS. Thou shalt with me to Iona SCOTT. 24. This would vex me, but it s. not SWIFT. I knew ..That she was uttering what she shouldn't 1872. 25. That s. I not said sir Dynadan MALORY. 26. He is not yet executed, nor I hear not when he s. 1615.

Shalloon (ʃălū·n). 1678. [a. F. *chalon*, adopted earlier as CHALON.] **1.** A closely woven woollen material chiefly used for linings. **b.** A wig-tie made of shalloon 1845. **2.** *attrib.* or *adj.* Made of s. 1665.

Shallop (ʃæ·ləp), *sb.*, †**shalloop.** 1578. [a. F. *chaloupe*, prob. a. Du. *sloep* (see SLOOP) or its source.] **1.** A large heavy boat fitted with one or more masts and carrying fore-and-aft or lug sails and sometimes furnished with guns; a sloop. **2.** A dinghy 1590.

1. A double S., well mann'd, with two guns 1666.

Shallot, shalot (ʃălǫ·t). 1664. [aphet. f. ESCHALOT. The spelling *shallot* is now usual.] A small onion, *Allium ascalonicum*, native to Syria and cultivated for use in flavouring salads, sauces, etc.

Shallow (ʃæ·lo͞u), *a.* and *sb.* late ME. [Early 15th c. *schalowe*, prob. related in some way to *schald* (OE. *sceald*): see SHOAL *a.*] **A.** *adj.* **1.** Not deep; having little extension in a downward direction: said e.g. of water, of a dish, of a depression in the ground. **b.** Of the soil of agricultural land: Forming only a thin stratum over rock 1733. **2.** Extending only a short distance inward from the surface or from the front towards the back. Of a lens: Having slight convexity or concavity. 1545. **3.** *fig.* Of thought, reasoning, observation, knowledge, or feeling Lacking depth, superficial 1586. **b.** Qualifying an agent-noun, or said of a person with ref. to knowledge, etc. 1601. **c.** Of persons and their attributes: Wanting in depth of mind, feeling, or character 1593. **4.** quasi-*adv.* To or at a slight depth 1662.

1. The River in Summer time is very ebbe and s. 1610. b. Poor light s. land 1760. 2. A s. bow-window 1886. 3. That were but s. policy SMOLLETT. b. O how hard it is to be s. enough for a polite audience! WESLEY. c. Out, idle words, servants to s. fools! SHAKS.

B. *sb.* **1.** A shallow part of a piece of water, of the sea, of a lake or river; shallow water; a shallow place (often *pl.*) 1571. **2.** A costermonger's barrow 1859.

1. By whose cunning guide We found the shalow of this Riuer Some 1596. *fig.* All the voyage of their life Is bound in Shallowes, and in Miseries SHAKS. Hence **Sha·llow-ly** *adv.*, **-ness.**

Shallow (ʃæ·lo͞u), *v.* 1510. [f. SHALLOW *a.*] To make or become shallow.

†**Shallow-brained,** *a.* 1592. [f. SHALLOW *a.*] Having no depth of intellect -1810.

Shaly (ʃē·li), *a.* 1681. [f. SHALE *sb.*² + -Y¹.] Composed of, or resembling shale.

Sham (ʃæm), *sb.*¹ and *a.* 1677. [Origin obsc.; perh. conn. w. *sham*, northern form of SHAME *sb.* and *v.*] **A.** *sb.* †**1.** A trick, hoax, fraud, imposture; a 'sell' -1821. **2.** Something that is intended to be mistaken for something else; spurious imitation, a counterfeit 1728. **3.** *spec.* A removable covering to give a specious appearance to an article, as *pillow-sham* 1721.

1. Phr. †*To put a s. upon*, to hoax, defraud. 2. For the pain of my thirst is no s. CAMPBELL. The greatest s.,..is he that would destroy shams CARLYLE. It's all s.—he's only afraid 1857.

B. *attrib.* and *adj.* (Sometimes with hyphen.) **1.** Pretended, feigned, false, counterfeit; not genuine or true 1681. **2.** Of a person: That pretends or is falsely represented to be (what is denoted by the sb.) 1683. **3.** Made in imitation of something else; made to appear to be what it is not; made of inferior or base materials 1699. †**4.** False, deceptive -1727.

1. *S. fight*, a mimic battle between two divisions of a military or naval force, either for exercise or display. 2. The s.-admirer is always more affected, than he that praises with sincerity 1756. 3. The s. coat of arms which Osborne had assumed 1848. Not one of the girls dared to wear a bit of s. jewellery 1876.

Sham (ʃæm), *sb.*² *slang.* 1849. Short for CHAMPAGNE.

Sham (ʃæm), *v.* 1677. [See SHAM *sb.*¹] †**1.** *trans.* To cheat, trick, deceive, delude with false pretences; to impose upon, take in, hoax -1821. †**b.** To put off, 'fob off' with something deceptive or worthless; to get rid of (a person) by some paltry excuse -1749. †**2.** To impose or attempt to pass off (something) *upon* (a person) by deceit; to palm *off* -1751. †**3.** *intr.* To practise deception or deceit -1689. **4.** *trans.*

a. To be or to produce a deceptive imitation of 1698. **b.** To assume the appearance of, counterfeit (a specified condition, action, etc.) 1775. **5.** *intr.* To make false pretences; to pretend to be, do, etc. what one is not, does not, etc.; to feign 1787. **6.** *To s. Abra(ha)m* (orig. *Naut. slang*), to feign sickness (see ABRAHAM-MAN) 1752. **b.** Hence *sham-Abra(ha)m* quasi-*sb.* malingering, deception. Also quasi-*adj.* hypocritical. 1828.

1. When they find themselves Fool'd and Shamm'd (as we say) into a Conviction 1692. 2. Don't go to s. your Stories off upon me DE FOE. 4. a. Phr. †*To s. one's glass*: to make a pretence of drinking; He keeps up his spirits bravely, and never shams his glass CHESTERF. b. Persons shamming an epileptic fit 1869. 5. What did you s. dead for? 1834. Wondering..whether those who lectured him were such fools as they professed to be, or were only shamming MACAULAY. Hence **Sha·mmer,** one who shams.

‖**Shama(h** (ʃā·mă). 1839. [Hindī *çāmā*.] An Indian song-bird, *Cittocincla tricolor.*

Shaman (ʃā·măn, ʃæ·măn), *sb.* (and *a.*). 1698. [a. G. *schamane*, Russian *shaman*, a. Tungusian *samân.*] **A.** *sb.* A priest or priest-doctor among various northern tribes of Asia. Hence applied to similar personages in other parts, esp. a medicine-man of some of the north-west American Indians. **B.** *adj.* (or *attrib.*) Of or pertaining to a s. or to Shamanism 1780. Hence **Shama·nic** *a.* akin to Shamanism.

Shamanism (ʃā·măniz'm, ʃæ·măniz'm). 1780. [f. prec. + -ISM.] The primitive religion of the Ural-Altaic peoples of Siberia, in which all the good and evil of life are thought to be brought about by spirits which can be influenced only by Shamans; hence applied to similar religions, esp. of north-west American Indians. Hence **Sha·manist, Sha·manite,** a believer in S. **Shamani·stic** *a.* pertaining to S. **Sha·manize** *v. intr.* to perform the incantations of a Shaman; *trans.* to imbue with Shamanistic beliefs.

Shamble (ʃæ·mb'l), *sb.*[1] [OE. *sc(e)amel*; a Com. WGer. adoption of L. *scamellum* dim. of *scamnum* bench.] †**1.** A stool, footstool –1483. **2.** *spec.* A table or stall for the sale of meat ME. **3.** *pl.* A place where meat (or occas. fish) is sold, a flesh- or meat-market. Now *local.* late ME. **4.** *pl.* A slaughter-house 1548. **5.** *transf.* and *fig.* A place of carnage or wholesale slaughter; a scene of blood. Chiefly *pl.* construed as *sing.*; rarely in sing. form. 1593.

3. Raw Meat is bought in the Shambles 1725. 4. He was felled like an ox in the butcher's shambles DICKENS. 5. I've fear'd him, since his iron heart endured To make of Lyons one vast human shambles COLERIDGE. Hence **Sha·mble** *v.*[1] *trans.* to cut up or slaughter as in the shambles (*rare*).

Shamble (ʃæ·mb'l), *sb.*[2] 1828. [f. SHAMBLE *v.*[2]] A shambling gait.

Shamble, *a. dial.* 1607. [prob. adj. use of SHAMBLE *sb.*[1]] Shambling, ungainly, awkward.

Shamble (ʃæ·mb'l), *v.*[2] 1681. [prob. f. SHAMBLE *a.*] *intr.* To go with an awkward ungainly gait, to walk awkwardly or unsteadily; usu. with adv. as *to s. along.*

Shambling (ʃæ·mbliŋ), *vbl. sb. rare.* 1681. [f. prec. + -ING[1].] An awkward motion in walking or progression.

Shambling (ʃæ·mbliŋ), *ppl. a.* 1690. [-ING[2].] That shambles or is characterized by an awkward, irregular gait or motion. **b.** *transf.* and *fig.* Often of metre and style, etc. 1802.

A s. pot-boy DICKENS.

Shame (ʃē¹m), *sb.* [Com. Teut.; OE. *sc(e)amu, sc(e)ǫmu* :—OTeut. **skamō.*] **1.** The painful emotion arising from the consciousness of something dishonouring, ridiculous, or indecorous in one's own conduct or circumstances (or in those of others whose honour or disgrace one regards as one's own), or of being in a situation which offends one's sense of modesty or decency. **2.** Fear of offence against propriety or decency, operating as a restraint on behaviour; modesty, shamefastness. late ME. **3.** Disgrace, ignominy, loss of esteem or reputation OE. **b.** An instance of disgrace ME. **c.** *spec.* Violation of a woman's honour, loss of chastity ME. †**4.** What is morally disgraceful or dishonourable; baseness in conduct or behaviour –1682. **5.** Used predic. (without article) for: A fact or circumstance which brings disgrace or discredit (*to* a person, etc.); matter for severe reproach or reprobation. Now *poet.* OE. **b.** Similarly *a. s., a great s.* Now common in colloq. use. late ME. **c.** Occas. in non-predic. use: A disgraceful thing, something to be ashamed of. *poet.* 1600. **6.** A person or thing that is a cause or source of disgrace 1586. **b.** *colloq.* A thing which is shockingly ugly or indecent, or of disgracefully bad quality 1764. †**7.** *concr.* The privy members –1611.

1. But for my part (in all humility And with no little s.) I ask your pardons 1623. *Sense of s.* guilty feeling; also, the right perception of what is improper or disgraceful. *Past s., dead to s.*, no longer capable of feeling s., grown callous to s. 2. Haue you no modesty, no maiden s., No touch of bashfulnesse? SHAKS. 3. Therfore beare thine owne s. COVERDALE *Ezek.* xvi. 52. b. Let his shames quickely Driue him tó Rome SHAKS. c. *Child, son of s.*, a child born out of wedlock. 5. It were s. to our profession were we to suffer it SCOTT. b. They..pay fifteen or twenty sometimes per cent. for their money which is a most horrid s. PEPYS. c. A peace that was full of wrongs and shames TENNYSON. 6. Erasmus, that great injured name, (The glory of the Priesthood, and the s.!) POPE.

Phrases. *To think s.*, to be ashamed. *To take s.* †a. To be disgraced, to incur disgrace. b. To feel ashamed; to acknowledge that one is in fault. More fully *to take s. to (unto, upon) oneself.* †*To do* (a person) *s.*: to inflict injury or dishonour, offer reproach or obloquy. *To put to s.*: to bring into disgrace, bring disgrace upon; also *fig.* to outshine, eclipse. *For s.*: from a sense of s., because one feels s.; also, for fear of s. b. esp. in adjuration or remonstrance; often as *int.* Also in ejaculatory formulæ of imprecation or indignant disapproval, as *Shame! Fie for s.!* etc. *To one's s.*, so as to cause one s. Also, parenthetically, with ellipsis of 'be it spoken'. *To cry s. on, upon*: to express vigorous reprobation of.

Shame (ʃē¹m), *v.* Pa. t. and pple. **shamed** (ʃē¹md). [OE. *sc(e)amian, sc(e)ǫmian*, f. *sc(e)amu, sc(e)ǫmu* SHAME *sb.*] **1.** *intr.* To feel or conceive shame; to become or be ashamed. *Obs.* exc. *dial.* **2.** *trans. impers.*, as in (*it*) *shames me* = I am ashamed. In later use only with *it.* Now *rare.* OE. **3.** To feel shame in regard to (a person or thing); to hold in awe or reverence; to dread or shun through shame. *Obs.* or *arch.* late ME. **4.** To make ashamed, fill with shame, cause to feel shame 1530. **b.** *pass.* To be ashamed. Now *poet.* ME. **5.** To inflict or bring disgrace upon, be a cause of disgrace to, dishonour ME. **6.** To put to shame by superior excellence; to outrival. late ME.

4. Nay, father,..s. me not Before this noble Knight TENNYSON. Phr. *To tell (say, speak) the truth and s. the devil*, to tell the truth boldly in defiance of strong temptation to the contrary. 5. This John..shamed the Churche of Rome wonderfully wᵗ his lyuing 1556. 6. She'll s. 'em with her good looks, yet DICKENS.

Shamefaced (ʃē¹·mfē¹st), *a.* 1555. [f. SHAME *sb.* + FACE *sb.* + -ED[2]; orig. an etymological misinterpretation of SHAMEFAST.] **1.** Modest, bashful, shy. **2.** Ashamed, abashed 1873.

1. He felt s. as a schoolboy before the great world 1873. Hence **Sha·mefaced-ly** *adv.*, **-ness.**

Shamefast (ʃē¹·mfast), *a. arch.* [OE. *sc(e)amfæst*, f. *sc(e)amu* SHAME *sb.* + *fæst* FAST *a.*] **1.** Bashful, modest. In a depreciatory sense: 'Sheepish'. **b.** Of actions, behaviour, appearance: Characterized by or indicating modesty or bashfulness ME. †**2.** Ashamed, abashed –1634.

1. Yf thy daughter be not s., holde her straitly COVERDALE *Ecclus.* xxvi. 10. b. Hir schamefast.. smyles 1611. Hence **Sha·mefast-ly** *adv.*, **-ness.**

Shameful (ʃē¹·mfŭl), *a.* OE. [f. SHAME *sb.* + -FUL 1.] †**1.** Modest, shamefaced –1625. †**2.** Ashamed –1772. **3.** That brings to shame; that causes or ought to cause shame; disgraceful, scandalous, degrading ME.

3. The s. close of all his mispent years COWPER. S.! Three against one! CARLYLE. Hence **Sha·meful-ly** *adv.*, **-ness.**

Shameless (ʃē¹·mlės), *a.* [OE. *sc(e)amlēas*; see SHAME *sb.* and -LESS.] **1.** Lacking shame; impudent, audacious, immodest; insensible to disgrace. **2.** Indicating or characterized by absence of shame or modesty. Of actions: Indicating absence of shame on the part of the agent, impudent. OE.

1. Though these men are so s. as to deny it 1683. 2. He..degraded the nobility by a s. sale of peerages 1874. Hence **Sha·meless-ly** *adv.*, **-ness.**

Shammy (ʃæ·mi). 1651. [Phonetic spelling of CHAMOIS 2.] **1.** In full **s.-leather:** a kind of soft, pliable leather. Also a piece of this, a wash-leather. 1714. **2.** *attrib.* or *adj.* Made of 'shammy' or chamois leather 1651.

2. I have got my cravat and s. shoes H. WALPOLE.

Shamoy (ʃæ·moi), *v.* 1837. [Phonetic spelling of CHAMOIS 2.] *trans.* To prepare (leather) by working oil or grease into the skin.

Shampoo (ʃæmpū·), *sb.* 1838. [f. next.] The act of shampooing; also, a 'wash' (or powder, *dry s.*) used for shampooing.

Shampoo (ʃæmpū·), *v.* 1762. [prob. a. Hindī *čāmpo*, imper. of *čāmpnā* to press.] **1.** *trans.* To subject (a person, his limbs) to massage. Now *rare* or *Obs.* exc. as designating a part of the process of a Turkish bath. **2.** To subject (the scalp, the hair) to washing and rubbing with some cleansing agent, as soap and water, shampoo powder, etc. 1860. Hence **Shampoo·er,** one who shampoos.

Shamrock (ʃæ·mrǫk). 1571. [a. Irish *seamróg* (= Gael. *seamrag*), dim. of *seamar* clover.] **1.** A plant with trifoliate leaves, used (according to a late tradition) by St. Patrick to illustrate the doctrine of the Trinity, and hence adopted as the national emblem of Ireland; a spray or leaf of this plant. (The name is now commonly applied to the lesser yellow trefoil, *Trifolium minus*, the plant worn as an emblem on St. Patrick's Day.)

Shandean (ʃæ·ndiăn, ʃændī·ăn), *a.* 1762. [f. (*Tristram*) *Shandy*, the title of a novel (1759–67) by Sterne + -AN.] Pertaining to *Tristram Shandy*, or the Shandy family there portrayed.

Shandrydan (ʃæ·ndridæn). 1820. [Origin obsc.] A kind of chaise with a hood. In later use, a joc. name for any rickety old-fashioned vehicle.

Shandygaff (ʃæ·ndigæf). 1853. [Origin unkn.] A drink composed of a mixture of beer and ginger-beer.

Shanghai (ʃæŋhəi·), *sb.* 1853. [f. *Shanghai* or *Shanghae*, one of the chief seaports of China.] **1.** A long-legged, large breed of domestic fowls, with feathered shanks, reputed to have been introduced from Shanghai; now developed into the brahmas and cochins. **2.** *Austral.* A catapult 1863.

Shanghai (ʃæŋhəi·), *v.* 1871. [f. as prec.] **1.** *trans. Naut. slang.* (orig. *U.S.*) To drug or otherwise render insensible, and ship on board a vessel wanting hands. **2.** *Austral.* To shoot with a 'shanghai' or catapult 1902.

Shank (ʃæŋk), *sb.* [OE. *sc(e)anca* :—WGer. **skankan-.*] **1.** That part of the leg which extends from the knee to the ankle; the tibia or shin-bone. Also (now *joc.*) the leg as a whole; chiefly *pl.*, one's legs. **b.** The lower part of the foreleg of some animals; *spec.* of a horse, the part between the so-called knee and the fetlock. Also, the tarsus of a bird; the tibia or fourth joint of the leg of an insect OE. **c.** As part of a joint of meat, e.g. in a ham, a leg of mutton, etc. 1806. **2.** *transf.* **a.** Each of the two portions of a pair of scissors between the bow and the joint 1833. **b.** *Arch. pl.* The plane spaces between the grooves of the Doric triglyph 1823. **c.** Each of the two cheeks or side-pieces of a spur 1891. **3.** The stem or straight part of anything. **a.** The stem of a goblet, glass, etc. 1553. **b.** The straight part of a nail or pin, between the head and the taper of the point. Also of a drill or borer. 1483. **c.** The stem of a plant; the pedicel or footstalk of a flower; the footstalk or connecting part of any organ in a plant 1513. **d.** The shaft or stem of an anchor, connecting the arms and the stock 1549. **e.** The straight part of a fish-hook, to which the line is attached 1613. **f.** *Typog.* The body of a type, as dist. from the shoulder, face, and foot 1683. **g.** The stem of a tobacco-pipe 1688. **h.** The blank part of a screw, or screw-bolt, between the thread and the head 1677. **i.** The tapering part of an oar between the handle and the blade 1857. **4.** A part or appendage by which something is attached; e.g. the wire loop by which some kinds of buttons are attached, that part of a ring which encircles the finger 1677. **5.** *Founding.* A clay-lined ladle having long handles, one of them T-shaped, in which to carry molten metal from the furnace to the mould 1843. **6.** *dial.*

and *U.S.* The latter end or part of anything 1828.

1. Sundry flowring bankes, To sit and rest the walkers wearie shankes SPENSER. *Shanks'* (or *Shanks's*) *mare, pony*, etc., one's own legs as a means of conveyance.

Comb. **s.-bone,** the tibia of an animal. Hence **Shank** *v. intr.* of a plant or fruit: to decay at the stem or footstalk; usu. *to shank off*; *trans.* (*Golf*) to strike (the ball) with the heel of the club. **Shanked** (ʃæŋkt) *a.* furnished with or having a s. or shanks.

Sha·nk-pai:nter. 1495. [PAINTER 2.] The rope or chain with which the shank and flukes of the anchor, when carried at the cathead, are confined to the ship's side.

Shanny (ʃæ·ni). 1836. [Origin obsc.] The smooth blenny. Also applied to several fishes of the genus *Chasmodes* of Eastern North America.

Shan't, sha'n't (ʃānt). 1664. Colloq. Contraction of *shall not*. Also used *subst.*

Shantung (ʃæntʊ·ŋ). 1882. [f. name of a province of North-east China where it is manufactured.] A soft undressed Chinese silk (formerly always undyed).

Shanty (ʃæ·nti), *sb.*[1] 1820. [prob. corruptly a. F. *chantier* CHANTIER.] 1. Chiefly *U.S.* and *Canada.* A small, mean, roughly constructed dwelling; a cabin, hut. 2. *Austral.* A public-house, esp. unlicensed 1864. Hence **Sha·nty** *v. intr.* to live in a s.; *Austral.* to frequent 'shanties' or public-houses.

Shanty (ʃæ·nti), *sb.*[2] Also **chant(e)y.** 1869. [perh. a corruption of F. *chantez*, imper. of *chanter* to sing.] A sailor's song, esp. one sung during heavy work.

Shape (ʃēⁱp), *sb.* [OE. *gesceap* creation, creature, make, form, f. Teut. **skap-* (cf. next).] 1. External form or contour; that quality of a material object (or geometrical figure) which depends on constant relations of position and proportionate distance among all the points composing its outline or its external surface; a particular variety of this quality. b. The contour or outlines of the trunk of the body. late ME. c. Impressed or represented form; a picture, image. *Obs.* exc. *dial.* late ME. †2. The appearance of a human or animal body or its parts, (often, of the general form as dist. from the face) considered as beautiful or the contrary –1734. 3. The visible form or appearance characteristic of a particular person or thing, or of a particular species of animate or supernatural beings OE. 4. A person's body considered with regard to its appearance 1601. b. An imaginary, spectral, or ethereal form; a phantom. Now *rare.* 1591. c. A figure dimly or uncertainly perceived 1834. 5. Assumed appearance, guise, disguise 1594. 6. *Theatr.* †a. A part, a character impersonated; the make-up and costume suited to a particular part. b. A stage dress or suit of clothes. 1603. 7. One of the forms or diversities of appearance, structure, or properties, in which a thing may exist 1667. 8. *In the s. of*: a. Represented by, embodied in (a person or thing) 1750. b. Of the nature of 1754. c. In the form of, existing or presenting itself as 1823. 9. Definite, regular or proper form; orderly arrangement 1633. †10. An attitude (in dancing, etc.) –1634. 11. orig. *Sport.* Condition with respect to efficiency, 'form' 1901. 12. *concr.* in techn. uses. a. *Cookery.* A mould for forming jelly, blanc-mange, etc., into a particular shape; a portion of jelly, blanc-mange, etc. moulded into an ornamental shape 1769. b. *Millinery.* The body of a straw bonnet or woman's hat or cap previous to trimming 1881. c. A portion of material cut or moulded so as to have a particular shape; *spec.* a piece of rolled or hammered iron of cross-section differing from that of merchant bar 1845. d. *Naut.* A cone, ball, or drum of metal or canvas used in signalling 1879.

1. I know the s. of 's Legge SHAKS. By pressure ice can be moulded to any s. TYNDALL. *To keep in s.*, to secure from change of s. *Out of s.*, changed from its proper s. 2. Hither come the Country Gentlemen to shew their Shapes 1700. 3. Thou com'st in such a questionable s. That I will speake to thee SHAKS. 4. b. Before the Gates there sat On either side a formidable s. MILT. 5. The brute Serpent in whose s. I Man deceav'd MILT. 7. Phr. *In any* (*no*) *s.* (*or form*), used loosely for: in any (no) manner, (not) at all. 8. b. I had nothing in the s. of food 1863. c. Recognition of his services in the s. of a small pension 1880. 9. Phr. *To take s.*; *to put into s.*

Shape (ʃēⁱp), *v.* Pa. t. **shaped** (ʃēⁱpt); pa. pple. **shaped** (ʃēⁱpt), *arch.* **shapen** (ʃēⁱ·p'n). [Com. Teut. str. vb.: OE. *scieppan* (*scōp*, *scapen*) :—OTeut. **skapjan.* In early ME. a new pres.-stem *shape* was formed on the analogy of the pa. pple. From the 16th c. onwards, *shape* has been a 'regular' wk. vb. (pa. t. and pple. *shaped*). Ult. etym. obsc.] I. To create, fashion, form. †1. *trans.* To create; in later use, to form, fashion (said of God or Nature) –1557. 2. To make, fashion out of pre-existing materials. In later use, to make by alteration of shape (as by moulding or carving) *out of* something else; to make in a definite shape. OE. b. To frame, fashion (an immaterial thing) ME. 3. *pass.* To have a certain shape OE. †4. *trans.* To cut out or fashion (clothing) –1828. †5. *intr.* To attain maturity of form and proportions. BACON. 6. *trans.* To trim, cut, or mould to a particular shape; to adapt in shape *to* 1457. 7. To give definite form to; to put *into* a certain form, to embody in words; also *refl.* 1589. b. Of events, etc.: To show a specified tendency 1865. 8. To give a direction and character to (one's life, conduct, etc.) 1823.

1. I was shapen in wickednesse BIBLE (Great) *Ps.* li. 5. 2. Come, to the Forge with it, then s. it SHAKS. 3. The head was well shapen 1884. 5. Young men, when they knit and s. perfectly, doe seldome grow to a further stature BACON. 6. Some [sleeves] are shaped to the elbow, and have cuffs 1861. 7. And there I shaped The city's ancient legend into this TENNYSON. The valleys..shaped themselves..into a succession of graceful curves 1869. Phr. *To shape an answer* (*to*).

II. To devise, plan, prepare. 1. To devise (a plan, a remedy). late ME. 2. *To s. one's course*: Naut., to steer *for*, *to* a place 1593. 3. To appear promising (chiefly *Sc.* and *dial.*). Often with ref. to physical exercises, as drill, rowing, etc.: To show signs of becoming efficient. 1865. b. Of a batsman: To get into the proper attitude and position for dealing with the bowling 1884. c. Of a horse: To exhibit capabilities; to develop *into* 1887.

2. *transf.* Minding now to s. my course so as I might winter in Italy EVELYN. Hence **Sha·p(e)able** *a.* capable of being shaped, plastic; shapely.

Shapeless (ʃēⁱ·plės), *a.* ME. [f. SHAPE *sb.* + -LESS.] 1. Without shape or form; having no definite or regular shape. 2. Unshapely 1588. 3. Without guidance or direction, aimless (*rare*) 1591.

1. Sunk are thy bowers in s. ruin all GOLDSM. 3. To..Weare out thy youth with shapelesse idlenesse SHAKS. Hence **Sha·pelessness.**

Shapely (ʃēⁱ·pli), *a.* late ME. [f. SHAPE *sb.* + -LY[1].] †1. Fit, likely, suitable; also, like (*to* something). late ME. only. 2. Of good or elegant shape, well-formed. late ME. b. Having definite form (*rare*) 1827.

1. Euerich..Was shaply for to been an Alderman CHAUCER. 2. Where the s. column stood COWPER. Hence **Sha·peliness.**

Shapen (ʃēⁱ·p'n), *ppl. a.* ME. [Strong pa. pple. of SHAPE *v.*] 1. Having a (specified) shape. *Obs.* exc. in *well s.* (arch.). 2. Furnished with a definite shape; fashioned 1483.

Shapen (ʃēⁱ·p'n), *v. rare.* 1535. [f. SHAPE *sb.* + -EN[5].] *trans.* To shape, impart a shape to.

Shaper (ʃēⁱ·pəɹ). ME. [f. SHAPE *v.* + -ER[1].] †1. The Creator or Maker (of the universe) –1496. 2. One who or something which makes (a thing) in the required shape; one who fashions (material). late ME. b. *spec.* in various trades as the designation of an operative 1881. 3. A machine or tool for shaping material; *spec.* a machine for shaping metal pieces and parts of machinery 1853.

‖**Shapoo** (ʃā·pu). 1858. [Tibetan *sha-pho* wild sheep.] A kind of sheep (*Ovis vignei*) found in Ládák (Kashmír) and Tibet.

Shard, sherd (ʃāɹd, ʃəɹd), *sb.*[1] [OE. *sceard* :—OTeut. **skardo-* cut, notched, diminished, f. **skar-* (:—**sker-*: **skur-*); see SHEAR *v.*] I. A gap in an enclosure, esp. in a hedge or bank. Now chiefly *dial.* II. A fragment of broken earthenware, POTSHERD OE.

Phr. *To break*, etc. *into sherds*, to reduce to fragments, break beyond repair. Hence **Shard** *v. trans.* to break into fragments (*rare*).

Shard (ʃāɹd), *sb.*[2] *Obs.* exc. *dial.* 1545. [app. cogn. w. dial. and Sc. *sharn* dung.] A patch of cow-dung.

Comb. **s.-beetle,** a beetle of the family *Geotrupidæ*, found under dung, a dor-beetle. Hence †**Sha·rded** *a.* of a beetle: living in dung. SHAKS.

Shard (ʃāɹd), *sb.*[3] 1755. [Evolved from a misunderstanding of SHARD-BORN in Shaks.] The elytron or wing-case of a coleopterous insect.

Sha·rd-born, -borne, *a.* 1605. [f. SHARD *sb.*[2] + BORN *a.*] a. Of a beetle: Born in dung; *spec.* applied to the SHARD-BEETLE. b. Used with the meaning (due to misinterpretation of Shaks.): Borne on shards (SHARD *sb.*[3]).

Ere..The shard-borne Beetle, with his drowsie hums, Hath rung Nightes yawning Peale SHAKS.

Share (ʃēᵊɹ), *sb.*[1] [OE. *scear*, *scær* (masc. or neut.), f. Teut. root **skar-*: **sker-*; see SHEAR *v.*] The iron blade in a plough which cuts the ground at the bottom of the furrow; a ploughshare. b. The analogous part of a seed-drill, or similar implement 1731.

Share (ʃēᵊɹ), *sb.*[2] [Late ME. *share*, *schar* :—OE. *scearu* cutting, division :—OTeut. **scaro-*, f. **sker-* to cut, divide; see SHEAR *v.*] 1. The part or portion (*of* something) which is allotted or belongs to an individual, when distribution is made among a number; also, the portion or quota which is contributed by an individual. b. In pregnant sense = One's due, proper, or fair share; one's full share (of something enjoyed or suffered in common with others) 1645. c. The measure or degree *of* a quality, condition, etc. which is allotted to an individual by nature or Providence 1722. 2. *Comm.* A definite portion of a property owned by a number in common; *spec.* each of the equal parts into which the capital of a joint-stock company or corporation is divided 1601. 3. A part taken in (an action, experience, etc.). Chiefly in phr. *to have, take, bear a* (*one's*, etc.) *s. in*, to have or take part in, participate in. 1592. †4. *gen.* A part, piece, or portion (*of* anything) –1772. †b. With etymol. ref. to *shear*: A piece hewn out, or cut or torn away –1776.

1. Taking our turns to row, of which..my share came to little less than 20 leagues EVELYN. There is gold here, my friend, and we must get our s. of it 1888. c. That amiable pity, of which your really superior woman always has such a s. to give away THACKERAY. 2. The ship, wherein my Father had halfe s. 1660. *Deferred, preference shares*: see DEFERRED, PREFERENCE. *Ordinary shares*, the shares which form the common stock and are without 'preference'.

Phrases. *S. and s. alike*, with equal shares, having each a like s. Also *to go s. and s. alike.* *To fall to one's s.*, to be assigned as one's portion; hence, to fall to one's lot (*to do*, etc.). *To go shares with* (another or others) *in* (a possession, enterprise, etc.), to enjoy a part in, participate in, contribute towards.

†**Share,** *v.*[1] 1553. [var. of SHEAR *v.*] *trans.* To cut into parts; to cut off –1735.

The sword..deep entring shar'd All his right side MILT.

Share (ʃēᵊɹ), *v.*[2] 1586. [f. SHARE *sb.*[2]] 1. *trans.* To divide and apportion in shares between two or more recipients. Now chiefly with *out.* 1590. b. To apportion to an individual as his share. Also with *out. arch.* 1586. c. To divide (what one has or receives) into portions, and give shares to others as well as one's self. Const. *with.* 1592. 2. Of two or more persons: To divide into shares and take each a portion. Also *absol.* 1594. 3. To grant or give another or others a share in. Also const. *with.* 1662. 4. To receive, possess, or occupy together with others 1592. †b. To take or receive as one's share. *poet.* –1618. †c. *To s. from*: to gain at the expense of. SHAKS. 5. To perform, enjoy, or suffer in common with others; to possess (a quality) which other persons or things also have. Const. *with.* 1590. 6. *intr.* To have a share (*in* something); to participate *in*, take part *in* 1598. b. To participate *with* (a person) *in* something (*rare*) 1594. c. Used in reduplicated form *s.* (*alike*, etc.): the phrase in SHARE *sb.*[2] being misapprehended grammatically 1821.

1. Suppose I s. my Fortune equally between my own Children and a Stranger SWIFT. b. He part of his small feast to her would s. SPENSER. 2. *Rich. III*, I. iii. 159. 3. Well may he then to you his Cares impart And s. his Burden where he shares his Heart DRYDEN. 4. He shares the frugal meal with those he loves 1804. *fig.* In vain doth Valour bleed While Avarice,

and Rapine s. the land MILT. **b.** *Rich. III*, v. iii. 268. **c.** What glory our Achilles shares from Hector SHAKS. **5.** A man that all his time Hath..Shar'd dangers with you SHAKS. **6. b** MILT. *P.L.* IX. 831. **d.** We all s. and s. alike in camp 1906. Hence **Shared** (ʃɛ̄ᵊɹd) *ppl. a.*, spec. in *Physics* of electrons (1923).

Shareholder (ʃɛ̄ᵊ·ɹhōᵘːldəɹ). 1828. [f. SHARE *sb.*[2] + HOLDER [1].] One who owns or holds a share or shares in a joint-stock company, or other joint fund or property. Hence **Sha·reholding** *vbl. sb.* the possession of shares; *pl.*, shares held in various undertakings.

Sharer (ʃɛ̄ᵊ·rəɹ). 1589. [f. SHARE *v.*[2] + -ER [1].] **1.** One who shares something (const. *of*) or shares *in* something 1603. †**2.** *spec.* A member of a company of players, who paid the expenses, and received the profits, and employed the 'journeymen' members of the company –1704. †**b.** A shareholder –1812.

Shark (ʃāɹk), *sb.*[1] 1569. [Origin obsc.] **1.** A selachian fish of the sub-order *Squali* of the order *Plagiostomi*; in popular language chiefly applied to the large voracious fishes of this sub-order, as the genera *Carcharodon*, *Carcharias*, etc. **b.** With defining word 1655. **c.** *transf.* **Freshwater s.**, (joc.) the pike, alluding to its voracity 1799. **2.** *fig.* (Cf. SHARK *sb.*[2]) One who enriches himself by taking advantage of the necessities of others; a rapacious usurer, an extortionate landlord, a financial swindler, etc. 1713. **b.** A customs officer; also *pl.* the press-gang 1785. **c.** *U.S.* An exceptionally capable person 1909. **3.** *Ent.* Any moth of the genus *Cucullia* (*Noctua*) 1819.

1. The S. hath not this name for nothing, for he will make a morsell of any thing he can catch, master, and devour 1655. **b. Angel-s.**, the monk-fish, *Squatina angelus*; **Gangetic s.**, *Carcharias gangeticus*, inhabiting some rivers; **Greenland s.**, the North Atlantic s., *Laemargus borealis* **Grey s.**, the sand-s., *Carcharinus americanus*; **Hammer-headed s.**, *Zygaena malleus*; **Sea-s.**, a s. of the high seas, esp. 'a large s. of the family *Lamnidæ*'; **Spine s.**, the Picked Dogfish, *Acanthias*; **Spinous s.**, a s. of the genus *Echinorhinus*, as *E. spinosus* **White s.**, a man-eating s., *Carcharodon rondeleti*. **2.** The slopsellers, and other sharks, at this port 1804.

Comb. **s.-fin**, the fin of a s., considered a delicacy by the Chinese; **-moth** = sense 3; **-ray**, the angel-fish, also a rhinobatid or beaked ray, **-toothed** *a.* applied to ornamentation suggesting shark's teeth. Hence **Sharking** *abl. sb.*, fishing for sharks.

†**Shark**, *sb.*[2] 1599. [Origin obsc.] A worthless and impecunious person who gains a precarious living by sponging on others, by executing disreputable commissions, cheating and petty swindling; a sharper –1700.

Shark (ʃāɹk), *v.* 1596. [Origin obsc.] **1.** *intr.* †**a.** *To s. on* or *upon*: to prey like a shark upon; to victimize, sponge upon, swindle; to oppress by extortion. **b.** To depend on or practise fraud or the arts of a 'shark', or sharper; to live by shifts and stratagems. Often *to s. for* (something). 1608. **2.** *trans.* **a.** *To s. up*: to collect hastily (a body of persons, etc.) without regard to selection. Now *arch.*, as an echo of *Haml.* I. i. 98. 1602. **b.** To steal, pilfer, or obtain by underhand or cheating means. *arch.* 1612.

1. **b.** To shift and sharke in every bie-corner for comfort 1641.

Sharp (ʃāɹp), *a.* and *sb.* [Com. Teut.; OE. *scearp* :—OTeut. **skarpo-*.] **A.** *adj.* **1.** Well adapted for cutting or piercing; having a keen edge or point; opp. to *blunt*. **b.** Of sand, gravel, etc.: Composed of materials having sharp points; hard, angular, gritty. Now *techn.* 1618. †**2.** Rough, rugged (chiefly as tr. L. *asper*) –1596. **3.** Acute or penetrating in intellect or perception. **a.** †(*a*) Keen-witted, sagacious. (*b*) Quick-witted, clever (said esp. of children). OE. **b.** Of reasoning or discourse: †Acute, sagacious. In later use, of remarks: Pointed, apt, witty. 1580. **c.** Of sight, hearing, the eyes or ears: Acute, keen OE. **d.** Hence of observation, an observer: Vigilant 1535. **e.** Businesslike, smart; often, quick to take unfair advantage of others 1697. **4.** Eager, impetuous, violent OE. **b.** (*a*) Of a hawk: Eager for prey, hungry. (*b*) Of the appetite: Keen. Of the stomach: Craving for food. 1486. **c.** Quick or active in bodily movement. Of movements: Brisk, energetic. 1440. **d.** Of a stream: Rapid. Now *rare*. 1655. **e.** Of winter, wintry weather, frost, wind, air: Cuttingly cold, keen. late ME. **5.** Severe, strict, harsh OE. **b.** Of pain, suffering, grief, etc.: Keen, acute, intense. Of experiences: Intensely painful. OE. †**c.** Of a mode of life: Austere –1611. **6.** Pungent in taste; also, having strong acid, alkaline, or caustic properties OE. **7.** Of sound: Penetrating, shrill, high-pitched. late ME. **b.** *Phonetics.* (*a*) Expressing the acoustic quality of high-front vowels 1532. (*b*) An antiquated designation for unvoiced consonants 1841. **8.** *Mus.* **a.** Of a note: Relatively high in pitch. **b.** Of a note, singing, an instrument: Above the regular or true pitch. **c.** *A, C, D*, etc. *s.*: the sound which is a semitone higher than A, C, D, etc. Also, the key or other contrivance in a musical instrument for producing such a note. d. Of an interval, †key, †scale: = MAJOR *a.* I. 2. e. Of a key. Having sharps in the signature. 1597. **9.** With ref. to form only (without implication of cutting or piercing). **a.** Tapering to a (relatively) fine point ME. **b.** Of an angle: †(*a*) = ACUTE *a.* 1 –1688. (*b*) Abrupt; involving sudden change of direction; so *s. turn* 1825. **c.** Of an ascent or descent, a rise or fall: Abrupt 1725. **d.** *Naut.* Of the shape of a vessel: Having a narrow and wedge-shaped bottom 1709. **e.** Of features: Emaciated, peaked, thin 1561. **10.** Having the angles or edges not rounded off or flattened; hence, clear or distinct in outline. Often of contrasts, distinctions, etc.: Abrupt, strongly marked. 1675.

1. A busshe full of s. thornes CAXTON. I know, his Sword Hath a sharpe edge SHAKS. *fig.* The s. edge ..of public curiosity 1807. Phr. *S. as a razor, as a needle*, etc. **b.** Clean but coarse s. sand 1859. 3. **a.** (*b*) A very s. lad 1870. **b.** He..alleadged Many sharpe reasons to defeat the Law SHAKS. **c.** The grey eye..is sharpest of sight 1630. **d.** Phr. *To keep a s. look-out.* **e.** They got a s. Newcastle attorney SCOTT. See also SHARP PRACTICE. Similarly, *s. work.* **4.** The contest between good and evil becomes s. and deadly 1845. **c.** A s. gallop 1842. Provb. phr. *Sharp's the word* (used as an injunction to promptitude). **e.** Though the air was s., he had been carrying his cloak over his arm 1894. **5.** Skelton a sharpe Satirist 1589. A rigorous and s. penance 1663. Phr. *To be s. upon*, to be hard or severe upon (now only by way of censure or criticism). **b.** Sharpe miserie had worne him to the bones SHAKS. S., lancinating pains 1843. **c.** *Cymb.* III. iii. 31. **6.** Wo was his cook, but if his sauce were Poynaunt and s. CHAUCER. **7.** S. Violins proclaim Their jealous Pangs DRYDEN. **9. a.** Hys nese at þe poynt es s. and smalle HAMPOLE. **c.** A very s. rise leads from the Pacific to the range of the Andes HUXLEY. **10.** The sharpest geographical contrast 1856.

B. *sb.* **1.** A sharp weapon; *spec.* a small sword; a rapier used for duelling as opp. to a 'blunt' or buttoned weapon. *Obs.* or *arch.* late ME. †**2.** A sharp edge; *spec.* the edge of a sword –1734. **3.** *Mus.* **a.** A high-pitched note (*rare*). **b.** A note raised half a tone above the natural pitch. **c.** In musical notation, the sign ♯ which indicates this raising of the note. *Double s.*: the sign × indicating that a note must be raised two semitones. **4. a.** = SHARPER 2 1797. **b.** *colloq.* An expert, connoisseur, a wise man or one professing to be so 1865. **5.** *pl.* The 'middlings' between bran and flour 1801. **6.** *pl.* One of the three grades of needles, including those of greatest length and most acutely pointed 1849.

1. Phr †*To fight, play*, etc. *at the s., at sharp(s*, to fight with unbated swords, to fight in earnest, in contradistinction to fencing; A combate of fensers (called *Gladiatores*) fighting at the sharpe NORTH. **2.** Phr. *The s. of the hand*, the edge of the hand. **3.** I chatter over stony ways, In little sharps and trebles TENNYSON. **4. a.** The sharps have queered me 1797.

Comb.: **s.-eyed** *a.*, keen of sight; *transf.* observant, penetrating; **-fanged** *a.*, having a s. tooth; *fig.* biting (in speech), caustic, sarcastic; **-featured** *a.*, peaked, thin; **-nosed** *a.*, having a pointed nose; *fig.* quick at fault-finding, captious; **-sighted** *a.*, having acute or quick sight; having acuteness of mental vision; **-tailed** *a.*, having a tapering tail or pointed tail-feathers, *spec.* in names of birds; **-tongued** *a.*, bitter of speech; **-toothed** *a.*, keen of tooth; *transf.* rending, tearing; **-witted** *a.*, sagacious, intelligent.

Sharp (ʃāɹp), *adv.* [OE. *scearpe*, f. *scearp* SHARP *a.*] **1.** In a sharp manner; †shrilly; †niggardly, stingily. **b.** Abruptly, suddenly 1836. **c.** In an invitation or appointment: Punctually, precisely (at the hour specified) 1840. **d.** *Look s.*: see LOOK *v.* I. 5. **2.** *Naut.* As near fore and aft as possible, trimmed as near as possible to the wind 1669.

1. If Flies and small Gnats bite sharpe and sore 1635. **b.** The horse..turns s. round and stands stock still 1860. **c.** They should dine that day at three o'clock s. THACKERAY. Hence **Sha·rp-ly** *adv.*, **-ness.**

Sharp (ʃāɹp), *v.* [OE. **scierpan*, *scẹrpan*, *scyrpan* :—OTeut. **skarpjan-*, f. **skarpo-* SHARP *a.*] **1.** *trans.* = SHARPEN *v.* 1. Now only *dial.* ME. †**2.** = SHARPEN *v.* 2. –1633. †**3.** *intr.* To play the sharper –1785. **4.** *trans.* **a.** To cheat, swindle, trick (a person) 1700. **b.** To obtain by swindling, to steal 1706.

Sharp-edged, *a.* (Stress variable). OE. Having a sharp edge or sharp edges.

fig. S. words have sharp edges to wound DICKENS.

Sharpen (ʃā·ɹp'n), *v.* 1450. [f. SHARP *a.* + -EN [5].] **1.** *trans.* To put a sharp edge or point upon; to furnish (a weapon, implement, etc.) with a cutting edge or fine point 1530. **2.** To make sharp or sharper. **a.** To render more acute (a person's wit, sight, appetite, etc.); to intensify (hostile feeling) 1450. **b.** To give an acid flavour or quality to, to make (a liquid) sour or bitter 1675. **c.** To increase the severity of (a law, punishment) 1709. †**d.** To exacerbate (persons, their temper) –1792. **e.** To aggravate (pain or suffering) 1768. **f.** To make (the features) sharp or thin 1835. **3.** *Mus.* To raise the pitch of a note sounded upon a musical instrument 1824. **4.** *Naut.* To brace sharp up 1841. †**5.** *intr.* To become sharp, to taper to a point; to grow thin –1851.

1. Flints sharpened by chipping 1890. **2. a.** My hearing..has been sharpened by my blindness SCOTT. **c.** A Law..for sharpening Laws against Papists 1709. **e.** An injury sharpened by an insult STERNE. **5.** His face..sharpened like the face of a sick man 1851. Hence **Sha·rpener,** one who or something which sharpens.

Sharper (ʃā·ɹpəɹ). 1567. [f. SHARP *v.* + -ER [1].] **1.** One who or something which 'sharps' or sharpens. **2.** A cheat, swindler, rogue; one who lives by his wits and by taking advantage of others; esp. a fraudulent gamester 1681.

Sharpie (ʃā·ɹpi). *U.S.* 1864. [app. f. SHARP *a.*] A long, sharp, flat-bottomed fishing-boat.

Sharp-pointed, *a.* (Stress variable.) 1530. **1.** Tapered or tapering to a point. **b.** *Bot.* Acuminate, mucronate 1565. **2.** Having a fine point adapted for piercing or stabbing 1594. **3.** Having irregular, sharp projections 1748.

Sharp practice. 1847. **1.** Work that demands brisk activity (*rare*). **2. a.** Hard bargaining; relentless pursuit of advantage. **b.** Dishonourable taking of advantage, trickery. 1847.

Sharp-set, *a.* (Stress variable.) 1540. [f. SHARP *a.* + SET *ppl. a.*] **1.** Eager or keen for food, very hungry. Also said of the stomach. **2.** *transf.* Keen, eager; having desire fixed *upon*, craving *after* 1580. †**b.** Having a craving for sexual indulgence –1794.

2. The town is s. on new plays 1711.

Sharpshooter (ʃā·ɹp,ʃūtəɹ). 1802. [f. SHARP *a.* + SHOOTER.] A marksman of accurate aim; *spec.* in naval and military use, a member of a division engaged in skirmishing and outpost work. Hence **Sha·rpshooting** *vbl. sb.*

Shaster (ʃæ·stəɹ), ‖ **Shastra** (ʃā·stră). 1630. [a. Hindī *çāstr*, Skr. *çastra*.] Any one of the sacred writings of the Hindus.

‖ **Shastri** (ʃā·strī). 1645. [Hindī *çāstrī*, Skr. *çāstrin*, f. *çāstra* SHASTER.] One who is learned in, or teaches, the shasters.

Shatter (ʃæ·təɹ), *sb.* 1640. [f. next.] **1.** *pl.* Fragments into which a thing is broken, rent, or torn. *Obs.* exc. *dial.* **2.** A shattered state of nerves (*rare*) 1777.

1. Phr. (*To break*, etc.) *into* or *to shatters*, (*to be*) *in shatters*; For the Ministry, it is all in shatters H. WALPOLE.

Shatter (ʃæ·təɹ), *v.* ME. [Obscurely related to SCATTER.] **1.** *trans.* To scatter, disperse; to cause (seed, leaves, etc.) to fall or to be shed. *Obs.* exc. *dial.* **2.** To break in pieces by a sudden blow or concussion; to dash into fragments, disrupt into parts 1450. **b.** To damage ruinously (a structure, a living organism, etc.) by battery or violent concussion; to damage or destroy by fracture of the parts 1513. **c.** *fig.*, or with immaterial object. Also, to damage or destroy the fortunes of (a person or body of persons). 1683. **d.** To wreck (a person's constitution, nerves, etc.) by sickness, hardship, or the like. Also, to wreck the health, strength, or spirits of (a person). 1785. **3.** *intr.* To become scattered or dispersed; to be shed or strewn about. Of grain, etc.: To drop out of the husk from over-ripeness. Of a flower: To drop its petals. Now *dial.* 1577. **4.** To become broken suddenly or violently into fragments or separate parts; to fly in pieces or asunder 1567. **b.** Of earth: To fall or crumble in pieces. *dial.* 1733. **5.** To dash or strike noisily against some hard object; to clatter, rattle (*rare*). late ME.

1. S. your leaves before the mellowing year MILT. 2. The bottles twain behind his back Were shatter'd at a blow COWPER. b. Cossack and Russian Reel'd from the sabre-stroke Shatter'd and sunder'd TENNYSON. c. The war or revolution that shatters a rotten system EMERSON. d. Shattered in mind, and perilously sick in body DICKENS. 4. Some Fragile Bodies breake but where the Force is; Some s. and fly in many Peeces BACON. 5. The casements s., tatter and clatter 1623.

Comb.: **s.-brain, -pate, -wit,** a person of 'cracked' brain or wandering wits; a giddy, thoughtless person; so **s.-brained, -pated, -witted,** *adjs.*, crazy, light-witted; giddy, thoughtless.

Sha·ttering, *ppl. a.* 1567. [f. prec. + -ING [2].] **1.** That is broken up suddenly or forcibly; falling in pieces or asunder. **2.** Ruinously destructive; that breaks or destroys by a sudden blow or concussion 1577. **b.** Of sound: Rending the air, ear-splitting 1842.

2. *fig.* Her answer to this was as s. as it was rapid DE QUINCEY. b. The s. trumpet shrilleth high TENNYSON. Hence **Sha·tteringly** *adv.*

Shattery (ʃæ·təri), *a.* 1728. [f. SHATTER *v.* + -Y [1].] Of rock, stone, or soil: Apt to break in pieces or crumble; friable.

Shave (ʃēⁱv), *sb.*[1] [OE. *sceafa* :—OTeut. *skaƀon-, f. *skaƀ-; see SHAVE *v.*] Any of various tools adapted for scraping, paring, or removing the surface of material in very thin slices; a drawing or paring knife; also, short for SPOKESHAVE, etc.

Shave (ʃēⁱv), *sb.*[2] 1604. [f. next.] **1.** Something shaved off; a shaving, paring, thin slice. **2.** An act of shaving the beard 1838. **3.** An act of swindling or extortion 1863. **b.** A premium paid for an extension of the time of delivery or payment, or for the right to vary a contract. 1864. **4.** *Mil. slang.* An unauthenticated report 1813. **5.** A slight or grazing touch; hence, a narrow escape from touching, more emphatically *a close, near s.* and the like 1834.

3. *Clean s.*, a complete swindle. 5. We passed clear; but it was a close s. 1856.

Shave (ʃēⁱv), *v.* Pa. t. **shaved**; pa. pple. **shaven, shaved.** [Com. Teut. (orig. str.) vb.; OE. *sceafan*, f. Teut. root *skaƀ-.] **1.** *trans.* To scrape, to scrape away the surface of, to cut down or pare away with a sharp tool, thereby removing very thin portions of the surface. Also with *off.* **b.** To scrape or pare (a skin, hide, etc.) 1467. **2.** To remove by scraping and paring; to cut off in thin slices or shavings; also *to s. off.* late ME. **3.** To cut off (hair, esp. the beard) close to the skin with or as with a razor. Also with *away, off.* ME. **4.** To cut off the beard, whiskers, or moustache from (a person, his chin, upper lip, etc.) with a razor ME. **5.** To remove the hair from (the head, crown, etc.) with a razor. Also (now *rarely*) with the person as object (= to s. the head of) ME. **b.** *esp.* To tonsure (a cleric). late ME. **6. a.** *absol.* Of a barber. late ME. **b.** *intr.* for *refl.* To shave oneself 1715. **7.** *trans.* †To strip (a person) clean of money or possessions; to practise exaction or extortion upon; to fleece. Also *absol.* Now *colloq.* or *slang.* late ME. **8.** To cut off cleanly or closely 1598. **b.** To cut off closely the growth of (ground, a lawn, etc.); also *transf.* of artillery fire 1764. **9.** To touch lightly in passing, to graze; hence, barely to escape touching 1513. **b.** intr. *To s. through*: to get through only by grazing (that which has to be passed); *fig.* to scrape *through* (an examination) 1860. **10.** trans. *U.S. slang.* To discount (a promissory note) at an exorbitant rate of interest; also *to s. paper* 1832.

3. With crowne and berde all fressh and newe y-shaue CHAUCER. Take my counsel, and s. off them mustachios, or they'll bring you into mischief THACKERAY. 4. Stepping into a barber's shop to be shaved SMOLLETT. 5. *Prov.* Enuy .. will offer to shaue an eg 1626. He shaved, however, only the fore part of his head 1770. 6. a. A poor Barber who shaves for Two-pence 1718. 7. We should never travel without—a case of good razors.. But no matter, I believe we shall be pretty well shaved by the way GOLDSM. 9. Three hansoms shaved him by an inch BARRIE.

Comb.: **s.-hook,** a plumbers' tool consisting of a blade, commonly triangular, set transversely in a handle, used for scraping metal before soldering.

Shavegrass (ʃēⁱ·vgrɑs). 1450. [f. prec. + GRASS *sb.*] A plant of the genus *Equisetum*; esp. *E. hyemale.*

Shaveling (ʃēⁱ·vliŋ), *sb.* (and *a.*). 1529. [f. as prec. + -LING [1].] **A.** *sb.* **1.** A contemptuous epithet for a tonsured ecclesiastic. **2.** A youth, young 'shaver' (*rare*) 1854. **B.** *adj.* Of, pertaining to, or characteristic of a tonsured ecclesiastic 1577.

A. 1. Counting up the number of shavelings still in France 1911.

Shaven (ʃēⁱ·v'n), *ppl. a.* ME. [Strong pa. pple. of SHAVE *v.*] **1.** Shaved. Chiefly of the head, crown, or of a person; often = tonsured. **2.** Of turf, grass: Closely cut 1632. **3.** Trimmed or polished by shaving 1660.

Shaver (ʃēⁱ·vəɹ). late ME. [f. SHAVE *v.* + -ER [1].] **1.** One who shaves with a razor. **2.** †**a.** One who pillages or plunders; an extortioner –1823. **b.** *U.S.* One who 'shaves' (SHAVE *v.* 10) 1813. **3.** = 'Fellow', 'chap'; also, a humorous fellow, joker, wag. Now commonly of a youth or boy, with the epithet *young, little.* 1592. †**4.** A shaving instrument or tool –1648.

2. a. *Cunning s.*, a swindler, sharper; The Devil is a cunning s. DE FOE. 3. Forty-five years ago I was just such a little s. as this 1887.

Shavian (ʃēⁱ·viăn), *a.* 1920. [f. *Shavius*, latinized f. proper name *Shaw*: see -IAN.] Of, pertaining to, or characteristic of George Bernard Shaw (1856–) or his plays or other writings.

Shaving (ʃēⁱ·viŋ), *vbl. sb.* ME. [f. SHAVE *v.* + -ING [1].] **1.** The action of removing the hair from the head or face with a razor; an instance of this. **2.** *concr.* A thin slice taken off the surface of anything with a sharp tool; esp. a thin slice of wood cut off with a plane. Chiefly *pl.* late ME. **3.** *slang.* The action or process of defrauding 1606. **b.** *U.S.* The discounting of bills at an exorbitant rate of interest 1834.

2. All shavings of horns..is good manure for land 1760.

Comb.: **s.-brush,** a brush used to put on the lather before shaving.

Shaw (ʃǭ). *arch.* and *dial.* [OE. *sc(e)aga*; related to *sceacga* SHAG *sb.*[1]] **1.** A thicket, a small wood, copse or grove. **2.** *spec.* A strip of wood or underwood forming the border of a field 1577.

1. Gaillard he was as Goldfynch in the shawe CHAUCER. A new-blawn plumrose in a hazle s. BURNS.

Shawl (ʃǭl), *sb.* 1662. [a. Pers. *shāl.*] **1.** An article of dress worn by Orientals (commonly as a scarf, turban, or girdle), consisting of an oblong piece of material manufactured in Kashmir from the hair of the Tibetan 'shawl-goat'. **2.** An oblong or square piece of any textile or netted fabric, whether of wool, cotton, silk, or mixtures of these; worn in Europe and the West, chiefly by women as a covering for the shoulders or the head 1767.

Comb.: **s.-dance,** an Eastern dance, in which a s. or scarf is waved; **-goat,** a goat of Tibet (*Capra lanigera*) which furnishes the wool for making the Indian shawls; **-wool,** the wool of the s.-goat.

Shawl (ʃǭl), *v.* 1812. [f. prec.] *trans.* To cover with a shawl, put a shawl on.

Shawm (ʃǭm), *sb.* [ME. *shallemelle*, a. OF. *chalemel* :—pop. L. *calamellus, dim. of *calamus* reed; also (*pl.*) *schalmeis, shalmys*, a. OF. *chalemie*, an unexplained deriv. of L. *calamus.*] A mediæval musical instrument of the oboe class, having a double reed enclosed in a globular mouthpiece.

With shaumes, and trompets, and with clarions sweet SPENSER. Hence **Shawm** *v. intr.* to play on the s. (*rare*).

Shawnee (ʃǭnī·). 1909. Name of a tribe of Algonquin Indians, used *attrib.* in **S.-haw,** the larger withe-rod, *Viburnum nudum*; **S.-wood,** the western catalpa or catawba-tree, *Catalpa speciosa.*

Shay (ʃēⁱ). 1717. [A back-formation from CHAISE (ʃēⁱz) mistaken for a pl.] = CHAISE.

It is n't everybody that can ride to heaven in a C-spring s. O. W. HOLMES.

She (ʃī, ʃi), *pers. pron.*, *3rd sing. fem. nom.* ME. [prob. an altered form of OE. fem. dem. pron. *sīo, sēo, sīe.*] **I.** As proper feminine pronoun of the third person, nominative case. **1.** The female being in question, or last mentioned. **b.** Used of animals of the female sex. Also (esp. in rustic use) of certain animals (e.g. the cat, the hare), the names of which have a quasi-grammatical feminine gender exc. when a male is specifically referred to. late ME. ¶**c.** Misused for *I* (also for *you* and *he*) in literary representations of Highland English 1450. **2.** Used (instead of *it*) of things to which female sex is conventionally attributed. late ME. **3.** Used pleonastically. Now only *arch.* and in uneducated use. 1440. **4.** Used for *her*, as obj. or governed by a prep. Now *rare* exc. *vulg.* 1530.

1. S. shalbe called woman, because shee was taken out of man *Gen.* ii. 23. 2. The Moone cannot shine except shee receiue light from the Sunne 1614. S. ..was a fine roomy ship 1748. Nature must not be hurried, and s. avenges herself of every attempt to do so SCOTT. 3. The Liner she 's a lady by the paint upon 'er face KIPLING. 4. I neuer saw a woman But onely Sycorax my Dam, and s. SHAKS. I have got rid of s. 1762.

II. As antecedent pronoun, followed by relative, etc. The or that woman, or person of the female sex (*that* or *who*...). ME.

Him that got thee, s. that gaue thee sucke SHAKS.

III. As demonstrative pronoun. late ME.

The Venus of the Medici?—s. of the diminutive head and the gilded hair? POE.

IV. As *sb.* (not changing in the objective). **1.** A female; a woman or girl; a lady-love 1538. **b.** A female animal 1556. **2.** Opp. to *he*: Female 1500.

1. Who ere she be, That not impossible s. That shall command my heart and me CRASHAW. Those are not shes — they're both men 1894.

V. *attrib.* passing into *adj.* Female. late ME.

‖**Shea** (ʃī, ʃī·ă). 1799. [Mandingo *si, se, sye.*] A sapotaceous tree of tropical Africa, *Bassia parkii*, from the kernels of which is obtained *s. butter*, a substance used as food by the natives and in Europe for the manufacture of soap, etc.

Sheading (ʃī·diŋ). 1577. [var. f. *shedding* vbl. sb.] Each of six administrative sub-divisions (three to each 'district') of the Isle of Man.

Sheaf (ʃīf), *sb.* [Com. Teut.; OE. *scēaf* :—OTeut. *skauƀo-, app. f. the root *skauƀ-: skeuƀ-: skuƀ-; see SHOVE *v.*] **1.** One of the large bundles in which it is usual to bind cereal plants after reaping. Also, a similar bundle of the stalks or blooms of other plants. **2.** A bundle or quiverful of 24 arrows ME. **3.** A representation of a sheaf (of corn, arrows, etc.). late ME. **4.** *gen.* A cluster or bundle of things tied up together; a quantity of things set thick together 1728. **b.** Emphatically in pl.: A large number, mass, or quantity 1865. **5.** *Physics* and *Math.* A bundle of rays, lines, etc. all passing through a given point 1863.

1. Corn reaped and standing in sheaves 1717. †*Tenth, ninth, third,* etc. *s.*, a specified proportionate part of the annual crop paid to the lord or to the church. 2. Half a shef of arwes LANGL.

Comb. **s.-binder,** one who binds sheaves, a machine which does this. Hence **Shea·fy** *a.* consisting of or resembling a sheaf or sheaves.

Sheaf (ʃīf), *v.* 1506. [f. prec.] *trans.* To bind into a sheaf or sheaves; also with *up.*

absol. They that reap must sheafe and binde SHAKS.

Shealing, var. of SHIELING.

Shear (ʃīᵊɹ), *sb.*[1] [prob. two formations: (1) OE. *scērero* pl.:—OTeut. *skǣrizō :—pre-Teut. *skēresā, f. root *sker-; see SHEAR *v.* (2) OE. *scēar*, f. the same root.] **1.** orig. (and still *Sc.* and *dial.*) = SCISSORS. In later use commonly applied to scissors of large size and to other cutting instruments which operate similarly. **a.** in pl. form, with pl. construction, either in sing. or pl. sense. When qualification by a numeral or an indef. article is required, *pair of shears* is used OE. **b.** in sing. form, = a pair of shears. Now *rare.* ME. **c.** *fig.*, esp. as attributed to the Fates 1590. **d.** *Mech.* Applied to various machines for cutting metals, more or less analogous to shears in manner of operation 1834. **e.** *Cloth-manuf.* The cutting apparatus of a cloth-cropping machine composed of a series of spiral blades on a revolving cylinder 1839. **2.** *pl.* (Often construed as sing.) A device used upon ships, and in dockyards and mines, for raising and fixing masts, boilers and other heavy gear, consisting of two (or occas. more) poles steadied (in a sloping position) by guys and fastened together at the top, from which the hoisting tackle depends, and with their lower ends separated as a base and secured to the deck or platform. Often spelt **sheers.** 1625.

1. a. For cutting thin sheet metal and wire, a pair of hand-shears 1902. *Prov.* †*There goes but a pair of shears between them*, they match each other as if cut from the same cloth; they are 'of a piece'. c. Comes the blind Fury with th' abhorred shears, And slits the thin spun life MILT.

Comb.: **s.-tail**, (*a*) *dial.* the Common Tern (*Sterna fluviatilis*); (*b*) a Peruvian bird (*Thaumastuar cora*).

Shear (ʃīəɹ), *sb.*[2] Now chiefly *dial.* 1614. [f. SHEAR *v.*] **I.** Action or result of shearing. **a.** A mowing of grass or corn, a crop 1794. **b.** Used in stating the age of sheep with ref. to the number of times the fleece has been shorn. *One s., two s.*, one, two years old. 1614. **II.** In scientific uses. **1. a.** *Physics* and *Mech.* (*a*) A kind of strain consisting in a movement of planes of a body that are parallel to a particular plane in a direction parallel to a line in that plane through distances proportional to their distances from that plane. (*b*) The stress called into play in a body which undergoes this kind of strain. 1850. **b.** *Geom.* The transformation produced in a plane figure by motion in which all the points of the figure describe paths parallel to a fixed axis and proportional in length to their distance from it 1885. **2.** *Geol.* Applied to the operation of transverse compression on a mass of rock, resulting in alteration of structure or breach of continuity 1888.

Shear (ʃīəɹ), *sb.*[3] Also **sheer.** 1812. [Origin obsc.] The bar, or one of the two parallel bars, forming the bed of a lathe on which the poppets slide.

Shear (ʃīəɹ), *v.* Pa. t. **sheared** (ʃīəɹd), **shore** (ʃōəɹ); pa. pple. **sheared, shorn** (ʃǭɹn). [Com. Teut. (orig. str.) vb.; OE. *sceran* (*scear, scǣron, scoren*); f. OTeut. **sker-, skar-, skǣr-, skur-* to cut, divide, shear, shave.] **1.** *trans.* To cut (something) with a sharp instrument. *Obs.* exc. *arch.* **b.** *absol.* or *intr.* Now chiefly, To cut *through* (an obstacle) with the aid of a weapon. ME. **c.** To cut (glass, tin-plate, etc.) with shears. Also, to cut (iron or steel bars, etc.) with shears. 1837. **2.** To remove (a part) from a body by cutting with a sharp instrument ME. **3.** To remove (the hair or beard) by means of some sharp instrument (also with *off, away*); to shave (the head or face); to cut (the hair) close or short; to cut or shave the hair or beard of (a person). Now *rare* exc. in pa. pple. *shorn*. OE. †**b.** To give the tonsure *to*. Usu. *pass.* –1653. **4.** pass. *To be shorn*: to be deprived *of* some part or appurtenance by or as by cutting. Chiefly *transf.* and *fig.* 1740. **5.** To cut the fleece from (an animal); also, to cut off (the fleece, wool, etc.) OE. **6.** To cut off (the superfluous nap of woollen cloth) in the process of manufacture; also, in hat-making, to remove (nap) by singeing or scouring ME. **7.** To cut down, to reap (grass, crops, etc.) with a sickle (†formerly also, with a scythe). Now *dial.* ME. **b.** *absol.* or *intr.* To cut standing crops; to use a sickle ME. **c.** To clip, cut, or trim (a tree or bush, a lawn) ME. **8.** To cleave, divide; said esp. of birds, ships, etc. ME. **b.** *intr.* for *refl.* *Where wind and weather* (or *water*) *shears*: on the ridge of a hill 1556. **9.** *Mech., Geol.*, etc. *trans.* To subject to a shearing stress; to distort or fracture by shear 1850.

1. As bright as if shorn by a file SMEATON. b. By a back stroke of his own cimeter shore through the cuirass LYTTON. 2. The plume was partly shorn away SCOTT. 3. They have shorn their bright curls off to cast on Adonis MRS. BROWNING. 4. Sadly I know I am shorn of my strength POE. *fig.* He cannot bear the thought of..appearing among the gentlemen of the neighbourhood shorn of his beams JOHNSON. 8. Like a plough that shears the heavy Land R. BRIDGES. Hence **Shea·rer**, a reaper of standing crops; one who or that which shears the fleece from an animal.

Shear-grass (ʃīə·ɹgrɑs). 1483. [f. prec.] Popular name of several kinds of sharp-edged grass or sedge, as the saw-grass.

Shearing (ʃīə·riŋ), *vbl. sb.* ME. [f. SHEAR *v.* + -ING[1].] **1.** The action or an act of cutting, clipping, or shaving with shears or some other sharp instrument. **2.** Something which is cut off with shears, etc. Now only *pl.* 1536. **3.** *dial.* A sheep after the first shearing, a shearling 1641. **4.** *Mining.* The vertical cutting of the ends of a portion of an undercut seam of coal 1875. **5.** *Physics*, etc. See SHEAR *v.* 9; the causing of a shear 1850.

2. It was like the s. of the Hogs, all Bristles 1673.

Comb.: **s. strain,** a strain of the nature of a shear; **s. strength,** power of resistance to s.; **s. stress,** a stress tending to produce or resist a shear.

Shear-legs. 1860. [SHEAR *sb.*[1]] A device consisting of three poles of wood or iron bolted together at their upper ends and extended below, carrying tackle for raising heavy weights for machinery.

Shearling (ʃīə·ɹliŋ). late ME. [f. SHEAR *v.* + -LING.] **1.** A sheep that has been once shorn. †**2.** The fleece of such a sheep –1680.

Shearman (ʃīə·ɹmăn). ME. [f. SHEAR *v.* + MAN *sb.*] **1.** One who shears woollen cloth. Now *Hist.* **2.** One who conducts the process of shearing metal 1881.

Shears *pl.*: see SHEAR *sb.*[1]

Shear steel. 1815. [f. SHEAR *sb.*[1]] Blister steel improved in quality by heating, rolling, and tilting; formerly used for shear-blades.

†**'Sheart.** 1596. A euphemistic shortening of *God's heart*, used as an oath or asseveration –1706.

Shearwater (ʃīə·ɹwǭːtəɹ). 1671. [f. SHEAR *v.* + WATER *sb.*] **1.** A bird of the genus *Puffinus*, esp. *P. anglorum*, the Manx Shearwater, and *P. major*, the Greater Shearwater. **2.** *U.S.* The Black Skimmer, *Rhynchops nigra* 1794.

Sheath (ʃīþ), *sb.* [OE. *scǣþ, sceāþ*:—OTeut. **skaiþjō*.] **1.** A case or covering into which a blade is thrust when not in use; usu. close-fitting and conforming to the shape of the blade, esp. of a sword, dagger, knife, etc. **2.** A sheath-like covering. *esp.* **a.** *Zool.* The tubular fold of skin into which the penis is retracted 1555. **b.** *Bot.* A tubular or enrolled part or organ that is rolled round a stem or other body, as the spathe of a flower, the lower part of the leaves of grasses, etc. 1671. **c.** *Bot.* 'A limiting layer of surrounding cellular tissue' 1884. **d.** *Anat.* The connective tissue covering which closely invests a part or elongated organ, and binds it together and holds it in place 1805. **e.** The elytron or outer hard wing-case of a coleopterous insect 1826. **f.** The fold of skin into which the claws of a feline animal are retracted 1774. **3.** A structure or banking of loose stones to prevent the overflow of a river 1850.

1. Handles, Scabbards, Sheaths for Knives 1669.

Comb.: **s. bill,** a sea-bird of the genus *Chionis*, having the basal part of the bill ensheathed in a horny case; **-knife,** a dagger-like knife encased in a sheath; **-winged** *a.*, having the wings encased in elytra, coleopterous, vaginipennate. Hence **Sheathed** (ʃīþt) *a.* *Nat. Hist.* having or surrounded by a s.; put in or capable of being withdrawn into a s. **Shea·thless** *a.* not encased in a s., having no s.

Sheathe (ʃīð), *v.* Also *techn.* **sheath** (ʃīþ). late ME. [f. prec.] †**1.** *trans.* To fit or furnish (a sword, etc.) with a sheath –1596. **2.** To put (a sword, dagger, etc.) into a sheath or scabbard. late ME. **b.** *transf.* To bury (a sword) as in a sheath (e.g. *in* an enemy's body). Also with obj. an animal's tusk, claw, etc. 1584. **c.** *fig.* To lay aside, cause to be laid aside (hostility, malice). Now *rare* or *Obs.* 1598. **d.** To retract or draw in (the claws) 1681. **3.** To cover or encase (esp. a person or part of the body) *in* (something, usu. protective) 1632. **4.** †**a.** *Med.* To mitigate the acridity or pungency of (a drug) by the use of an emollient vehicle –1811. **b.** *gen.* To mitigate the painfulness of 1820. **5.** (Often *sheath.*) **a.** To cover (a ship, door, roof, etc.) with a sheathing of metal 1615. **b.** To cover a telegraph cable with a protective envelope 1884. **6.** *Nat. Hist.* To surround with a 'sheath' or covering 1664.

1. Walters dagger was not come from sheathing SHAKS. 2. Phr. *To s. the sword* (fig.), to cease hostilities, to put an end to war or enmity; The sword should not be sheathed till he had been brought to.. punishment MACAULAY. b. 'Tis in my breast she sheaths her Dagger now DRYDEN. d. The Leopard ..always keeps the Claws of his fore-feet turned up from the ground, and sheath'd as it were in the Skin of his Toes 1681. 3. Warriors sheathed in complete steel SCOTT. Hence **Sheathed** (ʃīðd; *techn.* ʃīþt) *ppl. a.*, of a sword, etc., put into or encased in a sheath; of a ship, having the bottom covered with sheathing. **Sheather** (ʃī·ðəɹ), one who or that which sheathes.

Sheath-fish (ʃī·þfiʃ), **sheat-fish** (ʃī·t-). 1589. [The earlier form *sheath-fish* is prob. f. SHEATH; perh. so named from some fanciful resemblance to a cavalry scabbard. The later *sheat-fish* is app. ad. G. *scheidfisch*, f. *scheid*, of unkn. etym.] A large freshwater fish, *Silurus glanis*, common in the Danube and other rivers of eastern Europe. **b.** In extended use, as a name for the order *Siluridæ* or for a subdivision of it which includes the genus *Silurus* 1851.

Sheathing (ʃī·þiŋ, ʃī·ðiŋ), *vbl. sb.* 1499. [f. SHEATHE *v.* + -ING[1].] **1. a.** The action of putting into a sheath. **b.** The action of putting on a protective layer to a ship's bottom 1623. **2.** A protective layer or covering laid on the outside of the bottom of a wooden ship. Formerly of boards, etc., now usu. of thin plates of metal (copper). 1587. **b.** *gen.* A covering or envelope in which something is encased for protection or ornament; material prepared for use as an envelope or casing. Chiefly in techn. applications: e.g. a covering of boards, plates of metal, etc., fitted to the surface of a wall, roof, a piece of machinery, or the like 1859. **3.** A banking of loose stones to prevent the overflowing of a river 1867.

Sheave (ʃīv), *sb.* ME. [cogn. w. OS. *scīva*, mod.G. *scheibe*, etc.] **1.** A slice of bread. late ME. **2.** A wheel having a groove in the circumference to receive a cord passing over it, a pulley; esp. one of the pulleys connected in a block. Also, a wheel having a groove in the circumference to enable it to run on a rail or bar. ME. **b.** An eccentric or its disk 1887.

Sheave (ʃīv), *v.*[1] 1579. [f. SHEAF *sb.*] *trans.* To bring together, gather or put up (corn, etc.) into a sheaf or sheaves. Hence **Sheaved** *ppl. a.* put up or gathered into a sheaf or sheaves.

Sheave (ʃīv), *v.*[2] [perh. OE. *scēofan*, var. of *scūfan* SHOVE *v.*] *intr.* To back a boat.

Shebang (ʃĭbæ·ŋ). *U.S. slang.* 1867. [Origin unkn.] **1.** A hut, shed; one's dwelling, quarters. **2.** Any matter of present concern; thing; business 1895.

Shebeen (ʃĭbī·n). 1787. [orig. Anglo-Irish; origin obsc.] Chiefly in Ireland and Scotland: A shop or house where excisable liquors are sold without a licence; any low wayside public-house.

Shed (ʃed), *sb.*[1] [OE. (*ge*)*scēad*, altered f. (*ge*)*scēad*:—OTeut.*(*ga*)*skaiðōm*, f. root **skaið-* to divide; see SHED *v.*] †**1.** Distinction, discrimination, separation (of one thing from another) –1703. **2.** The parting made in the hair by combing along the top of the head; also, the part of the head thus indicated, the top of the crown. *Obs.* exc. *dial.* ME. **b.** A parting made in the wool of sheep in order to grease or anoint the skin 1523. **3.** A ridge of high ground dividing two valleys or tracts of lower country; a 'divide' 1530. **4.** *Weaving.* The opening made between the threads of the warp by the motion of the heddles for the shuttle to pass through 1792.

Shed (ʃed), *sb.*[2] 1481. [app. var. SHADE *sb.*] **1.** A slight structure built for shelter or storage, or for use as a workshop, either attached as a lean-to to a permanent building or separate; often with open front or sides. **b.** A similar structure, but large and strongly built; often consisting of a roof supported by columns. Also *Austral.*, short for WOOLSHED. 1840. **2. a.** *poet.* A hut, cottage, poor dwelling 1600. **b.** *gen.* A structure that affords shelter or covering; the hiding-place, lair, or nest of an animal 1616. **3.** In a telegraph-line insulator, a covering in the form of an inverted cup, a 'petticoat' 1859.

1. In such a season born when scarce a S. Could be obtain'd to shelter him or me From the bleak air

MILT. **2. a.** At last an hospitable House they found, A homely S. DRYDEN.

Comb.: **s.-roof,** a roof with only one slope (as in a lean-to s.). Hence **She·dding,** sheds collectively.

Shed (ʃed), *sb.*³ *rare.* 1648. [f. SHED *v.*¹] Something that is or has been shed; e.g. a silkworm's cocoon; a light fall of snow; the cast shell of a crab.

Shed (ʃed), *v.*¹ Pa. t. and pa. pple. **shed.** [Com. Teut. vb., orig. strong (redupl.): OE. *sc(e)ādan*, (*sceād*, *sceāden*), f. Teut. root **skaiþ*- (: **skīþ*-) and **skaiđ*- (: **skīđ*-); prob. related to Gr. σχίζειν to split, L. *scindere* to cut, cleave. In early ME. (12th c.) already conjugated *schēden*, *schedde*, *sched*, from which the mod. forms immediately derive.] **1.** *trans.* To separate, divide. Now only *dial.*, chiefly in farming uses: To separate (lambs) from the ewes, or (calves) from the cows; to separate (cattle, sheep) from the herd or flock. †**b.** *intr.* for *refl.* To part company, separate –1696. **2.** *trans.* **a.** To part (the hair; also, the hair or wool of an animal). Now *Sc.* and *dial.* **b.** *Weaving.* To divide (the warp-threads), to make a 'shed' in (a web) 1839. †**3.** To scatter, sprinkle; in later use only, to sow (seed) –1770. **b.** To throw off, repel (rain, sunlight, etc.). Now chiefly *dial.* late ME. †**c.** *refl.* and *intr.* To be dispersed, scatter –1650. **4.** *trans.* To pour, pour out; to emit, give forth ME. **5.** To cause (blood) to flow from the body by cutting or wounding; to let fall (a person's blood) on the ground, etc. ME. **b.** With pregnant sense ME. **6.** To emit and let fall in drops (tears, rain, dew, etc.) ME. **7.** To send forth as an emanation. **a.** To throw (light) *upon* something ME. **b.** To give forth, diffuse (fragrance, sound, heat, etc.); to pour out, impart (influence, blessings, qualities, etc.). Also with *abroad*, †*forth*, etc. ME. **8.** To cast off by natural process. **a.** To cast off as exuviæ; to undergo the falling of (hair, etc.) 1510. **b.** Of trees, plants: To lose, cast off (leaves, flowers, bark, etc.) 1598. **c.** Of plants: To let fall, cast (seed) out of the receptacle 1523. **d.** *colloq.* To drop, let go; to take off (a garment); to give away (something of no particular value) 1855. **9.** *intr.* for *refl.* †**a.** Of the hair: To fall out –1755. **b.** Of grain: To fall from the ear. Also of leaves or flowers: To drop off. 1557.

3. He..shede the seed into the erthe WYCLIF *Gen.* xxxviii. 9. **b.** As a shaggy dog sheds water from his coat 1885. **c.** Sike prayse is smoke, that sheddeth in the skye SPENSER. **4.** Roaches do then s. their Spawn 1630. As when a fountain sheds Dark waters streaming down a precipice 1870. **5. b.** *To s. the blood of* (another person or persons), to kill in a manner involving the effusion of blood; often *loosely*, to kill by violent means. So *to s. blood*, to destroy human life by violent means. *To s.* (one's own) *blood*, to undergo wounds or violent death in battle, martyrdom, or the like (*for* some person or cause, one's country, etc.). **6.** He could only s. childish tears of despair and terror 1862. **7. a.** The statement..sheds little light upon a situation still enveloped in mystery 1912. **8. a.** When hens are shedding their feathers they don't lay eggs 1845. *fig.* He sheds his bad reputation as a snake its skin 1910. Hence **She·dding** *vbl. sb.* the action of the verb; *concr.* (*pl.*) shed leaves, etc.

Shed (ʃed), *v.*² 1850. [f. SHED *sb.*²] *trans.* To place in a shed.

Shedder (ʃe·dəɹ). late ME. [f. SHED *v.*¹ + -ER¹.] **1.** One who sheds. **2.** *spec.* **a.** A female fish of the *Salmonidæ* after spawning 1588. **b.** A crab during the period when it is casting its covering integument or shell 1872.

Sheel (ʃīl), *v.* Now *dial.* 1440. [Related to SHALE *sb.*¹] *trans.* To shell; to take off the husk or outer covering of. Hence **Shee·ling** *vbl. sb.* the grain removed from the husk; the husks of oats, etc.

Sheen (ʃīn), *sb.* 1602. [f. next; assumed to be connected with SHINE *v.*] Shining, brightness. In recent use chiefly, gleaming, lustre, radiance as of a body reflecting light; a gleam. *rare* before 19th c. **b.** Gorgeous or bright attire 1802.

The azurn s. of Turkis blew MILT. **b.** In costly s. and gaudy cloak array'd BYRON.

Sheen (ʃīn) *a.* Now *poet.* [OE. *sciene* :—OTeut. **skauni*-, **skaunjo*-, f. root **skau*- to behold.] **1.** Beautiful. **2.** Bright, shining, resplendent OE.

1. Hayle be thou Mary, maydyn shen 1536. Narcissus will I twine, and lilies s. 1873. **2.** By fountaine cleere, or spangled star light sheene SHAKS.

Sheen (ʃīn), *v.* late ME. [f. prec.] *intr.* **a.** = SHINE *v.* Now only *Sc.* and *dial.* **b.** *poet.* To cast a gleam, glisten 1812.

b. This town, That, sheening far, celestial seems to be BYRON.

Sheeny (ʃī·ni), *sb. slang.* 1824. [Origin obsc.] Opprobrious term for: A Jew.

Sheeny (ʃī·ni), *a.* 1625. [f. SHEEN *a.* + -Y¹.] Covered with sheen, full of sheen; having a bright shiny surface.

Sheep (ʃīp). *Pl.* **sheep.** [WGer.: OE. (WS.) *scēap*, (Anglian) *scēp.*] **1.** Any animal of the ruminant genus *Ovis* (sometimes horned), closely allied to the goats; esp. of the widely domesticated species *Ovis aries*, of which there are many varieties, and which is reared for its flesh, fleece, and skin. **b.** With qualifying word denoting the species 1604. **2.** Similative (often passing into fig.) uses OE. **b.** *Lost s.*: one who has strayed from the right way 1611. **c.** *Black s.*: a bad character 1792. **3.** *fig.* In biblical and religious language, applied (as collective plural) to persons, in expressed or implied correlation with *shepherd*. Said, e.g. of Israel, the Church, or mankind generally, viewed as under the protection of God; also of those who are led by Christ as the Good Shepherd (John x. 1–16); etc. OE. **4.** A person who is as stupid, timid, or poor-spirited as a sheep 1542. **5.** *ellipt.* (For *s. leather.*) Leather made from the skin of the sheep: used in bookbinding 1705.

1. b. The Rocky Mountain s...is closely related to the chamois of Europe 1875. **2.** We have erred and strayed from thy wayes, lyke lost shepe *Bk. Com. Prayer.* Thou Wolfe in Sheepes array SHAKS. I will not..be flayed like a s. for the benefit of some pettifogging..attorney SCOTT. **c.** Provb. *There is a black s. in every flock.* Phr. *To return to our s.*: see MUTTON. **3.** In thy book record their groanes Who were thy S. MILT. **4.** I know he would not be a Wolfe, But that he sees the Romans are but Sheepe SHAKS.

attrib. and *Comb.*: as **s.-back** = *roche moutonnée* (see MOUTONNÉE); **-bot (fly),** the bot-fly *Œstrus ovis*; **†-counter,** a counter or token used in counting s.; **-dip,** (*a*) a preparation or solution used for washing sheep; (*b*) a place where sheep are washed; **-dog,** a dog that tends sheep; applied *spec.* to the Scotch collie and the bob-tailed English s.-dog; **-farm,** a tract of land devoted to sheep-rearing; so **-farm** *v.*, **-farmer, -farming; -gate,** (*a*) pasturage, or the right of pasturage for sheep (or a s.); (*b*) a gate for the passage of sheep; a hurdle for enclosing sheep; **-hook** (now *rare*), a shepherd's crook; **-kill, -laurel,** a N. Amer. shrub, *Kalmia angustifolia*, supposed to be very poisonous to sheep; **-louse,** a louse, *Trichodectes sphærocephalus*, which infests the wool of sheep; **-mark,** the mark used by a sheep-owner to distinguish his sheep, and app. formerly by illiterate persons as a substitute for their signature; **-pest,** (*a*) a common Australian weed, *Acæna ovina*, the booked spines of which catch in the wool of sheep; (*b*) = S.-TICK; **-pock, -pox,** a form of smallpox to which sheep are subject; **-rot,** (*a*) the rot in s., caused by the presence of flukes in the liver; (*b*) a name for plants supposed to cause disease in sheep, as butterwort and marsh pennywort; **-scab,** a skin-disease of sheep, due to an acarus; **-sorrel** = *sheep's sorrel*; **-walk,** a tract of grass-land used for pasturing sheep; **-wash,** the washing of sheep before shearing, the place where this is done; also, = *s.-dip* (a); **-weed,** soapwort; **-wool** = *sheep's wool.*

b. Combs. with genitive *sheep's*: **sheep's bit (scabious)** = *sheep's scabious*; **sheep's fescue (grass),** see FESCUE *sb.* 4; **sheep's gut(s** = CATGUT; **sheep's scabious,** *Jasione montana*; **sheep's sorrel,** *Rumex acetosella*; **sheep's wool** (*a*) wool from the fleece of a s.; (*b*) a W. Indian sponge, *Spongia equina*, var. *gossypina*; (*c*) *sheep's-wool fat*, lanoline. Hence **Shee·p-like** *a.* resembling a s. or that of a s.; *adv.* meekly, submissively, pusillanimously. **Shee·py** *a.* (*rare*).

Shee·p-bi:ter. 1548. **1.** A dog that bites or worries sheep. Now *rare.* †**2.** *fig.* A shifty, sneaking, or thievish fellow –1778. †**3.** One who runs after 'mutton'; a woman-hunter, whoremonger –1719.

2. There are Political Sheep-biters as well as Pastoral 1692.

Sheepcote (ʃī·pkōᵘt). late ME. [f. SHEEP + COTE *sb.*¹] A slight building for sheltering sheep; a sheep-house. So **Shee·pcot.**

Sheepfold (ʃī·pfōᵘld). late ME. [f. SHEEP + FOLD *sb.*¹] A pen or enclosure for sheep.

fig. The Prince of all Shepheards whose sheepefold is the world 1635.

Sheepish (ʃī·piʃ), *a.* (*adv.*). ME. [f. SHEEP + -ISH.] **1.** †**a.** Of, pertaining to, or concerned with sheep. **b.** Resembling sheep or their characteristics. Now *rare.* †**2.** Simple, silly –1692. †**b.** Excessively meek or submissive; mean-spirited –1711. **3.** Bashful or awkward in the presence of others, esp. in society to which one is unaccustomed; embarrassed or out of countenance from an excess of shyness or diffidence 1693.

Hence **Shee·pish·ly** *adv.*, **-ness.**

Shee·pman. 1591. †**1.** A shepherd –1641. **2.** *U.S.* A sheep-breeder, -owner, or -tender 1883.

Sheep's eye(s. 1529. **1.** Phr. *To cast* (or *throw*) *a sheep's eye at* or *upon*, now usu. *to cast sheep's eyes at*: to look lovingly, amorously, or longingly at. **2.** An amorous glance 1604.

1. I have often seen him cast a Sheep's Eye out of a Calf's Head at you SWIFT.

Sheepshank (ʃī·pʃæŋk), *sb.* 1627. **1.** The shank or leg of a sheep 1675. **2.** *Naut.* In full †*sheepshank(s) knot*: A knot cast on a rope for temporarily shortening it without cutting it or unfastening the ends. Hence **Shee·pshank** *v. trans.* to shorten (a rope) by means of a s.

Sheep's head. ME. **1.** The head of a sheep; a dish consisting of this. **2.** A fool, simpleton. †Also as *adj.*, stupid. 1542. **3.** A large and much esteemed food fish, *Archosargus* or *Diplodus probatocephalus* (*Sargus ovis*), abundant on the coasts of the U.S. 1676. **b.** A freshwater fish resembling the drumfish of the Mississippi and the Great Lakes; also locally in N. America applied to various other fishes 1836.

Shee·p-shea:rer. 1539. One who shears sheep. **b.** A machine for shearing sheep 1908.

Shee·p-shea:ring, *vbl. sb.* 1586. **1.** The act or practice of shearing sheep. **2.** The season for shearing sheep 1688. **3.** The feast held at the shearing-season 1611.

Shee·pskin. Also **sheep's skin.** ME. **1.** The skin of a sheep; *esp.* one used as a garment or in the making of a garment. **2.** The skin of sheep used for parchment, for the making of drumheads, in bookbinding, etc. ME. **b.** *U.S. slang.* A parchment diploma received on taking a degree; the holder of such a diploma 1843. **3.** *attrib.* or *adj.* Made or consisting of s. or parchment; written on parchment 1602.

3. So doth a sheepe-skin Bond make money breed 1624.

Shee·p-tick, †sheep's tick. late ME. [See TICK *sb.*¹ Cf. G. *schafsticke.*] A horny bristly wingless fly, *Melophagus ovinus*, which infests sheep, embedding its head in the skin and extracting the blood.

Sheer (ʃiᵊɹ), *sb.*¹ 1670. [f. SHEER *v.*¹] *Naut.* **1.** An abrupt divergence or deviation of a vessel from the line of her course; a swerve. **2.** An oblique position given to or taken by a vessel when under way or when riding at single anchor 1794.

2. Phr. *To break her s.*, of a vessel at anchor, to be forced by change of wind or current out of the position of s. in which she was placed.

Comb.: **s.-boom** *Lumbering*, a boom to catch floating logs and turn them in the desired direction; **-line,** in military bridges, the stretched hawser of a flying bridge along which the boat passes.

Sheer (ʃiᵊɹ), *sb.*² 1691. [perh. a use of SHEAR *sb.*²] *Naut.* **1.** The fore-and-aft upward curvature or rise of the deck or bulwarks of a vessel; the curve of the upper line of a vessel as shown in vertical section. **2.** = *s.-strake* 1841.

Comb.: **s.-draught** (**-draft**), the s.-plan; **-line,** the line of elevation of a ship's deck; **-plan,** the section of a ship which would be made by a vertical plane passing through the keel; **-strake, -wale,** the uppermost strake of the side planking or plating of a vessel.

Sheer (ʃiᵊɹ), *a.* and *adv.* [ME. *schere* :— OE. **scǣre* :—OTeut. **skairjo*-, related to **skīro*-, **skīrjo*-, f. root **skī*- to shine.] **A.** *adj.* †**1.** Exempt, free (from service or fealty). late ME. †**2.** Of light: Bright, shining. Of water, crystal, etc.: Clear and pure; translucent. –1871. **3.** Of textile fabrics, etc.: Thin, fine, diaphanous 1565. **4.** Of a material substance: Unmixed or unaccompanied with other matter. Esp. of strong drink: (*a*) Undiluted with water; (*b*) taken alone without solid food. 1596. **b.** Of an immaterial thing: Taken or existing by itself, ..alone. Now *rare* or *Obs.* 1622. **5.** Neither more nor less than (what is expressed by the sb.); that and nothing else; unmitigated, unqualified; downright, absolute, pure 1583. **6.** Of a descent or ascent, the face of a wall, cliff, etc.: Continued perpendicularly or very steeply down or up without break or halting-place 1800.

2. Afterward they began to yeeld sheere and cleere water in great aboundance HOLLAND. 3. Shear muslins fit for head dresses and neckcloths 1706. 4. If she say I am not xiiii. d. on the score for sheere Ale SHAKS. 5. Out of s. love and kindness to Lord Chatham *Junius Lett.* 6. This lake,..whose barriers drear Are precipices sharp and s. SCOTT.

B. *adv.* **1.** Completely, absolutely, altogether, quite 1600. **2.** Perpendicularly or very steeply up or down; straight up or down without break or halting-place 1829.

1. Thrown by angry Jove S. o're the Chrystal Battlements MILT. 2. It rose s. up above the contiguous roofs CARLYLE. Hence **Shee·r-ly** *adv.*, **-ness.**

Sheer (ʃīəɹ), *v.*¹ 1626. [perh. a use of SHEAR *v.*, but the sense development is obsc.] *Naut.* **1.** *intr.* Of a ship: To turn aside, alter its direction, swerve, in obedience to the helm. **b.** To swerve to either side irregularly or unsteadily, not in obedience to the helm. Also with *round.* 1635. **c.** *transf.* and *fig.* Chiefly with *off*: To change one's course; to depart, go away; to go off in a new direction or on another 'tack' 1704. **2.** *trans.* To cause (a vessel) to sheer; to direct (a vessel) obliquely towards a given point 1633.

1. Phr. *To s. alongside, to, up,* to bear up obliquely towards a vessel or other point.

Sheer (ʃīəɹ), *v.*² *rare.* 1851. [f. SHEER *a.*] *intr.* Of a rock-face: To rise or descend vertically or very steeply.

Sheer-hulk, shear-hulk. 1768. [f. *sheer* SHEAR *sb.*¹ 2 + HULK *sb.* 3.] The hulk or body of an old or disused ship fitted with shears, etc. for hoisting purposes; also, a vessel specially built and fitted with shears. (In the pop. fig. use of the word the first element is often misunderstood as *sheer* adj., and the compound written as two words.)

fig. Here, a sheer hulk, lies poor Tom Bowling DIBDIN. She had been built for a sheer-hulk 1799.

Sheer Thursday. *Hist.* [ME. *s(c)here t.*, English modification of Scand. forms repr. by *skere, skire t.*] Maundy Thursday.

Sheet (ʃīt), *sb.*¹ [OE. *sciete*, Anglian *scēte* :—pre-hist. **skautjōn-*, f. root **skaut-* (: *skeut-* : *skut-*; see SHOOT *v.*, SHOT *sb.*¹), of which one of the senses was to project.] **1.** †**a.** A napkin, cloth, or towel. **b.** A broad piece of linen or cotton stuff, canvas, or the like, for covering, swathing, protecting from injury, etc. (Now felt as a transf. use of 3.) **2.** = WINDING-SHEET OE. **3.** A large oblong piece of linen, cotton (or, formerly, hempen) cloth, used as an article of bedding, one being placed immediately above and one below the person ME. **b.** *pl.* in phrases with ref. to sexual intercourse 1604. **4.** A sail. Chiefly *poet.* late ME. **5.** An oblong or square piece of paper or parchment, *esp.* for writing or printing; *spec.* one of the pieces of definite size (varying according to the kind) in which paper is made, 24 (formerly also 25) going to a quire 1510. **b.** A piece of paper which is divided by means of perforations or the like into sections which may be torn or cut away as required 1776. **6.** In printing and bookbinding, such a piece of paper printed and folded so as to form pages of a required size (folio, quarto, etc.). Also, a quantity of printed matter equal to that contained in a sheet. 1589. **c.** *pl.* Pages or leaves of a book; esp. *these sheets, the following sheets* = the book now before the reader. Now *rare.* 1591. **d.** A newspaper. Now *rare.* 1749. **7.** A continuous extent or 'sweep' of something conceived as hanging, falling, or moving in a certain direction 1605. **8.** A broad expanse or stretch of something lying out flat, presenting a white or glistening surface, or forming a relatively thin covering or layer; *spec.* in *Geol., Anat., Path.* 1593. **9.** A relatively thin piece of considerable breadth *of* a malleable, ductile, or pliable substance 1675. **b.** A flat piece of tin, used for baking cakes, etc. 1747. **c.** Sheet iron or steel; a length of this 1884. **10.** quasi-*adj.* Rolled out in a sheet; esp. of metals, as *s. iron, lead, steel.* Also = printed on a single sheet or broadside, esp. *s.-almanac.* 1582.

1. She should..cover up every article of furniture ..with large dusting-sheets 1888. 2. Tybalt, ly'st thou there in thy bloudy s.? SHAKS. 3. *The sheets,* the pair of sheets belonging to a bed. *Between the sheets* (colloq.) in bed. b. My Daughters got 'tweene the lawfull sheets SHAKS. 4. The Boat was push'd off, the S. was spread 1712. 5. He had..managed to fill two sides of a s. of letter-paper 1857. *In sheets,* lying flat or expanded, not folded. 6. A Magazine s. is sixteen pages DICKENS. *In sheets,* (of books) not bound 1693. 7. A broad s. of lightning 1847. A heavy squall with sheets of rain 1894. 8. Sheets o' daisies white BURNS. 9. A s. of plate glass 1893.

attrib. and *Comb.*: **s. glass** (*a*) cylinder glass; (*b*) a vessel made of this glass; **-lightning,** lightning in a sheet-like form due to reflection by the clouds; **s. music,** music published in sheet form as opposed to book form. Hence **Shee·tful,** as much as a s. will contain. **Shee·ty** *a.* spreading in a broad s.: chiefly of water.

Sheet (ʃīt), *sb.*² ME. [OE. *scēata* SHEET *sb.*¹, also = lower corner of a sail.] **1.** A rope (or chain) attached to either of the lower corners of a square sail (or the after lower corner of a fore-and-aft sail), and used to extend the sail or to alter its direction. **2.** See quot. 1644.

1. A wet s. and a flowing sea CUNNINGHAM. *Three sheets in the wind,* very drunk; A thought tipsy..a s. or so in the wind, as folks say TROLLOPE 2. *Sheets,* the spaces in a rowing boat forward and abaft the thwarts, and named respectively *fore-sheets* and *stern-sheets* 1891.

Sheet (ʃīt), *v.*¹ 1606. [f. SHEET *sb.*¹] **1.** *trans.* To wrap or fold in or as in a sheet; now *spec.* to cover with a protecting sheet of canvas, tarpaulin, etc. 1621. **2.** To spread a sheet or layer of some substance upon (a surface); to cover with a sheet (e.g. of snow or ice) 1606.

1. [A racehorse] sheeted to the tail 1860. 2. When Snow the Pasture sheets SHAKS. Its roof was sheeted, like St. Peter's, with copper 1845.

Sheet (ʃīt), *v.*² 1797. [f. SHEET *sb.*²] trans. *To s. home*: to extend the sheets of (the topsails) to the outer extremities of the yards so that the clews are close to the sheet-blocks. Also *absol.*

Sheet-anchor (ʃī·tˌæ:ŋkəɹ). 1495. [Origin obsc.] A large anchor, formerly always the largest of a ship's anchors, used only in an emergency. **b.** *fig.* That on which one places one's reliance when all else has failed 1524.

b. It is Foreign Trade that is the main Sheet-Anchor of us Islanders 1676. Hence **Shee·t-cable** *Naut.*, the cable belonging to the s.

Sheeted (ʃī·tėd), *ppl. a.* 1604. [f. SHEET *sb.*¹ or *v.*¹] **1.** Wrapped in a sheet, *esp.* a winding-sheet; applied to the dead and ghosts. **b.** Enveloped in a sheet or sheets for protection against injury, etc. 1766. **2.** In the form of a sheet; expanded or spread out like a sheet: chiefly of rain, snow, lightning 1796. **3.** Of cattle: Having a broad band of white round the body 1834.

1. The s. dead Did squeake and gibber in the Roman streets SHAKS.

Sheeting (ʃī·tiŋ), *vbl. sb.* 1711. [f. SHEET *sb.*¹ or *v.*¹ + -ING¹.] **1.** Stout cloth of linen or cotton, such as is used for bed linen. **2.** A lining or covering of timber or metal, laid on a surface as a protection 1776. **3.** The action or process of making (lead) into sheets: the action of covering with sheets or laying in sheets 1778.

Sheffield (ʃe·fīld). late ME. Name of a manufacturing city of Yorkshire, famous for cutlery, used *attrib.* as *S. ware*; **S. plate,** plate made of copper coated with silver by a special process perfected in Sheffield (but now disused).

‖**Sheikh** (ʃēik, ʃīk). 1577. [Arabic *shaikh* properly 'old man', f. *shākha* to grow old.] **1.** The chief of an Arab family or tribe; the headman of an Arabian village; an Arab chief; †an Eastern governor, prince, king. Now also, among Arabs, a general title of respect. **2.** The head of a religious order or community; a great religious doctor or preacher; now *esp.* a saint having a local cultus 1613. **3.** In India, one of a dissenting sect of Mohammedans; now, a general term for Hindu converts to Islam. (Usu. *shekh, shaikh.*) 1883.

2. *S.-ul-Islam* (properly *Sheikhu 'l Islam*): the supreme authority in matters relating to religion and sacred law! in Turkey, the mufti; hence *Sheikh-ul-Islamate.*

Shekel (ʃe·kĕl). 1560. [a. Heb. *sheqel*, f. *shāqal* to weigh.] **1. a.** An ancient unit of weight of the Babylonians, and hence of the Phœnicians, Hebrews, and others, equal to one-sixtieth of a mina. **b.** A coin of this weight; *esp.* the chief silver coin of the Hebrews. **2.** *fig.* (*pl.*) Coin, money. *colloq.* 1883.

Shekinah, shechinah (ʃīkəi·nă). 1663. [a. late Heb. *shekīnāh*, f. *shākan* to rest, dwell.] The visible manifestation of the Divine Majesty, esp. when resting between the cherubim over the mercy-seat or in the temple of Solomon; a glory or refulgent light symbolizing the Divine Presence. **b.** *transf.* spec. applied to Jesus Christ 1682.

b. Truth indeed is veiled, But with a Schekinah of dazzling light 1834.

Sheld (ʃeld), *a. dial.* 1507. [ad. or cogn. w. MDu. *schillede* variegated, f. *schillen* to make different.] Particoloured, pied, piebald.

Sheld-duck, shell-duck (ʃe·ldɒk). 1707. [f. next, by substitution of *duck* for *drake.*] = next. So **Sche·ld-fowl.**

Sheldrake (ʃe·ldrēik). ME. [prob. f. SHELD *a.* + DRAKE ².] A bird of the genus *Tadorna* of the duck tribe, frequenting sandy coasts in Europe, North Africa, and Asia, and remarkable for its variegated colouring.

Shelf (ʃelf), *sb.*¹ *Pl.* **shelves** (ʃelvz). late ME. [app. ad. (M)LG. *schelf* shelf, set of shelves, cogn. w. OE. *scylfe* app. ledge, floor, and OE. *scylf* rugged rock, crag, pinnacle; perh. f. root *skelf-* to split. (Cf. next.)] **I. 1.** A slab of wood, etc. fixed in a horizontal position to a wall, or in a frame, to hold books, vessels, ornaments, etc.; one of the transverse boards in a bookcase, cabinet, or the like. **b.** *transf.* A shelf with ref. to its contents; the contents of a shelf (*esp.* of books) 1732. **2.** *Shipbuilding.* A timber on the inner side of the frame to support the deck-beams 1834.

1. Phr. (*fig.*) *On the s.*, (*a*) on one side, out of the way, in a position of inactivity or uselessness; esp. *to lay* (*put*, etc.) *on the s.*; (*b*) of women, without prospects of marrying. b. You may confute a whole s. of schoolmen BERKELEY.

II. Senses influenced by SHELF *sb.*² **1.** A ledge, platform, or terrace of land, rock, etc. 1809. **2.** *Mining* and *Geol.* Bed-rock 1671.

1. *Continental s.*, the relatively shallow belt of sea-bottom bordering a continental mass, the outer edge of which sinks rapidly to the deep ocean-floor.

attrib.: **s.-catalogue, -list,** a short-title catalogue of books in a library giving their shelf positions; **s.-mark** = PRESS-MARK. Hence **Shelf** *v. trans.* to lay on the s., shelve. **She·lf-ful,** a quantity sufficient to fill a s.: the contents of a s.

Shelf (ʃelf), *sb.*² 1545. [Origin obsc. Cf. OE. *scylf* sharp rock (cf. prec.).] A sandbank in the sea or river rendering the water shallow and dangerous. Also loosely applied to a submerged ledge of rock. Hence **She·lfy** *a.*¹ abounding in sandbanks lying near the surface of the water.

Shelfy, *a.*² *dial.* (Devon and Cornwall.) 1602. [f. dial. *shelf, shilf* broken slate.] Full of slaty rock.

Shell (ʃel), *sb.* [OE. *sciell, scill*, Anglian *scell* :—OTeut. **skaljō-*, f. **skal-*, whence also SCALE *sb.*¹, ², SHALE *sb.*¹] **I.** The hard outside covering of an animal, a fruit, etc. **1.** The calcareous or chitinous outer covering of crustaceans, molluscs, and other invertebrates. Freq. used allusively. **2.** A shell of this kind (or a vessel resembling one) used for a specific purpose. late ME. **3.** As tr. Gr. ὄστρακον, the potsherd or tile used in the OSTRACISM of the ancient Greeks 1565. **4.** *pl.* Burnt limestone before it is slaked 1743. **5.** Used as the second element of the name of a particular shellfish, as *razor-s.*; hence (chiefly *pl.*) = shellfish 1751. **6.** The hard calcareous envelope of a bird's egg. Also, the similar integument of the eggs of other creatures. OE. **7.** = NUTSHELL ME. **b.** The fibre-covered envelope of a coco-nut 1638. **8.** The outer covering of a seed. etc.; a husk, pod (e.g. *pea-s.*); putamen, pericarp 1561. **9.** The hard covering or 'house' of a snail. late ME. **b.** In fig. phrases, referring to avoidance of society or extreme reserve 1853. **10.** The hard covering of a tortoise or turtle; the material of which this is composed; cf. TORTOISESHELL 1545. †**b.** *poet.* A lyre (according to legend orig. a tortoise shell stringed); occas. 'lyric poetry' -1821. **11.** The integument of an armadillo, glyptodon, ostraciont, etc.; the elytron of an insect; the cast skin of a pupa 1774.

1. They used to gather up Shells on the Sea-Shore STEELE. **2.** By scaly Tritons winding s. MILT. Whiskey was served round in a s., according to the ancient Highland custom BOSWELL. **6.** *fig.* My young nouice..not yet crept out of the s. 1593. Phr. *In the s.*, (of an egg or a bird, etc.) unhatched; also *fig.* in embryo. **9. b.** Under the soothing influence of coffee and tobacco, he came out of his s. 1889. **10. b.** 'Twas Milton struck the deep-toned s. GRAY.

II. A shell-shaped object; something concave or hollow. **1.** *gen.* A hollow spherical, hemi-spherical, or dome-shaped object 1599. **2.** The semicircular guard of a sword 1685. **3.** The apsidal end of the school-room at Westminster School, so called from its conch-like shape. Hence, the name of the form (intermediate between the fifth and sixth) which orig. tenanted the 'shell' at this school, and *transf.* of forms (intermediate between forms designated by numbers) in other public schools. 1736. **4.** The outer ear 1847. **5.** *U.S.* A light narrow racing-boat 1873. **b.** The floating part of a racing boat 1895. **c.** In various techn. uses, e. g. a concave grinding tool, the outer wall of a mould in casting 1819. **III.** An exterior or enclosing cover or case. **1. a.** A covering (of earth, stone, etc.) 1667. **b.** The crust of the earth 1704. **2.** A case of metal, etc. in which powder and shot is made up, esp. for use as a hand-grenade 1644. **b.** Hence, an explosive projectile or bomb for use in a cannon or mortar. Also *collect. sing.* 1651. **c.** A cartridge case of paper or metal 1799. **3.** A wooden coffin, esp. a rough or temporary one. Also a thin coffin of lead or other material to be enclosed in a more substantial one. 1788.

2. b. The bomb-ship..plied the French with her shells 1767.

IV. A mere exterior or framework. **1.** The external part, exterior, or outward aspect, the externals (of something immaterial) 1652. **2.** An empty or hollow thing; mere externality without substance 1791. **3. a.** The outer part of an edifice or fabric, the interior of which has been removed or destroyed 1657. **b.** The skeleton or carcass of a building or a ship 1705. **c.** *U.S.* A rough, wooden structure, without decoration or furniture 1852.

1. The outward form and s. of religion 1774. **2.** Mere effigies and shells of men CARLYLE. **3. b.** I preached..in the s. of the new house WESLEY.

V. A scale or scale-like object. **1.** A scale of a fish or reptile; a hard epidermal excrescence (*rare*) OE. **2.** A scale or lamina (of stone, †bone, etc.) ME. **3.** Any of the thin pieces of metal composing scale-armour 1585. **4.** An epaulette 1848.

Comb.: **s.-back**, (*a*) *joc.* (a hardened or experienced) sailor; (*b*) a marine turtle; **-breaker**, an instrument used in lithotomy; **-fire**, (*a*) *dial.* phosphorescence or lambent fire seen enveloping or issuing from bodies; (*b*) the firing of shells from guns; **-flower**, *Molucella lævis*, the genus *Chelone*, and some species of *Alpinia*; **-game** (*U.S.*), a swindling game resembling THIMBLE-RIG; **-gland**, (*a*) an excretory organ beneath the shell in the lower crustaceans; (*b*) the shell-secreting gland of a mollusc; **-gold**, gold for painting or writing, laid in a mussel-shell; **-heap**, a mound of domestic remains consisting chiefly of refuse shells accumulated by aborigines who subsisted on shell-fish; **-jacket**, an undress tight-fitting military jacket, short in the back; **-lime**, lime made by burning sea-shells; **-money** = WAMPUM; **-mound** = *s.-heap*; **-plate**, one of the plates forming the outer shell of a vessel, boiler, etc.; **-pump** = *sand-pump* (see SAND *sb.*); **-sac** = *s.-gland*; **-shock**, derangement of the nervous system resulting primarily from exposure to shell-explosion at close quarters; so **-shocked** *a.*; **-work**, arrangement of shells in patterns for ornamentation; shells lining the walls of an artificial grotto. Hence **She·ll-less** *a.* without a s. or shells.

Shell (ʃel), *v.* 1562. [f. prec.] **1.** *trans.* To remove (a seed) from its shell, husk, or pod. Also with *out.* **b.** *intr.* Of grain, seed, etc.: To drop out of the shell or husk 1828. **2.** *trans.* To remove the shell, husk, etc. of 1694. **3.** *intr.* To come away or fall off as a shell, crust, or outer coat; to come *off* in thin pieces, peel or scale *off* 1676. **4.** *trans.* To enclose in, or as in, a shell; to encase 1637. **5.** To bombard with shells (also *absol.*); to drive *out of* a place by shelling 1827.

1. S. your pease just before you want them 1796. Phr. (colloq.) *S. out*, *trans.* to disburse, pay up, hand over; *intr.* to pay up. **2.** Some shrimps shelled 1806. **4.** S. thee with steel or brass.. Death from the casque will pull thy cautious head 1685. Hence **She·ller**, one who or that which shells.

Shellac (ʃĕlæ·k, ʃe·læk). 1713. [tr. F. *laque en écailles* lac in thin plates.] Lac melted and run into thin plates.

Shelled (ʃeld), *a.* 1577. [f. SHELL *sb.* + -ED [2].] **1.** Having a shell. **2.** Of ammunition: Contained in shells 1900.

Shelleyan (ʃe·liˌăn), *a.* (and *sb.*) 1849. [f. the name *Shelley* + -AN I. 1.] Pertaining, relating to, or characteristic of Percy Bysshe Shelley (1792–1822), his poetry, or the ideas expressed in his works. As *sb.*, an admirer of Shelley. So **She·lleyism** 1822. **She·lleyite.**

Shell-fish (ʃe·lfiʃ). [OE. *scilfisc* = ON. *skelfiskr.*] Any animal living in water whose outer covering is a shell, whether testaceous, as an oyster, or crustaceous, as a crab.

Shelling (ʃe·liŋ), *vbl. sb.* 1598. [f. SHELL *v.* + -ING [1].] **1.** The action of SHELL *v.* 1725. **2.** *concr.* (chiefly *pl.*) **a.** Husks or chaff 1598. **b.** Grain, etc. from which the husk has been removed 1705. **3.** The firing of shells, bombardment with shells 1860. **4.** The collecting of sea-shells 1861.

Shelly (ʃe·li), *a.* 1555. [f. SHELL *sb.* + -Y [1].] **1.** Abounding in (sea)shells; of a geological formation, consisting wholly or mainly of shells. **2.** Consisting of or of the nature of a shell; forming a covering resembling a shell; shell-like 1592. **3.** Of an animal: Having a shell; shell- 1593. **4.** Formed of a (sea)shell; consisting of (sea)shells or shell-fish 1716.

1. The s. shore POPE. Marle of the s. kind 1824. **2.** The shellie skin of the sea Vrchin HOLLAND. **3.** Animals of the s. tribe GOLDSM. **4.** S. Hautboys 1721.

S'help. 1904. = S'ELP.

Shelter (ʃe·ltəɹ), *sb.* 1585. [Origin obsc.; perh. f. *sheld* SHIELD *v.* + -TURE after words like *jointure.*] **1.** A structure affording protection from rain, wind, or sun; any screen or place of refuge from the weather. **b.** Something which affords a refuge from danger, attack, pursuit, or observation; a place of safety; *Mil.* a wall or bank behind which persons can obtain safety from gunshot 1605. **c.** Protection from the weather; trees, walls, or the like, which afford this 1613. **d.** A covering to protect an object from injury 1700. **e.** A place of temporary lodging for the homeless poor 1895. **2.** The state of being sheltered; protection from the elements; security from attack 1593.

1. Their tent was a sufficient s. from the rain DE FOE. *fig.* And thou shalt proue a s. to thy friends SHAKS. **e.** A Salvation Army s. 1895. **2.** Where..a ship might find good s. 1726. Phr. *To seek, find, take*, etc. *s.* *Under the s. of* = protected by.

Comb.: **s.-deck**, in a passenger vessel, a light deck more or less closed at the sides but open at the ends; **pit** *Mil.*, a small pit for one man only; **-tent**, a small ridged tent; a dog-tent. Hence **She·ltery** *a.*

Shelter (ʃe·ltəɹ), *v.* 1551. [f. prec.] **1.** *trans.* To be or provide a shelter for. **b.** *fig.* To screen from punishment, censure, etc. 1594. **c.** 'To succour with refuge, to harbour' (J.); to take under one's protection. Of a place: To be a secure home or refuge for. 1663. **2.** *refl.* To take shelter; to take refuge from pursuit or attack 1611. **b.** *fig.* Chiefly, to protect oneself from punishment or censure 1598. **3.** *intr.* for *refl.* To take shelter; to find a refuge 1602.

1. A wall of rock sheltered us from the north wind TYNDALL. Harbours and ports, which may s. the navy in the operations of war 1862. **b.** In vain I strove to..s. Passion under Friendship's Name PRIOR. **c.** These Ruines sheltered once His Sacred Head DRYDEN. **2. b.** Phr. *To s. oneself under, behind —*, to use the protection afforded by (what is specified). **3.** A company of buccaniers..s. here 1727. Hence **She·lterer**, one who takes shelter; one who shelters another.

Shelterless (ʃe·lterlės), *a.* 1714. [f. SHELTER *sb.* + -LESS.] **1.** Without a shelter or covering; unprotected from the elements. **2.** That affords no shelter 1760.

1. Now sad and s., perhaps, she lyes, Where piercing Winds blow sharp 1714.

Sheltie, shelty (ʃe·lti). *Sc.* 1654. [prob. repr. the Orkney pronunc. of ON. *Hjalti* Shetlander.] A Shetland pony; now, any small pony.

Shelve (ʃelv), *sb.*[1] 1582. A new sing. evolved from *shelves*, pl. of SHELF *sb.*[2], q.v.

Shelve (ʃelv), *sb.*[2] 1701. [f. SHELVE *v.*[1] I.] A ledge or shelf of rock, or mountain.

Shelve (ʃelv), *v.*[1] 1591. [f. *shelves* pl. of SHELF *sb.*[1]] †**1.** *intr.* To project like a shelf, overhang SHAKS. **2.** *trans.* To provide with shelves, *esp.* with bookshelves 1598. **3.** To place on a shelf or shelves; *esp.* to place or arrange (books) upon shelves 1650. **4.** *fig.* To lay aside as on a shelf, to put away or up as done with 1812.

4. Some of the present Government..will be shelved 1850. The Circumlocution Office..shelved the business DICKENS. Hence **She·lving** *vbl. sb.*[1] the action of the verb; shelves collectively.

Shelve (ʃelv), *v.*[2] 1587. [Origin obsc.] **1.** *intr.* Of a surface: To slope gradually 1614. †**2.** To have an inclined position -1763. **3.** *trans.* To tilt or tip up (a cart). *dial.* 1587.

1. The bank shelves away very fast from the Northern shore 1726. Hence **She·lving** *vbl. sb.*[2] the fact or condition of sloping; the degree of sloping; a sloping surface; a shelve. **She·lving** *ppl. a.* that shelves or slopes.

Shelvy (ʃe·lvi), *a.*[1] 1598. [f. SHELVE *sb.*[1] + -Y [1].] Of a shore: Having shelves or dangerous sand-banks; also †of a brook.

I had beene drown'd, but that the shore was sheluy and shallow SHAKS.

Shelvy (ʃe·lvi), *a.*[2] 1831. [f. SHELVE *sb.*[2] + -Y [1].] Projecting like a shelf; overhanging.

Shemite (ʃe·məit), *sb.* and *a.* 1659. [f. *Shem*, name of the eldest son of Noah (cf. Gen. vi. 10) + -ITE.] = SEMITE *a.* and *sb.* **Shemi·tic** *a.* and *sb.* **Shemi·tish** *a.* **She·mitism.**

Shemozzle ʃemǫ·z'l). orig. *East End slang.* Also **shle-.** 1899. [Yiddish.] A muddle or complication; a quarrel, 'row', mêlée.

Shend (ʃend), *v.* Now *dial.* and *arch.* Pa. t. and pa. pple. **shent** (ʃent). [OE. *scęndan* :— OTeut. **skandjan*, f. **skando-* ashamed. Since 15th c. almost always in the pa. pple. *shent.*] **1.** *trans.* To put to shame or confusion; to confound, disgrace. **2.** To blame, reproach, reprove; to revile, scold. In later use the passive often = to suffer for one's deeds, be punished. OE. **3.** To destroy, ruin. Also, in milder sense, to injure, damage, spoil. OE. †**b.** To disfigure, spoil; to defile, soil -1876. †**4.** To discomfit (in battle or dispute) -1829.

1. Debatefull strife, and cruell enmitie, The famous name of knighthood fowly s. SPENSER. **2.** Yet was his Loyalty shent, but not sham'd FULLER.

Shent (ʃent), *ppl. a.* *arch.* late ME. [pa. pple. of SHEND *v.*] Disgraced, lost, ruined.

She-oak. *Austral.* 1792. [See SHE V; cf. *he-oak.*] **1.** A tree of the genus *Casuarina.* **2.** *slang.* Colonial beer 1888.

‖**Sheol** (ʃī·oul, ʃī·ǫl). 1599. [Heb. *sheʾōl.*] The underworld; the abode of the dead or departed spirits, conceived by the Hebrews as a subterranean region clothed in thick darkness, return from which is impossible.

Shepherd (ʃe·pəɹd), *sb.* [OE. *scēaphirde*; see SHEEP and HERD *sb.*[2]] **1.** A man who guards, tends and herds a flock of sheep (grazing at large); usu. one so employed for hire; or one of a pastoral people who herds (his own) sheep, goats, etc. **b.** Applied to the rustic personages of pastoral poetry. Hence in pastoral poetry formerly often used to designate the writer and his friends or fellow-poets. 1591. **c.** Fr. Hist. *The Shepherds* [= F. *les Pastoureaux*]: those who took part in the peasant insurrections of 1251 ff. and 1320. 1759. **2.** *fig.* **a.** = A spiritual guardian or pastor of a 'flock' ME. **b.** In Biblical use, applied to God in relation to Israel or the Church; also to Christ (esp. with ref. to John x. 12). late ME. **c.** Applied to temporal rulers 1577. **3.** (With initial capital.) = SHEPHERD KING 1. 1813. **4.** *Austral* A miner who holds a claim but does not work it 1864.

1. b. If that the World and Loue were young, And truth in euery shepheards toung RALEIGH. **2. b.** Heare o thou shepherde of Israel, thou yt ledest Iacob like a flocke of shepe COVERDALE *Ps.* lxxix. 1.

attrib and *Comb.*: **s.-bird** = PASTOR *sb.* 4; **-dog** = *shepherd's dog*; **s. spider**, the harvest-spider; **s. tartan** = *shepherd's tartan.* **b.** Combs. with *shepherd's*: **shepherd's calendar**, a calendar containing weather predictions and seasonable instructions for shepherds (app. proverbially referred to as unreliable); hence adopted as the title of certain pastoral poems; **shepherd's check, plaid, tartan,** a woollen cloth with a black-and-white check pattern; **shepherd's dog,** a large variety of dog employed by shepherds to control and protect flocks of sheep; **shepherd's pie,** a pie made of mashed potatoes and minced meat, with a crust of mashed potatoes browned; **shepherd's pipe,** the pastoral oboe or musette; **shepherd's spider** = *s. spider*. **c.** In names of plants (chiefly *dial.*) **shepherd's calendar,** the scarlet pimpernel; **shepherd's club,** the common mullein, *Verbascum Thapsus*; **shepherd's needle,** †(*a*) crane's bill, (*b*) lady's comb; **shepherd's rod,** *Dipsacus pilosus*; **shepherd's staff,** (*a*) = *shepherd's rod*; (*b*) the common mullein. Hence †**She·pherdish** *a.* pastoral. **She·pherdize** *v.* (*rare*) *intr.* to pretend to lead the pastoral life. **She·pherdless** *a.* without a s.

Shepherd (ʃe·pəɹd), *v.* 1790. [f. prec.] **1.** *trans.* To tend, guard, and watch (sheep) as a shepherd. Also *absol.* **2.** *transf.* and *fig.* To tend, watch over, or guide as a shepherd does his sheep 1820. **3.** *Austral.* To watch over or guard (a mining claim) by working on it superficially (esp. by digging small pits) so as to retain legal rights. Also *intr.* 1861. **4.** *colloq.* or *slang.* To watch over, to follow closely and watchfully 1885. **b.** *Mil.* To force (a body of the enemy) into an unfavourable position 1900.

2. Arethusa arose From her couch of snows..Shepherding her bright fountains SHELLEY. **4.** Admiral Dowell is reported to be closely shepherding the Russian vessels in these seas 1885.

Shepherdess (ʃe·pəɹdės). late ME. [f. SHEPHERD *sb.* + -ESS [1].] A female shepherd; a woman or girl who tends sheep; also in pastoral poetry (see SHEPHERD 1 b). **b.** A representation (in painting, etc.; esp. in china or earthenware) of a shepherdess 1771.

Shepherd king. 1587. **1.** *pl.* [tr. Gr. βασιλεῖς ποιμένες, Manetho's rendering of the Egyptian designation which he transliterates as Ὑκσως (Hyksos).] The designation of a succession of kings of Egypt (the 15th and 16th dynasties of Manetho), belonging to some foreign people. (By historians often called *Hyksos.*) **b.** *gen.* A king who is a shepherd 1727.

Shepherdly (ʃe·pəɹdli), *a.* Now *rare.* 1559. [f. SHEPHERD *sb.* + -LY [1].] Pertaining to or befitting a shepherd (*lit.* and *fig.*); that has the characteristics of a shepherd; †that is a shepherd. †**b.** Pastoral, rural, rustic -1743.

b. I hate the country: I am past the s. age of groves and streams H. WALPOLE.

Shepherd's purse. late ME. [After med. L. *bursa pastoris*; cf. G. *hirtentasche.*] **1.** A common cruciferous weed, *Capsella Bursa-pastoris*, bearing pouch-like pods. **2.** *dial.* The fossil echinus found in the chalk 1893.

Sherardize (ʃe·răɹdəiz), *v.* 1904. [f. name of *Sherard* Cowper-Coles.] *trans.* To coat (iron articles) with zinc by a particular process.

Sheraton (ʃe·rătən), *a.* 1883. [Name of Thomas *Sheraton* (1751–1806), furniture-maker and designer.] Designating a severe style of furniture developed in England towards the end of the 18th c., chiefly by Thomas Sheraton.

Sherbet (ʃɔ̄·ɹbət). 1603. [a. Turk., Pers. *sherbet*, a. Arab. *sharbah*, f. *shariba* to drink.] **1. a.** A cooling drink of the East, made of fruit juice and water sweetened, often cooled with snow. **b.** A European imitation of this; now esp. an effervescing drink made of sherbet powder (see 2). **2.** In full *s. powder*: A preparation of bicarbonate of soda, tartaric acid, sugar, etc., variously flavoured, for making an effervescing drink 1856. **b.** *U.S.* A variety of water ice.

1. b. To bring in s., ginger-pop, lemonade 1845.

‖**Shereef** (ʃərī·f). 1560. [Arab. *sharīf* noble, glorious, f. *sharafa* to be exalted.] **1.** A descendant of Mohammed through his daughter Fatima. †Occas. *spec.* a Mohammedan priest. **2.** Hence used as the title of certain Arab princes, esp. the sovereign of Morocco; also, the chief magistrate, or local governor of Mecca 1600. ‖**Sheree·fa,** the wife of a Moroccan s., **-ee·fian** *a.* pertaining to the s. of Morocco.

Sheriff (ʃe·rif). [OE. *scīrgerēfa*, f. *scīr* SHIRE + *ȝerēfa* REEVE *sb.*[1]] **1. a.** *England* (and *Wales*). In England before the Norman Conquest, a high officer, the representative of the royal authority in a shire, who presided in the shire-moot, and was responsible for the administration of the royal demesne and the execution of the law. At the present time the sheriff of a county (more fully called *high s.*), appointed for one year by royal patent, is nominally responsible for the keeping of prisoners in safe custody, preparing the panel of jurors for the assizes, the execution of writs, and of the sentence of death. In addition to these duties, which are discharged by the under-sheriff, the high sheriff acts as presiding officer at parliamentary elections for the county, and is required to attend on the judges at assizes.

In *Ireland* (1542) and *U.S.* (1662) applied to similar officers (in U.S. usu. elective). Those boroughs and cities that are counties of themselves, and also the City of Oxford, have a sheriff (or in some instances two) chosen annually by the Corporation, the specific duties attached to the office varying in different towns. The City of London elects annually two sheriffs, who are also sheriffs of Middlesex.

b. *Scotland.* In early times, a high officer of a county with functions analogous to those of the English sheriff of the same period, together with a civil and criminal jurisdiction of very wide extent. The judicial duties of the office were performed by the *sheriff-depute*, who was necessarily a lawyer. Since the act 20 Geo. II, c. 43 (1747) the title of sheriff is given to the sheriff-depute, who is the chief local judge in a Scottish county, and popularly to the sheriff-substitute, who usu. hears cases in the first instance, subject to an appeal to the sheriff-depute. Both offices are now held for life, and the appointment rests with the crown. late ME.

Comb.: **sheriff's clerk,** *Sc.* **s. clerk,** the clerk of the sheriff's court; **sheriff's officer,** an official employed to execute the sheriff's writs, to distrain and arrest, etc. Hence **She·riffalty** (ʃe·rifălti) = SHRIEVALTY. †**She·riffhood,** the office of s. -1629. **She·riffwick** = next.

Sheriffdom (ʃe·rifdəm). late ME. [-DOM.] **1.** *Sc.* A district or territory under the jurisdiction of a sheriff. **2.** The office of sheriff 1596.

Sherris (ʃe·ris). *arch.* 1597. [a. Sp. (*vino de*) *Xeres* wine of Xeres.] next.

Comb.: **s.-sack,** 'sack' imported from Xeres.

Sherry (ʃe·ri). 1608. [A sing. form evolved from SHERRIS, mistaken for a pl.] Orig., the still white wine made near Xeres (now Jerez de la Frontera, near Cadiz); in mod. use, extended to a class of Spanish white wines of similar character, and to wines made elsewhere in imitation of Spanish sherry.

Comb.: **s.-cobbler**; see COBBLER 3.

Sherryvallies (ʃerivæ·liz), *sb. pl.* *U.S.* 1778. [app. adoption of some word of oriental origin signifying a kind of trousers; cf. Arab. *sirwāl*, now commonly *sharwāl*, whence Sp. *zaragüelles*, etc.] Overalls made of thick velvet or leather, buttoned on the outside of each leg, and worn over the trousers as a protection from mud, etc.

Sheth (ʃeþ). *local* and *techn.* [cogn. w. WFlem. *schet* rail, palisade, f. Teut.root **skaiþ-* (see SHED *v.*) SHEATH.] A bar, lath, esp. one of a series; *Mining* and *Agric.* one of a series of rows or workings.

Shetland (ʃe·tlănd). 1790. [Name of a group of islands to the north-north-east of the mainland of Scotland.] Used *attrib.*

S. pony, horse, etc., one of a breed (orig. from the Shetlands) of small hardy ponies having a rough coat and a long mane and tail. *S. wool*, a variety of wool spun in the Shetlands; hence applied to things made of this wool. Hence **She·tlander,** an inhabitant of the Shetland Isles; a S. pony.

Sheva (ʃəvā·). 1582. [Heb.] **1.** *Heb. Gram.* The sign ְ under a consonant letter to indicate (what Jewish grammarians regard as) the absence of a vowel. *Movable s.*: the neutral vowel (ə). **2.** *Phonetics.* (sometimes in G. form **schwa**). The neutral vowel-sound, *esp.* in comparative grammar 1888.

Shew, var. of SHOW *sb.* and *v.*

Shewbread (ʃōu·bred). 1530. [f. *shew* SHOW *sb.*, after G. *schaubrot* (Luther), repr. Heb. *leḥem pānīm*, LXX ἄρτοι ἐνώπιοι, Vulg. *panes propositionis.*] *Jewish Antiq.* The twelve loaves that were placed every Sabbath 'before the Lord' on a table beside the altar of incense, and at the end of the week were eaten by the priests alone.

Shewel (ʃū·əl). *Obs.* exc. *dial.* [Early ME. *scheules*, a deriv. of the vb. which appears as OHG. *sciuhen* (mod.G. *scheuen*) to scare.] A scarecrow. Also *Hunting*, something set up to keep a deer from entering a particular place, or from going in a particular direction.

‖**Shiah** (ʃī·ă). 1626. [Arab. *shīʿa*[h] sect, f. root *shāʿa* (in the third conjugation) to follow.] **a.** Properly, a collective name for the Mohammedan sect which maintains that Ali (Mohammed's cousin and son-in-law) was the true successor of the prophet, and regards the three first caliphs of the Sunnites as usurpers. **b.** Commonly, an adherent of this sect, a Shiite.

Shibboleth (ʃi·bŏleþ). ME. [a. Heb. *shibbōleth*; in the Vulg. transliterated *sciboleth.*] **1.** The Hebrew word used by Jephthah as a test-word by which to distinguish the fleeing Ephraimites (who could not pronounce the *sh*) from his own men the Gileadites (Judges xii. 4–6). **2.** *transf.* **a.** A word used as a test for detecting foreigners, or persons from another district, by their pronunciation 1658. **b.** *loosely.* A custom, habit, mode of dress, or the like, which distinguishes a particular class or set of persons 1806. **3.** *fig.* A catchword or formula adopted by a party or sect, by which their adherents or followers may be discerned, or those not their followers may be excluded 1638.

1. In that sore battel when so many dy'd Without Reprieve adjudg'd to death, For want of well pronouncing S. MILT. **3.** The fetters of party shibboleths 1862.

Shide (ʃəid). *Obs.* exc. *dial.* [OE. *scīd* :—OTeut. **skīđom*, f. root **skīđ-* to divide; see SHED *v.*] A piece of wood split off from timber, a block, billet; a board, plank, beam. As a quantity; Half a cubic foot of timber.

Shiel (ʃīl). *Sc.* and *north.* [Northern ME. *shāle*, *schēle*, of obsc. origin.] **1.** A temporary building, usu. of boards; a SHIELING. **2.** A small house, cottage, hovel ME.

Shield (ʃīld), *sb.* [Com. Teut.: OE. *sceld* :—OTeut. **skelduz.*] **I. 1.** An article of defensive armour carried in the hand or attached by a strap to the left arm of a soldier, as a protection from the weapons of the enemy. Sometimes *spec.* an article of this kind larger than the BUCKLER, and smaller than the PAVIS. **2.** *transf.* and *fig.* Something serving as a defence against attack or injury ME. **b.** Applied (as a Biblical Hebraism; see, e.g. Ps. xxxiii. 20), to a personal protector or defender (esp. to God) OE. **3.** *Her.* = ESCUTCHEON 1 ME. **4.** An ornamental piece of plate, more or less in the form of a shield, freq. offered for competition in an athletic or other contest 1868.

2. b. Thow be my sheld for þy benignite CHAUCER. **3.** *S.-of-arms*, an escutcheon with armorial bearings. *S. of pretence* = ESCUTCHEON *of pretence*.

II. A protective covering or shelter. **1.** Applied to certain parts of animal bodies. **a.** The thick tough skin upon the sides and flanks of the boar; *spec.* an article of food (in full, *s. of brawn*), made by placing a piece of this skin round the inside of a mould and filling up with meat, and cooking until soft and tender. late ME. **b.** *Zool.* A protective plate covering a part; a scute, a carapace, a plastron, or the like 1704. **2.** A framework erected for the protection of workmen engaged in boring or tunnelling and pushed forward as the work progresses; also, a watertight case used in submarine tunnelling to keep back quicksands and inrushes of water 1837. **3.** A protective device attached to a field-gun in order to shelter the gunners from rifle-fire 1898. **b.** A protective plate or screen in machinery generally 1888. **c.** Any protective device in clothing. **III.** Applied to things shaped like a shield. **1.** *Bot.* The apothecium of lichens 1796. **2.** *Cutlery.* A small metal plate fixed on the handle of a penknife or pocket-knife, for ornament or to be engraved with the owner's name 1876. **3.** *gen.* A flat or slightly convex surface more or less resembling a shield in shape 1849. **4.** A breed of pigeons of various colours 1855. **5.** *U.S.* A policeman's badge 1903.

Comb.: **s.-arm,** the left arm; **-bearer,** an attendant who carries the s. of a warrior; **-bud,** a bud and a portion of the bark surrounding it, used in grafting;

-**fern**, various forms of the genus *Aspidium*. Hence **Shie·ldless** *a.*, having no s.; unprotected by a s.

Shield (ʃīld), *v.* [OE. (*ge*)*scildan*, *scyldan*, f. *sceld* SHIELD *sb.*] **1.** *trans.* To protect (a person or object) by the interposition of some means of defence; to protect (an accused person, etc.) by authority or influence. **2.** *absol.* To offer a defence, to act as a shield OE. †**3.** To ward off, to keep away. Also with *off.* -1822. †**4.** In deprecatory phr. *God s.*, usu. with a clause or sentence as direct obj.; also *absol.* as an exclam.: = God forbid -1674.

1. Thow shalt bee shielded with my protection alway 1582. **2.** A desire to s. and save BYRON. **4.** God shilde that it sholde so bifalle CHAUCER.

Shielded (ʃī·ldėd), *ppl. a.* OE. [f. SHIELD *sb.* and *v.* + -ED [1].] **1.** Bearing a shield. **b.** *Nat. Hist.* In names of various animals characterized by a hard shield-like carapace or scute 1662. **2.** Furnished or hung with shields 1805. **3.** *techn.* Protected by a 'shield' 1855.

1. b. The s. tortoise 1662. **2.** The s. hall of Valhalla 1892.

Shieling, shealing (ʃī·liŋ). *Sc.* 1568. [f. SHIEL + -ING [1].] **1.** A piece of pasture to which cattle may be driven for grazing. **2.** A hut of rough construction erected on or near such a piece of pasture 1585.

Shift (ʃift), *sb.* [ME. *schift*, related to SHIFT *v.*] †**I.** A movement to do something, a beginning. ME. only. **II. 1.** An expedient, an ingenious device for effecting some purpose 1530. **b.** Faculty of contrivance, resourcefulness (*rare*). Cf. SHIFTLESS *a.* 1542. **2.** A fraudulent or evasive device, a stratagem; a piece of sophistry, an evasion, subterfuge 1545. **3.** An expedient necessitated by stress of circumstances 1647. **4.** *To make* (*a*) *shift.* **a.** To make efforts, bestir oneself. Now *dial.* 1460. **b.** To attain one's end by contrivance or effort; to succeed; to manage *to do* something 1504. **c.** To succeed with difficulty, to manage with effort *to do* something 1538. **d.** To do one's best *with* (inferior means), to be content *with*, put up *with* 1577.

1. Ile finde a thousand shifts to get away SHAKS. **b.** Hang them, say I, that has no S. SWIFT. **2.** Their whole life is a succession of shifts, excuses, and expedients HAZLITT. **3.** It were endless to recount the shifts to which I have been reduced JOHNSON. Phr. *One's* (or *the*) *last s.*, the last resource. *To be at one's last shift*(*s*, to be at the last extremity; so to *put, drive, reduce*, etc. *to the last shifts*. **4. d.** I cannot make s. nor bear fatigue as I used to do SWIFT. We..have to make a s. with cheap labour 1885.

III. Change, substitution, succession. †**1.** Change or substitution of one thing for another of the same kind -1625. **2.** Change (of clothing); *concr.* one of several suits of clothing, or garments of the same kind belonging to one person. *Obs.* exc. *dial.* 1570. **3.** A body-garment of linen, cotton, or the like; usu. a woman's 'smock' or chemise. Now *rare.* 1598. **4.** Each of the successive crops in a course of rotation 1787. **5.** A relay or change of workmen 1812. **b.** The length of time during which such a set of men work 1809. **6.** A change (of wind) 1594.

1. My going to Oxford was not merely for s. of air WOTTON. **5.** The night shifts receive so much higher pay for their labour 1912.

IV. Change of position, removal. **1.** A shifting, removal; a change of position or attitude; *dial.* a change of residence or employment 1826. **2.** *Mus.* In violin-playing, a change of the position of the hand on the finger-board 1771. **3.** *Building.* The arrangement of timbers, stones, etc. so that the joints of adjacent rows do not coincide 1805. **4.** *Mining.* A slight 'fault' or dislocation in a seam or stratum 1802.

Shift (ʃift), *v.* [OE. *sciftan* :—OTeut. **skiftjan*, f. Teut. root **skip-*.] **I.** To put in order, arrange. †**1.** *trans.* To appoint, assign, dispose in order. late ME. **2.** To apportion, distribute; to separate into shares, divide OE. †**3.** *intr.* To manage matters; to deal, bargain, make arrangements *with*; to make provision *for* ME. **4.** To manage to effect one's purposes; to succeed, get on (well or ill); to make shift 1532. **5.** To employ shifts or evasions; to practise or use indirect methods; to practise or live by fraud, or temporary expedients 1579. **6.** *To s. for oneself*, to provide for one's own safety, interests, or livelihood (implying either absence of aid, or, occas., want of concern for others); to depend on one's own efforts 1513.

3. Phr. †*To let* (persons) *s.* [= F. *laisser faire*] to let (them) take their own course, not to interfere. **4.** She that hath wit, may s. any-where MIDDLETON. Might not the colonists s. for the present with the southern island? 1865.

II. To change. †**1.** *trans.* To change, to replace by another of the kind. With pl. object: To quit one and take another of (the things indicated) -1864. **b.** *intr.* To undergo transmutation; to change 1605. **2.** To change (one's own or another's clothing). Also *refl.* and *intr.* for *refl.* Now chiefly *dial.* late ME. **3.** *trans.* To change (the scene) 1599. **b.** *intr.* Of a scene: To change 1828. †**4.** *trans.* To cause (a set of workmen) to change places with another set. Also said of a gang of workmen: To replace (another gang or set) as a relief; also *intr.* for *refl.* -1791.

1. There staid..till he shifted his horses PEPYS. Phr. †*To s. hands* = 'to change hands'; also, to change one's ground in argument; so *to s.* one's *ground.* **2.** I went immediately to s. my clothes DE FOE. **3.** The scene shifts to the latter place 1861.

III. To change the place of, to remove. **1.** *trans.* To transfer from one place to another; to remove; to alter the position of. late ME. **2.** *Naut.* **a.** To change or alter the position of (a sail, spar, the helm, etc.) 1667. **b.** Of a ship or a navigator: To undergo displacement of (cargo or ballast) 1854. **c.** *intr.* Of cargo, ballast: To move from its proper position, so as to disturb the equilibrium of the vessel 1797. **3.** *trans.* To alter the direction of 1698. **b.** *intr.* Of the wind: To change its direction 1645. **4.** *trans.* To change or alter (one's or its position, place); to change (one's lodging, abode, etc.) 1563. **5.** To get (a person) out of the way. Now *slang* or *colloq.*, to dislodge (a body of the enemy); of a horse, to throw (the rider); also *euphem.*, to 'put out of the way', murder. 1604. †**6.** To avoid, escape, elude -1816. **7. S. off.** †**a.** To put off, remove (a covering, a garment); *fig.* to remove from oneself or another (a burden) -1805. **b.** To evade, turn aside (an argument); to evade fulfilment of (a duty, a promise) 1577. **c.** To put (a person) off with an excuse or a subterfuge; to get rid of (a person) 1585. **8.** *intr.* To move from one place to another; esp. to change one's lodging 1530. **9.** To move about, to move from one position to another, to move slightly 1595. **10.** To move away, withdraw, depart; esp. to slip off unobserved. Now only with *away.* 1590.

1. Every man shifting the fault from himself CLARENDON. Cæsar had shifted his camp continually 1879. **3. b.** The wind has shifted round to due west 1885. **5.** Cassio came hither. I shifted him away. SHAKS. **10.** Oh Mistris, Mistris, s. and saue your selfe SHAKS. Hence **Shi·ftable** *a.*

Shifter (ʃi·ftəɹ). 1555. [f. prec. + -ER [1].] **1.** One who shifts something; *spec.* a scene-shifter. †**2.** One who resorts to petty shifts, or who practises artifice; an idle, thriftless fellow; a trickster, cozener, etc. -1670. **b.** One who uses evasive reasoning 1567. **3.** *Naut.* One who assists the ship's cook 1704. **4.** *Mech.* A contrivance used for shifting, e.g. a kind of clutch serving to transfer a belt from one pulley to another 1869.

1. He is no great s.; once a yeare his Apparel is ready to reuolt B. JONS. **2.** In worldly matters, practis'd and cunning Shifters MILT.

Shifting (ʃi·ftiŋ), *ppl. a.* 1479. [f. as prec. + -ING [2].] **1.** That shifts or changes position or direction. **2.** That uses shifts, tricks, deceit, expedients, subterfuges, or evasions 1581.

1. A whole parish was swallowed up by the s. sands SCOTT. Special collocations: **s. ballast**, ballast capable of being moved to trim the vessel; **s. centre** = METACENTRE; **s. use** *Law*, a use properly created for the benefit of one person, but so as to pass from him upon a specified contingency and vest wholly or in part in another. Hence **Shi·fting-ly** *adv.*, **-ness.**

Shiftless (ʃi·ftlės), *a.* 1562. [f. SHIFT *sb.* + -LESS.] †**1.** Helpless for self-defence; void of cunning or artifice -1698. **2.** Lacking in resource; incapable of shifting for oneself; hence, lazy, inefficient 1584. **b.** Of actions: Indicating shiftlessness; ineffective, futile 1613. **3.** Without a shift or shirt (*rare*) 1680.

2. Going to hunt up her s. husband at the inn HARDY. Hence **Shi·ftless-ly** *adv.*, **-ness.**

Shifty (ʃi·fti), *a.* 1570. [f. as prec. + -Y [1].] **1.** Full of shifts or expedients; well able to shift for oneself. **2.** Fond of indirect or dishonest methods; addicted to evasion or artifice; not straightforward, not to be depended on 1837. **3.** Changeable or changeful; wavering (*rare*) 1882.

1. The canny, s., far-seeing Scot, with that mingled daring and caution of his KINGSLEY. **2.** A most s. old fox he is 1841. I scorn your s. evasions DICKENS. Hence **Shi·fti-ly** *adv.*, **-ness.**

Shiite (ʃī·əit). 1728. [f. SHI(AH + -ITE [1] 1.] A member of the Shiah sect. Also *attrib.* or *adj.* Hence **Shii·tic** *a.*

Shikar (ʃikā·ɹ), *sb.* *Anglo-Ind.* 1613. [Urdū (from Pers.) *shikār*.] Hunting; sport (shooting and hunting); game. Hence **Shika·r** *v. trans.* and *intr.* to hunt.

Shikaree (ʃikā·rī). *Anglo-Indian.* 1827. [Urdū (from Pers.) *shikārī*, f. *shikār*.] A hunter or sportsman; esp. a native who brings in game on his own account, or accompanies European sportsmen as a guide.

Shillelagh (ʃilē·lă, -ē·li). 1772. [Name of a barony and village in Co. Wicklow.] An Irish cudgel of blackthorn or oak.

Shilling (ʃi·liŋ). [Com. Teut.: OE. *scilling* :—OTeut. **skilliŋgoz*. (Cf. SCHELLING, SCHILLING, SKILLING.) Ult. etym. obsc.] **1.** An English money of account, of the value of 12 pence or $\frac{1}{20}$ of a pound sterling. Abbrev. s. (= L. *solidus*; see SOLIDUS), formerly also sh., shil.; otherwise denoted by the sign /- after the numeral. **b.** Used in emphatic or rhetorical statements, where one wishes to be understood as deliberately reckoning every item, however small, of a given sum or expense 1737. **2.** A silver coin of the value of 12 pence. First issued in 1503, by Henry VII 1513. **b.** With defining word indicating a particular coinage 1699. †**3.** Used to render or represent the names of various foreign moneys -1776. **4.** With prefixed numerals, forming adjs. of price or value. Also in phr. denoting rate of payment. 1578.

1. Afterwards to ninepins, where I won a s. PEPYS. **b.** I will not engage to pay one s. more than the expenses really incurred by Hanover WELLINGTON. **3.** *Double s.*, a Dutch florin or guilder. **4.** Sold..in five s. and ten s. bottles SCOTT.

Phrases. *To cut off with a s.*, to disinherit deliberately. *To take the s., the King's* (or *Queen's*) *s.*, to enlist as a soldier by accepting a s. from a recruiting officer (a practice now disused).

Shillingsworth (ʃi·liŋzwəɹþ). Formerly **shillingworth** (now *rare*). ME. [WORTH *sb.*] The amount or quantity which may be bought for a shilling; as much as is worth a shilling or a (specified) number of shillings.

Shilly-shally (ʃi·liʃæ:li), *adv. phr.*, *a.*, *sb.* 1700. [orig. *shill I, shall I*, altered form of *shall I, shall I*. Cf. WISHY-WASHY.] **A.** *To stand shill I, shall I*: to vacillate, to be irresolute or undecided.

I'm for marrying her at once—Why should I stand s., like a Country Bumpkin? STEELE.

B. *adj.* Vacillating, irresolute 1734.

I am s. about it in my own mind 1743.

C. *sb.* Vacillation, irresolution 1755.

There can be no s. now GEO. ELIOT.

Shi·lly-sha:lly, *v.* 1782. [f. prec. adv. phr.] *intr.* To vacillate, be irresolute or undecided. Hence **Shi·lly-sha:llyer**, one who shilly-shallies.

Shim (ʃim), *sb. local.* 1723. [Origin unkn.] **1.** A piece of iron attached to an agricultural implement for scraping the surface of the soil. **2.** In full *s.-plough*: A kind of horse-hoe or shallow plough, used in Kent and elsewhere, for hoeing up weeds between rows of beans, hops, etc. 1736. **3.** A thin slip, usu. of metal, used to fill up a space between parts subject to wear, to aline or adjust the level of rails, etc. 1864. Hence **Shim** *v. intr.* to use the s. for hoeing; *trans.* to hoe (crops) with a s.

Shimmer (ʃi·məɹ), *sb.* 1821. [f. next. Cf. G. *schimmer*.] A shimmering light or glow; a subdued tremulous light.

Two silver lamps..diffused..a trembling..s. through the quiet apartment SCOTT.

Shimmer (ʃi·məɹ), *v.* [Late OE. *scymrian*; related to *scimian* to shine.] *intr.* To shine with a tremulous or flickering light; to gleam faintly. In early use also, to shine brightly, glisten.

Shimmy[1] (ʃi·mi). 1839. *dial.* and *U.S.* corruption of CHEMISE.

Shi·mmy.[2] 1919. *U.S.* [? = prec.] A kind of fox-trot accompanied by tremulous motions of the body. Also as *vb.*

Shin (ʃin), *sb.* [OE. *scinu* = OHG. *scina* skin, needle.] **1.** The front part of the human leg between the knee and the ankle; the front or sharp edge of the shank-bone. **b.** The lower part of a leg (of beef), the meat of which is lean and streaked 1736. **2.** Used, after G. *schiene*, for an iron plate or band 1747.

attrib. and *Comb.*, as *s.-guard, pad*, etc.; **s.-leaf,** the N. Amer. ericaceous plant *Pyrola elliptica* (also *P. rotundifolia*); **-plaster** *U.S. slang*, a piece of paper money, esp. one of a low denomination, depreciated in value.

Shin (ʃin), *v.* 1829. [f. prec.] **1.** *intr.* (orig. *Naut.*) To climb by using the arms and legs without the help of steps, irons, etc. **b.** *trans.* To climb up 1891. **2.** *US. intr.* To 'use one's legs'; to move quickly; to run *round* 1845. **3.** *trans.* To kick (a person) on the shins 1845.

1. We had to..s. up and down single ropes caked with ice 1840.

Shin-bone (ʃi·nbōun). [OE. *scinbān*; see SHIN *sb.* and BONE *sb.*] = TIBIA **1.**

Shindy (ʃi·ndi). 1821. [perh. alteration of SHINTY.] **1.** = SHINTY **1.** *local.* 1846. **2.** A spree, merrymaking 1821. **3.** A row, commotion, 'shine' 1845.

3. Phr. *To kick up a s.*

Shine (ʃəin), *sb.*[1] 1529. [f. SHINE *v.*] **1.** Brightness or radiance shed by a luminary or an illuminant. †**b.** A beam or ray; a halo –1654. **2.** Lustre or sheen of an object reflecting light, as metal, water, silk 1599. **b.** *Painting* and *Photogr.* Shininess; a shiny patch 1880. **c.** The polish given to a pair of boots by a bootblack; *transf.* a job of boot-blacking 1871. **3.** Sunshine, *esp.* as opp. to *rain*; hence, fine weather 1622. **4.** *fig.* Brilliance, radiance, splendour, lustre. †Also [after G. *schein*], a specious appearance, a 'show'. 1530. **b.** A brilliant display, a 'dash' 1819.

1. And mooned Ashtaroth..Now sits not girt with Tapers holy s. MILT. **2.** Dazled with the glittering s. of Gold 1667. **3.** Come storm, come s., whatever befall HENLEY. **4.** The bright s., and worthines of his auncestors 1586. **b.** Colloq. phrases. *To cut a s. To take the s. out of*, to deprive (a person or thing) of his or its brilliance or pre-eminence; to surpass.

Shine (ʃəin), *sb.*[2] 1830. [perh. uses of prec. sb., but cf. the senses of SHINDY.] **1.** A party, convivial gathering; usu. *tea-s.*, a 'tea-fight'. *dial.* 1838. **2.** A disturbance, row, fuss. *colloq.* 1832. **3.** *pl.* Capers, tricks. *U.S.* 1830. **4.** *To take a s. to* (U.S.): to take a fancy for 1848.

Shine (ʃəin), *v.* Pa. t. and pple. **shone** (ʃǫn). [Com. Teut. str. vb.: OE. *scīnan* (*scān, scinon, *scinen*) :—OTeut. **skīnan*, f. root **skī-* by means of the present-stem formative *n.*] **1.** *intr.* Of a heavenly body or an object that is alight: To shed beams of bright light; to give out light so as to illuminate; to be radiant. Also with *forth, out.* **b.** Of the day: To be sunny or bright; also, to dawn. Chiefly *poet.* late ME. **2.** Of a metallic, polished, smooth, or glassy object: To be bright or resplendent; to gleam, glisten, or glitter with reflected light OE. **b.** To be bright *with* 1606. **3.** To be radiant or brilliant with bright colouring; to be effulgent with splendour or beauty; to make a brave show OE. **4.** Of persons: To be conspicuous or brilliant in ability, character, achievement, or position; to be eminent or distinguished, to excel OE. **5.** Of something immaterial: To appear with conspicuous clearness; to be brilliantly evident or visible; to stand out clearly ME. **b.** To be clearly evident *through* an outward appearance 1590. **6.** *trans.* To cause (light) to shine, to emit (rays) 1588. **7.** *To s. down*: to surpass in brilliance 1613. **8.** To cause to shine, put a polish on; *U.S.* (inflected *shined*) to black (boots) 1613. **9.** *U.S.* (*Hunting.*) To throw the light of a lantern, etc. on (the eyes of an animal); to locate the position of (an animal) in this way 1845.

1. The fog became thin, and the sun shone through it TYNDALL. *To s. upon*, to look favourably upon, be favourable to, said of a star, or of the face of God. *fig.* As for them that dwel in the londe of the shadowe of death, vpon them shal the lyght s. COVERDALE. *Isa.* ix. 2. **b.** We can..dismiss thee ere the Morning s. MILT. †*It shines*, it is sunny. **2.** The huge hall-table's oaken face, Scrubb'd till it shone SCOTT. **3.** Her light foot Shone rosy-white TENNYSON. **4.** He.. never shone as an orator 1836. **5.** Princely counsel in his face yet shon MILT. **6.** She approached, shining smiles upon Esmond THACKERAY.

Shiner (ʃəi·nəɹ). ME. [f. SHINE *v.* + -ER [1].] **1.** An object that shines. **b.** *pl.* Coin, money, *esp.* sovereigns or guineas; occas. *sing.* a silver or gold coin. *slang.* 1760. **c.** A mirror; *spec.* one used by cheaters at cards. *slang.* 1812. **2.** One who shines (See SHINE *v.* 4.) 1810. **b.** A bootblack 1912. **3.** Applied to various small silvery fishes; the young of the mackerel; *U.S.* any of various small freshwater fishes, chiefly cyprinoids, as the dace 1836.

Shingle (ʃi·ŋg'l), *sb.*[1] [ME. *scincle, shyngle*, app. repr. L. *scindula*, later form of *scandula*, infl. by Gr. σχινδαλμός.] **1.** A thin piece of wood having parallel sides and one end thicker than the other, used as a house-tile. **b.** *gen.* A piece of board 1825. **c.** *U.S.* A small sign-board 1847. **d.** 'Shingled' hair; this manner of cutting the hair 1924. **2.** *attrib.* or *adj.* 1810.

1. Your house..covered with cedar shingles COBBETT. **2.** When the s. roof rang sharp with the rains. MRS. BROWNING. *Comb.* **s.-oak,** (*a*) the laurel-oak, *Quercus imbricaria*; (*b*) the she-oak.

Shingle (ʃi·ŋg'l), *sb.*[2] 1513. [Origin obsc.] **1.** Small, roundish stones; loose, waterworn pebbles such as are found collected upon the sea-shore; *collect. sing.* and *pl.* 1574. **2.** A beach or other tract covered with loose roundish pebbles 1513.

Shingle (ʃi·ŋg'l), *v.*[1] 1562. [f. SHINGLE *sb.*[1]] **1.** *trans.* To cover, roof (a house, etc.) with shingles 1562. **2.** orig. *U.S* To cut (hair), properly so as to give the effect of overlapping shingles, by exposing the ends of hair all over the head; to cut (women's hair) in a style in which it is made to taper from the back of the head to the nape of the neck; also *absol.* 1857.

1. *transf.* The..walls and roof are shingled with slate 1885. Hence **Shi·ngler**[1], one who shingles houses, etc.; also *U.S.* a machine which cuts and prepares shingles.

Shingle, *v.*[2] 1674. [ad. F. *cingler*, ad. G. *zängeln*, f. *zange* tongs, pincers.] *Iron-manuf. trans.* To subject (the puddled ball) to pressure and blows from a hammer so as to expel impurities. Hence **Shi·ngler**[2], one who or a machine which shingles puddled iron.

Shingles (ʃi·ŋg'lz), *sb. pl.* late ME. [repr. med.L. *cingulus*, var. of *cingulum* girdle, used to render Gr. ζώνη or ζωστήρ in the medical sense.] An eruptive disease (*Herpes zoster*) often extending round the middle of the body like a girdle (whence the name); usu. accompanied by violent neuralgic pain.

Shingly (ʃi·ŋgli), *a.* 1775. [f. SHINGLE *sb.*[2] + -Y [1].] Consisting of or covered with shingle; of the nature of shingle.

Shining (ʃəi·niŋ), *ppl. a.* OE. [f. SHINE *v.* + -ING [2].] **1.** That shines; luminous, lustrous, gleaming; also, of bright or brilliant aspect or exterior; resplendent. **2.** With ref. to intellectual or moral qualities: Eminent, distinguished, brilliant. Now *rare.* OE. **3.** Of looks: Radiant, beaming 1821.

1. Fish with thir Finns & s. Scales MILT. Phr. *S. light* (after John v. 35), a person conspicuous for some excellence *To improve the s. hour* (after Watts), to make good use of time. **2.** Men of the greatest and the most s. Parts 1711. **3.** A..s. sanguine face LAMB. Hence **Shi·ning·ly** *adv.*, **-ness.**

Shinny (ʃi·ni). 1672. [app. f. the cry used in the game *shin ye, shin you*, of obsc. origin.] A (north-country and American) game similar to hockey, played with a ball and sticks curved at one end; also, the stick and the ball used.

Shinto (ʃi·nto). 1727. [Japanese, f. Chinese *shin tao* way of the gods.] **1.** The native religious system of Japan, the central belief of which is that the mikado is the direct descendant of the sun-goddess and that implicit obedience is due to him. **2.** An adherent of Shinto beliefs 1829. Hence **Shi·nto,ism** = sense **1.** **Shi·nto,ist** = sense 2. **Shinto,i·stic** *a.* belonging to or characteristic of S.

Shinty (ʃi·nti). 1771. [Origin obsc.] = SHINNY.

Shiny (ʃəi·ni), *a.* (and *sb.*) 1590. [f. SHINE *sb.*[1] + -Y [1].] Full of light or brightness; luminous; having a bright or glistening surface.

Vpon a Sommers shynie day SPENSER S. boots, tall hat, go-to-meeting coat 1868. Hence **Shi·niness.**

B. *sb.* A shiny or bright object. *The s.* (slang), money. 1856.

Ship (ʃip), *sb.*[1] [Com. Teut.: OE. *scip*; ult. etym. uncertain.] **1.** A large sea-going vessel (opp. to a *boat*); *spec.* (in modern times) a vessel having a bowsprit and three masts, each of which consists of a lower, top, and topgallant mast. **b.** In rowing parlance, applied to the racing eight-oar boat; also used playfully of other craft 1878. **c.** *fig.* Applied to the state 1675. **2.** With qualifying word or phrase indicating the kind or use. late ME. **3.** In fig. and allusive phrases, *esp.* where *ship* typifies the fortunes or affairs of a person, etc. or the person himself in regard to them 1500. **4.** *transf.* Applied to various objects that are, or are conceived to be, navigated. late ME. **5.** A vessel, utensil, ornament, etc. shaped like a ship. late ME. **6.** A ship's company or crew ME.

1. A stately S. Of Tarsus, bound for th' Isles Of Javan or Gadier MILT. Phr. *To take s.* (see TAKE *v.* IV. 2 c). **b.** The..steadiness of their s...helped the Oxford men very much 1901. **2.** **King's s.** (now *Hist.*), one of the fleet of ships provided and maintained out of the royal revenue; a ship of the royal navy; later, a ship-of-war equipped at the public expense (opp. to *privateer*). For *flagship, steamship, warship*, etc., see these words. *When one's s. comes home* (or *in*), when one comes into one's fortune. **4.** An aeroplane or other form of aircraft. *S. of the desert, desert-s.*, the camel. *S. of Guinea, Guinea s.*, sailor's name for a floating medusa. **5.** A s. of silver for the almes disshe 1525. Two thuribles, with a s. for incense 1843.

attrib. and *Comb.*, as *s.-bell, -canal*, etc.; **ship('s) biscuit,** hard biscuit prepared for use on board ship, hard tack; formerly called **ship('s) bread; ship('s) boy,** a boy who serves on board ship; **-breaker,** a person who buys old vessels to break them up for sale; **s.-broker,** a mercantile agent who transacts the business of a ship when it is in port, or is engaged in buying and selling ships, or in procuring insurance on them; **-brokerage,** the business of a ship-broker; **ship('s) carpenter,** a carpenter employed in the building or repairing of ships; hence **-carpentry; ship('s) company,** the crew of a ship; **-fever,** a form of typhus fever, called also *gaol fever* and *hospital fever*; **-ladder,** a ladder used in boarding or leaving a ship; **-letter,** a letter carried by a private vessel and not by the ordinary mail boat; **-mate,** one who serves with another in the same ship; **-owner,** one who owns, or has a share in, a s. or ships; **-papers,** now usu. **ship's papers,** the documents (passport, muster-roll, charter party, log-book, etc.) with which a ship is required by law to be provided; **-plate,** an inferior grade of wrought iron plate; **-railway,** an inclined railway running into the water over which a ship may be drawn out on land for repairs, etc.; **-rigged** *a.* carrying square sails on all three masts; **ship('s) stores,** provisions and supplies for use on board ship; **-timber,** timber for shipbuilding; **ship('s) time,** the local mean time of the meridian where the ship is; **shipway,** (*a*) a way or bed on which ships are built or laid for examination; (*b*) a ship-canal. **b.** In the names of animals: **s.-borer** = *s.-worm*; **-rat,** a variety of rat found on board ship; **-worm,** any of the worm-shaped molluscs of the genus *Teredo* and allied genera, esp. *T. navalis.* **c.** Combs. with *ship's*: **ship's articles,** the terms according to which seamen take service on board ship; **ship's days,** the days allowed for loading and unloading a ship; **ship's husband** (see HUSBAND *sb.*). Hence **Shi·pful,** as much or as many as a s. will hold. **Shi·pless** *a.* unoccupied by ships; possessing no ships; deprived of one's ship or ships. **Shi·plet,** a small ship.

Ship, *sb.*[2] 1875. *Printing.* A colloq. abbrev. of COMPANIONSHIP [2].

Ship (ʃip), *v.* [Late OE. *scipian*, f. *scip* SHIP *sb.*[1] Later, directly f. SHIP *sb.*[1]] †**1.** *pass.* To be furnished with a ship or ships –1647. **2.** To put or take (persons or things) on board ship ME. **b.** Said of the ship 1800. †**3. a.** *pass.* Of a person: To have gone on board, to be embarked –1621. **b.** *refl.* To go on board ship, embark. *Obs.* or *arch.* late ME. **4.** *intr.* To go on board ship, embark. Now *rare.* ME. †**5.** To go by ship *to, into,* or *from* a place –1654. **6.** *trans.* To send or transport by ship. late ME. **b.** *transf.* To transport (goods) by rail or other means of conveyance. *U.S.* 1881. **c.** *fig.* To send *off*, send packing 1588. **7.** Of a vessel: To take in (water) over the side; to be submerged or flooded with (water) by waves breaking over it; esp. *to s. a sea.* Said also of the occupants of the vessel. 1698. **8.** To take or draw (an object) into the ship or boat to which it belongs 1630. **b.** To lift (an oar or scull) out of its rowlock, and (now, in sculling) to bring it into the boat. Also *absol.* as a command = 'ship oars!' 1700. **9.** orig. and esp. *Naut.* To put (an object) in position for performing its proper function; *spec.* to fix (an oar) in the rowlock, in readiness to row; hence, to put in position for any purpose 1616. **10.** To put on (clothing, etc.); also, to shoulder (a burden) 1829. **11.** To engage for service on a ship 1643. **b.** *intr.* To engage to serve on a ship 1829.

1. Is he well ship'd? SHAKS. 2. King Henry the fifth, was shipping his men for France 1640. b. A little vessel was shipping grain 1882. 3. a. Twenty to one then, he is ship'd already SHAKS. b. The Puritans.. shipped themselves off for America 1761. 4. I shipped at Rye, in Sussex 1517. 6. The third [son] was a Roué, and was shipped to the Colonies DISRAELI. 7. We shipt Seas over our Poop 1734. 8. b. The stranger came to the bank, shipped his sculls, and jumped out 1861. 9. A new rudder.., which was immediately shipped 1798.

-ship *suffix*, in OE. *-*sciepe*, -*scipe*, -*scype*:—OTeut. **skapiz*, f. **skap*- to create, ordain, appoint (see SHAPE *v.*).

1. Added to adjs. and pa. pples. to denote the state or condition of being so-and-so. The only survivals of this formation now in common use are HARDSHIP and WORSHIP.

2. Added to sbs. to denote the state or condition of being what is expressed by the sb., e.g. *authorship, fellowship, suretyship*. b. By extension, when the sb. is the designation of a class of human being, such compounds assume the sense of the qualities or character associated with, or the skill or power of accomplishment of, the person denoted by the sb.; e.g. *craftsmanship, kingship, workmanship*.

3. Added to sbs. designating an official or person of rank to denote the office, position, dignity, or rank of the person designated, as *ambassadorship, professorship*. etc. In the case of *fellowship, scholarship, postmastership* and the like, the connotation has come to include the emoluments, etc., pertaining to the office or position. b. With poss. pron. prefixed, the compounds *ladyship, lordship, worship*, have passed into honorific designations of the persons who are entitled to the style of 'Lady', 'Lord', 'the Worshipful'. Hence the suffix has been freely employed to form mock titles or humorous styles of address.

4. Added to sbs. to denote a state of life, occupation, or behaviour, relating to or connected with what is denoted by the sb. These compounds are now rare; COURTSHIP (first in Shaks.) is the chief instance.

5. Added to sbs. forming compounds having a collective sense. TOWNSHIP (OE *túnscipe* the inhabitants of a *tún*) is the one survival from the OE. period.

Shipboard (ʃi·pbōəɹd). ME. [f. SHIP *sb.*[1] + BOARD *sb.*] †**1.** The side of a ship (see BOARD *sb.* V.) –1848. **b.** *On s.*, on board ship 1470. †**2.** A plank of a ship –1560.

Shi·pbui:lder. 1700. One whose occupation is to design and construct ships; a naval architect. So **Shi·pbuilding** *vbl. sb.* the business or art of building ships; naval architecture.

Shi·p-cha:ndler. 1642. [See CHANDLER.] A dealer who supplies ships with necessary stores. Hence **Shi·p-cha:ndlery,** the business of, or goods dealt in by, a s.

Shi·p-load. 1706. A load (of persons or things) carried or capable of being carried by a ship.

Shipman (ʃi·pmæ̆n). *Pl.* **-men.** OE. [f. SHIP *sb.*[1] + MAN *sb.*] **1.** A seaman or sailor. Now *arch.* **2.** A master mariner; the master of a ship; a skipper. Also, a pilot. late ME.

Shi·pma:ster. late ME. [f. SHIP *sb.*[1] + MASTER *sb.* Cf. G. *schiffmeister.*] **1.** The master, captain, or commander of a ship; formerly also, a pilot, steersman. **2.** A man who owns the ship which he commands 1562.

Shipment (ʃi·pmĕnt). 1802. [f. SHIP *v.* + -MENT.] **1.** The act of shipping (goods, etc.) for transportation. **2.** That which is shipped; a consignment for transportation 1861.

Shi·p-mo:ney. Now *Hist.* 1636. An ancient tax levied in time of war on the ports and maritime towns, cities, and counties of England to provide ships for the king's service. It was revived by Charles I (with an extended application to inland counties), but was finally abolished by statute in 1640.

Shi·p-of-wa·r. Now *rare.* 1479. A ship equipped for warfare; a man-of-war, warship.

Shipper (ʃi·pəɹ). [Late OE. *scipere*, f. SHIP *sb.*[1] + -ER[1].] †**1.** A seaman –1728. †**2.** A skipper –1634. **3.** One who ships goods for transportation 1755. **b.** *U.S.* One who transports goods by rail or other means of conveyance 1903. **c.** A commodity that is shipped or is suitable for shipping 1883. **4.** *Mech.* A device for shifting a belt from one pulley to another 1869.

Shipping (ʃi·piŋ), *vbl. sb.* ME. [f. SHIP *v.* + -ING[1].] **1.** A ship or ships for the use or accommodation of a person or thing. **2.** Ships collectively; the body of ships that belong to a person's or country's fleet, that frequent a particular port or harbour, or that are used for a certain purpose 1591. †**3.** Navigation –1700. †**b.** A voyage, a sailing –1688. **4.** The action of putting persons or things on board ship or transporting them by ship 1483.

1. Phr. *To take s.* (now *arch.*), to embark; occas. pregnantly, to go abroad. 2. A river very commodious for s. DE FOE. 3. b. Phr. *God send you good s.!* used proverbially in the 16th and 17th c. as a wish for success in any venture. 4. A licence for the s. of his stores and provisions 1748.

Comb.: **s.-agent,** a licensed agent who transacts a ship's business for the owner; **-articles** = *ship's articles* (see SHIP *sb.*[1]); **-master,** an official who superintends the signing-on and discharging of seamen; **-office,** (*a*) an office where seamen sign on for a voyage; (*b*) an office where a s.-agent receives goods for shipment; **-papers** = *ship's papers.*

Shippon, -en (ʃi·pən). Now *dial.* [OE. *scypen*:—OTeut. **skupinī*, f. **skup*-; see SHOP *sb.* and -EN[2].] A cattle-shed, a cowhouse.

Shippound (ʃi·pˌpaund). 1545. [ad. MLG. *schippunt* or MDu. *schippond.*] A unit of weight used in the Baltic trade, varying from 300 to 400 pounds; = 20 lispounds.

Ship-shape (ʃi·pʃēᵉip), *a.* (*adv.*). 1644. [f. SHIP *sb.*[1] + SHAPEN (later reduced to *shape*).] Arranged neatly and compactly, as things on board ship should be; trim, orderly; orig. *Naut.* Occas. as *adv.*, in a seamanlike manner, in trim fashion.

It would have been more s. to lower the bight of a rope 1823. Neat s. fixings and contrivances BROWNING.

Shipwreck (ʃi·prek), *sb.* ME. Also †**shipwrack.** [f. SHIP *sb.*[1] + WRECK *sb.* (WRACK *sb.*[2])] **1.** What is cast up from a wreck; the remains of a wrecked vessel; wreckage. In later use chiefly *fig.* **2.** Destruction or loss of a ship by its being sunk or broken up by the violence of the sea, or by its striking or stranding upon a rock, etc. 1450. **b.** An instance of this 1548. **3.** *fig.* Destruction, total loss or ruin 1526.

2. †*To make s.*: see MAKE *v.* IX. 7. b. All in a shipwrack shift their severall way 1633. 3. A generall shipwrake of the Popes uniuersall power 1566. The S. of our Fortunes DE FOE.

Phr. *To make s. of* (arch.), to suffer the loss of, as in *to make s. of a good conscience* (cf. 1 Tim. i. 19); to bring to destruction or total ruin.

Shipwreck (ʃi·prek), *v.* 1589. [f. prec.] **1.** *trans.* To cause (a person) to suffer shipwreck; chiefly *pass.* to suffer shipwreck; also, to cause the loss of (goods) by shipwreck. **b.** To wreck (a vessel). Now *rare.* 1624. **c** *transf.* and *fig.* 1599. **2.** *intr.* To suffer shipwreck. *Obs.* or *arch.* 1607.

1. Shipwrack'd I floated on a driving Mast 1703. b. I..Who like a foolish Pilot have shipwrack't My Vessel MILT. c. Men, who have ship-wreck'd their fortunes as well as their reputations upon this rock 1721.

Shipwright (ʃi·prəit). OE. [f. SHIP *sb.*[1] + WRIGHT *sb.*] A man employed in the construction or repair of ships.

Shipyard (ʃi·pyāɹd). 1700. [f. SHIP *sb.*[1] + YARD.] An enclosure, adjoining the sea or a river, in which ships are built or repaired.

‖**Shiraz** (ʃiᵊ·ræz). 1634. Name of a city in Persia (formerly the capital); used *attrib.* as the designation of a wine made in the district; also *absol.* = Shiraz wine.

Shire (ʃəiᵊɹ), *sb.* [OE. *scīr* = OHG. *scīra* care, official charge.] †**1.** (OE. only.) Official charge; administrative office. †**2.** A province or district under the rule of a governor; the see of a bishop, the province of an archbishop, or the like; in wider sense, a country, region, district –1824. **3.** *spec.* In Old English times, an administrative district, consisting of a group of hundreds or wapentakes, ruled jointly by an ealdorman and a sheriff, who presided in the SHIRE-MOOT. Under Norman rule, the AF. *counté*, Anglo-Latin *comitatus*, was adopted as the equivalent of the English term. At the present day *shire* is current mainly as a literary synonym for *county* (chiefly restricted to those counties that have names ending in *-shire*). OE. **4.** As the terminal element in names of counties (as Berkshire, Derbyshire) and of certain other districts (as Hallamshire, Bedlingtonshire, etc.) which have from early times been regarded as separate unities. Pronounced (-ʃəɹ); in dialects often (-ʃiᵊɹ). OE. **5. The Shires. a.** A term applied to other parts of England by the inhabitants of East Anglia, Kent, Sussex, Essex, and Surrey; also *gen.* applied to those counties the names of which end in *-shire.* Usu. pron. (ʃiᵊɹz). 1796. **b.** *Foxhunting.* As the name of a hunting 'country' 1860. **6.** Short for next 1877.

3. How many suffer injurie, when one hundred of a Shiere is spoiled? 1549. 5. a. The Inhabitants of Kent, to express a person's coming from a great distance..will say, he comes a great way off, out of the shires 1796.

Comb.: †**s.-court** = COUNTY-COURT; **-hall** = *county-hall*; **-member,** a representative of a s. in parliament; **-oak,** an oak tree marking the boundary of a s. or a meeting place for a s.-court; **-reeve,** etymologizing form of SHERIFF; **-town,** a town which is the capital of a shire or county.

Shire, *a.* *Obs.* exc. *dial.* [OE. *scīr.*] = SHEER *a.* 2, 4, 5; also, thin, sparse.

Shire horse. Also **shires horse.** 1875. A horse of a heavy powerful breed, used for draught, chiefly bred in the Midlands.

Shi·re-moot. 1614. [f. SHIRE + MOOT *sb.*; after OE. *scīrgemōt.*] *Hist.* The judicial assembly of the shire in Old English times.

†**Shirk,** *sb.*[1] 1639. [perh. a. G. *schurke.*] A needy, disreputable parasite –1730.

Shirk (ʃɜ̄ɹk), *sb.*[2] 1818. [f. next.] **1.** One who shirks (work, obligations). **2.** An act or the practice of shirking (*rare*) 1877.

Shirk (ʃɜ̄ɹk), *v.* 1633. [Belongs to SHIRK *sb.*[1]; see SHARK *v.*[1]] †**1.** *intr.* To practise fraud or trickery, esp. instead of working as a means of living; to prey or sponge upon others –1850. **2.** To go evasively or slyly; to slink; to sneak *away, out*, etc. 1681. **3.** *trans.* To evade (a person, his conversation, acquaintance, etc.). Now *rare* or *Obs.* 1787. **b.** At Eton: To avoid meeting (a master, a sixth-form boy) when out of bounds. Also *absol.* 1821. **4.** To evade (one's duty, work, obligations, etc.) 1785. **b.** *U.S.* To shift (responsibility, etc.) *on to* or *upon* (another person). Also with *off.* 1845. **c.** *absol.* To practise evasion of work, one's duties, responsibilities, etc. 1853.

2. He and his comrades had been obliged to s. on board at night, to escape from their wives THACKERAY. One of the cities shirked from the league BYRON. 4. This trick..was intended..to s. responsibility 1880. c. The disposition to s. seems to be constitutional with the human race 1865. Hence **Shi·rker,** one who shirks (duty, work, etc.).

Shirley (ʃɜ̄·ɹli). 1886. [The name of *Shirley* Vicarage, Croydon, where the Rev. W. Wilks first cultivated the flower.] In full *S. poppy*: Any of certain varieties, grown in a great range of colours, of the single garden poppy.

Shirr (ʃɜ̄ɹ), *sb.* *U.S.* 1858. [Origin obsc.] **1.** Rubber thread woven into a fabric to make it elastic. **2.** A series of parallel gatherings 1891.

Shirr (ʃɜ̄ɹ), *v.* *U.S.* 1892. [app. back-formation from next.] *trans.* = GAUGE *v.* 8. Hence **Shirring** *vbl. sb.* (*a*) gathering in the form of shirrs; (*b*) elastic webbing made with shirrs.

Shirred (ʃɜ̄ɹd), *a.* *U.S.* 1847. [f. SHIRR *sb.* + -ED[2].] **1.** Having elastic threads woven into the texture. **2.** Gathered 1860. **3.** *Cookery.* Of eggs: Poached (in cream) 1883.

Shirt (ʃɜ̄ɹt), *sb.* [OE. *scyrte*:—OTeut. **skurtjōn*-, prob. f. **skurto*- SHORT *a.* Cf. SKIRT *sb.*] **1.** An undergarment for the upper part of the body, made of linen, flannel, silk, or other washable material; orig. worn next to the skin, now often over an undershirt or 'vest'. Formerly a garment common to both sexes, but now an article of male attire with long sleeves. Also, an infant's undergarment with short body and sleeves. **b.** Applied to a loose garment resembling a shirt 1553. **2.** A woman's blouse made in a severe style, with a collar, front, and cuffs, and so somewhat resembling a man's shirt 1896. **3.** *transf.* An inner casing or covering 1611.

1. *Boiled s.* (U.S.), a white linen s. as dist. from a coloured or flannel s. *Bloody s.*, a blood-stained s. exhibited as a symbol of murder or outrage. *S. of mail* [= F. *chemise de maille*]. *In one's s.*, in one's night attire; without one's coat and waistcoat. (To have) *not a s.* (*to one's back*), no goods or possessions, not even the necessaries of life. (To give away) *the s. off one's back*, i. e. all one's possessions. †*Not to tell one's s.*: to keep a matter strictly secret. *Near is my s. but nearer is my skin* = one's own interests come before one's nearest friend's. *To get* (a person's) *s. out*, to cause him to lose his temper. *To put one's s. on* (a horse), to bet all one's money on (*slang*). 3. The internal lining or s. of the furnace 1868.

Comb.: **s.-band** = BAND *sb.*² 4; also *dial.* the wrist-band of a s.; **-blouse** = sense 2; **-button,** a small-sized button usu. of linen or mother of pearl pierced with thread holes and used on shirt fastenings; **-frill,** a frill formerly worn on the front and wrist-bands of a s.; **s. front** = FRONT *sb.* 5 b; also *transf.* a white patch on the chest (of a dog); **-pin,** an ornamental pin used to fasten the s. at the throat. Hence **Shirt** *v. trans.* to clothe with or as with a s. **Shi·rtless** *a.* without a s.

Shirting (ʃɔ̄·ɹtiŋ). 1604. [f. SHIRT *sb.* + -ING ¹.] Material for shirts; *spec.* a kind of piece-goods of stout cotton cloth suitable for shirts which are to be subjected to hard wear.

Shirt-sleeve. 1566. A sleeve of a shirt. Chiefly *pl.*

Phr. *In one's shirt-sleeves*, with one's coat off.

Shirty (ʃɔ̄·ɹti), *a. slang.* 1859. [f. SHIRT *sb.* + -Y ¹.] Ill-tempered. Hence **Shi·rtiness.**

Shit (ʃit), **shite** (ʃəit), *sb.* Not now in decent use. OE. [Teut. root **skĭt-*.] **1.** Excrement from the bowels, dung 1585. **b.** A contemptuous epithet applied to a man 1508. †**2.** Diarrhœa, esp. in cattle –late ME. Also vb. *trans.* and *intr.*

‖**Shittah** (ʃi·tă). 1611. [Heb. *shiṭṭāh*.] *S. tree*: a tree belonging to some species of Acacia, from which SHITTIM wood was obtained.

Shittim (ʃi·tim). late ME. [a. Heb. *shiṭṭīm*, pl. of *shiṭṭāh*; see prec.] (More fully *S. wood.*) The wood of the shittah tree, acacia wood.

Shive ¹ (ʃəiv). Chiefly *dial.* [ME. *schive.* Cf. SHEAVE *sb.*] **1.** A slice (of bread; rarely of other edible). **2.** A thin flat cork for stopping a wide-mouthed bottle; also, a thin bung for a cask 1869. †**3.** A piece (of wood) split off, a billet –1786.

Shive ² (ʃiv). *Obs.* exc. *dial.* 1483. [= WFlem. *schif*, f. Teut. root **skīf-* to split, whence SHIVER *sb.*¹] A particle of husk; a splinter; a piece of thread or fluff on the surface of cloth, etc.; *pl.* the refuse of hemp or flax.

Shiver (ʃi·vəɹ), *sb.*¹ [Early ME. *scifre*, f. Teut. root **skĭf-* to split, whence SHIVE.²] **1.** A fragment, chip, splinter. Now *rare* exc. in phrases. **b.** *spec.* A flake or splinter of stone. Now *Sc.* and *dial.* 1600. **2.** [perh. a. G. *schiefer.*] Any kind of stone of a slaty or schistous character 1729.

1. Phr. *In shivers*, broken, in small fragments (so *to break, burst*, etc. *in* or *into shivers*); (*all*) *to shivers*, into small fragments.

Shiver (ʃi·vəɹ), *sb.*² [ME. *schivere*, f. Teut. root **skīb-* of SHEAVE *sb.*¹, SHIVE ¹.] †**1.** = SHIVE ¹ 1. –1753. **2.** SHEAVE *sb.*¹ 2. 1485.

Shiver (ʃi·vəɹ), *sb.*³ 1727. [f. SHIVER *v.*²] **1.** An act or condition of shivering; a quivering or trembling, esp. of the body from cold, emotion, etc. **2.** (*The*) *shivers*: an attack of shivering; often *spec.* the ague; also *transf.*, a feeling of horror or nervous fear 1861.

2. It gives me the cold shivers when I think what might have become of me 1888.

Shiver (ʃi·vəɹ), *v.*¹ ME. [f. SHIVER *sb.*¹] **1.** *trans.* To break or split into small fragments or splinters. **2.** *intr.* To fly into pieces; to split ME. **3.** [perh. after G. *schiefern.*] To split along the natural line of cleavage 1728.

1. Looking-Glasses had been..shivered into ten thousand Splinters STEELE. *S. my timbers*, a mock oath attributed in comic fiction to sailors. 2. As he crossed the hall, his statue fell, and shivered on the stones 1879.

Shiver (ʃi·vəɹ), *v.*² [Early ME. *chivere*; etym. obsc.] **1.** *intr.* To tremble, quake, quiver; esp. to tremble with cold or fear. **2.** *trans.* To pour out or give forth with a trembling motion 1821. **3.** *Naut.* **a.** *intr.* Of a sail: To flutter or shake (in the wind) 1769. **b.** *trans.* To cause (a sail) to flutter or shake in the wind; to bring a sail edge-on to the wind 1769. **4.** *intr.* To quiver, to tremble with a shrinking movement 1869.

1. Why stand we longer shivering under feares That show no end but Death? MILT. The dry rushes s. in the sand 1878. 3. b. S. the mizen, topsail or brail up the spanker 1875. Hence **Shi·vering** *ppl. a.*

Shivery (ʃi·vəri), *a.*¹ 1683. [f. SHIVER *sb.*¹ + -Y ¹.] Apt to split into flakes, brittle, flaky.

Shivery (ʃi·vəri), *a.*² 1747. [f. SHIVER *v.*² + -Y ¹.] **1.** Characterized by a shaking, quivering motion, or appearance of motion. **2.** Inclined to shiver 1837. **3.** Causing a shivering feeling, chilly 1839.

Shlemozzle, variant of SHEMOZZLE.

Shoad, shode (ʃōᵘd). *local.* 1602. [prob. f. OE. *scādan* to divide.] Loose fragments of tin, lead, or copper ore mixed with earth, lying on or near the surface and indicating the proximity of a lode. Also, one of these fragments. Hence **Shoa·ding,** the process of searching for shoad-ore by digging small pits.

Shoal (ʃōᵘl), *sb.*¹ ME. [absol. use of SHOAL *a.*] A place where the water is of little depth; a shallow; a sand-bank or bar.

Among the shoals and eddies with which the Sutlej abounds 1853. *fig.* Wolsey, that once..sounded all the Depths, and Shoales of Honor SHAKS.

Comb.: **s.-mark,** a buoy or other mark set to indicate a s.

Shoal (ʃōᵘl), *sb.*² 1579. [Late 16th c. *shole*; perh. a re-adoption of MDu. *schole* SCHOOL *sb.*²:—OTeut. **skulō*, f. **skul-*, wk. grade of **skel-* to divide.] **1.** = SCHOOL *sb.*² 1. Phr. *in a s.*, *in* or *by shoals.* **b.** Hence occas. used of a number of aquatic animals or floating objects 1593. †**2.** A flock of birds –1801. **3.** *transf.* A large number; a troop, crowd 1579.

1. Herrings offer themselves in shoals 1774. b. A s. of boats 1839. 3. Wherewith whole showls of martyrs once did burn 1610. Never-ending shoals of small troubles CARLYLE.

Shoal (ʃōᵘl), *a.* (and *adv.*). [OE. *sceald*:—prehist. **skalda-*.] **A.** *adj.* Of water: Not deep; shallow. **B.** *adv.* [ME. *schealde.*] To or at a slight depth ME.

A. Our shipps running all a-ground, it being so s. water PEPYS.

Shoal (ʃōᵘl), *v.*¹ 1574. [f. SHOAL *a.*] **I.** *intr.* Of water, a watercourse, harbour, sounding, etc.: To become shallow or more shallow.

It shoals suddenly from ten to two fathoms 1779. *To s. out*, to become gradually more shallow until no water is to be seen.

II. *trans.* **1.** *Naut.* To find (one's soundings) gradually more shallow; to pass from a greater into a less depth of (water), as shown by sounding 1670. **2.** To cause (a piece of water) to become shallow; also, to obstruct by shoals 1864. **3.** *Otter-hunting.* To drive (the otter) to the shallows 1897. Hence **Shoa·ler,** a vessel or a sailor in the coasting trade.

Shoal (ʃōᵘl), *v.*² 1610. [f. SHOAL *sb.*²] **1.** *intr.* Of fish: To collect or swim together in a shoal or shoals. **2.** *transf.* To crowd together, assemble in swarms 1618.

1. The mackerel shoaling in each bay 1901.

Shoaling (ʃōᵘ·liŋ), *vbl. sb.* 1574. [f. SHOAL *v.*¹ + -ING ¹.] **1.** The process of becoming shallow or more shallow; an instance of this 1633. **2.** *concr.* A place where the water becomes shallow 1574.

1. A sudden s. up of the port of discharge 1886.

Shoaly (ʃōᵘ·li), *a.* 1612. [f. SHOAL *sb.*¹ + -Y ¹.] Full of shoals or shallows.

[The river] hasting to his fall, his sholy grauell scowr's DRAYTON. Hence **Shoa·liness** (*rare*).

Shoat (ʃōᵘt). *dial.* and *U.S.* late ME. [Cf. WFlem. *schote, schoteling* a pig under one year old.] **1.** A young weaned pig. **2.** *transf.* An idle worthless person 1800.

Shock (ʃɒk), *sb.*¹ ME. [Corresponding to OS. *scok* a definite number of sheaves, MDu. *schok* shock of corn, sixty.] **1.** A group of sheaves of corn placed upright and supporting each other in order to permit the drying and ripening of the grain before carrying. **2.** *transf.* A crowd (of persons); a heap, bunch, bundle (of things). late ME.

1. He found Three hundred S. of Corn in the Fields 1746.

Shock (ʃɒk), *sb.*² Now *Hist.* 1583. [a. G. *schock*, Du. *schok*; prob. a special use of prec.] *Comm.* A lot of sixty pieces. (Used with ref. to certain articles of merchandise orig. imported from abroad.)

Shock (ʃɒk), *sb.*³ 1565. [app. a. F. *choc*, f. *choquer*; see SHOCK *v.*¹] **1.** *Mil.* The encounter of an armed force with the enemy in a charge or onset; also, the encounter of two mounted warriors or jousters charging one another. **2.** A sudden and violent blow, impact, or collision, tending to overthrow or to produce internal oscillation in a body subjected to it; also, the disturbance of equilibrium or the internal oscillation resulting from this 1614. **b.** *spec.* (= *earthquake s.*). A sudden and more or less violent shake of a part of the earth's surface; a single movement of the series of movements constituting an earthquake 1692. **3.** *transf.* and *fig.* A sudden and violent effect tending to impair the stability or permanence of something; a damaging blow (to a condition of things, a belief, etc.) 1654. **4.** A sudden and disturbing impression on the mind or feelings; usu., one produced by some unwelcome occurrence or perception, or by violent emotion, and tending to occasion lasting depression or loss of composure; in weaker sense, a thrill or start of surprise, or of suddenly excited feeling of any kind 1705. **b.** Used for: An occurrence, discovery, etc. that occasions a shock 1841. **c.** A feeling of being shocked; a pained sense of something offensive to morality or decorum 1876. **5.** *Med.* A sudden debilitating effect produced by over-stimulation of nerves, intense pain, violent emotion, or the like; the condition of nervous exhaustion resulting from this 1804. **6.** A momentary stimulation of a nerve. Also, a stimulation of nerves with resulting contraction of muscles and feeling of concussion; *spec.* = *electric s.* 1818.

1. This doubtfull shocke of Armes SHAKS. *transf.* The s. and encounter of thought 1879. 2. With twelve great shocks of sound, the shameless noon Was clash'd and hammer'd from a hundred towers TENNYSON. 3. The s. given to commercial credit 1833.

Comb.: **s.-absorber,** a device fitted to mechanically-propelled vehicles in order to absorb vibration; a device on an aeroplane to relieve strain when landing; **-action** *Mil.*, a method of attack esp. by a charge of cavalry, in which the force of the impact is principally relied upon; **-tactics** *Mil.*, tactics in which shock-action forms a principal part; **s. troops,** [tr. G. *stosstruppen*], units of men reserved for forlorn-hope service; in the British army, units specially formed for storming positions. **b.** In the U.S.S.R. applied to workers used for a specially arduous task, as *s.-brigade, -worker.*

†**Shock,** *sb.*⁴ 1638. [Cf. SHOUGH.] A dog having long shaggy hair, *spec.* a poodle –1800.

Shock (ʃɒk), *sb.*⁵ 1819. [perh. f. as next.] A thick mass (of hair).

Shock (ʃɒk), *a.* 1681. [perh. a back-formation from SHOCK-DOG.] Having rough thick hair. Of hair: Rough and thick, shaggy.

Shock (ʃɒk), *v.*¹ 1568. [app. a. F. *choquer*, of obsc. origin.] **1.** *intr.* To come into violent contact, to collide, clash *together*; esp. to encounter in the shock of battle. Now only *arch.* or as a Gallicism. 1576. †**2.** To assail with a sudden and violent attack, to charge (an enemy) with troops, etc. –1767. †**3.** To throw (troops) into confusion by an onset or charge; to damage or weaken by impact or collision; to destroy the stability of –1770. **4.** In early use, to wound the feelings of, offend, displease. Later: To affect with a painful feeling of intense aversion or disapproval; to outrage (a person's sentiments, prejudices, etc.). Often *pass.*, to be scandalized or horrified *at.* Also *absol.* 1656. **5.** To impart a physical shock to, to cause (a person or a part of the body) to suffer a nervous shock 1733. **b.** To give (a person) an electric shock 1746.

1. All at fiery speed the two Shock'd on the central bridge TENNYSON. 4. They are no more shocked at Vice and Folly, than Men of slower Capacities STEELE. Pope..was terribly shocked when he found himself accused of heterodoxy 1880. Hence **Sho·ckable** *a.* easily shocked. **Shocked** (ʃɒkt) *ppl. a.* scandalized, horrified 1861.

Shock (ʃǫk), *v.*² Now *dial.* late ME. [f. SHOCK *sb.*¹] **1.** *trans.* To arrange (sheaves) in a shock. Also with *up.* 1440. †**2.** *refl.* and *intr.* To crowd together –1622. Hence **Sho·cker,** a person or machine for piling sheaves in shocks.

†**Shock-dog.** 1673. [f. SHOCK *sb.*⁴] = SHOCK *sb.*⁴ –1845.

Shocker (ʃǫ·kəɹ). 1824. [f. SHOCK *v.*¹ + -ER ¹.] Something which shocks or excites; esp. a work of fiction of a sensational character.

Sho·ck-head. 1818. [f. SHOCK *a.*] A head covered with a thick crop of hair.

A. s. of red hair SCOTT. *attrib.* The s. willows TENNYSON. So **Shock-headed** *a.*

Shocking (ʃǫ·kiŋ), *ppl. a.* 1691. [f. SHOCK *v.*¹ + -ING ².] That shocks. *esp.* **1.** That gives offence; offensive. Also, causing unpleasant surprise. Now *rare* or *Obs.* **2.** Revolting to the feelings; exciting intense horror or repugnance 1704. **3.** 'Shockingly' bad, 'execrable' 1798. **b.** quasi-*adv.* Shockingly. *colloq.* 1831.

1. There is such a s. familiarity both in his railleries and civilities ADDISON. **2.** It is s. enough to see noble beasts ruthlessly mangled 1891. *hyperbolically.* S. To think we buy gowns lined with ermine For dolts BROWNING. **3.** The s. way those boys spell 1872. **b.** A s. bad road 1857. Hence **Sho·cking·ly** *adv.*, **-ness.**

Shod (ʃǫd), *ppl. a.* late ME. [pa. pple. of SHOE *v.*] **1.** Wearing shoes. Chiefly with qualifying adv., *well, neatly,* etc. **2.** Of things: Furnished with a shoe of metal, etc.; tipped, edged, or sheathed with metal 1565. **b.** Of cart wheels: Furnished with tires. Hence of a cart: Having shod wheels. 1481.

Shoddy (ʃǫ·di), *sb.* 1832. [Origin obsc.] **1.** Woollen yarn obtained by tearing to shreds refuse woollen rags, which, with the addition of some new wool, is made into a kind of cloth. **2.** A cloth composed of shoddy wool; more fully *s. cloth* 1847. **3.** *transf.* and *fig.* Worthless material made to look like material of superior quality; that which is worthless and pretentious in art, manufactures, ideas, etc.; the class of persons characterized by the endeavour to pass for something superior to what they really are 1862.

3. Theological s.,—old fragments of decaying systems woven into a web of the usual polish and flimsiness 1873.

Comb.: **s.-hole,** a place in which rubbish is deposited. Hence **Sho·ddyism,** pretentious vulgarity.

Shoddy (ʃǫ·di), *a.* 1862. [attrib. use of prec. 3.] **1.** Of a person: That pretends to a superiority to which he has no just claim. **2.** Of a thing: Having a delusive appearance of superior quality 1882. **3.** Of, pertaining to, or dealing in shoddy goods 1864.

1. That s. saviour of society, called L. Cornelius Cinna 1896. **2.** S. cottages..mere traps to catch rent 1891. **3.** Felting..made by some s. contractor 1874. Hence **Sho·ddily** *adv.*, **-ness.**

Shode, var. of SHOAD.

Shoder (ʃōu·dəɹ). 1763. [ad. F. *chauderet, chaudret.*] *Gold-beating.* The packet of skins into which the gold taken from the 'cutch' is placed and beaten out before its final beating in the 'mould'.

Shoe (ʃū), *sb. Pl.* **shoes** (ʃūz); *dial., poet.,* and *arch.* **shoon** (ʃūn). [Com. Teut.: OE. *scōh* (pl. *scōs*) :—OTeut. **skōhoz* or **skōhwoz.*] **1.** An outer covering for the human foot, normally made of leather (but often of other materials) and consisting of a more or less stiff sole and a lighter upper part. Chiefly in more specific sense (distinguished from *boot*), a 'low shoe', which does not reach above the ankle. **2.** A plate of metal, usually iron, nailed to the under-side of the hoof of a horse as a protection from injury; a horseshoe. late ME. **3.** Something resembling a shoe (sense 1 or 2) in shape, position, or function. **a.** A metal rim, ferrule, casing, or sheath, esp. for the end of a pile, pole, rod, or the like 1495. **b.** The receptacle beneath the hopper of a mill 1688. **c.** The short section which turns out the water at the foot of a water pipe 1769. **d.** A kind of drag or skid for the wheel of a vehicle; also, the concave part of a brake, which acts upon the wheel 1837. **e.** A strip of iron, steel, etc. fastened upon that part of a vehicle, machine, etc. which is liable to be worn out by friction 1837. **f.** A socket for the reception of a bolt, pin, or the like 1858. **g.** *Naut.* A block of wood for an anchor fluke 1750. **h.** A block, plate, etc. which serves as a socket or bearing for the foot of a pole, the legs of sheers, etc. to prevent slipping or sinking 1843. **i.** An iron plate shaped to receive the end of one or more pieces of timber in roof-construction 1842. **j.** An ingot of precious metal, somewhat in the form of a Chinese shoe, current in silver in China 1702. **k.** *Electr. traction.* A block attached to an electric car in such a position that it slides upon a conductor-wire or rail and collects the current for the propulsion of the car 1891.

1. The dull swayn Treads on it daily with his clouted shoon MILT. [She] felt..her heart sink to her shoes 1887. *High shoes,* boots with high uppers. *Shoes of swiftness,* the magic shoes of the giant in the story of Jack the Giant-killer; occas. used allus. *Old s.,* a type of something discarded as worn out, useless, or worthless. *Another pair of shoes* (predic.), quite a different matter or state of things. *To shake in one's shoes*: see SHAKE *v.* II. 3. *Over* (*the*) *shoes,* deeply immersed or sunk (*in* something). *To know best where the s. pinches*: see PINCH *v.* I. 1 b. *To be in* (another person's) *shoes,* to be in his position or place. *To step into the shoes of* (another person), to occupy the position vacated by him. *To wait for dead men's shoes,* to wait for the death of a person with the expectancy of succeeding to his possessions or office.

Comb.: **s.-beak, bill, bird,** a bird, *Balæniceps rex,* found in Central Africa; **s. buckle,** a fastening for a s., in the form of a buckle; also, an ornamental buckle worn on the front of a s.; **-lace** = *s.-string*; **s. pack** *U.S.*, a s. of tanned leather made without a separate sole after the manner of a moccasin; **-string,** a string or tie used to fasten or lace a s.; **-valve,** a valve at the foot of a pump-stock, or at the bottom of a reservoir. Hence **Shoe·less** *a.* without shoes.

Shoe (ʃū), *v.* Pa. t. and pa. pple. **shod** (ʃǫd), *rarely* **shoed** (ʃūd). [OE. *scōgan* :—OTeut. **skōhōjan,* f. **skōho-* SHOE *sb.*] **1.** *trans.* To put shoes on (one's feet); to put on (one's) shoes; to clothe or protect the feet with shoes; to provide (a person, oneself) with boots or shoes. **2.** To provide (a horse, etc.) with a shoe or shoes ME. **3.** To protect (the point, edge, or face of a thing, esp. something made of timber) with a plate, rim, ferrule, or sheath of metal, etc. ME. **4.** *transf.* To cover or protect as with a shoe or shoes 1639.

1. Shod with snow-shoes LONGF. **3.** Bootes..shodde vnderneath with yron 1585.

Shoeblack (ʃū·blæk). 1778. [f. SHOE *sb.* + BLACK *v.*] One who cleans boots and shoes for a living.

Shoe-horn (ʃū·hǭɹn). 1589. **1.** A curved instrument of horn, metal, etc. used to facilitate the slipping of one's heel into a shoe by placing it between shoe and heel. **2.** *fig.* = next 2. 1630.

Shoe·ing-horn. 1440. [f. *shoeing,* vbl. sb. f. SHOE *v.*] **1.** = prec. 1. **2.** *fig.* **a.** An appetizer for food or drink 1536. **b.** Something serving to facilitate a transaction, to bring on a condition, or to procure acceptance for something else 1584. **c.** A person used as a tool by another; esp. one employed as a decoy 1602.

Shoe·-leather. 1576. Leather for the making of shoes; the leather of which (one's) shoes are made 1660. **b.** Used for the wear of shoes in walking 1576.

As good a lad as ever stepped in s. 1818.

Shoemaker (ʃū·mēˑkəɹ). late ME. **1.** One whose trade it is to make shoes. **2.** In the names of fishes; as the Threadfish, *Blepharis crinitus,* the Runner, *Elagatis pinnulatus* 1688. So **Shoe·making** *vbl. sb.* the making of shoes.

Shoer (ʃū·əɹ). [OE. *scōere*; see SHOE *v.* and -ER ¹.] One who shoes. In OE. a shoemaker; later usu., one who shoes horses, etc.

Shog (ʃǫg), *sb.* Now *dial.* and *arch.* 1611. [f. next.] A shake, jerk.

Shog (ʃǫg), *v.* Now chiefly *dial.* [late ME. *shogge*; cf. JOG *v.*] **1.** *trans.* To shake or roll (something heavy) from side to side; to rock (a cradle); to shake, agitate (a liquid or the vessel containing it); to jolt or jar (some one or something). †**b.** To shake or jog (a person) –1651. **2.** To walk, ride or move with a succession of bumps or jerks; to jog along. Now usu., to travel steadily on. late ME. **b.** To go away. Also with *off. Obs.* exc. *dial.* 1599.

‖**Shogun** (ʃōu·gun). 1615. [Jap. *shōgun,* a sound-substitution for Chinese *chiang chün* (*chiang* to lead, *chün* army).] The hereditary commander-in-chief of the Japanese army, until 1867 the virtual ruler of Japan. Hence **Sho·gunal** *a.* **Sho·gunate,** the office or dignity of a s. or the shoguns.

‖**Shola** (ʃōu·lă). 1836. [Hindī *sholā* = Bengalī *solā.*] = SOLA.

Shone, pa. t. and pa. pple. of SHINE *v.*

Shoo (ʃū), *v.* 1622. [f. next.] **1.** *trans.* To scare or drive away (fowls, etc.) by calling out 'shoo'. **2.** *intr.* To cry out 'shoo' in order to frighten or drive away fowls, etc. 1746.

Shoo (ʃū), *int.*¹ 1483. [An instinctive exclam.] An exclam. used to frighten or drive away fowls or other intruders. Also as *sb.*

Shoo (ʃū, ʃu), **sho** (ʃō), *int.*² *dial.* and *U.S.* 1845. [Instinctive; cf. prec.] An exclam. indicating impatient or contemptuous rejection of a statement. Cf. PSHAW.

Shook (ʃuk), *sb.* Now chiefly *U.S.* 1768. [perh. f. next.] A set of staves and headings sufficient for one hogshead, barrel, cask, or the like, prepared for use and bound up compactly for convenience of transport. Also boxes similarly packed and prepared. Hence **Shook** *v. trans.* to pack in shooks.

Shook (ʃuk), *ppl. a.* In educated use only *arch.* 1695. [pa. pple. of SHAKE *v.*] = SHAKEN.

Shoon, *arch.* and *dial.* pl. f. SHOE.

Shoot (ʃūt), *sb.* 1450. [f. next.] **I.** An act of shooting; a discharge of arrows, bullets, etc. Now only *arch.* 1534. †**b.** Range, distance or reach of a shot; shooting distance –1719. **c.** A game-shooting expedition 1852. **d.** A shooting party 1885. **e.** The right to shoot game in a given area; also the area itself 1861. **f.** A shooting match or contest; a round of shots in such a contest 1892. **2.** The action of shooting, sprouting, or growing; the amount of growth (also *concr.* the new wood, etc. produced) in a certain period 1572. **b.** A young branch which shoots out from the main stock of a tree, plant, etc. 1450. **c.** *gen.* An offshoot; a growth or sprout from a main stock 1610. **3.** A motion or movement (of a thing) as though shooting or being shot in a particular direction; also, the space or distance covered by such a motion or by a push 1596. **b.** Of an immaterial thing: A sudden advance 1752. **c.** A short sharp twinge (of pain) 1756. **4.** *Weaving.* One movement or throw of the shuttle between the threads of the warp; the length of thread thus placed; also, the weft 1717. **5.** A heavy and sudden rush of water down a steep channel; a place in a river where this occurs, a rapid. (Confused with CHUTE 1.) 1613. **b.** An artificial channel for conveying water by gravity to a low level; or for the escape of overflow water from a reservoir, etc.; also for forcing water into a railway engine in rapid motion 1707. **6. a.** A sloping channel or conduit for letting down coal, ore, wheat, etc. into a lower receptacle 1844. **b.** A place where rubbish may be 'shot' 1851. **7.** *Mining.* A considerable and somewhat regular body or mass of ore in a vein, usu. elongated and vertical or inclined in position 1850.

1. How many a rogue would give his two crop ears to have a s. at either of us! STEVENSON. **c.** A big s. in the jungle 1895. **f.** Second-rate pigeon shoots 1892. **2.** *transf.* Ridges of barren land, that seemed like shoots of the adjacent Andes 1847. **b.** The French in Canada eat the tender shoots in spring as Asparagus 1812. **3.** Both [yachts] had a long s. up in the eye of the wind 1894. **5.** A single s. carried a considerable stream over the face of a black rock SCOTT.

Shoot (ʃūt), *v.* Pa. t. and pa. pple. **shot** (ʃǫt). [Com. Teut. str. vb.: OE. *scēotan* (*scēat, scuton, scoten*) f. OTeut. **skeut-*: *skaut-*: *skut-*; see SHEET *sb.*¹ and *sb.*², SHOT *sb.*¹, SHUT *v.* The mod. form *shoot* (displacing ME. *schete*) is due to the alteration of OE. *scēot-* to *sceót-*: cf. CHOOSE *v.* The pa. t. *shot* is prob. of mixed origin, but its permanence is mainly due to the influence of the pa. pple.] **I.** To go swiftly and suddenly. **1.** *intr.* To go or pass with a sudden swift movement through space; to be precipitated; to fly as an arrow from a bow. **b.** Of a 'star' or meteor: To dart across the sky ME. **c.** Of light, etc.: To be emitted in rays, to dart. Of a glance: To dart. 1693. **d.** *fig.* Of thoughts, etc.: To pass suddenly *into, across,* etc. a person's mind 1542. **e.** Of a person's feet: To slip suddenly *from under one.* late ME. **f.** *Naut.*

Of ballast: = SHIFT *v.* III. 2 c. 1678. **g.** Of a ball: To move with accelerated speed after its first impingement; esp. in *Cricket*, of a bowled ball: To move rapidly close to the ground after pitching 1833. **2.** To pass swiftly and suddenly from one place to another; to precipitate oneself, rush, dart OE. **3.** Of a vessel (hence of its commander or crew): To move swiftly in a certain direction. late ME. **4.** *trans.* With obj. denoting what is passed through, over, or under by 'shooting', e.g. a bridge, a rapid or cataract 1570. **b.** *Naut.* To succeed in sailing through (a dangerous strait, passage, gulf, etc.). Hence *to s. the gulf, Niagara* (fig.), provb. for any daring enterprise. 1622. **c.** *Racing.* To dash past (another competitor) 1868. **5.** *intr.* Of a pain: To pass in a sudden paroxysm along the nerves; to dart. Hence of a part of the body, a wound, etc.: To have darting pains. OE. **6.** Of a plant, bud, etc.: To emerge from the soil (also with *up*) or from the stem, etc.; to sprout, grow 1483. **b.** Of parts of animal bodies, teeth, hair, morbid growths 1607. **7.** To put forth buds or shoots, as a plant; to germinate 1560. **8.** To increase rapidly in growth (sometimes, to sprout and grow rapidly); to advance to maturity. Now only with *up*, etc.: To grow quickly tall, 'spring up' to a height (said of plants, young persons, buildings, etc.; also of immaterial things). 1530. **9.** Of a solution: To produce crystals. Also said of the crystals. Of a salt: To crystallize from solution or evaporation. 1626. **b.** *trans.* To form (crystals); of a solution, to deposit in the form of crystals. Also *refl.* and *pass.*, to crystallize; of a substance, to assume some definite form by internal movement. 1662. **10.** *intr.* To project, jut out; to extend in a particular direction OE.

1. The lambent lightnings s. Across the sky THOMSON. **b.** Certaine starres shot madly from their Spheares SHAKS. **c.** A gleam of anger shot along his features SCOTT. **2.** A lively young fellow in a fustian jacket shot by me STEELE. **3.** 'Tis..the boat, shooting round by the trees! M. ARNOLD. Phr. *To s. ahead*, of a vessel, to increase speed suddenly, so as to pass accompanying or competing vessels; hence *fig.* **4.** In half an hour I had shot Putney Bridge MARRYAT. *To s. the moon*, to remove household goods by night in order to avoid seizure for rent. **5.** *fig.* A pang of homesickness shot through him 1895. **6.** *fig.* Delightful task! to rear the tender thought, To teach the young idea how to s. THOMSON. **7.** The Cypress Tree..when cut down, never shoots again 1710. **8.** Great D'Ambois (Fortunes proud mushrome shot vp in a night) CHAPMAN. She had shot up into a woman all in a minute 1880. **10.** That Region [Cornwall].. shooteth out farthest into the West HOLLAND.

II. To send forth, esp. swiftly or by sudden impulse. **1.** *trans.* To throw suddenly or with violence. *Obs.* exc. as *transf.* from sense III. 1. OE. **b.** To empty out (gold, grain, earth, etc.) by overturning or tilting the receptacle; to dump (rubbish); to send (goods, debris, etc.) down a 'shoot'. late ME. **c.** *refl.* To throw or precipitate oneself; to rush. Now *rare.* 1587. **d.** To throw (rain, or running water) *from, off* the surface 1573. **e.** To put hurriedly and carelessly 1833. **2.** To launch (a vessel); to cast forth or let down (an anchor); to lower and place in position (a fishing net). Also *absol.* late ME. **b.** To cause (a vessel) to move forward suddenly or swiftly. late ME. **3.** To push or slide (a bar or bolt of a door or the like) into or out of its fastenings. Also, to force (a lock). OE. **b.** *intr.* Of a bolt: To slide *into* its fastenings; to admit of being shot 1886. **4.** *trans.* **a.** *Weaving.* To pass (the shuttle, the weft) between the threads of the warp 1603. **b.** To variegate by admixture of different coloured threads in the woof. Hence, to variegate (an expanse of colour) by interspersing streaks or flecks of some other colour. 1532. **5.** To emit swiftly and forcibly (rays, flames, etc.). late ME. **b.** To put forth, utter (words, sounds); chiefly with adv., *out, forth.* ME. **c.** To cause (a pain, an emotion, etc.) to pass rapidly *through* 1842. **6.** To thrust (one's hand, a limb, a weapon, etc.) *into* something. Also to thrust *out, forth, up*, etc. ME. **b.** *To s. out*: To protrude (the tongue, the lips), usu. as an expression of mockery 1535. †**7.** To eject from the body; *esp.* to discharge (excreta) -1775. **b.** Of a fish: To discharge (spawn). 1609. **8.** Of a plant: To put forth (buds, leaves, branches, etc.). Chiefly with *forth* or *out.* 1526. **9.** With ref. to stationary position: To throw out as a projection or protuberance; *refl.* to stand out, protuberate in a particular direction ME.

1. A more fractious horse..had finally shot him over his head 1858. **b.** A tract of suburban Sahara, where ..rubbish was shot DICKENS. **d.** A great Cap for my Head, with the Hair on the Outside to s. off the Rain DE FOE. **e.** He..shot his instrument into its case 1833. **2.** The nets were shot over the starboard 1894. **b.** Phr. *To s.* (a vessel) *to*, to bring it by 'shooting' to a required position. **4. b.** One couerlyt shot wyth blew and red 1566. His stiff, black hair a little shot with gray 1860. **5.** My sweet guide, who, smiling shot forth beams From her celestial eyes CARY. **6. b.** They shute out their lippes COVERDALE *Ps.* xxii. 7. **8.** Apt to make the wheat s. fresh ears 1766. **9.** Where Hibernia shoots Her wondrous causeway far into the main COWPER.

III. To send missiles from an engine. **1.** *trans.* To send forth, let fly (arrows, bolts, etc.) from a bow or other engine, or (bullets or shot) from a firearm OE. **b.** *transf.* To discharge, send forth like an arrow or a shot. Also *fig.* with obj. a glance, question, etc. 1612. **2.** *absol.* and *intr.* To send forth missiles from a bow, firearm, etc. OE. **b.** *transf. intr.* Formerly, to take a snapshot with a camera; now to take cinematic photographs. Also *trans.* to take a snapshot of; to photograph cinematically. 1890. **3.** *fig.* and in fig. context OE. **4.** Of a bow, engine, or firearm: **a.** *trans.* To send forth (a missile). late ME. **b.** *intr.* To send forth missiles; to 'carry' a certain distance. Also, of a gun, to be discharged, go off (e.g. in a salute). 1575. **5.** *trans.* To discharge (a bow, catapult, etc.), to fire (a gun or other firearm); also with *off, out.* 1482. **6.** To propel (a marble, pellet, etc.) as from the thumb and forefinger 1820. **7.** *Football.* To kick (the ball) at goal. In *Hockey, Lacrosse*, etc.: to hit or drive (the ball) at goal. 1882. **b.** *intr.* To kick or drive the ball at goal 1874.

1. A third [cannon ball]..said to have been shot into the wall at the siege of Padua 1756. *Phr. To have shot one's bolt* (fig.) to have done all that one can do. Provb. *A fool's bolt is soon shot*: see BOLT *sb.*[1] 1. **b.** The sullen and indignant glances which they shot at them SCOTT. **2.** Whose there?..speake quickly, or I shoote SHAKS. *Well shot!* an applauding exclam. when a shooter hits the mark. quasi-*trans. To s. a match*, to engage in a shooting-match. *To s. off a tie*, to decide a tie in a shooting-match by a supplementary contest. *To s. up*, to terrorize (a locality) by shooting (*U.S.*). **3.** If it is a Pleasure to be envyed and shot at, to be maligned standing,.. then it is a Pleasure to be great 1660. Phr. *To s. at*, (*a*) to aim at, to seek to have or accomplish; to aspire to, strive after (now *arch.*); †(*b*) to 'drive at', mean, have reference to; †(*c*) to aim at imitating. *To s. off one's mouth*, to talk indiscreetly or abusively (*U.S. slang*).

IV. To assail, wound, or kill with a shot. **1.** *trans.* To wound or kill with a missile from a bow or firearm (in early use, occas. with a spear or javelin). OE. **b.** To hit or wound with a shot *in* or *through* a part of the body ME. **2.** *intr.* To engage in or practise the sport of killing game with a gun (formerly with a bow or the like) ME. **3.** *trans.* With advs. and advb. phrases ME. **4.** slang or vulgar. *I'll be shot if—*, used as a strong expression of denial or refusal 1826. **5.** *transf.* fig. Of Cupid, love, etc. 1471. **6.** *intr. To s. over* or *to* (a dog), to train by use on a shooting expedition. *To s. over* (a cover, a tract of country), to kill game upon 1868. **b.** *trans.* To go over (a piece of country) shooting game 1833. **7.** *Mining.* To blast 1830.

1. My Lord himselfe had his horse shot under him 1617. I shot him dead 1863. **b.** Hambden..being shot into the shoulder with a brace of bullets CLARENDON. Phr. *To s. flying*, to shoot (birds) on the wing: now usu. *absol.*, as denoting a sportsmanlike accomplishment. **2.** Cadogan and Thomond are gone into the country to s. 1766. **3.** We shot away their middle mast 1632. His..equerry had his head shot off by a cannon ball 1859. *To s.* (a person) *down*, to kill by a shot (usu. with suggestion of merciless cruelty or determination). *To be shot by the board* (Naut.), of masts, etc., to be broken by the enemy's shot in a fight. *To be shot between wind and water*, of a vessel, to receive a shot causing a dangerous leak.

V. †**1.** *Sc.* To avoid, escape -1685. **b.** *dial. pass.* To be rid *of* 1802. **2.** *Carpentry* and *Joinery.* To plane accurately (the edge of a board), esp. with the aid of a shooting-board 1530.

1. **b.** Are you not glad to be fairly shot of him! SCOTT.

Comb. **s.-off**, the subsequent competition between tied contestants in a shooting-match.

Shooter (ʃū·təɪ). ME. [f. prec. + -ER[1].] **1.** One who shoots; now chiefly applied to a sportsman who shoots game. **2.** Something that shoots or is used for shooting, esp. *colloq.* or *slang.* A shooting instrument, *esp.* a revolver. 1812. **b.** *Cricket.* A ball which on touching the ground keeps very close to the turf, often with an increase of pace 1856.

Shooting (ʃū·tiŋ), *vbl. sb.* [f. SHOOT *v.* + -ING[1].] **1.** The action or practice of discharging missiles from a bow or gun. **b.** The sport of killing game with the gun 1642. **c.** An exclusive right to shoot game on a particular estate or tract of country. Hence also, a tract of country on which a person has such an exclusive right. Often *collect. pl.* 1848. **2.** The feeling of a sudden pain; a thrill or dart of pain 1528. **3.** In various senses of the verb 1464.

1. He daily practised s. at a mark 1727. **b.** But there's no s. (save grouse) till September BYRON. **c.** He rented the s. of Mixbury 1896. **2.** The s. of my Corn 1710. **3.** I have known the s. of a Star spoil a Night's Rest ADDISON.

Comb.: **s.-block, -board**, an appliance to facilitate the accurate planing of the edge of a board or stereotype plate; **s.-box**, a small country house in or adjacent to a shooting locality used as a residence while shooting; **-gallery**, a long room, or a booth at a fair, fitted up for the practice of shooting; **-ground**, (*a*) that part of a gun-factory where rifles, etc., are tested; (*b*) a place where rubbish is shot; **-iron**, a fire-arm, esp. a revolver; **-lodge** = *s.-box*; **-range**, a ground with butts for rifle practice; **-seat, -stick** = SEAT-*stick*; **-tool** *Mining*, a tool used in blasting.

Shooting star. 1593. [See SHOOT *v.* I.] **1.** A meteor, resembling a star, that darts across the sky. **2.** *U.S.* A Western name for the American Cowslip, *Dodecatheon Meadia* 1856.

1. *attrib.* The periodic shooting star shower known as the Leonids 1886.

Shop (ʃǫp), *sb.* [ME. *schoppe* :—OE. *sceoppa* :—prehist. *skuppan-, cogn. w. OE. *scypen* SHIPPON.] **1.** A house or building where goods are made or prepared for sale and sold. †**b.** *Banker's shop*: a bank. (Orig. the shop of a goldsmith or other tradesman who practised banking.) -1796. **2.** A building or room set apart for the sale of merchandise. late ME. **3.** A building or room set apart and fitted up for the carrying on of some particular kind of handiwork or mechanical industry; a workshop. Now often, a building or room in a factory, appropriated to some particular department or stage of the work carried on there. late ME. †**b.** *fig.* (Chiefly after L. *officina.*) A place where something is produced or elaborated, or where some operation is performed. Often said of the heart, liver, or other internal organs. -1737. **4.** *colloq.* or *slang.* A place of business; the place where one's ordinary occupation is carried on. Also used joc. for 'place'. *The S.* (Army slang): the Royal Military Academy, Woolwich. 1841. **b.** *Stage slang.* An engagement, a 'berth' 1888. **5.** Matters pertaining to one's trade or profession; discourse on matters of this kind, esp. as introduced unseasonably into general conversation; chiefly in phr. *to talk s.* 1814. **6.** *Stock Exch.* The inside influences affecting or controlling a company by the exercise of special knowledge; also a name for the S. African gold market 1889.

1. You are a gouldsmith and haue a lytle plate in your shoppe 1592. **2.** Phr. *To keep s.*: to exercise the calling of a shopkeeper; to take charge of a s. temporarily. *Shop!* an exclam. used to summon an attendant or shopkeeper. **3.** Engineering and repairing shops 1869. Phr. *The s.*, the workshop of a factory as dist. from the offices, etc. **b.** The sanctuary was now become..a s. of tyranny 1737. **4.** Senior Wrangler, indeed; that's at the other s. THACKERAY.

Phrases. *To set up s.*, to start a business. *To shut up s.*, to close business premises; hence, to bring any business to a close. *To smell of the s.*, (*a*) to indicate the spirit characteristic of a shopkeeper (*b*) of expressions, to savour unduly of the speaker's calling. *To come to the right* (or *wrong*) *s.*, to apply to the right or wrong person in order to obtain something. *All over the s.*, scattered about the place; following an erratic and undefined course.

Comb.: **s.-book**, a shopkeeper's or mechanic's account book; **-breaker**, a burglar who breaks into a s.; so **-breaking**; **-mark**, a private mark placed by a dealer upon his goods; **-soiled** *a.*, depreciated in value and appearance by being exposed for sale in a s.; **-walker**, an assistant exercising general supervision over a department of a s.; an attendant who directs customers to that part of the premises where the goods they require are to be found; **-worn** *a.* = *s.-soiled*. Hence **Sho·ppish** *a.* characteristic of persons connected with a s.

Shop (ʃǫp), *v.* 1583. [f. prec.] **1.** *trans.* To shut up (a person), to imprison. Of an informer, evidence, etc.: To 'get (a person) into trouble'. Now only *slang* or *dial.* **2.** To bring or take (an article) to a shop; to expose for sale in a shop 1688. **3.** *intr.* To visit a shop or shops for the purpose of making purchases or examining the contents 1764.

3. I thought..that you would be shopping 1845.

Sho·p-board. 1524. [f. BOARD *sb.*] **1.** A counter or table upon which a tradesman's business is transacted or upon which his goods are exposed for sale. **2.** A table or raised platform upon which tailors sit when sewing 1589.

Sho·pkeeper. 1530. [f. SHOP *sb.* + KEEPER.] One who carries on business in a shop.

A nation of shopkeepers, applied disparagingly to a nation whose chief interest and concern lies in commerce (esp. to England). So **Sho·pkeeping** *sb.* and *a.*

Sho·plifter. 1680. [f. SHOP *sb.* + LIFTER.] A person who steals from a shop, a shop-thief. So **Sho·plifting** *vbl. sb.* the action of stealing from a shop.

Shopman (ʃǫ·pmæ̆n). 1591. [f. SHOP *sb.* + MAN *sb.*] **1.** The owner of a shop. Now *rare.* **2.** An assistant in a shop 1758. **3.** A workshop hand 1926. So **Sho·p-woman** 1753.

Shopper (ʃǫ·pəɹ). 1862. [f. SHOP *v.* + -ER [1].] One who frequents a shop or shops for the purpose of inspecting or buying goods.

Shopping (ʃǫ·piŋ), *vbl. sb.* 1764. [f. SHOP *v.* + -ING [1].] The action of visiting a shop or shops for the purpose of inspecting or buying goods.

Shoppy (ʃǫ·pi), *a.* 1840. [f. SHOP *sb.* + -Y [1].] **1.** Of the nature of 'shop' or professional concerns or conversation. **2.** Characterized by having a number of shops, forming a centre for business 1851. **3.** Belonging to retail trade 1854.

1. A novel of clerical life written by a clergyman is apt to be..s. 1900. 3. don't like s. people MRS. GASKELL. Hence **Sho·ppiness.**

Shop-window. 1447. **1.** A window of a shop, in which goods are displayed for sale. **2.** *transf.* and *fig.* A display of anything, resembling the display of goods by a tradesman, intended to catch the attention 1905.

Shore (ʃōᵊɹ), *sb.*[1] [ME. *schore* a. or cogn. w. MLG. *schore, schare*, shore, MDu. *schore, schor* shore, sea-marsh; prob. f. the root of SHEAR *v.*, perh. with the sense 'division' (between land and water).] The land bordering on the sea or a large lake or river. **b.** In *Law*, usu. the tract lying between ordinary high and low water mark 1622. **c.** In vague or rhet. use (*sing.* or *pl.*): A sea-coast or the country which it bounds 1611. **d.** *transf.* and *fig.* 1599.

Canute..caus'd his Royal Seat to be set on the shoar, while the Tide was coming in MILT. **c.** You have since accompanied our Royal Master to other Shores 1691. **d.** Deposited upon the silent s. Of memory WORDSW.

Phrases. *On s.*, on the s., ashore, on land; *in s.*, near or nearer to the shore (from the water).

Comb.: **s.-anchor**, that which lies between the s. and the ship when moored; **-boat**, a small boat plying near the s. or between the s. and large vessels farther out; **-gun**, a gun for s.-shooting; **-gunner**, **-gunning** = *s.-shooter, -shooting*; **-line** (*a*) the line where s. and water meet; (*b*) = *s.-rope*; **-rope**, a rope connecting a net with the s.; **-shooter**, one who shoots birds on the s.; **-shooting**, the sport of shooting birds on the s. (as dist. from punt-shooting); **-side**, the edge of the s.; the part of the land or sea adjacent to the s.; **-weed**, a weed growing on the s., spec. *Littorella lacustris*.

b. With names of animals: **s.-bird**, a bird that frequents the sea-s. or estuaries; *spec.* the sand-martin, *Cotile riparia*; **-crab**, the common small crab, *Carcinus mænas*; **s.-fish**, a general name for fish whose habitat is near the s.; **s. lark**, *Otocorys* (formerly *Alauda*) *alpestris*; **s. pipit**, the rock pipit, *Anthus obscurus*; **s. sandpiper**, the ruff, *Machetes pugnax*; **s. snipe**, (*a*) the common sandpiper, *Totanus hypoleucus*; (*b*) *U.S.* the grey plover, *Squatarola helvetica*.

Shore (ʃōᵊɹ), *sb.*[2] [Late ME. *schore*, a. or cogn. w. MLG., MDu. *schore, schare* prop, stay. Ult. etym. obsc.] **1.** A piece of timber or iron set obliquely against the side of a building, of a ship in dock, etc., as a support when it is in danger of falling or when undergoing alteration or repair; a prop or strut. **2.** A prop or stake used for various purposes 1601.

1. *fig.* The true shoares of the unstable wheele of fortune 1603.

Shore (ʃōᵊɹ), *sb.*[3] 1598. [Usu. regarded as a var. of SEWER *sb.*[1] but prob. a use of SHORE *sb.*[1]] = SEWER *sb.*[1] **2.** Orig. in *common s.* = common sewer.

Olde receptacles, or common-shores of filthe SHAKS.

Shore (ʃōᵊɹ), *v.*[1] ME. [f. SHORE *sb.*[2]] **1.** *trans.* To prop, support with a prop. Often with *up*. †**2.** To lift up, raise (the eyes) -1617. †**3.** *intr.* To lean, slope, shelve -1621.

1. The old inn, long shored and trussed and buttressed STEVENSON. Hence **Shorer**, a thing (rarely a person) that shores up. **Sho·ring** *vbl. sb.* the action of the verb; *concr.* shores or props.

Shore (ʃōᵊɹ), *v.*[2] 1600. [f. SHORE *sb.*[1]] **1.** *intr.* To go ashore. **2.** *trans.* To put ashore; to land (passengers or goods); to beach (a vessel) 1611. **3.** To border as a shore 1832. **4.** *intr.* To sail *along* (a coast) 1632.

4. They had been *shoring*..to see if they could find anything worth their labour DE FOE.

Shore, pa. t. of SHEAR *v.*

Sho·re-going, *vbl. sb.* and *a.* 1895. Going ashore (from the sea); going, living, on shore.

Shoreless (ʃōᵊ·ɹlĕs), *a.* 1628. [f. SHORE *sb.*[1] + -LESS.] Having no shore. Of a sea, or what is compared to a sea: Boundless.

Lost upon that shorelesse Sea 1643. The s. tides of delirium KIPLING.

Shoreman (ʃōᵊ·ɹmæ̆n). Also *U.S.* (sense 2) **shoresman.** 1643. [f. SHORE *sb.*[1] + MAN *sb.*] **1.** A dweller on the seashore. **2.** One who is employed on shore in the business of a fishery 1690. **3.** One who makes his living by shooting on the shore; a shore-shooter 1882.

Shoreward (ʃōᵊ·ɹwə̆ɹd), *adv.* and *a.* 1582. [f. SHORE *sb.*[1] + -WARD.] **A. 1.** *advb. phr. To* (*the*) *s.*: in the direction of the shore. **2.** *adv.* In the direction of or towards the shore 1691. **B.** Situated or directed towards the shore 1804. So **Sho·rewards** *adv.* = A. 2.

Shorn, pa. pple. and ppl. a. of SHEAR *v.*

Short (ʃǭɹt), *a.*, *sb.*, and *adv.* [OE. *sc(e)ort* — OHG. *scurz* :—OTeut. **skurto-*, perh. an altered adoption of L. *curtus*.] **I.** With ref. to spatial measurement. **1.** Having small longitudinal extent; measuring little along its greatest dimension, or from end to end. Opp. to *long*. **b.** Const. *in*: Having a specified part short 1800. **c.** Of distance: Not great. Of a journey, flight, etc.: Extending over a short distance. 1597. **d.** *fig.* In Biblical expressions, said of a person's 'hand' or 'arm', implying inadequacy or limited range of power 1549. **e.** Of action, vision, etc.: Reaching but a little way. Hence *fig.* of mental powers, ideas, etc.: Contracted in range. late ME. **f.** Abbreviated in form (*for*).... **2.** Of persons: Low in stature; opp. to tall OE. **3.** *S. dung, manure*: manure containing short straw and in an advanced state of fermentation 1618. **4.** Of the sea, etc.: Having short waves; choppy 1834.

1. Thay beir verie schorte tailis 1596. The s. woolly hair of the Africans 1823. I see no reason why a governess..should not wear s. petticoats if she has good legs 1892. *To cut, trim s.*, to make s. by cutting, trimming, etc. **b.** My coat was..s. in the sleeves 1841. **c.** The way..to the Inne is..s. 1597. **d.** Is the Lords hand waxed s.? *Num.* xi. 23. **e.** Our s. views 1736. **2.** A man..somewhat s. of stature 1891. **4.** The shallow Baltic where the seas are steep and s. KIPLING.

II. With ref. to duration or serial extent. **1.** Having little extent in duration, lasting but little time, brief. *At s. intervals*: at times separated by brief intervals. OE. **b.** Occas. applied to conditions, qualities, etc. not usu. described in terms of duration: Not lasting a long time, soon over, short-lived. Somewhat *arch.* OE. **c.** Qualifying a sb. denoting a period of time, to indicate a pleased or regretful sense of its brevity 1715. **d.** Of a person's memory: Not long retaining anything ME. **2.** Of an appointed date in the future: Allowing but a short time, early, near at hand. late ME. **b.** Of notice: Given not long beforehand 1811. †**3.** Quick, speedy, immediate -1780. **4.** Of a speech, sentence, book, word, etc.: Having a small extent from beginning to end; brief OE. **b.** Of a speaker: Brief, occupying little time. Now *rare.* 1515. **5.** Of a style of writing or speaking, hence of a writer or speaker: concise, succinct 1487. **6.** Of utterances (occas. of gestures, etc.): Rudely, angrily, or sternly brief or curt. Of persons (chiefly *predic.*): Rudely or angrily curt in expression; returning short answers; snappish (const. *with* a person). late ME. **b.** Hasty in temper, easily provoked, irascible. Said also of the temper. 1599. **7.** Of breath, breathing: Coming in hurried gasps, impeded. Of a cough: Abrupt, checked; recurring abruptly at frequent intervals; dry, fast. Of a pulse: Making short beats, quick. late ME. **8.** Of a series or succession: Of small extent, having few members or terms. *Obs.* exc. in phrases. **9.** *Phonetics* and *Prosody*. Applied to a vowel (less freq. to a consonant) when its utterance has the less of the two measures of duration recognized in the ordinary classification of speech-sounds. Also, in *Prosody*, of a syllable: Belonging to that one of the two classes which is supposed to be distinguished from the other by occupying a shorter time in utterance. OE. **10.** colloq. *Something s.*: undiluted spirits 1823.

1. The lyf so s., the craft so long to lerne CHAUCER. So s. an acquaintance 1885. Phr. *To make s. work of* (occas *with*), to dispose of quickly. **c.** Seven s. weeks of quiet CARLYLE. **d.** Great men are apt to have s. memories 1839. **2.** Phr. *A s. day* (Law), (a bill) *at s. date* or *sight* (Comm.). **3.** There is no s. remedy for our disease BURKE. **4.** The s. and simple annals of the poor GRAY. Phr. *To make a long story s.* *S. story*, a prose work of fiction, shorter and less elaborate than a novel. *S. and sweet*, brief and pleasant; now usu. more or less *iron.* **5.** †*To be s.*: in short. **6.** No other answer but only a s. *yes* 1686. **b.** Prince Bismarck's s. temper 1885. **8.** Phr. *S. hour*, an hour indicated by a few strokes of the clock. *A s. purse*, a purse soon exhausted; scanty resources. *A s. kennel*, a small pack of hounds. **9.** *S.* †*accent, mark*, the mark(˘) placed over a vowel letter to indicate short quantity. **10.** A drop of summut s. HOOD.

III. Not reaching to some standard. **1.** Of things: Inadequate in quantity. late ME. **b.** Qualifying a sb. denoting a period of time, distance, number, quantity, etc., to indicate an extent less than that expressed by the sb. 1702. **c.** Qualifying a noun of action 1884. **2.** Of a throw, a missile, etc.: Travelling too short a distance, not reaching the mark 1545. **3.** *S. of*: Not fully attaining or amounting to (some condition or degree); not equalling (some other person or thing); inferior to; less than (a specified number or quantity) 1560. **4.** *predic.*, use, chiefly of persons: **a.** Defaulting in payments 1586. †**b.** Lacking in performance -1662. **c.** Having an insufficient supply of money, food, or something else implied by the context; *spec.* not having the means to meet one's engagements 1762. **d.** *S. of*: having an insufficient quantity of. Also, not possessing, lacking (something necessary or desirable); in want of (something to complete the desired number) 1697. **5.** *To run s.* **a.** Of persons: To 'run out' *of* (something). Also without const. 1752. **b.** Of supplies: To prove insufficient 1850.

1. *S. measure, weight*, defective quantity by measure or weight; also, a measuring rod, vessel, etc., or a scale-weight which defrauds the purchaser. *S. commons*: see COMMONS; so *s. allowance, rations*, etc. **b.** A s. league distant BORROW. **c.** *S. delivery, shipment* (Comm.), delivery or shipment of goods less in quantity than agreed on or invoiced. **3.** Cheese little s. of the best Parmeggiano EVELYN. And such a Constitution, little s. of miraculous CARLYLE. Nothing s. of that will do 1892. **4. b.** Very large in Pretence and Promise, but s. in Performance 1697. **c.** Phr. *To go s.*, to suffer privation, have less than enough. **d.** Allow me to take your hat—we are rather s. of pegs DICKENS.

IV. Not tenacious in substance, friable, brittle. (Prob. conn. w. branch I through the notion 'having little length of fibre'.) **1.** Of edible substances: Friable, easily crumbled. late ME. **2.** *gen.* Wanting in tenacity; friable, brittle. Of metals: cf. COLD-SHORT, RED-SHORT. 1607.

1. To make s. paste in Lent 1594. Phr. *To eat s.*, to break up or crumble in the mouth. **2.** Phr. *To work s.*, to break or crumble when being worked.

Comb.: **s.-coat**, a person wearing a s. coat; *pl.* the garments in which an infant is clothed when the long clothes are discarded; so as *v. trans.* to dress (an infant) in s. clothes; **s. division** (*Arith.*): see DIVISION 5; **-frock**, a s. garment, usu. worn in childhood; hence *fig.* in *pl.* habits, etc, associated with childhood; **-grained** *a.*, of wood: having a s.

fibre rendering it liable to snap easily; **-head,** *Anthropology*, a brachycephalic person; *Racing*, a distance less than the length of a horse's head; **s. heeled** *a.*, having a s. heel; *fig.* wanton: **s. metre,** a form of stanza used in hymn-writing, consisting of four lines, of which the first, second, and fourth are of six syllables and the third of eight, abbrev. S.M.; **S. Parliament** (see PARLIAMENT); **s. rib,** any of the lower ribs which do not attach to the sternum; also a piece of butcher's meat, esp. of pork, containing one or more of such ribs; **s. shrift** (see SHRIFT *sb.*); **s. staple** *a.*, having a short fibre; a commercial term applied to cotton of an inferior grade; also *absol.*; **s. suit** *Cards*, a suit of which one has less than four cards; **-sword,** a sword with a s. blade (*Hist.*); **-timer** (cf. TIMER 3); **s. title,** the abbreviated title by which an Act of Parliament is officially designated; **-waisted** *a.*, (of a person or garment) short in the waist; **s. wave,** spec. in *Wireless*, a wave having a wave-length of less than 100 metres. **b.** In names of animals, as **s.-hair,** one of a breed of short-haired cats; **-head,** a name given by sailors to the young of the whale; **-wing,** a diving-bird of the group *Brachypteri*. **c.** In *Cricket*: **s. ball,** a ball which pitches short of a length (see LENGTH *sb.*); **s. leg** (see LEG *sb.*); **s. pitch,** the pitch of a s. ball; **s. run,** (*a*) a run made when the ball does not travel far enough to give time for an easy run; (*b*) a run which does not count by reason of a batsman not having technically completed it; **s. slip** (see SLIP *sb.*[3]). **d.** *Comm.*, as **s. bill,** a bill having less than ten days to run; **-exchange,** exchange having a s. time (commonly thirty days or less) to run; **s. loan,** a loan repayable at an early date; **-money,** money to borrow or to lend upon s.-time loans; **-paper,** s. bills; **-payment,** payment at an early date after the completion of the transaction; **s. price,** a low price (in *Betting*, low odds).

B. quasi-*sb.* and *sb.* **I.** The neuter adj. used *absol.* **1.** With preps., forming advb. phrases. late ME. **2.** *The s.*: the total, the result, upshot; a brief summing up of something previously explained in full. Now *dial.* 1586.

1. *In s.*, briefly, concisely (now only parenthetically); These were, in s., the Orleans mob 1833. *For s.*, as an abbreviation; Father Dick—so they called him for s. 1845. 2. The s. of the matter is this WESLEY.

II. *sb.* **1.** Something that is short. **a.** *Prosody.* A short syllable 1795. **b.** *Electr.* = SHORT CIRCUIT 1906. **c.** Neat spirits: = 'something short' 1823. **2.** *Comm.* A broker who sells more stock than he has in his hands at the time of sale, intending to take advantage of a possible drop in prices to obtain the remainder 1881. **3.** *pl.* **a.** A mixture of the bran and coarse part of meal 1765. **b.** Knee-breeches, small-clothes. *Rowing-shorts*: short drawers worn by oarsmen; similarly *football, running*, etc. *shorts*. 1826. **c.** The refuse clippings or trimmings in certain manufactures, e.g. cuttings of tobacco 1840. **d.** What is 'short' or lacking; *esp.* that amount of stock which a broker who 'sells short' needs to cover his deficiency 1901. **4.** *colloq.* A short extract, piece, film, etc.

C. *adv.* **1.** Of a manner of speaking: Briefly, concisely, curtly. Now *rare* in educated prose use. ME. **2.** In various uses relating to size or distance: With short garments, appendages, etc.; to a short distance 1706. **3.** Abruptly, suddenly; esp. in phr. *to turn s.* (*round*) 1579. **b.** *To take* (a person) *s.* (*a*) To take by surprise, at a disadvantage; to come suddenly upon; *rarely* with *up*. Often *Naut.* of wind or bad weather. 1553. (*b*) To interrupt with a reply; not to allow to complete his speech or offer explanations. Often with *up*. 1565. **4.** On the hither side of the point aimed at or contemplated. Const. *of*. 1588.

1. Now to speak s. and plain 1681. 2. A..girl..big enough to be sixteen, and dressed s. enough to be eleven 1887. Phr. *To break, snap* (etc.) *s.* (*off*); to break straight across, so as to leave nothing beyond the plane of fracture; to break *off* close to the point of attachment. 4. He met me..in a Garden s. of the Town 1698. Phr. *To fall s.* (*of*): see FALL *v.* *To stop s. of*, not to go the length of (some extreme action).

Phrases: *To come s.*, to be imperfect or inadequate. *To come s. of*, to fail to reach (a standard); not to equal *in* some quality; to be something less than. †*To come s. home*, to return from an expedition in reduced numbers: hence, to fail to return. *To cut s.* [= F. *couper court*], to put a sudden end to (a person's life or career, a course of events, an action, speech, etc.); hence, to stop (a person) abruptly in a course of action or speech. *To sell s.* to effect a sale of stock or goods which the seller does not at the time possess, but hopes to buy at a lower price before the time fixed for delivery.

†Short, *v.*[1] [OE. *sc(e)ortian*, f. *sc(e)ort* SHORT *a.*] To grow or make short or shorter to shorten -1641.

Short, *v.*[2] *trans.* and *intr.* 1907. = SHORT-CIRCUIT *v.* (cf. SHORT *sb.* II. 1 b.)

Shortage (ʃǭ·ɹtėdʒ). orig. *U.S.* 1868. [f. SHORT *sb.* + -AGE.] Deficiency in quantity; the amount by which a sum of money, a supply of goods, or the like, is deficient.

Sho·rt-bread. 1801. [SHORT *a.* IV. 1.] A hard flat (often round) cake, the essential ingredients of which are flour, butter, sugar, mixed in such proportions as to make the cake 'short' when baked. Also *attrib.* as *s.-biscuit*.

Short-breathed (breþt), *a.* 1470. [f. SHORT *a.* + BREATH *sb.* + -ED[2].] Short of breath; suffering from difficulty of breathing, dyspnœic.

Sho·rt-cake. 1594. [SHORT *a.* IV. 1.] A thin flat cake made 'short' with butter or lard (the application varying locally).

Short circuit, *sb.* 1876. *Electr.* A circuit made through a small resistance, esp. one that acts as a shunt to a circuit of comparatively large resistance.

Short-circuit, *v.* 1873. [f. prec.] *trans.* **1.** *Electr.* **a.** To connect by a short circuit; to establish a short circuit in (an electric system). **b.** Of a conducting body: To be traversed by (a current) by way of short circuit. Also *refl.* of a current: To make a short circuit. 1882. **c.** To cut off the current from (part of an apparatus) by establishing a short circuit 1882. **2.** *Surg.* To form a direct communication between two portions of an intestine above and below an obstruction; to make a direct passage from (an organ) *into* some other part when the normal passage is obstructed; to avoid (an obstruction) by this means 1897.

Sho:rtco·ming, *vbl. sb.* 1680. [f. phr. *to come short*; see SHORT *adv.*] The condition or fact of coming short; an instance of this. **a.** Failure to come up to a standard or to fulfil a duty a defect. (Chiefly in *pl.*) **b.** Failure to reach an amount; a deficiency.

Short cut, *sb.*[1] 1568. [CUT *sb.*[2]] †**1.** A short passage or journey -1673. **2.** A path or a course which is shorter than the ordinary road taken between two places. Now often hyphened. 1618. **b.** *fig.* A compendious method of attaining some object 1589.

Short cut, *a.* and *sb.*[2] 1596. [f. *cut* pa. pple. of CUT *v.*] **A.** *adj.* Cut to a short length. **B.** *sb.* A kind of tobacco 1789.

Short-dated, *a.* 1815. [f. SHORT *a.* + DATE *sb.* + -ED[2].] Of bills, notes of hand, etc.: Falling due at an early date. So **Sho·rt-date** *a.* **Sho·rt-da:ter,** a short-dated bill, etc.

Shorten (ʃǭ·ɹt'n), *v.* 1513. [f. SHORT *a.* + -EN[5].] **1.** *trans.* To make shorter, to diminish the length of, to abridge, curtail. **b.** *fig.* In Biblical phrase, *To s. the arm* or *hand of*: to limit the power of 1535. **c.** To diminish in working length; to tighten (a rein); to hold (a weapon) nearer to the middle, in order to deal a more effective blow 1597. **d.** With reference to phonetic quantity 1589. **2.** *intr.* To grow shorter 1568. **b.** Of a price, odds: To be lowered or lessened 1884. **3.** *trans.* †**a.** To hold in check, restrain -1700. **b.** To keep from the attainment *of* 1837. **4.** *Naut.* **a.** *To s. sail(s*, to take in some of the sails of a vessel in order to slacken speed 1627. **b.** *To s. in*: to heave in (the cable) so that a shorter length remains overboard. Also *absol.* 1854. **5.** To make 'short' or friable. Also (of manure) *intr.* for *refl.* 1733. **6.** To put (a child) into short clothes 1871.

1. When Autumn..adds to Nights, and shortens Days DRYDEN. To s. my Story, she was married to another STEELE. 2. I am glad to see my labour s. MARVELL. 3. a. Here, where the Subject is so fruitful.. I am shorten'd by my Chain DRYDEN. 6. The blue sash he wore the day he was shortened 1871. Hence **Sho·rtener,** one who or something which shortens.

Shortening (ʃǭ·ɹt'niŋ), *vbl. sb.* 1542. [-ING[1].] **1.** The action or an act of the verb SHORTEN. **2.** *concr.* Fat used for 'shortening' pastry, cakes, etc. 1823.

Shorthand (ʃǭ·ɹthænd). 1636. [f. SHORT *a.* + HAND *sb.*] A method of speedy writing by means of the substitution of contractions or arbitrary signs or symbols for letters, words, etc.; brachygraphy, stenography. **b.** quasi-*adj.* Of the nature of shorthand; compendious 1822.

b. Every new short-hand mode of doing things 1822. *attrib.* as in *s. clerk, reports; s. typist*, a s. clerk who types.

Short-handed, *a.* (Stress variable.) 1794. Lacking a full complement of 'hands'; undermanned, understaffed.

Shorthorn (ʃǭ·ɹt,hǭɹn). 1847. [f. SHORT *a.* + HORN *sb.*] One of a breed of cattle having short horns, orig. bred in the north-eastern counties and now widely distributed over Great Britain and exported to other countries.

Shortish (ʃǭ·ɹtiʃ), *a.* 1800. [f. SHORT *a.* + -ISH[1].] Rather short.

Short-lived (ʃǭɹt,livd, -ləivd; stress variable), *a.* 1588. [f. SHORT *a.* + *live* LIFE + -ED[2]. Often apprehended as f. *lived* pa. pple. of LIVE *v.*] **1.** Having a short life. **2.** *transf.* Lasting only a short time, brief, ephemeral 1588.

1. The short lif'd days of flesh and blood 1645. 2. O short liu'd pride SHAKS.

Shortly (ʃǭ·ɹtli), *adv.* OE. [f. SHORT *a.* + -LY[2].] **1.** Briefly, concisely, in few words. **b.** Abruptly, curtly, sharply 1815. **2.** In a short time; soon OE. **3.** At a short time *after, before* 1548. **4.** For a short time (*rare*) 1809.

1. The Attorney General was heard s. in reply 1805. b. 'I think very differently', answered Elizabeth s. JANE AUSTEN. 2. A French ship..s. bound for Alexandria 1632. 3. On a given morning..shortly after noon 1886. 4. He 's been but s. in office SCOTT.

Shortness (ʃǭ·ɹtnės). OE. [f. SHORT *a.* + -NESS.] **1.** The quality or fact of being 'short', in various senses. **2.** Defective reach (of vision, memory, etc.) 1635. **3.** The condition of being 'short *of*' something; deficiency, want (esp. of money, food, etc.); also, scantiness (of a supply, a crop, etc.) 1669.

1. Such as the shortnesse of the time can shape SHAKS. *S. of breath*, breathlessness. 2. Their fatal s. of vision CARLYLE. 3. There was no s. of money 1882.

Short sight. 1822. [SHORT *a.* I. 1 e.] The defect of sight by which only near objects are seen distinctly; myopia.

Short-sighted, *a.* (Stress variable.) 1622. **1.** Having short sight; having the focus of the eye at less than the normal distance; unable to distinguish objects clearly at a distance; myopic. **2.** *fig.* Lacking in foresight or in extent of intellectual outlook 1622. **3.** Characterized by or proceeding from want of foresight or limited mental vision 1736.

2. So s. are politicians in power D'ISRAELI. A s. and suicidal policy KINGSLEY. Hence **Short-si·ghted-ly** *adv.*, **-ness.**

Short-tongued, *a.* (Stress variable.) 1575. Having a short tongue; hence (now *dial.*) inarticulate, stammering, lisping. Also *occas.* taciturn, unready in speech.

Short-winded, *a.* (Stress variable.) 1450. Short of breath; suffering from or liable to difficulty of breathing; that soon becomes out of breath with any exertion.

Short wool. 1728. **1.** Wool having a short staple or fibre. **2.** (Hyphened.) A sheep producing such wool 1837. **Short-woolled** *a.*

Shot (ʃǫt), *sb.*[1] [OE. *sc(e)ot, gesc(e)ot*:—OTeut. **skuto-*, **gaskutom*, f. root *skut-*; see SHOOT *v.*] **I.** The action of shooting. **1.** A rapid movement or motion (*rare*). **2.** A discharge, flux, or issue 1500. **3.** *Fisheries.* The spread or cast of a net; the throw and haul-in of a fishing-net 1859. **4.** The action of shooting with the bow, catapult, or firearms; the mechanical discharge of arrows or other projectiles as a means of attack; shots or discharges of missiles collectively. Now *arch.* late ME. **b.** An act of shooting OE. **c.** *Mining.* An explosion of a blasting charge 1881. **d.** The film record of a scene in cinematography 1923. **5.** The range of a shot, or distance to which a shot will go 1455. **6.** An attempt to hit with a projectile discharged from a gun 1653. **b.** *fig.* A remark aimed at some one, esp. in order to wound 1841. **7.** A random guess attempting to 'hit' the right answer 1840. **b.** An attempt or try 1756. **8.** An aim or stroke, esp. in a game, as tennis, golf, billiards, etc. 1868. **b.** A throw of a ball, stone, etc. 1852. **c.** In *Football, Hockey, Lacrosse*, an attempt to drive the ball into goal

1868. **d.** In *Boat-racing*, an attempt to 'bump' the boat in front 1868.

3. A second s. of the net produced eleven more [mullet] 1859. 4. Their admiral lost an eye by the s. of an arrow HUME. **b.** Phr. *To fire*, also (now *arch.*) *to make, shoot a s. A s. between wind and water* (cf. SHOOT *v.* IV. 3.). *Like a s.* (colloq.) at once, with rapidity; also, most willingly. *A s. in the eye* (colloq.), an ill turn. 5. Phr. *In, within, out of s.*: in, within, out of shooting distance. *transf. Haml.* I. iii. 35. 6. Phr. *To exchange shots*, said with ref. to a skirmish or a duel. *Not..by a long s.*, hopelessly out of reckoning. 7. Phr. *To make a s.*, to attempt an answer by guessing. **b.** Pinks is going to have a s. at the Wingfield Sculls 1912.

II. That which is discharged in shooting. †**1.** That which is discharged from a bow, an arrow or arrows; also, in early use, projectiles thrown by a catapult or other engine; ammunition for such an engine -1664. **2.** Projectiles (esp. balls or bullets, as dist. from explosive 'shells') designed to be discharged from a firearm or cannon by the force of an explosive 1474. **b.** A cannon-ball. Also (with numerals) as *collect. sing.* or uninflected pl. 1622. **c.** Hence, an iron globe like a cannon ball, used in the sport of 'putting the shot' (or 'weight'): see PUT *v.*[1] I. 2. 1881. **3.** Lead in small pellets, of which a quantity is used for a single charge of a sporting gun. Also (less frequently), a single pellet, a shot-corn (pl. *shot*, esp. with numerals; sometimes *shots*). 1770. **4.** *Mining.* The charge of powder sufficient for a blast in a mine (esp. a coal-mine); also the bored hole into which the charge is put 1851.

1. The Law of Arms doth bar The use of venom'd s. in War 1664. 2. *Bar-, chain-, grape-shot*, etc.: see the first words. **b.** Phr. *(Not) a s. in the locker*: see LOCKER *sb.* 3 b. *Small s.*, small pellets of lead, as dist. from bullets. 3. A strong silk-worm gut, with a s. or two on it 1833.

III. That which shoots. †**1.** Firearms -1727. †**2. a.** *collect. sing.* Soldiers armed with muskets or other firearms (rarely with bows) -1706. **3.** One who shoots; an expert in shooting 1780.

3. No, I am no s. DISRAELI. *Dead s.*: see DEAD *a.* V. 3.

IV. [Cf. OE. *scēotan* to pay, contribute.] Payment, share. The reckoning, amount due or to be paid, esp. at a tavern or for entertainment; a or one's share in such payment. Phr. *To stand s.*, to pay the bill (for all). Now *colloq.* 1475. **V. 1.** A division of land 1490. **2.** A corpse disinterred by body-snatchers 1828.

attrib. and *Comb.*: **s.-corn**, a small s., a grain of s.; **-hole**, a hole made by the passage of a s.; *arch.* a small hole in a fortified wall through which to shoot; *Mining*, a hole for the insertion of a blasting-charge; **-plug, -prop**, a tapered cone of wood to stop a s.-hole in a vessel's side, to prevent leakage; **-pouch**, a sportsman's pouch or bag, usu. of leather, for carrying s.; **-proof** *a.* impenetrable by s.; **-putter**, one who puts the s. in athletic sports; **-star**, (*a*) a shooting star; (*b*) the alga *Nostoc commune*; **-tower**, a tall round tower in which small s. are made by dropping molten lead from the top into water; **-window**, a window that can be opened and shut by turning on its hinges; a casement; a shutter with a few panes of glass at the top.

Shot (ʃɒt), *sb.*[2] 1883. [SHOT *ppl. a.*, used ellipt.] A 'shot' silken or other fabric.

Shot (ʃɒt), *v.* 1681. [f. SHOT *sb.*[1]] **1.** *trans.* To load (a fire-arm) with shot. **2.** To weight by attaching a shot or shots, so as to cause to sink in water 1857.

1. *fig.* Their every word was shotted with an oath 1884. Hence **Sho·tted** *ppl. a.* loaded with shot or ball as well as powder; weighted with shot, having a shot attached.

Shot (ʃɒt), *ppl. a.* late ME. [pa. pple. of SHOOT *v.*] **1.** Of a fish: Having discharged its spawn. **2.** Of a stalk, blade, etc.: That has grown or sprouted 1629. **3.** Of a bullet, arrow, etc.: That is discharged. Also of a bolt that has been pushed into or out of the lock. 1863. **4.** Hit, wounded or killed by a projectile discharged from a gun or bow 1837. **5.** Of a textile fabric: Woven with warp-threads of one colour and weft-threads of another, so that the fabric changes in tint when viewed from different points 1763. **b.** Of a colour, etc.: Changeable, variable 1824.

Shot-free, *a.* 1586. [f. SHOT *sb.*[1] + FREE *a.*] †**1.** Safe from shot, shot-proof -1778. **2.** = SCOT-FREE. Now *rare.* 1596.

Sho·t-gun, sho·tgun. orig. *U.S.* 1828. A smooth-bore gun (fowling-piece) used for firing small-shot, as dist. from a rifle for firing a bullet.

Shotten (ʃɒ·t'n), *ppl. a.* 1451. [pa. pple. of SHOOT *v.*] **1.** Of a fish (esp. a herring): That has spawned. **b.** *transf.* and *fig.* In *s. herring*, applied to a person who is exhausted by sickness or destitute of strength or resources. (*arch.*) Hence *gen.* †Thin, emaciated; worthless, good-for-nothing. 1596.

Should, pa. t. of SHALL *v.*

Shoulder (ʃōu·ldəɹ), *sb.* [OE. *sculdor* (cf. G. *schulter*, etc.).] **1.** Each of the two corresponding portions (right and left) of the human body, including the upper joint of the arm with its integuments and the portion of the trunk between this and the base of the neck; esp. the curved upper surface of this (*spec.*, as a military position in which the rifle is shouldered); in *pl.* often including the part of the back between the two. In quadrupeds, the upper part of the fore-limb and the adjacent part of the back. **b.** In fishes (*sing.* and *pl.*), the upper part of the trunk, adjoining the head 1820. **c.** The upper part of the wing or wing-case of a bird, beetle, butterfly, etc. adjoining the point of articulation 1735. **d.** = *s.-joint*: chiefly in *to put one's s. out.* 1611. **2.** As the part of the body on which burdens are carried; also, as the seat of muscular strength employed in carrying, pushing, etc. OE. **3.** The fore-leg and adjacent parts cut from the carcass of a deer, sheep or other animal; a joint consisting of this prepared for the table ME. **4.** That part of a garment which covers the wearer's shoulder 1473. **5.** A projection or protuberance resembling the human shoulder in shape, position or function 1545. **b.** A sudden inward curvature in the outline of something, from which it tapers to a point 1618. **c.** A rebate which serves as an abutment; a projection which serves as a support 1669. **d.** A comparatively gentle slope on the side of a hill and near the top 1817. **6.** An arched piece of wood or metal, or a frame of metal rods, placed inside the shoulders of a garment to be hung up in a wardrobe, etc. 1899.

1. Phr. *To put an old head on young shoulders*, to make a young person as staid or experienced as an elderly one. *To have a head upon one's shoulders* to have good sense. *S. to s.*, lit. of soldiers, so as to shoulder one another, in close conflict; also, in close formation; hence *fig.* of persons, with united effort. (*Straight*) *from the s.*, (of a blow) with the fist brought to the shoulder and then swiftly sent forward; made with the arm straight. *To rub shoulders with*: see RUB *v.* 5 b. See also COLD SHOULDER. 2. Make broad thy shoulders to receive my weight, And bear me to the margin TENNYSON. *fig.* All the debts are put upon my shoulders, on account of my known wealth THACKERAY. Phr. *His shoulders are broad* (*enough*), he is able to bear great burdens or responsibility. Phr. *To put* (*lay, set*) *one's s. to the wheel*, (lit.) so as to extricate the vehicle from the mire; hence *fig.* to set to work vigorously. *To open the shoulders*, to give free play to the muscles of the shoulders in making a stroke. 3. *S. of mutton fist*, A large, heavy, fleshy fist. *S. of mutton sail*, a triangular sail attached to a mast. 5. The neck [of the amphora] is not cylindrical, but slopes upon the shoulders 1857.

Comb.: **s.-belt** = BANDOLEER; **-brace**, a contrivance for flattening rounded shoulders; **-butt**, a pistol butt shaped for firing from the s.; **-clapper**, an officer charged with the arrest of an offender, a bailiff, sheriff's officer; **-girdle** *Anat.* (see GIRDLE *sb.*[1] 4 a); **-high** *a.* and *adv.*, as high as one's s.; **-joint**, the joint of the s.; the articulation by which the arm or fore-leg is connected with the trunk; **-shot, -shotten** *adjs.*, (of an animal (having a strained or dislocated s. (*arch.*); **s. slip**, a strain or dislocation of the s. joint; **-yoke**, a yoke for carrying pails.

Shoulder (ʃōu·ldəɹ), *v.* ME. [f. prec.] **1.** *trans.* To push against (a person or thing) with the shoulder; (of a crowd) to push shoulder against shoulder; hence, to push roughly, unceremoniously, or insolently; to thrust aside with the shoulder; to hustle, jostle. Now *rare* or *Obs.* exc. with adv. or advb. phr. **2.** *transf.* Of inanimate things 1590. **3.** *absol.* and *intr.* To push with the shoulder; to use the shoulders (in a struggle or contest). Const. *against, at.* 1440. **b.** To make one's way by pushing with the shoulders; more fully *to s. one's way*; also *refl.* 1581. †**4. a.** *trans.* To put (soldiers) shoulder to shoulder in close rank. **b.** *intr.* To stand shoulder to shoulder -1781. **5.** *trans.* To support with, bear up or carry on the shoulder or shoulders; to take or place on one's shoulder to be carried 1611. **b.** *fig.* To take upon oneself as a burden (expense, responsibility, etc.) 1900. **6.** *Mil.* To place (a weapon, etc.) upon the shoulder 1595. **7.** To furnish (a thing) with a shoulder; to cut shoulders or a shoulder on; to fit *into* with a shoulder. Also with *down, up.* late ME. **8.** Of inanimate things: To form a shoulder, project as a shoulder, or spread out into a shoulder; also with *up* 1611.

1. Around her, numberless, the rabble flowed, Shouldering each other, crowding for a view 1713. *fig.* Custom and prejudice..should'ring aside The meek and modest truth COWPER. 2. Walls of rock ..shouldering back the billows COLERIDGE. 3. All tramped, kicked, plunged, shouldered, and jostled SCOTT. 5. We shouldered our knapsacks, and started for the Lizard 1851. 6. Phr. *To s. one's* or *a rifle*, etc., often used for: to join the ranks, enlist as a soldier. *To s. arms*, to hold one's rifle in a vertical position, supported by the right hand at the lock, hence *at s. arms*, at the position directed by this word of command. 8. The hill shoulders up very steeply for three-fourths its height 1870. Hence **Shou·ldering** *vbl. sb.* the action of the vb.; *concr.* something which projects or supports as a shoulder.

Shou·lder-blade. ME. Each of the two flat triangular bones articulated with the humerus, and lying over the ribs in the upper part of the back in all mammals; the scapula.

Shou·lder-bone. ME. = prec.

Shouldered (ʃōu·ldəɹd), *ppl. a.* ME. [f. SHOULDER *sb.* and *v.* + -ED[1].] **1.** Having shoulders. Chiefly with qualifying adv. or advb. phr. Also ROUND-S. **2.** Having a shoulder or projection; made with a shoulder or with shoulders 1671. **3.** Placed and carried at, on, or over the shoulder; spec. *Mil. To stand s.*: to stand with shouldered arms 1760.

Shou·lder-knot. 1676. A knot of ribbon or lace worn on the shoulder by men of fashion in the 17th and 18th c.; also, a knot, formerly of ribbons of the family colours, now of lace, worn on the shoulder by some livery servants; a knot or bow of ribbon worn on the shoulder by a woman or child; also *Mil.* = AGLET 2.

Shou·lder-piece. 1580. **1. a.** *Antiq.* A piece of armour covering the shoulder. **b.** A piece or each of the pieces of material forming the shoulders of a garment 1611. **2.** The piece forming the shoulder (of a tool, etc.) 1811.

Shou·lder-strap. 1688. **1.** Each of the two short straps which go over the shoulders, connecting and supporting the fore and back parts of a garment. **2.** Each of the narrow straps fastened upon the shoulders of a military tunic; esp. an ornamental strap distinguishing the corps and grade of an officer 1840.

Shout (ʃaut), *sb.* late ME. [prob. f. root of SHOOT *v.*] **1.** A loud, vehement cry expressing joy, grief or pain, fear, triumph, warning, encouragement, etc.; a loud cry to attract attention at a distance; a tumultuous uproar made by a large body of people. **b.** *transf.* Applied to any loud noise or cry forcing itself upon the attention 1503. **2.** *Colonial slang.* A call to a waiter to replenish the glasses of the company; hence, a turn in paying for a round of drinks. Also, a free drink given to all present by one of the company; a drinking party. 1863.

1. This generall applause, and chearefull showt SHAKS. An involuntary s. of laughter 1809. **b.** Great was the s. of guns from the castles PEPYS.

Shout (ʃaut), *v.* late ME. [See prec.] **1.** *intr.* To utter a loud call, to make a loud outcry expressive of joy, exultation, etc. or to raise an alarm, to incite to action, etc. **b.** Of a place: To resound with shouts. Of an inanimate thing: To make a loud uproar. *rare.* 1513. **c.** *U.S.* To be loud in support of (a candidate) 1907. **2.** *trans.* To utter (something) with a loud voice 1500. **3.** *Austral. slang.* **a.** *intr.* To stand drinks 1859. **b.** *trans.* To call for (drinks, etc.) in order to treat the bystanders 1867.

1. The word of Peace is render'd: hearke how they showt SHAKS. *To s. at* (a person), to assail with shouts, *esp.* of derision or anger. *To s. down*, to reduce to silence by shouts of disapproval; to howl down. Hence **Shou·ter**, one who shouts.

Shove (ʃɒv), *sb.* ME. [f. next.] An act of shoving; a strong thrust or push to move a body away from the agent. Often *fig.*

fig. It would be such a fine thing for all the family: I could give all the boys such a s. 1873.

Shove (ʃʌv), *v.* Pa. t. and pa. pple. **shoved** (ʃʌvd). [Com. Teut. (orig. str.) verb: OE. *scúfan* (*scéaf, scufon, scofen*) :—OTeut. *skeuƀ-: skauƀ-: skŭƀ-.] (Generally equivalent to *thrust, push*; but now less dignified in use.) **1.** *trans.* To thrust away with violence; to precipitate; to 'cast' (into prison, etc.). *Obs.* exc. *arch.* **2.** To move (a heavy or resisting object) forward by the application of muscular strength from behind; to push along with effort ME. **b.** To force (a person, etc.) onwards by pushing. Also, to cause to fall *over* (a cliff, etc.) or *out of* (a place) by a push. late ME. †**c.** Of winds, etc.: To drive, propel, impel -1705. **3.** *spec.* To propel (a boat, etc.) either by pushing at the stern or with a pole worked from the inside. Also *absol.* 1513. **b.** With *out, off,* or const. *from.* (*a*) *trans.* To launch (a boat) by means of a steady push applied at the stern OE. (*b*) *absol.* To push one's vessel away from the bank. Also *transf.* of the boat. 1513. **4.** *trans.* Without the notion of difficulty. To push (something) so as to make it slide along a surface or in a groove or channel; also to move *up* or *down* by pushing 1633. †**b.** To put surreptitiously or improperly *in, on, under* -1773. **c.** (Chiefly *colloq.*) To put or thrust (carelessly or hastily) into a place or receptacle; also to thrust *aside, away* 1827. **d.** To push *out of* a position, *away*, by gradual encroachment 1629. **5.** *absol.* and *intr.* To push, to apply force against an object in order to move it from its position OE. **6.** *intr.* To push about or jostle in a crowd; to make one's way by jostling or elbowing ME. **b.** *refl.* To make one's way by shoving 1489. **7.** *trans.* To push (a person) with one's body or elbows; to knock against, jostle 1530.

2. He was the first to s. the gangway on to the vessel 1873. c. The Seas..s. the loaden Vessels into Port ADDISON. 3. The seamen towed, and I shoved SWIFT. b. The boats were shoved off MARRYAT. 4. b. To shorten man's duty..by shoving a commandment out of Moses's tables 1773. 5. Phr. *To s. at*, to push against (an object) in order to displace or overthrow. 7. Laughing and shoving each other about KINGSLEY.

Comb.: **s.-halfpenny**, *slang*, a gambling game similar to shovel-board.

Shove-groat. *Obs.* exc. *Hist.* 1488. [f. SHOVE *v.* + GROAT *sb.*] = SHOVEL-BOARD.

Shovel (ʃʌ·v'l), *sb.* [OE. *scofl* :—OTeut. *skŭflō, app. f. the root *skŭf-, *skŭƀ- of SHOVE *v.*] **1.** A spade-like implement, consisting of a broad blade of metal or other material (more or less hollow and with upturned sides), attached to a handle and used for raising and removing quantities of earth, grain, coal or other loose material. (In some dialects applied to a spade.) **2.** = SHOVEL HAT 1841. **3.** *Mil.* A contrivance fitted to a field-gun to act as a brake to lessen the recoil 1899.

attrib. and *Comb.*: **s.-bill** = SHOVELLER[2]; **s. head,** the bonnet-headed shark, *Reniceps tiburo*; **-nose,** a nose having the shape and fulfilling the functions of a s., also *attrib.* in the names of certain animals and fishes having this characteristic; hence **-nosed** *a.*; **-penny** = SHOVEL-BOARD; **-stirrup,** a stirrup with a broad rest for the foot, extending beyond the heel.

Shovel (ʃʌ·v'l), *v.*[1] 1440. [f. prec.] **1.** *trans.* To take up and remove with a shovel. **b.** *transf.* (With adv.) To remove as rubbish; to move about roughly and without consideration 1816. **2.** To excavate, dig up (the ground, etc.), dig (a hole, etc.) with a shovel 1470. **3.** To throw (quantities of some material) *into* a receptacle, to cast (earth, dust, etc.) *on* or *upon* something or somebody 1611. **4.** To gather (something) *up* in quantities as with a shovel 1685. **5.** *intr.* To use a shovel 1685. **6.** *trans.* To turn (something) over with a shovel 1775.

1. The men that s. the dirt out of the road 1791. 3. One of them..was shovelling tipsy-cake into his ample mouth 1913. 4. Store-keepers are simply shovelling up money 1879. 5. In relays, 3,000 of the Militia-men dig and s. night and day CARLYLE. Hence **Sho·veller**[1], one who shovels.

Shovel (ʃʌ·v'l), *v.*[2] Now *rare.* late ME. [app. frequent. of SHOVE *v.* Cf. SHUFFLE *v.*] *intr.* To make movements *with* the feet, without raising them from the ground; to walk languidly or lazily.

In walking he does not tread, but s. and slide CARLYLE.

†**Sho·velard.** 1440. [f. SHOVEL *sb.* + -ARD; perh. after MALLARD.] The spoonbill, *Platalea leucorodia* -1646.

Shovel-board (ʃʌ·v'l,bōəɹd), **shu·ffle-board.** 1532. [Unexplained alteration of †*shove-board*.] **1.** A game in which a coin or other disk is driven by a blow with the hand along a highly polished board, floor, or table marked with transverse lines. **b.** The table on which the game is played 1603. **2.** *transf.* A game played on shipboard by pushing wooden or iron disks with a cue (called a *shovel*) so that they may rest on one of nine squares of a diagram chalked on the deck 1877.

Comb.: †**s.-shilling,** a shilling (sometimes of Edw. VI) used in the game of s.

Shovelful (ʃʌ·v'lful). 1533. [-FUL **2.**] A quantity that fills a shovel; as much as a shovel can hold or take up at one time.

Shovel hat. 1829. A stiff broad-brimmed hat, turned up at the sides with a shovel-like curve in front and behind, worn by some ecclesiastics. Hence **Shovel-hatted** *a.*

Shoveller[2] (ʃʌ·v'ləɹ). 1460. [Alteration of SHOVELARD.] †**1.** = SHOVELARD -1796. **2.** Applied to the Spoonbill Duck, *Spatula clypeata*, a bird with a broad shovel-like beak. Also *s. duck*. 1674.

Shover (ʃʌ·vəɹ). 1500. [f. SHOVE *v.* + -ER[1].] **1.** One who or that which shoves. **2.** Jocular substitute for CHAUFFEUR 1908.

Show (ʃōu) *sb.* Also †**shew.** ME. [f. next.] **I. 1.** The action or an act of exhibiting to view or notice. Now *rare* exc. in specific use or phrase. **b.** A demonstration or display of military strength or of intention to take severe measures. Chiefly in phr. *to make a s.* 1548. **2.** The external aspect (of a person or thing). Now *rhet.* or *poet.* in gen. sense. 1555. **b.** *Theol.* and *Philos.* Used occas. as an equivalent for 'accident', 'phenomenon', 'species' 1560. **3.** With qualifying word: A (fine, striking, etc.) appearance. Also without qualification, a fine or striking appearance, imposing display. 1550. **b.** (Now *U.S.* and *Austral.*) An opportunity for displaying or exerting oneself; a chance, 'opening' 1579. **4.** In generalized sense: Ostentatious display 1713. **5.** An appearance or display (*of* something, a quality, activity, sentiment, etc.) to which there is at least some degree of reality to correspond. Chiefly in negative contexts, or with a limiting word. **b.** An indication, sign, or token *of* something; a trace or vestige *of*. Now only in neg. contexts. 1563. **c.** *U.S.* and *Austral.* An indication of the presence of metal in a mining ground, of oil in a well, etc. 1600. **6.** An unreal or illusory appearance (*of* something) 1547. **b.** In generalized sense: Empty appearance without reality 1583. **7.** An appearance (*of* some quality, feeling, activity, etc.) assumed with more or less intention to deceive; a simulation or pretence. Also, a half-hearted or inchoate attempt or 'offer' (*of* doing something). Formerly often *pl.* 1526.

1. Phr. *On s.*, in process of being shown or exhibited; on view. *S. of hands*, the holding up the hand above the head, as a means of indicating a vote or judgement on a proposition. 2. But I haue that Within, which passeth s.; These, but the Trappings, and the Suites of woe SHAKS. Phr. *In s.*, in appearance; often, in appearance only, ostensibly, seemingly. *To have a* (or *the*) *s. of*, to appear to be, appear to partake of; to look like, resemble. 3. Their names made a famous s. in the bills THACKERAY. b. Phr. *To give* (a person) *a s.* *To have* or *stand a* (or *no*) *s.* 4. A True Spaniard: Nothing but S. and Beggary ADDISON. 7. His refusal was cloked under a s. of feudal loyalty 1867. Phr. *To make* (*a*) *s.*, to make a pretence or feint; to pretend; Two little men, who did nothing, made a s. of doing it all DICKENS.

II. *concr.* Something shown or presented to view. **1.** A person or thing exhibited or gazed at as an object of admiration, curiosity, mockery, or the like 1535. **2.** *gen.* A sight, spectacle. Usu. with qualifying word. 1577. **3.** A phantasmal appearance; an apparition 1611. **4.** A display on a large scale of objects for public inspection 1837. **5.** A spectacle elaborately prepared or arranged; a pageant, masque, procession, or similar display on a large scale 1561. **b.** *gen.* Pageantry 1912. **6.** An exhibition of strange objects, wild beasts, dancers, acrobats, etc., held usu. in a booth or portable building, with a small charge for admission. Cf. PEEPSHOW, SIDESHOW. 1760. **b.** The booth or building (with its contents) 1840. **7.** Applied *colloq.* or *joc.* to any kind of public display; e. g. an exhibition of pictures, a theatrical performance, a fashionable gathering, a speech-making, etc. 1863. **8.** *slang.* A matter or affair, a concern. Also, a body or collection of persons. 1889.

1. [Venice] Perchance even dearer in her day of woe, Than when she was..a marvel, and a s. BYRON. 3. What you saw, was all a Fairy S. DRYDEN. 4. S. of Horses at the Agricultural Hall 1864. 5. A shew of gladiators 1770. *Lord Mayor's S.*: see LORD MAYOR. 6. The travelling menageries, or..'Wild-beast shows' DICKENS. 8. Phr. *To boss* or *run the s.*, to assume control. *To give the s. away*, to blab; to betray the deficiencies, pretentiousness, etc. of an affair.

III. Techn. uses. **1.** *Med.* A sanguino-serous discharge from the vagina prior to labour. Also, the first appearance of a menstrual flow. 1753. **2.** *Mining.* A lambent blue flame appearing above the ordinary flame of a candle or lamp when fire-damp is present 1851.

attrib. and *Comb.*, as *s.-bench, -keeper, -monster, -piece*, etc.; **s.-bill,** a bill or placard announcing a s., public sale, etc.; **-boat** (orig. *U.S.*), a steamboat in which theatrical performances are given; **-bottle,** a large glass bottle containing coloured liquid, to make a show in a druggist's window; **-box,** a box in which objects of curiosity are exhibited; **-card,** a card containing a tradesman's advertisement of goods, etc.; **-case,** a glass case for exhibiting articles in a shop or museum; **-glass,** a glass case for exhibiting valuable or delicate goods; **S.-Sunday,** (*a*) the Sunday before the Oxford Commemoration, on the evening of which a kind of University parade used to be held in the Broad Walk of Christ Church (*b*) among artists, the Sunday before 'sending-in day'; **-yard,** an enclosure in which live-stock, machinery, and other large objects are exhibited.

Show, shew (ʃōu), *v.* Pa. t. **showed, shewed** (ʃōud). Pa. pple. **shown, shewn** (ʃōun). [Com. WGer. wk. verb: OE. *scéawian* :—WGer. *skauwōjan, f. OTeut. *skau- to see, look. The spelling *shew* (which orig. represents a differentiated development of the OE. diphthong *éa*) is now rare or individual exc. in legal documents.] †**I.** *trans.* To look at, gaze upon, behold, view; to inspect, review; to look at mentally; to 'see', read, find (in a book) -ME. **II.** To cause or allow to be seen or looked at. **1.** *trans.* To bring forward or display (an object) in order that it may be looked at; to expose or exhibit to view ME. **b.** To display in a (specified) condition or with a (specified) appearance ME. **c.** To hold up or place (a light) where it can be seen (as a signal, to point out the way in the dark, etc.) ME. **d.** To exhibit (a sign, token). Hence, in Biblical language, to exhibit (a 'sign' or marvel), to work (a miracle). ME. **e.** To display (goods, wares, for sale or in an exhibition) ME. **f.** To display, hang out, unfurl (a banner, ensign, etc.) 1470. **g.** To exhibit (a spectacle, some interesting object) for the amusement of the public; to make a show of 1500. **h.** To exhibit threateningly. Hence *joc.*, to make the slightest possible application of. 1833. **2.** To produce or submit for inspection. **a.** To produce (a legal document, etc.) for official inspection; to exhibit (something) in proof that one possesses it ME. †**b.** To muster (soldiers); to make an array of (fighting cocks). **c.** *fig.* To (be able to) present to (physical or mental) view 1611. **3.** To let (a person) read or examine (a book, writing); to bring (it) to his notice 1677. **4.** To represent in sculpture or graphic art 1660. **5.** To display deliberately or ostentatiously in order to attract notice or win admiration 1509. **6.** To allow (a part of the body) to be seen ME. **7.** *refl.* To appear, allow oneself to be seen ME. **8. a.** Of plants, the seasons, etc.: To bring forth to view (fruit, flowers, etc.) ME. **b.** Of animals or plants: To display (their colours, beauties, etc.) 1667. **c.** Of a luminous body: To display (its light). late ME. **9.** To be the means of displaying, revealing to sight, or allowing to be seen. late ME. **b.** To be in such a state or position as to allow (something) to be seen 1848. **10.** To have visibly (some external feature or mark); to have (a part of itself) in a position exposed to view 1585. **b.** Of a list, a recording instrument, etc.: To be found to indicate 1866.

1. S. me your tongue—let me feel your pulse 1833. Phr. *To s. one's hand*, to display one's cards face upwards; *fig.* to allow one's plans or intentions to be

known. **c.** 'Light him down' said Sikes,..'s. him a light' DICKENS. **f.** The chase then shewed Hamburgh colours, and returned the fire SCOTT. **h.** To press the horse too suddenly up to the snaffle by showing the whip 1833. **2. a.** A call by the guard to 'shew tickets' 1866. *To have* (something) *to s. for* (one's labour, expenditure, etc.), to be able to exhibit as a result. *To s. up*, to hand up (a school-exercise, etc.), for inspection. **b.** Earth has not anything to s. more fair WORDSW. **3.** I showed Lord Steyne your pamphlet on Malt THACKERAY. **5.** Fools,..walking up and down to shew their new Cloaths 1693. Phr. *To s. off*, to display ostentatiously. **6.** Phr. *To s. one's face, head*, etc., joc. *to s. one's nose*, to allow oneself to be seen, make an appearance. *To s.* (a person) *one's heels, a clean* or *fair pair of heels*, to flee (from him). *To s. the cloven foot* (*hoof*), to betray something diabolic or sinister in one's character or motives. *To s. one's teeth*, to exhibit signs of resistance or attack. **8. c.** The sun..showed its broad disk above the eastern sea SCOTT. **9.** Very short petticoats, only not showing the knees 1859. *To. s. off, out*, to display in relief or by contrast; to set off, enhance in appearance (*rare*). **b.** *To s. daylight*, to have holes or openings through which light can be seen. **10.** Her planks s. signs of age 1883. **b.** His watch showed 7.30 p.m. 1910.

III. To guide another person's sight to (an object). **1.** To enable a person to discover or identify (a visible object) by pointing to it, or by conducting him to a place where it can be seen. Also, to direct a person's observation to the various parts or features of (a country, town, building, or any complex object). ME. **b.** To point out or indicate a place *where* (etc.) 1450. **2.** (With inverted const.) To guide or conduct (a person) *to, into* a particular place, room in a house, etc., *over* or *through* the rooms of a house. late ME.

1. I pray you shew my youth old Shylockes house SHAKS. *fig.* S. me a cavalry chief like him now that Murat is gone THACKERAY. *To s.* (a person) *the way*, to guide him in a required direction, by leading or accompanying him, or by giving him instructions. *To s.* (a person) *the door*, to order him to leave the room or house; to turn out of doors. **2.** The grim janitor..shewed me into a parlour SMOLLETT. Phr. *To s. up, upstairs*, to conduct (a person) upstairs. *To s. out*, to take (a person) to the exit door; to insist upon the departure of (a person) from the house. *To s. in*, to bring (a person) into a house or room. *To s. round*, to s. (a person) over a place, s. the 'sights'.

IV. To exhibit or manifest by outward signs. **1.** To exhibit, allow to be seen (some inward quality, feeling, condition, etc.) by one's outward appearance; occas. said of the appearance. Also with obj. cl. ME. **2.** To display (a quality, condition, feeling, etc.) by one's action or behaviour ME. **b.** With obj. cl.: To make it plain in regard to oneself (*that*) ME. **3.** *refl.* **a.** With compl. or inf.: To exhibit oneself in a (specified) light or character; to manifest or exemplify a (specified) quality, etc., in one's behaviour ME. **b.** Of a quality, condition, etc.: To manifest itself; to become evident by signs or tokens ME. **4.** To display (kindness, mercy, courtesy, malice, neglect, etc.) *to* a person by one's acts or behaviour; to accord or grant (favour, honour; a courtesy, etc.) ME. **†5.** To put forth, exert (one's power, strength). Also of things. –1595. **b.** To offer, attempt (resistance) 1634.

1. He showed all the outward signs of a mind at ease GEO. ELIOT. **2. b.** In both transactions he showed he was no fool (*mod.*). **3.** He shewed hym selfe a fermer frend to Zanzaber..then to me 1615. **4.** He is troubled that my wife shows my sister no countenance PEPYS. **5. b.** *To s. fight*, to display pugnacity or readiness to fight.

V. To make known by statement or argument. **1.** To point out, reveal, make known; to make evident or clear, explain, expound ME. **b.** With indirect obj.: To inform, instruct, teach (a person) *how to* (do something). Also with ellipsis of the inf. 1567. **2.** To communicate, announce, declare, narrate, state, tell (a fact, story, news, etc.); to describe, give an account of. Now *arch.* ME. **b.** To set forth, allege (in a legal document). Often in petitionary formulæ. late ME. **c.** To state, allege, plead (a cause, reason, etc.). Now chiefly in *Law.* ME. **3.** To prove, demonstrate (a fact, statement) by argument, reasoning, allegation of evidence or instances, experiment, etc. ME. **b.** With complementary obj.: To prove, make out (a person or thing) to be (something). Also with accus. and inf. 1563. **4.** Of a thing: To be a proof, evidence, sign or indication of ME. **5. S. up. a.** In school language: To report (a scholar) for punishment 1845. **b.** To disgrace or discredit by a thorough exposure; to expose (a person's faults, ignorance, misdeeds, etc.) 1826.

1. O let me liue, And all the secrets of our campe Ile shew SHAKS. The consequences of which a little time will shew EVELYN. **b.** Ile shew you how t'obserue a strange euent SHAKS. Phr. †*To s. one's mind*, to reveal one's thought or intention; to express one's opinion or judgement. **2.** My mouthe shall shewe forth thy prayse *Bk. Com. Prayer.* **3.** Many arguments are used to s., that motion is the source of life 1875. **4.** Nothing showing worse taste than to load your plate 1859. **5. b.** That mathematical mysticism, so mercilessly shown up by Berkeley MILL.

VI. *intr.* To be seen, be visible, appear. **1.** To be or become visible; to make an appearance ME. **b.** Of a thing: To be seen (*through, over, under*, etc.) something that partly covers or conceals it. Also, to be visible as a fault or defect. 1842. **2.** To appear in public, make a display in public. In mod. use chiefly *colloq.*: To appear in company or society; to make an appearance in an assembly, among guests, etc. 1625. **3.** With complement (*adj.* or †*sb.*): To look, seem, appear. *arch.* ME. **b.** With adv. or advb. phr. To present a (specified) appearance; to make a (good, bad, etc.) show. late ME. **c.** To look *like. arch.* 1578.

1. The fire i' th' Flint Shewes not, till it be strooke SHAKS. **b.** Cut underneath, where it won't s. 1852. The type shows through the page 1886. He meant more by the words than showed upon the face of them STEVENSON. **2.** I believe he never shews till just before dinner TROLLOPE. **3.** The wood when cut showed sound as a bell 1893. **b.** Becket never showed to more advantage than in moments of personal danger 1877.

With advs.: **S. off**: to act or talk for show; to make a deliberate or ostentatious display of one's abilities or accomplishments (*colloq.*). **S. up. a.** To appear conspicuously or in relief. **b** To become prominent, catch the eye. **c.** To put in an appearance; to be present or 'turn up' (*colloq.*).

Comb.: **s.-down**, in *Card-playing*, the act of laying down one's cards with their faces up; *fig.* an open disclosure of plans, means, etc. (chiefly *U.S.*); also, an exhibition of achievements or possibilities.

Shower (ʃauəɹ, ʃau·əɹ), *sb.*[1] [OE. *scúr* :— OTeut. **skūroz.*] **1.** A fall of rain, of short duration and (usu.) comparatively light. Also, a similar fall of sleet or hail, rarely of snow. **b.** In extended use: A copious downfall of anything coming or supposed to come from the clouds or sky; in recent use often of meteors. late ME. **2.** *transf.* A copious fall or discharge of water or other liquid in drops. Often of tears. late ME. **b.** *poet.* Of light, sound, etc. 1781. **c.** Short for SHOWER-BATH 1889. **d.** *Pyrotechny.* A device for producing a shower of small slow-burning 'stars', which fall from a rocket 1839. **3.** *fig.* A copious or liberal supply bestowed ME. **b.** *U.S. colloq.* A large number of gifts, usu. of a specified nature, given e.g. to a bride; an occasion when these are bestowed (a *s.-party*) 1926. **4.** A copious fall or flight of objects, esp. of missiles. Also of blows. OE.

1. A light s. drifted down the valley 1907. **b.** Meteoric showers 1835. **2.** This brought only another s. of tears 1846. **b.** What showers of gold the sunbeams rain! 1840. **3.** Sweet Highland Girl, a very s. Of beauty is thy earthly dower! WORDSW. A s. of..letters of hearty congratulation 1888. **4.** They were received with a s. of stones MACAULAY.

Comb.: **s.-cloud**, a cumulo-nimbus cloud.

Shower (ʃōu·əɹ), *sb.*[2] [OE. *scéawere* scout, watchman, f. *scéawian* to SHOW. Later, f. SHOW *v.* + -ER[1].] **1.** One who shows, points out, or exhibits ME. **†2.** Something which shows; an indicator –1668.

1. The breeders of Herefords have always been keen showers 1868. **2.** The second [finger] is cal'd..the shewer, or pointer 1668.

Shower (ʃauəɹ, ʃau·əɹ), *v.* 1573. [f. SHOWER *sb.*[1]] **1.** *intr.* To rain in a shower, or in showers. Chiefly *impers.* **2.** To fall down in a shower or showers, or as a shower of rain 1582. **3.** *trans.* To pour down or discharge in a shower or showers; to send down or pour out in abundance and rapidly 1582. **4.** To water with or as with a shower; to wet copiously with rain or with water in drops or spray; *transf.* to cover or strew as with rain 1667.

1. It showered all afternoon and poured..all night STEVENSON. **2.** Teares from her eies did s. 1601. *fig.* It rain'd downe Fortune showring on your head SHAKS. **3.** They showered him with special honours (*U.S.*). **4.** When God hath showrd the earth MILT. Ladies..bright In silks, with spangles shower'd KEATS.

Show·er-bath. 1803. A bath in which water from above is poured in a shower upon the person. Also an apparatus for producing such a bath.

Showery (ʃau·əri), *a.* 1591. [f. SHOWER *sb.*[1] + -Y[1].] **1.** Raining in showers; characterized by frequent showers of rain. **2.** Causing or producing showers; bringing showers 1697. **3.** Pertaining to, produced by, or resembling a shower or showers 1667.

2. 'Tis not s. south, nor airy wester 1871. **3.** Colours of the showrie Arch MILT. Hence **Show·eriness.**

Showing (ʃōu·iŋ), *vbl. sb.* OE. [f. SHOW *v.* + -ING[1].] **1.** The action of SHOW *v.*; with *pl.*, an instance of this. **2.** Manner of putting a case; in phrases *on this s., on one's own s.*, etc. 1857. **3.** A statement or presentation of figures, accounts, or the like. Chiefly *U.S.* 1868. **4.** *U.S.* An appearance or display of a specified kind 1890. **5.** Outward appearance (*arch.* or *Obs.*) ME.

4. Phr. *To make a* (good or bad) *s.*

†**Show·ish,** *a.* Common in the 18th c. 1671. [f. SHOW *sb.* + -ISH.] = SHOWY *a.* –1768.

Showman (ʃōu·măn). 1734. [SHOW *sb.*] One who exhibits or is proprietor of a show.

Show·manship. 1859. The art of being a showman; *transf.* the capacity for exhibiting one's wares, capabilities, etc.

Show·-place. 1579. **†1.** A place for public shows or spectacles; a theatre. (Used as tr. *θέατρον, circus*, etc.) –1647. **2.** A place (e.g. a large mansion or estate) which is regularly exhibited to visitors 1817.

Show·room. 1616. [f. SHOW *sb.*] **1.** A room used for the display of goods or merchandise. **2.** *pl.* The rooms in a large mansion which are regularly shown to visitors 1863.

Showy (ʃōu·i), *a.* 1712. [f. SHOW *sb.* + -Y[1].] Characterized by show. **a.** Of visible objects: Presenting an imposing or striking appearance; making a good display. **b.** Of immaterial things, qualities, etc.: Brilliant, striking, 'effective'. Of persons: Displaying brilliant talents, etc. 1728.

a. Inferior but s. watches 1832. **b.** Forming friendships with every shewy adventurer that comes in your way 1782. Hence **Show·i·ly** *adv.*, **-ness.**

Shrag (ʃræg), *sb.* *Obs.* exc. *dial.* 1552. [Cf. SCRAG *sb.*[2]] A twig; a branch lopped off. So **Shrag** *v. trans.* to lop, prune 1440.

Shrapnel (ʃræ·pnĕl), *sb.* 1804. [f. name of Gen. H. *Shrapnel*, its inventor.] A hollow projectile containing bullets and a small bursting charge which, when fired by the time fuse, bursts the shell and scatters the bullets in a shower. Also *s. shell.*

Shred (ʃred), *sb.* [OE. **scréad, scréade*, f. OTeut. **skraud-* (: *skreud-, skrūd-*) to cut. Cf. SCREED *sb.*] **1.** A fragment cut or broken off; a strip; a scrap. **2.** In OE., *pl.* Parings (of fruit, etc.); in mod. use, a narrow strip (of peel, vegetable, root, etc.) shaved so thin that it curls OE. **3.** A fragment or strip of textile material cut or torn off; a small piece of cloth, a fragment of clothing; *pl.* scanty or ragged garments. late ME. **b.** *transf.* (of cloud, mist, etc.) 1834. **4.** A length or end of gold or silver thread or lace. *arch.* 1450. **5.** A fragment, small piece, scrap (of something immaterial). late ME.

3. Her clothes became ragged, and she mended them with shreds of any colour 1850. Phr. *Of shreds (and patches)*, made up of rags or scraps; hence *allus.*; A King of shreds and patches SHAKS. *In, into shreds*, in or into small fragments. *To tear to shreds*, to rend into small pieces; also *fig.* to destroy.

Shred (ʃred), *v.* Pa. t. **shredded,** pa. pple. **shredded, shred.** [OE. *scréadian* f. OTeut. **skraud-*: see prec.] **†1.** *trans.* To rid (a tree, vine, vineyard) of superfluous growth; to prune –1762. **†2.** To lop *off* (branches), esp. in pruning –1725. **†b.** To cut or strip *off*; to cut (a piece) *from* or *out of* –1823. **3.** To cut or tear into shreds or small thin strips or slices. late ME. **4.** To divide *into* small portions 1660. **b.** *intr.* To be reduced to shreds 1646. **5.** *trans.* To cut in two, sever, as with scissors;

chiefly with ref. to severing the thread of life. Now *rare.* 1565.

3. S. very fine a pound of suet 1756. Machinery for washing and shredding rags 1890. 4. Indivisibles, such as can't be shread 1674. 5. When ye s. with fatall knife His line SPENSER. So **Shr·edding** *vbl. sb.* [OE. *scréadung*], †pruning or lopping of trees; *concr.* a fragment; a shred (now *rare*); †*pl.* or *collect. sing.* prunings or loppings of trees.

Shred-pie. *Hist.* 1580. [prob. f. *shred*, ppl. a. of SHRED *v.*] A mince-pie.

Shrew (ʃrū), *sb.*[1] [OE. *scréawa, scrǽwa*, not found elsewhere in Teut.] Any of the small insectivorous mammals belonging to the genus *Sorex* or the family *Soricidæ*, much resembling mice but having a long sharp snout; a SHREWMOUSE.

Shrew (ʃrū), *sb.*[2] and *a.* ME. [perh. a fig. use of prec., with ref. to the superstitions as to the malignant influence of the animal.] †1. A wicked, evil-disposed, or malignant man; a mischievous or vexatious person; a rascal, villain. *spec.* the Devil –1650. †2. A thing of evil nature or influence; something troublesome or vexatious –1620. 3. A person, *esp.* (now only) a woman given to railing or scolding or other perverse or malignant behaviour; freq. a scolding or turbulent wife ME.

1. Such as were shrewes to their wiues DEKKER. 2. Enmitie, hatred, and ill will is a s. 1620. 3. To be a shrewe in the kitchin, a saint in the Church 1589.

†B. *adj.* = SHREWD (in various senses); wicked, evil-disposed; shrewish –1638.

†**Shrew,** *v.* Also **'shrew.** ME. [app. f. prec.; cf. BESHREW *v.*] *trans.* To curse; = BESHREW 2. –1668.

O vile proude cherl I shrewe his face CHAUCER.

Shrewd (ʃrūd), *a.* [ME. *shrewede*, f. SHREW *sb.*[2] + -ED[2]. Cf. *crabbed, dogged.*] 1. Depraved, wicked; evil-disposed, malignant. Also, malicious, mischievous. *dial.* †b. Of children: Naughty –1645. †c. Of animals: Bad-tempered; vicious, fierce –1630. †2. Of material things (*esp.* animals): Mischievous, hurtful; dangerous, injurious –1621. †3. Of things: Of evil nature, character, or influence –1678. †b. Of reputation, opinion, meaning: Evil, bad, unfavourable –1664. †c. Poor, unsatisfactory –1616. †4. Of events, affairs, conditions: Fraught or attended with evil or misfortune; having injurious or dangerous consequences; vexatious, irksome, hard; (of a task) difficult, dangerous –1821. †5. As an intensive, qualifying a word denoting something in itself bad, irksome, or undesirable: Grievous, serious, 'sore' –1819 †6. Of persons and their actions: Severe, harsh, stern –1654. 7. Of a blow, etc.: Severe, hard. *arch.* 1481. 8. Of a weapon, pain, etc.: Sharp, piercing, keen. *arch.* 1642. †9. Of a sign, token, etc.: Of ill omen; hence, strongly indicative (of something unfavourable) –1732. 10. Of a piece of evidence: Hard to get over, 'awkward'. *arch.* 1606. †11. Given to railing or scolding; shrewish. Also of language. –1661. 12. †Cunning, artful. Now only: Clever or keen-witted in practical affairs; astute, penetrating, or sagacious in action or speech 1520. b. Of action, speech, etc.: †Cunning, artful; characterized by penetration or practical sagacity 1589. 13. Of a suspicion or guess: Coming 'dangerously' near to the truth of the matter 1588.

1. That shrew'd and knauish spirit Cal'd Robin Good-fellow SHAKS. Phr. *S. turn*, a mischievous or malicious act (*arch.*); †a piece of misfortune, an accident. b. *L. L. L.* v. ii. 12. 2. An Ant..is a s. thing, in an Orchard, or a garden BACON. 4. Ah fowle, shrew'd newes SHAKS. 5. That is a s. loss SCOTT. 7. Me thought hee made a s. thrust at your Belly SHAKS. 8. *advb.* The ayre bites s.; it is an eager and An nipping winde SHAKS. 9. When a man is against reason, it is a s. sign reason is against him BERKELEY. 11. His curst and s. wife COVERDALE. S. words are sometimes improved into smart blows betwixt them FULLER. 12. A s. observer 1867. A woman of s. intellect and masculine character 1880. 13. I have a s. idea that it is a humbug THACKERAY. Hence **Shrew·d-ly** *adv.*, **-ness.**

Shrewish (ʃrū·iʃ), *a.* late ME. [f. SHREW *sb.*[2] + -ISH.] †1. Wicked, malignant –1481. 2. Of a woman: Having the character or disposition of a shrew; given to or characterized by scolding 1565. b. In wider sense: Ill-natured, ill-tempered; cross-grained 1596.

2. Shee was a s. snappish bawd, that wold bite off a mans nose with an answere NASHE. Hence **Shrew·ish-ly** *adv.*, **-ness.**

Shrewmouse (ʃrū·maus). *Pl.* **-mice.** Also hyphened and as two words. 1572. = SHREW *sb.*[1] (See MOUSE *sb.* I. 1 b.)

Shrewsbury (ʃrū·z-, ʃrōu·zbəri). The name of the county town of Shropshire, used *attrib.*

S. cake, a flat round crisp biscuit-like cake.

Shriek (ʃrīk), *sb.* 1590. [f. next.] An act of shrieking; a shrill, piercing, or wild cry expressive of terror or pain. Also, an utterance of loud high-pitched laughter. b. Applied to the wild cry of birds, etc. 1765. c. The loud high-pitched piercing sound produced by an instrument of music, the whistle of a locomotive, etc. 1599. d. *fig.* A hysterical exclamation 1853.

Whose mournfull cryes and shreekes to heaven ascend KYD. d. Virtuous shrieks of 'flattery', 'meanness',..and so forth KINGSLEY.

Shriek (ʃrīk), *v.* 1567. [Cf. SHRIKE *v.*] 1. *intr.* To utter a loud sharp shrill cry. a. of a human being in terror or pain; also, said of loud high-pitched laughter 1577. b. of the characteristic cry of certain animals 1567. c. of inanimate things 1596. 2. *trans.* To utter (a shriek); to utter (words) with a shriek or shrieks 1592. 3. To bring (oneself) into a certain condition by shrieking 1642.

1. Ghosts did shrieke and squeale about the streets SHAKS. b. The Owle shriek'd at thy birth SHAKS. c. The winter wind, which shrieks through the bare branches RUSKIN. 3. I..shriekt my self awake 1642. Hence **Shrie·ker**, one who shrieks or utters a shriek.

Shrie·k-owl. Now *rare.* 1567. [f. prec. + OWL *sb.*] The screech-owl.

Shrieval (ʃrī·văl), *a.* 1681. [f. *shrieve*, obs. var. SHERIFF + -AL.] Of or belonging to a sheriff.

Shrievalty (ʃrī·vălti). 1502. [f. as prec. + *-alty*, repr. OF. *-alte* (F. *-auté*):—L. *-alitatem*, as in *admiralty*, etc.] The office or dignity of sheriff; a sheriff's jurisdiction or term of office.

Shrift (ʃrift), *sb.* Now *arch.* or *Hist.* [OE. *scrift*, vbl. n. f. SHRIVE *v.*] †1. Penance imposed by the priest after confession. –late ME. 2. In certain contexts = absolution OE. †3. A confessor –1638. 4. Confession to a priest; auricular confession; also, the sacrament of penance OE. 5. An instance of this; a confession on a particular occasion ME. 6. Confession (*of* sin or wrong); admission (*of* guilt); revelation (*of* something private or secret) ME.

2. I need no other s. Than mine owne conscience 1635. 4. *To come, go to s.*, to resort to confession, seek the ministry of a priest in the sacrament of penance. 5. Phr. *To make one's s., to hear a s. Short s.*, orig. a brief space of time allowed for a criminal to make his confession before execution; hence, a brief respite; *to give short s. to*, to make short work of. Hence **Shrift** *v. trans.* to shrive (*rare*).

Shri·ft-fa·ther. *Obs.* exc. *arch.* ME. [f. SHRIFT *sb.* + FATHER *sb.*] A confessor.

Shrike (ʃraik), *sb.*[1] *Obs.* or *dial.* late ME. [f. SHRIKE *v.*] = SHRIEK *sb.*

Shrike (ʃraik), *sb.*[2] 1544. [app. repr. OE. *scríc, scréc* (glossing L. *turdus*), perh. used gen. for birds having shrill cries.] Any of the birds of the numerous species of the family *Laniidæ*, characterized by a strong hooked and toothed beak; the majority of them are insectivorous, but several species, as the (Great or European) Grey Shrike, *Lanius excubitor*, prey upon mice and small birds. b. Applied to similar birds of other families (e.g. *Prionopidæ*), e.g. CUCKOO, DRONGO, SWALLOW s.

Shrike (ʃraik), *v.* *Obs.* exc. *dial.* ME. [perh. repr. an OE. **scrícan* (cf. prec.).] = SHRIEK *v.* †Of birds: To pipe.

Shrill (ʃril), *sb.* 1591. [f. SHRILL *v.*] A shrill sound, cry, whistle, etc.

Shrill (ʃril), *a.* and *adv.* [ME. *shrille*, related to LG. *schrell* of sharp tone or taste.] A. *adj.* 1. Of voice, sound: Of a sharp high-pitched piercing tone. late ME. 2. Emitting or producing a sound of this kind 1508. 3. Characterized or accompanied by sharp high-pitched sounds 1725. 4. *transf.* Keen, sharp, pungent; poignant 1608.

1. The s. Matin Song Of Birds MILT. 2. The first larum of the cock's s. throat COWPER. Churl and noble, fair lady and s. fish-wife 1866. The blast of a s. bugle SCOTT. 3. Let winds be s., let waves roll high BYRON.

B. *adv.* With a shrill voice or tone; shrilly. Now *rare.* ME. b. Qualifying a ppl. adj. used attrib. (usu. with hyphen) 1562.

Through the high wood echoing s. MILT. b. The ..s.-piping reed MORRIS. Hence **Shri·llish** *a.* **Shri·lly** *a.* (*poet.*) and *adv.* **Shri·llness.**

Shrill (ʃril), *v.* ME. [f. SHRILL *a.* Cf. G. *schrillen.*] 1. *intr.* Of a voice, cry: To sound shrilly. Hence of noises, the wind, or the like, or a place echoing with sound. 2. To speak, cry, or sing with a shrill voice; to make a shrill noise 1440. 3. *trans.* To utter, give forth (a sound, cry, words) in shrill tones; to exclaim or proclaim with a shrill voice 1595.

1. A wind, that shrills All night in a waste land TENNYSON. Breake we our pypes, that shrild as lowde as Larke SPENSER. The Ouzell shrills, the Ruddock warbles soft SPENSER. 3. Harke..How poor Andromache shrils her dolour forth SHAKS.

Shrimp (ʃrimp). ME. [prob. cogn. w. MHG. (MG.) *schrimpen* to shrink up.] 1. Any of the slender, long-tailed, long-legged (chiefly marine) crustaceans of the genus *Crangon* and allied genera, closely related to the prawns; esp. *C. vulgaris*, the common s., which inhabits the sand on the coasts of Great Britain and is an article of food. 2. A diminutive or puny person (*rarely* thing). Chiefly *contempt.* late ME.

2. When he was a babe, a childe, a shrimpe, Thus did he strangle Serpents SHAKS. Hence **Shri·mper,** one who catches shrimps; also, a vessel engaged in shrimping. **Shri·mping** *gerund* and *vbl. sb.* catching shrimps. **Shri·mpish** *a.* diminutive, puny, insignificant.

Shrine (ʃrəin), *sb.* [OE. *scrín*, ad. L. *scrinium* case or chest for books or papers.] †1. A box, coffer; a cabinet, chest –1658. 2. The box, casket, or other repository in which the relics of a saint are preserved. Also, a tomb-like erection of rich workmanship, enclosing the relics of a saint. OE. b. A receptacle containing an object of religious veneration; occas. a niche for sacred images 1526. 3. A case or casket for a dead body; also, a tomb or cenotaph of an elaborate kind. late ME. 4. *transf.* That which encloses, enshrines, or screens, or in which something dwells. late ME. 5. A place where worship is offered or devotions are paid to a saint or deity; a temple, church 1629. b. *fig.* in contexts referring to the veneration or idolizing of some person or thing 1575.

2. The Miracles at the Shrines and Sepulchres of the holy Martyrs 1638. 4. You living powres enclosed in stately s. Of growing trees SIDNEY. 5. Apollo from his s. Can no more divine MILT. b. Worshippers at the s. of Mammon! 1853.

Shrine (ʃrəin), *v.* ME. [f. prec.] 1. *trans.* To enclose (relics) in a shrine; to provide (a saint or deity) with a shrine or sanctuary. Now *rare.* 2. To enclose, envelop, engird, as a shrine or sanctuary does the body or the image of a saint 1577. 3. To enshrine in one's heart or thoughts 1579.

1. Believe a Goddess shrin'd in ev'ry tree POPE. 2. Th' Almightie Father where he sits Shrin'd in his Sanctuarie of Heav'n secure MILT In painting her I shrined her face Mid mystic trees ROSSETTI. 3. The man of real genius..has the feeling of truth already shrined in his own breast HAZLITT.

Shrink (ʃriŋk), *v.* Pa. t. **shrank** (ʃræŋk), pa. pple. **shrunk** (ʃrʊŋk). [OE. *scrincan* = MDu. *schrinken*, Sw. *skrynka* to wrinkle.] I. *intr.* †1. To wither or shrivel through withdrawal of vital fluid or failure of strength –1611. 2. To become reduced in size, volume, or extent; *esp.* to contract through heat, cold, or moisture. Also with *up, away.* ME. b. Of a textile fabric: To contract when wetted 1483. 3. To draw the limbs together, bring the body into a small compass; to cower, huddle *together*; (of the body) to contract as with pain, fear, or cold; (of a plant) to shrivel or curl *up* OE. 4. In immaterial sense: To be contracted or reduced in extent; to be drawn together *into* certain limits 1449. 5. To move *backward*, retire, or retreat *into* a cavity, shelter, or place of refuge; to draw oneself or itself *in.* late ME. 6. To withdraw *from* a place or position, esp. in a secret or furtive manner; to turn *aside, away, back*, etc. furtively or nimbly; to slip or slink *away.* Now *rare.* late ME. 7. To draw *back* or give way so as to avoid physical contact or conflict; to recoil through physical weakness or lack of courage or with abhorrence *from* 1513. †b. To give way; to collapse –1616. 8.

To refuse or hesitate to act in the face of anything irksome, grievous, horrible, or distasteful; to recoil mentally or morally 1470. †9. To be a deserter or rebel; to fall *away from* duty or allegiance, or *from* a person -1594.

1. His synewis shronke and withdrewe them CAXTON. 2. When a body of water is cooled, it shrinks in bulk HUXLEY. b. Patent flannel, which does not s. in washing 1879. 3. Isaac shrunk together, and was silent SCOTT. 4. Are all thy Conquests, Glories, Triumphes, Spoiles, Shrunke to this little Measure? SHAKS. 5. Jorian..shrunk in and became impenetrable as a hedgehog READE. 7. She shrunk back from his grasp SCOTT. b. *Cor.* v. iv. 20. 8. His herte is stablished, he wil not shrencke COVERDALE *Ps.* cxii. Opinions which he never shrunk from expressing 1891. 9. *Rich. III*, v. iii. 222.

II. *trans.* 1. To cause to contract or be reduced in size, volume, or extent; to cause to contract by moisture, heat, or cold; to cause (a limb, sinew, plant) to wither or (the skin) to wrinkle. Also with *up.* late ME. b. *spec.* To treat (a textile material) with water so that it may not shrink after it is made up 1856. c. *Mech.* To cause (a piece, e.g. the tire of a wheel) to be fixed tightly *on* (*to*) another (which it is intended to fit) by heating it, slipping it into place when sufficiently expanded, and then rapidly cooling it 1839. 2. To draw (the body, the limbs, oneself) into a smaller compass. late ME. 3. In immaterial sense: To reduce to smaller limits or compass 1628. †4. To cause to withdraw or disappear; to draw *in* (the horns, the claws); also with *back, up.* Hence *allus.* -1713. 5. To draw (the head, hand, etc.) *aside, back,* or *away* in a furtive, ashamed, or retiring manner. Now *rare.* 1489. †b. = SHRUG *v.* 3 -1720.

1. To shrinke mine Arme vp like a wither'd Shrub SHAKS. Return Alpheus, the dread voice is past, That shrunk thy streams MILT. 2. Her body huge she shrank MORRIS. 3. Logical cobwebbery shrinks itself together CARLYLE. 4. The Libyc Hammon shrinks his horn MILT. 5. b. Phr. *To s. up one's shoulders*: to shrug one's shoulders; *fig.* (with *at*) to regard with displeasure, aversion, or indifference. Hence **Shrink** *sb.* an act of shrinking or flinching. **Shri·nker,** one who shrinks or recoils from duty, danger, or the like. **Shri·nking-ly** *adv.*

Shrinkage (ʃri·ŋkėdʒ). 1800. [f. SHRINK *v.* + -AGE.] 1. The act or fact of shrinking; reduction in the size or volume of a substance or material due to contraction such as is caused by heat, cold, or wet. 2. The amount of such contraction or loss in bulk, volume, or measurement 1862. b. *Gun-making.* In shrinking on hoops or tubes, the difference between the inner diameter of the outer cylinder and the outer diameter of the inner cylinder 1891. 3. Of immaterial things: Diminution or reduction in quantity, amount, or size; depreciation or decrease in value; the amount of this 1879.

3. The failure is attributed to bad debts, s. in the value of goods, and the withdrawal of capital 1879.

Shrive (ʃrəiv), *v. arch.* Pa. t. **shrove** (ʃrōᵘv), pa. pple. **shriven** (ʃri·v'n). [Com. Teut.; OE. *scrīfan*; ad. L. *scribere* to write.] 1. *trans.* In OE. (const. dat.) To impose penance upon (a person); hence, to administer absolution to; to hear the confession of. b. *absol.* or *intr.* To perform the office of a confessor; to exercise the ministry of absolution; to hear confessions (*rare*) OE. 2. *pass.* To 'take shrift'; to be confessed; to make one's confession and receive absolution and penance OE. 3. *refl.* To make one's confession, go to confession, confess ME. 4. *intr.* To confess one's sins, go to confession ME. †5. *trans.* To reveal, disclose -1818. 6. To relieve (one) *of* a burden 1604.

1. Giue me leaue To shriue her; lest shee should dye vn-absolu'd 1633. 2. You ought first to bee shriven of one of the Monkes 1570. 3. Let me s. me clean, and die TENNYSON. 4. And who art thou, thou Gray Brother, That I should s. to thee? SCOTT. 6. A..tomb: Such as to look on shrives The heart of half its care R. BRIDGES. Hence **Shri·ver,** one who shrives, a confessor. **Shri·ving** *vbl. sb.* shrift.

Shrivel (ʃri·v'l), *v.* 1588. [Origin unkn.] 1. *intr.* To become contracted and wrinkled or curled up, as from great heat or cold. Also with *up, away.* b. *transf.* and *fig.* To be reduced to an inanimate or inefficient condition; (of a person) to shrink physically or mentally 1680. 2. *trans.* To cause to be shrunk into wrinkles. Often with *up.* 1608.

1. That his nose might be shrivelled with cold 1798. b. Undeveloped faculties that s. for want of using 1887. 2. A fire from heaven came and shrivell'd up Their bodies SHAKS. Hence **Shri·vel** *sb.* something shrivelled up.

Shriven (ʃri·v'n), *ppl. a.* 1846. [pa. pple. of SHRIVE *v.*] Confessed, absolved.

Shroff (ʃrǫf), *sb.* 1618. [Anglo-Ind. corruption of Pers. *saraf.*] A banker or money-changer in the East; in the Far East, a native expert employed to detect bad coin. Hence **Shroff** *v. trans.* to examine (coin) in order to separate the genuine from the base. **Shro·ffage,** the commission charged for shroffing coin.

Shroud (ʃraud), *sb.*¹ [OE. *scrūd,* f. OTeut. **skrūđ-*, lengthened wk.-grade of **skreuđ-* to cut (see SHRED *sb.*).] †1. A garment; an article of clothing; *sing.* and *pl.* (one's) clothes, clothing -1638. 2. The white cloth or sheet in which a corpse is laid out for burial; a winding-sheet 1570. ¶ By association with the black of mourning, *shroud* has received the epithet *sable* 1637. †3. A place or dwelling which affords shelter; a shelter, esp. one of a slight or temporary kind -1657. 4. *pl.* (rarely *sing.*) A crypt, vault. Now *Hist.* 1549. †5. Shadow, shade; *fig.* protection -1611. 6. A thing serving as a covering or protection; a covering, screen, veil, 'cloak', disguise. Now somewhat *rhet.* 1558. 7. *techn.* a. Either of the two annular plates at the periphery of a water-wheel, forming the ends of the buckets 1759. b. A rim or flange cast on the ends of the teeth of a gear-wheel 1797.

2. Bid fair peace be to my sable srowd MILT. Soon the grave must be your home And your only suit a s. COWPER. 3. Run to your shrouds, within these Brakes and Trees MILT. 4. A church vnder the ground, like to the shrouds in Pauls HAKLUYT. 5. *Ant. & Cl.* III. xiii. 71. 6. A grey s. of rain sweeping up from the westward 1850.

Comb.: **s.-brass,** a memorial brass in which the deceased is represented in his s.; **-plate** = 7 a.

Shroud (ʃraud), *sb.*² late ME. [prob. a use of prec.] *pl.* A set of ropes, usu. in pairs, leading from the head of a mast and serving to relieve the latter of lateral strain; they form part of the standing rigging of a ship. Also *collect. sing.* b. *sing.* Any one of these 1748.

Shroud (ʃraud), *sb.*³ Now *dial.* 1475. [Formally identical with SHROUD *sb.*¹, but in sense derived from the sense 'to cut' of the root.] a. *collect. sing.* and *pl.* Loppings of a tree. b. (chiefly *pl.*) A branch or bough.

Shroud (ʃraud), *v.*¹ ME. [f. SHROUD *sb.*¹] †1. *trans.* To clothe; to adorn, deck -1520. 2. To give shelter or housing to; to shelter. *arch.* 1450. b. *intr.* To take shelter or refuge. *arch.* 1579. †3. To cover so as to protect; to screen from injury or attack; to afford protection to -1810. †4. To conceal in a secret place or in a secret manner -1642. 5. To hide from view, as by a veil, darkness, cloud; to cover so as to conceal; to screen, veil. late ME. 6. In immaterial sense: To screen from observation; to veil under an appearance or 'show'; occas. with implication of disguise or concealment for an evil purpose. late ME. 7. To put a shroud on (a corpse), lay in a shroud; hence, to prepare for burial, bury 1577. 8. *Mech.* To furnish (a water-wheel, cogs) with shrouds 1834.

2. Ill wast thou shrouded then, O patient Son of God MILT. b. I will here shrowd till the dregges of the storme be past SHAKS. 4. I'll shrowde my selfe behinde the Arras SHAKS. 5. The hills, shrouded in grey mist 1902. 6. Its proceedings were impenetrably shrouded from the public eye 1838. 7. He has been showrded—full three hundred Years 1718. Hence **Shrou·ding** *vbl. sb.* the action of the vb. *Mech.* the shrouds of a water-wheel.

Shroud (ʃraud), *v.*² *local.* 1577. [f. SHROUD *sb.*³] *trans.* To lop (a tree or its branches); occas. *absol.*

Shrove Monday. 1450. [See SHROVE-TIDE.] The Monday before Shrove Tuesday.

†**Shrove Sunday.** 1463. [See next.] Quinquagesima Sunday -1843.

Shro·ve-tide. late ME. [Origin obsc.; the first element is conn. w. SHRIVE, and refers to the custom of being shriven in preparation for Lent.] The period comprising Quinquagesima Sunday and the two following days, 'Shrove' Monday and Tuesday.

Shrove Tuesday. 1500. [See prec.] The Tuesday immediately preceding Ash Wednesday; often called *pancake day.* †b. *allus.* A time of merriment -1621.

Shro·ving, *vbl. sb. Obs.* exc. *dial.* 1537. [f. *shrove-* in SHROVE-TIDE.] The keeping of Shrove-tide; the merrymaking characteristic of this season; festive rejoicing.

Shrub¹ (ʃrɒb). late ME. [app. repr. OE. *scrybb* shrubbery, underwood.] 1. A woody plant smaller than a tree; *spec.* in *Bot.* a perennial plant having several woody stems growing from the same root. †2. = SCRUB *sb.*¹ II. 2. -1690.

2. The Gyants in grace, as well as the weak and shrubs BUNYAN.

Shrub² (ʃrɒb). 1747. [perh. metathetic ad. Arab. *shurb* drink, draught.] 1. A prepared drink made with the juice of orange or lemon (or other acid fruit), sugar, and rum (or other spirit). 2. *U.S.* A cordial or syrup made from the juice of the raspberry, with vinegar and sugar 1860.

Shrubbery (ʃrɒ·bəri). 1748. [f. SHRUB¹ + -ERY.] 1. A plantation of shrubs; a plot planted with shrubs. 2. Shrubs collectively or in a mass 1777.

Shrubby (ʃrɒ·bi), *a.* 1540. [f. SHRUB¹ + -Y¹.] 1. Having the habit, growth, or size of a shrub 1581. b. In specific names of plants, often rendering L. *fruticosus* 1597. 2. Of the nature of or consisting of shrubs 1540. 3. Covered, planted, or overgrown with shrubs 1598. 4. Characteristic of a shrub 1776.

2. A lowe shrubbie boggie wood 1633. 3. Due west it rises from this s. point MILT.

†**Shruff.** 1541. [perh. ad. G. *schroff* fragment of mineral.] Old brass (or copper) -1825.

Shrug (ʃrɒg), *sb.* 1460. [f. SHRUG *v.*] †1. A tug, pull, shake. 2. A raising and contraction of the shoulders to express dislike, disdain, indifference, or the like 1594.

2. He is a lively man, full of chat, and foreign shrugs and gestures MME D'ARBLAY.

Shrug (ʃrɒg), *v.* late ME. [Origin obsc.] 1. *intr.* To shiver; to shudder for cold or fear. Now *rare* or *Obs.* 2. To raise (and contract) the shoulders, esp. as an expression of disdain, indifference, disclaiming responsibility, etc. 1450. 3. *trans.* To raise and contract (the shoulders) in this way 1547. †4. *intr.* (and *refl.*) To move the body from side to side as with uneasiness, or as a gesture of joy or self-satisfaction; to fidget about -1652. 5. To jerk, pull or tug *up. US.* 1807.

1. He will be chill, and s. for cold 1580. 2. I was quite shocked for her, and could only s. in dismay MME D'ARBLAY. 3. He..shrugs his shoulder when you talk of Securities STEELE.

Shrunk (ʃrɒŋk), *ppl. a.* 1530. [pa. pple. of SHRINK *v.*] Contracted or reduced in size; drawn together into a smaller compass. (Now *rare* in attrib. use.) So **Shru·nken** *ppl. a.* OE.

‖**Shuba** (ʃū·bă). 1591. [Russ.] A fur gown or greatcoat.

Shuck (ʃɒk), *sb.* Chiefly *dial.* and *U.S.* 1674. [Origin unkn.] 1. A husk, pod, or shell; *esp.* the outer coverings or strippings of Indian corn, chestnuts, hickory nuts, etc. b. The shell of an oyster or clam 1881. 2. As a type of something valueless 1847. 3. *pl.* As an interj. of contempt or indifference 1885.

Shuck, *v. U.S.* 1819. [f. SHUCK *sb.*] *trans.* To remove the shucks from (corn, etc.). **Shu·cker,** one who shucks oysters or clams.

Shudder (ʃɒ·dəɹ), *sb.* 1607. [f. next.] An act of shuddering; a convulsive tremor of the body occasioned by fear, repugnance, or chill. Phr. *To give one the shudders.*

Shudder (ʃɒ·dəɹ), *v.* [ME. *shod(d)re,* frequent. f. the root **skŭd-* to shake (see -ER⁵).] 1. *intr.* To have a convulsive tremor of the body caused by fear, abhorrence, or cold; hence, to tremble with horror or dread. 2. To move tremulously, vibrate, quiver 1849.

1. I shuddered, and drew involuntarily back, when ..I saw Mr. Burke MME D'ARBLAY. My mind shudders when I think of her awful, awful situation THACKERAY. Hence **Shu·dderingly** *adv.*

Shuffle (ʃɒ·f'l), *sb.* 1628. [f. next.] †1. A shifting from one place to another; an interchange of positions -1692. 2. A tricky exchange or alteration (of arguments, expedients, etc.) 1641. 3. An evasive trick, evasion, subterfuge 1628. 4. Movement of the feet along the ground without lifting them; a gait characterized by such movement 1847. 5. A dance of a rude kind, in which the feet are shuffled along the floor 1659. **6.** The act of shuffling playing-cards; also *ellipt.* (a player's) turn to shuffle 1651.

1. The unguided agitation and rude shuffles of Matter BENTLEY. 2. Life becomes a mere s. of expedients 1860. 3. You'll answer it now, yes or no, plain word and no s. 1893. 4. The bear ..dancing him from side to side in its heavy s. L. HUNT. 5. *Double s.*: one in which two movements of the same kind are made by each foot alternately; also *fig.*

Shuffle (ʃʌ·f'l), *v.* 1532. [ad. or cogn. w. LG. *schüffeln* to walk clumsily or with dragging feet; frequent. f. Teut. root **skuf-* (*skub-*) to SHOVE.] **1.** *intr.* To move the feet along the ground without lifting them, so as to make a scraping noise; to walk with such a motion of the feet; to go with clumsy steps or a shambling gait. Also said of the feet. 1598. **b.** To move restlessly or fidget in one's seat 1881. **c.** *trans.* To move (the feet) along the ground or floor without raising them 1576. **d.** To perform (a dance or a dance-step) with a shuffle. Also *absol.* or *intr.* 1818. **2.** To manipulate (the cards in a pack) so as to change their relative position. Formerly freq. in allusive use, *to s. the cards* = to manipulate matters. Also *absol.* and *intr.* 1570. **3.** To push along, about, or together in a disorderly mass or heap, or in a manner suggesting the shuffling of feet 1567. **4.** To huddle or jumble *together* indiscriminately, incongruously, or without order. 1570. **5.** To smuggle (a thing) *in* or *into* (something else); to thrust *in* somehow or other 1565. †**b.** To remove, put *aside* or *away* in a hurried, secret, or underhand manner -1754. **c.** To bring, put, or thrust *into* or *out of* a position or condition in a haphazard, underhand, or shirking manner, or by rough-and-ready means 1628. **d.** *To s. off*: to get rid of evasively; to shirk (a duty or obligation) 1601. **6.** *intr.* or *refl.* To get *in*, *into*, or *out of* a position or condition, by some means or other, in an underhand, shifty, or evasive manner 1565. **b.** *To s.* †*over*, *through*: to perform hurriedly or perfunctorily, get through somehow 1656. †**c.** To make scrambling efforts, scuffle -1625. **7.** To act in a shifting or evasive manner; to shift one's ground in argument, etc.; to make use of deceitful pretences or shifty answers 1598. †**8.** *To s. up*, to get or put together hastily or in a perfunctory manner -1659. **9.** To put (a thing) *off from* one *to* another, or *upon* a person 1612. **10.** To shift from one place to another; to move *about* this way and that 1694. **11.** To put (a thing) *into* a receptacle, put or take (a thing) *on*, *off*, etc. in a clumsy or fumbling manner 1694. **b.** *intr.* To get *into* an article of clothing in a clumsy or fumbling manner 1865.

1. The Bear..shuffling along at a strange Rate DE FOE. 2. [They] had shuffled their cards so cunningly as to be out of the reach of law 1643. They draw, they sit, they s., cut and deal CRABBE. 4. When Lots are shuffled in a Lap, Urn, or Pitcher 1685. Good Days, bad Days so shuffled together LAMB. 5. b. Her Mother..hath appointed That he shall likewise s. her away SHAKS. c. Thus was he shuffled into your father's Employment 1729. d. When we have shuffel'd off this mortall coile SHAKS. 6. He shuffles out of the consequences by vague.. charges of undue influence 1887. b. The service..was shuffled through..coldly and unfeelingly W. IRVING. c. Your life, good Master, Must s. for it selfe SHAKS. 7. I..am faine to s.: to hedge, and to lurch SHAKS. 9. Is he trying to s. off guilt from his own shoulders? 1875. 11. He shuffled off his slippers at the threshold DISRAELI. Hence **Shu·ffler**, one who acts in a shifty or evasive manner; one who shuffles cards. **Shu·ffling** *vbl. sb.* (in various senses).

Shuffle-board: see SHOVEL-BOARD.

Shu·ffling, *ppl. a.* 1596. [f. SHUFFLE *v.* + -ING[2].] **1.** That shuffles in walking. Hence, of a walk, pace, gait: Consisting of or characterized by a shuffle. **2.** Of persons: Given to shifty or evasive action or behaviour 1616. **b.** Of action, conduct, speech: Evasive, shifty 1644.

Hence **Shu·fflingly** *adv.*

Shun (ʃʌn), *v.* Pa. t. and pa. pple. **shunned** (ʃʌnd). [OE. *scunian* wk. vb., not found in other Teut. langs.] †**1.** *trans.* To abhor, detest, loathe -ME. †**2.** To seek safety by concealment or flight from (an enemy, his pursuit, etc.) -1638. †**b.** To evade (a blow, missile) -1667. **3.** To avoid (now always to avoid persistently or habitually) from repugnance, fear, or caution; to keep away from; to eschew, abstain carefully from ME. **4.** To escape (a threatened evil, an unwelcome task). Now *rare* or *Obs.* ME. †**5.** *intr.* To shrink back physically; to move or go aside (so as to escape or evade some person or thing); to fly (from an enemy, etc.); also with *aside*, *away* -1600.

2. b. I forewarn thee, s. His deadly arrow MILT. 3. I would say, s. late hours BERKELEY. The tim'rous hare..Scarce shuns me COWPER. They rode on all day, shunning towns and villages MACAULAY. *transf.* Scarcity and want shall s. you SHAKS. 4. No man of woman born Coward or brave, can s. his destiny 1870. Hence **Shu·nless** *a.* that cannot be shunned.

'Shun! Abbrev. of *attention!* as a word of command.

Shunt (ʃʌnt), *sb.* 1842. [f. next.] **1.** An act of shunting 1884. **2.** *Electr.* A derived circuit introduced to diminish the current flowing through the main circuit; esp. a resistance coil connected in parallel with a dynamo, etc.; more fully *s. circuit*, *coil* 1863. **b.** *Telegr.* A device for diverting the current from one line to another; a switch 1878. **3.** *Railways.* A switch 1842. **4.** *Ordnance.* Short for *s. rifled gun*, also, a curve in the rifling of a shunt rifled gun 1864.

2. *In s.*, connected so as to form a multiple current. *attrib.* and *Comb.*: **s. dynamo**, a s.-wound dynamo; **s. line, road**, a railway siding; **-rifling**, a method of rifling cannon so that the projectile undergoes a s. or lateral change of position in the process of loading; so *s.* (*rifled*) *gun*, etc.; **-wound** *a.* having the s. circuit wound in parallel with the main circuit.

Shunt (ʃʌnt), *v.* ME. [Origin obsc.; perh. a deriv. of SHUN *v.*] †**1.** *intr.* To start or go aside (so as to avoid some person or thing); to shy; to hang back -1550. **2.** *trans.* To shove or push aside or out of the way. Also *intr.* of a thing, to move from its proper position, to give way. Chiefly *dial.* 1706. **3.** To move (a train or some portion of it) from the main line to a side-track or from one line of rails to another; also to move *back* 1849. **b.** *fig.* To side-track; also, to get rid of 1858. **4.** *intr.* To move off the main line; to move from one line of rails to another 1851. **5.** *Electr.* To divert (a portion of an electric current) by means of a shunt; also, to divert current from (a galvanometer) 1873.

3. b. Practically, General Peel is not shunted, but shelved 1858. Hence **Shu·nter**, a railwayman who shunts trains; a mechanical device to facilitate shunting; (*slang*) an able organizer.

Shush, redupl. var. of SH *int.*; also (by contact with *hush*) as vb., to hush, be silent.

Shut (ʃʌt), *sb.* 1460. [f. next.] **1.** Something which shuts off or closes up; *esp.* a hinged or sliding door or plate for closing an aperture. **2.** The action, time, or place of shutting. Chiefly *poet.*, the close (of day), the closing in (of evening). 1667. **3.** A join, mend, splice; a weld, the line of junction of two pieces of welded metal 1721.

2. When the chill rain begins at s. of eve KEATS. 3. *Cold s.*, an imperfect weld due to chill; an imperfection in a casting, caused by the flow of liquid metal on a chilled surface.

Shut (ʃʌt), *v.* Pa. t. and pa. pple. **shut.** [OE. *scyttan* :—prehist. **skuttjan*, f. **skut-*, wk. grade of the root of SHOOT *v.*] †**1.** *trans.* To put (a lock, bar, bolt, etc.) in position so as to fasten a door, etc. -1633. †**2.** To fasten (a door or aperture) with a lock or bar- 1825. **3.** To bring (a door, gate, window, lid, etc.) into the position in which it closes the aperture ME. **b.** *intr.* for *refl.* Of a door, etc.: To close of its own accord, or by some unseen agency. Also, to admit of being shut, or of being shut in a specified manner 1470. **4.** *trans.* To close (the eyes, mouth) by bringing together the outward covering parts. ME. **5.** To close by folding up or bringing together of parts (e.g. a book, a clasp-knife, one's hand). Also *intr.* for *refl.* late ME. **6.** *trans.* To weld (cf. SHUT *sb.* 3) 1490. **7.** To close (an aperture) by placing something upon it or by drawing something across it; to stop up (a road) with obstacles or barriers. late ME. **8.** To prevent access to or egress from (a place, building, etc.) by closing the doors or apertures. Now *rare* exc. in *to s. a shop.* ME. **9.** To enclose, secure, or confine (a person or thing) *in* or *within* a place, building, or receptacle; to put *in* a place and shut the door. Also *refl.* ME. †**10. a.** To bar or exclude (a person) *from* some possession or enjoyment; to restrain *from* doing something -1719. **b.** To separate (one thing) *from* another; to cut off from view. Now *rare.* 1697. **11.** To set free *from*, relieve *of* (something troublesome). *Obs.* exc. *pass.* (*dial.* and *colloq.*) 1500.

3. The Gate used to be kept shut 1737 She..shut her own door briskly on herself THACKERAY. *transf.* Resistance to power, has shut the door of the House of Commons to one man BURKE 4. fig. *To s.* (*one's*) *eyes to*, *against*, *on*, to ignore, refuse to recognize or consider; That man is to be pitied who can s. his eyes to facts KINGSLEY. *To s.* (one's) *mouth*, to cease from speaking, to hold one's tongue; so (vulgar) *to shut* (one's) *head*, *face*. *To s.* (another's) *mouth*, to render unable to speak, reply, find fault, disclose secrets, etc. 5. The Scene Shuts DRYDEN. She.. shut the piano 1863. I can't s. the clasp of my journal 1905. 7. They would..for ever s. the Passage into Abyssinia JOHNSON. 8. Bank-Holiday with the shops of London shut 1886. *To s. one's purse*, etc., *against*, to refuse help to. 9. You s. yourselves within your park walls and garden gates RUSKIN. 10. b. A turn in the road shut them from his sight 1831. 11. Phr. *To be, get shut of*, *to s. one's hands of*: to be rid of, free from.

With advs. **S. down. a.** *intr.* To be closed with a lid; to come close down like a lid. Of fog, night: To come down and blot out the view. **b.** *trans.* To close by lowering, etc. **c.** To close (a manufactory). **d.** *absol.* To stop working. **S. in. a.** *trans.* To prevent access to or confine (a person or thing) by shutting a door, etc. or closing a receptacle. Also *refl.* **b.** To enclose with a barrier, hem in. †**c.** *intr.* Of the day, evening, etc.: To close in, grow dusk. **d.** To be closed in (to the view). **S. off. a.** *trans.* To prevent the passage of; to cut off (steam, etc.) by the closing of a valve or tap. **b.** To cut off, separate *from.* **S. out. a.** *trans.* To exclude (persons, also commodities, light, air) from a place, situation, circumstances, etc.; to deny (a person) right of entry to a place, etc. **b.** To screen from view. **S. to.** *trans.* To close (a door); †to shoot (a bolt); also *intr.* for *refl.* **S. up. a.** *trans* To place or store away in a closed box or other receptacle; to keep from view or use; to confine within bounds. **b.** (*a*) To confine (a person or animal) in prison or some kind of restraint; to keep in seclusion; to hem (a person) round in order to prevent his escape. Also, (chiefly *refl.*) to shut the door on (a person within a place, room, etc.) to prevent access; *pass.* to be closeted with. (*b*) In some games of skill: To surround (the pieces of an opponent) so that a move becomes impossible without capture. **c.** To close (an entrance, aperture, etc.); to pull (a door, window, etc.) to. Also *occas.* to shut permanently (the eyes, mouth). Now *rare.* **d.** To close, prevent access to or exit from (a place, house, shop, room, etc.); *Agric.* to close (a meadow) to pasture, in preparation for a hay crop; to close (a box or other receptacle); *Naut.* to stop the leaks in (a ship). *To s. up shop*, see SHOP *sb.* **e.** To close (something) by folding together; to fold (something) up. Also *intr.* for *refl.* **f.** *intr.* Of a person: To bring one's remarks to a close (now *rare*). **g.** *trans.* To cause (a person) to stop talking, to reduce to silence. **h.** *intr.* To shut one's mouth, to stop talking (*colloq.* or *slang*).

Shute (ʃūt). *dial.* 1790. [Partly a dial. form of SHOOT *sb.*, partly a variant spelling of CHUTE.] **1.** A channel or open trough for conveying water, esp. to a lower level; a gutter fixed beneath the eaves of a building. **2.** A steep (artificial) channel or enclosed passage, down which ore, coal, grain, etc. is 'shot' to reach a receptacle below 1847.

Shut-eye (ʃʌ·təi). *slang.* 1919. [f. SHUT *v.*] Sleep.

Shutter (ʃʌ·təɹ), *sb.* 1542. [f. SHUT *v.* + -ER [1].] **1.** *gen.* One who or something which shuts. **2.** *spec.* **a.** A movable wooden or iron screen, applied to the outside or the inside of a window, to shut out the light or to ensure privacy or safety 1683. **b.** A folding cover hinged to a picture-frame in order to protect the picture from light, dust, etc. 1700. **c.** *Photogr.* A device for opening and closing the aperture of a lens in order to regulate the duration of the exposure 1862. **d.** *Founding.* A gate or movable partition designed to cut off the passage to a mould from the channel in which the molten metal flows 1856. **e.** *pl. Organ-building.* The louvre boards forming one or more sides of the swell-box, which regulate the volume of sound from the swell-organ 1881. **f.** A lid or slide for obscuring the light of a lamp or lantern 1910.

2. a. *To put up the shutters*, to bring one's business to a close for the day or permanently. Hence **Shu·tter** *v. trans.* to close with a s.; *refl.* to close oneself *in*, shut oneself *off*, with shutters. **Shu·ttered** (ʃʌ·təɹd) *ppl. a.* closed or provided with shutters.

Shuttle (ʃʋ·t'l), *sb.*[1] [OE. *scytel* :—prehist. **skutil-*, f. Teut. root **skut-*; see SHOOT *v.*] †**1.** A dart, missile, arrow. OE. only. **2.** An instrument used in weaving for passing the thread of the weft to and fro from one edge of the cloth to the other between the threads of the warp ME. **3.** *transf.* **a.** A thread-carrying device in the form of a weaver's shuttle, used for knotting, tatting, and embroidery 1767. **b.** A reciprocating thread-holder in a sewing-machine, which carries the lower thread through the loop of the upper one to make a lock-stitch 1846. **c.** A curved type-bar (in some type-writers) guided into position by a race 1911. **4.** A shuttlecock. Also the game. *Obs.* exc. in *Badminton.* 1440. **5.** †**a.** A trochoid shell. **b.** In full *weaver's s.*, a shuttle-shell, esp. *Radius volva*; also, the shell of this gastropod. 1750.

Comb.: **s. armature** *Electr.* an armature shaped like an elongated shuttle, the wires being run longitudinally in grooves; **-box**, †(*a*) the cavity in the side of a s. to hold the spindle; (*b*) a tray or case at the end of the s.-race to receive the s.; **-race**, the ledge or track along which the s. passes; **-shell**, a gasteropod of the genus *Radius*; **-train**, a train running a short distance to and fro, as on a short branch-line.

Shuttle (ʃʋ·t'l), *sb.*[2] 1440. [f. SHUT *v.* + -LE.] **1.** A floodgate which opens to allow the flow and regulate the supply of water in a mill-stream. Also, a similar gate in a drain. **2.** A small gate through which metal is allowed to pass from the trough to the mould 1858.

Shuttle (ʃʋ·t'l), *v.* *Obs.* exc. *dial.* 1550. [f. SHUTTLE *sb.*[1]] **1.** *trans.* To move (a thing) briskly to and fro like a shuttle. Also, to throw swiftly. **2.** *intr.* To go or move backwards and forwards like a shuttle; to travel quickly to and fro 1823.

1. A face of most extreme mobility, which he shuttles about..in a very singular manner while speaking CARLYLE.

Shuttlecock (ʃʋ·t'lkɒk), *sb.* 1522. [f. SHUTTLE *sb.*[1] + COCK *sb.*[1]] **1.** A small piece of cork, or similar light material, fitted with a crown or circle of feathers, used in the game of 'battledore and shuttlecock', and also in badminton. **2.** The game (more fully *battledore and s.*) in which the shuttlecock is hit backwards and forwards between two players using the battledore, or by one player into the air as many times as possible without dropping it 1599. **3.** quasi-*adj.* Light, tossed hither and thither 1660.

1. *fig.* This Reform question ought not to be made the s. of party 1858. Hence **Shu·ttlecock** *v. trans.* to throw, send backwards and forwards or to toss like a s.; *intr.* to move or go backwards and forwards.

Shy (ʃəi), *sb.*[1] *Pl.* **shies.** 1791. [f. SHY *v.*[1]] A sudden start aside made by a horse, etc. when it sees an object that frightens it.

Shy (ʃəi), *sb.*[2] *colloq.* *Pl.* **shies**. 1791. [f. SHY *v.*[2]] **1.** A quick, jerking (or careless) throw, as of a stone, etc. **b.** *Coco-nut s.*: a form of amusement (with the attendant paraphernalia), which consists in throwing balls at coconuts 1903. **2.** *fig.* **a.** A 'fling' *at* a person or thing 1840. **b.** A trial, an experiment; a 'shot' 1848.

1. Jack-in-the-box—three shies a penny DICKENS. **2. b.** Have a s. at putting the case plainly to me 1881.

Shy (ʃəi), *a.* [OE. *scéoh* (*rare*) :—OTeut. **skeuhwo-*, f. Teut. root **skeuhw-* to fear, to terrify.] †**1.** Easily frightened or startled –1648. **b.** *dial.* Of a horse: Skittish; high-mettled 1787. **2.** Easily frightened away; difficult of approach owing to timidity, caution, or distrust; timidly or cautiously averse to encountering or having to do with some specified person or thing 1600. **3.** Fearful of committing oneself to a particular course of action; chary, unwilling, reluctant 1628. **b.** Averse from admitting (a principle), or from considering (a subject). Const *of.* 1641. †**4.** Cautiously reserved; wary in speech –1691. **5.** Shrinking from self-assertion; sensitively timid; retiring or reserved from diffidence bashful 1672. **6.** *transf.* **a.** Of plants, trees, etc.: Not bearing well 1823. **b.** *U.S.* Short (*of*), lacking 1895. **7.** *colloq.* or *slang* (now *rare* or *Obs.*) **a.** Of questionable character, disreputable, 'shady' 1849. **b.** Doubtful in amount or quality 1850.

2. Princes..are (by wisdome of State) somewhat shye of their Successors WOTTON. The cattle..were not s. of us 1748. Phr. *To be* or *look s. on* or *at*, to regard with distrust or suspicion. **3.** Be s. of loving frankly THACKERAY. Phr. *To fight s.*: see FIGHT *v.* **4.** *Meas. for M.* III. ii. 138. **5.** People too s. or too stupid to talk 1859. *transf.* S. recesses of the lake DE QUINCEY. **6.** The plant..seems to be a s. blossomer 1836. **7.** Gambling hells and s. saloons 1908. **b.** The dinner, I own, is s., unless I come and dine with my friends THACKERAY. **Shy·-ly** *adv.*, **-ness.**

Shy (ʃəi), *v.*[1] 1650. [f. prec.] **1.** *intr.* To take a sudden fright or aversion; to make a difficulty, 'boggle' about doing something; to recoil, shrink. Now usu. felt as *transf.* from 2. **2.** Of a horse: To shrink or start back or aside through sudden fear 1796. **3.** *To s. off*: to slip away in order to avoid a person or thing; *fig.* to find a means of evasion 1792. **4.** *trans.* To shun or avoid 1802. **5.** To render timid or shy; to frighten *off* 1845.

1. Finding I shied, he left me alone MME D'ARBLAY. **2.** The horse shyed from the boar SCOTT.

Shy (ʃəi), *v.*[2] Chiefly *colloq.* 1787. [Origin obsc.] **1.** *intr.* To throw a missile, esp. carelessly or by a jerk. Const. *at.* **2.** *trans.* To fling, throw, jerk, toss 1828.

1. To s. at a cow within six feet DE QUINCEY.

Shylock (ʃəi·lɒk). 1894. The name of the Jewish money-lender in Shaks. *Merchant of Venice*; hence *allus.*, an extortionate usurer.

Shyster (ʃəi·stəɹ). *U.S. slang.* 1856. Origin obsc.] A lawyer who practises in an unprofessional or tricky manner; esp., one who preys on petty criminals; hence, any one who conducts his business in a tricky manner.

Si (sī). 1728. [perh. from the initial letters of the words *S*ancte *I*ohannes in the sapphics quoted under UT.] *Mus.* In solmization, the seventh note of the scale.

Sial (səi·ăl). 1924. [f. SI(LICON + AL(UMINIUM.] *Geol.* That part of the crust of the earth (lithosphere) represented by the continental blocks.

Sialagogue (səi·ălăgɒg), *sb.* and *a.* Also **sialogogue.** 1783. [a. F., f. Gr. σίαλον saliva + ἀγωγός leading, drawing forth; cf. EMMENAGOGUE.] *Med.* **A.** *sb.* A medicine which produces a flow of saliva. **B.** *adj.* Inducing a flow of saliva 1855.

Siamang (səi·ămæŋ). 1822. [Malay, *si-(y)āmang*, f. *āmang* black.] A species of large ape (*Hylobates syndactylus*), with long black hair, found in Sumatra and the Malay Peninsula.

Siamese (səiămī·z), *a.* and *sb.* 1693. [f. *Siam* + -ESE.] **A.** *adj.* **1.** Of or pertaining to Siam or its inhabitants. **2.** *S. twins*, two male natives of Siam, Chang and Eng (1814–1874), who were united by a tubular band in the region of the waist 1829. **b.** Twin; closely connected or similar 1833. **B.** *sb.* **1.** A native of Siam 1693. **2.** The language of Siam 1808. Hence **Siame·se** *v. trans.* to join, unite, or couple, after the manner of the Siamese twins.

Sib (sib), *sb.*[1] Now *rare.* [Com. Teut.: OE. *sib(b*, related to next.] **1.** Kinship, relationship. †**2.** Peace, amity, concord –ME.

Sib (sib), *a.* and *sb.*[2] [OE. *sib(b*, = OFris. (and Fris.) *sib*, Goth. (*un*)*sibjis.*] **A.** *adj.* **1.** Related by blood or descent. Now chiefly *Sc.* or *arch.* **b.** *transf.* Closely related in some way 1500. **2.** Related by blood or kinship *to* (or †*with*) a person ME. **B.** *absol.* as *sb.* **a.** As *pl.* Kinsfolk, relatives OE. **b.** A kinsman or kinswoman OE.

A. 1. The deuyll and she be syb SKELTON. **B. b.** From goody, gossip, cater-cousin and s. BROWNING.

Si·bbens (also **-ans, -ins**). 1792. Variant of SIVVENS.

Siberian (səibī^ə·riăn), *a.* and *sb.* 1719. [f. *Siberia* + -AN.] **A.** *adj.* **1.** Of or belonging to, characteristic of, Siberia. **2.** In spec. applications, as *S. crab* (apple), *dog*, *pine*, etc. 1763. **B.** *sb.* **1.** A native of Siberia 1719. **2.** *pl.* Shares in Siberian gold-mines 1906.

Sibilant (si·bilănt), *a.* and *sb.* 1669. [a. L. *sibilant-*, *sibilans*, pres. pple. of *sibilare* to hiss, whistle.] **A.** *adj.* **1.** Having a hissing sound; of the nature of, characterized by, hissing. *spec.* in *Path.* **2.** Making a hissing or whistling sound 1802.

1. The dry bronchial rhonchus..includes two varieties, the s. and sonorous rhonchus 1833.

B. *sb.* A speech-sound having a hissing effect; a sound of the nature of *s.* 1822. Hence **Si·bilance** (*rare*), a hissing sound.

Sibilate (si·bileⁱt), *v.* Also †**sibillate.** 1656. [f. ppl. stem of L. *sibilare.*] *intr.* To hiss; to utter a hissing sound. Hence **Si·bilatory** (si·bilătəri) *a.* of the nature of, marked or expressed by, hissing.

Sibilation (sibilēⁱ·ʃən). Also †**sibill-.** 1626. [ad. late L. *sibilatio*, f. *sibilare.*] The action of hissing or whistling; a hissing or whistling sound.

The sharp fitful sibilations of the dry wiry grasses on the barren places 1892.

Sibilous (si·biləs), *a.* 1768. [f. L. *sibilus* adj. + -OUS.] Hissing, sibilant.

Sibling (si·bliŋ). 1897. [Modern use of OE. *sibling* relative; see SIB *sb.*[2] + -LING.[1]] *pl.* Children having one or both parents in common.

Sibyl (si·bil). ME. [a. OF. *Sibile*, or ad. med.L. *Sibilla*, L. *Sibylla*, a. Gr. Σίβυλλα.] **1.** One of various women of antiquity who were reputed to possess powers of prophecy and divination. (usu. with initial cap.) **2.** A prophetess; a fortune-teller, witch. (Now usu. with a small *s.*) 1589.

1. The spirit of deepe Prophecie she hath, Exceeding the nine Sibyls of old Rome SHAKS. **2.** Thou art no Sibyl, but from fury speak'st, Not inspiration; we reguard thee not 1632.

‖**Sibylla** (sibi·lă). ME. [L.] = prec. 1.

Sibylline (si·biləin), *a.* and *sb.* 1579. [ad. L. *Sibyllinus*, f. *Sibylla* SIBYL.] **A.** *adj.* **1.** Pertaining to, uttered or written by, one or more of the Sibyls. (usu. with initial cap.) **2.** Oracular, occult, mysterious 1817. **3.** Excessive, exorbitant. (In allusion to the Sibyl who sold three books to Tarquinius Superbus at the price of the original nine.) 1859. **4.** Resembling a Sibyl 1837.

3. My terms are Sybilline 1859.

B. *sb. pl.* The Sibylline books or oracles 1875.

Sibyllist (si·bilist). 1605. [ad. late Gr. Σιβυλλιστής; see SIBYL and -IST.] One who believes in the Sibylline prophecies; esp. applied to the early Christians who accepted the Sibylline writings as genuine.

Sic (sik), *a.* *Sc.* and *north.* late ME. [Reduced form of *swik*, *swilk*; see SUCH *a.*] = SUCH *a.*

‖**Sic** (sik), *adv.* 1887. [L. *sic* so, thus.] A parenthetical insertion used in printing quotations or reported utterances to call attention to something anomalous or erroneous in the original, or to guard against the supposition of misquotation.

‖**Sicca** (si·kă). *Anglo-Ind.* 1619. [a. Pers. (Arab.) *sikkah* a die for coining, the impression on money.] *S. rupee*, orig. a newly-coined rupee, and therefore of full standard weight; latterly, a rupee coined under the Government of Bengal from 1793, and legally current till 1836, of a greater weight than the East India Company's rupee. Also *ellipt.*

Siccative (si·kătiv), *a.* and *sb.* 1547. [ad. late L. *siccativus*, f. *siccare* to dry; see -ATIVE.] **A.** *adj.* Having the property of absorbing moisture. **B.** *sb.* A substance that dries up moisture, esp. as used in oil-painting; a dryer 1825. So †**Si·ccate** *v. trans.* to make dry. †**Sicca·tion**, the action or process of drying.

†**Si·ccity.** 1477. [ad. L. *siccitas*, f. *siccus* dry; see -ITY.] Dryness –1849.

The s. and drines of its flesh SIR T. BROWNE.

Sice (səis), **size** (səiz). late ME. [a. OF. *sis* (mod.F. *six*) :—L. *sex* six.] **1.** The number six marked upon dice; a throw in which the die turns up six. **2.** *Sice-point.* In backgammon, the sixth point from the inner end of each table 1552. †**3.** *slang.* Sixpence –1709.

1. *Sice cinque*, a throw with two dice turning up six and five. Similarly *s. quatre, trey, deuce.* *Size-ace*, *sice-ace*, a throw with two dice turning up six and one; also, †a variety of backgammon.

†**Sicer.** ME. [ad. late L. *sicera* CIDER.] Intoxicating liquor, strong drink –1623.

Sich(e, obs. or dial. ff. SUCH.

Sicilian (sisi·liăn), *a.* and *sb.* 1513. [f. L. *Sicilia* + -AN.] **A.** *adj.* Of or pertaining to Sicily or its inhabitants; characteristic of Sicily or the Sicilians 1611.

Sicilian Vespers, a general Massacre of all the French in Sicily, in the Year 1282; to which the first Toll that call'd to Vespers was the Signal 1728.

B. *sb.* **1.** A native of Sicily 1513. †**2.** = SICILIANA (*rare*) –1728.

‖ **Siciliana** (sisiliā·nă). Also pl. **-ane.** 1724. [It., fem. of *Siciliano* Sicilian.] A dance of the Sicilian peasantry, resembling a jig; the music for this.

‖ **Sicilienne** (sisilie·n). 1881. [F., fem. of *sicilien* Sicilian.] **1.** A fine poplin made of silk and wool. **2.** A mohair fabric 1908.

Sick (sik), *a.* and *sb.* [Com. Teut.; OE. *sēoc.*] **A.** *adj.* **I. 1.** Suffering from illness of any kind; ill, unwell. Now chiefly literary, official (e.g. in the services), and *U.S.* †**b.** Of parts of the body: Not in a sound or healthy state –1821. **2.** Having an inclination to vomit, or actually vomiting 1614.

1. In this meane while, king Henry waxed sicker and sicker GRAFTON. *fig.* Thou lyest in reputation sicke SHAKS. Phr. *S. man*, a term frequently applied, during the latter part of the 19th c., to the Sultan of Turkey. **b.** At last his Third Finger was s. 1700. **2.** O lend me a bason, I am sicke, I am sicke B. JONSON. *fig.* The noon of summer made The valleys s. with heat 1856.

II. †**1.** Spiritually or morally ailing; corrupt through sin or wrong-doing –1738. **2.** Deeply affected by some strong feeling, as sorrow, longing, envy, repugnance or loathing, producing effects similar or comparable to those of physical ailments OE. **b.** *slang.* Disgusted, mortified, chagrined 1853. **3.** Thoroughly tired or weary *of* a thing 1597.

1. *Hen. VIII*, II. iv. 204. **2.** Hope deferred maketh the heart sicke *Prov.* xiii. 12. The sad heart of Ruth, when s. for home She stood in tears amid the alien corn KEATS. **b.** How s. he was when the jury..gave five hundred pounds damages against him 1853. **3.** The world is s. of such societies 1842.

III. 1. Mentally affected or weak. Now *rare.* ME. **2.** Of things: Out of condition in some respect; corrupted or spoiled. late ME. **3.** Of a sickly hue; pale, wan 1592. **4.** Accompanied by illness or sickness; denoting sickness 1593. **5. a.** Appropriated or given up to, occupied by, one or more persons in a state of illness, as *s.-bay, -berth*, etc. 1748. **b.** Of or pertaining to, connected with, persons suffering from illness, as *s.-allowance, -club, -cookery*, etc. 1595.

2. Renish [wine]..commonly goes s. in June, if not rack'd 1703. *fig.* The enterprize is sicke SHAKS. **3.** *Rom. & Jul.* II. ii. 8. **4.** Now comes the sicke houre that his surfet made SHAKS. **5. a.** *S.-bay*, a place set apart in a ship for invalids or wounded men 1846.

B. *absol.* or as *sb.* **1.** *absol.* as pl. Those who, such as, are suffering from illness OE. †**2.** A person suffering from illness –1799. **3.** †A disease or illness; a fit of sickness; a sickening (*rare*). ME.

1. Ther is phisique for the seke GOWER. **2.** Then sayd he vnto the sicke of the palsey TINDALE *Matt.* ix. 6. Hence **Si·ckless** *a.* free from sickness or ill-health.

†**Sick,** *v.*¹ ME. [f. SICK *a.*] **1.** *intr.* To suffer illness; to fall ill, sicken –1597. **2.** *trans.* To cause to sicken; to make ill –1645.

Sick (sik), *v.*² Also **sic.** 1885. [dial. var. of SEEK *v.*] **1.** *trans.* Of a dog: To set upon, attack. Chiefly in imperative. 1890. **2.** To incite or encourage (a person) to attack. Const. with *on* adv. or prep. 1885.

Si·ck-bed. late ME. [SICK *a.*] A bed upon which a person lies ill.

Sicken (sik'n), *v.* ME. [f. SICK *a.* + -EN ⁵.] **1.** *intr.* To become affected with illness, to fall ill or sick. Also const. *of* or *with.* **2. a.** To feel faint with horror or nausea; to revolt or experience revulsion *at* something 1601. **b.** To grow weary or tired *of* a thing 1782. **c.** To pine with yearning; to long eagerly 1802. **3.** *trans.* To affect with illness; to make sick 1613. **4. a.** To give (one) a sickener; to make (a person) sick or tired *of* a thing 1797. **b.** To affect with nausea, loathing, or disgust 1825. **c.** To render faint with fear or horror 1821.

1. We s. to shun sicknesse when we purge SHAKS. *fig.* Speckl'd vanity Will s. soon and die MILT. **2. a.** I hate, abhor, spit, sicken at him TENNYSON. **c.** His strong heart..sickened with excess of love SHELLEY. **3.** His fetid breath sickened me 1902. *transf.* The pool was still; around its brim The alders sickened all the air 1876. **4. a.** The Blenheim,..gave us a respite, and sickened the Dons NELSON. Hence **Si·ckener,** something which nauseates or disgusts; an overdose or excess of anything; a sickening experience.

Sickening (si·k'niŋ), *ppl. a.* 1725. [f. prec. vb. + -ING ².] **1.** Falling or turning sick. **2.** That causes sickness, nausea, or faintness; that disgusts or revolts; repulsive, loathsome 1789. Hence **Si·ckeningly** *adv.*

Sicker (si·kəɹ), *a.* and *adv.* Now *Sc.* and *n. dial.* [OE. *sicor* (rare); early Teut. ad. L. *securus* SECURE *a.*] **A.** *adj.* **I. 1.** Free from danger or harm; secure, safe. **2.** That may be depended on; certain OE. **3.** Firm, unshaken, fast; stable ME. **4.** Indubitable; absolutely certain. late ME. **5.** Certain of its effect; effective ME. **II.** †**1.** Having assured possession or prospect *of* something. –1719. **2.** Fully assured or convinced ME. **B.** *adv.* †**1.** With security; safely; confidently –1440. **2.** Assuredly, certainly, without doubt ME. **3.** Effectively, strongly, firmly 1450. **4.** Securely; without risk of falling or shifting 1586. Hence **Si·ckerness,** the quality or state of being s. (*Obs.* exc. *Sc.*)

Si·ckerly, *adv.* Now *Sc.* and *n. dial.* [Late OE. *sicerlīce* (f. *sicer* SICKER *a.*).] †**1.** With certainty –1586. **2.** Without doubt; certainly ME. **3.** With assurance; confidently ME. **4.** Securely ME. **5.** In a stable or steady manner. late ME. **6.** With certainty of result ME. **7.** Sharply, severely, smartly 1596.

2. And sikurly sche was of gret disport CHAUCER.

Si·ckish (si·kiʃ), *a.* 1581. [f. SICK *a.* + -ISH.] **1.** Somewhat ill or sick; indisposed. **2.** Somewhat nauseating 1817.

2. A sweet, s. effluvium 1817. Hence **Si·ckish·ly** *adv.*, **-ness.**

Sickle (si·k'l). [OE. *sicol*, perh. ad. L. *secula*, f. *secare* to cut.] **1.** An implement resembling a reaping-hook, but with a serrated cutting-edge. **2.** Something having the curved or crescent form of a sickle; e.g. a form of spur or gaff for a fighting-cock 1459. **b.** Applied to the crescent moon, etc. 1657. **c.** A group of stars in the constellation Leo 1882.

1. Oft did the harvest to their s. yield GRAY. **2. b.** Ere the silver s. of that month Became her golden shield TENNYSON.

Comb.: **s.-bill,** any of various birds having a highly curved bill, e.g. a curlew; **-moon,** the crescent-moon; **-pod,** an Amer. species of rock-cress. Hence **Sickled** (sik'ld) *ppl. a.* provided with a s.; cut by means of a s. **Si·ckler,** a reaper.

†**Si·cklewort.** 1450. [f. prec.] **a.** The scarlet pimpernel. **b.** = SELF-HEAL. –1863.

Si·ck-list. 1794. [SICK *a.*] An official list of sick persons, esp. soldiers or sailors. Colloq. phr. *On the s.*, ill.

Sickly (si·kli), *a.* ME. [f. SICK *a.* + -LY ¹.] **1.** In a poor state of health; not robust or strong. **b.** Of the mind: Weak, disordered 1741. **2.** Of conditions, etc.: Connected with, arising from, characterized by, ill-health. late ME. †**3.** Pertaining to sickness or the sick –1814. **4.** Marked by the occurrence or prevalence of sickness; unhealthy 1602. **5.** Causing sickness or ill-health; producing discomfort or nausea 1604. **6.** Of light, colour, etc.: Faint, feeble 1695. **7.** Of feelings, etc.: Weak, mawkish 1766.

1. Feeble and s. children 1894. **2.** A s. Complaining Life they lead 1704. **3.** She at your s. Couch will wait SWIFT. **4.** This Physicke but prolongs thy s. dayes SHAKS. **5.** Dense gray mists..enshrouding the pretty village in their s. vapours 1882. **6.** The s. winter sun was feebly trying to shine 1888. **7.** The fastidiousness of s. taste 1805. Hence **Si·cklied** *a.* rendered s. or mawkish. **Si·ckli·ly** *adv.*, **-ness.**

Sickly (si·kli), *v.* 1602. [f. SICKLY *a.*] *trans.* **a.** To cover *over* with a sickly hue. Chiefly *fig.* and in direct echoes of Shaks. **b.** To render sickly or pale 1763.

1. a. The Natiue hew of Resolution Is sicklied o're, with the pale cast of Thought SHAKS. **b.** Sicklied with age, and sour'd with self-disgrace 1807.

Sickness (si·knės). OE. [f. SICK *a.* + -NESS.] **1.** The state of being sick or ill; the condition of suffering from some malady; illness, ill-health. **2.** A particular disease or malady OE. **b.** A defect in wines 1674. **3.** A disturbance of the stomach manifesting itself in retching and vomiting 1604. **4.** *fig.* Utter disgust or weariness 1779.

1. Noble Anthony, not sickenesse should detaine me SHAKS. **2.** The Causes..of ev'ry S. that infects the Fold DRYDEN. **4.** When the spirit is sore fretted, even tired to s. of the janglings..of the world LAMB.

Si·ck-nurse, *sb.* 1821. [SICK *a.*] A nurse who attends upon the sick. Hence **Si·ck-nurse** *v. intr.* to act as a s.

†**Sicle.** ME. [a. OF., ad. late L. *siclus*, a. Gr. σίκλος, σίγλος, ad. Heb. *sheqel*; see SHEKEL.] A shekel –1649.

‖ **Sida** (səi·dă). 1753. [mod.L., ad. Gr. σίδη some water-plant.] *Bot.* A genus of malvaceous plants of a woolly or downy character, indigenous to warm climates; a plant of this genus, esp. *S. rhombifolia* or Queensland hemp. Also *S.-weed.*

Si·ddow, si·dder, *a.* Now *dial.* 1602. [Origin unkn.] Soft, tender, mellow. Chiefly of peas, grain, or other vegetables.

Side (səid), *sb.*¹ [Com. Teut.; OE. *sīde.* Perh. conn. w. SIDE *a.*, and originally denoting the long part or aspect of a thing.] **I. 1.** Either of the two lateral surfaces or parts of the trunk in persons or animals, extending between the shoulders and the hips; the corresponding parts in fishes, reptiles, etc. **b.** Used with reference to generation or birth. (Cf. LOIN *sb.* 2 b.) *arch.* OE. **c.** In phrases denoting the effect of exertion in speaking (after L. *latera*), or boisterous mirth 1604. **2.** In phrases denoting close proximity to a person (properly to one hand or the other), as *by one's s.* OE. **3.** One of the lateral halves of the body of an animal, or the part about the ribs, used for cooking. Now chiefly in *s. of bacon.* ME.

1. His brawny sides, with hairy bristles arm'd SHAKS. *fig.* I haue no Spurre To pricke the sides of my intent SHAKS. **c.** Laughter holding both his sides MILT. **2.** Let us forth, I never from thy s. henceforth to stray MILT. Phr. *S. by s.*, close together and abreast of each other; in later use also of things. **3.** A great dish of s. of lamb PEPYS.

II. 1. One or other of the two longer (usually vertical) surfaces or aspects of an object, in contrast to the ends, or of the two receding surfaces or aspects, in contrast to the front and back OE. **b.** One or other of the bounding lines or surfaces of any right-lined figure or object. late ME. **c.** In a rounded, cylindrical, or spherical object, a part of the surface having a particular aspect OE. **2.** That part of the framework of a ship or boat extending from stem to stern between the gun-wale and the main-wale or the water-line OE. **3. a.** The slope of a hill or bank, esp. one extending for a considerable distance ME. †**b.** The outskirts of a wood, town, etc. –1750. **4. a.** The bank or shore of a river or water; also, the land or district bordering on a river ME. **b.** A surface serving to enclose or bound a space or hollow 1474. **5.** One or other of the two surfaces of a thing having little or no appreciable thickness; also, the inner or outer surface or aspect of a thing. late ME. **6. a.** A page of a book or writing. *Obs.* or *arch.* 1530. **b.** *Tanning.* Either half of a hide which has been cut down the middle of the back 1763. **7.** An aspect or view of something immaterial 1449.

1. I trow there are but two sides of a long table, and two ends 1628. **b.** The sides of each triangle 1863. **c.** Woodpeckers explore the sides Of rugged oaks for worms COWPER. **3. a.** The shatter'd s. Of thundring Ætna MILT. **4. a.** By the Silver s. Of some cool Stream DRYDEN. RIVER-, SEA-, WATER-*side*: see these words. **b.** Dauid and his men remained in the sides of the caue 1 *Sam.* xxiv. 3. **5.** I know on which syde my bread is buttred 1562. **7.** The ridiculous s. of everyone CARLYLE. **b.** *On the* (so-and-so) *side*, rather so-and-so.

III. 1. Place or direction with ref. to some central point; a point of the compass OE. **2.** One or other direction to either hand of an object, space, or imaginary line; the position, space, or area implied in this OE. **3.** The space lying to either hand *of*, or in any direction from, a specified place, point, etc. late ME. **4. a.** In phrases denoting position, movement, or inclination away from a central line or point, e.g. *on* or *to one's s.*, ASIDE. 1586. **b.** *Billiards.* Direction given to a ball by striking it at a point not directly in the middle 1873. **5.** A part *of* a place or thing lying in one or other direction from a centre or median line. late ME. **b.** A region or district, or the inhabitants of this. (Cf. *country-side.*) late ME. **c.** A portion of a building set apart for particular persons or purposes ME. **6.** The line or limit, on either side, up to which something extends ME.

1. *fig.* On that s. he multiplied his precautions, and

set double watch MACAULAY. Phr. *On each* or *every s.*, *on all sides.* **2.** Suppose the beam should dip on the wrong s. COWPER. Phr. *On either* or *each s.*, *on both sides.* **3.** On the East s. of the Groue SHAKS. *fig.* On the windy s. of Care SHAKS. *This s.*, used by Europeans and Americans for the side of the Atlantic on which they happen to be. Similarly, *the other s.* **4.** Phr. *On the s.* (orig. *U.S.*), as a subordinate occupation. **5.** The other s. a' th City is risen: why stay we prating heere? SHAKS. **c.** The female 'side' of a prison gives more trouble..than the male 1904.

IV. **1.** Used to denote the action, attitude, etc., of one person, or a set of persons, in relation to another or others ME. **b.** One of the two alternative views which may be taken of a question, problem, argument, etc. 1597. **c.** A division of a school devoted to a particular class of studies 1884. **2.** The position or interests of one person, party, etc., in contrast to that of an opposing one ME. **3.** Kinship or descent through father or mother. late ME. **4.** One of the parties in a transaction, battle, or debate; a political party; a faction. late ME. **b.** One of the parties in an athletic or sporting contest or game of skill. *No s.*, the announcement of the conclusion of a game of football. 1545. **5.** **a.** One of the two divisions of a choir 1519. **b.** At Cambridge, a body of students under the supervision of a college tutor 1852.

1. I was sorry on my s. for the occasion I had given him STERNE. **b.** There are two sides to the question 1884. **c.** The Classical s. 1884. **2.** To be ever of the loosing s. 1668. Phr. *On* (*one's*) *s.* *To take a* (or *one's*) *s.*, *take sides.* **3.** Distantly related to the Rochesters by the mother's s. C. BRONTE. **4.** 5000 of each s. killed on the place 1676.

attrib. and *Comb.* **1.** General: as *s.-aisle*, *-altar*, etc., *s. armour*, *-band*, *-comb*, etc.; *s.-bough*, *-branch*, *-shoot*, etc.; *s.-blow*, *-jump*, etc.; *s.-elevation*, *-front*, etc.; *s.-effect*, *-issue*, etc. **2.** Special: as **s.-arms** *Mil.*, weapons worn at the s., as dagger, sword, or bayonet; **-axe,** an axe with a handle slightly bent to one s.; **-bet,** a bet of one s. against another; **-car,** (*a*) a conveyance in which the seats face to the sides; a jaunting-car; (*b*) a car for passengers, attachable to the s. of a motor-cycle; (*c*) a kind of cocktail; **-dish,** a dish which is accessory to the principal one in a course; **-drawn** *a.*, sketched from the s.; **-drum,** a drum which is slung at the s. of the performer; **-face,** the human face in profile; a view or representation of this; **-hill** (now *U.S.*) a hillside, an acclivity; **-land,** a strip of land lying along the s. of a ploughed field; also *attrib.*, sloping; **-look,** an oblique look, a s.-glance; **-note,** a note made or placed at the s. of a page; **-pocket,** a pocket in the s. portion of a garment (esp. a coat or jacket); **-rail,** a rail placed or fixed at the s. of something; **-seat,** (*a*) the mode of sitting on horseback which accompanies a s.-saddle; (*b*) in a vehicle, etc. a seat in which the occupant has his back against the s. of the vehicle; **-splitter,** a very funny story, farce, etc.; **-splitting** *a.*, that convulses with merriment, extremely funny; also as *vbl. sb.*; **-stroke,** (*a*) a stroke used in swimming on the s., the arm remaining always in the water; (*b*) an incidental or subsidiary operation of an act; **-tackle** *U.S.*, in football, one or other of two players stationed at each end of the rush-line; **-tool,** a tool cutting on the s., used in wood-turning; **-view,** a view of anything obtained or taken from the s.; **-wheel** *attrib.*, of steamers, having paddle-wheels at the sides; hence *-wheeler*; **-work,** (*a*) in fortification, a lateral work; (*b*) the action of bounding sidewards, on the part of a horse.

Side (səid), *sb.*^{2} *slang.* 1878. [perh. identical with prec. Cf. next 3.] Assumption of superiority, swaggering conduct or attitude. Freq. *to put on s.*, to give oneself airs.

Side (səid), *a.* Now *Sc.* and *n. dial.* [OE. *sīd*, = ON. *síðr.*] †**1.** Large, ample, spacious, extensive –late ME. **2.** Extending lengthways; long OE. **3.** Haughty, proud 1508.

2. A street so 'syde-and-wyde' that there was elbow-room for everyone in Boulder in it 1876. **3.** The haire of their head long, their beards s. and overgrowne HOLLAND. †*Side-robe* = LONG ROBE.

Comb.: **s.-coat** (now *dial.*), a long coat, a great-coat.

†**Side,** *adv.* [OE. *side* (f. *sīd* SIDE *a.*).] **1.** To a great distance or length; far. Chiefly in *wide and s.*, far and wide. –1621. **2.** Low down; towards or on the ground –1538.

1. For the Grecian Colonies were diffused farre and neere, wide and s. 1621.

Side (səid), *v.* 1470. [f. SIDE *sb.*^{1}] **I.** *trans.* †**1.** To cut or carve (a pig or haddock) into sides –1854. **2.** To walk or stand by the side of; to be side by side with 1613. **b.** *fig.* To equal, match 1603. †**3.** To support or countenance (a person) –1618. **4.** *refl.* To take a side or party 1591. †**5.** To assign to one of two sides or parties. SHAKS. **6.** *dial.* To put in order, arrange; to clear or tidy *up* 1825. **b.** To clear *away* 1848. **7.** *Naut.* To draw (a rope) *over* or *out* 1834. **8.** To make of certain dimensions on the side; to square the sides of (timber) 1794. **9.** To furnish (a structure) with sides 1868.

2. The old benchers..might not be sided or jostled LAMB. **b.** He had sure read more..than any Man I ever knew, my Lord Falkland only excepted, who I think sided him CLARENDON.

II. *intr.* **1.** To take a side; to join or form sides or parties. Usu. const. *with.* 1600. **2.** To move or turn sideways 1668.

Hence **Si·der,** one who sides *with* a person or cause; a partisan, adherent.

Si·deband. 1926. [f. SIDE *sb.*^{1} + BAND *sb.*^{2}] *Wireless.* The band of frequencies on either side of the carrier frequency.

Si·de-bar. 1686. [SIDE *sb.*^{1}] **1.** *Law.* **a.** A former bar in the Outer Parliament House in Edinburgh. **b.** A former bar in Westminster Hall 1795. **2.** A lateral bar or longitudinal side-piece, as in a saddle, carriage, etc. 1875.

1. **b.** Phr. *S. rule*, a rule granted without formal application to the court; so called because moved for by the attorneys at the s. of the court.

Sideboard (səi·dbōᵊɹd). ME. [SIDE *sb.*^{1}] **1.** †**a.** A table (*esp.* for taking meals at) placed towards the side of a room, hall, etc. –1726. **b.** A piece of dining-room furniture for holding side-dishes, wine, plate, etc., and often having cupboards and drawers 1671. **2.** A board forming the side, or a part of the side, of any structure 1611.

Si·de-bone. 1819. [SIDE *sb.*^{1}] **1.** That part of the pelvis on either side of a bird or fowl which is easily separated from the backbone in carving; also sometimes, the scapula or shoulder-blade. **2.** Ossification of the side cartilages in a horse's foot 1886.

Si·de-box, *sb.* 1678. [SIDE *sb.*^{1}] A box or enclosed seat at the side of a theatre. †**b.** The occupants of a side-box –1732. Hence †**Side-box** *v. trans.* to gaze at from a side-box.

Sided (səi·dėd), *ppl. a.* late ME. [f. SIDE *sb.*^{1} and *v.*] **1.** Having sides; (esp. compounded with a numeral) furnished with (a specified number of) sides. **2.** *Naut.* Having a (specified) dimension in the direction contrary to that of the moulding 1794. **3.** Of timber: Dressed on one or more sides 1865.

1. A Pentagon, or five-sided Figure 1731. Hence **Si·dedness** (chiefly in combs.).

Side-door. (Stress var.) 1535. [SIDE *sb.*^{1} Cf. G. *seitentür.*] A door in the side of a building, garden, etc.; a door on one side of, or subsidiary to, the main door. Also *fig.* applied to indirect, oblique, or illegitimate action.

Si·de-glance, *sb.* 1611. [SIDE *sb.*^{1}] A glance directed sideways. **b.** *fig.* An indirect or slight reference 1831. So **Si·de-glance** *v.*

Si·de-light. Also **side light, sidelight.** 1610. [SIDE *sb.*^{1}] **1.** **a.** Light coming from the side. **b.** *fig.* Incidental light or information on a subject 1871. **2.** A window, or opening for light, in the side of a building, ship, lamp, etc. 1827. **b.** A side-portion of a large window; a window by the side of a door or other window 1851. **3.** *Naut.* A light carried on either side of a ship under way in the night 1887. **b.** The lamp on either side of a motor vehicle 1912.

1. **b.** The reader needs all the side-lights which can be thrown upon its translated forms 1871.

Si·de-line, *sb.* 1768. [SIDE *sb.*^{1}] **1.** A line extending along or towards one side of a thing or space; *spec.* in *Football*, *Tennis*, etc. either of two lines, bounding the pitch, court, etc., at the sides. **b.** A railway or tramway extending away from the main line 1898. **2.** A line used for securing an animal by tying together the fore and hind leg, on one side 1831. **3.** An auxiliary line of goods, trade, or occupation 1890. **b.** *fig.* Something subsidiary to the main subject, line of action, etc. 1927. Hence **Si·de-line** *v. trans.* to secure (cattle, etc.) with a s.

Sideling (səi·dliŋ), *sb.* late ME. [f. SIDE *sb.*^{1} + -LING^{1}.] †**1.** A strip or piece of land lying by the side of a larger portion or by a stream –1726. **2.** A slope, *esp.* one along the side of which a track or road runs. *local.* 1808.

Sideling (səi·dliŋ), *adv.* and *a.* ME. [f. SIDE *sb.*^{1} + -LING^{2}.] **A.** *adv.* **1.** With a sideward movement; in a side-long direction; sideways; obliquely. †**2.** On a side-saddle; facing to the side –1698.

1. Hee hath the witte yet to enter s., like a gentlewoman with an huge farthingall 1609. Crabs move s. SIR T. BROWNE. **2.** Queen Anne..being the first that taught women to ride s. on horseback 1612.

B. *adj.* **1.** Directed or moving sideways; oblique 1611. **b.** *fig.* Of speech, etc.: Indirect 1789. **2.** Having an inclination; sloping, steep 1611.

2. It is a good plan to plough sidling ground in a circle 1854. So **Si·delings** *adv.* = A.

Si·delong, *adv.* and *a.* Also **side-long.** 1523. [f. SIDE *sb.*^{1} + -LONG.] **A.** *adv.* **1.** Towards the side; sideways, obliquely 1580. **2.** To the side *of*; side by side; presenting the side *to* something 1643. **3.** On the side; with the side to the ground 1667. **4.** As *prep.* By or along the side of 1523.

3. Side-long the plough beside the field-gate lay MORRIS.

B. *adj.* **1.** In a slanting direction; in a sloping position; inclining to one side; lying on the side 1597. **b.** *spec.* Of ground: Sloping 1792. **2.** Directed to one side or sideways 1608. **b.** Glancing, moving, or extending sideways 1818. **3.** Indirect; not straightforward or open 1654.

2. He gives a dreadful s. glance of suspicion THACKERAY. **3.** Their s. Answers, and silly Excuses will not do 1697.

Si·de-post. 1535. [SIDE *sb.*^{1}] **1.** One of the posts at either side of a doorway; a door-post. (Chiefly in echoes of the Bible.) **2.** A post supporting a roof at or towards one side 1625.

1. Strike the lintel and the two side postes with the blood that is in the bason *Exod.* xii. 22.

-sider. 1841. Forming the second element in a comb as *near-s.*, a horse standing on the near side; *hillsider*, one living on a hillside.

Sideral (səi-, si·dĕrăl), *a.* 1594. [ad. L. *sideralis*, f. *sider-*, *sidus* star, etc.] **1.** Of or pertaining to the stars; sidereal, starry. **2.** Coming from, caused by, the stars. Chiefly of malign influences. 1611.

2. S. blast, Vapour, and Mist, and Exhalation hot MILT.

†**Si·derate,** *v.* 1623. [f. ppl. stem of L. *siderari* to be planet-struck, f. *sider-*, *sidus.*] *trans.* To strike with malign (sidereal) influence, to blast. Chiefly *pass.*, to be blasted, struck by lightning; *fig.* to be thunderstruck. –1679.

Sidera·tion. Now *rare.* 1612. [ad. L. *sideratio*, f. *siderari*; see prec.] **1.** Blasting of trees or plants 1623. **2.** Sudden paralysis; complete mortification of any part of the body 1612. **3.** *Path.* Erysipelas of the face or scalp 1828.

Sidereal (səidīᵊ·rĭăl), *a.* 1634. [f. L. *sidereus*, f. *sider-*, *sidus* + -AL^{1}.] **1.** Of or pertaining to the stars 1647. **2.** Star-like, lustrous, bright (*rare*) 1634. **3.** Of periods of time: Determined or measured by means of the stars. 1681. **4.** Of planetary or lunar motion: Relative to the stars 1815. **5.** Concerned with the stars 1833.

1. That general Astronomy which includes our whole s. system SPENCER. **3.** The Sydereal year is the space of time, in which the Sun returns to the same star from whence he departed 1681. The s. month is the interval between two successive conjunctions of the moon with the same fixed star 1868. Hence **Side·realize** *v. trans.* **Side·really** *adv.*

Siderite (si·dĕrəit, səidīᵊ·rəit). 1579. [orig. a. F., or ad. L. *siderites* m., *sideritis* f., a. Gr. σιδηρίτης, -ῖτις, f. σίδηρος iron; later, directly f. Gr. σίδηρος + -ITE^{1} 2 b.] *Min.* †**1.** Loadstone –1694. **2.** A steel-coloured stone, prob. sapphire 1623. †**3.** A phosphate of iron; pharmacosiderite, cube-ore –1805. **4.** A blue variety of quartz 1823. **5.** Rhombohedral carbonate of iron, native ferrous carbonate, spathic iron-ore 1850. **6.** A meteorite consisting mainly of iron 1875. So †**Sideri·tes** (in senses 1–3). **Sideri·tic** *a.* of the nature of s. (in sense 3).

Sidero- (si·dĕro, səidīᵊ·ro), comb. form of Gr. σίδηρος iron.

1. In various names of minerals, as *s.-calcite*, *-graphite*, etc. **2.** In miscellaneous combs., as **Si·derograph,** an engraving produced by siderography.

ŏ (Ger. Köln). ö (Fr. peu). ü (Ger. Müller). ü (Fr. dune). ɐ̄ (curl). ē (ēᵊ) (there). ē (ēⁱ) (rein). ĕ (Fr. faire). ə (fir, fern, earth).

Siderogra·phic, -al, *adjs.* pertaining to siderography. **Sidero·graphist,** 'one who engraves steel plates, or performs work by means of such plates'. **Sidero·graphy,** a method of engraving on steel, employed especially for bank-notes. **Si·deroscope,** an instrument used to detect minute quantities of iron by means of a combination of magnetic needles.

Siderolite (si·dĕrǒləit, səidiə·rǒləit). 1863. [f. prec. + -LITE.] A meteorite composed of a mixed mass of iron and stone. Hence **Sidero·li·thic** *a.* of the nature of a s.

‖ **Siderosis** (sidĕrōu·sis). 1880. [f. Gr. σίδηρος + -OSIS.] *Path.* Accumulation of oxide of iron in the lungs.

Siderostat (si·dĕrostæt). 1877. [f. L. *sider-, sidus* star, after *heliostat.*] *Astr.* An astronomical instrument by which a star under observation may be kept in the same part of the field of a telescope. Hence **Siderosta·tic** *a.*

Si·de-sa·ddle, *sb.* (and *adv.*). 1493. [SIDE *sb.*[1]] A saddle so contrived as to enable a woman to sit with both feet on one (usually the left or near) side of a horse; in mod. use *spec.* one with horns or crutches to support and give a hold to the knees of the rider, who sits facing forward with the right knee raised. **b.** as *adv.* On a side-saddle; sideways 1885.

attrib.: **s. flower (or plant),** (*a*) an Amer. swamp-plant of the genus *Sarracenia*, the leaves of which retain a considerable quantity of water; (*b*) the plant *Darlingtonia californica*. Hence **Si·de-saddle** *v.*

Si·de-show. 1855. [SIDE *sb.*[1]] A 'show which is subsidiary to a larger one; a minor attraction in an exhibition or entertainment; hence, a minor issue, a subordinate matter.

Si·de-slip, *sb.* 1872. [f. SIDE *sb.*[1] + SLIP *sb.* and *v.*] **1.** An illegitimate child. GEO. ELIOT. **2.** The action or fact of slipping sideways, *esp.* on the part of a cycle, motor-car, or aeroplane 1896. So **Si·de-slip** *v. intr.* to slip sideways; (of an aeroplane) to fall as the result of an excessive bank or roll 1887.

Sidesman (səi·dzmǣn). 1632. [f. SIDE *sb.*[1]] One of the persons elected as assistants to the churchwardens of a parish.

Si·de-step, *sb.* 1847. [SIDE *sb.*[1] or *adv.*] **1.** A step to one side. **2.** A step fixed to the side of a ship, vehicle, etc. 1867.

Hence **Si·de-step** *v. intr.*, to step to one side; *trans.*, to avoid by stepping sideways (*spec.* in *Football*).

Si·de-stick. 1683. [SIDE *sb.*[1]] *Printing.* One of a pair of wedge-shaped sticks, usu. of wood, with one side slanting, used in locking up a form.

Si·de-table. late ME. [SIDE *sb.*[1]] A table placed beside the wall of a room (*esp.* a dining-room), or to the side of a main or high table.

Si·de-track, *sb.* orig. *U.S.* 1881. [SIDE *sb.*[1]] A railway siding. Also *fig.*

Si·de-track, *v.* orig. *U.S.* 1881. [f. prec.] **1.** *trans.* To run or shunt (a train, etc.) into a siding. **2.** *intr.* To run into a siding 1888. **3.** *fig.* (*trans.* and *intr.*) To divert (be diverted) from the main course, line, object, etc. 1889.

Si·de-walk. 1667. [SIDE *sb.*[1]] **1.** A walk or path running parallel to a main or central one (*rare*). **2.** A (raised) path for foot-passengers along the side of a street, road, etc.; a footway or pavement. Now *U.S.* 1739.

Si·de-wall. late ME. A wall forming the side of a structure or an enclosure.

Sideward (səi·dwǫ̈ɪd), *adv.* and *a.* late ME. [f. SIDE *sb.*[1]] **A.** *adv.* Towards one side or the other. **B.** *adj.* Directed, moving, or tending towards one side 1831. So **Si·dewards.**

Si·deway, *sb.* Also **side-way.** 1552. [SIDE *sb.*[1]] **1.** A path or way diverging from, or lying to the side of, a main road; a byway. **2.** A (raised) path along the side of a road; a footway. Now *U.S.* 1738.

Si·deway, *adv.* and *a.* 1612. [SIDE *sb.*[1]] **A.** *adv.* = next *adv.* **B.** *adj.* Directed or moving towards or from one side; indirect 1800.

Sideways (səi·dwēɪz), *adv.* and *a.* 1577. [f. SIDE *sb.*[1] + -WAYS.] **A.** *adv.* **1.** From one side. **2.** Presenting the side instead of the face, front, or end; in the direction of the side; facing to the side, etc. 1598. **3.** In a lateral or sideward direction; towards one side; obliquely 1611. **4.** So as to incline to one side 1631. **5.** By an indirect way or route; indirectly 1723. **B.** *adj.* = SIDEWAY *a.* 1868.

A. 1. If the Wind be side-ways, it may do well enough 1725. **2.** Some side-ways, some head first, some stern first DICKENS. **3.** We listened and looked s. up! COLERIDGE.

Si·de-wind. Also **side wind, sidewind.** late ME. [SIDE *sb.*[1]] **1.** A wind blowing from one side, or on the side of a vessel, etc. **2.** *fig.* An indirect means, method, or manner. Chiefly in phr. *by a s.* 1648. **3.** *attrib.* as *adj.* Indirect, oblique; illegitimate 1680.

1. *fig.* Some sail to the port of their own praise by a s. 1642. **2.** Some Expressions, which by a S. reflected on me SWIFT.

Side-winder [1] (səi·dˌwi·ndəɪ). *U.S.* and *dial.* 1859. [f. SIDE *sb.*[1] + *winder* a blow.] A heavy blow with the fist delivered from or on the side.

Side-winder [2] (səi·dˌwəi·ndəɪ). *U.S.* 1888. [f. SIDE *sb.*[1] + WIND *v.*] A species of rattlesnake, *Crotalus cerastes.*

Sidewise (səi·dwəiz), *adv.* and *a.* 1571. [f. SIDE *sb.*[1] + -WISE.] **A.** *adv.* **1.** In a lateral direction; to one side; sidewards. **2.** = SIDEWAYS A. 2. 1608. **3.** On or from the side 1613. **4.** = SIDEWAYS A. 4. 1828. **B.** *adj.* Directed towards one side; sideward 1853.

1. Joltings, backwards, forwards, and s. 1854.

‖**Sidi** (sī·di). 1615. [a. Urdū *sīdī*, ad. Arab. *sayyidī* 'my lord', SAYYID.] Orig., a title of honour given in Western India to African Mohammedans holding high positions under the kings of the Deccan; in later use, an African, a negro. Now chiefly in comb. *s.-boy.*

Siding (səi·diŋ), *vbl. sb.* 1603. [f. SIDE *v.* or *sb.*[1] + -ING[1].] **I. 1.** The action of taking sides; party spirit, partisanship, factiousness; an instance of this. **2.** The action of tending or moving to a side 1646. **3.** *U.S.* The action of dressing or trimming the sides of timber 1875. **II. 1.** *U.S.* The boarding forming the sides of a timber building; weather-boarding; also (with *a* and *pl.*), a piece of this 1858. **2.** *Shipbuilding.* 'The size or dimensions of timber the contrary way to the moulding, or moulded side' 1797. **3.** A short piece of additional track parallel to the main line of a railway or tramway, and connected with it by switches, for enabling trains, trucks, etc., to pass each other or to lie by 1825.

Sidle (səi·d'l), *v.* 1697. [prob. a back-formation from SIDELING *adv.*, after verbs in -LE 3.] **1.** *intr.* To move or go sideways or obliquely; to edge along, esp. in a furtive or unobtrusive manner, or while looking in another direction; to make advances in this manner. **2.** *trans.* To move, turn, or direct sideways 1779.

1. Sir Harry..sidled to the door,..and then slipped out RICHARDSON. Hence **Si·dle** *sb.* an act of sidling, a sidelong or oblique movement. **Si·dlingly** *adv.*

Sidonian (səidōu·niăn), *sb.* and *a.* 1535. [f. L. *Sidonius*, a. Gr. Σιδώνιος, f. Σιδών, the Phœnician city of that name.] **A.** *sb.* A native or inhabitant of Sidon. **B.** *adj.* Of or pertaining to Sidon 1594.

A. They were farre from the Zidonians *Judges* xviii. 7.

Siege (sīdʒ), *sb.* ME. [a. OF., (mod.F. *siège*) :—pop. L. **sedicum*, f. **sēdem* (L. *sēdem*, *sēdes*) seat.] **I.** †**1.** A seat, *esp.* one used by a person of rank or distinction -1616. †**b.** An ecclesiastical see -1579. †**2.** A place in which a person has his seat or residence; a seat of rule, empire, etc. -1630. **b.** The station of a heron on the watch for prey 1452. †**3.** A privy -1555. †**b.** Evacuation -1700. †**c.** Excrement, ordure -1662. †**4.** The anus or rectum -1670. **5.** *techn.* **a.** The floor of a glass-furnace 1839. **b.** A hewer's table or bench 1854.

1. *fig.* I fetch my life and being, From Men of Royall Seige SHAKS. **2.** He [Constantine] made his s. Bizantium, that retaines his name ere since 1592.

II. 1. The action, on the part of an army, of investing a town, castle, etc., in order to cut off all outside communication and in the end to reduce or take it; an investment, beleaguering ME. **b.** Without article. late ME. **2.** *attrib.*, as *s.-artillery, -gun, -operations*, etc. 1450.

1. *fig.* Love stood the s., and would not yield his breast DRYDEN. **b.** *To lay s. to*: see LAY *v.* III. 3 c.

Siege (sīdʒ), *v.* ME. [f. prec., or aphetic f. ASSIEGE *v.*] **1.** *trans.* To besiege, beleaguer, lay siege to. †**2.** To place; to seat (oneself) -1594.

1. They sieg'd him a whole summer night SCOTT.

Sienese (siĕnī·z), *sb.* and *a.* Also **Siennese.** 1756. [f. *Siena, Sienna* + -ESE.] **A.** *sb.* An inhabitant or native of Siena, a city in Tuscany. **B.** *adj.* Of or pertaining to Siena 1830.

Sienna (siˌe·nă). 1787. [Elliptic for *terra di Sienna*; see SIENESE.] **a.** A ferruginous earth used as a pigment in oil and water-colour painting (called *burnt s.* when it has been exposed to a red heat). **b.** The colour of this pigment, a rich reddish brown.

‖**Sierra** (siˌe·ră). 1613. [Sp., :—L. *serra* saw.] **1.** In Spain and Spanish America: A range of hills or mountains, rising in peaks which suggest the teeth of a saw. **b.** *gen.* A mountain-range of this description 1850. **2.** *Astr.* = CHROMOSPHERE 1851.

1. The bleak winds of the s. gave an austerity to the climate 1843. Hence **Sie·rran** *a.*

‖ **Siesta** (siˌe·stă). 1655. [Sp. :—L. *sexta* sixth (hour); hence, in Sp. and Pg., the hottest part of the day, rest or sleep taken at this time.] An afternoon rest or nap; *esp.* that commonly taken during the hottest hours of the day in tropical countries.

Sieve (siv), *sb.* [OE. *sife* = MDu. *seve* (Du. *zeef*). The stem is that of SIFT *v.*] **1.** A utensil consisting of a circular frame with a finely meshed or perforated bottom, used to separate the coarser from the finer particles of any loose material, or as a strainer for liquids. **b.** In phr. denoting something that cannot be done, or that is waste of labour. late ME. **c.** *fig.* Of persons; *esp.* one who cannot keep a secret 1601. **2.** Used locally as a measure for various kinds of produce. 1440.

1. Sieves..to sift the Lime and Sand withal 1703. (Formerly often with ref. to its use for divination, and by witches for sailing in.) **b.** As he that fetcheth Water in a Sive 1477. **c.** Here's none but wee, I am no Sive? I prithee, Swain, be free QUARLES.

Comb.: **s.-cell, -disk, -pore, -tissue, -tube, -vessel,** botanical terms having reference to sieve-like openings in the walls or ends of plant-cells; **-plate,** (*a*) *Bot.* a sieve-like plate on the wall of a plant-cell; (*b*) in paper-making, a plate through which pulp is strained.

Sieve, *v.* 1499. [f. prec.] = SIFT *v.* 1, 4, 7.

‖**Siffleur** (sīflǫ̈r). 1703. [Fr.] **a.** An animal that makes a whistling noise, *spec.* the whistling marmot. **b.** (with fem. *-euse*). A whistling artiste 1923.

Sift (sift), *v.* [OE. *siftan, syftan*, = MDu. *siften, suften* (Du. *ziften*), etc. The stem is that of SIEVE *sb.*] **1.** *trans.* To pass (something) through a sieve, in order to separate the coarse from the fine particles, or to strain. **2.** *fig.* **a.** To make trial of (a person) ME. **b.** To subject to close questioning 1566. **3.** *fig.* To examine closely into, to scrutinize narrowly, so as to find out the truth 1573. **4.** To separate, to take or get *out*, by the use of a sieve. late ME. **b.** *fig.* To find *out*, get to know, by a process of elimination or close inquiry. 1586. **5.** To let fall through, scatter from or by means of, a sieve 1664. **6.** *intr.* To use a sieve; to do sifting. Chiefly *fig.*, esp. to pry *into*, make inquiry. 1535. **7.** To pass or fall as through a sieve 1599.

1. Two of the Fair Sex who are usually employed in sifting Cinders STEELE. *fig.* To s. the nations with the sieue of vanitie *Isa.* xxx. 28. **2. a.** Satan hath desired to haue you, that he may s. you as wheat *Luke* xxii. 31. **b.** You must speak with this wench,.. you must s. her a wee bit SCOTT. **4.** I have sifted out.. the flower of my fancye 1602. **b.** I endeavour'd to s. the Secret from him 1726. **5.** *fig.* From leaden skies the snow flakes were sifted over the land 1869. **6.** I will not s. into them too minutely 1699. **7.** Golden leaves were sifting down on the..floor 1867. Hence **Sift** *sb.* (*rare*) the act of sifting; the fact of falling as from a sieve; sifted material.

Sifter (si·ftəɪ). 1579. [f. SIFT *v.*] **1.** One who sifts. **2.** A sieve; also *dial.*, a fire-shovel, kitchen shovel 1611.

Sig. *dial.* and *U.S.* 1691. [Origin obsc.] Urine.

Sig., in printing, abbrev. of SIGNATURE.

Sigh (səi), *sb.* ME. [f. the vb.] **1.** A sudden, prolonged, deep and more or less audible respiration, following on a deep-drawn breath, esp. indicating or expressing dejection, weariness, longing, pain, or relief. **2.** *transf.* A sound made by the wind, suggestive of a sigh **1810.**

1. Stopping the Cariere Of Laughter, with a s. SHAKS. **2.** Autumn's hollow sighs in the sere wood SHELLEY.

Sigh (səi), *v.* Pa. t. and pple. **sighed** (səid). [ME. *sihen, siȝen*, prob. back-formation on *sihte, siȝte*, pa. t. of obs. *siche*:—OE. *sīcan.*] **1.** *intr.* To emit, give, or heave a sigh. **b.** Of the wind, trees, etc.: To make or give out a sound suggestive of a sigh **1757.** **2. a.** To express desire or longing by the utterance of sighs; hence, to wish or long ardently. Const. *for* (†*after*), or *to* with inf. **1549.** †**b.** To be sorry. Const. *that, to.* -**1734.** **3.** *trans.* To speak or utter (words, etc.) with a sigh **1553.** **b.** To emit, give out, impart, etc., by sighing **1593.** **4. a.** To spend, consume, or while away (time) by sighing **1599.** **b.** To bring into a certain state or condition by sighing **1603.** **5.** To lament (an event, circumstance, etc.) with sighing **1600.**

1. To s., and to wincke as thoughe he were a slepe **1560.** Nature from her seat Sighing through all her Works gave signs of woe MILT. **b.** Yon neglected shrub..That..sighs at every blast GOLDSM. **2. a.** Long have I sigh'd for a calm TENNYSON. **3. a.** Bvt wretch'd Iob, sigh't forth these words, and said, Ah me! QUARLES. **b.** Sapores..sighed out his affrighted ghost, at the age..of seventy one **1638.** **4. a.** Wearied I am with sighing out my dayes MILT. **b.** *refl.* The gale had sigh'd itself to rest SCOTT. **5.** I s. the lacke of many a thing I sought SHAKS. Hence **Si·gher**, one who sighs. **Si·ghing** *vbl. sb.*

Sighing (səi·iŋ), *ppl. a.* **1440.** [-ING [2].] **1.** Accompanied by, uttered with, a sigh. **2.** Of persons, etc.: That sigh(s) **1593.**

1. With dew all turned to tears; odour, to s. ruth SHELLEY. Hence **Si·ghingly** *adv.*

Sight (səit), *sb.* [OE. *sihð* (rare, usu. *gesihð, gesiht*), f. *sih-*, stem of SEE *v.* + -TH.] **I. 1.** A thing seen, esp. of a striking or remarkable nature; a spectacle. †**b.** A vision. *Book of sights*, the Apocalypse. -**1825.** **c.** *pl.* Those features or objects in a particular place or town which are considered to be specially worth seeing **1632.** **2.** A show or display *of* something; hence, a great number or quantity; a 'deal' or 'lot'. Also advb. Now *colloq.* or *slang.* late ME. †**3.** Aspect, appearance -**1680.**

1. White teeth is a good s. in a woman **1561.** Phr. *To be a s.*, to be an object of ridicule, horror, etc. *A. s. for sore eyes*, a welcome person or thing; esp. a welcome visitor. *S. unseen* (*U.S.* and *dial.*), without previous inspection. **2.** O ye Gods, what a s. of things do not I want? BURTON. You're a s. too clever for me **1889.**

II. 1. The perception or apprehension *of* something by means of the eyes; the presentation *of* a thing to the sense of vision ME. **b.** Without article, chiefly in phrases as *to catch, have, lose s. of* ME. **c.** The first perception or view *of* something. Usu. in phr. *at* or *upon* (*the*) *s. of.* **1471.** **d.** A position or point commanding or giving a view *of* something. Chiefly *in* or *within s. of.* **1533.** **2.** A view, look, or glimpse *of* something ME. **3.** With omission of the dependent genitive, in phrases related to **1 c.** ME. **4.** A look or glance (at something, or in a certain direction). Now *rare.* ME. **b.** An observation with a surveying or other similar instrument; an aim with a gun, etc. **1835.**

1. Therefore he never inform'd the Captain of the S. of Land **1743.** **b.** As if he dreaded losing s. of her **1898.** *To lose s. of* (fig.): not to bear in mind. **2.** You should have had a s. of the Copy **1692.** **3.** *At first s.* *At* or *on s.*, as soon as the person or thing is seen. *At* (formerly also *on* or *upon*) *s.*, used spec. with ref. to the payment of bills; also *after s.* *At* (so many) *days'* (etc.) *s.*, of bills. **4. b.** Some sights obtained for the chronometer gave the longitude 94° 40′ **1835.**

III. 1. The faculty or power of seeing, as naturally inherent in the eye; eyesight ME. **b.** *fig.* Mental or spiritual vision. See also SECOND SIGHT. ME. **2.** The sense or power of vision in relation to the individual possessing or exercising it; freq. approaching to a concrete use, = eye or eyes ME. **3.** The range or field of one's vision; chiefly in phr. *out of one's s.* Also *spec.*, the focal distance of a lens. ME. **b.** Without article, in the phrases *in s.*, *out of s.* ME. **4.** The exercise of the faculty of vision; the act of seeing or looking; esp. *by s.*, freq. denoting merely visual knowledge ME. **b.** Examination, inspection, scrutiny **1452.** **5. a.** Opinion, estimate, judgement; respect, regard, view. Now *rare.* ME. †**b.** Knowledge, skill, insight. Const. *in.* -**1600.**

1. Most Eyes have perfect S., tho' some be blind **1599.** **b.** To thee, O Lord most just, I lift my inward s. **1586.** **2.** Nor farther word she spoke, but closed her s. DRYDEN. Phr. *In one's s.*, before one's eyes. *To s.*, to the eye; so as to be seen. **3.** The two armies lay in s. of each other HUME. Phr. *Out of (all) s.*, immeasurably, beyond comparison. **4.** Lord Conway is barely known to me by s. **1831.** Phr. *Line of s.*, (*a*) an imaginary line between the sights of a gun and the object at which it is aimed; (*b*) an imaginary line drawn between the fovea of the eye and the point fixated by the two eyes in normal vision.

IV. 1. a. The pupil of the eye. Now *dial.* late ME. †**b.** A visor -**1666.** **c.** *pl.* Spectacles. Now *dial.* **1619.** **2.** An appendage to a surveying or observing instrument, serving to guide the eye **1559.** **b.** A device, of the nature of a projection or notch, on a fire-arm or piece of ordnance, etc., to assist in taking aim **1588.** **3.** The opening in a picture-frame; that part of the picture which shows in this **1850.**

1. b. Their eyes of fire, sparkling through sights of Steele SHAKS. **2.** An accurate land-surveyor, with his chain, s., and theodolite BURKE.

attrib. and *Comb.*: **s.-chase**, a chase in which the dogs hunt by s.; **-reader**, one who is able to read music at sight; †**-shot**, the range of vision; **-singing**, the practice or art of singing at sight; **-worthy** *a.*, worth seeing or visiting.

Sight (səit), *v.* **1556.** [f. prec.] **1.** *trans.* †**a.** *Sc.* To look at, view, inspect, examine, scrutinize -**1706.** **b.** To examine by taking a sight **1884.** **2.** To get or catch sight of, to see, to get or go within sight of (anything) **1602.** **3.** *intr.* To take a sight, *esp.* in shooting **1842.**

2. We sighted her one morning at daybreak **1887.** **3.** Together they sighted, and together they fired **1842.**

Sighted (səi·tėd), *ppl. a.* **1552.** [f. SIGHT *sb.* + -ED.] **1.** Having sight of a specified kind, as *dim-, long-, short-s.*, etc. **2.** Endowed with sight; able to see. Also *absol.* **1836.** **3.** Furnished or fitted with a sight or sights **1859.**

Sighter (səi·təɹ). **1897.** [f. SIGHT *v.*] A sighting shot in rifle or artillery shooting.

†**Si·ghtful**, *a.* late ME. [-FUL 1.] **1.** Visible -**1545.** **2.** Endowed with sight; seeing -**1613.** **3.** Sightly -**1571.** Hence †**Si·ghtfulness.**

Si·ght-hole. **1559.** [SIGHT *sb.*] A hole to see through, *esp.* in a surveying or other instrument.

Wee..Must..stop all sight-holes SHAKS.

Sighting (səi·tiŋ), *vbl. sb.* **1752.** [f. SIGHT *v.*] **1.** The action of SIGHT *v.*; *esp.* the action of giving to a gun the proper elevation and direction to hit the object aimed at. **2.** *attrib.*, esp. *s.-shot*, a preliminary shot allowed to each competitor in a shooting-match **1861.**

Sightless (səi·tlės), *a.* ME. [f. SIGHT *sb.* + -LESS]. **1.** Unable to see; without the power of sight; blind. **2.** Invisible, unseen, dark; impenetrable by vision **1589.** †**3.** Unsightly -**1632.** †**4.** Out of sight -**1816.**

1. A cruel mockery of his [Samson's] s. woe LONGF. **2.** The lark becomes a s. song TENNYSON. **3.** Vnpleasing blots, and sightlesse staines SHAKS. Hence **Si·ghtless-ly** *adv.*, **-ness.**

Sightly (səi·tli), *a.* (and *adv*). **1532.** [f. SIGHT *sb.*] **A.** *adj.* †**1.** Visible; conspicuous -**1579.** **b.** *U.S.* Of places: Open to the view; that may be seen from a distance; commanding a wide prospect **1828.** **2.** Pleasing to the sight; handsome, beautiful **1562.** **B.** as *adv.* Handsomely, finely **1591.**

2. The s. constellation of the southern cross **1850.** Hence **Si·ghtliness.**

Si·ght-see:ing, *vbl. sb.* **1847.** [f. SIGHT *sb.* I. 1 c.] The action or occupation of seeing sights. So **Si·ght-seer**, one who goes about to see the sights of a place or places.

Sightsman (səi·tsmæn). **1700.** [f. pl. or gen. sing. of SIGHT *sb.*] **1.** A local guide, a cicerone. **2.** One who reads or performs music at sight **1776.**

Sigil (si·dʒil). **1610.** [ad. late L. *sigillum* (in cl. L. *sigilla* neut. pl.), dim. of *signum*; see SIGN *sb.*] **1.** A seal or signet. **2.** *Astrol.* An occult sign or device supposed to have mysterious powers **1659.** **3.** *Rom. Antiq.* A small image **1738.**

2. Sign and s. well doth he know SCOTT.

‖**Sigillaria** (sidʒilē³·riă). **1831.** [mod. L., f. *sigillum* seal; see prec.] *Geol.* A fossil tree, the leaf-scars of which resemble the impressions of a seal, found chiefly in coal-deposits. Hence **Sigilla·rid.**

Sigillate (si·dʒilėˡt), *v.* **1471.** [f. late L. *sigillat-*, *sigillare*, f. *sigillum* SIGIL.] *trans.* To seal; to seal up. Hence **Si·gillated** *ppl. a.* impressed with a seal; esp. *sigillated earth*, Lemnian earth, sphragide. **Sigilla·tion.**

‖**Sigla** (si·glă). **1706.** [L., neut. pl., perh. a contracted form of *sigilla*; see SIGIL.] Letters (esp. initials) or other characters used to denote words; abbreviations or marks of abbreviation.

Sigma (si·gmă). **1607.** [L., Gr. σίγμα, the 18th letter of the Greek alphabet.] **1.** The name of the Greek letter Σ, σ, ς, the equivalent of the English S, s, in its uncial form having the shape of C. **2.** Something having the form of S or C **1788.** Hence **Si·gmate** *v. trans.* to add a s. or *s* to (a word, stem, etc.). **Sigmatic** (sigmæ·tik) *a.* characterized by the addition of s. or *s* to the stem. **Si·gmatism**, the marked use or repetition of *s*; an instance of this.

Sigmodont (si·gmŏdǫnt), *a.* and *sb.* **1877.** [f. Gr. σίγμα SIGMA + ὀδοντ-, ὀδούς tooth.] *Zool.* **A.** *adj.* Belonging to the *Sigmodontes*, a class of murine animals in which the molars exhibit sigmoid patterns. **B.** *sb.* An animal belonging to this class.

Si·gmoid (si·gmoid), *a.* and *sb.* **1670.** [ad. Gr. σιγμοειδής; see SIGMA and -OID.] Chiefly *Anat.* **A.** *adj.* **1.** Having the shape of the uncial sigma C; crescent-shaped, semicircular. Chiefly in *s. cavity, notch, valve.* **2.** Having a double curve like the letter S **1786.**

2. *S. flexure*, the last curving portion of the colon before terminating in the rectum.

B. *sb.* The sigmoid flexure of the colon **1891.** So **Sigmoi·dal** *a.* = A. **1666**; **-ly** *adv.*

Sign (səin), *sb.* ME. [a. F. *signe*, ad. L. *signum* mark, token, etc.] **I. 1.** A gesture or motion of the hand, head, etc., serving to convey an intimation or to communicate some idea. **b.** A signal **1601.** **2.** A mark or device having some special meaning or import attached to it, or serving to distinguish the thing on which it is put ME. **b.** A conventional mark, device, or symbol, used techn. (as in music, mathematics, botany) in place of words or names written in ordinary letters **1557.** †**3.** A mark of attestation (or ownership) written or stamped upon a document, seal, etc. -**1609.** †**4. a** A device borne on a banner, shield, etc.; a cognizance or badge -**1562.** **b.** Something displayed as an emblem or token; *esp.* an ensign, banner, standard -**1667.** **5.** A characteristic device attached to, or placed in front of an inn (†house) or shop, as a means of distinguishing it from others or directing attention to it; in later use commonly a board bearing a name or other inscription, with or without some ornament or picture **1467.**

1. Then Hudibras, with face and hand, Made signs for Silence BUTLER. **b.** Mark Antony, shall we giue signe of Battaile? SHAKS. **2.** *S. of the Cross*: cf. CROSS *sb.* 3. **b.** Two minus signs in arithmetic or algebra make a plus **1875.** **4. b.** The great Ensign of Messiah blaz'd Aloft by Angels born, his S. in Heav'n MILT. **5.** Putting up their pictures as signs for their taverns and ale-houses **1780.** Phr. *At the s. of* (*the Bell, Sun.* etc.). †*At the s. of the moon*, in the open air by night (after F. *à l'enseigne de la lune*).

II. 1. A token or indication (visible or otherwise) *of* some fact, quality, etc.; also *spec.* in *Med.* (= symptom), etc. ME. **b.** *U.S.* The trail or trace of wild animals, etc. (occas. in pl., but the sing. is the technical use) **1847.** **2.** A trace or indication *of* something; a vestige. Chiefly in neg. phrases. ME. †**b.** A mere semblance *of* something -**1693.** **3.** An indication of some coming event; *spec.* an omen or portent ME. **4.** An act of a miraculous nature, serving to demonstrate divine power or authority. (In biblical use, after L. *signum*, Gr. σημεῖον) ME. **5.** *Astr.* One or other of the twelve equal divisions of the Zodiac, each distinguished by the name of a constellation and freq. denoted by a special symbol ME.

1. What meanest thou by this word Sacrament? I meane an outward and visible signe, of an inward and spirituall grace. *Bk. Com. Prayer, Catechism* **1604.** [It was] no s. of grace, For folks in fear are apt to pray GRAY. Phr. *In s. of* (or *that*); In signe of truth, I kisse your Highnesse Hand SHAKS. **b.** We had noticed bear 'sign' in a thick patch of rose-bushes 1890. **2.** There is no s. of life in this wild place 1872. **b.** If it be but to punish that s. of a Husband there DRYDEN. **3.** These signs the coming mischief did foretell SHELLEY. **4.** Many wonders and signes were done by the Apostles *Acts.* ii. 43. **5.** I was looking..on that S. in the Heavens which is called by the Name of the Ballance STEELE.

Sign (səin), *v.*[1] ME. [ad. F. *signer* or L. *signare*, f. *signum* SIGN *sb.*] **I. 1.** *trans.* To mark, protect, consecrate, etc., *with* the sign of the cross. **b.** To cross (*esp.* oneself). late ME. **c.** To make the sign of (the cross) by a movement of the hand 1810. **2.** To place some distinguishing mark upon (a thing or person); to mark with a sign. late ME. †**3.** To put a seal upon (something). Also *intr.*, to use seals. -1638. **4.** To attest or confirm by adding one's signature; to affix one's name to (a document, etc.) 1477. **b.** To fix *down*, make *over*, give *away*, by signing 1589. **5.** *intr.* To affix one's signature (*to*) 1617. **6.** *trans.* To write or inscribe (one's name) as a signature 1817. **b.** *refl.* To denominate or designate (oneself) in a signature or signatures 1885. **c.** To engage by the signing of an agreement. Also with *on.* 1889.

1. He kissed the ground and signed himself with the cross 1878. **b.** Then, s. thyself, and peaceful go thy ways 1861. **2.** *fig.* Earth, Air, and Seas, with Prodigies were sign'd DRYDEN. **4.** I am not well, send the deed after me, And I will signe it SHAKS. *fig.* Turner always signs a locality with some given incident RUSKIN. **b.** Signing away vague and enormous sums of money DICKENS. **6.** Then you should s. your name in their presence 1858. **c.** The men can only be 'signed on' in the presence of the Board of Trade officer 1894. *To s. up* (U.S.), to enlist.

II. 1. a. To indicate, signify, betoken. late ME. †**b.** *intr.* To prognosticate, bode -1606. **2. a.** To make a sign or signs by some movement of the hand, etc. 1700. **b.** *trans.* To intimate, convey, by a sign 1719.

1. b. Musicke i' th' Ayre.. It signes well, do's it not? SHAKS. **2. b.** Upon this he sign'd to me, that he should bury them with Sand DE FOE. Hence **Si·gnable** *a.* **Signer** (səi·nəɹ), a signatory; *spec.* (*U.S.*), one of the signatories to the Declaration of Independence.

†**Sign**, *v.*[2] ME. [aphet. f. ASSIGN *v.*] *trans.* To assign, appoint -1582.

Signal (si·gnăl), *sb.* late ME. [a. F., = med.L. *signale*, a Rom. formation on L. *signum* SIGN; see -AL 2.] †**1. a.** A visible sign; a badge or symbol -1601. †**b.** A mark of distinction or honour -1685. **2.** A sign, token, or indication (*of* something) 1591. **3.** A sign agreed upon or understood as the occasion of concerted action, *esp*, one ordering the movement of troops or ships; also *fig.* an exciting cause 1593. **4.** A sign or notice, perceptible by sight or hearing, given esp. for the purpose of conveying warning, direction, or information 1598. **b.** An object serving to convey an intimation 1687. **c.** *Electr.* The intelligence, message, etc. conveyed in telegraphy or telephony.

2. The wearie sonne..Giues signall of a goodlie day to-morrow SHAKS. **3.** The s. of battle being given with two cannon shot we marched in order of battalia DE FOE. **4.** A bell rang which was a s...that a train was coming 1896. **b.** *Railway s.*, an apparatus by which engine drivers ascertain whether the line is clear.

attrib. and *Comb.*, as *s. apparatus, beacon, fire*, etc.; *s. box, cabin*, etc.; *s. corps, lieutenant*, etc.; **s. strength**, the strength of reception of wireless signals. Hence **Si·gnalist**, one who makes signals; one specially employed in signalling; a signaller.

Signal (si·gnăl), *a.* 1641. [f. L. *signum* SIGN *sb.* + -AL, after F. *signalé*, pa. pple. of *signaler* to distinguish.] **1.** Distinguished from the ordinary as by some sign or mark; notable. **2.** Constituting or serving as a sign 1655. Hence **Si·gnally** *adv.*

Signal (si·gnăl), *v.* 1805. [f. the sb.] **1.** *trans.* To make signals to (a person, ship, etc.); to summon, direct, or invite by signal. **2. a.** To communicate or make known by signalling; to notify or announce by signal(s) 1871. **b.** To mark out clearly 1869. **3.** To work (a railway) in respect of signals; to furnish with signalling apparatus 1888. **4.** *intr.* To give notice, warning, or information, or make any other communication, by signal 1864.

1. We were all signalled to be present at the Ferry Depôt 1892. **2. a.** Soon as..thine eyes shall s. a welcome 1871. **4.** They are signalling night and day ..by flag and fire 1864.

Signa·lity. Now *rare.* 1646. [f. SIGNAL *sb.* or *a.*] †**1.** The quality of a sign or indication. SIR T. BROWNE. †**2.** Signification; significance -1693. **3.** Notability 1650.

Signalize (si·gnălaiz), *v.* 1654. [f. SIGNAL *a.* + -IZE.] **1.** *trans.* To make signal; to distinguish; to render conspicuous, remarkable, or noteworthy. **b.** To display in a striking manner 1702. **2.** To characterize or mark conspicuously 1698. **3.** To point out, note or mention specially, draw attention to 1711. **4.** To make signals to; to communicate with by means of a signal 1824. **b.** *intr.* To make or send signals 1853.

1. She named Whitgift..,who had already signalised his pen in controversy HUME. **b.** Has he ever signalised his courage? 1702. **2.** The cheers which signalised the success of the Minister's speech 1882. **4.** They were signalising their consort with lights BYRON. Hence **Si·gnaller**, *U.S.* **signaler**, one who or that which signals.

Si·gnalman. 1737. [f. SIGNAL *sb.*] **1.** (Chiefly *Naval.*) A man employed to make, convey, display, or give signals. **2.** A railway employee who attends to the signals which show whether the line is clear or not 1840.

Signate (si·gnĕt), *a.* 1649. [ad. L. *signatus, signare* to mark.] Marked or distinguished in some way.

Signation (signēⁱ·ʃən). Now *rare.* 1607. [ad. late L. *signationem*, f. *signare* to sign.] **1.** The action of signing with the cross, or of marking with a seal. †**2.** A distinctive mark -1653.

Signatory (si·gnătəri), *a.* and *sb.* 1647. [ad. L. *signatorius*, f. *signat-, signare* to SIGN.] **A.** *adj.* †**1.** Used in sealing (*rare*) -1656. **2.** Forming one of those (persons or states) whose signatures are attached to a document 1870.

2. An understanding with the s. Powers 1870.

B. *sb.* One of those whose signatures are attached to a document of any kind 1866.

Signature (si·gnătiŭɹ, -tʃəɹ), *sb.* 1580. [ad. med.L. *signatura*, f. *signare* to sign, or a. F.] **1.** The name (†or special mark) of a person written with his or her own hand as an authentication of some document or writing. **b.** The action of signing one's name, or of authenticating a document by doing so 1621. †**2.** The action of impressing or stamping. BACON. **3.** A distinctive mark, a peculiarity in form or colouring, etc., on a plant or other natural object, formerly supposed to be an indication of its qualities, esp. for medicinal purposes. Now *Hist.* 1613. **b.** A distinguishing mark of any kind 1626. **c.** A stamp, impression 1649. **4.** An image; a figure; an imitative mark. Now *rare* or *Obs.* 1658. **5.** *Printing.* A letter or figure, a set or combination of letters or figures, etc., placed by the printer at the foot of the first page (and frequently on one or more of the succeeding pages) of every sheet in a book, for the purpose of showing the order in which these are to be placed or bound. Abbrev. *sig.* 1656. **b.** A sheet, as distinguished by its signature 1712. **6.** *Mus.* A sign, or set of signs, placed at the beginning of a piece of music, immediately after the clef, to indicate its key or time 1806.

1. I wish I had Miss MacWhirter's s. to a cheque for five thousand pounds THACKERAY. **3.** Whether men, as they say of plants, have signatures to discover their nature by, is hard to determine 1697.

Comb. **s.-tune**, a special tune used in broadcasting to announce a particular band, etc. Hence **Si·gnaturist** (*rare*), one who maintains the theory of signatures in plants.

Signature (si·gnătiŭɹ, -tʃəɹ), *v.* 1653. [f. the sb.] †**1.** *trans.* To indicate symbolically; to mark out, designate -1740. **2.** *Printing.* To put a signature on (a sheet) 1889. **3.** To put one's signature to; to authenticate or confirm by one's signature 1900.

Sign-board (səi·nbōᵊɹd). 1632. [SIGN *sb.* I. 5.] A board on which the sign of a shop, inn, or other place of business is painted or otherwise displayed.

Signet (si·gnĕt), *sb.* ME. [a. OF., or ad. med.L. *signetum*, dim. of OF. *signe*, L. *signum* seal, SIGN *sb.*] **1.** A small seal, usu. one fixed in a finger-ring. **2.** A small seal of this kind in formal or official use. late ME. **3.** *spec.* The smaller seal orig. used by the sovereigns of England and Scotland for private purposes and for certain documents of an official character. Also called *privy* or *King's* (*Queen's*) *s.* Hence *Clerk of* (or *to*), *Keeper of, the s.* late ME. **4.** An impressed seal or stamp; *esp.* the stamp or impression of a signet. late ME. **b.** *fig.* A mark, sign, stamp 1662.

1. Taking his s. from his finger 1770. **2.** She wrote a letter vnder Achabs name, and sealed it with his s. COVERDALE 1 *Kings* xxi. 8. *Writer to the s.* (Sc.): see WRITER. Hence **Si·gnet** *v. trans.* (*Sc.*), to stamp with a signet.

Si·gnet-ri·ng. 1681. [SIGNET *sb.*] A finger-ring containing a signet.

†**Si·gneur**, obs. var. of SENIOR *sb.* SHAKS.

Signifer (si·gnifəɹ). Now *rare.* late ME. [a. L., f. *signum* SIGN *sb.* + *-fer* bearing.] †**1.** The zodiac -1601. **2.** A standard-bearer, leader (*rare*) 1450.

1. And S. his kandles sheweth brighte CHAUCER.

Significance (signi·fikăns). 1450. [a. OF., or ad. L. *significantia*, f. *significare* to SIGNIFY.] **1.** The meaning or import *of* something. **b.** Without const.: Meaning; suggestiveness 1814. **2.** Importance, consequence 1725.

1. Empty sentences, that have..the s. of nothing pertinent MILT. **b.** A parting smile and nod of s. SCOTT. **2.** The omission is not of any real s. 1875.

Significancy (signi·fikănsi). 1595. [See prec. and -ANCY.] **1.** The quality of being highly significant. **2.** The quality of being significant, of having a meaning or import 1631. **b.** = prec. 1. 1641. **3.** = prec. 2. 1679.

1. Antiquated words..are never to be reviv'd, but when Sound or S. is wanting in the present Language DRYDEN.

Significant (signi·fikănt), *a.* and *sb.* 1579. [ad. L. *significant-, significare.*] **A.** *adj.* **1.** Full of meaning or import. **b.** Important, notable 1761. **2.** Signifying something 1597. **3.** Expressive or indicative *of* something 1793.

1. His words few, but s. and weighty 1668. A s. act followed these emphatic words 1874. **b.** A little man may be a very s. man 1857. **2.** Math. *To* (so many) *s. figures*: with the degree of accuracy indicated by the figures given, sequences of 0's at the end (of an integral number) or at the beginning (of a decimal fraction) not being counted.

B. *sb.* Something which conveys or expresses a meaning; a sign, symbol, indication 1588.

Since you are tongue-ty'd, and so loth to speake, In dumbe significants proclayme your thoughts SHAKS. So **Signi·ficantly** *adv.* in a s. manner 1577.

Significate (signi·fikĕt), *sb.* 1449. [ad. L. *significatum, significare.*] That which is signified or symbolized.

Signification (si:gnifikēⁱ·ʃən). ME. [a. OF., or ad. L. *significatio*, f. *significare.*] **1.** The fact or property of being significant or expressive of something. **b.** Importance, consequence, significance. Now *rare* or *dial.* 1670. **2.** That which is signified by something; meaning, import, implication. Freq. const. *of.* late ME. **3.** A thing, event, etc., which is significant or expressive of something ME. **4.** An indication or intimation of something. late ME. **b.** *spec.* Notification in proper legal form 1533.

1. The Rainbow hath in it two contrary significations, *viz.* of rain, and fair-weather 1643. **2.** Shewe me the dreame and the significacion of it COVERDALE *Dan.* ii. 6. **4.** Feeling myself inspired with courage by the s. of your noble desire..I stoutly fell to my taske 1638.

Significative (signi·fikătiv), *a.* and *sb.* late ME. [a. OF., or ad. late L. *significativus*; see SIGNIFY *v.* and -ATIVE.] **A.** *adj.* **1.** Serving to signify something; having a signification or meaning. **b.** Serving as a sign or indication *of* something 1637. **2.** Highly significant or suggestive 1677.

1. It does not appear that, like the bees, they emit any s. sounds 1816. **2.** A most s. and mysterious warning 1855.

B. *sb.* A thing or word serving to signify or indicate something 1641.

Hence **Signi·ficative·ly** *adv.*, **-ness.**

Significator (si·gnifikēⁱtəɹ). 1584. [a. med.L., f. L. *significare* to SIGNIFY.] **1.** *Astrol.* The planet by which the querent or the quesited is specially signified. **2.** That which signifies or indicates (*rare*) 1649.

1. The position of the S., or lord of the Ascendant, in the fixed sign Taurus 1895.

Significatory (signi·fikătəri), *a.* Now *rare.* 1579. [ad. late L. *significatorius.*] Serving to signify or intimate.

‖ **Significavit** (signifikēⁱ·vit). late ME. [L., 3rd sing. perf. indic. of *significare* to SIGNIFY.] *Eccl. Law.* A form of writ employed in ecclesiastical cases; *spec.* one formerly issued by Chancery for the arrest of an excommunicated person; also, the bishop's certificate on which such a writ is based.

Signify (si·gnifəi), *v.* ME. [ad. F. *signifier*, ad. L. *significare*, f. *signum* SIGN *sb.*] **1.** *trans.* To be a sign or symbol of; to represent, betoken, mean. Also *absol.* **b.** To foreshow, indicate as something that is to take place ME. **2.** Of words, etc.: To have the import or meaning of; to mean, denote. Also *absol.* ME. **3.** To make known, intimate, announce, declare ME. †**4.** To notify or inform (a person) -1690. **5.** *intr.* To be of importance or consequence; to have significance; to avail or matter 1661.

1. The secret grace which they [the sacraments] signifie and exhibit 1597. b. A gret sterre,..whiche synified gret sorw, & myschef þat fylle aftyrward 1475. 2. We now employ the term *Energy* to s. the power of doing work 1876. 3. Scott's wish as signified in the letter last quoted LOCKHART. 5. But it signify'd little 1686. His eye is still bloodshot, but nothing to s. 1817.

Sign-manual. late ME. [SIGN *sb.* + MANUAL *a.*] **1.** An autograph signature (*esp.* that of the sovereign) serving to authenticate a document. **2.** A sign made with the hand or hands 1841.

‖ **Signor** (sī·nyǫɹ). 1577. [It., reduced form of SIGNORE:—L. *seniorem*, acc. of *senior* SENIOR *a.* and *sb.* See also SEIGNEUR and SEIGNIOR.] **1.** The Italian term of respect placed before the name of a man in addressing him or speaking of him, now = English 'Mr.' 1584. **b.** Used without the name = 'sir' in English 1590. **c.** An Italian gentleman, *esp.* a singer 1779. **2.** A person of note or distinction; one having rank or authority; a gentleman or nobleman; an overlord. See also GRAND SIGNIOR. 1577.

1. A thousand thankes signior Gremio SHAKS. b. The stranger..said, 'S., your steps are watched' 1797.

‖ **Signora** (sinyǭ·rä). 1636. [It., fem. of next. Cf. SEÑORA, SENHORA.] The Italian term of respect applied to ladies, corresponding to 'Mrs.' and 'Madam' in English; hence (with *a*, *the*, etc.), a lady of Italian nationality.

‖ **Signore** (sinyǭ·re). 1594. [It., = Sp. SEÑOR, Pg. SENHOR.] = SIGNOR.

‖ **Signoria** (sīnyorī·a). 1549. [It.; cf. SIGNORY.] The governing body of some of the old Italian republics, *esp.* that of Venice.

‖ **Signorina** (sīnyorī·nă). 1820. [It., dim. of *signora.*] The Italian term of respect applicable to a young unmarried lady.

†**Si·gnorize,** *v.* 1588. [f. SIGNOR + -IZE.] **1.** *intr.* To rule, reign, have or exercise dominion (*in*, *over*) -1658. **2.** *trans.* To govern, control, exercise dominion or rule over -1602.

Signory (sī·nyŏri). late ME. [orig. a. OF. *signerie*, *signorie*, etc., vars. of *seignorie*, subseq. infl. by It. *signoria.*] **1.** Lordship, domination, rule. **2.** A lordship, domain, territory 1533. **3.** A governing body, *esp.* that of Venice or other mediæval Italian republic 1604.

2. His Sons..won them Lands and Signories in Germany MILT. Hence **Signo·rial** *a.*

Si·gn-post. 1620. [SIGN *sb.*] **1.** A post supporting a sign, usu. that of an inn or shop. **2.** A guide- or direction-post, set up to indicate the proper road to a place; a finger-post 1863.

1. When did the Lamb and Dolphin ever meet, except upon a Sign-Post? ADDISON.

Sike, syke (səik), *sb.*[1] *north.* and *Sc.* ME. [The northern form repr. OE. *sīc.*] A small stream of water, a rill or streamlet, esp. one flowing through flat or marshy ground, and often dry in summer; a ditch or channel through which a tiny stream flows.

Sike (səik), *v.* Now *dial.* ME. [var. of obs. *siche* SIGH *v.*] **1.** *intr.* To sigh. †**2.** *trans.* To emit (a sigh). ME. only. So **Sike** *sb.*[2] a sigh.

Sikh (sik, sīk). 1781. [Hindī *sikh* disciple.] **1.** A member of a military community belonging to the Punjab, where it was originally established as a religious sect by Nanak Shah in the early part of the 16th c. **2.** *attrib.* or *adj.* Of or pertaining to the Sikhs 1845. Hence **Si·khism,** the tenets of the Sikhs.

Silage (səi·lėdʒ). 1884. [Alteration of ENSILAGE, after SILO.] = ENSILAGE 2.

Sile (səil), *sb.*[1] *north.* and *Sc.* 1459. [a. ON. **sīl*; cf. SILE *v.*[2]] A strainer or sieve, esp. one for milk.

Sile (səil), *sb.*[2] *north.* and *Sc.* 1769. [Of Scand. origin.] Young herring.

Sile, *v.*[1] *Obs.* exc. *n. dial.* ME. [prob. of Scand. origin.] **1.** *intr.* To go, pass, move; to glide. **2.** To fall or sink (*down*). late ME. **3.** †**a.** Of tears, etc.: To flow -1878. **b.** *dial.* Of rain: To pour (*down*) 1703.

Sile, *v.*[2] Now *dial.* late ME. [Of Scand. origin; cf. MSw. *siila*, *sila*, Sw. and Norw. *sila* in the same sense.] *trans.* To strain; *esp.* to pass (milk) through a sieve or strainer.

Silence (səi·lėns), *sb.* ME. [a. OF., ad. L. *silentium*, f. *silere* to be silent.] **1.** The fact of abstaining or forbearing from speech or utterance; the state or condition resulting from this; muteness, reticence, taciturnity. Occas. with *a* or in pl. **b.** Used imperatively, = Be silent; make no noise 1590. **2.** The state or condition when nothing is audible; complete quietness or stillness; noiselessness. Also const. *of* (the night, etc.). late ME. **b.** Used allusively to denote the state beyond this life. Chiefly in pl. and with initial capital. 1803. **3.** Omission of mention, remark, or notice in narration 1513. **b.** Neglect or omission to write (about something); failure to communicate or reply 1617. **4.** *Mus.* A rest 1752.

1. Nor dream that I will..with my s. sanction tyranny SHELLEY. Phr. *To keep s.*, *to break s.*, *in s.* *To put to s.*, to silence by argument or prohibition; †to put to death. *S. gives consent*: see CONSENT *sb.* 1. b. S., ye troubl'd waves, and thou Deep, peace MILT. 2. Through the soft s. of the list'ning night MILT. b. Power to make Our noisy years seem moments in the being Of the eternal S. WORDSW. 3. Phr. *To pass with, pass over in, s.*

Silence (səi·lėns), *v.* 1560. [f. prec.] **1.** *trans.* To cause or compel (a person) to cease speaking on a particular occasion; also, to overcome in argument 1603. **b.** To cause (an animal or thing) to cease from giving out its natural sound; to still, quieten; (*colloq.*) to put to death 1604. **2.** To reduce (a person, etc.) to silence by restraint or prohibition, esp. in order to prevent the free expression of opinions 1597. **b.** To put down, repress (any expression of feeling, etc.) 1647. **3.** *Mil.* and *Naval.* To compel (a gun, battery, or ship) to cease firing; to disable by superior fire; to stop (the fire of a gun) 1748. **4.** *intr.* To cease speaking; to become silent or still (*rare*) 1560.

1. This learned priest has silenc'd the parson 1733. b. S. that dreadfull Bell, it frights the Isle, From her propriety SHAKS. 2. b. A threat of excommunication silenced the murmurs of the clergy 1874. 3. We silenced three of her lower deck guns 1755.

Silencer (səi·lėnsəɹ). 1635. [f. SILENCE *v.* + -ER [1].] **1.** One who, or that which, silences; a conclusive argument or retort. **2.** A piece of mechanism used to silence or reduce the sound caused by the working of a piece of machinery, as a motor vehicle, a maxim gun or rifle, a water cistern, etc. 1898.

Silene (səilī·ni). 1785. [mod.L. (Linn.), f. L. *Silenus.*] *Bot.* A genus of caryophyllaceous plants typifying the family *Silenaceæ*; a plant belonging to this genus; catchfly.

Silent (səi·lėnt), *a.* and *sb.* 1565. [ad. L. *silentem*, *silere.*] **A.** *adj.* **1.** Keeping silence; refraining from speech or utterance; mute, dumb. Also, taciturn, reserved. **2.** Of writers, books, etc.: Omitting mention of or reference to something in narration; containing no account or record 1601. **3.** Characterized by silence or absence of speech; performed, made, suffered, etc., in silence or without speaking 1592. **b.** Of letters: Not sounded; mute 1605. **4.** Characterized by the absence of sound or noise; quiet, noiseless, still 1588. **b.** Making or giving out little or no noise 1753. **5.** †**a.** Of the moon: Not shining -1727. **b.** Inactive, not operative 1745. **c.** Of distilled spirit: Possessing no flavour 1839.

1. He is as s. as a Stone 1580. The s. sow sups all the broth 1828. *fig.* My duty cannot be s., when I thinke your Highnesse wrong'd SHAKS. 2. As to the other shire..history is equally s. 1871. 3. *The s. system*, a method of discipline enforced in a prison, penitentiary, etc., which imposes complete silence on all occasions. b. The final *e* seems to have become s. 1869. 4. Three mountain-tops, Three s. pinnacles of aged snow TENNYSON. *Mod.* A s. film (opp. to *talkie*). 5. b. A volcano, after being s. for ages, may suddenly start forth into fresh life 1878. Hence **Si·lent-ly** *adv.*, **-ness.**

B. *sb.* †**1.** The time of silence. SHAKS. **2.** A device by which a clock or alarm may be prevented from striking or acting 1834. **3.** A s. film 1929.

1. Deepe Night, darke Night, the s. of the Night SHAKS.

Silentiary (səile·nʃiări). 1611. [ad. late L. *silentiarius*, f. L. *silentium*; see -ARY.] **1.** One who observes or recommends silence, *esp.* from religious motives. **2.** An officer of the Byzantine court, whose duty orig. was to obtain silence, but who frequently acted as a confidential adviser or agent. Now *Hist.* 1677. **b.** An official whose duty it is to command silence 1838.

‖ **Silenus** (səilī·nŏs). *Pl.* **Sileni** (səilī·nəi). 1710. [L., ad. Gr. Σειληνός.] **1.** *Gr. Myth.* The foster-father of Bacchus, and leader of the satyrs; also, a wood-god, a satyr. **2.** *Zool.* A species of macaque 1871.

Silesia (səilī·ʃiă). 1674. [Latinized form of G. *Schlesien*, a province in the east of Germany.] **1.** Used *attrib.* with *cloth*, *lawn*, etc. = SILESIAN. **b.** A fine linen or cotton fabric orig. manufactured in Silesia 1727. **2.** A variety of lettuce 1731. So **Sile·sian** *a.* of or pertaining to S.; *sb.* a native of S. 1645.

Silex (səi·leks). 1592. [L.] Flint, silica.

Silhouette (silu͡e·t), *sb.* 1798. [f. Étienne de *Silhouette* (1709–1767), a French author and politician.] **1.** A portrait obtained by tracing the outline of a profile, head, or figure, and filling in the whole with black; an outline portrait cut out of black paper; a figure or picture drawn or printed in solid black. **b.** *fig.* A slight verbal sketch in outline of a person, etc. 1819. **2.** A dark outline, a shadow in profile, thrown up against a lighter background 1847.

1. Phr. *En* (or *in*) *s.*, in outline, in profile.

Silhoue·tte, *v.* 1876. [f. prec.] **1.** *trans.* To represent in silhouette. **2.** *intr.* To show like a silhouette 1884.

1. I have seen it silhouetted hard against tornado-clouds 1897. Hence **Silhoue·ttist.**

Silica (si·likă). 1801. [f. L. *silic-*, SILEX, after *alumina*, etc.] An important mineral substance (the dioxide of silicon), which in the form of quartz enters into the composition of many rocks, and is contained in sponges and certain plants. Hence **Si·licide** *Chem.*, a compound of silicon with another element. **Silici·ferous** *a.* yielding or producing silex or s.

Silicate (si·likĕt). 1811. [f. prec. + -ATE [4].] A salt produced by the action of silicic acid.

Comb.: **s. board,** a board made incombustible by being saturated with s.; **s. cotton,** slag-wool. So **Si·licated** *a.* coated or impregnated with silex or silica. **Silica·tion,** combination with silica; silicification. **Silicatiza·tion,** silicification.

Sili·ceo-, comb. form of SILICEOUS, as in *s.-calcareous*, etc.

Siliceous (sili·ʃəs), *a.* 1656. [ad. L. *siliceus*, f. *silic-*, *silex* flint.] Containing or consisting of silica; of the nature of silica.

Silici- (si·lisəi), comb. form of SILEX or SILICA, as in *silicicalcareous*, etc.

Silicic (sili·sik), *a.* 1817. [f. SILICA (or L. *silic-* SILEX) + -IC.] *Chem.* Pertaining to, consisting of, or formed from silica. Chiefly in *s. acid* (H_4SiO_4).

Silicify (sili·sifəi), *v.* 1828. [f. L. *silici-* SILEX + -FY.] **1.** *trans.* To convert into, impregnate with, silica 1830. **2.** *intr.* To undergo silicification 1828.

1. Fossil wood which has been 'silicified' 1872. So **Sili·cified** *ppl. a.* converted into silica; chiefly in *silicified wood* 1822. **Sili·cifica·tion,** the process of becoming silicified, conversion into silica.

Silicious (sili·ʃəs), *a.* 1721. = SILICEOUS *a.*

Silicium (sili·ʃiŏm). 1808. [mod.L., f. L. *silic-* SILEX + -IUM.] = SILICON q.v.

Siliciuret (sili·siŭret). 1827. [f. prec.] *Chem.* = SILICIDE. Hence **Sili·ciure·tted** *a.* combined or impregnated with silicon.

Silicle (si·lik'l). 1785. [ad. F. *silicule* or L. *silicula.*] *Bot.* A small short seed-pod.

Silico- (si·liko), comb. form of SILICA or SILICON. **a.** With adjs., as *s.-alkaline, -fluoric*, etc. **b.** With nouns, as *s.-aluminate, -borate, -fluoride*, etc.

Silicon (si·likǫn). 1817. [f. L. *silic-* SILEX, after *boron*; replacing SILICIUM.] A non-metallic element, which in respect of its abundance in nature ranks next to oxygen, and is usu. found combined with this as *silica*; it may be obtained in the form of powder, scales, or crystals. Chemical symbol Si.

‖ **Silicula** (sili·kiŭlă). 1760. [L., dim. of SILIQUA.] *Bot.* A silicle. So **Si·licule** (*rare*).

Siliculose (sili·kiŭlōus), *a.* 1731. [ad. mod.L. *siliculosus*, f. *silicula.*] *Bot.* Bearing small short pods.

‖ **Siliqua** (si·likwă). *Pl.* **-æ.** 1704. [L., a pod.] *Bot.* A long pod-like seed-vessel. So **Silique** (silī·k). Hence **Sili·quiform** *a. Bot.* having the form of a s.

Siliquose (si·likwōus), *a.* 1693. [ad. mod. L. *siliquosus*, f. L. *siliqua.*] **1.** *Bot.* Bearing pods or siliques. **2.** Having the form of a silique 1821.

Si·liquous, *a.* Now *rare.* 1668. = prec. 1.

Silk (silk), *sb.* (and *a.*) [OE. *sioloc* (for earlier **siluc*), prob. f. (ult.) L. *sericus* or Gr. σηρικός silken, f. L. *Seres*, Gr. Σῆρες, the oriental people (perh. the Chinese) from whom silk was first obtained.] **1.** The strong, soft, lustrous fibre produced by the larvæ of certain bombycine moths which feed upon mulberry leaves, etc., and by certain spiders; silken thread or filament. **2.** The cloth or textile fabric woven or made from this OE. **b.** Used allus. to indicate the rank of a King's (or Queen's) Counsel, marked by the right to wear a silk gown. Also collectively, denoting the persons wearing such gowns. 1810. **c.** As the material of a jockey's jacket 1891. **3.** With *a* and *pl.* A particular make of silk cloth or fabric 1538. **b.** *pl.* Garments made of silk; silk stockings 1508. **c.** A lady's silk dress 1861. **d.** A King's (or Queen's) Counsel; a 'silk gown' 1884. **4.** *U.S.* The silk-like filiform styles of the female flower of unripe maize 1817. **5.** *attrib.* or as *adj.* Made of silk; silken ME. **b.** Clad in silk (*rare*) 1603. †**c.** Silky SHAKS.

1. *Artificial s.* [F. *soie artificielle*], thread or yarn manufactured from collodion or wood pulp; also, a fabric resembling silk made from this (abbrev. *art silk, artsilk*). 2. b. Phr. *To receive, obtain*, or *take s.*

Comb.: **s.-coal,** a variety of coal found in Shropshire; **-glue,** sericin; **s. gown** = sense 3 d; **-gut,** the gut in the silkworm from which the s. is produced; **s. hat,** a cylindrical hat having a light stiff body covered with s. plush or shag; **s. paper,** a kind of tissue-paper; **-shag,** a local name for young herring; **s. snapper,** a Bermudan fish; **s. stocking,** a stocking made of s.; *U.S. politics*, a member of a section of the Whig party in the early 19th c.; **-thrower, -throwster,** one who converts raw s. into s. thread. **b. s.-oak,** *Grevillea robusta*; **-tree,** a low-headed spreading Amer. tree (*Albizzia julibrissin*), with very graceful foliage. **c.** In the names of various s.-producing insects: †**s.-fly,** the silkworm moth; **s. moth,** *Bombyx mori*; **-spider,** one or other of various species of s.-spinning spiders. **d.** In the names of birds: **s.-bunting** *U.S.*, one or other of the buntings of the genus *Spiza*, esp. *S. americana*; **s. cock,** a species of domestic fowl, esp. *Phasianus gallus* or *Gallus lanatus*, native to eastern Asia; **s. fowl,** a s. cock or hen; **-hen,** the female of the s. cock; **s. starling,** a species of starling (*Sturnus sericeus*), native to China. Hence **Silk** *v. trans.* to clothe in or cover with s. **Si·lker,** one who works in or with s.

Silk-cotton. 1697. [f. SILK *sb.* + COTTON *sb.*[1]] **1.** The silky, elastic down or fibre obtained from various bombaceous and other tropical trees, and chiefly used for packing, stuffing pillows and cushions, making paper, etc. **2.** *S. tree*, any of various species of tropical trees belonging to the genera *Bombax, Eriodendron, Ochroma*, and *Pachira*, producing s. 1712.

Silken (si·lk'n), *a.* OE. [f. SILK *sb.* + -EN[4].] **I. 1.** Made or consisting of silk. †**2.** Worked in silk (*rare*) -1597. †**3.** Producing silk; characterized by the prevalence of silk -1820. **4.** Clad in silk 1640.

1. They would not suffer a man to were a Ring, or a woman a s. gown 1645.

II. 1. Silky, silk-like; soft; glossy, shining, lustrous 1513. **2.** Of words, etc.: Elegant; ingratiating, soft, flattering. So of persons, their looks, voice, etc. 1588. **3.** Effeminate, luxurious 1599. **4.** Soft, sweet, balmy; gentle 1599. **b.** Of sounds: Soft, low 1784.

1. All day..in silence The s. butterflies glide 1871. 2. Taffata phrases, s. tearmes precise SHAKS. 3. The s. son of dalliance GRAY. 4. b. The gray owl's s. flight. 1800. Hence **Si·lken** *v. trans.* to invest with a silky lustre.

Silk grass. Also **silk-grass.** 1620. [f. SILK *sb.* + GRASS *sb.*[1]] **1. a.** One or other of various species of lustrous grasses native to America and the West Indies, esp. *Bromelia* or *Nidularium Karatas*; also, the fibrous leaves produced by these. **b.** Applied to various species of aloe, agave, or yucca, or the fibre derived from these 1753. **2.** The grass *Oryzopsis cuspidata* of the western U.S., the glumes of which bear long silky hairs; also *Stipa comata* of the same region 1891.

Silkman (si·lkmæ̆n). 1553. [f. SILK *sb.* + MAN *sb.*[1]] One who makes or deals in silks. So **Si·lkwo:man** 1440.

Si·lkstone. 1867. A variety of coal obtained at *Silkstone*, near Barnsley in Yorkshire.

Si·lk-tail. 1685. [tr. G. *seidenschwanz*, f. *seide* silk + *schwanz* tail.] The waxwing or Bohemian chatterer, *Garrulus bohemicus.*

Si·lkweed. Also **silk-weed.** 1846. [f. SILK *sb.* + WEED *sb.*] *Bot.* **1.** *U.S.* A plant of the N. Amer. genus *Asclepias.* **2.** A plant of the genus *Conferva* 1857.

Si·lk-wi:nder. 1611. [f. SILK *sb.* + WINDER[1].] **1.** One who winds or coils silk filament or thread preparatory to weaving. **2. a.** A silk-reel. **b.** A machine by which silk thread in the hank is transferred to the bobbin before spinning. 1858.

Silkworm (si·lkwɒ̄ɹm). OE. [f. SILK *sb.* + WORM *sb.*] **1.** The caterpillar of the mulberry-feeding moth *Bombyx* (or *Sericaria*) *mori*, orig. a native of northern China, which on changing into the pupa state spins a cocoon made of silken filament; also, the caterpillar of any bombycid or other moth which thus yields silken cocoons of commercial value. **2.** *contempt.* One who wears a silken dress 1613.

attrib. and *Comb.*: **s. gut,** a fine, strong, light gut, made of the drawn-out glands of the s.; **s. moth,** any of the various bombycid moths, whose larvæ produce cocoons; **s. rot,** a fungous plant, *Botrytis bassiana*, which kills silkworms in great numbers.

Silky (si·lki), *a.* 1611. [f. SILK *sb.* + -Y[1].] **1.** Silken; made or consisting of silk. **2.** Having the delicate softness of silk 1666. **b.** Of liquor: Having a soft delicate taste 1743. **3.** Of speech, manners, etc.: = SILKEN II. 2. 1778. **4. a.** Having the gloss of silk 1730. **b.** Having a texture like that of silk 1757. **5.** *Bot.* Covered with fine, soft, close-set hairs having a silk-like gloss; sericeous 1776. **6.** *Nat. Hist.* Having silk-like hair, plumage, etc. 1781. Hence **Si·lkily** *adv.* **Silkiness.**

Sill[1] (sil). [OE. *syll, sylle*, = MDu. *sulle*, Da. *syld.*] **1.** A strong, horizontal timber (occas. a stone or iron substitute for this) serving as the foundation of a wall or other structure; hence, †a large beam or piece of squared timber. **b.** *dial.* and *U.S.* One of the lower framing-timbers of a cart or railway-car 1875. **2.** The piece of wood- or stone-work forming the lower horizontal part of a window-opening. late ME. **b.** *Naut.* A port-sill 1815. **c.** *Fortif.* The inner edge of the bottom of an embrasure 1859. **3.** The threshold of a door or gateway; the lower horizontal part of a door-case 1591. **b.** *Mining.* The floor of a gallery in a mine 1747. **c.** A horizontal timber (or structure) at the bottom of the entrance to a dock or canal-lock, against which the gates close 1789. **4. a.** A kind of clay found in coal-measures 1774. **b.** *Geol.* A bed, layer, or stratum of rock 1794. **5.** The foot or lower part *of* a title-page or title 1834.

Sill[2]. 1787. Dial. var. of THILL.

Sillabub, syllabub (si·lăbɒb). 1537. [Origin obsc.; cf. SILLIBOUK.] **1.** A drink or dish made of milk or cream, curdled by the admixture of wine, cider, or other acid, and often sweetened and flavoured. **2.** *fig.* Something unsubstantial and frothy; *esp.* floridly vapid discourse or writing 1706.

Sillery (si·ləri). 1680. [f. *Sillery*, in the department of the Marne, Champagne.] A high-class wine produced in and around the village of Sillery in Champagne.

Sillibouk. *dial.* 1573. [var. of SILLABUB.] A sillabub.

Sillimanite (si·limănəit). 1830. [f. Benjamin *Silliman*, an American chemist (1779–1864).] *Min.* A silicate of alumina, occurring in slender rhombic prisms or in fibrous masses.

Sillock (si·lək). *Sc.* 1654. [Orkney and Shetland dial.] A young coal-fish (saithe), at a certain stage of its first year.

Silly (si·li), *a., sb.*, and *adv.* [Later form of ME. *sely*, SEELY *a.*] **A.** *adj.* **1.** Deserving of pity, 'poor'. Now *north.* and *Sc.* **b.** Helpless, defenceless 1500. **2.** Feeble, frail; insignificant 1567. **b.** Weakly, ailing. *Sc.* and *north.* 1585. †**c.** Scanty, sorry, poor -1767. **3.** Unsophisticated, simple, ignorant. *Obs.* or *arch.* 1547. †**b.** Of humble rank; lowly -1647. **c.** Of things: Plain, simple, homely 1570. **4.** Feeble-minded, imbecile 1550. **5.** Foolish, empty-headed 1576. **b.** Of words, actions, etc.: Evincing or associated with foolishness 1588. **c.** *Cricket.* Applied to (the position of) point, mid-on, and mid-off, when they stand dangerously near the wicket 1900. **6.** Stunned, stupefied, dazed, as by a blow 1886.

1. Good wife, for your courtesie, Will ye lodge a s. poor man? 1724. **b.** His s. sheep, what wonder if they stray? COWPER. 2. Thou onely art The mightie God, but I a sillie worm HERBERT. **b.** She was but of a s. constitution 1821. **c.** 3 *Hen. VI*, III. iii. 93. 3. **c.** Perhaps their loves, or els their sheep, Was all that did their s. thoughts so busie keep MILT. 4. The King's uncle, being rather weak in intellect, was called S. Billy 1881. 5. Of this sort are they which creep into houses, and leade captiue s. women 2 *Tim.* iii. 6. **b.** This is the silliest stuffe that ere I heard SHAKS. Phr. *S. season*, the months of August and September, when newspapers supply the lack of real news by articles or discussions on trivial topics. 6. I..got knocked s. for my pains 1889. Hence **Si·llily** *adv.* **Si·lliness.**

B. *sb.* A silly or foolish person. *colloq.* 1858.

You are not to be a s. 1896.

C. *adv.* In a foolish or silly manner. Now *dial.* or *colloq.* 1704.

Silly-how. Now *Sc.* and *north.* 1574. [f. *sely*, SEELY *a.* + *how*, HOUVE.] A child's caul.

Silo (səi·lou), *sb.* 1835. [a. Sp., :—L. *sirum*, acc. of *sirus*, a. Gr. σιρός a pit to keep corn in.] **1.** A pit or underground chamber used for the storage of grain, roots, etc. **2.** *spec.* A pit, or an air- and water-tight chamber, in which green food is preserved for fodder by ensilage 1881. Hence **Si·lo** *v. trans.* to put (green food) into a s.; to turn into ensilage.

‖ **Silphium** (si·lfiŏm). 1753. [L., ad. Gr. σίλφιον.] A plant of the Mediterranean region, yielding a gum-resin or juice much valued by the ancients as a condiment or medicine; the juice obtained from this plant, also called LASER.

Silt (silt), *sb.* 1440. [app. denoting a salty deposit; cf. Da. and Norw. *sylt*, Norw. *sylta* salt-marsh, sea beach, f. **sult-*, ablaut-var. of **salt-*; see SALT *sb.*[1] and *v.*[1]] Fine sand, clay, or other soil, carried by moving or running water and deposited as a sediment on the bottom or beach; sometimes occurring as a stratum in soil.

Comb.: **s.-snapper,** a Jamaican fish. Hence **Si·lty** *a.* of the nature of or resembling s.; composed of or containing s.

Silt, *v.* 1799. [f. the sb.] **1.** *intr.* Of a channel, river-bed, etc.: To become filled or choked *up* with silt or sediment. **b.** To flow or drift *in* after the manner of silt. Also *transf.* to pass gradually *away.* 1863. **2.** *trans.* Of silt: To fill, block, or choke *up* (a channel, etc.) by gradual accumulation. Chiefly in pa. pple. 1825. **b.** To cover *up* or *over* with silt 1830.

Silure (siliū·ɹ). 1802. [a. F., ad. L. *silurus* SILURUS.] *Ichth.* A siluroid fish, esp. the sheath-fish (*Silurus glanis*).

Silurian (siliū·riăn), *a.* and *sb.*[1] 1708. [f. L. *Silures*, an ancient British tribe which inhabited the south-eastern part of Wales.] **1.** Of or belonging to the ancient Silures, or to the district inhabited by them. **2.** *Geol.* The name given to the system or series of Palæozoic rocks lying immediately below the Devonian or Old Red Sandstone; of or belonging to this formation, or to the period when it was deposited 1835. **b.** As *sb.* in *pl.* Silurian strata 1842. So **Si·lurist,** a native of the district formerly inhabited by the Silures 1650.

Silu·rian, *sb.*[2] 1842. [f. SILURUS + -IAN.] A siluroid fish. So **Silu·rid, Silu·ridan,** *a.* and *sb.* = SILUROID.

Siluro- (siliū·ro), used as a comb. form of SILURIAN *a.*, as *S.-Cambrian* adj.

Siluroid (siliū·roid), *a.* and *sb.* 1849. [f. SILURUS + -OID.] *Ichth.* **A.** *adj.* Belonging to the family *Siluridæ*, of the order *Physostomi*; characterized by the want of true scales; having only a naked skin or large bony plates. **B.** *sb.* A siluroid fish 1851.

Silurus (siliū·rɒs). *Pl.* **Siluri.** 1601. [a. L., a. Gr. σίλουρος.] *Ichth* A genus of fish typical of the family *Siluridæ*; a fish belonging to this genus, esp. the sly s. (*S. glanis*), or sheath-fish.

Silva, etc.: see SYLVA, etc.

Silver (si·lvəɹ), *sb.* and *a.* [Com. Teut.; OE. *siolfor, seolfor,* etc.; ult. origin obscure.] **A.** *sb.* **1.** One of the precious metals (in general use ranking next to gold), characterized in a pure state by its lustrous white colour and great malleability and ductility. Chem. symbol Ag. (Also applied to several natural or artificial substances resembling or imitating the real metal as *German, inflammable, mock s.*) **2.** The metal regarded as a valuable possession or medium of exchange; hence, silver coin; also (chiefly *Sc.*), money in general OE. **3.** Articles made of silver; silverware, silver plate ME. **4.** The metal as used for the ornamentation of textile fabrics; silver thread. late ME. **5.** As a tincture in heraldry, more commonly called ARGENT 1450. **6.** A silvery colour or lustre 1481. **7. a.** A variety of insect, fish, bird, etc., having silvery colouring or markings 1832. **b.** *Photogr.* A salt of silver, *esp.* nitrate of silver 1891.

3. For cups and s. on the burnish'd board Sparkled and shone TENNYSON.

B. *attrib.* passing into *adj.* **1.** Made or consisting of silver OE. **b.** Containing threads of silver, or some imitation of this 1728. **2.** Producing or yielding silver 1475. **3.** Of or pertaining to, connected with, characteristic of, silver or silver articles 1610. **b.** Denoting compounds of which silver forms a part 1797. **c.** Advocating, relating to, etc., the adoption of silver as a currency or standard 1890. **4.** Having the whiteness or lustre of silver; silvery. Chiefly *poet.* late ME. **5.** Of sounds: Having a clear gentle resonance like that of silver; soft-toned, melodious 1526. **b.** Eloquent, persuasive, sweet-spoken 1594. **6.** Of or pertaining to the silver age of Latin (SILVER AGE b.) 1889.

1. The British s. coinage 1858. **b.** *S.-lace,* wire coated with s. and woven into lace 1858. **2.** A rich s. mine 1789. **3.** Our gold and s. standards 1860. **b.** Gold of 20 carats with 4 carats of silver alloy 1879. **4.** Auncient men, upon whose siluer heads the Almond-tree hath blossomde NASHE. Faire Galatea, with thy silver Feet, O, whiter than the Swan DRYDEN. Provb. phr. *S. lining*; Don't let's be down-hearted! There's a s. lining to every cloud W. S. GILBERT. **5.** A Swaine ..Marrying his sweet Noates with their siluer sound 1613.

attrib. and *Comb.*: **s.-bath,** a solution, esp. of s. nitrate, used for sensitizing photographic plates and printing-paper; a dish to contain this; **s. bronze,** a metallic powder used in s. printing; **-glance,** a variety of s. ore; argentite; **-grain,** the lines of the medullary rays in longitudinal sections of some woods as elm, oak, etc.; **s. lustre,** a composition used for silvering potter's ware; **-point,** the process of making a drawing with a s. pencil on specially prepared paper; a drawing made in this way; **s. print,** a photograph produced by **s.-printing,** the process of producing a photograph on paper sensitized by a s. salt; **s. sand,** a fine white sand used in horticulture, etc.; **s. screen** (see SCREEN *sb.*); **-side,** the upper part of a round of beef; **s. steel,** a fine steel containing a small amount of s.; **-stick,** 'the name given to a field-officer of the Life Guards when on palace duty'; **s. streak,** the English Channel; **s. thaw,** the phenomenon of rain freezing as it falls and forming a glassy coating on the ground, trees, etc.; **s. wedding,** the twenty-fifth anniversary of a wedding; **s. weight,** (*a*) the weight used for s.; (*b*) the equivalent weight in s. **b.** In names of beasts, insects, etc.; **s. fox,** a North Amer. variety of the red fox with black s.-tipped hairs, the black fox; **-line(s),** a species of moth. **c.** In names of birds, as **s.-bill,** (*a*) one of several birds of the genus *Munia*; (*b*) a South Amer. tyrant bird of the genus *Lichenops*; **-dun,** a particular breed of domestic pigeon; **s. pheasant,** any pheasant of the species *Euplocamus nycthemerus*; also, a local name for the S.-spangled Hamburgh; **s. plover,** the gray plover, *Squatarola helvetica*, etc. **d.** In names of fishes, as **s.-belly, -bream,** a small fish, *Gerres ovatus*; **s. eel,** the Broad-nosed Eel, *Anguilla latirostris*. **e.** In names of plants or trees, as **s. bell (tree),** *Halesia tetraptera* of the southern U.S.; **-bush,** the plant Jupiter's beard; **s. chain,** the white laburnum; **-tree,** a tree with silvery lanceolate leaves (*Leucadendron argenteum*), native to Cape Colony. Hence **Si·lveriness,** silvery quality or character. **Si·lverize** *v. trans.* to silver; to treat with a preparation of s.; to render silvery in colour. **Si·lverless** *a.* without money; having no money.

Silver (si·lvəɹ), *v.* 1440. [f. the sb.] **1.** *trans.* To cover or plate with silver; to coat with silver-leaf. Freq. with *over.* **b.** To coat (glass) at the back with a mixture of tinfoil and quicksilver, esp. for use as a mirror 1635. **2.** To invest or suffuse with a silvery hue or lustre 1594. **b.** To turn (the hair, beard, etc.) white or silvery 1602. **3.** *intr.* **a.** To flow with a silvery gleam 1807. **b.** To take on a silvery lustre 1878.

1. My coach..is silvered over, but no varnish yet laid on PEPYS. **b.** The amalgam of tin is largely used in what is called silvering mirrors 1833. **2.** The moon..silvered the wood on one side 1797. **b.** His Beard was..A Sable Siluer'd SHAKS. **3. b.** The darkness silvers away, the morn doth break BRIDGES.

Silver age. 1565. The second age of the world, according to the Greek and Latin poets, inferior in simplicity and happiness to the first or golden age. **b.** The period of Latin literature from the death of Augustus to that of Hadrian 1736.

Silver-coloured, *a.* 1594. [SILVER *sb.*] Having the colour of silver; of a greyish white hue with a metallic lustre.

Silver fir. 1707. [SILVER *sb.*] **1.** A tall species of fir (*Abies* or *Picea pectinata*) native to southern and central Europe and to some parts of Asia, introduced into Britain in the 17th c. and extensively used for planting. **b.** A tree belonging to this species 1789. **2.** Applied to various other species of fir 1834.

Si·lver(-)fish. 1703. **1.** One of the various silver-coloured fishes found in different parts of the world. **2.** An insect of the genus *Lepisma*, esp. *L. saccharina* or *domestica*; a bristletail or springtail 1855.

Silver(-)foil. late ME. [SILVER *sb.*] Silver beaten out thin; silver-leaf.

Silver(-)gilt. late ME. **1.** Gilt silver or silverware. **b.** *attrib.* or as *adj.* 1705. **2.** An imitation of gilding, consisting of silver-foil varnished with a yellow lacquer 1891.

Si·lver grass. Also **silver-grass.** 1600. **a.** The striped or ribbon-grass. **b.** The Australasian grasses *Danthonia pallida* and *Poa cæspitosa*. **c.** *dial.* The silverweed.

Silver-grey, *a.* and *sb.* 1607. [SILVER *sb.*] **A.** *adj.* Of a silvery or silver-flecked grey colour; also, having silvery grey hair. **B.** *sb.* A silvery grey colour 1712.

Silver-haired, *a.* 1665. [SILVER *sb.*] **1.** Having hair silvered with age. **2.** Having hair naturally of a silver colour 1678.

2. Mounted upon a brown s. Gelding 1678. So **Silver-headed** *a.* (in sense 1) 1643.

Si·lvering, *vbl. sb.* 1710. [f. SILVER *v.* + -ING[1].] **1.** The action of SILVER *v.* 1738. **2.** *concr.* Silver plating; a coating of silver, silver nitrate, or quicksilver 1710.

Silver(-)lead. 1601. †**1.** A composition of lead and tin. **2.** Silver in combination with lead, esp. in the form of ore. Chiefly *attrib.* 1860.

Silver(-)leaf. 1728. Silver-foil; a piece of this. **b.** (In full *s. l. disease*) A disease incident to trees, esp. plum-trees, which causes the leaves to assume an unhealthy silvery colour 1890.

Si·lverling. Now *arch.* 1526. [ad. G. *silberling*.] A shekel.

Silverly (si·lvəɹli), *adv.* 1595. [f. SILVER *sb.* + -LY[2].] **1.** With a silvery appearance or colour. **2.** With a silvery sound 1752.

1 Let me wipe off this honourable dewe, That siluerly doth progresse on thy cheekes SHAKS.

Silvern (si·lvəɹn), *a.* Now *poet.* and *arch.* [OE. *seolfren, silfren*; see SILVER *sb.* and -EN[4].] **1.** Made of silver; consisting of silver. **2.** Silver-coloured (*rare*) 1885.

1. *fig.* Speech is s., Silence is golden CARLYLE.

Silver (-)ore. ME. An ore containing silver.

Silver paper. Also **silver-paper.** 1817. †**1.** A fine white tissue-paper –1873. **2.** Paper covered with silver-foil or an imitation of it 1875; also, loosely, tinfoil used as a wrapping for tobacco, etc. 1911. **3.** *Photogr.* Paper sensitized with a silver solution 1898.

Silver plate. Also **silver-plate.** 1526. **1.** A thin flat piece of silver. **b.** A silver dish in the form of a plate 1710. **2.** *collect.* Vessels or utensils made of silver 1610.

Silversmith (si·lvəɹsmiþ). OE. [f. SILVER *sb.* Cf. G. *silberschmied,* etc.] A worker in silver; one who makes silverware.

Silver-tongued, *a.* 1592. [f. SILVER *sb.*] Having a pleasant or melodious utterance; sweet-spoken; eloquent.

Si·lverware. 1860. [SILVER *sb.*] Articles, esp. tableware, made of silver.

Si·lverweed. Also **silver-weed, silver weed.** 1578. **a.** A common wayside plant of the genus *Potentilla*, with prostrate rooting stems and silvery leaves; goose-grass. **b.** Any East Indian shrub of the genus *Argyreia* 1829.

Si·lver-work. 1535. [SILVER *sb.*] **1.** Articles made of silver; silver vessels or ornaments; silverware. **2.** A place where silver is smelted 1674.

Silvery (si·lvəri), *a.* 1600. [f. SILVER *sb.* + -Y[1].] **1.** Having the hue or lustre of silver 1611. **2.** Having a clear gentle metallic resonance; silver-toned, melodious 1600. **3.** Producing silver; containing silver 1870.

1. One small bright s. likeness of a cloud RUSKIN. *S. iron,* an inferior kind of pig-iron, more commonly called *white iron*. **2.** In his ears one s. voice was ringing KINGSLEY.

Silvi-: see SYLVI-.

Sima (səi·mă). 1909. [f. SI(LICA + MA(GNESIA.] *Geol.* That portion of the earth's crust which forms the substratum of the ocean bed.

Simar (simā·ɹ). 1641. [ad. F. *simarre,* ad. It. *cimarra, zimarra.*] **1.** = CYMAR 1. **2.** = CHIMER[1]. 1840.

Simaruba (simărū·bă). 1753. [Native name in Guiana.] **1.** A tree of the genus *Simaruba*, esp. *S. amara* or *officinalis*, a native of northern Brazil, Guiana, etc. **2.** The bark of the root of *S. amara*, which contains quassine and is employed as a tonic or astringent 1778.

Simeonite (si·mĭənəit). 1823. [f. name of the Rev. Charles *Simeon* (1759–1836) + -ITE[1] 1.] A follower or adherent of Simeon or a supporter of his theological doctrines; a Low Churchman or Evangelical.

‖ **Simia** (si·miă). *Pl.* **simiæ** (si·mi,ī). 1753. [L., perh. f. *simus*, Gr. σιμός snub-nosed, flat-nosed.] The class of animals consisting of the apes and monkeys, and more specifically of the tailless apes only, or of certain kinds of these, as the orang-outang; also, an animal of this kind. Hence **Si·mial** *a.* (now *rare*). **Si·mious** *a.* belonging to the S.; having ape-like characteristics; typical of apes.

Simian (si·miăn), *a.* and *sb.* 1607. [f. prec. + -AN.] **A.** *adj.* **1.** Characteristic of apes; resembling that of apes; ape-like. **2.** Of or belonging to, comprising or consisting of, the apes or *Simiæ* 1863. **B.** *sb.* An ape or monkey 1880.

Similar (si·milăɹ), *a.* and *sb.* 1611. [ad. F. *similaire* or med.L. *similaris, f. L. *similis* like; see -AR[1] 1.] **A.** *adj.* †**1.** Of the same substance or structure throughout; homogeneous –1704. **2.** Having a marked resemblance or likeness; of a like nature or kind (*to*, †*with*) 1611. **3.** *Geom.* Applied to figures which may become congruous by adjusting their linear dimensions without changing their angles 1704. **b.** *Mus.* (See quot.) 1861.

3. *S. segments* of a Circle are such as contain equal Angles...*S. Triangles* are such as have all their three Angles respectively equal to one another. 1704. *S. Products* are those whose Corresponding Factors are Proportional 1706. **b.** *S. motion*, that in which two or more parts..ascend or descend at the same time 1861. Hence **Si·milarly** *adv.*

B. *sb.* A thing or person similar to or resembling another; a counterpart (*of*) 1654.

Similarity (similæ·rĭti). 1664. [f. SIMILAR *a.* + -ITY, or ad. F. *similarité*.] 1. The state or fact of being similar; likeness, resemblance. 2. *pl.* Points of resemblance 1838.

1. Certain insects escape danger by their s. to plants 1879.

†**Si·milary,** *a.* 1564. [See SIMILAR *a.* and -ARY [2].] = SIMILAR *a.* 1, 2. –1692.

Fat is a s. Body void of Life 1668.

Similative (si·milē̆tiv), *a.* 1883. [f. L. *similis* like, SIMILAR + -ATIVE.] Expressing likeness, applied e.g. to such compounds as *crystal-clear*.

Simile (si·milǐ). Also †**simily** (*pl.* **-ies**). late ME. [L., neut. of *similis* like.] A comparison of one thing with another, esp. as an ornament in poetry or rhetoric.

1. A s., to be perfect, must both illustrate and ennoble the subject JOHNSON.

Similitude (simi·litiūd). late ME. [a. OF., ad. L. *similitudo*, f. *similis* like.] 1. A person or thing resembling, or having the likeness *of*, some other person or thing; a counterpart or equal; †a similarity. 2. The form, likeness, or image *of* some person or thing. late ME. 3. †a. A sign or symbol; the symbolic representation of something –1558. b. A comparison drawn between two things or facts; the expression of such a comparison; †a simile. late ME. c. A parable; an allegory. (Chiefly in Biblical use.) late ME. 4. The quality or state of being like; resemblance, similarity. Now *rare.* late ME. †b. Likelihood –1548.

1. The shadow stood, s. exact Of Nestor COWPER. 2. Let us make now Man in our image, Man In our s. MILT. 3. b. London is often likened to Babylon; but the s. is a very unjust one 1875. 4. The s. of Passions, which are the same in all men HOBBES. b. Phr. †*By* or *of* (*all, any, some*) *s.*

Similize (si·milǝiz), *v.* Now *rare.* 1620. [f. L. *similis* or SIMILE; see -IZE.] †1. *trans.* To compare, liken –1670. 2. To symbolize; to express or describe in similes 1668. b. *intr.* To use a simile or comparison 1686.

1. Similizing the Braine to a Garden 1653.

Similor (si·milǭɹ). 1783. [a. F., f. L. *similis* like + F. *or* gold.] A very yellow kind of brass used in making cheap jewellery.

Si·mkin. *Anglo-Ind.* 1853. [Urdū corruption of *champagne.*] Champagne.

Simmer (si·mǝɹ), *sb.* 1809. [f. the vb.] The state or condition of simmering. Chiefly in phr. *on the* (or *at a*) *s.*

Simmer (si·mǝɹ), *v.* 1653. [Later form of SIMPER *v.*[1]] 1. *intr.* Of liquids: To make a subdued murmuring sound under the influence of continued heat; to be at a heat just below boiling-point. Also *transf.* of the containing vessel, etc. b. Of feelings, tendencies, etc.: To be in a state of gentle activity; to be on the verge of becoming active or breaking out 1764. c. Of persons, etc.: To be in a state of suppressed excitement or agitation 1840. 2. *trans.* To keep in a heated condition just below boiling-point 1823.

1. The water in the singing brass Simmer'd COWPER. b. The disaffection was already simmering in Devonshire FROUDE.

Simnel (si·mnĕl). Now *arch.* or *local.* ME. [a. OF. *simenel, seminel* (mod.F. dial. *simnel*), app. related in some way to L. *simila* fine flour.] A kind of bread or bun made of fine flour and prepared by boiling, sometimes with subsequent baking. Now *Hist.* b. A rich currant cake, usu. eaten on Mid-Lent Sunday in certain districts 1648. c. *attrib.*, as *s.-cake*, **-Sunday**, Mid-Lent or Mothering Sunday 1674.

Simoniac (simōu·niæ̆k), *sb.* and *a.* ME. [ad. med.L. *simoniacus*, f. *simonia* SIMONY.] A. *sb.* One who practises simony; a buyer or seller of benefices, ecclesiastical preferments, or other spiritual things. Freq. with initial capital. B. *adj.* = next 1632. So †**Simo·nian** [1] *a.* and *sb.* (*rare*).

Simoniacal (simŏnǝi·ăkăl), *a.* 1567. [f. prec. + -AL [1].] 1. Of the nature of, pertaining to, or involving simony. 2. Of persons: Guilty of or practising simony 1569. †3. Tainted or marked by simony –1641.

2. Away with such young mercenary striplings and their Simoniacall fathers MILT. Hence **Simoni·acally** *adv.*

Simonian [2] (sǝimōu·niăn), *sb.* and *a.* 1607. [ad. med.L. **Simonianus*, f. *Simon* (see def.).] A. *sb.* A member of an early Christian sect named after Simon Magus and regarded as heretical. B. *adj.* Pertaining to, characteristic of, the sect of the Simonians 1883.

Simon Pure (sǝi·mǝn piūǝɹ). *colloq.* 1815. [Name of a Quaker in *A bold stroke for a wife* (1717), who is impersonated by another character during part of the play.] *The* (*real*) *Simon Pure*, the real, genuine, or authentic person or thing. b. *attrib.* or as *adj.* Real, genuine, authentic 1889.

Simony (si·mŏni, sǝi·mŏni). ME. [a. OF. *simonie*, ad. med.L. *simonia*, f. the name of *Simon* Magus, in allusion to his offer of money to the Apostles (Acts viii. 18–19).] 1. Traffic in sacred things; *spec.* the act or practice of buying or selling ecclesiastical preferments, benefices, or emoluments. †2. The money paid in simony. Also *transf.* a tip (to a verger). –1707. Hence **Simo·nious** *a.* = SIMONIACAL (now *rare* or *Obs.*). **Si·monist,** one who practices or upholds s.

‖ **Simoom** (simū·m). Also **simoon.** 1790. [a. Arab. *semūm*, f. the root *samm* to poison. Cf. F. *simoun.*] A hot, dry, suffocating sand-wind which sweeps across the African and Asiatic deserts at intervals during the spring and summer.

Simous (sǝi·mǝs), *a.* 1634. [f. L. *simus*, Gr. σιμός; see -OUS.] †1. Bending or curving inward; concave –1697. 2. Having a flat nose; snub-nosed (*rare*) 1656.

Simper (si·mpǝɹ), *sb.* 1599. [f. SIMPER *v.*[2]] An affected and self-conscious smile; a silly smiling look; a smirk.

Si·mper, *v.*[1] *Obs.* exc. *dial.* 1477. [prob. imitative.] *intr.* To simmer.

Simper (si·mpǝɹ), *v.*[2] 1563. [With sense 1 cf. Da., Norw., and Sw. dial. *semper, simper*, G. *zimper, zimpfer* elegant, delicate.] 1. *intr.* To smile in a silly, self-conscious, or affected manner; to smirk. 2. *trans.* To say or utter with a simper 1801.

1. She..lisps affectedly, simpers designedly, and looks conceitedly MME D'ARBLAY. Hence **Si·mperer,** one who simpers. **Si·mperingly** *adv.*

Simple (si·mp'l), *a.* and *sb.* ME. [a. OF., ad. L. *simplus* or *simplex.*] A. *adj.* I. 1. Free from duplicity, dissimulation, or guile; innocent and harmless; undesigning, honest, open, straightforward. 2. Free from, devoid of, pride, ostentation, or display; humble, unpretentious ME. 3. Free from elaboration or artificiality; artless, unaffected; plain, unadorned ME. b. Of persons: Unsophisticated, unspoiled 1794.

1. Here wily Jesuits s. Quakers meet CRABBE. A s. innocent boy SHELLEY. 2. Lowly and symple is he, he rydeth vpon an asse COVERDALE. 3. The short and s. annals of the poor GRAY. b. Pastoral people.., S. and spirited; innocent and bold SHELLEY.

II. 1. Of persons, or their origin: Poor or humble in condition; of low rank or position; undistinguished, mean, common ME. 2. With designations or titles: Ordinary; not further distinguished in office or rank ME. 3. Of persons or their attire: Not marked by any elegance or grandeur; very plain or homely. late ME. b. So of living, diet, abode, etc. ME. 4. Small, insignificant, slight; of little account or value; also, weak or feeble. late ME. 5. Deficient in knowledge or learning; characterized by a certain lack of acuteness or quick apprehension ME. 6. Lacking in ordinary sense or intelligence; more or less foolish, silly, or stupid; also, half-witted (now *dial.*) 1604.

1. His place of birth a solemn Angel tells To s. Shepherds MILT. †Phr. *As s. as*, or *s. though, I stand here.* 2. This change affected however only the s. barons 1875. 3. b. Blest be those feasts, with s. plenty crown'd GOLDSM. *The s. life*, a mode of life in which anything of the nature of luxury is intentionally avoided. 4. I am a s. woman, much too weake T' oppose your cunning SHAKS. 5. The s. and unletter'd poor COWPER. 6. The good old Gentlewoman was not so s..; she began to smell a Rat 1713. *S. Simon*, a silly fellow (with ref. to nursery rhymes).

III. 1. With nothing added; considered or taken by itself; mere, pure, bare ME. 2. a. *Med.* Of wounds, diseases, etc.: Unaccompanied by complications. late ME. b. *Law.* Not specially confirmed 1546. 3. Consisting or composed of one substance, ingredient, or element; uncompounded, unmixed (or nearly so). late ME. 4. Not composite or complex in respect of parts or structure. late ME. 5. Not complicated or involved; presenting little or no complexity or difficulty 1555.

1. Yet s. Nature to his hope has giv'n..an humbler heav'n POPE. Phr. *Pure and s.* (often following the sb.): orig. a term of jurisprudence (e. g. 'a pure and simple obligation'); hence *gen.* unconditioned, mere (e. g. 'pure and s. robbery', 'robbery pure and s.'). 2. a. The Suppuration proceeding kindly, the Wound became a s. Wound 1758. b. *S. contract*, one made by word of mouth or not under seal. 3. A Needle is a s. Body, being made only of Steel; but a Sword or a Knife is a Compound 1724. 4. Those tenses are called s. tenses, which are formed of the principal, without an auxiliary verb 1824. The s. microscope may consist of one..or of two or three lenses; but these latter are so arranged as to have the effect only of a single lens 1867. Leaves..which are not divided into separate leaflets are termed s. 1872. *S. feast*, a feast which is not a double or a semi-double. *S. interest*: see INTEREST *sb.* II. 2. *S. machine*, any of the six or more elementary mechanical devices, e. g. the lever, wedge, etc. *S. sentence*, a sentence containing only one member having a subject and predicate of its own. *S. tense*, a tense formed with a single word. 5. *S. Quantities* in Algebra, are such as have but one Sign, whether Positive or Negative 1704. A S. Equation, is that which contains only one power of the unknown quantity, without including different powers 1798. A s. proposition is that in which one predicate is affirmed or denied of one subject MILL. We must prefer the simpler hypothesis to the more complicated 1884.

B. *absol.* as *sb.* 1. As *pl.* Persons in a humble or ordinary condition of life. Also as *sing.* a person of this class. ME. 2. As *pl.* Those who are unlearned, ignorant, easily misled, unsuspecting; also as *sing.* an ignorant or foolish person 1560. 3. A simple word; a verb in its simple form or without prefix 1530. 4. †A medicine or medicament composed or concocted of only one constituent, *esp.* of one herb or plant; hence, a plant or herb employed for medical purposes. Now *arch.* 1539. 5. A single uncompounded or unmixed thing; a substance free from foreign elements, *esp.* one serving as an ingredient in a composition or mixture 1560. b. A simple proposition, quantity, idea, etc. 1654. 6. *Weaving.* One of a number of lines or cords attached to the warp in a draw-loom 1731. b. A draw-loom 1875.

1. Gentle or semple shall not darken my doors the day my bairn 's been carried out a corpse SCOTT. 2. A snare to the s. of heart 1853. 4. From the knowledge of Simples, she had a Receipt to make white hair black SIR T. BROWNE. Hence **Simple** *v. intr.* to seek for or gather simples. **Si·mpler** (now *arch.*), one who collects or studies simples; a herbalist.

Simple-hearted, *a.* late ME. [f. SIMPLE *a.* + HEART *sb.*] Possessed of, or characterized by, a simple heart or spirit; ingenuous, sincere, unsophisticated; †ignorant, simple-minded.

Simple-minded, *a.* 1744. [f. SIMPLE *a.* + MIND *sb.*] Having a simple mind; possessing little or no subtlety of intellect; also, feeble- or weak-minded. Hence **Simple-mi·ndedness.**

Simpleness (si·mp'lnės). ME. [f. SIMPLE *a.* + -NESS.] The quality or state of being SIMPLE, in various senses.

Si·mplesse. *Obs.* exc. *arch.* ME. [a. OF.; see SIMPLE *a.* and -ESS [2].] = SIMPLENESS.

Simpleton (si·m'pltǝn). 1650. [Fancifully f. SIMPLE *a.*] One who is deficient in sense or intelligence; a silly or foolish person; a fool.

Simplex (si·mpleks), *a.* and *sb.* 1594. [a. L., = SIMPLE *a.*] A. *adj.* Consisting, or composed of, characterized by, a single part, structure, etc. B. *sb.* A single uncompounded word 1892.

‖ **Simpliciter** (simpli·sitǝɹ), *adv.* 1545. [L.] Absolutely, unconditionally; without any condition or consideration. Chiefly in *Sc. Law.*

Simplicity (simpli·sĭti). late ME. [a. OF. *simplicité*, or ad. L. *simplicitatem*; see -ITY.] 1. The state or quality of being simple in form, structure, etc.; absence of compositeness, complexity, or intricacy. 2. Want of ordinary knowledge or judgement; ignorance; rusticity 1514. b. A simple person; a simpleton (*rare*) 1633. 3. Freedom from artifice, deceit, or duplicity; sincerity, straightforwardness; also, absence of affectation or artificiality; plainness, naturalness 1526. b. Simple, unsophisticated ways or manners; plainness of life. Also (in *pl.*), an instance of this. 1585. 4. Of language or style: Absence or lack of elegance or polish; in later use, freedom from over-elaboration; plainness or directness of an attractive kind 1553. 5. Absence of ornament or decoration; freedom from useless accessories 1609.

1. In contriving machines, s. of parts should always be studied 1815. 2. That other s. which is only a euphemism for folly 1875. 3. Nathanael was..full of holy s., a true Israelite without guile 1649. b. The simplicities of cottage life WORDSW. 4. S. is become a very rare quality in a writer COWPER. 5. Give me a face, That makes s. a grace B. JONSON.

Simplification (simplifikēⁱ·ʃən). 1688. [a. F., f. *simplifier*.] The action or process of simplifying; the result of this.

Simplify (si·mplifəi), *v.* 1642. [ad. F. *simplifier*, ad. med.L. *simplificare*, f. L. *simplus* simple; see -FY.] *trans.* To make simple; to render less complex, elaborate, or involved; to reduce to a clearer or more intelligible form; to make easy. Also *absol.*

The laws of commerce..are simplified and expanded SYD. SMITH. In a state of nature man..does not s. and fix his motives J. H. NEWMAN.

Simplist (si·mplist). 1597. [f. SIMPLE B. 4 + -IST.] One who studies simples; a herbalist. Now *rare*. So **Simpli·stic** *a.*

Simply (si·mpli), *adv.* ME. [f. SIMPLE *a.* + -LY [2], with later contraction as in *gently*, *nobly*.] 1. With simplicity (of mind) or sincerity; in an honest or straightforward manner; also, in later use, unaffectedly, artlessly. 2. Humbly in respect of dress or surroundings. late ME. 3. In simple language; also, plainly, clearly. late ME. b. Without elaboration or complication 1746. †4. Poorly, badly, indifferently; meanly, inadequately; weakly -1754. 5. In a foolish, silly, or stupid manner; without common sense or sagacity. Also *s. disposed*, of a simple disposition. 1466. 6. Without addition or qualification. late ME. b. Without exception; absolutely. (Frequently used as an intensive.) 1590. Also, *simply and solely*.

1. By things deemd weak Subverting worldly strong, and worldly wise By s. meek MILT. 3. b. A fine massive piece of architecture, s. grand 1816. 5. If an elephant chance to meet with a man wandering s. out of his way HOLLAND. 6. If he take her, let him take her s. SHAKS. It is s. a question of degrees 1836. b. The plates are s. magnificent 1888.

Simulacre (si·miŭlǟkəɪ). *arch.* late ME. [a. OF., ad. L. SIMULACRUM.] 1. An image (of a god, etc.) to which honour or worship is rendered. 2. An image, a material or mental representation, *of* a person or thing 1483.

2. A knight, in whom Sir Osborne might easily distinguish the s. of himself 1830.

‖**Simulacrum** (simiŭlēⁱ·krŏm). *Pl.* **simulacra** and **-acrums**. 1599. [L., f. *simulare* to make like, to SIMULATE.] 1. A material image, made as a representation of some deity, person, or thing. 2. Something having merely the form or appearance of a certain thing 1805. b. A mere image, a specious imitation or likeness, *of* something 1833.

Simular (si·miŭlǟɪ), *sb.* and *a.* 1520. [irreg. f. L. *simulare* + -AR, perh. after SIMILAR *a.*] A. *sb.* One who, or that which, simulates, or puts on a false appearance (*of* something). B. *adj.* Simulated, pretended, counterfeited. Also, simulative *of* something. 1611.

I return'd with s. proofe enough, To make the Noble Leonatus mad SHAKS.

Simulate (si·miŭlĕt), *ppl. a. arch.* late ME. [ad. L. *simulatus*; see next.] Simulated.

Simulate (si·miŭleⁱt), *v.* 1652. [f. L. *simulat-*, *simulare*, f. *similis* like.] 1. *trans.* To assume falsely the appearance or signs of (anything); to feign, pretend, counterfeit, imitate; to profess or suggest (anything) falsely. b. To have the external features of 1661. c. *Biol.* = MIMIC *v.* 5. 1876. 2. *intr.* To pretend or feign 1823.

1. A government..in word and action simulating reform ARNOLD. b. If purely artificial it [a vault] doth most lively s. nature 1661.

Simulation (simiŭlēⁱ·ʃən). ME. [a. OF., ad. L. *simulationem*.] 1. The action or practice of simulating, with intent to deceive; false pretence, deceitful profession ME. b. Unconscious imitation 1870. 2. A false assumption or display, a surface resemblance or imitation, *of* something. late ME.

1. S. is a Pretence of what is not, and Dissimulation a Concealment of what is STEELE.

Simulative (si·miŭlĕtiv), *a.* 1490. [f. L. stem *simulat-*; see SIMULATE *v.* and -IVE.] Characterized by simulation or pretence.

Simulator (si·miŭleⁱtəɪ). 1835. [ad. L.] One who practises simulation.

Simultaneous (simŏltēⁱ·niəs), *a.* 1660. [ad. L. **simultaneus*, f. *simul* at the same time.] 1. Existing, happening, occurring, operating, etc., at the same time; coincident in time. 2. *spec.* in *Math.* as *s. equation* (see quot.), *function*, etc. 1816.

1. The s. use of both eyes 1879. 2. Pairs or sets of equations in which the same unknown symbols appear, which are assumed to possess the same values throughout, are called s. equations 1842. Hence **Simultaneity** (simŏltănī·iti), the quality or fact of being s.; occurrence at the same time. **Simulta·neous·ly** *adv.*, **-ness**.

‖**Simurgh** (simɜ̄·ɪg). 1786. [Pers., f. Pahlavi *sīn* eagle *murgh* bird.] A monstrous bird of Persian legend, imagined as rational and of great age.

Sin (sin), *sb.* [OE. *syn(n*, for original **sunjō*, related to OFris. *sende*, MDu. *sonde*, G. *sünde*. etc. Cf. L. *sons, sontis* guilty.] 1. A transgression of the divine law and an offence against God; a violation (esp. wilful or deliberate) of some religious or moral principle. b. *transf.* A violation of some standard of taste or propriety 1780. 2. Without article or pl. Violation of divine law; action or conduct characterized by this; a state of transgression against God or His commands OE. (See also DEADLY *a.* 5, MORTAL *a.* 5, VENIAL *a.* 1 a.)

1. Plenary remission of their synnes 1524. At present, for my sins, I live in a village of the plain BORROW. *The seven deadly sins*; The Seven curs'd deadly Sins..Pride, Envy, Sloth, Intemp'rance, Av'rice, Ire, And Lust 1711. *For my sins*: phr. often used trivially = as a judgement. *Like s.* (slang), vehemently, furiously. b. The many literary sins I know I must have committed 1907. 2. 'Tis s. to misemploy an hour DRYDEN. Phr. *Child*, or *man*, *of s.*; *as black*, or *ugly*, *as s.* *In s.*, in a state of free sexual union or adultery.

Comb.: **s.-eater**, one hired to take upon himself the sins of a deceased person by means of food eaten beside the dead body; **-flood** [after G. *sündflut*, an alteration of OHG. *sinvluot* general flood], the Deluge; †**-money**, money brought as an offering in expiation of s.

Sin (sin), *v.* [OE. *syngian* :—**sunigōjan*, f. **sunjō* (OE. *syn(n* SIN *sb.*).] 1. *intr.* To commit sin; to do a sinful act. b. *spec.* To commit fornication or adultery *with* (or †*on*) ME. c. To offend *against* some principle, standard, etc.; to be faulty or wrong 1704. 2. *trans.* To do, perform, or perpetrate sinfully; to commit (a sin) ME.

1. The Tempter, or the Tempted, who sins most? SHAKS. I am a man, More sinn'd against, then sinning SHAKS. c. Faces sinning Against proportion BYRON. 2. There remains so much to be sinned and suffered in the world 1859. Phr. *To s. one's mercies*, to be ungrateful for one's blessings or good fortune.

Sin (sin), *adv.*, *prep.*, and *conj.* Now *Sc.* and *north. dial.* ME. [contr. f. SITHEN. (Cf. SYNE.) In later use freq. written *sin'*, as if short for *since*.] A. *adv.* 1. Then, thereupon; thereafter, subsequently. 2. From that time onwards. late ME. 3. Ago; before now 1490. B. *prep.* From, after; subsequent to ME. C. *conj.* 1. From or since the time that ME. 2. Seeing or considering that ME.

Sinæan (səinī·ăn), *a. rare.* 1667. [irreg. f. late L. *Sinæ*, ad. Gr. Σῖναι (Ptolemy), prob. ad. Arab. *Ṣīn*, the empire of China.] Chinese.

Sinaic (səinē·ik), *a.* 1769. [f. *Sinai* + -IC.] = next.

Sinaitic (səinēⁱ,i·tik), *a.* 1786. [f. *Sinai* (a. Heb. *Sīnai*) + -ITIC.] Of, or pertaining to, Mount Sinai or the peninsula in which it is situated; given or promulgated at Mount Sinai.

The actual subdivision of the pages of the S. manuscript 1883.

Sinalbin (sinæ·lbin). 1875. [f. L. *sinapis* mustard + *alba* white.] *Chem.* A glucoside contained in white mustard-seed.

Sinamine (si·nămǝin). 1850. [f. L. *sinapis* + AMINE.] *Chem.* A basic compound obtained from thiosinamine.

Sinapate (si·năpeⁱt). 1857. [f. SINAPIC + -ATE [1] c.] *Chem.* A salt formed by the action of sinapic acid on an alkali.

Sinapic (sinæ·pik), *a.* 1857. [See next and -IC.] *Chem.* Of, pertaining to, or derived from sinapine.

S. acid, an acid derived from sinapine by the action of potash and soda.

Sinapine (si·năpin). 1838. [f. L. *sinapis* + -INE [5].] *Chem.* An unstable compound, existing as a sulphocyanate in white mustard-seed.

Sinapisine (sinæ·pisin). 1840. [irreg. f. L. *sinapis* + -INE [5].] *Chem.* A white, scaly, crystalline substance obtained from black mustard-seed by extraction with alcohol and ether.

Sinapism (si·năpiz'm). 1601. [a. F. *sinapisme*, or ad. L. *sinapismus*, Gr. σιναπισμα mustard plaster, f. σίναπι mustard.] *Med.* A plaster or poultice consisting wholly or partly of mustard flour; a mustard plaster.

Sinapoline (sinæ·polin). 1850. [f. L. *sinapis* + -OL + -INE [5].] *Chem.* An organic base obtained from cyanate of allyl.

Since (sins), *adv.*, *prep.*, and *conj.* (also *a.*). 1450. [Reduced form of SITHENCE, or f. SIN *adv.* + -S.] A. *adv.* †1. Then, thereupon; immediately afterwards -1568. 2. From that time till now. Often with *ever*. 1470. 3. At some or any time between then and now; subsequently, later 1549. b. As *adj.* That has been since (*rare*) 1598. 4. Ago; before now. With time specified, or preceded by *long*. 1489.

2. You know s. Pentecost the sum is due, And s. I haue not much importun'd you SHAKS. 3. It was written and s. is lost PURCHAS. b. My s. experience of Sunday evenings FROUDE. 4. He went out a little while s. 1862.

B. *prep.* 1. Ever or continuously from (a specified time, etc.) till now 1530. 2. During the period between (a specified time) and now; at some time subsequent to 1515.

1. He sleeps s. thirty years THACKERAY. 2. They seem to have changed s. Spenser's time 1880.

C. *conj.* 1. From the time that. late ME. †b. With vbs. of recollection: When; the time when -1690. 2. Because; seeing that; inasmuch as 1450. †b. So *s. that* -1682.

1. 'Tis an age since I saw you 1753. I have known him ever s. he was in petticoats 1877. b. *Mids. N.* II. i. 149. 2. But s. no reason can confute ye, I'll try to force you to your Duty 1664.

Sincere (sinsīᵊ·ɪ), *a.* 1533. [ad. L. *sincerus* clean, pure, sound. Cf. F. *sincère* (16th c.).] 1. Not falsified or perverted in any way; genuine, pure; veracious; exact 1536. 2. Pure, unmixed; free from any foreign element or ingredient 1538. b. *spec.* Unadulterated; genuine. *Obs.* or *arch.* 1557. 3. Containing no element of dissimulation or deception; not feigned or pretended; real, true 1539. 4. Characterized by the absence of all dissimulation or pretence; honest, straightforward 1533.

1. The syncere and pure doctrine of Goddes worde 1536. 2. Their enjoyments are s., unallayed with fears or suspitions 1676. Scarce any s. gall issued forth on incision 1763. 3. Weak grace, if s., shall always find acceptance with Christ 1703. 4. Master Wickliffe was noted..to be a man..of a very s. life 1533. She had not one s. friend left 1837. Hence **Since·re·ly** *adv.* (*Yours sincerely* a stereotyped formula used in concluding a letter), **-ness**.

Sincerity (sinse·riti). 1546. [ad. L. *sinceritas*, f. *sincerus*; see -ITY. Cf. F. *sincérité* (16th c.).] The character, quality, or state of being sincere. †1. Freedom from falsification, adulteration, or alloy; purity, correctness -1653. 2. Freedom from dissimulation or duplicity; honesty, straightforwardness 1557. b. Of feelings: Genuineness 1611. c. *pl.* Sincere feelings or actions 1840.

2. There is nothing so pitilessly..cruel as s. formulated into dogma 1870. b. The s. of his friendship has been suspected GIBBON.

Sinciput (si·nsipɒt). 1578. [L., for early **senciput*, f. *semi* half + *caput* head.] Chiefly *Anat.* The front part of the head or skull. Hence **Sinci·pital** *a.* of or pertaining to the s.

Sindon (si·ndən). Now *Hist.* 1450. [a. OF. *sindone*, or a. L. *sindon*, a. Gr. σινδών, prob. of Oriental origin.] 1. A fine thin fabric of linen; a kind of cambric or muslin. 2. A piece of this fabric used: a. As a shroud, *spec.* that in which the body of Christ was wrapped 1500. b. As a wrapper 1577. c. As a surgical appliance, being made up into a small roll or pledget, usu. with some medicament and used to fill up an open wound 1657. **3.** *attrib.* Made or consisting of sindon 1500.

2. b. There were found in it a Book, and a Letter; Both..wrapped in Sindons of Linnen BACON.

Sine (səin). 1591. [ad. L. *sinus* a bend; also, the bosom of a garment, and hence used as tr. the synonymous Arab *jaib*, applied in geometry as in sense 2.] †**1.** A gulf or bay. SYLVESTER. **2.** *Trig.* One of the three fundamental trigonometrical functions (cf. TANGENT, SECANT): Orig., the length of a straight line drawn from one end of a circular arc parallel to the tangent at the other end, and terminated by the radius; in mod. use, the ratio of this line to the radius, or (equivalently, as the function of an angle), the ratio of the side of a right-angled triangle opposite the given angle to the hypotenuse (the sine of an obtuse angle being numerically equal to that of its supplement). (Abbrev. *sin*) 1593. **b.** Const. *of* an angle 1728.

2. *Coversed, logarithmic, versed s.*: see the adjs.

Sinecure (səi·nĭkiūəɹ, si·n-), *sb.* and *a.* 1662. [ad. L. *sine cura* in the phr. *beneficium sine cura* (see def.), from *sine* without, *curā* abl. sing. of *cura* care.] **1.** An ecclesiastical benefice without cure of souls. **2.** Any office or position which has no work or duties attached to it, esp. one which yields some stipend or emolument 1676. **3.** *attrib.* or as *adj.* Of the nature of a sinecure; involving no duties or work 1761.

2. Many of the best institutions moulder into Sinecures 1800. **3.** I never could myself understand the difference between a Pension and a S. Place 1761. Hence **Si·necurism**, the practice of holding or permitting sinecures; the prevalence of sinecures in the church or any other sphere of work. **Si·necurist**, one who has or seeks a s.

‖**Sine die** (səi·nĭ dəi·ī). 1631. [L., *sine* without + *die*, abl. sing. of *dies* day.] Without any day being specified (for reassembling, resumption of business, etc.), indefinitely.

The *fête* was postponed *sine die* 1842.

‖**Sine qua non** (səi·nĭ kwē̆ nɒn). 1602. [L., *sine* without + *qua*, abl sing. fem. of *qui* which (agreeing with *causa*) + *non* not.] **1.** With adjectival force: Indispensable, absolutely necessary or essential 1615. **2.** Somebody or something indispensable 1602.

1. The Preliminary Article *sine quâ non*, was that ..he should surrender his Place of Recorder 1734. A ghost or a witch is a *sine qua non* ingredient in all the dishes of..my hobgoblin repast 1798. **2.** It was a *sine qua non* that the Indians should be included in the pacification 1814. Also (*Sc. Law*) **Sine quo non.**

Sinesian (səinī·ʃiăn), *a.* 1899. [f. late L. *Sinæ* (see SINÆAN) + -ESE + -IAN.] Of or pertaining to the Chinese and kindred races or to those parts of Asia inhabited by them.

Sinew (si·niu), *sb.* [OE. *seon o)we*, oblique form of *sionu, sinu.*] **1.** *Anat.* A strong fibrous cord serving to connect a muscle with a bone or other part; a tendon. **b.** A tendon taken out of an animal body and used for some purpose, esp. for binding or tying with; hence, a string in a musical instrument ME. **c.** Sinewy substance or material 1825. †**2.** A nerve -1621. **3.** Chiefly *pl.* Strength, energy, force 1560. **4.** The main strength, mainstay, or chief supporting force, *of* something. (More freq. in pl.) 1579.

1. c. The tassels had been fastened by split s. DARWIN. **3.** His authoritie hath no sinews 1617. **4.** *sing.* Achilles..The s., and the forehand of our Hoste SHAKS. *pl.* The discipline of the masses has hitherto knit the sinews of battle RUSKIN. Phr. *The sinews of war* [after L. *nervi belli pecunia* (Cicero)], i.e. money. Hence †**Si·newish** *a.* (*rare*) sinewy -1597.

Sinew (si·niu), *v.* 1592. [f. prec.] **1.** *trans.* To run through, tie together, cover over with, or as with, sinews (*rare*). **2.** To supply with sinews; to strengthen as by sinews; to nerve, harden 1614.

2. Christianity needs something to nerve and s. it 1852.

Sinewed (si·niūd), *ppl. a.* 1588. [f. SINEW *sb.* or *v.*] **1.** Having sinews of a specified kind. **2.** Strengthened with sinews; strong, firm, vigorous, powerful, sinewy 1604.

1. Strong sinew'd was the youth, and big of bone DRYDEN. **2.** The great Eagle..Whose s. wings.. Beat the thin air DRAYTON.

Si·newless, *a.* 1552. [f. SINEW *sb.* + -LESS.] Destitute of sinews; *fig.* lacking vigour; feeble, weak, powerless.

Sinewous (si·niuəs), *a.* 1495. [f. SINEW *sb.* + -OUS.] Sinewy; also *fig.*, strenuous, vigorous.

Sinewy (si·niui), *a.* late ME. [f. SINEW *sb.* + -Y [1].] **1.** Furnished with, full of, sinews. **2.** Having strong, well-developed, or prominent sinews. (Usu. implying strength, but occas. leanness.) late ME. **3.** Of the nature of sinews; tough, stringy 1578.

1. An awfully s. leg of beef 1885. **2.** Fainting as he touch'd the shore, He dropt his s. arms POPE. *transf.* The sinnowy vigour of the trauailer SHAKS. Nervous and s. Arguments 1641.

Sinful (si·nfŭl), *a.* and *sb.* OE. [f. SIN *sb.* + -FUL.] **1.** Of persons, etc.: Full of sin; wicked, corrupt. Also *absol.* **2.** Of acts, etc.: Involving sin; characterized or marked by sin ME. **b.** Highly reprehensible 1863.

1. What is man? Sinful and weak, in ev'ry sense a wretch. COWPER. **2.** Like that bad prophet at Bethel ..while he sat at his s. meat J. H. NEWMAN. Hence **Si·nful-ly** *adv.*, **-ness.**

Sing (siŋ), *v.* Pa. t. **sang** (sæŋ), **sung** (sɒŋ). Pa. pple. sung. [Com. Teut.; OE. *singan*. *Sang* is now the more common form of the pa. t.] **I.** *intr.* **1.** To articulate or utter words or sounds in succession with musical inflexions or modulations of the voice, so as to produce an effect entirely different from that of ordinary speech; *spec.* to do this in a skilled manner, as the result of training and practice. **b.** *transf.* and *fig.* To cry *out*; to make a noise, to boast *about* something. late ME. **2.** To tell *of* in song or verse OE. **b.** To compose in verse; to make poetry 1637. †**3.** To chant or intone, in the performance of divine service; to say mass -1599. **4.** Of birds: To produce tuneful or musical sounds; to warble OE. **b.** Of cocks: to crow (*out*) OE. **c.** Said of the raven, sea-mew, toad, etc., and of the cricket OE. **5.** Of things: To give out a ringing, murmuring, or other sound having the quality of a musical note OE. **b.** Of missiles, etc.: To sound in this way by reason of rapid motion through the air 1565. **6.** Of the ears: To ring, be filled with a humming sound 1621. **7.** To admit of being sung; to be usually sung 1728.

1. I sange by the morowe And now at eue I wepe 1400. When to the lute She sung SHAKS. **b.** They sholde singen, if that they were hent CHAUCER. S. out when we head right! SCORESBY. **2.** Minstrels, who sung of war and ladies love SCOTT. **b.** Who would not s. for Lycidas? he knew Himself to s., and build the lofty rhyme MILT. **3.** *Hen. V*, IV. i 319. **4.** Hearke, hearke, the Larke at Heauens gate sings SHAKS. **b.** The Bird of Dawning singeth all night long SHAKS. **5.** When the bagpipe sings i' the nose SHAKS. **b.** Whose bullet through the night-air sang? BYRON.

II. *trans.* **1.** To utter (a song, etc.) with musical modulations of the voice OE. **b.** With obj. denoting the key, voice, note, etc. late ME. **2.** To chant or intone (a lesson, mass, etc.) OE. **3.** To declare, relate, recount, or celebrate, in song or verse OE. **b.** To proclaim in a musical or resonant manner; to announce clearly or distinctly 1605. **c.** To call *out* 1833. **4. a.** To bring into a certain state, or to a certain place, by or with singing 1500. **b.** To drive, take, force, etc., by or with singing 1604. **c.** To make (one's way) with singing 1890.

1. The harper had songe his songe to the ende MALORY. **b.** A Frenchman who sung an admirable basse EVELYN. Phr. *To s. another song* or *a different tune*, to speak or act in a very different manner. *To s. the same* (or *one*) *song*, to harp on the same strain. *To hear a bird s.*, etc., denoting the receipt of private information. **3.** He sang the creation of the world, and the origin of man 1850. Phr. *To s. one's praises*, to be loud in laudation of (a person, etc.). **b.** I hear a tempest coming That sings mine and my kingdom's ruin FLETCHER. **c.** Moon and stars shining overhead, and the bell singing out the watch THACKERAY. **4.** This..swan, who..sings His soule and body to their lasting rest SHAKS. **b.** Oh she will s. the Sauagenesse out of a Beare SHAKS. Hence **Sing** *sb.*, an act of singing, a singing noise; **Si·ngable** *a.*

Singe (sindʒ), *sb.* 1658. [f. the vb.] The act or effect of singeing; a slight surface burn; a scorch.

Singe (sindʒ), *v.* [OE. *sencgan*, f. stem **sang-*, perh. related to SING *v.*, with ref. to the sound produced by violent singeing.] **1.** *trans.* **a.** Of persons: To burn (something) superficially or lightly, to burn the ends or edges of (hair, wings, etc.); *esp.* to subject (the carcase of a pig, fowl, etc.) to flame or fire in order to remove the bristles or hair. **b.** *techn.* To pass (a woven fabric) over a heated plate or roller or through gas flame, in order to remove superfluous fibres, or to dress the nap 1728. **2.** Of fire or flame: To burn (something) slightly or superficially. Also *techn.* ME. **3.** To take *off*, remove, by superficial burning 1590.

1. No man blameth the candle..though butter flyes sindge theyr winges in it 1626. *fig.* I go..to s. the King of Spain's beard KINGSLEY. **2.** *transf.* The scorching sky Doth s. the sandy wilds of spiceful Barbary DRAYTON. Hence **Singed** (sindʒd) *ppl. a.* **Singer** [2] (si·ndʒəɹ).

Singer [1] (si·ŋəɹ). ME. [f. SING *v.* + -ER [1].] **1.** One who sings; a trained vocalist. **b.** Of song-birds. (More freq. *songster*.) 1626. **2.** A composer of poetry or verse; a poet 1560.

2. Dauid.., the swete s. of Israel BIBLE (Geneva) 2 *Sam.* xxiii. 1. Hence †**Si·ngeress**, a female singer.

Singhalese, var. of SINHALESE.

Singing (si·ŋiŋ), *vbl. sb.* ME. [f. SING *v.* + -ING [1].] **1.** The action of the verb; an instance of this. **2.** A sound as of musical notes *in* the ears or head 1605. **3.** *attrib.*, as *s.-master, -school*, etc. late ME.

Singing, *ppl. a.* ME. [-ING [2].] **1.** That sings; giving forth song. **2.** That makes or gives out a sound of a musical character 1565. **3.** Of the nature of singing; having the musical qualities of song. late ME.

1. *S. man*, a man engaged to sing in an ecclesiastical choir. *S. bird*, a bird that sings; a songster (usu. applied to cage-birds; the pl. is also occas. used as a rendering of OSCINES 2). **2.** *S.-buoy*, a buoy having something attached which gives out a s. sound. Hence **Si·ngingly** *adv.* in a s. manner or tone.

Singing bread. late ME. [Cf. SING *v.* I. 3 and II. 2.] The wafer used in the celebration of the mass -1616.

Single (si·ŋg'l), *sb.* 1486. [SINGLE *a.* used subst.] **1. a.** *Falconry.* The middle or outer claw on the foot of a hawk or falcon. Now *arch.* **b.** *Hunting.* The tail of a deer 1576. **2.** *Sc.* and *n. dial.* A handful or small bundle of gleanings 1508. **3.** In various spec. or techn. senses.

a. A simple uncompounded word 1589. **b.** A form of change in bell-ringing 1684. **c.** A single (as opp. to a double) flower 1796. **d.** A silk thread consisting of a single strand 1831. **e.** *Cards.* Scoring the game after the other side has scored three or four up 1850. **f.** *Cricket*, etc. A hit for which one run is scored; a single point 1858. **g.** *Tennis*, etc. A game or match in which only one person on each side plays at one time 1884.

4. A single thing, person, etc. *In singles*, each one separately, singly. 1646.

Single (si·ŋg'l), *a.* ME. [a. OF. :—L. *singulum* (in class. L. only pl. *singuli*, etc.) one, individual, separate; the first syllable = *sim-* in *simplus* SIMPLE *a.*] **I. 1.** In predic. use: Unaccompanied or unsupported by others; alone, solitary. **2.** Individual, as contrasted with larger bodies or numbers of persons or things. late ME. **b.** Of, pertaining to, or connected with, one person only. Freq. with possessive pronoun 1592. **3.** Separate; distinct from each other or from others; not combined or taken together. late ME. **4.** Undivided, unbroken, absolute (*rare*) 1590. **5.** One only; one and no more. Occas. strengthened by *one*. 1538. **6.** Sole, only, solitary; †mere 1639. †**7.** Standing alone in comparison with other persons or things; unique -1817.

1. Misfortunes never come S. ADDISON. He is left alone, s. and unsupported 1780. **2.** Nor do those Ills on s. Bodies prey; But oft'ner bring the Nation to decay DRYDEN. **b.** With my s. fist Ile combat thee KYD. **3.** Dropped by s. pieces into the copper while in full boil 1826. **4.** Yet nought but s. darknes do I find MILT. **5.** Thus all will judge, and with one s. aim 1728. France had not possessed a s. man who dared to think for himself 1857. **6.** Heroes who carry victory with their s. presence SOUTHEY. **7.** I..am almost s. in not having been to see him 1770.

II. 1. Unmarried, celibate. Also *absol.* as pl. ME. **b.** Of, pertaining to, or involving celibacy, *esp.* in *s. life* 1549. †**2.** Of cloth, garments, etc.: Of one thickness of material; unlined -1670. **3.** Composed or consisting of only one part, feature, etc.; not double, compound, or complex; also, of the ordinary or small size, as dist. from DOUBLE A. **4.** late ME. **b.** Of flowers:

Having only one whorl or set of petals; also, of plants: Bearing such flowers; opp. to DOUBLE A. 1 d. 1551. c. Intended for or accommodating one person 1859. †4. a. Simple; plain; without further qualification or addition –1736. †b. Slight, poor, trivial –1638. 5. Of beer, ale, etc.: Weak, poor; small. Now *arch.* 1485. 6. Simple, honest, sincere, single-minded; free from duplicity or deceit 1519. b. Of the eye, after Biblical use 1526. 7. Of a combat or fight: Between two persons; man to man 1592. 8. In quasi-advb. use 1450.

1. Who that is s. and wyll have a wyfe, Right out of joy he shall be brought in stryfe 1509. *A s. man*, a bachelor. *A s. woman*, a spinster. b. *S. blessedness*: see BLESSEDNESS. 3. A s. line furnished with sidings to enable the laden waggons to pass the empty ones 1862. c. A strip of faded carpet stretched in front of a small s. bedstead 1867. 4. b. 2 *Hen. IV*, I. ii. 207. 6. S. Truth and simple Honestie Do wander up and downe despys'd of all SPENSER. b. When thine eye is s.: then is all thy body full of light TINDALE *Luke* xi. 34. 7. The two kings shall decide the matter by s. combat FREEMAN.

Comb., etc.: **s. court**, a court laid out for two players only; **-cut**, (of files) having but a single rank of teeth; **s. entry**, a method of book-keeping by which each item is entered to the debit or credit of a single account; **s. file**, a line of men, etc. one behind the other; **s. Gloucester**: see GLOUCESTER.

Single (si·ŋg'l), *v.* 1570. [f. the adj.] 1. *trans.* To separate or part from each other; to take asunder. Now *rare.* 2. *Hunting.* To separate (one deer, etc.) from the herd; to pick out and chase separately. Also with *forth* or *out.* 1575. 3. To separate (one person or thing) from others; to draw or take aside or apart. Also const. *from*, †*forth.* 1582. 4. To pick out or distinguish from others. Also with *out.* 1588. 5. To thin (seedling plants), so as to leave each plant separate; to pick *off* (shoots). Also const. *out.* 1731. 6. To render single, reduce to one, concentrate 1824. 7. *intr.* a. To go singly; to separate from others. Also with *out* and *off.* 1616. b. *U.S.* Of a horse: To be SINGLE-FOOTED 1864.

2. The hound had at length singled out a particular deer 1873. 3. Now Clifford, I haue singled thee alone SHAKS. 4. He, whom my jealousy..Hath singled for destruction! SMOLLETT. 7. a. Let..all go on At once. To s. is to weaken you. HOBBES.

Single-acting, *ppl. a.* 1825. [f. SINGLE *a.*] Acting in one direction or by one method, *spec.* of a steam-engine. Opp. to *double-acting.*

S. engine, an engine in which steam is admitted to one side only of the piston 1875.

Single-breasted, *a.* 1796. [f. SINGLE *a.*] Of a coat, waistcoat, etc.: Having only one thickness over the breast; not doubled by overlapping. Opp. to DOUBLE-BREASTED.

Single-eyed, *a.* 1705. [f. SINGLE *a.*] 1. *fig.* Having the eye single or sound; sincere, honest, straightforward. 2. *lit.* Having one eye or eye-like mark; monoculous 1839.

Si·ngle-foot. *U.S.* 1882. A particular gait of a horse, variously identified with the amble and the rack.

S. is an irregular pace,..distinguished by the posterior extremities, moving in the order of a fast walk and the anterior ones in that of a slow trot 1882. So **Single-footed** *a.* 1864.

Single-handed, *a.* 1709. [f. SINGLE *a.*] 1. a. Of actions: Carried on or performed by one person, ship, etc., alone or unaided, or by one person on each side. b. Adapted for using with one hand 1834. 2. Working alone or unassisted; by one's self; unaided 1768. So **Single-hand** *a.* Hence **Single-ha·nded-ly** *adv.*, **-ness.**

Single-hearted, *a.* 1577. [f. SINGLE *a.*] 1. Possessed of a single or sincere heart; straightforward, honest; simple-hearted. 2. Of actions, etc.: Proceeding from or characterized by sincerity of heart or purpose 1804. Hence **Single-hea·rted-ly** *adv.*, **-ness.**

Si·ngle-line, *a.* 1868. [f. SINGLE *a.*] 1. Consisting of or having only a single line of plants, rails, etc. 2. Occupying one line in writing or printing 1892.

Single-minded, *a.* 1577. [f. SINGLE *a.*] 1. Sincere in mind or spirit; honest; ingenuous. 2. Proceeding from or characterized by sincerity or honesty of mind 1836. 3. Having but one aim or purpose 1860.

Si·ngleness. 1526. [f. SINGLE *a.* + -NESS.] 1. Sincerity, straightforwardness, honesty, integrity; freedom from deceit, duplicity, or guile. 2. The condition of being unmarried, or of not marrying again; celibacy 1560. 3. The quality of being single; the fact of consisting of one in number or kind; oneness 1592. 4. The fact of standing alone; solitude, solitariness, isolation (*poet.*) 1805. 5. The quality or fact of having (one single aim or purpose) 1806.

5. His failure seems..due to a want of s. of aim 1886.

Si·ngle-stick, *sb.* Also **singlestick.** 1771. [f. SINGLE *a.* + STICK *sb.*] Fighting, fencing, or exercise with a stick provided with a guard or basket and requiring only one hand. b. A stick used for this 1837. Hence **Single-stick** *v. intr.* to fight or fence with a single-stick.

Singlet (si·ŋglėt). 1746. [f. SINGLE *a.* + -ET, after DOUBLET.] An unlined woollen garment (knitted or woven), now usu. close-fitting and worn as an undershirt or jersey.

Singleton (si·ŋg'ltən). 1876. [f. SINGLE *a.* Cf. SIMPLETON.] 1. *Cards.* In whist or bridge: The only card of a suit in a hand. 2. A single thing, as dist. from a pair 1887.

Si·ngle-tree. *U.S.* and *Austral.* 1847. = SWINGLE-TREE.

Si·ngle-wi·cket. 1736. [f. SINGLE *a.* I. 5.] A form of cricket in which there is only one wicket and consequently only one batsman at a time.

Singly (si·ŋgli), *adv.* ME. [f. SINGLE *a.* + -LY[2], with later contraction as in *simply*, etc.] 1. As a single person or thing; by oneself or itself; separately. b. Unassisted, single-handed 1608. 2. Solely, only; merely. Now *rare* or *Obs.* 1654. †3. Truly, honestly –1637.

1. He is greater then his subjects s. and apart 1673. b. Singlie of my selfe I will oppose all danger 1633. 2. People do not improve, s., by travelling, but by the observations they make CHESTERF.

Sing-sing. 1854. [Native name.] An African antelope, *Kobus sing-sing.*

Si·ng-song, *sb.* 1609. [f. SING *v.* + SONG *sb.*] 1. A ballad or a piece of verse of a monotonous or jingling character. 2. Verse or rhyme of this type 1693. b. Tone of voice marked by a monotonous rise and fall, with a kind of singing effect 1822. 3. An amateur concert of an informal nature; a convivial meeting where each person is expected to contribute a song 1769. 4. *attrib.* a. Of persons: Making mere jingling rhyme or monotonous verse 1687. b. Characterized by a jingling triviality or monotonous rise and fall 1734. c. Monotonous in cadence 1825.

2. b. The fine old Norfolk words, and twang, and squeaky s. have gone 1887. Hence **Sing-song** *v. trans.* to utter or express in a monotonous chant; *intr.* to sing, make verses, utter words, etc., in a s. manner.

Singular (si·ŋgiŭlăɹ), *a.*, *adv.*, and *sb.* ME. [a. OF. *singuler* and *singulaire*, or ad. L. *singularis*, f. *singuli* SINGLE *a.*] A. *adj.* I. †1. Alone; away from others; solitary –1787. 2. One only; one and no more; single. late ME. b. Unique, solitary, single. Also (with *the*), sole, only. 1555. 3. a. *Gram.* Denoting or expressing one person or thing. Chiefly in *s. number.* Opp. to PLURAL *a.* and DUAL *a.* late ME. b. *Logic.* Considered alone or as a single instance 1654. c. *Math.* Having properties not shared by other things of the same class 1845. †4. Of a combat: = SINGLE *a.* II. 7. –1826.

1. His way of living was s. and retired 1728. 2. b. He was the s. instance in Scotland 1715. 3. b. The proposition is s. when the subject is an individual name MILL. 4. Those in his high place fight no s. combats SCOTT.

†II. 1. Separate, individual, single –1719. 2. Of or pertaining to, connected with or affecting, the individual, in contrast to what is common or general; personal, private, one's own –1692. b. Special; peculiar *to* one –1710.

1. Every singuler persoone of the same chirche 1450. Phr. *All and s.*, every one. Also *each and s.* (rare, now *arch.*). 2. One that preferred the dignitee..of the commenweale, before his owne singulare avauntage 1542.

III. †1. Separate from others by reason of superiority or pre-eminence –1635. †b. Of persons: Eminent, distinguished, notable –1691. †c. Used in forms of address, esp. to a person of title –1638. 2. Above the ordinary in amount, extent, worth, or value; especially good or great; special, particular. Now *rare.* ME. †b. Of remedies, medicines, etc.: Excellent; highly efficacious or beneficial –1694. 3. Remarkable; extraordinary, unusual, uncommon. Hence, rare, precious. late ME. †4. Differing *from* others in opinion; standing alone; peculiar in this respect –1791. 5. Different from or not complying with that which is customary, usual, or general; strange, odd, peculiar 1684. †6. Quasi-*adv.* Singularly, especially, particularly –1693.

1. b. A s. Grecian, and an exact Philologer 1691. c. The Countesse of Arundell and Surrey, my s. good Ladie and Mistresse 1638. 2. Offices, or any other s. marke of the Soveraigns favour HOBBES. 3. A s. gift of Providence 1862. 4. Sir, he must be very s. in his opinion, if he thinks himself one of the best of men BOSWELL. 5. He was called strange and s. long before he was acknowledged to be great LANDOR. 6. A s. good principle CONGREVE.

B. *sb.* 1. a. An individual. Now *rare.* b. A single thing; a single point or detail 1615. c. (in *pl.*) Contrasted with a class or with universals 1640. 2. *Gram.* The singular number; a word in its singular form. late ME.

1. a. Eloquence would be but a poor thing, if we should only converse with singulars; speak with man and man together B. JONS.

Si·ngularist. 1593. [f. SINGULAR *a.* + -IST.] †1. One who affects singularity –1677. 2. *Eccl.* One who holds a single benefice, as contrasted with a PLURALIST (*rare*) 1799.

1. A clownish s., or non-conformist to ordinary usage, a stiff opiniatre 1677.

Singularity (siŋgiŭlæ·rĭti). late ME. [ad. F. *singularité* or late L. *singularitas*, f. *singularis* SINGULAR; see -ITY.] I. †1. A single or separate thing or entity; a unit –1708. 2. The quality or fact of being one in number or kind; singleness, oneness. Now *rare.* 1583.

1. 'Wee' importeth a multitude and not a singularitee 1548. 2. The s. in the number of God's Being 1850.

II. 1. A solitary instance 1814. †2. Distinction due to, or involving, some superior quality; special excellence or goodness –1632. 3. The fact or quality of differing or dissenting from others or from what is generally accepted, esp. in thought or religion; personal, individual, or independent action, judgement, etc. 1502. 4. a. Individuality; distinctiveness 1583. b. Peculiarity, eccentricity, oddity, strangeness 1768. 5. With *a* and *pl.* a. An instance of individual departure from common ideas or practice 1570. b. A distinctive, noteworthy, or curious thing; esp. *pl.*, notable features or objects 1570. c. A peculiar, exceptional, or unusual feature or characteristic 1663.

1. A friendship of forty years, I have found a rarity, though not a s. 1814. 3. So much the restless eagerness to shine, And love of s., prevail 1814. Avoid s. of opinion as well as of every thing else HAZLITT. 4. b. The s. of his manners had attracted as much notice as his eminence at the bar D'ISRAELI. 5. a. I pardon our religious Men the sad Singularitie of eating nothing but Herbs DRYDEN. b. Many haue wrote of the singularities of old Rome 1632.

Singularize (si·ŋgiŭlărəiz), *v.* 1589. [f. SINGULAR *a.* + -IZE.] 1. *trans.* To mark conspicuously; to make distinct or conspicuous. 2. To make singular or one; to individualize; to convert into the singular number (*rare*) 1663.

Singularly (si·ŋgiŭlaɹli), *adv.* ME. [f. SINGULAR *a.* + -LY[2].] 1. Singly; by oneself or itself; one by one, separately, individually. Now *rare.* †b. After one's own fashion; independently –1671. 2. In the singular number; so as to denote one. late ME. 3. Specially, particularly, unusually. late ME. †4. Excellently –1617. 5. Oddly (*rare*) 1752.

1. b. His lot who dares be s. good MILT. 3. A man of s. clear judgement and s. lofty spirit MACAULAY.

Si·ngult. *arch.* 1590. [ad. L.] = next –1661.

‖**Singultus** (siŋgʊ·ltʊ̆s). 1754. [L.] 1. *Path.* Hiccups, hiccuping. †2. A sob. BYRON.

Sinh (ʃin). *Math.* 1880. Abbrev. used for *hyperbolic sine.*

Sinhalese (sinhălī·z), *sb.* and *a.* Also **Singhalese, Singalese.** 1797. [f. Skr. *Sinhala* Ceylon + -ESE. Cf. CINGALESE.] A. *sb.* 1. As *pl.* The native inhabitants of Ceylon 1802. 2. The language spoken in Ceylon 1802. B. *adj.* Pertaining to Ceylon or its natives 1797.

Sinical (si·nikăl), *a.* 1593. [f. SINE + -ICAL.] *Math.* Of or relating to a sine or sines; employing or founded upon sines.

†*S. quadrant*, a former nautical instrument having intersecting sines drawn from each side.

Si·nigrin. 1876. [irreg. f. L. *sinapis* mustard + *nigra* black + -IN [1].] *Chem.* Myronate of potassium.

Sinister (si·nistəɹ), *a.* late ME. [a. OF. (mod.F.) *sinistre*, or L. *sinister* left, left-hand. Down to the time of Pope stressed *sini·ster.*] **I.** †**1.** Of information, advice, etc.: Given with intent to deceive or mislead; prompted by malice or ill-will –1601. †**2.** Of opinions, etc.: Prejudicial, unfavourable, darkly suspicious –1795. **3.** Of actions, practices, etc.: Dishonest, unfair; underhand; dark 1455. **4.** Corrupt, evil, bad, base 1474. **5.** Of omens, etc.: Portending or indicating misfortune or disaster; inauspicious, unfavourable 1579. **b.** Of looks, places, etc.: Suggestive of evil or mischief 1797. **6.** Attended with mishap, misfortune, or disaster; unlucky; adverse 1576. **7.** Unfavourable, harmful, or prejudicial *to* a person, his interests, etc. 1725.

3. Nimble and s. trickes and shiftes BACON. 4. All the evils came from the s. interests of the nobles 1871. 5. Guided by some s. starre 1600. **b.** The typical Irish immigrant, with his s. animal features 1864. 6. A trauailer that hath sustained harm by s. fortune LYLY.

II. 1. Situated on the left side of the body 1475. **b.** Lying on or towards the left hand 1483. **2.** *Her.* Forming, or situated on, the left half of a shield (regarded from the bearer's point of view). Also *absol.* See also BAR-, BEND-*sinister*. 1562. **3.** Directed to the left; characterized by moving or turning towards the left (*rare*) 1615.

1. My Mothers bloud Runs on the dexter cheeke, and this s. Bounds in my fathers SHAKS. **b.** The s. winge of the vangtuard 1600. 2. *S. bend* = BEND-*sinister*. Hence **Si·nister-ly** *adv.*, **-ness.**

Si·nistrad, *adv. rare.* 1803. [f. L. *sinistra* left hand + -AD II (see DEXTRAD).] To or towards the left side; sinistrally. Also with *of.*

Sinistral (si·nistrăl), *a.* 1475. [a. OF., or ad. med.L. **sinistralis*; see SINISTER and -AL 1.] †**I. 1.** Adverse; unlucky (*rare*). **2.** Likely, or designed, to cause mischief –1561. **3.** Darkly suspicious; very unfavourable –1572. **4.** Heterodox; unsound –1547. **II. 1.** Situated on the left side of the body; of or pertaining to the left hand or side 1803. **2.** *Conch.* Characterized by turning spirally from right to left; reversed, left-handed 1833. **3.** Of persons: Left-handed 1904.

3. Two per cent. of mankind are naturally s. 1904. Hence **Sinistra·lity,** s. state or quality. **Si·nistrally** *adv.* in a s. manner; towards the left.

Sinistro- (si·nistro), used as comb. form of SINISTER, in the sense 'on, situated in, directed or turning towards the left', as *s.-gyrate* adj.

Sinistrorse (si·nistrǫ̈ɹs), *a.* 1856. [ad. L. *sinistrorsus*, contr. f. **sinistrovorsus*, f. *sinister* left + *vertere* to turn.] **1.** *Bot.* Twining or turning spirally from right to left. **2.** Moving or going towards the left 1891. So **Sinistro·rsal** *a.* 1828, **-ly** *adv.*

The word has been used in two opposite senses, owing to a difference in the supposed position of the observer. Cf. DEXTRORSE.

Sinistrous (si·nistrəs, sini·strəs), *a.* 1560. [f. L. *sinistr-*, SINISTER + -OUS.] **I.** †**1.** Erroneous, perverse, heretical –1632. †**2.** Malicious, unfair, prejudiced –1751. †**3.** Underhand; dishonest; corrupt –1717. **4.** Betokening or attended with misfortune or disaster; ill-omened, unlucky; baleful, malign 1575.

4. Which to my soule s. signes impart 1607.

†**II. 1.** Pertaining to or situated on the left hand or side –1678. **2.** *fig.* Left-handed; slow SIR T. BROWNE. Hence **Si·nistrously** *adv.*

Sink (siŋk), *sb.* 1440. [f. SINK *v.*] **I. 1. a.** A pool or pit formed in the ground for the reception of waste water, sewage, etc.; a cesspool. **b.** A conduit, drain, or pipe for carrying away dirty water or sewage; a sewer. Now *rare.* 1499. **c.** A basin or receptacle made of stone, metal, etc. and having a pipe attached for the escape of water to a drain, etc.; *esp.* such a basin fitted in a kitchen or scullery 1566. **2.** *transf.* and *fig.* as in quots.

2. Hell is the Worlds s., and the receptacle of all the Filth in this Great Frame 1684. The Man..was the very s. of Fraud and Deceit 1707. Rome, that s. of sinks 1874. †*The sink(s) of the body*, the organs of digestion and excretion.

II. †**1.** The well of a ship. (= L. *sentina.*) –1711. **2.** *Mining.* A pit-shaft. Now *rare.* 1576. **3.** A flat, low-lying area, basin, etc., where waters collect and form a bog, marsh, or pool, or disappear by sinking or evaporation. Now *U.S.* 1596. **b.** = SINK-HOLE 2. Chiefly *U.S.* 1791. **III. 1. a.** *U.S.* An oblong boat used in wild-fowl shooting, which becomes submerged to the water-level and serves to conceal the sportsman 1857. **b.** = SINKER II. 2. 1865. **c.** *Theatr.* A part of the stage constructed to sink and rise by machinery 1859. **2.** A depression or hollow, esp. one in a flat surface 1875.

Sink (siŋk), *v.* Pa. t. **sank** (sæŋk), **sunk** (sɒŋk). Pa. pple. **sunk** (sɒŋk), **sunken** (sɒ·ŋk'n). [Com. Teut.; OE. *sincan.* In trans. use the form *sink* takes the place of OE. *sencan*, ME. *senchen.*] (The perf. and pluperf. tenses were formerly freq. conjugated with the vb. *to be* instead of *have.*) *Intr. uses.* **I. 1.** To become submerged in water; to go under or to the bottom; (of ships) to founder. **b.** To become partly or completely submerged in quicksand, marshy ground, snow, etc. ME. **2.** To subside or go down into, to be swallowed up by, the earth, etc. ME. **3.** To descend to a lower plane or level; to slip, drop, or fall *down*; to pass *in* by falling OE. **b.** To subside; to give way and go *down*, to fall *away*; to be beaten *in* 1530. **c.** Of the sun or moon: To descend in the sky; to move toward or pass beneath the horizon 1601. **d.** To pass out of sight; to disappear 1521. **e.** Of land, etc.: To have a downward lie or slope; to dip 1726. **4. a.** Of water, etc.: To go down; to fall to a lower level; to subside OE. **b.** Of flames, etc.: To die down; to go out 1611. **5.** To drop or fall gradually down to the ground, on a seat, etc., from want of power to remain erect; †to faint *away.* late ME. **b.** To fall down, fall *in* ruin; to give way through weakness or fatigue. Also of soil: To be soft or yielding. 1535. **c.** To drop down in a slow or easy manner into a lying or sitting posture 1825. **6.** Of water, etc.: To pass into or penetrate a substance, to be soaked up or absorbed ME. †**b.** Of paper: To absorb ink –1797. **7.** Of a weapon or blow: To make way *into* or *through* ME. **b.** To recede *into* 1530.

1. The boot was full of water and sanck CAXTON. **b.** They s. up to the Belly in the looser snow 1686. 2. Her gates are sunke into the ground *Lam.* ii. 9. 3. With that her head sunk down upon her brest MARSTON. **c.** So sinks the day-star in the Ocean bed MILT. 5. He was sinking with hardship, fatigue, and hunger 1879. **b.** Sunk are thy bowers in shapeless ruin all GOLDSM. 6. Nilus shal synke awaye, & be dronke up COVERDALE *Isa.* xix. 4. 7. The stone sunke into his forehead 1 *Sam.* xvii. 49.

II. 1. a. To penetrate *into* (†*to, unto, through*), enter or be impressed *in*, the mind, heart, etc. ME. **b.** To press or weigh *on* one 1764. **c.** To descend or fall (*up*)*on* a person or place; to settle down (*over*) a district 1808. **2.** To be immersed or plunged deeply *in* something; to dip deep *in.* Chiefly in *pa. pple.* ME. **3.** Contrasted with *swim*, to denote success, prosperity, etc., or (in later use) determination to do something without regard to consequences. late ME. **4.** To fall, lapse, or degenerate *into* some inferior or unsatisfactory state or condition. Also const. *from* (a better state). ME. **b.** To pass *into* oblivion, insignificance, etc., or *from* (notice) 1704. **c.** To change, be transformed *into* some lower form 1770. **5.** To pass or fall gently *into* (or *to*) sleep, rest, peace, etc. 1718. **b.** To lapse or fall *into* reverie, contemplation, etc. 1794. **6.** To give way *under* (or *beneath*) misfortune, affliction, etc.; to be weighed down or crushed 1592. **b.** To become depressed or dejected; to droop or languish 1605. **c.** To decline rapidly; to fail in health or strength; †also, to die. Freq. const. *under* (some trouble, etc.). 1718. **7.** To go downwards in the scale of fortune, success, or relative position 1599. **b.** To degenerate 1678. **c.** To fall in estimation; to decline in value or appreciation 1685. **8.** To fall low; to diminish or decrease; also, to disappear, to vanish 1655. **b.** Of sounds: To die away 1794.

1. These things s. into my heart 1852. **c.** Night sinks on the sea SWINBURNE. 2. They..were both sunk in the deepest sleep 1850. 3. I will be just and honest, s. or swim 1668. 4. The Republick sunk into those two Vices.., Luxury and Avarice ADDISON. **b.** Treatises..which are already sunk into..oblivion SWIFT. **c.** It is, indeed, possible..for men to s. into machines RUSKIN. 5. She at length sunk to repose 1794. 6. Vnder loues heauy burthen doe I sinke SHAKS. **b.** My heart as well as pursse being quite sunck 1655. **c.** His health began to s. under the vexations of his mind 1780. 7. It was his heauie fortune to sinke B. JONS. **c.** He had sunk by this time to the very worst reputation THACKERAY. 8. Towards the beginning of Harvest, prices sunk much 1801.

Trans. uses. **III. 1.** To cause (a vessel, etc.) to plunge or go down beneath the water; to submerge by rendering incapable of floating; to destroy in this way ME. **b.** To submerge; to put or thrust under water ME. **2.** To cause (a thing) to descend or fall to a lower plane or level; to force, press, or weigh down in any way ME. **b.** To allow (the hand, etc.) to fall lower 1680. **3.** To excavate (a well, pit-shaft, etc.) by digging vertically downwards; to lower (ground, etc.) by excavation. Also *absol.* ME. **4. a.** To excise or cut out; to form (a cavity, etc.) in this way, or by heavy pressure 1632. **b.** To lower by cutting away; to cut patterns or designs in (a die, etc.) 1679. **c.** To let in or insert into the substance of a thing by scooping, hollowing, or cutting 1825. **5.** To lower the level of (ground, water, etc.) 1627. **b.** To lose sight of (an object on the horizon) by sailing away 1762. **c.** To descend, move down (a slope, etc.) 1862.

1. If I take any of you vpon the Sea, I will sinke you 1623. **b.** The line is shotted so as just to s. it 1856. 2. Doth it not then our eyelids sinke? SHAKS. **b.** Each sentinel sunk his weapon SCOTT. 4. Any Place in the Ouze,..where a Ship may..s. herself a Place to lie in CHAMBERS. **c.** The holes for sinking the heads of..screws 1825. 5. You sunk the river with repeated draughts ADDISON. **b.** This island was sunk from the deck 1810.

IV. 1. To reduce or bring to ruin or a low estate; to overwhelm, destroy; to weigh down 1599. **b.** Used as an imprecation. *arch.* 1630. **c.** To swear. Now *dial.* or *arch.* 1663. **2.** To lower; to make of less repute or estimation 1601. **b.** To debase or degrade (a person) 1706. **c.** To reduce *to*, lose *in*, something lower 1751. **3.** To cause (a person, the mind, spirits, etc.) to become dejected or depressed 1630. **4.** To reduce in amount, value, or price 1700. **b.** To drop or lower (the voice) in speaking 1821. **5. a.** To abandon or cease to use; to give up; to allow to be merged *in* something else 1705. **b.** To avoid mentioning or alluding to (a person or matter). Also const. *upon* the person or persons spoken to. 1749. **c.** To suppress in pronouncing 1742. **d.** To set aside; to leave out of consideration 1860. **6.** To make away with; to appropriate (money, etc.) for one's own use 1713. **7.** To pay up or wipe out (a debt, etc.) 1727. **8.** To invest 1727. **9.** To invest or spend unprofitably; to lose (money) in unfortunate investment, etc. 1777.

1. If I haue a Conscience, let it sincke me,..if I be not faithfull SHAKS. **b.** S. them all for parsons TROLLOPE. **c.** We swear like Gentlemen of Rank, Curse, Damn, S. 1663. 2. I cannot say how it has sunk him in my opinion J. AUSTEN. **b.** Again I might..exalt the brute and s. the man BURNS. 5. **a.** I..have not sunk the lover in the husband 1809. **b.** Mr. Allworthy,..out of modesty, sunk everything that related particularly to himself FIELDING. **d.** A happy knack of sinking individual opinion 1884. 7. This windfall should properly go to s. the unfunded debt 1895. 9. The..amounts of cash, that had been sunk in that unhappy speculation! DE QUINCEY. Hence **Si·nkable** *a.* **Si·nkage,** the act of sinking; an instance of this; also, that which sinks or has sunk.

Sinker (si·ŋkəɹ). 1526. [f. SINK *v.* + -ER [1].] **I. 1.** One who engraves figures or designs on dies. Chiefly *Sc.* (Cf. *die-sinker.*) **2.** One who sinks a pit-shaft, well, or the like 1708. **3.** One who causes (something) to sink 1632. **II. 1.** In a stocking-frame or knitting-machine, a jack-sinker or a lead-sinker 1779. **2.** A weight of lead, stone, etc. for sinking a fishing-line or -net in the water 1844. **b.** A weight of lead or other metal for sinking a sounding-line, buoy, or mine in water 1882. **c.** *U.S.* A (heavy) dough-nut 1903. **3.** *attrib.* as *s.-bar, -wheel* (in a knitting-machine), *-bar, -rod* (in boring apparatus) 1834.

Sink-hole (si·ŋkhōᵘl). 1456. [f. SINK *sb.* + HOLE *sb.*] **1.** A hole or hollow into which foul matter runs or is thrown; †a sink, or a hole by which a sink is emptied. 2. A hole, cavern, or funnel-shaped cavity in the earth, freq. forming the course of an underground stream; a swallow-hole. Chiefly *U.S.* 1791.

Sinking (si·ŋkiŋ), *vbl. sb.* late ME. [f. SINK *v.* + -ING [1].] 1. The action of the vb. in intr. senses. b. A lowering or drooping of the spirits, etc. 1663. c. Decline of vital power 1730. 2. The action of the vb. in trans. senses 1605. 3. A depression, or the amount of this; a recess or worked hollow 1712.

1. c. That kind of sensation which patients describe by a s. 1776.

Si·nking fund. 1724. [See SINK *v.* IV. 7 and FUND *sb.*] A fund formed by periodically setting aside revenue to accumulate at interest, usu. for the purpose of reducing the principal of a national, municipal, or company's debt.

Sink-stone (si·ŋkstōun). Also **sinkstone.** 1865. [f. SINK *sb.* or *v.* + STONE *sb.*] A stone sinker for submerging a fishing-line or -net.

Sinless (si·nlės), *a.* OE. [f. SIN *sb.* + -LESS.] Free from, devoid of, without sin. Also const. *of.* Hence **Si·nless-ly** *adv.*, **-ness.**

Sinner (si·nəɹ). ME. [f. SIN *v.*] 1. One who sins; a transgressor against the divine law. 2. In trivial use: A reprobate, rogue; an offender against some rule or custom 1809.

1. Phr. *As I am a s.*; As I am a s. My eager stomach crokes, and calls for Dinner! 1682.

Sinnet (si·nėt). 1611. [Origin obsc. Cf. SENNIT.] *Naut.* A kind of flat braided cordage formed by pleating together several strands of rope-yarn, coarse hemp, grass, etc.

Sinn Fein (ʃin fē·n). 1907. [Ir., = 'we ourselves'.] A political society, party, or movement having as its object the political independence of Ireland, the revival of the Irish language, etc. Hence **Sinn Fei·ner.**

Sino- (si·no), comb. form of Gr. Σῖναι, L. *Sinæ* (see SINÆAN) the Chinese, as in **Sino·lo·gical** *a.* relating to the Chinese language or literature; **Sino·logist, Sinologue** (si·nǫlǫg), one versed in the Chinese language, or in the customs and history of China; **Sino·logy,** the study of things Chinese. b. Combined with another adj. = 'Chinese and', as **Sino-Japanese.**

Si·n-o·ffering. 1535. [f. SIN *sb.*, prob. after G. *sündopfer*, used by Luther as tr. Heb. *ḥaṭṭāth*, f. *ḥāṭā* to sin.] In the older Jewish religion, an offering (of an animal for sacrifice) made as an atonement for sin.

Sinon (səi·nǫn). 1581. [Name of the Greek who induced the Trojans to bring the wooden horse into Troy.] One who misleads by false tales; a perfidious person; a betrayer.

†Sinoper. late ME. [a. OF. *sinopre*, var. of *sinople* SINOPLE.] 1. A colour of some shade of red -1688. 2. a. A kind of red earth used as a pigment (orig. one brought to Greece from Sinope). b. Cinnabar. -1726.

Sinopic (sinǫ·pik), *a.* 1748. [ad. L. *Sinopicus*, a. Gr. Σινωπικός, f. Σινώπη, a Greek colony in Paphlagonia.] Obtained from Sinope or its neighbourhood.

Sinopite (si·nopəit). 1868. [ad. G. *sinopit*, f. L. *Sinopis* or *Sinope* (see next) + -ITE [1] 2 b.] *Min.* A ferruginous clayey earth of a brick-red color used by ancient races as a paint.

†Sinople. 1450. [a. OF., ad. L. *Sinopis*, a. Gr. Σινωπίς, f. Σινώπη, a Greek colony in Paphlagonia.] 1. = SINOPER 1. -1569. 2. = SINOPER 2. -1683. 3. The colour green; *spec.* in *Her.*, vert -1728. b. *attrib.* or as *adj.* Of a green colour -1698. 4. *Min.* A variety of ferruginous quartz -1836.

Sinter (si·ntər). 1757. [a. G., = Eng. *sinder* CINDER.] A hard incrustation or deposit formed upon rocks, etc., by precipitation from mineral waters; esp. *siliceous s.*, geyserite.

‖Sintoc (si·ntǫk). Also **sindoc.** 1842. [Malay *sintoq.*] The bark of *Cinnamomum sintoc.*

Sinuate (si·niuˌėt), *a.* 1688. [ad. L. *sinuatus*, *sinuare*, f. SINUS.] *Bot.* Of leaves: Having a margin made wavy or uneven by alternate rounded and somewhat large sinuses and lobes; sinuous. Similarly in *Ent.* of wing-cases, etc.

Sinuated (si·niuˌeitėd), *ppl. a.* 1578. [f. as prec. + -ED [1].] 1. *Bot.* = prec. 2. Sinuous 1859.

Sinuation (siniuˌēi·ʃən). 1653. [ad. late L. *sinuatio*, f. *sinuare*, f. SINUS.] 1. The act or fact of winding about, or pursuing a winding course. 2. A sinuosity 1676.

Sinuato- (si·niuˌēito), comb. form of SINUATE, with the sense 'sinuately', 'sinuate and', as *s.-dentate(d, -undulate*, etc.

Sinuose (si·niuˌōus), *a.* 1829. [ad. L. *sinuosus*, f. SINUS; see -OSE [1].] Full of or characterized by bends or windings; sinuous.

Sinuosity (siniuˌǫ·sĭti). 1598. [ad. F. *sinuosité*; see prec. and -ITY.] 1. The character, condition, or quality of being sinuous. 2. (Chiefly *pl.*) A curve or bend, *esp.* one of a series 1720. b. *fig.* A complexity or intricacy 1827. 3. A sinuous movement 1892.

1. Meander is a river..famous for the s. and often returning thereof DRAYTON. 2. Winding by a narrow path along the sinuosities of the valley SCOTT. b. The sinuosities of the discussion 1864.

Sinuoso- (siniuˌōu·so), comb. form of L. *sinuosus*, with the sense 'sinuately', 'sinuate and', as *s.-lobate*, etc.

Sinuous (si·niuəs), *a.* 1578. [ad. L. *sinuosus* (see SINUS and -OUS).] 1. Characterized by or abounding in turns, curves, or sinuosities; sinuate, curving. b. *transf.* Intricate, complex; roundabout 1853. c. *fig.* Deviating from the right; morally crooked 1850. 2. Of movements: Taking place in curves 1877.

1. Insect or Worme,..Streaking the ground with s. trace MILT. A s. band of highlands stretches almost continuously 1878. c. A man..who has acquired high station by no s. path 1850. Hence **Si·nuous-ly** *adv.*, **-ness.**

Sinupa·llial, -pa·lliate (siniu-), *adjs.* 1863. [f. *sinu-*, stem of SINUS + PALLIAL *a.*, PALLIATE *a.*] *Conch.* Of certain lamellibranchs: Having the pallial line deeply incurved or inflected beneath the impression of the posterior adductor muscles, for the retraction or expansion of the pallial siphons.

Sinus (səi·nǫ̆s). *Pl.* **sinuses.** 1597. [a. L., curve, bay, etc.] 1. *Path.* An imposthume, abscess, or sore, forming a narrow suppurating tract and having a small orifice; the cavity or hollow caused by this. 2. A curvature, flexure, or bend; *spec.* in *Zool.*, a curved recess in a shell 1615. b. *Bot.* One of a series of small rounded depressions on the margin of a leaf 1753. 3. *Anat.* a. Any of various venous cavities or reservoirs in different organs or parts of the body 1672. b. A natural hole, cell, or cavity in the substance of a bone or other tissue, and either closed or having a relatively small opening 1704. †4. A cavity or hole in the earth -1784. †5. A bay, gulf, or arm of the sea -1789.

Sinusoid (səi·nǫ̆soid). 1823. [a. F. *sinusoïde*, f. L. SINUS + -OID.] 1. *Math.* A curve of sines (CURVE *sb.* 1). 2. *Anat.* Venous meshwork in the tissues of an organ 1900. Hence **Sinusoi·dal** *a.* resembling, pursuing, flowing in, the wave-like course of a s.

Sip, *sb.* 1633. [f. next.] An act of sipping; a small quantity *of* some liquid taken in this way. b. *fig.* A mere taste *of* something 1728.

b. A s. is all that the public..ever care to take from reservoirs of abstract philosophy DE QUINCEY.

Sip, *v.* late ME. [perh. a modification of *sup.*] 1. *intr.* To take up liquid in small quantities with the lips; to drink by a sip or sips; freq. with *of* (a specified liquid). 2. *trans.* To drink (liquid, etc.) in very small draughts; to imbibe, or partake of, by sipping. Said also of bees, etc. 1602. b. *fig.* To take a mere taste of (something) 1618. 3. To take honey from (a flower) by sipping 1697.

1. Yee doe here but sippe of this cuppe, but then ye shall drinke up the dreggs of it for ever 1628. 2. *fig.* Weele drinke a health, while they two sip a kisse MARSTON. b. Pleasures he rather sipped than drank off 1639. 3. The Winged Nation..skim the Floods, and s. the purple Flow'rs DRYDEN.

Sipe (səip), *sb.* Chiefly *Sc.* and *U.S.* OE. [Related to SIPE *v.*] 1. The act of percolating or soaking through, on the part of water or other liquid; the water, etc., which percolates. 2. A small spring or pool of water 1825.

Sipe (səip), *v.* Chiefly *Sc.* and *n. dial.* [OE. *sipian*, = Fris. *sypje*, MLG. *sipen.* Cf. SEEP *v.*] *intr.* Of water, etc.: To percolate or ooze through; to drip or trickle slowly. Hence **Si·page,** leakage or oozing of water.

Siphon (səi·fən), *sb.* Also **syphon.** 1659. [ad. L. *siphon-*, *sipho*, ad. Gr. σίφων pipe, tube.] 1. A pipe or tube, bent so that one leg is longer than the other, and used for drawing off liquids. The head of liquid in the longer leg draws the liquid over the bend in the pipe, the column of liquid being sustained by atmospheric pressure. b. *transf.* A channel or tube through which water passes on this principle 1744. c. *ellipt.* A siphon-bottle, *esp.* one containing aerated water 1875. 2. *Zool.* a. = SIPHUNCLE 1. 1822. b. A tube-like organ serving as a canal for the passage of water or other fluid; also, a breathing-tube or suctorial organ 1826. c. In certain echinoids and annelids, a tube arising from the posterior extremity of the œsophagus and lying close to the inner margin of the intestine 1888. 3. *Bot.* One or other of a number of elongated cells which surround the large monosiphonous cell in the frond of certain florideous red algæ 1899. 4. *attrib.* In names of apparatus, etc., of which a s. forms a part, or which involve the principle or use of the s., as *s. barometer, bottle, condenser, cup, gauge, pump, trap*, etc. Also *s. pipe, tube*, = sense 1; **s.-shell,** a gasteropod having a s. Hence **Si·phonal** *a.* having the form or character of a s.; of or pertaining to a s. (Chiefly *Zool.*) **Si·pho·nic** *a.* of or pertaining to a s.; siphonal (*Zool.*); working by means of, or on the principle of, a s. **Siphoni·gerous** *a. Zool.* having a s.; siphonate.

Siphon (səi·fən), *v.* Also **syphon.** 1859. [f. prec.] 1. *trans.* To draw off or bring up (liquid, etc.) by means of a siphon. 2. To empty after the manner of a siphon 1892.

Siphonage (səi·fǫnėdʒ). Also **sy-.** 1855. [f. SIPHON *sb.* + -AGE.] The action of drawing off liquid by means of a siphon; also *spec.* the accidental emptying of a siphon-trap.

‖Siphonaria (səifǫnē°·riă). 1861. [mod.L., f. L. *siphon-* SIPHON.] A pulmonate gasteropod of the genus *Siphonaria*, distinguished by a siphon passing from the apex to the margin.

Siphonate (səi·fǫnėt), *a.* and *sb.* 1870. [f. SIPHON *sb.* + -ATE [2] 2.] A. *adj.* Of molluscs: Furnished with, or characterized by having, a siphon. B. *sb.* A mollusc furnished with a siphon 1877. So **Si·phonated** *a.* = A. 1851.

Siphonet (səi·fǫnet). 1826. [f. SIPHON *sb.* + -ET.] *Entom.* A small siphon or tube by which an aphis emits a sweet, honey-like fluid.

Siphono- (səi·fǫno), a. Gr. σιφωνο-, comb. form of σίφων SIPHON, used in various terms of *Zool.* and *Bot.*, as **Si·phonobra·nchiate,** *sb.* one of the *Siphonobranchiata*, a former order of gastropods, including those in which the branchial cavity terminates in a prolonged tube or siphon, by which the respiratory current of water is received and expelled; *adj.* having such a tube or siphon; belonging to the order *Siphonobranchiata.* **Siphono·phoran,** *sb.* **Si·phonophore** (-fō°ɹ) *sb.* a member of the *Siphonophora*, a group of colonial hydrozoans; *adj.* of or belonging to these. **Si·phonosto·matous** *a.*, of the shells of certain crustaceans: having the aperture of the shell notched in front. **Si·phonostome,** one of a family of crustaceans, having a siphon-shaped mouth for suction; also, applied to those gastropods which have the opening of the shell prolonged into a siphon.

Siphuncle (səi·fǫŋk'l). 1822. [ad. L. *siphunculus*, dim. of *sipho* SIPHON.] 1. *Zool.* A small canal or tube traversing and connecting the shell-chambers in certain cephalopods. 2. *Ent.* A small siphon or suctorial organ 1826. Hence **Si·phuncled** *a.* possessing or furnished with a s. **Siphu·ncular** *a.* of or pertaining to, acting or serving as a s. **Siphu·nculated** *a.* possessing or furnished with a s.

‖Siphunculus (səifǫ·ŋkiŭlǫ̆s). *Pl.* **-li.** 1752. [L., dim. of *sipho* SIPHON.] *Zool.* = prec. 1.

Sipper (si·pər). 1611. [f. SIP *v.* + -ER [1].] One who sips; hence, a drinker, toper.

Sippet (si·pėt). 1530. [app. a dim. of SOP *sb.*] A small piece of toasted or fried bread, usu. served in soup or broth, or with meat, or used for dipping into gravy, etc. b. *fig.* A fragment.

Sipple (si·p'l), *v.* 1566. [f. SIP *v.* + -LE 3.] **1.** *trans.* To drink (liquor, etc.) slowly or by sips; to sip *up.* **2.** *intr.* To sip liquor, etc. leisurely 1606.

Sipu·nculoid, *sb.* and *a.* 1857. [See next and -OID.] *Zool.* **A.** *sb.* A member of the group *Sipunculoidea* of gephyrean worms. **B.** *adj.* Of or belonging to the *Sipunculoidea* 1881.

‖**Sipunculus** (səipʊ·ŋkiŭlʊ̆s). *Pl.* **-li.** 1841. [L., var. of SIPHUNCULUS.] *Zool.* A gephyrean annelid with a retractile proboscis, belonging to the typical genus of the family *Sipunculidæ.*

‖**Si quis** (səi kwis). Also **si-quis, siquis.** 1597. [L. *si* if, *quis* any one (sc. *invenerit,* etc.), the opening words of the notice or bill (see def.), when written in Latin.] A public notice, freq. one exhibited on a post, door, etc., requesting information, advertising something lost, etc.; later only *Eccl.*, a notice, required in certain cases, intimating that a candidate seeks ordination, and asking if any one knows of any impediment.

Sir (sə̄ɹ), *sb.* ME. [Reduced form of SIRE *sb.*] **I. 1.** The distinctive title of honour of a knight or a baronet, placed before the Christian name. **2.** Applied retrospectively to notable personages of ancient, esp. sacred or classical, history. Now *arch.* ME. **3.** Used fancifully, or as a mock title. late ME. †**4.** Placed before the Christian name of ordinary priests (also that of a pope) –1635. †**5.** Used (as tr. L. *dominus*), with the surname of the person, to designate a Bachelor of Arts in some Universities –1822.

1. Sir Nich. Kemys was governour 1645. 2. Shall I Sir Pandarus of Troy become? SHAKS. 3. I am Sir Oracle, And when I ope my lips let no dog barke SHAKS. 5. Sir Wilkinson of Queen's 1714.

II. 1. Placed before a common noun, and forming with it a term of address, as *Sir clerk, knight,* etc. Now *arch.* ME. **b.** With contemptuous, ironic, or irate force. late ME. **2.** Used as a respectful term of address to a superior, or, in later use, an equal (sometimes with additions, as *dear, good,* etc.); also formally in addressing the Speaker of a legislative assembly ME. **b.** Used in beginning or subscribing letters. late ME. **3.** Used with scornful, contemptuous, indignant, or defiant force 1592. **4.** Applied to women. Now *dial.* 1578. **5.** A person of rank or importance; one who might be addressed as 'sir' ME.

1. I am one, that had rather go with sir Priest, then sir knight SHAKS. b. *Much Ado* v. i. 83. 2. 'Sir to you', said Mr. Foker politely THACKERAY. 5. A Lady to the worthiest Sir, that euer Country call'd his SHAKS.

Sir (sə̄ɹ), *v.* 1576. [f. prec.] **1.** *trans.* To address (a person) as 'sir'. **2.** *intr.* To use the term 'sir' in addressing a person 1798.

1. Don't *Sir* me! don't you know my name? 1890.

‖**Sirdar** (sə̄·ɹdāɹ, səɹdā·ɹ). 1615. [Urdū (Pers.) *sardār,* f. Pers. *sar* head + *dār* possessor.] In India and other Eastern countries, a military chief, a leader or general of a force or army; also *spec.* in recent use, the British commander-in-chief of the Egyptian army. Hence **Sirdarship.**

Sire (səiəɹ), *sb.* ME. [a. OF.:—pop. L. **seior,* for cl. L. *senior* SENIOR.] †**I. 1.** = SIR *sb.* I. 1, 2, and 4. –1492. †**2.** = SIR *sb.* II. 1. –1500. **3.** In early use = SIR *sb.* II. 2. Now only *arch.* (= 'your majesty') or as an echo of French usage. ME.

3. 'S.', said he, 'there has been a battle before Pavia' 1845.

II. 1. One who exercises dominion or rule; a lord, master, or sovereign. Now *rare* or *Obs.* ME. **2.** A person of some note or importance; an aged or elderly man. Also *gen.* man, fellow. late ME. **3.** A father; a male parent; also a forefather. Now chiefly *poet.* ME. **4.** A male parent of a quadruped; *esp.* a stallion: correl. to *dam* 1523.

2. At length a Reverend S. among them came MILT. 3. The sceptre of his sires he took COWPER. *fig.* S. of Insects, mighty Sol PRIOR. 4. So Kids and Whelps their Sires and Dams express DRYDEN. Hence **Si·reless** *a.*

Sire (səiəɹ), *v.* 1611. [f. SIRE *sb.*] *trans.* To beget or procreate; to become the sire of. **b.** *spec.* Of animals, esp. horses 1828.

Cowards father Cowards, & Base things Syre Bace SHAKS.

Siredon (səirī·dən). 1842. [a. late L., ad. Gr. Σειρηδών, late form of Σειρήν SIREN.] The axolotl.

Siren (səiə·rən). Also **syren.** ME. [ult. ad. Gr. Σειρήν, through L. *Siren* and late L. *Sirena.*] †**1.** An imaginary species of serpent –1520. **2.** *Greek* and *Latin Myth.* One of several fabulous monsters, part woman, part bird, who were supposed to lure sailors to destruction by their enchanting singing. late ME. **3.** One who, or that which, sings sweetly, charms, allures, or deceives, like the Sirens 1590. **4.** One or other of the eel-like gradient and tailed amphibians belonging to the family *Sirenidæ,* native to N. America; esp. the mud-iguana, *Siren lacertina* 1791. **5.** An acoustical instrument (invented by Cagniard de la Tour in 1819) for producing musical tones and used in numbering the vibrations in any note 1820. **b.** An instrument, made on a similar principle but of larger size, used on steamships, motor-vehicles, etc. for giving fog-signals, warnings, etc. 1879.

2. They hauing Sirens tongues and Crocodiles teares, thereby entic'd him to intangle him 1598. 3. Blest pair of Sirens,..Sphear-born harmonious Sisters, Voice and Vers MILT.

attrib., esp. in sense 'characteristic of, resembling that of, a Siren', as *s. air, beauty, note,* etc.; also *s. daughter, enemy,* etc.; *s.-voiced,* etc. Hence **Si·renize** *v. trans.* to delight or charm; to allure or enchant (now *rare*).

Sirenian (səirī·niăn), *sb.* and *a.* 1883. [f. mod.L. *Sirenia,* f. L. SIREN.] *Zool.* **A.** *sb.* Any member of the order *Sirenia* of fish-like aquatic mammals. **B.** *adj.* Pertaining to or having the characteristics of this order 1891.

Sirenic (səire·nik), *a. rare.* 1704. [f. SIREN *sb.* + -IC.] **1.** Melodious; charming, fascinating, alluring. **2.** Of persons: Sweet-singing 1797.

1. Spell-caught by their Syrenick Voice 1704. So **Sire·nical** *a.* 1599.

Sirian (si·riăn), *a.* 1591. [f. SIRIUS + -AN.] *Astr.* **1.** Of or belonging to Sirius. **2.** Having a spectrum like that of Sirius 1892.

‖**Siriasis** (sirəi·ăsis). 1601. [a. L., a. Gr. σειρίασις, f. σειριᾶν to be hot and scorching.] *Path.* A disease affecting children, characterized by inflammation of the brain and membranes, and burning fever. **b.** Sunstroke.

‖**Sirius** (si·riʊ̆s). late ME. [L., a. Gr. Σείριος.] *Astr.* A fixed star of the first magnitude, the chief of the constellation Canis Major or Great Dog, and the brightest in the heavens; the dog-star.

‖**Sirkar** (sə̄·ɹkāɹ). *Anglo-Ind.* 1619. [Urdū (Pers.) *sarkār,* f. Pers. *sar* head + *kār* agent, doer.] †**1.** The court or palace of a native king or prince –1626. **2.** A province; a revenue division 1627. **3.** The State or Government 1798. **4.** A house-steward (usu. native) 1772. **5.** A native clerk, accountant, or agent 1828.

Sirloin (sə̄·ɹloin). Also **surloin.** late ME. [ad. OF. **surloigne,* var. of *surlonge,* f. *sur* over, above + *longe* LOIN *sb.*] The upper and choicer part of a loin of beef, used for roasting. Also const. *of.* **b.** *transf.* Of persons 1648.

Sirmark (sə̄·ɹmaɹk). Also **surmark.** 1664. [perh. f. *sur-* over + MARK *sb.*[1]] *Shipbuilding.* One or other of several marks made upon a mould to indicate where the respective bevellings are to be applied to the frame-timbers of a vessel.

Siroc (səi·rǫk, sirǫ·k). 1775. [a. earlier F., (now *siroco*), or ad. It. *sirocco.*] = SIROCCO 1.

Sirocco (sirǫ·ko). 1617. [a. It. *sirocco, scirocco,* ad. Arab. *sharq* east, f. *sharaqa* (the sun) rose.] **1.** An oppressively hot and blighting wind, blowing from the north coast of Africa over the Mediterranean and affecting parts of Southern Europe (where it is also moist and depressing). Usu. with *the.* **b.** With *a* and *pl.* 1820. **2.** A sirocco drying-machine 1890.

attrib., as *s. blast, wind,* etc.; also **s. drying-closet, drying-machine, oven,** a closet, machine, or oven for drying hops or tea-leaves by means of a hot, moist current of air.

Sirrah (si·ră). Now *arch.* 1526. [f. SIR *sb.* The final syllable is of uncertain origin.] **1.** A term of address used to men or boys, expressing contempt, reprimand, or assumption of authority on the part of the speaker. †**2.** Applied to women (seriously or in jest) –1711.

1. S., I'll break your bones! MME D'ARBLAY. Give me a glass of brandy, s. host 1860. 2. You lose all your money at cards, s. Stella SWIFT.

Sir-re·verence. *Obs.* exc. *dial.* 1575. [Alteration of *save* (abbrev. *sa'*) *reverence.*] †**1.** *S. of,* with all respect for, with apologies to. Also without const. –1687. **2.** Human excrement 1592. **b.** With *a.* A lump or piece of this 1592.

1. A very reuerent body: I such a one, as a man may not speake of, without he say sir reuerence SHAKS.

Sirup, obs. and U.S. var. SYRUP.

‖**Sirvente** (sirvaṅt). 1819. [a. F., or ad. Prov. *sirventes, serventes,* app. f. *servir* to serve, but the connexion is obscure. The form *sirvente* has arisen by taking *sirventes* as a pl.] A form of poem or lay, usu. satirical, employed by the troubadours of the Middle Ages.

Sisal (si·săl, sisā·l). 1843. Name of a port in Yucatan, used attrib. to designate the prepared fibre of several species of *Agave* and *Fourcroya,* used in rope-making. Also *S. plant,* the aloe or other plant from which the fibre is obtained. Also *ellipt.*, chiefly *attrib.* 1883.

Siscowet (si·skǫ̆et). 1849. [Odjibwa, lit. = 'cooks itself'.] A variety of the great lake trout of N. America, found in Lake Superior.

Sisel (si·sĕl). 1880. [ad. G. *ziesel.*] A kind of ground-squirrel, *Spermophilus citillus.*

Siserary (siserē·ri). Now *dial.* Also siserara, etc. 1481. [Popular corruption of CERTIORARI.] †**1.** A writ of Certiorari –1761. **2.** *With a s.,* with a vengeance; suddenly, promptly 1607. **3.** A severe scolding; a sharp blow; a torrent *of* (language) 1771.

Siskin (si·skin). 1562. [ad. G. dial. *sisschen, zeischen,* a dim. form based on MHG. *zîsec,* MLG. *ziseke, sisek,* app. of Slavonic origin.] **1.** A small song-bird, in some respects closely allied to the goldfinch; also called ABERDEVINE. **2.** Applied with defining words to other small birds related to or resembling the siskin 1783.

2. *Chrysomitris pinus,*..American S. 1884.

attrib.: **s.-green,** a light green inclining to yellow.

Siss, *sb.*[1] *U.S.* Also **sis.** 1859. Abbrev. of *sister,* used in addressing girls and young women. So **Si·ssy** [-Y[6]] orig. and chiefly *U.S.*; also, an effeminate or inefficient man or boy.

Siss, *sb.*[2] 1870. [Cf. next.] A hissing sound.

Siss (sis), *v.* Now *dial.* and *U.S.* [ME. *cissen, sissen,* of imitative origin.] To hiss.

‖**Sissoo** (si·sū). 1810. [Urdū (Hindī) *sīsū.*] **1.** A valuable Indian timber-tree, *Dalbergia Sissoo.* **2.** The timber of this tree 1810.

Sist, *sb.* 1693. [f. next.] *Sc. Law.* A stay or suspension of some proceeding; *spec.* an 'order or injunction of the Lord Ordinary prohibiting diligence to proceed' (Bell).

Sist, *v.* *Sc.* 1652. [ad L. *sistere* to cause to stand.] **1.** *trans.* To stop, stay, or suspend (some proceeding, etc.), *esp.* by judicial decree. **2.** To cause or order (a person) to appear *before* a court; to summon or cite 1721.

1. The whole business of metaphysic..is summarily sisted 1881.

Sister (si·stəɹ), *sb.* [Com. Teut.; OE. *sweoster, swuster,* = ON. *systir* (whence prob. the current form). The Teut. stem **swestr-* is for original **swesr-* (L. *soror*).] **1.** A female in relationship to another person or persons having the same parents. (Also applied to animals.) Sometimes loosely used in the sense of HALF-SISTER, and in that of SISTER-IN-LAW. **2.** *fig.* One who is reckoned as, or fills the place of, a sister OE. **3. a.** A female member of a religious order, society, or gild; *spec.* a nun OE. **b.** A female fellow-member of the Christian Church as a whole, or of some body or association within this 1449. **c.** A member of a body of nurses; now *spec.* a head-nurse having charge of a ward in an infirmary or hospital 1552. **4. a.** Used to designate qualities, conditions, etc., in relation to each other or to some kindred thing ME. **b.** Applied to mythological or imaginary beings; esp. *the* (*fatal* or *three*) *sisters,* the Fates or Parcæ. late ME. **5.** A thing having close kinship or relationship to another 1613.

1. Daughter, s., wife, And mother of their Cæsars

GRAY. **2.** Sey to wisdam, My s. thou art WYCLIF *Prov.* vii. 4. **3. a.** One Isabell, a S. SHAKS. *Sister(s) of Charity, of Mercy*, etc. **4.** Thou with Eternal wisdom didst converse, Wisdom thy S. MILT. **b.** Begin then, Sisters of the sacred well MILT. **5.** Sparta..in laws and institutions is the s. of Crete 1875.

attrib. and *Comb.* †**a.** The old uninflected genitive remained in common use down to the 16th c. in terms of relationship, esp. *sister son*. **b.** *spec.*: **s.-block,** one of two blocks made of ash, and turned out of a solid piece, one above the other; **-hook,** a double hook in which the shanks of the respective portions form mousings for the fellow portions.

Si·ster, *v.* 1608. [f. prec.] **1.** *trans.* To stand to (a person or thing) in the relationship of a sister or sisters. **2.** To call (a person) sister; to address as a sister 1663.

Sister-german. late ME. [f. SISTER *sb.* + GERMAN *a.*[1]] A sister through both parents; a full sister.

Sisterhood (si·stəɹhud). late ME. [f. SISTER *sb.* + -HOOD.] **1.** The state or condition of being a sister; sisterly status or relationship. **2.** A society of sisters; *esp.* a society of women bound by certain vows and living together under conventual rule, or otherwise devoted to religious or charitable work as a vocation 1592. **b.** Used loosely to denote a number of females having some common characteristic or calling. Often in depreciatory sense. 1609.

1. She..left to doo the part Of s.. to doo that of a wife 1609. **2.** He dispose of thee, Among a S. of holy Nunnes SHAKS. **b.** Have the whole S. of Canting Females banished 1718. *fig.* A s. of churches 1883.

Sistering (si·stəriŋ), *ppl. a.* 1597. [f. SISTER *v.*] Having a relationship comparable in some way to that of a sister or sisters.

Si·ster-in-law. 1440. [See LAW *sb.*[1]] **a.** The sister of one's husband or wife. **b.** The wife of one's brother. **c.** The wife of one's husband's or wife's brother.

Sisterly (si·stəɹli), *a.* 1570. [f. SISTER *sb.* + -LY[1].] **1.** Of or pertaining to a sister; befitting or like a sister. **2.** Of or pertaining to a sisterhood 1883.

1. They..exchanged a s. kiss, and a s. good-night SCOTT. Hence **Si·sterliness.**

‖**Sistrum** (si·strə̆m). *Pl.* **sistra (sistrums).** late ME. [L., ad. Gr. σεῖστρον, f. σείειν to shake.] A musical instrument consisting of a thin oval metal frame furnished with transverse metal rods loosely fixed in it and a handle by which it was shaken.

Orig. peculiar to Egypt and the worship of Isis, but subseq. used in other Oriental countries.

Sisyphean (sisifī·ăn), *a.* 1635. [f. L. *Sisypheius*, ad. Gr. Σισύφειος, f. Σίσυφος Sisyphus, name of a king of Corinth, whose punishment in Hades was to roll a heavy stone up a hill; as he reached the top, the stone rolled down again.] Of or pertaining to Sisyphus; like (that of) Sisyphus; resembling the fruitless toil of Sisyphus; endless and ineffective. So **Sisy·phian** (sisi·fiăn) *a.* 1599.

Sit (sit), *sb.* 1776. [f. the vb.] **1.** The manner in which an article of dress, or some part of one, is disposed or fits the person. **2.** A spell of sitting 1832. **3.** A sinking or settling down (of a wall, the roof of a mine, etc.) 1808.

1. Long lectures about the s. of a cap 1776.

Sit (sit), *v.* Pa. t. and pa. pple. **sat** (sæt). [Com. Teut.; OE. *sittan*:—Teut. **sitjan*. The stem **set-*, pre-Teut. **sed-*, is represented in L. *sedere*, Gr. ἕζεσθαι.] **I.** *intr.* **1.** Of persons: To be or remain in that posture in which the weight of the body rests upon the posteriors; to be seated. **b.** *spec.* Used of persons seated (usu. at a table) for the purpose of, or while engaged in, eating, drinking, gaming, etc. ME. **2.** To occupy a seat in the capacity of a judge or with some administrative function OE. **b.** To occupy an episcopal, or the papal, see. late ME. **c.** To have a seat in, be a member of, a council or legislative assembly. Also const. *for* (a constituency). late ME. **3.** Of a legislative or other assembly: To hold a session; to be engaged in the transaction of business 1518. **4. a.** To place oneself in a position for having one's portrait painted or for being photographed. Also const. *for* (one's portrait), *to* (a painter, etc.). 1538. **b.** To serve as a model *for* a painting or a character in a novel 1673. **c.** To present oneself *for* examination; *Camb. Univ.* to be a candidate *for* a fellowship 1830. **5.** To be, to continue or remain, *in* a certain condition. Now *rare* or *Obs.* OE. **6.** To have one's seat, quarters, or place; to abide, dwell, remain (in a place) OE. **b.** To be tenant of, to occupy, a house, farm, etc.; to remain during a lease; to continue a tenancy. Usu. const. *at* (a certain rent), or with compl. 1598. **7.** To remain at a siege OE. **8.** Of birds: To perch or roost; also, to rest the body on the ground or other surface OE. **b.** To take up or continue in the posture necessary for the hatching of eggs. Also const. *on*. 1483. **9.** Of animals: To rest the body in a manner analogous to that of a seated person ME. **10.** To support the body *on the knees*. *Obs.* exc. *dial.* OE.

1. Like silly Beggars..sitting in the Stockes SHAKS. I sha'n't dare to sit cross-legg'd for you without offence 1754. I see them s., they linger yet GRAY. I had sat on pins during the inquisition 1885. *fig.* Thy rapt soul sitting in thine eyes MILT. *To s. on the* or *one's throne*, to reign. **2.** The summons was heard by the registrar, sitting as Deputy Chancellor 1896. Phr. *To s. in judgement*: see JUDGEMENT 1. **c.** You used to s. for Silverbridge TROLLOPE. **3.** In the House of Lords the presence of three members is sufficient to enable the House to s. 1863 **4. b.** *fig.* Airy dreams Sat for the picture COWPER. **5.** While Virtue, Valour, Wisdom s in want MILT. Conscience sat mistress over the whole earth 1833. **6.** *fig.* The lady..who sits, indeed, very near my heart FIELDING. **b.** S. wha like, I'll flitt 1844. **8. b.** *fig.* Thou..Dove-like satst brooding on the vast Abyss And mad'st it pregnant MILT. **10.** While he sat on his knees before me, mopping and mowing SCOTT.

II. 1. Of things: To have place or location; to rest or lie *on* OE. **b.** Of the wind: To blow from, be in, a particular quarter. **c.** In fig. phr. said of the effect of emotion, etc. *on* the mind, food *on* the stomach. late ME. **2.** Of clothes: **a.** With dative: To fit or suit (a person, etc.). *rare.* ME. **b.** To fit (well, tightly, etc.). late ME. †**3.** Usu. *impers.* To suit; to be fitting or proper –1579.

1. The Ship sat upright DE FOE. The village of Cocurès, sitting among vineyards and meadows STEVENSON. *fig.* Truth sits upon the lips of dying men M. ARNOLD. **b.** Sits the winde in that corner? SHAKS. **2.** A close dress of scarlet which sate tight to his body SCOTT. *fig.* A light stoicism sits gracefully on him CARLYLE.

III. 1. To seat oneself; to take a seat; to sit down OE. **2.** To rise *upright, on end*, move or lean *back*, in a sitting posture ME.

1. This said, he sat HOBBES.

With advs. **S. down. a.** To seat oneself; to take a seat. **b.** To establish oneself in some position or place; to settle, take up one's abode. Now chiefly *U.S.* (*b*) To encamp *before* a town, etc., in order to besiege it. (*c*) *fig.* Of persons or things, to settle down in some way. **c.** To put up, rest content, *with*, †to acquiesce *in*, something. **S. on.** To continue to sit, to remain, stay on. **S. out. a.** To sit apart from others, or to remain seated, so as to take no part in a game, dance, etc. **b.** To sit in the open air. **S. up. a.** To raise the body to (an upright) sitting posture. **b.** To defer the hour for retiring to bed until late; to wait up *for*; to watch through the night (or some part of it) *with* one. **c.** To be in a sitting posture, in contrast to lying in bed. *To s. up and take notice*: said orig. of a person beginning to recover from an illness; hence, to become aware of the state of things. **d.** *To make* (a person) *s. up* (*slang*), to astonish, startle, have a powerful effect on him. With preps. **S. on** or **upon. a.** To sit in judgement or council, to deliberate, on (a person or matter). **b.** To have a seat on (a jury, commission, etc.). **c.** *slang.* To squash, check, snub. **S. over. a.** To be occupied with (a matter etc.), while sitting; to pore over (a book). **b.** *Bridge.* To be on the left hand of, and so in an advantageous position over. **S. under,** to listen to, be a hearer of, attend the church of (a minister or preacher).

IV. 1. *refl.* To seat oneself OE.; esp. with *down* 1450. **2.** *trans.* To sit, or keep one's seat, on 1542. **b.** To sit on (eggs) 1600. **c.** To sit in (a boat) with proper poise 1866. **3.** To cause to sit *down, up*; seat in a certain place 1470. **4.** To resist, endure, put up with (*rare* or *Obs.*) late ME.

S. thee by our side SHAKS. I s. me down a pensive hour to spend GOLDSM. **2.** It was difficult to s. our horses WESLEY. **4.** I don't know how to s. it sometimes NEWMAN.

S. out. a. To remain seated and take no part in (a game, etc.). **b.** To remain sitting throughout the course of. **c.** To sit longer than (another) at a meeting, etc. **S.-down,** applied to a strike in which workmen occupy their place of employment while refusing to work or to allow others to do so.

Sitar (si·tāɹ). *Anglo-Ind.* 1845. [Urdū.] An Indian guitar.

Site (səit), *sb.* late ME. [a. AF., or ad. L. *situs* place, position, etc.] †**1.** The place or position occupied by some specified thing. Freq. implying original or fixed position. –1691. †**b.** With *a* and *pl.* –1716. †**c.** Without article: Place, position, situation –1697. †**d.** Attitude, position, or posture (of the body, etc.) –1746. **2.** The situation or position of a place, town, building, etc. Occas. without article. 1567. **3.** The ground or area upon which a building, town, etc., has been built, or which is set apart for some purpose. Also, a plot, or number of plots, of land intended or suitable for building. 1461. **b.** *transf.* The seat *of* (an industry); the scene *of* (some condition, etc.) 1637.

1. Of the providence and wisdome of God in the s. and motion of the Sun SIR T. BROWNE. **d.** The semblance of a lover, fix'd In melancholy s. THOMSON. **2.** The sublime s. of the Castle 1781. **3.** In rude and unsettled times, these insular sites afforded safe retreats 1863. *Plane of s.*, in *Fortif.*, a plane coinciding approximately with that of the ground occupied by a work.

Site (səit), *v.* 1598. [f. the sb., or back-formation from SITED *ppl. a.*] **1.** *trans.* To locate, to place. **2.** *intr.* To be situated or placed; to lie 1630.

Sited (səi·tėd), *ppl. a.* 1455. [f. SITE *sb.* or L. *situs* placed.] **1.** Of buildings, countries, etc.: Having a (certain) site or situation; situated. (Re-formed in the 20th c.) †**2.** Of things, persons, etc.: Having a particular place or position; placed, seated –1660.

1. A little howse..s. in midst of a small wood 1619.

Si·t-fast, sitfast, *sb.* and *a.* 1611. [f. SIT *v.* + FAST *adv.*] **A.** *sb. Farriery.* A hard excrescence, induration, or tumour, tending to ulceration, produced on the back of a horse by the uneven pressure or chafing of the saddle. **B.** *adj.* Marked or characterized by sitting firmly; fixed, firm 1807.

Which the cultivators of the soil have not yet been able to dig up from its sitfast hold 1807.

Sith, *adv., prep.,* and *conj.* Now *dial.* or *arch.* [Reduced f. OE. *siððan* SITHEN.] **A.** *adv.* †**1.** Then, thereupon; afterwards –1450. †**b.** Next in succession, order, or place. –late ME. †**2.** Continuously or ever from or since that time –1621. †**3.** = SINCE *adv.* 3, 4. –1549. †**B.** *prep.* = SINCE *prep.* –1593. **C.** *conj.* †**1.** From, subsequent to, or since the time that –1581. **2.** = SINCE *conj.* 2. Now *arch.* or *poet.* late ME. †**b.** So *s. that* –1678.

2. For s. the day is come þat I shal dye, I make pleynly my confession CHAUCER.

†**Sithe,** *sb.*[1] [OE. *sīþ*.] Journey; time, occasion.

Sithe (səið), *v.* Now *dial.* ME. [var. of SIGH *v.*] *intr.* To sigh. Also *trans.*, to say with a sigh. So **Sithe** *sb.*[2] a sigh.

†**Si·then,** *adv., conj.,* and *prep.* [OE. *siþþon, -an*, for earlier **sīð þon* (*þan*) 'subsequently to that', with shortening of the first vowel.] = SITH *adv.* (–1669), *conj.* (–1572), *prep.* (–1604).

Si·thence, *adv., conj.,* and *prep.* *Obs.* exc. *arch.* Also **sithens** (*arch.*). late ME. [f. prec. + *-es, -s*; cf. SINCE.] = prec., in all uses.

Sitio- (sitio), comb. form of Gr. σιτίον food made from grain, bread, as **Sitio·logy,** dietetics. **Sitioma·nia, Sitiopho·bia,** morbid repugnance or aversion to food.

Sito- (səito), comb. form of Gr. σῖτος food made from grain, bread, as **Sito·logy,** = SITIOLOGY. **Sitoma·nia, Sitopho·bia,** = SITIOPHOBIA; hence **Sitopho·bic** *a.*

‖**Sitringee** (sitri·ndʒī). *Anglo-Ind.* 1621. [ad. Urdū *shatranjī*, f. Pers. *shatranj* chess, with ref. to the original chequered pattern.] A carpet or floor-rug made of coloured cotton, now usually with a striped pattern.

Sitter (si·təɹ). ME. [f. SIT *v.* + -ER[1].] **1.** One who sits or occupies a seat; *esp.* one who sits to an artist, photographer, or sculptor, for a portrait, etc., or as a model. **b.** A passenger in a boat as dist. from the rowers or steersman; *spec.* at Eton 1653. **c.** One who has a séance with a medium or the like 1909. **2.** A female bird, *esp* a domestic hen, which sits on eggs for the purpose of hatching them 1614. **3.** *slang.* or *colloq.* An easy mark or shot (as at a sitting bird); a thing easily done, a certainty 1908.

Sittine (si·təin), *sb.* and *a.* 1829. [f. mod.L. *Sittinæ*.] *Ornith.* **A.** *sb.* A member of the *Sittinæ*, a sub-family of the Linnæan genus *Sitta*. **B.** *adj.* Of or pertaining to this family.

Sitting (si·tiŋ), *vbl. sb.* ME. [f. SIT *v.* + -ING [1].] **1.** The action of SIT *v.*; the fact of being seated; an instance of this. **2.** The action on the part of hen-birds of sitting on and hatching eggs; incubation. late ME. **b.** A number of eggs placed under a sitting bird for incubation; a clutch 1854. **3.** The fact of being engaged in the exercise of judicial, legislative, or deliberative functions; an instance or occasion of this; a meeting of a legislative or other body; the period of time occupied by this. late ME. **b.** A séance 1880. **4.** A thing or place on which one sits; a seat, *esp.* in later use, a seat for one person in a church, etc. late ME. **5.** A spell of sitting or of remaining seated 1596. **6.** With advs., as *down, out, up* 1535.

1. Why should a student indulge so much in the lazy and unhealthy habit of s.? 1874. 2. The Male ..amuses and diverts her with his Songs during the whole Time of her S. ADDISON. 3. The speaker was twenty hours in the chair, which was the longest s.,.. that is remembered 1764. 5. I am going to give Kneller my last s. 1829. Phr. *At a* or *one s.*, at one time or spell of continuous action, work, or study.

Comb.: **s.-room**, a room or apartment used for sitting in, esp. in contrast to a bedroom or kitchen; also, room or space in which to sit or available for sitting.

Situate (si·tiu,ĕt), *ppl. a.* 1523. [ad. late L. *situatus*, **situare*, f. L. *situs* SITE.] Situated.

Situate (si·tiu,eⁱt), *v.* Now *rare.* 1532. [f. ppl. stem of med.L. *situare*; see prec.] *trans.* To give a site to; to place, locate. **b.** To place in a certain situation 1896.

Situated (si·tiu,eⁱtėd), *ppl. a.* 1560. [f. as SITUATE *ppl. a.* + -ED [1].] **1.** Of places or things: Placed, located. **2.** Of persons: Placed in relation to, or in respect of, circumstances 1702.

1. *Oxford*, a city..s. on a gentle eminence 1808. 2. It was impossible for me to be thus s., and not feel.. the demon of my race at work within me 1857.

Situation (sitiu,ēⁱ·ʃən). 1490. [a. F., or ad. med.L. *situatio*, f. *situare*, f. L. *situs* site.] **I. 1.** The place, position, or location *of* a city, country, etc., in relation to its surroundings. **2.** †**a.** The place occupied by something; the site *of* a building, etc. –1730. **b.** A place, locality 1610. **3. a.** Place or position of things in relation to surroundings or to each other 1600. †**b.** A place or locality in which a person resides, or happens to be for the time –1825.

1. The s. of the cytie of Saba in Ethiopia vnder Egipt 1553. 2. **b.** The pleasant scituation called Beaulieu 1610. 3. **b.** Educated in a remote s. SCOTT.

II. 1. The position in life, or in relation to others, held or occupied by a person 1710. **b.** A post of employment; a position in which one works for wages 1813. **2.** Condition or state (*of* anything). *Obs.* or *arch.* 1710. **b.** Physical condition; state of health. In later use only *spec.* of women. 1749. **3.** Position of a person with regard to circumstances 1728. **4.** Position of affairs; combination of circumstances 1750. **b.** A particular conjunction of circumstances under which the characters are presented in the course of a novel or play 1779.

1. My s., as a soldier under command SCOTT. **b.** The s. of army-agent 1813. 2. **b.** Mrs. Bunny's in an interesting s...and has given the Lieutenant seven already THACKERAY. 3. The difficulties of his s. increased 1860. 4. The financial s. is perceptibly clearer 1884. **b.** There's s. for you! there's an heroic group! SHERIDAN.

‖ **Situs** (səi·tɒ̆s). *rare.* 1701. [L.] Situation, position.

Sitz bath (si·ts₁ bɑþ). Also **sitz-bath.** 1849. [ad. G. *sitzbad*, f. *sitzen* to sit.] **1.** A bath in which one sits; a hip-bath. **2.** A bath taken by means of this 1852.

Sivaism (sī·vă,iz'm). 1875. [f. Skr. *Siva* 'the auspicious one' (see def.) + -ISM.] The special worship of Siva, the third deity of the Hindu triad, to whom are attributed the powers of reproduction and dissolution.

‖ **Sivatherium** (sīvăþī·riɒ̆m). 1835. [mod. L., f. *Siva* the Hindu god + Gr. θηρίον wild beast.] *Palæont.* A fossil ruminant of great size, with four horns, discovered in the Siwalik or Sub-Himalayan hills in Northern India.

Si·vvens. *Obs.* exc. *Hist.* See also SIBBENS. 1762. [ad. local Gael. *suibhean* raspberry.] An infectious skin disease formerly prevalent in Scotland.

A loathsome and very infectious disease of the venereal kind, called the *Sivvens*...Sometimes a fungus appears in various parts of the body, resembling a raspberry, in the Erse language called *Sivven.* 1776.

Six (siks), *a.* and *sb.* [Com. Teut.; OE. *sex, six*, etc. Cognate forms occur in all the Indo-European langs. (as L. *sex*, Gr. ἕξ, etc.) and indicate an original **sueks*.] The cardinal number next after five, represented by the symbols 6, VI, or vi. **A.** *adj.* **1.** In concord with a sb. expressed. **b.** Followed by *hundred* or *thousand*, or the ordinals of these. Also, *six-sevenths, -tenths*, etc. six (parts, etc.) out of seven, ten, etc. OE. **c.** Coupled with a higher cardinal or ordinal numeral following, so as to form a compound number OE. **2.** With ellipsis of sb., which may usu. be supplied from the context OE.

1. The Creation of the world in the s. daies work 1662. *S. Nations* (of Amer. Indians), the Mohawks, the Oneidas, the Onondegas, the Cayugas, the Senecas, and the Tuscaroras. **b.** Into the valley of Death Rode the s. hundred TENNYSON. **c.** The sixe and thirtieth Chapter 1579. S.-and-twenty years of travel KINGSLEY. 2. At s. he was a charming child BYRON. The rule..was to rise and sup at s. 1834. A coach and s. 1849. Phr. *S. of one and half-a-dozen of the other*, denoting that there is no difference of choice between two (sets of) persons or things.

B. *sb.* **1.** The abstract number six, or the symbol denoting this. late ME. **2.** Chiefly *pl.* **a.** A set of six spots or pips on a die, domino, or card; also, a card, etc., having six pips or spots 1599. **b.** A set of six persons 1796. **3.** *pl.* In various elliptic uses. **a.** Lines of six syllables 1586. **b.** Gloves, shoes, etc., of the sixth size 1796. **c.** Six-pounder guns 1804. **d.** Candles weighing six to the pound 1825. **e.** Six-inch flower-pots 1851. **f.** Bonds bearing interest at six per cent. 1867.

2. **a.** 'Tis a hundred to one, if a man fling two Sixes COWLEY. 3. **g.** A six-cylinder motor car 1920.

Phr. *S. and seven, sixes and sevens*, etc., originally denoting the hazard of one's whole fortune, a carelessness as to the consequences of one's actions, and in later use the creation or existence of, or neglect to remove, confusion, disorder, or disagreement.

C. *Comb.* **1.** Combining (usually hyphened) with a sb. and forming an attrib. compound, as *six-bar* (gate), *six-bottle* (man) 1614. **b.** In phr. *six-year(s)-old* used attrib. or absol. 1630. **2.** In comb. with sbs. ending in *-er*, as *six-footer, -wheeler* 1844. **3.** In advb. sense, = 'in six parts', as *six-partite*, etc. **4.** Miscellaneous, as **s.-chamber**, a six-chambered revolver; **-oar**, a six-oared boat; **-shot, stroke**, a stroke in billiards counting six points; etc.

Sixain (sī·zeⁱn). 1575. [F.] A six-lined stanza.

Sixer (si·ksəɹ). *colloq.* 1870. [f. SIX *a.* + -ER [1].] Anything that counts as six (as a hit for six runs at cricket).

Si·xfoil. 1849. [f. SIX *a.*, after *cinquefoil*, etc.] *Arch.* and *Her.* An ornamental design (or opening) having the form of six leaflets or petals radiating from a common centre.

Sixfold (si·ksfōᵘld), *a.* OE. [f. SIX *a.* + -FOLD.] Consisting of six together; comprising six things, kinds, etc.; also, six times as great or as numerous; sextuple.

Si·x-foot, *a.* 1683. [See SIX C. 1.] **1.** Measuring six feet in length, breadth, or height. **2.** Containing six (metrical) feet 1891.

1. *Six-foot way*, the space between two parallel railway lines; also with ellipsis of *way*.

Sixpence (si·kspĕns). late ME. [f. SIX *a.* + PENCE.] **1.** A sum of money equal in value to six pennies. **2.** A British silver coin worth six pennies 1598.

Sixpenny (si·kspĕni), *a.* (and *sb.*) late ME. [SIX *a.*] **1.** *S. nail*, a nail orig. costing sixpence per hundred. **2.** Of persons: That may be hired for sixpence; earning no more than sixpence; worth only sixpence; paltry, petty 1561. **3.** Costing, or priced at, sixpence 1591. **b.** As *sb.* A book (*esp.* a novel) or magazine published at sixpence 1894. **4.** Amounting to, having the value of, sixpence 1592.

2. 1 *Hen. IV*, II. i. 82. 3. Bring him a s. bottle of ale B. JONSON. 4. *S. bit* or *piece* = SIXPENCE 2.

Six-pounder (si:kspau·ndəɹ). 1684. [f. SIX *a.* + POUNDER *sb.*[2] 1.] **1.** A cannon throwing shot six pounds in weight. **2.** A thing, e.g. a shot, weighing six pounds 1855.

Si·xscore, *a.* Now *arch.* ME. [f. SIX *a.* + SCORE *sb.*] One hundred and twenty.

Si·x-shoo·ter. 1856. [f. SIX C. 2.] A revolver capable of firing six shots without reloading; a six-chambered revolver.

Sixteen (sikstī·n, si·kstīn), *a.* and *sb.* [OE *syx-, six-, sextyne*; see SIX *a.* and -TEEN.] The cardinal number composed of ten and six, represented by the symbols 16, XVI, or xvi. **A.** *adj.* **1.** In concord with a sb. expressed. **2.** With ellipsis of sb. (esp. *years*), which may usu. be supplied from the context ME.

1. Some sixteene moneths SHAKS. 2. When I—was s. 1891.

B. *sb.* **1.** The abstract number sixteen OE. **2.** A sheet of sixteen leaves; a book in sixteenmo 1606. **3.** A girl of sixteen 1840.

Sixtee·nmo. 1847. [English reading of the symbol 16mo.] = SEXTO-DECIMO.

Sixteenth (sikstī·nþ, si·kstīnþ), *a.* and *sb.* ME. [f. SIXTEEN + -TH, repl. OE. *syxtēoða*, etc.] The ordinal numeral belonging to the cardinal sixteen. **A.** *adj.* **1.** In concord with a sb. expressed or implied. **2.** *S. note*, the sixteenth part of a semibreve; a semiquaver 1861. **B.** *sb.* **1.** A sixteenth part 1611. **2.** *Mus.* **a.** The interval of two octaves and a second. **b.** A sixteenth note. 1876.

Sixth (siksþ), *a.* and *sb.* [OE. *sixta*: see SIX *a.* and -TH [2].] The ordinal numeral belonging to the cardinal six. **A.** *adj.* **1.** In concord with a sb. expressed or implied. **b.** Following on the names of kings, popes, etc. late ME. **2.** *ellipt.* 1573.

1. And the euening and the morning were the s. day. *Gen.* i. 31. **b.** King James the S. 1857. 2. The sixt of May 1631.

B. *sb.* **1.** A sixth part 1557. **2.** *Mus.* A tone on the sixth degree above or below another, both tones being counted; the harmonic combination of two such tones; an interval comprising six degrees of the scale 1597. **3.** The sixth form in a school 1857. Hence **Si·xthly** *adv.* in the s. place.

Sixtieth (si·kstiĕþ), *a.* and *sb.* [OE. *sixteo-goða*, etc., f. *sixtig* SIXTY.] **A.** *adj.* The ordinal numeral belonging to the cardinal sixty. **B.** *sb.* A sixtieth part 1800.

Sixty (si·ksti), *a.* and *sb.* [OE. *siex-, syx-, sextig.*] The cardinal number equal to six times ten, represented by the symbols 60, LX, or lx. **A.** *adj.* **1.** In concord with a sb. expressed or implied. **2.** Followed immediately by a lesser numeral, as *sixty-one*, etc. 1597. **2.** Forming part of an ordinal number 1647. **b.** With *part*, or used absol. in this sense, esp. *sixty-fourth* 1768. **B.** *sb.* **1.** The abstract number sixty ME. **2.** Sixty years of age. Also *sixty-one*, etc. 1717. **3.** *pl.* The years from 60 to 69 in a century, or in a person's life; the period 1860–1869. 1886.

Comb.: *Sixty-fourmo*, the size of the page of a book in which each leaf is $\frac{1}{64}$ of a full sheet; abbrev. 64mo. *Sixty-fours*, a sheet in 64mo.

Sixtyfold (si·kstifōᵘld), *a.* (and *sb.*). OE. [-FOLD.] Sixty times as great or as much.

Sizar (səi·zăɹ). Also †**sizer.** 1588. [f. SIZE *sb.*[1] I. 4 + -AR [3], -ER [2].] In the University of Cambridge, and at Trinity College, Dublin, an undergraduate member admitted under this designation, and receiving an allowance from the college to enable him to study.

The name probably indicates that the person so admitted received his 'sizes' free. Formerly the sizar performed certain duties now discharged by the college servants. Hence **Si·zarship**, the position or status of being a s.

Size (səiz), *sb.*[1] ME. [a. OF. *sise, cise*, aphetic forms of *assise* ASSIZE, prob. due to *l'assise* being apprehended as *la sise.*] **I. 1.** = ASSIZE *sb.* 7, 8, 9. Now *dial.* †**2.** An ordinance fixing the amount of a payment or tax –1733. †**3.** = ASSIZE *sb.* 5. –1688. †**4.** A quantity or portion *of* bread, ale, etc.; *spec.* in Cambridge use (see quots.) –1785.

1. I will never..bring you to the sizes or sessions 1760. 4. 'Tis not in thee..to cut off my Traine,..to scant my sizes SHAKS. A s. is a portion of bread and drinke: it is a farthing which schollers in Cambridge have at the buttery: it is noted with the letter S as in Oxford with the letter Q for halfe a farthing 1617. *transf. Ant. & Cl.* IV. xv. 4.

II. 1. The magnitude, bulk, bigness, or dimensions *of* anything. late ME. **b.** In abstract use: Magnitude 1667. **2.** A particular magnitude or set of dimensions, *esp*, one of a series in manufactured articles, as boots, gloves, etc. 1591. **3.** Magnitude, extent, rate, amount, etc., as a standard of immaterial things 1530. **b.** Of persons in respect of mental or moral qualities, rank or position, etc.; †hence, class, kind, degree, order 1679. **c.** *pl.* As *adv.* Many times, far 1861.

1. *Of a* (or *one*) *s.*, of the same magnitude or dimensions. **b.** The books precisely matched as to s. DICKENS. **2.** *fig.* He was 'between sizes in politics' 1879. *ellipt.* A large s. plate 1889. **3.** He understood well the s. of their understandings BURNET. That seems to be about the s. of it 1860.

Comb.: **s.-roll** (*a*) a military roll showing the s. of each man; (*b*) a piece of parchment added to a roll; **-stick**, a shoemaker's measuring-stick to determine the length of feet.

Size (səiz), *sb.*[2] 1440. [perh. same word as prec.] †**1.** A glutinous or viscid wash applied to paper, parchment, etc., to provide a suitable ground for gilding, painting, or other work -1763. **2.** A semi-solid glutinous substance, prepared from materials similar to those which furnish glue, and used to mix with colours, to dress cloth or paper, etc. 1530. **3.** *attrib.*, as *s.-gelatin*, etc. 1603.

Size (səiz), *v.*[1] late ME. [f. SIZE *sb.*[1], or aphetic f. ASSIZE *v.*] †**1.** *trans.* To regulate or control, *esp.* in relation to a fixed standard -1771. **2.** In University use (at Cambridge, Harvard, and Yale): To enter as a 'size' upon the buttery or kitchen books; to score (an amount) against oneself in this manner 1598. **b.** *intr.* To order 'sizes', or have them entered against one 1598. **3.** To make of a certain size; to give size to; to adjust in respect of size. Also with *out.* 1609. **4.** To classify or arrange according to size. Also *transf.* to class or rank (*with* others). 1635. **b.** *Mil.* To arrange or draw up (men) in ranks according to stature 1802. **5.** *colloq.* (orig. *U.S.*) Usu. with *up*: To take the size or measure of; to regard so as to form an opinion of; to make an estimate of 1884.

4. The said broken products were then sized and separated 1886. **5.** The grey-haired..man who met us..mentally sized me up at once 1896. Hence **Si·zer**, a device for testing the size of articles or for separating them according to size.

Size (səiz), *v.*[2] 1667. [f. SIZE *sb.*[2]] *trans.* To cover, smear, prepare, treat, or stiffen with size. Hence **Sized** *ppl. a.*[2] treated or prepared in some way with size.

Sizeable, sizable (səi·zăb'l), *a.* 1613. [f. SIZE *sb.*[1] or *v.*[1] + -ABLE.] Of a fair (†proper or convenient) size; fairly large.

The people are fond of purchasing sizeable trees for building 1789. Halifax is a sizable place 1855.

Sized (səizd), *ppl. a.*[1] 1582. [f. SIZE *sb.*[1] or *v.*[1]] **1.** Having a specified or indicated size. †**2.** Matched in size. DRYDEN. **3.** Of a fair, proper, or standard size 1728.

1. *Fair-, large-, middle-s., moderately s.* With *the*, = the size of; The s. type most suitable 1824.

Sizing (səi·ziŋ) *vbl. sb.*[1] 1596. [f. SIZE *v.*[1]] **1.** In Univ. use: The action or practice of procuring 'sizes' from the buttery or kitchen; a portion or quantity so obtained; a size. **b.** *transf.* A share or allowance 1822. **2.** The action of separating and arranging according to size; also, singling of plants 1660.

Sizing (səi·ziŋ), *vbl. sb.*[2] 1635. [f. SIZE *v.*[2]] **1.** The action of applying size, or of preparing in some way with size. **2.** Size prepared for use; also, the materials from which size is prepared 1825.

Sizy (səi·zi), *a.* 1687. [f. SIZE *sb.*[2]] Resembling size; having the consistency of size; thick and viscous; glutinous. Hence **Si·ziness**, †**sizyness**.

Sizzle (si·z'l), *sb.* 1823. [f. the vb.] A hissing sound, *esp.* one produced by the action of frying or roasting; also, broiling heat.

Sizzle (si·z'l), *v.* 1603. [Imitative; cf. FIZZLE *v.*] **1.** *trans.* To burn or scorch so as to produce a hissing sound; to burn *up* with intense heat. **2.** *intr.* To make a kind of hissing sound, esp. in the process of frying, roasting, or burning 1825.

‖**Sjambok** (ʃæ·mbǫk), *sb.* 1804. [a. Cape Du., a. Malay *samboq, chamboq*, ad. Urdū *chābuk*; see CHABOUK.] A strong and heavy whip made of rhinoceros or hippopotamus hide, used in S. Africa for driving cattle and sometimes for administering chastisement. Hence **Sjambok** *v. trans.* to strike with a s.

Skail, *v. north.* ME. To scatter, *trans.* and *intr.*

Skald, scald (skǫld, skæld). ME. (Orm), 1763 (Percy). [a. ON., Icel. *skáld*, of unkn. origin.] An ancient Scandinavian poet.

Before taking the field of battle, it was the office of the S. to compose a poem suited to the occasion 1818. Hence **Ska·ldic, sc-**, *a.* of or pertaining to the skalds or their poetry.

‖**Skat** (skāt). 1864. [G.] A card-game.

Skate (skēⁱt), *sb.*[1] ME. [a. ON. *skata.*] A fish of the genus *Raia*; esp. the common species *Raia batis*, a very large, flat, cartilaginous fish much used for food.

Comb.: **s.-leech, -sucker**, a leech which infests the s.

Skate (skēⁱt), *sb.*[2] 1656. [orig. in pl. *schates, scates*, ad. Du. *schaats*, ad. ONF. *escache* (mod. *écache*) stilt. The alteration of sense has not been explained.] **1.** A steel blade mounted in a wooden sole, and fixed to the boot by means of a screw and straps, used for the purpose of gliding over ice; in later use a similar device made entirely of steel and clamped or strapped to the boot. Also = ROLLER-SKATE. Chiefly in *pl.* **b.** *pl.* = SKI *sb.* 1698. **2.** [from the vb.] An act or spell of skating 1853.

1. Over the Parke (where I first in my life..did see people sliding with their skeates, which is a very pretty art) PEPYS.

Skate (skēⁱt), *v.* 1696. [f. SKATE *sb.*[2]] **1.** *intr.* To glide over ice upon skates; to use skates as a means of exercise or pastime. Also with *over.* **b.** *transf.* To slide or glide along; to move lightly and rapidly 1775. **2.** *trans.* To contest (a match), to compete with (some one) by skating 1847.

1. b. Other insects merely dive into the water..or s. upon the surface 1891. Hence **Ska·ter.**

Skatol (skæ·tǫl). 1879. [f. Gr. σκατός, gen. of σκῶρ dung + -OL.] *Chem.* An aromatic substance produced by the decomposition of albumen in the intestinal canal.

†**Skayles.** 1566. [app. var. of KAYLES.] A form of the game of skittles or ninepins; also, one of the pins -1647.

Skedaddle (skĭdæ·d'l), *sb. colloq.* 1870. [f. the vb.] A hasty or precipitate flight; a scurry.

Skedaddle (skĭdæ·d'l), *v. colloq.* 1862. [prob. fanciful.] **1.** *intr.* Of soldiers, troops, etc.: To retreat or retire hastily or precipitately; to flee. (Orig. U.S. military slang.) **2.** *gen.* To run away, 'clear out' 1862. **b.** Of animals: To run off, stampede 1879.

Skeeball (skī·bǭl). 1923. [f. SKI + BALL *sb.*] A game consisting in throwing a ball along an alley in the centre of which is a bump which causes the ball to leap high in the air and enter a target.

Skeel (skīl). Now *dial.* ME. [a. ON. *skjóla* pail.] A wooden bucket, pail, tub, or similar vessel, used for holding milk or water.

Skee·ling. *Orkney dial.* 1578. [prob. of Scand. origin.] *S.-goose*, the sheldrake.

Skeet (skīt), *sb.* 1440. [Origin unkn.] A long-handled scoop or shovel; in later use *Naut.*, a scoop for throwing water over the planks of a ship's sides, etc. **Skeet** *v. trans.* to throw (water) over (sails) etc. with a s.

Skeg[1]. 1598. [a. ON. *skegg* beard.] **1.** *local.* A species of bearded oat, of inferior quality. **2.** *Shipbuilding.* The after part of the keel in a screw steamer; the triangular piece taking the place of the after part of the keel in a flat-bottomed boat 1625.

Skeg[2]. Now *dial.* 1601. [Origin obsc.] A species of wild plum, esp. the bullace (*Prunus insititia*) or the sloe (*P. spinosa*).

Skegger (ske·gəɹ). 1653. [Origin obsc.] A young salmon, a samlet; salmon fry.

Skein[1] (skēⁱn). ME. [ad. OF. *escaigne*, of unkn. origin.] **1.** A quantity of thread or yarn, wound to a certain length upon a reel, and usually put up in a kind of loose knot.

A skein of cotton consists of eighty turns of the thread upon a reel fifty-four inches in circumference.

2. *transf.* **a.** A small cluster or arrangement resembling a skein 1687. **b.** A flight of wild fowl 1851. **3.** *attrib.*, as *s.-silk*, etc. 1764.

1. *fig.* They disentangle from the puzzled s...The threads of politic and shrewd design COWPER. **2.** The mazy skeins of her shadowy hair T. HARDY.

Skein[2]. Also **skain.** 1837. [ad. Du. *scheen*, cog. w. SHIN *sb.*] **1.** A split of osier after being dressed for use in fine basket-work. **2.** *U.S.* A metal head or thimble protecting the spindle of a wooden axle 1862.

Ske·lder, *v. Obs.* exc. *arch.* 1599. [Cant term of unkn. origin.] **1.** *intr.* To beg; to live by begging. **2.** *trans.* To swindle, cheat, defraud (a person); also, to obtain (money) by cheating 1601.

Skeldraik, -drake, var. SHELDRAKE.

Ske·let. *Obs.* exc. *dial.* 1565. [ad. F. *squelette*, †*skel-*, or Gr. σκελετός, -όν.] = SKELETON.

Skeletal (ske·lĭtăl), *a.* 1854. [f. SKELETON *sb.* + -AL 1.] Of or belonging to, forming or formed by, forming part of, or resembling, a skeleton.

Ske·leto-, comb. form of Gr. σκελετός, -όν, as in **skeleto·genous** *a.*, producing, or helping to form, a skeleton; **skeleto·graphy**, a description of the skeleton; **skeleto·logy**, a treatise on the solid parts of the body.

Skeleton (ske·lĭtŏn). 1578. [a. mod.L. *sceleton, skeleton*, ad. Gr. σκελετόν (sc. σῶμα), neut. of σκελετός dried up, f. σκέλλειν to dry up.] **1.** The bones or bony framework of an animal body considered as a whole; also, more generally, the harder (supporting or covering) constituent part of an animal organism. **2.** *transf.* A very thin, lean, or emaciated person or animal 1629. **b.** *fig.* A mere outline; a thing having a bare, meagre, unattractive character 1607. **3.** The supporting framework of anything, as of buildings, etc. 1658. **4.** The bare outlines or main features, the most necessary elements, *of* something 1647. **b.** The outlines, plan, or scheme of a sermon 1724. **5.** *Mil.* The small number of men (and officers) representing a regiment which is far short of its full strength 1802. **6.** *attrib.* That is, or has the character of, a skeleton 1778.

1. Phr. *A s. in the closet, cupboard*, etc., a secret source of shame or pain to a family or person. *A s. at the feast* (or *banquet*), a reminder of serious or saddening things in the midst of enjoyment; a source of gloom or depression (in allusion to a practice of the ancient Egyptians). **2.** We are become an army of mere skellitons 1715. **3.** The s. or frame of a skin canoe 1817. **6.** *S. hand; s. map, plan, sermon*, etc.; *s. battalion, company, crew, regiment, staff*, etc.; **s. key**, a thin light key having a large part of the bits filed away so that it may open a number of locks as a master key; **s. shrimp**, a crustacean of the genus *Caprella*. A patched and much-soiled s. suit; one of those straight blue cloth cases in which small boys used to be confined DICKENS. **s. type**, a face of type with thin light lines.

This line is in Skeleton type.

Skeletonize (ske·lĭtŏnəiz), *v.* 1644. [f. SKELETON *sb.* + -IZE] **1.** *trans.* To reduce to a skeleton. **2.** To draw up in outline; to sketch out 1865. **3.** *intr.* To become a skeleton 1831. Hence **Ske·letonizer**, an insect which reduces leaves to a skeleton.

Skellum (ske·lŏm). 1611. [ad. Du. *schelm* (sχe·ləm), a. G. *schelm* rascal.] **1.** A rascal, scamp, scoundrel, villain. Now *arch.* (exc. in S. Africa). **2.** In S. African use applied to animals 1850.

Skelly (ske·li), *v. Sc.* and *n. dial.* 1776. [ad. ON. *skjelga*, f. *skalgr* adj. = OE. *sceolh* squint, skew.] *intr.* To squint.

Skelp, *sb.*[1] Chiefly *north.* and *Sc.* 1440. [Related to SKELP *v.*] A blow, *esp.* one given with the flat of the hand, or with something having a flat surface; a slap or smack; also, the noise made by such a blow.

Skelp, *sb.*[2] Also **scelp.** 1811. [perh. f. SKELP *v.* 1.] A thin narrow plate or flat strip of iron or steel, which by twisting and welding is converted into the barrel of a gun.

Skelp, *v.* Chiefly *north.* and *Sc.* late ME. [prob. imitative.] **1.** *trans.* To strike, beat, slap, smack, in later use *spec.* on the breech. **2.** *intr.* To skip, trip, walk, or run rapidly; to hurry. Also with *it.* 1721.

Skelter (ske·ltəɹ), *v.* 1852. [f. the second element in HELTER-SKELTER.] *intr.* To dash along, hurry, rush, skurry.

Sken, *v. dial.* 1611. [Cf. ASKANCE.] *intr.* To squint; to give a side-look; to glance.

Skene (skīn). Now *Hist.* or *arch.* Also **skean**, etc. 1527. [a. Irish (and Sc.) Gaelic *scian, sgian* knife.] 1. A form of knife or dagger, in former times one of the chief weapons of the Irish kerns, and also in use among the Scottish Highlanders. 2. a. *Skene-dhu* [Gael. *sgian dubh* black knife], a small dagger carried by Highlanders (now only as an ornament), frequently thrust into the stocking 1819. b. *Skene-ochles, ochil, -occle* [Gael. *achlais* arm-pit], a knife carried in the sleeve near the arm-pit 1754.

1. The good claymores, the dirks, skeans, and pistols 1879.

Skep. Also **skip.** [a. ON. *skeppa* basket, bushel.] 1. A specific quantity *of* grain, malt, charcoal, etc.; a skepful. 2. A basket or hamper ME. b. *Mining* = SKIP *sb.*[2] 1860. 3. A bee-hive 1494.

Skeptic, -al, etc.: see SCEPTIC, etc.

†**Skerry**, *sb.*[1] 1540. [Origin unkn.] A small punt or boat designed to carry two persons and used chiefly in fenny districts -1861.

Skerry (ske·ri), *sb.*[2] 1612. [Orkney dial., f. ON. *sker*, whence also Gael. *sgeir*.] A rugged insulated sea-rock or stretch of rocks covered by the sea at high water or in stormy weather; a reef.

Skerry (ske·ri), *a.* and *sb.*[3] 1800. [Origin unkn.] A. *adj.* Of the nature of shale; shaly, slaty. B. *sb.* Earth or stone of a shaly nature 1844.

Sketch (sketʃ), *sb.* 1668. [ad. Du. *schets* or G. *skizze*, ad. It. *schizzo*; supposed to be from L. **schedius*, Gr. σχέδιος done or made off-hand, extempore.] 1. A rough drawing or delineation of something, giving the outlines or prominent features without the detail, esp. one intended to serve as the basis of a more finished picture, or to be used in its composition; a rough draught or design. Also, in later use, a drawing or painting of an unpretentious nature. 2. A brief account, description, or narrative, not going into details; a short or superficial essay or study 1668. b. The general plan or outline, the main features, of anything (*rare*) 1697. 3. *Mus.* a. A short piece, usu. for the pianoforte, either slight in construction or vividly descriptive 1840. b. A preliminary study for a finished work or composition 1883. 4. A short play or performance of slight dramatic construction; also, a musical performance by one person in which playing, singing, and talking are combined 1861.

1. b. Something odd, ludicrous, or the like; a 'sight'. 2. Sketches by Boz DICKENS (*title*). *attrib. s.-block, -map*, etc.

Sketch (sketʃ), *v.* 1694. [f. prec.] 1. *trans.* To describe briefly, generally, or in outline; to give the essential facts or points of without going into details; to outline. Also with *out*. 2. To draw the outline or prominent features of (a picture, figure, etc.), esp. as preliminary to further development; to make a sketch or rough draught of (something); to draw or paint in this manner 1725. 3. *intr.* or *absol.* To practise sketching 1874.

2. The method of Rubens was to s. his compositions in colours REYNOLDS. Hence **Ske·tcher. Ske·tching** *vbl. sb.* (attrib. in *s. block*.)

Ske·tch-book. 1820. [f. SKETCH *sb.*] 1. A book having leaves of drawing-paper specially reserved or adapted for making sketches on. b. As the title of a book containing literary sketches 1820. 2. A notebook containing a composer's preliminary studies 1883.

1. b. The Irish Sketch-Book THACKERAY (*title*).

Sketchy (ske·tʃi), *a.* 1805. [f. SKETCH *sb.* + -Y[1].] 1. Giving only a slight or rough outline of the main features, facts, or circumstances without going into details. 2. Of pictures, etc.: Of the nature of, or resembling, a sketch; consisting or composed of outline without much detail 1817. 3. *colloq.* Light, flimsy, unsubstantial, fragmentary 1878.

1. Sketches of society,—very s. indeed 1828. 2. Landseer's very s. lions 1884. 3. A house with.. only very s. wooden window-shutters 1897. Hence **Ske·tchily** *adv.* **Ske·tchiness.**

Skew (skiū), *sb.*[1] ME. [ad. OF. *escu* (mod.F. *écu*) :—L. *scutum* shield.] †a. A stone specially intended or adapted for being placed with other similar ones to form the sloping head or coping of a gable, rising slightly above the level of the roof -1533. b. The line of coping on a gable. Chiefly *Sc.* 1789.

Skew (skiū), *sb.*[2] 1688. [f. SKEW *a.* or *v.*] A slant; a deviation from the straight line; an angle, esp. that at which a bridge spans a road or river; a sideward movement. b. *transf.* A slip, an error 1869.

On the (or *a*) *s.*, on the slant, slantwise.

Skew (skiū), *a.* and *adv.* 1609. [Cf. SKEW *v.* and ASKEW *adv.*] A. *adj.* 1. Having an oblique direction or position; turned to one side, slanting, squint. 2. In special collocations, denoting that the thing in question deviates from a straight line, or has some part not at right angles with the rest, as *s. arch, bridge, girder*, etc., or *s. bevel, chisel, facet, iron*, etc. 1678. B. *adv.* Obliquely, askew (*rare*) 1706. Also **Skew-whiff** *dial.* or *colloq.* 1754.

Skew (skiū), *v.* 1470. [ad. ONF. *eskiu(w)er, escuer*, var. of OF. *eschuer, eschever* ESCHEW *v.*] 1. To take an oblique course or direction; to turn *aside*, move sideways. b. To shy (as a horse), to swerve 1679. 2. To squint *at*, to look *at* (or *upon*) sideways, esp. in a suspicious or slighting manner; hence, to make side-hits *at*, reflect *upon*, something 1570. 3. To cut *off*, set *back*, insert, etc., obliquely 1611.

2. The cows stood round her..Skewing at her 1827.

Skew-back. 1703. [f. SKEW *sb.*[2] or *v.* + BACK *adv.*] 1. *Arch.* The springing-line of an arch; the sloping surface on which either extremity of an arch rests; a course of stone or brickwork, an iron plate, etc., immediately supporting the foot of an arch. 2. *Mech.* A cap or other casting made to receive the end of a diagonal rod or brace 1884.

Skewbald (skiū·bǫld), *a.* and *sb.* 1654. [Cf. PIEBALD.] A. *adj.* Of animals, esp. horses: Irregularly marked with white and brown or red, or some other colour. B. *sb.* A skewbald horse 1863. So **Skewed** (skiud) *a.* 1440.

Skewer (skiū·əɪ), *sb.* 1679. [var. of SKIVER *sb.*[1]] A long wooden or metal pin, used especially to fasten meat or the like together, to keep it in form while being cooked. b. Applied contemptuously to a weapon 1838.

Send up your Meat well stuck with Scewers, to make it look round and plump SWIFT.

Skewer (skiū·əɪ), *v.* 1701. [f. prec.] 1. *trans.* To fasten (meat, etc.) with a skewer or skewers. b. To run through, transfix, with a sword or other weapon 1837. 2. To fix, fasten, or secure to or into something else with, or as with, a skewer or skewers; to truss 1777. 3. To fix or thrust (*into* or *through* something) like a skewer or skewers 1869.

1. b. Perhaps *not* to part, but to fall mutually skewered through with iron CARLYLE. 3. He skewered his great eyes into mine 1869.

Ski (ʃī, skī), *sb.* *Pl.* **ski, skis.** 1885. [a. Norw., :—ON. *skíð* snow-shoe, billet of cleft wood, = OE. *scīd*.] One of a pair of long slender pieces of wood fastened to the foot and used as a snow-shoe, enabling the wearer to slide down hill with great rapidity. *Comb.* **ski-joring**, being drawn over snow or ice wearing skis. Hence **Ski** *v. intr.* to travel on s.

Skiagram (skəi·ăgræm). Also **scia-, skio-.** 1801. [f. Gr. σκιά shadow + -GRAM.] 1. An outline of the shadow of an object filled in with black; a picture painted or produced in this style. 2. A skiagraph, radiograph 1896.

Skiagraph (skəi·ăgraf), *sb.* Also **scia-, skio-.** 1896. [See prec. and -GRAPH.] A picture obtained by means of the Röntgen rays; a radiograph. Hence **Ski·agraph** *v. trans.* to photograph by this means. **Skia·graphy.**

Skid (skid), *sb.* 1609. [Origin obsc.] 1. A beam, plank, or piece of timber, *esp.* one of a number upon which something rests or is supported, or by which a thing is held in position. b. One of a number of beams, or pieces of stone, on which a vessel is built, or placed during repair 1856. 2. a. *Naut.* A wooden fender hung on the outside of a ship to protect it when hoisting in cargo, boats, etc. 1743. b. A plank or roller on which a heavy thing may be slid or pushed along 1846. c. *Lumbering.* One of a number of peeled logs, partially sunk into the ground, and forming a roadway down which logs are drawn or slid. *U.S.* 1851. d. Each of two runners attached to an aeroplane to facilitate landing or taxiing 1909. 3. A device for locking the wheel of a vehicle or for retarding its motion in descending a hill; *esp.* an iron shoe (a *s.-pan*) chained to the vehicle and placed in front of the wheel so as to be caught between it and the ground 1766. 4. [f. the vb.] An act of skidding; also, a side-slip 1909.

Skid (skid), *v.*[1] 1674. [f. SKID *sb.*] 1. *trans.* To apply or fasten a skid or brake to (a wheel) in order to retard its motion; to lock (a wheel) in this way. 2. *intr.* Of a wheel: To be retarded by a skid 1838. b. To slide forwards or backwards or sideways, esp. owing to the state of the road 1884. c. Of an aeroplane: To slip sideways from the centre of curvature while turning (cf. SIDE-SLIP *v.*) 1916.

Skid (skid), *v.*[2] *rare.* 1815. [var. of SCUD *v.*] *intr.* To run or go quickly, to scud.

Skidding (ski·diŋ), *vbl. sb.* 1859. [f. SKID *sb.* or *v.*[1]] 1. *concr.* Timber or planks used as a support for a gun, etc., or to facilitate its removal. 2. The action of SKID *v.*[1] 1889.

Skied (skəid), *ppl. a.* 1730. [f. SKY *sb.* or *v.*] †1. Seeming to touch the sky; lofty. THOMSON. 2. In combs.: Having a sky of a specified kind 1839. 3. *Cricket.* Of a ball: Hit or sent up high in the air. Also *transf.* of a stroke. 1868.

Skiey, var. of SKYEY *a.*

Skiff (skif), *sb.* 1575. [ad. F. *esquif*, Sp. or Pg. *esquife*, or It. *schifo*; prob. from OHG. *scif* ship, boat.] 1. A small sea-going boat, adapted for rowing and sailing; esp. one attached to a ship. Hence, a small light boat of any kind. 2. *spec.* A kind of clinker-built sculling- or pleasure-boat. Also, a long narrow racing-boat for one oarsman, outrigged, usually fitted with a sliding-seat, and covered in fore and aft with canvas. 1793.

Skiff (skif), *v.* 1625. [f. prec.] †1. *trans.* To cross, row or sail over (a river) in a skiff. 2. *intr.* To row or scull in a skiff; to go on a river in a pleasure-skiff 1869.

Skilful (ski·lfŭl), *a.* ME. [f. SKILL *sb.* + -FUL.] †1. Endowed with reason; rational -1440. †2. Reasonable, just, proper -1460. 3. Having practical ability; possessing skill; expert, dexterous, clever. Also const. *to*. ME. †b. Having a good knowledge *of* a subject -1631. 4. Displaying or requiring skill 1586.

3. A Captaine of the Sea, moste skylfull 1560. Skilfull in Astronomye 1555. 4. Irony..is one of those edged tools which require s. handling 1895. Hence **Ski·lful·ly** *adv.*, **-ness.**

Skill (skil), *sb.* ME. [a. ON. *skil*; cf. SKILL *v.*] †1. Reason as a faculty of the mind; the power of discrimination -1500. †2. That which is reasonable, proper, right, or just -1460. †3. Cause, reason, or ground. Also with *a* and *pl.* -1642. †4. In the phr. *can* (or *could*) *s.*, to have discrimination or knowledge, esp. in a specified matter. Usu. const. *of, in,* or *to* with inf. -1869. 5. Practical knowledge in combination with ability; cleverness, expertness ME. †b. An art or science -1667. c. A craft, an accomplishment (now *U.S.*). 6. Knowledge or understanding *of* something. Now *arch.* 1587.

2. It is reason and skyll, We your pleasure fulfyll SKELTON. 3. I thinke you haue As little s. to feare, as I haue purpose To put you to 't SHAKS. 4. Let them iudge that can s. 1581. Many such men as you are, can s. to giue good words 1601. 5. Utterly destitute of the s. necessary to the conduct of great affairs MACAULAY. No s. of speech have I SWINBURNE. b. Richard quickly got money, the sinews of warre, by a thousand princely skills 1647. Hence **Skil·less, Ski·ll-less** *a.*

Skill (skil), *v.* Now *arch.* ME. [a. ON. *skilja* to divide, distinguish, or *skila* to decide, related to MDu. and MLG. *schillen* and *schelen* to differ, make a difference, etc.] 1. a. *impers.* In negative or interrogative clauses: To make a difference, to be of importance, to matter 1460. b. *impers.* To avail, help 1528. 2. To understand, comprehend. Now *dial.* 1500. †b. *intr.* To have knowledge *of*, or skill *in*, something -1691. c. With inf.: To know how *to* do something. Also with *how.* 1586

1. a. What skilleth you though that he dye this

nyght? 1509. b. But what skills talking? 1880. 2. The speaker little skilleth the use of speech, or the rule of conversation 1677. c. They now skild not how from him to wend SIDNEY.

Skilled (skild), *ppl. a.* 1533. [f. SKILL *sb.* + -ED[2].] 1. Of persons: Possessed of skill or knowledge; properly trained or experienced. 2. Of work: Requiring or showing skill 1776.

1. To be well s. in the law 1552. Every physician and every s. artist does all things for the sake of the whole 1875. 2. Every branch of public administration is a s. business MILL.

Skillet (ski·lėt). late ME. [Origin obsc.] A cooking utensil of brass, copper, or other metal, usu. having three or four feet and a long handle, used for boiling liquids, stewing meat, etc.; a saucepan, stew-pan.

Skilligalee (ski:ligălī·). *slang.* 1819. [prob. fanciful.] 1. = SKILLY. 2. With neg.: A single coin of the smallest value 1833.

Skilling (ski·liŋ). *sb.*[1] late ME. [Origin obsc.] A shed or outhouse, *esp.* a lean-to, a penthouse.

‖ **Ski·lling,** *sb.*[2] 1700. [In sense 1 ad. Du. *schelling*; in sense 2 a. Da., Sw., or Norw. *skilling*.] †1. = SCHELLING. 2. A small copper coin and money of account formerly in use in Scandinavia 1793.

Skilly (ski·li). 1839. [Abbrev. of SKILLIGALEE.] A kind of thin, watery porridge, gruel, or soup, commonly made from oatmeal, and used esp. in prisons and workhouses.

Skim, *sb.* 1539. [f. SKIM *v.*] †1. = SCUM *sb.* 2 b. -1764. 2. An addition to the coulter of a plough by which the surface of the ground is pared off 1799. 3. *ellipt.* = SKIM-MILK 1. 1885. 4. The act of skimming or moving lightly 1851.

Skim, *v.* late ME. [prob. ad. OF. *escumer*; see SCUM *v.*] I. 1. *trans.* To clear (a liquid or a liquid mass) from matter floating upon the surface, usually by means of a special utensil; to deprive (milk) of cream by this method; to deal with (a pot, etc.) in this way. Also *absol.* (Cf. SCUM *v.* 1.) late ME. b. *Agric.* To plough (land) very lightly 1799. 2. To remove or collect by skimming 1651. 3. To cover with a thin layer, as with scum 1666. b. *intr.* To put on a thin layer 1865.

1. Are you not hee That..Skim milke? SHAKS. 2. We forget that the newspaper skims the scum of life 1894. 3. The Fountain of Trevi skimmed almost across with a glassy surface HAWTHORNE.

II. 1. *trans.* To deal with, treat, or study, in a cursory and superficial manner 1586. b. *esp.* To read rapidly or carelessly; to glance over without close attention 1799. 2. To move, glide, fly or float, lightly and rapidly over (the ground, etc.) 1697. 3. To cause to fly lightly; to throw (a thing, esp. one having a flat surface) so that it maintains an evenness of balance or poise in its flight 1611. 4. *intr.* To sail, glide, float, fly, run, etc., with a light and easy motion, on or close to some surface, or through the air 1591. b. To glance *over*, without reading closely 1738. c. To pass *over* lightly, without dwelling upon 1741. †5. To glance *round* the horizon. KEATS.

1. Such as love only to s. things, and have not the patience to keep their minds to a deep and close attention 1665. 2. Smooth as Swallows s. The new-shorn Mead 1735. 3. He skimmed his cocked-hat in the air SCOTT. 4. c. He skims over rather than dives into the subjects of which he treats 1824. Hence **Ski·mming** *ppl. a.* moving lightly along the surface; *fig.* not deep or thorough; **-ly** *adv.*

Ski·mble-ska·mble, *a.*, *sb.*, and *adv.* 1596. [f. SCAMBLE *v.*] A. *adj.* Confused, incoherent, nonsensical, rubbishy. (Now after Shaks.) B. *sb.* Confused or worthless discourse 1619. C. *adv.* Confusedly; in confusion 1775.

A. Such a deale of skimble-scamble Stuff SHAKS.

Ski·m-cou·lter. 1778. [f. SKIM *v.*] *Agric.* A coulter fitted with a plate of iron or steel which shaves off the top-layer of the ground and turns it into the furrow.

Skimmed (skimd), *a.* In senses of SKIM *v.*; *s. milk* = SKIM-MILK 1623; so *s. cheese.*

Skimmer (ski·məɹ). late ME. [ad. OF. *escumoir* and *escumeur*; see SCUMMER *sb.* In later use also f. SKIM *v.* + -ER[1].] 1. A shallow utensil, usually perforated, employed in skimming liquids; also, any utensil used for an analogous process. b. *U.S.* A clam or scallop, the shell of which may be used for skimming milk, etc. 1881. 2. One who skims, e.g. in reading 1611. 3. A bird of the N. American genus *Rhynchops*, esp. the black skimmer (*R. nigra*) 1785.

Ski·m-milk. 1596. [f. SKIM *v.* + MILK *sb.*] Milk with the cream skimmed off or otherwise removed. Also *attrib.*, as *s. cheese.*

Ski·mming, *vbl. sb.* 1450. [f. SKIM *v.*] 1. That which is removed or obtained by skimming. Usu. *pl.* 2. The action of SKIM *v.* in various senses 1611.

Ski·mming-dish. 1641. [SKIMMING *vbl. sb.*] A dish used for skimming with; *esp.* one used in skimming milk or in cheese-making.

Skimmington (ski·miŋtən). 1609. [Possibly from *skimming* -*ton* as in *simpleton*, with the object of simulating a personal name.] †1. The man or woman personating the ill-used husband or the offending wife in the procession (see 2) intended to ridicule the one or the other. Also *transf.* a husband whose wife is unfaithful to him, a shrewish woman. -1813. 2. A ludicrous procession, formerly common in villages and country districts, usu. intended to bring ridicule or odium upon a woman or her husband where the one was unfaithful to, or ill-treated, the other 1634.

2. *To ride* (*the*) *s.*, to hold a procession of this kind.

Skimp, *a.* 1775. [Origin unkn.] Scanty. So **Skimp** *v.* = SCRIMP *v.*

Skimpy (ski·mpi), *a.* 1847. [f. SKIMP *a.* + -Y[1].] Of a scrimp, meagre, scanty, or spare character; stinted or stunted in some respect. Hence **Ski·mpily** *adv.* **Ski·mpiness.**

Skin, *sb.* [Late OE., a. ON. *skinn.*] I. 1. The integument of an animal stripped from the body, and usu. dressed or tanned (with or without the hair), or intended for this purpose; a hide, pelt, or fur; also occas., an article made of this. 2. A complete hide of a sheep, calf, etc., or a part of one, specially prepared as parchment or vellum and used for writing or painting upon ME. 3. A vessel made of the hide of a small animal, such as a sheep or goat, and used for holding liquids, etc. 1547.

1. Skins of Beasts, the rude Barbarians wear DRYDEN. I do not like to divide the s. before we have caught the bear 1899. 2. The ponderous deed of eight skins of parchment 1870. 3. The best Xeres that ever smacked of the s. 1846.

II. 1. The continuous flexible integument forming the usual external covering of an animal body; also, one or other of the separate layers of which this is composed, the derma or epidermis ME. 2. A membrane covering any internal part of an animal body. late ME. 3. Anything which resembles skin in nature or use; an outer coat or covering of anything. late ME. b. *Arch.* The facing of a wall in contrast to the material in the heart of it 1884. 4. *Naut.* a. The planking, or iron plating, covering the ribs or frame of a vessel 1769. b. That part of a sail which is used as a cover for it when furled 1841.

1. Phr. *S. and bone(s)*, denoting extreme emaciation or leanness. *To sleep in a whole s.*, etc., to escape being wounded, to remain uninjured. *To the s.*, through all one's garments; hence, thoroughly, completely. *To jump*, etc., *out of one's s.* (with joy, etc.). *By* (or *with*) *the s. of one's teeth*, with difficulty, narrowly, barely. *To save one's* (*own*) *s.*, to save oneself from loss or injury. 2. See GOLD-BEATER'S *s.*

attrib. and *Comb.*: as *s.-disease*, etc.; *s.-boat*, *-bottle*, *-canoe*, etc.; also, **s.-bound** *a.*, having the s. tightly drawn; hide-bound; **s. effect** *Electr.*, the tendency of a high-frequency alternating current to be greater at the surface of the conductor than in its interior; **s. friction,** the friction developed between a solid and a fluid or gaseous body; the friction of the air with the roughnesses of an aeroplane's surface; **-graft** *v.*, to subject to the process of skin-grafting (see GRAFT *v.*[1] 6); **-plating,** metal plating forming the s. of a vessel; **-wool,** wool taken from the s. of a dead sheep.

Skin, *v.* 1547. [f. SKIN *sb.* Cf. Norw. *skinna* to cover with skin.] I. 1. *trans.* To furnish or cover (*over*) with skin; to cause skin to form or grow on; to heal by the formation of skin. b. *fig.* To cover (*over*) in some slight or superficial manner 1603. 2. *intr.* To form skin; to become covered with skin; to grow a new skin; to heal *over* in this way 1579.

1. It will but s. and filme the Vlcerous place SHAKS. b. Your Amsterdam affaires are rather skinned than cured 1650. 2. Her excoriated carkasse began to s. again 1654.

II. 1. *trans.* To strip or deprive of the skin; to flay; to peel 1591. b. To rub the skin off (a surface); to bark 1855. c. In phrases denoting excessive meanness or desire for gain, esp. *to s. a flint* 1694. 2. To strip or pull *off* (a skin, etc.); to remove by drawing off inside out 1658. 3. *intr.* To shed or cast the skin; to lose the skin by rubbing 1772. 4. *slang.* a. *trans.* To clean out (a person) at play 1812. b. To strip (*of* clothing or money); to fleece 1851. c. *To keep one's eyes skinned* (orig. U.S.): to keep a sharp look-out 1852. 5. *U.S. slang.* To copy or crib. *trans.* and *intr.* 1849.

1. A fishmonger who was skinning an eel alive BOSWELL. 4. b. Some new device is invented for enmeshing and skinning the investor 1898.

Skin-deep, *a.* and *adv.* 1613. [f. SKIN *sb.* + DEEP *a.* and *adv.*] A. *adj.* Penetrating no deeper than the skin; superficial, shallow.

Beauty that's only skin deep Must fade like the gowans of May 1725. *fig.* The s. joy of ungodly men 1730.

B. *adv.* Superficially, slightly 1633.

When I know her further than S. I'll tell you more of my mind STEELE.

Ski·nflint. 1700. [f. SKIN *v.* + FLINT *sb.*] One who would skin a flint to save or gain something; an avaricious, penurious, mean or niggardly person; a miser.

Ski·nful. 1650. [f. SKIN *sb.* + -FUL.] As much as a skin can or does hold; *transf.* a full allowance. *To have a s.* (slang): to be drunk.

Skink (skiŋk), *sb.*[1] 1590. [a. older F. *scinc* (now *scinque*), or ad. L. *scincus*, ad. Gr. σκίγκος.] *Zool.* A small lizard (*Scincus officinalis*) common in northern Africa and Arabia, formerly regarded as of great value in medicine for its stimulative qualities; also, any lizard belonging to the same family (the *Scincidæ*).

Skink, *v.* Now *dial.* or *arch.* late ME. [ad. MDu. or MLG. *schenken*, corresp. to OE. *scencan.*] 1. *trans.* To pour out or draw (liquor); to offer, present, serve (drink, etc.). 2. *absol.* To draw, pour out, or serve drink 1575. Hence **Skink** *sb.*[2] drink. **Ski·nker,** one who draws, pours out or serves liquor, a tapster.

Skinless (ski·nlės), *a.* ME. [-LESS.] Destitute or deprived of skin; having only a very thin skin.

Skinned (skind), *a.* [f. SKIN *sb.* or *v.*] 1. Having or covered with skin. late ME. 2. Stripped of skin 1673.

Skinner (ski·nəɹ). ME. [f. SKIN *sb.* or *v.* + -ER[1].] 1. One whose work or business is concerned with the preparation of skins for commercial purposes. 2. One who skins 1699.

1. The Principal Companies..are the Mercers,.. Skinners 1675.

Ski·nnery. 1480. A skinner's factory.

Skinny (ski·ni), *a.* 1573. [f. SKIN *sb.* + -Y[1].] 1. Consisting or formed of skin; resembling skin or film; cutaneous, membranous. 2. Having the skin prominently shown; lacking flesh; thin, lean, emaciated 1605. 3. Mean, miserly, niggardly, stingy 1833.

2. *Macb.* I. iii. 45. Hence **Ski·nniness.**

Skin-tight (ski·n,təit), *a.* 1885. [SKIN *sb.*] Fitting tightly to the skin; close-fitting.

Skip (skip), *sb.*[1] 1440. [f. SKIP *v.*[1]] I. An act of skipping; a slight bound or spring. 2. An act of passing from one thing or point to another with omission or disregard of what intervenes 1656. b. *Mus.* A passing from one note to another at a greater interval than one degree 1730. c. Matter in a book which may be skipped in reading 1833. 3. [prob. short for SKIP-KENNEL.] A footman, lackey, or manservant. Later *spec.* at Trinity College, Dublin, a college-servant, a scout. 1698.

1. *Hop, s., and jump* (see HOP *sb.*[2]). 2. d. *Wireless.* A silent belt between the point where the direct ray from a transmitting station becomes inaudible and the point where the reflected or indirect ray becomes audible. Also *attrib.*

Skip, *sb.*[2] 1815. [var. of SKEP *sb.* (q.v. for *skip* in other senses).] In mining or quarrying, a bucket, box, basket, cage, or wagon, in which materials or men are drawn up or let down. Also *attrib.*, as *s.-road*, *-shaft.*

Skip, *sb.*³ 1858. [f. SKIP *v.*²] 'In sugar-making in the West Indies, a charge or strike of syrup from the coppers' (Simmonds).

Skip *sb.*⁴, abbrev. of SKIPPER *sb.*² 1830.

Skip, *v.*¹ ME. [app. related to MSw. *skuppa, skoppa* in the same sense.] I. *intr.* 1. To raise oneself off the ground by a light and graceful movement; to spring or leap lightly and easily, *spec.* in the exercise of skipping with a rope. 2. To move or advance by a skip or skips ME. b. To hasten, hurry, move lightly and rapidly; to make off, abscond. Now *U.S. colloq.* ME. 3. To pass from one point, matter, etc., to another with omission of what intervenes; in mod. use *spec.* to do this in reading. late ME. b. So with *over.* Also occas., to pass *over* with very slight or superficial treatment. late ME. 4. Of things, in lit. or fig. senses. late ME. b. *Mus.* To pass from one note to another at an interval of more than one degree 1868.

2. They s. up stairs two at a time 1898. b. By Jove, you'd better s. for it MARRYAT. 3. The art of reading is to s. judiciously 1873. 4. In this wise skippeth venial in-to deedly synne CHAUCER.

II. *trans.* 1. To pass over in reading, etc. Also with *over*, and in fig. context. 1526. b. To pass over without mentioning, dealing with, taking into account, etc.; to omit 1531. c. To pass over, pass by, without touching or affecting in any way. Also with *over.* 1599. 2. a. To jump or leap lightly over (something); to go off, leave (rails) 1732. b. *U.S. colloq.* To flee (the country) 1884. 3. To cause to skip, bound, or jump 1683.

1. I do not think that I skipped a word of it [*sc.* a book] LAMB. b. Two virtues remain; shall we s. one and go to the other? JOWETT. c. Let not thy sword s. one: Pitty not honour'd Age for his white Beard SHAKS. 3. He had skipped pebbles on it 1894.

Comb.: **s. mackerel** *U.S.*, the blue-fish or skipjack. Hence **Ski·pping** *vbl. sb.* (attrib. in *s.-rope* 1836), **-ly** *adv.*

Skip, *v.*² 1818. [ad. Du *scheppen* to ladle, bale, dip, draw (water), etc.] *trans.* To transfer (sugar) from one vessel to another in the process of manufacture.

Skipjack (ski·pˌdʒæk), *sb.* and *a.* 1554. [f. SKIP *v.*¹ + JACK *sb.*¹] A. *sb.* 1. A pert shallow-brained fellow; a puppy; a conceited fop. Now *arch.* †2. A horse-dealer's boy; a jockey -1700. 3. A toy made of the merry-thought of a fowl and so contrived that it can be made to skip; the merrythought itself 1797. 4. Any of various fishes which have a habit of leaping out of the water, *esp.* the blue-fish (*Temnodon* or *Pomatomus saltator*) of tropical and subtropical seas 1703. 5. A beetle belonging to the family *Elateridæ*; a click-beetle or spring-beetle 1817. B. *adj.* 1. Having the qualities of a skipjack; foppish. Also *transf.* of things. 1597. 2. Hopping, jumping, skipping 1605.

†**Skip-kennel.** 1668. [f. SKIP *v.*¹ + KENNEL *sb.*²] One who has to jump over the kennels or gutters; a lackey, footman -1828.

Skipper (ski·pəɹ), *sb.*¹ 1440. [f. SKIP *v.*¹ + -ER ¹.] 1. One who or that which skips or jumps. †b. Applied contempt. to a youth. SHAKS. 2. *spec.* a. A skipjack or spring-beetle 1796. b. A butterfly of the family *Hesperiidæ* 1817. c. *dial.* and *U.S.* A cheese-maggot, or other small maggot, etc., of similar habits 1828. 3. *spec.* The saury pike 1674. 4. One who omits passages in reading 1824.

Skipper (ski·pəɹ), *sb.*² late ME. [ad. MDu. or MLG. *schipper*, f. *schip* SHIP *sb.*] 1. The captain or master of a ship, esp. of a small trading, merchant, or fishing vessel; †a shipman, seaman. b. *Skipper's daughters*, high white-crested waves 1888. 2. The captain or director of a sporting team or side 1830. Hence **Ski·pper** *v. trans.* to act as s. of.

Skirl (skɔ̄ɹl), *sb.* *Sc.* and *n. dial.* 1513. [f. the vb.] 1. A shrill cry, a shriek; shrill talk. 2. A shrill sound, *esp.* that characteristic of the bagpipe 1860.

Skirl (skɔ̄ɹl), *v.* *Sc.* and *n. dial.* late ME. [prob. of Scand. origin.] 1. *intr.* To scream, shriek, cry out shrilly. b. Of the bagpipe (or its music): To produce the shrill sounds by which it is characterized; to sound shrilly 1665. 2. To play the bagpipe 1828. 3. *trans.* To sing, utter, play, etc., in loud and shrill tones 1786. Hence **Ski·rling** *vbl. sb.* shrill crying, shrieking, etc.

Ski·rling, *sb.* *local.* 1776. [Origin unkn.] A young salmon; a samlet, sparling.

Ski·rmish (skɔ̄·ɹmiʃ), *sb.* late ME. [orig. aphetic ad. OF. *escar(a)moche, -muche*, ad. It. *scaramuccia*, of doubtful origin. The later forms *scar-, sker-, skirmish* have been influenced by those forms of the verb which are derived from OF. *eskirmiss-*; cf. SCRIMMAGE *sb.*] 1. An irregular engagement between two small bodies of troops, esp. detached or outlying portions of opposing armies; a petty fight or encounter. Also occas. without article, as a mode of fighting. 2. *transf.* a. Any contest or encounter 1576. b. An action or proceeding of a slight character; a slight display *of* something 1651.

2. a. They neuer meet, but there's a s. of wit between them SHAKS.

Skirmish (skɔ̄·ɹmiʃ), *v.* late ME. [In the earlier forms aphetic ad. OF. *escar(a)mucher, -mucier*, ad. It. *scaramucciare*; the forms in *-ish* are infl. by, or directly based on, OF. *eskirmiss-*, lengthened stem of *eskirmir*, ad. OHG. *skirman* to defend, f. *scirm* shield, defence.] 1. *intr.* To engage in a skirmish or irregular encounter; to fight in small parties. Freq. const. *with.* †2. To fence; to make flourishes with a weapon -1763. †3. *trans.* To engage or attack (an enemy) in or with a skirmish -1679.

Skirmisher (skɔ̄·ɹmiʃəɹ). ME. [f. prec. + -ER.] One of a number of soldiers taking part in a skirmish or acting in loose order. Also *transf.* and *fig.*

Skirr (skɔ̄ɹ), *v.* 1548. [Origin obsc.] 1. *intr.* To run hastily (*away*); to flee, make off. 2. To move, run, fly, sail, etc., rapidly or with great impetus. Sometimes implying a whirring sound accompanying the movement. 1567. 3. *trans.* To pass or go rapidly over, esp. in search of something or some one 1605. 4. To throw with a rapid skimming motion 1652.

3. Send out moe Horses, skirre the Country round SHAKS. Hence **Skirr** *sb.* a sound of a grating, rasping, or whirring character.

Skirret ¹ (ski·rit). [ME. *skirwhit(e*, app. an alteration by pop. etym. of OF. *eschervis* (mod.F. *chervis*), which is app. a var. of OF. *carvi* CARAWAY.] A perennial umbelliferous plant, *Sium sisarum*, a species of water parsnip, formerly much cultivated in Europe for its esculent tubers; the root of this plant.

Skirret ² (ski·rit). 1853. [?] An instrument for measuring land, aligning trenches, etc., working on a revolving centre-pin.

Skirt (skɔ̄ɹt), *sb.* ME. [a. ON. *skyrta* shirt; = OE. *scyrte*: see SHIRT *sb.*] I. 1. The lower part of a woman's dress or gown, covering the person from the waist downwards; also, a separate garment serving this purpose. b. A woman. Now *vulgar slang.* 1560. 2. The lower part of a man's gown or robe. Now chiefly *Hist.*, or with ref. to Eastern countries. ME. b. The bottom, lower portion, or tail of a coat or similar garment. Chiefly *pl.* 1598.

1. *Divided s.*, a form of s. divided in the middle and presenting the appearance of full knickerbockers; also, a s. made in two widths and open back and front, used in riding or cycling. 2. b. †*To sit (stick) in* or *upon* (a person's) *skirts*, to press hard upon, punish severely; A..gentleman..determined to stick in my skirts, and either ruin or marry me 1809.

II. 1. a. One of the flaps or lower portions of a saddle. Also *saddle s.* late ME. b. The rim or base of a bell or bee-hive 1555. c. The border, rim, outer portion, extremity, or tail-end of anything 1566. d. *Naut.* A side or leech of a sail 1627. †2. A rim or border; an edging (*rare*) -1713. 3. The diaphragm or midriff of an animal, *esp.* as used for food 1725.

1. a. This letter was sowen up in the s. of a saddle 1736. 2. This consists of a narrow lace, or a small s. of fine ruffled linnen, which runs along the upper part of the stays before ADDISON.

III. 1. The border, boundary, or outlying part *of* a territory, country, kingdom, etc. Chiefly in *pl.* 1470. b. *pl.* The suburbs *of* a town or city. Also rarely *sing.* 1598. c. *pl.* The parts *of* an army farthest distant from the centre or main body; the edge, border, or fringe *of* a crowd, etc. 1533. 2. The edge, margin, verge *of* a wood, lake, cloud, etc.; the foot or lower slopes *of* a mountain or hill 1598. 3. A number of trees, etc., surrounding or bordering a place 1617.

1. Upon the s. and fringe of our fair land TENNYSON. 2. I came to the S. of the Wood DE FOE. *fig.* I am a shadow now,..Upon the skirts of human-nature dwelling KEATS. 3. A s. of thickets hid the approach of the..enemy 1835.

attrib. and *Comb.*: **s.-board,** (*a*) a shaped board on which skirts, dresses, etc. are ironed or pressed; (*b*) = SKIRTING-BOARD; **-dancing,** a form of ballet dancing in which the steps are accompanied by the manipulation of long flowing skirts or drapery; so **s.-dance.**

Skirt (skɔ̄ɹt), *v.* 1602. [f. the sb.] I. *trans.* 1. To form the skirt or edge of; to lie alongside of; to bound or border. 2. To surround, edge, or border, *with* something 1667. 3. Of persons, ships, etc.: To go or pass along the border, edge, or side of (a country, district, etc.); to go round, in place of crossing 1735. b. To scour or search the outskirts of (a wood, etc.). *rare.* 1724.

1. Those vast and trackless forests that skirted the settlements W. IRVING. *fig.* So is man's narrow path By strength and terror skirted EMERSON. 3. We skirted a large reedy swamp 1865.

II. *intr.* 1. a. Of persons: To travel, move, hang about, etc., on the outskirts or confines of something, or in a casual manner 1623. b. Of hunting-dogs: To leave the pack when following the scent or in a chase 1781. 2. Of roads, rivers, etc.: To lie or run *along* or *round* the edge or border of a place, etc. 1776.

1. a. Then I set off up the valley, skirting along one side of it BLACKMORE. 2. A sandy desert..skirts along the doubtful confine of Syria GIBBON.

Skirter (skɔ̄·ɹtəɹ). 1781. [f. SKIRT *v.* + -ER ¹.] One who skirts, esp., *Hunting*, a hound which leaves the pack while following scent.

Skirting (skɔ̄·ɹtiŋ), *vbl. sb.* 1764. [f. SKIRT *v.*] 1. A border, edge, edging, or margin. 2. Material for skirts 1852. 3. *Carpentry.* The narrow boarding, edging of slate or cement, etc., placed vertically along the base of the wall of a room, or other place in a building, next to the floor. Also *collect.*, material suitable for this. 1825.

Ski·rting-board. 1759. [Cf. prec. 3.] The narrow board placed round the wall of a room, etc., close to the floor.

Skit, *sb.* 1572. [Related to SKIT *v.*] 1. A vain, frivolous, or wanton girl. Chiefly *Sc.* 2. A quizzing or satirical reflection *upon*, or hit *at*, a person or thing; a remark of this nature 1727. b. A piece of light satire, parody, or caricature 1820. 3. A slight shower 1847.

2. I know you mean all that as a s. upon my edication 1779.

Skit (skit), *v.* 1611. [perh. a. ON. *skytja f. *skut-, weak grade of *skjóta* to SHOOT.] 1. *intr.* To shy or be skittish; to move lightly and rapidly; to caper, leap, or spring. 2. a. *trans.* To cast indirect reflections or light satire upon (a person, etc.); to ridicule or caricature by means of a skit 1781. b. *intr.* To make satirical hits *at* a person or thing 1821.

Skittish (ski·tiʃ), *a.* late ME. [perh. f. a Scand. base *skyt- (see prec.) + -ISH ¹.] 1. Of disposition, etc.: Characterized by levity, frivolity, or excessive liveliness. 2. Of horses, etc.: Disposed or apt to start or be unruly without sufficient cause; unduly lively or spirited 1510. 3. Fickle, inconstant; tricky, difficult to deal with or manage 1601. 4. Spirited, active, lively; frolicsome 1592. 5. Inclined to show coyness or reserve 1648.

1. T'address The s. fancy with facetious tales COWPER. 2. Balancing our s. bark upon the green waters 1841. 3. Som men creepe in s. fortunes hall SHAKS. 4. She is like a frog in a parsley-bed, As s. as an eel 1592. Hence **Ski·ttishly** *adv.*, **-ness.**

Skittle (ski·t'l). 1634. [Origin unkn.] 1. *pl.* = NINEPINS 1. b. *colloq.* Nonsense, rubbish. Also as *int.* 1904. c. Chess not played seriously (*colloq.*) 1856. 2. One of the pins with which the game of skittles is played 1680.

1. Phr. (*Not*) *all beer and skittles*, etc., used to denote that something is (not) unmixed enjoyment. Hence **Ski·ttle** *v.* **Ski·ttler.** **Ski·ttling** *vbl. sb.* (esp. in chess).

Skive (skəiv), *sb.*¹ Also **skieve.** 1843. [ad. Du. *schijf* (sχəif), MDu. *schîve*; see SHIVE ².] A diamond-wheel.

Skive (skəiv), *sb.*² 1875. [f. the vb.] The surface part of a sheet of leather cut off by a skiving-machine; a skiver.

Skive (skəiv), *v.* 1825. [a. ON. *skífa*, related to ME. *schīve* SHIVE [2].] *trans.* To split or cut (leather, rubber, etc.) into slices or strips; to pare or shave (hides). Also with *off.*

Skiver (ski·vəɹ), *sb.*[1] Chiefly *dial.* 1664. [Origin unkn.] A skewer.

Skiver (skəi·vəɹ), *sb.*[2] Also **skyver.** 1800. [f. SKIVE *v.* + -ER [1].] **1.** A thin kind of dressed leather split from the grain side of a sheep-skin and tanned in sumach, used for bookbinding, lining hats, etc. **2.** One who or that which skives; *esp.* a workman who pares or splits leather 1875. Hence **Skiver** *v.*[2] *trans.* to cut or pare (leather).

Skiver (ski·vəɹ), *v.*[1] 1832. [f. SKIVER *sb.*[1]] *trans.* To pierce or stab with or as with a skewer; to fasten with a skewer.

Skiving (skəi·viŋ), *vbl. sb.* 1825. [f. SKIVE *v.*] **1.** The parings of hides; the piece or sheet of split leather from the inner, or flesh, side. **2.** The action of splitting leather, etc. 1884.

Skivvy (ski·vi). 1922. *colloq.* [Alteration of *slavvy*, SLAVEY.] Depreciatory term for a female domestic servant, esp. a rough 'general'.

Skua (skiū·ă). 1678. [ad. Færöese *skúgvur* = ON. *skúfr*, of unkn. origin.] A predatory gull belonging to the genus *Stercorarius*, esp. the largest European species, *S. catarrhactes*, which breeds in Shetland, the Færöes, and Iceland. Also *s.-gull.*

Skulk (skɒlk), *sb.* ME. [f. the vb.] **1.** One who skulks or hides himself; a shirker. †**2.** A number, company, or gathering (of persons or animals given to skulking) -1883.

2. We say a flight of doves.., a s. of foxes W. IRVING.

Skulk (skɒlk), *v.* Also **sculk.** ME. [Cf. Norw. *skulka* to lurk, lie watching, Da. *skulke*, Sw. *skolka* to shirk, play truant.] **1.** *intr.* To move in a stealthy or sneaking fashion, so as to escape notice. Usu. with *about, away, into*, or the like. **2.** To hide or conceal oneself, to avoid observation, esp. with some sinister motive or in fear of being discovered; to lurk ME. **b.** To hide, to withdraw or shelter oneself, in a cowardly manner 1621. **c.** To shirk duty; *spec.* to malinger 1781.

1. It is a poor thing for a fellow to get drunk at night, and sculk to bed JOHNSON. 2. Man is a yong Lyon,..lurking and sculking to doe mischiefe 1641. b. Ah! s. behind the women, do! 1877. Hence **Sku·lker**, one who skulks. **Sku·lkingly** *adv.*

Skull (skɒl). ME. [Origin obsc.] **1.** The bony case or frame containing or enclosing the brain of man or other vertebrate animals; also, the whole bony framework or skeleton of the head. **b.** The head as the proper seat of thought or intelligence. Commonly with allusion to dullness of intellect. 1523. **c.** A representation of a human skull, as an emblem or reminder of death or mortality 1826. †**2.** A skull-cap of metal or other hard material; a close-fitting head-piece -1674.

1. b. Your Sexe, Whose empty Sculles..your selues peruersely vexe 1632. c. She was a perpetual *memento mori*; a s. and cross-bones would hardly have been more efficacious 1826.

Comb.: **s.-fish**, a whalebone whale above two years of age.

Skull, var. or obs. f. SCULL *sb.* and *v.*

Skull-cap (skɒ·lkæp). 1682. [CAP *sb.*[1]] **1.** A light, close-fitting cap, usu. of silk, velvet, or other soft material, for covering the head or the crown of it. **2.** *Hist.* A steel or iron cap, a form of casque or helmet fitting closely to the head 1820. **3.** *Bot.* One or other of various species of plants belonging to the genus *Scutellaria*, in which the calyx finally assumes the appearance of a helmet 1760. **4.** *Anat.* The bony structure covering the brain; the top or roof of the head 1855.

2. There was a ferocious tyrant in a skullcap like an inverted porringer, and a dress of red baize 1824.

Skunk (skɒŋk), *sb.* 1634. [ad. Amer. Indian (Abenaki) *seganku* or *segongw.*] **1.** A N. American animal of the weasel kind, *Mephitis mephitica*, noted for emitting a very offensive odour when attacked or killed. **b.** *ellipt.* The fur of the skunk 1862. **2.** *colloq.* A thoroughly mean or contemptible person. Also in playful use. 1841.

attrib. and *Comb.*, *as s.-fur*, etc.; also, **s.-bird, -blackbird** *U.S.*, the bobolink, so called from a resemblance in the colours of the male bird to those of the s.; **-cabbage** *N. Amer.*, a perennial stemless plant of the arum family, *Symplocarpus fœtidus*, giving out an offensive odour, esp. when bruised; **-head** *U.S. local*, the Labrador duck; **-weed** *U.S.*, = *s.-cabbage*. Hence **Sku·nkish** *a.* resembling a s.; contemptible.

Skunk (skɒŋk), *v.* *U.S. slang.* 1848. [f. prec.] *trans.* To defeat an opponent so completely in a game of chance that he makes no score.

‖ **Skupshtina** (sku·pʃtină). 1862. [Serb, = assembly.] **a.** The national assembly of Serbia and of Montenegro. **b.** Now, the parliament of Jugoslavia.

Sky (skəi), *sb.* ME. [a. ON. *ský* cloud (:—**skiuja*), related to OS. *skio*, OE. *scéo.*] †**1.** A cloud -1550. **2.** *The skies*, the clouds (*obs.*); the upper region of the air; the heavens. Chiefly *poet.* ME. **b.** Used without *the*, in limited sense 1503. **3.** *The s.*, the apparent arch or vault of heaven; the firmament ME. **4.** *poet.* or *rhet.* **a.** The celestial regions; heaven; the heavenly power, the deity 1590. **b.** The sky (sense 3) of a particular region; hence, climate, clime 1701. **5. a.** The colour of the sky; sky-blue 1667. **b.** The representation of a sky in a painting, etc. 1747.

1. A certeyn wynde..blewe so hydously and hye, That hyt ne left not a skye In alle the welkene CHAUCER. 2. The skyes rang for schoutyng of the larkis DUNBAR. b. It was a dismal day with leaden skies overhead 1907. 3. Lead itself can fly, And pond'rous slugs cut swiftly thro' the s. POPE. *fig.* I, in the cleare Skie of Fame, o're-shine you SHAKS. *To the s.* or *skies*, to the highest possible degree, enthusiastically, extravagantly. *In the skies*, in an ecstasy, in the realms of fancy. 4. a. Now am I dead, now am I fled, my soule is in the s. SHAKS. 5. b. The s. is unusually careless RUSKIN.

Comb.: **s.-blink**, = ICE-BLINK 1; **-flyer**, an ambitious person; **-pilot** *slang* (*a*) a clergyman, *esp.* one who has a spiritual charge among seamen; (*b*) a licensed aviator; **-scape**, a view or painting of the sky; **-stone**, a meteorite; **-writing**, legible smoke-trails made by aeroplanes for advertising or in displays. Hence **Sky·ish**, *a.* lofty, approaching the s.; resembling that of the s.

Sky (skəi), *v.* Pa. t. and pa. pple. **skied.** 1802. [f. prec.] **1.** *trans.* **a.** *slang.* To throw or toss up (a coin). **b.** *Cricket*, etc.: To strike (a ball) into the air 1873. **2.** To hang (a picture, etc.) high up on the wall or near the ceiling, *esp.* at an exhibition 1865. **3.** To cover like the sky; to overshadow 1844.

3. Napoleon!..that great word..skied us overhead MRS. BROWNING.

Sky-blue, *sb.* and *a.* 1728. [SKY *sb.*] **A.** *sb.* **1.** A pure blue colour like that of the sky in daylight; a fabric of this colour 1738. **2.** Thin or watery milk, having a bluish tint 1798. †**3.** *slang.* Gin -1796. **B.** *adj.* Of the blue colour of the sky; azure 1728.

'Twas there gay Phylla..Glanc'd the soft passion from her s. eye 1773.

Skye (skəi). 1851. [Gael. *Sgith* (skī).] The name of the largest island of the Inner Hebrides used attrib., esp. in *S. terrier*, a small breed of dog, long-haired, long-bodied, and short-legged 1856. **b.** *ellipt.* A Skye terrier 1851.

Skyey (skəi·i), *a.* 1603. Also **skiey.** [f. SKY *sb.* + -(E)Y.] **1.** Of or pertaining to the sky; emanating from the sky. Also, lofty. **2.** Resembling the sky in colour; azure 1816.

1. A breath thou art, Seruile to all the skyie-influences SHAKS. The mountains..are of s. height COLERIDGE.

Sky-high, *adv.* and *a.* *colloq.* 1818. [SKY *sb.*] **A.** *adv.* As high as the sky; very high. **B.** *adj.* Reaching to the sky 1840.

Skylark (skəi·lāɹk), *sb.* 1686. [SKY *sb.*] **1.** The common lark of Europe, *Alauda arvensis*, so called from its habit of soaring towards the sky while singing. **2.** *U.S.* The Missouri pipit, *Anthus spraguei*; the prairie lark 1872.

Skylark (skəi·lāɹk), *v.* 1809. [f. prec.] *intr.* To frolic or play; to play tricks; to indulge in rough sport or horse-play. In early use chiefly *Naut.*

Skylarking, a term used by seamen, to denote wanton play about the rigging, and tops, or in any part of the ship 1815.

Skylight (skəi·ləit). Also **sky-light.** 1679. **1.** Light from the sky; light coming into a room, etc., from above. †**b.** = DAYLIGHT 3. -1824. **2.** A small opening in a roof, or in the ceiling of a room, filled in with glass, for admitting daylight; the framework and glass fitted to such an opening 1690.

Sky·-line. 1860. [SKY *sb.*] The line where earth and sky meet; the horizon. **b.** The outline of a building, etc. seen against the sky 1903.

Sky·-ro:cket. 1688. A rocket which ascends high into the sky before exploding.

Sky·-sail. Also **skysail.** 1829. [SKY *sb.*] *Naut.* In square-rigged vessels, a light sail set above the royal.

Sky·-scra:per. 1794. [SKY *sb.*] **1.** *Naut.* A triangular sky-sail. **2.** A high building of many stories, *esp.* one of those characteristic of American cities 1891.

Sky·-sign. 1880. [SKY *sb.*] **1.** *poet.* A celestial sign or portent. BROWNING. **2.** A sign of the nature of an advertisement, so constructed and placed that the letters, etc., usu. illuminated at night, stand out against the sky 1890.

Skyward (skəi·wǫ̈ɹd), *adv.* and *adj.* 1582. [SKY *sb.*] **A.** *adv.* Towards, in the direction of, the sky. **B.** *adj.* Leading to the sky; going towards the sky; heavenward 1838. So **Sky·wards** *adv.*

Slab (slæb), *sb.*[1] ME. [Origin obsc.] **1.** A flat, broad, and comparatively thick piece or mass of anything solid. **2.** A rough outside plank of timber cut from a log or tree-trunk preparatory to squaring the main portion, or sawing it into planks 1573. **3.** A flat piece of wood or stone used as a table, counter, etc.; a small table hinged to the wall in the passage or hall of a house 1739. Hence **Sla·bbing,** slabs collectively, slab-work. **Sla·bby** *a.*[2] of the nature of a s.; covered with slabs.

Slab (slæb), *sb.*[2] 1610. [app. of Scand. origin; cf. older Da. *slab* mud, mire, Icel., Norw., and Sw. *slabb* wet filth, etc.] **1.** A muddy place; a puddle. Now *dial.* **2.** Wet and slimy matter; ooze, sludge 1622.

Slab (slæb), *a.* 1605. [Related to SLAB *sb.*[2]] Semi-solid; viscid. (In mod. use entirely as an echo of Shakspere.)

Make the Grewell thicke, and s. SHAKS.

Slab (slæb), *v.* 1703. [f. SLAB *sb.*[1]] **1.** *trans.* To dress (timber) by removing the outside slabs; to clear of bark-wood. **2.** To convert into a slab or slabs 1868. **3.** To lay or pave with slabs 1832.

Slabber (slæ·bəɹ), *sb.*[1] 1718. [Related to SLABBER *v.*] **1.** Slaver; excessive saliva. **2.** Slobbering talk 1840.

Slabber (slæ·bəɹ), *sb.*[2] 1875. [f. SLAB *v.* + -ER [1].] **a.** A saw or machine for removing the outside slabs from timber, or dressing the outer portion of logs. **b.** A machine for dressing nuts or bolts.

Slabber (slæ·bəɹ), *v.* Now chiefly *dial.* 1573. [prob. of Du. or LG. origin. Cf. SLOBBER.] **1.** *trans.* To wet or befoul with saliva; to beslaver or beslobber 1579. **2.** To wet in a dirty or disagreeable manner 1573. **3.** To gobble *up*, swallow *down*, in a hurried or unrefined manner 1573. **4.** *intr.* To let saliva flow or fall from the mouth; to slaver, dribble; to disgorge water 1648.

1. He..slabber'd me all over from Cheek to Cheek, with his great Tongue 1712. 2. Her milke pan and creame pot, so slabbered and sost 1573. 4. Slabbering, whining, crying 1793. Hence **Sla·bbery** *a.* sloppy, slabby, slushy.

Slabby (slæ·bi), *a.*[1] 1542. [f. SLAB *sb.*[2] + -Y [1].] **1.** Wet, miry, muddy, slushy, sloppy. Now *dial.* **2.** Of liquids: Thick, ropy 1654.

2. They present you with a Cup, and you must drink of a s. stuff 1654. Hence **Sla·bbiness.**

Slabline (slæ·bˌləin). 1647. [prob. ad. Du. *slaplijn*, f. *slap* slack.] *Naut.* A small cord passing up behind the main-sail or fore-sail of a vessel and used to truss up the sail.

Slab-sided (slæ·bˌsəidėd), *a.* *U.S.* 1825. [f. SLAB *sb.*[1]] Having sides like slabs; flat-sided; long and lank.

Slack (slæk), *sb.*[1] *north.* and *Sc.* late ME. [a. ON. *slakki.*] **1.** A small shallow dell or valley; a hollow or dip in the ground; a depression in a hill-side or between two stretches of rising ground. **2.** A boggy hollow; a morass 1719.

Slack (slæk), *sb.*[2] 1440. [Origin obsc.] Small or refuse coal.

Slack (slæk), *sb.*³ 1756. [f. SLACK *a.* or *v.*] 1. A cessation in the strong flow of a current or of the tide. 2. An interval of comparative inactivity; a lull in business or in action of any kind 1851. 3. That part *of* a rope, sail, etc., which is not fully strained, or which hangs loose; a loose part or end 1794. 4. *dial.* and *U.S. colloq.* Impertinence, cheek 1842. 5. *pl.* Trousers (*dial.*); *spec.* trousers worn as part of military uniform instead of breeches and puttees 1822.

1. The tide was low water s., and the weather was fine and clear 1892. 4. Let 's have none of your s. 1876.

Slack (slæk), *a.* and *adv.* [Com. Teut.; OE. *slæc.* The stem is related to L. *laxus.*] A. *adj.* I. 1. Of persons: Lacking in energy or diligence; inclined to be lazy or idle; remiss, careless; negligent or lax in regard to one's duties. 2. Not busy; having little work 1834.

1. For in very dede he wil come, and not be slacke COVERDALE *Hab.* ii. 3.

II. 1. Of conduct, actions, etc.: Characterized by remissness or lack of energy OE. 2. Of pace: Slow; not smart or hurried OE. 3. Comparatively weak or slow in operation; deficient in strength or activity; dull. late ME. b. Of heat, etc.: Gentle, moderate 1495. c. Of wind, or tide: Blowing, or running, with very little strength or speed 1670. 4. Of work, etc.: Not brisk or active; also *transf.* of time 1813.

1. He becommeth poor that dealeth with a slacke hand *Prov.* x. 4. 2. Their pace was formal, grave, and s. DRYDEN. 3. By Study worn, and s. with Age PRIOR. b. Set them in a s. Oven till they are tender 1741. 4. When betting became s. 1813.

III. 1. Not drawn or held tightly or tensely; relaxed, loose ME. b. *Phonetics.* Of a vowel: Pronounced with relaxed muscles 1906. 2. Lacking cohesiveness or solidity; not compact or firm; crumbling, loose; soft 1440. 3. Of the hand: Not holding or grasping firmly 1667. b. Similarly of one's hold of anything 1836.

1. In the morning wee bore a s. saile 1621. 3. A s. hand had..been held upon them DE FOE.

Special collocations: **s. barrel, cask,** one made to hold dry goods; **s. jaw, s. lip,** tiresome or impertinent talk; **s. wire,** a wire not drawn tight, on which an acrobat performs. Hence **Sla·ck-ly** *adv.*, **-ness.**

B. *adv.* In a slack manner; slackly 1641.

Slack (slæk), *v.* 1520. [f. SLACK *a.*, in some senses replacing the earlier SLAKE *v.*] I. *trans.* 1. To be slack or remiss in respect of (some business, duty, etc.); to leave undone or not properly attended to 1530. †b. To neglect or let slip (an opportunity, etc.) -1697. †c. To lose or waste (time) -1633. 2. To cease to go on with, or prosecute, in a vigorous and energetic manner; to allow to fall off or decline 1520. b. To allow to mitigate or abate (*rare*) 1560. 3. a. To reduce the force or strength of; to make less active, vigorous, or violent 1589. b. To slake (one's thirst) 1631. 4. To make lax, neglectful, or remiss 1597. 5. To delay or retard; to render slower in respect of motion or progress. Also with *up.* Now *rare.* 1577. 6. To make slack or loose; to relax. Also *absol.* 1530. 7. To cause (lime) to disintegrate by the action of water or moisture; to slake 1703.

1. Whye slacke you your busynesse thus? PALSGR. b. Time calls you now,..S. not the good Presage DRYDEN. 2. I do not s. my labour. I can preach and write still. WESLEY. 3. I slack'd my Fire gradually DE FOE. 4. Love slack'd my Muse, and made my numbers soft MARLOWE. 5. I am nothing slow to s. his hast SHAKS. 6. Tak the..horse to the stable, and slack his girths SCOTT.

II. *intr.* †1. To delay, tarry (*rare*) -1611. 2. To be inactive or idle; to fail to exert oneself in a due manner. In mod. use *colloq.* 1543. b. To be backward or dilatory *to* do something. Now *rare.* 1560. 3. Of persons (or animals): To become less energetic, active, or diligent. Also with *off.* 1560. 4. To diminish in strength or speed; to moderate in some respect 1580. b. Of affairs, business, etc.: To fall off; to go more slowly; to be less brisk 1606. 5. To become less tense, rigid, or firm 1577. 6. Of lime, etc.: To become disintegrated under the action of moisture 1703.

2. b. Slack not my woords to remember 1582. 4. The breeze slacked, and we slowly worked up to the north 1865.

Slack-baked, *a.* 1823. [SLACK *adv.*] Of bread: Imperfectly or insufficiently baked.

Slacken (slæ·k'n), *v.* 1580. [f. SLACK *a.*] I. *trans.* 1. = SLACK *v.* I. 5. 2. To render less vigorous or eager; to cause or allow to fall off or decline 1631. 3. To relax in point of strictness or severity; to render less severe or stern 1605. 4. To give relaxation to (one's thoughts, etc.) 1643. 5. = SLACK *v.* I. 3 a. 1685. 6. To render, to allow to become, less tense, taut, or firm; to reduce the tension of 1611. 7. To make loose; to loosen 1815.

1. As the river approaches its mouth, the flow becomes slackened 1878. 2. Thy freeborn sons..Nor sloth can s., nor a tyrant bind 1807. 5. That consideration should..s. the fierce rages of grief 1685. 6. *fig.* In Spain, directly government slackened its hold, the nation fell to pieces 1861.

II. *intr.* 1. = SLACK *v.* II. 3. 1641. 2. = SLACK *v.* II. 4, 4 b. 1651. 3. To diminish in speed; to become slower 1721. 4. Of lime: To become slaked 1703. 5. = SLACK *v.* II. 5. 1850.

1. When the people s., and fall to loosenes and riot MILT. 2. Our exertions must not s. NELSON. When the demand for iron slackens 1832. 3. His pace slackened SCOTT. 5. The line for an instant slacken'd 1850.

Sla·cker. 1797. [f. SLACK *v.*] 1. A drawgate to hinder the passage of water in a sluice. 2. *colloq.* A person who shirks work, or avoids exertion, exercise, etc. 1898.

Sla·ck-rope. 1749. [f. SLACK *a.*] A rope, loosely stretched, on which an acrobat performs. (Contrasted with TIGHT-ROPE.)

Slack-water. Also **slackwater, slack water.** 1769. [f. SLACK *a.*] 1. The time at high or low water when the tide is not flowing visibly in either direction. 2. A stretch of comparatively still water in the sea, due to the absence of currents 1853. 3. A part of a river lying outside of the current, or one in which the flow is lessened by a lock or dam 1867.

attrib.: **s. navigation,** navigation carried on by the use of locks or dams on a river.

Sladang, variant of SELADANG.

Slade (slē¹d), *sb.*¹ [OE. *slæd* = Norw. dial. *slad* slope, hollow.] A valley, dell, or dingle; an open space between banks or woods; a forest glade; a strip of greensward or of boggy land.

Slade (slē¹d), *sb.*² 1867. [perh. related to SLIDE *v.*] The sole of a plough.

Slag (slæg), *sb.* 1552. [a. MLG. *slagge*, = G. *schlacke* (also *schlack*), of obsc. origin.] 1. A piece of refuse matter (see 2) separated from a metal in the process of smelting. 2. A vitreous substance, composed of earthy or refuse matter, which is separated from metals in the process of smelting; any similar product resulting from the fusion or distillation of other substances 1620. 3. *Geol.* A rough clinker-like lump of lava; lava in this form 1777. Hence **Sla·ggy** *a.* of the nature of s.; pertaining to or resembling s.

Sla·g-hearth. 1778. [SLAG *sb.*] A furnace for treating the slag-products of lead-smelting.

Sla·g-lead. 1668. [SLAG *sb.*] Lead obtained by re-smelting *grey slag*, i.e. slag from the Flintshire lead furnace, which is rich in lead.

Slake (slē¹k), *sb.* ME. [f. SLAKE *v.*] The act of slacking or slackening in some respect; an instance of this.

Slake (slē¹k), *v.* [OE. *slacian*, f. *slæc* SLACK *a.*] I. *intr.* †1. Of persons: To diminish the intensity of one's efforts; also, to undergo or manifest a weakening in some respect -1596. 2. †a. To become relaxed, slack, or loose -1599. b. Of lime: To become hydrated or slacked 1766. 3. To decrease in force or intensity; to become less violent, oppressive, or painful; to abate, moderate. Now *rare.* ME. b. Of fire: To burn less strongly; to die down, die away, go out ME. †4. To lessen, fall off -1614. †5. To become or grow less in number, quantity, or volume; to fall or subside -1613. II. *trans.* †1. To make slack or loose; to lessen the tension of; to allow to become slack or relaxed -1581. b. To disintegrate or slack (lime) 1662. †2. To reduce, diminish, lessen -1612. 3. To render less acute or painful; to abate, mitigate, or assuage. Now *rare.* ME. †4. To make less vehement, violent, or intense -1664. b. To allow to diminish in vehemence or vigour; to moderate (one's anger, etc.). Now *rare.* ME. 5. To appease, allay, or satisfy (desire, thirst, †hunger) ME. 6. To quench or extinguish (fire); to cause to burn less strongly 1566. 7. To cool or refresh by means of water or other fluid. late ME. b. To moisten, soak (*rare*) 1810. †8. To render less active or vigorous -1608.

1. b. The Lyonese builders..s. the lime by aspersion 1837. 4. b. He shall s. that loue which he now voweth to Cynthia LYLY. 5. His rage of lust, by gazing qualified; Slakt, not supprest SHAKS. 7. I reached a little patch of snow, and managed to s. my parched lips 1871. b. Oatmeal slaked with cold water SCOTT. 8. Now sleep yslaked hath the rout SHAKS. Hence **Sla·keless** *a.* incapable of being slaked, quenched, or mitigated; insatiable.

Slalom (slā·lǫm). 1921. In ski-ing, a race down a course defined by artificial obstacles, esp. flags.

Slam (slæm), *sb.*¹ 1672. [Related to SLAM *v.*¹] 1. A severe blow; a violent impact. 2. A violent closing of a door, etc., producing a resounding noise; the noise so made, or a noise of this nature 1837.

2. Closing his prayer-book with an angry s. 1871.

Slam (slæm), *sb.*² Also **slamm.** 1621. [Origin unkn.] †1. The card-game ruff and honours -1674. 2. The fact of losing or winning all the tricks in a game of cards, esp. in whist 1660. b. With the qualifying terms *grand* and *little*, chiefly in bridge 1892.

2. b. 'Grand s.', *i.e.* taking every trick, or 'minor s.', every trick but one 1899.

Slam (slæm), *v.*¹ 1691. [Possibly of Scand. origin; cf. Sw., Norw., and Icel. *slamra.*] 1. *trans.* To beat or slap vigorously. *dial.* 2. To shut (a door, window, etc.) with violence and noise; to bang; to close with unnecessary force 1775. b. To dash, throw, push, etc., with some degree of violence or force 1899. 3. *intr.* Of doors, etc.: To shut, or strike against anything, with violence and resounding noise 1823. 4. Used with advb. force: With a slam or heavy blow; suddenly and violently 1726.

2. He would s. the door to again 1873. b. Slamming every available man into the firing line 1899. 3. The huge Drawbridge slams down CARLYLE.

Slam (slæm), *v.*² 1746. [f. SLAM *sb.*²] 1. *trans.* To beat by winning a slam; also *dial.*, to trump. Hence *transf.* to beat completely. 2. *intr.* To win a slam 1833.

Slam-bang, *adv.*, *a.*, and *v.* Also **slam bang.** 1837. A. *adv.* With a slam and a bang; with noisy violence 1847. B. *adj.* Noisy, violent 1889. C. *vb. intr.* and *trans.* To slam and bang 1837.

Sla·mmakin, Sla·mmerkin, *sb.* and *a.* Chiefly *dial.* 1756. [Origin unkn.] A. *sb.* †1. A loose gown. 2. A slovenly female, a slattern 1785. B. *adj.* Untidy, slovenly 1794.

Slander (slɑ·ndəɹ), *sb.* [ME. *sclaundre*, ad. AF. *esclaundre*, OF. *esclandre*, an alteration of *escandle*, ad. L. *scandalum*; see SCANDAL *sb.*] 1. The utterance or dissemination of false statements or reports concerning a person, or malicious misrepresentation of his actions, in order to defame or injure him; calumny, defamation. 2. A false or malicious statement or utterance intended to injure, defame, or cast detraction on the person about whom it is made ME. †3. Discredit, disgrace, or shame, incurred by or falling upon a person or persons; evil name, ill repute, opprobrium -1678. †b. A source of shame or dishonour; a discreditable act; a disgrace; a wrong -1540 †c. A person who is a discredit, disgrace, or scandal to some body or set of persons -1596. †4. = SCANDAL *sb.* 1 b, OFFENCE *sb.* 2. -1586.

1. Shall S...Spit her cold venom in a dead man's ear? COLERIDGE. 2. His slanders were monstrous: but they were well timed MACAULAY. 3. c. That shamefull Hag, the slaunder of her sexe SPENSER.

Slander (slɑ·ndəɹ), *v.* ME. [ad. OF. *esclandrer*, f. *esclandre*; see prec.] †1. *trans.* In or after Biblical use: To be a stumbling-block to; to offend; to cause to lapse -1563. †2. To bring into discredit, disgrace, or disrepute -1603. 3. To defame or calumniate; to assail with slander; to speak evil of, traduce (a person, etc.) ME. †b. To accuse *of* something discreditable -1607. †4. To misrepresent or vilify (a thing) -1623. 5. *intr.* or *absol.* To speak or utter slanders. late ME.

1. If thyn eye sclaunder or shame thy self put hit fro the CAXTON. 3. Full ten years slander'd, did he once reply? POPE. b. *Two Gent.* III. ii. 38. 5. Let them rail, then, scoff, and s. BURTON. Hence **Sla·nderer**, one who slanders; a defamer, a calumniator.

Slanderous (sla·ndərəs), *a.* late ME. [ad. AF. **esclandrus*, = OF. *esclandreux*, f. *esclandre* SLANDER *sb.*; see -OUS.] †1. a. Of bad repute; discreditable, disgraceful, shameful –1589. b. Forming a source of shame or disgrace *to* some one (*rare*) –1595. c. Giving occasion for slander. SHAKS. 2. Of words, reports, language, etc.: Of the nature of, characterized by, or containing slander or calumny; calumnious, defamatory. late ME. 3. Of persons: Given to the use of slander or calumny; employing slander as a means of defaming or injuring others. Also *absol.* 1521.

1. b. If thou..wert grim, Vgly, and slandrous to thy Mothers wombe SHAKS. c. *Jul. C.* IV. i. 20. 2. The highest judge in the land is answerable..for s. language 1883. 3. Zealous..and pious, but..fierce and s. 1838. Hence **Sla·nderous-ly** *adv.*, **-ness.**

Slang (slæŋ), *sb.*[1] *dial.* 1610. [Origin unkn.] A long narrow strip of land.

Slang (slæŋ), *sb.*[2] 1756. [A word of cant origin; ult. source unkn.] 1. The special vocabulary used by any set of persons of a low or disreputable character; language of a low and vulgar type. (Now merged in c.) b. The cant or jargon of a certain class or period 1802. c. Language of a highly colloquial type, considered as below the level of standard educated speech, and consisting either of new words or of current words employed in some special sense 1818. 2. A travelling show 1859. b. *attrib.*, as **s. cove, cull**, a showman 1789.

1. Such grossness of speech, and horrid oaths, as showed them not to be unskilled in the s...of the lowest blackguards in the nation 1809. b. Correct English is the s. of prigs 1872. c. If I had ever talked s., I might have said that we chummed together famously 1887.

Slang (slæŋ), *sb.*[3] *Cant.* 1812. [app. a. Du. *slang* snake, etc.] 1. A watch-chain; a chain of any kind. 2. *pl.* Fetters, leg-irons 1812.

Slang (slæŋ), *a.* (and *adv.*). 1758. [Related to SLANG *sb.*[2]] 1. Of language, etc.: Having the character of, belonging to, expressed in, slang. †2. Given to the use of slang; of a fast or rakish character; impertinent –1864. †b. Of dress: Loud, extravagant –1858. c. Of tone, etc.: Slangy, rakish 1834. 3. *Costers' slang.* Of weights and measures: Short, defective 1812. b. *adv.* So as to give short measure 1851.

1. The cant language, commonly called the s. patter 1758. 2. Daring, saucy girls, s. and fast 1864.

Slang (slæŋ), *v. colloq.* or *slang.* 1812. [f. SLANG *sb.*[2] or *a.*] 1. a. *trans.* To defraud, cheat. b. *intr.* (also with *it*). To employ cheating; to give short measure. 2. To utter or use slang; to rail in abusive or vulgar language 1828. 3. *trans.* To abuse or scold violently 1844.

2. Mr. Carlyle slangs like a blaspheming pagan 1868. 3. He could..s. coal-heavers..better than any-one else in London 1844.

Slangwhang (slæ·ŋ,hwæŋ), *v.* Chiefly *U.S.* 1829. [f. SLANG *sb.*[2] 1 + WHANG *v.*] *trans.* and *intr.* To assail with, to make use of, violent language or abuse. So **Sla·ngwha:nger**, a noisy or abusive talker or writer 1807.

Slangy (slæ·ŋi), *a.* 1850. [f. SLANG *sb.*[2] 1.] 1. Of persons: a. Of a flashy or pretentious type. b. Given to the use of slang. 2. a. Of dress: Somewhat loud or vulgar 1861. b. Of language, etc.: Pertaining to, of the nature of, slang 1864. Hence **Sla·ngily** *adv.* **Sla·nginess.**

Slant (slɑnt), *sb.*[1] 1655. [conn. w. SLANT *adv.*, *a.*, and *vb.* Cf. SLENT *sb.*] 1. The slope *of* a hill, piece of ground, etc.; a sloping stretch of ground; an inclined plane or surface. b. A small surface, a short line, having an oblique position or direction 1711. c. A sloping beam or ray *of* light 1855. d. *Mining.* A heading driven diagonally between the dip and the strike of a coal-seam 1881. e. A vessel or surface having a sloping bottom or depression for paint-brushes or colours 1875. f. A bacteriological culture in a test-tube laid in a slanting position 1901. 2. Slope, inclination, obliquity. *On the s.*, aslant, obliquely. 1817. 3. *dial.* and *U.S.* a. A sly hit or sarcasm 1825. b. An opportunity, occasion 1837. c. A way of regarding a thing, point of view (*U.S.*) 1905.

Slant (slɑnt), *sb.*[2] 1596. [orig. *slent*, a. ON. **slent*, f. **slenta* to dash, throw, etc.] *Naut.* A slight breeze or spell *of* wind, etc.

Slant (slɑnt), *adv.* and *a.* 1495. [Aphetic for ME. *a-slonte*, *o-slante*, etc.; see ASLANT *adv.*] A. *adv.* In a slanting, sloping, or oblique manner or direction; slantingly, aslant. B. *adj.* 1. Of wind, etc.: Blowing or coming from the side; moving obliquely 1618. 2. Having an oblique or sloping position or direction; inclined from the perpendicular or horizontal; falling, lying, placed, etc. slantwise 1776. b. Of direction: Oblique 1793.

1. The s. Lightning, whose thwart flame driv'n down Kindles the gummie bark of Firr or Pine MILT. Hence **Sla·ntly** *adv.*

Slant (slɑnt), *v.* 1521. [Later var. of SLENT *v.*, prob. infl. by ASLANT *adv.*] 1. *intr.* To strike obliquely *on*, *upon*, or *against* something. 2. To be in, to have or take, an oblique direction or position; to slope 1698. b. Of light or shadow: To fall obliquely 1795. 3. Of persons: To travel, move, sail, etc. in an oblique direction; to diverge from a direct course. Also *U.S.*, to move off. 1692. b. Of things: To take an oblique course 1849. 4. *trans.* To give an oblique or sloping direction to (something); to cause to slope 1805.

2. That deep romantic chasm which slanted Down the green hill COLERIDGE. b. The shadows of the convent-towers S. down the snowy sward TENNYSON. 4. The rain came down in torrents, slanted by the wind 1891. Hence **Sla·nting** *ppl. a.* that slants or slopes; *adv.* obliquely. **Sla·ntingly** *adv.*

Slantindicular (slɑntindi·kiŭlăɪ), *a.* Also **slanting-, slanten-.** 1840. [f. *slanting*, after *perpendicular*; orig. U.S., and colloq. or humorous.] Slanting, sloping, oblique. So **Slant-indi·cularly** *adv.* 1834.

Slantways (slɑ·ntwēɪz), *adv.* 1826. [f. SLANT *a.* + -WAYS.] = next A.

Slantwise (slɑ·ntwəiz), *adv.* and *a.* 1573. [f. SLANT *a.* + -WISE.] A. *adv.* In a slanting or sloping direction or position; slantingly, obliquely. B. *adj.* Slanting, oblique 1856.

Slap (slæp), *sb.* 1648. [a. LG. *slapp*, of imitative origin.] 1. A smart blow, esp. one given with the open hand, or with something having a flat surface; a smack; an impact of this nature. b. A gust *of* wind 1890. 2. *transf.* a. A reprimand, reproof; a side-hit 1736. b. An attempt, venture, go, *at* something 1855.

2. b. Come, lads!..take another s. at them; we must get on deck somehow 1884.

Slap (slæp), *v.* 1632. [f. SLAP *adv.* or *sb.*] 1. *trans.* To strike or smack (a person or thing) smartly, esp. with the open hand or with something having a flat surface; to hit (a person) *on*, *upon*, or *over* (a certain part) in this way. b. *Pottery.* To work (clay) by flinging masses of it violently down 1786. 2. To strike, bring down (one's hand, etc.) *on* or *upon* something with a slap; to clap (the hands) *together* 1717. 3. To shut (a door, gate, etc.) sharply or with a slap. Also with *to.* 1708. 4. *intr.* Of a door, etc.: To slam (*rare*) 1796. 5. Of waves, water, etc.: To beat or strike *on* or *against* something with a slapping sound 1840.

1. He slapped his forehead as if he had hit upon something material GOLDSM.

Comb.: **s.-stick**, orig. and chiefly *U.S.*, the wand used by the harlequin in a pantomime; used *attrib.* to define knockabout comedy or the like, or slapdash methods.

Slap (slæp), *adv. colloq.* 1672. [ad. LG. *slapp*, of imitative origin.] 1. With, or as with, a slap or smart quick blow; suddenly, without warning or notice. 2. Directly, straight 1829.

1. Let us be serious and finish this comedy s. off 1852. 2. A turnstile leading s. away into the meadows DICKENS.

Slap-bang, *adv.*, *a.*, and *sb.* Also **slap bang.** 1785. [f. SLAP *adv.* + BANG *v.*] A. *adv.* With, or as with, a slap and a bang; without delay, immediately; without due consideration. B. *adj.* †1. *S. shop*, an eating-house or cook-shop where there is no credit given –1835. 2. Characterized by carelessness, heedlessness, or haste 1815.

1. Cow-heel or hot alamode from the s. shop 1838.

C. *sb.* 1. A slap-bang shop 1836. 2. Some kind of liquor. DISRAELI.

Slap-dash, *adv.*, *a.*, and *sb.* Also **slap dash, slapdash.** 1679. [f. SLAP *adv.* + DASH *adv.*] A. *adv.* With, or as with, a slap and a dash; in a hasty, sudden, or precipitate manner; *esp.* without much consideration, thought, ceremony, or care. B. *adj.* 1. Marked or characterized by haste, carelessness, or want of due preparation or consideration; done, performed, etc. in a dashing and haphazard manner or style 1792. 2. Of persons: Given to acting in this way 1833. C. *sb.* 1. Roughcast 1796. 2. Carelessness, roughness, or want of finish in style or workmanship; writing or work done in this style 1826. Hence **Sla·p-dash** *v. intr.* to write, work, etc. in a s. manner or style; *trans.* to roughcast.

Slape (slēɪp), *a.* **n.** *dial.* 1460. [a. ON. *sleipr* slippery.] Slippery; smooth. Also *fig.* crafty, cunning, deceitful.

S.-ale, plain ale as opp. to medicated or mixed ale (Ray); rich, soft, or smooth ale (Grose).

Slapjack (slæ·pˌdʒæk). Also **slap-jack, slap jack.** 1820. [f. SLAP *v.* + JACK *sb.*[1]] *U.S.* A griddle-cake.

Slapper (slæ·pəɪ). 1781. [f. SLAP *v.* + -ER[1].] 1. *dial.* A large person or object; a 'whopper'. 2. One who slaps; *spec.* in *Pottery* 1860. 3. An implement used for slapping with 1886.

Sla·pping, *ppl. a.* 1812. [f. SLAP *v.* + -ING[2].] 1. Of pace, etc.: Extremely fast; rapid, rattling. 2. Of horses: Big, powerfully built 1828. b. Of persons or things: Unusually large or fine; very good; strapping 1825. 3. That slaps 1898.

1. The first run was at a s. pace 1812.

Sla·p-up, *a. slang* and *colloq.* 1827. [SLAP *adv.*] Very or unmistakably good or fine; first-rate, first-class, grand.

Slash (slæʃ), *sb.*[1] 1576. [f. SLASH *v.*] 1. A cutting stroke delivered with an edged weapon or instrument, or with a whip. b. The debris of felled trees 1905. 2. A long and deep or severe cut; a gash; a wound of this character 1580. 3. A vertical slit made in a garment in order to expose to view a lining or under-garment of a different colour 1615.

1. *transf.* Rough slashes of sarcasm CARLYLE.

Slash (slæʃ), *sb.*[2] *U.S.* 1799. [Origin obsc.] A piece of wet or swampy ground overgrown with bushes. b. **s.-pine**, a loblolly or Cuban pine 1882.

Slash (slæʃ), *v.* late ME. [perh. ad. OF. *esclachier* to break; used only once, in the Wycliffite Bible, before the middle of the 16th c.] 1. *trans.* To cut or wound with a sweep or stroke of a sharp weapon or instrument; to gash, †hew. 2. *intr.* To deliver or aim cutting blows (also const. *at*); to make gashes or deep wounds 1548. b. To strike violently or at random; to lay about one with heavy blows; to move rapidly and violently, etc. 1654. 3. *trans.* To cut slits in (a garment) and so expose to view an under-garment or a lining of a contrasting colour; to vary *with* another material or colour in this way 1698. 4. To cut with a scourge or whip; to lash, thrash severely 1614. 5. To rebuke or assail cuttingly; to criticize severely. Also *absol.* 1653. 6. To crack (a whip); to bring down in a slashing manner 1660. 7. Used advb. to denote action or sound 1654.

1. b. *U.S.* To cut down or reduce severely 1906. 5. History must not cauterise, and s. with Malice, those Noble Parts 1653. Hence **Sla·shy** *a.* of a slashing nature (*rare*).

Slashed (slæʃt), *ppl. a.* 1633. [f. prec. + -ED[1].] 1. Of garments: Having vertical slits to show a contrasting lining; in mod. use, having a piece of a different colour inserted. 2. Gashed, cut; deeply wounded 1825. 3. *Bot.* Deeply cut; laciniate 1839.

1. Charles I. with ruff, ribband, and s. habit H. WALPOLE.

Slasher (slæ·ʃəɪ). 1559. [f. SLASH *v.* + -ER[1].] 1. One who slashes; a fighter, a bully; a slashing fellow. 2. A sword; a weapon for slashing 1815. b. A billhook 1882. 3. A severe criticism or review 1849. 4. A form of sizing-machine for yarn, so called on account of its rapid working 1862.

Slashing (slæ·ʃiŋ), *ppl. a.* 1735. [-ING[2].] Severely critical; spirited, dashing.

Slat (slæt), *sb.*[1] late ME. [ad. OF. *esclat* (mod.F. *éclat*) splinter, shiver, etc., related to

OF. *esclater* to burst, of doubtful origin.] 1. A roofing-slate; a thin slab of stone used for roofing. Now *dial.* 2. Slate used for roofing buildings. Now *dial.* late ME. 3. A long narrow strip of wood or metal, used for various purposes 1764.

3. Arranged in transverse rows, like slats on a blind 1885.

Slat (slæt), *sb.*[2] 1611. [f. SLAT *v.*[2]] 1. A slap; a slapping blow. Now *dial.* 2. A sudden gust or blast *of* wind 1840.

Slat (slæt), *sb.*[3] 1870. [perh. Irish.] A salmon out of season; a spent salmon.

Slat (slæt), *v.*[1] 1475. [f. SLAT *sb.*[1]] 1. *trans.* To cover with slates. Now *dial.* 2. To furnish, or make, with slats 1886.

Slat (slæt), *v.*[2] *local.* ME. [Origin unkn.] 1. *trans.* To cast, dash, impel quickly and with some force. 2. To strike, beat; to knock *out* 1577. 3. *intr.* To flap violently 1840.

2. *Men.* How did you kill him? *Mal.* Slatted his braines out. MARSTON.

Slat (slæt), *v.*[3] Now *dial.* 1607. [prob. ad. OF. *esclater* to break in pieces.] *intr.* and *trans.* To split.

†**Slatch.** 1625. [Related to OE. *slæc* SLACK *a.*] *Naut.* a. The slack of a rope –1627. b. A brief respite or interval; a short period or spell (*of* some kind of weather, etc.) –1769.

Slate (slēit), *sb.* Also (chiefly *north.* and *Sc.*) sclate. ME. [ad. OF. *esclate* fem., in the same sense as *esclat* masc., whence SLAT *sb.*[1]] 1. A thin, usu. rectangular, piece of certain varieties of stone which split readily into laminæ (see 4), used especially for covering the roofs of buildings. b. A slab of slate; a laminated rock 1601. 2. A tablet of slate, usually framed in wood, used for writing on. late ME. b. *fig.* A record of any kind concerning or against a person; esp. in phr. *a clean s.* 1868. c. *U.S.* A draft list of candidates to be proposed for nomination or for election 1877. 3. Roofing-slates collectively, or the material from which these are made ME. 4. An argillaceous rock of sedimentary origin, the different varieties of which have the common property of splitting readily into thin plates 1653.

Many varieties are distinguished, esp. in *Geol.*, by special terms, as *clay, hornblende, mica, talc s.*

b. With *a* and *pl.* A kind or variety of slaty rock 1704. 5. A bluish-grey colour like that of slate 1882.

1. Phr. *To have a s. loose* or *off*, to be weak in intellect. *slang* or *colloq.* 2. Take alle the signes,..& wryte hem in þy s. CHAUCER.

Comb.: s.-axe, an axe for shaping slates for roofing; **s. clay**, shale; **s. club**, a sharing-out club, whose accounts are nominally kept on a s.; **-galiot**, a vessel carrying slates; **-knife**, a knife used for splitting slates; **-nail, -peg, pin**, a nail, peg, or pin used to fix a s. on a roof; **-saw**, a machine for trimming the edges of slate-slabs to shape.

Slate (slēit), *v.*[1] 1530. [f. prec.] 1. *trans.* To cover or roof with slates. 2. To put down (a name, etc.) on a writing-slate; to set down, book, *for* something 1883. 3. To remove hair from (hides) 1897.

Slate (slēit), *v.*[2] *colloq.*, orig. *slang.* 1825. [app. f. as prec.] †1. *trans.* To knock the hat over the eyes of (a person). †2. To beat or thrash severely 1825. b. *Mil.* To punish (an enemy) severely 1854. 3. To assail with reproof or abuse; to rate or reprimand; to scold severely 1840. b. To criticize (a book or author) severely; to castigate 1848.

Slate (slēit), *v.*[3] *north.* and *Sc.* ME. [ad. ON. **sleita*, = OE. *slǣtan.*] 1. *trans.* To incite or set on (a dog). 2. To bait, assail, or drive, with dogs ME.

Sla·te-colour. 1826. [SLATE *sb.*] The bluish-grey colour of slate. So **Sla·te-coloured** *a.* of the colour of slate, usu. bluish-grey 1801.

Slate-pencil. 1759. [SLATE *sb.*] 1. A pencil, usu. made of soft slate, used for writing on a slate. 2. The material of which slate-pencils are made 1801.

Slater (slēi·təɹ). ME. [f. SLATE *sb.* or *v.*[1]] 1. One whose work consists in laying slates. 2. A wood-louse. Chiefly *Sc.* and *n. dial.* 1684.

Slating (slēi·tiŋ), *vbl. sb.*[1] 1579. [f. SLATE *v.*[1]] 1. The fixing of slates (on a roof or elsewhere); the business of fixing slates. 2. *collect.* The slates covering a roof 1816.

Slating (slēi·tiŋ), *vbl. sb.*[2] 1870. [f. SLATE *v.*[2]] 1. A severe punishment; a beating 1872. 2. A severe reprimand or scolding 1881. 3. A severe criticism or literary castigation 1870.

Slatter (slæ·teɪ). Now *dial.* late ME. [f. SLAT *sb.*[1] or *v.*[1]] = SLATER.

Sla·ttering, *ppl. a. dial.* 1674. [f. the dial. vb. *slatter* to spill, slop, waste, of unkn. origin.] Careless, slovenly.

Slattern (slæ·təɹn), *sb.* and *a.* 1639. [Related to prec.] A. *sb.* A woman or girl untidy and slovenly in person, habits, or surroundings; a slut.

Butterflies one day, and slatterns the next 1766.

B. *adj.* Slovenly, untidy, slatternly. Said of appearance, etc., or of persons. 1716.

A certain degree of s. elegance 1822.

Slattern (slæ·təɹn), *v.* 1747. [f. prec.] *trans.* To fritter or throw *away* (time, opportunity, etc.) by carelessness or slovenliness.

Slatternly (slæ·təɹnli), *a.* 1680. [f. SLATTERN *sb.*] 1. Of persons: Having the condition or habits of a slattern; slovenly; untidy. 2. Of appearance, etc.: Appropriate to, characteristic of, a slattern 1776. Hence **Sla·tternliness.**

Slaty (slēi·ti), *a.* 1529. [f. SLATE *sb.* + -Y[1].] 1. Composed of slate; resembling slate having the nature or properties of slate. Also of land: Lying upon slate. 2. Characteristic or typical of slate 1796. 3. Slate-coloured 1822.

2. The principal fracture is straight, s. 1854.

Slaughter (slǭ·təɹ), *sb.* [ME. *slahter*, a. early ON. **slahtr* neut., f. the stem **slah-*; see SLAY *v.*] 1. The killing of cattle, sheep, or other animals for food. 2. The killing or slaying of a person; murder, homicide, esp. of a brutal kind ME. 3. The killing of large numbers of persons in war, battle, etc.; massacre, carnage ME. b. Persons slain in battle, etc. (*rare*) 1757. 4. An instance of slaying or massacre 1483.

3. S. grows murder when it goes too far, And makes a Massacre what was a War DRYDEN. b. His body being found amidst a heap of s. GOLDSM.

Phr. *To* or *for the s.*; Wee are counted as sheepe for the s. *Ps.* xliv. 22. Hence **Slau·ghtery,** slaughter; a slaughter-house.

Slaughter (slǭ·təɹ), *v.* 1535. [f. prec.] 1. *trans.* To kill (cattle, sheep, or other animals), *spec.* for food. 2. To kill, slay, murder (a person), esp. in a bloody or brutal manner 1582. b. *U.S. colloq.* To defeat or demolish completely 1903. 3. To kill or slay (persons) in large numbers; to massacre 1589.

3. What do these Worthies, But rob.., s., and enslave Peaceable Nations MILT. fig. *Wint. T.* I. ii. 93. Hence **Slau·ghterer,** one who slaughters.

Slau·ghter-house. late ME. [SLAUGHTER *sb.*] 1. A house or place where animals are killed for food. 2. *transf.* A place or scene in which persons are killed or slaughtered 1578.

Slau·ghterman. ME. [f. SLAUGHTER *sb.*] 1. One who kills or slays; an executioner. 2. One employed in killing cattle, etc. for food.

Slaughterous (slǭ·tərəs), *a.* 1582. [f. SLAUGHTER *sb.* + -OUS.] Murderous, destructive. Hence **Slau·ghterously** *adv.*

Slav (slāv, slæv), *sb.* and *a.* late ME. [orig. *Sclave*, ad. med.L. *Sclavus*, = late Gr. Σκλάβος. Later forms in *Sl-* correspond to G. and F. *Slave*, med.L. *Slavus*, and are closer to the OSlav. and Russ. forms; see SLOVENE.] A. *sb.* A person belonging by race to a large group of peoples inhabiting eastern Europe and comprising the Russians, Bulgarians, Serbo-Croats, Poles, Czechs, Moravians, and Wends or Slovenes. B. *adj.* Belonging to, characteristic of, or originating with the Slavs; Slavic; Slavonian 1876. Hence **Sla·vdom,** the Slavonic race generally. **Sla·vism,** the collective qualities or racial character of the S. peoples.

Slave (slēiv), *sb.* ME. [ad. OF. *esclave* (also mod.F.), = med.L. *sclavus, sclava*, identical with the racial name *Sclavus* (see SLAV).] 1. One who is the property of, and entirely subject to, another person, whether by capture, purchase, or birth; a servant completely divested of freedom and personal rights. b. Used as a term of contempt. Now *arch.* 1537. †c. Rascal; fellow –1607. 2. *transf.* One who submits in a servile manner to the authority or dictation of another or others; a submissive or devoted servant 1521. b. *fig.* One who is completely under the domination *of*, or subject *to*, a specified influence 1559. 3. One whose condition in respect of toil is comparable to that of a slave 1774. 4. *Ent.* An ant captured by, and made to serve, ants of another species 1817.

1. Wee'll visit Caliban, my slaue, who neuer Yeelds vs kinde answere SHAKS. b. Thou pawnbroking s. SCOTT. *transf.* This yellow Slaue [*sc.* gold] Will knit and breake Religions SHAKS. 2. The head of a party, and consequently..the s. of a party MACAULAY. b. Giue me that man That is not Passions Slaue SHAKS. 3. The women..of these countries, are the greatest slaves upon earth GOLDSM.

Comb.: **s.-bangle,** a bangle of gold, silver, glass, etc., worn by women above the elbow; **-born** *a.*, born of a s. parent or parents; born in the condition of a s.; **-captain,** the captain of a s.-ship; **S. Coast,** a part of the west coast of Africa, from which slaves were exported; **-holder,** one who owns slaves; **-power,** a power based upon, or recognizing, slavery as an institution; **-ship** = SLAVER *sb.*[2] 1; **s. state,** one or other of the southern United States of America, in which s.-holding was legal. Hence **Sla·vedom,** (*a*) slavery, (*b*) the position of a s.

Slave (slēiv), *v.* 1559. [f. prec.] 1. *trans.* To enslave; to bring into subjection. 2. To treat as a slave; to employ in servile labour 1699. 3. *intr.* To toil or work hard like a slave 1719. b. *trans.* To wear *out*, etc., by severe toil 1864. †4. To traffic in slaves (*rare*) 1726.

3. b. I may s. my life out, and there isn't one of you will..help me 1864.

Sla·ve-me:rchant. 1747. [SLAVE *sb.*] One who traffics or deals in slaves; a slave-dealer.

Slaver (slæ·vəɹ), *sb.*[1] ME. [Related to SLAVER *v.*] Saliva issuing or falling from the mouth. b. *fig.* Drivel, nonsense; also, gross flattery 1825.

Of all mad creatures..It is the s. kills, and not the bite POPE.

Slaver (slēi·vəɹ), *sb.*[2] 1830. [f. SLAVE *sb.* + -ER[1].] 1. A vessel engaged in slave-traffic. 2. One who deals or traffics in, or owns, slaves 1842.

2. The Slaver's thumb was on the latch LONGF.

Slaver (slæ·vəɹ), *v.* ME. [app. of Scand. origin; cf. Icel. *slafra* in the same sense.] 1. *intr.* To let the saliva run from the mouth; to slabber. b. *fig.* To drivel; to fawn 1730. 2. *trans.* To wet with saliva; to slobber 1591. b. *fig.* To fondle or flatter, in a disgusting or sycophantic manner 1794. Hence **Sla·verer,** one who slavers; also *fig.* a servile flatterer.

Slavering (slæ·vəriŋ), *ppl. a.* 1576. [f. prec.] 1. Characterized or accompanied by the emission of slaver. 2. That slavers; allowing saliva to fall. Hence **Sla·veringly** *adv.*

Slavery (slēi·vəri), *sb.* 1551. [f. SLAVE *sb.* + -ERY.] 1. Severe toil like that of a slave; heavy labour, hard work, drudgery. 2. The condition of a slave; the fact of being a slave; servitude; bondage 1604. b. The condition of being entirely subject to, or dominated by, some power or influence 1577. c. A state of subjection or subordination comparable to that of a slave; also with *pl.*, an instance of this 1586. 3. The fact of slaves existing as a class in a community; the keeping of slaves as a practice or institution 1728.

2. Being taken..And sold to slauery SHAKS. b. Instilling their barren hearts with a conscientious s. MILT. c. The extream s. and subjection that courtiers live in EVELYN. 3. On this abstract question of s. there can..be but one opinion MRS. STOWE.

Slavery (slæ·vəri), *a.* late ME. [f. SLAVER *sb.*[1] + -Y[1].] Like slaver; befouled with slaver; characterized by, given to, slavering.

Sla·ve-trade. 1734. Traffic in slaves; *spec.* the former transportation of African negroes to America. So **Sla·ve-tra:der** = SLAVER *sb.*[2]

Slavey (slēi·vi, slæ·vi). *colloq.* 1812. [f. SLAVE *sb.* + -Y[6].] †1. A male servant or attendant –1855. 2. A female domestic servant, *esp.* one who is hard-worked 1821.

Slavic (slā·vik, slæ·vik), *a.* and *sb.* Also **Sclavic.** 1813. [f. SLAV *sb.* + -IC, after G. *slavisch.*] A. *adj.* Slavonian, Slavonic. B. *sb.* = SLAVONIC *sb.* 1866.

Slavish (slēi·viʃ), *a.*[1] 1565. [f. SLAVE *sb.* + -ISH[1].] 1. Of, belonging to, or characteristic of, a slave; befitting a slave; servile, abject. **2.** Having the character of slaves; of a submissive, unmanly disposition 1565. **3.** Vile, mean, ignoble 1593. **4.** Implying or involving slavery 1593. **5.** Servilely imitative 1753.

1. See how he lies..In s. habit, ill-fitted weeds MILT. 2. Scourge of thy people,..Sent in Jove's anger on a s. race POPE. 3. To lye is a s. Vice 1700. 4. *Rich. II*, II. i. 291. 5. There was no s. adherence to the old law 1861. Hence **Sla·vish-ly** *adv.*, **-ness.**

Slavish (slā·vĭʃ, slæ·vĭʃ), *a.*[2] and *sb.* 1834. [f. SLAV *sb.* + -ISH[1].] **A.** *adj.* Pertaining to or characteristic of the Slavs. **B.** *sb.* The Slavonic language.

Slavo- (slā·vo, slæ·vo), comb. form. of SLAV, as in *S.-Germanic*, *-Lithuanian*, etc.; also **Sla·vophil(e**, one who admires or favours the Slavs, Slavonic ideals, etc.; **Sla·vophobe**, one who has a morbid dread of these.

Slav(e)ocracy (slē̆ivǫ·krăsi). 1848. [f. SLAVE *sb.* + -OCRACY, but erron. applied.] The domination of slave-holders; slave-holders collectively as a dominant or powerful class.

Slavonian (slăvōu·niăn), *sb.* and *a.* †Also Scl-. 1577. [f. med.L. *S(c)lavonia* the country of the Slavs, f. *S(c)lavus* SLAV.] **A.** *sb.* **1.** The language of the Slavs; Slavic; Slavonic. **2.** A person of Slavonic origin; a Slav 1601. **B.** *adj.* **1.** Of or pertaining to the Slavs 1605. **2.** Of or pertaining to Slavonic countries, as *S. falcon, grebe* 1809. **3.** Coming from Slavonic regions 1812.

3. As snow..piled by rough Sclavonian blasts CARY.

Slavonic (slăvǫ·nik), *a.* and *sb.* 1614. [ad. med.L. *S(c)lavonicus*, f. *Slavonia*; see prec.] **A.** *adj.* Slavic; Slavonian. **B.** *sb.* A generic term for the languages of the Slavs 1668.

Old or *Church S.*, Old Bulgarian.

Slaw (slǫ). *U.S.* Also **slaugh.** 1864. [ad. Du. *sla*, shortened form of *salade* SALAD.] A salad made of sliced cabbage, etc.

Slay, sley (slēⁱ), *sb.* [OE. *slege* stroke, slaying, = OS. *slegi*, f. the stem of SLAY *v.*] An instrument used in weaving to beat up the weft; a reed.

Slay (slēⁱ), *v.* Pa. t. **slew** (slū). Pa. pple. **slain** (slēⁱn). Now mainly *literary* and *rhet.* [Com. Teut.; OE. *sléan* (pa. t. *slóg*, *slóh*, pa. pple. *slægen*, *slegen*.] †**I. 1.** *trans.* To smite, strike, or beat -ME. **2.** To strike (a spark, fire) from flint or other hard substance -1513. **II. 1.** To strike or smite so as to kill; to put to death by means of a weapon; also *gen.*, to deprive of life by violence OE. **2.** *absol.* To commit slaughter or murder OE. **3. a.** Of the Deity: To deprive (man, etc.) of life; to bring death upon, to destroy OE. **b.** Of natural forces, accidents, etc. Now *dial.* OE. †**4.** To put to death as a criminal; to execute -1667. **5.** To kill (a domestic animal or beast of game), *esp.* for food or as a sacrifice; to slaughter OE. †**b.** To destroy (vermin, etc.) by some means -1578.

1. The nombre of them that were slaine..was accompted a thousand 1560. *fig.* Sad souls are slain in merry company SHAKS. 2. The Parthian turn'd his Steed,..and as He fled, He slew PRIOR. 3. a. Lest I..set her like a drie land, and s. her with thirst *Hosea* ii. 3. b. There was above thirty Persons..slain by a Blast 1708. 4. Naild to the Cross By his own Nation, slaine for bringing Life MILT.

III. †**1.** To bring to spiritual death; to destroy with sin -1611. †**2.** To overcome with affliction or distress -1568. **3.** To destroy, put an end to, suppress completely (*esp.* something bad) ME. **4.** *intr.* Of grain: To become affected by smut, blight, or the like 1641.

1. *absol.* The lettre sleith, forsoth the spirit quykeneth WYCLIF *2 Cor.* iii. 6. 3. With this swerd shal I slen envie CHAUCER. In the very act of slaying the Bill 1884. Hence **Slay·er**[1], one who slays or kills. **Slay·ing** *vbl. sb.*[1] the action of the vb.; killing, slaughter.

Slaying, sleying (slēⁱ·iŋ), *vbl. sb.*[2] 1613. [f. SLAY *sb.* + -ING.[1]] The separating and arranging of the counts of warps to the different sets of slay, so as to preserve a uniformity of fabric in similar species of cloth. Hence **Sla·yer**[2], one who separates the threads and arranges them in a slay.

Sleave (slīv), *sb.* 1591. [See next and SLEAVE-SILK.] †**1.** A slender filament of silk obtained by separating a thicker thread; silk in the form of such filaments; floss-silk -1635. **2.** *transf.* and *fig.* 1605.

2. Sleepe that knits vp the rauel'd Sleeue of Care SHAKS.

Sleave (slīv), *v.* Now *dial.* 1628. [OE. *slǽfan*, f. *slāf-*, pret. stem. of *slīfan* SLIVE *v.*] **1.** *trans.* To divide (silk) by separation into filaments. **2.** To cleave, split, rend, tear apart 1828. So **Sleaved** *ppl. a.*, in *sleaved silk* 1577.

†**Sleave-silk.** 1588. [f. SLEAVE *v.* 1.] Silk thread capable of being separated into smaller filaments for use in embroidery, etc. -1703.

Sleazy, sleezy (slī·zi), *a.* 1644. [Origin unkn.] Thin or flimsy in texture; having little substance or body. **b.** *transf.* and *fig.* Slight, flimsy, unsubstantial 1645.

'Sleezy' silks, wispy surahs, or cottony velvets 1893. Hence **Slea·ziness** (*rare*), the fact or quality of being s.

Sled (sled), *sb.* Now chiefly *dial.* and *U.S.* late ME. [a. MFlem. or MLG. *sledde*.] **1.** = SLEDGE *sb.*[2] 2. **2.** A sledge or sleigh used as a vehicle in travelling or for recreation 1586.

Sled, *v.* Chiefly *U.S.* 1718. [f. prec.] **1.** *intr.* To travel in a sledge 1780. **2.** *trans.* To convey on a sled or sleds 1718.

Sle·dded, *a. rare.* 1602. [f. SLED *sb.*] **a.** Mounted on sleds. **b.** Made like a sled.

a. So frown'd he once, when in an angry parle He smot the s. Pollax on the Ice SHAKS.

Sle·dding, *vbl. sb. U.S.* 1755. [f. SLED *v.*] The action of using a sled; conditions favourable for this. **b.** *fig.* Work or progress in any sphere of action 1839.

Sledge (sledʒ), *sb.*[1] [OE. *slecg*. The stem **slagj-* is derived from that of the verb SLAY.] A large heavy hammer usu. wielded with both hands, esp. the large hammer used by a blacksmith; a sledge-hammer.

Sledge (sledʒ), *sb.*[2] 1617. [a. MDu. *sleedse*, conn. w. *sledde* SLED.] **1.** A carriage mounted upon runners instead of wheels, and gen. used for travelling over snow or ice; a sleigh. **2.** A simple form of conveyance, having runners instead of wheels, employed in the transport of goods over ice or snow or in heavy traffic unsuited to wheeled vehicles. Rarely, a similar vehicle with low wheels; a trolley. 1684. **b.** Formerly used for conveying condemned persons to execution 1651. **3.** *Rope-making.* A travelling structure of considerable weight to which the rope-yarns are attached at one end 1794. Hence **Sledge** *v. intr.* to travel in a s.; *trans.* to carry or convey on a s.

Sle·dge-ha·mmer. 1495. [f. SLEDGE *sb.*[1]] A large heavy hammer used by blacksmiths.

fig. Johnson's s. smashes his flimsy platitudes to pieces 1874.

Sleech (slītʃ). *dial.* 1587. [app. later form of dial. *slitch*, repr. OE. **slīc*.] Mud deposited by the sea or a river; soil composed of this.

Sleek (slīk), *a.* and *adv.* 1589. [Later var. of ME. *slīke* SLICK *a.*] **A.** *adj.* **1.** Of animals, their limbs, etc.: Having, or covered with, hair or fur which lies close and smooth, usually a sign of good condition or careful attention 1590. **b.** Of hair, etc., in this condition 1829. **2.** Of surfaces: Perfectly smooth and polished 1589. **b.** Of the sea or sky: Unruffled, tranquil (*rare*) 1603. **3.** Oily, fawning, plausible, specious 1599. **4.** Of persons: Having a smooth skin, esp. as the result of being in good condition; plump 1637. **B.** *adv.* In a smooth or sleek manner 1602.

A. 1. While I..sticke muske roses in thy s. smoothe head SHAKS. 2. b. On the sleeke waters waft her sayles along DRAYTON. 3. The smoothest and sleekest knaves in a country 1605. 4. S. well-fed blue-coat boys LAMB. Hence **Slee·k-ly** *adv.*, **-ness. Slee·ky** *a.* marked by s. condition; *Sc.* artful, plausible.

Sleek (slīk), *v.* 1440. [Later var. of ME. *slīke(n* SLICK *v.*] **1.** *trans.* To make sleek or smooth by rubbing or polishing. **b.** To reduce to smoothness 1513. **2.** To make (the skin, hair, etc.) smooth and glossy 1508.

1. b. S. eu'ry little Dimple of the Lake: Sweet Syrens DRAYTON. 2. He smooth'd his chin, and sleek'd his hair TENNYSON. *transf.* and *fig.* Gentle my Lord, sleeke o're Your rugged Lookes SHAKS. The perswasive Rhetoric That sleek't his tongue MILT. Musing how to smoothe And s. his marriage over to the Queen TENNYSON.

Sleep (slīp), *sb.* [OE. *slēp*, *slǣp*, = OFris. *slēp*, MDu. *slaep*, G. *schlaf*, the sb. corresponding to SLEEP *v.*] **1.** The unconscious state or condition regularly and naturally assumed by man and animals, during which the activity of the nervous system is almost or entirely suspended, and recuperation of its powers takes place; slumber, repose. **b.** Personified (after L. *Somnus*, Gr. Ὕπνος). late ME. **2.** A period or occasion of slumber ME. **b.** As an indication or division of time ME. **3.** *fig.* **a.** The repose of death OE. **b.** A state of inactivity or sluggishness (in persons or things) OE. **c.** The condition of being quiet and peaceful; complete absence of noise or stir 1807. **4. a.** *Bot.* A condition assumed by many plants, esp. during the night, marked by the closing of petals or leaves 1757. **b.** A state of numbness in a limb, produced by prolonged pressure upon it 1882.

1. S. comes as a medicine to weariness, as a repairer of decay 1658. Damn that boy, he 's gone to s. again DICKENS. *Dead s.*, s. so profound as to suggest death. b. The golden slepe me wrapt vndir his wyng 1460. 2. They are euen as a slepe and fade awaye sodenly like the grasse COVERDALE *Ps.* lxxxix. 5. b. Their division of time is by sleeps, and moons, and winters 1702. 3. b. He had put his doubts to s. 1889. c. The s. that is among the lonely hills WORDSW. Hence †**Slee·pish** *a.* somewhat sleepy.

Sleep (slīp), *v.* Pa. t. and pa. pple. **slept.** [OE. *slēpan*, *slǣpan*, = OFris. *slēpa*, (M)Du. *slapen*, G. *schlafen*.] **I.** *intr.* **1.** To take repose by the natural suspension of consciousness; to be in the state of sleep; to slumber. Also occas., to fall asleep. **b.** With *upon* or *on* (a matter), denoting the postponement of a decision till the following day 1519. **c.** With *in*: (*a*) To sleep in the house, or on the premises, where one is employed; (*b*) to oversleep (*Sc.* and *north.*) 1888. (*c*) To sleep late (*dial.* and *U.S.*) 1931. **2.** *fig.* To lie in the grave OE. **3.** *transf.* **a.** Of limbs: To be numb, esp. as the result of pressure OE. **b.** Of plants: To be in a quiescent or drooping condition 1797. **c.** Of a top: To spin so rapidly that the motion is imperceptible 1854. **4.** *fig.* To be dormant, inert, inactive, inoperative, or quiescent OE. **b.** To rest peacefully and quietly; to remain calm or motionless 1596. **5.** To be careless, remiss, or idle. late ME.

1. He that slepeth well thynketh no harme 1530. Phr. *To s. like a log, top*; Juan slept like a top, or like the dead BYRON. 2. Beneath those rugged elms..The rude Forefathers of the hamlet s. GRAY. 4. The restless enmity of the Angevin never slept 1869. b. How sweet the moonelight sleepes vpon this banke SHAKS.

II. *trans.* **1.** With cogn. obj.: To take rest in, continue in (sleep) OE. †**2.** To put off or delay; to disregard, pay no attention to -1792. **3. a.** With *off* or †*out*: To get rid of, remove the effects of, by sleeping 1552. **b.** With *away*: To remove, get rid of, lose, or waste by sleeping 1565. **c.** *refl.* To make (oneself) *sober* by sleeping. Also simply, to sleep. 1565. **4.** With *out* or *away*: To pass or spend (a certain time) in sleep 1565. **5.** To provide with sleeping accommodation 1884.

1. Phr. *To s. the sleep of the just.* (joc.), to s. soundly. *Not to s. a wink*: see WINK *sb.* 3. a. In the morning, after he had slept his wine off, he was very gay THACKERAY. b. To s. away Sorrow 1687. 5. The parents, owing to poverty, had to s. their children in the same bed as themselves 1895.

Sleep-at-noon. 1661. The goat's-beard, so called because its flowers close at midday.

Sleeper (slī·pəɹ). ME. [f. SLEEP *v.* + -ER[1].] **I. 1.** One who is inclined to sleep, or spends much time in sleep; one who sleeps (well or ill, etc.); also *fig.*, an indolent or inactive person. **2.** One who is asleep. Also *fig.*, a dead person. 1590. **b.** *spec.* in *pl.* (see SEVEN SLEEPERS) 1827. **3.** *Zool.* **a.** A dormouse. Now chiefly *dial.* 1693. **b.** As the name of various fishes 1668. **4.** A thing in a dormant or dead state 1625. **5.** A railway sleeping-car 1882.

1. b. A sleeping partner 1892. 3. b. *E[leotris] dormatrix*, the S., is a large fish 1854. 4. Let Penall Lawes, if they haue beene Sleepers of long..be by Wise Iudges confined in the Execution BACON.

II. 1. A strong horizontal beam or balk supporting a wall, joist, floor, or other main part of a building 1607. **2.** *Shipbuilding.* A strong internal timber in a ship 1626. **3. a.** *Mil.* A piece of timber forming one of the rests of a wooden platform for artillery 1688. **b.** A piece of timber or other material used to form a support (usually transverse) for the rails of a tramway or railway 1789. **c.** A strong longitudinal beam in a wooden bridge, supporting the transverse planks or logs 1823. **d.** *gen.* A horizontal beam, plank, etc., used to support any weighty body 1848.

2. *Sleepers*, pieces of compass timber fayed and bolted upon the transoms and timbers adjoining,..to strengthen the buttock of the ship 1850.

Sleepful (slī·pful), *a.* late ME. [f. SLEEP *sb.* + -FUL 1.] **1.** Sleepy (*rare*). **2.** Marked by sleep; restful through sleep 1827. Hence **Slee·pfulness**, sleepiness.

Sleeping (slī·piŋ), *vbl. sb.* ME. [f. SLEEP *v.*] The fact, state, or condition of being asleep; an instance or occasion of this.

transf. and *fig.* You euer Haue wish'd the s. of this busines SHAKS.

attrib., as *s. apartment, car*, etc.; *s.-bag, -sack*, etc.; in sense 'inducing sleep' (cf. SLEEPING *ppl. a.* 2), as *s. draught*; also **s. sickness**, now *spec.*, a fatal disease prevalent in some parts of Africa.

Sleeping (slī·piŋ), *ppl. a.* ME. [f. SLEEP *v.*] **1.** That is asleep; slumbering. Also *absol.* **b.** Seen in sleep 1781. †**2.** Inducing sleep, soporific (*rare*) -1597. **3.** Numb; devoid of sensation 1562. **4.** Inactive, torpid, quiescent 1538. **5.** Quiet, silent; motionless 1784.

1. A s. boy the Mother held the while CRABBE. 4. *S. table*, an immovable apparatus on which ore is washed. *S. rent*, a dead rent (see DEAD *a.* V. 2). *S. partner*, a partner in a business who takes no share in the actual working of it. 5. The moon-beam, sliding softly in between The s. leaves COWPER.

Sleepless (slī·plės), *a.* late ME. [f. SLEEP *sb.* + -LESS.] **1.** Deprived of sleep; unable to sleep. **2.** Yielding no sleep; marked by the absence or want of sleep 1633. **3.** Continually active or operative 1792. **b.** Unceasing in motion; ever-moving 1795.

3. b. Winds are rude in Biscay's s. bay BYRON. Hence **Slee·pless-ly** *adv.*, **-ness.**

Slee·p-wa:lker. 1747. [SLEEP *sb.*] One who walks while asleep; a somnambulist. So **Slee·p-wa:lking** *vbl. sb.* and *ppl. a.*

Sleepy (slī·pi), *a.* ME. [f. SLEEP *sb.* + -Y[1].] **1.** Inclined to sleep; having a difficulty in keeping awake; drowsy, somnolent. **b.** Given to sleep; lethargic, heavy. late ME. **2.** Characterized by, appropriate or belonging to, suggestive of, sleep or repose ME. **3.** Inducing sleep; soporific. Now *rare.* late ME.

1. Let a man sleep when he is s. 1874. **b.** There slepeth ay this god vnmerie, With his slepy thousande sones CHAUCER. *transf.* and *fig.* Love..oft..Awakes the s. Vigour of the Soul DRYDEN. An apple or pear beginning to rot is said to be s. 1790. 2. Surely It is a s. Language; and thou speak'st Out of thy sleepe SHAKS. Down the s. roadway..pipes a chaffinch MEREDITH. *S. sickness*, (*a*) misused for 'sleeping sickness' (SLEEPING *vbl. sb.*); (*b*) *Encephalitis lethargica.* 3. S. Poppies harmful Harvests yield DRYDEN.

Comb.: **s.-head**, a s. or lethargic person. Hence **Slee·pily** *adv.*, **-ness.**

Sleet (slīt), *sb.* ME. [prob. repr. OE. **slēt* (:—**slēatj-*), related to MLG. *slōte*, MHG. *slōze* (G. *schlosse*) hail.] Snow which has been partially thawed by falling through an atmosphere of a temperature a little above freezing-point, usu. accompanied by rain or snow. **b.** A storm or shower of sleet (*rare*) 1728.

transf. Shot Sharp s. of arrowie showers MILT.

Sleet (slīt), *v.* ME. [f. SLEET *sb.*] **1.** *intr.* **a.** *It sleets*, sleet falls. **b.** To fall as, or like, 1566. **2.** *trans.* To pour or cast like sleet 1786.

Sleety (slī·ti), *a.* 1725. [f. SLEET *sb.* + -Y[1].] **1.** Of storms, wind, etc.: Laden with, accompanied by, sleet. **b.** Sleet-like 1804. **2.** Of weather or time: Characterized by the presence or prevalence of sleet 1826.

1. A cold s. wind 1884. **b.** The flakes were..small and s. 1892. 2. It was mid-winter; snowy, foggy, s., wet 1826. Hence **Slee·tiness** (*rare*).

Sleeve (slīv), *sb.* [OE. *slīefe, slȳf*, = NFris. *slēv, slīv* sleeve.] **1.** That part of a garment which covers the arm. In early use freq. a separate article of dress which could be worn at will with any body-garment. **b.** A piece of armour for covering and protecting the arm. *Obs.* exc. *Hist.* 1465. **2.** [After F. *La Manche.*] The English Channel. *Obs.* exc. as *nonce-use.* 1574. †**b.** A channel or strait -1655. †**3.** *Mil.* A body *of* troops placed on the flanks of an army, battalion, etc.; a wing or flank -1604. **4.** *techn.* A tube, or hollow shaft, fitting over or enclosing a rod, spindle, etc., and designed to protect or strengthen it, or to connect one part with another. Also *attrib.* as *s.-axle, -coupling, -nut.* 1864.

1. Short was his gowne, with sleues longe and wyde CHAUCER. That Sleeue is mine, that heele beare in his Helme SHAKS. *Hippocrates' s.*, = HIPPOCRAS 2. Phrases. *To have in* or *up one's s.*, to have in reserve, at one's disposal, or ready for some need or emergency. †*To hang on, upon* (another's) *s.*, to depend or rely upon for support or assistance. *To laugh* or *smile in one's s.*: see LAUGH *v.* 1. *To pin.. on, upon*, or *to one's s.*: see PIN *v.* 3.

Comb.: **s.-board**, a shaped board on which sleeves are ironed or pressed; **-button**, a button for fastening a wristband or cuff; a s.-link; **-fish**, a fish of the family *Loligo*; esp. the squid, *L. vulgaris*; **-link**, two bars, buttons, or the like, linked together, for fastening a cuff or wristband; **-valve**, a valve in the form of a cylinder with sliding movement.

Sleeve (slīv), *v.* 1440. [f. SLEEVE *sb.*] **1.** *trans.* To provide with a sleeve or sleeves. †**2.** To provide (a body of troops) with a wing or wings -1613. †**b.** *intr.* To draw or line *up* on the flanks or wings -1635. **3.** To fix or fasten *on*, to couple, by means of a sleeve or tube 1875.

3. The motors are sleeved on the axles 1902.

Sleeved (slīvd), *ppl. a.* 1500. [f. SLEEVE *v.* or *sb.*] Fitted or provided with sleeves; having sleeves of a certain kind, as *long-, short-s.*

Sleeveless (slī·vlės), *a.* OE. [f. SLEEVE *sb.* + -LESS.] **1.** Of a garment: Having no sleeves; made without sleeves. **2.** †**a.** Of words, tales, answers, etc.: Futile, feeble; giving no information or satisfaction; irrelevant, trifling -1700. **b.** Of errands: Ending in, or leading to, nothing; having no adequate result or cause. Now *rare.* 1546. **c.** *gen.* Paltry, petty, frivolous; vain or unprofitable. *Obs.* exc. *arch.* or *dial.* 1550.

2. **a.** With no more but No, a sleevless reason,..to be sent home frustrat and remediless MILT. **b.** Shee . had of purpose sent them forth on sleeuelesse arrands DEKKER. **c.** The s. quarrel fixed on him SCOTT.

Sleezy, variant of SLEAZY.

Sleigh (slē^i), *sb.* Chiefly *U.S.* and *Canada.* 1703. [orig. U.S., ad. Du. *slee*, contr. f. *slede.*] **1.** A sledge constructed or used as a vehicle for passengers, usually drawn by one or more horses. **2.** A sledge or sled employed for the transport of goods over ice or snow 1748. **b.** *Mil.* A sledge or sled used for the transport of artillery 1797.

attrib. and *Comb.*: **s.-bell**, one of a number of small bells attached to a s. or to the harness of a horse drawing it. Hence **Sleigh** *v. intr.* to travel or ride in a sleigh.

Sleighing (slē^i·iŋ), *vbl. sb.* 1775. [f. SLEIGH *sb.* or *v.*] Riding in or driving a sleigh, esp. as a pastime; also, the state of the ground when this is possible.

When the s. arrives, it will be an affair of two days up and two days down 1780.

Sleight (sləit), *sb.* [Early ME. *slēȝþ*, ad. ON. *slœgð*, f. *slœg-r* SLY *a.* Cf. HEIGHT.] **1.** Craft or cunning employed so as to deceive; deceitful, subtle, or wily dealing or policy; artifice, strategy, trickery. Now *rare* or *Obs.* †**2.** Prudence; wisdom, knowledge. -late ME. **3.** Skill, skilfulness, cleverness, or dexterity in doing or making something, in handling a tool or weapon, etc. Now *rare.* late ME. **4.** The precise art or method, the special knack or trick, *of* (doing) something. Now *dial.* ME. **b.** *spec.* Skill in jugglery or conjuring; sleight of hand 1664. **5.** Adroitness, activity, smartness, nimbleness *of* mind, body, etc. late ME. **6.** A cunning trick; an artifice, ruse, stratagem, or wile. Now *rare.* ME. **b.** A feat of jugglery or legerdemain 1596. †**c.** A design or pattern. SPENSER.

1. Every interest did by right, or might, or s., get represented EMERSON. 4. **b.** The juggler's s., That with facility of motion cheats The eye 1850. 5. A new s. of tongue to make fools clap MACAULAY. 6. Unpractised in the sleights and artifices of controversy FRANKLIN. Hence †**Sleight** *a.* artful, crafty, wily; of juggling, etc., expert, deceptive. †**Slei·ghtful** *a.* (*rare*) characterized by craft or artifice; crafty, cunning. †**Slei·ghtness**, craftiness, subtlety.

Sleight of hand. Also **sleight-of-hand.** late ME. **1.** Dexterity or skill in using the hand or hands for any purpose; expertness in manipulation or manual action. **b.** In ref. to jugglery, conjuring, or the like 1622. **2.** With *a* and *pl.* A dexterous trick or feat; a piece of nimble juggling or conjuring 1605.

Sleighty (sləi·ti), *a.* Now *rare.* late ME. [f. SLEIGHT *sb.* + -Y[1].] **1.** Possessed of or making use of sleight or craft. **2.** Crafty, subtle. late ME. Hence †**Slei·ghtily** *adv.*

Slender (sle·ndəɹ), *a.* ME. [prob. from AF.] **I. 1.** Not stout or fleshy; slim, spare. (Freq. implying gracefulness of form.) **b.** Denoting absence of robustness. †Also *transf.* of age, etc.: Tender, immature. 1500. **2.** Of things: Small in diameter or width in proportion to length; long and thin; attenuated 1513. **3. a.** Slight or slim in size or structure 1444. †**b.** Of vowels: Narrow, close 1755. **4.** Of small extent, size, or capacity 1610.

1. These yer s. gals will bear half killin' to get their own way! 1852. 2. The s. line, nearly four miles long, which your army must make 1788. 3. **a.** A very s. book 1875. **b.** The s. *a*, or that heard in *lane* 1828.

II. †**1.** Moderate in power or strength; lax -1657. **2. a.** Of arguments, etc.: Lacking in cogency; unconvincing 1533. **b.** Having but slight foundation 1562. **3.** Slight, small, insignificant, trifling 1530. **4.** Small or limited in amount, number, range, etc. 1564. **b.** Of sounds: Weak, lacking in fullness 1784.

1. The s. and negligent execution of the Forest Lawes 1598. 2. **a.** The proofs were as s. as the crimes gross FULLER. **b.** Some claim (generally of the slenderest kind) 1886. 3. But what a s. answer is this 1641. He has but s. Parts 1687. 4. Her s. earnings were the sole support of the family LAMB. **b.** It gave one little s. squeak HAWTHORNE. Hence **Sle·nderize** *v.* to perform or subject to 'slimming' operations 1923. **Sle·nder-ly** *adv.*, **-ness.**

Slent, *sb.* Now *dial.* ME. [a. ON. **slent*, related to **slenta* SLENT *v.* (whence sense 2).] **1.** SLANT *sb.*[1] 1. †**2.** = SLANT *sb.*[1] 3a. -1612.

Slent, *v.* Now *dial.* ME. [a. ON. **slenta* to SLANT, slope, slip.] **1.** *intr.* To slip, fall, or glide obliquely; to strike or lie aslant. †**2.** To make sly hits or gibes -1579.

†**Sleuth**, *sb.*[1] [OE. *slǣwð*, f. *slāw* SLOW *a.* + -TH. In later use chiefly north. and Sc.] Sloth; laziness -1629.

†**Sleuth**, *sb.*[2] ME. [a. ON. *slōð* track, trail.] The track or trail of a person or animal; a definite track or path -1470.

Sleuth, *sb.*[3] orig. *U.S.* 1876. Short for next. Hence **Sleuth** *v. trans.* to track (a person); *intr.* to play the detective.

Sleuth-hound (slū·þ,haund). orig. *north.* and *Sc.* late ME. [f. SLEUTH *sb.*[2]] **1.** A species of bloodhound, formerly employed in Scotland. *Hist.* or *arch.* **2.** *transf.* A keen investigator; a tracker; *U.S.* a detective 1856.

Slew (slū), *sb.*[1] Also **slue, sleugh.** 1708. [var. spellings of *sloo*, ME. *slō*; see SLOUGH *sb.*[1]] **1.** *N. Amer.* A marshy or reedy pool, pond, small lake, backwater, or inlet. **2.** *Coal-mining.* A natural swamp in a coal seam 1883.

Slew (slū), *sb.*[2] Also **slue.** 1860. [f. SLEW *v.*] The act of turning, or causing to turn, without change of place; a turn, a twist; the position to which a thing has been turned.

Slew (slū), *v.* Also **slue.** 1769. [orig. *Naut.*; origin unkn.] **1.** *trans.* To turn (a thing) round upon its own axis, or without shifting it from its place; also loosely, to swing round. **b.** *fig.* To intoxicate; also in *pa. pple.*, beaten, 'done' 1888. **2.** *intr.* To turn about; to swing *round* 1823.

1. Slue the mast round 1882. A roller caught us and slued the boat round 1884. 2. The floe..began to 'slue' or revolve 1823.

Slewed (slūd), *ppl. a.* *slang.* 1834. [f. prec.] Intoxicated.

Sley, variant of SLAY, *sb.*

†**Slibber-sauce.** 1573. [perh. f. Flem. *slibber*, slime, ooze.] **1.** A compound or concoction of a messy, repulsive, or nauseous character, used esp. for medicinal purposes -1656. **2.** A preparation of this kind used as a cosmetic -1633.

Slice (sləis), *sb.*[1] ME. [ad. OF. *esclice* (mod.F. *éclisse*) splinter, shiver, small piece (of wood, etc.), f. *esclicer*; see SLICE *v.*] **I.** †**1.** A fragment, a splinter -1596. **2.** A relatively thin, flat, broad piece cut from anything. late ME. **3.** *transf.* A portion, share, piece, etc. 1550.

3. A fellow..who has spent a good s. of his life here 1857.

II. †**1.** A spatula used for stirring and mixing compounds -1686. **2.** One or other of several flattish utensils (sometimes perforated) used for various purposes in cookery, etc., as a *fish-s.* 1459. 3. A form of fire-shovel; also, an instrument for clearing the bars of a furnace when choked with clinkers 1465. 4. A flattish instrument, implement, etc., of various kinds 1483. 5. *Printing.* a. An ink-knife 1683. b. The sliding bottom of a s.-galley 1683. 6. *Shipbuilding.* One of the tapered pieces of wood driven between the bilgeways, etc., in preparation for launching a vessel 1791.

attrib. and *Comb.*: **s.-bar**, a hooked poker for removing slag and cinders from the grate-bars of furnaces; **-galley**, a galley having a movable false bottom or s.

Slice (sləis), *sb.*[2] 1611. [f. SLICE *v.*] †1. A sharp cut, a slash. COTGR. 2. *Golf.* A slicing stroke 1886.

Slice (sləis), *v.* late ME. [ad. OF. *esclicer* (mod.F. *éclisser*) to reduce to splinters or pieces, ad. OHG. *slîzan.*] 1. *trans.* To cut into slices; to cut into or through with a sharp instrument. 2. To cut *out* or *off* in the form of a slice or slices; to remove with a clean cut 1550. 3. *intr.* To cut cleanly or easily 1605. b. To use a slice or fire-shovel 1893. 4. *trans.* To make (a way) by slicing 1872. 5. *Golf.* To hit (the ball) a glancing blow so that it curves off to the right 1890. Hence **Sliced** *ppl.a.*, **Sli·cer.**

Slick (slik), *sb.* 1849. [f. SLICK *a.* or *v.*] 1. *Carpentry.* A wide-bitted paring chisel 1875. 2. a. *U.S.* A smooth place or streak on the surface of water, usually caused by the presence of some oily or greasy substance 1849. b. *Mining.* A smooth parting or plane of division in strata 1883.

Slick (slik), *a.* Now chiefly *dial.* and *U.S.* [ME. *slike*, prob. repr. OE. **slice*, related to *slician* SLICK *v.* Cf. SLEEK *a.*] 1. Of skin, hair, etc.: Smooth, glossy, sleek. 2. Of animals, etc.: Sleek in hair or skin; plump; well-conditioned. Now *rare.* 1440. 3. = SLEEK *a.* 3. 1599. 4. Adroit, deft, quick, smart; skilful in action or execution 1818. b. Smartly or cleverly done 1838. 5. First-class, excellent 1866.

1. Bent browis, smothe and slyke CHAUCER. 3. S. flattery and she Are twin-born sisters B. JONS. 4. I ain't..s. at the gruelling of sick folks 1830. Hence **Slick** *adv.* smartly, easily, quickly, completely 1825.

Slick (slik), *v.* [OE. *-slician* (in *nigslicod*); cf. SLEEK *v.*] 1. *trans.* To render smooth or glossy; to polish; to smooth with a slicker. b. *transf.* To polish up, make elegant or fine ME. 2. To make (the skin, hair, etc.) sleek or glossy, esp. by some special treatment ME.

1. c. *intr.* with *up.* (U.S.) To make oneself or a place neat and tidy; also *fig.* 1841.

Slickens (sli·kens). *U.S.* 1882. [perh. f. *slick* (a. G. *schlich*) finely pounded ore.] The pulverized matter from a quartz-mill; the fine soil of a hydraulic mill.

Slickenside (sli·k'nsəid). Also **-sides.** 1768. [f. dial. *slicken*, var. of SLICK *a.* + SIDE *sb.*[1]] 1. *Min.* A specular variety of galena found in Derbyshire. 2. *Geol.* A polished (and occas. striated) surface on the wall of a mineral lode, or on a line of fracture in a rock-mass; a smooth glistening surface produced by pressure and friction 1822.

Slicker (sli·kəɹ). 1851. [f. SLICK *a.* or *v.*] 1. a. A tool used for scraping or smoothing leather. b. A tool used for smoothing the surfaces of moulds in founding 1875. 2. *U.S.* A waterproof coat 1884.

Slicking (sli·kiŋ), *vbl. sb.* 1495. [f. SLICK *v.*] 1. The action of making sleek or smooth. 2. *Mining.* In *pl.* Narrow veins of ore 1843.

Sli·ckstone. *dial.* ME. Also **sleek-.** [SLICK *v.*] A stone for smoothing.

'Slid, *int. Obs.* exc. *arch.* 1598. Abbrev. of *God's lid*, used as a petty oath or exclam.

Sli·dder, *sb. dial.* 1793. [Cf. SLIDDER *a.* and *v.*] A trench or hollow running down a slope; a steep slope.

†**Sli·dder,** *a.* [OE. *slidor*, f. *slid-*, wk. grade of *slīdan* SLIDE *v.*] 1. Slippery –1578. 2. Inclined to slip or fall (*rare*) –1500. 3. Of a smooth or slippery nature –1686. So **Sli·ddery** *a.* (now *dial.*) slippery, uncertain, unstable.

Slidder (sli·dəɹ), *v.* Now *dial.* [OE. *slid(e)rian*, frequent. f. *slīd-* (see prec.).] 1. *intr.* To slide, slip. 2. *trans.* To make slippery or smooth. late ME.

1. With that he dragg'd the trembling Sire, Slidd'ring through clotter'd Blood, and holy Mire DRYDEN.

Slide (sləid), *sb.* 1570. [f. SLIDE *v.*] I. 1. The act or fact of sliding; an instance of this; also, the manner in which a thing slides. b. *Mus.* A grace consisting of two notes diatonically ascending or descending to a principal note; also = PORTAMENTO 1818. 2. An earth-slip, a landslip, an avalanche; a place on a hill-side, etc., where this has happened 1664. 3. *Mining.* a. A fracture in a lode resulting in the dislocation or displacement of a portion of it; a vein of clay, etc., marking such dislocation 1778. b. Matter dislodged by an earth-slip 1841. 4. a. A kind of sledge 1685. b. A runner on which a gun is mounted 1830.

1. My third Lieutenant broke his leg by a s. on the deck 1726. 4. b. Their guns..were fixed on slides.. to enable them to be fired over the bows MARRYAT.

II. 1. A sliding part of some mechanism; a part of an instrument or machine designed to be pulled in and out; a device which slides or may be slid 1608. 2. A kind of tongueless buckle or ring used as a fastener, clasp, or brooch; a small perforated object sliding on a cord, etc. 1779. 3. a. A slip of glass, etc., on which an object is mounted or placed to facilitate its examination by a microscope 1837. b. A picture prepared for use in a magic lantern or stereoscope 1846. c. *Photogr.* A flat case or receptacle within which plates are placed for the purpose of being inserted in a camera. Freq. *dark s.* 1856. 4. *Rowing.* A sliding seat 1875.

III. 1. A smooth surface, esp. of ice, for sliding on, or formed by being slid on; a slippery place 1687. 2. a. An inclined plane for the transit of heavy goods, esp. timber. Chiefly *Amer.* 1832. b. *Amer.* A sloping channel constructed to facilitate the passage of logs down stream; a chute 1858. 3. A device of the nature of a bed, rail, groove, etc., on or in which a thing may slide 1846. 4. The track of an otter 1894.

Slide (sləid), *v.* Pa. t. **slid.** Pa. pple. **slid** (**slided, slidden**). [OE. *slīdan*, = early LG. *slīden.*] I. *intr.* 1. To pass from one place or point to another with a smooth and continuous movement, *esp.* through the air or water or along a surface. b. To move in this manner while standing more or less erect upon a surface, *esp.* that of ice ME. 2. Of streams, etc.: To glide, flow. Now *rare.* late ME. 3. Of reptiles, etc.: To glide, crawl. Now *rare.* ME. 4. To move, go; to proceed unperceived, quietly, or stealthily; to steal, creep, slink, or slip *away*, *into*, or *out of* a place, etc. late ME. b. *colloq.* To make off. orig. *U.S.* 1859.

1. Fishes which through the flood..did softly slyde And swim away SPENSER. b. I had been sliding in Christ-Church meadow JOHNSON. 2. Where Thames and Isis heire By lowly Æton slides 1633. 4. Slouching my hat, I slid out of doors 1760.

II. 1. To pass away, pass by, so as to disappear, be forgotten or neglected, etc. Now *rare.* ME. b. With *let* (or *allow*). In later use freq., to let (something) take its own course. late ME. c. Of time: To pass, slip *away*, go *by*, imperceptibly or without being profitably employed. late ME. 2. To pass easily or gradually *into* some condition, practice, etc. late ME. b. To pass by easy or gradual change or transformation into some other form or character 1500. 3. To move, pass, make way, etc., in an easy or unobtrusive manner. late ME. b. *Mus.* To pass from one note to another without any cessation of sound or distinction between the intervals 1864. c. Of the eye or sight: To pass quickly from one object to another 1756.

1. Alack, how good men, and the good turns they do us, s. out of memory LAMB. b. Therefore..let the world s. SHAKS. c. So sholdestow endure, and laten slyde The tyme CHAUCER. 2. When an honourable man..slides into some dishonourable action 1847. b. Parts answ'ring parts shall s. into a whole POPE. 3. So desirous..of sliding through life to the end of it unnoted 1748.

III. 1. To slip; to lose one's foothold ME. b. Of the foot: To slip ME. 2. *fig.* To lapse morally; to commit some fault; to err or go wrong OE.

1. So sure, they walk on ice, and never s. CHURCHILL. b. Thou hast enlarged my goinge vnder me, and myne ankles haue not slyded COVERDALE 2 *Sam.* xxii. 37. 2. I find myself a learner yet, Unskilful, weak, and apt to s. COWPER.

IV. *trans.* 1. To cause to move with a smooth, gliding motion; to push over a level surface 1537. 2. With *in* or *into*: To introduce quietly or dexterously; to slip (something) *into* one's hand, etc. 1627. 3. To move over, traverse, descend, etc., in a sliding manner 1621.

1. *fig.* Madly sliding his splendid army, like a weaver's shuttle from his right hand to his left KINGLAKE. 2. He was..to s. the Letter into her Hand, but let no Body see STEELE. Hence **Sli·dden** *ppl. a.* that has slipped or slid down.

Slide-, the vbl. stem or the sb. in combs. (sometimes not hyphened): a. With names of apparatus, implements, parts of machines, etc., characterized by a sliding action, as *s.-bar, -bolt, -car, -lathe*, etc. 1763. b. Denoting something along which objects may slide or be slid, as *s.-ladder, -way* 1793. c. Misc., as *s.-centerer*; *s.-movement, -principle*; etc. 1846.

†**Slide-groat.** 1552. [f. SLIDE *v.* + GROAT.] Shove-groat, shovelboard –1635.

Slider (sləi·dəɹ). 1530. [f. SLIDE *v.* + -ER[1].] 1. One who slides. b. *U.S.* The red-bellied terrapin 1883. 2. A beam or plank on which something heavy may be slid; also *dial.*, a sledge 1582. 3. A thing or part which slides or may be slid; *esp.* a sliding part or device in some mechanical apparatus 1681.

Sli·de-rest. Also **slide rest.** 1839. [f. SLIDE *v.*] An appliance for holding tools in turning, enabling the tools to be variously held in relation to the material worked on.

Sli·de-rule. 1663. [f. SLIDE *v.*] A sliding rule.

Sli·de-valve. Also **slide valve.** 1802. [f. SLIDE *v.*] A valve having a sliding plate for opening and closing an orifice; *spec.* one which does this alternately and regularly.

Sliding (sləi·diŋ), *vbl. sb.* ME. [f. SLIDE *v.*] 1. The action of SLIDE *v.* 2. *attrib.*, as *s.-place*; *s. contact, motion, principle* 1611.

Sliding (sləi·diŋ), *ppl. a.* OE. [f. SLIDE *v.*] I. 1. *fig.* That slides or slips away; transitory; unstable, inconstant; passing. 2. Slippery ME. 3. That moves by sliding or slipping; flowing, gliding, etc. late ME. b. Accompanied by a sliding movement 1796. 4. Of language or music: Flowing easily 1627.

1. The Seasons of the s. Year DRYDEN. 3. Safelye slips away the slyding shippe 1562. Seuerall s. rills B. JONS. b. Craigengelt..made a s. bow to the Marquis SCOTT.

II. In special uses. 1. Of a knot: Made so as to slip along a cord; running 1591. 2. Designating parts of apparatus or machinery which slide, or are characterized by some sliding device, as *s.-bar, -collar, -joint*, etc. 1778. b. Designating doors, lids, panels, etc., which are opened or shut by sliding 1715. 3. *Naut.*, etc. a. *S. keel*, an extra deep keel which slides vertically through the bottom of a vessel. Also *attrib.* 1797. b. *S. seat*, a seat in an outrigger which moves backwards and forwards with the action of the rower 1874. 4. *S. rule*, a mathematical gauging or measuring instrument consisting of two graduated parts, one of which slides upon the other, and so arranged that when brought into proper juxtaposition the required result may be obtained by inspection 1663. 5. *S. scale*: a. A sliding rule 1706. b. A scale or standard (of payments, etc.) which rises or falls in proportion to, or conversely to, the rise or fall of some other standard 1843.

'Slife (sləif), *int. Obs.* exc. *arch.* 1634. Abbrev. of *God's life*, used as a petty oath or exclam.

Slight, obs. f. SLEIGHT.

Slight (sləit), *sb.* 1549. [f. SLIGHT *a.* and *v.*] †1. A very small amount or weight; a trifle –1678. 2. Display of contemptuous indifference or disregard; small respect *for* one 1701. 3. An instance of slighting or being slighted 1719.

Slight (sləit), *a.* and *adv.* [ME. (orig. north.) *slight, sleght*, ad. OScand. **sleht-* (ON. *sléttr*).] A. *adj.* 1. Smooth, glossy, sleek. *Obs.* exc. *dial.* 2. Of a small and slender form or build. late ME. 3. Of light, thin, or poor texture or material; rather unsubstantial. late ME. b. Lacking in solid or substantial qualities 1585. †4. Of persons: Of little worth or account; mean, low; humble in position –1700. 5. Small in amount, quantity, degree, etc. 1530. b. Unimportant, trifling 1548. c. Wanting in fullness or heartiness 1660. **d.** Performed with little exertion 1667.

2. E'en the s. hare-bell raised its head SCOTT. 3. For which price, but very s. work hath been furnished 1663. b. A good but rather s. story 1886. 5. Sleighte feares make women shrike 1601. b. Are we furious upon every sleight occasion? 1656. d. He..in contempt, At one s. bound high overleap'd all bound Of Hill or highest Wall MILT.

B. *adv.* †1. Poorly; slightly; contemptuously –1716. 2. Slimly, slenderly 1667. †3. Slightly; to a small extent –1746.

1. Think not so s. of glory MILT. 2. A s. made people 1800. 3. Come nearer, part not hence so s. inform'd MILT. Hence **Sli·ghtness.**

Slight (slait), *v.* ME. [f. SLIGHT *a.* In sense 2 ad. Du. *slechten*, or G. *schlichten* to level.] †1. *trans.* To make smooth or level –1620. †2. To level with the ground –1698. 3. To treat with indifference or disrespect; to disregard, disdain, ignore 1597. †b. To throw contemptuously. SHAKS. †4. To gloss or pass *over* carelessly or with indifference –1824.

2. *fig.* Christ our Lord..slighted and dismantled that mighty Garrison 1676. 3. He delighted in the conversation of men of science,..but the men of letters he slighted EMERSON. †*To s. off*, to put *off* disdainfully. Hence **Slighted** *ppl. a.*, **Sli·ghter.**

†**'Slight**, *int.* 1598. Abbrev. of *God's light*, used as a petty oath or exclam. –1668.

†**Sli·ghten**, *v.* 1605. [f. SLIGHT *a.* or *v.*] = SLIGHT *v.* 3. –1646.

Sli·ghting, *ppl. a.* 1632. [f. SLIGHT *v.* + -ING 2.] 1. Conveying or implying a slight; of a contemptuous or disdainful character. 2. Acting contemptuously or disdainfully 1684. Hence **Sli·ghtingly** *adv.*

Slightly (slai·tli), *adv.* 1521. [f. SLIGHT *a.* + -LY 2.] In various senses corresp. to those of the adj.; unsubstantially; carelessly, lightly; †easily; †slightingly; to a slight degree (1592).

Slighty (slai·ti), *a.* *Obs.* exc. *dial.* 1619. [f. SLIGHT *a.* + -Y 1.] †1. Superficial –1671. †b. Of persons: Negligent, careless –1661. †2. Slighting; light –1674. 3. Slight, trivial; also, unsubstantial, slender, weak. Now *dial.* 1669.

†**Slik(e**, *a. north.* ME. [a. ON. *slík-r*, for earlier **swa-līkr* 'so like'; see SUCH *a.*] Such.

Slily, variant of SLYLY.

Slim (slim), *a.* 1657. [a. Du. or LG., = MHG. *slim, slimm-* (G. *schlimm*), OHG. **slimb* crooked, perverse, bad, mean, etc.] 1. Slender, (gracefully) thin. b. Small, slight; of little substance; poor 1677. c. Meagre, scanty, sparse 1852. 2. Of persons, their actions, etc.: Sly, cunning, crafty, wily, artful 1674.

1. A s. young Girl of..Seventeen STEELE. b. The chances of your getting this [letter] are s. 1862. c. A very s. audience, not more than a dozen 1852. 2. The issue of the proclamation by the Boers..is regarded..as a 'slim' (crafty) move on the enemy's part 1899. Hence **Slim** *v. trans.* to make s.; see also SLIMMING. **Sli·m·ly** *adv.*, **-ness.**

Slime (slaim), *sb.* [Com. Teut.; OE. *slīm*. The stem is prob. related to L. *limus*.] 1. Soft glutinous mud; alluvial ooze; viscous matter deposited or collected on stones, etc. b. Applied to bitumen 1530. 2. A viscous substance or fluid of animal or vegetable origin; mucus, semen, etc. ME. b. Applied to star-jelly (see JELLY *sb.* 2b.) 1471. 3. *fig.* Applied to the human body, mankind, etc., or anything disgusting or repulsive ME. 4. *Mining.* Finely crushed metallic ore in the form of mud 1758.

1. The teeming Tide..Makes green the Soil with S., and black prolific Sands DRYDEN. *fig.* Lerne, thou erth & slyme, to humble the 1504. b. COVERDALE *Gen.* xi. 3. *Comb.*: **s.-eel**, *Myxine glutinosa*, which resembles the lamprey.

Slime (slaim), *v.* 1628. [f. SLIME *sb.*] 1. *trans.* To smear or cover with slime. 2. a. To make (one's way) in a slimy fashion. b. *intr.* To crawl slimily; to become slimy. 1842.

Sli·me(-)pit. 1530. 1. In or after Biblical use: A pit or hole yielding asphalt or bitumen. 2. *techn.* A pit or reservoir in which metallic slimes are collected 1778.

Slimming (sli·miŋ), *gerund* and *vbl. sb.* [f. SLIM *a.*] The practice of using special means such as dieting and exercises to reduce one's figure; often *attrib.*

Slimsy (sli·mzi, -si), *a.* *U.S.* 1845. [app. f. SLIM *a.*] Flimsy, frail.

Slimy (slai·mi), *a.* late ME. [f. SLIME *sb.* + -Y 1.] 1. Of the nature or consistency of slime; viscous. b. *techn.* Of ore: In the form of slime 1778. 2. Characterized by the presence of slime; covered with slime. late ME. 3. *transf.* and *fig.* Morally defiled or objectionable; vile, disgusting 1575.

1. b. Moving the s. Tin to and fro with a light hand 1778. 2. A pit of standing water..greene, slimie, and stinking 1613. Yea, s. things did crawl with legs Upon the s. sea COLERIDGE. Hence **Sli·mily** *adv.* **Sli·miness.**

Sling (sliŋ), *sb.1* ME. [app. of LG. or Scand. origin.] An implement or weapon for hurling stones, etc. by hand with great force or to a distance, consisting of a strap attached to two cords or strings, or to a stick or staff; the impulse is given by rapid whirling of the sling before discharging it. Also locally, a boy's catapult. b. A ballista. Now *Hist.* 1535.

Dauid orthrewe hym sone with his stone and his slyng 1450. *fig.* The Slings and Arrowes of outragious Fortune SHAKS.

Comb.: **s.-stone**, a stone or pebble used as a missile to be cast by a s.

Sling (sliŋ), *sb.2* ME. [perh. ult. the same word as prec. Immediate source unkn.] 1. A device for securing or grasping bulky or heavy articles while being hoisted or lowered, usually a belt, rope, or chain formed into a loop and fitted with hooks and tackle; a loop of this kind by which heavy articles are lifted, carried, or suspended. 2. *Naut.* The middle part of a yard 1670. 3. A leather strap attached to a rifle, etc., enabling it to be carried slung over the shoulder, or on the arm 1711. b. A strap, band, wire, etc., forming a kind of loop by which something is suspended or hung 1771. c. A piece of cloth or other material, formed into a loop and suspended from the neck so as to support an injured limb 1720.

1. *Shot s.*, a sling for carrying heavy shot or shell 1876. 2. *Slings*, that part of a yard encircled by the s.-hoop, which suspends it from the mast, or by which it is hoisted and lowered 1846. 3. c. He came ..with his arm in a s. 1860.

Comb.: **s.-cart** *Mil.*, a two-wheeled cart to which a cannon is slung in order to be transported; **-dog**, an iron hook with an eye at one end, through which a rope may be passed; **-hoop**, a ring which suspends the yard from the mast and by which it is hoisted or lowered.

Sling (sliŋ), *sb.3* 1530. [f. SLING *v.1*] 1. The act of slinging, throwing, etc.; a cast, fling, or throw. 2. *slang.* A drink or draught; a 'pull' (*rare*) 1788.

†**Sling**, *sb.4* 1566. A serpentine or culverin –1736.

Sling (sliŋ), *sb.5* 1807. [Of obscure origin.] 1. An American drink composed of brandy, rum, etc., and water, sweetened and flavoured. (Cf. GIN-SLING.) 2. The juice of the sugar-cane, as obtained in the manufacture of sugar 1826.

Sling (sliŋ), *v.1* Pa. t. and pa. pple. **slung** (slʌŋ). ME. [prob. ad. ON. *slyngva*.] I. *trans.* 1. To strike, to bring or knock *down*, by means of a sling (*rare*). b. To throw or cast (stones, etc.) by means of a sling ME. c. *absol.* To cast or discharge missiles by means of a sling; to use a sling 1440. 2. To throw, cast, hurl, or fling (a person or thing) in some direction or to some point. Now chiefly *dial.* or *colloq.* ME. b. Of sheep: To cast (a lamb) 1750. c. *absol.* To strike or launch *out* in boxing 1812. 3. In colloq. or slang uses, e.g. to hand round, distribute, dispense; to use or relate to a person. late ME.

1. b. All these colde s. stones at an heere breadth, and not faile BIBLE (Geneva) *Judges* xx. 16. 2. Brass Pieces that slung their Shot an incredible way 1698. 3. *To s. ink*, to write articles, etc. *To s. one's hook*, to make off, clear out; to pick pockets.

II. *intr.* 1. To move with some force or speed; to fly as if thrown by a sling; to fling oneself ME. 2. To advance, walk, etc., with long or swinging strides. Chiefly *Sc.* or *north.* and *Austral.* 1808.

Sling (sliŋ), *v.2* 1522. [f. SLING *sb.2*] 1. *trans.* To place in, or secure with, a sling or slings for hoisting or lowering; to raise up or let down by means of a sling or slings. 2. *Naut.* To pass chains or lashings round (a sail or yard) to secure it to the mast 1626. 3. To hang or suspend, to fix or fasten (something) about the person in a sling or in a loose manner so as to be carried easily 1688. 4. To hang up or suspend, esp. from one point to another; to put up (a hammock) 1697.

1. The horses were slung down into the stalls 1833. 3. The lance is slung on the left arm 1833. 4. *To s. the monkey*, a game played by sailors.

Sling, *v.3* *U.S.* 1836. [f. SLING *sb.5* 1.] *intr.* To drink or take sling.

Sling-, stem of SLING *v.1*, used in combs., as **s.-shot** *U.S.*, a catapult; **-trot**, a loose swinging trot or pace.

Sli·nger. late ME. One who slings, *esp.* a soldier armed with a sling. Now *rare.*

Sli·ng(s)man. 1579. [SLING *sb.2*] = prec.

Slink (sliŋk), *sb.* 1607. [Related to SLINK *v.*] I. An abortive or premature calf or other animal. Chiefly *dial.* b. The skin or flesh of a premature calf or other animal 1741. II. 1. A sneaking, shirking, cowardly fellow; a skulk. *dial.* or *colloq.* 1824. 2. A slinking, sneaking, or stealthy pace or tread 1853.

2. Those who went forth with the dog's trot might return with the cat's s. 1896.

Slink (sliŋk), *a. dial.* 1673. [Cf. SLINK *sb.* and *v.*] Lank, lean, poor, ill-conditioned.

Slink (sliŋk), *v.* Pa. t. and pa. pple. **slunk** (slʌŋk); †**slank**; †**slinked.** [OE. *slincan* to creep, crawl (of reptiles), = LG. *slinken*, G. *schlinken*.] 1. *intr.* Of persons or animals: To move or walk in a quiet, stealthy, or sneaking manner. late ME. 2. *trans.* Of animals, esp. cows: To bring forth (young) prematurely or abortively 1640. (Cf. SLING *v.1* 2 b.)

1. The wily Fox..slinks behind And slily creeps thro' the same beaten Track 1735. There were some few who slank obliquely from them as they passed LANDOR. *fig.* Seeing the sun quietly s. behind a mass of black clouds 1806. *transf.* Lady Castlemayne, who he believes has lately slunk a great belly away PEPYS. **Sli·nky** *a.*, gracefully slender and flowing.

Slip (slip), *sb.1* [OE. *slipa, slype*, of unkn. origin.] †1. A soft semi-liquid mass. OE. only. 2. Curdled milk. Now *U.S.* late ME. 3. *techn.* A semi-liquid material, made of finely-ground clay or flint, etc., mixed with water to about the consistency of cream, and used for making, cementing, coating, or decorating pottery, etc.; also, clay suitable for making this 1640.

Comb.: **s.-cheese**, soft cheese made without pressing out the whey; **-coat**, a soft cream cheese; chiefly in *s.-coat cheese.*

Slip (slip), *sb.2* 1440. [app. a. MDu. or MLG. *slippe* cut, strip, lappet, skirt.] I. 1. A twig, sprig, or small shoot taken from a plant, tree, etc., for the purpose of grafting or planting; a scion, cutting 1495. b. A scion or descendant 1588. 2. A young person of either sex, esp. one of small or slender build 1582. b. A thin or slender person 1703. 3. A sole of intermediate size 1881.

1. The Lab'rer cuts Young Slips, and in the Soil securely puts DRYDEN. b. He talk'd of bastard slips, and cursed his bed CRABBE. 2. Shusey Dogherty was a good-looking s. 1841. There was his wife, and the s. of a girl 1861. b. My Lady Shapely has by that thin S. eight Children STEELE.

II. †1. The edge, skirt, or flap of a robe or garment –1648. 2. A spoon-handle having the top cut off obliquely; a spoon with a handle or stem of this form. Now *Hist.* 1530. 3. A long and relatively thin and narrow piece or strip of some material 1555. 4. A strip, a narrow piece or stretch, *of* land, ground, etc. 1591. 5. An example or specimen *of* something having an elongated or slender form 1730. 6. A window, apartment, passage, etc., of an elongated form 1730. b. *U.S.* A narrow, doorless church-pew 1828. c. *pl.* The sides of the gallery in a theatre 1805. 7. A (narrow) piece of paper or parchment 1687. †b. A newspaper (or part of one) printed in the form of a long slip of paper –1727. c. *Typog.* A proof pulled on a long slip of paper, for revision before the type is made up into pages 1818. 8. A certain quantity *of* yarn, etc. Now *dial.* 1647.

5. A neat sanded s. of a coffee-room 1825.

Slip (slip), *sb.3* 1467. [f. (or related to) SLIP *v.1*] I. 1. An artificial slope of stone, etc., built or made beside a navigable water to serve as a landing-place. b. *Shipbuilding.* An inclined plane, sloping gradually down to the water, on which ships or other vessels are built or repaired 1769. c. A contrivance (patented in 1818) for hauling vessels out of the water in order to repair them 1830. **2.** *local.* A narrow roadway or passage 1739.

1. b. The largest of the available building slips is being prepared for the reception of the new vessel 1894.

II. 1. A leash for a dog, etc., so contrived that the animal can readily be released; esp. one used for a couple of greyhounds in coursing, by which they can be let go simultaneously 1578. **b.** *Bookbinding.* A cord used in fastening the back of a book 1875. **2. a.** A child's pinafore or frock (cf. *gym-slip*) 1690. **b.** An article of women's attire, formerly an outer garment, now worn under a gown of lace or other thin material. Also *transf.*, an infant's garment of this nature. 1761. **c.** A pillow-case 1800. **d.** *Upholstery.* A slot-hem in which a wire or the like may be inserted 1891. **3.** *pl.* The sidings of a theatrical stage, from which the scenery is slipped on, and where the actors stand before entering 1812. **4.** A cylindrical iron case, in which wood for making gunpowder is charred 1876.

2. e. *pl.* In full *bathing slips*: bathing-drawers.

III. 1. *To give* (a person) *the s.*: To evade or escape from (him); to elude, steal off, or slip away from unperceived 1567. **†b.** With punning allusion to SLIP *sb.*⁴ –1613. **†c.** An act of evading or escaping (*rare*) –1669. **2.** An act of slipping, sliding, or falling down 1596. **b.** *Naut.* The difference between the pitch of a propelling screw, and the actual advance of the vessel which it drives 1844. **3.** An error in conduct, procedure, argument, etc. 1579. **b.** A slight unintentional error or blunder in writing, speaking, etc. 1620. **4. a.** *Geol.* A slight fault or dislocation caused by the sinking of one section of the strata 1789. **b.** = LANDSLIP 1838. **5.** *Cricket.* A fielder who stands to the right of the wicket-keeper at a short distance behind the wicket; called esp. *short* or *first s.* to distinguish him from *long* or *second s.* 1833. **b.** The ground or position occupied or guarded by these players 1833.

1. b. You have given me a ninepence here, and I'll give you the s. for 't 1613. 2. By..some S. of my Foot..I fell down DE FOE. *Prov.* There 's many a s. between the cup and the lip. c. The loss of distance travelled by aircraft arising from the nature of the medium in which its propeller revolves 1897. d. *Electr.* The ratio of the difference between the operating and synchronous speed of an induction motor. 3. b. Phr. *A s. of the tongue, pen*, etc.

†Slip, *sb.*⁴ 1592. [perh. a special use of prec.] A counterfeit coin –1634.

Phr. *To nail up for a s.*, with reference to the exposure of spurious coin.

Slip (slip), *v.*¹ ME. [prob. ad. MLG. *slippen*. The stem *slip-* appears in OE. in the adj. *slipor*; see SLIPPER *a.*] **Intr. senses.* **I. 1.** To escape, get away, make off (*rare*). **2.** To pass or go lightly or quietly; to move quickly and softly, without attracting notice; to glide or steal. Used with various advs. and preps. late ME. **3. a.** To enter gradually or inadvertently *into* a theme, digression, opinion, etc. 1641. **b.** To pass *into* a certain state 1864. **4.** To pass *out of*, escape *from*, the mind, memory, etc. Also without const. ME. **5.** To break or escape *from* a person, the tongue, lips, etc. late ME. **b.** To leak *out* 1848. **6.** Of time: To go by quickly or imperceptibly; to pass unmarked; to run. Chiefly with advs., as *along, away, by.* 1564. **7. a.** To pass *over* (a subject or matter) without adequate attention or notice; to neglect, overlook 1577. **b.** To progress or travel *across, down, over*, a stretch of ground, etc., quickly 1864.

2. When slipping from thy Mothers eye thou went'st Alone into the Temple MILT. If the voters are apathetic and let a bad man s. in BRYCE. *fig.* Her memory..Went slipping back upon the golden days TENNYSON. 4. The experiments..were quite slipt out of my memory 1676. 5. The reply..slipp'd..glibly from my Tongue 1773. 6. As time was slipping by, ..he felt that he must act DICKENS.

II. 1. Of the foot: To slide; to lose its hold ME. **b.** = SLIDE *v.* III. 1. 1530. **c.** To fall into mistake, fault, or error; to err, †to sin. Also with *into* (error, etc.). ME. **d.** *U.S.* With *up*: To fail; to make a mistake 1856. **2.** To move out of place with an easy sliding motion; to fail to hold or stick; to slide. late ME. **b.** To enter or fall *into* by slipping or losing hold 1679. **3.** To glide or pass easily *out of* (or *from*) *one's hand* or *grasp, through* (or *between*) *one's fingers*, etc., so as to escape or be lost. late ME. **4.** To allow oneself to drop or fall with an easy, gliding motion; to slide *down* 1470. **b.** *fig.* (*colloq.*) usu. in *pres. pple.* To be failing in strength, etc.; to 'go downhill'. **5.** Of rivers, etc.: To run smoothly or gently; to flow, glide; to pass *into* the sea 1570. **6. a.** To get *out of* or *into* a garment, etc., in an easy or hurried manner 1500. **b.** To slide *in* or *into* a socket, etc. 1815. **7.** To move easily and smoothly 1680. **b.** To admit of being taken *off*, or put *on*, by a slipping process 1669. **c.** Of bark: To peel off 1788.

1. Better the foot s. then the tongue trip 1611. c. Great Masters..s. sometimes unawares 1638. 2. My axe slipped out of my hand, and slid..away from me TYNDALL. *To s. off the hooks*: see HOOK *sb.* 3. Hold her fast, She'll s. thorow your fingers like an Eel else 1622. 4. *To s. by the board*, to slip down by the ship's side 1867. 5. Where the grown-up river slips Into the sea STEVENSON. 6. a. He 's slipping into a clean shirt 1893. 7. b. I am grown somewhat fatter,..and my leathern coat slips not on so soon as it was wont SCOTT.

*** Trans. senses.* **III. 1.** To cause to move with a sliding motion; to draw or pull in this manner 1513. **2. a.** To strip or take off (a garment, etc.); to cast (the skin, etc.). Occas. with advs., as *down, off.* 1535. **b.** To put *on* (an article of apparel) hastily or carelessly 1590. **3.** To withdraw (one's head or neck) *out of* or *from* a collar, etc. 1583. **4.** To insert or introduce gently or surreptitiously. Const. *in, into.* 1688. **b.** *Cards.* To palm (a card) 1807. **c.** To give quietly or slyly 1841. **5.** To cause to slip or lose hold; *esp.* to undo (a knot) in this way 1606. **b.** To dislocate (a joint) 1727. **c.** To suffer an accidental slipping or sliding of (one's foot) 1769.

1. A Cinnamon-Tree..bears none but its Bark, which Slips itself off every Year 1707. 2. a. The snake slips off his skinne DEKKER. b. S. on your slippers and trip down the stairs 1660. 3. *Rich. III*, IV. iv. 112. 4. He had tried to s. a powder into her drink 1713. 5. The bonds of heauen are slipt, dissolu'd, and loos'd SHAKS. b. My horse, I fear, has slipped his shoulder 1842. c. He slipped his foot and fell 1874.

IV. 1. †a. To waste or lose (time) –1687. **b.** To allow (an occasion, opportunity, etc.) to slip or pass by; to neglect or fail to take advantage of 1592. **†c.** To fail in keeping (a prescribed time) –1707. **2.** To pass over, omit in speaking; to avoid mention or consideration of 1605. **b.** To neglect; to omit or fail to prosecute, perform, etc.; to skip, to miss 1592.

1. b. S. not thine oportunity MARLOWE. c. *Macb.* II. iii. 52. 2. I do slippe No action of my life, thus, but I quote it JONSON. b. To s. a lecture or so 1871.

V. 1. To elude or evade, esp. in a stealthy manner; to escape from; to give the slip to 1513. **b.** To get in front of; to outdistance 1856. **2.** To disengage oneself or get loose from (a collar, halter, etc.) 1579. **3.** To escape from (one's memory); to elude (one's notice, knowledge, etc.) 1652. **4.** To pass or escape inadvertently from (the pen, tongue, etc.) 1751.

1. He sees me; 'tis too late to s. him 1702. 2. Rascality has slipped its muzzle CARLYLE. 3. Reasons.. which have slipt my memory 1652.

VI. 1. To allow to escape (from one's hand, etc.); to loosen one's hold or grasp of, let go 1586. **b.** To allow to occur; to utter inadvertently. Also with *out.* 1591. **†c.** *To s. one's breath* or *wind*, to expire, die. *colloq.* or *dial.* 1819. **d.** *Knitting.* To pass (a stitch) from one needle to the other without knitting it 1880. **e.** To detach (the end carriage or coach) from an express or non-stopping train while running, in order to allow passengers to get out at a certain station 1866. **2.** To release (a greyhound, etc., or a hawk) from a leash or slip 1596. **3.** *Naut.* To allow (an anchor-cable, etc.) to run out, freq. with a buoy attached, when quitting an anchorage in haste; to drop or disengage (an anchor) in this way. Also *absol.* 1681. **b.** *To s. one's cable*, to die 1751. **4.** Of animals: To miscarry with; to drop prematurely 1665.

1. b. They..mortified us..by slipping out an oath GOLDSM. 2. When they grow ripe for marriage They must be slipt like Hawkes 1625. 3. *absol.* Vessels are obliged to s. and run for their lives on the first sign of a gale 1840. 4. The cheese may swell, or the cows may s. their calf GEO. ELIOT.

Slip (slip), *v.*² 1498. [a. MFlem. or MLG. *slippen* to cut, incise, cleave, etc.] **†1.** *trans.* To cut (a spoon-handle) obliquely at the end –1549. **2.** To part (a slip or cutting) from a stock, stalk, or branch, esp. for propagation; to divide (a plant, root, etc.) *into* slips 1530.

1. ij spones of sylver slipped at the endes 1538. 2. *absol.* I would I were a Gardiner, and had skill To digge and rake, and plant, and sowe, and slippe 1614.

Slip-, the stem of SLIP *v.*¹ in comb., as **s.-buoy,** a buoy attached to a cable when slipping an anchor; **-carriage, -coach,** a railway carriage detached at a station from a moving train; **-noose,** a noose which tightens and slackens by means of a slip-knot; **-rail** *Austral.* a fence-rail, forming one of a set which can be slipped out so as to leave an opening; chiefly *pl.*; **-stitch,** one slipped over the following stitch without being knitted. **2.** In comb. with advs., as **s.-on,** something that may be slipped on readily, *esp.* a great-coat or overall; so **-over.**

Slipe (sləip), *sb. Sc.* and *north.* 1470. [app. a. LG. *slîpe*, related to LG. *slîpen* to whet, and *slêpen* to drag.] A sledge or drag. **b.** *Mining. pl.* Sledge-runners, upon which a skip is dragged from the working breast to the tramway 1860.

Slip-knot (sli·pˌnǫt). Also **slip knot.** 1659. [f. SLIP *v.*¹] **a.** A knot which may readily be slipped or untied. **b.** A knot so constructed as to slip along the cord or line round which it is made; a running knot; also, a noose.

Slippage (sli·pėdʒ). 1850. [f. SLIP *v.*¹ + -AGE.] **a.** The act of slipping or subsiding. **b.** Amount or extent of slip.

Slipped (slipt), *ppl. a.* 1610. [SLIP *v.*²] *Her.* Represented as torn from the stem.

Slipper (sli·pəɹ), *sb.* 1478. [f. SLIP *v.*¹ + -ER¹.] **I. 1.** A light and sometimes heelless covering for the foot, capable of being easily slipped on, and worn chiefly indoors. **b.** *transf.* The lip or labellum of an orchid 1902. **2. a.** A form of skid used to retard the speed of a vehicle in descending a hill 1827. **b.** A device for conveying electricity from a conductor rail to a tram or train 1900. **II.** *Coursing.* The person appointed to slip the hounds at the proper moment 1825.

I. 1. If 'twere a kybe 'Twould put me to my s. SHAKS. A s. of his of red velvet, with a very low heel 1756. *Hunt the s.*: see HUNT *v.* *Comb.*: **s. animalcule,** a common infusorian of the genus *Paramecium*; **-bath,** a partially covered bath shaped somewhat like a s.; **s.-brake, -drag,** = sense I. 2 a; **s. limpet,** a limpet of the family *Acmæidæ*; **s. shell,** a shell of the genus *Crepidula*; **slipperwort,** the calceolaria or campanula.

Slipper (sli·pəɹ), *a. Obs.* exc. *dial.* [OE. *slipor*, related to SLIP *v.*] = SLIPPERY *a.*

As on a s. grounde, oft man doth fall or slide 1510. A s., and subtle knaue, a finder of occasion SHAKS.

Slippered (sli·pəɹd), *ppl. a.* 1600. [f. SLIPPER *sb.*] **1.** Wearing or shod with slippers. **2.** Characterized by the wearing of slippers 1817. **3.** Retarded by means of a slipper-brake 1905.

1. The leane and slipper'd Pantaloone SHAKS. 2. He leaned back..enjoying s. ease 1856.

Slippery (sli·pəri), *a.* 1535. [Alteration of SLIPPER *a.*, perh. after LG. *slipperig.*] **1.** Having a smooth, polished, or slimy surface, which renders foothold insecure. **2.** Of a soft oily or greasy consistency; having a smooth surface, so as to slip or slide easily; slipping readily from any hold or grasp 1551. **b.** Of persons: Difficult to catch or hold 1573. **3.** Of conditions, affairs, etc.: Unstable, uncertain, insecure; that cannot be relied upon as lasting or assured 1548. **4.** Of persons: Not to be depended on; shifty, deceitful 1555. **b.** Of actions, etc.: Characterized by shiftiness, deceitfulness, or want of sincerity 1579. **5.** Licentious, unchaste; of doubtful morality. *Obs.* or *arch.* 1586. **6.** Liable or prone to slip; readily giving way. Also of the memory, forgetful. 1548.

1. The rocks were steep and s. 1871. 2. The chiefest that is marked in the Ele is that it is slipperie 1567. *S. elm*, the N. Amer. red elm, *Ulmus fulva*, or the inner bark of this, used medicinally; also, a Californian shrub, *Fremontia Californica*, with similar bark. b. The slipp'ry God will try to loose his hold DRYDEN. 3. O slipp'ry State Of Human pleasures 1704. 4. The s. politicians in the capital FROUDE. b. He exercised a s. perseverance and a vindictive resolution THACKERAY. 5. He shall cause hir..to become slipperie & lascivious 1586. Hence **Sli·pperily** *adv.* **Sli·pperiness.**

Slippy (sli·pi), *a.* 1548. *dial.* or *colloq.* [f. SLIP *v.*¹ + -Y¹.] **1.** = SLIPPERY *a.*, in various senses. **2.** Of persons: Nimble, spry; sharp, quick; *esp.* in phr. *to be* or *look s.* 1847. Hence **Sli·ppiness.**

Slipshod (sli·pʃǫd), *a.* 1580. [f. SLIP *v.*[1] + SHOD *ppl. a.*, after SLIP-SHOE.] **1.** Wearing slippers or very loose shoes, in later use esp. such as are down at the heel. **b.** Of shoes: Loose or untidy; in bad condition; down at the heel 1687. **c.** In shabby condition 1818. **2.** *fig.* Slovenly, careless 1815.

1. With each foot in a cod's decapitated head and looking very slip-shod 1851. b. Old slip-shod shoes SCOTT. c. Half-bound and slip-shod volumes SCOTT. 2. She reigned supreme in a slip-shod household 1880.

Sli·p-shoe. *Obs.* exc. *dial.* 1555. [f. SLIP *v.*[1] + SHOE *sb.*] A light or loose shoe; a slipper.

Slip-slop (sli·pˌslǫp), *sb.* 1675. [f. SLOP *sb.*[2], with variation of vowel. In sense 2 with allusion to Mrs. Slipslop's blunders in *Joseph Andrews* (1742).] **1.** A sloppy compound used as a food, beverage, or medicine. **†2.** A blunder in the use of words, esp. the ludicrous misuse of one word for another; the habit of making such blunders –1837. **3.** Twaddle; loose or trifling talk or writing 1811.

2. One of the party (amongst other slipslops) saying instead of *Pasticcios*, he liked *Pistachios* 1826. Hence **Sli·p-slop** *a.* given to the use of slip-slops; of the nature of s. **Sli·p-slop** *v. intr.* to make blunders in the use of words; also, to move about in a sloppy manner or with a flapping sound.

Sli·p-string. Now *dial.* 1546. [f. SLIP *v.*[1] + STRING *sb.*] One who deserves to be hanged; a rogue or rascal, a shifty person.

Slip-way (sli·pweɪ). Also **slipway.** 1840. [f. SLIP- + WAY *sb.*] A sloping way leading down to the water; a slip.

Slit (slit), *sb.* ME. [f. SLIT *v.*] **1.** A straight and narrow cut or incision; an aperture resembling a cut of this description. **b.** A long narrow aperture in a wall; a window of this form 1607. **2.** *Coal-mining.* A short heading which connects two other headings 1860.

1. c. *spec.* A narrow opening in an optical instrument through which the light is admitted 1832.

attrib. and *Comb.*: **s.-eyed** *a.*, having long and narrow eyes; **-planting, -setting,** a mode of planting in which mere slits are made in the ground; **-pocket,** a side-pocket made with a vertical opening.

Slit (slit), *v.* Pa. t. and pa. pple. **slit.** [ME. *slitte* wk. vb., obscurely related to OE. *slītan.*] **1.** *trans.* To cut into, or cut open, by means of a sharp instrument or weapon; to divide or sever by making a long straight cut or fissure; also, to take *off* or *out* in this way. **b.** *fig.* To divide, separate, sever ME. **2.** *techn.* To cut (iron) into rods or (wood) into thin deals 1522.

1. Ile s. the villaines nose that would haue sent me to the Iaile SHAKS. b. Comes the blind Fury with th' abhorred shears, And slits the thin spun life MILT. Hence **Sli·tter,** one who or that which slits; *spec.* as the name of various instruments.

Slit, *ppl. a.* late ME. [f. prec.] **1.** Of garments: Rent, torn; slashed. **2.** Naturally divided or cloven 1607. **3.** Cut with a sharp instrument; divided by slitting 1611.

Slither (sli·ðəɹ), *v.* ME. [Later var. of SLIDDER *v.*; cf. *gather, hither,* etc.] **1.** *intr.* To slip, slide, glide, esp. on a loose or broken slope or with a clattering noise. **b.** *trans.* To make or cause to slide 1892. **2.** *intr.* To walk in a sliding manner; to slip along or away 1848. **3.** Of reptiles: To creep, crawl, glide 1839. Hence **Sli·ther** *sb.* a slipping or sliding.

Sli·tless, *a.* 1881. [f. SLIT *sb.*] Of a spectroscope: Made without the usual slit for admitting light.

Slitting (sli·tiŋ), *vbl. sb.* ME. [f. SLIT *v.* + -ING[1].] The action of making a slit or slits, or of cutting in this manner.

Comb.: **s.-mill** *Metall.*, a mill or machine by which iron bars or plates are slit into nail-rods, etc.; also, a saw-mill for slitting deals.

Slive (sləiv), *v.*[1] Now *dial.* [OE. **slīfan*, occurring in pa. t. *tó-slāf*; not represented in cogn. langs.] **1.** *trans.* To cleave, split, divide ME. **2.** To remove, to take *off*, by cutting or slicing. late ME. Hence **Slive** *sb.* a slice (now *dial.*).

Slive (sləiv), *v.*[2] Now *dial.* late ME. [app. var. of obs. *sleve* vb. (OE. *slēfan*).] **1.** *trans.* To cause to slip *down, over,* etc.; to slip *on* (a garment). **b.** To convey furtively or quietly 1821. **2.** *intr.* To slide; to slip 1440. **b.** To slip *off* or away; to sneak or hang about; to loiter, idle 1707.

Sliver (sli·vəɹ, sləi·vəɹ), *sb.* late ME. [f. SLIVE *v.*[1]] **1.** A piece cut or split off; a splinter, shiver, slice. **b.** *U.S.* The side of a small fish sliced off in one piece for use as bait 1880. **2.** A continuous ribbon or band of loose, untwisted, parallelized fibres of wool, cotton, flax, etc., ready for drawing, roving, or slubbing 1703. **3.** A slashing cut or stroke 1806.

1. An enuious sliuer broke, When downe the weedy Trophies, and her selfe, Fell in the weeping Brooke SHAKS.

Sliver (sli·vəɹ, sləi·vəɹ), *v.* 1605. [f. SLIVER *sb.*] **1.** *trans.* To separate or remove as a sliver; to cut, split, or tear into slivers. **b.** *intr.* To split, or split off 1880. **2.** *trans.* To convert (textile fibres) into slivers 1796.

1. Slippes of Yew, Sliuer'd in the Moones Ecclipse SHAKS.

Slob (slǫb), *sb.* 1780. [Mainly a. Irish *slab* (slǫb), mud, SLAB *sb.*[2] Chiefly with reference to Ireland.] **1.** Mud, esp. soft mud on the sea-shore; ooze; muddy land. **b.** A stretch of mud or ooze 1842. *Comb.*: **s.-land,** muddy ground; *esp.* alluvial land reclaimed from water. **2.** A large soft worm, used in angling 1815. **3.** A dull, slow, untidy person; a careless workman 1861.

Slobber (slǫ·bəɹ), *sb.* late ME. [Related to next. Cf. SLABBER *sb.*[1]] **1.** Mud or slime; slush, sleety rain; a sloppy mess or mixture. **2.** Slaver, slabber. Also *pl.*, a disease in rabbits marked by excessive salivation. 1755. **3.** A jelly-fish 1863.

Slobber (slǫ·bəɹ), *v.* late ME. [Related to SLABBER *v.*] **1.** *intr.* **a.** To feed in a slabbering manner. Now *dial.* **b.** To slaver 1733. **2.** *trans.* To wet in a dirty or disagreeable manner; to beslaver, befoul 1709. **3.** To utter thickly and indistinctly 1860. **4.** To execute carelessly or in a slovenly way. Usu. with *over.* 1694. Hence **Slo·bberer.**

Slo·bber-chops. 1667. [f. prec.] One who slobbers in eating, etc.

Slobbery (slǫ·bəri), *a.* late ME. [f. SLOBBER *sb.* or *v.*] **1.** Characterized by slobber or slobbering; disagreeably wet, slimy, or dirty. **2.** Slovenly, careless 1858.

1. I will sell my Dukedome, To buy a slobbery and a durtie Farme SHAKS.

Slock (slǫk), *v.* Chiefly *Sc.* ME. [f. ON. *slokinn* pa. pple., extinguished; the stem is related to that of SLACK *a.*] *trans.* To extinguish, quench (fire, thirst, etc.). **†b.** To slake (lime) –1655. So **Slo·cken** *v.* [a. ON. *slokna.*] *north.* and *Sc.*

Sloe (slōᵘ). [OE. *slā(h)*, *slāg*, perh. related to OSlav. and Russ. *sliva*, Lith. *slywas* plum.] **1.** The fruit of the blackthorn (*Prunus spinosa*), a small ovate or globose drupe of a black or dark-purple colour and sharp sour taste. **2.** The blackthorn, *Prunus spinosa* 1753.

Comb.: **s.-thorn, -tree,** the blackthorn.

Slog (slǫg), *sb. colloq.* 1888. [f. the vb.] **1.** Hard, steady work; a spell of this. **2.** A vigorous blow; a hard hit at cricket 1895.

Slog (slǫg), *v. colloq.* 1824. [Origin unkn.] **1.** *trans.* To hit or strike hard; to drive with blows; *fig.* to assail violently. **b.** *intr. Cricket* and *Boxing.* To hit hard and wildly 1880. **2.** To walk heavily or doggedly 1872. **3.** To deal heavy blows, to work hard (*at* something), to labour *away*, etc. 1888.

2. We 'slogged' on..for a mile or more 1907.

Slogan (slōᵘ·găn). 1513. [ad. Gael. *sluagh-ghairm*, f. *sluagh* host + *gairm* cry, shout.] A Highland or native Irish war-cry or battle-cry. **b.** *transf.* The distinctive note, phrase, cry, etc. of any person or body of persons 1704.

The Name of Hume have for their Slughorn (or S., as our Southern Shires terme it) a *Hume, a Hume* 1689. b. 'Duty, God, immortality',—the very s. of the pulpit 1880. c. Also in extended use.

Slogger (slǫ·gəɹ), *sb. colloq.* 1857. [f. SLOG *v.* + -ER[1].] One who slogs or delivers heavy blows. Also *fig.* an indefatigable worker.

Sloom (slūm), *sb. n. dial.* and *Sc.* [OE. *slūma.*] A gentle sleep or slumber; a light doze. So **Sloom** *v. intr.*

Sloo·my, *a. dial.* 1641. [Of Scand. origin.] **1. a.** Of grain: Not properly filled. **b.** Of corn, etc.: Laid through being soft and heavy; beginning to rot 1825. **2.** Sluggish, dull, spiritless. Also as *adv.* 1820.

Sloop (slūp). 1629. [ad. Du. *sloep*, possibly a. F. *chaloupe* or Sp. *chalupa.*] **1.** A small, one-masted, fore-and-aft rigged vessel, differing from a cutter in having a jib-stay and standing bowsprit. **b.** A relatively small ship-of-war, carrying guns on the upper deck only. Also *s.-of-war.* 1676. **†2.** A long-boat –1719.

Slop (slǫp), *sb.*[1] late ME. [Origin obsc.] **1.** An outer garment, as a loose jacket, tunic, cassock, mantle, gown, or smock-frock. **2.** *pl.* Wide baggy breeches or hose; loose trousers, esp. those worn by sailors. Now chiefly *dial.* 1481. **†b.** *sing.* in the same sense, or denoting only one leg of the garment –1652. **3.** *pl.* Ready-made clothing and other furnishings supplied to seamen from the ship's stores; hence, ready-made, cheap, or inferior garments generally 1663.

2. He would give an occasional hitch, Sailor-like, to his 'slops' 1842. b. Signior Romeo, *Bon iour*, there's a French salutation to your French s. SHAKS.

Comb: **s.-builder,** a jerry-builder; **s.-built** *a.*, jerry-built, *fig.* loosely built or made.

Slop (slǫp), *sb.*[2] late ME. [prob. repr. OE. **sloppe*, related to *slyppe* SLIP *sb.*[1], and *slūpan* to slip.] **†1.** A muddy place; a mud-hole. late ME. only. **b.** Slush 1796. **2.** An act of spilling or splashing; a quantity of liquid spilled or splashed 1727. **3.** Liquid or semi-liquid food of a weak, unappetizing kind; applied contemptuously to invalids' spoon-food, tea, etc. Now. usu. *pl.* 1657. **b.** *fig.* Weak or sickly sentiment 1924. **4.** Refuse liquid of any kind; rinsings of tea, coffee, etc.; the dirty water, etc., of a household. Usu. *pl.* 1815.

Comb.: **s.-basin,** a basin for holding slops; **-moulding,** a process in which the mould is dipped into water before it receives the clay.

Slop (slǫp), *sb.*[3] 1859. [For *ecilop*, back-slang for *police.*] A policeman.

Slop (slǫp), *v.* 1557. [f. SLOP *sb.*[2]] **1.** *trans.* To spill or splash (liquid); to dash or lay *on* carelessly. Also with *over.* **2.** To gobble *up.* Now *dial.* 1575. **3.** To make wet with spilled liquid 1721. **4.** To walk or travel *through* a place in mud or slush. Also with *along* or *on.* 1834. **5.** To run or flow *over*; to flow or dash *up* 1853. **b.** *fig.* With *over.* To overflow with expressions of weak sentiment, speak or act without restraint, gush (orig. *U.S.*) 1859.

Slope (slōᵘp), *sb.*[1] 1611. [Aphetic f. ASLOPE *adv.*] **1.** A stretch of rising or falling ground; a portion of the earth's surface marked by a gradual ascent or descent, whether natural or artificial 1626. **b.** An inclined surface of the nature of a bank, *esp.* one artificially constructed, as in fortification or engineering 1702. **c.** *Mining.* An inclined roadway 1874. **2.** Upward or downward inclination; deviation from the horizontal or perpendicular 1611. **b.** *Mil.* A position against the shoulder between perpendicular and horizontal (in the case of the rifle, with the hand under the butt) 1868. **3.** A slant; an inclined surface of any kind 1707.

1. A s. of country..very well wooded 1799. 3. b. *Bacteriol.* = SLANT *sb.*[1] 1 f. 1925. c. *Wireless.* Mutual conductance 1918. Hence **Slo·py** *a.* sloping.

Slope (slōᵘp), *sb.*[2] *colloq.* 1859. [f. SLOPE *v.*[2]] An act of making off, running, or slinking away, etc.

Slope (slōᵘp), *a.* Now *poet.* 1502. [f. as SLOPE *sb.*[1]] Sloping, slanting.

There the Water Rowleth, and Moveth,..with a Sloper Rise, and Fall BACON. Hence **†Slo·peness,** the condition of having a s.: sloping form or position. –1624. **Slo·peways** *adv.* in a sloping manner or position; so **Slo·pewise** *adv.*

Slope (slōᵘp), *v.*[1] 1591. [f. prec.] **1.** *intr.* To take, to move or proceed in, an oblique direction. **2.** To assume, to have or be in, a sloping or slanting position or direction 1707. **3.** *trans.* To bring into, to place or put in, a sloping or slanting position; to bend down; to direct downwards or obliquely 1605. **b.** *spec.* To bring (a weapon) into, or hold (it) in, a sloping position; now, to carry (a rifle) at the slope 1625. **4.** To cut, form, or make with a slope or slant 1611.

1. The sun was sloping down the sky COLERIDGE.

2. The corner where the mountain slopes down to the river 1877. 3. Though Pallaces and Pyramids do s. Their heads to their Foundations SHAKS.

Slope (slōᵘp), *v.*[2] *colloq.* 1839. [orig. U.S.; cf. SLOPE *v.*[1] I.] 1. *intr.* To make off, depart, decamp. b. To go loiteringly or saunteringly 1851. 2. *trans.* To leave (lodgings) without paying 1908.

1. If it is dull, they s. off 1861.

Slope (slōᵘp), *adv.* 1470. [Aphetic f. ASLOPE *adv.*] In a sloping or slanting manner or position. (In later use only *poet.*)

Hyperion..Came s. upon the threshold of the west KEATS.

Slope- in combs., repr. SLOPE *v.*[1] or *sb.*[1], with sbs., as *slope-desk*, *s. line*, and in parasynthetic compounds, as *slope-roofed* adj.

Sloping (slōᵘ·piŋ), *ppl. a.* 1610. [f. SLOPE *v.*[1]] That slopes.

With sloping masts and dipping prow..The ship drove fast COLERIDGE. Hence **Slo·ping-ly** *adv.*

Sloppy (slǫ·pi), *a.* 1727. [f. SLOP *sb.*[2] + -Y[1].] 1. Of ground, etc.: Very wet and splashy; covered with water or thin mud. 2. Of a semi-liquid consistency; watery and disagreeable 1794. 3. Splashed or soiled with liquid; wet from slopping; covered with slops; messy 1838. 4. Weak, feeble; lacking in firmness or precision; slovenly; feebly sentimental 1825. 5. Of dress: Loose, slack, ill-fitting 1825.

1. A wet, s., windy, October day 1890. 2. The rain began to fall, the ice to get s. 1846. 3. Idlers, playing cards or dominoes on the s., beery tables 1848. Hence **Slo·ppily** *adv.* **Slo·ppiness.**

Slo·p-seller. 1665. [SLOP *sb.*[1]] A dealer in slop-clothing.

The slop-sellers, and other sharks, at this port 1804.

Slo·p-shop. 1723. [SLOP *sb.*[1]] A shop where slop-clothing is sold.

Slo·p-work. 1849. [f. SLOP *sb.*[1]] 1. The making of slop-garments; the articles thus made. 2. Work cheaply and badly done 1861. So **Slo·p-wo:rker.**

Slosh (slǫʃ), *sb.* 1814. [Cf. next and SLUSH *sb.*[1]] 1. Slush, sludge. 2. Watery, weak, or unappetizing drink 1819. Hence **Slo·shy** *a.* slushy.

Slosh (slǫʃ), *v.* 1844. [f. prec. or imitative.] 1. *intr.* To splash about in mud or wet. 2. *U.S.* To move aimlessly; to loaf about 1854. 3. To make a splashing sound 1888.

Slot (slǫt), *sb.*[1] Chiefly *north.* and *Sc.* ME. [a. MDu. or MLG. *slot* (so Du. and LG.), from the weak grade of the stem **slūt*, *sliut-* to close (G. *schliessen*).] 1. A bar or bolt used to secure a door, window, etc., when closed. Now *dial.* 2. A metal rod; a flat wooden bar, esp. one forming a cross-piece. late ME.

Slot (slǫt), *sb.*[2] late ME. [ad. OF. *esclot* in sense 1; origin obsc.] 1. The slight depression or hollow running down the middle of the breast. Now *Sc.* and *rare.* 2. An elongated narrow depression or perforation made in the thickness of a piece of timber, etc., usually for the reception of some other part or piece, whether fixed or movable 1523. b. The opening in a slot-machine for the reception of a coin 1888. 3. *dial.* The open hem in which the strings of a purse, work-bag, night-cap, etc. run 1796.

attrib.: **s.-machine, -meter,** a machine or meter which is operated by inserting a coin in a s.

Slot (slǫt), *sb.*[3] 1575. [ad. AF., OF. *esclot* hoof-print of a horse, etc., prob. ad. ON. *slóð* track, SLEUTH *sb.*[2]] 1. The track or trail of an animal, esp. a deer, as shown by the marks of the foot; occas. misapplied to the scent of an animal; hence *gen.*, track, trace, trail. 2. A deer's foot 1876.

1. The s. of the bear is quite like that of a human being 1865.

Comb.: **s.-hound,** a sleuth-hound. Hence **Slot** *v.*[3] *trans.* to trace by the s.; to follow the track of (a stag, etc.).

Slot (slǫt), *v.*[1] Now *dial.* 1563. [f. SLOT *sb.*[1] I.] 1. *trans.* To bolt (a door). 2. To secure (a lock) by shooting a bolt 1904.

Slot (slǫt), *v.*[2] late ME. [f. SLOT *sb.*[2]] †1. *trans.* To pierce through the 'slot'. late ME. only. 2. To cut a slot or slots in; to furnish with a slot. Also with *out*. 1747. b. *Coal-mining.* To hole 1883. 3. To drop (a coin) through a slot in a slot-machine 1888. Hence **Slo·tted** *ppl. a.* having a slot or slots.

Sloth (slōᵘþ), *sb.* [Early ME. *slāwðe*, *slōwðe*, f. *slāw*, *slōw* SLOW *a.*; replacing OE. *slǣwð* SLEUTH *sb.*[1]] 1. Physical or mental inactivity; disinclination to action, exertion, or labour; sluggishness, indolence: as one of the seven deadly sins = L. *accidia*. 2. Slowness; tardiness. late ME. 3. A company *of* bears 1452. 4. An edentate arboreal mammal of a sluggish nature, inhabiting tropical parts of Central and South America 1613. b. Applied to other animals, as the sloth-bear, the koala or koolah, the slow lori or lemur, and the mylodon or megatherium 1790.

Combs.: **s.-animalcule,** a tardigrade; **-bear,** an Indian species of bear (*Melursus labiatus* or *ursinus*); **-monkey,** the slow lori or lemur.

Sloth (slōᵘþ), *v.* Now *rare.* late ME. [f. SLOTH *sb.*] †1. *trans.* To allow to slip through slothfulness or delay; to neglect -1708. †b. To pass *away* (time) in idleness -1676. 2. *intr.* To be or become indolent or lazy. late ME.

Slothful (slōᵘ·þful), *a.* late ME. [f. SLOTH *sb.* + -FUL.] 1. Of persons, etc.: Full of sloth; indisposed to exertion; inactive, indolent, lazy, sluggish. 2. Of habits, etc.: Characterized by sloth or disinclination to exertion. late ME.

1. Hee is the true Slothfull man that does no good DEKKER. Hence **Slo·thful-ly** *adv.*, **-ness.**

Slotting (slǫ·tiŋ), *vbl. sb.* 1841. [f. SLOT *v.*[2]] 1. The action of making or cutting a slot or slots 1844. b. *attrib.*, as *s.-machine(ry* 1841. 2. *Coal-mining. pl.* Coal cut away in the process of holing 1883.

Slouch (slautʃ), *sb.* 1515. [Origin unkn.] 1. An awkward, slovenly, or ungainly man; a lubber, lout, clown; also, a lazy, idle fellow. b. *U.S. slang.* A poor, indifferent, or inefficient place, thing, person, etc. 1869. 2. *ellipt.* A slouch hat or bonnet 1714. 3. A stooping, or bending forward of the head and shoulders, in walking; a loose, ungainly carriage or bearing; a walk or gait characterized by this 1725. Hence **Slou·chy** *a.* slouching, slovenly, untidy.

Slouch, *a. rare.* 1688. [f. the sb. or vb.] †1. Drooping or hanging loosely; slouching -1829. 2. *dial.* Clownish, loutish; slovenly 1837. 3. Slouched 1837.

Slouch (slautʃ), *v.* 1754. [app. f. the sb.] 1. *intr.* To move or walk with a slouch or in a loose and stooping attitude. b. To carry oneself with a slouch or stoop; to droop the head and shoulders 1755. c. Of a hat: To hang down, droop 1818. 2. *trans.* To put on, or pull down, (one's hat) in such a way that it partly conceals the face (cf. SLOUCH HAT and SLOUCHING *ppl. a.* 3) 1760.

1. b. He slouched over his oar very badly at the finish 1884. 2. His hat was unlooped and slouched SCOTT.

Slouched (slautʃt), *a.* 1779. [f. SLOUCH *sb.* or *v.* + -ED.] *S. hat* = next.

Slouch hat. 1837. A hat of soft or unstiffened felt or other material, esp. one having a broad brim which hangs or lops down over the face.

Slouching (slau·tʃiŋ), *ppl. a.* 1611. [f. SLOUCH *sb.* or *v.*] 1. Hanging down, drooping (*rare*). 2. Having an awkward, stooping, slipshod carriage or gait; moving with a slouch 1668. 3. Of a hat: Having a brim which hangs over the face 1691. 4. Characterized by a slouch 1773.

3. They wear the sombrero, or broad s. hat of Spain BORROW. Hence **Slou·chingly** *adv.*

Slough (slau), *sb.*[1] [OE. *slōh*; origin doubtful.] 1. A piece of soft, miry, or muddy ground; *esp.* a place or hole in a road or way filled with wet mud or mire and impassable by heavy vehicles, horses, etc. b. *fig.* A state or condition (esp. of moral degradation) in which a person, etc., sinks or has sunk ME. †2. The matter of which a slough is composed; soft mud or mire -1776. †3. A ditch, dike, or drain -1685. 4. *U.S.* (slū). A marsh or reedy pool, pond, small lake, backwater or inlet 1817.

1. Many a time enclos'd in the midst of sloughs and quagmires MILT. b. *S. of Despond*, after Bunyan's use: a state of despair or despondency.

attrib.: **s. grass,** a name in the Mississippi valley for *Muhlenbergia glomerata* and *M. mexicana.*

Slough (slʊf), *sb.*[2] [ME. type *slo(u)h*, *slo(u)ȝ*, perh. related to LG. *sluwe*, *slu* husk, peel, shell.] 1. The outer or scarf skin periodically cast or shed by a snake, adder, etc.; also generally, the skin of a serpent, eel, etc. b. The skin of a caterpillar, locust, etc. cast in the course of transformation, as from the nymphal to the imago stage 1681. c. *fig.* A feature, quality, etc. which is thrown off 1583. 2. A skin, caul, or membrane, enclosing or covering the body or some part of it ME. b. An enclosing or covering layer, coat, or sheath of some kind 1610. c. *dial.* The outer skin of certain fruits; a husk 1660. 3. *Path.* A layer or mass of dead tissue or flesh formed on the surface of a wound, sore, or inflammation; a sphacelus 1513.

1. c. Are we to give them..the s. of slavery, which we are not able to work off, to serve them for their freedom? BURKE.

Slough (slʊf), *v.* 1720. [f. SLOUGH *sb.*[2]] 1. *intr.* Of diseased tissue, etc.: To come *away* or *off*, to be shed, as a slough. b. To become covered with a slough; to form or develop necrosed tissue 1787. 2. *trans.* To eat *away*, to throw *off*, by the formation of a slough or sloughs 1762. 3. Of a serpent, etc.: To cast or shed (the skin) as a slough; to exuviate 1845. b. *fig.* To cast *off*, drop, discard, give up, get rid of (something) 1845. 4. To take *off* in grinding 1844.

1. The diseased part..sloughs away, and new and healthy skin is reproduced 1847. 3. b. She could s. off a sadness and replace it by a hope T. HARDY.

Sloughing (slʊ·fiŋ), *vbl. sb.* 1800. [f. SLOUGH *v.*] 1. *Path.* The process of forming a slough. 2. The action or process of casting a slough; exuviation 1835.

Sloughy (slau·i), *a.*[1] 1724. [f. SLOUGH *sb.*[1] + -Y[1].] Of the nature of or resembling slough; abounding in or full of slough; miry, muddy.

Sloughy (slʊ·fi), *a.*[2] 1483. [f. SLOUGH *sb.*[2] + -Y[1].] 1. Consisting or formed of slough or cast skin (*rare*). 2. *Path.* Of the nature of, resembling, a slough; marked or characterized by the presence of a slough or sloughs 1720.

Slovak (slǫvæ·k, slōᵘ·væk), *sb.* and *a.* Also **Slovac(k.** 1829. [a. Slovak and Czech *Slovák*, f. the stem *Slov-*; see SLOVENE.] A. *sb.* 1. A person belonging to a Slavonic race dwelling in the north-western part of Hungary. 2. The language or dialect spoken by this people 1862. B. *adj.* Of or belonging to the Slovaks, or their language 1887. Hence **Slova·kian** *a.* and *sb.*

Sloven (slʊ·v'n), *sb.* and *a.* 1450. [perh. an AF. formation on Flem. *sloef* dirty, squalid, or Du. *slof* careless, negligent.] A. *sb.* †1. A knave, rascal -1680. 2. An untidy or dirty person 1530. 3. One who works, etc. in a careless, perfunctory or slipshod manner; a writer who is careless in style or composition 1771.

2. Marriage often melts down a Beau into an errant S. 1700. 3. It must be conceded that we moderns are but slovens in composition LANDOR.

B. *adj.* Slovenly. Also *U.S.*, uncultivated, untrained. 1815. Hence **Slo·venry,** slovenliness (now *rare*) 1542.

Slovene (slovī·n), *sb.* and *a.* 1883. [a. G., ad. Styrian, etc. *Slovenec*, pl. *Slovenci*; app. derived from the stem of *slovo* word.] A. *sb.* A member of the Serbo-Croatian group of Slavonic peoples, dwelling in Styria, Carinthia, Carniola, and adjacent parts; a Wend. B. *adj.* Slovenian 1902.

Slovenian (slovī·niăn), *a.* and *sb.* 1844. [f. prec. + -IAN.] A. *adj.* Belonging or pertaining to the Slovenes. B. *sb.* The language of the Slovenes. So **Slove·nish** *a.* and *sb.*

Slovenly (slʊ·v'nli), *a.* 1515. [f. SLOVEN *sb.* + -LY[1].] †1. Low, base, rascally; lewd (*rare*) -1579. 2. Of persons: a. Careless in dress or appearance; untidy 1583. b. Careless or negligent in work of any kind 1781. 3. Of dress, appearance, habits, etc.: Marked or characterized by untidiness or want of attention to neatness and cleanliness 1568. 4. Marked or characterized by want of neatness, care, precision, or thoroughness 1621.

2. a. A thin, elderly man, rather threadbare and s. W. IRVING. b. Churchill.., Surly and s., and bold and coarse COWPER. 4. You must suppose it spoke

In a very slow and s. voice MME D'ARBLAY. Hence **Slo·venliness**, the state or quality of being s.

Slo·venly, *adv.* 1576. [f. SLOVEN *sb.* + -LY [2].] In a careless, negligent, or untidy manner. Now *rare*. So †**Slo·venness**, slovenliness.

Slow (slōu), *sb.* OE. [f. SLOW *a.* or *v.*] 1. A slow or slow-going person; a sluggard. 2. A slow-paced horse 1826. 3. *Cricket*. a. A slowly-bowled ball. b. A slow bowler. 1862. 4. [f. the vb.] *Slow-down, slow-up*, an act or instance of slowing a train, etc. 1891.

1. Hou longe, slowe, thou slepist? WYCLIF *Prov.* xxiv. 33.

Slow (slōu), *a.* [Com. Teut.; OE. *slāw* :—OTeut. **slaiwoz*. The stem is perh. the same as in L. *lævus*, Gr. λαιός left.] I. 1. Not quick or clever in apprehending or understanding a thing; obtuse, dull. 2. Constitutionally inert or sluggish; lacking in promptness or energy OE. b. *Med.* Torpid, sluggish 1896. 3. Not quick, ready, prompt, or willing *to* do something ME. 4. Tardy or dilatory in action; displaying a lack of promptitude or energy under particular circumstances; doing something in a slow or deliberate manner ME. 5. Not readily stirred or moved *to* something (esp. anger, revenge, etc.); not too ready, willing, or susceptible. Also with infin. late ME. †b. Inattentive *to* something -1746. 6. Of things, actions, etc.: Marked or characterized by slowness or tardiness ME. b. *Med.* Of the pulse: Below the average rapidity 1728. 7. Of a fire: That burns gently or slowly. Also *transf.* of heat. 1604. 8. *colloq.* Slow-going; behind the times; out of fashion; not smart or up-to-date 1827. b. Dull or tedious; tiresome; apt to bore one 1841. c. Of persons: Dull, lifeless, insipid; humdrum 1841.

1. Such reasoning had no effect on the s. understanding and imperious temper of James MACAULAY. 2. Is not Lead a mettall heauie, dull, and s.? SHAKS. 3. Freedom..came at length, tho' s. to come DRYDEN. 4. Seldom-readers are s. readers LAMB. He was a s. bowler 1833. 5. Vnmooued, could, and to temptation s. SHAKS. 6. With s. deliberation he unties His glitt'ring purse COWPER. 7. Let it stew on a s. fire 1769. b. Of an oven: That cooks slowly 1846.

II. 1. Taking or requiring a comparatively long time; very gradual ME. 2. a. Of fevers, etc.: Not rapidly developing into a serious form; not acute ME. b. Not rapid in operation or effect 1611. c. *Photogr.* Of a plate, etc.: That takes or receives impressions with comparative slowness; not quickly affected by light, and therefore requiring a longer exposure 1889. 3. Of time: Passing slowly or heavily. Also *transf.* of a dial. 1565. b. *S. time*, a rate of marching in which only 75 paces, of 30 inches each, are taken in a minute 1802. 4. Of clocks, etc.: Behind in time. Also of the sun: Behind mean time. 1696. b. Of local time: Less advanced than the standard to which it is referred 1894.

1. Sweet Flowres are s., and Weeds make hast SHAKS. Intellectual education is always s. 1876. 2. c. Also, of a lens. 3. When the s. dial gave a pause to care ROGERS. 4. From the 25th December to the 15th April the sun is always s. 1855.

III. 1. Moving, flowing, etc., in a slow or sluggish manner; having a relatively low speed or velocity. late ME. 2. a. Of pace, movement, etc.: Leisurely; not quick, fast, or hurried. late ME. b. Characterized by slowness of motion, progress, etc. 1709. c. Retarding, heavy 1873. d. Of a railway track: Utilized for traffic of low speed 1898.

1. The s. canal, the yellow-blossom'd vale GOLDSM. *N*[*ycticebus*] *tardigradus*, the common s. lemur or loris 1882. 2. a. With wandring steps and s. MILT. b. A needless Alexandrine..That, like a wounded snake, drags its s. length along POPE.

Comb.: as *s.-blooded, -hearted, -witted*, adjs.; **s.-hound**, a sleuth-hound; **-match**, a rope-match made so as to burn very slowly; **s.-motion**, applied to cinema films which exhibit action at a pace slower than the natural. Hence **Slow·ly** *adv.*, **-ness**.

Slow (slōu), *adv.* 1500. [f. SLOW *a.*] In a slow or tardy manner; slowly. Now chiefly comb. as *slow-burning, -going, -running* adjs. How s. This old Moon wanes SHAKS.

Slow (slōu), *v.* 1522. [f. SLOW *a.* Cf. OE. *slāwian* to be or become slow.] I. *trans.* †1. To lose (time) by delay; to put off (*rare*). 2. To delay, check, retard; to make slower in some respect 1557. b. To reduce the working rate or speed of (an engine); to ease. Also with *down*. 1839. c. To cause (a vessel, vehicle, or train) gradually to slacken in speed. Also with *down* or *up*. 1864.

2. b. By slowing her engines, she can stop and take soundings 1859.

II. *intr.* 1. To slacken in speed; to move or go more slowly. Also with *down, up*. 1594. b. Of a railway train: To move with slackening speed *into* a station, etc. 1877. 2. To become slower, less active or vigorous, etc. Also with *down*. 1879.

1. Slowing up, the..Cunarder..drew towards us 1881. b. He caught sight of her just as the train was slowing into the station 1877.

†**Slow·back.** 1577. [f. SLOW *a.* + BACK *sb.*[1]] 1. A slothful person; a sluggard -1639. 2. *attrib.* or as *adj.* Sluggish -1619.

Slow·-be·lly. 1607. [f. SLOW *a.*, after Gr. γαστέρες ἀργαί (Ep. Tit., in quot. from Epimenides).] A lazy, idle, or indolent person; a sluggard, laggard. Chiefly *pl.*

Slow·-coach. Also **slowcoach, slow coach.** 1837. [f. SLOW *a.*] One who acts, works, or moves slowly; a slow, idle, or indolent person.

Slow·-foot, *a.* 1642. [f. SLOW *a.*] Slow-footed; slow-paced.

The s. hope of the poor MORRIS. So **Slow-footed** *a.* slow of foot; that walks or goes slowly 1642.

Slow-paced, *a.* 1594. [SLOW *a.*] 1. Having a slow pace, gait, or motion. 2. Of time, etc.: Slow in coming or passing; tardy, lingering 1629.

2. Each slow-pac'd Minute seems to be a Year 1700.

Slow-worm (slōu·wɒ̄ɹm). [OE. *slāwyrm*; the first element is obscure.] A small harmless scincoid lizard, *Anguis fragilis*, native to most parts of Europe; the blindworm.

My supporters shall be two sloths, my crest a s. BURNS.

Sloyd (sloid). Also **slöjd.** 1885. [ad. Sw. *slöjd*, corresp. to ON. *slœgð* SLEIGHT *sb.*] A system of manual instruction or training in elementary woodwork, etc., orig. developed and taught in Sweden.

Slub (slʋb), *sb.*[1] Now chiefly *dial.* 1577. [perh. ad. MDu. *slubbe* in the same sense.] Thick sludgy mud; mire, ooze. Hence **Slub** *v.*[1] *trans.* to cover or plaster with mud.

Slub (slʋb), *v.*[2] Also **slubb.** 1774. [Origin unkn.] *trans.* To draw out and twist (wool, cotton, etc.) after carding, so as to prepare it for spinning. Hence **Slub** *sb.*[2], a slubbing of cotton or wool; a roving.

Slubber (slʋ·bəɹ), *sb.* 1825. [f. prec.] 1. One who manipulates a slubbing-machine 1835. 2. A slubbing-machine 1825.

Slubber (slʋ·bəɹ), *v.* Now chiefly *dial.* 1530. [prob. of Du. or LG. origin.] 1. *trans.* To stain, smear, daub, soil. b. *fig.* To sully (renown, etc.) 1600. 2. To perform, make, deal with, etc., in a hurried and careless manner 1550. 3. To run or skim *over* hurriedly and in a careless or slovenly manner 1592. 4. *intr.* To be lubberly; to slabber or slobber 1820.

1. b. If it be an honest end, That end 's the full reward and thanks but slubbers it 1625. 3. Sometimes I..s. over my Prayers 1716. Hence **Slu·bbering** *ppl. a.* **-ly** *adv.*

Slubberdegullion (slʋ·bəɹdɪgʋ·lyən). 1616. *arch.* [f. prec., with fanciful addition.] A slobbering or dirty fellow; a worthless sloven.

Slu·bbing, *vbl. sb.* 1779. [f. SLUB *v.*[2] + -ING [1].] 1. A process of drawing and twisting by which cotton or wool slivers are prepared for spinning. 2. One of the loosely-compacted threads obtained by this process 1786. 3. *collect.* Cotton or wool which has been slubbed 1836. 4. *attrib.*, in names of apparatus for s. as *s.-billy, -machine*, etc. 1795.

Sludge (slʋ·dʒ). 1649. [var. of SLUTCH.] 1. Mud, mire, or ooze, covering the ground or forming a deposit at the bottom of rivers, etc. b. *Naut.* Ice imperfectly formed, or broken up into minute pieces 1817. 2. Any earthy or slimy matter or deposit 1702. b. *Metall.* Finely crushed ore mixed with water; metalliferous slime 1757. c. The precipitate in sewage tanks 1877.

attrib.: **s.-hole**, the hand-hole, or manhole, in a steam boiler, through which sediment can be removed. Hence **Slu·dger**, an appliance for removing the s. from a bore-hole, or for boring in quicksand.

Sludgy (slʋ·dʒi), *a.* 1782. [f. as prec. + -Y [1].] 1. Muddy, oozy. 2. Consisting of newly formed particles of ice; full of sludge-ice 1853.

Slue, variant of SLEW.

Slug (slʋg), *sb.*[1] late ME. [Related to SLUG *v.*[1]] 1. A slow, lazy fellow; a sluggard. Also, †slothfulness. †2. A slow-sailing vessel -1734. 3. An animal, vehicle, etc., of a slow-moving or sluggish character 1618. 4. A slow-moving slimy gasteropod or land-snail (of the type represented by the families *Limacidæ* and *Arionidæ*), in which the shell is rudimentary or entirely absent 1704. 5. a. A slug-worm 1799. b. A sea-slug 1855.

2. [The Rose,] being a s., will never make a good man-of-war 1624.

Comb.: **s.-caterpillar**, a caterpillar of the genus *Limacodes*; **-fly**, the fly of the s.-worm; **-snail** = 4.

Slug (slʋg), *sb.*[2] 1622. [perh. same word as prec.] 1. A piece of lead or other metal for firing from a gun; a roughly-formed bullet. b. *slang.* Some kind of strong drink (*obs.*); a dram; a drink. Now *U.S.* 1756. 2. A heavy piece of crude metal, usually rounded in form; a nugget (of gold) 1891. 3. *Printing.* A metal bar used as a division, or one produced by a linotype machine for printing from (orig. *U.S.*) 1871. 4. *U.S.* †a. A fifty-dollar gold coin issued in 1849 and 1915. b. A piece of metal worth five cents. 5. A rudimentary horn of an ox or cow 1842.

Slug (slʋg), *v.*[1] Now somewhat *rare.* late ME. [perh. of Scand. origin.] 1. *intr.* To be lazy, slow, or inert; to lie idly or lazily. Also with *it*. 2. To move slowly; to loiter or delay 1565. 3. *trans.* To pass (time) in inactivity or idleness. Also with *out*. 1548. 4. To relax or slacken; to make inert or sluggish 1600. 5. To hinder, retard, delay 1605.

2. Their destruction sluggeth not 1565. 5. To.. slugge the Shippe from furder sayling BACON.

Slug (slʋg), *v.*[2] 1831. [f. SLUG *sb.*[2]] 1. *trans.* To load (a gun) with slugs. 2. *pass.* and *intr.* Of a bullet: To adapt its shape to that of the bore in the act of firing 1875.

Slug (slʋg), *v.*[3] Chiefly *north.* and *U.S.* 1862. [Cf. SLOG *v.*] *trans.* To strike, drive, throw, etc. heavily or violently; to slog.

Slug-a-bed (slʋ·găbed). Also **slug-abed.** 1592. [f. SLUG *v.*[1] 1 + ABED *adv.*] One who lies long in bed through laziness.

Get up, sweet S., and see The Dew-bespangling Herbe and Tree HERRICK.

Sluggard (slʋ·gāɹd), *sb.* and *a.* late ME. [f. SLUG *v.*[1] + -ARD.] A. *sb.* One who is naturally or habitually slow, lazy, or idle; a slothful or indolent person. B. *adj.* Sluggish, slothful, lazy 1593. Hence **Slu·ggard·ly** *a.*, **-ness.** †**Slu·ggardy**, slothfulness, indolence, laziness.

Sluggardize (slʋ·gāɹdəiz), *v.* 1591. [f. SLUGGARD *sb.* + -IZE.] 1. *trans.* To make idle or lazy. 2. *intr.* To play the sluggard 1837.

Slugger (slʋ·gəɹ). *U.S.* 1884. [f. SLUG *v.*[3]] 1. = SLOGGER. 2. A flat-surfaced boss, knob, or projection on a roll for crushing ore 1903.

Sluggish (slʋ·giʃ), *a.* 1440. [f. SLUG *sb.*[1] or *v.*[1] + -ISH.] 1. Of persons: Indisposed to action or exertion; inclined to be slow or slothful; not easily moved to activity. 2. Of the mind, disposition, etc.: Characterized by or exhibiting lack of vigour, alertness, or energy; slow in apprehension or decision; dull 1450. 3. Of conditions, etc.: Characterized by want of, or disinclination to, action or exertion 1561. 4. Of things: Not readily stirring or moving; slow to stir, act, or make progress in any way 1640. 5. Moving, flowing, etc., very slowly or tardily; slow in movement 1611. b. Of motion, etc.: Very slow or tardy 1648.

1. The Turke, and the Irish-man, are..the most s. liuers vnder the Sunne 1632. 2. Beating the track of the alphabet with s. resolution JOHNSON. S. imaginations require strong stimulants 1871. 3. A life of s. inaction 1838. 4. Matter is of it self a dull and s. thing 1640. A symptom of 's. liver' 1897. 5. b. His wry looks and s. pace..proclaimed his ill will to the task 1796. So **Slu·ggish·ly** *adv.*, **-ness.** †**Slu·ggy** *a.* (early ME.) sluggish, indolent -1608.

Slu·g-horn. 1770 (Chatterton). [erron. use of *slughorn* SLOGAN.] A trumpet.

Slu·g-worm. 1799. [f. SLUG *a.* or *sb.*[1] 4.] One or other of the slug-like and slimy larvæ of certain saw-flies (esp. those formerly classed in the genus *Selandria*).

Sluice (slūs), *sb.* ME. [Aphetic ad. OF. *escluse* (mod.F. *écluse*), = late and med.L. *exclusa* (also *sclusa*), fem. sing. of L. *exclusus*, *excludere* to shut out, EXCLUDE *v.*] **1.** A structure for impounding the water of a river, canal, etc., provided with an adjustable gate or gates by which the volume of water is regulated or controlled. Also, rarely, the body of water so impounded or controlled. **b.** A paddle or slide in a gate or barrier by which water is held back 1616. **c.** A device by which the flow of water, esp. into or out of some receptacle, is regulated 1617. **2.** A channel, drain, or small stream, *esp.* one carrying off overflow or surplus water 1538. †**3.** A gap, breach, opening, or hole; a gash or wound -1752. **4.** In gold-washing: An artificial channel or flume, into which a current of water is directed in order to separate the particles of gold from the auriferous earth 1862.

1. *fig.* So from the sluices of Ulysses' eyes Fast fell the tears POPE. The ball which opened in his breast the crimson s. of life 1800.

Comb.: **s.-box**, one of the long troughs of which a gold-washing s. is composed; a riffle-box; **-gate**, the gate of a s., the part which can be opened or shut to let out or retain the water; the upper gate of a lock; **-way**, a channel or water-way fed or controlled by means of a s. or sluices.

Sluice (slūs), *v.* 1593. [f. the sb.] **1.** *trans.* To let *out*, to cause to flow *out*, by the opening of a sluice. **b.** To let out or draw *from* some source or place in this manner. Usu. in pa. pple. 1593. **c.** To lead or draw *off* by, or as by, a sluice 1753. **2.** To draw off or let out water from (a pond, lake, etc.) by means of a sluice or sluices 1594. **3.** To cast, fling, or pour (something) as if through a sluice 1610. **4.** To throw or pour water over (a person or thing); to swill with water esp. in order to clean or wash 1755. **b.** *U.S.* and *Austral.* To wash (auriferous ore) in a gold-miner's sluice. Also with *out*. 1859. **5.** *intr.* To flow or pour *out* or down as through a sluice 1593.

1. b. A broad canal From the main river sluiced TENNYSON. **2.** My veins have been sluiced so often that they give me pain in writing SCOTT. **4.** His neck and face, which he had been sluicing with cold water 1861.

Sluicy (slū·si), *a.* Chiefly *poet.* 1697. [f. SLUICE *sb.* + -Y[1].] Of rain, etc.: Falling or pouring copiously or in streams, as if from a sluice; streaming, drenching. Also *transf.* and *fig.*

Oft whole sheets descend of slucy Rain DRYDEN.

Slum (slʋm), *sb.* 1812. [Of cant origin.] †**1.** A room -1824. **2.** A street, alley, court, etc., situated in a crowded district of a town or city and inhabited by people of a low class or by the very poor; a number of these streets or courts forming a thickly populated neighbourhood or district of a squalid and wretched character. Chiefly *pl.*, and freq. in the phr. *back slum(s.* 1825. †**3.** Nonsensical talk or writing; gammon, blarney. Also, gipsy jargon or cant. -1823. Hence **Slu·mmy** *a.*

Slum (slʋm), *v.* 1860. [Cf. SLUM *sb.*[1]] **1. a.** *intr.* To go into, or frequent, slums for discreditable purposes; to keep to back streets to avoid observation. **2.** To visit slums for charitable or philanthropic purposes, or out of curiosity, esp. as a fashionable pursuit 1884.

Slumber (slʋ·mbəɹ), *sb.* late ME. [f. SLUMBER *v.* Cf. Fris. *slûmer*, G. *schlummer*.] **1.** Sleep, repose. Chiefly *poet.* **2.** A period or occasion of sleep or repose; freq. a light or short sleep. late ME. **3.** *fig.* A state or condition of repose, inactivity, or quiescence 1552.

1. Ere theise eyes of mine take themselues to slomber SHAKS. **2.** Nor sleepe nor wake. But in a s. troublesome to both. 1611. **3.** The human mind awoke from a s. GODWIN. *attrib.* **s. cap**, a net cap worn when the wearer is in bed to keep the hair in order. Hence **Slu·mberless** *a.* obtaining or yielding no s.; sleepless. **Slu·mbery** *a.* slumberous, sleepy.

Slumber (slʋ·mbəɹ), *v.* [ME. *slūmeren*, f. *slūmen* vb. or *slūme* SLOOM *sb.*, corresp. to Fris. *slûmerje*, MHG. *slum(m)ern*.] **1.** *intr.* To sleep, *esp.* to sleep lightly; to doze or drowse. **b.** *fig.* To lie at rest in death or the grave 1588. **2.** *fig.* To live in a state of inactivity or negligence; to remain or be sunk *in* sin, sloth, etc.; to be dilatory or tardy *in* doing something. late ME. **3.** Of things, faculties, etc.: To be dormant, inoperative, or quiescent 1582. **b.** To be calm, peaceful, or still 1764. †**4.** *trans.* To cause to sleep; to render inactive or inoperative; to dull or deaden -1642. **5.** To pass, spend, or waste (time) in sleep or slumber. Const. *away*, *out*, *through*, etc. 1749.

1. He neyther slombrethe nor slepethe, but alwayes watchethe 1599. **3.** The might that slumbers in a peasant's arm 1799. **5.** She had slumbered away the day in order to sit up all night FIELDING. Hence **Slu·mberer**, one who sleeps or slumbers. **Slu·mbering** *vbl. sb.* and *ppl. a.* (whence **Slu·mberingly** *adv.*).

Slumberous, slu·mbrous (slʋ·mb(ə)rəs), *a.* 1495. [f. SLUMBER *sb.* + -OUS.] **1.** Inclined to slumber or sleep; unduly given to slumber; indolent, lethargic. **b.** Of the eyes or eyelids: Heavy or drooping with slumber or sleep 1828. **2.** Inducing sleep; soporific 1667. **3.** Calm, still, peaceful 1765. **4.** Appropriate to, characterized by, or suggestive of slumber 1818. **b.** Of places, etc.: Quiet, sleepy, tranquil 1863.

2. The slumbrous light is rich and warm TENNYSON. **3.** Faint heaves the s. wave 1765. *transf.* The slumbrous reign..became intolerable to the commonalty 1885. **b.** A sleepy town in a s. land 1883. Hence **Slu·mberous·ly** *adv.*, **-ness.**

Slumming (slʋ·miŋ), *vbl. sb.* 1884. [f. SLUM *v.*] The visitation of slums, esp. for charitable or philanthropic purposes.

Slump (slʋmp), *sb.*[1] *Sc.* 1718. [a. LG., heap, quantity.] **1.** A large quantity or number; chiefly in phrases *by* or *in* (*the*) *s.*, as a whole; in the lump 1795. **2.** *attrib.*, as **s. sum**, a lump sum 1718.

Slump (slʋmp), *sb.*[2] 1888. [f. SLUMP *v.*[2]] **1.** *Stock Exch.* A heavy fall or sudden decline in the price or value of commodities or securities. **2.** *transf.* A sudden or heavy decline or falling off; a collapse 1888.

2. There is..no 's.' in the matrimonial market 1896.

Slump (slʋmp), *v.*[1] Chiefly *Sc.* 1822. [f. SLUMP *sb.*[1]] *trans.* To lump; to put, place, regard, deal with, etc., as one quantity, mass, or group. Freq. *to s. together.*

Slump (slʋmp), *v.*[2] Chiefly *dial.* and *U.S.* 1677. [prob. imitative; cf. PLUMP *v.*[1]] **1.** *intr.* To fall or sink *in* or *into* a bog, swamp, muddy place, etc.; to fall *in* water with a dull splashing sound. **2. a.** Of the wind: To fall, drop 1855. **b.** Of stocks, values, etc.: To fall heavily or suddenly 1896. **3.** To move or walk in a clumsy, heavy, or laborious manner 1854. **4.** *trans.* To throw *down* heavily; to slam 1836. **b.** To cause to depreciate suddenly 1899.

1. Being in this swamp that was miry, I slumpt in and fell down 1684. **2. b.** Prices slumped from 2 to 5 points 1898.

Slumpy (slʋ·mpi), *a.* 1823. [f. dial. *slump* a marshy or muddy place; cf. LG. *schlump*.] Marshy, swampy, muddy, boggy.

Slung (slʋŋ), *ppl. a.* 1773. [f. SLING *v.*[2]] Placed in, hung or suspended by, a sling or slings.

Comb.: **s.-shot** *U.S.*, a shot, piece of metal, stone, etc., fastened to a strap or thong, and used as a weapon.

Slunk (slʋŋk), *ppl. a.* 1837. [f. SLINK *v.*] Of calves: Cast prematurely.

Slur (slɔ̄ɹ), *sb.*[1] 1598. [f. SLUR *v.*[2]] †**1.** A gliding movement in dancing -1673. †**2.** A method of cheating at dice (see SLUR *v.*[2] 1) -1680. **3.** A sliding piece of mechanism in a knitting-machine, serving to depress the sinkers 1796.

Slur (slɔ̄ɹ), *sb.*[2] 1609. [f. SLUR *v.*[1]] **1. a.** A deliberate slight; an expression or suggestion of disparagement or reproof. **b.** A mark, stain, or blot; a discredit (incurred by or cast upon a person, etc.); †a blunder 1654. **2.** *Printing.* A faulty or smeared impression 1771. **3.** *Mus.* A curved line placed over or under two or more notes of different degrees to show that they are to be played or sung smoothly and connectedly 1801. **4.** A slurred utterance or sound 1861.

1. My Lord Generall..hath received several slurs from the King PEPYS. Phr. *To cast, put, throw* (etc.) *a s. on* or *upon* (a person or thing).

Slur (slɔ̄ɹ), *v.*[1] 1602. [f. dial. *slur* thin or fluid mud.] **1.** *trans.* To smear, stain, smirch, sully. Now *dial.* **b.** *Printing.* To smudge or blur 1683. **c.** *U.S.* To cover (a wall) with plaster or rough-cast 1885. **2.** To disparage, calumniate, asperse 1660. **3.** To pass over lightly, without proper mention or consideration 1660. **b.** Freq. with *over*. Also with ref. to utterance. 1725. **4.** *Mus.* To sing or play (notes) in a smooth and connected manner; to mark with a slur 1746. **5.** To blur 1782. **6.** To go through hurriedly and carelessly. Also *intr.* with *through*. 1857.

2. To s. the descent of the house of York SCOTT. **3.** To silence a doubt, or s. a difference 1871. **b.** The little word, as, which is always slurred over SHERIDAN. **6.** They only slurred through their fagging 1857. Hence **Slurred** (slɔ̄ɹd) *ppl. a.* run together, rendered indistinct, blurred.

Slur (slɔ̄ɹ), *v.*[2] 1594. [perh. related to LG. *slurrn* to drag the feet, to shuffle.] †**1.** *trans.* To slip or slide (a die) out of the box so that it does not turn -1700. †**2.** To cheat or cozen -1731. **3.** *intr.* To slide, slide about. Now *dial.* 1617.

Slush (slʋʃ), *sb.*[1] 1641. [Origin unkn. Cf. SLOSH, SLUDGE, SLUTCH.] **1. a.** The watery substance resulting from the partial melting of snow or ice. **b.** Liquid mud or mire 1772. **2.** *Naut.* The refuse fat or grease obtained from meat boiled on board ship 1756. **3. a.** A mixture of grease and other materials used for lubricating 1847. **b.** A mixture of white lead and lime, used for painting parts of machinery to preserve them from oxidation 1864. **4.** Rubbishy discourse or literature; also, sentimental stuff, gush 1896. **5.** *U.S. slang.* (*a*) Illicit commission, bribery, corruption. (*b*) Forged paper money. 1924. **6.** *attrib.*, as *s. funds, melodrama.*

Slush (slʋʃ), *sb.*[2] 1880. [Echoic, or f. next.] A heavy splashing sound.

Slush (slʋʃ), *v.* 1807. [Partly f. SLUSH *sb.*[1] and partly echoic.] **I.** *trans.* **1.** To splash or soak with slush or mud. **2. a.** *Naut.* To grease (a mast) with slush. Also with *down*. 1823. **b.** To paint (machinery) with a mixture of white lead and lime 1864. **c.** To fill *up* or cover by dashing on mortar and cement 1875. **3.** To wash with a copious supply, or with dashing on, of water; to sluice. *dial.* 1854. **b.** To dash (water) *over* a person 1889. **II.** *intr.* **1.** Of pigs: To eat greedily and noisily 1833. **2.** To go or walk through mud, etc., with a dull splashing sound 1855. **3.** To rush (*down*) with a splashing sound 1883.

3. The filthy gutter slushes STEVENSON.

Slushy (slʋ·ʃi), *a.* 1791. [f. SLUSH *sb.*[1]] **1.** Covered with, consisting of, having the character of slush (in senses 1 a and b). **b.** Marked by the prevalence of slush 1848. **2.** Weak, washy 1839. **b.** *fig.* of emotion or the like 1889. **3.** Thick, indistinct 1861.

1. Mud under foot, alternating with s. snow 1857. **b.** S. splashy raw comfortless mornings in..winter 1871. **2. b.** A sloppy and s. sentimentalism 1894. **3.** He spoke in a s. voice DICKENS. Hence **Slu·shiness.**

Slut (slʋt). late ME. [Origin unkn.] **1.** A woman of dirty, slovenly, or untidy habits or appearance; a foul slattern. **b.** A kitchen-maid, drudge (*rare*) 1450. **2.** A woman of a low or loose character; a bold or impudent girl; a hussy, jade 1450. **b.** In more or less playful use 1664. **3.** A female dog, a bitch 1845.

1. She 's ugly, she 's old,..And a s., and a scold SHENSTONE. **2. b.** You're a wheedling s., you be so SWIFT.

Slutch (slʋtʃ). Now *dial.* 1669. [Cf. SLUDGE, SLUSH *sb.*[1]] Mud, mire, slush. Hence **Slu·tchy** *a.* muddy, slushy.

†**Sluttery.** 1586. [f. SLUT *sb.* + -ERY.] Sluttishness -1818.

Sluttish (slʋ·tiʃ), *a.* late ME. [f. SLUT *sb.* + -ISH.] **1.** Of persons: Dirty and untidy in dress and habits. Now *spec.* of women. †**b.** Of a low or lewd character -1606. **2.** Of things: Unclean, dirty; untidy 1549. **3.** Appropriate to, characteristic of, a slut or sluts 1561.

1. Why is thy lord so sluttissh, I the preye? CHAUCER. The..maid..is as lazy and s. as her mistress JOHNSON. **b.** *Tr. & Cr.* IV. v. 62. **2.** Suche hongrye doggs will slabbe vp sluttishe puddinges 1553. **3.** S. plenty deck'd her table PRIOR. Hence **Slu·ttish·ly** *adv.*, **-ness.**

Sly (slai), *a.*, *adv.*, and *sb.* [ME. *slēȝ*, ad.

ON. *slœg-r* clever, cunning, orig. 'able to strike', f. *slóg-*, pret. stem of *slá* to strike. Cf. SLEIGHT *sb.*] **A.** *adj.* **1.** Of persons: Skilful, clever, dexterous, or expert in doing something; skilled, knowing, wise. (Also occas. of animals.) *Obs.* exc. *n. dial.* †**2.** Showing skilfulness or ingenuity; cleverly or finely made –1721. **3.** Of persons: Adept or skilful in artifice or craft; deceitful, guileful, wily, underhand ME. **b.** Of animals, etc. 1640. **c.** Of looks: Expressive of slyness 1821. **4.** Of actions, things, etc.: Marked by, displaying or indicating, artifice, craft, or cunning; of an insidious or wily nature. late ME. †**b.** Of words, etc.: Full of duplicity or wile; subtle; disingenuous –1829. **5.** Characterized by secrecy or stealth; working, moving, etc., in an underhand manner. Also of places: Quiet, secret. 1440. **6.** Playfully mischievous or malicious; roguish; waggish 1764.

1. You..(whom grauer age And long experience hath made wise and slie) 1600. 3. He was, indeed, a little inquisitive; but I was s., sir; devilish s.! SHERIDAN. b. A s. old fish, too cunning for the hook CRABBE. 4. Envy..works in a s. and imperceptible manner 1755. 5. The slye slow houres shall not determinate The datelesse limit of thy deere exile SHAKS. 6. The s., delicate and..elegant pleasantry of La Fontaine 1805.

†**B.** *adv.* In a sly, skilful, or cunning manner; slyly –1802. **C.** *absol.* or as *sb.* in phr. *On* (*upon*, †*under*, or †*by*) *the s.*, in a secret or covert manner; without publicity or openness; stealthily 1812.

A certain farmer's man, who wired hares upon the s. 1866.

Sly-boots (slɔi·bŭts). *colloq.* 1700. [f. SLY *a.* + BOOTS 3.] A sly, cunning, or crafty person; one who does things on the sly. Freq. in mild or joc. use, and usu. in pl. form.

Sly-goose. *Orkney.* Also **slygoose.** 1776. [f. SLY *a.* + GOOSE *sb.*] The sheldrake, *Tadorna cornuta* or *T. vulpanser.*

Slyly, slily (slɔi·li), *adv.* ME. [f. SLY *a.* + -LY [2].] In a sly manner.

While we pursu'd the Horsmen of yᵉ North, He slyly stole away SHAKS. The clerk winked slily at Mr. Pickwick DICKENS. So **Sly·ness.**

Slype (slɔip). 1861. [Cf. WFlem. *slipe*, *slijpe* secret path.] *Arch.* A covered way or passage, esp. one leading from the cloisters and running between the transept and chapter-house of a cathedral or monastic church.

Smack (smæk), *sb.*[1] [OE. *smæc*, = OHG. *smac.*] **1.** A taste or flavour; the distinctive or peculiar taste of something, or a special flavour distinguishable from this. **2.** *transf.* A trace, tinge, or suggestion *of* something specified 1539. †**b.** A smattering –1791. **c.** A small quantity *of* liquor; a mouthful 1693. **d.** A touch or suggestion *of* something having a characteristic odour or taste 1848. †**3.** *fig.* Delight or enjoyment; inclination, relish –1620.

1. Midling Ale..that hath no burnt, musty, or otherwise ill s. 1710. 2. A s. of real earnestness in his tone 1874. d. A rough s. of resin was in the air STEVENSON. 3. She hath a very great s. of Courtship, and plays with everyone 1620.

Smack (smæk), *sb.*[2] 1570. [Related to SMACK *v.*[2]] **1.** A sharp noise or sound made by separating the lips quickly, esp. in kissing, and in tasting or anticipating food or liquor. **b.** A loud or sounding kiss 1604. **2.** The crack *of* a whip, lash, etc. 1781. **3.** A sounding blow delivered with the flat of the hand or something having a flat surface; a slap 1746. **b.** *colloq.* A slap or go *at* something 1889.

1. Tasting the Wine with a judicious S. STEELE. 3. *A s. in the face* (fig.), a sharp rebuff.

Smack (smæk), *sb.*[3] 1611. [prob. a. Du. *smak*, earlier *smacke.*] A single-masted sailing-vessel, fore-and-aft rigged like a sloop or cutter, and usually of light burden, chiefly employed as a coaster or for fishing, and formerly as a tender to a ship of war. **b.** *U.S.* A fishing-vessel having a well in which fish may be kept alive 1891.

Comb.: **sma·cksman**, one of the crew of a s., esp. of a fishing-s.; the owner of a s.

Smack (smæk), *v.*[1] ME. [f. SMACK *sb.*[1]] **1.** *trans.* Of persons: To perceive by the sense of taste. †Also *fig.* To experience, to suspect. **2.** *intr.* Of food, liquor, etc.: To taste (well or ill); to have a (specified) taste or flavour; to taste or savour *of* something. late ME. **b.** *fig.* To partake or savour *of*, to be strongly suggestive or reminiscent *of*, something 1595.

1. He soon smacked the taste of physic hidden in this sweetness CARLYLE. 2. *fig.* Indeede my Father did something s., something grow too; he had a kinde of taste SHAKS. b. All Sects, all Ages s. of this vice SHAKS.

Smack (smæk), *v.*[2] 1530. [prob. echoic; cf. MDu., MLG. *smacken.*] **1.** *trans.* To open or separate (the lips) in such a way as to produce a sharp sound; to do this in connexion with eating or drinking, esp. as a sign of keen relish or anticipation. Also *intr.* or *absol.* **b.** *trans.* To taste (wine or liquor) with keen relish or satisfaction 1822. **2.** To kiss noisily or loudly. Now *Obs.* or *dial.* 1570. **3.** To crack (a whip, thong, etc.) 1700. **4.** To bring, put, or throw *down* with a smack or slap; to clap (the hands) *together*; to slam (a door) *to* 1801. **5.** To strike (a person, part of the body, etc.) with the open hand or with something having a flat surface; to slap 1840. **6.** Used *advb.* **a.** With, or as with, a smack; suddenly and violently; slap 1782. **b.** Completely, entirely; directly 1828.

1. Tom..smacked his lips over the long-necked glass 1861. b. George,..filling himself a glass of wine, smacked it THACKERAY. 2. Phr. *To s. calf-skin* (slang), to kiss the Bible in taking an oath. 5. He smacked his leg with his hand, and burst out laughing 1881. 6. a. He..tumbled..s. on his face 1799.

Smacker (smæ·kəɪ). 1775. [f. prec. + -ER [1].] A smacking blow; a resounding kiss.

Smacking (smæ·kiŋ), *vbl. sb.* 1628. [f. SMACK *v.*[2]] The action of SMACK *v.*[2]; kissing, or the sound made by this.

Like the faint smackings of an after-Kiss DRYDEN.

Sma·cking, *ppl. a.* 1592. [f. as prec.] **1.** That smacks, in senses of the vb. **2.** Of a breeze: Blowing vigorously; spanking 1820.

Small (smǭl), *a.* and *sb.* [Com. Teut.; OE. *smæl.*] **A.** *adj.* **I. 1.** Of relatively little girth or circumference in comparison with length; slender, thin. Now *dial.* exc. of the waist. **b.** *spec.* Applied to the more slender portions of the intestines; esp. *s. gut(s)* OE. **2.** Having little breadth or width in proportion to length; narrow. Now *rare.* OE.

1. My sister..is as white as a lilly, and as s. as a wand SHAKS. He wor soa s. he luk'd like a walkin' clooas prop 1870.

II. 1. Of deficient or comparatively little size; not large (usu. without the emotional implication of *little*) OE. **b.** Of children, etc.: Not fully grown or developed; young ME. **c.** Of a family: Consisting of young children 1829. **2.** Used with collective nouns, denoting the limited size of the individual things, pieces, etc. late ME. **b.** Of money: Of little size and low value. *S. change*: coins of low denomination; hence *transf.* of little value. 1561. **3.** Little in amount or quantity ME. **b.** Of low numerical value or ordinal rank; low. late ME. **4.** Only a little or slight amount or degree of; not much; hardly any. late ME. **b.** *No s.*, great, considerable, marked; much, a good deal of 1548. **c.** Used in the superl. for emphasis: The least, the slightest 1596. **d.** *In the smallest*, in the least (*rare*) 1603. **5.** Of no great length; short, brief. late ME. **6.** Composed or consisting of, containing, few individual members; numerically little or weak 1470. **7. a.** Constituting a lower standard (of weight, size, etc.) than another having the same designation. **b.** Falling somewhat short of the proper or usual standard. 1554.

1. Herbes grete and smale CHAUCER. Rutland, the smallest of the English counties 1846. b. To the great delight of various s. boys 1896. 2. The quaking-asps..are in s. leaf 1902. b. Thou hast shewed vs none but s. money 1561. c. Her large s. family 1895. 3. My wages been ful streite and ful smale CHAUCER. I had gotten a s. cold SWIFT. 4. I kan but smal grammeere CHAUCER. They had indeed s. Hope of their Lives DE FOE. b. A matter of no s. momente 1548. c. He risked..life, if he betrayed the smallest suspicion 1797. d. Not molesting Prince Karl in the smallest CARLYLE. 5. For a s. moment haue I forsaken thee *Isaiah* liv. 7. 6. A s. but faithful Band Of Worthies DRYDEN. 7. b. After an ascent of a s. half hour we came to a..fountain of cold water 1753.

III. 1. Composed of fine or minute particles, drops, etc. In later use chiefly of rain. OE. **b.** Fine, as opp. to coarse OE. **2.** Of cloth, yarn, garments, etc.: Fine in texture or structure. *Obs.* exc. *dial.* OE. **3.** Of low alcoholic strength; light, weak 1440. **4.** Of sound or the voice: Gentle, low, soft; of little power or strength; not loud, harsh, or rough ME. †**b.** Of vowels: Narrow, close –1830. **5.** Of wind: Light, gentle 1542. **6.** Of the pulse: Beating weakly 1755.

1. Thick Fogs with s. Rain 1676. 3. Let me haue sacke for vs old men: For these girles and knaues s. wines are best 1605. 4. After the fire, a still s. voice *1 Kings* xix. 12. 5. A smal and softe wynde 1542.

IV. 1. Of persons: Low or inferior in rank or position; common, ordinary. Now *rare.* ME. **b.** Having but little land, capital, etc.; dealing, doing business, etc., on a small scale 1746. **2.** Of minor rank, note, or importance, in respect of some specified office, function, etc. ME. **b.** That is (such) to a small or limited extent, degree, etc. 1523. **c.** With negative, as in II. 4 b above 1551. **3.** Of things, etc.: Of little or minor consequence, interest, or importance; trifling, trivial ME. **4.** Not prominent or notable; humble, modest; unpretentious. In later use, chiefly in the phr. *in a s. way.* late ME. **5. a.** Base, low; mean, ungenerous 1824. **b.** Incapable of large views or great actions; small-minded, mean-souled 1837. **c.** With *feel*: Humiliated, mortified, injured in self-respect 1840.

1. Your Enemies are many, and not s. SHAKS. 2. A s. author, and smaller wit DISRAELI. 3. The fact..accounts..for certain s. recurrent defects 1893. 4. A composer in a s. way T. HARDY. 5. c. I should feel a little s. at being seen in such a place 1840.

Special collocations: **s. body,** in Printing, any size of type smaller than Long Primer; **s. capitals,** in Printing, capital letters differing little in size from the lower-case letters of the same fount; **s. cattle,** cattle below the size of oxen, as calves or sheep; **s. holding,** a holding smaller than an ordinary farm; also *spec.* land acquired by a council which exceeds one acre and either does not exceed fifty acres, or is of an annual value not exceeding fifty pounds; so **s. holder; s. people,** in local use, the fairies; **s. stuff** *Naut.*, applied to thin kinds of rope.

B. *absol.* or as *sb.* **1.** Persons or animals of small size or stature; little ones, children. (Now only with *the.*) ME. **2.** Persons of low or inferior rank or position, or of little ability or attainment. Chiefly in phr. *great and s.* ME. †**3.** Little, not much *of* –1640. **4.** *In s.* (rarely *the s.*), on a small scale; in little. In early use in ref. to painting, etc.: In miniature. 1611. **5.** The small, slender, or narrow part *of* something; *esp.* **a.** Of the leg 1489. **b.** Of the back 1536. **6.** Small coal; slack. In recent use also *pl.*, varieties of small coal. 1851. **7.** *pl.* Small clothes; breeches 1837. **b.** Small articles of laundry (*colloq.*). **8.** *pl.* At Oxford: The colloquial term for Responsions 1852. **9.** *S. and early*, a small evening party not intended to continue to a late hour. *colloq.* 1880.

3. Hauing s., yet doe I not complaine Of want SPENSER. 5. a. *L.L.L.* v. ii. 645. 7. Her footman, in large plush smalls and waistcoat THACKERAY. 8. He had been 'ploughed' for 'smalls' 1880. Hence **Sma·llness,** the fact, quality, or state of being s.

Small (smǭl), *adv.* OE. [f. SMALL *a.*] **1.** Into small pieces or morsels. †**2.** Not much; slightly –1637. **3.** Quietly, gently; in a small or low voice ME. **4.** In a fine or small manner; on a small scale, etc. 1637.

1. Geese will..fatten well on carrots cut s. 1759. 2. If thou dost weep.., it s. avails my mood SHAKS. 3. She..speakes s. like a woman SHAKS. Phr. *To sing s.*, to adopt a humble tone or manner; to use less assertive language; to say nothing.

Small (smǭl), *v. rare.* late ME. [f. SMALL *a.*] To †make, or become, small.

Smallage (smǭ·lėdʒ). ME. [f. SMALL *a.* + ACHE *sb.*[2]] One or other of several varieties of celery or parsley; *esp.* wild celery or water parsley, *Apium graveolens.* Now *rare.*

Sma·ll-arm. 1805. [Back-formation from next, at first in attrib. use.] **1.** *attrib.* **a.** Using or provided with small-arms. **b.** Intended or adapted for small-arms 1807. **2.** A fire-arm which may be carried in the hand 1875.

Sma·ll-arms. 1710. [f. SMALL *a.* + ARM *sb.*[2] 2.] Fire-arms capable of being carried in the hand, as contrasted with ordnance.

Small beer. 1568. [SMALL *a.* III. 3.] **1.** Beer of a weak, poor, or inferior quality. **2.** *transf.* **a.** Trivial occupations, affairs, etc.; matter(s or person(s of little or no consequence; nothing of importance 1777. **b.** *To think small* *beer of*, etc.: To have a poor or low opinion of. Chiefly with negs. *colloq.* 1825.

2. [To suckle Fooles, and chronicle small Beere SHAKS.]

Sma·ll-clothes. Also **smallclothes.** 1796. [SMALL *a.*] Breeches; knee-breeches.

Sma·ll coal. Also **small-coal.** 1638. [SMALL *a.* II. 2.] 1. Charcoal. *Obs.* exc. *Hist.* 2. Coal of small size; slack 1665.

Smallish (smǭ·liʃ), *a.* late ME. [f. SMALL *a.*] Somewhat small; rather little.

Smallpox (smǭ·lpǫks), *sb.* 1518. [orig. *small pokkes* pl. of *small pokke* (in late ME. *pokke smal*); see SMALL *a.* and POCK *sb.*[2] Long written as two words; the adj. distinguishes the disease from the pox proper, or *great pox.*] The pox or pustules on the skin which characterize the acute contagious disease sometimes called variola; hence commonly, the disease itself. (In later use, when denoting the disease, the word is construed as a singular.) b. *attrib.*, as *small-pox epidemic*, etc. 1775.

I am..expecting the doctor to give your little godson the s. They are rife in the country. BURNS. Hence **Sma·llpox** *v. trans.* **Sma·ll-poxed** *a.* marked by or suffering from s.

Sma·ll-sword. 1687. [SMALL *a.* I. 2.] A light sword, tapering gradually from the hilt to the point, and used esp. in fencing.

Sma·ll talk, *sb.* 1751. [SMALL *a.* IV. 3.] Light talk or conversation; chit-chat, gossip.

Sma·ll-ware(s. 1617. [SMALL *a.* II. 1.] Small textile articles of the tape kind; narrow bindings of cotton, linen, silk, or woollen fabric; plaited sash cord, braid, etc.; also, buttons, hooks and eyes, etc.

†**Sma·lly,** *adv.* ME. [f. SMALL *a.* + -LY [2].] 1. In or into small or minute pieces, fragments, etc.; finely –1662. 2. Sparsely, scantily –1604. 3. Not much, very little –1670. †4. Slightly, slenderly –1630.

Smalm, variant of SMARM.

Smalt (smǭlt), *sb.* and *a.* 1558. [a. F., ad. It. *smalto* SMALTO.] 1. A species of glass, usually coloured a deep blue by oxide of cobalt, etc., and after cooling finely pulverized for use as a pigment or colouring matter. 2. A deep blue colour like that of smalt 1881. 3. A piece of coloured glass. Cf. SMALTO. 1864. 4. *attrib.* *s.-glass, -works*, etc.; **-blue**, powder blue 1681. b. As *adj.* Deep blue 1880. **Sma·ltite** = next.

Smaltine (smǭ·ltəin). 1837. [f. SMALT *sb.* + -INE [5].] *Min.* Tin-white cobalt.

‖**Smalto** (sma·ltọ). Also *pl.* **smalti.** 1705. [It., of Teut. origin and related to SMELT *v.* Cf. AMEL *sb.*] Coloured glass or enamel used for mosaic work, etc.; a small cube or piece of this.

Smalts (smǭlts). 1610. [app. the pl. of SMALT taken as a sing.] = SMALT *sb.* 1.

Smaragd (smæ·rægd). Now *rare.* ME. [a. OF. *smaragde*, or ad. L. *smaragdus* SMARAGDUS. Cf. EMERALD.] An emerald.

Smaragdine (smăræ·gdin, -əin), *sb.* and *a.* late ME. [ad. L. *smaragdinus* of emerald, a. Gr., f. σμάραγδος; see SMARAGDUS.] A. *sb.* = prec. B. *adj.* 1. Of or belonging to, consisting of, a smaragd; resembling that of a smaragd; of an emerald green 1591. 2. *S. Table*, a mediæval Latin work on alchemy, *Tabula Smaragdina*, attributed to the Egyptian Hermes Trismegistus 1597.

Smaragdite (smăræ·gdəit). 1804. [a. F., f. Gr. σμάραγδος SMARAGD + -ITE [1] 2 b.] *Min.* A brilliant grass-green or emerald-green variety of amphibole or hornblende.

‖**Smaragdus** (smăræ·gdǒs). Now *rare.* late ME. [L., a. Gr. σμάραγδος; prob. connected with Skr. *marakata, marakta* emerald.] = SMARAGD.

Smarm, smalm (smāɹm, smām), *v. colloq.* 1847. [orig. dial.] 1. *trans.* To smooth *down* (as hair with pomade). 2. *intr.* To behave in a fulsomely flattering or toadying manner. Hence **Sma·rmy** *a.* inclined to do this.

Smart (smāɹt), *sb.*[1] [ME. *smierte, smerte*, app.:—OE. **smiĕrtu*, f. *smeart* SMART *a.*] 1. Sharp physical pain, esp. such as is caused by a stroke, sting, or wound. Also with *a* and *pl.* 2. Mental pain or suffering; grief, sorrow, affliction; sometimes, suffering of the nature of punishment or retribution ME. 3. *ellipt.* = SMART-MONEY 1802.

1. He..inflicted both corporall s. and pecuniary mulcts upon them 1641. 2. The very Eye betrays our inward s. COWLEY.

Smart (smāɹt), *sb.*[2] 1712. [f. SMART *a.*] 1. One who affects smartness in dress, manners, or talk. Now *Hist.* 2. Smartness in talk or writing 1845.

Smart (smāɹt), *a.* [OE. *smeart*, related to *smeortan* SMART *v.*] I. †1. Of a whip, rod, etc.: Inflicting or causing pain; sharp, biting, stinging –1671. †b. Severe or hard *on* or *upon* one –1648. 2. Of blows, strokes, etc.: Sufficiently hard or severe to cause pain ME. †3. Of pain, sorrow, wounds, etc.: Sharp, keen, painful, severe –1688. 4. Of words, etc.: Sharp, severe; cutting, acrimonious. Now *rare.* ME. 5. Brisk or vigorous; having a certain degree of intensity, force, strength, or quickness ME. †6. Sharp, abrupt, clearly outlined –1784. 7. Considerable (in number, amount, extent, etc.). Chiefly *dial.* and *U.S.* 1839.

2. How s. a lash that speech doth giue my Conscience? SHAKS. 3. The gospel..threateneth them with the heaviest and smartest judgments BUNYAN. 4. A Book written..against the Marriage in a s. and stinging Style 1625. 5. A s. and continued Rain 1692. Whisky,..very s. stuff it is KEATS. 6. A s. passage at arms 1885. 7. Madame..left a s. legacy to the..children THACKERAY.

II. †1. Pert, forward, impudent (*rare*) –1607. 2. Of persons: Quick, active; prompt ME. 3. Clever, capable, adept; quick at devising, learning, looking after oneself, etc. In later use chiefly *U.S.* 1628. 4. Clever in talk or argument; good at repartee 1639. b. Of sayings, etc.: Clever, pointed; witty 1656. 5. Alert and brisk; combining briskness with neatness or trimness of appearance 1602. b. Neatly and trimly dressed 1789. c. Of dress, etc.: Neat and trim; stylish 1716. 6. Fashionable, elegant, esp. in a very high degree 1718.

2. We were mighty s. getting under way 1899. 3. In America every s. man is expected to be able to do anything he turns his hand to 1888. A..s. catch at mid-on 1895. 4. b. He mistakes the question, that he may return a s. answer JOHNSON. 5. The s. lads of the city march'd downe the streets 1683. c. A collection of s...boots and shoes 1859. 6. I have seen plenty of s. society 1881. Hence **Smart, Sma·rt-ly** *advs.*, **-ness.**

Smart (smāɹt), *v.* [OE. *smeortan*; the stem is perh. related to Gr. σμερδνός, σμερδαλέος terrible, and L. *mordēre* to bite.] 1. *intr.* Of wounds, etc.: To be a source of sharp pain; to be acutely painful. 2. †With dative: To cause pain, be painful, to (a person, etc.) –ME. b. With sbs., passing into *trans.*: To affect with pain or smarting ME. 3. *intr.* To feel sharp pain or distress; to suffer acutely or severely ME. b. To bear the penalty, to suffer severely, *for* some offence, etc. 1548.

1. Here woundis sore did smerte 1400. 2. b. The smoke..smarted the nose 1884. 3. Countreys that yet smarted with the last years War 1670. b. He has done us a wrong, and should be made to s. for it 1884.

Smarten (smā·ɹt'n), *v.* 1815. [f. SMART *a.*] 1. *trans.* To make smart or spruce. Usu. with *up.* Also *absol.* 2. To brighten *up* 1864.

Sma·rt-mo·ney. 1693. [f. SMART *sb.*[1]] 1. A sum of money paid to sailors, soldiers, workmen, etc., as compensation for disablement or injuries received while on duty or at work. b. Any compensation made for injury or the like 1749. 2. Money paid to obtain the discharge of a recruit who has enlisted in the army 1760. b. Money paid on account of cancelling or not fulfilling a bargain or agreement, or in order to free oneself from some disadvantage, recover some lapsed privilege, etc. 1818.

1. b. (*U.S. law.*) *Smart-Money*...Damages beyond the value of a thing sued for, given by a jury in case of gross misconduct or cruelty on the part of a defendant 1851. So **Sma·rt-ti·cket**, a certificate given to wounded seamen entitling them to a pension or gratuity.

Sma·rtweed. Chiefly *dial.* and *U.S.* 1787. [f. SMART *sb.*[1] or *a.*] A name given to species of *Polygonum*, esp. the arsesmart or water-pepper, *P. Hydropiper.*

Smarty (smā·ɹti). *U.S.* 1880. [f. SMART *a.* II. 4.] A would-be smart or witty person.

Smash (smæʃ), *sb.*[1] 1779. [f. SMASH *v.*[1]] 1. *dial.* or *colloq.* A hard or heavy blow. b. *Lawn-tennis.* A hard and fast overhand volley 1882. 2. A shivered or broken-up condition 1798. Also *fig.* 3. A loud sound of breaking or crushing; a severe or extensive crushing, shivering, or breaking of anything, esp. accompanied by a crashing sound; a violent collision or impact 1808. b. *S.-up* [f. verbal phr.], a complete smash 1858. 4. Commercial failure; stoppage through insolvency; bankruptcy 1839. b. A crushing defeat or overthrow 1854. 5. An American beverage made of spirit, ice, water, sugar, and flavoured with mint 1859.

2. He determined .. to go to s. like a hero 1807. Phr. *to break, knock*, etc. *to s.* 4. b. It was a final s. to the enemy in the north BADEN-POWELL.

Smash, *sb.*[2] *Cant.* 1795. [Origin obsc.] Counterfeit coin.

Smash (smæʃ), *v.*[1] 1778. [prob. echoic.] I. *trans.* To break (a thing) in pieces violently; to dash to pieces; to crush, shatter, or shiver. b. *Bookbinding.* To flatten or compress (the sheets of a book) before binding 1875. 2. To dash or fling (a thing) with noise and violence; to batter; to cause to strike hard 1800. b. *Lawn-Tennis.* To strike (the ball) violently and swiftly in an overhand volley. Also *absol.* 1882. 3. To defeat utterly; to crush completely 1813. b. To render insolvent or bankrupt 1857.

1. The bottle is smashed, smashed to atoms! 1851. *absol.* in phr. *S.-and-grab*, applied to robbery consisting of smashing shop windows and grabbing the goods; also, of the thief. 2. I'll s. your face in 1852. It is asked that their grinders may be smashed in, broken off, or dashed out 1872. 3. A British expedition to 's.' the Mahdi 1884.

II. *intr.* 1. To move rapidly with shattering effect, dash violently, crash 1835. 2. *colloq.* To fail financially; to be ruined. Also with *up.* 1839. 3. To break or fly in pieces 1904.

2. A Glazier?—what if he should smash! HOOD. Phr. *To go s.*

Smash, *v.*[2] *Cant.* 1811. [Cf. SMASH *sb.*[2]] *trans.* To pass (counterfeit money). Hence **Sma·sher** [2], one who passes or utters counterfeit coin or forged notes.

Smasher [1] (smæ·ʃəɹ). 1794. [f. SMASH *v.*[1]] 1. *slang.* Anything uncommon, extraordinary, or unusual, *esp.* unusually large or excellent. 2. *colloq.* A severe or crushing reply, article, review, etc. 1828. 3. An appliance or machine which smashes or crushes; *spec.* a bookbinder's compressing-machine; a form of embossing-press 1822. 4. One who smashes 1884.

Smatch (smætʃ), *sb.* [ME. *smach*, var. development of OE. *smæc* SMACK *sb.*[1]] = SMACK *sb.*[1] So **Smatch** *v.* [OE. *smæccan*] = SMACK *v.*[1]

Smatter (smæ·təɹ), *v.* ME. [Origin obsc.] †1. *trans.* To dirty, smirch, pollute, defile –1600. †2. *intr.* To talk ignorantly or superficially, to prate or chatter, *of* something –1733. †b. Without const. –1691. 3. To have a slight or superficial knowledge or practice *of*; to dabble, to be a smatterer (*in* or *at* something) 1530. 4. *trans.* To talk or utter without proper knowledge or proficiency 1609.

2. b. Good Prudence, s. with your gossip, go SHAKS. 3. A man can but s. in six or seven languages 1573. 4. The barber smatters Latin, I remember B. JONS. Hence **Sma·tter** *sb.* superficial knowledge; a smattering. In *pl.*, scraps, trifles.

Smatterer (smæ·tərəɹ). 1519. [f. SMATTER *v.*] One who has only a slight or superficial knowledge *of* (now rare) or *in* a matter; a dabbler. Also used without const.

Sma·ttering, *vbl. sb.* 1538. [f. SMATTER *v.*] 1. A slight or superficial knowledge *in* or *of* something. †2. The action of discoursing or studying superficially (*rare*) –1692.

1. A s. of 'scholarship' 1874. 2. I would advise them to leave off this dabbling and s. in Philosophy 1692.

Smear (smiᵊɹ), *sb.* [In sense 1 Com. Teut.; OE. *sme(o)ru.* The later senses are f. the vb.] †1. Fat, grease, lard; ointment –1648. 2. A mark, smudge, or stain made by smearing, or suggestive of this; a layer or patch of some substance applied by smearing 1611. b. A small quantity of some substance smeared upon a slide for microscopical investigation 1903. 3. a. An application for smearing sheep 1802. b. *Pottery.* A mixture used for glazing 1875.

2. Roof, and walls..abounding in old smears of.. red-lead, and damp DICKENS.

Smear (smīᵊɹ), *v.* [Com. Teut.; OE. *smerian*, f. *smeru* SMEAR *sb.*] **1.** *trans.* To anoint with oil, chrism, etc., as a symbolic ceremony. In later use only contemptuous. **2.** To anoint, to rub or daub (a part of the body) with oil, grease, etc. Said also of the oil, etc. OE. **3.** To anoint medicinally; to treat (a wound, etc.) with a copious application of some thick or greasy medicament OE. **b.** To SALVE (sheep). late ME. **4.** To spread, daub, cover thickly or in patches *with* some unctuous, greasy, sticky, or dirty substance. Occas. said of the substance. Also without const. OE. **b.** *techn.* To glaze (pottery) by a process of evaporation 1839. **5.** To lay *on* in a thick or greasy layer ME. **6.** To rub *out* with a smear or smudge; to rub or draw in a smeary manner 1840.

2. The Groom..stript for Wrestling, smears his Limbs with Oyl DRYDEN. **4.** Slugs, pinched with hunger, smear'd the slimy wall 1763. *fig.* People smearing each other over with stupid flattery 1847.

Smear-dab. 1769. [perh. f. SMEAR *sb.* or *v.*] A variety of dab, also called lemon or smooth dab.

S., due to its being frequently covered with slime 1882.

Smeared (smīᵊɹd), *ppl. a.* 1584. [f. SMEAR *v.* + -ED [1].] Dirtied or soiled by smearing; bedaubed. **b.** *S. dagger*, a species of moth, *Apatella oblinita* 1883.

Smeary (smīᵊ·ri), *a.* 1529. [f. SMEAR *sb.* or *v.*] **1.** Marked or characterized by smears; bedaubed, begrimed. **2.** Tending to smear or soil; of a greasy or unctuous nature 1582. Hence **Smea·riness.**

Smeath (smīþ). *local.* 1622. [Related to SMEE.] The smee. Also *s. duck.*

Smectite (sme·ktəit). 1811. [f. Gr. σμηκτίς + -ITE [1] 2 b.] *Min.* A kind of fuller's earth.

Smectymnuan (smekti·mniuăn), *sb.* and *a.* 1646. [f. *Smectymnuus* (-vvs), a fictitious name made out of the initials of the five authors of *An Answer to a Book*, etc. (1641). See N.E.D.] **A.** *sb.* One or other of the authors of the work published under the name of Smectymnuus; also, one who accepted the views of these writers. **B.** *adj.* Pertaining to, connected with, or characteristic of, the Smectymnuans 1673.

Smeddum, variant of SMITHAM.

Smee (smī). *dial.* and *U.S.* 1668. [prob. later f. SMEATH.] A name for the smew, widgeon, pochard, and scaup-duck.

Smeek (smīk), *v.* Latterly *Sc.* and †*north.* [OE. *smēocan* and *smēcan*; related to SMOKE.] †**1.** *intr.* To emit smoke -1440. **2.** *trans.* To fumigate; to suffocate OE.

Smeeth (smīþ, smīð), *a.* and *sb.* *Obs.* exc. *dial.* [OE. *smǣðe*, *smēðe*, related to *smōð* SMOOTH *a.*] **A.** *adj.* Smooth; free from roughness. **B.** *sb.* A level space. *E. Anglian dial.* 1440. Hence **Smeeth** *v. trans.* to make smooth.

‖**Smegma** (sme·gmă). 1819. [L., a. Gr. σμῆγμα a detergent, f. σμήχειν.] *Phys.* A sebaceous secretion, *esp.* that found under the prepuce.

Smell (smel), *sb.* ME. [Cf. SMELL *v.*] **1.** The sense of which the nose is the organ; the faculty of smelling. Now usu. in *sense, organ*, etc., *of s.* **2.** That property of things which affects the olfactory organ; odour, perfume, aroma; stench, stink ME. **3.** *fig.* A trace, suggestion, or tinge *of* something. Also without article, or with adj. 1475. **4.** An act of smelling; a sniff 1560.

1. I have no s. yet, but my cold something better SWIFT. **2.** There was such a rich s. of pines 1847. There was a nasty s. about the premises 1885. **3.** Without the least s. or tang of imperfection BUNYAN.

Smell (smel), *v.* [Early ME. *smellen*, presumably of OE. origin. In pa. t. and pa. pple. *smelt* is now more freq. than *smelled.*] **I.** *trans.* **1.** To have perception of (an object, odour, etc.) by means of the olfactory sense. **b.** To inhale the odour or scent of (a thing); to sniff at; to examine in this way 1830. **2.** To perceive as if by smell; to suspect, to have an inkling of; to divine. late ME. **3.** To search or find *out* by, or as by, the sense of smell 1538. **4.** To distinguish (one thing *from* another) by the smell 1582. **5.** To find or make (one's way) by the sense of smell 1605.

1. Paris may be smelt five miles before you arrive at it 1779. *To s. powder*, to have actual experience of fighting. *To s. a rat*: see RAT *sb.* 1. **2.** The people never smelt the cheat 1798. *To s. the ground*, of ships, to slacken speed as the water becomes shallower. **3.** The Scots folks have an excellent nose to s. out their Countryfolks 1756. **5.** Go thrust him out at gates, and let him s. His way to Douer SHAKS.

II. *intr.* **1.** To exercise, employ, make use of, the sense of smell in relation to a specified object. Const. *at, of* (now *U.S.*), or *to.* ME. **2.** Without const. To possess or exercise the sense of smell; to be able to perceive odours, or to be engaged in doing this ME.

1. She smelt at her salts, and soon recovered that weakness READE. **2.** It will be the object of this Committee..to go smelling in Shoreditch 1898.

III. **1.** *intr.* To give out, send forth, or exhale an odour; to have a smell, scent, etc. ME. **b.** *spec.* To give out an offensive odour; to stink. late ME. **2.** To exhale or emit the odour *of*, to smell *of*, something. Also rarely *on* (now *dial.*). 1526. **b.** To have a touch, tinge, or suggestion *of* something 1526. **3.** *trans.* To have or emit a smell of (something) 1586.

1. Hee smels like a fish SHAKS. **b.** If he reach old Age..his Breath smells 1684. *fig.* Oh my offence is ranke, it smels to heauen SHAKS. **2.** One of the..men already smells of sherry DICKENS. **b.** Praises in an enemy are superfluous, or s. of craft MILT. Phr. *To s. of the candle, lamp, oil*, etc., of literary work, to show signs of being laboured and artificial. **3.** He smels April and May SHAKS.

Smeller (sme·lәɹ). 1519. [f. SMELL *v.* + -ER [1].] **1.** One who has or exercises the sense of smell; one who smells *out.* **2.** A feeler; a slender tactile organ, hair, etc.; *esp.* one of the whiskers of a cat 1665. **3.** *slang.* **a.** The nose; *pl.* the nostrils 1700. **b.** A blow on the nose; hence, a hard blow of any kind 1824.

Sme·ll-feast. 1519. [f. SMELL *v.* or *sb.* + FEAST *sb.*] **1.** One who scents out where feasting is to be had; one who comes uninvited to share in a feast; a parasite, a greedy sponger. Now *arch.* **b.** *attrib.* Parasitic, sponging 1566. **2.** 'A feast at which the guests are supposed to feed upon the odors only of the viands' 1864.

1. The Smell-feasts rouse them at the hint There's cookery in a certain dwelling-place BROWNING.

Smellfungus (sme·lˌfɒ·ŋgɒs). *Pl.* **-fungi.** 1807. [Sterne's name for Smollett, with reference to the captious tone of Smollett's *Travels through France and Italy* (1766).] A discontented person; a grumbler, faultfinder.

Smelling (sme·liŋ), *vbl. sb.* ME. [f. SMELL *v.*] **1.** The sense of smell. **b.** The act or fact of smelling. Also with *out.* 1509. †**2.** Odour, scent, smell -1611.

attrib.: **s.-bottle**, a phial or small bottle for containing smelling-salts or perfume ready for use; **-salts**, a preparation of carbonate of ammonia and scent for smelling, used as a restorative in cases of faintness or headache. So **Smelling** *ppl. a.* (chiefly in SWEET-SMELLING).

Smell-less (sme·lˌlės), *a.* 1612. [f. SMELL *sb.* + -LESS.] **1.** Giving out no smell; scentless. **2.** Having no sense of smell 1873.

Sme·ll-smock. 1550. [f. SMELL *v.* + SMOCK *sb.*] †**1.** A licentious man -1673. **2.** Dial. name for various plants 1876.

Smelly (sme·li), *a.* 1862. [f. SMELL *sb.* or *v.* + -Y [1].] Emitting a bad smell or smells; stinking.

Smelt (smelt), *sb.* [OE., = obs. G. *schmelt, schmelz*, Da. *smelt.*] **1.** A small fish, *Osmerus eparlanus*, allied to the salmon, and emitting a peculiar odour; the sparling or spirling. **b.** A fish of a related species, esp. *O. mordax* of the American coast 1836. **c.** Applied to the atherine or sand-smelt and other small fishes 1776. †**2.** *transf.* A simpleton -1625.

Smelt (smelt), *v.* 1543. [prob. ad. MDu. or MLG. *smelten.* The stem is app. a variation of that of MELT *v.*] *trans.* To fuse or melt (ore, etc.) in order to extract the metal; to obtain or produce (metal) by this means. Hence **Sme·ltery**, a place where ores are smelted.

Smelt-, the stem of SMELT *v.* in comb., as **s.-furnace, -house, -mill**, places where smelting is carried on.

Smelter (sme·ltәɹ), *sb.* 1455. [f. SMELT *v.* + -ER [1].] **1.** One who smelts; a workman engaged in smelting; an owner of smelting-works. **2.** Smelting-works; a smeltery. orig. *U.S.* 1877.

Smelting (sme·ltiŋ), *vbl. sb.* 1531. [f. SMELT *v.*] The action of SMELT *v.* Also *attrib.*, as *s.-furnace, works*, etc.

Smew (smiū). 1674. [Cf. SMEE.] A saw-billed duck (*Mergus* or *Mergellus albellus*) belonging to the merganser group; the white nun. The female is the *red-headed s.*

†**Smi·cker,** *a.* [OE. *smicer*; cf. OHG. *smehhar, smechar.*] Beautiful, handsome -1639. Hence **Smi·cker** *v. Sc. intr.* to look amorously or wantonly; to smile or smirk.

Smicket (smi·kėt). Now *dial.* 1685. [app. dim. of SMOCK *sb.*] A woman's smock or chemise; a small smock.

Smift. 1839. [Origin unkn.] *Mining.* A kind of fuse or slow match used in blasting.

Smilacin (smәi·lăsin). 1836. [a. F., f. *smilac-*, stem of SMILAX + -IN [1].] *Chem.* Parillin.

Smilax (smәi·læks). 1601. [a. L. (Pliny), a. Gr. σμῖλαξ bindweed.] *Bot.* **1.** A large genus of liliaceous plants typical of the order *Smilaceæ*, or a species of this genus, the tuberous rootstocks of which constitute the sarsaparilla of commerce. **2.** A climbing species of asparagus, *Myrsiphyllum asparagoides*, much used for decorative purposes 1870.

Smile (smәil), *sb.* 1562. [f. SMILE *v.*] **1.** An act of smiling; a slight and more or less involuntary movement of the countenance expressive of pleasure, amusement, affection, etc., or of amused contempt, disdain, incredulity, etc. (the characteristic features are a brightening of the eyes and an upward curving of the corners of the mouth). **2.** *colloq.* A drink, *esp.* of whisky. orig. *U.S.* 1859.

1. This sweet intercourse Of looks and smiles MILT. *transf.* and *fig.* Methought I stood not in the s. of Heauen SHAKS. Turn, Fortune, turn thy wheel with s. or frown TENNYSON. Hence **Smi·let** (*rare*) a little or slight s.

Smile (smәil), *v.* [ME. *smilen*; perh. a. MLG. **smîlen.*] **I.** *intr.* **1.** Of persons: To give to the features or face a look expressive of pleasure or amusement, or of amused disdain, scorn, etc. (see prec.). **2. a.** To look *on, upon, at*, or *to* a person with a smile or pleasant expression. late ME. **b.** To look *on* or *upon* one with favour, approval, or encouragement ME. **c.** To show by the features one's amusement (or pleasure) *at* something. late ME. **3.** Of physical features, things, etc.: To have or present an agreeable or pleasing aspect 1594. **4.** (*U.S.*) *slang.* To have or take a drink 1858.

1. Some that s., haue in their hearts I feare Millions of Mischeefes SHAKS. *transf.* and *fig.* Then let me not pass Occasion which now smiles MILT. The flower that smiles today Tomorrow dies SHELLEY. **2. a.** His mother on him smil'd HOBBES. **b.** Circumstances..seemed to s. on the project 1878. **3.** Cheard with the grateful smell old Ocean smiles MILT.

II. 1. a. To bring or convert into a specified condition by smiling. Const. *in, into, out of*, etc. 1588. **b.** To dismiss, get rid of, drive *away* (something) with a smile or smiles; to while *away* (time), dry *up* (tears), in or by smiling 1760. †**2.** To deride, laugh at. SHAKS. **3. a.** To exhibit, indicate, or express by smiling; to grant, bestow, etc., with a smile 1646. **b.** With cogn. obj.: To give (a smile, esp. one of a specified kind) 1837.

1. a. He does s. his face into more lynes, then is in the new Mappe SHAKS. **b.** A woman's reputation must not be smiled away 1885. **3. a.** She smiled disbelief 1880. **b.** Mr. Weller junior smiled a filial smile DICKENS. Hence **Smi·ling·ly** *adv.*, **-ness.**

Smileless (smәi·lˌlės), *a.* 1719. [f. SMILE *sb.*] **1.** Of persons, etc.: Exhibiting no smile; never smiling; grave, severe. **b.** Of words: Uttered without a smile 1810. **2.** Devoid of brightness or cheerfulness; dark, dull, cheerless 1858.

Smiler (smәi·lәɹ). late ME. [f. SMILE *v.*] **1.** One who smiles. **2.** *slang.* A kind of shandy-gaff 1892.

Smirch (smɔ̄ɹtʃ), *v.* 1495. [app. ad. OF. *esmorcher* to torment, with slight transference of sense.] **1.** *trans.* Of things: To make dirty, soil, sully, or discolour (something) by contact or touch. **2.** Of persons (or animals): To stain or befoul (the face, person, reputation, etc.) *with* or by means of something dirty, foul, or defamatory 1600.

1. *fig.* Lower thoughts as well as lower passions ..s. the human soul TROLLOPE. 2. Ile put my selfe in poore and meane attire, And with a kinde of vmber s. my face SHAKS. Hence **Smirch** *sb.* a dirty mark or smear, a stain; that which smirches or dirties.

Smirk (smɜ̄ɹk), *sb.* 1560. [f. SMIRK *v.*] An affected or simpering smile; a silly, conceited, smiling look.

He has the canonical s., and the filthy clammy palm of a chaplain WYCHERLEY. Hence **Smi·rky** *a. Sc.* and *U.S.* smart, neat, smiling; of the nature of a s.

Smirk (smɜ̄ɹk), *a.* and *adv.* 1530. [app. f. SMIRK *v.*; but cf. SMICKER *a.*] A. *adj.* Neat, trim, spruce in dress or appearance; pleasant, agreeable. Also *U.S.*, smug. Now chiefly *dial.*

Seest, how brag yond Bullocke beares, So smirke, so smoothe, his pricked eares? SPENSER.

†B. *adv.* Smirkingly. HEYWOOD.

Smirk (smɜ̄ɹk), *v.* [OE. *smearcian, smercian*; not in cogn. langs.] 1. *intr.* To smile; in later use, to smile in an affected, self-satisfied, or silly manner; to simper. 2. *trans.* To utter with a smirk. BROWNING.

1. The young perfumer came, smirking and scraping, into the room MME D'ARBLAY. Hence **Smi·rker.** **Smi·rkingly** *adv.* in a smirking manner.

Smite (smait), *sb.* ME. [f. next.] A stroke or heavy blow with a weapon, the hand, etc., or the sound made by this. Now chiefly *rhet.*

Smite (smait), *v.* Pa. t. **smote** (smōᵘt), †smit. Pa. pple. **smitten** (smi·t'n), **smit** (*arch.*), †smote. [OE. *smītan*, = OFris. *smīta*, (M)LG. *smīten* to throw, OHG. *smīzan* to strike.] I. *trans.* 1. To administer a blow to (a person, etc.) with the hand, a stick, or the like; to strike or hit; to beat or buffet; to slap or smack. Now *rhet.* and *rare.* b. To strike with the foot (†or spur). Also said of the foot. Now *rhet.* or *poet.* ME. c. To strike or touch (a harp, etc.) so as to produce musical sounds. Now *poet.* late ME. 2. Of the Deity, in or after biblical use: To visit with death, destruction, or overthrow; to afflict or punish in some signal manner OE. 3. To strike with a weapon, etc., so as to inflict serious injury or death ME. b. In or after Biblical use: To strike, or strike down, in battle; to kill, slay ME. 4. a. Of hail, lightning, flame, etc.: To strike and injure; to destroy, blast. late ME. b. To beat or dash against (something) 1440. c. Of sunlight, etc.: To beat or shine strongly upon 1588. 5. Of diseases, distempers, etc.: To attack or affect suddenly or grievously. Freq. in pa. pple., and const. *by* or *with* (a malady, etc.). ME. 6. To infect, imbue, impress, strike suddenly or strongly *with* some feeling or sentiment. Chiefly in pa. pple. ME. 7. Of the heart, conscience, etc.: To discompose or disquiet (one); to affect painfully. late ME. b. To distress or perturb (a person, the mind, conscience, etc.) 1470. 8. To strike or impress (the mind, etc.) favourably or attractively. Chiefly in pa. pple. and const. *with.* 1663. b. To inspire or inflame with love; to enamour. Chiefly in pa. pple. (*smitten*, also joc. *smit*) and const. *with* or *by.* 1663.

1. The Case was the same with Asa in his Anger, when he smote the Prophet 1675. c. Then smyte your tabur, and cry huff, huff, huff and make the fowle to spryng 1486. 2. The Lorde smote him, so yᵗ he dyed COVERDALE 1 *Sam.* xxv. 38. 3. I am so deeply smitten thro' the helm That without help I cannot last till morn TENNYSON. Phr. *To s...hip and thigh*: see HIP *sb.*¹ 4. b. With the din Smitten, the precipices rang aloud WORDSW. c. As thy eye beames, when their fresh rayse haue smot The night of dew SHAKS. 6. Wit strang dred he smiton was ME. 7. Dauids heart smote him, because he had cut off Sauls skirt 1 *Sam.* xxiv. 5. 8. Smit with the beauty of so fair a scene COWPER. b. Phillis one Day ..smote the Heart of a gay West-Indian STEELE.

II. *trans.* 1. To strike or cut *off* (the head, a limb, etc.) with a slashing blow ME. b. To strike or knock, to drive or force with a blow or stroke, *away, back, from, off, out, over*, etc. ME. 2. To knock, beat, or strike *down, to the earth* or *ground* ME. 3. a. To hew, cut, chop, or break in pieces, fragments, etc. ME. b. To bring *into* a certain condition by, or as by, striking (*rare*) ME. 4. To strike, deal, or give (a blow, stroke, etc.) ME. 5. To drive, hammer, knock, strike (a thing) with some degree of force *against, into, on*, etc. something else ME. b. To strike, dash, or clap *together* or *against* each other ME. †6. a. To make or contract (an agreement, etc.) –1596. †b. To strike or coin (money) –1535.

2. Surely they are smitten downe before vs *Judges* xx. 39. 3. b. If we look not wisely on the Sun it self, it smites us into darknes MILT. 5. Then Iael..went softly vnto him, and smote the naile into his temples *Judges* iv. 21.

III. *absol.* or *intr.* 1. To deal or give a blow or blows; to strike, deliver strokes. Also with advs. as *on, out.* ME. b. To strike *with* a hammer in doing smith-work; now *spec.* to strike with the sledge. late ME. †2. To come *together* in conflict –1590. b. To come *together* with some degree of force; to strike or dash *on* or *against* something ME. 3. To strike, to pass or penetrate, *in, into*, or *through* something ME.

1. Satan..Saw where the Sword of Michael smote MILT. 2. b. The heart melteth, and the knees s. together *Nahum* ii. 10. 3. But Arthur..Felt the light of her eyes into his life S. on the sudden TENNYSON. Hence **Smi·tten** *ppl. a.* that has been beaten or struck.

Smiter (smai·tər). ME. [f. prec. + -ER¹.] 1. One who smites; a beater, striker. †2. A weapon with which one smites; a sword, a scimitar. (Partly suggested by *simiter* 'scimitar'.) –1648. 3. A variety of fancy pigeon 1668.

Smith (smiþ), *sb.* [Com. Teut.; OE. *smið*.] One who works in iron or other metals; *esp.* a blacksmith or farrier; a forger, hammerman. Freq. in combs., as *black-, copper-, silver-, whitesmith.*

Smith (smiþ), *v.* [Com. Teut.; OE. *smiðian*, f. the stem of *smið* SMITH *sb.*] 1. *trans.* To make, construct, or fashion (a weapon, iron implement, etc.) by forging; to forge or smithy. b. To deal with by heating and hammering; to hammer or beat (a blade, etc.) on an anvil. late ME. 2. *intr.* To work at the forge; to practise smith-work ME.

1. b. After forging, the blade is smithed, or beaten on an anvil 1851. Hence **Smi·ther** (*rare*) a s.; a hammerman.

Smitham (smi·ðăm), **smeddum** (sme·dǝm). 1653. [OE. *smeduma*; later assoc. w. SMITH *sb.* or *v.*] 1. A fine powder. 2. *Mining.* The finest lead ore, usu. passed through a sieve, and afterwards ground to powder 1653. 3. *Sc.* Spirit, energy, go 1790.

Smi·thcraft. 1755. [f. SMITH *sb.* (Cf. OE. *smiðcræft*).] The work, craft, or art of a smith.

Smithereens (smiðərī·nz), *sb. pl. colloq.* and *dial.* 1841. [f. next, with Irish dim. ending.] Small fragments; atoms. Usu. in phrases *to knock* (etc.) *to* or *into, to go to, s.*

Smithers (smi·ðəɹz), *sb. pl.* Also sing. *colloq.* and *dial.* 1847. [Origin unkn.] = prec.

Smithery (smi·þəri). 1625. [f. SMITH *sb.* + -ERY.] 1. The trade, occupation, or art of a smith; smithcraft, smith-work. 2. The forge or workshop of a smith; a smithy; *esp.* in British Admiralty dockyards, the building in which smith-work is done 1755.

1. *fig.* From..this sonorous s. of harsh words..nothing adequate emerged DE QUINCEY.

Smithfield (smi·þfīld). 1599. [Name of a locality in London (orig. *Smethefeld*, f. SMEETH *a.*), long celebrated as a market for cattle, etc., and now the central meat-market.] 1. A cattle- or meat-market (*rare*). †2. *S. bargain*, a sharp or roguish bargain, or one in which the purchaser is deceived; also *transf.*, a mercenary marriage –1775.

2. To find myself made a mere S. bargain of at last! SHERIDAN.

Smithing (smi·þiŋ), *vbl. sb.* ME. [f. SMITH *v.*] The action of SMITH *v.*; the art or process of fashioning or forging metals; forging.

Smithsonite (smi·þsǝnait). 1835. [Named after James *Smithson* (1765–1829), who distinguished it from calamine.] *Min.* 1. Silicate of zinc. 2. *U.S.* Carbonate of zinc 1856.

Smithy (smi·ði), *sb.* Also *Sc.* and *n. dial.* **smiddy.** ME. [ad. ON. *smiðja*, = OE. *smiððe.*] 1. The workshop of a smith; a blacksmith's shop. Also occas., a portable forge. 2. Smithcraft (*rare*) 1804.

1. His blazing Locks..hiss'd, like red hot Iron within the S. drown'd DRYDEN. Hence **Smithy** *v. trans.* to forge or smith; *intr.* to practise smithing.

Smi·ttle, *a.* *n. dial.* and *Sc.* 1583. [f. dial. *smit* :—OE. *smittian*, f. *smītan* SMITE + -LE 1.] Infectious; contagious. So **Smi·ttle** *v. trans.* to infect.

Smock (smǫk), *sb.* [OE. *smoc.* The stem is prob. related to that of OE. *smūgan* to creep, ON. *smjúga* to creep into, put on, a garment.] 1. A woman's undergarment; a shift or chemise. Now *arch.* or *dial.* †b. Used allusively to denote a woman or womankind –1693. 2. = SMOCK-FROCK 1831.

1. Neare is my petticoat but nearer is my s. 1639. The colonel gave a s. for the young wenches to run for 1722.

attrib. and *Comb.*: **s.-face**, a pale and smooth or effeminate face; a person having a face of this description; so **-faced** *a.*; **-race**, a race in which a s. was offered as a prize to be run for by women or girls. Hence **Smo·ckless** *a.* having no s. or chemise.

Smock (smǫk), *v.* 1614. [f. the sb.] †1. *trans.* To render effeminate or womanish. SYLVESTER. †2. *intr.* To consort with women –1738. 3. *trans.* To dress in a smock 1847. 4. *Needlework.* To gather by means of sewing done in lines crossing each other diagonally at regular intervals after a honeycomb pattern common on smock-frocks 1888. Freq. in *vbl. sb.* (concr. the pattern so formed). Hence **Smo·cker**, one who smocks blouses, etc.

Smock-frock. 1800. [SMOCK *sb.*] A loose-fitting garment of coarse linen or the like, worn by farm-labourers over or instead of a coat and usu. reaching to mid-leg or lower. Hence **Smo·ck-frocked** (frǫkt) *a.* wearing a s.

Smokable (smōᵘ·kăb'l), *a.* and *sb.* Also **smokeable.** 1839. [f. SMOKE *v.* + -ABLE.] A. *adj.* That may be smoked; fit or suitable for smoking. B. *sb. pl.* Things which may be smoked 1849.

Smoke (smōᵘk), *sb.* [OE. *smoca* (cf. next) related to SMEEK *v.*] 1. The visible volatile product given off by burning or smouldering substances. b. *transf.* The pollen of the yew when scattered in a cloud 1868. 2. With *a* and *pl.* A volume, cloud, or column of smoke. In Amer. and Austr. use *spec.* one serving as a signal, sign of an encampment, etc. late ME. b. The smoke arising from a particular hearth or fireplace; hence, a hearth, fire-place, house. Now *rare.* 1591. 3. Fume or vapour caused by the action of heat on moisture. late ME. b. A mist, fog, or miasma 1648. 4. a. Tobacco. Now *rare* or *Obs.* 1612. b. A cigar or cigarette 1882. 6. [f. the vb.] A spell of smoking tobacco, etc. 1837. 7. *Cape s.*, a cheap kind of brandy drunk in South Africa 1849.

2. We..leave them a sign to know where we are by making one or more great Smoaks 1697. 6. Eager for a s. and a talk 1837.

Phrases. *There is no fire without s.* and *no s. without fire* (see FIRE *sb.* 1 b). †*Out of the s. into the fire*, *smother*, etc., out of a small danger into a great one. *To sell s.* (after L. *fumum vendere*), to swindle. *To come to, end in, vanish into, s.*, to come to nothing, be without result. *Like s.*, very quickly, rapidly.

attrib. and *Comb.*, as *s.-cloud, -ring, -wreath*; *s.-flue, funnel*; *s.-blue, -grey* (used as sbs. or adjs.); *s. quartz*, smoky quartz; *s.-consumer, -consuming*; *s.-proof, -tight* adjs.

Special combs.: **s.-arch** *U.S.*, the s.-box of a locomotive; **-bomb** = S.-BALL; **-box** *techn.* a chamber in a steam boiler between the flues and the chimney-stack; in a locomotive placed at the base of the funnel; **-farthing** *Hist.* an offering made at Whitsuntide by the householders of a diocese to the cathedral church; also, a hearth-tax; **-glass**, an eyepiece of smoked glass; **s. helmet**, a helmet used by firemen, enabling the wearer to see and breathe freely in the midst of smoke; **-house**, a room in a tannery, heated by smouldering spent tan, where hides are unhaired; a house or room used for curing meat, fish, etc., by means of s.; **-sail** (*Naut.*), a small sail put up to prevent the s. of the galley from being blown aft; **-screen** *Mil.*, s. diffused to hide operations; **-test**, a method of testing the state of drains and pipes by means of s.; **-tree**, the Venetian sumach, *Rhus cotinus*, which has a feathery inflorescence suggestive of s.; also, the American species *Rhus cotinoides.*

Smoke (smōᵘk), *v.* [OE. *smocian*, f. *smoca* SMOKE *sb.*] I. 1. *intr.* To produce or give forth smoke. b. Of a room, chimney, lamp, etc.: To be smoky, to emit smoke, as the result of imperfect draught or improper burning 1663. 2. To give off or send up vapour, dust, spray, etc.; *esp.* to steam. late ME. **b.** To rise, spread, or move, like smoke 1595. **c.** To ride, drive, sail, etc., at a rapid pace or great speed. Const. *along* (prep. or adv.). 1697. †**3.** To smart, to suffer severely –1773.

1. The houses fired and smoking farre of 1591. *fig.* Where hertes still burne and malice continually smoketh 1548. **2.** Which made his horse's flanks to s. COWPER. **c.** Proud of his Steeds he smoaks along the Field DRYDEN. **3.** Now I am resolv'd I will go see 'em, or some-body shall smoak for 't DRYDEN.

II. 1. *trans.* To fumigate (a person, place, etc.), esp. as a means of disinfecting OE. **b.** To expose or subject to smoke, so as to suffocate, stupefy, or make uncomfortable OE. **c.** To fill with, expose to, smoke, esp. so as to blacken, discolour, or render obscure 1611. **d.** To cure or preserve (bacon, fish, etc.) by exposure to smoke; to smoke-dry 1757. **2.** To drive *out* or *away* by means of smoke 1593. **3.** To get an inkling of, to smell or suspect (a plot, design, etc.). Also *absol.* Now *arch.* 1608. **4.** To make fun of, to jest at; to ridicule, banter, or quiz (a person). Now *arch.* 1700. **5.** To observe, take note of, 'twig'. Now *arch.* 1715.

1. I was smoaking a musty roome SHAKS. **b.** They then s. the bees until they are stupid 1900. **c.** I copy pictures and he smokes them and sells them as old masters 1883. **2.** Till we s. out of his earths the old fox Louis SCOTT. **4.** We hated her and smoked her and baited her and..drove her away KEATS. **5.** Kit, s. his eyes, how they glare 1826.

III. 1. *intr.* To inhale (and expel again) the fumes of tobacco, etc., from a pipe, cigar, or cigarette 1617. **2.** *trans.* To use (tobacco, etc.) as material for smoking 1687. **b.** To use (a pipe, cigar, etc.) in the act of smoking; to take (so many whiffs) 1706. **3.** To wear *out*, waste (*away*), bring *into* a certain state, etc., by smoking tobacco or some similar substance 1604. **4.** *intr.* Of a pipe: To admit of being smoked 1883.

1. Smoking vehemently on his black stump of a pipe CARLYLE. **2.** The bandits' custom of smoking banghi (wild hemp) 1878. **b.** See, I have smoked out your cigar 1842. **3.** Sweet youth, Smoake not thy time 1617.

Smo·ke-ball. 1753. [SMOKE *sb.* I.] **1.** *Mil.* A projectile filled with a preparation which, when ignited, sends out clouds of smoke, used to conceal military operations, etc. **2.** A ball used in trap-shooting, which, when struck by a shot, emits a puff of smoke 1881.

Smo·ke-black, *sb.* 1712. [BLACK *sb.* 2.] A form of lamp-black obtained by the combustion of resinous materials.

Smo·ke-dry, *v.* 1704. [SMOKE *sb.* I.] **1.** *trans.* To dry or cure (meat, fish, etc.) by exposure to smoke. **2.** *intr.* To become dried by the action of smoke 1855. So **Smo·ke-dried** *ppl. a.* 1653.

Smo·ke-hole. ME. [SMOKE *sb.* I.] The vent or external orifice of a flue; a hole in the roof of a hut through which the smoke of the fire escapes. **b.** = FUMAROLE 1899.

Smo·ke-jack. 1675. [JACK *sb.* II. 1.] An apparatus for turning a roasting-spit, fixed in a chimney and set in motion by the current of air passing up this.

Smokeless (smōu·klės), *a.* 1582. [f. SMOKE *sb.* + -LESS.] **1.** Emitting or producing no smoke. **2.** Free from, clear of, smoke 1631.

1. Tenants with sighs the smoakless towr's survey POPE. **2.** The sun shines..in s. mackerel-sky CARLYLE. Hence **Smo·keless-ly** *adv.*, **-ness.**

Smoker (smōu·kəɹ). 1599. [f. SMOKE *v.* + -ER[1].] **1.** One who cures fish, bacon, etc., by means of smoke. **2.** Something which emits smoke; e.g. a chimney, locomotive, etc. 1700. **3.** One who smokes tobacco, opium, or the like 1617. **4. a.** A railway carriage or compartment assigned for the use of those travellers who wish to smoke 1883. **b.** A concert at which smoking is permitted 1891.

Smo·ke-stack. 1862. [SMOKE *sb.*] **1.** *U.S.* **a.** The funnel of a steamboat. **b.** The chimney of a locomotive 1875. **2.** The chimney of a stove; a chimney-stack 1871.

Smoking (smōu·kiŋ), *vbl. sb.* 1530. [f. SMOKE *v.*] The action of the vb. **b.** *attrib.*, as *s.-carriage, -concert*; **s.-bean** *U.S.*, the catalpa bean, the pods of which are smoked by boys; **-room,** a room in a house, hotel, etc. set apart in which to smoke.

Smoking (smōu·kiŋ), *ppl. a.* ME. [f. SMOKE *v.*] In the senses of the vb. **b.** quasi-*adv.* in *s.-hot* 1816. Hence **Smo·kingly** *adv.* smokily.

Smoky (smōu·ki), *a.* and *sb.* ME. [f. SMOKE *sb.* + -Y[1].] **A.** *adj.* **1.** Emitting smoke in considerable volume. **b.** Of a chimney: Inclined to send out smoke into the room 1639. **2.** Of vapour, mist, etc.: Having the character or appearance of smoke; smoke-like. late ME. **3.** Full of, or charged with, smoke; rendered offensive or disagreeable by the presence of smoke. late ME. **b.** Blackened or begrimed by smoke 1552. †**4.** *fig.* Having the obscuring, objectionable, or unsubstantial qualities of smoke –1633. **5.** Having the flavour or odour of smoke; tasting or smelling of smoke 1542. **6.** Of the colour of smoke; dark, dusky; *spec.* of a brownish or bluish shade of grey 1555. **7.** Steaming, reeking; rising in fine spray 1590. **8.** Addicted to, associated with, the smoking of tobacco 1596. †**9.** Shrewd, sharp, suspicious –1784. **10.** *U.S.* Foggy, misty 1768.

1. In Sympathizing Night he rowls his smoaky Fires 1663. **2.** The light and s. mist COWPER. **3.** O, he is..Worse then a smoakie House SHAKS. **b.** In lowly sheds With s. rafters MILT. **6.** S. quartz is a transparent..variety, having a s. color 1837. **8.** A s. man must write s. farces LAMB.

B. *sb.* **1.** *dial.* The hedge-sparrow 1889. **2.** *Sc.* A smoked haddock 1891. **3.** A smoke-blue cat 1898. Hence **Smo·kily** *adv.* **Smo·kiness.**

Smolt (smōult), *sb.* orig. *Sc.* and *north.* 1469. [Origin unkn.] **1.** A young salmon in the stage intermediate between the parr and the grilse, when it becomes covered with silvery scales and migrates to the sea for the first time. **2.** *transf.* A small person or thing 1808.

Smooch (smūtʃ), *v.* Latterly *U.S.* 1631. [Cf. SMUTCH *v.*] *trans.* To sully, dirty.

Smoot (smūt). *Printers' slang.* 1683. [Obscure.] *intr.* To do casual work in a house where one is not regularly employed.

Smooth (smūð), *sb.* 1440. [f. the adj.] **1.** †**a.** = SMEETH *sb.* **b.** *Naut.* A stretch of comparatively smooth or calm water in a rough sea 1840. **2.** The smooth part or surface *of* something; smoothness 1551. **b.** Smooth water or ground 1667. **c.** The agreeable or pleasant part, side, or aspect of anything. (Opp. to *rough.*) 1612. **3.** An act of smoothing 1848. **4.** A smoother; a smooth file 1879.

2. Like the silver-wing'd dove was the s. of her hair 1805.

Smooth (smūð), *a.* [OE. *smōð*.] **I.** Having a surface free from projections, irregularities, or inequalities; presenting no roughness or unevenness to the sight or touch. **b.** Free from hairs or bristles. late ME. **c.** *Bot.* Of leaves: Free from hairs or any sort of roughness 1688. **2.** Of ground, ways, etc.: Not rugged, rough, or broken; free from obstructions; easy to traverse. late ME. **3.** Of water, the sea, etc.: Not broken or turbulent; free from big waves or roughness; running or flowing evenly, calmly, or gently. Hence, of a passage, etc.: Accompanied by or performed in good weather. late ME. **4.** Of wind or weather: Not rough or stormy; agreeable, pleasant. Now *rare.* late ME. **5.** Of liquids, etc.: Having a uniform or even consistency; free from lumps or knots 1450. **b.** Of liquor: Soft to the taste; free from sharpness or acidity 1743. **6.** Of looks, words, etc.: Pleasant, affable, polite; seemingly amiable or friendly; having a show of sincerity. late ME. **b.** Of the tongue, or of persons: Speaking fair or smoothly; using specious or attractive language; plausible, bland, insinuating, flattering. (Usu. in an unfavourable sense.) 1450. **7.** Of style or diction: Flowing gently or easily; nicely modulated; not harsh or rugged; polished 1589. **b.** Of writers: Having an easy, polished style 1670. **8.** Free from disturbance or excitement 1756. **9.** Free from, unaccompanied by, obstruction, interruption, impediment, or difficulty. Also in phr. *to make s.* 1792. **10.** Of sounds: Soft; not harsh or grating 1775. **b.** *S. breathing*: see BREATHING *vbl. sb.* 9.

1. Brows as pale and s. As those that mourn..In deathless marble TENNYSON. **b.** Beholde, my brother Esau is rough, and I am s. COVERDALE *Gen.* xxvii. 11. **2.** The road to wickedness is s. and very short 1875. **3.** *S. chance* or *spell*, a stretch of calm water in a rough sea; Watching for 's. chance' 1840. **5. b.** More tuns of marsh water..than combs of s. ale 1896. **6.** Colour'd with a s. pretence Of specious love and duty DRYDEN. **b.** A s. Preacher, and a rank Whigg 1708. **7.** Their style is clear, masculine, and s., but not florid SWIFT. **8.** Hence have I S. passions, s. discourse, and joyous thought WORDSW. **9.** Consider too whether he had s. times of it CARLYLE.

Comb. Forming parasynthetic adjs., as *s.-bellied, -browed, -chinned*, etc.; **s.-spoken** *a.*, smooth-tongued. Hence **Smooth·ly** *adv.*, **-ness.**

Smooth(e (smūð), *v.* ME. [f. SMOOTH *a.*; repl. *smēðen* SMEETH *v.*] **1.** *trans.* To make (a surface or substance) smooth, even, or level; to remove or reduce the roughness, irregularity, inequality, or unevenness of 1440. **b.** To iron (linen, etc.). Now *dial.* 1617. **c.** To cause (feathers, hair, etc.) to lie smooth and even 1634. **2.** To make (a way) easy or plain; to free from obstruction, difficulty, or impediment 1582. **b.** To diminish or clear away (an obstruction, difficulty, etc.) 1599. **3.** To render (the brow) free from wrinkles, lines, frowns, etc., by natural effort; to invest with, replace by, a calm or placid expression 1593. **4. a.** To make smooth, plausible, or specious ME. †**b.** To refine (a person or his manners) –1749. **c.** To render smooth to the ear; to polish 1667. †**5.** To use smooth, flattering, or complimentary language to (a person). Also *absol.* –1718. **6. a.** To allay, assuage, mitigate the force of (passion, trouble, etc.) 1589. **b.** To render (the mind, etc.) calm or tranquil; to soothe 1604. **7.** To hush up, gloss over, make less conspicuous or offensive 1592. **8.** *intr.* To become smooth, calm, or tranquil 1837. **9.** With advs. and preps. 1584.

1. To s. the yce, or adde another hew Vnto the Raine-bow SHAKS. **c.** Smoothing the Raven doune Of darknes till it smil'd MILT. **2.** Useful for smoothing a man's way through the world 1779. **3.** Grim-visag'd Warre, hath smooth'd his wrinkled Front SHAKS. **4. a.** An open grave their throat, their tongue they s. MILT. **c.** Great Spencer first..Smoothed our old Metre, and refined our Lays 1724. **5.** Because I cannot flatter,..Smile in men's faces, s., deceiue, and cogge SHAKS. **6. a.** Whereof hee soon aware, Each perturbation smooth'd with outward calme, Artificer of fraud MILT. **b.** What could the world afford.. Which did not s. my soule 1604. **7.** Oh had 't beene a stranger..To s. his fault I should haue beene more milde SHAKS. **8.** I trust that things are smoothing now 1864. **9.** *To s. over* (fig.) to gloss over. This he smoothed over to his conscience SCOTT. Hence **Smoo·ther,** one who or that which smooths; a refiner, pacifier; an ironer; a smoothing-iron, etc.

Smoo·th(-)bore. 1848. [f. SMOOTH *a.* + BORE *sb.*[1]] **1.** A cannon or gun of which the barrel is made with a smooth or unrifled bore. **2.** *attrib.* **a.** Having a smooth or unrifled bore 1859. **b.** Adapted for guns having a smooth bore 1859.

Smoothen (smū·ð'n), *v.* 1635. [f. SMOOTH *a.* + -EN[5].] = SMOOTH *v.*

Smooth-faced, *a.* 1580. [SMOOTH *a.*] **1.** Of persons: Having a face free from hair, wrinkles, etc.; clean-shaven, beardless. **b.** *fig.* Having or assuming a bland, ingratiating, or insinuating expression; plausible in manner 1595. **2.** *fig.* Of words, etc.: Specious, plausible 1620. **3.** Of things: Having a smooth face or surface 1647.

1. *transf.* Let thy Heires..Enrich the time to come, with Smooth-fac'd Peace, With smiling Plenty SHAKS.

Smoothing (smū·ðiŋ), *vbl. sb.* 1577. [f. SMOOTH *v.*] The action of the verb; an instance of this. **b.** *Phonology.* The reduction of a diphthong to a monophthong 1888. **c.** *Wireless.* Levelling out of fluctuation in the supply of current.

attrib.: **s.-iron,** a flat-iron; an iron slicker used for smoothing leather; **-plane,** a small fine-set plane used in finishing; **-trowel,** a trowel used in plastering.

Smooth-tongued, *a.* 1592. [f. SMOOTH *a.*] **1.** Smooth or plausible in speech; using fair or flattering words; smooth-spoken. **2.** Marked or characterized by, of the nature of, plausibility or speciousness 1761.

1. Those Jesuits are so s. to women 1829.

Smore (smōəɹ), *v.* Now *Sc.* and *n. dial.* [OE. *smorian.*] = SMOTHER *v.*

Smored and styfled, theyr breath failing, thei gaue vp to God their innocent soules 1513.

Smother (smʌ·ðəɹ), *sb.* [Early ME. *smorðer*, f. the stem of OE. *smorian* SMORE *v.*] **1.** Dense, suffocating, or stifling smoke, such as is produced by combustion without flame.

(Freq. coupled with *smoke.*) b. A smouldering state or condition; a smouldering or slow-burning fire 1597. 2. Dense or suffocating dust, fog, etc., filling the air 1697. b. A confused turmoil or welter of foam or water 1840.

1. Thus must I from the smoake into the s. SHAKS. b. Men should remedy Suspicion, by procuring to know more, and not to keep their Suspicions in S. BACON.

Comb.: **s.-kiln**, a kiln in which pottery in process of firing is blackened by smoke. Hence **Smo·thery** *a.* tending to smother.

Smother (smʊ·ðəɹ), *v.* ME. [f. SMOTHER *sb.*] I. *trans.* 1. a. To suffocate with smoke. b. To suffocate by the prevention of breathing; to deprive of life by suffocation 1548. c. Used hyperbolically to denote an effusive welcome, etc., or the gaining of a complete or overwhelming victory 1676. 2. †a. To conceal by keeping silent about; to hush up (a matter, etc.). (Cf. 6 below.) –1752. b. To cover up, so as to conceal or cause to be forgotten 1585. c. To repress (feeling, etc.) by the exercise of self-control 1591. 3. To cover up so as to prevent from having free play or development; to suppress or check in this way 1590. b. To prevent (words, etc.) from having full utterance; to render indistinct or silent 1601. 4. a. To deaden or extinguish (fire, etc.) by covering so as to exclude the air; to cause to smoulder 1591. †b. To cook in a close vessel 1809. 5. To cover up, cover over, densely or thickly by some thing or substance 1598. 6. With *up.* a. = sense 2 a. 1589. b. To cover up in a close, dense, or suffocating manner, etc. 1590.

1. b. The helpless traveller..smother'd in the dusty whirlwind dies ADDISON. 2. c. She smothered her own grief 1891. 3. Ability..smothered by pomposity and vulgar pride 1882. 4. a. S. the fire with wet cloathes CAPT. SMITH 5. The small stations we passed were smothered in green foliage 1872.

II. *intr.* 1. To be suffocated or stifled; to be prevented by smoke or other means from breathing freely 1520. 2. To smoulder; to burn slowly. Now *dial.* 1600.

Smouch (smautʃ), *sb.*[1] Now *dial.* 1578. [Cf. G. *schmutz.*] A kiss. Hence **Smouch** *v.*[1]

Smouch (smautʃ), *sb.*[2] 1873. [perh. var. of SMUTCH *sb.*] A smudge, a dirty mark.

Smouch (smautʃ), *v.*[2] Now *U.S.* 1826. [perh. f. SMOUCH, var. of SMOUSE.] 1. *trans.* To acquire dishonestly; to pilfer. 2. *intr.* To deal unfairly or dishonestly 1848.

Smoulder (smōu·ldəɹ), *sb.* ME. [Origin obsc.] 1. Smother; smoky vapour; the result of smouldering or slow combustion. 2. A slow-burning fire or the ashes of this 1548.

Smoulder (smōu·ldəɹ), *v.* 1481. [f. prec.] †1. *trans.* To smother, suffocate –1586. 2. *intr.* To burn and smoke without flame 1529.

2. The floor was smouldering in several places 1859. *fig.* The Civil War..had continued during some time to s. MACAULAY. Hence **Smou·lderingly** *adv.*

Smouse (smauz), **smouch** (smautʃ). 1705. [ad. Du. *smous.*] 1. *slang.* A Jew. 2. *S. Afr.* An itinerant trader 1849.

Smudge (smʊdʒ), *sb.*[1] 1768. [Related to SMUDGE *v.*[1]] 1. A dirty mark or stain, esp. such as is caused by a smear or by trying to rub out a previous mark. b. *transf.* A blurred indistinct mass or area 1871. 2. A smeary condition, substance, etc.; the result of smearing or dirtying 1830. b. *techn.* The scum of paint 1823. 3. Very small coal; fine slack 1883.

Smudge (smʊdʒ), *sb.*[2] 1767. [Related to SMUDGE *v.*[2]] 1. A suffocating smoke. Now *U.S.* 2. A heap of combustibles ignited and emitting dense smoke, usually made with the object of repelling mosquitoes, etc. Chiefly *U.S.* and *Canada.* 1842.

Smudge (smʊdʒ), *v.*[1] late ME. [Origin obsc.] 1. *trans.* To soil, stain, blacken, smirch; to mark with dirty stains or smears. b. To rub out or in, to paint or lay on, etc., in a smearing or daubing manner 1865. 2. To bungle, make a mess of (something) 1864.

Smudge (smʊdʒ), *v.*[2] Now *dial.* and *U.S.* 1599. [Origin unkn.] 1. *trans.* †a. To cure (herring) by smoking. NASHE. b. *U.S.* To make a smoky fire in (a tent, etc.); to fill with smoke from a smudge 1891. 2. *intr.* To smoulder 1825.

Smudgy (smʊ·dʒi), *a.* 1859. [f. SMUDGE *sb.*[1] or *v.*[1]] 1. Grimy, dirty; marked with smudges. 2. Smeared, smeary; blurred, indistinct 1865. Hence **Smu·dgily** *adv.* **Smu·dginess.**

Smug (smʊg), *a.* 1551. [Origin obsc.] 1. Of persons: Trim, neat, spruce, smart; in later use, having a self-satisfied, conceited, or consciously respectable air. 2. Of the face (person, etc.): Smooth, sleek; also, in later use = sense 4. 1582. 3. Of things: Smooth, clean, neat, trim, or tidy; in later use, having an appearance suggestive of complacency or respectability 1596. 4. Indicative of, characterized by, complacency or conscious respectability 1851.

1. A s. officer of the United States Government THACKERAY. 2. Sleek their heads And s. their countenances COWPER. 3. The s. and scanty draperies of his style DE QUINCEY. 4. Addressing the audience.. in the most s. and self-satisfied tone 1859. Hence †**Smug** *sb.* a quiet hardworking student (*slang*); a s. or self-satisfied person. **Smu·g-ly** *adv.*, **-ness.**

Smug (smʊg), *v.* 1588. [f. prec.] 1. *trans.* To smarten *up* (oneself or another, one's appearance, etc.); to make trim or gay. Also *absol.* †2. To smarten up (a thing); to fit *up* (a room, etc.) neatly or nicely (*rare*) –1751.

1. Your..master..has been smugging up his pretty face 1750.

Smuggle (smʊ·g'l), *v.* 1687. [orig. *smuckle*; app. of LG. or Du. origin; cf. LG. *smuggeln* (G. *schmuggeln*).] 1. *trans.* To convey (goods) clandestinely into (or out of) a country or district, in order to avoid payment of legal duties, or in contravention of some enactment; to bring *in*, *over*, etc. in this way. b. *intr.* To practise smuggling 1697. 2. *transf.* a. *trans.* To get possession of by stealth 1766. b. To convey, etc., in a stealthy or clandestine manner. Const. with *away, in, into, off, out of*, etc. 1783. c. *intr.* To make *off* stealthily 1865.

1. To *S. Goods*, to run them ashore, or bring them in by stealth, without paying the Custom 1706. b. The temptation to s. was diminished 1845. 2. b. A single Plebeian could not be smuggled in 1783.

Smuggler (smʊ·gləɹ). 1661. [ad. LG. *smukkeler* or *smugg(e)ler.*] 1. One who smuggles commodities; *esp.* one who makes a trade or practice of smuggling. 2. A vessel employed in smuggling 1799.

Smut (smʊt), *sb.* 1664. [Related to SMUT *v.* Cf. LG. *schmutt*, G. *schmutz.*] 1. A fungous disease affecting cereals, etc., which are spoiled by the grain being wholly or partly converted into a blackish powder; also, one or other of the fungi (species of *Ustilagineæ*) causing the disease 1665. 2. A black mark or stain; a smudge 1664. 3. *Coal-mining.* Bad, soft, earthy coal 1686. 4. Soot or sooty matter 1693. b. A particle of sooty matter 1806. c. A very minute insect 1899. 5. Indecent or obscene language 1698.

5. The gentlemen talked s., the ladies laughed GOLDSM.

Phr. *Ditto, brother s.*, a tu quoque retort to criticism.

attrib.: **s.-ball**, a single grain of wheat or other cereal affected by smut or bunt; a cohesive body of smut.

Smut (smʊt), *v.* 1587. [Cf. MHG. *smutzen* (G. *schmutzen*) to smear, dirty.] 1. *trans.* To mark with some black or dirty substance; to blacken, smudge. 2. To affect (grain) with smut 1626. b. *intr.* Of grain: To be affected by smut 1657. 3. *trans.* To make obscene 1722. 4. *intr.* Of fish: To rise at, or feed on, smuts 1889.

1. *fig.* What is the cause why some one sinne doth so blot and s. the most excellent men? 1601.

Smutch (smʊtʃ), *sb.* 1530. [Related in some way to SMUDGE.] 1. A black or dirty mark; a stain; a smudge. b. *fig.* A moral stain 1648. c. A slight mark or indication; semblance; also, a slight or light touch 1776. 2. Soot, smut, grime, dirt 1790.

1. c. Without a shadow, a relish, a s., a tinge,..of anger BURKE.

Smutch (smʊtʃ), *v.* 1611. [See prec. and cf. SMOOCH *v.*] *trans.* To blacken, make dirty, smut, smudge. b. *fig.* To stain, sully, besmirch, etc., morally or otherwise 1640.

b. The passion..is never smutched by sensuality 1865.

Smutty (smʊ·ti), *a.* 1597. [f. SMUT *sb.* or *v.*] 1. Of grain: Affected by smut. 2. Soiled with, full of, characterized by, smut, dirty; blackened 1645. 3. Of the colour of smut; dusky; dark 1648. 4. Having the appearance or form of smut 1667. 5. Indecent, obscene, 'dirty' 1668.

5. He is s., and vulgar and low 1851. Hence **Smu·ttily** *adv.* **Smu·ttiness.**

Smyrna (smə̄·ɹnă). 1735. [L. *Smyrna*, Gr. Σμύρνα.] Name of the chief port of Asia Minor, situated at the head of the gulf of the same name, used *attrib.* in: *S. cotton*, an Indian cotton cultivated in the Levant; *S. wheat*, a kind of wheat with an extremely large ear. b. *ellipt.* (*pl.*) Smyrna raisins 1845. **Smyrnæ·an** [L. *Smyrnæus*, Gr. Σμυρναῖος] = next 1598.

Smyrniote (smə̄·ɹniᵒut), *sb.* and *a.* 1670. [f. SMYRNA; see -OTE, and cf. *Cypriote.*] A. *sb.* An inhabitant or native of Smyrna. B. *adj.* Of or pertaining to Smyrna 1869.

Snack (snæk), *sb.* late ME. [f. next. Cf. MDu. *snac(k*, in sense 1.] 1. A snap or bite, esp. that of a dog. Now *dial.* 2. A share, portion, part 1683. 3. a. A mere taste of liquor 1685. b. A mere bite or morsel of food, as contrasted with a regular meal; a light or incidental repast 1737. 4. Comb. *s.-bar, -basket.*

2. *To go snacks* (†or *s.*), to have a share *in* (something), to divide profits; 'Tis about a thousand pounds; we go snacks 1701.

Snack (snæk), *v.* ME. [Cf. MDu. *snacken* to snap (of a dog).] 1. *intr.* To bite or snap (at). *north.* and *Sc.* 2. *trans.* To share, divide 1707. 3. *intr.* To lunch, take a snack 1807.

Snaffle (snæ·f'l), *sb.* 1533. [perh. conn. w. (M)Du., (M)LG. *snavel*, OHG. *snapal* beak.] A simple form of bridle-bit, having less controlling power than one provided with a curb.

Phr. *To ride* (a person) *in, on,* or *with the s.*, to rule easily, to guide with a light hand.

Snaffle (snæ·f'l), *v.* 1559. [f. prec.] 1. *trans.* To put a snaffle on (a horse, etc.); to control or guide with a snaffle. 2. *slang.* To arrest; to seize; to acquire by means or machinations not strictly lawful, purloin 1725.

Snag (snæg), *sb.* 1577. [prob. of Scand. origin; cf. Norw. dial. *snag* sharp point, projection, stump, spike, etc.] 1. A short stump standing out from the trunk, or from a stout branch, of a tree or shrub, esp. one left after cutting or pruning. b. A trunk or large branch of a tree imbedded in the bottom of a river, lake, etc., with one end directed upwards (forming an impediment or danger to navigation). Orig. *U.S.* 1807. c. *fig.* An impediment or obstacle (now usu. unexpected) 1830. 2. A sharp, angular, or jagged projection 1586. b. A broken piece or stump of a tooth; a large or unshapely tooth 1612. c. A tine or branch of a deer's horn, *spec.* one which is short or imperfectly developed 1673.

1. c. He's a s. in the Devil's way 1830.

Comb.: **s.-boat**, 'a steamboat fitted with an apparatus for removing snags, or obstructions to navigation in rivers'; **-tooth**, = 2 b.

Snag (snæg), *v.* 1807. [f. prec.] 1. *trans.* a. In passive: To be caught, pierced, or damaged by a snag. Chiefly *U.S.*, and esp. of river-steamers. b. *fig.* To occupy or block as with a snag 1863. 2. To cut roughly, or so as to leave snags 1811. b. To tear on or by a sharp projection. *dial.* 1854. 3. To clear (a river, etc.) from snags 1882.

2. Blazing the trees and snagging the bushes with our tomahawks 1812.

Snagged (snæ·gd), *ppl. a.* 1658. [f. SNAG *sb.* or *v.*] 1. Having projecting points or jagged protuberances; jagged, ragged. 2. Caught or impaled upon a snag 1872.

Snaggy (snæ·gi), *a.* 1566. [f. SNAG *sb.* + -Y.[1]] 1. Having snags or sharp protuberances; jagged, knotty; snag-like. 2. Resembling or full of snags 1703.

1. His stalking steps are stayde Vpon a s. Oke SPENSER.

Snail (snēl), *sb.* [OE. *snægel* = G. *schnägel.*] 1. One or other of the terrestrial or freshwater gasteropods having a well-developed spiral or whorled shell capable of housing the whole body; also formerly, a slug.

The common types of the true snail belong to the

genus *Helix* (esp. *H. aspersa* or *hortensis*, the common garden snail, and *H. pomatia*, the edible snail). **b.** Applied to various animals allied to, or resembling, the snails or slugs 1541. **2.** Used with ref. to the exceptionally slow motion of the snail OE. **b.** A slow or indolent person; a sluggard 1590. †**3. a.** A structure or formation resembling a snail-shell; a testudo –1610. †**b.** *Mil.* = LIMAÇON **1.** –1591. **4.** *pl.* A species of medick (usu. *Medicago scutellata*) having snail-shaped seed-pods 1629. **5.** *Mech.* A flat, spirally-curved piece of metal; *esp.* a toothed disk of this shape forming part of the striking mechanism of a clock; a spiral cam 1696.

2. Phr. *Snail's gallop, pace*, an excessively slow pace, rate of progress or motion, etc. **b.** Dromio, thou Dromio, thou snaile, thou slug SHAKS.

Comb.: **s.-bore** *U.S.*, a shell-fish (*Urosalpinx cinerea*) which injures oysters by boring; **-fish**, a fish related to the lumpsucker; **-flower**, *Phaseolus Caracalla*; **-plant**, = sense 4; **-slow** *a.* that is as slow as a s., very sluggish or tardy in motion. Hence **Snai·lery**, a place where (edible) snails are bred or reared.

Snail (snēⁱl), *v.* 1548. [f. SNAIL *sb.*] †**1.** *intr.* Of soldiers: To form into a 'snail' or 'snails'. HALL. **2.** To move, walk, or travel lazily or sluggishly; to go very slowly. Also with *on*. 1582. **3.** *trans.* To make or construct after the spiral form of a snail-shell. Now *spec.* in clockmaking 1591. **b.** To finish off with curved eccentric lines 1884. **4.** To clear of, keep free from, slugs or snails 1661.

Snai·l-like, *a.* and *adv.* 1607. [f. SNAIL *sb.* + -LIKE.] **A.** *adj.* **1.** Like or resembling a snail in appearance, habits, etc. **2.** Slow, tardy 1639.

2. The s. siege of Ptolemais 1639.

B. *adv.* With the slow motion characteristic of a snail; tardily, sluggishly 1825.

Snai·l-paced, *a.* 1594. [SNAIL *sb.*] **1.** Slow, sluggish, or tardy in pace, progress, or motion; slothful, slow-moving. **2.** Marked by tardiness, slowness, or sluggishness 1601.

1. Goe..bid the snaile-pac'd Aiax arme SHAKS.

†**'Snails,** *int.* 1590. An abbrev. of *God's nails*, used as an oath –1828.

Snai·l-shell. 1530. = COCHLEA 3.

Snake (snēⁱk), *sb.* [OE. *snaca*, = MLG. *snake*.] **1.** One or other of the limbless vertebrates constituting the reptilian order *Ophidia* (characterized by a greatly elongated body, tapering tail, and smooth scaly integument), some species of which are noted for their venomous properties; an ophidian, a serpent. Also, in pop. use, applied to some species of *Lacerta*, and to certain snake-like amphibians. **b.** A representation, figure, or image of a snake 1579. **2.** In fig. or allus. uses 1593. **3.** Applied to persons, esp. with opprobrious force 1590. **4.** Applied to objects resembling a s. 1676. **5.** A species of mediæval war vessel 1864.

1. *Great snakes!* used as an exclam. **2.** Phr. *A s. in the grass* (after Virgil *Ecl.* iii. 93. *Latet anguis in herba*): used to denote some lurking danger, suspicious circumstance or persons, etc. *To see snakes*, to have delirium tremens (*U.S. slang*). **3.** *Poor s.*, a poor, needy, or humble person; a drudge.

Comb.: *s.-charmer*; **s.-bird**, a bird belonging to the genus *Plotus*, esp. the Amer. species *P. anhinga*, characterized by its long s.-like neck; *dial.* the wryneck; **-boat**, a canoe of great length used in the East; **-fence** *U.S.*, a fence made of roughly-split rails laid zigzag; **-fish**, one or other of certain fishes having some resemblance to a s.; **s. juice** *Austral. slang*, whisky; **-poison** *U.S.*, whisky; **s.-story**, an incredible tale about a s. esp. in regard to its great length or size. Also in collocations with **snake's**, chiefly in plant names as *snake's tail, tongue*.

Snake (snēⁱk), *v.* 1815. [f. SNAKE *sb.*] **I. 1.** *trans.* **a.** *Naut.* (See quot.) 1815. **b.** To move, stretch out, (the head, etc.) after the manner of a snake. Also *refl.* 1887. **2.** *intr.* To move in a creeping, crawling, or stealthy manner suggestive of the movements of a snake 1848. **3.** To wind, twist, curve, etc., in a snake-like manner 1875. **4.** *trans.* To make (one's way) in a sinuous or creeping manner 1879.

1. a. *S.*, to pass small stuff across a seizing at the outer turns by way of finish. To attach lengths of rope between two stays or backstays. 1846.

II. *U.S.* To drag, pull, or draw; *spec.* in *Lumbering*, to haul (logs) along the ground lengthwise by means of chains or ropes 1833. **b.** *transf.* To drag or pull forcibly or quickly 1897.

Sna·ke(-)head. 1845. [SNAKE *sb.*] **1. a.** The N. Amer. plant *Chelone glabra*. **b.** The snake's head or common fritillary 1884. **2.** *U.S.* The loose bent-up end of one of the thin iron rails formerly used on railroads 1848. **3.** A representation of a snake's head 1865. **4.** A fish (*Ophiocephalus*) or turtle having a snake-like head 1891.

Sna·ke-like, *a.* 1612. [f. SNAKE *sb.*] Like or resembling a snake or that of a snake; having the characteristic form of a snake; long and slender.

fig. This is a snakelike world, And always hath its tail within its mouth 1839.

Sna·ke(-)root. 1635. [f. SNAKE *sb.*] **1.** The root or rhizome of one or other of several Amer. plants reputed to possess properties antidotal to snake-poison, *esp.* the dried root of *Polygala Senega* and *Aristolochia serpentaria* used largely in medicine; the medicinal preparation obtained from this. **b.** One or other of these plants 1712. **2.** One or other of several plants so called from a fancied resemblance to a snake in some respect; e.g. *Polygonum Bistorta* 1856.

Snake's(-)head. Also **snakeshead.** 1739. [f. SNAKE *sb.*] **1.** *attrib.* **a.** *S. iris*, an iris of the Mediterranean region, *Hermodactylus tuberosus*. **b.** *S. fritillary, lily* (see 2 b) 1899. **2. a.** *U.S.* = SNAKE-HEAD 1 a. **b.** The common fritillary, *Fritillaria meleagris*; so called from the fancied resemblance of the bud to the head of a snake 1859. **3.** *U.S.* = SNAKE-HEAD 2. 1848.

Sna·ke(-)stone. 1661. [f. SNAKE *sb.*] **1.** An ammonite. Now *dial.* **2.** A porous or absorbent substance regarded as efficacious in curing snake-bite or as a remedy against poison; a serpent-stone 1694. **3.** A small perforated stone (cf. *adder-stone*, ADDER *sb.*[2]) 1700. **4.** A kind of hone slate or whetstone, obtained in Scotland; also known as Ayr stone 1850.

Sna·ke-weed. Also **snakeweed.** 1597. [SNAKE *sb.*] **1.** The plant bistort, *Polygonum Bistorta*. **2.** = SNAKE-ROOT 1. 1631.

Sna·ke-wood. 1598. [SNAKE *sb.*] **1. a.** A tree or shrub belonging to the genus *Strychnos*, esp. *S. colubrina* of the East Indies; the wood of one or other of these trees used as a remedy for snake-poison. **b.** The East Indian plant *Ophioxylon serpentinum*. **2.** One or other of various trees formerly classed under the genus *Colubrina*, or of the West Indian trees *Cecropia peltata*, the trumpet tree, and *Plumieria rubra*, the red jasmine 1832. **3.** The wood of the S. American timber-tree *Brosimum Aubletii*, so called from its snake-like markings; letter-wood; also, the tree producing this wood 1843.

Snakish (snēⁱ·kiʃ), *a.* 1532. [f. SNAKE *sb.*] Snake-like, snaky.

Snaky (snēⁱ·ki), *a.* 1567. [f. SNAKE *sb.* + -Y [1].] **1.** Formed or composed of snakes. **2.** Entwined with snakes. Said of the caduceus. 1591. **3.** Of or pertaining to a snake; freq. in allusive use, venomous, guileful, deceitful, treacherous 1586. **4.** Resembling the form of a snake; long and winding or twisting; sinuous, tortuous 1596. **5.** Of places: Infested with snakes 1856. **6.** Relating to snakes 1882.

1. The Furies fell Theyr s. heads doe combe SPENSER. **2.** In his Hand He holds the Virtue of the S. Wand DRYDEN. **3.** So to the Coast of Jordan he directs His easie steps; girded with s. wiles MILT. **4.** Huge woolly camels..thrust out their shaggy s. necks 1887. Hence **Sna·kily** *adv.* **Sna·kiness.**

Snap (snæp), *sb.* 1495. [Related to SNAP *v.* Cf. Du. *snap*, LG. *snap*.] **I. 1.** A quick or sudden closing of the jaws or teeth in biting, or of scissors in cutting; a bite or cut made in this way. **2.** *slang.* A share (cf. SNACK *sb.* 2.); something worth securing or getting hold of; an odd chance; a good place or job 1561. **3.** A small piece or portion; a scrap, fragment, or morsel. Now *dial.* 1610. **4.** A slight or hasty meal or mouthful; a snack. Now *dial.* 1642. **5.** A sudden snatch or catch at something; a quick movement or effort 1631. **b.** A method of fishing for pike 1651. **c.** A card-game, in which the call of 'snap' under certain conditions gives one player the right to take cards from another. (Cf. SNIP-SNAP-SNORUM.) 1882. **6.** A curt or sharp speech or manner of speaking; an angry dispute 1648. **7.** A brief and sudden spell *of* cold, winter, etc. orig. *U.S.* 1740. **b.** A sharp and sudden frost; a short spell of cold weather. Chiefly in *cold s.* 1829. **8.** = SNAP-SHOT 1, 2. 1851. **9.** Alertness, energy, vigour, 'go'. orig. *U.S.* 1872.

1. He had the scent of a slow-hound..and the s. of a bull-dog SCOTT. Also = *soft s.*, an easy pleasant job; a profitable business or undertaking (*U.S.*) 1909. **6.** The moment I ventured to speak I was at once contradicted with a s. GOLDSM.

II. 1. a. An instrument or implement that snaps 1611. **b.** A snap-hook 1839. **c.** A device or implement used for rounding the head of a rivet 1869. **2.** A spring-catch, clasp, or fastening, or one closing with a snapping or clicking sound 1815. **III. 1.** A quick, sharp sound or report 1611. **2.** The act of snapping or breaking suddenly 1755. **3.** *Sc.* and *n. dial.* A small, usu. round, cake or biscuit of crisp gingerbread; a ginger-snap (cf. *brandy-s.*) 1818. **4.** *pl.* (*U.S.*) Also *s.-beans*, French beans 1842.

Snap (snæp), *v.* 1530. [app. ad. MDu. or MLG. *snappen*.] **I. 1.** *intr.* Of animals: To make a quick or sudden bite *at* something; to feed *on* in this way. Also without const. **2.** To utter sharp, tart, or cutting words or remarks; to speak irritably or abruptly. Usu. with *at*. 1579. **b.** *trans.* To utter (words) in an angry, sharp, or peevish manner or tone. Also with *out*. 1683. **3.** To snatch, to make a quick or eager catch, *at* a thing 1673. †**b.** *To s. short*, to fail to get or obtain –1738.

1. A little Lap-Dog, that barked and snapped at every one ADDISON. **2. b.** To s. out a refusal 1888. **3.** His resignation was eagerly snapped at SCOTT.

II. 1. (freq. with *up*) *trans.* To catch, capture, or seize quickly, suddenly, or by surprise. Now chiefly *dial.* 1568. **b.** To snatch for one's own use; to take to oneself with a quick movement; to steal or purloin in this manner 1624. **c.** To catch or seize with a quick bite or snap. Also *fig.* 1687. **d.** To secure the passing or giving of (decisions, legislation, etc.) without allowing due time for consideration or discussion 1883. **2.** With *off*. To bite off (a limb, etc.) sharply and quickly. Also *transf.*, to drink off quickly. 1590. **3.** To catch or take (a person) *up* with an abrupt or sharp remark. Also with *short*. 1647. **b.** To interrupt or snub, to cut *short*, in an abrupt or peevish manner. Also with *off*. 1687. **4. a.** To take (an instantaneous photograph); to snap-shot 1890. **b.** *intr.* To take instantaneous photographs 1891.

1. c. The Ægyptian dogs, when they drink at the Nile, are said to run all the while, for fear of being snapped by the Crocodiles 1760. **2.** Phr. *To s. (a person's) nose* or *head off*, to speak to a person in a curt, sharp, or angry manner; Old G. snapped my nose off for saying I had sent for him 1742. **3. b.** Your ladyship did s. and snub her confoundedly 1796.

III. 1. *trans.* To close (the jaws, mouth, etc.) suddenly or with a snap 1573. **2.** To pull the trigger of or fire (a pistol); to strike (a flint, etc.) 1673. **3.** To cause (something) to make or give out a sharp sound of the nature of a click or crack; to close or fasten, to open or shut, etc., with this sound; to crack (a whip); to jerk *out* with a snap 1714. **b.** To cause (the fingers) to make a sharp noise by striking the ball of the thumb, esp. as a sign of delight or contempt 1742. **4.** *intr.* Of things: To make or emit a sharp cracking sound or report; to crack, crackle 1673. **b.** To move or slide *into* place, to close or shut, to fit *home*, with a snap 1793. **5. a.** Of the eyelids or eyes: To open and close quickly in an angry manner 1870. **b.** Of jaws, etc.: To close with a snap 1899.

2. He snapped a pocket-pistol at him, which missed him 1798. **3.** Tyranny..Slips the slave's collar on, and snaps the lock COWPER. **b.** Phr. *To s. one's fingers at*, to treat with indifference or contempt; to disregard or ignore. **4.** Cedar..makes a brisk fire, but is..subject to s. and fly 1768.

IV. 1. *intr.* To break suddenly and (usually) with a sharp noise or report; to give way or part suddenly owing to strain or tension 1602. **b.** To be broken *off* with a snap 1806. **2.** *trans.* To break (something) suddenly and cleanly; to break in two; to cause (a rope, etc.) to part or give way 1679. **b.** To break *off* with a snap 1808.

1. *fig.* When the so-called Bonds of Society s. asunder CARLYLE. **2.** From the roof the sleeper fell, And snapped the spinal joint and waked in hell POPE. *fig.* And now this spell was snapt COLERIDGE.

V. *advb.* With, or as with, a snap; quickly, smartly. Freq. in phr. *to go s.* 1583.

Snap-, the stem of SNAP *v.* used in comb., as **snap-action gun**, a gun which, as the hinged barrel closes, is fastened by a spring catch; **s.-beetle, bug**, a click-beetle; **-sound** *Path.*, a snapping sound heard in auscultation; **-weed**, *Impatiens fulva*. **b.** In the names of things or appliances operating, closing, fastening, fitting, etc., with a snap or by means of a catch, as *s.-bolt, -catch, -flask, -gun, -lock*. **c.** In combs. relating to or connected with the use of a snap-hook in fishing, as *s.-angling; s.-bait, -tackle*. **d.** Formed, taken, performed, etc., hastily or rapidly, as *s. exposure, -firing, -judgement*, SNAP-SHOT, etc. **e.** In parliamentary usage, as *s. dissolution, division, vote*, one obtained or taken unexpectedly or without notice, often when comparatively few members are present.

Snapdragon (snæ·pdræ:gən). 1573. [f. SNAP *v.* + DRAGON.] **1.** A popular name for one or other of the plants belonging to the genus *Antirrhinum*, esp. *A. majus*, a hardy plant bearing showy flowers, freq. grown in gardens. **b.** Applied to various other plants having personate flowers 1753. **2.** A figure or representation of a dragon, esp. one so constructed as to open and shut the mouth, used in mayoral or civic shows or processions. *Obs.* exc. *Hist.* 1611. **3.** A game (usually played at Christmas) in which the players try to snatch raisins out of a bowl or dish of burning brandy or other spirit and to eat them while alight; a bowl or quantity of the liquor, etc., used in this game 1704.

1. The flowers..fashioned like..a dragon's mouth; from whence the women haue taken the name S. 1597.

Snape (snēip), *v. techn.* 1794. [perh. identical with dial. *snape*, a. ON. *sneypa* to dishonour.] **1.** *trans.* To cause or make to taper; *spec.* in *Shipbuilding*, to bevel the end of. **2.** *intr.* To taper (*off*) 1794. Hence **Snape** *sb.* (*rare*) a tapering, a bevel, an act of snaping.

Snapha(u)nce (snæ·phɑns). Now *Hist.* 1538. [repr. Du., Flem. *snaphaan*, f. *snappen* SNAP *v.* + *haan* cock. It is not clear whether the sense is 'snapping cock' or 'cock-snapper' (i.e. cock-stealer).] †**1.** An armed robber or marauder; a freebooter or highwayman; a desperate fellow or thief –1609. **2.** An early form of flint-lock used in muskets and pistols; also, the hammer of this 1588. **3.** A musket, gun, etc., fitted with a lock of this kind, in use in the 16–17th centuries 1580.

3. [He] had borne a snap-hance on his shoulder as a volunteer 1860.

Snap(-)head. 1869. [f. SNAP *sb.*] **1.** A round head to a rivet, bolt, etc. **2.** A tool used to shape the head of a rivet 1875.

Snap-hook. 1688. [f. SNAP-.] **1.** *Angling.* A device consisting of three or four hooks connected in a special manner. **2.** A hook with a spring snap by which it is prevented from accidental unhooking 1875.

Snapper (snæ·pəɹ). 1577. [f. SNAP *v.*] **1.** A thing which snaps or produces a sharp cracking sound: **a.** A pistol (*rare*). †**b.** *pl.* Bones; castanets 1605. **c.** *U.S.* A word, sentence, verse, etc., used as a finishing touch or wind-up 1857. **d.** *U.S.* A cracker on the end of a whip-lash. Also *fig.*, a sharp or caustic remark. 1882. **3.** One who snaps *up* or seizes upon a thing quickly 1611. **4.** A snappish person; one who speaks or answers snappishly or roughly 1648. **5. a.** One or other of various fishes, esp. the West Indian *Lutjanus Blackfordii* or *L. vivanus* or other fish of this group, the N. American rose-fish, *Sebastes marinus*, and the Australian *Pagrus unicolor* 1697. **b.** With distinctive epithets, as *alligator, bastard, black s.* 1775. **c.** A snapping-turtle 1872. **d.** A woodpecker 1847. **e.** *U.S.* A flysnapper 1891.

3. My Father..was likewise a snapper-vp of vnconsidered trifles SHAKS.

Sna·pping, *ppl. a.* 1642. [f. SNAP *v.*] **1.** Sharp, curt, snappish; peevish, petulant. **2.** That snaps or breaks suddenly 1823. **3.** That snaps with the jaws or beak 1873.

3. *S.-turtle*, one or other of the N. American fresh-water tortoises of the family *Chelydridæ*, esp. *Chelydra serpentina*, the alligator terrapin. *S. beetle* (or *bug*), any beetle of the family *Elateridæ*; the skip-jack (*U.S.*). So **Sna·ppingly** *adv.* 1567.

Snappish (snæ·piʃ), *a.* 1542. [f. SNAP *v.* + -ISH.] **1.** Of persons: Using, or apt to use, sharp, harsh, or uncivil language; peevish, testy, or ill-natured in speech or reply. **b.** Of manner, etc.: Marked or characterized by sharpness or curtness of speech 1836. **c.** Of the sea: Somewhat choppy or rough 1867. **2.** Of words, language, etc.: Sharp, curt, peevish, ungracious 1551. **3.** Of a dog, etc.: Inclined or prone to snap 1700.

1. I found him morose and s. BORROW. **b.** A..s. tone of voice 1885. **2.** Vexed at a s. answer Madame Williams did give me PEPYS. Hence **Sna·ppish-ly** *adv.*, **-ness.**

Snappy (snæ·pi), *a.* 1834. [f. SNAP *v.* + -Y [1].] **1.** = SNAPPISH *a.* **2.** Of the nature of, producing or emitting, a snap or crack; crackling 1878. **3.** *colloq.* Cleverly smart, bright, or pointed; full of 'go'; brisk 1873. **b.** Neat and elegant; smart, 'natty' 1881. **4.** Quick, sudden, instantaneous; jerky 1872.

1. S. and disagreeable..in their replies 1858. **2.** The birch..makes a hot, s., cheerful fire 1894. **3. b.** A s. team of grays 1897. Hence **Sna·ppily** *adv.*

Snap-shot (snæ·pˌʃɒt), *sb.* Also **snap shot, snapshot.** 1808. [f. SNAP-.] **1.** A quick or hurried shot taken without deliberate aim, esp. one at a rising bird or quickly moving animal. **b.** One who fires such a shot 1887. **2.** An instantaneous photograph, esp. one taken with a hand-camera 1890.

2. *transf.* Your Yankee interviewer is a s. incarnate 1897. Hence **Sna·p-shot** *v. intr.* or *absol.* to take snap-shots with a camera; *trans.* to take a s. of or at (a person or thing).

Snare (snēəɹ), *sb.* OE. [In sense 1, a. ON. *snara* noose, snare. Sense 2 is prob. from the Du. or LG. forms.] **1.** A device for capturing small wild beasts or birds, usu. consisting of a string with a running noose in which a foot or the head may be caught. **b.** *Surg.* A device, on the principle of a snare, for removing morbid growths 1884. **2.** One of the strings of gut or rawhide which are stretched across the lower head of a side-drum 1688.

1. The..time..For stalking Cranes to set the guileful S. DRYDEN. *fig.* The snares of deep play 1779. Hence **Sna·ry** *a.* of the nature of, resembling, a s.; ensnaring.

Snare (snēəɹ), *v.* late ME. [f. prec. Cf. Norw. *snara.*] **1.** *trans.* To capture (small wild beasts or birds) in a snare; to catch by entangling. **b.** *fig.* To entangle, entrap. late ME. **2.** *Surg.* and *Path.* To catch in a loop, *esp.* in order to remove; to cut off with a snare 1884.

1. I..will..instruct thee how to s. the nimble Marmazet SHAKS. **b.** Be thow not snairde in Venus snair 1567. Hence **Sna·rer**, one who snares or traps.

Snark (snāɹk), 1879. [Invented by 'Lewis Carroll' (C. L. Dodgson) in *The Hunting of the Snark* (1876).] An imaginary animal.

Snarl (snāɹl), *sb.*[1] late ME. [f. SNARE *sb.* or *v.*; see -LE 1.] **1.** A snare, gin; a noose. *Obs.* exc. *dial.* **2.** A tangle, knot, ravel 1609. **3.** A knot in wood (*dial.*) 1881.

Snarl (snāɹl), *sb.*[2] 1613. [f. SNARL *v.*[2]] An act of snarling; a display of the teeth accompanied by an angry sound.

Snarl (snāɹl), *v.*[1] late ME. [Cf. SNARL *sb.*[1]] **1.** *trans.* To catch in a snare or noose; to entangle or secure with a cord, rope, etc.; to strangle. Now *dial.* **b.** *fig.* To ensnare, entangle, entrap. late ME. **2.** To tangle; to twist together confusedly; to make a tangle of. Now chiefly *dial.* and *U.S.* 1440. **3.** *intr.* To become twisted or entangled; to get into, or form, tangles or knots 1600.

2. The Daughter had..her Hair snarled and matted together 1687. **3.** The yarn tends to 's.' and curl, and cannot be drawn out straight 1884.

Snarl (snāɹl), *v.*[2] 1589. [f. †*snar* vb. (prob. imitative) + -LE 3.] **1.** *intr.* Of dogs, etc.: To make an angry sound accompanied by showing the teeth. **2.** Of persons: To quarrel; to grumble viciously; to show strong resentment or ill-feeling 1594. **3.** *trans.* To utter in a harsh, rude, or ill-natured manner 1693.

1. A dog snarls at a stone, but looks not at the hand that cast it 1732. *fig.* I hear the angry trumpet snarling 1866. Hence **Sna·rler** [1].

Snarl (snāɹl), *v.*[3] *techn.* 1688. [perh. f. SNARL *sb.*[1] 3.] *trans.* To raise, or force *up*, into bosses or projections by the use of the snarling-iron. Hence **Sna·rler** [2], one who works with a snarling-iron; a snarling-iron. **Sna·rling** *vbl. sb.* a method of producing raised work in metal by means of indirect percussion; chiefly *attrib.* in *snarling-iron, tool.*

Snatch (snætʃ), *sb.* ME. [f. SNATCH *v.*] †**1.** A hasp or fastening (*rare*) –1528. †**2.** A trap, snare, entanglement –1655. **3.** A hasty catch or grasp; a sudden grab or snap *at* something 1577. †**b.** A catch, check, or hesitancy. SHAKS. **4.** A brief period, short space (*of* time, etc.) 1563. **5.** A hasty meal or morsel; a snack 1573. **6.** A small amount or portion (†taken hurriedly); a mere fragment or disconnected piece 1592. **7.** A short passage, a few words, *of* a song, etc.; a small portion, a few bars, *of* a melody or tune 1602. **b.** *ellipt.* in the same senses 1823. †**8.** A quibble, a captious argument –1687. **9.** *ellipt.* Any open lead for a rope. (See SNATCH-*block.*) 1850.

3. Here and there he made guesses and snatches at the truth M. ARNOLD. Phr. *By* or *in snatches*, by hasty, unsustained efforts; hurriedly, by fits and starts; intermittently, interruptedly. **4.** Then after a shower to weeding a s. 1573. **6.** Snatches of reading ..will not make a Bentley or a Clarke JOHNSON. **7.** She chaunted snatches of old tunes SHAKS.

Snatch (snætʃ), *v.* ME. [Origin obsc.] **1.** *intr.* **a.** To make a sudden snap or bite (*at* something). **b.** To make a sudden catch *at* a thing, in order to secure possession or hold of it 1530. **2.** *trans.* To seize, to take or lay hold of, suddenly, smartly, or unexpectedly ME. **b.** With immaterial object: To take, obtain, acquire, etc., in a hasty or improper manner, or so as to take advantage of a momentary chance 1563. **3.** To seize, take, or remove hastily 1555. **b.** To remove quickly *from* sight, etc.; to remove suddenly from this world or life; to save or rescue *from* or *out of* danger, etc., by prompt and vigorous action 1582. **4.** *Naut.* To place (a line) in a snatch-block 1769.

1. **b.** This looke of thine will hurle my Soule from Heauen, And Fiends will s. at it SHAKS. **2.** The Sarazin..Snatcheth his sword, and fiercely to him flies SPENSER. **b.** Let us s. what happiness is yet in our power LYTTON. **3.** The Moones an arrant theefe, And her pale fire, she snatches from the Sunne SHAKS. I snatched his Hat off his Head STEELE. **b.** This youth that you see heere, I snatch'd one halfe out of the iawes of death SHAKS. Several who are snatched away by untimely death BERKELEY. Hence **Sna·tchy** *a.* consisting of, characterized by, snatches; irregular; spasmodic; *spec.* of rowing.

Snatch-, the stem of SNATCH *v.* used in comb.: **a.** *Naut.* Denoting devices capable of rapid attachment, or to which a rope can be quickly attached, as *s.-cheek, -hook, sheave*; **s.-block**, a block having a hole in one side to receive the bight of a rope. **b.** In objective combs., as *s.-grace*. **c.** = SNAP- e.

Snatcher (snæ·tʃəɹ). 1575. [f. SNATCH *v.*] One who or that which snatches; a thief, a robber. **b.** A body-snatcher 1831.

Sna·tchingly, *adv.* 1552. [f. *snatching*, pres. pple. of SNATCH *v.*] In a snatching manner; hurriedly; by snatches.

Snath (snæþ). Chiefly *dial.* and *U.S.* Also **snathe, sneath** 1574. [var. of next.] = next.

Snead (snīd), **sned** (sned). Now *dial.* [OE. *snǣd.*] The shaft or pole of a scythe.

Sneak (snīk), *sb.* 1643. [app. f. SNEAK *v.*] **1. a.** A sneaking, mean-spirited, paltry, or despicable person; one who acts in a shifty, shabby, or underhand manner. **b.** One who robs or steals in a sneaking manner, or who enters places clandestinely for that purpose 1785. **2.** *Cricket.* A ball bowled so as to roll along the ground; a daisy-cutter 1862.

1. **a.** We call him tuft-hunter, lickspittle, s. THACKERAY. Hence **Snea·ky** *a.* of persons: like or resembling a s.; mean, paltry, sneaking; characterized by, partaking of sneaking. **Snea·kiness.**

Sneak (snīk), *v.* 1590. [Origin obsc.] **I.** *intr.* **1.** To move, go, walk, etc., in a stealthy or slinking manner; to creep or steal furtively, as if ashamed or afraid to be seen; to slink, skulk. **b.** Freq. used to denote want of courage, independence or straightforwardness, without ref. to place or movement 1633. **2.** To cringe or be servile *to* (a person, etc.) 1660. **3.** *School slang.* To peach, inform, tell tales 1897.

1. I hope he will not sneake away with all the money DEKKER. b. He sneak'd like a Cock, that hangs down his wings when he 's beaten 1699. 2. We s. to the regicides, but we boldly trample on our poor fellow-citizens BURKE.

II. *trans.* 1. To turn or draw *aside*, to put or thrust *in* or *into*, to move or slide *to*, etc., in a stealthy manner 1648. b. To pass *through* in an underhand or stealthy manner 1891. 2. *colloq.* To steal in a sneaking or stealthy manner; to filch 1883.

1. I lay stirless, softly sneaking my right hand to the pistol 1889. 2. Those who sneaked umbrellas 1883.

Sneak-, the sb. or vb.-stem used in comb., as **s.-boat** *U.S.*, a boat by which one may readily move or approach unobserved; *esp.* a sneak-box; **-box** *U.S.*, a small, flat, shallow boat used in wild-fowl shooting, and when in use masked with brush or weeds; **-current** *Electr.*, current which escapes or strays owing to leakage or imperfect insulation; **-thief** (orig. *U.S.*), one who thieves by sneaking into houses through open or unfastened doors, etc.

Sneak-cup. 1596. app. error for SNEAK-UP.

Sneaker (snī·kəɹ). 1598. [f. SNEAK *v.*] 1. A person or animal that sneaks; a sneak. 2. †a. A small bowl (*of* punch) -1775. b. A glass *of* brandy 1805.

Sneaking (snī·kiŋ), *ppl. a.* 1582. [f. SNEAK *v.*] 1. That sneaks; moving, walking, acting, etc., in a furtive or slinking manner 1590. †b. *S.-budge*, one who steals or robs alone -1751. †c. Niggardly, mean, near -1773. 2. Mean, contemptible 1582. 3. Of feelings, affection, etc.: Unavowedly cherished or entertained; undemonstrative 1748.

1. Lurking footpads and s. pickpockets 1824. 3. I can't help having a s. regard for him 1842. Hence **Snea·king-ly** *adv.*, **-ness** (*rare*).

Snea·ksby. Now *rare.* 1580. [See -BY 2.] A mean-spirited person; a paltry fellow.

Sneak-up (snī·kᵢʋp). 1596. [f. SNEAK *v.*] A mean, servile, or cringing person; a sneak; a shirk.

Sneap (snīp), *v.* Now *dial.* and *arch.* 1588. [Later form of dial. *snape*, a. ON. *sneypa.*] 1. *trans.* To nip or pinch. 2. To check, repress; to snub, reprove, chide 1611.

2. My lord Archbishop sneaps us for our sloth 1865. Hence **Sneap** *sb.* a snub, check; a rebuke, reproof.

Sneb, *v.* Now *dial.* 1440. [var. of SNIB *v.*] *trans.* To reprimand, reprove; to snub. Also *absol.*

Thou heardst euen now a yong man s. me sore SIDNEY.

Sneck (snek) *sb.* Chiefly *Sc.* and *n. dial.* ME. [Origin obsc.] The latch of a door or gate; the lever which raises the bar of a latch; †a catch. Hence **Sneck** *v. trans.* to latch (a door or gate); to close or fasten by means of a s.; *intr.* of a door or gate: to latch. **Sne·cket,** a s.; *transf.* a noose, halter.

Sne·ck-draw:er. Now *Sc.* and *north.* late ME. [f. SNECK *sb.* + DRAWER *sb.*[1]] One who draws or lifts a sneck or latch (in order to enter stealthily); a crafty, flattering, or sly fellow. So **Sne·ck-draw.**

Sned, *v.* In later use *Sc.* and *n. dial.* [OE. *snǣdan*, related to *sniðan.*] 1. *trans.* To cut or lop off (a branch). Also with *off.* b. To prune (a tree); to divest of branches 1595. 2. To cut; to form, or sever, by cutting 1789.

Snee (to cut): see SNICKERSNEE.

Sneer (snīᵊɹ), *sb.* 1707. [f. the vb.] An act of sneering; a look or expression implying derision, contempt, or scorn; a disdainful or scornful remark or utterance, esp. one of a covert or indirect nature.

A s. at my understanding GOLDSM. Hence **Snee·rful** *a.* of persons, given to sneering; of words, etc., of the nature of a s.; scornful.

Sneer (snīᵊɹ), *v.* 1553. [prob. imitative.] 1. *intr.* Of a horse: To snort. Now *dial.* 2. To smile scornfully or contemptuously; to express scorn, derision, or disparagement in this way; to speak or write in a manner suggestive of contempt or disparagement 1680. †3. To laugh foolishly or smirkingly; to grin -1719. 4. *trans.* To utter with a sneer or in a sneering tone 1693. 5. To deride or decry (a person or thing). *Obs.* exc. *dial.* 1707. 6. To affect in a certain way by sneering; to force by means of sneers or scornful speech or manner 1737.

2. Walpole sheltered himself behind..a pension to s. at the tragi-comedy of life 1874. 4. He sneered some contemptuous word 1904. 6. Nor sneer'd nor brib'd from Virtue into Shame 1737. Circles which s. down Voltaire LYTTON. Hence **Snee·rer,** one who sneers. **Snee·ringly** *adv.* in a sneering or scornful manner; with a s.

Sneeshing (snī·ʃiŋ). *Sc.* (*Ir.*) and *n. dial.* 1686. [Alteration of SNEEZING *vbl. sb.*] Snuff; a pinch of snuff.

Sneeze (snīz), *sb.* 1632. [f. the vb.] 1. A powder or preparation for inducing sneezing. Also *attrib.*, as *s.-box, -horn*, etc. *Obs.* exc. *n. dial.* 2. An act of sneezing; a sudden and involuntary expiration of breath through the nose and mouth, accompanied by a characteristic sound 1646. Hence **Snee·zy** *a.* characterized by sneezing, causing one to sneeze.

Sneeze (snīz), *v.* 1493. [app. an alteration of obs. *fnese* vb., due to misreading or misprinting.] 1. *intr.* To drive or emit air or breath suddenly through the nose and mouth by an involuntary and convulsive or spasmodic action, accompanied by a characteristic sound. 2. *colloq.* With *at.* To regard as of little value, worth, or consideration; to despise, disregard, underrate. Chiefly in the neg. phrase *not to be sneezed at.* 1806. 3. *trans.* To utter with a sneeze. Also with *out.* 1851.

1. Being unused to Snuff, some Grains from off her upper Lip made him s. aloud STEELE. 2. A thousand pounds..was not..to be sneezed at 1891. Hence **Snee·zer,** one who sneezes; (*slang*) something exceptionally good, great, strong, violent, etc., in some respect.

Snee·ze(-)weed. 1856. [f. SNEEZE *v.*] *U.S.* The plant *Helenium autumnale*, or other species of the same genus.

Snee·ze(-)wood. 1834. [f. as prec., after Cape Du. *nieshout.*] A South African timber tree, *Ptæroxylon utile*; also, the wood of this tree; *attrib.* as *s. tree.*

Snee·ze(-)wort. 1597. [f. SNEEZE *v.*] The plant *Achillea Ptarmica*, bastard or wild pellitory, the dried leaves of which are powdered and used as a sternutatory.

Sneezing (snī·ziŋ), *vbl. sb.* 1495. [f. SNEEZE *v.*] 1. The action of the vb.; an instance of this. †2. A preparation or powder inducing sternutation; an errhine or sternutatory -1653. †b. = SNEESHING -1812.

Snell (snel), *sb. U.S.* 1859. [Origin obsc.] A short line of gut or horsehair by which a fish-hook is attached to a longer line. Hence **Snell** *v.* (*U.S.*) *trans.* to tie or fasten (a hook) to a line.

Snell (snel), *a.* and *adv.* In later use *Sc.* and *north.* [Com. Teut.; OE. *snel, snell.*] A. *adj.* 1. Quick in movement or action; prompt, smart, active, strenuous; †good. 2. Keen-witted, clever, sharp, acute, smart. late ME. 3. Severe, sharp, unsparing. late ME. 4. Of weather: Keen, bitter, severe ME. 5. Grievous, heavy, stinging; rigorous; painful ME.

1. That horny-handed, s., peremptory little man 1859. 4. The wintry air is s. and keen 1822. 5. That was a s. law SCOTT.

B. *adv.* 1. Quickly, promptly, swiftly ME. 2. Vigorously, strongly, keenly ME.

†**Snew,** *v.* [OE. *sniwan*, related to SNOW *sb.*[1]] *intr.* To snow -1746.

1. *fig.* It snewed in his hous of mete and drynke CHAUCER.

Snib (snib), *v.* Now *dial.* and *Sc.* ME. [Of Scand. origin; cf. older Da. *snibbe*, MSw. *snybba.* Cf. SNUB.] 1. *trans.* To reprove, reprimand, rebuke, check sharply or severely. 2. To check by some repressive action 1500.

1. Hym wolde he snybben sharply for the nonys CHAUCER. Hence **Snib** *sb.* (latterly *Sc.*) a check, sharp rebuke, or snub.

Snick (snik), *sb.*[1] 1775. [f. SNICK *v.*[2]] 1. A small cut; a nick, notch. b. An act of snipping or light cutting 1898. 2. *Cricket.* A light, glancing blow given to the ball by the batsman, sending it in the direction of the slips or to leg; a ball so hit 1879.

Snick (snik), *v.*[1] *Obs.* exc. *dial.* 1599. [Origin unkn.] Used with *go*, or imperatively, and always followed by *up*, in the sense of 'go hang'.

We did keepe time sir in our Catches. Snecke vp! SHAKS.

Snick (snik), *v.*[2] 1700. [prob. suggested by SNICK AND SNEE, etc.] 1. *trans.* To cut, snip, clip, nick. Also *intr.* 2. To strike or hit sharply 1880. b. *Cricket.* To strike (the ball) lightly so that it glances off in the slips or to leg; to obtain (so many runs) in this way 1880. 3. *colloq.* To cut or slip across or along (a road) quickly or sharply 1883.

Snick (snik), *v.*[3] 1828. [Echoic.] 1. *trans.* To cause to click or sound sharply. 2. *intr.* To make a sharp, clicking noise 1892.

2. Ye may hear a breech-bolt s. where never a man is seen KIPLING. Hence **Snick** *sb.*[2] a sharp noise, a click.

Snick and snee, Snick-a-snee: see SNICKERSNEE.

Snicker (sni·kəɹ), *sb.* 1857. [f. SNICKER *v.*] A smothered laugh; a snigger.

Snicker (sni·kəɹ), *v.* 1694. [Imitative; cf. SNIGGER *v.*] 1. *intr.* To laugh in a half-suppressed or smothered manner; to snigger. 2. Of horses: To neigh, nicker 1824. Hence **Sni·ckeringly** *adv.*

Snickersnee (snikəɹsnī·), *v.* and *sb. Obs.* or *arch.* 1613. Also †**snick or snee,** †**snick and snee,** †**snick-a-snee.** [Earlier *steake* or *stick or snee*, repr. Du. *steken* to thrust, stick, and *snijen, snijden* to cut, with assimilation of the *st-* of the first word to the *sn-* of the second.] †A. As *vb.* To thrust or cut in fighting with a knife; to use a knife in this manner, to fight with knives -1802. B. *sb.* 1. The practice of fighting or a combat with cut-and-thrust knives 1670. †2. *transf.* Used to denote one or other of two possible alternatives or courses -1680. 3. A cut-and-thrust knife (in forms *snick-a-snee, snickersnee*) 1760.

Snide (snəid), *a.* and *sb. Cant.* 1862. [Origin unkn.] A. *adj.* Counterfeit, sham, bogus. B. *sb.* Counterfeit jewellery; base coin 1885.

A. [To] get ready for the trial, and look up the 'snyde witnesses' 1862.

Snider (snəi·dəɹ). 1868. [See def.] *S. rifle*, a form of breech-loading rifle invented by Jacob Snider. Also *ellipt.* for this.

Sniff (snif), *sb.* 1767. [f. the vb.] 1. An act of sniffing; the sound made in doing this. 2. An act of sniffing in order to express or show contempt, disdain, incredulity, etc. 1837. 3. An act (or habit) of clearing the nose by a short inhalation 1860.

2. Miss Miggs gave a great s. to the same effect DICKENS.

Sniff (snif), *v.* ME. [Imitative.] 1. *intr.* To draw air through the nose with short or sharp audible inhalations; to clear the nose in this way, esp. when under the influence of emotion. 2. To do this in smelling; to smell with a sniff or sniffs. Said esp. of animals. 1788. 3. To show or express contempt, disdain, disparagement, incredulity, etc., by sniffing 1729. 4. *trans.* To take *up*, draw *in* (air, etc.) by inhaling through the nostrils 1796. 5. a. To smell (a thing) 1845. b. *fig.* To perceive as if by smell; to smell or smell out (a plot, etc.); to suspect 1864. 6. To utter with a (scornful) sniff; to express by means of a sniff 1859.

2. A curious old ewe came to s. at him 1883. 5. b. It is not only Rome that sniffs heresy in independent thought or action 1873. 6. Fastidious Edinburgh sniffs disdain 1865. Hence **Sni·ffing** *vbl. sb.* the action of the vb.; an instance of this, a sniff.

Sniffle (sni·f'l), *sb.* 1825. [f. next.] 1. *The sniffles*, the snuffles. Also *U.S. slang*, a fit of low spirits. 2. An act of sniffling; a slight snivel or snuffle 1880.

Sniffle (sni·f'l), *v.* 1819. [Imitative.] *intr.* To snivel or snuffle slightly; to sniff. Also *transf.* of a breeze.

Sniffy (sni·fi), *a. dial.* and *colloq.* 1871. [f. SNIFF *v.* + -Y [1].] Prone or inclined to sniff; contemptuous, disdainful; disagreeable. Hence **Sni·ffily** *adv.* **Sni·ffiness.**

Snift (snift), *v.* Now chiefly *dial.* 1703. [Imitative.] 1. *intr.* To sniff, in various senses. b. Of an engine, etc.: To blow out air or steam 1865. 2. *trans.* To draw *up* by sniffing; to sniff the smell of (*rare*) 1736.

1. More steamers came along snorting and snifting at the buoys KIPLING. Hence **Snift** *sb. techn.* the waste in bottling aerated waters.

Snifter (sni·ftəɹ). Chiefly *Sc.* and *n. dial.*

1789. [Imitative.] 1. A strong or rough breeze or wind. 2. *pl.* A bad cold in the head, or the stoppage in the nostrils caused by this; the snuffles. Also, a disease of poultry. *Sc.* 1808.

Sni·fting, *ppl. a.* 1744. *S. valve*, a valve through which air may be expelled from the cylinder of a condensing steam-engine.

Sni·fty, *a.* 1889. [f. SNIFT *v.* + -Y[1].] Sniffy.

Snig (snig). 1483. [Origin unkn.] A young or small eel; a grig.

Snigger (sni·gəɪ), *v.* 1706. [Echoic.] 1. *intr.* To laugh in a half-suppressed, light or covert manner; to snicker. 2. *trans.* To utter with a snigger 1857. Hence **Snigger** *sb.* a slight or half-suppressed laugh. **Sni·ggeringly** *adv.*

Sniggle (sni·g'l), *v.*[1] 1671. [See SNIGGLING *vbl. sb.*] 1. a. *intr.* To fish *for* eels by the method known as sniggling. b. *trans.* To fish for, catch, pull out (an eel or eels) in this way 1844. 2. To catch (fish) by means of striking a hook into them 1834. Hence **Sni·ggle** *sb.* a baited hook or other device used in sniggling for eels, etc.

Sniggle (sni·g'l), *v.*[2] 1815. [Echoic.] *intr.* To snigger or snicker. Hence **Sni·ggle** *sb.*

Sniggling (sni·gliŋ), *vbl. sb.* 1661. [perh. related to SNIG *sb.*] The action or practice of fishing for eels by means of a baited hook or needle thrust into their holes or haunts.

Snip (snip), *sb.* 1558. [Related to SNIP *v.*, and in some senses perh. directly of LG. origin.] I. 1. A small piece or slip, esp. of cloth, cut off or out; a shred. 2. A white or light mark, patch, or spot on a horse, esp. on the nose or lip 1562. 3. A small amount, piece, or portion, a little bit (*of* something) 1588. b. Applied to persons in depreciation or contempt. In later use: A young, slight, or diminutive person. 1625. †4. A share or portion; a snack -1702.

3. b. This s. of an attorney MASSINGER.

II. 1. A small cut or incision made by, or such as that made by, a pair of scissors; a wound of this nature 1596. 2. An act of snipping; a single cut or clip *of* scissors, etc. 1676. 3. *slang* or *colloq.* A tailor. Also as an allusive personal name for a tailor. 1599. 4. *pl.* Hand shears, as contrasted with bench shears 1846.

3. Sir, here's S. the Taylor Charg'd with a riot 1634.

Snip (snip), *v.* 1586. [prob. of Du. or LG. origin; cf. Du., Flem., LG. *snippen*, etc.] †1. *trans.* To take (something) quickly or suddenly; to snap or snatch. Also *absol.* -1720. 2. To cut, to cut up or off, by or as by scissors or the like. Also *absol.* 1593. 3. To snub, check, repress. Now *dial.* 1601.

1. The captain seldom ordered anything..but I snipped some of it for my own share DE FOE. 2. He has snipt off as much as he could pinch from every author of reputation LANDOR.

Snipe (snəip), *sb.* ME. [Corresponds to a Scand. *snīpa* recorded in Icel. *mýrisnípa*, Norw. *myr-*, *strandsnipa*. See N.E.D.] 1. One or other of the limicoline birds of the genus *Gallinago* (formerly included in the Linnæan genus *Scolopax*), characterized by having a long straight bill, and by frequenting marshy places; esp. *G. cœlestis* or *media*, the common English species. b. Applied to species of birds resembling the snipe 1785. c. Without article, in collective sense 1842. 2. As an opprobrious or abusive term 1604.

1. The s. flies screaming from the marshy verge 1794. See also GUTTER-, HALF-, JACK-, WOODSNIPE. c. I have..seen flocks of s. crossing the bay 1845.

Comb.: **s.-fish**, any fish of the genus *Centriscus*; esp. the trumpet-fish, bellows-fish or sea-s.

Snipe (snəip), *v.* 1782. [f. SNIPE *sb.* 1.] 1. *trans.* To shoot or fire at (men, etc.), one at a time, usu. from cover and at long range; to pick off (a person) in this manner. 2. *intr.* To fire as in snipe-shooting; to shoot at an enemy in this manner. Also with *at* and *away*. 1832.

2. Three hundred Boers hung on the rearguard, sniping but refusing battle 1901.

Sni·pe-bill. Also **snipe's bill.** 1678. [SNIPE *sb.* 1.] 1. A narrow moulding-plane with a sharp arris, for forming or cutting quirks. 2. *U.S.* The bolt connecting the body of a cart with the axle. (Also written *snibel.*) 1860.

Sniper (snəi·pəɪ). 1824. [f. SNIPE *v.*] 1. One who snipes, or shoots from concealment, etc.; a sharp-shooter. 2. A snipe-shooter 1840. 3. *U.S.* A prospector for gold or the like 1902.

Sniping (snəi·piŋ), *ppl. a.* 1821. [f. SNIPE *v.*] That snipes, or shoots from cover.

S. fire, individual and irregular shooting from a concealed position.

Snipped (snipt), *ppl. a.* 1578. [f. SNIP *v.*] 1. *Bot.* Irregularly notched or serrated; incised. 2. That has been subjected to snipping; jagged or irregularly cut 1601.

Sni·pper. 1593. 1. *pl.* Scissors. 2. One who snips or clips; *spec.* a tailor 1611.

Sni·pper-sna·pper. Now *dial.* 1590. [Cf. *snip-snap.*] A whipper-snapper.

Sni·ppet. 1664. [f. SNIP *v.* + -ET.] A small piece cut off; a small fragment or portion. b. *spec.* A short passage taken from a literary work; a short scrap of literary matter 1864.

fig. That is a poor s. of malicious gossip STEVENSON. Hence **Sni·ppety**, **-etty** *a.* of the nature of, composed of, a s. or snippets.

Snip-snap (sni·p,snæp), *sb.* 1597. [f. SNIP *sb.* + SNAP *sb.*, used with imitative effect.] †1. The action of snipping or clipping with a pair of scissors or the like; an instance of this -1638. 2. Smart remark or reply; sharp repartee 1727.

Snip-snap (sni·p,snæp), *a.* 1600. [Cf. prec.] †1. Making a snipping sound; working or acting by snipping or clipping -1643. 2. Of the nature of snip-snap; characterized by snip-snap or smart repartee 1673.

2. With volleys of small shot, or s. wit 1702.

Sni·p-snap, *v.* 1593. [Cf. SNIP-SNAP *sb.*] 1. *intr.* To indulge in snip-snap or smart repartee; to speak in a snappy manner. 2. To snip; to clip with a snipping sound 1906. So †**Snip-snap** *adv.* (and *int.*) with snip and snap; with a snipping, snapping sound 1588.

Snip-snap-sno·rum. 1755. [a. LG. *snipp-snapp-snorum* (also *-snurr*).] A round game of cards, in which the players on turning up the requisite cards respectively call 'snip', 'snap', and 'snorum'.

Snipy (snəi·pi), *a.* 1825. [f. SNIPE *sb.*] 1. Characterized by having a long pointed nose or muzzle suggestive of a snipe's bill. 2. Snipe-like 1888. 3. Frequented by snipe 1903.

Snitch (snitʃ), *sb. slang.* 1676. [?] †1. A filip (on the nose) -1700. 2. The nose 1700. 3. An informer 1785. So **Snitch** *v. intr.* to inform *upon* a person; to peach (1801); *trans.* to catch in a noose or loop (1900). **Sni·tcher.**

Snite (snəit), *sb.* [OE. *snite.*] = SNIPE *sb.* 1.

Snite (snəit), *v.* Now *dial.* and *Sc.* [OE. *snýtan*; the stem *snūt-* is prob. the same as that of SNOUT *sb.*] 1. a. *intr.* To clean or wipe the nose; to cast away mucus. b. *trans.* To remove by wiping, etc. 2. *trans.* To clean or clear (the nose) from mucus, esp. by means of the thumb and finger only; to blow. Also *fig.*, to tweak or pull. ME.

Snivel (sni·v'l), *sb.* late ME. [f. SNIVEL *v.*] 1. Mucus collected in, or issuing from, the nose. 2. A slight sniff indicating, or intended to suggest, suppressed emotion 1848. b. A show or pretence of emotion; hypocritical expression of feeling 1878.

Snivel (sni·v'l), *v.* ME. [OE. **snyflan*, f. *snofl* mucus.] 1. *intr.* To run at the nose; to emit mucus from the nose; also, to draw up mucus audibly. 2. To make a sniffing or snuffling sound expressive of real or assumed emotion; to be in, or affect, a tearful state 1690. 3. *trans.* a. To affect in some way by snivelling; to address in a snivelling manner (*rare*) 1668. b. To utter with a snivelling or sniffing sound, to shed (tears) snufflingly 1780.

2. Every woman in the house was snivelling at the time THACKERAY. Hence **Sni·veller**, one who snivels or whines; a cold breeze (causing one to snivel).

Snob (snǫb), *sb.* 1781. [orig. slang; origin unkn.] 1. *dial.* or *colloq.* A shoemaker or cobbler; a cobbler's apprentice. †2. *Cambridge slang.* Any one not a gownsman; a townsman -1865. †3. A person belonging to the lower classes of society; one having no pretensions to rank or gentility -1852. †b. A vulgar or ostentatious person -1859. c. One whose ideas and conduct are prompted by a vulgar admiration for wealth or social position. Also *transf.* of intellectual superiority. 1848. †4. = BLACKLEG 3. 1859.

3. c. He was..such a s., he felt pleased his clerks should hear a butler ask for a situation 1882. 4. Those who work for lower wages during a strike are called snobs, the men who stand out being 'nobs' DE QUINCEY. Hence **Sno·bbism** [whence F. *snobisme*], the characteristic qualities of a s.; snobbishness. **Sno·bby** *a.* snobbish. **Sno·bling**, a little, young, or petty s. **Snobo·cracy**, the class of snobs as having some power or exerting some influence. **Snobo·grapher**, a writer on, a describer of, snobs.

Snobbery (snǫ·bəri). 1833. [f. SNOB *sb.* 3.] 1. The class of snobs. †2. Snobbishness; vulgar ostentation; an instance of this 1843.

Snobbish (snǫ·biʃ), *a.* 1840. [f. SNOB *sb.* 3.] 1. Of, pertaining to, or characteristic of a snob. 2. Having the character of a snob 1849. Hence **Sno·bbish-ly** *adv.*, **-ness.**

Snod (snǫd), *a. Sc.* and *north. dial.* 1480. [Origin unkn.] 1. Smooth, sleek; even. 2. Neat, tidy, trim 1691. 3. Snug, cosy 1695. Hence **Snod** *v. trans.* to make smooth, trim, or neat; to tidy, put in order.

Snood (snūd), *sb.* [OE. *snōd.*] 1. A fillet, band, or ribbon, for confining the hair; latterly, in Scotland, etc., the distinctive hair-band worn by young unmarried women. 2. a. In sea-fishing: One of a number of short lines, each carrying a baited hook, attached at regular distances along the main line 1682. b. *Angling.* A hair or catgut line attaching the hook to the rod line 1823.

1. Yet ne'er again to braid her hair The virgin s. did Alice wear SCOTT.

Snood (snūd), *v.* 1725. [f. prec.] 1. *trans.* To bind *up*, fasten *back*, or secure (the hair) with a snood. 2. *Angling.* To attach (a hook) to a snood 1840. Hence **Snoo·ded** *ppl. a.* wearing a snood; bound by a snood.

Snook (snūk), *sb.* 1697. [ad. Du. *snoek* pike.] A name given to various fishes, esp. the sergeant-fish, *Elacate canada*, and the robalo, *Centropomus undecimalis.*

Snooker (snū·kəɪ). 1889. [Origin unkn.] A game, played with balls on a billiard table, combining pool and pyramids. Also *snooker('s) pool.*

Snooks (snūks). Also **snook.** 1879. [Origin unkn.] A derisive gesture consisting in placing the thumb against the nose and extending the fingers.

Snoop (snūp), *v.* orig. *U.S.* 1848. [ad. Du. *snoepen.*] 1. *trans.* To appropriate. 2. *intr.* To go round in a prying manner 1864.

Snooze (snūz), *v. colloq.* 1789. [App. a cant or slang word.] *intr.* To sleep; to slumber, to doze. Hence **Snooze** *sb.* a sleep, nap, doze; *slang.* a lodging, bed.

Snore (snōᵊɪ), *sb.* ME. [f. the vb.] †1. A snort; snorting (*rare*) -1513. 2. The snuffles 1585. 3. An act of snoring; a harsh or noisy respiration through the mouth, or through the mouth and nose, during sleep 1605. 4. *transf.* A sound resembling that of a snore; a loud roaring or droning noise 1709.

3. Thou do'st s. distinctly, There's meaning in thy snores SHAKS.

Snore (snōᵊɪ), *v.* late ME. [prob. echoic.] 1. *intr.* Of animals, *esp.* horses: To snort. Now *dial.* 2. To make harsh or noisy sounds in sleep by breathing through the open mouth or through the mouth and nose; to breathe in this manner during sleep. Also *poet.* and *rhet.*, to sleep heavily. 1440. 3. *trans.* With *out* or *away*: To spend or pass (time) in snoring 1597. 4. To utter with a snore or with a sound resembling this. Also with cogn. obj. 1790.

3. He dranke the Night away..then snor'd out all the Day 1746. Hence **Sno·rer**, one who snores. **Sno·ring** *vbl. sb.* the action of the vb.

Snort (snǭɪt), *sb.* 1619. [f. the vb.] †1. A snore -1622. 2. An act of snorting; a loud sound made by a horse or other animal in driving breath through the nostrils with some force 1808. b. A similar sound made by persons in order to express contempt, disdain, or other feeling 1865.

Snort (snǭɪt), *v.* late ME. [prob. echoic.] †1. *intr.* Of the nose: To turn *up*, as in sniffing. CHAUCER. †2. To snore; to sleep heavily or sluggishly -1680. 3. Of a horse: To make a characteristic loud or harsh sound by violently driving the breath through the nostrils, esp. when excited or frightened. Also said of other animals. late ME. 4. *transf.* Of things, esp. in later use of a railway engine: To make or emit a sound resembling or suggestive of a snort 1582. 5. Of persons: **a.** To express contempt or indignation by a snorting sound 1818. **b.** *dial.* and *U.S.* To laugh loudly or roughly 1825. 6. *trans.* **a.** To utter with a snort 1634. **b.** To eject or discharge through the nostrils with a snort; to spout *out* in this way 1818.

4. The little circular railway puffed and snorted 1879. 5. **a.** Duncan..snorted thrice, and prepared himself to be in a passion SCOTT. 6. **a.** 'Dat is gut! haw! haw!' snorted the Baron THACKERAY.

Snorter (snǭ·ɹtəɹ). 1601. [f. SNORT *v.*] 1. One who or that which snorts (†or snores); a person who utters a snort in scorn, indignation, etc.; also, a pig. **b.** *dial.* The wheatear 1802. 2. *slang* or *colloq.* **a.** A stiff or strong wind; a gale 1855. **b.** Anything exceptionally remarkable for size, strength, severity, etc. 1859. So **Sno·rting** *ppl. a.* used *advb.* = remarkably.

Snot (snǫt), *sb.* [ME. *snotte* or *snot*, = Fris. *snotte, snot.*] 1. The snuff of a candle; the burnt part of a candle-wick. Now *n. dial.* 2. The mucus of the nose. Now *dial.* or *vulgar.* late ME. 3. *dial.* and *slang.* Applied to persons as a term of contempt or opprobrium 1809. Hence **Sno·tter**[1], s. or nasal mucus.

Snot (snǫt), *v.* Now *n. dial.* and *Sc.* late ME. [f. prec.] 1. *trans.* To snuff (a candle). 2. To blow or clear (the nose) 1576. 3. *intr.* To sniff or snivel; to snort 1662.

Sno·tter[2]. 1769. [Origin unkn.] 1. A rope secured to a yard-arm with an eye forming a becket to which a tripping-line is bent, used in sending down topgallant and royal yards 1846. 2. A loop or ring of rope in which the lower end of the sprit rests 1769.

Sno·tty, *sb. slang.* 1903. A midshipman.

Snotty (snǫ·ti), *a.* 1570. [f. SNOT *sb.*] 1. Foul with snot or nasal mucus. **b.** Dirty, mean, paltry, contemptible, etc. Now *dial.* or *slang.* 1681. **c.** *dial.* or *slang.* Angry, curt, short-tempered; pert, impudent; proud, conceited 1870. 2. Consisting of snot; mucous; of the nature of, or resembling snot; viscous, slimy. 1656. Hence **Sno·ttily** *adv.* **Sno·ttiness**; **Sno·tty-nosed** *a.* having a s. nose; *fig.* contemptible.

Snout (snaut), *sb.* [ME. *snūt(e*, = MLG. *snūt(e*, G. *schnauze.*] 1. **a.** The trunk of an elephant. **b** = MUZZLE *sb.* I. 1; the proboscis or rostrum of an insect; etc. ME. 2. Contemptuously: The nose in man, esp. when large or badly shaped ME. 3. The end of a ship's prow; the beak or rostrum of a vessel. late ME. 4. A structure, formation, projecting part, etc., resembling or suggestive of a snout; a nozzle or the like. late ME. **b.** A projecting point of land, rock, etc. 1536. **c.** The front portion or termination of a glacier 1841. 5. One or other of various species of moths characterized by having abnormally long palpi projecting in front of the head; esp. the snout-moth, *Hypena proboscidalis* 1819.

Comb.: **s.-beetle**, one or other of several species of beetles characterized by having the head prolonged into a rostrum or proboscis. Hence **Snou·ty** *a.* resembling a s. or muzzle; having a pronounced or prominent s.; *colloq.* overbearing, insolent.

Snout (snaut), *v.* 1753. [f. SNOUT *sb.*] 1. *trans.* To finish *off* with a snout. 2. *trans.* and *intr.* To root, dig up, or grub, with or as with the snout 1857.

Snouted (snau·tėd), *ppl. a.* late ME. [f. SNOUT *sb.*] 1. Of things: Furnished with a snout or distinct terminal part. 2. Of persons or animals: Provided or furnished with a snout, muzzle, or rostrum 1536. 3. Shaped or fashioned like a snout; snout-like 1866.

Snow (snōu), *sb.*[1] [Com. Teut.; OE. *snāw* :—OTeut. **snaiwoz*. Cf. L. *nivis* (*nix*), Gr. *νίφα* (acc.) snow.] I. 1. The congealed vapour of the atmosphere falling in flakes characterized by their whiteness and lightness; the fall of these flakes, or the layer formed by them on the surface of the ground. **b.** Taken as a type of whiteness or brightness OE. **c.** With adjs. of colour, denoting snow tinged by various foreign substances, or the alga, etc., to which the colouring is due 1678. 2. A fall of snow; a snowstorm. Now *rare.* OE. **b.** As marking a period of time; a winter 1825. 3. *pl.* An accumulation, expanse, or field, of snow. late ME. **b.** *pl.* The arctic regions EMERSON.

1. Chaste as the Isicle That's curdied by the Frost, from purest S. SHAKS. S. is white and opaque in consequence of the air entangled among its crystals 1878. **b.** So is my sweet, much paler than the snowe 1593. **c.** The green s. (*Protococcus viridis*) and the red (*P. nivalis*) are..the same plant 1842. A..fall of ..black s. 1898. 2. Next come the snows, and rain, And frosts, and storms SHELLEY. *transf.* A fragrant s. of blossoms KINGSLEY. **b.** Through four sweet years.., from s. to s. TENNYSON. 3. Yonder, where the far snows blanch Mute Mont Blanc BROWNING.

II. 1. Applied to various things or substances having the colour or appearance of snow 1597. 2. **a.** The white hair of age. Also *pl.* 1638. **b.** White bloom or blossom; spray or foam 1859. 3. The pure white colour of snow; snow-white. Chiefly *poet.* 1745. 4. Cocaine (*slang*) 1921.

1. Argentine s., or flowers of antimony 1815. Whip the whites of six eggs to a hard s. 1864. 2. If my passions be cooled by the s. of my head, I have then never a white hair 1638. The May rain still on their petalled s. 1900. 3. Her eye sae bright..—Her breast o' mountain snaw 1843.

attrib. and *Comb.*: 1. General: as *s.-bed, -berg, -blast, -crystals*, etc.; *s.-boot, -fence, -spectacles*, etc.; *s. cake*, etc.; *s.-bound, -capped, -crested* adjs. 2. Special: **s.-blink**, the reflection from s. or ice-fields in polar regions; **-break**, (*a*) a rush of loose or melting s.; (*b*) a narrow strip of forest serving as a protection against s.; (*c*) the breaking of trees by the weight of s.; an area over which this happens; **-broth**, melted s.; water produced or obtained by the melting of s., esp. from natural causes; **-bucking** *U.S.*, the action of forcing a railway-train through a s.-drift; **-clad** *a.*, clad or covered with s.; **-cold** *a.*, as cold as s.; **-craft**, the art of traversing or dealing with s. in mountaineering; **-field**, an extensive stretch or expanse of s.; **-hole**, a hole or opening in the burner of a pyrites kiln; **-limit**, the limit (towards the equator) for the fall of s. at sea-level; **-scape**, a snow scene; **-sheen**, = *s.-blink*; **-sleep**, a somnolent condition induced by walking in s.; **-wreath**, a heap of s. blown together by the wind; a s.-drift. **b.** In names of animals, insects, etc., as **s.-flea, -fly, -gnat, -insect**, one or other of several species of small insects freqenting s.; **-leopard**, the ounce; **-mouse**, *Arvicola nivalis*; also, *Cuniculus torquatus*, a lemming of Arctic America which turns white in winter; **-panther**, = *s.-leopard*; **-worm**, a worm frequenting or living among s. **c.** In names of birds, as **s.-bunting**, a fringilline bird, *Plectrophanes nivalis*, widely distributed in Arctic regions; **-cock**, a s.-partridge, s.-pheasant, *Tetraogallus*; **-finch**, a species of mountain-finch; **-fleck**, the s.-bunting or Lapland bunting; **-goose**, a northern (American) goose of the genus *Chen*, esp. *C. hyperboreus*, characterized by its pure white plumage; **-grouse**, †**hen**, the ptarmigan; **-owl**, the snowy owl; **-partridge**, (*a*) the s.-pheasant; (*b*) a Himalayan gallinaceous bird, *Lerwa nivicola*; **-pheasant**, one or other of several species of the genus *Tetraogallus*, esp. *T. himalayensis*; also, several species of the genus *Crossoptilum*; **-pigeon**, a pigeon of Northern India and Tibet, *Colomba leuconota*; **-quail** *U.S.*, the white-tailed ptarmigan, *Lagopus leucurus*. **d.** In names of plants or fruits, as **s.-flower**, (*a*) = SNOWDROP 1; (*b*) = SNOWDROP-TREE 1; **-glory**, a hardy garden-plant of the genus *Chionodoxa*; **s.-pear**, a variety of pear, esp. *Pyrus nivalis*, which comes into season after snow has fallen; **-plant**, (*a*) a s.-alga; (*b*) a plant of the Sierra Nevada in California (*Sarcodes Sanguinea*), with a dense spike of flowers of a blood-red colour. Hence **Snow·less** *a.* free from s.; characterized by the absence of s.

Snow (snōu), *sb.*[2] 1676. [ad. Du. *sna(a)uw* or LG. *snau.*] A small sailing-vessel resembling a brig, carrying a main and fore mast and a supplementary trysail mast close behind the mainmast; formerly employed as a warship.

Snow (snōu), *v.* Pa. t. and pa. pple. **snowed** (snōud). ME. [f. SNOW *sb.*[1], taking the place of OE. *snīwan* SNEW *v.*] 1. *intr.* *It snows*, snow falls. Also occas. with *snow* as subject. 2. To fall, descend, etc., in the manner of snow ME. 3. *trans.* To let fall as snow; to cause to descend in the manner of snow; to shower down. late ME. 4. To strew or cover with or as with snow. late ME. 5. To cause (the hair, etc.) to turn white like snow; to invest with white hair 1598. 6. **a.** With *up.* To block, obstruct, incommode, imprison, etc., with snow. Usu. in pa. pple. 1815. **b.** With *under.* To bury in snow; *fig.* to submerge, overwhelm, overpower, etc. Orig. *U.S.* 1880.

1. Whan it snoweth, it is good syttynge by a good fyre 1530. 2. Away shot the cards..snowing upon the audience in the front rows 1894. 3. *fig.* 'Till age s. white hairs on thee DONNE. 6. **a.** News came from the country of trains snowed-up 1862.

Snowball (snōu·bǫl), *sb.* late ME. [f. SNOW *sb.*[1] + BALL *sb.*[1]] 1. A ball of snow, esp. one made for throwing by hand. 2. *Cookery.* One or other of various dishes or confections intended to resemble a ball of snow in appearance 1769. 3. The Guelder rose, *Viburnum Opulus*, or one of its clusters of white flowers 1799. 4. = *s.-contribution, letter* (= CHAIN *letter*), etc.

1. My bellies as cold as if I had swallow'd snowbals SHAKS. The Caravan like a snow-ball, increases in bulk as it rolls on 1845.

attrib.: **s.-contribution, -system**, one which increases by a kind of geometrical progression; **-tree**, the Guelder rose.

Snowball (snōu·bǫl), *v.* 1684. [f. prec.] 1. *intr.* To form balls or masses of snow. **b.** *fig.* To accumulate by degrees like a rolling snowball 1929. 2. *trans.* and *intr.* To pelt or have a pelting-match with snowballs 1855. So **Snow·balling** *vbl. sb.*

Snowberry (snōu·beɹi). 1760. [f. SNOW *sb.*[1]] A name given to various plants or shrubs bearing white berries, as *Chiococca racemosa*, a rubiaceous shrub of the West Indies and Florida, and *Symphoricarpus racemosus*, a caprifoliaceous shrub native to N. America and Mexico. **b.** The fruit of these shrubs 1837.

Creeping s., U.S., a trailing evergreen plant (*Chiogenes hispidula*) common in bogs and woods.

Snow·-bird. Also **snow bird, snowbird.** 1688. [f. SNOW *sb.*[1]] 1. One or other of various small European or American birds, *esp.* the snow-bunting, snow-finch, or snow-sparrow (*Junco hiemalis*). 2. The ivory gull, *Pagophila eburnea* 1831.

Snow·-blind, *a.* Also **snowblind.** 1748. [f. SNOW *sb.*[1]] Having the eyes or sight affected by exposure to the glare of snow. So **Snow·-blindness**, blindness or defective vision caused by exposure of the eyes to the glare of snow.

Snowdon (snōu·dən). 1450. [See note.] *S. herald*, one of the six Scottish heralds.

Snowdon was occas. used as a name for Stirling, but Jamieson cites statements that the designation of the herald was derived from 'Snowdoune castle of the county of Rosse'. N.E.D.

Snow·(-)drift. ME. [f. SNOW *sb.*[1]] 1. A heap or mass of snow driven together, or piled up, by the action of the wind. 2. A driving mass or cloud of snow; snow driven before the wind 1836.

Snowdrop (snōu·drǫp). 1664. [f. SNOW *sb.*[1]] 1. An early-flowering bulbous plant (*Galanthus nivalis*), having a white pendent flower; also, a flower, bulb, or single plant of this. 2. Used as a name for a variety of wheat or potato 1844.

Snow·drop tree. 1731. [f. prec.] 1. The Virginian fringe-tree, *Chionanthus virginica.* 2. A N. Amer. styraceous tree or shrub, *Halesia tetraptera* 1823.

Snow(-)fall (snōu·fǭl). 1821. [f. SNOW *sb.*[1]] 1. A fall of snow; a quantity of snow falling during a certain time. 2. The amount of snow falling at a particular place 1875.

Snow(-)flake (snōu·flēik). 1734. [f. SNOW *sb.*[1] + FLAKE *sb.*[2]] 1. One of the small masses in which snow commonly falls. 2. The snow-bunting 1770. 3. One or other species of *Leucojum* 1798. 4. A method of weaving woollen cloth, by which small knots are formed upon the 'right' side 1882.

Snow·-line. 1835. [f. SNOW *sb.*[1]] The general level on mountains, etc., above which the snow never completely disappears; the lower limit of perpetual snow, or (more rarely) of snow at a particular season.

Snow·-man. 1827. [f. SNOW *sb.*[1]] A mass of snow made into the figure of a man.

Snow·-plough. 1792. [f. SNOW *sb.*[1]] An implement or machine for clearing away snow from a road, railway track, etc.

Snow·(-)shoe, *sb.* 1674. [f. SNOW *sb.*[1]] **a.** A kind of foot-gear enabling the wearer to walk on the surface of snow, *esp.* one of a pair of racket-shaped frames of light wood, strung and netted with narrow strips of raw hide, used by the Indians and others in North America. **b.** One of a pair of ski 1864. Hence **Snow·-**

shoe *v. intr.* to travel on snow-shoes or ski. **Snow·-shoer**, one who uses, or travels on, snow-shoes. **Snow·-shoeing** *vbl. sb.* the action or practice of travelling on snow-shoes, esp. as an exercise or sport.

Snow·(-)storm. 1800. [f. SNOW *sb.*[1]] A storm accompanied by a heavy fall of snow.

Snow-white (stress var.), *a.* and *sb.* OE. [f. SNOW *sb.*[1] + WHITE *a.*] **A.** *adj.* White as snow; pure white. **B.** *sb.* Pure white; a kind of wool of this colour 1890.

A. Two s. and waxen hyacinths 1877.

Snowy (snōu·i), *a.* OE. [f. SNOW *sb.*[1]] **1.** Of weather, time, etc.: Characterized by the presence or prevalence of snow. **2.** Composed of melted snow; consisting, formed, or made of snow ME. **3.** Covered with snow; abounding in snow 1548. **4.** Resembling the colour of snow; snow-white 1590. **b.** Used to qualify *white* or *whiteness* 1785. **5.** In the specific names of birds or animals 1777.

1. A cold, s., uncomfortable month 1748. **3.** His slanting ray Slides ineffectual down the s. vale COWPER. **4.** So shewes a S. Doue trooping with Crowes SHAKS. *transf.* There did he loose his s. Innocence 1646. **5.** S. plover *Ægialites nivosus*, a small ring-plover of the Pacific and Mexican Gulf coasts of the United States 1891. *S. egret* or *heron*, an entirely white egret (*Ardea candidissima*) ranging from New York to Chile 1895. The..s. owl (*Nyctea scandiaca*) 1895. Hence **Snow·ily** *adv.* **Snow·iness.**

Snub (snɒb), *sb.*[1] 1537. [f. SNUB *v.*] **1.** An act or instance of snubbing; a remark or action intended to repress or rebuke a person. †**2.** A check, stay or hindrance –1672.

Snub (snɒb), *sb.*[2] and *a.* 1830. [See SNUB NOSE.] **A.** *sb.* A snub nose. **B.** *adj.* **1.** Of the nose: Short and turned up 1844. **2.** Snub-nosed 1883. Hence **Snu·bby** *a.* somewhat s.; short, stumpy.

Snub (snɒb), *v.* ME. [a. ON. *snubba.*] **1.** *trans.* To check, reprove, or rebuke in a sharp or cutting manner; in later use, to treat or receive (a person, suggestion, etc.) in a way calculated to repress or mortify. Also *absol.* †**b.** To take *up* sharply or severely; to order *about* in a sharp fashion –1797. **2.** †**a.** To check or restrain (a thing); to prevent from having free course or development –1688. **b.** *Naut.* and *U.S.* To check or stop (a rope or cable) suddenly while running out; to stop or bring *up* (a boat, etc.) sharply or suddenly, esp. by passing a rope round a post; to fasten or tie (*up*) 1841. **3.** To check the growth of; to shorten; to cut, nip, or break *off*, the end of (a thing). Now *rare*. 1615. **Snu·bbing** *vbl. sb.*

Snub-, the stem of SNUB *v.* used in comb., in †**s.-devil** (*slang*), a clergyman; **s-line, -post** *U.S.*, a snubbing-line or -post, etc.

Snub(-)nose. 1724. [f. SNUB *v.* 3.] A short stumpy nose turned up and flattened at the tip. **Snu·b-nosed** *a.* having a snub nose.

Snu·bber. 1925. [f. SNUB *v.*] A shock-absorber.

Snudge (snɒdʒ), *sb.* Now *dial.* 1545. [Cf. SNUDGE *v.*] A miser, a niggard; a sneaking or sponging fellow.

Snudge (snɒdʒ), *v.* 1540. [Origin unkn.] †**1.** *intr.* To be miserly, stingy, or saving. Also with *it*. –1611. **2.** To walk in a stooping or meditative attitude. Now *dial.* 1677.

Snuff (snɒf), *sb.*[1] late ME. [Origin obsc. Cf. G. *schnuppe.*] **I. 1.** That portion of a wick, etc., which is partly consumed in the course of burning and requires to be removed at intervals; †a candle-end. **b.** In comparisons, used to describe what is faint, feeble, or on the point of extinction 1534. †**2.** A heel-tap –1738.

1. *fig.* Let me not liue..After my flame lackes oyle, to be the snuffe Of yonger spirits SHAKS. **b.** Thy soul, which..Scarce glimmers like a dying s. SWIFT.

II. 1. †**a.** *To take..in* (*the*) *s.* (or *to snuff*), to take (a matter) amiss, to take offence at, to resent –1716. **b.** *To take s.*, to take offence or umbrage (*at* a thing). *Obs.* exc. *arch.* 1565. **2.** A fit of indignation; a huff, rage or passion. Now *Sc.* 1592.

1. a. This matter the Justice tooke sore to snuffe, and was very angry 1570. **b.** Jupiter took S. at the Contempt, and Punish'd him for't 1692. **2.** He went away in snuffe, and I followed him B. JONS.

Snuff (snɒf), *sb.*[2] 1570. [f. SNUFF *v.*[2]] **1.** An (*or* the) act of snuffing, esp. as an expression of contempt or disdain. **2.** Smell, odour, scent 1763. **3.** A sniff *of* something 1822.

A derisive and defiant s. C. BRONTË.

Snuff (snɒf), *sb.*[3] 1683. [prob. ad. Du., Flem. *snuf* or *snuif* in the same sense; app. an abbrev. of *snuiftabak.*] **1.** A preparation of powdered tobacco for inhaling through the nostrils. **b.** Any powder used like snuff, esp. for medicinal purposes; a sternutatory or errhine. (*rare.*) 1861. **2.** A pinch of snuff 1724. **b.** Used to denote something of small value 1809.

1. He took s. with everybody DICKENS. Phrases. *Up to s.*, knowing, sharp, not easily deceived. *In high s.*, in high feather; elated. *To give* (one) *s.*, to deal sharply or severely with; to punish.

attrib. and *Comb.*: **s.-coloured** *a.* of the colour of s.; brown, brownish; **-dipper**, *U.S.*, one who habitually takes s.

Snuff (snɒf), *v.*[1] 1450. [f. SNUFF *sb.*[1]] **1.** *trans.* To free (a candle, wick, etc.) from the snuff, by pinching or cutting this off, or removing it with a special instrument. **b.** *fig.* To make clearer or brighter; to purge 1574. **2.** With *out*: **a.** To extinguish, put out; to cause to go out or disappear from sight 1687. **b.** To eclipse, efface, wipe out 1852. **3.** *intr.* To die. *slang* or *colloq.* 1865.

1. b. By exact definitions first snuffed, and purged from ambiguity HOBBES. **2. a.** 'Tis strange the mind..Should let itself be snuff'd out by an article BYRON.

Snuff (snɒf), *v.*[2] 1527. [prob. ad. MDu. *snoffen, snuffen* to snuffle, either imitative in origin, or related to MDu. *snuven* to snuff or sniff.] **I.** *trans.* **1.** To draw *up* or *in* through the nostrils by the action of inhalation. **2.** To inhale, draw up, into or through the nostrils 1547. **3.** To detect, perceive or anticipate, by inhaling the odour of 1697. **4.** To smell at, examine by smelling 1859.

2. The leading Highlander snuffed the wind like a setting spaniel SCOTT. Phr. †*To s. pepper*: see PEPPER *sb.* 4. **3.** The old bull snuffed danger in the wind 1863. **4.** He [a dog]..snuffed him all over 1859.

II. *intr.* **1.** To draw air, etc., into the nostrils by an effort of inhalation; to do this in order to smell something 1530. **b.** Const. *up* one's nose 1714. **2.** To express scorn, disdain, or contempt by snuffing; to sniff. Freq. const. *at* a thing or person. Now *rare* or *Obs.* 1544. **3.** To inhale powdered tobacco; to take snuff 1725.

1. Like a wild Asse..that snoffeth and bloweth COVERDALE *Jer.* ii. 23. **b.** Tricks such as snuffing up his nose CHESTERF. Hence **Snu·ffer**[2], one who takes s.; *U.S. local*, a porpoise.

Snu·ff-box. 1687. [SNUFF *sb.*[3] 1.] **1.** A box for holding snuff, usu. small enough to be carried in the pocket. **2.** *slang.* The nose 1853.

1. *Musical s.*, one fitted with mechanism capable of playing tunes.

Snuffer[1] (snɒ·fəɹ). 1465. [f. SNUFF *v.*[1]] **1.** An instrument for snuffing, or snuffing out, candles, etc. In later use only in pl. form (also *a pair of snuffers*). **2.** One who snuffs candles 1611.

Snuffle (snɒ·f'l), *sb.* 1764. [f. the vb.] †**1.** An (*or* the) act of snuffling. **2.** *pl.* A stopped condition of the nose, through a cold in the head, etc., causing a snuffling sound in the act of respiration 1770. **3.** A nasal tone in the voice 1820.

2. She has at present a little London cold, but her Grace says it is 'only the snuffles' 1770. **3.** With a hypocritical s., and a sly twinkle of his eye SCOTT.

Snuffle (snɒ·f'l), *v.* 1583. [prob. ad. Du. and Flem. *snuffelen.*] **I.** *intr.* †**1.** To show dislike or disdain by snuffing; to sniff *at* a thing in contempt –1662. **2.** To draw air into the nostrils in order to smell something; to snuff or smell *at* a thing 1600. **3.** To speak through the nose; to have a nasal twang. (Occas. taken as indicating hypocrisy or canting.) 1600. **4.** To draw up air or mucus through the nostrils in an audible or noisy manner 1600. †**5.** Of the wind: To blow in fitful gusts –1781.

3. Snuffling through the nose with an harmonious twang 1756.

II. *trans.* **1.** To inhale, to clear, to search out or examine, by snuffing 1599. **2.** To utter, say, declare, etc., in a snuffling or nasal tone 1641.

2. Even the old Marquis snuffles approval CARLYLE. Hence **Snu·ffler**, one who snuffles or speaks through the nose; one who speaks cantingly. **Snu·fflingly** *adv.*

Snuffy (snɒ·fi), *a.*[1] 1678. [f. SNUFF *sb.*[1] or *v.*[2]] Annoyed, displeased; ready to take offence.

Snuffy (snɒ·fi), *a.*[2] 1789. [f. SNUFF *sb.*[3]] **1.** Like, or resembling snuff or powdered tobacco in colour or substance. **2. a.** Of persons: Given to taking snuff; bearing marks of this habit 1790. **b.** Of things: Soiled with snuff 1840.

2. a. A little odd-looking s. old man, with a brown scratch wig DISRAELI. Hence **Snu·ffiness.**

Snug (snɒg), *sb.*[1] 1665. [Origin obsc.] **1.** A snag (*rare*). **2.** *techn.* A projection or ridge cast on a plate, bolt, etc., in order to keep something in position, prevent rotation, or for some similar purpose 1843.

Snug (snɒg), *sb.*[2] 1768. [f. SNUG *a.*] **1.** *The s.*, that which is comfortable, quiet, or private (*rare*). **2.** *dial.* or *slang*. = SNUGGERY 1 b. 1864.

Snug (snɒg), *a.* and *adv.* 1595. [Origin obsc.] **A.** *adj.* **1.** *Naut.* Of a ship or her parts: Trim, neat, compact; properly prepared for, or protected from, bad weather. **b.** *transf.* Of persons: Neat, trim. Now *Obs.* or *dial.* 1714. **2.** In a state of ease, comfort, or quiet enjoyment 1630. **3.** Of places, buildings, etc.: Comfortable and warm, cosy; esp. combining comfort with neatness and compactness 1718. **4. a.** Enabling one to live in comfort and comparative ease 1735. **b.** Moderately well-to-do; comfortably off; 'warm'. Chiefly *Irish dial.* 1802. **c.** Fairly large or substantial 1833. **5.** Comfortable, cosy 1766. **6.** In concealment or hiding; out of sight or observation. Chiefly with *lie* vb. 1687. †**b.** Secret –1766. **7.** Used as an interjection asking for or commanding secrecy, esp. in phr. *snug 's the word* 1700.

1. She will be..s. for any gale 1883. **2.** On southern banks the..sheep Lay s. and warm COWPER. You might sit as s. as a bug in a rug 1833. **3.** Your s. warm bed 1806. **4. a.** A good s. business they've got 1867. **c.** Having a s. legacy from Miss Crawley THACKERAY. **5.** He liked s. dinners of all things in the world THACKERAY. **6.** Be sure..[To] Lie s., and hear what critics say SWIFT.

B. *adv.* Snugly 1674.

He eyes the centre, where his friends sit s. GOLDSM. Hence **Snu·g·ly** *adv.* in a s. manner; **-ness.**

Snug (snɒg), *v.* 1583. [Origin unkn.] **1.** *intr.* Of persons (or animals): To lie or nestle closely or comfortably, esp. in bed; to snuggle. Now *rare* or *dial.* **2.** *trans.* To place or put snugly, neatly, or comfortably 1754. **3.** To make snug, comfortable, or tidy; to set nicely in order 1787. **b.** To put or stow *away* snugly 1859. **4.** *Naut.* To make (a ship, etc.) snug or trim, esp. by lashing or stowing movables, furling or reducing sails, lowering topmasts, etc., in preparation for bad weather; to furl (a sail) 1881.

1. The loving couple lay snugging together 1692. **3.** The tent was shut, and everything snugged up 1888. **4.** The men were employed in snugging the decks 1881.

Snuggery (snɒ·gəri). 1815. [f. SNUG *a.* + -ERY.] **1.** A cosy or comfortable room, esp. one of small size, into which a person retires for seclusion or quiet; a bachelor's den. **b.** *spec.* The bar-parlour of an inn or public-house 1837. **2.** A snug, comfortable, or cosy house or dwelling 1833. **b.** A snug place, position, feature, etc. 1850. **3.** A sinecure (*rare*) 1839.

Snuggle (snɒ·g'l), *v.* 1687. [Cf. SNUG *v.* and -LE.] **1.** *intr.* Of persons, esp. children: To lie snug or close, esp. for warmth or comfort; to settle down cosily or comfortably; to get or press close to a person, esp. as a mark of affection; to nestle. **2.** *transf.* Of buildings, etc.: To lie in a sheltered or snug situation; to nestle 1862. **3.** *trans.* To hug or cuddle (a person, etc.) 1775.

So (sōu), *adv.* and *conj.* [Com. Teut.; OE. *swa, swā* (also *swǣ, swē*, etc.); ult. origin unkn.] **I. 1.** In the way or manner described, indicated, or suggested; in that style or fashion. **2.** With the verbs *do, say, think*, etc., latterly assuming the function of an object and passing into the sense of 'that' OE. **b.** With auxiliary verbs in elliptic use (requiring the addition of *do* or *to do*) OE. **c.** In this way; thus; as follows ME. **3.** Used as predicate with the verb *be* OE. **b.** With auxiliary verbs in elliptic use (requiring the addition of (*to*) *be*, (*to*) *have it*, etc.)

OE. **c.** Followed by a clause introduced by *that* ME. **d.** In clauses of supposition (sometimes with omission of *that*) ME. **4.** Representing a word or phrase already employed: Of that nature or description; of or in that condition, etc. OE. **b.** With verbs of thinking, considering, etc.: To be such, as such ME. **c.** With *call*, *name*, etc.: By that name or designation 1608. **5.** In various elliptic uses: **a.** After adverbs and conjunctions, as *how so?* *not so*, *if so*, etc. ME. **b.** As an introductory particle. Also *so, so.* 1593. **c.** As an expression of approval, or a direction to do something in a particular manner. Also in phr. *so best.* 1598. †**d.** = Let it be so; it is well. SHAKS. **e.** With ellipse of 'says' or 'writes' 1613.

1. There was the woman at Pau; and that girl..at Vienna. He went on just so about them all. THACKERAY. 2. I cannot doubt that they think so COLERIDGE. Some State legislatures have affected so to do 1888. b. *Brut[us].* Repaire to th' Capitoll. *All.* We will so. SHAKS. c. For so the Lord sayd vnto me; I will take my rest *Isa.* xviii. 4. 3. You argue from fact to necessity; 'Tis so, therefore it must be so 1697. No! Is that so? 1880. b. You are a welcome guest, if so you please 1594. c. Yet so it is, that People can bear any Quality in the World better than Beauty STEELE. d. Thus love I thee, so be thou loue me 1638. 4. To make men happy, and to keep them so POPE. b. Her Attractions would indeed be irresistible, but that she thinks them so STEELE. c. My son Johnny, named so after his uncle SWIFT. 5. a. 'I know China as well as any living Englishman.' 'Quite so.' 1896. b. So, let me see: my apron 1602. So, so, ma'am! I.. beg pardon SHERIDAN. c. So, thus, keep her thus 1669. d. If it please you, so: if not: why so SHAKS. e. So he; doubting..the truth of his witnesses 1613.

II. Placed at the beginning of a clause with continuative force, and freq. preceded by *and.* **1.** Used to confirm or strengthen a previous statement OE. **2.** Denoting similarity, parallelism, or identity in some respect between two facts, actions, etc. OE. **3.** For that reason, on that account, accordingly, consequently, therefore ME. **b.** As an introductory particle, without a preceding statement (but freq. implying one) 1710. **4.** Denoting sequence, freq. without implication of manner, and hence passing into: Then, thereupon, thereafter, subsequently ME.

1. My father's birthday? Why, so it is! 1898. 2. The Mayor looked blue; So did the Corporation too BROWNING. 3. A shelter..is all I seek for. So name your rent. SCOTT. b. So one of my nephews is a wild rogue, hey? SHERIDAN. 4. Then we marched out..to the drum, and so to bed 1892.

III. To that extent; in that degree. **1.** With adjs. or advs. (or equivalent phrases) in neg. and interrog. clauses OE. **2.** In affirmative clauses, with adj. followed by *a*, etc., and with verbs. Freq. as mere intensive. ME.

1. A voice so thrilling ne'er was heard WORDSW. What am I to say in answer to conduct so preposterous? NEWMAN. 2. The bones of so dogged Contentions 1626. So barefaced a blunder 1845. I held back because I loved you so 1884.

IV. Introducing one or both of two clauses expressing comparison or correspondence. †**1.** After relative pronouns or advs.: So ever -1593. †**2.** *So..so* = As..so -1667. **3.** In adjurations or asseverations: In that way; to that extent OE. **4.** *So..as, so as*, in such or the same way, manner, etc., as ME. **5.** *So..as*, to the same extent, in the same degree, as: a. In neg. or interrog. clauses ME. **b.** In affirmative clauses: As..as. Now *arch.* or *dial.* late ME. **c.** With *as* taking the place of an object to the following verb 1555. **6.** *As..so*: **a.** Denoting more or less exact correspondence, similarity, or proportion ME. **b.** Denoting a simple parallelism between two different acts, concepts, etc., and sometimes approaching the sense of 'not only ..but (also)' ME.

1. Commaund What so thy mind affectes MARLOWE. 2. So high as heav'd the tumid Hills, so low Down sunk a hollow bottom MILT. 3. This seat..I claim as my right—so prosper me God and St. Barr! SCOTT. *So help*: see HELP *v.* 1. 4. Do euen so as thou hast spoken COVERDALE *Gen.* xviii. 5. 5. a. Women were never soe usefull as now 1646. b. The one is become so old as the other 1621. c. Is our Perfection of so frail a Make, As ev'ry Plot can undermine or shake? DRYDEN. 6. a. For as he thinketh in his heart, so is he *Prov.* xxiii. 7. b. As we rose with the sun, so we never pursued our labours after it was gone down GOLDSM. As in the arts, so also in politics, the new must always prevail over the old 1881.

V. 1. *So that*, denoting result or logical consequence; also sometimes = 'in order that' OE. **2.** *So..that*, in such a way, to such an extent, that: **a.** With adjs. and advs., and vbs. OE. **b.** With *but* (= that..not) 1842. **3.** With omission of *that*, = prec. sense ME. **b.** With the *so*-clause placed after that stating the consequence or result ME. **4.** *So (that)*, in limiting sense: On condition that, provided that, so long as, if only OE. **b.** In the event that, in case that (*rare*) OE.

2. So frownd the mighty Combatants, that Hell Grew darker MILT. So ill that she could hardly speak 1802. b. There was no heart so bold, But sore it ached MACAULAY. 3. He..treads so light, he scarcely prints the Plains DRYDEN. b. Friends he has few, so high the madness grows DRYDEN. 4. I'll swiftly go.. Nor care what land thou bear'st me to, So not again to mine BYRON.

VI. 1. *So..*, or *so..as*, *so as*, followed by an infinitive denoting result or consequence. late ME. **2.** *So as*, in such a way that, so that. Now *dial.* 1523. **b.** *So..as*, in similar use 1548. **c.** *So..as that, so as that*, = b. 1583. **3.** *So as*, provided that, etc. 1585.

1. Be so good to continue to favour me with your letters 1767. To repair the drain so as to abate the nuisance 1896. 2. b. So posted, as they were not to be surprized 1738. c. When both flames have approached so near as that they join GOLDSM.

Phrases. 1. *So to speak*: see SPEAK *v.* I. 3. **And so on,** an abbreviating phrase to avoid further description or enumeration of details. *And so forth*: see FORTH *adv.* **Or so,** or the like; or thereabout. 2. With various adjs. and advs. of quantity, number, etc. **So far**: see FAR *adv.* 5, FAR-FORTH *adv.* *In so far as* (see IN *prep.* Phr.). *To be so far from..that*, and, by illogical ellipsis, simply *so far from*, are used to distinguish a contrasted statement or supposition. *So far, so good*, used to express satisfaction with matters up to a certain point. **So long**: see LONG *adv.* 1. **So much. a.** *adj.* So great, extensive, or abundant; so large a quantity or number of, etc.; an equal sum or amount of (something). **b.** *adv.* Followed by *the* and a comparative (and sometimes with *by* preceding): To that extent, in that degree. Also, To such an extent; in such a degree. **c.** *sb.* An equal amount; as much; a certain unspecified amount, sum, etc.; thus much, thus far (used to sum up or dismiss a matter); such an amount, quantity, etc. **So much (so)..as** or **that. a.** With *as* in ordinary comparative use. **b.** Used to emphasize a negation (e.g. *not so much as a penny*). **c.** With *that* denoting result or consequence.

Soak (sōᵘk), *sb.* 1598. [f. the vb.] **1. a.** The condition or process of being or becoming soaked; a spell of soaking. Chiefly in the phr. *in s.* **b.** A liquid used for maceration; a steep 1850. **c.** A vat in which hides are macerated 1876. **2.** A percolation of water; water which has oozed through or out of the ground, strata, etc. 1707. **3.** A heavy drinker; a tippler 1820. **4.** A prolonged draught or drinking-bout 1851.

Soak (sōᵘk), *v.* Pa. pple. **soaked,** †**soaken.** [OE. *socian*, f. wk. grade of the stem of *sūcan* to SUCK.] **I.** *intr.* **1.** To lie immersed in a liquid for a considerable time, so as to be saturated or permeated with it; to become thoroughly wet or soft in this manner. **2.** To percolate; to penetrate by saturation or infiltration; to ooze. Also with *in*, *through*, etc. 1440. **b.** With cogn. object: To make (way) by percolation 1815. **3.** To drink immoderately; to saturate oneself with liquor 1687.

1. As soon as the goose was killed, the liver was put to s. in milk and honey 1853. *fig.* Now, put these little hints 'to s.', as they say out here 1874. 2. The water ..soaked under the wall and wetted the mud below it 1884. b. The rivulet..soaked its way obscurely through wreaths of snow SCOTT.

II. *trans.* **1.** Of liquid or moisture: To permeate thoroughly; to saturate with wet ME. **2.** To lay or place in, to wet with, a liquid so as to produce thorough saturation; to steep. late ME. **b.** *refl.* with ref. to excessive drinking 1818. **3.** To bake (bread, etc.) thoroughly 1686.

2. Phr. *To s. one's clay* (colloq. or slang), to drink (heavily). c. Phr. *U.S. slang.* To strike hard, pummel; also *fig.* to 'slate'. *To s. it*, to 'give it hot', administer punishment to 1896. d. To impose upon (a person) by an extortionate charge or price (*slang*) 1899.

III. 1. To draw *out*, cause to ooze *out*, by means of soaking. late ME. **b.** To draw or suck *out* 1577. †**c.** To drain, exhaust, impoverish. Also *to s. dry* or *up.* -1687. **2.** To allow to sink in; to absorb; to take in by absorption. Also with *up.* 1553. **b.** To drink, imbibe, esp. to excess 1697.

1. Put half the Planks into Water..to s. out their Sap 1733. c. A Woman that sokes up a Man 1687. 2. b. The quantity of port soaked there 1865.

Soakage (sōᵘ·kėdʒ). 1766. [f. prec. + -AGE.] **1.** Liquid which has filtered or oozed out. **2.** Liquid or moisture absorbed 1830. **3.** The process of percolating or soaking through 1867. **4.** The fact of lying in soak 1855.

Soaker (sōᵘ·kəɹ). 1577. [f. SOAK *v.* + -ER[1].] †**1.** A drainer, exhauster -1641. **2.** A drunkard 1593. **3.** *Old s.*, an old hand at anything; *spec.* at drinking 1589. **4.** One who soaks something 1611. **b.** A drenching rain 1839. **5.** A sheet of lead used in roofing to keep out heavy rains 1895.

Soaking (sōᵘ·kiŋ), *vbl. sb.* 1440. [f. SOAK *v.*] **1.** The action of the vb. **b.** *pl.* Liquid which has soaked through 1846. **2.** In iron-working: A special process by which the heat of an ingot is equally distributed through the mass, in order to fit it for rolling 1884.

Soaking (sōᵘ·kiŋ), *ppl. a.* 1440. [f. SOAK *v.*] †**1.** Taking in moisture, absorbent; *fig.* drawing to oneself, tending to drain or exhaust -1611. **2.** *Printing. S. pull*, a long and easy pull over of the bar-handle of a printing press 1683. †**3.** Percolating; sinking in; flowing slowly -1699. **4.** Drenching; wetting thoroughly 1641. **5.** Saturated, drenched 1864. **6.** Quasi-*adv.*, in *s. wet* 1847.

1. Conceit is s., will draw in More then the common Blocks SHAKS. 4. The rain was coming down in a s. drizzle 1894. 5. The suns of August sucked up the venom from the emerald s. swamp 1882. Hence **Soa·kingly** *adv.*

Soam (sōᵘm). *Sc.* and *north.* late ME. [prob. a. OF. *some* pack-saddle, horse-load.] **1.** A rope or chain, attaching a draught-horse, etc., to a wagon, plough, etc.; a trace-rope. **2.** *Coal-mining. pl.* Traces for drawing coal in tubs along the roads 1789.

So-and-so, *sb.*, *a.*, and *adv.* 1596. **A.** *sb.* An indefinite phrase (= 'such a thing, person, number, etc.') used in place of a more lengthy statement, or as a substitute for an expression or name not exactly remembered or stated.

Number s. in such-and-such a street 1861.

B. *adj.* Paltry, worthless; indifferent; poor in health or circumstances; so-so. Now *dial.* 1655. **C.** *adv.* **1.** To a certain number or degree 1631. **2.** In a certain manner or way 1653. **3.** With only moderate prosperity, success, etc. 1844.

2. Vertue and Vice are nothing else but the Soul so and so affected or modified 1678.

Soap (sōᵘp), *sb.* [Com. WGer.; OE. *sāpe* = MDu. *seepe* (Du. *zeep*), (M)LG. *sêpe*, OHG. *seifa* (G. *seife*). L. *sapo* (and the Rom. forms), Finnish *saipio*, etc. are from Teut. The word occurs also in some of the Tartar langs.] **1.** A substance formed by the combination of certain oils and fats with alkaline bases, and used for washing or cleansing purposes. **b.** *slang.* Flattery (cf. SOFT SOAP *sb.* 2) 1859. **c.** *U.S.* Money; now esp. that used in bribery 1860. **2.** With distinguishing terms, denoting a particular kind or make of soap, as CASTILE S., *hard s.*, SOFT S.; also *s. of soda*, etc. late ME. **3.** With *a* and *pl.* A kind of soap 1562.

1. c. If thy father hath 'the s.', Do not wash your hands of me 1860. 2. Fixed oil, in combination with soda, forms the finest kind of hard s. 1813.

Comb.: **s.-box,** a box in which soap is packed; used, esp. in U.S., as a makeshift stand for a street orator; *attrib.* characteristic of s.-b. oratory; hence as *vb.*; also **soapboxer; s. cerate,** a cerate composed of lead, soap, and the acetates of lead and soda, used to allay inflammation; †**-earth,** soapstone; **-fat,** the refuse of kitchens, used in making s.; **-fish,** either *Rhypticus saponaceus* or *Promicropterus maculatus*; **-liniment,** a liniment composed of s., camphor, and spirits of rosemary; **s. plaster,** a healing plaster chiefly composed of s.; **-saver,** a wire receptacle with a handle in which remnants of soap are utilized for producing a lather. **b.** Forming names of plants or trees, or their products: **s.-bark,** a vegetable principle obtained from certain trees, as the *Quillaja Saponaria* of Chili, the common Soapwort, *Saponaria officinalis*, and allied species, and used as a substitute for s.; saponin; **-fruit,** = SOAPBERRY 1; **-nut,** = SOAPBERRY; **-plant** *U.S.*, an American liliaceous plant, *Chlorogalum pomeridianum*, used as a detersive; also, the soapberry; **-root,** either of two plants, the Egyptian Soap-root (*Gypsophila struthium*), and the Spanish Soap-root (*G. Hispanica*), both used for washing; **-tree,** one or other of various trees or plants, of which the roots, leaves, or fruits yield a substitute for s.

Soap (sōᵘp), *v.* 1585. [f. SOAP *sb.*] **I.** *trans.*

To rub, smear, lather, or treat with soap. Also with *up*. **2.** *slang*. To address with smooth or flattering words; to flatter 1853.

Soapberry (sōᵘ·pbe:ri). Also **soap-berry, soap berry.** 1629. [SOAP *sb.*] **1.** The fruit or nut of various species of *Sapindus* (esp. *S. Saponaria*), or of *Acacia concinna*, used in certain countries as a substitute for soap; a soap-nut. **2.** Any of the trees bearing this fruit 1716.

Soa·p-boi·ler. 1594. [SOAP *sb.*] **1.** One who boils (the ingredients of) soap; a soap-maker. **2.** A pot used for boiling soap; a soap-pan 1863. So **Soa·p-boi·ling** *vbl. sb.* the business, occupation, or process of boiling soap.

Soa·p-bu·bble. 1815. [SOAP *sb.*] An iridescent bubble composed of a thin film of soap and water.

fig. The talk has been mere soap-bubbles EMERSON.

Soapery (sōᵘ·pəri). 1674. [f. †*soaper*: see -ERY.] A soap-factory.

Soa·p-ma·ker. 1483. [SOAP *sb.*] One who makes soap; a soap-boiler.

Soap(-)stone (sōᵘ·pˌstōᵘn). 1681. [SOAP *sb.*] *Min.* A massive variety of talc, of which various kinds are found in several countries, having a smooth greasy feel, and used for various economical or ornamental purposes (occas. as a soap); steatite; also loosely applied to certain soft clays, etc.

Soap(-)suds. 1611. [SOAP *sb.*] Water impregnated with dissolved soap, *esp.* water in which clothes have been washed; in attrib. use freq. *soap-sud*.

Soapwort (sōᵘ·pwɒɹt). 1548. [f. SOAP *sb.*] **1.** One or other of the herbaceous plants belonging to the genus *Saponaria*, which yield a saponaceous principle; esp. the common species, *S. officinalis*; also, the genus itself. **2.** Any plant of the order *Sapindaceæ* 1846.

Soapy (sōᵘ·pi), *a.* 1610. [f. SOAP *sb.* + -Y [1].] **1.** Smeared with soap; covered with soap-suds or lather. **2.** Impregnated with soap; containing soap in solution 1721. **3.** Of the nature of soap; having the soft or greasy feel of soap; soap-like 1722. **4.** Of appearance, feel, etc.: Resembling that of soap; suggestive of soap 1732. **b.** Having a taste of soap 1892. **5.** *slang*. Ingratiating, suave, unctuous 1865. Hence **Soa·pily** *adv.* **Soa·piness.**

Soar (sōᵊɹ), *sb.* 1596. [f. SOAR *v.*, perh. partly after F. *essor.*] **1.** The altitude attained in soaring; range of flight upwards. **2.** The act of soaring or rising high 1817.

1. Within soare Of Towring Eagles MILT. **2.** It is ill whistling for a hawk when she is once on the s. SCOTT.

Soar (sōᵊɹ), *v.* late ME. [ad. F. *essorer* (= It. *sorare*) to fly up, to soar, repr. pop. Lat. **exaurare*, f. *aura* air.] **I.** *intr.* **1.** Of birds: To fly or mount upwards; to ascend to a towering height; also loosely, to sail or skim at a great height. Occas. with *up*. **2.** *fig.* To mount, ascend, or rise to a higher or more exalted level in some respect 1593. **3.** Of inanimate objects: To ascend, rise up to a height 1697. **b.** Of a mountain, building, etc.: To rise majestically or imposingly to a great altitude. Also with *up*. 1812.

1. A flight of Condors soaring in circles in a particular spot 1830. *transf.* O, in what orbe thy mightie spirit soares 1602. **b.** *Aeronautics.* To fly without motor power and without loss of altitude 1897. **2.** How high a pitch his resolution soares! SHAKS. When men of infamy to grandeur s. YOUNG.

II. *trans.* **1.** To perform or accomplish (a flight) by rising high 1659. **2.** To attain or reach (a height) by upward flight; to fly up through (the air, etc.) 1667.

2. They summ'd thir Penns, and soaring th' air sublime, With clang despis'd the ground MILT. Hence **Soa·rer. Soa·ring** *ppl. a.*, **-ly** *adv.*

Sob (sɒb), *sb.* late ME. [f. SOB *v.*[1]] **1.** An act of sobbing, a convulsive catching of the breath under the influence of grief. **b.** A similar act or sound expressive of pain or exertion 1480. †**c.** An act, on the part of a horse, of recovering its wind after exertion; an opportunity allowed to it of doing this; hence *fig.*, a rest or respite. Chiefly in the phr. *to give.. a s.* -1658. **2.** *transf.* A sound resembling that of a sob 1765.

1. The syghes, the sobbes, the diepe and deadly groane SACKVILLE. **b.** The tremulous s. of the complaining owl WORDSW. **c.** *Com. Err.* IV. iii. 25. **2.** With sea-sobs warning of the awakened wind 1897.

attrib.: **s.-stuff**, orig. *U.S. slang*, exaggerated pathos; sentimental talk or writing. So **s.-story.**

Sob (sɒb), *v.*[1] ME. [app. echoic.] **1.** *intr.* To catch the breath in a convulsive manner as the result of violent emotion, esp. grief; to weep in this fashion. **b.** To make a sound resembling sobbing 1676. **2.** *refl.* To bring (oneself) *into* a certain state (e.g. *to sleep*), with sobbing 1658. **3.** *trans.* **a.** To send *out*, bring *up*, etc., by sobbing or with sobs 1718. **b.** To utter with sobs. Usu. with *out*. 1782.

1. See how my wretched sister sobs and weeps SHAKS. **3. b.** Sobbing out their entreaties on their knees FROUDE. Hence **So·bbing** *vbl. sb.* the action of giving vent to sobs; the sound produced by this; freq. in *pl.* **So·bbingly** *adv.*

Sob, *v.*[2] Now *dial.* and *U.S.* 1625. [Origin unkn.] *trans.* To soak, saturate, sop. (Usu. in pa. pple.) So **So·bby** *a.* soaked 1611.

The high lands are sobbed and boggy 1859.

Sobeit (sōᵘˌbī·it), *conj.* 1583. [So *adv.* I. 3 d.] Provided *that*; if only.

Sober (sōᵘ·bəɹ), *a.* ME. [a. OF. (and mod. F.) *sobre*, ad. L. *sobrius* (opp. to *ebrius*).] **I. 1.** Moderate, temperate, avoiding excess, in matters of appetite, diet, conduct, etc. **2.** Not addicted to the use of strong drink; abstemious. late ME. **3.** Free from the influence of intoxicating liquor; not intoxicated; not drunk. late ME.

1. Of Arthure men say..he was..sobre & honest 1338. The Vintage of the Sabine Grape,..in s. Cups shall crown the Feast 1743. **2.** Men moste enquere.. Wher she be wys, or sobre, or dronkelewe CHAUCER. **3.** Very vildely..when hee is s., and most vildely.. when hee is drunke SHAKS.

II. 1. Of demeanour, speech, etc.: Grave, serious, solemn; indicating a serious mind or purpose. late ME. **2.** Quiet or sedate in demeanour; of grave, dignified, or discreet deportment; serious or staid. late ME. **3.** Of natural forces, etc.: Quiet, gentle, peaceful. late ME. **4.** Of living, etc.: Characterized by temperance, moderation, or seriousness 1552. **5.** Not readily excited or carried away; of a calm, dispassionate judgement 1564. **6.** Of colour, dress, etc.: Subdued in tone; not glaring, gay, or showy; neutral-tinted 1596. **b.** Unexciting; dull 1838. **7.** Free from extravagance or excess 1607. **b.** Moderate, sensible; not fanciful or imaginative 1619. **8.** Guided by sound reason; sane, rational 1638.

1. Phr. *In s. earnest* or †*sadness*. **2.** What damned error, but some s. brow Will blesse it? SHAKS. **4.** Men..Live to no s. purpose, and contend That their Creator had no serious end COWPER. **5.** Far from the madding crowd's ignoble strife, Their s. wishes never learn'd to stray GRAY. The s. and patient spirit of the English intellect 1862. **6.** Twilight gray Had in her s. Liverie all things clad MILT. **7.** With such s. and vnnoted passion He did behooue his anger ere 'twas spent SHAKS. **8.** Mad all his life, at least not s. BOSWELL. Hence **So·berize** *v.* = SOBER *v.* **So·ber-ly** *adv.*, **-ness.**

Sober (sōᵘ·bəɹ), *v.* late ME. [f. SOBER *a.*] *trans.* and *intr.* To make or become sober, in various senses. Also with *down*.

Shallow draughts intoxicate the brain, And drinking largely sobers us again POPE. When..solemn speeches s. down a dinner 1877.

Sober-minded, *a.* 1534. [SOBER *a.*] **1.** Of a sober mind; temperate; self-controlled; rational; sensible. Also *absol.* with *the*. **2.** Characterized by soberness of mind 1815. Hence **So:ber-mi·ndedness.**

Sobersides (sōᵘ·bəɹsəidz). 1705. [f. SOBER *a.*] A sedate, serious-minded person.

‖**Soboles** (sɒ·bolīz). Also as pl. 1722. [L., f. *sub* under + **olere* to grow.] *Bot.* †**1.** A shoot, a sprout. LISLE. **2.** A creeping underground stem 1832. So **Soboli·ferous** *a. Bot.* bearing shoots.

Sobriety (sŏbrəi·ĕti). late ME. [ad. F. *sobriété*, or L. *sobrietas*, f. *sobrius*.] **1.** The quality of being sober or moderate in the indulgence of appetite; *spec.* moderation in the use of strong drink. **2.** Moderation in any respect; avoidance of excess or extravagance 1582. **3.** Staidness, gravity, seriousness; soundness or saneness of judgement, etc. 1548.

1. Let the sad consequences of Noah his intemperance give caution for s. unto all ancient persons 1655. **2.** S. of dress must be enforced 1884. **3.** Delicacy of feeling and s. of judgement 1841.

‖**Sobriquet** (sōᵘ·brikĕ, ‖sobrīke). See also SOUBRIQUET. 1646. [F.] An epithet, a nickname.

Soc (sɒk). Now *Hist.* ME. [var. of SOKE.] **1.** A right of local jurisdiction (see SAC [1]). **2.** = SOKE 2 (*rare*) 1728.

Socage (sɒ·kėdʒ). Now *Hist.* ME. [a. AF., (Anglo-Lat. *socagium*) f. *soc* SOC + -AGE.] The tenure of land by certain determinate services other than knight-service. **b.** An estate held in socage (*rare*) 1464. **c.** A payment made to the superior by one holding land in socage 1859. **d.** *attrib.*, as *s. freehold*, tenure 1467.

Free or *common* (also *free and common*) *s.*, the ordinary form of this tenure. Hence **So·cager,** one holding land by s. tenure.

So-called, so called, *ppl. a.* 1657. **1.** In predic. use (prop. without hyphen): Called or designated by that name. **2.** In attrib. use (hyphened): Called or designated by this name or term, but not properly entitled to it or correctly described by it 1837.

Soccer (sɒ·kəɹ). Also **socker.** orig. *University slang*. 1891. [f. *Assoc.* (short for *Association*) + -ER [6].] Association football.

Sociability (sōᵘʃăbi·lĭti). 1475. [f. next + -ITY.] The character or quality of being sociable; friendly disposition or intercourse.

Sociable (sōᵘ·ʃăb'l), *a.* and *sb.* 1553. [a. F., or ad. L. *sociabilis*, f. *sociare* to unite, associate; see -ABLE.] **A.** *adj.* **1.** Naturally disposed to be in company with others of the same species. **2.** Inclined to seek and enjoy the company of others; disposed to be friendly or affable in company; willing to converse in a pleasant manner 1573. **3.** Characterized by, pertaining to, contact, intercourse, or companionship with others, esp. in a pleasant or friendly manner 1573. †**4.** Capable of being combined or joined together -1679.

1. Man is said to be a S. Animal ADDISON. **2.** We had a s. company in the cabin 1771. **3.** The harvesting of potatoes was a s. toil 1898. †*S. coach*; see B. 1 a. **4.** Another Law there is, which toucheth them as they are s. parts united into one body HOOKER.

B. *sb.* **1. a.** An open, four-wheeled carriage having two seats facing each other and a box-seat for the driver 1794. **b.** A tricycle or aeroplane having two seats side by side 1882. **2.** *U.S.* An informal evening party; *esp.* a social church meeting 1826. Hence **So·ciableness,** sociability. **So·ciably** *adv.*

Social (sōᵘ·ʃăl), *a.* and *sb.* 1562. [a. F., or ad. L. *socialis*, f. *socius*.] **A.** *adj.* †**1.** Capable of being associated or united *to* others (*rare*). †**2.** Associated, allied, combined -1686. **3.** Of war: Occurring between allies or confederates; *spec.* (with *the*), in Roman Hist., the war between Rome and the Italian allies, 90–89 B.C.; in Gr. Hist., the war between the Athenians and their confederates, 357–355 B.C. 1665. **4.** Marked or characterized by mutual intercourse, friendliness, or geniality; enjoyed, taken, spent, etc., in company with others, esp. with those of a similar class or kindred interests 1667. †**b.** Sympathetic -1745. **5.** †**a.** United by some common tie. POPE. **b.** Sociable 1729. **c.** Consisting or composed of persons associated together in, or for the purpose of, friendly intercourse 1849. **6.** Living, or disposed to live, in companies or communities desirous of enjoying the society or companionship of others 1722. **b.** *Zool.* Living together in more or less organized communities; belonging to a community of this kind 1831. **c.** *Bot.* Of plants: Growing in a wild state in patches or masses with other members of the same species, so as to cover a large area 1834. **d.** Of ascidians, etc.: Compound 1860. **7.** Pertaining, relating, or due to, connected with, etc., society as a natural or ordinary condition of human life 1729. **8.** Concerned with, interested in, the constitution of society and the problems presented by this 1841.

4. Thou..Best with thy self accompanied, seek'st not S. communication MILT. *S. evening*, an evening meeting of a society, etc. of the nature of an entertainment; an evening on which such a meeting is held. **5. a.** The s. shades the same dark journey go POPE. **b.** His own friendly and s. disposition JANE AUSTEN. **c.** The club is strictly a 's.' one 1892. **6.** Man not being..accidentally gregarious, but essentially s. 1853. **7.** Forgetfulness of s. duties JOHNSON. Enjoying..an equality of s. rank 1849. *S. contract*, the mutual agreement which, according to Rousseau's *Contrat social* (1762), forms the basis of human society. *S. evil*, prostitution. *S. service*, any activity designed to promote social welfare. 8. *S. Democrat*, a member of a political party having socialistic views.

B. *sb.* A social gathering or party, esp. one held by members of a club or association 1876. Hence **So·cialness** = SOCIALITY 1.

Socialism (sōᵘ·ʃăliz'm). 1839. [a. F. *socialisme* (1832), or f. SOCIAL *a.* + -ISM.] A theory or policy of social organization which advocates the ownership and control of the means of production, capital, land, property, etc. by the community as a whole, and their administration or distribution in the interests of all.

Christian s., a doctrine advocating a form of s. on a Christian basis. *State s.*: see STATE *sb.*

Socialist (sōᵘ·ʃălist). 1833. [Cf. prec.] One who advocates or believes in the theory of socialism; an adherent or supporter of this.

attrib. The worst of all S. plans..is that all have within them..a damning desire to shirk work 1848. Hence **Sociali·stic** *a.* of, pertaining to, characteristic of, or based on socialism; favouring socialism.

Sociality (sōᵘʃiæ·lĭti). 1649. [ad. F. *socialité* or L. *socialitas*; see SOCIAL *a.* and -ITY.] 1. The state or quality of being social. b. With *pl.* A social act or function 1825. 2. The action or fact on the part of individuals of forming a society or of associating together; the disposition to do this 1775. 3. Companionship or fellowship *in* or *with* a thing or person 1806.

Socialize (sōᵘ·ʃăləiz), *v.* 1828. [f. SOCIAL *a.* + -IZE.] 1. *trans.* To render social. 2. To render socialistic in nature; to establish or develop according to the theories or principles of socialism 1846. Hence **So:cializa·tion.**

Socially (sōᵘ·ʃăli), *adv.* 1642. [f. SOCIAL *a.*] †1. As a member of a body or society. (Opp. to *severally*.) *rare.* -1647. 2. In a social manner; sociably 1763. 3. In respect of or with regard to society 1871.

†**So·ciate**, *sb.* 1450. [ad. L. *sociatus*; see next.] An associate or colleague; a companion or comrade -1788.

So·ciate, *pa. pple.* and *ppl. a. arch.* 1501. [ad. L. *sociatus, sociare.*] 1. *pa. pple.* Associated *with* or *to* some thing or person; joined or united *together*. †2. *ppl. a.* Associated, joint. DE FOE.

†**So·ciate**, *v.* 1578. [f. L. *sociat-, sociare* to unite, combine, etc., f. *socius* companion.] 1. *trans.* To associate, join, or unite together; to form into a society or association -1654. 2. *intr.* To associate *with* others -1719.

Sociative (sōᵘ·ʃiĕtiv), *a.* 1871. [ad. F. *sociatif, -ive*; see SOCIATE *v.* and -IVE.] *Gram.* Denoting or expressing association.

Societarian (sŏsəi,ĕtēᵊ·riăn), *a.* and *sb.* 1822. [f. SOCIETY, after words in -ARIAN.] A. *adj.* Societary; socialistic.

The all-sweeping besom of s. reformation LAMB.

B. *sb.* 1. A socialist 1842. 2. One who moves in or is a member of fashionable society 1891.

Societary (sŏsəi·ĕtări), *a.* 1847. [f. SOCIETY + -ARY.] Of, pertaining to, concerned or dealing with, society or social conditions; social.

Society (sŏ̆səi·ĕti). 1531. [ad. OF. *societe* (mod.F. *société*), ad. L. *societas*, f. *socius* companion, ally.] I. 1. Association with one's fellow men, esp. in a friendly or intimate manner; companionship or fellowship. Also rarely of animals. †b. With *a* and *pl.* An instance of association or companionship with others (*rare*) -1780. c. *concr.* Persons with whom one has, or may have, companionship or intercourse. Also *transf.* of plants. 1605. 2. The state or condition of living in association, company, or intercourse with others of the same species; the system or mode of life adopted by a body of individuals for the purpose of harmonious coexistence or for mutual benefit, defence, etc. 1553. 3. The aggregate of persons living together in a more or less ordered community 1639. b. The aggregate of leisured, cultured, or fashionable persons regarded as forming a distinct class or body in a community; *esp.* those persons collectively who are recognized as taking part in fashionable life, social functions, entertainments, etc. Also with *a* and *the*. 1823. c. Personified 1784.

1. S., without which man's life is unpleasant 1531. b. *Merry W.* III. iv. 9. c. For all s. he had two friends RUSKIN. 2. In the earliest stages of s. there are many arts, but no sciences 1862. 3. S. has only one law, and that is custom 1873. b. Who *is* Mr. Gascoyne and who *is* Mr. Thistleton?..Are they in s.? 1893. c. S. shrugged its shoulders 1877.

†II. 1. Participation in some thing or action -1758. 2. The fact or condition of being connected or related -1771. 3. The state or condition of being politically confederated or allied; confederation -1665. 4. Partnership or combination in or with respect to business or some commercial transaction -1650. III. 1. A number of persons associated together by some common interest or purpose, united by a common vow, holding the same belief or opinion, following the same trade or profession, etc.; an association 1548. b. A corporate body of persons having a definite place of residence 1588. 2. A collection of individuals composing a community or living under the same organization or government 1577. b. Less widely: A company; a small party. Now *rare* or *Obs.* 1590. 3. A number of persons united for the promotion of a common purpose by means of meetings, publications, etc. 1665. b. *U.S.* = CONGREGATION *sb.* 6. 1828.

1. An old lady of the S. of Friends SCOTT. b. The S. of the Inner Temple CLARENDON. 2. b. Therefore be abhorr'd, All Feasts, Societies, and Throngs of men SHAKS. 3. He always runs to a disputing s. JOHNSON. The English Historical S. was just being formed 1844.

attrib. and *Comb.*, as *s. meeting*, etc.; *s. journal, man*, etc.; also, **s. hand**, a workman belonging to a trade s.; **s. house**, an establishment conforming to the rules of a trade s.

Socinian (sŏsi·niăn), *sb.* and *a.* 1645. [ad. mod.L. *Socinianus*, f. *Socinus*.] A. *sb.* One of a sect founded by Lælius and Faustus Socinus, two Italian theologians of the 16th c., who denied the divinity of Christ. B. *adj.* Pertaining to the Socinians or their creed 1694. Hence **Soci·nianism**, the doctrines or special views of the Socinians 1643. **Soci·nianize** *v.* to make or become S.

Socio- (sōᵘ·siŏ), comb. form (on Greek analogies) of L. *socius* fellow, in sense 'society'.

Sociologic (sōᵘsiŏlǫ·dʒik), *a.* 1861. [ad. F. *sociologique.*] Of or pertaining to sociology; concerned or connected with the organization, condition, or study of society. So **Sociolo·gical** *a.*, **-ly** *adv.* **Socio·logist**, a student of sociology.

Sociology (sōᵘsiǫ·lŏdʒi). 1843. [ad. F. *sociologie*; see SOCIO- and -LOGY.] The science or study of the origin, history, and constitution of human society; social science.

Sock (sǫk), *sb.*[1] [OE. *socc*, ad. L. *soccus* light low-heeled shoe or slipper.] 1. A covering for the foot, of the nature of a light shoe, slipper, or pump. Now *rare* or *Obs.* 2. A short stocking covering the foot and usually reaching to the calf of the leg; half-hose ME. 3. *spec.* A light shoe worn by comic actors on the ancient Greek and Roman stage; hence *allus.* comedy or the comic muse 1597. 4. *techn.* A loose inner sole for a shoe 1851.

2. Phr. *To pull up one's socks*: to brace oneself for an effort. 3. Great Fletcher never treads in buskins here, Nor greater Jonson dares in socks appear DRYDEN. *S. and buskin*, comedy and tragedy, the drama or theatrical profession as a whole. Hence **Sock** *v.*[2] *trans.* to provide with socks; to put socks on. **So·ckless** *a.* without socks; wearing no socks.

Sock, *sb.*[2] *north.* and *Sc.* late ME. [a OF. *soc*, prob. of Celtic origin.] A ploughshare.

Phr. *S. and scythe*, ploughing and mowing.

Sock, *sb.*[3] *Eton slang.* 1825. [Origin unkn.] Eatables, esp. dainties.

Sock, *sb.*[4] *slang.* 1700. [Cf. next.] A blow, beating; esp. *pl.* in *to give* (a person) *socks*.

Sock, *v.*[1] *slang.* 1700. [Origin unkn.] 1. *trans.* To beat, strike hard, hit. b. To drive or strike *into* something; to 'give it' *to* a person 1892. 2. *intr.* To strike out, deliver blows; to pitch *into* a person 1856.

1. We socks 'im with a stretcher-pole KIPLING.

Sockdolager (sǫkdǫ·lădʒəɹ). *U.S. slang.* 1836. [prob. fanciful.] 1. A heavy or knock-down blow; a finisher. 2. 'A patent fish-hook, having two hooks which close upon each other by means of a spring as soon as the fish bites' (Bartlett) 1848. 3. Something exceptional in any respect; esp. a large fish 1869.

Socker, var. SOCCER.

Socket (sǫ·kĕt), *sb.* ME. [a. AF. *soket*, dim. of *soc* SOCK *sb.*[2]] †1. A lance- or spear-head having a form resembling that of a ploughshare -1535. 2. A hollow part or piece, usually of a cylindrical form, constructed to receive some part or thing fitting into it 1448. 3. The part of a candlestick or chandelier in which the candle is placed 1440. 4. *Anat.* A cavity in which some part or articulation (as a tooth, eye, bone, etc.) is inserted 1601.

attrib. and *Comb.*, as *s.-bar, -bit, -chisel, -pole*, etc. Hence **So·cket** *v. trans.* to place in, or fit with, a s.; *Golf*, to strike (the ball) with the heel of the club. **So·cketed** *ppl. a.* **So·cketless** *a.*

Socle (sǫ·k'l, ‖ sokl'). 1704. [a. F., ad. It. *zoccolo*, repr. L. *socculus*, dim. of *soccus* SOCK *sb.*[1]] A low plain block or plinth serving as a pedestal to a statue, column, vase, etc.; also, a plain plinth forming a foundation for a wall.

Socman (sǫ·kmæn). 1579. [ad. Anglo-L. *socmannus*, var. of *sokemannus* SOKEMAN.] One who holds lands in socage. Hence **So·cmanry**, = SOKEMANRY.

Socotrine (sǫ·kŏ̆trin, sōᵘ·k-, -əin), *a.* late ME. [f. *Socotra* or *Socotora*, name of an island in the Indian Ocean.] 1. *S. aloes*, a drug prepared from the juice of the *Aloe socotrina* (or *perryi*), and orig. obtained from the island of Socotra. 2. *S. aloe*, the plant yielding the drug 1778.

Socratic (sŏ̆kræ·tik), *a.* and *sb.* 1637. [ad. L. *Socraticus*, ad. Gr. Σωκρατικός, f. Σωκράτης.] A. *adj.* Of or pertaining to, characteristic of, Socrates the Athenian philosopher, or his philosophy, methods, character, etc.

By questions aptly proposed in the S. method 1741.

B. *sb.* A follower of Socrates 1678.

Plato and Aristotle, the two Socratics 1886. So **Socra·tical** *a.* 1581, **-ly** *adv.* **Socra·ticism**, **So·cratism**, the philosophy of Socrates or some aspect of this. **Socratize** (sǫ·krătəiz) *v. intr.* to philosophize or live after the manner of Socrates.

Sod (sǫd), *sb.*[1] late ME. [app. ad. MDu. *sode*, or MLG. *sode* (*sade*).] 1. A piece or slice of earth together with the grass growing on it, cut out or pared off from the surface of grass land; a turf. Also const. *of* (grass, turf, etc.). 2. A pair of these used as a saddle. *Sc.* and *north.* 1586. 3. The surface of the ground, esp. when turfy; the sward. Freq. *poet.* or *rhet.* 1729.

1. For a monument they only raysed a turffe or greene Sodd of the earth 1618. 3. Tender bluebells, at whose birth The s. scarce heaved SHELLEY.

Comb.: **s.-worm**, the larva of certain moths, as *Crambus exsiccatus*, which destroys the roots of grass and corn. Hence **Sod** *v. trans.* to cover or build up, to provide or lay, with sods or turfs; to turf.

Sod, *sb.*[2] *vulgar.* 1880. Abbrev. of SODOMITE, used as a term of abuse or joc.

Sod (sǫd), *pa. pple.* and *ppl. a.* ME. [Pa. pple. of SEETHE *v.*] †1. Of food, liquor, etc.: Boiled -1658. †b. *Twice s.* [after L. *crambe repetita*], stale, unpalatable -1641. 2. *S. oil*, a greasy matter extracted in the treatment of sheepskins 1883.

Soda (sōᵘ·dă). 1558. [a. med.L., of unkn. origin.] 1. An alkaline substance, now manufactured artificially from common salt, or occurring in a mineral state as a deposit, esp. in certain lakes, or in solution in the water of such lakes (natron); soda-ash; sodium carbonate (Na_2CO_3). b. Sodium bicarbonate, used largely for domestic purposes; baking or cooking soda 1851. 2. *Chem.* Sodium oxide (Na_2O) 1826. 3. Soda-water 1842.

1. *Caustic s.*, sodium hydroxide or hydrate (NaOH).

attrib. and *Comb.*: in *Photogr.* for hyposulphite of soda, as *s. developer, -pyro, -solution*, etc.; **s.-ash**, the sodium carbonate of commerce; = SODA 1; **-lye**, a solution of hydrate of s., employed in the manufacture of hard soap; **s. waste**, the insoluble oxisulphide of calcium, left as a useless residue, when the soda salts have been dissolved out by water. b. Connected or dealing with sodium carbonate or its manufacture, as *s.-apparatus, -furnace, -manfacture*, etc. c. Used for, or containing, soda-water, as *s.-bottle, -fountain* (orig. U.S.), *-tumbler*, etc. d. Made with or containing sodium bicarbonate, as *s.-biscuit, -cake*. Hence **Sodaic** (sodē·ik) *a.* containing s. or sodium bicarbonate.

Sodalite (sōᵘ·dăləit). 1810. [f. SODA + -LITE.] *Min.* A vitreous, transparent or translucent silicate of aluminium and sodium containing sodium chloride, usually of a greenish blue colour and occurring in certain igneous rocks.

Sodality (sodæ·liti). 1600. [a. F. *sodalité* or ad. L. *sodalitas*, f. *sodalis* mate, companion.] **1.** Association or confederation *with* others; brotherhood, companionship, fellowship. **2.** *R. C. Ch.* A religious guild or brotherhood established for purposes of devotion or mutual help or action; the body of persons forming such a society 1600. **b.** A chapel used by a religious sodality 1667. **3.** A society, association, or fraternity of any kind 1633.

Sodamide (sōu·dăməid). 1838. [f. SODA + AMIDE.] *Chem.* A white solid formed by treating sodium with gaseous ammonia.

Soda(-)water. 1802. [f. SODA + WATER *sb.*] **1.** Water containing a solution of sodium bicarbonate, or, more generally, charged under pressure with carbon dioxide (carbonic acid gas), strongly effervescent, and used as a beverage or stimulant. **2.** Water containing a solution of sodium carbonate for cooling or wetting metal-working tools 1891.

Sodden (sǫ·d'n), *pa. pple.* and *ppl. a.* ME. [Strong pa. pple. of SEETHE *v.*] **1.** Boiled. Now *rare* or *Obs.* **2.** Of persons, their features, etc.: Having the appearance of that which has been steeped or soaked in water; rendered dull, stupid, or expressionless, esp. owing to indulgence in intoxicants; pale and flaccid 1599. **b.** Characterized by heaviness, dullness, or want of vivacity 1851. **3.** Of food: Heavy, doughy; spoiled through over-boiling or imperfect baking 1800. **4.** Saturated or soaked with water or moisture 1820.

2. His complexion was pale and s. 1841. 4. Don't work the ground when it is s., muddy, or rendered sticky by a recent frost 1856.

Sodden (sǫ·d'n), *v.* 1812. [f. prec.] **1.** *trans.* To make sodden; to soak in, or saturate with, water. **b.** To render (the faculties) dull or stupid 1863. **2.** *intr.* To become soaked or saturated with water or moisture; to grow soft or rotten in this way 1820.

Soddy (sǫ·di), *a.* and *sb.* 1611. [f. SOD *sb.* + -Y [1].] **A.** *adj.* Abounding in sods; consisting or composed of sods; of the nature of a sod. **B.** *sb.* A house made of sods. *U.S.* 1893.

Sodio- (sōu·dio), comb. form of SODIUM, denoting the presence of that substance or its salts, as *s.-aluminic* adj.; *s.-salicylate.*

Sodium (sōu·diŏm). 1807. [f. SODA + -IUM.] *Chem.* An elementary alkaline metal (isolated by Davy in 1807), forming the basis of SODA, closely resembling potassium in its appearance and properties, and occurring most commonly in the chloride (common salt). Symbol Na (for Natrium).

attrib. **a.** In the names of chemical compounds or groupings, as *s.-alcohol, -amyl, bicarbonate, bromide, carbonate* 1857. **b.** Misc., as *s.-compound, -flame, -light*; **s.-amalgam**, a compound of mercury and sodium; **s. soap**, soda soap. Hence **So·dic** *a.* of, containing, or composed of s.

Sodom (sǫ·dəm). 1605. [The name of the early city beside the Dead Sea, the destruction of which is recorded in Gen. xviii–xix.] An extremely wicked or corrupt place.

S. apple, Apple of Sodom (see APPLE *sb.* 3.) 1615.

Sodomite (sǫ·dəməit). ME. [a. OF., or ad. L. *Sodomita* (Gr. Σοδομίτης), f. SODOM; see -ITE [1] 1 a.] †**1.** Sodomy. ME. only. **2.** One who practises or commits sodomy. late ME. **3.** An inhabitant of Sodom 1474.

Sodomitical (sǫdəmi·tikăl), *a.* 1546. [f. L. *Sodomiticus*, + -AL 1.] **1.** Of persons: Guilty of, committing, or practising sodomy. †**b.** With whom sodomy is committed –1634. **2.** Of the nature of, characterized by, consisting in, or involving sodomy 1550. †**3.** Of places, etc.: Polluted or infected by sodomy –1632. So **Sodomi·tic** *a.* (*rare*) 1630. **Sodomi·tical-ly** *adv.*, **-ness.**

Sodomy (sǫ·dəmi). ME. [a. OF. (also mod.F.) *sodomie*; see SODOM and -Y [3].] An unnatural form of sexual intercourse, esp. that of one male with another.

Soe (sōu). Now *dial.* late ME. [a. ON. *sár.*] A large tub.

Soever (so₁e·vəɹ), *adv.* Also *poet.* **soe'er** (so₁ē·ɹ). 1557. [See SO *adv.* and EVER *adv.*] Used with generalizing or emphatic force after words or phrases preceded by *how, what, which, whose*, etc.

Whose tongue so ere speakes false SHAKS. To all who are perplexed in any way s. 1835.

Sofa (sōu·fă). 1625. [= F., ad. Arab. *ṣoffah.*] **1.** In Eastern countries, a part of the floor raised a foot or two, covered with rich carpets and cushions, and used for sitting upon. **2.** A long, stuffed seat with a back and ends or one end, on which to recline or sit; a form of lounge or couch 1717.

2. Convenience next suggested elbow-chairs, And luxury th' accomplish'd S. last COWPER.

Comb.: **s.-bed, -bedstead**, a piece of furniture so constructed as to form a s. or bedstead as required.

Soffit (sǫ·fit). 1613. [after F. *soffite*, a. It. *soffitta*, f. *sof-* (L. *sub*) under + pa. pple. of *figgere* to fix.] *Arch.* The under horizontal face of an architrave or overhanging cornice; the under surface of a lintel, vault, or arch; a ceiling.

†**So-forth.** 1611. [See FORTH *adv.*] Such and such a thing.

They 're here with me already; whisp'ring, rounding: Silicia is a s. SHAKS.

Soft (sǫft), *sb.* ME. [f. the adj.] †**1.** That which is agreeable, pleasant, or easy; comfort, ease (*rare*) –1677. **2.** That which is soft or yielding; the soft part *of* something; softness 1593. **b.** *pl.* Soft coal; also, soft woollen rags 1883. **3.** *Phonetics.* A 'soft' consonant (see next, 3 b) 1846. **4.** *U.S.* **a.** A member of a local party which advocated a 'soft money' or paper currency. **b.** A member of one or other party holding moderate views. Cf. SOFT-SHELL. 1847. **5.** A soft, simple, or foolish person; a 'softy'. Chiefly *dial.* or *colloq.* 1854.

Soft (sǫft), *a.* [Late OE. *sǫ́ft(e*, var. of the older *sēfte.*] **I. 1.** Producing agreeable or pleasant sensations; characterized by ease and quiet enjoyment; of a calm or placid nature. †**b.** Pleasing *in* taste; free from acidity or sharpness. Also of odour: Not pungent, strong, or heavy. –1826. **c.** Pleasing to the eye; free from ruggedness or asperity. Also of colour, or with reference to this: Not crude or glaring; quiet, subdued 1702. **2.** Involving little or no discomfort, hardship, or suffering; easily endured or borne ME. **b.** Involving little or no exertion or effort. Now chiefly *colloq.*, easy, lazy, idle. 1639. **3.** Of a sound, the voice, etc.: Low, quiet, subdued. Also, melodious, pleasing to the ear, sweet. ME. **b.** *spec.* in *Phonetics*, voiced (opp. to HARD *a.* III. 4). Now disused. 1636. **c.** Of musical instruments: Making or emitting a soft sound 1561. **4.** Of weather, seasons, etc.: Free from storms or rough winds; genial, mild, balmy ME. **b.** Of the sun, rain, wind, etc.: Shining, falling, or blowing gently; not strong, violent, or boisterous. late ME. **c.** Of the sea, streams, etc.: Smooth, calm; running calmly or gently 1450. **5.** Of pace, progression, or movement: Leisurely, easy; slow; not hasty or hurried. Now *arch.* ME. †**6.** Of a fire: Burning slowly or gently; moderate in heat or intensity; slow –1738. †**7.** Of a slope, ascent, etc.: Gentle, gradual –1819.

1. Where young Adonis oft reposes, ..In slumber s. MILT. Many a joy could he from Night's s. presence glean BYRON. c. S. scenes of solitude no more can please POPE. 2. After ten years s. durance in all plenty, ..He dyed 1661. b. A s. and easy life these ladies lead! BROWNING. The..idea that romance is 'a s. job' 1894. You wanted a s. time of it 1905. 3. Her voice was euer s., Gentle, and low, an excellent thing in woman SHAKS. The s. rustle of a maiden's gown KEATS. c. Anon they move..to the Dorian mood Of Flutes and s. Recorders MILT. 4. In a s. Air and a delicious Situation ADDISON. b. In a somer sesun whon softe was þe sonne LANGL. c. In thee fresh brooks, and s. streams glance MILT. 5. A s. pace goes far 1663. 7. S. declivities with tufted hills COWPER.

II. 1. Of persons: Gentle or mild in nature or character; inclined to be merciful, lenient, or considerate in dealing with others; compassionate, kind, tender-hearted ME. **b.** Of animals: Gentle, docile; lacking in spirit ME. **c.** Not rigid or severe; lax, yielding 1715. **2.** Of disposition, look, qualities, feelings, etc.: Gentle, mild ME. **3.** Of words, language, etc.: **a.** Ingratiating, soothing, bland; tender, sentimental. late ME. **b.** Free from roughness or harshness; tending to tone down or minimize something unpleasant. late ME. **c.** Expressive of what is tender or peaceful 1704. **4.** Of actions, means, etc.: Gentle or moderate in character; carried on, performed, etc., without harshness, severity, or violence 1495. **5.** Of the hand, etc.: Touching lightly or gently 1650. **6.** Of drink: Non-alcoholic. orig. *dial.* and *U.S.* 1880.

1. At the first impulse of passion be silent, till you can be s. CHESTERF. He..was very s. and gentle with the children THACKERAY. 2. Sadde of his semblaunt and of s. chiere LANGL. S. pity enters at an iron gate SHAKS. 3. a. The lippes of an harlot are a droppinge hony combe, and hir throte is softer then oyle COVERDALE *Prov.* v. 3. b. You have s. words for hard meanings RICHARDSON. 4. They are disposed to try s. means at first 1888. 5. Through the temple..He went with s. light feet SHELLEY.

III. 1. Yielding readily to emotions of a tender nature; impressionable. Also *absol.* of persons. ME. **2.** Easily influenced or swayed; facile, compliant. Also *absol.* of persons. ME. **b.** Weak, effeminate, unmanly 1593. **c.** Refined, delicate (*rare*) 1601. **3.** Of a weakly or delicate constitution; incapable of much physical endurance or exertion 1661. **4.** *The soft(er sex*, the female sex 1648. **5.** More or less foolish, silly, or simple; lacking ordinary intelligence or common-sense; easily imposed upon or deceived. Also *dial.* or *colloq.*, mentally deficient, half-witted. 1621. **b.** *colloq.* Foolishly kind, benevolent, etc. 1890.

1. Loues feeling is more s. and sensible, Then are the tender hornes of..Snayles SHAKS. Phr. *To be s. on* or *upon* (a person), to be in love with; to regard amorously or sentimentally. 2. A heart too s. from early life To hold with fortune needful strife SCOTT. c. An absolute gentleman,..of very s. society, and great showing SHAKS. 5. Your greatest Students are commonly..silly, s. fellows 1621.

IV. 1. Presenting a yielding surface to the touch; not offering absolute resistance to pressure ME. **2.** Of cloth, hair, etc.: Of a yielding texture, pleasant to the feel or touch; also, capable of being easily folded, or put into a different form; flexible ME. **b.** *U.S.* Of paper money. (Cf. HARD *a.* I. 2.) 1831. **3.** Of a bed, pillow, etc.: Readily yielding to the weight of the body; into or upon which one sinks or settles down comfortably ME. **4.** Of ground: **a.** Insufficiently hard; allowing a vehicle, etc., to sink in, esp. through excess of wet 1523. **b.** Of a fall: Made on a soft substance, or in such a way as to escape injury 1587. **5.** Of a yielding consistency. late ME. **b.** Of a semi-fluid consistency 1703. **6.** Relatively inferior or deficient in hardness 1599. **7.** Applied to water, such as rain or river water, which is more or less free from calcium and magnesium salts 1755. **8.** Rainy, wet. Chiefly *Sc.* and *n. dial.* 1812.

1. Softer to the touch, than down of Swans DRYDEN. 2. Satin smooth, Or velvet s. COWPER. *S. wares*, or *goods*, woollen or cotton fabrics, such as cretonne, chintz, lace, muslin, velvet, etc., or articles made of these. 3. A good s. Pillow for that good white Head SHAKS. *transf.* Good cheer and s. lodging SCOTT. 4. a. The match was played on a s. wicket (*mod.*). 5. c. Of rays: Of a low penetrating power 1902. 6. A head and face rudely carved in a s. stone 1847. *S. coal*, bituminous coal.

attrib. and *Comb.*: *s.-billed, -finned* adjs.; **s.-eyed** *a.*, having s. or gentle eyes; **-footed** *a.*, having feet which tread softly; **s. grass**, velvet-grass; **s. pedal**: see PEDAL *sb.* 1 b (*b*); hence as *vb. intr.* to play with the soft pedal down; *trans.* to 'tone down'; **-spoken** *a.*, having, speaking with, a s. or gentle voice; plausible, affable; **-wood**, wood which is relatively s. or easily cut; sap-wood, alburnum. **b.** In names of animals: **s. crab**, a soft-shelled crab; **s. tortoise**, any tortoise of the genus *Trionyx*. Hence **So·ftish** *a.* somewhat s.; rather tender.

Soft (sǫft), *adv.* [OE. *sǫ́fte*, orig. adv. of *sēfte* soft.] **1.** Softly; gently; without harshness or roughness; quietly; not hastily or hurriedly. †**2.** *S. and fair(ly)*, softly, gently, leisurely –1736. **3.** Used as an exclam. with imperative force, either to enjoin silence or deprecate haste. Now *arch.* 1550.

1. I will..sleepe as s. As Captaine shall SHAKS. How s. the poplars sigh 1896. 2. S. and Fair goes far 1700. 3. Not too fast: s., s. SHAKS. S.—who is that stands by the dying fire? M. ARNOLD.

†**Soft,** *v.* ME. [f. the adj.] **1.** *trans.* To render soft, in various senses –1594. **2.** *intr.* To become or grow soft. ME. only.

1. Yet cannot all these flames..her hart more harde then yron s. awhit SPENSER.

‖ **Softa** (sǫ·ftă). Also **sophta.** 1613. [Turk. *sōfta*, ad. Pers. *sūhtah* lighted, set on fire.] In Turkey, a Moslem theological student; also *gen.*, a pupil engaged in professional studies at a secondary school.

Soften (sǫ·f'n), *v.* late ME. [f. Soft *a.* + -en 5. Cf. Soft *v.*] **I.** *trans.* **1.** To mitigate, assuage, or diminish; to render less painful or more easy to bear. **2. a.** To render more impressionable or tender. late ME. **b.** To enervate, weaken, render effeminate 1581. **c.** To make more gentle, delicate, or refined. Also with *into.* 1709. **3.** To mollify or appease; to render less harsh or severe 1450. **4.** To make physically soft or softer; to lessen the hardness of (a substance) 1530. **5.** To modify or tone down; to render less pronounced or prominent 1670. **6.** To make softer in sound 1736.

1. That blisful sight softneth al my sorwe Chaucer. 2. Misfortune, adversity, s. the human heart 1874. b. Troops softened by luxury 1828. c. Though some divine thought softened all her face Morris. 3. To s. the anger of an offended deity 1835. 4. With Fire he..softens iron 1796. 5. Others proposed to send a deputation to s. the harshness of his removal 1879. 6. He spoke to her in accents somewhat softened from their usual harshness 1794.

II. *intr.* **1.** To become soft or softer in various non-physical senses; *esp.* to become more gentle, tender, or emotional; to grow fainter or less pronounced 1611. **2.** To become physically soft 1626. Hence **So·ftener,** one who or that which softens; a mollifier; *spec.* a painting-brush of soft hair.

So·ftening, *vbl. sb.* 1568. [f. prec.] **1.** The action of making soft. Also with *a* and *pl.* **b.** *Path.*, esp. in *s. of the brain* (encephalomalacia) 1830. **2.** *spec.* In Painting, the mixing and diluting of colours with the brush or pencil 1728.

1. b. *S. of the brain*, pop. name for progressive dementia with general paresis; When s. of the brain is accompanied by an increase of bulk 1835.

So·ft-head. 1650. [f. Soft *a.* + Head *sb.*] One who has a soft head; hence, a simpleton. So **Soft-headed** *a.*

Soft-hearted, *a.* 1593. [Soft *a.*] Having a soft or susceptible heart; tender-hearted. Hence **Soft-heartedness** 1580.

Softling (sǫ·ftliŋ). 1547. [f. Soft *a.* + -ling 1 2.] **1.** An effeminate or unmanly person; a weakling. **2.** A small soft object 1817. **3.** *attrib.* Of a soft nature 1732.

2. Each s. of a wee white mouse Browning.

Softly (sǫ·ftli), *adv.* ME. [f. Soft *a.* + -ly 2.] **1.** In a soft manner, in various senses. **2.** Used imperatively: = Soft *adv.* 3. 1596.

Phr. *Fair and s.*: see Soft *adv.* 2. So **So·ftness.** late OE.

Soft-sawder (sǫft,sǭ·dəɹ), *v. colloq.* 1843. [f. *soft sawder*; see Sawder *sb.*] *trans.* and *absol.* To flatter; = Sawder *v.*

Soft-shell. 1853. [f. Soft *a.*] **1.** *attrib.* In the specific names of animals: Having a soft shell 1860. **2.** *attrib.* That adopts or advocates a moderate or temperate course or policy. *U.S.* 1859. **3.** *U.S. ellipt.* **a.** = Soft *sb.* 4 b. 1853. **b.** A soft-shelled lobster 1884. So **Soft-shelled** *a.* (freq. of a shell-less egg) 1611.

Soft(-)soap, *sb.* 1634. [f. Soft *a.*] **1.** A smeary, semi-liquid soap, made with potash lye; potash soap. **b.** With pl. A make or kind of this 1783. **2.** *slang.* Flattery; blarney; 'soft sawder' 1848. Hence **Soft(-)soap** *v. trans.* to flatter, 'soft-sawder' (*slang*).

Softy (sǫ·fti). *dial.* or *colloq.* 1863. [f. Soft *a.* + -y 6.] A weak-minded or silly person; a simpleton, noodle.

Soggy (sǫ·gi), *a.* Chiefly *dial.* and *U.S.* 1722. [f. dial. *sog* a swamp, etc.] **1.** Of land: Soaked with moisture; boggy, swampy, marshy. **2.** Of things: Saturated with wet; soppy, soaked 1863. **3.** Of bread: Sodden, heavy 1868. **4.** Of persons: Dull, spiritless 1896. **5.** Moist, close, sultry 1896.

5. We rattled along through the bush,..all the time in deep, s. heat 1896. Hence **So·gginess.**

Soh = Sol 2, in tonic-sol-fa notation.

Soh (sōu), *int. Obs.* or *arch.* 1814. [Of exclamatory origin.] **1.** An exclam. denoting anger, scorn, reproof, surprise, etc., on the part of the speaker. **2.** Used in soothing a restive horse, = Gently! Softly! Easy! 1820.

Soho (sǫuhōu·), *int.* and *sb.* ME. [An AF. hunting call, prob. of exclamatory origin.] **1.** A call used by huntsmen to direct attention to a hare which has been discovered or started, or to encourage the dogs; hence used as a call to draw the attention of any person, announce a discovery, or the like. **b.** As *sb.* 1572. **2.** = prec. 1825.

1. b. Such sohoes, whoopes and hallowes 1589. Hence **Soho·** *v. intr.* to shout s.; *trans.* to announce the starting of (a hare) by this shout.

‖ **Soi-disant** (swadizaṅ), *a.* 1752. [F., f. *soi* oneself + *disant*, pr. pple. of *dire* to say.] **1.** Of persons: Calling oneself; self-styled, would-be. (Usually with implication of pretence or deception.) **2.** Of things: Said to be such, without really being so; pretended 1845.

2. The modern s. science of political economy Ruskin.

Soil (soil), *sb.*1 late ME. [a. AF., app. repr. L. *solium*, taken in the sense of *solum* (F. *sol*) ground.] **I. 1.** The earth or ground; the face or surface of the earth. **2.** A piece or stretch of ground; a place or site. Now *rare* or *Obs.* late ME. **3.** A land or country; a region, province, or district. Now *Obs.* or *arch.* late ME. **4. a.** The place of one's nativity; one's (native) land or country. late ME. †**b.** One's domicile or place of residence –1643.

1. The precise spot where his foot first touched the s. 1838. 3. Is this the Region, this the S., the Clime, ..That we must change for Heav'n? Milt. 4. a. You..To shun my sight, your Native S. forego Dryden. b. Phr. *To change one's s.*

Phrases. *Lord of the s.*, the owner of an estate or domain. *Child* (*son*, etc.) *of the s.*, a native of a place or country; also, one closely connected with the cultivation of the ground.

II. 1. The ground with respect to its composition, quality, etc., or as the source of vegetation. late ME. **2.** Without article: Mould; earth 1440. **3.** With *a* and *pl.* A particular kind of mould or earth 1560.

1. Most subiect is the fattest Soyle to Weedes Shaks. 3. *fig* No. s. like poverty for growth divine Cowper.

Comb.: **s.-bound** *a.*, (*a*) 'clagged', clodded; (*b*) bound or attached to the s.; **-cap** *Geol.*, a layer of s. and detritus covering strata or bedrock. Hence **Soi·lless** *a.* destitute of, devoid of, s. or mould.

Soil (soil), *sb.*2 late ME. [Partly a. OF. *soille, f. OF *soiller*, F. *souiller*; partly f. Soil *v.*1] **I.** †**1.** A miry or muddy place used by a wild boar for wallowing in –1611. **2.** A pool or stretch of water, used as a refuge by a hunted deer or other animal. Freq. in the phr. *to take s.* late ME.

2. He..Then takes the S., and plunges in the Flood Precipitant 1735. *fig.* The King..singles out the Archbishop, and hunts him to s. at Rome 1647.

II. 1. Staining or soiling; the fact of being stained or soiled; a stain or discolouring mark 1501. **2.** *fig.* Moral stain or tarnish 1597.

2. For all the soyle of the Atchieuement goes With me, into the Earth Shaks.

III. 1. Filth; dirty or refuse matter 1608. **2.** Filth usually carried off by drains; sewage 1601. **3.** Ordure, excrement; the dung of animals used as a compost; manure. Cf. also Night-soil. 1607.

Comb.: **s.-pipe**, a sewage or waste-water pipe.

Soil (soil), *v.*1 ME. [ad. OF. *soill(i)er*, (mod.F. *souiller*), app.:—pop. L. *suculare, f. L. *suculus*, dim. of *sus* pig.] **I.** *trans.* **1.** To defile or pollute with sin or other moral stain. Also *absol.* **2.** To make foul or dirty, esp. on the surface; to begrime, stain, tarnish ME. **3.** *fig.* To sully or tarnish; to bring disgrace or discredit upon (a person or thing) 1593. **4.** *intr.* To become dirty or stained; to take on a stain or tarnish 1530.

1. My soule was soyld with foule iniquitie Spenser. 2. Much handling soileth things 1638. Phr. *To s. one's hands* (fig.). 3. Black falsehood has ineffaceably soiled her name Carlyle. 4. Silver soils sooner than gold 1882.

II. 1. *intr.* and †*refl.* Of a wild boar or deer: To roll or wallow in mud or water. late ME. **2.** Of a hunted stag: To take to water or marshy ground; †to swim *down.* late ME. Hence **Soiled** (soild) *ppl. a.* ME.

†**Soil,** *v.*2 ME. [ad. OF. *soille*, pres. subj., or *soil*, pres. ind. of *soldre*, *soudre*:—L. *solvere* to release, loosen; see Assoil *v.*] **1.** *trans.* = Assoil *v.* 1. –1530. **2.** To set free *of*, release from, an obligation, etc. late ME. only. **3.** To resolve, clear up, expound, or explain; to answer (a question) –1611. **4.** To refute (an argument or objection); to overcome by argument –1567.

†**Soil,** *v.*3 1593. [f. Soil *sb.*2] *trans.* To supply or treat (land) with dung, etc.; to manure –1692.

Just as they Soyl their Ground, not that they love the Dirt, but that they expect a Crop 1692.

Soil (soil), *v.*4 1605. [perh. f. Soil *sb.*2] *trans.* To feed (horses, cattle, etc.) on fresh-cut green fodder, orig. for the purpose of purging; †to feed up or fatten (fowls).

Soilure (soi·liŭɹ). ME. [a. OF. *soilleure* (mod.F. *souillure*), f. *soillier* Soil *v.*1] **1.** Soiling, sullying, staining. **2.** A stain, blot, or blemish 1829.

1. *fig.* He merits well to haue her, that doth seeke her, Not making any scruple of her soylure, With such a hell of paine Shaks.

Soily (soi·li), *a.* Now *rare.* 1575. [f. Soil *sb.*2 or *v.*1] †**1.** Apt to soil or stain –1605. **2.** Soiled, stained, dirty 1631. Hence **Soi·liness.**

‖ **Soirée** (swa·re). 1820. [F., f. *soir* evening :—L. *serum* late hour, neut. of *serus* late. Cf. Swarry.] An evening party, gathering, or social meeting.

‖ **Soixante-quinze** (swasaṅt kæ̃nz). [F. = 75.] = *seventy-five* (see Seventy A. 2).

Sojourn (sǫ·dʒɒɹn, -əɹn, sɒ·-), *sb.* ME. [a. OF. *sojorn*, vbl. sb. from *sojorner*: see Sojourn *v.*] **1.** A temporary stay at a place. **2.** A place of temporary stay ME.

2. Thee I re-visit now.., Escap't the Stygian Pool, though long detain'd In that obscure s. Milt.

Sojourn (sǫ·dʒɒɹn, -əɹn, sɒ·-), *v.* ME. [a. OF. *sojorner* (also mod.F. *séjourner*), f. pop. L. *subdiurnare, f. *diurnum* daily, day.] **1.** *intr.* To make a temporary stay in a place; to remain or reside for a time. †**2.** To make stay; to tarry, delay –1594. †**3.** *trans.* To lodge; to rest or quarter (horses); to have as a lodger –1690.

1. They soiourned there a vij nyghte Malory. *fig.* Mirth is farre away, Nor may it soiourne with sad discontent Drayton. 3. [They] are sojourned there by one Thomson 1690. Hence **So·journment.**

Sojourner (sǫ·-, sɒ·dʒəɹnəɹ). late ME. [f. prec. + -er 1.] **1.** One who sojourns; a temporary resident. †**2.** A guest or lodger; a visitor –1660. †**b.** A boarder living in a house, school, or college, for the purpose of receiving instruction –1785.

2. b. [Grocyn] became a Sojournor in Exeter Coll. 1691.

Soke (sōuk). Now chiefly *Hist.* ME. [ad. med.L. *soca*, ad. OE. *sócn* Soken.] **1.** A right of local jurisdiction; = Soken 3. 1598. **2.** A district under a particular jurisdiction; a local division of a minor character ME. **3.** = Soken 2 b. 1609. **4.** *attrib.*, as *s.-mill* ME.

Sokeman (sōu·kmæ̆n). *Hist.* 1603. [a. AF., or ad. Anglo-L. *sokemannus*, f. OE. *sócn*.] A tenant holding land in socage; a socman. So **So·kemanry**, the tenure of land by a s.; also, the sokemen collectively.

Soken (sōu·k'n). Now *Hist.* [OE. *sócn*, f. *sōk-* stem of *sécan* to Seek.] †**1.** An attack or assault. OE. only. †**2.** Resort to, or visiting of, a place; habitual going or haunting –1440. †**b.** *spec.* Resort of tenants or others to a particular mill to have their corn ground; the right of the mill to such custom –1591. †**3.** Right of prosecution, legal investigation, or jurisdiction. OE. only **4.** = Soke 2. OE.

2. b. Gret s. hath this meller.., With whete and malt, of al the lond aboute Chaucer.

‖ **Soko** (sōu·kōu). 1870. [Native Afr. name.] A species of anthropoid ape discovered by Livingstone near Lake Tanganyika.

Sol 1 (sǫl). late ME. [L., = Gr. ἥλιος.] **1.** The sun (personified) 1450. †**2. a.** *Alch.* Gold –1758. **b.** *Her.* = Or *sb.* –1709.

Sol 2 (sǫl, sōul). ME. [First syllable of L. *solve*; see Ut.] *Mus.* The fifth note of Guido's hexachords, and of the octave in modern solmization; the note G in the natural scale of C major.

‖ **Sol** 3 (sǫl). Now *Hist.* 1583. [OF. *sol* (now *sou* Sou) :—L. *solidum*, acc. of *solidus* (sc. *nummus*) a gold coin.] A former coin and money of account in France, etc., equal to the twentieth part of a livre, but of varying actual value.

||**Sol**⁴ (sǭul). *Pl.* **soles.** 1884. [Sp. *sol* sun; see SOL *sb.*[1]] A Spanish American (now Peruvian) silver coin worth about two shillings.

Sol⁵ (sǫl). 1899. [Short for *solution*; cf. GEL.] *Phys. Chem.* A liquid solution or suspension of a colloid.

|| **Sola** (sǭu·lă). Also **solah.** 1845. [Urdū and Bengālī *solā* = Hindī *sholā*; see SHOLA.] A tall leguminous swamp-plant (*Æschynomena aspera* or *paludosa*) of India; the pith of this used in making light hats. Also *attrib.*

||**Sola** (sǭu·lă), *a.* 1660. [L., fem. of *solus* SOLUS, and It. *sola*, fem. of *solo* SOLO.] **1.** Of females: Sole, solitary, alone. **2.** *Comm.* A single bill, as dist. from one of a 'set' 1866.

†**Sola,** *int.* [Cf. SOHO *int.* and *hola* HOLLA.] A call or cry to attract attention. SHAKS.

Solace (sǫ·lĕs), *sb.* [ME. *solas*, a. OF. *solas* :—L. *solatium*, f. the stem of *solari* to comfort, console.] **1.** Comfort, consolation; alleviation of sorrow, distress, or discomfort. †**2.** Pleasure, enjoyment, delight; entertainment, recreation, amusement –1667. **3.** That which gives comfort, †brings pleasure or enjoyment, etc. ME. **4.** *Printing.* A penalty imposed by the chapel for any breach of its rules 1683.

1. Sorrow would [have] sollace, and mine Age would ease SHAKS. 2. Great joy he promis'd to his thoughts, and new S. in her return MILT. 3. To have thee by my side..an individual s. dear MILT. Hence **So·lacement,** solace, solacing, consolation.

Solace (sǫ·lĕs), *v.* ME. [ad. OF. *solacier*, f. *solas* SOLACE *sb.*] **1.** *trans.* To cheer, comfort, console; †to entertain or recreate. Also *refl.* **b.** To make (a place) cheerful or pleasant 1667. **c.** To allay, alleviate, assuage, soothe 1667. †**2.** *intr.* To take comfort or consolation, recreation or enjoyment –1728. **3.** *trans.* Of printers: To punish (a person) corporally for non-payment of a 'solace' 1683.

1. We will with some strange pastime s. them SHAKS. b. The smaller Birds with song Solac'd the Woods MILT. c. A little hint to s. woe TENNYSON.

†**Sola·cious,** *a.* late ME. [a. OF. *solacieus*, f. *solas* SOLACE *sb.*] Affording solace –1675.

Old Friends to trust, old Gold to keep, old Wine To drink; are a s. good old Trine 1675.

Solan (sǭu·lăn). Also **soland.** 1450. [f. ON. and Icel. *súla* gannet; perh. + ON. *ǫnd, and-* duck. Orig. Sc.] The gannet (*Sula bassana*), a large sea-fowl resembling a goose, which frequents a few rocks and small islands of Britain, the Færöes, Iceland, and Canada. Also attrib., *solan goose.*

Solanaceous (sǫlănē¹·ʃəs), *a.* 1804. [f. mod. L. *Solanaceæ*, f. L. *solanum* nightshade.] *Bot.* Belonging to the *Solanaceæ*, a family of gamopetalous plants which includes the genera *Solanum, Capsicum, Atropa, Hyoscyamus*, etc.

Solander (sǒlæ·ndəɹ). 1788. [f. D. C. *Solander*, the Swedish botanist (1736–1782).] A box made in the form of a book, used for holding botanical specimens, papers, maps, etc.

Solania (sǒlē¹·niă). 1830. [f. SOLANUM + -IA.] *Chem.* An alkaloid found in the woody nightshade.

Solanicine (sǒlæ·nisin). 1868. [f. as prec. + -IC + INE⁵.] *Chem.* A base produced by the action of hydrochloric acid on solanine. So **Sola·nidine** *Chem.*, a base produced by the action of acids on solanine.

Solanine (sǫ·lănin). Also **solanina, solanin.** 1838. [a. F., f. SOLANUM + -INE⁵.] *Chem.* A poisonous alkaloidal glucoside found in various plants of the genus *Solanum.*

||**Solano** (sǫlā·nǫ). 1792. [Sp.:—L. *solanus*, f. *sol* sun.] In Spain, a hot south-easterly wind.

Solanoid (sǫ·lănoid), *a.* 1851. [f. SOLANUM + -OID.] *Path.* Resembling a raw potato: applied to a form of cancer.

||**Solanum** (sǒlē¹·nǒm). 1578. [L., nightshade.] A plant of the nightshade family, or the genus of gamopetalous plants of which this is the type; some amount or preparation of the plant used for medicinal purposes.

attrib. Solanaceæ.—The S. or Potato Order 1861.

Solar (sǭu·lăɹ), *a.* and *sb.* 1450. [ad. L. *solaris*, f. *sol* sun.] **A.** *adj.* **1.** Of or pertaining to the sun, its power, light, heat, etc. **b.** Of time: Determined by the course of the sun; fixed by observation of the sun 1594. **c.** Indicating time in relation to, or by means of, the sun 1728. **d.** Of mechanism, etc.: Operating by means of, or with the aid of, the light or heat of the sun 1740. **2. a.** *Astrol.* Subject to the influence of the sun; having a nature or character determined by the sun 1626. **b.** Sacred to the sun; connected or associated with the worship of the sun 1774. **c.** Representing or symbolizing the sun 1807. **d.** Sprung or descended from the sun 1788. †**3.** *S. earth, metal*, gold. **b.** *S. metal*, a coloured metal. –1800. **4.** Of light, heat, etc.: Proceeding or emanating from the sun 1698. **5.** Resembling that of the sun; comparable to the sun 1754.

1. In climes beyond the s. road GRAY. The spots were..s. phenomena 1878. b. The mean interval of time between the sun's passing the meridian one day, and his passing it the next, is called a mean s. day 1816. d. The s. microscope is..a magic lantern, the light of the sun being used instead of..a lamp 1831. 2. a. They haue denominated some Herbs S. and some Lunar BACON. b. The assumption of Stonehenge having been a s. temple 1906. 4. A means of filtering the s. beam 1871. 5. He was in this respect a s. man: he drew after him his own firmament of planets 1861.

Special collocations: **s. apex,** the point in space, situated in the constellation Lyra, towards which the sun is moving; the apex of the s. way; **s. compass,** (*a*) a magnetic instrument turning under the influence of the sun's rays: (*b*) an instrument used in surveying for easy determination of the meridian; **s. eye-piece,** a device used in observations of the sun to diminish its light and heat; **s. ganglion,** = *s. plexus*; **s. lamp,** (*a*) an argand lamp; (*b*) a grade of electric lamp; **s. myth,** a myth resulting from a personification of the sun and describing its course or attributes as those of some god or hero; **s. oil,** commercial name for the heavier portions of petroleum and shale-oil; **s. phosphorus,** a substance which emits light as the result of exposure to sunlight; **s. plexus,** a complex of nerves situated at the pit of the stomach; the epigastric plexus; **s. print,** a photograph made by sunlight; **s. spot,** a sunspot; **s. system,** the sun together with all the planets and other bodies connected with it; **s. tables,** tables by which the position of the sun may be ascertained.

B. *sb. Photogr.* A solar print 1889.

Solari- (sǫlē·ri), comb. form of L. *solaris* SOLAR *a.*

Solarism (sǭu·lăriz'm). 1885. [f. SOLAR *a.* + -ISM.] The theory of solar myths; excessive use of, or adherence to, this theory. So **So·larist,** one who holds this theory, esp. to an excessive degree.

||**Solarium** (sǒlēᵊ·riǒm). *Pl.* **solaria.** 1842. [L., f. *sol* sun.] **1.** A sun-dial. **2.** A terrace, balcony, or room exposed to the rays of the sun, *spec.* one used for treating illness by means of sun-baths 1891.

Solarization (sǭu:lărəizē¹·ʃən). 1853. [f. next + -ATION.] *Photogr.* The injurious effect produced by over-exposing a negative to the action of light, resulting in the reversal of the image; a similar effect produced by over-printing sensitized paper, etc.

Solarize (sǭu·lărəiz), *v.* 1855. [f. SOLAR *a.* + -IZE.] **1.** *trans.* To affect or modify by the influence of the sun or the action of its rays; *spec.* in *Photogr.*, to injure by over-exposure to light. **2.** *intr.* To be affected by solarization. 1868.

†**So·lary,** *a.* 1588. [ad. L. *solaris*; see -ARY².] **1.** Of or belonging to, pertaining to, or connected with, the sun –1716. **b.** Of time: = SOLAR *a.* 1 b. –1697. **2.** *Alch.* and *Astrol.* Of the nature of the sun; subject to the influence of the sun –1671.

|| **Solatium** (sǒlē¹·ʃiǒm). 1817. [L., related to *solari* to console.] **1.** A sum of money, or other compensation, given to a person to make up for loss or inconvenience. **2.** *spec.* in *Law.* A sum of money paid, over and above the actual damages, as a solace for injured feelings 1832.

|| **Solazzi** (sola·tsi). 1861. [Italian maker's name.] *S. juice*, a kind of liquorice.

†**Sold,** *sb.* [ME. *soude*, a. OF., L. *solidum* :— acc. sing. of *solidus*; see SOL *sb.*³ and SOU.] Pay (esp. of soldiers); wages, salary –1630. Hence †**Sold** *v. trans.* to pay; to enlist or retain for service by payment.

Sold (sǭuld), *ppl. a.* 1535. [pa. pple. of SELL *v.*] **1.** Disposed of by sale. **2.** Denoting a sale effected 1862.

2. Those pictures which have 's.' tickets 1862.

|| **Soldado** (soldā·dǫ). 1586. [Sp. (and Pg.) = It. *soldato*, f. *soldo* military pay; see SOLD *sb.*] **1.** A soldier. **2.** The S. American heron 1852. **3.** The squirrel-fish (*Holocentrus ascensionis*) of the West Indies, etc. 1902.

Soldan (sǫ·ldăn). Now *arch.* or *Hist.* [ME. *soudan*, a. OF., ad. Arab. *sultān*; see SULTAN.] **1.** The supreme ruler of one or other of the great Mohammedan powers or countries of the Middle Ages; *spec.* the Sultan of Egypt.

The *S.* is sometimes contrasted with the (*Great*) *Turk* and with the *Sophy* of Persia.

2. With *a* and *pl.* A Mohammedan ruler; one having the rank of sultan ME.

1. Where Champions bold..at the Soldans Chair Defi'd the best of Panim chivalry To mortal combat MILT.

|| **Soldanella** (sǫldăne·lă). 1579. [mod.L., a. It.] *Bot.* †**1.** A species of convolvulus or bindweed, *Convolvulus soldanella* –1712. **2.** A primulaceous plant of the genus *Soldanella*, native in Alpine districts 1629.

Solder (sǫ·ldəɹ, sǭu·dəɹ, sǫ·dəɹ), *sb.* [ME. *soudour*, a. OF. *soudure*, f. *souder* :—L. *solidare* to make solid or firm, f. *solidus*. See also SAWDER.] **1.** A fusible metallic alloy used for uniting metal surfaces or parts. †**2.** *transf.* Any binding or uniting substance (*rare*) –1610. **3.** *fig.* A quality, principle, etc., which unites in any way; a bond or means of union 1599. **4.** *Soft s.*: **a.** A common kind of solder, usually made from tin and lead 1594. **b.** = SOFT SAWDER 1848.

Solder (sǫ·ldəɹ, sǭu·dəɹ, sǫ·dəɹ), *v.* late ME. [f. prec.] **1.** *trans.* To unite or fasten by means of a metallic solder. **b.** *transf.* To unite firmly or closely, to cause to adhere strongly, by means of some substance or device 1601. †**2.** *Med.* To cause (wounds) to close up and become whole; to reunite (tissues or bones) –1788. **3.** *fig.* To unite, to cause to adhere, in a close, firm, or intimate manner 1597. **4.** *fig.* To bring or restore to a sound or unimpaired condition; to repair, patch up again 1607. **5.** *absol.* To perform the operation of uniting with solder 1588. **6.** *intr.* To adhere, unite, grow together 1470.

3. Friendship..of equalls is ever best soldered 1646. 6. The Tripple Crown could never s. with the English, nor it with that 1647. Hence **So·lderer.**

So·ldering, *vbl. sb.* 1466. [f. SOLDER *v.*] **1.** The action of the vb. **2.** Solder; material used for soldering 1648. **3.** *attrib.*, chiefly in the names of tools or apparatus used for soldering, as *s. iron* 1675.

Soldier (sǭu·ldʒəɹ), *sb.* [ME. *souder*, etc., a. OF. *soud(i)er, soldier*, f. *soude* SOLD *sb.* (cf. med. L. *solidarius*).] **1.** One who serves in an army for pay; one who takes part in military service or warfare; *spec.* one of the ordinary rank and file of an army; a private. **b.** A man of military skill and experience 1603. **2.** *fig.* (usu. with ref. to spiritual service or warfare) ME. **b.** *To come the old s. over*, to impose upon 1824. **3.** *transf.* Used as a name for various animals. **4.** A disease of swine characterized by red patches on the skin 1882.

1. As he is a Gentleman and a Soldiour SHAKS. *Common s.*: see COMMON *a.* II. 3. *Private s.*: see PRIVATE *a.* 1 b. *Foot-soldier*, a s. in an infantry regiment. *S. of Fortune*: see FORTUNE *sb.* 1. b. So great a s. taught us there, What long-enduring hearts could do TENNYSON. 2. To make them Soldiers of Christ 1737. 3. a. The soldier-crab or hermit-crab 1666. b. A fighting ant or termite; also *Austral.*, a species of large red ant 1781. c. The red gurnard 1846. d. *slang.* A red herring 1811. e. A red spider; a small red beetle; a ladybird 1848.

attrib. and *Comb.*: **s.-fish** *U.S.*, *Pæcilechthys cæruleus*, called also Blue Darter, Rainbow Darter; **-fly** *U.S.*, a name given to flies of the family *Stratiomydæ*; **-moth,** *Euschema militaris*; **-orchis,** an orchis (*Orchis militaris*), having a fancied resemblance to a s. Hence **So·ldieress,** a female s. **So·ldierize** *v. intr.* to serve as a s.; *trans.* to make into a s. **So·ldiership,** the state or condition of being a s.; the qualities of a s.; military experience or skill.

Soldier (sǭu·ldʒəɹ), *v.* 1647. [f. the sb.] *intr.* To act or serve as a soldier. Also with *it.* **b.** To feign illness, to malinger; to make a mere show of working; to shirk (*slang*) 1840. **c.** *Mil. slang.* To furbish up accoutrements, etc. 1885.

b. Finding fault with some fellow for 'sogering', as it is called 1890.

So·ldier-crab. 1668. The hermit-crab.

Soldiering (sǭu·ldʒəriŋ), *vbl. sb.* 1643. [f. the vb.] **1.** The action of serving as a soldier;

the state of being a soldier; military service. **2.** Malingering, shirking 1894.

So·ldierlike, *a.* and *adv.* 1542. [f. SOLDIER *sb.*] **A.** *adj.* **1.** Having the character or bearing of a soldier. **2.** Appropriate to, worthy of, becoming or befitting, a soldier 1553.

1. You are also to be vastly careful..to make them appear always neat and clean, and soldier-like WASHINGTON.

B. *adv.* In a manner befitting a soldier 1571.

Soldierly (sōu·ldʒəli), *a.* and *adv.* 1577. [f. SOLDIER *sb.* + -LY.] **A.** *adj.* **1.** Becoming or appropriate to a soldier or soldiers. **2.** Having the qualities of a soldier 1610.

1. They had fought rather with beastlie furie, then with any souldierly discipline SIDNEY.

B. *adv.* = SOLDIERLIKE *adv.* 1585.

Soldiery (sōu·ldʒəri). 1570. [f. SOLDIER *sb.* + -Y³.] **1.** Soldiers collectively; the military; a military class or body. **2.** Military training; knowledge or science of military matters 1579.

1. The Souldiery..all flockt unto him 1635.

‖ **Soldo** (sǫ·ldo). *Pl.* **soldi.** 1599. [It. :— L. *solidum*; see SOL³.] An Italian coin and money of account, the twentieth part of a lira, now equal in value to an English halfpenny.

Sole (sōul), *sb.*¹ ME. [a. OF., = pop. and med.L. *sola*, for L. *solea* sandal, shoe.] **I. 1.** The under surface of the foot; †the mark made by this upon the ground. **b.** *Farriery.* The concave plate of horn which surrounds the frog 1610. **2.** The bottom of a boot, shoe, etc.; that part of it upon which the wearer treads (freq. exclusive of the heel); one or other of the pieces of leather, etc., of which this is composed. (See also *stocking-sole.*) Also, a properly shaped piece of felt, etc. placed in the bottom of a boot, shoe, etc. 1440. **b.** With punning allusion to SOUL *sb.* 1603.

1. We've but naked soles to run with 1871. 2. *Haml.* II. ii. 234. b. Not on thy s., but on thy soul, harsh Jew, Thou mak'st thy knife keen SHAKS.

II. 1. †**a.** The foundation of a building; the site of a city, etc. (*rare*) -1634. **b.** The bottom, floor, or hearth of an oven or furnace 1615. **c.** *Naut.* A protective lining attached to the rudder, bilgeways, etc. to prevent them from being worn away 1850. **2. a.** = SILL *sb.*¹ 1 and 2. Now *rare.* late ME. **b.** *Naut.* and *Fortif.* The bottom of an embrasure 1769. **c.** *Mining.* A horizontal piece of timber set underneath a prop as a support 1839. **d.** A flat tile used as a rest or support for a draining-tile or drain-pipe 1843. **3.** The inner circle of a water-wheel 1673. **4.** The lower part, bottom, or under surface of anything 1615. **b.** *esp.* The under part or surface of a plane-stock, plough, rudder, electrical instrument, etc. 1607. **5. a.** *Mining.* The bottom or floor of a vein, level, or working 1653. **b.** The bottom or lowest part *of* a valley, etc. 1880. Hence **So·leless** *a.* of boots, shoes, etc. having no soles; without soles.

Sole (sōul), *sb.*² ME. [a. OF. (also mod. F.) *sole*, of the same origin as prec., agreeing in sense with L. *solea.*] **1.** A common British and European flat-fish (*Solea vulgaris* or *solea*), highly esteemed as food; one or other of the various fishes of the genus *Solea.* **b.** In collect. sing. 1661. **2.** With distinguishing terms, as *common s., spotted s.*, see also LEMON². 1668. **3.** In American and Australasian use: One or other of various fishes belonging to related genera (esp. *Achirus*) or to the family *Pleuronectidæ* 1882.

Sole (sōul), *a.* late ME. [a. OF. *sol* (fem. *sole*) (mod.F. *seul, seule*) :—L. *solum*, acc. sing. of *solus* alone.] **1.** Having no husband or wife; single, unmarried; †celibate. Chiefly in legal use and freq. of women. Now *rare* or *Obs.* †**b.** Of life: Pertaining to or involving celibacy -1598. **2.** Without companions; alone, solitary. Usually predicative. late ME. **b.** Of places: Solitary, lonely; secluded 1598. **3.** Being, or consisting of, one person only. late ME. †**4.** In predicative or quasi-advb. use: With no other person or persons; without participation, etc., in something -1671. **5.** One and only 1497. **b.** Singular, unique, unrivalled. late ME. †**6.** Of things, qualities, etc.: Standing alone -1622. **7.** Of things, rights, duties, etc.: Pertaining or due to, possessed or exercised by, vested in, etc., one person or corporate body to the exclusion of all others; exclusive 1597. **8.** Uniform or unvaried (*local*) 1845. **9.** quasi-*advb.* Solely 1562.

1. *Woman s.* = *feme-sole* s. v. FEME. If a woman s. shall doe homage COKE. b. Some [men] like a s. life, others thinke it no life without a companion 1598. 2. I am oft times s., but seldom solitary 1650. 3. *Corporation s.*: see CORPORATION 3. 4. I, when no other durst, s. undertook The dismal expedition MILT. 5. I believe my s. crime was candour LYTTON. The s. manager of these estates 1839. 7. The right of s. succession 1766. *Comb.* **s.-coloured** *a.* of a single uniform colour; self-coloured.

Sole (sōul), *v.* 1570. [f. SOLE *sb.*¹] **1.** *trans.* To provide (a boot, shoe, stocking, etc.) with a sole. **b.** To fit the head of a golf-club with a sole 1905. **2.** *Golf.* To place the sole of (a club) on the ground in preparing for a stroke. Also *absol.* 1909.

‖ **Solea** (sōu·liă). 1858. [Byzantic Gr. σολέα.] *Eccl.* A raised floor before the entrance of a chancel or chapel.

Solecism (sǫ·lĭsiz'm). 1577. [ad. L. *solœcismus*, ad. Gr. σολοικισμός, f. σόλοικος speaking incorrectly.] **1.** An impropriety or irregularity in speech or diction; a violation of the rules of grammar or syntax; properly, a faulty concord. **b.** Without article 1583. **2.** A breach or violation of good manners or etiquette; an impropriety *in* manners, etc. 1599. **3.** An error, incongruity, inconsistency, or impropriety of any kind 1599. **b.** Without article (*rare*) 1649.

1. The last part of the Sentence not agreeing nor answering to the first; which is the proper definition of a Solœcism 1699. b. A wary man he is in grammar, very nice as to s. or barbarism DRYDEN. 2. In those days smoking in the streets was an unpardonable s. 1884. 3. Where a fat jovial Franciscan would be a s. 1850. So **So·lecist** (*rare*), one who uses solecisms. **Soleci·stic** *a.* of the nature of or involving solecism. **Soleci·stical** *a.*, **-ly** *adv.*

Solecize (sǫ·lĭsəiz), *v.* Now *rare* or *Obs.* 1627. [ad. Gr. σολοικίζειν, f. σόλοικος; see SOLECISM.] *intr.* To make use of, or commit, solecisms in language, behaviour, conduct, etc.

Soled (sōuld), *ppl. a.* 1480. [SOLE *sb.*¹, *v.*] Having a sole or soles (of a specified kind).

So·le-lea:ther. late ME. [f. SOLE *sb.*¹ 2 + LEATHER *sb.*] Leather of a thick or strong kind used or suitable for the soles of boots, shoes, etc.

Solely (sōu·l,li), *adv.* 1495. [f. SOLE *a.* + -LY².] **1.** As a single person (or thing); without any other as an associate, partner, etc.; alone; occas. without aid or assistance. **2.** Only, merely, exclusively; also (contextually), entirely, altogether 1588.

1. Who meanes to sit solie on Olympus, must suffer no climers LODGE. 2. Hote furious spirits..who delight soly in fights and vproares 1628.

Solemn (sǫ·ləm), *a.* [ME. *solempne*, a. OF. *solempne, solemne*, or ad. L. *sol-, sollemnis* established, customary.] **1.** Associated or connected with religious rites or observances; performed with due ceremony and reverence; having a religious character; sacred; *spec.* of church rites performed with full ceremonial. **2.** Of days or seasons: Marked by the celebration of special observances or rites (esp. of a religious character); distinguished by, or set apart for, special ceremonies ME. **3.** Performed with, accompanied by, due formality or ceremony; of a formal or ceremonious character. late ME. †**b.** Formal; regular, uniform -1704. †**c.** Customary; carefully observed. B. JONS. †**4. a.** Grand; imposing; sumptuous -1589. †**b.** Of great dignity or importance -1596. **5.** Of a formal and serious or deliberate character ME. **6.** Of a grave or earnest character 1449. **7.** Impressive, awe-inspiring. late ME. †**b.** Gloomy, dark, sombre -1625.

1. [They] with cursed things His holy Rites, and s. Feasts profan'd MILT. 2. Þat feyris nor markets had no place in þe kirk in solempne tymis 1400. 3. Being the King's birth day, there was a solemne ball at Court EVELYN. 4. a. In solempne robes they glad shall goe 1586. b. There was..A limitour, a ful solempne man CHAUCER. 5. Makyng a grete & a solempne oath CAXTON. *S. League and Covenant*: see COVENANT *sb.* 8. 6. The sad and solemne Priests SHAKS. What Virgins these..That bend to earth their s. brow GRAY. 7. In solem silency this vapour rose From this drad Dale 1642. b. Customary suites of solemne Blacke SHAKS. Hence **So·lemn·ly** *adv.*, **-ness**; also (more usu.) **So·lemness.**

Solemnity (sǫle·mnĭti). [ME. *solempnete*, a. OF. *solempneté, -ité*, ad. L. *sol-, sollem(p)nitas* (post-classical), f. *sol-, sollem(p)nis* SOLEMN *a.*; see -ITY.] **1.** Observance of ceremony or special formality on important occasions. **2.** An occasion of ceremony; an observance of special importance; a festival or other similar occasion ME. **3.** *Law.* Necessary formality, such as is requisite to make an act or document valid 1588. **4.** The state or character of being solemn or serious; impressiveness; gravity; a solemn utterance or statement 1712.

1. If a female child be borne, there is small solemnitie PURCHAS. Phr. *With* or *in* (*great*, etc.) *s.* (now *rare*); Wee'll hold a feast in great solemnitie SHAKS. 2. Among other solemnities, they roasted an Oxe in the middest of the field for the people 1617. 3. Not being sealled be the seall of the partie, quilk was ane essentiall solemnitie of contracts 1665. 4. That S. of Phrase, which may be drawn from the Sacred Writings ADDISON.

Solemnization (sǫ:ləmnəizēⁱ·ʃən). 1447. [a. OF. *solem(p)nisation, -ization*, or ad. med.L. *solempnizatio*; see next and -ATION.] The action of solemnizing or celebrating in a ceremonial manner. **b.** *spec.* The celebration or performance *of* a marriage 1497.

Solemnize (sǫ·ləmnəiz), *v.* Also **solemnise.** late ME. [ad. OF. *solem(p)niser, -izer*, or med.L. *solemnizare*; see SOLEMN *a.* and -IZE.] **1.** *trans.* To dignify or honour by ceremonies; to celebrate with special formality. **2.** To celebrate (a marriage) with proper ceremonies and in due form; also, to perform the ceremony of (marriage). late ME. **3.** To hold, observe, perform, †proclaim, etc., with some amount of ceremony or formality 1483. †**4.** To laud or glorify -1687. **5.** To make solemn; to render serious or grave 1726.

1. These two enraged Princes solemniz'd their mutuall fury by the death of so many thousands 1652. 2. The mariage whiche was solempnised betwene his maiestie, and..the lady Catherine 1533. 3. The..peasantry were compelled to s. the obsequies of every Bacchiad 1835. 4. My hart is bent..God's name to s. 1586. 5. Holy horrors s. the shade POPE.

Solen (sōu·lĕn). 1661. [a. L. *solen*, or Gr. σωλήν pipe, shell-fish, etc.] **1.** *Zool.* The razor-fish, *Solen ensis* or *siliqua.* **2.** *Surg.* A frame-work to prevent the bedclothes from touching an injured limb 1693. Hence (from sense 1) **Solena·cean** *sb.* and *a.* **Solena·ceous** *a.*

Soleness (sōu·lnĕs). Now *rare.* 1449. [f. SOLE *a.*] †**1.** Solitude; solitariness -1618. **2.** The state or condition of being sole, alone, or apart 1587.

Solenette (sōulne·t, sǫlĕne·t). 1839. [irreg. f. SOLE *sb.*² + -(*n*)ETTE.] The little sole, *Monochirus linguatulus* or *Solea minuta.*

So·lenite. 1828. [a. F. *solénite*; see SOLEN *sb.* and -ITE¹ 2 a.] A fossil razor-fish or solen.

Soleno- (solī·no), comb. form of Gr. σωλήν channel, pipe, etc., as **Sole·nocyte,** one of the cells found in the nephridia of certain polychætan worms; **Sole·nodon(t,** one or other of certain insectivorous mammalian rodents native to the West Indies and America, as the agouta or the almiqui; **Solenosto·matous** *a.*, of, belonging to, or resembling the genus *Solenostomus* of lophobranchiate fishes.

Solenoid (solī·noid, sōu·lĕnoid). 1832. [a. F. *solénoïde*, f. Gr. σωλήν; see SOLEN *sb.*] **1.** *Electr.* An electro-dynamical spiral, formed of a wire with the ends returned parallel to the axis; a series of elementary circuits arranged on this principle. **2.** *Med.* A cage to enclose a patient during medical treatment 1901.

‖ **Solera** (solē·ra). 1851. [Sp.] **1.** A blend of sherry wine. **2.** A wine-cask, usu. containing a double butt 1863.

‖ **Soleus** (solī·ŭs, sōu·lĭ,ŭs). 1676. [mod.L., f. L. *solea* SOLE *sb.*¹] *Anat.* A muscle of the calf of the leg, situated between the gastrocnemius and the bone.

Sol-fa (sǫlfā·, sǫ·lfā·), *sb.* 1548. [From the syllables *sol* (SOL *sb.*²) and *fa* (FA) of the scale; see GAMUT.] *Mus.* The set of syllables 'do (or ut), re, mi, fa, sol, la, si', sung to the respective notes of the major scale; the system of singing notes to these syllables; a musical scale or exercise thus sung. †Occas. in the phr. *to sing s.* *Tonic s.*: see TONIC *a.*

Sol-fa (sǫlfā·, sǫ·lfā·), *v.* 1568. [See prec.] **1.** *trans.* To sing (a tune, air, etc.) to the sol-fa syllables. **2.** *intr.* To sing in this manner; to use the sol-fa syllables in singing 1584.

1. You shall not find a musicion..able to *sol fa* it right 1597. So **Solfaing** *vbl. sb.* 1549.

‖ **Solfatara** (sǫlfātā·rā). 1777. [Name of a sulphurous volcano near Naples, f. It. *solfo* sulphur.] A volcanic vent, from which only sulphurous exhalations and aqueous vapours are emitted, incrusting the edge with sulphur and other minerals.

‖**Solfeggio** (sǫlfe·dʒio). *Pl.* **solfeggi**(-ed₁dʒi), **solfeggios.** 1774. [It., f. *sol-fa* SOL-FA.] An exercise for the voice, in which the sol-fa syllables are employed; †also *transf.*, an exercise for a musical instrument.

Solferino (sǫlfĕrī·no). 1865. [f. the place-name *Solferino* in Italy, because discovered shortly after the battle fought there in 1859.] The bright crimson dye-colour rosaniline.

Solicit (sǒli·sit), *v.* 1450. [ad. OF. *sol-, solliciter*, or ad. L. *sollicitare* (*sol-*), f. *sollicitus*, f. *sollus* whole, entire + *citus, ciere* to put in motion.] **I.** *trans.* †**1.** To disturb, disquiet, trouble; to make anxious, fill with concern –1788. **2.** To entreat or petition (a person) for, or to do, something; to urge, importune 1530. **3.** To incite or move to some act of lawlessness or insubordination 1565. **4.** To incite, draw on, allure, by some specious representation or argument 1591. **b.** To court or beg the favour of (a woman), *esp.* with immoral intention 1591. **c.** Of women: To accost and importune (men) for immoral purposes 1710. **5.** Of things: **a.** To affect (a person or thing) by some form of physical influence or attraction. Now *rare.* 1601. **b.** To tempt, allure; to attract or draw by enticement, etc. 1663. †**6.** To endeavour to draw out (a dart, etc.) by the use of gentle force –1784. **7.** *Med.* To seek to draw, to induce or bring on, esp. by gentle means 1732.

1. Hath any ill solicited thine ears Befall'n my Myrmidons? CHAPMAN. 2. The charge of sollliciting the Government for the moneys 1719. 3. Boadicea.. sollicited the Britains..to a Revolt 1683. 3. Solicite Henry with her wonderous praise. Bethinke thee on her Vertues. SHAKS. b. *Much Ado* II. i. 70. 5. a. Then gently sleep sollicited each eye HOBBES. b. That Fruit, which with desire..Sollicited her longing eye MILT. 6. But good Agenor gently from the wound The spear sollicits POPE.

II. †**1.** To push forward or prosecute (business, affairs, etc.) –1789. **b.** To conduct (a law-suit, etc.) as a solicitor; to transact or negotiate in the capacity of a law-agent. 1606. †**2. a.** To urge or plead (one's suit, cause, etc.) –1769. **b.** To urge or press (a matter) –1704. **3.** To request, petition, or sue for (some thing, favour, etc.); to desire or seek by petition 1595. **b.** To seek after 1717. **4.** Of things: To call or ask for, to demand (action, attention, etc.) 1592.

1. b. The attorney-at-law who solicited the suits 1839. 3. How could he s. her hand? 1797. b. I.. Repent old pleasures and s. new POPE. 4. The formation of a new government solicited his attention 1817.

III. *intr.* **1.** To make request or petition; to beg or entreat 1509. **2.** To act or practise as a solicitor 1596. †**3.** To petition *against*, to make intercession *for*, a person or thing –1741.

1. If you bethinke your selfe of..Grace, Solicite for it straight SHAKS. 2. We are at a great distance from the King's Court, and have no body there to s. for us SWIFT. Hence **Soli·cit** *sb.* an entreaty or solicitation.

Solicitant (sǒli·sitănt), *sb.* and *a.* 1802. [ad. L. *sol-, sollicitant-*, pres. ppl. stem of *sollicitare* SOLICIT *v.*] **A.** *sb.* One who solicits or requests earnestly. **B.** *adj.* That solicits; making petition or request 1886.

Solicitation (sǒlisitē¹·ʃən). 1492. [a. OF., or ad. L. *sol-, sollicitatio*; see SOLICIT *v.* and -ATION.] †**1.** Management, transaction, or pursuit of business, legal affairs, etc. –1722. **2.** The action of soliciting, or seeking to obtain by earnest request; entreaty, petition, diligent or importunate asking. Also, an instance of this. 1500. **b.** The action of soliciting a person of the other sex 1604. **3.** The exertion or operation of a physically attracting influence or force 1626. **4.** The action of some attractive, enticing, or alluring influence 1676. †**5.** Anxiety; solicitude –1725.

2. At her s. the trustee lent the fund to the husband and it was lost 1883. b. *Oth.* IV. ii. 202. 3. The solicitations of Jupiter's attractive force are..urgent on a swiftly rushing body 1884. 4. Vicious sollicitations of appetite, if not checked, will grow more importunate JOHNSON.

Solicitor (sǒli·sitəɹ). late ME. [ad. OF. *sol-, solliciteur* (mod.F. *solliciteur*), f. *solliciter* SOLICIT *v.*; see -OR 2.] †**1.** One who urges, prompts, or instigates –1722. †**b.** A thing serving to instigate, etc. –1751. †**2.** One who conducts, negotiates, or transacts matters on behalf of another or others; a representative, agent, or deputy –1741. **3.** One properly qualified and formally admitted to practise as a law-agent in any court; formerly, one practising in a court of equity, as dist. from an *attorney* 1577. **b. Solicitor-General**, a law-officer (in England ranking next to the Attorney-General, in Scotland to the Lord-Advocate), who takes the part of the state or crown in suits affecting the public interest 1533. **4.** One who entreats, requests, or petitions; one who solicits or begs favours; a pleader, intercessor, advocate 1551. **b.** *transf.* of things 1579. †**5.** One who, or that which, draws on or entices –1655. **6.** *U.S.* One who solicits business, contributions, or help of any kind 1903.

So †**Soli·citer** (in senses 3, 4). Hence **Soli·citorship.** †**Soli·citress,** †**Soli·citrix,** a female solicitor.

Solicitous (sǒli·sitəs), *a.* 1563. [f. L. *sol-, sollicitus* (f. *sollus* whole, entire + *citus, ciere* to put in motion) + -OUS.] †**1.** Anxious, apprehensive –1741. **2.** Troubled, anxious, or deeply concerned, on some specified account 1570. **3.** Extremely or particularly careful or attentive 1609. **4.** Anxious, eager, desirous 1628. **5.** Marked or characterized by anxiety, care, or concern 1563. **6.** Of features: Suggestive of solicitude or anxiety 1868.

2. Much s. how best He may compensate for a day of sloth COWPER. Sollicitous chiefly for the peace of my own country BURKE. 4. The Prince..was..most impatiently sollicitous to bring it to pass CLARENDON. 5. An attentive, s., perhaps painful exercise of their understanding about it BUTLER. Hence **Soli·citous-ly** *adv.*, **-ness.**

Solicitude (sǒli·sitiūd). late ME. [a. OF., or ad. L. *sol-, sollicitudo*, f. *sollicitus.*] **1.** The state of being solicitous or uneasy in mind; disquietude, anxiety; care, concern. **2.** Anxious, special, or particular care or attention 1535. **3.** *pl.* Cares, troubles, anxieties 1490.

1. Free from s., because free from wants 1833. 2. Never had such s. been lavished on human being DISRAELI. 3. Wearied with perpetual sollicitudes and labours 1750.

Solicitudinous (sǒlisitiū·dinəs), *a.* 1682. [f. L. *sol-, sollicitudin-*, stem of *sollicitudo* SOLICITUDE.] †**1.** Filled with anxiety, care, or concern. SIR T. BROWNE. **2.** Characterized by solicitude or anxiety 1829.

Solid (sǫ·lid), *sb.* 1495. [f. next, or ad. F. *solide*, ad. L. *solidum* neut.] **1.** *Geom.* A body or magnitude of three dimensions; one having length, breadth, and thickness. **2.** A solid substance or body 1698. **b.** *Physiol.* A solid part or constituent of the body. Used in pl. Now *Obs.* or *rare.* 1704. **c.** *Building.* A solid mass of masonry or other construction, esp. that between windows or doors; a pier of a bridge 1736. **3.** *The s.*, the unbroken mass, the main part or body, of something 1776.

1. *S. of revolution*, one formed by the revolution of a plane figure. 3. Actuated by cams turned from the s. 1908.

Solid (sǫ·lid), *a.* late ME. [a. OF. *solide* or ad. L. *solidus.*] **I. 1.** Free from empty spaces, cavities, interstices, etc.; having the interior completely filled in or up. Opp. to *hollow.* **b.** *spec.* in *Bot.* Fleshy and uniform; not hollow or furnished with internal cavities of any kind 1753. **c.** *Typog.* Having no leads between the lines; unleaded 1808. **d.** Of a wall, etc.: Having no opening or window; unbroken, blank 1865. **2.** *Math.* Of a body or figure: Having three dimensions. late ME. †**b.** Of number or measure: = CUBIC *a.* –1705. **c.** Of, relating or pertaining to, a geometrical solid or solids (†or to cubic numbers) 1570. **3.** Of material substances: Of a dense or massive consistency; composed of particles which are firmly and continuously coherent; hard and compact 1532. **b.** Solidified; frozen 1697. **c.** Of clouds, the atmosphere, etc.: Having the appearance of a solid or unbroken mass; dense, thick, compact. Chiefly *poet.* 1807. **4.** Of states, conditions, etc.: Characterized by solidity or compactness 1597. **5.** Of rain, etc.: Steady, drenching; continuous. Also, of a day: Characterized by rain of this kind. 1621. **6.** Having the property of occupying a certain amount of space (cf. SOLIDITY 4) 1690.

1. This was hollow, the other s. PURCHAS. 2. *S. Angle*, the angle made by the meeting of three or more planes which join in a point. b. There are in a s. Foot 1728 s. Inches 1705. 3. Oh that this too too s. Flesh would melt, Thaw, and resolue it selfe into a Dew SHAKS. *transf.* Asses..in Judgement sit In s. Deafness, on the Works of Wit 1746. b. O'er s. seas, where Winter reigns 1786. c. Yonder gap in the s. gray Of the eastern cloud BROWNING. 5. A sad and sollid shewer without intermission 1621. 6. Even a particle of water is s. 1794.

II. 1. Of a strong, firm, or substantial nature or quality; not slight or flimsy 1586. **2. a.** Combined; consolidated; united (*rare*) 1596. **b.** Unanimous, undivided. Orig. *U.S.* 1884. **c.** Of persons: Regular or steady in attendance, politics, voting, etc. Chiefly *U.S.* 1883. **3.** Of a day, hour, etc.: Whole, entire, complete. Now *colloq.* 1718. **4.** Entirely of the same substance or material (as that specified); of (gold, etc.) and nothing else 1710. **5.** Of persons, their constitution, etc.: Strong, healthy, sturdy 1741.

1. A Bottle or two of good s. Edifying Port STEELE. Faith is gone, having no s. support 1770. The s. cities of the Greeks and Romans 1870. 2. b. The vote of the s. South 1884. c. I'm s. for Mr. Peck every time 1888. 3. I walked him up and down,..for a s. hour 1890. 4. The..statues..were of s. gold 1844. 5. He walks there, with s. step CARLYLE.

III. 1. Of persons: **a.** Of sound scholarship or sober judgement in matters of learning or speculation 1600. **b.** Sober-minded, of reliable judgement, in practical matters; steady, sedate, staid 1632. **2.** Of qualities: Well founded or established; of real value or importance; substantial 1601. **3.** Of arguments, reasons, writings, etc.: Having a sound or substantial foundation; based upon sound principles or indisputable facts 1615. **4.** Marked by, or involving, serious study or intention; not light, frivolous, or merely amusing 1647. **5.** Of judgement, etc.: Of a sober, sound, or practical character 1662. **6.** Characterized by a high degree of religious fervour or seriousness –1769. **7.** Thorough, downright, vigorous, etc. Used with intensive force and freq. strengthened by *good, right*, etc. 1830.

1. A s. and well-read man 1709. b. The s., and sad man, is not troubled with the floods and ebbes of Fortune 1632. 2. Having a very s. Respect for humane Nature STEELE. A man of s. learning 1882. 3. If there were no s. defence to the claim the plaintiff would ..obtain his order 1894. 4. Romances debauch the taste for s. reading 1845. 5. He who is..cold in affection may have solider judgement, and steadier resolution 1805. 7. Swear your innocency with a good s. oath STEVENSON.

IV. Quasi-*adv.* In a body or as a whole; unanimously. In phrases with ref. to voting, esp. *to go s.* (*for* or *against* some thing or person). 1884.

The fleet seems to have gone..s. against him 1891. Hence **So·lid-ly** *adv.*, **-ness.**

Solidago (sǫlidē¹·go). 1771. [med.L.] **a.** A large composite genus of perennial plants; golden-rod. **b.** A plant of this genus, esp. *S virgaurea*, a European and British species, formerly in repute for its medicinal properties.

Solidarity (sǫlidæ·rĭti). 1848. [ad. F. *solidarité*, f. *solidaire* solid; see SOLIDARY *a.*] **1.** The fact or quality, on the part of communities, etc., of being perfectly united or at one in some respect, esp. in interests, sympathies, or aspirations. **2.** Community or perfect coincidence *of* (or *between*) interests 1874. **3.** *Civil Law.* A form of obligation involving joint and several responsibilities or rights 1875.

1. They have s., or responsibleness, and trust in each other EMERSON. Each is responsible to the Czar, but they have no sort of s. 1877.

Solidary (sǫ·lidări), *a.* 1818. [ad. F. *solidaire*; see SOLID *a.* and -ARY [1].] **1.** *Civil Law.* Joint and several. **2.** Characterized by or having solidarity or community of interests 1848.

2. Regarding as s., or indissolubly connected together, all the members of the great human family 1848.

Solidate (sǫ·lidēɪt). *Hist.* 1610. [ad. med. L. *solidata* (*terræ*), f. SOLIDUS.] A piece of land of the annual value of a solidus.

So·lidate, *v.* Now *rare.* 1640. [f. L. *solidat-*, *solidare* to make solid.] **1.** *trans.* To make solid or firm; to consolidate. †**2.** = CONSOLIDATE *v.* 4. –1684.

Solid-hoofed, -hooved, *a.* 1842. [f. SOLID *a.*] Having the hoof whole or undivided; solidungulate, soliped; *spec.* as the designation of certain swine.

Solidify (sǒli·difəi), *v.* 1799. [ad. F. *solidifier*; see SOLID *a.* and -(I)FY.] **1.** *trans.* To render solid; to make firm, hard, or compact. **2.** *intr.* To become solid; to change from a liquid or gaseous to a solid state 1837.

1. We cannot as yet s. alcohol 1871. *transf.* Disraeli..sought to s. them into a party 1885. Hence **Soli·difi·able** *a.* capable of solidification. **Soli·difica·tion,** the action or process of solidifying; consolidation, concentration. **Soli·difier.**

Solidism (sǫ·lidiz'm). 1832. [f. SOLID *sb.* + -ISM.] *Med.* The doctrine or theory which refers all diseases to the state of, or to morbid changes in, the solid parts of the body. So **So·lidist,** one who believes in s.

Solidity (sǒli·dĭti). 1532. [ad. F. *solidité* or L. *soliditatem*, f. *solidus* SOLID; see -ITY.] **1.** The quality of being solid or substantial, in various fig. or transf. senses. **2.** The quality or condition of being materially solid; compactness and firmness of texture, structure, etc. 1603. **3. a.** *Geom.* The amount of space occupied by a solid body; volume, cubic or solid content 1570. **b.** Relative density or mass 1698. **4. a.** The property of occupying a certain amount of space 1690. **b.** Extension in the three dimensions of space 1855. **5.** A solid thing or body. 1602. **6.** = SOLIDARITY 3. 1706.

1. Establishing their assertions with great s. SIR T. BROWNE. Assure me of the s. of your recovery 1788. The Persians are unthinking, perpetually joking, and deficient in s. 1821. 2. They have the s. of the hardest bone GOLDSM. The château..strikes the spectator by its s. and magnificence 1833. 4. a. The s. of matter..expresses that property which every body possesses of not permitting any other body to occupy the same place with it at the same time 1815. 5. Heauens face doth glow, Yea this s. and compound masse. Is thought-sicke SHAKS.

Solidungulate (sǫlidʊ·ŋgiŭlĕt), *a.* and *sb.* 1839. [f. L. *solidus* SOLID *a.* + *ungulatus*, f. *ungula* hoof.] = SOLIPED *sb.* and *a.* So **Solidu·ngular** *a. rare.* **Solidu·ngulous** *a.* 1650.

‖ **Solidus** (sǫ·lidǒs). *Pl.* **solidi** (sǫ·lidəi). late ME. [L. *solidus* (sc. *nummus*) SOLID *a.*, used subst.] **1. a.** A gold coin of the Roman empire, orig. worth about 25 denarii. †**b.** A shilling. **2.** A sloping line used to separate shillings from pence, as 12/6; a shilling-mark; used also in writing fractions and for other separations of figures and letters 1891.

Solifidian (sǭuˡlifi·diăn), *sb.* and *a.* 1596. [f. L. *soli-*, comb. form of *solus* alone + *fides* faith.] **A.** *sb.* One who holds that faith alone, without works, is sufficient for justification.

The doctrine is based on Rom. iii. 28, where Luther rendered πίστει by 'allein durch den Glauben' (only by faith).

B. *adj.* **1.** Consisting of, pertaining to, the doctrine of justification by faith alone 1605. **2.** Of persons, etc.: Accepting or maintaining this doctrine 1628. Hence **Solifi·dianism,** the doctrine or tenet of justification by faith alone.

Soliform (sǭuˡlifǫɪm), *a.* 1678. [ad. L. type **soliformis* [f. *sol* sun), after Gr. ἡλιοειδής.] Resembling the sun; sun-like. Also *absol.*

Eye never yet beheld the sun, that was not s. 1806.

‖ **Soliloquium** (sǫlilǭu·kwiǒm). Now rare. 1597. [L.] = SOLILOQUY.

Soliloquize (sǒli·lǒkwəiz), *v.* 1759. [f. SOLILOQUY + -IZE.] **1.** *intr.* To engage in soliloquy; to talk to oneself. **2.** *trans.* To utter, address or apostrophize in, soliloquy 1805. Hence **Soli·loquizer.**

Soliloquy (sǒli·lǒkwi). 1604. [ad. L. *soliloquium*, f. *soli-*, *solus* alone + *loqui* to speak.] **1.** An instance of talking to or conversing with oneself, or of uttering one's thoughts aloud without addressing any person. **b.** A literary production representing or imitating a discourse of this nature 1641. **2.** Without article: The act of talking to oneself; soliloquizing 1668.

1. b. The soliloquies of Hamlet..must have been lost upon the groundlings 1873. 2. He confounds s. and colloquy 1839. So **So·liloque** (*rare*).

Soliped (sǫ·liped), **-pede** (-pīd), *sb.* and *a.* 1646. [ad. med. or mod.L. *soliped-*, *solipes*, f. *soli-*, *solus* alone, only + *pes* foot, or alteration of L. *solidipes.*] **A.** *sb.* An animal having a whole or uncloven hoof. **B.** *adj.* Having a whole hoof; solid-hoofed 1656. So **Soli·pedal, Soli·pedous** *adjs.*

Solipsism (sǫ·lipsiz'm). 1881. [f. L. *solus* alone + *ipse* self.] *Metaph.* The view or theory that self is the only object of real knowledge or the only thing really existent. So **So·lipsist,** one who accepts this theory.

Solitaire (sǫ·litēəɪ, sǫlitē·ɪ). 1716. [a. F., or ad. L. *solitarius* SOLITARY *sb.* and *a.*] **1.** A person who lives in seclusion; a recluse. **2.** A precious stone, usually a diamond, set by itself. Also *ellipt.*, a solitaire ring. 1727. **3.** A game which can be played by one person: **a.** One of various card-games. **b.** A game played on a board with marbles or pegs, which have to be removed by jumping as in draughts. 1746. **4.** A loose neck-tie of black silk or broad ribbon worn by men in the 18th c. 1731. **5.** *Ornith.* **a.** A large flightless bird (*Pezophaps solitarius*) formerly existing in the island of Rodriguez 1797. **b.** A Jamaican bird (*Myiodectes solitarius*) 1847. **6.** *attrib.* Intended for one person only 1885.

2. I saw the evening star hanging like a s. from the ..western firmament 1886. 4. He ties a vast s. around his neck 1882. 6. A variety of..s. breakfast sets 1885.

Solitary (sǫ·litări), *sb.* late ME. [Subst. use of next.] **1. a.** One who retires into, or lives in, solitude from religious motives; a hermit or recluse. **b.** One who lives by himself in seclusion or retirement; one who avoids, or is deprived of, the society of others 1763. †**2.** = SOLITAIRE *sb.* 3. –1806.

1. b. Hardy pioneers, solitaries who had lived on far-off creeks 1898.

Solitary (sǫ·litări), *a.* ME. [ad. L. *solitarius*, f. *solus* alone.] **1.** Quite alone or unaccompanied; destitute or deprived of the society of others. **b.** Keeping apart from society; living alone. late ME. **c.** Standing alone or by itself; not accompanied or paralleled in any way 1633. **d.** With *a*, *one*, etc.: Single, sole 1742. **2.** Of places: Marked by solitude; remote, unfrequented, secluded, lonely. late ME. **3.** Characterized by the absence of all companionship or society. late ME. **4.** *Zool.* In names of various insects, birds, etc., which live alone or in pairs only 1600. **5.** *Bot.* Of parts or of plants: Growing singly or separately; not forming clusters or masses 1796.

1. I am made as sparow s. in þe hous HAMPOLE. He travels on, a s. Man; His age has no companion WORDSW. b. Those rare and solitarie, these in flocks Pasturing at once MILT. d. Poor moralist! and what art thou? A s. fly. GRAY. 2. He sodaynly turned into a s. wood next adioyning 1548. 3. Satan..toward the Gates of Hell Explores his s. flight MILT. 4. S. Sandpiper, *Tringa solitaria* 1813. *Scolopax major.* S. Snipe 1843. 5. Bearing..flowers in a peculiar spike, which is either s. or double 1807. Hence **So·litarily, -ness.**

Solitude (sǫ·litiūd). late ME. [a. OF., or ad. L. *solitudo*, f. *solus* alone.] **1.** The state of being or living alone; loneliness, seclusion, solitariness (of persons). †**b.** The fact of being sole or unique –1646. **2.** Loneliness (of places); remoteness from habitations; absence of life or stir 1585. **3.** A lonely, unfrequented, or uninhabited place 1570. **4.** A complete absence or lack (*rare*) 1605.

1. For sollitude best fits my cheereles mood KYD. b. Nor will the s. of the Phœnix allow this denomination, for many there are of that species SIR T. BROWNE. 2. The s. of the infinite sea 1873. 3. That busy scene was converted into a silent s. GIBBON. 4. Thomas Coventry.., who made a s. of children wherever he came LAMB. So **Solitudina·rian,** a recluse.

Solivagant (soli·văgănt), *a.* and *sb.* 1621. [f. L. *solivagus*, f. *solus* + *vagari* to wander; see -ANT.] **A.** *adj.* Wandering about alone; characterized by going alone 1641. **B.** *sb.* One who wanders about alone 1621. So **Soli·vagous** *a.* (*rare*).

Sollar (sǫ·lăɪ), *sb.* Also **solar.** [OE. *solor*, *soler-*, ad. L. *solarium*, f. *sol* sun.] **1.** An upper room or apartment in a house or other dwelling; in later use, a loft, attic, or garret (orig. one open to the sun). Now *arch.* or *dial.* **b.** An elevated chamber or loft in a church, in later use *spec.* in a steeple or belfry ME. **2.** *Cornish mining.* **a.** A platform in a mine, *esp.* one supporting a ladder 1778. **b.** A raised floor under which air is admitted to a working 1778. Hence **So·llar** *v. trans.* to furnish with a s.

Solleret (sǫ·ləret). Also **soleret(te.** 1826. [a. OF. *sol(l)eret*, dim. of *sol(l)er* (mod.F. *soulier*) shoe.] *Archæol.* A shoe composed of steel plates or scales, forming part of a knight's armour in the 14th and 15th centuries.

Solmization (sǫlmizē̆·ʃən). Also **solmisation.** 1730. [ad. F., f. *solmiser*, f. *sol* SOL[2] + *mi* MI.] The action or practice of solfaing. So **So·lmizate** *v.* to express by, or employ, s.

Solo (sǭu·lo), *sb.* and *a.* *Pl.* **solos** (also, as a musical direction, **soli**). 1695. [It., :—L. *solum*, *solus* SOLE *a.*] **A.** *sb.* **I. 1.** *Mus.* An instance of a song, melody, or other piece of music being rendered or performed by one singer or player; a piece of vocal or instrumental music performed, or intended for performance, by a single person. **2.** Performance by one singer or player 1779. **3.** A dance by one person 1794. **b.** *Aviation.* A solo flight 1920. **II.** *Cards.* Any of various games in which one player plays without a partner against the others; esp. in *s. whist*, in which a player undertakes to make five out of the thirteen tricks; also, the call made by such a player 1878.

Comb. **s. organ,** one of the divisions of a larger organ, for producing solo effects; so **s. stop.**

B. *adj.* **1.** Alone; without a companion or partner 1712. **2.** Made to accommodate one person 1774. **3.** Of musical instruments, or the players of these: Playing or taking the solo part 1880. **4.** *Aviation.* Alone, i.e. without an instructor or a mechanic 1914.

3. [He] was..s. euphonium 1901.

So·lo *v.*, to perform by oneself; to fly solo. **Soloist** (sǭu·loˌist), one who performs a solo; one who flies solo.

Solomon (sǫ·lǒmǫn). Also †**Salomon.** 1554. [The name of the Jewish king *Solomon*, ad. Heb. *Sh'lōmōh.*] One who resembles, or is comparable to, Solomon, esp. in respect of wisdom or justice; a sage; also ironically, a wiseacre.

British, *English*, or *Scotch S.*, King James VI of Scotland and I of England. Hence **Solomo·nic** *a.* ascribed to, originating with, S.; characteristic of S.

Solomon's seal. 1543. [tr. med.L. *sigillum Solomonis.*] **1.** A plant, *Polygonatum multiflorum*, the stems of which bear on the upper part broad sessile leaves and drooping green and white flowers. **2.** Applied to various other plants, as *Smilacina*, False Solomon's Seal, *Convallaria trifoliata*, Three-leaved Solomon's Seal 1760.

Solon (sǭu·lǫn). 1625. [a. L., Gr. Σόλων, the early Athenian legislator and one of the seven wise men of Greece.] A sage; a wiseacre. Hence **Solo·nian, Solo·nic** *adjs.*

So long: see LONG *adv.* 1.

‖ **Solpuga** (sǫlpiū·gă). 1601. [L., also *solipuga*, *solifuga.*] **1.** A venomous ant or spider mentioned by classical authors. **2.** *Ent.* A genus of tropical or semi-tropical spiders belonging to the group *Solpugidæ* or *Solifugæ*; a weasel-spider 1815. Hence **Solpugid** (sǫlpiū·dʒid), one of the *Solpugidæ.*

Solstice (sǫ·lstis). ME. [a. OF., ad. L. *solstitium.*] **1.** One or other of the two times in the year, midway between the two equinoxes, when the sun, having reached the tropical points, is farthest from the equator and appears to stand still, i.e. about 21st June (the summer s. of the northern hemisphere and winter s. of the southern) and 22nd December (the winter s. of the northern hemisphere and summer s. of the southern). **b.** *spec.* The summer solstice, or the heat of this 1643. **2.** A solstitial point 1601. **3.** *fig.* A turning, culminating, or stopping point; a farthest limit; a crisis 1631. **4.** *transf.* A standing still (*of* the sun). SIR T. BROWNE.

Solstitial (sǫlsti·ʃăl), *a.* and *sb.* 1559. [a. F. *solsticial* or ad. L. *solstitialis*, f. *solstitium*; see prec.] **A.** *adj.* **1.** Of or belonging to, connected with, a solstice or solstices. **2.** Occurring, taking place, etc., at the time of a solstice 1610. 3. Of heat, etc.: Characteristic of the summer solstice. Also as an epithet of the sun, etc., in this connexion. 1642. 4. †a. Of plants (after L. *solstitialis herba*): Coming up at the summer solstice; growing or fading rapidly –1783. b. Of insects, etc.: Appearing about the time of the summer solstice 1812. 5. Connected with the observation of the solstices 1834.

3. From the South to bring S. summers heat MILT.

†B. *sb.* A solstice (*rare*) –1612.

Solstitium (sǫlsti·ʃiŭm). *Pl.* **-ia.** 1515. [L., f. *sol* sun + ppl. stem of *sistere* to stand still.] = SOLSTICE.

Solubility (sǫliŭbi·lĭti). 1628. [f. next + -ITY.] 1. The quality or property of being soluble. 2. *Bot.* Capability of easy separation into parts 1832. 3. Capability of being solved or explained 1882.

1. The s. of salt in water 1794.

Soluble (sǫ·liŭb'l), *a.* late ME. [a. OF., ad. L. *solubilis*, f. *solvere* to loosen, dissolve, etc.] 1. *Med.* a. Of the bowels, etc.: Free from constipation or costiveness; relaxed. Now *rare* or *Obs.* †b. Laxative –1704. 2. Capable of being melted or dissolved. late ME. b. Dissolving, solvent (*rare*) 1846. 3. Capable of being untied or loosed (*rare*) 1613. 4. Capable of being solved or explained 1705. 5. Reducible *into* 1826.

1. a. Dry figges and old make the bodye s. 1539. 2. There results a soap which is s. in water 1794. 3. More s. is this knot, By gentleness than war TENNYSON. 4. Questions not very s. at present CARLYLE. Hence †**So·lubleness.**

‖ **Solus** (sōu·lǫs), *a.* 1599. [L.] Of male persons: Alone; by oneself. Also of females.

The Famous Blunder in an old Play of *Enter a King and two Fidlers S.* ADDISON.

Solute (sǒl·lū·t), *ppl. a.* 1440. [ad. L. *solutus*, *solvere* SOLVE *v.*] †1. Of loose open texture or composition –1653. †2. Of discourse: Free, loose, discursive –1680. †3. Relaxed, free from care. YOUNG. 4. *Bot.* Not adhering; separate 1760. 5. Dissolved; in a state of solution 1890. B. *sb.* A dissolved substance 1904.

2. A s. and lax discourse 1680. 3. A brow s., and ever-laughing eye 1742. Hence †**Solu·teness**, want of solidity.

†**Solu·te**, *v.* 1533. [f. L. *solut-*, *solvere* SOLVE *v.*] 1. *trans.* To solve, explain, clear up –1654. 2. To dissolve, nullify (*rare*) –1550.

1. Of the loosing or soluting of Fallacies 1654.

Solution (sǒlĭū·ʃən), *sb.* late ME. [a. OF., or ad. L. *solution-*, *solutio*, f. *solut-*, *solvere* SOLVE *v.*] I. 1. The action or process of solving; the state, condition, or fact of being solved. b. A particular instance or method of solving or settling; an explanation, answer, or decision. late ME. c. *Med.* The termination or crisis of a disease 1851. †2. The action of releasing or setting free; deliverance –1659. †3. The action of paying; a payment –1722.

1. A difficult problem of mixed law and fact for s. by the judges 1879. b. It provides a s. for every difficulty 1854.

II. 1. The action of dissolving, or changing from a solid or gaseous to a liquid state, by means of a fluid or solvent; the state or fact of being so dissolved. late ME. b. *transf.* Fusion, combination (*poet.*) *rare.* 1820. 2. A more or less fluid substance produced by the process of solution; a liquid or semi-liquid preparation obtained by the combination of a solid with a solvent 1594. 3. A dissolved state or condition. Freq. *state of s.* 1802.

1. Mechanical agitation facilitates s. 1800. b. The rose Blendeth its odour with the violet,—S. sweet KEATS. 2. A good solucion of salt in oile 1594. b. In full *rubber solution*: a liquid preparation of caoutchouc, used chiefly in repairing rubber tyres 1894.

III. 1. *S. of continuity*: a. *Med.* (Also *of connexion*, *of unity*.) The separation from each other of normally continuous parts of the body by external or internal causes 1541. b. *transf.* and *fig.* A breach, break, or interruption 1654. 2. The action of breaking up or separating; dissolution; bringing to an end 1655.

1. a. A Wound or S. of Continuity is worse then a Corrupt Humor BACON. b. Magnificent gradations of color, one fading into another without s. of continuity 1863. 2. Easie and frequent Solutions of Conjugal Society LOCKE. Hence **Solu·tion** *v. trans.* to treat with, fasten or secure by, a s.

†**Solu·tive**, *a.* and *sb.* 1564. [ad. med.L. *solutivus*, f. *solut-*, *solvere* SOLVE *v.*] A. *adj.* 1. Laxative, relaxing –1750. 2. Capable of releasing or setting free. EVELYN. 3. Capable of dissolving –1732. B. *sb.* 1. A laxative or purgative medicine –1674. 2. A solvent –1712.

Solvable (sǫ·lvăb'l), *a.* Also †**solvible.** 1647. [f. SOLVE *v.* + -ABLE, or a. F.] †1. Able to pay; solvent –1773. 2. Capable of being solved 1676. 3. Capable of being dissolved. Also *absol.* 1669. 4. Capable of being resolved *into* something 1804.

1. Imprisonment was imposed by law on persons not s. 1655. Hence **Solvabi·lity. So·lvableness.**

Solvate (sǫ·lveit), *sb.* 1910. [f. SOLVE *v.* + -ATE [1].] *Phys. Chem.* A compound of a dissolved substance with the solvent. So **So·lvate** *v. intr.* of a solute: to enter into combination with the solvent. **Solva·tion.**

Solve (sǫlv), *v.* 1440. [ad. L. *solvere.*] †1. *trans.* To loosen; to break –1450. 2. To explain, clear up, resolve, answer 1533. b. *Math.* To find the answer or solution to (a problem, etc.); to work out 1737. 3. To clear off; to pay or discharge 1558. 4. To dissolve, put an end to, settle 1667. 5. To dissolve; to melt. Now *rare.* 1662.

2. That Theban Monster that proposed Her riddle, and him, who solv'd it not, devour'd MILT. 3. Minos returned.. And solved his vows 1866. 4. *P.L.* VIII. 55. Hence **So·lver**, one who solves.

†**So·lvend.** 1738. [ad. L. *solvendum*, *solvere.*] Something to be dissolved –1867.

Solvent (sǫ·lvĕnt), *a.* and *sb.* 1653. [ad. L. *solvent-*, *solvens*, *solvere* SOLVE *v.*] A. *adj.* 1. Able to pay all one's debts or liabilities. 2. Dissolving; causing solution 1686. 3. Helping to solve or explain 1872.

1. *Comb.*: A s. looking gentleman, solus in a buggy, is the very thing for a highwayman 1852.

B. *sb.* 1. A substance (usually a liquid) having the power of dissolving other substances 1671. b. *fig.* A dissolving or disintegrating influence 1841. 2. Something which solves, explains, or settles 1865. 3. A laxative; a loosener 1815. 4. A person able to pay all his debts 1825.

1. Water..is found the most universal s. of the food of man and other animals 1756. 2. That only universal s., a cash payment 1890. 3. He took it [tobacco], he would say, as a s. of speech LAMB. Hence **So·lvency**, the state of being s. **So·lvently** *adv.*

‖ **Soma** [1] (sōu·mă). 1827. [Skr. *sōma.*] 1. An intoxicating drink holding a prominent place in Vedic ritual and religion. 2. *S. plant*, the plant (perh. *Asclepias acida* or *Sarcostemma viminale*) yielding the soma-juice. Also *ellipt.* 1827.

‖ **Soma** [2] (sōu·mă). 1889. [a. Gr. σῶμα body.] *Biol.* The body of an organism in contrast to the germ-cells. Also *attrib.* in *soma-plasm.* Hence **So·mal** *a.*

Somatic (somæ·tik), *a.* and *sb.* 1775. [ad. Gr. σωματικός, f. σωματ-, σῶμα body.] A. *adj.* 1. Of or pertaining to the (or a) body; bodily, corporeal, physical. b. *Anat.* and *Phys.* of parts of the body 1859. c. *spec.* Pertaining to the soma 1888. 2. Affecting the body 1835.

1. Motions and emotions, both . and psychical 1884. b. The termination of the s. nerves 1899. 2. Hypnotism could do nothing in s. affections 1899.

B. *sb. pl.* Somatology 1816. Hence **Soma·tical** *a.* corporeal, bodily, substantial; **-ly** *adv.*

Somatist (sōu·mătist). 1676. [f. Gr. σῶμα, σώματ- SOMA [2] + -IST.] †1. A materialist –1694. 2. *attrib.* Pertaining to, connected with, the soma 1908.

Somato- (sōu·măto), a. Gr. σωματο-, comb. form of σώματ-, σῶμα body (see SOMA [2]), as in **so·matocyst**, a sac forming the proximal end of the hydrosoma in oceanic hydrozoa; **so·matoplasm**, soma-plasm; **so·matopleure**, the upper (or outer) leaf of the blastoderm, as giving rise to the body-walls; **somatopleu·ric** *a.*, of or belonging to the somatopleure; **somato·tomy**, anatomy.

Somatology (sōumătǫ·lŏdʒi). 1736. [f. SOMATO- + -LOGY.] 1. A treatise or science dealing with the properties of bodies. 2. A treatise or science dealing with the human body in some respect 1851. Hence **So:matolo·gical** *a.*, **-ly** *adv.* **Somato·logist.**

Sombre (sǫ·mbəɹ), *a.* and *sb.* 1760. [a. F., app. f. *sombrer to shade :—pop. L. *subumbrare*, f. *sub* + *umbra* shade.] A. *adj.* 1. Of inanimate natural objects and their attributes: Characterized by the presence of gloom or shadow; depressingly dark, dusky, or obscure. 2. Of persons, etc.: Gloomy, lowering, dark and sullen or dejected 1767. b. Of thoughts, feelings, etc.: Melancholy, dismal, darksome 1821. 3. Conveying gloomy ideas or suggestions 1768. 4. Of colours or colouring: Of a dark shade or tinge; dark, dull 1805. b. Of things in respect of colour 1829.

1. This coast..dark, gloomy, and silent;—a savage s. air spread over the whole YOUNG. 2. The man.. was a s. ill-looking fellow 1865. b. In s. mood 1821. 4. b. A s. garb was worn by the nuns 1872.

B. *sb.* Sombre character; sombreness (*rare*) 1795. Hence **So·mbre·ly** *adv.*, **-ness.**

Sombre (sǫ·mbəɹ), *v.* 1787. [f. SOMBRE *a.*] To make, or become, sombre.

Day again had sombred into night 1893.

‖ **Sombrero** (sǫmbrēə·ro). 1598. [Sp., f. *sombra* shade.] †1. An Oriental umbrella or parasol –1727. 2. A broad-brimmed hat, usually of felt or some soft material, of a type common in Spain and Spanish America 1770.

Sombrous (sǫ·mbrəs), *a.* 1730. [ad. F. *sombreux*, app. f. *sombrer (see SOMBRE *a.*).] Sombre.

Where..the s. pine And yew-tree o'er the..rocks recline WORDSW. Hence **So·mbrous·ly** *adv.*, **-ness.**

Some (svm), *indef. pron.*, *a.*, *adv.*, and *sb.* [Com. Teut.: OE. *sum*, = OFris. *sum*, MDu. *som*, *zom*; the stem is also found in Gr. ἀμο- (as ἀμόθεν from some place), and Skr. *sama* any, every.] A. *indef. pron.* I. In sing. uses. †1. One or other of a number of persons; some one, somebody. In later use also in phr. *s. or other.* –1729. 2. A certain indeterminate part of something; a portion. Also *s...., s.* OE.

1. Whan somme good cometh to somme, it ought not to be reffused CAXTON. S. or other hath abused him in this Letter 1664. Phr. *S. of these* (..) *days*, some day soon; before very long. 2. Bate me s., and I will pay you s. SHAKS. S. of it, much of it, has ceased to be alive for us now 1872.

II. In pl. senses. 1. An indefinite or unspecified (but not large) number of persons, animals or things; certain persons not named or enumerated OE. 2. *S....*, *s.*, = Some..., others OE. b. So *S....*, *others* (†*other*) OE. †3. *S. and s.*, a few at a time, gradually –1769.

1. And the while he soweth, sum felden byside the weye WYCLIF *Matt.* xiii. 4. Neuer was Woolfe seene, many nor s. SPENSER. 2. S. are gold, s. silver 1750. b. S. have a smacke of Christ, others of Mahomet 1634. 3. The swallow kind disappear s. and s., gradually, as they come 1769.

B. *adj.* I. With sing. nouns. †1. A certain (person or place) –1578. 2. One or other; an undetermined or unspecified OE. †3. Used with an indefinite or generalizing force similar to that of the plural –1638. 4. A certain (unspecified) amount, part, degree, or extent of (something), freq. implying 'not little, considerable' OE. b. With adjs., as *little*, *small*, *considerable*, etc. late ME. c. *U.S.* Of some account; deserving of consideration (cf. PUMPKIN 2 b) 1848. 5. *S. other* (see OTHER *a.* 5 b) OE. 6. Followed by *certain* or *one* with limiting force 1561.

2. He hopis sum day to see his sone 1550. Som neighbour Wood-man, or..Som roaving Robber MILT. He must write s. day or other 1881. 4. 'Twixt which Regions There is s. space SHAKS. Where he feathered his nest to s. purpose MARVELL. b. S. brief time hence SCOTT. c. She 's 's.' now, that is a fact 1848. d. In attrib. use: Such in the fullest sense, 'something like a', worthy of the name (*U.S.* and *slang*) 1914. 5. Sette scolers to scole or to sum oþer craft LANGL. 6. In s. one Excellence their Merit lies 1746.

II. With pl. nouns. 1. Certain (taken individually) OE. 2. A certain number of; a few at least ME. 3. Used with numbers to indicate an approximate amount or estimate, and passing into an adv. with the sense 'about, nearly, approximately' OE. b. With numerals denoting the time of day 1596. c. Hence with singular nouns expressing time, distance, etc. 1592.

1. S. certaine dregges of conscience are yet within mee SHAKS. 2. S. flaggons of rich wine, s. very white bisket, s. pruines and raisins 1617. For s. few gasping moments KEATS. 3. I have s. three hundred pistoles by me DRYDEN. b. 'Tis now s. seuen a clocke SHAKS. c. S. halfe musket shot distance 1617.

III. With *other*, *one*, *few*, etc., used absol. in sing. or pl. OE.

S. certaine of the Noblest minded Romans SHAKS.

C. *adv.* 1. With comparatives: A little; slightly; somewhat. Chiefly *Sc.* and *north.* 1560. 2. With vbs.: a. A certain amount; a little 1699. b. *U.S.* To some extent; in some degree; somewhat 1825. c. *U.S.* In emphatic use: Very much, very well 1866. 3. *dial.* and *U.S.* With adjs.: Somewhat 1817.

2. a. I hunt s., and snake a little 1834. c. Thet night, I tell ye, she looked *some*! 1866. 3. His clothes were s. bloody 1817.

D. *sb.* An unspecified amount, person, thing, etc. (*rare*) 1830.

-some, *suffix* 1, repr. OE. *-sum,* = OFris. *-sum,* related by ablaut to OS. and OHG. *-sam* (G. *-sam*), etc., used to form adjs. from nouns and adjs., as *fulsome, gladsome, loathsome, winsome,* rarely from verbs, as *tiresome, wearisome,* etc. (cf. BUXOM).

-some, *suffix* 2, repr. OE. *sum* after numerals in the genitive pl. In ME. the inflexion disappeared, and the pronoun was finally treated as a suffix to the numeral, chiefly with the simple numbers from two to ten. See TWOSOME, THREESOME, etc.

-some, *suffix* 3, later variant of *-sum,* repr. Scand. *sum, som,* as in †*whosome* (= whoever); cf. SOMEVER.

Somebody (sʊ·mbǫdi). Also †**some body.** ME. [f. SOME *a.* + BODY *sb.*] 1. A person unknown, indeterminate, or unnamed; some one, some person. b. Used as a substitute for a personal name 1825. 2. A person of some note, consequence, or importance. Freq. *depreciatory* or *sarcastic.* 1566. b. With *a* and *pl.* 1601. 3. A person whose name is intentionally suppressed; occas., the Devil 1606.

1. I heard some body at a Distance hemming after me ADDISON. *S. else,* some other person. b. General S. ordered him to bring up his guns 1842. 2. A desire to be s...seems to be the rule of his life 1704. b. People who are somebodies MARRYAT. 3. There is a deeper impression of Somebody's Hoof here DICKENS.

Somedeal (sʊ·mˌdīl), *sb.* and *adv.* Now *arch.* or *dial.* [OE., f. *sum* SOME *a.* + *dæl* DEAL *sb.*[1]] A. *sb.* Some part or portion *of* some thing or things; some, somewhat.

Somdeale of our birth our countrey, somedeale our parentes..do claime 1553.

B. *adv.* In some degree or measure; to some extent; somewhat; partly OE.

I doubte not..but that it doth some deal vexe you 1533.

Somehow (sʊ·mhau), *adv.* 1664. [f. SOME *a.* + HOW *adv.*] 1. In some manner or by some means not understood or defined; one way or another; someway 1740. 2. In phr. *S. or other, or another* 1664.

1. Somewhere, s., there was a fault BYRON. 2. We contrived at last, s. or other, to agree 1875.

Some one, someone (sʊ·mwʊn), *pron.* (and *sb.*). ME. [f. SOME *a.* + ONE.] Some person, somebody.

Some one intent on mischief MILT.

Somersault (sʊ·məɪsǫlt), *sb.* Also †**-saut.** 1530. [ad. OF. *sombresaut, -sault,* alteration of *soubresault,* f. L. *supra* above + *saltus* leap.] A leap or spring in which a person turns heels over head in the air and alights on his feet; esp. such a feat as performed by acrobats or tumblers; a pitchpoll. Hence, a turning over in this fashion; a complete overturn, upset, etc.

fig. The summersaults, spells, and resurrections wrought by the imagination EMERSON. Hence **So·mersault** *v. intr.* to make or turn a s.

Somerset (sʊ·məɪset), *sb.* 1591. [Alteration or corruption of *somersaut*; see prec.] = prec. Hence **So·merset** *v. intr.* to somersault; *trans.* to cause (a person) to turn a somersault.

Something (sʊ·mþiŋ), *sb.*, (*adj.*,) and *adv.* OE. [f. SOME *a.* + THING *sb.*[1] Orig. written as two words.] A. *sb.* 1. Some unspecified or indeterminate thing (material or immaterial). b. Used as a substitute for a name or part of one, or other particular, which is not remembered or is immaterial, etc. 1764. c. Some liquor, drink, or food; esp. in phr. *to take s.* 1778. d. Used (with *between*) to denote an intermediate stage or grade 1821. e. Used to denote an undefined or unknown occupation, or a person in respect of this 1874. 2. A certain part, portion, amount, or share (*of* some thing, quality, etc.); freq. a small part or amount, a slight trace ME. 3. Followed by an adj. (see below). late ME. 4. In more emphatic use: A thing, fact, person, etc., of some value, consideration or regard 1582. 5. As *adj.* Used euphemistically for 'damned' or other expletive 1859.

1. Yet s. must be done for examples sake 1638. *S. like,* see LIKE A. 2. *S. or other,* one thing or another; anything whatever; a thing which it is unnecessary to specify. *Or s.,* vague addition to a word or phrase = 'or the like'. b. Lady S. Grey is here 1764. e. The restless gentlemen who are 's. in the city', but no one knows what 1886. 2. S. of the tone, and manners, and feeling of a gentleman SCOTT. *S. of a(n,* to a certain extent or degree a (person or thing of the kind specified). 3. Slang or colloq. phr. *S. damp* or *short,* a drink; spirits. *S. good,* a good racing tip. 4. *S. in the wind*: see WIND *sb.* *There's s. in it,* etc. *To make s. of,* to make important or useful; to improve in some way; to succeed in utilizing to some extent. 5. It's the somethingest robbery I ever saw in my life 1859.

B. *adv.* In some degree; to some extent; somewhat; rather, a little ME.

Conies..s. resemble a wilde Cat 1634. Our Guide being s. before us DE FOE. Sir George is s. nervous 1791. 'O!' said I, s. snappishly DICKENS. Now this song..is s. less than just to me STEVENSON. Hence **So·mething** *v. trans.* used *colloq.* in pa. pple. as a euphemism for 'damned' or the like. **So·methingness,** the fact or state of being s.; entity. **Somethingth** (sʊ·mþiŋþ) *a.* used to supply the place of an ordinal number which is not remembered or is immaterial.

Sometime (sʊ·mtəim), *adv.* (and *a.*). ME. [f. SOME *a.* + TIME *sb.*] 1. At one time or another, with the possibility of recurrence; now and then; occasionally. Now *rare* or *Obs.* 2. †a. At a certain time in the past; once –1661. b. At one time; in former times, formerly ME. 3. At some future time; on a future occasion. Also in phr. *s. or other.* late ME. 4. At some indefinite or indeterminate point of time; at some time or other 1590. 5. With *since,* = some time ago (*rare*) 1700.

1. My heart is s. heavy, when I smile 1622. 2. a. Let the power speak, which s. said, 'Lazarus arise!' 1653. b. Of Inde Somtyme ther was a nobyll kyng 1440. Our s. constable, the tipsiest..of men 1824. 3. You may s. or other come to Bath BERKELEY. *attrib.* The s. resurrection of the body 1805. 4. It was s. in the 11th century SOUTHEY.

Sometimes (sʊ·mtəimz), *adv.* 1526. [f. SOME *a.* + *times* pl. of TIME *sb.*] 1. On some occasions; at times; now and then. 2. = SOMETIME 2 a, b –1665. †3. *At s.,* = sense 1. –1719.

1. Hither s. the King repaires 1634. Somtimes sighingly, and somtimes comfortably BUNYAN. S. The Devil is a gentleman; At others a bard SHELLEY. 2. Farewell old Gaunt, thy s. brothers wife..must end her life SHAKS.

†**Some·ver,** *adv.* 1440. [f. ME. *sum* (Scand. *sum, som* rel. adv.) + EVER *adv.*] = SOEVER 2; cf. dial. *whatsomever,* etc.

Someway (sʊ·mweⁱ), *adv.* Now *rare* exc. *dial.* Also **some way.** 1450. [f. SOME *a.* + WAY *sb.*] 1. In some way or manner; by some means; somehow. 2. At some distance. Also *transf.* of time. (Usu. as two words.) 1859.

1. We s. think that contentment is to feel no want 1890. So **Someways** (sʊ·mweⁱz) *adv.* (in sense 1); now chiefly *dial.* 1440.

Somewhat (sʊ·mhwǫt), *sb.* and *adv.* ME. [f. SOME *a.* + WHAT *pron.* Freq. written as two words down to the end of the 16th c.] = SOMETHING *sb.* and *adv.* A. *sb.* 1. A certain amount, esp. in the way of statement, information, etc. Freq. with *of* (= concerning). Now *arch.* b. Some (material or immaterial) thing of unspecified nature, amount, etc. Now *arch.* or *dial.* ME. 2. With dependent genitive: Some part, portion, amount, etc., *of* something ME. b. *S. of a(n, = something of a(n* (see SOMETHING A. 2.) 1841. 3. A thing, quality, etc., worth considering; a person of importance. late ME. 4. With *a, the,* etc., and *pl.* A certain undefined or unknown thing, quality, amount, etc. 1598.

1. It is strange, how long some Men will lie in wait, to speake s., they desire to say BACON. b. He's.. turned miser, or s. 1855. 2. By quitting s. of his royal prerogative HUME. 3. The fool is a handsome fool, that's s. DRYDEN. 4. Thus achievement lacks a gracious s. BROWNING.

B. *adv.* In a certain degree or measure; to some (slight or small) extent; slightly, a little; rather ME.

Ye be diligent To forthren me somwhat in my labour CHAUCER. His vtterance was somewhat vnready 1595. Tell me.., in s. plainer terms, what you mean! 1875.

Somewhen (sʊ·mhwen), *adv.* ME. In mod. use casual and freq. jocular. [f. SOME *a.* + WHEN *adv.*] At some (indefinite or unknown) time; sometime or other.

Somewhere (sʊ·mhwēᵊɪ), *adv.* and *sb.* ME. [f. SOME *a.* + WHERE *adv.*] A. *adv.* 1. In or at some place unspecified, indeterminate, or unknown. 2. To some (unspecified or unknown) place. Usu. with *go.* late ME. 3. In some part or passage of a book, etc.; in some work or other 1634. 4. a. At some time *about* or *in* (a certain specified year, date, etc.) 1839. b. *S. about,* approximately 1846.

1. What malicious Foe..somwhere nigh at hand Watches MILT. 3. As some one s. sings about the sky BYRON. 4. b. S. about two months 1846.

B. *sb.* Some unspecified or indefinite place 1647. So **So·mewheres** *adv.* (*dial.* or *vulgar*).

Somewhile (sʊ·mhwəil), *adv.* Now *rare.* ME. [f. SOME *a.* + WHILE *sb.*] 1. †a. At or in some former time; formerly –1654. b. *attrib.* or *adj.* Former, sometime 1860. †2. Once; at one time –1631. 3. At some (unspecified) time; at one time or other; at times, sometimes ME.

1. b. Richard Doyle, s. illustrator of *Punch* 1888. 3. Tho vnder colour of shepeheards, s. There crept in Wolues, ful of fraude and guile SPENSER. So **So·mewhiles** (*dial.* or *arch.*) ME.

Somewhither (sʊ·mhwiːðəɪ), *adv.* late ME. [f. SOME *a.* + WHITHER *adv.*] 1. In some direction. 2. To some place 1530.

2. Like ghosts waiting for Charon to take them s. 1877.

Somewise (sʊ·mwəiz), *adv.* Now *arch.* 1440. [f. SOME *a.*; see -WISE.] In some way or manner; to some extent. In recent use with *in.*

I..knew In s. he was well awake SWINBURNE.

Somite (sōᵘ·məit). 1869. [f. Gr. σῶμα body, SOMA [2] + -ITE.] *Zool.* One or other of the more or less distinct segments into which the bodies of many animals are divided. Hence **So·mital, Somi·tic** *adjs.* of or pertaining to, having the form or character of, a s.

Somn-, comb. form of L. *somnus,* used in words based on L. *ambulare* to walk. **Somna·mbulance,** sleep-walking. **Somna·mbulant** *a.,* walking in sleep; *sb.,* a somnambulist. **Somna·mbular** *a.,* of or pertaining to sleep-walking; also *erron.,* connected with, of the nature of, sleep. **Somna·mbulate** *v. intr.,* to walk during sleep; *trans.,* to walk along (a place) while asleep. **Somna·mbula·tion,** the action or fact of walking in sleep. **Somna·mbulator,** = next. **Somna·mbule** [a. F.], a somnambulist. **Somna·mbulic** *a.,* of the nature of or pertaining to somnambulism; walking during sleep. **Somna·mbulism,** the fact or habit of walking about and performing other actions while asleep; sleep-walking. **Somna·mbulist,** one who walks, etc., while asleep; **Somna·mbuli·stic** *a.,* somnambulic.

†**Somne,** *v.* ME. [var. of *somony,* etc., SUMMON *v.*] *trans.* To summon –1530.

†**So·mner.** ME. [f. *somene* SOMNE *v.*] An official summoner –1608.

Somni-, comb. form of L. *somnus* sleep, occurring in a number of L. compounds, as *somnifer, somnificus,* and in English adaptations or imitations of these.

Somni·loquence, = *somniloquy.* **Somni·loquent** *a.,* talking in sleep. **Somni·loquism,** = *somniloquy.* **Somni·loquist,** one who speaks or talks while asleep. **Somni·loquous** *a.* apt to talk in sleep. **Somni·loquy,** the act or habit of speaking during sleep. **Somni·pathy,** sleep induced by mesmerism. **Somni·pathist,** a person in a state of somnipathy.

Somnial (sǫ·mnial), *a. rare.* 1693. [a. obs. F., or ad. L. *somnialis,* f. *somnium* dream.] Of or relating to dreams.

The S. magic superinduced on..the active powers of the mind COLERIDGE.

†**So·mniate,** *v.* 1657. [f. L. *somniat-, somniare,* f. *somnium* dream.] 1. *trans.* To dream (something). †2. To stupefy, make drowsy. DE FOE. Hence †**So·mniative** *a.* relating to, or producing, dreams. †**So·mniatory** *a.* of or pertaining to dreams or dreaming (*rare*).

Somni·culous, *a. rare.* 1656. [ad. L.

somniculosus, f. *somnus* sleep.] **a.** Drowsy, sleepy. **b.** Inducing sleep.

Somniferous (sǫmni·fĕrəs), *a.* 1602. [f. L. *somnifer* (f. *somni-* + *-ferre* to bring) + -OUS.] **1.** Inducing sleep; soporific. **2.** Somnolent 1798.

1. The wine had exerted its s. influence DICKENS.

Somnific (sǫmni·fik), *a.* 1721. [ad. L. *somnificus*.] Causing sleep; somniferous.

Somnolence (sǫ·mnŏlĕns). late ME. [a. OF. *sompnolence* (mod.F. *somnolence*), or ad. L. *somnolentia*, f. *somnolentus*; see next.] Inclination to sleep; sleepiness, drowsiness. So **So·mnolency.**

Somnolent (sǫ·mnŏlĕnt), *a.* 1475. [a. OF. *sompnolent* or ad. L. *somnolentus*, f. *somnus* sleep.] **1.** Tending to cause sleepiness or drowsiness; inclining to sleep. **b.** Marked by sleepiness or slowness 1812. **2.** Of persons: Inclined to sleep; drowsy. Also *transf.* 1547.

1. b. He served me well in his own s. fashion 1877. Hence **So·mnolently** *adv.* sleepily.

‖ **Somnus** (sǫ·mnŏs). 1599. [L., sleep, also personified as a divinity.] The god of sleep.

†**Sompnour.** late ME. Variant of SOMNER. –1555.

Son (sɒn). [Com. Teut.; OE. *sunu*. The root *su-* is identical with that of Gr. *υἱός*.] **1.** A male child or person in relation to either or both of his parents. Sometimes said of animals. **b.** = SON-IN-LAW 1533. **2.** *Theol.* The second person of the Trinity OE. **3.** One who is regarded as, or takes the place of, a son OE. **b.** Used as a term of affectionate address to a man or boy by an older person or by one in a superior (esp. ecclesiastical) relation OE. **4.** *S. of God* **a.** Jesus Christ OE. **b.** A divine being; an angel. late ME. **c.** One spiritually attached to God OE. **5.** *S. of man*: **a.** One of the human race; a mortal OE. **b.** *spec.* Jesus Christ OE. **6.** A male descendant *of* some person or representative *of* some race OE. **b.** One who inherits the spirit, or displays the character, *of* some person, etc. late ME. **c.** A member or adherent of a religious body or order, or a follower of the founder of one. late ME. **7. a.** One who is characterized by the presence, possession, influence, use, etc., *of* some quality or thing OE. **b.** A person regarded as the product or offspring *of* a certain country or place 1595. **c.** In terms of abuse or contempt. (See GUN *sb.*, WHORE *sb.*)

1. Lord Colchester, s. to the earl of Rivers 1764. Phr. *S. and heir.* 2. We seeme more inwardly to knowe the Sonne 1628. 3. For thy children dead I'll be a s. to thee! WORDSW. b. 'Prove thy strength, my s., in the name of God!' said the preacher SCOTT. 4. a. Beyond compare the S. of God was seen Most glorious MILT. b. The Angels..are the Sons of God by temporal Creation 1643. 5. a. Deciduous Forests that die and are born again..like the sons of men CARLYLE. b. Shall the stones cry out..that they are the only pillows where the S. of Man can lay His head? RUSKIN. 6. Adams sonnes are my brethren SHAKS. b. Thay were the sones of Belial, that is, the devel CHAUCER. 7. a. Certain Sons of Parchment, call'd Solicitors and Barristers 1700. b. We, the sonnes and children of this Isle SHAKS. *fig.* Easie..thou s. of night, Pass by his troubled senses FLETCHER. *S. of the soil.* see SOIL *sb.*[1] Hence **So·nhood** = SONSHIP.

Sonance (sōᵘ·năns). 1599. [f. L. *sonare* to sound + -ANCE.] Sound; quality of sounding.

Let the Trumpets sound The Tucket Sonuance SHAKS.

Sonant (sōᵘ·nănt), *a.* and *sb.* 1846. [ad. L. *sonant-*, *sonans*, *sonare*.] *Phonetics.* **A.** *adj.* Uttered with voice or vocal sound; voiced.

Final *a* is changed to *o* before all s. consonants 1846.

B. *sb.* A sonant articulation or letter 1875.

Hence **Sonantal** (sōᵘnæ·ntăl) *a.*

Sonata (sŏnā·tă). 1694. [It., fem. pa. pple. of *sonare* to sound.] †**1.** A musical composition for instruments (opp. to a *cantata*). **2.** An instrumental piece of music, usually for the pianoforte, in several (commonly three or four) movements 1801. **b.** Without article: The class of music represented by sonatas 1883.

2. *Double s.*, a s. for two solo instruments, as pianoforte and violin, or two pianofortes 1880.

Sonatina (sǫnătī·nă). 1801. [It., dim. of prec.] A short, simple form of sonata.

Song (sǫŋ). [Com. Teut.; OE. *sang*, *sǫng* :—OTeut. *sangwoz, f. ablaut-var. of stem of *singwan SING *v.*[1]] **1.** The act (†or art) of singing; the result or effect of this, vocal music; that which is sung (in general or collective sense). **b.** The musical utterance of birds OE. **c.** *transf.* A sound as of singing 1822. **2.** A poem, lay; also *gen.* poetry, poetical composition. Now *arch.* OE. **3.** A metrical composition adapted for singing, esp. one having a regular verse-form; such a composition as actually sung OE. **b.** A musical setting or composition of the character of or suggestive of a song, e.g. Mendelssohn's 'Songs without Words' 1871. **4.** *transf.* and *fig.* OE. **b.** A fuss or outcry *about* something 1843. **5.** Used to denote a very small sum, amount, or value, or a thing of little worth or importance 1601.

1. The world is full of s.! 1878. b. The night-warbling Bird, that now awake Tunes sweetest his love-labor'd s. MILT. 2. Our sweetest songs are those that tell of saddest thought SHELLEY. *The S. of Solomon, S. of Songs*, one of the books of the O.T. 3. We'll hear that s. again SHAKS. My Book of Songs SHAKS. 4. Out on ye, Owles, nothing but Songs of Death SHAKS. Phr. *To change one's s., sing another* (or *a different*) *s.*, to 'change one's tune'. b. She had foreborne likewise and no one made a s. about it 1863. 5. They were acquired 'for an old s.' 1889.

Comb.: **s.-box**, the syrinx of a bird; **-form** *Mus.*, the simplest form of instrumental composition, consisting of one or more melodic themes as in a vocal song; **-grosbeak**, one or other species of the American genus *Zamelodia*; **-sparrow**, a common North American bird of the genus *Melospiza*, esp. *M. fasciata* (or *melodia*) and *cinerea*; **-thrush**, the common thrush (*Turdus musicus*). Hence **So·ngful** *a.* abounding in s.; musical, melodious. **So·ngless** *a.* devoid of s.; not singing; (of birds) lacking the power of s.

So·ng-bird. 1774. [SONG.] A bird having the power of song; a singing-bird.

So·ng-book. OE. **1.** A book of hours with music. *Hist.* **2.** A book of songs 1489.

So·ng-school. 1537. A school devoted to the teaching of singing or the practising of vocal music.

So·ng-smith. 1795. [SONG.] A composer or maker of songs. Also as a book-title.

Songster (sǫ·ŋstəɹ). OE. [See SONG *sb.* and -STER.] **1.** One who sings, a singer; orig. a female singer, a songstress. **2.** A poet; a writer of songs or verse 1585. **3.** A bird that sings; a song-bird 1700. Hence **So·ngstress**, (*a*) a female singer; a poetess; (*b*) a female singing-bird.

Soniferous (sǫni·fĕrəs), *a.* 1713. [f. L. *soni-*, comb. form of *sonus* sound + -FEROUS.] Sound-bearing; conveying or producing sound.

Son-in-law (sɒ·nˌinˌlǭ). ME. [SON and LAW *sb.*[1]] A daughter's husband.

How should you like him for a s.? 1811.

Sonless (sɒ·nlĕs), *a.* late ME. Having no son; destitute of a son or sons.

Sonlike (sɒ·nləik), *a.* 1583. [f. SON.] Resembling that of a son; filial.

Sonnet (sǫ·nĕt), *sb.* 1557. [a. F., or ad. It. *sonetto*, dim. of *suono* sound.] **1.** A piece of verse (properly expressive of one main idea) consisting of fourteen decasyllabic lines, with rhymes arranged according to one or other of certain definite schemes. **2.** A short poem or piece of verse; in early use esp. one of a lyrical or amatory character. Now *rare* or *Obs.* 1563.

1. He is a fool which cannot make one S., and he is mad which makes two DONNE. 2. Some thinke that all Poemes (being short) may be called Sonets GASCOIGNE.

Sonnet (sǫ·nĕt), *v.* 1589. [f. prec.] **1.** *intr.* To compose sonnets; to sonnetize. **2.** *trans.* To celebrate in a sonnet or sonnets 1598.

1. Come, now, you're sonnetting again TENNYSON.

Sonneteer (sǫnĕtī°·ɹ), *sb.* Also **sonnetteer.** 1665. [ad. It. *sonettiere* (f. *sonetto*), or f. SONNET *sb.* + -EER.] A composer of sonnets; freq. in disparaging sense, a minor or indifferent poet.

Our little Sonnettiers..have too narrow Souls to judge of Poetry DRYDEN. Hence **Sonnetee·r**, **Sonnettee·r** *v. trans.* to celebrate in sonnets; *intr.* to compose sonnets.

Sonnetize (sǫ·nĕtəiz), *v.* 1798. [f. SONNET *sb.*] **1.** *intr.* To compose a sonnet or sonnets. **2.** *trans.* To celebrate in a sonnet or sonnets 1799.

Sonny (sɒ·ni). *colloq.* Also **sonnie.** 1870. [f. SON *sb.* + -Y [6].] A familiar term of address to a boy or to a man younger than the speaker.

Sonometer (sonǫ·mĭtəɹ). 1808. [f. *sono-*, used as comb. form of L. *sonus* sound + -METER.] **1.** An instrument for determining the number of vibrations made by a sonorous cord. **2.** An instrument for testing the sense of hearing 1849. **3.** *Electr.* A telephone attached to an apparatus for testing metals by means of an induction-coil 1879.

Sonority (sŏnōᵊ·rĭti, sŏnǫ·rĭti). 1623. [a. F. *sonorité*, or ad. L. *sonoritas*, f. *sonorus*; see -ITY.] The quality of being sonorous.

The richness and s. of his [Milton's] language 1876.

Sonorous (sŏnōᵊ·rəs, sǫ·nŏrəs), *a.* 1611. [f. L. *sonorus*, f. *sonor*, *sonoris* sound; see -OUS.] **1.** Of things: Giving out, or capable of giving out, a sound, esp. of a deep or ringing character. **b.** Of places, etc.: Resounding, roaring, noisy 1729. **2.** Of sounds: Having a loud, deep, or resonant character 1668. **3.** Of language, diction, etc.: Having a full, rich sound; strong and harmonious 1693. **b.** Of persons: Having a full and rich style or voice 1728.

1. S. mettal blowing Martial sounds MILT. b. The s. Shore 1729. 2. Nestor, brave Gerenian, with a voice S. COWPER. S. vibrations convey the sensation of sound to the ear 1839. 3. The Italian Opera..has something beautiful and s. in the Expression ADDISON. b. Santerre, the s. Brewer of the Suburb Saint-Antoine CARLYLE. Hence **Sonorous·ly** *adv.*, **-ness.**

Sonship (sɒ·nʃip). 1587. [f. SON + -SHIP.] The position, state, or relation of a son.

Sonsy (sǫ·nsi), *a.* orig. *Sc.*, *Ir.*, and *n. dial.* 1533. [f. *sonse*, ad. Gael. *sonas* good fortune, etc.] **1.** Bringing luck; lucky, fortunate. **2.** Plump, buxom, comely and pleasant; comfortable-looking, etc. 1725. **3.** Of animals: Tractable, manageable 1786.

2. Twa s. lasses, young and fair 1725. Trousers of s. grey homespun 1870.

‖ **Soojee** (sū·dʒī). Also **-y, -ie.** 1810. [Hindi *sūjī*.] A flour obtained by grinding Indian wheat; a nutritious food prepared from this.

Soon (sūn), *adv.* [OE. *sōna*, = OFris. *sôn*, OS. *sâno*.] **1.** Within a short time (after a particular point of time specified or implied), before long, quickly; without delay, forthwith, straightway. **2.** Early, betimes; before the time specified or referred to is much advanced ME. **b.** At an early stage, date, period 1615. **3.** *So s.*, so quickly, so early ME. **4.** *As* or *so s. as*: **a.** At the very time or moment when, whenever ME. **b.** As quickly, as early (as). 1548. **c.** As readily, as willingly, (as) 1590. **d.** With as much reason or probability 1591.

1. Small lights are s. blown out, huge fires abide SHAKS. S. I must drink the poison 1875. S. afterwards a direct charge of plagiarism was made 1875. 2. I went s. To bedde CHAUCER. Late and s., Getting and spending, we lay waste our powers WORDSW. 3. What, all so soone asleepe? SHAKS. 4. a. This Law..fell into disuse as soon as made 1710. c. For he'll abuse a stranger just as s. as his best friend SHERIDAN. d. *Two Gent.* II. vii. 19. Hence **Soo·nness.**

Soon (sūn), *a.* late ME. [attrib. use of prec.] Taking place, coming about, happening, etc., soon or quickly; early, speedy.

Soone sowing sometime deceaveth 1546.

Sooner (sū·nəɹ), *adv.* ME. [comp. of SOON *adv.*] Earlier, more readily; preferably, rather (1457). So **Soo·nest** superl. ME.

Phr. *Sooner or later*, at some time or other (usu. with ref. to the future). *With the soonest*: †**a.** Rather, or very, early. †**b.** As soon as possible. **c.** *dial.* Too soon. *At* (*the*) *soonest*, at the earliest.

Soot (sut), *sb.*[1] [OE. *sót*, = ON., Icel. *sót*, related to Lith. *súdis*.] **1.** A black carbonaceous substance or deposit consisting of fine particles formed by the combustion of coal, wood, oil, or other fuel. **2.** With *a* and *pl.* **a.** A particular kind of soot 1601. **b.** A flake of soot; a smut 1906.

1. *fig.* Al sugre and hony, al minstralsy..ben but s. and galle in comparison T. USK.

†**Soot**, *a.*, *sb.*[2] and *adv.* [OE. *swót*, var. of *swéte* SWEET *a.*, infl. by *swóte* adv.] Sweet –1614.

1. As þe fayre and swoote rose spryngeth amonge þe thornes 1430.

B. *sb.* That which is sweet; a person of sweet disposition –1682. **C.** *adv.* Sweetly –1579.

Soot (sut), *v.* 1602. [f. SOOT *sb.*[1]] **1.** *trans.* To smear, smudge, or foul with soot; to cover with or as with soot. 2. To sprinkle or manure with soot 1707.

2. Part was dunged; part, sooted 1778.

Sooterkin (sū·təɹkin). Now *rare*. 1530. [In sense 1 app. ad. early Du. or Flem. **soetekijn*, f. *soet* sweet. In sense 2 perh. f. SOOT *sb.*[1]] †1. Sweetheart, mistress. 2. An imaginary kind of afterbirth formerly attributed to Dutch women 1658. b. *transf.* Applied to persons; sometimes = Dutchman 1680. c. Applied to literary compositions, etc., of a supplementary or imperfect character 1668.

2. There goes a Report of the Holland Women, that together with their Children, they are delivered of a S., not unlike to a Rat, which some imagine to be the Off-spring of the Stoves 1658. c. Fruits of dull Heat, and Sooterkins of Wit POPE.

Sooth (sūþ), *sb. arch.* [OE. *sōð*, f. the adj.; see next.] I. Without article. Truth, verity. Also *personif.*

Phrases *S. to say. To speak s. In s. In good* or *very s.* (also with ellipsis of *in*). *By my, your*, etc. *s.* (also with ellipsis of *by*).

II. With article (or pronoun). 1. *The s.*, the truth; the real or actual facts, circumstances, etc. Freq. with the verbs *say, speak, tell*, etc. OE. †2. A true thing or saying; a truth –1641. †3. Soothsaying; prognostication –1582.

1. He goth ful neigh the soth CHAUCER. To say the s.,..My people are with sickness much enfeebled SHAKS. 3. Time..taught me..: The soothe of byrds by beating of their wings SPENSER.

†III. assoc. w. senses of SOOTHE *v.*: Blandishment, flattery; a smooth or plausible word or speech. Also *personif.* –1609.

When *signior* s. here does proclaime peace, He flatters you, makes warre vpon your life SHAKS.

Sooth (sūþ), *a. arch.* [OE. *sōð* :—**sonþ-*, *sanþ-* (pre-Teut. **sont-*), related by ablaut to Goth. *sunjis, sunja* truth, and Skr. *satyas* true.] †1. True, veritable, real, genuine –ME. 2. True; in accordance with truth; not false or fictitious OE. 3. Of persons, etc.: Telling or speaking the truth; truthful. Also const. *in* (speech, etc.), *of* (one's word). ME. 4. *poet.* Soothing, soft; smooth. KEATS.

2. If thy speech be s. SHAKS. 3. Melibœus.., The soothest Shepherd that ere pip't on plains MILT. 4. Jellies soother than the creamy curd KEATS. Hence **Soo·th-ly** *adv.* (now *arch.*); †**-ness** –1587.

Sooth (sūþ), *adv.* Now *arch.* and *rare.* [OE. *sōðe*, f. the adj.; see prec.] Truly; truthfully; in truth.

And s., men say that he was not the sonne Of mortall Syre SPENSER.

Soothe (sūð), *v.* [OE. *sōðian*, f. *sōð* SOOTH *a.*] †1. *trans.* To prove or show (a fact, statement, etc.) to be true; to verify, demonstrate –1588. †2. To declare (a statement) to be true; to uphold as the truth; to corroborate, support –1616. †b. To maintain or put forward (a lie or untruth) as being true –1616. †3. To support, or back *up*, (a person) in a statement or assertion –1623. †4. To confirm, encourage, or humour (a person) *in* something by expressing assent or approval. Also with *up.* –1705. †5. To blandish, cajole, or please (a person) by agreement or assent; to flatter in this way; to humour. Also with *up.* –1814. †6. To smooth or gloss over (an offence, etc.). Also with *up.* –1645. 7. To render (an animal, a person, the feelings) calm or quiet; to mollify or appease 1697. 8. To bring to a calm or composed condition; to affect in a tranquillizing and agreeable manner 1742. 9. To reduce the force or intensity of (a passion, pain, etc.); to allay, assuage, mitigate, etc. 1711. 10. *absol.* To have or exercise a soothing or tranquillizing influence 1728.

5. Like shrill-tongued tapsters answering every call, Soothing the humour of fantastic wits SHAKS. 6. 3 *Hen. VI*, III. iii. 175. 7. *transf.* The loveliness of heaven Soothes the unquiet sea SHELLEY. 8. Poetry of a certain kind soothed him 1891. 9. An intimate Friend..will..s. and asswage their secret Resentments ADDISON. 10. 'Twill s. to be where thou hast been BYRON. Hence **Soo·ther**, one who or that which soothes. **Soo·thingly** *adv.*

Soothfast (sū·þfɑst), *a.* and *adv. arch.* [OE. *sōðfæst*; see SOOTH *sb.* and FAST *a.*] A. *adj.* 1. Of persons: Veracious, truthful; true, faithful, loyal. 2. In accordance with the truth; true, veracious; †just, equitable OE. †3. Truly or actually that which the name implies; true, real, veritable, very. Said esp. of God or of the persons of the Trinity. –1470.

1. Edie was ken'd to me..for a true, loyal, and s. man SCOTT. 2. It was a southfast sentence..That hastye men shal never lacke much woe 1559.

B. *adv.* Soothfastly OE. Hence **Soo·thfast-·ly** *adv.*, **-ness.** Now *arch.*

Soothsay (sū·þsēⁱ), *sb.* 1549. [f. SOOTHSAYER or SOOTHSAYING.] †1. A true or wise saying; a proverb, saw. LATIMER. 2. A prediction, prognostication, or prophecy; an omen or portent 1582. b. Without article. (Good) omen; soothsaying, prognostication (*rare*) 1590.

2. Shewes, visions, sooth-sayes, and prophesies SPENSER. b. God turne the same to good s. SPENSER. So **Soo·thsay** *v. intr.* to make predictions; to prophesy (*rare*).

Soothsayer (sū·þsēⁱ:əɹ). ME. [f. SOOTH *sb.* or *a.* + SAYER *sb.*] †1. One who speaks the truth –1642. 2. One who claims or pretends to the power of foretelling future events; a predicter, prognosticator. late ME. 3. An insect of the family *Mantidæ*; a mantis 1855.

Soothsaying (sū·þsēⁱ:iŋ), (*vbl.*) *sb.* 1535. [f. SOOTH *sb.* or *a.* + SAYING (*vbl.*) *sb.*] 1. The practice of foretelling the future or the course of future events; prediction, prognostication. 2. A prediction or prophecy 1535.

1. Soythsayenge, witchcraft, sorcery, and dreaminge is but vanyte COVERDALE *Ecclus.* xxxiv. 5. 2. Hearkning to impious South-sayings 1653.

Sooty (su·ti), *a.* ME. [f. SOOT *sb.*[1] + -Y[1].] 1. Foul or dirty with soot; covered or smeared with soot; full of soot. †b. Of the soul: Foul with sin –1680. †c. Of grain: Affected by smut; blackened DRYDEN. 2. Resembling soot in colour; dusky or brownish black 1593. †b. *fig.* Black, dismal. –1673. 3. Of colours: Having a dark, dusky, blackish, or dirty tinge 1597. 4. Consisting of soot; of the nature of soot 1651.

1. In thunder Jove his s. bolt down threw HOBBES. 2. Not like that s. devil of Othello's BYRON. The S. Tern (*Sterna fuliginosa*) inhabits the bays and gulfs of the Mediterranean 1870. 3. By the heat of the sun the skin is scorched, and so acquires a s. hue JOHNSON. Hence **Soo·tied** *pa. pple.* made s., blackened. **Soo·tily** *adv.* **Soo·tiness.**

Sop (sǫp), *sb.* [OE. *sopp*, *sop-*, app. f. wk. grade of *sūpan* SUP *v.*[1]] 1. A piece of bread or the like dipped or steeped in water, wine, etc., before being eaten or cooked. b. Const. *in* (or †*of*) the liquid in which the bread, etc., is dipped or steeped. late ME. c. A dish composed of soaked bread 1845. 2. *transf.* and *fig.* †a. A thing of small value –1526. †b. Used of persons in respect of some pervading quality or property –1605. c. = MILKSOP. 1625. d. A person or thing thoroughly soaked or steeped in some way 1594. e. Something given to appease or pacify the recipient; a bribe (see CERBERUS) 1665. 3. A copious collection or accumulation of some liquid; soppy or soaked condition 1700.

1. A s., in honey steep'd DRYDEN. b. Thanne he taketh a sope in fyne clarree CHAUCER. 2. b. *Lear* II. ii. 35. d. The bounded Waters Should..make a soppe of all this solid Globe SHAKS. e. This bill..is a s. given to the priests 1845. 4. A great pool and s. of blood HAWTHORNE.

Sop (sǫp), *v.* [OE. *soppian*, f. *sopp* SOP *sb.*] 1. *trans.* To dip, soak, or steep (bread, etc.) in some liquid. Also *absol.* b. To drench with moisture; to soak; also *fig.*, to intoxicate 1682. 2. *intr.* a. To be, or become, soaking wet 1831. b. Of moisture: To soak *in* or *through* 1844. 3. [f. prec. 2 d.] *trans.* To propitiate; to bribe 1837.

2. b. The water just sops through the turf 1894. 3. Danton and needy corruptible Patriots are sopped with presents of cash CARLYLE. Hence **So·pper**, one who sops (*rare*).

Soph (sǫf). *colloq.* 1661. [abbrev. of SOPHISTER and SOPHOMORE.] 1. = SOPHISTER 3. (In early use also at Oxford.) 2. *U.S.* = SOPHOMORE 1 b. 1778.

‖ **Sophia** (sǫ·fiă). 1649. [L., a. Gr. σοφία, f. σοφός wise.] Wisdom, knowledge; *spec.* the Divine Wisdom (freq. personified).

Sophic (sǫ·fik), *a.* 1709. [ad. Gr. σοφικός, f. σοφία wisdom.] †1. Obtained by some secret process. †2. Conveying, or full of, wisdom; learned –1773. 3. Pertaining to knowledge or speculation 1898. So **So·phical** *a.* 1601. **So·phically** *adv.*

Sophism (sǫ·fiz'm). Also †**sophim(e.** ME. [a. OF. *soff-*, *sophime*, *-isme* (mod.F. *sophisme*), or ad. L. *sophisma*, a. Gr. σόφισμα a clever device, trick, σοφίζεσθαι to devise, f. σοφός wise, clever.] A specious but fallacious argument, either used deliberately in order to deceive or mislead, or employed as a means of displaying ingenuity in reasoning. b. Without article: Sophistry 1768.

But no s. is too gross to delude minds distempered by party spirit MACAULAY. b. All that s. and equivocation wherewith it has been..overclouded 1768.

Sophist (sǫ·fist). 1542. [ad. L. *sophista*, *sophistes*, ad. Gr. σοφιστής, f. σοφίζεσθαι to become wise or learned.] 1. In ancient Greece, one specially engaged in the pursuit or communication of knowledge; *esp.* one who gave instruction in intellectual and ethical matters in return for payment. 2. A wise or learned man 1614. 3. One who makes use of fallacious arguments; a specious reasoner 1581.

1. The very Sophists themselves..have declar'd him no S., but a Philosopher BENTLEY. 3. Thou art and thou remain'st a s., liar 1871. *attrib.* I laugh..At the s. schools EMERSON.

Sophister (sǫ·fistəɹ). late ME. [a. OF. *sohpistre*, ad. L *sophista* SOPHIST.] †1. = SOPHIST 1. –1710. 2. = SOPHIST 3. late ME. 3. At Cambridge, a student in his second or third year. Now *Hist.* 1574. 4. At Trinity College, Dublin, a student in his third or fourth year 1841.

Sophistic (sǒfi·stik), *a.* and *sb.* 1549. [ad. L. *sophisticus*, ad. Gr. σοφιστικός, f. σοφιστής SOPHIST.] A. *adj.* 1. Of persons: Given to the use or exercise of sophistry. 2. Of or pertaining to sophistry or sophists; of the nature of sophistry 1591. b. Pertaining to, characteristic of, the ancient sophists 1835.

2. A mystery indeed in their S. Subtilties, but in Scripture a plain Doctrin MILT.

B. *sb.* 1. Sophistic argument or speculation as a subject of instruction. Also **Sophi·stics.** 1862. 2. Sophistry, deceptiveness 1868.

Sophistical (sǒfi·stikăl), *a.* 1483. [See prec. and -ICAL.] 1. = prec. A. †2. Employed for the purpose of adulteration or deception –1680.

1. He is fluent and s.,—a sure token of feeble wisdom 1863. So **Sophi·stically** *adv.* late ME.

Sophisticate (sǒfi·stikĕt), *ppl. a.* late ME. [ad. med.L. *sophisticatus*, *sophisticare*; see next.] = SOPHISTICATED *ppl. a.*

Sophisticate (sǒfi·stikeⁱt), *v.* late ME. [f. the ppl. stem of med.L. *sophisticare*, f. *sophisticus* SOPHISTIC *a.*] 1. *trans.* To mix (commodities) with some foreign or inferior substance; to adulterate. Now somewhat *rare*. b. To deal with in some artificial way (*rare*) 1611. c. To render artificial; to convert *into* something artificial 1796. 2. To corrupt or spoil by admixture of some baser principle or quality; to render less genuine or honest 1604. 3. To corrupt, pervert, mislead (a person, the understanding, etc.) 1597. 4. To falsify by misstatement or by unauthorized alteration 1598. 5. *intr.* To practise sophistication 1664.

1. b. His hair, never sophisticated by a comb,..resembled dark sea-weed 1831. 2. It is the manner of the world..to s. ever the best things with hypocrisy 1626. 3. It alwaies behoueth men to take good heede, lest affection..s. the true and sincere iudgement 1597. 4. Thou..shalt testifie..What now thy shame-lesse lips s. 1598. Hence **Sophi·sticator**, one who sophisticates or adulterates.

Sophisticated (sǒfi·stikeⁱtėd), *ppl. a.* 1603. [f. prec.] 1. Mixed with some foreign substance; adulterated; not pure or genuine 1607. 2. Altered from, deprived of, primitive simplicity or naturalness 1603. 3. Falsified in a greater or less degree 1672.

3. I love not a s. truth, With an allay of lye in't DRYDEN.

Sophistication (sǒfistikēⁱ·ʃən). late ME. [a. OF., or ad. med.L. *sophisticatio*, f. *sophisticare* SOPHISTICATE *v.*] 1. The employment of sophistry; the process of investing with specious fallacies or of misleading by means of these; falsification. b. A sophism, a quibble, a fallacious argument 1491. 2. Disingenuous alteration or perversion *of* something 1564. 3. a. An adulterated article. b. A substance used in adulteration. late ME. 4. Adulteration (of commodities, etc.) 1540.

1. If you asked her opinion upon any subject you got it, without s. 1882. 2. The s. of the human intellect formed..language HAWTHORNE. 4. Food free from s. 1871.

Sophistry (sǫ·fistri). ME. [a. OF. *sophistrie*, or ad. med.L. *sophistria*; see SOPHIST and -RY.] 1. Specious but fallacious reasoning; employment of arguments which are intentionally deceptive. b. A sophism 1673. 2. The use or practice of specious reasoning as an art or dialectic exercise. late ME. †3. Cunning, trickery, craft -1657. 4. The type of learning characteristic of the ancient sophists; the profession of a Sophist 1837.

1. The parson's cant, the lawyer's s. POPE. 4. Euripides was nursed in the lap of s. 1837.

Sophoclean (sǫfǫ̆klī·ăn), *a.* 1649. [f. L. *Sophocleus*, ad. Gr. Σοφόκλειος, f. Σοφοκλῆς, -κλέης.] Of or pertaining to, characteristic of, Sophocles, the Athenian tragic poet, or his works, style, etc.

Sophomore (sǫ·fǫ̆mōᵊɹ). Now *U.S.* Also **sophimore.** 1688. [app. f. *sophom*, SOPHISM + -OR.] 1. A student of the second year: †a. At Cambridge -1795. b. In American universities and colleges 1726. 2. *attrib.*, passing into adj., as *s. class, year*, etc. 1778.

1. a. The Freshman's year being expired, the next distinctive appellation conferred is A Soph Mor 1795. Hence **Sophomo·ric, -al** *adjs.*, *U.S.*, of or pertaining to, befitting or resembling, characteristic of, a s.; hence, pretentious, bombastic; immature, crude, superficial.

‖**Sophora** (sofōᵊ·ră). 1753. [mod.L. (Linn.).] *Bot.* A genus of leguminous trees, shrubs, or plants, characterized by having odd-pinnate leaves and racemose or paniculate flowers, many species of which are cultivated for their ornamental properties; a tree of this genus.

Sophy (sōᵘ·fi). Now *Hist.* or *arch.* 1539. [ad. Pers. *çafī*, surname of the ruling dynasty of Persia from *c* 1500 to 1736, derived from the Arabic epithet *çafī-ud-dīn* 'purity of religion', given to an ancestor of the founder of the dynasty.] 1. A former title or designation of the supreme ruler of Persia; the Shah. Also *Grand S.* 2. With *a* and *pl.* A Persian monarch or king 1606. b. *transf.* A ruler; a great person 1599.

Sopite (soᵘpəi·t), *v.* Now *rare.* 1542. [f. L. *sopit-*, *sopire* to deprive of sense, render unconscious, put to sleep, etc.] 1. *trans.* To put or lull to sleep; to render drowsy, dull, or inactive. Also *transf.* (with ref. to the mental or moral faculties). 2. To put an end to, to settle (a dispute, question, etc.) in some way. Also, to pass over or suppress (something discreditable). 1628.

2. A meeting of the bishops..about sopiting..the controversies of this present time 1628. So **Sopi·te** *pa. pple. rare* put to sleep; settled. †**Sopi·tion**, the action of sopiting.

Sopor (sōᵘ·pǫ̆ɹ). 1658. [a. L., related to *somnus* sleep.] 1. A deep, lethargic, or unnatural sleep or state of sleep. In later use *Path.* 1675. †2. *fig.* A state of mental or moral lethargy or deadness -1693.

Soporiferous (sōᵘpŏri·fĕrəs, sǫp-), *a.* Now *rare.* 1590. [f. L. *soporifer* (f. *sopor* + *-fer* bearing); see -FEROUS.] †1. Of a disease, morbid state, etc.: Characterized by unnatural or excessive sleep; soporose; lethargic -1681. 2. = next A 1. 1601. †3. = next A 3. -1624.

2. S. Medecines applyed unto them, provoke sleep BACON. Hence **Sopori·ferous-ly** *adv.*, **-ness.**

Soporific (sōᵘpŏri·fik, sǫp-), *a.* and *sb.* 1690. [f. L. type **soporificus* (f. *sopor* sleep; see -FIC).] A. *adj.* 1. Inducing or tending to induce sleep; causing a person to sleep or slumber. 2. Of the nature of, characterized by, belonging to, sleep or sleepiness 1754. 3. Drowsy, sleepy, somnolent 1841.

1. Its [opium's] s. or anodyne virtues LOCKE. I thought of all sleepy sounds and all s. things SOUTHEY. 2. The s. tendencies of..a portion of the congregation 1896.

B. *sb.* A substance, esp. a medicament, which induces sleep 1746.

Soporose (sōᵘ·pŏrōᵘs, sǫ·p-). *rare.* 1710. [f. L. *sopor* + -OSE [1].] *Med.* Of diseases, states, etc.: Marked or characterized by morbid sleep or stupor. So **So·porous** *a.* 1684.

Sopping (sǫ·piŋ), *ppl. a.* 1866. [f. SOP *v.* + -ING.[2]] Soaking wet; also *advb.*

Soppy (sǫ·pi), *a.* 1611. [f. SOP *sb.* or *v.* + -Y [1].] †1. Full of or containing sops. 2. Soaked or saturated with water or rain; soft with moisture; drenched, sodden 1823. 3. Of the season or weather: Very wet or rainy 1872. 4. Sloppy, slovenly 1899. 5. *slang.* 'Soft', foolishly sentimental.

2. It [Yarmouth] looked rather spongey and s. DICKENS. Hence **So·ppiness.**

Soprano (sŏprā·no), *sb.* (and *a.*). *Pl.* **sopranos**, also **soprani.** 1730. [a. It., f. *sopra* above.] *Mus.* 1. The highest singing voice in women and boys, having a compass from about middle C to two octaves above it; the quality or range of this voice. b. A part for or sung by such a voice 1801. 2. A singer having a soprano voice; one who sings the soprano part 1738. 3. *attrib.* or as *adj.* a. Of persons: Having a soprano voice; singing a soprano part 1730. b. *transf.*, as *s. cornet, trombone* 1856. 4. Of or belonging to the soprano 1801.

4. **S. clef**, the C-clef upon the first line of the treble stave. Hence **Sopra·nist**, a s. singer.

Sops-in-wine. 1573. [See SOP *sb.* Cf. F. *soupe-en-vin*.] †1. The clove-pink or gillyflower -1625. 2. A variety of apple 1764.

Sora (sōᵊ·ră). 1705. [prob. native name.] The Carolina rail (*Porzana carolina*). Also *attrib.* with *gallinule, rail.*

Sorabian (sŏrēⁱ·biăn), *a.* and *sb.* 1788. [f. med.L. *Sorabi*; see SORB [2].] A. *adj.* Of or belonging to the Slavonic race formerly dominant in Saxony; Sorbian. B. *sb.* A Sorb; the Sorbian language.

†**So·rance.** 1440. [f. SORE *a.*[1] + -ANCE, prob. after GRIEVANCE 4.] A sore, or a morbid state producing a sore, in an animal, esp. in a horse -1749.

Sorb [1] (sǭɹb). 1530. [a. F. *sorbe*, or ad. L. *sorbum* service-berry, *sorbus* service-tree.] 1. The fruit of the service-tree (*Pyrus domestica*); a service-berry. 2. a. The service-tree 1555. b. = SERVICE-TREE 2. 1777. c. The rowan-tree 1796. Hence **So·rbin** *Chem.*, = SORBITOL.

Sorb [2] (sǭɹb). Also **Sorbe.** 1843. [ad. G. *Sorbe*, var. of *Serbe*, repr. the national designation *Serb* (pl. *Serbjo*); cf. SERB.] 1. A member of the Slavonic race inhabiting Lusatia in the east of Saxony; a Wend. 2. The language spoken by this race 1862. Also **So·rbian** 1836.

So·rb-a·pple. 1548. [ad. G. *sorbapfel*; see SORB [1].] The fruit of the service-tree, or the tree itself.

Sorbate (sǭ·ɹbĕt). 1823. [See SORBIC *a.* and -ATE [1] 1 c.] *Chem.* A salt of sorbic acid.

Sorbefacient (sǭɹbĭfēⁱ·ʃiĕnt), *a.* and *sb.* 1847. [f. L. *sorbere* to absorb + -FACIENT.] A. *adj.* Causing or promoting absorption. B. *sb.* A substance or preparation causing absorption.

Sorbet (sǭ·ɹbĕt). 1585. [a. F., ad. It. *sorbetto*, ad. Turk. *shorbet* (see SHERBET), perh. infl. by It. *sorbire* to imbibe.] 1. = SHERBET. 2. A variety of sweetmeat or ice 1864.

Sorbic (sǭ·ɹbik), *a.* 1815. [f. SORB [1] + -IC.] *Chem.* Contained in or derived from the berries of the mountain-ash, *Sorbus* (now *Pyrus*) *aucuparia.* Chiefly in *s. acid.*

Sorbile (sǭ·ɹbəil), *a.* Now *rare.* 1620. [ad. L. *sorbilis*, f. *sorbere* to drink.] That may be drunk or supped; liquid.

Sorbite (sǭ·ɹbəit). 1867. [f. SORB [1] + -ITE.] *Chem.* = SORBITOL. Hence **Sorbi·tic** *a.*

Sorbitol (sǭ·ɹbitǫl). 1895. [f. SORBITE + -OL.] *Chem.* An unfermentable saccharine principle found in the berries of the mountain-ash.

Sorbonist (sǭ·ɹbŏnist). Also †**-onnist.** 1560. [ad. mod.L. *Sorbonista* or F. *Sorboniste*; see next.] A doctor or student at the Sorbonne.

Sorbonne (sǭɹbǫ·n, Fr. sorbon). 1560. [F., f. the place-name *Sorbon* in the Ardennes.] A theological college at Paris founded by Robert de Sorbon early in the 13th c.; the faculty of theology in the old University of Paris, of great importance down to the 17th c.; later, (the seat of) the university of Paris.

‖**Sorbus** (sǭ·ɹbŏs). 1706. [L. Cf. SORB [1].] A Linnæan genus (now placed under *Pyrus*) including the service-tree, mountain-ash, etc.; a tree of this genus.

Sorcerer (sǭ·ɹsərəɹ). 1526. [Extension of *sorcer*, ad. OF. *sorcier*:—pop. L. **sortiarius*, f. *sort-*, *sors* lot, SORT *sb.*[1]; see -ER [1].] One who practises sorcery; a wizard, magician.

The sorserar Elemas..withstode them TINDALE *Acts* xiii. 8.

Sorceress (sǭ·ɹsərĕs). late ME. [a. AF. *sorceresse*, fem. of *sorcer* (see prec.).] A female sorcerer; a witch. b. In playful use 1800.

Sorcerous (sǭ·ɹsərəs), *a.* 1546. [f. SORCERER + -OUS.] 1. Of the nature of, pertaining to or connected with, sorcery. 2. Dealing in or exercising sorcery 1550. Hence **So·rcerously** *adv.*

Sorcery (sǭ·ɹsəri). ME. [a. OF. *sorcerie*, f. *sorcier*; see SORCERER.] 1. The use of magic or enchantment; the practice of magic arts; witchcraft. b. *pl.* Particular forms or instances of this ME. 2. *transf.* and *fig.* 1576.

1. By enchauntement and sorssery she hath ben the destroyer of many good knyghtes MALORY. 2. What drugs, what sorceries..doe our curious Dames vse to inlarge our withered beauties? 1592.

‖**Sordes** (sǭ·ɹdīz). 1640. [L. (pl., rare in sing.) filth, etc., related to *sordere* to be dirty or foul. Construed either as sing. or pl.] 1. Dirt, filth; foul or feculent matter; refuse or rubbish removed or separated by or during the treatment, manufacture, or working of something. 2. Filthy or feculent matter attaching to, or collecting on or in, the bodies of persons or animals 1670. b. Impure matter collecting about the teeth, gums, etc.; *spec.* in *Path.*, the foul crusts formed upon the teeth and lips in typhoid or other fevers 1746.

Sordid (sǭ·ɹdid), *a.* 1597. [a. F. *sordide*, or ad. L. *sordidus* foul, base, mean, f. *sordere* to be dirty; cf. prec.] I. *Path.* a. Of suppurations, etc.: Corrupt, foul, repulsive; of the nature of sordes. b. Of an ulcer, wound, etc.: Yielding or discharging matter of this kind 1597. 2. Dirty, foul, filthy; in later use, mean and squalid 1611. †3. Of persons (or animals): Dirty or sluttish in habits or appearance -1712.

2. Their houses..within are poore and s. 1634. Tattered raiment, and all the outward signs of s. misery 1850. 3. The Person he chanced to see was ..an old s. blind Man ADDISON.

II. †1. Of a coarse, gross, or inferior character or nature; menial -1751. 2. Of actions, habits, etc.: Of a low, mean, or despicable character; marked by or proceeding from ignoble motives, esp. of self-interest or monetary gain 1611. b. Low, coarse, rough 1668. 3. Of persons, their character, etc.: Inclined to what is low, mean, or ignoble; *esp.* moved by mercenary motives; influenced only by material considerations 1636.

2. His courage, his abilities,..had made him, in spite of his s. vices, a favourite with his brethren in arms MACAULAY. 3. He s. is, who..dies wrangling in a worthlesse cause 1636. Hence **Sordi·dity** (*rare*) sordidness 1584. **So·rdid·ly** *adv.*, **-ness.**

Sordine (sǭ·ɹdīn). 1591. [ad. It. *sordina*, *-dino*, f. L. *surdus*, deaf, mute; see SURD *a.*] †1. A small pipe or mouthpiece placed in a trumpet or bugle in order to muffle or reduce the sound; a trumpet fitted with this -1611. 2. *Mus.* = MUTE *sb.*[1] 4 a. 1776.

Sordor (sǭ·ɹdǭɹ). 1823. [a. L. type **sordor*, corresp. to *sordidus* as *squalor* to *squalidus*.] Physical or moral sordidness.

Sore (sōᵊɹ), *sb.*[1] [OE. *sár*; see SORE *a.*] †1. Bodily pain or suffering -1583. †2. Sickness, disease; a disease, ailment, or bodily affliction -1648. 3. A bodily injury; a wound. *Obs.* exc. *dial.* OE. 4. A place in an animal body where the skin or flesh is diseased or injured so as to be painfully tender or raw; a sore place, such as that caused by an ulcer OE. 5. In fig. uses, esp. coupled with *salve* ME. †6. Mental suffering, pain, or trouble; grief, sorrow, anxiety, or the cause of this -1575.

4. Another [hound] licking of his wound, 'Gainst venom'd sores the only sovereign plaster SHAKS. 5. That infectious soare of iealowsie GREENE.

Sore (sōᵊɹ), *sb.*[2] late ME. [subst. use of SORE *a.*[2]] †1. *Venery.* A buck in its fourth year -1865. 2. *Falconry.* A hawk in its second year. Also *transf.* 1600.

Sore (sōᵊɹ), *a.*[1] [Com. Teut.; OE. *sár*:—OTeut. **sairoz.*] I. Now mainly *arch.* or *dial.*

1. Causing or involving bodily pain; painful, grievous; distressing or severe in this respect. 2. Causing, involving, or accompanied by mental pain, trouble, or distress OE. b. Of manifestations of grief: Bitter, painful ME. 3. Involving great hardships, painful exertion, unusual difficulty, etc. OE. b. Of battle, etc.: Severe, fierce, hot. late ME. 4. Pressing hardly upon one; difficult to bear or support 1500. b. In intensive use: Very great or serious 1555. 5. Severe, stern, hard, or harsh 1526. 6. Of a strong, severe, or violent character in respect of operation or effect 1449. †7. Strong, weighty, valid –1551. 8. *dial.* = SORRY *a.* 4. 1825.

1. The Lord with his s. and great and strong sworde *Isa.* xxvii. 1. 2. b. They mourned with a great and very s. lamentation *Gen.* l. 10. 3. Sleepe,..The death of each dayes Life, s. Labors Bath SHAKS. b. In that s. battel when so many dy'd MILT. 4. Man is to man the sorest, surest ill YOUNG. b. Henry was now in s. want of money 1875. 6. Soch a s. snowe & a frost 1556.

II. 1. Of parts of the body: In pain; painful, aching. Now *spec.*, having the skin broken or raw. OE. b. Of the eyes, throat, etc.: Painful through inflammation or other morbid condition. late ME. 2. Of persons: Suffering pain (from wounds, disease, etc.). Also *absol.* ME. 3. Afflicted with sorrow or grief; pained, distressed ME. 4. Of persons or their feelings: Inclined to be irritated or grieved; irritable, sensitive 1694.

1. I'm tyr'd, my Bones are s. 1704. *A bear with a s. head*, used allusively for a type of sullen irritability, peevishness, or sensitiveness. b. May not honey's self be turn'd to gall..by marriage, and s. eyes? GRAY. *Clergyman's sore-throat*, chronic follicular pharyngitis 1898. 4. Malice and hatred are.. apt to make our minds s. and uneasy 1694. *S. point, spot*, a matter in respect of which one is easily annoyed or grieved. Hence **So·reness.**

Sore, *a.*² *Obs.* exc. *Hist.* late ME. [a. AF. and OF. *sor, saur(e.*] 1. *Falconry.* Applied to a hawk of the first year that has not moulted and still has its red plumage (now called a *red hawk*); hence applied to the plumage itself; occas. extended to other birds of prey, as the kite and eagle 1450. †2. Of a horse: Of a reddish-brown colour –1679.

Sore (sōᵊɹ), *v.* In mod. use *U.S.* ME. [f. SORE *a.*¹] *trans.* To make sore; to give (physical or mental) pain to; †to wound.

Sore (sōᵊɹ), *adv.* Now chiefly *arch.* and *dial.* [OE. *sáre* (f. *sár* SORE *a.*¹).] 1. Severely, dangerously, seriously. 2. With verbs of grieving, annoying, etc.: So as to cause mental pain or irritation; deeply, intensely OE. 3. With great grief, distress, or perturbation of mind; in such a manner or to such an extent as to involve or manifest this. (Passing into a mere intensive.) OE. 4. To a painful or distressing degree OE. 5. With great exertion or effort; laboriously, toilsomely, hard ME. b. Severely 1483. 6. Eagerly, earnestly ME. 7. To a great extent; greatly, very much 1440.

1. Fast his blood was flowing And he was s. in pain MACAULAY. 2. It griev'd him s. COWPER. 3. And the people..lift vp their voices, and wept s. *Judges* xxi. 2. 4. The torrid Clime Smote on him s. besides MILT. 6. Because thou s. longedst after thy fathers house *Gen.* xxxi. 30. 7. A shameless wight, S. given to revel and ungodly glee BYRON.

Soredi- (sŏrī·di), comb. form of SOREDIUM, as in **Sore·dial** *a.*, of the nature of, pertaining to, a soredium; **Sore·diate** *a.*, bearing or characterized by the presence of soredia; **Soredi(i)·ferous** *a.*, bearing soredia; caused by producing soredia; etc.

‖ **Soredium** (sŏrī·diŏm). *Pl.* **-ia.** 1829. [mod. L., f. Gr. σωρός a heap.] *Bot.* A thallus-bud or cell in lichens. Usu. in *pl.*

So·re-head, *a.* and *sb.* 1862. [See SORE *a.*¹] **A.** *adj.* Irritable or out of temper 'like a bear with a sore head'; discontented, dissatisfied. **B.** *sb. U.S. political slang.* A dissatisfied or disappointed politician 1862.

Sorely (sōᵊ·ɹli), *adv.* [OE. *sárlice*; see SORE *a.* and -LY ².] In a manner involving pain, grief, distress, or oppression; hardly, severely; (chiefly with words expressing injury, evil, or want) greatly, highly.

Sorghum (sǫ·ɹgŏm). Also †**sorgum.** 1597. [mod.L., f. It. *sorgo*, med.L. *surgum.*] 1. a. The cereal plant known as Indian millet, Guinea-corn, durra, etc. (*Andropogon Sorghum*, also called *Holcus Sorghum* and *Sorghum vulgare*). b. The Chinese sugar-cane (*Andropogon saccharatus*). Usually *Sweet s.* 1859. 2. A genus of grasses belonging to the tribe *Andropogoneæ* and including the species mentioned above; also, with *a* and *pl.*, a variety belonging to this genus 1842. 3. *U.S.* A kind of molasses made from sorghum-juice 1883. So **So·rgho.**

‖ **Sorites** (sŏrəi·tīz). 1551. [L., ad. Gr. σωρείτης, f. σωρός a heap.] 1. *Logic.* A series of propositions in which the predicate of each is the subject of the next, the conclusion being formed of the first subject and the last predicate. b. An instance of this type of syllogism. 1581.

In the GOCLENIAN form, the subject of each proposition is the predicate of the next, the conclusion being formed of the last subject and the first predicate.

2. *transf.* A series, chain, or accumulation *of* some thing or things 1664. 3. A sophistical argument turning on the definition of a 'heap' 1768.

1. The S. can be resolved into as many simple syllogisms as there are middle terms between the subject and predicate of the conclusion 1838. Hence **Sori·tic, -al** *adjs.*

Sorn (sǭɹn), *v. Sc.* 1563. [f. SORREN.] †1. *trans.* To exact 'sorren' from –1589. 2. *intr.* To take up free quarters or exact maintenance unjustifiably; to sponge *upon* 1575. So **So·rner,** a sponger 1449.

Sororal (sŏrōᵊ·răl), *a.* 1654. [f. L. *soror* sister + -AL.] 1. By one's sister; on a sister's side (*rare*). 2. That is a sister. LAMB. 3. Of, pertaining to, or characteristic of a sister or sisters; sisterly 1854.

Sororicide¹ (sŏrǫ·risəid). 1656. [ad. L. *sororicida*, f. *soror* sister; see -CIDE 1.] One who kills his or her sister.

Sororicide² (sŏrǫ·risəid). 1727. [ad. late L. *sororicidium*, f. *soror*; see -CIDE 2.] The action of killing one's sister. Hence **Soro·ricidal** *a.*

Sorority (sŏrǫ·rĭti). 1532. [ad. med.L. *sororitas*, or f. L. *soror* + -ITY, after *fraternity.*] 1. A body or company of women united for some common object, esp. for devotional purposes. 2. *U.S.* A women's society in a college or university 1900.

Sororize (sǫ·rŏrəiz), *v. rare.* 1875. [f. L. *soror* + -IZE, after *fraternize.*] *intr.* To associate *with* a person or persons as a sister or sisters; to form a sisterly friendship.

‖ **Sorosis** (sŏrōᵘ·sis). 1831. [mod.L., f. Gr. σωρός a heap.] 1. *Bot.* A spike or raceme converted into a fleshy fruit by the cohesion in a single mass of the ovaria and floral envelopes. 2. *U.S.* A woman's society or club.

Sorrel (sǫ·rĕl), *sb.*¹ late ME. [a. OF. *surele, sorele* (mod.F. *surelle*), f. OF. *sur* adj., a. G. *sur* SOUR *a.*] 1. One or other of certain small perennial plants belonging to the genus *Rumex*, characterized by a sour taste, and to some extent cultivated for culinary purposes; esp. the common wild species, *R. acetosa* 1440. 2. The leaves of species of *Rumex* used in cookery or medicine, or as a salad; a decoction or drink made from one or other of these plants. late ME. †3. *S. de boys*, = WOOD-SORREL –1647. 4. With distinguishing epithet: One or other of various plants of other genera in some way resembling sorrel 1753. 5. *pl.* Species of sorrel; sorrel plants 1596. 6. *Salt of s.*, binoxalate of potash 1800.

4. S., Indian or red, *Hibiscus Sabdarifa* 1864. *Oxyria reniformis*..Mountain S. 1843.

Comb.: **s.-tree,** the sour-wood or elk-tree of N. America, *Oxydendron arboreum.*

Sorrel (sǫ·rĕl), *a.* and *sb.*² late ME. [a. OF. *sorel*, f. *sore* SORE *a.*²] **A.** *adj.* Of a bright chestnut colour; reddish brown 1469.

Behind him there were horses, red, s., and white BIBLE (1884) *Zech.* i. 8.

B. *sb.* 1. A horse of a bright chestnut colour; also as the name of a horse. late ME. 2. A buck in its third year. Now *Obs.* or *arch.* 1486. 3. A sorrel or reddish-brown colour 1530.

Sorren (sǫ·rən). *Sc.* and *Ir.* Now *Hist.* ME. [ad. obs. Ir. *sorthan*, 'free quarters, living at free expense'. Cf. SORN *v.*] A service formerly required of vassals in Scotland and Ireland, consisting in giving hospitality to the superior or his men; a sum of money or other contribution given in lieu of this.

Sorrow (sǫ·rōᵘ), *sb.* [Com. Teut.; OE. *sorh, sorg.*] 1. Distress of mind caused by loss, suffering, disappointment, etc.; grief, deep sadness or regret; also, that which causes grief or melancholy; affliction, trouble. Occas. *personified.* 2. With *a* and *pl.* An instance or cause of grief or sadness; an affliction or trouble OE. b. Applied to persons 1637. 3. In phrases of imprecation or emphasis ME. 4. The outward expression of grief; lamentation, mourning; *poet.*, tears ME.

1. A countenance more in s. then in anger SHAKS. S.,..the mother and daughter of melancholy BURTON. 2. When sorrowes come, they come not single spies, But in Battaliaes SHAKS. *The Man of Sorrows*, Jesus Christ (after *Isa.* liii. 3). 3. S. on thee, and all the packe of you SHAKS. 4. She nothing said but, ..wept a rain Of sorrows at his words KEATS.

Comb., as *s.-blinded, -bound, -laden*, etc. Hence **So·rrowless** *a.* free from s.

Sorrow (sǫ·rōᵘ), *v.* [OE. *sorgian*, f. *sorg, sorh* SORROW *sb.*] 1. *intr.* To feel sorrow or sadness; to regret or grieve; also, to exhibit signs of grief, to mourn. 2. *trans.* To think of with sorrow; to feel sorrow on account of; to lament ME. 3. To give pain to; to grieve, make sorrowful ME.

1. The miserable change..Lament nor s. at SHAKS. I shall..So send them forth, though sorrowing, yet in peace MILT. 2. The redde rose waxed..pale when the vyrgyn sorowed the dethe of her sonne 1450. 3. The bitterness of her tone sorrowed him 1890. Hence **So·rrower,** one who sorrows; a mourner.

Sorrowful (sǫ·rŏful), *a.* [OE. *sorh-, sorgful*, f. *sorh, sorg* SORROW *sb.*] 1. Full of or oppressed by sorrow or grief; sorrow-laden, grieved. Also *absol.* (chiefly *pl.*). 2. Indicative or expressive of sorrow or grief ME. 3. Distressing, lamentable, doleful OE. 4. quasi-*adv.* Sorrowfully. late ME.

1. I rent my holy garmentes, and..sat me downe sorowfull & heuy COVERDALE 1 *Esdras* viii. 71. 2. Sorowfull blacke apparell 1565. 3. Sounds and odours, s. Because they once were sweet SHELLEY. Hence **So·rrowful-ly** *adv.*, **-ness.**

Sorry (sǫ·ri), *a.* [OE. *sárig*, f. *sár* SORE *sb.*¹ The change of ā to ō and subsequent shortening have given the word an apparent connexion with SORROW *sb.*] 1. Pained at heart; distressed or sad; full of grief or sorrow. (In later use freq. expressing mere sympathy or apology, as in the phrase 'I'm sorry'.) †2. Expressive or suggestive of distress or sorrow –1567. †3. Causing distress or sorrow; painful, grievous, dismal –1605. 4. Vile, wretched, mean, poor; of little account or value ME.

1. No soryer man in erth may dwel Than I 1430. I do not wonder that they are s. BURKE. 2. A sory song we myght all synge CHAUCER. 3. This is a s. sight SHAKS. 4. One s. room in a miserable tavern 1716. One man, with a couple of s. horses HUME. The baron..grew fat and wanton, and a s. brute EMERSON. Hence **So·rrily** *adv.* **So·rriness** (now *rare*). **So·rryish** *a.* somewhat s.

†**Sort,** *sb.*¹ ME. [a. OF., or ad. L. *sort-, sors.*] Lot, fate, destiny; share, portion –1606.

Part is not to thee, nethir s., in this word WYCLIF *Acts* viii. 21. Make a Lott'ry, And by deuice let blockish Aiax draw The s. to fight with Hector SHAKS.

Sort (sǫɹt), *sb.*² late ME. [a. OF. (mod.F.) *sorte* :—pop.L. **sorta*, alteration of L. *sort-, sors.*] I. A (definite or specified) kind, species, variety, or description of persons or things. 1. Preceded by *of.* 2. Followed by *of*: A particular kind, etc., *of* thing(s) or person(s) 1526. b. Used collectively, after *kind of* (see KIND *sb.* II) esp. with *these* or *those* 1551. 3. *ellipt.* or *absol.* a. A particular class, order, or rank of persons 1529; a kind, variety, etc., of thing(s) 1523. b. *Typog.* One or other of the characters or letters in a fount of type. Usu. in *pl.* 1668. †4. Without article: Rank, class. MILT.

1. *Of a* (certain) *s.*, of a certain kind, etc.; The moment a topic of that solemn s. is started 1787. *Of* (various) *sorts*; Plays of all sorts ADDISON. †*Of s.*, of (high) quality or rank; Persons of good S. and Credit DE FOE. *Of a s.*, of the same kind or description (now *dial.*). *Of sorts*: (*a*) of different or various kinds (now *rare*); They [*sc.* bees] haue a King, and Officers of sorts SHAKS; (*b*) *colloq.* of a kind which is not very satisfactory; rather poor. *Something of the s.*, something similar to that previously indicated, mentioned, or specified. *Nothing*

of the s., no such thing. **2.** A fair specimen of the s. of letter they ought not to write TROLLOPE. *All sorts of* (things or persons) = things or persons of all kinds or descriptions. All sorts of Ven'son DRYDEN. *A s. of* = something in the nature of. So *a* (or *some*) *s. of a*... *In a s. of way*, imperfectly. *No s. of*.., used as an emphatic neg. phrase to denote the complete absence of anything of the kind specified. *That* or *this s. of thing*, used to denote in a general way a thing, quality, etc., of a like or similar nature to that specified. **b.** These s. of details gave my poor father great delight 1798. Such s. of questions..are not merely innocent subtleties SYD. SMITH. **3. a.** All sorts and conditions that stood by..bore witness to the prophecy BROWNING. There 's a shop of all sorts, that sells every thing HOOD. Phr. *A* (*bad, good*, etc.) *s.*, applied to a single person. (*colloq.*). *Out of sorts*: (*a*) not in the normal condition of good health or spirits; slightly unwell; (*b*) †out of or without certain kinds of articles or goods (*rare*).

II. †**1.** A number of persons associated together in some way; a band, company, group, or set of persons (or animals) -1612. **2.** A (great, good, etc.) number or lot of persons or things; a considerable body or quantity; a multitude. Now *dial.* 1475. †**3.** A (great, etc.) part or portion *of* a number of persons or things -1669.

1. †*In s.*, in a body or company. **2.** See what a s. of rebels are in arms MIDDLETON.

III. Manner, method, or way. *arch.* **1.** In phrases with *in* 1533. **2.** *After this, what*, etc., *s.*, *after a* (..) *s.* 1551.

1. Phr. *In this, that, such,* (*the*) *like, what*, etc., *s.* (now *arch.*) *In good, honest*, etc. *s.* (now *rare*). *In some* or *a s.*, in a certain undefined or unknown way; to some extent or degree. †*In no s.*, in no way, to no extent, not at all. **2.** Captain Dampmartin..who loves the Reign of Liberty, after a s. CARLYLE.

Sort (sǭɹt), *v.* ME. [Partly ad. L. *sortiri* to divide or obtain by lot, f. L. *sort-, sors* lot. In most senses closely related to prec. Cf. also F. *assortir* ASSORT *v.*] **I.** †**1.** *trans.* To allot, apportion, or assign -1599. †**b.** To dispose, ordain, order (events). Also *absol.* (*rare*). -1596. †**2.** To arrive at, attain to, result in, or reach (an effect, end, etc.) -1656. †**3.** *intr.* Of events, etc.: To come about, to fall or turn out, in a certain way or with a certain result -1653. †**b.** To come to effect; to be successful (*rare*) -1626. †**4. a.** To come or attain *to* an end, conclusion, effect, etc. -1659. **b.** To end in coming or leading *to* a specified result -1624. **c.** To fall *to* a person as a right or duty (*rare*) -1677. **5.** *trans.* To answer or correspond to, to befit or suit. Now *rare.* 1587.

3. The Experiment sorted in this Manner BACON. **b.** It was tried in a Blowne Bladder..and it sorted not BACON. **5.** Well sorting your high place 1587.

II. 1. *trans.* To arrange (things, etc.) according to kind or quality, or after some settled order or system; to classify; to assort. Also *absol.* ME. †**b.** To separate or distinguish (*from* something else). *rare.* -1599. **2.** To place in a class or sort; to give a place to; to classify 1486. **3.** With *out*: To take *out*, remove, or separate (certain sorts from others) 1534. **b.** To choose or select in this way. Now *rare* or *Obs.* 1553. **c.** To arrange according to sort 1713. **4.** *refl.* **a.** To form sets or groups by some process of combination or separation 1570. **b.** To associate or consort *with* another or others. Now *dial.* 1579. **5.** To adapt, to fit, to make conformable *to* or *with* some thing or person. Now *rare* or *Obs.* 1561. †**6.** To choose or select (time, opportunity, etc.) as fitting or suitable -1634. †**b.** To choose (a thing or person) from others -1638. **7.** *Sc.* and *north.* **a.** (Also with *up.*) To arrange or put in order; to put to rights in some respect 1816. **b.** To deal effectively with (a person) by way of punishment, repression, etc. 1815.

1. Wee have sorted what papers I could at present find 1684. **2.** A bony, yellow, crab-like hand..easy to s. with the square gaunt face GEO. ELIOT. **3.** They will s. out the good from the evil BURKE. **5.** My will is something sorted with his wish SHAKS. **6.** 1 *Hen. VI*, II. iii. 27. **b.** *Rom. & Jul.* iv. ii. 34. **7. b.** Bid them bring up the prisoner—I trow I'll s. him SCOTT.

III. 1. *intr.* To fit, suit, or agree; to be in harmony or conformity Now *arch.* 1590. †**b.** Without const.: To be fitting; to accord; to be in place, to exist -1667. **2.** To associate, consort, go in company *with* others or *together*. Also with *among* and without const. Now *rare* or *dial.* 1592.

1. For diff'rent styles with diff'rent subjects s. POPE. **b.** Among unequals what societie Can s., what harmonie or true delight?—MILT. **2.** A company, with whom I may not s., Approaches CARY. Hence †**So·rtable** *a.* suitable or appropriate; of a cargo, properly assorted. †**So·rtance**, agreement, correspondence. **So·rtment**, the action or process of sorting; an assortment.

Sorter (sǭ·ɹtəɹ). 1554. [f. prec. + -ER.] One who sorts, arranges, selects, or classifies; *esp.* a wool-sorter. **b.** *spec.* A letter-sorter 1700.

Sortie (sǭ·ɹti). 1795. [a. F., a going out, f. *sortir.*] **1.** A dash or sally by a besieged garrison. Freq. in phr. *to make a s.* **2. a.** A sally-port. **b.** An outlet (of a river). 1848.

Sortilege (sǭ·ɹtilėdʒ). late ME. [a. OF., or ad. med.L. *sortilegium*, f. L. *sortilegus* diviner.] **1.** Divination by lots; †sorcery, magic, witchcraft. **2.** An act of this 1600.

2. A woman infamous for sortileges and for witcheries SCOTT. Hence †**Sortile·gious** *a.* of the nature of, relating to, or connected with s. **So·rtileger**, a diviner, fortune-teller. **So·rtilegy**, sortilege.

Sortition (sǫɹti·ʃən). 1597. [ad. L. *sortitio*, f. *sortiri* to cast or draw lots.] **1.** The casting or drawing of lots; selection, choice, or determination by lot. **2.** With *a* and *pl.* An act or instance of determining by lot 1634.

‖**Sorus** (sōᵊ·rɒ̆s). *Pl.* **sori** (sōᵊ·rəi). 1832. [mod.L., ad. Gr. σωρός a heap.] **1.** *Bot.* A cluster of capsules or spore-cases on the under surface of fern-leaves. **2.** A similar formation in algæ, lichens, or fungi 1842.

SOS (eːsǭuːeˑs). 1910. [Arbitrary.] A wireless code-signal of extreme distress, used esp. by ships at sea. Also *transf.*

So so, so-so (sōᵘ·sōᵘ), *adv.* and *a.* 1530. [So *adv.*] **A.** *adv.* In an indifferent, mediocre, or passable manner or degree; indifferently, not quite satisfactorily.

Clo. Art rich? *Will.* Faith sir, so, so SHAKS. He ..said he had been but so so 1820.

B. *adj.* **1.** Indifferent, mediocre, of middling quality; neither very good nor very bad, but usu. inclining towards bad 1542. **2.** Of persons 1592.

1. Your white or Clarret Is but so so he cares not greatly for it 1616. As in some Irish houses, where things are so so, One gammon of bacon hangs up for a show GOLDSM. *attrib.* You will..make but a so so Figure, as..a Husband 1767. **2.** Mrs. Harris—a so-so sort of woman 1775. Hence **So-so·-ish** *a.*

Soss, *sb.*[1] Now *dial.* 1691. [perh. imitative of the sound of lapping.] **1.** A sloppy mess or mixture; a dish of food having this character. **2.** A sloven 1611.

Soss (sǫs), *sb.*[2] Chiefly *dial.* 1718. [Echoic.] **1.** The sound made by a heavy, soft body falling upon or otherwise coming into contact with a surface; a heavy, awkward fall. Chiefly in the phr. *with a s.* **2.** The sound made by impact upon water 1885.

Soss, *v.* Now *dial.* and *Sc.* 1711. [Cf. prec.] †**1.** *trans.* To put *up* so as to rest softly. SWIFT. †**2.** *intr.* To move gently; to lounge -1723. **3.** To fall with a thud or heavy impact 1789. **4.** *trans.* To throw heavily 1855. So **Soss** *adv.* with a heavy fall or dull thud.

‖**Sostenuto** (sǫstėnū·to), *a.* Abbrev. **sost.** 1724. [It., pa. pple. of *sostenere* SUSTAIN *v.*] **1.** Of music: To be sung or played in a sustained manner. **2.** Marked or characterized by being sustained or held on 1835.

Sot (sǫt), *sb.* and *a.* OE. [a. OF. *sot* masc., *sote* fem. (mod.F. *sot, sotte*).] **A.** *sb.* †**1.** A foolish or stupid person; a blockhead, dolt -1745. **2.** One who dulls or stupefies himself with drinking; a soaker 1592.

1. The one is ever..a s., an ideot for any use that mankind can make of him MILT. **2.** A s., a beast, benumbed and stupefied by excess BERKELEY. Hence †**So·ttery**, a piece of foolishness or folly.

†**B.** *adj.* Foolish, stupid -1648.

Sot (sǫt), *v.* late ME. [f. SOT *sb.*] **I.** *trans.* †**a.** To render foolish or doltish; to besot -1700. **b.** With *away*. To waste or squander by sottish conduct 1746. **2.** *intr.* To play the sot; to drink to excess; to soak 1633.

1. b. I must..have destroyed my health and faculties by sotting away the evenings CHESTERF. **2.** Writers that s. over beer 1815. So **So·tted** *ppl. a.* rendered sottish or stupid; besotted.

Sotadean (sōᵘtădī·ăn), *a.* and *sb.* 1774. [f. L. *Sotadeus*, f. *Sotades.*] = SOTADIC *a.*

Sotadic (sotæ·dik), *sb.* and *a.* 1645. [ad. L. *Sotadicus*, f. *Sotades*, Gr. Σωτάδης.] **A.** *sb.* **1.** A satire after the manner of Sotades, an ancient Greek poet noted for the coarseness and scurrility of his writings. **2.** *Pros.* A catalectic tetrameter composed of ionics *a majore* 1830. **B.** *adj.* **1.** Characterized by a coarseness or scurrility like that of Sotades 1716. **2.** Palindromic 1814. **3.** *Pros.* (see A. 2.) 1830.

Soteriology (sotīᵊriǫ·lŏdʒi). 1864. [f. Gr. σωτηρία salvation + -LOGY.] *Theol.* The doctrine of salvation. Hence **Sote:riolo·gical** *a.* of or pertaining to s. or salvation.

Sothiac (sōᵘ·þiăk), *a.* 1834. [ad. F. *sothiaque*; see next.] = next. So **Sothi·acal** *a.*

Sothic (sǫ·þik, sōᵘ·þik), *a.* 1828. [f. Gr. Σῶθις, an Egyptian name of Sirius, the dog-star.] **1.** *S. cycle* or *period*, a period of 1460 full years, containing 1461 of the ancient Egyptian ordinary years. **2.** *S. year*, a year of 365¼ days, in contrast to the ordinary Egyptian year of 365 days 1828.

‖**Sotnia** (sǫ·tniă). 1863. [Russ. *sotnya* hundred, f. *sot-*, related to Skr. *çatam*, L. *centum*, OE. *hund.*] A squadron of Cossack cavalry. So ‖**So·tnik**, a commander of a s.; a local Cossack official 1799.

‖**Sottise** (sotīz). 1673. [F., f. *sot* SOT *a.*] A silly remark or saying; a foolish action.

Sottish (sǫ·tiʃ), *a.* 1566. [f. SOT *sb.* + -ISH.] †**1.** Foolish, doltish, stupid -1796. **2.** Given to, characterized or affected by, excessive drinking or coarse self-indulgence 1632.

1. How ignorant those s. pretenders to astrology are in their own concerns SWIFT. **2.** His face was sallow and s. 1871. Hence **So·ttish-ly** *adv.*, **-ness.**

‖**Sotto voce** (sǫ·to vō·tʃe), *adv.*, *a.*, and *sb.* 1737. [It. *sotto* under + *voce* voice.] **1.** In a subdued or low voice. **2.** *fig.* Quietly, privately. SCOTT. **3.** as *adj.* Uttered, etc., in an undertone 1809. **4.** as *sb.* A remark made in an undertone 1868.

‖**Sou** (sū). 1556. [F., earlier *soul, sol* SOL *sb.*[3]] A French coin, formerly the twentieth part of a livre, now used to designate the five-centime piece.

‖**Soubise** (subīz). 1776. [From Charles de Rohan *Soubise* (1715–1787), French general and courtier.] †**1.** A kind of cravat. **2.** A kind of onion-sauce. (Often in F. form *Sauce S.*) 1822.

‖**Soubrette** (subrɛ̄t). 1753. [F., ad. Prov. *soubreto*, fem. of *soubret* coy, reserved, f. *soubra* to set aside.] **1.** *Theatr.* A maidservant or lady's maid as a character in a play or opera, usually one of a pert, coquettish, or intriguing character; an actress or singer taking such a part. **2.** A lady's maid; a maidservant 1824.

‖**Soubriquet** (sū·brikeⁱ, ‖subrikɛ̄), *sb.* 1818. [a. older F.] = SOBRIQUET.

‖**Soucar** (sau·kāɪ). 1785. [ad. Urdū (Hindī) *sāhūkār* great merchant.] A Hindoo banker or moneylender.

The Indian Sowcar has..a notoriety hardly surpassed by that of the European Jew 1883. Hence **Sou·caring**, moneylending.

Souchong (sūʃǫ·ŋ). 1760. [ad. Chinese *siao-chung* small sort.] One of the finer varieties of black tea.

Soudan, Sudan (sudā·n). 1875. [Arab. *sūdān*, pl. of *sūdā* black.] The part of Africa lying between the Sahara and the Equator. Hence **Soudane·se** *sb.* an inhabitant of the S. (also as *pl.*); *adj.* of or pertaining to the S.

‖**Souffle** (sufl'). 1879. [F.] *Path.* A murmuring or breathing sound.

‖**Soufflé** (sū·fleⁱ, sufle), *sb.* and *a.* 1813. [F., pa. pple. of *souffler*:—L. *sufflare*, f. *sub* under + *flare* to blow.] **A.** *sb.* A light dish, either sweet or savoury, made by mixing materials with white of egg beaten up to a froth, and heating the mixture in an oven until it puffs up. **B.** *adj.* Of ceramic ware: Having liquid colour applied by means of blowing 1878.

‖**Souffleur** (suflǒr). [F., f. *souffler* to blow.] A prompter.

Sough (sau, sɒf, *Sc.* suχ), *sb.*[1] [ME. **swōh*, *swōȝ*, from the verb *swōȝen*; see SOUGH *v.*[1]] **1.** A rushing or murmuring sound as of wind, water, or the like, esp. one of a gentle or soothing nature. **2.** A deep sigh or breath. late ME. **3.** A rumour; a report 1716.

1. Pinewood's steady sugh WORDSW. **2.** From the loch would come the s. of a porpoise 1885. **3.** There was a s. in the country about it SCOTT.

Phr. *To keep a calm* (or *quiet*) *s.*, to say little or nothing, to keep quiet (Sc.).

Sough (sʊf), *sb.*[2] ME. [Origin obsc.] **1.** A boggy or swampy place; a small pool. **2.** A drain, sewer, trench 1440. **3.** An adit of a mine 1619.

Sough (sau, sʊf, *Sc.* suχ), *v.*[1] [OE. *swōgan*, = OS. *swōgan* to move with a rushing sound.] **1.** *intr.* To make a rushing, rustling, or murmuring sound. **2.** To draw the breath heavily or noisily; to sigh deeply 1475. **b.** With *away*: To breathe one's last. *dial.* 1816. **3.** *trans.* **a.** To hum (a tune) 1711. **b.** To utter in a sighing or whining tone 1816.

1. The wind soughed through the..branches..in long monotonous swell 1884.

Sough (sʊf), *v.*[2] 1688. [f. SOUGH *sb.*[2]] **1.** *trans.* **a.** To face or build up (a ditch) *with* stone, etc. **b.** To make drains in (land); to drain by constructing proper channels. Also *absol.* **2.** *intr.* To reach, or get into, a sough 1898.

Sought (sǭt), *ppl. a.* ME. [pa. pple. of SEEK *v.*] That is, or has been, searched for, desired, etc.

Soul (sōul), *sb.* [Com. Teut.; OE. *sáwol, sáwl*, = Goth. *saiwala*.] **I.** †**1.** The principle of life in man or animals; animate existence –1697. **2.** The principle of thought and action in man, commonly regarded as an entity distinct from the body; the spiritual part of man in contrast to the purely physical. Also occas., an analogous principle in animals. Freq. in connexion with or in contrast to *body*. OE. **3. a.** The seat of the emotions, feelings, or sentiments; the emotional part of man's nature OE. **b.** Intellectual or spiritual power; high development of the mental faculties 1604. **4.** *Metaph.* The vital, sensitive, or rational principle in plants, animals, or human beings. Freq. distinguished as *vegetative, sensitive,* and *rational* or *reasonable*. ME. **5.** *fig.* Applied to persons: **a.** As a term of endearment or adoration 1581. **b.** The personification *of* some quality 1605. **c.** The inspirer or leader of some business, cause, movement, etc. 1662. **6.** *fig.* Of things: **a.** The essential or animating part, element, or feature *of* something 1596. **b.** An element, principle, or trace *of* something 1599. **c.** *The s. of the world* [after L. *anima mundi*, Gr. ψυχὴ τοῦ κόσμου], the animating principle of the world, according to early philosophers 1600. **d.** The essential part or quality *of* a material thing 1658.

1. þei hated her soules, þat is to say, her bodely lyues, þat þei mi3t kepe hem in to lif euerlasting 1450. **2.** Who can tell yf that the sowle of man ascende, Or with the body of it dye? 1547. So much..as will hold s. and body together SCOTT. God is s., souls I and thou BROWNING. **3. a.** Is it not strange that sheepes guts should hale soules out of men's bodies? SHAKS. Phr. *Heart and s.*, with all one's energy and devotion; entirely. **b.** The mouse that..trusts to one poor hole, Can never be a mouse of any s. POPE. From that moment he could not call his s. his own 1889. **4.** Shall wee rowze the night-Owle in a Catch, that will drawe three soules out of one Weauer? SHAKS. **5. a.** Hang there like fruite, my soule, Till the Tree dye SHAKS. **b.** My brother..was the s. of honour GOLDSM. **c.** He was the author and the s. of the European coalition MACAULAY. **6. a.** Breuitie is the Soule of Wit SHAKS. **b.** There is some soule of goodnesse in things euill SHAKS. **c.** The prophetick soule Of the wide world, dreaming on things to come SHAKS. **d.** The s. of a ship is her engines 1890.

II. 1. The spiritual part of man considered in its moral aspect or in relation to God and His precepts OE. **2.** The spiritual part of man regarded as surviving after death and as susceptible of happiness or misery in a future state OE. **3.** Used in various asseverative phrases or as an exclam. late ME.

1. I begin to think of setting things in order, which I pray God enable me to put both as to s. and body PEPYS. **2.** Beseechinge him to have mercye on my sowle 1536. **3.** *By, for, on* or *upon* (one's) *s.*, etc.; Vpon my Soule, a Lye; a wicked Lye SHAKS.

III. 1. The disembodied spirit of a (deceased) person, regarded as a separate entity, and as invested with some amount of form and personality OE. **2.** A person, an individual; †a living thing. Chiefly in enumeration, or with *every*. ME. **3.** Used with defining adj. to denote a person of a particular character or in respect of some quality; freq. with a touch of contempt, compassion, or familiarity 1519. **4.** One in whom the spiritual or intellectual qualities predominate (*rare*) 1814.

1. It was beleved certenly that dead mens soules dyd walke after they were buried 1560. Devils and damned Souls in hell Fry in the fire with which they dwell 1683. **2.** There were about three hundred souls on board 1894. All alone, without a s. to say a word to 1897. **3.** For his errors, poor s.! were venial 1811.

IV. In spec. or techn uses. **1.** The lungs of a goose. Now *dial.* 1530. †**2.** The bore of a cannon. (So F. *l'âme d'un canon.*) –1669. **3.** The sound-post of a violin 1838.

attrib. and *Comb.*, as *s.-concern(ment; s.-curer; s.-adorning, -afflicting, -amazing, -conquering, -saving, -searching* adjs.; *s.-benumbed, -blinded, -felt* adjs.; also, †**s.-ale**, a dirge ale; †**s. chaplain**, = *s.-priest*; **s. pence**, money subscribed by members of a guild to pay for s.-masses; †**s.-priest**, a priest having the special function of praying for the souls of the dead.

Soul (sōul), *v.* late ME. [f. the sb.] †**1.** *trans.* To endow or endue with a soul. Also *fig.* –1646. **2.** *intr.* To go about collecting doles, properly on the eve of All Souls' Day. Chiefly in the phr. *to go a-souling*. 1779.

Sou·l(-)bell. 1599. [f. SOUL *sb.* II. 2.] The passing-bell.

The great Soul Bell of St. Swithun's was sobbing in the winter wind 1893.

Souled (sōuld), *ppl. a.* 1602. [f. SOUL *sb.*] As the second element of parasynthetic combs.: Endowed with a soul of a specified kind, as *great-, high-, large-, mean-s.* adjs.

Soulful (sōu·lfŭl), *a.* 1863. [f. SOUL *sb.* + -FUL 1.] **1.** Full of soul or feeling; in recent use freq. affectedly or unduly æsthetic or emotional. **2.** Expressive or indicative of deep feeling or emotion 1868.

1. Who can be s. and an athlete? 1882.

Soulish (sōu·liʃ), *a.* 1550. [f. SOUL *sb.* + -ISH.] **1.** = PSYCHICAL *a.* 2. **2.** Soul-like 1581.

Soulless (sōu·l,lės), *a.* 1553. [f. SOUL *sb.* + -LESS.] **1.** Having no soul; from whom or which the soul has departed. **2.** Of persons: Destitute of the noble qualities of the soul; lacking spirit, courage, or elevation of mind or feeling 1587. **b.** Of the eyes: Lacking animation or expression; dull 1835. **3.** Of things, qualities, etc.: Characterized by a lack of animation, ardour, or vivacity; dull, insipid, uninteresting 1632. **b.** Of writings, etc.: Devoid of inspiration or feeling 1856.

1. A brainlesse head and a soule-lesse body 1599. **2.** Trembling, and Soul-less half the Nation stood DE FOE. **3.** I see things as they are, bleak and bare, and s. 1833. Hence **Sou·lless-ly** *adv.*, **-ness.**

Sou·l-mass. Now *Hist.* or *dial.* 1450. [f. SOUL *sb.* II. 2 + MASS *sb.*[1]] **1.** A mass for the soul of a dead person 1488. **2.** *Soul-mass* (*Day*), All Souls' Day, 2 Nov. 1450.

Sou·l-scot. *Hist.* 1670. [f. SOUL *sb.* II. 2 + SCOT *sb.*[2]] A due paid on behalf of a deceased person to the church of the parish to which he belonged; a mortuary.

Sou·l-shot. *Hist.* 1647. [f. SOUL *sb.* + SHOT *sb.*] = prec.

Sou·l-sick, *a.* 1598. [f. SOUL *sb.*] **1.** Of persons: **a.** Suffering from spiritual indisposition or depression. **b.** Sick at heart; deeply dejected 1609. **2.** Characterized by dejection of spirit 1880.

2. A soul-sick longing comes over us for the silent heather hill 1899. So **Sou·l-sickness.**

Soum (sʊm). *Sc.* (*Hist.*) 1500. [app. identical with SUM *sb.*] The amount of pasturage that will support one cow or a proportional number of sheep; the number of sheep or cattle so maintained.

Sound (saund), *sb.*[1] [Partly OE. *sund* swimming, water, sea, and partly a. ON. *sund* swimming, strait, f. the stem of SWIM *v.*] **I.** †**1.** The action or power of swimming –ME. **2.** The swimming bladder of certain fish, esp. of cod or sturgeon ME.

2. This day dined..upon a fin of ling and some sounds PEPYS.

II. A relatively narrow channel or stretch of water, esp. one between the mainland and an island, or connecting two large bodies of water; a strait. Also, an inlet of the sea. ME. **b.** *The S.*, the strait between Denmark and Sweden which connects the Cattegat with the Baltic Sea 1633.

Sound (saund), *sb.*[2] ME. [a. AF. *soun*, OF. (mod.F.) *son* :—L. *sonum*, acc. of *sonus* sound. The -*d* is excrescent.] **1.** The sensation produced in the organs of hearing when the surrounding air is set in vibration in such a way as to affect these; also, that which is or may be heard; the external object of audition, or the property of bodies by which this is produced. **2.** The particular auditory effect produced by a special cause ME. **b.** The distance or range over which the sound of something is heard. In phr. *in* or *within* (*the*) *s. of* (something). 1617. **3.** A particular cause of auditory effect; an instance of the sensation resulting from this ME. **4.** In restricted sense: The auditory effect produced by the operation of the human voice; utterance, speech, or one of the separate articulations of which this is composed ME. **b.** The audible articulation(s) corresponding to a letter, word, name, etc. late ME. **c.** Used with implication of richness, euphony, or harmony 1553. †**d.** Import, significance –1719. **e.** Mere audible effect, without significance or real importance 1605. **5.** Fame or knowledge, report or rumour, news or tidings (*of* some thing or person). *Obs.* exc. *arch.* late ME.

1. He loudly brayd with beastly yelling s. SPENSER. Linnets fill the Woods with tuneful S. DRYDEN. **2.** The sowne Of swarming Bees SPENSER. After s. of trumpets and silence made EVELYN. **b.** Whether he first sees light..in s. of the swallowing sea M. ARNOLD. **3.** Oft in the Winds is heard a plaintive S. Of melancholy Ghosts ADDISON. **4.** Idle words,..Unprofitable sounds SHAKS. **b.** The very s. of the name of a royal maiden SCOTT. **c.** Woordes that fill the mouthe and haue a s. with them 1553. **e.** A Tale Told by an Ideot, full of s. and fury, Signifying nothing SHAKS.

attrib. and *Comb.*, as *s.-carrier, -wave; s.-conducting, -producing* adjs.; also **s.-body** *Mus.*, the hollow part of a stringed instrument which strengthens its s.; **-bow**, the thickest part of a bell, against which the hammer strikes; **-box**, s.-body; in a gramophone, the box which carries the reproducing or recording stylus; **-change** *Philol.*, the passage of one sound into another; so **-law**; **-house**, a marine alarm station from which audible alarms or signals are given in foggy weather; **-proof** *a.* (see PROOF *a.* 1 b). **b.** Denoting instruments, etc. for the recording of sound or the resulting record, as *s. camera, record*; **s.-film**, a cinema film with audible dialogue, music, etc.

Sound, *sb.*[3] Now *dial.* late ME. [var. *swoun(d* SWOON *sb.*] A swoon or fainting-fit.

Sound (saund), *sb.*[4] 1584. [app. f. (ult.) OE. or ON. *sund* SOUND *sb.*[1], or f. SOUND *v.*[2]] **1.** An act of sounding with the lead; also *fig.*, power of sounding or investigating (*rare*). **2.** *Surg.* An instrument for probing parts of the body, usually long and slender and having a slightly enlarged end 1797.

Sound (saund), *a.* [ME. *sund*, repr. OE. *gesund* (= G. *gesund*).] **I. 1.** Of persons, animals, etc.: Free from disease, infirmity, or injury; having or enjoying bodily health; healthy, robust. Usu. predicative. Also *absol.* **b.** Said of appetite, health, etc. 1591. **2.** Not affected by disease, decay, or injury ME. **3.** Free from damage, decay, or special defect; unimpaired, uninjured; in good condition or repair ME. **b.** Of air, liquor, or food: Not spoiled or vitiated in any way; hence, wholesome, good and strong 1460. **c.** Financially safe 1601. **4. a.** Of things or substances: Solid, massive, compact. late ME. **b.** Of land: Dry in subsoil; not boggy or marshy. Now *dial.* 1523. **5.** Of sleep, etc.: Deep, profound; unbroken or undisturbed. Hence with *sleeper*. 1548. **6.** Of a solid, substantial, ample, or thorough nature or character 1565. **b.** Of blows, a beating, etc.: Dealt or given with force or severity 1607.

1. They were known to be all s. and in good health DE FOE. Phr. *As s. as a bell.* **b.** Things unsavory to s. appetites 1591. **2.** A s. heart is the life of the flesh: but enuie is the rotting of the bones BIBLE (Geneva) *Prov.* xiv. 30. A prince of..sound intellectuals EVELYN. **3.** Our men healthy, and our ships s. DE FOE. *fig.* My loue to thee is s., *sans* cracke or flaw SHAKS. **b.** Some s. old ale, and a glass of stiff negus SCOTT. **c.** He lent his money..with s. securities and at usurious interest 1879. **4.** A small Gothic chapel, hewn..out of the s. and solid rock SCOTT. **5.** This sleepe is s. indeede SHAKS. **6.** School-friendships are not always..permanent and s. COWPER. **b.** A s. rap on the pate 1607.

II. 1. In full accordance with fact, reason, or good sense; free from error, fallacy, or logical defect; good, strong, valid 1440. **b.** Theologically correct; orthodox 1575. †**c.** Of a book or writing: Accurate, correct –1700. **2.** Of judgement, sense, etc.: Based on or characterized by well-grounded principles or good practical knowledge 1577. **3.** Of persons, disposition, etc.: Morally good; honest, straightforward 1580. **b.** Sincere, true; trusty, loyal 1581. **c.** Having a healthy national or moral tone 1822. **4.** Of persons: Orthodox, esp. in regard to religious belief 1526. **5.** Of sober or solid judgement; well-grounded in principles or knowledge; thoroughly versed and reliable 1615.

1. Remarks..as s. as they are acute and ingenious BURKE. Their..theory, s. or unsound, was..complete and coherent MACAULAY. **b.** He ordinarily preach'd s. doctrine EVELYN. **2.** It is a Maxim of the soundest Sense 1718. **4.** He came from Scotland s. as a bell on the five points of Calvinism 1874. **5.** As s. in iudgement as ripe in experience 1615. Hence **Sou·nd-ly** *adv.* late ME, **-ness** late ME.

Comb., as *s.-headed*, *-hearted*, *-minded*, adjs.

Sound (saund), *adv.* late ME. [f. prec.] Soundly.

So s. he slept, that nought mought him awake SPENSER. *S.* (*asleep*), fast asleep.

Comb., as *s.-judging*, *-thinking*, adjs.

Sound (saund), *v.*[1] ME. [ad. OF. *suner*, *soner* (mod.F. *sonner*) :—L. *sonare*, f. *sonus* sound.] **I.** *intr.* **1.** Of things: To make or emit a sound. **b.** To resound; to be filled with sound ME. **c.** Of instruments: To give a call *to* arms, battle, etc. 1705. **2.** Of persons: To make a sound by blowing, or playing upon, some instrument. late ME. **3.** To strike the ears, to be heard, as a sound. late ME. **b.** To be mentioned or spoken of 1635. **4.** To convey a certain impression or idea by the sound; to appear to have a certain signification when heard (or read). late ME. †**5.** To have a suggestion or touch of, a tendency towards, some connexion or association with, a specified thing –1661. **6.** *To s. in damages*, in legal use, to be concerned only with damages 1780.

1. The Trumpet alwaies sounding when the meat was carried up 1662. **b.** The street sounds to the soldiers' tread 1896. **c.** The trumpets sounded to horse DE FOE. **3.** I hear the far-off Curfeu s. MILT. As if the words of an oracle sounded in his ears SCOTT. **b.** Wherever I went my name sounded DISRAELI. **4.** I tell you 'twill s. harshly in her eares SHAKS. **5.** I promise you that this matter sowndeth moche to your dishonour 1530.

II. *trans.* **1.** To cause (an instrument, etc.) to make a sound; to blow, strike, or play on ME. **2.** To utter in an audible tone; to pronounce or repeat. Sometimes implying loudness of tone. ME. †**b.** To express in words (*rare*). –1592. **c.** To utter or pronounce in a certain way 1542. **3.** To give intimation of, a signal or order for (something) by the sound of a trumpet, drum, etc.; to announce, order, or direct by such means 1568. **b.** To blow (a blast) 1806. **4.** To declare, announce, proclaim; to make known or famous; to celebrate. late ME. †**5.** Of words: To signify or mean; to import or imply –1671. **6.** To examine (a person) by auscultation 1887.

1. Or say we s. The trump of liberty GRAY. **2.** Hearing these tearmes of hell and eternall, so often souned in our eares 1593. **b.** No words can that woe s. SHAKS. **3.** The besieged sounded a retreat 1734. **4.** To him The Sabbath bell sounds peace 1804.

Sound (saund), *v.*[2] ME. [ad. OF. *sonder*, f. *sonde* SOUND *sb.*[4]] †**1.** *intr.* To sink in, penetrate, pierce. –late ME. **2.** *Naut.* To employ the line and lead, or other means, in order to ascertain the depth of the sea, a channel, etc., or the nature of the bottom 1485. **b.** *fig.* To make inquiry or investigation 1793. **3. a.** Of the lead: To go down; to touch bottom 1610. **b.** Of a whale: To go deep under water; to dive 1839. **4.** *trans.* To investigate (water, etc.) by the use of the line and lead or other means, in order to ascertain the depth or the quality of the bottom; to measure or examine in some way resembling this 1460. **b.** To measure (depth) in this way 1628. **5.** In fig. contexts: To measure, or ascertain, as by sounding 1589. **6.** To examine or question (a person) in an indirect manner 1575. **b.** To investigate (a matter, a person's views, etc.), esp. by cautious or indirect questioning; to make trial of in this way 1579. †**7.** To understand; to fathom –1655. **8.** *Surg.* To examine by means of a sound, esp. for the stone; †to probe 1597.

2. There sounding with our plummet, sand of Amber stuck thereto 1617. Men went overboard with poles in their hands, sounding..for deeper water DE FOE. **b.** His thoughts..had sounded into the depths of his own nature CARLYLE. **3. a.** And deeper then did euer Plummet s. Ile drowne my booke SHAKS. **b.** The whale suddenly disappears; he has 'sounded' 1839. **4.** It is so deepe in some places that it cannot be sounded 1604. **5.** He..sounded the depth of my character 1824. **6.** It is better to s. a person..a farre off, then to fal vppon the pointe at first BACON. Hence **Sou·ndable** *a.* (*rare*) of the sea, capable of being sounded. †**Sou·ndage**, a due paid for the taking of soundings. **Sou·nder**[3], an apparatus for sounding the sea.

Sound, *v.*[3] Now *dial.* late ME. Variant of SWOON *v.*

Sou·nd-board. 1500. [SOUND *sb.*[2]] **1.** A thin board or plate of wood forming part of a musical instrument and placed in such a position as to strengthen or increase its sound. **2.** = SOUNDING-BOARD **1.** 1766.

1. As in an Organ from one blast of wind To many a row of Pipes the s. breaths MILT.

Sounder[1] (sau·ndəɹ). late ME. [a. OF. *sundre*, *sonre*, of Germanic origin.] A herd of wild swine.

Sounder[2] (sau·ndəɹ). 1591. [f. SOUND *v.*[1]] **1.** One who causes or utters a sound or sounds; one who causes something, esp. an instrument, to sound. **2.** A telegraphic device which enables the communications or signals to be read by sound 1860. **b.** A telegraphist who operates or has experience with this 1887. **3.** A device which gives a signal, etc., by sounding; also, the signal so given 1884.

Sou·nd-hole. 1611. [SOUND *sb.*[2]] **1.** *Mus.* Either of the curvilinear openings in the belly of a stringed instrument, one on each side of the bridge. **2.** *Arch.* An opening in a tower or belfry 1848.

Sounding (sau·ndiŋ), *vbl. sb.*[1] late ME. [f. SOUND *v.*[1]] **1.** The fact of giving out a sound or sounds, or the power of doing this; the sound produced by something. **2.** Vocal utterance or pronunciation; resonant or sonorous quality of this. late ME. **3.** The (or an) act of causing a trumpet, bell, etc., to sound; the blowing *of* a bugle or trumpet, esp. as a signal 1523. **4.** The action of examining by percussion; *spec.* auscultation 1883.

1. A blast so hye, That made an eckow in the ayer and sowning through the sky 1557.

Comb.: **s.-post**, = SOUND-POST.

Sounding (sau·ndiŋ), *vbl. sb.*[2] ME. [f. SOUND *v.*[2]] **1.** The action of sounding or ascertaining the depth of water by means of the line and lead; an instance of this. **b.** *fig.* Investigation 1592. **2.** A place or position at sea where it is possible to reach the bottom with the ordinary deep-sea lead. Chiefly *pl.* late ME. †**b.** *spec.* with *the.* Such places in the mouth of the English Channel 1666. **3.** *pl.* The depths of water in the sea or (rarely) in a river, ascertained by sounding with the line and lead; also, the entries in a log-book, etc., giving these, together with particulars of the nature of the bottom reached by the lead 1570. **4.** *Surg.* The action of examining with a sound or probe 1597. **5.** *attrib.*, chiefly in sense **1**, as *s.-machine*, *-plumb*, *-plummet* 1555.

2. We were soon out of soundings, and well into the Bay of Biscay MARRYAT.

Sounding (sau·ndiŋ), *ppl. a.* ME. [f. SOUND *v.*[1]] **1.** Having a sound; causing, emitting, producing a sound or sounds, esp. of a loud character; resonant, sonorous; reverberant. **2.** Of language, names, titles, etc.: Having a full, rich, or imposing sound; high-sounding, pompous, bombastic 1683.

1. The s. cataract Haunted me WORDSW. **2.** The orator has been apt to..deal in s. commonplaces 1888.

Sou·nding-board. 1766. [SOUNDING *vbl. sb.*[1]] **1.** A board or screen placed over or behind a pulpit, etc., in such a manner as to reflect the speaker's voice towards the audience. **2.** *Mus.* = SOUND-BOARD **1.** 1776.

Sou·nding-lead. late ME. [SOUNDING *vbl. sb.*[2]] *Naut.* The lead or plummet attached to the sounding-line.

Sou·nding-line. ME. [f. as prec.] *Naut.* A line used in sounding the depth of water; also, material forming this.

Soundless (sau·ndlės), *a.*[1] 1586. [f. SOUND *v.*[2]] That cannot be sounded; unfathomable. *lit.* and *fig.*

Soundless (sau·ndlės), *a.*[2] 1601. [f. SOUND *sb.*[2]] **1.** Having, making, etc., no sound; quiet, silent. **2.** In which no sound is heard; still 1816.

2. A s. waste, a trackless vacancy! WORDSW. Hence **Sou·ndless-ly** *adv.*, **-ness.**

Sou·nd-post. 1687. [f. SOUND *sb.*[2] + POST *sb.*[1]] A small peg of wood fixed beneath the bridge of a violin or similar instrument, serving as a support for the belly and as a connecting part between this and the back.

Soup (sūp), *sb.* 1653. [ad. F. *soupe* sop, broth; see SOP *sb.*] **1.** A liquid food prepared by boiling, usually consisting of an extract of meat with other ingredients and seasoning. **2.** *colloq.* or *slang.* **a.** Briefs for prosecutions given to members of the Bar at Quarter Sessions or other courts; the fees attaching to such briefs. Also in *pl.* 1856. **b.** *In the s.*, in a difficulty. orig. *U.S.* 1889.

Comb.: **s.-house**, **-kitchen**, an establishment for preparing s. and distributing it to the poor or unemployed, either free or at a very low charge; **-ticket**, a ticket given to poor people enabling them to receive s. from a s.-kitchen. Hence **Soup** *v. trans.* to provide with s. **Sou·py** *a.* like s.; having the appearance or consistency of s.

‖**Soupçon** (supson̄). 1766. [F., repr. OF. *soupeçon*, *souspeçon* :—late L. *suspection-*, *suspectio* for *suspicio* SUSPICION.] A suspicion, a suggestion, a very small quantity or slight trace, *of* something.

Souper (sū·pəɹ). 1851. [f. SOUP *sb.* or *v.*] **1.** In Ireland, a Protestant clergyman seeking to make proselytes by dispensing soup in charity. **2.** One converted to Protestantism by the receipt of soup or other charity 1871.

Soup maigre (sūp‚ mē·gəɹ). 1754. [ad. F. *soupe maigre*; see SOUP *sb.* and MAIGRE *a.*] Thin soup, made chiefly from vegetables or fish. So †**Soup-mea·gre** 1737.

Sour (sauəɹ), *a.* and *sb.* [Com. Teut.; OE. *sūr.*] **A.** *adj.* **I. 1.** Having a tart or acid taste, such as that of unripe fruits or vinegar. (Opp. to *sweet*, and dist. from *bitter.*) **b.** *transf.* Producing tart or acid fruit OE. **c.** In fig. or allusive uses. late ME. **2.** Rendered acid by fermentation or similar processes; fermented; affected or spoiled in this way by being kept or exposed too long OE. **b.** Of smell, breath, eructations, etc. ME. **3. a.** Of land, etc.: Cold and wet; uncongenial through retaining stagnant moisture 1532. **b.** Of pasture: Having a harsh, unpleasant taste; coarse, rank. Now *dial.* 1654.

1. [The fox] sayd these raysyns ben sowre CAXTON. More sowr then the strongest Vinegar 1666. **b.** The soure crabtree 1560. **c.** *Provb.* He has given me sweet Meat, but sowr Sauce 1687. *Sour grapes*, in allusion to Æsop's fable of 'The Fox and the Grapes', when a person disparages something which it is suspected he would be glad to possess if he could. **2.** *fig.* Ephraim is ioyned to idoles:..Their drinke is sowre *Hosea* iv. 18.

II. 1. Extremely distasteful or disagreeable; bitter, unpleasant ME. **2.** Having a harsh, morose, or peevish disposition; sullen, austere; gloomy, discontented, embittered ME. **3.** Displaying, expressing, or implying displeasure or discontent; peevish, cross 1440. **b.** Wry, distorted 1611. **4.** Of weather, etc.: Cold and wet; inclement. Now *Sc.* 1582. **5.** Of animals: Heavy, coarse, gross. *dial.* 1713.

1. Al though it be soure to suffre, þere cometh swete after LANGL. **2.** His temper was s., arrogant, and impatient of opposition MACAULAY. **3.** He..from his sower Looks is commonly called Vinegar Jones 1720. A s. discourse on the wickedness of the others 1851. **b.** Make what s. mouths he would for a pretence LAMB. **4.** The Earth..weeps and blears itself, in s. rain, and worse CARLYLE.

Comb.: **s. cake**, an oat- or rye-cake made of fermented dough; **s. gourd**, (the fruit of) the Baobab, *Adansonia digitata*, or the related species *A. gregorii*; **s. grass**, (*a*) the grass *Paspalum*; (*b*) sorrel; **s. gum** *U.S.*, *Nyssa villosa* or *multiflora*, also called tupelo; **s. plum,** *Owenia acidula*; **s. wood** *U.S.*, the sorrel-tree. Hence **Sou·r-ly** *adv.*, **-ness** OE.

B. *sb.* **1.** That which is sour OE. **2.** In bleaching and tanning, a bath or steep of an acid character 1756. **3.** *U.S.* An acid drink, usu. whisky or other spirit with lemon added 1885.

1. The sweets we wish for, turne to lothed sowrs SHAKS.

Sour (sauəɹ), *adv.* [ME. *sūre*, f. *sūr* SOUR *a.*] †**1.** Bitterly, dearly; severely –1450. **2.** Disagreeably, unpleasantly; crossly, gloomily, unfavourably. Chiefly in phr. *to look s.* 1500.

Sour (sauəɹ), *v.* ME. [f. SOUR *a.*] **1.** *intr.* To become sour; to acquire a sour taste. **b.** To become embittered, morose, or peevish 1748. **c.** *To s. on*, to take a dislike to. orig. *U.S.* 1862. **2.** *trans.* Of leaven: To cause fermentation in (dough, etc.) ME. **3.** To make sour or acid; *esp.* to cause to have a tart or sour taste; to spoil in this way 1460. **b.** To make (land) cold and wet 1842. **c.** *Bleaching.* To subject to the action of diluted acids 1756. **4.** To render sour, gloomy, or morose; to embitter (the mind, temper, etc.) 1599. †**b.** To invest with a sour expression. SHAKS.

1. Milk when it sours on the Stomach 1632. *fig.* Hote loue often after wil soure ME. **b.** She sour'd To what she is: a nature never kind! TENNYSON. **2.** *fig.* Sowred with the leauen of their superstition 1611. **3.** *fig.* This sowers all thy sweets, sads all thy Rest 1645. **4.** A man..whose conscience..had soured him 1878. Physical and mental misery,..soured her disposition 1882. **b.** *Ven. & Ad.* 185.

Source (sōᵊɹs). ME. [a. OF. *sors*, **sours* masc., and *surse*, *source* (mod.F. *source*) fem., subst. uses of the pa. pple. of *sourdre* to rise or spring; see SOURD *v.*] †**1.** 'A support or underprop' –ME. †**2.** *Hawking.* The act of rising on the wing, on the part of a hawk or other bird –1612. **3.** The fountain-head or origin of a river or stream; the spring or place from which a flow of water takes its beginning. late ME. **b.** With *a* and *pl.* A spring; a fountain 1477. **4.** *fig.* The chief or prime cause *of* something of a non-material or abstract character; the quarter whence something of this kind originates. late ME. **b.** The origin, or original stock, *of* a person, family, etc. 1669. **c.** The originating cause or substance *of* some material thing or physical agency 1803. **d.** A work, etc., supplying information or evidence (esp. of an original or primary character) as to some fact, event, or series of these 1788. **5.** *Physics.* A point or centre from which a fluid or current flows 1878.

2. Right as an hauk upon a sours Upspringeth into thaer, right so prayeres..Maken her sours to Goddis eeres tuo CHAUCER. **3.** The flouds do gaspe, for dryed is theyr sourse SPENSER. **b.** Like torrents from a mountain s. TENNYSON. **4.** O swerd of knighthod, sours of gentilesse! CHAUCER. This s. of ideas, every man has wholly in himself LOCKE.

Comb. **s.-book** [tr. G. *quellenbuch*], a book or collection of 'sources' or original documents serving as materials for the historical study of a subject.

Sour(-)crout. 1617. [Anglicized form of SAUERKRAUT.] A fermented preparation of cabbage.

†**Sourd,** *v.* late ME. [ad. OF. *sourdre* (also mod.F.), *sordre*, *surdre* :—L. *surgere* to rise.] **1.** *intr.* Of conditions, events, etc.: To arise, take rise, spring or issue –1567. **2.** Of fountains, etc.: To spring up, to issue from the ground –1606.

1. Now myghte men axe, wher-of that pride sourdeth and spryngeth CHAUCER.

Sour(-)dock. Now *dial.* ME. [SOUR *a.* and DOCK *sb.*[1]] Common sorrel.

Sour-dough (sauᵊ·ɹ,dōu). ME. [See SOUR *a.* and DOUGH *sb.*] **1.** Leaven. Now *dial.* and *rare.* **2.** *Amer.* One who has spent one or more winters in Alaska 1902.

Souring (sauᵊ·riŋ), *vbl. sb.* late ME. [f. SOUR *v.*] **1.** A substance which renders sour or acid; *spec.* leaven, lemon-juice, or vinegar. Now chiefly *dial.* **2.** The process or fact of becoming or making sour 1579. **3.** *spec.* The process of subjecting cloth, wool, skins, etc., to the action of diluted acids 1756. **4.** A sourish variety of apple; *dial.* a crab-apple 1846.

2. *fig.* Hazlitt's cynicism is the s. of a generous nature 1874.

Sourish (sauᵊ·riʃ), *a.* late ME. [f. SOUR *a.* + -ISH.] Somewhat sour, in various senses. Bread brownish and sowrish, and made with aniseeds 1617. Hence **Sou·rish-ly** *adv.*, **-ness.**

Sour-sop. 1667. [f. SOUR *a.* + SOP *sb.*] **1.** The fruit of the West Indian tree *Anona muricata.* **2.** The tree itself 1753.

Sou·r-sweet, *a.* and *sb.* 1591. [f. the adjs.] **A.** *adj.* Sweet with an admixture or aftertaste of sourness. **B.** *sb.* Something which is sour-sweet; *spec.* an acid sweetmeat 1603.

‖**Sous-** (sū, sūz), *prefix*, repr. OF. and mod. F. *sous* (:—L. *subtus*) 'under', 'sub-', in words directly adopted from French, as *s.-lieutenant*, *-ministre*, *-officier*, *-prefect.*

Souse (saus), *sb.*[1] Now *dial.* and *U.S.* late ME. [a. OF. *sous* (*soulz*), or *souce*, ad. OHG. *sulza*, or directly f. the Germanic stem *sult-* (see SILT *sb.*).] **1.** Various parts of a pig or other animal, esp. the feet and ears, prepared or preserved for food by pickling. **b.** *transf.* The ears; also in *sing.*, an ear 1658. **2.** A liquid employed as a pickle 1502.

Souse (saus), *sb.*[2] Now *dial.* 1480. [perh. echoic.] A heavy blow; a thump.

†**Souse,** *sb.*[3] 1486. [Alteration of SOURCE *sb.* 2.] *Hawking.* **1.** Phr. *at* (*the*) *s.*: (of a hunted bird) in the act of rising from the ground and giving the hawk an opportunity to strike. –1620. **2.** The act of a hawk, in swooping down upon a hunted bird –1638.

2. As a Faulcon faire That once hath failed of her s. full neare SPENSER.

†**Souse,** *sb.*[4] 1502. [a. OF. *sous*, pl. of *sout*, *solt*, later *sol* SOL *sb.*[3] and *sou* SOU.] **1.** A sol or sou –1823. **2.** Taken as a type of a small coin or amount, with an expressed or implied negative –1815.

Souse (saus), *sb.*[5] 1741. [f. SOUSE *v.*[1]] **1.** An act of sousing; a plunge into, immersion in, or drenching with, water; *dial.* a wash. **b.** An act of getting drunk (*slang*) 1930. **2.** A sound as of water surging against something 1883.

Souse (saus), *v.*[1] late ME. [f. SOUSE *sb.*[1]] **I.** *trans.* **1.** To prepare or preserve (meat, fish, etc.) by steeping in some kind of pickle, esp. one made with vinegar or the like. **2.** To plunge or immerse (a person, etc.) deeply or thoroughly *in* or *into* water, etc. 1470. **3.** To drench or soak with water, etc. 1542. **4.** To dash or pour (a quantity of water or something containing this). Const. *into*, *on*, etc. 1859.

1. A sheepes heade sawsed in ale 1500. *fig.* Sowse us..in the Powdering-Tub of thy Mercy, that we may be Tripes fit for the Heavenly Table 1704. **2.** To be soused over head and ears in cold water 1660. **3.** Then the engines arrived and soused the burning houses 1871.

II. *intr.* **1.** To soak; to be or become soaked or drenched; to go plunging or sinking in water, etc. **b.** To get drunk (*slang*) 1923. †**2.** To flow or fall in copious streams –1648.

1. Down I soused into the water THACKERAY. **2.** The surging seas came sousing in againe DRAYTON.

Souse (saus), *v.*[2] Now *dial.* 1550. [Related to SOUSE *sb.*[2]] **1.** *trans.* To strike, smite, or beat severely or heavily. †**2.** *absol.* To deliver heavy blows. SPENSER. **3.** *intr.* To fall heavily or with some weight 1596.

1. Soundly did he s. my pate 1787. **2.** Both..souce so sore, that they the heauens affray SPENSER.

Souse (saus), *v.*[3] Now *arch.* 1583. [f. SOUSE *sb.*[3] 2.] **1.** *intr.* Of a hawk, etc.: To swoop down; to descend with speed and force. **2.** *trans.* To swoop or pounce upon (something) in a hostile manner 1595.

1. The sacred eagle..sousing on the quivering hare POPE. **2.** The gallant Monarch..like an Eagle, o're his ayerie towres, To sowsse annoyance that comes neere his Nest SHAKS.

Souse (saus), *adv.*[1] Now chiefly *dial.* 1680. [f. SOUSE *sb.*[3] or *v.*[3]] **1.** Suddenly; without warning. **2.** With a direct and rapid course 1690. **3.** With strong or violent impact 1694.

3. Gundling comes s. upon the ice with his sitting-part CARLYLE.

Souse (saus), *adv.*[2] 1706. [f. SOUSE *sb.*[1] or *v.*[1]] With a deep or sudden plunge.

S. he went into the sea 1882.

Souslik, var. of SUSLIK.

‖**Soutache** (sutaʃ). 1856. [F., corruptly ad. Hungarian *szuszak* a pendant curl of hair, etc.] A narrow flat ornamental braid of wool, silk, or the like, usually sown upon fabrics in fanciful designs.

‖**Soutane** (sutan). 1838. [F., ad. It. *sottana*, f. *sotto* :—L. *subtus* under.] **1.** An ecclesiastic's cassock. **2.** *transf.* An ecclesiastic 1890.

2. A confederacy of soutanes and petticoats 1890.

‖**Souteneur** (sutnör). 1906. [Fr. 'protector'.] A man who cohabits with and lives on the earnings of a prostitute.

Souter (sū·təɹ). Now *Sc.* and *n. dial.* [OE *sūtere*, ad. L. *sutor*, f. *suere* to sew, stitch.] A shoemaker or cobbler.

The s. tauld his queerest stories BURNS. Hence †**Sou·terly** *a.* resembling a s.; common, vulgar; appropriate to a s.

Souterrain (sū·tərēⁱn). 1735. [a. F., f. *sous* under + *terre* earth, after L. *subterraneus.*] An underground chamber, store-room, passage, etc.

South (sauþ), *adv.*, *prep.*, *sb.*, and *a.* [Com. Teut.; OE. *sūð* = OFris. *sûth*, OS. *sûth*, OHG. *sund-*, *sunt-*, ON. *suðr.*] **A.** *adv.* **1.** Towards, or in the direction of, that part of the earth or heavens which is directly opposite to the north. **2.** From the south 1626. **3.** quasi-*sb.* = B. 1. ME. **4.** *ellipt.* as *prep.* At, in, or to the south of 1607.

1. Steering s. and s. by west 1743. **2.** In a Faire and Dry Day,..And when the Wind bloweth not S. BACON. **3.** To S. the Persian Bay MILT. †*By s.*, in the s.; on the s. side. **4.** The Chimney Is S. the Chamber SHAKS.

B. *sb.* (Usu. with *the.*) **1.** That one of the four cardinal points which is opposite to the north ME. **2.** The southern part of a country or region; *spec.* **a.** Of England (below the Wash), Great Britain, Scotland, or Ireland; the south country ME. **b.** The southern lands of Europe, etc. late ME. **c.** The southern States of America. orig. *U.S.* 1779. **3.** The southern part *of* a particular country, etc. late ME. **4.** *transf.* The inhabitants of a southern region or district ME. **5.** The south wind. Chiefly *poet.* ME. **b.** A south wind 1699.

1. The wyndes of the S. Ben most of alle debonaire GOWER. **2. a.** In the S. we usually call marygolds simply *golds* 1691. **b.** Dark-browed cavaliers from the sunny s. 1890. **4.** Between the North and S. here will be feelings of implacable hatred 1861. **5.** Wake North, and com O South, and on my garden blowe 1587. **b.** My wind is turned to bitter north, That was so soft a s. before CLOUGH.

C. *adj.* **1.** With proper names: Situated or dwelling in the south; southerly OE. **2.** With common nouns: Lying towards the south; situated on the side next the south OE. **3.** Of the wind: Blowing from the south OE. **4.** Of or pertaining to the south; belonging or native to the south 1470. **5.** Facing the south 1527. **6.** Tending towards the south 1839.

1. The second Kingdome of the Heptarchy, was of the S. Saxons 1643. They were lordes of Granada in s. Spaine 1600. **2.** The fort near the s. end of the city 1792. **3.** The Southwind rose,..with black wings Wide hovering MILT. *transf.* The South-Fog rot him SHAKS. **4.** For what says the s. proverb SCOTT. **5.** Carnations and mignonette blooming in the s. window 1867. **6.** In a s. direction 1886. Also in comp. †**Sou·ther** *a.*, whence **Sou·thermost** *a.* (now *rare* or *Obs.*).

South (sauþ), *v.* 1659. [f. SOUTH *adv.* or *sb.*] **1.** *intr.* To cross the meridian of a place. **2.** To veer, move, or turn towards the south; to blow more from the south 1725.

2. About sun-down the wind southed 1898.

South- (sauþ), comb. form repr. SOUTH *sb.* or *adv.*, with the sense 'to or towards, in or on, the south', as in *s.-going*, etc.; *s.-bounded*, *-turned*, etc.

Southard (sɒ·ðəɹd), *adv.* and *sb.* 1470. Reduced form of SOUTHWARD.

Southco·ttian, *sb.* and *a.* Also **-cotian.** 1842. [See def.] **A.** *sb.* A believer in the claims or teaching of Joanna Southcott (1750–1814), who announced herself as the woman spoken of in Rev. xii. **B.** *adj.* Of or pertaining to Joanna Southcott or her followers 1843.

South country. late ME. [SOUTH *a.* 2.] The southern part of any country; the district or region towards the south; *spec.* of Great Britain (south of the Tweed), of England (south of the Wash), or of Scotland (south of the Forth). Also *attrib.* (freq. hyphened).

Southdown (sau·þdaun). Also **South Down, South-down.** 1787. [See def.] **1.** One of a breed of sheep, noted for its short, fine wool and for the good quality of its mutton, orig. reared on the South Downs of Sussex and Hampshire. Chiefly in *pl.* **2.** This breed of sheep. Chiefly with *the.* 1827. **3.** *ellipt.* Mutton from this breed of sheep 1859.

South-east (saup,ī·st), *adv.*, *sb.*, and *a.* [OE. *sūðēast* (see SOUTH *adv.* and EAST *adv.*).] **A.** *adv.* **1.** In the direction lying midway between south and east. **2.** quasi-*sb.* ME.

1. We..stood off to sea, steering still s. DE FOE. The district east and s. of Charter 1896. 2. Faced all round with a..Rock, except a Bay at South-East 1707.

B. *sb.* **1.** The direction or point of the horizon lying between south and east. late ME. †**2.** The south-east wind –1725. **3.** The south-eastern part of a country 1778.

1. He made the signal..to..steer to the s. 1806. 3. Sardinia rising to invade the Southeast 1837.

C. *adj.* **1.** Lying or situated in or towards, directed to, the south-east 1548. **2.** Of the wind, currents, etc.: Blowing or running from the south-east. late ME.

2. The strong southeast swell 1898. Hence **South-ea·ster**, a wind or gale blowing from the s.

South-ea·sterly, *a.* and *adv.* 1708. [f. SOUTH + EASTERLY.] **A.** *adj.* **a.** Lying, etc., in the direction of south-east. **b.** Blowing or running from the south-east. **B.** *adv.* Towards the south-east 1884.

South-ea·stern, *a.* 1577. [f. SOUTH + EASTERN.] **1.** Lying on the south-east side; situated in the south-east. **b.** Of or pertaining to the south-east of England 1886. **2.** Of the wind: Blowing from the south-east 1842.

South-ea·stward, *adv.*, *sb.*, and *a.* 1528. [f. SOUTH-EAST + -WARD.] **A.** *adv.* In a south-easterly direction; towards the south-east. **B.** *sb.* The south-east quarter or direction 1555. **C.** *adj.* Situated towards or leading to the south-east 1766. Hence **South-ea·stwardly** *adv.* towards the south-east; on the south-east side.

Souther (sau·þəɹ), *sb.* 1862. [f. SOUTH *a.* + -ER [1].] A south wind or gale.

Souther (sɒ·ðəɹ), *v.* 1628. [f. SOUTH *adv.* + -ER [5].] *intr.* To shift, turn, or fly to the south; of the wind, to south.

Southerly (sɒ·ðəɹli), *a.* 1551. [f. SOUTH; cf. *northerly*, etc.] **1.** Situated in or towards the south; southern. **2.** Of the wind: Blowing from the south 1602. **3.** Tending or facing southwards 1789. Hence **Sou·therliness.**

Southerly (sɒ·ðəɹli), *adv.* 1577. [Cf. prec. and -LY [2].] **1.** To the southward; in or towards the south; on the south side. **2.** From the direction of the south 1642.

2. The Wind chop'd up S. 1642.

Southern (sɒ·ðəɹn), *a.* and *sb.* [OE. *sūðerne*, f. *sūð* south + *-erne* (:—OTeut. *-ronjo-*). See also SOUTHRON.] **A.** *adj.* **1.** Of persons: Living or originating in, coming from, the south, esp. of Great Britain (= English), of England, or of Europe. **b.** *U.S.* Belonging to the Southern States 1839. **2.** Of the wind: Blowing from the south OE. **3.** Situated or lying to the southward or in the south; having a position relatively south OE. **b.** *Astron.* In the names of constellations, as *S. Cross*, *Fish*, etc. 1594. **4.** Of things: Pertaining or belonging to, produced by, found in, characteristic of, the south OE. **b.** *S. lights*, the Aurora Australis 1775. **5.** Facing or directed towards the south 1706. **6.** As *adv.* Towards the south 1678.

3. b. *S. Cross*, see CROSS *sb.* 11. 6. All S., from yon Hills, the Roman Camp Hangs o'er us black and threatning DRYDEN.

B. *sb.* **1.** Southern men (*rare*). late ME. **2.** A native of the south (see A. 1) 1721.

1. The S. on this side, for Yorke 'a Warwicke' cry 1622. Hence **Sou·thern** *v. intr.* to become more southerly. **Sou·therner**, a native of the south. **Sou·thernly**, *a.* and *adv.* = SOUTHERLY *a.* and *adv.* **Sou·thernmost** *a.* furthest south.

Southernwood (sɒ·ðəɹnwud). [OE. *sūðerne* SOUTHERN *a.*, and *wudu* WOOD *sb.*] A hardy deciduous shrub, *Artemisia Abrotanum*, having a fragrant aromatic smell and a sour taste, orig. native to the south of Europe, and formerly much cultivated for medicinal purposes. Also, the genus of *Compositæ* of which this is the type.

Southing (sau·ðiŋ, sau·þiŋ), *vbl. sb.* 1659. [f. SOUTH *adv.* or *v.* + -ING [1].] **1.** Of heavenly bodies: The action of crossing or approaching the meridian of a place. **2.** Progress or deviation towards the south made in sailing, travelling, etc.; difference in latitude due to moving southward. Chiefly in *Navigation.* 1669.

Sou·thland. Now *arch.* or *poet.* Also **south land, south-land.** [OE. *sūðland*; see SOUTH *adv.* and LAND *sb.*] **1.** A land lying in or towards the south. **2.** The southern part of a country or district; the South OE. **3.** *attrib.* or as *adj.* 1470. Hence **Sou·thlander,** a southerner.

†**Sou·thly,** *a.* and *adv.* 1440. [f. SOUTH + -LY.] **A.** *adj.* Southern. **B.** *adv.* Towards or in the south; facing or from the south –1590.

Southmost (sau·þməst, -moᵘst), *a.* OE. [f. SOUTH *adv.*; see -MOST.] Most southerly; southernmost.

Sou·thness. 1852. [f. SOUTH + -NESS.] The quality of indicating the south; the state of being relatively south.

Southron (sɒ·ðrə̆n), *a.* and *sb.* 1470. [Alteration of *Southren* SOUTHERN *a.*] **A.** *adj.* **1.** Belonging to or dwelling in the south, esp. of Britain; southern; *esp.* English as dist. from Scottish. Chiefly *Sc.* **2.** Of or pertaining to, characteristic of, the south; situated in or on the south 1470.

2. A s. mode of speech 1891.

B. *sb.* **1.** A native of the south of Great Britain; an Englishman 1470. **b.** In pl. sense, = Englishmen. Freq. with *the.* 1470. **2.** A native or inhabitant of the south of England, of Europe, etc. 1848.

South Sea. late ME. †**1. a.** The sea to the south of Europe; the Mediterranean. TREVISA. †**b.** The English Channel –1478. **2.** *pl.* The seas of the southern hemisphere; *esp.* the South Pacific Ocean 1528. **3.** The South Pacific Ocean; †the Pacific Ocean as a whole 1555. **b.** *ellipt.* for 'South Sea bonds', etc. 1717.

3. *fig.* One inch of delay more, is a South-sea of discouerie SHAKS. b. The nation then too late will find..South Sea, at best, a mighty bubble SWIFT.

attrib.: **South Sea bubble** = *South Sea scheme*; **South Sea Company,** a company incorporated in 1711 for the purpose of exclusive trade with the South Seas, and of taking up the unfunded National Debt; **South Sea scheme,** a stock-jobbing scheme which was inaugurated by this company in 1720 for taking up the whole National Debt, but which collapsed in the same year.

South-side. [orig. repr. ME. *sūðside*; but in later use felt merely as a collocation of SOUTH *a.* and SIDE *sb.*[1]] The side situated in or lying towards the south.

South-south-east, *adv.* late ME. In or from the direction lying midway between south and south-east. Also as *sb.* and *adj.*

South-sou·therly. 1814. [Imitative of its cry.] *Amer.* The long-tailed duck, *Harelda glacialis.*

South-south-west, *adv.* 1513. In or from the direction situated midway between south and south-west. Also as *sb.* and *adj.*

Southward (sau·þwə̆ɹd, *Naut.* sɒ·ðəɹd), *adv.*, *sb.*, and *a.* [OE. *sūðweard*, f. SOUTH *adv.* + -WARD.] **A.** *adv.* **1.** Towards the south; in a southern direction. **2.** quasi-*sb.* = B. 1842.

1. S. they set their faces TENNYSON. Half a mile s. of the town lies a..rising ground 1896. 2. So came he far to s. MACAULAY.

B. *sb.* That direction or part which lies to the south of a place, etc. 1555.

It looked black at the s. and eastward 1840.

C. *adj.* That has a southerly situation or direction; lying, facing, moving, etc., towards the south 1611.

With the s. swallow SWINBURNE. Hence **Sou·thwardly** *adv.* in a s. direction; *adj.* situated in or directed towards the south; of the wind, blowing from the south.

Sou·thwards, *adv.* and *sb.* [OE. *sūðweardes*; see -WARDS.] = prec. A, B.

South-west (saupwe·st), *adv.*, *sb.*, and *a.* [OE. *sūðwest* (see SOUTH and WEST).] **A.** *adv.* **1.** In the direction situated midway between south and west. **b.** From this direction 1725. **2.** quasi-*sb.* **a.** *At s.* = 1. **b.** = B. 1. 1555.

2. a. The wind at s., and the thermometer at 58½ 1777.

B. *sb.* **1.** The direction, district, or region situated between south and west OE. **2.** The (or a) south-west wind 1610.

2. A Southwest blow on yee, And blister you all ore SHAKS.

C. *adj.* **1.** Of the wind: Blowing from the south-west. late ME. **2.** Lying in or situated to the south-west 1440. **3.** Directed towards the south-west 1756.

South-we·ster. Also **southwester.** 1831. [f. prec. + -ER [1].] **1.** A wind or gale blowing from the south-west 1833. **2.** (usu. *sou'wester.*) A large oilskin or waterproof hat or cap worn orig. by seamen to protect the head and neck during wet or rough weather. Also *attrib.* 1831.

South-we·sterly, *a.* and *adv.* 1708. [f. SOUTH-WEST.] **A.** *adj.* **a.** Of the wind: Blowing from the south-west. **b.** Tending south-westward. **B.** *adv.* South-westwardly 1792.

South-we·stern, *a.* and *sb.* [OE. *sūðwesterne* (see SOUTH *adv.* and WESTERN *a.*).] **A.** *adj.* **1.** Of the wind: Blowing from the south-west. **2.** Situated or extending towards the south-west; of or pertaining to the south-west 1828. **B.** *sb.* A wave from the south-west. TENNYSON.

A. 1. Western and s. gales 1835. 2. The main marks of s. English 1863.

South-we·stward, *adv.* and *sb.* 1548. [f. SOUTH-WEST + -WARD.] = SOUTH-WEST *adv.* and *sb.* So **South-we·stwards** *adv.*

South-we·stwardly, *adv.* 1796. [f. prec.] = SOUTH-WEST *adv.*

Souvenir (sū·vənīəɹ). 1775. [a. F. *souvenir* memory, keepsake, sb. use of the inf. *souvenir* :—L. *subvenire* to come into the mind.] **1.** A remembrance, a memory. **2.** A token of remembrance; a keepsake 1782.

Sou'-we·st, -we·ster, reduced ff. SOUTH-WEST, -WESTER.

Sov (sɒv). 1850. Colloquial abbrev. of SOVEREIGN *sb.* 3 b.

†**Sovenance.** 1477. [a. OF. *souvenance*, *sov-*, (F. *souvenance*), f. *so(u)venir*; see SOUVENIR.] Remembrance; memory –1625.

Sovereign (sɒ·vrėn), *sb.* and *a.* ME. [a. OF. *soverain*, *souverein*, etc. (mod.F. *souverain*) :—pop.L. **superanus*, f. *super* above. The spelling *-eign*, which appears in the 14th c., is due to the influence of *reign.*] **A.** *sb.* **1.** One who has supremacy or rank above, or authority over, others; a superior; a ruler, governor, lord, or master (*of* persons, etc.). Freq. applied to the Deity in relation to created things. **b.** A person or thing which excels or surpasses others of the kind. Now *rare.* 1500. **2.** *spec.* The recognized supreme ruler of a people or country under monarchical government; a monarch; a king or queen ME. **3. a.** A gold coin minted in England from the time of Henry VII to Charles I, orig. of the value of 22*s.* 6*d.* but later worth only 10*s.* or 11*s.* 1503. **b.** A current British gold coin of the value of twenty shillings 1817.

1. Thy husband is thy Lord, thy life, thy keeper, Thy head, thy soueraigne SHAKS. b. This Soveraigne of her Sexe 1635. 2. How darst thou thus oppose thy Soveraignes will 1652. *fig.* Weak Verses, go, kneel at your Sovereign's feet SHELLEY.

B. *adj.* †**1.** Of persons: Standing out above others or excelling in some respect –1688. **2.** Of things, qualities, etc.: Supreme, paramount; principal, greatest, or most notable ME. **b.** Qualifying *good.* (Freq. = *summum bonum.*) ME. **c.** Of contempt: Supreme, unmitigated 1749. **3.** Of remedies, etc.: Efficacious in a superlative degree. Freq. in fig. use. late ME. **4.** Of persons: Having superior or supreme rank or power; *spec.* holding the position of a ruler or monarch ME. **b.** Of states, communities, etc. 1595. **5.** Of power, authority, etc.: Supreme 1532. **6.** Of or belonging to, characteristic of, supremacy or superiority 1600.

2. This is his s. Charm against Fear in an Engagement 1706. b. The knowledge of Truth..is the Soueraigne Good of humane Nature BACON. 3. A soueraine simple against disquiet and feare GREENE. 4. Partly because, being members of the s. body, they would have it so BENTHAM. b. A State is called a s. *State* when this supreme power resides within itself 1868. 6. Full many a glorious morning haue I seene, Flatter the mountaine tops with soueraine eie SHAKS. Hence **So·vereignly** *adv.* in a s. manner.

†**So·vereignize,** *v.* 1601. [f. SOVEREIGN *sb.* + -IZE.] *intr.* To exercise supreme power; to rule as a sovereign –1680.

Sovereignty (sɒ·vrėnti). ME. [a. AF. *sovereyneté*, = OF. *souveraineté* (mod.F. *souv-*

raineté); see SOVEREIGN and -TY.] **1.** Supremacy or pre-eminence in respect of excellence or efficacy. **2.** Supremacy in respect of power, domination, or rank; supreme dominion, authority, or rule. late ME. **3.** *spec.* The position, rank, or power of a supreme ruler or monarch; royal authority or dominion. late ME. **b.** *transf.* The supreme controlling power in communities not under monarchical government; absolute and independent authority 1860. **4.** A territory under the rule of a sovereign, or existing as an independent state 1715.

1. *L. L. L.* IV. iii. 234. 2. The Romans..had acquired the S. of the Sea 1718. 3. Hee wanne the soueraignty not meerely by the sword 1625. 4. The United States, with thirty governors, for thirty independent sovereignties 1849.

Soviet (sōᵘ·viet, soᵘvie·t). 1917. [Russ., = council.] A Russian soldiers' or workmen's council of delegates; since the Russian revolution of 1917 also a congress consisting of representatives of the local soviets (hence *attrib.* as in 'Soviet Republic'); (with *the*) the system of government by soviets. Also *transf.* of similar organizations elsewhere. Hence **So·vietism,** the system of government by soviets. **So·vietize** *v. trans.* to organize on a soviet basis.

Sovran (sǫ·vrăn), *a.* and *sb.* Chiefly *poet.* 1634. [Milton's spelling of SOVEREIGN, after It. *sovrano.*] = SOVEREIGN *a.* and *sb.* Hence **So·vranly** *adv.* **So·vranty,** sovereignty.

Sow (sau), *sb.* [OE. *sugu*, related to OHG. and MHG. *sû* (G. *sau*) and ON. *sýr*, also L. *sus*, Gr. ὗς, Zend *hu.*] **1.** The female of swine; a full-grown female pig, esp. a domestic one used for breeding. **2.** Applied to persons (male or female) as a term of abuse, esp. to a fat, clumsy, or slovenly woman 1508. **3.** *Mil.* A movable structure having a strong roof, used to cover men advancing to the walls of a besieged town or fortress, and to protect them while engaged in sapping and mining or other operations. Now *Hist.* ME. **4.** A wood-louse or sow-bug. Now chiefly *dial.* late ME. **5.** *techn.* A large oblong mass of solidified metal as obtained from the blast- or smelting-furnace 1481. **b.** In general use: A bar or mass of metal; an ingot. Now *Obs.* or *rare.* 1570. **c.** One of the larger channels, or the main channel, in the hearth of an iron-smelting furnace, serving as a feeder to the smaller channels or 'pigs' 1843. **d.** A mass of metallic iron which has congealed in the hearth of a lead-furnace; a salamander 1871.

Phrases. *To get, have,* or *take the wrong* (or *right*) *s. by the ear,* to get hold of, hit upon, the wrong (or right) person or thing; to arrive at a wrong (or right) conclusion, solution, etc. *As drunk as David's s.* or *as a s.,* blind-drunk.

Sow (sōᵘ), *v.* Pa. t. **sowed** (sōᵘd). Pa. pple. **sowed, sown** (sōᵘn). [Com. Teut.; OE. *sáwan.*] **1.** *intr.* or *absol.* To perform the action of scattering or depositing seed on or in the ground so that it may grow. **2.** *trans.* To scatter seed on or upon (land, etc.) in order that it may grow; to supply with seed OE. **b.** To strew or sprinkle (land, etc.) *with* something as in the sowing of seed 1611. **c.** Of seed: To be sufficient for (a certain area) 1440. **3.** To cover or strew (a place, etc.) thickly *with* something. Chiefly in pa. pple. late ME. **4.** To scatter or deposit (seed) on or in the ground, etc., for growth, usually by the action of the hand; to place or put (seed) in the ground; to plant (a crop) in this way OE. **b.** *transf.* with ref. to fish, bacilli, etc. 1854. **5. a.** Used with *seed*, etc., in transf. and fig. senses OE. **b.** Contrasted with *reap* in fig. uses. late ME. **6.** *fig.* To disseminate or spread; to endeavour to propagate or extend OE. **7.** To scatter after the manner of seed; to sprinkle, throw or spread about, in this way. late ME. **b.** To distribute or disperse (*rare*) –1535.

1. [I] Plough water, s. on rocks, and reap the wind 1687. 2. The whole was sowed with barley 1846. *fig.* The daily strife..Which sows the human heart with tares SHELLEY. **b.** And Abimelech..beat downe the citie and sowed it with salt *Judges* ix. 45. 3. Thick as the Galaxy with Stars is sown DRYDEN. 4. When to turn The fruitful Soil, and when to sowe the Corn DRYDEN. *To s. one's wild oats*: see OAT 3. 5. **a.** In all this the seeds of the Conquest were sowing 1868. **b.** What Darkness sowed, the Light shall reap 1878. *To s. the wind and reap the whirlwind*: see WHIRLWIND. 6. Between the best of Peoples and the best of Restorer Kings they would s. grudges CARLYLE. He sow'd a slander in the common ear TENNYSON. 7. Not sowing hedgerow texts and passing by TENNYSON. Hence **Sown** *ppl. a.*

‖ **Sowar** (sɒˌwā·ɪ). *Anglo-Ind.* 1802. [Urdū (Pers.) *sawār* horseman.] A native horseman or mounted orderly, policeman, etc.; a native trooper, esp. one belonging to the irregular cavalry.

Sowarry (sɒˌwā·ri). *Anglo-Ind.* 1776. [Urdū (Pers.) *sawārī*, f. prec.] The mounted attendants of a person of high rank, a state official, etc.; a number of these forming a cavalcade.

Sow·-back (sau-). 1874. [f. SOW *sb.*] *Geol.* A ridge of glacial origin suggestive of the back of a sow. So **Sow·-backed** *a.* 1728.

Sow·-bread (sau-). Also **sowbread.** 1550. [f. SOW *sb.* + BREAD *sb.*, after med.L. *panis porcinus* or G. *saubrot.*] A plant of the genus *Cyclamen*, esp. *C. europæum*, the fleshy tuberous root-stocks of which are eaten by swine.

Sow·-bug (sau-). 1750. [f. SOW *sb.* 4.] **a.** A wood-louse of the genus *Oniscus*, esp. *O. asellus.* **b.** *U.S.* A small marine crustacean of the genus *Idotea.*

Sowens (sōᵘ·ĕnz, sū·-), *sb. pl. Sc.* (and *Ir.*). 1582. [app. ad. Gael. *súghan, súbhan*, the liquid used in preparing 'sowens', f. *súgh, súbh* sap.] An article of diet formerly in common use in Scotland (and some parts of Ireland), consisting of farinaceous matter extracted from the bran or husks of oats by steeping in water, allowed to ferment slightly, and prepared by boiling.

Sower (sōᵘ·əɪ). OE. [f. SOW *v.* + -ER [1].] One who, or that which, sows.

Sow·-ge·lder (sau-). 1515. [f. SOW *sb.*] One whose business it is to geld or spay sows.

Sowl (saul, sūl), *v.* Now *dial.* 1607. [Origin obsc.] **1.** *trans.* To pull, seize roughly, etc., *by* the ear or ears. In later use esp. of dogs: To seize (a pig) by the ears. **2.** To pull or lug (the ears) 1654.

Sow·-me·tal (sau-). 1674. [f. SOW *sb.* 5.] Cast iron in sows or large ingots as it comes from the blasting- or smelting-furnace.

Sown, pa. pple of SOW *v.*

Sow·-pig (sau-). 1548. [f. SOW *sb.*] A young female pig, esp. one that has been spayed; a sow.

Sow-thistle (sau·þi:s'l). Also **sowthistle.** [Early ME. *suȝepistel.*] One or other of the species of *Sonchus*; a plant belonging to this genus, esp. *S. oleraceus* and *S. asper*, common European weeds characterized by their sharply-toothed thistle-like leaves and milky juice.

Soy (soi). 1696. [a. Japanese *soy* (also *shoy*), colloq. f. *shō-yu*, ad Chinese *shi-yu*, f. *shi* salted beans or the like, used as condiments + *yu* oil.] **1.** A sauce prepared chiefly in Japan, China, and India, from the beans of *Soja hispida* (*Dolichos soja*), and eaten with fish, etc. **2.** The soy-bean, *Soja hispida* 1880.

attrib.: s.-bean = 2.

Soya (soi·ă). 1679. [a. Du. *soya, soja*; see prec.] = SOY.

Sozzle (sǫ·z'l), *sb. dial.* and *U.S.* 1823. [Cf. SOSS *sb.*[1]] **1.** *dial.* A sloppy spoon-meat or medicine. **2.** *U.S.* A slattern; a state of sluttish confusion or disorder 1854. So **So·zzle** *v. trans.* to mix or mingle in a sloppy manner; *U.S.* to splash; to perform sluttishly or lazily (also *intr.*). **So·zzled** *ppl. a.* (*slang*) intoxicated.

Spa (spā, spǭ), *sb.* 1565. [A place-name.] **1.** With capital. The name of a watering place in the province of Liége, Belgium, celebrated for the curative properties of its mineral springs. **b.** In generalized sense 1610. **2.** A medicinal or mineral spring or well 1626. **3.** A town, locality, or resort possessing a mineral spring or springs; a watering-place of this kind 1777. Hence **Spa** (also **spaa**), *v. trans.* to subject to spa-treatment; *intr.* to frequent or visit a s. or spas.

†**Spaad.** 1594. [ad. obs. G. *spad, spade*, varr. of *spat* SPATH.] *Min.* A variety of talc, gypsum, or spar, or a powder prepared from one or other of these, mainly used to form moulds for casting metal objects –1738.

Space (spēⁱs), *sb.* ME. [ad. OF. *espace* (also mod.F.), ad. L. *spatium* (med.L. also *spacium*).] **I.** Denoting time or duration. **1.** Without article: Lapse or extent of time between two definite points, events, etc. Chiefly with *long, short, small*, etc. ME. †**b.** Delay (*rare*) –1554. †**2.** Time, leisure, or opportunity for doing something. Chiefly in *to have* or *give s.* –1675. **3.** With *the* (*that*, etc.): **a.** The amount or extent of time comprised or contained in a specified period ME. **b.** The amount of time already specified or indicated, or otherwise determined ME. **4.** With *a* and *pl.*: A period or interval of time ME.

1. Short s. ensued; I was not held..Long in expectance CARY. 2. Come on, thou art granted s. SHAKS. Phr. *Time and s., s. and time.* 3. **a.** In the s. of a tide, the salt water has not time to..return 1793. **b.** In less than the s...mentioned, the Count..came back SCOTT. †*In the mean s.*, meantime. 4. He and his defended themselues..a long s. 1568. Phr. (*for*) *a s.*, for a moderate period of time.

II. Denoting area or extension. *Without article, in generalized sense.* **1.** Linear distance; interval between two or more points or objects. late ME. **2.** Superficial extent or area; also, extent in three dimensions. late ME. **b.** Extent or area sufficient for some purpose; room. Also const. *to* with inf. late ME. **c.** Extent or room in a letter, periodical, book, etc., available for or occupied by written or printed matter 1530. **3.** *Metaph.* Continuous, unbounded, or unlimited extension in every direction, regarded as void of matter, or without reference to this. Freq. coupled with *time.* 1656. **4.** *Astr.*, etc. The immeasurable expanse in which the solar and stellar systems, nebulæ, etc., are situated; the stellar depths 1667. **b.** In more limited sense: Extension in all directions, esp. from a given point 1827.

1. 'Twixt Host and Host but narrow s. was left, A dreadful interval MILT. 2. Affrica in his kynde haþ lasse s. TREVISA. The more it is heated, the more s. it takes up 1815. **b.** Crime that leaves no s. for penitence! 1869. **c.** I write no more to you, for lacke of s. 1530. 3. All our conceptions are defined by conditions of time and s. 1892.

In particularized or limited senses. **5.** A certain stretch, extent, or area of ground, surface, sky, etc.; an expanse ME. **6.** A more or less limited area or extent; a small portion of space (in senses II. 2, 4 b). late ME. **b.** A division, section. late ME. **c.** A void or empty place or part 1837. **7.** An interval; a length of way; a distance. late ME. **b.** A short distance 1813. **8.** The dimensional extent occupied by a body or lying within certain limits 1530. **9.** *Mus.* One or other of the degrees or intervals between the lines of a staff 1597. **10.** An interval or blank between words, or lines, in printed or written matter 1676. **b.** *Typog.* One or other of certain small pieces of cast-metal, of various thicknesses and shorter than a type, used to separate words (or letters in a word), and also to justify the line 1676.

5. The s. around the building was silent 1794. *fig.* Oh indistinguished s. of Womans will SHAKS. 6. A viscid secreting s. called the stigma 1845. 7. The s. which separates the stars 1842. Phr. †*From s. to s.*, at (regular) intervals. 8. The things do not fill up that s., which the idea of them seemed to take up in his mind LAMB. 10. Leaving a s. for his own name 1908.

attrib. and *Comb.*: **s.-nerve,** 'that portion of the auditory nerve which supplies the semicircular canals of the inner ear'; **-telegrapher,** one concerned or connected with s.-telegraphy; **-telegraphy,** wireless telegraphy; **-time,** a fusion of the concepts of s. and time regarded as a continuum in which the existent exists. Hence **Spa·ceful** *a.* (*rare*) spacious, commodious; wide, extensive.

Space (spēⁱs), *v.* 1548. [f. prec., or ad. F. *espacer* to space, etc. :—L. *spatiari* to walk, to extend.] **1.** *trans.* To limit or bound in respect of space; to make of a certain extent. **2.** †**a.** To divide into spaces or sections (*rare*) 1578. **b.** *dial.* To measure (ground, etc.) by pacing 1808. **3.** To set, to arrange or put, at determinate intervals or distances. Also with *out.* 1703. **4.** *Typog.* **a.** With *out*: To extend to a required length by inserting additional space between the words (or lines) 1683. **b.** To separate (words, letters, or lines) by means of a space or spaces; occas. = a 1771. †**5.** *intr.* To walk, ramble, or roam –1599.

5. That Wolues, where she was wont to s., Should harbour'd be SPENSER.

Spaceless (spēⁱ·slės), *a.* 1606. [f. SPACE *sb.* + -LESS.] 1. That is not subject to or limited by space; infinite, boundless. 2. Occupying no space 1825.

1. There timeless, s., dwells the Eternal One 1819.

Spacer (spēⁱ·səɹ). 1884. [f. SPACE *v.* + -ER [1].] A device or piece of mechanism for spacing words; a piece of metal, etc., for making a space, interval, or division.

Spacious (spēⁱ·ʃəs), *a.* late ME. [ad. L. *spatiosus* (med.L. *spaciosus*), f. *spatium* SPACE *sb.*] 1. Of lands, etc.: Of vast, large, or indefinite superficial extent or area; wide, extensive. 2. Of dwellings, rooms, roads, etc.: Having or affording ample space or room; large, roomy, commodious. late ME. b. quasi-*adv.* Spaciously. MILTON. 3. Of things: Presenting, having, or covering a comparatively wide surface; large, ample, expansive 1631. 4. *fig.* Great, extensive, ample 1595. 5. Characterized by greatness, breadth, or comprehensiveness of character, style, or outlook 1600. 6. †Prolonged 1642.

1. Ouse, slow winding through a level plain Of s. meads COWPER. 2. The log burnt on the s. hearth 1832. 4. You may Conuey your pleasures in a s. plenty, And yet seeme cold SHAKS. 5. The s. times of great Elizabeth TENNYSON. Hence **Spa·cious-ly** *adv.*, **-ness.**

Spade (spēⁱd), *sb.*[1] [OE. *spadu*, *spada*, *spade* = OFris. *spada*, OS. *spado*; not in OHG. or MHG.] Related to Gr. σπάθη wooden blade, paddle, sword, etc., whence L. *spatha*; see next and SPATHE.] 1. A tool for digging, paring, or cutting ground, turf, etc., now usually consisting of a flattish rectangular iron blade socketed on a wooden handle which has a grip or cross-piece at the upper end, the whole being adapted for grasping with both hands while the blade is pressed into the ground with the foot. b. The depth of a spade-blade; a spit 1674. 2. An implement resembling a spade in form or use; *esp.* a spade-like knife used in flensing a whale 1820.

1. Phr. *To call a s. a s.*, to call things by their real names, without any euphemism; to use plain or blunt language; to be straightforward to the verge of rudeness or indecency.

Comb.: **s.-bayonet**, a broad-bladed bayonet, which may be used in digging shelter-holes or rifle-pits; **-bone**, the shoulder-blade; **-fish**, a fish resembling a s. in form; now *spec.* the moon-fish, *Chætodipterus faber*; **-foot**, (*a*) the foot used in pressing a s. into the ground; (*b*) a toad having a foot specially adapted for digging; **-guinea**, a guinea coined from 1787 to 1799, on which the shield bearing the arms has the form of a pointed s.; **-(s)man**, a labourer accustomed to work with a spade; **-work**, *lit.* work done with a spade; *fig.* pioneer work.

Spade (spēⁱd), *sb.*[2] 1598. [ad. It. *spade*, pl. of *spada* SPADO [2], used as a mark on playing-cards.] 1. One or other of the black spade-shaped marks by which one of the four suits in a pack of playing-cards is distinguished; hence *pl.*, the cards belonging to or forming this suit. 2. A card belonging to the spade-suit 1745.

Spade (spēⁱd), *v.*[1] 1594. [f. SPADE *sb.*[1]] †1. *trans.* To cut in the form of a spade. NASHE. 2. To dig up or remove with a spade 1647. 3. To cut or flense with a whaling-spade 1887. 4. *intr.* To work with a spade 1869.

†Spade, *v.*[2] 1611. [f. *spaid*, *spayed*, pa. pple. of SPAY *v.*, perh. assoc. w. L. *spado* SPADO [1].] *trans.* To spay –1816.

Spa·de-beard. 1598. [f. SPADE *sb.*[1] + BEARD *sb.*] A spade-shaped beard; a beard cut or trimmed to the shape of a (pointed or broad) spade-blade.

Spadeful (spēⁱ·dful). Also **-full.** 1643. [f. SPADE *sb.*[1] + -FUL.] A quantity that fills a spade; as much as a spade can hold or take up at one time.

Spader (spēⁱ·dəɹ). 1647. [f. SPADE *v.*[1] + -ER [1].] One who works with a spade; an implement which digs, etc., by means of spades; also *dial.*, a breast-plough.

Spadiceous (spēⁱdi·ʃəs), *a.* Now *Bot.* 1646. [ad. mod.L. *spadiceus*, f. L. *spadic-*, *spadix* SPADIX.] 1. Of a reddish or brownish colour. 2. Having the nature or form of a spadix 1760. So **Spa·dicose** *a.* (in sense 2).

Spadici- (spēⁱdəi·si), comb. form of SPADIX, used in a few terms of *Bot.*, as *spadicifloˑral*, *-form* adjs.

‖**Spadille** (spădi·l). 1728. [F., ad. Sp. *espadilla*, dim. of *espada* sword, SPADE *sb.*[2]] The ace of spades in ombre and quadrille. Also †‖**Spadi·llo** [ad. Sp.].

‖**Spadix** (spēⁱ·diks). *Pl.* **spadices** (spēⁱdəi·sīz), and **spa·dixes.** 1760. [L., a. Gr. σπάδιξ palm-branch, palm-coloured.] 1. *Bot.* A form of inflorescence consisting of a thick fleshy spike, closely set with flowers, and enclosed in a spathe; a succulent spike, whether enclosed in a spathe or not. 2. *Zool.* A part in cephalopods and hydrozoans having some analogy to a spadix in plants 1871.

‖**Spado** [1] (spā·*do*). late ME. [L., ad. Gr. σπάδων.] A eunuch.

†‖**Spado** [2] (spā·*do*). 1711. [Altered from It. *spada* or Sp. *espada*:—L. *spatha*, ad. Gr. σπάθη; see SPADE *sb.*[1]] A cut-and-thrust sword –1785.

Spadroon (spădrū·n). *Obs.* exc. *Hist.* 1798. [ad. Genevan dial. *espadron*, = F. *espadon.*] A sword much lighter than a broadsword, and made both to cut and to thrust.

Spae (spēⁱ), *v.* orig. *north.* and *Sc.* ME. [a. ON. *spá*, of uncertain origin.] To foretell, prophesy. Chiefly *trans.* So **Spae** *sb.*

Spae·man. *Sc.* 1480. [a. Scand. *spámann*, f. *spá* SPAE *v.*] A soothsayer, wizard.

Spae·wife. *Sc.* 1774. [f. SPAE *v.* + WIFE *sb.*] A female fortune-teller; a sybil; a witch.

‖**Spaghetti** (spăge·ti). 1888. [It. pl. of dim. of *spago* string.] An Italian variety of alimentary paste made in solid cords intermediate in thickness between macaroni and vermicelli.

Spagyric (spădʒi·rik), *sb.* and *a.* *Obs.* exc. *Hist.* 1593. [ad. early mod. L. *spagiricus* (used, and prob. invented, by Paracelsus).] A. *sb.* †1. The science of alchemy or chemistry –1605. 2. An alchemist 1593. B. *adj.* Pertaining to alchemy 1596. So **Spagy·rical** *a.*, **-ly** *adv.*

Spagyrist (spæ·dʒirist). 1652. [ad. mod L. *spagirista.*] An alchemist.

‖**Spahi** (spā·hī). 1562. [ad. Turk. (Pers.) *sipāhī*; see SEPOY.] 1. A horseman forming one of a body of Turkish cavalry which was to some extent organized on a feudal basis. Now *Hist.* 2. A native Algerian horseman serving under the French Government 1863.

Spake, obs. poet. or arch. pa. t. of SPEAK *v.*

Spald, *v.* *north.* and *Sc.* late ME. [ad. MLG. *spalden*, = OHG. *spaltan* (MHG. and G. *spalten*) to split.] a. *trans.* To splinter, split, break up, lay open or flat. b. *intr.* To go apart, to splay out. Hence **Spa·lding,** a split and dried fish. **Spalding-knife.**

Spale (spēⁱl), *sb.*[1] *Sc.* and *north.* 1470. [Origin obsc.] A splinter or chip, a thin piece or strip, of wood.

Spale, *sb.*[2] 1867. [Cf. SPALL *sb.*[3]] *Shipbuilding. pl.* Temporary cross beams used as internal strengthening.

Spall (spǭl), *sb.*[1] Also **spawl.** 1440. [Cf. SPALE *sb.*[1]] A chip or splinter, esp. of stone.

Spall, *sb.*[2] *rare.* 1590. [ad. It. *spalla.*] A shoulder.

Spall (spǭl), *sb.*[3] Also **spawl.** 1895. [Cf. SPALE *sb.*[2]] A cross-spall; a cross-piece used in staging.

Spall (spǭl), *v.*[1] 1758. [Related to SPALL *sb.*[1]] 1. *trans.* a. *Mining.* To break (ore) into smaller pieces. b. To dress (stones) roughly with a hammer 1793. 2. To split or chip. Also with *off.* 1841. 3. *intr.* To break *off* in fragments or chips 1853.

Spall (spǭl), *v.*[2] 1850. [Related to SPALL *sb.*[3]] *trans.* To fix (ship-frames) at the proper breadth by means of cross-spalls.

Spalpeen (spælpī·n). *Irish.* 1780. [a. Ir. *spailpín* of unknown origin.] 1. A common workman or labourer; a farm-worker or harvester. 2. A low or mean fellow; a scamp, a rascal 1815. 3. A youngster 1891.

Spalt, *a.* Now *dial.* 1567. [Related to next.] Of wood: Brittle, short-grained; breaking easily through dryness or decay.

Spalt (spǭlt), *v.* *dial.* 1733. [prob. ad. Du. and Flem. *spalte*, = G. *spalzen*, related to SPALD *v.*] *intr.* and *trans.* To split, tear, splinter.

Span (spæn), *sb.*[1] [OE. *span(n*, = MDu. (and Du.) *spanne*, ON. *spann-*, app. related to *spannan* SPAN *v.*[2]] 1. The distance from the tip of the thumb to the tip of the little finger, or sometimes to the tip of the forefinger, when the hand is fully extended; the space equivalent to this taken as a measure of length, averaging nine inches. 2. The hand with the thumb and fingers extended, esp. as a means of measuring. *Obs.* exc. *arch.* 1535. 3. A thing, piece, etc., of the length of a span; a very small extent or space ME. 4. A short space of time, esp. as the duration of human life; the (short) time during which a person lives 1599. 5. The distance or space between the abutments of an arch, the supports of a beam, the piers of a bridge, the walls carrying a roof, etc.; the stretch or extent of this 1725. 6. An arch of a bridge; a section between two piers. Also *transf.*, the vault of the sky. 1806. b. A stretch, line, or extent *of* something 1894.

1. Ehud made him a two edged dagger of a spanne longe COVERDALE *Judges* iii. 16. 2. Who hath measured heauen with his spanne? COVERDALE *Isa.* xl. 12. 4. Tymon is dead, who hath out-stretcht his s. SHAKS. 5. The maximum lateral dimension of an aeroplane or of a wing 1910.

Span (spæn), *sb.*[2] 1769. [a. Du. and LG., f. *spannen* to unite, fasten.] 1. *Naut.* One or other of various ropes or chains used as fastenings or means of connexion. 2. *U.S.* and *Canada.* A pair of horses harnessed and driven together, *esp.* a pair as nearly alike in colour and size as possible 1769. 3. *S. Africa.* A team of oxen or other draught animals consisting of two or more yokes 1812.

1. *S.*, a rope with both ends made fast, for a purchase to be hooked to its bight DANA. *S.*,..a double rope with thimbles seized betwixt the two parts, stretched across the rigging as a fair-leader for ropes 1846.

Span (spæn), *v.*[1] late ME. [f. SPAN *sb.*[1]] I. *trans.* †1. To grasp, lay hold of, seize –1513. 2. To measure by means of the outstretched hand; to cover with the hand in this way 1560. †b. To measure in any way –1717. †c. To measure out; to set a limit or bound to (life, etc.) –1657. d. To encircle or encompass (the wrist, waist, etc.) with the hand or hands 1781. 3. Of the rainbow, a bridge, etc.: To form an arch across or over (the sky, a river, etc.); to cross from side to side 1633. 4. To throw a bridge across (a river, etc.); to bridge over 1861.

2. My right hand hathe spanned the heauens BIBLE (Geneva) *Isa.* xlviii. 13. b. How to s. Words with just note and accent MILT. c. My life is spand already SHAKS. d. And oft..her wrist she spanned COLERIDGE. 3. A rainbow spanned the lake SHELLEY. Its waters are spanned by a fine stone bridge 1869. *transf.* Chaucer's life..spans rather more than the latter half of the fourteenth century 1879.

II. *absol.* To make a span *over* something; to reach with or as with a span; to stretch or range *from* one place or point *to* another. Chiefly *fig.* 1535.

Span (spæn), *v.*[2] 1550. [ad. Flem., Du., or LG. *spannen*, = OE. *spannan* to fix or fasten, to join, to draw tight.] 1. *trans.* To harness or yoke (horses, oxen, etc.); to attach to a vehicle. See also INSPAN *v.* and OUTSPAN *v.* b. *dial.* To fetter or shackle (a horse); *transf.* to enclose or confine 1844. 2. To stretch, extend, make taut or tight; to draw (a bow). Now *arch.* 1597. 3. †a. To wind up the wheel-lock of (a pistol or musket) by means of a spanner –1672. b. To screw tight with a spanner 1859. 4. *Naut.* To fix, fasten, attach, or draw tight in some way. Also with *in.* 1781 5. *U.S. intr.* Of horses: To form a span or pair; to match in colour and size 1828.

1. We left Berea, and spanned out on the flat 1836. 2. New bows I s., new arrows fill my quiver 1878. 5. The horses s. well 1828.

Span, *a.*: see SPICK AND SPAN.

Span-, stem of SPAN *v.*[1] and SPAN *v.*[2], used in various technical combs., as **s.-dog,** either of a pair of dogs linked together, used to lift timber; **-piece** *dial.*, the collar-beam of a roof; **-shackle,** a large bolt with a triangular ring attached to which anchors or spars are lashed; **-worm** *U.S.*, a caterpillar of the *Geometræ* of Linnæus; a geometer.

Spanæmia (spæniˑmiă). Also (*U.S.*) -emia. 1845. [mod.L., f. Gr. σπανο-, comb. form of σπανός (usu. σπάνιος) scarce, scanty + -αιμία (as in ἀναιμία ANÆMIA), f. αἷμα blood.] *Path.* A morbid condition of the blood characterized by a deficiency of red corpuscles; poorness of the blood. Hence Spanæˑmic *a.* of or relating to, inducing, s.; also *sb.* a medicine inducing s.

Spancel (spæˑnsĕl), *sb.* 1610. [ad. Flem., Du., or LG. *spansel*, f. *spannen* SPAN *v.*[2]] A rope or fetter for hobbling cattle, horses, etc.; *esp.* a short, noosed rope for fettering the hind legs of a cow during milking. Hence Spaˑncel *v. trans.* to fetter or hobble with a s. or spancels.

†Span-counter. 1566. [f. SPAN *sb.*[1] or *v.*[1] + COUNTER *sb.*[3] 1.] A game in which the object of one player was to throw his counters so close to those of his opponent that the distance between them could be spanned with the hand –1815.

Spandrel (spæˑndrĕl). 1477. [app. a dim. of AF. *spaundre, -dere*; perh. identical with (*e*)*spandre* to expand, extend.] 1. The triangular space between the outer curve of an arch and the rectangle formed by the mouldings enclosing it; any similar space between an arch and a straight-sided figure bounding it; also, the space included between the shoulders of two contiguous arches and the moulding or string-course above them. b. *transf.* The support of a set of steps; the material with which the space between a stair and the floor is filled in 1833. 2. An inner border or frame for a picture 1862.

Spane (spēⁱn), *v. north.* and *Sc.* ME. [ad. OF. *espanir* or MDu. and MLG. *spanen*, app. related to OE. *spana* teat.] 1. *trans.* To wean (an infant, lamb, etc.). 2. *intr.* Of corn: To begin to take root and cast off the seed 1843.

†Span-farthing. 1688. [f. SPAN *sb.*[1] or *v.*[1] + FARTHING *sb.*] A game played with farthings after the same manner as span-counter –1777.

Spang, *sb.*[1] late ME. [prob. ad. MDu. *spange* clasp, buckle, spangle.] †1. A small, glittering ornament; a spangle –1625. 2. *techn.* A stain due to defective bleaching 1839.

1. The same horse Harneis were sette full of tremblyng spanges 1548.

Spang (spæŋ), *sb.*[2] Chiefly *Sc.* and *north.* 1513. [Cf. SPANG *v.*[2]] 1. A jerk. 2. a. A spring, bound, leap 1818. b. A strong kick 1863.

†Spang, *v.*[1] 1552. [f. SPANG *sb.*[1]] *trans.* To spangle; to ornament as with spangles –1621.

Spang (spæŋ), *v.*[2] *Sc.* and *north.* 1513. [Origin obsc.] 1. *intr.* To spring, leap, bound; to move rapidly. 2. *trans.* To cast, throw, jerk, bang 1513.

1. The trout slipped off, spanged down the bank, and..was lost 1833.

Spangle (spæˑŋg'l), *sb.* late ME. [f. SPANG *sb.*[1] + -LE.] 1. A small round thin piece of glittering metal (usu. brass or steel) with a hole in the centre to admit a thread, used for the decoration of textile fabrics and other materials. b. *transf.* A star (*poet.*) 1591. c. A glitter as of spangles (*rare.*) 1830. 2. A condensed particle reflecting light, as of hoar-frost, snow, or dew 1590. b. A glittering point or speck of light 1821. 3. A small or minute glittering particle, esp. of a mineral substance 1611. 4. A scale, spot, or marking suggestive of a spangle 1796. b. An oak-spangle. 1842.

1. A tawdry scarf of yellow silk, trimmed with tinsel and spangles SCOTT. c. Overhead was the s. of the stars 1893. 2. The wintry clouds..drop spangles on the mountains 1862. Hence Spaˑngly *a.* resembling spangles, covered with spangles.

Spangle (spæˑŋg'l), *v.* 1548. [f. prec.] 1. *trans.* To decorate (a garment or the like) with spangles. b. To adorn as with spangles; to cause to glitter as if so decorated. Const. *with.* 1591. 2. Of things: To dot or cover (something) as if with spangles 1596. 3. In passive: To present an appearance as if decorated with spangles; to be dotted or spotted *with* something suggestive of spangles 1667. 4. *intr.* To glitter or sparkle with, or in the manner of, spangles 1639.

1. b. A hundred torches play'd, Spangling the wave with lights SCOTT. 2. What stars do s. heauen with such beautie? SHAKS. 3. The meadows, spangled with yellow flowers 1874. 4. Sparks flashing and spangling 1857. Hence Spaˑngler, one who or that which spangles.

Spangled (spæˑŋg'ld), *ppl. a.* 1584. [f. SPANGLE *sb.* or *v.* + -ED.] 1. Adorned with or as with spangles. 2. Speckled 1586.

Spanglet (spæˑnglĕt). 1610. [f. SPANGLE *sb.* + -ET.] A little spangle.

Sweet star..S. of light on evening's shadowy veil SHELLEY.

Spaniard (spæˑnyăɹd), *sb.* (and *a.*). late ME. [ad. OF. *Espaignart, Espaniard*, f. *Espaigne* SPAIN; see -ARD.] 1. A native of Spain; one of Spanish descent. Occas. (with *the*) in collect. sing. = the Spanish nation or people. 2. A Spanish ship or vessel 1537. 3. a. New Zealand bayonet- or spear-grass 1851. b. A species of willow 1871. 4. *attrib.* (or as *adj.*) 1485.

Spaniel (spæˑnyĕl), *sb.* (and *a.*) late ME. [ad. OF. *espaignol, espaigneul* (mod.F. *épagneul*) 'Spanish dog'.] 1. A small or medium-sized variety of dog characterized by large drooping ears, long silky hair, keen scent, and affectionate nature, some breeds of which are used for sporting purposes, esp. for starting and retrieving game, while others are favourite pet- or toy-dogs. 2. *fig.* a. One who pries into, or searches out, something 1562. b. A submissive, cringing, or fawning person 1592. 3. *attrib.*, passing into *adj.* in the sense 'meanly submissive, cringing, fawning', etc. 1601.

1. For, as a spaynel, she wol on hym lepe CHAUCER. *Alpine, Blenheim, cocker, English, King Charles, Norfolk* (etc.) *s.* 2. b. You are the Spaniels of the court HEYWOOD. Hence Spaˑniel *v. rare, intr.* to act like a s., to be meanly submissive or subservient; *trans.* to follow, or fawn upon, like a s.

Spaniolize (spæˑniŏlǝiz), *v.* Now *rare.* 1598. [f. Romanic **Spaniolus* SPANISH + -IZE.] *trans.* To make Spanish; to imbue with Spanish notions or tendencies; to cause to follow Spanish fashions. (Chiefly in pa. pple.) So Spaˑniolate *v. trans.* (*rare*) 1577.

Spanish (spæˑniʃ), *a.* (*adv.*) and *sb.* ME. [f. SPAIN + -ISH, with later shortening of the first element.] A. *adj.* 1. Of or pertaining to Spain or its people; inhabiting, native to, characteristic of, Spain. 2. Of things: Of actual or attributed Spanish origin; made, manufactured, or produced in Spain (or Spanish America); associated or connected with Spain on this account 1483. b. Of articles of dress, etc.: Made in Spain, of Spanish materials, or after the Spanish fashion 1530. 3. Of a type or kind characteristic of, or exemplified by, the Spaniards 1530. 4. Of or pertaining to, dealing or connected with, the language or literature of Spain 1599.

1. *S. Main*, the mainland of America adjacent to the Caribbean Sea, esp. that portion of the coast stretching from the Isthmus of Panama to the mouth of the Orinoco; in later use also, the sea contiguous to this, or the route traversed by the Spanish register ships. Now *Hist.*

Special collocations. **S. black**, a pigment obtained by burning cork in closed vessels. **S. brown**, a kind of earth having a reddish brown colour, used as a pigment; also, the colour which this imparts. **S. burton** *Naut.*, a purchase composed of three single blocks, or two single blocks and a hook. A double S. burton has one double and two single blocks. **†S. chalk**, a variety of steatite found in Spain. **S. fox** *Naut.*, a rope-yarn twisted contrary to the lay. **S. juice, liquorice** (see LIQUORICE 1). **S. red**, an ochre resembling Venetian red, but slightly yellower. **S. reef** *Naut.*, a form of reefing in which the yards are lowered on the cap of the mast to reduce the spread of square sails; also, a knot tied in the head of the jib to reduce its area. **S. white**, (*a*) finely powdered chalk used as a pigment or for its cleansing properties; (*b*) a fine quality of flour. **S. windlass** *Naut.*, a windlass with an iron bolt inserted through the bight of the rope to serve as a lever.

b. In the specific names or designations of animals; esp. **S. fly**, = CANTHARIDES. **S. mackerel** (see MACKEREL[1] 1).

c. In the names of plants, trees, etc. denoting either varieties or distinct species found in Spain or Spanish America (esp. the West Indies). **S. bayonet** (see BAYONET *sb.*). **S. bean**, (*a*) a variety of broad bean; (*b*) *U.S.*, the scarlet runner. **S. chestnut**, *Castanea vesca*, a native of Asia Minor and the region eastward of the Himalayas. **S. dagger**, a West Indian name for *Yucca aloifolia*. **S. elm**, an evergreen timber-tree (*Cordia Geraschanthus*) of the West Indies. **S. grass**, esparto grass. **S. iris**, a bulbous iris of the genus *Xiphium*, esp. *X. vulgare*. **S. moss**, *U.S.*, the epiphytic plant, *Tillandsia usneoides*, of the Southern States; long-beard. **S. needles**, the American plant *Bidens bipinnata* or its prickly fruit. **S. nut**, (*a*) an iridaceous plant, *Moræa Sisyrinchium*, the bulbs of which are eaten in Spain; (*b*) a variety of hazel-nut, *Corylus Colurna*. **S. potato** (see POTATO *sb.* 1.).

B. *sb.* or *ellipt.* The Spanish language 1485.

C. *adv. U.S. To walk S.*, to (cause to) walk under compulsion, prop. with some one holding the collar and the seat of the trousers 1848.

Spanish broom. 1562. [SPANISH *a.*] The plant *Spartium junceum* (or *Cytisus junceus*) common to the Mediterranean region, the rush-like branches or twigs of which are used in basket-work and yield a fibre employed in the manufacture of cords, coarse cloth, etc.

Spanishly (spæˑniʃli), *adv.* 1641. [f. SPANISH *a.* + -LY [2].] Towards Spain or Spanish policy; like Spanish; in a characteristically Spanish manner.

Spank (spæŋk), *sb.* *dial.* or *colloq.* 1785. [f. SPANK *v.*[1]] A smart or sounding blow, esp. one given with the open hand; a slap or smack. b. The sharp sound produced by this 1833.

Spank (spæŋk), *v.*[1] *dial.* and *colloq.* 1727. [prob. echoic.] 1. *trans.* To slap or smack (a person, esp. a child) with the open hand. Also *absol.* 2. *intr.* a. To drop or fall with a spank or smack 1800. b. Of a boat: To pound, beat, or slap the water in sailing (*rare*) 1891.

Spank (spæŋk), *v.*[2] *dial.* and *colloq.* 1807. [prob. a back-formation from SPANKING *ppl. a.* 2.] 1. *intr.* To move or travel with speed and elasticity; to go quickly and vigorously; to ride or drive at a sharp trot and in a smart or stylish manner. b. *spec.* Of horses, or of persons driving or riding them 1811. c. Of ships: To sail quickly and smartly; to bowl *along* 1834. 2. *trans.* To drive (horses) quickly and smartly 1825.

2. How knowingly did he s. the horses along THACKERAY.

Spanker (spæˑŋkǝɹ). 1663. [Related to SPANKING *ppl. a.* or (in later use) f. SPANK *v.*[2]] †1. *slang.* A gold coin; usu. in *pl.*, coin, money –1785. 2. *dial.* and *colloq.* Anything exceptionally large or fine 1751. b. A heavy blow or smack 1772. 3. *Naut.* A fore-and-aft sail, set with a gaff and boom at the aftermost part of the ship 1794. 4. *dial.* A person who takes long rapid strides 1808. 5. *dial.* and *colloq.* A fast-going horse 1814.

Comb.: s.-boom *Naut.*, the boom on which the s. is set.

Spanking (spæˑŋkiŋ), *vbl. sb.* 1854. [f. SPANK *v.*[1]] The action of beating or slapping with the open hand by way of punishment.

Spanking (spæˑŋkiŋ), *ppl. a.* Chiefly *dial.* and *colloq.* 1666. [Origin obsc.] 1. Very big, large, or fine; exceptionally good in some respect. 2. Of horses; *esp.* in later use: Moving or travelling at a rapid pace and in a smart and vigorous manner 1738. 3. Of a breeze: Blowing strongly or briskly; rattling 1849. 4. Of a pace, etc.: Rapid, smart, vigorous 1857.

4. The wheelers in a s. trot, and leaders cantering 1857.

Spanless (spæˑnlĕs), *a.* 1847. [f. SPAN *v.*[1]] That cannot be spanned.

Spaˑn-long, *a.* 1593. [f. SPAN *sb.*[1] + LONG *a.*] Having the length of a span; hence, brief, short.

White faies..And span-long elves that dance about a pool B. JONS.

Spanner (spæˑnǝɹ). 1639. [ad. G. *spanner*, f. *spannen* SPAN *v.*[2]] †1. An instrument by which the spring in a wheel-lock firearm was spanned or wound up –1863. 2. A hand-tool, usually consisting of a small bar of steel, having an opening, grip, or jaw at the end which fits over or clasps the nut of a screw, a bolt, coupling, etc., and turns it or holds it in position; a wrench 1790. 3. *Mech.* A bar or lever for opening the valves of a steam-engine 1773.

Span-new (spæˑn₁niū), *a.* Now chiefly *dial.* Also span new. ME. [ad. ON. *spán-nýr*, f. *spánn* chip + *nýr* new.] Quite or perfectly new.

A maker of s. governments and religions COBBETT.

Span-roof (spæˑn₁rūf). 1823. [SPAN *sb.*[1]] A roof consisting of two inclined sides.

Spar (spāɹ), *sb.*[1] [ME. *sperre, sparre*; cf.

OHG. *sparro* (G. *sparren*), ON. *sperra.*] **1.** One of the common rafters of a roof. Now chiefly *dial.* **2.** A pole or piece of timber of some length and moderate thickness; *spec.* an undressed stem of fir, etc., under six inches in diameter. late ME. **3.** †**a.** A bar of wood used to fasten a gate or door -1668. **b.** A spoke, bar, or cross-bar 1687. **4.** *Naut.* A general term for masts, yards, booms, gaffs, etc. 1640.

4. b. Each of the main lateral members of the wing of an aeroplane 1913.

Comb.: **s.-buoy**, a buoy designed with a s. or mast which stands almost perpendicularly out of the water; **-deck**, a light upper deck in a vessel; **-torpedo**, a torpedo fastened on the end of a s. projecting from the bows of the boat.

Spar (spāɹ), *sb.*² 1581. [ad. MLG. *spar, sper*, related to OE. *spæren* gypsum, *spærstān* SPAR-STONE.] *Min.* **1.** A general term for a number of crystalline minerals more or less lustrous in appearance and admitting of easy cleavage. **b.** *pl.* Different varieties of this 1668. **2. a.** A fragment or particle of spar. Also *transf.* 1855. **b.** An ornament made of spar 1851.

1. *Calcareous, Derbyshire, Iceland s.*: see these words and CALC-, FELD-, FLUOR-SPAR.

Spar (spāɹ), *sb.*³ late ME. [f. SPAR *v.*²] †**1.** A thrust. late ME. only. **2.** A boxing-match; a display of boxing; a motion of sparring 1814. **3.** A cock-fight 1849. **4.** *transf.* A wordy contest or dispute. *colloq.* 1836.

Spar (spāɹ), *v.*¹ [ME. *sperren, sparre*, app. ad. MDu. *sperren*, f. the stem *sparr-* SPAR *sb.*¹] **1.** *trans.* To fasten (a door or gate) with a bar or bolt; to shut securely. Also occas. with *up.* Now *arch.* †**2.** *gen.* To close, fasten, secure, lock (*up*), etc. -1615. †**3.** To confine, enclose, or imprison; to shut *up*, in a place -1600. †**4.** To shut (a person or thing) *in* or *out* -1535.

1. Sperre the yate fast for feare of fraude SPENSER.

Spar (spāɹ), *v.*² ME. [OE. *spierran.*] †**1.** *intr.* To dart or spring; to strike or thrust rapidly -1450. **2.** Of cocks: To strike with the feet or spurs; to fight 1570. **b.** *trans.* To cause (a cock) to spar; to exercise in sparring 1686. **3.** To engage in or practise boxing; to make the motions of attack and defence with the arms and fists; to box. Also const. *at.* 1755. **4.** To dispute; to bandy words 1698.

2. A young cock will s. at his adversary before his spurs are grown 1776. **Spa·rring** *vbl. sb.* attrib. *s. partner*, a boxer employed to practise with another.

Spar (spāɹ), *v.*³ 1657. [f. SPAR *sb.*¹] **1.** *trans.* To furnish, make, or close *in*, with spars. **2.** *Naut.* **a.** In pa. pple: Provided with spars 1840. **b.** To fix spars across (the rigging) preparatory to rattling down 1860.

Sparable (spæ·răb'l). 1627. [Reduced form of SPARROW-BILL.] A small headless wedge-shaped iron nail (stouter than a *sprig*), used in the soles and heels of boots and shoes.

†**Sparadrap.** 1543. [a. F., of unkn. origin.] *Med.* A piece of linen or other cloth dipped in, or spread with, some ointment or medicament for use as a bandage or plaster -1728.

†**Spa·rage.** 1565. [a. OF., ad. L. *asparagus.* Cf. SPARROW-GRASS.] Asparagus -1612. So †**Spa·ragus** 1543.

Spare (spēᵊɹ), *sb.* ME. [f. SPARE *v.* and *a.*] †**1.** The fact of leaving unhurt or unharmed; sparing; leniency, mercy -1633. **2.** The exercise of economy, frugality, or moderation. Chiefly in the phr. *to make* (*no*, etc.) *s.* 1577. **3.** *ellipt.* A spare or reserve sum of money; a spare room; a spare part, tool, tire, etc., carried esp. by motorists to replace a breakage, etc. 1642. **4.** In skittles and ten-pins (*U.S.*): The knocking down of all the pins with two bowls (thus leaving one 'to spare'), or with the first bowl (= *double s.*); the score for doing this 1879.

1. Cut them off..and make no s. of any of them 1633. 2. At our meal there was no spare of liquor 1655.

Spare (spēᵊɹ), *a.* and *adv.* late ME. [Connected w. next.] **I. 1.** Not in actual or regular use at the time spoken of, but carried, held, or kept in reserve for future use or to supply an emergency; orig. *Naut.*; additional, extra. †**b.** Of land, ground, etc.: Uncultivated, unoccupied, vacant -1669. **2.** That can be spared, dispensed with, or given away, as being in excess of actual requirements; superfluous 1553. **b.** Of time: Leisure 1610.

1. A small s. Mast, Such as sea-faring men prouide for stormes SHAKS. One or more s. beds for lodging of strangers 1702. A spare part (1897), room (1837). 2. When I..have enough s. gold To boil away, you shall be welcome to me 1613. **b.** The female world.. have more s. time upon their hands ADDISON.

II. †**1.** Of speech: Sparing; marked by reticence or reserve (*rare*) -1460. **2.** Of persons, their limbs, etc.: Having little flesh; not fat or plump; lean, thin 1548. **b.** Const. *in* or *of* (flesh) 1632. **c.** *poet.* Growing thinly or sparsely 1815. †**3.** Of persons: Sparing *of* or *in* something, esp. diet or speech -1697. †**b.** Not lavish, liberal, or profuse; frugal, niggardly; abstemious -1633. **4.** Characterized by meanness, bareness, economy, or frugality, esp. in regard to food 1560. **b.** Of diet, fare, meals, etc.: Consisting of a comparatively small amount of food, esp. of a plain kind; not plentiful 1570. **c.** *poet.* Scanty, meagre, rare 1813. **5.** As *adv.* Sparely; with spare diet. SCOTT.

2. O, giue me the s. men, and spare me the great ones SHAKS. **c.** Grey rocks did peep from the s. moss SHELLEY. 3. Are they s. in diet SHAKS. 4. As it is a s. life..it fits my humor well: but as there is no more plentie in it, it goes much against my stomacke SHAKS. **b.** S. feast!—a radish and an egg! COWPER. 5. The warrior..Feeds hard and s., and seldom sleeps SCOTT. Hence **Spa·re-ly** *adv.*, **-ness.**

Spare (spēᵊɹ), *v.* [Com. Teut.; OE. *sparian*, f. stem *spar-* of uncertain relationship. The Teut. word is the base of OF. *espargner* (mod. F. *épargner*).] **I. 1.** *trans.* To leave (a person) unhurt, unharmed, or uninjured; to refrain from inflicting injury or punishment upon; to allow to escape, go free, or live. **b.** To allow to be free or exempt *from* some task -1794. **c.** To deal leniently or gently with 1535. **d.** To refrain from afflicting or distressing 1794. **2.** *absol.* To exercise or show mercy, forbearance, or leniency ME. **3.** *trans.* **a.** To abstain from visiting (a sin, etc.) with due punishment; to forgive or pardon. late ME. **b.** To preserve or save (life) in place of destroying; to allow to continue or last 1594. **4.** To abstain from destroying, removing, damaging, or injuring (a thing) OE.

1. Spare my gray-beard, you wagtaile? SHAKS. Whom ev'n the savage Beasts had spar'd, they kill'd DRYDEN. **c.** My lady used not to s. Colonel Esmond in talking of him THACKERAY. 2. He will not s. in the day of vengeance *Prov.* vi. 34. 3. **b.** He hoped that the squire's life would be long spared TROLLOPE. 4. Shee..was now about to put out his eyes, which all this while were spared SIDNEY.

II. 1. To refrain from using or consuming; to use in a frugal or economical manner. Now *rare.* OE. †**b.** To save, hoard, or store up -1683. **c.** *absol.* To use or practise economy or frugality; to be parsimonious or niggardly; to live or act sparingly. late ME. **d.** In passive: To be left over or unused 1577. **2.** To abstain from using, employing, exercising, etc.; to forbear, omit, or avoid the use or occasion of; also, to use or deal in, with moderation, economy, or restraint OE. **b.** *ellipt.* To refrain from doing something. Now *rare* or *Obs.* late ME. **3.** To avoid incurring or being involved in, to save (expense or labour) ME. **b.** To avoid, shun, keep clear of. Now *rare.* late ME. **4.** To dispense with; to part with to another or others, esp. without inconvenience or loss to oneself; to do without ME. **b.** To set aside *for* some particular use or purpose; to keep in reserve ME. **c.** To set apart, save, or give (time) from one's usual duties or avocations; to have (time) free 1548. **5.** With direct and indirect object: **a.** To give or grant; to supply (a person) with (something) out of a stock, quantity, etc. 1593. **b.** To save or relieve (a person, one's feelings, etc.) from (something) 1681.

1. Free Nature's bounty thriftily they spent, And spared the Stock COWLEY. **c.** I, who at some times spend, at others s. POPE. 2. Had he but spared his tongue and pen, He might have rose like other men SWIFT. S. the rod and spoil the child 1841. 3. No time, trouble, or expense has been spared in the matter 1892. **b.** Shun me and I will s. your haunts SHAKS. 4. Kirke could s. no soldiers; but he had sent..some experienced officers MACAULAY. **c.** Let all the citizens who can s. time hear..such causes 1875. 5. And now A word, but one,..Not one to s. her TENNYSON. **b.** I was, however, spared this infliction 1893.

III. *intr. To s. for*: **a.** To desist or refrain from some action because or on account of (difficulty, opposition, loss, etc.). Now *arch.* ME. **b.** With neg.: To refrain from action in order to save (expense, trouble, etc.); to be sparing of or in (something). late ME.

a. S. not for spoiling of thy steed SCOTT. **b.** S. for no cost MARLOWE. Hence **Spa·reable** *a.* 1688.

†**Spa·reful,** *a.* 1565. [f. SPARE *sb.* or *v.*] Sparing, frugal -1600. Hence †**Spa·reful-ly** *adv.*, †**-ness.**

Spareless (spēᵊ·ɹlės), *a.* and *adv.* late ME. [f. as prec.] †**1.** Unstinted, unlimited -1450. **2.** Unsparing, merciless 1589. **3.** As *adv.* Without stint 1567.

Spare-rib (spēᵊ·rib, spæ·rib). 1596. [prob. ad. MLG. *ribbespêr*, subseq. assoc. w. SPARE *a.*] A cut of meat, esp. of pork, consisting of part of the ribs somewhat closely trimmed.

Sparge (spāɹdʒ), *v.* 1560. [app. ad. OF. *espargier* or L. *spargere* to sprinkle; but in sense 1 answering to PARGET *v.*] **1.** *trans.* To plaster; to rough-cast. **2.** To dash, splash, or sprinkle (water) about 1785. **3.** *Brewing.* To sprinkle (malt) with hot water. Also *absol.* 1839. Hence **Sparge** *sb.*, sprinkling; *Brewing*, the spray of water with which the malt is sprinkled. **Spa·rger,** an appliance for sprinkling water, esp. in brewing.

Spargefication (spāɹdʒėfikēⁱ·ʃən). Also **-ification.** 1835. [f. L. *spargere*; see -FICATION.] The action of sprinkling or scattering. So **Spargefa·ction.** SWIFT.

Sparhawk (spā·ɹhǭk). Now *arch.* or *dial.* [OE. *spearhafoc*, f. the stem of *spearwa* SPARROW + *hafoc* HAWK.] A sparrowhawk.

Sparing (spēᵊ·riŋ), *ppl. a.* and *adv.* ME. [f. SPARE *v.*] **1.** Inclined to save, niggard; restrained in discourse or statement; scanty, limited; forbearing, merciful. †**2.** As *adv.* Sparingly -1742. Hence **Spa·ring-ly** *adv.*, **-ness.**

Spark (spāɹk), *sb.*¹ [OE. *spærca, spearca*, = MDu., (M)LG., *sparke.*] **1.** A small particle of fire or an ignited fragment, thrown off from a burning body or remaining in one almost extinguished, or produced by the impact of one hard body on another. **b.** *fig.* and in fig. context; freq. with allusion to the beginning or immediate cause of a fire or conflagration OE. **2.** A small trace, indication, or portion *of* some quality, feeling, sentiment, etc., in some way comparable to a spark, esp. in respect of its latent possibilities OE. **b.** A small remnant, fragment, piece, atom, or amount *of* something 1548. **3.** The vital or animating principle in man; a trace *of* life or vitality. Freq. in *vital s., s. of life.* late ME. **4. a.** A small ruby or diamond: orig. *diamond* or *ruby s.* and *s. of diamond*, etc. 1629. **b.** A (glittering) fragment or particle *of* some metal, ore, or mineral 1560. **5.** A bright or glittering flash or gleam of light. Also *transf.*, a bright glance. 1542. **6.** *Electr.* In full *electric(al) s.*: A brilliant streak or flash of light produced by a discontinuous discharge of electricity between two conductors at a short or moderate distance apart 1748. **b.** *spec.* An electric spark serving to fire the explosive mixture in the oil-engine of a motor.

1. Yet man is borne vnto trouble, as the sparkes flie vpward *Job* v. 7. **b.** Left alone they might have remained quiet; but they only wanted the s. DISRAELI. Phr. *A s. in one's throat* (slang), a constant thirst. 2. They still kept alive the sparks of future friendship 1820. 4. **a.** All the haft twinkled with diamond sparks TENNYSON. **b.** This bluish stone was filled with sparks of virgin copper 1796. 6. *fig.* Animated by the electric s. of genius 1846. *Sparks* (slang), a wireless operator.

attrib. and *Comb.*: **s.-arrester,** a device for arresting sparks in locomotive funnels or chimneys; **-gap,** a space between two terminals through which an electric spark passes; **-plug** *U.S.* = sparking-plug. Hence **Spa·rker,** a s.-arrester.

Spark (spāɹk), *sb.*² 1513. [prob. a fig. use of prec.] †**1.** A woman of great beauty, elegance, or wit -1676. **2.** A young man of an elegant or foppish character; one who affects smartness. 1513. **3.** A beau, lover, suitor (*arch.*) 1706.

1. The louely sparke, the bright Laodice CHAPMAN. 2. Hark'ee, my s., none of your grinning! MISS BURNEY. 3. A very woman..daring death..for the sake of thee, her handsome s.! BROWNING.

Spark (spāɹk), *v.*¹ ME. [Related to SPARK

sb.[1]] **1.** *intr.* To emit or give forth a spark or sparks; to sparkle. **2.** To issue, come forth, fall, etc., as or in the manner of sparks 1513. **3.** *trans.* **a.** To send *out*, or emit, in or as sparks 1596. **b.** *Electr.* To affect, act or operate upon, by the emission or transmission of electric sparks. Also *absol.*, to send a spark *across*, etc. 1889.

1. *transf.* Her eyes did sparke, At every glance, like Diamonds in the darke QUARLES. Hence **Spa·rking** *vbl. sb.*, esp. in *sparking-plug*, a device for firing the explosive mixture in a motor engine.

Spark (spāɹk), *v.*[2] 1676. [f. SPARK *sb.*[2]] †**1.** *intr.* With *it.* To play the spark or gallant; to show off –1709. **2.** *U.S.* To engage in courtship; to play the suitor, wooer, or beau. Also with *it.* 1807. **b.** *trans.* To court 1888.

2. He used to go sparkin' round among the girls 1884.

Sparkish (spā·ɹkiʃ), *a.* 1641. [f. SPARK *sb.*[2] + -ISH.] **1.** Of persons: Having the character, airs, or manner of a spark or gallant. **2.** Of things: Characteristic of, or appropriate to, a spark; of a smart or elegant make 1657. Hence **Spa·rkish-ly** *adv.*, **-ness.**

Sparkle (spā·ɹk'l), *sb.* ME. [f. SPARK *sb.*[1] + -LE 1.] **1.** A small spark; an ignited or luminous particle. **b.** *fig.* and in fig. context; freq. with allusion to the kindling of a fire or conflagration. late ME. **2.** A slight beginning, trace, indication, or manifestation *of* something. late ME. †**3.** A vital or animating principle (*rare*). late ME. †**4.** A small ruby or diamond (*rare*) –1704. **5.** A glittering or flashing point of light. Also *fig.* 1490. **b.** A flashing or fiery glance 1590. **6.** Glittering or flashing appearance or quality; lively brightness 1589. **b.** Liveliness of spirit; smartness; wittiness 1611. **c.** *spec.* The appearance characteristic of certain wines, due to the presence of carbonic-acid gas 1833. **7.** A small piece, part, spot, etc. *of* something; now only, a (glittering) particle 1570.

1. Smoak and bickering flame, and sparkles dire MILT. **b.** Some unlucky s. from a Tory paper set Steele's politicks on fire JOHNSON. **2.** Sparclis of grace þat we felen WYCLIF. **5.** Swift as the S. of a glancing Star MILT. **6.** The occasional s. of the long line of spears SCOTT. **7.** Sparkles of blood on the white foam are cast SHELLEY.

Sparkle (spā·ɹk'l), *v.*[1] ME. [f. SPARK *sb.*[1] + -LE 3.] **I.** *intr.* **1.** To issue, fly, spring *out* or *forth* in sparkles or small particles. **2.** To emit sparks or sparkles of fire 1480. **b.** Of the eyes: To flash with anger or rage 1593. **3.** To reflect or emit numerous separate rays or points of light; to glitter or flash. late ME. **b.** To move, proceed, flow, etc., in a glittering or sparkling manner 1823. **4.** Of wines, etc.: To effervesce with small glittering bubbles. late ME. **5. a.** Of feelings, etc.: To appear or be evident *in* (or *through*) the eyes by the brightness or animation of these 1592. **b.** Of the eyes: To be bright or animated; to shine; to glisten 1700.

1. When some heat of difference sparkled out TENNYSON. **2. b.** Mine eyes should s. like the beaten Flint SHAKS. **3.** Sparkles this Stone as it was wont? SHAKS. *fig.* His Wit sparkles as well as his Eyes 1699. **b.** To trace your..waters sparkling through green Hertfordshire LAMB. **5. a.** Disdaine and Scorne ride sparkling in her eyes SHAKS. **b.** A burly man..whose little eyes seemed always sparkling with unclerical humour 1883.

II. *trans.* **1.** To cause to sparkle or glitter 1553. **2.** To emit or eject (fire, etc.) as or like sparks 1588. **b.** Of the eyes: To indicate (a feeling) by brightness or animation 1601.

1. Aurora now..Sparkled with rosy light the dewy lawn POPE. **2.** Womens eyes..sparcle still the right promethean fire SHAKS. Hence **Spa·rkling-ly** *adv.*, **-ness.**

Spa·rkle, *v.*[2] *Obs.* or *dial.* late ME. [Alteration of SPARPLE *v.*] **1.** *intr.* Of persons: To scatter, disperse 1440. **2.** *trans.* To cause to scatter or disperse; to drive in different directions 1470. **3.** To cast abroad; to scatter, sprinkle, or strew 1440. **4.** To sprinkle, bestrew or bespatter *with* something; to dot thickly. late ME. **5.** To disseminate or diffuse; to spread or circulate 1532.

2. Then went the kyng..and sparcled them then so That North they went 1470. **4.** The pauement of the temple is all sparcled with bludde 1555.

Sparkler (spā·ɹklər). 1713. [f. SPARKLE *v.*[1] + -ER.] **1.** One who sparkles; *esp.* a vivacious, witty, or pretty young woman. **2.** A bright or sparkling eye. Chiefly *pl.* Latterly *colloq.* or *slang.* 1746. **3.** A sparkling gem; a diamond; esp. *pl.* 1822. **4.** Something which shines or sparkles; a sparkling firework which is noiseless 1879. **5.** A tiger-beetle 1860.

Sparkless (spā·ɹklės), *a.* 1821. [f. SPARK *sb.*[1] + -LESS.] Free from or devoid of sparks; emitting no sparks; *spec.* in *Electr.*

Sparklet (spā·ɹklėt). 1689. [f. as prec. + -LET.] **1.** A small spark or sparkle. **2.** A small sparkling ornament for a dress 1902. **3.** (*pl.*) Trade name for a capsule containing carbonic acid gas under pressure used with a siphon for making aerated water 1904.

Sparkling (spā·ɹkliŋ), *ppl. a.* ME. [f. SPARKLE *v.*[1]] **1.** That emits sparks or sparkles. **2.** Of the eyes: Flashing, bright, animated. late ME. **3.** Reflecting or emitting rays of light; flashing, glittering, brilliant, resplendent. late ME. **4.** Characterized by brilliancy and liveliness; brilliant, animated, sprightly 1647. **5.** Of pleasure: Characterized by a high degree of delight or enjoyment 1789.

1. A large s. fire of turf and bog-wood SCOTT. **2.** His s. Eyes, repleat with wrathfull fire SHAKS. **3.** Drynke grene wyne, clere, sharpe and sparklynge in tempure 1422. **4.** A piece of s...rhetoric CARLYLE. Hence **Spa·rkling-ly** *adv.*, **-ness** (*rare*).

Sparling (spā·ɹliŋ). Now chiefly *north.* and *Sc.* ME. [ad. OF. *esperlinge* (later *esperlan*, mod.F. *éperlan*), of Teut. origin.] **1.** The common European smelt, *Osmerus eperlanus.* **2.** Applied to other small fish; †**a.** The sprat, *Clupea sprattus* (*rare*) –1740. **b.** *U.S.* A young or immature herring 1884.

Sparoid (spæ·roid, spēᵊ·roid), *a.* and *sb.* 1836. [ad. mod.L. *Sparoides*, f. SPARUS.] Of or belonging to, characteristic of, the *Sparidæ* or sea-bream family; a fish of this family.

†**Sparple,** *v.* Also **sparpoil,** etc. ME. [ad. OF. *esparpeillier* (mod.F. *éparpiller*), of uncertain origin.] = SPARKLE *v.*[2] –1819.

Sparred (spāɹd), (*ppl.*) *a.* 1805. [f. SPAR *sb.*[1] or *v.*[3]] **1.** Made or constructed of, having or fitted with, spars, narrow boards, or planks, set with intervals or spaces between them. **2.** Of a ship: Furnished with spar 1905.

Sparrow (spæ·roᵘ). [OE. *spearwa*, = Goth. *sparwa*, MHG. *sparwe.*] **1.** A small brownish-grey bird of the family *Fringillidæ*, indigenous to Europe, where it is very common, and naturalized in various other countries; esp. the house-sparrow, *Passer domesticus.* **2.** With distinguishing terms, denoting varieties of the true sparrow, or other small birds in some way resembling these 1668.

2. *Field-, house-, Java, Savannah, song-, swamp-s.*, HEDGE-, REED-, TREE-SPARROW: see these words.

Comb.: **s.-bunting,** *Zonotrichia albicollis*, differing from the true bunting in having exposed nostrils; **-owl,** one or other of various small owls, esp. of the genus *Glaucidium*: **-pie, -pudding,** a dish proverbially supposed to make the eater sharp-witted; **-wort,** *Erica passerina*, native to South Africa.

Spa·rrow-bill. 1629. [f. prec.] = SPARABLE.

†**Spa·rrow-bla:sting.** 1589. [f. SPARROW, with joc. or contemptuous force.] The fact of being blasted or blighted by some mysterious power, sceptically regarded as unimportant or non-existent –1633. So †**Spa·rrow-blasted** *a.* balefully stricken or blighted; dumbfounded.

Spa·rrow(-)grass. Now *dial.* or *vulgar.* 1649. [Earlier *sparagrass*, corruption of SPARAGUS.] Asparagus.

Spa·rrow-hawk. late ME. [f. SPARROW; cf. SPARHAWK.] **1.** A species of hawk (*Accipiter nisus*) which preys on small birds, common in the British Islands and widely distributed in northern Europe and Asia. Occas., one or other species of hawk resembling this. **2.** A small anvil used in silver-working 1869.

Sparry (spā·ri), *a.* 1695. [f. SPAR *sb.*[2]] **1.** Consisting of or abounding in spar; of the nature of spar. **b.** Of places: Rich in spar 1789. **2.** In specific terms denoting mineral substances of the nature of or containing spar, as *s. iron* (*ore*) 1796. **3.** Of lustre, etc.: Resembling that of spar 1792.

Sparse (spāɹs), *a.* 1727. [ad. L. *sparsus*, pa. pple. of *spargere* to scatter.] **1.** *Sc.* Of writing: Having wide spaces between the words. **2.** Separated by fairly wide intervals or spaces; thinly scattered; placed or set here and there over a relatively extensive area; not crowded, close, or dense 1753. **3.** Characterized by wide distribution or intervals 1801. **b.** Characterized by sparseness or scantiness 1871.

2. A wide-spread though s. population 1870. A man with s. grey hair 1875. **3. b.** The gleaning has been somewhat s. 1889. Hence **Spa·rse-ly** *adv.*, **-ness. Spa·rsity,** s. state or condition; comparative scarcity or fewness.

†**Sparse,** *v.* 1535. [f. L. *spars-*, *spargere* to scatter.] **1.** *absol.* To scatter *abroad* in giving –1614. **2.** *trans.* To spread or disseminate (a rumour, doctrine, etc.). Freq. with *abroad.* –1651. **3.** To break up, scatter; to dispose, sprinkle, etc., in a scattered manner –1614. Hence **Spa·rsedly** *adv.* (now *rare*), sparsely.

‖ **Sparsim** (spā·ɹsim), *adv.* 1586. [L.] In various places; here and there; sparsely.

Spart (spāɹt). 1600. [ad. L. *spartum* or Sp. *esparto.*] Esparto. Also *s.-grass.*

Spartacist (spā·ɹtăsist). 1916. [a. G., f. *Spartacus*, name of the leader in the servile war against Rome (73–1 B.C.); see -IST.] A member of the Spartacus group of communistic revolutionists in Germany.

Spartan (spā·ɹtăn), *sb.* and *a.* late ME. [ad. L. *Spartanus*, f. *Sparta* (Gr. Σπάρτα, Σπάρτη), capital of the ancient Doric state of Laconia.] **A.** *sb.* **1.** A native or inhabitant of Sparta; a Laconian or Lacedæmonian. **2.** One who resembles the ancient Spartans in character 1810. **B.** *adj.* **1.** Of or pertaining to Sparta or its inhabitants; Laconian, Lacedæmonian 1582. †**b.** *S. dog*, etc.: A kind of bloodhound –1697. **2.** Characteristic or typical of Sparta, its inhabitants, or their customs; *esp.* distinguished by simplicity, frugality, courage, or brevity of speech 1644.

1. **b.** *fig.* Oh Sparton Dogge: More fell then Anguish, Hunger, or the Sea SHAKS. **2.** The fare is S. in its extreme frugality 1885.

Sparteine (spā·ɹtīin). 1850. [f. mod.L. *Spartium* broom; see -INE [5].] *Chem.* An alkaloid obtained from common broom, used to some extent in medicine.

Sparth. *Obs.* exc. *Hist.* ME. [ad. ON. *sparða*, of obscure origin.] A long-handled broad-bladed battle-axe, used esp. by the Irish down to the 16th c.

He hath a s. of twenti pound of wighte CHAUCER.

Spartiate (spā·ɹʃiĕt). *rare.* late ME. [ad. L. *Spartiates*, a. Gr. Σπαρτιάτης, f. Σπάρτη Sparta.] A Spartan.

‖ **Sparus** (spēᵊ·rɒs). *Pl.* **spari** (spēᵊ·rəi). 1668. [L., ad. Gr. σπάρος.] A sea-bream or gilt-head.

Spasm (spæ·z'm). late ME. [a. OF. *spasme*, or ad. L. *spasmus* masc., *spasma* neut., a. Gr. σπασμός, σπάσμα, f. σπᾶν to draw, tug, etc.] **1.** Sudden and violent muscular contraction of a convulsive or painful character. **2.** With *a* and *pl.* A convulsive twitch or throe 1477. **3.** *fig.* Any sudden or convulsive movement of a violent character; a convulsion 1817.

3. As with an earthquake's s. SHELLEY. A mere s. of suspicious jealousy 1874. So †‖**Spa·sma** (in senses 1 and 2). †‖**Spa·smus. Spasma·tic, Spa·smic** *adjs.* spasmodic, convulsive.

Spasmodic (spæzmǫ·dik), *a.* 1681. [ad. med. or mod.L. *spasmodicus*, f. Gr. σπασμώδης, f. σπασμός or σπάσμα SPASM.] **1.** Of the nature of a spasm; characterized by spasms or convulsive twitches; marked by jerkiness or suddenness of muscular movement; *spec.* in *Path.* **2.** Occurring or proceeding by fits and starts; irregular, intermittent; not sustained 1837. **3.** Agitated, excited; emotional, highly-strung; characterized by a disjointed or unequal style of expression 1848.

1. The use of ipecacuan in s. asthma 1811. **2.** Acquiescence in disorder would be followed by a s. severity 1856. So **Spasmo·dical** *a.*, **-ly** *adv.*

Spastic (spæ·stik), *a.* 1753. [ad. L. *spasticus* (Pliny), a. Gr. σπαστικός, f. σπᾶν to draw; cf. SPASM.] **1.** *Path.* Of the nature of a spasm or sudden contraction; characterized or affected by spasmodic symptoms or movements. **2.** *Physiology.* Performing involuntary contractile movements 1822. Hence **Spasti·city**, s. condition or quality.

Spat (spæt), *sb.*[1] 1634. [perh. related to SPIT *v.*[1]] 1. The spawn of oysters or other shell-fish. Freq. used in *pl.* 1667. †2. The eggs of bees –1657.

Spat (spæt), *sb.*[2] Chiefly *dial.* or *colloq.* 1804. [prob. echoic; cf. SPAT *v.*[2]] 1. A tiff or dispute; a quarrel. Orig. *U.S.* 2. A smart blow, smack, or slap 1823. 3. A sharp smacking sound 1881.

Spat (spæt), *sb.*[3] 1802. [Abbrev. of SPATTERDASH.] A short gaiter worn over the instep and reaching only a little way above the ankle, usually fastened under the foot by means of a strap. Chiefly in *pl.*

Spat (spæt), *sb.*[4] 1876. [app. a. Du., in the same sense.] A small splash *of* something.

Spat (spæt), *v.*[1] 1667. [f. SPAT *sb.*[1]] *intr.* and *trans.* Of oysters: To spawn.

Spat (spæt), *v.*[2] 1809. [prob. imitative.] 1. *intr.* To start *up* sharply or actively; to engage in a dispute. *U.S.* 2. *trans.* To clap, slap, or smack 1832. 3. *intr.* To administer slaps or pats; to strike sharply; to spatter. Also used advb. 1868.

2. The little Isabel leaped up and down spatting her hands 1845. 3. Bill fired again..and I heard the ball go 's.!' 1890.

Spatangoid (spætæ·ŋgoid), *sb.* and *a.* 1857. [ad. mod.L. *Spatangoides*, f. *Spatangus* (late L. *spatangius*, Gr. σπατάγγης); see -OID.] *Zool.* A. *sb.* A sea-urchin belonging or related to the genus *Spatangus* (heart-urchins). B. *adj.* Having the characteristics of this.

Spatch-cock, spatchcock (spæ·tʃkǫk), *sb.* 1785. [According to Grose (1785), abbrev. of *dispatch cock*, an Irish dish prepared in an emergency.] A fowl split open and grilled after being killed, plucked, and dressed in a summary fashion.

Spatchcock (spæ·tʃkǫk), *v.* 1865. [f. prec.] 1. *trans.* To cook as, or in the manner of, a spatchcock. 2. To insert, interpolate, or sandwich (a phrase, sentence, etc.) 1901. b. To add to, or modify, by interpolation 1901.

2. We read phrases of apparent sincere religious fervour spatchcocked in between these bloodthirsty expressions 1903. ¶ Also used for SPITCHCOCK *v.*

Spate (spēⁱt), *sb.* Orig. *Sc.* and *north.* late ME. [Origin obsc.] 1. A flood or inundation; *esp.* a sudden flood or rising in a river or stream caused by heavy rains or melting snow. Also *transf.* and *fig.*, esp. a sudden outburst, rush, or 'flood'. 2. Without article: Flooding or inundation, swollen condition *of* water, etc.; copious downpouring *of* rain. Now usu. without const. 1513. Hence **Spate** *v. trans.* and *intr.* to flood.

1. Heaps of drifted rubbish..to mark the tide-line of the winter spates 1889. 2. *In s.*, in flood.

Spath (spæþ). Now *rare.* 1763. [a. G., var. sp. of *spat, spad*, MHG. and MLG. *spat.*] = SPAR *sb.*[2] Hence **Spa·thic** *a.* = SPATHOSE.

‖**Spatha** (spēⁱ·pă). *Pl.* -æ (-ī). 1753. [L., ad. Gr. σπάθη broad blade, spatula, etc.] 1. *Bot.* A spathe. 2. A flat blade-shaped implement 1881.

Spathaceous (spăpēⁱ·ʃəs), *a.* 1760. [a. mod.L. *spathaceus*; see SPATHA and -ACEOUS.] *Bot.* Furnished with or enclosed by a spathe; of the nature of or resembling a spathe.

Spathe (spēⁱð). 1785. [ad. L. *spatha* or Gr. σπάθη; see SPATHA.] 1. *Bot.* A large bract or sheathing-leaf enveloping the inflorescence (usu. a spadix) of certain plants, as arums, palms, etc., in such a way as completely to enclose it before expansion. 2. *Zool.* A spatulate or spoon-shaped part, process, etc. 1891. Hence **Spa·thal** *a.* furnished with a s. **Spathed** (spēⁱðd) *a.* having a s. **Spa·thiform** *a.*[2] having the form of a s.

Spathiform (spæ·pifǭɹm), *a.*[1] 1793. [f. SPATH + -(I)FORM.] *Min.* Resembling spath or spar in form or appearance; lamellar.

The s., or uranite spar 1793.

Spathose (spæþōᵘ·s), *a.* 1776. [f. SPATH + -OSE [1].] *Min.* 1. Of the nature of or resembling spath or spar; abounding in, consisting of, spar; foliated or lamellar in structure or texture; sparry. †2. Derived from fluor-spar –1811.

1. *S.-iron, iron-ore, ore* = SIDERITE 6. 2. *S. acid*, hydrofluoric acid.

Spathulate (spæ·piŭlĕt), *a.* 1821. [f. L. *spathula* + -ATE [2].] Chiefly *Bot.* Spatulate, spatular. So **Spa·thulated** *ppl. a.* (*rare*).

Spatial (spēⁱ·ʃăl), *a.* 1847. [f. L. *spatium* SPACE *sb.* + -AL.] 1. Having extension in space; occupying or taking up space; consisting of or characterized by space. 2. Of, pertaining, or relating to space; subject to, or governed by, the conditions of space. Chiefly *Metaph.* and opp. to *temporal.* 1857. 3. Happening or taking place in space; caused or involved by space 1866. 4. Of faculty or sense: Apprehending or perceiving space or extension 1886.

1. An independent s. world 1886. 2. Ideas..which have been formed from a vast quantity of temporal and s. experience 1886. 4. The origin of the s. faculty 1886. Hence **Spa·tially** *adv.* as regards, in or with reference to, or by means of space.

Spatiate (spēⁱ·ʃiĕⁱt), *v.* 1626. [f. ppl. stem of L. *spatiari*, f. *spatium* SPACE *sb.*] *intr.* To walk about; to stroll, wander, range, or roam.

Spattee (spætī·). 1926. [f. SPAT *sb.*[3] + -EE.] A kind of gaiter for women and girls made in imitation of Highland stockings. Chiefly *pl.*

Spatter (spæ·təɹ), *sb.* 1797. [f. next.] A slight splash or sprinkle; a spattering.

Spatter (spæ·təɹ), *v.* 1582. [app. a frequentative of the stem found in Du. and LG. *spatten* to burst, spout; or simply imitative.] I. *trans.* 1. To scatter or disperse in fragments. b. With *out*: To sputter, or cause to sputter 1586. c. To dash, cast, send flying, in drops or small particles 1721. 2. To splash or stain with drops of fluid, mud, etc.; to bespatter; *fig.* to assail with obloquy or detraction 1645. b. To cover in a dispersed manner 1647. 3. Of fluids, etc.: To fall or strike upon (something) in scattered drops 1837.

1. With..my battle-axe..To s. his brains TENNYSON. c. The..puffs of wind spattered the snow against the windows 1852. 2. Bend all your force to s. merit GAY. b. Natures carelesse pencill dipt in light With sprinkled starres hath spattered the Night 1647.

II. *intr.* 1. To spring, fly, or spirt in drops or particles; to throw off drops or small fragments 1600. b. To fall, descend, strike, in heavy drops or with a sound suggestive of these 1675. 2. To eject small drops of saliva or particles of food, etc., from the mouth; to splutter while speaking; to cause spattering in any way 1618. b. To scatter drops of ink 1640. 3. To walk or tread in some splashy substance 1806.

1. b. The musket-balls spattering in the water 1887. 2. That mind must needs be irrecoverably deprav'd, which..tasting but once of one just deed, spatters at it, and abhorrs the relish ever after MILT.

Comb.: **s.-dock**, the yellow pond-lily, *Nuphar.*

Spatterdash (spæ·təɹdæʃ). 1687. [f. SPATTER *v.* + DASH *v.*] A kind of long gaiter or legging of leather, cloth, etc., to keep the trousers or stockings from being spattered, esp. in riding. Chiefly in *pl.* Hence **Spa·tterdashed** (dæʃt) *ppl. a.* clad in, provided with, spatterdashes.

Spattle (spæ·t'l), *sb.*[1] *Obs.* exc. *dial.* [OE. *spātl*, f. *spāt-*, stem of *spǣtan* to spit.] Spittle.

Spattle (spæ·t'l), *sb.*[2] 1440. [Anglicized f. SPATULE.] 1. A spatula. Now *rare* or *Obs.* 2. *techn.* A tool for mottling a moulded article with pigment 1875.

†**Spa·ttle**, *v.*[1] [OE. *spātlian*, f. *spātl* SPATTLE *sb.*[1]] *intr.* and *trans.* To spit –1611.

Spattle (spæ·t'l), *v.*[2] Now *techn.* and *dial.* 1611. [Related to SPATTER *v.*] *trans.* To spatter or sprinkle; to mottle.

‖**Spatula** (spæ·tiŭlă). 1525. [L., var. of *spathula*, dim. of *spatha* SPATHA.] A simple instrument of wood, ivory, or metal, having a flat elongated form with various modifications of shape and size, used for a variety of purposes: *esp.* a. For stirring mixtures, spreading ointments or plasters, etc. b. For minor surgical operations or for the medical examination of certain organs 1684. So **Spa·tule**. late ME.

Spatulate (spæ·tiŭlĕt), *a.* 1760. [ad. mod. L. *spatulatus*, f. *spatula*.] Having a broadened and rounded end like that of a common form of spatula. So **Spa·tulated** *a.*

Spatulous (spæ·tiŭləs), *a.* 1828. [f. SPATULA + -OUS.] Resembling a spatula in form; spatulate. So **Spa·tulose** *a.*

Spauld (spǭld). Now *Sc.* and *north.* ME. [a. OF. *espalde, espaule* (mod.F. *épaule*) shoulder :—L. *spatula* shoulder-blade.] 1. The shoulder in man or animals; a shoulder of an animal used for food. 2. *transf.* A limb, leg, etc.; any joint of the carcass of a beast or bird 1500.

Spavin (spæ·vin). late ME. [ad. OF. *espavain*, var. of *esparvain* (mod.F. *éparvin, épervin*), of unkn. origin.] *Farriery.* 1. A hard bony tumour or excrescence formed at the union of the splint-bone and the shank in a horse's leg, and produced by inflammation of the cartilage uniting those bones; a similar tumour caused by inflammation of the small hock bones. b. A malady of horses due to the above cause 1500. 2. With distinguishing terms, as *blood s.*, a soft swelling of the hock vein caused by the accumulation of blood; freq. taken as synonymous with *bog s.* (see BOG *sb.*[1]); *dry* or *bone s.* (see BONE *sb.*) 1523.

Spavined (spæ·vind), *a.* late ME. [f. prec.] Of horses, etc.: Affected with spavin; having a spavin. b. *fig.* Lame, halting 1647.

Spa·-wa:ter. 1589. Water from a mineral spring (orig. from the springs at Spa).

Spawl (spǭl), *v. arch.* 1598. [Origin obsc.] 1. *intr.* To spit copiously or coarsely; to expectorate. 2. *trans.* To utter in a coarse manner 1616.

1. Why must he sputter, s., and slaver it In vain.. against the people's fav'rite? SWIFT.

Spaw·ling, *vbl. sb. arch.* 1609. [f. SPAWL *v.*] 1. The action of the vb.; expectoration. 2. *pl.* Spittle, spittings, saliva 1614.

Spawn (spǭn), *sb.* late ME. [f. next.] †1. The milt of a fish –1450. 2. The minute eggs of fishes and various other oviparous animals, usu. extruded in large numbers and forming a more or less coherent or gelatinous mass; also, the young brood hatched from such eggs, while still in an early stage of development 1491. b. With *a* and *pl.* A fish-egg; an undeveloped fish 1563. 3. A brood; a numerous offspring. Chiefly *fig.* 1590. 4. *fig.* A person contemptuously regarded as the offspring of some parent or stock 1589. b. So in collective use 1601. 5. *fig.* A product, result, or effect *of* something 1624. 6. *fig.* The source or origin *of* something 1591. 7. The mycelium of mushrooms or other fungi 1731.

4. Thou s. of the old serpent, fruitful in nothing but in lies DRYDEN. 5. Libels are her spawns 1646.

attrib. and *Comb.*: **s.-brick**, a brick-shaped mass of compost containing mushroom-spawn **-eater** *U.S.*, the smelt (*Leuciscus hudsonicus*).

Spawn (spǭn), *v.* late ME. [app. for *spaund, ad. AF. *espaundre*, = OF. *espandre* (mod.F. *épandre*) to shed, spill, pour out :—L. *expandere* EXPAND *v.*] I. *intr.* 1. Of fish, etc.: To cast spawn. 2. To increase or develop after the manner of spawn; to become reproductive 1607. 3. To issue or come forth like or after the manner of spawn 1657. 4. To swarm or teem *with* something 1818.

1. The sun comes forth, and many reptiles s. SHELLEY. 4. The rivers and the surrounding sea s. with fish EMERSON.

II. *trans.* 1. To produce or generate as spawn or in large numbers; also, in contemptuous use, to give birth to (a person) 1603. 2. To engender, produce, bring forth, give rise to 1594. b. *spec.* in contemptuous use with reference to literary work, utterances, etc. 1631. 3. To supply with spawn or mycelium 1786. 4. To extract spawn from (fishes) 1884.

2. b. The Press..hath Spawn'd so many Blasphemous ..Pamphlets 1713. Hence **Spawned** *ppl. a.* cast or deposited as spawn; that has emitted spawn, spent.

Spawner (spǭ·nəɹ). 1601. [f. SPAWN *sb.* or *v.*] 1. A female fish, esp. at spawning time †b. Applied to a woman –1675. 2. One who, or that which, spawns, produces, etc., in various senses 1650.

Spay (spēⁱ), *v.* late ME. [ad. AF. *espeier*, = OF. *espeer* to cut with a sword, f. *espee* (F. *épée*) sword.] †1. *trans.* To pierce or cut (a deer) so as to kill. late ME. only. 2. To operate upon (a female, esp. the female of certain animals) so as to remove the ovaries and destroy the reproductive power. late ME.

Spaya(r)d, spayd. Now *arch.* late ME. [Origin obsc.] A male deer in its third year.

Speak (spīk), *v.* Pa. t. **spoke** (spǭuk), *arch.* or *poet.* **spake.** Pa. pple. spoken (spǭu·k'n). [OE. *sprecan*, later *specan*, = OFris. *spreka*, OHG. *sprehhan* (G. *sprechen*).] **I.** *intr.* **1.** To utter or pronounce words or articulate sounds; to exercise the faculty of speech; to express one's thoughts in words. Also said of the mouth. **b.** To hold talk with others or with each other. Also, in mod. use, to be on speaking terms. OE. **c.** To deliver a speech or formal address; to express one's opinions or views in an assembly of any kind 1577. **2. a.** Followed by direct quotation of the words uttered OE. **b.** In pa. t. used in narrative poetry (after L. *dixit*) at the end of a speech 1667. **3.** Of a writer, literary composition, etc.: To make a statement or declaration in words; to state or say ME. **4.** *fig.* Of things: To be expressive or significant; to make some revelation or disclosure 1535. **b.** To take effect legally; to be valid 1837. **5.** *transf.* **a.** Of musical instruments, etc.: To emit a sound; *spec.* to utter a full and proper note. Chiefly *rhet.* or *techn.* 1602. **b.** Of natural forces, etc.: To emit noise, make a sound; to reverberate 1604. **c.** Of firearms: To emit a report on being fired 1706. **d.** Of a hound: To give tongue; to bay 1826.

1. I speake but as I finde SHAKS. Christ bids the dumb tongue s.; it speakes CRASHAW. I had taught my Poll, as I noted before, to s. DE FOE. I am speaking like a book 1875. b. Going a side, they spake among them selues N.T. (Rhem.) *Acts* xxvi. 31. There is Courtown, but we do not s. DISRAELI. c. Heere..Come I to speake in Cæsars Funerall SHAKS. 2. a. Again th' Almightie spake: Let there be Lights MILT. b. He spoke, and headlong..plunged to endless night GRAY. 3. A law of the Twelve Tables at Rome speaks to the same effect 1869. Phr. with advb., e. g. *to s. generally, generally speaking*, to make a general statement. *So to s.* 4. His words were ended, but his meek aspect Silent yet spake MILT. b. A will now speaks from the death of testator 1845. 5. a. Let the Kettle to the Trumpets speake SHAKS.

Comb. with preps. **Speak for —. a.** To make a speech in place of or on behalf of (a person); *esp.* to plead for. **b.** To beg or request; to ask for. **c.** To order; to bespeak; to engage. **d.** To indicate. **e.** *To s. for itself*, to be significant or self-evident. **S. of —. a.** To mention, or discourse upon, in speech or writing. **b.** In the phr. *to s. of* (in later use = 'worth mentioning'). Chiefly in neg. constructions. **c.** With vbl. sbs.: To suggest, propose, hint at (doing something). **S. to —. a.** To address words or discourse to (a person); to talk to, converse with. *To s. to*: so as to have personal conversation with. **b.** To apply to (a person) for a special purpose, esp. for help or service; to influence or bribe. **c.** To treat of or deal with (a subject) in speech or writing. **d.** To give (†or constitute) evidence regarding (a thing); to attest, bear testimony to. **e.** To address with reproof; to admonish. **S. with —. a.** To converse with, talk to; to consult or confer with. **b.** *Naut.* To hold communication with (another vessel).

With advs. **S. out.** *a.* To talk in a loud voice. **b.** To talk freely or unreservedly. **S. up. a.** To speak strongly *for* (= on behalf of, in defence of) a person. **b.** To raise the voice in speaking; to talk boldly; to break into speech.

II. *trans.* **1.** With cognate object: To articulate or utter (a word or words); to utter, make, or deliver (a speech, statement, etc.) OE. **2.** To utter or say (something) by way of a remark or statement OE. **3.** To utter or express (truth, falsehood, etc.) in words or speech OE. **4.** To declare in words; to make known by speech; to tell (of) OE. **b.** To state or declare in writing, etc. ME. **c.** *transf.* Of musical instruments: To announce, indicate, or proclaim by sound 1702. **5.** To use as a language; to talk ME. †**6.** To make mention of (a person); to speak of or mention in a certain way; to commend (a person) *to* another –1657. **7.** To indicate, denote, or betoken; to reveal, make known 1588. **b.** Of the countenance, eyes, etc.: To indicate or manifest by expression 1601. **8.** To manifest or show (a person, thing, etc.) to be or do a certain thing, or to possess a certain quality or character. Now *arch.* 1605. **b.** To term; to describe as (*rare*) 1617. **c.** To describe (a person). Now *arch.* 1623. **9.** To express or signify. Now *rare.* 1645. **10.** To send *to*, to cause to pass or enter *into* (another state, condition, or position) by speaking 1684.

1. Phr. *To s. not a word of*, to make no mention or suggestion of. *To s. a good* (*word*) *for*: see WORD *sb.* I. 2 d. Speeches are spoken..audible within doors and without CARLYLE. *fig.* He speakes all creame, skimd B. JONS. 2. To s. the matter in a word 1662. 3. Beleeue it (Page) he speakes sence SHAKS. That Vision spake Fear to my Soul WORDSW. 4. Phr. *To s. one's mind*: see MIND *sb.* I. 2. c. These Trumpets s. his Presence 1702. 5. Can they s. Dutch? DE FOE. 6. *Hen. VIII*, IV. ii. 32. 7. The loud laugh that spoke the vacant mind GOLDSM. b. Her look spoke affection 1859. 8. His whole Person is finely turned, and speaks him a Man of Quality STEELE. 9. Phr. *To s. volumes*: see VOLUME *sb.* I. 3. 10. Too just to wink, or s. the guilty clear COWPER.

III. 1. To talk or converse with; to address OE. **b.** To communicate with (a passing vessel) at sea, by signal, speaking trumpet, etc. 1792. **2.** *To s.* (a person) *fair*, to address (a person) courteously or kindly. late ME.

1. b. We saw several vessels, but spoke none 1816. 2. *fig.* Heaven speaks me fair DRYDEN.

IV. Speak out. *trans.* To utter, declare openly or plainly. late ME.

Comb.: **s.-easy** *U.S. slang*, an illicit liquor-shop.

Speakable (spī·kăb'l), *a.* 1483. [f. prec. + -ABLE.] **1.** That may or can be spoken; fit to be expressed in speech. †**2.** Having the power of speech, able to speak (*rare*) –1676.

2. Redouble then this miracle, and say, How cam'st thou s. of mute? MILT.

Speaker (spī·kəɹ). ME. [f. SPEAK *v.* + -ER [1].] **1.** One who speaks or talks. **b.** *spec.* One who addresses an audience; an orator. late ME. **2.** The member of the House of Commons who is chosen by the House itself to act as its representative and to preside over its debates. Also called *Mr. S.* late ME. **b.** More fully in *S. of* (*the*) *Parliament* 1460. **c.** The presiding officer or chairman of the House of Lords, now the Lord Chancellor, or one acting as his deputy or substitute 1660. **d.** A similar president in other assemblies 1656. †**3.** One who proclaims or celebrates. SHAKS. **4.** As a title of books containing pieces adapted for recitation or reading aloud 1774.

1. Let not an euill s. be established in the earth *Ps.* cxl. 11. We of the Lower House..have likewise the most able speakers MISS BURNEY. **Loud s.**, a device for converting electrical energy into sound energy with the object of producing a large volume of sound. Hence **Spea·kership**, the office of Speaker in a legislative or other assembly.

Speakie (spī·ki). *U.S.* 1928. = TALKIE.

Speaking (spī·kiŋ), *vbl. sb.* ME. [f. SPEAK *v.*] **1.** The action of the vb.; talking, discoursing. **b.** Speech-making 1763. **2.** With possessive prons., etc.: Speech, talk; conversation, discourse ME. **b.** An instance or occasion of speech or talk; a discourse, discussion, etc. ME. **3.** *attrib.*, as *s. acquaintance, voice*, etc. 1687.

2. b. A s. to instruction and edification CROMWELL. Phr. *On* (*upon*) *s. terms*: see TERM *sb.* III. 2.

Comb.: **s.-front**, an organ-front composed of pipes which actually sound, as contrasted with dummy pipes.

Speaking (spī·kiŋ), *ppl. a.* ME. [f. as prec.] **1.** That speaks; capable of articulate speech. **2.** *fig.* and *transf.* esp. **a.** Expressive, significant, eloquent 1586. **b.** Of the eyes, countenance, etc.: Highly expressive 1592. **3.** Of a likeness: Faithful or true (so that it gives the impression of one speaking) 1582.

1. The s. head which uttered its oracular responses at Lesbos 1832. 2. a. Still borne Silence..Admirations speakingst Tongue 1653. b. I vow she has s. eyes! RICHARDSON. 3. Anybody..could still draw a s., nay scolding, likeness of Keate 1844. Hence **Spea·kingly** *adv.* in a s. manner; strikingly.

Spea·king-tru·mpet. (Also unhyphened.) 1671. [SPEAKING *vbl. sb.*] A kind of trumpet (chiefly used at sea), so contrived as to carry the voice to a great distance, or to cause it to be heard above loud noises.

Spea·king-tu·be. (Also unhyphened.) 1833. [SPEAKING *vbl. sb.*] **1.** A tube or pipe for speaking, or communicating orders, from one room, building, etc., to another. **2.** A speaking-trumpet 1889.

Spear (spīəɹ), *sb.*[1] [OE. *spere*, = OFris. *spiri, spere*, OHG. *sper* (G. *speer*).] **1.** A thrusting weapon consisting of a stout wooden staff of some length, on which a sharp-pointed head, usually of iron or steel, is socketed or otherwise fixed; also, a shorter weapon of this kind used for throwing. **b.** Without article, freq. in a collective sense ME. **c.** One of the transverse spikes or poles of a cheval-de-frise 1823. **2.** A spearman. Now *arch.* ME. **3.** A sharp-pointed weapon used for various purposes; esp. one for catching fish, a leister 1551. **4. a.** *pl.* The thorns or prickles of a plant, the spines or spikes of a hedgehog, sharp fins of a fish, etc. Chiefly *poet.*; now *rare.* 1607. **b.** The sting of a reptile or insect, esp. of a bee. Now *Sussex dial.* 1608.

1. His S., to equal which the tallest Pine Hewn on Norwegian hills..were but a wand MILT. *fig.* Slanders venom'd speare SHAKS. The s. of Butler's reasoning M. ARNOLD. Phr. †*To sell at the s., to put*, etc., *under the s.*, to sell by auction. †*To pass under the s.*, to 'come under the hammer'. †*Stroke of the s.*, the feather of a horse (see FEATHER *sb.* III. 1). b. They shall lay hold on bowe and speare *Jer.* vi. 23. 3. Abounding in trouts catch'd by speare in the night EVELYN. *Eel-, fish-, salmon-, trout-s.*

attrib. and *Comb.*: as *s.-point, -shaft* (OE. *sperescreaft*), *-staff*; **s.-axe**, a s. with an axe-shaped head; †**-foot**, the off hind foot of a horse; **-hand**, the hand with which a s. is usually held, thrown, etc.; the right hand or side; **-side** (after OE. *on sperehealfe*), the male line of descent. **b.** In names of plants, etc.: **s.-thistle**, *Cnicus lanceolatus*; **-wood**, *Acacia doratoxylon*, also *Eucalyptus doratoxylon*. **c.** In names of fishes: **s.-dog**, *Spinax acanthias*; **-fish**, *Tetrapturus albidus*, also called Bill-fish.

Spear (spīəɹ), *sb.*[2] 1490. [irreg. var. of SPIRE *sb.*[1]] †**1.** A spire of a church or other building; a pyramid –1755. **2.** The plumule or rudimentary shoot of a seed; *spec.* the acrospire of grain 1647. **b.** A blade, shoot, or sprout (*of* grass, etc.) 1841.

2. Tell me the motes, dust, sands, and speares Of Corn, when Summer shakes his eares HERRICK.

Spear (spīəɹ), *sb.*[3] 1543. [var. of SPIRE *sb.*[2]] **1.** A young tree, esp. a young oak; a sapling. Also *attrib.* in *s. oak, tree.* **2.** *techn.* A pump-rod. Also *attrib.* 1729.

Spear (spīəɹ), *sb.*[4] *rare.* 1903. [f. SPEAR *v.*[2]] The act of spearing or striking with a spear, *spec.* in pig-sticking.

Spear (spīəɹ), *v.*[1] 1573. [irreg. var. of SPIRE *v.*[1]] *intr.* Of corn, etc.: To sprout, germinate. Also with *out.*

Spear (spīəɹ), *v.*[2] 1755. [f. SPEAR *sb.*[1]] **1.** *trans.* To pierce or transfix with a spear. **2.** *intr.* To rise *up* like a spear 1822.

1. The King saw his men speared and shot down 1869. *transf.* The sparrow [is] spear'd by the shrike TENNYSON.

Spearer (spīə·rəɹ). 1573. [f. SPEAR *sb.*[1] or prec.] One who is armed with, or strikes with, a spear.

Spea·r-grass. Also as one or as two words. 1548. [f. SPEAR *sb.*[1]] A name for many grasses or grass-like plants having spear-like parts.

†1. = SPEARWORT 2. –1596. 2. One or other of various British grasses, *esp.* couch-grass (*Triticum repens, Agrostis*, etc.) 1784. 3. *Amer.* One or other of several species of meadow-grass, esp. *Poa pratensis* 1747. 4. One or other of many Australasian and Asiatic grasses 1847.

Spea·r-head. Also as one word. late ME. [f. SPEAR *sb.*[1]] **1.** The sharp-pointed head or blade forming the striking or piercing end of a spear. **b.** *fig.* A person or body of persons chosen to lead a thrust or attack 1929. **2.** *transf.* A thing having the pointed form characteristic of the head of a spear 1894.

Spea·rman. ME. [f. SPEAR *sb.*[1]] **1.** A soldier armed with a spear; one who carries a spear as a weapon. **2.** A spearer of fish. SCOTT.

Spearmint (spīə·ɹmint). 1539. [f. SPEAR *sb.*[1]] The common garden mint, *Mentha viridis*, much used in cookery; (with pl.) †a plant of this. Also *attrib.*

Spea·r-shaped, *a.* 1763. Resembling a spear in shape; pointed like a spear.

Spearwort (spīə·ɹwɒɹt). OE. [f. as prec.] †**1.** Elecampane –ME. **2.** One or other of several species of ranunculus, esp. *R. Flammula* (lesser or small s.) and *R. Lingua* (great s.). late ME. **b.** Mentioned as used by beggars to produce artificial sores –1673.

Speary (spīə·ri), *a.* 1577. [f. SPEAR *sb.*[1]] †**1.** Of grass: Hard and stiff –1653. **2.** Resembling a spear or spears; slender and sharp-pointed; keen 1820. **3.** Consisting of spears; waged with spears 1810.

2. S. sleet and driving snow 1855.

Spec (spek), *sb. colloq.* or *slang*; orig. *Amer.* 1794. [Short for SPECULATION.] A commercial speculation.

Phr. *A good* (*bad*, etc.) *s.* *On s.*, on the chance of obtaining something, gaining some profit, etc.

†Spece. ME. [ad. OF. *espece* (mod.F. *espèce*), ad. L. *species* SPECIES.] **1.** Appearance, form –1490. **2. a.** A spice. **b.** A medical substance, drug. –1605. **3.** A species, kind –1647.

Special (spe·ʃăl), *a.*, *adv.*, and *sb.* ME. [Aphetic ad. OF. *especial* (see ESPECIAL *a.*) or L. *specialis* individual, particular, f. *species* SPECIES.] **A.** *adj.* **1.** Of such a kind as to exceed or excel in some way that which is usual or common; exceptional in character, quality, or degree. **2.** Of friends: Admitted to particular intimacy; held in particular esteem ME. **3.** Marked off from others of the kind by some distinguishing qualities or features; having a distinct or individual character; also, in weakened sense, particular, certain ME. **b.** Additional to the usual or ordinary 1840. **4.** Of persons: **a.** Appointed or employed for a particular purpose or occasion ME. **b.** Devoted to a particular or limited field of study or research 1899. **5.** Having an individual, particular, or limited application, object, or intention; concerning a single person, thing, or circumstance, or a particular class of these ME. **6.** Having close, intimate, or exclusive connexion or relationship with one person or thing (or set of these); peculiar. late ME. **7.** *Law.* Used to denote particular or distinctive instances or cases of the thing, action, or person in question, as *s. bail, bailiff, bastard(y, occupant, tail, verdict* 1495.

1. She's a s. favourite 1854. Men of no s. celebrity 1867. **3.** Aristotle saith, a man is the most speciall 1620. A s. Idea is call'd by the Schools, a Species 1725. **b.** S. Trains may be engaged for large Parties 1847. **4. a.** The s. correspondent of the 'Times' in the Crimea 1856. **b.** Some well-known (and not too s.) specialist 1899. **5.** It is a s. purpose, specially consulted throughout 1802. *S. intention*: see INTENTION II. 4. **6.** The Lord thy God hath chosen thee to be a s. people vnto himselfe *Deut.* vii. 6. Each region has its s. treasures 1870.

B. *adv.* **1.** In a special manner; especially, particularly. Now only *colloq.* or *dial.* ME.

1. Great plenty of dates, which..are speciall good 1600.

C. *sb.* **†1.** A particularly intimate or favourite friend, associate, or follower –1660. **†2.** A particular point, part, detail, concept, statement, thing, or article –1628. **†b. 2. In s.:** (*a*) Specially, particularly –1680. (*b*) In detail –1573. **†3.** Species, kind –1654. **4.** *ellipt.* A special constable, correspondent, etc.; an advocate at a special fee 1837. **b.** A special train, examination, prize, etc. 1866. Hence **Spe·cialness,** the quality of being s.

Specialism (spe·ʃăliz'm). 1856. [f. prec. + -ISM.] **1.** Restriction or devotion to a special branch of study or research; limitation to one department or aspect of a subject. **2.** With *a* and *pl.* A special study or investigation; an instance of specializing 1868.

1. The evils of s. [in medicine] 1891.

Specialist (spe·ʃălist). 1856. [f. as prec. + -IST.] **1.** A medical practitioner or authority who specially devotes his attention to the study or treatment of a particular disease or class of diseases. **2.** *gen.* One who specially or exclusively studies one subject or one particular branch of a subject 1862.

1. He was a famous nerve s. 1889. Hence **Speciali·stic** *a.* of or pertaining to specialism or specialists.

Speciality (speʃiæ·lĭti). late ME. [ad. OF. *specialite*, or late and med.L. *specialitas*, f. *specialis* SPECIAL *a.*] **1.** A special, particular, or individual point, matter, or item; freq. *pl.*, particulars, details. **2.** The quality of being special, limited, or restricted in some respect (occas. implying particularity of application or treatment) 1456. **3.** A special or distinctive quality, property, characteristic, or feature; a peculiarity 1625. **b.** With *the*: The distinctive quality, etc., *of* a particular thing or class 1829. **4.** *Law.* = SPECIALTY II. 3. 1681. **5.** A special aptitude, skill, occupation, or line of business 1867. **b.** A special subject of study or research; that branch of work in which one is a specialist 1858. **c.** A thing or article specially characteristic of, produced or manufactured by, a particular place, business firm, etc. 1863. **6.** A thing or article of a special kind, as dist. from what is usual or common 1867.

1. A practical position..chains the mind to specialities and details 1865. **2.** Phr. *In s.*, especially, particularly. **3.** Think of this, Sir,..apart from the specialities..of prejudice DICKENS. **b.** It is the s. of all vice to be selfishly indifferent to..injurious consequences 1882. **5. b.** His s. was Entomology 1880.

Specialization (spe:ʃăləizē^i·ʃən). 1843. [f. next + -ATION.] The action or process of specializing or of becoming specialized. **a.** Of language, legislation, etc. **b.** *Biol.* Of animals or plants, or of the parts or organs of these 1862. **c.** Of employments, studies, etc. 1865.

c. The increasing specialisation of all employments ..is not without inconveniences 1865.

Specialize (spe·ʃăləiz), *v.* 1613. [ad. F. *spécialiser*; see SPECIAL *a.* and -IZE.] **1.** *trans.* To mention or indicate specially; to specify, particularize 1616. **b.** *absol.* To enter into particulars or details 1613. **2.** To render special or specific; to invest with a special character or function 1628. **b.** *spec.* in *Biol.* In pa. pple.: Adapted to a special function or environment; modified by development tending to this end 1851. **3.** To make narrower and more intensive 1855. **4.** *intr.* **a.** To engage in special study or some special line of business, etc. 1881. **b.** To develop in a special direction 1889.

1. b. First lash the Great-ones; but if thou be wise, In generall and doe not speciallize 1613. **4. a.** They will not allow their scholars to s. 1881.

Specially (spe·ʃăli), *adv.* ME. [f. SPECIAL *a.* + -LY[2].] **1.** In a special manner; particularly. **2.** Of special purpose; expressly ME. **3.** In a supreme degree; pre-eminently ME. **†4.** With particularity or detail –1620.

1. The military results..were not s. glorious 1871. **2.** It is better to make them s. for each patient 1879. **3.** Phr. *And s.*, used to introduce a clause following upon a previous statement; In the Writings of Divines, and s. in Sermons HOBBES.

Special pleader. 1804. [See PLEADER.] **1.** *Law.* A member of an Inn of Court who devotes himself mainly to the drawing of pleadings and to attending at Judges' chambers. **2.** One who uses special pleading; a disingenuous or sophistical disputant 1809.

Special pleading. 1684. [See PLEADING *vbl. sb.*] **1.** A pleading drawn with particular reference to the circumstances of a case, as opposed to general pleading. **2.** The putting forward of special pleadings; the art or science of drawing pleadings 1768. **b.** *fig.* Ex-parte or one-sided argumentation; disingenuous pleading; sophistry 1872.

Specialty (spe·ʃălti). ME. [ad. OF. (*e*)*specialté*, f. (*e*)*special* SPECIAL *a.*; see -TY.] **I.** **†1.** Particularity or detail in description or discussion –1577. **2.** *In s.*, in a special or particular manner or degree 1451. **3.** Special or particular character or quality; a special feature or characteristic 1575. **b.** The quality of being limited or determined by special cases or circumstances 1619. **c.** Special knowledge; tendency to specialism 1868.

3. The s. of Rule hath beene neglected SHAKS. **c.** The favorite charge against the academies is their 'one-sidedness' or s. 1868.

II. **†1.** A thing specially belonging or attached to one person; a special possession, distinction, favour, or charge –1628. **2.** A special or particular matter, point, or thing. late ME. **3.** *Law.* A special contract, obligation, or bond, expressed in an instrument under seal 1482. **4.** A special line of work or business; a special manufacture or product; an article specially dealt in or stocked 1860. **b.** A special subject of study or research 1861.

3. Marriage-settlements, mortgage-deeds, and specialties of various kinds 1781. **4.** The brass work of Birmingham has long been one of its specialties 1883. **b.** He had selected as his s. currency and finance 1883.

Specie (spī·ʃi, spī·ʃī, spī·ʃiī). 1551. [a. L., abl. sing. of *species* SPECIES, orig. adopted in the phr. *in specie*.] **I.** In the phr. **in specie** **1.** In kind; in respect of kind; specifically 1562. **2.** In the real, proper, precise, or actual form; without any kind of substitution. In later use only in *Law.* 1551. **3. †a.** In the actual coin specified –1630. **†b.** Of coin or money: In the actual form of minted pieces of metal –1714. **c.** Of sums or amounts: In actual coin; in money 1636. **†4.** Of goods, etc.: In kind –1738. **†b.** *transf.* Of requital or repayment: In a similar fashion; with like treatment –1772.

2. The covenant will be decreed to be performed in s. 1818. **3. b.** Our Coin..whether we send it in S., or whether we melt it down here to send it in Bullion LOCKE. **c.** He has wealth in s. DRYDEN. **4. b.** Kindnesses are to be paid in S. as well as Money 1702.

II. 1. Coin; coined money 1671. **2.** Species; kind. Now *rare* or *Obs.* 1711.

1. Money may mean either s., or bank-notes 1864. **2.** A very large s. of gull 1800.

Species (spī·ʃīz, -iz, spī·ʃiīz). *Pl.* **species.** 1551. [a. L., appearance, form, kind, f. *specere* to look, behold. Cf. SPICE *sb.*] **I.** **†1.** Appearance; outward form –1651. **b.** *Geom.* Form, irrespective of size 1660. **2.** *Eccl.* The sensible form of the consecrated bread and wine in the sacrament of the Eucharist; one or other of these (cf. KIND *sb.* II. 4) 1579. **†3.** The outward appearance or aspect, the visible form or image, *of* something, as constituting the immediate object of vision –1700. **†b.** The image of something as cast upon, or reflected from, a surface; a reflection –1790. **†4.** A thing seen; a spectacle; *esp.* a phantom or illusion –1661. **†5.** *Metaph.* A supposed emission or emanation from outward things, forming the direct object of cognition for the various senses or for the understanding –1756. **†b.** A mental impression; an idea –1711. **†6.** In Platonic philosophy, = IDEA *sb.* 1. –1792.

1. b. A triangle is said to be given in s. when its angles are given 1881. **2.** The Ceremony of mixing a Particle of the Host with the S. of Wine in the Chalice 1737. **3.** As the two Eyes, two S. entertain 1700. **5. b.** There are certain moral Species or Appearances so striking..that..they bear down all contrary Opinion 1711.

II. 1. *Logic.* The second of the five predicables (q.v.), connoting the common attributes or essential qualities of a class of persons or things as dist. from the genus on the one hand and the individual on the other 1551. **†b.** The essential quality or specific properties *of* a thing –1651. **2.** A class composed of individuals having some common qualities or characteristics, freq. as a subdivision of a larger class or genus 1630. **3.** A distinct class, sort, or kind, of something specifically mentioned or indicated. Freq. const. *of.* 1561. **b.** *A s. of*, a kind of (cf. KIND *sb.* I. 7); also with *the* 1620. **c.** Applied to individuals as unique or as typical of a class 1644. **d.** *The s.*, the human race 1711. **4.** *Zool.* and *Bot.* A group or class of animals or plants (usu. constituting a subdivision of a genus) having certain common and permanent characteristics which clearly distinguish it from other groups 1608. **†5. a.** *pl.* The separate materials or ingredients used in compounding a perfume, drug, or the like –1693. **†b.** *pl.* Spices. CRASHAW. **†6. a.** A particular kind or sort of coin or money –1756. **b.** Coinage, coin, money, bullion –1804. **c.** Metal (gold or silver) used for coinage. BURKE. **†7.** *pl. Naut.* Sorts of provisions –1806.

1. That common nature which is communicable to several Individuals, is called S., Sort or special kind 1668. **2.** A s. is any class regarded as forming part of the next larger class 1870. **3.** Aristotle..divides mankind into two distinct species: that of freemen and that of slaves BENTHAM. Such history is a distinct s. of composition 1845. **b.** Their gratitude is a s. of revenge JOHNSON. **c.** The Phœnix Pindar is a vast S. alone COWLEY. **d.** If individuals were happy, the s. would be happy GODWIN.

Specifiable (spe·sifəiăb'l), *a.* 1661. [f. SPECIFY *v.*] Capable of being specified.

Specific (spĕsi·fik), *a.* and *sb.* 1631. [ad. med.L. *specificus*, f. *species* SPECIES; see -FIC.] **A.** *adj.* **1.** Having a special determining quality. **2.** Of qualities, properties, effects, etc.: Specially or peculiarly pertaining to a certain thing or class of things and constituting one of the characteristic features of this 1650. **b.** Peculiar *to*, characteristic *of*, something 1667. **3. a.** *Med.* Of remedies, etc.: Specially or exclusively efficacious for, or acting upon, a particular ailment or part of the body 1677. **b.** *Path.* Of a distinct or characteristic kind 1804. **4. a.** Precise or exact in respect of fulfilment, conditions, or terms; definite, explicit 1740. **b.** Exactly named or indicated, or capable of being so; precise, particular 1766. **5.** *Zool.* and *Bot.*

Of or pertaining to, connected with, etc., a distinct species of animals or plants; esp. in *s. character, name* 1753.

2. The s. taint or peculiar cause of the malady BERKELEY. This feature in the case..constitutes the s. difference between justice, and generosity MILL. Phr. *S. gravity, heat*: see GRAVITY II. 1 c, HEAT *sb.* 2. *S. difference* = DIFFERENTIA. 3. a. Garlick..I believe is ..a Specifick Remedy of the Gout 1680. b. The s. irritation of the skin termed scabies 1843. 4. a. A command must by its very nature be s. 1871. b. The s. cause of the quarrel 1880. c. Of a duty or tax: Assessed by quantity or amount without reference to its value 1845.

B. *sb.* 1. A specific remedy. (See A. 3 a.) 1661. 2. A specific difference, quality, statement, subject, disease, etc. 1697.

1. How did you light on your specifick for the tooth-ach? JOHNSON. *transf.* and *fig.* A more infallible s. against tedium and fatigue 1779. Hence **Speci·fical** *a.* (now *rare*) = A.; *sb.* = B. 1. **Speci·fically** *adv.* **Speci·ficness**, s. character or quality (*rare*).

Specificate (spėsi·fikeᶦt), *v.* Now *rare* or *Obs.* 1620. [ad. med.L. *specificat-*, *specificare* SPECIFY *v.*] 1. *trans.* To distinguish as belonging to a particular species, group, or kind; to determine specifically. 2. To apply specifically or especially *to*; to confine or limit *to* 1631. 3. To give specific or explicit details of or concerning; to mention specifically or in detail; to particularize or specify 1649. 4. To render specific in character or qualities 1650. 5. *intr.* To become specific COLERIDGE. Hence **Speci·ficate** *sb.* something specified.

Specification (spe:sifikēᶦ·ʃən). 1615. [ad. med.L. *specificationem*, f. *specificare*.] †1. The action of investing with some specific or determinate quality; conversion to something specific –1701. b. *Roman* and *Scots Law.* The formation of a new species of property out of material belonging to another by converting it into a different form 1651. †2. A specific character, quality, or nature –1710. 3. Specific definition or description 1633. 4. Specific, explicit, or detailed mention, enumeration, or statement *of* something 1642. b. *spec.* A document, drawn up by the applicant for a patent and submitted to the proper authority, giving an explicit description of the nature, details, construction, and use of an invention 1791. c. *techn.* A detailed description of the particulars of some projected work in building, engineering, or the like, giving the dimensions, materials, quantities, etc., of the work, together with directions to be followed by the builder or constructor; the document containing this 1833. d. A specified article, item, or particular 1828.

3. The second element in the s. of a force is its direction..The third element in the s. of a force is its magnitude 1879. 4. By demanding a S. of the powers claimed 1719.

Specificity (spesifi·sĭti). [f. SPECIFIC *a.* + -ITY.] Chiefly *Med.* The quality or fact of being specific.

Specify (spe·sifəi), *v.* ME. [a. OF. *specifier* (mod.F. *spécifier*), ad. med.L. *specificare* to describe, mention, etc.] †1. *intr.* To speak or make relation *of* some matter fully or in detail –1489. 2. *trans.* To mention, speak of, or name (something) definitely or explicitly; to set down or state categorically or particularly; to relate in detail ME. 3. To invest with a specific character 1645.

2. There must many requisites be observed, which the statute specifies BLACKSTONE. Take..double the quantity above specified 1799. Hence **Spe·cified** *ppl. a.*

Specimen (spe·simĕn). 1610. [a. L. *specimen*, f. *specere* to look, look at.] †1. A means of finding out; an experiment. †2. A pattern or model –1697. 3. An example, instance, or illustration *of* something, from which the character of the whole may be inferred 1659. 4. A single thing selected or regarded as typical of its class; a part or piece *of* something taken as representative of the whole 1654. b. *spec.* An animal, plant, or mineral, a part or portion of some substance or organism, etc., serving as an example of the thing in question for purposes of investigation or scientific study. Also *transf.* 1765. 5. Of persons as typical of certain qualities or of the human species. Also *colloq.* or *slang.* with derogatory force. 1817. 6. *attrib.*, passing into *adj.* (freq. hyphened): Serving as or intended for a specimen; typical. (Often implying 'exceptionally large or fine'.) 1860.

3. Our English Bible is a wonderful s. of the strength and music of the English language EMERSON. 4. Things..of which they had brought specimens DE FOE. b. I have found..a s. of another yellow trefoil 1765. 5. There were some curious specimens among my visitors 1854. *A bright, fine, poor, sad s.* 6. A number of 's.' fish have lately been caught in the Thames 1896.

Specio-, comb. form of L. *species*, as in *speciology*, the doctrine of species, etc.

Speciosity (spīʃiǫ·sĭti). Now *rare.* 1470. [ad. late L. *speciositas* beauty, good appearance, f. *speciosus* SPECIOUS; see -ITY.] †1. The quality of being beautiful; beauty. Also, a beautiful thing. –1731. 2. The quality of being specious; speciousness 1608. b. *pl.* Specious actions, promises, etc. CARLYLE.

2. S. in all departments usurps the place of reality ..; instead of performance, there is appearance of performance CARLYLE.

Specious (spī·ʃəs), *a.* late ME. [ad.L. *speciosus* fair, fair-seeming, etc., f. *species* SPECIES.] †1. Fair or pleasing to the eye or sight; beautiful, handsome, lovely; resplendent with beauty –1818. 2. Having a fair or attractive appearance or character, but in reality devoid of the qualities apparently possessed; *occas.*, merely apparent 1612. 3. Of language, statements, etc.: Fair, attractive, or plausible, but wanting in genuineness or sincerity 1651. b. Of reasoning, etc.: Plausible, apparently sound or convincing, but in reality sophistical or fallacious 1651. 4. Of material things: Showy, but of little intrinsic worth (*rare*) 1816. 5. Of persons: Characterized by conduct, actions, or reasoning of a specious nature; †outwardly respectable 1740. †6. Of algebra: Performed by means of, expressed in, letters –1728. 7. *Psychol.* Appearing to be actually known or experienced 1890.

1. Successive acquists of fair and s. Plants SIR T. BROWNE. There is thy Saviour..looking like a s. Bridegroom 1670. 2. Traiterous requests..he was now willing to maske with the s. pretext of iustice and deuotion 1611. It appeared that this plan, though s., was impracticable MACAULAY. A policy which had a s. show of liberality MACAULAY. 3. The meaning latent under this s. phrase MACAULAY. b. This s. reasoning is nevertheless false HOBBES. 5. You are a s. fellow,.. and carry two fans under your hood DICKENS. Hence **Spe·cious-ly** *adv.*, **-ness.**

Speck (spek), *sb.*[1] [OE. *specca*, not found in cogn. langs.] 1. A small spot of a different colour or substance from that of the material or surface upon which it appears; a minute mark or discoloration. b. Applied to things rendered extremely small by distance or by comparison with their surroundings 1656. c. Applied to a very small or distant cloud. Freq. in fig. context. 1726. 2. A small or minute particle *of* something. late ME. b. A small piece, portion, etc., of ground or land 1538. 3. A small spot as indicative of a defective, diseased, or faulty condition; a blot, blemish, or defect 1825.

1. The smallest s. is seen on snow GAY. b. We find ..that the whole solar system is but a mere s. in the universe 1868. 2. These bunches frequently containing strings and specks of ore 1839. He..deemed it a duty..to magnify faults and dwindle virtues to specks 1883. 3. The..little pitted s. in garner'd fruit TENNYSON. *fig.* Can all the pearls of the East atone for a s. upon England's honour? SCOTT.

Speck (spek), *sb.*[2] Now *U.S.* and *S. African.* 1633. [a. Du. *spek* or G. *speck*, related to OE. *spic* SPICK *sb.*[1]] 1. a. Fat meat, esp. bacon or pork. b. The fat or blubber of a whale 1743. c. The fat of a hippopotamus 1863. 2. *attrib.* in the names of tackle or apparatus used in dealing with whale-s., as *s.-block*, *-purchase* 1820.

Speck (spek), *v.* 1580. [f. SPECK *sb.*[1]] 1. *trans.* To mark with specks; to dot after the manner of specks. b. In passive: To be covered, marked, or diversified *with* (or *by*) specks or spots 1667. 2. To go over (a woven fabric) and remove specks or other blemishes 1895. 3. To convert into a mere speck. MEREDITH.

1. b. Each Flour of slender stalk, whose head though gay Carnation, Purple, Azure, or spect with Gold, Hung drooping unsustained MILT. 3. Specked overhead, the imminent vulture wings At poise MEREDITH.

Speckle (spe·k'l), *sb.* 1440. [See SPECK *sb*[1] and -LE.] 1. A speck, small spot, or mark, esp. one occurring on the skin or body; a natural marking of this nature; a small patch or dot of colour. 2. Speckled colouring, speckling. HAWTHORNE.

1. An huge great Serpent all with speckles pide SPENSER.

Comb.: **s.-belly**, (*slang*) a Nonconformist or Dissenter; (*U.S.*) one or other of various birds or fishes having speckled markings on the abdomen. Hence **Spe·ckly** *a.*, full of or covered with speckles; speckled or spotted; freckly.

Speckle (spe·k'l), *v.* 1570. [f. SPECKLE *sb.* or back-formation from next.] 1. *trans.* To mark with, or as with, speckles; to cover or dot (a surface, etc.) as if with speckles. 2. *intr.* To form speckles; to be dotted about like speckles. (*rare.*) 1820.

Speckled (spe·k'ld), (*ppl.*) *a.* and *pa. pple.* late ME. [Corresponds to MDu. and WFlem. *spekelde* adj. and *gespekeld* pa. pple.] Covered, dotted, or marked with (numerous) speckles or specks; variegated or flecked with spots of a different colour from that of the main body; spotted. 1. In predicative use. 2. In attrib. use 1482. b. *fig.* Of sin, vice, etc.: Characterized by, full of, moral blemishes or defects 1603. c. *colloq.* Of a mixed character or nature; motley 1845.

1. She usually lays but one [egg], which is s. GOLDSM. Trophies..s. with blood SCOTT. 2. A clean old woman ..talking to some s. fowls GEO. ELIOT. b. And speckl'd vanity Will sicken soon and die MILT. c. They are usually a s. lot 1909. Hence **Spe·ckledness**, the state of being s.; spottiness.

Spe·ckless, *a.* 1788. [f. SPECK *sb.*[1]] Having no speck or speckle; free from specks, blemishes, flaws, etc. b. Free from specks of dirt, dust, etc.; spotlessly clean 1827. Hence **Spe·ckless·ly** *adv.*, **-ness.**

Specksioneer (spekʃənīᵊ·ɹ). 1820. [ad. Du. *speksnijer*, colloq. form of *speksnijder*, f. *spek* SPECK *sb.*[2] + *snijden* to cut.] *Whale-fishing.* A harpooner, usu. the chief harpooner, of a whaler, who directs the operation of flensing the whale or cutting up the blubber.

Specky (spe·ki), *a.* late ME. [f. SPECK *sb.*[1] + -Y[1].] Covered or marked with specks; having specks or spots of disease, discoloration, etc.

Spec(k)s. 1807. [dial. or colloq. abbrev. of pl. of next II. 2.] Spectacles for the eyes.

Spectacle[1] (spe·ktăk'l). ME. [a. OF. *spectacle* (also mod.F.), or ad. L. *spectaculum*, f. *spectare* to look.] I. 1. A specially prepared display of a more or less public nature (esp. one on a large scale), forming an impressive or interesting show for those viewing it. Also without article. 2. A person or thing exhibited to the public gaze as an object either of curiosity or contempt, or of marvel or admiration. late ME. 3. A thing seen or capable of being seen; a sight. late ME. b. The sight or view *of* something 1625. 4. A sight, show, or exhibition *of* a specified character or description 1484.

1. They abhorred Theaters, and publique spectacles, especially of blood 1641. 2. We are made a s. to the world, and to Angels and men N.T. (Rhem.) 1 *Cor.* iv. 9. 3. *A.Y.L.* II. i. 44. b. The s. of their hurried and harassed retreat SCOTT. 4. A s. of suffering royalty BURKE.

II. †1. A means of seeing; something made of glass; a window or mirror –1630. †b. *fig.* A mirror, model, pattern, or standard –1575. †c. An illustrative instance –1656. 2. A device for assisting defective eyesight, or for protecting the eyes from dust, light, etc., consisting of two glass lenses set in a frame which is supported on the nose, and freq. kept in place by 'legs' passing over the ears. Usu. in *pl.* late ME. b. *fig.* A means or medium through which anything is viewed or regarded; a point of view, prepossession, prejudice, etc. late ME. 3. *pl.* A batsman's score of two zeros or 'duck's eggs' in a cricket match of two innings. Freq. in *a pair of spectacles.* 1892.

2. Reading much, yet never used s. or other help 1640. I this evening did buy me a pair of green spectacles PEPYS. b. False informations, which are rightly called the spectacles of error 1606.

attrib. and *Comb.*: **s.-case**, a case of leather, etc., in which spectacles are kept when not in use; **s. owl**, *Strix perspicillata*; **s. warbler**, a bird of the family *Sylviidæ*, having naked yellowish wrinkled skin round the eye suggesting spectacles.

‖ **Spectacle**[2] (spe·ktakl'). 1749. [F.; see prec.] 1. = prec. I. 1. 2. *spec.* A piece of stage-display or pageantry, as contrasted with real drama 1752.

Spectacled (spe·ktăk'ld), *a.* 1607. [f. SPECTACLE[1].] 1. Provided with or wearing spectacles. 2. In names of birds, animals, etc., having spectacle-shaped markings or the appearance of wearing spectacles 1829.

1. The bleared sights Are spectacled to see him SHAKS. 2. Named S. Serpent, from a black line drawn on the widened part of its disk in the form of spectacles 1831. The S. Bear, *Ursus ornatus*..inhabits the Cordilleras of the Andes in Chili 1835.

Spectacular (spektæ·kiŭlăɹ), *a.* 1682. [f. L. *spectaculum* SPECTACLE[1].] 1. Of the nature of a spectacle or show; striking or imposing as a display. b. *absol.* That which appeals to the eye 1876. 2. Pertaining to, characteristic of, spectacles or shows 1864. 3. Addicted to spectacles 1894.

1. The Lord Mayor's Show was a more..s. pageant than ever 1884. 3. The most s. nation in the world 1894. Hence **Specta·cularly** *adv.*

Spe·ctant, *a.* 1688. [a. L. *spectant-*, *spectare* to look.] *Her.* At gaze, looking forward.

Spectator (spektē¹·təɹ). 1586. [a. L.] 1. One who sees, or looks on at, some scene or occurrence; a beholder, onlooker, observer. 2. *spec.* One who is present at, and has a view or sight of, anything in the nature of a show or spectacle 1590. 3. Used as the title of various periodical publications 1711.

1. There is a true saying, 'That the s. oft times sees more than the gamester' 1645. 2. Gods..sit Amus'd spectators of this bustling stage COWPER. Hence **Spectato·rial** *a.* pertaining to, characteristic of, a s.; having the characteristics of one or other of the periodicals bearing the title of *Spectator*. **Spectatress, Specta·trix,** a female s.

Spectatorship (spektē¹·təɹʃip). 1607. [f. prec.] †1. Presentation to the eyes of spectators. SHAKS. 2. The state of being a spectator; the fact of (merely) looking on 1712.

Spectral (spe·ktrăl), *a.* 1718. [ad. L. **spectralis*, f. *spectrum* SPECTRE, SPECTRUM.] †1. Capable of seeing spectres. 2. Having the character of a spectre; ghostly, unsubstantial, unreal 1815. b. Resembling or suggestive of a spectre or spectres. Also *spec.* in *Zool.* 1828. 3. Characteristic of or appropriate to a spectre 1820. 4. Produced merely by the action of light on the eye or on a sensitive medium 1839. 5. a. Of or pertaining to, appearing or observed in, the spectrum 1832. b. Carried out by means of the spectrum. Freq. in *s. analysis.* 1862.

2. A wild vision of a pair of s. horses apparently in mid-air 1877. b. The old s. Lombard friezes RUSKIN. *Strix cinerea*,..S. Owl 1884. 3. A s. voice, Which shook me in a supernatural dream BYRON. 5. a. S. colours, when re-united, produce white 1832. b. S. observations on stars 1881. Hence **Spe·ctrally** *adv.*

Spectre (spe·ktəɹ). Also (now *U.S.*) **specter.** 1605. [a. F., or ad. L. *spectrum*, f. *specere* to look, see.] 1. An apparition, phantom, or ghost, esp. one of a terrifying nature or aspect. b. *fig.* A phantasm of the brain (*rare*) 1711. c. *fig.* An object or source of dread or terror, imagined as an apparition 1774. d. *transf.* One whose appearance is suggestive of an apparition or ghost 1807. 2. One of the images or semblances supposed by the Epicurean school to emanate from corporeal things 1785. 3. An image or phantom produced by reflection or other natural cause 1801. 4. *Zool.* Any insect or animal distinguished by the epithet *spectre-* (see combs.), esp. an insect of the family *Phasmidæ* 1797.

1. A terror..As when a sudden s. at mid-day Meets us 1871. c. That same cloud-capt, fire-breathing S. of Democracy CARLYLE. 3. Before each of us..stood a spectral image of a man...We stretched forth our arms; the spectres did the same TYNDALL.

Comb.: **s.-bat,** a tropical species of bat (*Vespertilio* or *Phyllostoma spectrum*); **-candle,** a belemnite; **-crab,** a glass-crab; **s. insect,** an insect of the genus *Phasma*; **-lemur,** = *spectre tarsier*; **-shrimp,** a slender-bodied amphipod of the genus *Caprella*; **s. tarsier,** a small lemuroid animal (*Tarsius spectrum*).

Spectro- (spe·ktro), comb. form (on Gr. analogies) of SPECTRUM, chiefly employed in a number of recent terms, as **Spe·ctrogram,** a photograph of a spectrum; **-graph,** (*a*) an instrument for photographing a spectrum; (*b*) = *spectrogram*; **-he·liograph,** an instrument for photographing the sun; **-heliogra·phic** *a.*, **-phone, -photo·meter, -te·lescope,** etc.

Spectrology (spektrǫ·lŏdʒi). *rare.* 1820. [f. SPECTRO- + -LOGY.] 1. The science or study of spectres. 2. The scientific study of spectra 1862. Hence **Spectrolo·gical** *a.* of or pertaining to s.

Spectrometer (spektrǫ·mĭtəɹ). 1874. [ad. G. *spektrometer.*] An instrument used for measuring the index of refraction. Hence **Spectrome·tric** *a.* **Spectro·metry.**

Spectroscope (spe·ktrŏskōᵘp), *sb.* 1861. [ad. G. *spektroskop* or a. F.] An instrument specially designed for the production and examination of spectra. Hence **Spe·ctroscope** *v. trans.* to examine by means of a s. **Spectroscopist** (spektrǫ·skŏpist), one who pursues researches with the s. **Spectroscopy** (spektrǫ·skŏpi), the art of using the s.; that branch of science which involves the use of the s.

Spectroscopic (spektrŏskǫ·pik), *a.* 1864. [f. prec.] 1. Performed by means of the spectroscope. 2. Presented or afforded by, pertaining or belonging to, the spectroscope 1869. 3. Occupied or dealing with spectroscopy 1871. So **Spectrosco·pical** *a.*, **-ly** *adv.*

Spectrous (spe·ktrəs), *a.* 1652. [f. SPECTRE 1.] Spectral.

Spectrum (spe·ktrŏm). *Pl.* **spectra** (also **-ums**). 1611. [L.; see SPECTRE.] 1. An apparition or phantom. 2. An image or semblance (*rare*) 1693. 3. The coloured band into which a beam of light is decomposed by means of a prism or diffraction grating 1671. 4. The image retained for a time on the retina of the eye when turned away after gazing fixedly for some time at a bright coloured object 1786. 5. *attrib.*, as *s.-analysis* (cf. SPECTRAL *a.* 5 b); *s.-band*, *-line*, *microscope* 1866.

4. This appearance in the eye we shall call the ocular s. of that object 1786.

Specular (spe·kiŭlăɹ), *a.* 1577. [ad. L. *specularis*, f. *speculum* SPECULUM; or, in branch II, f. L. *speculari* to spy, observe, *specula* watch-tower.] I. 1. *S. stone* (after L. *specularis lapis*): a transparent or semi-transparent substance formerly used as glass or for ornamental purposes; a species of mica, selenite, or talc; a piece or flake of this. *Obs.* exc. *arch.* †2. Of vision: Obtained by reflection only; not direct or immediate. (Based upon 1 *Cor.* xiii. 12.) –1704. 3. Having the reflecting property of a mirror; presenting a smooth, polished, and reflecting surface; of a brilliant metallic lustre. Now *Min.* 1661. 4. Of a telescope: Fitted with a speculum; reflecting 1676. 5. Performed by means of a surgical speculum 1898.

3. *S. iron* or *iron ore*, hæmatite, esp. the brilliant crystalline form of this. 5. In every case in which there is probability of rectal disease digital or s. examination must be made 1898.

II. 1. Of or pertaining to sight or vision; esp. *s. orb* (poet.), the eye 1656. 2. *poet.* Of heights, etc.: Affording a wide view 1671.

2. Look once more e're we leave this s. Mount Westward MILT.

Speculate (spe·kiŭleᵗt), *v.* 1599. [f. L. *speculat-*, *speculari* to spy out, watch, etc., f. *specula* a look-out, watch-tower, f. *specere* to see, look.] 1. *trans.* To observe or view mentally; to consider or reflect upon with close attention; to contemplate; to theorize upon. *Obs.* or *arch.* †2. To look at (something); to examine or observe closely or narrowly –1805. b. *spec.* To observe (the stars, heavens, etc.), esp. as an object of study 1630. 3. *intr.* To engage in thought or reflection, esp. of a conjectural or theoretical nature, *on* or *upon*, *about*, *as to*, etc., a subject 1677. 4. To engage in the buying and selling of commodities or effects in order to profit by a rise or fall in their market value; to undertake, or take part or invest in, a business enterprise or transaction of a risky nature in the expectation of considerable gain 1785. b. To count or reckon *on* something as probable or certain 1797.

1. If we do but s. the folly and indisputable dotage of avarice SIR T. BROWNE. 2. b. The sun and moon, which, he said, he was born to s. 1890. 3. Nearly every body whose death was worth speculating about 1847. 4. Would he be what he is if he hadn't speculated? DICKENS.

Speculation (spekiŭlē¹·ʃən). late ME. [ad. late L. *speculationem*, f. *speculari*. Cf. OF. *speculation*, F. *spéculation.*] I. 1. The faculty or power of seeing; sight, vision, *esp.* intelligent or comprehending vision. Now *arch.* 1471. †2. The exercise of the faculty of sight; the action, or an act, of seeing, viewing, or looking on or at; examination or observation –1774. †b. Observation of the heavens, stars, etc. –1652. †3. An observer or watcher; a spy. SHAKS.

2. †*Top* or *turret of s.* (after L. *turris speculationis*), one from which a wide view is obtained.

II. 1. The contemplation, consideration, or profound study *of* some subject. Now *rare* or *Obs.* late ME. 2. An act of speculating, or the result of this; a conclusion, opinion, view, or series of these, reached by abstract or hypothetical reasoning. late ME. b. A conjectural consideration or meditation; an attempt to ascertain something by probable reasoning 1796. 3. Without article: Contemplation of a profound, far-reaching, or subtle character; abstract or hypothetical reasoning on subjects of an abstruse or conjectural nature; freq. in disparaging use, usu. with adjs.; also simply = conjecture, surmise 1450. b. *In s.*, in conjecture or theory; not actually or practically; also, under consideration, in view 1638. 4. The action or practice of buying and selling goods, stocks and shares, etc., in order to profit by the rise or fall in the market value, as distinct from regular trading or investment; engagement in any business enterprise or transaction of a venturesome or risky nature, but offering the chance of great or unusual gain 1774. 5. An act or instance of speculating 1776. 6. *Cards.* A round game of cards, the chief feature of which is the buying and selling of trump cards, the holder of the highest trump card in a round winning the pool 1804.

2. In consequence of these speculations, I ordered a well to be sunk near the middle of the peninsula 1793. 3. Your courtier theorique..doth..know the court, rather by s., than practice B. JONSON. Because slavery is of all things the greatest clog and obstacle to s. SWIFT. The mere romantic s. of political dreamers 1861. 4. That species of gambling named s. 1834. Phr. *On s.*, on chance; on the chance of gain or profit.

Speculatist (spe·kiŭleᵗtist). 1613. [f. SPECULATE *v.*] 1. One who speculates, or indulges in abstract reasoning; a theorist. 2. One who speculates in commerce or finance 1812.

1. The s. is only in danger of erroneous reasoning JOHNSON.

Speculative (spe·kiŭlătiv), *a.* and *sb.* late ME. [a. OF. *speculatif*, *-ive* (mod.F. *spéculatif*, *-ive*), or ad. L. *speculativus*, f. *speculat-*, *speculari* to SPECULATE.] A. *adj.* 1. Of the nature of, based upon, or characterized by speculation or theory in contrast to practice or positive knowledge. 2. Given to speculation or conjectural reasoning 1546. †b. Given to pry or search *into* something. BACON. 3. Of life, etc.: Spent in, devoted to, speculation –1849. 4. Of faculties, etc.: Adapted for or exercised in speculation 1604. 5. Suitable for observation or watching. Chiefly *poet.* 1709. 6. a. Of persons: Given to or engaging in commercial or financial speculation 1763. b. Of the nature of, characterized by, or involving speculation 1799.

1. She has a world of knowledge: knowledge s., as I may say, but no experience 1748. He..had a languid s. liking for republican institutions MACAULAY. 2. Too s. a writer 1813. 4. Thoughts speculatiue, their vnsure hopes relate SHAKS. 5. High on her s. tower Stood Science WORDSW. 6. a. A s. bookseller SCOTT. b. Heavy s. transactions 1907. Hence **Spe·culative-ly** *adv.*, **-ness.**

B. *sb.* †a. Speculation; hypothetical reasoning; theory. (After late L. *speculativa* sb.) –1509. †b. *pl.* Speculative matters; the speculative sciences –1678. c. With *the*: That which rests only on speculation 1877.

Speculator (spe·kiŭleᵗtəɹ). 1555. [a. L., f. *speculari.*] 1. One who speculates on abstruse or uncertain matters; one who devotes himself to theoretical reasoning. 2. A watchman, sentry, or look-out 1607. †3. One who engages in occult observations or studies –1691. 4. One who engages in commercial or financial speculation 1778.

1. The most enthusiastic s. cannot suppose a greater increase MALTHUS.

Speculatory (spe·kiŭlătəri), *sb.* and *a.* Now *rare.* 1569. [ad. L. *speculatorius*; see SPECULATE *v.* and -ORY.] A. *sb.* †1. The observation or study of occult phenomena –1676. †2. = SPECULATOR 2. –1775. B. *adj.* †1. Of the nature of or pertaining to, occult speculation –1676. 2. Serving for observation; affording an outlook or view 1781.

Speculatrix (spe·kiŭlātriks). 1611. [a. L.] A female speculator.

Speculist (spe·kiŭlist). 1707. [f. SPECULATE *v.* + -IST.] = SPECULATIST.

‖ **Speculum** (spe·kiŭlŏm). *Pl.* **specula** and -**ums**. 1597. [L., f. *specere* to look (at), observe.] 1. A surgical instrument for dilating orifices of the body so as to facilitate examination or operations. 2. A mirror or reflector (of glass or metal) used for some scientific purpose; †a lens 1646. b. *spec.* A metallic mirror forming part of a reflecting telescope 1704. 3. *Ornith.* A lustrous mark on the wings of certain birds; = MIRROR *sb.* III. b. 1804.

attrib.: **s.-forceps**, long, slender forceps, used for dressing wounds or operating on parts not accessible except through a speculum. **s. metal**, an alloy of copper and tin used for making specula.

Speech (spītʃ), *sb.* [OE. *sprǽc*, *sprēc* (later *spǽc*, *spēc*), f. ablaut-stem of *sprecan*, *specan* SPEAK *v.* The forms with *spr-* did not survive beyond the 12th c.] I. 1. The act of speaking; the natural exercise of the vocal organs; the utterance of words or sentences. b. *transf.* The speaking or sounding of a musical instrument, organ-pipe, etc. 1862. 2. Talk, speaking, or discourse; colloquy, conversation, conference. Commonly const. *with* or *of* (a person). OE. b. With possess. pron., or *the* and genitive: The opportunity of speaking or conversing with a person; an audience or interview with a person. Now *arch.* or *Obs.* OE. c. Mention *of* a thing. Also with *no*. Now *rare*. ME. 3. Common or general talk; report, rumour, or current mention *of* something. Now *rare* or *Obs.* ME.

1. Men..express their thoughts by s. BERKELEY. 2. Deserue well at my hands, by helping mee to the s. of Beatrice SHAKS. He desires Some priuate s. with you SHAKS. 3. Dr. Clement, what's he? I haue heard much s. of him B. JONS. †*In s.*, spoken about, mentioned.

II. 1. The form of utterance peculiar to a particular nation, people, or group of persons; a language, tongue, or dialect OE. 2. The faculty or power of speaking, or of expressing thoughts by articulate sounds OE. 3. Manner or mode of speaking; *esp.* the method of utterance habitual to a particular person OE.

1. The Iewes speche COVERDALE 2 *Kings* xviii. 26. The several families who understood one another's s. kept together DE FOE. 2. The s. of the dying man failed MACAULAY. 3. Thou art a Galilean, and thy speach soundeth euen alike COVERDALE *Mark* xiv. 70.

III. 1. The result of speaking; that which is spoken or uttered OE. 2. A certain number of words uttered by a person at one time; *esp.* a more or less formal utterance or statement with respect to something OE. †b. A talk or discourse between persons or *with* another -1633. c. A more or less formal discourse delivered to an audience; an oration; also, the manuscript or printed copy or report of this 1583. d. A school composition declaimed on speech-day 1886. †3. a. A report or rumour -1660. †b. A current saying or assertion -1642. †c. A phrase, term, or idiom -1675. †4. A law-plea -1450.

1. Blessed be thy speach, and blessed be thou COVERDALE 1 *Sam.* xxv. 33. Ten Kabs of s. descended into the world, and the women took away nine of them 1647. 2. Many have been the wise speeches of fools, though not so many as the foolish speeches of wise men FULLER. c. *King's S.*, the sovereign's address to parliament at its opening and closing; His Majesty's s. of 13th November 1770 *Junius Lett.* 3. b. The common s. is, spend and God will send GASCOIGNE.

Comb.: **s.-centre**, the nervous brain-centre controlling the power of speech; **-craft**, the knowledge or science of s.; **-day**, the day at the end of the school year on which exercises are declaimed and the annual prizes distributed in certain public schools; also, a similar day in other schools marked by prize-giving and s.-making; **-reading**, the action on the part of deaf and dumb persons of comprehending s. by watching the movements of a speaker's mouth.

Speech (spītʃ), *v.* 1682. [f. prec.] 1. *trans.* To say or state in a speech or speeches (*rare*). 2. To make a speech to; to address in a speech 1818. 3. *intr.* To make a speech or speeches. Now *rare*. 1684.

Speechful (spī·tʃfŭl), *a.* 1842. [f. SPEECH *sb.*] Full of speech; possessing the power of speech; loquacious, talkative. b. Of the eyes, etc.: Full of expression; speaking 1849. Hence **Spee·chfulness**.

Speechification (spī:tʃifikē¹·ʃən). 1809. [f. SPEECHIFY *v.*; see -FICATION.] 1. An instance or occasion of speech-making; a speech, oration, harangue. 2. The action of making speeches; oratory 1825.

Speechifier (spī·tʃifəi,əɹ). 1778. [f. next.] One who speechifies or delivers speeches; one given to, or having some aptitude for, public speaking.

Speechify (spī·tʃifəi), *v.* Chiefly *joc.* or *depreciatory*. 1723. [f. SPEECH *sb.* + -IFY.] 1. *intr.* To make a speech or speeches; to 'hold forth'; to speak or talk at some length or with some degree of formality. 2. *trans.* To address in a speech or speeches 1862.

Speechifying (spī·tʃifəi,iŋ), *vbl. sb.* 1723. [f. prec.] 1. The action of making speeches; the practice of oratory. b. The action of speaking or talking, esp. in a formal manner or at excessive length 1777. 2. An instance or occasion of public speaking 1843.

1. Then came the feast, and afterwards the meeting, with music and s. in the church C. BRONTË.

Speeching (spī·tʃiŋ), *vbl. sb.* 1664. [f. SPEECH *sb.* or *v.*] The action or practice of making speeches; the art of speaking; a speech.

Speechless (spī·tʃlės), *a.* [Late OE. *spǽcléas*, f. *spǽc* SPEECH *sb.*] 1. Destitute of the faculty of speech; naturally or permanently dumb. b. Of a state or condition: Characterized by the lack of speech 1593. 2. a. Unable to speak on account of illness, injury, or extreme exhaustion ME. b. Deprived for the time being of speech through astonishment, fear, etc., or through excessive drinking; temporarily dumb. late ME. 3. Refraining from speech; silent. Also, reticent, taciturn. late ME. †4. Not uttered or expressed in speech. SHAKS. 5. Of an emotion, etc.: Characterized by loss of speech 1593. 6. Free from, unaccompanied or undisturbed by, speech 1726. 7. *poet.* Incapable of expression in or by speech 1813.

1. They mouthes, but speechlesse, have; Eyes sightlesse 1586. b. As pure as s. infancy! SHELLEY. 2. a. Some powere strike me s. for a time! 1591. b. S. with surprise 1891. 3. *transf.* A silence in the Heauens,..The bold windes speechlesse SHAKS. 4. For in her youth There is a prone and speechlesse dialect, Such as moue men SHAKS. 5. She gave herself up to s. joy 1794. 6. The great..darkness Of the speechless days that shall be! LONGFELLOW. Hence **Spee·chless-ly** *adv.*, **-ness**.

Spee·ch-ma:ker. 1710. [f. SPEECH *sb.*] One who makes a speech or speeches, esp. in public; an orator. So **-ma:king** 1718.

Speed (spīd), *sb.* [OE. *spéd*, earlier *spǽd* (= OHG. *spōt*), f. OE. *spōwan*, OHG. *spuon* to prosper, succeed.] I. 1. Success, prosperity, good fortune; profit, advancement, furtherance. *Obs.* exc. *Sc.* or *arch.* †2. a. Assistance, aid, help -1500. †b. One who, or that which, promotes success or prosperity -1681.

1. The king wished us good s. DE FOE. 2. b. Good-manners be your speede SHAKS. Christ be our s. 1681.

II. 1. Quickness in moving or making progress from one place to another, usually as the result of special exertion; celerity, swiftness; also, power or rate of progress OE. b. Of things: Swiftness, rapidity, velocity, of direct or circular movement; rate of motion or revolution ME. 2. Quickness, promptness, or despatch in the performance of some action or operation OE. b. *Photogr.* The relative rapidity with which a plate, film, etc., is acted upon by light or by a developer 1892. 3. A section of a cone-pulley giving a particular rate of speed 1881.

1. Madam, I goe with all conuenient s. SHAKS. b. The slowness of the s. 1857. Phr. †*At s.*, at a rapid rate of movement. *At* (or †*on*) *full s.*, or, simply, *full s.*, with the utmost s. possible. *To make s.*, to hurry, make haste. †*To have*, or *get*, *the s. of*, to outdistance, to get ahead of (a person). 2. Get them transcribed by good hands with all s. 1701.

attrib. and *Comb.*: a. In the names of devices or apparatus for regulating or indicating s., as *s.-check*, *-clock*, *-cone*, *-gauge*. b. Denoting the attainment of, or capacity for, high s., as *s.-boat*, *-car*, *lathe*. c. Miscellaneous, as *s.-capacity*, *-limit*, *-trial*. **s.-cop** *U.S. slang*, a policeman who is detailed to observe the s. of motorists; **-gear**, a device for regulating the s. of a bicycle, etc.; **-man**, a cyclist who rides at a high rate of s.; **-merchant**, orig. *U.S. slang*, one who indulges in motoring, etc. at high s.; **-way** *U.S.*, a special track for rapid cycling or motoring.

Speed (spīd), *v.* Pa. t. and pa. pple. **sped**. [OE. *spēdan*, = OHG. *spuoten*, f. stem **spōd-*; see prec.] I. 1. *intr.* Of persons: To succeed or prosper; to attain one's purpose or desire. Now *arch.* †b. Const. *of*: To succeed in getting, obtaining, or accomplishing -1643. 2. *impers.* To go or fare (well or ill) *with* a person, etc. ME. 3. Of things: To prove successful; to thrive ME. 4. *trans.* To further or assist (a person); to cause to succeed or prosper. Now *arch.* ME. †b. Const. *of* or *with*: To provide or furnish (a person) with something. Chiefly in *pa. pple.* -1665. 5. In *pa. pple.*: a. Furthered or brought to the end or condition desired; so dealt with as to be satisfied or well situated ME. b. In contexts implying an evil plight or awkward situation 1530. c. Appointed or elected *to* (or as) something (*rare*) ME. 6. To promote or further (a matter); to accomplish or carry out ME. b. *spec.* To promote, expedite, prosecute (a bill, plea) as a matter of official or legal business. late ME. 7. *arch.* a. †To deal with, finish, or dispatch (a matter) ME. b. To dispatch, destroy, kill (a person, etc.) 1594.

1. Soonest he spedes, that most can lye and fayn WYATT. 2. It has constantly sped worse with philosophy, instead of speeding better 1854. 3. Philip's suit no longer sped so favorably as before 1855. 4. For let the Gods so s. mee, as I loue The name of Honor, more then I feare death SHAKS. Phr. *God s. the plough*, etc. 5. b. We three are married, but you two are sped SHAKS. c. His father got him to be sped a Kings-scholar at Westminster 1691. 6. S. his hunting with thy Pow'r divine DRYDEN. b. To s. the action, that is to prosecute the action with due diligence 1884. 7. a. Go, s. thine office quickly, sirrah SCOTT. b. 'Yes. I am sped,' he said in a faint voice 1845.

II. 1. *trans.* To send with speed or haste; also, to force to go ME. b. To send out, cast, discharge, or direct, with some degree of quickness and force 1569. c. To enable (a person) to make speed in departing or travelling; to further the going or progress of; sometimes simply, to bid farewell to 1725. 2. To give speed to (a course, etc.); to hasten; to cause to be rapid in movement ME. b. To press or urge on, *esp.* in order to bring to an early result or termination; to expedite. late ME. c. To cause (time) to pass (*away*) quickly 1818. d. To increase the working rate of. In recent use chiefly with *up*. 1856. e. To give a specified speed to (a machine) 1881. 3. *refl.* a. To go with speed. Now *literary*. ME. b. To act with speed; to make haste in doing, or to do, something. Now *arch.* ME. 4. *intr.* a. To go or move with speed. late ME. b. Of time: To pass quickly ME. c. To make haste *to* do something; to be speedy in action. late ME. d. To drive a motor vehicle at a high rate of speed. Chiefly in *vbl. sb.* Also *trans.* 1904.

1. The cry in all thy ships is still the same—S. us away to battle and to fame COWPER. b. His last arrow is sped TENNYSON. c. I..Welcome the coming, s. the going guest POPE. 2. The king..Repels their hordes, and speeds their flight afar 1807. b. Command thy maids to s. the work 1870. e. Similar automatic machines, speeded alike 1897. 4. a. Streams sped downwards, falling over the rocks 1860. *fig.* Your wit 's too hot, it speeds too fast, 'twill tire SHAKS. c. First to Watch, and then to S. BACON.

Speeder (spī·dəɹ). late ME. [f. prec.] 1. One who speeds, aids, or furthers; a helper or forwarder. Now *arch.* †2. One who prospers, *esp.* in a suit -1671. 3. A device for quickening or regulating the speed of machinery; also, a kind of roving-machine used in cotton-manufacture 1875.

Spee·dful, *a.* ME. [f. SPEED *sb.* + -FUL.] †1. Profitable, advantageous, expedient, helpful, efficacious -1573. 2. Speedy, quick, swift, rapid. Now *rare*. late ME. **Spee·dfully** *adv.*

Speedless (spī·dlės), *a.* ME. [f. SPEED *sb.* + -LESS.] Profitless, ineffectual, unsuccessful.

Speedometer (spīdǫ·mĭtəɹ). 1904. [f. SPEED *sb.* + *-ometer* -METER.] A speed-indicator, esp. one affixed to an automobile.

Speedster (spī·dstəɹ). 1918. [f. as prec. + -STER, after *roadster*.] a. A person who drives, etc. at high speed. b. A fast motor car, etc.

Speedwell (spī·d,wĕl). 1578. [app. f. SPEED *v.* I. 1 + WELL *adv.*, in ref. to the fugacious petals.] Any herb of the genus VERONICA.

Speedy (spī·di), *a.* late ME. [f. SPEED *sb.*] †1. Advantageous, expedient, helpful -1449. 2. Moving, or able to move, with speed; swift.

Now *rare*. late ME. **3.** Acting with speed; active, prompt, quick 1504. **4.** Characterized by speed of motion or action. late ME. **b.** Rapidly brought to pass or to an end; quickly accomplished, arrived at, or obtained 1607. **5.** quasi-*adv.* Speedily 1601.

2. The Barbary Horse is more s. than the rest 1630. **3.** Speak out, and be s. SCOTT. **4.** Some s. remedy should be applied 1764. Favourable winds seemed ..to promise them a s. navigation 1797. **b.** I will wish her s. strength SHAKS.

Comb.: **s. cut**, an injury on the inner side of a horse's fore leg, near the knee, caused by the foot of the opposite leg when in motion; also as *vb.* and *attrib.* So **Spee·di-ly** *adv.* ME., **-ness.**

†**Speer,** *sb.* Also **spear.** 1607. [var. of SPIRE *sb.*[1]] A branch or prong of a deer's horn -1774.

Speer (spīəɹ), *v.*[1] Also **speir.** Chiefly *Sc.* and *north.* [Com. Teut.; OE. *spyrian*, = OS. **spurian*, OHG. *spurigen, spurien.*] **I.** *intr.* **1.** To put a question or questions; to ask. †**2.** To inquire one's way -1615.

1. S. as little about him as he does about you SCOTT.

II. *trans.* **1.** With objective clause: To inquire or ask *how, what, who*, etc. OE. **2.** To make inquiries concerning, to ask questions regarding (a thing or fact) ME. **3.** To trace or find out by inquiry. Usu. with *out.* late ME. **4.** To ask (a question) 1460. **5.** To question or interrogate (a person) ME.

Speer (spīəɹ), *v.*[2] *dial.* and *U.S.* 1866. [perh. identical w. prec., infl. by PEER *v.*] *intr.* To peer.

†**Speight.** 1450. [Either repr. OE. **speht*, or a. MDu. or MLG. *specht.*] The green woodpecker -1656.

Speiss (spəis). 1796. [ad. G. *speise* in the same sense, a special use of *speise* (:—pop. L. *spesa*, L. *expensa*) food.] **1.** An impure metallic compound, containing nickel, cobalt, iron, etc., produced in the smelting of certain ores; *esp.* an arsenide obtained in the manufacture of smalt and used as a source of nickel. **2.** **Speiss-cobalt**, tin-white cobalt; smaltine 1872.

‖**Spek-boom** (spe·kbōm). Also **speck-.** 1823. [S. Afr. Du., f. *spek* SPECK *sb.*[2] + *boom* tree.] The purslane-tree (*Portulacaria Afra*) of South Africa; the wood of this.

Spelæan (spĭlī·ăn), *a.* Also **spelean.** 1839. [f. mod.L. *spelæus*, f. L. *spelæum*, ad. Gr. σπήλαιον cave.] **1.** Inhabiting a cave or caves; frequenting caverns; cave-dwelling. **2.** Of the nature of a cave 1882.

Spelæology (spīliǫ·lŏdʒi). Also **speleo-.** 1895. [ad. F. *spéléologie*; see prec. and -LOGY.] The scientific study of caves. Hence **Speleo·lo·gical** *a.*, **-lo·gically** *adv.* **Speleo·logist.**

Spelding (spe·ldiŋ). *Sc.* 1537. [f. Sc. *speld* vb. to split open + -ING[1].] A small split fish, preserved by being dried in the sun.

Spelk. Chiefly *north.* and *Sc.* [OE. *spelc* (also *spilc*), = LG. *spalke*, Icel. *spelka.*] **1.** A surgical splint. **2.** A splinter or chip; a small strip of wood 1440. **3.** A thatching-rod 1563.

Spell (spel), *sb.*[1] [OE. *spel(l*, = OS., OHG. *spel, spell-*, Goth. *spill* recital, tale. Cf. GOSPEL.] †**1.** Without article: Discourse, narration, speech; *occas.* idle talk, fable. -late ME. †**2.** A discourse or sermon; a narrative or tale -1653. **3.** A set of words, a formula or verse, supposed to possess occult or magical powers; a charm or incantation 1579. **b.** *transf.* and *fig.* An occult or mysterious power or influence; a fascinating or enthralling charm 1592.

3. She workes by Charmes, by Spels, by th' Figure, & such dawbry as this is SHAKS. **b.** The s. is removed; I see you as you are JANE AUSTEN. Hence **Spe·llful** *a.* full of, abounding in, spells or magical power.

Spell (spel), *sb.*[2] Now *dial.* 1545. [Cf. G. *spellen* to split, cleave.] **1.** A splinter, chip, fragment. **2.** A bar, rail, or rung 1559. **3.** The trap used in the game of *s. and knur* 1781.

Spell (spel), *sb.*[3] 1593. [Related to SPELL *v.*[3]] **1.** A set of persons taking a turn of work in order to relieve others; a relay, relief-gang, or shift. Now *rare.* **2.** A turn of work taken by a person or set of persons in relief of another 1625. **3.** A continuous course or period *of* some work, occupation, or employment; a turn or bout *at* something. Also without const. 1706. **4.** A period or space of time of indefinite length 1728. **b.** A period having a certain character or spent in a particular way 1830. **5.** A continuous period or stretch *of* a specified kind of weather 1728. **6.** *U.S.* A period of being indisposed, out of sorts, or irritable 1856.

1. Yet I sent them an other fresh s. of men 1628. **2.** The men gave way..with a good will, the passengers taking spells to help them STEVENSON. **3.** The Termagant Sloop..has had a long s. of service NELSON. *S. oh!* (or *ho!*), a call or signal, usu. to rest or cease working. **4.** I hope to take a pretty long s. in town GIBBON. **b.** A grievous s. of eighteen months on board the French galleys 1885. **5.** A severe s. of cold weather 1775. No man ever knew so winter-like a s. so early in the year 1740.

Spell, *v.*[1] *Obs.* or *dial.* [OE. *spellian*, f. *spel* SPELL *sb.*[1]] **1.** *intr.* To discourse or preach; to talk, converse, or speak. **2.** *trans.* To utter, declare, relate, tell OE.

Spell (spel), *v.*[2] Pa. t. and pa. pple. **spelled, spelt.** ME. [ad. OF. *espeller* (also *espeler*, mod. F. *épeler*), f. the Germanic stem *spell-*; see SPELL *sb.*[1]] **I.** *trans.* **1.** To read (a book, etc.) letter by letter; to peruse, or make out, slowly or with difficulty. **2.** *fig.* **a.** To find out, to guess or suspect, by close study or observation 1587. **b.** To make out, understand, decipher, or comprehend, by study 1635. **c.** To consider, contemplate, scan intently 1633. **3.** To name or set down in order the letters of (a word or syllable); to denote by certain letters in a particular order 1588. **b.** Of letters: To form (a word) 1738. **4.** To amount to; to signify, imply, or involve 1661.

1. He was spelling the paper, with the help of his lips THACKERAY. **2. a.** That there should be a God, heathens might s. out 1879. **b.** He..spells a horse's teeth divinely 1820. **c.** Will great God measure with a wretch? Shall he thy stature s.? G. HERBERT. **3.** What is Ab speld backward with the horn on his head? SHAKS. **c.** *U.S.* To put to the test in spelling; to put (a person) *down* in spelling 1853.

II. *intr.* **1.** To form words by means of letters; to repeat or set down the letters of words; to read off the separate letters forming a word or words. late ME. **b.** *fig.* To engage in study or contemplation *of* something. *poet.* 1632. **2.** To intimate or suggest a desire *for* something; to ask *for*, either by hints or direct request 1790.

1. A foolish opinion..that we ought to s. exactly as we speak SWIFT. **b.** The..Mossy Cell, Where I may sit and rightly s. Of every Star that Heav'n doth shew MILT. **2.** It will be observed..that he 'spelled' for the curacy 1860.

Phrases: *To s. able* (U.S. slang.), to be able; to have all the ability and strength needed (for some particular purpose). †*To s.* (a person) *backward*, to misrepresent, to pervert. *To s. short*, to express by a blunter term. Hence **Spe·llable** *a.* capable of being spelled or denoted by letters.

Spell (spel), *v.*[3] 1595. [Later form of dial. *spele* vb., of obsc. origin.] **1.** *trans.* To take the place of (a person) at some work or labour; to relieve (another) by taking a turn at work. Now *U.S.* **b.** To relieve by an interval of rest; to rest (*esp.* a horse). Chiefly *Austral.* 1846. **2.** *Naut.* To take a turn or turns of work at (the pump, etc.) 1769. **3.** *intr.* **a.** To replace one set of workers by another; to take turns 1861. **b.** *Austral.* To take an interval of rest 1880.

1. Sometimes there are two ostensible boilers to s. and relieve one another 1823.

Spell (spel), *v.*[4] 1591. [f. SPELL *sb.*[1] 3.] **1.** *trans.* To charm, fascinate, bewitch, bind by (or as by) a spell; to act as a spell upon. **b.** To protect (a person) *from*, to drive *away*, by means of a spell or charm 1691. **2.** To invest with magical properties 1697.

1. When..thy roses came to me My sense with their deliciousness was spell'd KEATS. **b.** Thy soft voice spelled away All my dearth 1876. **2.** This,..spell'd with Words of Pow'r, Dire Stepdames in the Magick Bowl infuse DRYDEN.

Spell-bind (spe·lbəind), *v.* 1808. [f. SPELL *sb.*[1] 3, after next.] *trans.* To bind by, or as by, a spell; to fascinate, enchant. So **Spe·ll-binder** *U.S.* a speaker capable of holding an audience spell-bound.

Spell-bound (spe·lbaund), *ppl. a.* 1799. [f. SPELL *sb.*[1] 3.] Bound by, or as by, a spell; fascinated, enchanted, entranced.

Speller (spe·ləɹ). 1440. [f. SPELL *v.*[2]] **1.** One who spells; an authority on spelling. **2.** *U.S.* A spelling-book 1864.

Spelling (spe·liŋ), *vbl. sb.* 1440. [f. SPELL *v.*[2]] **1.** The action, practice, or art of naming the letters of words, of reading letter by letter, or of expressing words by letters. **2.** Orthography; a particular instance of this 1661.

Comb.: **s.-book,** a book designed to teach s.

Spelt, *sb.* [OE. *spelt*, a. late L. *spelta* (= older L. *far*).] A species of grain (*Triticum Spelta*) related to wheat, formerly much cultivated in southern Europe and still grown in some districts.

Spelt (spelt), *v.* Now *dial.* 1570. [Cf. G. *spelzen* to husk.] *trans.* To husk or pound (grain); to bruise or split (*esp.* beans).

Spelter (spe·ltəɹ). 1661. [Related to PEWTER.] **1.** Zinc. (Now only *Comm.*) **2.** An alloy or solder of which zinc is the principal constituent 1815.

Speluncar (spelʊ·ŋkăɹ), *a.* 1855. [f. L. *spelunca* + -AR.] Having relation or reference to a cave.

Spence (spens). late ME. [Aphetic ad. OF. *despense* (mod.F. *dépense*) DISPENSE *sb.*] **1.** A room or separate place in which victuals and liquor are kept; a buttery or pantry; a cupboard. Now *dial.* or *arch.* **2.** *Sc.* An inner apartment of a house; a parlour 1783.

1. In one large aperture, which the robber facetiously called his *s.* (or pantry) SCOTT.

†**Spencer**[1]. ME. [a. AF. *espenser*, var. of *despenser*, OF. *despensier* DISPENSER.] A steward or butler -1580.

Spencer[2] (spe·nsəɹ). 1700. [From the family name *Spencer*. In sense 1 prob. from that of Charles *Spencer*, third Earl of Sunderland (1674–1722); in sense 2 from that of George John *Spencer*, second Earl Spencer (1758–1834).] †**1.** A kind of wig -1753. **2.** A short double-breasted overcoat without tails worn by men in the end of the 18th c. and the beginning of the 19th 1796. **b.** A kind of close-fitting jacket or bodice commonly worn by women and children early in the 19th c., and since revived 1803. **c.** A short coat or jacket 1851.

Spencer (spe·nsəɹ), *sb.*[3] 1840. [perh. f. the name of Mr. Knight *Spencer.*] *Naut.* A fore-and-aft sail, set with a gaff, serving as a trysail to the fore or main mast of a vessel.

Spencerian (spensīə·riăn), *a.* and *sb.* 1881. [f. name of the philosopher Herbert *Spencer* (1820–1903).] **A.** *adj.* Of or pertaining to Herbert Spencer or his philosophical views. **B.** *sb.* A follower of Spencer 1888.

Spend (spend), *sb.* 1688. [f. SPEND *v.*] The action of spending money. Only in phr. *on* or *upon the s.*

Spend (spend), *v.* Pa. t. and pa. pple. **spent.** [OE. **spendan*, ad. L. *expendere*, or aphetic ad. OF. *despendre* DISPEND *v.*] **I.** *trans.* **1.** Of persons: To pay out or away; to disburse or expend; to dispose of, or deprive oneself of, in this way. †**b.** To levy charges on (a person). Only in phr. *s. me and defend me.* -1596. **2.** *absol.* To exercise, make, or incur expenditure of money, goods, means, etc. ME. **3.** To expend or employ (labour, material, thought, etc.) in some specified way ME. **4.** To employ, occupy, use, or pass (time, one's life, etc.) *in* or *on* some action, occupation, or state ME. **b.** *ellipt.* To pass (the day, evening, etc.) in social intercourse or entertainment, or as a guest 1697. **5.** To use up; to exhaust or consume by use; to wear out. In later use freq. with *force, fury*, etc., as object. ME. **b.** To bring to a violent end; to destroy; to consume by destruction or wasting; to reduce or convert *into* something. late ME. **c.** *refl.* Of persons or things: To exhaust or wear out (oneself or itself); to become incapable of further activity; to cease to operate 1593. **6.** To suffer the loss of (blood, life, etc.); to allow to be shed or spilt ME. †**b.** *Naut.* To lose or incur the loss of (a mast, yard, sail, etc.) through bad weather or by some accident -1694. **7.** To use for food or drink; to consume in this way; to eat or drink. late ME. **b.** *Agric.* To use (a crop, hay, etc.) as food or fodder for cattle; to eat off 1733. **8.** To make use of; to use or employ. Now *rare.* late ME. **9.** To expend or employ (speech or language); to utter or emit (a word, sound, etc.). late ME. †**b.** *To s. the mouth, tongue,* etc. Of hunting dogs: To bark or give tongue on finding or seeing the game -1682. c. To shed (tears, blood, or the like). *arch.* 1602. 10. To consume, employ, use superfluously, wastefully, or with undue lavishness; to waste or squander; to throw away. late ME. †b. To waste (time) -1720. 11. To allow (time, one's life, etc.) to pass or go by; to live or stay through (a certain period) to the end. late ME. †12. To cause or involve expenditure of (something) -1703. †b. To involve the expenditure of (time) -1649.

1. I have..spent very many hundred powndes 1574. Wherefore doe yee s. money for that which is not bread? *Isa.* lv. 2. 2. He spendeth a pace and getteth nothyng 1530. 3. I s. my Breath in Groans 1696. Why do you s. many words..on this subject? 1875. 4. He spent his time in training horses 1802. 5. The Thunder..Perhaps hath spent his shafts MILT. c. Man after man spends himself in this cause CARLYLE. 7. b. To spend all the stover, straw, and turnips on the land 1823. 9. b. *absol.* For then reason like a bad hound spends upon a false sent SIR T. BROWNE. 10. I am a fool..to s. my words upon an idle..unintelligent boy SCOTT. 11. I have been spending six weeks in Ireland 1854.

II. *intr.* †1. Of time, the season, etc.: To pass, elapse -1681. †2. To be consumed, dispersed, exhausted, or used up; to pass off or *away* -1704. 3. Of foodstuffs, wheat, hay, etc.: To turn out or prove in use to be of a certain quality; to last or hold out *well*. Now *dial.* 1673. †4. Of a liquid: To flow or run -1811.

2. The Sound spendeth, and is dissipated in the Open Aire BACON. 3. Meat that spends well 1687. Hence **Spe·ndable** *a.* that can be spent.

Spe·nd-all. Now *rare.* 1553. [f. SPEND *v.* + ALL *sb.*] One who spends all his goods, money, etc.; a spendthrift.

Spender (spe·ndəɹ). late ME. [f. SPEND *v.* + -ER[1].] 1. One who spends; *spec.* a spendthrift. 2. One who, or that which, consumes, employs, or uses up; a consumer or waster *of* something 1565. 3. *Tanning.* A pit in which the bark is leached. Also *attrib.* in *s. pit.* 1882.

Spending (spe·ndiŋ), *vbl.sb.* OE. [f. SPEND *v.* + -ING[1].] 1. The action of SPEND *v.*, in various senses. †2. That which may be expended or spent; means of support; goods, money, cash -1650.

Spe·nding-mo:ney. 1598. [f. SPENDING *vbl. sb.*] Money used or available for spending; a sum allowed for this purpose; pocket-money.

Spendthrift (spe·ndþrift), *sb.* (and *a.*). 1601. [f. SPEND *v.* + THRIFT *sb.*[1]] 1. One who spends money profusely or wastefully; one who wastes his patrimony by foolish or lavish expenditure; an improvident or extravagantly wasteful person (freq. connoting moral worthlessness). 2. *transf.* A prodigal consumer, user up, or waster, *of* something 1610. 3. *attrib.* passing into *adj.* a. Acting as or like, having the qualities of, a spendthrift 1607. b. Wasteful 1790.

2. Fie, what a spend-thrift is he of his tongue SHAKS. 3. a. These rich plebeians are a harvest for us spendthrift nobles 1834. b. The improvident resource of a s. sale BURKE. Hence **Spe·ndthri·fty** *a.* prodigal or wasteful in expenditure.

Spenserian (spensīə·riăn), *a.* and *sb.* 1818. [f. name of the poet Edmund *Spenser* (? 1552–1599) + -IAN.] A. *adj.* Of or belonging to, characteristic of, Spenser or his work.

S. stanza, the stanza employed by Spenser in the *Faerie Queen*, consisting of eight decasyllabic lines and a final Alexandrine, with the rhyming scheme *ab ab bc bcc.*

B. *sb.* 1. A Spenserian stanza, or a poem in this metre 1818. 2. A follower or imitator of Spenser; a poet of Spenser's school 1894.

Spent (spent), *pa. pple.* and *ppl. a.* 1440. [f. SPEND *v.*] I. In predicative uses. 1. Of material things: Expended, consumed, used up completely. 2. Passed, gone; come to an end; over 1528. 3. Of persons or animals: Deprived of force or strength; tired or worn out; completely exhausted 1591. 4. Of things: Exhausted of the active or effective power or principle 1596.

1. Their powder and ball were s. MACAULAY. 2. The time is farre spente 1560. The raine is s. 1634. 3. Now thou seest me S., overpower'd, despairing of success ADDISON. 4. Though their lustre now was s. and faded SHELLEY.

II. In attrib. uses. 1. Of persons or animals: = sense I. 3. 1568. b. Of fish: Exhausted by spawning; having recently spawned 1864. 2. Of things: Exhausted, worn out, used up; no longer active, effective, or serviceable 1697.

1. The talke of a s. old man ASCHAM. 2. Heaps of s. Arrows fall and strew the Ground DRYDEN. The s. liquor..is discharged into the stream 1877.

‖**Speos** (spī·ǫs). 1843. [Gr. σπέος cave.] *Egyptol.* A cave temple or tomb, esp. one of some architectural importance. Hence **Speo·logy**, the study of caves.

†**Spe·rage.** 1440. [a. OF., var. SPARAGE.] Asparagus -1760.

Spe·rate, *a. Obs.* or *arch.* 1551. [ad. L. *speratus, sperare* to hope.] 1. Of debts: Having some likelihood of being recovered; not desperate. 2. *gen.* Giving or leaving room for hope; of a promising nature 1808.

Spere, obs. f. SPHERE.

Sperling, variant of SPARLING.

Sperm (spəɹm). late ME. [ad. OF. *esperme* (F. *sperme*), or L. *sperma*, a. Gr. σπέρμα, f. stem of σπείρειν to sow.] I. 1. The generative substance or seed of male animals (esp. of vertebrates). b. A spermatozoon 1904. †2. Offspring, brood (of persons). MILT. 3. *transf.* The generative matter or source from which anything is formed or takes its origin 1610. II. (Short for SPERM WHALE or SPERMACETI.) 1. a. *S. oil*, an oil found together with spermaceti in the head of various species of whales 1839. b. *S. candle*, a spermaceti candle 1856. 2. A sperm whale. Also *collect.* and *attrib.* 1840. 3. Sperm candles or oil 1856.

‖**Sperma** (spə̄·ɹmă). Now *rare. Pl.* **spermata.** late ME. [a. L. or Gr.; see prec.] Sperm; seed. Hence **Sperma-**, comb. form.

Spermaceti (spəɹmăse·ti, -sī·ti). 1471. [med.L., f. *sperma* sperm + *ceti*, gen. sing. of *cetus* (ad. Gr. κῆτος) whale, through an erroneous notion as to the nature of the substance.] A fatty substance, which in a purified state has the form of a soft white scaly mass, found in the head (and to some extent in other parts) of the sperm-whale (*Physeter macrocephalus*) and some other whales and dolphins; it is used largely in medicinal preparations, and in the manufacture of candles. Also *attrib.*, as *s.-candle*, etc.; s. whale, the sperm whale.

Spermaduct (spə̄·ɹmădɒkt). 1847. [f. SPERMA- + DUCT.] *Zool.* A spermatic or seminal duct or passage in a male animal. Also **Spe·rmaphore** *Bot.*, = SPERMOPHORE.

Spermary (spə̄·ɹmări). 1864. [Anglicized f. mod.L. *spermarium* (f. *sperma* sperm), also used; see -ARY[1].] The organ or gland in which spermatozoa are generated in male animals.

‖**Spermatheca** (spəɹmăþī·kă). *Pl.* **-thecæ** (þī·sī). 1826. [f. SPERMA + THECA.] A receptacle in the oviduct of female insects and invertebrates, in which fecundation of the ova takes place. Hence **Spermathe·cal** *a.*

Spermatic (spəɹmæ·tik), *a.* (and *sb.*). 1539. [ad. med.L. *spermaticus*, ad. Gr. σπερματικός, f. σπέρμα sperm.] 1. Containing, conveying, or producing sperm or seed; seminiferous. b. Full of sperm; generative, productive 1619. 2. Of the nature of sperm; resembling sperm 1541. †3. Directly derived from sperm (according to old physiological views) -1728. 4. Of qualities: Characteristic of, peculiar to, or derived from, sperm 1642. 5. Existing in sperm 1837. 6. As *sb.* in *pl.* The spermatic vessels 1690.

1. A disease of the s. chord 1797. b. Spermatick Nile, which brings Choise Monsters forth 1648. 4. Spermatick Vigour spreads the poison'd Race DE FOE. 5. S. animalcules 1837. So †**Sperma·tical** *a.* (in senses 1–4); **-ly** *adv.*

Spermatin (spə̄·ɹmătin). 1836. [a. F. *spermatine*, f. L. *spermat-, sperma* + *-ine* -IN[1].] *Chem.* An albuminic constituent of the spermatic fluid.

Spermatium (spəɹmēi·ʃiŏm). *Pl.* **-atia.** 1856. [mod.L., ad. Gr. σπερμάτιον, dim. of σπέρμα seed.] *Bot.* A minute linear sporule forming part of the reproductive system of lichens and fungi. (Chiefly in *pl.*)

Spermato- (spə̄·ɹmăto, spəɹmătǫ·), repr. Gr. σπερματο-, comb. form of the stem of σπέρμα SPERM, employed in terms (chiefly of recent origin) relating to the reproductive organs or activities of animals and plants. Some of these have alternative forms in *sperma-* or *spermo-*. a. In terms denoting special reproductive organs, or parts of these, as **Spe·rmatoblast, -cyst, -cyte, -ge·mma, -gone, -go·nium, -mere, -spore.** b. In some other sbs. and adjs. with second elements of obvious meaning, as **Spermatoge·nesis, -gene·tic** *a.*, **-ge·nic** *a.*, **-o·logy, -o·phoral** *a.*, **-o·phorous** *a.*, **-rrhœ·a, -spore.**

‖**Spe·rmatocele** (-sīl). 1693. [med.L.; see prec. and CELE.] *Path.* A swelling of the testes or epididymis, from an accumulation of semen.

Spe·rmatophore (-fōəɹ). 1847. [f. SPERMATO- + -PHORE.] 1. *Biol.* In certain of the lower forms of animal life, a structure containing a compact mass of spermatozoa. 2. *Bot.* A part of the spermogonium of lichens or fungi, on which the spermatia are borne 1861.

Spe·rmatozoid (-zōu·id). 1857. [f. next + -ID.] 1. *Bot.* A minute fertilizing body or cell in Cryptogamia and Algæ. 2. *Phys.* = next 1861.

‖**Spe·rmatozoon** (-zōu·ǫn). *Pl.* **-zoa.** 1836. [f. SPERMATO- + Gr. ζῷον living thing, animal.] One of the numerous minute and active filaments present in the seminal fluid, by which the fecundation of the ovum is effected. Hence **Spe·rmatozo·al** *a.*

Spermi-, irreg. comb. form of L. *sperma* SPERM, as in **Spe·rmiduct** (= SPERMADUCT).

Spermism (spə̄·ɹmiz'm). 1889. [f. SPERMA + -ISM.] *Biol.* The theory that the male sperm contains the whole germ of the future animal.

Spermo-, irreg. comb. form (for SPERMATO-) of L. *sperma* or Gr. σπέρμα SPERM, used in various terms of *Phys.*, *Zool.*, and *Bot.*

Spe·rmoderm [mod.L. *spermoderma, -dermis* (De Candolle)] *Bot.*, the combined outer and inner integuments of a seed, or the outer of these by itself. ‖**Spermogo·nium** [mod.L.], (*a*) *Bot.* one of the receptacles in lichens and fungi in which the spermatia are produced; (*b*) *Phys.* a sperm-cell. **Spe·rmophile** [mod.L. *Spermophilus* (Cuvier)] *Zool.*, a rodent belonging to the squirrel-like genus *Spermophilus*; a pouched marmot. **Spe·rmophore** [mod.L. *spermophorum*] *Bot.*, the placenta in plants. **Spe·rmophyte** *Bot.*, a seed-bearing plant. **Spermophy·tic,** *a.* 'capable of producing true seeds'. **Spe·rmospore** *Phys.*, a compound cellular mass from which sperm filaments are developed. **Spermoto·xin** *Chem.*, a serum destructive to spermatozoa.

Sperm whale. Also **sperm-whale.** 1830. [Short for *spermaceti whale*; cf. SPERM II.] The spermaceti whale; = CACHALOT. b. Applied, with distinguishing epithets, to species of whales resembling, or related to, this 1882. Hence **Sperm-whaler**, a person or vessel engaged in the capture of sperm-whales.

‖**Speronara** (sperǫnā·ră). 1783. [It.] A large rowing and sailing boat used in southern Italy and Malta.

Sperse (spə̄ɹs), *v.* Now *arch.* 1580. [Aphetic f. DISPERSE *v.*] 1. *trans.* To cause to scatter or disperse; to drive in different directions. 2. *intr.* To take different directions 1819.

Spessartine (spe·săɹtin). 1850. [ad. F. *spessartine*, f. *Spessart* the district in Bavaria where it is found.] *Min.* A species of manganese garnet. So **Spe·ssartite.**

Spet, *v.* Now *dial.* late ME. [Alteration of SPETE *v.*, after pa. t. and pa. pple. *spet(te).*] *intr.* and *trans.* To spit. Hence **Spet** *sb.* spit.

Spetch (spetʃ). 1611. [Later f. north. dial. *speck.*] A piece or strip of undressed leather, a trimming of hide, used in making glue or size.

†**Spete,** *v.* [OE. *spǣtan*, f. stem **spāt-*.] To spit. -late ME.

†**Spettle.** late ME. [repr. OE. *spǣtl*; cf. prec.] Spittle -1693.

Spew (spiū), *sb.* Also †**spue.** 1609. [f. the vb.] That which is spewed or cast up from the stomach; vomit.

Spew (spiū), *v.* Also †**spue.** [repr. two OE. forms; (1) the strong verb *spīwan, spȳwan*; (2) the weak verb *spēowan, spīowan.* Cf. L. *spuere*, Gr. πτύειν, Lith. *spiauti.*] 1. *intr.* To bring up and discharge the contents of the stomach through the mouth; to vomit. Not now in polite use. 2. *trans.* To bring up (food or drink) from the stomach and eject through the mouth; to cast up or vomit; to cast out or discharge (blood, poison, etc.) from the mouth OE. 3. To cast *out* (†or *up*), to eject or reject, with abhorrence, contempt, or loathing. late ME. 4. To eject, cast or throw up or out, as if by vomiting; *spec.* to eject by volcanic action 1594. 5. *intr.* Of water, liquids, etc.: To flow, pour, or run in a more or less copious stream; to ooze or be forced *out* or *up*. Now chiefly *dial.* 1670. b. Of ground: To swell through excess of moisture; to slip or run when left unsupported 1839.

2. *fig.* My sonne, beholde you deserue to be burnt quicke.., Spewing forth..this Fæminine Latine 1632. 3. Because thou arte..nether colde ner hott, I wil s. the oute of my mought TINDALE *Rev.* iii. 16. 4. A crater-crust which may crack and spue fire any day C. BRONTË. Phr. *To s. the oakum*, said of a vessel when the oakum starts out from the seams of her planks. 5. b. In constructing a 'sike' for the drainage of land, gravelly earth will often break edge, and spew 1876. Hence Spew·er OE.

Spewy (spiū·i), *a.* 1669. [f. prec. + -Y[1].] Of ground: Tending to excessive wetness; from which water oozes out. Chiefly *Agric.* Hence **Spe·winess** s., boggy, or undrained condition (of land) 1653.

Sphacelate (sfæ·sĭleᵗt), *v.* 1653. [f. med. or mod.L. *sphacelat-*, *sphacelare*, f. SPHACELUS.] *Path.* 1. *trans.* To affect with sphacelus; to cause to gangrene or mortify. 2. *intr.* To become gangrenous or mortified 1684. So **Spha·celated** *ppl. a.* (*a*) *Path.* mortified, gangrened 1612; (*b*) *Bot.* withered, dead.

Sphacelation (sfæsĭlēⁱ·ʃən). 1657. [f. as prec.] *Path.* The fact or process of becoming mortified; the formation of a sphacelus.

‖ **Sphacelia** (sfæsī·liă). 1879. [mod.L., f. *sphacelus*, with reference to its effects when eaten.] *Bot.* The first stage of the fungus which produces ergot in rye.

‖**Sphacelus** (sfæ·sĭlŏs), *a.* 1575. [med. or mod.L., ad. Gr. σφάκελος gangrene.] *Path.* 1. Necrosis, mortification; an instance of this. 2. A mass of mortified tissue; a slough 1880. Hence **Spha·celous** *a.* necrotic.

‖**Sphæridium** (sfiəri·diŏm). *Pl.* **-idia.** 1877. [mod.L., f. *sphæra* SPHERE *sb.*] *Zool.* One of the numerous minute rounded bodies attached to certain parts of sea-urchins.

Sphæro- (sfī·*ro*), ad. Gr. σφαιρο-, comb. form of σφαῖρα ball, SPHERE, as in **Sphæ·rospore** *Bot.*, the quadruple spore of some algals.

Sphærosiderite (sfiərosi·dərait). 1837. [f. SPHÆRO- + SIDERITE[1].] *Min.* A variety of siderite which occurs in spherical concretions.

Sphagnous (sfæ·gnəs), *a.* 1828. [f. next.] 1. Of the nature of, consisting of, sphagnum. 2. Producing, or abounding in, sphagnum 1845.

‖ **Sphagnum** (sfæ·gnŏm). *Pl.* **-a, -ums.** 1753. [mod.L., f. Gr. σφάγνος a kind of moss.] *Bot.* 1. A genus of mosses growing in boggy or swampy places; bog-moss, peat-moss; also, one or other of the species or plants composing this genus. 2. The mossy substance of which plants of this genus are composed 1840.

Sphalerite (sfæ·lĕrəit). 1868. [f. Gr. σφαλερός deceptive + -ITE[1] 2.] *Min.* Zinc-blende.

‖ **Sphendone** (sfe·ndŏnī). 1850. [a. Gr. σφενδόνη.] *Archæol.* A head-band or fillet, shaped like a common form of sling, worn by women in ancient Greece.

Sphene (sfīn). 1815. [a. F. *sphène*, f. Gr. σφήν wedge, from the shape of its crystals.] *Min.* = TITANITE.

Sphenethmoid (sfīne·þmoid), *sb.* and *a.* 1875. [f. Gr. σφήν wedge + ETHMOID.] *Zool.* One of the cranial bones in batrachians, situated at the base of the skull; the girdle bone. Also *s. bone.*

Spheniscan (sfĭni·skăn). 1840. [f. mod. L. *Spheniscus* (Brisson) + -AN.] A penguin of the genus *Spheniscus*; a jackass penguin.

Spheno- (sfī·*no*), a. Gr. σφηνο-, comb. form of σφήν wedge.

1. *Anat.* In adjs. which designate something belonging to the sphenoid bone together with the part specified by the second element of the compound, as **S.-ba·silar, -maxi·llary, -te·mporal.** 2. In names of genera of animals or plants, as **Sphe·nodon,** a New Zealand lizard, called also *Tuatera* or *Hatteria*; **Sphenophy·llum,** a genus of fossil plants peculiar to the coal measures and the transition formations.

Sphenoid (sfī·noid), *a.* and *sb.* 1732. [ad. mod.L. *spheno(e)ides*, a. Gr. σφηνοειδής, f. σφήν wedge; see -OID.] A. adj. *S. bone*, a bone of irregular form situated at the base of the skull, where it is wedged in between the other bones of the cranium. B. *sb.* 1. *Anat.* The s. bone; one or other of the separate parts of this 1828. 2. *Cryst.* A wedge-shaped crystal bounded by four equal and similar triangular faces 1855.

Sphenoidal (sfĭnoi·dăl), *a.* 1726. [ad. mod.L. *sphenoidalis*, f. *sphenoides* SPHENOID.] 1. *S. bone*, the sphenoid bone. 2. Of or pertaining to, connected with, this bone 1726.

Sphenotic (sfĭnǫ·tik), *a.* and *sb.* 1872. [f. SPHEN(O)- + OTIC *a.*] *Zool.* A. *adj.* Of or pertaining to, formed by combination of, the sphenoid bone and otic structures in certain fishes and in birds 1884. B. *sb.* The sphenotic bone or ossification 1872.

Spheral (sfī·răl), *a.* 1571. [ad. late L. *spher-*, *sphæralis*, f. *sphæra* SPHERE *sb.*; see -AL 1.] 1. Of or pertaining to a sphere or round body; having the rounded form of a sphere; spherical. b. *fig.* Symmetrically rounded or perfect 1841. 2. Of or pertaining to the cosmic spheres or the heavenly bodies 1829.

1. b. There is somewhat s. and infinite..in every genius EMERSON. 2. As the Ancients fabled of the S. Music CARLYLE.

Sphere (sfīəɹ), *sb.* ME. [orig. *sper(e*, ad. OF. *espere*; later *sphere* (mod.F. *sphère*), ad. late L. *sphera*, earlier *sphæra*, ad. Gr. σφαῖρα ball.] I. 1. The apparent outward limit of space, conceived as a hollow globe enclosing (and at all points equidistant from) the earth; the visible vault of heaven, in which the celestial bodies appear to have their place. b. A globe or other construction illustrating the place and motions of the celestial bodies. late ME. 2. One or other of the concentric, transparent, hollow globes imagined by the older astronomers as revolving round the earth and respectively carrying with them the several heavenly bodies (moon, sun, planets, and fixed stars). late ME. b. In ref. to the harmonious sound supposed to be produced by the motion of these spheres. late ME. c. A place of abode different from the present earth or world; a heaven 1592. 3. One or other of the concentric globes formerly supposed to be formed by the four elements, earth, water, air, and fire. Now *Hist.* late ME. 4. With possess. pron. or genitive: The particular sphere (in sense 2) appropriate to, or occupied by, each of the planets (or the fixed stars). late ME. 5. A place, position, or station in society; an aggregate of persons of a certain rank or standing 1601. b. The group of persons with whom one is directly in contact in society 1839. 6. A province or domain in which one's activities or faculties find scope or exercise, or within which they are naturally confined; range or compass of action or study 1606. 7. The whole province, domain, or range *of* some quality or activity 1602.

1. Sweet Echo,..Sweet Queen of Parly, Daughter of the Sphear MILT. *fig.* God is our circumambient S. KEN. *Oblique, parallel, right s.*: see OBLIQUE *a.* 2 b, PARALLEL *a.* 1 b, RIGHT *a.* I. 3. b. *Armillary s.*: see ARMILLARY. 2. b. His voyce was propertied As all the tuned Spheres SHAKS. 3. The principle that each element seeks its own place, led to the doctrine, that, the place of fire being the highest, there is, above the air, a s. of fire 1837. 4. Certaine starres shot madly from their Spheares SHAKS. 5. The young lady,.. seemed to have dropped amongst them from another s. of life SCOTT. 6. A village is..too narrow a s. for him 1776. 7. In this course, he came within the s. of the trade wind 1777. The s. of architecture proper RUSKIN. Phr. *S. of action, influence*, or *interest*, a region or territory within which a particular nation is admitted to have a special interest for political and economic purposes; also *ellipt.*

II. 1. *Geom.* A figure formed by the complete revolution of a semicircle about its diameter; a round body of which the surface is at all points equidistant from the centre. late ME. 2. A body of a globular or orbicular form; a globe or ball. late ME. b. The rounded mass *of* such a body 1555. 3. †a. = GLOBE *sb.* 4. -1548. b. An orb of the mundane system; a planet or star 1598.

2. Of Celestial Bodies first the Sun A mightie Spheare he fram'd MILT. b. Until the flat surface is nearly equal to the diameter of the s. of the ball 1858.

Sphere (sfīəɹ), *v.* Chiefly *poet.* 1605. [f. prec.] 1. *trans.* To enclose in or as in a sphere; to encircle, engirdle 1607. 2. To make into a sphere; to fill up or 'crown' *with* liquor 1605. b. *fig.* To form into a rounded or perfect whole 1615. 3. To place in a sphere or among the spheres; to set in the heavens 1606. b. *fig.* To set aloft or aloof 1615. 4. To send *about* in a circle; to turn *round* in all directions 1648.

1. Spreading all our reaches As if each private arm would s. the earth CHAPMAN. 2. An urn sphered with wine B. JONS. 3. Therefore is the glorious Planet Sol In noble eminence, enthron'd and spear'd Amid'st the other SHAKS. b. Maiestie should be spear'd Beyond the common Eye 1649.

Sphereless (sfī·əɹlès), *a.* 1819. [f. SPHERE *sb.* + -LESS.] a. Having no proper sphere; wandering. b. Starless.

Spheric (sfe·rik), *a.* and *sb.* 1559. [ad. late L. *spher-*, *sphæricus*, ad. Gr. σφαιρικός, f. σφαῖρα SPHERE *sb.*] A. *adj.* 1. Of or relating to the sphere as a geometrical figure. 2. = next 1. 1610. 3. Of, pertaining to, or connected with, the spheres or heavenly bodies 1648.

1. Cutting the Equinoctiall at right Spherick Angles 1594. 3. We shall leap up..To join the s. company MRS. BROWNING.

B. *sb.* (Chiefly *pl.*) The mathematical study or science of the sphere; spherical geometry and trigonometry 1660.

Spherical (sfe·rikăl), *a.* 1523. [f. as prec.; see -ICAL.] 1. Having the form of a sphere (or a segment of a sphere); globular. b. Of form or figure: Characteristic of a sphere 1527. 2. *Math.* a. Of lines or figures: Drawn in, or on the surface of, a sphere; esp. *s. triangle* 1571. b. Dealing with the properties of the sphere or spherical figures 1728. c. Of or pertaining to, characteristic of, or arising from the sphere or its properties 1840. 3. Of or pertaining to the celestial spheres 1605.

1. †*S. number*, a number whose powers always terminate in the same digit as the number itself, viz 5, 6, and 10. 2. c. *S. aberration, excess, harmonic, inversion*, etc.: see the sbs. 3. As if we were..Knaues, Theeues, and Treachers by Sphericall predominance SHAKS. Hence **Spherica·lity**, the quality of being s. **Sphe·rical·ly** *adv.*, -ness (*rare*).

Sphericity (sferi·sĭti). 1625. [ad. mod.L. *spher-*, *sphæricitas*; see SPHERIC *a.* and -ITY.] The quality of being spherical or having the form of a sphere.

The S. of the drops of Rain 1719.

Spherico- (sfe·riko), used as comb. form of SPHERIC *a.*, as in *s.-cylindrical, -tetrahedral, -triangular* adjs.

Spheriform (sfī·rifǭɹm), *a.* 1678. [See SPHERE *sb.* and -FORM.] = SPHERICAL *a.* 1.

Sphero- (sfī·*ro*), var. of SPHÆRO-, used as comb. form of SPHERE *sb.*, as in **Spheroco·nic** *Math.*, the section of a sphere by a quadric cone having its vertex at the centre of the sphere. **Sphe·rograph** *Naut.*, a device serving to facilitate the calculation of spherical problems. **Spheroma·niac**, one who is passionately fond of playing at ball-games, esp. bowls.

Spheroid (sfī·roid), *sb.* and *a.* 1664. [ad. L. *sphæroides*, ad. Gr. σφαιροειδής, f. σφαῖρα ball; see -OID.] A. *sb.* A body approaching in shape to a sphere, *esp.* one formed by the revolution of an ellipse about one of its axes. B. *adj.* = next 1767.

Spheroidal (sfĭroi·dăl, sfe-), *a.* 1781. [f. SPHEROID *sb.* + -AL 1.] 1. Of form, figure, etc.: Approximately spherical. 2. Having the form of a spheroid 1798. 3. Dealing with the properties of spheroids 1876.

1. *S. condition* or *state*, the condition in which a liquid, as water, assumes drops of a s. form on being placed on a highly-heated surface, the drops being supported by a thin badly-conducting layer of vapour. 3. S. Trigonometry 1876. Hence **Spheroi·dally** *adv.* after a s. manner so as to form spheroids.

Spheroidical (sfĭroi·dikăl, sfe-), *a.* 1698. [f. SPHEROID *sb.* + -ICAL.] = prec. 1, 2. Hence **Spheroi·dically** *adv.* **Sphe·roidi·city**, the state or character of being spheroidal.

Spherometer (sfĭrǫ·mĭtəɹ, sfe-). 1827. [ad. F. *sphéromètre*; see SPHERO- and -METER.] An instrument for measuring the sphericality or curvature of bodies or surfaces.

Spherule (sfe·riul). 1665. [ad. L. *spher-*, *sphærula*, dim. of *sphæra* SPHERE *sb.*] A little sphere; a small or minute spherical body. Hence **Sphe·rular** *a.* having the form of a s.

Spherulite (sfe·riŭləit). 1823. [f. L. *sphærula* SPHERULE + -ITE[1] 2 a and 2 b.] **1.** *Min.* A concretionary substance found in small spherular masses in certain rocks. **b.** A spherular concretion of this nature 1863. **2.** *Palæont.* A genus of fossil molluscs 1834.

Spherulitic (sferiŭli·tik), *a.* 1833. [f. prec. + -IC.] *Geol.* and *Min.* **1.** Of rocks, etc.: Containing, or composed of, spherulites. **2.** Pertaining to or characteristic of spherulites 1878.

Sphery (sfīə·ri), *a.* 1590. [f. SPHERE *sb.*] **1.** Of or pertaining to, connected with, the spheres or heavenly bodies; sphere-like. **2.** Having the form of a sphere 1600.

1. Hermias s. eyne SHAKS. Love vertue,..She can teach ye how to clime Higher then the Spheary chime MILT.

‖ **Sphex** (sfeks). *Pl.* **spheges** (sfī·dʒīz). 1797. [a. Gr. σφήξ (pl. σφῆκες) wasp.] *Entom.* A genus of digger-wasps; a wasp of this genus.

Sphincter (sfi·ŋktəɪ). 1578. [a. L. *sphincter*, ad. Gr. σφιγκτήρ band, contractile muscle, f. σφίγγειν to bind tight.] *Anat.* A contractile muscular ring by which an orifice of the body (in man or animals) is normally kept closed. **b.** *attrib.*, as *s.-fibre*, *-muscle*, *-power* 1615.

The Fibres that compose the S. of the Bladder 1691. Hence **Sphincte·ric** *a.* of or pertaining to, of the nature of, a s.

Sphinx (sfiŋks). *Pl.* **sphinges** (sfi·ndʒīz), **sphinxes.** late ME. [a. L. *Sphinx*, a. Gr. Σφίγξ (stem Σφιγγ-), app. f. σφίγγειν to draw tight. In generalized senses usu. with small initial; otherwise with capital S.] **1.** *Gr. Myth.* A hybrid monster, usually described as having the head of a woman and the (winged) body of a lion, which infested Thebes until the riddle it propounded was solved by Œdipus; also, any monster of a similar form and character. **b.** *transf.* One who propounds or presents a difficult question or problem 1603. **c.** *fig.* A thing or subject of an inscrutable or mysterious nature 1610. **2.** A sculptured, carved, or moulded figure of an imaginary creature having a human head and breast combined with the body of a lion 1579. **b.** *spec.* The colossal stone image of this kind near the pyramids of El-Gizeh in Egypt 1613. **3.** A kind of ape; in mod. use, a sphinx-baboon 1607. **4.** An insect belonging to the lepidopterous genus *Sphinx* or to the family represented by this, so called from the attitude frequently assumed by the caterpillar 1753.

1. Subtill as S., as sweet and musicall, As bright Apollos Lute SHAKS. **b.** Mr. Dodson has for many years been a political s. 1884. **2.** He had a S. of Yvory geven him by Verres NORTH.

attrib. and *Comb.*, as *s.-enigma*, *-form*, *-question*, etc.; *s.-like* adj.; **s.-baboon**, the Guinea baboon (*Cynocephalus* or *Papio Sphinx*); **-moth** = sense 4.

Sphragistic (sfrădʒi·stik), *sb.* and *a.* 1836. [ad. F. *sphragistique* or Gr. σφραγιστικός, f. σφραγίς seal.] **A.** *sb. pl.* The scientific study or knowledge of seals or signet rings. **B.** *adj.* Of or pertaining to, relating to or dealing with, seals or signet rings 1884.

Sphygmic (sfi·gmik), *a.* 1707. [ad. mod. L. *sphygmicus*, Gr. σφυγμικός, f. σφυγμός.] Of or pertaining to the pulse. Also *sb. pl.*

Sphygmo- (sfi·gmo), a. Gr. σφυγμο-, comb. form of σφυγμός pulse.

Sphy·gmogram, a diagram of pulse-beats as traced by the sphygmograph. **Sphy·gmograph**, an instrument which records the movements of the pulse by means of tracings; hence **Sphy·gmograph** *vb.* **Sphygmogra·phic** *a.*, of or pertaining to, effected or produced by, the sphygmograph. **Sphygmo·graphy**, the scientific description of the pulse or registration of pulse-beats. **Sphy·gmomano·meter**, **Sphygmo·meter**, an instrument for measuring the force or rate of the pulse. **Sphygmome·tric** *a.*, relating to the measurement of the pulse. **Sphy·gmophone**, an instrument by which pulsations are rendered audible. **Sphy·gmoscope**, an instrument for examining the pulse.

‖ **Sphyræna** (sfəirī·nă). 1849. [mod.L., a. L., ad. Gr. σφύραινα, f. σφῦρα hammer.] *Zool.* A pike-like fish belonging to the genus *Sphyræna* or the family represented by this; one of the common species is the barracuda. Hence **Sphyræ·noid** *a.* related to or resembling the genus *S.*; *sb.* a fish of this kind.

†**Spi·al.** late ME. [Aphetic f. ESPIAL.] **1.** Spying; observation, watch -1611. **2.** A spy, scout -1837.

‖ **Spica** (spəi·kă). late ME. [L. = ear of grain, etc. In senses 3 and 4 after Gr. στάχυς.] †**1.** *Oil of s.*, oil of spike. -late ME. **2.** *Bot.* A flower-spike 1693. **3.** *Astr.* A bright star in the constellation Virgo 1728. **4.** *Surg.* A form of bandage, the arrangement of which is suggestive of an ear of wheat or barley 1731.

Spicate (spəi·kĕt), *a.* 1668. [ad. L. *spicatus* furnished with spikes, pointed, f. *spica* SPIKE *sb.*[1]] *Bot.* and *Zool.* Having the form of a spike; arranged in a spike. So **Spi·cated** *a.* having the form of a spike; furnished with spikelets 1661.

Spice (spəis), *sb.* ME. [ad. OF. *espice* (mod.F. *épice*), ad. L. *species* SPECIES.] **1.** One or other of various strongly flavoured or aromatic substances of vegetable origin, obtained from tropical plants, commonly used as condiments, etc. **b.** An odour or perfume arising from, or resembling that of, spices 1560. **2.** Without article, as a substance or in collective sense ME. †**3.** A sort, kind, or species -1601. **4.** A slight touch or trace, a dash, *of* something 1479.

1. Let our Merchants answer, which owe their Spices to Arabia 1625. *fig.* Variety 's the very s. of life, That gives it all its flavour COWPER. **b.** The woodbine spices are wafted abroad TENNYSON. **2.** A man all vertue, like a pye all s., will not please 1694. **3.** The spices of penitence ben thre CHAUCER. **4.** The horse..had a considerable s. of devil in his composition 1835.

attrib. and *Comb.*, as *s.-bag*, *-bread*, *-merchant*, etc.; **s.-bush** *U.S.*, wild allspice, fever-bush (*Benzoin odoriferum*); **-islands**, the islands in the East from which spices were imported; **-nut**, a gingerbread nut; **-tree**, a s.-bearing tree; **-wood**, (*a*) *U.S.*, the s.-bush; (*b*) wood of s.-bearing shrubs.

Spice (spəis), *v.* late ME. [ad. OF. *espicer* (mod.F. *épicer*), f. *espice* SPICE *sb.*; or from the sb.] **1.** *trans.* To prepare or season (food, etc.) with a spice or spices. **b.** *fig.* To season, to affect the character or quality of, by means of some addition or modification. Usu. const. *with.* 1529. **2.** †**a.** To embalm, to preserve with spices -1598. †**b.** To perfume with or as with spices -1648. **c.** To dose (a horse) with spice in order to mislead the buyer 1841.

1. Consume the flesh, and s. it well, and let the bones be burnt *Ezek.* xxiv. 10. **b.** O, why should Love..S. his fair banquet with the dust of death? TENNYSON. Hence **Spi·cer**[2], one who seasons with s.

Spi·ce-box. 1527. [SPICE *sb.*] **1.** A box having several compartments, to keep spices in. **2.** A small decorated box, usually of Oriental workmanship 1880.

Spi·ce-cake. 1530. [SPICE *sb.*] A cake seasoned with spice; *dial.* a rich fruit cake.

Spiced (spəist), *ppl. a.* ME. [f. SPICE *sb.* or *v.*] **1.** Seasoned or flavoured with spice or spices; cured with spices. †**2.** Of conscience, etc.: Nice, dainty, delicate; over scrupulous -1631. **3.** Fragrant, aromatic; spice-laden 1590.

1. Carmela seeing her brother refuse his spicete drinke, thought all was not well 1589. **3.** In the s. Indian aire SHAKS.

†**Spi·cer**[1]. ME. [ad. OF. *espicier* (mod.F. *épicier*), f. *espice* SPICE *sb.*] A dealer in spices; an apothecary or druggist -1609.

Spicery (spəi·səri). ME. [ad. OF. *espicerie* (mod.F. *épicerie*), f. *espice* SPICE *sb.*] **1.** *collect. sing.* or *pl.* Spices. **2. a.** The department of the royal household connected with the keeping of spices; esp. in *Clerk of the S.* Now *Hist.* late ME. **b.** A room or part of a house set apart for the keeping of spices. Now *Hist.* 1536.

1. While on the veined pavement lie The honied things and s. MORRIS.

Spici- (spəisi), comb. form of L. *spica* ear of corn, SPIKE *sb.*[1], as in **Spici·ferous** *a.* [L. *spicifer*], bearing ears of corn. **Spi·ciform** *a.*, having the form of a (flower-) spike. **Spi·cilege**, ‖ **Spicile·gium** [L. *spicilegium*], a gleaning; a collection or anthology.

Spick(-)and(-)span, *a.*, *sb.*, and *adv.* 1665. [Shortening of next.] **A.** *adj.* Particularly neat, trim, or smart; suggestive of something quite new or unaffected by wear.

1. New spicke and span white shoes PEPYS. A dog-cart,..driven by a spick-and-span groom 1886.

B. *sb.* That which is quite new or particularly trim and smart 1758. **C.** *adv.* In a spick and span manner 1815. Hence **Spick-span** *a.*

Spick(-)and(-)span new. Also †**speck-.** 1579. [Emphatic extension of SPAN-NEW.] Absolutely or perfectly new; brand-new; perfectly fresh or unworn.

Spicket (spi·kėt). late ME. Now *dial.* and *U.S.* = SPIGOT *sb.*

†**Spi·cous**, *a.* 1658. [f. L. *spica* spike.] *Bot.* Spicate; spiky, pointed -1775.

‖ **Spicula** (spi·kiŭlă). *Pl.* **-læ** (-lī). 1747. [mod.L., dim. of L. *spica*; cf. SPICULUM.] **1.** A sharp-pointed or acicular crystal or similar formation. **2.** A small sharp-pointed process on some part of a plant or animal; a prickle 1753. **3.** *Bot.* A floral spikelet (*rare*) 1760. **4.** A slender pointed fragment *of* bone, etc. 1835. **5.** = SPICULUM 3. 1845. Hence **Spi·cular** *a.* of the nature of a spicule or s.; slender and sharp-pointed; also, characterized by the presence of spicules.

Spiculate (spi·kiŭlĕt), *a.* 1832. [ad. L. *spiculatus*, f. SPICULUM.] *Bot.* Covered with spicules; composed of several spicules crowded together.

Spiculated (spi·kiŭlēted), *a.* 1738. [f. as prec. + -ED[1].] **1.** Containing spiculæ -1794. **2.** Having the form of a spicula; slender and sharp-pointed 1744. **3.** Furnished with sharp points or spikelets 1762.

Spicule (spi·kiul). 1785. [a. F.] **1.** *Bot.* A floral spikelet. **2.** One or other of the points of the basidia or sporophores in fungals 1843. **3.** = SPICULUM 3. 1846. **4.** *Zool.* A needle-like or sharp-pointed process or part 1861. **5.** A fine-pointed piece, splinter, or fragment of some hard substance; a spicula or spiculum 1878.

Spiculi- (spi·kiŭli), comb. form, after L. models, of SPICULA, SPICULE, and SPICULUM, occurring in a few *Zool.* terms, as **Spiculi·ferous** *a.*, bearing spicules. **Spi·culiform** *a.*, formed like a spicule; sharp-pointed. **Spiculi·genous** *a.*, containing spicules.

‖ **Spiculum** (spi·kiŭlŏm). *Pl.* **-la.** 1746. [L., dim. of *spica* SPIKE *sb.*] **1.** = SPICULA 1. **2.** *Zool.* A sharp-pointed process or formation 1762. **b.** The excitatory dart in snails 1838. **3.** One of the calcareous or siliceous needles found in sponges. Usu. in *pl.* 1842. **4.** = SPICULA 4. 1872.

Spicy (spəi·si), *a.* 1562. [f. SPICE *sb.*] **1.** Having the characteristic qualities of spice; of the nature of spice. **b.** Flavoured or mixed with spice 1632. **2.** Having the fragrance of spice; sweet-scented, aromatic 1650. **3.** Containing or producing, abounding in, spices 1648. **b.** Consisting of spice; conveying spice 1712. **4.** Of qualities: Appropriate to, or characteristic of, spices 1652. **5.** *slang.* **a.** Full of spirit, smartness, or 'go' 1828. **b.** Smart-looking; neat 1846. **6.** Of writing or discourse: Smart and pointed; having a flavour of the sensational or scandalous; somewhat improper 1844.

1. Whence Merchants bring Thir spicie Drugs MILT. **b.** The S. Nut-brown Ale MILT. **2.** Led by new stars, and borne by s. gales! POPE. The s. myrtle sent forth all its fragrance 1797. **3.** The spicie shoare Of Arabie the blest MILT. **b.** The s. traffick of the East 1712. **5. a.** A remarkably s. team 1828. **b.** *advb.* That young Tom! He've come to town dressed that s. MEREDITH. **6.** The articles were so clever, and so very 's.' 1844. Hence **Spi·cily** *adv.* **Spi·ciness.**

Spider (spəi·dəɪ). [OE. *spīþre* :—**spin-þre*, f. *spinnan* SPIN *v.*] **1.** One or other of the arachnids belonging to the insectivorous order *Araneidæ*, many species of which possess the power of spinning webs in which their prey is caught.

The cunning, skill, and industry of the spider, as well as its power of secreting or emitting poison, are frequently alluded to in literature.

b. Applied to persons as an opprobrious or vituperative term 1568. **2.** Applied to other allied species of *Arachnida* resembling spiders in appearance; esp. the harvest-spider; the spider-mite. See also RED *spider*, SEA SPIDER. 1665. **3.** A kind of frying-pan having legs and a long handle; also loosely, a frying-pan. Orig. *U.S.* 1830. **b.** *U.S.* A trivet or tripod; a griddle 1875. **4.** *Naut.* An iron outrigger to keep blocks clear of the ship's side. Cf. *s.-hoop*. 1860. 5. *techn.* One or other of various parts or pieces of machinery, *esp.* one consisting of a framework or metal casting with radiating arms or spokes suggestive of the legs of a spider 1875. 6. A lightly-built cart, trap, or phaeton with a high body and disproportionately large and slender wheels. Orig. *S. Afr.* 1879. 7. Short for *s.-cell, -rest, -table* 1893.

Comb.: **s.-cell,** (*a*) *Biol.* a bacillus having the appearance of a s.; (*b*) *Anat.* one of the characteristic cells of the neuroglia, having numerous delicate processes resembling the legs of a s.; **-hoop** *Naut.*, a hoop passing round a mast in order to secure the shackles to which the futtock-shrouds are attached; **-rest,** a billiard-rest with legs of sufficient length to allow of its being placed over a ball without touching it; **-shanks,** a person having long thin legs; **-table,** a slightly-constructed occasional table with s.-like legs; **-work,** work having the characteristics or appearance of a spider's web.

b. In the names of beasts, insects, birds, etc. which bear some resemblance to or are associated with spiders: **s.-ant,** an insect of the genus *Mutillæ*; **-fly,** a pupiparous dipterous insect, as a bee-louse, bat-louse, sheep-tick, etc.; **-hunter,** = next 2 (*b*); **-mite,** (*a*) a parasitic mite of the family *Ganasidæ*; (*b*) a small mite injurious to plants; **-shell,** any shell of the genus *Pteroceras*; a scorpion-shell. Hence **Spi·dered** *a.* infested by spiders, cobwebbed.

Spi·der-ca:tcher. 1579. [SPIDER *sb.*] 1. One who catches spiders. Chiefly *fig.*, and freq. as a vague term of abuse (*obs.*). 2. One or other of certain birds which catch or eat spiders, as (*a*) the wall-creeper; (*b*) any East Indian sunbird of the genus *Arachnothera* 1668.

Spi·der-crab. 1710. [SPIDER *sb.*] One or other of several crabs belonging to the group *Oxyrhyncha*, esp. to the family *Maioidea*, and characterized by their long slender legs and spider-like appearance; a maia or maioid crab.

Spi·der-leg. 1760. [SPIDER *sb.*] 1. A thin long leg like that of a spider. 2. *transf.* A long irregular marking, crack, etc., resembling in shape the leg of a spider. Also *attrib.* in *s. gold.* 1873.

Spi·der-like, *adv.* and *a.* 1604. [f. SPIDER *sb.*] A. *adv.* In or after the manner of a spider; with the power or faculty (real or supposed) of a spider. B. *adj.* Like or resembling a spider or that of a spider; spidery 1653.

Spi·der-line. Also **spider's line.** 1829. [SPIDER *sb.*] One of the threads or filaments of spider-web used to form the reticle of various optical instruments, esp. of micrometers, and serving to obtain minute measurements; also loosely, any slender thread or wire used for this purpose.

Spi·der(-)mo:nkey. 1764. [SPIDER *sb.*] One or other of the monkeys belonging to the South and Central American genus *Ateles*, characterized by their long spider-like limbs and prehensile tail.

Spi·der-web. Also **spider's web.** 1535. 1. A cobweb. 2. *transf.* and *fig.* Something resembling a cobweb in nature or appearance 1700.

1. His confidence shalbe destroyed, for he trusteth in a spyders webbe COVERDALE *Job* viii. 14.

Spi·derwort. 1597. †1. One or other plant of the liliaceous genus *Anthericum* (earlier *Phalangium*) –1763. 2. Any plant belonging to the genus *Tradescantia*, or (later) to the family *Commelynaceæ*, which includes this genus 1629.

Spidery (spəi·dəri), *a.* 1837. [f. SPIDER *sb.* + -Y [1].] 1. Like a spider in appearance or form. 2. Of legs or arms: Resembling those of a spider; long and thin 1845. b. Suggestive of the appearance of a spider with long and thin legs 1862. c. Like a spider-web in formation 1860. 3. Suggestive of that of a spider, in respect of entanglement, cunning, etc. 1843. 4. Infested by spiders 1889.

1. That hideous s. crustacean, the crab 1881. 2. b. The marchesa wrote..in her long s. characters 1862.

‖ **Spiegeleisen** (ʃpī·gəl,əi:zən). 1868. [G., f. *spiegel* mirror + *eisen* iron.] A crystalline and lustrous variety of white manganiferous cast-iron much used in the Bessemer process for the manufacture of steel. So (semi-translated) **Spiegel iron.**

Spiffing (spi·fiŋ), *a.* *colloq.* and *dial.* 1872. [Cf. next and *ripping, topping.*] Excellent, first-rate, very good. Also as *adv.*

Spiffy (spi·fi), *a.* *colloq.* and *dial.* 1860. [Origin obsc.] Smart, spruce.

Spif(f)licate (spi·flikeit), *v.* *joc.* or *colloq.* 1785. [prob. fanciful.] *trans.* To treat or handle roughly or severely; to crush, destroy. Hence **Spiflica·tion,** complete destruction.

Spignel (spi·gnĕl). 1502. [Origin obsc.] †1. The aromatic root of the umbelliferous plant *Meum athamanticum*, used, when dried and ground, in medicine as a carminative or stimulant, or as a spice in cookery –1718. 2. The plant itself; meum; baldmoney 1548.

Spigot (spi·gɵ̆t), *sb.* late ME. [prob. ad. Prov. *espigot, f. *espiga* SPIKE *sb.*[1]] 1. A small wooden peg or pin used to stop the vent-hole of a barrel or cask; a vent-peg; a similar peg inserted into the opening or tube of a faucet and used to regulate the flow of liquor. b. *fig.* That which controls, lets out, or restrains 1780. †2. A faucet –1725. 3. A plain end of a pipe entering an enlargement of another as a means of forming a joint. Chiefly in attrib. phrases, as *s. and faucet joint*, etc. 1797. 4. *attrib.*, as **s.-joint,** a spigot and faucet joint 1611.

1. b. Something which he called the rudder of Government, but which was rather the s. of Taxation CARLYLE. Hence **Spi·got** *v. trans.* to thrust a s. into.

Spike (spəik), *sb.*[1] late ME. [ad. L. *spica* ear of corn, plant-spike.] 1. An ear of grain. Chiefly *poet.* b. Astr. *The Virgin's s.* [tr. L. *spica Virginis*], = SPICA 3. 1559. 2. *Bot.* A form of inflorescence consisting of sessile flowers borne on an elongated simple axis 1578. †3. French lavender (*Lavandula Spica*) –1712.

3. *Oil of s.*, an essential oil obtained by distillation from *Lavandula Spica* (and *L. Stœchas*), employed in painting and in veterinary medicine 1577.

attrib. and *Comb.*, as *s. corn, -lavender, -stalk*; **s.-grass,** *Uniola paniculata*; **-oil,** = *oil of s.*; **-rush,** any sedge of the genus *Eliocharis.*

Spike (spəik), *sb.*[2] ME. [ult. f. L. *spica* SPIKE *sb.*[1], perh. through Sw. and Norw. *spik* nail.] 1. A sharp-pointed piece of metal (esp. iron) or wood used for fastening things together; a large and strong kind of nail. b. A pointed piece of steel used for driving into the touch-hole of a cannon in order to render it unserviceable 1617. 2. A sharp-pointed piece of metal (or other hard material) which is, or may be, so fixed in something that the point is turned outwards; a stout sharp-pointed projecting part of a metal object 1470. b. *transf.* A stiff sharp-pointed object or part 1718. c. [back-formation f. SPIKY *a.*[2] 2 b.] A 'spiky' churchman or churchwoman 1902.

2. b. Then shot up on high A steady s. of light MORRIS.

attrib. and *Comb.*, as *s. bit, gimlet, rod*; **s.-buck** *U.S.*, a buck in its first year; **-fish** *U.S.*, the sail-fish (*Histiophorus americanus*); **-tail** *U.S.*, a dress-coat; **-team** *U.S.*, a waggon drawn by three animals, arranged as one leader and two wheelers. Hence **Spi·kelet**[2] a small s. or spike-shaped object; a prickle or thorn.

Spike (spəik), *v.*[1] 1624. [f. prec.] 1. *trans.* With *up.* a. To fasten or close firmly with spikes or strong nails. †b. *spec.* = sense 2. –1799. 2. To render (a gun) unserviceable by driving a spike into the touch-hole; also, to block or fill up (the touch-hole) with a spike 1687. 3. To fix or secure by long nails or spikes 1703. 4. To provide, fit, or stud with spikes 1716. 5. To pierce with, or as with, a spike 1687.

2. *fig.* All the batteries of noise are spiked 1871.

Spike (spəik), *v.*[2] 1711. [f. SPIKE *sb.*[1] 2.] *intr.* Of plants: To form a spike or spikes of flowers. Also with *up.*

Spiked (spəikt), *a.*[1] 1597. [f. SPIKE *sb.*[1]] Of plants: Having an inflorescence in the form of a spike; bearing ears, as grain.

Spiked (spəikt), *a.*[2] 1681. [f. SPIKE *sb.*[2]] Provided with spikes or sharp points.

Spikelet[1] (spəi·klĕt). 1793. [f. SPIKE *sb.*[1]] *Bot.* 1. A small group of florets in grasses, forming part of the spike. 2. A subdivision of an ear of grain 1860.

Spi·ke-nail. ME. [f. SPIKE *sb.*[2]] A large and strong nail, now *spec.* one upwards of three (or four) inches in length, with a small head.

Spikenard (spəi·knaɹd). ME. [ad. late or med.L. *spica nardi* (see SPIKE *sb.*[1] and NARD *sb.*), rendering Gr. νάρδου στάχυς; perh. partly after OF. *spicanarde* fem., *spica-, spiquenard* masc.] 1. An aromatic substance (employed in ancient times in the preparation of a costly ointment or oil) obtained from an Eastern plant, now identified as the *Nardostachys Jatamansi* of Northern India. 2. The plant yielding this substance 1548. 3. With defining term, applied to other fragrant plants, as American S., *Aralia racemosa*, Ploughman's S., *Inula Conyza.* 1597. 4. *Oil of s.*, a name given to various fragrant oils 1565.

Spiky (spəi·ki), *a.*[1] 1578. [f. SPIKE *sb.*[1]] Having the form of a flower-spike; characterized by the production of spikes or ears.

Spiky (spəi·ki), *a.*[2] 1720. [f. SPIKE *sb.*[2]] 1. Fitted with a spike or spikes; having sharp projecting points. 2. Having the form of a spike or spikes; stiff and sharp-pointed 1742. b. *fig.* Extremely sharp or aggressive; (*slang*) extreme and uncompromising in Anglo-Catholic belief or practice 1881.

1. The s. Wheels thro' Heaps of Carnage tore; And thick the groaning Axles dropp'd with Gore POPE. 2. A dozen s. thorns sticking into him 1894.

Spile (spəil), *sb.*[1] 1513. [a. MDu., MLG. *spile* splinter, wooden pin or peg, skewer.] 1. *north.* and †*Sc.* A splinter, chip, or narrow strip, of wood; a spill. 2. A small plug of wood for stopping the vent of a cask; a vent-peg; a spigot. Chiefly *dial.* 1707. b. *U.S.* A small wooden or metal spout for conducting sap from the sugar-maple 1875.

Spile (spəil), *sb.*[2] 1513. [app. an alteration of PILE *sb.*[1]] = PILE *sb.*[1] 3. b. *Mining.* A sharp-pointed post used in sinking by means of cribs 1841. Hence **Spile** *v.*[2] *trans.* = PILE *v.*[1] 1.

Spile (spəil), *v.*[1] 1691. [f. SPILE *sb.*[1]] 1. *trans.* To stop up (a hole) by means of a spile. Also with *up.* 2. To draw (liquid) from a cask by spiling or broaching. Now *dial.* 1772. 3. To provide (a cask, tree, etc.) with a spile, in order to draw off liquid. Now *dial.* or *U.S.* 1832.

Spiling (spəi·liŋ), *vbl. sb.* 1841. [Origin obscure.] *Naut. pl.* The dimensions of the curve or sny of a plank's edge 1846.

Spill (spil), *sb.*[1] ME. [Origin obsc.; related to SPILE *sb.*[1]] 1. A splinter; a sharp-pointed fragment of wood, bone, etc.; a slip or sliver. 2. A thin slip of wood, a folded or twisted piece of paper, used for lighting a candle, pipe, etc. 1839. 3. A small peg or pin for stopping a hole 1875.

Spill (spil), *sb.*[2] 1594. [app. a. Du. *spil* or LG. *spille* spindle, axis, stalk, perh. for original **spinla*, f. *spin-* SPIN *v.*] †1. A spool –1615. 2. A rod or stalk of wood, metal, etc. 1594. 3. A pin or slender rod on which anything turns; a spindle 1730.

Spill (spil), *sb.*[3] 1845. [f. SPILL *v.*] 1. A throw from a horse or vehicle; a fall or tumble; an upset. 2. A downpouring or dropping of liquid; a quantity spilled 1848.

Spill (spil), *v.* Pa. t. and pple. **spilled** (spild); **spilt.** [OE. *spillan*, = MDu., Du. *spillen.*] I. 1. *trans.* To destroy by depriving of life; to put (or bring) to death; to slay or kill. Now *arch.* †b. *absol.* To cause death; freq. contrasted with *save, spare*, etc. –1627. 2. To destroy or put an end to (life). Now *arch.* OE. †3. To destroy, ruin, or overthrow (a person); to bring to ruin or misery –1642. †4. To wreck, destroy, or devastate; to spoil or ruin by demolition, etc. –1623. 5. To spoil by injuring or damaging in some way; to render imperfect or useless; to destroy the goodness or value of (a thing). Now *dial.* ME. †6. To waste by scattering, squandering, or misusing; to employ or expend wastefully –1786. †7. *intr.* To perish; to be destroyed or lost –1592. 8. To fall off or decline in respect of good qualities; to degenerate or deteriorate; to spoil. *Obs.* exc. *dial.* ME.

1. Caring no more in their fury to s. a man, then to kill a dogge 1612. 2. You must carry your body steadily, or else s. your life 1668. 3. *Haml.* IV. v. 20.

II. 1. *trans.* To shed (blood) ME. 2. To allow or cause (a liquid) to fall, pour, or run out (esp. over the edge of the containing vessel), usually in an accidental or wasteful manner; to lose or waste in this way ME. **3.** To scatter, esp. by emptying from some receptacle or the like; to disperse ME. **b.** *To s. the beans, s. it*: to reveal or divulge something. *U.S. slang.* 1919. **4.** *Naut.* To empty (the belly of a sail) of wind in order that it may be reefed or furled more easily 1625. **b.** To discharge (wind) from a sail 1875. **5.** *colloq.* To cause to fall from a horse or vehicle; to throw or throw out. So in other contexts. 1731. **6.** *intr.* To flow or run over the brim or side; to escape or be wasted in this manner 1655. **b.** *Naut.* To become void of wind 1762. **7.** *trans.* To divulge (*U.S. slang*) 1920.

1. The red life spilt for a private blow TENNYSON. 2. Their arguments are as fluxive as liquor spilt upon a table B. JONS. 3. As ruthless Winds the tender Blossoms s. 1710. 4. b. *Spilling-line*, a line to s. the wind out of a sail, by keeping it from bellying out when clewed up 1875. 5. I..call'd to the Coachman, Pray, Friend, don't s. us SWIFT. 6. The Mettal may s. or slabber over the Mouth of..the Mold 1683.

Spill- (spil), the stem of SPILL *v.* in comb., *esp.* in the sense 'constructed for (or by) the passage of surplus water, for receiving overflow liquid, etc.', as *s.-box, channel, -trough, -way.*

Spiller[1] (spi·ləɹ). 1530. [f. SPILL *v.* + -ER[1].] One who sheds or spills; *esp.* a shedder of blood.

Spiller[2] *arch.* 1576. [Altered f. *espeler* (1486).] A branchlet of a deer's horn.

Spiller[3] (spi·ləɹ). Chiefly *Cornish dial., Ir.,* and *Amer.* Also -(i)ard. 1602. [Origin obsc.] A long fishing-line provided with a number of hooks; a trawl-line. So **Spi·llet.**

Spillikin (spi·likin), **spellican** (spe·likăn). 1734. [app. dim. of SPILL *sb.*[1]] **1.** *pl.* A game played with a heap of slips or small rods of wood, bone, or the like, the object being to pull off each by means of a hook without disturbing the rest. **b.** One of the slips with which this is played 1883. **2.** *fig.* In *pl.*, Splinters, fragments 1857.

Spilt (spilt), *ppl. a.* of SPILL *v.* late ME.

Phr. *To cry over s. milk* (or variants of this), to fret about some loss, mistake, etc., that cannot be remedied.

Spilth (spilþ). 1607. [See -TH[1].] That which is spilled; the action or fact of spilling.

To avenge..The s. of brother's blood 1830.

Spin (spin), *sb.* 1831. [f. the vb.] **1.** An act or spell of spinning; also *techn.*, capacity for being twisted or spun; the product resulting from spinning 1853. **2.** An act or spell of revolving or whirling round; a circular or rotatory movement 1831. **b.** *Cricket*, etc. A twisting motion given to the ball when bowled, thrown, or hit 1862. **3.** The act of causing something to spin 1840. **b.** The act of spinning a coin 1882. **4.** A spell of continuous movement by way of exercise or pastime; a fairly rapid ride or run of some duration 1856. **b.** A spell of quick rowing or sailing 1875. **5.** *Aviation.* An act of spinning (see SPIN *v.* II. 4c, quots.) 1915.

4. A ten-mile s. with a greatcoat on 1890.

Spin (spin), *v.* Pa. t. **spun** (spʊn), **span** (spæn). Pa. pple. **spun.** [Com. Teut.; OE. *spinnan*; the stem is perh. related to that of SPAN *v.*[2]] **I. 1.** *intr.* To draw out and twist the fibres of wool, flax, etc., so as to form a continuous thread; to be engaged in or to follow this occupation. **b.** Of insects: To produce glutinous threads from the body by means of special organs 1511. **2.** *trans.* To draw out (wool, flax, etc.) and convert into threads either by the hand or by machinery OE. **b.** To convert (or *intr.*, to admit of being converted) *into* thread, etc., by spinning 1669. **3.** To form or fabricate (a thread, etc.) by the process of drawing out (and twisting) some suitable material; to prepare the material for (a fabric or garment) by this process ME. **4.** *fig.* **a.** Of the Fates or other powers: To devise or appoint (one's destiny or fortune). late ME. **b.** To evolve, produce, contrive, or devise, in a manner suggestive of spinning 1555. **c.** To draw out, prolong 1629.

1. When Adam dalve, and Eve span, Who was than a gentleman? 1560 2. The farmers' wives began..to s. their wool from their own sheeps' backs 1874. b. It will not s. into good yarn 1842. c. To convert (a viscous solution or pulp) into artificial silk; to form (artificial silk filaments) 1894. 3. All the yearne she spun in Vlisses absence SHAKS. *transf.* and *fig.* Insects s. silk for his service 1660. [A grave] so fresh made that the spring had scarce had time to s. a coverlet for it THACKERAY. *To s. a yarn* (to tell a story): see YARN *sb.* 4. a. On David's head, God doth not s. good hap 1606. b. Many secret agents..were spinning their dark intrigues D'ISRAELI.

S. off: *trans.* To finish or clear *off* (a distaff, etc.) by spinning. **S. out:** *trans.* **a.** To protract, prolong. **b.** To spend or occupy (time) in inactivity or without effect. **c.** To evolve or devise by mental effort; to express at length. **d.** To draw out, prolong, in length or duration. **e.** To cause to last out; to use sparingly. **f.** *intr.* To run out; to extend; to last out.

II. 1. *intr.* To shoot or spring *up*; to grow or rise rapidly (*rare*). late ME. **2.** Of blood, etc.: To issue in a rapid stream; to gush or spurt. late ME. **3.** To move rapidly; to run quickly; now *esp.* to ride or drive at a rapid and even rate. late ME. **b.** To pass or be spent quickly 1850. **c.** *trans.* To cause to pass *away*; to carry *away* or convey rapidly 1696. **4.** *intr.* To revolve or gyrate; to whirl *round* 1667. **b.** Of the brain or head: To whirl; to be giddy or dazed 1819. **5.** *trans.* To cause to turn or revolve rapidly; to twirl or whirl 1612. **b.** To shape (articles of sheet-metal) by pressure applied during rotation on a lathe 1853. **6.** *Angling.* **a.** *trans.* To cause (a minnow or other bait) to revolve in the water by fastening it on the hook in a particular manner 1814. **b.** *intr.* To fish with a spinning bait 1863. **c.** *trans.* To fish (a pool, etc.) by means of a spinning bait 1886. **7.** *slang.* To reject (a candidate) at an examination; to plough. Usu. in *pass.* 1860.

2. One raz'd Achilles' hand; the spouting blood Spun forth POPE. 3. b. The young one is making the money s. THACKERAY. 4. The Earth..With inoffensive pace that spinning sleeps On her soft Axle MILT. c. *Aviation.* (*a*) *intr.* To make a diving descent combined with a continued rotation of the aeroplane 1915; (*b*) *trans.* to make (an aeroplane) perform this evolution 1918. d. Of a motor clutch: To continue to revolve after being disengaged 1918. 5. When you spun tops and snapped marbles EMERSON. *To s. a coin* (also absol.): to toss a coin with a spinning motion (see TOSS *v.* III. 3).

‖**Spina** (spəi·nă). late ME. [L. *spina* SPINE.] **1.** The backbone. Now only *Path.* in *spina bifida*, dropsy of the spine. **2.** *Rom. Antiq.* The barrier running up the middle of a Roman circus 1766.

Spinaceous (spinē[i]·ʃəs), *a.* 1822. [f. mod. L. *Spinacia* spinach.] Belonging to the spinach family.

Spinach (spi·nėdʒ). Also †**spinage.** 1530. [ad. OF. *espinage*, (*e*)*spinache* (also -*ace*), of doubtful origin.] **1.** A plant (*Spinacia oleracea*) belonging to the family *Chenopodiaceæ*, extensively cultivated for culinary purposes; the succulent leaves of this plant used as a vegetable. **b.** Applied (with distinguishing terms) to other species of *Spinacia*, or to plants in some way resembling or taking the place of this, as *Australian, mountain, New Zealand, wild s.* 1710. **2.** *ellipt.* As a moth-name 1832.

1. b. The Orach, or Mountain S., *Atriplex hortensis* 1822. New Zealand S., *Tetragonia expansa* 1824. Australian S. (*Chenopodium erosum*) 1866.

Spinal (spəi·năl), *a.* 1578. [ad. late L. *spinalis*, f. *spina* SPINE.] **1.** Of or pertaining to, forming part of, or located in, the spine or backbone. **2.** Of diseased conditions: Affecting the spine 1838. **3.** Resembling a spine or backbone in form or function 1841. **4.** Of qualities: Arising from or seated in the spine 1855. **5.** Of appliances: Adapted to or intended for application to the spine 1864.

1. The spinall marrow, which is but the braine prolonged SIR T. BROWNE. *S. artery, bone, canal,* etc. 2. S. hemorrhage 1878. 3. Everywhere else the s. ridge seemed unbroken 1856. 5. *S. brace*, a brace for remedying posterior curvature of the spine 1875.

Spindle (spi·nd'l), *sb.* [OE. *spinel*, f. stem of *spinnan* SPIN *v.*] **I. 1.** A simple instrument employed in spinning by hand, consisting of a slender rounded rod (usually of wood), tapering towards each end, which is made to revolve and twist into thread the fibres drawn out from a bunch of wool, flax, etc. **b.** In a spinning frame, one of many steel rods, by each of which a thread is twisted and wound on a bobbin 1790. **c.** A spool or bobbin 1837. **2.** *fig.* In allusion to the Fates imagined as spinning the thread of life or destiny 1577. **3.** Such an amount of thread or yarn as can be prepared on a spindle at one time; hence, a certain measure or quantity of yarn, varying according to the material 1452. **4. a.** *Her.* = FUSIL[1] 1486. **b.** *Anat.* A dilatation of the fœtal aorta resembling a spindle in shape; the spindle-shaped part of a muscle 1898.

II. 1. A rod, usually of iron or other metal, serving as an axis upon which, or by means of which, something revolves or is turned round ME. **2. a.** A cylindrical rod or bar provided with grooves so as to act as a screw; *spec.* that by which the platen of a hand printing-press is lowered and raised. late ME. **b.** A revolving frame used for stirring a mixture 1793. **c.** A rod upon which the core of a gun-shell is moulded 1842. **3.** A machine for recessing an aeroplane spar (cf. SPINDLE *v.* 4) 1920. †**4.** A stalk, stem, or shoot of a plant, esp. of cereals –1750. **5.** *Naut.* The upper part or section of a made wooden mast 1597.

Comb.: **s. cross** *Her.*, a cross having arms shaped somewhat like a s.; **-shell,** (*a*) = *s.-stromb*; (*b*) a gasteropod of the genus *Fusus*; **-stromb,** any marine gasteropod of the genus *Rostellaria*; **-wood,** the s.-tree, or the wood of this; **-worm** *U.S.*, the maize-eating larva of a noctuid moth, *Achatodes zeæ*.

Spindle (spi·nd'l), *v.* 1577. [f. the sb.] **1.** *intr.* Of cereals: To shoot up into the slender stalks on which the ear is formed. **b.** Of flowering plants: To form the stalk or stem on which the flowers are produced 1601. **c.** With *up* or *upward*(*s*). In later use sometimes implying too slender a growth. 1601. **2.** To shoot out or up, to develop by rapid growth or attenuation, *into* something thin or unsubstantial 1784. **3.** *trans.* To fit with or fix upon a spindle or axis 1833. **4.** To recess and taper (an aeroplane spar) 1919.

2. That fairest variety of mortal grass which with us is apt to s. so soon into a somewhat sapless womanhood 1854.

Spindleage (spi·nd'lėdʒ). 1921. [See -AGE.] The total number of cotton spindles in use at a given time and in a specified area.

Spi·ndle-legged, *a.* 1710. [SPINDLE *sb.*] Having long and slender legs.

Spindle(-)shank. 1570. **1.** A long and slender leg. (Chiefly *contempt.* and in *pl.*) **2.** *transf.* A spindle-legged person 1602. So **Spi·ndle-shanked** *a.*

Spi·ndle-shaped, *a.* 1776. Fusiform.

Spi·ndle-side. 1851. [f. SPINDLE *sb.*, after OE. *spinelhealf*.] The female line of descent.

Spi·ndle-tree. 1548. [f. SPINDLE *sb.*, after G. *spindelbaum*.] **1.** An ornamental European shrub (*Euonymus europæus*), furnishing a hard fine-grained yellowish wood formerly much used for spindles. **2.** *pl.* The family *Celastraceæ*, to which the genus *Euonymus* belongs 1846.

Spi·ndling, (*vbl.*) *sb.* 1626. [f. SPINDLE *sb.* or *v.*] **1.** The formation of a stem, stalk, or shoot, in plants. **2.** A spindly plant, animal, etc. 1842.

2. Half-conscious of the garden-squirt, The spindlings look unhappy TENNYSON.

Spi·ndling, *ppl. a.* 1750. [f. SPINDLE *v.*] **1.** Of plants: Growing or shooting out into (long) stalks or stems, esp. of a slender or weakly kind. **2.** Of things: Slender, spindly 1858.

1. Five s. pines stand in the midst of a sandy waste 1885.

Spindly (spi·ndli), *a.* 1651. [f. SPINDLE *sb.*] **1.** Of plants: Of a slender and weakly growth. **b.** Of growth: Characterized by slimness or attenuation and weakness 1856. **2.** *gen.* Having a slender elongated form implying, or suggestive of, weakness 1827.

Spi·ndrift. orig. *Sc.* 1600. [var. of SPOONDRIFT, app. due to local Sc. pronunciations of *spoon*.] Continuous driving of spray.

Spine (spəin). late ME. [ad. OF. *espine* (mod.F. *épine*), or directly ad. L. *spina* thorn, prickle, backbone.] **I. 1.** *Bot.* A stiff sharp-pointed process produced or growing from the wood of a plant, consisting of a hardened or irregularly developed branch, petiole, stipule, or other part; a thorn; a similar process developed on fruit or leaves. Cf. PRICKLE *sb.* 2. **2.** *Anat.* One or other of several sharp-pointed slender processes of various bones 1706. **3.** *Zool.* A stiff, pointed, thorn-like process or appendage developed on the integument of certain fishes, insects, or lower forms of animal life 1721. **b.** One of the prickles of a hedgehog, the quills of a porcupine, or similar growth on other animals 1753. **c.** *Ichth.* A spinous or spiny fin-ray; a fin-spine 1774. **4.** Any natural formation having a slender sharp-pointed form 1750. **II. 1.** The spinal or vertebral column in man and vertebrates; the backbone. late ME. **b.** *transf.* A part or formation having the function of a backbone 1665. **2.** The heart-wood or duramen of a tree 1630. **3.** A ridge or elevated stretch of ground, rock, etc., having a position analogous to that of the backbone, or resembling it 1796. **4.** The 'back' of a book 1922

Comb.: **s.-bill**, one or other of two species of Australian honey-eaters, characterized by their long spine-like bills; **-bone**, the spine; **-eel**, a spiny eel; **-oak**, the heart-wood of an oak. Hence **Spined** (spəind), *a.*, (*a*) having, provided with, or covered with, spines; spinous, spiny; (*b*) having a spine or spinal column.

Spinel (spi·nĕl). 1528. [ad. F. †*espinelle* (mod.F. *spinelle*).] **1.** A gem or precious stone of a red or scarlet colour closely resembling the true ruby, now classed as belonging to the typical species of the spinel group of minerals. More fully *s. ruby*. **2.** *Min.* The typical species of a group of minerals (the *s. group*) which are compounds of sesquioxides with protoxides, and crystallize in the isometric system 1807. **b.** Any mineral belonging to this group 1837.

Spineless (spəi·nlės), *a.* 1827. [f. SPINE.] **1.** Having no spines or sharp-pointed processes; not spinous. **2.** Having a weak or diseased spine; deprived of the natural support of the spine; exhausted, limp 1860. **b.** Lacking moral force or vigour; irresolute, flabby 1885.

2. b. We are sick of this s. way of treating violators of law 1885.

Spinelle (spine·l). 1555. = SPINEL.

Spinescent (spəine·sĕnt), *a.* 1793. [ad. mod.L. *spinescent-*, *spinescere* to grow thorny, f. *spina* SPINE.] **1.** *Bot.* Developing into or terminating in a spine or thorn; also, bearing or covered with spines; spiniferous. **2.** *Zool.* Tending to become a spine or spinous process; spinous, spinulous 1856. Hence **Spine·scence.**

Spinet[1] (spi·nėt, spine·t). Also **spinette.** 1664. [ad. F. †*espinette* (mod.F. *épinette*), = It. *spinetta*, *-etto*; prob. from the name of the inventor, Giovanni *Spinetti* of Venice.] A keyed musical instrument, common in England in the 18th c., closely resembling the harpsichord, but smaller and having only one string to each note.

†Spi·net[2]. 1603. [ad. L. *spinetum* (f. *spina* thorn).] A thicket; a spinney –1848.

Spi·ne-tail. 1839. [SPINE.] One or other of several birds of unrelated genera characterized by their stiff, spine-like, or mucronate tail-feathers. So **Spi·ne-tailed** *a.* 1802.

Spi·n-house. Now *Hist.* 1700. [ad. Du. *spinhuis*. Cf. SPINNING-HOUSE.] A house or building in which persons are employed in spinning; (in ref. to Continental usage) a house of correction for women.

Spini- (spəi·ni), comb. form of L. *spina* spine, as in *s.-acute*, *-dentate*, *-spirulate* adjs.

Spiniferous (spəini·fĕrəs), *a.* 1656. [f. L. *spinifer*, f. *spina* SPINE] Bearing, covered with, or having spines; spinose. Chiefly *Zool.* or *Bot.*

‖**Spinifex** (spei·nifeks). 1846. [mod.L., f. L. *spina* SPINE + *-fex* maker, f. *facere*.] *Bot.* One or other of a number of coarse grasses (now classed in the genus *Tricuspis*) which grow in dense masses on the sand-hills of the Australian deserts, and are characterized by their sharp-pointed spiny leaves; esp. the porcupine-grass, *Triodia irritans*.

Spiniform (spəi·nifǫım), *a.* 1833. [ad. mod.L. *spiniformis*; see SPINE and -FORM.] *Bot.* and *Zool.* Having the form of a spine or spinous process.

Spinigerous (spəini·dʒĕrəs), *a.* 1852. [f. L. *spiniger* spine-bearing.] *Bot.* and *Zool.* = SPINIFEROUS *a.*

Spink (spink), *sb.* Now *dial.* late ME. [prob. imitative of the note of the bird.] **1.** One or other of the finches; esp. the chaffinch. **2.** Used to imitate or represent the characteristic note or cry of certain birds 1898. Hence **Spink** *v. intr.*

Spinnaker (spi·năkəı). 1866. [Said to be a fanciful formation on *spinx*, mispronunciation of *Sphinx*, name of the first yacht that carried the sail.] A large three-cornered sail carried by racing-yachts, boomed out at right angles to the vessel's side opposite to the mainsail, and used in running before the wind.

Spinner (spi·nəı). ME. [f. SPIN *v.* + -ER[1].] **I. 1.** A spider, esp. one which spins a web. **2.** One who spins cotton, wool, yarn, etc.; *esp.* one whose occupation it is to do this; one who attends to or works a spinning machine. late ME. **b.** A manufacturer engaged in spinning, esp. cotton-spinning; a master-spinner 1834. **3.** *fig.* One who spins, tells, or relates (a story, yarn, etc.) 1770. **4. a.** = next 1815. **b.** *techn.* A spinning-machine 1875.

3. I am a s. of long yarns HAWTHORNE.

II. 1. *Angling.* **a.** One or other of several flies, or imitations of these, used esp. in trout-fishing 1787. **b.** An angler who uses spinning-tackle 1836. **2. a.** A teetotum; a top 1794. **b.** A cricket-ball bowled with a spin 1895. **3.** *Aircraft.* A metal fairing attached to the propeller boss and revolving with it 1924.

Spinneret (spi·nəret). 1826. [dim. of SPINNER; see -ET.] An organ or process by which the silk, gossamer, or thread of certain insects, esp. silkworms and spiders, is produced; a spinning-organ; *spec.* (*a*) one of the pores or tubules on the lower lip of a silkworm or caterpillar; (*b*) one of the nipple-like mamillæ on the abdomen of a spider. **b.** *Artificial Silk Manuf.* A tube, or a small plate with fine holes, through which the viscous solution passes into the solidifying medium to form filaments 1894.

Spinney (spi·ni). ME. [ad. OF. *espinei*, *-oi*, *-oy* masc., *-oie*, *-aye* (mod. F. *épinaie*) fem., a place full of thorns or brambles, f. *espine* SPINE.] **†1.** A thorn-hedge (*rare*). **2.** A small wood or copse, esp. one planted or preserved for sheltering game-birds; a small clump or plantation of trees 1597.

Spinning (spi·niŋ), *vbl. sb.* ME. [f. SPIN *v.* + -ING[1].] **1.** The action of SPIN *v.*; an instance of this. **2.** The thread or yarn spun 1511.

attrib., as *s.-engine*, *-factory*, *-mill*, *-organ*, *-top*; **s.-gland**, one of the glands which form the material for spinning the thread of silkworms, etc.; **-top**, = TOP *sb.*[2] 1.

Spi·nning, *ppl. a.* 1634. [f. SPIN *v.* + -ING[2].] **1.** That spins or produces thread. **2.** That revolves, gyrates, or turns round 1854.

Spi·nning-house. 1463. [SPINNING *vbl. sb.*] **1.** A room or building set apart for the purpose of spinning. **2.** A house of correction for women, esp. at Cambridge 1803.

Spi·nning-je·nny. 1783. [f. SPINNING *vbl. sb.* or *ppl. a.* + JENNY.] An early form of spinning-machine in which several spindles were set in motion by a band from one wheel.

Spi·nning-wheel. late ME. [f. SPINNING *vbl. sb.*] A simple apparatus for spinning, formerly in common use, in which the formation of the thread is carried out by the help of a wheel worked either by the hand or foot.

Spino- (spəi·no), used as comb. form of L. *spina* spine, in a few terms of *Anat.*, *Bot.*, etc.

Spinode (spəi·nǭud). 1852. [irreg. f. L. *spina* SPINE *sb.* + NODE *sb.*] *Geom.* A stationary point on a curve; a cusp.

Spinose (spəinǭu·s), *a.* 1660. [ad. L. *spinosus*, f. *spina* thorn.] = SPINOUS 2, 3.

Spinosity (spəinǫ·sĭti). 1605. [ad. late L. *spinositas*; see prec. and -ITY.] **†1.** *fig.* The quality of being spinose or thorny –1660. **2.** A disagreeable remark; an argument or theory of a difficult and unprofitable character 1653.

2. Amid the dry spinosities and tortuous labyrinths of theology 1836.

Spinous (spəi·nəs), *a.* 1638. [ad. L. *spinosus* SPINOSE *a.*] **1.** *fig.* Resembling or suggestive of a thorn or thorns in respect of sharpness and aridity; unpleasant and difficult or unprofitable to handle or deal with. **2.** *Bot.* Furnished with spines or thorns; thorn-bearing, thorny 1668. **3.** Spinigerous. Chiefly *Zool.* 1774. **4.** Having the form of a spine or thorn; slender and sharp-pointed 1732.

4. *S. process*, a process or apophysis of a spine-like form, esp. one of those on the vertebræ.

Spinozism (spinǭu·ziz'm). 1728. [f. the name of the philosopher Baruch or Benedict de *Spinoza* (1632–77). So F. *spinosisme*.] The philosophical doctrines of Spinoza, or the general principles underlying these; pantheism as represented by Spinoza.

Spinozist (spinǭu·zist). 1728. [f. as prec. + -IST. So F. *spinosiste*.] One who accepts or advocates the philosophical doctrines of Spinoza. Hence **Spinozi·stic, -osistic** *a.* of, pertaining to, or characteristic of Spinoza or his philosophical views.

Spinster (spi·nstəı). late ME. [f. SPIN *v.* + -STER.] **1.** A woman (or, rarely, a man) who spins, *esp.* as a regular occupation. **b.** A spider, or other insect that spins (*rare*) 1636. **2.** Appended to the names of women, orig. to denote their occupation, but subsequently as the proper legal designation of one unmarried. late ME. **b.** An unmarried woman; *esp.* an 'old maid' 1719.

1. Ther were..ther dwelling..dyuers good spynsters & carders 1543. **2.** Joan Lambe, widow of London, spynster 1564. I write myself s., because the laws of my country call me so 1719. **b.** Plain little spinsters with a knack of making themselves useful 1882. Hence **Spi·nsterdom** = next. **Spi·nstry,** the art or occupation of spinning, the product of spinning.

Spi·nsterhood. 1823. [f. prec. 2 b.] **1.** The condition of being an unmarried woman, esp. one advancing in years. **2.** The collective body of spinsters 1844.

Spinstress (spi·nstrės). 1643. [f. SPINSTER + -ESS.] **1.** A female spinner. **2.** A maiden lady; a spinster 1716.

Spi·n-text. 1693. [f. SPIN *v.* + TEXT *sb.*, orig. as a suggestive surname.] A parson, *esp.* one who preaches long or weak sermons.

Spintha·riscope. 1903. [irreg. f. Gr. σπινθαρίς spark; see -SCOPE.] An instrument in which the rays emitted from the metal radium are evidenced by the production of tiny sparks.

Spinule (spəi·niul). 1752. [ad. L. *spinula*, dim. of *spina* SPINE *sb.*] **1.** A small or minute spine or thorn-like formation, esp. in lower forms of animal life. **2.** A particular kind of larva 1857. Hence **Spinule·scent** *a.* having a tendency to produce small spines. **Spi·nulous** *a.* = SPINULOSE *a.*

Spi·nuli-, comb. form of L. *spinula* spinule, as in *spinuli·ferous*, *spinu·liform* adjs.

Spinulose (spəi·niulǭus), *a.* 1819. [ad. mod.L. *spinulosus*, f. *spinula* SPINULE.] *Zool.* and *Bot.* **1.** Furnished or covered with spinules. **2.** Having the form of spinules 1848. So **Spinulo·so-**, comb. form.

Spiny (spəi·ni), *a.* 1586. [f. SPINE *sb.* + -Y[1].] **1.** Having the characteristics of a thorn or thorns. **b.** Thin and hard or dry; spare, lean 1598. **2.** Abounding in, furnished or thickly set with, thorns 1604. **3.** Furnished or set with spines 1615. **4.** Having the form of a spine; stiff and sharp-pointed 1828.

1. And so much for this little s. objection COWLEY. **2.** The spiney Desarts of Scholastic Philosophy 1727. **3.** Two..lizards with remarkable spiney skins 1883. **4.** S. developments of the epidermis HUXLEY. Hence **Spi·niness.**

Spiracle (spəi·răk'l). late ME. [ad. L. *spiraculum* SPIRACULUM.] **†1.** Breath, spirit. (orig. after L. *spiraculum vitæ* in Gen. ii. 7, vii. 22) –1654. **2.** A small opening by which a confined space has communication with the outer air; *esp.* an air-hole or air-shaft 1620. **b.** *spec.* A volcanic vent-hole 1671. **3. a.** A breathing-pore in the epidermis of plants; a stoma (*rare*) 1774. **b.** *Zool.* A special aperture, orifice, or pore, chiefly in lower forms of animal life, by which respiration is effected 1775. **c.** The blow-hole of a cetacean (and of certain sharks) 1796. Hence **Spira·cular** *a.* of, pertaining to, or serving as a s. or spiracles.

‖**Spiraculum** (spəiræ·kiŭlŏm). *Pl.* **-acula.** 1668. [L., f. *spirare* to breathe.] = prec. 2, 2 b, 3 b.

Spiræa (spəirī·ă). Also **spirea.** 1669. [L. ad. Gr. σπειραία, app. f. σπεῖρα SPIRE *sb.*[3]] *Bot.* **1.** One or other species of an extensive genus of rosaceous plants or shrubs, many of which are largely cultivated for their handsome foliage and flowers. **b.** With *a* and *pl.* A single plant or shrub, or one particular species, of this genus 1731. **2.** The genus composed of these plants 1753.

Spiral (spəiə·răl), *sb.* 1656. [Subst. use of next.] **1.** *Geom.* A continuous curve traced by a point moving round a fixed point in the same plane while steadily increasing (or diminishing) its distance from this. **2.** A curve traced by a point moving round, and simultaneously advancing along, a cylinder or cone; a helix or screw-line 1670. **b.** The degree in which the successive circles of such a curve approach each other 1846. **3. a.** A piece of wire coiled into a spiral form 1825. **b.** *Bot.* A spiral vessel in plants 1837. **c.** *Astr.* A spiral nebula 1866. **d.** *gen.* Any object having a spiral form 1853. **e.** *Aviation.* A spiral mode of ascent or descent 1918. **4.** One of the separate circles or coils of a spiral or helical object 1728.

1. *S. of Archimedes*, a curve traced by a point moving uniformly along a line which at the same time revolves uniformly round a fixed point in itself. *Equiangular, Logarithmic s.*: see these words. **3. d.** The staircase was of those narrow, twisting spirals 1853. **e.** When I came out of my s. 1918.

Spiral (spəiə·răl), *a.*[1] 1551. [ad. med.L. *spiralis*, f. *spira* SPIRE *sb.*[1]] **1.** Forming a succession of curves arranged like the thread of a screw; coiled in a cylindrical or conical manner; helical. **2.** Curving continuously round a fixed point in the same plane, at a steadily increasing (or diminishing) distance from it 1639.

1. As woodbine..In s. rings ascends the trunk COWPER. Where upward..The noisy bittern wheeled his s. way LONGF.

Special collocations: *s. gearing, spring, staircase*; Bot., *s. cell, tube, vessel.* Hence **Spira·lity**, s. character, the degree of a s. curve. **Spi·rally** *adv.*

Spiral (spəiə·răl), *a.*[2] 1658. [f. SPIRE *sb.*[1] + -AL.] Rising like a spire; tall and tapering or pointed.

Spiral (spəiə·răl), *v.* 1834. [f. SPIRAL *sb.*] **1.** *intr.* To wind or move in a spiral manner; to form spiral curves; *Aviation*, to fly in a spiral. **2.** *trans.* To twist spirally 1867.

Spirant (spəiə·rănt), *sb.* and *a.* 1866. [a. L. *spirant-*, *spirare* to breathe.] *Phonetics.* A consonant uttered with a continued emission of breath, so that the sound is capable of being prolonged. Also *attrib.* or as *adj.* = **Spira·ntal** *a.*

Spi·rated, *ppl. a.* 1871. [f. L. *spira* SPIRE *sb.*[3]] Spirally twisted.

The males..have long straight s. horns DARWIN.

Spiration (spəirē·ʃən). 1526. [ad. L. *spiration-*, *spiratio*, f. *spirare* to breathe.] **1.** *Theol.* †**a.** The creative function of the Deity conceived as the action of breathing -1765. **b.** The procession of the Holy Ghost regarded as an emanation of spirit 1602. †**2.** The action of breathing or drawing breath in man and animals -1674.

Spire (spəiəɹ), *sb.*[1] [OE. *spīr*, = MLG., MHG. *spīr* (G. *spier, spiere*), sprout, shoot, sprig.] **1.** A stalk or stem of a plant, esp. one of a tall and slender growth. Now *rare.* **b.** The tapering top of a tree 1657. **c.** A flower-spike 1850. **d.** Reeds; a reed. Now *south.* or *s. w. dial.* ME. **2.** *Mining.* The tube carrying the train to the charge in the blast-hole 1875. **3.** A young or tender shoot or sprout; *esp.* the rudimentary shoot of a seed; the acrospire of grain ME. **b.** A blade or shoot *of* grass, etc. Now *rare.* 1646. **4.** A long slender and tapering growth in a plant; *esp.* the awn or beard of grain. Now *Obs.* or *dial.* 1530. **5.** An elongated or pointed shoot or tongue of fire or flame 1450. **6.** A conical, tapering, pointed body or part of something; a sharp point 1551. **b.** A prong of a deer's horn 1607. **7.** A tall, slender, sharp-pointed summit, peak, rock, or column 1586. **8.** A tall structure rising from a tower, roof, etc., and terminating in a slender point; *esp.* the tapering portion of the steeple of a cathedral or church 1596. †**9.** *fig.* The highest point, summit, or top *of* something -1611.

1. Tall spires of windlestrae SHELLEY. **c.** Where ..asphodel is pale with spires of faintest rose 1874. **3.** As an oke comyth of a littil s. CHAUCER. **5.** The flames Drivn backward slope their pointing spires MILT. **6.** The narrow'r end I sharpen'd to a s. POPE. **7.** These two Pyramides, the mighty spires and steeples whereof..do arise out of the very water HOLLAND. **8.** And that sweet city with her dreaming spires.. Lovely..she lies M. ARNOLD. **9.** The s., and top of prayses SHAKS. Hence **Spi·relet**, a small s.

Spire, *sb.*[2] Chiefly *Sc.* and *n. dial.* late ME. [app. of Continental origin.] †**1.** A spar or pole of timber; a bar or moderately long piece of wood -1609. **2.** A young tree suitable for making into a spar; a sapling. late ME.

Spire (spəiəɹ), *sb.*[3] 1572. [a. F. *spire*, or ad. L. *spira*, ad. Gr. σπεῖρα coil, twist, winding.] **1.** One of the series of complete convolutions forming a coil or spiral. **2.** A spiral; a series of spiral curves or coils 1611. **3.** *Conch.* The upper convoluted portion of a spiral shell, consisting of all the whorls except the body-whorl 1822.

Spire (spəiəɹ), *v.*[1] ME. [f. SPIRE *sb.*[1]] **1.** *intr.* Of seeds, grain, etc.: To send forth or develop shoots, esp. the first shoot or acrospire; to germinate, sprout. Now *rare* or *Obs.* **2.** Of plants, corn, etc.: To run up into a tall stem, stalk, or spike; to grow upwards instead of developing laterally. Now *dial.* late ME. **3.** To rise or shoot up into a spire or spire-shaped form; to mount or soar aloft 1591.

3. The crowded firs S. from thy shores, and stretch across thy bed COLERIDGE.

†**Spire**, *v.*[2] late ME. [ad. OF. *spirer*, *espirer*, or L. *spirare* to breathe.] **1.** *intr.* or *absol.* To breathe; to blow gently; to come *forth* or *out* as breath -1535. **2.** *trans.* To breathe (air, etc.). Const. *into.* -late ME. **3.** To breathe forth or out, to create or produce by the agency of the breath -1645.

Spire (spəiəɹ), *v.*[3] 1607. [f. SPIRE *sb.*[3]] *intr.* To curl, twist, or wind spirally; to make a spiral curve; *esp.* to mount or soar with spiral movement.

Spired (spəiəɹd), (*ppl.*) *a.* 1610. [f. SPIRE *sb.*[1]] **1.** Having a tapering, sharp-pointed top; peaked 1611. **b.** Of a steeple, tower, etc.: Provided with or carrying a spire 1610. **2.** Of plants: Stemmed, spiked 1780.

†**Spire-steeple.** 1559. [SPIRE *sb.*[1]] A steeple surmounted by a spire; a church spire -1809.

Spiricle (spəiə·rik'l). 1891. [dim. of SPIRE *sb.*[3]] *Bot.* A minute coiled thread in the coating of certain seeds and achenes, which uncoils when moistened.

Spirifer (spəiə·rifəɹ). 1835. [mod.L., f. L. *spira* SPIRE *sb.*[3] + -FER bearing.] *Palæont.* A genus of fossil brachiopods, characterized by long highly developed spiral appendages; a member or species of this genus, or of the family *Spiriferidæ* of which it is the type.

Spiriform (spəiə·rifǭɹm), *a.* 1841. [ad. mod.L. *spiriformis.*] Having the form of a spire or spiral.

Spirillum (spəiri·lŏm). *Pl.* **-a.** 1875. [mod.L., dim. of L. *spira* SPIRE *sb.*[3]] *Bacteriology.* A genus of bacteria characterized by a spiral structure; any member of this genus, esp. the species found in the blood in relapsing fever. Hence **Spiri·llar** *a.*

Spiring (spəiə·riŋ), *ppl. a.* 1538. [f. SPIRE *v.*[1]] **1.** That spires or rises up taperingly to a point; soaring aloft or reaching to a great height. freq. *poet.* or *rhet.* **2.** Of grass or plants: Shooting, sprouting; running up into a spire or stem 1612.

1. The lofty, s. tops of the spruce and fir 1857. **2.** The s. grass DRAYTON.

Spirit (spi·rit), *sb.* ME. [a. AF. *spirit*, or ad. L. *spiritus* breathing, breath, air, related to *spirare* to breathe.] **I. 1.** The animating or vital principle in man (and animals); that which gives life to the physical organism, in contrast to its purely material elements; the breath of life. **b.** In contexts relating to temporary separation of the immaterial from the material part of man's being, or to perception of a purely intellectual character. Chiefly in phr. *in s.* late ME. **c.** Incorporeal or immaterial being, as opp. to *body* or *matter*; being or intelligence conceived as distinct from, or independent of, anything physical or material. late ME. **2.** The soul of a person, as commended to God, or passing out of the body, in the moment of death. late ME. **b.** = SOUL III. 1. late ME. **3.** A supernatural, incorporeal, rational being or personality, usually regarded as imperceptible at ordinary times to the human senses, but capable of becoming visible at pleasure, and freq. conceived as troublesome, terrifying, or hostile to mankind ME. **b.** A being of this nature imagined as possessing and actuating a person. late ME. **c.** With *the* and qualifying term, denoting some particular being of the above nature. late ME. **4.** A being essentially incorporeal or immaterial ME.

1. The s. when it is gone foorth returneth not; neither the soule receiued vp, commeth againe *Wisd.* xvi. 14. **b.** In S. perhaps he also saw Rich Mexico..And Cusco in Peru MILT. **c.** The Egyptians are men and not God, and their horses flesh and not s. *Isaiah* xxxi. 3. **2.** Father, into thy hands I commend my s. *Luke* xxiii. 46. **b.** Where I may..unsphear The s. of Plato MILT. **3.** For Spirits when they please Can either Sex assume, or both MILT. As if God bade some s. plague a world BROWNING. Phr. *Evil, familiar, guardian, wicked s.*, etc. **b.** Sum wenche hauynge a s. of dyuynacioun WYCLIF *Acts* xvi. 16. **c.** The Evil S. is pulling you towards him 1842. **4.** Man *has* a body, but he *is* a s. 1876.

II. 1. *The S. of God* (or *the Lord*), the active essence or essential power of the Deity, conceived as a creative, animating, or inspiring influence ME. **b.** *The Holy S., the S., the S. of truth*, etc. = HOLY GHOST 1. ME. **2.** The active or essential principle or power *of* some emotion, frame of mind, etc., as operating on or in persons. late ME. **b.** With *a*: A tendency, inclination, or impulse, *of* a specified kind. late ME. **3.** A particular character, disposition, or temper existing in, pervading, or animating, a person or set of persons; a special attitude of mind characterizing men individually or collectively 1561. **b.** The disposition, feeling, or frame of mind with which something is done, considered, or viewed 1601. **4.** A person considered in relation to his character or disposition; one who has a spirit of a specified nature 1591. **5.** The essential character, nature, or qualities *of* something; that which constitutes the pervading or tempering principle of anything 1690. **b.** The prevailing tone or tendency *of* a particular period of time 1820. **c.** The broad intent or meaning *of* a statement, enactment, etc.; opp. to *letter* 1802.

1. The Spirit of the Lord is God the Holy Ghost 1875. **2.** O s. of Loue, how quicke and fresh art thou SHAKS. **b.** A slight s. of mockery played over his speech DISRAELI. **3.** The money-making s. was.. driven back 1856. **b.** It is not thy works. but only the S. thou workest in, that can have worth or continuance CARLYLE. **4.** Let thirsty Spirits make the Bar their Choice 1746. **5.** The s. of the hills is action, that of the lowlands repose RUSKIN. **b.** It is the s. of the age, and we are all infected with it SHELLEY.

III. 1. The immaterial, intelligent, or sentient part of a person, freq. in implied or expressed contrast to the body. late ME. **2.** The emotional part of man as the seat of hostile or angry feeling. late ME. **3.** Mettle; vigour of mind; courage; disposition to assert oneself or hold one's own 1596. **4.** A brisk or lively quality, vivacity or animation, in persons or things 1588.

1. My spirite reioyseth in god my sauiour BIBLE (1551) *Luke* i. 47. Saddened and humbled in s. THACKERAY. **2.** She was prepared for war and her s. was hot within her 1862. **3.** A man of more s. than discretion 1715. Phr. *With s. A man of s.* **4.** Wine hath Briskness and S. in it 1686. The absence of Dr. Johnson..took off the s. of the evening MME D'ARBLAY.

IV. 1. A movement of the air; a wind; a breath (of wind or air). Now chiefly *poet.* late ME. **b.** *Gram.* An aspirate or breathing; a conventional mark indicating this; *spec.* in the writing or printing of Greek 1555. †**2.** One of certain subtle highly-refined substances or fluids (dist. as *natural, animal*, and *vital*) formerly supposed to permeate the blood and chief organs of the body. Chiefly used in *pl.* late ME. **b.** *pl.* Vital power or energy; the normal operation of the vital functions. late ME. **3.** *pl.* The mind or faculties as the seat of action and feeling, esp. as liable to be depressed or exalted by events or circumstances. late ME. **b.** Vigour or animation of mind; cheerfulness, vivacity, liveliness 1716. †**4.** *pl.* The faculties of perception or reflection -1697. †**b.** Disposition. SHAKS. †**5.** A subtle or intangible element or principle in material things -1725.

1. The balmy s. of the western gale POPE. **b.** The book has neither spirits..nor accents 1861. **2. b.** Thy spirits have a fainter flow, I see thee daily weaker grow COWPER. **3.** Depressed in spirits 1893. Phr. *In good, high*, etc. *spirits.* **b.** I..have had spirits enough to go and see all that is curious in the town 1716. *In spirits*, in a cheerful mood. *Out of spirits*, low-spirited. **4. a.** His Spirits should hunt After new Fancies SHAKS.

V. †1. One or other of four substances so named by the mediæval alchemists; *spec.* mercury -1728. 2. A liquid of the nature of an essence or extract from some substance, esp. one obtained by distillation; a solution in alcohol of some essential or volatile principle 1610. b. Without article: Liquid such as is obtained by distillation, *spec.* that which is of an alcoholic nature. Also *pl.* 1610. c. orig. *pl.* Strong alcoholic liquor for drinking, obtained by distillation from various substances; *sing.* any particular kind of this 1684. 3. An essence, distilled extract, or alcoholic solution *of* a specified substance. Freq. *pl.*, esp. in later use. 1700. b. *Dyeing.* Any of various solutions used as mordants 1875.

2. b. M. Palm..shot one, and forwarded it to Batavia in s. 1863. c. He gave me also..a little Bottle of Spirits BUNYAN. Quilp..drank three..glassfulls of the raw s. DICKENS. 3. Aromatic S. of Ammonia 1871. Sweet Spirits of Nitre 1871. See also TURPENTINE 3, VITRIOL 1, WINE *sb.* 5.

attrib. and *Comb.*: *s. flask*, *grocer*, **s. fresco**, a method of fresco-painting, in which the colours are ground in a medium of wax, elemi, rosin, artist's copal, oil of spike or spirits of turpentine; **-gum**, a quick-drying gum used in theatrical make-up; **-licence**, a legal permit to sell spirits; **-merchant**, a vendor of spirits; **-stove**, a stove fed by methylated or other s.; **s. varnish**, a varnish prepared by dissolving a resin in s.; also as vb.

Spirit (spi·rit), *v.* 1599. [f. SPIRIT *sb.*] I. 1. *trans.* To make (the blood, a liquor) of a more active or lively character. 2. To infuse spirit, life, ardour, or energy into (a person); to inspirit, animate, encourage 1608. b. To excite, instigate, or stir up (*rare*) 1680. †3. To invest with a spirit or animating principle -1741. 4. With *up*: To stimulate, animate, encourage, stir up, or excite (a person) 1712.

1. And shall our quick blood, spirited with Wine, Seeme frostie? SHAKS. 2. Spirited with this advantage, he pushed onwards 1758. Phr. *To spirit* (a person) *on*, to urge him on by encouragement. 3. Thy high commands must s. all our wars POPE. 4. Spiriting them up to heroic deeds W. IRVING.

II. 1. To carry off or away; to make away with or remove in a mysterious or dexterous manner 1666. 2. With *away*: To kidnap, carry off, or abduct (a person) 1670. b. To take away or carry off by some mysterious means or power; to transport with speed 1696. c. Said of the action of spirits 1825.

1. [He] seemed to s. the things off the table without sound or effort 1858. 2. The archbishop spirited away the preacher into Kent 1858. b. She was spirited away in a moment 1861.

†**Spi·rital**, *a.* 1598. [a. OF. (*e*)*spirital*, or ad. L. *spiritalis*.] Of the nature of spirit; of or pertaining to the spirit -1707.

Spirited (spi·rited), *a.* 1599. [f. SPIRIT *sb.*] †1. Impregnated with spirit or active properties -1677. 2. Of persons: Full of spirit or animation; lively, energetic; prompt to act in a worthy manner 1599. b. Of horses, etc.: Mettlesome 1774. 3. Of things: Characterized by, displaying, or suggestive of spirit, animation, vigour, or energy 1715. †4. Of persons: Occupied or possessed by a (good or evil) spirit (*rare*) 1667.

2. The s. little garrison 1852. b. A remarkably fine and s. horse 1828. 3. A very s. critique upon the party JANE AUSTEN. What clearly cut, s. features! C. BRONTË. 4. So talk'd the s. sly Snake MILT.

Freq. as second element of parasynthetic combs.; as *high-*, *low-*, *mean-*, *public s.* Hence **Spi·rited-ly** *adv.*, **-ness.**

Spi·ritful, *a.* *Obs.* or *dial.* 1546. [f. SPIRIT *sb.*] 1. Having a spiritual or refined character. 2. Of persons: Spirited, vigorous, energetic 1598. 3. Of actions, etc.: Performed with, characterized by, spirit or vigour 1614. 4. Of liquor: Spirituous 1608.

1. The spiritfull and orderly life of our grown men MILT. 2. Miss Howe is..confoundedly smart and s. RICHARDSON. Hence †**Spi·ritful-ly** *adv.* †**-ness.**

Spi·riting, *vbl. sb.* 1768. [f. SPIRIT *v.*] The action or work of a spirit; the ministering of spirits.

Spiritism (spi·ritiz'm). 1864. [f. SPIRIT *sb.* + -ISM.] = SPIRITUALISM 3.

Spi·ritist. 1858. [f. SPIRIT *sb.* + -IST.] 1. One who believes in spiritism; a spiritualist. Also *attrib.* 2. = SPIRITUALIST 3. 1878. Hence **Spiriti·stic** *a.*

Spi·rit(-)lamp. 1802. [SPIRIT *sb.* V. 2.] A lamp fed by methylated or other spirits, and used esp. for heating or boiling.

Spi·ritless, *a.* 1570. [f. SPIRIT *sb.* + -LESS.] 1. Deprived of the spirit or animating principle; not having or possessing a spirit; lifeless. 2. Devoid of lively or cheerful spirits; dejected, dull or melancholy 1597. 3. Destitute of spirit, animation, or courage; lacking ardour or boldness 1628. b. Destitute of energy or enterprise (*rare*) 1799. 4. Marked or characterized by lack of animation, vivacity, or energy 1651.

1. The s. Body should be restored to the Earth 1705. 2. Euen such a man, so faint, so spiritlesse, So dull SHAKS. 3. As a swordless and s. nation SWINBURNE. 4. The evening was passed in s. conversation MME D'ARBLAY. Hence **Spi·ritless-ly** *adv.*, **-ness.**

Spi·rit(-)le:vel. 1768. [f. SPIRIT *sb.* + LEVEL *sb.* 1.] A levelling instrument used for determining a horizontal line or surface, usu. consisting of a hermetically-sealed glass tube filled with spirit and containing an air-bubble, which when the tube lies exactly horizontal, occupies a position midway in its length.

†**Spi·ritous**, *a.* 1605. [f. SPIRIT *sb.* + -OUS.] 1. Of the nature of spirit; having the qualities of an essence; highly refined or dematerialized -1766. b. Of liquors: Alcoholic -1836. 2. Of persons: Lively, vivacious, high-spirited -1763.

Spi·rit-ra:pper. 1854. [f. next.] One who professes that he can induce spirits to communicate with him by means of rapping.

Spi·rit-ra:pping. 1853. [f. SPIRIT *sb.* + *rapping* vbl. sb.] 1. *pl.* Rappings alleged to be made by spirits in answer to questions addressed to them. 2. Professed communication from or with spirits by means of raps made by them 1854.

Spi·rit-sti:rring, *a.* 1604. That stirs or animates the spirits.

Spiritual (spi·ritiŭăl), *a.* and *sb.* ME. [a. OF. *spirituel*, or ad. L. *spiritualis*, f. *spiritus* SPIRIT *sb.*] A. *adj.* 1. Of, pertaining to, affecting or concerning, the spirit or higher moral qualities, esp. as regarded in a religious aspect. (Freq. dist. from *bodily*, *corporal*, or *temporal*.) late ME. b. Applied to material things, substances, etc., in a fig. or symbolical sense. late ME. †c. Of songs, etc.: Devotional, sacred -1660. 2. Of, belonging or relating to, or concerned with sacred or ecclesiastical persons or things, as dist. from secular; pertaining to the church or the clergy; ecclesiastical ME. 3. Of persons: a. Standing to another in a relationship based on a sacred or religious obligation. late ME. b. Ecclesiastical, religious. Freq. in *s. lords* and *s. man* (or *person*). late ME. c. Devout, holy, pious; morally good; having religious tendencies or instincts. late ME. 4. Of, pertaining to, or consisting of spirit, regarded in either a religious or intellectual aspect; of the nature of a spirit or incorporeal supernatural essence; immaterial ME. 5. Consisting of pure essence or spirit; volatile; alcoholic. Now *rare* or *Obs.* 1477. 6. Of or pertaining to, emanating from, the intellect or higher faculties of the mind; intellectual 1725. 7. Characterized by a high degree of refinement of thought or feeling. (Cf. SPIRITUEL *a.*) 1784. 8. Clever, smart, witty. (Cf. SPIRITUEL *a.*) 1791. 9. Concerned with spirits or supernatural beings 1841.

1. For they doo spiryteull and also corporall werkis CAXTON. b. The Spirituall and sincere milke of the word 1611. 2. The duties of life, which are either s. or secular DE FOE. *S. court*, a court having jurisdiction in matters of religion or ecclesiastical affairs. 3. a. He preferrs his own parish priest..as being his s. father 1697. b. The Lords S. and Temporal form one legislative assembly 1863. 4. Millions of s. Creatures walk the Earth Unseen MILT. 6. Blunting the keenness of his s. sense With narrow schemings and unworthy cares SHELLEY. 7. Those sad eyes were s. and clear KEATS. 8. We French are extremely s., and..are never at a loss for an answer 1872. Hence **Spi·ritual-ly** *adv.*, **-ness.**

B. *sb.* 1. a. A spiritual or spiritually-minded person 1532. b. *Eccl. Hist.* (With initial capital.) A member of the Congregation of Narbonne, a branch of Franciscans, pronounced schismatic in 1318, which advocated a stricter observance of the rule of poverty and simplicity of dress 1791. 2. *pl.* a. Spiritual matters, affairs, or ideas 1582. b. Matters which specially or primarily concern the church or religion 1647. c. Spiritual or ecclesiastical goods or possessions; spiritualities 1827. 3. A 'spiritual' song of American negro origin 1870.

2. a. Such was the prevailing tone of English belief in temporals; what was it in spirituals? MILL. b. It did not belong to the secular power to meddle in spirituals 1794.

Spiritualism (spi·ritiŭăliz'm). 1831. [f. SPIRITUAL *a.* + -ISM.] 1. Tendency towards, or advocacy of, a spiritual view of things, esp. as a leading principle in philosophy or religion 1836. 2. The belief that the spirits of the dead can hold communication with the living, or make their presence known to them in some way, esp. through a 'medium'; the system of doctrines or practices founded on this belief 1855. 3. Belief in the existence and influence of spiritual beings 1871.

2. Witchcraft, demonology, possession, and the like, revived in the modest phrase of S. 1860.

Spiritualist (spi·ritiŭălist). 1649. [f. as prec. + -IST.] 1. One who regards things from a spiritual point of view; one whose ideas and doctrines have a purely spiritual basis or tendency. 2. An adherent of spiritualism as a philosophical doctrine 1836. 3. A believer in spiritualism (sense 2); a spiritist 1859.

Spiritualistic (spi:ritiŭăli·stik), *a.* 1852. [f. prec. + -IC.] 1. Of or pertaining to, characterized by, philosophical or theological spiritualism; of the nature of spiritualism. 2. Of or pertaining to, associated or connected with, spiritualism (sense 2); spiritistic 1865.

Spirituality (spi:ritiŭæ·lĭti). late ME. [a. OF. (*e*)*spiritualite*, *-alete* (mod.F. *spiritualité*), or ad. late L. *spiritualitas*, f. *spiritualis* SPIRITUAL *a.*; see -ITY.] 1. The body of spiritual or ecclesiastical persons; the clergy. Now *Hist.* 1441. 2. That which has a spiritual character; ecclesiastical property or revenue held or received in return for spiritual services. Now *arch.* 1456. b. *pl.* Spiritual or ecclesiastical things; ecclesiastical possessions, rights, etc., of a purely spiritual character. Now *Hist.* late ME. 3. The quality or condition of being spiritual 1500. b. With *a* and *pl.* A spiritual thing or quality as distinct from a material or worldly one 1676. 4. The fact or condition of being spirit or of consisting of an incorporeal essence 1681.

1. He blamed both S. and laity 1709. 2. b. They [the Dean and Chapter] are Guardians of the Spiritualities during the Vacancy of the Bishoprick 1726. 3. His Life..is full of excellent Lessons of S. 1753. 4. That He is invisible is accounted for by His s. 1884.

Spiritualization (spi:ritiŭăləizē¹·ʃən). 1665. [f. next + -ATION.] 1. The action of changing into spirit; conversion or transformation of a corporeal or material substance into a spiritual condition. 2. The action of spiritualizing; the state of being spiritualized 1809.

Spiritualize (spi·ritiŭăləiz), *v.* 1631. [f. SPIRITUAL *a.* + -IZE.] 1. *trans.* To render spiritual; to raise or change to a spiritual (a more spiritual) condition. b. To convert into, invest with, a spiritual sense or meaning; to expound in a spiritual sense; to explain *away* in this manner. Also *absol.* 1645. c. To render spiritual in appearance; to refine in a high degree 1889. 2. †a. To render volatile or spirituous -1741. b. To invest with the nature of a spirit 1659.

1. Christ more spirituallized their Joy, rather to rejoyce that their Names were written in Heaven FULLER. b. To spiritualise away the pains of what is technically called Hell 1833. c. The softened light spiritualises the landscape 1889. Hence **Spi·ritualizer**, one who spiritualizes.

Spi·ritual-mi·ndedness. 1647. [After *spiritually-minded* (Tindale), tr. *geistlich gesinnet* (Luther).] The quality or state of being spiritually-minded or of having the mind set on spiritual things.

Spiritualty (spi·ritiŭălti). late ME. [ad. OF. *spiritualte*; see SPIRITUAL *a.* and -TY.] = SPIRITUALITY 1, 2, 2 b, 3.

‖**Spiritue·l, -e·lle**, *a.* 1673. [F. *spirituel* masc., *-elle* fem.; see SPIRITUAL *a.*] Of a highly refined character or nature, esp. in conjunction with liveliness or quickness of mind.

Spirituosity (spiritiuǫ·sĭti). 1669. [f. next + -ITY.] The state or quality of being spirituous, esp. through distillation.

Spirituous (spi·ritiu̯əs), *a.* 1599. [f. L. *spiritus* + -OUS, or ad. F. *spiritueux.*] **1.** Spirited, animated, lively, vivacious. Now *rare.* **2.** Of the nature of, having the properties of, spirit; containing spirit or volatile principle in a natural state 1605. **3.** Containing or impregnated with spirit or alcohol obtained by distillation; containing an infusion of alcohol; alcoholic, ardent 1681. **4.** Of or belonging to spirit or alcohol; like or resembling that of spirit 1667. †**5.** = SPIRITUAL, in various senses -1745.

1. The Emir in his s. humour, and haughty familiar manners 1888. 3. Strong Waters or S. liquors 1732. Hence **Spi·rituousness** = SPIRITUOSITY.

Spirketting (spə̄·ɹkėtiŋ). Also †**spirkiting, spar-.** 1748. [f. †*spirket*, †*spurket* pl. spaces between the rungs along a ship's side.] *Naut.* Inside planking between the waterways and the ports of a vessel.

Spirling (spə̄·ɹliŋ). Now only *Sc.* late ME. [a. MLG. *spirling*; cf. SPARLING, SPURLING.] The smelt, *Osmerus eperlanus.*

Spiro- (spəi·ro), comb. form of L. *spira*, Gr. σπεῖρα SPIRE *sb.*[3], as in: **Spirobacte·ria,** bacteria with spirally twisted cells; **Spirochæte** (-kī·tī), a genus of bacteria having a highly twisted spiral form.

Spirometer (spəirǫ·mǐtəɹ). 1846. [irreg. f. L. *spirare* to breathe; see -OMETER.] An instrument for measuring the breathing power of the lungs. Hence **Spirome·tric, -al** *adjs.*

Spirometry (spəirǫ·mǐtri). 1859. [See prec. and -METRY.] Measurement of breathing-power; the use of the spirometer.

Spirt (spə̄ɹt), *sb.*[1] 1550. [Origin obsc.] †**1.** A brief period of time; a short space -1612. **2.** *Naut.* A short or slight spell *of* wind 1726. **3.** A sudden outbreak or brief spell of activity or exertion; a spurt 1829.

Spirt (spə̄ɹt), *sb.*[2] 1716. [f. SPIRT *v.*[1]] **1.** A jet or slender spout of water or other liquid. **2.** A sudden jet of fire or puff of smoke 1851.

1. A great s. of blood DICKENS. 2. Little spirts of fire 1851.

Spirt (spə̄ɹt), *v.*[1] 1582. [Origin obsc.] **1.** *intr.* Of liquids (or small objects): To issue in a jet. **2.** *trans.* To send out in a jet or slender rapid stream; to squirt 1582.

Spirt (spə̄ɹt), *v.*[2] 1599. [f. SPIRT *sb.*[1]] *intr.* To make a spurt; to exert oneself for a short time.

Spirtle (spə̄·ɹt'l), *sb. dial.* 1881. [Cf. next.] A small spirt or jet; a sprinkle.

Spirtle (spə̄·ɹt'l), *v.* Now *dial.* 1603. [f. SPIRT *v.*[1] + -LE.] **1.** *trans.* To sprinkle, spatter, or splash *with* something. **2.** To cause to spatter or splash; to disperse in small particles 1612. **3.** *intr.* To become dispersed or scattered 1725.

‖**Spirula** (spəi·riŭlă). 1835. [mod.L., dim. of L. *spira* SPIRE *sb.*[3]] *Zool.* A genus of cephalopods having a flat spiral shell in the hinder part of the body; an animal of this genus, or one of the shells. So **Spi·rule.**

Spiry (spəi·ri), *a.*[1] 1602. [f. SPIRE *sb.*[1]] **1.** Of grass or other plants, stems, etc.: Forming slender pointed shoots. **b.** Of trees: Rising in a tapering form without much branching 1664. **2.** Having the characteristic form of a spire; tapering up to a point 1664. **3.** Of form: Resembling that of a spire 1777. **4.** Of places: Full of spires; spire-crowned 1728. **5.** Characterized by slenderness or slimness of growth or form 1853.

1. Heath and Spirie Grasse 1602. **b.** A range of meadows, set with s. poplars STEVENSON. 2. London's s. turrets THOMSON. Two s. cliffs..bound the lake 1840. 4. The s. habitable city STEVENSON.

Spiry (spəi·ri), *a.*[2] 1676. [f. SPIRE *sb.*[3]] Curving or coiling in spirals.

Hid in the s. volumes of the snake, I lurked within the covert of a brake DRYDEN.

†**Spiss,** *a.* 1530. [ad. L. *spissus.*] Thick, dense, compact, close -1784.

Boil these to a spisse Cataplasme 1658.

Spissitude (spi·sitiu̯d). Now *rare.* 1440. [ad. L. *spissitudo*, f. *spissus* SPISS *a.*] Density, thickness, compactness.

Spit (spit), *sb.*[1] [OE. *spitu*, = MDu. *spit*, *spet*, MLG. *spit*, *spet.*] **1.** A slender sharp-pointed rod of metal or wood, used for thrusting into or through meat which is to be roasted at a fire; a broach. †**2.** = OBELISK *sb.* 2. -1627. **3.** *Printing.* An iron rod carrying the wheel by which the carriage of a hand-press is run out or in 1728. **b.** A rod or skewer on which fish are strung and hung up to dry 1833. **4.** A sword. (Chiefly contemptuous.) 1642. **5.** A small, low point or tongue of land, projecting into the water; a long narrow reef, shoal, or sandbank extending from the shore 1673.

4. Out with your s. without delay! You've but to lunge and I will parry 1871. 5. Above the third buoy ..lies a dangerous s. 1802.

Spit (spit), *sb.*[2] ME. [f. SPIT *v.*[2]] **1.** The fluid secreted by the glands of the mouth, esp. when ejected; saliva, spittle; a clot of this. See also CUCKOO-SPIT. **2.** The act of spitting; an instance of this 1658. **3.** *The very s. of*, the exact image, likeness, or counterpart of (a person, etc.). *colloq.* 1825. **4.** A slight sprinkle or shower of rain or snow 1849.

2. *A s. and a stride* (dial.), a very short distance. 3. A daughter,..the very s. of the old Captain 1825.

Spit, *sb.*[3] 1507. [a. MDu., MLG. *spit*; see SPIT *v.*[3]] **1.** Such a depth of earth as is pierced by the full length of a spade-blade; a spade-graft. **b.** A thrust *of* the spade in digging 1844. **2.** A layer of earth of a spade's depth 1663. **3.** The quantity of earth taken up by a spade at a time; a spadeful 1675. **b.** A series of spadefuls taken in a line 1722.

1. The ground is delved two s. deep 1670.

Spit, *v.*[1] ME. [f. SPIT *sb.*[1]] **1.** *trans.* To put on a spit; to thrust through with a spit. **b.** *transf.* To pierce, transfix, or stab with a sharp weapon, etc.; to impale *on* or *upon* something sharp. late ME. **2.** To fix (herrings, etc.) on a spit or rod for drying or smoking 1617.

1. He lighted a fire, spitted a leg of mutton SMOLLETT. **b.** Your naked Infants spitted vpon Pykes SHAKS.

Spit, *v.*[2] Pa. t. **spit, spat.** Pa. pple. **spit, spat.** [Northern OE. *spittan*, = G. dial. *spitzen*, of imitative origin; cf. OE. *spǣtan.*] **I.** *trans.* †**1.** To eject saliva on (a person) as a sign of contempt -ME. **2.** To eject from the mouth by the special effort involved in expelling saliva OE. **3. a.** To emit, cast, throw, in a manner similar to the ejection of saliva. late ME. **b.** To extrude or lay (eggs or spawn) 1847. **4.** With *out* (or †*forth*): To utter in a proud, spiteful, plain, or unreserved manner. Also without adv.: To speak (a language). 1595.

2. The wulf..spytte blood CAXTON. fig. *To s. venom, poison, fire*, etc. *To s. in one's face, teeth*, etc. (chiefly *fig.*); He bit off his tongue and s. it in her face 1636. 3. **a.** The Canons..ready mounted..to s. forth Their Iron indignation gainst your walles SHAKS. 4. Thus Michael spits out bitter reproaches against David 1657. He spits French like a Magpy 1701.

II. *intr.* **1.** To eject saliva (at or on a person or thing) as a means of expressing hatred or contempt OE. **2.** To eject saliva from the mouth; to expectorate ME. **b.** Of certain animals when angry 1668. **3.** To sputter 1611. **4.** Of rain or snow: To fall in scattered drops or flakes. (Usu. impers.) 1567. **5.** *S. and polish*, the occupation of cleaning up or furbishing, as part of the work of a sailor or soldier 1895.

Spit, *v.*[3] Now *dial.* [OE. *spittan*, = MDu. and MLG. *spitten*, perh. related to SPIT *sb.*[3]] **1.** *intr.* To dig with a spade; to delve. late ME. **2.** *trans.* To plant with a spade 1610. **3.** To dig (*up*) with a spade; also, to turn up with a plough OE.

Spital (spi·tăl). 1634. [Late respelling of SPITTLE *sb.*[1] after HOSPITAL.] **1.** = SPITTLE *sb.*[1] 1, 2. **b.** *S. sermon*: see SPITTLE *sb.*[1] 1755. **2.** *fig.* A foul or loathsome place. SMOLLETT. **3.** A shelter for travellers. WORDSW.

1. Defrauding the Poor..or, to see it under the most opprobrious Colours, robbing the Spittal FIELDING.

Spi·t-ball. *U.S.* **1.** Paper chewed and rolled into a ball, to be thrown as a missile. Also *fig.* 1846. **2.** *Baseball.* A pitched ball moistened on one side with saliva 1912.

Spitchcock (spi·tʃkǫk), *sb.* 1597. [Origin obsc. Cf. SPATCHCOCK.] †**1.** A method of preparing an eel for the table (see sense 2) -1771. **2.** An eel cut into short pieces, dressed with bread-crumbs and chopped herbs, and broiled or fried 1601.

Spitchcock (spi·tʃkǫk), *v.* 1675. [f. prec.] **1.** *trans.* To prepare (*esp.* an eel) for the table as, or after the manner of, a spitchcock. **2.** To deal with (a person) in a similar manner; *fig.* to handle severely 1674. So **Spitchcocked** (spi·tʃkǫkt) *ppl. a.* 1643.

Spite (spəit), *sb.* †Also **spight.** ME. [Aphetic f. DESPITE *sb.*] †**1.** Action arising from, or displaying, hostile or malignant feeling; outrage, injury, harm; insult, reproach -1658. **2.** A strong feeling of (†contempt,) hatred, or ill-will; intense grudge or desire to injure; rancorous or envious malice ME. **b.** *fig.* Of fortune, nature, the elements, etc. 1562. **3.** With *a* and *pl.* A particular instance of malignant or rancorous feeling directed towards a special object. late ME. †**4.** An annoying matter, affair, or thing; a feeling of irritation -1670.

2. Much have I borne from canker'd critic's s. GRAY. Phr. *For* or *in spite.* **b.** He defied the spight of Fortune 1562. 3. Phr. *To have a s. at*; This Preacher ..hath some s. at me 1612. *Phr.* **In s. of** (also, now *arch.*, **s. of**), in defiance (†scorn or contempt) of; in the face of; notwithstanding. 5. *attrib.* **s. fence** *U.S.* an unsightly fence erected for the purpose of injuring a neighbour.

Spite (spəit), *v.* ME. [Aphetic f. DESPITE *v.*; cf. prec.] †**1.** *trans.* To regard with contempt or spite -1690. **2.** To treat spitefully or maliciously; to annoy or thwart in a spiteful manner 1592. **3.** To fill with spite or vexation; to annoy, offend, irritate 1563. †**4.** *intr.* To be angry or annoyed; to cherish spite -1580.

2. Not caring what they suffer themselves, so they may s. their enemy 1658. Phr. *To s.* (*one*), in order to vent spite or spleen upon (another); with the object of vexing or annoying. 3. There is nothing spites us more, than to heare a man commend himselfe 1581.

Spiteful (spəi·tfŭl), *a.* 1440. [f. SPITE *sb.* + -FUL.] †**1.** Expressive of, characterized by, contempt or disdain -1700. †**b.** Bringing contempt or opprobrium; disgraceful, shameful -1586. **2.** Full of, possessed or animated by, spite; malicious, malevolent. Also *fig.* of things 1490. †**3.** Distressing, annoying, vexing -1633.

2. A s. Saying gratifies so many little Passions ADDISON. Hence **Spi·teful-ly** *adv.*, **-ness.**

Spitfire (spi·tfəiəɹ), *a.* and *sb.* 1600. [f. SPIT *v.*[2]] **A.** *adj.* **1.** That spits fire; fire-spitting; *fig.* irascible; displaying anger or hot temper. **2.** Naut. *S.-jib*: in cutters, a small storm-jib of very heavy canvas 1867.

1. Where..spit-fire cats their midnight revels keep 1791.

B. *sb.* **1.** A thing which emits or vomits fire; *esp.* a cannon 1611. **2.** One whose temper is fiery; a passionate quick-tempered person 1680. **3.** A cat in an angry state 1825.

1. That s., the Rock of Gibraltar 1785. 2. What a little s. was this Nancy of mine! 1881.

Spi·tful. 1842. [f. SPIT *sb.*[3]] A spadeful.

†**Spi·tous,** *a.* and *adv.* ME. [Aphetic ad. AF. *despitous*, f. *despit*; see SPITE *sb.*]. **1.** = DESPITOUS *a.* -1481. **2.** As *adv.* = DESPITOUSLY *adv.* -1400. So †**Spi·tously** *adv.*

†**Spi·tter**[1]. 1565. [app. f. SPIT *sb.*[1]] A young deer with simple unbranched horns; a brocket or pricket -1661.

Spitter[2] (spi·təɹ). late ME. [f. SPIT *v.*[2]] One who spits or ejects saliva. Also *fig.*

Spi·tter[3]. Now *dial.* 1600. [f. SPIT *v.*[3]] **1.** A spade or spud. **2.** A spademan; a delver or digger 1648.

†**Spittle,** *sb.*[1] [ME. *spit(t)el*, repr. (ult.) an aphetic form of HOSPITAL, modified after native words in *-el, -le.*] **1.** A house or place for the reception of the indigent or diseased; a charitable foundation for this purpose, *esp.* one chiefly occupied by persons of a low class or afflicted with foul diseases; a lazar-house. (Now written SPITAL.) -1839. **2.** Phr. *To rob the s.*, to make gain in a particularly mean or dastardly manner -1708. **3.** *fig.* A foul receptacle or collection. Const. *of.* -1652.

2. Of all men, Vs'rers are not least accurst; They robb the S.; pinch th' Afflicted worst QUARLES.

Comb.; **s.-house** = sense 1; **S. sermon**, one of the sermons preached on Easter Monday and Tuesday from a special pulpit at St. Mary Spital (afterwards at St. Bride's and finally at Christ Church in the City).

Spittle (spi·t'l), *sb.*[2] 1480. [f. SPIT *v.*[2]] **1.** Saliva, spit. **2.** The frothy secretion of an insect. Cf. CUCKOO-SPIT. 1821.

Phr. †*S. of the stars*, honey-dew, nostoc. †*S. of the the sun*, gossamer.

Comb.: **s.-fly, -insect,** *U.S.*, an insect forming, or bred in, a frothy secretion.

Spi·ttle, *sb.*³ Now *dial.* [OE. *spitel*, related to SPIT *sb.*³ and *v.*³] **1.** A spade or small spade; a spud. **2.** A hoe or scraper 1832.

Spittle (spi·t'l), *v.*¹ *rare.* ME. [orig. f. SPIT *v.*² + -LE; later f. SPITTLE *sb.*²] *intr.* To eject spittle; to spit.

Spittle, *v.*² *rare.* 1727. [f. SPITTLE *sb.*³] *trans.* To dig (*in*), to pare, etc., with a spittle.

Spittoon (spitū·n). 1840. [f. SPIT *v.*² + -OON.] A receptacle for spittle; usually a round flat vessel of earthenware or metal, sometimes having a cover in the form of a shallow funnel with an opening in the middle, and frequently containing sawdust.

‖**Spitz** (spits). 1845. [G. (also *spitzhund*), special use of *spitz* pointed, peaked.] A species of dog having a very pointed muzzle; a Pomeranian dog.

Spla·cknuck. 1726. [Invented by Swift.] An imaginary animal of Brobdingnag; a strange animal or person.

Your modern ladies shriek at a pipe as if they saw a 's.' TENNYSON.

Splanchnic (splæ·ŋknik), *a.* and *sb.* 1681. [ad. med. or mod.L. *splanchnicus*, ad. Gr. σπλαγχνικός, f. σπλάγχνον, usu. pl. σπλάγχνα, the inward parts, esp. the heart, lungs, liver, and kidneys.] **A.** *adj.* **1. a.** Situated in, connected with, the viscera or intestines. Freq. in *s. nerve(s.* 1694. **b.** Occupied by the viscera (esp. in *s. cavity*); of a visceral character 1830. **2.** Affecting, pertaining or relating to, the viscera 1681. **B.** *sb.* A splanchnic nerve. Chiefly in *pl.* 1840.

Splanchno- (splæ·ŋkno), comb. form of Gr. σπλάγχνον (see prec.), as in:

Splanchno·graphy, an anatomical description of the viscera. **Splanchnopleu·ral** *a.*, pertaining to the splanchnopleure. **Spla·nchnopleure,** one of the two layers or divisions of the mesoblast. **Splanchnopleu·ric** *a.*, = *splanchnopleural.* **Splanchnoske·letal** *a.*, relating or belonging to the visceral skeleton. **Splanchnoske·leton,** the visceral skeleton, consisting of hard or bony parts developed in the viscera or sense-organs. **Splanchno·tomy,** dissection or anatomy of the viscera.

Splanchnology (splæŋknǫ·lŏdʒi). 1706. [See prec. and -LOGY.] **1.** The scientific study of the viscera. **2.** The visceral system 1842.

Splash (splæʃ), *sb.* 1736. [f. SPLASH *v.*] **1.** A quantity of some fluid or semi-liquid substance dashed or dropped upon a surface. **b.** The fragmentary metal resulting from the shattering of bullets upon impact 1865. **2.** *colloq.* A striking or ostentatious display, appearance, or effect; a dash 1806. **3.** The act or result of suddenly and forcibly striking or dashing water or other fluid; the sound produced by this 1819. **4.** The act, result, or sound of water falling or dashing forcibly upon something 1832. **5.** A large or irregular patch of colour or light 1832.

2. Phr. *To make* or *cut a s.* **3.** That pebble which falls into the water with a s. 1898. **5.** [The light] fell in a great s. upon the thicket STEVENSON.

Splash (splæʃ), *v.* 1715. [Alteration of PLASH *v.*²] **I.** *trans.* **1.** To bespatter, to wet or soil, by dashing water, mud, etc. 1722. **b.** To stain, mark, or mottle with irregular patches of colour or light. Chiefly in *pa. pple.* 1833. **2.** To cause (a liquid or semi-liquid substance) to fly about 1762. **3.** To cause (something) to dash or agitate a liquid, esp. so as to produce a sound 1879. **4.** To make (one's way) with splashing 1830.

3. Splashing their oars, and making as much noise as possible FROUDE.

II. *intr.* To cause dashing or noisy agitation of a liquid; to move or fall with a splash or splashes 1715. **2.** Of liquids: To dash or fly in some quantity and with some degree of force 1755. **3.** Of bullets: To throw off fragments on striking an object 1894. Hence **Splash** *adv.* in a splashing manner; with a splash or splashing sound.

Splash-, the stem of SPLASH *v.*, as in **s. lubrication, method, system,** a method of keeping machinery oiled by regular splashing of oil from a receptacle; **s.-net,** a small fishing-net; hence *splash-netting* vbl. sb.; **-paper,** paper coloured in irregular patches; **-work,** spatter-work.

Spla·sh(-)board. 1842. [f. prec.] **1.** A guard or screen in front of the driver's seat on a vehicle, to protect him from being splashed with mud from the horse's hoofs. **2.** A board fixed over or beside a wheel to intercept splashings 1850. **3.** *Naut.* A screen above the deck-line 1907.

Splasher (splæ·ʃəɹ). 1848. [f. SPLASH *v.*] **1. a.** A guard placed over or beside a wheel to prevent splashing or accidental contact. **b.** A splash-board 1887. **2.** A flat board strapped to the foot for walking on soft ground or mud 1859.

Spla·shy, *a.*¹ 1727. [Alteration of PLASHY *a.*¹] Full of shallow pools or puddles; wet and soft.

Splashy (splæ·ʃi), *a.*² 1834. [f. SPLASH *sb.* or *v.*] **1.** Of a splashing character; falling, etc., with a splash or in splashes 1856. **2.** Of sounds: Such as are made by a splash 1834. **3.** Making a show or stir; sensational 1836. **4.** Done in splashes; not even or regular 1880.

1. Brown leaves, s. rains, and winds moaning CARLYLE. **4.** Fine, but s., sketches 1880.

Spla·tter, *v.* Chiefly *dial.* and *U.S.* 1784. [Imitative.] **1.** *intr.* To splash continuously or noisily. **2.** *trans.* To spatter or sputter (something); to cause to spatter 1785.

Splay (splēi), *sb.* 1507. [f. SPLAY *v.*¹] *Arch.* A slope or bevel; applied esp. to the sides of a door or window by which the opening widens from the door or window toward the face or faces of the wall. **b.** The degree of bevel or slant given to the sides of an opening, etc. 1860. **c.** The outward spread of a bowl or cup 1874.

Splay, *adv.* and *a.* 1734. [Back-formation f. SPLAY-FOOTED.] **A.** *adv.* **a.** = SPLAY-FOOT 3. **b.** In an oblique manner; slantingly. **B.** *adj.* Oblique; awry; off the straight 1876.

In the German mind, as in the German language, there does seem to be something s. M. ARNOLD.

Splay (splēi), *v.*¹ ME. [Aphetic f. DISPLAY *v.*] †**1.** *trans.* = DISPLAY *v.* **1.** –1594. **2.** To spread out, expand, extend; to open out in a spreading manner. late ME. †**b.** = DISPLAY *v.* 3. –1575. **3.** *trans.* To bevel or make slanting; to construct with a splay 1598. **4.** *intr.* **a.** To have, take, or lie in, an oblique or slanting direction 1725. **b.** To spread out in an awkward manner 1848.

1. Swerd or septer..There was none nor baners splayde wyde LYDG. **3.** The simplest method..is to s. the jambs and arch of the window 1878.

Splay, *v.*² Now *dial.* 1601. [Alteration of SPAY *v.*] *trans.* To spay (female animals).

Splay(-)foot. 1548. [f. SPLAY *v.*¹] **1.** A flat, spread out, clumsy foot, esp. one which turns outwards. †**2.** *attrib.* = next –1766. **3.** As *adv.* In a splay-footed manner 1626.

Splay-footed, *a.* 1545. [f. as prec.] Having splay feet. **b.** *fig.* Clumsy, awkward; sprawling 1716.

†**Splay-mouthed,** *a.* 1651. [f. SPLAY *v.*¹] Having a wide or wry mouth –1812. So †**Splay-mouth** a distorted mouth. DRYDEN.

Spleen (splīn), *sb.* ME. [ad. OF. *esplen*, or L. *splen*, a. Gr. σπλήν, related to Skr. *plīhan*, L. *lien.*] **1.** *Anat.* An abdominal organ consisting of a ductless gland of irregular form, which in mammals is situated at the cardiac end of the stomach and serves to produce certain changes in the blood; the milt or melt. †**b.** Regarded as the seat of melancholy or morose feelings –1665. †**c.** Regarded as the seat of laughter or mirth –1681. †**2.** Merriment, gaiety, sport. SHAKS. †**3. a.** A sudden impulse; a whim or caprice –1625. **b.** Caprice; changeable temper. SHAKS. †**4.** Hot or proud temper; high spirit, courage, resolute mind –1605. †**b.** Impetuosity, eagerness. SHAKS. **5.** Violent ill-nature or ill-humour; irritable or peevish temper 1594. **6.** With *a*: **a.** A fit of temper; a passion. *Obs.* exc. *arch.* 1589. †**b.** A grudge –1722. **7.** Excessive dejection or depression of spirits, gloominess and irritability; moroseness; melancholia. Now *arch.* 1664.

1. c. Come burst your spleens with laughter to behold A new found vanity QUARLES. **2.** *Tam. Shr.* Induct. i. 137. **3. a.** A thousand spleens bear her a thousand ways SHAKS. **b.** 1 *Hen. IV*, II. iii. 81. **4.** *Rom. & Jul.* III. i. 163. **5.** Whereat Geraint flash'd into sudden s. TENNYSON. **6. a.** *Mids. N.* I. i. 146. **7.** This quiet room gives me the s. LYTTON. He is the victim of English s. 1860. Hence **Splee·nish** *a.* somewhat spleenful or splenetic; **-ly** *adv.*, **-ness.**

†**Spleen** *v.* 1629. [f. the sb.] **1. a.** *trans.* To regard with spleen; to have a grudge at –1675. **b.** To fill with spleen; to make angry or ill-tempered –1801. **2.** *trans.* To deprive of the spleen 1735.

Spleenful (splī·nfŭl), *a.* 1588. [f. SPLEEN *sb.*] Full of spleen; passionate, irritable, peevishly angry.

My selfe haue calm'd their spleenfull mutinie SHAKS. Then rode Geraint, a little s. yet, Across the bridge TENNYSON.

Spleenless (splī·nlės), *a.* *rare.* late ME. [f. SPLEEN *sb.*] **1.** Destitute of a spleen. †**2.** *fig.* Mild, gentle 1615.

Spleenwort (splī·nwɒɹt). 1578. [f. SPLEEN *sb.*, after L. *splenion* or *asplenon*, a. Gr. σπλήνιον, ἄσπληνον, f. σπλήν spleen.] **1. a.** One or other of various ferns belonging to the genus *Asplenium*; also, the genus itself. †**b.** Hart's-tongue; scolopendrium –1796. **2.** *U.S.* A species of cactus 1846.

Spleeny (splī·ni), *a.* 1604. [f. SPLEEN *sb.*] Spleenful, splenetic.

Splen-, var. of SPLENO- bef. vowels, as in **Splena·lgia,** pain in the spleen, etc.

†**Splenative,** *a.* 1592. Also †**spleen-.** [f. SPLEEN *sb.*] **1.** Acting on the spleen. NASHE. **2.** Of a hot or hasty temper –1660.

Splendacious (splendē¹·ʃəs), *a.* 1843. [Fancifully f. SPLEND(ID + -ACIOUS.] Very splendid.

Splendent (sple·ndĕnt), *a.* 1474. [a. L. *splendent-*, *splendens*, *splendere* to be bright or shining.] **1.** Shining brightly by virtue of inherent light. Also *fig.* **2.** Reflecting light with great brilliancy; bright, gleaming, resplendent 1578. **b.** Extremely brilliant, gorgeous, or magnificent 1567. **3.** *fig.* Having qualities comparable to material brightness or brilliancy; pre-eminently beautiful, grand, or great 1509.

1. Whan the golden sterres clere were s. 1503. **2.** The best Grey-hound hath..a neate sharpe head, and s. eyes 1607. **b.** Giants, s. in gold-lace and grenadier-caps CARLYLE. **3.** The s. brightnes of the Trueth, which burnes..so gloriously 1599. Hence †**Sple·ndently** *adv.*

Splendid (sple·ndid), *a.* 1624. [ad. L. *splendidus*, f. *splendere* to be bright.] **1.** Marked by much grandeur or display; sumptuous, grand, gorgeous. **b.** Of persons: Maintaining, or living in, great style or grandeur 1658. **2. a.** Resplendent, extremely bright, in respect of light or colour (*rare*) 1634. **b.** Magnificent in material respects 1685. **c.** Having or embodying some element of material grandeur or beauty 1815. **3.** Impressive by greatness, grandeur, or some similar excellence 1653. **b.** Dignified, haughty, lordly 1833. **4.** Excellent; very good or fine 1644. **5.** Used, by way of contrast, to qualify nouns having a different connotation 1667.

1. Accommodation so s. I know not that I should desire were I a prince 1797. **b.** Ambitious of s. acquaintance 1779. **2. a.** The topaz is a most s. and famous stone 1750. **b.** A s. Hindoo temple 1863. **c.** The splendider scenery of the Alps 1851. **3.** Persons of..splendider fortunes 1653. **b.** A s. contempt for female intellect 1833. **4.** A s. shot 1882. **5.** Our state Of s. vassalage MILT. Hence **Sple·ndid-ly** *adv.*, **-ness.**

†**Splendi·dious,** *a.* late ME. [f. L. *splendidus* + -IOUS.] Splendid, magnificent, brilliant –1653. So †**Sple·ndidous** *a.*

Splendiferous (splendi·fĕrəs), *a.* 1460. [orig. f. med.L. **splendifer* (for late L. *splendorifer*). In mod. use joc. and orig. *U.S.*] †**1.** Full of or abounding in splendour –1546. **2.** *colloq.* Remarkably fine 1843.

Splendorous (sple·ndŏrəs), *a.* Also †**splendrous.** 1591. [f. L. *splendor.*] Full of splendour; resplendent, bright.

In splendrous Armes he road DRAYTON.

Splendour (sple·ndəɹ). Also (now *U.S.*) **splendor.** 1450. [ad. AF. (*e*)*splendur*, *-our*, or L. *splendor*, f. *splendere* to shine.] **1.** Great brightness; brilliant light or lustre. **2.** Magnificence; great show of riches or costly things; pomp, parade 1616. **3.** Brilliant distinction, eminence, or glory; impressive character 1604. **4.** Brilliant or ornate appearance or colouring 1774.

1. And swift and swift beyond conceiving The splendor of the world goes round 1871. 2. The antique s. of the ducal house 1837. 3. The s. of the present progress had not..been equalled D'ISRAELI. 4. *Comb.* Like s.-winged moths SHELLEY.

Splenetic (splǐne·tik), *a.* and *sb.* 1544. [ad. late L. *spleneticus*, f. *splen* SPLEEN. Until the beginning of the 19th c. the stress was on the first syllable.] A. *adj.* 1. Of or pertaining to, connected with, the spleen; splenic. Also *fig.* †2. Affected with disease or disorder of the spleen; in later use, affected with melancholia or hypochondria –1766. †b. Characterized by, tending to produce, melancholy or depression of spirits –1781. 3. Having an irritably morose or peevish disposition or temperament; ill-humoured, testy, irascible 1592. 4. Characterized by, arising from, displaying or exhibiting, spleen or ill-humour 1693. †5. Of medicines: Acting on the spleen –1728.

1. The Splenetick Vein, or Artery 1722. 2. If he be s., he may..meet companions..with whose groans he may mix his own GOLDSM. b. Our cloudy and s. country EVELYN. 3. A s. woman, who must have somebody to find fault with RICHARDSON. 4. The overflowing of a s. moment 1775.

B. *sb.* 1. One who has a splenetic disposition; a splenetic, peevish, or ill-humoured person 1703. †2. A splenetic medicine or remedy –1718. Hence †**Splene·tical** *a.* and *sb.*, -**ly** *adv.*

Splenial (splī·niăl), *a.* and *sb.* 1848. [f. L. *splenium* (Pliny), ad. Gr. σπλήνιον bandage or compress.] *Zool.* and *Anat.* A. *adj.* 1. *S. bone* or *piece*, a splint-like bone or process applied to the inner side of the lower mandible in certain classes of vertebrates below Mammalia. 2. *S. border*, the posterior border of the corpus callosum 1891. B. *sb.* The splenial bone or process 1854.

Splenic (sple·nik), *a.* 1619. [ad. L. *splenicus*, ad. Gr. σπληνικός, f. σπλήν SPLEEN *sb.*] 1. *Anat.* Of, pertaining to, connected with, or situated in the spleen. b. *S. flexure*, the bend of the colon near the spleen 1808. 2. *Path.* Of diseases, etc.: Of or affecting the spleen; esp. *s. fever*, malignant anthrax 1867. Hence †**Sple·nical** *a.*

‖ **Splenitis** (splǐnəi·tis). 1753. [a. Gr. σπληνῖτις, f. σπλήν SPLEEN *sb.*; see -ITIS.] *Path.* Inflammation of the spleen, or a particular form of this.

‖ **Splenius** (splī·niŏs). 1732. [mod.L., f. Gr. σπλήνιον; cf. SPLENIAL *a.*] *Anat.* A broad muscle, or either of the two portions (the *splenius capitis* and *colli*) composing it, which occupies the upper part of the back of the neck and is attached to the occipital bone.

Splenization (splenizē¹·ʃən). 1849. [a. F. *splénisation*, or ad. mod.L. *splenisatio*, f. *splen* SPLEEN *sb.*] *Path.* The conversion of substance into tissue resembling that of the spleen; *esp.* the diseased condition of the lungs when this has taken place.

Spleno- (splī·no), a. Gr. σπληνο-, comb. form of σπλήν SPLEEN *sb.*, as in: **Sple·nocele**, a rupture of the spleen. **Spleno·graphy**, a description of the spleen. **Spleno·logy**, the science of the spleen. **Spleno·tomy**, dissection or anatomy of the spleen.

Spleuchan (splū·yăn). *Sc.* (and *Ir.*). 1785. [a. Gael. *spliùchan*, Ir. *spliuchăn*.] A tobacco pouch, freq. used as a purse.

Splice (spləis), *sb.* 1627. [f. the vb.] 1. A joining or union of two portions of rope, cable, cord, etc., effected by untwisting and interweaving the strands at the point of junction. Chiefly *Naut.* b. *techn.* A joining of two pieces of wood, etc., formed by overlapping and securing the ends; a scarf-joint 1875. 2. *slang.* Union by marriage; a marriage, wedding 1830.

attrib. and *Comb.*: **s.-grafting**, a method of grafting in which the scion and stock are cut obliquely and bound firmly together; whip- or tongue-grafting; hence **Splice-graft** *vb.*; -**joint**, the connecting joints between rails on railways; -**piece**, a fish-plate or break-joint piece at the junction of two rails.

Splice (spləis), *v.* 1524. [ad. MDu. *splissen*, perh. related to SPLIT *v.*] 1. *trans.* To join (ropes, cables, lines, etc.) by untwisting and interweaving the strands of the ends so as to form one continuous length; to unite (two parts of the same rope) by interweaving the strands of one end into those of another part so as to form an eye or loop; to repair (rigging) in this way. Also *absol.* Chiefly *Naut.* b. To form (an eye or knot) in a rope by splicing 1773. 2. To join (two pieces of timber, etc.) by overlapping or scarfing the two ends together in such a way as to form a continuous length; to fasten *together* in this way; to graft by a similar process 1626. b. *transf.* To unite in this manner by means of surgery or natural healing 1755. c. To unite, combine, join, mend 1803. 3. *slang.* To join in matrimony; to marry. Chiefly *pass.* 1751.

1. Phr. *To s. the main-brace*: see MAIN-BRACE¹.

Spline (spləin), *sb.* 1756. [orig. E. Anglian dial.; perh. related to SPLINTER *sb.*] 1. A long, narrow, and relatively thin piece or strip of wood, metal, etc.; a slat. b. *spec.* A flexible strip of wood or hard rubber used by draftsmen in laying out broad sweeping curves, especially in railroad work 1891. 2. *techn.* A rectangular key fitting into grooves in a shaft and wheel or other attachment so as to allow longitudinal movement of the latter 1864. Hence **Spline** *v. trans.* to fit with a s. **Spli·ning** *vbl. sb.*, used attrib. in *splining-machine*, one for cutting key-seats and grooves.

Splint (splint), *sb.* ME. [a. MDu. *splinte* or MLG. *splinte*, *splente* metal plate or pin. Cf. prec.] 1. One of the plates or strips of overlapping metal of which certain portions of mediæval armour were sometimes composed; *esp.* one of a pair of pieces of this nature used for protecting the arms at the elbows. 2. A slender, moderately long and freq. flexible, rod or slip of wood cut or cleft off and serving for some particular purpose, esp. as a lath or wattle, or prepared for use in some manufacture ME. 3. A splinter of wood or stone; a chip or fragment. Now chiefly *n. dial.* late ME. 4. *Surg.* A thin piece of wood, etc., used to hold a fractured or dislocated bone in position during the process of reunion; hence, any appliance serving this purpose. late ME. 5. *Farriery.* A callous tumour developing into a bony excrescence on the metacarpal bones of a horse's or mule's leg, occurring usually on the inside of the leg along the line of union of the splint-bones with the cannon-bone 1523. b. The growth of this, as a specific malady in horses 1594. 6. A laminated, coarse, hard coal. (See also SPLINT COAL.) 1789.

1. The knees and feet were defended by splints, or thin plates of steel, ingeniously jointed upon each other SCOTT.

Splint (splint), *v.* late ME. [f. the sb.] †1. *trans.* To cover, furnish, or construct with splints or thin strips of wood, etc. –1639. 2. To adjust, bind, or fit a surgical splint to (a fractured bone, etc.); to put into splints; to secure by means of a splint or splints 1543. b. *transf.* and *fig.* To strengthen or support as if with splints 1634. †3. To cut or split (wood, etc.) into splints or splinters; to cleave apart –1600.

Splint(-)bone. Also †**splent bone.** 1704. [SPLINT *sb.*] *Farriery.* †a. = SPLINT *sb.* 5. b. Either of the two small metacarpal bones of the foreleg of a horse, lying behind and in close contact with the cannon-bone or shank.

Splint coal. 1789. [Cf. SPLINT *sb.* 6.] Coal with a more or less splintery fracture; orig. a less bituminous variety of Scotch cannel coal; now chiefly, a hard and highly bituminous coal burning with great heat.

Splinter (spli·ntəɹ), *sb.* late ME. [a. MDu. *splinter*, *splenter*, = LG. *splinter*, *splenter*, related to SPLINT *sb.*] 1. A rough (usu. comparatively long, thin, and sharp-edged) piece of wood, bone, etc., split or broken off, esp. as the result of violent impact; a chip, fragment, or shiver. b. Used (chiefly with negs.) to denote a very small piece or amount, or something of little or no value 1606. 2. A surgical splint. *Obs.* or *dial.* 1597. 3. A comparatively thin piece or slender strip of wood prepared or used for some particular purpose 1648. b. Used as a torch, or dipped in tallow and used as a candle 1751. 4. *ellipt.* = SPLINTER-BAR 2. (*rare*) 1794.

1. The bomb,..a s. of which struck the lady 1711. Phr. *In* or *into splinters*. b. The Grecian Dames are sun-burnt, and not worth The s. of a Lance SHAKS. 3. b. Perusing a hymn-book by the light of a pine s. 1862.

attrib. and *Comb.*: **s. net**, -**netting** *Naut.*, a net or netting of small rope spread on board a warship during action to protect the men from falling splinters; -**new** *a.* (*dial.*) quite new.

Splinter (spli·ntəɹ), *v.* 1582. [f. the sb.] 1. *trans.* To break or split into splinters or long narrow pieces, or in such a way as to leave a rough jagged end or projections. †2. = SPLINT *v.* 2. Also with *up.* –1720. 3. *intr.* To split 1625. b. *poet.* To pierce *through* in the form of, or after the manner of, splinters 1821.

1. A strong bull..splintered with his horns the upper post 1806. *fig.* The Courtier, Scholler, Souldier, all in him, All dasht and splinterd thence SHAKS. 3. b. The moon..Splinters through the broken glass CLARE. Hence **Spli·nterless** *a.* that will not s.

Splinter-bar. Also **splinter bar.** 1765. [SPLINTER *sb.*] 1. A swingle-tree or whippletree. 2. A cross-bar in a carriage, coach, etc., which is fixed across the head of the shafts, and to which the traces are attached 1794.

Spli·nter-proof, *sb.* and *a.* 1805. [See PROOF *a.*] *Mil.* A. *sb.* A structure serving for protection from the splinters of bursting shells. B. *adj.* Of sufficient strength to ward off the splinters of bursting shells 1834.

Splintery (spli·ntəri), *a.* 1796. [f. SPLINTER *sb.* and *v.* + -Y¹.] 1. *Min.* Of fracture: Characterized by the production of small splinters. 2. Of stone, minerals, etc.: Liable to split into splinters; breaking or separating easily into splinters; *spec.* having a splintery fracture 1807. b. Of rocks, etc.: Marked by splintering; rough or jagged 1829. 3. Of the nature of a splinter; resembling a splinter in shape or form 1839. 4. Full of splinters 1857.

Split (split), *sb.* 1597. [f. SPLIT *v.* and *ppl. a.*] 1. A narrow break or opening made by splitting; a cleft, crack, rent, or chink; a fissure. b. *techn.* An angular groove cut on glass vessels 1850. 2. A piece of wood separated or formed by splitting. Now *U.S.* 1617. b. *techn.* In the leather trade, a section of a skin obtained by splitting it into several thicknesses 1858. 3. A rupture, division, or dissension in a party or sect, or between friends 1729. 4. *Mining.* A division of a ventilating air-current 1883. 5. *slang.* An informer; a detective 1812. 6. *colloq.* a. A split soda; a bottle of mineral water half the usual size 1884. b. A split roll or bun 1905. c. A split vote 1894.

The splits: the acrobatic feat of lowering oneself to the floor with the legs in a straight line 1861.

Split (split), *v.* Pa. t. and pa. pple. **split** (also †**splitted**, †**splitten**). 1590. [ad. MDu. *splitten* (Du. *splitten*, WFris. *splitte*).] I. *trans.* 1. Of storms, rocks, etc.: To break up (a ship); to cause to part asunder. Chiefly in *pass.* b. Of persons: In *pass.*, to suffer shipwreck. Also *fig.* 1602. 2. To divide longitudinally by a sharp stroke or blow; to cause to burst or give way along the grain or length; to cleave or rend 1593. b. *Naut.* Of wind: To rend or tear (a sail). Also of persons or a vessel: To have (a sail) rent or torn by the wind. 1625. 3. *fig.* a. Of violent grief or pain 1594. b. Of loud noise 1602. c. Of excessive laughter 1687. 4. a. To divide or apportion to, or between, two or more persons 1670. b. To divide or break up into separate parts or portions 1706. c. To divide or separate (persons) into parties, factions, groups, etc. 1712. d. To divide or separate by the interposition of something 1824. 5. *slang.* To disclose, reveal, let out 1850.

1. Our helpefull ship was splitted in the midst SHAKS. 2. At Cajeta, in Italy, a mountain was split in this manner by an earthquake GOLDSM. *fig.* Blow, and s. thyself SHAKS. b. We split our maintop-sail 1748. 3. a. Let sorrow s. my heart, if euer I Did hate thee SHAKS. b. The air was split with shrill outcries 1865. c. He laughed ready to s. his sides 1809. 4. a. Not worth splitting a guinea;..toss who shall pay for both DICKENS. b. He..falls to splitting his Text most methodically 1706. c. They are easily split into parties by intrigue 1861. d. Mrs. Williamson splits her infinitives 1895.

Phrases. *S. me* (or *my windpipe*), used as an imprecation. *To s. a hair* or *hairs*, *straws*, *words*, to make fine or subtle distinctions, to be over-subtle or captious. *To s. the difference*, to halve an amount in dispute between two parties; to take the mean between two sums or quantities; to compromise on this basis.

II. *intr.* †1. As predicate to *all*: To go to pieces –1611. 2. Of a ship: To part or break by striking on a rock or shoal, or by the violence of a storm 1593. b. Of persons: To suffer shipwreck in this manner. Freq. *fig.* 1610. 3. To part asunder, to burst, to form a fissure or fissures, esp. in a longitudinal direction 1625. b. Used hyperbolically to denote the effect of excessive laughter, pain, or repletion 1677. c. To admit of being cleft 1846. 4. To part, divide, or separate in some way 1712. b. To break up into separate groups or parties 1824. 5. To break up *into* factions, sects, etc.; to separate through disagreement or difference of opinion; to fall out or disagree 1730. b. *slang.* To break or quarrel *with* a person 1835. 6. *slang.* To turn evidence or informer; to peach; to betray confidence 1795.

1. *Mids. N.* I. ii. 32. 2. This is the most dangerous Rock to s. upon, in all the Archipelago 1718. b. Mercy on vs. We s., we s. SHAKS. 3. b. I laugh'd till I thought I should s. SWIFT. My head was like to s. 1756. c. The wood splits clean and easy 1846. 4. At the point where Hermon splits into its two parallel ranges 1856. 5. 'Don't let us s. on a small point of detail,' he began 1890. 6. If anybody is to s., I had better be the person DICKENS.

Split-, the verbal stem in combs., as **s.-farthing** *a.*, mean, miserly.

Split (split), *ppl. a.* 1648. [f. SPLIT *v.*] 1. That has undergone the process of splitting; divided in this manner; riven, cleft. b. Of a surface: Exposed by splitting 1715. c. *Bot.* Cleft or divided very deeply 1832. 2. Separated, divided, parted, or apportioned in some way 1839.

Special collocations: **s. brilliant**, a brilliant the foundation squares of which are divided horizontally into two triangular facets; **s. infinitive** (see INFINITIVE); **s. peas**, peas shelled, dried, and split for making pease-puddings, soup, etc.; **-pin**, a pin or cotter split at one end; **-ring**, a metal ring split spirally, on which keys, etc. may be hung; **s. second(s**, applied to chronographs having two independent centre second hands, one under the other; **-shot, -stroke**, in various games, a shot or stroke which sends in divergent directions two or more balls placed in contact; **-tail**, (*a*) a Californian fish of the carp family; (*b*) the pintail duck.

Splitter (spli·təɹ). 1623. [f. SPLIT *v.* + -ER[1].] One who, or that which, splits or cleaves, in various senses 1648. b. *spec.* One employed in splitting fish 1623.

Splodge (splǫdʒ). 1854. [Imitative.] A thick, heavy, or clumsy splotch. Hence **Splo·dgy** *a.*

Splosh (splǫʃ), *adv.* [Contamination of *splash* and *plop.*] With a heavy fall or blow.

Splotch (splǫtʃ), *sb.* 1601. [perh. imitative.] A large irregular spot or patch of light, colour, or the like. Hence **Splotch** *v. trans.* to cover with splotches; to splash or stain in patches. **Splo·tchy** *a.* covered with or having the appearance of splotches.

Splurge (splɜ̄ɹdʒ), *sb. U.S.* 1834. [Imitative.] 1. An ostentatious display or effort. 2. A heavy splash or downpour 1879. So **Splurge** *v. U.S. intr.* (*a*) to make an ostentatious display, to show off; (*b*) to splash heavily.

Splutter (splʋ·təɹ), *sb.* 1677. [Imitative.] 1. A noise or fuss. b. Violent and confused declamation, discourse, or talk; an instance of this 1688. 2. A loud or violent sputter or splash 1815.

1. b. Dinner..with a confused s. of German to the neighbours on my right HUXLEY. 2. A couple of ducks..made away with a great s. 1873.

Splutter (splʋ·təɹ), *v.* 1728. [f. prec.] 1. *trans.* To utter hastily and indistinctly 1729. 2. a. To scatter in small splashes 1835. b. To bespatter (a person) 1869. 3. *intr.* To talk or speak hastily and confusedly 1728. 4. To make a sputtering sound or sounds 1818. 5. Of a pen: To scatter ink in writing 1837. 6. To fly in small splashes or pieces 1849.

1. King James spluttered out his alarm at Jesuit plots in clumsy Latin 1870. 4. Waning candles s. in the sockets 1860.

Spode (spōᵘd). 1893. The surname of a maker of china, Josiah *Spode* (1754–1827), used *attrib.* to designate ware made by him. Also *ellipt.*, = Spode-ware.

‖**Spodium** (spōᵘ·diǒm). Now *rare.* late ME. [L., ad. Gr. σπόδιον, = σποδός ashes.] A fine powder obtained from various substances by calcination.

Spodo- (spǫ·do, spǫdǫ·), a. Gr. σποδο-, comb. stem of σποδός ashes, dross, as in **Spodoge·nic** *a.*, **Spodo·genous** *a.*, *Path.* characterized by the production of waste organic matter. **Spo·domancy**, divination by means of ashes. **Spodoma·ntic** *a.*

Spodumene (spǫ·diumīn). Also **spodumen.** 1805. [a. F. *spodumène*, G. *spodumen*, ad. Gr. σποδούμενος, σποδοῦσθαι to be burnt to ashes, f. σποδός.] *Min.* A silicate of aluminium and lithium, of varying colour, found both in crystals and massive.

Spoil (spoil), *sb.* ME. [ad. OF. *espoille*, f. *espoillier*, or directly f. SPOIL *v.* In branch II after L. *spolium*, pl. *spolia.*] I. 1. Goods taken from an enemy or captured city in time of war; the possessions of which a defeated enemy is deprived by the victor; any goods, property, territory, etc., seized by force, acquired by confiscation, or obtained by similar means; booty, loot, plunder. b. *transf.* That which is or has been acquired by special effort or endeavour; esp. objects of art, books, etc. so acquired 1750. c. The public offices or positions of emolument distributed among the supporters of a successful political party on its accession to power. Chiefly *U.S.* and in *pl.* 1770. 2. The action or practice of pillaging or plundering; rapine, spoliation. *Obs.* or *arch.* 1532. †3. A marauding expedition or raid –1646. 4. An object or article of pillage, plunder, or spoliation; a prey 1594.

1. Why did they not..preserve the spoiles of the cloisters for publick and charitable uses? 1654. He led his army back..laden with the s. of Locris 1838. *fig.* New islands..are sometimes formed from the spoils of the continent GOLDSM. Phr. *The spoils of war.* b. But Knowledge to their eyes her ample page Rich with the spoils of time did ne'er unroll GRAY. c. My vote was counted in the day of battle, but I was overlooked in the division of the s. GIBBON. 2. So was the citie of Constantinople..for that time saued from saccage and spoile 1603. Phr. *To make s. of*, to pillage or plunder. 4. Oh, Greece! thy flourishing cities were a s. Unto each other 1821.

II. 1. The arms and armour of a slain or defeated enemy as stripped off and taken by the victor; a set or suit of these. Usu. *pl.* 1547. b. A single article acquired in this way 1697. 2. The skin of a snake (or of any animal) stripped or cast off; the slough. Also *pl.* Now *Obs.* or *arch.* 1601. b. *pl.* The remains of an animal body; the parts left intact or uneaten 1695.

1. That Hector..Which erst returnd clad with Achilles spoiles 1547. 2. Like the old Skin, or Spoile of Serpents 1638. Skins of Beasts, the rude Barbarians wear; The Spoils of Foxes, and the furry Bear DRYDEN. b. Numbers of flies, whose spoils lay scattered before..his [the spider's] palace SWIFT.

III. 1. The action or fact of spoiling or damaging; damage, harm, impairment, or injury, esp. of a serious or complete kind. Now *rare.* 1572. †2. An act or instance of this –1722. 3. *techn.* Earth or refuse material thrown or brought up in excavating, mining, dredging, etc. 1838.

1. Sir John Wallop..did much s. upon the French 1648.

Comb.: **spoils system**, the system or practice of a successful political party giving government or public offices, etc., to its supporters. Hence **Spoi·lsman** *U.S.*, one who obtains, or seeks to obtain, a share of political spoils.

Spoil (spoil), *v.* Pa. t. and pple. **spoiled, spoilt.** ME. [ad. OF. *espoillier*:—L. *spoliare*, f. *spolium*; see SPOIL *sb.* II.] I. 1. *trans.* To strip or despoil (a dead or helpless person); *esp.* to strip (a defeated or slain enemy) of arms and armour. Now *arch.* 2. To strip (persons) of goods or possessions by violence or force; to plunder, rob. Now *rare* or *arch.* ME. 3. To pillage or plunder (a country, city, house, ship, etc.); to clear of goods or valuables by the exercise of superior force; to ravage or sack. Now *arch.* late ME. 4. To seize (goods) by force or violence; to carry off as spoil; to rob or steal; to take away improperly. *arch.* late ME. 5. *absol.* To commit or practise spoil or pillage; to plunder, ravage. *arch.* late ME.

1. The Greeks with shouts press on, and s. the dead POPE. 2. Thy hands..have spoyl'd The hopelesse Widdow 1624. 3. To slay the folk, and s. the land TENNYSON. 4. No man can..spoile his goods, except he will first bind the strong man *Mark* iii. 27. 5. On this manner he went spoyling through Fraunce 1597.

II. 1. To strip (a person, body, etc.) *of* arms, clothes, or the like. Now *arch.* ME. 2. To deprive, despoil, or rob *of* something, *of* some quality, distinction, etc. late ME.

2. When you do this, you s. it of every thing sublime BURKE.

III. †1. To destroy, bring to an end –1726. †b. To inflict serious bodily injury upon (an animal or person). Now merged in next. –1665. 2. To damage, impair, or injure, esp. to such an extent as to render unfit or useless; to mar or vitiate completely or seriously 1563. 3. With immaterial obj.: To affect injuriously or detrimentally, esp. to an irretrievable extent 1578. 4. To injure in respect of character, esp. by over-indulgence or undue lenience. Also, to treat with excessive consideration or kindness. 1694. 5. *intr.* To become unfit for use; to deteriorate; to go bad, decay 1692.

1. For Gods sake take a house, This is some Priorie, in, or we are spoyl'd SHAKS. 2. A great flood, all grass spoyl'd 1692. 3. If the sudden coming of the King of Barma, had not spoiled his markets 1652. Phr. *To s. all* or *everything.* 4. I swear, my dear, you'll s. that child CONGREVE. 5. Cargoes that are liable to s., such as all kinds of grain SOUTHEY. Phr. *To be spoiling for* (a fight, etc.), to long for, desire ardently (orig. *U.S.*). Hence **Spoi·lable** *a.* that may be spoiled; capable of being spoilt.

Spoil-, the stem of SPOIL *v.* in comb. with sbs., as **s.-five**, a round game of cards which is said to be 'spoiled' if no player wins three out of a possible five tricks; †**-paper**, a petty author; **-sport**, one who acts so as to spoil the sport or plans of others.

Spoilage (spoi·lėdʒ). 1816. [f. SPOIL *v.* + -AGE.] 1. The action of spoiling; the fact of being spoilt. 2. That which is or has been spoilt, *spec.* applied to sheets of paper which have been spoiled in printing 1888.

Spoil(-)bank. *local.* 1830. [f. SPOIL *sb.*] A bank or large mound consisting of refuse earth or similar waste material.

†**Spoi·lful**, *a.* 1590. [f. SPOIL *sb.* + -FUL.] Causing or characterized by destruction or pillage; plundering, spoliatory –1670.

Spoke (spōᵘk), *sb.* [OE. *spáca*, = OFris. *spêke*, OS. *spêca.*] 1. One of the set of staves, bars, or rods radiating from the hub or nave of a wheel and supporting the felloes or rim. Also *fig.*, esp. in ref. to the wheel of Fortune. b. One of a set of radial handles projecting from a cylinder or wheel (esp. a steering-wheel) 1648. 2. A bar or rod of wood, esp. one used or shaped for a particular purpose; a stake or pole; a handspike; a weaver's beam 1467. b. A round or rung of a ladder, etc. 1658. c. A contrivance for locking a wheel in descending a hill 1858.

1. The wheel of fortune keeps turning for the comfort of those who are at the lowest s. 1834.

Phrases. *To put in one's s.*, etc., (*a*) to attempt to give advice or have some say in a matter; (*b*) to attempt to advance a person's interests (*rare*). *To put a s. in* a person's *wheel*, to act in a manner calculated to thwart, obstruct, or impede his actions or purposes; so *a s. in* a person's *wheel*, an impediment or obstacle.

Comb.: **s.-bone** *Anat.*, = RADIUS 1 b.

Spoke (spōᵘk), *v.* 1720. [f. the sb.] 1. *trans.* To furnish or provide with spokes or bars; to mark *with* spoke-like lines or rays. 2. To thrust a spoke into (a wheel, etc.) in order to check movement; *fig.* to block, impede, or obstruct 1854. 3. To force (a wheel or vehicle) *forward* by pushing the spokes 1860.

Spoken (spōᵘ·k'n), *ppl. a.* 1460. [Pa. pple. of SPEAK *v.*] 1. As the second element in combs.: Speaking or given to speaking in a specified way, as *broad-*, *civil-*, *out-*, *plain-spoken.* 2. Of language, words, etc.: Uttered in speech, oral. Also, colloquial as dist. from *literary.* 1837. b. Expressed, declared, made known by speech or utterance 1851. c. Of a phrase in or in connexion with a song: Uttered with the ordinary speaking voice; also *ellipt.* a phrase or part of this nature 1865.

2. b. There is a vast difference between the silent and the s. protest 1879. c. A comic song..with 'S.' in it DICKENS.

Spokeshave (spōᵘ·kʃēᵗv), *sb.* 1510. [f. SPOKE *sb.* + SHAVE *sb.*[1]] A form of drawing-knife or shave used for shaping and finishing spokes; a transverse plane. Hence **Spo·ke-shave** *v. intr.* to use a s.

Spokesman (spōu·ksmǣn). 1540. [irreg. f. *spoke*, pa. pple. of SPEAK *v.*, after *craftsman*, etc.] **1.** One who speaks for or on behalf of another or others, *esp.* one deputed to voice the opinions of a body, etc.; a mouthpiece. **b.** *transf.* The chief representative or exponent *of* a movement, period, etc. 1828. **2.** A public speaker 1663.

1. He hath been an earnest s. in your cause 1585. b. Dante is the s. of the Middle Ages CARLYLE. 2. There is many an excellent S. that makes a bad Writer 1693.

Spokeswoman (spōu·kswu:măn). 1654. [Cf. prec.] A woman who speaks for another or others; a female advocate or representative.

Spoliate (spōu·liēⁱt), *v.* 1722. [f. L. *spoliat-*, *spoliare* to spoil, f. *spolium.*] *trans.* To spoil or despoil; to rob or deprive *of* something.

Spoliation (spōuliēⁱ·ʃən). late ME. [ad. L. *spoliatio*, f. *spoliare*, or a. F.] **1.** The action of spoliating; seizure of goods or property by violent means; depredation, robbery. Also, the condition of being despoiled or pillaged. **b.** An act or instance of despoiling or plundering; a robbery; an exaction of a spoliatory nature 1800. **2.** *Eccl.* A writ or suit brought by one incumbent against another holding the same benefice by an illegal or questionable title 1498. **b.** The action on the part of one incumbent of depriving another of the emoluments of a benefice 1726. **3.** *Law.* The action of destroying a document, or of injuring or tampering with it in such a way as to destroy its value as evidence 1752. **4.** The action of spoiling or injuring 1867.

1. He brought Rome into a state of poverty and s. hitherto unexampled 1832.

Spoliative (spōu·liētiv), *a.* 1876. [See SPOLIATE *v.* and -IVE.] *Med.* Having the effect of seriously diminishing the amount of the blood 1876.

Spoliator (spōu·liēⁱtəɹ). 1831. [a. L., f. *spoliare*, or ad. F. *spoliateur.*] One who commits spoliation; a pillager; a spoiler.

Spoliatory (spōu·liătəri), *a.* 1790. [f. L. *spoliat-*, *spoliare* + -ORY [2].] Of the nature of or characterized by, spoliation or robbery; pillaging, plundering.

Spondaic (spǫndēⁱ·ik), *a.* and *sb.* 1722. [ad. F. *spondaïque* or L. *spondaicus.*] **A.** *adj.* **1.** Of verses (or parts of these): **a.** Composed of spondees. **b.** Having a spondee in positions where a different foot is normal; *esp.* of hexameters, having a spondee in the fifth foot. **2.** Characterized by a spondee or spondees 1751. **3.** Of words: Consisting of two long syllables 1849. **B.** *sb.* A spondaic foot or line 1839.

Spondee (spǫ·ndī). late ME. †Also in L. form. [ad. L. *spondeus*, incorrectly *spondæus* (sc. *pes*), ad. Gr. σπονδεῖος, f. σπονδή solemn drink-offering; or a. F. *spondée.*] *Pros.* A metrical foot consisting of two long syllables. Hence **Sponde·an** *a.* (*rare*).

Spondulicks (spǫndiū·liks). *slang*. orig. *U.S.* Also **-ics, -ix.** 1857. [Fanciful.] Money, cash.

Spondyl(e (spǫ·ndil). Now *rare*. late ME. [a. F. *spondyle*, or ad. L. *spondylus*, *sphondylus*, ad. Gr. σπ-, σφόνδυλος.] †**1.** One or other of the joints of the spine; a vertebra –1667. †**2.** A joint *of* a wheel, vessel, etc. –1662. **3.** *Zool.* = next 1668.

‖ **Spondylus** (spǫ·ndilŏs). *Pl.* **-li.** 1601. [L.; see prec.] *Zool.* One or other of the species of bivalves belonging to the genus *Spondylus*, characterized by foliaceous spines.

Sponge (spʊndʒ), *sb.*[1] Also †**spunge.** [OE. *sponge*, *spunge*, ad. L. *spongia*, *spongea*, a. Gr. σπογγιά, later deriv. of σπόγγος sponge.] **I. 1.** The soft, light, porous, and easily compressible framework which remains after the living matter has been removed from various species of porifers, characterized by readily absorbing fluids and yielding them on pressure, and much used in bathing, cleansing surfaces, etc. **2.** Without article: The material of which this is composed. late ME. **3.** *Zool.* One or other of various aquatic (chiefly marine) animals (or colonies of animals) of a low order, belonging to the group *Porifera*, characterized by a tough elastic skeleton of interlaced fibres 1538. **4.** A moistened piece of the above substance (sense 1) as used for wiping a surface in order to obliterate writing, etc. Also *fig.* 1555. **b.** A method of cancelling or wiping off debts without payment 1717. **5.** A kind of mop or swab for cleansing a cannon-bore after firing 1625.

1. Phr. *To throw up the s.* (of a boxer or his attendant) to throw the s. used between rounds into the air in token of defeat; *fig.* to submit or yield; to abandon a contest or struggle. 3. The finest type of all, the Levant toilet or Turkish cup-sponge (*Spongia officinalis*) 1883. *Glass-sponge*, the genus *Hyalonema*. 4. b. A spunge..is the only needful and only availing remedy BENTHAM. Phr. *To pass the s. over*, to agree to forget (an offence, etc.).

II. 1. a. = BEDEGUAR 2. 1608. **b.** The soft fermenting dough of which bread is made. Freq. in the phr. *to set* (or *lay*) *the s.* 1822. **c.** A stretch of ground of a swampy nature 1856. **d.** *techn.* Metal in a porous or sponge-like form, usu. obtained by reduction without fusion 1861.

III. *fig.* **1.** An immoderate drinker; a soaker 1596. **2.** One who or that which absorbs, drains, or sucks up, in a sponge-like manner 1603. **b.** *spec.* One who or that which appropriates or absorbs material or other advantages, wealth, etc.; a person of this kind as a source from which something may be recovered or extracted 1601. **c.** An object of extortion; a source of profit or pecuniary advantage 1625. **3.** A sponger 1838.

1. I will doe any thing Nerrissa ere I will be married to a spunge SHAKS. 2. *Haml.* IV. ii. 12. He is a s. full of knowledge, which you may squeeze at your leisure 1779. c. Thy monarchs..in distress Found thee a goodly s. for Power to press COWPER.

attrib. and *Comb.*, as *s.-bag*, *-bath*, *-bed*, *-fishery*; **s.-biscuit**, a biscuit of a similar composition to sponge-cake; **-cloth**, (*a*) a peculiar kind of cloth, moist with oil, for cleaning machinery and fire-arms; (*b*) a soft, loosely-woven fabric with a roughish surface; **-finger**, a long, narrow sponge-biscuit; **-gold**, gold as it remains after the silver has been removed in the process of 'parting'; **-iron**, iron ore rendered light and porous by the removal of foreign matter.

Sponge, *sb.*[2] 1693. [f. the vb.] **1.** The act of living parasitically on others. **2.** An act of wetting or wiping (off) with or as by means of a sponge 1720.

Sponge (spʊndʒ), *v.* late ME. [f. SPONGE *sb.*[1], or ad. OF. *esponger* (mod.F. *éponger*), late L. *spongiare.*] **I. 1.** *trans.* To wipe or rub with a wet sponge for the purpose of cleaning. **b.** To swab the bore of (a cannon), esp. after a discharge. Also *absol.* 1625. **c.** To wipe, wet, or moisten, *with* some liquid applied by means of a sponge 1800. †**2.** With *up*: To make spruce, smart, or trim –1626. **3.** To remove with a sponge 1624. **4.** To convert (flour or dough) into 'sponge' 1772. **5.** *intr.* To issue or rise in a spongy form; to foam 1790.

1. Planning how her..gown..might be sponged, and turned MRS. GASKELL. c. The patient should be..sponged with tepid water 1876. 5. She did not even s. at her mouth 1867.

II. *fig.* **1.** To rub or wipe out; to efface or obliterate 1548. **2. a.** To drain or empty; to clear out (*rare*) 1610. †**b.** To deprive (a person) *of* something by sponging; to press (a person) *for* money; to squeeze –1724. **3.** To get from another in a mean or parasitic manner 1676. **4.** *intr.* To live *on* others in a parasitic manner; to obtain assistance or maintenance by mean arts 1673. **5.** To go about in a sneaking or loafing fashion, esp. in order to obtain something 1825.

1. Its gloom saturated the forest rim, and then sponged it out of sight 1887. 2. b. Those Hogs hee must feed, till they spunge him of all his substance 1631. 3. They spunged up my money while it lasted GOLDSM. 4. Humbugs, ready to..s. upon his benevolence 1902.

Spo·nge-cake. 1808. [SPONGE *sb.*[1]] A very light sweet cake made with flour, milk, eggs, and sugar.

Spongelet (spʊ·ndʒlĕt). 1835. [f. SPONGE *sb.*[1] + -LET.] **1.** *Bot.* = SPONGIOLE. **2.** A small sponge 1887.

Spongeous (spʊ·ndʒəs), *a.* late ME. [ad. L. *spongeosus*, f. *spongea* SPONGE *sb.*[1]] **1.** Of the nature or character of a sponge; porous, spongy. **2.** Characterized by porousness or sponginess 1600.

Sponger (spʊ·ndʒəɹ). 1677. [f. SPONGE *v.* or *sb.*[1] + -ER [1].] **1.** One who lives meanly at another's expense; a parasite. **2.** One who uses a sponge, esp. in order to cleanse the bore of a cannon 1828. **3.** A gatherer of, a diver or fisher for, sponges 1880.

Spongi- (spʊ·ndʒi), comb. form, after L. types, of SPONGE *sb.*[1], as in **Spo·ngiculture**, **Spongi·ferous** *a.*, **Spo·ngiform** *a.*

Spongin (spʊ·ndʒin). 1868. [f. SPONGE *sb.*[1] + -IN.] = KERATOSE *sb.*

Sponginess (spʊ·ndʒinĕs). 1610. [f. SPONGY *a.* + -NESS.] **1.** Spongy or porous character, nature, or quality. **2.** *Path.* The characteristic soft fungous condition of the gums in scurvy 1873.

Sponging (spʊ·ndʒiŋ), *vbl. sb.* 1575. [f. SPONGE *v.* or *sb.*[1]] **1.** The action of SPONGE *v.* **2.** The practice or occupation of gathering sponges 1868.

Spo·nging-house. 1700. [f. prec.] A house kept by a bailiff or sheriff's officer, formerly in regular use as a place of preliminary confinement for debtors.

His creditors..become more pressing, and at last he gets into a s. 1874.

Spongio- (spǫ·ndʒio), comb. form, on Gr. analogies, of Gr. σπογγιά, L. *spongia* SPONGE *sb.*[1], as in **Spongio·logist** (ǫ·lŏdʒist), **-logy**, = SPONGOLOGIST, -LOGY.

Spongiole (spʊ·ndʒ-, spǫ·ndʒiōul). 1832. [a. F., ad. L. *spongiola* asparagus-root, rose-gall, dim. of *spongia* SPONGE *sb.*[1]] *Bot.* The tender extremity of the radicle of a plant, characterized by loose sponge-like cellular tissue.

Spongiopiline (spʊ:ndʒiopəi·ləin, -in). Also **-ene**, **-in.** 1851. [f. SPONGIO- + Gr. πῖλος felt + -INE.] *Med.* Wool or cloth felted together with small pieces of sponge and having an impermeable back, used as a substitute for a poultice when moistened with hot water.

Spongiose (spʊ·ndʒiōus), *a.* 1755. [ad. L. *spongiosus*, f. *spongia.*] Of a spongy texture; porous.

Spongious (spʊ·ndʒiəs), *a.* Now *rare*. late ME. [ad. L. *spongiosus* (see prec.).] **1.** Of the nature of a sponge; spongy. **2.** Of or pertaining to a sponge 1846.

1. The s. bones of the upper jaw 1778.

Spongo- (spǫ·ŋgo, spǫŋgǫ·), a. Gr. σπογγο-, comb. form of σπόγγος sponge, as in **Spo·ngoblast**, one of the pear-shaped cells which secrete the hyaline lamellæ in sponges. **Spongo·logist**, an authority on sponges. **Spongo·logy**, the science or knowledge of sponges.

Spongoid (spǫ·ŋgoid), *a.* Also **spungoid.** 1808. [f. Gr. σπόγγος SPONGE *sb.*[1] + -OID.] **1.** *S. inflammation*, a kind of soft cancer or morbid growth. **2.** Having the form or structure of a sponge 1833. **3.** Like that of a sponge 1847.

Spongy (spʊ·ndʒi), *a.* 1539. [f. SPONGE *sb.*[1] + -Y [1].] **1.** Having a soft elastic or porous texture resembling that of a sponge; deficient in solidity or firmness, so as to be readily compressible. **2.** Of hard substances: Having an open porous structure resembling that of a sponge 1591. **3.** Resembling a sponge in respect of moisture or capacity for containing moisture; absorbent 1598. **4.** *fig.* Of diction or style: Deficient in substance or solidity 1603. **5.** Of texture or other qualities: Resembling that of a sponge 1611. **6.** Resembling that pressed from a sponge 1605.

1. The ground..being very spungy in wet weather 1677. The muscular, s. flesh of the tongue GOLDSM. Spungy rushes hide the plashy green CRABBE. 2. A Splent is a spungy harde grissell or bone, growing fast on the inside of the shin-bone of a Horse 1607. This Ice becometh..spungy by the dashing of the Sea 1694. 3. The spungy South SHAKS. There is no Lady ..More spungie, to sucke in the sense of Feare SHAKS. 4. To set a petty Gloss upon a spungy Conjecture 1665. 5. The soil may be of a spungy nature 1765. 6. With a s. moisture diffused through the atmosphere HAWTHORNE.

Sponsal (spǫ·nsăl), *a.* 1656. [ad. L. *sponsalis*, f. *sponsus*, *-a*, spouse.] Of or pertaining to marriage; spousal; wedded.

Sponsible (spǫ·nsĭb'l), *a.* Now *dial.* 1721. [Aphetic f. RESPONSIBLE *a.*] Responsible, reliable. Hence †**Sponsibi·lity** (*rare*).

Sponsion (spǫ·nʃən). 1632. [ad. L. *sponsio*, *spondere* to promise solemnly.] **1.** A solemn or formal engagement, promise, or pledge, freq. one entered into or made on behalf of another person 1677. **b.** *International Law.* An engagement made on behalf of the supreme authority by a person not having a commission to make such engagement 1776. **2.** *Rom. Law.* An engagement to pay a certain sum to the other party in a suit, in the event of not proving one's case 1632. Hence †**Spo·nsional** *a.* entering into an engagement or pledge.

Sponson (spǫ·nsən), *sb.* 1835. [Origin obsc.] **1.** *Naut.* One or other of the triangular platforms before and abaft the paddle-boxes of a steamer. **2.** A gun platform standing out from the side of a vessel 1862. Hence **Spo·nson** *v. trans.* to support, or set *out*, on a s.

Sponsor (spǫ·nsǝ̆ɪ), *sb.* 1651. [a. L., f. *spondere*; cf. SPONSION.] **1.** *Eccl.* One who answers for an infant at baptism; a godfather or godmother. **2.** One who enters into an engagement on behalf of another; a surety 1677. **3.** A business firm or person who pays for a broadcast programme which introduces advertisements of a commercial product 1931.

Hence **Spo·nsor** *v. trans.* to be surety for, to support strongly; also in ref. to sense 3 above. **Spo·nsorship,** the state of being a s.; the office of a s.

Sponso·rial, *sb.* and *a.* 1797. [f. prec.; see -ORIAL.] **A.** *sb.* A baptismal sponsor 1836. **B.** *adj.* Of or pertaining to a sponsor 1797.

Spontaneity (spǫntănī·ĭti). 1651. [ad. L. **spontaneitas*, f. *spontaneus*.] **1.** Spontaneous, or voluntary and unconstrained, action on the part of persons; the fact of possessing this character or quality. **2.** Spontaneous or voluntary action or movement on the part of animals (or plants); activity of physical organs in the absence of any obvious external stimulus 1721. **3.** The fact or quality in things of being spontaneous in respect of production, occurrence, etc. 1751. **b.** The fact or quality of coming without deep thought or premeditation 1826.

1. Actions performed without the s. of the agent, are automatic 1804. **3. b.** Poets who, delighted with the s. of their ideas, never reject any that arise 1839.

Spontaneous (spǫntē¹·nǐəs), *a.* 1656. [f. L. *spontaneus*, f. *sponte* of one's own accord, willingly.] **1.** Arising, proceeding, or acting entirely from natural impulse, without any external stimulus or constraint; voluntary. **2.** Of motion: Arising purely from or entirely determined by the internal operative or directive forces of the organism 1659. **3.** Of natural processes: Having a self-contained cause or origin 1664. **4. a.** *S. generation*, the development of living organisms without the agency of pre-existing living matter, usually considered as resulting from changes taking place in some inorganic substance 1656. **b.** *S. combustion*, the fact of taking fire or burning away, through conditions produced within the substance itself; *spec.* the alleged occurrence of this fact in persons addicted to the excessive use of alcohol 1795. **5.** Growing or produced naturally without cultivation or labour 1665. **b.** Produced, developed, or coming into existence by natural processes or changes 1732. **6.** Quasi-*adv.* Spontaneously 1667.

1. That all voluntary actions,..are called also s., and said to be done by a man's own accord HOBBES. **2.** Vegetables..have in some instances s., though we know not that they have voluntary, motion 1807. **3.** Regions of s. fertility JOHNSON. **4. a.** The idea of a s. generation of organic bodies is now exploded 1857. The first and simplest plants had no ancestors; they arose by s. generation 1882. **b.** The s. combustion.. of masses of tow, cotton, or rags saturated with oil 1863. **5.** When men lived on the s. fruits of the earth 1839. **6.** Chariots wing'd..now came forth S. MILT. Hence **Sponta·neous-ly** *adv.*, **-ness.**

Spontoon (spǫntū·n). Now *Hist.* 1708. [a. F. *sponton*, ad. It. *spontone*, *spuntone*, f. *puntone*, *punto* point.] A species of half-pike or halberd carried by infantry officers in the 18th c.

Spoof (spūf), *sb. slang.* 1889. [Invented by Arthur Roberts (1852–), comedian.] **1.** A game of a hoaxing and nonsensical character. Also, a round game of cards in which certain cards when occurring together are termed 'spoof'. **2.** Hoax, humbug; an instance of this 1897. **3.** *attrib.* Hoaxing, humbugging 1895. Hence **Spoof** *v. trans.* to hoax or humbug. **Spoo·fer. Spoo·fery.**

Spook (spūk). 1801. [ad. Du. *spook*, G. *spuk*.] A spectre, ghost. Hence **Spoo·kish** *a.*

Spool (spūl), *sb.* ME. [ad. ONF. *espole* or the source of this, MLG. *spôle*.] **1.** A small cylindrical piece of wood or other material on which thread is wound as it is spun, esp. for use in weaving; a bobbin. **b.** A reel 1852. **c.** Any cylinder on which cord, wire, tape, etc., is wound for convenience or for a special purpose 1864. **2.** A mesh-pin used in net-making 1838. **3.** *attrib.*, as *s.-stand*, *-ticket*, *-wheel* 1538.

Spool (spūl), *v. rare.* 1603. [f. prec.] **a.** *intr.* To wind spools. **b.** *trans.* To wind (thread) on spools. So **Spoo·ler,** one engaged in winding thread on spools 1554.

†**Spoom,** *v.* 1620. [Alteration of SPOON *v.*[1]] *intr.* To run *before* the sea, wind, etc.; to scud –1830.

fig. When vertue spooms before a prosperous gale, My heaving wishes help to fill the sail DRYDEN. Hence **Spoo·ming** *ppl. a.* foaming.

Spoon (spūn), *sb.* [Com. Teut.; OE. *spôn*. In OE. the word has only the general sense of 'chip'; sense 2 is specifically Scand.] †**1.** A thin piece of wood; a chip, splinter, or shiver –1513. **2.** A utensil consisting essentially of a straight handle with an enlarged and hollowed end-piece (the bowl), used for conveying soft or liquid food to the mouth, or employed in the culinary preparation or other handling of this (often distinguished as *dessert-*, *sugar-*, *tea-s.*) ME. **3.** An implement of the form described above, or something similar to this, used: **a.** As a surgical instrument. late ME. **b.** In melting, heating, or assaying substances 1496. **c.** A wooden golfing-club having a slightly concave head 1808. **d.** A kind of artificial bait having the form of the bowl of a spoon, used in spinning or trolling 1851. **4.** The student last in each class in the list of mathematical honours at Cambridge; *spec.* the 'wooden spoon' (see WOODEN *a.*) 1824. **5.** *slang.* or *colloq.* A shallow, simple, or foolish person; a simpleton, ninny, goose 1799.

2. A spone of golde, full of hony swete SKELTON. Phrases. *He should have a long s. that sups with the Devil. To be born with a silver s. in one's mouth*, to be born in affluence or under lucky auspices. *To make a s. or spoil a horn*, to make a determined effort to achieve something, whether ending in success or failure (orig. *Sc.*). †*S. of the brisket*, the hollow at the lower end of the breast-bone. **5.** Phr. *To be spoons with* or *on* (slang), to be sentimentally in love with (a girl).

Comb.: **s.-bait, -hook,** = sense 3 d; **-wood,** *Kalmia latifolia*, the Mountain Laurel of America.

Spoon, *v.*[1] *Obs.* exc. *arch.* 1576. [Origin obsc.] *Naut.* **1.** *intr.* In sailing, to run *before* the wind or sea; to scud. **2.** To move rapidly *on* or *upon* another vessel 1608.

1. We went spooning away large with the wind for one of the islands DE FOE.

Spoon (spūn), *v.*[2] 1715. [f. SPOON *sb.*] **I. 1.** *trans.* To lift or transfer by means of a spoon. **2.** In games: **a.** *Croquet.* To push (a ball) without an audible knock 1865. **b.** *Cricket.* To hit or lift (the ball) up in the air with a soft or weak stroke 1879. **c.** *Golf.* To hit (a ball) in putting so as to lift it 1896. **3.** *intr.* To lie close together, fit into each other like spoons 1887. **4.** *trans.* To hollow out, make concave, after the fashion of a spoon 1897.

1. *fig.* A pewter age,..An age of scum, spooned off the richer past MRS. BROWNING.

II. 1. *intr.* To make love, esp. in a sentimental or silly fashion. *colloq.* 1831. **2.** *trans.* To court or pay addresses to (a person), esp. in a sentimental manner 1877.

Spoonbill (spū·nbil). 1678. [f. SPOON *sb.* + BILL *sb.*[2], after Du. *lepelaar*, f. *lepel* spoon.] **1.** One or other of various species of birds belonging to the widely distributed genus *Platalea*, characterized by having a long spatulate or spoon-shaped bill; esp. the common white species, *P. leucorodia*. **b.** *pl.* The genus *Platalea* 1819. **2.** A spatulate or spoon-shaped bill 1802. **3.** The paddle-fish 1892.

Comb.: **S. Duck,** the Scaup Duck; also, the Shoveller, *Spatula clypeata*. So **Spoo·n-billed** *a.*, having a spoon-shaped bill 1668.

Spoondrift (spū·ndrift). 1769. [f. SPOON *v.*[1] + DRIFT *sb.*] Spray swept from the tops of waves by a violent wind and driven continuously along the surface of the sea. Now commonly SPINDRIFT.

Spoonerism (spū·nəriz'm). 1900. [f. the name of the Rev. W. A. *Spooner* (1844–1930).] An accidental transposition of the initial sounds, or other parts, of two or more words.

Spoon-feed (spū·nfīd), *v.* 1615. [f. SPOON *sb.* + FEED *v.*] *trans.* To feed with a spoon. Chiefly *fig.*, esp. in *pa. pple.* **Spoo·n-fed,** fed with a spoon like a child or an invalid; artificially nourished or supported; encouraged by doles or the like.

Spoonful (spū·nful). ME. [f. SPOON *sb.* + -FUL.] As much as fills a spoon; such a quantity as can be lifted in a spoon. **b.** *transf.* A very small quantity or number 1531.

Throw this mixture by spoonfuls into a crucible 1800.

Spoo·n-meat. 1555. [f. SPOON *sb.* + MEAT *sb.*] Soft or liquid food to be taken with a spoon, esp. by infants or invalids. Also with *a* and *pl.*

A fortnight's s. reduced me to inanity 1884.

†**Spoo·nwort.** 1578. [f. SPOON *sb.*, after the L. name or Du. *lepelblad*.] The common scurvy-grass, *Cochlearia officinalis* –1760.

Spoony (spū·ni), *sb.* Also **spooney.** 1795. [f. SPOON *sb.*] **1.** A simple, silly, or foolish person; a noodle. **2.** One who spoons or is foolishly amorous 1857.

1. What the deuce can she find in that spooney? THACKERAY.

Spoony (spū·ni), *a.* Also **spooney.** 1812. [f. SPOON *sb.*] **1. a.** Of persons, etc.: Foolish, soft, silly. **b.** Of things: Characterized by foolishness or silliness 1843. **2.** Sentimentally or foolishly amorous 1836. **b.** Expressive of sentimental fondness 1882.

1. a. Then you think that Priests are bound to be mild and s.? 1876. **2.** They are not a bit a spooney couple 1882. Hence **Spoo·ni·ly** *adv.*, **-ness.**

Spoor (spūᵊɪ), *sb.* 1823. [a. Du. (in S. Afr. use). The stem is also represented in OE. *spyrian* SPEER *v.*[1]] **1.** The trace, track, or trail of a person or animal, esp. of a wild animal pursued as game. **b.** *collect.* (without article) 1850. **2.** The track of a vehicle 1850.

Spoor (spūᵊɪ), *v.* 1850. [f. prec. or ad. Du. *sporen*.] **1.** *trans.* To trace (an animal) by the spoor. **2.** *intr.* To follow a spoor or trail 1865. Hence **Spoo·rer,** a tracker.

Sporadic (spŏræ·dik), *a.* 1689. [ad. med. L. *sporadicus*, a. Gr., f. σποραδ-, σποράς scattered, f. the stem of σπορά, σπόρος sowing.] **1.** *Path.* Of diseases: Occurring only here and there; not epidemic. **2.** Scattered or dispersed in respect of locality or local distribution 1830. **b.** Occasional 1847. **c.** Of single persons or things: Accidental; isolated 1821. **3.** Characterized by occasional or isolated occurrence, appearance, or manifestation 1842.

1. A man who died of s. cholera 1845. **2. b.** The continuance of s. troubles in Basutoland 1882. So **Spora·dical** *a.* 1654. **Spora·dically** *adv.*

Sporange (sporæ·ndʒ). 1857. [perh. a. F.] *Bot.* = SPORANGIUM.

Sporangiophore (sporæ·ndʒiofōᵊɪ). 1875. [See next and -PHORE.] *Bot.* A structure bearing sporangia.

‖**Sporangium** (sporæ·ndʒiŏm). 1821. [mod. L., f. Gr. σπορά SPORE- + ἀγγεῖον vessel.] *Bot.* A receptacle containing spores; a spore-case or capsule. Hence **Spora·ngial** *a.*

Spore (spōᵊɪ). 1836. [ad. mod.L. *spora*, a. Gr. σπορά sowing, seed.] **1.** *Bot.* One of the minute reproductive bodies characteristic of flowerless plants. **2.** *Zool.* and *Biol.* A very minute germ or organism 1876.

attrib., as *s.-capsule*, *-cell*, etc.; **-case** (*Bot.*), a receptacle containing spores; a sporangium.

Sporidiiferous (sporidii·fĕrəs), *a.* Also **sporidiferous.** 1836. [f. SPORIDIUM + -(I)FEROUS.] *Bot.* Bearing sporidia.

‖**Sporidium** (spori·diŏm). 1821. [mod.L., dim. (after Gr. types) of σπορά SPORE.] *Bot.* **a.** A case or cell containing sporules. **b.** A sporule.

Sporiferous (spori·fĕrəs), *a.* 1836. [f. mod.L. *spora* SPORE + -(I)FEROUS.] *Bot.* Bearing spores. So **Sporifica·tion,** the process of forming spores. **Spori·genous** *a.* producing spores.

Sporo- (spǫ·ro, sporǫ·), comb. form of Gr. σπορά SPORE, employed in many scientific terms relating to the spores of plants or elementary forms of animal life, as **Spo·roblast, -o·genous,** *a.* **-o·phorous,** *a.*

Spo·rocarp [Gr. καρπός fruit] *Bot.*, a fructification containing sporangia; a spore-case. **Spo·rocyst,** (*a*) *Zool.* a cyst or capsule containing spores, forming a stage in the development of Trematodes, etc.; (*b*) *Bot.* the spore-case of algals. **Spo·rophore,** (*a*) a spore-bearing process or stalk; (*b*) the asexual generation of plants. **Spo·rosac** *Zool.*, a simple form of gonophore.

Sporran (spǫ·răn). Also **sporan.** 1818. [a. Sc. Gael. *sporan*, Ir. *sparán* purse.] A pouch or large purse made of skin, usu. with the hair left on and with ornamental tassels, etc., worn by Scottish Highlanders in front of the kilt.

Sport (spōᵊɹt), *sb.* 1440. [Aphetic f. DISPORT *sb.*] I. 1. Pleasant pastime; amusement; diversion. †b. Amorous dalliance or intercourse -1796. c. *spec.* Pastime afforded by the endeavour to take or kill wild animals, game, or fish 1653. d. Participation in games or exercises, esp. those pursued in the open air; such games collectively 1863. 2. Jest, jesting; mirth or merriment 1671.

1. Great s. to them was jumping in a sack 1821. c. The higher an angler goes up the Thames, ..the more s...he will meet with 1787. 2. Thrice I deluded her, and turn'd to s. Her importunity MILT.

Phr. *In s.*, in jest or joke; not seriously. *To make s.*: (*a*) to provide entertainment or diversion; (*b*) to furnish oneself with, or find, recreation or diversion.

II. 1. A matter affording entertainment; a jest or joke 1450. 2. An occupation or proceeding of the nature of a pastime or diversion 1526. b. *spec.* A game, or particular form of pastime, esp. one carried on in the open air 1523. c. *pl.* A series of athletic contests engaged in or held at one time and forming a spectacle or social event 1594. †d. A theatrical performance -1593. †3. *S. of nature*, = LUSUS NATURÆ -1827. b. A plant (or part of a plant), animal, etc., which exhibits abnormal variation from the parent stock or type in some respect, esp. in form or colour; a new variety produced in this way 1842. 4. That with which one plays or sports; that which forms the sport *of* some thing or person 1667. 5. One concerned with or interested in sport. a. *U.S. slang.* A gambler 1861. b. = SPORTSMAN 1, 3. 1873.

1. Especially, it is a S. to see, when a Bold Fellow is out of Countenance BACON. Phr. †*To make a s. of*, to make a jest of. 2. Your present kindness Makes my past miseries sports SHAKS. Phr. †*A s. of terms, wit, words*, a playing upon or trifling with terms, etc.; a passage or piece of writing characterized by this. b. In such a state of things hunting might be a s. FREEMAN. c. The Oxford and Cambridge Sports 1892. d. *Mids. N.* III. ii. 14. 4. The s. and prey Of racking whirlwinds MILT.

Comb. with *pl.*: **sports-car,** an open low-built fast motor car; **-coat, -jacket,** a loose-fitting coat or jacket such as is worn for some games.

Sport (spōᵊɹt), *v.* late ME. [Aphetic f. DISPORT *v.*, or f. prec.] I. †1. *refl.* To amuse, recreate (oneself); to take one's pleasure. Also *transf.* of things. -1779. 2. *intr.* To amuse or recreate oneself, *esp.* by active exercise in the open air; to take part in some game or play; to frolic or gambol. Also *transf.* and *fig.* 1483. b. To engage in or practise field-sports, etc.; to hunt or shoot for sport or amusement 1812. 3. To indulge in sport, fun, or ridicule *at, over,* or *upon* a person or thing 1533. b. To deal *with* in a light or trifling way; to trifle, dally, or play *with* something 1630. 4. †a. Of Nature: To produce or develop abnormal or irregular forms or growths as if in sport -1769. b. Of plants, animals, etc.: To vary abnormally from the parent stock or specific type; to exhibit or undergo spontaneous mutation 1768. †5. *trans.* To amuse or divert (a person); to provide with sport; to cheer, enliven -1763. 6. To pass (time) in sport or amusement 1760. 7. To take or cast *away* in or as in sport; to scatter or squander. Now *rare.* 1713.

2. See the Children s. upon the shore WORDSW. The wind sported with her gown HAWTHORNE. b. Any fellow who has sported on the estate at Bradford Wood 1812. 3. I find there simple folke, at whom I maie s. 1533. b. My misery is too great to be sported with 1861. 4. b. All flowers, as we know, easily s. a little in colour 1882. 6. Laughing and sporting Life away 1760. 7. He had sported away thirty thousand lives 1778.

II. In slang or colloq. uses. †1. To invest or stake (money) in some sport or in a highly speculative undertaking; to bet or wager. Also, to lay or make (a bet). -1850. b. To spend (money) freely or extravagantly and with ostentation 1859. 2. To display or exhibit, esp. in public or company. Freq. with implication of some degree of parade. 1712. b. To display on the person; to wear 1778. c. To set up, go in for, keep, support, or use (a carriage, etc.) 1806. 3. To keep (one's door) shut as a sign that one is absent or does not wish to be disturbed; now only in Univ. slang, *to s. one's oak.* Also formerly *refl.* and *pass.* of a person. 1785. 4. To entertain or treat (a person) with food or drink by way of compliment or hospitality (*rare*) 1828.

1. The chaps will win your money as sure as you s. it THACKERAY. 2. If a man..sports loose views on morals at a decent dinner party,..he is not invited again FROUDE. b. Sported my Peninsular medal this day at the Queen's Levée 1849. c. We hope some day to s. buttons 1858. 3. b. His door was always sported; he had but little intercourse with the other Fellows 1889.

Sporter (spōᵊ·ɹtəɹ). 1611. [f. SPORT *v.* + -ER [2].] One who is given to or takes part in sport of any kind; a gamester; a sportsman or sporting man.

The beast [a horse] was too keen a s. to choose any other way than that which the stag followed 1751.

Sportful (spōᵊ·ɹtfŭl), *a.* late ME. [f. SPORT *sb.*] 1. Yielding sport; having an element of recreation, play, or frolic. b. Devised or carried on merely in sport; not serious 1601. c. Of movements: Lively, frolicsome 1691. 2. Of persons, their minds, etc.: Having an inclination or tendency to engage in sport or play; sportive, playful. Also of animals, etc. 1593.

1. A young fool, bent on s. pursuits instead of serious CARLYLE. b. Though 't be a sportfull Combate, Yet in this triall much opinion dwels SHAKS. c. The s. leap of a trout 1848. 2. The s. fawn 1768. They who were then s. on the green are now serious in the church CARLYLE. Hence **Spo·rtful-ly** *adv.*, **-ness.**

Sporting (spōᵊ·ɹtiŋ), *vbl. sb.* 1480. [f. SPORT *v.*] The action of the verb; an instance or occasion of this.

attrib. and *Comb.*, as *s. celebrity; s. magazine; s. dog, gun*; also, **s. box,** a small residence for use during the sporting season; **-house,** a house, hotel, or inn frequented by sportsmen; *U.S.* a betting or gambling house; a brothel or disorderly house.

Sporting (spōᵊ·ɹtiŋ), *ppl. a.* 1600. [f. SPORT *v.*] In the senses of the verb.

Special collocations: **s. chance** *colloq.*, a chance such as is met with or taken in sport; one of an uncertain or doubtful nature; so *s. offer*; **s. man,** now used to denote a sportsman of an inferior type or one who is interested in sport from purely mercenary motives. Hence **Spo·rtingly** *adv.*

Sportive (spōᵊ·ɹtiv), *a.* 1590. [f. SPORT *sb.* or *v.* + -IVE.] 1. Inclined to jesting or levity. b. Characterized by lightness or levity; not serious 1593. 2. Of the nature of or inclined to amorous sport or wantonness. *arch.* 1594. 3. Disposed to be playful or frolicsome 1637. 4. Of or pertaining to, marked or characterized by sport; of the nature of sport or amusement; affording or providing diversion 1705. b. Undertaken, given, etc., in (mere) sport 1743. 5. Produced in or as in sport; *spec.* of the nature of a sport or abnormal variation; anomalous. Now *rare* or *Obs.* 1796. b. Of plants, etc.: Liable to vary from the true type 1850.

1. I am not in a sportiue humor now: Tell me, and dally not, where is the monie? SHAKS. b. Severall select Pieces of s. Wit 1655. 2. *Rich. III*, I. i. 14. 3. A shoal of s. dolphins 1762. 4. b. It was now not a s. combat, but a war to the death MACAULAY. Hence **Spo·rtive-ly** *adv.*, **-ness.**

Spo·rtless, *a.* 1621. [f. SPORT *sb.* + -LESS.] Destitute or devoid of sport; marked by the absence of sport.

Sportsman (spōᵊ·ɹtsmæn). 1706. [f. SPORT *sb.*] 1. A man who follows, engages in, or practises sport; esp. one who hunts or shoots wild animals or game for pleasure. 2. *U.S.* A gambler, betting man 1848. 3. *transf.* One who displays the typical good qualities of a sportsman 1894. Hence **Spo·rtsmanlike** *a.* resembling a s.; like that of a s.; consonant with the character or conduct of a s. **Spo·rtsmanship,** skill in, or knowledge of, sport; conduct characteristic or worthy of a s. So **Spo·rtswo:man.**

Sporulate (spǫ·riŭleⁱt), *v.* 1885. [f. SPORULE + -ATE [3].] 1. *trans.* To convert into spores. 2. *intr.* To form spores or sporules 1891. So **Sporula·tion,** conversion into spores; spore-formation 1876.

Sporule (spǫ·riul). 1819. [a. F., or ad. mod.L. *sporula*; see SPORE and -ULE.] 1. *Bot.* and *Zool.* A spore or spore-granule. 2. *fig.* A germ 1861. Hence **Sporuli·ferous** *a.*

Spot (spǫt), *sb.* [ME. = MDu. *spotte, spot*, ON. *spotti.*] I. 1. *fig.* A moral stain, blot, or blemish; a stigma or disgrace. Also applied to persons. 2. A small discolouring or disfiguring mark; a speck or stain ME. 3. In special senses: †a. A mark or speck on the eye; also, a disease characterized by this -1639. b. An eruptive or other disfiguring mark on the skin. late ME. c. A dark mark on the face of the sun, moon, or a planet. (Cf. *sun-spot.*) 1605. d. A discoloration produced by various fungi upon the leaves or fruit of a plant 1852.

1. Spottes they are and filthynes TINDALE 2 *Pet.* ii. 13. This s. of synne god dothe away 1526. Sublimely mild, a Spirit without s. SHELLEY. 2. The Moone was like a glasse all voyd of s. 1591. An innocent hand, Not painted with the Crimson spots of blood SHAKS. 3. c. The spots, which have served for determining the period of the rotation of Mars 1854.

II. 1. A small, usu. roundish, mark of a different colour from the main surface ME. †b. A patch worn on the face; a beauty-spot -1735. 2. A variety of domestic pigeon, having white plumage with a spot of another colour above the beak 1672. b. A spotted textile material 1798. c. *U.S.* The red fish or red drum 1882. 3. *Billiards.* a. One or other of the three marked places on a billiard-table, esp. the one at the upper end on which the red ball is placed. b. *ellipt.* The spot-ball, or the person who plays it; a spot-stroke, or the score obtained by this 1844.

1. Like as the man of Inde maye chaunge his skynne, & the cat of the mountayne hir spottes COVERDALE *Jer.* xiii. 23. Phr. *To knock* (*the*) *spots off* or *out of*, to beat thoroughly (orig. *U.S.*).

III. 1. A small piece, amount, or quantity; a particle, a drop. Usu. with *of.* late ME. †b. A piece *of* work -1821. c. A drop *of* liquor; hence, a small amount *of.* *slang* or *colloq.* 1885. 2. A particular place or locality of limited extent. late ME. b. A small space or extent *of* ground, etc. 1440. 3. A particular small area, part, or definite point in any surface or body 1827. 4. *Comm.* a. *ellipt.* as *adv.* At immediate cash rates; for cash payment 1884. b. *pl.* and *collect. sing.* Goods at immediate cash rates 1890.

1. A few spots of rain 1881. 2. The most pleasant s. in Italy EVELYN. Phr. **On** (or **upon**) **the s.**: a. Without having time to move from the place; straightway, at once. b. At the very place in question. c. Doing exactly what is necessary. d. In a position prearranged for one's assassination. *U.S. slang. Off the s.*, inexact, irrelevant. b. Lab'ring well his little S. of Ground DRYDEN. 3. *Soft, sore, tender s.*, a point on which one is touchy or easily affected; Mr. Ambrose touched a very tender s. in Camilla's heart 1887. 4. a. Linseed oil..s...18s. 7½d. 1884.

attrib. and *Comb.*, as *s.-break, -stroke; s. cash, price, sale*; **s.-barred** *a. Billiards*, (a game) in which only one winning hazard is allowed to be made in the top pockets; **-lens,** a lens having the central portion obstructed by a s.; **s. light,** a light that is or can be played upon a particular s.; also as vb., to direct a spot light upon; **s. pigeon** = sense II. 2.

Spot (spǫt), *v.* late ME. [f. prec.] I. 1. *trans.* To stain, sully, or tarnish, in respect of moral character or qualities. †b. To asperse or vilify -1718. 2. To mark with spots; to stain in spots 1440. 3. *intr.* To be liable to spots; to become spotted 1879.

1. Who might be spotted merely with the errors introduced by Luther 1855. 2. It spotteth and staineth the linnen so mightily, as that such staines will neuer be got out 1600.

II. 1. *trans.* To mark, cover, or decorate with spots 1591. †b. To ornament (the face) with a patch or patches -1711. c. *U.S.* To mark (a tree) by cutting out a piece of the bark 1792. 2. To form or appear as spots upon (a surface); to stud 1801. 3. *Billiards.* To place (a ball) on some particular spot 1844. 4. *impers.* of rain falling in scattered drops 1849.

2. Many ships spotting the dark blue deep SHELLEY.

III. 1. *Cant.* To mark or note as a criminal

or suspected person 1718. 2. *colloq.* a. To single out beforehand (the winner in a race) 1857. b. To catch sight of; to recognize or detect; to mark or note the position of 1860.

1. At length he became 'spotted'. The police got to know him. 1851. 2. a. I spotted a few winners 1888. b. *spec.* (*Mil.*) To locate (the fall of a shot or an enemy position) 1914.

Spotless (spǫ·tlės), *a.* late ME. [f. SPOT *sb.*] 1. Free from spot or stain; of a pure or uniform colour. 2. *fig.* Immaculate, pure 1577.

1. Vntrodden snow is not so s. 1606. 2. How have ye..banisht from mans life..Simplicitie and s. innocence MILT. Hence **Spo·tless-ly** *adv.*, **-ness.**

Spotted (spǫ·tėd), *a.* and *ppl. a.* ME. [f. SPOT *sb.* and *v.*] 1. Marked or decorated with spots. b. *Mining.* Having the ore irregularly distributed through the workings 1874. 2. Disfigured or stained with spots 1532. b. *fig.* Morally stained or blemished 1522. c. Marked, suspected 1864.

1. *S. Dick* (colloq.), a boiled pudding with currants in it; plum-duff. *S. dog,* (*a*) a white dog with black spots; (*b*) = s. Dick. *S. fever,* a fever characterized by the appearance of spots on the skin; now *spec.* epidemic cerebro-spinal meningitis, and typhus or petechial fever. So *s. death, pestilence, sickness.* Often in specific names of animals and plants. b. The ground is s. and very rich in places 1874. Hence **Spo·ttedness,** s. quality or state.

Spotter (spǫ·təɹ). 1611. [f. SPOT *v.* or *sb.*] 1. One who makes spots. 2. *U.S.* A spy or detective, esp. one employed by a company to keep watch on employees, or one who watches for infringements of the prohibition-laws 1878. 3. In target practice, one who notes the point where a shot strikes; one who 'spots' the position of a naval or military unit, etc. 1893. 4. An aviator detailed to locate enemy positions 1914.

Spotty (spǫ·ti), *a.* ME. [f. SPOT *sb.* + -Y [1].] 1. Full of, marked with, spots; spotted. 2. Patchy; lacking in uniformity or harmony 1812. 3. Occurring in spots; characterized by such occurrence 1821. **Spo·tti-ly** *adv.*, **-ness.**

Spou·sage. *Obs.* exc. *arch.* ME. [ad. AF. *esposage,* OF. *espousage,* f. *espo(u)ser* SPOUSE *v.*] 1. Wedlock. 2. = next 2. ME.

Spousal (spau·zăl), *sb.* ME. [ad. OF. *espousaille* (freq. in pl.); see ESPOUSAL.] †1. The condition of being espoused or married; the married state; wedlock –1621. 2. The action of espousing or marrying; the celebration of a marriage or betrothal; an instance or occasion of this. Freq. in pl. Now *arch.* ME.

2. My hoped day of spousall shone SPENSER. With the morrow the Church blessed the spousals 1874.

Spousal (spau·zăl), *a.* 1513. [attrib. use of prec.] 1. Of, pertaining or relating to, espousal or marriage; nuptial, matrimonial. 2. Of a hymn, poem, etc.: Celebrating or commemorating an espousal or marriage 1596.

1. There shall we Consummate our Spousall rites SHAKS. So **Spou·sally** *adv.* 1501.

Spouse (spauz), *sb.* ME. [a. OF. *spous,* var. of *espous*; see ESPOUSE *sb.*] 1. A married woman in relation to her husband; a wife; †a bride. 2. A married man in relation to his wife; a husband; †a bridegroom ME. 3. *fig.* In religious use: a. Applied to the Church, or to a woman who has taken religious vows, in relation to God or Christ ME. b. Applied to God or Christ in relation to the Church (or its members), or to women of religion ME.

1. So qualified, as may beseeme The S. of any noble Gentleman SHAKS. 2. The lady thus address'd her s. COWPER. 3. a. Their..religious sister..a moste chaste s. of Christ 1610. The Church, the holy s. of God 1827. Hence †**Spousess.**

Spouse (spauz), *v.* *Obs.* exc. *arch.* ME. [ad. OF. *espouser*; see ESPOUSE *v.*] †1. *trans.* To join in marriage or wedlock. Chiefly in *pass.* –1667. 2. To give in marriage; to promote or procure the marriage of; to marry (*esp.* a woman *to* a man) ME. 3. To take (a woman) as a wife; to marry, wed ME.

1. It was not lawfull for a Christian woman and virgin to be maried, or spoused to a paynime 1565. 2. I haue spoused you to one husband 1565. 3. To Faerie land; Where he her spous'd, and made his ioyous bride SPENSER.

†**Spou·se-breach.** ME. [f. SPOUSE *sb.* + BREACH *sb.*] Adultery –1637.

Spousehood (spau·zhud). Now *arch.* ME. [f. SPOUSE *sb.* + -HOOD.] The married state; matrimony; wedlock.

Spouseless (spau·zlės), *a.* 1460. [f. SPOUSE *sb.*] 1. Of a person: Having no spouse; bereaved or deprived of a spouse. 2. Characterized by the absence of a spouse 1812.

Spout (spaut), *sb.* [Late ME. *spowte, spoute,* of doubtful origin; cf. SPOUT *v.*] I. 1. A pipe by which rain-water is carried off or discharged from a roof. b. A pipe or similar conduit through which water or other liquid flows and is discharged. late ME. †c. = SPOUT-HOLE 1. –1774. d. *Mining.* A short passage connecting an air-head with a gate-road 1839. 2. A tubular or lip-like addition to, or projection from, a vessel to facilitate the pouring out of liquid from it 1444. 3. A contrivance having the form of a trough or box with open ends by which flour, grain, coals, etc., are discharged from or conveyed to a receptacle; a shoot 1557. 4. A lift formerly in use in pawnbrokers' shops, up which the articles pawned were taken for storage. Also *transf.*, a pawnshop. 1837.

1. A S...from the Roof down to the Ground, to carry off..the Water 1823. b. She dreampt..she saw my Statue, Which like a Fountaine with an hundred spouts Did run pure blood SHAKS. 4. Phr. *To put* (or *shove*) *up the s.*, to pawn. *Up the s.*, pawned, pledged; also *fig.*, in a hopeless condition.

II. 1. A waterspout 1555. b. A heavy downpour (*of* rain). Now *rare.* 1648. 2. A discharge of water or other liquid, in some quantity and with some degree of force, from the mouth of a pipe or similar orifice 1500. b. *Agric.* A spring of water forcing its way up through the soil 1791. c. The column of spray thrown into the air by a whale in the act of respiration 1650. 3. An outpour or rush of water falling from a higher to a lower level, esp. in a detached stream; a waterfall or cascade of this kind 1700. b. A similar fall of earth or rock 1883.

1. The dreadfull s., Which Shipmen doe the Hurricano call SHAKS. 2. c. Its s...flashes up from the ocean just like smoke 1850.

Comb.: **s.-fish,** a mollusc which spouts or squirts out water, *esp.* a razor-fish; **-shell** *Zool.*, any shell of the genus *Aporrhais* or family *Aporrhaïdæ*; **-whale,** a spouting whale. Hence **Spou·tless** *a.* deprived of a s., having no s. **Spou·ty** *a.* given to spouting or discharging water.

Spout (spaut), *v.* [ME. *spouten,* = MDu. *spouten,* Du. *spuiten.* The stem *spūt-* appears also in ON. and Icel. *spýta* to spit.] I. *intr.* 1. To discharge a liquid or other substance in a copious jet or stream; to gush with water, blood, etc. b. *spec.* Of a whale: To throw up spray in the act of respiration; to blow 1796. 2. Of liquids: To issue with some force and in some quantity from a narrow orifice; to spurt copiously. Also with *out* or *up.* 1500. 3. *fig.* To engage in declamation or recitation; to make a speech or speeches, esp. at great length or without much matter 1756.

2. A ribbon of white surf, which spouts up in pillars of foam 1885. 3. The far-sounding Street-orators cease, or s. milder CARLYLE.

II. *trans.* 1. To discharge, cast out, or pour forth (water, etc.) in a stream of some force or volume. Also with *out* or *up.* ME. 2. To wet or drench by a stream of liquid 1575. 3. To utter readily or volubly; to talk (a language); to declaim or recite 1594. 4. [f. SPOUT *sb.*]. To pawn. *slang.* 1811. 5. To fit or furnish with spouts 1853.

1. Who kepte Ionas in the fisshes mawe Til he was spouted vp at Nynyuee? CHAUCER. The Parish Engine spouts excessive Streams To quench the Blaze 1739. 3. Pray s. some French BEAUM. & FL. I heard Macaulay s. the first chapter of Isaiah RUSKIN. 4. The dons are going to s. the college plate HUGHES.

Spouter (spau·təɹ). 1760. [f. SPOUT *v.*] 1. A spouting whale 1830. b. A whaling-vessel 1840. 2. †a. A reciter or amateur actor –1809. b. A fluent or voluble declaimer or speaker 1782. 3. A spouting oil-well 1886.

Spou·t-hole. 1694. [f. SPOUT *v.*] 1. The blow-hole or spiracle of a whale or other cetacean. 2. A natural opening in rocks through which the sea spouts 1849.

Sprack (spræk), *a.* Chiefly *dial.* 1747. [Cf. SPRAG *a.*] Brisk, active; alert, smart; in good health and spirits.

Sprag (spræg), *sb.*[1] 1706. [Origin obsc.] †1. A lively young fellow. 2. a. A young salmon 1790. b. A young cod 1875.

Sprag, *sb.*[2] 1841. [Origin obsc.] 1. *Mining.* A prop used to support the coal or roof during the working of a seam. 2. A stout piece of wood used to check the revolution of a wheel (or roller), usually by inserting it between two of the spokes 1878; also, in a motor vehicle 1902.

Sprag, *a. rare.* 1598. [Cf. SPRACK *a.*] Smart, clever. (Only in Shaks. and imitators.)

M. Pag. He is a better scholler then I thought he was. *Eu.* He is a good sprag-memory. SHAKS.

Sprag, *v.* 1841. [f. SPRAG *sb.*[2]] 1. *trans.* To prop up or sustain (esp. coal in a mine) with a sprag or sprags. 2. To check or stop (a wheel) by inserting a sprag 1878.

Sprain (sprēⁱn), *sb.* 1601. [prob. f. SPRAIN *v.*] 1. A severe wrench or twist of the ligaments or muscles of a joint, causing pain and swelling of the part. 2. Without article: The condition of being sprained 1805.

2. The analogy of common s. to gout 1805.

Sprain (sprēⁱn), *v.* 1622. [Origin obsc.] *trans.* To wrench or twist (a part of the body) so as to cause pain or difficulty in moving.

He would see my leg. It was sprained sore, and swelled at the ankle. READE.

Spraints, *sb. pl.* late ME. [ad. OF. *espraintes* (mod.F. *épreintes*), f. *espraindre* to squeeze out.] The excrement of the otter.

Sprat (spræt), *sb.* 1597. [Later form of OE. *sprot.*] 1. A small sea-fish, *Clupea Sprattus,* common on the Atlantic coasts of Europe. b. *collect.* Fish of this species 1611. 2. One or other of various small fishes, usually one resembling a sprat 1603. 3. *fig.* a. Applied to persons, usually as a term of contempt 1601. b. In phrases denoting the venturing of a small expenditure in the hope of a large gain 1856. 4. *slang.* A sixpence 1839.

3. a. When his disguise and he is parted, tell me what a s. you shall finde him SHAKS. b. Give a S. to catch a Mackarel 1864.

Comb.: **s.-borer,** the young of the Red-throated Diver, *Colymbus septentrionalis*; **-diver** (see DIVER); **-loon,** the Speckled Diver; **-mowe,** the herring-gull. Hence **Sprat** *v. intr.* to fish for sprats.

Spra·t-ba·rley. 1523. [perh. f. SPRAT *sb.*] A species of barley, *Hordeum zeocriton,* with short broad ears and long awns.

Sprawl (sprǭl), *sb.* 1719. [f. SPRAWL *v.*] 1. The, or an, act of sprawling; an awkward or clumsy spreading out of the limbs. b. A straggling array or display *of* something 1827. 2. *dial.* and *U.S.* Activity, energy, go 1888.

1. To the iron porch they glide, Where lay the Porter, in uneasy s. KEATS.

Sprawl (sprǭl), *v.* [OE. *spreawlian,* = NFris. *spraweli.*] 1. *intr.* To move the limbs in a convulsive effort or struggle; to toss about or spread oneself out; later, to be stretched out on the ground, etc., in an ungainly or awkward manner. b. To crawl from one place to another in a struggling or ungraceful manner. Also *fig.*, to proceed, issue. 1582. 2. Of things: To spread out, extend, climb, etc., in a straggling fashion 1745. 3. *trans.* To spread or stretch out (something) in a wide or straggling manner. Usu. with *out.* 1541.

1. Before the child can crawl, He learns to kick.. and s. PRIOR. 2. His long mis-shapen legs sprawling abroad SCOTT. Is it not a sweet name? It sprawls over half the paper. THACKERAY. Hence **Spraw·ler,** one who or that which sprawls. **Spra·wling** *ppl. a.* **Spra·wly** *a.* of a sprawling character; straggly.

Spray (sprēⁱ), *sb.*[1] ME. [perh. conn. w. dial. *sprag* twig.] 1. *collect.* Small or slender twigs of trees or shrubs, either as still growing or as cut off and used for fuel, etc.; fine brushwood. Also with *the* (or †*that*). 2. A slender shoot or twig. late ME. b. *pl.* Hazel, birch, or other twigs used in thatching 1520. c. A graceful shoot or twig of some flowering or fine-foliaged plant or tree, used for decoration or ornament; an artificial imitation of this 1862. 3. A metal casting resembling a set of twigs 1831.

1. Majestic trees..with spreading tortuous branches and s. 1852. 2. No more the birds shall..hearken from the sprays POPE. c. He would never meet me without some s. of roses, or some boughs of lemon 1873.

attrib.: **s. drain,** a drain formed by burying the branches of trees under the earth.

Spray (sprēⁱ), *sb.*[2] †Also **spry(e.** 1621. [app. related to MDu. *sprayen, spraeyen,* = MHG. *spræjen, spreien* to sprinkle.] 1. Water blown from or thrown up by the waves of the sea in the form of a fine shower or mist. **b.** Water or other liquid dispersed by impact, etc., in fine mist-like particles 1750. **2.** A jet of medicated vapour or the like, used esp. as a disinfectant or a deodorizer 1875. **b.** An instrument used for applying such a jet 1881.

1. In great storms the s. of the sea has been carried more than 50 miles from the shore 1813.

Spray (sprē¹), *v.* 1829. [f. SPRAY *sb.*²] **1.** *trans.* To diffuse or send in the form of spray; to scatter in minute drops. **2.** To sprinkle with or as with spray; to wet with fine particles of water or other liquid, esp. by means of a special apparatus 1861. **3.** *absol.* To scatter or throw up spray 1891.

1. Where the nich'd snow-bed sprays down Its powdery fall M. ARNOLD.

Sprayer (sprē¹·əɹ). 1891. [f. prec.] One who or that which sprays; *esp.* a machine for diffusing insecticides over plants and trees.

Spread (spred), *sb.* 1626. [f. the verb.] **I. 1.** The act of spreading in space; degree or extent of this. **b.** With *the*: The extent, expanse, or superficial area *of* something 1691. **c.** Capacity for spreading 1772. **d.** Increased girth of the body 1930. **e.** The difference between two rates or prices 1919. **2.** With *a*: An expanse or stretch *of* something 1712. **b.** *Naut.* A display *of* sails 1849. **3.** The fact of being spread abroad, diffused, or made known; diffusion, dispersion 1675. **4.** *U.S. Stock Exchange.* = STRADDLE *sb.* 2. 1911.

1. No Flower hath that kinde of S. that the Woodbine hath BACON. **b.** Under the immense s. of the starry heavens STEVENSON. **2.** I have got a fine S. of improveable Lands ADDISON. **b.** A..ship..carrying a large s. of canvas 1889. **3.** The translation..had a wonderful s. among the people 1732.

II. 1. *colloq.* A banquet, feast, meal 1822. **2.** A bed-cover, coverlet. orig. *U.S.* 1852.

Spread (spred), *v.* Pa. t. and pple. **spread** (spred). [OE. *sprǣdan* (in compounds, and *sprǣdung*), = OHG. *spreitan*; ult. etym. unkn.] **I.** *trans.* **1.** To stretch or draw out (a cloth, etc.) so as to display more or less fully; to open out or lay out so as to cover or occupy some space ME. **b.** *spec.* To expand, unfurl, or set (sails) ME. **c.** To display in wide extension 1600. **d.** To flatten out; to make of a thin flat form 1704. **†2.** To draw or stretch out (the limbs or a person) in some form of punishment or torture -1526. **3. a.** To send out in various directions so as to cover or extend over a larger space ME. **b.** To hold out, stretch out, extend (the hands or arms) ME. **c.** To extend, open out (the wings, etc.). late ME. **d.** To extend, make larger or wider (*rare*). late ME. **4.** To distribute or disperse (a substance or a number of things) over a certain superficies or area; to scatter ME. **b.** To distribute in a thin layer; *esp.* to smear 1558. **c.** To place in an open or expanded manner; to distribute *over* a certain space, time, etc. 1592. **d.** To lay out (a meal, banquet, etc.) 1784. **5.** In *pass.* of persons, animals, etc.: To be distributed over or throughout some area ME. **6.** To disseminate or diffuse; to cause to become prevalent or (more) widely existent, present, known, felt, etc. ME. **7.** *refl.* **a.** To extend, expand, etc., in various senses ME. **b.** *U.S.* To exert oneself; also, to show off 1857. **8.** To cover, overlay, deck, or strew, *with* something. Also without const. ME. **b.** To lay (a table) for a meal or other purpose 1460. **c.** To cover with a thin layer of some soft substance, esp. butter; to prepare in this way 1579. **9. †a.** To overrun or overspread (an area) -1722. **b.** To cover, extend over. *poet.* 1700.

1. He spread the newspaper on the table before him 1902. **b.** He spreads his canvas; with his pole he steers DRYDEN. **c.** The Euxine spread its waters before their eyes THIRLWALL. **d.** The Diamond weighing near 11 Grains, well spread, and of a perfect Water 1706. **3. a.** Pleasant the Sun When first on this delightful Land he spreads His orient Beam: MILT. **b.** Trent, who like some earth-born Giant spreads His thirsty Armes MILT. **4.** The flourie lap Of som irriguous Valley spread her store MILT. **b.** *1 Kings* vi. 32. **c.** The repayment of the money to be borrowed shall be spread over a series of years 1885. **e.** *U.S.* To record, enter in a documentary record 1858. **5.** This sect was now wonderfully spread EVELYN. **6.** Missionaries for spreading the gospel among their countrymen BERKELEY. His arrival spread dismay through the whole English population MACAULAY. **8.** Silence spreads the couch of ever welcome rest BYRON. **b.** A Table richly spred, in regal mode, With dishes pil'd MILT. **c.** Every old woman..can ..s. a plaster SCOTT. **9. a.** The Gangren..had spread her whole Body DE FOE. **b.** A purple carpet spread the pavement wide POPE.

II. *intr.* **1.** To receive extension or expansion; to cover or occupy a wider space by this means ME. **b.** Of conditions, qualities, etc. 1565. **c.** To become larger; to increase in size 1630. **d.** To go apart; to separate 1839. **2.** Of immaterial things: To become diffused or disseminated ME. **3.** Of flowers, leaves, etc.: To unfold, expand ME. **4.** To extend by growth; *spec.* of trees, to grow outwards ME. **5.** To extend over a larger area by increase or by separation; to disperse ME. **6.** To stretch out, extend ME.

1. A fire broke out and spread with great rapidity 1885. **b.** The mortification seemed to s. DE FOE. **d.** The toes s. widely upon soft ground 1890. **2.** I am informed that this Fashion spreads daily ADDISON. His fame may s., but in the past Her spirit finds its centre WORDSW. **3.** To sen these flouris agen the sunne to sprede CHAUCER. **4.** The she oaks were more inclined to s. than grow tall 1802. **5.** So the men of armes sprad abrode 1523. **6.** Below their breezy crowns..Spreadeth the infinite smile of the sunlit sea R. BRIDGES. Hence **Sprea·dingly** *adv.*

Spread eagle, *sb.* Also **spread-eagle.** 1570. [*spread* ppl. adj.] **1.** A representation of an eagle, with body, legs, and both wings displayed, esp. as the emblem of various states or rulers, or as an inn-sign. **2.** A person secured with the arms and legs stretched out, esp. in order to be flogged 1785. **3.** A fowl flattened out for broiling 1854. **4.** *attrib.* Bombastic, ridiculously boastful, esp. in laudation of the United States. *U.S.* 1858.

1. At the Spread Eagle (commonly called the Spread Crow) 1685. **b.** *U.S. Stock Exchange.* = STRADDLE *sb.* 2. 1857. **4.** 'The spread-eagle style'—a compound of exaggeration, effrontery, bombast, and extravagance 1858. Hence **Spread-ea·gleism,** extravagant laudation of the United States; tendency to bombast or grandiloquence in this or similar connexions.

Spread-eagle, *v.* 1829. [f. prec.] **1.** *trans.* To tie up (a person) for punishment. **b.** To fasten, pin firmly, stretch out, etc., in the form of a spread eagle 1894. **2.** To beat completely, esp. in racing 1864. **3.** *intr.* To speak or act in a spread-eagle fashion 1866.

Spreader (spre·dəɹ). 1843. [f. SPREAD *v.*] **I. 1.** One who spreads, strews, or scatters. **2.** A diffuser, disseminator, or promulgator *of* something 1551. **3.** A piece of wood, metal, etc., by which things or parts are stretched out or kept asunder 1839. **b.** *Naut.* A bar attached to the mast of a yacht in order to tighten the shrouds 1895. **4.** An apparatus or device by which something is spread or scattered 1853. **II. 1.** Something which spreads or grows outwards 1639. **2.** A catch which operates by spreading 1884.

1. The oak is naturally a wide s. 1845.

Sprea·d-o·ver. 1923. [f. verbal phr. *spread over.*] The accommodation of a limited number of working hours to the requirements of special needs.

Spreagh (spreχ). 1809. [conn. w. Gael. *spréidh* cattle.] A cattle-raid; a foray. Hence **Sprea·ghery,** cattle-raiding; plunder. SCOTT.

Spree (sprī). Chiefly *colloq.* 1804. [A slang word of obscure origin.] **1.** A lively or boisterous frolic; an occasion or spell of noisy enjoyment (freq. accompanied by drinking). **b.** *spec.* A drunken carousal 1811. **2.** Rough amusement, merrymaking, or sport; prolonged drinking or carousing; indulgence or participation in this 1808.

1. Phr. *On a s., on* or *upon the s.*

Sprenge (sprendʒ), *v. Obs.* exc. *arch.* in pa. t. and pa. pple. sprent. [OE. *sprengan* :—**sprangjan*, f. ablaut var. of stem of *springan* SPRING *v.*] **1.** *trans.* To sprinkle (a liquid, etc.). Also *absol.* **b.** To scatter, disperse, distribute, spread abroad or about. Also *absol.* OE. **2.** To sprinkle (a person or thing) with some liquid OE. **3.** In *pa. pple.* and const. *with*: Besprinkled, besprent. late ME.

3. All the ground with purple bloud was sprent SPENSER. The cheek grown thin, the brown hair sprent with grey M. ARNOLD.

Sprew (sprū). *S. Afr.* 1897. [ad. Du. *spreeuw* starling.] A bird belonging to the genus *Spreo* (of the family *Sturnidæ*), esp. *S. bicolor*, a glossy starling.

Sprig (sprig), *sb.*¹ ME. [Origin obsc.] **1.** A small slender nail, either wedge-shaped and headless, or square-bodied with a slight head on one side. **b.** *Naut.* A small eye-bolt, ragged at the point 1794. **c.** A wedge-shaped piece of tin used to hold glass in a sash until the putty dries 1823. **2.** A small projecting part or point 1679.

attrib., as *s.-nail*; **s.-awl, -bit,** a bradawl.

Sprig (sprig), *sb.*² late ME. [Origin obsc.] **1.** A shoot, twig, or spray of a plant, shrub, or tree; †a rod. **b.** A small spray *of* a particular plant 1563. **2.** *fig.* **a.** An offshoot, a minor development, part, or specimen, of something 1576. **b.** Applied to persons (usu. in disparagement): A scion *of* some person, class, institution, etc. 1601. **c.** Without const.: A stripling; a young fellow 1661. **3. †a.** A branch of a nerve, vein, etc. -1730. **b.** A piece of some substance or material resembling a sprig of a plant 1660. **4.** An ornament in the form of a sprig or spray; in later use esp. one made of diamonds 1591. **b.** A design, imitative of a sprig, embroidered, woven, or stamped on a textile fabric, or applied to ceramic ware, etc. 1771. **c.** A small detached piece of pillow-lace, made separately for subsequent use in composite work 1851.

1. Where there are several Sprigs upon one Stem, as in Fenil, Hemlock, and the like 1676. **b.** Sprigs of Rosemarie SHAKS. **2. a.** The following s. of sepulchral poetry SCOTT. **b.** The illustrious sprigs of our Nobility 1768. **c.** A s. whom I remember with a whey face and a satchel not so very many years ago SCOTT. **3. b.** Half-a-score Sprigs of Coral BOYLE.

Sprig, *v.*¹ 1713. [f. SPRIG *sb.*¹] **1.** *trans.* To fasten with sprigs or brads. **2.** *intr.* To drive in sprigs 1898.

Sprig, *v.*² 1731. [f. SPRIG *sb.*²] *trans.* To decorate or cover with designs representing sprigs.

A blue satin tie sprigged with gold 1850.

Sprigged (sprigd), *ppl. a.* 1613. [f. SPRIG *sb.*² or *v.*²] **1.** Adorned or ornamented with sprigs. **2.** Having the form of a sprig or sprigs; minutely branched 1714.

Spriggy (spri·gi), *a.* 1597. [f. SPRIG *sb.*²] Abounding in sprigs or small branches; suggestive of a sprig or sprigs.

Spright (sprəit), *sb.* 1533. [var. of SPRITE *sb.*, after words in *-ight.*] **†1.** = SPIRIT *sb.* in various senses -1700. **2.** A disembodied spirit, a ghost; a supernatural being, goblin, fairy, etc. 1533.

My weryed spryght 1563. Come Sisters, cheere we vp his sprights, And shew the best of our delights SHAKS. **2.** Glad was Huon when he had loste the syghte of the spryghte 1533. And sweete Sprights beare the burthen SHAKS. Hence **†Spright** *v. trans.* to haunt, as by a s. SHAKS. **†Spri·ghtless** *a.* devoid of spirit or animation -1710.

Sprightful (sprəi·tfŭl), *a.* Now *rare.* 1591. [f. SPRIGHT *sb.*] **1.** Of persons: Full of spirit; animated, lively. **†b.** Of horses: Spirited -1674. **2.** Of actions, sounds, etc.: Marked by spirit, animation, or liveliness 1628. **†3.** Of liquids, etc.: Impregnated with spirit; spirituous -1669.

1. Spoke like a sprightfull Noble Gentleman SHAKS. **b.** The Horses were..The noblest, sprightfulst breed COWLEY. **2.** The right jolly and sprightfull tune of *Ca Ira* W. IRVING. Hence **Spri·ghtful-ly** *adv.*, **-ness.**

Sprightly (sprəi·tli), *a.* and *adv.* 1596. [f. SPRIGHT *sb.* + -LY.] **A.** *adj.* **1.** Of persons: Full of vivacity or animation; cheerful, gay, brisk. **b.** Of animals: Lively, sportive 1735. **2.** Characterized by animation or cheerful vivacity 1606. **3.** Of things: Having lively qualities or properties; naturally brisk; suggestive of animation or gaiety 1605. **†4.** Ghostly, spectral. SHAKS.

1. Seest thou that s. youth? MARSTON. **b.** The crowing of the s. cock 1830. **2.** My bones are full of unctious marrow, and my blood, of s. Youth 1646. Gay s. land of mirth and social ease GOLDSM. **3.** Let ..Bacchus fill the s. Bowl PRIOR. It is a noble, s. Sound. The Trumpet's Clangor, and the Clash of Arms! DRYDEN.

B. *adv.* In a sprightly manner; with vigour and animation 1604. Hence **Spri·ghtlily** *adv.* (*rare*). **Spri·ghtliness.**

Spri·g tail, spri·gtail. 1676. [f. SPRIG

sb.[1]] **1.** A short pointed tail. **2.** *U.S.* = PIN-TAIL 1. 1782. So **Sprig-tailed** *a.* 1676.

Spring (spriŋ), *sb.*[1] [OE., f. the stem *spring-, sprang-, sprung-*; see SPRING *v.*] **I. 1.** The place of rising or issuing from the ground; the source or head, *of* a well, stream, or river; the supply of water forming such a source. Now *rare.* **2.** A flow of water rising or issuing naturally out of the earth; a similar flow obtained by boring, etc. ME. **b.** A flow of water possessing special properties, esp. of a medicinal or curative nature 1787. **c.** *pl.* A place or locality having such springs to which invalids or pleasure-seekers resort 1849. **3.** *fig.* A source or origin *of* something. Also occas. without const. ME.

1. Great riuers, whose mouthes are knowne, but not their springs 1600. 2. It has also some Springs of good Water 1665. *fig.* When old age approaches, ..the springs of life dry up 1771. b. *Chalybeate, hot, mineral, thermal, warm,* etc. *springs.* 3. The S., the Head, the Fountaine of your Blood Is stopt SHAKS. Language reveals the deepest springs of thought 1892.

II. 1. The action or time of rising or springing into being or existence: **a.** The first sign *of* day, morning, etc.; the dawn. Also, the beginning of a season. Now *Obs.* exc. *poet.* ME. †**b.** *S. of the leaf,* the time when trees begin to burst into leaf again -1670. **2.** orig. †*Spring of the year* (1530): The first season of the year, or that between winter and summer, reckoned astronomically from the vernal equinox to the summer solstice; in pop. use in Great Britain comprising the months of February, March, and April, or (according to some) March, April, and May. Also *transf.*, a season resembling this in some respect. 1547. **b.** The first or early stage or period *of* life, youth, etc. 1590. **c.** Contrasted with *fall* (cf. FALL *sb.*[1] I. 2). Now *arch.* 1643. **d.** This season in a particular year 1621.

1. It came to passe about the s. of the day 1 *Sam.* ix. 26. 2. O, Wind, If Winter comes, can S. be far behind? SHELLEY. b. Oh, how this s. of loue resembleth The vncertaine glory of an Aprill day SHAKS. d. I am going to the same place I went last s. 1711.

attrib. in senses 'of or pertaining to the s.', 'appearing, happening, etc., in the s.', as *s.-ague*; **s. pottage, soup,** pottage or soup made of or from fresh green vegetables; 'sown or suitable for sowing in the s.', as *s. barley, onion, wheat.*

Comb.: **s.-beauty,** any plant of the genus *Claytonia*; **-grass,** *Anthoxanthum odoratum,* a native of Britain; **-herring,** the alewife.

III. †**1. a.** A young growth on a tree, plant, or root; a shoot, sprout, sucker; a small branch, sprig, or twig; the rudimentary shoot of a seed -1660. **b.** A growth of this nature cut or slipped off, esp. for planting -1657. **2.** A copse, grove, or wood consisting of young trees springing up naturally from the stools of old ones; a plantation, esp. one inclosed and used for rearing or harbouring game. Now *dial.* late ME. **b.** *collect.* Young growth, shoots, or sprouts, esp. the under growth of trees or shrubs. Now *dial.* 1482. **3.** A springing up, growing, or bursting forth of plants, vegetation, etc.; also, a race or stock of persons. Now *rare.* 1624.

2. Yonder S. of Roses intermixt With Myrtle MILT.

IV. †**1.** Rise, beginning, first appearance, or birth (*of* something) -1682. **2.** †**a.** The rising *of* the sea (to an exceptional height) at particular times -1585. **b.** = SPRING-TIDE 2. Chiefly *pl.* 1584. **3.** An act of springing or leaping; a bound, jump, or leap 1450. **b.** A recoil or rebound 1680. **c.** A quick, convulsive, or elastic movement made by certain plants or animals in dispersing or depositing seed, eggs, etc. 1801. **d.** A distance capable of being covered by a spring or leap 1817. **4.** A flock *of* teal. Now *arch.* 1450. **5.** A cut or joint of pork consisting of the belly or lower part of the forequarter. *Obs.* exc. *dial.* 1598. **6.** *Naut.* A split or opening in a †vessel, mast, or spar, esp. one of such a size as to render it unsafe to carry the usual amount of sail 1611. **7.** The quality or capacity of springing; elastic energy or force; elasticity 1660. **b.** Elasticity or springiness as possessed by persons or the limbs; buoyancy and vigour in movement 1700. **8.** *transf.* Buoyancy, activity, vigour *of* mind, temper, etc.; active power or faculty 1682. **9.** *Arch.* The point at which an arch or vault springs or rises from its abutment or impost; the commencement of curvature in an arch 1726. **10.** *Naut.* The sheer, the upward curvature or rise, of the deck planking of a vessel or boat 1838.

1. Phr. *To take* (..) *s. from* or *out of*, to have source or origin in, to rise or originate in. 2. b. The tide rises six feet on the springs 1779. 3. *fig.* When Science was pausing for the s. she has since made 1878. b. The s. of a well-drawn bow 1853. 6. We.. ..discover'd a great S. in the Foremast 1744. 7. The air's s. or elasticity GOLDSM. Yielding few..woods that have sufficient s. for the construction of the bow 1874. b. Th' elastic s. of an unwearied foot COWPER. 8. A selfish villain may possess a s. and alacrity of temper HUME.

V. 1. An elastic contrivance or mechanical device, usu. consisting of a plate or strip of steel (or a number of these) suitably shaped or adjusted, which, when compressed, bent, coiled, or otherwise forced out of its normal shape, possesses the property of returning to it; used chiefly for imparting motion, regulating movement, or for lessening or preventing concussion. late ME. **2.** *fig.* That by which action is produced, inspired, or instigated; a moving, actuating, or impelling agency, cause, or force; a motive. Freq. const. *of* action (or conduct). 1616. **3.** *Naut.* A rope put out from the end or side of a vessel lying at anchor, and made fast to the cable 1744. **b.** A hawser laid out to some fixed object to slew a vessel in any required direction 1769.

1. A helical s. has coils of decreasing diameter as they approach the center KNIGHT. 2. These men are..able..to put all the springs of a perfect culture in motion 1767. It is difficult..to come at the true springs of action 1779.

attrib.: in senses 'fitted with a spring or springs', 'acting like a spring', 'of or pertaining to a spring', as *s.-arbor, -balance, -bar, -barrel, -bed*; 'having springs, hung or suspended on springs', as *s.-ambulance, -carriage -cart*; in similar combs. used attrib., as *s.-blade knife*; in parasynthetic combs. as *s.-framed, -jointed* adjs.; *spring-heeled Jack,* a person who from his great activity or agility is imagined to have springs in the heels of his boots.

Spring (spriŋ), *sb.*[2] late ME. [prob. related to OF. *espring(u)er, -ier* to dance; see SPRING *v.*[1]] †**1.** Some kind of dance -1460. **2.** A tune upon the bagpipes or other musical instrument, esp. a quick or lively tune; a dance-tune. Chiefly, and now only, *Sc.* 1475.

2. *fig.* I've play'd mysel a bonie s., An' danc'd my fill! BURNS.

Spring, *sb.*[3] *Obs.* exc. *dial.* 1604. [Alteration of SPRINGE *sb.*] A snare or noose.

I set no springs for Woodcocks 1604.

Spring (spriŋ), *v.*[1] Pa. t. **sprang** (spræŋ), **sprung** (sprɒŋ). Pa. pple. **sprung.** [Com. Teut.; OE. *springan*, = OFris. *springa*, MDu. *springen.*] **I.** **Intr. senses.* **1.** Of things: To change place or position by sudden and rapid movement without contact; to move with a sudden jerk or bound (in later use esp. by resilient force); to dart or fly. **b.** To be resilient or elastic; to shift or move on account of this 1667. **c.** To rise or come suddenly *to, into* the eyes, lips, etc. 1848. †**2.** Of fame, rumour, etc.: To spread, extend -1578. **3. a.** Of persons or animals: To bound or leap. Const. with advs. or preps. Also *spec.*, of partridges, to rise from cover. ME. **b.** To rise quickly, or with a bound, from a sitting or recumbent posture 1474. **4.** To fly asunder or in pieces; to burst, break, crack, or split; to give way. Also *fig.* of the heart. ME. **b.** In pa. pple. †(*a*) Of horses: Foundered -1696. (*b*) Of planks, masts, etc.: Split, cracked 1704. (*c*) *slang.* Of persons: Intoxicated 1826. **c.** Of mines: To go off, explode 1658. **5.** To swell *with* milk; to give signs of foaling or calving. Now *dial.* 1607.

1. As fire ys wont to quyk and goo From a sparke spronge amys CHAUCER. c. An indignant refusal sprang to his lips 1891. 3. a. Like Pallas springing arm'd from Jove COWPER. b. Good news caused me to s. from my bed 1860. 4. Splicing a favourite old fives'-bat which had sprung 1857. b. (*b*) It will not be possible to race this cutter..owing to her mast being sprung 1894.

II. 1. To issue or come forth suddenly, to break out, esp. in a jet or stream. Freq. with *forth* or *out.* OE. **b.** *esp.* Of water: To rise or flow in a stream out of the ground. Freq. with *out* or *up.* ME. **2.** Of morning, etc.: To come above the horizon; to begin to appear ME.

1. The perspiration which sprung from his brow SCOTT. b. I have sene the place where Temmes springeth 1530. 2. When the day began to s. *Judges* xix. 25. *fig.* The Gentiles shal come to thy light, & kynges to the brightness y[t] springeth forth vpon y[e] COVERDALE *Isa.* lx. 3.

III. 1. Of vegetation: To grow; to arise or develop by growth OE. **2.** Of conditions, qualities, etc.: To take rise, to originate or proceed ME. **3.** Of persons (or animals): To originate by birth or generation; to issue or descend. Usu. const. *from, of,* or *out of.* ME. **b.** To come into being 1667. **c.** To arise as an offshoot *from* a society 1782. **4.** To grow (*up*); to increase or extend in height or length; to grow out *from* some thing or part. late ME. **b.** To attain to a certain height or point by growth. late ME. **c.** Of arches, etc.: To take a curving or slanting upward course *from* some point of support. Also without const. 1739. **5.** With *up.* Of a breeze: To begin to blow 1719.

1. From the cedar tre..euen vnto the hyssope that springeth out of the wall BIBLE (Geneva) 1 *Kings* iv. 33. For her the green grass shall not s. TENNYSON. 2. The scholastic philosophy sprung up in the schools of Paris 1874. Out of the union of wisdom and temperance with courage, springs justice 1875. 3. Thou, sprung of the seed of the seas As an ear from a seed of corn SWINBURNE. b. The isles of Greece!.. Where Delos rose, and Phœbus sprung! BYRON. 4. b. Corne as yet not sprong To the full height 1627. c. Doubtless an arched roof sprung from the side walls SCOTT. 5. As the breeze is now springing up from the NW. NELSON.

** *Trans. senses.* **IV. 1.** †**a.** = SPRENGE *v.* 1. -1581. **b.** = SPRENGE *v.* 2. Usu. const. *with.* *Obs.* exc. *dial.* late ME. †**2.** To produce, bring forth. Also *fig.* -1697. **3.** To cause (a bird, *esp.* a partridge) to rise from cover. Also *fig.* 1531. **4.** *Naut.* Of a vessel, or those on board: To have (a mast, yard, etc.) split, cracked, or started 1595. **b.** To have or make (a leak) open or start 1611. **5. a.** *Mil.* To explode (a mine) 1637. **b.** To sound (a rattle) 1812. **6.** †**a.** To start (something); to set going -1700. **b.** *colloq.* To give, pay, or disburse (a sum of money); to buy (a certain amount); also (*slang*), to afford to buy 1851. **c.** To bring (an announcement, etc.) suddenly *upon* a person or persons 1884. **7.** To cause (a thing) to spring, move suddenly, fly with a jerk, etc. 1665. **b.** *Mil.* To shift (a weapon, etc.) smartly from one position to another 1780. **c.** To cause (some mechanism, etc.) to work with a sudden movement; to force open by pressure 1828. **d.** To apply or adjust by force applied to some elastic or resilient body 1842. **e.** To bend or deflect from a straight line 1873. **8.** *Arch.* To commence the curve of (an arch) 1703.

2. If, as we dream, Egyptian earth, impregnated with flame, Sprung the first man DRYDEN. 3. We sprang Ducks and Snipes 1682. 4. b. The vessel sprang a leak 1851. 5. a. *fig.* He springs the hushed Volcano's mines WORDSW. 6. c. The..arrangement by which Sir Henry Peek's resignation was sprung upon the constituency 1884. 7. c. He would s. all their traps 1897.

V. To leap over; cover with a spring 1825.

Spring, *v.*[2] 1843. [f. SPRING *sb.*[1]] **1.** *trans.* To give spring or elasticity to. **2.** To provide or fit with a spring or springs 1884.

Spring-, the stem of SPRING *v.* used in a few specific names, as **s.-beetle,** a skipjack; **-hare,** the jumping hare of S. Africa; **-jack,** = *s.-beetle.*

Spri·ngal(d[1]. *Obs.* exc. *Hist.* ME. [ad. OF. *espringale, -alle,* app. f. OF. *espringuer* SPRING *v.*[1]] An engine of the nature of a bow or catapult, used in mediæval warfare for throwing heavy missiles; also, a missile thrown by an engine of this kind.

Spri·ngal(d[2]. Now *arch.* 1440. [perh. f. SPRING *v.*[1] Revived by Scott.] **1.** A young man, a youth, a stripling. **2.** *attrib.* or as *adj.* Youthful, adolescent 1614.

1. Sure the Devil..is in this Springald BEAUM & FL.

Spri·ng-beam. 1797. [f. SPRING *sb.*[1] or *v.*[1]] The distinctive name of certain strong timbers forming part of the fittings of an engine or paddle-box.

Spri·ng-board. 1866. [f. SPRING *sb.*[1] or *v.*[1]] **1.** A projecting board or plank, from the end of which a person may jump or dive. **2.** An elastic board used to assist in vaulting 1875.

‖**Springbok** (spri·ŋbǫk). Also †**-bock, -boc.** 1775. [Cape Du., f. *springen* to spring + *bok* goat, antelope.] A species of antelope,

Antilope euchore, abounding in S. Africa, characterized by a habit of springing almost directly upwards when excited or disturbed. **b.** *pl.* A nickname for South Africans. So **Spri·ngbuck** 1775.

Spring-cleaning. 1887. [f. SPRING *sb.*^{1}] The general cleaning of a house, etc., usually performed in the spring. Hence **Spring-clean** *v.* and *sb.*

Springe (sprin^{d}ʒ), *sb.* ME. [app. repr. OE. **spręncg*, related to SPRENGE *v.* and SPRING *v.*^{1}] A snare for catching small game, esp. birds. Freq. *fig.*

fig. Springes to catch Woodcocks SHAKS. He wanted to catch me in his springes of words 1875.

Springe (sprin^{d}ʒ), *v.* 1616. [f. prec.] **1.** *trans.* To catch in a springe or snare. **2.** *intr.* To set snares 1895.

Springer (spri·ŋəɹ). late ME. [f. SPRING *v.*^{1}] **I.** †**1.** A source or origin. CHAUCER. **2. a.** A fish which springs or leaps; now *spec.* a newly-run salmon 1753. **b.** *Zool.* The springbok. Also *s. antelope.* 1781. **3.** One who springs or leaps 1775. **4.** *Arch.* The support from which an arch springs; the impost at each end of an arch 1611. **5.** A cow or heifer near to calving 1844. **II. 1.** One of the larger varieties of spaniel 1808. **2.** One who fires or sets off a mine 1861.

Spri·ng-flood. late ME. [f. SPRING *sb.*^{1} + FLOOD *sb.*] †**1.** = SPRING-TIDE **2.** –1648. **2.** A river-flood occurring in spring-time 1823.

Spring(-)gun. 1775. [SPRING *sb.*^{1}] A gun capable of being discharged by one coming in contact with it, or with a wire or the like attached to the trigger; formerly used as a guard against trespassers or poachers, and placed in concealment for this purpose.

Steel traps and spring guns seemed writ in every wrinkle SHERIDAN.

Springhalt. 1613. [app. an alteration of STRINGHALT, through association with SPRING *v.*^{1}] = STRINGHALT.

Spri·ng-head. 1555. [f. SPRING *sb.*^{1}] The source or fountain of a river. Also *fig.*

Springing (spri·ŋiŋ), *vbl. sb.* ME. [f. SPRING *v.*^{1}] **1.** The action or process of one who or that which springs, in various senses. **2. a.** *Arch.* = SPRING *sb.*^{1} IV. 9. 1703. **b.** The point of growth from the trunk of a tree 1825. **3.** The action of exploding a mine 1665.

1. Thou makest it soft with showres, thou blessest the s. thereof *Ps.* lxv. 10.

Springle (spri·ŋg'l), *sb.* 1602. [perh. f. SPRING *sb.*^{3}] A springe or snare.

Springle (spri·ŋg'l), *v.* Now *rare* or *arch.* 1502. [perh. var. of SPRINKLE *v.*] *trans.* To sprinkle. Also *absol.*

Springlet (spri·ŋlėt). 1808. [f. SPRING *sb.*^{1} + -LET.] A small spring or fountain.

From out the..hill Oozes the slender s. still SCOTT.

Spri·ng-lock. 1485. [f. SPRING *sb.*^{1}] A common form of lock in which a spring presses the bolt outwards, thus rendering it self-locking except when secured by a catch.

Spri·ng-tail. 1797. [SPRING *sb.*^{1}] *Zool.* One or other of various species of insects which leap or spring by means of their tail.

Spring-tide. 1530. [SPRING *sb.*^{1}] **1.** The season of spring; spring-time. **2.** A tide occurring on the days shortly after the new and full moon, in which the high-water level reaches its maximum 1548. **3.** *transf.* A copious flow or large quantity *of* something 1593.

1. *fig.* Happy youth, that shalt possesse Such a spring-tyde of delight 1640. **2.** A sudden land-flood, met by a spring-tide, surrounded and overwhelmed the town 1776. **3.** Woe, wonder, and sensation high, In one spring-tide of ecstasy! SCOTT.

Spri·ng(-)time. 1495. [SPRING *sb.*^{1}] **1.** = prec. **1.** **2. a.** The earlier period of a person's life; youth 1593. **b.** A time or period comparable in some way to spring. Usu. const. *of.* 1764.

1. As Bees In spring time..Poure forth thir populous youth about the Hive In clusters MILT.

Spri·ng(-)wa·ter. 1440. [SPRING *sb.*^{1} I. 2.] Water issuing or obtained from a spring or fountain.

Spri·ng-well. ME. [f. as prec. + WELL *sb.*] A spring or well of water; a spring-head or fountain.

Spri·ng-wood. 1523. [f. SPRING *sb.*^{1} III. 2.] **1. a.** Wood growing in a spring or copse of young saplings. **b.** A copse or wood of springs or young trees 1623. **2.** A ring or layer of wood formed round a tree each spring 1884.

Springy (spri·ŋi), *a.* 1641. [f. SPRING *sb.*^{1} and *v.*^{1}] **1.** Characterized by the presence of springs of water. **2.** Endowed with spring or elasticity 1660. **b.** Elastic to the tread 1797. **3.** Marked or characterized by spring, elasticity, or resilience 1669. **b.** *esp.* Of the bearing or movements of persons or animals 1818.

1. Lowe, moist, and s. groundes are the best to increase milke in an ewe 1641. **2.** A laughing schoolboy..Riding the s. branches of an elm KEATS. **3. b.** The s. step..reminded Henry Warden of Halbert SCOTT. Hence **Spri·ngily** *adv.* **Spri·nginess.**

Sprinkle (spri·ŋk'l), *sb.* late ME. [Related to SPRINKLE *v.*] †**1.** A sprinkler, *esp.* one for sprinkling holy water –1647. **2.** An (or the) act of sprinkling; a quantity which is sprinkled 1596. **b.** A small number or quantity; a sprinkling 1768. **3.** *techn.* A colour effect produced by sprinkling; a mixture for producing this 1835.

2. Baptizing the Christian infant with a solemne s. MILT.

Sprinkle (spri·ŋk'l), *v.* late ME. [Related to Du. *sprenkelen*, G. *sprenkeln.*] **1.** *trans.* To scatter in drops; to let fall in small particles here and there; to strew thinly or lightly. **b.** *fig.* To disperse, distribute, or scatter here and there 1514. **2.** To bedew, bespatter lightly, or powder (a thing or surface); to besprinkle. Usu. const. *with.* late ME. **b.** To dot, intersperse, diversify *with* something. Usu. in *pass.* 1591. **c.** To colour with small specks or spots. (Chiefly in *pass.*, or *techn.* in bookbinding.) 1750. **3.** *intr.* **a.** To spring or fly *up* in fine drops 1594. **b.** To rain or fall in fine or infrequent drops 1778.

1. S. sordid Ashes all around DRYDEN. **b.** Besides cities, many private dwellings were sprinkled on mount Ephraim FULLER. **2.** The floor was merely sprinkled with rain, and not saturated 1878. **3. a.** It will make the Water friske and sprinckle vp, in a fine Dew BACON. **b.** The rain..continued to s. 1858.

Sprinkler (spri·ŋkləɹ). 1535. [f. SPRINKLE *v.*] **1.** A vessel or other device used for sprinkling water, etc. **b.** A machine or vehicle used for this purpose, esp. one for watering the roadway or extinguishing fire 1879. **2.** A brush for sprinkling holy water 1577. **3.** A person who sprinkles 1613.

Spri·nkling, *vbl. sb.* 1440. [f. SPRINKLE *v.*] **1.** The action of the verb in various senses. **2.** A small quantity sprinkled or to be sprinkled 1657. **3.** *fig.* A small or slight quantity or amount 1594. **b.** A small number scattered or distributed here and there 1621. **4.** *attrib.* as *s.-brush, -can, -cart, -machine* 1596.

1. Baptism..may be perform'd even by Effusion or S. 1726. **2.** A s. of Rain 1700. **3.** Some little S. of Grammer learning NASHE. **b.** A s. of gray hairs 1706.

Sprint (sprint), *sb.* 1865. [f. SPRINT *v.*] A short spell of running, rowing, etc., at full speed. Also *attrib.*, as *s. course, race.*

Sprint (sprint), *v.* 1566. [a. early Scand. **sprinta.*] †**1.** *intr.* To dart or spring. **2.** To run, row, etc., at full speed, esp. for a short distance; to race in this manner 1871.

2. By running and walking, or rather sprinting, the whole time 1889. Hence **Spri·nter,** one who sprints or engages in sprint-racing. **Spri·nting** *vbl. sb.*

Sprit (sprit), *sb.*^{1} [OE. *spréot*, ult. related to SPROUT *v.*] **1.** A pole, *esp.* one used for propelling a boat; a punting-pole; †**a** spear. **2.** *Naut.* A small boom or pole which crosses the fore and aft sail diagonally from the mast to the upper hindmost corner of the sail, which it extends and elevates. Also *attrib.* late ME.

Sprit (sprit), *sb.*^{2} 1622. Now *dial.* [f. the vb.] A shoot, sprout. **Sprit** *v.* [OE. *sprytan*] *intr.* to sprout.

Sprite (sprəit), †**sprit,** *sb.* ME. [ad. OF. *esprit*, or similarly reduced from OF. *esperit(e*, AF. *spirit(e* SPIRIT *sb.*] †**a.** = SPIRIT *sb.* in various senses –1847. **b.** A disembodied spirit, a ghost ME. †**c.** The spirit of God; the Holy Spirit –1600.

His sprete was moved in hym TINDALE *Acts* xvii. 16. Forth with jocund s., I run SHENSTONE. **b.** Where must I lye anights? For I am monstrous fraid of Sprites COTTON. **c.** Governe me with thy holy s. 1600.

Spritsail (spri·tsēil, spri·ts'l). 1466. [f. SPRIT *sb.*^{1} Cf. Du. *sprietzeil*, WFris. *-seil.*] A sail extended by a sprit; formerly also a sail attached to a yard slung under the bowsprit of large vessels.

attrib., as *s. brace, clewline*; *s. barge, vessel*; **s. yard,** a yard slung under the bowsprit to support a s.

Sprocket (sprǫ·kėt). 1536. [Origin obsc.] **1.** *Carp.* and *Build.* A triangular piece of timber used in framing, esp. one fastened on the foot of a rafter in order to raise the level of the eaves. **2.** A projection (either forked or simple) from the rim of a wheel, engaging with the links of a chain. Also *attrib.* in *s. wheel.* 1750. **b.** *ellipt.* A sprocket-wheel, esp. that of a cycle 1886. **3.** *Naut.* One of the teeth of a pawl-rim 1903.

Sprod. *n. dial.* 1617. [Origin obsc.] A salmon in its second year.

Sprout (spraut), *sb.* ME. [Related to SPROUT *v.*] **1.** A shoot from a branch, root, or stump of a tree, shrub, or plant; a new growth developing from a bud into a branch, stalk, sucker, etc. **b.** A rudimentary shoot of a seed; the acrospire of grain 1610. **c.** *pl.* Young or tender shoots or side-growths of various vegetables, esp. of the cabbage kind 1639. **d.** *ellipt.* for *Brussels sprouts* 1858. **2.** *fig.* Applied to persons: A scion 1725. **3.** The action of sprouting or of putting forth new growths (*rare*) 1586.

2. That resuscitated s. of Saxon royalty SCOTT.

Sprout (spraut), *v.* [OE. **sprūtan*, = WFris. *sprute*, MDu. *spruten.* Cf. OE. *sprytan* (rare), *spryttan* SPRIT *v.*] **1.** *intr.* To grow, issue, or proceed as a sprout or sprouts; to shoot forth or spring up by natural growth. **b.** Of persons: To originate or spring 1582. **2.** Of a tree, plant, seed, etc.: To put forth, throw up or out, a sprout or sprouts; to develop new growths or shoots; to bud. ME. **b.** *spec.* To germinate, begin to grow, prematurely 1685. **3.** *transf.* Of earth, a surface, etc.: To bear, bring forth, or produce sprouts or sprout-like growths. Freq. const. *with* (a growth). 1591. **4.** *trans.* To cause (branches, leaves, etc.) to grow or shoot; to bear or develop, to put or throw *forth* or *out*, as sprouts 1601. **5.** To cause or induce (plants, seeds, etc.) to develop sprouts or shoots, esp. before planting or sowing them 1770. **b.** *dial.* and *U.S.* To rub or break off the sprouts of (potatoes) 1828.

1. Verse sprouting from verse as simply as leaf from leaf 1879. **2.** *fig.* Should his money s. and yield a thousand fold 1856. **4.** *fig.* When you think he has exhausted his battery of looks,..suddenly he sprouts out an entirely new set of features LAMB.

Spruce (sprūs), *sb.* late ME. [Alteration of PRUCE Prussia.] †**1.** The country of Prussia. Also *Spruce-land.* –1656. †**b.** *attrib.* in the sense 'brought or obtained from Prussia', as *S. board, canvas* –1875. **2.** *ellipt.* †**a.** Spruce leather –1611. **b.** Spruce beer 1741. **3.** *ellipt.* = SPRUCE FIR 1670. **b.** A species, or a single tree, of spruce fir 1832. **c.** The wood of the spruce fir 1853.

1. b. A Broker, in a s. leather ierkin NASHE. *Spruce-leather*, a sort of Leather corruptly so call'd for Prussia leather 1706. **3.** The black s. is used only for beer...Of this s., is made the essence, which is as well known in Europe as in America. 1792.

attrib., as *s. bark, -bough, -cone*; **s.-borer, bud, worm,** U.S. names of insects which attack s. trees; **s. grouse, partridge,** the spotted Canada grouse.

Spruce (sprūs), *a.* and *adv.* 1589. [perh. f. SPRUCE *sb.* 1 b in the collocation *spruce* (*leather*) *jerkin.*] **A.** *adj.* †**1.** Brisk, smart, lively –1749. **2.** Trim, neat, dapper; smart in appearance 1599.

1. A s., lively air, fashionable dress; and all the glitter that a young fellow should have CHESTERF. **2.** A Neat, s., affecting Courtier, one that weares clothes well, and in fashion B. JONS. The s. Night-cap of his Valet STEELE. The Cathedral [of Salisbury], which was finished 600 years ago, has even a s. and modern air EMERSON.

B. *adv.* Sprucely (*rare*) 1618. Hence **Spru·cely** *adv.*, **-ness.**

Spruce (sprūs), *v.* 1594. [f. prec.] **1.** *trans.* To make spruce, trim, or neat. Also with *up.* **2.** With *up* (or †*out*): To make oneself spruce 1709.

2. His Father and grandfather are..profess'd Sparks,

and s. up in Cherry and other gaudy colour'd silk Stockings 1709.

Spruce beer. 1500. [SPRUCE *sb.*] †**a.** Beer from Prussia. **b.** A fermented beverage made with an extract from the leaves and branches of the spruce fir.

Spruce fir. 1731. [SPRUCE *sb.*] **1.** A distinct species of fir (*Pinus* or *Abies*) comprising several clearly marked varieties, as *black, red, white, Canadian, Norway spruce*; one or other of these varieties. **2.** A tree belonging to this species 1768.

Sprue[1] (sprū). 1825. [ad. Du. *spruw*, perh. related to Flem. *spruwen* to sprinkle.] †**1.** = THRUSH[2] 1. (In Dicts.) **2.** A disease characterized by sore throat, raw tongue, and digestive disturbance, occurring esp. in tropical countries; psilosis 1888.

Sprue[2] (sprū). 1875. [Origin obsc.] *Founding.* One of the holes through which metal is poured into the mould.

Sprue[3] (sprū). 1846. [Origin obsc.] A poor or inferior quality of asparagus. Also *s. grass.*

‖**Spruit** (spræt). *S. Afr.* 1863. [Du., = SPROUT *sb.*] A small stream or watercourse, usu. almost dry except in the wet season.

Sprung (sprʊŋ), *ppl. a.*[1] 1575. [pa. pple. of SPRING *v.*[1]] **1.** That has sprung up or arisen. **2.** Cracked, split 1597. **3.** Made to fly up, as *a s. partridge* 1598.

Sprung[2], irreg. ppl. adj. of SPRING *v.*[2]

S. rhythm, a modern form of poetical rhythm based on that of medieval alliterative verse.

Sprunt (sprʊnt), *v.* Now *dial.* 1601. [app. related to SPRENT *v.* and SPRINT *v.*] *intr.* To spring or start; to move in a quick or convulsive manner; to dart or run. Hence **Sprunt** *sb.* a convulsive movement; a start, spring.

Spry (sprəi), *a.* 1746. [Origin obsc.] **1.** Active, nimble, brisk; full of health and spirits. **2.** *dial.* Spruce, neat, smartly dressed 1806. Hence **Spry·ly** *adv.*, **-ness.**

Spud (spʊd), *sb.* 1440. [Origin obsc.] †**1.** A short and poor knife or dagger -1824. **2. a.** A digging or weeding implement of the spade-type, having a narrow chisel-shaped blade 1667. **b.** A digging fork with three broad prongs 1805. **c.** A small instrument with an enlarged end used in ocular and other surgery 1869. **3.** A short or stumpy person or thing 1687. **4.** *slang* and *dial.* A potato 1860.

2. a. We..begun with a spudd to lift up the ground PEPYS. **3.** That baby..everlastingly holds out its spuds of arms 1900.

Spud (spʊd), *v.* 1652. [f. prec. 2.] **1.** *trans.* To dig *up* or *out*, to remove, by means of a spud. **2.** To dig with a spud. Also *intr.* 1828. **3.** To drill (a hole) by a special process in the early stages of sinking an oil-well 1886.

Spulyie (spü·lyi, spö·li), *v.* Chiefly *Sc.* Now *arch.* late ME. [ad. OF. *espoillier* SPOIL *v.*] **1.** *trans.* To despoil or plunder (persons, etc.). **2.** To take as spoil or plunder 1470. **3.** *intr.* To commit spoliation 1834. So **Spu·lyie** *sb.* [ad. OF. *espoille*] spoiling, spoil 1464.

Spume (spiūm), *sb.* late ME. [ad. OF. *spume, espume*, or L. *spuma.*] **1.** Foam, froth, frothy matter. **b.** *spec.* Foam of the sea 1440. †**2.** = LITHARGE 1. -1661.

1. *fig.* These foul snails..leaving their s. and filth on the fairest flowers of literature RUSKIN. **b.** My forehead was wet with the s. of the spray 1805.

Spume (spiūm), *v.* late ME. [ad. L. *spumare* f. *spuma* SPUME *sb.*] **1.** *intr.* To foam or froth. Also with *out.* **2.** *trans.* To send or cast *forth* like foam 1859.

Spumescence (spiūme·sĕns). 1796. [See next and -ENCE.] Frothiness; the state of being foamy. So **Spume·scent** *a.* having the appearance of froth or foam (*rare*).

Spumous (spiū·məs), *a.* late ME. [ad. L. *spumosus.*] **1.** Of the nature of or resembling froth or foam. **2.** Marked by foam; foaming 1854. So **Spu·mose** *a.* 1576.

Spumy (spiū·mi), *a.* 1582. [f. SPUME *sb.* + -Y[1].] **1.** Covered with, throwing up, or of the nature of sea-foam. **2.** Of a frothy consistency or character; characterized by the presence of froth 1618.

1. The s. Waves proclaim the wat'ry War DRYDEN.

Spun (spʊn), *ppl. a.* 1486. [pa. pple. of SPIN *v.*] **1.** That has undergone the process of spinning; formed, fabricated, or prepared by spinning. **b.** Of butter or sugar: Drawn out or worked up into a thread-like form, esp. for ornamenting confectionery, etc. 1834. **c.** *ellipt.* Spun silk or yarn 1868. **2.** With *out.* Unduly protracted or prolonged 1879. **3.** Tired out, exhausted. *slang.* 1924.

1. *Spun-silk*, a..material produced from short-fibered and waste silk, in contradistinction to the long fibers wound from the cocoon 1875. *S. gold, silver*, a silk thread wound with gold, silver-gilt, or silver wire.

Spunge, var. of SPONGE.

Spunk (spʊŋk). 1536. [prob. related to FUNK *sb.*[1]] **1.** A spark, in various senses. *Sc.* and *dial.* **2.** Touchwood; tinder, match, or amadou prepared from this 1582. **3.** One or other of various fungi or fungoid growths on trees, esp. those of the species *Polyporus*, freq. used in the preparation of tinder 1665. **4.** A match, a lucifer. *Sc.* and *north.* 1755. **5.** Spirit, mettle; courage, pluck 1773.

2. A spark of fire is seen and caught in a piece of s. 1841. **5.** The squire has got s. in him GOLDSM. Phr. *Fellow, man*, etc. *of* (..) *s.* Hence **Spu·nky** *a.* full of s. or spirit; courageous, mettlesome.

Spun(-)yarn. late ME. [f. SPUN *ppl. a.*] **1.** Yarn fabricated by the process of spinning. **2.** *Naut.* Line composed of two or more rope-yarns not laid but simply twisted together by a winch or by hand 1627. **b.** A line or cord of this kind 1685.

Spur (spɜ̄ɹ), *sb.* [Com. Teut.; OE. *spora, spura.* The stem is possibly the same as that of SPOOR *sb.*] **I. 1.** A device for pricking the side of a horse in order to urge it forward, consisting of a small spike or spiked wheel attached to the rider's heel. **b.** *Her.* The representation of a spur 1688. **2.** A stimulus, incentive, or incitement. Also const. *of* (the particular influence) and *to* (a person or persons). 1548.

1. A pair of Spurs taken from Buonaparte WELLINGTON. They..Set lance in rest, strike s., suddenly move TENNYSON. *Gilt* (or †*gilded*) *spurs*, as the distinctive mark of a knight (now *Hist.*). **2.** With the spurre of Courage, and the bitte of Respect SIDNEY. Avarice, the s. of industry HUME.

Phrases. *On* or *upon the s.* (arch.), at full speed, in or with the utmost haste. *On* (or *upon*) *the s. of the moment* (or *occasion*, etc.), without premeditation; on a momentary impulse; impromptu, suddenly, instantly. *To win one's spurs*, to gain knighthood by some act of valour; hence, to achieve one's first honours. *To put* or *set spurs to*, to impel or urge on by spurring.

II. 1. *Zool.* A sharp, hard process or projection on the tarsus of the domestic cock and certain other fowls and birds; a back-claw 1548. **b.** *Zool.*, *Anat.*, and *Path.* A sharp-pointed or spur-like process, formation, or growth on some part of the body 1681. **2. a.** A sharp-pointed projection from the prow of a war-vessel 1604. **b.** A metal needle or gaff for fastening to the leg of a gamecock for fighting purposes 1688. **c.** *Whaling.* One of a number of metal spikes in a boot-sole to prevent slipping 1820. **d.** Any sharp or short projection, point, or spike suggestive of a spur 1872. **3. a.** A short or stunted branch or shoot, esp. one likely to produce fruit 1700. **b.** *Bot.* A tubular expansion, resembling a cock's spur in form, of some more or less foliaceous part of a flower; a calcar 1731. **c.** = ERGOT 1. 1763.

1. *fig.* Though we are cockerels now, we shall have spurs one day 1571.

III. 1. A short strut or stay set diagonally to support an upright timber; a shore, prop, or sustaining pillar; a sloping buttress 1529. **b.** *Naut.* (*a*) A curved piece of timber serving as a half-beam to support the decks, where a whole beam cannot be placed; (*b*) A piece of timber fixed on the bilge-ways, its upper end being bolted to the vessel's sides above the water; (*c*) A prong or projection on the arm of an anchor to assist in catching hold of the bottom. 1769. **2.** One of the principal roots of a tree 1610. **3.** †**a.** *Fortif.* An angular outwork or projection from the general face of a curtain or wall, to assist in its defence -1702. †**b.** An angular end of the pier of a bridge -1742. **c.** An artificial projection from a river-bank serving to deflect the current 1818. **4.** A range, ridge, mountain, hill, or part of this, projecting for some distance from the main system or mass; an offshoot or offset 1652. **b.** A branch of a lode, railway, etc. 1833.

2. *Temp.* v. i. 47. **4.** A s. or rising ground at the base of the hills 1863.

Comb.: **s. box**, a special form of horseman's boot-heel, to which the rims of the spurs are affixed; **-fowl**, pop. name of *Galloperdix lunulosa*; **s. gear, gearing** *Mech.*, gearing consisting of spur-wheels; **s. line** (cf. 4 b); **s.-nut** *Mech.*, a small spur-wheel; **s. pepper**, *Capsicum frutescens*, a native of the East Indies; **-way**, a bridle-path (*dial.*); **-wheel**, a gear wheel which has cogs or teeth on the periphery projecting radially from the centre; a cog-wheel.

Spur (spɜ̄ɹ), *v.* [ME. *spure, spore*, f. SPUR *sb.*] **I.** *trans.* **1.** To prick (a horse, etc.) with the spur in order to urge to a faster pace; to urge on by the use of spurs. Also *absol.* **2.** *fig.* To drive on or hasten; to incite, impel, or stimulate; to urge or prompt. Freq. const. *to* (do something, or some course of action). ME. **3.** To provide with a spur or spurs; to furnish with gaffs ME. **4.** Of a bird: To strike or wound with the spur. Also *transf.* 1631.

1. He could scarcely make his horse go, though he spurred him continually 1770. He spurred his horse into the waves GIBBON. **2.** Ire, that spurr'd him on to deeds unjust CARY. **3.** They..began to boot and s. one another 1694.

II. *intr.* **1.** To ride quickly by urging on one's horse with the spur 1590. **b.** *transf.* To hasten; to proceed hurriedly 1513. **2. a.** To strike out with the foot; to kick 1590. **b.** Of cocks, etc.: To fight with the spur; to strike *at* 1722.

1. Parthians..spurring from the Fight, confess their Fear DRYDEN. *fig.* Obstinacy spurs on in spight of all perswasions 1659. **2. a.** All day, between his..sleeps, he [an infant] sputters and spurs EMERSON.

III. *trans.* **1.** To support or prop up (a post, etc.) by means of a strut or spur; to strengthen with spurs 1733. **2.** To prune in (a side-shoot, etc.) so as to form a spur close to the stem. Chiefly with *in* or *back.* 1840. **3.** To affect with ergot 1896.

Spu·r-gall, *v. Obs.* exc. *arch.* 1555. [f. SPUR *sb.* + GALL *v.*[1]] **1.** *trans.* To gall (a horse, etc.) with the spur in riding; to injure or disable in this way 1565. **2.** *fig.* To gall severely, in various senses 1555.

Spurge (spɜ̄ɹdʒ), *sb.* late ME. [ad. OF. *espurge* (F. *épurge*), f. *espurgier* SPURGE *v.*] **1.** One or other of several species of plants belonging to the genus *Euphorbia*, many of which are characterized by an acrid milky juice possessing medicinal properties. **2.** A particular species or plant of this. Chiefly in *pl.* 1715.

attrib.: **s. flax**, *Daphne Gnidium*; **-nettle**, *Cnidoscolus stimulosus*; **-olive**, the shrub *Daphne Mezereum.*

Spurge, *v. Obs.* exc. *dial.* ME. [ad. OF. *espurgier* :—L. *expurgare.*] †**1.** *trans.* To cleanse, purify (a person, the body, etc.); to rid *of* impurity. Also *fig.* to clear of guilt. -1546. **2.** *intr.* Of ale, wine, or other fermenting liquor: To emit or throw off impure matter by fermentation; to cleanse or purify itself in this way; to ferment or 'work' 1440.

Spurge laurel. Also hyphened. 1597. [SPURGE *sb.*] One or other of the shrubs belonging to the genus *Daphne*, esp. *D. Laureola*, the dried bark of which is used in medicine.

Spu·rge-wort. 1562. [f. SPURGE *sb.* or *v.*] †**1.** The plant *Iris fœtidissima* -1588. **2.** *Bot.* Any plant belonging to the order *Euphorbiaceæ* 1647.

Spurious (spiūə·riəs), *a.* 1598. [f. L. *spurius* illegitimate, false.] **1.** Of persons: Begot or born out of wedlock; illegitimate, bastard, adulterous. **b.** Characterized by bastardy or illegitimacy 1770. **2.** Having an illegitimate or irregular origin; not properly qualified or constituted 1601. **3.** Superficially resembling or simulating something; not true or genuine; false, sham, counterfeit 1615. **4.** Of a writing, passage, etc.: Not really proceeding from its reputed origin, source, or author; not genuine or authentic; forged 1624. **5.** Characterized by spuriousness or falseness 1840.

1. Henry came of the s. stock of John of Gaunt 1768. **3.** S. gems our hopes entice COWPER. Statesmen..exist by every thing which is s., fictitious, and false BURKE. Morbid conditions..known as s. dropsies 1877. **4.** The vexed question concerning his reputed works—what are genuine, what s. EMERSON. Hence **Spu·rious·ly** *adv.*, **-ness.**

Spu·r-leather. 1598. [f. SPUR *sb.* + LEATHER *sb.*] **1.** A leather strap for securing a spur to the foot. 2. *Under spur-leather*, a subordinate, an attendant, a menial. Now *arch.* 1685.

Spurless (spɒ̄·ɹlės), *a.* ME. [f. SPUR *sb.* + -LESS.] 1. Lacking a spur; having no spurs. 2. Of birds or their legs: Devoid of spurs 1819. 3. *Bot.* Having no spur or calcar 1839.

Spurling. 1471. var. of SPIRLING.

Spurn (spɒ̄ɹn), *sb.*[1] ME. [f. SPURN *v.*] †1. A trip or stumble -1535. 2. A stroke with the foot; a kick ME. b. The act of kicking or spurning 1641. 3. The act of treating with disdain or contemptuous rejection; an instance of this 1602.

2. *fig.* Death with an equall s. The lofty Turret and low Cottage beats 1612. 3. The insolence of Office, and the Spurnes That patient merit of the vnworthy takes SHAKS.

Spurn (spɒ̄ɹn), *sb.*[2] 1601. [var. of SPUR *sb.*, prob. after prec.] 1. An outward-growing root or rootlet; one of the main roots *of* a tree. *Obs.* exc. *dial.* 2. A slanting prop or stay; a spur or spur-stone 1620. b. *Mining.* A small pillar of coal left within the seam as a temporary support during holing 1837.

Spurn (spɒ̄ɹn), *v.* [OE. *spurnan.* The stem is prob. that of SPUR *v.*] I. *intr.* †1. To strike against something with the foot; to trip or stumble -1734. †2. To strike or thrust with the foot; to kick (*at* something) -1740. 3. *fig.* To kick *against* or *at* something disliked or despised; to manifest opposition or antipathy, esp. in a scornful or disdainful manner 1526.

2. Folly it is to spurne against a pricke CAMDEN. 3. They spurned at danger, and made several vigorous sallies on the enemy 1781.

II. *trans.* 1. To strike or tread (something) with the foot; to trample or kick. late ME. 2. To reject with contempt or disdain; to treat contemptuously; to scorn or despise OE.

1. He with his feet wol spurne adoun his cuppe CHAUCER. You spurne me hence, and he will spurne me hither SHAKS. 2. Every offer tending to conciliation had been spurned FREEMAN.

Comb.: s.-water *Naut.*, a low barrier on the ends of a deck to prevent water from coming aboard.

Spurner (spɒ̄·ɹnəɹ). 1562. [f. SPURN *v.*] †1. One who strikes with the foot -1611. 2. One who rejects or despises; a scorner 1863.

2. Traitor and trickster, And s. of treaties TENNYSON.

Spurred (spɒ̄ɹd), *a.* late ME. [f. SPUR *sb.*] 1. Wearing or provided with a spur or spurs. 2. Furnished with sharp and hard spikes, claws, or the like 1611. 3. Of rye, etc.: Affected with ergot or spur 1763. 4. *Bot.* Of the nature of, provided with, a spur or calcar; calcarate 1824.

1. Others came forth on foot, booted and s. FREEMAN.

Spurrer (spɒ̄·rəɹ). 1632. [f. SPUR *v.*] One who spurs or urges.

Spurr(e)y (spɒ·ri). 1577. [a. Du. *spurrie*, prob. related to med.L. *spergula.*] 1. One or other of various species of herbaceous plants or weeds of the genus *Spergula*; esp. the common species corn spurrey (*S. arvensis*), occas. used as fodder for sheep and cattle; also, the genus to which these species belong. 2. Applied to various species of plants allied to or resembling the genus *Spergula* 1753.

Spurrier (spɒ·riəɹ). ME. [f. SPUR *sb.* + -IER.] A spur-maker.

Spur-rowel. 1611. [f. SPUR *sb.*] The rowel of a spur.

Spur-royal. Now *Hist.* or *arch.* Also -rial. 1588. [f. SPUR *sb.* + ROYAL *sb.*] A gold coin of the value of fifteen shillings, chiefly coined in the reign of James I; so called from having on its reverse the form of the sun with rays, resembling a spur-rowel.

Spurry (spɒ̄·ri), *a. rare.* 1611. [f. SPUR *sb.* + -Y[1].] †a. Radiating like the points of a spur-rowel. b. Of the nature of a spur or prop 1863. c. Having spur-like projections 1875.

Spurt (spɒ̄ɹt), *sb.*[1] 1566. [var. of SPIRT *sb.*[2]] 1. †a. A short spell *of* (something) -1699. b. A short space of time; a brief period. Now *dial.* 1591. 2. A brief and unsustained effort; a sudden and short spell of activity or exertion 1591. b. A short spell of rapid movement; a marked or sudden increase of speed attained by special exertion 1787. c. *transf.* A marked increase or improvement in business; a sudden advance or rise of prices, etc.; also, the period during which this lasts 1814. 3. *Naut.* A short spell *of* wind 1699.

1. b. Herschel has been in town for short spurts, and back again, two or three times MME D'ARBLAY. 2. Quinine..has given me a s. for the last two days 1885. b. Their boat..dipped a little when they put on anything like a severe s. HUGHES. Phr. *By* or *in spurts*, in or with brief, unsustained or spasmodic efforts; in intermittent jets.

Spurt (spɒ̄ɹt), *sb.*[2] 1775. [f. SPURT *v.*[1]] 1. A stream or shower of water, etc., ejected or thrown up with some force and suddenness. b. A spatter or splash made by a pen 1871. 2. A sudden manifestation *of* feeling or energy 1859.

2. A sudden s. of woman's jealousy TENNYSON.

Spurt (spɒ̄ɹt), *v.*[1] 1570. [var. of SPIRT *v.*[1]] = SPIRT *v.*[1] 1, 2.

The milk went on spurting and fizzing into the pail 1833. 2. *fig.* His stream of meaning..is ever and anon spurting itself up into epigrams CARLYLE.

Spurt (spɒ̄ɹt), *v.*[2] 1664. [f. SPURT *sb.*[1] 2.] *intr.* To make a spurt, put on increased speed or make greater exertions, for a short time.

Spurtle (spɒ̄·ɹt'l). *v.* 1633. [f. SPURT *v.*[1] + -LE.] 1. *trans.* To besprinkle or bespatter (*rare*). 2. *intr.* To burst or fly out in a small quantity or stream with some force or suddenness; to spirt 1651.

Spu·r-wing. 1842. [Cf. next.] A spur-winged water-hen, goose, etc.

Spu·r-winged, *a.* 1668. [f. SPUR *sb.*[1]] *Ornith.* Having one or more stiff claws or spurs projecting from the pinion-bone of the wing. In specific names, as *s. goose, plover, lapwing.*

Spute, *v. Obs.* or *dial.* ME. [Aphetic f. DISPUTE *v.*] *intr.* To dispute; to contend in disputation. Usu. const. *with.*

Sputter (spɒ·təɹ), *sb.* 1673. [f. SPUTTER *v.*] 1. = SPLUTTER *sb.* 1 b. b. A state of bustling confusion or excitement 1823. 2. The action or an act of sputtering; the emission of small particles with some amount of explosive sound; the noise characteristic of this. Freq. *fig.* 1837.

1. But he must make some s. rather than be held to the terms of the Question MARVELL. 2. Nothing breaking the silence but the occasional s. of the rushlight 1845.

Sputter (spɒ·təɹ), *v.* 1598. [= Du. *sputteren*, WFris. *sputterje*, of imitative origin.] 1. *trans.* To spit out in small particles and with a characteristic explosive sound or a series of such sounds. 2. To utter hastily and with the emission of small particles of saliva; to ejaculate in a confused, indistinct, or uncontrolled manner, esp. from anger or excitement 1677. 3. *intr.* Of persons: To eject from the mouth, to spit out, food or saliva in small particles with some force and in a noisy explosive manner 1681. 4. To speak or talk hastily and confusedly or disjointedly 1681. 5. To make or give out a sputtering sound or sounds, esp. under the influence of heat 1692.

2. Without the least pretended incitement [to] s. out the basest and falsest accusations SWIFT. 3. His tongue was too large for his mouth; he stuttered and sputtered 1878. 4. The Servants..sputter'd in Dutch, which they understood not 1696. 5. Like the Green Wood That sputtring in the Flame works outward into Tears DRYDEN. The candle..was sputtering with the rain-drops 1845.

‖ **Sputum** (spiū·tǒm). *Pl.* **sputa** (spiū·tă). 1693. [L., spit, spittle.] *Med.* Saliva or spittle mixed with mucus or purulent matter, and expectorated in certain diseased states of the lungs, chest, or throat; a mass or quantity of this.

Spy (spəi), *sb.* ME. [ad. OF. *espie* ESPY *sb.* In sense 3 partly f. SPY *v.*] 1. One who spies upon or watches a person or persons secretly; a secret agent whose business it is to keep a person, place, etc., under close observation; esp. one employed by a government in order to obtain information relating to the naval, military or aeronautical conditions of other countries, or to collect intelligence of any kind. 2. *Mil.* A person employed in time of war to obtain secret information regarding the enemy; in early use esp. one venturing in disguise into the enemy's camp or territory ME. 3. The action of spying; an instance or occasion of this. Chiefly in phrases. 1450.

1. Theeves have their spies..in all Innes 1617. I come no Spie With purpose to explore..The secrets of your Realm MILT. 2. In the early romances, no disguise is so frequently used by a s. as that of a minstrel 1846.

attrib. and *Comb.*, as *s.-system*, etc.; -**money**, payment for the services of a s.; **S. Wednesday**, in Irish use, the Wednesday before Easter Sunday (in allusion to Judas). Hence **Spy·ism**, espionage.

Spy (spəi), *v.* ME. [ad. OF. *espier* ESPY *v.*] I. *trans.* 1. To watch (a person, etc.) in a secret or stealthy manner; to keep under observation with hostile intent; to act as a spy upon (a person). b. To make stealthy observations in (a country or place) from hostile motives. Also with *out.* ME. c. To (seek to) discover or ascertain by stealthy observation ME. 2. To look at, examine, or observe closely or carefully; to see or behold; in mod. use *spec.* to investigate with a spy-glass or telescope ME. 3. To catch sight of; to descry or discover; to notice or observe ME. 4. To find *out*, to search or seek *out*, by observation or scrutiny 1530.

1. b. The men, whom Moses sent forth to spye out the lande COVERDALE *Numb.* xiii. 16. c. Goe and spie where he is, that I may send and fetch him 2 *Kings* vi. 13. 2. I spied the whole ground, and never saw a beast 1893. 3. Feare seeing all, feares it of all is spy'd DRAYTON. By dilating the pupil, the animal..is enabled to s. its prey..in the dark GOLDSM. 4. I felt ashamed of myself for spying out their follies THACKERAY.

II. *intr.* 1. To make observations (now *spec.* with a telescope); to keep watch; to be on the look out ME. 2. To make stealthy or covert observations; to play the spy; to pry 1456.

2. I confesse it is my Natures plague To s. into Abuses SHAKS. I am come to s. upon your vanity and ambition GOLDSM.

Spy-, the stem of SPY *v.* used in combs. in the sense 'that spies', as *s.-all*, or 'from or through which one may spy', as *s.-hole, -tower, -window*, etc.

Spy-glass. 1706. [f. SPY *v.* + GLASS *sb.*] A telescope; a field-glass.

Squab (skwǫb), *sb.* 1640. [Of uncertain origin.] 1. A newly-hatched, unfledged, or very young bird. Also *fig.* of a person. b. *spec.* A young pigeon 1694. 2. A short fat person 1700. 3. A sofa, ottoman, or couch 1664. 4. A thick or soft cushion, *esp.* one serving to cover the seat of a chair or sofa 1687. b. A cushion forming part of the inside fittings of a carriage 1794.

2. He is a fat, sallow s. of a man 1823. 3. On her large s. you find her spread, Like a fat corpse upon a bed POPE. 4. She was poking the little fists into the s. of the sofa 1881.

Squab (skwǫb), *a.* 1675. [Cf. prec.] 1. Of persons: Short and stout; squat and plump. b. Having a thick clumsy form 1723. 2. Young and undeveloped; *esp.* of young birds, unfledged or not fully fledged, newly or lately hatched 1706. †3. Abrupt, blunt, curt -1759.

1. A Dutch woman is s. 1703. b. Turning his s. nose up in the air SCOTT. 2. A nest-full of little s. Cupids W. IRVING. 3. We have returned a *squab* answer, retorting the infraction of treaties H. WALPOLE. So **Squa·bbish** *a.* somewhat s. or squat. **Squa·bby** *a.* squat, thick-set.

Squab (skwǫb), *v.* 1668. [Cf. SQUAB *sb.*] 1. *trans.* To squash. 2. To stuff or stuff up 1819. 2. *intr.* To fall or hang in a full or heavy manner 1755.

Squab, *adv.* 1692. [Imitative.] With a heavy fall or squash.

The Eagle took him up a matter of Steeple-high into the Air, and..dropt him down, S. upon a Rock 1692.

Squabash (skwǫbæ·ʃ), *sb.* 1818. [A combination of *squash* and *bash.*] A crushing blow; a squashing. Hence **Squaba·sh** *v. trans.* to crush, squash, demolish.

Squabble (skwǫ·b'l), *sb.* 1602. [prob. imitative.] A wrangle, brawl; a petty quarrel.

Squabble (skwǫ·b'l), *v.* 1604. [See prec.] 1. *intr.* To wrangle or brawl; to engage in a petty quarrel or dispute; to argue disagreeably or with heat. 2. *trans.* In *Typog.*, to throw (type) out of line; to disarrange or disorder; to twist or skew so as to mix the lines 1674. b. *intr.* Of type: To get into disorder 1683.

1. Drunke? And speake Parrat? And s.? Swagger? SHAKS. It agreeth to children..to s. 1677. The Devil comes..and squabbles with him 1677. Hence **Squa·bbler.**

Squab-pie. *local* (*w. and s.w.*). 1708.

[Cf. SQUAB *sb.*] A pie with a thick crust composed of mutton, pork, apples, and onions.

Squacco (skwa·kko). 1752. [Local It.] A small crested species of heron, *Ardea ralloides* or *comata.*

Squad (skwǫd), *sb.* 1649. [ad. F. *escouade*, earlier *esquade*, var. of *esquadre* square, company, squadron.] **1.** *Mil.* A small number of men, a subdivision or section of a company, formed for drill, or told off for some special purpose. Also in phr. *awkward s.* **2.** A small number, group, or party of persons 1809. **3.** A particular set or circle of people 1786.

1. The awkward s. consists not only of recruits at drill, but of formed soldiers that are ordered to exercise with them, in consequence of some irregularity under arms 1802. 2. Phr. *Flying s.*, a police detachment equipped for rapid pursuit with motor-cars, cycles, etc. 3. A rowing s., football s. (*U.S.*).

Squad (skwǫd), *v.* 1802. [f. prec.] **1.** *trans.* To divide or form into squads; to draw up in a squad. **2.** To assign or allocate to a squad 1802.

1. I say, lads, s. your men and form on the road 1841.

Squadron (skwǫ·drən), *sb.* 1562. [ad. It. *squadrone*, f. *squadra* square.] †**1.** *Mil.* A body of soldiers drawn up or arranged in square formation -1656. **2.** *Mil.* A relatively small body or detachment of men 1579. **b.** *spec.* A body of cavalry, usu. composed of between one and two hundred men 1702. **3.** A division of a fleet forming one body under the command of a flag-officer; a detachment of warships told off for some particular duty. Also, a unit of a definite number of aeroplanes with its officers and men. 1588. **4.** A comparatively large group or number of people or animals; an organized body of persons 1617. †**b.** *transf.* A multitude *of* things (*rare*) -1680. **5.** A body of cardinals hovering between the main factions in a conclave 1670.

2. Trump nor pibroch summon here Mustering clans, or squadrons tramping SCOTT. 3. *Flying s.*: see FLYING *ppl. a.* 4. phr. 5. Cardinal de Retz and Cardinal Azzolino were of the s. 1906. **S.-commander, -leader,** officers of the Royal Air Force. Hence **Squa·droned** *ppl. a.*, formed into squadrons; drawn up in a s.

Squail (skwēⁱl), *sb.* 1847. [Origin unkn.] **1.** *pl.* Ninepins, skittles. *s.w. dial.* **2.** *pl.* A table-game in which counters or disks are propelled towards some mark by snapping 1862. **b.** A disk or counter used in this game 1862.

Squail, *v.* Chiefly *dial.* 1626. [Origin obsc.] **1.** *intr.* To throw a (loaded) stick or similar missile (*at* some object). **2.** *trans.* To strike or hit by throwing a stick or squailer 1844. **3.** To cast or throw 1876. Hence **Squai·ler,** a loaded stick, esp. used for throwing at small game or apples.

Squalid (skwǫ·lid), *a.* 1591. [ad. L. *squalidus*, f. *squalere* to be rough, dirty.] **I. 1.** Naturally foul and repulsive because of the presence of slime, mud, etc., and the absence of all cultivation or care. **b.** *gen.* Repulsive or loathsome to look at 1620. **2.** Foul through neglect or want of cleanliness; repulsively mean and filthy 1596. **3.** Of qualities, conditions, etc.: Marked or characterized by filth, dirt, or squalor 1621. **4.** *fig.* Wretched, miserable, morally repulsive or degraded 1660.

1. S. fields of mud and thistles 1887. 2. 'Tis a s. den made in the rock EVELYN. The poorest and most s. savage 1875. 3. Winter is..vgly, foule, s. BURTON.

II. †**1.** Dry, parched; marked by drought -1661. †**2.** Rough, shaggy, unkempt -1722. **3.** Having a pinched and miserable appearance, or a dull unhealthy look. 1661.

3. His complexion sallow and s. LYTTON. Hence **Squa·lid·ly** *adv.*, **-ness.**

Squalidity (skwǫli·dĭti). 1668. [ad. L. *squaliditas.*] The quality or character of being foul or squalid; filthiness, squalidness.

Squall (skwǭl), *sb.*[1] 1709. [f. SQUALL *v.*] A discordant or violent scream; a loud harsh cry. **b.** The action or habit of squalling or talking in a shrill voice 1755.

The crowing pheasant..Betrays his lair with awkward squalls 1821.

Squall (skwǭl), *sb.*[2] 1719. [perh. conn. w. prec.] **1.** A sudden and violent gust, a blast or short sharp storm, of wind. orig. *Naut.* **2.** *fig.* A disturbance or commotion; a quarrel 1813.

1. A very violent and sudden S. took us quite a-head 1745. A *black s.* is attended with a dark cloud, in distinction from a *white s.*, where there are no clouds, and a *thick s.*, accompanied with hail, sleet, &c. CRABB. 2. Phr. *To look out for squalls*, fig. to anticipate and be on one's guard against sudden danger, disturbance, or trouble.

Squall (skwǭl), *v.* 1631. [Imitative; cf. SQUEAL *v.* Direct connexion with Scand. forms having the stem *skval-* is doubtful.] **1.** *intr.* Of birds or animals: To scream loudly or discordantly. Also in common usage, of persons, esp. children. (Freq. with a suggestion of contempt.) 1687. **2.** *trans.* To utter or sing in a loud discordant tone 1703.

1. The parrot scream'd, the peacock squall'd TENNYSON. 2. She sung, or rather squalled, a song of Sacchini's 1779. Hence **Squa·ller.**

Squally (skwǭ·li), *a.* 1719. [f. SQUALL *sb.*[2]] **1.** Characterized by the prevalence of squalls. **2.** Of the wind: Blowing in sudden and violent gusts or blasts 1748. **3.** *fig.* Stormy, troublous, threatening. Chiefly *U.S.*, esp. in the phr. *to look s.* 1814.

1. S. Weather, with Hail and Snow 1745. 3. But for some hours things looked s. enough 1853.

Squalodon (skwēⁱ·lŏdǫn). 1872. [mod.L., f. L. *squalus* SQUALUS + Gr. ὀδοντ-, ὀδούς tooth.] *Palæont.* A genus of fossil cetaceans found in Miocene and early Pliocene formations; a cetacean of this genus. So **Squa·lodont.**

Squaloid (skwēⁱ·loid), *a.* and *sb.* 1836. [f. L. *squalus* SQUALUS; see -OID.] **A.** *adj.* Shark-like; comprising the sharks. **B.** *sb.* A fish of the shark family 1836.

Squalor (skwǫ·lǭɹ). 1621. [a. L., f. *squalere* to be dry, rough, dirty.] The state or condition of being physically squalid; a combination of misery and dirt. **b.** *fig.* The quality of being morally squalid 1860.

Hovel piled upon hovel,—s. immortalized in undecaying stone HAWTHORNE. **b.** The s. of Mesmerism, the deliration of rappings EMERSON.

‖**Squalus** (skwēⁱ·lŏs). *Pl.* **-li** (ləi). 1753. [L., some sea-fish.] A shark.

‖**Squama** (skwēⁱ·mă). *Pl.* **-mæ** (mī). 1706. [L., scale.] **1.** *Zool.* A scale as part of the integument of a fish, reptile, or insect. **b.** *Path.* A small portion of epidermis morbidly developed in the form of a scale 1876. **2.** *Anat.* A thin scaly portion of a bone, esp. of the temporal bone 1728. **3.** *Bot.* = SCALE *sb.*[2] 3 c. 1738. Hence **Squama·ceous** *a.* furnished with scales.

Squamate (skwēⁱ·mēⁱt), *a.* 1826. [ad. L. *squamatus*, f. *squama* SQUAMA.] *Zool.*, etc. Provided or covered with squamæ or scales.

Squamation (skwămēⁱ·ʃən). 1881. [f. SQUAMA; see -ATION.] *Zool.* The condition or character of being covered with scales; a special mode or form of this.

Squame (skwēⁱm). late ME. [ad. OF. *esquame* or L. *squama* SQUAMA.] †**1.** A scale (of iron, or on the skin or eyes) -1661. **2.** *Zool.* = SQUAMA 1. 1877.

Squami·ferous (skwă-), *a.* 1748. [f. L. *squamifer*; see SQUAMA and -FEROUS.] *Zool.* and *Bot.* Bearing or provided with scales; squamigerous. So **Squami·gerous** *a.* 1656.

Squamiform (skwēⁱ·-), *a.* 1828. [ad. mod. L. *squamiformis*; see SQUAMA and -FORM.] *Zool.* and *Bot.* Having the shape of a scale or scales.

Squamo- (skwēⁱ·mo), used as comb. form of SQUAMA, chiefly in terms of *Anat.* relating to the squamous bones, as *s.-occipital, -temporal.*

Squamosal (skwămōᵘ·săl), *a.* and *sb.* 1848. [f. next + -AL.] *Anat.* **A.** *adj.* **1.** *S. bone*, the squamous bone 1849. **2.** Of or pertaining to the squamous bone 1863. **B.** *sb.* The squamosal bone or squamous portion of the temporal bone 1848.

Squamose (skwēⁱ·mous), *a.* 1661. [ad. L. *squamosus*, f. *squama* scale.] **1.** Covered or furnished with scales; scaly. **2.** *Anat., Bot., Path.* = SQUAMOUS *a.* 1 a, b 2, 5. 1708.

Squamoso- (skwămōᵘ·so), used as comb. form of prec., in the sense 'squamous and —', as *s.-dentated*; or in terms of *Anat.* relating to the squamous bones, as *s.-maxillary, -zygomatic.*

Squamous (skwēⁱ·məs), *a.* 1541. [ad. L. *squamosus*, f. *squama* SQUAMA.] **1.** *Anat.* **a.** *S. bone, part, portion*, the thin and scaly part of the temporal bone, situated in the temple 1541. **b.** Of a suture: Formed by thin overlapping parts resembling scales 1709. **2.** *Bot.* Furnished or covered with, composed of, squamæ or scales 1658. **3.** = SQUAMOSE *a.* 1. 1668. **4.** Of substances: Composed of scales 1728. **5.** *Path.* Of skin-diseases: Characterized by the development of scales or laminæ of skin 1843. **6.** Of armour: Scaly; laminated 1845.

2. The bracts are described as s. or *scaly* 1870. 3. Blue bellied, s. lizards 1796. 4. S. epithelium generally consists of many layers of cells, one over the other 1872. Hence **Squa·mous·ly** *adv.*, **-ness.**

‖**Squamula** (skwēⁱ·miŭlă). 1754. [L., dim. of *squama* scale.] *Zool., Ent., Bot.* A small scale. So **Squa·mule.**

Squamulose (skwēⁱ·miŭlōᵘs), *a.* 1846. [ad. mod.L. *squamulosus*; see SQUAMULA and -OSE.] *Bot.* Furnished or covered with small scales.

Squander (skwǫ·ndəɹ), *sb.* 1709. [f. next.] The act of squandering; extravagant expenditure; an instance of this.

Squander (skwǫ·ndəɹ), *v.* 1593. [Origin obsc.] **1.** *trans.* In pa. pple. **a.** Of things: To be scattered over a comparatively wide surface or area 1596. **b.** Brought to disintegration or dissolution 1610. **2.** To cause to scatter or disperse 1657. **3.** To use (money, goods, etc.) recklessly, prodigally, or lavishly; to expend extravagantly, profusely, or wastefully. (The most common usage.) 1593. **4.** To spend or employ (time) wastefully; to waste 1693. **5.** To spend profusely, without securing an adequate return; to use in a wasteful manner 1716. **6.** *intr.* To roam about; to wander 1630. **7.** To scatter 1823.

1. **a.** In many thousand Islands that lye squandred in the vast Ocean 1645. 2. All along the sea They drive and s. the huge Belgian fleet DRYDEN. 3. The public money is squandered away in pensions 1763. 4. They considered the time occupied in learning as so much squandered away BORROW. 5. If he s. his Talents in Luxury 1716. Hence **Squa·nderer. Squa·ndering** *vbl. sb.* and *ppl. a.* **-ly** *adv.*

Squandermania (skwǫndəɹmēⁱ·niă). 1920. [f. SQUANDER *v.* + -MANIA.] A craze for extravagant expenditure.

Squarable (skwēᵊ·răb'l), *a.* and *sb.* 1706. [f. SQUARE *v.*] **A.** *adj.* Capable of being squared. **B.** *sb.* A person who can be 'squared'.

Square (skwēᵊɹ), *sb.* Also †**squire.** ME. [ad. OF. *esquire* and *esquare* (mod. F. *équerre*):— pop. L. **exquadra.* Also partly f. SQUARE *a.*] **I. 1.** An implement or tool for determining, measuring, or setting out right angles, etc., usually consisting of two pieces or arms set at right angles to each other, but sometimes with the arms or sides hinged or pivoted so as to measure any angle; esp. one used by carpenters and joiners. Freq. without article in phr. *by s.* †**b.** *fig.* In phr. *by the s.*, with extreme accuracy; precisely, exactly -1633. †**2.** *fig.* A canon, criterion, or standard; a rule or guiding principle; a pattern or example -1809.

1. A poet does not work by s. or line, As smiths and joiners perfect a design COWPER. *Bevel-s.* = BEVEL *sb.*; *mitre-s., set-s., T-* or *tee-s., trial-* or *try-s.*: see these words. **b.** *L.L.L.* v. ii. 475. 2. To governe the body..by the s. of prudence, and rule of reason 1604. Is merit everywhere else made the exact s. of preferment? FULLER.

II. †**1.** Rectangular or square shape or form -1663. †**2.** A side of a square, rectangle, or polygon; a face of a cube -1753. **3.** A square or quadrilateral space, esp. one of several marked out on a board, paper, etc., for playing certain games or for purposes of measurement, etc.; a square surface or face 1440. †**b.** *fig.* Affairs, events, matters, proceedings. Only in the phr. *how* (*the*) *squares go.* -1828. **4.** *Geom.* A plane rectilinear and rectangular figure with four equal sides 1551. †**b.** A rectangle with only the opposite sides equal, spec. called *long* or *oblong s.* -1842. †**c.** *Geometrical s.*: two graduated sides of a square marked in the rectangular corner of a quadrant to facilitate its use -1728. **d.** *Logic.* A square diagram used to illustrate the four kinds of logical opposition 1864. **5.** *Math.* The product of a number multiplied by itself; the second power (*of*) 1557. **6.** *Mil.* A body of troops drawn up in a square formation, either with solid ranks or leaving an open space in the centre 1591. **7.** †**a.** A square piece of material covering the bosom; the breast-piece of a dress –1710. b. A square or rectangular piece, block, etc. 1601. c. A rectangular pane of glass. Now *dial.* 1687. 8. A square or rectangular area or piece of ground; *spec.* a garden plot of this shape 1615. 9. An open space or area (approximately quadrilateral and rectangular) in a town or city, enclosed by buildings or dwelling-houses, esp. of a superior or residential kind, freq. containing a garden or laid out with trees, etc.; more generally, any open space resembling this, esp. one formed at the meeting or intersection of streets; also, the group of houses surrounding an area of this kind 1687. b. A rectangular building or block of buildings; *U.S.* a block of buildings bounded by streets 1700. 10. An area of a hundred square feet, forming the measure or standard by which the price of flooring, roofing, tiling, or the like is reckoned 1663. †11. *Astrol.* and *Astron.* Quartile aspect; quadrature (*rare*) –1690. 12. In various techn. uses denoting square parts or structures; also *ellipt.* for *s. cap, dance, drink,* etc. 1688.

1. fig. *Ant. & Cl.* II. iii. 7. 3. The queen gives a check in the black queen's second s. 1735. *Magic s.*: see MAGIC *a.* b. He..then ask'd him how Squares went at Rome 1692. 5. The law of the inverse s. in electric action 1885. 6. He..no practise had In the braue squares of Warre SHAKS. *Hollow S.*, a Body of Foot drawn up with an empty space in the middle for the Colours, Drums, and Baggage 1702. *Solid S.*, is a body of foot, where both ranks and files are equal 1802. Men are formed into s. to resist attacks of cavalry 1859. 7. a. *Wint. T.* IV. iv. 212. b. He.. bolted his food down his capacious throat in squares of three inches SCOTT. 8. Within a s. of tall trees, is a basilisc of copper EVELYN. 9. Going early from his house in the s. of St James EVELYN.

†III. A quarrel, dispute, wrangle; discord, dissension, quarrelling –1627.

They did agree without any S. at all 1627.

Phrases. *To break s.*: see BREAK *v.* *To break no s.*, to make no difference. †*At s.*, at variance; esp. *to be* or *to fall at (a) s.*, to quarrel or wrangle. *Out of s.*, out of the true, proper, or normal state or condition; out of (right) order or rule.

Square (skwēᵊɹ), *a.* ME. [ad. OF. *esquarre*, pa. pple. of *esquarrer* SQUARE *v.*] I. 1. Having a rectilinear and rectangular form of equal length and breadth; contained by four equal sides at right angles to each other; quadrate. late ME. 2. Having an equilateral rectangular section ME. b. Having a form more or less approximating to a cube; rectangular and of three dimensions. late ME. 3. Of limbs, the body, etc.: Approximating to a square section or outline; stoutly and strongly built; solid, sturdy. late ME. 4. Of a (stated) length on each of the four sides forming a square. late ME. 5. †a. Of an angle: Right. RECORDE. b. At right angles; rectangular in position or direction; perpendicular (*to* something) 1571. 6. Even, straight, level 1814. b. *fig.* On equal terms; with all accounts settled 1859. c. *Golfing.* Having equal scores 1887.

1. EIGHT-, *six*-, THREE-SQUARE: see these words. *S. inch, foot, yard*, etc., a rectangular space measuring an inch, etc., either way, or any equivalent area. *S. measure*, a unit of measurement consisting of a square space; a system of measures based on such units. *S. number*, the product of a number multiplied by itself. *S. root*, the number or quantity constituting such a base of a given number or quantity as to produce this when multiplied by itself. 2. *fig.* I should but be..the s. man in the round hole TENNYSON. 3. He is a S. well-set Man 1709. 4. The whole were reared in a back-yard not ten feet s. 1854. 5. b. A long low vessel.. with immensely square yards 1833. 6. b. 'To be s. with a man', to be revenged 1859. c. They were all s. at the 18th 1898.

II. 1. Of actions: Just or equitable; fair, honest, honourable, straightforward. Also *gen.* 1591. 2. Of persons: †a. Not readily moved or shaken in purpose; steady, reliable –1710. b. Honourable, upright 1646. 3. Precise, exact 1590. b. Straight, direct 1804. c. Right; in good order; on a proper footing 1836. d. Of meals: Full, solid, substantial. Of a drink: Copious; of full measure. orig. *U.S.* 1868.

1. She 's a most triumphant Lady, if report be s. to her SHAKS. Phr. *S. †play* or *dealing, a s. deal, the s. thing*. 3. Oh what formalitie, what s. obseruance: liues in a little roome 1590. His ideas being s., solid and tangible HAWTHORNE. b. Opportunity for a s. talk 1896. c. Phr. *To call (it) s.*, to regard as balanced or settled. d. The one 's. meal' of the day 1876.

Phr. *On* or *upon the s.* a. With a square front; face to face; directly, openly (now *rare*). b. Without artifice, deceit, fraud, or trickery. †c. Upon terms of equality or friendship *with* another or others; also, even or 'quits' *with* another. d. In predic. use without const.: Free from duplicity or unfairness; honest, straightforward, upright (now *slang*). e. *To set on* or *upon the s.*, at right angles; in a square or solid form; *fig.* to put in proper order (*rare*).

Comb., as *s.-bodied, -built, -faced, -set, -shouldered, -sterned, -tailed* adjs.; **s. bracket** (see BRACKET *sb.* 5); **-headed** *a.* having the head or top of a s. form; **s. hit**, a hit at right angles to the wicket, esp. to square leg; **-knot**, = *reef-knot*; **-leg**, the position in the cricket-field to the left of the batsman and nearly in a line with the wicket; the fielder stationed at this point; hence as *vb.*; **-rig** *Naut.*, rig in which the lower sails are suspended from horizontal yards, as dist. from *fore-and-aft* rig; so **-rigged** *a.*; **-roof**, one in which the principal rafters meet at a right angle. Hence **Squa·re-ly** *adv.*, **-ness**.

Square (skwēᵊɹ), *adv.* 1570. [f. prec.] †1. Steadily, copiously –1608. 2. Fairly, honestly; in a direct manner. Now *slang* or *colloq.* 1577. b. *colloq.* Solidly, without reserve 1867. 3. So as to be square; in a rectangular form or position; directly in line or in front 1631. 4. At right angles 1680.

2. 'I reckon the boy means s.', muttered the old man 1891. b. N. C. comes out 's.' for the Republican party 1867. 3. He walked burly and s. LAMB. 4. Pivot men..face s. into the new direction 1847.

Square (skwēᵊɹ), *v.* late ME. [ad. OF. *esquarrer*:—pop. L. **exquadrare*, f. L. *ex* out + *quadra* square.] I. *trans.* 1. To make (a thing) square; to shape by reduction to straight lines and right angles. b. To make (timber, etc.) square or rectangular in cross-section. late ME. c. To mark out as a square or in rectangular form; to convert into or draw up in a square; to mark *off* or *out* in squares 1440. d. To form by making square; to cut in square or rectangular form 1584. 2. a. To multiply (a number) by itself 1571. b. To convert (a circle) into an equivalent square; to measure exactly in terms of a square 1624. c. To calculate in square measure 1811. 3. a. *Naut.* To lay (the yards) at right angles to the line of the keel by trimming with the braces; to set at right angles to or parallel with some other part 1625. b. To adjust so as to make rectilinear or rectangular or to set at right angles to something else 1690. c. *Astrol.* To stand in quartile aspect in relation to (another sign) 1697. d. To set or place (some part of the body) squarely 1819.

1. Those who..squared the Portland stone for Saint Paul's MACAULAY. 2. a. Then do I s. 6, and it is 36 1674. b. Circles to s., and Cubes to double, Would give a Man excessive Trouble PRIOR. 3. b. *fig.* I feel me..Well squar'd to fortune's blows CARY. c. The Icy Goat, the Crab which s. the Scales 1697. d. The Saxon domestics squared their shoulders SCOTT.

II. 1. *fig.* To regulate, frame, arrange, or direct, *by, according to*, or *on* some standard or principle of action 1531. b. To adjust or adapt, to cause to correspond *to* or harmonize *with* something 1583. c. To arrange, adjust, render appropriate or exact 1596. 2. To bring to an equality on both sides; to balance 1815. b. To put (a matter) straight; to settle satisfactorily, to compound. *colloq.* 1853. c. With *up*: To settle (a debt, etc.) by payment 1862. d. *intr.* (*Golf*) To make the scores equal 1923. 3 *slang* or *colloq.* To conciliate, satisfy, or gain over (a person), *esp.* by some form of bribery or compensation; to get rid of in this way 1859.

1. He who squares his actions by this rule can never do amiss BERKELEY. b. Eie me, blest Providence, and s. my triall To my proportion'd strength MILT. 2. She would accept benefits..but then she insulted her benefactors, and so squared accounts THACKERAY. b. We always s. it with the usher 1872. 3. Rich offenders..'s. the reporters' 1885.

III. *intr.* †1. To deviate or diverge, to vary (*from* something) –1609. †2. To fall out, to be at variance or discord, *with* a person, etc. –1561. 3. To accord, concur or correspond, to agree or fit, *with*, †*to*, †*unto*, something 1592. b. *Golf.* To equalize the scores 1923. 4. To strut or swagger. *Obs.* exc. *dial.* 1590. 5. To put oneself into a posture of defence; to assume a boxing attitude 1820. 6. a. To measure (so much) on each of four sides forming a square; to yield a square of (the dimensions specified) 1789. b. To become square in form 1902. c. *Naut.* To sail *away* with the yards squared 1887.

1. The prophetes somtyme..dyd s. from the trouthe 1521. 3. There is no Church, whose every part so squares unto my Conscience SIR T. BROWNE. 4. At another time, malapert boldnesse will s. it out CAMDEN. 5. He squared up to his adversary and..struck him a heavy blow 1893. 6. c. We squared away to a spanking breeze 1899. Hence **Squa·ring** *vbl. sb.*

Square cap. 1584. [SQUARE *a.*] An academic cap with a square top; a mortar-board, trencher.

Square-cut, *a.* 1622. [SQUARE *a.* or *adv.*] 1. Cut to or into a square form. 2. *absol.* A coat with square skirts 1893.

1. The grave man..with s. antique waistcoat 1848. There 's the s. chancellor KEATS.

Squarer (skwēᵊ·rəɹ). late ME. [f. SQUARE *v.*] 1. a. One who reduces wood, stone, etc., to a square form. b. One who aims at squaring the circle 1852. †2. A contentious or quarrelsome person. SHAKS.

Square sail. 1600. [SQUARE *a.*] a. A four-sided sail supported by a yard slung across the vessel. b. A flying sail set on the fore-mast of a schooner or the mast of a sloop or cutter.

Square-toed, *a.* 1785. [SQUARE *a.*] 1. Of shoes: Having broad square toes. 2. *fig.* Old-fashioned, formal, precise 1795.

2. We old people must retain some s. predilection for the fashions of our youth BURKE.

Squa·re-toes. 1771. [SQUARE *a.*] A precise, formal, old-fashioned person; one having strict or narrow ideas of conduct. Freq. qualified by *old* and usu. with initial capital.

Old Square-toes was obliged to go out of town immediately 1785.

Squa·rewise, *adv.* 1546. [See -WISE.] †1. Rectangularly –1725. 2. In the form of a square 1611.

Squarish (skwēᵊ·riʃ), *a.* 1742. [f. SQUARE *a.*] Somewhat, more or less, or approximately, square.

Squarrose (skwæ·rōᵘs, skwǫ·rōᵘs), *a.* 1760. [ad. L. *squarrosus*, scurfy, scabby.] 1. *Bot.* a. Composed of or covered with, scales or other processes standing out at right angles or more widely. b. Of scales: Standing out at right angles or to a greater degree 1829. 2. *Ent.* Cut into laciniæ which are elevated above the plane of the surface 1826.

Squarro·so-, comb. form of prec., as in *s.-dentate, -laciniate* adjs.

Squarson (skwā·ɹsən). 1857. [joc. combination of SQUIRE *sb.* and PARSON.] A parson who is also the squire in his parish. Hence **Squa·rsonry.**

Squash (skwǫʃ), *sb.*[1] 1590. [Related to SQUASH *v.*] I. 1. The unripe pod of a pea. Also applied contemptuously to persons. *Obs.* exc. *arch.* †2. *S. pear*, a variety of pear. *S. perry*, a beverage made from this. –1826. 3. A soft india-rubber ball used in a form of the game of rackets (orig. at Harrow). b. Also short for **s. rackets**, a game resembling rackets, played with rackets and soft india-rubber balls in a walled court. 1886.

1. As a s. is before 'tis a pescod SHAKS. This Kernell, This s., this Gentleman SHAKS.

II. 1. †a. The act of squashing; the fact or sound of some soft substance being crushed or dispersed –1739. b. The shock or impact occasioned by a soft heavy body falling upon a surface; the sound produced by this. Now *rare.* 1654. 2. A crush or crowd of persons, etc.; a large number 1884. 3. Short for *lemon-squash* (LEMON *sb.*[1]) 1894.

1. a. Phr. *To go to s.*, to become squashed or ruined. b. Hearing a s., he cried, Damn it, what 's that? 1812.

Squash (skwǫʃ), *sb.*[2] 1643. [abbrev. of Narragansett Indian *asquutasquash*, f. *asq* raw, uncooked. (The *-ash* is a pl. ending.)] 1. A gourd produced by plants of the genus *Cucurbita*, esp. a fruit of the bush gourd, *C. Melopepo.* 2. Any species of the genus *Cucurbita* producing the above fruit 1661.

attrib., as *s. pie, vine*; **s.-bug**, one or other of various insects infesting or injurious to squashes; **s. gourd, (-melon) pumpkin**, the common bush gourd or squash, *Cucurbita Melopepo.*

†**Squash,** *sb.*[3] 1678. [Aphetic f. MUSQUASH.] The musk-rat or musquash, *Fiber zibethicus* –1824.

Squash (skwǫʃ), *v.* 1565. [ad. OF. *esquasser, esquacer*, = It. *squassare*:—pop. L. **exquassare*; see QUASH *v.*] 1. *trans.* To squeeze, press, or crush into a flat mass or pulp; to beat to, or dash in, pieces. **b.** To quash; to suppress or put down; to undo or destroy in a complete or summary manner. Often *colloq.* To silence or discomfort (a person) in a crushing fashion. 1762. **2.** *intr.* To emit or make a splashing sound; to move, walk, etc., in this way; to splash 1671. **3.** To be pressed into a flat mass on impact; to flatten *out* under pressure 1858.

2. Our feet 'squashing' as we step, for our boots are full of rain-water 1893. Hence **Squa·sher.**

Squash, *adv.* 1766. [f. prec.] With or as with a squash. Freq. in *to go s.* (also *transf.*).

Squash-, the vbl. stem used in combs., in the sense 'having the appearance of being squashed', as **squash hat.**

Squashy (skwǫ·ʃi), *a.* 1698. [f. SQUASH *v.* or *sb.*[1]] **1.** Of fruit, etc.: Having a soft or pulpy consistency; lacking in firmness. **2.** Of ground, etc.: Soft with, full of, water; soaking, marshy 1751. **3.** Of the nature of a squash or squashing 1865. Hence **Squa·shiness,** s. condition or character.

Squat (skwǫt), *sb.*[1] ME. [f. SQUAT *v.*] **1.** A heavy fall or bump; a severe or violent jar or jolt. Now *n. dial.* **b.** A bruise, contusion, or wound, esp. one caused by a fall; a dent or indentation. Now *dial.* 1578. †**2.** *At* (*the* or *a*) *s.*, in a squatting or crouching attitude, esp. that assumed by a hare when sitting –1732. **3.** The act of squatting, *spec.* on the part of a hare 1584. †**4.** The place where an animal squats; *spec.* the form or lair of a hare –1673. **5.** A squatting attitude or posture 1886.

1. Bruises and squats and falls which often kill others can bring little grief or hurt to those that are temperate G. HERBERT.

Squat, *sb.*[2] *Cornwall.* 1671. [perh. same word as prec.] A small bunch of ore in a vein.

Squat (skwǫt), *pa. pple.* and (*ppl.*) *a.* late ME. [pa. pple. of SQUAT *v.*] **I. 1.** In predic. use: Seated in a squatting or crouching posture; sitting close to the ground. **2.** Hidden from observation; quiet, still. *dial.* 1841.

1. Him there they found S. like a Toad, close at the eare of Eve MILT. The shrub lies s. to the ground 1853.

II. 1. Short and thick; disproportionately broad or wide; podgy 1630. **2.** Characterized by squatness of form or structure 1774.

1. She is a broad, s., pursy, fat thing, quite ugly RICHARDSON. The arches are circular, and the columns s. 1828. Hence **Squa·t-ly** *adv.*, **-ness.**

Squat (skwǫt), *v.* ME. [ad. OF. *esquatir, esquater*, f. *es-* Ex- + *quatir* to beat or press down.] **I.** *trans.* To crush, flatten, or beat out of shape; to smash or squash; to bruise severely. Now *dial.* **b.** To dash down heavily or with some force. Now *dial.* late ME. **II. 1.** *refl.* To seat (oneself) upon the hams or haunches; to take one's seat in a crouching attitude or posture. late ME. **2.** *intr.* Of hares: To sit close to the ground in a crouching attitude; to crouch or cower down, esp. in order to escape observation or capture. late ME. **3.** Of persons: To sit down with the legs closely drawn up beneath the hams or in front of the body; *esp.* to sit on the ground in this way or in a crouching attitude. Also *joc.*, to sit down. 1573. **4.** *trans.* To cause to squat; to put into, place in, a squatting attitude or posture (*rare*) 1600. **5.** *intr.* †**a.** To sink *into* (something lower or less important). MILT. **b.** To sink in or down 1687. **6.** To settle upon new, uncultivated, or unoccupied land without any legal title and without the payment of rent. orig. *U.S.* 1800. **b.** *Austral.* To rent or take up government or crown land for pasturage as a squatter 1828.

1. The Prince at last squatted himself on the corner of a form MME D'ARBLAY. 2. The coy hare squats nestling in the corn 1821. 3. Down on the grass the Doctor squatted 1812. 6. He was a Kentucky man, of the Ohio, where he had 'squatted' MARRYAT. Hence **Squa·tty** *a.* somewhat squat.

Squatarole (skwæ·tărōul). Also **-olle.** 1819. [ad. mod.L. *Squatarola*, a. local It. *squatarola.*] The grey or Swiss plover, *Squatarola helvetica.*

Squatter (skwǫ·təɹ), *sb.* 1788. [f. SQUAT *v.*] **1.** *U.S.* A settler having no normal or legal title to the land occupied by him, *esp.* one thus occupying land in a district not yet surveyed or apportioned by the government. **b.** An unauthorized occupant of land 1849. **2.** *Austral.* One occupying a tract of pastoral land as a tenant of the crown; a grazier or sheep-farmer, esp. on a large scale 1840. **3.** A squatting person or animal 1824.

1. b. Hundreds of squatters from the neighbouring parts of Sutherland and Ross 1860.

attrib.: **s. sovereignty** *U.S.*, the right claimed by the inhabitants of newly-formed territories to settle for themselves the question of slavery, etc.

Squatter (skwǫ·təɹ), *v.* 1611. [prob. imitative.] †**1.** *trans.* To scatter, disperse, spill –1653. **2.** *intr.* To fly or run, to struggle along or make one's way, among water or wet with much splashing or flapping 1785. **b.** To flutter, flap, or struggle among water or soft mud 1808.

2. A little callow gosling squattering out of bounds without leave C. BRONTE.

Squaw (skwǭ). 1634. [a. Narragansett Indian *squaws*, Massachusetts *squa* woman.] **1.** A North American Indian woman or wife. **b.** Applied by Indians to white women 1642. **2.** *transf.* An effeminate or weak person 1807. **3.** *Old s.*, the long-tailed duck 1884.

attrib., as **s.-root,** *Conopholis*, cancer-root; †**-sachem,** a squaw chief in certain American Indian tribes; **-weed,** *Senecio aureus.*

Squawk (skwǭk), *sb.* 1850. [f. next.] **1.** A loud grating call or cry; a hoarse squall. **2.** *U.S.* The *Nyctiardea*, or Night Heron 1872.

Squawk (skwǭk), *v.* 1821. [Echoic.] **1.** *intr.* To call or cry with a loud harsh note; to squall or screech hoarsely. **b.** Of things: To creak or squeak harshly 1859. **2.** *trans.* With *out*: To utter with or as with a squawk 1856.

Squeak (skwīk), *sb.* 1664. [f. the vb.] **1.** The act of squeaking. **2.** A short or slight sound, of a thin high-pitched character, made by animals or persons 1700. **b.** A thin, sharp sound produced by a musical instrument 1805. **3. a.** A slight, narrow, or bare chance *for* something 1716. **b.** A narrow escape, a close shave; usu. with qualifying adjs. *narrow, near*, etc. 1822.

3. a. See all ready with the boat, . . it may give us a s. for our lives, if a little one 1868. **b.** We had a near s., the wind suddenly coming calm 1889.

Squeak (skwīk), *v.* late ME. [Echoic.] **1.** *intr.* To emit a short or slight sound of a thin high-pitched character. **2.** *slang.* To confess; to turn informer; to 'split' or 'peach' 1690. **3.** *trans.* To utter, sing, or play in a squeaking manner or with a squeaky voice. Usu. derisively. 1577.

1. The sheeted dead Did squeake and gibber in the Roman streets SHAKS. Shrill Fiddles s., Hoarse Bagpipes roar 1740. Rats began to s. and scuffle in the night time DICKENS. 2. If he be obstinate, put a civil Question to him upon the Rack, and he squeaks I warrant him DRYDEN. 3. Ye s. out your Coziers Catches without any mitigation or remorse of voice SHAKS. Hence **Squea·kingly** *adv.*

Squeaker (skwī·kəɹ). 1641. [f. the vb.] **1.** One who, or that which, squeaks. **2.** One or other of various birds characterized by their squeaking call 1817. **3.** *colloq.* A (young) pig 1861.

2. *Strepera Anaphonensis*, Grey Cow-Shrike; . . S. of the Colonists 1848.

Squeaky (skwī·ki), *a.* 1862. [f. SQUEAK *sb.* or *v.*] Characterized by squeaking sounds; tending to squeak.

Squeal (skwīl), *sb.* 1747. [f. the vb.] A more or less prolonged sharp cry; a shrill scream. **b.** A sharp shrill sound 1867.

Squeal (skwīl), *v.* ME. [Echoic.] **1.** *intr.* To utter (or give *out*) a more or less prolonged sharp cry, esp. by reason of pain or sudden alarm; to scream shrilly. **2.** Of things: To emit or produce a shrill or strident sound 1596. **3.** *slang.* To turn informer; to inform or 'peach' *on* a person 1865. **4.** *trans.* To utter or produce with a shrill, grating, or squeaking sound 1675.

1. Ghosts did shrieke and squeale about the streets SHAKS. 2. Here tortur'd cats-gut squeals amain 1727. Phr. *to make* (a person) *s.*, to blackmail him. 4. 'Here, sir,' squealed Timothy 1833.

Squealer (skwī·ləɹ). 1854. [f. prec.] **1.** One who or that which squeals. Also *transf.* 1865. **b.** *slang.* An informer 1865. **c.** *U.S.* A complainer 1889. **2.** Freq. in bird-names 1854.

2. The Swift. . . This bird's loud piercing cry has obtained for it the name of the *s.* 1879. Harlequin Duck, . . known also as S. 1888.

Squeamish (skwī·miʃ), *a.* 1450. [var. of *squaymes, squemes* SQUEAMOUS *a.*, by alteration of suffix.] **I. 1.** Readily affected with nausea; easily turned sick or faint; physically unable to support or swallow anything disagreeable. **2.** Slightly affected with or inclined to nausea 1660. †**3.** Characterized by a feeling of nausea (*rare*) –1748.

1. Art thou so squemish that thou canst not see wine but thou must surfet? GREENE. *fig.* The stomach of his Holinesse not being so s., but that he would take a good almes from dirty hands FULLER. 2. This day. . the wind grew high, and . . I began to be dizzy and s. PEPYS.

II. †**1.** Averse, unwilling, or reluctant *to* do something –1589. **2.** Averse to freedom or familiarity of intercourse; distant, reserved; coy, cold. Now *dial.* 1561. †**b.** Of actions, etc.; Characterized by coldness or coyness –1603. **3.** Easily shocked; prudish 1567. †**b.** Sensitive; shrinking from contact with anything rude or rough –1785. **4.** Sensitively or excessively fastidious, scrupulous, punctilious, or particular, with regard to standards of action or belief 1581. **b.** Marked or characterized by fastidiousness or scrupulousness 1593. **5.** Fastidious or dainty with respect to what one handles, uses, or comes in contact with 1608.

3. Riddles more or less good, some coarse, and some profane; but the age was not s. 1892. 4. Trifles magnified into importance by a s. conscience MACAULAY. They are not so s. as to what they say about us 1865. 5. If delicacies could invite My s. courtier's appetite 1746. **Squea·mish·ly** *adv.*, **-ness.** So **Squea·my** *a.*

Squea·mous, *a.* Now *n. dial.* ME. [a. AF. *escoymous*; origin unkn.] = SQUEAMISH *a.*

†**Squea·sy,** *a.* 1583. [Alteration of QUEASY *a.*] **1.** Of times: Troublous, disturbed –1662. **2.** Of the stomach: Readily nauseated; easily upset –1656. Hence †**Squea·siness** –1687.

Squeegee (skwī·dʒī, skwīdʒī·), *sb.* 1844. [perh. f. *squeege*, strengthened form of SQUEEZE *v.*] **1.** A scraping implement, usu. a straight-edged blade of india-rubber, gutta-percha, or the like, attached to the end of a long handle, for removing water, mud, etc. **2.** *Photogr.* A strip of rubber mounted on a wooden frame which serves as a handle, for squeezing moisture from a print or pressing a film closer to its mount; a rubber roller serving this purpose; a squeezer 1878.

Squeegee, *v.* 1883. [f. the sb.] **1.** *trans.* To press, squeeze, or force, with a squeegee. **2.** = SQUILGEE *v.* 1886.

Squeezable (skwī·zăb'l), *a.* 1813. [f. SQUEEZE *v.*] **1.** Capable of being compressed or squeezed. **2.** Capable of being constrained or coerced to yield or grant something 1837. **b.** *esp.* From which money may be extracted 1840.

2. b. The result of their industry is only that they become more s. for taxes 1880.

Squeeze (skwīz), *sb.* 1611. [f. SQUEEZE *v.*] **1.** An act of squeezing; an application of strong or heavy pressure, or of force sufficient to compress. **b.** The pressure *of* a crowd of persons; a crush 1802. **c.** *colloq.* A strong financial or commercial demand or pressure 1830. **2.** A strong or firm pressure of the hand as a token of friendship or affection 1736. **b.** A close embrace; a hug 1790. **3. a.** A (small) quantity or amount squeezed out; a few drops pressed out by squeezing 1761. **b.** A forced exaction or impost made by Asiatic officials or servants; a percentage taken upon goods bought or sold; an illegal charge or levy 1858. **4.** *colloq.* A crowded assembly or social gathering 1779. **5.** *Coal-mining.* A gradual coming together of the floor and roof of a gallery or working; a place where this has occurred; a creep 1789. **6.** A moulding or cast of an object obtained by pressing some plastic substance round or over it; *spec.* in *Archæol.*, an impression or copy of an inscription, design, etc., taken by applying wet paper or other soft material in this way 1857. **7.** Without article: Pressure; constraint used to obtain a concession or gift 1862.

1. d. In full *s. play* (Bridge), leading winning cards until opponent is forced to discard an important card 1928. 3. a. A s. of lemon-juice 1864. 4. The weather is getting terribly hot for squeezes 1808. 6. I saw squeezes of this stone for the first time 1870.

Squeeze (skwīz), *v.* 1599. [perh. a

strengthened form of *Quease* vb.] **1.** *trans.* To press or compress hard, esp. so as to flatten, crush, or force together 1601. **b.** With complement: To reduce to, or bring into, a specified condition by pressure 1660. **c.** To press (the hand) in token of friendship or affection; also, to hug 1687. **2.** To force by pressure. Const. with advs. and preps. 1683. **3. a.** To press upon (a person, etc.) so as to exact or extort money; to fleece. Also const. *of.* 1639. **b.** To subject to strong constraint or pressure 1888. **4.** With *out*: To press or force out 1599. **5. a.** To extort or exact, to obtain by force or pressure, *from* or *out of* a person, etc. Also without const. 1602. **b.** To extract (juice or the like) by pressure 1611. **c.** To put or drop *in* (a fluid extracted by pressure) 1725. **6.** *absol.* **a.** To press hard, esp. with the hand 1692. **b.** To take a squeeze or facsimile impression 1890. **7.** *intr.* To yield to pressure; to admit of being squeezed 1683. **8.** To force a way; to press or push; to succeed in passing by means of compression. Const. with advs. and preps. 1704.

1. *fig.* The six hundred millions of Debt..are now squeezing the borough-mongers 1823. Phr. †*To s. wax*, to set one's seal to a document. *A squeezed orange*, fig. a person or thing from whom or which nothing more can be obtained. **b.** To be squeezed flat against a wall 1871. **2.** Crowl was squeezed into a corner behind a pillar 1892. **3. a.** The Church had been so often squeezed by him 1700. **4.** Lady Kew could..s. out a tear over a good novel too THACKERAY. **5. a.** The above..was the sum squeezed by the judge out of the clerk BENTHAM. **6. a.** He [the fox] squeez'd hard to get out again; but the Hole was too Little for him 1692. **7.** Bran squeezes much more—But plaister of Paris not at all 1771. **8.** The old duke..squeezing into the circle SMOLLETT. Hence **Squee·zy** *a.*

Squeezer (skwī·zəɹ). 1611. [f. SQUEEZE *v.*] **1.** One who squeezes, in various senses. **2.** A mechanical device or apparatus, an implement, by which pressure can be applied 1839. **b.** *spec.* An apparatus by which a ball of puddled iron is reduced to a compact mass 1843.

Squee·zing, *vbl. sb.* 1611. [f. SQUEEZE *v.*] **1.** The action of pressing or compressing; the fact of being compressed. †**b.** That which is squeezed out –1719. **2.** The action of oppressing by exactions or extortion; the practice of extorting excessive or illicit gain 1681.

Squelch (skwelᵗʃ), *sb.* 1620. [Echoic.] **1.** A heavy crushing fall or blow acting on a soft body; the sound produced by this. **2.** A thing or mass that has the appearance of having been squelched or crushed 1837. **3.** The sound made by a liquid when subjected to sudden or intermittent pressure 1895.

1. I heard a heavy s. and a howl 1829.

Squelch (skwelᵗʃ), *v.* 1624. [f. as prec.] **1.** *trans.* To fall, drop, or stamp upon (something soft) with crushing or squashing force; to crush in this way. **b.** *fig.* To squash or crush; to put down or suppress thoroughly or completely 1864. **2.** *intr.* **a.** To fall with a squelch. Now *dial.* 1755. **b.** To emit a squelch or squelches; to spout in squelches 1834. **c.** To walk or tread heavily in water or on wet ground, or with water in the shoes, so as to make a splashing sound 1849.

1. Oh 'twas your luck and mine to be squelch'd FLETCHER. **b.** It would be so nice to s. that pompous impostor HUXLEY. **2. c.** You'd..pass all your time in squelching about soppy fields 1849. Hence **Sque·lcher** (*colloq.*), a crushing blow, newspaper article, etc.

Squelch, *adv.* 1772. [f. as prec.] With or as with a squelch or heavy splash.

Squench, *v.* Now *dial.* and *colloq.* 1535. [f. QUENCH *v.* with prosthetic *s-*.] **1.** *trans.* To extinguish (a fire, etc.). **2.** To suppress, put an end to; to quell or stifle 1577. **3.** To satisfy (the appetite); to slake (thirst) 1598. **4.** *intr.* To become extinguished 1643.

Squeteague (skwetī·g). *U.S.* Also **squetee.** 1838. [Narragansett Indian.] The weakfish or sea-salmon, *Cynoscion regalis*, of the eastern United States.

Squib (skwib), *sb.* 1525. [perh. imitative of an explosive sound.] **1.** A species of firework, in which the burning of the composition is usu. terminated by a slight explosion 1530. **2.** †**a.** An explosive device used as a missile or means of attack –1686. **b.** *Mining.* A tubular case filled with a priming of gunpowder used to fire a charge 1881. **3.** A smart gird or hit; a sharp scoff or sarcasm; a lampoon 1525. †**4.** Applied to persons: A mean, insignificant, or paltry fellow –1653. **5.** A squirt. Now *dial.* 1583. **6.** A small measure or quantity (*of* strong drink). Now *dial.* 1766.

1. The literary gentleman having finished, like a damp s. with a good bang, resumed his seat 1847. *fig.* In 1841 he had thrown a few squibs in the Examiner at Sir Robert Peel and the Tories 1882. **3.** No one was more faithful to his early friends..particularly if they could write a s. DISRAELI. **4.** Out steps me an infant s. of the Innes of Court NASHE.

Squib (skwib), *v.* 1579. [f. the sb.] **I.** *intr.* **1.** To use smart or sarcastic language; to utter, write, or publish a squib or squibs. **2.** To let off squibs; to shoot 1691. **3.** To move *about* like a squib 1760.

1. To s. in the journals, and write for the stage 1825. **3.** A battered unmarried beau, who squibs about from place to place GOLDSM.

II. *trans.* **1. a.** To cast or throw *forth*, *off*, *out* (a remark, quip, etc.) after the manner of a squib 1596. **b.** To let off (a squib); to fire (a gun, etc.), esp. with the priming or powder only; †to shoot (an arrow) 1603. **2.** To assail or attack (a person) with squibs or witty sarcasm; to lampoon or satirize smartly 1631. **3.** To spatter with a squib or squirt 1840.

1. a. Hook squibbed off a few pleasantries 1853. **2.** The mendicant parson, whom I am so fond of squibbing J. R. GREEN.

Squid (skwid), *sb.* 1613. [Origin obsc.] **1.** One or other of various species of cephalopods belonging to the family *Loliginidæ*, *Teuthididæ*, or *Sepiidæ*, more esp. to the genus *Loligo*; a calamary, cuttle, or pen-fish. **b.** Without article, esp. as a bait or food-stuff 1865. **2.** *Bone-s.*, an artificial bait made to imitate a squid 1883.

attrib. and Comb.: **s. fish,** = sense 1; **s.-hound,** a name in New England for large sea-going specimens of the Striped Bass. Hence **Squid** *v. intr.* to fish with squid-bait *U.S.*

Squiffer (skwi·fəɹ). *slang.* 1911. [?] A concertina.

Squiffy (skwi·fi), *a. slang.* 1874. [Fanciful.] Intoxicated, drunk.

Squiggle (skwi·g'l), *v.* Chiefly *dial.* and *U.S.* 1804. [Imitative.] **1.** *intr.* To work wavy or intricate embroidery. **2.** To writhe about; to squirm or wriggle 1816. **Squi·ggle** *sb.* a wriggly twist or curve. **Squi·ggly** *a.* wavy, wriggly.

Squilgee (skwi·ldʒī, skwildʒī·), *sb.* Also **squillage, squiligee.** 1850. [Origin obsc.] *Naut.* = SQUEEGEE 1. **Squilgee** *v.* to use a s.; to swab, clean, or press with a s.

Squill (skwil). late ME. [ad. L. *squilla*, var. *scilla*, a. Gr. σκίλλα.] **1.** A bulb or root of the sea-onion or other related plant (see 2). Chiefly in *pl.* **b.** In names of preparations made from these bulbs 1652. **c.** *Pharm.* Without article, as a substance 1725. **2.** *Bot.* The bulbous-rooted sea-shore plant *Scilla* (or *Urginea*) *maritima*; the sea-onion; also, any other species of the genus *Scilla* 1440. **b.** A plant of the sea-onion or related species. Chiefly *pl.* as a collective term. 1601. **3.** *Zool.* The mantis-shrimp, *Squilla mantis* 1710.

1. b. Galen..gave it to a Dram in Oxymel or Honey of Squills 1712.

‖ **Squilla** (skwi·lă). *Pl.* **-æ** (*ī*). 1516. [L. (see prec.).] †**1.** = prec. **2.** –1611. **2.** = prec. 3. 1658.

†**Squilli·tic,** *a.* 1544. [ad. med.L. *squilliticus*, var. of *scilliticus*, f. *scilla* SQUILL.] Made of squills; containing squill –1725.

Squinacy (skwi·năsi). Now *dial.* ME. [var. of SQUINANCY, by elision of the second *n*.] = SQUINSY.

Squi·nancy. Now *rare.* late ME. [ad. med.L. *squinancia*, *-antia*, app. formed by confusion of Gr. συνάγχη and κυνάγχη CYNANCHE, both denoting diseases of the throat.] **1.** Quinsy. **2.** = SQUINSY 2. 1596.

Comb.: **s. berry,** the black currant, *Ribes nigrum*; **s.-wort,** the quinsy-wort or small woodruff, *Asperula cynanchica.* So †**Squi·nance** –1730.

Squinch (skwinʃ). 1500. [var. *scunch*, shortened f. SCUNCHEON.] *Arch.* †**1.** A stone cut to serve as a scuncheon –1518. **2.** A straight or arched support constructed across an angle to carry some superstructure 1840. **3.** A small structure, with two triangular faces, sloping back from an angle of a tower against the superimposed side of a spire 1848.

Squinny (skwi·ni), *v.* Now *dial.* Also **squiny.** 1605. [Related to SQUINT *v.*] **1.** *intr.* To squint, look askance; to peer with part'y closed eyes. **2.** *trans.* To direct (the eyes) obliquely; to close *up* partly in a short-sighted manner 1825.

Squi·nsy. Now *dial.* 1499. [Reduced f. SQUINACY.] **1.** *Path.* Quinsy; suppurative tonsillitis. **2.** A form or attack of this 1591.

Squint (skwint), *sb.* 1652. [f. SQUINT *a.* or *v.*] **1.** A permanent tendency in the eye to look obliquely or askant; defective coincidence of the optic axes; strabismus. **2.** A directing of the eyes obliquely; a sidelong look or glance; a hasty or casual look; a peep 1673. **3.** An inclination or tendency towards some particular object; a drift or leaning; a covert aim 1736. **4.** An oblique or perverse bent or tendency 1774. **5.** *Arch.* = HAGIOSCOPE 1839.

2. To give damages for all opprobrious language, and especially for all hints, squints, innuendoes, leers, and shrugs SWIFT. **3.** A s. towards radicalism 1895.

Squint (skwint), *a.* 1579. [perh. inferred from SQUINT-EYED *a.*] **1.** Of eyes: Looking obliquely; having a cast or squint; affected with strabismus. Now *rare.* **b.** *fig.* (with *eye* = 'look, regard', and usu. hyphened) 1623. **2.** Characterized by oblique vision 1611. †**3.** Indirect –1681. **4.** Oblique; slanting 1703.

1. He was syrnamed..Strabo, for his s. eyes HOLLAND. **2.** I..gladly banish s. suspicion MILT.

Squint (skwint), *v.* 1599. [Aphetic f. ASQUINT *adv.*] **1.** *intr.* To have the axes of the eyes not coincident; to be affected with strabismus 1611. **b.** Of the eyes 1836. **2.** To look with the eyes differently directed; to glance obliquely; also, to glance hastily or casually, to peep 1610. **b.** *fig.* To have a private eye to something 1642. **c.** To glance *at*, *on*, or *upon* (a person or thing) with dislike or disapproval, or by means of some covert allusion, hint, or suggestion 1652. **3.** *fig.* To refer or bear indirectly; to incline or tend 1599. **4.** To move or branch off in an oblique direction 1721. **5.** *trans.* To give a permanent or temporary cast to (the eye); to cause to look asquint or obliquely 1605. **b.** To cast or direct (a look, etc.) in a sidelong manner 1631.

1. Can any one be call'd beautiful that squints? WYCHERLEY. **2. b.** Pity but his eyes were out that squints at his own ends in doing God's work FULLER. **3.** The document squints towards treason 1895. **5.** The foule Flibbertigibbet..squints the eye, and makes the Hare-lippe SHAKS. Hence **Squi·nter.**

Squint-eye(**s.** 1653. [See SQUINT *a.* 1.] A person who has squinting eyes.

Squint-eyed (skwi·nt,əid), *a.* 1589. [f. SQUINT *a.*] **1.** Of persons: Having squint eyes; affected with squint or strabismus. **2.** Characterized by squint or oblique vision 1598.

1. *fig.* Heart-gnawing Hatred, and Squint-ey'd Suspition QUARLES.

Squi·nting, *vbl. sb.* 1611. [f. SQUINT *v.*] **1.** The action of looking with a squint or sidelong glance. **2.** *spec.* = SQUINT *sb.* 1. 1626. So **Squi·nting** *ppl. a.*, **-ly** *adv.* 1593.

Squirage (skwəiə·rėdʒ). Also **squireage.** 1837. [f. SQUIRE *sb.* + -AGE.] The body of country squires; a book containing a list or account of these.

Squiralty (skwəiə·rălti). Also **squirealty.** 1856. [f. SQUIRE *sb.*] **a.** The existence of squires as an institution. **b.** The body or class of squires. **c.** The position or status of a squire.

Squire (skwəiə̆ɹ), *sb.* ME. [ad. OF. *esquier* ESQUIRE *sb.*[1]] **1.** In the military organization of the later middle ages, a young man of good birth attendant upon a knight (= ESQUIRE 1 a); one ranking next to a knight under the feudal system of military service and tenure. **b.** A personal attendant or servant; a follower. Also *transf.* late ME. †**c.** In contemptuous use –1618. **2.** Applied to personages of ancient history or mythology holding a position or rank similar to that of the mediæval squire ME. **3.** A gallant or lover 1590. **4.** Employed as a title and prefixed to the surname of a country gentleman. Now chiefly *colloq.* 1645. **b.** A country gentleman or landed proprietor, *esp.*

one who is the principal landowner in a village or district 1676. **5.** *U.S.* A Justice of the Peace; also, a lawyer or judge 1817.

1. Each knight was attended to the field by four squires or archers on horseback GIBBON. **b.** †*S. of* (or *for*) *the body* (or *household*), an officer charged with personal attendance upon a sovereign, nobleman, etc. **c.** *Trencher-s.*: see TRENCHER [1]. **2.** And Saul seyde to his squyer, Draw3e out thi swerd WYCLIF 1 *Chron.* x. 4. **3.** *S. of dames* (Spenser) or *ladies*, one who devotes himself to the service of ladies or pays marked attentions to them. Hence **Squi·ress,** a female s.; the wife of a s.

Squire (skwəiəɹ), *v.* late ME. [f. SQUIRE *sb.*] **1.** *trans.* Of a man: To attend (a lady) as, or after the manner of, a squire; to escort. †**b.** *transf.* To act or serve as an escort or guard to; to convoy -1632. **2.** *intr.* With *it*: To act as a squire; to play the squire; to rule or domineer *over* as a country squire 1672.

1. To 'squire a royal girl of two years old SWIFT.

Squirearch (skwəiəˑraɹk). 1831. [f. SQUIREARCHY, after *monarch*, etc.] A member of the squirearchy; a squire as a local magnate. Hence **Squirea·rchal** *a.* of or belonging to, characteristic of, the squirearchy or a s.

Squirearchy (skwəiəˑraɹki). Also **squirarchy.** 1804. [f. SQUIRE *sb.*, after *hierarchy*, *monarchy*, etc.] **1.** The collective body of squires, landed proprietors, or country gentry; the class to which squires belong, regarded especially in respect of political or social influence. **b.** A class, body, or number of squires 1830. **2.** Rule or government by a squire or squires 1861.

Squiredom (skwəiəˑɹdəm). 1650. [f. SQUIRE *sb.* + -DOM.] **1.** The dignity, position, or status of a squire. **2.** The body of squires; squires collectively 1842.

1. I always direct to you as 'Mr. Barton' because I know not if Quakers ought to endure S. FITZGERALD.

Squireen (skwəiərīˑn). orig. *Irish.* 1809. [f. SQUIRE *sb.* + *-een*, Ir. Gael. *-ín*, dim. suffix.] A petty squire; a small landowner or country gentleman.

Squirehood (skwəiəˑɹhud). 1680. [f. SQUIRE *sb.*] **1.** The position or status of a squire or esquire; squireship. **2.** The body of squires; the squirearchy 1792.

Squireling (skwəiəˑɹliŋ). 1682. [f. SQUIRE *sb.*] **1.** A petty squire. **2.** A young squire 1834.

Squirely (skwəiəˑɹli), *a.* 1612. [f. as prec. + -LY [1].] Of, belonging or relating to, a squire or the squirearchy; befitting a squire.

Squireship (skwəiəˑɹʃip). 1613. [f. SQUIRE *sb.* + -SHIP.] **1.** The state, position, or dignity of a squire or esquire; squirehood. **2.** The personality of a squire 1786.

Squirm (skwɔ̄ɹm), *sb.* 1839. [f. the vb.] **a.** A squirming or writhing movement; a wriggle. **b.** *Naut.* A twist in a rope.

Squirm (skwɔ̄ɹm), *v.* 1691. [app. symbolic.] **1.** *intr.* To wriggle or writhe. **2.** To move, proceed, or go with a wriggling or writhing motion 1759. **3.** *fig.* To be painfully affected or sharply touched by something; to writhe under reproof, sarcasm, etc. 1804. **4.** *trans.* With *out*: To utter with a squirm 1889.

1. This harmless snake frequents the branches of Trees and very nimbly squirms among the leaves 1743. These poor little mortals..s. and squall 1890. **3.** I'll write my Lord..such a letter as shall make him s. 1894.

Squirr, *v.* Also **squir.** 1710. [var. of SKIRR *v.*] *trans.* To throw or cast with a rapid whirling or skimming motion.

Squirrel (skwiˑrĕl). late ME. [ad. AF. *esquirel*, OF. *esquireul* (mod.F. *écureuil*), = med.L. (*e*)*scurellus, scurellius*, dims. from pop. L. **scurius*, for L. *sciurus*, ad. Gr. σκίουρος, app. f. σκιά shade + οὐρά tail. Formerly pron. (skweˑrel) and (skwɒˑrĕl).] **1.** One or other of various species of rodents (characterized by a long bushy tail, furry coat, and bright eyes), belonging to the genus *Sciurus*, or to the widely-distributed sub-family *Sciurina* including this; *esp.* the common species *Sciurus vulgaris*, native to Britain, Europe, and parts of Asia. **b.** Applied to other animals or to persons, usu. with contemptuous force 1566. **2.** With *the*, in generalized sense; also, the genus *Sciurus* or the sub-family *Sciurina* to which this belongs. Also *pl.* 1591. **b.** = squirrel-skin, squirrel-fur. late ME. **3.** One or other of various species of fish belonging to the family *Holocentridæ*, esp. *Holocentrus erythræus* 1734.

1. b. A little, cheery, agile, red s. of a Man 1865.

attrib. and *Comb.*: **s.-cage,** a cylindrical cage in which squirrels are confined, and which revolves as they move; also *transf.* a structure resembling this, *spec.* in *Electr.*; **-corn,** *Dicentra canadensis*; **-fish** = sense 3; **-hake,** *Physis tenuis*, also called White Hake (*U.S.*); **-hawk,** the Californian species, *Archibuteo ferrugineus*; **-headed, -minded** *adjs.*, shallow-brained; **-monkey,** one or other of various species of monkeys belonging to the genus *Chrysothrix*.

†**Squi·rrel-tail.** Also **squirrel's tail.** late ME. **1.** The tail of a squirrel. †**2.** A species of lob-worm -1839. **3.** *Squirrel-tail grass*, one or other of various species of grasses belonging to the genus *Hordeum*. Also *ellipt.* 1777. So **Squi·rrel-tailed** *a.* having a tail like that of a squirrel in form or character.

Squirt (skwɔ̄ɹt), *sb.* 1460. [f. SQUIRT *v.*] **1. a.** Diarrhœa; looseness of the bowels; an attack of diarrhœa. Now *dial.* in *pl.* **2.** A small tubular instrument by which water may be squirted; a form of syringe 1530. **b.** A larger instrument of the same type, used esp. as a fire-extinguisher 1590. **3.** A small quantity of liquid that is squirted; a small jet or spray; an act of squirting 1626. **4.** A paltry or contemptible person; a whipper-snapper; a fop. (Chiefly *U.S.* and *dial.*) 1848.

Squirt (skwɔ̄ɹt), *v.* 1460. [app. symbolic or onomatopœic.] **I.** *intr.* **1.** To eject or spirt out water in a jet or slight stream. **b.** To void thin excrement; to have diarrhœa 1530. **2.** To move swiftly or quickly; to dart or frisk 1570. **3.** To issue or be ejected in a jet-like stream; to spirt or spurt 1858.

2. Comes master doctor Glister, as his manner is, squirting in suddenly MIDDLETON.

II. *trans.* **1.** To cause (liquid) to issue or stream (*out*) in a jet from a squirt or syringe 1583. **b.** To eject or propel in a stream from a small orifice, etc. 1601. **2.** To inject (a liquid) by means of a squirt or in a similar manner 1550. **3.** To moisten or cover (a surface) with liquid by means of spirting or squirting; to bring into a certain state in this way 1601. **4.** *techn.* To force or press (a viscous or ductile material) through a small orifice; to form or fashion in this way 1881.

1. *fig.* Versifiers squirting out careless rhapsodies of harmonious billingsgate 1768. **b.** The emphatic way in which..they squirted their tobacco-juice on the deck 1849. Hence **Squi·rter,** one who or that which squirts.

Squish (skwiʃ), *sb.* 1874. [f. next.] **1.** *Univ. slang.* Marmalade. **2.** A squishing sound 1902. **3.** *slang.* Nonsense, 'rubbish', 'rot', 'bilge' 1912.

Squish (skwiʃ), *v.* 1647. [Echoic.] **1.** *trans.* To squeeze, to squash. Now *dial.* **2.** *intr.* Of water, soft mud, etc.: To give out a peculiar gushing or splashing sound when walked in or on; to gush up, squirt out, with such a sound 1825.

Squitch (skwitʃ). 1785. [Altered f. QUITCH *sb.*] **1.** Couch-grass, *Triticum repens*. **2.** Applied to certain species of *Agrostis* and other similar plants 1792.

Squi·tter, *sb.* Now *dial.* 1664. [f. the vb.] Usu. *pl.* Diarrhœa.

Squi·tter, *v.* Now *dial.* 1596. [Echoic.] **1.** *trans.* and *intr.* To squirt; to spatter, splutter. **2.** *intr.* To void thin excrement 1611.

St (st), *int.* 1552. [repr. a checked sibilation.] **1.** = HIST, HUSH, WHIST. **2.** An exclam. used to drive away an animal, or to urge it to attack 1552.

St. *Abbreviations.* **a.** (with cap.) = SAINT prefixed to a name; **b.** (with cap. or small initial) = STREET preceded by a defining word; **c.** (chiefly with small initial) in references (*a*) = STANZA; (*b*) = STATUTE; **d.** (with small initial) = STONE (weight).

Stab (stæb), *sb.*[1] 1440. [Related to STAB *v.*] **1.** A wound produced by stabbing. **2.** An act of stabbing; a thrust with some sharp-pointed instrument 1530. **3.** *Billiards.* A short, stiff stroke which causes the striker's ball to remain dead or to travel but slowly after striking the object ball; more fully *s. stroke*; hence *s. cannon, screw*, a cannon or screw made with this stroke 1873.

1. An important punctured wound, such as the s. of a bayonet 1826. *A s. in the back*, an act of treachery. **2.** A s. that touched the vitals DE FOE. *fig.* A s. was attempted on my reputation BURKE. Phr. *The s.*, death by stabbing. *To have* or *make a s. at*: to try, attempt, make a shot at (*colloq.*, orig. *U.S.*).

Comb.: **s.-awl,** a shoemaker's tool used for piercing leather; **-culture,** a CULTURE (3) in which the medium is inoculated by means of a needle thrust deeply into its substance.

Stab, *sb.*[2] 1865. *Printer's slang.* = ESTABLISHMENT II. 4.

Stab (stæb), *v.* ME. [orig. Sc. Related to the synonymous *stob* (1529).] **1.** *trans.* To wound (often to kill) with a thrust of a pointed weapon (chiefly, with a short weapon, as a dagger) 1530. **2.** *absol.* and *intr.* To use a pointed weapon to wound or kill. late ME. **3.** *trans.* To thrust (a weapon) into a person 1610. **4.** *Bookbinding.* To pierce (a collection of sheets) in order to make a hole for a binding thread or wire; to fasten the sheets of (a pamphlet, etc.) together in this way instead of by sewing 1863.

1. Stabbed to the heart by the hand of an obscure villain CLARENDON. *fig.* He fabricates The sword which stabs his peace SHELLEY. Phr. *To s. in the back*, to slander; to behave treacherously towards. **2.** *fig.* Shee speakes poynyards, and euery word stabbes SHAKS. Hence **Sta·bber,** one who or that which stabs. **Sta·bbingly** *adv.*

‖**Stabat Mater** (stēⁱˑbæt mēⁱˑtəɹ, stāˑbæt māˑtəɹ). 1867. [From the opening words, L. *stabat mater dolorosa* 'Stood the mother, full of grief'.] A sequence, composed by Jacobus de Benedictis in the 13th c., in commemoration of the sorrows of the Blessed Virgin Mary. Also, a musical setting of this sequence.

Stabile (stēⁱˑbil, -əil), *a.* 1797. [ad. L. *stabilis*; see STABLE *a.*] **1.** Firmly established, enduring, lasting. (Used to express more unequivocally the etymological sense of STABLE *a.*) *rare.* **2.** Fixed in position 1896.

†**Sta·biliment.** late ME. [ad. L. *stabilimentum*, f. *stabilire* to render stable, f. *stabilis*; see STABLE *a.* and -MENT.] Something which gives stability or firmness; stay, support -1684.

In the Trailing of the Trunk, they [the Claspers] serve for s., propagation and shade 1673.

Stabilimeter (stæbiliˑmītəɹ). 1907. [f. STABILITY + -METER.] *Aeronautics.* A contrivance for ascertaining the stability of a model airship or aeroplane.

Stabilitate (stăbiˑlitēⁱt), *v. rare.* 1642. [f. L. *stabilitat-*, *stabilitare*, f. *stabilitas*.] *trans.* To give stability to.

Stability (stăbiˑlĭti). [ME. *stablete*, a. OF. (*e*)*stableté*, semi-pop. ad. L. *stabilitas*, f. *stabilis* STABLE *a.*; see -TY.] The quality or condition of being stable. **1.** Of a person, his character or disposition: The condition of 'standing fast'; fixity of resolution or purpose; firmness, steadfastness. **2.** In physical senses. **a.** Power of remaining erect; freedom from liability to fall or be overthrown. late ME. **b.** Fixity of position in space; freedom from liability to changes of place 1625. **c.** Capacity for resistance to displacement; the condition of being in stable equilibrium, tendency to recover the original position after displacement. Also, of a body in motion: Freedom from oscillation, steadiness. 1542. **d.** Of a system of bodies: Permanence of arrangement; power of resisting change of structure 1855. **e.** Of a chemical compound or combination: Capacity to resist decomposition or disruption 1862. **f.** Of a colour: Permanence 1791. **3.** Of an immaterial thing: Immunity from destruction or essential change; enduring quality 1470.

1. The s. of England is the security of the modern world EMERSON. **2. a.** The S. of a Pyramid 1746. **b.** The doctrine of the motion of the earth and the s. of the sun 1831. **c.** *spec.* with ref. to aircraft.

Stabilizator (stēⁱˑbiləizēⁱˑtəɹ, stæˑb-). 1902. [ad. F. *stabilisateur*, f. *stabiliser*; see next and -ATOR.] *Aeronautics.* = STABILIZER.

Stabilize (stēⁱˑbiləiz, stæˑb-), *v.* 1861. [ad. F. *stabiliser*, f. L. *stabilis*; see STABLE *a.* and -IZE.] **1.** *trans.* To give stability to (a ship or aircraft). **2.** To give a stable character or value to 1875. **b.** To establish a scale of (payments, prices, or the like) 1918. So **Stabiliza·tion.**

Sta·bilizer. 1909. [f. prec.] 1. *Aeronautics.* A stabilizing apparatus or device. 2. A substance added to an explosive to render it less liable to spontaneous decomposition 1911.

Sta·bilizing, *ppl. a.* 1911. [f. STABILIZE *v.* + -ING[2].] That stabilizes or gives stability; *spec.* in *Aeronautics*, that gives stability (to an aeroplane, etc.); that acts or may be used as a stabilizer.

Stable (stēⁱ·b'l), *sb.* ME. [a. OF. *estable* stable (mod.F. *étable* cowhouse) :—L. *stabulum* stable, stall, lit. standing place, f. *sta-* root of *stare* to stand.] 1. A building fitted with stalls, loose boxes, rack and manger and harness appliances, in which horses are kept. Formerly, a building in which domestic animals, as cattle, goats, etc., are kept. b. See AUGEAN *stable* 1903. 2. A collection (of horses) belonging to one stable 1576. 3. An establishment where race-horses are trained; a racing-stable. Also, the horses belonging to a particular racing-stable; the proprietors and staff of such an establishment 1810. 4. *Mil.* Used in *pl.* for: Duty or work in the stables; also the bugle-call for this duty, stable-call 1885.

1. Ful many a deyntee hors hadde he in s. CHAUCER. b. Suggestions as to how this particular 's.' must be swept out 1909.

Comb.: **s.-boy,** a boy or man employed in or about a s.; **-call** *Mil.*, a bugle-call to stables (see 4); **s. companion,** a horse from the same s.; *transf.* (colloq.) a member of the same school, club, etc.; **-fly,** any species of the genus *Stomoxys*, esp. *S. calcitrans*; **-lad** = *s.-boy*; **stableman,** one who is employed in a s. to groom, feed, and otherwise look after the horses; **s. room,** stabling; **-yard,** the yard attached to a s.

Stable (stēⁱ·b'l), *a.* ME. [a. OF. *stable, estable* (mod.F. *stable*) :—L. *stabilem*, f. *sta-, stare* to stand; see -BLE.] 1. Able to remain erect; secure against falling or being overthrown. b. Of a support or foundation: Firm, not likely to give way ME. c. Firm in consistency, solid. Now *rare.* 1666. 2. Stationary, keeping to one place ME. 3. Of a material thing or its condition: Able to maintain its place or position; presenting resistance to displacement; not easily shaken or dislodged 1560. b. Of a system of bodies: Having a permanent structure or constitution; not liable to disintegration 1839. c. Of a chemical compound or combination: Not readily decomposing 1850. 4. Not liable to fail or vary; securely established; firm ME. 5. Of persons and their dispositions. a. Steadfast in purpose or resolution; settled in character, not fickle, changeable, or frivolous ME. †b. Of God or a deity: Unchangeable –1700.

1. He which is tottering himselfe, had neede leane unto a s. thing 1591. b. It often affords a s. mooring to a ship 1820. 2. Some seventy miles from the nearest s. ice 1853. 3. Phr. *S. equilibrium*: see EQUILIBRIUM 1. 4. Men..deemed present institutions s., because they had never seen them shaken 1849. An accurate and s. definition of wealth RUSKIN. The s. forces of nature 1878. 5. a. Things to make me s. In what I have began to take in hand BUNYAN. b. He perfect, s.; but imperfect We, Subject to Change, and diff'rent in Degree DRYDEN. Hence **Sta·bleness** (now *rare*), = STABILITY.

†**Stable,** *v.*[1] ME. [var. of ESTABLE *v.*, a. OF. *establir* :—L. *stabilire*, f. *stabilis* STABLE *a.*] *trans.* To make stable –1545.

Stable (stēⁱ·b'l), *v.*[2] ME. [f. STABLE *sb.*] 1. *trans.* To put (a horse) into a stable, or into a place which is used as a stable. b. Of a building: To afford stabling for 1903. 2. *intr.* Of an animal: To live in a stable 1508.

2. *transf.* In thir Palaces..Sea-monsters whelp'd And stabl'd MILT.

Stable door. ME. The door of a stable.

Prov. *To shut (lock, etc.) the s. when the horse is stolen*, to take preventive measures too late.

Stabler (stēⁱ·blər). Now *Sc.* late ME. [a. OF. *establier*, f. *estable* STABLE *sb.*; see -ER[2].] A stable-keeper.

†**Stable-stand.** 1598. [f. *stable* var. STABLY *sb.* + STAND *v.*] The position of a man found in a forest standing, with bow bent, ready to shoot at a deer, or standing by a tree with greyhounds in leash, ready to let slip.

Stabling (stēⁱ·bliŋ), *vbl. sb.* 1481. [f. STABLE *v.*[2] + -ING[1].] The action of placing or accommodating (horses) in a stable; stable accommodation; stable-buildings collectively.

Stablish (stæ·bliʃ), *v.* Now *arch.* ME. [var. of ESTABLISH *v.*] = ESTABLISH *v.*

And s. quietnesse on euery side SHAKS. As hee went to s. his dominion 1 *Chron.* xviii. 3. He stablishes the strong, restores the weak COWPER.

Stablishment (stæ·bliʃmĕnt). *arch.* late ME. var. of ESTABLISHMENT.

†**Sta·bly,** *sb.* ME. [a. AF. *establie*, f. *establir* to ESTABLISH.] 1. *Hunting.* A besetting of a wood with men, hounds in leash, nets, etc., for the purpose of taking deer, etc. –late ME. 2. A stand, halt (of armed men)–1450.

Stably (stēⁱ·bli), *adv.* ME. [f. STABLE *a.* + -LY[2].] In a stable manner, firmly, †steadfastly, †constantly.

†**Stacca·do.** 1612. [Alteration of Sp. *estacada*, f. *estaca*, of Teut. origin; see STAKE *sb.*] = STOCKADE –1777.

‖**Staccato** (stăkā·to), *a.* (*adv.*, *sb.*). 1724. [It., pa. pple. of *staccare*, shortened f. *distaccare*; see DETACH *v.*] *Mus.* Detached, disconnected, *i.e.* with breaks between successive notes. Used *adj.* or *advb.* as a direction; also as *sb.*, a succession of disconnected notes.

The monotonous s. of the guitar BECKFORD. Hence **Stacca·to** *v. trans.* to play (a piece of music) in a s. manner.

Stack (stæk), *sb.* ME. [a. ON. *stakkr* haystack :—OTeut. type **stakkoz*, prob. :—pre-Teut. **stognos*; cf. Russ. *stog* haystack.] 1. A pile, heap, or group of things, esp. such a pile or heap with its constituents arranged in an orderly fashion. 2. A pile of grain in the sheaf, of hay, straw, fodder, etc., gathered into a circular or rectangular form, and usu. with a sloping thatched top to protect it from the weather ME. 3. A pile of sticks, faggots, firewood, poles, etc. late ME. b. A measure of volume for wood and coal, usu. 4 cubic yds. (108 cubic feet) 1651. 4. A number of chimneys, flues, or pipes, standing together in one group 1667. b. A chimney of a house, factory, etc.; the chimney or funnel of a locomotive or steamship; also = *stack-furnace* 1825. 5. *dial.* A columnar mass of rock, detached by the agency of water and weather from the main part of a cliff, and rising precipitously out of the sea 1769. 6. Often in *pl.* = 'heaps' (*slang*) 1903.

1. b. A structure of bookshelves for compact storage of books; also, a building containing such a structure. 2. While the Cock..to the s., or the Barn Dore, Stoutly struts his Dames before MILT.

Comb.: **s.-furnace,** a tall circular blast-furnace; **-guard,** a temporary covering to protect a s. of hay or grain in process of formation; **-stand,** a raised staging for a s. of hay or grain, to keep it dry and free from the ravages of vermin; **-yard,** a rick-yard.

Stack (stæk), *v.* ME. [f. prec. sb.] 1. *trans.* To pile (corn, fodder, etc.) into a stack; to make a stack of, to pile (something) up in the form of a stack. 2. *absol.* and *intr.* To put corn or hay into stacks; to make a stack or stacks 1722. 3. *trans.* To make a pile of (weapons, etc.) by leaning one against another 1841. 4. To fill *with* stacks of 1652.

1. At the far end, fleeces of wool stacked up GEO. ELIOT. *To s. the cards* (orig. U.S.), to cheat by shuffling the cards in a particular way; *fig.* to take an unfair advantage. 3. The men [military cyclists], having dismounted and stacked their machines 1887. Hence **Sta·cker.**

Sta·ck-garth. *north.* ME. [a. ON. *stakkgarðr*; see STACK *sb.* and GARTH[1].] A stack-yard, rick-yard.

Stacking (stæ·kiŋ), *vbl. sb.* 1531. [f. STACK *v.* + -ING[1].] The action or an act of STACK *v.*

attrib.: **s. stage,** a scaffold used in the building of stacks.

‖**Stacte** (stæ·ktī). ME. [L., a. Gr. στακτή, fem. of στακτός distilling in drops, f. σταγ-, στάζειν to drop.] a. A fragrant spice referred to by ancient writers; prop., the finest kind of myrrh, the exudation of the living tree, but the name was also applied to a mixture of storax with fat. In the Bible used as tr. Heb. *nāṭāph*, one of the ingredients of the incense prescribed for the Tabernacle worship, variously conjectured to be opobalsamum, myrrh, storax, or tragacanth. †b. *Pharmacy.* Applied to LIQUIDAMBAR and perh. other preparations.

Stactometer (stæktǫ·mĭtər). Also **stakto-**. 1842. [f. Gr. στακτός (see prec.) + -METER.] *Hydrodynamics.* An appliance consisting of a glass tube having a hollow bulb in the middle, used for measuring liquids in drops.

‖**Stad** (stat). *S. Africa.* Also **stadt.** 1896. [Du.] A town or village.

Staddle (stæ·d'l), *sb.* Also †**stadle.** [OE. *staðol* foundation, support, trunk of a tree :—OTeut. **staþloz* :—pre-Teut. **statlos*, f. *sta-* to STAND + *-tlo-* instrumental suffix.] †1. A foundation –ME. 2. A young tree left standing when others are cut down. Also *dial.* the root or stump of a tree that has been felled. 1559. 3. a. The lower part of a stack of corn, hay, etc. 1581. b. A platform of timber, stone, etc., on which a stack or rick is placed. Also, in some districts, = *s.-stones.* 1729.

Comb.: **s.-stones,** the stones on which a s. or stack-frame is supported.

Stade (stēⁱd). *arch.* 1537. Anglicized f. STADIUM.

Stadholder, stadtholder (stæ·thǫᵘldər). 1668. [ad. Du. *stadhouder* one who occupies another's place, 'locum tenens', lieutenant, f. *stad* place + *houder* HOLDER.] 1. *Netherlands Hist.* a. orig., A viceroy or lieutenant-governor of a province or provinces. b. The title borne by the chief magistrate of the Dutch republic. 2. Used as tr. G. *statthalter*, Da. *statholder*, lieutenant-governor, viceroy 1704. Hence **Sta·dholderate,** the office or dignity of s., a state ruled by a s. **Sta·dholdership.**

Stadia (stēⁱ·diă). 1865. [History obsc.; prob. f. STADIUM, or the pl. *stadia.*] An apparatus for measuring distance by optical means. a. *Mil.* A glass plate, or a brass plate with an opening in the form of an isosceles triangle, marked with figures showing the distance at which a foot- or horse-soldier will be when his image covers a certain height on the instrument held at arm's length. b. *Surveying.* An apparatus consisting of a rod or staff placed at one end of the distance to be measured and a pair of horizontal lines, hairs or wires on the diaphragm of a telescope placed at the other end.

Stadiometer (stēⁱdiǫ·mĭtər). 1862. [f. Gr. στάδιον STADIUM + -METER.] a. *Mil.* = STADIA a. b. A surveying instrument. In *U.S.* A self-recording theodolite in which the directions are marked upon a small sheet.

‖**Stadium** (stēⁱ·diŏm). *Pl.* **stadia** (stēⁱ·diă); †also **stadias, stadiums,** etc. late ME. [L., ad. Gr. στάδιον.] 1. An ancient Greek and Roman measure of length, most commonly = one-eighth of a Roman mile. (In the English Bible rendered by *furlong.*) 2. A race-course for foot-racing, orig. a stadium in length; hence *occas.* foot-racing as an exercise. In mod. use freq., a place for athletic exercises. 1603. 3. A stage of a process, disease, etc. 1669. 4. *Surveying.* = STADIA b. 1861.

‖**Stadthaus** (ʃtat,haus). 1839. [G., f. *stadt* town + *haus* HOUSE *sb.*] A German town-hall.

Stadthouse (sta·t,haus). 1646. [Anglicization of G. *stadthaus* or Du. *stadhuis.*] A town-hall.

Staff (staf), *sb.*[1] *Pl.* **staves** (stēⁱvz), **staffs** (stafs). [Com. Teut.; OE. *stæf* :—OTeut. **staðoz.*] I. 1. A stick carried in the hand as an aid in walking or climbing. Now chiefly *literary.* b. *joc.* as a type of thinness or leanness. late ME. †c. A shepherd's crook –1577. d. A rod or wand used as an instrument of magic or divination 1610. 2. A stick, pole, or club used as a weapon. (Cf. QUARTERSTAFF.) OE. 3. a. The shaft of a spear or lance. *arch.* ME. †b. A spear, lance, or similar armed weapon –1868. 4. *fig.* Something which serves as a support or stay. late ME. b. In the Biblical phr. *to break the s. of bread* (literally from Heb.), to diminish or cut off the supply of food. late ME. c. Hence *the s. of life* = bread (or similar staple food) 1638. 5. Part of the insignia of the episcopal office, consisting of a rod or pole of wood, metal or ivory supporting a crook, or, in the case of metropolitans, a cross OE. 6. A rod or wand, of wood or ivory, borne as an ensign of office or authority; *spec.* as the badge of certain chief officers of the Crown 1535. 7. A pole from which a flag is flown 1613. †8. A strong stick, pole, bar, rod or stake used for various purposes; e.g. for carrying burdens, to support a canopy, the stems of plants, etc. -1708. **9.** *Surveying.* A rod for measuring distances and heights 1556. **b.** The gnomon of a sun-dial 1669. **10.** *Her.* A representation of a stick, stake, bar, etc.; *spec.* = BATON 3, FISSURE *sb.* 2c. See also RAGGED STAFF. 1486. **11.** *Surg.* A grooved steel instrument used to guide the knife in lithotomy 1698. **12. a.** A rung of a ladder ME. **b.** A round cross-bar connecting the handles or stilts of a plough, or the legs of a chair. Also, each of the handles of a plough. *Obs.* or *dial.* 1523. **†c.** A bar or rail used in the construction of a gridiron, gate, cart, cage, etc. -1601. **d.** *Watchmaking.* An arbor or axle 1860.

1. I..dug my s. deeply into the snow TYNDALL. **b.** 2 *Hen. IV*, v. i. 71. **d.** I'le breake my staffe *Temp.* v. 54. **2.** I..with an Oak'n s. will meet thee MILT. **3. b.** Come, put mine Armour on: giue me my Staffe SHAKS. *To break a s.*, to tilt or contend *with* (an antagonist). With defining word, as *Jedburgh* (*Jedworth*, *Jedwood*, etc.) *s.* **4.** The boy was the verie staffe of my age, my verie prop SHAKS. **12. a.** How many mount Fortunes ladder, and break the staves as they go up 1657.

Phrases. *S. and staple*, the chief elements or ingredients. *To set up* (or †*in*) *one's s.* (*of rest*), to settle down in a place, take up one's abode. *To have the s. in* (*one's*) *own hand*, to keep possession of one's property, to retain authority and obedience.

II. Letter, verse, musical staff. **†1.** A written character, a letter. Cf. RUNE-STAVE. -ME. **2. †a.** A line of verse -1540. **†b.** A stanza or set of lines -1697. **c.** A 'verse' or stanza of a song. Now STAVE. 1598. **3.** *Mus.* A set of horizontal lines (now five in number) on, and in the spaces between which, notes are placed so as to indicate pitch. Also STAVE. 1662.

2. b. Mr. Cowley had found out that no kind of S. is proper for a Heroick Poem DRYDEN.

III. (Pl. always *staffs*.) **1.** *Mil.* A body of officers appointed to assist a general, or other commanding officer, in the control of an army, brigade, regiment, etc., or in performing special duties (as the *medical s.*). *General s.*, a body of officers controlling an army from headquarters under the commander-in-chief. [App. of continental Teut. origin, and prob. developed from the sense 'baton' (= 6 above).] 1781. **2.** *gen.* A body of persons employed, under the direction of a manager or chief, in the work of an establishment or the execution of some undertaking (e.g. a newspaper, hospital, government survey); *esp.* the body of servants (*domestic s.*) employed in any establishment 1837.

attrib. and *Comb.* **a.** In sense 'of or belonging to a military staff', as *s. appointment, pay, surgeon, uniform*; **s. cap**, a flat-topped cap with a peak, such as forms part of various uniforms; **s. college**, a college in which officers are trained for s. appointments; **s. corps**, a body of officers and men organized to assist the commanding officer and his s. in various special departments; in India, a corps formed in each of the three presidencies to supply officers for service; **s.-ride**, a name for exercises on the ground without troops, as a means of teaching strategy. **b.** In the Navy used to designate a senior class of officers, as *s. captain*, etc. **c.** Special: **s.-angle** *Plastering*, a piece of wood fixed to the external angle of the two upright sides of a wall for floating the plaster to, and for defending the angle against accidents; **-head**, the upper end of a s., carved, tipped with metal, etc.; the top of the tripod which supports a theodolite, etc.; **-man**, a workman employed in silk-throwing; **sling**, a sling the strings of which are attached to the end of a staff (*Obs.* exc. *Hist.*); **-tree**, the genus *Celastrus*; **-vine**, *Celastrus scandens* of U.S.

Staff (stɑf), *sb.*[2] 1892. [Origin obsc.] A building material consisting of plaster mixed with fibre, used for temporary ornamental work.

Staff (stɑf), *v.* 1859. [f. STAFF *sb.*[1]] *trans.* To provide with a staff of officers, teachers, servants, etc.

Staffette (stæfe·t). *Obs.* exc. *Hist.* 1545. [ad. It. *staffetta*, dim. of *staffa* stirrup.] A mounted courier. Cf. ESTAFETTE.

†Staffier. 1532. [ad. It. *staffiero*, *-ere*, f. *staffa* stirrup, a. OHG. *stapho*; see STEP *v.*] An attendant; a footman -1734.

†Sta·ffish, *a.* 1500. [f. STAFF *sb.*[1] + -ISH.] **a.** Rigid, stiff, hard. **b.** *fig.* Stubborn, unmanageable. -1802.

Staff officer. 1702. **†1.** A high officer of the royal household, or minister of state, bearing a white staff. See STAFF *sb.*[1] I. 6. -1728. **2.** *Mil.* **†a.** A non-commissioned officer -1727. **b.** An officer doing duty with the general or departmental staff of an army, division, or brigade 1777. **c.** In the U.S. navy, an officer not exercising military command 1891.

Stafford (stæ·fəɹd). 1460. Name of the county town of Staffordshire, England; used *attrib.* in †*S. blue* (a cloth), †*S. law* ('club law'). So **Sta·ffordshire,** the distinctive name of a kind of earthenware and porcelain 1784.

Stag (stæg), *sb.* ME. [prob. repr. OE. **stacga* (*stagga*); cf. *docga* dog, *frocga* frog. Properly, a male animal in its prime.] **1.** The male of a deer, esp. the red deer; spec. a hart or male deer of the fifth year. **b.** In the names of various species of the genus *Cervus*, as *Axis S.*, an Indian deer (*C. axis*), *Carolina S.*, the N. Amer. Wapiti (*C. canadensis*) 1859. **2.** *north.* and *Sc.* A young horse, esp. one unbroken ME. **3.** An animal castrated when full-grown. **a.** A bull; more fully *bull s.* Now *dial.*, *Sc.*, and *Austr.* 1680. **b.** A boar, hog, or ram. *dial.* 1784. **4.** Applied to the male of various birds; *esp.* a cock. Also *spec.* in *Cockfighting*, a cock less than one year old. 1730. **5.** *slang.* An informer; esp. in phr. *to turn s.* 1725. **b.** A shilling 1857. **c.** *U.S. slang.* A man who goes to a social gathering unaccompanied by a female partner; phr. *to go stag*; also = *stag-party*; attrib., as *s.-dance*, *-party*, etc. 1848. **6.** *Comm. slang.* A person who applies for an allocation of shares in a joint-stock concern solely with a view to selling immediately at a profit 1845. **7.** *attrib.* and *Comb.* **a.** quasi-*adj.* = male, as *s.-bird*, *-hog*, *-moose*, etc. 1606. **b.** (See 5 c.)

Comb.: **s.-evil**, of a horse, lockjaw; **s. fern**, = staghorn fern (see STAG-HORN 2c); **-hafted**, **-handled** *adjs.*, furnished with a haft or handle of stag-horn; **-hog** = BABIROUSSA; **†-match** (*Cockfighting*), a match for young cocks.

Stag (stæg), *v.* 1796. [f. STAG *sb.*] **1.** *slang.* **a.** *trans.* To observe; to take particular notice of; to watch; also, to find out or discover by observation, to detect. Also *absol.* or *intr.* **b.** *intr.* To turn informer; to inform *against* 1839. **2.** *Comm. slang.* To deal in shares as a stag (see STAG *sb.* 6.) 1845.

Sta·g-bee·tle. 1681. A beetle of the genus *Lucanus*, the males of which have large denticulated mandibles resembling the horns of a stag; esp. *L. cervus*, and, in U.S., *L. elaphus*.

Stage (stēɪdʒ), *sb.* ME. [ad. OF. *estage*, (mod.F. *étage*) = It. *staggio* station:—pop. L. **staticum*, f. L. *stare* to stand.] **I.** Standing-place; something to stand upon. **1.** Each of the portions into which the height of a structure is divided; a horizontal partition; *esp.* a story or floor of a building. **b.** A shelf; *spec.* a tier of shelves for plants; *Geol.* two or more sets of beds; *U.S.* a level (of water) 1465. **†2.** Station, position, seat, esp. with reference to relative height; each of a number of positions or stations one above the other -1625. **†3.** A degree or step in the 'ladder' of virtue, honour, etc.; a 'step' on Fortune's wheel -1634. **4.** A raised floor, platform, scaffold. **a.** A floor raised above the level of the ground for the exhibition of something to be viewed by spectators. Now *rare* or *Obs.* ME. **†b.** A scaffold for execution or exposure in the pillory -1781. **c.** A scaffold for workmen and their tools, materials, etc.; also, each of the levels of scaffolding 1440. **d.** A platform, etc., for drying fish 1535. **e.** A platform used as a gangway, landing place, support or stand for materials, etc. 1773. **f.** A raised plate, ledge, or shelf to support an object, slide, etc., in a microscope or other instrument 1797. **5.** The platform in a theatre upon which spectacles, plays, etc., are exhibited; esp. a raised platform with its scenery upon which a theatrical performance takes place 1551.

3. From the highest S. of Honour, to the lowest staire of disgrace 1622. **4. a.** *Haml.* v. ii. 389. **5.** Then to the well-trod s. anon, If Jonsons learned Sock be on MILT. *fig.* All the world's a s., And all the men and women, meerely Players SHAKS. Phr. *To go on the s.*, to take up the profession of an actor. *To bring* (a person) *on* or *to the s.*, to present (him) as a character in a play. *To bring, put* (an opera, a tragedy, etc.) *on the s.*, to produce (it) in public. *To take the s.*, of an actor, to walk with dignity across the stage after concluding an impressive speech; hence, to assume the chief part, as in a play.

II. Division of a journey or process. **1.** A place in which rest is taken on a journey; *esp.* a regular stopping place on a stage-coach route where horses are changed and travellers taken up and set down 1603. **2.** As much of a journey as is performed without stopping for rest, a change of horses, etc.; each of the several portions into which a road is divided for coaching or posting purposes; the distance travelled between two places of rest on a road 1603. **b.** Short for STAGE-COACH 1671. **3.** A period of a journey through a subject, life, course of action, etc. 1608. **4.** A period of development, a degree of progress, a step in a process 1818. **b.** *Med.* A definite period in the development of a disease, marked by a specific group of symptoms 1747.

2. We proceeded leisurely and by easy stages 1898. **b.** 'Tis like a parcel sent you by the s. COWPER. **3.** The love that cheers life's latest s. COWPER. **4.** It is necessary that at some s. of the Bill the consent of the Crown should be signified 1863. **b.** I found him in the last s. of a dropsy 1780.

attrib. and *Comb.*: **s.-box**, each of the boxes over the proscenium of a theatre; **-craft**, that part of the art of dramatic composition which is concerned with the conditions of representation on the stage; **s. direction**, a direction inserted in a written or printed play where it is thought necessary to indicate the appropriate action, etc.; **-door**, the entrance to that part of a theatre used by the actors; **-fright**, extreme nervousness experienced by an actor on the stage, esp. on his first appearance; hence *transf.*; **-name**, a professional name assumed by an actor; **-property** = PROPERTY *sb.* 3; **-setting**, the disposition of the persons of a play and the accessories on the stage; **-struck** *a.*, smitten with love for the stage or drama or with the desire to become an actor; **†-wagon**, one of the wagons belonging to an organized system of conveyance for heavy goods and passengers by road; **-wait**, a delay or hitch in the course of a theatrical performance; also *transf.*; **-whisper**, a conventional whisper used on the stage, purposely made audible to the spectators; hence any very audible whisper. Hence **Sta·gery**, exhibition on the s.; s. arrangements or contrivances.

Stage (stēɪdʒ), *v.* ME. [f. STAGE *sb.*] **†1.** To build, erect. ME. only. **2.** To furnish with a stage or staging; freq. with *about*. Now *rare* or *Obs.* 1506. **3.** To put (a person) into a play; to satirize in drama; to represent (a character, incident) on the stage. Sometimes in phr. *to s. to the crowd* or *show*. 1601. **b.** To put (a play, etc.) upon the stage 1879. **4.** To put (plants) on a stage; to exhibit (plants, etc.) at a show. Also *absol.* 1850. **5.** *intr.* To travel by stage or stage-coach; to journey *over* by stages 1695. **6.** Of a play: To lend itself to presentation; esp. *to s. well, badly*, etc. 1924.

3. *Ant. & Cl.* III. xiii. 30. **c.** *U.S.* To arrange to take place dramatically; to make a setting for 1924. **5.** Riding, driving, or staging to London COLERIDGE.

Stage-coach. 1658. [STAGE *sb.* II. 2.] A coach that runs daily or on specified days between two places for the conveyance of parcels, passengers, etc. Hence **Stage-coachman**, the driver of a stage-coach.

Stage-manager. 1817. One whose office it is to superintend the production and performance of a play, and to regulate the arrangements of the stage. So **Stage-manage** *v.*, **Stage-management.**

Stage play. 1513. A dramatic performance; also, a dramatic composition adapted for representation on the stage. **b.** Play-acting 1872. So **Stage-player** (1556), = PLAYER 2, **-playing** (1597).

Stager (stēɪ·dʒəɹ). 1570. [f. STAGE *sb.* + -ER[1]. See N.E.D.] **1.** *Old s.*: one who has become graduated or qualified by long experience; a veteran, an old hand. Also occas. of animals. **b.** Hence *stager* simply, and with other adjs., as *cunning, sly*. Also (rarely) *young s.*, one of small experience, a beginner. 1664. **2.** A stage-player. *Obs.* exc. *arch.* 1580. **3.** A stage-coach or stage-coach horse 1852.

Staggard (stæ·gāɹd). *arch.* late ME. [f. STAG *sb.* + -ARD.] A stag in its fourth year.

Stagger (stæ·gəɹ), *sb.* 1577. [f. STAGGER *v.*] **1.** An act of staggering; a tottering or reeling motion of the body as if about to fall, as through feebleness, tripping, giddiness, or intoxication. **b.** In a biplane, etc., the amount of advance of the entering edge of an upper wing over that of a lower 1915. **2.** *pl.* (const. as *sing.*) A name for various diseases affecting domestic animals, of which a staggering gait is a symptom 1577.

1. *fig.* I will throw thee from my care for euer Into

the staggers, and the carelesse lapse Of youth and ignorance SHAKS. **2.** Phr. (*To have*) *the staggers*, inability to walk steadily.

attrib.: **s. bush** *U.S.*, the shrub *Andromeda mariana*; **-grass**, the atamasco-lily, *Zephyranthes Atamasco*; **staggerwort**, the ragwort, *Senecio Jacobæa*.

Stagger (stæ·gəɹ), *v.* 1530. [Altered f. dial. *stacker* vb. to reel, a. ON. *stakra* to stagger, freq. of *staka* to push, stagger.] **I.** *intr.* **1.** Of a person or animal: To sway involuntarily from side to side when trying to stand or walk erect; to totter or reel as if about to fall; to walk with a swaying movement. **b.** Said of the legs or feet 1665. **c.** As the result of a blow or encounter, or of carrying a heavy load. Const. *under*. 1547. **d.** *transf.* Of a ship: To move unsteadily and with difficulty; esp. *under* a press of sail 1840. **2.** *fig.* To begin to doubt or waver in an argument, opinion, or purpose; to become less confident or determined; to hesitate or waver *at*. Now *rare*. 1533. **b.** Of purpose, opinion, faith, etc. 1617. **3.** Of an army, line of battle, etc.: To waver, become unsteady, give way 1544. **4.** Of a material thing: To sway or rock from side to side; to shake, rock, or swing violently; to totter 1530.

1. Hee maketh them to s. like a drunken man *Job* xii. 25. **c.** The bearers s. under the heavy coffin 1874. **d.** We are staggering along under all sail 1853. **2.** If you shal haue faith, and s. not N.T. (Rheims) *Matt.* xxi. 21. **b.** At whose immensity Even soaring fancy staggers SHELLEY.

II. *trans.* **1.** To cause (a person or animal) to reel or totter, esp. from a blow 1593. **2.** *fig.* **a.** To bewilder, perplex, nonplus; to render helpless by a shock of amazement (or *occas.* horror). In *pass.* to be perplexed or astonished *at*. 1556. **b.** To shake the stability of (a country, a condition of things) 1613. **c.** To shake, unsettle, cause to waver or falter (a person's faith, opinion, purpose, etc.) 1617. **d.** To cause (a person) to falter or waver (*in* his faith or purpose) 1627. †**e.** To throw doubt upon (a doctrine) –1833. **3.** To cause to waver, throw into confusion (troops) 1721. **4.** *Mech.* To arrange in zig-zag order, or in positions alternately on either side of a median line 1856. **b.** To arrange in such a way that one part is farther forward than another; *spec.* cf. STAGGER *sb.* 1 b. 1909.

1. *Rich. II.* v. v. 110. **c.** Phr. *To s. belief*: to be incredible. **e.** He .. staggereth the immortality of the soul SIR T. BROWNE. **4. c.** To arrange (working hours) so that some businesses open and close at different times from others, or so that employees enter and leave in batches at intervals instead of all at the same time (orig. *U.S.*) 1918. Hence **Sta·ggerer** (*lit.* and *fig.*).

Stag-headed, *a.* 1683. **1.** Of an animal: Having a head like that of a stag. **2.** Of a tree or forest of trees: Having the topmost branches bare and withered 1769.

2. Some oaks are old and s. at 100 years 1882.

Stag-horn. Also **stag's horn.** 1663. [STAG *sb.*] **1. a.** *pl.* The horns of a stag. **b.** *sing.* The horn of a stag as a material. **2.** In the names of plants. **a.** The American or Virginian sumach, *Rhus typhina*. More fully *stag('s horn tree, sumach*. 1753. **b.** A kind of moss, esp. *Lycopodium clavatum*. More fully *stag's horn* (also *staghorn*) *moss*. 1741. **c.** A fern of the genus *Platycerium*. In full *staghorn fern*. 1882. **3.** In the names of insects, etc. 1816.

3. The s. capricorn beetle (*Prionus cervicornis*, F.) in America 1816. Among the true stony corals are the S. corals (*Madrepora cervicornis*, *prolifera*, and *palmata*) 1884. Hence **Stag-horned** *a.* (*a*) epithet of a beetle; (*b*) = STAG-HEADED *a.* 2.

Staghound (stæ·ghaund). 1707. [f. STAG *sb.* + HOUND *sb.*] = DEER-HOUND.

Stagiary (stē¹·dʒiări), *sb.*[1] 1868. [ad. med.L. *stagiarius*, f. *stagium* term of residence of a canon, ad. OF. *estage*; see STAGE *sb.*] *Eccl. Hist.* A canon residentiary.

Stagiary (stē¹·dʒiări), *sb.*[2] and *a.* 1836. [ad. F. *stagiaire*, f. after med.L. *stagiarius*; see prec.] **A.** *sb.* A French law student. **B.** *adj.* In *s. school*, a school in which, according to the French law of 1850, assistants could be employed who had no certificate of capacity, but only a certificate of three years' service (F. *stage*).

Staging (stē¹·dʒiŋ), *vbl. sb.* Also †**stageing.** ME. [f. STAGE *sb.* and *v.* + -ING[1].] **1.** *concr.* **a.** A temporary platform or structure of posts and boards for support; scaffolding. **b.** *Arch.* The stages of a buttress collectively 1865. **2.** The action, process, or art of putting a play on the stage; stage-setting 1884. **3.** The business of running or managing stage-coaches; the action of travelling by stage-coach or by stages (chiefly *Anglo-Ind.*) 1850.

2. The s. of a play is in itself a work of true art 1884.

Stagirite (stæ·dʒĭrəit). 1595. [ad. L. *Stagirites* (also *Stagerites*), ad. Gr. Σταγειρίτης, f. Στάγειρος, also Στάγειρα neut. pl.; see -ITE.] A native or inhabitant of Stagira, a city of Macedonia; *spec.* the philosopher Aristotle, who was born there.

Welcome, great S., and teach me now All I was born to know COWLEY.

Stagnancy (stæ·gnănsi). 1659. [f. STAGNANT *a.*; see -ANCY.] †**1.** The condition of being stagnant or without motion, flow, or circulation. **2.** Anything stagnant 1681.

Stagnant (stæ·gnănt), *a.* 1666. [ad. L. *stagnantem*, *stagnare*; see STAGNATE *v.*] †**1.** Of a fluid: That is at rest in a vessel –1721. **2.** Not flowing or running, of water, air, etc.; without motion or current, as a pool. Often involving unwholesomeness. 1669. **3.** *fig.* Void of activity, excitement, or interest 1749.

3. Immur'd, and buried in perpetual Sloth, That gloomy Slumber of the s. Soul JOHNSON. Trade is s. CARLYLE. Hence **Sta·gnantly** *adv.*

†**Sta·gnate,** *a.* 1706. [ad. L. *stagnatus*; see next and -ATE[2].] = prec. –1845.

The s. sea Under the torrid zone HOOD.

Stagnate (stæ·gnē¹t), *v.* 1669. [f. ppl. stem of L. *stagnare*, f. *stagnum* pool; see -ATE[3].] **1.** *intr.* To be or become stagnant; to cease to flow, to stand without motion or current; *transf.* of a person or people: to subside into a stagnant mode of existence. **2.** *trans.* To cause to be or become stagnant 1693. **3.** To astonish. *dial.* and *U.S.* 1784.

1. The Air that stagnated in the Shaft 1691. The blood tends to accumulate and to s. in the capillaries and veins 1878. *fig.* Nothing tends more to the corruption of science than to suffer it to s. BURKE. **2.** We have neither bogs nor marshes to s. our waters 1750. *fig.* His credit, the life and blood of his trade, is stagnated DE FOE.

Stagnation (stægnē¹·ʃən). 1665. [f. prec.; see -ATION.] **1.** The condition of being stagnant; an instance of this. **2.** *fig.* Unhealthy absence of activity, energy, etc. 1711.

1. If the water runneth, it holdeth clear..; but s. turneth it into a noisome puddle 1677. They are subject to a S. of blood 1707. **2.** The dulness and s. of a French country town 1907.

Stagy, stagey (stē¹·dʒi), *a.* 1860. [f. STAGE *sb.* + -Y[1].] **1.** Of or pertaining to the stage; theatrical in appearance, manner, style, etc. (Chiefly in a depreciatory sense.) **2.** Of a seal or its skin: Out of condition from undergoing the change of coat 1885.

1. A stage hero in stagey heroics MEREDITH. Fechter, the tragedian,—an agreeable man, and not at all stagey LONGF. Hence **Sta·gily** *adv.* **Sta·giness.**

Stagyrite, erron. f. STAGIRITE.

Stahlian (stā·liăn), *a.* and *sb.* 1790. [f. name of G. E. *Stahl*, a German chemist (1660–1734) + -IAN.] **A.** Pertaining to Stahl or his doctrines, esp. his theory of vital action and of disease. **B.** A follower of Stahl; an animist.

‖**Stahlhelm**: see *Steel Helmet* s.v. STEEL *sb.*

Staid (stē¹d), *a.* 1541. [adj. use of *stayed*, STAY *v.*] **1.** Of beliefs, institutions, etc.: Fixed, permanent; settled, unchanging. Of a person's gaze: Fixed, set. Now *rare*. †**b.** Of persons: Settled in faith, purpose, etc. –1812. **2.** Settled in character; of grave or sedate deportment; dignified and serious in demeanour or conduct; free from flightiness or caprice 1557. **b.** Characterized by or indicating sedateness 1567. **3.** Of the intellect, etc.: Sober, steady, well-regulated; free from extravagance or caprice 1555.

1. His s. opinion 1863. **2.** By his stayed life God hath bene glorified NORTH. Ore laid with black s. Wisdoms hue MILT. A s. and quiet palfrey SCOTT. **3.** A s. and considerate understanding 1870. Hence **Stai·d·ly** *adv.*, **-ness.**

Stail(e, var. ff. STALE *sb. dial.* handle.

Stain (stē¹n), *sb.* 1563. [f. STAIN *v.*] †**1.** The action of staining; pollution, disgrace –1607. **2.** A discoloration produced by absorption of or contact with foreign matter; usually, one that penetrates below the surface and is not easily removable 1583. **b.** A mark or discoloration on the skin; a blotch or sore 1595. **c.** *transf.* A spot or patch of colour different from the ground. Common in *Nat. Hist.* 1704. †**d.** A slight tinge *of*. SHAKS. **3.** *fig.* (Often in phrases like *to wash*, *purge a s.*) **a.** A grave blemish on a person's reputation; a mark of infamy or disgrace; a stigma 1591. **b.** A person or thing that causes disgrace. Now *rare* or *Obs.* 1589. †**c.** One who eclipses or casts into the shade –1605. **4.** A dye or colouring matter used in staining. **a.** A thin liquid preparation used to colour wood, etc. 1758. **b.** A dye or pigment used to render minute and transparent structures visible, or to differentiate tissue elements by colouring, for microscopic purposes; or to produce specific microchemical reactions 1880.

1. *Timon* v. i. 176. **2.** Staynes in thinne silkes and woollen clothe 1583. **b.** You do remember This staine [a mole] vpon her? SHAKS. **c.** Swift trouts, diversified with crimson stains POPE. **d.** You haue some staine of souldier in you SHAKS. **3. a.** The probable s. on their birth FREEMAN. **b.** Staine to thy countrymen, thou hear'st thy doom SHAKS. **c.** Staine to all Nimphs, more louely then a man SHAKS.

Stain (stē¹n), *v.* late ME. [Aphetic a. OF. *desteign-*, *desteindre* (mod.F. *déteindre*), f. *des-* DIS- + *teindre* to dye; see DISTAIN *v.* Some of the Eng. senses are difficult to account for.] †**1.** *trans.* To deprive of colour –1589. †**b.** Of the sun, etc.: To deprive (feebler luminaries) of their lustre. Also *fig.* of a person or thing: To eclipse. –1649. †**c.** To obscure the lustre of –1657. †**2.** *intr.* To lose colour or lustre –1614. **3.** Of something dyed or coloured: To impart its colour to (something in contact). Also in wider use (e.g. said of a chemical reagent), to alter the colour of (something to which it is applied) 1440. **b.** *transf.* Of the blood: To suffuse with colour. Also *pass.*, to be (naturally) spotted or streaked with colour. 1557. **c.** To absorb colouring matter, take a stain 1877. **4.** *trans.* To damage or blemish the appearance of (something) by colouring a part of its surface; to discolour by spots or streaks of blood, dirt, or other foreign matter not easily removed. In poetic use occas.: To colour, defile (a river) with blood. late ME. **b.** *Hunting.* = FOIL *v.*[1] 2. 1798. **5.** *fig.* **a.** To defile or corrupt morally; to taint with guilt or vice 1446. **b.** To be a permanent reproach to, inflict a stigma upon; to blemish, soil (a person's reputation, honour, conscience, etc.). Also *intr.* of the conscience: †To suffer stain. 1513. †**c.** *To s.* (a person's) *blood*: (*a*) to prove (him) of base descent; (*b*) to cause 'corruption of blood' (see CORRUPTION 2). –1766. †**6.** To ornament with coloured designs or patterns –1615. **7.** To colour (esp. textile fabrics, paper, wood, stone) by the application of pigment that more or less penetrates the substance instead of forming a coating on the surface, or by means of chemical reagents. In microscopical and histological research: To colour (tissues, etc.) with some pigment so as to render the structure clearly visible. 1655. **b.** To colour (glass) with transparent colours. Also to depict in stained glass (*rare*). 1797.

1. b. O voice that doth the Thrush in shrilnesse staine SIDNEY. **2.** Suns of the world may staine when heauens sun staineth SHAKS. **3.** The rouge on her neck had stained her collar 1901. [Flint] stained ferruginous from adjacent red clay 1912. **4.** The walls were stained and discoloured DICKENS. **5. a.** The British kings were stained with every vice 1847. **b.** I have..stain'd the glory of my Royal House DRYDEN. A reputation which his later cruelties might s., but could not efface 1879. **7.** There were rolls of vellum or papyrus, stained saffron-colour at the back 1891.

Stained (stē¹nd), *ppl. a.* late ME. [f. STAIN *v.* + -ED[1].] In the senses of the vb.; freq. in comb. with a prefixed sb., as BLOOD-STAINED.

S. glass, transparent coloured glass, formed into decorative mosaics, used in windows (esp. of churches); also, less correctly, glass which has been decorated with vitrified pigments; so *s. window*.

Stainer (stē¹·nəɹ). late ME. [f. STAIN *v.*; see -ER[1].] One whose employment is staining; one who colours wood, etc., with pigments which penetrate below the surface. See also PAINTER-STAINER, PAPER-STAINER.

Stainless (stē¹·nlės), *a.* 1586. [f. STAIN *sb.* + -LESS.] Without stain, spot, or blemish; in trade use, that does not become stained.

The s. mirror of the lake SHELLEY. The very care

he took to keep his name S. CRABBE. Hence **Stai·n·less-ly** *adv.*, **-ness.**

Stair (stēᵊɹ). [OE. *stǽger* :—OTeut. type **staigri*, f. **staig-*: **stīg-* to climb; see STY *v.*[1]] **1.** An ascending series or 'flight' of steps leading from one level to another, esp. from one floor to another in a house; a staircase. **b.** *fig.* A means of ascending in rank, power, moral excellence, etc. 1570. †**c.** An ascending series, scale. SIR T. BROWNE. **2.** One of a succession of steps leading from one floor of a building to another 1530. †**b.** *fig.* A step or degree in a (metaphorical) ascent or in a scale of dignity –1640. **3.** *collect. pl.* (of sense 2) = sense 1. Also, in generalized sense, the steps of staircases. late ME. †**b.** construed as *sing.* A flight of steps, a staircase –1830. **c.** *fig.*; *esp.* applied to the means by which a person rises in rank or power. Now *rare* or *Obs.* 1576. **4.** *pl.* (rarely †*sing.*). A landing-stage, esp. on the Thames in and near London 1517.

1. A S. of 20 Steps 1730. 2. I ascended the same by two hundred and forty staires of marble 1617. b. The elder he growes, hee is a stayer lower from God EARLE. 3. *Pair, flight of stairs*: see PAIR *sb.* II. 1 b, FLIGHT *sb.*[1] 6. *Back stairs*: see BACKSTAIRS. *Above stairs*: on or to the ground floor or upper floors of a house. *Below stairs*: on or to a lower floor, esp. below the ground floor; hence, in the servants' quarters. *Down, up stairs*: see DOWNSTAIRS, UPSTAIRS. b. It is a good way to any bed-chamber, and the stairs is steep 1776. 4. Just opposite, on the riverside, were the Millbank stairs 1904.

Comb., as *s.-carpet*; **s.-pit** *Mining*, a shallow shaft or staple in a mine fitted with a ladder or steps; **-rod,** a metal or wooden rod, fixed in eyes, to secure a stair-carpet in the bend of each step; **-step,** one of the steps in a flight of stairs.

Staircase (stēᵊ·ɹkēⁱs). 1624. [f. STAIR + CASE *sb.*[2]] **1.** Orig., the inclosure of a flight of stairs; now usu. a flight (or series of flights) of stairs, with their supporting framework, balusters, etc. **2.** *Phys.* A continuous series of responses to nerve stimuli 1882.

1. Who lived in the same s. with me at Christchurch WESLEY.

Comb.: **s.-shell,** a shell of the genus *Solarium*, any member of the family *Solariidæ*.

Stai·r-foot. Also rarely **stairs-, stair's-.** 1470. The foot of a staircase; the level space in front of the lowest step of a flight of stairs.

Stai·r-head, stai·rhead. 1534. The level space at the top of a staircase or flight of stairs.

Stairway (stēᵊ·ɹwēⁱ). 1767. [f. STAIR *sb.* + WAY *sb.*] A way up a flight of stairs, a staircase.

He walked up the grim s. of the hotel 1872.

Staithe (stēⁱð). Now *local.* Also **staith.** [In sense 1, repr. OE. *stæþ* :—OTeut. **staþo*, f. **sta-*; see STAND *v.* In senses 2 and 3 the word prob. represents ON. *stǫð* fem. (:—**staþwō*) landing-stage.] †**1.** The land bordering on water, a bank, shore –ME. **2.** A landing-stage, wharf; esp. a waterside depôt for coals brought from the collieries for shipment, furnished with staging and shoots for loading vessels ME. **3.** An embankment 1698. Hence **Stai·th(s)man,** one who superintends the shipping of coal.

Stake (stēⁱk), *sb.*[1] [OE. *staca*, f. **stak-* ablaut-var. of **stek-* to pierce, thrust in; see STICK *v.*] **1.** A stout stick or post, usually of wood, with a pointed end for driving into the ground; used e.g. to mark a boundary or site, to support a plant, etc. **b.** A post upon which persons were bound for execution, esp. by burning. Hence *the s.* = the punishment of death by burning. ME. **c.** The post to which a bull or bear was fastened to be baited 1546. **d.** A post pointed at both ends for use in military defensive work ME. **2.** *collect. sing.* Stakes used as a framework or support in fencing and hedging; esp. as a basis for the intertwining, wattling, or plashing of brushwood or other materials 1457. **3.** *techn.* **a.** A small anvil used by metal workers, esp. one with a tang for fitting into a socket on a bench 1660. **b.** *Leather-manuf.* A wooden stake in the top of which is set a broad steel blade over which the skins are drawn to soften and stretch them 1853. **c.** Each of the stanchions or posts which fit into sockets or staples on a trolley, wagon or boat to prevent the load from slipping off 1875. **d.** *Basket-making.* Each of the longest foundation-rods of a basket or the like 1911. **4.** In the Mormon Church: A territorial division; the see or jurisdiction of a Mormon bishop. [perh. suggested by Isa. liv. 2, 3.] 1882.

1. b. Curse Miscreant, when thou comst to the s. SHAKS. c. Let vs do so: for we are at the s., And bayed about with many Enemies SHAKS.

attrib. and *Comb.*: **s.-boat,** a boat moored or otherwised fixed to serve as a starting-point or mark for racing boats; **-driver** *U.S.*, the bittern, *Botaurus mugitans*; **-head,** in *Rope-making*, a s. with wooden pins in the upper side to keep the strands apart; **-presidency,** the presidency of a Mormon s. (see sense 4).

Stake (stēⁱk), *sb.*[2] 1540. [perh. f. STAKE *v.*[2]] **1.** That which is placed at hazard; esp. a sum of money, etc. deposited or guaranteed, to be taken by the winner of a game, race, contest, etc. **2.** In certain phrases: The condition of being staked 1592. **3.** *pl.* in *Horse-racing, Coursing*, etc., the sums of money staked or subscribed by the owners who enter horses or dogs for a contest, the whole to be received as the prize by the owner of the winner or divided among the owners of the animals 'placed'. Hence in *sing.* (cf. SWEEPSTAKE) a race for money thus staked or subscribed. Also in *pl.* with defining words as the designation of particular races or classes of races in which the sum of money staked is the prize as dist. from a Plate, Cup, or the like 1696.

1. Our landlord here shall hold stakes SCOTT. *fig.* The Sword, Which for no less a S. than Life you Draw DRYDEN.

Phrases. *To have a s. in* (an event, concern, etc.): to have something to gain or lose by the turn of events; esp. in *to have a s. in the country* (said of those who hold landed property). *To draw stakes*, to withdraw what is staked as a wager, etc. 2. †*To be, lay down* or *set* (a thing) *at s.* or *at the s.* *To be at s., to have at s.*; I see my reputation is at s. My fame is shrowdly gored SHAKS. 3. *Produce stakes*: (*a*) in *Horse-racing*, a race in which the runners must be the offspring of horses named and described at the time of entry; a produce race; (*b*) in *Coursing*, a race for puppies, i.e. for dogs of from one to two years of age; also called *Puppy stakes*. *Subscription stakes*: in *Horse-racing*, a race for which subscribers of a fixed amount annually have the right to enter one or more horses.

Comb.: **s.-holder,** one who holds the s. or stakes of a wager, etc.

Stake (stēⁱk), *v.*[1] ME. [f. STAKE *sb.*[1]] **1.** *trans.* To mark (land) with stakes. Also with *off, out.* **2.** To protect, support, or obstruct with stakes. Also, to shut *in, off, out, up* with stakes. 1500. **b.** To put a stake or stakes to (a plant) 1664. **3.** To secure with or as with a stake 1544. **4.** To impale (a person) on a stake. Also with *up.* Also, to transfix and fasten down (a person) with a stake. 1577. **b.** *pass.* Of a horse, etc.: To be injured by impalement on a hedge or fence stake. Also *refl.*; hence *trans.*, to cause a horse to stake himself. 1687.

2. Order was giuen that the camp should be entrenched and staked SAVILE. On the bank of loose stones above the mud and stakes that staked the tide out DICKENS. 3. Our horses were unsaddled and staked on the open plain MAYNE REID. *fig.* I haue a soale of Lead So stakes me to the ground, I cannot moue SHAKS. 4. Stak'd through the body like a paltry Thief 1786.

Stake (stēⁱk), *v.*[2] 1530. [perh. a. Du. *staken* to fix, place.] **1.** *intr.* To wager, hazard money, on the event of a game or contest. Now felt as absol. use of sense 3. **2.** trans. *To s. down*: to deposit (a sum of money) as a wager or stake on the result of a game or contest. Also *absol.* 1565. **3.** To put at hazard (a sum of money, an article of value, etc.) upon the cast of dice, the result of a competition or game, the event of a contingency, etc.; to wager 1591. **4.** *fig.* To risk the loss of, to hazard 1670.

2. *Gra.* Weele play..for a thousand ducats. *Ner.* What and s. downe? SHAKS. 3. He..No lesser of her Honour confident..stakes this Ring SHAKS. 4. Mary had staked all on her union with Darnley 1874.

Stalactic (stălæ·ktik), *a.* 1756. [ad. Gr. σταλακτικός, f. σταλακ-, σταλάσσειν to let drop, to drop, drip.] Deposited by dripping water; pertaining to or consisting of stalactites. So **Stala·ctical** *a.* (now *rare*) 1714.

Stalactite (stæ·lăktəit, (*U.S.*) stălæ·kteit). 1677. [Anglicized f. next.] **1.** An icicle-like formation of calcium carbonate, depending from the roof or sides of a cavern and produced by the dropping of waters which have percolated through, and partially dissolved, the overlying limestone. **b.** A similar formation of other material 1801. **2.** A general term for limestone found in this formation 1796.

1. b. Delicate stalactites and stalagmites of lava 1890. 2. White crusts of s. 1908. Hence **Stala·ctiform, Stalacti·tiform** *adjs.* having the form of a s.

‖ **Stalactites** (stælăktəi·tīz). Now *rare. Pl.* stalactitæ (-tī). 1681. [mod.L., f. Gr. σταλακτός dropping, dripping, after names of stones in *-ites*; see -ITE[1].] = prec.

Stalactitic (stælăkti·tik), *a.* 1770. [f. STALACTITE + -IC.] **1.** Having the form or structure of a stalactite; resembling or pertaining to stalactites. **2.** Covered with, containing or consisting of, stalactites 1845. So **Stalacti·tical** *a.*

‖ **Stalagma** (stălæ·gmă). 1693. [mod.L., a. Gr. στάλαγμα drop, drip, f. σταλακτ-, σταλάσσειν; see STALACTIC *a.*] **1.** A distilled liquor (*rare*). **2.** = next 2. 1903.

Stalagmite (stæ·lăgməit, *U.S.* stălæ·gməit). 1681. [a. mod.L. *stalagmites*, f. Gr. στάλαγμα STALAGMA.] **1.** An incrustation or deposit, more or less like an inverted stalactite, on the floor of a cavern, formed by the dropping from the roof of some material in solution. **2.** Limestone deposited in this manner 1815.

attrib.: **s. marble,** onyx marble. Hence **Stalagmi·tic, -al** *adjs.* formed in the same way as a s., composed of stalagmites or having their form or character. **Stalagmi·tically** *adv.*

Stale (stēⁱl), *sb.*[1] Now *dial.* [OE. *stalu*, related by ablaut to the synonymous *stela* STEAL *sb.*[1]] **1.** †Each of the two upright sides of a ladder. Also (now *dial.*) a rung or step of a ladder; the stave of a rack in a stable. **2.** A handle, esp. a long, slender handle, as the handle of a rake. Also, the stem of a pipe, etc. ME. **3.** The stem of an arrow or spear 1553.

Stale (stēⁱl), *sb.*[2] 1440. [prob. a. AF. *estale*, *estal*, applied to a pigeon used to entice a hawk into the net. Of Teut. origin; prob. from the root of OE. *steall* place (STALL *sb.*[1]), *stellan* to place.] **1.** A decoy-bird; a living bird used to entice other birds of its own species, or birds of prey, into a snare or net. Also, a stuffed bird or figure of a bird used for the same purpose. (Now *dial.*) †**2.** *transf.* and *fig.* A deceptive means of allurement; a person or thing held out as a lure or bait to entrap a person –1692. †**3.** A person who acts as a decoy; esp. the accomplice of a thief or sharper –1633. †**4.** More fully *common s.*: a prostitute of the lowest class, employed as a decoy by thieves –1641. †**5.** = STALKING-HORSE 2, 2 b. –1774. †**6.** A lover or mistress whose devotion is turned into ridicule for the amusement of a rival or rivals –1635.

1. Like vnto the fowlers, that by their stales draw other birdes into their nets NORTH. 2. *Temp.* IV. i. 187. 4. *Much Ado* II. ii. 26. 5. Had he none else to make a s. but me? SHAKS. 6. *Com. Err.* II. i. 101.

†**Stale,** *sb.*[3] ME. [a. OF. *estal*, a. OHG. *stal*; see STALL *sb.*[1]] **1.** A fixed position or station –1485. **2.** An ambush –1627. **3.** A body of armed men posted in a particular place for ambush, etc., or detached for reconnoitring, etc. Also, the main body of an army. –1579.

Stale (stēⁱl), *sb.*[4] late ME. [perh. f. STALE *v.*[1]] Urine; now only of horses and cattle.

†**Stale,** *sb.*[5] late ME. [a. AF. *estale*, perh. f. *estaler* STALE *v.*[3]] = STALEMATE –1656.

Stale (stēⁱl), *a.* ME. [prob. f. (ult.) the Teut. root **sta-* to STAND.] †**1.** Of malt liquor, mead, wine: That has stood long enough to clear; freed from dregs or lees; hence, old and strong –1743. **2.** That has lost its freshness; altered by keeping. (Of bread: opp. to *new.*) 1530. **3.** *fig.* Of an immaterial thing: That has lost its freshness, novelty, or interest; hackneyed, worn out; effete 1562. **b.** *Law.* Of a claim or demand: That has been allowed to lie dormant for an unreasonable time 1769. †**4.** Of persons: Past the prime of life; having lost the vigour or attractiveness of youth. Of a bachelor or spinster: Past the fitting season for marriage. –1858. **5.** *Sport.* Of an athlete, a racing animal, etc.: Out of condition through over-severe training or exertion too long continued 1856.

1. Good reed wine þat be s. 1400. 2. The egg becomes s. or addled 1829. The bread should be s. 1878. 3. How weary, s., flat, and vnprofitable Seemes

to me all the vses of this world? SHAKS. Hence **Sta·le·ly** *adv.* (rare), **-ness.**

Stale (stēⁱl), *v.*¹ *Obs.* exc. *arch.* and *dial.* late ME. [Proximate source obsc.; perh. a. OF. *estaler* = It. *stallare*; cf. Du., LG., HG. *stallen*, Sw. *stalla*, Da. *stalle* to make water (said of horses).] **1.** *intr.* To urinate, said esp. of horses or cattle. †**2.** *trans.* To pass (blood) in the urine –1647.

Stale (stēⁱl), *v.*² 1440. [f. STALE *a.*] **1.** *trans.* To render (beer or ale) 'stale'. **b.** *intr.* Of beer: to become 'stale' or old 1742. **2.** *trans.* To render stale, out of date or uninteresting; to diminish interest in 1599. †**b.** To lower (oneself, one's dignity) in estimation by excessive familiarity –1843. **c.** *intr.* To grow stale, get out of fashion, become uninteresting 1897.

2. Age cannot wither her, nor custome s. Her infinite variety SHAKS. **b.** Not content To s. himselfe in all societies, He makes my house here common as a mart B. JONS.

Stale, *v.*³ 1470. [prob. a. AF. *estaler*, perh. of Eng. origin.] *Chess.* **a.** *trans.* = STALEMATE *v.* **b.** *intr.* To undergo stalemate 1585.

Stalemate (stēⁱ·lmēⁱt), *sb.* 1765. [f. STALE *sb.*⁵ + MATE *sb.*¹] *Chess.* A position in which the player whose turn it is to move has no allowable move open to him, but has not his king in check.

According to modern rules, the game which ends in s. is drawn. See N.E.D.

Stalemate (stēⁱ·lmēⁱt), *v.* 1765. [f. prec.] *Chess. trans.* To subject to a stalemate.

Stalk (stǭk), *sb.*¹ [ME. *stalke*, app. a dim. with *k* suffix f. *stal-* in STALE *sb.*¹] **1.** The main stem of a herbaceous plant, bearing the flowers and leaves; also, a scape or flower-stem rising directly from the root. **2.** The comparatively slender connecting part by which a vegetable organ is attached to the plant; the petiole of a leaf, the peduncle or pedicel of a flower, fruit, or inflorescence, the stipe of an ovary, etc. ME. **b.** A similar slender connecting part by which an animal organ or structure is attached or supported 1826. **3.** The shaft of a chimney. (Cf. STACK *sb.* 4.) 1821. **4.** The main part of anything long and slender, as dist. from the extremities; e.g. †the shaft of a quill; the tube or stem of a thermometer 1530. **5.** A slender upright support; the stem of a wineglass 1864. **6.** *Arch.* An ornament in the Corinthian which resembles the stalk of a plant 1842.

1. A long green reed, like the s. of the maize 1839. The rough tangle of stalks and stems 1910. **2. b.** The 's.' of the tumour 1899. **5.** Old drinking-glasses, with tall stalks HAWTHORNE.

Comb.: **s.-borer** *U.S.*, the larva of a moth, *Gortyna nitela*, destructive to plants; **-eyed** *a.*, having the eye at the end of a s., podophthalmate.

Stalk (stǭk), *sb.*² 1450. [f. STALK *v.*] **1.** An act of stalking game. **2.** A striding gait; a stately or pompous mode of walking 1590.

2. An vgly feend,..The which with monstrous stalke behind him stept SPENSER.

Stalk (stǭk), *v.* [ME. *stalke* :—OE. **stealcian* :—prehist. **stalkōjan*, freq. f. **stal-* : **stel-*, see STEAL *v.*] †**1.** *intr.* To walk softly, cautiously, or stealthily –1587. **2.** †To go stealthily *to, towards* (an animal) for the purpose of killing or capturing it. Hence, to pursue game by the method of stealthy approach, esp. by the use of a stalking-horse or of some similar device. late ME. **3.** *trans.* **a.** To pursue (game) by stealthy approach 1823. **b.** To go through (a tract of country) stalking game 1860. **4.** *intr.* To walk with stiff, high, measured steps, like a long-legged bird. Usu. with disparaging notion, implying haughtiness, sullenness, or the like. Freq. said of ghosts, animals, etc. 1530. **b.** *trans.* To march proudly through (a country, etc.) 1610.

1. There stalkte he on, as softe as foote could tread 1587. **2.** One vnderneath his Horse, to get a shoot doth stalke DRAYTON. *fig.* O I, stalke on, stalke on, the foule sits. I did neuer thinke that Lady would have loued any man. SHAKS. **3.** And for shooting him from behind a wall, it is cruelly like to stalking a deer SCOTT. **b.** To s. the bush on foot 1890. **4.** About them round A Lion now he [Satan] stalkes with fierie glare MILT. The Fen-men, stalking through the marshes on their stilts 1787. No heron was seen stalking on the usual haunts of the bird SCOTT. The plague was stalking grimly up and down the land 1889. **b.** Like a hideous phantom stalking the streets at noon-day 1841.

Stalked (stǭkt), *a.* 1731. [f. STALK *sb.*¹ + -ED².] Having a stalk or stalks; in *Nat. Hist.*, *Path.*, etc. opposed to *sessile*. Also in parasynthetic combs., *long-s.*, *red-s.*, etc.

One species of S. Barnacle 1863. The s. Crinoids 1874.

Stalker (stǭ·kəɹ). late ME. [f. STALK *v.* + -ER¹.] †**1.** A kind of net used by poachers. Also *s. net.* –1667. **2.** One who stalks game. late ME. **3.** One who walks with long measured steps 1585.

Sta·lking-horse. 1519. [f. *stalking* vbl. sb.] **1.** A horse trained to allow a fowler to conceal himself behind it or under its coverings in order to get within easy range of the game without alarming it. Hence, a portable screen made in the figure of a horse, similarly used. **2.** *fig.* A person whose participation in a proceeding is made use of to prevent its real design from being suspected 1612. **b.** An underhand means for making an attack or attaining some sinister object; usu., a pretext put forward for this purpose 1579.

1. Giovanni d'Udine..is thought to have been the inventor of the s., which poachers now use 1706. **2. b.** He uses his folly like a s. SHAKS.

Stalkless (stǭ·klės), *a.* 1698. [f. STALK *sb.*¹ + -LESS.] Having no stalk; chiefly of vegetable organs, sessile.

Stalklet (stǭ·klėt). 1835. [f. as prec. + -LET.] A small stalk; in *Bot.* = PEDICEL.

Stalky (stǭ·ki), *a.* 1552. [f. as prec. + -Y¹.] Consisting of or abounding in stalks; of the nature of a stalk or stalks; long and slender like a stalk.

Stall (stǭl), *sb.*¹ [Com. Teut. (wanting in Gothic); OE. *steall* standing, place, stall for cattle:—OTeut. **stallo-*, repr. an older **stadlo-*, f. **sta-* to STAND.] †**1.** *gen.* Standing-place, place, position; place in a series, degree of rank; in OE. occas., state, condition –1618. **2.** [Cf. mod.F. *stalle*.] A standing-place for horses or cattle; a stable or cattle-shed; also each division for one animal in a stable, cattle-shed, or cow-house; also, a manger OE. †**3.** A seat of office or dignity –1638. **4.** [Cf. med. L. *stallus*, OF. *estal(e*, mod.F. *stalle*.] A fixed seat enclosed, either wholly or partially, at the back and sides, esp. each of a row of seats in the choir of a church for the use of the clergy or religious, and, in a chapter-house, for the canons; also, each of the seats appropriated to knights of the higher orders of chivalry (e.g. the Knights of the Garter in St. George's Chapel, Windsor, etc.). Hence *occas.* the office, status, dignity or emolument connected with the occupancy of a (cathedral) stall; a canonry or the like. late ME. **b.** A long seat or doorless pew in a church; also, a 'sitting' 1580. **c.** Each of the chair-like seats arranged in rows in front of the pit in a theatre; also each of the corresponding seats in other places of entertainment 1828. **5.** [Cf. OF. *estal*, Flem. *stal*.] A bench, table, board, or the like, esp. one in front of a shop, upon which goods are exposed for sale; a booth or covered stand for the sale of wares at a market, fair, or in the open street; a stand at a Fancy Fair. late ME. †**b.** The booth or shed to shelter a cobbler at his work –1762. **6.** Applied to a sheath or receptacle of various kinds 1483. †**7.** Each of a series of 'screen' book-cases set at right angles to the walls of a library, each pair forming a bay or alcove –1886. **8.** *Metall.* A 'walled area' or compartment between low walls in which ores are roasted 1887. **9.** [perh. a distinct word.] *Coal-mining.* A working place in a mine, left between pillars in the pillar-and-stall system of mining 1665.

1. Phr. *In stead and s.*, everywhere, continually. **2.** I haue..Sixe-score fat Oxen standing in my stalls SHAKS. At the west end is a s. for one horse 1782. **4.** The eleven vacant stalls of the Most Honorable Order of the Bath 1788. But Wolsey was not satisfied ..with six prebendary stalls 1873. **c.** From our places in the stalls we could see our four friends..in the loge THACKERAY. **9.** *Pillar* (or *post*) *and s.*, a method of working coal, etc., in which pillars of coal are left during the first stage of excavation.

Comb.: **s.-edition,** a cheap edition of a work offered for sale on the bookstalls; **s. gate,** the road from a s. to the main road in a coal-mine; **-holder,** (*a*) the holder of an ecclesiastical s.; (*b*) one who is in charge of a s. at a bazaar, etc.; **-literature,** the cheap literature of the bookstalls; **-man,** (*a*) a keeper of a bookstall; (*b*) a man who contracts for and works a s. in a coal-mine; also each of a company of men associated for that purpose; **-plate,** a plate of gilt copper on which the arms of a Knight of the Garter are engraved; **-reader,** one who peruses the books on a bookstall.

Stall (stǭl), *sb.*² 1500. [a. AF. *estal*, var. of *estale*; see STALE *sb.*²] †**1.** A decoy-bird. Chiefly *fig.* –1592. **2.** A pickpocket's helper who distracts the attention of the victim whose pocket is being rifled; also the action or an act of stalling 1591.

Stall (stǭl), *sb.*³ 1918. [f. STALL *v.*¹] *Aviation.* An act of stalling.

Stall (stǭl), *v.*¹ ME. [Partly repr. a ME. adoption of OF. *estaller*, *estaler* (see STALE *v.*), and partly an Eng. formation on STALL *sb.*¹] **I.** To place. **1.** *intr.* To have one's abode, dwell. *Obs.* exc. *dial.* in *To s. with*, to get on with (another). **2.** *trans.* To assign a particular place to (a person or thing); to place. late ME. †**3.** To agree to the payment of (a debt) by instalments; to fix (days) for payment by instalments –1670.

1. *Ant. & Cl.* v. i. 39. **3.** *fig.* Thou canst never promise thyself to sin..thriftly..and s. the fine DONNE.

II. To place in a 'stall'. †**1.** = INSTALL *v.* **1.** –1661. **2.** To put (an animal) in a stall; to keep in a stall, esp. for fattening. late ME. **b.** *intr.* Of cattle: To be lodged in stalls 1805.

1. Where Kings were stall'd, disthron'd .. and crown'd 1632. **2.** I much prefer penning to stalling the sheep 1850. *fig.* Praie you leaue mee, s. this in your bosome, and I thanke you for your honest care SHAKS.

III. To come or bring to a stand. **1.** *trans.* To bring to a stand or standstill 1591. **b.** esp. in *pass.* To become stuck (in mud, mire, a snowdrift, etc.). Now *U.S.* or *dial.* 1460. **c.** *intr.* Of a flying machine: To lose flying speed 1914. Also *trans.* To cause (a flying machine) to stall 1913. **2.** *trans.* To take away (a person's) appetite; to satiate, surfeit *with*, *of*. Now *dial.* and *Sc.* 1583. **b.** To cause aversion in, cause to turn away. Also with *off*. Now *rare.* 1642.

1. When as thine eye hath chose the dame, And stall'd the deer that thou shouldst strike 1599. **b.** A teamster whose waggon was stalled in a place where it was somewhat swampy 1897. **2.** Ain't you fairly stalled of waiting? 1875.

IV. To furnish (a choir, etc.) with stalls 1516.

Stall (stǭl), *v.*² *slang.* 1592. [f. STALL *sb.*²] **1.** *trans.* To screen (a pickpocket or his operations) from observation; also with *off*. Also, to close *up* or surround and hustle (a person who is to be robbed). **2.** *To s. off.* **a.** To get rid of by evasive tactics, a trick, plausible tale, or the like; also, in sporting parlance, to keep the upper hand of (a competitor) 1812. **b.** To get off or extricate (a person) by artifice 1812.

2. a. His very preface should have stalled off denunciations of this kind 1905.

Stallage (stǭ·lėdʒ). late ME. [ad. Anglo-L. *stallagium*, AF. *estalage* (mod.F. *étalage*), f. *estal* STALL *sb.*¹] A tax or toll levied for the liberty of erecting a stall in a fair or market; also *attrib.*, as *s. rent.*

Stalled (stǭld), *ppl. a.* 1560. [f. STALL *sb.*¹ and *v.*¹ + -ED.] †**1.** Of a person: Endowed with or occupying a (church) stall –1829. **2.** Of an animal: Confined to a stall; fattened in a stall for killing 1560. **3.** Divided into stalls for animals 1825. **4.** Of a vehicle, etc.: That has stuck fast 1839. **5.** Glutted, satiated 1740.

2. Better is a dinner of grene herbes where loue is, then a s. oxe and hatred therewith BIBLE (Geneva) *Prov.* xv. 17.

Staller (stǭ·ləɹ). *Hist.* [ad. late OE. *stallere*, **steallere*, prob. f. *steall* STALL *sb.*¹] The title of a high officer in the reign of Edward the Confessor, equivalent to CONSTABLE **1.**

Sta·ll-fed, *ppl. a.* 1554. [f. STALL *sb.*¹ + FED *ppl. a.*] Fed in a stall; hence, luxuriously nurtured.

Sta·ll-feed, *v.* 1763. [Backformation from prec.] **1.** *trans.* To feed (an animal) in a stall. **2.** *intr.* Of an animal: To undergo feeding or fattening in a stall 1766.

Stalling (stǭ·liŋ), *vbl. sb.* late ME. [f. STALL *v.*¹ + -ING¹.] †**1.** Installation –1535. †**2.** The action of agreeing for the payment of a debt by instalments, or of fixing dates for payment; also, an instance of this -1640. **3.** Stall-accommodation (of or for an animal) 1535. **4.** *Aeronautics.* (Cf. STALL *v.*[1] III. 1 c.) 1916.

3. *A.Y.L.* I. i. 11.

Stallion (stæ·lyən). late ME. [a. OF. *estalon* (mod.F. *étalon*), corresp. to It. *stallone* :—pop. L. **stallonem*, f. Teut. **stallo-* stable, STALL *sb.*[1]] **1.** A male horse not castrated, an entire horse, esp. one kept for the purpose of serving mares. †**2.** Applied to a person: A man of lascivious life; in later use, a woman's hired paramour -1796. †**3.** A courtesan -1670.

2. What are you, her S., and her Bravo too? SHADWELL. 3. *Haml.* II. ii. 616.

†**Stall net.** ME. [prob. f. STALL *sb.*[1]] A net laid across a river, esp. for sprat-fishing.

Stalwart (stǭ·l-, stæ·lwəɹt), *a.* Now *literary.* late ME. [16th c. Sc. form of STALWORTH *a.*, brought into Eng. use by Scott.] **A.** *adj.* **1.** Strongly and stoutly built, sturdy, robust 1450. **2.** Of inanimate things: Firmly made or established, strong. Now *rare.* late ME. **3.** Of persons, their attributes, etc.: Resolute, unbending, determined. Chiefly *mod.* late ME. **4.** Valiant in fight, brave, courageous. late ME.

1. A tall and s. bagpiper LOCKHART. 3. S. opponents of superstition 1905. 4. A s. knight TENNYSON.

B. *sb.* **1.** A strong and valiant man. (Now only as nonce-use, after 2.) 1470. **2.** A sturdy, uncompromising partisan; esp. as a political designation 1881.

2. *attrib.* The 's.' section of militant Dissent 1907. Hence **Sta·lwart-ly** *adv.*, **-ness** (*rare*).

Sta·lworth, *a.* and *sb.* *Obs.* exc. *arch.* [OE. *stǣlwierðe*, f. *stǣl* place + *wierðe* WORTH *a.*] **A.** *adj.* †**1.** Of things: Serviceable. OE. only. **2.** Of persons and animals: = prec. *a.* **1.** OE. **3.** Of persons, their actions, etc.: Brave, courageous, valiant, mighty ME. †**B.** *sb.* A strong and valiant man -1500. Hence †**Sta·lworthness,** s. quality. -late ME.

Stamen (stēⁱ·mĕn). *Pl.* **stamens**; also (now *rarely*) stamina (stēⁱ·mină). 1650. [a. L., the warp in an upright loom, a thread of the warp, a thread or fibre in general; formally corresp. to Gr. στήμων warp, στῆμα some part of a plant, Skr. *sthāman* station, place :—Indo-Eur. **st(h)āmon-, -en-*, f. **st(h)ā-* to STAND.] †**1.** The warp of a textile fabric (*rare*) -1681. †**2.** **a.** The thread spun by the Fates at a person's birth -1753. **b.** The supposed germinal principle or impulse in which the future characteristics of any nascent existence are implicit -1725. **c.** The fundamental or essential element of a thing -1794. **3.** *Bot.* The male or fertilizing organ of a flowering plant, consisting of two parts, the *anther*, which is a double-celled sac containing the pollen, and the *filament*, a slender footstalk supporting the anther 1668. Hence **Sta·mened** *a.* having stamens.

†**Sta·min.** ME. [a. OF. *estamin, -ine*, app. f. *estame* :—L. *stamina* pl. warp threads.] A coarse worsted cloth; in earliest use usu. an under garment made of this worn by ascetics; later a kind of woollen or worsted cloth, for which Norfolk was formerly noted -1664.

Stamina (stæ·mină). 1676. [a. L., pl. of *stamen*; see STAMEN 2 c.] †**1.** As *pl.* The native or original elements and constitution of anything; the nature, structure, and qualities of an organism, as existing potentially in its nascent state; the rudiments or germs from which living beings or their organs are developed -1824. †**2.** As *pl.*; rarely as *sing.* The congenital vital capacities of a person or animal, on which (other things being equal) the duration of life was supposed to depend; natural constitution as affecting the duration of life or the power of resisting debilitating influences -1863. **3.** orig. as *pl.*; now chiefly as *sing.* Vigour of bodily constitution; power of sustaining fatigue or privation, of recovery from illness, and of resistance to debilitating influences; staying power 1726. †**4.** As *pl.* and *sing.* Source of strength, main support, 'backbone' -1799.

1. *fig.* Enmity to us..is wrought into the very s. of its constitution BURKE. 3. Had he been possessed of less s. and less vitality he must have succumbed 1880. *fig.* The British Constitution has considerable s. 1865.

Staminal (stæ·mĭnăl), *a.* 1798. [f. L. *stamin-* STAMEN, STAMINA + -AL.] **1.** Belonging to the stamina or natural constitution of a person or thing. **2.** *Bot.* Pertaining to or consisting of stamens 1845.

Staminate (stæ·minĕt), *a.* 1845. [ad. L. *staminatus* consisting of threads, f. *stamin-, stamen*; see STAMEN and -ATE[2].] *Bot.* Furnished with or producing stamens. Of certain flowers: Having stamens but no pistils.

Stamineous (stămi·nĭəs), *a.* 1668. [f. L. *stamineus* consisting of threads, f. *stamin-* STAMEN; see -EOUS.] *Bot.* Consisting of, bearing, or pertaining to a stamen or stamens.

Staminiferous (stæmini·fĕrəs), *a.* Also stameniferous. 1761. [f. L. *stamin-* STAMEN; see -FEROUS.] *Bot.* Having or bearing stamens, applied to a flower having stamens but no pistils.

Staminodium (stæminōᵘ·diǒm). 1821. [mod.L., f. L. *stamin-* STAMEN + mod.L. *-odium* (see -ODE).] *Bot.* **a.** A sterile or abortive stamen, or an organ resembling an abortive stamen, without its anther. **b.** The antheridium of a cryptogam 1848. So **Sta·minode.**

Stammel (stæ·mĕl). Now *arch.* or *Hist.* 1530. [Corresponds to F. *estamel*, either f. *estame* + *-el, -elle*, or f. *estamine* STAMIN, by substitution of suffix.] **1.** A coarse woollen cloth or linsey-woolsey, usually dyed red; an undergarment of this, worn by ascetics. **2.** More fully *s. colour*: the shade of red in which the cloth was commonly dyed. (Sometimes vaguely = 'red'.) 1567.

Stammer (stæ·məɹ), *sb.* 1773. [f. the vb.] A stammering mode of utterance.

Stammer (stæ·məɹ), *v.* [OE. *stamerian*, *stǫmrian* :—WGer. **stamrōjan*, f. **stamro-*, f. **stam-*.] **1.** *intr.* To falter or stumble in one's speech; *esp.* to make one or more involuntary repetitions of a consonant or vowel before being able to pass from it to the following sound. (Cf. STUTTER *v.*) **2.** *trans.* To utter or say with a stammer 1587. **3.** *intr.* To stagger in walking; said esp. of horses. Now *dial.* late ME.

1. The eloquent tongue forgot its office. Cicero stammered, blundered, and sat down. FROUDE. *fig.* That I may dare, in wayfaring, To s. where old Chaucer used to sing KEATS. 2. I stammer'd that I knew him TENNYSON. *transf.* I stammered out a bow, and..went home LAMB. Hence **Sta·mmerer,** one who stammers. **Sta·mmeringly** *adv.*

Stammering (stæ·məriŋ), *vbl. sb.* ME. [-ING[1].] **1.** The action of STAMMER *v.*; hesitation and involuntary repetition in speech; also (now *dial.*) staggering and stumbling in gait. **2.** *transf.* in certain *Path.* uses 1855.

2. S. of the Fingers 1855. The s. with the bladder occurs in just the same conditions as the stammering speech 1868. S. with the organs of deglutition 1868.

Stamp (stæmp), *sb.* 1465. [Partly f. STAMP *v.*, partly ad. MF. *estampe* (mod.F. *estampe*, *étampe*), f. *estamper*; see STAMP *v.*] **I.** An act of stamping; a forcible downward blow with the foot 1590.

The repeated stamps of the heel of his heavy boot SCOTT.

II. An instrument for stamping. **1.** An instrument for making impressions, marks, or imprints, on other bodies; a stamping-tool, an engraved block or die 1465. **b.** *esp.* A die or the apparatus used in stamping a device upon a coin, token, medal, or the like 1572. **2.** A printing type or types (collectively); hence, a printing press. *To put to s.*, to print 1548 (later, printer's slang). **3.** A bookbinder's tool for embossing bindings. Also *transf.* an ornament produced by this. 1811. **4.** A machine for shaping articles made of sheet-metal; a drop-hammer 1839. **5.** An iron-shod pestle of a mill for stamping ores, esp. each of the several pestles forming a battery; chiefly in *pl.*, a battery of stamps, a stamp-mill 1674.

1. My old silver s., with the double G upon it SCOTT. *fig.* His Sword, Deaths stampe, Where it did marke, it tooke from face to foot SHAKS.

III. The result of stamping. **1.** The mark, impression, or imprint made with an engraved block or die 1542. **2.** *fig.* **a.** A certifying mark or imprint 1611. **b.** The imprint or sign (*of* what is specified) 1596. **c.** Character, fashion, type 1573. **3.** An embossed or impressed mark placed by a government office on paper or parchment to certify that the duty chargeable in respect of what is thereon written or printed has been paid. Hence also, in recent times, an adhesive label (printed with a distinctive device) which is issued by the government for a fixed amount, and which serves the same purpose as an impressed stamp. 1694. **b.** *spec.* = POSTAGE STAMP 1837. **c.** *pl.* (*U.S. slang.*) Money, (properly, paper money) 1872. †**4.** Something marked with a device; a coin, medal -1633. †**5.** A picture produced by printing from an engraved plate, an engraving, print. *In s.*, by means of engraving. [After It. *stampa*, F. *estampe.*] -1780. **6.** *Metall.* 'The pieces into which the rough bars shingled from the finery ball are broken, to be piled for subsequent rolling into sheet-iron' (Raymond) 1880.

1. He sold goods, that were not marketable without the s. ARBUTHNOT. The dollar, under its new s., has preserved its name and circulation 1871. The s. acts as a kind of hall-mark 1883. *fig.* The rank is but the guinea's s.—The man's the gowd for a' that BURNS. 2. **a.** Truth its radiant s. Has fixed..Upon her children's brow SHELLEY. **b.** The s. of merit SHAKS. **c.** A yong maid, truly of the finest s. of beautie SIDNEY. Men of the s. of a Washington or a Hampden 1869. 4. *Merry W.* III. iv. 16. *fig. Rich. III*, I. iii. 256. 5. The stamps are extremely beautiful, and are representations of the gods and heroes of antiquity 1780.

Comb., as *s.-album*; **S. Act,** each of the various Acts of Parliament for regulating the s. duties; esp. that of 1765 for levying s. duties in the American colonies; also, that of 1712 imposing a s. duty on newspapers; **battery,** a series of stamps in a stamp-mill; **-collecting,** (*a*) *sb.* = PHILATELY; (*b*) *adj.* that practises philately; **-collector,** (*a*) a collector or receiver of s. duties; (*b*) a PHILATELIST; **-cutter,** an engraver of dies; **-distributor,** an official who issues or sells government stamps; **s. duty,** any of the duties collected by means of stamps impressed on or affixed to the articles taxed; **s. edging,** the gummed marginal paper of a sheet of postage stamps; **s. gold,** gold ore for stamping; **-hammer,** the hammer of a stamping machine; **-head,** the head of a pestle of a s.-mill; **-mill,** (*a*) the apparatus used to crush ores by means of a pestle or series of pestles operated by machinery; (*b*) an oil-crushing mill of similar construction; **s. note,** a permit from a Custom House official granting permission for the loading of goods on board ship; **s. office,** an office where government stamps are issued and where s. duties are received; **s. paper,** (*a*) paper having a government revenue s. impressed on or affixed to it; (*b*) = *s.-edging*; **s. rock,** ore suitable for treatment by stamping; **-tax,** a tax imposed by a s. act. Hence **Sta·mpless** *a.*

Stamp (stæmp), *v.* [Early ME. *stampen* :—OTeut. **stampōjan*, f. **stampoz* pestle, mortar. The Teut. root **stamp-* is prob. a nasalized form of **stap-* to tread (cf. branch II).] **I.** †**a.** *trans.* To bray in a mortar; to beat to a pulp or powder; to pound. Also *absol.* -1764. †**b.** To crush or press (fruit, esp. crabs) to extract the juice; to press (wine) out of grapes -1618. **c.** To crush (ore); in mod. use, by means of the machine called a 'stamp' 1568. **d.** To drive in (a blasting charge) 1899.

a. S. good store of ripe Sloes 1579.

II. To bring down the foot heavily. **1.** *intr.* **a.** To bring the sole of one's foot suddenly and forcibly down (*upon* the ground or floor, etc.), with the object of crushing or beating down something ME. **b.** To strike the ground or floor forcibly with the sole of the foot; *esp.* as an instinctive expression of fury. late ME. **c.** To walk with a heavy, 'pounding' tread; to tramp 1489. **2.** *trans.* **a.** With compl.: To affect in the specified way by stamping; *esp.* to trample violently *down, to the ground* 1470. **b.** To bring down the sole or heel forcibly upon. Now somewhat *rare.* 1602.

1. Shouting clans or squadrons stamping SCOTT. **b.** I have only to s. with my foot, he said,..to raise legions from the soil of Italy 1850. The Queen..went stamping about, and shouting 'Off with his head!' 'L. CARROLL'. **c.** And Bahrâm, that great Hunter—the Wild Ass Stamps o'er his Head, and he lies fast asleep FITZGERALD. 2. Phr. *To s. one's foot* = sense II. 1. *To s. out*, to extinguish (a fire) by trampling on it; hence, *transf.* to extirpate (a disease, a heresy, etc.), suppress (a rebellion); *occas.* to exterminate (a people). **b.** He frets, he fumes, he stares, he stamps the Ground DRYDEN.

III. To strike an impression on something. **1.** To impress with an embossed or intaglio device or lettering by means of a die and the impact of a hammer or machinery; to make (a coin, a medal) by this process 1560. **b.** To impress (a device, lettering, etc.) by means of a die 1589. **c.** To make by cutting out with a die 1798. **2.** To mark (paper or textile material) with a device either impressed in relief or intaglio, imparted to the surface by ink or pigment, or produced by both processes combined. Also, to impress (a device) on paper, etc. by means of a die or engraved plate. 1604. †b. [Cf. It. *stampare.*] To print (a book, etc.). –1624. 3. To impress with a device or lettering indicating genuineness, quality, or official inspection and approval; to impress (a device, etc.) on merchandise, weights or measures, or the like, for this purpose 1564. 4. To impress with an official stamp or mark indicating that a duty or tax has been paid. In later use also, to attach an adhesive 'stamp' to. 1765. 5. *fig.* a. To show to be of a certain quality or nature 1599. b. To impress with some conspicuous characteristic 1780. c. To impress or fix permanently (an idea, etc.) on the mind or memory 1662.

1. Also they [the Irish] had silver groats,..stamped with the Popes tripple Crowne 1617. b. *fig.* What stamps the wrinkle deeper on the brow? BYRON. 2. This jacket..was stamped in various places with the government broad arrow 1885. The address..was also stamped on the envelope 1908. 4. We..made another attempt to get the deed stamped 1907. 5. a. *Leo[nato]* Are they [*sc.* the newes] good? *Old[Man].* As the euents stamps them. SHAKS. b. Its beauty was..stamped with..sadness 1838. The picture of the streets..remained forever stamped upon his memory 1885.

Stamp and go. 1830. [The vbs. in imperative.] *Naut. phr.*

Stamp and go! the order to step out at the capstan, or with hawsers, topsail-halyards, etc., generally to the fife or fiddle (ADM. SMYTH).

Stampede (stæmpī·d), *sb.* 1834. [orig. U.S.; ad. Mexican Sp. *estampida*, a peculiar use of Sp. *estampida*, also *estampido* crash, uproar.] A sudden rush and flight of a body of panic-stricken cattle. b. *transf.* A sudden or unreasoning rush or flight of persons in a body or mass; in U.S. politics, a sudden unconcerted rush of a political convention for a candidate who seems likely to win 1846.

The shells..only causing a s. among the mules and horses 1884.

Stampede (stæmpī·d), *v.* 1847. [f. the sb.] 1. *trans.* To cause a stampede amongst (cattle); to cause a stampede of (a person's) cattle. b. *transf.* and *fig.* To cause (a body of persons) to fly or rush away through fear or common impulse; in U.S. politics, to induce (a political convention) to vote suddenly in a body (for a particular candidate) 1868. 2. *intr.* Of a herd of cattle: To become panic-stricken and take to flight 1859. b. Of a company of persons: To rush with a common impulse 1849.

1. b. Efforts of the Bears to S. the New York Market 1889. 2. b. The new regiment broke, stampeded into the other, and threw it into confusion 1884.

Stamper (stæ·mpəɹ). late ME. [f. STAMP *v.* + -ER [1].] 1. One who stamps. 2. An instrument used in stamping; *esp.* (chiefly *pl.*) each of the pestles in a crushing or pounding machine, esp. in a stamping-mill 1483.

Stamping (stæ·mpiŋ), *vbl. sb.* ME. [-ING [1].] 1. The action of STAMP *v.* 2. *concr.* a. *pl.* The materials pounded or crushed 1594. b. An article fashioned by stamping 1862.

attrib. and *Comb.*, as *s.-die, -machine, -mill*, etc.; **s. ground** *U.S.*, an animal's habitual place of resort.

Stance (stæns). Now chiefly *Sc.* and *north.* 1532. [a. F., ad. It. *stanza* station, stopping-place, room, etc.; see STANZA.] 1. A standing-place, station, position. b. *Golf*, etc.: The position of the player in playing a stroke 1897. 2. A site; esp. an area for building upon. Also *building-s.* 1631.

Stanch, staunch (stanʃ, stǭnʃ), *sb.*[1] late ME. [f. STANCH *v.*] †1. That which stops or allays, also a stopping –1790. 2. Something used for stanching blood, a styptic. late ME. 3. A kind of after-damp in mines, etc. 1693.

Stanch, staunch (stanʃ, stǭnʃ), *sb.*[2] 1767. [a. OF. *estanche*, related to *estanc* STANK *sb.*] A lock or dam in a river.

Stanch, staunch (stanʃ, stǭnʃ), *v.* ME. [ad. OF. *estanchier* (mod.F. *étancher*) to stop the flow of:—Com. Rom. **stancare*, perh. a contr. of pop. L. **stagnicare*, f. *stagnum* pool, pond (whence STAGNATE *v.*, etc.).] 1. *trans.* To stop the flow of (water, etc.). Now only *poet.* (*rare*). 1481. 2. To stop the flow of (blood or other issue from the body); to stop the flow of blood from (a wound). Also *intr.* for *refl.* ME. †3. To quench, allay, satisfy (thirst, hunger, desire, etc.); also, to repress, extinguish (appetite, rebellion, anger, etc.) –1828. 4. To arrest the progress of (a disease); to allay (pain); to relieve (a person) *of* pain. late ME. 5. To stop up, to render water-tight or weather-proof. [After F. *étancher.*] 1776.

1. I will staunch his floudes COVERDALE *Ezek.* xxxi. 15. 2. The bleeding was stanched, the wound was closed SCOTT. 4. Aloe..stancheth the heade ake 1551. 5. The gathered sticks to staunch the wall Of the snow-tower, when snow should fall EMERSON. Hence **Sta·ncher**, one who or that which stanches. **Sta·nchless** *a.* that may not be stanched.

Stanchel (sta·nʃĕl). Now *Sc.* 1586. [perh. a. OF. *estanchele* the name of an object used in some game.] = next.

Stanchion (sta·nʃən), *sb.* late ME. [a. OF. *estanchon, estançon* (mod.F. *étançon*), f. *estance* prop:—pop. L. **stantia*, f. *stare* to stand.] An upright bar, stay, or support, as for a ship's deck, awning, etc.; *spec.* of a window.

S., a sort of small pillar of wood or iron used for various purposes in a ship; as to support the decks, the quarter-rails, the nettings, the awnings, &c. 1769. *attrib.*: **s.-gun**, a gun mounted in a boat for wild-fowl shooting.

Stanchion (sta·nʃən), *v.* 1528. [f. prec.] *trans.* To provide with stanchions, strengthen or support with stanchions.

Stand (stænd), *sb.*[1] OE. [f. STAND *v.*] I. Action or condition of standing. †1. A pause, delay (*rare*). OE. only. 2. The action or an act of standing or coming to a position of rest; a pause, halt, esp. in the phr. *to make a s.* Now *rare* or *Obs.* 1592. b. *Theatr.* Each halt made on a tour to give performances 1896. †3. A standing in ambush or in cover –1621. 4. A holding one's ground against an opponent or enemy; a halt (of moving troops) to give battle or repel an attack; esp. in the phr. *to make a* (or *one's*) *s.* 1590. 5. A state of checked or arrested movement; a standstill; *spec.* the rigid attitude assumed by a dog on finding game 1618. 6. A state of being unable to proceed in thought, speech, or action; a state of perplexity or nonplus 1599. 7. A state of arrested progress (of affairs, institutions, natural processes, or the like). Chiefly in the phrases *to be at a s., to come to a s.* 1614. 8. Manner of standing (of a thing). Now *techn.* 1700.

2. Why he stalkes vp and downe like a Peacock, a stride and a s. SHAKS. 3. 3 *Hen. VI*, III. i. 3. 4. Instead of making any S. they retreated continually 1736. *fig.* To make a s. against oppression 1833. 5. Phr. *To be at a s., to come to a s., to bring* or *put to a s.* 6. There is one point however that puts me to a s. 1734. 7. Public business was at a s. 1789.

II. Place of standing. 1. A place of standing, position, station; also in phr. *to take one's s.* ME. 2. The post or station of a soldier, sentinel, or watchman 1513. 3. The standing-place from which a hunter or sportsman may shoot game. late ME. †4. *Hawking.* An elevated resting place of a hawk; *spec.* as a 'fault', a position of rest from flight –1678. 5. A stall or booth 1508. 6. A plot of land (*S. Afr.*), the position, site, or building for a business (*U.S.*) 1787. 7. A station for a row of vehicles plying for hire; also, the row of vehicles occupying a station 1692. 8. A raised platform for spectators at open-air sports as race-meetings, football matches, or for a company of musicians or performers 1615. 9. An elevated standing place for a speaker; a rostrum, pulpit; *U.S.* the place where a witness stands to testify in court, more fully *witness-s.* 1840.

1. Come, I haue found you out a s. most fit, Where you may haue such vantage on the Duke He shall not passe you SHAKS. *fig.* Their opponents take their s. on a quibble 1850. 3. Like an old decayed oak.., where the keepers in England take *a s.*,..to shoot a deer DE FOE. 7. A shabby s. Of Hackney coaches SHELLEY. 8. *Band s.*: see BAND *sb.*[3] *Grand s.*: see GRAND *a.*

III. An appliance to stand something on. 1. A base, bracket, stool or the like upon which a utensil, ornament, or exhibit may be set; the base upon which an instrument is set up for use 1664. 2. A frame or piece of furniture upon which to stand or hang articles 1692.

IV. Something which stands. 1. *Sc.* and *Anglo-Ir.* A complete set (of things); *Mil.* a set (of arms, colours) 1450. 2. *S. of pikes*: a compact group of pikemen. *Obs.* exc. *Hist.* 1598. 3. *Sporting.* An assemblage or group (of certain game birds) 1881. 4. *U.S.* A standing growth or crop (of wheat, cotton, etc.) 1868.

attrib. and *Comb.*: **s. camera**, a camera for use on a tripod or other stand, as dist. from a hand camera; **s. cock** = STAND-PIPE; **-house**, the grand stand of a race-course with the buildings attached to it.

Stand (stænd), *sb.*[2] *Obs.* exc. *dial.* ME. [f. root of next.] 1. An open tub; a barrel set on end. 2. A certain weight (of pitch, coal) 1706.

Stand (stænd), *v.* Pa. t. and pa. pple. **stood** (stud). [Com. Teut.; OE. *standan, stōd, stōdon, gestanden*, f. root **sta-*: *stō-*; cf. Skr. *sthā*, Gr. ἱστάναι, L. *stare, sistere.*] I. Of persons and animals. 1. *intr.* To assume or maintain an erect attitude on one's feet (opp. to *sit, lie, kneel*, etc.). Also said of the feet. Freq. *fig.* b. With predicate: To be of a (specified) height when holding oneself upright. Said also of quadrupeds, etc. 1831. 2. Of a horse: To be kept in a stable or stall. Phr. *To s. at livery.* 1465. 3. To remain motionless on one's feet; to cease walking or moving on OE. b. In imper., a command to come to a halt 1513. c. *Hunting.* Of a dog: To point. Const. *upon* (game). 1823. 4. With predicative extension: To remain erect on one's feet in a specified place, occupation, position, condition, etc. OE. 5. *Cricket*, etc.: To act as umpire in the field. Also *To s. umpire.* 1846. 6. To remain firm or steady in an upright position, to support oneself erect on one's feet. Often in neg. contexts. OE. b. *fig.* To remain steadfast, firm, or secure ME. 7. To take up an offensive or defensive position against an enemy; to present a firm front; to await an onset and keep one's ground without budging. Of soldiers: To be drawn up in battle array. OE. 8. To appear as a candidate, to offer oneself as a candidate 1551. 9. *Card-playing.* To be willing to play with one's hand as dealt 1824. 10. *U.S.* To **stand pat.** (*a*) In *Poker*, to play, or declare one's intention of playing, a hand just as it has been dealt, without drawing other cards. (*b*) *transf.* To adhere to an existing state of things or to an avowed policy (esp. a high tariff), refusing to consider proposals for change or reform. Hence **Stand-patter.** 1882. 11. Uses in which the force of the verb is weakened and approaches that of a copula, the stress being on the complement or predicative extension. late ME. 12. *fig.* In betting, commercial speculation, etc.: To be in the position of being reasonably certain *to* (win or lose something or a specified amount); to have *to* (win or lose a certain amount in a specified contingency) 1861.

1. Oure fete shal stonde in thy gates, O Jerusalem COVERDALE *Ps.* cxxi. 2. Kneele, and repeate it, I will s., and so shall Trinculo SHAKS. *fig.* phrases. *To s. on one's own feet* or *legs, upon a* (specified) *footing, not to have a leg to s. on, to s. in a person's* or *one's own light* (see LIGHT *sb.* 1 e), *in* (another person's) *shoes* (see SHOE sb.), *in the way* (*of* a person or thing: see WAY *sb.*). b. Six foot two, as I think, he stands TENNYSON. 3. All but Nausicaa fled; but she fast stood CHAPMAN. b. He order'd him to S. and Deliver 1714. 'S., Bayard, s.!'—the steed obeyed SCOTT. 4. The salvage Linxes listning stood DRYDEN. *To s. at attention, at ease, at gaze, on one's own bottom,* (*on*) *tiptoe, upright*, see these words. *To s. on one's head*, to take up a position with the crown of the head on the ground and heels in the air; *fig.* (to be ready) to do this as a sign of extreme delight. *To s. sentinel, sentry*, see the sbs. 6. b. They had stood true to the honour of Ireland 1888. Phr. *To s. or fall*, often used *fig.* of a person or thing, to indicate that his or its fate is contingent on the fate of some other person or thing, or must be governed by some event or rule; const. *with* (a person or thing), *together*, also *by* (a rule, an uncertain event). 7. *T. s. fast, firm; to s. at bay, in the breach, on* or *upon one's guard, on* or *upon the defensive* or *offensive*. *To s. upon one's trial*, to submit to judicial trial. 8. How many s. for Consulships? SHAKS. He did not s. for a fellowship 1890. *To s. for a constituency* or *for Parliament*: to offer oneself for election as the representative of a constituency in the House of Commons. 11. *To s. security, surety. To s. godfather, sponsor.* †*To s.* (a person's) *good lord. To s. committed, indebted, pledged. I s. corrected*, I accept or acknowledge the correction. So *I s. reproved. To s. well* or *high* (= to be in high favour or esteem) *with* a person. *To s. fair* (= to be favourably situated) *for* something or *to do* something. *How do you s.* (financially)? 12. She stood to lose all round 1880.

II. Of things. **1.** To be in an upright position with the lower part resting on or fixed in the ground or other support; opp. to *lie* OE. **b.** Of plants: To grow erect. Said esp. of grass, corn, etc., when left uncut to ripen. OE. **c.** Of the hair: To grow stiff and erect like bristles. *To s. on end*, †*up*, *upright*: to rise up on the head as a result of fright or astonishment. late ME. **2.** More loosely: To be set, placed, or fixed; to rest, lie (with more or less notion of firmness and steadiness). Of a dish or its contents: To rest flat or on a flat base. ME. **3.** Of a place, country, piece of ground, dwelling, etc.: To be situated in a specified position or aspect. Now chiefly of a town or village. OE. **4.** With predic. extension or complement, indicating the manner or condition OE. **5.** To be inscribed, drawn, †painted, etc. (on a list, sheet, or the like). Hence of words or literary matter: To be set down, recorded, composed in a (specified) context or form. OE. **b.** esp. of numerical figures: To be set down or entered in a list, account, ledger, or the like. Hence of a sum, price, score; also of the game or player whose score is recorded. Const. *at* (a certain figure). 1537. **c.** Of an account: To show a (specified) position of the parties with regard to debit and credit. Also, to continue on the books unsettled. 1710. **d.** Of a word, clause, etc.: To occupy a specified place in a verse or context; to be used in a specified inflexion or construction 1693. **6.** Of water, etc.: To have the surface at a specified level. Of the mercury (or other liquid) in a thermometer, barometer, etc.: To reach to a certain height; hence said of the instrument itself. ME. **7.** Of an edifice, or the like: To remain erect and entire; to resist destruction or decay OE. †**b.** Of the world: To exist; to remain stable, last –1598. **8.** *Naut.* (See quots.) 1669. **9.** Of a pigment or dye: To keep its colour; also, not to blot or run 1811. **10.** Of liquids: To cease flowing; *esp.* of water, to collect and remain motionless, be stagnant OE. **b.** Of land, a ditch, etc.: *To s. with*, to be full of (stagnant water) 1601. **11.** Of tears: To remain collected (in the eyes) without falling. Of a humour, esp. perspiration: To remain in drops (*on* the skin, etc.). 1530. **12.** Of a liquid, etc.: To be kept in a vessel without shaking 1467. **13.** Of a star: To appear fixed in the heavens. Of the sun or a planet: To be seen apparently motionless at any point of its course. late ME. **14.** Of a piece of machinery, a timepiece, an implement, a vehicle, etc.: To remain still or motionless; to cease moving, working, or turning. late ME. **b.** Of a mine, factory, etc., also of the men employed: To stop working; to be at a standstill 1733. **c.** Printing. *To be standing*: (of type) to remain undistributed 1888. **15.** Of the wind: To blow from a quarter indicated; also simply, to blow favourably, to continue to blow. Similarly of the weather. *arch.* ME. **16.** *Naut.* Of a vessel (hence of the commander, sailors, etc.): To sail, steer, direct one's course (in a specified direction, to sea, into harbour, etc.) 1627. **17.** With adv., advb. phr., or adj. predicate: To be or remain in a specified condition, relation, situation, etc. OE. **b.** With a relative or demonstrative adv. as predicate; e.g. *the case stands thus, as things s.* (= under present circumstances) OE. **18.** Of a condition, process, or the like: To remain stationary or unchanged, neither progressing nor receding; to be at a standstill. late ME. **19.** To endure, last; to continue unimpaired; to flourish OE. **20.** To be or remain valid or of force, hold good. Freq. with complement or predic. extension, as *to s. good, in force.* OE.

1. Behind the town-hall..stood the parish church 1886. **b.** White wheats should s. somewhat longer 1847. 2. Some food stood on the table SCOTT. 3. The village stands pleasantly 1792. 4. *To s. high, firm, ajar*, etc.; The Gate stood open STEELE. Phr. Of a thing: *As it stands* (= with all its accessories). 5. Let this pernitious houre S. aye accursed in the Kalender SHAKS. **b.** The score standing at 123 for five wickets 1890. The balance at the Bank stands..at £50 1913. **c.** Let me know how accounts s. SWIFT. 6. The thermometer now stood at 20 Fah. 1891. 7. She had only a foremast standing at day-light 1798. **b.** Whill the worlde stondeth TINDALE 1 *Cor.* viii. 13. 8. *To let all s.*, to leave a ship fully rigged. *All standing*, without dismantling or unrigging; *transf.* with one's clothes on, dressed. *To be brought up all standing*, to be suddenly checked or stopped, without any preparation. *Paid off all standing*, dismissed without unrigging or waiting to return stores. 11. Cold drops stood on my brow 1849. 13. Full-faced above the valley stood the moon TENNYSON. 14. The ploughe standeth, there is no worke done 1549. 15. The wind stood most easterly 1635. 16. We discovered a fleet..standing *athwart* us, i.e. steering across our way FALCONER. We took sail, and stood into the river 1823. 17. My life stoode in ieopardie HALL. *To s. in awe, in need; s. condemned*, etc. 18. And while his Fate is in thy Hands, The Bus'ness of the Nation stands SWIFT. 20. A written Contract..would s. DE FOE. That charge of murder will not s. law 1890.

III. To cost late ME.

Phr. *To s.* (a person) *in* (a price, etc.) (the ordinary construction; now restricted in currency, being partly fashionable slang, partly dial.); It stands me in eight shillings a bottle THACKERAY. Now *rare*.

IV. Trans. senses. **1.** To confront, face, oppose, encounter; to resist, withstand, bear the brunt of ME. **2.** To endure, undergo, be submitted to (a trial, test, ordeal, or the like). Usu., to come through or sustain successfully, (be able) to bear (a test, etc.). 1606. **b.** To submit to, offer to abide by (a judgement, decision, vote); to expose oneself to the chances of (a contested election) 1700. **3.** To face, encounter without flinching or retreating (an issue, hazard, etc.). Also, in weaker sense, to be exposed or liable to (hazard, fortunes). 1594. †**4.** To withstand, disobey, hold out against (a command). (*rare*). –1800. **5.** To endure (a physical trial, hardship, etc.) without hurt or damage, without succumbing or giving way 1756. **6.** To put up with, tolerate; (to be able or willing) to endure 1626. **7.** To bear the expense of, make a present of, pay for (a treat). Const. *to* or dat. of the recipient. *colloq.* 1835. **8.** *Racing*, etc. To bet on the success of, back (a horse) 1890. **9.** *Hunting*. Of a dog: To set (game) 1863. **10.** *causative*. To cause to stand; to place or leave standing; to set (a thing) upright; to place firmly or steadily in a specified position. Only *colloq.* or in familiar writing. 1837.

1. She was ready to s. fire rather than retreat 1891. 2. He has stood the ordeal of a London audience 1825. Phr. *To s. one's trial*, to be tried by a court for an offence; also *slang*, in the same sense, *to s. the patter*. **b.** All through his career he never stood a contested election 1891. *To s. one's chance*, to take one's chance, submit to what may befall one. 3. A gallant fellow, who had..stood the hazards of many a bloody day 1792. 4. *Lear* IV. i. 71 (Qo.). 5. These dyes will not s. water 1890. Drivers have to s. all weathers 1891. 6. She..was not going to s. that kind of thing TROLLOPE. 7. I'll s. you a dinner 1890. Phr. *To s. shot (to)*, rarely *to s. the shot*, to meet the expenses, pay the bill (for all); see SHOT *sb.* So *to s. Sam, treat*. 10. I stood my rifle against a tree 1878.

Phrases. *To s. one's ground*, to maintain one's position against attack or opposition. *To s. a chance* (also *a good, poor, little, some, no chance*), to be likely to meet with some piece of fortune, danger, good or ill luck. *To s. watch, to s. a* or *one's watch*: to keep watch, perform the duty of a watch; now chiefly *Naut.*, to take part in the duty of a watch during the prescribed time.

With preps. **S. against —.** To s. and face (an antagonist, etc.); to withstand, oppose, resist. Freq. to resist successfully. **S. at —.** To stick, hesitate, or scruple at; to allow oneself to be deterred, impeded, or checked by. **S. before —. a.** To come or be brought into the presence of, to confront (a person or assembly, a king, judge, tribunal, etc.). **b.** To confront (an adversary). Usu. with *can*, etc. negatively or interrogatively: To maintain one's ground against. **S. by —. a.** *lit.* To station oneself or remain stationed beside (a person); usu. as a helper, advocate, sympathizer, etc. **b.** *Naut.* To prepare to work (a gun, rope, etc.). **c.** *fig.* To support, assist, protect, defend (a person, a cause, etc.); to uphold the interests of, take the side of, be faithful or loyal to. **d.** To adhere to, maintain, abide by (a statement, agreement, or the like). **S. for —. a.** To uphold, defend (a cause, etc.); to support, take the part of (a person). **b.** To be reckoned or alleged for; to be counted or considered as; to serve in lieu of. *To s. for nothing*, to be worthless, of no avail; *to s. for something*, to have some value or importance. **c.** To put up with, 'stand'. *U.S.* **d.** To represent, do duty for. **e.** *Naut.* To sail or steer towards. **f.** To represent by way of symbol or sign; to be an emblem of. **g.** To represent by way of specimen. **S. in —. a.** To be dressed in, to be actually wearing. †**b.** To remain steadfast or obstinate in (a state, course of action, purpose, opinion, assertion). **c.** Of things: To rest or depend upon (something) as its ground of existence (*arch.*). **S. on —. a.** To base one's arguments or argumentative position on, 'take one's stand on'. **b.** Of an immaterial thing: To be grounded or based on. †**c.** To give oneself to, practise (some kind of action or behaviour). **d.** To be meticulously careful or scrupulous about, raise difficulties about (nice points, ceremony, etc.). **e.** To assert, claim respect or credit for (one's rights, qualities, dignity, etc.). †**f.** To value, set store by (something external to oneself). †**g.** To insist on, as essential or necessary, urge, press for, demand. †**h.** *impers.* (It) behoves. **S. over —.** To stand close by and watch or control (one who is seated, lying down, or on a lower level). **S. to —.** †**a.** To submit oneself to, abide by (a trial, award); to obey, accede to, be bound by (another's judgement, decision, opinion, etc.). †**b.** To leave oneself dependent upon (another's mercy, courtesy, etc.). **c.** To apply oneself manfully to (a fight, contest, etc.). *Obs.* exc. in *to s. to it*, to fight stoutly; also, to toil without flagging at painful or severe labour. **d.** Mil. *To s. to one's arms*, also *to s. to*: to stand with one's weapon in readiness for action. *To s. to one's guns, colours*: to maintain one's position, not to retire before an attack. **e.** To confront, present a bold front to (an enemy). †**f.** To abide by (the issue or consequences of an event). †**g.** To endure, bear, put up with (harm, pain); to make good, bear the expense of (damage, loss); to defray, be answerable for (expenses); to accept liability for (a tribute or tax). **h.** To side with, back, help, support (a person); to maintain, uphold (a cause, interest, etc.); to remain faithful or loyal to. **i.** To adhere to, abide by, carry out (a promise, vow, bargain, etc.). **j.** (*a*) To adhere to (a statement, etc.); to persist in affirming or asserting. (*b*) *To s. to it*: to insist upon or maintain a statement or assertion. **k.** *It stands to reason* (dial. *to sense*): it is reasonable, it is natural, evident, or certain (*that*). **l.** To be related to. **S. under —. a.** To be exposed or subject or obnoxious to; to undergo, bear the burden or weight or incidence of; (to be able) to sustain (a charge, etc.). **b.** *Naut.* To make sail with (a specified display of canvas). **c.** Mil. *To s. under arms*, to be ready for action. **S. upon —. a.** In fig. phrases of which the wording is literal. *To s. upon thorns*: see THORN *sb.* *To s. upon the defensive, upon one's guard*, etc.: see sense I. 7. **b.** To rely upon, depend on, trust to. *Obs.* exc. in the sense: To take one's stand upon an argument, argumentative position, etc. **c.** Of an immaterial thing (also *impers.*): To be grounded or based upon. **d.** *To s. upon terms*: (*a*) to be on a specified footing or in a specified situation or condition; (*b*) to insist upon conditions; also, *to s. upon conditions*; (*c*) to take a high line, to hold one's own, refuse to knuckle under. **e.** To be careful or scrupulous in regard to (forms, ceremonies, etc.); to be attentive to or observant of; to allow oneself to be unduly influenced or impeded by. **f.** To pride or value oneself upon; to urge, assert, make the most of, claim respect or consideration for, insist on the recognition of (one's qualities, rank, rights, possessions, dignity, etc.). †**g.** To attach importance to, give prominence or weight to; to value, set store by. †**h.** To dwell with emphasis or at length upon (a topic, argument, etc.). †**i.** *impers.* (It) concerns, behoves, is incumbent upon, is the duty of, is urgent or necessary for (a person). Const. *to* (do something). Usu. in the form *it stands* (a person) *upon* = he ought, he must needs. *Obs.* or *dial.* **S. with —.** To be consistent or consonant with, agree or accord with. *Obs.* exc. *arch.*

With advs. **S. about.** Of a number of persons: To stand here and there, in casual positions or groups. Of an individual: To remain about a locality without a fixed position or definite object. **S. aloof.** To s. at, or withdraw to, some distance (*from*), keep away (*from*). Also *fig.* **S. apart.** To stand separate or at a distance (*from* another or others). **S. away. a.** To withdraw to some distance. **b.** *Naut.* To sail or steer away (from some coast, quarter, enemy, etc.). **S. by. a.** To s. near at hand; to be present. Now chiefly, to be present as an unconcerned spectator. **b.** To draw back and s. apart from the general company or from what is going on. **c.** *Naut.* To hold oneself in readiness, be prepared (*for* something, *to do* something). Often in imper. = be ready! Also *gen.* **S. down. a.** Of a witness: To step down and leave the box after giving evidence. **b.** *Sport.* To withdraw from a game, match, or race; to give up one's place in a team, crew, or 'side'. **c.** *Naut.* To sail with the wind or tide. **S. in. a.** To go shares *with*, join, be a partner (*with*); in wider sense, to have a friendly or profitable understanding with, be in league with, be on good terms with. Also, to share chances with others *for* (a speculative event). **b.** *Naut.* To direct one's course towards the shore. **S. off. a.** To remain at or retire to a distance; to draw back, go farther away. Chiefly in commands. †**b.** *fig.* To be separated in quality, differ. **c.** *fig.* To hold aloof; to be 'distant', uncomplying or unaccommodating. **d.** Of a thing: To project, protrude, jut out (*from* a surface, etc.). Of a picture: To appear as if in relief. Also *fig.*, to be conspicuous. **e.** *Naut.* To sail away from the shore. **f.** *trans.* To keep off; keep at a distance; to repel, hold at bay. *U.S. colloq.* **g.** To dispense with the services of (an employee) temporarily. **S. off and on.** *Naut.* Alternately to recede from and approach the land while sailing by the wind. **S. on.** *Naut.* To keep one's course, continue on the same tack. **S. out. a.** To move away (from a company, shelter, etc.) and stand apart or in open view. **b.** Not to take part in (an undertaking, joint action, etc.); to refuse to come in or join others; now *esp.* not to take part in a match, game, or dance. **c.** To resist, refuse to yield or comply, hold out. Const. *against* (an opponent, proposal, etc.), *with* (an opponent). **d.** *To s. out for*: to declare oneself for, contend on behalf of. **e.** To haggle; to make an obstinate demand *for* (certain terms). **f.** *Naut.* To sail in a direction away from the shore. Usu. *to s. out to sea.* Hence *gen.*, to start on a journey. **g.** To jut out, project, protrude (*from* a surface); to be prominent. **h.** To be conspicuous; to be seen in contrast or relief *against* a dark object or background. Of figures in painting: To appear as if in relief. **i.** *fig.* To be prominent or conspicuous to the mental gaze. **j.** *trans.* To remain standing throughout (a performance). Also *Naut.* To 'stand watch' during (a specified time). **k.** To endure to the end, hold out under or against (a trial, ordeal, severe weather, etc.); to last out (a period of time). **l.** With object-cl.: To maintain, insist, persist in asserting (*that*). **S. over. a.** *Naut.* To leave one shore and sail towards another. **b.** To be left or reserved for treatment, consideration or settlement at a later date. †**S. together.** To agree, be consistent, harmonize. **S. up. a.** To assume an erect position; to rise, get up on one's feet. **b.** To take part in a dance; to dance *with* (a partner). **c.** Of things: To be set upright; to be or become erect. Of hair, spines, etc.: To grow stiff and erect. **d.** To hold oneself boldly erect to confront an opponent; to make a stand *against*. **e.** *To s. up for*: to defend, support, champion (a person, a cause, etc.). **f.** *To s. up to*: to confront or encounter boldly. Also *U.S.*, to meet (an obligation or promise). **g.** *To s. up in* (only in rel. clause), to be actually wearing. **h.** Of an animal: To hold out, endure (in a race, etc.).

Comb.: **s.-easy**, an assumption of the attitude directed by the command 'stand easy'; *fig.* a period of relaxation.

Standage (stæ·ndėdʒ). 1777. [f. STAND *v.* + -AGE.] **1.** Arrangements or accommodation for standing. **2.** *Mining.* An underground reservoir for water 1842.

Standard (stæ·ndăɹd), *sb.* ME. [Aphetic a. OF. *estandard* (mod.F. *étendard*); prob. f. Com. Rom. *estendere* (L. *extendere* to stretch out; see EXTEND *v.*) + -ARD. The senses of group III are affected by association with STAND *v.*] **A.** *sb.* **I.** A military or naval ensign. **1.** A flag, sculptured figure, or other conspicuous object, raised on a pole to indicate the rallying point of an army (or fleet), or of one of its component portions; the distinctive ensign of a king, great noble, or commander, or of a nation or city. **2.** In a more restricted sense, a military or naval flag of some particular kind usu. rectangular. late ME. **3.** = STANDARD-BEARER. ME. **4.** *Bot.* = VEXILLUM. 1776. **5.** *Ornith.* Each of the two lengthened wing-feathers characteristic of certain birds 1859.

1. Then in the name of God and all these rights, Aduance your Standards, draw your willing Swords SHAKS. Phr. *To raise one's s.*, to take up arms. *Under the s. of*, serving in the army of; so *to join the s. of* **2.** Barges garnished with standardes, stremers and penons HALL. 3. *Temp.* III. ii. 19.

II. Exemplar of measure or weight. **1.** The authorized exemplar of a unit of measure or weight; e.g. a measuring rod of unit length; a vessel of unit capacity, or a mass of metal of unit weight, preserved in the custody of public officers as a permanent evidence of the legally prescribed magnitude of the unit. late ME. **b.** The substance or thing which is chosen to afford the unit measure of any physical quantity, such as specific gravity 1805. **2.** (orig. *fig.* from prec.) An authoritative or recognized exemplar of correctness, perfection, or some definite degree of any quality 1477. **b.** A criterion, measure 1563. **3.** Legal rate of intrinsic value for coins; also, the prescribed degree of fineness for gold or silver 1463. **b.** (orig. †*s. of commerce.*) A commodity, the value of which is treated as invariable, in order that it may serve as a measure of value for all other commodities 1683. **4.** A definite level of excellence, attainment, wealth, or the like, or a definite degree of any quality, viewed as a prescribed object of endeavour or as the measure of what is adequate for some purpose 1711. **b.** In British elementary schools: Each of the recognized degrees of proficiency according to which school children are or have been classified 1876. **5.** A definite quantity of timber, differing in different countries 1858. **6.** The market price per ton of copper in the ore 1855. **7.** *Dyeing.* Short for *s. solution* (see B. I. 1 b) 1882.

1. These standards were kept in the royal exchequer 1871. **b.** Water is the s. with which all other bodies are compared 1805. **2.** We always return to the writings of the ancients, as the s. of true taste 1777. **b.** Personal interest is often the s. of our belief, as well as of our practice GIBBON. **3.** The standards for gold are 22 and 18 carats of pure metal in every ounce... The coinage is of the higher s... The lower s. is used for all manufacturing purposes. 1638. **4.** *S. of living, of comfort*, the view prevailing in a community or class with regard to the minimum of material comfort with which it is reasonable to be content.

III. Senses assoc. w. the verb *stand.* †**1.** A lofty erection of timber or stone, containing a vertical conduit pipe with spouts and taps, for the supply of water to the public –1854. **2.** A tall candlestick. Now *spec.* a tall candlestick (also, latterly, an upright gas or electric candelabrum) rising directly from the floor of a church. late ME. **3.** An upright timber, bar, or rod; e.g. an upright scaffold pole; an upright support or pedestal in various machines. In recent use often, a slender and lofty iron pillar carrying an electric or gas lamp, overhead electric wires, or the like. 1450. **b.** *Naut.* An inverted knee-timber, having the vertical portion turned upwards 1748. **4. a.** *Forestry.* A tree or shoot from a stump left standing when a coppice is cut down 1473. **b.** *Gardening.* A tree or shrub growing on an erect stem of full height, not dwarfed or trained on a wall or espalier 1625. †**5.** A large packing-case or chest –1663. **6.** †**a.** Something permanent; something that has lasted a long time –1655. **b.** One who has been long in a position; an old resident, official, servant, etc. Now only *old s.* (rare exc. dial.). 1661.

1. This paradise, five miles from the s. at Cornhill THACKERAY. 4. **b.** [Gardens] part laid out for flowers, others for fruits; some standards, some against walls or palisadoes 1685.

Comb.: **s.-bred** *a.*, of horses, etc. bred up to the s. of excellence prescribed by some authority; **-high** *a.*, of the height of a standard shrub; **s. lamp**, a lamp with a tall s. resting on the floor.

B. *adj.* [attrib. use of sb.] **I. 1.** Serving as a standard of measurement, weight, or value; conformed to the official standard of a unit of measure or weight 1622. **b.** Having the prescribed or normal size, amount, power, degree of quality, etc. 1807. **2.** Of precious metals, coins: Conforming to the legal standard of fineness or intrinsic value. Also said of value or fineness. 1677. **3.** Serving or fitted to serve as a standard of comparison or judgement 1724. **b.** Of a book, an author: That has a permanent rank as an authority, or as an exemplar of excellence 1645. **c.** Of a maxim, etc.: Constantly repeated 1805.

1. **b.** *S. gauge* (Railways): '4' 8½" between centers of rails'. 3. Applied to a language 1858. *S. English*: that form of the English language which is spoken (with modifications) by the generality of cultured people in Gt. Britain. So *S. American*, etc.

II. 1. Upright, set up on end or vertically 1538. **2.** Of a tree: Grown as a 'standard', not dwarfed or trained on a wall 1685.

2. A tall s. Rose 1908.

Sta·ndard·bea:rer. 1450. **1.** An officer or soldier who bears the standard. **b.** One who carries a banner in a procession 1495. **2.** *fig.* Chiefly, a conspicuous advocate of a cause; one who is in the forefront of a political or religious party 1561.

Standardize (stæ·ndăɹdəiz), *v.* 1873. [f. STANDARD *sb.* and *a.* + -IZE.] **1.** *trans.* To bring to a standard or uniform size, strength, form of construction, proportion of ingredients, or the like. **2.** To test by a standard 1881. Hence **Sta:ndardiza·tion**, the action of standardizing. **Sta·ndardizer**, one who or that which standardizes.

Sta·ndard-wing. 1869. [STANDARD *sb.* I. 5.] **1.** A species of Bird of Paradise (*Semioptera wallacei*) discovered by Wallace in the island of Batchian. **2.** *attrib.* or *adj.* Of certain birds: Characterized by the possession of 'standards' 1872. So **Standard-winged,** *a.*

Sta·nd-by. 1796. [f. vbl. phr. *stand by*; see STAND *v.*] **1.** *Naut.* **a.** A vessel kept in attendance for emergencies. **b.** An order or signal for a boat to stand by; *attrib.* in *s. bell*, the ringing of a bell in the engine-room of a vessel as a signal to stop the engines 1896. **2.** One who stands by another to render assistance; esp. *fig.* one who upholds or seconds another; a staunch adherent or partisan 1801. **3.** Something upon which one can rely; a main support; a chief resource 1861. **4.** *attrib.* or *adj.*

3. Art and marriage are two very good stand-by's STEVENSON.

Standel (stæ·ndĕl). 1543. [perh. an alteration of STADDLE influenced by STAND *v.*] A young tree left standing for timber.

Stander (stæ·ndəɹ). late ME. [f. STAND *v.* + -ER[1].] **1.** One who stands. †**2.** A person of long standing (in a profession or place); an old hand, an old resident –1832. †**3.** An upright support; a supporting pillar, stem, etc.; also a candlestick –1860. †**4.** = prec. –1712.

S.-by, one who stands by; one who looks on and abstains from interfering; occas. a bystander (now *rare*).

Standergrass (stæ·ndəɹgrɑs). 1578. [f. *stander-* (alteration of *standel-*, f. root of STAND *v.*) + GRASS *sb.*] The male orchis (*Orchis mascula*) and allied plants.

Standing (stæ·ndiŋ), *vbl. sb.* late ME. [f. STAND *v.* + -ING[1].] **1.** The action of STAND *v.*; an instance of this. **b.** The condition of being at a standstill. Also *s. still.* 1440. **c.** Erect position; condition of not falling or being overthrown. Now *rare* or *Obs.* 1709. †**2.** Manner of standing. **a.** Relative position –1733. **b.** Situation, site, aspect –1682. **c.** Posture, attitude; position of a thing –1801. **3.** An act of standing erect on one's feet; a period during which a person keeps a standing position 1653. **4.** A standing-place, station; standing-room. late ME. **5.** A position for or occupied by a booth, stall, or the like; a booth or stall occupying such position. Now *dial.* 1547. **6.** Degree of antiquity. (Now only of immaterial things.) Chiefly in phrases, *of old, ancient s.* 1656. **7.** Length of service, experience, or residence; position as determined by seniority 1580. **8.** Status in society, a profession, or the like 1607.

1. He cursed him in sitting, in s., in lying 1840. **4.** Keep all your standings and not stir a foot MARLOWE. *fig.* Some of them believed this; and so kept their s. in the Church 1676. **6.** Tuberculosis of long s. 1891. **7.** One of the fellows, and of Johnson's s. 1790. **8.** Men of some s. in the neighbourhood 1889.

Comb.: **s. room**, space in which to stand; accommodation for persons or a person standing.

Standing (stæ·ndiŋ), *ppl. a.* late ME. [f. STAND *v.* + -ING[2].] **I.** That stands upright or on end. **1.** Of a person, an animal, a statue: That keeps an upright stationary position on the feet 1576. **b.** *transf.* Of an action: Performed in a standing posture 1637. **2.** Of vegetation: That stands erect (in growth); growing. late ME. **3.** Of an inanimate thing: That stands up, upright, or on end; that is set in a vertical position 1539. **b.** Remaining erect; not fallen or overthrown 1700. **4.** Having a foot or feet, a base, or a stem and base upon which to stand, esp. in *s. bowl, cup, piece* (of plate). late ME. **5.** Of a piece of furniture: That rests upon its base when set up for use. 1485. **6.** *Naval Arch.* Of a bevel or bevelling: Forming an angle greater than a right angle; obtuse 1754.

1. Ye shall make you no Idoles..neither reare you vp a s. image *Lev.* xxvi. 1. **b.** That Warr..sometimes on firm ground A s. fight MILT. **2.** Sheets of Lightning blast the s. Field DRYDEN. **3.** Let vs haue s. Collers, in the fashion 1611. **5.** A s. screen which perpetually belies its name 1806. *S. ladder* = step-ladder.

II. That remains at rest or in a fixed position. **1.** Of air, water, a piece of water: Still, stagnant. late ME. **2.** Of a thing: At a standstill. Of a machine, tool, etc.: Not in operation. 1585. **3.** That is used in a fixed position 1634. **4.** That remains in one spot; stationary. *Obs.* exc. *Mil.* in *s. camp.* 1469. **5.** That remains stationary while another part, or other parts, move; esp. *Naut.* 1680.

1. A sort of men, whose visages Do creame and mantle like a s. pond SHAKS. **2.** Ixion..leans attentive on his s. Wheel DRYDEN. **4.** We got back to our s. camp..about mid-day 1896. **5. S. rigging**, the fixed part of a vessel's rigging which serves as a support for the masts and is not hauled upon, as dist. from the running rigging; **s. ropes** *pl.*, the ropes composing the s. rigging; **s. part** (of a rope, sheet, etc.), that end of a thing which is made fast as dist. from the end hauled upon.

III. That stands or continues. **1.** Continuing without diminution or change; constant, permanent. Of colours: unfading. late ME. **2.** Of employment, wages, prices, attributes, etc.: Fixed, settled; not casual, fluctuating, or occasional 1473. **3.** That continues in existence or operation; that continues to be (what the noun specifies); that does not pass away 1662. **4.** Habitually used; stock 1492. **5.** Permanently and authoritatively fixed or set up; stated, established, organized, regular 1549. **b.** Of a legislative, administrative, or other body: Permanently constituted 1625. **c.** Of troops: Maintained on a permanent footing; esp. in *s. army* 1603. **d.** Of an official: Holding permanent office 1656.

2. My s. allowance from Michaelmas last till Christmas 1670. Two s. characteristics of the Professor's style 1835. 3. This is the s. joke nightly repeated 1864. *S. order* (Parliament), a continuing regulation for the guidance and order of parliamentary proceedings. *S. order, rule,* (Mil.), any one of certain general rules and instructions which are to be invariably followed, and are not subject to the temporary intervention of rank. 4. The s. excuse of a bad headache 1861. Phr. *s. dish* (at a meal). 5. A s. caravan commerce with Phenicia 1846. b. I commend also s. Commissions; as for Trade; for Treasure BACON. d. There should be a s. treasurer 1656.

Sta·nding-place. 1440. [f. STANDING *vbl. sb.*] **1.** A place prepared or assigned for a person or thing to stand in; a place to accommodate persons standing. **2.** A place where a person takes his stand 1736.

Sta·nding stone. ME. [STANDING *ppl. a.*] A large block of stone set upright; a menhir, monolith.

Standish (stæ·ndiʃ). *Obs.* exc. *Hist.* or *arch.* 1474. [Said to be f. STAND *v.* + DISH *sb.*; but evidence is wanting for such a use of *dish.*] A stand containing ink, pens and other writing materials and accessories; an inkstand; inkpot.

He wanted pen, ink, and paper. There was an old s. on the high mantel shelf containing a dusty apology for all three. DICKENS.

Sta·nd-off, *attrib. phr.* and *a.* 1837. [f. vbl. phr. *stand off*; see STAND *v.*] That holds aloof from familiar intercourse; contemptuously distant in manner; reserved, unsocial. **b.** *S. half,* in Rugby football, the half-back who stands away from the scrum 1909. Hence **Stand-o·ffish** *a.*, **-ness.**

Stand-patter: see STAND *v.* I. 10.

Sta·nd-pipe, *sb.* 1790. [f. STAND *v.*] **1.** A vertical pipe for the conveyance of water, gas, steam, etc. to a higher level. **2.** A pipe for attachment to a water-main furnished with a spout or nozzle to which a hose may be fixed or with a tap 1850.

Standpoint (stæ·ndpoint). 1829. [f. STAND *v.* + POINT *sb.*[1], after G. *standpunkt.*] A fixed point of standing; the position at which a person stands to view an object; a point of view. Hence, a mental point of view.

Sta·nd(-)still, *sb.* and *a.* 1702. [f. vbl. phr. *to stand still*; see STILL *a.*] **A.** *sb.* **1.** A state of cessation of movement; a halt, pause. **2.** The state of being unable to proceed, owing to exhaustion 1811.

1. Phr. *To come, bring to a s., to be at a s.* 2. To *ride* (a horse) *to a s., to row* (a competitor) *to a s.*

B. *adj.* That stands still; that is deficient in advancement or progress 1856.

Sta·nd-up, *a.* 1811. [f. vbl. phr. *stand up*; see STAND *v.*] **1.** That stands erect; esp. of a collar, upright, not 'turn-down' 1812. **2.** Performed in a standing posture. Of a meal, etc.: Taken standing. 1862. **3.** *Pugilism.* Of a contest: In which the combatants stand up fairly to one another, without wrestling, flinching, or evasion; esp. in (*a fair, square,* etc.) *s. fight* 1811.

Stang (stæŋ), *sb.*[1] *dial.* ME. [a. ON. *stǫng*, cogn. w. OE. *stæng, stęng* pole, OS. *stanga.* The OTeut. types are **stangō*, **stangjō*, **stangiz*, f. the root **steng-* to pierce; see STING *v.*] **1.** A pole or stake, a wooden bar or beam. †**2.** A measure of land -1777.

1. *To make* (a person) *ride the s.*, a method of expressing popular disapproval by having an offender carried on a s. for public derision.
Comb.: **s.-ball,** a variety of bar-shot.

Stang, *sb.*[2] *Sc.* and *north.* ME. [f. next.] A sting; a sharp pain.

Stang (stæŋ), *v.*[1] ME. [a. ON. *stanga* to prick, goad, spear (fish), etc., f. *stang, stǫng* STANG *sb.*[1]] *trans.* To sting. Also *absol.*

Stang (stæŋ), *v.*[2] 1674. [f. STANG *sb.*[1]] †**1.** To cause to ride the stang -1777. **2.** To carry (produce) on stangs 1829.

Stanhope (stæ·nəp). 1825. [Proper name.] A light open one-seated vehicle, formerly made with two wheels, but now commonly with four. First made for The Hon. the Rev. Fitzroy *Stanhope* (1787–1864). Often written with small initial.

Comb.: **s. horse,** one suitable for a s.
S. lens, a lens of small diameter with two convex faces of different radii, inclosed in a metallic tube (invented by Charles 3rd Earl *Stanhope* 1753–1816); **S. press,** a hand printing-press invented by the 3rd Earl *Stanhope.*

Staniel, stannel (stæ·nyĕl, stæ·nĕl). [OE. *stānegella, stāngella,* lit. 'stone-yeller', f. *stān* STONE + **gella,* agent-n. f. *gellan* to YELL.] The kestrel, *Tinnunculus alandarius.* Also applied contemptuously to a person, in allusion to the uselessness of the kestrel for the purposes of falconry.

‖**Stanitza** (stăni·tsă). 1662. [Russ.] A Cossack community or township.

Stank (stæŋk), *sb.* ME. [a. OF. *estanc* (mod.F. *étang*) :—Com. Rom. **stanco,* prob. vbl. noun f. **stancare* to dam up (:—pop. L. **stagnicare,* f. *stagnum* pond); see STANCH *v.*] **1.** A pond or pool. Also a ditch or dyke of slowly-moving water, a moat. Now *Sc.* and *dial.* **2.** A dam to hold back water, a weir or flood-gate. Now *dial.* and *techn.* 1604.

Comb.: **s.-hen,** the moor-hen, *Gallinula chloropus*; **-meadow,** a meadow containing a pool. Hence **Stank** *v. trans.* to dam or strengthen the banks of a stream (*dial.* and *techn.*).

Stannary (stæ·nări). 1455. [ad. med.L. *stannaria,* f. L. *stannum* tin; see -ARY.] **1.** *The Stannaries*: The districts comprising the tin mines and smelting works of Cornwall and Devon formerly under the jurisdiction of the Stannary courts; also, the customs and privileges attached to the mines. **2.** Tin; tin-ware; a locality in a mart or fair appropriated to the sale of tin-ware. *Obs.* exc. *Hist.* 1668.

attrib.: **S. courts,** the courts of law for the administration of justice in the Stannaries. So **Stanna·tor,** a member of the S. convocation or parliament.

Stannic (stæ·nik), *a.* 1790. [f. STANNUM + -IC.] *Chem.* Of a compound: Containing tin as a quadrivalent element.

Stannite (stæ·nəit). 1851. [f. STANNUM + -ITE.] **1.** *Chem.* A salt of stannous acid. **2.** *Min.* Sulphide of tin, copper, iron and zinc, found in steel-grey masses 1896.

Stanno- (stænǫ), bef. a vowel also **stann-,** used in *Chem.*, as comb. form of late L. *stannum* tin, as stannamyl, stannofluoride, etc.

Stannoso- (stænōu·sǫ), *Chem.*, used as comb. form of mod.L. *stannosus* STANNOUS.

Stannotype (stæ·nǫtəip). 1883. [f. late L. *stannum* tin + Gr. τύπος impression, print, TYPE.] A form of photo-mechanical engraving in which a mould obtained from a positive instead of a negative is coated with tinfoil.

Stannous (stæ·nəs), *a.* 1849. [f. STANNUM + -OUS.] *Chem.* Of a compound: Containing tin as a bivalent element.

‖**Stannum** (stæ·nǫm). *rare* in Eng. context. 1783. [mod.L. use of late L. *stannum* tin, orig. an alloy of silver and lead; app. an altered form of *stagnum,* whence OF. *estain* (mod.F. *étain*), etc.] *Chem.* The chemical Latin name for tin. (Hence the symbol Sn.) Hence **Sta·nnate** *Chem.* a salt of stannic acid. **Stanni·ferous** *a.* producing or containing tin.

Stanza (stæ·nză). 1588. [a. It., stopping-place, room :—pop. L. **stantia,* f. L. *stantem, stare* to stand.] **1.** *Prosody.* A group of lines of verse (usu. not less than four), arranged according to a definite scheme which regulates the number of lines, the metre, and (in rhymed poetry) the sequence of rhymes; normally forming a division of a song or poem consisting of a series of such groups constructed according to the same scheme. Also, any of the particular types of structure according to which stanzas are framed. **2.** In Italy, an apartment, chamber, room; *spec.* in pl. ‖ *stanze* (sta·ntse), applied to certain rooms in the Vatican 1648.

1. I have adopted the s. of Spenser SHELLEY. Hence **Stanzaic** (stænzē¹·ik), **-al** *adjs.* of, belonging to, or of the nature of poetry composed in the form of stanzas.

Stap. 1696. Affected pronunciation of STOP *v.*, in the phr. *S. my vitals,* used as an exclam. of surprise, anger, etc., or as an asseveration.

Well, 'tis Ten Thousand Pawnd well given — s. my Vitals VANBRUGH.

Stapedial (stăpī·diăl), *a.* 1875. [f. mod. L. *stapedius* (see next) + -AL.] *Anat.* Pertaining to the stapes.

‖**Stapedius** (stăpī·diǫs). 1788. [mod.L., ellipt. use of *stapedius* adj. (sc. *musculus*), f. *staped-* STAPES.] *Anat.* (More fully *s. muscle.*) The small muscle attached to the neck of the stapes.

‖**Stapelia** (stăpī·liă). 1785. [mod.L. (Linn.), f. name of Jan Bode von *Stapel,* a Dutch botanist (died 1636); see -IA.] *Bot.* A S. Afr. genus of asclepiadaceous plants, remarkable for the fetid smell of the flowers, whence one species (*S. hirsuta*) is called Carrion-flower. Also, a plant of this genus.

‖**Stapes** (stē¹·pīz). 1670. [mod.L. use of med.L. *stapes* (*staped-*) stirrup.] The innermost of the three ossicles in the tympanum of the ear in mammals; named from its stirrup-like shape.

Staphyline (stæ·filəin), *a.* 1820. [ad. late Gr. σταφύλινος, f. σταφυλή bunch of grapes.] *Min.* = BOTRYOIDAL *a.*

Staphylinid (stæfili·nid), *sb.* and *a.* 1848. [ad. mod.L. *Staphylinidæ,* f. *Staphylinus,* a. Gr. σταφυλῖνος a kind of insect, prob. f. σταφυλή bunch of grapes; see -ID.] *Entom.* **A.** *sb.* An insect belonging to the *Staphylinidæ* or rove-beetles, a coleopterous order of which the typical genus is *Staphylinus.* **B.** *adj.* Belonging to the *Staphylinidæ.*

‖**Staphylococcus** (stæfiloko·kǫs). *Pl.* **-cocci** (-ko·ksəi). 1887. [mod.L., f. Gr. σταφυλή bunch of grapes + κόκκος berry.] *Bacteriol.* A form of pus-producing bacteria composed of cocci grouped in irregular masses.

‖**Staphyloma** (stæfilōu·mă). 1597. [mod. L., a. Gr. σταφύλωμα a disease of the eye, f. σταφυλή bunch of grapes.] *Path.* Protrusion of the cornea or sclera, resulting from inflammation. Hence **Staphylo·matous** *a.*

Staphyloplasty (stæ:filoplæ·sti). 1846. [f. Gr. σταφυλή + -PLASTY.] A plastic operation for the closure of cleft palate.

Staphylorrhaphy (stæfilǫ·răfi). 1846. [f. Gr. σταφυλή + ῥαφή sewing, suture.] *Surg.* The surgical closure of a cleft palate.

Staple (stē¹·p'l), *sb.*[1] [OE. *stapol* :—OTeut. **stapuloz* something supporting.] †**1.** A post, pillar, column (of wood, stone, metal). -late ME. **b.** *Mining.* A pillar of coal left as a temporary support for a superincumbent mass 1839. **2.** A short rod or bar of iron, etc. bent into the form of a U or of three sides of a rectangle, and pointed at the ends, to be driven into a surface, in order to serve as a hold for a hasp, hook, or bolt to secure a door or box, or as an attachment for a rope or the like. Also any similar contrivance, as the box or case into which the bolt of a lock is shot. ME. **b.** A snout-ring 1688. **c.** A piece of thin wire, driven through papers, etc., and clinched to bind them 1911.

Comb.: **s.-ring** = sense 2 b.

Staple (stē¹·p'l), *sb.*[2] late ME. [a. OF. *estaple* emporium, mart (mod.F. *étape* halting-place) :—med.L. *stapula,* also *staplus,* ad. MLG. *stapol*; see prec.] **1.** A town or place appointed by royal authority, in which was a body of merchants having the exclusive right of purchase of certain classes of goods destined for export; also, the body of merchants so privileged. Now *Hist.*

From about 1390 to 1558 the chief s. was at Calais, which is often called 'The S.' There were also staples in many important towns of England, Wales, and Ireland.

b. †(*a*) A town or country which is the principal market or entrepôt for some particular class of merchandise. (*b*) A commercial centre (Now *arch.*). late ME. †**c.** An authorized place of trade for merchants of a foreign country -1892. **2.** [Short for *staple-ware,* etc. (see 3), and ellipt. use of STAPLE *a.*] A staple commodity. **a.** A principal industrial product of a country, town, or district; *occas.* the commodity principally dealt in by a person or class of persons 1616. **b.** *transf.* and *fig.* The thing chiefly 'dealt in'; the principal object of employment, thought, or discourse. Sometimes: The chief component element, the 'substance', 'bulk'. 1826.

1. *Mayor of the S.*: orig., an official specially appointed by the king; latterly, the mayor of some boroughs was *ex officio* mayor of the staple. 2. a. The manufacture of cotton..has long been the s. of this county 1806.

attrib.: **s.-house,** a warehouse where commodities chargeable with export duties were stored; **†-ware(s,** such goods as were the monopoly of the S.

Staple (stē¹·p'l), *sb.*³ 1481. [perh. a back-formation from STAPLER, the sorting of wool according to quality being part of the business of the stapler.] **1.** The fibre of wool (in later use also of cotton, flax, etc.) considered with regard to its length and fineness; a particular length and degree of fineness in the fibre of wool, cotton, etc. **b.** A lock of wool 1805. **c.** Unmanufactured wool 1885. **2.** The fibre of which a thread or a textile fabric is composed. Hence *gen.* the material of which anything is made. 1588. **3.** The stratum of vegetable mould overlying the rock; a particular depth or quality of this 1722.

1. The s. of mohair is from five to six inches long 1879. 2. He draweth out the thred of his verbositie finer then the s. of his argument SHAKS.

Comb.: **s.-threaded** *a.*, composed of thread of selected s.

Staple (stæ·p'l), *sb.*⁴ *north.* Also **stapple.** 1818. [Origin obsc.] **a.** A small shaft joining two different levels in a mine. **b.** A small pit.

Staple (stē¹·p'l), *a.* 1586. [Extension of attrib. use of STAPLE *sb.*², as in *staple-ware.*] orig., qualifying *commodity* or the like: Having a foremost place among the products exported by a country or place. Hence: Having the chief place among the articles of production or consumption, the industries, employments, etc., of a place, a people, or an individual, or among the constituent elements of anything. 1615. **†b.** Of a book, an author: Standard -1745.

The s. commodities are cotton woolles..chamolets, salt and sope-ashes 1615. The s. trade of Keswick 1872. Phr. In STATUTE STAPLE (the adj. replaces the phr. *of the staple*, on the analogy of *statute merchant*); so *Recognizance s.*, a recognizance taken before the mayor of the s.

Staple (stē¹·p'l), *v.*¹ 1470. [f. STAPLE *sb.*¹] To secure with or as with a staple. Hence **Sta·pler¹, Sta·pling-machine,** a machine for binding papers together with staples.

Staple (stē¹·p'l), *v.*² Now *Hist.* 1472. [f. STAPLE *sb.*²] *trans.* To receive (export goods) at a staple; to cause to be weighed, etc., in accordance with the regulations of the staple.

Stapled (stē¹·p'ld), *a.* 1594. [f. STAPLE *sb.*³] Having a staple (of a certain kind).

Stapler² (stē¹·plər). 1513. [f. STAPLE *sb.*² + -ER¹.] **1.** (More fully *merchant s.*) A merchant of the Staple. **2.** = WOOL-STAPLER 1552.

Star (stāɹ), *sb.*¹ [Com. WGer.; OE. *steorra* :—OTeut. type **sterron-*, f. **ster-* cogn. w. L. *stella* (:—**ster-la*), Gr. ἀ-στερ-, ἀστήρ, ἀ-στρ-ον, Skr. *star.* cf. STERN *sb.*²] **1.** Any one of the many celestial bodies appearing as luminous points in the night sky. Now usu. restricted to the *fixed stars* as dist. from planets (exc. in EVENING-STAR, MORNING-STAR), comets, and meteors (exc. in FALLING STAR, SHOOTING STAR). See also SEVEN STARS. Freq. *fig.* **b.** With ref. to the pagan belief that the souls of illustrious persons after death appear as new stars in the heavens. late ME. **c.** *poet.* = LODE-STAR, POLE-STAR. 1599. **2.** In extended use, any one of the heavenly bodies, including the sun and moon; sometimes in *pl.* as a vague designation for the abode of departed spirits. Chiefly *poet.*; cf. L. *sidus.* ME. **3.** In *Astrol.*, used of the planets and zodiacal constellations, as supposed to influence human affairs ME. **b.** *transf.* A person's fortune, rank, or destiny, disposition or temperament, viewed as determined by the stars 1601. **4.** *fig.* A person of brilliant reputation or talents. **a.** *Theatr.*, etc. An actor, singer, etc. of exceptional celebrity, or one whose name is prominently advertised as a special attraction to the public 1824. **b.** *gen.* (Chiefly *colloq.*) One who 'shines' in society, or is distinguished in some branch of art or science 1850. **5.** An image or figure of a star ME.

It is conventionally represented by a number of rays diverging from a central point or circle, or by a geometrical figure of five or more radiating points, such as is formed by producing the sides of a pentagon, hexagon, etc.

6. *Pyrotechny.* A small piece of combustible composition, used in rockets, mines, etc., which as seen burning high in the air resembles a star 1634. **7.** An ornament, usu. of precious metal, representing a star, worn as part of the insignia of an order of knighthood, or as a military decoration. Also occas. applied to the holder or wearer of this decoration. 1712. **8.** A natural object resembling or likened to a star; e.g. the open corolla (or corolla and disk) of a flower 1635. **b.** A spot or patch of white hair on the forehead of a horse or ox. late ME. **c.** A star-like crystalline pattern which appears on the surface of antimony in the process of refining 1660. **d.** *Zool.* A star-shaped zoophyte or its cell. Also, a stellate sponge-spicule. 1755. **9.** = ASTERISK 3. (Cf. F. *étoile.*) late ME. **b.** In lists of stockholders, an asterisk prefixed or appended to a person's name when his holding exceeds a certain amount 1845. **10.** Applied to various objects having the conventional form of a star 1672. **11.** A person having a star as a badge 1859. **12.** *Billiards.* The act of 'starring' (see STAR *v.* 7.) 1850.

1. And tell us whence the stars; why some are fix'd, And planetary some COWPER. Thy soul was like a S., and dwelt apart WORDSW. *fig.* Quixote—the errant S. of Knighthood LAMB. Phr. *S. of the sea* = *Stella maris*, a title given to the Virgin Mary. *To see stars* (colloq.), to have a sensation as of flashes of light, produced by a sudden jarring of the head, as by a direct blow. **b.** Heauens make a Starre of him! SHAKS. **c.** Loue..is the s. to euery wandring barke SHAKS. **2.** *Diurnal s., s. of day, of noon*: the sun; Ere this diurnal Starr Leave cold the Night MILT. **3.** You were borne vnder a charitable starre SHAKS. *One's s.* or *stars* the planet or constellation which, by its position at the moment of a man's birth, sways his destinies, moulds his temperament, etc. *My stars!* usu. a trivial expression of astonishment. **b.** Lord Hamlet is a Prince out of thy Starre SHAKS. **5.** *Stars and stripes*, the popular name for the United States flag, which originally contained 13 stripes and 13 stars, representing the 13 States of the Union; it now contains 13 stripes and 48 stars. **8. b.** She Kiss'd the white s. upon his noble front TENNYSON.

attrib. and *Comb.*, as *s.-galaxy*; *s.-watcher*; *s.-embroidered*, *-led*, adjs., etc.; *-eyed*, adj., etc.; *s.-craft*, *-love*, etc. With the sense 'marked or distinguished by a star or asterisk', as *s. days*, *routes*, *prisoners*, etc. In sense 4, as *s. part*, *soprano*, etc.

Comb.: **s.-beam** *poet.*, a ray of starlight; **s.-chart,** a chart which shows the stars in a certain portion of the sky; **-cluster,** a number of stars closely grouped together; **s. connexion** *Electr.*, in a polyphase system, an arrangement by which the coils or circuits have a common junction; **-crossed** *a.*, thwarted by a malign s.; **-cut** *a.*, cut with s.-facets; *sb.*, this style of cutting; **-facet,** one of the small triangular facets which surround the table of a brilliant; **-fort,** a small fort having alternate salient and re-entrant angles; **s. fracture** *Med.*, a fracture with radiating fissures; **-gauge,** (*a*) a determination by the average of a number of observations of the number of stars visible in a given portion of the heavens; (*b*) a gauge with radiating steel points for measuring the bore of a cannon at any part of its length; **-headed** *a.*, headed with a s.; *spec.* as an epithet of certain stellate flowers; **-lit** *ppl. a.*, lit up or lighted by the stars; **s. lot,** an item in a sale catalogue added after the numbering is completed, and therefore designated by a starred number; **-pagoda,** an Indian gold coin (cf. PAGODA 3); **-proof** *a.*, impervious to starlight; **-pulley** = *s.-wheel*; **-shake,** a shake in timber consisting of radial fissures; **-shell** *Mil.*, a shell which on bursting releases a shower of stars, to illuminate the enemy's position at night; **-shine** = STAR-LIGHT; **-shower,** a shower of falling meteors; **s. system** *Theatr.*, the method of relying on one or two stars to make up for a weak company; **s. turn,** the chief attraction of a performance, company, display, etc.; **-wheel,** a wheel with radial projections or teeth, used in winding-machines, clock-work, etc.; **-worship** = SABAISM. **b.** In names of animals and plants: **s. anemone,** *Anemone stellata* (or *hortensis*); **-anise,** *Illicium anisatum* or its fruit (from the stellate arrangement of the carpels); **-buzzard,** an American hawk of the genus *Asturina*; **-coral,** a coral of the family *Astræidæ*; **-cucumber,** *Sicyos angulatus* of N. America; **-hyacinth,** *Scilla amœna*; **-jelly, -slough,** nostoc. **c. Star of Bethlehem,** the genus *Ornithogalum*, esp. *O. umbellatum*, abundant in Palestine, with white stellate flowers; applied also to other plants; **s. of the earth,** *Plantago Coronopus*; **s. of Jerusalem,** *Tragopogon pratensis* or *T. porrifolius*. **d.** In names of precious stones which exhibit asterism, as *s. diamond, quartz, ruby, sapphire*; STAR-STONE.

Star, *sb.*² Now *dial.* ME. [a. ON. *stjorr.*] A name given locally to various coarse seaside grasses and sedges, as *Psamma arenaria* and *Carex arenaria*. Also *s.-grass*.

Star (stāɹ), *v.* 1592. [f. STAR *sb.*¹] **†1.** *trans.* To mark (a horse) with a star. GREENE. **2.** To adorn with an ornament likened to a star or a number of stars; to bespangle as with stars 1718. **3.** To make a radiating crack or fracture in (a surface of glass, ice, etc.) 1788. **b.** *intr.* To become fractured in this way 1842. **c.** *trans.* (*Geol.*) To diversify (strata) by cracks or veins radiating from a centre 1839. **4. a.** To produce the 'stars' on (antimony) in the process of refining. **b.** *intr.* Of antimony: To form 'stars' when solidifying. 1889. **5.** To distinguish (a word, name, etc.) by an affixed star or asterisk. Hence, to single out for notice or recommendation. 1897. **6.** *intr.* Of an actor, singer, distinguished personage, etc.: To appear as a 'star', perform the leading part; to make a tour in the provinces as the 'star' of a dramatic company. Also quasi-trans. *to s. the provinces.* 1824. **7.** *Billiards.* In the game of Pool, to buy an additional life or lives. Similarly in *Dominoes*. Also quasi-*trans.* 1850.

2. Like a sable curtain starr'd with gold YOUNG. The primroses starred the banks 1884. 5. He maintained that..if the Government meant to proceed with these Bills they ought to have 'starred' them 1897.

Star-apple (stā·ræ:p'l). 1697. The fruit of any tree of the genus *Chrysophyllum*; the tree itself (also *s. tree*).

The fruit is the size of a large apple, and when cut across shows ten cells forming a star-like figure.

Starboard (stā·ɹbəɹd, -bōᵊɹd), *sb.* (and *a.*). [OE. *stéorbord*, f. *stéor* steering paddle, rudder, STEER *sb.* + *bord* BOARD *sb.*

The etym. sense of the word refers to the mode of steering the early Teut. ships, by means of a paddle worked over the right side of the vessel.]

A. *sb.* The right-hand side of a ship, as dist. from the LARBOARD or PORT side; the side upon which in early types of ships the steering apparatus was worked. **b.** as *adv.* To or on the starboard side 1634. **B.** *attrib.* or *adj.* Of, belonging to or situated on the right side of a boat or vessel 1495.

Starboard (stā·ɹbəɹd, -bōᵊɹd), *v.* 1598. [f. the sb.] *trans.* To put over or turn (the helm) to the starboard side of the ship. Chiefly in the command *S.* (*the helm*)!

Starbolins, starbowlines (stā·ɹbǫlinz), *pl.* 1769. [perh. for **starboardlings*, f. STARBOARD *sb.* + -LING¹.] *Naut.* The men of the starboard watch.

Sta·r-bright, *a.* Chiefly *poet.* 1560. Bright as a star; bright with stars.

Florence!..Thou brightest star of star-bright Italy! COLERIDGE.

Starch (stāɹtʃ), *sb.* 1440. [In 15th c. *sterche*, f. *sterche* STARCH *v.* to stiffen.] **1.** A substance obtained from flour by removing some of its constituents (now also from other vegetable sources containing 'starch' in sense 2) used, in the form of a gummy liquid or paste made with water, to stiffen linen or cotton fabrics, to give a finish to the surface of textile materials, to size paper, etc. Also, the paste made from this substance to prepare it for use. **2.** *Chem.* An organic compound found in plant-cells (a member of the amylose group of carbohydrates) being the chief constituent of starch as described in sense 1. 1812. **3.** *fig.* Stiffness, esp. of manner or conduct 1705.

attrib. and *Comb.*, as **s. bandage,** a bandage rubbed with s. paste, to serve as a splint; **s. bath,** a medicinal bath or lotion made with s.; **-gum** = DEXTRIN; **s. sugar** = DEXTROSE; **-water,** a solution of starch and water; **starchwort,** *Arum maculatum*.

Starch (stāɹtʃ), *a.* Somewhat *arch.* 1717. [f. prec.] Of a person, his bearing, etc.: Stiff, unbending; formal.

The s. and unpliant habits of the times H. WALPOLE. Hence **Sta·rch·ly** *adv.* in a stiff or formal manner, **-ness.**

Starch (stāɹtʃ), *v.* [Late ME. *sterche* :—OE. **stercan* to make rigid, f. *stearc* stiff, rigid; see STARK *a.*] **1.** To stiffen (a thing, linen, etc.) with starch. **†b.** *fig.* To make rigid, formal, or precise; to frame (a discourse) in formal or pretentious terms. Also *absol.* -1814. †2. To fasten or stick with starch paste -1721.

Sta·r-cha·mber, †starred chamber. late ME. [f. STAR *sb.*[1], STARRED *a.* So called 'because at the first all the roofe thereof was decked with images of starres gilted' (Sir T. Smith's conjecture).] 1. An apartment in the royal palace at Westminster, in which during the 14th and the 15th c. the chancellor, treasurer, justices, and other members of the king's council sat to exercise jurisdiction. 2. (More fully *Court of S.*) A court, chiefly of criminal jurisdiction, developed in the 15th c. from the judicial sittings of the King's Council in the Star Chamber at Westminster and abolished by the Long Parliament in 1641. From its abuse under James I and Charles I it has become proverbial as a type of an arbitrary and oppressive tribunal. 1487.

2. *attrib.* I will make a Star-Chamber matter of it SHAKS.

Starched (stāɹtʃt), *ppl. a.* 1599. [f. STARCH *v.* + -ED[1].] 1. Stiffened with or as with starch 1617. 2. *fig.* Stiff, formal, precise 1599. Hence **Sta·rched-ly** *adv.*, **-ness.**

Starcher (stā·ɹtʃəɹ). 1515. [f. STARCH *v.* and *sb.* + -ER[1].] 1. One whose employment or trade is to starch linen. 2. A starched neckcloth 1818. 3. A starching machine 1893.

Starchy (stā·ɹtʃi), *a.* 1802. [f. STARCH *sb.* + -Y[1].] 1. Of or belonging to starch; resembling starch or containing starch grains. 2. *fig.* Of a person: Stiff, formal, precise 1828. Hence **Sta·rchily** *adv.* **Sta·rchiness.**

Sta·r-dust. 1844. 1. *Astr.* Innumerable minute stars, likened, as seen in the telescope, to particles of dust. 2. Meteoric matter in fine particles supposed to fall upon the earth from space; 'cosmic dust'. GEIKIE.

Stare (stēəɹ), *sb.*[1] *arch.* and *dial.* [OE. *stær* :—OTeut. **staroz*, *starŏn-*, cogn. w. L. *sturnus.*] = STARLING[1].

Stare (stēəɹ), *sb.*[2] late ME. [f. STARE *v.*] †1. Power of seeing. late ME. only. †2. A condition of amazement, horror, admiration, etc., indicated by staring -1610. 3. An act or a habit of staring; a fixed gaze with the eyes wide open 1700.

2. Why stand you In this strange s.? SHAKS. 3. A stony British s. TENNYSON.

Stare (stēəɹ), *v.* [OE. *starian*, f. OTeut. **staro-* rigid (whence OE. *stær(e)blind*).] 1. *intr.* To gaze fixedly and with eyes wide open. Said also of the eyes. Also quasi-*trans.* with complement. (In mod. use the verb ordinarily implies rudeness.) b. *transf.* and *fig.* Of things: To be obtrusively conspicuous 1657. 2. Used with implication of a mental state. †a. To open the eyes wide in madness or fury; to glare -1837. b. To open the eyes wide in astonishment; hence, to be amazed. late ME. 3. Of hair, a horse's coat, feathers, fibres of any kind: To stand on end. Now chiefly *techn.* 1523.

1. Her bright eyes gan ope, And starde upon him MARSTON. Panurge star'd at him like a dead Pig 1694. I sat for hours together staring on the fire 1806. Phr. *To s.* (a person) *out of countenance*, to disconcert by staring at. *To s.* (a person) *in the face*, to stare at (his) face; *fig.* of a thing, to be glaringly obvious. *To s.* (a person) *up and down*, to survey with a stare from head to foot. 2. a. Some laught, some swore, some star'd and stamp'd and curst 1615. b. Mac-Morlan will s. when he sees the bill SCOTT. 3. The affected cows were restless and irritable; their coats 'stared' 1888. Hence **Sta·rer**, a person who stares. **Sta·ring** *ppl. a.*, **-ly** *adv.*

Star(-)fish (stā·ɹfiʃ). *Pl.* **-fish, -fishes.** 1538. [cf. SEA-STAR 2.] 1. Any echinoderm of the genus *Asterias* or of the class *Asteroidea*, having a flattened body, normally consisting of lobes or rays (usually five) radiating from a central disk. These rays are occas. very short or altogether absent, the body having the form of a pentagonal disk. The common star-fish is *Asterias rubens.* 2. *transf.* A name for certain species of Stapelia 1840.

Sta·r-flo·wer. 1629. A name given to a number of plants with bright stellate flowers, as *Ornithogalum umbellatum* and other species, (in U.S.) *Trientalis americana*, etc. Also, a book-name for *Stellaria* and *Aster.*

Sta·r-gaze, *v.* 1626. [Back-formation from next.] *intr.* To gaze at or study the stars or something compared to a star.

Sta·r-ga:zer. 1560. 1. One who gazes at the stars. Often used as a familiar or contemptuous substitute for *astrologer* or *astronomer.* 2. Applied to various fishes; esp. *Uranoscopus scaber*, which has eyes set on the top of the head and directed vertically; also, any fish of this genus or of the family *Uranoscopidæ* 1661. So **Sta·r-ga:zing** *vbl. sb.* the action of gazing at or studying the stars 1576; *ppl. a.* that gazes at the stars 1593.

Sta·r-grass. 1687. [STAR *sb.*[1]] A name for various grass-like plants with stellate flowers or stellate arrangement of leaves; as *Aletris farinosa*, *Callitriche verna* and *C. aquatica*, *Hypoxis erecta.*

Stark (stāɹk), *a.* and *adv.* [Com. Teut.; OE. *stearc* :—OTeut. **starku-.*] **A.** *adj.* 1. Hard, unyielding. *Obs.* exc. *arch.* 2. Violent, harsh, severe. *Obs.* exc. *arch.* or *dial.* OE. 3. Strong, stout, powerful ME. 4. Rigid, stiff, incapable of movement ME. b. Rigid, stiff (in death) 1592. c. Of landscape or an object in a landscape: Stiff in outline or formation; hence, bare, barren, desolate 1833. 5. Sheer, absolute, unqualified. late ME. b. Qualifying an unfavourable appellation of a person: Arrant, thorough, unmitigated. late ME. 6. = STARK-NAKED 1762.

1. Against Tallow-plots, however, the Whig government was s. 1836. 2. He is..s. as death To those that cross him TENNYSON. The season is early, the weather s. and unpromising 1913. 3. S. beer boy, stout and strong beer FLETCHER. The dragoons were s. fellows 1895. 4. That little pug-dog stands s. and stiff 1838. b. Each part depriu'd of supple gouernment, Shall stiffe and starke, and cold appeare like death SHAKS. c. Among rigid crater rims and s. fields of volcanic sand 1872. 5. It was s. midnight before they landed W. IRVING. b. Beauty is often incident to s. fools 1711. 6. They bore me to a cavern..And one did strip me s. SHELLEY.

B. *adv.* 1. In a stark manner; strenuously, vigorously; boldly ME. 2. To the fullest extent or degree; absolutely, utterly, quite 1489.

2. His conscience accuseth him, hee is stroke starke dumbe NASHE. I am distracted! I am s. raving mad! FIELDING. Hence **Stark** *v.* (*arch.*) to make or †become stiff or rigid. **Sta·rk-ly** *adv.*, **-ness.**

Stark blind, *a.* late ME. [f. STARK *adv.* 2; an alteration of *stareblind* (after next).] Quite blind.

Stark dead, *a.* late ME. [prob. orig. STARK *a.* (sense 4); afterwards taken as STARK *adv.* 2.] Quite dead.

Starken (stā·ɹk'n), *v.* Now *dial.* late ME. [f. STARK *a.* + -EN[5].] = STARK *v.*

Stark-naked, *a.* and *sb.* 1530. [f. STARK *adv.* 2; altered f. earlier START-NAKED.] **A.** *adj.* Of a person: Absolutely without clothing.

Rather on Nylus mudde Lay me starke-nak'd SHAKS.

B. *sb.* Unadulterated spirit; esp. raw gin. *slang.* 1820.

Stark naught, *a.* Now *rare* and *arch.* 1543. [STARK *adv.* 2.] Utterly worthless or valueless; †utterly bad, vicious, hurtful, etc.

Starless (stā·ɹlės), *a.* late ME. [-LESS.] Destitute of stars or starlight; having no stars visible.

Blacker then a starlesse night COWLEY. The Czar ..wore but a s. blue coat BYRON.

Starlet (stā·ɹlėt). 1830. [-LET.] 1. A small star. Also *transf.* of a flower. 2. A star-fish of the genus *Asterina* 1854.

Sta·rlight, *sb.* and *a.* late ME. **A.** *sb.* The light of the stars.

By fountaine cleere, or spangled star-light sheene SHAKS.

B. *attrib.* and *adj.* Of or pertaining to starlight; bright as the stars; appearing or accompanied by starlight; lighted by the stars 1585.

A Star-light Evening, and a Morning fair DRYDEN.

Sta·r-like, *a.* 1591. 1. Resembling a star; shining like a star. 2. Shaped like a conventional star; stellate, radiate 1611.

1. Those two starrlike eyn 1591. *fig.* You, Whose Starre-like Noblenesse gaue life and influence To their whole being? SHAKS. 2. A star-like yellow blossom C. BRONTË.

Starling[1] (stā·ɹliŋ). [OE. *stærlinc*, f. *stær* STARE *sb.*[1]; see -LING[1].] 1. Any bird of the passerine genus *Sturnus*, esp. *S. vulgaris.* Now, more widely, any bird of the family *Sturnidæ.* b. Applied to birds of the American family *Icteridæ* 1731. 2. A kind of pigeon. Also *s.-pigeon.* 1867.

1. The Rose S. or Shepherd-bird (*Pastor roseus*) 1869.

Starling[2] (stā·ɹliŋ). Also **†sterling.** 1684. [perh. a corruption of *staddling* (dial.). N.E.D.] An outwork of piles, projecting in front of the lower part of the pier of a bridge, so as to form a protection for the pier against the force of the stream or to secure it from damage by the impact of vessels or floating objects.

‖ **Starosta** (sta·rǫstă). *Pl.* **-ti** (ti). 1591. [Russ. and Polish, lit. 'elder'.] 1. In Russia, the head man of a village community. 2. In the former kingdom of Poland, a noble holding a castle and domain bestowed by the Crown 1670.

‖ **Starosty** (sta·rǫsti). 1710. [ad. G. *starostei* or F. *starostie*, f. *starost* STAROSTA.] In the former kingdom of Poland, the domain of a starosta.

Starr. *Hist.* 1614. [ad. med.L. *starrum*, ad. late Heb. *sh'ṭār* a writing.] A Jewish deed or bond, esp. one of release or acquittance of debt.

Starred (stāɹd), *ppl. a.* ME. [f. STAR *sb.*[1] and *v.* + -ED.] 1. Of the heavens, the sky, etc.: Studded with stars, starry. 2. Marked with the representation or figure of a star; studded with star-like figures. Of a horse or cow: Having a star on the forehead. late ME. b. Decorated with the star of an order 1826. c. Marked with an asterisk 1893. d. Of glass or ice: see STAR *v.* 3. 1849. 3. Star-shaped; stellate. Chiefly *Bot.* 1725. 4. Influenced by the stars; born under a (lucky or unlucky) star; only with defining adv. or in parasynthetic comb. (as ILL-STARRED) 1611. 5. Of a person: Made into a star or constellation; elevated to the region of the stars 1632.

1. On a s. night, Prince Lucifer uprose MEREDITH. 2. b. Gartered peers, and s. ambassadors DISRAELI. 4. My third comfort (Star'd most vnluckily) SHAKS. 5. That Starr'd Ethiope Queen MILT.

Starry (stā·ri), *a.* late ME. [f. STAR *sb.*[1] + -Y[1].] 1. Of the sky, night, etc.: Full of stars, spangled or lit up with stars. 2. Of or relating to the stars; consisting of stars 1594. 3. Shining like a star or stars, bright as a star, star-like 1608. 4. Shaped like the conventional figure of a star; arranged in the form of a star; in *Bot.* = STELLATE 1606. 5. Sprinkled or studded with star-like forms. Chiefly *Nat. Hist.* 1611.

1. The s. heaven which we behold JOWETT. 2. The s. system 1878. 3. Sublime their s. fronts they rear GRAY. Hence **Sta·rrily** *adv.* **Sta·rriness** (*rare*).

Sta·r-shot. Also **†-shoot, -shut.** 1653. [SHOT *sb.*[1]] A pop. name for nostoc, which is supposed to fall from the stars, or to be the remains of a shooting star. *Obs.* or *dial.*

Star-spangled, *ppl. a.* 1591. Spangled with stars; *s. banner*, the U.S. flag.

Sta·r-stone. 1658. [STAR *sb.*[1]] 1. A name for the pentagonal or star-shaped vertebral joints of pentacrinites. 2. A precious stone which exhibits asterism 1798.

Start (stāɹt), *sb.*[1] [Com. Teut.; OE. *steort* :—OTeut. **stertoz.*] †1. The tail of an animal -ME. 2. A handle (of a vessel, handbell, broom, etc.). Now *dial.* ME. †3. The footstalk of a fruit -1672. †4. An outgrowth, a projecting point or spur; *esp.* the point of a stag's horn -1721. 5. *Mech.* a. The innermost segment of the bucket of a water-wheel 1547. b. The shaft or lever of a horse-mill 1771.

Start (stāɹt), *sb.*[2] ME. [f. the vb.] †1. A short space of time, a moment -1620. 2. A sudden and transient effort of movement; in early use, †a leap, a rush. late ME. †b. A sudden journey; a sudden flight, invasion, etc. *To take the s.*: to decamp. -1894. c. A sudden acceleration of progress or growth 1817. 3. A sudden involuntary movement of the body, occasioned by surprise, terror, joy or grief, or the recollection of something forgotten. late ME. 4. A starting into activity; a sudden and transient effort or display of energy 1605. b. A sudden fit of passion, grief, joy, madness, etc.; an outburst of wit, humour, or fancy.

Now *rare* or *Obs.* 1596. **c.** A sudden broken utterance or burst of sound 1601. **5.** A beginning to move; a setting out on a journey or race; the beginning of a career, of a course of action, a series of events, etc. 1566. **b.** An act of setting in motion; an impulse to movement; a signal for starting in a race, etc. 1602. **c.** An opportunity or an assistance given for starting on a career or course of action. Often *a s. in life.* 1849. **6.** Advantage gained by starting first in a race or on a journey; in wider sense, position in advance of competitors whether obtained at the beginning or in the course of a race, etc. Hence *gen.* 1580. **7.** *Mining.* = LEAP *sb.*[1] 5. 1778. **8.** *slang.* = GO *sb.* 3. 1837.

2. Phr. †*At a s.*, with a bound, in an instant; This duc his courser with his spores smoot And at a stert he was bitwix hem two CHAUCER. 3. Phr. *To give a s.*; He gave a s. of astonishment, and stood still 1863. *To give* (a person) *a s.*, to startle. 4. Such vnconstant starts are we like to have from him SHAKS. *By starts, by fits and starts* (see FIT *sb.*[2] 4 a). **b.** 1 *Hen. IV*, III. ii. 125. **c.** She did speake in starts distractedly SHAKS. 5. *False s.*, in *Racing*, a wrong start, necessitating return to the starting-point; hence *gen.* an unsuccessful attempt to begin something. *Flying s.*, a start in a race in which the actual starting-point is passed when one is travelling at full speed; also *fig. From s. to finish.* **b.** The s. shall be by word of mouth 1897. 6. Phr. *To get, have,* †*take the s.* (*of* a competitor), freq. with words indicating the amount of the advantage as in *ten minutes s., ten yards s.* 8. That 's the rummest s. I ever knew 1880.

Start (stāɹt), *v.* Pa. t. and pa. pple. **started.** [OE. *styrtan* :—OTeut. **sturtjan* to overthrow; to rush, fall headlong; the Northern ME. *sterte* suggests an OE. **steortian* corresponding to MHG. *sterzen* to set up stiffly, move briskly.] **I.** *intr.* †**1.** To leap, jump, caper –1567. **2.** To move with a bound or sudden violent impulse from a position of rest. Also with *out.* Freq. *fig.* ME. **b.** To move suddenly from one's place, as to avoid a danger; hence *fig.* to flinch or recoil *from* something in alarm or repugnance. Chiefly with adv. ME. **c.** To awake suddenly *from, out* of; to emerge suddenly *into*, etc. late ME. **3.** Of an inanimate thing: To issue suddenly and violently; to fly, flow, or be projected by a sudden impulse. Of tears: To burst *out* suddenly; to rise suddenly *to* the eyes. late ME. **b.** Of the eyes: To burst out, escape *from* their sockets. Chiefly hyperbolical, expressing the effect of horror or fury. 1526. **c.** *S. out*: to project; to become visible or conspicuous, burst into view 1825. †**4.** To go or come swiftly or hastily; to rush, hasten –1637. **5.** To undergo a sudden involuntary movement of the body, resulting from surprise, fright, sudden pain, etc. Hence *occas.*, to feel startled. 1529. †**6.** To desert or revolt *from* (a leader, a party); to swerve *from* (a cause, purpose, principle); to withdraw *from* (a promise, treaty). Also with *aside, back.* –1781. **7.** Of a material thing: To break away from its place; to be displaced by pressure or shrinkage; to get loose. Chiefly in techn. uses. 1526. **8.** To set out from the starting-point in a race 1645. **9.** To set out, to begin a journey; to begin to move, to leave the point of departure in any kind of progression. Said of a person or animal; also of a vehicle, ship, etc. 1821. **10.** To begin a career, course of action, process, etc. Also of a process: To begin. 1798.

2. Vpon my feet incontinent I s. 1605. Out of tne wood he starts in wonted shape MILT. I started out of my Reveries as if I had awak'd from a..Dream 1737. **b.** The horse, too, upon which the lady rode, started back SCOTT. **c.** When all creation started into birth COWPER. The characters s. into light, life, and identity 1863. 3. 'Tis said, at times the sullen tear would s. BYRON. *fig.* Fear, pity, justice, indignation s. GOLDSM. **b.** His eyes were starting..and his hair rose up on end 1863. 5. He starts at every Noise 1695. His fiery steeds Started aside with fright 1870. 7. Just as the ship floated several rivets started 1869. 8. Phr. *To s. fair*, to start on equal terms. 9. Next morning I started with this man up the valley TYNDALL. 10. Each bowler started with a maiden 1868. Phr. *To s. from* or *with*, (in reasoning) to assume as the point of departure. *To s. in business*, to begin one's career. *To s. in* (U.S. colloq.), to begin. *To s. out*, to set oneself, begin *to do* something.

S. up. a. To rise suddenly; to spring to an erect position; *fig.* to bestir oneself. †**b.** To become suddenly conspicuous. **c.** Of things: To come suddenly into being or notice, to spring up.

II. *trans.* †**1.** To cause to start or flinch; to startle –1871. **2.** *Hunting.* To force (an animal, esp. a hare) to leave its lair, form, or resting-place. late ME. **3.** To propound (a question, an objection); to introduce (a subject of discussion) 1643. **4.** To discharge the contents of, empty (a vessel); to pour or shoot (liquids, coal, etc.) from one vessel into another 1700. **5.** To cause (a material thing) to 'start' or break away from its place; to displace by pressure or strain. Of a ship: To suffer the starting or giving way of (a plank, etc.). 1676. **6.** To cause (a person, an animal, a vehicle) to start or set out in a race, on a journey; to cause to begin moving in any kind of progression. Also with *off.* 1725. **7.** To cause to begin to act or operate; to initiate; *esp.* (freq. **s. up**) to set (machinery) in motion 1666. **b.** To begin to keep as part of one's establishment; to set up (e.g. a horse, carriage) 1851. **8.** To begin (some action or operation). Also said of a thing. 1833.

1. And now..dost thou come To s. my quiet SHAKS. 2. Little dogs s. the hare, the great one gets her 1659. *transf.* Do but s. An eccho with the clamor of thy drumme SHAKS. 3. Will you give me liberty to s. one difficulty here? DE FOE. 4. A small place..wherein the powder is started 1850. 5. The damage..was trifling,..not a rivet was started 1840. 7. He started a discourse of a talk he hears about the town PEPYS. The plan for starting the cottager in business 1854. **b.** He is sure to s. a yacht 1873. 8. The young fellow..started another ballad 1873. Hence **Sta·rtful** *a.* timorous, fitful. **Sta·rting** *ppl. a.* that starts; **-ly** *adv.* by starts. **Sta·rtish** *a.* apt to jib.

Starter (stā·ɹtəɹ). 1536. [f. START *v.* + -ER [1].] **1.** One who or something which starts. **2.** One who sets out in a race or journey 1818. **3.** A dog trained for starting game 1748. **4.** One who gives the signal to start 1622.

Sta·r-thi:stle. 1578. [STAR *sb.*[1]] A name for the weed *Centaurea Calcitrapa*, the flowers of which are surrounded by radiating spines; also for *C. solstitialis*, and as a book-name for the whole genus.

Sta·rting, *vbl. sb.* late ME. [f. START *v.* + -ING [1].] The action of the vb.

Phr. *At s.*: at the beginning or outset.

Comb.: **s.-bolt** *Naut.*, a bolt used to drive out another; it is usually a trifle smaller; **-gate,** a removable barrier for securing a fair start in horse races; **-place,** the place occupied at starting by a competitor in a race; the place from which a person or thing starts; **-point,** the point from which a person or thing starts; a point of departure in a journey, argument, development, etc.; **-post,** a post marking the place from which competitors in a race should start; **-price,** (*a*) the price at which the bidding at an auction starts; (*b*) *Racing*, the final odds on a horse at the time of starting.

†**Sta·rting-hole.** 1530. [f. STARTING *vbl. sb.*] **1.** A place in which a hunted animal or person takes refuge –1618. **2.** *fig.* A means of evasion; a loophole –1801.

Startle (stā·ɹt'l), *sb.* 1714. [f. STARTLE *v.*] An experience of being startled; a start or shock of surprise or alarm. Also (predic.), something that startles.

Burton's death..was quite a s. to me 1836.

Startle (stā·ɹt'l), *v.* [OE. *steartlian* :— **startlōjan*, f. **start-*; see START *v.*] †**1.** *intr.* To kick, struggle. OE. only. **2.** To rush, move swiftly; to caper. Now *dial.* ME. **3.** †**a.** To start. Of a horse: To shy. **b.** To feel sudden astonishment or alarm. Now *rare* or *Obs.* (repl. by passive of sense 4). 1530. †**c.** To awake with a start; to move or change as if surprised or frightened –1847. **4.** *trans.* To cause to start; to frighten; to surprise greatly; †to shock 1595.

2. We see oxen goe to the shambles leaping and startling 1637. 3. **b.** The cloister startles at the gleam of arms WORDSW. **c.** The grass that sprung Startled and glanced and trembled even to feel An unaccustomed presence SHELLEY. 4. The garrison, startled from sleep, found the enemy already masters of the towers W. IRVING. *fig.* To hear the Lark..singing s. the dull night MILT. Hence **Sta·rtler,** one who or something which startles. **Sta·rtlingly** *adv.* **Sta·rtlish** *a.* easily startled; apt to take fright; esp. said of a horse.

Start-naked, *a. Obs.* exc. *dial.* ME. [app. f. START *sb.*[1] + NAKED *a.*; lit. naked to the tail.] = STARK NAKED *a.*

Startup (stā·ɹtɒp), *sb.*[1] *Obs.* exc. *dial.* and *Hist.* 1517. [f. vbl. phr. *start up* (see START *v.*).] Orig., a kind of 'high-low' or boot, worn by rustics; in later use, a kind of gaiter or legging. Chiefly in *pl.*

†**Start-up,** *ppl. a.* and *sb.*[2] 1557. [f. *start*, pa. pple. of START *v.* + UP *adv.*] = UP-START *a.* and *sb.* –1801.

A new S. Sect 1762. A. s. baron of yesterday 1801.

Starvation (stāɹvēⁱ·ʃən). 1778. [f. STARVE *v.* + -ATION.] **1.** The action of starving or subjecting to famine. **2.** The condition of being starved or having too little food to sustain life or health 1802. **b.** *transf.* Insufficient supply of something necessary to life 1866.

2. **b.** Oxygen s. and carbonic acid poisoning..are at work together 1866.

attrib.: **s. wages,** wages which are barely sufficient to keep the recipient from s.

Starve (stāɹv), *v.* [Com. WGer. str. vb.; OE. *steorfan*, f. Teut. root **sterƀ-*. The weak conjugation appears in the 15th c.] **I.** *intr.* †**1.** To die. In late use app. to die a lingering death, as from hunger, cold, grief, or slow disease. Also, in spiritual sense, of the soul. –1657. **2.** With various constructions, specifying the cause of death. In later use: To be brought gradually nearer to death, to be in process of being killed; to suffer extremely. Now *dial.* ME. †**3.** Of plants or their parts: To die, wither. Of a material substance: To lose its characteristic quality, spoil, deteriorate. –1722. **4.** [orig. *ellipt.*] To die of hunger; to perish or be in process of perishing from lack or insufficiency of food; to suffer extreme poverty and want; more emphatically *to s. to death.* Also hyperbolically in colloq. use: To be extremely hungry. 1578. **5.** [orig. *ellipt.*] To die of exposure to cold; chiefly hyperbolical, to be benumbed or 'dead' with cold. Now *north.* 1602.

2. In paril for to sterue For hungyr CHAUCER. To s. for Food, to perish In Penury SYLVESTER. His Office keeps your Parchment fates entire, He starves with cold to save them from the fire POPE. 4. No: on the barren Mountaine let him sterue SHAKS. *fig.* I at home starue for a merrie looke SHAKS. 5. Whether they s. in the snows of Lapland, or burn in the sands of Guinea? 1772.

II. *trans.* †**1.** To cause to die, to kill, destroy –1707. **2.** To cause to perish of hunger; to deprive of or keep scantily supplied with food. Also *transf.* and *fig.* 1530. **b.** To subdue by famine or low diet; also to force *into* (a course of action) by starvation 1625. **c.** To cure (a disease) by abstemious diet 1617. **3.** To produce atrophy in (a plant, an animal or vegetable organ, a morbid growth) by withholding nutriment 1633. **4.** To cause to die of cold, to kill with cold; also hyperbolically, to benumb with cold. Chiefly *pass. Obs.* exc. *dial.* 1600.

1. Aches contract, and sterue your supple ioynts SHAKS. 2. To s. a man, in law is murther PRIOR. *transf.* We must starue our sight, From louers foode, till morrow deepe midnight SHAKS. **b.** They..were to be starved into compliance 1775. **c.** He had been ..starving a cold 1839. 4. There is not a window or door that shuts; I am starved to death at my fire side 1770. Hence **Sta·rvedly** *adv.* **Sta·rver,** one who or that which starves.

Starveling (stā·ɹvliŋ), *sb.* and *a.* 1546. [f. STARVE *v.* + -LING.] **A.** *sb.* A starved person, animal, etc.; one who habitually starves or is stinted of food; one who is emaciated for lack of nutriment.

If I hang, old Sir Iohn hangs with mee, and thou know'st hee 's no Starueling SHAKS.

B. *adj.* **1.** That lacks a sufficiency of food; hence, lean and weak for want of nutriment; ill-fed, hungry 1597. **2.** Poverty-stricken. Of circumstances, etc.: Characterized by or exhibiting poverty. 1638. **3.** *fig.* Poor in quality or quantity, lean, thin, meagre, scanty 1641.

1. Staruling Famine comes of large expence 1597. 3. A s. and comfortless religion COLERIDGE.

Starwort (stā·ɹwɒɹt). late ME. [f. STAR *sb.*[1] + WORT *sb.*] **1.** The genus *Stellaria*, with white starry flowers; esp. *S. Holostea.* **2.** A book-name for the genus *Aster*; esp. *A. Tripolium*, Sea Starwort; *A. Amellus*, Italian Starwort 1578. **3.** *Water Starwort*, the genus *Callitriche* 1597. **4.** A moth, *Cucullia Asteris* 1819.

‖**Stasimon** (stæ·simɒn). *Pl.* **stasima, stasimons.** 1861. [Gr. στάσιμον neut. (agreeing with μέλος song) of στάσιμος stationary, f. στα- to stand.] In ancient Greek tragedy, a song of the Chorus, occurring after the PARODE, continued without the interruption of dialogue or anapæstics.

||Stasis (stēi·sis). 1745. [mod.L., a. Gr. στάσις standing, f. στα- to stand.] *Path.* A stagnation or stoppage of the circulation of any of the fluids of the body, esp. of the blood in some part of the blood-vessels.

-stat, the terminal element in certain names of scientific instruments, *aerostat, heliostat, hydrostat, thermostat*, etc. The earliest example of this formation is *heliostat*, ad. mod.L. *heliostata*, app. repr. an assumed Gr. type *ἡλιοστάτης, intended to mean an instrument for causing the sun to appear stationary, f. ἥλιος sun + -στατης, agent-n. f. στα- root of ἱστάναι to cause to stand. The later words have been formed on the analogy of *heliostat*, app. with some ref. to the Gr. στατός standing, stationary.

Statable (stēi·tăb'l), *a.* Also **stateable.** 1802. [f. STATE *v.*] Capable of being stated.

Statant (stēi·tănt), *a.* 1500. [app. irreg. f. L. *stat-, stare* + -ANT.] *Her.* Of an animal, esp. a lion: Standing in profile with all four feet on the ground.

State (stēit), *sb.* ME. [Partly var. of ESTATE *sb.*, a. OF. *estat* (mod.F. *état*), ad. L. *status*, f. *sta-, stare* to stand; partly directly ad. L. *status.*] **I.** Condition, manner of existing. **1.** A combination of circumstances or attributes belonging for the time being to a person or thing; a particular manner or way of existing, as defined by the presence of certain circumstances or attributes; a condition. **b.** *colloq.* Implying a state of dirt, untidiness, etc. 1879. **2.** A condition (of mind or feeling) 1538. **b.** *colloq.* An agitated or excited state of mind or feeling 1837. **3.** The mode of existence of a spiritual being; a particular mode or phase of (spiritual) existence ME. **4.** Physical condition as regards internal make or constitution, molecular form or structure, and the like. Also, one of several forms or conditions in which an object—animal, vegetable, or mineral—is found to exist; a phase or stage of existence. ME. †**5.** The height or chief stage of a process; the condition of full vigour. Chiefly *Path.*, the crisis or 'acme' of disease -1717. †**6.** *Rhet.* (after L. *status.*) The point in question or debate between contending parties, as it emerges from their pleadings; the issue or main question. In full *s. of the cause, of the plea.* -1776. **7.** *Semitic Gram.* Applied to certain formal and syntactical conditions (see N.E.D.) 1752. **8.** *Engraving.* An impression taken from a plate at a particular stage of its progress and recognizable by special marks 1874. **b.** *Bibliography.* One of two or more differing portions of a single edition of a book 1931.

1. I all alone beweepe my out-cast s. SHAKS. Ye violent & desperate s. of their affairs H. WALPOLE. The crowded s. of the port 1890. He attempted to deceive his patient as to her s. 1908. *S. of nature*: see NATURE *sb.* IV. 2. *S. of siege*, the condition of undergoing investment by a hostile army. **b.** Just look what a s. I am in! 1879. **2.** A foolish and unreasonable s. of mind 1728. The term *S.* has.. been applied to all modifications of mind indifferently 1837. **3.** From s. to s. the spirit walks TENNYSON. *Future s.*: see FUTURE *a.* **4.** Water, in the s. of vapour 1815. The most perfect and useful s. of it [iron] is that of ochreous stain RUSKIN. 8. The best states of the old plates now procurable RUSKIN.

Phrases. *The* (or *a*) *s. of things* or *affairs*, the way in which events or circumstances stand disposed (at a particular time or in a particular sphere). *The s. of the case*, the facts and circumstances of a particular affair, question, etc. †*In s.*, later *in a s.* (now *in a fit s.*) followed by infinitive: fit, likely, ready *to do* or *be* something. *In a great state*, very excited or agitated.

II. Status; high rank; pomp. †**1.** A person's condition or position in life; a person's natural, social, or legal status, profession or calling, rank or degree -1741. †**b.** *Man's s.* = manhood; cf. ESTATE *sb.* 1 b. 1580. **c.** Condition or status as married or single. late ME. †**2.** *contextually* and *pregnantly.* A high rank or exalted position; an office of power or importance -1642. †**b.** High rank, greatness, power -1640. **3.** Costly and imposing display, such as befits persons of rank and wealth; splendour, magnificence ME. **4.** Dignity of demeanour or presence. Now *rare.* 1586. †**5.** A raised chair with a canopy, etc.; a throne -1712. †**b.** A canopy -1828.

1. Having died in the s. of apparency 1741. **2. b.** The glories of our blood and s. 1640. †*To bear* (*great*) *s.*, to hold (high) office; *fig.* (of a thing), to be of importance, involve great consequences. **3.** The gilded coach, indeed, which is now annually admired by the crowd, was not yet a part of his s. MACAULAY. Phr. *of s.*; as in *bed* or *chair of s.* *In s.*, with great pomp and solemnity; with a great train. *To lie in s.*, of a dead body, to be ceremoniously exposed to view before interment. **4.** There is a s. sometimes in decent plainnesse 1642. Phr. *To keep s., one's s.*, to keep one's dignity, behave in a dignified manner (now *rare*). *To hold one's s.*, to appear in pomp and splendour (*arch.*). **5.** This Chayre shall bee my S. SHAKS.

III. A class, rank; a person of rank. †**1.** A class, rank, order, sort or body *of* persons; a 'condition', profession, or occupation; the members of a class or profession collectively. (Cf. ESTATE *sb.* 5 and F. *état.*) -1625. †**2.** An ESTATE of the realm -1700. **3.** *pl.* The 'estates of the realm' met to form a constitutional assembly; the princes, dukes, nobles, etc., together with the delegates or representatives of the several ranks, orders, chief cities, etc. of a country, assembled in a parliament or diet. Now *Hist.*, exc. as the title of the legislatures of Jersey and Guernsey. See also STATES GENERAL. late ME. †**b.** Delegates or members of the Dutch government as individuals -1767. †**4.** A person of standing, importance or high rank -1667. †**5.** *pl.* The dignitaries or authorities of a town or district -1609. †**6.** *collect. sing.* The rulers, nobles, or great men of a realm; the government, ruling body, grand council, or court -1617.

2. In full assembly of the three States 1641. **3.** The French States at no time attained the regularity of the English Parliament 1844. In Jersey, besides the Royal Court, there is only one Assembly. It is called the States. 1862. **4.** The bold design Pleas'd highly those infernal States MILT. **6.** *Oth.* I. ii. 96.

IV. Commonwealth, polity. †**1.** The condition of the Church, a country, realm, etc. in regard to its welfare and polity. Occas., a condition of prosperity, of order and settled government. -1651. †**2.** A particular form of polity or government -1701. **3.** *The state*: the body politic as organized for supreme civil rule and government; the political organization which is the basis of civil government; hence, the supreme civil power and government vested in a country or nation 1538. **b.** dist. from 'the church' or eccl. organization and authority. In the phr. *church and s.* the article is dropped. 1589. **4.** A body of people occupying a defined territory and organized under a sovereign government. Hence *occas.* the territory occupied by such a body. 1568. **5. a.** The territory, or one of the territories, ruled by a particular sovereign. *Hereditary states*: spec. (= G. *Erbstaaten*) the kingdoms or principalities held hereditarily by any head of the Holy Roman Empire 1602. **b.** *pl.* (*Hist.*) Applied (perh. after It. *stati*) to the cities and territories included in an Italian principality or republic, esp. the grand-duchy of Tuscany and the republic of Venice. Also in *States of the Church, Papal States* (also *sing.*), titles of the former temporal dominions of the Holy See. 1797. **c.** One of a number of polities, each more or less sovereign and independent in regard to internal affairs, which together make up a supreme federal government; as in the U. S. of America, the Commonwealth of Australia 1774. **d.** *The States*: the United States of America 1777. **6.** (Without article.) All that concerns the government or ruling power of a country; the sphere of supreme political power and administration 1582.

1. *Rich. II*, IV. i. 225. **2.** Phr. †*The popular s.*, democracy. †*S. royal*, a monarchy. **3.** The S. is properly.. the nation in its collective and corporate capacity M. ARNOLD. **4.** Never any S. was.. so open to receive Strangers, into their Body, as were the Romans BACON. States are sovereign within their own territories, independent of other states, and equal as between themselves 1880. **6.** *Reason of S.*: see REASON *sb.* II. 1. *Secretary of S.* (Gt. Britain), a minister in charge of a Government office (defined as *for Foreign Affairs, for War*, etc.); (U.S.) the Foreign Minister. *Department of S., S. Department* (U.S.): see DEPARTMENT 2.

V. Interest in property; possessions. †**1.** *Law.* = ESTATE *sb.* 9 (in a property); right or title to property -1660. †**2.** *Law.* Possession (of property). Chiefly *Sc.* -1768. †**3.** Property, possessions; one's private means -1899.

3. A great s. left to an heire, is as a lure to al the birds of prey round about, to seise on him BACON.

VI. (perh. partly from STATE *v.*) †**a.** A statement; a detailed report of particulars -1818. **b.** *Mil.* A report of the numbers of a corps, regiment, etc. in the field, with details of casualties 1802.

attrib. and *Comb.*, as *s.-bed, s. occasion, entry*, etc.; *s. religion, education, S. Railways*, etc.; *s.-crime, -criminal, -trial.* **s.-cabin** = STATE-ROOM 2, 3; **-church**, a church established by the s.; hence **-churchman**; **-hospital** *U.S.*, a public asylum for the insane under the direction of a S.; **-paper**, an official document in which some matter concerning the government or the nation is published or expounded; also *attrib.* in *S. Paper Office*; **-prison**, (*a*) a prison for political offenders; (*b*) *U.S.* and *Austral.*, a prison maintained by a S. for the penal confinement of criminals; in *U.S.* also *state's prison*; so **s. prisoner**, a person under arrest for felony, also a political prisoner; **S. rights**, the rights and powers vested in the separate States under the Federal constitution of the U.S.A.; also **States rights**; **s. secret**, a matter kept secret by the government; *joc.* an important secret. **s. socialism**, a form of socialism which advocates utilizing the power of the state to improve the condition of the working-classes by pensions, etc., and by state administration of industries, railways, etc.; hence **s.-socialist, -socialistic** *a.* Combinations of the genitive or pl.: **State's Attorney** *U.S.*, a lawyer commissioned to represent the S. in the Courts, esp. in criminal actions; **states-system** [tr. G. *staaten-system*], the federation of a number of states with the object of preserving the actual balance of power. Hence **Sta·tehood** (chiefly *U.S.*), the condition or status of a political s.

State (stēit), *v.* 1590. [f. prec.] **1.** *trans.* To place, station (*rare*). †**2.** To give a certain rank or position to, to rank; also in *pass.* -1715. †**3.** To place in a specified condition; in early use chiefly to settle, place in safety or quiet -1786. **4.** To set out (a question, problem, etc.) in proper form; spec. in *Logic* 1641. **5.** To declare in words; to represent (a matter) in all the circumstances of modification; to set out fully or in a definite form 1647. **b.** To specify (a number, price, etc.) 1789.

4. An argument thus stated regularly and at full length, is called a Syllogism 1826. Phr. *To s. a case*, to set out the facts of a matter or pleading for consideration by a court. *To s. an account* or *accounts*, to set down formally the debits and credits arising in a course of business transactions. **5.** The contents of the deed were falsely stated 1891.

Statecraft (stēi·tkraft). 1642. [f. STATE *sb.* + CRAFT.] The art of conducting state affairs; statesmanship.

Stated (stēi·tėd), *ppl. a.* 1641. [f. STATE *v.* + -ED[1]. In early use perh. rather f. L. *status* appointed, fixed, regular + -ED[1].] **1.** Fixed, regular; settled by authority, agreement or prearrangement. **b.** Of a functionary, an employment: Recognized, regular, official 1752. **2.** Of a law, rule, penalty: Formulated, explicitly set forth 1681. **b.** Narrated, alleged as fact 1787. **c.** *S. account*: a statement of account that has been agreed to by the parties to a suit 1765. **d.** Law. *S. case, case s.*: A summary of the points in dispute, drawn up by agreement of the parties to an action, to be presented to a court or an arbitrator in order to facilitate a speedy decision 1899.

2. A penalty in the nature of s. damages; as a rent of 5 *l.* an acre for ploughing up antient meadow BLACKSTONE. Hence **Sta·tedly** *adv.* with regularity, constantly.

Stateful (stēi·tfŭl), *a.* Now *rare* or *Obs.* 1591. [f. STATE *sb.* + -FUL.] Full of state or dignity, stately.

Thou lookest down from heaven, thy s. throne 1624.

Sta·te-house. 1593. [f. STATE *sb.* + HOUSE *sb.* Cf. Du. *stathuis* STADTHOUSE.] †**1. a.** A house of state; a building appropriated to state-ceremonies. **b.** = SENATE-HOUSE 1. -1614. †**2.** A town hall -1756. **3.** *U.S.* The building in which the legislature of a State of the Union has its sessions, or in which, formerly the public affairs of a colony or province were transacted 1639.

Stateless (stēi·tlės), *a.* 1609. [f. STATE *sb.* + -LESS.] **a.** Without a state or political community. **b.** Destitute of state or ceremonial dignity.

Stately (stēi·tli), *a.* and *adv.* late ME. [f. STATE *sb.* + -LY.] **A.** *adj.* **1.** Of persons or personal appearance or demeanour. In early use, Befitting or indicating high estate, princely, noble, majestic. In later use, Imposingly dignified. **b.** Of movement, a person or animal in movement: Dignified, deliberate 1593. **2.** Of persons, etc.: †**a.** Haughty, domineering, arrogant -1607. **b.** Showing a sense of superiority; repellently dignified; not affable or approachable 1625. **3.** Of things: Appertaining to or befitting a person of high estate; magnificent, splendid. late ME. **4.** Imposing or majestic in size and proportions 1450. **5.** Of speech or writing or its style; hence of a speaker or writer: Elevated in thought or expression, dignified, majestic 1579.

1. She was..the stateliest of dames 1877. 2. b. Their ladyships made three s. curtsies THACKERAY. 3. A s. dinner both of Fish and Flesh 1648. Armorial bearings s. TENNYSON. 4. Woods high and decked with Stately trees 1586. Garrick and statelier Kemble, and the rest TENNYSON. The s. calmness of the wood-dove's note KINGSLEY. 5. Choice word and measured phrase..; a s. speech WORDSW.

B. *adv.* In a stately manner. late ME.

A figure..Appeares before them, and with sollemne march Goes slow and s. SHAKS. Hence **Sta·telily** *adv.* (now *rare*). **Sta·teliness.**

Statement (stē¹·tmĕnt). 1775. [f. STATE *v.* + -MENT.] **1.** The action or an act of stating; the manner in which something is stated 1789. **b.** *Mus.* A presentation of a subject or theme in a composition 1883. **2.** Something that is stated; an allegation, declaration 1775. **3.** A written or oral communication setting forth facts, arguments, demands, or the like 1787. **b.** *Comm.* (More fully *s. of account*): a document setting out the items of debit and credit between two parties 1897. **4.** *Comm.* In certain branches of industry, a document periodically issued, setting forth the prices to be paid to workmen for various kinds of piece-work. Also *attrib.* as *s. price, wages.* 1889.

1. In s., the late Lord Holland was not successful MACAULAY. A model of cautious and accurate s. (*mod.*). 2. The s., that truth is appearance only JOWETT.

Sta·te(s)-monger. *Obs.* exc. *arch.* 1616. [See MONGER.] A projector of political constitutions; a pretender to political science.

‖ **Stater**¹ (stē¹·təɹ). late ME. [a. L., a. Gr. στατήρ, f. στα-, ἱστάναι (see STAND *v.*) in the sense 'to weigh'.] *Antiq.* **1.** An ancient weight equal to half an ounce. **2.** A name of various ancient coins, esp. the Persian stater or DARIC, a gold coin worth about £1 1*s.* 3*d.* late ME.

Stater² (stē¹·təɹ). 1702. [f. STATE *v.* + -ER¹.] One who states. *Average s.* = average-adjuster; see AVERAGE *sb.*²

State-room. 1660. **1.** A state apartment; a room in a palace, great house, hotel, etc., splendidly decorated and furnished, and used only on ceremonial occasions. **2.** A captain's or superior officer's room on board ship 1660. **3.** *U.S.* A sleeping apartment with one or two berths on a passenger steamer 1837. **b.** *U.S.* A private compartment in a railway train 1867.

States General. 1585. [= F. *états généraux*, Du. *staaten generaal.*] *Hist.* A legislative assembly representing the three estates, viz. clergy, nobles, and commons or burghers of a whole realm, principality, or commonwealth: **a.** in France before the Revolution; **b.** in the Netherlands from the 15th c. to 1796.

Sta·teship. *Irish Hist.* 1917. = TUATH.

Statesman (stē¹·tsmăn). 1592. [f. *state's*, gen. of STATE *sb.* + MAN *sb.*, after F. *homme d'état.* In sense 2 f. STATE *sb.* V. 1.] **1.** One who takes a leading part in the affairs of a state or body politic; esp. one who is skilled in the management of public affairs. **2.** *dial.* A small landowner 1787.

1. He..in the course of one revolving Moon, Was Chymist, Fidler, States-man, and Buffoon DRYDEN. *Elder statesman*, in Japan: see ELDER *a.* [Lord Dufferin's] wide and varied training had made him not a politician but a s. able to take Imperial views 1891. 2. A s., which means in Cumberland phrase one who owns the fee-simple of his land, but works on it himself 1813. Hence **Sta·tesmanlike** *a.* having the qualities characteristic of a s.; befitting or worthy of a s. **Sta·tesmanly** *a.* pertaining to or characteristic of a s.; befitting a s.

Sta·tesmanship. 1764. [-SHIP.] The activity or skill of a statesman; skilful management of public affairs.

Stateswoman (stē¹·tswumăn). *Pl.* **-women** (-wimĕn). 1609. [f. *state's* gen. of STATE *sb.* + WOMAN, after STATESMAN.] A woman who takes part in the conduct of public affairs; a woman with statesmanlike ability.

The Queen is a theologian as well as a s. 1885.

Static (stæ·tik), *a.* and *sb.* 1570. [ad. mod. L. *staticus*, a. Gr. στατικός causing to stand, also, pertaining to weighing, f. στα-, ἱστάναι to cause to stand, to weigh. The sb. is ad. mod. L. *statica*, ad. Gr. στατική (sc. τέχνη) the art of weighing.] **A.** *adj.* †**1.** Of or pertaining to weighing or the use of the balance -1734. †**2.** Pertaining to the effect of weight or the conditions of the equilibrium of weight. Of a power or principle: Operative in the production of equilibrium. -1775. **3.** Pertaining to forces in equilibrium, or to bodies at rest; opp. to *dynamic* 1850. **b.** Applied *spec.* to designate frictional as opp. to voltaic electricity 1839. **4.** *transf.* and *fig.* = next 5. 1856. **5.** *Path.* and *Phys.* Structural or organic, as opp. to *functional* 1855. **6.** *Machinery.* Of an electric transformer or generator: Having all its parts stationary, non-rotary 1903. **7.** Applied to minor disturbances of an electric current 1911.

1. *S. chair*, the Sanctorian weighing chair (see SANCTORIAN *a.*) for determining the amount of insensible perspiration by weighing the body. 3. I have used..the terms dynamic and s. to represent the different states of magnetism 1850. 4. Revelation, like inspiration, is a process, not a s. condition 1909.

B. *sb.* **1.** = STATICS. Now *rare.* 1570. **2.** = STATICS b (*U.S.*) 1913.

Statical (stæ·tikăl), *a.* 1570. [f. as prec. + -AL 1.] †**1.** = prec. A. 1. -1780. **2.** Of or pertaining to STATICS 1660. †**3.** Of analysis, etc.: Gravimetrical -1813. **b.** Pertaining to the metrology of weight 1846. **4.** = prec. A. 3, 3 b. 1802. **5.** *transf.* and *fig.* Of or pertaining to a fixed or stable condition, as dist. from a state of progress or change 1855. **6.** *Math.* Concerned with magnitude alone, without regard to direction (*rare*) 1859. **7.** *Med.* Structural, organic 1896.

4. The s. attributes, shape, size and position 1868. 5. The fund by which the life of the human race..is sustained is never in a s. condition 1886. Hence **Sta·tically** *adv.*

‖ **Statice** (stæ·tisī). 1731. [L., a. Gr. στατική, orig. fem. of στατικός causing to stand still, in the sense 'stopping flow of blood'.] A genus of plumbaginaceous perennial herbs, typical of the *Staticeæ*; a plant of this genus, esp. Sea Lavender.

Statics (stæ·tiks). 1656. [Alteration of STATIC *sb.*, after names of sciences in -ICS.] Orig., the science relating to weight and its mechanical effects, and to the conditions of equilibrium as resulting from the distribution of weight. In mod. use, the branch of physical science concerned with the action of forces in producing equilibrium or relative rest, in contradistinction to *Dynamics* as the science of the action of forces in producing motion. **b.** *Wireless Telegr.* = ATMOSPHERICS 1918.

Phr. *Social s.*; Social philosophy may be aptly divided..into s. and dynamics; the first treating of the equilibrium of a perfect society, the second of the forces by which society is advanced towards perfection SPENCER.

Stating (stē¹·tiŋ), *vbl. sb.* 1652. [f. STATE *v.* + -ING¹.] The action of STATE *v.*

Many of our..peevish wranglings are kept up by the ill s. of the Question JER. TAYLOR.

Station (stē¹·ʃən), *sb.* late ME. [a. F., ad. L. *stationem*, f. *sta-*, *stare* to stand.] **I.** Action or condition of standing. **1.** The action or posture of standing on the feet; manner of standing. Now mainly *techn.* 1526. **2.** The condition or fact of standing still; assumption of a continuance in a stationary condition: opp. to *motion.* Now *rare.* 1606. **3.** A halt; a stand. Now *rare* or *Obs.* 1604. **4.** *Astr.* The apparent standing still of a planet at its apogee and perigee. late ME.

1. A S., like the Herald Mercurie New lighted on a heauen kissing hill SHAKS. *S.*,..the manner of standing or the attitude of live stock, particularly of exhibition game fowls 1891. 2. His life is a progress, and not a s. EMERSON.

II. Standing-place, position. In lit. applications. **1.** A place to stand in; *esp.* a position assigned to a man on duty, or in games 1556. **b.** A point at which one may stand to obtain a view 1822. **c.** *Boat-racing.* The position (at one side or the other of the river) occupied by a competing crew at starting 1864. **d.** The correct position of a vessel in a squadron 1911. **2.** *Surveying.* Each of the selected points at which observations are taken 1571. **3.** The place in which a thing stands or is appointed to stand. Now *rare* or *Obs.* 1440. **b.** *Biol.* The kind of place in which an animal or a plant is fitted to live, the nature of its habitat 1721. **4.** *Naut.* **a.** More fully *naval s.* In early use, a port, harbour, or roadstead for ships. In mod. use, a place at which ships of the Navy are regularly stationed. late ME. **b.** A place or region to which a government ship or fleet is assigned for duty 1666. **5.** *Mil.* A place where soldiers are garrisoned, a military post 1609. **b.** In India, a place where the English officials of a district, or the officers of a garrison (not in a fortress) reside. Also, the aggregate society of such a place. 1860. **6.** The locality to which an official is appointed for the exercise of his functions 1632. **7.** A place where men are stationed and apparatus set up for some particular kind of industrial work, scientific research, or the like 1823. **b.** = POLICE-STATION 1889. **8.** *Austral.* A stock-farm 1833.

1. I got a s...at the doore of the lobby to the House, and heard much of the debate EVELYN. Phr. *To take* (*up*), *keep one's s.* 4. a. A large Recess,..A S. safe for Ships, when Tempests roar DRYDEN. b. She was fit for service on the Australasian S. 1912. 5. b. Who asked the S. to dinner? 1866. 6. I am glad my s. is to be here, near my own home PEPYS. 7. *Fishing, seismological, telegraph, zoological s.*; A wireless telegraph s. at Barfleur 1912.

In fig. applications. **9.** *gen.* A metaphorical standing-place or position, e.g. in a class, in a scale of dignity; and the like 1605. **10.** A person's position in the world; a state of life as determined by outward circumstances or conditions; *spec.* a calling, office, employment. Now *rare* or *Obs.* exc. in *private s.*, an unofficial position. 1675. **11.** Position in the social scale, as higher or lower 1682. **b.** *spec.* Elevated position, high social rank 1731.

9. If you haue a s. in the file, Not i' th' worst ranke of Manhood SHAKS. 11. Content may dwell in all Stations SIR T. BROWNE. b. Many other gentlemen of s. and fortune 1832.

III. A stopping-place. **1.** A stopping-place on a journey; a place of temporary abode in a course of migration. Also (chiefly *U.S.*), a place on a coach route where a stop is made for change of horses and for meals. 1585. **2.** (More explicitly *railway s.*) A place where railway trains regularly stop for taking up and setting down passengers or for receiving goods for transport. Also, and more frequently, a building or group of buildings erected at such a place for purposes connected with the transport of passengers and goods. 1830. **b.** Also with reference to a service of omnibuses, etc. **IV.** Ecclesiastical uses. **1.** *Hist.* A service at which the clergy of the city of Rome assembled at one of a certain number of churches within the city, each of which had its fixed day in the year for this celebration. late ME. **2.** Each of a number of holy places visited by pilgrims in fixed succession; esp. each of those churches in the city of Rome at which 'stations' (see prec. sense) were held, and to the visiting of which on certain days indulgences were attached. Also, a visit to such a holy place, or an assembly held there for purposes of devotion on the appointed day. late ME. **3.** *Stations* (*of the Cross*): the series of images or pictures (usually fourteen in number) representing successive incidents of the Passion, placed in a church (or sometimes in the open air) to be visited in order for meditation and prayer; the series of devotional exercises appointed to be used on this occasion 1553. **4.** A special service held at a holy place 1447. **5.** *Hist.* The bi-weekly fast (on Wednesday and Friday) anciently observed 1637. **6.** *Ireland.* A visit of a Roman Catholic parish priest and his curate to the house of a parishioner on a weekday, to give to those in the neighbourhood the opportunity of confession 1830.

Phr. *To go, make, perform one's* (or *the*) *stations, to go on* or *for stations*, to perform the prescribed acts of devotion in succession at certain holy places, or at the Stations of the Cross.

Comb.: **s.-bill** *Naut.*, a list containing the appointed posts of the ship's-company, when navigating the ship; **-hand** *Austral.*, a man employed on a s.; **-line** *Perspective*, the vertical line drawn through the point of sight; -pointer *Surveying*, an instrument for placing the observer's position on the chart from angles taken between three objects, the relative positions of which are known; -staff *Surveying*, a levelling staff; †s. time *Eccl.*, the time when a s. is celebrated.

Station (stēⁱ·ʃən), *v.* 1748. [f. prec. Cf. F. *stationner.*] 1. *trans.* To assign a post, position or station to (a person, troops, ships, etc.); to place or post (a sentinel, etc.) in a station. b. To place in a certain position in a list 1865. c. *refl.* To take up one's station, post oneself. Also *pass.* Said occas. of a thing. 1780. 2. *Shipbuilding.* To determine the proper position for (timbers) 1797.

1. The troops stationed near London 1849.

Stational (stēⁱ·ʃənăl), *a.* 1610. [ad. L. *stationalis*, f. *stationem* STATION *sb.*; see -AL 1.] Of or pertaining to a station or stations.

Stationary (stēⁱ·ʃənări), *a.* and *sb.* late ME. [ad. L. *stationarius*, in class. L. 'belonging to a military station', f. *stationem* STATION *sb.*; see -ARY.] A. *adj.* 1. Having a fixed station or place. a. Not itinerant or migratory 1670. b. Not moving 1784. c. *Astr.* Said of planets at the portions of their orbits in which they have no apparent motion. late ME. d. Having a fixed position. Of a machine, etc.: That remains in one spot when in operation. 1648. 2. *transf.* Remaining unchanged in condition, quality, or quantity; neither advancing nor retrograding 1628. 3. Of or belonging to a station or stations 1571.

1. A passion for field sports had..kept his brother s. MME D'ARBLAY. b. The sun, being s., could not be said to stand still or to move 1862. *S. air*, the amount of air which remains constantly in the lungs in ordinary respiration. d. *S. engines* are used for effecting the ascent and descent of carriages along inclined planes 1840. 2. It would never do if the world remained s. 1898.

B. *sb.* †a. A planet when stationary. HOLLAND. b. One of a force of permanent or stationary troops. *Obs.* exc. *Rom. Hist.* 1698. c. A politician hostile to progress 1831. Hence **Sta·tionari-ly** *adv.*, **-ness.**

Stationer (stēⁱ·ʃənəɹ). late ME. [ad. L. *stationarius* (see prec.), in med.L. used subst. for a tradesman (chiefly, a bookseller) who has a station or shop, as dist. from an itinerant vendor.] 1. a. A bookseller *Hist.* †b. A publishing bookseller, publisher –1673. 2. A tradesman who sells writing materials, etc. 1656.

The Company of Stationers (or *the Stationers' Company*): one of the Livery Companies of the City of London, founded in 1556, comprising booksellers, bookbinders, and dealers in writing materials, etc. *Stationers' Hall*: the hall of the Stationers' Company, at which a register of copyrights is kept.

Stationery (stēⁱ·ʃənəri). Also †-ary. 1727. [f. STATIONER + -Y³.] 1. The articles sold by a stationer; writing materials, writing-table appurtenances, etc. 2. *attrib.* as in *s. business, trade, ware* 1679.

2. **S. Office**, an office in London through which government offices are supplied with s., and which issues the reports, etc. published by the government.

Sta·tion-house. 1836. 1. The lock-up attached to a police-station 1836. 2. A railway station; now only, a small country station 1838. 3. *Austral.* The house belonging to a station 1894.

Stationmaster (stēⁱ·ʃənmāːstəɹ). 1857. [f. STATION *sb.* + MASTER *sb.*] The official who has the control of a railway station. So **Sta·tion-mi·stress.**

Statist (stēⁱ·tist). 1584. [f. L. *status* STATE *sb.*; see -IST.] 1. A person skilled in state affairs, one having political knowledge, power, or influence; a politician, statesman. Now *arch.* 2. One who deals with statistics, a statistician 1803.

1. Art thou a S., in the van Of public conflicts trained and bred? WORDSW.

Statistic (stăti·stik), *a.* and *sb.* 1789. [ad. G. *statistik* sb., *statistisch* adj., ad. mod.L. *statisticus*, f. **statista* STATIST.] A. *adj.* 1. = next. Now *rare.* 2. Of or pertaining to status 1871. B. *sb.* 1. = STATISTICS 1 (*rare*) 1796. 2. = STATISTICIAN 1804.

Statistical (stăti·stikăl), *a.* 1787. [f. prec. + -AL 1.] Of or pertaining to statistics, esp. with reference to economic, sanitary, and vital conditions. b. Of a writer, etc.: Dealing with statistics 1787.

The..moral and s. features of the period 1841. b. Some respectable s. writers 1787. Hence **Stati·stically** *adv.*

Statistician (stætisti·ʃăn). 1825. [f. STATISTIC + -IAN.] One versed in or engaged in collecting and tabulating statistics.

Statistics (stăti·stiks). 1787. [pl. of STATISTIC.] 1. Construed as *sing.* In early use, that branch of political science dealing with the collection, classification, and discussion of facts bearing on the condition of a state or community. In recent use, the department of study that has for its object the collection and arrangement of numerical facts or data, whether relating to human affairs or to natural phenomena. 2. Construed as *pl.* Numerical facts or data collected and classified 1837.

Stative (stēⁱ·tiv), *a.* and *sb.* 1631. [ad. L. *stativus*, f. *stat-*, *stare* to stand.] A. *adj.* 1. Stationary, fixed, having a permanent situation, a fixed recurring date, or the like. Now *Rom. Antiq.* in *s. camp*, etc. 2. *Heb. Gram.* Epithet of verbs which express a state or condition [= mod.L. *verba stativa*] 1874. B. *sb. Heb. Gram.* A stative verb 1874.

Stato- (stæto), repr. Gr. *στατό-ς* standing, used (mainly as virtual comb. form of STATIC, STATICS) in scientific words, chiefly *Biol.*, as **Sta·toblast**, a reproductive gemmule developed in some Polyzoa and Sponges and liberated after the death of the parent organism; hence **Statobla·stic** *a.* **Sta·toscope**, a form of aneroid barometer adapted for recording minute variations of atmospheric pressure.

Stator (stēⁱ·təɹ). 1902. [a. L., f. *sta-*, *stare* to stand.] 1. *Electr.* The stationary portion of an electric generator or motor, esp. of an induction motor. 2. The casing enclosing the revolving blades of a steam turbine 1911.

†Sta·tua. late ME. [a. L.] = STATUE *sb.* –1691.

I stood A verie S., dull as my owne Mudde 1646.

Statuary (stæ·tiu̯ări), *sb.* and *a.* 1563. [ad. L. *statuarius* adj., f. *statua* STATUE *sb.*] A. *sb.* 1. One who practises the art of making statues 1581. 2. Sculpture composed of statues, statues collectively. †Also pl., works of sculpture. 1673. 3. [L. *statuaria*, sc. *ars.*] The art of making statues, sculpture 1563.

1. If Statuaries could By the foote of Hercules set downe punctually His whole dimensions MASSINGER.

B. *adj.* 1. Of or pertaining to the making of statues 1627. 2. Consisting of statues or a statue; sculptured 1629. 3. Of materials: Suitable for statues or statuary work; esp. *s. marble*; *s. vein*, a variety of statuary marble 1815.

Statue (stæ·tiu), *sb.* late ME. [a. F., ad. L. *statua*, f. *sta-*, *stare* to stand.] A representation in the round of a living being, sculptured, moulded or cast in marble, metal, plaster, etc.; esp. a figure of a deity, allegorical personage, or eminent person, usu. of life-size proportions. Also *transf.* and *similative*, as a type of silence or absence of movement or feeling.

And to remember what he does, Build his S. to make him glorious SHAKS. Still as a s...He stood BYRON. Hence **Sta·tueless** *a.*

Statue (stæ·tiu), *v.* 1607. [f. prec.] *trans.* To represent in a statue or in statuary; to honour (a person) by erecting a statue of him. Now only in *nonce-use.*

Statued (stæ·tiūd), *ppl. a.* 1806. [f. STATUE *v.* and *sb.* + -ED.] 1. Furnished or ornamented with statues or statuary. 2. Represented in a statue or in statuary 1839.

1. Vased and s. terraces 1806. 2. The s. satyrs seemed to grin and jibber 1839.

Statuesque (stætiu̯e·sk), *a.* 1834. [f. STATUE *sb.* + -ESQUE, after *picturesque.*] Having the qualities of a statue or of sculpture.

The s. native soldiers who stand as sentries 1905. Hence **Statue·sque-ly** *adv.*, **-ness.**

Statuette (stætiue·t). 1843. [a. F., dim. of *statue*; see -ETTE.] A small statue; a statue less than life-size.

Stature (stæ·tiŭɹ, -tʃəɹ), *sb.* ME. [a. OF., ad. L. *statura*, f. *sta-*, *stare* to stand; see -TURE.] 1. The height of an animal (esp. the human) body in its normal standing position; *transf.* esp. of a tree. †2. An effigy, statue –1653.

1. *Two Gent.* IV. iv. 163. *fig.* The men are of meaner moral s. 1875. Hence **Sta·ture** *v.* (*rare* exc. in pa. pple.) *trans.* to give s. to. **Sta·tured** *a.* having (a certain kind of) s.

Status (stēⁱ·tŏs). *Pl.* (*rare*) **status** (stēⁱ·tiūs). 1693. [a. L., f. *sta-*, *stare* to stand.] ‖1. *Path.* a. The height or acme of a disease. Now *rare* or *Obs.* b. Used (with the sense 'state, condition') in many mod.L. combinations with adj., as *s. arthriticus*, *epilepticus*, *lymphaticus*, etc. 1883. 2. *Law.* The legal standing or position of a person as determined by his membership of some class of persons legally enjoying certain rights or subject to certain limitations; condition in respect, e.g. of infancy or majority. Also applied to things. 1791. 3. Position or standing in society, a profession, and the like 1820. 4. Condition of things 1860. b. *Finance.* A particular grouping of the conditions bearing on the continuance of an annuity 1838.

2. The legal s. of the Gipsies 1910. The s. of enemy merchant vessels 1914. 4. The present s. of photography (*mod.*).

‖ **Status quo** (stēⁱ·tŏs kwōᵘ·). 1833. [L.; 'state in which'. See ‖IN 16.] The existing state of things.

Statutable (stæ·tiutăb'l), *a.* 1636. [f. STATUTE *sb.* + -ABLE.] 1. Prescribed, authorized, or permitted by statute. 2. Satisfying the requirements of the statutes; †*transf.* of standard quality; that will pass muster 1661. 3. Recognized by statute; legally punishable 1792.

1. They do not carry with them..any statuteable authority EVELYN. 2. One s. acre of ground 1758. Hence **Sta·tutably** *adv.*

Statute (stæ·tiūt). ME. [a. F. *statut*, ad. late L. *statutum* decree, subst. use of neut. pa. pple. of *statuere* to set up, f. *sta-*, *stare* to stand.] I. 1. A law or decree made by a sovereign or a legislative authority. Now *rare* or *Obs.* in gen. sense. b. Applied to an ordinance or decree of God, a deity, fate, etc. late ME. c. An enactment made by a corporation for its government. late ME. 2. An enactment, containing one or more legislative provisions, made by the legislature of a country at one time, and expressed in a formal document; the document in which such an enactment is expressed. late ME. †b. *By* (*the*) *s.*: according to the measure, price, or rate appointed by statute –1781. 3. In international law, [= F. *statut personnel, réel*] *Personal s.*: the system of law to which an alien party to a process is personally subject, as dist. from *real s.*, the system of law to which the particular transaction is otherwise subject 1907.

1. b. Praysed be thou O Lorde, O teach me thy statutes COVERDALE *Ps.* cxviii. 12. c. Oxford..is still governed by the statutes of Archbishop Laud EMERSON. 2. The famous s., called the Declaration of Right BURKE.

II. Uses originating in ellipsis. †1. Applied to certain legal instruments or procedures based on the authority of a statute. a. A STATUTE MERCHANT or STATUTE STAPLE –1701. b. *S. of bankrupt*, *s. of lunacy*: the process by which a person was declared a bankrupt or a lunatic –1742. 2. (*sing.* and *pl.*) [Short for †*statute-sessions.*] A fair or gathering held annually in certain towns or villages for the hiring of servants. Also called *statute-fair*, *-hiring.* 1600.

1. a. He that marries her shall give the other a s. upon his estate for two thousand pounds 1701.

III. Misused for STATUE *sb.* late ME.

attrib. and *Comb.*: quasi-*adj.*, with the senses 'fixed by statute', 'recognized by statute', 'statutory'; also *transf.*; as *s.-interest*, *s.-hospitality*, etc.; designating a unit of measure or weight as fixed by statute, as in *s. acre, mile, ton*, etc. Special comb.: **s.-barred** *a.*, (of debts, claims) barred by the statute of limitations; †**-cap**, the woollen cap ordered by 13 Eliz. c. 19 to be worn on Sundays and holy days by all persons not of a certain social or official rank; **s. fair, s. hiring** = sense II. 2; **s. labour**, a definite amount of labour on works of public utility, formerly required by statute to be performed by the residents in the district interested; so *s. labourer*; **s. law**, a law contained in a statute; also, the system of law contained in statutes, as dist. from common law; **s. money**, money paid as commutation for statute labour; **-roll**, the roll on which the statutes are engrossed; often = next; **-work** = *s. labour.*

Sta·tute-book. 1648. The book containing the statutes of a nation or state; usu. (*sing.*, occas. *pl.*) the whole series of volumes forming the official record of the statutes. Phr., *on the s.*

Statute merchant. 1442. Now *Hist.*

[ellipt. use of **statute of merchants** = med.L. *statutum de mercatoribus*, AF. *estatut marchand*, med.L. *statutum mercatorium*, whence the powers of summary execution of this kind of instrument were derived.] *Law.* A bond of record, acknowledged before the chief magistrate of a trading town, giving to the obligee power of seizure of the land of the obligor if he failed to pay his debt at the appointed time.

Statute staple. 1444. Now *Hist.* [ellipt. use of **statute of the staple**; see STAPLE *sb.*[2], and cf. prec.] *Law.* A bond of record, acknowledged before the mayor of the staple, conveying powers similar to those given by the statute merchant.

Statutory (stæ·tiŭtəri), *a.* 1766. [f. STATUTE *sb.* + -ORY[2].] Pertaining to or consisting in statutes; enacted, created, or appointed by statute; conformable to the provisions of a statute.

S. treason, an offence made treasonable by statute. *S. declaration*, a declaration in accordance with the Statutory Declaration Act (1835), which substituted simple affirmations for the oaths or solemn affirmations formerly required on certain occasions.

Staunch, stanch (stǭnʃ, stānʃ), *a.* late ME. [a. OF. *estanche*, fem. of *estanc* (mod.F. *étanche*), f. Com. Rom. **stancare*; see STANCH *v.* In British use the spelling *staunch* is the more common for the adj., *stanch* for the vb.] **1.** Impervious to water, not leaking; watertight. Also occas. air-tight. **2.** Of strong or firm construction, in good or firm condition, substantial 1455. **3.** Of a sporting dog: That may be trusted to find or follow the scent, or to mark the game; dependable 1576. **4.** Of a person: Standing firm to one's principles or purpose, not to be turned aside, determined 1623. **b.** Of personal qualities, actions, etc.: Showing determination or resolution, unwavering 1690.

1. Our ship was staunch, and our Crew all in good Health SWIFT. 2. The wall of the tower is still stanch and strong HAWTHORNE. 3. A dog that is stanch on a covey 1883. 4. In Politicks, I hear, you'r stanch PRIOR. Hence **Sta(u)·nchly** *adv.* **Sta(u)·nchness.**

Stauro- (stǭ·ro, stǭrǫ·), bef. a vowel **staur-**, comb. form of Gr. σταυρός cross.

Staurolite (stǭ·rŏləit). 1815. [a. F.; see prec. and -LITE.] Silicate of aluminium and iron, found frequently in cruciform twins. Hence **Stauroli·tic** *a.*

Stauroscope (stǭ·roskōup). 1875. [f. Gr. σταυρός cross (see STAURO-) + -SCOPE.] An instrument used for the microscopic examination of rocks. Hence **Staurosco·pic** *a.*

Staurotide (stǭ·rotəid). 1802. [a. F., app. f. Gr. σταυρωτός cruciform, f. σταυρός cross.] *Min.* = STAUROLITE.

Stave (stēⁱv), *sb.* ME. [A back-formation from *staves*, pl. of STAFF *sb.*] **I. 1.** Each of the thin, narrow, shaped pieces of wood which, when placed together side by side and hooped, collectively form the side of a cask, tub or the like. **2.** A rod, bar, pole or the like; e. g. a rung (of a ladder); a cross-bar to the legs of a chair. *local.* ME. **II. 1.** A 'verse' or stanza of a poem, song, etc. 1659. **2.** *Mus.* A set of lines for musical notation 1800.

II. 1. Phr. *To tip* (a person) *a s.*, to sing a song to; *joc.*, to send a line to.

Stave (stēⁱv), *v.* Pa. t. and pa. pple. **staved;** also (chiefly *Naut.*) †**stove.** 1595. [f. prec.] **1.** *trans.* To break up (a cask) into staves; to break into and let out the contents. **b.** To destroy (wine, etc.) by breaking up the cask 1615. **2.** *trans.* To break a hole in (a boat); to break *to pieces*; also, to break (a hole in a boat). *To s. in*, to crush inwards, make a hole in. 1628. **b.** *intr.* for *refl.* of a boat: To break up; hence *trans.* to break a hole in 1743. **3.** *transf.* (*trans.*) To burst in, crush inwards. Chiefly with *in.* 1716. **4.** To renew the staves of (a bucket); to put together the staves of (a cask, etc.) 1627. **5.** To drive off or beat with a staff or stave; esp. in *to s. off*, to beat off (a dog in bear- or bull-baiting; also *transf.* a human combatant); to keep back (a crowd). Now *arch.* 1609. **6.** *fig.* Chiefly *to s. off.* †**a.** To keep (a person) *from* (doing something); to divert *from* (an object, practice, etc.) –1684. **b.** To put off as importune or inopportune; to treat with evasion 1646. **c.** To ward off (something undesirable or hurtful); to prevent the occurrence or event of; to keep back, delay 1662. **7.** *intr.* To go with a rush or dash; to 'drive'. *Sc.* and *U.S.* 1819. **8.** *Forging.* To thicken (bar-iron) by heating and hammering, to UPSET. Also *absol.* **b.** *intr.* Of the iron: To undergo staving 1906.

1. Hogsheads of French wine..were publickly staved 1679. **b.** He..staves all prohibited goods 1694. 2. A sea..stove in the quarter gallery 1748. **b.** Like a vessel of glass, she stove and sank LONGF. 3. To break open and s. trunks and chests 1753. 5. S. off the crowd upon the Spaniard there TENNYSON. 6. **b.** This staved the fellows off for a while 1887. **c.** A little fish sufficed to s. off hunger 1879.

Staved (stēⁱvd), *ppl. a.* 1481. [f. STAVE *v.* or *sb.* + -ED[1].] **1.** Furnished with a stave or staves. **b.** Of a ladder: Furnished with rungs 1603. **c.** *Arch.* Of a column: Having a round convex moulding or bead in the lower part of the fluting 1664. **2.** Broken; also *s. in* 1699. **4.** *Forging.* Thickened by hammering 1906.

Stavesacre (stēⁱ·vzēⁱ:kəɹ). late ME. [ad. L. *staphisagria*, a. Gr. σταφὶς ἀγρία wild raisin.] A ranunculaceous plant of the species *Delphinium Staphisagria*, native in Southern Europe and Asia Minor; the seeds of this plant, used to destroy vermin, and formerly as an emetic.

Staving (stēⁱ·viŋ), *vbl. sb.* 1491. [f. STAVE *v.* and *sb.* + -ING[1].] **1.** The action of STAVE *v.* 1633. **2.** Staves collectively 1491.

Stay (stēⁱ), *sb.*[1] [OE. *stæg* :—OTeut.**stago-*, f. Teut. root **stah-* : *stag-* to be firm (in **stahlo-* STEEL *sb.*, etc.) :—pre-Teut. **stak-* or **stok-*. (The Teut. word has been adopted in Rom. languages.)] *Naut.* A large rope used to support a mast, and leading from its head down to some other mast or spar, or to some part of the ship. **b.** *transf.* A guy or rope supporting a flagstaff, or a pole of any kind 1533.

Phrases. *In stays*, said of a ship when her head is being turned to windward for the purpose of tacking. *To miss, lose stays*, of a ship, to fail in the attempt to go about. See *also* BACKSTAY, FORESTAY.

Comb.: **s.-block**, a block buried in the ground as an attachment for the s. of a telegraph pole; **-tackle**, a large tackle attached to the mainstay, and used to hoist heavy bodies in and out of the ship; **-wire**, a wire forming part of a s. for a telegraph pole.

Stay (stēⁱ), *sb.*[2] 1515. [prob. f. STAY *v.*[2]] **1.** Something that supports or steadies something else; esp. an appliance for holding up or securing in position some part of a structure; a prop, pedestal, bracket, buttress, or the like. **b.** *fig.* A thing or a person that affords support; an object of reliance. Also, in abstract sense: Support. 1530. **2.** *spec.* Applied to various kinds of supports in technical and mechanical use 1577. **3.** *pl.* (Also *pair of stays.*) = CORSET 2. Rarely in *sing.* 1608.

1. **b.** From that hour Gerard was looked upon as the s. of the family READE. 3. The s. he has an invincible aversion to 1731. The deceased died of apoplexy, produced by her stays being too tightly laced 1831.

Comb.: **s.-bar**, a bar for keeping a casement window open at a certain angle; **-bolt**, a bolt connecting plates of a boiler, to secure them against internal pressure; **-rod**, a rod serving to give support, or to connect two parts of a machine or structure to prevent displacement. Hence **Stayed** *a.* provided with stays.

Stay (stēⁱ), *sb.*[3] 1525. [f. STAY *v.*[1]] **1.** The action of stopping or bringing to a stand or pause; the fact of being brought to a stand or delayed; a stoppage, or suspension of action; a check, set-back 1537. **b.** *Law.* Suspension of a judicial proceeding 1542. †**2.** Control; restraint; self-control –1622. **3.** A coming to a stand; a cessation of progress or action; a pause, halt 1530. †**4.** Delay, postponement, waiting –1707. †**5.** A cause of stoppage; an obstacle, hindrance –1665. †**b.** A demur, hesitation, scruple –1567. **6.** The action or fact of staying in a place, continued presence; an instance of this, a sojourn 1538. †**b.** Continuance in a state, duration –1700. **c.** Staying power. Now *rare.* 1586. **7.** A stationary condition, a standstill. Now *arch.* 1525.

1. A conqueror who no s. will brook 1862. **b.** The prisoner's counsel then moved for a s. of execution 1856. 3. Trauailing both day and night without any rest or s. 1585. 5. Not grudging, that thy lust hath bounds and staies G. HERBERT. 6. Her s. in London was longer than mine in Paris 1789. **b.** Alas, what s. is there in human state DRYDEN. 7. Man that is borne of a woman..neuer continueth in one staye *Bk. Com. Prayer, Burial of Dead.* Phr. †*To set in* or *at s.*, to settle. Also *to set a s.*, *to set stays*, to settle matters.

Stay (stēⁱ), *v.*[1] Pa. t. and pa. pple. **stayed** (stēⁱd), †**staid.** 1440. [prob. a. OF. (*e*)*stai-*, (*e*)*stei-*, flexional stem of *ester* (:—L. *stare*) to stand.] **I.** *intr.* *To cease moving, halt. †**1.** To cease going forward; to stop, halt; to arrest one's course and stand still –1777. **b.** To stop, halt, pause *and* (do something), or in order *to* (do something). Now *rare.* 1577. **2.** To cease or desist from some specified activity. *Obs.* or *arch.* 1576. **b.** In *imper.* used as an injunction to pause, arrest one's course, not to go on doing something. Hence often = give me time to consider, decide, etc.; wait for me to make some remark or give some order. 1590. **3.** Of an action, activity, process, etc.: To be arrested, to stop at a certain point, not to go forward. *Obs.* or *arch.* 1563.

1. And the Sunne stood still, and the Moone stayed, vntill the people had auenged themselues vpon their enemies *Josh.* x. 13. 2. He hearkned, and did s. from further harmes SPENSER. **b.** S., stand apart, I know not which is which SHAKS. S., there is one way FIELDING. 3. Neither did the matter s. here 1570.

To remain stationary. **4. To remain in a place or in others' company (as opp. to going on or going away) 1575. **b.** With inf.: To remain in order *to* (do something). Also *to s. to* (dinner, etc.). 1591. **c.** Const. *for*: To await in a place, remain to take part in or witness 1554. **5.** Of a thing: To remain (in a place or position); to remain (as opp. to being lost, changing its nature, etc.). Now *rare.* 1593. **b.** Of food, etc.: To be retained by the stomach after swallowing 1643. **6.** With predicative extension: To remain in the specified condition 1573. **7.** With emphasis or contextual colouring: **a.** To delay (as opp. to going on). Chiefly with neg. 1500. **b.** To stand one's ground. Now *rare.* 1593. **8.** To reside or sojourn in a place for a longer or shorter period; to put up *with* a person as his guest 1554. †**9.** To remain inactive or quiet; to wait; to put off action (*until*) –1751. **10.** *Sport.* To last or hold out in a race or run. Also, to hold out for (a specified distance). 1834. **11.** *Poker.* To remain *in* the game when the ante has been raised; so *to s.* out 1882.

4. He comes for half an hour, and stays an hour RICHARDSON. I wish you would s. and talk 1885. 5. A lesson learned with strokes, staies with the scholler 1593. 6. I can bend them up and down and they s. bent RUSKIN *To s. put* (orig. U.S.): see PUT *v.*[1] II. a. 7. And Ionathan cryed after the ladde, Make speed, haste, stay not 1 *Sam.* xx. 38. **b.** And giue them leaue to flye, that will not s. SHAKS. 8. He stayed at Rippon one night 1617. While she staid with her uncle 1823. Phr. *To come to s.*, to become permanent or established, to come into regular use or recognition; to assume a secure position in public favour (*colloq.*) 9. Madam: dinner is ready, and your father staies SHAKS. 10. [Alcohol] may enable a man 'to spurt' but not 'to s.' 1897.

II. quasi-*trans.* and *trans.* uses derived from I. **1.** quasi-*trans.* To remain for, to remain and participate in or assist at (a meal, ceremony, prayers, etc.); to remain throughout or during (a period of time) 1570. **2.** quasi-*trans.* with *out.* To remain to the end of; to remain and witness the end of. Also, to outstay. 1639. **3.** *trans.* To wait for, await (a person, his coming, an event, etc.); to wait upon, serve (a person's leisure); to abide, sustain (a question, onset). Now *arch.* 1586.

1. I stay'd yᵉ sermon 1661. I'm obliged to ask them to s. tea 1888. 2. It seemed as if we had stayed our English welcome out HAWTHORNE. 3. They basely flie and dare not s. the field SHAKS.

III. *trans.* To stop, arrest, check. **1.** To detain, hold back, stop (a person or thing); to hinder from going on or going away; to keep in a fixed place or position. Now *literary.* 1440. **2.** To render motionless or keep immovable; to fix, hold fast 1627. **3.** To prevent, hinder, stop (a person or thing) from doing something; to check restrain; esp. *to s.* (one's own or another's) *hand* (chiefly *fig.*, to cease or cause to cease from attack or working). Now *arch.* 1560. **4.** To stop, arrest, delay, prevent (an action or process, something which is begun or intended). Freq. in legal parlance. 1525. **b.** To arrest the course or growth of (a disease, something noxious or destructive) 1563. **5.** To leave off, discontinue (doing something, an activity of one's own). Also, to delay, withhold (one's good opinion, thanks). Now *rare* or *Obs.* 1538. 6. To appease, allay (strife, tumult); to bring under control (rebellious elements). Now *rare.* 1537. 7. *To s. the stomach*: to stave off hunger. Similarly *to s. one's longing, hunger, appetite,* etc. 1608.

1. And here shal it staye thy proud waues BIBLE (Geneva) *Job* xxxviii. 11. The wet and uncomfortable weather staying us from church EVELYN. 2. Each Galley doe foure anchors s. 1627. 3. Rivers are dried, winds stay'd M. ARNOLD. My tongue is tied and my hand is stayed 1880. 4. I do order..that until such indemnity be given all further proceedings be stayed 1856. b. That the plague may be stayed from the people 2 *Sam.* xxiv. 21. 5. S. your Thanks a while, And pay them when you part SHAKS. 6. Old men..Bless'd him who staid the civil strife SCOTT.

Stay (stēi), *v.*[2] Pa. t. and pa. pple. **stayed** (stēid). 1526. [a. OF. *estayer* (mod.F. *étayer*) to prop up, prob. an extended use of the nautical vb. *estayer* (mod.F. *étayer*) = next.] 1. *trans.* To support, sustain, hold up (a person or thing). Const. *on, upon,* †*unto.* Now chiefly in sense 3. Also *transf.* and *fig.*, to strengthen, comfort. 2. *fig.* To cause to rest *on, upon* or *in* (a firm support, base or ground); to base or ground *upon*, set firmly *in* 1565. †b. *refl.* with *upon*: To rely or build upon, rest or act upon; to abide by; to content oneself with –1709. 3. (*spec.* and *techn.*) To support, strengthen or secure with stays. Also with *up.* 1556.

1. Because on the bones of the English the English Flag is stayed KIPLING. 2. Thou wilt keepe him in perfect peace, whose minde is stayed on thee *Isa.* xxvi. 3. b. They..staie them selues vpon the God of Israel BIBLE (Geneva) *Isa.* xlviii. 2. 3. Watch an old building with anxious care..s. it with timber where it declines RUSKIN.

†**To s. on, upon.** a. *intr.* To lean upon, support oneself by (a staff, etc.); of a thing, to be supported by. b. To trust to, have confidence in; to depend on. Hence **Stayed** *ppl. a.*, **-ness.**

Stay, *v.*[3] Pa. t. and pple. **stayed** (stēid). 1613. [f. STAY *sb.*[1]] *Naut.* 1. *trans.* To secure or steady by means of stays; to incline (forward, aft, or to one side) by means of stays 1627. 2. To put (a ship) 'in stays'; to put on the other tack 1625. 3. *intr.* To go about in stays; to turn to windward in order to tack 1613.

Stay-at-home, *a.* and *sb.* 1806. [f. STAY *v.*[1]] A. *adj.* That stays at home, not given to travelling or to gadding abroad; hence untravelled. B. *sb.* One who stays at home 1841.

Stayer[1] (stēi·əɪ). 1591. [f. STAY *v.*[1] + -ER[1].] 1. One who stays or remains. b. *Sport.* A person or animal having great staying power 1862. 2. One who or something which stops or restrains 1597.

Stayer[2] (stēi·əɪ). 1579. [f. STAY *v.*[2] + -ER[1].] One who stays or supports. b. With reference to the title of Jupiter Stator 1611.

b. Thou Iupiter, whom we do call the S. Both of this Citie, and this Empire B. JONS.

Staying (stēi·iŋ), *vbl. sb.* 1546. [f. STAY *v.*[1] + -ING[1].] The action of STAY *v.*[1] in various senses.

Comb.: **s. power,** in a race or other contest, power to 'stay' or continue in action for a long time; power of persistent effort; hence *gen.*

Staylace (stēi·lēis), *sb.* 1720. [f. STAY *sb.*[2] + LACE *sb.*] A lace or cord used to draw together a woman's stays or bodice. Hence **Stay·lace** *v. trans.* to lace up with staylaces.

Stayless (stēi·lės), *a.*[1] 1572. [f. STAY *sb.*[3] + -LESS.] 1. Not to be stayed or stopped, ceaseless 1578. 2. Without stay or permanence, ever-changing 1572.

Stay·less, *a.*[2] 1587. [f. STAY *sb.*[2] + -LESS.] 1. Without stay or support. 2. Unsupported by stays or corsets 1880.

Staysail (stēi·seil, stēi·s'l). 1669. [f. STAY *sb.*[1]] *Naut.* A triangular sail hoisted upon a stay.

Stay-ship (stēi·ʃip). 1567. [f. STAY *v.*[1]] = REMORA.

Stay·-tape. 1698. [STAY *sb.*[2]] Tape used by tailors as a support or binding.

‖**Stchi** (ʃtʃī). 1833. [Russ.] Cabbage soup.

Stead (sted), *sb.* [Com. Teut.; OE. *stęde* :—OTeut. **stadiz* :—pre-Teut. **stəti-s* (cf. Skr. *sthíti* standing, position, Gr. στάσις standing, stoppage, L. *statim* advb. accus., *statio* STATION *sb.*), f. wk.-grade of *sta-* to STAND.] I. A point or tract in space. †1. A locality; = PLACE *sb.* 2. –1596. †2. An inhabited place –1577. †b. **The Steads** [= MLG. *de Steden*]: the Hanse Towns. Also, the corporation of Hanse merchants in London. –1558. 3. Chiefly with *possessive.* The place assigned to, belonging to, or normally occupied by a thing; appointed or natural place; †a seat. *Obs.* exc. *arch.* OE. †b. The place where a body of soldiers is stationed; a military position –1627. 4. A property or estate in land; a farm ME. 5. A site for a building; the land on which a building stands. (Cf. *farmstead*, etc.) ME. †6. The framework which supports the bedding of a bed. (Cf. BEDSTEAD.) –1858.

1. Great God it planted in that blessed sted With his almightie hand SPENSER. 3. The mast in its s. we 'stablished and hauled the sails in air MORRIS. 5. Messuage steads and cottage steads 1773.

II. The place, 'room', 'lieu', or function (of a person or thing) as held by a substitute or a successor. Only in certain phrases. ME.

Phr. *In the s. of* (now *arch.*), (*a*) in the room of, in succession to (one who has died, has retired from or is superseded in an office); (*b*) in lieu of; (*c*) predicatively, *to be in the s. of*, to make up for the want of. *In his*, etc., *s.* (now literary), (*a*) as a successor in his room; (*b*) as his deputy or representative (*arch.*); (*c*) instead of him.

III. Advantage, profit, service, support; esp. in *to stand in s.*; *to do s.* Now *arch.* ME.

Stead (sted), *v.* ME. [f. *stude, stede* STEAD *sb.*] I. To stand in stead. 1. *trans.* a. *impers.* or with subj. clause, inf., etc.: To avail, profit, be of use to (a person). Also *absol.* Now *arch.* b. Of a thing: To be useful or advantageous to. Also *absol.* Now *arch.* (*rare.*) 1594. c. With subj. a person: To succour, help, render service to. Now *rare.* 1582. †2. *To s. up*: to fulfil in the stead of another. SHAKS.

1. a. So it steed you, I will write..a thousand times as much SHAKS. b. No adjectives would s. me 1891. c. It 's like I may pleasure you, and s. your father in his extremity SCOTT. 2. *Meas. for M.* III. i. 260.

II. To place. †1. To establish, fix, place. Chiefly *pass.*, to be situated, stand –1821. †2. *pass.* To be placed *in* a certain (evil or difficult) plight or condition; to be burdened *with* (sickness), beset *with* (enemies, etc.) –1818.

1. But it is done..To honour thee..To s. thee as a verse in English tongue KEATS. 2. Sen we are stad with enemys on ilk syd 1470. We are cruelly sted between God's laws and man's laws SCOTT.

Steadfast (ste·dfāst), *a.* (*adv.*) [OE. *stędefæst*, f. *stęde* (see STEAD *sb.*) + *fæst* FAST *a.*] A. *adj.* 1. Fixed or secure in position. Of a person, esp. a soldier in battle: Maintaining his ground. c. Of a foundation, etc.: Firmly fixed OE. 2. Of persons: Unshaken, immovable in faith, resolution, friendship, etc. Also said of belief, purpose, or affection. ME. †b. Applied to God: Unchanging –1611. 3. Of a law, a treaty, an institution, a condition of things: Firmly settled, established, unchangeable ME. 4. Of sight, the eye (occas. of the mind): Steadily directed ME.

1. These Elements In mutinie had from her Axle torn The stedfast Earth MILT. 2. COVERDALE *Prov.* xii. 4. b. *Dan.* vi. 26. 4. MILT. *Hymn Nativ.* 70.

†B. *adv.* Steadfastly –1887. Hence **Stea·dfast-ly** *adv.*, **-ness.**

Steading (ste·diŋ). *Sc.* and *north.* 1472. [f. STEAD *sb.* + -ING[1].] 1. A farm-house and outbuildings; the outbuildings in contrast to the farm-house. 2. A site for a building 1822.

Stea·dy, *sb.* 1792. [f. STEADY *a.* and *v.*] 1. Something which is steady or which steadies. 2. *U.S. slang.* A regular sweetheart 1900.

Steady (ste·di), *a.* (and *adv.*) 1530. [app. f. STEAD *sb.* + -Y[1].] A. *adj.* †1. Fixed or immovable in position; not liable to give way or become displaced –1683. b. Of affairs: Stable. Of a rule, etc.: Settled, established. 1571. 2. Firm in standing or movement; not tottering, rocking, or shaking; that is in stable equilibrium 1574. 3. Of a person or his mind: Not easily perturbed or discomposed; balanced. Of the head: Free from giddiness. Of the eye: Not diverted from its object; unwavering. 1602. b. Of troops, their attributes or actions: Firm, disciplined; not liable to panic or loss of self-control. Also *ellipt.* = 'be steady'. 1670. c. Of a hound: Not easily diverted from the scent. Of a horse: Not nervous, skittish, or excitable; also, that travels at a moderate and even pace. 1735. 4. Regular in operation or intensity; uniform, equable 1548. b. Of weather, temperature: Free from sudden changes, settled. Of climate: Having little variation of temperature. Hence said of an instrument for recording variations of weather. 1700. c. *Comm.* Of prices: Free from sudden rise or fall; hence of the market, goods, shares, etc. 1889. 5. Persistent, unwavering in resolution, attachment, or in a course of action; persistently devoted *to* a cause, etc. 1602. 6. Not given to frivolity; staid 1759. 7. Regular in habits; not given to dissipation or looseness in conduct 1832.

1. b. Their union should be deferred no longer than until Butler should obtain some s. means of support SCOTT. 2. The hand that held the candle was as s. as a rock 1865. 3. With folded arms and s. eyes SHELLEY. b. They're coming up: s., boys; s. now LEVER. c. As a rule, there were four s. horses and a good driver, rarely drunk RUSKIN. 4. There was a s. trade in all descriptions of barley 1855. The s. rise in the price of wool 1874. c. Glorious s. weather EVELYN. d. Corn opened s. 1896. 5. A trusty counsellor and s. friend SMOLLETT. Their own serious and s. attachment to the laws 1818. 6. A very grave, s. person 1818. Hence **Stea·di-ly** *adv.*, **-ness.**

B. *adv.* In a steady manner, steadily. Chiefly *Naut.* 1605. b. *ellipt.* Chiefly *Naut.* = 'steer steady' 1620. c. *Comb.*, as *steady-going* adj.

Steady (ste·di), *v.* 1530. [f. STEADY *a.*] 1. *trans.* To keep from rocking, shaking, tottering, or similar movement. b. To keep from falling 1848. c. *intr.* for *refl.* 1849. 2. *trans.* To make (one's mind, troops, etc.) steady 1530. 3. *Naut.* To keep (a vessel) to the direct line of her course. Also *absol.* and *intr.* for *refl.* 1627. 4. To bring to a more regular rate of progress. Also *intr.* for *refl.* 1812. 5. To keep (a person) from irregularity of conduct. Also *intr.* for *refl.*; also with *down.* 1848. 6. *Comm.* intr. To become more free from fluctuation; also with *up* 1913.

1. The chronic drunkard, who takes a glass of spirits to 's. the hand' 1899. 3. She doth not tack from side to side..Withouten wind, withouten tide She steddies with upright keel COLERIDGE. 5. He breaks off..from folly;..he steadies down 1848. Hence **Stea·dy** *sb.* something which is steady; something which steadies, *spec.* a device for holding steady an object in process of being fashioned. **Stea·diment,** a means of studying steady conditions.

Steak (stēik). late ME. [a. ON. *steik*, cogn. w. *steikja* to roast on a spit, *stikna* to be roasted.] A thick slice or strip of meat cut for grilling, frying, or stewing, sometimes used in a pie or pudding; esp. a piece cut from the hind quarters of the animal; without qualification = BEEF-STEAK. b. A thick slice (of cod, salmon, halibut, or hake) 1883. c. *transf.* and *fig.* Now *rare* or *Obs.* 1607.

Steal (stīl), *sb.*[1] *Obs.* exc. *dial.* [OE. *stela*, f. OTeut. **stel-*, ablaut-var. of **stal-*, whence STALE *sb.*[2]] 1. The stalk or stem of a plant, leaf, flower, or fruit. 2. The handle of a tool or utensil (e. g. a hammer, pot, spoon). late ME.

Steal (stīl), *sb.*[2] 1825. [f. STEAL *v.*] 1. The, or an, act of stealing; a theft; the thing stolen. Chiefly *U.S. colloq.* b. *U.S.* and *Colonial.* A piece of dishonesty or fraud on a large scale; a corrupt or fraudulent transaction in politics 1884. 3. a. *Golf.* 'A long putt holed unexpectedly.' b. *Base-ball.* A stolen run from one base to another. 1842.

Steal (stīl), *v.* Pa. t. **stole** (stōul), †**stale.** Pa. pple. **stolen** (stōu·lən). [Com. Teut. str. vb.; OE. *stelan, stæl, stǣlon, stolen*, f. OTeut. **stel-* (: *stal-* : *stǣl-* : *stul-*). *Stole* has been the accepted form of the pa. t. since the 17th c.] I. To take dishonestly or secretly. 1. *trans.* To take away dishonestly (portable property, cattle, etc., belonging to another); *esp.* to do this secretly or unobserved by the owner or the person in charge. b. In wider sense: To take or appropriate dishonestly (anything belonging to another, whether material or immaterial) ME. c. *esp.* To plagiarize; to 'borrow' improperly (words, expressions). Also *absol.* 1544. 2. *absol.* or *intr.* To commit or practise theft OE. 3. *trans.* To take (*away*) by stratagem or by eluding observation (something that is in the possession or keeping of another) OE. b. To carry off, abduct, kidnap (a person) secretly. Now *rare.* late ME. 4. With immaterial obj.

a. To cause the loss of, take away (e.g. happiness, a person's life, etc.). late ME. b. To take without permission (esp. a kiss). late ME. c. To take (time) by contrivance *from* its ordinary employment, sleep, etc. to devote to some other purpose 1526. d. To gain possession of, or to entice away (a person's heart, affections, etc.) 1526. 5. To effect or accomplish clandestinely or unperceived 1625. b. To direct (a look), breathe (a sigh) furtively 1586. 6. To place, move, or convey stealthily. Now somewhat *rare.* ME. b. Of a hen: To make (her nest) in a concealed place 1854.

1. Yes; I stole money from Philemon, my beloved master 1891. b. No man like you for stealing other men's inventions SCOTT. c. It was stolen as Phidias stole from Homer 1841. 2. To give short weight or measure, is to s. 1871. 3. Thou who stealest fire From the fountains of the past TENNYSON. 4. a. How soon hath Time the suttle theef of youth Stoln on his wing my three and twentith yeer! MILT. c. They must frequently s. an hour to converse with him whom they love 1758. d. So did she steale his heedelesse hart away SPENSER. 5. He did not s. an interview 1857. *S. runs*, to get a run for a hit, when no run seems reasonably possible 1897. †*To s. a marriage*, to get married secretly. *To s. a march*, Mil. to succeed in moving troops without the knowledge of the enemy; hence *gen.* to get a secret advantage over a rival or opponent. b. And, now and then, a Sigh he stole DRYDEN. 6. Slily s. thy bonnet on,..And wander out with me CLARE.

II. To go secretly or quietly. †1. *refl.* To withdraw oneself secretly or quietly. Chiefly with *away*. -1725. 2. *intr.* To depart or withdraw secretly or surreptitiously from a place ME. b. With advb. accus., *to s. one's way.* Now *rare.* late ME. c. Hunting. *To s. away.* Of a hunted animal: To leave its lair unperceived and gain a start of the pursuers. late ME. 3. To go or come secretly or stealthily; to walk or creep softly so as to avoid observation ME. b. To come stealthily *on* or *upon* a person for the purpose of attack or injury ME. 4. Of things. a. Of time (with *on, away*): To come or go unobserved. late ME. b. Of a condition, esp. sleep, infirmities, etc.: To come insensibly *over* or *on* a person. late ME. c. Of a stream, tears, a body of vapour, a ship, etc.: To glide, or move gently or almost imperceptibly 1626. d. Of sound, fragrance, light: To become gradually perceptible. Const. *on, upon* (the sense). 1634. †e. To develop by insensible degrees *from*; to change insensibly *into, to* something else -1826.

2. Other Captains secretly stole home FULLER. c. There was a rustle amongst the long grass, and a fine dog fox..stole away 1872. 3. Her feet beneath her petticoat, Like little mice stole in and out SUCKLING. *fig.* Calm, independent, let me s. thro' life 1763. b. The cat that steals on her prey SCOTT. 4. a. The houre steales on, I pray you sir dispatch SHAKS. b. A kind of pleasant stupor was stealing over me C. BRONTË. c. The white ships swim, And s. to havens far R. BRIDGES. e. A bright sun-shiny afternoon was stealing into twilight DISRAELI. Hence **Stea·ling** *vbl. sb.* the action of the vb.; concr. in *pl.* gains made by stealing. **Stea·lingly** *adv.* stealthily, furtively (now *rare*).

Stealer[1] (stī·ləɹ). 1500. [f. STEAL *v.* + -ER [1].] One who steals; now only, one who steals something specified.

Stealer[2] (stī·ləɹ). Also **steeler.** 1805. [The same word as prec.] *Shipbuilding.* The foremost or aftmost plank in a strake, which is dropped short of the stem or stern-post.

Stealth (ste·lþ). [Early ME. *stalðe, stelthe*; :—OE. **stǣlþ*, f. OTeut. **stǣl-*, ablaut-var. of **stel-*; see STEAL *v.* and -TH.] †1. The action or practice of stealing; theft -1781. †b. An instance of stealing; a theft -1797. †c. Plagiarism -1653. †d. Cunning thievishness. SHAKS. †2. Something stolen; something to steal; plunder -1655. †3. The action of stealing into or out of a place; the action of stealing or gliding along unperceived -1788. †4. Furtive or underhand action; an act accomplished by eluding observation or discovery -1797. 5. *By s.* †a. With ref. to taking: By an act of theft; secretly and without right or permission b. In mod. use: Secretly, clandestinely. late ME.

1. Safeguarded from sand and s., by a defensive wall 1638. 2. Next morning he was apprehended with his stealths about him 1638. 3. I told him of your s. vnto this wood SHAKS. 4. *Meas. for M.* I. ii. 158. Hence **Stea·lthful** *a.* (*poet.*) stealthy; -**ly** *adv.*

Stealthy (ste·lþi), *a.* 1605. [f. prec. + -Y [1].] Of movement or action: Taking place by stealth; proceeding by imperceptible degrees; furtive. Of persons or things: Moving or acting by stealth or secretly; stealing on by imperceptible degrees.

Wither'd Murder..With his s. pace..towards his designe Moues like a Ghost SHAKS. Hence **Stea·lthily** *adv.* **Stea·lthiness.**

Steam (stīm), *sb.* [OE. *stēam* :—OTeut. **staumoz*, of obsc. origin.] 1. A vapour or fume given out by a substance when heated or burned. b. *spec.* An odorous exhalation or fume OE. †2. A vapour or exhalation produced as an 'excrement' of the body, e.g. hot breath, perspiration, etc. -1731. b. Close and hot air arising from persons crowded together. *arch.* 1609. 3. An exhalation or watery vapour rising from the earth or sea 1612. †4. Matter in the state of gas or vapour; any impalpable emanation or effluvium -1704. 5. The vapour into which water is converted when heated. In pop. language, applied to the visible vapour which floats in the air in the form of a white cloud or mist. (Also occas. applied to the vapour arising from other liquids when heated.) In mod. scientific and techn. language, applied only to water in the form of an invisible gas. 1440. 6. The vapour of boiling water used, by confinement in specially contrived engines, for the generation of mechanical power. Hence, the mechanical power thus generated. 1699. b. *fig.* Energy, 'go', driving power, and the like 1826. 7. Short for *s.-coal* 1897.

1. b. The savoury steams of roast and stew..pervaded the mansion 1827. 2. b. The dust and din and s. of town TENNYSON. 3. The Steams and Damps of Mines are detrimental to Health 1695. 5. *Dry s.*, in Steam-engine working, steam containing no suspended vesicles of water; opp. to *wet s.* 6. Phrases. *By s.*, (to travel) by steamer. *Under s.*, worked by steam (as opp. to *under sail*). (*At*) *full, half*, etc. *s.*; *with full* or *all one's s. on*; *to have* (all, much, etc.) *s. on*; *to get up, put on s.*; *to blow off, shut off, turn off s.* *Under s., with s. up, in s.*, with the engine working or ready to start working. b. Phr. *to get up s.*; *to put on, let off, work off s.*

attrib. and *Comb.*: with reference to operations performed by s., contrivances for managing s. in a steam-engine, or locomotion by s.-power, as *s. chamber, cock, gauge, laundry, packet, tram*; **s.-boiler**, a vessel in which water is heated to generate s., esp. for working a steam-engine; **-car**, a car driven or drawn by s., e.g. a motor-car worked by s. instead of petrol; *U.S.* a railway-carriage; †**-carriage**, a carriage driven or drawn by s.: **-coal**, coal suitable for heating water in s.-boilers; **-colour**, a colour developed and fixed in the cloth by steaming; **-jacket**, a jacket or casing filled with steam in order to preserve the heat of the vessel round which it is placed; **-kettle**, a kettle used in sick-rooms to create a moist warm atmosphere; **-navvy**, a machine for digging or excavating by s.; **-organ**, = CALLIOPE; **-road**, a road prepared for s.-traction; *U.S.* a railroad; **-room**, **-space**, the space above the water-level in a s.-boiler; **-tight** *a.*, tight enough to resist the ingress or egress of s.; also quasi-*adv.*; **-tug**, a s.-boat specially constructed for towing vessels; **-vessel**, †(*a*) a vessel for holding s.; (*b*) a steamboat or steamship; †**-wheel**, the rotary steam-engine; **-whistle**, a powerful whistle worked by a jet of s. (usu. from a s.-boiler), used as a signal.

Steam (stīm), *v.* [OE. *stēman, stȳman* :—pre-hist. **staumjan*, f. **staum-* STEAM *sb.*] I. *intr.* †1. To emit a scent or odour. Of a scent: To be emitted or exhaled. -1847. 2. Of vapour, etc.: To be emitted or exhaled; to rise or issue in the form of steam 1582. 3. To emit, give off, exhale steam or vapour 1614. 4. Of a surface: To become covered with condensed vapour 1892. 5. To generate steam for mechanical purposes: said of an engine or boiler 1860. 6. To move or travel by the agency of steam 1831.

2. The reek of the labouring horses steamed into it DICKENS. *fig.* A waking Dream, Such as from ill-digested Thoughts doth s. 1692. 3. Several damp gentlemen, whose clothes..began to s. DICKENS. 5. Some engines s. best with a low fire 1877. Phr. *To s. up*, to turn on steam or set it working; hence *fig.* 6. Every mile we steamed, the lake assumed a new character 1844. The train was steaming into the station 1863.

II. *trans.* 1. To exhale (steam or other vapour); to send out in the form of vapour 1666. 2. To expose to the action of steam; to treat with steam for the purpose of softening, cooking, heating, disinfecting, etc. 1798. b. *Calico-printing.* To fix (colours) by the steam-process 1862.

2. Potatoes that are either broiled or steamed 1798. She might easily s. open the envelope 1911.

Stea·mboat. 1787. A boat propelled by steam; esp. a coasting or river steamer of considerable size, carrying either passengers or goods.

Stea·m-e·ngine. 1751. An engine in which the mechanical force of steam is made available as a motive power for driving machinery, etc. b. A locomotive engine 1815. c. Often in joc. or hyperbolic comparisons 1833.

c. Daniel Webster struck me much like a s. in trousers 1840.

Steamer (stī·məɹ), *sb.* 1814. [f. STEAM *v.* and *sb.* + -ER [1].] 1. One who is employed in some process of steaming 1832. 2. An apparatus for steaming; a vessel in which articles are subjected to the action of steam, as in washing, cookery, etc. 1814. 3. A vessel propelled by steam; a steamboat, steamship 1825. 4. a. A steam-propelled road-locomotive, traction-engine, or the like (*rare*). b. A motor-car driven by steam. 1837. 5. a. A fire-engine the pumps of which are worked by steam 1876. b. A steam thrashing-machine 1898. 6. (*transf.* from sense 3.) The duck *Tachyeres* (*Micropterus*) *cinereus* (*brachypterus*) of the Falkland Islands; the loggerhead or race-horse. Also *s.-duck.* 1827.

attrib.: **s.-chair**, a lounge-chair such as is used on the deck of a s. (*U.S.*). Hence **Stea·mer** *v. intr.* to travel by steamboat.

Stea·m-ro·ller. 1866. A heavy locomotive engine with wide wheels used for crushing road-metal and levelling roads. b. *fig.* (*colloq.*) A crushing power or force 1902. Also as vb.

b. At last Kitchener..set his s. in motion and rolled the enemy flat 1902.

Stea·mship. 1819. A ship propelled by steam.

Steamy (stī·mi), *a.* 1644. [f. STEAM *sb.* + -Y [1].] 1. Consisting of, abounding in, or emitting steam; resembling steam. 2. Covered with condensed vapour. *Path.* Of the cornea: Covered or apparently covered with condensed vapour. 1869.

1. The climate is s. and enervating 1899. Hence **Stea·mi·ly** *adv.*, **-ness.**

Stean (stīn). [OE. *stǣne* = OHG. *steinna* stone jug :—OTeut. **stainjō*(*n-*, f. **staino-* (OE. *stān*) STONE *sb.*] A vessel for liquids (or, in later use, for bread, meat, fish, etc.), usu. made of clay, with two handles or ears; a jar, pot, pitcher, urn. Now *dial.* and *arch.*

Steapsin (sti,æ·psin). 1896. [f. Gr. στέαρ fat, after PEPSIN.] *Phys. Chem.* A ferment of the pancreatic juice which saponifies fat.

Stearate (stī·ăreᵗt). 1841. [f. as next + -ATE.] *Chem.* A salt of stearic acid.

Stearic (sti,æ·rik), *a.* 1831. [ad. F. *stéarique*, f. Gr. στέαρ fat, tallow; see -IC.] *Chem.* Derived from or containing stearin. *S. acid*, an organic acid, $C_{18}H_{36}O_2$, prepared from stearin.

Stearin (stī·ărin). Also **-ine.** 1817. [ad. F. *stéarine*, f. Gr. στέαρ stiff fat, tallow, suet; see -IN.] 1. *Chem.* A general name for the three glycerids (monostearin, distearin, tristearin) formed by the combination of stearic acid and glycerine; chiefly applied to tristearin, which is the chief constituent of tallow or suet. 2. The solid portion of any fixed oil or fat, in contradistinction to OLEIN 2. 1910. 3. (Chiefly spelt *stearine.*) The commercial name of a preparation consisting of purified fatty acids, used for making candles, and formerly also as a material for statuettes 1839. Hence **Ste·ariform** *a.* resembling s.

Stearo- (stī·ăro), used as a comb. form of STEARIC or STEARIN, with the sense 'containing or derived from stearin', e.g. *stearoglucose.*

Stearone (stī·ărōᵘn). 1836. [f. STEARIN + -ONE.] *Chem.* A ketone obtained from stearic acid.

Stearoptene (stī,ărǫ·ptīn). 1836. [ad. mod. L. *stearoptenum*, f. Gr. στέαρ solid fat + πτηνός winged (taken as = 'volatile').] The solid crystalline component of a volatile oil, in contradistinction to the liquid part or *elæoptene*; a camphor.

Stearyl (stī·ăril). 1868. [f. STEARIN + -YL.] The radical of stearic acid.

Steatite (stī·ătəit). 1758. [ad. L. *steatitis*

or -*ites*, a. Gr. *στεατῖτις, -ίτης (λίθος) a stone resembling tallow, f. στεατ-, στέαρ tallow, suet; see -ITE.] *Min.* A massive variety of talc, commonly of a grey or greyish-green colour, with an unctuous or soapy feel; soapstone. Hence **Steatitic** (stīăti·tik) *a.* of or composed of s., of the nature of s.

Steato- (stīăto, -ǫ·), used as comb. form of Gr. στεατ-, στέαρ stiff fat, tallow, suet, in many scientific terms, chiefly Medical, as **Stea·togene, -o·genous** *adjs.*, tending to produce steatosis; etc.

‖ **Steatoma** (stīătōu·mă). 1599. [L., a. Gr. στεάτωμα, f. στεατοῦσθαι to be converted into fat, f. στεατ-, στέαρ fat.] *Path.* An encysted fatty tumour. Hence **Steatomatous** (-ǫ·mătəs) *a.* of the nature of or resembling a s.

‖ **Steatopyga** (stīătǫpəi·gă). 1822. [mod. L., f. Gr. στεατ-, στέαρ fat + πυγή rump.] *Phys.* A protuberance of the buttocks, due to an abnormal accumulation of fat in and behind the hips and thighs, found (esp. in women) as a racial characteristic of certain peoples, esp. the Hottentot Bushmen of S. Africa. So ‖**Steatopygia** (-pi·dʒiă), the condition of having a s. **Steatopygous** (stīătǫ·pigəs, stīătǫpəi·gəs) *a.* pertaining to or characterized by a s.

‖ **Steatosis** (stīătōu·sis). 1860. [mod.L.; f. Gr. στεατ- STEATO- and -OSIS.] *Path.* Fatty degeneration.

Steed (stīd). [OE. *stēda* :—OTeut. **stōdjon-*, f. **stōdō* (OE. *stōd*) STUD *sb.*[2]] †**a.** In OE., a stud-horse, stallion. †**b.** In ME. and early mod. Eng., a high-mettled horse used on state occasions, in war, or in the lists; a great horse, as dist. from a palfrey. **c.** From the 16th c. used only *poet.* or *rhet.* for: A horse, usu. one for riding.

Thenne they broughte hym a rede spere and a rede stede MALORY. Mounted vpon a hot and fierie S. SHAKS.

Steek (stīk), *v.*[1] Chiefly *Sc.* and *north.* [ME. *steke.*] To shut.

Steek (stīk), *v.*[2] Now dial. [ME. *steke.*] To pierce; to fix.

Steel (stīl), *sb.* [OE. *stȳle* :—OTeut. **stahljom*, f. **stahlo-* steel. The root is app. Teut. **stah-*: **stag-* (:—pre-Teut. **stak-*) to be firm or rigid; see STAY *sb.*[1]] **1.** A general name for certain artificially produced varieties of iron, dist. from those known as 'iron' by certain physical properties, esp. greater hardness and elasticity, which render them suitable as material for cutting instruments, etc. **b.** A particular variety or sort of steel 1839. **2.** Similative and fig. uses, in which steel is taken as the type of hardness ME. **b.** *Sport.* Power of endurance or sustained effort 1850. **3.** Steel in the form of weapons or cutting tools (occas. spurs, a trap, etc.) Hence used for: A †sword, lance, bayonet, or the like. OE. **4.** Steel as the material of defensive armour ME. **5.** As a material for plates engraved with drawings or designs to be reproduced by printing. Hence, as a trade term: A steel engraving. 1843. **6.** Iron as used medicinally; chalybeate medicine 1647. **7.** The steel part of anything 1450. **8.** As the name of instruments made of steel. **a.** A piece of steel shaped for the purpose of striking fire with a flint ME. **b.** A rod of steel, fluted or plain, fitted with a handle, used for sharpening table or butchers' knives 1541. **c.** A needle; a knitting-needle. *dial.* 1784. **9.** *Dress.* A strip of steel used to give stiffness or support, or to expand a dress 1608. **10.** *pl.* (*Finance.*) Shares in steel-manufacturing companies 1912.

1. b. Self-hardening and other special steels 1891. 2. Like a man of Steele SHAKS. Phr. *True as s.* (said of persons, rarely of things, statements, etc.). †*S. to the* (*very*) *back*, thoroughly robust; thoroughly trustworthy. 3. The stern joy which warriors feel In foemen worthy of their s. SCOTT. *Cold s.*, cutting or thrusting weapons, as dist. from bullets. 4. In compleat steele SHAKS. *fig.* She that has that [chastity], is clad in compleat s. MILT. 6. *Flowers of s.*, iron chloride prepared by heating s. filings, etc. with salammoniac. *Tincture of s.*, tincture of iron chloride.

attrib. and *Comb.*: = made of s., as *s. spring*; in similative, objective, or instrumental combs., as *steel-blue, -bound, -clad, -lined, -worker*; **s.-concrete**, concrete reinforced with steel; **-engraving**, the art of engraving upon a s. plate; a print or impression from such a plate; similarly **-engraver**; **s. grain**, a granular texture like that of s.; **-hardened** *a.*, case-hardened; **-head**, the rainbow-trout of N. America, *Salmo iridens*; **-hearted** *a.*, courageous; hard-hearted, obdurate; **S. Helmet** [tr. G. *stahlhelm*], the designation of an organization of German ex-service men drawn mainly from the Nationalist Party and having a strong conservative bias; also, a member of this; **s. trap**, a trap with jaws and spring of s.

Steel (stīl), *v.* OE. [f. prec.] **1.** *trans.* To overlay, point, or edge with steel. †**b.** To back (a mirror) with steel -1630. **c.** To cover (an engraved metal plate) with a film of iron by electrolysis to render it more durable 1880. **2.** To cause to resemble steel. **a.** *fig.* To make hard, unbending, or strong as steel, to render insensible to impression, to make obdurate, to nerve or strengthen; also to fortify *against* 1581. **b.** To make like steel in appearance (*rare*) 1807.

†**Steel-bow**[1], **stee·l bow.** 1607. [Bow *sb.*[1]] A bow made of steel; a cross-bow -1671.

Steelbow[2] (stī·lbōu). *Obs.* exc. *Hist.* late ME. [f. STEEL *sb.* (used fig. = rigidly fixed) + *bow* farmstock (ON. *bú*).] *Sc. Law.* **a.** A quantity of farming stock, which a tenant received from his landlord on entering, and which he was bound to render up undiminished at the close of his tenancy. **b.** The species of tenancy or contract by which farming stock is hired on the condition that the tenant renders up on the expiration of his tenancy the same quantity and value that he received; esp. in phr. *in s.*

Steelify (stī·lifəi), *v.* 1662. [f. STEEL *sb.* + -(I)FY.] †**1.** *trans.* To add steel to, imbue with the properties of steel. **2.** To convert into steel 1807. Hence **Stee:lifica·tion.**

Steeling (stī·liŋ), *vbl. sb.* 1819. [f. STEEL *v.* + -ING[1].] **1.** The giving a steel edge or point to iron, etc. **2.** Conversion into steel 1860. **3.** In *Engraving*, the process of covering a metal plate with steel to render it more durable 1871. **4.** The steel part of a machine 1869.

Steel pen. 1636. **1.** A pen made of steel, split at the tip like a quill. **2.** *colloq.* Applied to the 'swallow-tail' or evening-dress tail-coat 1873.

Steel plate. 1680. A plate of steel used for engraving, for the armour of warships, etc.

Steely (stī·li), *a.* 1509. [f. STEEL *sb.* + -Y[1].] **1.** Of or belonging to, made or consisting of, steel 1586. **2.** Resembling steel in appearance, colour, hardness, or some other quality 1596. **b.** Of corn, esp. barley: Very hard and brittle 1580. **3.** Of a person, his qualities, etc.: **a.** Hard and cold as steel, unimpressionable, inflexible, obdurate 1509. **b.** Strong as steel 1648.

1. Again the foe discharge the s. show'r POPE. 2. The s. heavens 1874. 3. a. That she would unarme her hart of that s. resistance against the sweet blowes of Love SIDNEY. Hence **Stee·liness**, s. quality or condition.

Steelyard[1] (stī·lyaɹd). *Hist.* 1474. [f. STEEL *sb.* + YARD *sb.*[1]; a mistranslation of MLG. *stâlhof*, f. *stâl* sample, pattern + *hof* courtyard.] The place on the north bank of the Thames above London Bridge where the Merchants of the Hanse had their establishment. Also, the merchants collectively. **b.** A similar establishment in a provincial town 1474. **c.** A tavern within the precincts of the Steelyard where 'Rhenish wine' was sold 1592.

Steelyard[2] (stī·lyaɹd). 1639. [f. STEEL *sb.* + YARD *sb.*[2]] A balance consisting of a lever with unequal arms, which moves on a fulcrum; the article to be weighed is suspended from the shorter arm, and a counterpoise is caused to slide upon the longer arm until equilibrium is produced, its place on this arm (which is notched or graduated) showing the weight; = *Roman balance.*

†**Steem**, *v.* 1590. [Aphetic var. of ESTEEM *v.*] *trans.* To estimate, value -1642.

Steen (stīn), *v.* [OE. *stǣnan*, f. OTeut. **stainoz* STONE *sb.*] †**1.** *trans.* To stone (a person); to put to death by stoning -1450. **2.** To line (a well or other excavation) with stone, brick, or other material 1723. Hence **Stee·ning** *vbl. sb.* (*concr.*) the lining of a well or other excavation.

‖ **Steenbok** (stē·nbǫk). 1775. [Du., f. *steen* STONE + *bok* BUCK *sb.*[1]] A small S. African antelope, *Rhaphiceros campestris.*

Steenkirk, steinkirk (stī·nkəɹk). *Hist.* 1694. [a. F. (*cravate à la*) *Steinkerke, Steinkerque*, from the victory of Steenkerke (Belgium) gained by the French over the English and their allies on 3 Aug. 1692.] A kind of neckcloth (worn both by men and women), having long lace ends hanging down or twisted together, and passed through a loop or ring.

Steep (stīp), *sb.*[1] ME. [f. STEEP *v.*] **1.** The process of steeping or soaking; the state of being steeped, esp. in phr. (*to lay*) *in s.* **2.** The liquid in which a thing is placed to undergo soaking or maceration; a prepared liquor used as a dyeing bath or cleansing wash; in *Agric.* a wash for seeds 1759. **3.** = RENNET *sb.*[1] 1688.

Steep (stīp), *a.*, *sb.*[2], and *adv.* [OE. *stēap* :—OTeut. **staupo-*, f. Teut. root **steup-*: *staup-*: *stŭp*; see STOOP *v.*] **A.** *adj.* †**1.** Elevated, lofty -1738. **2.** †**a.** Of eyes: Projecting, prominent; staring; glaring with passion -1555. †**b** Of jewels, eyes, stars: Brilliant -1577. **3.** Of a hill, mountain, cliff: Having an almost perpendicular face or slope; precipitous. Of a gradient or slope, a staircase, etc.: High-pitched. ME. **b.** *transf.* of movement. *poet.* 1603. †**c.** Of water: Having a headlong course, flowing precipitously -1659. **d.** *Coal-mining.* Of a seam or measure: Having a high inclination 1883. **4.** *fig.* **a.** Of an aim, an undertaking, etc.: Arduous, ambitious 1598. †**b.** Of a difficulty: Hard to surmount. MILT. †**c.** = HEADLONG *a.* 4. -1667. **d.** Of inequalities, contrasts: Violent, extreme 1856. **5.** *slang.* Excessive, extravagant, 'stiff', 'tall'. Of a price or amount: Exorbitant. Of a story, etc.: Exaggerated, incredible. 1856.

1. To a roome they came, Steepe, and of state CHAPMAN. 3. The whole herd of swine ranne violently downe a steepe place into the Sea *Matt.* viii. 32. b. [He] Throws his s. flight in many an Aerie wheele MILT. c. And the gilded Car of Day, His glowing Axle doth allay In the steep Atlantick stream MILT. 5. This is rather a s. statement, even for a party that exists on credit 1895.

B. *sb.* The declivity or slope of a mountain, hill, cliff; a steep or precipitous place 1555. **b.** *poet.* of the sky 1697.

Why art thou heere Come from the farthest steepe of India? SHAKS. b. Behold the new morning glittering down the eastern steeps CARLYLE.

†**C.** *adv.* With a steep slope, abruptly 1548. Hence **Stee·pish** *a.* somewhat s., rather precipitous. **Stee·p·ly** *adv.*, **-ness.**

Steep (stīp), *v.* [Late ME. *stepe, stipa*, perh. repr. OE. **stīepan*, **stēpan* :—OTeut. **staupjan*, perh. f. **staupom* (OE. *stēap*) vessel for liquor.] **1.** *trans.* To soak in water or other liquid; chiefly, to do so for the purpose of softening, altering in properties, cleansing, or the like. **b.** To plunge or bathe (one's face, eyes, limbs, etc.) in water. Somewhat *rare.* 1579. **c.** *transf.* Of mist, vapour, smoke, light: To 'bathe', envelop like a flood 1798. **2.** To soak, saturate, thoroughly moisten 1590. **b.** To soak or imbrue (a weapon, etc.) *in* blood, poison, etc. 1594. **c.** *hyperbolically.* To 'soak' in alcoholic liquor; chiefly *pass.* Also, to deaden, stupefy (one's memory, senses), to drown (grief, etc.) *in* liquor. 1592. **3. a.** To 'bathe' (the heart, head, limbs, etc.) in slumber or rest 1591. **b.** To soak and stupefy or deaden (grief, the senses) *in* (sleep, etc.) 1597. **c.** To involve deeply in a state or condition; to imbue (with some quality); to make profoundly acquainted (with a subject of study); to absorb *in* (a pursuit). Chiefly *pass.* 1603. **4.** *intr.* To undergo the process of soaking in liquor. late ME.

1. S. your ham all night in water 1769. c. A rivermist is steeping The trees BRIDGES. 2. a. A Napkin, steeped in the harmlesse blood Of sweet young Rutland SHAKS. b. With tongue in Venome steep'd SHAKS. c. When thirsty griefe in Wine we steepe LOVELACE. 3. a. Sleep; Which..In quiet rest his molten heart did s. SPENSER. b. O Sleepe,..thou no more wilt..steepe my Sences in Forgetfulnesse SHAKS. c. The whole of modern thought is steeped in science HUXLEY. 4. *fig.* In a loch at Moy the stars were steeping 1914. Hence **Stee·per**, one who steeps; *spec.* one who carries out the operation of

steeping flax, wool, etc.; a vessel used in steeping or infusing.

Stee·p-down, *a. Obs.* exc. *poet.* 1530. [f. STEEP *a.* + DOWN *adv.*] Precipitous.
Wash me in steepe-downe gulfes of Liquid fire SHAKS.

Steepen (stī·p'n), *v.* 1847. [f. STEEP *a.* + -EN[5].] **1.** *intr.* To become steep or steeper. **2.** *trans. fig.* To increase, 'pile on', 'heap up' 1909.

†Stee·piness. 1612. [f. STEEPY *a.* + -NESS.] Steepness -1771.

Steeple (stī·p'l). [OE. *stēpel, stȳpel* :— prehist. **staupil-*, f. **staup-* STEEP *a.*] **†1.** A tall tower; a building of great altitude in proportion to its length and breadth -1660. **2.** A lofty tower forming part of a church, temple, or other public edifice (often serving to contain the bells); such a tower together with the spire or other superstructure by which it is surmounted ME. **3.** A spire on the top of the tower or roof of a church or similar edifice. Also *spire s., broach s.* 1473.
attrib. and *Comb.*: **s.-clocked** *a.*, having steeple-shaped clocks (CLOCK *sb.*[2]); **-crown,** a crown of a hat rising to a point in the middle; also a hat with a s.-crown; hence *s.-crowned* adj.; **s. jack,** a man who climbs steeples or tall chimneys to repair them; **-roofed** *a.*, having very high roofs; **-top,** (*a*) the top of a s.; (*b*) the bowhead, or great polar whale (*Balæna mysticetus*), so called from the spout-holes terminating in a sort of cone. **b.** In names of plants: **s. bells, s. bell-flower,** *Campanula pyramidalis*; **-bush** = HARDHACK. Hence **Stee·pled** *ppl. a.* having the form of a s.; having a s. or steeples. **Stee·ple-wise** *adv.* after the manner of a s.; in a conical or pyramidal form.

Stee·plechase, *sb.* 1793. [f. prec. + CHASE.] **1.** A horse-race across country or on a made course with artificial fences, water-jumps, and other obstacles. Formerly, a race having a church steeple in view as goal, in which all intervening obstacles had to be cleared. **b.** A parlour game simulating this 1895. **2.** *transf.* A foot-race across country or over a course furnished with hurdles, ditches, etc. 1864. Hence **Stee·plechase** *v. intr.* to ride or run in a s.; to practise riding in steeplechases. **Stee·plechaser,** one who rides or runs in a s.; a horse trained for steeplechasing.

Stee·ple-house. 1644. A building with a steeple: used by the early Quakers instead of 'church', on the ground that that word ought not to be applied to a building.

Stee·p-to, *a.* 1748. [f. STEEP *a.* + TO *adv.*] *Naut.* Of a shore: Descending very steeply into the water.

Stee·p-up, *a. arch.* 1565. [f. STEEP *a.* + UP *adv.* Cf. STEEP-DOWN.] Precipitous; perpendicular.
And hauing climb'd the steepe-vp heauenly hill SHAKS.

Steepy (stī·pi), *a. Obs.* exc. *arch.* 1561. [f. STEEP *a.* + -Y[1].] Steep; full of steep places; precipitous.
Now take thy s. flight from Heav'n DRYDEN. *fig.* Ages steepie night SHAKS.

Steer (stiəɹ), *sb.*[1] [OE. *stēor* :—OTeut. **steuroz* :—pre-Teut. *(*s*)*teuros*, f. Indo-Eur. root **st*(*h*)*eu-* to be fixed or rigid.] A young ox, esp. one which has been castrated.
In the U.S. and the colonies applied to male beef-cattle of any age.

Steer, *sb.*[2] *Obs.* exc. in *Comb.* [OE. *stēor*, see next.] **1.** The action of directing or governing; guidance, control, rule, government -1596. **2.** A rudder, helm -1625.
Comb.: **s.-oar,** an oar used at the stern for steering a boat.

Steer (stiəɹ), *v.* [Com. Teut.; OE. *stieran* :—OTeut. **steurjan*, f. **steurō* rudder, STEER *sb.*[2]] **1.** *trans.* To guide the course of (a vessel) by means of a rudder, or of an oar or paddle used like a rudder. **b.** *transf.* of animals. late ME. **c.** To guide (a vessel) to a specified point or in a specified direction 1470. **2.** *absol.* and *intr.* To guide a vessel by means of a rudder or the like OE. **b.** *intr.* in passive sense. Of a ship: To admit of being steered; to answer the helm (well or ill) 1627. **c.** Of a ship: To be guided by the helm in a certain direction 1667. **3.** *trans.* In extended sense, to guide something that is in motion OE. **b.** To guide, lead, 'pilot' (a person) through a crowd, along an intricate path, etc. Also *absol.* Also (*U.S. slang*) to manœuvre or decoy (a person) to a place, or into doing something. 1859. **4.** *intr.* To shape one's course (on land, in the air). Also *trans.* with cogn. obj. 1500. **b.** Of an inanimate thing: To travel in a set course 1692. **†5.** To conduct (one's life) -1699. **†b.** Of reasons, indications, influences: To guide -1683. **c.** *intr.* To direct one's course of action (*by* guiding indications). Often, to find a safe course *between* two evils or two extremes. 1658. **†6.** To govern, rule -1678. **†b.** To manage, administer (government); to conduct (business, negotiations, etc.) -1647.
1. Whanne a fool stereth a barge, Hym self and al the folke is shent 1400. *To s. a* (*one's*) *course*; You must s. a middle course HAZLITT. **c.** When Cook.. Steer'd Britain's oak into a world unknown COWPER. **2.** Two skilful helmsmen on the poop to s. 1762. They steered by the guidance of the stars GIBBON. *fig.* Yet I..still bear vp and s. Right onward MILT. Phr. *To s. clear of*, to avoid completely. **c.** As when a Ship ..where the Wind Veres oft, as oft so steers, and shifts her Saile MILT. **3.** Tapp was the jockey..and 'steered him to victory' 1890. He feeds the pigs and steers the plough 1914. **4.** He was bravely steering his way across the continent W. IRVING. **b.** Thou busy sunny river..Through woodlands steering CLOUGH. **5. c.** Rational animals should use their reason, and s. by it 1722. **6. b.** The great persons who steered the public affairs CLARENDON. Hence **Stee·rable** *a.* that may be steered or guided, dirigible.

Steerage (stiə·rėdʒ). 1450. [f. prec. + -AGE.] **1.** The action, practice, or method of steering a boat or ship; the guidance of a balloon or airship, *rarely* of a carriage. **b.** Of a ship: The action, method, or ability of answering to the helm 1653. **2. a.** The direction or government of affairs, the State, one's life 1592. **b.** A course held or steered, esp. a course of conduct 1625. **3.** The steering apparatus of a boat, etc. 1697. **4.** That division of the after part of a ship which is immediately in front of the chief cabin; the second cabin. Also called *†s. room*. (orig. the place from which the ship was steered.) 1612. **5.** That part of a passenger ship allotted to the passengers who travel at the cheapest rate. Also quasi-advb. in *to go, travel s.* 1804.
1. These Pilots by their ill s. did split their Vessels 1654. **b.** She..made bad S. 1745. **2. a.** But he that hath the stirrage of my course, Direct my sute SHAKS. **5.** He travelled s. with a ship of emigrants 1906.
attrib. and *Comb.*: **s. passenger,** one who occupies a berth in the s. of a passenger-vessel; **-way,** a way or motion sufficient for the helm to have effect.

Steerer (stiə·rəɹ). late ME. [f. STEER *v.* + -ER[1].] **†1.** A rudder -1633. **2.** A steersman 1585. **3.** *U.S. slang.* A swindler whose business it is to lead his victims to the rendezvous 1883. **4.** A thing which directs its course: **a.** of a ship with adj. referring to its power of answering to the helm or rudder 1887. **b.** Of a cycle, with prefix indicating the position of its steering-wheel 1883.
4. a. The ship is a bad s. 1887. **b.** A front-steerer 1883.

Steering (stiə·riŋ), *vbl. sb.* ME. [f. STEER *v.* + -ING[1].] The action of STEER *v.*
Comb.: **s.-lock,** the turning movement of the wheels of a motor-vehicle; **-wheel,** (*a*) *Naut.* a vertical wheel by which motion is communicated to the rudder through the medium of a tiller-rope or other device; (*b*) a hand-wheel for guiding a motor-vehicle; (*c*) the wheel of a cycle by which steerage is effected.

Stee·ring, *ppl. a.* 1903. [-ING[2].] *S. committee* (U.S.), a committee of management.

†Stee·rless, *a.* [OE. *stēorlēas*; see STEER *sb.*[2] and -LESS.] **1.** Not amenable to guidance or control -ME. **2.** Without a rudder -1639.

Stee·rling. 1648. [-LING[1].] A young steer.

Steersman (stiə·ɹzmăn). [OE. *stēoresman*, f. *stēores* gen. of *stēor* STEER *sb.*[2] + MAN *sb.*] One who steers a boat or ship. **b.** *transf.* One who drives and guides a machine 1828. So **Stee·rman** (now *rare*). **†Stee·rsmate** (*rare*).

Steeve (stīv), *sb.*[1] 1794. [f. STEEVE *v.*[1]] *Naut.* The upward inclination of a bowsprit, cathead, etc.; the amount of this.

Steeve (stīv), *sb.*[2] *U.S.* 1840. [perh. f. STEEVE *v.*[2]] *Naut.* A long derrick or spar, with a block at one end, used in stowing cargo.

Steeve (stīv), *v.*[1] 1644. [Origin obsc.] *Naut. intr.* Of a bowsprit, etc.: To incline upwards at an angle instead of lying horizontally. Also *trans.* to set (a bowsprit) at a certain upward inclination.

Steeve (stīv), *v.*[2] 1482. [a. F. *estiver* :— L. *stipare.*] Chiefly *Naut. trans.* To compress and stow (wool, cotton, or other cargo) in a ship's hold, etc.; also, to pack tightly.

Steganography (steganǫ·grăfi). *Obs.* exc. *Hist.* 1569. [ad. mod.L. *steganographia*, a. Gr. *στεγανογραφία, f. στεγανός covered; see -GRAPHY.] The art of secret writing; cryptography. Also, cryptographic script, cipher. Hence **Stegano·grapher, Stegano·graphist,** a cryptographer. **Steganogra·phical** *a.*

Steganopod (ste·gănopǫd), *sb.* and *a.* 1842. [ad. mod.L. *Steganopodes*, a. Gr. στεγανοποδ-, -όπους web-footed, f. στεγανός covered + ποδ-, πούς foot.] *Ornith.* **A.** *sb.* A bird belonging to the group *Steganopodes*, which comprises the pelicans, cormorants, frigate-birds, gannets, tropic-birds, and snake birds. **B.** *adj.* Of a bird: Belonging to the group *Steganopodes*. Hence **Stegano·podan, Stegano·podous** *adjs.* belonging to the group *Steganopodes*.

Stego- (stego), used as comb. form of Gr. root στεγ- of στέγειν to cover, στέγη covering, στέγος roof, in certain modern scientific terms.
Stegocephalian (-sĭfē·liăn) [Gr. κεφαλή head], *a.* = STEGOCEPHALOUS; *sb.*, a member of the order *Stegocephala* of fossil Batrachians, characterized by having the skull protected by bony plates. **Stegoce·phalous** *a.*, pertaining to or having the characteristics of the order *Stegocephala*. **Ste·gosaur,** ‖**Stegosau·rus** [Gr. σαῦρος lizard], a genus of dinosaurs, characterized by the completeness of their armour; hence ‖**Stegosau·ria** *pl.*, the order of which this genus is typical; **Stegosau·rian** *a.* and *sb.*

‖**Stein** (ʃtəin). Chiefly *U.S.* 1901. [G., lit. 'stone'.] An earthenware mug, esp. for beer.

Steinbock (stəi·nbǫk). Also **-boc.** 1683. [a. G., 'wild goat', f. *stein* STONE *sb.* + *boc* BUCK *sb.*[1]] A wild goat of the genus *Ibex*; the Alpine Ibex (*Capra ibex*).

Steinkirk: see STEENKIRK.

‖**Stela** (stī·lă). *Pl.* **stelæ** (stī·li), *rarely* **stelas.** 1776. [L., ad. Gr. στήλη.] = next **1.**

Stele (stīl, ‖ stī·li). 1820. [As a disyllable, repr. Gr. στήλη standing block or slab, f. root **stă-* to stand. As a monosyllable, anglicized form of the Gr. word.] *Antiq.* **1.** An upright slab bearing sculptured designs or inscriptions. Occas. loosely, any prepared surface on the face of a building, a rock, etc., covered with an inscription. **2.** *Bot.* The axial cylinder in the stems and roots of vascular plants, developed from the plerome 1895.

Stell (stel), *v.* [OE. *stęllan* :—WGer. **stalljan*, f. OTeut. **stallo-* place, STALL *sb.*] **†1.** *trans.* To set (an example); to establish (a law) -ME. **2.** *Sc.* To fix, post, place 1470. **3.** To portray, delineate. *Obs.* exc. *arch.* 1598.
3. Mine eye hath play'd the painter and hath steeld Thy beauties forme in table of my heart SHAKS.

‖**Stella** (ste·lă). *Pl.* **stellæ** (-ī). 1828. [L., 'star'.] **a.** *Zool.* A star-shaped projection on the surface of a coralline; also, a star-shaped sponge-spicule. **b.** *Crystall.* A stellate crystal 1844.

Stellar (ste·lăɹ), *a.* 1656. [ad. late L. *stellaris*, f. L. *stella* star.] **1.** Pertaining to the stars or a star; of the nature of a star. **2.** Star-shaped, stellate: chiefly of crystals 1670.
1. These soft fires..shed down Thir s. vertue on all kinds that grow On Earth MILT. **2.** A clump of planting of a s. form 1844. So **†Ste·llary** *a.*

Stellate (ste·lět), *a.* and *sb.* 1500. [ad. L. *stellatus*, f. *stella* star; see -ATE[2].] **1.** Of the sky: Studded with stars. *poet.* **2.** Star-shaped; arranged or grouped in the form of a conventional star or stars; (chiefly in scientific use) radiating from a centre like the rays of a star 1661. **B.** *sb.* A stellate sponge-spicule 1880.
2. The uniform s. form of snow 1755. S. cells 1899. So **Ste·llated** *a.* **Ste·llately** *adv.*

†Ste·lled, *a. rare.* 1605. [f. L. *stella* + -ED[1].] Stellar, starred. -1656.
The Sea..Would have buoy'd vp, And quench'd the S. fires SHAKS.

Stellenbosch (ste·lənbǫʃ), *v. Mil. slang.* 1900. [f. *Stellenbosch*, a military base in Cape Colony.] *pass.* 'To be relegated, as the result of incompetence, to a position in which little harm can be done' (Pettman).

Stellerid (ste·lĕrid). 1835. [ad. F. *stelléride*, app. irreg. f. L. *stella* star; see -ID [3].] *Zool.* A star-fish. Also **Stelle·ridan** [see -IDAN], †**Stelleri·dean, -ian.**

Stelliferous (steli·fĕrəs), *a.* 1583. [f. L. *stellifer*; see -FEROUS.] Bearing stars. **b.** *Biol.* Having star-shaped markings.

Stelliform (ste·lifǫɹm), *a.* 1796. [ad. mod.L. *stelliformis*, f. L. *stella* star; see -FORM.] Shaped like a star; existing in the form of star-shaped crystals.

Stellify (ste·lifəi), *v.* late ME. [a. OF. *stellifier*, ad. med.L. *stellificare*, f. *stella* star; see -FY.] **1.** *trans.* To transform (a person or thing) into a star or constellation; to place among the stars. †**b.** *fig.* To extol –1721. †**2.** To set with stars, or with something compared to stars –1658. So **Stellifica·tion,** the action of stellifying.

‖ **Stellio** (ste·lio). late ME. [L. form of next.] = next. Now only *Zool.* as generic name.

Stellion (ste·liŏn). late ME. [ad. L. *stellionem*, *stellio*; according to Pliny f. *stella* star.] In early use, a kind of lizard with star-like spots, mentioned by ancient writers. In mod. use, a lizard of the genus *Stellio* or family *Stellionidæ*, native in Southern Europe and Asia.

Stellionate (ste·liŏnēt). 1622. [ad. L. *stellionatus*, f. *stellionem* a fraudulent person, perh. transf. use of *stellio* STELLION.] *Sc. Civil Law.* (See quot.)

The crime of s...includes every fraud which is not distinguished by a special name; but is chiefly applied to conveyances of the same numerical right, granted by the proprietor to different disponees 1754.

Stellular (ste·liŭlăɹ), *a.* 1796. [f. late L. *stellula*, dim. of *stella* star + -AR.] Having the form of a small star or small stars.

Stem (stem), *sb.*[1] [OE. *stęmn*, *stęfn* :—OTeut. **stamniz*; prob. f. root *sta-* to STAND + *-mn-* suffix.] **1.** The main body of the portion above ground of a tree, shrub, or other plant; a trunk, stock, stalk. (Ordinarily implying more slenderness than *stock* or *trunk*.) **b.** *Bot.* The ascending axis (whether above or below ground) of a plant, in contradistinction to the descending axis or root 1807. **2.** The stalk supporting a leaf, flower, or fruit; a peduncle, pedicel, or petiole. Also *transf.* in *Anat.* and *Path.* 1590. **3.** The stock of a family; the main line of descent from which the 'branches' of a family are offshoots; the descendants of a particular ancestor. Also *abstr.*, ancestry, pedigree. 1540. **b.** An ethnic stock, a race 1540. †**c.** *fig.* A branch or offshoot of a family –1634. **4.** Applied to various objects resembling the stem of a plant or of a flower, etc. **a.** *Calligraphy* and *Printing.* The upright stroke of a letter 1676. **b.** *Mus.* The vertical line forming part of a minim, crotchet, quaver, etc. 1806. **c.** The long cylindrical body of an instrument, etc., as dist. from the 'head', or from branches or projections; the tube of a thermometer or similar instrument; the tube of a tobacco-pipe 1815. **d.** The upright cylindrical support of a cup, a wineglass, or other vessel 1835. **e.** *Watch-making.* The pendant-shank of a watch 1866. **f.** The SHAFT of a hair, of a feather 1845. **5.** *Philol.* That part of an inflected word that remains unchanged (except for euphonic variations) in the process of inflexion; the theme of a word, to which the flexional suffixes are attached 1851.

1. The sea eryngo..has a s. about a foot high 1850. **2.** Two louely berries molded on one s. SHAKS. **3.** There shall come forth a rod out of the stemme of Iesse *Isa.* xi. 1. Where ye may all that are of noble stemm Approach MILT. **b.** The Danishe governement beganne..to bee..hatefull, as a thinge moste..pestilent to the Englishe name and stemme 1540. **c.** This is a S. Of that Victorious Stock SHAKS.

Comb.: **s.-bed** *Geol.*, a stratum containing stems of trees; **-composition** *Philol.*, composition of word-stems, as dist. from syntactical combination of words; **s. stitch** *Needlework*, a stitch usu. employed for stems and single lines in embroidery and lace-making; **-winder** *U.S.* (*a*) a keyless watch; (*b*) a geared logging locomotive; (*c*) *slang*, a person or thing that is first-rate; **-winding,** *a. U.S.* (of a watch) that is wound up by means of a s. Hence **Stem** *v.*[3] *trans.* (*Tobacco-manuf.*) to remove the stalk and midrib from tobacco-leaf. **Ste·mless** *a.* having no s. **Ste·mlet,** a small s. **Ste·mmy** *a.* having long bare stems; containing stems.

Stem (stem), *sb.*[2] [OE. *stęmn*, *stęfn*, orig. spec. use of STEM *sb.*[1] in sense 'tree-trunk'.] *Naut.* †**1.** The timber at either extremity of a vessel, to which the ends of the side-planks were fastened; the 'stem' (in the mod. sense) or the stern-post. Hence, the prow or the stern. –1497. **2.** The curved upright timber or piece of metal at the bow of a vessel, into which the planks of the bow are scarfed 1538. **3.** The prow, bows, or the whole forepart of a vessel 1555.

2. Phr. *From s. to stern*, along the whole length of a ship. *S. on*, so as to strike with the s. *S. to s.*, (of ships) with their stems facing each other. *To give* (a ship) *the s.*, to ram.

Stem (stem), *v.*[1] 1450. [a. ON. *stemma* :—OTeut. **stamjan*, f. **stam-*, root of STAMMER *v.*] **1.** *trans.* To stop, check; to dam up (a stream, or the like). **2.** To set (one's limbs, hand) firmly 1827. **3.** *Mining.* To plug or tamp (a hole for blasting) 1791. Hence **Ste·mmer** (*Mining*), a metal bar used for stemming.

Stem (stem), *v.*[2] late ME. [f. STEM *sb.*[2]] **1.** *trans.* Of a vessel, a navigator: To urge the stem against, make headway against (a tide, current, gale, etc.). Hence of a swimmer, a bird, etc.: To make headway against (water or wind), to breast (the waves, the air). 1593. **b.** *transf.* and *fig.* To go counter to, make headway against (something compared to a stream) 1675. **c.** To direct the head of (a vessel) *on* a place; to keep (a vessel) on a fixed course 1594. **d.** *intr.* Of a vessel or a navigator: To head in a certain direction, keep a certain course. late ME. †**2.** *trans.* To dash against with the stem of a vessel; to ram –1810. †**3.** To furnish (a ship) with a stem –1590.

Stem, *v.*[3] 1577. [f. STEM *sb.*[1]] †**1.** *intr.* To rise erect like a stem –1786. **b.** *fig.* (*U.S.*) To have or trace one's origin *in*; to spring *from* or *out*. **2.** *trans.* To remove the stalk from (a leaf, etc.) 1844.

‖ **Stemma** (ste·mă). *Pl.* **stemmata** (ste·mătă). 1826. [L., a. Gr. στέμμα garland, f. στέφειν to crown.] **1. a.** *Rom. Antiq.* The recorded genealogy of a family. **b.** A genealogical tree; *transf.* the tree of descent of a text. 1879. **2.** *Zool.* A simple eye, or a single facet of the compound eye, in invertebrates 1826.

Stemson (ste·msən). 1769. [f. STEM *sb.*[2], after *keelson* KELSON.] *Naut.* In a wooden vessel, the timber fitted into the angle formed by the junction of stem and kelson.

Stench (stenʃ), *sb.* [OE. *stęnc* :—OTeut. **stankwiz*, f. **stankw-*, ablaut-var. of **stinkw-* STINK *v.*] †**1.** An odour, a smell; also, the sense of smell. OE. only. **2.** A foul, disgusting, or noisome smell, an offensive odour, a stink OE. **3.** without article. Evil-smelling quality or property, offensive odour, stink ME. **4.** Something that smells offensively 1595.

2. In Köhln..I counted two and seventy stenches. All well defined, and several stinks! COLERIDGE. **3.** A narrow winding street, full of offence and s. DICKENS. **4.** Thou odoriferous s., sound rottennesse SHAKS.

attrib. and *Comb.*: **s.-pipe,** an extension of a soil-pipe to a point above the roof of a house, to allow foul gases to escape; **-trap,** a device in a drain, etc. to prevent the upward passage of noxious gas. Hence **Ste·nchy** *a.* emitting a s., foul-smelling.

†**Stench** (stenʃ), *v.* [OE. *stęncan* :—**stankwjan*, f. **stankwiz* STENCH *sb.*] **1.** *intr.* To have an ill smell, to stink –1570. **2.** *trans.* To cause to emit a stench, to make to stink, render offensive –1838.

Stencil (ste·nsĭl), *sb.* 1707. [orig. *stanesile*, app. f. ME. *stansel* vb. to ornament with various colours.] **1.** A thin sheet of metal, cardboard, etc., in which one or more holes have been cut, of such shape that when a brush charged with pigment is passed over the back of the sheet, a desired pattern, letter, or figure is produced upon the surface upon which the sheet is laid. **2.** A pattern or design produced by stencilling 1899. **3.** The colouring matter used in stencilling. Also (*Ceramics*), a composition used in transfer-printing and enamelling, to protect from the oil those portions of the pattern that are to be left uncoloured. 1853.

Comb.: **s.-brush,** the brush used in stencilling; **-plate** = sense 1.

Stencil (ste·nsĭl), *v.* late ME. [In sense 1, a. OF. *estanceler*, f. *estencele* (mod.F. *étincelle*) :—pop. L. **stincilla*, metathesis of *scintilla* spark. In sense 2, a late deriv. of prec.] †**1.** *trans.* To ornament with bright colours or pieces of precious metal. late ME. only. **2. a.** To produce (an inscription, design, etc.) by using a stencil 1861. **b.** To mark or paint (a surface) with an inscription or design by means of a stencil 1833. Hence **Ste·nciller.**

‖ **Steneosaurus** (stenīǫsǭ·rŏs). 1836. [mod. L., badly formed (after *Teleosaurus*) on Gr. στενός narrow + σαῦρος lizard.] A fossil genus of saurians characterized by a narrow beak.

Steno- (steno), comb. form of Gr. στενός narrow, as in **Stenocephalic** (-sĭfæ·lik) *a.*, (of a skull) characterized by abnormal or excessive narrowness. **Stenoderm** (ste·nodəɹm), a bat of the genus *Stenoderma* or of the family *Stenodermata*, the members of which are characterized by having a contracted wing-membrane. **Stenode·rmine** *a.*, resembling a stenoderm; *sb.* a stenoderm. **Stenophyllous** (-fi·ləs) *a.*, having narrow leaves. **Stenopæic** (-pī·ik) *a.* [Gr. ὀπή opening], of an eye-piece, having only a narrow translucent aperture.

Stenog (stenǫ·g). *U.S. colloq.* 1906. = STENOGRAPHER. Hence **Ste·nog** *v.*

Stenograph (ste·nŏgraf), *v.* 1821. [Back-formation from next.] *trans.* To write in shorthand, to represent by stenography; also *absol.*

Stenographer (stĭnǫ·grăfəɹ). 1809. [f. next + -ER [1].] A shorthand writer.

Stenography (stĭnǫ·grăfi). 1602. [f. Gr. στενός narrow + -GRAPHY.] The art of writing in shorthand. Hence **Stenogra·phic, -al** *adjs.* of, pertaining to, or expressed in s.; **-ly** *adv.* by means of shorthand.

‖ **Stenosis** (stĭnōᵘ·sis). *Pl.* **stenoses** (īz). 1866. [mod.L., a. Gr. στένωσις narrowing, f. στενοῦν to narrow, f. στενός.] *Path.* The contraction or stricture of a passage, duct, or canal. Hence **Steno·tic** *a.* pertaining to, characterized by or resulting from s.

Stenting (ste·ntiŋ), *sb.* Also **stenton.** 1812. [Origin obsc.] *Mining.* A passage between two winning headways.

Stentor (ste·ntǫɹ). 1600. [Gr. Στέντωρ (*Iliad* v. 785).] **1.** The name of a Greek warrior in the Trojan war, 'whose voice was as powerful as fifty voices of other men'; applied allusively to a man of powerful voice. ‖ **2.** mod.L.] A genus of Protozoa; an individual of this genus, a trumpet-shaped protozoan 1863. Hence **Stento·rious** *a.* = next.

Stentorian (stentōᵊ·riăn), *a.* 1605. [f. prec. + -IAN.] **1.** Of the voice: Loud, like that of Stentor; very loud and far-reaching; hence, of uttered sounds. **2.** That utters such sounds 1690.

1. 'Hold' exclaimed the general, in s. tones 1872. **2.** S. lungs 1875. *S. trumpet* = STENTOROPHONIC *trumpet.*

Stentorophonic (ste:ntŏrofǫ·nik), *v.* 1678. [ad. mod.L. *Stentorophonicus* (f. Gr. Στεντορόφωνος having the voice of a Stentor, f. Στεντορ-, STENTOR + φωνή voice).] †**1.** *S. horn, trumpet, tube*: a speaking trumpet –1831. **2.** †Loud as a speaking trumpet; in later use (echoed from Hudibras) = prec. 1. 1678.

Stentorphone (ste·ntǫɹfōᵘn). 1921. [f. STENTOR + Gr. φωνή voice.] A specially powerful loud speaker.

Step (step), *sb.* [OE. *stæpe*, *stępe* :—OTeut. **stapiz*, f. root **stap-*; see STEP *v.*] **I.** Action of stepping. **1.** An act of bodily motion consisting in raising the foot from the ground and bringing it down again in a fresh position; usu., an act of this kind as constituting by repetition the progressive motion of a human being or animal in walking, running, or climbing. **b.** *contextually.* A footstep or footfall considered in regard to its audibility 1605. **c.** Manner of stepping or treading; one's stride OE. **d.** One of the various paces taught in drill; as *slow* or *quick s.* 1798. **e.** *Dancing.* Any one of the various paces taught by the master; esp. the gliding movement formerly used in the quadrille, etc. Also, a person's individual manner of pacing in the dance. 1678. **2.** *pl.* Progress by stepping or treading; a person's movements, his goings and comings, the course which he follows OE. **3.** *fig.* An action or movement which leads towards a result; one of a series of proceedings or measures 1549. **4.** In phrases which refer to the action of walking evenly with another 1613. **5.** The space traversed by the movement of one foot beyond the other in walking or running; a pace. Hence as a measure of length or distance. OE. **b.** With limitation or negative: A very short distance OE. **6.** A degree in an ascending scale; a remove in an upward process; a grade in rank or promotion OE. **b.** *Mus. By s.*: by progression through a single degree of the scale (i. e. a tone or semitone) 1889. **7.** A footprint ME.

1. If you will walk a few steps this way SCOTT. *False s.*: see FALSE *a.* 6. *Hop, s., and jump*: see HOP *sb.*² 3. **b.** Thou sowre and firme-set Earth Heare not my steps SHAKS. **2.** Honour attend thy steps 1598. Phr. *To bend* or *direct* one's *steps* (to a place, etc.); *to retrace* one's *steps* (see RETRACE *v.*); *to guide, dog* a person's *steps.* **3.** The next s. was to assert the royal supremacy 1860. **4.** Phr. *In, out of, s.* (*with*); *s. for s.* (*with*); *to keep s.* (*with*; also *to* music, etc.). **5.** The military s. of 30 inches, of which there are 2112 to a mile 1862. **b.** There is but one s., said Napoleon, from the sublime to the ridiculous 1831. **6.** *To get the* or *one's s.* (Mil.), to be promoted to the next higher grade.

S. by s. a. Moving one foot after the other continuously; *fig.* by gradual and regular progress. **b.** Keeping pace with another. **c.** *attrib.* or quasi-*adj.* = that moves or advances s. by s. **To make** or **take a s. a.** To perform the act of moving the foot as in walking or climbing. †**b.** To make a short journey *to.* **c.** *fig. To take a s.* or *steps*: to perform a move or moves in a course of action; to take action towards attaining an end. *To take the necessary steps*: often, to take the action prescribed by law as necessary to attain some implied object.

II. Something on which to place the foot in ascending or descending. **1.** A flat-topped structure, normally made of wood or stone and some six or seven inches high, used, singly or as one of a series, to facilitate a person's movement from one level to another OE. **b.** The height or depth of this 1662. **c.** A foothold cut in a slope of earth or ice 1860. **d.** A flat projecting foot-piece, fixed or made to let down when wanted, for entering or alighting from a vehicle 1837. **e.** *Fortif.* = BANQUETTE 1. 1672. **2.** A rung or stave of a ladder; each of the flat cross-pieces of a step-ladder OE. **b.** *pl.* A step-ladder; also *a pair* or *set of steps. colloq.* 1693.

1. Adèle and I sat down on the top s. of the stairs to listen C. BRONTE. **c.** He cut steps down one side of a *strac* 1871.

III. Transferred uses of sense II. 1. **1.** *Geol.* A fault or dislocation of strata 1789. **2.** An offset or part resembling a step in outline, singly or in a series; e.g. in the bit of a key 1674. **3.** *Naut.* The block in which is fixed the heel of a mast or capstan OE. **4.** *Mech.* **a.** The lower bearing or block on which a vertical pivot, shaft, or the like rotates 1814. **b.** The lower brass of a journal-box or pillow-block in which a horizontal shaft revolves 1875.

Comb.: **s.-board,** the tread or flat part of a wooden s.; **-collar,** a collar with a V-shaped opening at the junction of the collar and lapel; **-cut** = TRAP-CUT; also as *adj.*; **-dance,** a dance intended for the display of special steps by an individual performer; **-fault** *Geol.*, one of a series of parallel faults with successive falls like steps; **-wheel,** a wheel with an edge formed in twelve steps arranged spirally, used in striking-clocks; **-wise** *adv.* like a series of steps.

Step (step), *v.* Pa. t. and pa. pple. **stepped** (stept). [Com. WGer. strong vb.: OE. *stæppan, steppan, stōp,* (*be*)*stapen,* :—OTeut. **stapjan* (**stōp-,* **stapan-*). Weak forms are found from the close of the 13th century, and from the 16th are universal.] **I.** *intr.* **1.** To lift the foot and set it down again on the ground in a new position; to lift and set down the feet alternately in walking; to pace, tread. With adv.: To use a (specified) gait or motion of the feet (often of a horse). **b.** To move with measured paces in a dance. Also quasi-*trans.*, to go through the steps of, perform (a dance) 1698. **2.** To move to a new position by extending the foot to a higher or lower level or across an intervening object or space; with adv. or prep., as *across, in, into, off, out of, on* or *upon, over, up* OE. **3.** To go or proceed on foot. Now chiefly, to go a 'step' or short distance for a particular purpose: often in polite formulas of request or direction to another person. OE. †**b.** *fig.* To advance, proceed (in an action, argument, etc.) –1644. †**4.** In pa. pple.: **a.** (*Well, far,* etc.) *stepped in age, in* or *into years*: advanced in years, elderly –1629. †**b.** *Far stepped*: far advanced *in* (an action, etc.) –1605. **5.** *colloq.* To go away, make off. late ME. **6.** Of a horse: To go at a good pace. Also joc. of persons. 1856. **7.** *Naut.* and *Mech.* Of a mast or other upright: To be fixed *in* its step. Of other parts: To be fixed or jointed *in* or *into* (a groove, etc.); to rest securely *on* or *against* (a support). 1791.

1. Phr. *As good* (etc.) *a man as ever stepped* (*in shoe-leather*). **b.** He stepped a minuet gravely and gracefully 1893. **2.** *To s. short,* to make an insufficiently long stride, so that the foot fails to reach the intended position. **3.** *To s. lively* (orig. *U.S. slang*), to hurry up. **4. b.** I am in blood Stept in so farre SHAKS. **5.** Well, I must be stepping.. It 's getting late 1902.

II. *trans.* (causal, or by omission of prep.) **1.** To move (the foot) forward or through a specified step. Phr. *To s. foot in* (a place). Now only *U.S.* 1540. **2.** To measure (a distance) by stepping over it. Also with *off, out.* 1832. **3.** *Naut.* and *Mech.* To fix (a mast or other upright) *in* or *into* its step; to fit (a piece) *into* (a groove, etc.); to fix securely *on* or *against* (a support) 1711. **4.** *Mech.* To cut steps in (a key); to arrange (the teeth of a toothed wheel or rack) stepwise 1856.

With preps. (*intr.*) **S. between —.** To come between (two persons, a person and thing, etc.) by way of severance, interruption, or interception. **S. into —. a.** See sense I. 3 and INTO *prep.* **b.** To walk into (a vehicle, etc.) by taking one or more steps up or down. **c.** To obtain possession of (an estate, a place, or office) at a single step; to succeed at once to (the place of another person or thing). †**d.** To enter suddenly and incautiously into (a course of action, etc.). **S. over —.** To walk or stride across (an intervening space, cavity, or obstacle); *fig.* to OVERSTEP, transgress; to 'skip', miss, or neglect in passing; also *Mil.* to be promoted to a position above (another who is considered to have a prior claim).

With advs. **S. aside.** *intr.* **a.** To go a little distance away from one's place or from the path one is following; to withdraw or retire for a short distance; to take one or more steps to one's right or left. †**b.** To abscond. **S. back. a.** To go back a little distance. **b.** To go one or more paces backwards without turning the body round. **S. down. a.** To go from a higher level to a lower, esp. by treading on a step or stairway. Also, to go a short distance to a place which is or is regarded as lower. **b.** *trans.* in *Electr.* To lower the voltage of (a current) by means of a transformer. Hence **s.-down,** used attrib. or as adj. designating a transformer that does this. **S. forth.** *intr.* To advance a short distance from one's place or position; to come out to the front or into the midst; to advance with some immediate purpose in view. **S. forward** = *s. forth.* **S. in. a.** To come or go indoors; to enter a house or apartment casually or for a short time. Also, to enter a boat, vehicle, etc. **b.** To come forward and join in what is going on; to enter the fray; to intervene in an affair, a dispute, etc. **c.** In *Wrestling,* to bring one's leg round an opponent's. In *Cricket,* of a batsman: To advance a step to meet a ball. Hence **step-in,** applied to garments made without fastenings, so that one must step into them. **S. off.** *Mil.* To begin to march at a prescribed pace. **S. out. a.** To go or come out from a place, usu. for a short distance or for a short time; esp. to leave the house, go out of doors. Also, to leave a boat or vehicle. Also, to move one or more paces away from one's position. **b.** *Mil.* To lengthen the pace in marching. **c.** To walk with a vigorous step or stride. **S. up. a.** To go up from a lower position to a higher; to mount, ascend (also *fig.*); *spec.* to go up by treading on a step or stairway. Also, in later use, to go a short distance, or pay a short visit, to a place which is regarded as higher. **b.** To mount a pulpit, rostrum, or the like. **c.** To come forward for some purpose; to leave one's place and come close *to* (a person). **d.** *U.S.* To raise the status, rate, quality, etc. (as by 'steps') 1920. **e.** *Electr.* To increase the voltage of (a current) by means of a transformer. Hence **S.-up,** used attrib. or as adj. designating a transformer that does this.

Step-, OE. *stēop-,* corresp. to OFris. *stiap-, stiep-,* OHG. *stiuf-,* ON. *stjúp-* :—OTeut. **steupo-*; a Com. Teut. combining element, prefixed to terms of relationship to designate the degrees of affinity resulting from the remarriage of a parent.

Stepbrother (ste·pbrʊːðəɹ). 1440. [STEP-.] A son of one's stepfather or stepmother.

Stepchild (ste·pˌtʃəild). [OE. *stēopcild*; see STEP-.] †**1.** An orphan. OE. and ME. only. **2.** A stepson or stepdaughter ME.

Stepdame (ste·pdēˈm). Now *arch.* late ME. [f. STEP- + DAME *sb.* 8.] A stepmother.

Stepdaughter (ste·pdǭːtəɹ). [OE. *stēopdohtor*; see STEP-.] A daughter, by a former marriage, of one's husband or wife.

Stepfather (ste·pfāːðəɹ). [OE. *stēopfæder*; see STEP-.] The husband of one's mother by a subsequent marriage.

‖ **Stephanion** (stɪfēˈniǫn). *Pl.* **-ia, -ions.** 1878. [mod.L. use of Gr. στεφάνιον, dim. of στέφανος crown.] *Craniometry.* The point where the coronal suture crosses the temporal ridge.

Stephanite (ste·fănəit). 1849. [ad. G. *stephanit,* named after the Archduke *Stephan* of Austria; see -ITE.] *Min.* Sulphantimonide of silver, black in colour and very brittle.

Stephanotis (stefănōᵘ·tis). 1870. [mod. L., a. Gr. στεφανωτίς fem. adj., fit for a crown or wreath, f. στέφανος crown.] **1.** ‖**a.** *Bot.* A genus of tropical asclepiadaceous twining shrubs having fragrant white flowers. **b.** A plant of this genus; a flower of such a plant. **2.** A perfume said to be prepared from the flowers of *Stephanotis floribunda* 1907.

Ste·p-laːdder. 1751. [STEP *sb.*] A ladder which has flat steps instead of rungs.

Stepmother (ste·pmʊːðəɹ), *sb.* [OE. *stēopmōdor*; see STEP-.] The wife of one's father by a subsequent marriage. **b.** *transf.* Said of a bird that hatches another bird's eggs 1567. Hence **Ste·pmother** *v. trans.* (*a*) to provide with a s.; (*b*) to behave as a s. to, esp. with suggestion of unfairness or cruelty. **Ste·pmotherly** *a.* pertaining to or characteristic of a s.

Stepney (ste·pni). 1907. [Said to be from the name of *Stepney*-street, Llanelly, the place of manufacture.] A spare wheel with ready inflated tyre but no spokes, carried by motorists.

Steppe (step). 1671. [a. Russ. *stepĭ.*] **1.** One of the vast treeless plains of south-eastern Europe and Siberia. **2.** *transf.* An extensive plain, usu. treeless 1837.

Stepped (stept), (*ppl.*) *a.* 1833. [f. STEP *sb.* and *v.* + -ED.] Having a step or steps; formed in a series of steps.

In this style we have the simple gable of two lines.. and the s. gable 1833. A wheel with s. teeth 1869.

Stepper (ste·pəɹ). 1835. [f. STEP *v.* + -ER ¹.] A horse with good paces and showy action. Often with *good, sure,* etc. Cf. HIGH-STEPPER.

Ste·pping-stone. ME. [f. *stepping,* vbl. sb. f. STEP *v.*] **1.** A stone for stepping upon. **a.** A stone placed in the bed of a stream or on muddy or swampy ground, to facilitate crossing on foot. Chiefly *pl.* **b.** A raised stone on which the foot can be placed to facilitate a climb or ascent (*rare*) 1837. **c.** *transf.* A place for a break of journey 1849. **2.** *fig.* Something that is used as a means of rising in the world, or of making progress towards some object; often, a position, etc. that affords opportunity for further advancement 1653.

1. Once he fell into the brook crossing at the stepping-stones SCOTT. **2.** I held it Truth..That men may rise on stepping-stones Of their dead selves to higher things TENNYSON. These obstacles his genius had turned into stepping stones MACAULAY.

Stepsister (ste·psiːstəɹ). 1440. [STEP-.] A daughter of one's stepfather or stepmother.

Stepson (ste·psʊn). [OE. *stēopsunu*; see STEP-.] A son, by a former marriage, of one's husband or wife.

-ster, *suffix,* repr. a WGer. type *-strjōn-,* forming fem. agent-nouns, prob. a deriv. of the OTeut. *-stro-* forming nouns of action, as in ON. *bakstr* act of baking.

In OE. *-estre* was freely used to form fem. agent-nouns, usu. by being appended to the pres.-stems of verbs. The few instances in which it is used as a masc. are renderings of the Latin designations of men exercising functions which among the English were peculiar to women, as *byrdistre* embroiderer (gl. *blaciarius*), *bæcestre* baker (gl. *pistor*), *sēamestre* tailor (gl. *sartor*).

In the south the suffix continued to be predominantly feminine throughout the ME. period, while in the north it came very early to be used, indiscriminately with -ER[1], as an agential ending irrespective of gender; from the 16th c. onwards the older words in *-ster*, so far as they have survived, have been regarded as masculines, in several instances giving rise to feminines in *-ess*, as *seamstress, songstress, huckstress*, etc. In the modern English period the suffix has been freely used, but it is doubtful whether any of the new formations are really derived from verbs; they are usually associated rather with sbs. than with vbs.

Stercobilin (stɔ̄ɹkoˌbəiˑlin). 1880. [irreg. f. L. *stercus* (*stercor-*) dung + *bilis* BILE + -IN.] The colouring matter of the fæces.

Stercoraceous (stɔ̄ɹkŏrēiˑʃəs), *a.* 1731. [f. L. *stercoraceus*, f. *stercor-, stercus* dung; see -ACEOUS.] **1.** Consisting of, containing, or pertaining to fæces. **b.** *Path.* Of vomiting: Consisting of fæces, fæcal 1754. **2.** *Ent.* Of certain beetles, flies, etc.: Frequenting or feeding on dung 1891.

Stercoral (stɔ̄ˑɹkŏrăl), *a.* 1758. [f. L. *stercor-, stercus* dung + -AL[1].] *Path.* = prec.

Stercoranism (stɔ̄ˑɹkŏrăniz'm). 1728. [f. as next + -ISM.] *Eccl. Hist.* The beliefs of the Stercoranists.

Stercoranist (stɔ̄ˑɹkŏrănist). 1686. [ad. med.L. *stercoranista*, irreg. f. L. *stercor-, stercus* dung + -IST.] *Eccl. Hist.* A nickname given to one who holds that the consecrated elements in the Eucharist undergo digestion in, and evacuation from, the body of the recipient.

Stercorarious (stɔ̄ɹkŏrēəˑriəs), *a.* 1656. [f. L. *stercorarius* (see next) + -OUS.] = STERCORACEOUS 1, 2.

Stercorary (stɔ̄ˑɹkŏrări), *a.* and *sb.* 1664. [ad. L. *stercorarius*, f. *stercor-, stercus* dung; see -ARY.] **A.** *adj.* Of or pertaining to dung. Of insects: Living in or feeding on dung. **B.** *sb.* A place where manure is stored, a dung-heap. Now *rare* or *Obs.* 1759.

Stercorate (stɔ̄ˑɹkŏreit), *v.* 1623. [f. L. *stercorat-, stercorare*, f. *stercor-, stercus* dung.] *trans.* To manure or dung. So **Stercoraˑtion**, manuring with dung; †dung, manure 1605.

Stercorin (stɔ̄ˑɹkŏrin). 1873. [a. F. *stercorine*, f. *stercor-, stercus* dung; see -IN.] A fæcal extractive resembling biliary cholesterin.

Stercorous (stɔ̄ˑɹkŏrəs), *a.* 1542. [ad. L. *stercorosus*, f. *stercor-, stercus* dung; see -OUS.] Stercoraceous, excrementitious.

‖**Sterculia** (stəɹkiūˑliă). 1771. [mod.L., f. *Sterculius* the god of manuring, f. *stercus* dung.] **1.** *Bot.* A genus of polypetalous plants (typical of the family *Sterculiaceæ*); a plant of this genus. (Some of the species have a fetid odour, whence the name.) **2.** *Ent.* A beetle of the family *Xantholinidæ* 1874. Hence **Sterculiaˑceous** *a. Bot.* pertaining to the *Sterculiaceæ*; **Stercuˑliad**, a sterculiaceous plant.

Stere, ‖**stère** (stīəɹ, F. stēr). 1798. [F. *stère*, f. Gr. στερεός solid.] The unit of the metric system for solid measures; a cubic metre, equal to about 35·3 English cubic feet.

Sterelminthous (sterelmiˑnþəs), *a.* 1843. [f. mod.L. *Sterelmintha* (irreg. f. Gr. στερεός solid + ἑλμινθ-, ἕλμινς intestinal worm) + -OUS.] *Zool.* Of or pertaining to the *Sterelmintha*, Owen's name for a division of the Entozoa comprising the endoparasitic worms having a solid body with no visceral cavity. So **Sterelmiˑnthic** *a.*

Stereo[1] (stīəˑrio, steˑrio). 1823. abbrev. of STEREOTYPE; also *attrib.*, as *s. forme, matter.*

Stereo[2] (stīəˑrio, steˑrio). 1876. abbrev. of STEREOSCOPE, STEREOSCOPIC.

Stereo- (stīəˑrio, steˑrio), bef. a vowel prop. stere-, comb. form repr. Gr. στερεός solid, in various (chiefly recent) scientific and technical terms. (In some instances serving as comb. form of *stereoscope* or *stereoscopic*.)

Steˑreobate *Arch.*, a solid mass of masonry serving as a base for a wall or a row of columns; hence **Stereobaˑtic** *a.* **Steˑriochrome**, stereochromy; also, a picture produced by this. **Steˑriochroˑmy**, a process of mural painting in which water-glass is used as a preservative against atmospheric influences. †**Steˑreo-eleˑctric** *a.*, applied to a (thermo-electric) current produced by contact of solids (opp. to HYDRO-ELECTRIC 2). **Steˑreomoˑnoscope**, an instrument with two lenses by which an image of an object is projected upon a screen of ground glass so as to appear solid, as in a stereoscope. **Steˑreoplaˑsm**, (*a*) *Biol.* Nägeli's term for the denser or more solid part of protoplasm (dist from HYGROPLASM); (*b*) *Zool.* an endothecal structure in corals, enveloping or connecting the septa, or forming a mass in the interior. **Stereoˑpticon**, a double magic lantern arranged to combine two images of the same object or scene upon a screen, so as to produce the appearance of solidity as in a stereoscope. **Steˑreostaˑtic** *a., Mech.* applied to an arch constructed to sustain the pressure of a mass of solid matter, as a geostatic arch. **Steˑreostaˑtics**, the statics of solid bodies.

Stereochemistry (stīəːrio-, steːriokeˑmistri). 1890. [f. STEREO- + CHEMISTRY.] That department of chemistry which deals with theoretical differences in the relative position in space of atoms in a molecule, in relation to differences in the optical and chemical properties of the substances. So **Steːreo-cheˑmical** *a.*

Stereogram (stīəˑrio-, steˑriogræm). 1866. [f. STEREO- + -GRAM.] **1.** A diagram representing a solid object on a plane; esp. a drawing in which the inequalities or curvature of a surface are indicated by contour lines or shading 1868. **2.** = next 1. 1866.

Stereograph (stīəˑrio-, steˑriograf). 1859. [f. STEREO- + -GRAPH.] **1.** A picture (or pair of pictures) representing the object so that it appears solid, a stereoscopic photograph. **2.** An instrument for making projections or geometrical drawings of skulls or similar solid objects 1877.

Stereographic (stīəːrio-, steːriogræˑfik), *a.* 1704. [ad. mod.L. *stereographicus*, f. Gr. στερεός solid + -γραφικός; see -GRAPHIC.] **1.** Delineating or representing a solid body on a plane; applied *spec.* to a kind of projection used in maps, etc., in which the centre of projection is a point on the surface of the sphere, and the whole sphere is represented once on an infinite plane, circles being represented as circles, and the angles being retained. **2.** Pertaining to stereoscopic photography 1859. So **Stereograˑphical** *a.* 1675; **-ly** *adv.* 1679.

Stereography (stīəri-, sterịǫˑgrăfi). 1700. [ad. mod.L. *stereographia*, f. Gr. στερεός solid + -γραφία; see -GRAPHY.] The art of delineating or representing the forms of solid bodies on a plane, as in perspective.

Stereometer (sterịǫˑmītəɹ). 1801. [a. F. *stéréomètre*, f. Gr. στερεός solid + -μέτρον; see -METER.] **1.** An instrument for measuring the specific gravity of porous or pulverulent bodies. **2.** An apparatus consisting of a frame of bars and columns with sliding rods and wires, for illustrating problems in solid geometry 1884.

Stereometry (sterịǫˑmėtri). Now *rare.* 1570. [ad. mod.L. *stereometria*, a. Gr. στερεομετρία, f. στερεός solid + -μετρία; see -METRY.] **1.** The art or science of measuring solids; that branch of geometry which deals with solid figures, solid geometry; the practical application of this to the measurement of solid bodies. **2.** The art of measuring specific gravities with a STEREOMETER (sense 1) 1886. Hence **Stereomeˑtric, -al** *adjs.* pertaining to s.; relating to or existing in three dimensions of space.

Stereoscope (stīəˑrio-, steˑrioskōup). 1838. [f. Gr. στερεός solid + -SCOPE.] An instrument for obtaining from two pictures of an object, taken from slightly different points of view (corresponding to the positions of the two eyes), a single image giving the impression of solidity or relief, as in ordinary vision of the object itself. Hence **Steːreoscopic** (-skǫˑpik) *a.* of, pertaining to, or adapted to the s.; having an appearance of solidity or relief like an object viewed in a s.; so **Steːreoscoˑpically** *adv.* **Stereoscopist** (-ǫˑskŏpist), one skilled in the use of the s.; a maker of stereoscopes. **Stereoˑscopy**, the art or practice of using the s.

Stereotomy (sterịǫˑtŏmi). 1728. [ad. F. *stéréotomie*, f. Gr. στερεός solid + -τομία -TOMY.] The science or art of cutting, or making sections of, solids; that department of geometry which deals with sections of solid figures; the art of cutting stone or other solid bodies into measured forms, as in masonry. Hence **Steːreotoˑmic, -al** *adjs.* pertaining to s.; **Stereoˑtomist**, one skilled in s.

Stereotype (stīəˑrio-, steˑriotəip), *sb.* and *a.* 1798. [a. F. *stéréotype* adj., f. Gr. στερεός solid + τύπος TYPE *sb.*] **A.** *sb.* **1.** The method or process of printing in which a solid plate of type-metal, cast from a papier-mâché or plaster mould taken from the surface of a forme of type, is used for printing from instead of the forme itself. **2.** A stereotype plate 1817. **b.** In generalized sense 1823. **3.** *fig.* Something continued or constantly repeated without change; a stereotyped phrase, formula, etc.; stereotyped diction or usage 1850.

2. b. The mode of casting s. 1823. 3. The s. of school, newspaper and department prevails 1908.

Comb.: **s.-block**, (*a*) a s. plate; (*b*) a block of iron or wood on which a s. plate is fixed.

B. *adj.* **1.** *lit.* Of an edition: Printed by the process described in A. 1. Also used as an epithet of the process. 1801. **2.** *fig.* = STEREOTYPED b. Now somewhat *rare.* 1824.

2. He..answers now always with a kind of s. formula CARLYLE.

Stereotype (stīəˑrio-, steˑriotəip), *v.* 1804. [ad. F. *stéréotyper*, f. *stéréotype*; see prec.] **1.** *trans.* To cast a stereotype plate from (a forme of type); to prepare (literary matter) for printing by means of stereotypes. Also *absol.* **2.** *fig.* To fix or perpetuate in an unchanging form 1819.

2. Shakespeare and the Bible have stereotyped English 1874. **Steˑreotyːper**, one who makes stereotype plates; one who fixes unchangingly.

Steˑreotyped (-təipt), *ppl. a.* 1820. [f. prec. + -ED[1].] **a.** Cast in the form of, or prepared for printing by means of, stereotype (*rare*). **b.** Usu. *fig.* Fixed or perpetuated in an unchanging form.

b. Uttering..s. commonplaces MRS. GASKELL.

Stereotypic (stīəːrio-, steːriotiˑpik), *a. rare.* 1801. [f. STEREOTYPE *sb.* + -IC.] Pertaining to or having the character of a stereotype.

Stereotypy (stīəˑrio-, steˑriotəiːpi). 1891. [ad. F. *stéréotypie*, f. *stéréotype* STEREOTYPE *a.*] **1.** The process of making stereotype plates; stereotyping. **2.** *Path.* Persistence of a fixed or stereotyped idea, mode of action, etc., in cases of insanity 1909.

Sterhydraulic (stɔ̄ɹhəidrǭˑlik), *a.* 1866. [ad. F. *stérhydraulique*, irreg. f. Gr. στερεός solid + F. *hydraulique*.] Applied to a form of hydraulic press in which pressure is generated by displacement of the contained liquid by a solid body, as a rod, screw, or rope, introduced with a continuous movement through a packed opening.

Steric (steˑrik), *a.* 1898. [irreg. f. Gr. στερεός solid + -IC.] *Chem.* Pertaining or relating to the arrangement in space of the atoms in a molecule.

‖**Sterigma** (stĕriˑgmă). 1866. [mod.L., a. Gr. στήριγμα support.] *Bot.* A stalk or filament: variously applied.

Sterile (steˑrəil, steˑril), *a.* 1552. [ad. L. *sterilis*, cogn. w. Skr. *starī*, Gr. στεῖρα barren cow, στέριφος barren.] Barren; not producing fruit or offspring. **1.** Of soil, a country, etc.: Unproductive of vegetation 1572. **2.** Producing no offspring; incapable of producing offspring. (Chiefly of females.) 1552. †**b.** Causing sterility. SHAKS. **3.** Of a plant: Not bearing fruit 1626. **4.** Mentally or spiritually barren. Also, fruitless; barren *in* or *of* (something sought or desired). 1642. **5.** *Biol.* **a.** Of an organ or structure that would normally contain reproductive elements: Barren, infertile 1646. **b.** Of cells, etc.: Not capable of reproduction 1856. **6.** Free from micro-organisms. Now often of surgical instruments, etc. = STERILIZED. 1877.

1. Leane, stirrill, and bare Land SHAKS. Very S. Yeares BACON. 2. Women frequently become s. after a miscarriage 1741. 3. *Potentilla Fragaria* (S. Strawberry) 1845. 4. He seems..to be very steril of Invention 1665. 5. a. Flowers having stamens only, are staminiferous, staminal, or s. 1849. 6. A s. needle or lancet 1898. Hence **Steˑrile·ly** *adv.*, **-ness.**

Sterility (stĕriˑlĭti). late ME. [ad. L. *sterilitas*, f. *sterilis* STERILE *a.*] **1.** The quality of being sterile, barrenness. Also *fig.* **2.** The state of being free from micro-organisms 1877.

Sterilize (steˑriləiz), *v.* 1695. [f. STERILE *a.* + -IZE.] **1.** *trans.* To cause to be unfruitful; to destroy the fertility of. **2.** To deprive of fecundity; to render incapable of producing offspring 1828. **3.** *Biol.* To render (organs) sterile 1891. **4.** *fig.* To make mentally or spiritually barren; to render unproductive, unprofitable or useless 1880. 5. To render free from micro-organisms 1878.

1. *absol.* The practice of sowing with salt, in order to s., is alluded to in the Old Testament 1910. 5. The milk should be sterilized 1899. Hence **Ste·riliza·tion**, the action of sterilizing. **Ste·rilized** *ppl. a.* **Ste·rilizer.**

Sterlet (stɜ̄·ɹlėt). 1591. [a. Russ. *sterlyadt.*] A small species of sturgeon, *Acipenser ruthenus*, found in Russia.

Sterling (stɜ̄·ɹliŋ), *sb.* and *a.* ME. [prob. a late OE. formation; perh. **steorling* 'coin with a star' (f. *steorra* star), some of the early Norman pennies having on them a small star: see N.E.D.] **A.** *sb.* 1. The English silver penny of the Norman and subsequent dynasties. Often in *pound of sterlings*, orig. a pound weight of silver pennies, afterwards a name for the English pound (240 pence) as a money of account. Also in *mark, shilling*, etc. *of sterlings. Obs.* exc. *Hist.* **b.** Applied to the Scottish penny. late ME. †2. = PENNYWEIGHT –1776. 3. Money of the quality of the sterling or standard silver penny; genuine English money 1565. 4. English money as dist. from foreign money. Formerly often in contrast to *currency*, i.e. the depreciated pounds, shillings, and pence of certain colonies. 1601. **b.** *attrib.* Related to or payable in sterling 1894. †5. Standard degree of fineness –1724.

1. Paid in starlings which were pence so called 1598. 3. *fig.* You haue tane his tenders for true pay, Which are not starling SHAKS. 4. The Tenants are obliged by their Leases to pay S., which is Lawful Current Money of England SWIFT. b. S. exchange 1912. 5. Gold and Silver of the Right S. and Standard SWIFT.

B. *adj.* (Formerly often abbreviated *ster., sterl.*) 1. In *pound*, etc. *s.*, altered from the older *pound*, etc. (*of*) *sterlings* (see A. 1), and orig. used in the same sense. Hence, in later use, appended to the statement of a sum of money, to indicate that English money is meant. 1444. 2. Prefixed as the distinctive epithet of lawful English money or coin. Now *rare.* late ME. †**b.** *fig.* That has course or currency –1593. 3. Of silver: †Having the same degree of purity as the penny. Hence, in later use: Of standard quality. 1488. 4. Of character, principles, qualities, occas. of persons: Thoroughly excellent, capable of standing every test 1645.

1. Many millions s. 1838. 2. A pennie loafe of Breade (of English starling money) was worth a crowne of gold 1590. Phr. *To pass for* (later *as*) *s.* (chiefly *fig.*). b. *Rich. II*, IV. 264. 3. *S. mark, stamp*, the hall-mark guaranteeing s. quality; The s. mark upon plate 1776. 4. Many sound and s. principles of conduct 1828. A young man of s. worth, and Spanish gravity W. IRVING.

Stern (stɜ̄ɹn), *sb.*[1] [OE. *stearn.*] A sea-bird; the tern, esp. the black tern (*Hydrochelidon nigra*).

Stern (stɜ̄ɹn), *sb.*[2] ME. [prob. a. ON. *stjórn* steering, f. OTeut. **steurjan* STEER *v.*] †1. The steering gear of a ship, the rudder and helm together; but often applied to the rudder only –1671. †**b.** *fig.* That which guides or controls affairs, actions, etc.; also, (from the metaphor of the ship of state) government, rule –1708. 2. The hind part of a ship or boat (as dist. from the bow and midships); in restricted sense, the external rear part of a ship's hull; also *spec.* in vessels of ordinary type, the overhanging portion of the hull abaft the stern-post ME. 3. The buttocks of a person (chiefly *joc.* and *vulgar*) or beast; the hinder part of any creature 1614. 4. The tail of an animal, esp. of a sporting-dog or a wolf 1575.

1. b. I intend to . . sit at chiefest Sterne of publique Weal SHAKS. 2. Phr. *Down by the s.*: see BY A. 1 d. *S.-foremost*, backwards, with the s. (senses 2, 3) first. *S. on*, with the s. presented. 3. We don't want to . . fancy them cherubs without sterns FURNIVALL.

attrib. and *Comb.*: **s.-frame**, the framework of a ship's s.; **-knee** = STERNSON; **-port**, a port or window in the s. of a vessel; **s. sea**, a following sea.

Stern (stɜ̄ɹn), *a.* (*adv.*) [OE. (WS.) *styrne.* The ME. forms point to an OTeut. type **sternjo-*, which is represented only in Eng.] **A.** *adj.* 1. Of persons and things personified, their dispositions, etc.; Severe, inflexible; rigorous in punishment or condemnation. **b.** Rigorous in morals or principles; uncompromising, austere. late ME. **c.** Of personal attributes, actions, feelings, etc.: Severe, strict, hard, grim, harsh ME. 2. Of battle, debate, etc.: Stubbornly-contested, fierce, hard ME. †3. In a bad sense: Merciless, cruel –1600. 4. Of looks, bearing, gait: Indicating a stern disposition or mood; expressing grave displeasure; resolute, austere, gloomy. late ME. **b.** *transf.* Of a building: Severe in style; gloomy or forbidding in aspect 1822. 5. Of the voice: Expressive of a stern disposition or mood ME. †6. Of things, in transf. uses; *esp.* of blows, weapons: Inflicting severe pain or injury –1805. 7. Of a country, or its physical features, the soil, etc.: Unkindly, inhospitable; forbidding in aspect, frowning, gloomy 1812. 8. Of circumstances and conditions: Oppressive, hard, inexorable; esp. *s. necessity, s. reality* 1830.

1. The s. ambitious, military old bishop 1841. b. Lord Nithsdale, who was a s. Catholic 1835. c. Ambition should be made of sterner stuffe SHAKS. The s. policy that dictated his execution 1820. 3. How many Lambs might the sterne Wolfe betray SHAKS. 4. Gods and men Fear'd her s. frown MILT. 7. Mountains s. and desolate WORDSW.

B. *adv.* or *quasi-adv.* Sternly, resolutely, severely, harshly. (*Obs.* or *arch.*) ME.

He shook his Miter'd locks, and s. bespake MILT. Hence **Ste·rn-ly** *adv.*, **-ness.**

Stern (stɜ̄ɹn), *v.* late ME. [f. STERN *sb.*[2]] †1. *trans.* and *intr.* To steer, govern –1648. 2. *trans.* To propel (a boat) stern foremost; also *intr.* to go stern foremost 1845. 3. To place astern, in the phr. *s. the buoy* 1711.

Sternad (stɜ̄·ɹnæd), *adv.* 1803. [f. STERNUM + -AD II (cf. DEXTRAD, etc.).] *Anat.* Towards the sternum or the sternal aspect.

†**Ste·rnage.** 1599. [f. STERN *sb.*[2] + -AGE.] The sterns of a fleet collectively. SHAKS.

Sternal (stɜ̄·ɹnăl), *a.* (and *sb.*) 1756. [ad. mod.L. *sternalis*, f. STERNUM; see -AL.] *Anat.* and *Zool.* 1. Of, pertaining to, or connected with the sternum or breast-bone. 2. Situated on the same side as the sternum; anterior (in man) or inferior (in other animals); ventral; hæmal. (Opp. to *dorsal, tergal,* or *neural.*) 1803. 3. Of or pertaining to a sternum or sternite in Arthropoda; sternitic 1835. **B.** as *sb.* A sternal bone 1901.

Sternbergite (stɜ̄·ɹnbɜ̄ɹgəit). 1826. [f. name of Count Caspar *Sternberg*; see -ITE.] *Min.* A native sulphide of silver and iron, occurring in brown flexible laminæ with metallic lustre.

Ste·rn-board. 1815. [f. STERN *sb.*[2] + BOARD *sb.*] 1. A board forming the flat part of the stern of a small boat, punt, etc. 1849. 2. *Naut.* In phr. *to make a s.*, to go backwards as the result of tacking; also, to force a ship astern with the sails 1815.

Ste·rn-chase. 1627. [f. STERN *sb.*[2] + CHASE *sb.*[1]] *Naut.* 1. A chase in which the pursuing ship follows directly in the wake of the pursued. †2. The chase-guns arming the stern of a warship –1798.

1. *Prov.* A stern chase is a long chase 1849.

Ste·rn-cha:ser. 1815. *Naut.* A gun belonging to the STERN-CHASE (sense 2).

‖**Sternebra** (stɜ̄·ɹnĭbră). *Pl.* **-æ** (-ī). 1846. [mod.L. f. STERNUM, with ending of VERTEBRA.] *Anat.* Any one of the segments of the sternum, each corresponding to a pair of ribs. Hence **Ste·rnebral** *a.* pertaining to or constituting a s.

Sterned (stɜ̄ɹnd), *a.* 1611. [f. STERN *sb.*[2] + -ED[2].] Having a stern. Only in combs., as *black-s., square-s.*

Ste·rn-fast. 1569. [f. STERN *sb.*[2] + FAST *sb.*[2]] *Naut.* A rope by which a vessel's stern is moored.

Sternite (stɜ̄·ɹnəit). 1868. [f. STERNUM + -ITE.] *Zool.* The under or ventral part of each somite or segment of the body of an insect or other arthropod.

Sternmost (stɜ̄·ɹnmoust, -məst), *a.* 1622. [f. STERN *sb.*[2] + -MOST.] 1. Farthest in the rear, last in a line of ships. 2. Nearest the stern 1838.

1. He came alongside the s. ship SOUTHEY.

Sterno- (stɜ̄ɹno), bef. a vowel **stern-**, comb. form repr. Gr. στέρνον or L. STERNUM, occurring in several terms, usu. denoting muscles, etc. connected with the sternum and some other part.

‖**Sternalgia** (-æ·ldʒiă) [Gr. ἄλγος pain], pain in the region of the sternum; spec. *angina pectoris.* **Ste·rnoclavi·cular** *a.*, pertaining to or connecting the sternum and the clavicle. **Sternoco·stal** [L. *costa* rib] *a.*, pertaining to or connecting the sternum and the ribs. **Sterno-hy·oid** *a.*, pertaining to or connecting the sternum and the hyoid bone; the name of each of the two muscles serving to depress the larynx; also as *sb.* **Sternoma·stoid** *a.*, pertaining to or connecting the sternum and the mastoid process of the temporal bone; also as *sb.* (*sc.* muscle). **Ste·rno-maxi·llary** *a.*, pertaining to or connecting the sternum and lower jaw-bone. **Sternothy·roid** *a.*, pertaining to or connecting the sternum and the thyroid cartilage; also as *sb.* (*sc.* muscle). **Sterno-ve·rtebral** *a.*, connected with the sternum and the vertebræ.

Ste·rn-post. late ME. [f. STERN *sb.*[2] + POST *sb.*[1]] *Naut.* A more or less upright beam, rising from the after end of the keel and supporting the rudder. **b.** *attrib.*, as *s.-knee* (= STERNSON) 1845.

Ste·rn-sheet. 1481. [f. STERN *sb.*[2] + SHEET *sb.*[2]] *Naut.* 1. *sing.* and *pl.* The internal stern portion of a boat; *spec.* that part abaft the hindmost thwart. 2. *pl.* **a.** The flooring boards in the after portion of a boat or small ship 1644. **b.** The seats with which the after portion of a boat is furnished 1912.

Sternson (stɜ̄·ɹnsən). 1846. [f. STERN *sb.*[2], after KELSON.] *Naut.* In a wooden vessel, the knee-shaped timber fitted into the angle formed by the junction of stern-post and kelson in order to secure the joint. **b.** S.-knee (in the same sense) 1849.

Sternum (stɜ̄·ɹnɒ̆m). *Pl.* **sterna, sternums.** 1667. [mod.L., ad. Gr. στέρνον chest, breast.] *Anat.* and *Zool.* 1. The breast-bone; a long bone or series of bones, occurring in most vertebrates except snakes and fishes, extending along the middle line of the front or ventral aspect of the trunk, usu. articulating with some of the ribs, and with them completing the wall of the thorax. 2. *Zool.* The ventral part of any somite of an arthropod; opp. to *tergum* 1835.

Sternutation (stɜ̄ɹniutē¹·ʃən). 1545. [ad. L. *sternutationem*, f. *sternutare*, freq. f. *sternuere* to sneeze, cogn. w. Gr. πτάρνυσθαι (:—**pstrnu-*).] The action of sneezing; a sneeze. (Chiefly *Med.* and *Path.*; otherwise, in mod. use, *joc.*)

Sternutative (stɜɹniū·tātiv), *a.* and *sb.* Now *rare.* 1666. [f. L. *sternutat-, sternutare*; see prec. and -IVE.] = next.

Sternutatory (stɜɹniū·tătŏri), *a.* and *sb.* 1616. [f. as prec. + -ORY[2].] **A.** *adj.* 1. Causing or tending to cause sneezing. 2. Of or pertaining to sneezing 1842. **B.** *sb.* A substance that causes sneezing; *esp.* an errhine 1634.

Ste·rn-wheel. 1816. [STERN *sb.*[2]] A paddle-wheel placed at the stern of a small river or lake steamer. Hence **Ste·rnwhee:ler**, a boat propelled by a s.

Sterol (ste·rǫl). 1913. *Biol. Chem.* The ending of CHOLESTEROL, ERGOSTEROL, etc., used as a separate word to denote one of a group of allied complex solid alcohols of importance in the synthesis of vitamins.

Ste·rro-me:tal (ste·ro). 1865. [Gr. στερρός stiff, hard.] An alloy of copper and zinc, with a small amount of iron and tin. Also *sterro.*

Stertor (stɜ̄·ɹtǫɹ). 1612. [mod.L., f. L. *stertere* to snore.] A heavy snoring sound accompanying inspiration in profound unconsciousness.

Stertorous (stɜ̄·ɹtŏrəs), *a.* 1802. [f. prec. + -OUS.] Characterized by or of the nature of stertor or snoring.

Hence **Ste·rtorously** *adv.* **Ste·rtorousness.**

Stet (stet). 1821. [L., 3rd sing. pres. subj. of *stare.*] *Printing.* 'Let it stand'; a direction on a proof or MS. that matter which has been altered or struck out is to remain uncorrected. Hence as *v. trans.*, to cancel a correction by writing 'stet' in the margin and underlining the words with a series of dots.

Stetho- (steþo), bef. a vowel **steth-**, comb. form repr. Gr. στῆθος breast, chest, occurring in medical terms. **Stethe·ndoscope** [Gr. ἔνδον within + -SCOPE], an instrument for examining the inside of the chest by means of Röntgen rays.

Stethograph (ste·þǒgraf). 1876. [f. STETHO- + -GRAPH.] An instrument for automatically recording the movements of the chest in breathing; a recording stethometer; also called *pneumograph*.

Stethometer (stĭþǫ·mĭtəɹ, steþ-). 1850. [f. STETHO- + -METER.] An instrument for measuring the extent of the movement of the walls of the chest in breathing. So **Stethome·tric** *a.* pertaining to or obtained by means of the s. **Stethometry** (-ǫ·mĕtri), measurement by a s., the use of the s.

Stethoscope (ste·þǒskoup), *sb.* 1820. [a. F. *stéthoscope*, fr. Gr. στῆθος chest + σκοπεῖν to observe; see -SCOPE.] An instrument used for examining the chest or other part by auscultation, the sound of the heart, lungs, or other internal organs being conveyed by means of it to the ear of the observer. Hence **Ste·thoscope** *v. trans.*, to apply a s. to; to examine with a s. **Stethoscopic** (-skǫ·pik), **-al** *adjs.* pertaining to, of the nature of, observed or obtained by a s.; **-ly** *adv.* by means of the s. **Stethoscopist** (-ǫ·skŏpist), one who uses a s. **Stetho·scopy.**

Stetson (ste·tsən). 1924. [Name of maker.] A slouch hat worn by soldiers of the Australian and New Zealand forces.

Stevedore (stī·vĭdōəɹ), *sb.* 1788. [a. Sp. *estivador*, f. *estivar* to stow a cargo; see STEEVE *v.*[2]] A workman employed either as overseer or labourer in loading and unloading the cargoes of merchant vessels. Hence **Ste·vedore** *v. trans.* to stow (cargo) in a ship's hold; to load or unload the cargo of (a ship).

Steven (stev'n). *Obs.* exc. *dial.* [OE. *stefn*, *stemn.*] **1.** = VOICE in various applications. In mod. dial. use chiefly: A loud voice. **2.** Outcry, noise, tumult, din. late ME.

1. Sche cryeth 'systyr' with ful loude a steuene CHAUCER.

Stew (stiū), *sb.*[1] late ME. [a. OF. *estui*, f. *estuier* to shut up, keep in reserve.] †**1.** In phr. *in s.* [= OF. *en estui*], said of fish kept in confinement, to be ready for the table -1573. **2.** A pond or tank in which fish are kept until needed for the table. late ME. **3.** An artificial oyster-bed 1610.

Stew (stiū), *sb.*[2] ME. [a. OF. *estuve*, a Com. Rom. word; ult. etym. obsc.] **I.** A stove, heated room. †**1.** A vessel for boiling, a caldron -1603. †**2.** A heated room; a room with a fireplace -1572. **3.** A heated room used for hot air or vapour baths: hence, a hot bath. *Obs.* exc. *Hist.* or *arch.* late ME. **4.** *pl.* A brothel. (Developed from sense 3, on account of the frequent use of the public hot-air baths for immoral purposes.) *Hist.* late ME. †**b.** (*sing.* and *pl.*) A bawd or prostitute -1650.

4. He strongly censured the licensed stews at Rome BOSWELL.

II. Senses derived from STEW *v.* **1.** A preparation of meat slowly boiled in a stew-pan, usually containing vegetables, etc. 1576. **2.** A state of excitement, esp. of great alarm or anxiety 1806. **3.** *colloq.* A state of being overheated or bathed in perspiration 1892.

1. *Irish s.*, a dish composed of pieces of mutton, potatoes, and onions stewed together. 2. Poor Mr. Allen is in a s. about his sermon 1809.

Stew (stiū), *v.* late ME. [a. OF. *estuver*, related to prec.] †**1.** *trans.* To bathe in a hot bath or a vapour bath -1665. **2.** *Cooking.* **a.** *trans.* To boil slowly in a close vessel; to cook (meat, fruit, etc.) in a liquid kept at the simmering-point. late ME. **b.** *intr.* Of meat, fruit, etc.: To undergo stewing 1594. **c.** In fig. phrases, with the sense: To be left to suffer the natural consequences of one's own actions 1656. **3.** *transf.* †**a.** *trans.* To bathe in perspiration -1687. †**b.** *fig.* To soak, steep, imbue -1822. **c.** To confine in close or ill-ventilated quarters. Chiefly with *up.* 1590. **d.** *intr.* To stay excessively long in bed. Also, to remain in a heated or stifling atmosphere; hence *slang*, to study hard. 1671.

2. **a.** Pour it on your pippins, and s. them till they are quite tender 1770. **c.** Phr. *to s. in one's own juice* [cf. F. *cuire dans son jus*]. He would let them s. in their own..juice 1885. 3. **b.** *Haml.* III. iv. 93. **d.** Stewing over his books 1866.

Steward (stiū·əɹd), *sb.* [OE. *stīweard*, f. *stig*, of uncertain meaning + *weard* WARD *sb.*] **1.** An official who controls the domestic affairs of a household, supervising the service of his master's table, directing the domestics, and regulating household expenditure; a major-domo. *Obs.* exc. *Hist.* **b.** A member of a college who supervises the catering or presides at table 1749. **c.** A servant of a college who is charged with the duty of catering. Also, the head servant of a club or similar institution 1518. **d.** An officer in a ship who, under the direction of the captain or the purser, keeps the stores and arranges for the serving of meals; now applied to any attendant who waits upon the passengers 1450. **2.** As the title of an officer of a royal household. **a.** *gen.* Orig., an officer with similar functions to the 'steward' of an ordinary household (see sense 1). *Obs.* exc. *Hist.* OE. **b.** **(Lord) S. of the King's Household.** A peer whose nominal duty it is to control the King's household above stairs, and to preside at the Board of Green Cloth. late ME. **3.** One who manages the affairs of an estate on behalf of his employer. late ME. **b.** The administrator, often with merely nominal duties, of certain estates of the Crown, as †*S. of the Duchy of Lancaster* 1444. **c.** In Scotland: A magistrate orig. appointed to administer the crown lands forming a STEWARTRY. late ME. **4.** *fig.* (from senses 1 and 3.) An administrator and dispenser of wealth, favours, etc.; esp. one regarded as the servant of God or of the people OE. **5.** In various societies and corporations, the title of certain officers (e. g. *city s.*; *s. of the Jockey Club*) OE. **6. High S.** In the Universities of Oxford and Cambridge, the title (in academic Latin *seneschallus*) of a judicial officer, in whom is vested the jurisdiction belonging to the university in causes of treason and felony 1459. **b.** In certain English cities, a municipal title of dignity, usu. borne by a nobleman or royal prince 1563. **7.** A person appointed to supervise the arrangements or maintain order at a race meeting, exhibition, dinner, ball, concert, public gathering, etc. 1703. **8.** An overseer of workmen ME. **9.** Among Methodists, a layman appointed to manage the financial affairs of a congregation or of a circuit 1741.

1. Antonio Bologna, s. of the household to the Duchess 1611. **d.** *Bath-, cabin-, deck-, table-s.*; *captain's s.*, etc. 2. **(Lord High) S. of England.** The title of a high officer of state, the earlier *seneschallus Angliæ*; since the accession of Henry IV appointed only on the occasion of a coronation, at which he presides, or for the trial of a peer. **(Lord High) S. of Scotland.** *Hist.* The first officer of the Scottish King in early times. 3. *S. of the manor*, one who transacts the financial and legal business of a manor on behalf of the lord; he holds the manor-court in the lord's absence, and keeps a copy of its rolls, whence the name *s. of copyhold.* So *S. of the leet*, *s. of the hundred*, etc. **b.** *S. of the Chiltern Hundreds*: see CHILTERN. 4. A man of business and a vigilant s. of the public money MACAULAY. 5. The Stewards and Members of the Jockey Club 1831. Hence **Stew·ard** *v. trans.* to manage, administer; *intr.* to do the duties of a s. **Stew·ardly** *adv.* (*rare*) like a s., with the care of a s. **Stew·ardship**, the office of a s.; conduct of the office of s., administration.

Stewardess (stiū·əɹdės). 1631. [-ESS [1].] A female who performs the duties of a steward. **b.** Now chiefly: A female attendant on a ship whose duty it is to wait on the women passengers 1837.

Stewartry, stewardry (stiū·əɹtri, stiū·əɹdri). Chiefly *Sc.* 1473. [See STEWARD *sb.* and -RY.] **1.** A former territorial division of Scotland under the jurisdiction of a steward. **2.** The office of steward in such a territory 1483.

Stewed (stiūd), *ppl. a.* [-ED [1].] Cooked by slow boiling in a closed vessel. Of tea: made strong and bitter by being kept too long in the pot.

Stewpan (stiū·pæn). 1651. [f. STEW *sb.*[2] or *v.* + PAN *sb.*] A saucepan for stewing.

Stewpot (stiū·pǫt). 1628. [f. as prec. + POT *sb.*] A covered pot for stewing meat, etc.

Sthenic (sþe·nik), *a.* 1788. [ad. mod.L. *sthenicus*, f. Gr. σθένος strength; after *asthenicus.*] *Path.* Applied to diseases characterized by a normal or excessive accumulation of 'excitability' or vital power in the system. In later use, of diseases, symptoms, etc.: Marked by normal or excessive vital or nervous energy. Opp. to *asthenic.*

Stib-. 1852. Used in *Chem.* as comb. form of STIBIUM: cf. STIBIO-.

Stibic (sti·bik), *a. rare.* 1609. [f. STIBIUM + -IC.] Of or belonging to antimony; antimonic.

Stibiconite (sti·bikǒnəit). 1843. [f. STIBIUM + Gr. κόνις dust + -ITE.] *Min.* A hydrous oxide of antimony, sometimes found in a pulverulent form.

Stibine (sti·bəin). 1843. [f. STIBIUM + -INE.] **1.** *Min.* = STIBNITE. **2.** *Chem.* Any of the antimony-compounds on the type of ammonia, SbH_3. 1852.

Stibio- (sti·bio). 1857. Comb. form of STIBIUM, used in *Chem.* and *Min.*

Stibium (sti·biǒm). late ME. [a. L.] 'Black antimony', i.e. trisulphide of antimony calcined and powdered, used as a cosmetic for blackening the eyelids and eyebrows. †Formerly used also for metallic antimony or any of its salts, esp. as a poison or an emetic.

Stibnite (sti·bnəit). 1854. [f. STIBINE + -ITE.] *Min.* Native trisulphide of antimony, 'gray antimony', the most common ore of the metal.

Sticcado (stikā·do). 1776. [perh. ad. It. *steccato.*] *Mus.* A kind of xylophone.

Stich (stik). 1723. [ad. Gr. στίχος row, line, verse.] A portion or division of prose or verse writing, of a measured or average length; a line, verse.

Stichic (sti·kik), *a.* 1864. [ad. Gr. στιχικός, f. στίχος STICH.] **1.** Pertaining to or consisting of verses or lines. **2.** *Pros.* Consisting of successive lines of the same metric form 1886. So **Sti·chical** *a.* (in sense 1) 1787.

Stichidium (stiki·diǒm). *Pl.* **-ia** (-iă). 1855. [mod.L., f. Gr. στίχος STICHOS + dim. suffix *-idium* (= Gr. -ίδιον).] *Bot.* A pod-like receptacle for tetraspores in some rose-spored Algæ.

Stichocrome (sti·kokrōum). 1899. [f. Gr. στίχος + χρῶμα colour.] *Phys.* Any nerve-cell having the chromophilic bodies arranged in more or less regular layers.

Stichometrical (stikome·trikăl), *a.* 1845. [f. next + -ICAL.] Of or pertaining to stichometry; characterized by measurement by *stichoi* or lines. So **Stichome·tric** *a.* **Stichome·trically** *adv.*

Stichometry (stikǫ·mĕtri). 1754. [ad. late Gr. στιχομετρία, f. στίχος STICHOS + -μετρία -METRY.] *Palæogr.* **a.** The measurement of a manuscript text by *stichoi* or lines of fixed or average length into which the text is divided. Also, a list or appendix stating this length. **b.** Occas. used for: The practice of writing a prose text in lines of nearly equal length corresponding to divisions in the sense. Also, *stichoi* collectively. 1875.

b. S. was really nothing but a cumbrous substitute for punctuation 1881.

‖ **Stichomythia** (stikomi·þiă). Also **stichomuthia** (miū·þiă). 1861. [mod.L. a. Gr. στιχομυθία, f. στίχος STICHOS + μῦθος speech, talk.] In classical Greek Drama, dialogue in alternate lines, employed in sharp disputation, and characterized by antithesis and rhetorical repetition or taking up of the opponent's words. Also applied to modern imitations of this.

‖ **Stichos** (sti·kǫs). *Pl.* **stichoi** (sti·koi). 1863. [a. Gr. στίχος STICH.] **1.** In the Greek Ch., a verse or versicle. **2.** *Palæogr.* A line of a stichometrically written text; a line of average length assumed in measuring the contents of a text or codex 1885.

Stick (stik), *sb.*[1] [OE. *sticca* :—OTeut. **stikkon-*, f. Teut. root **stik-* to pierce, prick; see STICK *v.*[1]] **I.** A rod or staff of wood. **1.** A short piece of wood, esp. a piece cut and shaped for a special purpose. **2.** A slender branch or twig of a tree or shrub, esp. when cut or broken off. Now *rare.* OE. **b.** *pl.* Pieces of cut or broken branches, also pieces of cut and chopped wood, used as fuel ME. **c.** A twiggy bough or long rod stuck in the ground for a plant to 'run' upon 1577. **3.** A stem or thick branch of a tree cut and trimmed and used as timber for building, fencing, etc.; a stave, stake. late ME. 4. A long and relatively slender piece of wood, whether in natural form or shaped with tools, cut or broken of a convenient length for handling. late ME. b. A staff, club, cudgel used as a weapon. late ME. c. (Chiefly *the s.*) A beating with a stick. *colloq.* 1856. d. = WALKING-STICK 1620. e. A rod of dignity, or office, a baton; also the bearer of such a stick 1688. The rod of a sky-rocket 1651. 5. *spec.* in various games. a. A staff for striking or pushing, as in Hockey; also applied to a billiard cue, a golf club, etc. 1674. b. Hence in Hockey, *Sticks*, the word used by the umpire in declaring a breach of rule committed by improperly handling the stick; a breach of rule of this kind 1896. c. *Cricket.* pl. The stumps of a wicket, the wicket. *rare* in *sing.* Also *Football* the goalposts 1862. 6. A timber-tree; also, a tree-trunk when cut for timber; more fully *s. of timber* 1748. 7. *Naut.* A mast or portion of a mast; also a yard. *The sticks*, the masts and yards. 1802.

2. b. Come, Hostis,..lay a few more sticks on the fire WALTON. 3. *Every s.* (*and stone*), the whole materials of a building. 4. *Cleft s.*: see CLEFT *ppl. a.* c. Come in,..or I'll give you the s. 1856.

II. Transf. uses. 1. A piece of material rolled, moulded, or cut for convenience of use into a long and slender form like that of a stick: e.g. of sweetstuff; of glass; of lac or sealing-wax 1460. 2. The stem of a culinary plant when trimmed for use, e.g. a root of celery with its blanched leaf-stems; a leaf-stem of rhubarb; a young shoot of asparagus 1756. 3. a. A support for a candle, a candlestick 1540. b. = COMPOSING-*stick* 1683. c. A violin bow, a fiddlestick 1600. d. *pl.* The thin pieces of ivory, bone, or other material upon which the folding material of a fan is mounted 1701. e. A joy-stick 1914. 4. *slang.* a. *pl.* Furniture, household goods; more fully *sticks of furniture*. Rarely *sing.* in *every s.*, every article of furniture. 1809. b. (Now *U.S.* and *colonial.*) *With a s. in it*: said of tea, coffee, etc., with a dash of brandy 1804. 5. Applied to a person, as *tough s.*, *queer s.* 1682. b. A 'wooden' person; one lacking in capacity for his work, or in geniality of manner; *Theatr.* an indifferent actor 1800.

1. Pink sticks of barley-sugar THACKERAY. 5. *Crooked s.*, a perverse, cross-grained person. Phr. (*To have* or *get*) *the right* or *the wrong end of the s.*, to have the advantage or the contrary in a bargain or a contest. Also, *to have got hold of the wrong end of the s.*, to have got a story wrong, not know the facts of the case. *To hold sticks with*, to compete on equal terms with.

Comb.: **s.-bug** *U.S.* (*a*) = *s.-insect*; (*b*) a predaceous reduvioid bug, *Emesa longipes*; **-caterpillar**, **-looper**, a geometrid larva resembling a bit of stick; **s. chimney** *U.S.*, a log-house chimney composed of sticks piled up crosswise and cemented with mud or clay; **-insect**, any insect of the family *Phasmidæ*, from its resemblance to the branches and twigs of the trees in which it is found.

Stick (stik), *sb.*^{2} *Obs.* exc. *Hist.* OE. [Origin obsc.] A measure of quantity in small eels (app. 25 or 26).

Stick (stik), *sb.*^{3} 1646. [f. next.] 1. A temporary stoppage, a hitch; a boggle. *Obs.* exc. *arch.* 2. Something which causes hindrance or delay, a difficulty, an obstacle. *Obs.* exc. *arch.* 1657. 3. The power of adhering or of causing a thing to adhere 1853. 4. A batsman who is not easily 'got out' 1863.

1. When we came at the Hill Difficulty, he made no s. at that BUNYAN.

Stick (stik), *v.*^{1} Pa. t. and pa. pple. **stuck** (stʌk). [OE. *stician* wk. vb., f. Teut. root **stik-*:—Indo-Eur. **stig-* (: **steig-*) in Gr. στίζειν, στίγμα STIGMA, L. *instigare* INSTIGATE.] I. To pierce, thrust. 1. *trans.* To stab, pierce, or transfix with a thrust of a spear, sword, knife, or other sharp instrument; to kill by this means. Not now in dignified use. b. To kill (an animal, esp. a pig) by thrusting a knife into its throat ME. c. *Sport.* To spear (a salmon). *To s. a pig*: (in India) to hunt the wild boar with a spear. 1820. 2. To thrust (a dagger, a spear, a pointed instrument) *in, into, through.* late ME. 3. To thrust, push forward, protrude (one's head, hand, etc.) *in, into, out* (*of*), *over* 1627. b. *intr.* To project, protrude. Now only const. *from, out of.* 1580.

1. Like a Storme suddenly, The English Archery Stuck the French Horses DRAYTON. 2. Thou stick'st a dagger in me SHAKS. 3. A lean old gentleman.. stuck his head out of the window 1907.

II. To remain fixed. 1. *intr.* Of a pointed instrument: To remain with its point imbedded; to be fixed by piercing OE. †2. Of things: To be fastened in position; to be fixed in or as in a socket; to be attached –1673. b. In phr. with *full, close*, expressive of crowding to the utmost. *colloq.* 1776. 3. Chiefly of persons: To continue or remain persistently in a place. Now only *colloq.* OE. b. *fig.* Of feelings, thoughts, etc.: To remain permanently in the mind ME. †4. To remain firm, continue steadfast, stand *fast*; to be determined *to do* something; to persist *in* (an opinion, etc.); to be persistently engaged *upon* –1698. b. To keep persistently *at* 1886. c. *trans.* (*slang.*) To put up with, endure association with, tolerate (a person or thing). Also *to s. it* (*out*), to continue what one is doing without flinching. 1899. 5. *intr.* Of things: To remain attached or fastened by adhesion, to adhere, hold, cleave 1558. b. *fig.* Of a fact, a saying: To abide in one's memory. Of an imputation: To be fastened upon a person. Of opinions, feelings, habits: To be fixed, not to be shaken off. 1535. 6. Of a living creature: To cling *to, on, upon*. *To s. on, to* (a horse), to keep one's seat on. Also *absol.* 1596. 7. To be set fast or entangled in sand, clay, mud, mire, or the like; similarly of a boat, to become fixed or grounded on sand, a rock, etc.; more explicitly *to s. fast* OE. 8. To become fixed or stationary in or on account of some obstruction, to be arrested or intercepted. Of a thing made to run, swing, or slide: To become unworkable, to jam. 1531. b. Of food, etc.: To lodge (in the throat) 1553. c. Of words, *To s. in one's throat*, †*teeth*: 'to resist emission' (J.) 1605. 9. Of a matter: To be at a stand, to suffer delay or hindrance 1530. b. Of a person or thing: To remain in a stationary condition, to be unable to make progress. Of a commodity, etc.: Not to 'go off'; to remain unsold. 1641. 10. To be in difficulty or trouble; to stop or stand in a state of perplexity; to be embarrassed, puzzled, or nonplussed 1577. b. To be unable to proceed in narration or speech, through lapse of memory or embarrassment 1579. 11. To hesitate, scruple, be reluctant or unwilling. Const. *to* (do something). Only with neg. Now *rare.* 1532.

1. By the light he spies Lucrecias gloue, wherein her needle sticks SHAKS. 3. I'll s. where I am, for here I am safe as to food and shelter HARDY. b. His speech stickes in my heart SHAKS. 4. c. Sergeant Chambers shouted back, 'Go to hell!' and to his men he cried 'S. it!' 1905. 5. *Provb.* If you throw mud enough, some of it will s. 1911. Phr. *To s. to a person's fingers*, said *fig.* of money dishonestly retained. b. A bad character sticks to a country as well as to an individual 1845. Phrases..which s., like barbed arrows, in the memory of every reader KINGSLEY. 7. They ranne the shippe a ground, and the forepart stucke fast *Acts* xxvii. 41. Phr. *To s. in the mud*, now usu., to remain content in a mean or abject condition. (Cf. STICK-IN-THE-MUD.) 8. c. Amen stuck in my throat SHAKS. 10. b. He always stuck in the middle, everybody recollecting the latter part excepting himself W. IRVING. 11. They will not sticke to say, you enuide him SHAKS.

III. To fix, cause to adhere. 1. *trans.* To fasten (a thing) in position by thrusting in its point ME. b. To secure (a thing) by thrusting the end of it *in, into, behind, through* (a receptacle) 1664. c. To fix on a point ME. 2. *gen.* To fasten in position; also in weaker sense, to place, set, put. Now chiefly, to place obtrusively, inappropriately, or irregularly. late ME. b. To fasten as an adornment or garnishing. late ME. c. *Joinery.* To work (moulding, a bead) with a plane fashioned for that purpose 1769. 3. To set (a surface) *with*, to furnish or adorn with on the surface, to cover or strew with ME. b. *Cookery.* To set with a garnish 1530. 4. To cause to adhere; to fasten, fix, secure (a thing) *against, on, upon, to* (a surface) by means of an adhesive, pins, etc. Also said of the adhesive. late ME. b. *fig.* To fasten (one's choice, opinion, an imputation, a nickname, dishonour, etc.) *on, upon* 1601. 5. *colloq.* To bring to a stand, render unable to advance or retire. Chiefly *pass.* 1829. b. *colloq.* To pose, nonplus 1884. 6. *slang* and *colloq.* a. To cheat (a person) out of his money, to cheat or take in in dealing; to 'saddle' *with* something counterfeit or worthless in purchase or exchange 1699. b. To 'let in' *for* 1895. c. *To s. it in* or *on*: to make extortionate charges 1844. d. *To be stuck on* (U.S. slang): to be captivated with 1886.

1. Then s. a skewer into it 1756. b. Sticking his pen behind his ear SCOTT. 2. Two pitch bals stucke in her face for eyes SHAKS. 3. My shrowd of white, stuck all with Ew, O prepare it SHAKS. *fig.* Supposition, all our liues, shall be stucke full of eyes SHAKS. b. A good piece of beef, stuck with Rose-mary 1611. 4. *S. no bills*, the usual form of the notice placed on a building forbidding placards to be posted upon it. b. His foul esteeme Sticks no dishonor on our Front MILT. 6. I'm stuck with a counterfeit note 1848. b. I'm awfully sorry I stuck you for such a lot 1915.

With preps. (*intr.*) **S. at** —. a. To scruple at; to hesitate to accept or believe, to take exception to, to be deterred by. (Chiefly neg.) *To s. at nothing*, to be unscrupulous. b. To be impeded or brought to a stand at (a difficulty). **S. by** —. a. To remain resolutely faithful to (a person) as a follower, partisan, or supporter. †b. Of a thing: To remain with, cling to (a person); to remain in (a person's) memory. c. To hold to, be constant to (a principle, one's word). Now *rare*. **S. to** —. a. To remain resolutely faithful to (a person or party), not to desert. Now chiefly *colloq.* b. To adhere, keep, or hold to (an argument, demand, resolve, opinion, bargain, covenant, and the like); to refuse to renounce or abandon; to persist in. c. To refuse to be enticed, led or turned from; to attend unremittingly to (an occupation, course of action, work, etc.). d. To keep exclusively to. e. To remain by or in (a place, etc.); to refuse to desert or leave. f. To follow closely (an original, etc.). g. To keep close to (in a pursuit or race). h. To keep possession of, refuse to part with.

With advs. **S. down.** To put down in writing (*colloq.*). **S. out** a. *intr.* To jut out, project. b. To be prominent or conspicuous (*colloq.*). c. To persist in resistance; to hold out. *To s. it out*, to endure to the end. c. To persist in one's demand *for* (*colloq.*). **S. together.** a. Of things: To adhere one to another. b. Of persons, etc.: To keep together; chiefly *fig.*, to make common cause. **S. up.** a. *intr.* To stand out from a surface; to project. b. *To s. up for*; to defend the cause of, to champion (*colloq.*). c. To offer resistance *to* (colloq.). d. To set up in position, to set up (a stake, etc.) on its own point, or (a head, body) by impalement. Also, to put up (one's hands) in surrender. e. To affix or post. f. To stop and rob on the highway; also, to rob (a bank, etc.). g. To hinder from proceeding (on a journey, in work, etc.); hence to puzzle, nonplus. h. *Austral.* To bring (an animal) to bay.

Comb.: **s.-culture**, a bacterial culture made by thrusting a platinum needle into the culture medium; **-jaw** *colloq.*, a pudding or sweetmeat difficult of mastication; **-pin** *U.S.*, a pin that is merely stuck in as an ornament; **-seed**, a plant of the genus *Echinospermum*, the seeds of which are furnished with hooked adhesive prickles; **sticktight**, a composite weed, *Bidens frondosa*, whose flat achenia bear two barbed awns; also, one of the seeds.

Stick (stik), *v.*^{2} Pa. t. and pa. pple. **sticked** (stikt). 1573. [f. STICK *sb.*^{1}] 1. *trans.* To lay sticks between (pieces of timber) in stacking them. 2. To furnish (a plant) with a stick as a support 1636. 3. *intr.* To gather fallen wood for firewood: chiefly in *to go sticking*. *local.* 1870.

Sticker (sti·kəɹ). 1585. [f. STICK *v.*^{1} + -ER.] One who or that which sticks. 1. One who sticks or stabs, esp. one who kills swine by sticking. 2. A weapon used for piercing or stabbing; as dist. from cutting or slashing; esp. a sticking-knife, a fishing-spear, an angler's gaff. Chiefly *colloq.* 1896. 3. One who remains constant; one who persists in a task 1674. 4. Something which causes a person to stick or to be at a nonplus; a poser. *colloq.* 1849. 5. A rod in the mechanism of an organ or pianoforte 1845. 6. *U.S.* An adhesive label; *spec.* = PASTER 2. 1872.

Sti·ckful. 1683. [STICK *sb.*^{1}] As much type as a composing-stick will hold.

Stickiness^1 (sti·kinės). 1727. [f. STICKY *a.*^{2} + -NESS.] The quality of being sticky; adhesiveness, glutinousness.

Stickiness^2 (sti·kinės). 1910. [f. STICKY *a.*^{1} + -NESS.] Stiffness, woodenness.

Sticking (sti·kiŋ), *vbl. sb.* late ME. [-ING^1.] 1. The action of STICK *v.*^{1} 2. *concr.* a. *Mining.* = SELVAGE 3. 1653. b. *pl.* Coarse, bruised, inferior meat; *spec.* the portions damaged by the butcher's knife 1851.

Sticking (sti·kiŋ), *ppl. a.* ME. [f. STICK *v.*^{1} + -ING^2.] That sticks.

Comb.: **s.-grass** = CLEAVERS; **-piece**, the lower

part of the neck-piece of a carcass of beef; **-place,** the place in which a thing stops and holds fast; **-plaster,** a material for covering and closing superficial wounds, consisting of linen, silk, etc., spread with an adhesive substance; **-point** = *s.-place.*

Sti·ck-in-the-mu:d. 1733. [f. phr. *to stick in the mud*; see STICK *v.* II. 7.] A helpless or unprogressive person; one who lacks resource or initiative. Also, a contemptuous substitute for WHAT'S-HIS-NAME.

Stickit (sti·kit), *a. Sc.* 1787. [Sc. form of *sticked* ppl. a. f. STICK *v.*[1]] 1. Of a task, a product of labour: Imperfect or bungled, unfinished. 2. That has relinquished his intended profession from want of ability or means to pursue it 1815.

Sticklac (sti·klæk). 1704. [f. STICK *sb.*[1] + LAC[1].] Lac in its natural state of incrustation on twigs.

Stickle (sti·k'l), *v.* 1530. [app. identical with ME. *stiȝtle*, freq. of *stiȝte*, OE. *stihtan* to set in order.] †1. *intr.* a. To act as an official regulator of a tournament, wrestling match, or the like, in order to ensure fair play. b. Hence, to act as mediator or umpire; to interpose or intervene (*between* or *among* combatants, etc.). –1692. †2. *trans.* To compose (a dispute, disputants); to stop, quell (a strife or contest) –1630. †3. *intr.* To be busy, stirring, or energetic; to strive or contend pertinaciously; to take an active part (*in* a cause, affair) –1706. †b. To strive *to* (do something) –1732. 4. S. for —. a. To strive or contend for (a desired object, an issue, principle, etc.) 1642. †b. To take the part of, stand up for (a person) –1748. 5. To make difficulties, raise objections, haggle (*about*); to be tardy in givingone's acceptance; to hesitate, scruple, take offence *at* 1819.

1. The same Angel..when half of the Christians are already kill'd..stickles between the Remainders of God's Host, and the Race of Fiends DRYDEN. 3. Oh how we can s. in our own causes! 1630. b. The Devil.. will s. to *do* as much mischief as he can among you 1680. 4. a. The plot..will..please those who s. for happy endings 1905. b. When Fortune (as she 's wont) turn'd fickle And for the foe began to s. 1663. 5. Flying for life, one does not s. about his vehicle CARLYLE.

Sti·ckleback. late ME. [f. OE. *sticel* prick, sting + BACK *sb.*[1]] A small spiny-finned fish of the genus *Gasterosteus* or family *Gasterosteidæ*. The common three-spined s., *G. aculeatus*, is found in both fresh and salt water.

Stickler (sti·klər). 1538. [f. STICKLE *v.* + -ER[1].] 1. A moderator or umpire at a tournament, a wrestling or fencing match, etc. (*Obs.* exc. *s.w. dial.*) †2. An active partisan; a (great, chief, etc.) agent, mover, or instigator –1728. †b. In unfavourable sense: A factious, seditious, or pragmatic contender; a wrangler; a busybody –1696. †3. One who fights or contends *against* (a person, cause, etc.); an opponent, antagonist; one who makes difficulties or raises objections –1846. 4. With *for*: One who pertinaciously supports or advocates (a cause, principle, person, etc.); one who insists on or stands out for (a form, ceremony, etc.) 1644. †5. A second or backer in a contest –1828.

4. Beaufort was no s. for pedantic rules 1879. 5. Their fathers were honest men and sticklers to their lawful Prince 1711.

Stick-up, *a.* and *sb.* 1857. [f. phr. *to stick up*; see STICK *v.*[1]] A. *adj.* That sticks up; esp. of a collar = STAND-UP *a.* 1. 1873. B. *sb.* Something which sticks up; *esp.* a stand-up collar 1857. b. A thief armed with a revolver who orders his victims to put their hands up; also, a job performed by this type of criminal, a hold-up; also *attrib.* (*U.S.*) 1905.

Sticky (sti·ki), *a.*[1] 1577. [f. STICK *sb.*[1] + -Y[1].] 1. Of plant-stems: Like a stick; woody. 2. *Painting.* Characterized by hardness of outline 1753.

Sticky (sti·ki), *a.*[2] 1727. [f. STICK *v.*[1] + -Y[1].] Having the property of sticking or adhering; adhesive; also, viscid, glutinous. b. *Racing* and *Cricket.* Of a course, a wicket: Having a yielding surface owing to wet 1888.

Everything s. except postage-stamps LONGF. Hence **Sti·cky** *v. trans.* to smear with something s. (*colloq.*).

Stiff (stif), *a.*, *sb.*, and *adv.* [OE. *stif*:—OTeut. **stīfo-* :—pre-Teut. **stīpo-*, cogn. w. L. *stipare* to crowd, *stipes* stake.] A. *adj.* I. 1. Rigid; not flexible or pliant. 2. Of the body, limbs, joints, muscles, etc.: Lacking suppleness, unable to move without pain ME. b. Rigid in death. Often predic. in fig. phr. *to bore* (one) *s.*, to bore 'to death' (*colloq.*). ME. c. Of machinery, etc.: Working with excessive friction; hard to move 1848. 3. Rigid as the result of tension; taut. Now *rare* or *Obs.* late ME. 4. Of a semi-liquid substance: Thick or viscous, so as to flow with difficulty or to be capable of retaining a definite shape. late ME. 5. Of soil: Heavy, dense; not porous or friable; difficult to work 1523. 6. Tight, closely packed. Now *hyperbolically* in colloq. use: Densely crowded (*with*). 1683. 7. Of a ship: Offering a high resistance to deflexion from the vertical or normal floating position; stable, not crank 1627. 8. *fig.* Inflexible of purpose, steadfast, resolute, firm, constant ME. b. In a bad sense: Obstinate, stubborn, not amenable to reason. Now *rare.* 1526. c. Of a battle, debate, etc.: Stubbornly contested, hard ME. 9. Formal, constrained, lacking ease or grace 1608. 10. Of price, charges, rates, etc.: Unyielding, firm; having an upward tendency. Hence of a commodity or the dealers in it. 1883.

1. The Gown with s. Embroid'ry shining PRIOR. With sleet and rain, ropes s., and sails half set, very squally, she works like a Cutter 1801. 2. You and I, ma'am, I think, are too s. to dance THACKERAY. Phr. *To have a s. neck*, to suffer from a rheumatic affection of the neck in which the head cannot be moved without pain. b. *S. one*, *s. 'un*, a corpse (*slang*). 4. Then work it up into a s. paste MRS. GLASSE. 8. b. S. in Opinions, always in the wrong DRYDEN. 9. Too s. a carriage of his fortune WOTTON. S. rectangular walks 1779. His diction..was..pronounced s. and pedantic MACAULAY. Several letters..directed in a s., careful..hand 1885.

Colloq. phrases. *S. as a poker*; *s. in the back*, firm, resolute; *to keep* (*carry*, *have*) *a s. upper lip*, to be firm or unyielding, esp. in bearing pain or sorrow.

II. Strong. 1. Of living creatures: Stout, stalwart, sturdy. *Obs.* exc. *dial.* ME. 2. Of natural agencies: a. Strong, violent (of wind); also applied to a steady wind of moderate force ME. †b. Of news: Formidable, grave. SHAKS. 3. Of liquors: Strong, potent. Now only of spirits and water. 1813.

2. a. The winde being contrary, and a stiffe gale 1565. 3. A good s. glass of brandy grog 1883.

III. Hard, difficult. 1. Of an ascent or descent: Steep so as to be difficult. In *Hunting*: Difficult (said of an obstacle or a tract of country presenting many obstacles). 1704. 2. That requires considerable effort; severe; laborious, toilsome 1862. 3. Of a price, demand, etc.: Unusually high, excessive 1824.

1. The next day's climb proved a stiff one 1903. 2. A s. examination in the History School 1886. 3. He naturally thought 3s. an hour pretty s. boat hire 1903.

Comb.: **s.-leaf** *Arch.*, the foliage of conventional form, with stiff leaf-stems, characteristic as a decoration in the Early English style.

B. *sb.* 1. *slang.* Paper; a document, esp. a promissory note or bill of exchange; a clandestine letter 1823. 2. *slang.* A corpse 1859. 3. *slang.* A penniless man; a wastrel 1899.

1. I wish you'd do me a bit of s. THACKERAY.

C. *adv.* Stiffly, tightly, hard, etc. late ME.

Phr. *To give it to someone* (*pretty*) *s.*, to speak severely to, to rate. Hence **Sti·ff-ly** *adv.*, **-ness.**

Stiffen (sti·f'n), *v.* 1500. [f. STIFF *a.* + -EN[5].] To make or become stiff or stiffer. 1. *trans.* To make stiff or rigid, e.g. by means of starch, or by the addition of a lining or a support 1622. b. *Naut.* To increase the initial stability of a ship; to render less liable to heel 1706. 2. To render stiff in consistency; to thicken, coagulate 1627. b. *intr.* To become stiff in consistency; to harden. Also *fig.*, to assume a more definite or permanent form or character. 1697. 3. *trans.* To make more steadfast, unyielding, or obstinate; *Mil.* to increase the fighting value of a force by the admixture of soldiers of better quality 1500. b. *intr.* To become hard or unyielding in temper 1732. 4. *trans.* To make rigid; to take away the natural suppleness or mobility of (the limbs, joints, muscles, etc.); also *fig.* to make a corpse of, kill (*slang*) 1599. b. *intr.* Of persons: To become stiff or rigid; also, to die 1714. 5. *trans.* To make (a person) formal, cold, or constrained in manner; to make (an artistic composition) pedantic, laboured, or overloaded 1763. b. *intr.* To become formal, cold, or constrained 1864. 6. a. Of prices, the market, etc.: To become stiffer. b. *trans.* To render (prices, etc.) stiffer. 1855. 7. *intr.* Of wind: To increase in strength or violence 1844. 8. Of an ascent: To become more steep or difficult 1877.

2. The polar oceans being almost continually stiffened into ice GOLDSM. b. *fig.* But gradually the favour will s. into a right 1883. 3. The Home Secretary wants stiffening 1898. 4. S. the sinewes, commune [*sic*] vp the blood SHAKS. 5. I pity Kings.. Whom Education stiffens into state COWPER. Hence **Sti·ffener,** a workman who stiffens (cloth, hats, etc.); something serving to s.; a reviving drink.

Stiffening (sti·f'niŋ), *vbl. sb.* 1614. [f. prec. + -ING[1].] 1. The action of the vb.; the process of making or becoming stiff; *concr.* a stiffened substance. 2. Something that serves to stiffen 1620. b. An admixture of soldiers of better quality 1900.

Stiffish (sti·fiʃ), *a.* 1733. [-ISH[1].] Rather stiff.

Stiff-necked (stress var.), *a.* 1526. [f. *stiff neck* + -ED[2]; after Gr. σκληροτράχηλος 'hard of neck'.] Having a stiff neck. Chiefly *fig.* of persons, with Biblical ref.: Obstinate, stubborn, inflexible, haughty.

Ye stiffenecked and of vncircumcised hertes and eares TINDALE *Acts* vii. 51. Hence **Sti·ffne·cked-ly** *adv.*, **-ness.**

Stifle (stəi·f'l), *sb.*[1] ME. [Origin obsc.] The joint at the junction of the hind leg and the body (between the femur and the tibia) in a horse or other quadruped: corresponding anatomically to the knee in man.

Comb.: **s.-bone, -cap, -pan,** the patella of a horse, the bone in front of the stifle-joint; **-joint** = *stifle.*

Stifle (stəi·f'l), *sb.*[2] *rare.* 1823. [f. next.] The fact of stifling or condition of being stifled.

Stifle (stəi·f'l), *v.*[1] [Late ME. *stuf*(*f*)*le*; cf. OF. *estouffer* to stifle, smother.] 1. *trans.* To kill by stopping respiration; to kill or deprive of consciousness (a person or animal) by covering the mouth and nose, by depriving of pure air or by introducing an irrespirable vapour into the throat and lungs; to suffocate. Also *absol.* 1513. b. In hyperbolic or exaggerated use. late ME. †2. To suffocate by immersion; to drown –1705. 3. To stop the passage of (the breath); to suppress, prevent the emission of, choke in the utterance (the voice, a cry, sob, cough, etc.) 1495. b. To make mute or inaudible through intervening space or obstructing medium 1833. 4. In various fig. uses; *esp.* to conceal, keep from becoming known, suppress (a fact, report, movement; a document, letter) 1577. 5. To smother or extinguish (a flame) 1726. †6. To choke up, impede the flow of (running water); to obstruct the passage of, absorb, quench (rays of light) –1794. 7. *intr.* To be or become suffocated; to perish by stoppage of breath. In weaker sense: To feel in danger of suffocation, to feel almost unable to breathe 1594.

1. Shall I not then be stifled in the Vault? SHAKS. b. He almost stifled her with caresses 1832. 3. He attempted to raise an alarm, but they stifled his cries 1885. b. The fog..stifled the roar of the traffic of London KIPLING. 4. Their former piety was after a manner stifled HOLLAND. This Insurrection was stifled in its very beginning 1705. The rumour may s. the truth for a short time SCOTT. Hence **Sti·fling** *ppl. a.*

Stifle (stəi·f'l), *v.*[2] 1580. [f. STIFLE *sb.*[1]] *Farriery.* (*trans.*) To affect (a horse, etc.) with dislocation of the stifle-bone. Chiefly *pass.*

Stifled (stəi·f'ld), *ppl. a.* 1643. [f. STIFLE *v.*[1] + -ED[1].] 1. Suffocated, smothered, suppressed, etc. 2. Devoid of fresh air, close, stuffy 1824.

2. We were shown into a small, s. parlor HAWTHORNE.

Stifler (stəi·flər). 1642. [f. STIFLE *v.*[1] + -ER[1].] One who or something which stifles, suffocates, etc. b. *Thieves' slang.* The gallows 1818.

Stigma (sti·gmă). *Pl.* **stigmata** (sti·gmătă) or **stigmas** (sti·gmăz). 1596. [a. L., a. Gr. στίγμα, mark made by a pointed instrument, brand, f. root **stig-* in στίζειν (:—**stigy-*) to prick, puncture; see STICK *v.*] 1. A mark made upon the skin by burning with a hot iron (rarely, by cutting or pricking), as a token of infamy or subjection; a brand. 2. *fig.* A mark of disgrace or infamy; a sign of severe censure or condemnation, regarded as impressed on a person or thing; a 'brand' 1619. **b.** A distinguishing mark or characteristic (of a bad or objectionable kind); in *Path.* a sign of some specific disorder, as hysteria 1859. **3.** *pl.* Marks resembling the wounds on the crucified body of Christ, said to have been supernaturally impressed on the bodies of certain saints and other devout persons 1632. **4.** *Path.* A morbid spot, dot, or point on the skin, esp. one which bleeds spontaneously 1661. **5.** *Zool.* and *Anat.* **a.** Each of the respiratory openings or breathing-pores in insects and other invertebrates; a spiracle. Also applied to other small openings or pores, as that of the pneumatocyst in *Hydrozoa.* (Pl. usu. *stigmata.*) 1747. **b.** The part of an ovisac or Graafian follicle where it ruptures to discharge the ovum 1890. **c.** A natural spot or mark, as one formed by enlargement of a nervure on the fore-wings of certain insects (*pterostigma*), or the pigment- or eye-spot of an infusorian 1826. **6.** *Bot.* That part of the pistil in flowering plants which receives the pollen in impregnation, of very various form, situated either directly on the ovary, or at the summit of the style. Also applied to an analogous structure in cryptogams. (Pl. usu. *stigmas.*) 1753.

1. His flinty Front my S. shou'd retain 1778. 2. Branded with the s. of illegitimacy 1882. 3. St. Frances with his inuisible Stigmata 1632.

‖ **Stigmaria** (stigmēᵊ·riă). *Pl.* **-æ**(*i*). 1845. [mod.L., f. prec., in ref. to the marks or scars on the fossil.] *Geol.* A former genus of fossil plants, whose remains are found abundantly in the coal-measures; they are now commonly believed to be the roots of *Sigillaria* and possibly other trees.

Stigmat (sti·gmæt). 1901. [app. back-formation from STIGMATIC *a.*] *Photogr.* A stigmatic lens or combination of lenses.

Stigmatic (stigmæ·tik), *a.* and *sb.* 1594. [ad. med.L. *stigmaticus*, f. L. *stigmat-* STIGMA; see -IC.] **A.** *adj.* **1.** Constituting or conveying a stigma; branding with infamy; ignominious; severely condemnatory 1607. †**2.** Marked with a 'stigma' or brand, branded -1628. †**3.** Marked with or having a deformity or blemish; deformed, ill-favoured, ugly -1827. **4.** Pertaining to or accompanying the stigmata (see STIGMA 3) 1871. **5.** *Path., Zool., Bot.* Pertaining to, constituting, characterized by, or having the nature of a stigma 1830. **6.** [Back-formation from ASTIGMATIC.] Applied to a photographic lens or combination of lenses constructed so as to correct the astigmatic aberration 1896. **B.** *sb.* [the adj. used ellipt.] **1.** A person branded as a criminal; a profligate, villain. *Obs.* (or *rare arch.*) †**2.** A person marked with some physical deformity or blemish -1633. **3.** A person marked with the 'stigmata' (see STIGMA 3) 1885. So †**Stigma·tical** *a.* 1589.

Stigmatism (sti·gmătiz'm). 1664. [f. assumed Gr. *στιγματισμός, f. στιγματίζειν to STIGMATIZE.] †**1.** Branding; *collect.* marks made by branding, or by tattooing or the like. **2.** *Path.* The condition of being affected with stigmata (see STIGMA 4) 1900. **3.** Absence of astigmatism 1890.

Stigmatist (sti·gmătist). 1607. [f. *stigmata*, pl. of STIGMA + -IST.] †**a.** = STIGMATIC B. 1. **b.** = STIGMATIC B. 3.

Stigmatize (sti·gmătəiz), *v.* 1585. [a. med. L. *stigmatizare*, a. Gr. στιγματίζειν, f. στιγματ- STIGMA; see -IZE.] **1.** *trans.* To mark with a 'stigma' or brand; to brand; also, to tattoo. Now *rare.* **b.** *transf.* To mark with a stain, scar, or blemish 1632. **c.** *Path.* To mark or affect with stigmata; to produce stigmata upon 1822. **d.** To mark with the stigmata: see STIGMA 3. 1844. **e.** To imprint as a brand (*rare*) 1644. **2.** *fig.* To set a stigma upon; to mark with a sign of disgrace or infamy; to 'brand'; *esp.* to characterize by a term implying severe censure or condemnation 1619.

1. God stigmatized him on the forehead with a letter of his own name 1737. e. Letters stigmatized in slaves foreheads 1647. 2. As to their white wines, he stigmatizes them as mere substitutes for cider W. IRVING. Hence **Sti·gmatiza·tion**, the action of stigmatizing, or condition of being stigmatized.

Stigmatose (sti·gmătous), *a.* 1840. [f. L. *stigmat-* STIGMA; see -OSE.] **1.** *Bot.* Said of a style bearing the stigma on some specified part, as along the side instead of (as usual) at the summit. **2.** *Path.* Covered or affected with stigmata 1894.

Stigmatypy (sti·gmătəipi). 1875. [f. Gr. στίγμα (here taken as = στιγμή point, dot) + -*typy*.] The art or process of printing portraits, etc. with small types bearing dots of different sizes, so as to produce an effect of light and shade.

Stilbene (sti·lbīn). 1868. [f. Gr. στίλβειν to glitter + -ENE.] *Chem.* A hydrocarbon produced by the action of heated lead oxide on toluene, and in other ways: used in dye-stuffs. So **Sti·lbin** [see -IN] in same sense.

Stilbite (sti·lbəit). 1815. [a. F., f. as prec.; see -ITE.] *Min.* A hydrous silicate of aluminium and calcium, in oblique prismatic crystals with pearly lustre.

Stile[1] (stəil). [OE. *stigel*, f. Teut. root *stig- to climb; see STY *v.*[1]] An arrangement of steps or the like, contrived to allow passage over or through a fence to one person at a time, while forming a barrier to sheep or cattle.

There was a s. to pass from this field into the next SWIFT. I can..help a lame dog over a s. 1857. *fig.* A lift over the s. at a crisis 1884.

Stile[2] (stəil). 1668. [perh. a. Du. *stijl* pillar, prop, door-post.] *Carpentry*, etc. An upright in a framing or structure, carrying a cross-piece; e.g. each of the vertical bars of a wainscot, sash, panel door, etc.

Stiletto (stile·to), *sb.* *Pl.* **-oes.** 1611. [a. It., dim. of *stilo* dagger, STYLUS; see -ET.] **1.** A short dagger with a blade thick in proportion to its breadth. **2.** *Needlework*, etc. A small pointed instrument for making eyelet-holes 1828.

Comb.: †**s. beard**, a pointed beard. Hence **Stile·tto** *v. trans.* to stab, esp. mortally, with a s.

Still (stil), *sb.*[1] 1533. [f. STILL *v.*[2]] **1.** An apparatus for distillation, consisting essentially of a close vessel (alembic, retort, boiler) in which the substance to be distilled is subjected to the action of heat, and of arrangements for the condensation of the vapour produced. Also applied to the alembic or retort separately. 1562. **2.** †**a.** = STILL-ROOM. **b.** A distillery. 1533. **3.** A chamber or vessel for the preparation of bleaching-liquor by the action of hydrochloric acid on manganese dioxide, or for the preparation of chlorine, of alkalis, etc. 1853.

Comb.: **s. burnt** *a.*, of alcoholic spirits, damaged by burning in the process of distillation; **-house**, a distillery.

Still (stil), *a.* and *sb.*[2] [Com. WGer.; OE. *stille* :—OTeut. **stiljo-*, **steljo-*, f. **stel-* to be fixed, stand; see STEAL *sb.*[1]] **A.** *adj.* **1.** Motionless; stationary; also, remaining in the same position or attitude, quiescent; *spec.* of a photograph, opp. to *moving, motion, picture.* **b.** Of wine and other beverages: Not sparkling or effervescing 1833. **2.** Silent OE. †**a.** *predic.*, of a person -1604. **b.** Habitually silent, taciturn (*dial.*) 1729. **3.** Of a voice, sounds, utterances: Subdued, soft, not loud. Now *arch.* and chiefly after 1 *Kings* xix. 12. OE. †**b.** *esp.* of music; hence of instruments, performers, etc. -1816. **4.** Free from commotion. **a.** Of water: Having an unruffled surface; motionless or flowing imperceptibly OE. **b.** Of the air, weather: Quiet. Of rain: Unattended by wind, gentle. late ME. **5.** In mixed sense of 2 and 4. Of places, times, conditions: Characterized by absence of noise and movement; quiet, calm ME. **b.** *contextually* (*poet.*) = That has become still; no longer active or audible 1485. †**6.** Of a child: Dead before birth -1607. †**7.** Constant; continued until now -1615.

1. Hah, no more mooning? S. as the Graue. SHAKS. The charmed water burnt alway A s. and awful red COLERIDGE. b. S. champagne 1858. 2. Phr. *To be (hold oneself) s.*, to hold one's peace, refrain from speaking. b. Phr. *To keep a s. tongue in one's head.* 3. And after the fire a s. small voice 1 *Kings* xix. 12. The s. voice of law and reason was seldom heard or obeyed GIBBON. b. The s. flutes sound softly MARSTON. 4. a. The deep s. Pool 1735. *Provb.* Hers was a case of 'S. waters run deep' 1895. b. But our widows sorrow is no storm but a s. rain FULLER. 5. Now came s. Eevning on MILT. She comes from another stiller world of the dead TENNYSON. b. O for the touch of a vanish'd hand, And the sound of a voice that is s.! TENNYSON. 7. *Rich. III*, IV. iv. 229.

B. *sb.* †**1.** A calm -1626. **2.** Stillness, quiet. Now only *poet.* or *rhet.* 1608. **3.** A 'still' photograph 1918.

1. There is no better sign of *omnia bene*, than when the court is in a s. BACON. 2. The s. of the night 1608.

Still (stil), *v.*[1] Pa. t. and pa. pple. **stilled** (stild). [OE. *stillan*, related to WGer. **stilljo-* STILL *a.*] To make or become still. Now chiefly *poet.* and *rhet.* **I.** *trans.* **1.** To quiet, calm (waves, winds, etc.). **b.** To subdue, allay (sedition, tumult) 1570. **2.** To relieve (pain); to assuage, allay (an appetite, desire) OE. **3.** To quiet, calm (a person's mind); to subdue (agitation, emotion) ME. **b.** To appease (anger) ME. †**4.** To lull, soothe (a child); to induce (a person) to cease from weeping -1660. **5.** To silence, cause (a sound) to cease. Also *fig.* To cause the cessation of (murmurs, complaints, etc.) late ME. †**b.** To impose silence on -1665. **6.** In occas. uses: To stop the movement or activity of 1850.

1. To s. the wilde winds when they roar MILT. 2. He tries..to s., or at least to deaden, the undying pain of his spirit 1856. 3. A turne or two, Ile walke To s. my beating minde SHAKS. 5. The monks stilled their chant SCOTT. 6. She stilled her feet 1866.

II. *intr.* To become still or calm OE.

At length the winds began to s. 1851.

Still (stil), *v.*[2] ME. [Aphetic f. DISTIL *v.*] †**1.** *intr.* = DISTIL *v.* 1. -1690. †**2.** *trans.* To exude, discharge, or give forth in minute drops -1693. †**b.** To cause to distil or fall in drops -1719. **3.** To subject to the process of distillation. Now *rare* or *Obs.* late ME. †**4.** To extract or produce by distillation -1707.

Still (stil), *adv.* [OE. *stille* :—OTeut. **stillō*, related to WGer. **stilljo-* STILL *a.*] †**1.** Without noise or commotion; quietly; in a low voice, softly -1560. **2.** At rest, motionless; without change of place or attitude. With certain verbs. OE. **3.** With ref. to action or condition: Without change, interruption or cessation; continually, constantly; invariably; always. *Obs.* exc. *poet.* ME. **b.** †*S. and anon*, †*s. an end*: constantly from time to time. SHAKS. **c.** With words denoting increase or progress: Ever more and more 1596. **4.** Indicating the continuance of a previous action or condition. **a.** Now (or at the time in question) as formerly 1535. **b.** Now (or at the time in question) in contrast to the future; as yet 1632. **c.** After as before some points of time; further. *Obs.* or *arch.* 1526. **d.** In addition; after the apparent ending of a series 1790. **5.** In a further degree; yet 1593. **6.** With adversative notion. **a.** After or at the same time with some event or condition implied to be adverse; even then 1699. **b.** Quasi-*conj.*: In spite of what has been stated or conceded; notwithstanding, yet. Sometimes preceded by *but*, or followed by *however.* 1722. **7.** *Comb.* and quasi-*Comb.* = 'always, ever'; 'now as before' 1593.

2. *To stand s.*; I paused, and my heart stood s. LYTTON. *To sit, lie s.*; I rose at six, tired of lying s. MRS. CARLYLE. 3. One generacion passeth awaye, another commeth, but the earth abydeth s. COVERDALE *Eccl.* i. 4. Howbeit these..Devise new things and good, not one thing s. SWINBURNE. b. *Two Gent.* IV. iv. 67. c. Thus s. his courage, with his toils encreas'd POPE. 4. a. For as you were when first your eye I eyde, Such seemes your beautie s. SHAKS. I wrote a similar epitaph for my wife, though s. living GOLDSM. c. Poore haue I been, and poore I am, and poore s. shall I bee 1577. 5. Next day, he heard the sound s. louder than before 1832. 6. a. For e'en though vanquished, he could argue s. GOLDSM. b. S., however, there was another extreme, which..was also to be avoided MACAULAY. 7. That s.-closed booke of secrets 1603. Your many acts of s.-continued friendship COWPER.

Stillage (sti·lėdʒ). 1596. [app. a. Du. *stellagie, stellaedsie* now written *stellazje, stellage* scaffold, stand, f. *stellen* to place + Fr. suffix *-age*; see -AGE.] **1.** *Brewing.* A stand for casks. **2.** In various industries, a stand for keeping something from the ground 1875.

Stillatitious (stilăti·ʃəs), *a.* 1656. [f. L. *stillaticius* falling in drops + -OUS.] **1.** Falling in drops. Also, †produced by falling in drops, as stalactites. †**2.** Produced by distillation -1704.

Stillatory (sti·lătəri). late ME. [ad. med. L. *stillatorium*, f. L. *stillare* to drip, distil; see -ORY[1].] **1.** A still. *Obs.* exc. *Hist.* and *fig.* **2.**

A place where distillery is carried on; a still-room; a distillery 1602.

Still-birth. 1785. [f. STILL *a.* + BIRTH, after next.] Birth of a still-born child; an instance of this. (Cf. next.)

Still-born (stress var.), *a.* 1597. Born lifeless; dead at birth; abortive Also, born in a state of suspended animation.

[His] works one and all fell s. from the press 1894.

Stiller[1] (sti·ləɹ). 1608. [f. STILL *v.*[1] + -ER[1].] One who or something which makes still, quiet, or tranquil.

Stiller[2] (sti·ləɹ). 1580. [f. STILL *v.*[2] + -ER[1].] One who distils; a distiller.

Still hunt, *sb. U.S.* 1860. [f. STILL *a.* + HUNT *sb.*] 1. A pursuit for game in a stealthy manner or under cover; stalking. 2. *transf.* The pursuit of any object quietly and cautiously 1890. So **Sti·ll-hunt** *v. trans.* and *intr.* **Sti·ll-hunter** 1831. **Sti·ll-hunting** *vbl. sb.* 1831.

Stillicide (sti·lisəid). 1626. [Anglicized f. next.] 1. A falling of water, etc. in drops; a succession of drops. Now *rare.* 2. *Civil* and *Scots Law.* The dropping of rain-water from the eaves of a house upon another's land or roof; the right or the servitude relating to this 1656.

‖ **Stillicidium** (stilisi·diŏm). *Pl.* **-cidia.** 1727. [L., f. *stilla* drop + *cid-*, weakened root of *cadere* to fall.] 1. *Civil Law.* = prec. 2. 2. *Path.* A morbid dropping or trickling 1791.

Stilling (sti·liŋ). 1604. [perh. corruptly a. Du. *stelling* stand, scaffold, f. *stellen* to place.] A stand for a cask, a gantry.

Stillion (sti·liən). 1803. [perh. var. of prec.] 1. = prec. 2. A trough to catch yeast 1826.

Still life. 1695. [f. STILL *a.* + LIFE *sb.*, after Du. *stilleven.*] Inanimate objects, such as fruit, flowers, dead game, vessels, etc., as represented in painting.

Stillness (sti·lnės). [OE. *stilnes, -nys*, f. *stille* adj.] The condition or quality of being still. 1. Absence of movement or physical disturbance; motionlessness. 2. Freedom from agitation, tranquillity OE. 3. Silence; freedom from noise; †taciturnity OE. †4. Freedom from turbulence or self-assertion -1745.

1. The s. of the Weather SWIFT. 2. On my Mind A passive s. is enjoined WORDSW. 3. Soft stilnes, and the night Become the tutches of sweet harmonie SHAKS. 4. In Peace, there 's nothing so becomes a man, As modest stillnesse, and humilitie SHAKS.

Sti·ll-room. 1710. [STILL *sb.*[1]] a. *Hist.* Orig., a room in a house in which a still was kept for the distillation of perfumes and cordials. b. Later, a room in which preserves, cakes, liqueurs, etc. are kept, and tea, coffee, etc. are prepared. Also *attrib.* in *s. maid*, etc.

A hundred years ago, every lady in the country had her still-room THACKERAY.

Sti·ll-stand. 1597. [f. STILL *a.* + STAND *sb.*] 1. A stand-still (*rare*). †2. *spec.* [After G. (*waffen*)*stillstand.*] An armistice -1819.

Sti·ll wa·ter. 1626. [f. STILL *a.* + WATER *sb.*] = SLACK-WATER 1.

Stilly (sti·li), *a.* ME. [f. STILL *a.* + -LY[1].] †1. Secret. ME. only. 2. Characterized by stillness. Chiefly *poet.* 1776.

2. The s. murmur of the distant Sea COLERIDGE. Oft, in the s. night, Ere Slumber's chain has bound me MOORE.

Stilly (sti·li), *adv.* [OE. *stillīce*, f. *stille* STILL *a.* + *-līce* -LY[2].] In a still manner; silently, quietly; †secretly.

From Camp to Camp,..The Humme of eyther Army s. sounds SHAKS.

Stilpnomelane (stilpnǫ·mĭlēⁱn). 1850. [ad. G. *stilpnomelan*, f. Gr. στιλπνός glittering + μελαν-, μέλας black.] *Min.* A hydrous silicate of iron and aluminium, occurring in thin scales, or as a velvety coating, of a black or bronze colour.

Stilt (stilt), *sb.* [ME. app. f. Teut. root **stelt-*; cf. LG. *stelte*, G. *stelze.*] 1. The handle of a plough. *Obs.* exc. *dial.* 2. A crutch. *Obs.* exc. *dial.* ME. 3. Each of a pair of props, usu. slender wooden poles with a foot-rest some distance above the lower end, for enabling a person to walk with the feet raised from the ground, the upper end being held by the hand or under the arm, or strapped to the legs 1440. b. *transf.* Applied to long slender legs of an animal, esp. a bird 1597. 4. *techn.* a. Each of a set of posts or piles on which a building (esp. of primitive construction) is raised from the ground, or which are fixed under water to support the pier of a bridge, etc. 1697. b. *Arch.* A vertical course of masonry placed beneath and continuous with an arch or vault so as to raise the springing of it above the general level, or for a similar purpose beneath or above a column 1835. 5. Any bird of the genus *Himantopus*, characterized by very long slender legs and slender sharp bills, and inhabiting marshes; a long-legged plover 1831.

3. Fen-men..who stalking on high upon stilts, apply their mindes, to grasing, fishing and fowling HOLLAND. *fig.* Ambition is but Avarice on stilts and masked LANDOR.

attrib. and *Comb.*: **s.-bird,** (*a*) = sense 5; (*b*) any long-legged wading bird, a grallatorial bird; **-plover** = sense 5; **s. sandpiper,** a long-legged N. Amer. species of sandpiper, *Micropalama himantopus*; **-shank** = sense 5.

Stilt (stilt), *v.* 1649. [f. prec.] 1. *trans.* To raise as on stilts; to elevate artificially. b. *Arch.* To raise (an arch, vault, etc.) above the ordinary level by a 'stilt' or other course of masonry beneath 1835. c. *Bookbinding.* To bind (a book) so as to make it range with one of larger size 1824. 2. *intr.* To walk on stilts 1861.

Stilted (sti·ltėd), *ppl. a.* 1615. [f. STILT *sb.* and *v.* + -ED.] 1. Furnished with or having stilts; raised artificially as if on stilts. b. *Arch.* Raised above the general level by a course of masonry beneath, as an arch, vault, etc. 1835. c. Of animals, esp. birds: Having very long slender legs resembling stilts 1869. 2. *fig.* Of (or in ref. to) language, style, or manner: Artificially or affectedly lofty; unnaturally elevated; formally pompous 1820.

2. You are taken in by that false, s., trashy style BYRON.

Stiltified (sti·ltifəid), *a.* Not in dignified use. 1820. [f. as prec. + -(I)FY + -ED[1].] = prec. 2. So **Sti·ltify** *v. trans.* = STILT *v.* 1.

Stilton (sti·ltən). 1736. [Name of a village in Huntingdonshire.] *S. cheese*: a rich quality of cheese made at various places in Leicestershire; so called from having been originally largely sold to travellers at a coaching inn at Stilton. Also *ellipt.* as *sb.*

Stilty (sti·lti), *a.* 1826. [f. STILT *sb.* + -Y[1].] 1. Resembling stilts. 2. *fig.* Characterized by stiltedness 1846.

Stimulancy (sti·miŭlănsi). Now *rare.* 1799. [f. next; see -ANCY.] Stimulating quality.

Stimulant (sti·miŭlănt), *a.* and *sb.* 1728. [ad. L. *stimulantem, stimulare*; see next.] A. *adj.* 1. Stimulating, rousing 1803. 2. *Phys.* and *Med.* a. Exciting an organ, or the organism, to increased activity; quickening some vital function or process 1772. b. Acting as a stimulus; exciting the functional activity of an organ (*rare*) 1785. B. *sb.* 1. Something that stimulates, rouses, or incites to action. Now *rare* exc. with some fig. notion of sense 2. 1794. 2. *Phys.* and *Med.* Something that temporarily quickens some vital process, or the function of some organ 1728. b. *spec.* Applied to alcoholic drinks 1865.

1. The pecuniary remuneration..is the direct and immediate s. to exertion and enterprise 1847. 2. b. The..craving for stimulants LIVINGSTONE.

Stimulate (sti·miŭlēⁱt), *v.* 1548. [f. L. *stimulat-, stimulare*, f. *stimulus* STIMULUS.] †1. *trans.* To prick, sting, afflict. HALL. 2. To rouse to action or exertion as by pricking or goading; to spur on; to incite (a person) *to do* something; to impart additional energy to (an activity, a process) 1619. 3. *Phys.* To act as a stimulus to (see STIMULUS 1, 3). Also *absol.* 1662. 4. *intr.* for *refl.* To indulge in (alcoholic) stimulants. Now only *U.S. colloq.* Also *pass.*, To be affected by alcoholic drinks. 1800.

2. To s. production by useful..labour 1832. To..s. him to fresh exertions DICKENS. 4. We were all slightly stimulated before a move was made 1882. Hence **Sti·mulating** *ppl. a.*

Stimulation (stimiŭlēⁱ·ʃən). 1526. [ad. L. *stimulationem*, f. *stimulare* to STIMULATE.] 1. The action of stimulating or condition of being stimulated. 2. *Phys.* and *Med.* The action of a stimulus. a. Excitation to increased activity, quickening of some vital function or process. b. Excitation of an organ or tissue to its specific activity. 1733.

Stimulative (sti·miŭlētiv), *a.* and *sb.* 1747. [See STIMULATE *v.* and -IVE.] A. *adj.* Having the property of stimulating; of a stimulating nature or character 1791. B. *sb.* Something having a stimulating quality. Now *rare.* 1747.

Stimulator (sti·miŭlēⁱtəɹ). 1614. [a. L.; see STIMULATE *v.*] One who or that which stimulates.

Stimulatory (sti·miŭlătŏri), *a.* and *sb. rare.* 1758. [f. L. *stimulare* STIMULATE; see -ORY.] A. *adj.* = STIMULATIVE *a.* B. *sb. Phys.* and *Med.* = STIMULANT B. 2.

Stimulose (sti·miŭlōus), *a.* 1866. [ad. mod. L. *stimulosus*; see -OSE.] *Nat. Hist.* Covered with stings or stinging hairs.

Stimulus (sti·miŭlŏs). *Pl.* **-li** (-ləi). 1684. [orig. a mod.L. use of L. *stimulus* goad, of obsc. origin.] 1. *Phys.* Something that acts as a 'goad' or 'spur' to a languid bodily organ; an agency or influence that stimulates, increases, or quickens organic activity. b. Stimulating property, action, or effect; stimulation or quickening of organic activity 1684. 2. *gen.* An agency or influence that stimulates to action or (const. *to*) that quickens an activity or process 1793. b. A quickening impulse; also, stimulation 1794. 3. *Phys.* Something that excites an organ or tissue to a specific activity or function; a material agency that produces a reaction in an organism 1793. b. Influence or effect in calling forth some specific reaction of a tissue; irritation of a nerve or other sensitive structure 1785. 4. *Nat. Hist.* A sting, a stinging hair (*rare*, and perh. only as L.) 1760.

3. c. *Psychology.* A process of stimulation or excitement which affects the area of a sense-organ (*external s.*), or which originates within a sense-organ (*internal s.*). Also *attrib.* 1894.

Sting (stiŋ), *sb.* OE. [f. next.] 1. a. The act of stinging. b. The fact or effect of being stung; the wound inflicted by the *aculeus* of an insect, the telson of a scorpion, the fang of an adder, etc.; the pain or smart of such a wound. c. The smart or irritation produced by touching a nettle or similar plant 1878. 2. A sharp-pointed organ in certain insects and other animals (e. g. bees, wasps, scorpions) capable of inflicting a painful or dangerous wound. Applied also to the fang or venom-tooth (and erron. to the forked tongue) of a poisonous serpent. late ME. 3. *Bot.* A stiff sharp-pointed tubular hair, which emits an irritating fluid when touched. †Also applied to a thorn. 1567. 4. *fig.* Something which inflicts acute pain; an acute pain or sharp wound inflicted on the mind or heart; the 'point' of an epigram or sarcasm; something which goads to action or appetite. late ME. b. *gen.* Stinging quality, capacity to sting or hurt; a (specified) degree or amount of this 1863.

2. Beware the secret Snake that shoots a S. DRYDEN. 4. The renewed s. of iealosie SIDNEY. They never worked till they felt the s. of hunger MACAULAY. b. When once collared the Yorkshire bowling lacks s. 1896.

Comb.: **s.-bull,** the greater weever, *Trachinus draco*; **-fish,** (*a*) the lesser weever, *Trachinus vipera*; (*b*) the sea-scorpion, *Cottus scorpius*; **-moth,** the Australian moth, *Doratifera vulnerans*, the larva of which is able to sting; **-tail,** (*a*) a tail tapering to a point, as in the pointer; (*b*) *U.S.* = STING-RAY. Hence **Sti·ngless** *a.* having no s.

Sting (stiŋ), *v.* Pa. t. and pa. pple. **stung** (stɒŋ). [OE. *stingan*, corresp. to ON. *stinga* to stick, stab, pierce, f. Teut. root **steng-*, **stang-*, **stung-* to pierce.] †1. *trans.* To pierce with a sharp-pointed weapon or instrument -1485. 2. 'To pierce or wound with a point darted out, as that of wasps or scorpions' (J.). Also *absol.* OE. b. *transf.* and *fig.* To inflict a sharp or mortal hurt upon. late ME. c. *slang.* To rob or cheat, impose upon 1812. 3. Of certain plants, etc.: To produce by contact a kind of rash or inflammation, accompanied with a burning sensation and itching, in (a person's skin). Also *absol.* 1548. 4. *transf.* To affect with a tingling pain, a burning sensation, or the like. Also *absol.* 1615. 5. *fig.* To affect with a sudden sharp mental pain or an access of painful emotion or irritation; to goad or stimulate *to* or *into* (action, rage, etc.). late ME. 6. *intr.* To smart 1848.

2. With doubler tongue Then thine (thou serpent) neuer Adder stung SHAKS. b. Two fired..'stinging' one man in the leg 1878. 3. A pricking of the intire skin, as if stung with Nettles 1665. 5. Remember'd folly stings JOHNSON. Stung to madness by defeat 1836.

Stingaree (stiŋgărī·, sti·ŋgărī). *U.S.* and *Austral.* 1811. [Corruption of STING-RAY.] A sting-ray, esp. *Trygon centrura* (*Dasyatis centrurus*).

Stinger (sti·ŋəɹ). 1552. [f. STING *v.* + -ER[1].] 1. One who stings; applied *fig.* to Death. 2. An animal or plant that stings 1593. 3. Something that stings or smarts, e.g. a smart blow; something that causes sharp distress; a pungent speech or crushing argument. Now *colloq.* 1576.

2. The..Nilgiri nettle, a most virulent s. 1880. 3. I wrote him back a s. 1900.

Stinging (sti·ŋiŋ), *ppl. a.* ME. [-ING[2].] 1. That stings, that has power to sting; used (often as a specific designation) of animals or plants. 2. *transf.* That produces a sharp pain or tingling smart, a burning sensation, or the like. Said also of the pain or sensation. late ME. 3. *fig.* That causes sharp mental pain or irritation, poignant; that goads or stimulates. Of speech: Biting, pungent. ME.

1. Like s. Bees in hottest Sommers day SHAKS. The common s. nettle (*Urtica dioica*) 1887. 2. Fierce showers of s. hail 1866. 3. A s. rejoinder 1885. Hence **Sti·nging-ly** *adv.*, **-ness.**

Stingo (sti·ŋgo). *slang.* 1635. [f. STING *v.* (in allusion to the sharp taste) + *-o* of obsc. origin.] Strong ale or beer. b. *fig.* Energy, vim.

Sti·ng ray. 1624. [STING *sb.*] Any fish of the genus *Trygon* or family *Trygonidæ*, esp. *T. pastinaca*. The long tapering tail is armed near the middle with a flattened sharp-pointed bony spine, serrated on both sides, capable of inflicting a severe wound.

Sti·ngy (sti·ŋi), *a.*[1] 1615. [f. STING *sb.* or *v.*] Having a sting; stinging, sharp, virulent. †Often *fig.* of controversy, etc.

Stingy (sti·ndʒi), *a.*[2] 1659. [Origin uncertain; perh. f. dial. *stinge* (:—OE. **stenge*) sting.] 1. Bad-tempered, irritable, peevish, cross. *dial.* 1787. 2. Of persons, actions, etc.: Niggardly, penurious, mean, close-fisted 1659. b. Betokening meanness; doled out sparingly or grudgingly 1849. 3. Scanty, poor in quantity or amount 1854.

1. Those virulent and stingie Pamphlets 1657. 2. Liberal in promises, and s. in performances 1770. Hence **Sti·ngi-ly** *adv.*, **-ness.**

Stink (stiŋk), *sb.* ME. [f. the vb.] 1. A foul, disgusting, or offensive smell. 2. Evil-smelling quality, offensive odour ME. 3. *pl.* Univ. and Public School slang for Natural Science (orig., for Chemistry) as a subject of study or university examinations 1869.

Comb.: **s.-ball, -bomb,** a missile contrived for the purpose of emitting a suffocating vapour when thrown among the enemy; **-rat** *U.S.* = STINK-POT 4; **-shad,** the mud-shad *Dorosoma cepedianum*; **-trap** = STENCH-TRAP; **-turtle** = STINK-POT 4.

Stink (stiŋk), *v.* Pa. t. **stank** (stæŋk). Pa. pple. **stunk** (stʊŋk). [Com.WGer.: OE. *stincan* :—WGer. **stinkwan*, f. **stinkw-* (: **stankw-* : **stunkw-*); see STENCH *sb.* and *v.*] †1. *intr.* To emit a smell or vapour of any kind; to smell (sweetly or otherwise) –ME. 2. To emit a strong offensive smell; to smell foully. (In ordinary polite use avoided as unpleasantly forcible.) OE. b. *fig.* To be offensive; to be abhorrent; to savour offensively *of* something. Phr. *to s. in* (a person's) *nostrils.* ME. 3. *trans.* To fill (an animal's earth) with suffocating fumes. Also, to drive (animals or persons) *out* of a place by stench or suffocating fumes. 1781. 4. To cause to stink ME.

2. b. The name of the vngodly shal stynke COVERDALE *Prov.* x. 7.

Stinkard (sti·ŋkəɹd). 1600. [f. STINK *v.* + -ARD.] 1. One who stinks. Formerly often as a term of abuse. Now *rare* or *Obs.* 2. A name given to various ill-smelling animals 1774. 3. A shark of the genus *Mustelus* 1883. 4. = STINK-POT 3. 1850.

Stinker (sti·ŋkəɹ). 1607. [f. STINK *v.* + -ER[1].] One who or something which stinks. 1. = prec. 1. *vulgar.* 2. A sailor's name for the giant fulmar (*Ossifraga gigantea*) and other ill-smelling petrels 1837. 3. Anything that emits an offensive smell. *vulgar.* 1898.

Stink-horn (sti·ŋk,hǭɹn). 1724. [f. STINK *sb.* + HORN *sb.*] A name for various ill-smelling fungi.

†**Sti·nkibus.** *slang.* 1706. [f. STINK *sb.* + *-ibus*, Latin ending of dat. pl.] Bad liquor, esp. adulterated spirits.

Stinking (sti·ŋkiŋ), *ppl. a.* OE. [-ING[2].] That stinks; offensively smelling. b. Used as a vague epithet connoting intense disgust and contempt. Now *vulgar.* ME.

Phr. *To cry s. fish*: see CRY *v.* 5.

Special collocations: **s. badger** = TELEDU; **s. cedar,** any species of *Torreya*; **s. ill,** a disease of sheep. **s. polecat,** one of the skunks or *Mustelidæ*; **s. yew** = *s. cedar*. Hence **Sti·nkingly** *adv.*

Sti·nk-pot. 1665. [f. STINK *sb.* + POT *sb.*, after Du. *stinkpot.*] †1. A pot or jar containing a disinfectant. 2. A hand-missile charged with combustibles emitting a suffocating smoke, used in boarding a ship for effecting a diversion while the assailants gain the deck 1669. 3. A sailor's name for a petrel 1865. 4. The musk turtle, *Cinosternum odoratum* or *Aromochelys odorata* 1844.

Sti·nkstone. 1804. [f. STINK *sb.* + STONE *sb.*, after G. *stinkstein.*] *Min.* A name given to various limestones which give out a fetid odour on being scratched or struck.

Sti·nkweed. 1793. [f. STINK *sb.* + WEED *sb.*] a. The cruciferous plant *Diplotaxis muralis.* b. *U.S.* The Thorn Apple, *Datura Stramonium.*

Sti·nkwood. 1731. [f. STINK *sb.* + WOOD *sb.*] A name given in certain colonies to various trees, the wood of which has an unpleasant odour; the wood of any of these trees.

Stint (stint), *sb.*[1] ME. [f. STINT *v.*] I. The action of STINT *v.* †1. Cessation of action or motion, pause, –1613. 2. Limitation, restriction, esp. excessive restriction in the supply of the necessaries or comforts of life; the condition of being kept scantily supplied 1593.

1. Phr. *To make a s.*, to stop. 2. Phr. *Without s.*, with no fixed limit of amount, unstintedly; His.. children had money lavished on them without s. 1876.

II. Limited or fixed amount. 1. An allotted amount or measure; an allowance. Now *rare* or *Obs.* 1447. 2. A measure, rate, gauge of amount, price, size, etc. fixed by authority. Chiefly in the phrases *to set*, etc. *at one s.*, *to appoint, set a s. Obs.* or *dial.* 1485. 3. The limited number of cattle, according to kind, allotted to each definite portion into which pasture or common land is divided, or to each person entitled to the right of common pasturage; also, the right of pasturage according to the fixed rate 1437. 4. An allotted portion of work; a definite task 1530. †5. Prescribed, destined, or customary limit 1509.

1. Phr. *One's s.*, an amount which one has resolved not to exceed; My s. [of wine] in company is a pint at noon, and half as much at night SWIFT. 2. A child's s...for braiding nets..is four-pence a day 1794. 4. Their stent was mair than they cou'd well mak out 1789. 5. Every one of our passions and affections hath its natural s. and bound 1729.

Stint (stint), *sb.*[2] 1466. [Origin obsc.] Any one of the smaller Sandpipers (genus *Tringa*), esp. the Dunlin.

Stint (stint), *v.* [OE. *styntan* to blunt, dull :—OTeut. **stuntjan*, f. **stunto-* STUNT *a.*] I. To cut short, stop. 1. *intr.* To cease action; to desist, forbear. Now only *arch.* and *dial.* ME. †2. Of processes, conditions, impersonal agencies: To cease, abate, come to an end –1681. 3. To cease moving, pause in a journey, to halt, stop ME. †4. *trans.* To cause (a person) to cease action, to cause to desist –1653. 5. To discontinue (an action); to hold in check, restrain (one's own actions or organs of action). Now *arch.* and *dial.* ME. †6. To cause to cease, check, stop (an event or state of affairs, actions of others) –1763. †b. To assuage, quench (grief, pain, appetite) –1666. 7. To cause (a fluid, etc.) to stop flowing or emanating; esp. to staunch (blood). *Obs.* exc. *dial.* late ME. 8. To check the growth of (an animal, plant); to arrest (growth); to force (a plant) *into* bloom by restricting its supply of nourishment 1735.

1. Pretty foole it stinted, and said I SHAKS. 2. Ther saw I how the tempest stent CHAUCER. 3. But come on, what s. ye for? SCOTT. 5. We must not. s. Our necessary actions, in the feare To cope malicious Censurers SHAKS. 8. The laborious Chace Shall s. his [a young hound's] growth 1735.

II. To limit, apportion, or appoint definitely. 1. *trans.* To set bounds to, to limit in extent or scope, to confine to certain limits. Now *rare.* 1513. 2. To limit (the pasturage of common land) to a certain number of cattle; also, to assign a limited right of pasturage to (a person). late ME. 3. To restrict (a person, his share or right) with respect to quantity or number; to limit in amount of allowance or indulgence 1567. 4. To limit unduly in supply; to keep on short allowance, to scant. Const. of. 1722. b. To limit (a supply) unduly; to give in scanty measure 1838. 5. *dial.* To apportion a 'stint' of work to (a person); also, to fix upon a definite portion of work as a stint 1794. 6. *pass.* Of a mare: To be served (by a horse). Also of a ewe: To conceive. 1823.

1. The law of nations does not s. the right of executing justice 1863. 3. We ought to s. our selves in our most lawful Satisfactions ADDISON. 4. They s. themselves in their meals 1885. Hence **Stinted** *ppl. a.* **Sti·nted-ly** *adv.*, **-ness. Sti·nter,** one who or something which stints.

Stintless (sti·ntlės), *a.* 1587. [f. STINT *sb.*[1] + -LESS.] †1. That may not be stinted or caused to cease; that may not be assuaged or satisfied –1657. 2. Supplied without stint 1844.

1. See heere. The lasting panges: the stintlesse greefes the teares 1587. 2. S. charity RUSKIN.

Stipe (stəip). 1785. [a. F., ad. L. *stipes* (*stipit-*) log, post, tree-trunk.] 1. *Bot.* A footstalk; = STIPES 1. 2. *Anat.* 'A stem: applied to two branches, anterior and posterior, of the zygal or paroccipital fissure of the brain' 1891. 3. *Zool.* = STIPES 2. 1891.

Stipend (stəi·pend), *sb.* late ME. [a. OF. *stipende, stipendie*, ad. L. *stipendium*, f. *stipem* money payment, wages, alms, f. *pendere* to weigh, (hence) to pay.] 1. The pay of a soldier. Now *rare.* 2. A salary or fixed periodical payment, made (annually or at shorter intervals) to a clergyman, teacher, or public official, in requital of his services. late ME. †3. *gen.* Payment for services, wages –1863. 4. A fixed periodical payment of any kind, e.g. a pension or allowance, †a tax 1545.

1. Cicero..earned under the auspices of Strabo his first and only 's.' 1875. 2. The s. of the teacher was precarious enough 1883. 3. For the s. and wages of sin is death 1629. The boys are generally taken away from school as soon as they are able to earn some small s. 1856. 4. Hiring is always for a price, a s., or additional recompense BLACKSTONE. Hence †**Sti·pend** *v. trans.* to provide with a s., salary, or pension. **Sti·pendless** *a.* that has no s.

†**Stipendary,** *a.* and *sb.* 1530. [f. prec. + -ARY.] = next –1660.

Stipendiary (stəipe·ndiări, stip-), *a.* and *sb.* 1545. [ad. L. *stipendiarius*, f. *stipendium* STIPEND; see -ARY.] A. *adj.* 1. That receives a stipend. Of a soldier (now *rare*): Serving for pay, mercenary. 2. Pertaining to a stipend or stipends; of the nature of a stipend. Also of services: Paid for by a stipend. 1659.

1. To make the king a mere s. officer STUBBS. *S. magistrate*, in England, a salaried official exercising judicial functions similar to those exercised by the unpaid justices of the peace. 2. His application for an augmented s. grant 1844.

B. *sb.* One who receives a stipend; a salaried clergyman or teacher; †a pensioner 1584. b. A stipendiary magistrate 1875.

I know but three ways of living in society: you must be either a beggar, a robber, or a s. 1849.

Stipendiate (stəipe·ndieᵢt), *v.* Now *rare* or *Obs.* 1656. [f. L. *stipendiat-*, *stipendiari* to be in receipt of pay.] *trans.* To pay a stipend to.

‖**Stipes** (stəi·pīz). *Pl.* **stipites** (sti·pitīz). 1760. [L.] 1. *Bot.* A stalk, esp. of some special kind, other than an ordinary leaf- or flower-stalk; e.g. one supporting a carpel or other part of a flower, or the pappus of the 'seed' or fruit of some composites; that of the frond of a fern or sea-weed (also, the stem or caudex of a tree-fern); that supporting the pileus or cap of certain fungi. 2. *Zool.* A part or organ resembling a stalk; *esp.* the footstalk or second joint of the maxilla of an insect; also applied to certain parts of the mouth-appendages in myriapods 1826.

Stipiform (stəi·pifǭɹm), *a.* 1821. [ad. mod. L. *stipiformis*, f. L. *stipi-*, *stips*, collateral f. *stipit-* STIPES; see -FORM.] *Bot.* and *Zool.* Having the form or character of a stipe: applied esp. to the stems of certain dicotyledonous trees, of simple structure like those of lower classes.

Stipitate (sti·pitēɪt), *a.* 1785. [ad. mod.L. *stipitatus*, f. L. *stipit-* STIPES; see -ATE ².] *Bot.* and *Zool.* Having or furnished with a stipes or stipe; stalked.

Stipitiform (sti·pitifǭɹm), *a.* 1859. [ad. mod.L. *stipitiformis*, f. L. *stipit-* STIPES; see -FORM.] *Bot.* and *Zool.* = STIPIFORM.

Stipple (sti·p'l), *sb.* 1669. [In sense 1 prob. a. Du. *stippel*, dim. of *stip* point; in sense 2 f. next.] †1. *pl.* Dots or small spots, used in shading a painting, engraving, etc. 2. The method of painting, engraving, etc. by means of dots or small spots, so as to produce gradations of tone; the effect so produced; dotted work done with the point of a brush, a pencil, or a graver. Also *transf.* applied to natural appearances resembling this. b. In full *s. engraving*: An engraving thus produced 1864.

Stipple (sti·p'l), *v.* 1675. [a. Du. *stippelen*, freq. of *stippen* to prick, speckle, f. *stip* a point.] 1. *trans.* To paint, engrave, or otherwise design in dots; to produce gradations of shade or colour in a design by means of dots or small spots. Also *intr.* or *absol.* 2. *transf.* in ref. to natural processes or effects resembling this kind of painting or engraving 1774.

2. The Virginia-creeper stipples the church walls with green in summer and..scarlet in winter 1894.

‖ **Stipula** (sti·piŭlă). *Pl.* **-læ** (lī), **-las** (lăz). 1762. [mod.L. use of L. *stipula* straw, STUBBLE.] *Bot.* and *Ornith.* = STIPULE *sb.*

Stipulaceous (stipiŭlēɪ·ʃəs), *a.* 1760. [f. mod.L. *stipulaceus*, f. *stipula*; see -ACEOUS.] Of the nature of or composed of stipules; having large stipules.

Stipulant (sti·piŭlănt). 1880. [ad. L. *stipulantem.*] *Rom. Law.* = STIPULATOR 1.

Stipular (sti·piŭlăɹ), *a.* 1793. [ad. mod.L. *stipularis*; see STIPULA and -AR.] *Bot.* Of, belonging to, or furnished with stipules; situated on, near, or in the place of a stipule. Hence **Sti·pulary** *a. Bot.* occupying the place of stipules; formed of stipules.

Stipulate (sti·piŭlĕt), *a.* 1776. [ad. mod. L. *stipulatus*, f. STIPULA; see -ATE ².] *Bot.* Having stipules; with scales that are degenerate stipules.

Stipulate (sti·piŭlēɪt), *v.* 1624. [f. L. *stipulat-*, *stipulari*, of doubtful origin.] 1. *intr.* a. *Rom. Law.* To make an oral contract in the verbal form (of question and answer) necessary to give it legal validity. Said *spec.* of the party who asks the question 1656. †b. *gen.* To contract, make a bargain settle terms, covenant (*with* a person or persons) -1785. 2. *trans.* Of an agreement, or of both contracting parties: To specify (something) as an essential part of the contract 1645. 3. Of one of the parties to an agreement, or a person making an offer: To require or insist upon (something) as an essential condition. Now only with clause or inf. as obj. 1685. 4. *intr.* To make an express demand *for* something as a condition of agreement 1790. 5. *trans.* To promise, give surety for, guarantee. Now only (somewhat *rare*) with clause or inf. as obj. 1737.

1. a. That mutes can neither s. nor promise is quite plain 1880. 2. The marriage-contract..stipulates a dowry of twelve ounces of gold and twenty camels GIBBON. 3. All I s., is to know the day SCOTT. 4. I had stipulated for ten minutes' sleep on reaching the summit TYNDALL.

Stipulation¹ (stipiŭlēɪ·ʃən). 1552. [a. L. *stipulationem*, f. *stipulari* STIPULATE *v.*; see -ATION.] The action or an act of stipulating. †1. An engagement or undertaking to do something -1719. †2. A contract, agreement, treaty -1818. b. *Rom. Law.* The action of making a contract or agreement in the verbal forms legally binding; a contract or agreement so made 1623. 3. A giving security for the performance of an undertaking. (Now only in the language of the Admiralty Courts.) 1648. 4. The action of specifying as one of the terms of a contract or agreement; a formulated term or condition of a contract or agreement 1750. 5. The action of stipulating for something as a condition of agreement; an instance of this; a condition stipulated for 1792.

4. Next follow the terms or stipulations..upon which the grant is made BLACKSTONE. 5. Pensions were thrown about indiscriminately...The only s. was, 'Give us your vote'. 1792.

Stipulation² (stipiŭlēɪ·ʃən). 1760. [ad. mod.L. *stipulationem*; see STIPULA and -ATION.] *Bot.* The arrangement of the stipules.

Stipulator (sti·piŭlēɪtəɹ). 1610. [a. L., f. *stipulari.*] *Roman Law.* The person who asks the question (see STIPULATE *v.* 1 a) 1611.

Stipulatory (sti·piŭlĕtəri), *a.* Now *rare.* 1658. [ad. mod.L. *stipulatorius*, f. *stipulari*; see -ORY ².] Of the nature of or characterized by stipulation.

Stipule (sti·piŭl), *sb.* 1793. [a. F., ad. mod.L. STIPULA.] 1. *Bot.* A lateral appendage (often resembling a small leaf or scale) borne in pairs upon the leaf-base of certain plants. 2. *Ornith.* A newly sprouted feather; a pin-feather 1891. Hence **Sti·puled** *a.* furnished with stipules, stipulate.

Stir (stəɹ), *sb.*¹ late ME. [f. STIR *v.*] The action or an act of stirring. 1. Movement, regarded as an interruption of rest; slight or momentary movement; movement of disturbance, agitation 1470. 2. Active or energetic movement of a number of persons (or animals); bustle, activity 1586. 3. Commotion, disturbance, tumult; general excitement; fuss. Now usu. with *a*; the pl. was formerly common, esp. in the sense 'publick disturbance, tumultuous disorder' (J.), riot, insurrection. late ME. 4. *fig.* Movement of feeling or thought; emotion; intellectual activity 1563. 5. An act of stirring something; *fig.* a rousing 1818.

1. No s. in the air, no s. in the sea SOUTHEY. 2. Above the smoak and stirr of this dim spot, Which men call Earth MILT. 3. For one slight trespass all this s.? COWPER. 4. *Cymb.* I. iii. 12.

Stir (stəɹ), *sb.*² *slang.* 1851. A prison.

Stir (stəɹ), *v.* Infl. **stirred** (stəɹd), **stirring** (stə·riŋ). [OE. *styrian* :—OTeut. **sturjan*, related to **sturiz*, disturbance.] I. *trans.* 1. To move, set in motion; *esp.* to give a slight or tremulous movement to; to shake, agitate. b. To move (a limb); now almost always, in neg. expressions, to make any or the slightest movement with ME. c. To move (something) from its place; to shift, displace. Chiefly (now always) with negative or its equivalent (implying ineffectual effort): (to be unable) to move or shift in the slightest degree. Now *rare* or *Obs.* OE. d. To rouse or disturb with a push 1590. 2. *refl.* To move oneself or one's limbs; to take bodily exercise; to move from one's place. Now *rare* or *Obs.* OE. 3. To agitate with the hand or an implement so as to alter the relative position of the parts of: a. a liquid; *esp.* to agitate with a more or less circular continuous movement, as with a spoon OE. b. a collection of solid bodies or particles; *esp.* to poke (burning coals, a fire) so as to promote combustion ME. c. Soil or earth, as with an agricultural implement. Also *absol.* 1483. 4. *fig.* To move from a fixed or quiet condition; to disturb, trouble, molest; to put into tumult or confusion; to upset. *Obs.* exc. *dial.* OE. 5. To rouse from rest or inaction ME. 6. To move to action, urge, incite, instigate, stimulate. Also formerly: To prompt, induce, persuade. OE. 7. To excite to feeling, emotion, or passion; to move, affect ME. b. To move strongly (a person, his spirit, 'blood', etc.) 1489. 8. To excite, occasion (passion, anger, †laughter, etc.) OE. 9. To bring into notice or debate; to move, raise, moot (a subject or question). Now *rare.* OE.

1. The shrill sea-wind, whose breath idly stirred My hair SHELLEY. b. Unable to arise, or foote or hand to styre SPENSER. 'I will not s. a foot', said the Countess, obstinately SCOTT. *To s. one's stumps*: see STUMP *sb.*¹ 1 c. 3. a. Idly stirring her little cup of black coffee 1905. b. Seizing the poker and stirring the fire vigorously 1888. 5. Follow forth your own..objects, without stirring a nest of hornets SCOTT. 6. An Ate, stirring him to bloud and strife SHAKS. Can ye not s. his mind to any pastimes? SCOTT. 7. The story of a great man's life still stirs the heart 1889. 8. A fault which stirs the critic's rage 1760. 9. That..a doubt once decided may be stirred no more PALEY.

II. *intr.* †1. To move; to be in motion; *spec.* to move as a living being -1633. 2. To pass from rest to motion, to begin to move; to move at all or in the least (chiefly with neg.); *occas.* to show signs of life or consciousness (after sleep or a faint) OE. b. To go out (from a house or place of abode); almost always with neg. 1567. c. *fig.* To begin to show signs of 'life' or activity (as an intellectual movement or the like) 1873. 3. To move about in a place, to 'be about'; chiefly in *pres. pple.* (often *spec.* = out of bed, up and about) ME. b. *transf.* To be in circulation, be current; chiefly in *pres. pple.* Now somewhat *rare.* late ME. c. To go on, happen, take place; chiefly in *pres. pple.* = going on, 'on foot' 1526. 4. To move briskly or energetically; to be on the move, bestir oneself ME. b. *fig.* To be active or occupied *about* something; to begin to act ME. c. To rise in revolt or insurrection. Now *rare* and merely contextual. ME. 5. To be roused or excited, as feeling, passion, etc. OE.

1. While rocks stand, And rivers stirre G. HERBERT. 2. Not a Mouse stirring SHAKS. b. I came home at seven, and have never stirred out SWIFT. 3. When no one in the house was stirring, and the lights were all extinguished DICKENS. b. He asked..if there were any news stirring 1850. c. No ill luck stirring but what lights a my shoulders SHAKS. 4. Her husband stirred and bustled about until the requisite leave was obtained THACKERAY. 5. My Blood stirs at the very thought on 't CIBBER.

Stir up. a. *trans.* To set in motion, agitate; to push or poke so as to displace, disturb, or mix the parts of. b. To rouse to action, activity, or emotion; to incite, instigate, stimulate. c. To excite, provoke, induce; to raise, set on foot (strife, disturbance, etc.); to arouse (feeling or emotion).

Stirabout (stə·răbaut). 1682. [See STIR *v.* and ABOUT *adv.*] 1. a. Porridge made by stirring oatmeal, etc. in boiling water or milk. (orig. *Anglo-Irish.*) b. *fig.* A bustle, a state of confusion 1905. 2. A bustling person 1870.

Stire (stəiəɹ). 1483. [Origin obsc.] A kind of cider apple; also, the cider made from it.

Stirk (stəɹk). *dial.* [OE. *stirc*, *stiorc*, app. a dim. f. *stéor* STEER *sb.*¹ + *-ic*, a var. of *-oc*, *-uc*; see -OCK.] 1. A young bullock or heifer, usu. between one and two years old. 2. Used as a term of abuse: a foolish person 1590.

Stirless (stə·ɹlės), *a.* 1816. [f. STIR *sb.* and *v.* + -LESS.] Not stirring, motionless.

Mountains..s. as death CARLYLE.

Stirp (stəɹp). 1502. [ad. L. *stirpem* stock, stem.] 1. The stock of a family; a line of descent; the descendants of a common ancestor. Now somewhat *rare.* 2. *Eugenics.* The total of the germs which are found in the newly fertilized ovum 1875.

Stirpiculture (stə·ɹpikɒltiŭɹ, -tʃəɹ). 1870. [f. L. *stirpi-* STIRP + *cultura* CULTURE *sb.*] The production of pure races or stocks by careful breeding. Hence **Stirpicu·ltural** *a.* **Stirpicu·lturist.**

‖**Stirps** (stəɹps). *Pl.* **stirpes** (stə·ɹpīz). 1681. [L.] 1. *Law.* A branch of a family; the person who with his descendants forms a branch of a family. Chiefly in L. phr. *per stirpes*; also *in stirpes.* 2. *Zool.* Used variously (often vaguely) as a term of classification; a family, subfamily, group, etc. 1863.

Stirrer (stə·rəɹ). late ME. [f. STIR *v.* + -ER ¹.] One who or something which stirs; an instigator; †an agitator; one who moves about; an active person; an instrument or appliance for stirring a liquid or the like.

Stirring (stə·riŋ), *ppl. a.* OE. [f. STIR *v.* + -ING ².] That stirs; that is in motion, or capable of motion; active; energetic in action; that excites or incites.

S. times for you English LYTTON. Cheerful and s. music 1873. Hence **Sti·rringly** *adv.*

Stirrup (sti·rɒp), *sb.* [OE. *stigráp*, f. *stig-*, wk. grade of *stīgan* to rise, climb + *ráp* ROPE *sb.*] 1. A contrivance suspended from the side of a saddle to serve as a support for the foot of the rider; now, an arched piece of metal (rarely of wood, leather, etc.) closed by a flat plate to receive the sole of the boot. 2.

Applied to various kinds of foot-rest analogous to the stirrup, e.g. in *Shoemaking*. late ME. **3.** *Anat.* = STAPES 1615. **4.** Something shaped like a stirrup; e.g. a U-shaped clamp or support ME. **5.** *Naut.* One of the ropes supporting the foot-ropes 1495.

1. Instead of stirrups we had ropes tied with a loope to put our feete in EVELYN. Phr. *To hold the s.*, lit. in helping a person to mount, esp. as a manifestation of homage or reverence; hence *fig.* to be subservient.

attrib. and *Comb.*: **s.-bone** = sense 3; **-cup**, a cup of wine or other drink taken by one already on horseback setting out for a journey; a parting drink; **-iron** (now *rare*), the metal portion of a stirrup, as dist. from the strap; **-leather**, the leather strap by which a stirrup hangs from the saddle; **-vase** [misrendering of G. *bügelkanne*, formed after *bügeleisen* flat-iron], *Archæol.* a 'pseudamphora' with a square-cut handle on either side of the false spout.

Stirrup (sti·rŏp), *v.* 1610. [f. prec.] **1.** *trans.* To supply with or as with stirrups. **2.** To flog with a stirrup-leather or with a shoemaker's stirrup. *slang.* 1735. **3.** *Naut.* To attach stirrups to 1748.

Stitch (stitʃ), *sb.*¹ [OE. *stice* :—OTeut. **stikiz*, f. **stik-*, root of STICK *v.*] **I.** A thrust, stab. †**1.** A prick, puncture, or stab, inflicted by a pointed instrument. OE. only. **2.** A sharp sudden local pain, like that produced by the thrust of a pointed weapon; esp. (now only) an acute spasmodic pain in the intercostal muscles, called more fully *a s. in the side* OE. †**3.** *fig.* A grudge, dislike, spite -1679.

2. If you..will laughe your selues into stitches, follow me SHAKS. The agonising s. of pleurisy 1898.

II. A movement in sewing or the like. **1. a.** Each of the movements of a threaded needle in and out of a fabric which is being sewn. Also, a like movement with the awl in shoemaking. ME. **b.** The portion or loop of thread or yarn left in the material as a result of this movement, and forming the means by which the parts of the sewn materials are held together. late ME. **c.** In machine sewing, a single motion of a needle and shuttle carrying the thread through the fabric; the loop or interlocked thread thus produced 1844. **d.** In emphatic phrases with a negative or the like: A single movement with the needle; *fig.* a 'stroke' of work of any kind 1581. **2.** *Surgery.* The movement of the needle through the edges of a wound when it is being sewn up; each loop of thread or other material fastened in the skin or flesh as a result of this operation 1525. **3.** A single complete movement of the needle or other implement used in knitting, crochet, embroidery, lace-making, etc.; the portion of the work produced by such a movement 1599. **4.** A particular mode of using the needle or other implement, in sewing, knitting, embroidery, etc.; the kind or style of work thus produced 1624. **5.** A loop of thread or yarn as an ultimate constituent of a sewn or woven material; hence, the least piece of fabric or clothing 1500. **6.** *A good s.*: a considerable distance (in walking). *dial.* 1684.

1. *Proverb.* A s. in time saves nine. **b.** A s. or two had broke out in the gathers of my stock STERNE. **d.** He never will do a s. of work before Wednesday morning 1768. 3. Phr. *To drop, take up a s.* 4. While she is engaged in teaching them a new s. JOHNSON. BACK-, CHAIN-, CROSS-, FEATHER-, HEM-S.; see these words; also LOCK *sb.*², etc. 5. I haven't a dry s. on my back! 1883. *Every s.*, all the clothes one is wearing; every available piece (of sail); A boat.. with every s. of canvas set DISRAELI. 6. You have gone a good s., you may well be a weary BUNYAN.

Stitch (stitʃ), *sb.*² Now *dial.* 1493. [prob. orig. identical w. prec.] A ridge or balk of land; esp. a strip of ploughed land between two water-furrows.

Men at plow..that draue earth here and there, And turnd vp stitches orderly CHAPMAN.

Stitch (stitʃ), *v.*¹ ME. [f. STITCH *sb.*¹] †**I.** *trans.* To stab, pierce; *transf.* to afflict with a 'stitch' or sharp sudden pain -1620. **II.** To fasten or adorn with stitches. **1.** *trans.* To fasten together (pieces of textile material, leather, etc.) by stitches; to make or mend (a garment, etc.) by thus joining its parts ME. **2.** *Surgery.* To unite the edges of (a wound) by drawing stitches through the flesh 1580. **3.** *Bookbinding.* To fasten together (a number of sheets or sections) by passing the thread or wire through all the sheets at once 1566. **4.** To fasten or attach (something) by sewing 1530. **b.** To enclose *in* or *into* a cover or receptacle secured by stitching 1848. **5.** To ornament with stitches; to embroider 1529. **6.** *absol.* and *intr.* To make stitches; to work with a needle and thread 1697.

1. Court Ladies will..s. a Gown, to pass the time away 1709. 6. She..stitched in silence 1865.

Stitch up. *trans.* **a.** To make or put together by sewing. **b.** To close (an orifice, a wound), to mend (a rent), by sewing the edges together. **c.** To enclose *in* a cover or receptacle and secure it by sewing. Hence **Sti·tcher**, one who stitches or sews; †(*contempt.*) a tailor; a tool or machine used for stitching.

Stitch (stitʃ), *v.*² *dial.* 1805. [Goes w. STITCH *sb.*²] *trans.* To turn up (the ground) in ridges in order to cover or protect the roots of potatoes, etc.; to earth *up*.

Stitchery (sti·tʃəri). 1607. [f. STITCH *v.*¹ or STITCHER; see -ERY 2. (App. coined by Shaks.)] Needlework.

Stitching (sti·tʃiŋ), *vbl. sb.* 1521. [f. STITCH *v.*¹ + -ING¹.] **1.** The action of STITCH *v.*¹ **2.** *concr.* **a.** Stitches collectively; i.e. the portions or loops of thread, etc. fastened in the material sewn as the result of sewing. Also, a series of stitches. **b.** The thread, silk, etc., of which stitches are made. Also *pl.* 1614.

Stitchwort (sti·tʃwɒɹt). ME. [f. STITCH *sb.*¹ + WORT.] A name for *Stellaria Holostea*. Also, a book-name for the genus.

Stithy (sti·ði), *sb.* ME. [a. ON. *steði* :—prehist. **staþjan-*, f. Teut. root **sta-* to STAND.] **1.** An anvil. †**2.** *Anat.* = INCUS 1 (*rare*) -1615. **3.** A forge, smithy 1602.

3. My imaginations are as foule As Vulcans s. SHAKS. Hence †**Sti·thy** *v. trans.* to forge.

Stive (stəiv), *sb.* 1793. [a. Du. †*stuive*, related to *stuiven* to rise as dust.] Dust; esp. the floating dust of flour during the operation of grinding.

Stive (stəiv), *v.*¹ Now chiefly *Sc.* ME. [a. OF. *estiver*.] *trans.* To compress and stow (cargo) in a ship's hold. Also *transf.* to pack tightly; to crowd (with things or people). Also with *up*.

Stive (stəiv), *v.*² late ME. [app. a var. of STEW *v.*, a. OF. *estuver*.] †**1.** *trans.* = STEW *v.* (*rare*) -1743. **2.** To shut up in a close hot place; to stifle, suffocate 1722. **3.** *intr.* To 'stew', suffocate 1806.

2. I have one half of the house to myself..while.. the two musty nieces are stived up in the other half RICHARDSON.

Stiver (stəi·vəɹ), *sb.* 1502. [a. Du. *stuiver*; origin obsc.] **1.** A small (orig. silver) coin of the Low Countries; now applied to the nickel piece of 5 cents of the Netherlands, in value about a penny English. **2.** Used as a type of a coin of small value, or of a small amount of money; occas. a small quantity of anything. *Not a s.* = nothing.

‖**Stoa** (stōᵘ·ă). *Pl.* **stoas** (stōᵘ·ăz), **stoai** (stōᵘ·əi). 1603. [Gr. στοά.] *Gr. Antiq.* A portico, roofed colonnade; *spec.* the great hall at Athens (adorned with frescoes of the battle of Marathon), in which Zeno lectured, and from which his disciples were called Stoics.

Stoat (stōᵘt). 1460. [Origin unkn.] The European ermine, *Putorius ermineus* or *Mustela erminea*, esp. when in its brown summer coat.

Stoccado (stǫkā·do), *sb.* *Obs.* exc. *arch.* 1569. [Corruptly a. It. *stoccata*, f. *stocco* point of sword, dagger; cf. -ADO 2.] A thrust or stab with a pointed weapon. Also as vb.

Stochastic (stokæ·stik), *a.* Now *rare* or *Obs.* 1662. [ad. Gr. στοχαστικός, f. στοχάζεσθαι to aim at a mark, guess, f. στόχος aim, guess.] Pertaining to conjecture.

Stock (stǫk), *sb.*¹ [OE. *stoc(c* :—OTeut. **stukkoz*.] **I.** Trunk or stem. **1.** A tree-trunk deprived of its branches; the lower part of a tree-trunk left standing, a stump. *Obs.* or *arch.* †**b.** A log, block of wood -1806. **c.** As the type of what is lifeless, motionless, or void of sensation. Hence, a senseless or stupid person. ME. **d.** Applied contempt. to an idol or graven image OE. **2.** The trunk or stem of a (living) tree, as dist. from the root and branches ME. **b.** *Bot.* = RHIZOME 1831. **3.** *fig.* **a.** The source of a line of descent; the progenitor of a family or race. In *Law*, the first purchaser of an estate of inheritance. late ME. †**b.** The original from which something is derived -1756. **c.** A line of descent; the descendants of a common ancestor; a family, kindred. late ME. **d.** A race, ethnical kindred; a race or family (of animals or plants); a related group or 'family' (of languages). Also, an ancestral type from which various races, species, etc. have diverged. 1549. †**e.** Pedigree -1657. **f.** Kind, sort. Now *dial.* 1450. **4.** A stem in which a graft is inserted. late ME. †**5.** The 'trunk' of a human body -1590. †**6.** A post, stake -1688. **7.** *pl.* An instrument of punishment now disused, in which the person to be punished was placed in a sitting posture in a frame of timber, with holes to confine the ankles between two planks (and sometimes others for securing the wrists) ME. **8.** [perh. *transf.* from 7.] A frame in which a horse is confined for shoeing 1875.

1. The magpye, lighting on the s., Stood chatt'ring SWIFT. **c.** I am not so credulous to thinke every S. a Stoicke 1640. **d.** *Phr. Stocks and stones* = gods of wood and stone. 2. Strong Stocks of Vines it will in time produce DRYDEN. *fig.* The blessid stoke þat ytt on grew Ytt was Mary, that bare Jhesu. *Carol.* 3. **a.** Hee that was the stocke of all mankinde 1594. To constitute a new s. of descent a very real possession was necessary 1886. **c.** The Crabbs were of a very old English s. THACKERAY. **d.** A population, sprung from the English s., and animated by English feelings MACAULAY. 4. He..grafted apples upon the wild stocks 1903. 7. The pillory, the stocks, and the ducking-stool 1769. fig. *The shoe-maker's stock* (joc.), tight boots.

II. A supporting structure. †**1.** A gun-carriage -1748. **2.** The outer rail of a bedstead; the side of a bed away from the wall; *pl.* a bedstead. *Obs.* exc. *Sc.* 1525. **3.** *pl.* The framework on which a ship or boat is supported while in process of construction. late ME. **b.** *fig.* esp. in phr. *on the stocks*, said e.g. of a literary work planned and commenced 1659. **4.** *dial.* = HOB *sb.*² 1. 1592. **5.** *Brick-making.* **a.** = *s.-board* -1753. **b.** Short for *s.-brick* 1738. **6.** The support of the block in which the anvil is fixed, or of the anvil itself ME.

3. **b.** Until my other Play be finished, which is now on the Stocks 1669.

III. (More fully *fulling-s.*) In a fulling-mill: orig., the wooden trough or box in which the cloth is placed to be beaten by the 'faller' or mallet; hence, this receptacle with the 'faller'. In mod. use, often the 'faller' itself. late ME.

IV. The more massive portion of an instrument or weapon; usu., the body or handle to which the working part is attached. **1.** The heavy cross-bar (orig. wooden) of an anchor ME. **2.** The block of wood from which a bell is hung 1474. **3.** The 'hub' of a wheel 1585. **4.** The wooden portion of a musket or fowling-piece; the handle of a pistol 1541. **5.** The handle (of a whip, fishing-rod, etc.) 1695. **6.** (More explicitly *bit-stock*.) A carpenter's boring tool, a brace 1688. **7.** An adjustable wrench for holding screw-cutting dies 1862. **8.** The shorter and thicker of the two pieces composing a T-square or an L-square 1815. **9.** In a plane, the block in which the plane-iron is fitted 1815. **10.** The wooden case of a lock 1833. **11.** *Flax-dressing.* One of the beaters in a scutching-mill 1776.

1. *S. and fluke* (Naut.), the whole of anything. 4. Phr. *S., lock, or lock, s., and barrel*, the whole of a thing; also *advb.*, every whit, entirely.

V. Concrete senses of uncertain or mixed origin. **1.** A stocking. Now only *dial.* 1456. **2.** A swarm of bees 1568. **3.** The portion of a tally which was given to the person making a payment to the Exchequer 1601. **4.** [Short for *S.-gilliflower*.] **a.** Any plant of the cruciferous genus *Matthiola*. **b.** *Virginia(n) s.*: the cruciferous plant *Malcolmia maritima*, having flowers somewhat resembling those of the s.-gilliflower. 1664. **5.** A kind of stiff close-fitting neckcloth, formerly worn by men generally, now only in the army 1700. **b.** An article of clerical attire, consisting of a piece of black silk or other fabric (worn on the chest and secured by a band round the neck) over which the linen collar is fastened 1883.

4. To smell the sucklins and the stocks and to see the new trees grow 1664. 5. My neckcloths being all worn out, I intend to wear stocks COWPER. The wearing of Stocks may be dispensed with on the line of March 1868.

VI. A fund, store. †1. A sum of money set apart to provide for certain expenses; a fund –1718. †2. A capital sum to trade with or to invest; capital or principal –1760. †b. An endowment for a son; a dowry for a daughter –1686. †c. *fig.* phrase. *Upon the s. of*: on the ground or basis of –1821. †3. An estate or property that produces income; a person's total property –1771. †b. The aggregate wealth of a nation –1825. †4. The business capital of a trading firm or company –1844. b. In bookkeeping by double entry, the heading (more fully *s. account*) of the ledger account which summarizes the assets and liabilities of the trader, firm, or company to whom the books belong 1588. †5. Money, or a sum of money, invested by a person in a partnership or commercial company –1710. 6. The subscribed capital of a trading company, or the public debt of a nation, municipal corporation, or the like, regarded as transferable property held by the subscribers or creditors, and subject to fluctuations in market value. Also, a kind of stock, a particular fund in which money may be invested. 1692. 7. A collective term for the implements (*dead s.*) and the animals (*live s.*) employed in the working of a farm, an industrial establishment, etc. See also ROLLING STOCK. 1519. 8. *spec.* = LIVE STOCK; the animals on a farm; also, a collective term for horses, cattle, and sheep bred for use or profit 1523. †b. Applied to slaves –1837. 9. A quantity (of something specified, whether material or immaterial) accumulated for future use; a store or provision to be drawn upon as occasion requires 1638. 10. The aggregate of goods, or of some specified kind of goods which a trader has on hand as a provision for the possible future requirements of customers 1696. 11. The liquor made by boiling bones or meat (with or without vegetables, etc.) and used as a foundation for soup 1764. b. *gen.* The raw material from which anything is made 1873. 12. *Card-playing.* a. In certain games, the portion of the pack of cards which is not dealt out, but left on the table to be drawn from according to the rules of the game 1584. b. The set of cards used in a particular game (whether a pack, or one or more incomplete packs) 1584. †c. = HAND *sb.* V. 1. –1657.

6. In modern British use, the subscribed capital of a company is called *shares* when it is divided into portions of uniform amount, and s. when any desired amount may be bought or sold. When there is no specific indication, *s.* is usually taken to refer to those portions of the National Debt, the principal of which is not repayable, the government being pledged only to the payment of interest in perpetuity. N.E.D. Phr. (*fig.*) *To take s. in*, to be interested in, attach importance, give credence to (*colloq.* or *slang*). 9. You have not yet exhausted the whole s. of human infelicity JOHNSON. Phr. *To lay in a s.* 10. **Take s.**, In commercial use, to make an inventory of the merchandise, furniture, etc. in one's own (*rarely* in another's) possession, recording its quantity and present value. Hence *fig.*, to make a careful estimate of one's position with regard to resources, prospects, or the like. *To take s. of*, to reckon up, evaluate; also *colloq.*, to scrutinize (a person) with suspicion or interest. See also 6 above. *In s.*, in the possession of the trader.

Combs. a. Similatively (with ref. to sense I. 1 c): **s.-blind, -dead, -deaf** *adjs.*, as blind (etc.) as a stock. b. In sense VI. 6: **s. certificate**, a document issued by the Treasury, entitling the holder to a certain amount of a particular government stock. c. In sense VI. 8: *s.-breeder, -raiser, -run*; indicating an animal selected for breeding purposes, as *s.-dog, -mare*; **s.-rider** *Austral.*, a man employed to ride after cattle on an unfenced station; **-riding**, the occupation of a s.-rider; **-whip** *Austral.*, a whip for driving cattle. d. In names of birds: **s. annet**, the common sheldrake, *Tadorna cornuta*; **s. drake, duck**, the mallard or wild duck, *Anas Boscas*; **s. pigeon** = STOCK-DOVE. e. Special comb.: **s. account** *Book-keeping* (see VI. 4 b); **-book**, a book in which an account is kept of goods in s.; **-board**, the wooden board which forms the bottom of a brick-mould; **-brick**, a hard solid brick, pressed in the mould; **-company**, a company the capital of which is represented by s.; **-lock**, a lock enclosed in a wooden case, usu. fitted on an outer door; **-market**, (*a*) a place where stocks or securities are bought and sold; the traffic at such a place; (*b*) a cattle-market; trade in live-s.; **-pot**, a pot in which s. for soups is boiled and kept; **-purse**, a fund for the common purposes of a group of persons; **-room**, (*a*) a room in which reserve s. is stored; (*b*) a room in a hotel in which commercial travellers display their samples; **-tackle** *Naut.*, a tackle used for raising the s. of an anchor perpendicular.

B. *adj.* (in attrib. use only). That is kept in stock. 1. Kept regularly in stock for sale; **s. size**, a size (of ready-made garments) regularly kept in stock; used *attrib.* or predicatively to designate a person whom such a size fits 1625. b. Designating a medicinal or chemical preparation which is kept ready for use, or the vessel in which such a preparation is stored 1861. 2. *Theatr.* **s. piece, play**, etc., one which forms part of a *répertoire*; **s. company**, a company who regularly act together at a particular theatre 1761. 3. *fig.* In ref. to conventional, intellectual, or literary topics: Kept in stock for use; commonly used or brought forward in conversation, discussion, or composition; hence, commonplace, trite 1738.

3. The s. arguments against utilitarianism MILL. S. quotations from the fathers 1895.

†Stock, *sb.*[2] 1513. [a. F. *estoc*, ad. It. *stocco*, prob. of Teut. origin.] 1. A thrusting sword –1572. 2. *Fencing.* A thrust with a pointed weapon –1604.

2. *Merry W.* II. iii. 36.

Stock (stǫk), *v.*[1] ME. [f. STOCK *sb.*[1]] I. †1. *trans.* To set in the stocks; to punish by confining in the stocks; in early use, to subject to rigorous imprisonment –1694. 2. To fasten to or fit with a stock: esp. a. To fix (a bell) to its stock 1483. b. To fit (a gun, †crossbow) with a stock 1539. c. To fix the stock upon (an anchor) 1769. d. Naut. *To s. to*: to haul (an anchor) into a perpendicular position by means of a stock-tackle 1815. †3. To cover (hose) with some stronger material; to strengthen (stockings) with pieces of cloth sewn on –1691. II. To root up (trees, stumps, weeds, etc.); to extirpate by digging or grubbing; to fell (a tree) by digging round and cutting its roots 1440. b. *transf.* To pull up (stones, a fence); to break up or loosen (the surface of the ground with a pick) 1802. III. To check in growth; to stiffen. 1. To stunt, check in growth (a plant or animal). Chiefly in pa. pple. *stocked*. Also *intr.*, to be stunted in growth. *dial.* 1607. 2. *local.* To indurate (stone) by exposure to the weather 1712. IV. To supply with a 'stock', fund, or store. 1. *trans.* To supply or provide with stock or with a stock; to furnish (a farm, estate, etc.) with live or dead stock; to fill (a pond, river) with fish; to store or supply with goods, commodities, appliances, etc. 1622. 2. To lay up in store; to form a stock or supply of (a commodity). Also with *up*. 1700. b. *esp.* To keep (goods) in stock for sale 1884. 3. *absol.* To provide stock; to lay in a stock or supply. Also with *up*. 1850.

1. The Fish wherewith you s. the Waters 1683. The country was plentifully stocked with provisions GIBBON. The cellar was stocked with Rhenish Wine 1899. 2. b. Wholesale Houses regularly S. it 1888.

V. Techn. and dial. senses. 1. *pass.* Of a female animal: To be impregnated 1478. 2. *trans.* To leave (a cow) unmilked in order that she may make a good show at market 1683. 3. To sow (land) with grass or clover. Also with *down*: To lay down to grass, etc. *U.S.* 1828. 4. To cause to be cropped or eaten by cattle; to use (land) as pasture 1794. 5. a. To put (playing cards) together in a pack. b. To arrange or shuffle fraudulently. 1735.

Stock (stǫk), *v.*[2] Now *dial.* 1625. [Cf. STOCK *sb.*[2]] †1. *trans.* To strike or hit with a thrust of a pointed weapon. 2. Of a bird: To peck, peck at; to make (a hole) by pecking. Also, to root *up* with the beak. Also *intr.* To peck *away* (*at*). 1653.

Stockade (stǫkēⁱ·d), *sb.* 1614. [a. F. †*estocade*, corruption of *estacade*, a. Sp. *estacada*.] 1. A defensive barrier of stakes or piles placed across a harbour or river, around a building, village, or the like; *spec.* in *Fortification*, a barricade for entrenchments and redoubts, usu. made of timber, furnished with loopholes for gun-fire. b. *transf.* An enclosure, or pen, made with posts and stakes 1858. 2. *Hydraul. Engin.* Piling which serves as a breakwater 1891.

Comb. **s. fort** *Brit. N. Amer.* and *U.S.*, a fortified trading station. Hence **Stocka·de** *v. trans.* to protect or fortify with a s.

†Stocka·do, *sb.* 1609. [Altered f. STACCADO, as if f. STOCK *sb.*[1]] = prec. *sb.* 1. –1809. Hence **†Stocka·do** *v.* = STOCKADE *v.*

Sto·ck-bro:ker, sto·ckbro:ker. 1706. [STOCK *sb.*[1]] A broker who, for a commission, buys and sells stock on behalf of clients.

Sto·ck-dove. ME. [Cf. Flem. †*stockduive*, G. *stocktaube*. Prob. so named as living in hollow trees.] The wild pigeon, *Columba œnas*.

Stocker (stǫ·kəɹ). 1641. [f. STOCK *sb.*[1] + -ER [1].] 1. A workman who makes or fits stocks, esp. gun-stocks. 2. *U.S.* and *Canada*. An animal sold to be finally butchered, but kept as stock until matured or fattened 1881.

Sto·ck excha:nge. 1773. A market for the buying and selling of public securities; the place or building where this is done; an association of brokers and jobbers who transact business in a particular place or market.

Often with capital initials as the name of a particular building, esp. that in the City of London.

Sto·ck-fish. ME. [prob. a. (M)Du. *stokvisch*, f. Du. *stok* STOCK *sb.*[1]] A name for cod and other gadoid fish cured without salt by splitting open and drying hard in the air. b. In fig., proverbial and joc. expressions (often with ref. to the beating of the fish before cooking) 1515. c. In contemptuous address to a person. SHAKS.

b. Mute as a s. DICKENS. London is as dead as a s. MEREDITH.

Sto·ck-gi:llyflower. 1530. [Cf. Flem. *stokvioliere* 'viola lignescens'.] The plant *Matthiola incana*; so called as having a woody stem, in distinction from clove-gillyflower.

Sto·ckho:lder. 1753. 1. One who is a proprietor of stock in the public funds or the funds of a joint-stock company, etc. Also (now *U.S.*) used more widely to include the meaning of 'shareholder'. 2. *Austral.* An owner of large herds of cattle or flocks of sheep 1819.

Stockinette (stǫkine·t). Also **-et.** 1824. [prob. a perversion of the older *stocking-net*.] 1. A knitted silk or woollen textile fabric of considerable elasticity. 2. A garment made of stockinette 1837.

Stocking (stǫ·kiŋ), *sb.* 1583. [f. STOCK *v.*[1] I. 3 + -ING [1].] 1. A close-fitting article of clothing covering the foot and the leg, and made of knitted or woven material. Freq. *pl.* 2. A stocking used: a. as a receptacle for storing one's money; hence, a store of money 1873; b. as a receptacle for the presents supposed by children to be deposited in it by 'Father Christmas' (or, latterly, by Santa Claus) on Christmas Eve 1853. 3. a. A surgical appliance resembling a stocking. b. A bandage for the leg of a horse. 1875. 4. *transf.* Applied to the surface or coat of the leg (or the lower part of it) of a bird or beast, when of different colour from the body 1821.

2. a. She had a 's.' gathered to to meet the wants of an evil day 1876. 3. a. *Elastic s.*, a covering of elastic webbing worn as a remedial support for the leg, esp. when affected with varicose veins. 4. A very handsome.. bay, with a white s. on his off hind leg 1856.

Comb.: **s.-needle**, a darning-needle; **†-net** = STOCKINETTE; **-sole**, that part of the s. which comes under the tread of the foot; *in one's s. soles*, without one's shoes (cf. STOCKING-FOOT).

Stocking (stǫ·kiŋ), *v.* 1755. [f. prec.] *trans.* To furnish with stockings.

Stockinged (stǫ·kiŋd), *ppl. a.* 1608. [f. STOCKING *sb.* or *v.* + -ED.] 1. Furnished with stockings or with a stocking. 2. Of the foot: Covered with a stocking only 1862. 3. Of a bird: Feathered on the shank 1855.

Stockinger (stǫ·kiŋəɹ). 1741. [f. STOCKING *sb.* + -ER [1].] One who works at a stocking hand-loom; a framework-knitter, stocking-weaver.

Sto·cking-foot. 1766. That part of a stocking which covers the foot. b. As a receptacle for money laid by. Chiefly *fig.* 1894.

In (*on*) *one's stocking feet*, with only one's stockings on one's feet, without one's shoes.

Sto·cking-frame. 1710. A machine for producing material composed of the looped stitch used in knitting; a knitting machine.

Stock-in-trade. 1762. [Earlier †*stock for* or *of trade*.] The goods kept on sale by a dealer, shopkeeper, or pedlar. Also, a workman's tools, appliances, or apparatus.

Such charges were the standing material, the s. of every orator DE QUINCEY.

Stockish (stǫ·kiʃ), *a.* 1596. [f. STOCK *sb.*[1] + -ISH.] Resembling a stock or block of wood; esp. of a person, excessively dull, stupid, or 'wooden'.

1. Naught so s., hard, and full of rage, But musicke for time doth change his nature SHAKS.

Stockist (stǫ·kist). 1923. [f. STOCK *sb.*[1] or *v.*[1] + -IST.] A tradesman who keeps (specified goods) in stock.

†**Stock-job**, *v.* 1697. [Back-formation from next.] a. *trans.* To apply the methods of stock-jobbing to, employ in stock-jobbing -1721. b. *intr.* To practise stock-jobbing -1721.

Sto·ck-jo:bber. 1626. A member of the Stock Exchange who deals in stocks on his own account.

Sto·ck-jo:bbing, *vbl. sb.* and *ppl. a.* 1692. A. *vbl. sb.* The business of a stock-jobber; buying and selling of stock as practised by a jobber; *loosely*, speculative dealing in stocks and shares. (Often with implication of rash or dishonest speculation.) B. *ppl. a.* That deals in stocks and shares; concerned with this business or traffic 1692.

Sto·ckman. 1806. 1. A man employed to look after cattle or other live stock. Chiefly *Austral.* 2. One who raises live stock; a stock-farmer 1856.

Stock still, stock-still, *a.* 1470. [STOCK *sb.*[1]] As still as a stock or log; quite motionless.

Sto·ck-ta:king. 1858. [STOCK *sb.*[1]] A periodical examination, inventorying, and valuation of all the stock or goods in a shop, warehouse, etc. Also *fig.* So **Sto·ck-ta:ker.**

Sto·ck-work. 1839. [repr. G. *stockwerk.*] *Mining.* A deposit (esp. of tin) in which the ore is distributed through a large mass of rock.

Stocky (stǫ·ki), *a.* 1622. [f. STOCK *sb.*[1] + -Y[1].] 1. Of a plant: Of stout and sturdy growth. b. Of a root: Woody, as dist. from fibrous 1915. 2. Of a person, etc.: Short and thick-set 1676.

2. Sturdy and s. as a Jersey bull 1888.

Stodge (stǫdʒ), *sb.* 1825. [f. next.] I. A thick liquid mixture. a. Thick, tenacious mud or soil. b. Food of a semi-solid consistency, esp. stiff farinaceous food 1841. 2. a. 'Stodging', gorging with food. b. A heavy, solid meal. Chiefly *school slang.* 1894. 3. 'Stodgy' notions. *slang.* 1902.

Stodge (stǫdʒ), *v.* 1674. [Origin obsc.] 1. *trans.* To fill quite full, to fill to distension. b. esp. To gorge with food. *slang.* 1854. 2. *pass.* To be stuck in the mud, to be bogged 1873. 3. *intr.* To work steadily *at* (something 'stodgy' or tedious). *colloq.* 1889. 4. To walk or trudge through mud or slush, or with short heavy steps; also *trans.* to trample (mud). *dial.* or *colloq.* 1854. **Sto·dger**, a stodgy person.

Stodgy (stǫ·dʒi), *a.* 1823. [f. prec. + -Y[1].] 1. Of a thick, semi-solid consistency. b. *dial.* Of food, esp. of farinaceous food: Thick, glutinous 1858. c. Of food or a meal: Heavy, solid, hard to 'get through' 1884. 2. *fig.* Dull, heavy; wanting in interest, gaiety, or brightness 1887. 3. Of a person: Bulky in figure (usu. connoting stiffness and clumsiness in movement) 1854. 4. Of things: Bulky, 'fat'; distended 1860.

1. b. This cannibal meal was succeeded by s. pudding 1890. 2. The wedding was a s. affair 1904. S. sonnets to the moon 1907.

‖**Stœchas** (stī·kæs). 1548. [L., a. Gr. στοιχάς.] The plant French Lavender.

Stœch-: see STOICH-.

‖ **Stoep** (stūp). *S. Afr.* 1822. [Du., related to STEP *sb.* and *v.*] A raised platform or verandah running along the front and sometimes round the sides of a house of Dutch architecture.

Stogy (stōᵘ·gi), *a.* and *sb.* *U.S.* 1847. [orig. *stoga*, short for *Conestoga*, name of a town in Pennsylvania.] A. *adj.* The distinctive epithet a. of a rough heavy kind of boots or shoes; b. of a long, slender, roughly made kind of cigar or cheroot. B. *sb.* a. A 'stogy' boot 1853. b. A 'stogy' cigar 1892.

Stoic (stōᵘ·ik), *sb.* and *a.* late ME. [ad. L. *stoicus*, a. Gr. στωϊκός, f. στοά 'the Porch' in which Zeno lectured; see STOA.] A. *sb.* 1. One of a school of Greek philosophers (founded by Zeno, fl. *c* 300 B.C.), characterized by the austerity of its ethics and practices on account of which the name has become proverbial (see 2). 2. One who practises repression of emotion, indifference to pleasure or pain, and patient endurance 1579.

2. I..smile a hard-set smile, like a s...and let the world have its way TENNYSON.

B. *adj.* 1. Of or belonging to the school of the Stoics or to its system of philosophy 1607. 2. = next 2 1596.

Stoical (stōᵘ·ikăl), *a.* late ME. [f. L. *stoicus* (see prec.) + -AL.] 1. Of or belonging to the Stoics; characteristic of the Stoic philosophy. 2. a. Of temper or disposition, or its manifestations: Conformable to the precepts of the Stoic philosophy; characterized by indifference to pleasure and pain 1571. b. Of a person: Resembling a Stoic in austerity, indifference, fortitude, repression of feeling, or the like 1577.

2. a. He looked around him in agony, and was surprised..to see the s. indifference of his fellow-prisoners SCOTT. Hence **Sto·ically** *adv.*

Stoicheiology (stoikəiǫ·lŏdʒi), **stœchiology** (stīkiǫ·lŏdʒi). *rare.* 1837. [f. Gr. στοιχεῖον element + -LOGY.] The science of elements. a. In Oken's use: A treatise on, or the theory of, elementary substances 1847. b. *Logic.* The division of Logic which treats of its elementary or constituent processes 1837. c. *Phys.* The study of the principles of animal tissues; a system of therapeutics based on this 1875. Hence **Stoicheiolo·gical, stœchiolo·gical** *a.*

Stoicheiometry (stoikəiǫ·mėtri), **stœchiometry** (stīkiǫ·mėtri). 1807. [f. as prec. + -METRY.] *Chem.* The process or art of calculating or determining the equivalent and atomic weights of the elements participating in any chemical reaction; the science of estimating chemical elements; the branch of science concerned with the determination of atomic weights. Hence **Stoicheio-, stœchiome·tric, -al** *adjs.*

Stoicism (stōᵘ·isiz'm). 1626. [ad. mod.L. *stoicismus*, f. L. *stoicus* STOIC; see -ISM.] 1. The philosophy of the Stoics. 2. Stoic conduct or practice; austerity, repression of feeling, fortitude 1630. So †**Stoi·city**, a stoical attitude. B. JONS.

Stoke (stōᵘk), *v.* 1683. [Back-formation from STOKER.] 1. *trans.* To feed, stir up, and poke the fire in (a furnace); to tend the furnace of (a boiler). Also with *up.* 2. *transf.* (*joc.*) To feed oneself or another as if stoking a furnace; to 'shovel' food into one's mouth steadily and continuously. Also *absol.* 1882.

Stokehold (stōᵘ·khōᵘld). 1887. [f. prec. + HOLD *sb.*[2]] *Naut.* The compartment containing a ship's boilers, where the stokers tend the furnaces.

Sto·ke-hole. 1660. [Partly ad., partly tr. Du. *stookgat*, f. *stoken* to stoke + *gat* hole.] The space in front of a furnace where the stokers stand to tend the fires; the aperture through which the fire is fed and tended.

Stoker (stōᵘ·kəɹ). 1660. [a. Du. *stoker*, f. *stoken* to stoke.] 1. One who feeds and tends a furnace. 2. *pl.* Small particles of black gritty matter which escape through the funnel of a steam-engine 1899.

1. *Mechanical s.*, an apparatus for automatically feeding fuel into a furnace.

‖ **Stola** (stōᵘ·lă). 1728. [L., ad. Gr. στολή; see STOLE *sb.*[1]] *Antiq.* A long robe worn by Greek and Roman women; chiefly referred to as the distinctive dress of Roman matrons.

Stole (stōᵘl), *sb.*[1] OE. [ad. L. *stola*, ad. Gr. στολή, orig. equipment, array, clothing, hence a robe, garment, f. root of στέλλειν to place, array.] 1. A long robe. Chiefly used in translation from Gr. and L., ref. to classical antiquity; also *poet.* and *rhet.* ¶b. Some writers have carelessly or ignorantly supposed the ecclesiastical 'stole' (sense 2) to be a gown or surplice 1805. 2. *Eccl.* A vestment consisting of a narrow strip of silk or linen, worn over the shoulders (by deacons over the left shoulder only) and hanging down in front or crossed over the breast OE. 3. A woman's fur or feather garment, or the fabric collar of a dress or coat, made somewhat in the shape of an ecclesiastical stole, and worn over the shoulders 1889.

1. b. Behind, four priests, in sable s., Sung requiem for the warrior's soul SCOTT.

Stole (stōᵘl), *sb.*[2] 1455. [prob. var. of STOOL *sb.*[1]] 1. *Groom of the s.*: the title of a high officer of the king's household, ranking next below the vice-chamberlain of the household. Also †*yeoman of the s.* 2. The office of Groom of the Stole 1911.

1. Groom of the S., which hath the..benefit of being first Gentleman of the Bed-Chamber CLARENDON.

Stole (stōᵘl), *sb.*[3] 1806. [irreg. ad. L. STOLO.] *Bot.* = STOLON.

Stole (stōᵘl), *v.* 1824. [f. prec.] *intr.* Of a plant: To develop stolons.

Stole, pa. t. and pa. pple. of STEAL *v.*

Stoled (stōᵘld), *ppl. a.* 1546. [f. STOLE *sb.*[1] + -ED.] Wearing a stole (in various senses of the sb.).

The sable-stoled Sorcerers MILT.

Stolen (stōᵘ·lən), *ppl. a.* ME. [Pa. pple. of STEAL *v.*] 1. Obtained by theft. 2. Accomplished or enjoyed by stealth; secret. late ME. †3. Of time: Obtained by contrivance -1611.

Stolid (stǫ·lid), *a.* 1600. [ad. L. *stolidus*, related to *stultus* foolish, f. root *stel- to stand or cause to stand still.] Dull and impassive; having little or no sensibility; incapable of being excited or moved. Also, of actions, demeanour, etc. Hence **Sto·lidly** *adv.*

Stolidity (stǒli·dĭti). 1563. [ad. L. *stoliditatem*, f. *stolidus* STOLID *a.*] The attribute of being stolid; dull impassiveness; incapacity for feeling.

The look of complacent and pompous s. DISRAELI.

‖ **Stolo** (stōᵘ·lo). *Pl.* **stolones** (stǒlōᵘ·nīz). 1725. [L.; see next.] *Bot.* and *Zool.* = next. *S. prolifer*, the germ-stock of certain compound organisms.

Stolon (stōᵘ·lǫn). 1601. [ad. L. *stolonem*, *stolo* sucker of a plant.] 1. *Bot.* (see quot.) 2. *Zool.* Each of the connecting processes of the cœnosarc of a compound organism 1846.

1. A S. is a prostrate or reclined branch which strikes root at the tip, and then develops an ascending growth, which becomes an independent plant 1880.

Stoloniferous (stōᵘ-, stǫlŏni·fĕrəs), *a.* 1777. [See prec. and -FEROUS.] *Bot.* and *Zool.* Producing stolons.

‖ **Stoma** (stōᵘ·mă). *Pl.* **stomata** (stǫ·mătă). 1684. [mod.L., a. Gr. στόμα mouth.] 1. *Anat.* and *Zool.* A small opening in an animal body; an aperture, orifice, pore (as of a lymphatic or other vessel, an air-tube, etc.). 2. *Bot.* One of the minute orifices in the epidermis of plants, esp. of the leaves, occurring as a slit between two (or more) cells of special structure (guard-cells), and opening into intercellular spaces in the interior tissue so as to afford communication with the outer air; a breathing-pore 1837.

Stomach (stʋ·măk), *sb.* late ME. [a. OF. *estomac, stomaque* (mod.F. *estomac*), ad. L. *stomachus*, a. Gr. στόμαχος, orig. the throat, gullet, hence the mouth or orifice of any organ, esp. of the stomach, and later the stomach itself; f. στόμα mouth.] 1. In a human or animal body: The internal pouch or cavity in which food is digested. b. Viewed as the organ of digestion. Often with epithet, as *weak, strong*, etc. late ME. c. as the seat of hunger, nausea, discomfort from repletion, etc. late ME. d. as the part of the body that requires food; hence, put for the body as needing to be fed 1530. 2. The part of the body containing the stomach, the belly, abdomen; occas. (formerly often) applied to the chest. late ME. 3. Appetite or relish for food. Now somewhat *arch.* (const. *for*). late ME. b. *fig.* Relish, inclination, desire (for something immaterial) 1513. †4. Used to designate the inward seat of passion, emotion, secret thoughts, affections, or feelings -1721. †5. Temper, disposition; state of feeling with regard to a person -1610. b. With various adjs. (e.g. *bold, high, proud*) or other qualifying words 1510. 6. In various senses relating to disposition or state of feeling. †a. Spirit, courage, valour, bravery -1663. †b. Pride, haughtiness; obstinacy, stubbornness -1765. †c. Anger, irritation; malice, ill-will, spite; vexation, pique -1825.

1. Phr. *On an empty s.*, fasting. *On a full s.*, immediately after a copious meal. c. Phr. *To lie (heavy) on one's s.*, (of food) to cause indigestion. d. An army marches on its s. 1904. 2. Good crawled

upon his s. 1888. 3. Heaven send us all as good food as I have a good s. 1841. b. You cram these words into mine eares, against the stomacke of my sense SHAKS. I had no s. for more mysteries 1902. 5. b. His s. is too high for that now LYTTON. 6. a. Lustie and couragious captaines, valiaunt men of stomacke 1571. c. Others of the nobility..took s. against him 1643.

attrib. and *Comb.*: **s.-cough**, a cough supposed to proceed from indigestion; **-pump**, a kind of pump or syringe for emptying the s. (esp. in cases of poisoning) or for introducing liquids into it; **-staggers**, a variety of staggers caused by distension of the s.; **-syringe** = *s.-pump*; **-tube**, (*a*) a siphon used in washing out the s.; (*b*) a feeding-tube; **-worm**, a common intestinal round worm, *Ascaris lumbricoides*, sometimes found in the human s.

Stomach (stʊ·măk), *v.* 1523. [f. prec. Cf. L. *stomachari* to be resentful.] †1. *trans.* To be offended at, resent –1825. †b. To be offended with (a person) –1671. †c. *intr.* To take offence, feel resentment –1706. 2. *trans.* To turn the stomach of, to nauseate (*rare*) 1796. 3. To endure, put up with, tolerate 1677.

1. An Englishman would have stomached it, and been sulky JOHNSON. 3. The study of the Latin language..he could not s. 1887.

Stomach-ache (stʊ·măk,ēⁱk). 1763. Pain in the stomach or abdomen. Also *fig.*

Stomachal (stǫ·măkăl), *a.* 1582. [ad. mod.L. *stomachalis*, f. L. *stomachus* STOMACH *sb.*; see -AL.] 1. Pertaining to the stomach, gastric; of the nature of or serving the purpose of a stomach. †2. Of remedies: Good for the stomach –1707.

Stomacher¹ (stʊ·măkəɹ, stʊ·mătʃəɹ). 1450. [app. f. STOMACH *sb.* + -ER¹.] †1. A kind of waistcoat worn by men –1715. 2. An ornamental covering for the chest (often covered with jewels) formerly worn by women under the lacing of the bodice 1535.

2. Their stomatchers some were all Diamonds 1710.

Stomacher² (stʊ·măkəɹ). 1814. [f. STOMACH *sb.* + -ER¹.] *Pugilism.* A blow on the stomach.

†**Sto·machful,** *a.* 1600. [f. as prec. + -FUL¹.] Full of 'stomach'. 1. Obstinate, self-willed. (Often said of horses; also of children.) –1828. 2. Resentful, angry, malignant –1765. 3. Spirited, courageous –1809. Hence †**Sto·machful·ly** *adv.*, †**-ness.**

Stomachic (stomæ·kik), *a.* and *sb.* 1656. [ad. L. *stomachicus*, a. Gr. στομαχικός, f. στόμαχος STOMACH *sb.*; see -IC.] A. *adj.* 1. Of or pertaining to the stomach; gastric. 2. Good for the stomach 1665.

1. The author..treats..of the great s. gland 1799.

B. *sb.* A stomachic medicine 1735. So **Stoma·chical** *a.* (now *rare*) 1601.

Stomaching (stʊ·măkiŋ), *vbl. sb.* 1549. [f. STOMACH *v.* + -ING¹.] The action of STOMACH *v.*; †feeling or cherishing indignation or bitterness.

Tis not a time for priuate stomacking SHAKS.

Stomachless (stʊ·măklės), *a.* 1626. [f. STOMACH *sb.* + -LESS.] †1. a. Having no appetite. b. Unresentful –1727. 2. Destitute of a stomach 1865.

†**Sto·machous,** *a.* 1547. [ad. L. *stomachosus*, f. *stomachus* STOMACH *sb.*; see -OUS.] a. Spirited, courageous. b. Resentful, bitter, irascible; stubborn, obstinate. –1658.

Who..with sterne lookes, and s. disdaine, Gaue signes of grudge SPENSER.

Stomachy (stʊ·măki), *a. dial.* 1825. [f. STOMACH *sb.* + -Y¹.] 1. Ready to take offence, irritable. 2. High-spirited 1896. 3. Paunchy 1889.

3. A little, bald, solemn, s. man STEVENSON.

Stomapod (stǫ·măpǫd), *a.* and *sb.* 1833. [f. mod.L. *Stomapoda* neut. pl., irreg. f. Gr. στόμα mouth + ποδ-, πούς foot.] *Zool.* = STOMATOPOD.

Stomatal (stǫ·mătăl), *a.* 1861. [f. Gr. στοματ-, στόμα STOMA + -AL.] *Bot.* and *Zool.* Pertaining to or connected with a stoma or stomata; of the nature of a stoma; *loosely*, having stomata, stomatous.

Stomate (stōᵘ·mēt). 1835. [app. an Eng. sing. for the pl. **stomata** (see STOMA).] *Bot.* = STOMA 2.

Stomatic (stomæ·tik), *a.* and *sb.* 1656. [ad. mod.L. *stomaticus*, a. Gr. στοματικός, f. στοματ-, στόμα STOMA; see -IC.] †1. a. *adj.* Of a medicine: Good for diseases of the mouth. b. *sb.* A 'stomatic' medicine. –1857. 2. *Bot.* and *Zool.* = STOMATAL 1835.

Stomatiferous (stǫmăti·fĕrəs), *a.* 1866. [f. mod.L. *stomat-*, STOMA + -(I)FEROUS.] *Bot.* Bearing stomata.

‖ **Stomatitis** (stǫmătəi·tis). 1859. [mod.L., f. Gr. στοματ-, στόμα + -ITIS.] *Path.* Inflammation of the mucous membrane of the mouth. Hence **Stomatitic** (i·tik) *a.*

Stomato- (stǫ·măto), repr. Gr. στοματο-, στόμα mouth (see STOMA): occurring in modern scientific terms, chiefly zoological.

Stomatodæ·um, *Embryol.* = STOMODÆUM. ‖**Sto:matode·ndron** (pl. **-dendra**) [Gr. δένδρον tree], each of the dendritic branches bearing minute polyps in the family *Rhizostomidæ* of hydrozoans. **Sto:matoga·stric** [GASTRIC] *a.*, pertaining to or connected with the mouth and stomach; applied to a system of visceral nerves in invertebrates. **Sto·matopla:sty** [-PLASTY], plastic surgery of the mouth (or of the *os uteri*); hence **Sto:matopla·stic** *a.*, pertaining to stomatoplasty. **Sto·matosco:pe** (-skōᵘp) [-SCOPE], an instrument for examining the interior of the mouth.

Stomatode (stǫ·mătoᵘd), *a.* and *sb.* 1870. [f. mod.L. *Stomatoda* neut. pl., irreg. f. Gr. στοματ-, στόμα mouth, after *Nematoda*, etc.] *Zool.* A. *adj.* Pertaining to the *Stomatoda*, a group of *Protozoa* characterized by having a mouth. B. *sb.* A member of the *Stomatoda*.

Stomatopod (stǫ·mătopǫ:d), *a.* and *sb.* 1877. [f. mod.L. *Stomatopoda* neut. pl.; cf. STOMAPOD.] *Zool.* A. *adj.* Belonging to the *Stomatopoda*, an order of malacostracous crustaceans, orig. (in form *Stomapoda*) synonymous with *Gastrura*, now restricted to the family *Squillidæ*. B. *sb.* A s. crustacean.

Stomatous (stǫ·mătəs), *a.* 1880. [f. mod. L. *stomat-* STOMA + -OUS.] Having or furnished with stomata.

‖ **Stomodæum, -eum** (stǫmodī·ɒ̆m). *Pl.* **-æa, -ea** (-ī·ă). 1876. [mod.L. irreg. f. Gr. στόμα mouth + ὁδαῖος that is on or by the road.] *Embryol.* and *Zool.* The anterior portion of the digestive tract, beginning as an invagination of the epiblast. Hence **Stomodæ·al, -e·al** *a.* belonging to or constituting a s.

Stone (stōᵘn), *sb.* [Com. Teut.; OE. *stán* :—OTeut. *stainoz, cogn. w. Gr. στία, στῖον pebble.] I. 1. A piece of rock or hard mineral substance (other than metal) of a small or moderate size. †b. A rock, cliff, crag; a mass of rock; rocky ground –1700. 2. The hard compact material of which stones and rocks consist; hard mineral substance other than metal ME. b. as material for lithography 1806. c. A particular kind of rock or hard mineral matter. late ME. d. *spec.* = PHILOSOPHER'S STONE. late ME. †e. A mirror. SHAKS. 3. As a type or emblem of motionlessness or fixity, hardness, insensibility, stupidity, etc. ME. 4. *transf.* and *fig.* Something resembling stone or a stone. late ME. 5. A piece of stone of a definite form and size (usu. artificially shaped), used for some special purpose, e.g. for building, paving, as a memorial, etc. OE. b. *spec.* = GRAVESTONE, TOMBSTONE. ME. c. A rounded stone or pebble formerly used as a missile in war ME. d. A shaped piece of stone for grinding or sharpening something, as a GRINDSTONE 2, MILLSTONE 1. 1578. e. A flat slab or tablet for grinding something upon, or for smoothing or flattening something; also a slab of stone for lithography. late ME. f. A heavy stone used in athletic sports. Phrases. *To cast, put,* or *throw the s.* ME. 6. A precious stone OE. 7. A lump of metallic ore. *Obs.* exc. in *s. of tin*, a lump of tin ore. OE. †b. = LOADSTONE 1. –1631. †8. = HAILSTONE –1753. 9. = CALCULUS 1. Also, the disease caused or characterized by the formation of a calculus; lithiasis. OE. 10. A testicle; chiefly in *pl. Obs.* exc. in vulgar use. ME. 11. The hard woodlike endocarp of a *s.-fruit* or drupe, enclosed by the pulpy pericarp, and enclosing the seed or kernel. Also, applied to the hard seeds of some pulpy fruits, as the grape. 1523. 12. A measure of weight, usu. equal to 14 pounds avoirdupois, but varying with different commodities from 8 to 24 pounds. The stone of 14 lb. is the common unit used in stating the weight of a man or large animal. (Collective pl. usu. *stone.*) late ME.

1. Aerolites, called also Meteoric Stones 1833. 2. c. Semitransparent Stones, as Agat 1731. d. Lend me a Looking-glasse, If that her breath will mist or staine the s., Why then she liues SHAKS. 3. Me thynketh myn hert ys harder than a ston 1400. She was deaf as a s. 1841. 4. Nor wept, for all Within was S. GRAY. The widow's lamentations.. would have pierced a heart of s. DICKENS. 5. The stones on Salisbury-plain, which can never be settled to any certain number ADDISON. Horses clattered on the uneven stones DICKENS. Built up, s. by s., from the level of the earth 1867. b. The s. closes over Harry the Fourth THACKERAY. c. Like..a s. from a sling 1867. 6. Sparkles this S. as it was wont? SHAKS. 12. Of Sugar and Spice 8 pound make the s. 1674. A drayman weighing about eighteen s. 1887.

Phrases. *To kill two birds with one s.*, to accomplish two different purposes by the same act or proceeding. *To leave no s. unturned*, to try every possible expedient in order to bring about a desired result. *To set a s. rolling*, to start a course of action which may lead to unforeseen, esp. disastrous, consequences. Prov. *A rolling s. gathers no moss*: see MOSS *sb.* II. 1, ROLLING STONE 1. *To throw* (*cast*) *a s.* or *stones* (*at*), to make an attack (upon) or bring an accusation (against); so *to cast the first s.* (in allusion to John viii. 7). *S. of stumbling* (arch.), an occasion of scandal or stumbling, a stumbling-block (Vulg. *petra scandali*).

II. *attrib.* passing into *adj.* a. Consisting of stone; made or built of stone OE. b. Made of stoneware; also, *transf.* of ginger-beer contained in stoneware bottles OE. c. Applied to substances in a solid or massive (as dist. from liquid or powdered) form, as *stone alum, stone ochre*, etc. 1608. d. Of, pertaining or relating to stone or stones (in various senses) 1826. e. *ellipt.* Belonging to the STONE AGE 1864. f. (from 10.) Of male domestic animals: Not castrated, entire; †hence allus. of men: lascivious, lustful 1602. g. With preceding numeral, forming an attrib. or adj. phrase, in sense (*a*) set with a (specified) number of (precious) stones; (*b*) weighing (so many) stone; hence *transf.* applied to the prize in a race in which the horses carry the specified weight 1683.

a. The lion on your old s. gates TENNYSON. b. Beate them well in a s. morter 1600. While I sipped my stone-ginger 1904. e. The earlier S. folk are known to us only by their graves 1880. g. A Seven S. Diamond Ring 1683.

Comb.: **s.-bark** *Bot.*, bark consisting chiefly of hardened and thickened cells; **-blue,** a compound of indigo with starch or whiting, used by laundresses; **-boat,** a boat (*U.S.* a sled) for transporting stones; **-boiling,** the primitive process of boiling water by putting hot stones in it; **-breaker,** a person employed in, or a machine used for, breaking stones; so **-breaking**; **-broke** *a. slang*, = *stony-broke*; **-butter** [after G. *steinbutter*], alum occurring in soft masses greasy to the touch; **-canal** *Zool.*, a canal forming part of the water-vascular system in Echinoderms, usu. with calcareous walls, leading from the madreporic plate to the circumoral water-vessel; **-cast** = STONE'S THROW; **-cell** *Bot.*, one of a number of greatly hardened and thickened cells occurring in certain plants; **-china,** a variety of earthenware in common domestic use; **s. circle** *Archæol.*, = CIRCLE *sb.* II. 2; **-coal,** †(*a*) mineral coal as dist. from charcoal; (*b*) any hard variety of coal, esp. anthracite; **-colour,** the (usual) colour of s., a yellowish or brownish grey, also *attrib.*; **-crusher,** a machine for crushing or grinding s., a s.-breaker; **-dike, -dyke,** a dike constructed of s.; a s. fence or embankment; **-dresser,** one who dresses or shapes s. for building; also, a machine for this purpose; **-engraving,** the art or process of engraving on s., lithography; **s. era** = STONE AGE; **-fall,** a fall of meteoric stones, or of loose stones on a mountain slope; **s. fence,** (*a*) a fence made of stones, a s. wall; (*b*) *U.S. slang*, name for various intoxicating drinks; **-ground** *a.*, ground by means of millstones; **-hammer,** a hammer for breaking or rough-dressing stones; **-heading** *Coal-mining*, a heading driven through s. or rock; **-horse** (now *dial.*), an uncastrated horse, a stallion; **-lily,** a fossil crinoid or encrinite, from its resemblance to a lily on its stalk; **-mill,** (*a*) a mill for grinding; (*b*) a machine for dressing stones; (*c*) a mill in which millstones (not rollers) are used for grinding the flour; so **-milled** *a.* = *s.-ground*; **-oil,** a kind of bitumen; petroleum or rock-oil; **s. period** *Archæol.*, = STONE AGE; also, a portion of the Stone age; **-pit,** a quarry; †**-pitch,** pitch in the solid form, hard or dry pitch; **-pock** *Path.*, a hard suppurating pimple; a disease characterized by such pimples, as acne; **-saw,** a saw, usu. without teeth, for cutting stone into blocks or other shapes for building, etc.; **-shot,** (*a*) stones used as missiles, esp. as shot for cannon; (*b*) = STONE'S-THROW; **-shower,** a shower or fall of meteoric stones; **-slate,** a roofing slate made of thin s.; **-weight,** = sense I. 12; also, a piece of metal of this

weight, used in weighing; **-yard**, a yard in which s.-breaking or s.-cutting is done.

b. In names of animals, as **s.-bass**, a fish of the genus *Polyprion* (family *Serranidæ*), characterized by a bony ridge on the operculum and serrated spines on the anal and ventral fins; **-bird**, (*a*) the vinous grosbeak; (*b*) = *s.-snipe* (*a*); **-borer**, a bivalve mollusc that bores into stones or rocks; **-buck** = STEINBOCK; **-cat**, a N. Amer. freshwater cat-fish of the genus *Noturus*; **-coral**, hard or sclerodermatous (as dist. from sclerobasic), or massive (as dist. from branching) coral; **-crab**, (*a*) a name for various species of crab; (*b*) applied locally in *U.S.* to the dobson or hellgrammite, the larva of a neuropterous insect, used as a bait in angling; **-crawfish**, a European species of crawfish or crayfish, *Astacus torrentium*; **s. curlew**, see CURLEW 3; **-eater**, = *s.-borer*; **s. falcon** [G. *steinfalke*], the merlin; **-fly**, an insect of the family *Perlidæ*, whose larvæ are found under stones in streams, esp. *Perla bicaudata*, much used as a bait in angling; also, an artificial fly made to imitate this; **-hawk**, = *s. falcon*; **-marten**, the beech-marten (*Mustela foina*), or its fur; **-plover**, see PLOVER 2; **-roller**, name for two N. Amer. freshwater fishes, *Catostomus nigricans*, and *Campostoma anomalum*; **-runner**, the ringed plover or the dotterel; also applied to some species of sandpiper; **-smatch**, **-smitch** = STONECHAT; **-snipe**, (*a*) the s.-curlew, *Œdicnemus scolopax*; (*b*) a large N. Amer. bird of the snipe family, *Totanus melanoleucus*; also applied to other species of *Totanus*.

c. In names of plants (either growing in stony places, or having some part hard like stone), or their fruits; as **s. basil**, the wild basil, *Calamintha Clinopodium*, or basil-thyme, *C. Acinos*; **s. bramble**, a species of bramble, *Rubus saxatilis*, growing in stony places, and having bright red fruit; **-break** = SAXIFRAGE; **-fern**, *Asplenium Ceterach*; also applied to other ferns growing in stony places; **-mint**, the Amer. dittany, *Cunila Mariana*.

Stone (stōun), *v.* [Early ME. *stanen*, f. *stan* STONE *sb.*] 1. *trans.* To throw stones at, pelt with stones; *esp.* to put to death by pelting with stones. †2. To turn into stone, or make hard like stone; to petrify. (Chiefly *fig.*) –1853. 3. To furnish or fit with stones; to pave, or build up, with stone or stones 1600. 4. To rub or polish with a stone; to sharpen on a whetstone; in *Leather Manuf.* to scour and smooth with a stock-stone 1688. 5. To take the stones out of (fruit) 1639. 6. *intr.* Of a fruit (drupe): To form a stone in the process of growth 1842.

1. Cowards were stoned to death GIBBON. 2. O periur'd woman, thou do'st s. my heart SHAKS. 5. S. a pound and a half of cherries 1769. Hence **Sto·ner**[1], one who pelts with stones, esp. so as to kill.

Sto·ne age. 1864. *Archæol.* The period or stage in the development of human culture which is marked by the exclusive or greatly predominant use of stone as material for weapons and implements, in contradistinction to the later 'ages' in which bronze or iron was used.

The *Stone age* is divided into the PALÆOLITHIC and NEOLITHIC periods N.E.D.

Sto·ne-axe. OE. 1. A two-edged axe used for hewing stone. 2. An axe made of stone 1864.

Stone-blind (stōu·n,bləi·nd), *a.* (*sb.*) late ME. [STONE *sb.*] Blind as a stone; completely blind.

Stone-bow (stōu·nbōu). OE. 1. An arch of stone. *Obs.* exc. as the name of one of the gates of Lincoln. †2. A kind of cross-bow or catapult used for shooting stones –1660.

Stonechat (stōu·n,tʃæt). 1783. [f. STONE *sb.* + CHAT *sb.*[2], from its alarm note which resembles the striking together of two pebbles.] A small bird, *Pratincola* (or *Saxicola*) *rubicola*, inhabiting heaths, commons, etc. in Britain and various parts of Europe. (Also called *s. warbler*.) Also improperly applied to the whinchat, *P. rubetra*, and the wheatear, *S. œnanthe*, etc.

Stonecrop (stōu·nkrǫp). [OE. *stāncrop*; see STONE *sb.* and CROP *sb.* 6.] The common name of *Sedum acre*, a herb with bright yellow flowers and small cylindrical fleshy sessile leaves, growing in masses on rocks, old walls, etc.; also applied to other species of *Sedum*, and of allied genera, as the N. Amer. *Penthorum*.

Stone-cutter (stōu·n,kʋtəɹ). 1540. 1. One who cuts or carves stone; one who carves figures or inscriptions on stone. b. A machine for cutting or shaping stone 1875. †2. A lithotomist –1787.

1. *Stone-cutter's disease*, an affection of the lungs, incident to stone-cutters, caused by inhaling the fine dust of the stones. So **Sto·ne-cu·tting**, the process or art of cutting or shaping stone.

Sto·ne-fruit. 1523. 1. A fruit having the seed or kernel surrounded by a 'stone' or hard endocarp within the pulp; a drupe. (Also collectively.) 2. (As two words.) Imitation fruit made of stoneware, used as chimney ornaments 1851.

Stonehatch (stōu·nhætʃ). 1852. [STONE *sb.*] The ring-plover or stone-plover, *Ægialitis hiaticula*.

Stonehenge (stōu·nhe·ndʒ). OE. [f. STONE *sb.*; the second element may have meant something 'hanging' or supported in the air; cf. OE. *hengeclif* 'præruptum'.] Name of a celebrated stone circle on Salisbury Plain; hence applied allus. to similar structures elsewhere.

Stone(-)jug. 1596. 1. A jug made of stoneware. 2. *slang.* A nickname for Newgate prison, or for a prison in general 1796.

Stonemason (stōu·n,mēⁱs'n). 1809. [f. STONE *sb.* + MASON *sb.*] = MASON *sb.* 1.

Sto·ne-pa·rsley. 1548. The umbelliferous herb *Sison Amomum*; also applied to *Seseli Libanotis* and other species.

Sto·ne-pine. 1759. [= F. *pin de pierre.* The name has been supposed to refer to the hardness of the seeds.] A species of pine-tree, *Pinus Pinea*, a native of Southern Europe and the Levant, having edible seeds. Also applied to *P. Cembra* (Swiss S.), etc.

Stoner[2] (stōu·nəɹ). 1862. [f. STONE *sb.* + -ER[1].] In comb. with prefixed numeral: A person weighing, or a horse carrying, (so many) stone.

Stonesfield (stōu·nzfīld). 1839. Name of a village in Oxfordshire; used *attrib.* in **S. slate** *Geol.*, a stratum of thin-bedded limestone and calcareous sandstone forming part of the Great Oolite series in Oxfordshire and Gloucestershire.

Stone's throw (stōu·nz,þrōu). 1581. [THROW *sb.*[2] II. 1.] The distance that a stone can be thrown by the hand; vaguely used for a short or moderate distance.

Stone-still, *adv.* and *predic. a.* ME. [See STONE *sb.* and STILL *adv.* and *a.*] As still as a stone; perfectly still and motionless.

Stone-wall, *sb.* Now usu. as two wds. OE. 1. A wall built of stones; now esp. of rough stones without mortar, as a fence between fields, etc. 2. *Austral. Polit. slang.* Parliamentary obstruction, or a body of obstructives 1876. Hence **Stonewall** *v.* (*a*) *intr.*, *Cricket slang*, to block balls persistently; to play solely on the defensive; (*b*) *Polit. slang*, orig. and chiefly *Austral.*, to obstruct business by lengthy speeches, etc., to practise obstruction; also *trans.* to obstruct (business). **Stonewa·ller.**

Stoneware (stōu·nwēəɹ). (Also, with hyphen, or as two wds.) 1683. A hard dense kind of pottery ware, made from very siliceous clay, or a mixture of clay with much flint or sand.

Stonework (stōu·nwʋɹk). Also, with hyphen, or occas. as two wds.) OE. [Cf. OS. *stēnwerk.*] 1. Work built of stone; masonry. b. Artistic work of any kind executed in stone 1910. 2. The process of working in stone, as in building; the labour or task of a mason 1793. b. *Coal Mining.* The work of driving headings through stone or rock 1883. Hence **Stoneworker, -works.**

Stonewort (stōu·nwʋɹt). 1585. [f. STONE *sb.* + WORT.] †1. The fern *Asplenium Ceterach*, also called *stone fern* –1647. 2. With defining words, applied to species of *Sison* and other umbelliferous plants 1796. 3. A book-name for the genus *Chara*, from the calcareous deposits on the stem; also, extended to the family *Characeæ* 1816.

Stonify (stōu·nifəi), *v. rare.* 1610. [f. STONE *sb.* or STONY *a.* + -FY.] *trans.* To make stony, or turn into stone; to petrify.

†Sto·nish, *v.* 1470. [Aphetic f. ASTONISH *v.*] To stun mentally, shock, surprise –1612.

Stony (stōu·ni), *a.* [OE. *stānig* :—OTeut. **stainago-*, *-aꭓo-*, f. **staino-* STONE *sb.*; see -Y[1].] 1. Abounding in, or having the character of, stone or rock; full of rocks; rocky. Now *rare* or *Obs.* b. Full of or abounding in stones. late ME. †c. Of fruits: Having a stone; also, abounding in stone-like seeds –1784. 2. †a. Made of stone –1776. b. Of the nature of stone 1695. c. Consisting of stones. Chiefly *poet.* 1586. 3. Pertaining or relating to stone or stones (*rare*) 1847. 4. Resembling stone in consistence; hard like stone; very hard 1523. b. Of a quality (as hardness, colour): Like that of stone 1565. 5. *fig.* a. 'Hard', insensible, or unfeeling, as if consisting of stone; hardened, obdurate ME. b. Rigid, fixed, motionless; destitute of movement or expression: esp. of the eyes or look 1642. c. Of fear, grief, etc.: 'Petrifying', stupefying; having no relief 1590. d. *slang.* Short for *s.-broke* 1890.

1. Some [seed] fell on a s. grounde TINDALE *Mark* iv. 5. b. I chatter over s. ways TENNYSON. 2. b. Ordinary earthy or s. matter FARADAY. c. Batter Cadmus walls with s. showers GRAY. 4. S. haile 1586. 5. a. A stonie adversary, an inhumane wretch, Vncapable of pitty SHAKS. b. A s. British stare TENNYSON. c. A s. speechless sorrow 1882.

Comb.: **s.-broke** *a.*, *slang*, 'hard up', without any money, ruined; **s. coral** = *stone-coral.* Hence **Sto·ni·ly** *adv.*, **-ness.**

†Sto·ny, *v.* ME. Aphetic f. ASTONY *v.* (Prob. sometimes confused with STUN *v.*) –1688.

Stony-hearted (stress var.), *a.* 1569. Having a stony heart; unfeeling, merciless.

So then, Oxford Street, s. stepmother..at length I was dismissed from thee! DE QUINCEY.

Stook (stuk), *sb.* [Late ME. *stouk*, a. or cogn. w. MLG. *stūke* (WFlem. *stuik*).] 1. = SHOCK *sb.*[1] 1. ¶b. Used for: A pile, mass 1865. 2. A bundle of straw. *dial.* 1571. 3. *Coal-mining.* [perh. a different word.] The portion of a pillar of coal left to support the roof 1826.

Stook (stuk), *v.* 1575. [f. prec.] *trans.* To set up (sheaves) in stooks. Also with *up.* Also *absol.*

Stool (stūl), *sb.* [Com. Teut.; OE. *stōl* :—OTeut. **stōloz*, prob. f. root **stō-* : *sta-* to STAND.] †1. Any kind of seat for one person; often, a chair of authority, state, or office; esp. a royal or episcopal throne –1818. †b. A seat for an offender. See CUCKING-, DUCKING-STOOL, *s. of* REPENTANCE. –1750. 2. A wooden seat (for one person) without arms or a back; a piece of furniture consisting in its simplest form of a piece of wood for a seat set upon legs, usu. three or four in number, to raise it from the ground. late ME. b. A high seat of this kind for convenience of writing at a high desk; more fully *office s.* Hence, a situation as clerk in an office. 1837. c. A low short bench or form upon which to rest the foot, step, or kneel. Chiefly = FOOTSTOOL. ME. 3. A seat enclosing a chamber utensil; a commode; more explicitly *s. of ease.* Also, a privy. late ME. b. In phrases originally meaning 'the place of evacuation', now (without *the*) the action of evacuating the bowels 1542. c. With dem. or poss.: act of discharging fæces 1533. d. A discharge of fæcal matter of a specified colour, consistency, etc.; the matter discharged (chiefly *pl.*) 1597. †4. A frame upon which to work embroidery or tapestry –1548. 5. *Naut.* a. A minor channel abaft the main channels, for the dead-eyes of the backstays 1711. b. The lowest transome of a vessel's stern frame 1797. 6. *Brick-making.* A brick-moulder's shed or workshop; also, the gang of workmen employed in one shed; also, a moulder's bench 1693. 7. *Arch.* The sill of a window. *Obs.* exc. *U.S.* 1663. 8. A base or stand upon which a thing is set to raise it above the ground or general surface 1481. 9. [Cf. Du. *stoel.*] a. The stump of a tree which has been felled; also, the head of the stump from which new shoots are produced 1577. b. *Forestry.* A stock or stump of a tree felled or headed for the production of coppice-wood, underwood, saplings, or young timber. Also, a set or group of stumps. 1722. c. *Forestry* and *Horticulture.* The base of a plant cut down to produce shoots or branches for layering 1789. d. *Horticulture.* The base containing the latent buds in plants which annually throw up new stems or foliage to replace the old 1790. e. A cluster of stems or foliage springing from a stool or from the same root; the complement of stalks produced by one grain of corn 1712. f. A shoot or layer from the stump or base of a plant. [Confused with L. *stolo*; see STOLON.]

1818. 10. *U.S.* A decoy-bird (perh. short for *s.-pigeon*), esp. one used in shooting wild-fowl; also a perch upon which a decoy-bird is set 1859.

Phrase. *To fall, come to the ground,* or *sit between two stools,* to incur failure through vacillation between two different courses of action.

Comb.: **s. pigeon** *U.S.*, a pigeon fastened to a s. as a decoy; chiefly *fig.* of a person employed, especially by gamblers, as a decoy.

Stool (stūl), *v.* 1545. [f. prec.] **1.** *intr.* To evacuate the bowels; also *trans.*, to evacuate as excrement. **2.** Of a plant: To throw up young shoots or stems; of corn, grass, herbage, to throw out lateral shoots producing a thick head of stems or foliage. Also with *out, forth.* 1789. **3.** *U.S.* (*trans.*) To entice (wild-fowl) by means of a decoy-bird; also *intr.* (of a bird) to come (well) to a decoy 1859.

Stoo·l-ball. 1475. [f. STOOL *sb.* + BALL *sb.* 1] **1.** An old country game somewhat resembling cricket, played chiefly by young women, or, as an Easter game, between men and women for a 'tansy' as the stake. The 'stool' was the wicket. **2.** A ball used in this game 1690.

Stoop (stūp), *sb.*¹ Now only *dial.* [late ME. *stulpe, stolpe,* a. ON. *stolpe.*] **1.** A post, pillar. **2.** *fig.* A person or thing that supports or sustains; a 'prop', 'pillar'. *Sc.* 1572.

Stoop (stūp), *sb.*² 1571. [f. STOOP *v.*] **1.** An act of stooping; a bending of the body forwards; a bow. **b.** *fig.* A condescension, a voluntary descent from superiority or dignity 1636. **2.** A stooping attitude; a temporary or permanent bent position of the back or shoulders 1716. **3.** The action of descending from a height; *spec.* the swoop of a bird of prey on its quarry or the descent of the falcon to the lure 1586.

1. b. Can I, can any Loyal Subject see With Patience, such a S. from Sovereignty? DRYDEN. **2.** A tall thin man, with a slight s. 1904.

Stoop (stūp), *sb.*³ *U.S.* and *Canada.* 1789. [a. Du. *stoep* STOEP.] A raised, uncovered platform before the entrance of a house, approached by means of steps. Sometimes incorrectly used for *porch* or *veranda.*

Stoop (stūp), *v.* Pa. t. and pa. pple. **stooped** (stūpt). [OE. *stūpian* wk. vb. corresp. to MDu. *stūpen*; related by ablaut to OTeut. **staupo-* STEEP *a.*] **I.** To bow down, to descend. **1.** *intr.* Of a person: To lower the body by inclining the trunk or the head and shoulders forward, sometimes bending the knee at the same time. Often with *down.* **b.** Said of the head or shoulders. late ME. †**c.** Of a quadruped: To crouch -1625. **d.** Of a dog: To put its nose to the ground to find a scent 1523. **2.** *fig.* **a.** To 'bow' to superior power or authority; to yield obedience. Const. *to, under.* Now somewhat *rare.* 1530. †**b.** To submit *to* something burdensome -1647. **c.** To condescend *to* one's inferiors or *to* some position or action below one's rightful dignity 1579. **d.** To lower or degrade oneself morally 1743. **3.** Of a thing: To incline from the perpendicular; to bend down; to slope; to hang over OE. **4.** To stand or walk with the shoulders bent or the upper part of the body inclined forwards; esp. to have habitually or permanently this kind of attitude ME. †**5.** To descend from a height -1847. **6.** Of a hawk or other bird of prey: To descend swiftly on its prey, to swoop (const. *at, on*); also, to descend to the lure 1575. †**b.** *trans.* = To stoop at or on -1618.

1. Angels..stoope down with their faces towards the mercy Seat 1649. **2. a.** Early or late, They s. to fate, And must give up their murmuring breath SHIRLEY. **c.** She stoops to conquer GOLDSM. (*title*). **d.** Incapable of stooping to an act of baseness MACAULAY. **3.** The grasse stoops not, she treads on it so light SHAKS. **4.** Cissy, my Love, don't s. so LYTTON. **6.** *fig.* Whether the priest had stooped at the lure of a cardinal's hat.. I know not 1717.

II. Causative uses. **1.** *trans.* To cause to bow down, bring to the ground; *fig.* to humiliate, subdue. Now *rare.* ME. **2.** To bow (the head, †face, neck, knee); to incline (one's ear) 1634. **b.** *fig.* To condescend to apply (one's thoughts, etc.) to something unworthy 1598. †**3.** To let down, lower, 'vail'. Often *Naut.* and *Mil.* to lower (a sail, an ensign). -1697. **4.** To tilt (a cask). Now *dial.* 1670. **5.** To train (a dog) to 'stoop' for a scent 1781.

1. Shoote, shoote, and stoope his pride CHAPMAN. **2.** MILT. *Comus* 333. **b.** None stoop'd a Thought to base inglorious Flight POPE. Hence **Stooped** (stūpt) *ppl. a.*, that has swooped down; of the head or shoulders: bent downwards; also of a person: stooping. **Stoo·per,** a wedge for tilting a barrel (*dial.*); one who stoops; one who has a stoop. **Stoo·ping** *ppl. a.*, **-ly** *adv.*

†**Stoop-gallant.** 1551. [f. STOOP *v.* + GALLANT *sb.* – F. *trousse-galant.*] Something that humbles 'gallants'; orig., a name for the 'sweating sickness'; also *fig.* -1862.

†‖**Stoo·ter.** 1598. [Du.] A Dutch coin worth two stuivers and a half -1811.

Stop (stǫp), *sb.* 1450. [f. next.] **I.** Action of stopping. **1.** The action or an act of impeding, obstructing, or arresting; the fact of being impeded or arrested; a check, arrest, or obstruction (of motion or activity) 1544. **2.** *spec.* A veto or prohibition (*against*); an embargo (*upon* goods, trade); a refusal to pass tokens; an order stopping payment of a bank note, cheque, or bill 1634. **3.** The act of filling or closing up an aperture 1593. **4.** The act of coming to a stand; a halt; a cessation of progress or onward movement. Phr. *to make a s.* 1575. **b.** A stay or sojourn made at a place, esp. in the course of a journey 1650. **c.** A place at which a halt is made; a stopping-place 1889. **5.** A block or obstruction of traffic caused by the overcrowding of vehicles 1626. **6.** A cessation, coming to a pause or end (of any activity, process, etc.) 1483. **b.** A pause or breaking-off made by one speaking 1561.

1. If people only made prudent marriages, what a s. to population there would be! THACKERAY. Phr. *To put a s. to,* to check, restrain; to arrest the progress of; to bring to an end, abolish. **4.** Many a s. and stay he makes WORDSW. **b.** From thence [they] rode Post to Paris, where they made some s. 1659. **6.** The band came to a s. 1889. **b.** The smiling and unconscious look of Florence brings him to a dead s. DICKENS.

II. Something that stops, arrests, or blocks. †**1.** Something that hinders motion or activity; an impediment, obstacle -1725. **2.** †**a.** A weir or dam across a river; a sluice or floodgate -1800. **b.** A blind alley in a maze 1666. **3.** A piece of mechanism (e.g. a pin, bolt, shoulder, a strip or block of wood) which checks the motion or thrust of anything, keeps a part fixed in its place, determines the position to which a part shall be brought, etc. 1523. **b.** *Joinery.* Each of the pieces of wood nailed on the frame of a door to form a rebate against which the door shuts 1833. **c.** *Clockwork.* A contrivance to prevent over-winding 1675. **4.** *Naut.* **a.** A piece of small line used to fasten or secure anything 1846. **b.** A projection at the upper part of a mast 1846. **5.** *Arch.* An ornamental termination to a chamfer 1825. **6.** *Optics.* A perforated plate or diaphragm used to cut off marginal rays of light round a lens 1831. **7.** Something that stops an aperture; a plug 1770.

III. *Music.* **1.** In an organ, a graduated set of pipes producing tones of the same quality 1500. **b.** The handle or knob by which a set of organ pipes is turned on or off; a stop-knob, draw-stop 1585. **c.** In the harpsichord, a handle controlling a lever by which the position of a jack can be varied so as to modify the tone produced 1730. **2. a.** The closing of a finger-hole or ventage in the tube of a wind-instrument so as to alter the pitch. Also, a metal key used for this purpose. Also, the hole or aperture thus closed. 1500. **b.** The act of pressing with the finger on a string of the violin, lute, etc., so as to raise the pitch of its tone. Also, the part of the string where pressure is made in order to produce a required note, sometimes mechanically marked, as by frets. *Full s.*, a chord in producing which all the strings are stopped. 1530. **3.** *fig.* or *transf.* Now chiefly with ref. to the organ. 1576.

1. All Organs of sweet s. MILT. Flourishes..on the trumpet s. RUSKIN. **2. a.** He touch'd the tender stops of various Quills MILT. **b.** *Much Ado* III. ii. 62. **3.** Sweet as stops Of planetary music heard in trance SHELLEY.

IV. *Grammar.* **1.** A mark or point of punctuation 1590. **2. Full stop. a.** The end of a sentence; the single point or dot used to mark this; a period, full point 1596. **b.** *transf.* and *fig.*, as, a complete halt, stoppage, check, or termination 1628. **3.** *Phonetics.* †**a.** The complete closure of the orinasal passages in articulating a mute consonant 1669. **b.** A consonantal sound in the formation of which the passage of the breath is completely obstructed; a stopped consonant, a mute 1873.

2. b. The story..comes unexpectedly to a full s. 1798.

V. 1. a. *Pugilism.* A guard or attack that prevents a blow from getting home 1812. **b.** *Wrestling.* A counter to any particular fall or hold 1840. **2.** A hole in the ground in which the doe-rabbit secures her litter 1669. **3.** *Shooting.* A person posted in order to keep the game within range 1897. **4. a.** The indentation in the face of a dog between the forehead and the nose 1867. **b.** In a cavy: A white marking on the hind feet 1902. **5.** *Card-playing.* In Pope Joan and similar games, a card which stops a sequence. Hence *pl.*, the game of Newmarket. 1808. **b.** *Bridge.* A card that can reasonably be counted on, in conjunction with other cards in the same suit, to take a trick in that suit 1920.

Comb.: **s.-block, -buffer,** a buffer at the termination of a railway-line; **-drill,** a drill with a shoulder or collar to limit the depth of penetration; **-gate,** (*a*) a gate placed across a railway; (*b*) a gate by which the water in one section of a canal can be shut off from the next in case of damage to the bank; **-knob,** the handle which is pulled out to open a particular s. in an organ; **-net,** (*a*) a net thrown across a river or tidal channel to intercept fish; (*b*) a net to stop the ball, in various games; **-order,** (*a*) an order issued by the Court of Chancery to stay payment of funds in the custody of the Court; (*b*) an order directing a broker to buy or sell stock at a specified price, in order to limit loss; **-piece, -pin,** a piece or pin serving to arrest some moving part; **-quoin, -coin,** a quoin used for keeping a gun steady; **-stroke** *Croquet,* a stroke which drives a croqueted ball to a distance, while leaving the striker's ball more or less stationary; **-tap** = STOPCOCK; **-thrust** *Fencing,* a thrust delivered at the opponent at the moment when he advances for attack; **-valve,** a valve which closes a pipe against the passage of fluid; **-work,** a mechanism to prevent the overwinding of the spring of a watch, etc. Hence **Sto·pless** *a.* without a s. or stops.

Stop (stǫp), *v.* Pa. t. and pa. pple. **stopped** (stǫpt), **stopt.** ME. [OE. **stoppian* (in *forstoppian*); a Com. WGer. adoption of pop. L. or Rom. **stuppare* to stop or stuff with tow or oakum. The sense 'bring or come to a stand' is a specially English development.] **I.** To fill up, plug, close up. **1.** *trans.* To close up (an aperture) by stuffing something into it, by building it up, or by placing something before it. late ME. **b.** Said of the obstruction: To block, choke up. Also *pass.*, to be choked up *with* (dirt, etc.). Now chiefly with *up.* 1508. **2.** To make (a way) impassable by blocking up its passage or outlet ME. **3.** To fill up, repair, make good (a breach, hole, crevice or defective place of any kind). Also with *up.* So *to s. a leak.* late ME. **b.** To plug (the seams of a boat) with oakum, tow, or other caulking material; †to caulk (a ship). Also *to s. up.* 1535. **c.** *Plastering, House-painting,* etc. To fill up or make good the holes in (a surface to be covered with a wash, paint, etc.); †to close (the joints of brick-work), to 'point' 1557. **d.** *Dentistry.* To fill the cavity of (a decayed tooth) with a stopping: now generally superseded by *fill* 1592. †**4.** To stanch the bleeding of, bind up (a wound) -1602. **5.** To close (a vessel or receptacle) by blocking its mouth with a cover, plug, or other stopper; similarly, to close (the mouth of a vessel); also, to shut up (something) *in* a stoppered vessel. Also with *down, up.* late ME. **6.** To obstruct the external orifice of (a bodily organ) by putting something in or on it or by pressing the parts together OE. **7.** To close up, choke, obstruct (a canal, duct, passage or pipe in the animal body); to block the passage or passages of (a bodily organ). Also with *up.* late ME. †**8.** To shut up, block up (a person or thing *in* a place) -1693. **9.** To press down (the tobacco in a pipe) with or as with a tobacco-stopper 1848.

1. S. the holes of the doore with double Matts 1632. S. all the holes, lest the fox should bolt out unseen 1781. **b.** One of the stack pipes was stopped up with leaves and dirt 1885. **2.** The Countess of Avon's carriage stopping the way 1831. Phr. *To s. one's way,* to stand in one's way, bar one's passage, oppose one. **3.** *To s. a gap,* see GAP *sb.* **c.** The walls..of a light buff colour, rubbed down and stopped 1842. **4.** *fig.* Now ciuill wounds are stopp'd, Peace liues agen SHAKS. **5.** Keep it close stopped in a Bottle for Use 1737. **6.** Phr. *To s.* (one's own or another's) *ear* or *ears*; also *fig.*, to render oneself deaf *to* something, close one's mind against arguments, etc. *To s.* (one's own or another's) *mouth*, lit., as with a gag or muzzle; *fig.* to compel or induce to be silent. 7. The smoulder stops our nose with stench 1573. 8. *Rich. III*, I. iv. 38.

II. To bring to a stand. 1. *trans.* To prevent the passage of by blocking a channel or outlet. late ME. **b.** To intercept (light, air, heat, etc.). late ME. **c.** To stanch (bleeding, blood) 1573. **2.** To arrest the onward movement of (a person or thing); to bring to a stand or state of rest; to cause to halt on a journey; also, to prevent the departure or starting of 1440. **b.** To bring down (a bird) with the gun. Also, to arrest the rush of (a charging enemy or wild beast) with rifle-fire. (Said also of the bullet and of the wound produced.) 1862. **c.** *Fencing, Pugilism*, etc. To check (an adversary, his stroke, weapon, etc.) with a counter movement or stroke; to counter (a blow, a manœuvre in wrestling, etc.) 1714. 3. *Cricket.* (*a*) Of a batsman: To play (a ball) defensively, without attempting to hit it away. Also *absol.* (*b*) *absol.* Of a fieldsman: To field the ball, to act as fieldsman. *To s. behind*, to act as longstop. 1744. 4. To intercept and detain in transit 1604. 5. To withhold (a sum of money) in paying wages or other debt, on the ground of some counterclaim. late ME. †**b.** To withhold (goods) as security or in lieu of payment -1865. **6.** To give instructions to a banker not to cash (a bank-note, bill, or the like). Similarly *to s. payment* (of a cheque, etc.). 1713. 7. To cause (a person) to desist from or pause in a course of action or conduct. Also, *to s. short*, to check abruptly. late ME. **b.** To cause (a person) to break off in narrative or speech. Also *to s. short.* 1545. **c.** To cause (a thing) to cease action. Now *rare.* late ME. 8. To restrain or prevent (a person) from a contemplated action 1470. †**b.** *Law.* To bar, hinder, preclude -1711. **c.** *Law.* To stay, suspend (proceedings); to prevent (a decree, etc.) from taking effect 1690. †9. To hamper the course or progress of (affairs, a project, etc.); to hinder (a person) in action or in some proceeding -1721. 10. To cause to cease, put an end to (a movement, activity, course of events). late ME. **b.** To prevent the coming-on of 1538. 11. To cease from, discontinue (an action, allowance, employment) 1525. 12. To cause (a machine or mechanism) to cease working or going 1538. 13. *Mus.* To press down (a string of a violin, lute, or the like) with the finger (*rarely* with a key) in order to shorten its vibrating length and thereby produce certain intermediate sounds; hence, to produce (a note, sound) by this means; to use (a finger) for this purpose 1500. 14. *Naut.* To bring (a ship) to anchor by gradually checking the cable 1627. **b.** To tie up with thin rope. Also *to s. up.* 1770. 15. *Horticulture.* To pinch out the head of (a plant); to remove (a shoot or portion of it) by pinching. Also *to s. back.* 1699. 16. *Arch.* To cause (a rib, shaft, chamfer, etc.) to terminate (in a specified form or position) 1835. 17. *Phonetics.* To check the flow of (breath or voice) in articulation 1867.

1. By the labour of the Persians, the course of the river was stopped below the town, and the waters were confined GIBBON. Phr. *To s. the breath of*, to prevent the respiration of, to suffocate, stifle, choke; hence, to cause to die. 2. I was at length stopped by the dislocated ice TYNDALL. The responsibility of stopping a train..is given..to the engine-driver 1876. *S. thief!* a cry for help to arrest an escaping thief. *To s. a bullet*, to be shot. 5. Nor stops, for one bad cork, his butler's pay POPE. 7. What can be done to s. him from running headlong on ruin? SCOTT. **c.** Hold, s. your murd'ring hands 1672. 8. If any one likes to go, nobody will s. them RUSKIN. **b.** *K. John* II. i. 562. 10. For God's sake s. the grunting of those Pigs! SHELLEY. **b.** With thousand doubts How I might s. this tempest ere it came SHAKS. 11. She has..stopped his..pocket-money DICKENS. The clock stopped striking 1860. Phr. *To s. payment*, to declare oneself unable to meet one's financial obligations. 12. Phr. *To s. the press*, to suspend the operation of printing (esp. in order to give opportunity to make some insertion). 14. Phr. *To s. the cable*, to prevent it running out too fast. *S. her!*, an order to check the running out of the cable; also, on small steamers and motor-boats, the command to s. the engine. *To s. the tide*, to prevent the ship being carried with the tide.

With advs. **Stop down.** *trans.* To reduce the aperture of (a lens) by means of the stops. **S. off.** (*a*) In *Moulding*, to adapt (a mould) to a new design by shortening or obliterating some part of it. (*b*) In *Etching*, etc. = *s. out.* **S. out.** In *Etching*, to obliterate or cover with a varnish (the parts of a plate which are to be kept from the acid in the process of biting in). Also *absol.*

III. To come to a stand, cease to move or act. 1. *intr.* To cease from onward movement, to come to a stand or position of rest. More emphatically *to s. dead*, *s. short.* 1530. 2. To make a halt on a journey, esp. to halt and remain for rest and refreshment. Of a coach, train, boat, etc.: To halt at a specified place to pick up or set down passengers, etc. 1743. **b.** *To s. over*: to make a halt (*at* a place) and proceed by a later conveyance. So *to s. off. U.S.* 1884. 3. To remain, prolong one's stay in a place; to stay (*to* dinner, *at* home, *with* a person). Also quasi-*trans.*, to remain for (a ceremony, a meal, etc.). 1801. **b.** To sojourn as a visitor, resident, or guest 1797. 4. To leave off doing what one is actually engaged in for the moment 1594. **b.** To pause in speech or narrative; to break off in the middle of a sentence 1579. **c.** *imper.* Also in the phr. *s. a moment!* 1570. 5. To leave off, stay, desist (in a course of action or a pursuit, or from one's customary action or employment) 1689. **b.** To limit one's activity *at* a certain point; to refrain from exceeding a certain degree or extent 1737. **c.** To stay in action, to hesitate, 'stick'. Const. *at.* 1676. 6. Of a thing: To cease its motion or action. Of a process: To come to a pause or end. 1529. **b.** Of a machine, etc.: To cease working or going 1789. 7. Of an immaterial thing: To have its limit of operation at a specified point. Of a series: To come to an end. 1733.

1. A saw a Coach s. at my Door 1709. 2. The postilions stopped at the convent..to take up Blanche 1794. 3. But you'll s. and take a bit of dinner with us? 1858. Phr. *To s. on*, to continue in one place or employment. *To s. up*, (*a*) to remain 'up' at one's college or university; (*b*) to sit up instead of going to bed. 4. **b.** *To s. short*, to pause abruptly. 5. **b.** His charity would willingly have stopped short at Ashby SCOTT. **c.** *To s. at nothing*, to be prevented by no obstacle. 6. The ulceration stops and heals 1830. **b.** My watch has stopped DICKENS. 7. But the severities exercised against catholics did not s. there 1741.

IV. 1. [from STOP *sb.*] *trans.* To furnish with stops, to punctuate 1776. 2. *Versification.* To conclude or divide (a line of verse) with a 'stop' or sense pause. Also *intr.* 1857.

Comb.: **s.-over** *U.S.*, the act of 'stopping over' or breaking one's journey to go on by a later conveyance; also *attrib.*; **-press**, an interruption of the printing in order to insert a late piece of news (see II. 12); also *attrib.* or *adj.* of a newspaper (of an issue of a newspaper, etc.), containing late news inserted after printing has begun; **-water** *Naut.*, (*a*) something fixed or towed overboard to retard the motion of a ship; (*b*) a plug, etc., for making a joint watertight.

Stopcock (stǫ·pkǫk). 1584. [f. STOP *sb.* or *v.* + COCK *sb.*[1]] A tap or short pipe furnished with a valve operated from the outside by turning a key or handle, for the purpose of stopping or permitting as required the passage of liquid, air, steam, gas or the like. (Sometimes improperly applied to the key or handle by which the valve is turned.)

Stope (stōᵘp), *sb.* 1747. [app. cogn. w. STEP *sb.*] *Mining.* †1. A step or notch in the side of a pit, or in an upright beam, to receive the end of a stemple or cross-piece -1836. 2. A step-like working in the side of a pit 1747. **b.** *attrib.*, as in **s. drill**, a portable rock-drill, used in stoping 1908. Hence **Stope** *v. trans.* to cut (mineral ground) in stopes; to excavate horizontally, layer after layer; to extract (ore) by this process.

Sto·p-gap. 1684. [f. STOP *v.* + GAP *sb.*[1]] 1. Something that temporarily supplies a need; a makeshift. Also, of a person: One who temporarily occupies an office, etc. until a permanent appointment can be made. 1691. 2. An utterance intended to fill up a gap or an awkward pause in conversation or discourse 1684. 3. *attrib.* passing into *adj.* 1684.

1. Moral prejudices are the stopgaps of virtue 1827. 3. What will be known in history as the 'S.' Government J. CHAMBERLAIN.

Stoppage (stǫ·pėdʒ). 1465. [f. STOP *v.* + -AGE.] The action of stopping; the condition of being stopped. 1. Deduction from payments; a sum 'stopped' from the pay of a soldier, workman, or servant. 2. Obstruction of a road, passage, stream, or current 1540. **b.** A 'block' of the traffic in a street 1727. 3. *Path.* Obstructed condition of a bodily organ 1575. 4. Arrest or detention of a traveller, or of goods being conveyed from place to place 1621. 5. The action of stopping or causing to cease 1657. **b.** Discontinuance of supply 1865. 6. Cessation of movement or activity; a stop or halt in a journey 1794. 7. *Comm.* The action of stopping payment 1817. **b.** A strike or lock-out 1902.

Stopped (stǫpt), *ppl. a.* 1440. In the senses of STOP *v.*; *spec.* in *Phonetics*, of a consonant sound: Formed by complete closure of the orinasal passages; explosive.

Bridge. A Suit is Stopped when you can make one trick in it, or can compel the adversary to quit it and lead something else 1901.

Stopper (stǫ·pəɹ), *sb.* 1480. [f. STOP *v.* + -ER [1].] 1. A person who stops (see the senses of the verb). 2. Something that stops up a hole or passage 1591. **b.** *spec.* A plug for closing the neck of a bottle, the end of a tube, or the hole for the egress of fluid from any vessel 1667. 3. The upper pad of the sole of a greyhound's foot 1853. 4. Something that causes to cease or brings to a stand 1828. 5. *West Indian.* A tree of the genus *Eugenia* 1884. 6. *Naut.* A short piece of rope, usu. knotted at one or both ends, used to suspend or secure something 1626. 7. *Bridge.* = STOP *sb.* V. 5 **b.** 1901.

4. Phr. *To put a s. on*, to put a stop to (*colloq.*).

Comb.: **s.-bolt** *Naut.*, a ring-bolt in the deck of a ship to which the stoppers are secured; **-knot** *Naut.*, a kind of knot used for the ends of stoppers.

Stopper (stǫ·pəɹ), *v.* 1769. [f. prec.] 1. *trans. Naut.* To secure with a stopper. 2. To close or secure (a bottle, etc.) with a stopper. Also with *down.* 1868. 3. To fit with a stopper 1827. 4. *slang.* To stop; to 'put the stopper on' 1821. **Sto·ppered** *a.* fitted with a stopper.

Stopping (stǫ·piŋ), *vbl. sb.* late ME. [f. STOP *v.* + -ING [1].] 1. The action of STOP *v.* in various senses. †2. *Path.* Obstructed conditions of an organ -1741. 3. Something inserted to stop a hole, crevice, or passage 1585. **b.** *Farriery.* A pad charged with grease inserted within the shoe for the purpose of keeping the horse's foot moist 1580. **c.** A composition used to stop holes or crevices; *Dentistry*, the material used for stopping a hollow tooth, latterly called *filling* 1823. 4. *Mining.* A partition of boards, etc. in an air passage 1708.

attrib. and *Comb.*: **s.-ground** *Etching*, a mixture used to cover the parts of a plate which are bitten-in enough; **s. mixture** *Etching*, a composition to be used as a stopping-ground; **s.-place**, each customary point on their route at which vehicles carrying passengers stop to allow them to mount or alight.

Stopping (stǫ·piŋ), *ppl. a.* late ME. [-ING [2].] †1. *Med.* Tending to cause stoppage; astringent -1666. 2. That stops 1529.

S. train, a train which stops at some or all intermediate stations on a particular line.

Stopple (stǫ·p'l), *sb.* late ME. [Partly from STOP *v.* + -EL [1], -LE; partly aphetic f. ESTOPPEL.] 1. An appliance for closing the orifice of a vessel, tube, etc.; a stopper, cork or plug. Now *rare.* †2. The action of stopping; a stoppage, prohibition -1651. Hence **Sto·pple** *v. trans.* to put a s. on; to close with a s.

Sto·p-watch. 1737. A watch which indicates fractions of a second by a hand that may be instantly stopped by pressure on a spring or catch, so as to record an exact moment or period of time; chiefly used for timing races.

Storage (stōᵊ·rėdʒ). 1612. [f. STORE *v.* + -AGE.] 1. Capacity or space for storing. 2. The action of storing; the condition or fact of being stored 1828. **b.** The conversion of electric energy into chemical energy from which electricity may be generated again 1881. 3. A place where something is stored 1775. 4. Rent paid for warehousing 1775.

2. *Cold s.*, the storing of provisions in refrigerating chambers as a means of preserving them from decay.

Comb.: **s. battery**, a secondary battery in which a supply of electricity is accumulated; **s. cell**, an electrical accumulator; **s. heater**, a heating apparatus for railway carriages, operating by means of stored heat; **s. tank**, a tank for s.; **s. tuber**, a tuber forming a reservoir of nourishment for the plant.

Storax (stōᵊ·ræks). late ME. [a. L., ad. Gr. στύραξ STYRAX.] 1. A fragrant gum-resin described by ancient writers. In early mod. use applied to the resin of the tree *Styrax officinalis*; in later commercial and pharmaceutical use to the balsam of the tree *Liquidambar orientale* (more explicitly *liquid s.*). 2. The tree *Styrax officinalis* 1694.

Store (stōᵊɹ), *sb.* [ME. *stor*, aphetic f. ASTORE *sb.*, a. OF. *estor*, vbl. noun f. *estorer*; see STORE *v.*] 1. a. *sing.* (without indef. art.) That with which a household, camp, etc., is stored; food, clothing, and other necessaries, collected for future use. Now *rare*. b. *collective pl.* Articles (such as food, clothing, arms, etc.) serving for the equipment and maintenance of an army, a ship; occas. of a household, etc. Cf. MARINE STORES. 1636. †2. Live stock -1697. 3. Sufficient or abundant supply (*of* something needful) 1471. †b. Plenty; abundance (of food or necessaries) -1712. c. Used *advb.*, or as postpositive or predicative adj. = 'in store', in plenty, abundant(ly). Also *good, great s.* Now *arch.* and *dial.* 1569. 4. A person's collective possessions; accumulated goods or money. Now *arch.* or *poet.* ME. 5. In phrases with the sense 'to value, esteem, prize; make account of': †*To tell, make, hold, set* (*great, little, no*) *s. of*. *To set* (*great*, etc.) *s. by, upon*. late ME. 6. A stock (of anything material or immaterial) laid up for future use. Phr. *to lay in a s.* 1487. b. *collect. pl.* Stocks, reserves; often in immaterial sense, treasures, accumulated resources 1520. 7. Storage, reserve. Now *rare* exc. in phr. *in s.* (*for*). 1487. 8. A sheep, steer, cow, or pig acquired or kept for fattening 1620. 9. A place where stores are kept, a warehouse; a storehouse 1667. 10. A place where merchandise is kept for sale. a. Chiefly *U.S.* and *colonial*. orig., A shop on a large scale, and dealing in a great variety of articles. Now, the usual equivalent for SHOP *sb.* 2. 1740. b. In Great Britain from about 1850, current in *co-operative store(s)*, the shop in which a co-operative trading society exposes goods for sale. Now commonly in *pl.* ('The Stores'), applied esp. to the establishment of any of the larger co-operative societies of London and other cities, which consists of a number of departments, each dealing in a separate class of goods. In imitation of this, often adopted as the designation of a trading establishment resembling these. 1852. 11. *attrib.* a. Denoting a receptacle, repository, depot or transport for stores or supplies, as *s.-cellar*, STORE-HOUSE, STORE-ROOM 1507. b. Designating animals kept for breeding or as part of the ordinary stock of a farm, also animals bought lean to be fattened; as *s. beast, cattle*; **s. farm**, a farm on which cattle are reared 1602. c. *U.S.* and *Colonial*. Of or belonging to a store or shop; purchased or purchasable at a store, as *s. goods* 1741. d. Pertaining to 'the Stores', as *s. price(s)* 1889.

1. Small s. will serve, where s., All seasons, ripe for use hangs on the stalk MILT. b. The docks were full of triremes and naval stores JOWETT. 3. Thou hast given them s. Of flowers M. ARNOLD. Prov. *S. is no sore*, i.e. abundance does no harm. b. Starving in the Midst of S. SWIFT. c. Wolves there are great s. 1694. 4. Increase thy Wealth, and double all thy S. DRYDEN. 5. The precious metal, on which they set so high a s. 1797. 6. My desk usually contained a s. of most miscellaneous volumes SCOTT. A s. of energy 1881. b. The Stores of Learning 1699. 7. The vse of things is all, and not the S. B. JONS. Phr. *To keep* (young animals) *for s*. *In s.*, in reserve, laid up for future use; hence (of events or conditions in the future) *in s. for*, awaiting (a person); What such surprise can be in s. for me? DICKENS.

Store (stōᵊɹ), *v.* ME. [Aphetic var. of ASTORE *v.*, a. OF. *estorer* :—L. *instaurare*.] 1. *trans.* To furnish, supply, stock (a person, place, etc.) *with* something. 2. To keep in store for future use; to collect and keep in reserve; to form a store, stock or supply of; to accumulate, hoard 1600. b. *spec.* To deposit (goods, furniture, etc.) in a store or warehouse for temporary safe-keeping 1899. 3. Of a receptacle: To hold, keep, contain, have storage-accommodation for 1911.

1. I have storyd my parkes and my pondes 1530. These studies..s. a man's mind with valuable facts W. IRVING. 2. My capital secret, in what part my strength Lay stor'd MILT. But Dora stored what little she could save TENNYSON. b. I shall s. my furniture and spend a year in travelling (*mod.*). 3. A single cell can s. 2000000 foot-pounds of energy 1911.

Hence **Stored** (stōᵊɹd) *ppl. a.* laid up in store, accumulated, hoarded; stocked, furnished or supplied with a store. **Sto·rer**, one who or a thing which stores or keeps in store.

Sto·rehouse. ME. [f. STORE *sb.* + HOUSE *sb.*] 1. A building in which goods are stored. 2. *transf.* and *fig.* Often, a store or treasury from which something may be obtained in plenty; an abundant source (*of*) 1578.

1. Which nether have stoore housse ner barne TINDALE *Luke* xii. 24. 2. Memory, which is as it were the Store-house of our Ideas LOCKE.

Storekeeper (stōᵊ·ɹ₁kīpəɹ). 1618. 1. One who has charge of a store or stores; *spec.* an officer in charge of naval or military stores. 2. *U.S.* and *Colonial*. A shopkeeper 1741.

Sto·re-room. 1746. 1. A room set apart for the storing of goods or supplies, esp. those of a ship or household. 2. Room or space for storage 1783.

Sto·re-ship, sto·reship. 1693. A government ship employed to carry naval or military stores.

Storey, Storeyed: see STORY *sb.*², STORIED *a.*²

‖ **Storge** (stǭ·ɹgī). 1637. [Gr. στοργή, related to στέργειν to love.] Natural affection; usu., that of parents for their offspring.

Storiation (stōᵊri₁ēⁱ·ʃən). 1884. [f. STORY *v.* + -ATION.] Decoration with artistic designs representing historical, legendary, or emblematic subjects. Hence **Sto·riate** *v.*

Storied (stōᵊ·rid), *a.*¹ and *ppl. a.* 1481. [f. STORY *sb.*¹ and *v.* + -ED.] 1. Ornamented with scenes from history or legend by means of sculpture, painting or other art; also, inscribed with a legend or memorial record. 2. Celebrated or recorded in history or story 1725.

1. S. Windows richly dight, Casting a dimm religious light MILT. 2. The s. Past TENNYSON.

Storied (stōᵊ·rid), *a.*² Also **storeyed.** 1624. [f. STORY *sb.*² + -ED.] Having stories, divided into stories.

†**Sto·rier.** late ME. [Aphetic var. of *historier*.] A chronicler, historian -1640.

Storify (stōᵊ·rifəi), *v. rare.* 1616. [f. STORY *sb.*¹ + -FY.] *trans.* To picture, delineate, or record (a historical event or fact); to celebrate in history or story. Also *absol.*

Storiology (stōᵊriǫ·lŏdʒi). 1860. [f. STORY *sb.*¹ + -(O)LOGY.] The systematic study of popular tales and legends, with regard to their origin and development. Hence **Sto:riolo·gical** *a.* **Storio·logist.**

Stork (stǭɹk). [OE. *storc* :—OTeut. **sturkoz*.] 1. A large wading bird of the genus *Ciconia*, allied to the ibis and heron; characterized by having long legs and a long stout bill.

Usually the name denotes the White Stork (*Ciconia alba*), which stands over three feet high, and has brilliant white plumage with black wing-coverts and quills, and red legs.

b. Applied to birds of allied genera 1869. c. *fig.* and *allus.* 1555. 2. The bird or its flesh as an article of food 1460. 3. A variety of the domestic pigeon. More fully *s. pigeon*. 1855.

1. b. The Giant Storks (*Mycteria*) 1869. The Field Storks (*Arvicolæ*) 1869. c. Like Æsops folish Frogges ..if hee proue a Storke, they croke and rayle Against him as a tyranne MASSINGER.

Stork's bill. 1562. [Cf. G. *storchschnabel* in sense 1.] 1. A book-name for a plant of the genus *Erodium* (family *Geraniaceæ*), esp. *E. cicutarium* or *E. moschatum*. 2. A plant of the genus *Pelargonium* (*Geraniaceæ*) 1825.

Storm (stǭɹm), *sb.* [Com. Teut.; OE. *storm* :—OTeut. **sturmoz*, f. root **stur-* of STIR *v.*] I. 1. A violent disturbance of the atmosphere, manifested by high winds, often accompanied by heavy falls of rain, hail, or snow, by thunder and lightning, and (at sea) by turbulence of the waves. Hence sometimes applied to a heavy fall of rain, hail, or snow, or to a violent outbreak of thunder and lightning, unaccompanied by strong wind. b. Used *spec.* as the distinctive appellation of a particular degree of violence in wind. In mod. *Meteorology*: An atmospheric disturbance which in the Beaufort scale is classed as intermediate between a whole gale and a hurricane, having a wind-force estimated at 10-11 and a limit of velocity at from 56-57 miles per hour. 1801. c. *Magnetic s.*: a magnetic disturbance observed simultaneously over a considerable portion of the globe 1860. 2. *transf.* A heavy discharge or downfall (of missiles, blows) OE. 3. *fig.* and in fig. context. a. A violent disturbance of (political, social, etc.) affairs; commotion, sedition, tumult OE. b. A tumultuous rush (of sound, tears, etc.); a vehement utterance (of words); a violent outburst (of censure, ridicule, etc.); a passionate manifestation of feeling 1602. c. Commotion or unrest (of mind, etc.); a tumultuous assemblage (of thoughts, feelings) 1569. 4. *Path.* A paroxysm, violent access (of pain or disease) 1545.

1. Heres..another Storme brewing, I heare it sing ith' winde SHAKS. The wind setting in at South-west, blew a s. DE FOE. Prov. phr. *A s. in a tea-cup*, a great commotion in a small community or about a trifling matter. 2. The Sulphurous Hail Shot after us in s. MILT. 3. a. Here's to the pilot that weather'd the s.! [i.e. Pitt] CANNING. b. The s. of music shakes th' astonish'd crowd COWPER. The s. of invective which burst upon him MACAULAY. A s. of weeping 1891. *S. and stress* [G. *Sturm und Drang*], designation of the movement in German literature about 1770-82, due to a school of young writers characterized by extravagance in the representation of passion, and by energetic repudiation of the 'rules' of the French critics. 4. *Brain s.*, a succession of sudden and severe phenomena, due to some cerebral disturbance 1894.

II. [f. STORM *v.*] *Mil.* A violent assault on a fortified place 1645.

To take by s., to take possession of by a sudden attack, to carry by assault; also *fig.*; The Franciscans ..were taking the world by s. 1889.

attrib. and *Comb.*: **s.-area**, the area of the earth's surface over which a s. spreads itself; **-belt**, a belt or zone in which storms occur periodically; **s. centre**, the central area of a cyclonic storm, characterized by comparative calmness; *fig.* the central point around which a s. of controversy, trouble, etc. rages; the seat of disease, sedition, or the like; **-cloud**, a heavy cloud which threatens or comes with rain; also *fig.*; **-collar**, a collar fitted to a garment and specially adapted for protection against wind and rain; **-cone**, = CONE *sb.* 5; **s. door** *U.S.*, an outer or supplementary door for use in stormy weather; **-glass**, a hermetically sealed tube containing a solution which becomes flocculent on the approach of a s.; **-proof** *a.*, (*a*) impervious to s.; (*b*) proof against storming or assault; **-sail**, 'a sail made of stout No. 1 canvas, of reduced dimensions, for use in a gale'; **-shutter**, an outside window-shutter for use in stormy weather; **-signal**, a signal exhibited at coastguard stations, etc., to give warning of the approach and direction of dangerous winds; also *fig.*; **-system**, a group of low-pressure areas constituting a cyclonic s.; **s. track**, the path traversed by the centre of a cyclonic s.: **-troops** = *shock troops* (SHOCK *sb.*³); **-wind**, the wind which accompanies a s.; **-window**, an outer window to protect the inner from the effects of storms; **-zone**, = *s.-belt*. b. In names of certain birds, the movements or cries of which are supposed to presage a s.; **s.-cock**, the missel-thrush; also locally applied to the fieldfare and the green woodpecker; **-finch**, **-petrel**, *Procellaria pelagica*; **s. thrush**, the missel-thrush. Hence **Sto·rmful** *a.* abounding in or subject to storms; **-ly** *adv.*, **-ness**. **Sto·rmless** *a.* free from storms.

Storm (stǭɹm), *v.* late ME. [f. prec. (OE. had *styrman*).] 1. *intr.* Of the elements or weather: To be tempestuous or stormy, to rage. b. *impers.* To blow violently; also to rain, snow, etc. heavily. Now only *U.S.* 1530. c. *transf.* To rush with the violence of a storm 1842. 2. *trans.* To make stormy. Also *fig.*, to trouble, vex, disturb. 1597. 3. *intr.* To complain with rough and violent language; to rage. Const. *at, against* (a grievance or person). 1553. 4. *Mil.* To make a vigorous assault on (a fortified position); to take or attempt to take by storm or assault 1645. 5. *intr.* a. *Mil.* To rush to an assault or attack 1632. b. *transf.* To rush with violence 1837.

1. b. It is now snowing and storming furiously 1858. 3. Why looke you how you storme, I would be friends with you SHAKS. I do not want to s. at the man 1889. 4. They stormed Dundie, and caried the towne 1651. He basely resolves to s. her chastity 1652. 5. a. All the Norman foot Are storming up the hill TENNYSON. Hence **Sto·rmable** *a.* that can be taken by storm. **Sto·rmer.**

Storming (stǭ·ɹmiŋ), *ppl. a.* 1557. [-ING².] 1. That storms or rages. 2. That attacks in order to take by storm; chiefly in *s. party* 1802.

Stormy (stǭ·ɹmi), *a.* ME. [f. STORM *sb.* + -Y¹.] 1. Of the weather, season, air, sky, sea, etc.: Characterized by storm or tempest; tempestuous. Of a place or region: Subject to storms. 2. *fig.* Of persons, their temper or looks; of times, events, circumstances, etc. ME.

3. Associated or connected with storms; indicative, predictive, or symbolical of storms. *poet.* 1560.

1. Beyond the s. Hebrides MILT. 2. Nothing shall hide me from thy s. looke 1592. A s. session 1831. The discussion was long and s. 1891. 3. *S. Petrel*, the bird *Procellaria pelagica*; also *fig.*, a person who delights in strife, or whose appearance on the scene is a harbinger of coming trouble. Hence **Sto·rmi-ly** *adv.*, **-ness.**

‖**Stornello** (stǫrne·lo). *Pl.* **-li** (-lī). 1873. [It.] A short popular Italian lyric, usu. improvised.

Storthing (stǭə·ɹtiŋ). 1834. [Norw. *storting*, formerly *-thing*, f. *stor* great + *ting, thing*, assembly.] The Norwegian parliament.

Story (stōə·ri), *sb.*[1] *Pl.* **stories** (stōə·riz). ME. [a. AF. *estorie* :—L. *historia* HISTORY.] I. †1. A historical narrative or anecdote -1642. †2. A historical work, a book of history -1756. †3. Historical writing or records; history as a branch of knowledge, or as opp. to fiction. Also, the events recorded or proper to be recorded by historians. -1768. 4. A recital of events that have or are alleged to have happened; a series of events that are or might be narrated. late ME. b. With possessive: A person's account of the events of his life or some portion of it 1604. c. With possessive or followed by *of*: The series of events in the life of a person, or in the past existence of a thing, country, institution, etc., considered as narrated or as a subject for narration 1700. 5 A narrative of real or, more usu., fictitious events, designed for the entertainment of the hearer or reader; a series of traditional or imaginary events forming the matter of such a narrative; a tale; *spec.* a nursery or folk tale 1500. b. Traditional, poetic, or romantic legend or history 1794. c. Succession of incidents, 'plot (of a novel, poem, or drama) 1715. d. An incident, real or fictitious, related in order to amuse or interest, or to illustrate some remark made; an anecdote 1679. ¶e. Used for: A subject of story. Also, a theme for mirth, a dupe. 1603. 6. An allegation, statement; an account or representation of a matter; a particular person's representation of the facts in a case 1601. †b. A mere tale, a baseless report -1796. c. *U.S.* A narrative or descriptive article in a newspaper; the subject or material for this 1892. 7. Euphemism for: A lie. *colloq.* 1697.

2. Examples of this, we have both in Holy Writ, and also in other Stories 1684. 3. Who is so unread ..in s., that hath not heard of many sects refusing books as a hindrance MILT. 4. A mournful s. of domestic woes POPE. *transf.* Better the rudest work that tells a s...than the richest without meaning RUSKIN. b. And then she told him her whole s. 1894. c. The S. of Creation 1888. 5. Now wee haue Arcadia, and the Faery Queene, and Orlando Furioso, with such like friuolous stories 1597. b. Or die in fight, to live in s. 1839. d. Phr. *Good s.*, often, an amusing anecdote. e. *Meas. for M.* I. iv. 30. 6. Phr. *The s. goes that..*, it is reported. *To be all in one s., to be in the same s.*, (of a number of persons) to agree in their account of a matter (usu. implying collusion). *The whole s.*, the full account of the matter, all that there is to be said. (*That is*) *another s.*, an entirely different matter; a matter requiring different treatment. 7. You were always good Children, and never told stories WESLEY. *You s.!* = you story-teller, liar (*vulgar* and in nursery use).

†II. A painting or sculpture representing a historical subject. Hence, any work of pictorial or sculptural art containing figures. -1700.

Comb.: **s.-book**, a book containing stories, esp. children's stories; also *occas.* a novel or romance; **-writer**, a historian; a writer of tales. Hence **Storye·tte**, a very short story.

Story, *sb.*[2], **storey** (stōə·ri). *Pl.* **stories, storeys.** late ME. [First in AngloL. form *historia*; hence prob. the same word as STORY *sb.*[1]] 1. Each of the stages or portions one above the other of which a building consists; a room or set of rooms on one floor or level. b. *transf.* and *fig.* Anything compared to a story of a building 1625. 2. Each of a number of tiers or rows (of orders, columns, window mullions or lights, etc.) disposed horizontally one above another. late ME.

1. b. *The* or *one's upper s.*, used joc. for the head as the seat of the mind or intellect; I wuz born weak in th' upper s. 1884.

Story (stōə·ri), *v.* late ME. [f. STORY *sb.*[1]] 1. *trans.* In early use, †to record historically; in later use, to tell as a story, to tell the story of. Now *rare.* 1450. 2. To decorate with paintings or sculpture; to represent in painting or sculpture. late ME.

1. Daphnis..storied to her what he had seen 1657.

Sto·ry-te:ller. 1709. [f. STORY *sb.*[1] + TELLER.] 1. One who is accustomed to tell stories or anecdotes in conversation. 2. Euphemistically: A liar. *colloq.* 1748. 3. One whose business it is to recite legendary or romantic stories 1777. 4. Applied to a writer of stories 1814. 5. The teller of a particular story 1851.

1. He was also a *bon-vivant*, a diner-out, and a s. 1862. So **Sto·ry-te:lling** *sb.* the action of telling stories 1709. **Sto·ry-te:lling** *a.* that tells stories; *colloq.* lying, mendacious.

‖**Stoss** (stǫs, as G. ʃtos). 1891. [G., = thrust, push.] Applied to the side or end (*s. side, s. end*) of an object that meets the impact of a moving body.

Stot (stǫt). [OE. *stot(t*; the root may be OTeut. **stut-*, ablaut-var. of **staut-* to thrust, push.] †1. A horse -1440. 2. A young castrated ox, a steer. *north.* ME. 3. A heifer. *north.* 1677.

Stound (staund, stūnd), *sb.*[1] [Com. Teut. OE. *stund* :—OTeut. **stundō*.] 1. A time, while; a short time, moment. *Obs.* exc. *dial.* 2. †a. Contextually: A hard time, a time of trial or pain -1590. b. Hence, a sharp pain, a pang; a fierce attack, a shock. Chiefly *north.* ME. c. Roar, violent noise 1627.

Stound (staund, stūnd), *sb.*[2] Now *dial.* 1567. [app. f. STOUND *v.*[2]] A state of stupefaction or amazement.

Stound, *v.*[1] ME. [f. STOUND *sb.*[1]] †1. *intr.* To remain, stay. -late ME. 2. †a. *trans.* To affect with a 'stound' or pang; to cause great pain to. b. *intr.* To be acutely painful; to smart, throb. Only *Sc.* and *north.* 1500.

Stound (staund, stūnd), *v.*[2] Now *dial.* ME. [Aphetic var. of ASTOUND *v.*] *trans.* To stun as with a blow; to stupefy, benumb; to stupefy with astonishment.

Stoup (stūp). late ME. [a. ON. *staup* = OE. *stēap* :—OTeut. **staupo-*.] 1. A pail or bucket; also *water-s.* Now only *Sc.* 2. A drinking-vessel; a cup, flagon, tankard. Also as a measure of definite quantity; often with defining word, as *gill, pint, quart s.* Now *Sc.* and *north.* and as a literary archaism. 1452. 3. A vessel to contain holy-water; often a stone basin set in or against the wall of the church-porch, or within the church close to the entrance-door 1500.

Stour (stūr). ME. [a. AF. *estur*, OF. *estour, estor* = It. *stormo*, a. Teut. **sturmoz* STORM *sb.*] I. 1. An armed combat or conflict; esp. a contest in battle; a fight. *Obs.* exc. *arch.* †2. *fig.* A conflict waged with immaterial weapons; a struggle with pain or adversity -1810. †3. Used by Spenser and his imitators for: Time of turmoil or stress -1811. †b. Used by Greene, Lodge, and others for: Occasion, place -1600. 4. Tumult, uproar; commotion, fuss. Now *Sc.* and *dial.* 1440. b. A (driving) storm. *Sc.* and *north.* 1827.

1. When joins yon host in deadly stowre SCOTT. 3. I haue beene trained vp in warlike stowre SPENSER. b. Oft from her lap at sundry stoures, He leapt, and gathered Sommer flowres LODGE.

II. Flying dust raised by the rapid movement of a person or thing, or by the wind; hence, a deposit of dust; also, dust from material undergoing mechanical treatment. *Sc.* and *north.* 1456.

Stout (staut), *sb.*[1] Now *dial.* [OE. *stūt*; etym. obsc.] A gadfly, horse-fly; also applied to a gnat.

Stout (staut), *sb.*[2] 1677. [prob. ellipt. for *stout ale* or *stout beer.*] †a. 'A cant name for strong beer' (J.). b. In present use, a strong variety of porter.

Stout (staut), *a.* and *adv.* ME. [a. OF. *estout* brave, fierce, proud; of Teut. origin (cf. MLG. *stolt* stately, proud, mod.G. *stolz* proud :—WGer. **stulta-*).] A. *adj.* I. †1. Proud, haughty, arrogant -1851. †2. Fierce, furious -1600. 3. Valiant, brave; undaunted in conflict. Now *arch.* (chiefly *attrib.* of soldiers). ME. b. Of courage, the 'heart', etc.: Undismayed 1508. c. Of a conflict, assault, or resistance: Vigorous 1582. †4. Of persons: Firm in resolve, unyielding, determined -1815. b. Of utterances or demeanour: Resolute, defiant. *arch.* late ME. c. Of a partisan, an advocate, an enemy: Uncompromising 1586. 5. a. Of a fox: Capable of long runs 1714. b. Of a horse: Of great staying power: contrasted with *speedy* 1773.

1. As s. and proud as he were Lord of all SHAKS. 2. Sterne Strife, and Anger s. SPENSER. 3. A stouter Champion neuer handled Sword SHAKS. b. To quell the valour of the stoutest heart COWPER. c. He.. Smote fiercest, where resistance was most s. CARY. 4. Askelon was s., and would not surrender FULLER. b. Your words haue bin s. against me, saith the Lord *Mal.* iii. 13. c. Johnson, who was a s. unbeliever in Rowley 1850.

II. Physical senses. 1. Strong in body; of powerful build. *arch.* b. In robust health, 'strong'. *Obs.* exc. *Sc.* 1697. 2. Of buildings, rocks, trees, etc.: Capable of defying attack; strong. late ME. b. Of a ship: Strongly built; capable of bearing rough weather 1622. 3. Of plants and their parts: Strong in growth; thick, not slender 1573. †4. Of liquor: Having 'body' or density. Chiefly of ale or beer: cf. STOUT *sb.*[2] -1826. 5. Of persons: Thick in the body and limbs; not lean or slender; inclined to corpulence; often *euphem.* = corpulent, fat 1804. 6. Of a material object or substance: So thick as to be strong or rigid 1765.

1. The Millere was a s. carl for the nones Ful byg he was of brawn, and eek of bones CHAUCER. 2. The s. dam with its marble bridge 1909. b. A s. fighting ship 1868. 5. Uncle looks very well, but he grows very s., I think 1866. 6. A s. pair of scissors 1875. Very s. cardboard 1891.

B. *adv.* Stoutly. Now *rare.* ME.

Comb.: **s.-hearted** *a.* courageous, undaunted; †stubborn, intractable. Hence **Stou·ten** *v. trans.* and *intr.* to make or grow stout. **Stou·tish** *a.* somewhat s. **Stou·t-ly** *adv.*, **-ness.**

Stout (staut), *v.* ME. [f. STOUT *a.*] †1. *intr.* To be defiant; to act in a defiant or stubborn manner -1616. 2. quasi-*trans.* a. †*To s. it* = sense 1. -1670. b. *To s. it out*: to persist in a defiant attitude; to 'brave it out'. Now *rare.* 1587.

Stovaine (stōu·veˌəin). 1904. [a. F. *stovaïne*, f. STOVE *sb.* (tr. F. *fourneau*) after *cocaïne.*] A local anæsthetic, discovered by Fourneau in 1903. (Proprietary term.)

Stove (stōuv), *sb.* 1456. [app. a. MLG. or MDu. *stove* (Du. *stoof*) = OHG. *stuba* (MHG. *stube* heated room, mod.G. *stube* sitting-room), etc.] †1. A hot air bath; a sweating-room -1756. †2. A sitting-room or bedroom heated with a furnace. Chiefly with ref. to Germany, the Low Countries, Scandinavia, or Russia. -1706. 3. A hothouse for plants 1695. 4. A heated chamber or box for some special purpose 1640. 5. An apparatus for heating (orig. for heating a 'stove' in sense 1 or 2). a. A closed box or vessel of earthenware, porcelain, or (now more usu.) of metal, portable or fixed, to contain burning fuel: often with defining word, as *cooking, electric, gas s.* 1618. b. Applied to the metal structure of a more or less open fireplace; a 'grate' 1756. c. [after Du. *stoof*] A foot-warmer containing burning charcoal 1716.

1. As they were rubbing of him with oile in his stooue or hotte house NORTH. 2. How tedious is it to them that liue in Stoues & Caues halfe a yeare together; as in Island, Muscovy, or vnder the Pole it selfe BURTON. 5. c. Under her feet was a wooden s. 1883.

Comb. **s.-grate** = sense 5 b; **-house** = sense 3; **-polish**, black lead or other substance used for polishing stoves.

Stove (stōuv), *v.* 1456. [f. prec.] †1. *trans.* To subject (a person) to a hot-air bath; to sweat (a gamecock) -1686. 2. To put (plants) in a hothouse 1625. †3. To keep (persons) in heated rooms -1802. 4. To dry in a stove or heated chamber; *Naut.* to dry (ropes) in this manner to prepare them for tarring 1625. 5. To stew (meat or vegetables). Now *Sc.* and *north.* 1738. 6. To fumigate with sulphur; to disinfect with sulphur or other fumes 1805.

Sto·ve-pipe. 1699. 1. Each of the pipes by which hot air is conveyed in a 'stove' or hothouse. 2. A metal pipe attached to a stove to carry off the smoke 1858. 3. *colloq.* or *slang.*

(orig. *U.S.*) A tall hat of cylindrical shape, a 'top hat', 'chimney-pot'. Also *s. hat.* 1851.

Stover (stōu·vəɹ). Now *dial.* ME. [Aphetic var. of ESTOVER.] †1. The provision of food (for persons or animals) necessary for a journey or for a sojourn. ME. only. 2. †a. *gen.* Winter food for cattle –1674. b. *spec.* In various applications according to locality: Hay made from clover; broken straw, etc. from the threshing-floor; stubble 1669.

2. a. Thy Turphie-Mountaines, where liue nibling Sheepe, And flat Medes thetchd with Stouer, them to keepe SHAKS.

†Stow, *sb.*[1] [OE. *stów* :—OTeut. **stōwō*, f. **stō-* (*sta-*); see STAND *v.*] = PLACE *sb.* in various senses –ME.

Stow (stōu), *sb.*[2] *Obs.* exc. *techn.* 1614. [var. of STOVE *sb.*] †1. In various senses of STOVE *sb.*: A hot-air bath; a heated room or chamber; a hothouse for plants; a closed fireplace –1731. 2. *Tin-plate making.* A raised structure containing the furnace, etc. 1839.

Stow (stōu), *v.* Pa. t. and pa. pple. **stowed** (stōud). late ME. [f. STOW *sb.*[1]] †1. *trans.* To place; to put in a certain place, position, or situation –1594. b. To lodge, quarter, find room for (persons). Now only in derogatory sense. 1604. †2. To invest (money); to apply (money or goods) to a particular purpose; to spend –1762. 3. To place in a receptacle to be stored or kept in reserve 1456. 4. *Naut.* To place (cargo) in proper order in the hold or other receptacles in a ship; also, to store (provisions, etc.) between decks 1555. †b. To fasten down (persons) under the hatches for confinement or safety –1644. c. To put (guns, oars, furniture, etc.) in the proper receptacles on board 1595. d. To furl (a sail) 1644. †e. Of a ship: To have stowage-room for; to hold –1645. 5. a. *Naut.* To fill (the hold of a ship, etc.) with cargo; to load (a ship). Also, to fit up (a ship), supply with necessaries. 1692. b. *transf.* To fill (a receptacle), to pack (*full, close*) with things or persons; to crowd with contents 1710. 6. *slang.* †a. *intr.* To cease speaking, 'shut up'. b. *trans.* To desist from. 1567.

1. Till sable Night..in her vaultie prison, stowes the daie SHAKS. b. Oh thou foule Theefe, Where hast thou stow'd my Daughter? SHAKS. 3. Raftered lofts to s. the hay 1874. 4. The human cargoes were stowed close in the holds of small vessels MACAULAY. b. The Marriners all vnder hatches stowed SHAKS. 5. b. The House was stowed as full as possible, but still many were constrained to stand without WESLEY.

Stow away. a. *trans.* To remove and store until required; to put (a thing) in a secret or not easily accessible place or where it will be out of the way; occas. to put or lodge (a person) in out-of-the-way quarters; *joc.* to 'put out of sight', 'dispose of', eat up (quantities of food). b. *intr.* for *refl.* to conceal oneself on board a ship, to be a STOWAWAY.

Stowage (stōu·ėdʒ). late ME. [f. prec. + -AGE.] 1. The action or operation of stowing cargo on board ship, or goods in a warehouse, etc. b. Manner in which the contents of a ship are stowed 1769. 2. The condition or process of being stowed or placed in a receptacle 1611. 3. Room or accommodation for stowing anything; internal capacity of a warehouse or receptacle of any kind 1547. b. *joc.* Capacity for food 1651. 4. A place in which something is stowed 1641. 5. That with which a vessel is or is to be stowed 1622.

1. We had finished the s. of the holds 1784. b. Losses by bad s. or deficient dunnage 1867. 3. The small s. necessary for the silver 1748. 4. A room under the s. or cooling-room 1848.

Stowaway (stōu·ăwē¹). 1854. [f. vbl. phr. *stow away*; see STOW *v.*] A person who hides in a ship in order to escape payment of passage-money, or to get to sea unobserved. b. *gen.* Something stowed away; also the place 1913.

Stow-blade. Also **stoblade.** 1681. [f. *stow* = STOWCE.] *Mining.* Each of two upright pieces of wood, a foot in length, connected at the top with the sole-trees of a stowce.

Stowce (stōus). 1664. [Origin obsc.] *Mining. sing.* and *pl.* A kind of windlass for drawing up ore; also, a model of this, intended not for working, but to comply with the old law which provides that the presence of an owner's 'stowce' on a mining tract secures his right of possession. Hence **Stowce** *v. trans.* to mark (a 'meer' of ground) with 'a pair of stowces'.

Strabism (strē¹·biz'm). 1656. Anglicized f. STRABISMUS.

‖ **Strabismus** (străbi·zmǒs). 1684. [mod.L., ad. Gr. στραβισμός, f. στραβίζειν to squint, f. στραβός squinting.] *Path.* An affection of the eyes in which the axes of vision cannot be coincidently directed to the same object; squinting, a squint. b. *fig.* Perversity of intellectual perception 1844.

Convergent or *internal s.*, a turning inward of the eyes, CROSS-EYE; *divergent* or *external s.*, a turning outward of one or both eyes. Hence **Strabi·smal, Strabi·smic** *adjs.* of, pertaining to, or affected by s. **Strabismometer** (strē¹bizmǫ·mǐtəɹ), an instrument for measuring the degree of s.

Strabotomy (străbǫ·tŏmi). 1857. [ad. F. *strabotomie* (mod.L. *strabotomia*), f. *strabo-* taken as comb. form of STRABISMUS; see -TOMY.] *Path.* The operation of dividing one or more of the muscles of the eye as a remedy for strabismus.

‖ **Stracchino** (strakī·no). 1832. [It.] *S. cheese*, a variety of very soft cheese made in the north of Italy.

Strad (stræd). *colloq.* 1884. Short for STRADIVARIUS.

Straddle (stræ·d'l), *sb.* 1611. [f. next.] 1. The action of walking, standing, or sitting with the legs wide apart. b. The distance between the feet or legs of one who straddles 1864. 2. *U.S. Exchange slang.* A 'privilege' or speculative contract in any one market or class of commodities giving the holder the right at his option (1) of calling, within a specified number of days, for delivery of an ascertained quantity of the commodity at a stated price, or (2) of delivering to the person to whom the consideration had been paid an ascertained quantity of another (or, less usu., of the same) commodity at a stated price. Hence, applied to an analogous contract on the Stock-exchange. Also called *spread-eagle.* 1883. 3. *U.S. Politics* (*colloq.*). An attempt to take an equivocal or noncommittal position in a party platform 1883. 4. *Poker.* A doubling of the 'blind' or stake by one of the players 1882.

Straddle (stræ·d'l), *v.* 1565. [frequent. f. *strād-* ablaut-var. of *strīd-* STRIDE *v.*; see -LE.] 1. *intr.* To spread the legs wide apart in walking, standing, or sitting. b. Of the legs: To stand wide apart 1634. c. *transf.* of a thing, esp. of a thing having legs; also, to sprawl 1596. d. *spec.* Of the spokes of a wheel: To stand with the ends staggered 1875. 2. To walk with the legs wide apart; *dial.* 'to swagger, strut' 1825. 3. *trans.* To set (the legs) wide apart (in standing or walking) 1565. 4. To sit, stand, or walk with one leg on either side of; to stride over; to bestride 1823. b. *transf.* To stand or lie across or on both sides of (something) 1890. 5. *U.S. colloq.* To occupy or take up an equivocal position in regard to; to appear to favour both sides of. Also *intr.* 1884. 6. *Poker.* To double (a stake, bet). Also *absol.* 1882. 7. *Gunnery.* To find the range of (an object) by placing shots first on one side of it and then on the other 1916.

4. Straddling a chair..may be pardonable in a bachelor's rooms 1859. 5. He never straddled the negro question 1884. Hence **Stra·ddling** *ppl. a.* that straddles; *Bot.* divaricate.

Stradiot (stræ·diǫt). 1533. [ad. It. *stradiotto*; see ESTRADIOT.] *Hist.* = ESTRADIOT.

Stradivarius (strædivē⁰·riǒs). 1833. [a. L. *Stradivarius*, latinized f. the name of Antonio *Stradivari.*] A violin or other stringed instrument made by Stradivari or his pupils.

Strafe (strāf), *v. slang.* 1915 [From G. phr. *Gott strafe England* 'God punish England', supposed to be a salutation in Germany in 1914 and the following years.] *trans.* Used (orig. by British soldiers in the war of 1914–18) in various senses: To punish; to do damage to; to attack fiercely; to heap imprecations on. Also *absol.* Hence **Strafe** *sb.* a fierce assault; a period of heavy shell-fire. **Stra·fer.**

Straggle (stræ·g'l), *sb.* 1470. [f. next.] †1. Phr. *At, to* (*the*) *s.*, in straggling order. *Sc.* –1549. 2. A body or group of scattered objects; an irregular or fitful emergence (*of* something) 1865.

Straggle (stræ·g'l), *v.* late ME. [Of uncertain etym.] 1. *intr.* To wander or stray *from* the proper road, one's companions, etc.; to rove without fixed direction; to go up and down dispersedly. Often conjugated with *be.* b. *spec.* of a soldier: To wander from the line of march, stray from one's company. Also of a ship: To stray from the line of battle. Of a sailor: To be absent from his ship without leave or to overstay his leave. 1529. c. *transf.* and *fig.* (of persons and things) 1588. d. Of a plant, branch, etc.: To grow irregularly or loosely; to spread or shoot too far. Similarly of hair. 1693. e. Of inanimate objects: To be arranged dispersedly or irregularly. Of a town, building, etc.: To be built irregularly and without compactness. Of a road, river, fence, etc.: To wind in an irregular course. 1611. 2. *pass.* To be placed stragglingly. *U.S.* 1898.

1. [They] runne strag1ing and rouing..from towne to towne 1583. b. They sickened or straggled or frankly deserted 1913. c. Children..cannot keep their Minds from straggling LOCKE. e. A little hamlet which straggled along the side of a creek SCOTT. Hence **Stra·ggling** *ppl. a.*, **-ly** *adv.*

Straggler (stræ·gləɹ). 1530. [f. prec. + -ER[1].] 1. One who wanders or roves without fixed direction; one who strays from his companions or from the regular route; †a gadabout; †a camp-follower, a tramp, vagabond. 2. *Mil.* A soldier who leaves the line of march or falls out of the ranks. †Also, a scout or skirmisher. 1589. b. *Naut.* A sailor who is absent from his ship without leave or who overstays his leave 1670. 3. An animal that strays from its habitat or companions; esp. a migratory bird found at a place outside its usual range 1552. 4. A plant, branch, etc., that grows irregularly or shoots too far; also, a plant, fruit, etc., found growing singly or apart from others of its kind. Similarly, a stray lock of hair. 1553.

1. Let's whip these straglers o're the Seas againe SHAKS. The vast pleasure-grounds were cleared of the last s. 1883. 4. Sometimes his pruning-hook corrects the vines, And the loose stragglers to their ranks confines POPE.

Straggly (stræ·gli), *a.* 1866. [f. STRAGGLE *v.* and *sb.* + -Y[1].] Characterized by straggling.

Straight (strē¹t), *a.*, *sb.*, and *adv.* [ME. *stregt, stragt*, orig. an adjectival use of the pa. pple. of *strecchen* to STRETCH.] A. *adj.* †1. As ppl. adj.: Extended at full length –1596. 2. Not crooked; free from curvature, bending, or angularity ME. b. Of a human form, a back: Erect, not crooked or stooping 1599. c. Of a limb, etc.: Held with the joint not flexed 1765. d. Of hair: Not curly or waved 1748. e. *Anat.* The distinctive epithet of certain structures (= mod.L. *rectus*) 1585. 3. Direct, undeviating. late ME. b. *colloq.* Of an utterance: Outspoken, unreserved 1894. 4. *S. angle.* †a. A right angle; b. in mod. use, an angle of 180° 1601. 5. Of conduct: Free from crookedness; honest. Hence used of persons and their attributes. Now *colloq.* 1530. b. Of a person: Well-conducted, steady. Chiefly in *to keep s.* Of a woman: Virtuous, chaste. 1868. 6. Not oblique; either vertical or horizontal. Hence, *a s. eye*: ability to see whether an object is placed straight. 1600. b. *Cricket.* Of the bat: Held so as not to incline to either side 1843. 7. *predic.*: In proper order, not ruffled or disarranged 1831. b. *colloq.* Of accounts: Settled up, leaving nothing owing 1613. c. Of a person: Having settled one's differences (*with* another); also, having balanced one's account, 'even' 1730. 8. *U.S.* a. Unmixed, undiluted; of spirits, 'neat'. Also qualifying a designation of a political party: Strict, rigid, extreme. 1856. b. *S. Poker, Whist,* etc.: the game in its unmodified form. *S. five*: a sequence or rotation of fives. *S. flush*: a sequence of five cards, all of the same suit. 1882. 9. Of or pertaining to the legitimate drama 1928.

2. And bent the wand that might have growen ful streight 1563. Panicle stiff and s. 1796. *S. line*, a line uniform in direction throughout its length; *Geom.* the shortest distance between two points. b. A daughter of our meadows..S., but as lissome as a hazel wand TENNYSON. 3. Prepare the waye of the Lorde, and make his pathes s. COVERDALE *Luke* iii. 4. *The s. tip* (colloq.): see TIP *sb.*[4]. b. *S. talk*, a piece of plain speaking. 5. A s. man, true to his cloth and calling 1893. 6. *S. play*, play with the bat held s. 7. Phr. *To keep one's face s.* (colloq.), to refrain from laughing. 8. a. *To vote the s. ticket* (U.S.), to vote for all the official candidates of one's party.

Comb.: *s.-edged*, *-legged*, *-limbed*, *-veined* adjs.; s.

arch, an arch having radiating joints but a straight intrados and extrados line; **s. fight,** a direct contest between two candidates; **s. play,** a play in which there is plain dialogue without music, etc.; **-side** *a.*, having straight sides, *spec.* of a pneumatic automobile tyre.

B. quasi-*sb.* and *sb.* **1.** The adj. used *absol.* (quasi-*sb.*) in certain phrases. late ME. **2.** A straight form or position; a level 1645. **3.** A straight portion, e.g. of a racecourse (*the s.*), a railway 1846. **4.** *Geom.* A straight line (*rare*) 1892. **5.** In Poker, etc.: A series of five cards in sequence but not of the same suit 1882.

1. *On the s.*, (*a*) along a straight line, not following irregularities of contour; (*b*) parallel with the side, as opp. to 'on the cross' = diagonally; (*c*) *slang*, behaving reputably. *Out of s.*, deviating from the required s. form or position; not duly rectilinear, level, or perpendicular; awry.

C. *adv.* **1.** In a straight course; directly to or from a place; in a straight line, not crookedly ME. **b.** In a straight direction; directly to a mark or object, or following a moving object without deviation 1535. **c.** With additional notion, which sometimes becomes the substantive sense: All the way, continuously to the end; 'right' *across, through*, etc. 1446. **2.** Immediately, without delay. Now *poet.* or *arch.* ME. **3.** In an erect posture, upright 1535. **4.** Honestly, honourably 1845. **5.** Frankly, outspokenly. Also *s. out.* 1877.

1. We took our way streight to Jerusalem 1687. I cannot write straighter in bed, so you must be content SWIFT. **b.** He..looked this time s. into my eyes 1886. **c.** Apertures..cut s. through a wall 1840. **2.** She burst into tears, and s. quitted the room 1760. *S. away, s. off*, immediately, at once, without deliberation or preparation. **3.** *S. set up*, having an erect figure. **4.** As a rule I believe they [*sc.* jockeys] run very s. 1888. **5.** Speak right s. out and do not be afraid 1877.

Straight (strēit), *v.* late ME. [f. STRAIGHT *a.*] †**1.** *trans.* To stretch (e.g. a body on the rack); to extend, stretch forth (a spear) –1800. **2.** To make straight, straighten. In later use chiefly *Sc.*, to straighten (a stream, a boundary); to lay out (a corpse). 1530.

Strai·ghtaway, *a.* and *sb.* 1874. [phr. *straight away* (STRAIGHT C. 2) used *attrib.*] **A.** *adj.* Of a shot: Aimed at a bird flying 'straight away'. Also said of the bird. Of a ride, a course in rowing or sailing: Continuous in direction and time. **B.** *sb.* A race-course which is without turn or curve 1895.

Strai·ght-edge. 1812. A narrow strip of hard wood, steel, or brass, with one edge cut perfectly straight, used to test the accuracy of a plane surface, or as a guide for a cutting instrument.

Straighten (strēit'n). 1542. [f. STRAIGHT *a.* + -EN [5].] **1.** *trans.* To make straight (what is bent or crooked). Also with *out.* **2.** To unravel, disentangle, clear up (what is confused or intricate). Now chiefly with *out.* 1577. **3.** To put in order, tidy up 1867. **4.** *intr.* To become straight. *To s. up* (orig. U.S.): to rise to an erect posture; also *slang* to adopt an honest course of life. 1891.

1. The crooked Scythes are streightned into Swords DRYDEN. **3.** I'll send Granny up here to s. things a bit 1901. Hence **Strai·ghtener,** one who or something which straightens.

Straight forth, strai·ghtforth, *adv.* Now *rare.* 1530. [STRAIGHT *adv.*] **1.** Directly in front or onwards. **2.** Immediately, at once 1577.

Straight forward, straightfo·rward, *adv.* and *a.* 1806. [STRAIGHT *adv.*] **A.** *adv.* Directly in front or onwards; in direct order 1809. **B.** *adj.* **1.** Of movement, vision, etc.: Proceeding or directed straight forward 1807. **2.** Of language, narrative, or exposition: Direct, without circumlocution or digression 1806. **3.** Of an action or process: Continuous in one direction, undeviating 1817. **4.** Presenting a clear course; free from difficulties 1833. **5.** Of persons, their dispositions or conduct: Consistent, undeviating in purpose, single-minded. Also (now usu.), free from duplicity or concealment; frank, outspoken. 1834. Hence **Straightfo·rward-ly** *adv.*, **-ness.**

Straight-lined (stress var.), *a.* 1571. Composed of or containing straight lines; having the form of a straight line; rectilinear.

Straightly (strēitli), *adv.* late ME. [f. STRAIGHT *a.* + -LY [2].] **1.** In a straight manner; in a straight line; directly. **2.** Straightway, immediately. *poet.* (*rare*) 1830.

Straightness (strēitnės). 1530. [-NESS.] The quality of being straight.

Strai·ght-out, *a.* and *sb.* Chiefly *U.S.* 1840. [attrib. use of the phr. *straight out.*] **A.** *adj.* Unrestrained; going all lengths. In party politics = STRAIGHT *a.* 8. 1856. **B.** *sb.* One who votes a 'straight' party ticket, an uncompromising partisan 1840.

Straightway (strēit·twē¹), *adv.* 1461. [f. STRAIGHT *a.* + WAY *sb.*] †**1.** By a direct course –1587. **2.** Immediately; at once. Now only *literary.* 1526.

2. She s. sat down and indited a long letter DICKENS. So **Strai·ghtways** *adv.* (in sense 2). Now *rare* or *Obs.*

Strain (strēin), *sb.*[1] [OE. *strēon, strīon*, aphetic f. *gestrēon, gestrīon*, f. prehistoric **streu-* to pile up; cf. L. *strues* pile, *struere* to build.] †**I.** Gain, acquisition; treasure –ME. **II.** †**1.** Begetting, generation. ME. only. †**2.** The germinal vesicle in the yoke of an egg –1764. **3.** Offspring, progeny. *Obs.* exc. *arch.* ME. **4.** Pedigree, lineage, ancestry, descent ME. **5.** The descendants of a common ancestor; a race, stock, line ME. **b.** Any one of the various lines of ancestry united in an individual or a family; an admixture of some racial or family element in a genealogy 1863. **6.** A race, breed; a variety developed by breeding 1607. **7.** Inherited character or constitution 1603. **b.** An inherited tendency or quality; hence, in wider sense, an admixture in a character of some quality somewhat contrasting with the rest 1598. **8.** A kind, class, or sort (of persons), as determined by community of character, conduct, or degree of ability. Now *rare.* 1598. **b.** A kind, class, or grade (of things) 1612.

4. Hee is of a noble straine, of approued valour, and confirm'd honesty SHAKS. **5.** Charlemain, And the long Heroes of the Gallic S. PRIOR. **b.** Horses which had any s. of hackney..blood 1897. **6.** Two Kids..Both fleck'd with white, the true Arcadian S. DRYDEN. Begonias, gold medal s. 1908. **7. b.** There was..a s. of insanity in the family 1906. **8.** Thou, who lately of the common s., Wert one of us DRYDEN.

Strain (strēin), *sb.*[2] late ME. [f. STRAIN *v.*[1]] †**I.** A strainer –1655. **II.** Action or result of straining. †**1.** Constraint; compulsion –1648. **2.** A result of straining; an injury done to a limb or part of the body through being forcibly stretched beyond its proper length; often = SPRAIN 1. 1558. **3.** A stretch, extreme degree, height, pitch (of a quality, activity, etc.). Now *rare.* 1576. †**4.** A strained construction or interpretation –1731. **5.** A strong muscular effort; †*spec.* an effort to vomit, a retching; a straining at stool 1590. **b.** Extreme or excessive effort; a straining *at* or *after* some object of attainment 1683. **6.** A forcible stretching of a material thing; force tending to pull asunder or to drag from a position. Later, in wider sense: Force or pressure tending to cause fracture, change of position, or alteration of shape; also, the condition of a body or a particle subjected to such force or pressure 1602. **b.** *Physics.* Any definite change of volume or figure exhibited by a solid or liquid mass 1850. **7.** Pressure or exigency that severely taxes the strength, endurance, or resources of a person or thing, or that imperils the permanence of a feeling, relation, or condition 1853.

3. It is, indeed, a high S. of Generosity in you, to think of making me easy all my Life POPE. **5.** Phr. *At* (*full, utmost*) *s.*, *on the s.*, straining, using strong effort; Adonis..spear in hand, with leashed dogs at s. R. BRIDGES. **b.** There shall be strenuousness without s.! 1905. **6.** Table of Breaking Strains 1888. **7.** He had been often driven to borrow money of Sir Ralph ..but their friendship had stood the s. 1894. The s. of his responsibility had been too much for him 1897.

III. 1. *Mus.* A definite rhythmical section of a piece of music, divided from what follows by a double bar 1575. **2.** In wider sense, a musical sequence of sounds; a melody, tune; often *collect. pl.* 1579. **b.** *transf.* A passage of song or poetry 1563. †**c.** A stream or flow of impassioned or ungoverned language –1742. **3.** Tone, style, or turn of expression; tone or character of feeling expressed; tenor, drift, character, or general tendency (of a composition or discourse) 1622.

2. That s. I heard was of a higher mood MILT. **b.** Till old experience do attain To something like Prophetic s. MILT. **c.** The Strains of ancient Eloquence HUME. **3.** But his letters to England were in a very different s. MACAULAY.

Strain (strēin), *v.*[1] [ME. *streyne*, a. OF. *estrein-, estreign-*, stem of *estreindre* to bind tightly, clasp, squeeze:—L. *stringere*; see STRINGENT *a.*] **I.** To bind tightly; to clasp, squeeze. †**1.** *trans.* To bind fast; to confine in bonds –1532. **b.** To fasten, attach firmly. *Obs.* exc. (*rarely*) with the sense: To attach by compulsion. late ME. **2.** To clasp tightly in one's arms. *Obs.* exc. as in **b.** late ME. **b.** esp. *to s.* (a person) *to one's bosom, heart*, and the like 1789. **3.** To clasp tightly in the hand. *Obs.* or *arch.* 1518. †**b.** Of a bird (esp. a hawk) or beast: To seize (its prey) in its claws. Chiefly *absol.* –1596. **4.** To constrict painfully, as with an encircling cord. late ME. †**5.** To press hard upon, afflict, distress –1730. †**6.** To bridle, control, restrain –1595. †**7.** To force, press, constrain (*to* a condition or action) –1603. †**b.** To urge, insist upon (a thing). Also *absol.* –1604. †**8.** To extract (liquor or juice) by pressure; to squeeze out. Also *intr.* Of a juice: To exude. –1781. †**b.** To extort (money, confessions, etc.) –1699.

2. *Hen. VIII*, IV. i. 46. **3.** The one in hand an yron whip did strayne, The other brandished a bloudy knife SPENSER. **4.** Was it..For this with fillets [you] strain'd your tender head? POPE. **7.** *John* III. iii. 46. **8.** The Bard..strains, from hard-bound brains, eight lines a year POPE. **b.** The quality of mercy is not strain'd SHAKS.

II. To tighten, draw tight, stretch. **1.** To extend with some effort; to subject to tension, to stretch ME. **b.** To tighten up (the strings of a musical instrument) so as to raise the pitch. Also with *up.* late ME. **2.** *fig.* **a.** To force the meaning or sense of (words, an ordinance, decree, etc.) 1449. **b.** To transgress the strict requirements of (one's conscience), to violate the spirit of (one's oath) 1592. **c.** To force (prerogative, power, etc.) beyond its legitimate extent or scope 1605. †**d.** To apply or use (a thing) beyond its province –1647. **e.** *To s. a point*: to exceed one's usual limits of procedure; to do more than one is bound to do or go further than one is entitled to go in a matter 1596. †**f.** To insist upon unduly –1711. †**g.** To raise to an extreme degree –1697. **h.** To raise to a high state of emotional tension 1667. **i.** To make excessive demands upon, tax severely (resources, credit, friendship, etc.) 1609. **3.** To stretch (sinews, nerves, muscles) beyond the normal degree (as the supposed condition of intense exertion); hence, to force to the utmost (one's limbs, organs, powers) 1446. **4.** To injure or alter by excessive tension 1612.

1. There may be a danger in straining too strongly the bonds of government BURKE. The barbed wire fence ..was strained to posts..6 ft. high 1893. **2. a.** Defective laws should be altered by the legislature, and not strained by the tribunals MACAULAY. **c.** The Crown retains prerogatives at present which would be fatal to it if strained 1883. **d.** *Much Ado* IV. i. 254. **i.** The King had strained his private credit in Holland to procure bread for his army MACAULAY. **3.** Phr. *To s. every nerve* (fig.), to use one's utmost endeavours. **4.** I have strained the thumb of my left hand with pulling him SWIFT. The ship had strained herself a good deal, owing to the heavy cargo of railway-iron she had stowed in her hold 1868.

III. To press through a filtering medium, to filter. **1.** To press (a liquid) through a porous or perforated medium so as to keep back the denser portions or the solid matter held in suspension; to free (solid matter) from the contained or accompanying liquid by this process; to purify or refine by filtration. Also *absol.* late ME. **b.** To remove (liquid) by filtration, drain off 1558. ¶**c.** To take out (something) from a liquid by straining 1526. **2.** *intr.* for *refl.* To filter; to trickle 1588.

1. *fig. Tr. & Cr.* IV. v. 169. **c.** Ye blinde gydes which strayne out a gnat and swalowe a cammyll TINDALE *Matt.* xxiii. 24. **2.** The Sea water passing or Strayning through the Sandes, leaueth the Saltnesse BACON.

IV. 1. *refl.* To exert oneself physically. In later use, to exert oneself so as to be in danger of injury. Now *rare* or *Obs.* late ME. **2.** *intr.* To make violent and continuous physical effort ME. **b.** *transf.* of a thing viewed as endowed with power to make effort 1819. c. To pull forcibly (*at* a rope, leash, rein) 1791. 3. *intr.* To use one's utmost endeavours; to strive vigorously 1593. 4. †a. To retch, make efforts to vomit -1727. b. To make efforts to evacuate the bowels; more fully *to s. at stool* 1645. 5. *To s. at*: to make a difficulty of 'swallowing' or accepting (something); to scruple at 1609. (This use is due to misunderstanding of the phr. 'strain at a gnat' meaning properly 'which strain the liquor if they find a gnat in it', in Matt. xxiii. 24.)

2. The patience with which he had seen a boatman on a canal s. against an adverse eddy MACAULAY. b. The wind sung, cordage strain'd, and sailors swore BYRON. 3. Straining after novelty 1797.

†V. a. *trans.* To use (the voice) in song; to play upon (an instrument) -1648. b. To utter in song -1648. c. *intr.* To sing -1612.

b. It is the Larke that sings so out of tune, Straining harsh Discords, and vnpleasing Sharpes SHAKS. Hence †**Strai·nable** *a.* coercive, compulsive; violent, exerting great force (chiefly of wind and weather).

†**Strain**, *v.*[2] 1450. [Aphetic f. DISTRAIN *v.*] *Law.* = DISTRAIN *v.* II. 1-3. -1718.

Strained (strēind), *ppl. a.* late ME. [f. STRAIN *v.*[1] + -ED[1].] In the senses of the verb: Subjected to physical tension; done or produced under compulsion or by an abnormal effort; of conduct, demeanour, etc., artificial, forced, not spontaneous or natural; of language, etc., wrested or distorted from the natural meaning or intention; pressed, forced; injured by over-exertion or excessive tension, etc.

S. ropes 1640. A strange, and very..strained interpretation HOBBES. A s. and powerful voice SCOTT. The s., eye-shirking talk at dinner KIPLING. Hence **Strai·ned-ly** *adv.*, **-ness.**

Strainer (strēi·nəɹ). ME. [f. STRAIN *v.*[1] + -ER[1].] A utensil or device for straining, filtering, or sifting; a filter, sieve, or the like. b. Applied to natural structures or processes which perform the function of filtering 1626. 2. A device for stretching or tightening 1527.

Straining (strēi·niŋ), *vbl. sb.* ME. [f. STRAIN *v.*[1] + -ING[1].] 1. The action of the verb, in various senses. 2. *concr.* Something strained or extracted by straining; usu. a strained liquor 1580.

attrib. and *Comb.*: **s.-arch**, an arch designed to resist end-thrust; **-beam, piece**, a piece of timber placed between *queen-posts*, at their upper ends, to withstand the thrust of the principal rafters.

Straint (strēint). *rare.* 1534. [a. OF. *estrainte, estreinte*, f. *estreindre* to STRAIN.] Application of force or pressure.

Strait (strēit), *a.*, *sb.*, and *adv.* [ME. *streit*, a. OF. *estreit* tight, close, narrow, also as sb. :—L. *strictus* STRICT, pa. pple. of *stringere*; see STRAIN *v.*, STRINGENT *a.*] A. *adj.* I. Tight, narrow. 1. Of a garment, etc.: Tight-fitting *Obs. exc. dial.* 2. Affording little room; narrow. Of bounds, limits: narrow. Now *rare* exc. in *too s.* ME. b. Of a place of confinement 1460. 3. Of a way, passage, or channel: So narrow as to make transit difficult. Now *rare* in lit. sense. ME.

2. Myn hous is streit CHAUCER. 3. The s. passe was damm'd With dead men SHAKS. *fig.* Entre ȝe bi the streyt ȝate WYCLIF *Matt.* vii. 13.

Special collocations: **s. jacket** *sb.* and *v.* = STRAIT WAISTCOAT *sb.* and *v.*; **s. work**, the system of getting coal by headings or narrow work.

II. †1. Strict, rigorous (of conditions, sufferings, of modes of living, a religious order, etc.) -1642. †2. Of a person, an agent: Severe, strict, exacting in actions or dealings -1612. b. Strict or scrupulous in morality or religious observance. *arch.* 1526. 3. Of a commandment, law, penalty, vow: Stringent, allowing no evasion. *Obs.* exc. *arch.* late ME. 4. †a. Of actions, proceedings: Conducted with strictness -1599. b. Of guard, watch, imprisonment: Rigorous, strict. Now *rare.* late ME.

1. The streit administration of Justice 1550. Neither let them keepe any straight Diette 1582. 2. His Creditors most straite SHAKS. b. After the most straytest secte of oure laye lived I a pharisaye TINDALE *Acts* xxvi. 5. 3. His..s. charge to all posteritie, that one man should cleaue to one wife 1612. 4. a. S. inquisition and search is made 1599.

III. 1. Of fortune, circumstances, etc.: Limited (so as to cause hardship or inconvenience). *arch.* †2. Strictly specified, exact, precise, definite -1638. 3. Of friendship, alliance, etc.: Close, intimate. Now *rare.* 1530. †4. Reluctant and chary in giving; close, stingy; narrow -1760.

1. My wages been ful streite and ful smale CHAUCER. 4. I begge cold comfort, and you are so straight.., you deny me that SHAKS.

B. *sb.* 1. A narrow confined place or space or way generally. Now *rare* or *Obs.* ME. 2. *fig.* A narrow or tight place; a time of sore need or of awkward or straitened circumstances; a difficulty or fix. Now *rare* in *sing.*; still common in *pl.* 1544. b. occas. in generalized sense: Privation, hardship 1837. 3. A comparatively narrow water-way or passage connecting two large bodies of water. (As a geographical proper name, usu. *pl.* with sing. sense.) late ME. b. *pl.* Short for *Straits Settlements*, the British possessions in the Malay peninsula collectively, so named because near the Straits of Malacca 1884. †4. A narrow pass or gorge between mountains; a defile, ravine -1778. 5. *poet.* An isthmus. Now *rare.* 1562. 6. A narrow part (of a river); *pl.* 'narrows'. Now *rare* or *Obs.* late ME. †7. A narrow lane, alley, or passage -1622. 8. The narrow part (of anything tubular); a narrow passage in the body 1558. †9. *pl.* Cloth of single width, as opp. to BROADCLOTH -1706.

1. He brought him through a darksome narrow s. To a broad gate SPENSER. 2. He keept them in great straits for money 1756. Take me: I'll serve you better in a s. TENNYSON. 3. They returned home by the pillars and streights of Hercules..called now the straights of Gybralter RALEGH. *transf.* Where the scattered stars are seen In hazy straits the clouds between WORDSW. *The Straits*, in 17-18th c. usu. = the Straits of Gibraltar; now chiefly = the Straits of Malacca. 4. The streight of Thermopilæ 1753. 5. A chapel..That stood on a dark s. of barren land TENNYSON.

C. *adv.* 1. Tightly. *Obs.* exc. *dial.* ME. †2. Close; with narrow opening -1641. †3. In strait or careful keeping, securely; in strict custody -1611. 4. Severely, oppressively; so as to cause hardship. Now *rare.* ME. †5. With strictness -1590.

†**Strait**, *v.* ME. [f. STRAIT *a.*] I. *trans.* As tr. Vulg. *coartare, artare*, to press together, contract. -late ME. 2. To narrow -1615. 3. To shut up in or force into a narrow space -1641. b. To bring into straits, subject to hardship -1654. c. *pass.* To be hard put to it, to be at a loss -1647. 4. To restrict; to keep ill supplied, stint -1669.

Straiten (strēi·t'n), *v.* 1523. [f. STRAIT *a.* + -EN[5].] 1. *trans.* To render strait or narrow; to narrow, contract (an opening, a passage, road, stream, etc.). Now somewhat *rare.* 1552. 2. *intr.* To become narrow, to narrow 1601. †3. *trans.* To tighten (a knot, cord, bonds) -1742. †b. To render more strict or rigorous -1753. 4. To confine in or force into a narrow space; to hem in closely. Now *rare.* 1570. 5. To narrow or restrict the freedom, power, or privileges of (now *arch.*); to narrow in range, scope, or amount 1586. †b. To abridge *of* (a possession or privilege) -1647. 6. To reduce to straits; to subject to privation, hardship, or distress 1611. b. To inconvenience by insufficiency of something specified (as time, space, supplies of any kind). Now only in *pass.* (somewhat *arch.*). 1620. c. To render short of money or supplies 1699. †7. To hamper, impede in action -1726.

1. An ancient grant..that a way leading to their common should not be streightened COKE. 4. Waters, when they..are straitned (as in the falls of Bridges;) ..giue a Roaring Noise BACON. If this be our condition, thus to dwell In narrow circuit strait'nd by a Foe MILT. 5. Is the Spirit of the Lord straitned? *Micah* ii. 7. They had no design to s. the rights of the Holy See 1855. 6. The siege and straitnesse, wherewith their enemies..shall s. them *Jer.* xix. 9. c. If straitened for provisions, they ate the chargers which carried them to battle J. H. NEWMAN. Often in pa. pples, esp. *straitened circumstances.*

Strait-lace, *v.* 1636. [Back-formation from next.] *trans.* and *intr.* (for *refl.*) To lace tightly, confine.

Strait-laced (strēit,lēst; stress var.), *a.* 1546. [f. STRAIT *adv.* + LACED *ppl. a.*] †1. Wearing stays or bodice tightly laced -1698. 2. *fig.* †a. Of things: Narrow in range or scope -1686. †b. Of persons: Shut up within oneself, uncommunicative, morose -1691. †c. Obstinate; grudging in gifts or concessions -1601. d. Of persons, their habits, opinions, etc.: Excessively rigid or scrupulous in matters of conduct; over-precise; prudish 1554.

1. We should as certainly have no perfect children born, as we have few well-shaped that are strait-laced LOCKE. 2. d. Had these strait-lac'd Gentlemen once gain'd their Point against Plays 1707.

Straitly (strēi·tli), *adv.* ME. [f. STRAIT *a.* + -LY[2].] 1. Tightly. *Obs.* exc. *arch.* 2. Narrowly; within narrow limits. late ME. 3. Strictly, rigorously, stringently (now only *arch.* with respect to commands, questions, etc.) ME. 4. With ref. to alliance or union: Closely, intimately. *arch.* 1480.

Straitness (strēi·tnės). ME. [f. STRAIT *a.* + -NESS.] 1. The quality of being strait; *esp.* straitened condition (of circumstances). late ME. †2. Want of room -1775. 3. Hardship, distress; privation, straitened circumstances. *arch.* ME.

Strait waistcoat, *sb.* 1753. A garment for the upper part of the body with or without sleeves, made of strong material and admitting of being tightly laced, used for the restraint of violent lunatics or prisoners, and sometimes as a means of punishment. Hence **Strait-waistcoat** *v. trans.* to confine in a strait waistcoat.

Strake (strēik), *sb.*[1] [ME. *strake*, app. belonging to the OTeut. root **strak-*, whence **strakjan*, OE. *streççan* STRETCH *v.*] 1. A section of the iron rim of a cart-wheel. 2. A stripe of different colour from the rest of the surface of which it forms part. late ME. 3. *Naut.* Each of the several continuous lines of planking or plates, of uniform breadth, in the side of a vessel, extending from stem to stern. Hence, the breadth of a plank used as a unit of vertical measurement in a ship's side. late ME. 4. A stretch of ground travelled over. Also, length of stride; pace. Now *dial.* 1558.

2. Alabaster is a white stone with strakes of diuerse coloure TREVISA. 3. *Garboard s.*: see GARBOARD.

Strake (strēik), *sb.*[2] 1758. [perh. same word as prec.] *Mining.* a. A shallow pit for the purpose of washing ore. b. A wooden box without ends, used for the same purpose. c. *Gold-mining.* An apparatus for concentrating the stamped ore 1887.

†**Strake** (strēik), *v.*[1] 1537. [f. STRAKE *sb.*[1]] 1. *trans.* To mark with lines, to streak -1718.

Strake (strēik), *v.*[2] 1778. [f. STRAKE *sb.*[2]] *Mining. trans.* To wash (ore) in a strake. Also *Gold mining*, to concentrate (ore) by means of strakes.

Stramash (strămæ·ʃ), *sb.* Chiefly *Sc.* 1819. [Belongs to next.] 1. An uproar, state of noise and confusion; a 'row' 1821. 2. A state of ruin, a smash 1819.

Stramash (strămæ·ʃ), *v. dial.* 1788. [app. onomatopæic; cf. SMASH.] *trans.* To smash.

Stramineous (strămi·nĭ,əs), *a.* 1621. [f. L. *stramineus* (f. *stramen* straw) + -OUS.] 1. Consisting of or relating to straw; *fig.* valueless. 2. *Bot.* Straw-coloured; dull pale yellow 1845.

Stramonium (strămōu·niŏm). 1677. [a. mod.L., of uncertain origin.] 1. The solanaceous plant *Datura Stramonium*, the THORN-APPLE. 2. A narcotic drug prepared from this plant 1802.

Stramony (stræ·mŏni). 1842. Anglicized form of prec.

Strand (strænd), *sb.*[1] [OE. *strand* = OFris. *strŏnd*, MLG. *strant*, ON. *strǫnd* border, edge, coast.] The land bordering a sea, lake, or †river; in a more restricted sense, that part of a shore which lies between the tide-marks; sometimes vaguely, coast, shore. Now *poet.*, *arch.*, or *dial.* †b. A quay, wharf, or landing-place by the side of navigable water -1859. c. Used vaguely for country, region, esp. a foreign country. Chiefly *poet.* late ME.

On the bare s. Upon the sea-mark a small boat did wait SHELLEY. *The Strand*, a street in London, orig. so called as occupying the 'strand' or shore of the Thames between the cities of London and Westminster. c. Let Freedom and Peace flee far To a sunnier s. SHELLEY.

Comb.: **s. fishery**, a coast fishery pursued from the shore.

Strand (strænd), *sb.*[2] 1497. [Origin obsc.] 1. Each of the strings or yarns which when twisted together or 'laid' form a rope, line, cord, or cable. Also, a ply (of worsted). *dial.* **b.** Each of the lengths of twisted wire used to form a wire-rope, cable, or electric conductor 1860. **2.** Each of the threads or strips of a woven material; hence, a thread or strip drawn from such material 1802. **3.** *transf.* A tress or filament of hair 1870. **b.** A thread or filament in animal or vegetable structure 1877.

1. A Cabell is a three-s. Roape 1644. *fig.* The dusky s. of Death inwoven here With dear Love's tie TENNYSON.

Strand (strænd), *v.*[1] 1621. [f. STRAND *sb.*[1]] **1.** *trans.* To drive or force aground on a shore, esp. on the sea-shore; also *rarely* of a river, to leave aground (by the ebbing of the tide). **2.** *transf.* and *fig.* Chiefly *pass.* 1837. **3.** *intr.* To run aground 1687.

1. The vessel was stranded in a gale 1843. 2. I am left utterly stranded and alone in life RUSKIN.

Strand (strænd), *v.*[2] 1780. [f. STRAND *sb.*[2]] **1.** *intr.* Of a rope: To break one or more of its strands. Also *trans.*, to break one or more of the strands of (a rope). **2.** *trans.* To form (a rope) by the twisting of strands 1886. **3.** To insert a strand or filament in (a texture); also *absol.* 1895.

3. Time..has..stranded her..hair with grey 1914.

Strange (strēindʒ), *a.* ME. [a. OF. *estrange*:—L. *extraneus* external, foreign, f. *extra* outside, etc.] †**1.** Of persons, language, customs, etc.: Of or belonging to another country; foreign, alien –1755. †**b.** Of a country, etc.: Situated outside one's own land –1722. **2.** Belonging to some other place or neighbourhood; unknown to the particular locality specified or implied. Of a place or locality: Other than one's own. ME. †**3.** Belonging to others; not of one's own kin or family –1533. **4.** *S. woman*, a harlot 1535. †**5.** Added or introduced from outside, adventitious, external –1672. **6.** Unknown, unfamiliar; not known, met with, or experienced before ME. **7.** Exceptionally great (in degree, amount, intensity, etc.), extreme. late ME. **8.** Unfamiliar, abnormal, or exceptional to a degree that excites wonder or astonishment; queer, surprising, unaccountable. late ME. **b.** quasi-*int.* 'An expression of wonder' (J.): an elliptical expression for *it is strange* 1670. †**9.** Of persons: **a.** Unfriendly; having the feelings alienated. **b.** Distant or cold in demeanour; reserved; not affable, familiar, or encouraging. –1763. **10.** Of a person: Unfamiliar or unacquainted with something (specified or implied); fresh *to*; unpractised or unskilled *at* 1561.

1. Ancient Bards, and Poets in s. toungs 1621. b. And Palmeres for to seken straunge strondes CHAUCER. 2. A s. Dog happens to pass through a Flesh-Market SWIFT. 5. Cleanse the Wound first from all s. Bodies 1672. 6. Among new men, s. faces, other minds TENNYSON. 7. Taking Devilish long Strides, and shuffling along at a s. Rate DE FOE. 8. 'Tis s.—but true; for truth is always s.; Stranger than fiction BYRON. Phr. *S. to say*, etc., used parenthetically. 9. I should haue beene more s., I must confesse SHAKS. Phr. †*To look s.*, to look at a person as if one did not know him. 10. I am..As s. vnto your towne, as to your talke SHAKS. [I] am s. to the work 1911.

Phrases. †*To make* (*it*) *s.*, to make difficulties, be unwilling; to be distant or unfriendly; to affect coyness; to pretend not to understand; to affect or feel surprise, dislike, indignation, etc. Const. *of* (=about) a matter, etc.; *to* (do something); also *to make s. at.*

Strange, *v.* late ME. [ad. OF. *estranger* ESTRANGE *v.*] †**1.** = ESTRANGE *v.*, in various senses –1715. **2.** To be surprised, wonder. *Obs.* or *dial.*

Strangely (strēi·ndʒli), *adv.* late ME. [f. STRANGE *a.* + -LY[2].] †**1.** In an unfriendly or unfavourable manner; coldly, distantly –1707. †**2.** In an uncommon or exceptional degree; very greatly, extremely –1719. **3.** Surprisingly, unaccountably, oddly 1450.

1. Look not s. upon him because he differs from thee in some opinions 1707. 2. Hee was straungely importunate with me to give him leave to goe 1618. 3. They vanish'd s. SHAKS. This fellow runs s. in my head SHERIDAN. So **Stra·ngeness**, the quality of being strange; quasi-*concr.* something strange; a strange circumstance, object, event, or the like.

Stranger (strēi·ndʒəɹ), *sb.* (and *a.*). late ME. [Aphetic a. OF. *estrangier* :—pop. L. **extranearius*, f. L. *extraneus*; see EXTRANEOUS and STRANGE *adjs.*] **1.** One who belongs to another country, a foreigner; chiefly, (now exclusively), one who resides in or comes to a country to which he is a foreigner; an alien. Now somewhat *rare.* †**b.** Something that comes from abroad; *esp.* an exotic plant –1732. **2.** One who is not a native of, or who has not long resided in, a country, town, or place 1447. **3.** A guest or visitor, in contradistinction to the members of the household. Now chiefly with mixture of sense 4. late ME. **b.** Any of the things which are popularly imagined to forebode the coming of an unexpected visitor, e.g. a floating tea-leaf in the cup; a piece of soot flapping on the bar of the grate 1838. **4.** An unknown person; also, a person with whom one is not yet well acquainted. late ME. **b.** Said playfully of a newborn child 1829. **c.** *vocatively.* (formerly, in rustic use in the U.S., the customary mode of address to one whose name is unknown.) 1817. **d.** Predicatively, said of one whose visits have long ceased 1530. **5.** A non-member of a society. Now *rare.* late ME. **b.** *Parliament.* One who is not a member or official of the House, and is present at its debates only on sufferance 1809. **6.** A person not of one's kin; more fully, *s. in blood.* Also, a person unconnected by ties of friendship or the like. 1535. **7.** *Law.* One not privy or party *to* an act. Also, one not standing towards another in some relation implied in the context. 1543. †**8.** Something alien (*to* a class, the nature of a thing, a person's character, etc.) –1838. **9.** Predicatively, *a s. to* —: Unacquainted with, ignorant of 1697. **10.** *attrib.*, passing into *adj.* **a.** That is a stranger (in senses 1–5). Often hyphened. late ME. **b.** Pertaining to a stranger or strangers; also, situated abroad; foreign 1593. **c.** Not one's own (or its own); alien (*rare*) 1577.

1. In a generation or two the s. ceased to be a s. The foreign spoiler..insensibly changed into the son of the soil. FREEMAN. 2. I cannot show you the way, for I am almost a s. here 1794. 3. Phr. *To make a s. of*, to treat with ceremony, not as one of the family. 4. The Duke..hath known you but three dayes, and already you are no s. SHAKS. Phr. *A perfect, a total, an utter s.* d. I am surprized to see you, you have been so long a S. DE FOE. 5. b. *I spy strangers*, the formula used by a member in demanding the expulsion of strangers from the House. 6. To be told.. that henceforth they must be for ever strangers 1860. 7. No man ought to be bound by proceedings to which he was a s. 1842. 8. *Macb.* IV. iii. 125. 9. They are strangers to all discipline 1796. 10. a. What think'st thou of our s. guest? SCOTT. b. You cousin Herford ..Shall..tread the s. pathes of banishment SHAKS. c. The roofs, that heard our earliest cry, Will shelter one of s. race TENNYSON. Hence **Stra·nger** *v. trans.* †To make a stranger of, alienate; to make strange.

Strangle (stræ·ŋg'l), *sb.* late ME. [f. next.] †**1.** The action of strangling: strangulation –1641. **2.** = *strangle-hold* 1890.

Comb.: **s.-hold** *Wrestling*, a hold which stops the adversary's breath; also *fig.*

Strangle (stræ·ŋg'l), *v.* ME. [a. OF. *estrangler*:—L. *strangulare*, a. Gr. στραγγαλᾶν, f. στραγγάλη halter, cogn. w. στραγγός twisted.] **1.** *trans.* To kill by external compression of the throat, esp. by means of a rope or the like passed round the neck. **b.** To constrict painfully (the neck or throat) 1450. **2.** In wider sense: To kill by stoppage of breath; to smother, suffocate, choke. Now *rare.* ME. †**b.** To kill by poison or the like; *rarely*, by the sword –1607. †**c.** said of a wild beast, a devil –1751. **3.** *transf.* To choke, hinder the growth of (a plant) by crowding; to impede the action of (an internal bodily organ) by compression; to suppress (a laugh, a yawn). late ME. **b.** *fig.* To prevent the growth or rise of; to hamper or destroy by excessive restrictions; to suppress 1611. **4.** *intr.* To be choked or suffocated ME.

1. He strangles Alexius with the Bowstring 1663. *fig.* They would be eager to s. this insurrection in the birth 1870. 2. Shall I not then be stifled in the Vault? ..And there die strangled ere my Romeo comes SHAKS. c. The lyon wold haue strangled hym CAXTON. 3. b. Her surest way to s. thought MEREDITH. 4. He came down..strangling in a tight, cross-barred cravat THACKERAY. Hence **Stra·ngler**, one who or something which strangles.

Strangles (stræ·ŋg'lz), *sb. pl.* 1600. [orig. pl. of STRANGLE *sb.*] †**1.** = STRANGULLION 1. –1686. **2.** An infectious febrile disease of equine animals, caused by the bacterium *Streptococcus equi* 1706.

Strangulate (stræ·ŋgiŭlĕt), *a.* 1866. [ad. L. *strangulatus*, *strangulare* STRANGLE *v.*] *Bot.* = STRANGULATED *ppl. a.* 3.

Strangulate (stræ·ŋgiŭleit), *v.* 1665. [f. L. *strangulat-*, *strangulare* STRANGLE *v.*] †**1.** *trans.* To choke, stifle, suffocate. **2.** *Path.* and *Surg.* To constrict or compress (an organ, duct, etc.) so as to prevent circulation or the passage of fluid; to remove (a growth) by constricting it with a ligature 1771. **b.** To choke (a plant); to prevent the flow of sap in (a tree) 1835. **3.** = STRANGLE *v.* (*rare*) 1829.

Strangulated (stræ·ŋgiŭleitėd), *ppl. a.* 1771. [f. prec. + -ED[1].] **1.** *Path.* and *Surg.* Of a vessel, an intestine: Congested by constriction and the arrest of circulation. **2.** *Ent.* Of the head, abdomen, or thorax of an insect: Constricted or greatly narrowed 1819. **3.** *Bot.* Of a plant-stem: Contracted by or as if by a ligature 1849.

1. *S. hernia*, a hernia so constricted that the circulation in the protruded part is arrested.

Strangulation (strængiŭlē·ʃən). 1542. [ad. L. *strangulationem*, f. *strangulare* STRANGLE *v.*] **1.** The action or process of strangling. the condition of being strangled. **2.** *Path.* and *Surg.* Constriction (of a bodily organ, duct, etc.) so as to stop circulation or the passage of fluids 1749. **3.** *transf.* Excessive constriction of a channel or passage 1882. **4.** *concr.* A strangulated part; a constriction. *spec.* in *Nat. Hist.* 1828. So **Stra·ngulative** *a.*, that strangles.

Strangullion (stræŋgʊ·lyən). 1481. [a. OF. *stranguillon*, *estranguillon*, ad. It. *stranguglione*:—pop. L. **strangulionem*, f. L. *strangulare* to STRANGLE; see -ION.] **1.** A disease of horses, characterized by inflammation and swelling of the glands of the throat. †¶**2.** Used incorrectly for STRANGURY –1678.

Strangurious (stræŋgiūə·riəs), *a.* 1733. [ad. late L. *stranguriosus*; see next and -OUS.] Of, pertaining to, or characteristic of strangury; affected with strangury.

Strangury (stræ·ŋgiŭri). late ME. [ad. L., *stranguria*, a. Gr. στραγγουρία, f. στραγγ-, στράγξ drop squeezed out + οὖρον urine.] **1.** A disease of the urinary organs characterized by slow and painful emission of urine; also the condition of slow and painful urination. ¶**2.** Erroneously taken to mean a disease due to strangling or choking; chiefly *fig.* 1698.

Strany (stræ·ni). *local.* 1804. The Common Guillemot.

Strap (stræp), *sb.* 1573. [dial. form of STROP *sb.*] **1.** A leather band, thong; in recent use, a flat band or strip of leather or other material of uniform breadth used for securing, holding together, etc. 1685. **b.** as used for flogging. Hence, the application of the strap as an instrument of punishment. 1710. **2.** *Naut.* = STROP *sb.* 2. 1625. **3.** A narrow strip of leather, cloth, or other material fitted with a buckle as a fastening and for adjustment 1688. **4. a.** A short band formerly attached to the bottom of each leg of a pair of pantaloons or trousers passing from side to side under the instep of the boot. Now used on leggings, regimental trousers, etc. Chiefly *pl.* 1837. **b.** = SHOULDER-STRAP 2. 1802. **5.** A looped band of leather for a particular use, e.g. to draw a boot on, to steady oneself in a moving vehicle, etc. 1601. **6.** *Mech.* = BAND *sb.*[2] 6. 1790. **7.** A razor-strop. *Obs.* exc. *dial.* 1758. **8.** A narrow band of iron or other metal used in the form of a plate, loop, or ring for fastening a thing in position, holding together timbers, parts of machinery, etc. 1620. **9.** A projection on a metal article, narrowed and flattened for screwing down to a wooden surface or for slipping under a metal plate; esp. each or one of the leaves of a strap-hinge 1831. **10.** *Bot.* **a.** An appendage to the leaf in some grasses. **b.** = LIGULE. 1796. **11.** *Anglo-Ir.* A term of abuse applied to a woman or girl 1842. **12.** *slang.* Credit, trust. Phr. *on* (*the*) *s.* 1828.

1. b. A lively Cobler, that..had scarce passed a Day in his Life without giving her the Discipline of the S. ADDISON.

Comb.: **s.-bolt** *sb.*, a bolt with a flattened end for screwing down to a surface; *v. trans.*, to fasten *down* with a s.-bolt; **s. brake**, a brake consisting of a friction s. applied to a cylindrical bearing surface; esp. a dynamometer brake on this plan; **straphanger**, *slang* or *colloq.*, a passenger who is compelled to stand and hold on by the s. in a full omnibus, etc.; so **s.-hang** *v. intr.*; **s. hinge,** a hinge with long leaves or flaps for screwing down to a surface; also, a hinge with one leaf lengthened for insertion into an iron plate; **-oil,** *slang*, flogging with a strap; **-rail** *U.S.*, a flat railroad rail laid upon a continuous longitudinal sleeper; hence **s. railroad, railway, road** *U.S.*, a railroad constructed with s.-rails; **-worm,** a cestoid worm of the family *Ligulidæ*.

Strap (stræp), *v.* 1711. [f. prec.] **1.** *trans.* To furnish with a strap; to fasten, bind, or secure with a strap or with straps. **b.** *Surg.* To apply straps of adhesive plaster to (a wound, etc.); to fasten (dressing) *on* with plaster; *to s. up*, to dress and bandage (a wound or a person, *i.e.* his wound) 1843. **c.** To fasten, bind, or secure (a strap) tightly 1818. **2.** To beat with a strap or leather thong 1735. **3.** = STROP *v.* Now *rare* or *Obs.* 1785. **4.** *intr.* To work closely and energetically (*at* a task); to buckle *to* one's work (*slang*) 1823. **5.** *trans.* To groom (a horse) 1854.

‖**Strapontin** (straponťæň). 1926. [Fr.] A bracket seat, such as are used in carriages and cars; also, a similar seat used in play-houses.

Strappado (străpē·do, -ā·do), *sb. Obs.* exc. *Hist.* 1560. [ad. F. *strapade, estrapade*, ad. It. *strappata*, f. *strappare* to drag, pull, snatch; see -ADO.] **1.** A form of punishment or of torture to extort confession in which the victim's hands were tied across his back and secured to a pulley; he was then hoisted from the ground and let down half way with a jerk; also, an application of this punishment or torture; also, the instrument used. ¶**2.** Erron. taken to mean 'chastisement by blows' (J.) 1668.

2. He gave me the s. on my shoulders, and the bastinado on the soles of my feet BICKERSTAFFE. Hence †**Strappa·do** *v. trans.* to torture or punish with the s.

Strapper (stræ·pəɹ). 1675. [f. STRAP *v.* + -ER [1].] **1.** A 'strapping' person. (Chiefly applied to women.) **2.** One who grooms horses 1828. **3.** *slang.* An unremitting worker 1851.

Stra·pping, *ppl. a.* 1657. [f. STRAP *v.* + -ING [2].] Orig. of a young woman: †Full of activity, vigorous, lusty. Now of a person of either sex: Strongly and stoutly built, robust, sturdy. **b.** *transf.* Big, 'whopping' (*rare*) 1819.

They..are..all well-built, s. fellows 1902.

†**Stra·pple,** *sb.* [OE. *strapul*, of obsc. origin.] A covering for the lower part of the leg, consisting of a fillet or band laced or bound round the limb -1483.

Stra·pple, *v. Obs.* exc. *dial.* 1607. [f. prec.] †**1.** *trans.* To furnish with 'strapples' or coverings for the legs. CHAPMAN. **2.** To bind or make fast with bands. Now *dial.* 1611.

Strasburg (stræ·zbɒɪg, ‖ʃtrāsburχ). 1642. [G. *Strassburg*, F. *Strasbourg*.] The name of the principal town of Alsace, used *attrib.*

S. linen, a kind of linen imported from Strasburg. *S. pie*, a pie made of fatted goose liver.

Strass (stræs). 1820. [a. G. *strass*, F. *stras*; from the name of the inventor, Josef Strasser.] A vitreous composition used as a basis in the manufacture of artificial stones; = PASTE *sb.*[1] 5.

Strata, pl. of STRATUM.

Stratagem (stræ·tădʒĕm). 1489. [a. F. *stratagème*, ad. L. *strategema*, a. Gr. στρατήγημα a piece of generalship, stratagem, f. στρατηγεῖν to be a general, f. στρατηγός STRATEGUS.] **1.** An operation or act of generalship; usu., an artifice or trick designed to outwit or surprise the enemy. **b.** *gen.* Military artifice 1599. **2.** Any artifice or trick; a device or scheme for obtaining an advantage 1588. **b.** *gen.* Skill in devising expedients; artifice, cunning 1588. †**3.** Used loosely for: A deed of blood or violence -1606.

1. He was advertised by spies what stratagems the enemy would use against us 1653. **b.** *Hen. V*, iv. viii. 113. **2. b.** 'Tis pollicie and stratageme must doe That you affect SHAKS. **3.** 3 *Hen. VI*, II. v. 89. Hence †**Stratagema·tic,** †**-al** *adjs.*, relating to, versed in, s. or strategy -1650.

†**Stratagemical** (strætă͵dʒe·mikăl), *a.* 1585. [irreg. f. STRATAGEM + -IC + -AL.] Concerned with, of the nature of, stratagem -1838.

Strategetic (strætī͵dʒe·tik), *a.* 1848. [ad. Gr. στρατηγητικός (f. στρατηγεῖν).] = STRATEGIC. So **Stratege·tical** *a.* 1828.

Strategic (străte·dʒik, -ī·dʒik), *a.* and *sb.* 1825. [a. F. *stratégique* or ad. Gr. στρατηγικός of or pertaining to a general, f. στρατηγός STRATEGUS.] **A.** *adj.* Of or belonging to strategy; useful or important in regard to strategy.

S. point [= F. *point stratégique*], a position determined as important in a plan of campaign.

B. *sb.* The strategic art, strategy. *sing.* (rare) and *pl.* 1852. So **Strate·gical** *a.*, **-ly** *adv.*

Strategist (stræ·tī͵dʒist). 1838. [a. F. *stratégiste*, f. *stratégie* STRATEGY.] One versed in strategy.

Strategus (strătī·gɒs). *Pl.* **-gi** (-dʒəi). Also **strategos** (strătī·gɒs), *pl.* **-oi.** 1656. [L., a. Gr. στρατηγός, f. στρατός army + -αγ-, ἄγειν to lead.] *Gr. Hist.* A commander-in-chief or chief magistrate at Athens and in the Achæan league.

Strategy (stræ·tīdʒi). 1688. [a. F. *stratégie*, ad. Gr. στρατηγία office or command of a general, generalship, f. στρατηγός.] †**1.** A government or province under a strategus. **2.** The art of a commander-in-chief; the art of projecting and directing the larger military movements and operations of a campaign 1810. **b.** An instance or species of this 1833. **3.** *Gr. Hist.* The office of a STRATEGUS (*rare*) 1869.

2. S. differs materially from *tactic*; the latter belonging only to the mechanical movement of bodies, set in motion by the former 1810.

Strath (stræþ). *Sc.* 1540. [a. Gael. *srath*.] A wide valley; a tract of level or low-lying land traversed by a river and bounded by hills or high ground. †**b.** *loosely.* A stretch of flat land by the water-side -1730.

Strathspey (stræþspē·). 1653. [f. the Sc. place-name *Strathspey* (= the strath of the river Spey).] **a.** A lively Scotch dance or reel for two dancers. **b.** The music or tune (usu. in common time) used to accompany this dance.

Straticulate (străti·kiŭlĕt), *a.* 1880. [f. mod.L. **straticulum* (dim. of L. *stratum* STRATUM) + -ATE [2].] *Geol.* and *Min.* Arranged in thin layers. So **Straticula·tion,** arrangement in thin layers.

Stratification (stræ:tifikē·ʃən). 1617. [ad. med.L. *stratificationem*, f. *stratificare* STRATIFY *v.*; see -FICATION.] †**1.** The action of depositing something in layers -1882. **2.** *Geol.* The formation, by natural process, of strata or layers one above the other; the fact or state of existing in the form of strata, stratified condition; also, the manner in which something is stratified 1795. **b.** *Biol.* and *Path.* The thickening of a tissue by the deposition or growth of successive thin layers 1875. **c.** *Electr.* The striated appearance assumed by an electric discharge passing through a highly rarefied gas 1856. **d.** *transf.* and *fig.*, chiefly with ref. to the geological use 1860.

2. d. By exact observation of s., eight more periods have been distinguished by the explorer of Cnossus 1910.

Stratified (stræ·tifəid), *ppl. a.* 1802. [f. STRATIFY *v.* + -ED [1].] Disposed in strata or layers; *spec.* in *Geol.* and *Electr.*

Stratiform (stræ·tifǭɹm), *a.* 1805. [ad. F. *stratiforme*; see STRATUM and -FORM.] **1.** *Geol.* Disposed in the form of strata; showing apparent stratification. **2.** Forming or formed into strata or layers 1834.

Stratify (stræ·tifəi), *v.* 1661. [ad. F. *stratifier*, ad. mod.L. *stratificare*, f. *stratum* STRATUM; see -FY.] **1.** *trans.* 'To range in beds or layers' (J.); *spec.* in *Metall.*, to range in alternate layers (metals and reagent substances) in a crucible. **2.** *Geol.* Of natural agencies: To deposit (rocks) in strata or beds; to produce (a portion of the earth's crust) in the form of strata; to form strata in. Chiefly *pass.* 1794. **3.** *intr.* To assume the form of strata 1856.

2. *fig.* Society stratifies itself everywhere O. W. HOLMES.

Stratigraphy (străti·grăfi). 1865. [f. L. *strati-* comb. form of *stratum* STRATUM; see -GRAPHY.] **1.** The branch of geology that is concerned with the order and relative position of the strata of the earth's crust. **2.** The stratigraphical features (of a country, etc.); the order and relative position of the strata 1882. Hence **Strati·grapher,** one versed in s. **Stratigra·phic, -al** (1817) *adjs.* pertaining to s.; **-ly** *adv.* **Strati·graphist.**

Stratiote (stræ·tiōut). 1656. [ad. Gr. στρατιώτης, f. στρατία army.] *Gr. Hist.* A soldier.

Strato- (strē·to), comb. form of STRATUS, used to form names for mixed types of cloud-structure in which the 'stratus' form is present as an element modifying one of the other forms. **Strato-ci·rrus,** a cloud resembling cirro-stratus, but more compact in structure; hence **Strato-ci·rrous** *a.* **Strato-cu·mulus** = *cumulo-stratus*; hence **Strato-cu·mulous** *a.*

Stratocracy (strătǫ·krăsi). 1652. [f. Gr. στρατός army + -κρατία; see -CRACY.] Government by the army; military rule; a polity in which the army is the controlling power. Hence **Stratocra·tic** *a.* pertaining to s.

Stratose (strē·tous), *a.* 1881. [f. STRATUM + -OSE.] *Bot.* Stratified; arranged in layers.

Stratosphere (strē·tǫsfīəɹ). 1908. [f. STRATUM + -O- + (ATMO)SPHERE.] That stratum of the atmosphere, lying above the troposphere, in which the temperature is nearly uniform at any height.

Stratum (strē·tɒm). *Pl.* **strata** (strē·tă); *rarely* **stratums.** 1599. [mod.L. use of L. *stratum*, lit. something spread or laid down, neut. pa. pple. of *sternere*.] **1.** *gen.* A quantity of a substance or material spread over a nearly horizontal surface to a more or less uniform thickness; a layer or coat; esp. one of two or more parallel layers or coats successively superposed one upon another. **2.** A bed of sedimentary rock, usu. consisting of a series of 'layers' or 'laminæ' of the same kind, representing continuous periods of deposition 1671. **3.** A region of the atmosphere, of the sea, or of a quantity of fluid, assumed for purposes of calculation as bounded by horizontal planes 1787. **4.** *Biol.*, etc. One of a number of layers composing an animal or vegetable tissue 1741. **5.** *fig.* (in various applications, chiefly after sense 2) 1807.

1. The broken or perforated s. of new snow TYNDALL. **2.** The..Laurentian strata..are seen to underlie..the Silurian beds 1875. **3.** The temperature of the lower strata of the air 1858. **5.** The habit of reading spread to a lower social s. 1902.

Stratus (strē·tɒs). 1803. [a. L. *stratus*, f. *stra-*, *sternere* to spread, lay down. Cf. prec.] *Meteorol.* One of the simple forms of cloud, having the appearance of a broad sheet of nearly uniform thickness.

†**Stra·vagant,** *a.* and *sb.* 1565. [ad. It. *stravagante*; see EXTRAVAGANT.] **A.** *adj.* Irrelevant, unsuitable, extraordinary -1613. **B.** *sb.* **a.** Something irrelevant. **b.** A vagrant. -1608.

Straw (strǭ), *sb.* [Com. Teut.: OE. *stréaw* :—OTeut. **strawo-*, f. root **strau-* : **streu-*: see STREW *v.*] **I.** *collect. sing.* **1.** The stems or stalks of certain cereals, chiefly wheat, barley, oats, and rye. Used e. g. as litter and as fodder for cattle, as filling for bedding, as thatch, etc. **b.** *fig.* with ref. to the small value of straw in comparison with the grain, or to its ready inflammability. late ME. **2.** Applied to the stalks of certain other plants, chiefly pease and buckwheat ME. **b.** *U.S.* Pine needles 1856. **3.** As a material (plaited or woven) for hats and bonnets; a kind or variety of this material, or an imitation of it 1730.

1. A lioun and an oxe schulen ete stree WYCLIF. *Isa.* lxv. 25. Their lean and flashy songs Grate on their scrannel Pipes of wretched s. MILT. **b.** Strongest oathes, are s. To th' fire ith' blood SHAKS. **3.** Plain Dunstable straws continue to be worn 1859.

Phrases. *To make bricks without s.*, (to be required) to produce results without the means usu. considered necessary. *In the s.*, in childbed, lying-in; so *out of the s.*, recovered after childbearing. *To die in the s.* (of warriors, esp. vikings), to die in bed, as opp. to the coveted death in battle. *To run to s.*: see RUN *v.* *Man of s.*, a person or thing compared to a straw image; a counterfeit, sham, 'dummy'; (*b*) an imaginary adversary, or an invented adverse argument, adduced in order to be triumphantly refuted; (*c*) a person of no substance; (*d*) a fictitious or irresponsible person fraudulently put forward as a surety or as a party in an action.

II. A single stem of a cereal, etc. **1.** A stem of any cereal plant, esp. when dry and separated from the grain; also, a piece of such a stem ME. **b.** *poet.* A pipe made of an oaten straw (*rare*) 1588. **c.** A straw, or a similar slender tube made of paper, etc. through which drinks are sucked up 1872. **2.** A small particle of straw or chaff, a 'mote' OE. **3.** Used as a type of what is of trifling value or importance ME. **b.** A trifle 1692. **4.** *Cheese s.*: a thin stick of pastry containing cheese 1877.

1. *Jul C.* I. iii. 108. *To draw, gather, pick straws*: (of the eyes) to be sleepy. Provbs. and allusive phrases: A drowning man will catch at a s. RICHARDSON. The last s. breaks the laden camel's back DICKENS. Sunstroke may act as 'the last s.' 1897. Such straws of speech show how blows the wind READE. b. When Shepheards pipe on Oaten strawes SHAKS. 3. Phr. *Not to care a s.* (*two, three straws*). b. My passions will not.. be irritated by straws MISS BURNEY.

III. A straw hat 1863.

attrib. and *Comb.*: *s.-roofed, -thatched*, ppl. adjs.; = made of straw, as *s. hat*; **s. bail**, bail given by 'men of s.'; insufficient or worthless bail **-bid** *U.S.*, a worthless bid; one not intended to be taken up; **-board**, coarse yellow millboard made from straw pulp; **s. cat**, the pampas cat; **s. colour**, the colour of straw, a pale yellow; **-coloured** *a.* pale yellow; **-drain**, a drain filled with s.; **-dynamite**, a mixture of nitro-glycerine and nitro-cellulose made from s.; **s. hat**, a hat made of plaited or woven straw; **-needle**, a long thin needle used for sewing together s. plaits; **s. paper**, paper made from s. bleached and pulped; **s. plait, plat**, a plait or braid made of s., used for making s. hats, etc.; **s. rope**, a rope made of twisted or plaited s.; **-stem**, a wine-glass stem pulled out of the substance of the bowl; hence, a wine-glass having such a stem; **s. vote** *U.S.*, an unofficial vote taken before an election in order to discover the trend of public opinion; **-worm**, the caddis-worm; **s. yard**, a yard littered with s., in which horses and cattle are wintered.

Straw (strǭ), *v.*[1] Pa. t. and pa. pple. **strawed** (*rarely* pa. pple. **strawn**). *Obs.* exc. *arch.* ME. [OE. *stréawian*: see STREW *v.*] = STREW *v.*

Straw (strǭ), *v.*[2] 1440. [f. STRAW *sb.*] *trans.* To supply with straw.

Strawberry (strǭ·bĕri). [OE. *stréaw-, stréowberige*, f. *stréaw* STRAW *sb.* + *berige* BERRY *sb.*] **1.** The 'fruit' of any species of the genus *Fragaria*; a soft bag-shaped receptacle, scarlet to yellowish in colour, full of juicy pulp, and dotted over with small yellow seed-like achenes. **2.** The plant which bears this fruit OE.

1. We may say of Angling as Dr. Boteler said of Strawberries; Doubtless God could have made a better berry, but doubtless God never did WALTON. To Godstow bound..For strawberries and cream 1788.

attrib. and *Comb.* *s. bed, ice, jam*; *s.-coloured, crushed s.* etc. **s. bass** *U.S.*, the fish *Pomoxys sparoides*; **s. blite**, *Blitum capitatum* and *B. virgatum*, the fruit of which resembles the s.; **s. bush**, (*a*) = *s. shrub*; (*b*) the shrub *Euonymus americanus* with crimson and scarlet pods; **s. finch**, the amadavat; **s. mark**, a birth-mark or nævus resembling a s.; **s. pear**, the fruit of the W. Indian cactus *Cereus triangularis*, or the plant itself; **s. perch** *U.S.* = *s. bass*; **s. shrub** *U.S.* = CALYCANTHUS; **s. tomato**, *Physalis Alkekengi* **-tree**, †(*a*) = sense 2; (*b*) = ARBUTUS; (*c*) *U.S.* = *s-bush* (*b*); **s. vine** = sense 2.

Strawberry leaf. ME. The leaf of the strawberry plant. **b.** In allusion to the row of conventional figures of the leaf on the coronet of a duke, marquis, or earl 1827.

Straw·-breadth, straw's breadth. Now *rare.* 1577. The breadth of a straw. Formerly, a typically small distance.

Strawy (strǭ·i), *a.* 1552. [f. STRAW *sb.* + -Y[1].] **1.** Consisting of, of the nature of, full of, straw. **2.** Made with straw; filled, thatched, or strewed with straw 1568. **3.** Resembling straw in colour, texture, etc. 1668. †**4.** *fig.* Light, empty, or worthless as straw –1662.

4. *Tr. & Cr.* v. v. 24.

Stray (strēⁱ), *sb.* 1440. [(1) a. AF. *stray, estrai*, vbl. noun f. AF., OF. *estraier* STRAY *v.*; (2) f. STRAY *v.*] **I. 1.** *Law.* = ESTRAY *sb.* 1498. **2.** An animal that has strayed from its flock, home, or owner 1440. **b.** *fig.* One who has gone astray in conduct, opinion, etc. 1605. **c.** A homeless, friendless person; an ownerless cat or dog 1649. **d.** Something that has strayed from its usual or proper place; something separated from the main body; a detached fragment, an isolated specimen 1798. †**e.** *collect.* A number of stray beasts; a body of stragglers from an army –1717.

1. No Fowle can be a s. but a Swan COKE. *Waifs and strays*: see WAIFS. 2. d. Not found in the Gulf of Mexico, unless as a s. 1888. If a telephone be used as a telegraphic receiver, strays (atmospheric discharges) may sometimes be distinguishable from signals 1908. e. 2 *Hen. IV*, IV. ii. 120.

II. †**1.** The action of straying or wandering –1793. **2.** The right of allowing cattle to stray and feed on common land. *north.* 1736. **b.** = COMMON *sb.* 3. 1889. **3.** *Naut.* = STRAY-LINE 1628. Hence **Stray·ling**, a stray thing or person.

Stray (strēⁱ), *a.* 1607. [Partly aphetic var. of ASTRAY; partly attrib. use of prec.] **1.** Of an animal: That has wandered from confinement or control; that has straggled from a flock; that has become homeless or ownerless. **2.** Of a cable: Loose, slack 1791. **3.** Of a person or thing: Separated from the main body; occurring away from the regular course or habitat; isolated 1796. **4.** *Electr.* (see quot.) 1893.

4. *s. Power*, the proportion of the energy wasted in driving a dynamo, which is lost through friction or other hurtful resistances 1893.

Stray (strēⁱ), *v.* ME. [Aphetic var. of ASTRAY, ESTRAY *vbs.*, a. OF. *estraier*:—Rom. **estragare*, repr. L. *extra vagari* to wander outside.] **1.** *intr.* To escape from confinement or control, to wander away from a place, one's companions, etc. Also of inanimate things. late ME. **2.** To wander up and down free from control; to roam about. late ME. †**b.** Of a stream: To meander –1754. **3.** *intr.* To wander from the direct way; to deviate 1561. **4.** *fig.* **a.** To wander from the path of rectitude, err ME. **b.** To wander or deviate in mind, purpose, etc. Said also of the mind or thoughts. late ME.

1. Here too, 'tis sung, of old Diana stray'd POPE. b. Boughs, that stray'd Beyond their Ranks DRYDEN. 2. Ah fields belov'd in vain, where once my careless childhood stray'd GRAY. *fig.* Their sober wishes never learn'd to s. GRAY. c. Where Thames amongst the wanton Vallies strays DENHAM. 4. a. We have erred and strayed from thy ways like lost sheep *Bk. Com. Prayer.* b. But, sir, I ask pardon, I am straying from the question GOLDSM. Hence **Stray·er**, one who strays.

Stray·-line. 1769. [f. STRAY *a.* (or STRAY *sb.* II. 1) + LINE *sb.*] *Naut.* Deviation (of a sounding line) from the perpendicular.

Streak (strīk), *sb.* [OE. *strica*, f. weak-grade of Teut. root **strīk-*; see STRIKE *v.*] †**1.** A line, mark, stroke; esp. a character in writing, or a unit or degree in measurement –1735. **2.** A thin irregular line of a different colour or substance from that of the material or surface of which it forms a part 1577. **b.** A line of colour, less firm and regular than a stripe, occurring as a distinctive mark on the coat of an animal, the plumage of a bird, or the body or wings of an insect 1567. **c.** *Min.* The line of coloured powder produced by scratching a mineral or fossil, or the mark made by rubbing it on a harder surface 1794. **d.** *Biol.* A linear mark, stria. Also, a narrow tract in a tissue. 1837. **3.** A faint line of light (esp. of the dawn) diversifying the darkness 1592. **b.** A flash of lightning, etc. 1781. **4.** A long irregular narrow strip of land, water, etc.; a line of colour representing a distant object in a landscape 1727. **5. a.** The horizontal course of a stratum of coal. **b.** A stratum or vein (of metal ore). 1672. **6.** An intermixture (of some contrasting or unexpected quality); an inherited strain 1647. **b.** A temporary run (of luck) 1882.

2. For streaks of red were mingled there, Such as are on a Katherne Pear SUCKLING. 3. The West yet glimmers with some streakes of Day SHAKS. 4. That black s. is the belfry BROWNING. *The silver s.*, the English Channel. 6. A s. of eccentricity in his character 1865.

Streak (strīk), *v.* 1440. [f. prec.] †**1.** *trans.* To cancel by drawing a line or lines across –1595. **2.** To mark with lines or stripes of a different colour, substance, or texture; to form streaks on or in 1595. **3.** *intr.* Of lightning: To flash forth in a streak 1849. **4.** To become streaked or streaky 1870. **5.** To move fast, like a 'streak' of lightning 1927.

2. Some pieces of Rock streaked with gold and silver 1660.

Streaked (strīkt), *ppl. a.* 1596. [f. prec. + -ED[1].] **1.** Marked with streaks; striped, striate. **b.** Of bacon, etc.: = STREAKY 2 b. 1687. **2.** *U.S. dial.* Confused, agitated; scared, uneasy 1833.

Streaky (strī·ki), *a.* 1670. [f. STREAK *sb.* + -Y[1].] **1.** Of the nature of a streak or streaks; occurring in, consisting of, streaks. **2.** Marked with streaks; streaked 1745. **b.** Of flesh-meat, esp. bacon: Having lean and fat in alternate streaks 1838. **3.** *fig.* Variable, uneven (in character or quality); changeable, uncertain. *colloq.* 1898. **4.** *slang.* **a.** Ill-tempered, irritable. **b.** *U.S.* = prec. 2. 1848.

2. The blushes of the s. west 1745. Hence **Strea·kily** *adv.*, **-ness.**

Stream (strīm), *sb.* [Com. Teut.: OE. *stréam*:—OTeut. **straumoz*:—pre-Teut. **sroumos*, f. Indo-Eur. root **srou-* (: **sreu-* : **srū-*) to flow.] **1.** A course of water flowing continuously along a bed on the earth, forming a river, rivulet, or brook. **b.** *pl.* The waters (of a river). *poet.* 1500. **c.** A rivulet or brook, as contrasted with a river 1806. **2.** Flow or current of a river; force, volume, or direction of flow. late ME. **b.** A current in the sea. Cf. GULF STREAM. late ME. **c.** The middle part of a current or tide, as having the greatest force of flow. late ME. **3.** A flow or current of water or other liquid issuing from a source, orifice, or vessel. Often *hyperbolically* in sing. or pl. for a great effusion of blood or tears. OE. **b.** A current or flow of air, gas, electricity 1722. **4.** *transf.* An uninterrupted succession of persons, animals, or things, moving constantly in the same direction 1600. **5.** *fig.* in various applications: e. g. a continuous flow of words; an outflow (of beneficence, etc.); an influx (of wealth) OE. †**b.** The prevailing direction of opinion or fashion –1669. †**6.** A ray or beam of light; the tail of a comet –1700.

1. For there the streme of Isis breaketh into many armelets LELAND. 2. Soon after, the River had the wonted s. and was Navigable again 1653. Phrases. *Against, with the s.* (often in fig. context). *Down, up* (*the*) *s.* 3. Traitors..That would..make poore England weepe in Streames of Blood SHAKS. Wine and ale..flowed in streams 1899. 4. He followed the s. of people JOHNSON. A constant s. of emigration 1849. 5. This flowing streame of wordes 1585. The quit-rents..will pour large streams of wealth into the royal coffers JOHNSON. To..hear the mighty s. of tendency Uttering, for elevation of our thought, A clear sonorous voice WORDSW. 6. Holes..to resseyuen the stremes of the sonne by day CHAUCER.

Comb.: **s.-anchor**, an anchor intermediate in size between the bower and the kedge, used to moor a ship in a sheltered position; **-cable**, the cable or hawser of the s.-anchor; **-gold**, gold in alluvial deposits; **-ice**, pieces of drift ice joining each other in a continuous ridge and following the line of current; **-ore**, ore in alluvial deposits; **-tin**, tin ore found in pebble-like lumps in alluvial beds; **-work(s**, the operation of washing detrital deposits for metal, esp. tin; a place where this is done. Hence **Strea·mless** *a.* having no streams; of water, having no current.

Stream (strīm), *v.* ME. [f. prec.] **I.** *intr.* **1.** Of a body of liquid: To flow or issue in a stream; to flow or run in a full and continuous current. **b.** Of a road, or of land which seems to move in the opposite direction to one who passes along it 1833. **2.** *transf.* and *fig.* Of light, air, vapour, immaterial effluences, etc.: To be carried or emitted in a full and continuous current ME. **b.** Of a star or meteor: To form a continuous trail of light as it moves in its course 1838. **3. a.** Of a flag, or the like: To wave or float outwards in the wind 1560. **b.** Of hair, a garment, etc.: To hang loose and waving; to trail *out, behind* 1784. **4.** Of persons (or animals): To move together continuously in considerable numbers; to flock 1735. **5.** To pour off or exude liquid in a continuous stream; to run, drip, overflow with moisture. late ME. **6.** Of a luminous body: To emit a continuous stream of beams or rays of light. Also *spec.* of a comet, with ref. to its 'tail': To issue in a widening stream of light. late ME. **b.** To be suffused *with* (radiant light) 1830.

1. The river Ock streameth by Stow 1630. She suffered the tears to stream down her cheeks unconcealed 1849. 2. *All's Well* II. iii. 82. The morning sun was streaming in at the window 1852. 3. a. Th' Imperial Ensign..Shon like a Meteor streaming to the Wind MILT. b. Adorn'd with..ribbands streaming gay COWPER. 4. People..streamed to it from all quarters SCOTT. Flocks of little Auk streaming south 1853. 5. He was streaming with perspiration 1875. 6. b. The mountain tops began to s. with golden light 1830.

II. *trans.* **1.** To cause to flow; to pour forth, discharge, or emit in a stream (a liquid, rays of light, etc.); also with adv. as *out, forth, down.*

late ME. **2.** To suffuse or overspread (a surface) *with* flowing moisture 1526. †**3.** To ornament with flowing lines or rays -1626. **4.** To cause (a flag) to float outwards in the wind; to wave (a handkerchief) 1593. **5.** *Naut.* *To s. the buoy*: to throw the anchor-buoy overboard before casting anchor 1769. **6.** *Mining.* To flush (a detrital deposit) with a stream of water, in order to carry off the earthy matter, and leave the ore exposed; usu. absol. *to s. for* (tin, copper, etc.) 1778.

1. It may so please, that she at length will streame Some deaw of grace into my withered hart SPENSER. 3. The Heralds Mantle is streamed with Gold BACON. 4. *Rich. II*, IV. i. 94.

Streamer (strī·məɹ), *sb.* ME. [f. prec. + -ER[1].] **1.** A flag streaming or waving in the air; *spec.* a long and narrow pointed flag or pennon. **2.** *transf.* **a.** Something long and narrow, that hangs loose in the manner of a streamer 1810. **b.** A long narrow strip of vapour, snow, etc. 1871. **3.** †**a.** A luminous heavenly body emitting a continuous stream of light -1647. **b.** A ray proceeding from the sun; esp. *pl.*, the radiation of the sun's corona seen in eclipses 1697. **c.** *pl.* The Aurora Borealis 1735. **4.** *Mining.* One who washes detrital deposits to procure the ore they contain 1619.

1. Like a stately Ship..With all her bravery on, and tackle trim, Sails fill'd, and streamers waving MILT. 2. Tying up a bouquet..with long streamers of pale yellow ribbon 1889. Hence **Strea·mer** *v. trans.* to furnish or fill with streamers.

Streaming (strī·miŋ), *vbl. sb.* late ME. [f. STREAM *v.* + -ING[1].] The action of STREAM *v.* in various senses; an instance of this. **b.** *Biol.* A peculiar flowing motion of protoplasm in a cell 1875.

Streamlet (strī·mlĕt). 1552. [-LET.] A small stream; a brook, rill, or rivulet.

Strea·m-line, *sb.* 1873. **1.** *Hydrodynamics.* See quot. **2.** = *S. form* 1909.

1. A 'line of motion' or 's.' is defined to be a line drawn from point to point, so that its direction is everywhere that of the motion of the fluid 1906.

attrib.: **s. form,** that shape of a solid body which is calculated to meet with the smallest amount of resistance in passing through the atmosphere. Hence **Stre·am-line** *v. trans.* to give a s. form to (a motor-car, etc.) **Strea·m-lined** *ppl. a.*

Streamy (strī·mi), *a.* late ME. [f. STREAM *sb.* + -Y[1].] **1.** Abounding in or full of running streams. **2.** Of water, etc.: Flowing in a stream, running 1586. **b.** Of hair, etc.: Flowing 1813. **3.** Of the nature of, having the appearance of, or issuing in, a stream 1718.

1. Fair Scotia's s. vales 1806. 3. His nodding Helm emits a s. Ray POPE. Hence **Strea·miness.**

Streek, streak (strīk), *v.* Now *Sc.* and *dial.* [Northern ME. *strēk-*, corresp. to Southern ME. *strēch-*:—OE. *stręccan* STRETCH *v.*] = STRETCH *v.*, in various senses.

Streel (strīl), *v.* Chiefly *Anglo-Ir.* 1839. [Cf. Ir. *straoillim*, to trail, drag along on the ground.] *intr.* To trail on the ground; to float at length. Also of persons, to stroll, wander aimlessly. Hence **Stree·ling** *ppl. a.*

Street (strīt), *sb.* [OE. *stræt*; a Com. WGer. adoption of late L. *strata*, used ellipt. for *via strata* paved road.] †**1.** A paved road; a highway. *Obs.* exc. as surviving in the proper names of certain ancient roads, as Watling S., Icknield S. †**b.** Used vaguely for: A road, way, path -1547. **2.** A road in a town or village (comparatively wide, as opp. to a 'lane' or 'alley'), running between two lines of houses or shops. Also, the road together with the adjacent houses. (As part of the proper name of a street, abbrev. *St.*) OE. **b.** Used for: The inhabitants of the street; also, the people in the street. late ME. **c.** *transf.* A passage between continuous lines of persons or things. late ME.

2. Broadway is undoubtedly the handsomest s. in America 1798. I am sure I could not live again in a s. DISRAELI. *S. of houses* or *shops*, a number of houses or shops built in a double line with a road in the middle, forming a s. Phr. *The s.*: some particular s. to which the merchants or financiers of a city resort for business intercourse. In mod. use primarily *U.S.* (with cap.), applied to Wall S., New York. Hence, the money market. Also, in London, *in the s.* is said with ref. to business done or prices quoted after the hour of closing of the Stock Exchange. *In the street(s*, outside the house, out of doors. *To be on the streets*, to be a prostitute; hence, *the street(s*, as designating a life of prostitution. *To walk the street(s*, to go about on foot in a town; also with ref. to prostitution. *The man in the s.*, the ordinary man as dist. from the expert or the man who has special opportunities of knowledge. *Not to be in the same s. with* (colloq. or slang), to be far behind, far inferior to (a person); so *to be streets ahead, better*, to be far ahead of, far superior to. **b.** There was a mystery about him which the whole s. had tried its skill in fathoming 1856.

attrib. and *Comb.*: *s.-corner*, *-lamp*, *-singer*, *-sweeper*; **s.-Arab** (also written with small *a*), a homeless vagrant (usu. a child) living in the streets (see ARAB *sb.*); **-boy,** a homeless or neglected boy who lives chiefly in the streets; **-car,** *U.S.* a tram-car; **-orderly,** a s.-sweeper or scavenger; **-porter,** a porter employed to lift or carry heavy packages in the s.; **-railway,** a tramway; **-refuge** = REFUGE *sb.* 3; **-urchin,** a mischievous little s.-boy; **-way,** a paved road or highway, the roadway of a s. (now only *poet.*). Hence **Street** *v. trans.* to furnish or provide with streets, to lay out in streets.

Street-door. 1563. The chief external door of a house or other building, opening on the street.

Stree·t-wa:lker. 1592. **1.** One who walks in the street 1618. **2.** *spec.* A common prostitute whose field of operations is the street 1592.

Streetward (strī·twǫɹd), *a.* and *adv.* 1596. [f. STREET *sb.* + -WARD.] **A.** *adv.* Towards the street. **B.** *adj.* Facing or opening on the street.

Strelitz (stre·lits). 1603. [a. Russ. *strielets* archer.] A soldier belonging to a body of Russian troops composed of infantry raised by the Tsar Ivan the Terrible (1533–84) and abolished by Peter the Great in 1682.

Strelitzia (strĕli·tsiă). 1789. [f. *Strelitz* (after Charlotte of Mecklenburg-Strelitz, queen to Geo. III) + -IA.] A genus of herbaceous plants (of the family *Musaceæ*), natives of S. Africa; also, a plant of this genus.

Strengite (stre·ŋəit). 1881. [a. G. *strengit* (named after A. *Streng*); see -ITE[1] 2b.] *Min.* Hydrous phosphate of iron, found as a drusy incrustation of a red colour.

Strength (streŋþ), *sb.* [OE. *strengðu*:—OTeut. **strangiþo*, f. **strango-* STRONG *a.*; see -TH[1] b.] **1.** The quality or condition of being strong. **a.** Power of action in body or limbs; ability to exert muscular force. **b.** Bodily vigour in general; efficiency of the bodily powers OE. **c.** Power in general, whether physical, mental, or due to the possession of resources; ability for effective action OE. **d.** Capacity for moral effort or endurance; firmness (of mind, character, will, purpose) OE. **e.** Power of contending in warfare; now chiefly, military power derived from numbers, equipment, or resources OE. **f.** In a fortification, fortified place, etc.: Power of withstanding assault or capture. late ME. **g.** In things, material or immaterial: Operative power; capacity for producing effects OE. **h.** Power to sustain the application of force without breaking or yielding. late ME. **i.** Intensity and active force (of movement, wind, fire, a stream, current of electricity, or the like); intensity (of a physical condition, colour, sound, etc.) ME. **j.** Vigour, intensity (of feeling, conviction, etc.). Also, emphasis, positiveness (of refusal). 1550. **k.** Intensity of the specific property, or proportionate quantity of the active ingredient in a substance; potency (of drugs, liquors) 1588. **l.** Of soil: Firmness 1573. **m.** Demonstrative force or weight (of arguments, evidence); amount of evidence for (a case) 1593. **n.** Energy or vigour of literary or artistic conception or execution; forcefulness (of delineation, versification, expression) 1687. **o.** *Cards.* Of a hand (or its holder): Effectiveness due to the value of the cards held; also, the condition of being strong *in* (a specified suit). Of a suit: Number and value of the cards held by a player 1862. **p.** *Billiards.* The measure of force used to make a stroke 1788. **q.** *Comm.* Firmness, steadiness in prices 1891. **2.** Used for: A source of strength; that which makes strong OE. †**3.** Legal power; authority -1689. **4.** A stronghold, fastness, fortress. Now *arch.* or *Hist.*, chiefly with ref. to Scotland. ME. †**b.** A defensive work, fortification -1661. †**c.** One's strong position; the place within which one is most secure -1714. †**5. a.** *collect. sing.* Troops, forces -1703. **b.** A body of soldiers; a force -1627. **6.** *Mil.* and *Naval.* The number of men on the muster-roll of an army, a regiment, etc.; the body of men enrolled; the number of ships in a navy or fleet 1601. **7.** A sufficient number (of persons or things) for some purpose. Now *dial.* 1607. †**8.** The aggregate resources (of a nation) -1711. **9.** Strongest part; *spec.* the strongest part of a stream or current 1530.

1. **a.** Sampson loste hys streyngthe therfore 1400. You have s., I have brains 1888. **b.** My s. was gone, and..I required to rest once more TYNDALL. **c.** His s. lay in accurate verbal scholarship rather than in philosophy 1894. **d.** If..Thou hast the s. of will to slay thy selfe SHAKS. **f.** An old town, formerly of considerable s. BORROW. **g.** Great is the s. Of words SHELLEY. **h.** The brittle s. of bones MILT. Tensile s. 1876. **i.** The s. of the pulse 1866. **j.** If you did know..You would abate the s. of your displeasure SHAKS. **k.** T' allay the S...of the Wine DRYDEN. **m.** The s. of his opponent's case 1895. **n.** The easy vigour of a line, Where Denham's s., and Waller's sweetness join POPE. 2. The Lord, my S. and Righteousness WESLEY. 4. To lay down their Arms, and surrender Chester and other Strengths 1661. 6. His s. at sea now [is] very small 1718. The fighting s. of the regiment 1894. Phr. *Under s.*, having less than the standard or normal number. *On the s.*, entered on the rolls of a regiment; also said of those soldiers' wives whose marriage has been approved by the authorities and who have therefore a recognized position; opp. to *off the s.* 8. The Woollen Manufacture is the British S., the staple Commodity..of our Country ADDISON.

Phr. *On the s. of*, encouraged by, relying on, or arguing from. Hence †**Strength** *v. trans.* to give s. to, to make strong or stronger; to strengthen, fortify, confirm -1614. **Stre·ngthful** *a.* full of or characterized by s. **Stre·ngthless** *a.* destitute of s.

Strengthen (stre·ŋþ'n), *v.* ME. [f. prec. + -EN[5].] **1.** *trans.* To give moral support, courage or confidence, to. **2.** To give physical strength to (a person); to make stronger or more robust; to give defensive strength to (a town, etc.), make strong against attack; to reinforce (some material thing) by an additional support, added thickness, etc. 1452. **3.** To make stronger in influence, authority, or security of position 1579. **4.** To add strength or intensity to; to increase the strength or force of (reasons, etc.); to make more effective or powerful 1586. **5.** *intr.* To become strong or stronger; to grow in strength or intensity 1610.

2. Wine..taken in moderation..strengthens the stomach 1789. 3. He loved to s. his family by a good alliance GEO. ELIOT. 4. Additional Arguments to s. the Opinion which you have..delivered 1712. 5. The young disease..Grows with his growth, and strengthens with his strength POPE. Hence **Stre·ngthener,** one who or something which strengthens. **Stre·ngthening** *vbl. sb.* and *ppl. a.*

Strengthily (stre·ŋþili), *adv.* *rare.* 1456. [f. next + -LY[2].] Strongly.

Strengthy (stre·ŋþi), *a.* Chiefly *Sc.* and *north.* ME. [f. STRENGTH *sb.* + -Y[1].] †**1.** Strong, powerful; difficult to overthrow -1596. **2.** Physically or muscularly strong. Now *rare* exc. *dial.* 1456.

Strenuity (strĭniū·ĭti). Now *rare.* late ME. [ad. L. *strenuitas*; see next and -ITY.] The quality of being strenuous, strenuousness.

Strenuous (stre·niu,əs), *a.* 1599. [f. L. *strenuus* (related to Gr. στρηνής strong, hard, rough) + -OUS.] **1.** Vigorous in action, energetic; 'brave, bold, active, valiant' (J.). Now usu.: Unremittingly and ardently laborious. **b.** Zealous, earnest, 'strong' as a partisan or opponent 1713. †**2.** Of inanimate things: Strong in operation -1633. **b.** Of voice, etc.: Powerful, loud. *arch.* 1680. **3.** Of action or effort: Vigorous, energetic; now, persistently and ardently laborious. Of conditions, periods, etc.: Characterized by strenuous exertion. 1671.

1. A s. and an expert Souldier 1631. The s. metropolis 1899. **b.** A s. supporter of Mary Stuart 1774. 3. To love Bondage more then Liberty; Bondage with ease than s. liberty MILT. *S. idleness* (= L. *strenua inertia* Hor. *Ep.* I. xi. 28), busy activity to no useful purpose. Hence **Stre·nuous-ly** *adv.*, **-ness.**

Strepent (stre·pĕnt), *a.* *rare.* 1750. [ad. L. *strepentem*, *strepere* to make a noise.] Noisy.

Strepitant (stre·pitănt), *a.* 1855. [ad. L. *strepitantem*, *strepitare*, freq. of *strepere.*] Making a great noise, noisy.

Strepitous (stre·pitəs), *a.* 1681. [ad. mod. L. **strepitosus*, f. L. *strepitus* noise, f. *strepere.*] Noisy, accompanied with much noise. (Now used chiefly in musical criticism.)

Strepsipterous (strepsi·pterəs), *a.* 1817. [f. mod.L. *Strepsiptera* (f. Gr. στρεψι-, comb. form of στρέφειν to twist + πτερόν wing) + -OUS.] *Ent.* Belonging to the order *Strepsiptera* of insects (named from the twisted front wings). So **Strepsi·pteral** *a.*; **Strepsi·pteran** *a.*, also *sb.* an insect of the order *Strepsiptera*.

Strepto- (stre·ptǫ), bef. a vowel **strept-**, comb. form of Gr. στρεπτός twisted (freq. taken to mean 'chain'), f. στρέφειν to turn, twist; used in many scientific terms.

Stre·ptobaci·lli [BACILLUS] *sb. pl.*, bacilli arranged in chains. **Stre·ptobacte·ria** [BACTERIUM] *sb. pl.*, bacteria linked together like a chain. ‖**Streptoca·rpus**, a genus of African gesneraceous plants bearing pistils or fruits spirally-twisted towards the point; a plant of this genus, esp. the Cape Primrose. **Stre·ptocyte** [-CYTE], an amœbiform body occurring in bead-like strings from the vesicles of foot-and-mouth disease. **Streptomycin** (-mai·sin) [Gr. μύκης fungus. -IN], an antibiotic similar in action to penicillin. **Streptoneu·ral, -neu·rous** *adjs.*, pertaining to the *Streptoneura*, a branch of gasteropoda in which the loop of visceral nerves is twisted into a figure-of-eight, **Stre·ptothrix**, genus of bacteria comprising organisms having branching filaments growing in interlacing masses; a micro-organism of this type.

‖ **Streptococcus** (streptǫkǫ·kǫ̆s). *Pl.* **-cocci** (-kǫ·ksəi). 1877. [mod.L., f. STREPTO- + Gr. κόκκος berry.] *Bacteriol.* A form of bacterial organism in which the cocci are arranged in chains or chaplets. Hence **Streptococcal** (-kǫ·kăl), **-coccic** (kǫ·ksik), **-coccous** (-kǫ·kǫ̆s), *adjs.* pertaining to or produced by s.

Stress (stres), *sb.* ME. [prob. an aphetic form of DISTRESS *sb.*] **I.** †**1.** Hardship, straits, adversity, affliction -1704. †**2.** Force or pressure exercised on a person for the purpose of compulsion or extortion -1655. **3.** The overpowering pressure *of* some adverse force or influence. Chiefly in *s. of weather*. 1513. **b.** A condition of things compelling or characterized by strained effort; occas. coupled with *storm* 1637. **4.** Strained exertion, strong effort. Now *rare*. 1690. **5.** Physical strain or pressure exerted upon a material object; the strain *of* a load or weight. Now *rare* exc. in scientific use. 1440. **b.** Strain upon a bodily organ or a mental power 1843. †**6.** Testing strain or pressure on a support or basis; weight (of inference, confidence, etc.) resting upon an argument or piece of evidence; amount of risk ventured on some assurance; degree of reliance. Chiefly in phr. *to lay s. on* or *upon*, to rely on, rest a burden of proof upon. -1765. †**b.** Weightiest part, essential point (of a business, argument, question) -1791. †**c.** Argumentative force -1784. **7.** Exceptional insistence on something; emphasis. Chiefly in phr. *to lay s. upon*. 1756. **8.** Relative loudness or force of vocal utterance; a greater degree of vocal force characterizing one part of a word as compared with the rest. Also, superior loudness of voice as a means of emphasizing one or more of the words of a sentence. 1749.

1. [He] began to be reduced to the utmost s. 1704. 3. b. This age of s. and transition 1883. Phr. *Storm and s.*: see STORM *sb.* 4. Though the faculties of the mind are improved by exercise, yet they must not be put to a s. beyond their strength LOCKE. 6. I always put a great deal of s. upon his judgment DE FOE. 7. Do you consider the forms of introduction, and the s. that is laid on them, as nonsense? JANE AUSTEN.

II. *Law.* A distraint; also, the chattel or chattels seized in a distraint. *Obs.* exc. *dial.* 1440. Hence **Stre·ssful** *a.* full of, or subject to, s. or strain. **Stre·ssless** *a.* having no s., unstressed.

Stress (stres), *v.* ME. [orig. prob. a. OF. *estrecier*:—pop. L. **strictiare*, f. L. *strictus*; see STRAIT *a.* In mod. use f. STRESS *sb.*] †**1.** *trans.* To subject (a person) to force or compulsion; to constrain or restrain -1581. †**b.** To confine, incarcerate -1556. †**2.** To subject to hardship; to afflict, harass, oppress; *pass.*, to be 'hard up' -1824. **3.** To subject (a material thing, a bodily organ, a mental faculty) to stress or strain; to overwork, fatigue. Now chiefly *Sc.* 1545. **4.** To lay the stress or emphasis on, emphasize (a word or phrase in speaking); to place a stress-accent on (a syllable) 1859. **b.** *fig.* To lay stress on, emphasize (a fact, idea, etc.). Chiefly *U.S.* 1896.

3. A metal structure..must not be stressed to more than one-third of its ultimate breaking stress 1892. 4. Stressing the epithet to increase the defiance MEREDITH.

Stretch (stretʃ), *sb.* 1558. [f. next.] **1.** The action or an act of stretching physically; the fact of being stretched 1600. **b.** An act of 'stretching one's legs'; a walk taken for exercise 1761. **c.** The condition of being stretched; state of tension 1673. **d.** Capacity for being stretched 1875. **2.** In immaterial sense: A stretching or straining something beyond its proper limits; e. g. an unwarranted exercise *of* power; a straining *of* the law 1689; an undue extension of scope or application 1849. **3.** *Furthest, utmost s.*: the utmost degree to which a thing can be extended. Now *rare* or *Obs.* 1558. **4.** Strain or tension of mental or bodily powers; strained exertion 1622. **5.** Extent in time or space. **a.** An unbroken continuance of some one employment, occupation, or condition, during a period of time; an uninterrupted 'spell' of work, rest, prosperity, etc. 1689. **b.** A (more or less long) period of time 1698. **c.** A continuous journey or march. Now *colloq.* 1699. **d.** *Naut.* A continuous sail on one tack 1675. **e.** A continuous length or distance 1661. **f.** An expanse of land or water (usu., of a uniform character) 1829. **g.** *slang.* A term of hard labour; twelve months as a term of imprisonment 1821. **6.** *Mining* and *Geol.* Course or direction of a seam or a stratum with ref. to the points of the compass 1799.

1. Sometimes he thought to swim the stormy Main, By S. of Arms the distant Shore to gain DRYDEN. He gave a yawn and a s. 1856. **c.** Phr. *On, upon the s.*; An instrument, whose cords, upon the s.,..Yield only discord in his Maker's ear COWPER. 2. These stretches of power naturally led the lords and commons into some degree of opposition GOLDSM. *S. of language*, the use of words or expressions with undue latitude of meaning. 4. *On the* (†*full*) *s.*, in a state of mental strain, making intense effort. 5. **a.** Phr. *At one* or *a s.*, *upon* or *on a s.*, rarely *at the s.*, without intermission, continuously (during the time specified or implied). **b.** Fretted out of..your mind, for a s. of months together DICKENS. **d.** In the evening, we made a s. toward the land 1823. **e.** This range [Lebanon] has an unbroken s. of a hundred miles 1908. **f.** Windsor, with its wide stretches of park and woodland and river 1885.

Stretch (stretʃ), *v.* [Com.WGer.; OE. *strecan*:—WGer. **strakkjan*, f. **strakko-* straight, rigid, stiff.] **I.** To place at full length. **1.** *trans.* To prostrate (oneself, one's body); to extend (one's limbs) in a reclining posture; *refl.* to recline at full length. **b.** To lay (a person) flat ME. **2.** To extend (the arms) laterally; to expand (the wings), esp. for flight ME. **3.** *refl.* To straighten oneself; to rise to full height; also, to draw up the body, as from a stooping, cramped, or relaxed posture; to straighten the body and extend the arms, as a manifestation of weariness or languor (chiefly coupled with *yawn*). Also *intr.* for *refl.* ME.

1. There..His listless length at noontide would he s. GRAY. **b.** Andremon first..Of life bereft, lay stretch'd upon the sand 1757. 3. Mop [the dog]..rose and stretched himself 1858. Phr. *To s. one's legs*, to straighten them from a sitting position; usu., to relieve by walking the stiffness or fatigue caused by sitting; to take a walk for exercise.

II. To put forward, protrude. **1.** *trans.* To put forth, extend (the hand, an arm or leg, the neck, head). Now almost always with adv., e. g. *forth, out, forward*. OE. **2.** To hold out, hand, reach (something). Now only *Naut.* 1450.

1. He stretcht his hand, and into it, the Herald put the lot CHAPMAN.

III. To direct a course. **1.** *intr.* To make one's way (rapidly or with effort) ME. **2.** *Naut.* To sail (esp. under crowd of canvas) continuously in one direction 1687.

1. I s. over Putney Heath, and my spirit resumes its tranquillity THACKERAY. 2. I stretched over for California 1726.

IV. To (make to) reach; to give or have a certain extent. **1.** *trans.* To place (something) so as to reach from one point to another, or across an interval in space ME. **2.** *intr.* (rarely *pass.*) and †*refl.* To have a specified extent in space; to be continuous to a certain point, or over a certain distance or area. late ME. **b.** To have its length in a specified direction. late ME. †**3.** *fig.* **a.** To have a specified measure in amount, degree, power, etc.; to be adequate for some purpose -1648. **b.** To have a specified extent or range of action or application -1659. †**4.** To tend, be serviceable (to some object) -1621.

1. A piece of clothes line, stretched across the room 1907. 2. A steep slope stretches down to the Mer de Glace TYNDALL. *transf. Ant. & Cl.* I. i. 46. 3. **a.** 1 *Hen. IV*, I. ii. 62.

V. To tighten by force, to strain. **1.** *trans.* To pull taut; to bring to a rigid state of straightness or evenness by the application of tractive force at the extremities. late ME. **2.** To pull (a person's) limbs lengthwise; esp. to torture by so doing; to rack. In early use, to place with extended limbs on a cross. ME. **3.** †**a.** *To s. a halter, rope*: to be hanged -1708. **b.** *To s.* (a person, his neck): to hang 1595. †**c.** *intr.* To be hanged -1676. **4.** *To s. a point* = to strain a point; see STRAIN *v.* II. 2 e. 1565. †**5.** *fig.* To strain (one's powers) -1660. †**b.** *refl.* and *intr.* To strain, press forward, use effort -1738.

1. Each eager Hound exerts His utmost Speed, and stretches ev'ry Nerve 1735. 2. He hates him, That would vpon the wracke of this tough world S. him out longer SHAKS. 5. **b.** Phr. *To s. to the oar, to the stroke*, to put forth one's strength in rowing.

VI. 1. *trans.* To lengthen or widen (a material thing) by force; to pull out to greater length or width; to enlarge in girth or capacity by internal pressure. late ME. **b.** To open wide (the eyes, mouth, nostrils) 1599. **2.** *fig.* To enlarge or amplify beyond proper or natural limits; to extend unduly the scope, application, or meaning of (a law, rule, word, etc.) 1553. **b.** To exaggerate in narration; chiefly *absol.* (colloq.) 1674. **3.** *intr.* To be or admit of being forcibly lengthened or dilated without breaking 1485.

1. Gentlemen, You'l breake your wits with stretching them 1632. My business..is to s. new boots for millionaires 1889. **b.** Now set the Teeth, and s. the Nosthrill wide SHAKS. 2. To Love an Enemy is to s. Humanity as far as it will go 1670. **b.** They call anything that is 'stretched' a Yankee story 1883. 3. I tell you their consciences are like chiuerell skins, that will stretch euery way 1597.

Comb.: **s.-bench** *Leather-manuf.*, a bench on which the stretching of hides is performed; **-wood**, a wooden hand upon which a glove is stretched to dry in dyeing. Hence **Stre·tchable** *a.* capable of being stretched.

Stretcher (stre·tʃəɹ). late ME. [f. prec. + -ER[1].] **I.** One who or something which stretches. **1.** One who stretches; *spec.* a worker employed in various industries to stretch fabrics. **2.** An exaggerated story or yarn; *euphem.* or *joc.* a lie 1674. **II.** Techn. senses. †**1.** *Falconry.* A toe of a hawk or falcon -1677. **2.** An instrument or appliance for expanding material, making it taut, removing its wrinkles, and the like 1532. **b.** A frame upon which an artist's canvas is stretched 1847. **c.** An instrument for easing the fit of boots, gloves, hats, etc. 1858. **3.** A bar serving as a stay or brace. **a.** A buttress in masonry; a tie-beam in joinery; in trench timbering, a temporary strut 1774. **b.** A bar or rod used as a tie or brace in the framework of an article; esp. a cross-piece between the handles of a plough or the legs of a chair 1844. **4.** A bar or rod used to expand and to keep expanded something collapsible; e. g. each of the rods pivoted to the ends of the ribs and the sleeve which slides upon the stick of an umbrella 1843. **5.** A foot-rest in a rowing-boat 1609. **6.** A kind of litter composed of two poles separated by cross-bars upon which canvas is stretched, used to transport a sick or wounded person. Also, a shutter, gate, etc. used in the same way. 1845. **7.** A folding bed or bedstead chiefly for camp or hospital use. Also *pl.* the trestles for a bed. 1841. **8.** *Building.* A brick or stone laid with its length in the direction of the wall. Also *Fortif.*, a sod laid in a similar position. 1693. **9.** *Angling.* The artificial fly at the extremity of a casting line to which two or more flies are attached 1837.

attrib. and *Comb.*: **s.-bearer**, a man who helps to carry a s.; esp. a soldier who assists in carrying the wounded from a battle; **-party** *Mil.*, a party of men equipped with stretchers and appliances for assisting and removing the wounded; **-pole**, a pole of an ambulance.

Stretching (stre·tʃiŋ), *vbl. sb.* ME. [-ING[1].] The action or an act of STRETCH *v.*

Comb.: **s.-bond**, a bond (BOND *sb.*[1] 13) in which stretchers, not headers, are used; **-course**, a course of bricks or stones laid in the direction of the wall.

Stretching (stre·tʃiŋ), *ppl. a.* 1547. [-ING².] That stretches, in the senses of the verb.

Comb.: **s.-beam**, a tie-beam or brace used in building.

Stre·tchy, *a. colloq.* 1854. [f. STRETCH *v.* + -Y¹.] **1.** Having the quality of stretching; elastic. **b.** Liable to stretch unduly 1885. **2.** Inclined to stretch oneself or one's limbs 1872.

‖ **Stretto** (stre·tˌto), *adv.* and *sb. Pl.* **stretti** (stre·tˌti), also **strettos.** 1753. [It. = narrow.] *Mus.* **A.** *adv.* A direction: In quicker time. **B.** *sb.* (See quot.) 1854.

In a fugue the s. is an artifice by which the subject and answer are, as it were, bound closer together, by being made to overlap 1869.

Strew (strū), *sb. rare.* 1578. [f. next.] A number of things strewed over a surface or scattered about.

Strew (strū), *v.* Also (now *arch.* and *dial.*) **strow** (strōu). Pa. t. and pple. **strewed, strowed;** pa. pple. also **strewn, strown.** [Com. Teut. wk. vb.; OE. *strewian, stréowian, stréawian,* f. OTeut. root **strau-*.] **1.** *trans.* To scatter, spread loosely; to sprinkle over a surface. **2.** To cover (the ground, a floor, any surface) with something loosely scattered or sprinkled ME. **3.** To be spread or scattered upon (a surface) 1513. **4. a.** To spread (a cloth or the like) as a covering. **b.** To cover (a bed) *with* a coverlet. **c.** To make or lay (a bed). *rare.* 1615. **5.** To level with the ground, lay low, throw down, prostrate. Chiefly *poet.* 1460. **6.** To level, calm (stormy waves); to allay (a storm). *arch.* and *poet.* (Cf. L. *sternere æquor*) 1594.

1. The newspapers which were strewn upon the table DICKENS. *fig.* The cleare moone strowes siluer in our path 1602. **2.** All the ground With shiverd armour strow'n MILT. Wild tornadoes, Strewing yonder sea with wrecks COWPER. *transf.* The coast is thickly strewn with islands 1879. **3.** The boulders that strewed the mountain-side 1893. **4.** Hands unseen thy Couch are strewing SCOTT. **5.** They..would have strown it, and are fall'n themselves TENNYSON. Hence **Strew·ing** *vbl. sb.*, the action of the vb. *concr.* something strewed (now *rare* or *Obs.*). **Strew·ment** (*rare*), something strewed or for strewing; *pl.* flowers, etc. strewed on a grave.

'Strewth. *vulgar.* 1892. Short for *God's truth*, used as an oath.

‖ **Stria** (strəi·ă). *Pl.* **striæ** (strəi·ī). 1563. [L., furrow, flute of a column.] **1.** *Arch.* A fillet between the flutes of columns, pilasters, and the like. **2.** Chiefly in scientific use. A small groove, channel, or ridge; a narrow streak, stripe, or band of distinctive colour, structure, or texture; *esp.* one of two or of a series 1673. **b.** *pl. Electr.* The alternate bright and dark bands observed in vacuum-tubes (Geissler tubes) upon the passage of an electrical discharge 1881.

Striate (strəi·ĕ't), *a.* 1678. [ad. mod.L. *striatus*, f. L. *stria* STRIA; see -ATE².] Marked or scored with striæ, showing narrow structural bands, striped, streaked, or furrowed.

Striate (strəi·eⁱt), *v.* 1709. [ad. mod.L. *striat-, striare*, f. *stria* STRIA; see -ATE³.] *trans.* To mark or score with striæ; to furrow or streak.

Striated (strəi·eⁱtĕd), *ppl. a.* 1646. [f. prec. + -ED¹.] **1.** = STRIATE *a.* **2.** *Arch.* Chamfered, channelled, grooved 1727. **3.** Constituting striæ 1854.

1. A deep, thin.. finely s. Shell 1705. *Picus striolatus.* The S. Woodpecker. 1840.

Striation (strəiˌēⁱ·ʃən). 1849. [f. as prec.; see -ATION.] **1.** Striated condition or appearance 1851. **2.** One of a set or system of striæ, a streak, a marking; esp. *Geol.*, one of the grooves or glacial marks found on rock-surfaces; *Min. pl.* the fine parallel lines on a crystalline face; *Electr. pl.* (cf. STRIA 2 b).

Striato- (strəiˌēⁱ·to), used in *Zool.* and *Bot.* as comb. form of mod.L. *striatus*, prefixed to adjs. in the sense 'striate and —', as *s.-rugose, -tubular.*

Striature (strəi·ătiŭɹ). 1728. [ad. L. *striatura*, f. *stria.*] Disposition of striæ, striation; also, one of a set of striæ.

Strick (strik), *sb.* late ME. [f. **strik-*, wk. grade of root of STRIKE *v.*] **1.** A bundle of broken hemp, flax, jute, etc. for heckling. **2.** A measure of capacity for corn, coal, etc.; also the measuring vessel. Now *dial.* late ME. **3.** A piece of wood with which measures of grain are made level. Now *dial.* late ME.

Strick (strik), *v.* late ME. [f. prec.] **1.** *trans.* To strike off (corn, etc.) level with the rim of the measure. **2.** To prepare (lint) for heckling; also, to heckle (flax, etc.) 1808.

Stricken (stri·k'n), *pa. pple.* and *ppl. a.* late ME. [pa. pple. of STRIKE *v.*] **A.** *pa. pple.* in special sense. (For other uses see STRIKE *v.*) **S. in years:** advanced in years. *arch.* **B.** *ppl. a.* **1.** Of a deer, etc.: Wounded in the chase 1513. **2.** Struck with a blow 1538. **b.** Of a sound, musical note: Produced by striking a blow 1820. **3.** Of a person, community: Afflicted with disease or sickness; overwhelmed with trouble, sorrow, or the like: esp. in *fever-, panic-s.* Of the face: Marked with or exhibiting great trouble. 1611. **b.** Of the mind, heart, soul: Afflicted with frenzy, madness, grief, or the like 1795. **4.** Of a measure: Having its contents levelled with the rim of the measuring vessel, as dist. from *heaped* 1495. **5.** *S. field*: a joined engagement between armed forces or combatants; a pitched battle 1700.

1. Let the s. deere goe weepe SHAKS. **2.** Out of s. helmets sprang the fire TENNYSON. **b.** *S. hour*, (arch.), a full hour as indicated by the striking of the clock; General —..sat talking a s. hour or thereabouts HAWTHORNE. **3.** A drawn, s. face 1896. **5.** I never had the good fortune to see a s. field SCOTT.

Strickle (stri·k'l), *sb.* late ME. [OE. *stricel* pulley, f. Teut. **strik-*: see STRIKE *v.*] **1.** A straight piece of wood with which surplus grain is struck off level with the rim of the measure. **b.** Applied to instruments used for similar purposes in casting or moulding 1688. **2.** A tool with which a reaper whets or sharpens his scythe 1641. Hence **Stri·ckle** *v. trans.* (*Founding*) to strike *off* with a s. (the superfluous sand) in moulding; to shape (a core) or form (a mould) by means of a s.; also *absol.*

Strict (strikt), *a.* 1578. [ad. L. *strictus*, *stringere* to draw or bind tight.] **I.** Physical senses. †**1.** Drawn tightly together; tight, close –1781. **2.** Restricted as to space or extent; narrow, drawn in. Now *rare* or *Obs.* 1597. **3.** Straight and stiff. *Obs.* exc. *Bot.* and *Zool.* 1592.

1. She wildly breaketh from their s. imbrace SHAKS. **2.** S. passage, through which sighs are brought WORDSW. **3.** The s. stem of some corals 1891.

II. Fig. senses. **1.** Of personal relations, alliance, etc.: Close, intimate. Now *rare* or *Obs.* 1600. **2.** Of correspondence, agreement, or connexion between facts, ideas, etc.: Close, exactly fitting 1715. †**3.** Restricted in amount, meaning, application, etc. –1737. **4.** Accurately determined or defined; exact, precise, not vague or loose 1631. **b.** Law. *S. settlement*: see quot. 1710. **5.** Of confinement or imprisonment: Rigorous; severely restricted in regard to space or liberty of movement 1667. **6.** Of watch and ward, authority, discipline, obedience, etc.: Rigorously maintained, admitting no relaxation or indulgence 1602. **7.** Of a law, ordinance, etc., or its execution: Stringent and rigorous in its demands or provisions, allowing no evasion 1578. **8.** Of an art or science, its procedure, etc.: In rigid conformity to rules or postulates 1638. **9.** Of a quality or condition, an attitude or line of action: Maintained to the full, admitting no deviation or abatement; absolute, entire 1588. **b.** Of truth, accuracy, etc.: Rigidly observed; exactly answerable to fact or reality 1748. **10.** Rigorous and severe in rule and discipline, in administering justice, etc. 1596. **11.** Of persons: Holding a rigorous and austere standard of living; stern to oneself in matters of conscience and morality 1578. **b.** Of virtue, chastity, etc. 1589. **12.** Undeviating in adherence to the principles or practice implied by the designation 1660. **13.** Of inquiry, investigation, inspection, observation, calculation, and the like: Characterized by close and unrelaxing effort, so as to let nothing escape notice 1596.

2. The strictest explanation is the truest PUSEY. **3.** *Cymb.* v. iv. 17. **4.** The s. Import of the Word 1692. **b.** When land is settled..by a limitation to the parent for life, and after his death to his first and other sons in tail, and trustees are interposed to preserve the contingent remainders, this is called a *s. settlement* 1841. **6.** His temper was under s. government MACAULAY. **7.** This purdah system is strictest in the north 1913. **8.** The only concords recognized in s. counterpoint 1869. **9.** I generally go about In s. incognito SHELLEY. A man of the strictest prudence 1860. **10.** S. disciplinarians 1850. **11.** My mother and sisters are dissenters, and very s. THACKERAY. **12.** The feeling on the subject among s. churchmen 1868. **13.** Upon a s. review, I blotted out several passages SWIFT. Hence **Stri·ct-ly** *adv.*, **-ness.**

Striction (stri·kʃən). 1875. [ad. L. *strictionem*, f. *stringere.*] **1.** The action of straining (*rare*) 1889. **2.** *Geom.* In a skew surface, *curve* or *line of s.*: the line that cuts each generator in that point of it that is nearest to the succeeding generator 1875.

Stricture (stri·ktiŭɹ, -tʃəɹ), *sb.*¹ late ME. [a. L. *strictura*, f. *strict-, stringere*, really two verbs; the one with the sense to bind tightly, strain; the other with the senses to touch lightly, to gather (flowers), to draw (a sword).] **I.** A binding, tightening. **1.** *Path.* A morbid narrowing of a canal, duct, or passage, esp. of the urethra, œsophagus, or intestine. **2.** *gen.* The action of binding or encompassing tightly; tight closure; restriction (*rare*) 1649. †**II.** A spark, flash of light. *lit.* and *fig.* –1674.

Rays and strictures of the divine Glory 1651.

III. A touching slightly or in passing. †**1.** A touch, slight trace –1695. **2.** An incidental remark or comment; now always, an adverse criticism 1655.

2. We may now and then add a few strictures of reproof JOHNSON. Hence **Stri·cture** *v. trans.* to criticize, censure (*rare*). **Stri·ctured** *ppl. a.* affected with s. **Stri·cturing** *vbl. sb. Path.* formation of a s.

†**Stri·cture,** *sb.*² [f. STRICT *a.* + -URE.] Strictness. SHAKS.

Strid (strid). 1807. [app. repr. OE. *stride*; see next.] The proper name of the narrowest part of the channel of the Wharfe between level rocks at Bolton Priory; hence, any similar gorge or chasm.

Stride (strəid), *sb.* [Two formations: (1) OE. *stride*, f. **strid-*, wk.-grade of the root of STRIDE *v.*; (2) the surviving word, f. the present stem of the vb.] **1.** An act of striding; a long step in walking ME. **b.** The distance covered by a stride; the normal length of a stride used as a measure of distance OE. **2.** A striding gait 1671. **3.** An act of progressive movement of a horse, etc., completed when all the feet are returned to the same relative position which they occupied at the beginning; also, the distance covered by such a movement 1614. **b.** The regular or uniform movement (of a horse) in a race. Also *transf.* 1883. **4.** Divergence of the legs when straddled; also, the distance between the feet when the legs are stretched apart laterally to the utmost 1599.

1. Ile..turne two minsing steps Into a manly s. SHAKS. *fig.* Simplicity flies away, and iniquity comes at long strides upon us SIR T. BROWNE. **2.** I know him by his s. MILT. **3. b.** Phr. *To take in his s.*, of a horse or his rider, to clear (an obstacle) without checking his gallop; *fig.* to deal with (a matter) incidentally, without interrupting one's course of action, argument, etc. *To get into one's s.*: to settle down to one's pace or rate of progress.

Stride (strəid), *v.* Pa. t. **strode** (strōud), occas. **strided,** pa. pple. **stridden** (strid'n). [OE. *stridan* :—Teut. root **strīd-*.] †**1.** *intr.* To stand or walk with the legs widely diverging; to straddle –1638. **b.** *transf.* (Often said of an arch.) 1598. **2.** To walk with long steps; to stalk ME. **3.** To take a long step; to advance the foot beyond the usual length of a step; to pass *over* or *across* an obstacle by a long step or by lifting the feet ME. **4.** *trans.* To step over with a stride 1572. **5.** To walk about (a street, etc.) with long steps; to pace; hence, to measure by striding 1577. **6.** To bestride ME.

1. b. The arches, striding o'er the new-born stream BURNS. **2.** He then rose up, strided to the fire, and stood for some time laughing and exulting BOSWELL. **3.** They that s. so wide at once will go farre with few paces FULLER. **4.** A hedge to clamber or a brook to s. CLARE. **6.** The tempest is his steed, he strides the air SHELLEY.

Strident (strəi·dĕnt), *a.* 1656. [ad. L. *stridentem, stridere* to creak.] **1.** Making a harsh, grating, or creaking noise; loud and harsh, shrill. **2.** *transf.* and *fig.* 1876.

1. Old Steyne's s. voice THACKERAY. **2.** S. colour 1907. Hence **Stri·dency,** the quality of being s. **Stri·dently** *adv.*

Stridor (strəi·dǭɹ). 1632. [a. L. *stridor*, f. *stridere*; see prec.] **1.** A harsh, high-pitched sound, a shrill grating or creaking noise. **2.** *Path.* A harsh vibrating noise produced by a bronchial, tracheal, or laryngeal obstruction 1876.

Stridulate (stri·diu̇leit), *v.* 1838. [f. mod. L. *stridulat-*, *stridulare*, f. L. *stridulus* STRIDULOUS.] *intr.* To make a harsh, grating, shrill noise; said *spec.* of certain insects. So **Stri·dulant** *a.* that stridulates.

Stridulation (stridiu̇lēⁱ·ʃən). 1838. [a. F., f. mod. L. *stridulare*; see prec.] The action of prec. vb.; the stridulous noise produced by certain insects.

Stridulator (stri·diu̇leⁱtəɹ). 1880. [f. STRIDULATE *v.* + -OR.] **a.** An insect that stridulates. **b.** A stridulating apparatus.

Stridulatory (stri·diu̇lătəri), *a.* 1838. [f. as prec. + -ORY [2].] Pertaining to, causing, or caused by stridulation; also, capable of stridulating.

Stridulent (stri·diu̇lĕnt), *a.* 1874. [f. L. *stridulus* (see next) + -ENT.] = next.

Stridulous (stri·diu̇ləs), *a.* 1611. [f. L. *stridulus* (f. *stridere*) + -OUS.] **1.** Emitting or producing a shrill grating sound. **2.** Of voice, sound: Harsh, shrill, grating 1646. **3.** *Path.* Pertaining to or affected with stridor 1822.

1. S. guitar with wiry twang 1819. 2. In piercing accents s. COWPER. Hence **Stri·dulous·ly** *adv.*, **-ness.**

Strife (strəif). ME. [a. OF. *estrif*, related to *estriver* STRIVE *v.*] **1.** The action of striving together; a condition of antagonism, enmity, or discord; contention, dispute. **b.** An act or instance of contention or antagonism; a contest, quarrel, or dispute ME. **c.** A subject of contention (*rare*) 1535. **2.** Competition, emulation; a contest of emulation 1530. **3.** The act of striving; strong effort (*rare*) 1601.

1. A fell woman and full of s. ME. The diuell hath cast a bone..to set stryfe Betweene you 1546. *transf.* Safe amidst the elemental s. BYRON. *At s.*, at variance. *To make s.*, to cause dissension. **b.** A mere s. of words JOWETT. **c.** Thou hast made vs a very s. vnto our neghbours COVERDALE *Ps.* lxxix. [lxxx.] 6. **2.** Let our s. be, which can best serve our country 1836. **3.** As if these Mystic Authors made it their s. to imitate Nature 1687. Hence **Stri·feful, Stri·feless** *adjs.*

Strift. 1612. [f. STRIVE *v.* after *drift*, *thrift*, etc.] The action of striving; an instance of this; also, contention, strife. *Obs.* exc. in the traditional phraseology of the Society of Friends.

Strig (strig). 1565. [Origin obsc.] **1.** The stalk of a leaf, fruit, or flower; a petiole, peduncle, or pedicel. Also, the stem of the hop cone. **2.** A long thin appendage in various tools; the tang of a sword-blade; the stem of a marking-gauge; or the like 1703.

‖**Striga** (strəi·gă). *Pl.* **strigæ** (strəi·dʒi). 1760. [L.] †**1.** *Arch.* = STRIA 1. -1771. **2.** *Bot.* A row of stiff bristles; now, a stiff bristle (chiefly *pl.*) 1760. **3.** *Ent.* A transverse streak 1826.

Strigate (strəi·gĕt), *a.* 1891. [ad. L. *strigatus*, f. *striga* furrow, swath of hay or corn, etc.] = STRIGOSE *a.* 2. So **Striga·ted** *a.* having a channelled surface 1728.

‖**Striges** (strəi·dʒiz), *sb. pl.* 1563. [L., *striæ*, *strigæ*.] The channels of a fluted column.

Strigil (stri·dʒil). 1581. [ad. L. *strigilis*, f. *strig-*, *stringere* to touch lightly.] **1.** *Antiq.* An instrument with a curved blade, for scraping the sweat and dirt from the skin in the hot-air bath or after gymnastic exercise. Also *transf.* a flesh-brush or other instrument used for the same purpose. **2.** *Ent.* (See quot.) 1873.

2. The sixth segment [of the male *Corixa*] bearing on its upper side a small stalked plate (*strigil*)..furnished with rows of teeth 1910.

Strigillose (stridʒi·lōᵘs), *a.* 1857. [f. mod. L. *strigilla*, dim. of STRIGA.] *Bot.* Finely strigose.

Strigose (strəi·gōᵘs), *a.* 1793. [ad. mod. L. *strigosus*, f. L. *striga*; see -OSE.] **1.** *Bot.* Covered with strigæ or stiff hairs. Also of hairs: Having the character of strigæ. **2.** *Ent.* Having strigæ, streaked 1826.

Strigous (strəi·gəs), *a. rare.* 1776. [ad. mod. L. *strigosus*; see prec. and -OUS.] = prec. 1.

Strike (strəik), *sb.* ME. [f. next.] **1.** = STRICK *sb.* 1. late ME. **2. a.** = STRICKLE *sb.* 1. late ME. **b.** An instrument, usu. a rod or narrow board, used in brickmaking, casting, plumbing, etc., for levelling a surface by striking off the superfluous material 1683. **3.** A denomination of dry measure (not now officially recognized); usu. identical with the bushel, but in some districts equal to a half-bushel, and in others to two or four bushels. Also, the cylindrical wooden measuring vessel containing this quantity. ME. †**4.** The unit proportion of malt in ale or beer -1820. **5.** An act of striking 1587. **6.** *Fishing.* **a.** The jerk by which the angler secures a fish that is already hooked 1840. **b.** A large catch (of fish) 1887. **7.** *Mining* and *Geol.* The horizontal course of a stratum; direction with regard to the points of the compass 1829. **8.** A concerted cessation of work on the part of a body of workers, for the purpose of obtaining some concession from the employer or employers. Formerly occas. *s. of work.* 1810. **9.** An act of 'striking oil'; a discovery of a rich vein of ore in mining. Also *fig.* a stroke of success. 1883. **10.** *U.S. Baseball.* An act of striking at the ball, characterized as *fair* or *foul s.*; a 'foul s.' 1874. **11.** *Printing.* A type matrix struck from the punch 1871. **12.** *Coining.* The amount struck at one time 1891. **13.** *Soap-making.* The proper crystalline or mottled appearance of a soap, indicating complete saponification 1884.

8. It appeared there was a s. for higher wages 1815. Phr. *On s.* **14.** *U.S. Political slang.* The introduction of a bill (a *s. bill*) hostile to some moneyed interest in the hope of being paid to withdraw it 1885.

Comb.: **s.-breaker,** a workman who consents to work for an employer whose workmen are on s., thus contributing to the defeat of the s.; **-pay,** the periodical payment made by a trade-union for the support of men on s.

Strike (strəik), *v.* Pa. t. **struck** (strʌk); pa. pple. **struck,** *arch.* (also *U.S.* in sense III. 2) **stricken** (stri·k'n); see also STRIKED. [Com. WGer. str. vb.; OE. *strīcan*, *strāc*, *stricen*, f. OTeut. **strīk-* (: **straik-* : **strik-*):—Indo-Eur. **streig-* (: **stroig-* : **strig-*), found in L. *stringere*; cf. STRIGIL.] **I. 1.** *intr.* To make one's way, go. In early use chiefly *poet.* Later, chiefly with adv. (*forth*, *forward*, *over*) or phr. indicating the direction. *Obs.* exc. *arch.* ME. **2.** To proceed in a new direction; to make an excursion; to turn in one's journey *across*, *down*, etc. 1615. **b.** of a road, stream, etc. 1584. **c.** Of a boundary, path, mountain-range, etc.: To take a (specified) direction 1456. **d.** trans. *To s. a line* or *path*: to take a direction or course of movement 1867.

1. The Jews were not long of striking forward STEVENSON. **2.** It began raining, and I struck into Mrs. Vanhomrigh's, and dined SWIFT. We struck across the island DARWIN. **b.** A bridle road..struck into the fields 1883. **c.** A range of hills strikes southerly 1881.

II. To stroke, rub lightly, smooth, level. **1.** *trans.* To go over lightly with an instrument, the hand, etc.; to stroke, smooth; to make level. Also *absol.* Now *dial.* OE. †**2.** To smear (soap, blood, etc.) on a surface; also, to spread (a surface) with (something); to coat (a surface) *over* with oil, a wash, etc. -1799. **3.** To make (grain, etc.) level with the rim of the measure by passing a strickle over it. Also with the measure as obj. late ME. **b.** To level (sand) in moulding 1779. **4.** *Bricklaying.* To level up (a joint) with mortar; to spread (mortar) along a joint 1668. **b.** To cut off the superfluous mortar from the edges of (tiling) 1693. **5.** *Tanning.* To smooth and expand (skins) 1764. **6.** *Carpentry.* To fashion (moulding) with a plane 1842.

III. To mark with lines; to draw a line. **1.** To draw (a straight line) esp. by mechanical means; to draw (a circle, an arc) with compasses; †to make (a stroke, written mark) 1611. **2.** To cancel or expunge with or as with the stroke of a pen. *Obs.* exc. in *s. off*, *s. out*, *s. through*, and in the phr. *to s.* (a name, a person) *off* or (now rarely) *out of* a list. late ME. **3.** To form (a jury) by cancelling a certain number of names from the list of persons nominated to serve; similarly, to form (a committee), to make (a new register of voters) 1715. **4.** To make or cut (a tally) 1626. **5.** *Agric.* To mark off (land, a ridge) by ploughing once up and down the field; to make (furrows) in this manner; also *absol.* 1573. **b.** To make (a row of holes) with a dibble 1797.

1. Accustome your self to s. your strokes firm and bold 1662. **2.** He has struck Thomas out of his will THACKERAY. **3.** The Committee was struck late in the summer 1896.

IV. To lower (sails, masts), and derived senses. **1.** *Naut.* To lower or take down (a sail, mast, yard, etc.); esp. to lower (the topsail) as a salute and, more rarely, as a sign of surrender in an engagement ME. **b.** To haul down (a flag), esp. as a salute or as a sign of surrender. Chiefly in the phrases *to s.* (*the*) *flag*, *to s. one's colours*. Also *to s.* one's *flag* (said of an admiral): see FLAG *sb.*[4] 2. 1628. **c.** *absol.* To lower sail, haul down one's flag. late ME. **2.** trans. *Naut.* To lower (a thing) into the hold by means of a rope and tackle. Chiefly *to s. down* (also *absol.*). Also, *to s. out*, to hoist out from the hold and lower to the dock. 1644. **3.** *Building.* **a.** To remove (scaffolding); in trench-work, to remove (the timbers with which the sides have been secured) 1694. **b.** To remove (the centre or centering of an arch) 1739. **4.** *Shipbuilding.* To cause (a vessel) to slide *down*, *off* (the slipway); to release (a boat from the cradle) 1647. **5.** To discharge (a load); to empty (a vessel) of its load 1627. **b.** *Sugar-boiling.* To empty (the liquor, the tache) 1793. **6.** To let down (a tent) for removal; to remove the tents of (a camp or encampment) 1707. **7.** To unfix, put out of use 1793. **b.** *Theatr.* To remove (a scene); to remove the scenery, etc. of (a play); to turn down (a light) 1889. **8.** *intr.* Of an employee: To refuse to continue work; esp. of a body of employees, to cease working by agreement among themselves or by order of their society or union 1768. **b.** More explicitly *to s. work*, †*tools* (cf. sense 7 above) 1803. **c.** *trans.* Of a workmen's society or union: To order a strike of workmen against (a firm); to order (a body of workmen) to strike 1891.

1. Now s. your sailes ye iolly Mariners, For we be come vnto a quiet rode SPENSER. *fig.* He boarding her, she striking sail to him POPE. **3. a.** On striking the scaffolding, part of the south transept..came down 1868. **6.** Next morning we struck camp and turned homewards 1891. **7.** Arrange..the hour for..striking wickets 1851. **8.** The London omnibus men struck in a body 1892.

V. To deal a blow, to smite with the hand (*occas.* another limb), a weapon or tool. **1.** *trans.* To deal (a person, an animal) a blow; to hit with some force either with the hand or with a weapon. Also with double obj. *to s.* (a person) *a blow.* ME. **b.** *absol.* and *intr.* To deal or aim a blow with the fist, a stick, etc. 1509. **2.** *trans.* To hit, smite (a material, an object) with an implement, esp. with one designed for the purpose. Also with cogn. obj. ME. **b.** *absol.* and *intr.* To make a stroke with a hammer or other implement; spec. in *Smithing* ME. **c.** trans. *To s.* (a prisoner) *in the boots*, to crush the limbs by driving wedges between them and the iron boots as a form of torture. *Obs.* exc. *Hist.* 1715. **3.** With complementary adv. or phr.: To remove or drive with or as with a blow of an implement or the hand. Now somewhat *rare.* 1450. **4.** To stamp with a stroke. **a.** To impress (a coin, medal, etc.) *with* a device by means of a die; to coin (money); also †*absol.* 1449. **b.** To impress (a device) *upon*; also to impress (a die, etc.) with a device 1551. **c.** To impress or print by means of type, an engraving or the like. *Obs.* exc. in *to s. off.* 1759. †**d.** *fig.* To imprint on the mind -1709. **5.** To tap, rap, knock 1470. **b.** To beat or sound (a drum, etc.); to sound (an alarm) on a drum (said also of the drum). Also *to s. up.* Also *absol. Obs.* exc. *Hist.* 1572. **c.** To touch (a string, a key of an instrument) so as to produce a musical note; *poet.* to play upon (a harp, lyre, etc.) 1565. **6. a.** (*a*) To produce (fire, a spark) by percussion, esp. by the percussion of flint and steel. Chiefly in the phr. *to s. fire.* 1450. (*b*) *transf.* (in recent use). To cause (a match) to ignite by friction. Also *intr.* of a match: To admit of being struck. 1880. **b.** To produce (music, a sound, note) by touching a string or playing upon an instrument; hence *gen.* to sound (a particular note). Also said of the instrument. 1597. **7.** To pierce, stab, or cut (a person, etc.) with a sharp weapon. Also with double obj. Now *rare*. ME. **b.** *fig.* Of a feeling, etc.: To pierce (a person *to* the heart, *to* the quick). late ME. **8.** *absol.* and *intr.* (also with cogn. obj.). To deliver a cut or thrust with a sharp weapon. Also said of the weapon. ME. **b.** *fig.* esp. in *to s. at*, to aim at the overthrow, destruction, or defeat of. late ME. **9.** In various spec. uses of sense V. 7; *esp. Angling.* to cause the hook to pierce the mouth of (a fish) by a jerk; to hook; also said of the hook or the rod. late ME. **10.** To hit with a missile, a shot, etc. Also said of the missile. late ME. **11.** *intr.* To use one's weapons; to fight. Also with cogn. obj. 1579. **b.** *trans.* To fight (a battle). late ME. **c.** *Mil. intr.* To attack. Const. *at.* Also *trans.* to attack (in flank, etc.). 1606. **12.** *trans.* **a.** To deliver a blow with (the hand or something held in the hand), to bang, slap (the fist, hand), to stamp (the foot) *on, upon, against.* Also, to strike a horse with (the spur). Const. *to, against.* 1548. **b.** To cause (a tool, etc.) to make the required stroke. In *Bookbinding*, To cause (a hot tool) to make an impression in tooling. 1600. **13.** Of a serpent, etc.: To wound (a person) with its fangs or sting. Also *absol.* late ME. **14.** Of an animal: To wound or attack with the heels, horns, tusks, claws, or any natural weapon. Also *absol.* Now *rare.* 1538. **b.** *intr.* To aim a blow with a natural weapon; to lash *out* (with the feet, etc.) 1565. **15.** *trans.* †**a.** Of a bird of prey: To dart at and seize (its quarry or prey) –1879. **b.** *intr.* Of a fish: To seize the bait 1891. **16.** Of a piece of mechanism: To make a stroke, hit or beat something 1610. **17.** *intr.* and *trans.* with cognate obj. Of a clock: To make one or more strokes on its sounding part. Hence *trans.* to indicate (the hour of day) by a stroke or strokes; also with obj. a numeral designating the hour. late ME. **b.** *intr.* in passive sense. Of the hour: To be indicated by the striking of the clock. late ME. **c.** *trans.* To cause (a clock, etc.) to sound the time; to cause (bells) to sound *together* 1675. **18.** Of lightning, thunder, a thunderbolt: To descend violently upon and blast (a person or thing). late ME. **b.** *absol.* and *intr.* 1750. **19.** *trans.* Of God: To visit with lightning, esp. as a punishment. Also *to s. dead.* 1577. **20.** To bring suffering or death upon (a person, etc.) as with a blow; to afflict suddenly (*with, by* sickness, infirmity, death), esp. as a punishment. (Said chiefly of God or a deity.) late ME. **b.** Of a disease, etc.: To attack or afflict (a person) suddenly; to make infirm, lay low. Chiefly *pass.* 1530. **c.** *pass.* Of a crop, of cattle: To be tainted or infected with a disease 1750. **21.** To deprive (a person) suddenly of life, or of one of the faculties, as if by a physical blow. Often with compl., as *to s. dead, blind*, etc. Also *pass.*: To become suddenly *blind, dumb*, etc. 1534. **b.** *hyperbolically*, expressing the temporary effect of fear, amazement, etc. 1533. **c.** Vulgarly used in joc. forms of imprecation, as *s. me blind* (*if, but* —), etc. 1696. **d.** To turn as by enchantment *into* 1609. **22.** To prostrate mentally; in weaker sense, to shock, depress. *Obs.* exc. in *To s. all of a heap* (colloq.). 1598. **b.** To cause (a person) to be overwhelmed or seized *with* (terror, amazement, grief, etc.). Also of the feeling: To seize. 1533. **c.** To cause (a feeling, etc.) to fall or come suddenly. Const. *into*, †*in*, †*to*. 1583.

1. [He] struck the boy a violent blow 1824. **b.** His dwarf..Struck at her with his whip TENNYSON. **2.** *fig.* Wit now and then, struck smartly, shows a spark COWPER. **b.** Phr. *To s. while the iron is hot*, to make one's effort while opportunity serves. **3.** [They] now prepared to s. the weapon from his hand 1797. **4.** A fine Medal was struck..on Occasion of the Victory 1736. **c.** Send it to the printer to s. off a certain number of proofs 1892. **5.** He struck the table a blow 1889. **b.** The kettledrums struck up MACAULAY. **c.** But hark! he strikes the golden lyre! POPE. **6. a.** Phr. *To s. a light*, to produce a flame with flint and steel or by the friction of a match. (*b*) Matches that s. only on the box 1892. **b.** Such musick sweet..As never was by mortall finger strook MILT. **7. b.** The News of the loss of Bologna, struck Pope Julius the 2d to the Heart 1712. **8.** The Fellow..struck at the Spaniard with his Hatchet DE FOE. **b.** The Revolution..began to s. at Church and King 1892. Phr. *To s. at the root* or *foundation*, to attempt or tend to the utter destruction or overthrow (*of* something). **9.** He that strikes The Venison first, shall be the Lord o' th' Feast SHAKS. High authorities say that salmon should not be struck at all 1892. **11.** To s. one blow for the King 1847. **c.** The French centre..was marching to s. it in flank 1893. **12.** He struck the stock of his gun violently upon the ground 1862. **13.** A hideous snake..had uplifted its triangular head to s. 1893. **14. b.** They s. with their claws, they bite each other GOLDSM. **17.** The clocke hath strucken twelue vpon the bell SHAKS. *fig.* This day my years s. fiftie 1605. **b.** I will sit up 'till twelve strikes 1787. **c.** I struck my repeater again 1893. **18.** The house had been struck with lightning 1808. Phr. *To s. dead, blind.* **19.** Heau'n with Lightning s. the murth'rer dead SHAKS. **20. b.** The Duke had been stricken by paralysis 1891. **c.** They [lambs] have been struck with the fly 1840. **21.** Some Planet s. him dead 1628. **b.** Her beauty will certainly s. me dumb SHERIDAN. **22. b.** Rebecca's appearance struck Amelia with terror THACKERAY. **c.** His appearance will s. terror into his enemies JOWETT.

VI. To make a vigorous movement (as if striking a blow). **1.** *intr.* To make a stroke with the limbs in swimming. Also *to s. out.* 1660. **b.** To make a stroke with one's oar 1725. **2.** Of a horse: To put down his fore feet *short, close*, etc. 1683. **b.** *trans.* Of a horse: To alter his pace into (a faster movement). Also *intr.* To quicken his pace *into.* Also, to put (a horse) *into* a quicker pace. 1816. **3.** To thrust (the hand, etc.) with a sudden movement. Also *intr.* 1607. **4.** *intr.* To move quickly, dart, shoot 1639. **b.** To start suddenly *into* (a song, tune) 1819. **c.** To thrust oneself suddenly or vigorously *into* (a quarrel, debate, etc.) 1828. **d.** *trans.* (= *s. into*) in phr. *to s. an attitude*: see ATTITUDE 2. 1825. **5.** *intr.* **a.** Of light: To pierce *through* (a medium), break *through* (clouds, darkness) 1563. **b.** Of cold: To go *through*, penetrate *to.* Also of the wind, something damp or cold, *to s. chill, damp*, etc.; also *trans.* 1569. **6.** *trans.* To cause to penetrate, impart (life, warmth, dampness) *to, into, through* 1611. **7.** Of a plant, cutting, etc.: To send down or out (its roots); to put forth (its root or roots) 1707. **b.** *intr.* To put forth roots. Of a root: To penetrate the soil. 1682. **c.** *trans.* To cause (a cutting, etc.) to root; to propagate (a plant) by means of a cutting, etc. 1842. **8.** To change the colour of (a substance) by chemical action *into* (a specified colour); to produce or assume (a specified colour) by this means 1664. **9. a.** *trans.* To cause (a colour, dye) to take or sink in 1769. **b.** *intr.* Of a dye: To sink in; also, to spread, run 1790. **10.** *trans.* To cause (herrings) to become impregnated with salt, or (pork) with saltpetre in curing 1780.

1. He..struck out, and swam for a few yards 1888. **2. b.** He struck his horses into a gallop 1823. **4.** A sudden pain..struck across my heart 1719. **b.** The Jester next struck into another carol SCOTT. **5. b.** The..damp of the place struck to his marrow 1889.

VII. To impinge upon. **1.** *intr.* Of a moving body: To impinge upon or come into collision or contact with something else. Const. *on, upon, against.* ME. **2.** *trans.* To come into forcible contact or collision with 1626. **b.** *fig.* (chiefly after Latin *ferire cælum, sidera*) 1605. **3.** *spec.* Of a ship: **a.** *intr.* To hit (*on* or *upon* a rock, etc.), to run aground 1518. **b.** *trans.* To hit or run upon (a rock, the ground, a mine) 1587. **4.** Naut. *To s. ground, soundings*: to reach the bottom with a sounding line. Also *transf.* of a swimmer: To touch (bottom). 1726. **5.** *trans.* Of a beam or ray of light or heat: To fall on, catch, touch 1586. **b.** *intr.* Of light: To fall, impinge *on* 1662. **6.** *trans.* Of a sound, report, etc.: To fall on, reach, or catch (the ear) 1596. **b.** *intr.* with *on, upon* 1848. **7.** *trans.* Of a thought, an idea: To come into the mind of, occur to (a person) 1606. **8.** To impress or arrest (the eye, view, sight) 1700. **9.** Of something seen or heard: To impress strongly (a person); to appear remarkable to 1672. **b.** *intr.* To make an impression (*on* the mind, senses, observation) 1732. **c.** *trans.* To impress in a specified way 1701. **d.** To impress or catch (the senses, fancy, etc.) 1697. **e.** To catch the admiration, fancy, or affection of (one of the opposite sex) 1599. **10.** *intr.* To hit or light *on, upon* 1616. **11.** *trans.* To come upon, reach in travelling; to come to in the course of one's wanderings. Chiefly *U.S.* and *Colonial.* Also of a line: To hit, come upon (a specified point). 1798. **b.** To come across unexpectedly; also, to hit upon (the object of one's search). Chiefly *U.S.* 1851.

1. Birds killed striking [against the glass of a light-house] 1901. **2.** His stool-legs were so loosened that when he sat down he struck the floor with a crash 1899. **b.** Bass, and treble voices s. the skies POPE. **2.** The yacht had struck bow on 1890. **6.** [A] scraping sound struck his quick ear 1891. **7.** It struck me immediately that I had made a blunder SWIFT. Hold.. a thought has struck me! SHERIDAN. **9.** His attendant was struck by the unusual change in his deportment SCOTT. **b.** On diff'rent senses, diff'rent objects s. POPE. **c.** Phr. *To s. one as* —, to appear to one as —, to give one the impression of being —. **e.** *To be struck on* (vulg.); I'm glad you're struck on her 1893. **10.** You s. on truth in all things, sir 1616. **11.** At length we successfully struck the spoor BADEN-POWELL. **b.** Phr. *To s. a bonanza* (cf. BONANZA 1). *To s. it rich*, to find a rich mineral deposit. *To s. oil*: see OIL *sb.*[1] 3.

VIII. 1. *To s. hands* (said of two parties to a bargain): to take one another by the hand in confirmation of a bargain; hence, to ratify a bargain *with* (another) 1440. †**b.** *To s.* (a person) *luck*: to give him a 'luck-penny' on making a bargain –1677. **2.** To settle, arrange the terms of, make and ratify (an agreement, treaty, truce, †marriage, †peace, etc.); esp. in phr. *to s. a bargain* 1544. **3.** *trans.* To balance (a book or sheet of accounts) 1539. **4.** To determine, estimate (an average, a mean) 1729. †**5.** *To s. a docket*: see DOCKET *sb.* –1852. **6.** *slang.* †**a.** *trans.* To steal (goods), rob (a person); also *absol.* and with cogn. obj. –1622. †**b.** *intr.* To borrow money –1700. **c.** To beg; also in phr. *to s. it* 1898. **d.** *trans.* To make a sudden and pressing demand upon (a person *for* a loan, etc.). Also *absol.* or *intr.* 1751. **7.** *intr.* In the *U.S.* army: To act as an officer's servant 1891.

3. *To s. a balance*: see BALANCE *sb.* 16.

With advs. **S. down. a.** *trans.* To fell to the ground with a blow. **b.** *intr.* Of the sun: To send down its heat oppressively. **S. home.** *intr.* To make an effective stroke or thrust with a weapon or tool. **b.** Of words, etc.: To tell powerfully to produce a strong impression. **S. in.** †**a.** *intr.* To join *with* as a co-worker, etc.; to fall in agreement *with.* †**b.** To enter a competition *for.* **c.** Of an eruption, disease: To disappear from the surface or the extremities with internal effects. **d.** To interpose actively in an affair. **e.** To interpose in a discussion, etc., with a remark, an expression of opinion, etc. **S. off. a.** *trans.* To cancel by or as by a stroke of the pen; to remove from a list or record. **b.** To cut off with a stroke of a sword, axe, etc. **c.** To produce (a picture, literary composition, etc.) quickly or impromptu. **S. out. a.** *trans.* = *Strike off* a. **b.** To produce or elicit as by a blow or stroke. **c.** To produce by a stroke of invention (a plan, scheme, fashion, etc.). **d.** To represent in a working drawing or plan. Also, to sketch rapidly. **e.** To open up, make for oneself (a path, course, line). **f.** *intr.* To go energetically. **g.** To lay about one (with the fists, a weapon, etc.). **S. up. a.** (*a*) *trans.* To begin to play or sing (a piece of music, a song); (*b*) *intr.* (or *absol.*) To begin playing or singing; (*c*) *intr.* Of music: To begin to be played. **b.** To make and ratify (an agreement, treaty, bargain, etc.). In recent use slightly *contempt.* **c.** To start (a friendship, a conversation, trade, etc. *with* another). **d.** *intr.* To rise up quickly, dart or spring up. **e.** *U.S.* in *pass.* (*a*) To be bewildered. (*b*) To be fascinated *with* or 'gone' *on* (a person of the opposite sex).

Striked (strəikt), *ppl. a.* 1581. [f. prec. (II. 3) + -ED [1].] Of a measure: Levelled with a strike or strickle: opp. to *heaped.*

Striker (strəi·kəɹ). ME. [f. STRIKE *v.* + -ER [1].] **I.** †**1.** One who roams as a vagrant. late ME. only. †**b.** A footpad –1611. **2.** A person (or animal) that strikes. **a.** *gen.* ME. **b.** In indecent sense. Hence, a fornicator. –1665. **c.** One who 'strikes' fish with a spear or harpoon 1697. **d.** In metal-working, the assistant operator who wields the heavy sledge-hammer 1831. **e.** In various games: The player who is to 'strike' 1699. **f.** A workman who 'strikes' or is 'on strike' 1850.

2. a. Against which no blow can be struck but it recoils on the s. EMERSON. **c.** The natives are excellent hunters and strikers of fish 1827. **e.** *S.-out* (in *Tennis*, etc.) the one who plays the ball when first served.

II. A thing that strikes or is used for striking. **1.** *gen.* 1644. **2.** = STRICKLE *sb.* 1. a, b. 1693. **3.** A clock or watch that strikes 1778. **4.** A harpoon 1858. **5.** A steam-hammer designed as a substitute for the blacksmith's 'striker' 1869. **6.** The piece of mechanism in a gun, fuse, etc. which explodes the charge 1824. **7.** The part of a bell, clock, etc. which strikes 1872.

Striking (strəi·kiŋ), *vbl. sb.* late ME. [f. STRIKE *v.* + -ING [1].] The action of STRIKE *v.*, in various senses.

attrib. and *Comb.*: **s. distance**, the distance within which it is possible to strike a blow; **-iron**, a kind of harpoon; **-plate**, the metal plate against which the end of a spring-lock bolt strikes, when the door or lid is being closed.

Striking (strəi·kiŋ), *ppl. a.* 1611. [f. STRIKE *v.* + -ING [2].] That strikes, esp. that strikes the attention of an observer; telling, impressive. Hence **Stri·king-ly** *adv.*, **-ness.**

String (striŋ), *sb.* [OE. *streng* :—OTeut. **strangiz.*] I. A line, cord, thread. **1.** A line for binding or attaching anything; normally one composed of twisted threads of spun vegetable fibre. †**a.** In early use occas. a rope or cord of any thickness. In 16–18th c. applied joc. to the hangman's rope. –1840. **b.** Chiefly applied to a line of smaller thickness than that connoted by *rope*. In mod. use: A thin cord or stout thread. ME. **c.** Thin cord or stout thread used for tying parcels and the like 1827. **d.** A cord used as a snare (*rare*) ME. **e.** A cord for leading or dragging along a person or an animal; a leading-string, a leash ME. **f.** A thread on which beads, pearls, etc. are strung 1612. **g.** A cord for actuating a puppet 1860. **2.** *transf.* A natural string or cord. **a.** A ligament, tendon, nerve, etc.; an elongated muscle or muscular fibre; the frænum of the tongue. *rare* exc. in *s. of the tongue.* OE. **b.** In plants: A cord, thread, or fibre; a 'vein' of a leaf; the tough piece connecting the two halves of a pod (in beans, etc.); a root-filament. late ME. **c.** A tendril; a runner. Now *dial.* 1585. **3.** A cord or line (composed of vegetable fibre, gut, or fine wire) adapted to produce a musical sound when stretched and caused to vibrate OE. **b.** *fig.* and in fig. context 1583. **c.** *pl.* Stringed instruments; now only, such as are played with a bow. Also, in mod. use, the players on these (in an orchestra or band). ME. **4.** A bowstring OE. **5.** A piece of cord, tape, ribbon, etc. for tying up or fastening some portion of dress, for binding the hair, for closing a bag or purse, etc. ME. †**b.** *pl.* The short cords, ribbons, or leather straps, formerly often attached (in pairs) to the edges of book-covers, to be tied in order to keep the book closed (now called *ties*) –1663. †**6.** A cord or ribbon worn as a decoration; the ribbon of a knightly order –1814. †**7. a.** The cord or chain wound on the barrel of a watch. **b.** A chain or cord for carrying a watch. –1701.

1. d. We walk in a world of Plots; strings universally spread, of deadly gins and fall-traps CARLYLE. **e.** fig. *To lead in a s., to have in* or *on a s.*: to be able to do what one likes with. Also *U.S.* a limitation or restriction attached to something 1897. **g.** fig. *To pull the strings*, to control the course of affairs, to be the concealed operator in what is ostensibly done by another. **2. b.** *fig.* The Enquirye concerning the Rootes of Good and euill, and the strings of those Rootes BACON. **3. b.** But why touch I this s. agayne? 1655. *To harp on one* (*the same*, etc.) *s.*: see HARP *v.* 1. **4.** They make ready their arrow vpon the s. *Ps.* xi. 2. fig. *To have two* (*many*, etc.) *strings to one's bow*, to have two (etc.) alternative resources. *Second s.*, a second resource available if the first should fail; 'First,' 'second,' and 'third' strings are the first, second, and third men chosen to represent a club in any event 1897. **5.** Thou..who hast had my purse, As if yᵉ strings were thine SHAKS.

II. A number of objects strung on a thread; hence, a series, succession. **1.** A thread or file with a number of objects strung upon it; a number (of beads, herrings, etc.) strung on a thread. Also, a number of things (e.g. sausages) linked together in a line. 1488. **2.** A number of animals driven in single file tied one to the other; a train of animals, vehicles, or persons one behind the other 1686. **b.** A flock (of birds) flying in single file 1801. **3.** A set or stud of horses, beasts of draught or burden, †slaves 1734. †**b.** A set (of persons); a band, a faction –1699. **4.** A number of things in a line; a row, chain, range 1683. **5.** A continuous series or succession (e.g. of stories, questions, incidents) 1710. **b.** A continuous utterance, a 'screed'. *contempt.* 1766. **c.** The 'thread', sequence (of a narrative). *rare.* 1833.

1. I haue sent you..a s. of Corall Beads 1620. **2.** Smugglers and their strings of pack-horses DARWIN. **5.** I had a s. of questions ready to ask 1797. **b.** It sounds like a s. of mere gabble HAWTHORNE.

III. *transf.* **1.** *Mining.* A thin vein of ore or coal; a ramification of a lode 1603. **2.** *U.S.* A line of fencing 1794. **3.** *Carpentry.* = *s.-board* 1711. **4.** *Arch.* = *s.-course* or *-moulding* 1817.

Comb.: **s.-bean** *U.S.*, the French or kidney bean; **-board,** a board which supports the ends of the steps in a wooden staircase; also *collect. sing.*; **-course,** a distinctive horizontal course, carried round a building; **-galvanometer,** one consisting of a fine conducting fibre, for measuring rapidly-fluctuating currents; **-moulding,** a moulding carried horizontally along a wall; **-piece,** a long piece of timber serving to connect and support a framework (e.g. a floor, bridge); a longitudinal railway-sleeper (*U.S.*); a heavy squared timber carried along the edge of a wharf-front.

String (striŋ), *v.* Pa. t. and pa. pple. **strung** (strɒŋ). late ME. [f. prec.] **1.** *trans.* **a.** To fit (a bow) with its string; to 'bend' or prepare for use by slipping the loop of the bow-string into its notch, so that the string is drawn tight. **b.** To fit or furnish with a string or strings. Also *poet.* to tighten the strings of (a musical instrument) to the required pitch; to tune. 1530. **2.** To furnish (the body) with nerves or sinews; *spec.* to furnish (the tongue) with its frænum 1632. **3.** *fig.* To make tense, brace, give vigour or tone to (the nerves, sinews, the mind, its ideas, etc.) 1599. **b.** with *up* 1845. **c.** To brace *to*, rarely *for* (action) or *to* (do something) 1748. **d.** To bring to a (specified) condition of tension or sensitiveness 1860. **4.** To bind, tie, fasten, or secure with a string or strings 1613. **5.** To thread or file (beads and the like) on or as on a string 1612. **b.** To hang or suspend by a connecting string 1890. **c.** *fig.* To put together in connected speech 1605. **6.** To hang, kill by hanging. Usu. with *up.* 1727. **7.** To deprive (a bean-pod) of its string or strings; to remove the runners from (a strawberry-bed) 1664. **8.** To furnish, equip, or adorn *with* something suspended or slung 1845. **9.** To draw up in a line or row; to extend in a string or series. Also with *out, up.* 1670. **10.** To extend or stretch (something flexible or rigid) from one point to another. Also with *out.* 1838. **11.** *intr.* To move or progress in a string or disconnected line; spec. in *Hunting*, of the hounds 1824. **12.** To form into strings, become stringy 1839. **13.** *trans.* To deceive, humbug. *U.S. slang.* 1901.

1. He tipt his arrow, strung his bow, and shot 1788. **b.** Orpheus Lute was strung with Poets sinewes SHAKS. **2.** Art neuer strung her tongue 1632. **3.** Toil strung the Nerves and purifi'd the Blood DRYDEN. **d.** Too highly strung for banter 1863. **5. c.** It is easy..to s. platitudes together 1884. **6.** They strung him up after a fair trial before Judge Lynch 1893. **10.** Stringing booms across the river—obstructing navigation 1908. **11.** However good the scent, they [staghounds] s. out 1905.

Stringed (strind), *a.* OE. [f. STRING *sb.* + -ED [2].] **1.** Having a string or strings; *spec.* of musical instruments such as the violin and guitar. **b.** *Her.* Used in specifying the tincture of a string; e.g. *s. argent* 1572. **2.** *transf.* Produced by strings or stringed instruments 1629.

1. A one-stringed banjo 1873. **2.** Divinely-warbled voice Answering the s. noise MILT.

Stringency (stri·ndʒĕnsi). 1844. [f. next; see -ENCY.] The quality of being stringent; strictness, rigour. **b.** Of reasoning: Compulsive force 1864. **c.** *Comm.* 'Tightness' in the money-market 1877.

Stringent (stri·ndʒĕnt), *a.* 1605. [ad. L. *stringentem, stringere.*] **1.** Astringent, constrictive, styptic, esp. with ref. to taste. **2.** Tightly enfolding or compressing (*rare*) 1736. **3.** Of reasoning: That compels assent, convincing 1653. **4.** Of regulations, procedure, obligations, etc.: Rigorous, strict, thorough-going; rigorously binding or coercive 1846. **5.** Of the money-market: Tight 1891.

1. Harsh and s. to the palate, as..unripe fruit 1858. **4.** A more s. test was now added MACAULAY. Hence **Stri·ngent-ly** *adv.*, **-ness.**

Stringer (stri·ŋəɹ). late ME. [f. STRING *v.* and *sb.*] †**1.** One who makes strings for bows –1688. **b.** The workman who fits a musical instrument with strings 1842. **2.** *fig.* One who strings words together 1774. **3.** *Building*, etc. **a.** A horizontal timber connecting uprights in a framework, supporting a floor, or the like; a tie or tie-beam 1838. **b.** *Shipbuilding.* An inside strake of planking or plating, secured to the ribs and supporting the ends of the beams 1830. **c.** *U.S.* A longitudinal railway sleeper 1881. **4.** *Mining* and *Geol.* A narrow vein of mineral traversing a mass of different material 1874. **5.** *pl.* Handcuffs (*slang*) 1893.

Stringhalt (stri·ŋhǭlt). 1523. [app. f. STRING *sb.* + HALT *a.* and *sb.*[2] See also SPRINGHALT.] An affection of the hind legs of a horse which causes certain muscles to contract spasmodically.

Stringing (stri·ŋiŋ), *vbl. sb.* 1620. [-ING [1].] **1.** The action of STRING *v.* **2.** *concr.* **a.** Strings collectively 1722. **b.** Material for the string-board of a staircase, or for string-courses on a building 1833. **c.** Straight or curved inlaid lines in cabinet work 1812.

Stringless (stri·ŋlės), *a.* 1591. [-LESS.] Having no string; lacking strings.

His tongue is now a stringlesse instrument SHAKS.

Stringy (stri·ŋi), *a.* 1669. [f. STRING *sb.* + -Y [1].] **1.** Resembling string or fibre; consisting of string-like pieces. Chiefly of vegetable or animal tissue, esp. meat when its fibres have become tough. **2.** Of a person, the body, etc.: Thin; exhibiting sinew rather than flesh 1833. **3.** Of liquid or viscous matter: Containing or forming glutinous thread-like parts; ropy 1694.

1. Bits and gobbets of lean meat..tough and s. morsels HAWTHORNE. Hence **Stri·nginess.**

Stringy-bark. *Austral.* 1802. A name for many species of *Eucalyptus* (e.g. *E. gigantea*), which have a tough fibrous bark. **b.** The bark of any of these trees 1859. **c.** quasi-*adj.* Belonging to the 'bush' or uncultivated country 1833.

Strip (strip), *sb.*[1] Now only *U.S.* 1516. [a. AF. *estrepe.*] *Law.* = ESTREPEMENT.

Strip (strip), *sb.*[2] 1459. [a. or cogn. w. MLG. *strippe* strap, perh. f. Teut. root **strĭp-*; see STRIPE *sb.*[2]] **1.** A narrow piece (primarily of textile material, paper, or the like; hence *gen.*) of approximately uniform breadth. **b.** A long narrow tract of land, wood, etc. 1816. †**2.** An ornamental article of attire worn, chiefly by women, about the neck and upper part of the chest –1658. **3.** *Metall.* **a.** An ingot prepared for rolling into plates 1876. **b.** A narrow flat bar of iron or steel; hence, iron or steel in 'strips' (more fully *s. iron, steel*) 1887. **4.** *Mining.* An inclined trough for separating ores by washing 1875.

1. No carpet, except little strips by the bed 1856. Strips of wood about 2½ in. wide 1907.

attrib.: **s. ticket**, a ticket for a journey by a public conveyance, printed with a number of similar tickets on a strip of paper.

Strip (strip), *sb.*[3] 1844. [f. STRIP *v.*[1]] *pl.* Tobacco-leaf with the stalk and midrib removed. Also *s.-leaf.*

Strip (strip), *v.*[1] Pa. t. and pa. pple. **stripped** (stript), **stript**. [ME. *stripe, strepe, strupe* :—OE. **striepan*, **strȳpan* :—WGer. **straupjan*; the Teut. root **straup-* : **strup-* prob. occurs also in MHG. *strupfen* to strip off, and possibly in STROP *sb.*] I. To unclothe, denude. **1.** *trans.* To divest (a person, body) of clothing; to undress, make bare or naked. Const. *of* (one's clothing). Also *intr.* for *refl.* **b.** To divest (a person, oneself) of outer garments, or of some specified outer garment. Const. *of.* Also *intr.* for *refl.* spec. of an athlete, etc.: To take off one's ordinary wearing apparel in preparation for a contest. late ME. **c.** *trans.* To deprive *of* armour, insignia, ornaments. late ME. **d.** To remove the clothing of (a race-horse); also *intr.* of a horse, to undergo this process 1730. **2.** *fig.* **a.** To divest or dispossess (a person, oneself) *of* attributes, titles, honours, offices, etc. ME. **b.** To denude or divest (a thing) *of* attributes 1597. **c.** To expose the character or nature of (a person or thing) 1619. **3.** To plunder, spoil; to render destitute ME. **b.** To deprive or rid (a substance or thing) *of* 1675. **4.** To denude (a thing) of its covering, esp. (a tree) of its bark, (a seed) of its skin, (a fruit) of its rind ME. †**5.** To skin (an animal) –1770. **6.** To deprive (a plant *of* its foliage or fruit); to remove (seed or grain *from* the straw) 1697. **7.** To empty, make bare, clean out (a place, thing) *of* its contents, ornaments, etc.

1616. 8. To take away the accessories, equipment, or furniture of; to dismantle 1683.

1. For there they began to s. her of her clothes SIDNEY. *refl.* The Nymph..Stript her self naked to the skin PRIOR. *transf.* (joc.) Therefore on, or strippe your sword starke naked SHAKS. b. He had already stripped himself of his wrappings 1865. c. The mutineers were stripped of their uniforms 1866. d. The mare stripped beautifully, as fine as a star 1857. 2. a. Of his Godhead he could not s. himself BUNYAN. b. Your friend, sir, must at least s. his proposals of their fine gilding SCOTT. c. He hides behind a magisterial air His own offences, and strips others bare COWPER. 3. His fate was to be strip'd of all he had in Sweden 1737. 5. An hart or a bucke is flayed, a hare strypped 1575. 7. I stripped the house for a sale BRIDGES. 8. To s. a muzzle-loader, first remove the lock 1881.

II. To doff, take off, peel away. 1. To remove (the clothes, a garment, trappings, hair) from a person, body ME. †2. To take as plunder or spoil –1791. 3. To remove (an adhering covering of skin, bark, lead, paper, etc.); to pull off (leaves, fruit) from a tree, etc. Also *to s. off.* late ME. b. *intr.* Of bark, membrane: To lend or adapt itself to the process of peeling or decortication. Of a layer of metal: To become detached. 1877. †4. To remove, roll up (a sleeve) –1815. 5. To slip off (a jewel) from the arm, (a ring) from the finger 1611.

1. As she spoke she stripped off her gloves 1895. 2. *Hen. V*, I. i. 11. 3. Gather your currants.., s. them from the stalks 1769. The covers were stripped from the..chair-bottoms 1780. 4. Then will he s. his sleeue, and shew his skarres SHAKS. 5. *Cymb.* II. iv. 101.

III. Technical uses. 1. *Tin-washing.* To remove tin from (the gravel). Also, to wash out, (gold). 1674. 2. *Tobacco-manuf.* To remove the leaves from the stems of (tobacco) 1688. b. To remove the stalk and midrib from (tobacco-leaf) 1844. 3. *Mech.* To tear off (the thread from a screw or bolt, the teeth from a wheel) 1873. b. To rip off the screw thread of (a cannon-ball or bullet); to render incapable of receiving the rotatory direction from the rifling of the barrel. Also *intr.* for *refl.* 1839. 4. *Mining.* To lay bare (a mineral deposit, etc.) 1839. 5. To smooth (a metal surface) by filing or the like; to smooth the surface of (a file-blank) preparatory to cutting the teeth 1831. 6. *Carding.* To remove fluff, etc. from the teeth of (a card) 1891. 7. *Electrometallurgy.* To remove (the plating from a plated article, the metal from a positive pole, etc.) by electrolysis. Also *intr.* of a plating: To come off. 1877. Hence **Stri·pping** *vbl. sb.* the action of the vb.; *concr.* something stripped off.

†Strip, *v.*[2] late ME. [f. Teut. root *strip-; see STRIPE *sb.*[2]]. 1. *intr.* To move or pass swiftly –1616. 2. *trans.* = OUTSTRIP *v.* –1774.

1. As the Westerne side shee stript along 1616. 2. Before he reacht it, he was out of breath, And then the other stript him 1613.

Strip (strip), *v.*[3] 1610. [cogn. w. STRIPE *sb.*[1]; cf. WFlem. *strippen.*] 1. *trans.* To extract (the milk from a cow's udder). Now *spec.* to extract the milk remaining in the udder after the normal milking, esp. by a particular movement of the hand. 2. To draw between the finger and thumb, through the closed hand, etc.; e.g. to press out with the hand the ripe roe or milt from (a fish) 1884.

Strip (strip), *v.*[4] 1885. [f. STRIP *sb.*[2]] *trans.* To cut into strips.

Stripe (strəip), *sb.*[1] 1440. [prob. from LG. or Du.; cf. mod.Du. *strippen* to whip; also MLG. *strippe* strap, whip-lash.] †1. A blow or stroke with a staff, sword, or other weapon, with a missile, with the claws or hoofs of an animal, etc. –1596. †b. A touch on the keys of an instrument; hence, measure, strain –1616. 2. A stroke or lash with a whip or scourge. Now *arch.*, chiefly in *pl.* 1485. †3. The mark left by a lash; a weal (*rare*) –1746.

2. Of the Iewes five tymes receaved I every tyme .xl. strypes saue one TINDALE. Labor exacted with stripes—how do you fancy that? 1839.

Stripe (strəip), *sb.*[2] 1626. [Either a back-formation from STRIPED *a.*, or prob. a. MLG. or MDu. *strīpe*, corresp. to OHG. **strīfo*, MHG. *strīfe*. The Teut. root **strīp-* (: **straip-*) :—pre-Teut. **streib-* seems to have been nearly synonymous with **strīk-* :—pre-Teut. **streig-* (see STRIKE *v.*).] 1. In textile fabrics, hence *gen.*, a portion of the surface long in proportion to its breadth, of uniform width, and differing in colour or texture from the adjacent parts. 2. A narrow strip of cloth, braid, or gold lace, sewn on a garment of different colour. Pop. applied to the chevrons worn by a non-commissioned officer, to good conduct badges worn by soldiers on the sleeve, etc. 1827. 3. A striped textile fabric 1751. 4. *Geol.* A narrow band of rock interposed between strata of differing character 1799. 5. A long narrow tract of land (*occas.* of ice) 1801. 6. A strip, shred; a narrow piece cut out 1785. 7. *U.S.* A particular shade or variety of political or religious doctrine; in wider sense, a sort, class, type 1853.

1. Waistcoat, blue and yellow stripe, each s. an inch in depth 1860.

Stripe (strəip), *v.*[1] 1460. [Belongs to STRIPE *sb.*[1]] †1. *trans.* To beat, whip –1533. 2. To punish with stripes (*rare*) 1843.

Stripe (strəip), *v.*[2] 1471. [f. STRIPE *sb.*[2]] 1. *trans.* To ornament (cloth, a garment) with narrow pieces of material or with stripes of colour. 2. To mark with a narrow band or with bands of colour; to mark with alternate stripes of colour 1597. b. *intr.* Of a plant: To become variegated. Also *trans.* To produce variegation in (a plant). 1725. 3. To finish (a surface) with grooves or ridges 1842.

2. A goodly Tulip, Stript In Gold and Purple 1645.

Striped (strəipt), *ppl. a.* 1617. [f. STRIPE *v.*[2] + -ED[1], or perh. ad. Du. *strijpt* or MLG. *striped.*] Marked with a stripe or stripes, having a band or bands of colour, streaked. b. In specific names of animals, plants, and minerals 1629. c. Of muscular fibre: Divided by transverse bands into striations 1854. d. Of a person: Entitled to wear a (good-conduct, etc.) stripe 1890.

Stripling (stri·pliŋ). late ME. [prob. f. STRIP *sb.*[2] + -LING; as if 'one who is slender as a strip', one whose figure is not yet filled out.] 1. A youth, one just passing from boyhood to manhood. 2. *attrib.* passing into adj. 1553.

1. *transf.* I'm but a s. In the Trade of War DRYDEN. 2. The s. Thames at Bab-lock-hithe M. ARNOLD.

Stripper (stri·pəɹ). 1581. [f. STRIP *v.*[1] + -ER[1].] 1. One who strips or strips off. 2. A machine or appliance for stripping 1835. 3. *pl. Gaming.* 'High cards cut wedge-shape, a little wider than the rest, so as to be easily drawn in a crooked game' (Farmer) 1887.

Stripy (strəi·pi), *a.* 1513. [f. STRIPE *sb.*[2] + -Y[1].] Having, marked with, or suggestive of stripes or bands of colour.

Strive (strəiv), *v.* Pa. t. **strove** (strōᵘv), pa. pple. **striven** (stri·v'n). [ME. *striven*, a. OF. *estriver* to quarrel, contend; of disputed origin. The strong conjugation is on the analogy of *drive*, etc.] †1. *intr.* To be in a state of variance or mutual hostility –1829. 2. To quarrel, wrangle. Now *rare* (*poet.*). ME. 3. To contend, carry on a conflict of any kind ME. b. To fight against temptation or the like; to wage spiritual warfare. late ME. c. To struggle *with* disease or suffering, †hindrances 1594. d. Of things: To come into conflict *with*. late ME. †4. To contend in arms, fight *with* –1706. †5. To contend in words, dispute –1600. †6. To contend in rivalry; to seek to surpass another or each other –1725. †b. To vie, to be equal or comparable *with* –1700. 7. To offer obstinate resistance, struggle *against* ME. 8. To struggle physically. *Obs.* exc. *dial.* of a horse: To be restive. late ME. b. To struggle against a natural force, e.g. winds, waves. Const. *with, against.* ME. 9. To endeavour vigorously, use strenuous effort ME. b. *transf.* of things 1586. 10. To make one's way with effort 1586.

1. They say you cannot live in Rome and s. with the Pope SCOTT. 2. And still they strove and wrangled TENNYSON. 3. Two Pretenders oft for Empire s. DRYDEN. b. In vain I strove Against the Tempter 1816. 4. How a knyght & a dwarf stroof for a lady MALORY. 6. *fig.* Patience and sorrow strove Who should express her goodliest SHAKS. 8. b. To stryve agenst the streame CROMWELL. 9. Habits are soon assum'd; but when we s. To strip them off, 'tis being flay'd alive COWPER. He for whose applause I strove TENNYSON. She strove to keep her self-control 1885. 10. He..Strives through the surge, bestrides the beach BYRON. Hence **Stri·ver**, one who strives with others, a contender; one who makes strenuous effort.

Stroam, strome (strōᵘm), *v. Obs.* exc. *dial.* 1796. [perh. after *stroll* and *roam.*] *intr.* To walk with long strides. Also, to wander about idly.

‖**Strobila** (strobəi·lă). *Pl.* **strobilæ** (-lī). 1842. [mod.L., a. Gr. στροβίλη plug of lint twisted into the shape of a fir-cone.] *Zool.* 1. A stage in the development of certain Hydrozoa. 2. A segmented tape-worm, consisting of a scolex and a chain of proglottides 1864.

Strobilaceous (strobilēⁱ·ʃəs), *a.* 1802. [f. STROBILUS; see -ACEOUS.] *Bot.* Relating to, or resembling, a strobilus.

Strobilation (strobilēⁱ·ʃən). 1878. [f. STROBILA + -ATION.] *Zool.* The formation of strobilæ in Hydrozoa, tapeworms, etc.

Strobile (stro·bəil, strōᵘ·bəil, -bil). 1777. [a. F. *strobile* or ad. L. *strobilus*, Gr. στρόβιλος STROBILUS, also στροβίλη STROBILA.] 1. *Bot.* = STROBILUS 1. 2. *Zool.* = STROBILA 2. 1855.

Strobiliform (strobi·lifǭɹm), *a.* 1830. [ad. mod.L. *strobiliformis*, f. STROBILUS; see -FORM.] *Bot.* Shaped like a strobilus.

Strobiline (stro·biləin), *a.* 1842. [ad. Gr. στροβίλινος of a fir-cone, f. στρόβιλος STROBILUS.] *Zool.* and *Bot.* Relating to or of the nature of a strobila or strobilus; strobilaceous.

Strobilization (stro:biləizēⁱ·ʃən). 1884. [f. STROBILA + -IZE + -ATION.] *Zool.* = STROBILATION.

Strobiloid (stro·biloid), *a.* 1865. [f. STROBILA or STROBILUS + -OID.] *Zool.* and *Bot.* Resembling, or of the nature of, a strobila or strobilus.

‖**Strobilus** (strobəi·lŏs). *Pl.* **strobili** (-ləi). 1753. [a. L., a. Gr. στρόβιλος anything twisted up, fir-cone.] 1. *Bot.* A fir-cone, or any fruit resembling a fir-cone; an inflorescence made up of imbricated scales, as that of the hop. b. In cryptogams: An aggregation of sporophylls resembling a fir-cone 1891. 2. *Zool.* = STROBILA 2. 1876.

Stroboscope (stro·bŏskōᵘp). 1836. [f. Gr. στρόβος a twisting or whirling round + -SCOPE.] a. A scientific toy which produces the illusion of motion by a series of pictures viewed through the openings of a revolving disc. b. An instrument for observing the successive phases of a periodic motion by means of light periodically interrupted 1896. Hence **Strobosco·pic, -al** *adjs.* relating to, of the nature of, the s.

Stroke (strōᵘk), *sb.*[1] [ME. *strōk*, prob. repr. OE. **strāc* :—OTeut. **straikoz*, f. **straik-*, ablaut-var. of **strīk-*; see STRIKE *v.*] 1. An act of striking; a blow given or received. a. A blow with the hand or a weapon (occas. with the paw of an animal, etc.) inflicted on or aimed at a living being. Sometimes (now rarely) applied to the thrust of a pointed weapon. b. A blow struck at an inanimate object; e.g. with a hammer, axe, etc. late ME. c. In various games: An act of striking the ball; a hit or an attempted hit. Also, manner of striking. 1744. †d. Discharge of an engine of war; the impact of a missile –1771. e. †Shock or forcible impact of a moving body; impact or incidence of moving particles, light, etc. (now *rare*) 1534. 2. *fig.* a. With conscious metaphor: An act which causes pain, injury, or death; often, an act of divine chastisement or vengeance ME. b. A calamitous event 1700. †c. An offensive movement in warfare –1777. †d. *To have, bear, carry the s.*: to prevail, rule, have authority; to be highest in excellence –1731. 3. A damaging or destructive discharge (of lightning) 1542. 4. An attack of disease; an apoplectic or (now more usu.) paralytic seizure 1599. 5. The striking of a clock; the sound produced by each striking of the clapper or hammer upon the bell, etc. late ME. †6. A touch on a stringed instrument; manner of playing a musical instrument; hence, a tune, strain –1773. 7. A pulsation, beat (of the heart, pulse) 1538. 8. A movement of beating time; a beat, measure; metrical ictus, rhythm. Now *rare* or *Obs.* 1576. 9. a. In neg. context: A minimum amount of work 1568. b. A large or considerable amount *of* work, business, trade 1712. 10. A movement like that of striking a blow. a. A single movement of the legs in walking or running, of the wings in flying, etc. 1618. b. In swimming, the combined movement of the limbs forming a single impulse of progression; also, any particular manner of effecting this, as the breast-s., side-s. 1800. **c.** A single complete movement in either direction of any piece of machinery having a reciprocating motion (e.g. of a piston, piston-rod, etc.); also, the amplitude or length of such a movement 1731. **11.** *Rowing.* **a.** A single pull of the oar 1583. †**b.** *To keep s.*: to keep time in rowing –1652. **c.** Style of rowing, manner of handling the oars, esp. with regard to the length, speed, or frequency of the 'strokes' 1870. **d.** The oarsman who sits nearest to the stern of the boat, and whose 'stroke' sets the time for the other rowers. Also quasi-*adv.* in *to pull, row s.* 1825. **e.** The station occupied in a boat by the stroke-oarsman 1901. **12.** A vigorous attempt to attain some object; a measure, expedient, or device adopted for some purpose 1699. **b.** In a game: An effective move or combination 1735. **13.** A feat, achievement; a signal display *of* art, genius, wit, etc. 1672. **b.** *S. of luck*: an unexpected piece of good fortune 1853. **14.** A movement of the pen, pencil, graver, etc., in writing, printing, drawing, etc.; a single movement of a brush, chisel, knife, file, etc. over the surface operated on 1668. †**b.** Manner of handling the pencil, graver, etc. –1717. **15.** A linear mark; a mark traced by the moving point of a pen, pencil, etc.; a component line of a written character (cf. *up-, down-s.*); also, a dash (in writing or print) 1567. **b.** *Bacteriology.* A line formed by drawing the point of an infected wire over the surface to be inoculated 1893. †**16.** Lineament, line of a face or form –1638. †**b.** *fig.* A characteristic; a trait of character –1780. **c.** *fig.* A felicitous or characteristic expression or thought in literary composition; a 'touch' of description, satire, pathos, or the like 1666. **17.** *Agric.* (See quot.) 1765. **18.** = STRIKE *sb.* 3. 1532.

1. He slewe and bette downe..all that came within his s. 1533. He suddenly..aimed a rapid and furious s. at the woodman's head 1849. Phr. *At one s., at a s.*, with a single blow; *fig.* all at once. **b.** With many strokes is an oke ouerthrowen 1539. **c.** A ball may, under a penalty of two strokes, be lifted out of a difficulty of any description 1879. **d.** The Stroak of an Arrow convinc'd Alexander, that he was not the Son of Jupiter 1678. **2.** Till the mortal s. shall lay me low BURNS. The s. of calamity 1858. **3.** The oak, Rent by the lightning's recent s. SCOTT. **4.** He has had a s., like that of an apoplexy JOHNSON. **5.** *On* or *upon the s.* (*of* a specified hour), on the point of striking; It is on the s. of twelve now C. BRONTE. **9. a.** Work! ..thank God, I have never done a s. of work since I was born 1867. **b.** A good s. of business 1825. **10.** A gnat's wings make ten or fifteen thousand strokes per second H. SPENCER. **c.** A new pump..for raising water with a perpendicular s. 1741. **11. c.** Rowing a long easy s. 1870. **e.** University..with Huntley at s. 1901. **12.** Phr. *S. of policy, of business. S. of state*: tr. F. *coup d'état* (see COUP *sb.*[3]). **b.** Any of the finer strokes of play 1862. **13.** It is filled with strokes of wit and satire in every line GOLDSM. **14.** Phr. *With a s. of the pen*, often used *hyperbolically*; He changed with a s. of the pen the general aspect of affairs 1804. *Finishing s.* (lit. and fig.); see FINISHING *ppl. a.* **b.** Paulo's free s., and Titian's warmth divine POPE. **16. b.** He discovers in almost every body, some Strokes of vanity LAW. **c.** How bold, how masterly, are the strokes of Virgil! DRYDEN. **17.** Each time land is crossed with harrows it is said to have received a s. or line 1891.

attrib.: **a.** *Golf*, in terms relating to the method of scoring by strokes instead of by holes, as *s.-competition, -game, -play*; **b.** *Bacteriology*, as *s.-culture, -inoculation*; **c.** **s.-haul**, an apparatus used for illegal capture of fish, formed of three hooks joined back to back, and weighted with lead; hence as *vb.*; **-oar,** (*a*) the oar nearest the stern of a rowing-boat; (*b*) the rower who handles this oar; **-oarsman** = sense 11 d; **-side,** the side of a rowing-boat on which the s. oarsman sits.

Stroke, *sb.*[2] 1631. [f. STROKE *v.*[1]] A stroking movement of the hand, †esp. for purposes of healing.

Stroke (strōuk), *v.*[1] Pa. t. and pa. pple. **stroked** (strōukt). [OE. *strácian*, f. Teut. **straik-* (see STROKE *sb.*[1]), ablaut-var. of **strīk-* (see STRIKE *v.*).] **1.** *trans.* To rub softly with the hand or some implement; *esp.* to pass the hand softly in one direction over, by way of caress or as a method of healing. Also *absol.* **b.** said of an animal using a foot or paw 1621. **c.** With adv., etc.: To bring into a specified position, condition, etc. by such action 1594. **2.** To draw (a cutting instrument) along a surface in order to sharpen or whet it. *Obs.* or *arch.* late ME. **3.** To milk (a cow); esp. to draw the last milk from (a cow) by pressing the teat 1538. **4.** *Masonry.* To work the face of (a stone) in such a manner as to produce a sort of fluted surface 1842. **5.** *Needlework.* To dispose (small gathers) in regular order and close succession by drawing the point of a blunt needle from the top of each gather downwards 1875.

1. His only gesture is that of stroking his beard GIBBON. *absol.* A good groom will rather s. than strike BERKELEY. *fig.* With these faire Promises he stroked the Senators 1629. Phr. *To s. against the hair, the wrong way* (*of the hair*), to rub (an animal) in the direction opposite to the natural lie of its hair; *fig.* to irritate, ruffle, cross (a person). **c.** With his hands so full that he cannot even s. out his splendid whiskers 1859.

Stroke (strōuk), *v.*[2] 1597. [f. STROKE *sb.*[1]] **1.** *trans.* To mark with streaks or stripes. **2.** To draw the horizontal line across the upright of (the letter *t*) 1894. **3.** To row stroke in (a boat); to act as stroke to (a crew) 1866.

Stroker (strōu·kəɹ). 1632. [f. STROKE *v.*[1] + -ER[1].] **1.** One who strokes; *spec.* one who cures diseases by stroking. **2.** An implement used for some operation likened to stroking 1884.

Strokesman (strōu·ksmæ̆n). 1712. [f. genit. of STROKE *sb.*[1] + MAN *sb.*] †**1.** A rubber or masseur. STEELE. **2.** One who pulls the stroke-oar in a boat 1769.

Stroking (strōu·kiŋ), *vbl. sb.* 1587. [-ING[1].] **1.** The action of STROKE *v.*[1], in various senses. **2.** *pl.* The last milk drawn from a cow; 'afterings' 1602.

Stroll (strōul), *sb.* 1623. [Belongs to next.] **1.** = STROLLER. *Obs.* exc. *U.S.* (*rare*). **2.** A walk or ramble taken leisurely, a saunter 1814.

Stroll (strōul), *v.* 1603. [Origin obsc.] †**1.** *intr.* To roam from place to place without any settled habitation –1765. **2.** To walk or ramble in a careless, haphazard or leisurely fashion as inclination directs, often simply to take a walk 1680. †**3.** *trans.* To walk or pace along (a path) or about (a place) –1810.

1. These Mothers..are forced to employ all their time in Stroling, to beg Sustenance for their helpless Infants SWIFT. **2.** They..then strolled along the sands towards the cliff 1827.

Stroller (strōu·ləɹ). 1608. [f. prec. + -ER[1].] One who strolls. **1.** A vagabond, vagrant; an itinerant beggar or pedlar. Now chiefly *Sc.* 1679. **2.** An itinerant actor; a strolling player 1608. **3.** A saunterer; a casual traveller or visitor 1738.

Strolling (strōu·liŋ), *ppl. a.* 1621. [-ING[2].] That strolls; roving, itinerant; chiefly in *s. actor, player*, an actor who wanders about the country, giving performances in temporary buildings or hired rooms.

Strom (strǫm), **strum** (strʊm). *Obs.* exc. *dial.* late ME. [Origin obsc.] **1.** *Brewing.* An oblong wicker basket, placed over the bung-hole within the mash-tub to prevent the grains and hops passing through when the liquor is drawn off. **2.** *Mining.* A kind of iron sieve placed round the suction-pipe of a pump to prevent obstruction 1849.

‖ **Stroma** (strōu·mă). *Pl.* **stromata** (strōu·mătă). 1832. [mod.L. use of L. *stroma* bed-covering, a. Gr. στρῶμα anything spread or laid out for lying or sitting upon, f. στρω- root of στρωννύναι to spread.] **1.** *Anat.* The fibrous connective sustentacular tissue or substance of a part or organ. Also, the framework containing the alveoli of cancer-cells. 1835. **b.** The spongy colourless framework of a red blood corpuscle or other cell 1872. **2.** *Bot.* A structure containing the substance in which perithecia or other organs of fructification are immersed 1832. Hence **Stro·mal** *a.* of, pertaining to, or of the character of the s. (sense 1). **Stroma·tic** *a.* of the nature of or resembling a s.

Stromb (strǫm, strǫmb). 1835. [Anglicized form of STROMBUS.] A gasteropod of the family *Strombidæ*, esp. a wing-shell of the genus *Strombus*.

Strombite (strǫ·mbəit). 1811. [f. prec. + -ITE[1].] A fossil stromb or some similar shell.

Stromboid (strǫ·mboid), *a.* and *sb.* 1859. [f. as prec. + -OID.] **A.** *adj.* Resembling or related to a stromb or strombus. **B.** *sb.* A stromb 1891.

Strombuliform (strǫmbiū·lifǫɹm), *a.* 1846. [ad. mod.L. *strombuliformis*, f. **strombulus*, dim. of L. *strombus* STROMBUS; see -(I)FORM.] **a.** *Geol.* Shaped like a top. **b.** *Bot.* Twisted in a long spire, so as to resemble the convolutions of the shell *Strombus*.

‖ **Strombus** (strǫ·mbʊ̆s). 1601. [mod.L. use of L. *strombus* spiral shell, a. Gr. στρόμβος anything spirally twisted.] *Zool.* The typical genus of the family *Strombidæ* of gasteropods; a species or individual of this genus, a wing-shell or fountain-shell.

Stromeyerite (strōu·məiˌĕrəit). 1835. [Named after Fr. *Stromeyer*, a German chemist; see -ITE.] *Min.* Sulphide of silver and copper, of steel-gray colour and metallic lustre.

Strong (strǫŋ), *a.* [OE. *strang, strǫng*:—OTeut. **strango-*.] **1.** Of living beings, their body or limbs: Physically powerful; able to exert great muscular force. **b.** Of an action: Performed with muscular strength. late ME. **c.** Of a runner, swimmer, etc.: Having great staying power. Hence, of his 'going' or pace: Maintained with vigour; that does not flag 1854. **2.** Physically vigorous or robust; capable of physical endurance or effort; not readily affected by disease; hale, healthy ME. **b.** of the vital organs and their functions, the nerves, brain, etc. late ME. **c.** of a plant or its parts. late ME. **d.** *A s. head*: capacity for taking much drink without becoming intoxicated 1822. **3.** Having great moral power for endurance or effort; firm in will or purpose; brave, resolute, steadfast OE. **b.** Of actions or attributes ME. **c.** Of looks, voice, etc.: Indicative of strength of character 1815. **d.** Of a statesman, judge, commander: That makes his authority felt 1879. **4.** Of the mind or mental faculties: Powerful. Of the memory: Tenacious, retentive. late ME. **5.** Having great controlling power over persons and things, by reason of the possession of authority, resources, or inherent qualities OE. **b.** *absol.* OE. **c.** Of things, sometimes personified ME. **d.** Having great financial resources, rich 1622. **6.** Eminently able or qualified to succeed in something; well skilled or versed *in* some branch of knowledge or practice OE. **b.** *One's s. point*: that in which one excels, one's forte 1875. **c.** In athletic contests, of a side, crew, etc.: Formidable as an opponent or competitor 1860. **7.** Powerful in arms; formidable as a fighting force (or as a commander) ME. **b.** Of an individual: Powerful or formidable as a combatant 1450. **c.** Of a warlike operation: Performed or prosecuted with a powerful fighting force 1560. **d.** With prefixed numerical determination: Powerful to the extent of (a specified number of men, ships, etc.). Hence *gen.*, having the specified number. 1589. **e.** Of a body of persons or things, a sect or party: Numerous 1617. **f.** Abundantly supplied with persons or things of a specified kind. Const. *in*. 1621. **8.** Of a fortress, town, country, or military position: Powerful for resistance; difficult to capture or invade OE. **b.** Of a place of confinement, receptacle for valuables and the like: Difficult to escape from or break into ME. **9.** Of material things: Capable of supporting strain or withstanding force; not easily broken, torn, injured, or forced out of shape; solidly made, massive, stout OE. **b.** Of soil: Firm, tenacious, compact OE. **c.** Of food: Solid, hard of digestion 1526. **d.** *Mining.* Of a vein: Thick, massive 1839. **e.** Of wool: Broad-haired or coarse-fibred 1885. **10.** Powerful in operative effect OE. **11.** Severe, burdensome, oppressive OE. †**b.** Of a crime, evil quality. Gross, flagrant. Of a malefactor: Flagrantly guilty. –1818. **c.** Of a course of action or a measure: Extreme, high-handed 1838. **d.** *colloq.* Of a payment, a charge: Heavy, 'stiff' 1669. **12.** Of movements or conditions: Intense; energetic; powerful OE. **b.** Of the voice, a sound: Powerful, loud and firm OE. **c.** Of illumination, light, shadow, colour: Vivid, intense 1658. **d.** Of feeling, conviction, belief: Intense, fervid. Of party views or principles: Uncompromising, thoroughgoing. ME. **e.** Of a person: Firmly convinced, decided in opinion;

colloq. laying great stress *on* something 1526. **13.** Having its specific property in a high degree OE. **b.** *S. of*: largely or greatly impregnated or flavoured with (*dial.*) 1617. **14.** Affecting the sense of taste or smell in a high degree; strong-smelling; strong-tasting, rank; *spec.* having a powerful unpleasant smell OE. **15.** Having a powerful effect on the mind or will; hard to resist or overthrow ME. **b.** Of a case: Well supported by evidence or precedent 1698. **16.** Having legal force; †valid; effectual 1450. **17.** Vividly perceptible; marked, definite 1697. **b.** Of a line: Broad, thick. Also, vivid in colour. 1731. **c.** *Photogr.* Of a negative: Having marked contrasts of light and shade; dense 1892. **18.** Of language, an expression, a word: Emphatic; signifying or implying much; not moderate. *S. language*: see LANGUAGE *sb.* 3. 1697. **b.** Of a protest, recommendation, etc.: Emphatic, strongly-worded, urgent 1733. **19.** Of literary or artistic work: Vigorous or forceful in style or execution 1746. **20.** *Comm.* Of prices: Tending to steadiness or to a rise 1870. **21.** *Gram.* (Opp. to *weak.*) **a.** Of Teut. sbs. and adjs., their inflexions, etc.: Belonging to any of those declensions in which the OTeut. stem ended otherwise than in *n* 1841. **b.** Of Teut. vbs. and their inflexions: Forming the pa. t. and pa. pple. by means of vowel-gradation in the root-syllable, as the Eng. *give, break.* Hence, occas. used with ref. to other Indo-European langs., e. g. in *s. aorist*, applied in Gr. grammar to the 'second aorist' (ἔλιπον) in contradistinction to the 'weak' or sigmatic aorist (ἔλειψα). 1841. **c.** In Skr. grammar, applied to the unreduced form of noun-stems, and to those cases which are formed on the 'strong' stem 1863. **22.** *Phonetics* and *Prosody.* Of a syllable: Bearing stress or metrical ictus. Of a consonant-sound: Characterized by force of utterance. Also in *Music*, Accented. 1792. **23.** *Card-playing.* Of a player: Holding commanding cards (*in* a specified suit). Of a hand or suit: Composed of commanding cards. Of a card: Of high and commanding value. 1862.

1. He is as s. as a horse 1861. *fig.* The s. arm of the law 1873. *The stronger sex*, the male sex. **2.** Old Nanny..was now quite s. again MARRYAT. **b.** Persons even with s. stomachs 1833. Wearying even to the strongest nerves 1863. **3.** Be s. and prosperous In this resolue SHAKS. **b.** To conquer Sin and Death.. By Humiliation and s. Sufferance MILT. **c.** The lady with the s. face, and the piercing grey eyes 1891. **d.** He wants to show..that he too can be a 'S. Man' on a pinch 1879. **4.** He was not a man of s. sense MACAULAY. **5.** What King so s. Can tie the gall vp in the slanderous tong? SHAKS. **b.** It was a reign of minority, when the strongest had the best right SCOTT. **c.** The old Adam was too s. for her 1865. **d.** 'S. people'—that is, people who can wait..for a rise 1885. **6.** I am not very s. in spelling THACKERAY. **7.** Pompey is s. at Sea SHAKS. **d.** The garrison, thirteen hundred s. MACAULAY. **f.** The king was s. in horse DE FOE. **8.** The king was in Wales, which was a Countrey s. by reason of the Mountaines STOW. **b.** Our prison s. MILT. **9.** S. outer walls for defence were discarded 1861. **c.** Soche as haue nede off mylke, and not of stronge meate TINDALE. Hence *s. meat*, doctrine, etc., suitable only for 'digestion' by vigorous or well-prepared minds. **d.** The vein is very s., and carries a very large proportion of quartz 1877. **10.** The spring is always strongest when first wound up 1675. I hate him like s. poison SCOTT. Only traces of it can be seen under a s. lens. 1887. **11.** A s. shuddering fit SCOTT. **b.** Oh heinous, s., and bold Conspiracie SHAKS. **12.** By a stronger heat they are decomposed 1857. *S. breeze*, that which reduces a ship to double-reefed topsails, jib, and spanker. *S. gale*, that strength of wind under which close-reefed topsails and storm-staysails are usually carried when close-hauled. The pulse may be s. or weak 1876. **c.** The southern sash admits too s. a light COWPER. **d.** Hate stronger, under shew of Love well feign'd MILT. S. Free-trade views 1881. **e.** A very s. Papist 1679. Mary, who is so s. on the proprieties 1883. **13.** Ale & bere of the strongest TINDALE. S. antiseptic solution 1899. **b.** German sausages, s. of garlick DICKENS. **14.** They say poore Suters haue s. breaths SHAKS. As s. as Mustard 1659. **15.** A man of..s. passions 1779. A s. impulse SHELLEY. The evidence as to this is too s. to be discarded 1892. **b.** Shakespeare has made out a s. case for Shylock 1863. **16.** One heynous Article ..cracking the s. Warrant of an Oath SHAKS. The old laws..received a stronger sanction 1838. **17.** The local traditions..are still very s. 1894. A very s. family likeness amongst them 1879. A s. Breton accent 1890. **18.** He expressed his indignation in the strongest terms 1836. **19.** What the publishers call a 's.' book 1905. **20.** Coal is very s. in price 1890. **23.** A s. hand is difficult to define, further than as one likely to make many tricks 1864.

Comb.: **a.** in parasynthetic adjs., as *s.-armed, -backed, -brained*, etc. **b.** *s.* **bark**, a tree or shrub of the genus *Bourreria*, found in the W. Indies and tropical America.

Strong (strǫŋ), *adv.* [OE. *strange, strǫnge*; see STRONG *a.*] Qualifying a verb or predication = STRONGLY *adv.* *Obs.* exc. as in b, c. **b.** Used regularly with certain verbs, as *blow, flow, grow, run, smell*, etc. late ME. **c.** In colloq. phrases 1812.

The Bow-string touch'd her Breast, so s. she drew DRYDEN. **b.** The Whig peers..mustered s. MACAULAY. **c.** *To come it s.*, to go to great lengths; to make statements which are hard to credit. *To come out s.*, to make a big display or impression; to 'launch out'; to declare oneself vigorously. *To go it s.*, to act vigorously or recklessly. *To be going s.*, to be vigorous, thriving, or prosperous. *To pitch it s.*, to indulge in 'tall' talk.

Comb., as *s.-built, -knit, -made*, etc.; *s.-beating, -growing, -smelling*, etc.

Stro·ng-box. 1684. A strongly-made chest or safe for money, documents, or other valuables.

Strong drink. late ME. Intoxicating liquor, alcoholic liquors generally. Also, drink of more than ordinary alcoholic strength.

Strong hand. Now *rare.* late ME. The exercise of superior power; the use of force.

I carried it with the strongest hand possible SWIFT.

Strong-headed (stress var.), *a.* 1603. **1.** Headstrong. **2.** Endowed with strong intellectual faculties 1849. Hence **Stro·nghea·dedness**, obstinacy.

Stronghold (strǫ·ŋ,hǭᵘld). late ME. [f. STRONG *a.* + HOLD *sb.*] A strongly fortified place of defence, a secure place of refuge or retreat, a fastness.

fig. The Northern counties..were the s. of the papal party 1856.

Strongish (strǫ·ŋiʃ), *a.* 1799. [f. STRONG *a.* + -ISH.] Somewhat strong.

Strongly (strǫ·ŋli), *adv.* [OE. *stranglīce*, f. *stranglīc* adj. strong, f. *strang* STRONG *a.*; see -LY [1], [2].] **1.** In a strong manner; powerfully; forcibly; firmly, securely; violently, vehemently; with fortitude; resolutely; emphatically. **2.** In a strong degree; with strength or intensity of the condition or quality predicated. late ME.

2. He s. resembles her CARLYLE. Sea-water is always s. salt to the taste 1880.

Strong-minded (stress var.), *a.* 1791. Having a strong, vigorous, or determined mind. **b.** Applied (usu. in disparagement) to women who have or affect the qualities of mind regarded as distinctively masculine 1854.

Strong room. 1761. A room made specially secure for the custody of persons or things; esp. a fire- and burglar-proof room in which valuables are deposited for safety, e. g. at a bank.

Strong water. 1580. [tr. med.L. *aqua fortis.*] †**1.** = AQUAFORTIS –1694. **2.** Any form of alcoholic spirits used as a beverage. Now only in *pl.* (somewhat *arch.*) 1613.

Strongyle [1] (strǫ·ndʒil). 1847. [ad. mod.L. *strongylus*, ad. Gr. στρογγύλος round.] A thread-worm of the genus *Strongylus* (or the family *Strongylidæ*, of which this is the type), common as a disease-producing parasite in various animals.

Strongyle [2] (strǫ·ndʒil). 1887. [ad. Gr. στρογγύλη fem. (agreeing with ῥάβδος RHABDUS) of στρογγύλος round.] *Zool.* A sponge-spicule of the rhabdus type, rounded at both ends.

Strongyloid (strǫ·ndʒiloid), *a.* and *sb.* 1879. [f. mod.L. *strongylus* STRONGYLE [1]; see -OID.] *Zool.* **A.** *adj.* Resembling a strongyle. **B.** *sb.* A strongyloid worm.

Strontia (strǫ·nʃiă). 1802. [f. next; see -IA.] *Chem.* One of the alkaline earths, the monoxide of strontium. Also *attrib.* in *s. water*, the aqueous solution of strontium hydroxide.

Strontian (strǫ·nʃiăn). 1789. [Name of a parish in Argyllshire, where are the lead mines in which the mineral was discovered.] (orig. *s. earth, lime, mineral, spar.*) Properly, native strontium carbonate, but applied loosely to strontia, occas. to strontium. Not now in scientific use. *S. yellow*: a yellow colour produced by adding potassium chromate to a solution of a strontium salt.

Strontianite (strǫ·nʃiănəit). 1794. [f. prec. + -ITE.] *Min.* Native strontium carbonate.

Strontium (strǫ·nʃiŏm). 1808. [f. STRONTIA; see -IUM.] *Chem.* The metallic base of strontia; a dark-yellow metal, fusible at red heat. Symbol Sr.

Strop (strǫp), *sb.* [OE. *strop*, prob. a. WGer. adoption of L. *struppus, stroppus* strap, band.] †**1.** A band, thong; a loop or noose of leather, etc. –1723. **2.** A ring or band of hide or of rope with its ends spliced together, used upon a mast, yard, etc., as a fastening or as a purchase for tackle; esp. a band of rope, iron, or chain fastened round a pulley or block. Chiefly *Naut.* ME. **3.** A strip of leather (or of a special textile), or a strip of wood covered with leather or other suitable material, used for sharpening a razor; a razor-strop 1702.

Strop (strǫp), *v.* 1841. [f. prec.] **1.** *trans.* To sharpen or smooth the edge of (a razor) with a strop. **2.** *Naut.* To furnish (a block) with a strop 1860. Hence **Stro·pping** *vbl. sb. concr.* (*Naut.*) rope for making strops.

‖ **Strophanthus** (strŏfæ·nþŏs). 1888. [mod. L., f. Gr. στρόφος twisted cord + ἄνθος flower.] **a.** *Bot.* A genus of plants (family *Apocynaceæ*), native to tropical Africa and Asia, having strongly poisonous qualities; a plant of this genus. **b.** A poisonous drug extracted from the seeds of various species of this genus; in recent pharmacy used as a cardiac tonic. Hence **Stropha·nthin**, a glucoside obtained from this.

Strophe (strǭᵘ·fi). *Pl.* **strophes** (-fiz), **strophæ** (strǭᵘ·fī). 1603. [a. Gr. στροφή, f. στροφ-, στρέφειν to turn.] **1.** In Greek choral and lyric poetry: A series of lines forming a system the metrical structure of which is repeated in a following system called the ANTISTROPHE. Also, one of two or more metrically corresponding series of lines forming divisions of a lyric poem. Hence occas. (after Fr.) used as = STANZA. **2.** *Bot.* Applied to a spiral development of leaves 1846. Hence **Strophic** (strǫ·fik) *a.* pertaining to strophes; consisting of strophes; belonging to the s. as dist. from the antistrophe. **Stro·phical** *a.*, **-ly** *adv.*

Strophiolate (strǫ·fiŏlět), *a.* 1821. [ad. mod.L. *strophiolatus*, f. *strophiolum*; see next and -ATE.] *Bot.* Furnished with a strophiole.

Strophiole (strǫ·fiǭᵘl). 1839. [a. mod.L. *strophiolum*, a use of L. *strophiolum*, dim. of *strophium* chaplet, ad. Gr. στρόφιον, f. στροφ-, στρέφειν to turn, twist.] *Bot.* An excrescence or tubercle surrounding the hilum of certain seeds.

Strophoid (strǫ·foid). 1880. [ad. F. *strophoïde*, f. Gr. στρόφος twisted cord; see -OID.] *Geom.* The locus of the intersection of two straight lines which rotate uniformly about two fixed points in a plane. Hence **Strophoi·dal** *a.* and *sb.*

‖ **Strophulus** (strǫ·fiŭlŏs). 1808. [app. a. corruption of med.L. *scrophulus*, corruption of L. *scrophulæ* (SCROFULA), misapplied to an eruptive disease.] *Path.* A papular eruption on the skin of infants; known popularly as *red-gum, white-gum, tooth-rash*, etc.

†**Stro·sser.** 1598. [Origin obsc.] = TROUSER –1637.

Stroud (straud). Now *rare* or *Obs.* 1683. [perh. f. *Stroud* in Gloucestershire.] **1.** A blanket manufactured for barter or sale in trading with the N. Amer. Indians. **2.** The material of which these blankets were made 1759.

Stroy (stroi), *v.* *Obs.* or *dial.* ME. [Aphetic f. DESTROY *v.*] *trans.* To destroy.

Struck (strɒk), *pa. pple.* and *ppl. a.* 1594. [pa. pple. of STRIKE *v.*] †**A.** *pa. pple.* in special use = STRICKEN A. –1787. **B.** *ppl. a.* = STRICKEN *ppl. a.* in various uses 1627.

S. jury, a special jury selected by striking from the pannel of jurors, a certain number by each party, so as to leave a number required by law to try the cause 1856. So **Stru·cken** *pa. pple.* and *ppl. a.* (now *Sc.* and *north.*).

Structural (strɒ·ktiŭrăl, -tʃərăl), *a.* 1835. [f. STRUCTURE *sb.* + -AL.] Of or pertaining to structure. **1.** Of or pertaining to the art or practice of building; chiefly in *s. iron, steel*, iron or steel intended for building construction 1867. **2.** Of or pertaining to the structure of a building as dist. from its decoration or fittings 1877. **3.** Of or pertaining to the arrangement and mutual relation of the parts of any complex unity 1870. **4. a.** *Phys.* and *Path.* Of or pertaining to the organic structure of an animal or plant, or a portion of an animal or vegetable body 1845. **b.** *Geol.* Pertaining to the structure of the earth's crust, of a rock, formation, mountain, or the like 1855. **c.** Of a branch of science: Concerned with the study of the structures of natural products 1835.

2. *S. load*, the load due to a structure itself, as dist. from the imposed load. 4. **a.** *S. disease*, one involving tissue and causing change visible to the naked eye or the microscope; also, organic disease in contradistinction to functional disease 1898. **c.** *S. botany*, botany dealing with the structure and organization of plants. *S. chemistry*, chemistry treating of the arrangement or order of attachment of atoms in the molecules of compounds. Hence **Stru·cturally** *adv.* with regard to structure.

Structure (strʊ·ktiŭɪ, -tʃəɪ), *sb.* 1440. [ad. L. *structura*, f. *struct-*, *struere* to build; see -URE.] **1.** The action, practice, or process of building or construction. Now *rare* or *Obs.* **2.** Manner of building or construction; the way in which an edifice, machine, etc. is made or put together 1650. **3.** The mutual relation of the constituent parts or elements of a whole as determining its peculiar nature or character; make, frame 1615. **4.** *concr.* That which is built or constructed; a building or edifice of any kind, esp. one of considerable size and imposing appearance 1615. **5.** More widely: A fabric or framework of material parts put together 1677. **6.** An organized body or combination of mutually connected and dependent parts or elements. Chiefly in *Biol.*, applied to component parts of an animal or vegetable organism. 1830.

1. The progress and s. of the Edystone Lighthouse SMEATON. 2. They..show purchased dirks, of an improved s. CARLYLE. 3. Of the internal S. of the Earth GOLDSM. The s. of society 1803. The story itself is in s. extremely simple 1887. 4. A church..which is, indeed, a most stately s. GRAY. 5. This moveable s. of shelves,..charg'd with octavos and twelves COWPER. 6. The general law of organization..is that distinct duties entail distinct structures SPENCER. Hence **Stru·cture** *v. trans.* (*rare*) to build or form into a s. **Stru·ctureless** *a.* lacking organic s.

Struggle (strʊ·g'l), *sb.* 1692. [f. next.] **1.** An act of struggling; a resolute contest; a continued effort to resist force or free oneself from constraint; a strong effort under difficulties. **b.** A strong effort to continue to breathe, as in the death-agony 1794. **2.** *gen.* Contention, determined effort or resistance 1706.

1. The Horrors of an hopeless Soul, and the Struggles and Agonies of one sinking under the dismal Apprehensions of the divine Wrath 1716. Phr. *S. for existence, for life*, in *Biol.* used metaphorically to describe the relation between co-existing organic species when the causes tending to the survival of one tend to the extinction of another; also *gen.*, an effort under difficulties to obtain the means of livelihood. **b.** He died..without a groan or s. 1854. 2. The subject of love at s. with death 1901.

Struggle (strʊ·g'l), *v.* [Late ME. *strugle*, *strogel*, a frequentative formation of obscure origin.] **1.** *intr.* To contend (*with* an adversary) in a close grapple as in wrestling; also, to make violent bodily movements in order to resist force or free oneself from constraint. **b.** To make violent efforts to breathe (usu. *to s. for breath*); to be in the agony of death 1674. **2.** *fig.* To contend resolutely, esp. with an adversary of superior power; to offer obstinate resistance; to make violent efforts to escape from constraint. late ME. **3.** quasi-*trans.* with adv. or phr. expressing the result of struggling 1633. **4.** *intr.* To make great efforts in spite of difficulties; to contend resolutely *with* (a task, burden); to strive *to do* something difficult 1597. **5.** To make progress with difficulty *to*, *into*, *out of*, *through*. Also with adv. *along*, *forward*, *on*. 1700.

1. In strugling with him for the knife..hee hurt himselfe therwith 1603. The wind was adverse.. and they struggled against it without much assistance from the tide SCOTT. 2. The sunbeams..struggling with the smoky air SCOTT. The Netherlands are struggling vainly for their liberties 1855. 3. When the light began to appear, the Ass had strugled her self out 1660. 4. Phr. *To s. for existence*: cf. STRUGGLE *sb.* 1. 5. He struggled to his feet 1888. Phr. *To s. on*, occas. to maintain existence, or continue one's course of action, with difficulty. Hence **Stru·ggler**, one who struggles. **Stru·gglingly** *adv.*

Struldbrug (strʊ·ldbrʊg). 1726. [Arbitrary.] In Swift's *Gulliver's Travels*, given as the native appellation of 'the immortals' in the kingdom of Luggnagg, who were incapable of dying, but after the age of eighty continued to exist in a state of decrepitude, regarded as legally dead, and receiving a small pittance from the state. Also *allus.* Hence **Struldbru·ggian** *a.* **Stru·ldbrugism.**

Strum (strʊm), *v.* 1775. [Echoic.] **1.** *trans.* To play on (a stringed instrument) carelessly or unskilfully; to produce (notes, a tune, etc.) by such playing. **2.** *intr.* To play carelessly or unskilfully on a stringed instrument. Said also of an instrument: To sound when strummed upon. 1785. **3.** quasi-*trans.* with advb. extension 1777.

1. Sitting at the piano strumming a music-hall ditty 1894. 3. To..s. your father to sleep after a Fox Chase SHERIDAN. Hence **Strum** *sb.* the action of strumming.

‖**Struma** (strū·mă). *Pl.* **strumæ** (-ī). 1565. [mod.L. use of L. *struma* scrofulous tumour.] **1.** *Path.* **a.** = SCROFULA. **b.** A scrofulous swelling or tumour. Also, a goitre, bronchocele (*rare*). 1654. **2.** *Bot.* A cellular dilatation on a leaf-stalk at the point where the petiole joins the lamina or where the midrib joins the leaflets of a compound leaf 1832. Hence **Struma·tic** *a.* (*rare*) suffering from s. **Stru·miform** *a. Bot.* having the appearance of a s.; *Path.* resembling s. **Stru·mose** *a. Bot.* having a s.

Strumous (strū·məs), *a.* 1590. [ad. L. *strumosus*; see prec. and -OUS.] **1.** Affected with struma; characteristic or indicative of a scrofulous disposition. **2.** Of the nature of or caused by struma 1590. **3.** *Nat. Hist.* Having a natural protuberance on some part of the body 1802.

Strumpet (strʊ·mpĕt), *sb.* ME. [Origin obsc.] A debauched or unchaste woman; a harlot, prostitute. **b.** *fig.* and of things personified 1545. **c.** as *adj.* That is a strumpet 1596.

b. That s. Fortune SHAKS. **c.** *Merch. V.* II. vi. 16.

†**Stru·mpet**, *v.* 1590. [f. prec.] **1.** *trans.* To bring to the condition of a strumpet –1687. **2.** To repute as a strumpet; to debase (a woman's fame, name, virtue) to that of a strumpet –1633.

Strung (strʊŋ), *ppl. a.* 1687. [pa. pple. of STRING *v.*] **1.** Furnished or fitted with strings or a string. Now *rare* or *Obs.* 1695. **2.** Threaded on a string 1687. **3. a.** Of nerves, etc.: In a state of tension. **b.** With prefixed adj., *finely-*, *highly-s.*: said of persons with ref. to their nervous organization or condition. 1840.

Strut (strʊt), *sb.*[1] 1587. [(ult.) f. Teut. root **strūt-*; proximate origin obsc.] A bar, rod, or built-up member, of wood, iron, etc., designed to resist pressure or thrust in a framework.

Strut (strʊt), *sb.*[2] 1607. [f. STRUT *v.*[1]] A manner of walking with stiff steps and head erect, affecting dignity or superiority; a stiff self-important gait.

Strut (strʊt), *sb.*[3] 1880. [f. STRUT *v.*[2]] The act of strutting; deflexion (of the spoke of a wheel) from the perpendicular.

Strut (strʊt), *v.*[1] Infl. **strutted, strutting.** ME. [OE. *strūtian* (meaning somewhat obsc.), prob. f. **strūt* (ME. *strut* strife, contention).] †**1.** *intr.* To bulge, swell; to protrude on account of being full or swollen –1854. †**b.** *trans.* To distend, make protuberant; to puff *out* –1740. †**2.** *intr.* To contend, strive, quarrel, bluster. -late ME. †**3.** To protrude stiffly from a surface or body; to stand *out* –1809. †**b.** *trans.* To protrude, stick *out*, stretch *out* –1681. †**4.** *intr.* To behave proudly or vaingloriously; to triumph, swagger –1754. †**5.** To thrust up one's head and stand erect; to perk *up* –1807. **6.** To walk with an affected air of dignity or importance, stepping stiffly with head erect 1518. (The current sense.) **b.** quasi-*trans.* with cogn. or advb. obj. 1605. **c.** *trans.* To walk upon or over (a floor, space) with a strut 1749.

5. Johnson did not s. or stand on tiptoe: He only did not stoop BOSWELL. 6. Do's he not hold vp his head (as it were?) and s. in his gate? SHAKS. While the Cock..Stoutly struts his Dames before MILT. *fig.* Big passions strutting on a petty stage WORDSW. **b.** A poore Player, That struts and frets his houre vpon the Stage SHAKS.

Strut (strʊt), *v.*[2] 1828. [f. STRUT *sb.*[1]] **1.** *trans.* To brace or support by a strut or struts; to hold in place or strengthen by an upright, diagonal, or transverse support. **2.** *intr.* To be fixed diagonally or slantwise; to be bent so as to form a sharp turn or angle 1841.

Struthiin (strū·þi,in). 1835. [f. mod.L. (*Gypsophila*) *Struthium* the oriental soapwort (ad. Gr. στρουθίον soapwort); see -IN.] *Chem.* = SAPONIN.

Struthioid (strū·þi,oid), *a.* and *sb.* 1879. [ad. mod.L. *struthioides*, f. L. *struthio* ostrich; see next and -OID.] **A.** *adj.* Ostrich-like, struthious. **B.** *sb.* A struthious bird.

Struthious (strū·þiəs), *a.* 1773. [f. L. *struthio* ostrich, a. Gr. στρουθίων.] *Zool.* Related to or resembling the ostrich.

Struvite (strū·vəit). 1850. [ad. G. *struvit*, f. name of *Struve*, Russian minister at Hamburg.] *Min.* Hydrous phosphate of ammonium and magnesium, found in small yellowish-brown or greyish crystals.

Strychnia (stri·kniă). 1826. [f. STRYCHNOS; see -IA.] *Chem.* = STRYCHNINE.

Strychnic (stri·knik), *a.* 1840. [f. STRYCHNOS + -IC.] *Chem.* Pertaining to strychnine. *S. acid* = IGASURIC ACID.

Strychnine (stri·knīn, -in). 1819. [a. F., f. L. *strychnos* STRYCHNOS; see -INE[5].] *Chem.* A highly poisonous vegetable alkaloid $C_{21}H_{22}N_2O_2$, obtained chiefly from *Strychnos Nux-vomica* and other plants of the same genus. Used in medicine as a stimulant and tonic. **b.** *attrib.*, as in *s. poisoning*; **s.-tree,** *Strychnos psilosperma* 1879.

‖**Strychnos** (stri·knǫs). Also **strychnus**, *pl.* **strychni.** 1836. [mod.L. use of L. *strychnos*, a. Gr. στρύχνος a kind of nightshade.] *Bot.* A genus of plants of the family *Loganaceæ*, including the nux vomica (*S. Nux-vomica*), the St. Ignatius' bean (*S. Ignatia*), and other species. Also, a plant or a species of this genus.

Stub (stʊb), *sb.* [OE. *stub(b* :—OTeut. **stubboz.*] **1.** A stump of a tree or, more rarely, of a shrub or smaller plant; the portion left fixed in the ground when a tree has been felled; also, †a trunk deprived of branches. †**b.** The part of a tree-trunk close to the ground –1637. †**2.** *fig.* A blockhead. MILT. **3.** A short piece of a broken branch remaining on the stem. late ME. **4.** = STUBBLE *sb.* Also *pl.* Now *dial.* ME. **5.** A splinter or thorn in the flesh. Now *dial.* 1531. **6.** A short thick nail; a worn horse-shoe nail, esp. in *pl.* as material for making stub-iron. late ME. **7.** Something that looks stunted or cut short, e.g. a rudimentary tail or horn 1670. **b.** A short thick piece of wood 1833. **8.** *Mech.* A stud or projection; *spec.* in a lock, a stud which acts as a detent for the tumblers when their slots are engaged with it 1561. **9.** The remaining portion of something that has been broken or worn down; a stump, fag-end 1530. †**b.** = *s.-pen* –1829. **10.** *U.S.* A counter-foil 1876.

1. Old stockes and stubs of trees, Whereon nor fruit nor leafe was euer seene SPENSER. 4. But ill it suits thee in the stubs to glean CLARE. 9. A fellow..smoking an old s. of a clay pipe 1898.

attrib. and *Comb.*: **s. book** *U.S.*, a book containing only the counterfoils of cheques or other documents; **-end**, the butt end of a connecting-rod, a weapon, etc.; **-iron**, a tenacious kind of iron, orig. made out of old horse-shoe nails; **-nail** = sense 6; **-pen**, orig. a worn quill pen; hence a broad-pointed pen; **-twist**, a material for fine gun-barrels, composed of a ribbon of stub-iron twisted into a spiral shape.

Stub (stʊb), *v.* Infl. **stubbed** (stʊbd), **stubbing.** 1440. [f. prec.] **1.** *trans.* To dig up by the roots; to grub up (roots). Chiefly with *up*. **2.** To cut down (a tree, etc.) close to the root 1594. **3.** To remove the stubs from (land). Also, to clear (land) of trees, furze, etc. by uprooting. Chiefly with *up*. 1464. **4.** To reduce to a stub or stump 1577. **5.** To cause (a horse) to be wounded with a stub. Also *refl.* of the horse. 1686. **6.** To strike (the toe) violently against anything in walking or running. orig. *U.S.* 1848. Hence *intr.* to go heedlessly (*U.S. colloq.*). 7. To cover with stubs 1878. 8. To extinguish (a cigarette) by pressing the lighted end of the stub against a hard object; also with *out* 1927.

Stubbed (stʋbd), *ppl. a.* 1529. [f. STUB *v.* + -ED [1].] 1. Of trees: Cut down to a stub; cut off near the ground; also, deprived of branches or pollarded 1575. 2. Short and thick, stumpy. *Obs.* exc. *dial.* 1529. 3. Reduced to a stub; (of hair) cut close to the skin, stubbly 1621. 4. Blunted at the point 1610. 5. Abounding in stubs 1855.

2. The Tartar is a s. squat fellow, hard bred 1630. 5. Then came a bit of s. ground, once a wood BROWNING.

Stubble (stʋ·b'l), *sb.* ME. [a. OF. *stuble*, *estuble*:—pop. L. **stupla* = late L. *stupula*, for class. L. *stipula* STIPULA.] 1. Each of the stumps or lower ends of grain-stalks left in the ground after reaping. Now only in *pl.* 2. *collect. sing.* The stumps or lower parts of the stalks of wheat or other grain left in the ground by the sickle or reaping-machine ME. b. *transf.* A rough surface or short growth likened to this; *esp.* the short bristly growth on a man's unshaven face 1596. 3. The straw of grain-stalks, etc. gathered after the crop has been harvested. late ME. 4. A field that has been reaped and not yet ploughed again; a stubble-field. Chiefly *pl.* 1792.

1. Every withered stem and s. rimed with frost EMERSON. 2. I suppose, that you..Know by the s., what the Corne hath bene CHAPMAN. b. Bristly with the s. of a coarse hard beard DICKENS. 3. One night as I lay on my bed of s. 1760.

attrib. and *Comb.*: **s. goose**, (*a*) a goose fed on the s.; (*b*) the grey-lag goose, *Anser cinereus*. Hence **Stu·bble** *v. trans.* to clear (land) of s. **Stu·bbled** *a.* covered with s., stubbly.

Stubbly (stʋ·bli), *a.* 1600. [f. prec. + -Y [1].] 1. Covered with stubble. 2. Resembling stubble; *esp.* of hair, bristly 1849.

Stubborn (stʋ·bəɹn), *a.* late ME. [Etym. obsc. The earliest form is *stiborn*.] 1. Of persons or animals: Pertinacious or dogged in refusing obedience or compliance; unyielding, inflexible, obstinate; chiefly in bad sense, unreasonably obstinate. b. Of dispositions, resolves, speech or action: Characterized by obstinacy 1526. 2. Of things: Intractable, refractory to treatment; difficult to subdue, work, cure, etc. 1514. 3. Of material things: Hard, stiff, rigid. *Obs.* exc. of wood or stone (with some notion of sense 2) 1577.

1. A disputatious..and s. female will always offend 1767. The people were as s. as their King GREEN. b. Stout were their hearts, and s. was their strife SCOTT. 2. An old S. Pain in the Back WESLEY. The s. glebe GRAY. *Prov.* Facts are s. things. Hence **Stu·bborn** *v.* (only *poet.*) *trans.* to make s.; to harden. **Stu·bborn-ly** *adv.*, **-ness.**

Stubby (stʋ·bi), *a.* 1572. [f. STUB *sb.* + -Y [1].] 1. Of the nature of a stub; short and thick or broad. 2. Abounding in or full of stubs. Chiefly of the hair or beard: Composed of short, stiff bristles. 1604. Hence **Stu·bbiness.**

Stubwort (stʋ·bwʋɹt). 1541. [f. STUB *sb.* + WORT.] The Wood-sorrel, *Oxalis Acetosella*.

Stucco (stʋ·ko[u]), *sb.* 1598. [It.; perh. ad. the Teut. word represented by OHG. *stukki* fragment, piece, crust.] 1. a. A fine plaster, esp. one composed of gypsum and pulverized marble, used for covering walls, ceilings, and floors, and for making cornices, mouldings, and other decorations. b. A coarse plaster or calcareous cement used chiefly for covering the rough exterior surfaces of walls in imitation of stone; also called *common s.*; *spec.* the third or last coat of plastering 1779. c. Plaster of Paris 1839. 2. The process of ornamenting walls, ceilings, cornices, etc. with stucco; also, work or ornamentation produced by this process 1697. 3. *attrib.* or *adj.* 1744.

3. S. houses with asphalte terraces in front THACKERAY.

Stucco (stʋ·kou), *v.* Infl. **stuccoed, stuccoing.** 1726. [f. prec.] *trans.* To coat or plaster (a cornice, wall, etc.) with stucco; to ornament with stucco-work. b. In mod. building: To coat or plaster (a wall, building) esp. in imitation of stone-work 1790. c. *transf.* and *fig.* 1774.

c. Ye must s. and whitewash your faces 1776. Hence **Stu·ccoer,** a modeller in stucco.

†**Stuck,** *sb.* 1601. [perh. var. of STOCK *sb.*[2]] *Fencing.* A thrust or lunge -1614.

Stuck (stʋk), *ppl. a.* 1702. [str. pa. pple. of STICK *v.*] 1. Of an animal: That has been stabbed or had its throat cut. Chiefly in provb. phr. *to stare like a s. pig.* 2. Unable to go further, 'stickit' 1885.

Stuck-up (stress var.), *a. colloq.* 1829. [pa. pple. of *stick up*, STICK *v.*[1]] Assuming an unjustified air of superiority, or pluming oneself unduly on real superiority; offensively pretentious.

'He's a nasty stuck-up monkey..' said Mrs. Squeers 1839.

Stud (stʋd), *sb.*[1] [OE. *studu, studðu*:—OTeut. **stuð-*, **stuþ-*:—pre-Teut. **stut-* prop, support.] I. A post, prop. 1. †A wooden post of any kind; one of the upright timbers in the wall of a building; now chiefly = QUARTER *sb.* IV. 1. b. *collect. sing.* Laths to be used as the uprights in partition walls or the walls of lath-and-plaster buildings 1535. †2. *fig.* A prop or support -1652. 3. *U.S.* The height of a room from floor to ceiling 1850. 4. †a. A stem, trunk (of a tree) -1621. b. A short branch, spur (*rare*) 1657.

4. a. Seest not thilke same Hawthorne studde? SPENSER.

II. Something fixed in and projecting from a surface. 1. An ornamental round knob; a boss or large nail-head standing out on a surface, for decoration or protection. late ME. b. *Arch.* A sculptured disk such as was used in the ornamentation of mouldings in the Late Norman period of English architecture 1686. 2. A kind of button which is passed through one or more eyelet-holes, either in order to fasten some article of dress, or merely for ornament 1555. 3. *Machinery.* a. A lug or projecting socket to receive the end of an axle, pin, etc. 1683. b. A short rod or pin fixed in or projecting from something, and serving as a support, axis, or stop 1694. c. *Gunnery.* One of a number of protuberances on the surface of a projectile to be fired from a rifled gun, placed spirally to make the shot receive rotatory movement from the grooving of the gun 1866. d. = *s.-bolt* 1887. e. *Naut.* A transverse bar of cast-iron inserted in the middle of each link of a chain-cable 1863.

1. A belt of straw and Iuie buds, With Corall clasps and Amber studs MARLOWE. 2. The s. in his shirt sleeve 1772.

Comb.: **s.-bolt,** a cylindrical bolt, threaded at both ends, one end to be screwed into a hole tapped in a casting or the like, while the other end passes through a hole in the cover-plate, which is secured by a nut.

Stud (stʋd), *sb.*[2] [OE. *stōd*:—OTeut. **stōdom*, **stōðo*, f. root **stō-*: **sta-* (see STAND *v.*).] 1. An establishment in which stallions and mares are kept for breeding. Also, the stallions and mares kept in such an establishment. †b. A collection of mares kept for breeding -1607. †c. A breed, race (of horses); also *transf.* -1557. 2. In early use: The horses bred by and belonging to one person. In later use: A number of horses (esp. race-horses or hunters) belonging to one owner. Also *transf.* 1661. 3. *U.S.* [Short for STUD-HORSE.] A stallion 1803.

1. A third [order] establishes a Government S. in the district of Tirhút 1898. 2. He kept a hunting s. to the last 1910. *transf.* A large s. of sows 1813. His ..s. of motor-cars 1907.

Comb.: **s.-book,** a book giving the pedigree of thoroughbred horses; also, a similar book relating to dogs, etc.; **-groom,** the head groom attached to a s.; **-poker** *U.S.*, a variety of the game of poker.

Stud (stʋd), *v.* 1505. [f. STUD *sb.*[1]] 1. *trans.* To supply with studs or upright timbers; to build with studs. 2. To ornament or cover with or as with studs, bosses, or nail-heads 1570. 3. To set (a surface) with a number of protuberant or conspicuous objects 1790. b. *rarely* in immaterial sense 1849. 4. Of things: a. To be fixed in (a surface) in the manner of studs. b. To be placed at intervals over (a surface) 1652. 5. To insert or place (a number of things) at intervals over a surface 1856. 6. *Mech.* To secure with studs 1911.

2. Their harnesse studded all with Gold and Pearle SHAKS. A strong door of oak, studded with nails SCOTT. 3. b. Conversation..studded with execrable jokes 1849. 4. Coaling-stations s. the ocean highways of the world 1906.

Studding (stʋ·diŋ), *vbl. sb.* 1588. [f. STUD *v.* + -ING [1].] 1. The woodwork of a lath and plaster wall or partition; also *pl.* wood cut into battens for use as studs. 2. That with which a surface is studded 1844. 3. *U.S.* = STUD *sb.*[1] I. 3. 1884.

Stu·dding sail. 1549. [Origin obsc.] A sail set beyond the leeches of any of the principal sails during a fair wind.

Student (stiū·dĕnt). [Late ME. (*a*) *studiant*, *-ient*, a. OF. *estudiant*, subst. use of pr. pple. of *estudier* to STUDY; (*β*) *student(e*, ad. L. *studentem*, *studere*.] 1. A person who is engaged in or addicted to study. 2. A person who is undergoing a course of study and instruction at a university or other place of higher education or technical training. late ME. 3. a. At Christ Church, Oxford: A member of the foundation, corresp. to the 'fellow' or 'scholar' of other colleges (now restricted to the senior members) 1651. b. A person who receives emoluments, during a fixed period, to enable him to pursue his studies and as a reward of merit 1800.

1. I am not..leane enough to bee thought a good Studient SHAKS.

Comb.: **s. interpreter,** a civil servant who is appointed to undergo a course of instruction in foreign languages in order to qualify for a post in the diplomatic or consular service; **s.-teacher,** a student who teaches in a school as part of his training for a teacher's diploma. Hence **Stu·dentry** (*rare*), students collectively.

Studentship (stiū·dĕnt,ʃip). 1782. [-SHIP.] 1. A position, usu. stipendiary, the holding of which constitutes a person a 'student'; see prec. 3 a, b. 2. *gen.* The condition or fact of being a student 1881.

1. A travelling s. for travel and study abroad, of the value of £200. 1883.

Stu·d-horse. OE. [f. STUD *sb.*[2] + HORSE.] A stallion kept for breeding.

Studied (stʋ·did), *ppl. a.* 1530. [f. STUDY *v.* + -ED [1].] 1. Produced or acquired by study, carefully contrived or excogitated; premeditated; deliberate, intentional 1606. 2. Of a person: Learned, deeply read, skilled, practised, versed 1530. †b. Prepared by study or cogitation -1658.

1. Expressed..in terms of s. ambiguity 1769. A s. discourtesy 1859. 2. *Merch. V*, II. ii. 205. b. I..am well s. for a liberall thanks, Which I do owe you SHAKS. Hence **Stu·died-ly** *adv.*, **-ness.**

Studier (stʋ·diəɹ). late ME. [f. STUDY *v.* + -ER [1].] †1. A student -1466. 2. One who studies a specified subject. Now *rare* or *Obs.* 1593. 3. One who strives after or pursues (an object or end). Now *rare.* 1597.

2. A s. of character JANE AUSTEN. 3. The merest S. of Pleasure 1710.

Studio (stiū·dio). 1819. [a. It.; cf. STUDY *sb.*] †1. *Fine Art.* = STUDY *sb.* 10. SHELLEY. 2. The work-room of a sculptor or painter; also that of a photographer 1819. b. A room or building for the making of a cinematographic film or for wireless broadcasting 1912.

1. The original s. by Michael Angelo of the 'Day of Judgment' SHELLEY.

Studious (stiū·diəs), *a.* late ME. [ad. L. *studiosus*, f. *studium* STUDY *sb.*; see -OUS.] 1. Assiduous in study; devoted to the acquisition of learning. b. Of the nature of, pertaining to, or concerned with learning or study 1526. c. Of a place: Devoted or suited to study 1591. 2. Giving careful attention; intent on a purpose or object, heedful, solicitous 1450. b. Characterized by or exhibiting careful attention 1532. c. Planned with care; studied, deliberate 1750.

1. Master Tindall..was..a man of ryght good lyuynge, studyouse & well lerned in scrypture 1528. *absol.* The S. ought to have stated times for Exercise WESLEY. b. Persons of s. habits 1832. c. But let my due feet never fail, To walk the s. Cloysters pale MILT. 2. The work she plied; but s. of delay, By night revers'd the labours of the day POPE. b. Agrippa paid s. court to the Jews 1879. c. For the frigid villany of s. lewdness,..what apology can be invented? JOHNSON. Hence **Stu·dious-ly** *adv.*, **-ness.**

Stu·d-mare. OE. [f. STUD *sb.*[2] + MARE.] A mare kept for breeding purposes; a brood-mare.

Stu·d-sail. 1850. [Etym. obsc.] = STUDDING SAIL.

Study (stʋ·di), *sb.* ME. [a. OF. *estudie*, = It. *studio*, ad. L. *studium*, related to *studere* to be zealous, study.] †**1.** (Chiefly in translations from Latin): Affection, friendliness, devotion to another's welfare; partisan sympathy; desire, inclination; pleasure or interest felt in something –1697. †**2.** An employment, occupation –1610. †**3.** A state of mental perplexity or anxious thought –1689. **b.** A state of reverie or abstraction. *Obs.* exc. in BROWN STUDY. late ME. **4.** Thought or meditation directed to the accomplishment of a purpose; studied or deliberate effort or contrivance; also, the object or aim of (a person's) solicitous endeavour. late ME. **5.** Application of mind to the acquisition of learning ME. **b.** The cultivation of a particular branch of learning or science. Often *collect. pl.*, a person's work as a student. 1477. **6.** The action of studying (something specified or implied); mental effort in the acquisition *of* (some kind of learning) ME. **b.** *Theatr.* The action of committing to memory one's part in a play. Hence, *to have* or *be a quick, slow*, etc. *s.*, to be quick, slow, etc. in learning by heart. 1590. **7.** That which is studied; the object of one's study. Chiefly with *poss.* 1535. **b.** Something worth studying, or that requires to be studied; an object presenting effects of colour (and the like) attractive to an artist 1766. **8.** A room furnished with books and used for private study, reading, writing, or the like. Often applied to the private room or office of the master of the house, however it may be used. ME. †**9.** A seat of learning. *General s.*, *s. general* (= med.L. *studium generale*), a university. –1673. **10.** An artistic production executed for the sake of acquiring skill or knowledge, or to serve as a preparation for future work; a careful preliminary sketch for a work of art, or (more usu.) for some detail or portion of it. Also, occas., a drawing, painting, or piece of sculpture designed to bring out the characteristics of the object represented, as they are revealed by especially careful observation. 1769. **b.** A discourse or literary composition devoted to the detailed consideration of some question, or the minute description of some object; a literary exercise or experiment 1866. **11.** *Mus.* A composition intended to develop a player's powers of execution 1875.

4. The acquisition of a fortune is the s. of all 1803. 5. Of studie took he mooste cure and moost heede CHAUCER. Much studie is a wearinesse of the flesh *Eccles.* xii. 12. b. He gave a considerable time to sacred studies 1756. 6. The s...of the effect of art on the mind of nations RUSKIN. *To make a s. of*, to study, observe carefully. 7. The proper s. of mankind is Man POPE. b. The harpist, whose nose is a s. in purples 1894. 8. Doe you obserue this gallerie?.. Here are a couple of studies, at each end one. B. JONS. 10. A clever s. of a calf being fed 1884.

Study (stʋ·di), *v.* Pa. t. and pa. pple. **studied** (stʋ·did). [ME. *studie*, a. OF. *estudier*, ad. med.L. *studiare*, f. L. *studium* STUDY *sb.*] **I.** *intr.* **1.** To apply the mind to the acquisition of learning, whether by means of books, observation, or experiment. **b.** To follow one's studies at a university, college, or the like; to be a student of some science or art *under* a professor or master 1450. **2.** To think intently; to meditate; to reflect, try to recollect something or to come to a decision. *Obs.* exc. *dial.* and *U.S. colloq.* ME. †**b.** With indirect question: To debate with oneself, deliberate, consider –1788. †**c.** To search, 'cast about' *for* –1748. **3.** To endeavour, make it one's aim, set oneself deliberately *to do* something. *arch.* ME.

1. I wolde fayne be a great clerke, but I love not to studye 1530. b. Vandyke studied under Rubens 1758. 2. You make me s. of that: She was of Carthage, not of Tunis SHAKS. b. I haue beene studying how I may compare This prison where I liue, vnto the world SHAKS. c. I found a Moral first and studied for a Fable SWIFT. 3. No body did ever s. to hurt him 1715.

II. *trans.* **1.** To apply one's mind to the acquiring of (a science, art, language, etc.) 1445. **2.** To be occupied with (a specific branch of learning) as the subject of one's educational course or professional training 1569. **3.** To read (a book, a passage, an author) with close attention. late ME. **b.** Of an actor: To commit to memory and exercise oneself in the rendering of (a part) 1601. **4.** To examine in detail, seek to become minutely acquainted with or to understand (a phenomenon, a state of circumstances, a person's character, etc.); to investigate (a problem) 1600. **b.** To scrutinize (a visible object) in order to ascertain its nature or to be familiar with its appearance; *loosely*, to look at as if examining minutely 1662. **5.** To aim at, seek to achieve. Now only, to aim at (some quality in one's own action). 1606. **6.** To devise, excogitate. Now only with *out*. 1559. **7.** To exercise thought and deliberation in (an action, composition, etc.) 1668. **8.** To 'consider' (a person's wishes, feelings, or interests); hence *colloq.* to humour (a person) 1758.

1. If a Gentleman be to s. any Language, it ought to be that of his own Country LOCKE. 3. The Learned Men who s. Aristotle DE FOE. One cannot be always studying one's own works M. ARNOLD. b. *Twel. N.* I. v. 190. 4. The more he studied the situation, the more apparent it became that..he was in a cleft stick 1885. b. By seizing and studying the contents of my dearest portmanteaus KINGLAKE. 5. The three Villains studied nothing but Revenge DE FOE. 6. The temple itself is nobly and magnificently studied WARTON. 8. With no husband to s., housekeeping is mere play MRS. CARLYLE.

Stuff (stʋf), *sb.* [ME. *stoffe*, *stof*, a. OF. *estoffe*; ult. etym. obscure.] **I.** Equipment, stores, stock. *Obs.* exc. *Sc.* and *north.*, and in HOUSEHOLD-STUFF *arch.* **II.** Material of which something is or may be made. **1.** Material to work with or upon 1440. **b.** *collect.* Materials for a piece of work, esp. building materials. late ME. †**c.** A manufactured material –1626. **2.** *transf.* and *fig.* 1553. **3.** In various operative trades, applied *spec.* to the kind of material used in the trade. **a.** *Carpentry* and *Joinery*. Timber 1544. **b.** *Paper-making.* Pulp or paper-stock ground ready for use 1745. **c.** *Mining.* Material of rock, earth, or clay containing ore, metal, or precious stones 1853. **4.** Material for making garments; woven material of any kind 1462. **b.** In particularized sense: A kind of stuff; a textile fabric 1604. **c.** *spec.* A woollen fabric 1643. **d.** As the material for the gown worn by a junior counsel. Hence *rarely*, A 'stuff gownsman', i. e. a junior counsel, as dist. from a 'silk' (see SILK *sb.* 3 d) 1889.

1. Let Phidias haue rude & obstinate stuffe to carue, ..his worke will lacke that bewtie which otherwise.. it might haue had HOOKER. b. A small cotage, poore for the stuffe, and rude for the workemanship ASCHAM. 2. We are such stuffe As dreames are made on SHAKS. He was not naturally of the s. that martyrs are made of HAWTHORNE. 3. a. Panel s. should be treated in a similar manner 1879. c. About 10 tons of s. are washed per hour 1887. 4. *Tam. Shr.* IV. iii. 119. b. The walls were covered with the stuffs of the East LYTTON. c. He dresses himself according to the Season in Cloth or in S. STEELE.

III. Matter of an unspecified kind. **1.** The general designation for solid, liquid, or (rarely) gaseous matter of any kind: used indefinitely instead of the specific designation, or where no specific designation exists. Often applied to a preparation or composition used for some special purpose. 1580. **b.** Applied to medicine, esp. liquid mixtures. More definitely *doctor's s.* Now only *colloq.* 1611. **c.** Applied to articles of food or drink 1597. **d.** In certain operative trades e.g. *Plastering*, applied *spec.* to some particular preparation used in the work 1812. **e.** Cultivated produce of a garden or farm; natural produce of land 1687. **f.** In commercial and industrial use, applied *spec.* to the particular commodity dealt in 1708. **2.** *transf.* and *fig.* in non-physical senses. **a.** Literary or artistic matter. Now *rare* exc. disparagingly, and *colloq.* among journalists and professional authors = 'copy'. 1542. **b.** Applied to a person 1588. **3.** What is worthless; rubbish 1668. **b.** Worthless ideas, discourse, or writing; nonsense, rubbish. Freq. in interjectional use. 1579. **4.** *slang.* **a.** Money, cash. Chiefly with article, *the s.* 1775. **b.** Stolen goods 1865.

1. For stuffe to kille myce..ij[d] 1617. b. Your very kind letter..did me more good, I think, than any of my doctor's s. 1779. c. *Good s.*, *the s.* (colloq.), whisky. War slang, *That's the s.* (*to give the troops*); often fig. 2. b. *Hot s.* (slang), applied to (*a*) a lustful person; (*b*) a person of fiery courage; (*c*) a strong competitor. 3. b. It is sad s., Sir, miserably written, as books in general then were JOHNSON. Phr. *S. and nonsense.* — *and s.*, and such-like useless or dull matters (*colloq.*). 4. a. But has she got the s., Mr. Fag; is she rich, hey? SHERIDAN.

Comb.: **s. gown**, a junior counsel (see II. 4 d above); so also **s. gownsman**; **s. heap**, a heap of coals and slack raised from a mine; **s. mark**, a weaver's mark woven into goods to identify them or attest their quality.

Stuff (stʋf), *v.* late ME. [a. OF. *estoffer* :—Rom. **stoffare*; ult. etym. obsc.] †**1.** *trans.* To furnish (a fortified town, an army, a commander, etc.) with men, munitions, and stores; to garrison (a town) –1640. †**b.** To furnish (troops) with support; to support, aid (a war) –1560. †**2.** To supply (a person) with arms, provisions, money, etc. –1656. †**3.** To furnish (a place) with accessories, stock, inhabitants; to store with provisions, etc. –1626. †**b.** To store (goods) in a receptacle or place; to keep (flocks) in a place –1606. **4.** To line or fill with some material as a padding; to distend or expand with padding; esp. to fill (a bed-tick, cushion, etc.) with packing in order to furnish a yielding support 1450. **b.** Of material: To serve as padding or stuffing 1530. †**c.** To distend, expand (as if by padding) –1678. **5.** *Cookery.* To fill (the inside of a bird or animal, a piece of meat, etc.) with forcemeat, herbs, etc. as a stuffing. late ME. **6.** To fill out (the skin of a beast, bird, etc.) with material so as to resemble the living creature 1555. **7.** To fill (a receptacle); esp. to fill by packing the materials closely together, to cram full 1440. **b.** Said of the filling material 1664. **c.** To crowd, cram (a vehicle, room *with* persons). Also *intr.* for *pass.* To be crammed. Now *rare.* 1571. **d.** *U.S.* To put fraudulent votes into (a ballot-box) 1872. **8.** *fig.* **a.** To fill, crowd (speech, etc.) *with* something; to fill (a person, his mind, etc.) with ideas, feelings, etc. 1531. **b.** *slang.* To 'cram', hoax, humbug (a person). Also with *up.* 1844. **9.** To fill (oneself, one's stomach) to repletion with food. Also said of the food. late ME. **b.** To cause (a patient) to eat to repletion. Also, to treat (a disease) by feeding up the patient. 1789. **c.** *intr.* for *refl.* To gorge oneself with food 1726. **d.** *trans.* To gorge (food). Also with *down.* 1743. **10.** To fill (an aperture, cavity, etc.) by thrusting something tightly in; hence, to stop up, to plug. Also of a material: To fill *up* so as to block (an aperture). 1593. †**11.** Of bodily humours: To clog, choke *up* (the body, its organs, vessels, etc.) –1750. †**b.** To cause stuffiness in (the head or nose) –1620. **12.** To thrust (something, esp. loose materials) tightly into a receptacle or cavity 1579. **b.** To pack tightly (a person) in a confined space; to crowd (a number of persons *together*) 1728. **13.** *Leather-manuf.* To dress (a skin) with a coating of dubbing or stuffing 1844.

2. A Gentleman..Stuft as they say with Honourable parts SHAKS. 3. b. In Iuory cofers I haue stuft my crownes SHAKS. 4. Giue me your Doublet, and stuffe me out with Straw SHAKS. b. *Much Ado* III. ii. 47. c. Their very sighs might serve to s. the sail 1631. 5. As shee went to the Garden for Parseley to stuffe a Rabit SHAKS. 7. In 's Hand a Wallet stuff'd with Papers 1705. c. The room as full as it could s. 1799. 8. The lies and fables with which his work is stuffed WALPOLE. Don't s. up your head with things you don't understand 1889. 9. Stuffed himself till his hide was stretched as tight as a sausage skin 1903. b. S. a cold and starve a cold are but two ways 1849. c. Let them neither starve nor s. SWIFT. 10. *Rich. II*, I. i. 44. 11. b. I am stuft cosin, I cannot smell SHAKS. 12. With hands stuffed into his front pockets SURTEES. b. There I was..stuffed down between Godmamma and the Marquis's mother 1900. Hence **Stuffed** (stʋft) *ppl. a.* **Stu·ffer,** one who stuffs or fills; a machine or implement used for stuffing.

Stuffiness (stʋ·finės). 1611. [-NESS.] †**1.** Thickness or closeness of texture. COTGR. **2.** The condition of being close or ill-ventilated 1859. **3.** The state or sensation of stoppage and obstruction in the nose or throat 1862.

Stuffing (stʋ·fiŋ), *vbl. sb.* 1530. [-ING[1].] **1.** The action of STUFF *v.*, or the result of this action 1533. **b.** Obstruction of the throat, nose, or chest by catarrh; the sensation produced by this 1601. **2.** The material with which a receptacle is stuffed 1530. **b.** *Cookery.* Forcemeat or other seasoned mixture used to stuff meat before cooking 1538. †**c.** *fig.* (e.g. literary 'padding') –1804. **3.** *Leather-manuf.* The process of rubbing with a mixture of fish-oil and tallow; the mixture used for this 1851.

1. These cowled gentry, that think of nothing but quaffing and s.! SCOTT. 2. Phr. *To knock, beat, take the s. out of* (an animal, person, etc.), to reduce to a state of weakness or flabbiness, take the strength or conceit out of (*colloq.*)

Comb.: **s.-box** *Machinery*, a chamber packed with fluid-tight elastic material, through which a piston-rod or shaft is made to pass in order to prevent leakage at the orifice through which it leaves or enters a vessel; similarly *s.-gland, s. ring*; **s. wheel**, a revolving hollow drum in which leather is subjected to 'stuffing'.

Stuffy (stʌ·fi), *a.* 1551. [f. STUFF *sb.* + -Y[1].] †1. Full of stuff or substance –1667. 2. Of a room, etc.: Ill-ventilated, close. Of the air: Wanting in freshness; oppressive to the lungs and head. Of persons: Addicted to living in stuffy conditions. 1831. b. *transf.* Lacking in freshness, interest, or smartness 1843. 3. Of persons: Affected with a sensation of stoppage in the nose or throat. Said also of the sensation 1847. 4. *U.S. colloq.* Angry, sulky 1825. 5. *slang.* Easily offended or shocked 1926.

2. b. Listening to a s. debate in the Senate 1909.

Stull (stʌl). 1778. [perh. ad. G. *stollen* support, prop.] *Mining.* A platform or framework of timber covered with boards to support workmen or to carry ore or rubbish; also, a framework of boards to protect miners from falling stones.

Stulm (stʌlm). 1684. [perh. a. G. *stolln, stollen.*] *Mining.* An adit or level in a mine.

Stultification (stʌ:ltifikē¹·ʃən). 1832. [f. next; see -FICATION.] The action of STULTIFY *v.*; the state of being stultified; an instance of this.

Stultify (stʌ·ltifəi), *v.* 1766. [ad. late L. *stultificare*, f. *stultus* foolish, fool; see -FY.] 1. trans. *Law.* To allege or prove to be of unsound mind; esp. *refl.*, to allege one's own insanity in order to evade some responsibility. 2. To cause to be or appear foolish, ridiculous, or absurdly inconsistent 1809. b. To render nugatory, worthless, or useless 1865. 3. To regard as a fool or as foolish (*rare*) 1820.

2. This witness, however, stultified himself by admitting that he was too far off to hear what Clement said 1871. b. The blind folly of his servants had stultified his efforts 1888. 3. The modern sciolist stultifies all understanding but his own, and that which he conceives like his own HAZLITT.

Stultiloquence (stʌlti·lŏkwĕns). 1721. [ad. L. *stultiloquentia*, f. *stultiloquus*, f. *stultus* foolish + *-loquus* that speaks.] Foolish or senseless talk, babble, twaddle. So **Stulti·loquent** *a.* (*rare*) talking foolishly; **-ly** *adv.*

Stultiloquy (stʌlti·lŏkwi). 1653. [ad. L. *stultiloquium*, f. *stultiloquus*; see prec.] A speaking foolishly, a foolish babbling.

Stum (stʌm), *sb.* 1662. [a. Du. *stom*, subst. use of *stom* dumb. Cf. F. *vin muet* in the same sense.] 1. Unfermented or partly fermented grape juice, must; esp. must in which the fermentation has been prevented or arrested by fumigation with sulphur. b. Must as used for renewing vapid wines. Also occas. applied to apple-juice similarly used. 1679. 2. Vapid wine renewed by the mixture of stum 1664.

1. b. Let our Wines without mixture, or S. be all fine 1692. *fig.* Thy bellowing Renegado Priests, That.. with thy Stumm ferment their fainting Cause DRYDEN.

Stum (stʌm), *v.* Infl. **stummed, stumming.** 1645. [ad. Du. *stommen*, f. *stom* STUM *sb.*] 1. *trans.* To renew (wine) by mixing with stum or must and raising a new fermentation. 2. To fumigate (a cask) with burning sulphur, in order to prevent the contained liquor from fermenting; to stop the fermentation of (new wine) by fumigation 1787.

Stumble (stʌ·mb'l), *sb.* 1547. [f. next.] 1. An act of stumbling; a missing one's footing; a blunder, slip. b. A moral lapse 1702. c. A stumbling or coming by accident upon something 1865. 2. *gen.* The action of stumbling 1641.

1. b. One s. is oftentimes enough to deface the character of an honourable life 1702.

Stumble (stʌ·mb'l), *v.* [ME. *stomble, stumble* (the *b* is euphonic), corresp. to Norw. *stumla* to grope and stumble in the dark, Da. dial. *stumle*, Sw. dial. *stomla*. The root is an ablaut-var. of **stam-*; see STAMMER *v.*] 1. *intr.* To miss one's footing, or trip over an obstacle, in walking or running, so as to fall or be in danger of falling. b. To knock or jostle *against* (a person or thing) involuntarily 1440. 2. *fig.* a. To trip morally ME. b. To make a slip in speech or action; to blunder through inadvertence or unpreparedness 1450. c. To come *on* or *upon* by chance and unexpectedly; to come *in* or *into* (a place) by chance 1555. d. To take offence; to find a stumbling-block or obstacle to belief 1526. 3. To walk unsteadily and with frequent stumbles. late ME. b. *fig.* To proceed, speak, or act in a blundering or hesitating manner. late ME. 4. *trans.* (causatively). †a. To trip up, overthrow –1652. b. To puzzle; to give pause or offence to; to embarrass, nonplus 1605. †c. To shake (a resolve, an opinion) –1651.

1. How oft to night Haue my old feet stumbled at graues SHAKS. The horse stumblinge threw them both 1659. *To s. at* (*on*) *the threshold*, chiefly *fig.* to fail, take offence, meet with an ominous check at the beginning of an enterprise. Phr. 2. a. They sinned and stumbled..with debt, with drink THACKERAY. b. T'is better s. with thy feet Then s. with thy tongue 1607. c. The founders..appear to have stumbled upon their discovery by a kind of accident 1874. d. In case the Prelacy for England should s. at the Supremacy of Rome 1647. 3. But..blind be blinded more, That they may s. on, and deeper fall MILT. b. My tongue should s. in mine earnest words SHAKS. 4. b. By these..Reproaches, many were stumbled at his Testimony 1724. Hence **Stu·mbler**, one who, or something which stumbles; a cause of stumbling, a 'poser'. **Stu·mblingly** *adv.*

Stu·mbling-block. 1526. [f. *stumbling* vbl. sb.] Something to stumble at or over; a cause of stumbling. Chiefly *fig.*

That no man putt a stomblinge blocke or an occasion to faule [Gr. πρόσκομμα ἢ σκάνδαλον] in his brothers waye TINDALE *Rom.* xiv. 13.

Stumer (stiū̆·məɪ). *slang.* 1890. [?] A worthless cheque; a counterfeit note or coin. b. A race-horse fraudulently run; also, a dud.

Stump (stʌmp), *sb.*[1] [Late ME. *stompe*, a. or cogn. w. MLG. *stump, stumpe*, subst. use of MLG. *stump* mutilated, blunt, dull.] 1. The part remaining of an amputated or broken-off limb or portion of the body. b. A rudimentary limb or member, or one that has the appearance of being mutilated 1555. c. *joc.* A leg. Chiefly in *to stir one's stumps*, to walk or dance briskly. 1460. d. A wooden leg 1679. 2. The portion of the trunk of a felled tree that remains fixed in the ground; also, a standing tree-trunk from which the upper part and the branches have been cut or broken off 1440. b. The base of a growing tree 1902. 3. = STUB *sb.* 9. 1516. b. The part of a broken tooth left in the gum. late ME. c. A docked tail 1544. d. *Naut.* The lower portion of a mast when the upper part has been broken off or shot away 1725. e. The remaining portion of a leaf cut out of a volume; the counterfoil of a cheque 1887. 4. A blockhead; a man of short stumpy figure 1601. 5. The stalk of a plant (esp. cabbage) when the leaves are removed 1819. b. *pl.* Hair cut close to the skin. Also, remains of feathers on a plucked fowl. 1584. 6. A post, a short pillar not supporting anything 1700. 7. *Cricket.* Each of the three (formerly two) upright sticks which, with the bails laid on the top of them, form a wicket 1735. 8. A projecting stud in a lock or a hinge 1808. 9. orig. *U.S.* a. In early use, the stump (sense 2) of a felled tree used as a stand or platform for a speaker 1775. b. Hence, a place or an occasion of political oratory 1816.

1. The stumps that beggars thrust into coaches to excite charity and miscarriages H. WALPOLE. 2. b. Phr. *To buy* (timber) *on the s.*, before felling. 3. A black s. of a tobacco-pipe was in his mouth 1829. Phr. (*To wear*) *to the stumps* (chiefly *fig.*; *rare* or *Obs.*). 5. b. He said..that the Stumps of my Beard were ten times stronger than the Bristles of a Boar SWIFT. 7. *To draw* (*the*) *stumps*, to pull up the stumps, as a sign of the discontinuance of play or of the termination of a match or game. 9. b. The first of our Presidents who has descended to the s. 1866. Phr. *To go on the s.*, *to take the s.*, to go about the country making political speeches, whether as a candidate or as the advocate of a cause.

Comb.: **s. bed, bedstead**, a bedstead without posts **s.-end,** (*a*) the end of the s. of a tail; (*b*) the remnant of a cheque-book containing the 'stumps'.

Stump (stʌmp), *sb.*[2] 1778. [perh. ad. F. *estompe.*] A kind of pencil consisting of a roll of paper or soft leather, or of a cylindrical piece of india-rubber or other soft material, usu. cut to a blunt point at each end, used for rubbing down hard lines in pencil or crayon drawing, for blending the lines of shading, and for other similar purposes.

Stump (stʌmp), *sb.*[3] 1690. [f. STUMP *v.*[1]] 1. A heavy step or gait, as of a lame or wooden-legged person 1770. b. Reiterated, with echoic intention. Also quasi-*adv.*, (to go, come) *s.*, *s.* 1690. 2. *U.S. colloq.* A challenge to do something difficult or dangerous 1871.

Stump (stʌmp), *a.* 1563. [Partly from attrib. use of STUMP *sb.*[1], perh. partly ad. Du., LG. *stomp.*] 1. Worn down to a stump 1624. 2. Said of mutilated or malformed limbs 1563.

2. *S. foot*, a club-foot. *S. leg*, a leg without a foot or with a club foot.

Comb.: **s.-tail**, a stump-tailed dog; also *Austral.* a stump-tailed lizard (*Trachysaurus*).

Stump (stʌmp), *v.*[1] ME. [f. STUMP *sb.*[1]] †1. *intr.* To stumble over a tree-stump or other obstacle –1607. 2. To walk clumsily, heavily, or noisily, as if one had a wooden leg 1600. b. *slang.* 'To go on foot'; also *s. it* 1841. 3. *trans.* To reduce to a stump; to truncate, mutilate 1596. 4. *Colonial.* To stub; to dig up by the roots 1790. 5. To remove the stumps from (land). Also *absol.* 1796. 6. *Cricket.* Of the wicket-keeper: To put (a batsman) out by dislodging a bail (or knocking down a stump) with the ball held in the hand, at a moment when he is off his ground. Also with *out.* 1744. 7. *slang.* To render penniless. Chiefly in *pass.*, to be 'stony broke'. 1828. 8. *U.S. colloq.* To strike (the toe) unintentionally against a stone or something fixed 1828. 9. orig. *U.S.* To cause to be at a loss; to nonplus 1807. 10. *U.S.* To challenge, 'dare' (a person) to do something 1766. 11. Chiefly *U.S.* a. *intr.* To make stump speeches; to conduct electioneering by public speaking 1838. b. *trans.* To travel over (a district) making stump speeches; to canvass or address with stump oratory 1856.

6. He caught three batsmen at the wicket and stumped one 1884. 9. That beastly Euclid altogether stumps me 1854. 11. a. Stumping it through England for seven years made Cobden a consummate debater EMERSON.

S. up. a. *trans.* To dig up by the roots. b. *slang.* (*a*) To pay down, 'fork out' (money). *rare.* (*b*) *absol.* or *intr.* (*c*) *trans.* To wear out, exhaust (a horse) by excessive strain.

Stump (stʌmp), *v.*[2] 1807. [app. ad. F. *estomper.*] *Drawing. trans.* To tone or treat with a 'stump'.

Stumpage (stʌ·mpėdʒ). *local U.S.* 1848. [f. STUMP *sb.*[1] + -AGE.] 1. The price paid for standing timber; also, a tax charged in some states for the privilege of cutting timber on State lands. 2. Standing timber considered with reference to its quantity or marketable value 1854.

2. We assume a pine s. of 5000 feet to the acre 1894.

Stumper (stʌ·mpəɪ). 1776. [f. STUMP *v.*[1] + -ER[1].] 1. One employed or skilled in stumping trees 1828. 2. *Cricket.* A wicket-keeper 1776. 3. Something that 'stumps' one; a poser 1807. 4. *U.S.* A stump speaker 1863.

Stumpy (stʌ·mpi), *sb.* 1828. [f. STUMP *sb.*[1] + -Y[6].] 1. A spritsail barge 1881. 2. *slang.* Money 1828.

Stumpy (stʌ·mpi), *a.* 1600. [f. STUMP *sb.*[1] + -Y[1].] 1. Like a stump; short and thick. Of grass, etc. Full of stumps or short hard stalks. 2. Worn down to a stump 1794. 3. *U.S.* Of ground: Full of stumps 1838.

1. Turner was a s., ill-dressed man, with a red face 1862. Hence **Stu·mpi·ly** *adv.*, **-ness.**

Stun (stʌn), *sb.* 1727. [f. STUN *v.*] 1. The act of stunning; a stunning effect; stunned condition. 2. A flaw on the surface of a piece of stone 1850.

Stun (stʌn), *v.* ME. [Aphetic a. OF. *estoner* ASTONE.] 1. *trans.* To deprive of consciousness or of power of motion by a blow, a fall, or the like. 2. To daze or astound with some strong emotion or impression ME. 3. To daze or bewilder with noise or din. Also *absol.* 1621. 4. a. To bruise or loosen the surface of (stone, a mineral), so that it splinters or exfoliates. Also, to scratch or tear (a saw) in sawing. b. *intr.* Of stone, etc.: To exfoliate, peel off in splinters or laminæ. 1676.

1. She was as one stunned into unconsciousness;..

she hardly breathed 1853. **2.** The multitude,..are captivated by whatever stuns and dazzles them MACAULAY. I sat stunned with my good fortune 1886. **3.** The ear is stunned by the not unmusical roar of the Falls 1910.

Stundist (ʃtu·ndist, stu·ndist). 1878. [a. Russ. *štundist*, f. G. *stunde* hour, said to be used by the German settlers as the name for their religious meetings; see -IST.] A member of a large Evangelical sect (called *štunda*) which arose among the peasantry of South Russia about 1860, as a result of contact with German Protestant settlers. Hence **Stu·ndism**, the teaching and practice of the Stundists.

Stung (stɒŋ), *ppl. a.* ME. [See STING *v.*] Wounded or hurt by a sting.

Stunner (stɒ·nəɹ). 1847. [f. STUN *v.* + -ER.] **1.** Something that stuns or dazes, that amazes or astounds. **2.** *colloq.* A person or thing of extraordinary excellence or attractiveness 1848.

2. The cook..was really a s. for tarts THACKERAY.

Stunning (stɒ·niŋ), *ppl. a.* 1667. [-ING [2].] **1.** That stuns or stupefies; dazing, astounding; deafening. **2.** *colloq.* Excellent, first-rate, 'splendid', delightful; extremely attractive or good-looking 1849.

2. Those regular s. slap-up out-and-outers THACKERAY. The most s. girl I ever set my eyes on 1856. Hence **Stu·nningly** *adv.*

Stunsail (stɒ·ns'l). 1762. *Naut.* Contraction, repr. the ordinary pronunciation, of STUDDING-SAIL.

His ears large and outstanding, like a couple of stunsails 1913.

Stunt (stɒnt), *sb.*[1] 1725. [f. STUNT *v.*[1]] **1.** A check in growth; also, a state of arrested growth or development 1795. **2.** A creature which has been hindered from full growth or development 1725. **3.** *dial.* A fit of sulkiness or obstinacy; in phr. *to take* (*the*) *s.* 1837.

Stunt (stɒnt), *sb.*[2] *colloq.* 1878. [orig. American college slang; origin obsc.] **a.** An 'event' in an athletic competition or display; a feat undertaken as a defiance in response to a challenge; an act which is striking for the skill, strength, or the like, required to do it; a feat; something performed as an item in an entertainment. **b.** In recent use, An enterprise set on foot with the object of gaining reputation or signal advantage. In soldiers' use often vaguely: An attack or advance, a 'push', 'move'. **c.** In wider use, an enterprise, performance 1913.

Hence **Stunt** *v.*[2] *intr.* to perform stunts; *spec.* of a motorist, an airman, etc., to perform spectacular and daring feats. **Stu·nter. Stu·ntist.**

Stunt, *a.* *Obs.* exc. *dial.* [OE. *stunt* foolish :—OTeut. **stunto-* short, truncated, perh. repr. pre-Teut. **stṃdo-*, f. root **stem-*.] †**1.** Foolish, stupid -ME. **2.** Obstinate, stubborn; rudely or angrily curt or blunt 1581. **3.** Stunted. **a.** Short and thick 1788. **b.** Dwarfed in growth 1819. **4.** Of a turn, bend: Abrupt 1851.

Comb.: **s.-head** *Engineering*, the vertical timbered end of a trench which has been excavated for the purpose of laying a sewer or a water-main.

Stunt (stɒnt), *v.*[1] 1583. [f. prec.] †**1.** *trans.* **a.** To irritate, provoke to anger. †**b.** To bring to an abrupt stand; to nonplus. -1642. **2.** To check the growth or development of (a person, plant, etc.); to decrease (growth or production); hence, to dwarf 1659. †**3.** *intr.* To become arrested in growth -1796.

2. *transf.* When by a cold penury, I blast the abilities of a nation, and s. the growth of it's active energies, the ill I may do is beyond all calculation BURKE. Hence **Stu·nted** *ppl. a.*, **-ly** *adv.*, **-ness.**

‖ **Stupa** (stū·pă). 1876. [Skr.] A Buddhist monument; = TOPE *sb.*[4]

Stupe (stiūp), *sb.*[1] late ME. [ad. L. *stupa*, *stuppa* tow.] A piece of tow, flannel, or the like, wrung out of hot liquor and medicated, for fomenting a wound or ailing part. Hence **Stupe** *v.* *trans.* to foment with a s. or stupes.

Stupe (stiūp), *sb.*[2] *colloq.* Now chiefly *dial.* 1762. [Shortened f. STUPID.] A stupid person, a fool.

Stupefacient (stiūpĭfē̆·ʃĕnt), *a.* and *sb.* 1669. [ad. L. *stupefacientem*, *stupefacere* STUPEFY *v.*] *Med.* **A.** *adj.* Stupefying, producing stupor. **B.** *sb.* A medicine producing stupor (*rare*) 1855.

Stupefaction (stiūpĭfæ·kʃən). 1543. [a. F. *stupéfaction*, or ad. mod.L. *stupefactionem*; see STUPEFY *v.* and -FACTION.] **1.** The action of stupefying or state of being stupefied. **2.** Overwhelming consternation or astonishment 1597.

1. Tobacco is the delight of Dutchmen, as it diffuses a torpor and pleasing s. BURKE.

Stupefactive (stiū·pĭfæktiv), *a.* and *sb.* 1527. [a. F. *stupéfactif*, ad. med.L. *stupefactivus*, f. L. *stupefact-*, *stupefacere* STUPEFY *v.*] = STUPEFACIENT *a.* and *sb.* Now *rare* or *Obs.*

Stupefy (stiū·pĭfəi), *v.* Also **stupify** (now unusual). 1596. [a. F. *stupéfier*, ad. L. *stupefacere*, f. *stupere* to be struck senseless, be amazed.] **1.** *trans.* To make stupid or torpid; to deprive of apprehension, feeling, or sensibility; to benumb, deaden. Also *absol.* 1600. **2.** To stun with amazement, fear, or the like; to astound 1596. **3.** *intr.* To become stupid or torpid; to grow dull or insensible. Now *rare.* 1631.

1. Those [drugs] she ha's, Will stupifie and dull the Sence a-while SHAKS. **2.** He sat, stupified with shame and remorse 1779.

Stupend (stiupe·nd), *a.* *Obs.* exc. *joc.* 1621. [ad. L. *stupendus* STUPENDOUS.] Stupendous.

The s. Variety of Human Faces 1702.

†**Stupe·ndious,** *a.* 1547. [irreg. f. L. *stupendus*, after adjs. in -IOUS.] Stupendous -1800.

Stupendous (stiŭpe·ndəs), *a.* 1666. [f. L. *stupendus*, gerundive of *stupere* to be struck senseless, be amazed at; see -OUS.] Such as to cause stupor or astonishment; amazing, astounding; marvellous, prodigious; amazingly large or great.

All are but parts of one s. whole POPE. The man who thinks to outwit three women..must indeed be a s. ass 1863. Hence **Stupe·ndous-ly** *adv.*, **-ness.**

Stupent (stiū·pĕnt), *a.* *rare.* 1843. [ad. L. *stupentem*, *stupere.*] That is in a state of stupor or amazement.

Stupeous (stiū·pĭəs), *a.* Also **stuppeous** (stɒ·pĭəs). 1826. [f. L. *stupeus*, *stuppeus* made of tow, f. *stupa*, *stuppa* STUPE *sb.*[1]; see -OUS.] *Zool.* and *Bot.* Having, or covered with, matted or tufted hairs or filaments.

Stupid (stiū·pid), *a.* and *sb.* 1541. [ad. L. *stupidus*, f. *stupere.*] **A.** *adj.* **1.** Having one's faculties deadened or dulled; in a state of stupor, stupefied, stunned; esp. *hyperbolically*, stunned with surprise, grief, etc. *Obs.* exc. *arch.* (*poet.*) 1611. †**2.** As the characteristic of inanimate things: Destitute of sensation, consciousness, thought, or feeling -1744. **3.** Wanting in or slow of mental perception; lacking ordinary activity of mind; slow-witted, dull 1541. **b.** Of attributes, actions, ideas, etc.: Characterized by or indicating stupidity or dullness of comprehension 1621. †**c.** Of the lower animals: Irrational; senseless, dull -1867. **4.** Void of interest, tiresome, boring, dull 1778.

1. Is he not s. With Age, and altring Rheumes? Can he speake? heare? Know man, from man? SHAKS. **2.** Matter is incapable of acting, passive only, and s. 1722. **3.** No man who knows aught, can be so s. to deny that all men naturally were borne free MILT. **b.** Let us not..persist in such a s. error 1707. **4.** We were quartered at a s. sea-port town 1862. If my letter is very s., forgive me 1884.

B. *sb.* A stupid person. *colloq.* 1712. Hence **Stu·pid-ly** *adv.*, **-ness.**

Stupidity (stiupi·dĭti). 1541. [ad. L. *stupiditas*, f. *stupidus* STUPID; see -ITY.] †**1.** Numbness, incapacity for sensation -1737. †**2.** A state of stupor -1831. †**3.** Incapacity for emotion; apathy, indifference -1748. †**b.** Insensibility to pain or sorrow; blameable absence of resentment under injury or insult -1673. **4.** Dullness or slowness of apprehension; gross want of intelligence 1541. **b.** A stupid idea, action, etc. 1633.

4. With S. and sound Digestion man may front much CARLYLE. **b.** The dull stupidities and senseless flippancies of Roman architecture 1851.

Stupor (stiū·pəɹ; as scientific L. ‖stiū·pǭɹ). late ME. [a. L., f. *stupere.*] **1.** A state of insensibility or lethargy; spec. in *Path.*, a disorder characterized by great diminution or entire suspension of sensibility. **b.** = DEMENTIA **1.** 1899. **2.** A state of mental stupefaction; apathy or torpor of mind (now only torpor due to sorrow, painful surprise, or the like) 1672. **b.** Admiring wonder. Also (after med.L. *stupor mundi*), the object of wonder, 'the marvel *of*' (the world, etc.). 1482.

1. James sank into a s. which indicated the near approach of death MACAULAY. **2.** With her mouth wide open, staring vacantly at the collector, in a s. of dismay DICKENS. Hence **Stu·porous** *a.* affected with or characterized by s.

Stupose (stiū·pōᵘs), *a.* 1835. [ad. med.L. *stuposus*, *stupposus*, f. L. *stupa*, *stuppa* tow; see -OSE.] *Bot.* = STUPEOUS.

Sturdy (stɒ̄·ɹdi), *a.* and *sb.* ME. [a. OF. *estourdi* stunned, dazed, reckless, violent, pa. pple. of OF. *estourdir* :—vulgar L. **exturdire*, of obsc. origin.] **A.** *adj.* **I.** Giddy. Said of sheep affected with the 'sturdy': see B. **1.** Now *dial.* 1641. **II.** †**1.** Impetuously brave, fierce in combat -1684. †**2.** Recklessly violent, furious, ruthless, cruel -1603. †**b.** Of waves, a stream, a storm, etc.: Violent, rough -1823. †**3.** Of countenance, speech, demeanour: Stern, harsh, rough, surly -1611. †**4.** Hard to manage, intractable, refractory; rebellious, disobedient -1781. †**b.** Obstinate -1781. **c.** Epithet of beggars or vagabonds who are able-bodied and apt to be violent. late ME. **5.** Of material things: Refractory, defiant of destructive agencies or force; strong, stout. late ME. **b.** Of a plant: Hardy 1695. **6.** Of persons or animals: Solidly built; stalwart, strong, robust, hardy. late ME. **b.** Of movements, etc.: Displaying physical vigour 1697. **7.** *transf.* Of persons, their actions and attributes: Robust in mind or character; 'downright', uncompromising 1775. **b.** Of expressions: Vigorous, lusty 1822.

4. The most s. and refractory Non-conformists FULLER. **b.** Your blund'rer is as s. as a rock COWPER. **c.** Like s. Beggars, that intreat For Charity at once, and threat 1680. **5.** On the vext Wilderness, whose ..sturdiest Oaks Bow'd thir Stiff necks MILT. **b.** Lichen and moss and s. weed C. ROSSETTI. **6.** A rugged land..well fitted to produce a s. race JOWETT. **b.** With s. steps he walks PRIOR. **7.** I respect that fine old s. fellow Hobbes HAZLITT. **b.** Here crash'd a s. oath of stout John Bull BYRON.

B. *sb.* **1.** A brain-disease in sheep and cattle, which makes them run round and round; the turnsick 1570. **2.** A name for darnel or some similar stupefying weed 1683. **3.** A sturdy person 1704.

Sturgeon (stɒ̄·ɹdʒən). ME. [a. AF. *sturgeon*, *esturgeoun*, a. Com. Rom. word :—pop.L. *sturionem* (*sturio*), a. OTeut. **sturjon-*.] A large fish of the family *Acipenseridæ*, having an elongated, almost cylindrical, body protected by longitudinal rows of bony scutes and a long tapering snout, found widely distributed in the rivers and coastal waters of the north temperate zone; esp. a fish belonging to either of the genera *Acipenser* and *Scaphirhynchops*, *A. sturio* being the common s. of the Atlantic. It is a 'royal' fish (see FISH *sb.*[1]), esteemed as an article of food, and the source of caviar and isinglass. **b.** With qualifying word, as **black, lake, Ohio, red, rock, stone s.,** *Acipenser rubicundus*, the s. of the great lakes of N. America; **great white, isinglass, Russian s.,** *A. huso*, the BELUGA or HUSO; **small** or **Ruthenian s.,** the STERLET.

Sturionian (stiūᵒɹiōᵘ·niăn). 1835. [f. mod. L. *Sturiones* (pl. of pop.L. *sturio* STURGEON) + -IAN.] A fish belonging to the *Sturiones*, a former order of fishes including the sturgeons (*Acipenseridæ*) and related families.

‖ **Sturm und Drang** [G.]: see STORM *sb.* 3.

Sturnoid (stɒ̄·ɹnoid), *a.* 1874. [f. L. *sturnus* starling + -OID.] *Ornith.* Resembling the *Sturnidæ* or Starlings in form or characteristics.

Sturt (stɒ̄ɹt). 1849. [perh. var. of START *sb.*[2]] *Tin-mining.* A great profit made by a 'tributer' in tribute mining.

Stut (stɒt), *v.* *Obs.* exc. *dial.* [Late ME. *stutten*, f. Teut. root **stut-*, ablaut var. of **staut-*.] *intr.* To stutter.

Stu·tter, *sb.*[1] *Obs.* exc. *dial.* 1529. [f. prec. + -ER [1].] = STUTTERER.

Stutter (stɒ·təɹ), *sb.*[2] 1854. [f. next.] An act or a habit of stuttering.

Stutter (stɒ·təɹ), *v.* 1570. [freq. f. STUT *v.*; see -ER [5].] **1** *intr.* To speak with continued involuntary repetition of sounds or syllables owing to excitement, fear, or constitutional nervous defect; to stammer. **2.** *trans.* To say or speak with a stutter 1645.

1. And though you hear him stut-tut-tut-ter, He barks as fast as he can utter SWIFT. Hence **Stu·tterer. Stu·tteringly** *adv.*

Sty (stəi), *sb.*[1] *Pl.* **sties** (stəiz). [OE. *stī*, prob. identical with *stig* hall; corresp. to ON. *stí*; repr. OTeut. *stijom, f. root *stī-: *stai-.] **1.** An enclosed place where swine are kept, usu. a low shed with an uncovered forecourt, a pigsty. **2.** *transf.* and *fig.* **a.** A human habitation (or sleeping-place) no better than a pigsty 1598. **b.** An abode of bestial lust, or of moral pollution generally. late ME.

2. b. The painted booths and sordid sties of vice and luxury BURKE.

Sty (stəi), *sb.*[2] 1617. [prob. a back-formation from STYANY (interpreted as *sty-on-eye*).] An inflammatory swelling on the eyelid.

†Sty, *v.*[1] [OE. *stigan* (*stāh, stigon, stigen*), a Com. Teut. str. vb.:—OTeut. *stīg- (: *staig-) :—Indo-Eur. *steigh- (: *stoigh- *stigh-) to go, repr. by Skr. *stigh to step, stride, Gr. στείχειν to go, στοῖχος, στίχος a row, line, L. *ve-stigium* footstep, trace.] **1.** *intr.* To ascend, rise or climb to a higher level –1652. **2.** With *down* adv., etc.: To descend. Also *gen.* To ascend or descend. -ME.

1. From this lower tract he dar'd to stie Up to the clowdes SPENSER.

Sty (stəi), *v.*[2] [OE. *stigian*, f. *stī* STY *sb.*[1]] **1.** *trans.* To place or confine (swine) in a sty. **b.** *transf.* To confine as in a sty; to pen *up* 1610. **2.** *intr.* To share a sty *with*; to dwell as in a sty 1748.

1. b. And here you s. me In this hard Rocke SHAKS.

Styan (stəi·ăn). Now *dial.* [OE. *stīgend* (lit. 'riser'), f. *stīgan* STY *v.*[1]] = STY *sb.*[2]

Styany (stəi·əni). Now *dial.* 1440. [f. prec. + EYE *sb.*] = STY *sb.*[2]

Styca (stəi·kă). 1705. [Assumed sing. from ONorthumb. *stycas*, dial. pl. of OE. *stycce* piece (of money).] *Numism.* A small copper coin current in Northumbria in the seventh, eighth, and ninth centuries.

Stygian (sti·dʒiăn), *a.* 1566. [f. L. *Stygius* (a. Gr. Στύγιος, f. Στυγ- STYX) + -AN.] **1.** Pertaining to the river Styx or to the infernal regions of classical mythology. **b.** Of an oath: Supremely binding, like the oath by the Styx, which the gods themselves feared to break 1608. **2.** Infernal, hellish 1601. **3.** Black as the river Styx; dark or gloomy as the region of the Styx 1599.

1. *S. Jove, Jupiter*, Pluto, the god of the lower world; Thus will I pay my Vows, to S. Jove DRYDEN. **3.** Will I not turne a glorious bridall morne Unto a S. night? MARSTON.

Phr. †*S. water, liquor* [tr. mod.L. *aqua Stygia*], in Old Chemistry, a name for nitrohydrochloric acid and other strong mineral acids.

Stylar (stəi·lăɹ). 1614. [ad. mod.L.*stylaris, f. *stylus* STYLE *sb.*; see -AR.] **†1.** Pertaining to the 'style' or gnomon of a dial –1668. **2.** 'Having the character of or pertaining to a style for writing' 1891.

‖ **Stylaster** (stəilæ·stəɹ). 1831. [mod.L., f. Gr. στῦλος column + ἀστήρ star.] *Zool.* A genus of hydrozoa, closely related to the *Millepora*; a species or an animal of this genus, or of the family *Stylasteridæ*, of which it is the type.

Stylate (stəi·lĕt), *a.* 1866. [ad. mod.L. *stylatus*, f. *stylus* STYLE *sb.*; see -ATE.] **a.** *Bot.* Having a persistent style. **b.** *Zool.* Having a style or stylet. Also, having the form of a pen or pin, styliform, styloid.

Style (stəil), *sb.* ME. [a. OF. *style, stile*, ad. L. *stilus* a stake or pale, pointed instrument for writing, style of speaking or writing; f. root *sti-; cf. STIMULUS.] **I.** Stylus, pin, stalk. **1.** *Antiq.* An instrument made of metal, bone, etc. having one end sharp-pointed for incising letters on a wax tablet, and the other flat and broad for smoothing the tablet and erasing what is written. Also applied to similar instruments in later use. **b.** Used as a weapon of offence, for stabbing, etc. 1669. **c.** *fig.*, or as a symbol of literary composition 1579. **2.** An engraving-tool; a graver 1662. **3.** *Surg.* A blunt-pointed probe 1631. **4.** A hard point for tracing, in manifold writing; the marking point in a telegraph or phonograph 1871. **5.** *gen.* A fixed pointer, pin, or finger for indicating a point or position 1555. **6.** The pin, rod, or triangular plate which forms the gnomon of a sun-dial 1577. **7.** *Bot.* A narrowed prolongation of the ovary, which, when present, supports the stigma at its apex 1682. **8.** *Ent.* **a.** A slender bristle-like process in the anal region. **b.** The bristle or seta of the antenna of a dipter. 1826. **9.** *Zool.* A small slender pointed process or part; a stylet 1851. **b.** A sponge-spicule pointed at one end 1879.

1. Phr. †*To turn one's s.*, to change *to* another subject; also, to speak on the other side. [So *stilum vertere* in late L.]

II. Writing; manner of writing (hence also of speaking). **†1.** A written work or works; literary composition –1595. **†b.** An entry, clause, or section in a legal document –1649. **2.** The manner of expression characteristic of a particular writer (hence of an orator), or of a literary group or period; a writer's mode of expression considered in regard to clearness, effectiveness, beauty, and the like ME. **3.** *gen.* Those features of literary composition which belong to form and expression rather than to the substance of the thought or matter expressed. Often used for: Good or fine style. 1577. **4.** A manner of discourse, or tone of speaking, adopted in addressing others or in ordinary conversation 1567. **†5.** A form of words, phrase, or formula, by which a particular idea or thought is expressed –1736. **6.** *Scots Law.* The authorized form for drawing up a deed or instrument 1480. **b.** *gen.* Legal technicality of language or construction 1743. **7.** A legal, official, or honorific title; the proper name or recognized appellation of a person, family, trading firm, etc.; the ceremonial designation of a sovereign ME. **b.** *gen.* Any distinguishing or qualifying title, appellation, or denomination. Now *rare* or *Obs.* late ME.

2. Proper words in proper places, make the true definition of a s. SWIFT. The incomparable s. of Mr. Ruskin SWINBURNE. **3.** S. is the dress of thoughts CHESTERF. **4.** He talked in his usual s. with a rough contempt of popular liberty BOSWELL. **7.** The Kings Stile, is now no more of England, but of Britaine BACON. I have always been shy of assuming the honourable s. of Professor M. ARNOLD. **b.** The S. of *Maritime Powers*, by which our Allies, in a sort of contemptuous manner, usually couple us with the Dutch SWIFT.

III. Manner, fashion. **†1.** A method or custom of performing actions or functions, esp. one sanctioned by usage or law –1773. **2.** A particular mode or form of skilled construction, execution, or production; the manner in which a work of art is executed; one of the modes recognized in a particular art as suitable for the production of beautiful or skilful work 1706. **b.** *gen.* Often used for: Beauty or loftiness of style 1801. **c.** A definite type of architecture, distinguished by special characteristics of structure or ornamentation 1777. **d.** *Printing.* The rules and methods, in regard to typography, display, etc., observed in a particular printing-office 1871. **3.** A kind, sort, or type, as determined by manner of composition or construction, or by outward appearance 1794. **b.** *transf.* Said predicatively of a person or thing: What suits (a person's) taste; the 'sort' that (a person or set of persons) would choose or approve 1811. **4.** Manner of executing a task or performing an action or operation. Often with ref. to athletics, racing, games: The manner of action of a particular performer, racehorse, etc. 1774. **b.** Used *absol.* for: Good or fine style 1864. **5.** A mode of deportment or behaviour; a mode or fashion of life, esp. in regard to expense, display, etc. 1770. **b.** Used *absol.* for: Fashionable air, appearance, deportment, etc. 1807. **6.** A particular mode or fashion of costume 1814. **7.** A person's characteristic bearing, demeanour, or manner, esp. as conducing to beauty or striking appearance 1826.

1. The S. of Court is properly the Practice observ'd by any Court in its way of Proceeding 1726. I like to give them a hearty reception in the old s. at my gate GOLDSM. **2.** At Lausanne we only stopped for dinner (which we obtained in sufficiently bad s. at the *Lion d'Or*) 1832. **c.** A very handsome church..in the Gothic stile 1777. **3.** There was something in her s. of beauty to please them [*i.e.* men] particularly JANE AUSTEN. **b.** She is not the s. of the day at all, you know 1880. **4.** A barge was coming up in fine s. 1833. The s. in which he [*sc.* a horse] ran, his nose almost sweeping the ground 1833. **5.** The society is noisy and in bad s. 1792. That gentleman..lived in what is called great s. SCOTT. **b.** A plain German city, with little or no pretensions to s. 1835. Phr. *In s.*, splendidly, showily, according to fashionable requirements. **6.** His daughters look very well in their better s. of dress 1833. **7.** Most amusing, delightful girl, great s.! DISRAELI.

IV. A mode of expressing dates. *Chiefly*, Either of the two methods of dating that have been current in the Christian world since the introduction of the Gregorian calendar in 1582: viz., the *New Style* (abbrev. N.S.), which is the result of the Gregorian reform, and the *Old Style* (O.S.) which follows the unreformed calendar. The New Style is occas. called the *Roman Style*, and the Old Style the *English Style*. In historical dates earlier than 1582, however, *Roman Style*, as used by modern writers, means only that the year mentioned is to be understood as beginning on 1 January. 1590.

The Julian calendar assumed that the tropical year consisted of 365¼ days. To give the average calendar year this length, it was provided that the normal year should contain 365 days, but every fourth year 366 days. In England the beginning of the legal year was 25 March.

The Julian estimate of 365¼ days for the length of the year was too great by about 11 minutes, an error which amounts to one day in about 128 years. Hence in 1581 the date of 21 March for the vernal equinox, assumed since the early 4th c. in the rule for computing Easter, was 10 days too late. To remedy this, Pope Gregory XIII ordained that in A.D. 1582 the day after 4 Oct. should be reckoned as 15 Oct., and that in future the years which had a number ending in two cyphers should not be leap years unless the number were divisible by 400. The Julian date for the beginning of the year, viz., 1 Jan., was retained.

In England and Scotland the Gregorian calendar was established by the Act 24 Geo. II. c. 23 (1751), which provided that the year 1752 and all future years should begin on 1 Jan. instead of 25 Mar., that the day after 2 Sep. 1752 should be reckoned the 14 Sep., and that the reformed rule for leap year should in future be followed.

Style (stəil), *v.* 1563. [f. prec.] **1.** *trans.* To give a name or style to; to call by a name or style. **†2.** To relate or express in literary form –1605. **3.** To execute (a design) with a stylus on a prepared ground 1864.

Stylet (stəi·lĕt). 1697. [a. F., ad. It. *stiletto* STILETTO.] **1.** *Surg.* A slender probe. Also, a wire run through a catheter or canula in order to stiffen it or to clear it. **2. †a.** *Bot.* = STYLE *sb.* I. 7. –1723. **b.** *Zool.* = STYLE *sb.* I. 8, 9. 1834. **3.** A kind of pencil for the use of the blind 1819. **b.** A pointed marking instrument; a graving tool 1853. **4.** A stiletto, dagger 1820.

3. b. The strong hieroglyphics graven as with iron s. on his brow C. BRONTË.

‖ **Stylidium** (stəili·diŏm). 1829. [mod.L., f. Gr. στῦλος column + -ιδιον dim. suffix (here used loosely).] *Bot.* A genus of gamopetalous plants, native in Australia, India, and Ceylon, remarkable for the irritability of the column formed by the union of the stamens and style.

Styliferous (stəili·fĕrŏs), *a.* 1826. [f. mod. L. *stylifer*, f. *stylus*; see -FEROUS.] *Bot.* and *Zool.* Bearing a style or styles.

Styliform (stəi·lifǭɹm), *a.* 1578. [ad. mod. L. *styliformis*, f. *stylus*; see -FORM.] *Anat.*, *Zool.*, *Min.* Shaped like a stylus.

Stylish (stəi·liʃ), *a.* 1797. [f. STYLE *sb.* + -ISH.] **1.** Of persons, their appearance or manners, also of dress, equipage, etc.: Noticeable for 'style' or conformity to the fashionable standard of elegance; showily fashionable. **2.** In occas. uses: Having 'style' (in various senses: see STYLE *sb.*) 1892.

2. A most patient and s. innings of 65. 1895. Hence **Sty·lish-ly** *adv.*, **-ness.**

Stylist (stəi·list). 1795. [f. STYLE *sb.* + -IST.] A writer who is skilled in or cultivates the art of literary style; a writer as characterized by his style.

[Addison] while notably distinguished, as a s., for ease,..combines with it the extreme of inexactness 1873.

Stylistic (stəili·stik), *a.* and *sb.* 1860. [f. STYLE *sb.* + -IST + -IC; after G. *stilistisch* adj., *stilistik* sb.] **A.** *adj.* Pertaining to literary style. **B.** *sb.* The science of literary style; the study of stylistic features. Also (more commonly) **Styli·stics.** 1882.

Stylite (stei·ləit). Also in Gr. form **stylites** (stəiləi·tīz). 1638. [ad. eccl. Gr. *στυλίτης*, f. *στῦλος* pillar; see -ITE.] *Eccl. Hist.* An ascetic who lived on the top of a pillar. Also *attrib.* or as *adj.*

Peter à Metra, a famous S., or Pillar-Monk 1638. Hence **Styli·tic** *a.* **Sty·litism**, the mode of life or the ascetic principles of the Stylites.

Stylize (stəi·ləiz), *v.* 1898. [f. STYLE *sb.* + -IZE, after G. *stilisiren*.] *trans.* To conform (an artistic representation) to the rules of a conventional style; to conventionalize. Chiefly in pa. pple.

Stylo (stəi·lo). 1890. Short for STYLOGRAPH or STYLOGRAPHIC (*pen*).

Stylo- (stəi·lo), bef. a vowel **styl-**, used as comb. form of Gr. *στῦλος* pillar in scientific words.

Styloglo·ssal [Gr. *γλῶσσα* tongue], *a.* pertaining to the styloid process and the tongue; *sb.* = *styloglossus*. ‖**Styloglo·ssus**, a muscle arising from the styloid process and inserted in the tongue. **Stylohy·al**, *a.* epithet of one of the bones of the hyoid arch, constituting in man the styloid process of the temporal bone; *sb.* this bone. **Stylohy·oid**, *a.* of or pertaining to the stylohyal and the hyoid bone; *sb.* the stylohyoid muscle, a muscle connecting the styloid process and the hyoid bone. ‖**Stylomandi·bular, Stylomaxi·llary**, *adjs.* used to designate a ligament which connects the styloid process and the lower jaw-bone. **Styloma·stoid**, *a.* common to the styloid and mastoid processes of the temporal bone. **Stylommato·phorous** [Gr. *ὀμματ*, *ὄμμα* eye, *-φόρος* bearing], *a.* belonging to the suborder *Stylommatophora* of pulmonate gasteropods (land-snails and slugs) which have eyes borne on the tips of a pair of retractile tentacles. ‖**Stylopo·dium**, *Bot.* the double fleshy disk from which the style of the *Umbelliferæ* arises. **Sty·lospore**, *Bot.* one of the naked spores in certain fungals, which are produced at the tips of short thread-like cells. ‖**Styloste·gium** [Gr. *στέγη* roof], **Stylote·gium** [Gr. *τέγος* roof], the inner corona enveloping the style in some asclepiads.

Stylobata (stəilǫ·bătă). 1563. [a. L., ad. Gr. *στυλοβάτης*, f. *στῦλος* pillar + *-βατης*, f. *βαίνειν* to walk.] *Arch.* = next.

Stylobate (stəi·lŏbēit). 1694. [ad. L. *stylobata*; see prec.] *Arch.* A continuous basement upon which a row of columns is supported.

Stylograph (stəi·lŏgraf). 1866. [f. mod. L. *stylus*, incorrect form of L. *stilus* STYLE + -GRAPH.] †**1.** Any drawing or writing made with a style. **2.** A stylographic pen. Also *s. pen.* 1882.

Stylographic (stəilŏgræ·fik), *a.* 1808. [f. as prec. + -GRAPHIC.] †**1.** Relating to stylography or writing with a style –1854. **2.** *S. pen*: a variety of fountain pen, having no nib, but a fine perforated writing-point fed with ink from the reservoir in the stem; in this point is fitted a fine needle, which when pushed back in the act of writing opens a valve so as to permit the flow of ink 1880.

Stylography (stəilǫ·grăfi). Now *rare* or *Obs.* 1840. [f. as prec. + -GRAPHY.] A method of writing, drawing, or engraving with a style.

Styloid (stəi·loid), *a.* 1709. [ad mod.L. *styloides*, a. Gr. *στυλοειδής* like a style, f. *στῦλος* pillar; see -OID.] *Anat.* and *Zool.* Resembling a style in shape; styliform. Applied chiefly to several slender pointed processes of bone, e. g. the spine that projects from the base of the temporal bone.

Stylolite (stəi·lŏləit). 1866. [f. Gr. *στῦλος* pillar + -LITE.] *Geol.* A cylindrical or columnar formation in some limestones, marls, etc. 'varying in length up to more than four inches, and in diameter to two or more inches'. Hence **Styloli·tic** *a.*

‖**Stylus** (stəi·lŏs). Also **stilus.** 1728. [a. L. *stylus*, incorrect form of *stilus*.] **1.** = STYLE *sb.* I. 1. 1807. **2.** The tracing-point applied to the record of a phonograph or gramophone 1875. **3.** The gnomon of a sun-dial 1796. **4.** *Bot.* = STYLE *sb.* I. 7. 1728. **5.** *Zool.* A style or stylet 1856.

Stymie (stəi·mi), *sb.* 1857. [Origin obsc.] *Golf.* An opponent's ball which lies on the putting green in a line between the ball of the player and the hole he is playing for, if the distance between the balls is not less than six inches; also, the occurrence of this; often in phr. *to lay a s.* Hence **Sty·mie** *v. trans.* to put (one's opponent or oneself) into the position of having to negotiate a s.; freq. *fig.*; also *intr.* (of a ball) to intervene as a s.

Stymphalian (stimfēi·liăn), *a.* 1653. [f. L. *Stymphalius* (f. *Stymphalus* or *-um*, a. Gr. *Στύμφαλος*) + -AN.] *Myth.* Of or belonging to Stymphalus, a district in Arcadia haunted by a species of odious birds of prey, the destruction of which was the sixth of the 'labours' of Hercules. So **Sty·mphalid** *a.* and *sb.* 1560.

Styphnate (sti·fnēt). 1857. [f. STYPHNIC + -ATE [1].] *Chem.* A salt of styphnic acid.

Styphnic (sti·fnik), *a.* 1850. [f. supposed Gr. **στυφνός* (a mistake for *στρυφνός*) astringent + -IC.] *Chem. S. acid*, a dibasic astringent acid obtained by the action of nitric acid on asafœtida and other gum resins. Also called *oxypicric acid.*

‖**Stypsis** (sti·psis). 1890. [Late L., a. Gr. *στύψις*, f. *στύφειν*.] *Med.* The application or use of styptics.

Styptic (sti·ptik), *a.* and *sb.* late ME. [ad. late L. *stypticus*, a. Gr. *στυπτικός*, f. *στύφειν* to contract.] **A.** *adj.* Having the power of contracting organic tissue; having an austere or acid taste; harsh or raw to the palate; having a binding effect on the stomach or bowels. **b.** Of a medicament, etc.: That arrests hæmorrhage. late ME. **B.** *sb.* A substance having the power of contracting organic tissue. late ME. So **Sty·ptical** *a.* 1528.

Stypticin (sti·ptisin). 1910. [f. STYPTIC + -IN.] The phthalate of cotarnine used as a hæmostatic and an analgesic. So **Styptol** (sti·ptǫl), the hydrochloride of cotarnine, similarly used 1908.

Stypticity (stipti·sĭti). late ME. [ad. med. L. *stypticitas*, f. *stypticus* STYPTIC.] Styptic quality; astringency.

Styracin (stəiə·răsin). 1838. [a. F. *styracine*, f. L. *styrac-*, STYRAX; see -IN, -INE.] *Chem.* A crystalline substance obtained from storax and balsam of Peru.

Styrax (stəiə·ræks). 1558. [a. L., a. Gr. *στύραξ* storax, storax-tree.] **1.** = STORAX 1. **2.** A styrax-tree 1832.

Comb.: **s.-tree**, a tree of the genus *Styrax*, esp. *S. officinalis*.

Styrian (sti·riăn), *a.* and *sb.* 1621. [f. *Styria* + -AN.] Of or belonging to, an inhabitant of, the province of Styria, formerly a crown-land and duchy of the Austrian empire.

Styrol (stəiə·rǫl). 1845. [f. STYRAX + -OL.] *Chem.* An oil obtained from storax and the resin of balsam of Peru; oil of storax.

Styrolene (stəiə·rŏlīn). 1881. [f. prec. + -ENE.] *Chem.* = prec.

Styrone (stəiə·roun). 1852. [f. STYRAX + -ONE.] *Chem.* An alcohol in crystalline form obtained from the decomposition of styracin; used as an antiseptic and a bleaching agent.

Styryl (stəiə·ril). 1852. [f. STYRAX + -YL.] *Chem.* The radical, C_9H_9, of styrone. Also *attrib.*, as in *s. alcohol* = STYRONE.

Stythe, styth (stəið, stəiþ). *dial.* 1708. [Origin obsc.] **1.** = CHOKE-DAMP. **2.** A suffocating smell 1823.

‖**Styx** (stiks). late ME. [L., a. Gr. *Στύξ* (*Στυγ-*) related to *στυγεῖν* to hate, *στυγνός* gloomy.] *Myth.* A river of the lower world or Hades, over which the shades of the departed were ferried by Charon, and by which the gods swore their most solemn oaths.

Suable (siū·ăb'l), *a.* Now chiefly *U.S.* 1623. [f. SUE *v.* + -ABLE.] Capable of being sued, liable to be sued; legally subject to civil process. Hence **Suabi·lity**, liability to be sued.

Suade (swēi·d), *v.* Now *rare* or *dial.* 1531. [Partly ad. L. *suadere*; partly by aphæresis from PERSUADE.] = PERSUADE *v.*

Suant (siū·ănt), *a.* Now *dial.* 1547. [a. AF. *sua(u)nt*, OF. *suiant*, *sivant*, pr. pple. of *sivre* to follow :—L. **sequere* for *sequi*.] Working or proceeding regularly, smoothly, or easily; even, smooth, regular. Also *advb.* Hence **Su·antly** *adv.* (now *dial.*) 1547.

Suasible (swēi·sĭb'l), *a. rare.* 1582. [ad. L. **suasibilis*; f. *suas-*, *suadere* to SUADE; see -IBLE.] Capable of being persuaded; that is easily persuaded.

Suasion (swēi·ʒən). late ME. [ad. L. *suasionem*, f. *suadere*.] **1.** The act or fact of exhorting or urging; persuasion. **2.** An instance of this. late ME.

1. *Moral s.*, persuasion exerted or acting through and upon the moral nature or sense.

Suasive (swēi·siv), *a.* and *sb.* 1601. [ad. L. **suasivus*, f. *suas-*; see SUASIBLE.] **A.** *adj.* Having or exercising the power of persuading or urging; consisting in or tending to suasion; occas. const. *of*, exhorting or urging to. **B.** *sb.* A suasive speech, motive, or influence 1670.

A. Thanks to the s. influence of British gold 1897. Hence **Sua·sive·ly** *adv.*, **-ness.**

Suasory (swēi·səri), *a.* Now *rare.* 1576. [ad. L. *suasorius*, f. *suas-*; see SUASIBLE and -ORY.] Tending to persuade; persuasive.

Suave (swēiv, swāv), *a.* 1560. [a. F. :— L. *suavis* sweet, agreeable :—**swādwis*, f. *swād-* (see SWEET *a.*).] **1.** Pleasing or agreeable to the senses or the mind; sweet. **2.** Of persons, their manner: Blandly polite or urbane; soothingly agreeable 1847. Hence **Sua·vely** *adv.*

Suaviloquence (sweivi·lŏkwĕns). *rare.* 1649. [ad. L. *suaviloquentia*, f. *suaviloquens*, f. *suavis* + *loquens*, *loqui* to speak.] Pleasing or agreeable speech or manner of speaking.

Suavity (swæ·vĭti, swēi·vĭti). 1450. [ad. L. *suavitas* (partly through F. *suavité*), f. *suavis* SUAVE; see -ITY [1].] †**1.** Sweetness or agreeableness to the senses –1661. †**b.** Sweetness (of sound, harmony, expression) –1821. **2.** Pleasurableness, agreeableness; *pl.* delights, amenities. Now only as coloured by sense 3. 1594. **3.** The quality or condition of being suave in manner or outward behaviour; bland agreeableness or urbanity 1815.

2. The common suavities of social life 1823. **3.** These words, delivered with a cutting s. DICKENS.

Sub (svb), *sb.* 1696. [Short for various subst. compounds of SUB-.] **1.** = SUBORDINATE. **b.** For various titles of subordinate officials, as *sub-editor*, *sub-lieutenant*, *sub-warden* 1837. **2.** = SUBALTERN *sb.* 2. 1756. **3.** = SUBSTITUTE; *U.S.* esp. of substitute printers 1830. **4.** = SUBSCRIPTION 1903. **5.** = SUBSIST (*money*): money in advance on account of wages due at the end of a certain period. *local.* 1866.

Sub (svb), *v.* 1879. [Short for various vbl. compounds of SUB-; or f. prec.] **1.** *intr.* To work as a printer's substitute. **2.** To pay or receive 'sub' 1886. **3.** = SUB-EDIT 1890.

‖**Sub** (svb). 1592. The L. prep. *sub* (with the ablative) 'under', in a few legal and other phrases, now or formerly in common use.

sub dio, under the open sky, in the open air. **sub forma pauperis** = *in forma pauperis* (see ‖IN). **sub hasta**, lit. 'under a spear', i. e. by auction. **sub Jove frigido**, under the chilly sky, in the open air. **sub judice**, lit. 'under a judge'; under the consideration of a judge or court; undecided, still under consideration. **sub lite**, in dispute. **sub modo**, under certain conditions, with a qualification, within limits. **sub rosa**, 'under the rose' (see ROSE *sb.* II), in secret, secretly. **sub sigillo**, under the seal (of confession); in confidence, in secret. **sub silentio**, in silence, without remark being made. **sub voce**, under the word (so-and-so); abbrev. s. v.

Sub- (svb, səb) *prefix*, repr. L. *sub-* = the prep. *sub* under, close to, up to, towards, used in composition with various meanings.

The *b* of L. *sub-* remained unchanged when it preceded a radical beginning with *s*, *t*, or *v*; before *m* and *r* it was frequently assimilated (see e. g. SUMMON, SURROGATE), and before *c*, *f*, *g*, and *p* it was almost invariably assimilated (see e. g. SUCCEED, SUFFER, SUGGEST, SUPPOSE). A by-form *subs-* was normally reduced to *sus-* in certain compounds with words having initial *c*, *p*, *t* (see SUSCEPTION, SUSPEND, SUSTAIN); and before *sp-* the prefix becomes *su-* (see SUSPECT, SUSPICION).

The original force of the prefix is either entirely lost sight of or to a great extent obscured in many words derived from old L. compounds, such as *subject*, *suborn*, *subscription*, *subserve*, *subsist*, *substance*. As a living prefix in English it bears a full meaning of its own and has become capable of being prefixed to words of native English or any other origin.

Under, underneath, below, at the bottom (of). **1–4.** Forming adjs. in which *sub-* is in prepositional relation to the sb. implied in the second element, as in L.

subaquaneus = that is *sub aqua* under water, *subterraneus* = that is *sub terra*, SUBTERRANEOUS.

a. Compounds of a general character (mainly nonce-words), and miscellaneous scientific terms. **Subae·rial,** taking place, existing, operating, or formed in the open air or on the earth's surface. **Suba·stral,** situated beneath the stars, mundane, terrestrial. **Su·bcarboni·ferous,** *Geol.* designating the mountain-limestone formation of the carboniferous series or that lying beneath the millstone grit, lower carboniferous. **Subgla·cial,** existing or taking place under the ice. **Submu·ndane,** existing beneath the world. **Subpe·ctoral,** emanating from the depths of the chest. **Subse·nsible,** below or deeper than the range of the senses; so **Subse·nsual, Subse·nsuous. Subso·lar,** *Meteorol.* directly underneath the sun, having the sun in the zenith. **Subtarta·rean,** below or living under Tartarus. **Su·bterrane** (now *rare*) **†Subterra·neal,** = SUBTERRANEAN; also as *sb.*

b. *Anat.* (*Path., Surg.*) and *Zool.* = Situated or occurring under or beneath (occas. behind) the part or organ denoted by the radical element, or lying on the ventral side of it or ventrally with respect to it; as in (late) L. *subocularis.*

In most of these compounds the meaning is readily inferred from that of the prefix and of the second element; as *subabdo·minal* (= situated or occurring under, below, or beneath the abdomen), *-ara·chnoid* (the arachnoid membrane), *-clavi·cular, -conjuncti·val* (the conjunctiva), *-cra·nial, -cuti·cular, -du·ral* (the dura mater), *-epide·rmal, -ic, -epithe·lial, -glo·ttic* (the glottis), *-intesti·nal, -lo·bular* (a lobule of the liver), *-me·ntal* (the chin), *-mu·scular, -notocho·rdal, -o·cular, -pe·ctoral, -peritone·al, -pi·al* (the pia mater), *-pleu·ral, -pu·bic, -spi·nal, -spi·nous, -tenta·cular* (the tentacles or tentacular canal), *-u·ngual, -vagi·nal, -ve·rtebral, -zo·nal* (the zona pellucida of an ovum). (*b*) in derived advs.; e.g. *subdu·rally, subperio·steally.*

c. *Bot.* in the same sense as **b**; e.g. *subpe·tiolar.*

d. *Anat.* In adj. compounds in L. form, designating parts of the body, used absol. by ellipsis of sb. (e.g. *musculus* muscle, *membrana* membrane). **‖Su·bancone·us,** a small muscle arising from the triceps and humerus above the elbow-joint and inserted in the posterior ligament of the elbow. **‖Subcrure·us,** a small band of muscular fibres extending from the anterior surface of the femur to the synovial membrane of the knee-joint.

e. With sbs. forming attrib. compounds. **Subatla·ntic,** under the Atlantic. **Sub-tu·rbary,** found under turf-ground.

f. With sbs. forming sbs. designating a part, organ, or substance lying under the part denoted by the radical element. **Subli·ngua,** in some animals, a process consisting of a fold of mucous membrane under the tongue. **Subme·ntum,** *Ent.* the basal part of the labium. **Subumbre·lla,** *Zool.* the internal ventral or oral disk of a hydrozoan; the concave muscular layer beneath the umbrella of a jelly-fish.

g. Forming vbs., as in L. *subjugare* to SUBJUGATE.

2. With adverbial force (= underneath, below, down, low, lower), prefixed to adjs., vbs., and pples. (and less freq. to sbs.), as in *subadja·cent* adj.; *subaera·ted, -concea·led* pples.; *subi·rrigate* vb. **Su·blinea·tion,** underlining. **Subna·scent** *a.* growing under or up from beneath. **Subnota·tion** = RESCRIPT 2.

b. Hence = in or into subjection, as in *subicere* to SUBJECT.

3. Prefixed to sbs. with adjectival force = lying, existing, occurring below or underneath, under-(hence, by implication) underground; e.g. *sub-armour; sub-current, -deposit; sub-note, -text; sub-crossing, -railway*; in designations of architectural features, indicating a secondary member, feature, chamber, etc. placed under one of the same kind, e.g. *sub-basement, -member, -shaft*; so *subtrench.* Also SUB-ARCH, etc. (Stress even, or on the prefix.)

b. *Anat.* (*a*) Designating the lowest or basal part of the organ denoted by the second element; e.g. *subface, subilium.* (*b*) Denoting a part concealed or encroached upon; e.g. *subfissure, subgyre.*

c. *Agric.* Short for *subsoil-*, as *sub-pulverizer.*

4. *Mus.* With adj. force combining with sbs. to form terms designating: (*a*) an interval of so much below a given note; e.g. *subdiapente*; (*b*) a note or an organ-stop an octave below that denoted by the original sb.; e.g. SUBOCTAVE; *sub-bass, -diapason*; (*c*) a note lying the same distance below the tonic as the note designated by the radical sb. is above it; e.g. SUBDOMINANT, SUBMEDIANT.

5–9. Subordinate, subsidiary, secondary; subordinately, subsidiarily, secondarily. (Stress on the prefix.) **5.** Having a subordinate or inferior position; of inferior or minor importance or size; subsidiary, secondary. **a.** of persons; e.g. *sub-advocate, -substitute.* **b.** of material objects; e.g. *sub-affluent, -constellation, -piston.* **c.** of something immaterial, a quality, state, or action; e.g. *sub-appearance, -cause, -commission, -element, -flavour, -plot, -type.*

6. With names of officials, etc., forming titles designating one immediately subordinate to the chief official; e.g. *sub-abbot, -captain, -collector, -commissioner, -delegate, -governor, -king, -minister, -preceptor, -prefect, -rector, -vicar, -warden.* **Su·b-al·moner,** a subordinate almoner, one of the officials of the Royal Almonry. **Su·bma·rshal,** a deputy or under-marshal, an official in the Marshalsea acting as the knight-marshal's deputy (*Obs.* exc. *Hist.*). (*b*) in derived adjs.; e.g. *subsecretarial* pertaining to a sub-secretary. **b.** In the designation of corresponding offices or functions; e.g. *sub-administration, -inspectorship.*

7. Compounded with sbs., to express division into parts, sections, or branches. **a.** Of material objects; e.g. *sub-cavity*, one of the smaller cavities into which a cavity is divided. **Su·b-atom,** *Chem.* a constituent part of an atom; hence **Subato·mic** *a.* **b.** Of a body or assembly of people, as in SUBCOMMITTEE, or of a division of animals or plants, as in SUBGENUS; e.g. *subdenomination, -group, -tribe.* (*b*) in derived adjs.; e.g. *subsynodical* pertaining to a sub-synod. **c.** Of a region or an interval of time, as in *sub-age* a division of an age, *-zone*, SUB-DISTRICT. **d.** = branch-; e.g. *sub-bureau* a bureau depending on the principal bureau, *sub-office*, a branch office.

8. With advb. force, combined with adjs. and vbs. = in a subordinate or secondary manner or capacity, by subsidiary means.

9. (*a*) On the analogy of SUBDIVIDE and SUBDIVISION, *sub-* is used to denote a further division or distinction; e.g. *sub-classify; sub-articulation*; (*b*) on the analogy of SUBCONTRACT *sb.* and *v.*, SUBLET, to denote a second or further action or process of the same kind as that denoted by the radical; e.g. *subcolonize* to colonize from a colony, *sub-infer* to draw as a further inference, *sub-rent* to rent from one who himself rents *sub-purchaser*, one who purchases from a previous purchaser; *sub-secession* a secession from a body that has seceded; *subtenure*, the subfeudation of land.

10. *Math.* Compounded with adjs. expressing ratio, *sub-* denotes a ratio the opposite of that expressed by the radical element, as in late L. *submultiplus* SUBMULTIPLE; e.g. *subdecuple* the ratio 1 : 10, *subtriple.* Analogously, in SUBDUPLICATE, etc., the prefix is employed to express the ratio of the square (etc.) roots of quantities; e.g. *subtriplicate* (of the cube roots of the quantities).

11–18. Next below, near or close (to); subsequent (to). (As a living prefix *sub-* is restricted in this sense to prepositional uses; the advb. use is seen in SUBSEQUENT.) **11.** Near to (a particular region or point, as in L. *suburbanus* SUBURBAN; e.g. *suba·pical, -basal, -caudal, -dorsal, -lateral, -littoral, -marginal.*

12. *Geog.* and *Geol.* **a.** Lying about the base of or subjacent to mountains designated by the second element, hence, of less height than mountains of similar height to these, characteristic of regions of such altitude; e.g. *sub-Andean, -Etnean, -Himalayan.* **Suba·pennine,** applied to a series of strata of Pliocene age, such as are characteristic of the flanks of the Apennines in Italy; belonging to or characteristic of these strata. **b.** Denoting a region or zone adjacent to or on the borders of that designated by the second element; e.g. *subantarctic, -frigid, -torrid.*

13. *Mus.* Designating a note next to or next below some principal note; e.g. SUBTONIC. (Cf. 4.) **Subse·mitone,** the leading note of a scale.

14. Combined with adjs. with the sense 'of lower condition or degree (or size) than' that denoted by the original adj.; e.g. *sub-angelical, -elementary, -judicial, -regal.*

15. *Zool.* In names of divisions of animals regarded as having only imperfectly developed the characteristics denoted by the word to which *sub-* is prefixed, as *Subungulata*, etc.; also, in derivatives; e.g. *subostracean*, a mollusc of the family *Subostracea.*

16. In craniometry, forming adjs. designating a type of skull having an index next below that of the type denoted by the second element; e.g. *subbrachycephalic* (hence *-cephaly*).

17. In the names of certain sectaries, = after, consequent upon: opp. to SUPRA- e.g. SUBLAPSARIAN.

18. In designations of periods immediately 'below' or posterior to a particular period. **Subaposto·lic,** belonging to or characteristic of the period in the history of the Church immediately following that of the apostles.

19–23. Incomplete(ly), imperfect(ly), partial(ly). **With adverbial meaning.* **19.** Prefixed to adjs. or pples. of a general character; e.g. *subanalogous* somewhat similar, *subaudible* imperfectly, slightly, or barely audible, *subobscure, subtypical.* (The force of *sub-* may vary contextually from 'only slightly' to 'not quite, all but'.)

20. In techn. use, chiefly *Nat. Hist.* **a.** With adjs. of colour; e.g. *sub-pale, -red, -vivid.* **b.** With adjs. denoting surface texture, contour, or marking, substance, consistency, composition, taste, odour; e.g. *subacrid, -astringent, -cartilaginous, -coriaceous, -fossil, -granular, -spinous, -stony, -villose, -villous,* etc. **c.** With adjs. expressing shape, conformation, or physical habit; e.g. *sub-acuminate, -angular, -arborescent, -arcuate, -equal, -globular, -globose, -hooked, -lunate, -orbicular, -oval, -ovate, -ovoid, -ramose, -rotund, -sessile.* **d.** With adjs. denoting position, as in SUBCENTRAL, SUBLATERAL; e.g. *subcrect, -internal, -terminal.* **e.** With adjs. designating geometrical forms; e.g. *subcylindric(al, -pentagonal* (= five-sided but not forming a regular pentagon), *-oblong, -spherical, -triangular,* etc. **f.** With adjs. denoting a numerical arrangement or conformation; e.g. *subbifid* imperfectly bifid, *-bipinnate, -dichotomous* somewhat divided or branched. **g.** *Med.* e.g. *subacute, subchronic* not entirely chronic, more chronic than acute; **subconti·nued,** almost continuous, remittent; *subfebrile.* **h.** Forming advs. corresponding to adjs. of any of the above classes, e.g. *subacutely.*

21. With vbs., as in L. *subaccusare* to accuse somewhat; e.g. *sub-blush, -cachinnate, -indicate, understand.* **Subo·dorate** (*rare*) to smell or scent out.

***With adjectival meaning.* **22.** With sbs. denoting action or condition, in the sense partial, incomplete, 'slight'; e.g. *sub-animation, -saturation*; *Med.* often = 'less than the normal, mild, gentle'; e.g. *sub-delirium, -purgation*; also occas. with sbs. denoting material objects, e.g. *sub-relief.* **Subima·go,** *Entom.* in Ephemeridæ, the stage immediately preceding the imago; the insect at this stage. **Subluxa·tion,** a partial dislocation, a sprain.

23. *Chem.* In names of compounds *sub-* indicates that the ingredient of the compound denoted by the term to which it is prefixed is in a relatively small proportion, or is less than in the normal compounds of that name; e.g. *subacetate*, an acetate in which there are fewer equivalents of the acid radical than in the normal acetate, a basic acetate, *subsalt* a basic salt.

24. Secretly, covertly, as in L. *subornare* to SUBORN. **†Subai·d** *v.* (*rare*), to give secret aid to. **†Subingre·ssion,** subtle or unobserved entrance. **Su·bintrodu·ce** *v.* to introduce in a secret or subtle manner. **Subtru·de,** to thrust itself in stealthily.

25. From below, up, (hence) away; e.g. SUCCOUR, SUGGEST, SUSPICION, etc. **b.** Hence *sub-* implies taking up so as to include, as in SUBSUME.

26. In place of another, as in L. *substituere* to SUBSTITUTE.

27. In addition, by way of or as an addition, after L. *subjungere* to SUBJOIN; e.g. *subinsert* vb.

Subacid (sʊbæ·sid), *a.* and *sb.* 1669. [ad. L. *subacidus*; see SUB- 20 b and ACID.] **A.** *adj.* **1.** Somewhat or moderately acid. **b.** *Chem.* Containing less than the normal proportion of acid 1808. **2.** Of character, speech, etc.: Somewhat acid or tart; verging on acidity or tartness 1765.

2. An excellent temper, with a slight degree of s. humour SCOTT.

B. *sb.* **1.** Subacid quality or flavour 1838. **2.** A subacid substance 1828.

1. The s. of the strawberry 1884. Hence **Subaci·dity.**

†Suba·ct, *v.* 1614. [f. L. *subact-*, *subigere*, f. *sub-* SUB- 2, 25 + *agere* to bring.] **1.** *trans.* To work up, as in cultivating the ground, kneading, the process of digestion, etc. –1822. **2.** To bring into subjection; to subdue –1680. So **†Suba·ction,** the action of working up, reducing, or kneading –1822.

Su·b-a:gent. 1683. [SUB- 6.] A subordinate agent; the agent of an agent; *spec.* in *U.S. Law.* Hence **Su·b-a:gency,** the position, condition, or residence of a s.

‖Subah (sū·ba). *Anglo-Ind.* 1753. [Urdū = Arab *çūbah*.] **1.** A province of the Mogul empire. **2.** = next 1753. Hence **Su·bahship** = sense 1. 1753.

‖Subahdar (sūbadā·ɹ). *Anglo-Ind.* 1698. [Urdū *çūbahdār*, f. prec. + Pers. *dār* possessor, master.] **1.** A governor of a subah or province. **2.** The chief native officer of a company of sepoys 1747.

attrib.: **s.-major,** the native commandant of a regiment of sepoys. Hence **Subahdary** (sūbadā·ri), subahship.

Suba·lpine, *a.* 1656. [ad. L. *subalpinus*; see SUB- 12 and ALPINE.] **1.** Belonging to regions lying about the foot of the Alps. **2.** Partly alpine in character or formation; pertaining to or characteristic of elevations next below that called *alpine*; belonging to the higher slopes of mountains (of an altitude of about 4,000 to 5,500 feet) 1833.

Subaltern (sʊ·băltəɹn, sʊbǭ·ltəɹn), *a.* and *sb.* 1581. [ad. late L. *subalternus*; see SUB- 11–18, ALTERN *a.*] **A.** *adj.* **†1.** Succeeding in turn (*rare*) –1762. **b.** Logic. *S. genus* (or *species*): a genus that is at the same time a species of a higher genus 1654. **2.** Of inferior status, quality, or importance 1581. **3.** *S. officer*: an officer of junior rank in the army, i.e. below that of captain. Hence *s. rank*, etc. 1688. **4.** Of a vassal: Holding of one who is himself a vassal. Hence of a feu or right. 1681. **5.** *Logic.* Of a proposition: Particular, in relation to a universal of the same quality 1656.

1. b. Iron-ore is a s. species or genus, being both the genus of magnet, and a species of mineral 1826. **2.** All such s. actors as played between the acts 1734. Fighting his way through every s. degree of his profession 1817. 5. *S. opposition*, opposition between a universal and a particular of the same quality.

B. *sb.* 1. A person (or †thing) of inferior rank or status; a subordinate 1605. 2. A subaltern officer in the army 1690. 3. *Logic.* A subaltern proposition 1826.

Subalternate (sʌbǫltə·nĕt), *a.* (*sb.*) late ME. [ad. late L. *subalternatus*, *subalternare*; see -ATE².] †1. Subordinate, inferior –1874. †2. [f. SUB- 20 d and ALTERNATE *a.*] *Nat. Hist.* Alternate, but with a tendency to become opposite 1829.

1. The several kinds of s. Species of Plants 1704.

B. *sb. Logic.* A particular proposition 1826.

Subalternation (sʌ·bǫltəɹnē¹·ʃən). 1597. [ad. med.L. *subalternatio*, *-onem*.] †1. Subordination. †2. Succession by turn –1627. 3. *Logic.* The relation between a universal and a particular of the same quality; also, an immediate inference from a universal to a particular under it 1650.

Subalternity (sʌbǫltə·ɹnĭti). 1620. [f. SUBALTERN + -ITY.] Subordinate position.

Subaqua·tic, *a.* 1789. 1. [SUB- 1 a.] = next 1. Also, pertaining to plants growing under water. 2. [SUB- 20 c.] *Zool.* and *Bot.* Partly aquatic 1844.

Subaqueous (sʌbē¹·kwiəs), *a.* 1677. [SUB- 1 a.] 1. Existing, formed, or constructed under water. b. Performed or taking place under water; adapted for use under water 1774. 2. Reflected as if in depths of water 1798.

1. Vast s. precipices 1774. b. *Sub-aqueous Helmet*, a diver's head-dress, supplied with air by pump from above 1875.

Su·b-arch. 1835. [SUB- 3, 5 b.] *Arch.* A subsidiary or secondary arch; one of two or more arches grouped in a larger arch; the lowest member in an arch of two or more 'orders'.

Suba·rctic, *a.* (*sb.*) 1854. [SUB- 12 b.] Nearly arctic; somewhat south of the arctic circle or regions; belonging to such a region. Also *sb.*, *pl.*, subarctic regions.

Su·barcua·tion. 1845. [SUB- 2.] *Arch.* The construction of two or more subordinate arches under a main arch; the system of arches so constructed. Hence **Suba·rcuated** *a.* having two or more such arches under a main arch.

Subarrhation (sʌbarē¹·ʃən). 1623. [ad. med.L. *subarr(h)ationem*, f. *subarr(h)are*, f. *sub-* SUB- 1 g + *arr(h)a* pledge.] An ancient form of betrothal in which pledges in the form of money, rings, etc. were bestowed by the man upon the woman.

‖ **Subashi** (sūbā·ʃi). 1599. [Turk. *sūbāshī* and *çūbāshī*, f. *çū* water + *bāsh* head, chief.] A Turkish official in command of a district or village; a 'police magistrate under the timariot system' (Redhouse).

Subaudition (sʌbǫdi·ʃən). 1798. [ad. L. *subauditionem*, f. *subaudire*, f. *sub-* SUB- 24 + *audire* to hear.] Chiefly *Gram.* The act of mentally supplying something that is not expressed; something that is mentally supplied or understood; implied or understood meaning.

'Policeman' has no evil s. 1859.

‖ **Subauditur** (sʌbǫdəi·tʊ̆ɹ). 1803. [L., = 'it is understood'.] = prec. Phr. *In a s.*: by implication.

Suba·xillary, *a.* (*sb.*) 1769. [SUB- 1 b, c.] 1. *Zool.* Situated beneath the axilla; *Ornith.* = AXILLARY. 2. *Bot.* Beneath the axil or the angle made by a branch with the stem or a leaf with the branch 1802.

S·ub-base. 1826. 1. [SUB- 3.] a. *Arch.* The lowest part of a base which is divided horizontally. b. A base placed under the bottom of a machine or other apparatus to raise it higher from the ground 1904. 2. [SUB- 5 b.] A secondary base 1903.

Subbra·chial, *a.* 1836. [ad. mod.L. *subbrachialis*; see SUB- 1 b and BRACHIAL.] 1. *Ichth.* Situated under or near the pectoral fins; (of a fish) having the ventral fins so situated. 2. Under the pectoral muscles 1896. 3. Beneath the brachium (in cerebral anatomy) 1913. So **Subbra·chian** *a.* = sense 1; *sb.* a s. fish; one of the *Subbrachiati*.

Subcele·stial, *a.* and *sb.* 1561. [SUB- 1 a.] A. *adj.* Situate or existing beneath or below the heavens; chiefly *transf.* terrestrial, mundane, sublunary. B *sb.* A subcelestial being 1652.

Subce·ntral, *a.* 1822. 1. [SUB- 11, 20 d.] Nearly or not quite central; near or close to the centre. 2. [SUB- 1 a.] Being under the centre 1828. 3. [SUB- 1 b.] *Anat.* Beneath the central sulcus of the brain; beneath the centrum of a vertebra 1882.

Su·bcha·nter. 1515. [f. SUB- 6 + CHANTER.] A precentor's deputy, succentor; now, a vicar-choral or lay-clerk of a cathedral, who assists in chanting the litany.

Subche·late, *a.* 1852. [SUB- 20 c.] Imperfectly chelate.

Subclass (sʌ·bklɑs). 1819. [SUB- 7 b.] A subdivision of a class; *Nat. Hist.* a group of orders ranking next to a class. So **Su·bclass** *v. trans.* to place in a s.

†‖ **Subcla·via.** 1733. [mod.L. *subclavia* (sc. *arteria*), fem. of SUBCLAVIUS.] *Anat.* The subclavian artery –1771.

Subclavian (sʌbklē¹·viăn), *a.* and *sb.* 1646. [f. mod.L. SUBCLAVIUS + -AN.] A. *adj.* Lying or extending under the clavicle 1681. b. Pertaining to the s. artery, vein, or muscle 1646.

S. artery, the principal artery of the root of the neck, being the main trunk of the arterial system of the upper extremity. *S. muscle* = SUBCLAVIUS. *S. vein*, the continuation of the axillary vein from the first rib until it joins the internal jugular vein.

B. *sb.* A s. vessel, nerve, or muscle 1719.

‖ **Subclavius** (sʌbklē¹·viʊ̆s). 1704. [mod.L. *subclavius* (sc. *musculus*), f. *sub-* SUB- 16 + *clavis* key.] *Anat.* In full *s. muscle*: A small muscle extending from the first rib to the clavicle.

Su·bcommi:ttee. 1610. [SUB- 7 b.] A committee formed from and acting under a main committee; a part of a committee appointed for special purposes.

Subconscious (sʌbkǫ·nʃəs), *a.* 1832. [SUB- 19.] 1. *Psych.* a. Partially or imperfectly conscious; belonging to a class of phenomena resembling those of consciousness but not clearly perceived or recognized. b. Belonging to that portion of the mental field the processes of which are outside the range of attention. 2. Partly or imperfectly aware 1864.

1. *transf.* A sketch of himself..has a s. humour one would not have suspected 1899. Hence **Subco·nscious-ly** *adv.*, **-ness.**

Sub-co·nstable. Now *Hist.* 1512. [SUB- 6.] An under-constable, *esp.* in the Royal Irish Constabulary.

Su·bco:ntinent. 1863. [SUB- 5 b.] A land mass of great extent, but smaller than those usu. called continents; a large section of a continent having a certain geographical or political independence; in recent use, *spec.* South Africa.

Su·bco:ntract, *sb.* 1817. [SUB- 9.] A contract, or one of several contracts, for carrying out a previous contract or a part of it.

Subcontra·ct, *v.* 1605. [SUB- 9.] †1. *pass.* To be betrothed for the second time. SHAKS. 2. *intr.* To make a subcontract 1842. 3. *trans.* To make a subcontract for 1898. Hence **Subcontra·ctor**, one who enters into a subcontract.

Su:bcontrari·ety. 1697. [f. next.] *Logic.* The relation existing between subcontrary propositions.

Subco·ntrary, *a.* and *sb.* 1603. [ad. late L. *subcontrarius*, tr. late Gr. ὑπεναντίος; see SUB- 19 and CONTRARY *a.*] A. *adj.* 1. Somewhat or partially contrary. 2. *Logic.* Applied to particular propositions (or the relation of opposition between them) agreeing in quantity but differing in quality 1656. 3. *Geom.* a. Applied to the relative position of two similar triangles having a common angle at the vertex and their bases not parallel, so that the basal angles are equal but on contrary sides 1704. b. Applied to any circular section of a quadric cone in relation to the base or to another circular section not parallel to it 1706. B. *sb.* 1. *Logic.* A s. proposition 1697. 2. *Geom.* A s. section of a cone 1842.

Subco·rtical, *a.* 1815. [SUB- 1 a.] 1. Lying, situated, or formed under the bark of a tree; (of insects) living or feeding under bark. 2. Situated under or pertaining to the region underlying (*a*) the cortex of a sponge, (*b*) the cortex of the brain 1887.

Subco·stal, *a.* and *sb.* 1733. [ad. mod.L. *subcostalis*; see SUB- 1 b and COSTAL.] A. *adj.* 1. *Anat.* Situated below a rib or beneath the ribs; lying on the under side of a rib, as a groove for an artery 1872. 2. *Entom.* Situated behind or near the costal vein or nervure of an insect's wing 1826. B. *sb.* A s. muscle (usu. in L. form *subcostalis*); a s. artery or nervure 1733.

Subcutaneous (sʌbkiutē¹·niəs), *a.* 1651. [f. late L. *subcutaneus*, f. *sub-* SUB- 1 b + *cutis* skin + *-aneus*; see -EOUS.] 1. Lying or situated under the skin 1656. 2. Living under the skin 1664. 3. Of operations, etc.: Performed or taking place under the skin; characterized by application of a remedy beneath the skin; hence, of instruments by which such operations are performed or remedies administered; hypodermic 1651.

3. The s. administration of anti-toxic serum 1899. Hence **Subcuta·neously** *adv.*

Subdeacon (sʌbdī·kən). ME. [a. AF., OF. *soudiakene*, *subdiakne*, f. *sou(s)-*, *sub-* (see SUB- 6) + *diakne* DEACON *sb.*, after eccl. L. *subdiaconus*, eccl. Gr. ὑποδιάκονος.] *Eccl.* 1. The name of the order of ministers in the Christian church next below that of deacon.

The duty of subdeacons is to assist in the celebration of the Eucharist by preparing the sacred vessels and (in the Western Church) by reading the epistle. The subdiaconate does not exist in the Church of England.

2. The cleric (orig. one in subdeacon's orders) or clerk who acts as assistant next below the deacon at a solemn celebration of the Eucharist; the 'epistoler' 1440. Hence **Subdea·conate**, †**-dea·conry**, **-dea·conship** = SUBDIACONATE.

Subdean (sʌbdī·n). late ME. [a. AF. **sodean*, **subdene* = OF. *sou(z) deien*, f. *sou(s)-*, *sub-* (see SUB- 6) + *deien* DEAN¹, after med.L. *subdecanus*.] An official immediately below a dean in rank, and acting as his deputy. Hence **Subdea·nery**, the office, position, or residence of a s.

Subdeca·nal, *a. rare.* 1846. [f. med.L. *subdecanus* SUBDEAN + -AL 1.] Of or pertaining to a subdean or subdeanery.

Subdia·conate. 1725. [ad. med.L. *subdiaconatus*.] The office or rank of subdeacon.

Su·bdi:alect. 1642. [SUB- 7.] A subordinate dialect; a division of a dialect.

Subdisju·nctive, *a.* and *sb.* 1656. [SUB- 19.] *Logic* and *Gram.* A. *adj.* Partly disjunctive. B. *sb.* A subdisjunctive proposition or word 1656.

In English we use the conjunction *or* indifferently as a disjunctive or s.; that is, we say 'Alexander *or* Paris', whether Alexander and Paris be two different persons, or only two different names for the same person 1818.

Subdisti·nction. 1636. [In sense 1, ad. late L. *subdistinctio*, f. *subdistinguere* to put a comma or one of the lesser stops. In senses 2 and 3, f. SUB- 5 c and 7 b + DISTINCTION.] †1. A comma or semicolon –1825. 2. A subordinate distinction 1655.

†**Subdisti·nguish**, *v.* 1620. [SUB- 9.] *trans.* To distinguish into subordinate kinds, classes, species, etc. –1789.

Su·b-di:strict. 1816. [SUB- 7 c.] A division or subdivision of a district.

Subdivide (sʌbdivəi·d), *v.* late ME. [ad. late L. *subdividere*; see SUB- 9 and DIVIDE *v.*] 1. *trans.* To divide (a part of a divided whole); to divide again after a first division. 2. *intr.* To break up into subdivisions 1597.

1. The army formed in two grand divisions, each of which was subdivided into a battle and two wings 1823. The use of machinery tends still further to s. labour 1868. Hence **Subdivi·der**, one who subdivides; *spec.* one who settles on a portion of an estate. **Subdivi·sible** *a.*

Subdivision (sʌbdivi·ʒən). 1553. [ad. late L. *subdivisio*, *-onem*, f. *subdivis-*, *subdividere*.] 1. The act or process of subdividing, or the fact of being subdivided 1599. b. An instance of this 1577. 2. One of the parts into which a whole is subdivided; part of a part; a section resulting from a further division; *Nat. Hist.* a subordinate division of a group 1553. b. *Mil.* The half of a division. Also, at various times, the half of a company; in the artillery, a gun with its waggons (now called SUBSECTION). 1625.

1. The increase of wealth had produced its natural effect, the s. of labour MACAULAY. 2. The Gnosticks and the severall subdivisions of them 1662. Hence **Subdivi·sional** *a.* of the nature of s.; pertaining to s., or a s.; consisting of a s.

Subdivi·sive, *a.* 1838. [f. L. *subdivis-*, *subdividere* + -IVE.] Resulting from subdivision.

Subdolous (sɒ·bdŏləs), *a.* Now *rare.* 1588. [f. L. *subdolus* (f. *sub-* SUB- 19 + *dolus* cunning) + -OUS.] Crafty, cunning, sly. Hence **Su·bdolous·ly** *adv.*, **-ness.**

Subdo·minant, *sb.* 1793. [SUB- 14.] *Mus.* The note next below the dominant of a scale; the fourth note in ascending and the fifth in descending a scale.

Subdo·minant, *a.* 1826. [SUB- 14.] Less than dominant, not quite dominant.

Subduable (sŏbdiū·ăb'l), *a.* *rare.* 1611. [f. SUBDUE *v.* + -ABLE.] That may be subdued.

Subdual (sŏbdiū·ăl). 1675. [f. SUBDUE *v.* + -AL.] The act of subduing or state of being subdued; subjection.

†**Subdu·ce**, *v.* 1542. [ad. L. *subducere*, f. *sub-* SUB- 25 + *ducere* to lead, bring.] 1. *trans.* To take away, withdraw -1761. b. *refl.* (occas. *intr.*) To withdraw oneself or itself *from*; to secede -1660. 2. To subtract, as a mathematical operation -1676.

Subduct (sŏbdɒ·kt), *v.* Now *rare.* 1571. [f. L. *subduct-*, *subducere* to SUBDUCE.] 1. *trans.* To take away from its place or position, withdraw from use, consideration, influence, etc. 1614. 2. To take away (a quantity) *from*, †*out of* another; to subtract, deduct 1571. †b. *intr.* To take something away *from* -1798. 3. To take away or remove surreptitiously or fraudulently. Also *absol.* 1758. 4. To draw up 1837.

2. When we..s. the vapour pressure from the barometric height 1881. b. Nature..from my side subducting, took perhaps More then enough MILT. 3. Purchased with money subducted from the shop JOHNSON.

Subduction (sŏbdɒ·kʃən). Now *rare.* 1579. [ad. L. *subductio, -onem*, f. *subducere* to SUBDUCE.] 1. The action of subducting; subtraction, withdrawal. 2. The action of subduing or fact of being subdued 1670.

Subdue (sŏbdiū·), *v.* [Late ME. *sodewe, subdewe*, repr. AF. **soduer*, **su(b)duer* = OF *so(u)duire* (used with the meanings of L. *seducere*) to deceive, seduce :—L. *subducere*. Presumably the AF. form took over the sense of 'subdue' from L. *subdere*.] 1. *trans.* To conquer (an army, an enemy, a country or its inhabitants) in fight and bring them into subjection. †b. To overcome (a person) by physical strength or violence -1604. 2. To bring (a person) into mental, moral, or spiritual subjection; to render (a person or animal) submissive; to prevail over, get the better of. Const. *to* (that which exercises control, the control exercised). 1509. b. With a person's body, soul, mind, actions, etc. as obj. 1520. †c. To bring *to* a low state, reduce. SHAKS. 3. To bring (land) under cultivation 1535. †4. In medical use: To reduce, allay -1829. 5. To reduce the intensity, force, or vividness of (sound, colour, light); to make less prominent or salient 1800.

1. Iohn of Gaunt, Which did s. the greatest part of Spaine SHAKS. b. If he do resist S. him, at his perill SHAKS. 2. Swords Conquer some, but Words s. all men PRIOR. b. My heart and hands thou hast at once subdu'd SHAKS. c. *Lear* III. iv. 72. 5. The warm colours of distance, even the most glowing, are subdued by the air RUSKIN. Hence **Subdue·d** *ppl. a.* reduced to subjection, overcome; reduced in intensity, force, or vividness; toned down. **Subdue·ment** (*rare*), subdual. **Subdu·er**, one who or that which subdues.

Subduple (sɒbdiū·p'l, sɒ·bdiup'l), *a.* 1598. [ad. late L. *subduplus*; see SUB- 10 and DUPLE *a.*] *Math.* That is half of a quantity or number; denoting a proportion of one to two; (of a ratio) of which the antecedent is half the consequent.

Subdu·plicate, *a.* 1656. [SUB- 10.] *Math.* Of a ratio or proportion: Being that of the square roots of the quantities; thus, 2 : 3 is the subduplicate ratio of 4 : 9.

Sub-e·dit, *v.* 1862. [Back-formation from next.] *trans.* To edit (a paper, periodical, etc.) under, to prepare (copy) for, the supervision of a chief editor.

Sub-e·ditor. 1837. [SUB- 6.] A subordinate editor; one who sub-edits. Hence **Su·b-edito·rial** *a.*

‖ **Suber** (siū·bəɹ). 1859. [L., = cork, cork-oak.] *Bot.* (*Chem.*) The bark or periderm of the cork-tree; cork. Also, a vegetable principle found in this. So **Suberate**, *Chem.* a salt of suberic acid. **Sube·reous** (siubīə·riəs) *a.* suberous, suberose. **Su·berin**, *Chem.* the cellular tissue which remains after cork has been exhausted by various solvents. **Su·berize** *v.* *Bot.* *pass.* to be converted into cork-tissue by the formation of suberin. **Su·berone**, *Chem.* an aromatic oil formed by the distillation of suberic acid with lime. **Su·beryl**, *Chem.* the diatomic radical of suberic acid.

Suberic (siube·rik), *a.* 1799. [ad. F. *subérique*; see SUBER and -IC.] *Chem.* Of or pertaining to cork. *S. acid*, a white crystalline dibasic acid prepared by the action of nitric acid on cork, paper, linen rags, fatty acids, and other bodies.

Subero- (siū·bĕrο), comb. form of SUBER in names of chemical compounds containing or obtained from suberic acid.

Suberose (siū·bĕrōᵘs), *a.* 1845. [ad. mod. L. *suberosus*; see SUBER and -OSE¹.] *Bot.* Having the appearance of cork; like cork in form or texture. So **Su·berous** *a.* 1679.

Su·bfa:mily. 1833. [SUB- 7 b.] *Nat. Hist.* A primary subdivision of a family.

Subfief (sɒ·bfīf), *sb.* 1845. [f. SUB- 9 + FIEF *sb.*] A fief which is held of an intermediary instead of the original feoffor; *spec.* in Germany, a minor state, holding of a more important state instead of directly of the German crown. Hence **Subfie·f** *v. trans.* to grant as a s.

Subfusc, -fusk (sɒbfɒ·sk), *a.* and *sb.* 1710. [ad. L. *subfuscus*; see SUB- 20 a + FUSK.] Of dusky, dull, or sombre hue 1763. b. (*a*) *absol.* with *the*; (*b*) as *sb.* subfusc colour 1710. So **Subfu·scous** *a.* (*rare*).

Subgeneric (sɒbdʒĕne·rik), *a.* 1836. [f. next after *generic*.] Of or pertaining to a subgenus; having the characteristics of, constituting, or typifying a subgenus.

Su·bge:nus. *Pl.* **su·bge:nera.** 1813. [SUB- 7 b.] A subordinate genus; a subdivision of a genus of higher rank than a species.

Subhastation (sɒbhæstē·ʃən). *Obs.* exc. *Hist.* 1600. [ad. L. *subhastatio, -onem*, f. *subhastare*, f. *sub hasta* under the spear, from the Roman practice of setting up a spear where an auction was to be held.] A public sale by auction.

Su·b-hea·d. 1588. [SUB- 5, 6.] 1. An official next in rank to the head (of a college, etc.). *rare.* 2. One of the subordinate divisions into which a main division of a subject is broken up 1673. 3. A subordinate heading or title in a book, chapter, article, etc. 1875. So **Su·bheading** (in senses 2, 3).

Sub-hu·man, *a* 1793. [SUB- 14, 19.] 1. Not quite human, less than human; *occas.* almost human. 2. Belonging to or characteristic of the part of creation that is below the human race 1837.

‖ **Subiculum** (siubi·kiŭlŏm). 1836. [mod. L., dim. f. *subic-*, stem of late L. *subices* (pl.) supports, f. *subicere* (see SUBJECT).] 1. *Bot.* In certain fungi, the modified tissue of the host bearing the perithecia. 2. *Anat.* The uncus or uncinate gyrus 1891.

Subindu·ce, *v.* *rare* or *Obs.* 1623. [Partly ad. late L. *subinducere*, partly f. SUB- 24 + INDUCE.] 1. *trans.* To insinuate, suggest indirectly 1640. 2. To induce by indirect or underhand means 1623. 3. To bring about (a thing) as a result of or in succession to another 1855.

Su:binfeuda·tion. 1730. [See SUB- 9 (*b*) and INFEUDATION.] 1. The granting of lands by a feudatory to an inferior to be held of himself on the same terms as he held them of his superior; the relation or tenure so established. 2. An instance of this; also, an estate or fief created by this process 1766. So **Subinfeu·d** *v. trans.* to grant (estates) by s.; to give (a person) possession *of* estates by s.

‖ **Subintelligitur** (sɒ:binteli·dʒitŏɹ). 1649. [L., 3rd pers. sing. pres. indic. pass. of *subintelligere*, f. *sub-* SUB- 24 + *intellegere*.] An unexpressed or implied addition to a statement, etc. (Cf. SUBAUDITUR.)

We pray to God as a Person, a larger self; but there must always be a s. that He is not a Person JOWETT.

Subintrant (sɒbi·ntrănt), *a.* (*sb.*) 1684. [ad. L. *subintrantem, subintrare* to steal into; see SUB- 24.] *Path.* Of fevers: Having paroxysms so rapidly that before one is over another begins; also said of the paroxysms. B. *sb.* A s. fever 1899.

Subitaneous (sɒbitē·niəs), *a.* Now *rare.* 1651. [f. L. *subitaneus* sudden (f. *subitus*) + -OUS.] Sudden, unexpected; hastily produced or constructed. So †**Subitany** *a.* 1603.

‖ **Subito** (su·bito), *adv.* 1724. [It.] *Mus.* A direction: Quickly; usu. in phr. *volti subito*, turn quickly.

Subjacent (sɒbdʒē·sĕnt), *a.* 1597. [ad. L. *subjacentem, subjacere*; see SUB- 2.] 1. Situated underneath or below; underlying. b. *transf.* and *fig.* Forming the basis or substratum 1677. 2. Lying or situated at a lower level, at or near the base (e.g. of a mountain) 1650. 3. Taking place underneath or below (*rare*) 1862.

1. The skin and s. cellular membrane 1813. S. and intercalated beds GEIKIE. 2. The rivers that water the s. plains 1760. Hence **Subja·cently** *adv.*

Subject (sɒ·bdʒĕkt), *sb.* ME. [a. OF. *suget, soget, subject*, ad. L. *subjectus* masc., *subjectum* neut., subst. uses of pa. pple. of *subicere* (see next).] I. 1. One who is under the dominion of a monarch or reigning prince; one who owes allegiance to a government or ruling power, is subject to its laws, and enjoys its protection. †b. *collect. sing.* The subjects of a realm. SHAKS. †2. One who is bound to a superior by an obligation to pay allegiance, service, or tribute; *spec.* a feudal inferior or tenant; a vassal, retainer; a dependant, subordinate; an inferior -1681. 3. A person (rarely, a thing) that is in the control or under the dominion of another; one who owes obedience *to* another ME. 4. *Law.* A thing over which a right is exercised 1765. b. *Sc.* A piece of property 1754.

1. I have the honour to be a British s. BENTHAM. The..kings of our own day very much resemble their subjects in education and breeding JOWETT. b. transf. *Per.* II. i. 53. 3. By Nature woman was made mans subiect KYD. 4. By the s. of a right is meant the thing..over which the right is exercised. My house, horse, or watch is the s. of my right of property. 1875.

II. Senses derived ultimately (through L. *subjectum*) from Aristotle's use of τὸ ὑποκείμενον in the threefold sense of (1) material out of which things are made, (2) subject of attributes, (3) subject of predicates. †1. The substance of which a thing consists or from which it is made -1775. 2. *Philos.* The substance in which accidents or attributes inhere. late ME. †b. A thing having real independent existence. SHAKS. 3. *Logic.* a. That which has attributes; the thing about which a judgement is made 1551. b. The term or part of a proposition of which the predicate is affirmed or denied 1620. 4. *Gram.* The member or part of a sentence denoting that concerning which something is predicated (i.e. of which a statement is made, a question asked, or a desire expressed); a word or group of words constituting the 'nominative' to a finite verb 1638. 5. *Mod. Philos.* More fully *conscious* or *thinking s.*: The mind, as the 'subject' in which ideas inhere; that to which all mental representations or operations are attributed; the thinking or cognizing agent; the self or ego. (Correl. to OBJECT *sb.* 6.) 1796.

2. Two Contraries can never subsist in the same S. 1728. 5. Every state of consciousness necessarily implies two elements at least; a conscious s., and an object of which he is conscious 1851.

III. 1. The subject-matter of an art or science 1541. 2. A thing affording matter for action of a specified kind; a ground, motive, or cause 1586. b. That which can be drawn upon or utilized, means of doing something (*rare*) 1752. 3. That which is or may be acted or operated upon; a person or thing towards which action or influence is directed 1592. **b.** An object with which a person's occupation or business is concerned or on which he exercises his craft; that which is operated upon manually or mechanically 1541. **c.** A body used for anatomical examination or demonstration; a dead body intended for or undergoing dissection 1694. **d.** A person who presents himself for or undergoes medical or surgical treatment; hence, one who is affected with some disease 1822. **e.** A person upon whom a psychic or other experiment is made 1883. **f.** With epithet: A person in respect of his conduct or character (*rare*). (Cf. F. *mauvais sujet.*) 1848. **4.** That which forms or is chosen as the matter of thought, consideration, or inquiry; a topic, theme 1586. **b.** An object of study in relation to its use for pedagogic or examining purposes; a particular department of art or science in which one is instructed or examined 1843. **5.** The theme *of* a literary composition; what a book, poem, etc. is about 1586. **b.** The person of whom a biography is written 1741. **6.** An object, a figure or group of figures, a scene, an incident, etc., chosen by an artist for representation 1614. **7.** *Mus.* The theme or principal phrase of a composition or movement; in a fugue, the exposition, dux, or proposition 1753.

1. All sciences have a s., number is the s. of arithmetic JOWETT. 2. Which had never given..the least s. of complaint SCOTT. 3. To be Shames scorne, and subiect of Mischance SHAKS. The S. of Conversation at Several Tea-Tables STEELE. d. Phr. *A good* (*bad*) *s.*, a patient who has (has not) good prospects of improvement or recovery. 4. As for politics, it was a s. far beyond the reach of any female capacity 1780. b. If an officer only pass in the subjects necessary for a subaltern 1887. 6. The next thing is to make choice of a S. beautifull and noble DRYDEN. Subjects after Watteau 1867.

attrib. and *Comb.*, as (sense III. 5, chiefly with ref. to cataloguing books according to their subjects) *s. catalogue, index, list, reference*; **s. picture,** a genre painting.

Subject (sɒ·bʒėkt), *a.* ME. [a. OF. *suget, subject*, repr. L. *subjectus*, pa. pple. of *subicere, subjicere*, f. *sub-* SUB- 3 + *jacere* to throw, cast.] **I. 1.** That is under the dominion or rule of a sovereign, or a conquering or ruling power; owing allegiance or obedience *to* a sovereign ruler or state, a temporal or spiritual lord, or other superior. **b.** *to* a law, a jurisdiction. late ME. **2.** *transf.* and *fig.* In a state of subjection or dependence; under the control or influence of something; subordinate ME. **b.** *to* the power, law, command, etc. of another. late ME.

1. All round about are subiect vnto the King of Tunis 1600. The relations between..governing race and s. race MORLEY. 2. The military power ought always to be s. to the civil BURNET. b. He would no longer be s. to the caprice of any woman 1876.

II. (Const. *to.*) **1.** Exposed or open *to*; prone *to* or liable to suffer from something damaging, deleterious, or disadvantageous. late ME. **b.** Exposed *to* violent treatment, damaging weather, or the like 1490. **c.** Liable *to* disease 1577. **2.** Liable *to* the incidence or recurrence of an action, process, or state 1559. **b.** *absol.* Without *to*, in bookselling parlance: Subject to discount 1906. †**3.** Having a tendency, prone or disposed, *to* an action, or *to do* something -1793. †**4.** That may be brought under the operation of a faculty or sense -1668. **5.** Dependent upon a certain correcting or modifying condition; conditional upon. Freq. *advb.*, conditionally upon, with the assumption of. 1832.

1. Lord! what miseries are mortal men s. to EVELYN. b. This Region is very moist and subiect to raine 1604. c. He became s. to epileptic fits FROUDE. 2. A man of my Kidney..that am as subiect to heate as butter SHAKS. 3. A widdow, husbandles, subiect to feares SHAKS. 4. Be subiect to no sight but thine, and mine SHAKS. 5. All other business should be transacted by single judges s. to appeal 1883.

III. 1. Lying in the neighbourhood below a certain level, as that of a spectator; subjacent. *Obs.* or *arch.* late ME. †**2.** Forming the substratum or substance. Chiefly in *matter s.*: see SUBJECT-MATTER. -1744.

1. Long he them bore aboue the subiect plaine SPENSER.

Subject (sɒbdʒe·kt), *v.* late ME. [ad. OF. *subjecter, -getter*, or L. *subjectare*, freq. f. *sub(j)icere, subject-* (see prec.).] **1.** *trans.* To make (persons, a nation or country) subject *to* a conquering or sovereign power; to bring into subjection *to* a superior; to subjugate. *Obs.* or *arch.* **b.** *to* the rule, government, power, or service of a superior 1552. **2.** To render submissive or dependent. late ME. †**3.** *intr.* To submit *to* -1720. †**4.** *trans.* To make subjacent *to.* Chiefly *pass.* -1807. †**b.** To lay before a person's eyes. Const. *to.* -1776. **5.** To lay open or expose to the incidence, occurrence, or infliction of, render liable *to* something. †Also *occas.* to render susceptible *to*, predispose *to.* 1549. †**6.** *pass.* To be attributed *to*, inhere *in* a subject (SUBJECT *sb.* II. 2) -1690. **7.** *Logic.* To make the subject of a proposition 1628. **8.** To bring under the operation of an agent, agency, or process; to submit *to* certain treatment; to cause to undergo or experience something 1794.

1. Men..consequently may s. themselves, if they think good, to a Monarch HOBBES. b. Subjecting them to an unheard of tyranny 1839. 2. He..was unwilling to s. himself to that which was exacted in polite society SCOTT. 4. b. In one short view subjected to our eye Gods, Emp'rors, Heroes, Sages, Beauties, lie POPE. 5. Clauses, subjecting the whole to forfeiture, in case the prohibition was infringed 1758. 8. When people began to s. the principal historical religions to a critical analysis 1870.

Subjected (sɒbdʒe·ktėd), *ppl. a.* 1586. [f. L. *subjectus* or SUBJECT *v.* + -ED[1].] **1.** Placed or set underneath; underlying, subjacent. *Obs.* or *arch.* 1597. **2.** Reduced to a state of subjection; under the dominion or authority of another. Hence, submissive, obedient. 1586.

1. The hastning Angel..Led them direct, and down the Cliff as fast To the s. Plaine MILT. Hence **Subje·cted-ly** *adv.*, **-ness.**

Subjectify (sɒbdʒe·ktifəi), *v.* 1868. [f. SUBJECT *sb.* + -IFY.] *trans.* To identify with or absorb in the subject; to make subjective.

Subjection (sɒbdʒe·kʃən). ME. [a. OF., or ad. L. *subjectio, -onem*, f. *subicere* (see SUBJECT *a.*).] †**1.** The act, state, or fact of exercising lordship or control; dominion, domination, control -1667. **b.** Phr. *In, into,* †*to,* †*under s.*: in, into, under the dominion or control of a superior power ME. **2.** The act or fact of being subjected, as under a monarch, etc.; the state of being subject to, or under the dominion of, another; hence *gen.*, subordination. late ME. †**3.** Submission; obedience; homage -1674. **4.** Subjugation (*rare*) 1597. †**5.** The condition of a subject, and the obligations pertaining to it -1635. **6.** Legal or contractual obligation or liability 1450. †**7.** The condition of being under some necessity or obligation; a duty or task; an 'infliction' -1719.

2. Now we read no where of the s. of one Bishop and his charge to an other 1641. The s. of women 1869. 6. The obligation of civil s., whereby the inferior is constrained by the superior to act contrary to what his own reason and inclination would suggest BLACKSTONE. Hence **Subje·ctional** *a.* (*rare*) involving or based upon s.

Subjective (sɒbdʒe·ktiv), *a.* (*sb.*) 1450. [ad. late L. *subjectivus*, f. *subjectus, -um* SUBJECT *sb.*] †**1.** Pertaining or relating to one who is subject; belonging to or characteristic of a political subject; hence, submissive, obedient -1706. **2.** Pertaining to the subject as that in which attributes inhere; inherent; hence, pertaining to the essence or reality of a thing; real, essential 1642. **3.** Relating to the thinking subject; proceeding from or taking place within the subject; having its source in the mind; (in the widest sense) belonging to the conscious life. (Correl. to OBJECTIVE *a.* 2 b.) 1707. **4.** Pertaining or peculiar to an individual subject or his mental operations; personal, individual 1767. **6.** *Art* and *Literature.* Expressing, bringing into prominence, or deriving its materials mainly from, the individuality of the artist or author 1840. **c.** Excessively introspective or reflective 1842. **d.** Existing in the mind only; illusory, fanciful 1869. **e.** *Physiol.* and *Path.* Due to internal causes and discoverable by oneself alone; said of sensations, symptoms, etc. 1855. **5.** Having the character of the subject of a sentence as expressing the doer of an action 1864. **6.** *absol.* with *the*: That which is subjective; rarely *sb.*, a subjective fact or thing 1817.

3. The motives to consider a proposition as true, are either objective, i. e. taken from an external object,..or..s., i. e. they exist only in the mind of him who judges 1801. *S. idealism*: see IDEALISM 1. *S. method*, the method of investigation which starts from conceptions and *a priori* assumptions, from which deductions are made. 4. b. The whole s. scheme (damn the word!) of the poems I did not like E. FITZGERALD. e. The boomings in the ear and the s. buzz 1876. 5. The confounding of s. with objective genitives 1864. Hence **Subje·ctive-ly** *adv.*, **-ness.**

Subjectivism (sɒbdʒe·ktiviz'm). 1857. [f. prec. + -ISM.] **1.** The philosophical theory according to which all our knowledge is merely subjective and relative, and which denies the possibility of objective knowledge. **2.** The subjective method (see prec. 3) 1882. **3.** A theory or method based exclusively on subjective facts 1865. **b.** An ethical theory which conceives the aim of morality to be based upon, or to consist in, the attainment of states of feeling 1897. So **Subje·ctivist,** one who believes in or advocates s.

Subjectivity (sɒbdʒėkti·vĭti). 1821. [f. as prec. + -ITY.] **1.** Consciousness of one's perceived states. **b.** A conscious being 1830. **2.** The quality or condition of viewing things exclusively through the medium of one's own mind or individuality; hence, individuality, personality 1827. **b.** That quality of art which depends on the expression of the personality or individuality of the artist; the individuality of an artist as expressed in his work 1830. **3.** = SUBJECTIVISM 1. 1839. **4.** The quality or condition of resting upon subjective facts or mental representation; the character of existing in the mind only 1877.

4. The pure s. of Religion 1884.

Subjectivize (sɒbdʒe·ktivəiz), *v.* 1868. [f. as prec. + -IZE.] *trans.* To make subjective.

Subjectivo- (sɒbdʒėktəi·vo), comb. form of SUBJECTIVE = subjective and ..., subjectively.

Su·bjectless, *a.* 1803. [f. SUBJECT *sb.* + -LESS.] Having no subject or subjects.

Su·bject-ma:tter. (Earlier *matter subject*: see SUBJECT *a.* III. 2.) 1542. [f. SUBJECT *a.* + MATTER *sb.*; tr. late L. *subjecta materia*, repr. Gr. ἡ ὑποκειμένη ὕλη (Aristotle).] **I. 1.** The matter operated upon in an art, a process, etc.; the matter out of which a thing is formed. †**2.** The ground, basis, or source *of* something -1683. **II. 1.** Material for discourse or expression in language; facts or ideas as constituting material *for* speech or written composition, occas. for artistic representation 1702. **2.** The subject or theme of a written or spoken composition 1598. **3.** The substance of a book, speech, etc. as dist. from the *form* or *style* 1633. **4.** That with which thought, deliberation, or discussion, a contract, undertaking, project, or the like is concerned; that which is treated of or dealt with 1657. **b.** That with which a science, law, etc. deals 1660. **c.** *Law.* The matter in dispute 1843.

1. Subject-matter for his satyrical muse, he never wanted 1759. 4. If subject-matters more than one are included in the deed, mention them accordingly BENTHAM.

Subject-object. 1821. *Philos.* A subjective object; the immediate object of cognition presented to the mind as dist. from the real object; applied by Fichte to the ego.

Subjoin (sɒbdʒoi·n), *v.* 1573. [In early use Sc.; ad. obs. F. *subjoindre*, ad. L. *subjungere*; see SUB- 27 and JOIN *v.*] **1.** *trans.* To add at the end of a statement, argument, or discourse; *occas.*, to add (a note) at the bottom of a page. **2.** To place in immediate sequence or juxtaposition; to add as a concomitant or related element 1668.

1. According to your request I s. my Epitaph on Dr. Johnson COWPER.

Subjugate (sɒ·bdʒŭgeᶦt), *v.* late ME. [f. L. *subjugat-, subjugare*, f. *sub-* SUB- 1 g + *jugum* yoke.] **1.** *trans.* To bring under the yoke or into subjection; to reduce to the condition of a subject country or people. **2.** *transf.* and *fig.* To bring into bondage or under complete control; to make subservient or submissive 1589.

1. The special commissions given to the children of Israel to s. the land of Canaan 1845. 2. Aristotle.. had subjugated the minds of generation after generation D'ISRAELI. Hence **Su·bjugate** *pa. pple.* (*Obs.* or *arch.*) subjugated.

Subjugation (sɒbdʒŭgēᶦ·ʃən). 1658. [ad. late L. *subjugatio, -onem*, f. *subjugare*; see prec.] **1.** The action of subjugating or condition of being subjugated. **2.** *transf.* and *fig.* Intellectual or moral subjection; reduction to a state of subserviency or submission 1785.

Subjugator (sɒ·bdʒŭgeⁱtəɹ). 1834. [ad. late L.] One who subjugates; a conqueror.

Subjunction (sɒ̆bdʒɒ·ŋkʃən). Now *rare.* 1633. [ad. late L. *subjunctio, -onem.*] The action of subjoining; the condition of being subjoined.

Subjunctive (sɒ̆bdʒɒ·ŋktiv), *a.* and *sb.* 1530. [ad. L. *subjunctivus*, f. *subjunct-, subjungere* to SUBJOIN.] **A.** *adj. Gram.* That is subjoined or dependent 1583. **b.** Designating a mood (L. *modus subjunctivus*, Gr. ὑποτακτικὴ ἔγκλισις) the forms of which are employed to denote an action or a state as conceived (and not as a fact) and therefore used to express a wish, command, exhortation, or a contingent, hypothetical, or prospective event. Also, belonging to this mood, e.g. *s. present* or *present s.* (So named because it was regarded as specially appropriate to 'subjoined' or subordinate clauses.) 1530. **c.** Characteristic of what is expressed by the subjunctive mood; contingent, hypothetical 1837.

b. No s. mood existed in the common Sanskrit 1853.

B. *sb. Gram.* The subjunctive mood; a form of a verb belonging to the subjunctive mood 1532. Hence **Subju·nctively** *adv.* in the s. mood.

Su·bki:ngdom. 1825. [SUB- 7 b.] One of the primary groups into which the animal and vegetable kingdoms are divided.

Sublapsarian (sɒblæpsēᵊ·riăn), *sb.* and *a.* 1633. [f. mod.L. *sublapsarius*, f. L. *sub-* SUB- 17 + *lapsus* LAPSE; see -IAN.] *Theol.* **A.** *sb.* = INFRALAPSARIAN A. 1656. **B.** *adj.* = INFRALAPSARIAN B. 1633. Hence **Sublapsa·rianism,** the s. doctrine.

Sublate (sɒ̆blēⁱ·t), *v.* 1548. [f. L. *sublat-*, f. *sub-* SUB- 25 + *lat-*, pa. ppl. stem of *tollere* to take away.] †**1.** *trans.* To remove, take away -1672. **2.** *Logic.* To deny, contradict, disaffirm; opp. to POSIT 2. 1838. **3.** *Hegelian Philos.* (tr. G. *aufheben*, used by Hegel as having the opposite meanings of 'destroy' and 'preserve') 1865.

Sublation (sɒ̆blēⁱ·ʃən). 1626. [ad. L. *sublatio, -onem* (see prec.).] The act of taking away, removal. **b.** *Logic.* (See prec. 2.) 1864. **c.** *Hegelian Philos.* (See prec. 3.) 1865.

Su·b-lease, *sb.* 1826. [f. SUB- 9 (*a*).] A lease granted by one who is a lessee or tenant, an underlease.

Sub-lea·se, *v.* 1828. [f. SUB- 9 (*b*).] *trans.* To sub-let. So **Sub-lessee·**, one who holds or receives a sub-lease; **Sub-le·ssor,** one who grants a sub-lease.

Sub-le·t, *v.* 1766. [f. SUB- 9 (*b*) + LET *v.*[1]] *trans.* To let (property, a tenement) to a sub-tenant; to lease out (work, etc.) under a sub-contract; to underlet, sub-lease. Hence **Su·b-let** *sb.* a sub-lease.

†**Subleva·tion.** 1556. [ad. L. *sublevatio, -onem*, f. *sublevare*, f. *sub-* SUB- 25 + *levare* to raise.] **1.** The action of raising or lifting; elevation; also, a particular point of elevation or height -1708. **2.** A rising, revolt -1699.

Su:b-lieute·nant. 1702. [SUB- 6.] **1.** An army officer ranking next below a lieutenant; formerly, an officer in certain regiments of the British Army, corresponding to the ensign in others. **2.** An officer in the British Navy ranking next below a lieutenant. Formerly called *mate.* 1804. Hence **Sub-lieute·nancy.**

Sublimable (sɒ̆bləi·măb'l), *a.* Now *rare.* 1666. [f. SUBLIME *v.* + -ABLE.] Capable of sublimation or of being sublimated. Hence **Subli·mableness** 1661.

Sublimate (sɒ·blimĕt), *sb.* 1543. [ad. L. *sublimatum, sublimare* to SUBLIME.] **1.** A solid product of sublimation, *esp.* in the form of a compact crystalline cake 1626. **b.** *fig.* A refined or concentrated product 1683. **2.** 'Mercury s.'; mercuric chloride (bichloride or perchloride of mercury), a white crystalline powder, which acts as a violent poison 1543. **b.** Now usu. *corrosive s.* 1685. **c.** *attrib.* = containing or impregnated with corrosive s., as *s. gauze, lotion* 1753.

†**Su·blimate,** *pa. pple.* and *ppl. a.* late ME. [ad. L. *sublimatus, sublimare* to SUBLIME.] **A.** *pa. pple.* Raised, elevated, exalted -1646. **B.** *ppl. a.* **1.** *Mercury s.*: = prec. 2. -1799. **2.** Refined, purified; elevated, sublime -1720.

Sublimate (sɒ·blimeⁱt), *v.* 1566. [f. L. *sublimat-, sublimare* to SUBLIME.] †**1.** *trans.* = SUBLIME *v.* 7. -1637. **2.** = SUBLIME *v.* 1. Now *rare.* 1591. **b.** *gen.* To act upon (a substance) so as to produce a refined product 1601. †**3.** = SUBLIME *v.* 2. -1644. **b.** *pass.* and *intr.* To be produced as the result of sublimation 1682. **4.** To exalt or elevate *to* a high or higher state 1599. **5.** = SUBLIME *v.* 5. 1624. **6.** To refine away *into* something unreal or non-existent; to reduce to unreality 1836.

2. b. The heat of Milton's mind may be said to s. his learning JOHNSON. **4.** Moral ideas in a thousand forms have been sublimated, enlarged and changed 1869. **5.** Their understandings were too direct to s. absurdities into mysteries FROUDE.

Sublimated (sɒ·blimeⁱtėd), *ppl. a.* 1599. [f. prec. + -ED [1].] **1.** Produced by sublimation 1605. **2.** *fig.* Exalted, elevated; raised to a high degree of purity or excellence; lofty, sublime 1599. **3.** Of physical things: Purified, refined, rarefied (*rare*) 1676.

2. In words, whose weight best sute a s. straine DRAYTON. **b.** *Psychoanalysis.* (Cf. next, 3 c.) 1920. **3.** The s. air, diffusing itself by its mobility 1860.

Sublimation (sɒblimēⁱ·ʃən). late ME. [a. F., or ad. late L. *sublimatio, -onem*, f. *sublimare.*] **1.** The chemical action or process of subliming or converting a solid substance by means of heat into vapour, which resolidifies on cooling. **b.** *Geol.* Applied to a (supposed) analogous process by which minerals are thrown up in a state of vapour from the interior of the earth and deposited nearer its surface 1829. **c.** (The condition of) being in the form of vapour as the result of sublimation 1808. **2.** A solid substance deposited as the result of the cooling of vapour arising from sublimation or a similar process 1646. **3.** Elevation to a higher state or plane of existence; transmutation into something higher, purer, or more sublime 1615. **b.** An elated or ecstatic state of mind 1816. **4.** The result of such elevation or transmutation; the highest stage or point (*of*) 1691.

3. c. *Psychoanalysis.* The action of directing an obstructed impulse away from its primitive aim to activities of a higher order 1916.

†**Sublimatory,** *a.* 1605. [ad. med.L. *sublimatorius*, f. *sublimat-*; see SUBLIMATE and -ORY [2].] **1.** Suitable for subliming. **2.** Used in sublimation -1666.

Sublime (sɒ̆bləi·m), *a.* and *sb.* 1586. [ad. L. *sublimis*, perh. f. *sub* up to + *limen* lintel.] **A.** *adj.* **1.** Set or raised aloft, high up. *arch.* 1604. **b.** Of flight; only in fig. context with implication of senses 4-7. 1684. **c.** *Anat.* Of muscles: Lying near the surface, superficial 1855. **2.** Of buildings, etc.: Rising to a great height, lofty, towering. *arch.* 1635. **3.** Of lofty bearing or aspect; in a bad sense, haughty, proud. Chiefly *poet.* 1596. †**b.** Exalted in feeling, elated. MILT. **4.** Of ideas, truths, subjects, etc.: Belonging to the highest regions of thought, reality, or human activity 1634. **5.** Of persons, their attributes, feelings, actions: Standing high above others by reason of nobility or grandeur of nature or character; of high intellectual, moral, or spiritual level. Hence: Supreme, perfect; freq. *mod. colloq.* with ironical force 1643. **6.** Of language, style, or a writer: Expressing lofty ideas in a grand and elevated manner 1586. **7.** Of things in nature and art: Calculated to inspire awe, deep reverence, or lofty emotion, by reason of beauty, vastness, or grandeur 1700. **8.** Of rank, status: Very high, exalted. *arch.* 1702. **b.** As an honorific title of the Sultan or other potentates; also *transf.* of their actions. Cf. *Sublime Porte* (see PORTE). 1820. **c.** Refined; now used in trade names to designate the finest quality 1694.

1. Hee on the wings of Cherub rode s. On the Crystallin Skie MILT. **3.** The proud Souldan with.. countenance s. and insolent SPENSER. His fair large Front and Eye s. declar'd Absolute rule MILT. **4.** England's sublimer battle cry of 'Duty' 1853. **5.** Others more s... Have sunk, extinct in their refulgent prime SHELLEY. A s. piece of impertinence (*mod.*). **6.** The s. Dante COLERIDGE. **7.** A very s. and stately Corinthian columne EVELYN. **8.** Meek Newton's self bends from his state s. GRAY.

B. *sb.* **1.** Now always with *the*: That which is sublime; the sublime part, character, property, or feature *of* 1679. **2.** With *the*: The highest degree or point, summit, or acme *of.* Now *rare.* 1813.

1. The S. of Nature is the Sky, the Sun, Moon, Stars, &c. POPE. The s. of Homer in the hands of Pope becomes bloated and tumid COWPER. **2.** With that s. of rascals your attorney BYRON. Hence **Subli·me·ly** *adv.*, **-ness.**

Sublime (sɒ̆bləi·m), *v.* late ME. [a. OF. *sublimer*, ad. L. *sublimare*, f. *sublimis* SUBLIME *a.*] **1.** *trans.* To subject (a substance) to the action of heat in a vessel so as to convert it into vapour, which is carried off and on cooling is deposited in a solid form. **2.** To cause to be given off by sublimation or an analogous process (e.g. volcanic heat); to carry over as vapour which resolidifies on cooling; to extract by or as by sublimation 1460. **3.** *intr.* **a.** To undergo this process; to pass from the solid to the gaseous state without liquefaction 1622. **b.** To be deposited in a solid form from vapour produced by sublimation 1682. **4.** *trans.* To raise to an elevated sphere or exalted state; to make (esp. morally or spiritually) sublime 1609. **5.** To transmute *into* something higher, nobler, or more excellent. Also *intr.* 1669. **6.** To raise up or aloft, to cause to ascend 1632. **b.** To cause (vapour, etc.) to ascend, as by the action of the sun's heat 1633. †**c.** To cause (the juices of a plant, etc.) to rise, and thereby rarefy and purify them -1712. †**7.** To exalt (a person), raise to a high office or degree -1638.

4. A judicious use of metaphors wonderfully raises, sublimes, and adorns oratory GOLDSM. The blest sherbet, sublimed with snow BYRON. A soul sublimed by an idea above the region of vanity and conceit 1866. **5.** His very selfishness therefore is sublimed into public spirit MACAULAY. Hence **Subli·ming** *vbl. sb.* freq. *attrib.* as *subliming-glass, -tube.*

Sublimed (sɒ̆bləi·md), *ppl. a.* late ME. [f. prec. + -ED [1].] **1.** That has undergone the chemical process of sublimation; produced by sublimation. †**2.** *fig.* Elevated, exalted, sublime; purified, refined -1823.

1. *S. mercury*, mercury sublimate.

Sublimification (sɒ̆bli:mifikēⁱ·ʃən). 1791. [f. as prec. + -(I)FICATION.] The act or fact of making or being made sublime.

Subliminal (sɒ̆bli·minăl), *a.* 1886. [f. SUB- 1 a + L. *limin-, limen* threshold + -AL 1; coined to represent Herbart's *unter der Schwelle* (sc. *des Bewusstseins*) under the threshold (of consciousness).] *Psych.* Below the threshold (see LIMEN) of sensation or consciousness: said of states supposed to exist but not strong enough to be recognized. Also, pertaining to 'the s. self'. **b.** *absol.* That which is s.; the s. self 1901.

Sublimity (sɒ̆bli·mĭti). 1526. [ad. L. *sublimitas, -tatem*, f. *sublimis* SUBLIME; see -ITY.] The state or quality of being sublime. **b.** An instance of this; a sublime thing or being 1642.

S. is produced by aggregation, and littleness by dispersion JOHNSON. Bursts of rapture and of unparalleled s. PALEY. **b.** He loved to talk of great sublimities in religion 1715.

Sublinear (sɒbli·niăɹ), *a.* 1777. **1.** [SUB- 20 c.] *Bot.* and *Zool.* Nearly linear. **2.** [SUB- 1 a.] Placed below a written or printed line 1868.

Sublingual (sɒbli·ŋgwăl), *a.* (*sb.*) 1661. [ad. mod.L. *sublingualis*; see SUB- 1 a, b and LINGUAL.] **A.** *adj.* †**1.** *Med.* Of a pill, etc.: That is placed under the tongue to be sucked -1666. **2.** *Anat.* Situated under the tongue or on the under-side of the tongue 1694. **B.** *sb.* A s. gland, artery, etc. 1720.

2. *S. gland*, the smallest salivary gland situated at the side of the jaws and underneath the tongue. So *s. artery*, supplying the s. gland, side of the tongue, etc.

Sublunar (sɒ̆blᶦū·năɹ), *a.* and *sb.* 1610. [ad. mod.L. *sublunaris*; see SUB- 1 a and LUNAR.] **A.** *adj.* = next A. Now *rare.* †**B.** *sb.* = next B -1686.

Sublunary (sɒ·blᶦunări, sɒ̆blᶦū·nări), *a.* (*sb.*) 1592. [f. mod.L. *sublunaris*; cf. LUNARY.] **A.** *adj.* **1.** Existing or situated beneath the moon; lying between the orbit of the moon and the earth; hence, subject to the moon's influence 1613. **2.** Of or belonging to this world; earthly, terrestrial 1592. †**3.** Characteristic of this world and its affairs; mundane; material, gross; temporal, ephemeral -1814.

1. The s. Aereal Heavens 1692. 2. The uncertainty of all s. things 1650. 3. Can ye hope to finde rest in any of these s. contentments? 1648.

†B. *sb.* A s. thing or creature -1748.

Sub-man (sʊ·bmæn). 1921. [SUB- 5.] A human being of a subnormal type. (Opp. to SUPERMAN.)

Submarine (sʊ·bmărīn, *in the adj. also* sʊbmărī·n), *a.* and *sb.* 1648. [SUB- 1 a.] A. *adj.* 1. Existing or lying under the surface of the sea 1668. 2. Operating or operated, constructed or laid, intended for use under the surface of the sea 1648.

1. A sub-marine Plant 1668. S. volcanoes 1877. 2. S. cables 1855. *S. boat*, a boat so designed that it can be submerged, and navigated when under water. *S. mine*, a charge of explosives moored at or beneath the surface of the sea and exploding on impact.

B. *sb.* 1. A submarine creature; †a submarine plant, coral, etc. 1703. 2. A submarine mine 1886. 3. A submarine boat 1899. Hence **Su·bmarine** *v trans.* to attack with a s.; **Su·bmarining** *vbl. sb.* **Su·bmariner.**

‖ **Submaxilla** (sʊbmæksi·lă). 1891. [mod. L.; see SUB- 3 and MAXILLA.] *Anat.* The lower jaw or jaw-bone.

Submaxi·llary, *a.* (*sb.*) 1787. [f. mod.L. *submaxillaris*; see SUB- 1 b and MAXILLARY.] *Anat.* 1. Situated beneath the inferior maxilla; pertaining to the s. gland; also as *sb.* 2. [f. prec.] Pertaining to the submaxilla 1884.

1. *S. gland*, a salivary gland situated on either side below the lower jaw.

Subme·dial, *a.* 1849. 1. [SUB- 11, 20 d.] Near the middle or median line; almost medial. 2. *Geol.* [SUB- 1 a.] Lying below the middle group of rocks 1855. So **Subme·dian** *a.* near or behind a median part.

Subme·diant. 1806. [SUB- 4 (*c*).] *Mus.* The sixth note of a scale, lying midway between the subdominant and the upper tonic.

Submerge (sŏbmɔ̄·ɹdʒ), *v.* 1606. [ad. L. *submergere*, var. of *summergere*; see SUB- 2 and MERGE *v.*] 1. *pass.* To be covered with water; to be sunk under water. 2. *trans.* To cause to sink or plunge into water; to place under water 1611. 3. *intr.* To sink or plunge under water; to undergo submersion: now freq. of submarines 1652.

1. Continents submerged, and..ocean bottoms lifted up to become mountains 1880. 2. The shallow and tideless Baltic has scarcely a sounding that could s. St. Paul's Cathedral 1870. 3. He submerged, and we lost sight of him 1863.

Submerged (sŏbmɔ̄·ɹdʒd), *ppl. a.* 1799. [f. prec. + -ED [1].] Sunk under water; covered or overflowed with water; *Bot.* growing entirely under water. Now freq. of submarines.

S. tenth (fig.), that part of the population which is permanently in poverty and misery.

Submergence (sŏbmɔ̄·ɹdʒĕns). 1832. [f. SUBMERGE *v.* + -ENCE.] The condition of being submerged or covered with water (also *Geol.*, with glacier ice); the state of being flooded or inundated. b. *fig.*, e.g. a being plunged in thought; the 'swamping' of one thing by another; a sinking out of sight or into obscurity 1872.

Submerse (sŏbmɔ̄·ɹs), *v. rare.* 1837. [f. L. *submers-*, *submergere* to SUBMERGE.] *trans.* To submerge, drown. So **Submersed** (sŏbmɔ̄·ɹst) *pa. pple.* and *ppl. a.* (now chiefly *Bot.*) submerged 1727.

Submersible (sŏbmɔ̄·ɹsib'l), *a.* and *sb.* 1866. [f. L. *submers-*, *submergere.*] A. *adj.* That may be submerged, covered with, plunged into, or made to remain under water; *esp.* of a boat. B. *sb.* A submersible boat 1900.

Submersion (sŏbmɔ̄·ɹʃən). 1572. [ad. L. *submersio*, *-onem*; see prec.] The action of submerging or condition of being submerged; plunging into, sinking under, or flooding with water; *occas.* drowning.

Subminister (sŏbmi·nistəɹ), *v.* Now *rare.* 1601. [ad. L. *subministrare*; see SUB- 8 and MINISTER *v.*] 1. *trans.* To supply or furnish (sometimes in a secret manner). †2. *intr.* To minister *to* (lit. and fig.) -1692.

2. Our Passions..S. to the Best, and Worst of Purposes, at once 1692.

Submiss (sŏbmi·s), *a.* 1570. [ad. L. *submissus*, *submittere* to SUBMIT.] 1. = SUBMISSIVE. *Obs.* exc. *arch.* †2. Of the voice, speech: Low, uttered in an undertone, subdued -1787.

1. With aw In adoration at his feet I fell S. MILT. A Simple, S., Humble Style 1702. Hence **Submi·ssly** *adv.*, -ness (*arch.*).

Submission (sŏbmi·ʃən). late ME. [ad. OF., or L. *submissio*, *-onem*, f. *submittere* to SUBMIT.] 1. *Law.* Agreement to abide by a decision or to obey an authority; reference to the decision or judgement of a (third) party; in recent use *spec.*, the referring of a matter *to* arbitration. b. In wider use, the act of submitting a matter *to* a person for decision or consideration 1911. c. The theory of a case put forward by an advocate 1922. 2. The condition of being submissive; submissive conduct or bearing; deference; †*occas.* humiliation, abasement. *arch.* 1449. b. *pl.* Acts of deference or homage; demonstrations of submissiveness. *arch.* 1617. 3. The action of submitting *to* an authority, a conquering or ruling power; the act of yielding to the claims of another, or surrendering to his will or government; the condition of having submitted 1482. †4. Used for: Admission, confession. SHAKS.

2. Luther..writeth to the Bishop of Rome letters full of s. 1560. †Phr. *With* (*great*) *s.*, subject to correction. 3. To save his own life..by s. to the enemy HOBBES. *transf.* I learn'd at last s. to my lot COWPER. 4. *Rom. and Jul.* III. i. 76.

Submissive (sŏbmi·siv), *a.* 1586. [f. L. *submiss-*, *submittere* to SUBMIT.] Disposed or inclined to submit; yielding to power or authority; marked by submission or humble and ready obedience.

A lowe submissiue reuerence SHAKS. Pious and s. prayers SCOTT. As little s. to lawful authority as his forefather FREEMAN. Hence **Submi·ssive·ly** *adv.*, -ness.

Submit (sŏbmi·t), *v.* late ME. [ad. L. *submittere*, var. of *summittere*, f. *sub-* SUB- 2 + *mittere* to send, put.] I. 1. *refl.* and *intr.* To place oneself *under* the control of a person in authority or power; to become subject, surrender oneself, or yield *to* a person or his rule, etc. 2. To surrender oneself *to* judgement, criticism, correction, a condition, treatment, etc.; to consent to undergo or abide by a condition, etc. late ME. †b. Const. *to* with inf. or gerund: To yield so far as *to do* so-and-so, consent *to*; *occas.* to condescend *to* -1852. †3. *refl.* To expose oneself *to* danger, etc. -1601.

1. When a man maketh his children, to s. themselves ..to his government HOBBES. To thy Husband's will Thine shall s. MILT. 2. Submitting to what seemd remediless MILT. b. Where the mortgagee submits to be redeemed 1818. 3. *Jul. C.* I. iii. 47.

II. 1. *trans.* To bring under a certain control, government, or rule; to make subject, cause to yield *to* a person; to cause (a thing) to be subordinated *to* another. Now *rare.* late ME. 2. To subject *to* a certain condition or treatment. Now *rare.* 1450. b. To subject *to* an operation or process 1815. 3. To bring under a person's view, notice, or consideration; to refer *to* the decision or judgement of a person; to bring up or present *for* criticism, consideration, or approval 1560. b. In *Sc. Law*, to refer to arbitration 1799. 4. To put forward as a contention or proposition; to urge or represent with deference (*that* ...). Now freq. in legal parlance. 1818.

1. We submitte our reason to our fayth 1558. 2. b. When alcohol is submitted to distillation 1857. 3. Dare to be true, s. the rest to Heaven PRIOR. Such proceedings may be submitted for the sanction of Parliament 1905. 4. Counsel,..submitted that the plaintiff was entitled to recover damages 1907.

†III. *trans.* To let or lay down, lower, sink, lay low; to place (one's neck) under the yoke or the axe. -1807.

Will ye s. your necks, and chuse to bend The supple knee? MILT. Hence **Submi·tter,** one who submits.

Submo·ntane, *a.* 1819. 1. [SUB- 1 a.] Passing under, or existing below, mountains. 2. [SUB- 12 a.] Lying about the foot of mountains; belonging to the foot-hills of a range; belonging to the lower slopes of mountains 1830.

Submu·cous, *a.* 1684. [ad. mod.L. *submucosus.*] 1. *Path.* [SUB- 20.] Somewhat mucous; partly consisting of or attended by mucus; of an indistinctly mucous character. 2. [SUB- 1 b.] a. *Anat.* Situated beneath the mucous membrane; pertaining to the areolar tissue so situated 1835. b. *Path.* and *Surg.* Occurring or introduced under the mucous membrane; affecting the submucous areolar tissue 1875.

Submu·ltiple, *a.* and *sb.* 1696. [ad. late L. *submultiplus*; see SUB- 10 and MULTIPLE.] A. *adj.* Of a ratio: In which the antecedent is an aliquot part of the consequent: the converse of *multiple.* Of a number, etc.: That is an aliquot part *of* another. Now *rare* or *Obs.* B. *sb.* A submultiple or aliquot part (*of*) 1758.

†**Subne·ct,** *v.* 1583. [ad. L. *subnectere*; see SUB- 2, 27.] 1. *trans.* To subjoin. Also *absol.* -1704. 2. To fasten underneath. POPE.

Su·bnormal, *sb.* 1710. [ad. mod.L. *subnormalis* (sc. *linea* line); see SUB- 1 and NORMAL.] *Geom.* That part of the axis of abscissas which is intercepted between the ordinate and the normal at any point of the curve.

Subno·rmal, *a.* 1890. [SUB- 14.] Less than normal, below the normal. Chiefly *Med.* Hence **Subnorma·lity** 1890.

Subocci·pital, *a.* 1733. [ad. mod.L. *suboccipitalis*; see SUB- 1 b.] *Anat.* 1. Situated under the occiput or below the occipital bone. 2. Situated on the under surface of the occipital lobe of the brain 1889.

1. *S. nerve*, the first cervical nerve.

Subo·ctave. 1659. †1. [SUB- 10.] An eighth part (*rare*) -1705. 2. *Mus.* [SUB- 4 (*b*).] The octave below a given note. Also *attrib.* in *s. coupler.* 1659.

Su·b-o:fficer. 1618. [SUB- 6.] A subordinate officer.

Subope·rcular, *a.* (*sb.*) 1854. [f. next + -AR [1].] *Ichth.* Designating a bone in the lower part of the operculum of a fish; pertaining to the suboperculum.

‖ **Suboperculum** (sʊbopɔ̄·ɹkiŭlɒm). 1834. [mod.L., f. *sub-* SUB- 2 b (*a*) + OPERCULUM.] 1. *Ichth.* The bone situated below the operculum in the gill-cover of a fish. 2. *Anat.* The part of an occipital orbital gyre which overlies the insula of Reil 1889.

Subo·rbital, *a.* and *sb.* 1822. [SUB- 1 b.] A. *adj.* Situated below or under the orbit of the eye; infraorbital. B. *sb.* A s. structure; a s. bone, cartilage, nerve, etc. 1834. So **Subo·rbitar, -o·rbitary** *adjs.* and *sbs.*

Su·border. 1826. 1. [SUB- 7 b.] *Zool.* and *Bot.* A subdivision of an order; a group next below an order in a classification of animals or plants. 2. [SUB- 5 b.] *Arch.* A secondary or subordinate 'order' in a structure of arches 1890.

Subordinacy (sʊbǭ·ɹdinăsi). 1627. [f. SUBORDINATE *a.*; see -ACY.] The state of being subordinate; subordination.

Lifted out of s. into supremacy 1893.

Subo·rdinal, *a.* 1870. [f. mod.L. *subordo*, *-ordinis* (see SUB- 7, ORDER *sb.*) + -AL 1.] Of, pertaining to, or of the rank of, a suborder.

Subo·rdinary. 1791. [f. SUB- 5 + ORDINARY *sb.*] *Her.* A charge of frequent occurrence but considered of less importance than an ordinary; a subordinate ordinary.

Subordinate (sʊbǭ·ɹdinĕt), *a.* and *sb.* 1456. [ad. med. L. *subordinatus*, *subordinare* to SUBORDINATE.] A. *adj.* 1. Belonging to an inferior rank, grade, class, or order, and hence dependent upon the authority or power of another. So of power, position, etc. 2. Of things, material and immaterial: Dependent upon or subservient *to* the chief or principal thing. Chiefly in techn. use. 1588. 3. Of inferior importance; not principal or predominant; secondary, minor 1661. 4. *Geol.* Underlying; subjacent 1833.

1. The s. officer must receive the commands of his superior GOLDSM. In his s. official position 1862. 2. A S. End is that which is referred to some farther End 1697. When a s. clause acts the part of object to a verb 1844. 3. My expectations from it were of a s. nature only 1786. 4. Consisting..partly of clay and sand, with s. beds of lignite 1833.

B. *sb.* 1. A subordinate person; one in a position of subordination; one who is under the control or orders of a superior 1640. 2. A subordinate thing, matter, etc. 1839.

1. What the jurisdiction of bishops over their subordinates is to be BURKE. Hence **Subo·rdinate·ly** *adv.*, -ness (*rare*).

Subordinate (sŏbǭ·ɹdinēᶦt), *v.* 1597. [f. late L. *subordinat-, subordinare*, f. *sub-* SUB- 2 + *ordinare* to order, ORDAIN.] **1.** *trans.* To bring into a subordinate position; to render subordinate, dependent, or subservient. Now *rare* with personal obj. **2.** To place in a lower order, rank, etc.; to make secondary or consider as of less importance or value 1624. **3.** *Arch.* To arrange (arches) in 'orders' 1878.

1. He to whose will our wills are to be subordinated CARLYLE. 2. The teacher, who subordinates prudence to virtue COLERIDGE.

Subo·rdinating, *ppl. a.* 1751. [-ING [2].] That subordinates; involving subordination.

S. conjunction, (Gram.) one that serves to join a subordinate to a principal clause.

Subordination (sŏbǭɹdinē^i·ʃən). 1616. [ad. late L. *subordinatio, -onem*; see prec.] **1.** The arrangement *of* persons or things in a series of successively dependent ranks or degrees. Also, †an instance of this. Now *rare* or *Obs.* †**b.** A rank in a graded series –1751. **2.** The condition of being subordinate, inferior, or dependent; subjection, subservience 1651. **b.** *Gram.* The dependence of one clause upon another 1857. **3.** The condition of being subservient *to* some end, object, or need 1673. **4.** The condition of being duly submissive to authority or discipline; submission or subjection to the rule of a superior officer or the government of a higher power 1736. **5.** *Arch.* The act or fact of forming arches into 'orders' 1878.

1. The s. of superior and vassal having soon ceased to be strict 1758. b. An insolent leveller,..eager..to confound the subordinations of society JOHNSON. 2. Their independent spirit disdained the yoke of s. GIBBON. 3. A certain s. of individual actions to social requirements 1862. 4. S. must be preserved in the Army 1760. Hence **Subordina·tionism** *Theol.*, the doctrine that the Second and Third Persons of the Trinity are inferior, in order or in essence, to the First Person.

Subo·rdinative, *a. rare.* 1642. [f. SUBORDINATE *v.* + -IVE.] Tending to subordinate, involving subordination. **b.** *Gram.* Containing a subordinate clause or clauses 1857.

Suborn (sŏbǭ·ɹn), *v.* 1534. [ad. L. *subornare*, f. *sub-* SUB- 24 + *ornare* to equip.] **1.** *trans.* To bribe, induce, or procure (a person) by underhand or unlawful means *to* commit a misdeed. When used *absol.* often = to draw away from allegiance, corrupt the loyalty of. **2.** *spec.* To bribe or unlawfully procure (a person) *to* make accusations or give evidence; to induce *to* give false testimony or *to* commit perjury. Also, to procure (evidence) by such unlawful means. 1557. **b.** To procure the performance or execution of (a thing) by bribery or other corrupt means 1817. †**3.** To prepare, provide, or procure, *esp.* in a secret, stealthy, or underhand manner –1721. †**4.** To furnish, equip, adorn –1605. †**5.** To introduce or bring to one's aid with a sinister motive –1677.

1. Different persons were suborned to cut off the duke by assassination 1783. 2. Then they suborned men, which sayd, We haue heard him speake blasphemous wordes *N.T.* (Geneva) Acts vi. 11. 3. In a golden boule She then subornd a potion CHAPMAN. Hence **Subo·rner.**

Subornation (sɒbǫɹnē^i·ʃən). 1528. [ad. L. *subornatio, -onem*, f. *subornare* to SUBORN.] **1.** The act of inducing or procuring a person to commit an evil action, by bribery, corruption, or the like; an instance of this. Also, †underhand action. 1548. **2.** The act of procuring a person to give false evidence. Also, an instance of this. 1528.

1. Without Bribery, or S., he had attain'd to the dignity of the Purple 1670. 2. A perjury as bloody as that of Oates and Bedlow;—a s. as audacious BURKE. Phr. *S. of perjury*, the act of procuring a witness on oath to commit perjury.

‖**Subpœna** (sŏbpī·nă, sŏpī·nă), *sb.* late ME. [Law-L., = L. *sub pœna* under a penalty, being the first words of the writ.] *Law.* **1.** A writ issued by chancery commanding the presence of a defendant to answer the matter alleged against him. Also *writ of s.* **2.** A writ issued from a court of justice commanding the presence of a witness under a penalty for failure 1467. **b.** *attrib.* in *s. office* 1688. Hence ‖**Subpœ·na** *v. trans.* to serve with a writ of s.; to summon as a witness in a court of justice.

Subpo·lar, *a.* 1826. [Cf. Sp. *subpolar.*] **1.** [SUB- 12 b.] Adjacent to the poles or polar sea. **2.** [SUB- 1 a.] Beneath the pole of the heavens 1876.

Su·b-pre:fect. 1845. [SUB- 6.] An assistant or deputy prefect; *spec.* an administrative official of a department of France immediately subordinate to the prefect; the administrator of a province of Peru. Hence **Subprefe·cture,** the office of a s., a division of a prefecture.

Su·bpri:ncipal. 1597. **1.** [SUB- 6.] A vice-principal of a university, etc. **2.** *Arch.* [SUB- 5 b.] An auxiliary rafter or principal brace 1842. **3.** *Mus.* [SUB- 13.] An open diapason sub-bass 1876.

Su·bpri:or. ME. [a. OF. *subprieur*, med. L. *subprior*, var. of *supprior*; see SUB- 6 and PRIOR *sb.*] A prior's assistant and deputy. So **Su·bpri:oress.**

Su·bre:gion. 1864. [SUB- 7 c.] A division or subdivision of a region, *esp.* of a geographical region, with ref. to the distribution of animals.

Subreption (sŏbre·pʃən). 1600. [ad. L. *subreptio, -onem*, f. *subripere*, f. *sub-* SUB- 24 + *rapere* to snatch.] **a.** *Eccl. Law.* The suppression of the truth or concealment of facts with a view to obtaining a faculty, dispensation, etc. (Opp. to *obreption.*) **b.** A fallacious or deceptive representation; an inference derived from such a misrepresentation 1865.

Subreptitious (sɒbrepti·ʃəs), *a.* 1610. [f. L. *subrepticius, -itius* (f. *subrept-, subripere*); see prec. and -ITIOUS [1].] **a.** *Law.* Obtained by subreption. **b.** Clandestine, SURREPTITIOUS. Hence **Subrepti·tiously** *adv.* by subreption.

Subreptive (sŏbre·ptiv), *a.* 1611. [ad. late L. *subreptivus*, f. *subrept-, subripere.*] Surreptitious; *spec.* in *Kantian Philos.*

Subrogate (sɒ·brŏgēᶦt), *v.* 1538. [f. L. *subrogat-, subrogare* (var. *surr-*), f. *sub-* SUB- 26 + *rogare* to ask, offer for election.] †**1.** *trans.* To elect or appoint in the place of another; to substitute in an office –1728. **2.** To substitute (a thing) for another. Now *rare.* 1548. **3.** *Law.* To put (a person) *in the place of*, or substitute (him) *for*, another in respect of a right or claim; to cause to succeed *to* the rights of another; see next 2. 1818.

Subrogation (sɒbrŏgē^i·ʃən). late ME. [ad. L. *subrogatio, -onem*; see prec.] †**1.** Substitution –1681. **2.** *Law.* The substitution of one party for another as a creditor; the process by which a person who pays a debt for which another is liable succeeds to the rights of the creditor to whom he pays it; the right of such succession 1710.

Sub rosa: see ‖SUB.

Subscapular (sɒbskæ·piŭlăɹ), *a.* 1831. [ad. mod.L. *subscapularis*; see next.] **a.** *Anat.* Situated below, or on the under surface of, the scapula. **b.** *Path.* Occurring under the scapula 1897.

a. *S. muscle* = next. So **Subsca·pulary** *a.* 1705.

‖**Subscapularis** (sɒ:bskæpiŭlē^ə·ris). 1704. [mod.L., see SUB 1 d and SCAPULAR.] *Anat.* In full *s. muscle*: A muscle originating in the venter of the scapula and inserted in the lesser tuberosity of the humerus.

Subscribable (sŏbskrəi·băb'l), *a.* 1824. [f. next + -ABLE.] Capable of being subscribed.

Subscribe (sŏbskrəi·b), *v.* late ME. [ad. L. *subscribere*, f. *sub-* SUB- 2 + *scribere* to write.] **1.** *trans.* To write (one's name or mark) on, orig. at the bottom of, a document, esp. as a witness or consenting party; to sign (one's name) *to.* Now *rare.* **b.** To write, set down, or inscribe below or at the conclusion of something. Now *rare.* 1579. †**c.** To put (a person) down *for* so much. SHAKS. **2.** With compl.: **a.** *refl.* To put oneself down as so-and-so, at the foot of a letter or other document. Now *rare.* 1678. †**b.** *trans.* To 'write (a person) down' so-and-so. SHAKS. **3.** To sign one's name to; to signify assent or adhesion to, by signing one's name; to attest by signing 1440. †**4.** To give one's assent or adhesion to; to countenance, support, favour, sanction, concur in –1781. †**5.** To sign away, yield up. SHAKS. **6.** *intr.* To write one's signature; *esp.* to put one's signature *to* in token of assent, approval, or testimony; to sign one's name as a witness, etc. 1535. **7.** To give one's assent *to* a statement, opinion, proposal, scheme, or the like; to express one's agreement, concurrence, or acquiescence 1549. **b.** To agree or be a party *to* a course of action or condition of things; to give approval, sanction, or countenance *to*; also *occas.* to consent or engage *to*; to agree *that...* Now *rare* or *Obs.* 1566. **8.** To give one's adhesion or allegiance, make one's submission *to* another; *gen.* to submit, yield, give in. Now *rare* or *Obs.* 1590. †**b.** To submit or subject oneself *to* law or rule; to conform or defer *to* a person's will, etc. –1772. †**c.** To admit one's inferiority or error, confess oneself in the wrong. SHAKS. **9.** Const. *to*: **a.** To admit or concede the force, validity, or truth of. Now *rare* or *Obs.* 1591. †**b.** To make acknowledgement or admission of. SHAKS. †**10.** To vouch or answer *for* a person. SHAKS. **11.** *trans.* To promise over one's signature to pay (a sum of money) *for* shares in an undertaking, or *to* or *towards* a particular object; to undertake to contribute (money) in support of any object. Also, to take up (shares). 1640. **12.** *absol.* or *intr.* To undertake to contribute money *to* a fund, *to* a society, party, etc. 1642. **b.** *To s. for*: to put one's name down as a purchaser of shares, a periodical, newspaper, or book, etc. 1711. **13.** *Book trade.* **a.** Of a bookseller: To agree beforehand to take (a certain number of copies of a book); also *s. for.* Also occas. *intr.* Of a book: To be taken by the trade. 1867. **b.** Of a publisher: To offer (a book) to the trade 1910.

1. They must all s. their names as witnesses BLACKSTONE. c. *Rich. II.* I. iv. 50. 2. b. *Much Ado* V. ii. 59. 3. He subscribed the will as a witness in the same room 1818. 4. *Tr. & Cr.* II. iii. 156. 6. He proceeded in Divinity, having..subscribed to the 34 Articles WOOD. 7. If ye all doo s. to this opinion 1549. b. Shall..I..tamely s. to my own degradation? 1844. 8. *Tr. & Cr.* IV. v. 105. b. Sir, to your pleasure humbly I s. SHAKS. c. I will s., and say I wrong'd the Duke SHAKS. 9. a. I must warmly s. to the learning..of Mr. Hume's history GOLDSM. 11. The large sum of 10,000*l.* was subscribed at once 1871. 12. I s. to the club here DICKENS. b. The maids of honour..are teazing others to s. for the book SWIFT. 13. a. Of Mr. Disraeli's 'Lothair' 1500 copies were at first subscribed 1873.

Subscriber (sŏbskrəi·bəɹ). 1599. [f. prec. + -ER [1].] **1.** One who subscribes, or affixes his signature *to*, a letter or document, articles of religion, etc. **2.** One who subscribes *to* a specified object or institution, the funds of a company, etc., *for* shares, a book, etc. 1697.

Subscript (sɒ·bskript), *sb.* and *a.* 1704. [ad. L. *subscriptus, subscribere* to SUBSCRIBE.] **A.** *sb.* **1.** That which is written underneath; a writing at the bottom or end of a document, etc.; a signature. **2.** A subscript letter or symbol 1901. **B.** *adj.* Written underneath; chiefly in *iota s.* (see IOTA 1), the small ι written underneath in ᾳ, ῃ, ῳ 1861.

Subscription (sŏbskri·pʃən). 1450. [ad. L. *subscriptio, -onem*, f. *subscript-, subscribere* to SUBSCRIBE.] **1.** A piece of writing at the end of a document, *e.g.* the concluding clause or formula of a letter with the writer's signature, the colophon of a book, etc. †**b.** Something written or inscribed underneath, *e.g.* a number written under another, an inscription or title underneath –1814. **2.** A signature, signed name 1483. **3.** A signed declaration or statement; *Rom. Antiq.*, a rescript signed by the emperor. *Obs.* exc. *Hist.* 1599. **4.** The action or an act of affixing a signature; the signing *of* one's name or *of* a document 1492. **5.** A declaration of one's assent *to* articles of religion, or some formal declaration of principles, etc. by signing one's name; *spec.* in the Church of England, assent to the Thirty-nine Articles 1588. †**6.** Assent, approval. Also, an instance of this. –1650. †**b.** Submission, allegiance. SHAKS. **7.** The action or an act of subscribing money to a fund or for stock; the raising of a sum of money for a certain object by collecting contributions from a number of people; †a scheme for raising money in this way. Also, an undertaking or agreement to subscribe so much. 1647. **8.** A contribution of money for a specified object; *spec.* the fixed sum promised or required as a periodical contribution by a member of a society, etc. to its funds, or for the purchase of a periodical publication, or in payment for a book published 'by subscription' 1679. b. A sum of money subscribed by several parties; a fund. Now chiefly in phr. *to raise, get up a s.*, U.S. *to make* or *take up a s.*, to make a collection. 1730. †c. *spec.* A share in a commercial undertaking or a loan. Also *collect. sing.* -1762. 9. *Book-trade.* a. A method of bringing out a book, by which the publisher or author undertakes to supply copies of the book at a certain rate to those who agree to take copies before publication. Freq. in phr. *by s.* 1706. b. (*a*) The taking up of a book by the trade; (*b*) The offering of a book to the trade. 1895. c. *U.S.* The house-to-house sale of books by canvassers 1880.

1. The s. of the first epistle to the Corinthians states that it was written from Philippi PALEY. 6. b. I neuer gaue you Kingdome, call'd you Children; You owe me no s. SHAKS.

attrib. and *Comb.* in the sense 'supported by subscription', as *s. concert*; **s. book,** (*a*) a book containing the names of subscribers to any object (with the amounts of their subscriptions); (*b*) *U.S.* a book sold from house to house by canvassers; **-list,** a list of subscribers' names (often with the amounts of their subscriptions); **s. price,** (*a*) the price at which a book is offered before publication to those who promise to take copies; (*b*) the price at which a periodical publication is supplied to those who promise to take so many numbers; **s. room,** a room (e.g. belonging to a club, an exchange) which is open to subscribers only.

Subscriptive (sŏbskri·ptiv), *a. rare.* 1748. [f. L. *subscript-*, *subscribere* to SUBSCRIBE + -IVE.] 1. Pertaining to the 'subscription' of a letter. 2. Pertaining to the subscribing of money 1897.

Subsecive (sʊ·bsĭsiv), *a.* Now *Obs.* or *rare.* 1613. [ad. L. *subsecivus* cut off and left remaining, f. *sub-* SUB- 25 + *secare* to cut.] Remaining over, spare: chiefly in *s. hours.*

Su·bsection. 1621. [f. SUB- 7 + SECTION.] A division of a section. b. *Nat. Hist.* A subordinate division of a section or group 1826. Hence **Su·bsectioned** *a.* divided into subsections.

‖**Subsellium** (sŏbse·liŏm). *Pl.* **-ia** (-iă). 1701. [L., f. *sub-* SUB- 3 + *sella* seat.] 1. *Rom. Antiq.* A seat in an amphitheatre. 2. *Church Arch.* = MISERICORD 2 c. 1806. So ‖**Subse·lla** (in sense 2).

Subsequence (sʊ·bsĭkwĕns). 1500. [f. next; see -ENCE.] 1. That which is subsequent; a subsequent event; the sequel. 2. The condition or fact of being subsequent 1668.

2. With such an order of precedence and s. as their natures will bear 1668.

Subsequent (sʊ·bsĭkwĕnt), *a.* and *sb.* 1460. [a. F. *subséquent*, or ad. L. *subsequens, -entem*, *subsequi*, f. *sub* -closely + *sequi* to follow.] A. *adj.* 1. Following in order or succession; coming or placed after, *esp.* immediately after. 2. Following or succeeding in time; existing or occurring after, *esp.* immediately after, something expressed or implied; coming or happening later 1503.

1. But more of this in a s. chapter SCOTT. 2. The day from which all his s. years took their colour MACAULAY. It was long s. to the death of both his parents 1871. Phr. *Condition s.*: see CONDITION *sb.*

†B. *sb.* A person or thing that follows or comes after another -1824. Hence **Subse·que·ntial** *a.*, **-ly** *adv.* **Su·bsequently** *adv.*

Subserous (sŏbsĭə·rəs), *a.* 1833. [f. SUB- + SEROUS.] 1. [SUB- 1 b.] a. *Anat.* Situated or occurring beneath a serous membrane, as *s. tissue.* b. *Path.* Affecting the subserous tissue. 2. [SUB- 20 b.] Somewhat serous 1891.

Subserve (sŏbsɔ̄·ɪv), *v.* 1619. [ad. L. *subservire*, f. *sub-* SUB- 8 + *servire* SERVE *v.*] 1. *intr.* To be subservient *to.* 2. *trans.* To be instrumental in furthering or assisting (a purpose, object, action, function, or condition); to promote or assist by supplying an instrument or means 1677. b. To be instrumental in furthering the purpose, interest, or function of (a person or thing). *rare.* 1661. †3. *intr.* To act in a subordinate position. MILT.

1. It subserves..to the Trade of this Place 1759. 2. It might s. the double purpose of ridding us of a nuisance, and relieving the public pressure 1815. b. Portions of bone are also developed to protect and otherwise s. the organs of the senses 1854. 3. Not made to rule, But to s. where wisdom bears command MILT.

Subservience (sŏbsɔ̄·ɪviĕns). 1676. [f. next; see -ENCE.] 1. The condition or quality of being serviceable, as a means *to* an end. 2. A condition of subordination or subjection *to* another. Now *rare* exc. as implied in 3. 1701. 3. Subservient behaviour, attitude, or conduct; servile subordination, submissiveness, obsequiousness 1819.

1. To order al means and affaires in s. to his end and designe 1677. 3. A young Persian monarch, corrupted by universal s. around him 1849. So **Subse·rviency** 1651.

Subservient (sŏbsɔ̄·ɪviĕnt), *a.* 1632. [ad. L. *subserviens, -entem, subservire.*] 1. Being of use or service as an instrument or means; serviceable. 2. Acting or serving in a subordinate capacity; subordinate, subject 1641. 3. Of persons, their actions, etc.; Slavishly submissive; truckling, obsequious 1794.

1. Scarce ever reading any thing which he did not make s. in one kinde or other 1661. Every particular affection..is s. to self-love 1729. 2. Can we think he will be patient thus to be made s. to his enemy? 1667. 3. The lawyers had been s. beyond all other classes to the Crown GREEN. Hence **Subse·rvient-ly** *adv.*

Subside (sŏbsəi·d), *v.* 1681. [ad. L. *subsidere*, f. *sub-* SUB- 2 + *sidere* to sit down.] 1. *intr.* To sink down, fall to the bottom, precipitate. 2. To sink to a low or lower level, *esp.* of liquids or soil sinking to the normal level; (of valleys) to form a depression; (of a swelling or something inflated) to be reduced so as to become flat 1706. b. Of a mass of earth, etc.: To fall or give way as the result of dynamic disturbance, etc. 1773. c. Of persons: To sink down *into* or *on to* a chair, etc. 1879. 3. Of the sea, wind, storm: To sink to rest, abate 1721. 4. Of strong feeling, excitement, clamour, and the like: To cease from agitation, fall *into* a state of quiet or of less violence or activity 1700. b. Of a condition: To die down, pass away, wear off. Of an action: To be discontinued. 1751. 5. Of persons: To fall *into* an inactive or less active or efficient state 1728. b. To cease from activity; *esp.* to lapse into silence 1871. 6. To be merged *in*; to pass *into* (rare) 1781.

2. The waters of the Nile had subsided 1863. 3. The wind had already subsided 1839. 4. Our desire of revenge had by this time subsided EVELYN. The hubbub gradually subsides 1892. 5. b. Being told that he must keep quiet or be arrested he subsided 1880.

Subsidence (sʊ·bsidĕns, sŏbsəi·dĕns). 1646. [ad. L. *subsidentia* sediment, f. *subsidere* to SUBSIDE; see -ENCE.] †1. A sediment, precipitate -1890. 2. The settling (of solid or heavy things) to the bottom, formation of sediment, precipitation 1656. 3. The sinking (of liquids) to a normal or lower level; also, a fall in the level of ground 1669. b. A fall in rhythm or accent 1824. 4. A sinking *into* inactivity or quiescence 1731. 5. (orig. *Geol.*) A gradual lowering or settling down of a portion of the earth due to dynamic causes, mining operations, or the like 1802. 6. *attrib.*, applied to vessels in which liquids are put in order to precipitate their suspended solid matter 1858.

2. Separate the liquid part by filtration or by s. 1800. 4. A decided s. of her animosity DICKENS. So **Subsidency** (stress var.).

Subsidiary (sŏbsi·diări), *a.* and *sb.* 1543. [ad. L. *subsidiarius*, f. SUBSIDIUM.] 1. Serving to help, assist, or supplement; auxiliary, tributary, supplementary. (Chiefly of things.) b. Of a stream: Tributary. Similarly of a valley. 1834. 2. Subordinate, secondary 1831. 3. †a. Consisting of a subsidy or subsidies -1640. b. Depending on a subsidy or subsidies: in *s. treaty* 1755. c. Maintained by subsidies 1802.

2. *S. company*, a company controlled by another holding more than 50 per cent of its issued share capital.

B. *sb.* A subsidiary thing; something which furnishes assistance or additional supplies; an aid, auxiliary. Now *rare.* 1603. b. An assistant 1807. c. *Stock Exch.* A subsidiary company 1898. d. *Polo.* A subsidiary goal 1903.

‖**Subsidium** (sŏbsi·diŏm). *Pl.* **-ia** (iă). 1640. [L.; see SUBSIDY.] A help, aid, subsidy.

Subsidize (sʊ·bsidəiz), *v.* 1795. [f. next + -IZE.] 1. *trans.* a. To make a payment for the purpose of securing the services of (mercenary or alien troops). b. To furnish (a country, nation, princes) with a subsidy for the purpose of securing their assistance or their neutrality in war 1797. 2. *transf.* a. To secure the services of by payment or bribery 1815. b. To support by grants of money: now *esp.* of the government or some central authority contributing to the upkeep of an institution, etc. 1828.

1. a. He..subsidized a corps of 8000 Swiss 1838. b. To s. one power against another 1860. 2. a. To s. a venal pen 1815. b. The schools..have been subsidised by grants from the county magistrates 1885.

Subsidy (sʊ·bsĭdi), *sb.* late ME. [a. AF. *subsidie* = OF. *subside*, ad. L. *subsidium.*] 1. Help, aid, assistance. Also with *a* and *pl. Obs.* or *arch.* 2. *Eng. Hist.* A pecuniary aid granted by parliament to the sovereign to meet special needs. late ME. b. *transf.* A pecuniary aid exacted by a prince, lord, etc. 1450. 3. A grant or contribution of money. a. *gen.* late ME. b. A sum of money paid by one country to another for the promotion of war or the preservation of neutrality 1668. c. Financial aid furnished by a state or a public corporation in furtherance of an undertaking or the upkeep of a thing 1867.

2. The perils of her reign drove her at rare intervals to the demand of a s. 1874. 3. a. A S. for a Prince in Misfortune STEELE. c. Subsidies as a means of restoring American shipping 1882. Hence **Su·bsidy** *v. trans.* and *intr.* to subsidize. CARLYLE.

†**Subsi·gn,** *v.* 1572. [ad. L. *subsignare*, f. *sub-* SUB- 2 + *signare* to SIGN.] 1. *trans.* To sign one's name under, subscribe, attest *with* one's signature or mark. Also, to subscribe (one's name). -1700. 2. *absol.* or *intr.* To append one's signature; (with clause) to testify *that*... -1653. So †**Subsigna·tion,** signature; affixing a seal -1726.

Subsist (sŏbsi·st), *sb.* 1855. [Short for SUBSISTENCE.] Payment of wages on account. *attrib.*: **s. money,** = SUBSISTENCE MONEY 1; **s. week,** a week for which s. money is paid.

Subsist (sŏbsi·st), *v.* 1549. [ad. L. *subsistere* to stand still, stand firm, cease, etc., f. *sub-* SUB- 25 + *sistere* to stand.] I. 1. *intr.* To have an existence as a reality; to exist as a substance or entity. 2. To have its being or existence *in* a certain manner, form, or state, or *by* a certain condition. *Obs.* or *arch.* 1594. 3. †a. *Philos.* To exist *in* a substance or *in* accidents -1821. b. *gen.* To consist, lie, or reside *in* some specified thing, circumstance, fact, etc. 1633. 4. To preserve its existence or continue to exist; to remain in existence, use, or force 1600. †b. To continue in a condition or position; to remain (so-and-so) -1650. †5. Of physical objects: To be or live in a certain place or state -1813. 6. Of a condition or quality: To exist 1729.

1. Matter abstractly consider'd cannot have subsisted eternally BENTLEY. 2. By ceaseless action all that is subsists COWPER. 4. So long as braine and heart Haue facultie by nature to s. SHAKS. Which charter subsists to this day, and is called Magna Charta CHESTERF. 6. Granted upon a condition which did not yet s. 1777.

II. †1. To make a stand, stand firm, hold out -1726. †2. To cease, stop at a certain point -1680.

1. Firm we s., yet possible to swerve MILT.

III. 1. *trans.* To provide sustenance for; to maintain, support, keep: said of provisions, funds, etc., or of the persons dispensing them 1683. b. To maintain, provide for, provision (troops) 1687. 2. *intr.* and *refl.* To maintain or support oneself; to live *upon* food or money, or *by* a particular occupation 1646. †3. *intr.* To support life, keep alive, live -1794.

1. Cultivating just as much land as would s. them 1854. b. The Charge of Subsisting these Officers and Men must be very great 1704. 2. From that time he subsisted by literature 1885. 3. It is difficult to conceive how man can s. without a News-paper JOHNSON.

Subsistence (sŏbsi·stĕns). late ME. [ad. late L. *subsistentia*, f. *subsistens* SUBSISTENT; see -ENCE.] I. 1. Existence as a substance or entity; substantial, real, or independent existence. 2. A thing that has substantial or real existence 1605. 3. Continued existence; continuance. Now *rare.* 1616. †4. *Theol.* = HYPOSTASIS 5. -1685.

1. He believed the soul had a distinct s. BURNET. 3. This barbarous outrage committed during the s. of truce 1769.

II. 1. The provision of support for animal life; the furnishing of food or provender. Now *rare* exc. in *means of s.* 1645. **b.** The upkeep *of* an army; the provision of supplies for troops 1746. **2.** Means of supporting life in persons or animals; means of support or livelihood 1639. **b.** A living, livelihood 1690. †**c.** Food-supply, food, provender –1788. **d.** = SUBSISTENCE MONEY 1. 1702.

1. b. I have always taken most especial care of the s. of my troops WELLINGTON. 2. The country..but just affording s. 1760. b. You offered your labour in return for a s. paid out of our capital 1832. c. The seal ..being their principal s. 1788.

Comb.: **s. diet**, the minimum amount of food requisite to keep a person in health.

Subsistence money. 1687. **1.** Money paid in advance to soldiers, workmen, etc. to supply their needs until the regular pay-day. **2.** An allowance for maintenance granted under special circumstances 1720.

†**Subsi·stency.** 1592. [ad. late L. *subsistentia*.] = SUBSISTENCE I. –1768.

Subsistent (sŏbsi·stĕnt), *a.* and *sb.* Now *rare* or *Obs.* 1526. [ad. L. *subsistens, -ent-, subsistere* to SUBSIST.] **A.** *adj.* **1.** Existing substantially or really; existing of or by itself 1617. †**2.** Inherent or residing *in* –1692. **3.** Subsisting at a specified or implied time 1832.

1. Those which deny there are spirits s. without bodies SIR T. BROWNE. 2. How..those iii persones be s. in one deite 1526. 3. Serious indications of s. evil 1849.

B. *sb.* **1.** A being or thing that subsists 1656. †**2.** *Theol.* = HYPOSTASIS 5. –1802.

Subsistential (sɒbsiste·nʃăl), *a.* 1620. [f. late L. *subsistentia* SUBSISTENCE + -AL 1.] Pertaining to subsistence, *esp.* to the divine subsistence or hypostasis.

Subsizar (sɒ·bsəi:zăɹ). 1590. [SUB- 6.] In the University of Cambridge (now only at Trinity and Emmanuel colleges) an undergraduate (having special need of pecuniary assistance and formerly performing menial offices) ranking below a sizar.

Subsoil (sɒ·bsoil), *sb.* 1799. [f. SUB- 3 + SOIL *sb.*[1]] **1.** The stratum of soil lying immediately under the surface soil. **2.** *attrib.* as *s. cultivator, draining* 1831. **b.** *fig.* with adj. force = penetrating deep down 1882.

2. b. German is used by s. research men 1882. Hence **Su·bsoil** *v. trans.* to plough so as to cut into the s., use a s. plough upon.

Subsoil plough, *sb.* 1831. A kind of plough with no mould-board, used in ploughed furrows to loosen the soil at some depth below the surface without turning it up. Hence **Subsoil-plough** *v. trans.* to use a subsoil plough upon.

Su·bspe:cies. 1699. [mod. L.] A subdivision of a species; a more or less permanent variety of a species. Chiefly *Nat. Hist.* Hence **Subspeci·fic** *a.* of, pertaining to, or of the nature of a s.

Substage (sɒ·bstēˡdʒ). 1859. **1.** [SUB- 7.] *Geol.* A subdivision of a stage. **2.** [SUB- 3.] An apparatus fixed beneath the ordinary stage of a compound microscope for the purpose of supporting mirrors and other accessories 1885.

Substance (sɒ·bstăns). ME. [a. OF., ad. L. *substantia*, f. *substans, -ant-*, pr. pple. of *substare* to stand or be under, be present, f. *sub-* SUB- 2 + *stare*.] **1.** Essential nature, essence; esp. *Theol.*, with regard to the being of God, the divine nature or essence in respect of which the three Persons of the Trinity are one. **2.** *Philos.* A being that subsists by itself; a separate or distinct thing; hence *gen.*, a thing, being ME. **3.** *Philos.* That which underlies phenomena; the permanent substratum of things; that which receives modifications and is not itself a mode; that in which accidents or attributes inhere. late ME. †**4.** That which underlies or supports; a basis, foundation; a ground, cause –1595. **5.** The matter, subject-matter, subject (of a study, discourse, written work, etc.). late ME. **6.** That of which a physical thing consists; the material of which a body is formed and in virtue of which it possesses certain properties. late ME. **b.** of incorporeal things ME. **7.** The matter or tissue composing an animal body, part, or organ. late ME. **b.** The muscular tissue or fleshy part of an animal body 1695. **8.** Any particular kind of corporeal matter. late ME. **b.** A species of matter of a definite chemical composition 1732. **c.** *Anat.* and *Zool.* With qualifying word or phr. forming specific designations 1815. **9.** A piece or mass of a particular kind of matter; a body of a specified composition or texture. Now *rare*. 1595. **10.** A solid or real thing, as opp. to an appearance or shadow. Also, reality. 1576. **11.** What is embodied in a statement; the meaning or purport of what is expressed in writing or speech; what a writing or speech amounts to. late ME. †**12.** The vital part –1605. **13.** That which gives a thing its character; that which constitutes the essence of a thing; the essential part, essence 1585. **b.** in legal use 1592. †**14.** The amount, quantity, or mass (*of* a thing) –1596. †**15.** The greater number or part, the majority, mass, or bulk *of* –1553. **16.** Possessions, goods, estate; means, wealth. *arch.* ME. †**17.** A supply or provision *of* –1535. **18.** Substantial or solid qualities, character, etc. late ME. **b.** That which makes a material firm, solid, and hard-wearing 1833.

1. That Essence or S. of the Godhead, which all the Three Persons or Hypostases agree in CUDWORTH. 2. Substances are usually distinguished as Bodies or Minds 1843. *First* (*primary*) *s.*, *second* (*secondary*) *s.*; The first s. (οὐσία πρώτη) is the individual, which can neither exist in nor be predicated of another. Second s. is the universal, which, as such, does not exist in another, but may be predicated of another. 1903. 3. *transf.* Thise Cookes, how they stampe, and streyne and grynde And turnen substaunce in-to Accident CHAUCER. 5. Vnto your Grace doe I in chiefe addresse The s. of my Speech SHAKS. 6. Surely not in vain My S. from the common Earth was ta'en FITZGERALD. 8. Thus, from the mixture of two perfectly transparent substances, we obtain an opaque one 1860. c. Adipose s. 1815. 10. He takes false shadowes, for true substances SHAKS. 11. The s. of what I said to them was this RUSKIN. 12. *Tit. A.* I. i. 374. 13. b. The s. of this contract consisteth in the thing solde, and in the price thereof 1592. 14. *Merch V.* IV. i. 328. 15. Phr. *Sum and s.*: see SUM *sb.* 16. Thy s., valued at the highest rate, cannot amount vnto a hundred Markes SHAKS. 18. This fact gave great strength and s. to the pretensions of Russia KINGLAKE. b. You must learn from the French to give your fabrics more s. 1833.

Phrases. **In s. a.** In reality. **b.** In essentials, substantially. **c.** In effect, virtually. **Of** (..) **s.** (often *of good* or *great s.*). Substantial, well-to-do, wealthy. Hence **Su·bstanceless** *a.* devoid of s., unsubstantial.

Substanced (sɒ·bstănst), *pa. pple. rare.* 1615. [f. prec. + -ED [2].] †**1.** Furnished with wealth. CHAPMAN. **2.** Made into a substance, made substantial 1873. **3.** Of a specified kind of substance 1624.

Substant (sɒ·bstănt), *a. rare.* 1660. [ad. L. *substans, -ant-, substare* (see SUBSTANCE).] **1.** Subsistent. **2.** Underlying 1883.

Substantial (sŏbstæ·nʃăl), *a.* and *sb.* ME. [ad. late L. *substantialis* (f. *substantia* SUBSTANCE).] **A.** *adj.* **1.** That is, or exists as, a substance; having a real existence; subsisting by itself. late ME. **2.** *Philos.* Of, pertaining or relating to, or inherent in substance (esp. as opp. to *accident*); that is substance. late ME. **3.** Relating to or proceeding from the essence of a thing; essential. Now *rare* or *Obs.* late ME. **4.** That is, constitutes, or involves an essential part, point, or feature; essential, material. late ME. **b.** *Law.* Belonging to or involving essential right, or the merits of a matter 1843. **5.** Of food, a meal: Affording ample or abundant nourishment. (In later use the notion of solidity or quantity is predominant.) ME. **6.** Of structures, etc.: Of solid material or workmanship. late ME. **7.** Of ample or considerable amount, quantity, or dimensions 1454. **8.** Based upon a solid substratum; not easily disturbed or damaged; of solid worth or value; weighty, sound. late ME. †**9.** Of acts, measures, etc.: Having weight, force, or effect; effective, thorough –1683. **10.** Possessing 'substance', property, or wealth; well-to-do, wealthy; hence, of weight or influence 1450. **11.** Of real worth, reliability, or repute; of good standing or status 1449. **12.** Having a corporeal form; consisting of solid matter. *Obs.* or *rare.* 1589. **13.** Having substance; not imaginary, unreal, or apparent only; true, solid, real 1592. **14.** Pertaining to the substance or tissue of the body or a part or organ 1611. **15.** That is such in the main; real or true for the most part 1771.

1. This hypothesis, that no s. and indivisible thing ever perisheth 1652. 2. *S. form*, the nature or distinctive character in virtue of possessing which a thing is what it (specifically or individually) is. 4. Securing them from s. error RUSKIN. b. The judge will consider what is the s. fact to be made out 1883. 5. A s. dinner at three 1902. 6. Some rich Burgher, whose s. dores, Cross-barrd and bolted fast, fear no assault MILT. 7. S. reinforcements 1780. 8. In great matters aske substancial counsell 1547. S. reasons.. why there should be such differences 1687. The s. comforts of a good coal fire 1814. 9. That s. Order be taken forthwith for the pulling down all Altars 1551. 10. The Knights, Aldermen, and substantiall Citizens of London 1642. 11. A sound and s. scholar 1814. 13. All this is but a dreame, Too flattering sweet to be substantiall SHAKS. 15. The s. genuineness of the text 1875.

B. *sb.* **1.** *pl.* The things belonging to or constituting the substance; the essential parts or elements; the essentials. late ME. **2.** *pl.* Substantial or solid things 1653. **3.** *pl.* The substantial or solid parts of a meal 1751.

1. His judgement in substantials, like that of Johnson, is always worth having LOWELL. Hence **Substa·ntial-ly** *adv.*, **-ness.**

Substantialism (sŏbstæ·nʃăliz'm). 1881. [f. prec. + -ISM.] *Philos.* The doctrine that there are substantial realities underlying phenomena. So **Substa·ntialist**, one who holds a philosophical doctrine of s.; also, a Flacian.

Substantiality (sŏbstænʃiæ·lĭti). 1545. [ad. late L. *substantialitas*, f. *substantialis* SUBSTANTIAL.] **1.** The quality or state of being substantial; existence as a substance or substratum; substantial or real existence. **2.** Soundness, genuineness; solidity of position or status 1660. **3.** Solidity (of a structure) 1790. **4.** *concr.* (*pl.*) = SUBSTANTIAL B. 3. 1813.

1. The ascription of independent s. to each of the different phases of intellectual life 1877. 3. A ham and other substantialities composed our meal 1842.

Substantiate (sŏbstæ·nʃiēˡt), *v.* 1657. [f. mod.L. *substantiat-, substantiare*, f. *substantia* SUBSTANCE; see -ATE [3].] **1.** *trans.* To give substance or substantial existence to, make real or substantial. **2.** To give solidity to, make firm, strengthen 1792. **3.** To give substantial form to, embody, body forth 1784. **4.** To demonstrate or verify by proof or evidence; to make good 1803.

1. Faith substantiateth things not yet seen 1657. 4. If the Court should wish it, it can be substantiated by evidence WELLINGTON.

Substantiation (sŏbstænʃiēˡ·ʃən). 1760. [f. prec.; see -ATION.] **1.** Embodiment (*rare*). **2.** The substitution of substance for shadow 1863. **3.** The making good or proving a statement, etc. 1861.

3. He failed to cite a single case in s. of his words 1886.

Substantival (sɒbstăntəi·văl), *a.* 1832. [f. next + -AL 1.] **1.** *Gram.* Of, belonging to, or consisting of, a substantive or substantives. **2.** Existing substantially 1884. Hence **Substanti·vally** *adv.* as a substantive.

Substantive (sɒ·bstăntiv), *a.* and *sb.* late ME. [a. OF. *substantif*, ad. late L. *substantivus*, f. *substantia* SUBSTANCE; see -IVE.] **A.** *adj.* **1. a.** Of persons, nations, etc.: That stands of or by itself; independent, self-existent, self-sufficient 1470. **b.** Of immaterial subjects: Having an independent existence or status; not dependent upon, subsidiary to, or referable to something else 1561. **c.** Of a dye: That attaches itself directly to the stuff, without the necessity of using a mordant 1794. **d.** *Mil.* Definitely appointed to the rank specified; also of an appointment or rank 1883. **2.** *Gram.* Denoting a substance; *noun s.* (late L. *nomen substantivum*): = B. 1. 1509. **b.** Of the nature of, equivalent to, or employed as a substantive; substantival 1668. **3.** *Gram.* Expressing existence; in *s. verb*, formerly *verb s.*: the verb 'to be' (late L. *verbum substantivum*, tr. Gr. ῥῆμα ὑπαρκτικόν) 1559. **4.** Belonging to the substance of a thing; essential 1858. **b.** Of law: Relating to or consisting of the rules of right administered by a court, as opp. to the forms of procedure (*adjective law*) 1786. **5.** Existing as a substance or individual thing; having an actual or real existence; not imaginary or illusory; real 1830. **6.** Having a firm or solid basis; not slight, weak, or transitory 1809. **7.** Having a value or effect because of numbers or quantity; of considerable amount or quantity 1821. 8. Relating to or affecting the substance or tissue of an organ 1875.

1. That Spain is not a s. power: That she must lean on France, or on England BURKE. b. A mere title..rather than a s. office and function 1850. 2. b. S. clauses, expressing the subject, are placed at the commencement of the sentence 1857. 4. As a s. part of their message 1858. 6. Strength and magnitude are qualities which impress the imagination in a powerful and s. manner HAZLITT. 7. A poem of s. length (above 600 lines) SOUTHEY.

B. *sb.* (for *noun s.*) That part of speech which is used as the name of a person or thing; a noun. late ME. Hence **Substa·ntively** *adv.* as a s. or noun; substantially, inherently. **Su·bstantivize** *v. trans. Gram.* to convert into a s.

Substituent (sɒbsti·tiuĕnt). 1895. [ad. L. *substituens, -entem, substituere.*] *Chem.* An atom or group of atoms taking the place of another atom or group in a compound.

Substitute (sɒ·bstitiūt), *sb.* late ME. [ad. L. *substitutus, -um*, masc. and neut. of pa. pple. of *substituere* (see next).] **I. 1.** One exercising deputed authority; a deputy, delegate. †**b.** *By s.*: by proxy. SHAKS. **2.** *Law.* A person nominated in remainder 1758. **3.** *Mil.* One who for a remuneration agrees to serve in place of another balloted for the militia 1802. **4.** *gen.* One who acts in place of another 1836.

1. My Substitutes I send ye, and Create Plenipotent on Earth MILT. 4. In China, where a Criminal can buy a s. to be executed in his stead 1873.

II. A thing put in the place of another. **1.** That which is used or stands in place of something else 1589. **2.** *techn.* **a.** An artificial foodstuff intended to supply the place of a natural food; also, a cheaper article or ingredient substituted for one that is recognized or patented 1879. **b.** *Chem.* A new compound formed by substitution 1852.

Substitute (sɒ·bstitiūt), *v.* 1532. [f. L. *substitut-, substituere*, f. *sub-* SUB- 26 + *statuere* to set up.] †**1.** *trans.* To appoint (a person) *to* an office as a deputy or delegate –1712. †**b.** To set up or appoint as a ruler or official *in the place* (*stead, room*) *of* another –1831. †**c.** To depute, delegate –1700. **2.** To put (one) in place of another 1588. **3.** *Law.* To nominate in remainder 1560. **4.** To take the place of, replace. (orig. in *pass.* Now regarded as incorrect.) 1675. **b.** *intr.* To act as a substitute. *U.S.* 1888.

1. b. The Pope substituted John de Columna, a Cardinall, Legate in the place of Pelagius FULLER. 2. For real wit he is obliged to s. vivacity GOLDSM. The reader by substituting various terms can easily make propositions 1870. 4. A means of judging how far touch can s. sight 1855. Hence **Su·bstituted** *ppl. a.* put in place of another; created or produced by substitution.

Substitution (sɒbstitiū·ʃən). late ME. [a. OF., or ad. late L. *substitutio, -onem*, f. *substituere* to SUBSTITUTE.] †**1.** The appointment of a deputy (or successor); deputation, delegation –1758. **2.** The putting of one person or thing in place of another 1612. **b.** With ref. to the principle in religious sacrifices of replacing one kind of victim by another or a bloody by an unbloody offering; *esp.* in *Christian Theol.* used to designate a doctrine of the Atonement according to which Jesus Christ suffered punishment vicariously for man 1836. **3.** *Law.* The designation of a person or series of persons to succeed as heir or heirs on the failure of a person or persons previously named 1590. **4.** *Alg.* **a.** The method of replacing one algebraic quantity by another of equal value but differently expressed. **b.** The operation of passing from the primitive arrangement of *n* letters to any other arrangement of the same letters. 1710. **5.** *Chem.* The replacement of one or more equivalents of an element or radical by a like number of equivalents of another 1848. **6.** *Biol.* The replacement of one organ or function by another 1870. **7.** *Philol.* A sound-change consisting in the replacement of one vowel or consonant by another 1876. 8. *Trade.* The dishonest replacement of one article of commerce by another, usu. of inferior quality; the passing off of one manufacturer's goods for another's 1902.

1. *Temp.* I. ii. 103. 2. A mere s. of words for reasons PALEY. The s. of a yellow-stained belt for a plain uncoloured one 1876. Hence **Substitu·tional** *a. Theol.* of or pertaining to, based upon the principle of, sacrificial s.; involving a s.; constituting or forming a substitute; **-ly** *adv.* **Substitu·tionary** *a.* substitutional.

Substitutive (sɒ·bstitiūtiv), *a.* 1600. [ad. late L. *substitutivus*, f. *substitut-* (see SUBSTITUTE *v.*) + -IVE.] †**1.** Belonging to, characteristic of, or involving the appointment of a substitute or deputy –1640. **2.** Taking, or fitted to take, the place of something else 1668. **b.** *Logic.* Of a proposition or judgement: = CONDITIONAL *a.* 2. 1656. **3.** *Theol.* Involving a theory of substitution 1865. **4.** Dependent upon a designation of heirs in remainder 1853.

Substract (sɒbstræ·kt), *v.* Now *illiterate.* 1550. [f. med.L. *substract-, substrahere*, alteration of *subtrahere* SUBTRACT *v.* after *abstrahere* ABSTRACT *v.*] = SUBTRACT *v.* So **Substra·ction.** †**Substra·ctor**, a calumniator. SHAKS.

Substrate (sɒ·bstreɪt). 1810. [ad. mod.L. *substratum.*] = next.

‖**Substratum** (sɒ̆bstrēɪ·tɒ̆m). *Pl.* **substrata** (sɒ̆bstrēɪ·tă); also **substratums.** 1631. [mod. L., pa. pple. neut. sing. of L. *substernere* to spread underneath, f. *sub-* SUB- 2 + *sternere* to lay down, strew.] **1.** *Metaph.* That which is regarded as supporting attributes or accidents; the substance in which qualities inhere 1653. **2.** That which underlies, or serves as the basis or foundation of, an immaterial thing, condition, or activity; the basis on which an immaterial 'structure' is raised 1631. **3.** That upon which a material thing is 'built up' or from which it is created; the subject-matter or matter operated upon 1676. **4.** An under-layer of any material substance 1730. **b.** An under-layer of soil or earthy matter 1730. **c.** In immaterial sense 1855.

1. Something..which we take to be the *s.*, or support, of those Idea's we do know LOCKE. 4. c. Children belonging to the s. of society 1876.

Substruct (sɒ̆bstrɒ·kt), *v. rare.* 1847. [f. L. *substruct-, substruere*, f. *sub-* SUB- 2 + *struere* to build, erect.] *trans.* To construct beneath; to lay as a foundation.

Substruction (sɒ̆bstrɒ·kʃən). 1624. [ad. F., or L. *substructio, -onem* (see prec.).] **1.** *Arch.* The under-structure of a building or other work. **2.** *fig.* A basis, foundation 1765.

1. The massy substructions of the Capitoline temple 1838. 2. A scaffolding or s. for the doctrine 1822.

Substructure (sɒ·bstrɒktiŭɹ, -tʃəɹ). 1726. [f. SUB- 3 + STRUCTURE, after prec.] *Arch.* That part of a building which supports the superstructure; an under-structure, substruction. Hence **Substru·ctural** *a.* of the nature of a s.

Substylar (sɒ·bstəilăɹ), *a.* (*sb.*) 1669. [ad. mod.L. *substylaris* (sc. *linea* line); see SUB- 1 and STYLAR.] *S. line* = next. Also *ellipt.* as *sb.*

Substyle (sɒ·bstəil). 1593. [See prec. and STYLE.] In dialling, the line on which the style or gnomon stands.

Subsultory (sɒ̆bsɒ·ltəri), *a.* 1638. [f. L. *subsult-, subsilire* (see next) + -ORY.] Making or moving by sudden leaps, bounds, or starts. So **Subsu·ltive** *a.* (*rare*).

‖**Subsultus** (sɒ̆bsɒ·ltɒ̆s). 1806. [mod.L., f. L. *subsult-, subsilire*, f. *sub-* SUB- 25 + *salire* to leap.] *Path.* A convulsive or twitching movement. Often short for *s. tendinum*, a convulsive twitching of the muscles and tendons present in certain fevers.

Subsu·mable, *a. rare.* 1882. [f. next + -ABLE.] Capable of being subsumed.

Subsume (sɒ̆bsiū·m), *v.* 1535. [ad. mod. L. *subsumere*, f. *sub-* SUB- 2, 25 b + *sumere* to take.] †**1.** *trans.* To bring (a statement, instance, etc.) under another; to subjoin, add –1660. **2.** intr. *Logic.* To state a minor premiss: freq. with the words of the proposition following 1589. **3.** trans. *Logic.* To state as a minor proposition or concept *under* another 1697. **4.** To bring (one idea, principle, term, etc.) *under* another, (a case, instance) under a rule; to take up *into*, or include *in*, something larger or higher 1812. †**5.** *gen.* To assume; to infer –1694.

3. In the judgment, 'all horses are animals', the conception 'horses' is subsumed under that of 'animals' 1876. 4. A principle under which one might s. men's most strenuous efforts after righteousness PATER.

Subsumption (sɒ̆bsɒ·mᵖʃən). 1639. [ad. mod.L. *subsumptio, -onem*, f. *subsumere* to SUBSUME.] **1.** *Logic.* A proposition subsumed under another; a minor premiss; *gen.*, an assumption 1651. b. Sc. Law. *S. of the libel*, a narrative of the alleged crime 1639. **2.** Chiefly *Logic* and *Philos.* The bringing of a concept, cognition, etc. *under* a general term or a larger or higher concept, etc.; the instancing of a case *under* a rule, etc. 1652.

1. It is the nature of a syllogisme to haue the s. in the second proposition 1672. 2. A casuistry, that is, a s. of the cases most frequently recurring in ordinary life DE QUINCEY.

Subsumptive (sɒ̆bsɒ·mᵖtiv), *a. rare.* 1834. [ad. mod.L. *subsumptivus*, f. *subsumpt-, subsumere* to SUBSUME; see -IVE.] Involving subsumption.

Subsurface (sɒ·bsɒ̄ːɹfės). 1778. [SUB- 1–4.] **1.** That which lies immediately below the surface, e.g. the subsoil. **2.** *Math.* In five-dimensional geometry, a three-dimensional continuum 1873. **3.** as *adj.* [see SUB- 1 e.] Existing, lying, or operating under the surface (as of the earth or water) 1875.

3. The construction of sub-surface torpedo boats 1902.

Su·bta:ngent. 1715. [ad. mod.L. *subtangens, -entem*; see SUB- 1 and TANGENT.] *Math.* That part of the axis of a curve which is contained between the tangent and the ordinate.

Su·bte:nancy. 1861. [f. next.] The status, right, or holding of a subtenant.

Subtenant (sɒ·bte:nănt). 1445. [SUB- 9 (*b*).] One who holds of a tenant; an undertenant. Hence **Su·bte:nancy.**

Subtend (sɒ̆bte·nd), *v.* 1570. [ad. L. *subtendere*, f. *sub-* SUB- 2 + *tendere* to stretch.] **1.** trans. *Geom.* To stretch or extend under, or be opposite to: said *esp.* of a line or side of a figure opposite an angle; also, of a chord or angle opposite an arc. Also in *Astron.* and *Optics.* **2.** *Bot.* To extend under, so as to embrace or enfold 1871.

1. Standing upon a semicircular tract of ground, subtended by the great bay or roadstead KINGLAKE.

Subtense (sɒ̆bte·ns). 1614. [ad. mod.L. *subtensa* (sc. *linea* line), fem. pa. pple. of *subtendere* to SUBTEND.] *Geom.* A subtending line; *esp.* the chord of an arc.

attrib.: **s. method,** a method of tacheometry in which the angle at the instrument is variable and the distance base is either constant or specially measured.

Subter- (sɒ·btəɹ) *prefix*, repr. L. *subter-* = the adv. and prep. *subter* below, underneath, used in composition = (1) below, beneath; (*a*) advb. as in *subterfluere* to flow beneath, (*b*) prep. as in *subtercutaneus* lying under the skin; (2) secretly, as in *subterfugere* to flee secretly (see SUBTERFUGE); and, in some rare Eng. compounds, = (3) lower or less than (cf. SUB- 14).

Subtera·queous, *a.* living, situated, performed, etc. under water (*rare*). **Su·btercuta·neous** *a.* = SUBCUTANEOUS *a.* **Su·btererogation**, the performing of less than is required. †**Subterflu·ent,** †**Subte·rfluous** *adjs.*, flowing underneath. **Subterna·tural,** *a.* below what is natural, less than natural.

Subterfuge (sɒ·btəɹfiūdʒ). 1573. [ad. L. *subterfugium*, f. *subterfugere*, f. *subter-* SUBTER- (2) + *fugere* to flee.] **1.** An artifice or device to which a person resorts in order to escape the force of an argument, to avoid condemnation or censure, or to justify his conduct; an evasion or shift. Chiefly of discourse, argument, debate, but also of action in general. **b.** contextually: A means of escape (*from* censure, etc.); an excuse 1755. †**2.** A place to which a person escapes; a retreat, refuge –1844. †**3.** That which conceals; a 'cloak' –1733.

1. Do not affect little shifts and subterfuges to avoid the force of an argument WATTS. b. The queen of Scots had no other s. from these pressing remonstrances HUME. 2. They depended on these under ground subterfuges 1737.

Subterranean (sɒbtĕrēɪ·nĭăn), *a.* and *sb.* 1603. [f. L. *subterraneus* (f. *sub-* SUB- 1 a + *terra*) + -AN.] **A.** *adj.* **1. a.** Of inanimate objects: Existing, lying, or situated below the surface of the earth; formed or constructed underground, either by nature or the hand of man; underground 1610. **b.** Of animate beings: Living or working under ground 1621. **c.** Of physical phenomena, forces or movements, actions, etc.: Operating or performed under ground 1603. **d.** *Bot.* Of parts of a plant: Growing under ground 1839. **2.** Existing under the earth; belonging to the lower regions or underworld 1619. **3.** *fig.* Existing or working out of sight, in the dark, or secretly 1651.

1. His taste in cookery, formed in s. ordinaries and *Alamode* beefshops, was far from delicate MACAULAY. **b.** S. colliers, tinners, [&c.] RICHARDSON. **c.** A noise like s. thunder SCOTT. **2.** The celestial, terrestrial, and s. deities EVELYN. **3.** The entire town..was honeycombed with s. revolt 1891.

B. *sb.* **1.** One who lives under ground; a cave-dweller 1625. **2.** An inhabitant of the lower regions 1836. **3.** An underground cave, chamber, or dwelling 1797. Hence **Subterra·neanly** *adv.* So **Su·bterrane** *a.* and *sb.* (now *rare*).

Subterraneous (sʊbtĕrēⁱ·nĭəs), *a.* Now *rare.* 1607. [f. L. *subterraneus* (see prec.) + -OUS.] = prec. A. Hence †**Subterrane·ity** the condition of being s. (*rare*). **Subterra·neous·ly** *adv.*, **-ness** (*rare*).

Subterra·nity. *Obs.* or *rare.* 1646. Irregular var. of SUBTERRANEITY.

†**Su·bterrany,** *a.* (*sb.*) *rare.* 1626. [ad. L. *subterraneus.*] = SUBTERRANEAN -1656.

Subterrene (sʊbtĕrī·n), *a.* and *sb.* 1610. [ad. L. *subterrenus*; see SUB- 1 a and TERRENE.] **A.** *adj.* = SUBTERRANEAN A. **1, 2.** **B.** *sb.* An underground dwelling, etc.; (with *the*) the underworld 1854.

Subterrestrial (sʊbtĕre·striăl), *a.* and *sb.* Now *rare.* 1613. [See SUB- 1 a and TERRESTRIAL.] **A.** *adj.* **1.** = SUBTERRANEAN A. **1.** †**2.** = SUBTERRANEAN A. 2. -1702. **B.** *sb.* A creature living under ground 1800.

Subtile (sʊ·til, sʊ·btil), *a.* late ME. [a. F. *subtil,* latinized refashioning of OF. *s(o)util* SUBTLE *a.*] **1.** Chiefly of fluids: Not dense, thin, rarefied; penetrating, etc. by reason of tenuity. **2.** Of fine or delicate texture; also, delicately formed or moulded. late ME. **3.** = SUBTLE *a.* 3, 4, 5, 6, 9, 10. late ME. **4.** Of feeling, sense: Acute, keen 1610.

1. The belief in ghosts, or spirits of s. bodies HALLAM. **3.** Many a subtil resoun forth they leyden CHAUCER. Frenchemen are ryght subtyl in gyuyng of good counsell BERNERS. The Goats were so shy, so s., and so swift of Foot DE FOE. Arachne's s. line POPE. Their s. shades of meaning 1888. **4.** A secret S. sense crept in of pain LONGF. Hence †**Su·btileness** -1676.

†**Subti·liate,** *v.* late ME. [f. med.L. *subtiliat-, subtiliare,* f. *subtilis* SUBTLE *a.*; see -ATE [3].] *trans.* To make thin or tenuous; *esp.* to rarefy (a fluid); to sublime; to refine, purify -1678. Hence †**Subtilia·tion** -1685.

Subtility (sʊ̆bti·lĭti). late ME. [a. OF. *soutilite, subtilite,* ad. L. *subtilitas, -atem,* f. *subtilis* SUBTLE *a.* Now used as the noun of quality of SUBTILE chiefly in the physical senses.] **1.** = SUBTLETY 1. †**2.** = SUBTLETY 3. -1761. **3.** (Excessive) nicety or refinement in argument, etc. late ME. **4.** An instance of this 1589. **5.** = SUBTLETY 7. late ME.

3. This same vnprofitable subtilitie or curiositie is of two sorts BACON. **4.** The subtilities of philosophers 1845.

Subtilization (sʊ·btiləizēⁱ·ʃən). 1603. [ad. med.L. *subtilizatio, -onem,* f. *subtilizare* to SUBTILIZE.] **1.** The action of SUBTILIZE *v.*; the sublimation or rarefaction of a substance. **2.** The drawing of subtle distinctions; over-refinement of argument, etc. 1755.

2. The oriental subtilizations about points of faith 1812.

Subtilize (sʊ·btiləiz), *v.* 1592. [ad. med.L. *subtilizare,* f. *subtilis* SUBTLE *a.*; see -IZE.] **1.** *trans.* To render thin or rare, less gross or coarse, more fluid or volatile; to rarefy, refine. Now *rare* or *Obs.* 1597. **2.** *fig.* To exalt, elevate, sublime, refine 1638. **3.** To render (the mind, the senses, etc.) acute or penetrating 1642. **4.** To render subtle, introduce subtleties or nice distinctions into; also, to argue subtly upon 1599. **5.** *intr.* To make subtle distinctions; to argue or reason in a subtle manner; to split hairs 1592.

1. Fire only subtilizes and attenuates the earthy matter 1758. **5.** Men..who s. upon the commonest Duties until they no longer appear binding GOLDSM.

Subtilly, subtilely (sʊ·btili), *adv.* Now *rare* or *Obs.* late ME. [f. *subtil* SUBTILE *a.* + -LY [2].] **1.** Thinly; finely; in a rarefied manner or form. **2.** = SUBTLY, in various senses. late ME.

Subtilty (sʊ·btilti). late ME. [Alteration of ME. *sutilte* SUBTLETY, after SUBTILE. Now used as an occasional var. of SUBTLETY in moral and intellectual senses.] †**1.** = SUBTLETY 1. -1748. **2.** = SUBTLETY 2. late ME. †**3.** = SUBTLETY 3. -1734. †**4.** = SUBTLETY 7. -1815. **5.** Excessive nicety or refinement in argument, etc. 1550. **b.** An instance of this, esp. *pl.* = SUBTLETY 6. 1474. †**6.** Delicacy, fineness (of physical objects, movements) -1794.

1. A better stratagem, than any that can proceed from s. of Wit HOBBES. **5.** These reasons savour of a wonderful s. 1818. **b.** Conversant in subtilties of Logick, Philosophy, and the Schoolmen 1668.

Su·b-ti:tle, *sb* 1878. [SUB- 5 b.] **1.** A subordinate or additional title of a literary work. **2.** A repetition of the chief words of the full title of a book at the top of the first page of text; also, a half-title 1890. **3.** *Cinema.* Any of the series of captions which constitute the running commentary on a moving picture. So **Su·btitle** *v. trans.* to furnish with a specified s.; to furnish (a film) with sub-titles.

Subtle (sʊ·t'l), *a.* ME. [a. OF. *soutil, sotil, sutil*:—L. *subtilem,* f. *sub* under + **texla, tela* woven stuff, web.] **1.** Of thin consistency, tenuous; not dense, rarefied; hence, penetrating, pervasive or elusive by reason of tenuity (now chiefly of odours). late ME. **2.** Of fine or delicate texture or composition. *Obs.* exc. *arch.* late ME. †**3.** Of small thickness or breadth; thin, slender, fine -1680. †**4.** Finely powdered; (of particles) fine, minute -1753. **5.** Of immaterial things: Not easily grasped, understood, or perceived; †intricate, abstruse ME. **6.** Fine or delicate, esp. to such an extent as to elude observation or analysis 1639. **7.** Of craftsmen, etc.: Skilful, clever, expert, dexterous. *arch.* ME. **b.** Of animals (*rare*) 1605. †**8.** Of things: Characterized by cleverness or ingenuity in conception or execution; cleverly designed or executed, artfully contrived -1667. **9.** Of persons, their faculties, actions: Characterized by penetration, acumen, or discrimination. Now with implication of (excessive) refinement or nicety of thought, speculation, or argument. ME. †**10.** Of persons or animals: Crafty, cunning; treacherously or wickedly cunning, insidiously sly, wily -1781. †**b.** Of actions, thoughts, etc. -1671. †**c.** Of ground: Tricky -1630. **11.** Working imperceptibly or secretly, insidious 1601.

1. The material theory supposes heat to be..a s. fluid stored up in the inter-atomic spaces of bodies TYNDALL. **2.** Thinner than the subtlest lawn KEBLE. **3.** *Tr. & Cr.* v. ii. 151. **5.** Things remote From use, obscure and suttle MILT. **6.** The seven are in a most s. alternating proportion RUSKIN. **8.** From the arched roof Pendant by suttle Magic many a row Of Starry Lamps MILT. **9.** The s. dexterity of a scholastic metaphysician 1769. **10.** How soon hath Time the suttle theef of youth, Stoln on his wing my three and twentith yeer! MILT. **b.** Is not thy kindnesse s., couetous? SHAKS. **c.** Like to a Bowle vpon a s. ground I haue tumbled past the throw SHAKS. Hence **Su·btleness,** subtlety.

Subtlety (sʊ·t'lti). ME. [a. OF. *su-, soutilte*:—L. *subtilitas, -atem,* f. *subtilis* SUBTLE.] **1.** Of persons, the mind, etc.: Acuteness, sagacity, penetration: in mod. use chiefly with implication of delicate or keen perception of fine distinctions or nice points. **2.** Craftiness, cunning, esp. of a treacherous kind; guile, treachery. late ME. †**3.** An ingenious contrivance; a crafty or cunning device; an artifice; *freq.* in unfavourable sense, a wily stratagem or trick -1671. **4.** *Cookery.* A highly ornamental device, wholly or chiefly made of sugar. *Obs.* exc. *Hist.* late ME. †**5.** Abstruseness, complexity, intricacy; also *pl.,* abstruse or intricate matters -1591. **6.** A refinement or nicety of thought, speculation, or argument; a fine distinction; a nice point 1654. **7.** Thinness, tenuity, exility; penetrativeness arising from lack of density 1691. **8.** Fineness or delicacy of nature, character, manner, operation, or the like; an instance of this 1820.

2. The laws were violated by power, or perverted by s. GIBBON. **6.** Curious in Subtleties, and ignorant in things of solid Knowledge 1680. **8.** Religious controversy sharpens the understanding by the s. and remoteness of the topics it discusses HAZLITT.

Subtly (sʊ·tli), *adv.* ME. [f. SUBTLE *a.* + -LY [2].] **1.** Cleverly, dexterously, skilfully; ingeniously, artfully, cunningly. *arch.* **2.** With subtle thought or argument; with nice or fine-drawn distinctions ME. †**3.** With craft or guile -1727. **4.** Delicately, finely 1732. **5.** In a manner that defies observation, analysis, or explanation 1854.

1. Thou seest How suttly to detaine thee I devise MILT. **3.** The same dealte suttely with oure kynred COVERDALE *Acts* vii. 19. **4.** The Pisan front is far more s. proportioned RUSKIN. **5.** Apology and demonstration are s. blended throughout his appeal 1879.

Subtonic (sʊbtǫ·nik), *a.* and *sb.* 1833. [f. SUB- 19, 13.] **A.** *adj. Phonetics.* Of sounds: Having properties analogous to those of the tonics, but inferior in degree. **B.** *sb.* **1.** *Phonetics.* A subtonic sound 1833. **2.** *Mus.* The note a semitone immediately below the upper tonic of a scale; the leading note 1854.

Subtract (sʊ̆btræ·kt), *v.* 1540. [f. L. *subtract-, subtrahere,* f. *sub-* SUB- 25 + *trahere* to draw, carry.] **1.** *trans.* To withdraw or withhold (a thing that is or may be used or enjoyed). *Obs.* exc. *arch.* 1548. †**2.** To remove *from* a place or position -1676. **b.** *refl.* 1540. **3.** *Math.* To take away or deduct (one quantity *from,* †*out of* another): see SUBTRACTION **2.** Also *absol.* or *intr.* 1557.

3. Podex can..Adde, Multiply, S., Divide 1652. *transf.* That is what I suppose you to say,..you may, if you wish, add or s. anything JOWETT.

Subtraction (sʊ̆btræ·kʃən). late ME. [ad. late L. *subtractio, -onem,* f. *subtrahere* to SUBTRACT.] **1.** The withdrawal or withholding *of* something due, necessary, or useful. Also, an instance of this. *Obs.* exc. *arch.* 1450. **b.** *Law.* The withdrawal or withholding from a person of any right or privilege to which he is lawfully entitled 1660. **c.** *Logic* The exception of one class from another in which the excepted class is naturally included 1909. **2** *Math.* The taking of one quantity *from* (†*out of*) another; the operation of finding the difference between two quantities, the result being termed the *remainder.* Also, an instance of this. late ME. **b.** *transf.* and *fig.* Abstraction, deduction, removal 1534.

1. **b.** Ecclesiastical laws relate to..s. and right of tythes, oblations, &c. COKE.

Subtractive (sʊ̆btræ·ktiv), *a.* 1690. [ad. med.L. *subtractivus*; see SUBTRACT *v.* and -IVE.] Involving or denoting subtraction, deduction, or diminution; (of a mathematical quantity) that is to be subtracted, negative, having the minus sign.

Subtrahend (sʊ·btrăhend). 1674. [ad. L. *subtrahendus* (sc. *numerus* number), gerundive of *subtrahere* to SUBTRACT.] *Math.* The quantity or number to be subtracted. **b.** *transf.* A sum of money to be deducted 1845.

Su·b-trea:surer. 1546. [SUB- 6.] An assistant or deputy treasurer. (The specific designation of an official of Hereford and Truro Cathedrals, and of the Inner Temple; in *U.S.* of the official in charge of a subtreasury.)

Su·b-trea:sury. 1837. [SUB- 7 d.] A subordinate or branch treasury; *U.S.* the organization by which the separate safe keeping of the public funds is entrusted to specially appointed officers; any of the branches of the Treasury established in certain cities of the States for the receipt and safe-keeping of public monies.

Su·btro:pic, *a.* and *sb.* 1886. [SUB- 12 b, 19.] **A.** *adj.* = next 1891. **B.** *sb. pl.* **Subtropics**: the regions adjacent to or bordering on the tropics 1886.

Su·btro:pical, *a.* 1842. [SUB- 12 b, 19.] **1.** Bordering on the tropics 1865. **2.** Characteristic of subtropical regions; almost tropical 1842.

Subulate (siū·biŭlēt), *a.* 1760. [ad. mod. L. *subulatus,* f. L. *subula* awl; see -ATE [2].] *Bot.* and *Zool.* Awl-shaped; slender and tapering to a point. So **Su·bulated** *a.* 1752.

Subuliform (siubiū·lifǭim), *a.* 1859. [ad. mod.L. *subuliformis,* f. L. *subula* awl; see -FORM.] Subulate.

Suburb (sʊ·bɒɪb). late ME. [a. OF. *sub(b)urbe,* ad. L. *suburbium,* f. *sub-* SUB- 11 + *urbs* city.] **1.** *collect. pl.* The country lying immediately outside a town or city; more particular-

ly, those residential parts belonging to a town or city which lie immediately outside and adjacent to its walls or boundaries. **2.** Any of such residential parts, having a definite designation, boundary, or organization. late ME. **3.** *transf.* and *fig.* (*pl.*, rarely *sing.*) Outlying parts, outskirts, confines, purlieus. late ME. **4.** *attrib.* and *Comb.* **a.** = SUBURBAN. Now *rare.* 1592. †**b.** = Belonging to or characteristic of the suburbs (of London) as a place of inferior, debased, and *esp.* licentious habits of life –1668.

1. That part of the Suburbs of London commonly called Covent Garden 1665. 2. I went to the Ghetto, where the Jewes dwell as in a suburbe by themselues EVELYN. 3. In the Suburbs and expectation of sorrowes JER. TAYLOR. [Bees] Flie to and fro, or on the smoothed Plank, The s. of thir Straw-built Citadel, . .confer Thir State affairs MILT. 4. a. From the slope side of a s. hill KEATS. b. *S. sinner*, a loose woman, a prostitute.

Suburban (sŏbɒ̄·ɹbăn), *a.* and *sb.* 1625. [ad. L. *suburbanus*, f. *sub-* SUB- 11 + *urbs* city; see -AN.] **A.** *adj.* **1.** Of or belonging to a suburb or the suburbs of a town; living, situated, operating, or carried on in the suburbs. **2.** *transf.* Having characteristics that are regarded as belonging especially to life in the suburbs of a city; having the inferior manners, the narrowness of view, etc., attributed to residents in suburbs 1817.

1. S. villas, highway-side retreats COWPER. 2. A fifth's look 's vulgar, dowdyish, and s. BYRON.

B. *sb.* A s. residence. **b.** A resident in the suburbs. 1856. Hence **Subu·rbanite,** a resident in the suburbs. **Suburba·nity,** the condition of being s., an instance of this. **Subu·rbanize** *v. trans.* to render s.

Suburbia (sŏbɒ̄·ɹbiă). 1896. [f. SUBURB + -IA [1].] A quasi-proper name for: The suburbs (*esp.* of London).

†**Subu·rbian,** *a.* and *sb.* 1606. [f. as prec. + -AN.] **A.** *adj.* Suburban: in 17th c. often with ref. to the licentious life of the (London) suburbs –1810. **B.** *sb.* A resident in the suburbs –1825.

Suburbican (sŏbɒ̄·ɹbikăn), *a.* 1659. [ad. L. **suburbicanus*, f. *suburbium*, after *suburbicarius*.] = next.

Suburbicarian (sŏbɒ̄ɹbikē·riăn), *a.* 1654. [f. late L. *suburbicarius*, f. *suburbium* SUBURB.] Applied to the dioceses (now six in number) around Rome, and to their churches, etc., which are subject to the jurisdiction of the Pope as metropolitan and the bishops of which form the body of cardinal bishops. So **Subu·rbicary** *a.* 1654.

Su·bvari:ety. 1802. [SUB- 7 b.] A subordinate or minor variety, *esp.* of a domestic animal or cultivated plant.

Subvention (sŏbve·nʃən), *sb.* late ME. [a. OF. *subvencion, -tion*, ad. late L. *subventio, -onem*, f. *subvenire*, f. *sub-* SUB- 25 + *venire* to come.] **1.** A subsidy levied by the state. *Obs.* exc. *Hist.* †**2.** The provision of help, support, or relief. Also, an instance of this. –1737. **3.** A grant of money for the support of an object or institution; *occas.* a grant in aid of necessitous persons; now *esp.* a grant from government or some other authority in support of an enterprise of public importance 1851. **4.** The granting of pecuniary aid for the support of an undertaking 1868.

3. The Crown-Prince..begged some dole or s. for these poor people CARLYLE. 4. The s. of rural roads 1894. Hence **Subve·ntion, Subve·ntionize** *vbs. trans.* to support or assist by the payment of a s.

Subverse (sŏbvə̄·ɹs), *v. rare.* 1590. [f. L. *subvers-, subvertere* to SUBVERT.] *trans.* To subvert, upset.

Subversion (sŏbvə̄·ɹʃən). late ME. [a. OF., ad. late L. *subversio, -onem*, f. *subvertere* to SUBVERT.] **1.** Overthrow, demolition (of a city, stronghold, etc.). Now *rare* or *Obs.* **2.** The turning (of a thing) upside down or uprooting it from its position; overturning, upsetting (of an object). Now *rare.* 1670. **3.** In immaterial senses: Overthrow, ruin. late ME.

2. The s. of woods and timber..through my whole estate..is almost tragical EVELYN. 3. The decaye of healthe, and subuersion of reason 1558. The s. of several powers and states upon the continent 1798. Hence **Subve·rsionary** *a.* (*rare*) = next.

Subversive (sŏbvə̄·ɹsiv), *a.* 1644. [ad. L. **subversivus*, f. *subvers-, subvertere* to SUBVERT; see -IVE.] Having a tendency to subvert or overthrow; tending to subversion.

There is a poignant delight in study, often s. of human happiness 1812.

Subvert (sŏbvə̄·ɹt), *v.* late ME. [ad. L. *subvertere*, f. *sub-* SUB- 25 + *vertere* to turn.] †**1.** *trans.* To overthrow, raze to the ground (a town or city, a structure, edifice) –1792. †**2.** To upset, overturn (an object); *occas.* to break up (ground) –1700. **3.** To undermine the character, loyalty, or faith of, corrupt, pervert (a person). Now *rare.* late ME. **4.** To disturb (the mind, soul); to overturn, overthrow (a condition or order of things, a principle, law, etc.) late ME. **5.** To bring about the overthrow or ruin of (a †person, people, or country, a dynasty, etc.) 1529.

4. This cursed opynion..wyll s. all good lawes 1530. *absol.* They have a power given to them,..to s. and destroy BURKE. 5. By things deemd weak Subverting worldly strong MILT. Hence **Subve·rter,** one who subverts or overthrows. **Subve·rtible** *a.* capable of being subverted.

Subway (sɒ·bwēⁱ). 1828. [SUB- 3.] An underground passage for conveying water-pipes, gas-pipes, telegraph wires, etc.; an underground tunnel which enables pedestrians to get from one point to another by passing below a road, railway, etc., and thus avoiding its traffic. **b.** *U.S.* An underground railway 1904.

Succade (sɒkē·d). 1463. [a. AF. *sukade* = OF. *succade*, of unkn. origin (see -ADE 1 c).] Fruit preserved in sugar, either candied or in syrup; *pl.* sweetmeats of candied fruit or vegetable products. Now *Obs.* or *rare.* **b.** S. gourd, the vegetable marrow 1866. So †**Succate** –1715.

†**Succeda·neous,** *a.* 1646. [f. L. *succedaneus*, f. *succedere* to SUCCEED.] Taking, or serving in, the place of something else; acting as a succedaneum or substitute.

‖**Succedaneum** (sɒksīdē·niɒ̆m). *Pl.* **-ea, -eums.** 1643. [mod.L., neut. sing. of L. *succedaneus* (see prec.).] **1.** A thing which (*rarely*, a person who) replaces or serves in the place of another; a substitute 1662. **2.** *Med.* A drug, frequently of inferior efficacy, substituted for another 1643. †**3.** Misused for: A remedy, cure –1789.

1. In lieu of me, you will have a charming s., Lady Harriet Stanhope H. WALPOLE.

Succedent (sŏksī·dĕnt), *a.* and *sb.* Now *Obs.* or *rare.* late ME. [ad. L. *succedens, -ent-*, *succedere* to SUCCEED.] **A.** *adj.* **1.** Following, succeeding, subsequent 1450. **2.** Astrol. *S. houses*: the 2nd, 5th, 8th, and 11th houses 1591. **B.** *sb.* †**1.** A thing that follows another –1608. **2.** *Astrol.* A 'succedent house'. late ME.

Succeed (sŏksī·d), *v.* late ME. [a. OF. *succeder* or ad. L. *succedere*, to go under, go up, come close after, go near, f. *suc-* = SUB- 11–18 + *cedere* to go.] **1.** *intr.* To come next after and take the place of another, either by descent, election, or appointment, in a position of rule or ownership; to be the immediate successor in an office or in an estate. **b.** *transf.* Const. *to* (†*into*): To follow another in the enjoyment or exercise of; to be the next to share or take part in 1612. **2.** *trans.* To take the place of, as successor in an office or heir to an estate; to be successor or heir to 1503. †**3.** To fall heir to, inherit, come into possession of –1725. **4.** *intr.* To come next in an order of individual persons or things; to follow on; also, †to occupy the space vacated by something. late ME. **5.** To follow or come *after* in the course of events, the sequence of things, the order of development, etc.; to take place or come into being subsequently 1450. †**b.** To follow as a consequence *of* or *upon*; to proceed *from* a source; to ensue, result –1710. †**6.** To follow *in*, or come *into, the place of* someone or something –1701. **b.** Const. *to*: To take the place of 1700. †**7.** Of an estate, etc.: To descend in succession; to devolve *upon*, to come down *from.* Chiefly *Sc.* –1604. **8.** *trans.* To come after in the course of time or the sequence of events 1525. †**9.** *intr.* To happen, come to pass –1653. †**10.** Of an enterprise, etc.: To have a certain issue; to turn out (well or ill, etc.) –1684. **11.** To have the desired or a fortunate issue; to turn out successfully 1450. **b.** Of growing plants: To do well, thrive 1812. **12.** Of persons: To attain a desired end or object; to be successful in an endeavour; to bring one's labours to a happy issue. Also formerly, with adv., to have 'good' or 'ill success'. 1509. †**13.** *trans.* To give success to; to prosper, further –1843. †**14.** To come up or near *to*, approach (*rare*) –1697.

1. When Sir Ralf died, Sir John succeeded 1891. b. The christian saints succeeded..to the honours 1782. 2. Richard Cromwell succeeded his father 1860. 4. There was another Malefactor to succeede EVELYN. 5. Enjoy, till I return, Short pleasures, for long woes are to s. MILT. 6. b. Revenge succeeds to love, and rage to grief DRYDEN. 7. *All's Well* III. vii. 23. 8. Shame succeeds the short-liv'd pleasure COWLEY. 10. But euery day things now succeeded worse DANIEL. 11. I only used it in two instances, in both of which it succeeded 1808. 12. Alike my scorn, if he succeed or fail POPE. She succeeded in finding an empty carriage 1898. 13. Pallas..succeeds their enterprise POPE. 14. Will you to the cooler cave s.? DRYDEN. Hence **Succee·der,** a successor (now *rare*); one who is successful.

Succeeding (sŏksī·diŋ), *vbl. sb.* 1450. [-ING [1].] **1.** Successful issue, success. †**2.** Succession –1679. †**3.** Consequence. SHAKS.

Succentor (sŏkse·ntǫɹ). 1642. [a. late L., f. L. *succinere* to sing to, accompany, 'chime in', agree, f. *suc-* = SUB- 8 + *canere* to sing. In sense 2, assoc. with SUB- 6.] †**1.** A chanter who takes up the chant after the precentor, or who presides over the left choir –1817. **2.** A precentor's deputy 1642.

‖**Succès** (sükse). 1859. [F., = success.] In *s. d'estime*, a cordial reception given to something out of respect rather than from admiration; *s. fou*, a success marked by wild enthusiasm; *s. de scandale*, the success of a thing, e.g. of a work of art, dependent upon its scandalous character.

Success (sŏkse·s). 1537. [ad. L. *successus*, f. *succedere* (*success-*) to SUCCEED.] †**1.** That which happens in the sequel; the termination (favourable or otherwise) of affairs; the result –1733. †**b.** An event –1753. †**c.** The result (of an experiment), the effect (of a medicine) –1756. **2.** The fortune (good or bad) befalling anyone in a particular situation or affair. *Good s.* = sense 3; *ill s.*: failure, misadventure, misfortune. *arch.* 1548. †**b.** In particularized use. –1764. **3.** (= the older *good s.*) The prosperous achievement of something attempted; the attainment of an object according to one's desire: now often with particular ref. to the attainment of wealth or position 1586. **b.** An instance of this; a successful undertaking or achievement 1666. **c.** *transf.* One who or a thing which succeeds or is successful 1882. †**4.** Succession or sequence in time or occurrence –1690. †**5.** Succession as of heirs, etc. –1611.

1. *All's Well* III. vi. 86. †*In the s.*, eventually. 2. Perplex'd and troubl'd at his bad s. MILT. b. After diuers unfortunat successes in warre DRAYTON. 3. Giue but success to mine attempting spirit KYD. That argument of s. which is always powerful with men of the world GEO. ELIOT. c. Mrs. Hartwell's dance was a great s. 1885. 5. Our Parents Noble Names, In whose successe we are gentle SHAKS.

Successful (sŏkse·sfŭl), *a.* 1588. [f. prec. + -FUL.] **1.** Of persons: That succeeds or achieves success, *esp.* (in recent use), that attains to wealth or position, that 'gets on'. Also *transf.* of things. **2.** Of actions, conditions, etc.: Attended with, characterized by, or resulting in success 1588.

1. A s. play 1848. It failed; we tried again, and were s. TYNDALL. 2. And welcome Nephews from succesfull wars SHAKS. Hence **Succe·ssful·ly** *adv.*, **-ness.**

Succession (sŏkse·ʃən). ME. [ad. OF., or L. *successio, -onem*, f. *succedere.*] **I. 1.** The action of a person or thing following, or succeeding to the place of, another; the coming of one thing or person after another; also, the passing from one act or state to another; an instance of this. late ME. †**2.** The course, lapse, or process *of time* –1655. **3.** The transmission (or mode of transmission) *of* an estate, royal or official dignity, or the like ME. **4.** The process by which one person succeeds another in the occupation or possession of an estate, a throne, or the like; the act or fact of succeeding according to custom or law *to* the rights and liabilities of a predecessor; the conditions or principles in accordance with which this is done 1513. **b.** *pregnantly* for: The line or order of succession 1533. **5.** (A person's) right or privilege of succeeding to an estate or dignity 1461. **6.** The act of succeeding to the episcopate by the reception of lawfully transmitted authority by ordination 1565.

1. By reflecting on the appearing of various Ideas, one after another in our Understandings, we get the Notion of S. LOCKE. Phr. *In s.*, one after another in regular sequence, successively. 3. So long as the Earl of Warwick lived, he was not certaine of the Kingdoms s. 1641. 4. He swore consent to your S. SHAKS. Phr. *The s.*, the conditions under which successors to a particular estate, throne, etc. are appointed. *War of S.*, a war to settle a dispute as to the s. to a particular throne. *By s.*, according to the customary or legal principle by which one succeeds another in an inheritance, an office, etc. by inherited right. b. He was in the s. to an earldom MACAULAY. 5. The right to make wills or settlements or successions is the creation of positive law 1894. 6. *Apostolic(al) s.* (or *the s.*), the continued transmission of the ministerial commission, through an unbroken line of bishops from the Apostles onwards.

II. †1. Successors, heirs, or descendants collectively; progeny, issue -1697. **†2.** A generation (of men); chiefly *pl.* (future or successive) generations -1720. **†b.** Posterity -1704. **3.** A series of persons or things in orderly sequence; a continued line (*of* sovereigns, heirs to an estate, etc.); an unbroken line or stretch (*of* objects coming one after another) 1579. **†b.** The followers collectively, or a sect of followers, of a school of thought (tr. Gr. διαδοχή) -1699. **4.** A set of persons or things succeeding in the place of others 1647. **†5.** That to which a person succeeds as heir (*rare*) -1751.

1. Their young S. all their Cares employ: They breed, they brood, instruct and educate DRYDEN. 3. A s. of victories MACAULAY. Every progress of Elizabeth..was a s. of shows and interludes 1874.

III. *techn.* **a.** *Mus.* The order in which the notes of a melody proceed. Also = SEQUENCE 3 b. 1752. **b.** *Agric.* and *Hort.* (*a*) The rotation (of crops); (*b*) the maturing of crops of the same kind by a system of successive sowings so that as one is declining another is coming on 1778. **c.** *Geol.*, etc. The continued sequence in a definite order of species, types, etc.; *spec.* the descent in uninterrupted series of forms modified by evolution or development 1834.

attrib.: **s.-crop**, a crop of some plant coming in s. to another; **s. duty**, a duty assessed upon s. to estate; **s. house**, one of a series of forcing-houses having regularly graded temperatures into which plants are moved in s.; **s. powder**, a poison supposed to have been made of lead acetate; **S. States**, the states resulting from the dismemberment of Austria-Hungary under the Treaty of Versailles; **s. tax**, a tax similar to s. duty.

Successional (sŏkse·ʃənăl), *a.* 1600. [f. prec. + -AL 1.] **1.** Pertaining to, characterized by, or involving the succession of persons as heirs, rulers, or the like; passing or proceeding by succession or descent; often with special ref. to the apostolic succession. **2.** Of things: Following one upon another; occurring in succession; involved in a succession 1685.

2. A useful s. crop of flowers 1881. Hence **Succe·ssionally** *adv.* by succession.

Successionist (sŏkse·ʃənist). 1846. [f. as prec. + -IST.] One who maintains the validity or necessity of a succession; *esp.* one who upholds the doctrine of the Apostolic Succession.

Successive (sŏkse·siv), *a.* late ME. [ad. med.L. *successivus*, f. *success-*, *succedere* to SUCCEED.] **1. a.** With pl. or compound sb.: Coming one after another in an uninterrupted sequence; following one another in order. **b.** With sing. sb.: Following another of the same kind in a regular sequence or series. Somewhat *rare*. 1597. **2.** Characterized by or involving succession; brought about or produced in succeeding stages 1685. **†3.** = HEREDITARY -1726.

1. a. Three s. Bishops..excommunicated him 1606. b. And three..he assailes;..each s. after other quailes DANIEL. 2. Doctrine of s. development not confirmed by the admission that man is of modern origin 1835. 3. Pleade my Successiue Title with your Swords. I was the first borne Sonne. SHAKS. Hence **Succe·ssive·ly** *adv.*, **-ness.**

Successless (sŏkse·slės), *a.* Now *rare.* 1584. [f. SUCCESS + -LESS.] Without, or having no, success; unsuccessful.

How mighty men made foul s. war Against the gods PEELE. Hence **Succe·ssless-ly** *adv.*, **-ness.**

Successor (sŏkse·səɹ). ME. [a. OF. (AF.) *successour*, ad. L. *successor, -orem*, f. *success-*, *succedere* to SUCCEED.] One who succeeds another in an office, function, or position. (Correlative to *predecessor*.) Also *transf.* of a thing.

A gift to such a corporation, either of lands or of chattels, without naming their successors, vests an absolute property in them so long as the corporation subsists BLACKSTONE. So **Succe·ssorship.** **†Succe·ssory** *a.* hereditary -1641.

Succiferous (sɒksi·fĕrəs), *a. rare.* 1655. [f. mod.L. *succiferus*, f. SUCCUS; see -FEROUS.] *Bot.* Producing or bearing sap.

Succin- (sɒksin), comb. form (bef. a vowel) of L. *succinum* amber, in the names of various amide and anilide derivatives of SUCCINIC acid, e.g. *succinamic acid, succinanil.*

Succinate (sɒ·ksineɪt). 1790. [ad. F.; see SUCCINIC and -ATE 4.] *Chem.* A salt of succinic acid.

Succinct (sŏksi·ŋkt), *pa. pple.*, *ppl. a.*, and *a.* late ME. [ad. L. *succinctus*, *succingere*, f. *suc-* = SUB- 2, 25 + *cingere* to gird.] **A.** *pa. pple.* and *ppl. a.* **1.** Girt, engirdled. **2.** Of garments, etc.: Girded up; confined by or as by a girdle. Also of persons. 1604. **3.** *Ent.* Of certain pupæ: supported by a silken filament round the middle 1891.

2. The Priest..s. for sacrificial feast 1866.

B. *adj.* **1.** Of a narrative, etc.: Compressed into small compass; brief and concise 1585. **2.** Of persons, their speech, style, etc.: Characterized by verbal brevity and conciseness; terse 1603. **3.** Of garments: Not ample or full, close-fitting, scant. *arch.* or *poet.* 1667. **4.** Of short duration, brief, curt 1796.

1. A full, though s. and sober Narrative 1711. 2. A s. and dry writer 1759. 3. Some novelties of dress, viz., very low stays, and very s. petticoats 1755. 4. With a s. bow..he took a hasty leave MME D'ARBLAY. Hence **Succi·nct-ly** *adv.*, **-ness.**

‖ **Succinea** (sŏksi·niă). *Pl.* **-eæ, -eas.** 1840. [mod.L., fem. of *succineus*, f. *succinum* amber.] *Zool.* Any gasteropod of the genus of this name: so called from the transparent texture and amber colour of the shell.

Succinic (sŏksi·nik), *a.* 1790. [ad. F. *succinique*, f. L. *succinum* amber; see -IC 1 b.] **1.** Chem. *S. acid*: a dibasic acid obtained by the dry distillation of amber. (Formerly called *salt* or *spirit of amber*.) **b.** So *s. anhydride*, etc. 1805. **2.** Found in amber, as an insect 1836.

Succinimide (sɒksi·nimɜid). 1857. [f. prec. + IMIDE.] *Chem.* A crystalline substance obtained by the action of dry ammonia gas on succinic anhydride.

Succinite (sɒ·ksinɜit). 1816. [f. SUCCINUM + -ITE.] **1.** *Min.* **a.** A granular garnet of the colour of amber. **b.** Amber 1854. **2.** *Chem.* The insoluble resinous element in amber 1868.

Succino- (sɒ·ksino), used as comb. form (bef. a consonant) of L. *succinum* amber.

Succinol (sɒ·ksinǫl). 1913. [f. L. *succinum* + -OL.] Purified amber tar-oil, used in the treatment of skin-diseases.

Succinous (sɒ·ksinəs), *a. rare.* 1658. [f. next + -OUS.] Of or pertaining to amber.

‖ **Succinum** (sɒ·ksinɒ̆m). 1608. [L.] Amber.

Succinyl (sɒ·ksinil). 1868. [f. SUCCINIC + -YL.] *Chem.* The radical of succinic acid. Hence **Succiny·lic** *a.* = SUCCINIC.

Succise (sŏksɜi·s), *a.* 1880. [ad. L. *succisus*, *succidere*.] *Bot.* Shaped as if abruptly cut or broken off at the lower end.

Succory (sɒ·kəri). 1533. [Alteration of *cicoree, sichorie, sycory*, old forms of CHICORY.] **1.** The plant *Cichorium Intybus* (family *Compositæ*), with bright blue flowers, found wild in England, esp. by roadsides. Also, its leaves and roots used medicinally and as food. **2.** Applied with qualifying words to other composites, chiefly of the tribe *Cichoriaceæ* 1538.

Succose (sɒ·kous), *a. rare.* 1859. [ad. L. *succosus*, f. *succus* juice.] *Bot.* Full of juice or sap. So **†Succo·sity**, juice, moisture 1530-1579.

Succotash (sɒ·kŏtæʃ). 1778. [a. Narragansett *msiquatash* (inanimate pl.).] A dish of N. Amer. Indian origin, usu. consisting of green maize and beans boiled together.

Succour (sɒ·kəɹ), *sb.* Also (now *U.S.*) **succor.** [ME. *sucurs, socurs, socours*, etc., a. OF. (AF.) *sucurs, soc(c)ours*:—med.L. *succursus*, f. *succurrere* to SUCCOUR. The final *-s* was taken early as the pl. suffix and a new sing. (*succour*) came into existence, the pl. of which is identical with the old singular.] **1.** Aid, help, assistance. **2.** One who or that which helps; a means of assistance; an aid ME. **3.** Military assistance in men or supplies; *esp.* auxiliary forces; reinforcements ME. **4.** Shelter, protection; a place of shelter, sheltered place, refuge. *Obs.* exc. *dial.* ME.

1. I can no mor, but aske of hem socours 1460. The devotion of life or fortune to the s. of the poor JOHNSON. 2. Thou art my socoure, haist the to helpe me COVERDALE *Ps.* xxi. 19. 3. Our watchful General had discern'd from far This mighty s., which made glad the Foe DRYDEN.

Succour (sɒ·kəɹ), *v.* Also (now *U.S.*) **succor.** ME. [a. OF. (i) *socorre, suc(c)urre, secourre*:—L. *succurrere*, f. *suc-* = SUB- 25 + *currere* to run; (ii) *suc(c)urir* (with change of conjugation), mod.F. *secourir*.] **1.** *trans.* To help, assist, aid (a person, etc.). **2.** To furnish with military assistance; to bring reinforcements to; *spec.* to relieve (a besieged place) ME. **†3.** To relieve or remedy (a state of want, weakness, etc.); to relieve (a diseased condition) -1645. **4.** To shelter, protect. Now *dial.* late ME. **5.** *Naut.* To strengthen, make firm or taut 1688.

1. He is able to sucker them that are tempted TINDALE *Heb.* ii. 18. *transf.* Yet not for me, shine sun to s. flowers 1599. 2. I will socoure hym with all my puyssaunce MALORY. 3. That so the Parliament May ..s. our just Fears MILT. 5. To S. a Cable 1706. So **Su·ccourable** *a.* affording succour, helpful (*Obs.* exc. *arch.*). **†Su·ccourer**, one who, or that which aids or assists -1686.

Succourless (sɒ·kəɹlės), *a.* Now *rare.* late ME. [-LESS.] Of persons or conditions: Without help, helpless; *freq.* without resources or means of subsistence, destitute.

Succous (sɒ·kəs), *a. rare.* 1694. [ad. L. *succosus*, f. *succus* juice.] Containing juice or sap; juicy.

‖ **Succuba** (sɒ·kiŭbă). *Pl.* **-bæ** (bī). 1587. [Late L. = strumpet, f. *succubare*, f. *suc-* = SUB- 2 + *cub-* to lie.] = SUCCUBUS.

Succubous (sɒ·kiŭbəs), *a.* 1857. [f. L. *suc-* = SUB- 2 + *cub-* (*-cumbere*) to lie + -OUS.] *Bot.* Having the upper margin of each leaf covered by the lower margin of the one succeeding it; applied to some of the *Jungermanniaceæ*.

‖ **Succubus** (sɒ·kiŭbɒ̆s). *Pl.* **-bi** (bɜi), **†-busses.** late ME. [med.L., masc. form (with fem. meaning) corresp. to SUCCUBA, after INCUBUS.] **1.** A demon in female form supposed to have carnal intercourse with men in their sleep. **2.** *transf.* **a.** A demon, evil spirit; *occas.* a familiar spirit 1601. **b.** A strumpet, whore 1622.

1. For forty years, he had kept up an amatory commerce with a S., called Hermeline 1818. Hence **Su·ccubine** *a.* (*rare*) of or pertaining to a s.

Succulence (sɒ·kiŭlĕns). 1787. [f. as next; see -ENCE.] The quality or condition of being succulent; juiciness. Also, succulent part. So **Su·cculency** 1616.

Succulent (sɒ·kiŭlĕnt), *a.* and *sb.* 1601. [ad. L. *succulentus*, f. *succus* juice; see -LENT, -ULENT.] **A.** *adj.* **1.** Full of juice; juicy. **2.** *transf.* and *fig.* 'Juicy', 'sappy', rich 1626.

1. The fruit, which..is s. in the peach 1785. Rich, deep black, s. mud 1877. 2. His air of rather s. patronage MEREDITH.

B. *sb. Bot.* A succulent plant 1825. Hence **Su·cculently** *adv.*

Succumb (sŏkɒ·m), *v.* 1489. [a. OF. *succomber*, ad. L. *succumbere*, f. *suc-* = SUB- 2 + *-cumbere* to lie.] **†1.** *trans.* To bring down, bring low, overwhelm -1549. **2.** *intr.* To yield to pressure or give way to superior force, authority, etc.: said properly of persons or communities, and *transf.* of conditions, designs; occas. of material things 1604. **3.** *spec.* To sink under the attacks of a disease, the effects of wounds, an operation, etc.; hence, to die 1849.

2. Pardon me if I do not s. to curiosity 1825. 3. He succumbed in a few months to fever LIVINGSTONE.

†Succu·mbent, *a. rare.* 1645. [ad. L. *succumbens, -entem*, *succumbere*.] Subject, submissive *to* -1660. Hence **Succu·mbency** (*rare*), submission.

Succursal (sŏkɒ̄·rsăl), *a.* and *sb.* 1844. [ad. F. *succursal*, only in fem. *succursale* (sc. *église* church), ad. L. *succursalis*, f. *succursus* SUCCOUR.] **A.** *adj.* Subsidiary; applied *esp.* to a religious establishment dependent upon a principal one.

Its Cathedral, surrounded by its s. churches 1855.

B. *sb.* A subsidiary establishment; a branch institution, society, business, etc. Also in F. form **succursale.** 1859.

‖ **Succus** (sɒ·kɒ̆s). *Pl.* **succi** (sɒ·ksəi). 1719. [L.] A juice; in scientific terminology applied to (*a*) fluid secretions in an animal or vegetable body, (*b*) juices extracted from plants.

†**Succussa·tion.** 1646. [ad. L. **succussatio*, *-onem*, f. *succussare*, f. *succuss-*, *succutere*, f. *suc-* = SUB- 25 + *quatere* to shake.] Shaking up, violent shaking, jolting –1774. **b.** Trotting (of a horse) –1681.

Succussion (sŏkɒ·ʃən). 1622. [ad. L. *succussio*, *-onem*, f. *succuss-*, *succutere* (see prec.).] The action of shaking or the condition of being shaken, esp. with violence; an instance of this. **b.** *spec.* (*Med.*) An act or method of diagnosis in pneumothorax, etc., which consists in shaking the thorax to detect the presence of fluid 1747. So **Succu·ss** *v. trans.*

Successive (sŏkɒ·siv), *a. rare.* 1742. [f. L. *succuss-*, *succutere.*] Characterized by shaking.

Such (sɒtʃ), *dem. adj.* and *pron.* [OE. *swelc*, *swilc*, *swylc* :—OTeut. **swalīko-*, **swilīko-*, f. *swa* So *adv.* + **līko-* body, form (cf. LIKE *a.*). OE. *swylc*, *swulc* became in ME. *swülch*, *swulch*, which, by the absorption of *w* and loss of *l*, gave *such*, the modern standard form. The variants *sech* and *sich* are widespread locally.] **I.** **1.** Of the character, degree, or extent described, referred to, or implied in what has been said. (With a concrete sb., or an abstract sb. used in a particularized sense, now always *s. a* exc. *poet.*) **2.** Standing predicatively at the head of a sentence or clause, and referring summarily to a statement or description just made ME. **3.** Of the same kind or class as something mentioned or referred to; of that kind; similar, the like. *Obs.* or *arch.* exc. in collocation with a numeral, indef. adj., etc. ME. **4.** Equivalent to a descriptive adj. or adv. on which it follows closely and the repetition of which is thus avoided. (*So* is now preferred.) OE. **5.** The previously described or specified; the (person or thing) before mentioned. (In this sense usu. *s.* (not *s. a*) with a sing. sb.). late ME.

1. She thinks not fit s. he her face should see CRASHAW. S. Joy my Soul, s. Pleasurs fill'd my Sight DRYDEN. Thou didst ill to speak to s. a man of s. matters SCOTT. 2. Lo sich it is to haue a tunge loos CHAUCER. Phr. *S. is life!*, now often used trivially as an expression of resignation or acquiescence in things as they are. 3. Of rotchets, whitings or s. common fish 1613. 4. A heroic poem, truly s. DRYDEN. 5. For default of *s.* issue, viz. that issue which is before mentioned 1818.

II. Where the meaning is determined by ref. to a correlative or dependent clause. **1. a.** With *s.* in both clauses; now *s. as . . s.* = L. *qualis . . talis* OE. **b.** With *what* as the correlative in the dependent clause (*rare*) 1834. †**c.** With advb. *as* as the correlative in the dependent clause –1790. **2.** With correlative *as* pron., also *as that* ME. *S. as* = Of the kind or degree that; the kind of (person or thing) that OE. **3.** In uses marked by special word-order. **a.** In predicative use ME. **b.** *S. as one* or *it is*: having the character that he (it) has; chiefly depreciatory or contemptuous, or apologetic ME. **c.** In attrib. use after its sb. OE. **d.** Hence *s. as* is used to introduce examples of a class: = for example, *e.g.* 1695. **4.** The principal clause may be reduced to *s.* and the words qualified by it for the purpose of producing a terse (exclamatory) form. late ME. **b.** The clause introduced by *as* may be reduced to the subj. only; when this is a pron., it may be either nom. or accus., *e.g.* 's. as *me*' or 's. as *I*' (*sc.* am) OE. **c.** *There is s. a thing as*: a phr. used to hint that the thing referred to exists and therefore must be taken into account often used *colloq.* to convey a veiled threat 1729. **5.** *S. . . as* (OE. *swā*): the . . that, *pl.* those . . that; any or all . . that; as many (or as much) . . as OE. **6.** With relative *who*, *which* (*whence*, etc.) or *that*: = 'such . . as'. Now *rare* and regarded as incorrect. OE. **7.** Followed by a dependent clause introduced by *that*, *as that* (now *rare*), etc., or by *as to* (†*to*) with infin., expressing a consequence. The meaning of *s.* tends to be intensive = so great, etc. OE. **b.** predicative ME. **c.** In attrib. use after its sb. 1771. **d.** With the clauses in reverse order, that containing *s.* being explanatory of what precedes. late ME. **8.** By suppression of the clause expressing comparison or relativity, *s.* acquires emphatic force = so great, so eminent, and the like OE. **b.** *colloq.* Used as an absolute intensive 1553. **9.** Preceding an adj. used attrib., *s.*, *s. a* becomes advb. = so, so . . a 1522.

1. **a.** S. as is the tree s. is the fruit 1586. *Prov.* S. master, s. man. **c.** As the man is, soch is also his strength COVERDALE *Judges* viii. 21. **2.** We'll each of us give you s. a thrashing as you'll remember HUGHES. **3. a.** Her conduct was s. as might have been expected from the weakness of her principles MRS. RADCLIFFE. **b.** But, s. as the rooms were, there were plenty of them HARDY. **c.** Tears s. as Angels weep MILT. **d.** Many large gold coins, s. as the . . doubloon 1875. **4.** S. a dinner as we had to-day! 1779. **b.** Others s. as he SHAKS. **c.** There are s. things as horsewhips 1889. **5.** S. ale as he hath brued, let him drynke him self 1539. **6.** S. suffering Soules That welcome wrongs SHAKS. **7.** This filled my Mind with s. a huddle of Ideas, that . . I fell into the following Dream ADDISON. He . . had borne himself with s. gallantry as to attract the attention of his superior officers 1892. **d.** You still shall liue (s. vertue hath my Pen) SHAKS. **8.** *Merry W.* II. i. 45. **b.** It's ever s. a way off 1803. **9.** This mighty army . . collected from s. distant parts 1742.

III. 1. Used to indicate or suggest a name, designation, number or quantity, instead of the specific term that would be required in a particular instance 1460. **2.** *Comb.* (parasynthetic) 1591.

1. That the feoffour pay to the feoffee . . s. a sume at s. a day 1544. Phr. *S. and s.*; Number so-and-so in s.-and-s. a street 1861. **2.** S. a coulour'd Perrywig SHAKS.

IV. Absolute and pronominal uses. †**1.** The persons or things before mentioned; those, they; also with sing. ref., that person or thing –1655. **2.** Persons or things such as those mentioned, described, or referred to OE. **3.** With dependent rel. pron.: Such people *as*, those (people) *who*, *whose*, etc.; all or any *that* OE. **b.** People of the same kind *as* 1823. **4.** Such a thing; the thing mentioned or referred to OE. **5.** *S. and s.*: such and such persons or things; also *sing.*, this and this 1450.

2. To s. my errand is MILT. Phr. *And s.*, and suchlike, and the like. **3.** S. whose fathers were right worshipful MASSINGER. **b.** S. as I are free in spirit when our limbs are chained SCOTT. **4.** A forest became s. by a stroke of the pen, not by any physical change 1912. **5.** We have done s., and s., and s. 1893

Phrases, *Many* (*more*), *some*, *all*, *every*, *s.*, many (etc.) . . of the (same) kind, many . . like this. *S. another*, *another s.*, another . . of the kind, another similar. **No s.** *adj.*, **none s.** *absol.* or as *pron.* **a.** No (person or thing) of the kind; none of the kind. **b.** No great; advb. qualifying an adj. = not (a) very, not a. **c.** *No s.* †*matter* or *thing*: nothing of the kind; also exclamatorily, = not at all, not a bit of it, quite the contrary. **S. a(n) one. a.** One of that kind. **b.** Followed by rel. pron. *as*: One of the kind that; one who, a thing which. **c.** Followed by rel. adv. *as*: One of the same kind as; one like (so-and-so). **d.** So-and-so. *Obs.* or *arch.* **As s. a.** In that capacity. **b.** Hence: Accordingly, consequently, thereupon. *colloq.* or *vulgar.* **c.** In itself; *quâ* (so-and-so). *S. kind of*, of s. a kind. *S. time as* (or *that*), the time when, the moment at which.

Su·ch-like, su·chlike, *a.* and *pron.* late ME. [f. prec. + LIKE *a.*] **A.** *adj.* Of such a kind; of the like or a similar kind; of the before-mentioned sort or character. **b.** Having forward ref., usu. with correl. *as* (*rare*) 1591.

Many other suche lyke thinges ye do TINDALE *Mark* vii. 8. **b.** Such like petty crimes as these SHAKS.

B. *pron.* Usu. *pl.* Such-like persons or things; also *sing.*, something of that kind. Chiefly in *and s.*, *or s.* late ME.

These Bushes, Brakes, and suchlike 1669. A smooth marble hearth-stone, or such like GOLDSM.

Suchness (sɒ·tʃnės). Chiefly *Philos.* OE. [f. SUCH *a.* + -NESS.] The condition or quality of being such; quality.

Suchwise (sɒ·tʃ,wəiz), *adv. rare.* late ME. [Short for *in such wise.*] In such a manner.

Suck (sɒk), *sb.* ME. [f. next.] **I. a.** The action or an act of sucking milk from the breast; the milk or other fluid sucked at one time. **b.** The application of suction by the mouth either to an external object (e.g. a wound, a pipe) or internally 1760. **2.** A small draught of liquid; a drink 1625. †**3.** Milk sucked (or to be sucked) from the breast; mother's milk –1655. **4.** The drawing of air by suction; *occas.* a draught or current of air; *spec.* in *Coal-mining*, the backward suction of air following an explosion of fire-damp 1667. **5.** The sucking action of eddying or swirling water; the sound caused by this; *locally*, the place at which a body of water moves in such a way as to suck objects into its vortex ME. **6.** *slang.* A deception; a disappointing event or result. Also *s.-in.* 1856. **7.** *pl.* Sweetmeats. Also *collect. sing. colloq.* 1858.

1. **a.** Phr. *At s.*, engaged in sucking. **b.** I saw the cut, gave it [*sc.* my finger] a s., wrapt it up, and thought no more about it STERNE.

To give s.: see SUCK *v.* III. 2.

Suck (sɒk), *v.* Pa. t. and pple. **sucked.** [OE. *sūcan*, corresp. to L. *sugere*, f. root **sūg-*. Related by ablaut to *soak.*] **I. 1.** *trans.* To draw (liquid, *esp.* milk from the breast) into the mouth by contracting the muscles of the lips, cheeks, and tongue so as to produce a partial vacuum. **b.** of flies, etc., drawing blood, of bees extracting honey from flowers ME. **2.** To imbibe (qualities, etc.) *with* the mother's milk 1586. **3.** To extract or draw (moisture, goodness, etc.) *from* or *out of* a thing; to absorb into itself. late ME. **4.** To derive or extract (information, comfort, profit, etc.) *from*, †*of*, or *out of* 1535. †**5.** To draw (air, breath) into the mouth; to inhale (air, smoke, etc.) –1717. **6.** To draw (water, air, etc.) in some direction, esp. by producing a vacuum 1661. **7.** To draw in so as to swallow up or engulf. (Now *rare* or *Obs.*) 1523. **b.** *fig.* To draw *into* a course of action, etc. 1771.

1. The milke thou suck'st from her did turne to Marble SHAKS. *fig.* Death that hath suckt the honey of thy breath SHAKS. *To s. the blood of* (fig.), to exhaust the resources of, drain the life out of. **3.** *Rich. II*, III. iv. 38. **4.** There out sucke they no small auauntage COVERDALE *Ps.* lxxii. 10. **5.** Tobacco suckt through water by long canes or pipes 1634. **7.** When a whirle-poole sucks the circkled waters 1590.

II. 1. To apply the lips to (a teat, breast, the mother, nurse, or dam) for the purpose of extracting milk; to draw milk from with the mouth OE. **b.** Of flies, bees, etc. late ME. **2.** To apply the lips and tongue (or analogous organs) to (an object) for the purpose of obtaining nourishment; to extract the fluid contents of by such action of the mouth; to absorb (a sweetmeat) in the mouth by the action of the tongue and the muscles of the cheeks ME. **b.** To apply the tongue and inner sides of the lips to (one's teeth) so as to extract particles of food 1595. **3.** *transf.* To draw the moisture, goodness, etc. from 1693. **b.** To work (a pump) dry 1753. **4.** To draw money, information, or the like from (a person); to rob (a person or thing) of its resources or support; to drain, 'bleed' 1558. **5.** With predicative adj.: To render so-and-so by sucking 1530.

2. *To s.* a person's *brains*: see BRAIN *sb.* **3. b.** Phr. *To teach one's grandmother to s. eggs*: said of those who offer advice to others who are more experienced. *To s. the monkey*: see MONKEY *sb.* Phrases. **4.** The land sucked of its nourishment, by a small class of legitimates EMERSON. **5.** Phr. *To s. dry*, to extract all the moisture out of by suction; *fig.* to exhaust.

III. 1. *intr.* Of the young of a mammal: To perform the action described in sense I. 1; to draw milk from the teat; to feed from the breast or udder OE. **b.** of flies drawing blood, etc. 1610. **2.** To give suck (occas. †*to give to s.*): to give milk from the breast or udder, to suckle. Const. simple dat. or *to*. Now *arch.* (*Suck*, properly infin., is now felt as a sb.) ME. **3.** *To s. at*: (*a*) to take a draught of; to inhale; (*b*) to take a pull at (a pipe, drinking vessel) 1584. **4.** Of inanimate objects: To draw by suction ME. **5.** Of a pump: To draw air instead of water, as a result of the exhaustion of the water or a defective valve. Also *fig.* 1627.

1. To see my Ewes graze, & my Lambes sucke SHAKS. **b.** Where the Bee sucks, there s. I SHAKS. **2.** *Macb.* I. vii. 54. **5.** *fig.* Even Byron's pump sucks sometimes, and gives an unpleasant dry wheeze LOWELL.

With advs. **S. in. a.** *trans.* To draw into the mouth by suction; to inhale (air, etc.); *occas.* to draw in (one's breath) etc. **b.** To imbibe (qualities, etc.) *with* one's mother's milk, *with* a draught. **c.** *gen.* To draw or take in (*lit.* and *fig.*); to absorb. **d.** *dial.* and *slang.* To 'take in', cheat, deceive. **S. out.** *trans.* To draw out by or as by suction. **S. up. a.** *trans.* To draw up into the mouth by suction. **b.** To draw up by suction or the creation of a vacuum; to absorb (liquid); to draw up (moisture) by heat; also, to draw up moisture from. **c.** To swallow up. **d.** intr. *To s. up to*, to curry favour with; to toady *to*. *Schoolboy slang.*

Suck-, the vb.-stem used in comb., as in **s.-bo·ttle**, an infant's feeding-bottle; a tippler; **s.-fish** = SUCKER *sb.* II. 2; **s.-(a)-thumb**, a child that sucks its thumb.

Su·ck-egg. 1609. [f. SUCK- + EGG *sb.*] **a.** An animal that is reputed to suck eggs, e.g. a weasel, cuckoo; *fig.* an avaricious person. **b.** A young fellow; *slang*, 'a silly person'.

Sucken (sɒ·kən). *Sc.* late ME. [var. of SOKEN; orig. 'resort' (*sc.* to a particular mill).] **1.** The duty and liability of tenants within a district astricted to a mill. **2.** The lands astricted to a mill; also, the population of such lands 1754. **b.** *transf.* The area of a bailiff's jurisdiction; the district within which one practises or carries on business 1688.

Hence **Su·ckener**, one who is bound to have his corn ground at a certain mill.

Su·ckeny. *Hist.* late ME. [a. OF. *soucanie*, of Slavonic origin.] A smock.

Sucker (sɒ·kəɹ), *sb.* late ME. [f. SUCK *v.* + -ER [1].] **I. 1.** A young mammal before it is weaned; now *spec.* a sucking-pig; a young whale-calf. **b.** *fig.* A greenhorn, simpleton. *U.S.* 1857. **2.** One who or that which sucks with the mouth 1440. **3.** One who lives at the expense of another; one who draws profit or extorts subsistence from some source; *U.S. slang*, a sponger, parasite 1500. **4.** A shoot thrown out from the base of a tree or plant, which in most cases may serve for propagation; now *esp.* such a shoot rising from the root under ground, near to, or at some distance from, the trunk; also, (now *rare*) a runner (as of the strawberry); also, a lateral shoot; in the tobacco plant, an axillary shoot 1577. **b.** *fig.* (freq. with ref. to the withdrawal of nourishment from the parent stem) 1591. **5.** An organ adapted for sucking or absorbing nourishment by suction, *e.g.* the proboscis of an insect 1685. **6.** Any fish having a conformation of the lips which suggests that it feeds by suction; *esp.* N. Amer. cyprinoid fishes of the family *Catostomidæ* 1772. **b.** *U.S.* An inhabitant of the state of Illinois 1833. **7.** Used as a book-rendering of *Suctoria*, the name of various groups of animals having a sucking apparatus 1835. **8.** The embolus, piston, or rising-valve of a pump; the piston of a syringe or an air-pump 1611. **9. a.** A pipe or tube through which anything is drawn by suction; *locally*, a hood over a fire-place 1755. **b.** An air-hole fitted with a valve; a valve for the regulation of the flow of air 1797. **c.** *Bot.* = HAUSTORIUM 1849.

2. In names of animals, as BLOOD-SUCKER, GOAT-SUCKER, HONEYSUCKER. **3.** Flatterers to the kyng.. suckers of his purse and robbers of his subiectes HALL. **4. b.** If thou payest nothing, they will count thee a s., no branch FULLER.

II. 1. A part or organ adapted for adhering to an object; the adhesive pad of an insect's foot, etc.; a suctorial disk, foot, etc. 1681. **2.** Any fish characterized by a suctorial disk by which it adheres to foreign objects; *e.g.* fishes of the genus *Cyclopterus*, the genus *Liparis* (sea-snails or snail-fishes), and the remora (*Echeneis*) 1753. **3.** A toy, consisting of a round piece of leather with a string attached at the centre, which, laid wet upon a solid surface and drawn up by the string, adheres by reason of the vacuum created 1681.

attrib. and *Comb.*: **s.-cup, -foot**, a cup or foot acting as a s.; **-fish** = senses I. 6, II. 2; **-rod**, a pump rod. Hence **Su·ckered** *ppl. a.* of an organ: provided with suckers.

Sucker (sɒ·kəɹ), *v.* 1660. [f. prec.] †**1.** *trans.* To fit or provide with a sucker or valve. **2.** To remove superfluous young shoots from (tobacco or maize plants); also, †to remove (the shoots) 1661. **3.** *intr.* To throw up suckers. Also occas. *pass.*, to be thrown up as a sucker. 1802.

†**Su·cket.** 1481. [Altered f. SUCCATE after SUCK *v.* and -ET.] = SUCCADE -1751.

Sucking (sɒ·kiŋ), *vbl. sb.* late ME. [f. SUCK *v.* + -ING [1].] **1.** The action of SUCK *v.*; suction. Also, an instance of this. **2.** *pl.* What is obtained by suction (*rare*). late ME.

attrib. and *Comb.*: **s.-cushion, -pad**, a lobulated mass of fat occupying the space between the masseter and the external surface of the buccinator; †**-tooth** = MILK-TOOTH; **-tube**, a tube through which liquid is sucked into the mouth.

Sucking (sɒ·kiŋ), *ppl. a.* OE. [f. SUCK *v.* + -ING [2].] **1.** That sucks milk from the breast, that is still being suckled, unweaned. **2.** Of an animal that is still sucking its dam. late ME. **b.** Of a bird: That is still with its mother. Now chiefly in *s. dove*, echoed from Shaks. 1590. **3.** *fig.* Not come to maturity; not fully developed 1648. **4.** That sucks down, under water, into a whirlpool, etc. 1513.

2. My enemies are but s. critics, who would fain be nibbling ere their teeth are come DRYDEN. **b.** I will roare you as gently as any s. Doue SHAKS.

Su·cking-fish. 1697. A fish furnished with a sucker or adhesive organ. **a.** The REMORA, *Echeneis remora*. **b.** Applied to other fishes, e.g. the Cornish sucker, the lump-sucker 1776.

Su·cking-pig. 1566. A new-born or very young pig; a young milk-fed pig suitable for roasting whole. (Formerly often called *roasting pig*.)

Su·cking-pump. 1660. †**1.** An air-pump. BOYLE. **2.** A suction pump. Now *rare*. 1660.

Suckle (sɒ·k'l), *v.* late ME. [perh. a back-formation from SUCKLING *sb.*] **1.** *trans.* To give suck to; to nurse (a child) at the breast. **b.** *fig.* To nourish *with*, bring up *on* 1654. **2.** To cause to take milk from the breast or udder; to put to suck 1523. **3.** *intr.* To suck *at* the breast (*rare*) 1688.

1. The brests of Hecuba When she did s. Hector, look'd not louelier Then Hectors forhead SHAKS. **b.** A Pagan suckled in a creed outworn WORDSW.

Suckler (sɒ·kləɹ). 1473. [f. SUCKLE *v.* + -ER [1].] **1.** An unweaned mammal (rarely an infant); *esp.* a sucking calf. **2.** An animal that suckles its young, a mammal (*rare*) 1850.

Suckling (sɒ·kliŋ), *sb.*[1] 1440. [f. SUCK *v.* + -LING [1].] **a.** An infant that is at the breast or is unweaned. **b.** = prec. **1.** 1530.

Suckling (sɒ·kliŋ), *sb.*[2] 1440. [app. f. *suckle*, short for HONEYSUCKLE.] **1.** Clover. (Also *lamb-sucklings*.) *dial.* **2.** = HONEYSUCKLE 2 (*Lonicera Perichymenum*). *Obs.* exc. *dial.* 1653.

Sucrate (siū·kreⁱt). 1868. [a. F., f. *sucre* SUGAR + -ATE [4].] *Chem.* A compound of a substance with sucrose.

‖ **Sucre** (sū·kre). 1886. [f. name of Antonio José de *Sucre*, a S. Amer. patriot.] A silver coin of Ecuador of the value of two shillings.

Sucro- (siū·kro), used as comb. form of F. *sucre* sugar.

Sucrose (siū·krous). 1862. [f. F. *sucre* SUGAR + -OSE [2].] *Chem.* Any one of the sugars having the composition ($C_{12}H_{22}O_{11}$) and properties of cane-sugar; = SACCHAROSE.

Suction (sɒ·kʃən). 1626. [ad. L. *suctio*, *-onem*, f. *suct-*, *sugere* to SUCK.] **1.** The action of sucking with the tongue and lips (or analogous organs). Also, an instance of this. **b.** Imbibing strong drink, drinking. *slang.* 1817. **2.** The production of a more or less complete vacuum with the result that external atmospheric pressure forces fluid into the vacant space or causes the adhesion of surfaces 1658. **3.** Short for *s.-pipe* 1886.

attrib. and *Comb.*: **s. box, chamber**, a chamber in a pump into which the liquid is conveyed by a s.-pipe; **s. pipe**, (*a*) the pipe leading from the bottom of a pump barrel to the reservoir from which fluid is to be drawn; (*b*) a pipe for the extraction of dust from tow; **s. pump**, a pump of the type in which the barrel is placed above the level of the reservoir, and is connected therewith by a s. pipe; **s. stop**, any of the 'clicks' peculiar to certain S. Afr. languages; **s. valve**, (*a*) the valve at the bottom of the cylinder of a s. pump, below the piston; (*b*) the valve in a steam engine through which the water is drawn from the hot-well into the feed-pump. Hence **Su·ctional** *a.* (*rare*) having a power of s.

Suctorial (sɒktōᵊ·riăl), *a.* 1833. [f. mod. L. *suctorius* (n. pl. *Suctoria*, sc. *animalia*, the name of various zoological groups), f. *suct-*, *sugere* to SUCK *v.*] *Zool.* Of an organ: Adapted for sucking. Of an animal: Having organs adapted for sucking or having the power of suction; belonging to any of the groups named *Suctoria* in which the mouth is adapted for sucking, or which possess sucking disks or the like. Of a habit, etc.: Involving or characterized by suction. So **Sucto·rian**, a member of the *Suctoria*; *esp.* a cyclostomous fish. **Sucto·rious** *a.* (now *rare*), suctorial 1815.

‖ **Sudamina** (siudæ·mină), *sb. pl.* 1671. [mod. L., pl. of *sudamen*, f. *sudare* to sweat.] *Path.* Minute whitish vesicles or pustules caused by the accumulation of sweat in the upper layers of the skin after copious perspiration, esp. in certain fevers. Hence **Suda·minal** *a.*

Sudan, -ese, variety of SOUDAN, -ESE.

‖ **Sudarium** (siudēᵊ·riǒm). 1601. [L.; see next.] **1.** A napkin or cloth for wiping the face; a handkerchief; *spec.* the cloth with which, according to legend, St. Veronica wiped the face of Christ on the way to Calvary, and on which his features were impressed; hence, a portrait of Christ on a cloth. **2.** = SUDATORIUM 1852.

Sudary (siū·dări). *Obs.* or *arch.* ME. [ad. L. *sudarium*, f. *sudor* sweat; see -ARY [1] 2.] **1.** A napkin or handkerchief used to wipe sweat or tears from the face; a sweat-cloth; *esp.* such a napkin venerated as a relic of a saint. **2.** The napkin which was about Christ's head in the tomb; hence, a shroud or winding-sheet ME. **3.** *Eccl.* A ceremonial cloth of linen or silk, often fringed; *esp.* a humeral veil. *arch.* late ME.

‖ **Sudatorium** (siudătōᵊ·riǒm). 1756. [L., neut. sing. of *sudatorius*; see next and -ORIUM.] A room in which hot-air or steam baths are taken to produce sweating; a sweating-room; esp. *Rom. Antiq.*

Sudatory (siū·dătəri), *a.* and *sb.* 1597. [ad. L. *sudatorius*, f. *sudat-*, *sudare* to sweat; see -ORY.] **A.** *adj.* Producing, accompanied by, or connected with sweating (*rare*). **B.** *sb.* = prec. 1615.

‖ **Sudd** (sɒd). Also **sadd.** 1874. [Arab. *sudd*, n. of action f. *sudd* to obstruct.] An impenetrable mass of floating vegetable matter which obstructs navigation on the White Nile. **b.** *transf.* A temporary dam constructed across a river 1900.

Sudden (sɒ·d'n), *a.*, *adv.*, and *sb.* ME. [a. AF. *sodein*, *sudein* = OF. (mod.F.) *soudain* :— pop. L. **subitanus*, for L. *subitaneus*, f. *subitus*.] **A.** *adj.* **1.** Happening or coming without warning or premonition; taking place or appearing all at once. **b.** Of a turning, etc.: Abrupt, sharp. In *Zool.* and *Bot.* applied to parts that are sharply marked off from the neighbouring parts. late ME. **c.** Of physical objects: Appearing or discovered unexpectedly. Now *arch.* or *poet.* 1460. **2. a.** Of actions, feelings: Unpremeditated, done without forethought. *Obs.* or *arch.* ME. **b.** Of persons: Acting without forethought or deliberation; hasty, impetuous, rash. *Obs.* or *arch.* late ME. **3.** Performed or taking place without delay; speedy; prompt, immediate. *Obs.* exc. of death. late ME. †**4.** Of persons: Swift in action, quick to perform, prompt, expeditious. Also, peremptory, sharp. -1753. †**b.** Of mental faculties: Quick, sharp -1742. †**c.** Of the eye: Glancing quickly -1651. **5.** Made, provided, or formed in a short time. *Obs.* or *arch.* 1599. **6.** Prompt in action or effect; producing an immediate result. *poet.* 1586. †**7.** Done, performed, or prepared on the spur of the moment; extempore, impromptu -1741. †**8.** Brief, momentary -1595. †**9.** Happening at an early date; shortly to come or to be -1749.

1. Hayle, rain, and suddaine darknesse EVELYN. A s. start of surprise SCOTT. **c.** See lilies spring, and s. verdure rise POPE. **2. a.** If one kill another upon a suddaine quarrell, this is manslaughter BACON. **b.** Some men..are more s. in their tempers than others NEWMAN. **3.** Expecting your s. answer, I rest, Your servant, Oliver Cromwell 1650. **4.** Caska be sodaine, for we feare preuention SHAKS. **5.** Neuer was such a sodaine Scholler made SHAKS. **6.** *Rom. & Jul.* III. iii. 45. **7.** *Two Gent.* IV. ii. 12. **9.** To morrow, in my judgement, is too s. SHAKS.

B. *adv.* **1.** Suddenly. Chiefly *poet.* late ME.

2. When qualifying an adj. in the attrib. position *sudden* is often hyphened to it 1730.

1. The day with cloudes was suddeine ouercast SPENSER. 2. The sudden-starting tear THOMSON.

C. quasi-*sb.* and *sb.* **1.** In advb. phr. formed with preps. = Suddenly 1558. †**2.** A sudden need, danger, or the like; an emergency -1704. †**3.** *For a s.*: for an instant. BUNYAN.

1. *Of a s.* (†*of the s.*); now usu. with preceding *all*; Is it possible That loue should of a sodaine take such hold? SHAKS. *On* or *upon a* (or *the*) *s.* (arch.); On a s. a gleam of hope appeared MACAULAY. †*On such a s.*, so suddenly. 2. At such a S. I knew not what to doe 1704. Hence **Su·dden-ly** *adv.*, **-ness.**

Suddenty (sʊ·d'nti). Chiefly *Sc. Obs.* exc. *dial.* late ME. [a. OF. *sodeinete*, f. *sodein* SUDDEN; see -TY.] **1.** Unexpectedness; suddenness; *occas.* an instance of this, an unexpected attack. **2.** (In Sc. legal language.) An unpremeditated outburst of passion 1469.

‖ **Sudder** (sʊ·dəɹ), *a.* (*sb.*) *Anglo-Ind.* 1787. [a. Urdū = Arab. *çadr* foremost or highest part of a thing, chief place or seat, etc., used in comb. with adj. sense.] Chief, supreme: applied esp. to high government departments or officials. **b** *ellipt.* as *sb.*, = S. Court 1834.

Sudoral (siū·dŏrăl), *a. rare.* 1876. [f. L. *sudor* sweat + -AL.] *Path.* Characterized by a disturbance of the function of sweating.

‖ **Sudoresis** (siūdŏrī·sis). 1834. [mod.L., irreg. f. L. *sudor* + *-esis* as in DIAPHORESIS.] Sweating, exudation.

Sudoriferous (siūdŏri·fĕrəs), *a.* 1597. [f. mod.L. *sudoriferus*; see -FEROUS.] **1.** = next A. 1. **2.** = SUDORIPAROUS 1713.

2. The s. Glands and Vessels 1713.

Sudorific (siūdŏri·fik), *a.* and *sb.* 1626. [ad. mod.L. *sudorificus*; see -FIC.] **A.** *adj.* **1.** Promoting or causing perspiration; diaphoretic. **2.** Connected with the secretion and the exudation of sweat; sudoriparous, perspiratory 1720. **3.** Consisting of sweat (*rare*) 1807.

1. S. toil 1850. 2. The Sudorifick Pores 1720.

B. *sb.* A medicine or remedy which promotes perspiration; a diaphoretic 1667.

Sudoriparous (siūdŏri·părəs), *a.* 1851. [f. mod.L. *sudoriparus*, f. L. *sudor* sweat; see -PAROUS.] *Phys.* Secreting sweat. **b.** Used loosely for: Connected with the production of sweat or with the sweat-glands 1899.

Sudorous (siū·dŏrəs), *a. rare.* 1646. [f. late L. *sudorus*, f. L. *sudor* sweat; see -OUS.] Sweaty.

‖ **Sudra** (sū·dra). *Anglo-Ind.* 1630. [a. Skr. *çūdra*, of doubtful etym.] A member of the lowest of the four great Hindu castes.

Suds (sʊdz), *sb. pl.* 1548. [Etym. unc.] †**1.** Dregs, leavings; hence, filth, muck -1645. †**2.** Flood-water; the water of the fens; water mixed with drift-sand and mud; drift-sand left by a flood -1851. **3. a.** Water impregnated with soap for washing, esp. when hot. **b.** The frothy mass which collects on the top of soapy water in which things are washed; in early use *esp.* a barber's lather. (More fully SOAP-SUDS.) 1581. **c.** *sing.* A soap solution 1835. **4.** Foam, froth. Also *sing.* 1592.

Phr. **In the suds:** chiefly in *to lie* or *be in the suds; to lay, leave in the suds.* **a.** In difficulties; in embarrassment or perplexity. *Obs.* or *slang.* †**b.** Done for; in disgrace. **c.** In the sulks in the blues. *dial.* †**d.** Unfinished. **e.** Being washed, 'in the wash'.

Sue (siū), *v.* ME. [a. AF. *suer*, *siwer* = OF. *sivre*:—pop. L. **sequere*, for L. *sequi* to follow.] **I.** *trans.* †**1.** To follow (a person or thing in motion) -1590. †**2. a.** To follow (a person's steps, a track, path). **b.** To go in pursuit of (a person); to chase, pursue -1596. †**c.** To follow in time or as a consequence -1559. †**3.** To follow as an attendant, companion, or adherent; *occas.* to follow (a banner or the like); to frequent (a person's company) -1522. †**4.** To take as guide, leader, or pattern; to follow as a disciple or imitator -1509. †**5.** To comply with (a person's will), follow (another's advice or one's own devices) -1767. †**6.** To follow, adopt, put in practice (a form of belief, a manner of life, a virtue or vice, an occupation or profession); to occupy oneself with (a pursuit) -1799. †**7.** To prosecute (an action); to pursue (a subject); also, to follow up (an achievement) -1596. †**8.** To take (legal action); to institute (a legal process); to plead (a cause) -1572. **9.** To institute a suit for, make a legal claim to; hence *gen.* to petition or appeal for; to seek to obtain. Now *rare* (repl. by *s. for*). ME. **b.** Const. inf. (occas. gerund): To petition to be allowed, (hence) to seek *to do* or *to be* something. *arch.* late ME. **10.** *spec.* To make application before a court for the grant of (a writ or other legal process): often with implication of further proceedings being taken upon the writ, etc.; hence, to put in suit, to enforce (a legal process). More freq. to *s. out*, †*forth.* ME. **11.** To institute legal proceedings against (a person); to prosecute in a court of law; to bring a civil action against. In full, *to s. at law.* late ME. **12.** To petition, appeal to (*rare*) 1521. **13.** To woo, court. *arch.* 1596.

2. c. Shame sueth sinne, as rayne drops do the thunder 1559. 3. Phr. †*To serve and s.*: to give 'suit and service to' (see SUIT *sb.* I. 2). 6. Since errant armes to sew he first began SPENSER. 9. b. Many sued to haue had her to maryage 1509. 10. *Hen. VIII*, III. ii. 341. It putteth him to s. out his pardon of course BACON. Phr. *To s., s. out, s. forth* (*one's*) *livery*: see LIVERY *sb.* 5. 11. My opinion is that he will not pay a peny till he is sued 1670. 13. They would s. me, and woo me, and flatter me TENNYSON.

II. *intr.* †**1.** To follow after a person or thing in motion; to follow as an attendant or adherent; to go in chase or pursuit; freq. with *after, on, upon* -1555. †**2.** To do service or homage; chiefly in phr. *serve and s.* -1590. †**3. a.** To follow in time or in a succession of persons. Nearly always in pr. pple. -1642. **b.** To follow in the sequence of events, as a consequence or result -1597. **4.** To make legal claim; to institute legal proceedings; to bring a suit. late ME. **5.** To make one's petition or supplication *to* a person *for* a person or thing; to plead, appeal, supplicate. late ME. **6.** To be a suitor *to* a woman. *arch.* 1588.

2. What bootes thy seruice bace To her, to whom the heauens do serue and sew? SPENSER. 4. Infant executors may s. by attorney 1817. To s. for a debt 1858. 5. We were not borne to s., but to command SHAKS. 6. *Two Gent.* II. i. 143.

‖ **Suède** (swēd). 1884. [F. = Sweden.] Orig. in *s. gloves* (= F. *gants de Suède*), gloves made of tanned kid-skin; hence *suède* is used for the material and the colour of it, also for a fabric woven to imitate suède.

Suet (siū·ėt). late ME. [app. a. AF. **suet*, **sewet*, f. *su*(*e*, *seu* = OF. *seu*, *sieu* (mod.F. *suif*) :—L. *sebum* tallow, suet, grease.] The solid fat round the loins and kidneys of certain animals, *esp.* that of the ox and sheep, which, chopped up, is used in cooking, and, when rendered down, forms tallow. (Occas. applied to the corresponding fat in the human body.) †**b.** *Hunting.* The fat of deer -1700.

attrib., as *s.-chopper, dumpling*; **s. face,** a face of a pale podgy appearance; **s. pudding,** a pudding made of flour and chopped or shredded s. and usu. boiled in a cloth or basin.

Suety (siū·ėti), *a.* 1730. [f. prec. + -Y[1].] **1.** Of the nature of suet. **b.** *fig.* Pale-faced 1801. **2.** Full of suet; made with suet 1807.

2. I always spell plumb-pudding with a *b*, p-l-u-m-*b* —I think it reads fatter and more suetty LAMB.

Sueve (swīv). 1901. = next B.

Suevian (swī·viăn), *a.* and *sb.* 1617. [f. L. *Suevus*, var. *Suebus* + -IAN.] **A.** *adj.* Of or belonging to a confederation of Germanic tribes called by the Romans *Suevi* (*Suebi*), which inhabited large territories in Central Europe to the east of the Rhine. **B.** *sb.* Any individual of these tribes.

Suffect (sŏfe·kt), *a.* (*sb.*). 1862. [ad. L. *suffectus*, *sufficere* to substitute.] *Rom. Antiq.* Applied to the office of those additional consuls (or to the consuls themselves) who were elected, as under the Empire, during the official year. Also *sb.*, a consul s.

Suffer (sʊ·fəɹ), *v.* ME. [a. AF. *suffrir*, = OF. *sof*(*f*)*rir* :—pop. L. **sufferire*, for *sufferre*, f. *suf-* = SUB- 25 + *ferre* to bear.] **I.** To undergo, endure. **1.** *trans.* To have (something painful, distressing, or injurious) inflicted or imposed upon one; to submit to with pain, distress, or grief. **2.** To go or pass through, be subjected to, undergo, experience (now usu. something evil or painful) ME. **3.** *intr.* To undergo or submit to pain, punishment, or death ME. **b.** *from* or (now *rare*) *under* a disease or ailment 1800. **4.** To be the object of an action, be acted upon, be passive. Now *rare.* late ME. †**5.** To endure, hold out, wait patiently -1611. **6.** *trans.* To endure, bear, stand. *Obs.* exc. *dial.* late ME. **7.** To be affected by, subjected to, undergo (an operation or process, *esp.* of change). Now only as *transf.* of 1. late ME. **8.** *intr.* To undergo the extreme penalty; to be put to death, be executed. Now *rare* in literary use exc. of martyrdom. 1570. †**b.** To be killed or destroyed. SHAKS. **9.** To sustain injury, damage, or loss; to be injured or impaired 1600. **10.** *causative.* To inflict pain upon. *Obs.* exc. *dial.* 1500.

1. I suffered thryse shipwracke TINDALE 2 *Cor.* xi. 25. For feare that hee should s. thirst 1617. The plaintiff had suffered no loss 1891. 2. Three more.. suffered the same fate 1839. 3. A brave man suffers in silence 1889. b. He had suffered from delirium tremens 1884. 4. To be weak is miserable Doing or Suffering MILT. 5. Love suffreth longe, and is courteous TINDALE 1 *Cor.* xiii. 4. 7. Nothing of him that doth fade, But doth s. a Sea-change Into something rich, & strange SHAKS. 8. Edward Transham.. suffered at Tyburn 1877. b. But let the frame of things dis-ioynt, Both the Worlds s. SHAKS. 9. How must he in the meantime be suffering in her opinion? SCOTT. 10. 2 *Hen. VI*, v. i. 153.

II. To tolerate, allow. **1.** *trans.* To bear with, put up with, tolerate. *arch.* or *dial.* ME. †**b.** To admit of -1793. **2.** Const. *acc.* and *inf.* or *clause*: To allow or permit a person, animal, or inanimate thing to be or to do so-and-so ME. **3.** *refl.* or †*intr.* To allow oneself, submit *to be* treated in a certain way; to endure, consent *to be* or *to do* something ME. **4.** *trans.* To permit or allow (a person) to do a certain thing; †to let alone. Also occas. *absol. arch.* late ME. †**5.** *intr.* **a.** Of a person (*transf.* of a thing): To allow a certain thing to be done -1613. †**b.** Of a condition of things: To allow or admit of a certain thing being done -1612.

1. That nolde she suffre by no wey CHAUCER. We s. religion, and endure the laws of God but we love them not JER. TAYLOR. He suffered his grandmother with a good-humoured indifference THACKERAY. 2. S. mee, that I may feele the pillars whereupon the house standeth *Judges* xvi. 26. I was not suffered to stir far from the house, for fear I should run away GOLDSM. 3. Why rather suffre ye not youre selves to be robbed? TINDALE 1 *Cor.* vi. 7. *intr.* I must not s. to have the laws broken before my face GOLDSM. 5. b. And saye the Lordes prayer, yf the tyme will suffre *Bk. Com. Prayer.*

Sufferable (sʊ·fərăb'l), *a.* *Obs.* exc. *arch.* ME. [a. OF. *suffrable*, ad. med.L. *sufferabilis*, f. *sufferre* to SUFFER.] †**1.** Patient, long-suffering. Also const. *of*: Willing to submit to. -1611. **2.** That can be 'suffered' or put up with; bearable, tolerable. Also, tolerably good. ME. †**3.** Permissible -1653.

1. And sith a man is moore resonable Than womman is, ye moste been suffrable CHAUCER. Hence **Su·fferably** *adv.* (*rare*) patiently; tolerably.

Sufferance (sʊ·fərăns). ME. [a. AF., OF. *suf*(*f*)*rance*, *soffrance*, ad. late L. *sufferentia*, f. *sufferre* to SUFFER; see -ANCE.] **I. 1.** Patient endurance, forbearance, long-suffering. *arch.* **2.** The suffering *of* pain, trouble, wrong, etc. *arch.* late ME. †**b.** The suffering of a penalty -1640. **c.** Damage, injury (*rare*) -1823. **3.** A painful condition; pain suffered. *arch.* late ME. †**4.** Capacity to endure, endurance -1823.

1. The best apology against false accusers is silence and s. MILT. 2. Calm in the s. of wrong 1856. c. *Oth.* II. i. 23. 3. The poore Beetle that we treade vpon In corporall s., finds a pang as great, As when a Giant dies SHAKS. 4. The two chiefest parts of a soldier, Valour and S. 1604.

II. 1. Sanction, consent, or acquiescence, implied by non-intervention; toleration, indulgence. Now *rare* exc. as in b. ME. **b.** *On* or *upon s.*: by virtue of a tacit assent but without express permission; under conditions of passive acquiescence or bare tolerance 1562. †**c.** An instance of this, a licence -1645. **d.** *Customs.* In full, *bill of s.*: a licence to ship or discharge cargoes at specified ports 1670. **2.** *Law.* The condition of the holder of an estate who, having come in by lawful right, continues to hold it after the title has ceased without the express leave of the owner. Phr. *tenant, estate at s.* 1579. †**3.** Suspension, delay; respite. (Chiefly after OF. or med.L.) -1738.

1. The Company.. possessing their privileges through his s. 1817. †*S. of peace*, a grant of peace, truce. b. They were a Ministry on s. when they appealed

to the country 1879. **2.** *transf.* This is no highway, but a way of S., by favour 1633. **3.** To treat for a peace, and sufferaunce of warr 1523.

attrib.: **s. goods,** goods shipped or landed under a s.; **s. quay, wharf,** a quay or wharf at which cargo could be shipped or landed under a s.

Sufferer (sʊ·fərəɪ). 1450. [f. SUFFER *v.* + -ER [1].] **1.** One who suffers pain, tribulation, injury, wrong, loss, etc.; one who suffers *from* disease or ill health. **b.** One who suffers death; one who is killed (now only in ref. to martyrdom) 1721. **c.** A patient. Now *rare.* 1809. †**2.** One who permits something to be done –1627.

1. Sad suff'rer under nameless ill COWPER. **c.** At the bedside of the unfortunate s. 1809.

Suffering (sʊ·fəriŋ), *vbl. sb.* ME. [f. SUFFER *v.* + -ING [1].] †**1.** Patient endurance; long-suffering. -late ME. **2.** The bearing or undergoing of pain, distress, or tribulation ME. †**b.** Execution; martyrdom –1700. **3.** A painful condition; pain suffered. late ME. **b.** In particularized use, chiefly *pl.* 1609. **c.** In the Society of Friends, the hardships of those who were distrained upon for tithes, etc. 1657.

2. I..to the evil turne My obvious breast, arming to overcom By s. MILT. **3.** Far less shall be Our S., Sir GRAY. **b.** She is callous to his sufferings 1877.

Su·ffering, *ppl. a.* ME. [-ING [2].] †**1.** That endures patiently; inured to suffering; submissive –1694. †**2.** Passive –1792. **3.** That suffers, or is characterized by the suffering of, pain, affliction, or distress 1597. **b.** In Puritan use, with ref. to hardships endured for the sake of religion, esp. in *s. saint* 1661. **c.** [After F. *souffrant.*] Ill, indisposed (*rare*) 1885.

3. Gentle maid Haue of my s. youth some feeling pitty SHAKS. Hence **Su·fferingly** *adv. rare.*

Suffete (sʊ·fīt). 1600. [ad. L. *suffes, sufes, -et-*, of Phœnician origin.] *Antiq.* One of the supreme executive magistrates of the ancient republic of Carthage.

Suffice (sŏfəi·s), *v.* ME. [f. OF. *suffis-*, pres. stem of *suffire*:—L. *sufficere*, f. *suf-* = SUB- + *facere* to make do.] **1.** *intr.* To be enough, sufficient, or adequate for a purpose or the end in view. †**2.** *impers.* It is enough –1530. **b.** Const. inf. or clause with (or †without) anticipatory subject *it.* Now chiefly in the subj., *S. it*, occas. short for *S. it to say.* late ME. **c.** With dat. pron. *arch.* late ME. †**3.** To have the necessary ability, capacity, or resources for doing something; to be competent or able *to do* something –1823. **4.** *trans.* To be enough for; to meet the desires, needs, or requirements of (a person); to satisfy. *arch.* late ME. **b.** *pass.* To be satisfied or content. *arch.* late ME. †**5.** To provide enough food for, satisfy the appetite of; also, to satisfy (the appetite). Chiefly *pass.* –1791. †**6.** To satisfy, meet the 'calls' of (a desire, need, sense, emotion, etc.) –1737. †**7.** To make or be sufficient provision for; to supply *with* something. Also, to replenish (a supply). –1700. †**8.** To supply, furnish (a product, etc.) –1725.

1. Twixt such friends as wee, Few words s. SHAKS. The fog..every trace of which a few minutes sufficed to sweep away TYNDALL. **2. b.** S. it, that perchance they were of fame BYRON. **4.** The good old rule Sufficeth them WORDSW. **b.** Not half suffic'd, and greedy yet to kill DRYDEN. **6.** Scarce all my herds their luxury s. POPE. **8.** The Iuyce, as it seemeth, not being able to s. a Succulent Colour, and a Double Leafe BACON.

Sufficience (sŏfi·ʃĕns). *arch.* late ME. [a. OF., or ad. late L. *sufficientia*, f. *sufficient-, -ens*, SUFFICIENT; see -ENCE.] **1.** The quality or condition of being sufficient or enough; sufficient supply, means, or resources. †**2.** Capacity; ability; competence. Also, a capable or competent person. –1676. †**3.** That which suffices for one's needs; satisfaction of one's needs; sustenance –1620.

1. This full and perfect s. of life was abruptly disturbed MORLEY.

Sufficiency (sŏfi·ʃĕnsi). 1495. [ad. L. *sufficientia* (see prec. and -ENCY).] †**1.** Sufficient means or wealth; ability to meet pecuniary obligations –1747. **b.** A sufficient supply; a competence 1608. **c.** Adequate provision of food or bodily comfort 1796. **2.** The condition or quality of being sufficient for its purpose or for the end in view; adequacy 1565. **3.** A sufficient number or quantity *of*; enough 1531. **4.** Sufficient capacity *to* perform or undertake something; adequate qualification; ability, competency. *Obs.* or *arch.* 1567. †**b.** An instance of this; also, an accomplishment –1713. **5.** = SELF-SUFFICIENCY 2. *arch.* 1638.

1. In the fulnesse of his sufficiencie, he shalbe in straites *Job* xx. 22. **b.** An elegant s., content, Retirement, rural quiet THOMSON. **2.** There is a doubt about the s. of the assets 1884. **3.** S. of wood for fuel 1832. **4.** We haue there a Substitute of most allowed sufficiencie SHAKS.

Sufficient (sŏfi·ʃĕnt), *a.* (*adv.*, *sb.*) late ME. [a. OF., or ad. L. *sufficiens, -ent-, sufficere* to SUFFICE.] **A.** *adj.* **1.** Of a quantity, extent, or scope adequate to a certain purpose or object. **b.** *impers.* with dependent clause or inf. 1538. **c.** Achieving its object; effective (*rare*) 1831. **2.** In techn. language, of legal documents, securities, etc. 1461. †**3.** Qualified by talent or ability; competent, capable, able –1817. †**4.** Of persons: Of adequate means or wealth; having a competence; well-to-do; hence, qualified by means or status for an office or duty –1782. †**5.** Of things: Of adequate quality; of a good standard; substantial; in good condition –1800. †**6.** In full, *s. for oneself*: = SELF-SUFFICIENT **1.** –1502. †**7.** = SELF-SUFFICIENT 2. –1709.

1. What thanks s...have I to render thee? MILT. The publiq armoury..s. for 30,000 men EVELYN. Even a threatened interference with a plaintiff's rights..is s. to justify him in taking proceedings 1890. **b.** They thought it not sufficiente in their life time to deserue prayse 1553. **2.** This our Lettre shalbe your s. discharge for the same 1551. *S. grace* (Theol.): see GRACE *sb.* II. (*Principle* or *law of*) *s. reason* (mod. Philos.), the principle that nothing happens without a reason why it should be so rather than otherwise. **3.** Those that..have a s. Gardener 1719. **4.** An honest and s. farmer 1672. **7.** A s. self-conceited Coxcomb STEELE.

†**B.** *adv.* = Sufficiently –1826. **C.** *sb.* †**1.** The quality or condition of being sufficient –1600. **2.** A sufficient quantity or supply; sufficient means; enough 1470.

2. We saw s. to account for the noise TYNDALL. Hence **Suffi·ciently** *adv.* in a s. manner.

Sufficing (sŏfəi·siŋ), *ppl. a.* 1606. [f. SUFFICE *v.* + -ING [2].] That suffices *for* a purpose or object; sufficient, adequate, satisfying.

Draw thy sword, and giue mee, Sufficing strokes for death SHAKS. Hence **Suffi·cing-ly** *adv.* so as to suffice; **Suffi·cingness,** sufficiency.

†**Su·ffisance.** late ME. [a. OF. *suff-, soffisance*, ad. late L. *sufficientia* SUFFICIENCE.] **1.** Enough to supply one's needs –1632. **2.** = SUFFICIENCY 3. –1544. **3.** Ample means, wealth –1574. **4.** Ability –1627. **5.** Satisfaction, contentment –1590. **b.** A source of satisfaction –1502.

5. S., that seketh no riche metes ne drinkes CHAUCER. **b.** She was, that swete wife, My suffisaunce, my luste, my lyfe CHAUCER.

†**Su·ffisant,** *a.* ME. [a. OF. *suffisant, soufisant*, pr. pple. of *suffire* to SUFFICE.] **1.** = SUFFICIENT, in various senses –1570. **2.** Of things (chiefly immaterial): Satisfactory in quality or efficacy; effective –1455.

Suffix (sʊ·fiks), *sb.* 1778. [ad. mod.L. *suffixum*, subst. use of neut. of *suffixus, suffigere*, f. *suf-* = SUB- 2 + *figere* to FIX.] **1.** *Gram.* A verbal element attached to the end of a word to form an entirely new word (e.g. *short, shortage, short-en, short-er, short-ly*) or as an inflexional formative (e.g. *ox, ox-en*). **2.** *Math.* An inferior index written to the right of a symbol 1842. Hence **Suffi·xion** [after PREFIXION], the act of suffixing or state of being suffixed. **Su·ffixment,** use as a s.

Suffix (sŏfi·ks), *v.* Chiefly in *pa. pple.* 1604. [Partly f. L. *suffixus* (see prec.), partly f. prec.] **1.** *trans.* To fix or place under; to subjoin. **2.** To add as a suffix 1778. So **Suffi·xed** *ppl. a.* used as a suffix.

Sufflaminate (sŏflæ·minėɪt), *v.* Now *rare.* 1656. [f. L. *sufflaminat-, -are*, f. *sufflamen, -min-*, f. *suf-* = SUB- 2 + **flamen* :—**flagmen* (cogn. w. BALK *sb.*) beam, balk.] *trans.* To put an obstacle in the way of, obstruct.

†**Suffla·te,** *v.* 1616. [f. L. *sufflat-, sufflare*, f. *suf-* = SUB- 25 + *flare* to blow.] *trans.* To blow up, inflate –1791.

†**Suffla·tion.** 1599. [ad. L. *sufflatio, -onem*, f. *sufflare* (see prec.).] The action of blowing (up); inflation (*lit.* and *fig.*); distension with wind; inspiration (by the 'breath' of the Holy Ghost); expiration –1817.

Sufflue (sʊflū·). 1562. [Origin unkn.] *Her.* A bearing resembling a clarion.

†**Su·ffocate,** *pa. pple.* and *ppl. a.* 1460. [ad. L. *suffocatus, suffocare* (see next).] **1.** Suffocated by deprivation of air –1632. **2.** Smothered, overwhelmed –1606.

1. For Suffolkes Duke, may he be s. SHAKS.

Suffocate (sʊ·fŏkeɪt), *v.* 1526. [f. L. *suffocat-, suffocare*, f. *suf-* = SUB- 1 + *fauces* throat.] **1.** *trans.* To kill (a person or animal) by stopping the supply of air through the lungs, gills, or other respiratory organs 1599. **2.** To interrupt or impede respiration in (a person); to stifle, choke. Also, †to throttle (the windpipe), stifle (the breath). 1599. **3.** To destroy as if by the exclusion of air; to smother, overwhelm, extinguish 1526. **4.** *intr.* To become stifled or choked 1702.

1. Half suffocated with the loss of breath 1791. **2.** Let not Hempe his Windpipe s. SHAKS. **3.** The plants..will s. every kind of weed near them 1793. That..superstition which..had suffocated the higher truths of religion 1868. Hence **Su·ffocating** *ppl. a.*, **-ly** *adv.*

Suffocation (sʊfŏkēɪ·ʃən). 1549. [ad. L. *suffocatio, -onem*, f. *suffocare* (see prec.).] The act of suffocating or condition of being suffocated. †**b.** In full *s. of the womb, matrix, mother*: hysteria –1719.

Suffocative (sʊ·fŏkeɪtiv), *a.* 1605. [See SUFFOCATE *v.* and -IVE.] Tending to suffocate; causing or inducing suffocation; attended by suffocation. (Chiefly *Med.*, esp. in *s. catarrh* = capillary bronchitis.)

Suffolk (sʊ·fək). The name of a county of East Anglia; used attrib. in designations of things produced in or peculiar to the county, as *S. cow, pig*; **S. coprolite,** a phosphatic nodule occurring in the Red Crag of Suffolk; **S. crag,** a Pliocene formation occurring in Suffolk; **S. punch,** a small but strong and hardy horse bred largely in Suffolk. **b.** *absol.* = Suffolk brick, cow, horse, pig, sheep, etc. 1831.

Suffragan (sʊ·frăgăn), *sb.* and *a.* late ME. [a. AF., OF. *suffragan*, corresp. to med.L. *suffraganeus*, f. stem of *suffragium* SUFFRAGE.] **A.** *sb.* **1.** A bishop considered in regard to his relation to the archbishop or metropolitan, by whom he may be summoned to attend synods and give his suffrage. **2.** An assistant or subsidiary bishop; in the Church of England, a bishop appointed to assist a diocesan bishop in a particular part of his diocese. late ME. †**3.** A coadjutor, assistant; a deputy, representative –1760. **B.** *adj.* **1.** *Bishop s., s. bishop*: = A. **1,** **2.** 1475. **2.** Of a see or diocese: Subordinate *to* a metropolitical or archiepiscopal see 1712. Hence **Su·ffraganship,** the office or status of a s.

†**Su·ffragant,** *sb.* and *a.* 1603. [a. F., ad. L. *suffragans, -ant-, suffragari* (see next).] **A.** *sb.* One who gives his suffrage or vote; a voter; hence, a supporter, witness –1697. **B.** *adj.* **1.** Auxiliary, subordinate. FLORIO. **2.** Giving support or witness –1656.

†**Su·ffragate,** *v.* 1600. [f. L. *suffragat-, suffragari*, f. stem of *suffragium* SUFFRAGE.] **1.** *trans.* To delegate, appoint. **2.** *intr.* To testify, to bear witness *to* –1676. **3.** To vote (*for*) –1691.

Suffrage (sʊ·frėdʒ), *sb.* late ME. [ad. L. *suffragium*, partly through F. *suffrage.*] **1.** *collect. pl.* and *sing.* Prayers, *esp.* intercessory prayers, intercessions. *arch.* **b.** *spec.* Prayers for the souls of the departed; *esp.* in phr. *to do s.* (*arch.*) 1440. **c.** *pl.* Liturgical intercessory petitions; *esp.* in the Book of Common Prayer, (*a*) the intercessory petitions pronounced by the priest in the Litany; (*b*) a set of versicles and responses 1532. †**2.** Help, support, assistance. Also, one who helps, a support. –1613. **3.** *orig.* A vote given by a member of a body, state, or society, in assent to a proposition or in favour of the election of a person; in extended sense, a vote for or against any controverted question or nomination 1534. **b.** An object, as a pebble, a marked paper, or the like, used to indicate a vote given (*rare*) 1534. **4.** *gen.* A vote in support of or an opinion in favour of some person or thing; hence (now *Obs.* or *arch.*), in neutral sense, an opinion 1594. **5.** Approval, sanction, consent. Const. *to. arch.* 1598. †**b.** An instance of this; an expression or token of approval -1829. **6.** The collective vote of a body of persons 1610. **7.** The collective opinion of a body of persons; hence, contextually, consensus of opinion; (common or general) consent 1576. **8.** The casting of a vote, voting; the exercise of a right to vote; election by voting 1665. **9.** The right or privilege of voting as a member of a body, state, etc. (orig. *U.S.*) 1789. **b.** With prefixed word denoting the extent, as *female, household, manhood s.*, etc. 1706.

1. Of what use to you then the suffrages of the saints? KINGSLEY. **b.** Their prayers and suffrages for the dead 1848. **c.** After the s. for the Church, those for the ecclesiastical orders usually come first 1855. **3.** The manner of choosing Magistrates..was by plurality of suffrages HOBBES. **b.** The Grand Master had collected the suffrages SCOTT. **4.** He that finds his knowledge narrow,..and by consequence his s. not much regarded JOHNSON. **5.** I'll giue no s. to 't B. JONS. **6.** The election of a new emperor was referred to the s. of the military order GIBBON. **7.** To prefer their own judgment to the general s. of mankind 1794. **8.** The right of s. is not valued when indiscriminately bestowed 1887. **9.** The s., or qualification of electors, is very various COBBETT. **b.** The universal s. of France 1877.

†**Su·ffrage,** *v.* 1613. [f. prec.] **1.** *intr.* To vote *for* or *against*; hence, to agree or side *with*, to give support *to* -1661. **2.** *trans.* To elect by vote; hence, to give support to; to side with -1838.

Suffragette (svfrădʒe·t). 1906. [irreg. f. SUFFRAGE *sb.* + -ETTE.] A female supporter of the cause of women's political enfranchisement, *esp.* one of a violent or 'militant' type.

Suffragism (sv·frădʒiz'm). 1888. [f. next + -ISM.] The advocacy of an extension of the suffrage, e. g. to women.

Suffragist (sv·frădʒist). 1822. [f. SUFFRAGE + -IST.] An advocate of the extension of the political franchise, *esp.* (since about 1885) to women.

I am a woman and a s. 1914.

‖ **Suffrago** (svfrē·go). 1842. [L.] *Anat.* The 'heel' at the junction of the tibia and the tarsus in quadrupeds and birds.

Suffrutescent (svfrute·sĕnt), *a.* 1816. [ad. mod.L. *suffrutescens, -ent-*, f. *suf-* = SUB- 20 c + *frutescens* FRUTESCENT.] *Bot.* Somewhat woody or shrubby at the base.

‖ **Suffrutex** (sv·fruteks). *Pl.* **suffrutices** (svfrū·tisīz). 1567. [mod.L., f. *suf-* = SUB- 22 + FRUTEX.] *Bot.* A plant having a woody base, but a herbaceous annual growth above.

Suffruticose (svfrū·tikoᵘs), *a.* 1793. [ad. mod.L. *suffruticosus*, f. *suffrutic-* SUFFRUTEX + -OSE.] *Bot.* Of the character of a suffrutex; woody at the base but herbaceous above.

Suffumigate (svfiū·migeᶦt), *v. rare.* 1588. [f. pa. pple. of L. *suffumigare*, f. *suf-* = SUB- 2, 25 + *fumigare* to FUMIGATE.] *trans.* To fumigate from below.

Suffumigation (svfiūmigēᶦ·ʃən). Now *arch.* or *Hist.* late ME. [ad. L. *suffumigatio, -onem* (see prec.).] The action of suffumigating; an instance of this; chiefly *concr.* (usu. *pl.*) fumes or vapours generated by burning herbs, incense, etc.; also *occas.*, a substance used for this purpose. †**b.** *gen.* A fume, vapour -1651.

Suffuse (svfiū·z), *v.* 1590. [f. L. *suffus-*, *suffundere*, f. *suf-* = SUB- 2, 25 + *fundere* to pour.] **1.** *trans.* To overspread as with a fluid, a colour, a gleam of light. **2.** To pour (a liquid) over a surface. Chiefly in fig. context. 1734.

1. His eies vnclos'd, with teares suffus'd 1600. You hazy ridges.. Climbing suffused with sunny air WORDSW. *fig.* The amused expression suffused the lawyer's face 1876. Hence **Suffu·sedly** *adv.*

Suffusion (svfiū·ʒən). late ME. [ad. L. *suffusio, -onem*, f. *suffus-* (see prec.).] **1.** The defluxion or extravasation of a fluid or 'humour' over a part of the body; †*concr.* the fluid itself; *spec.* in *Old Med.*, cataract. **2.** The action of suffusing a surface with fluid, moisture, or colour; the condition of being suffused or overspread. Also, an instance of this. 1611. **3.** A colouring or tint spread over a surface, *esp.* over the skin by the action of the blood, etc.; *freq.* a flush of colour in the face, a blush 1700.

1. So thick a drop serene hath quencht thir Orbs, Or dim s. veild MILT. **2.** The s. of the eyes with tears DARWIN. **3.** Would she not be much more modest without that ambiguous S.? STEELE.

‖ **Sufi** (sū·fi). 1653. [a. Arab. *çūfī* lit. 'man of wool', f. *çūf* wool.] One of a sect of Mohammedan ascetic mystics who in later times embraced pantheistic views. Hence **Su·fic** *a.* pertaining to the Sufis or their mystical system.

Sufiism (sū·fiiz'm). 1817. [f. prec. + -ISM.] The mystical system of the Sufis. Also **Su·fism** 1836.

Sugar (ʃu·gəɹ), *sb.* ME. [a. OF. *çucre*, *zuchre*, etc., mod.F. *sucre*, ad. med.L. *zuccarum*, *succarum*, ad. Arab. *sukkar*.] **1.** A sweet crystalline substance, white when pure, obtained from a great variety of plant juices, but chiefly from those of the sugar-cane and sugar-beet, and forming an important article of human food. **b.** With qualifying adj., sb., or phr., indicating place of origin, colour, stage of boiling, purification, or crystallization at which, or the form in which, the particular kind is produced, its use, or the plant from which it is made. late ME. **c.** *pl.* Kinds of sugar; also, †cargoes or stocks of sugar 1570. †**d.** = SUGAR-CANE -1785. **2. a.** Sweetness; also, sweet or honeyed words. late ME. **b.** Phr. *To be neither s. nor salt, not to be made of s. or salt*, not likely to be injured by a wetting, not afraid of wet weather 1842. **c.** *slang.* Money 1862. **3.** *Chem.* **a.** In old terminology, applied (with qualification) to certain compounds resembling sugar in form or taste. *S. of lead*: lead acetate. *Acid* (or *essence*) *of s.*: oxalic acid. 1652. **b.** In mod. terminology, a chemical compound having the composition of ordinary sugar and forming a constituent of many substances; also, more widely (with distinctive qualifying word), any member of the saccharose and glucose groups of carbohydrates, all of which are soluble in water, more or less sweet to the taste, and either directly or indirectly fermentable 1826.

1. **b.** *Brown, white s.; burnt, caramel, clarified, crystal, granulated, lump, moist, raw, refined s.; coffee, preserving s.*; BEET *s.*, CANE *s.*; etc. **d.** I have not told you..that S. is a grass of the first division 1785. **2. a.** She was all s. and honey 1895.

attrib. and *Comb.*: **s.-almond**, a sweetmeat consisting of an almond coated with s.; **-cake**, a rich cake made with s., butter, and cream; **-camp** *U.S.*, a place in a maple forest or plantation where the sap is collected and boiled for s.; **-caster, -castor** (see CASTOR 2); **-coat** *v.*, to coat with s.; *fig.* to make palatable; *esp.* in **s.-coated** *ppl. a.* (of pills); **-cone**, a conical mould used in making loaf-sugar; **-disease**, diabetes; **-house**, a s.-factory, s.-works; **-house molasses**, a low-grade molasses produced at s.-factories, now chiefly used in the preparation of certain medicines and chemicals; **-lime**, lime formed in the process of preparing s. from beetroot; **-orchard** *U.S.* = SUGAR-BUSH 1; **-stick**, a stick of sweetstuff; **-tongs**, a metal implement for taking hold of pieces of lump s. (to put them into a beverage), consisting of two limbs connected by a flexible back (or a hinge) and furnished at each end with claws or a spoon-shaped plate; **-vinegar**, vinegar made from the waste juice and washings in s.-manufacture; **-water** *U.S.*, the sap of the s.-maple. **b.** In names of birds, insects, and other animals that feed upon or infest s. or sweet things; **s.-mite**, (*a*) a springtail or silver-fish, *Lepisma saccharii*; (*b*) a mite of the genus *Tyroglyphus* or *Glyciphagus*; **-squirrel**, a species of flying-squirrel found in Australia, which lives partly on honey. **c.** In the names of plants or fruits, so called on account of their sweetness or their yielding s.; **s. beet**, any variety of the beetroot plant from which s. is manufactured; **-berry**, the N. Amer. nettle-tree, *Celtis occidentalis*; **-fungus**, the fungus of yeast, *Saccharomyces cerevisiæ*; **-grass**, (*a*) = SORGHUM 1 b; (*b*) the Australian grass *Pollinia fulva* or *Erianthus fulvus*; **-gum**, the Australian *Eucalyptus corynocalyx* and *E. Gunnii*; **-tree**, (*a*) = SUGAR-MAPLE; (*b*) = SUGAR-BUSH 2; (*c*) an Australian shrub, *Myoporum platycarpum*; **-wood** = SUGAR-MAPLE.

Sugar (ʃu·gəɹ), *v.* late ME. [f. prec.] **1.** *trans.* To mix, cover, sprinkle, or sweeten with sugar 1530. **b.** *intr.* To spread sugar mixed with beer, gum, etc. upon trees or the like in order to catch moths. Also *trans.* with the tree as obj. 1857. **2.** *fig.* (*trans.*) To make sweet, agreeable, or palatable. late ME. **3.** *intr.*, usu. *s.-off*: in U.S. and Canada, in the manufacture of maple-sugar, to complete the boiling down of the syrup in preparation for granulation 1836. **4.** *Cambridge Univ. Rowing slang.* To shirk while pretending to row hard 1890. **5.** *pass.* Euphemistic substitute for an imprecation. *slang.* 1891.

1. Rum and water..sugared to the utmost SOUTHEY. *fig.* One dram whereof is able to s. the most wormwood affliction FULLER. **2.** Then I perceiue there 's treason in his lookes That seem'd to s. o're his villanie SHAKS. Hence **Su·garless** *a.* without s., unsugared.

Su·gar-ba:ker. 1650. †**1.** A confectioner. **2.** A sugar-refiner. *Obs.* exc. *Hist.* 1688.

Su·gar-bird. 1688. Applied to various small birds which feed (or were supposed to feed) on the nectar of flowers. †**1.** = CANARY-BIRD 1. **2.** A bird of the genus *Certhiola*, belonging to the family *Cærebidæ*, in the W. Indies and S. America; also applied to the genera *Certhia* and *Dacnis* 1787. **3.** Applied to various members of the family *Nectariniidæ* or Sun-birds of Africa 1822.

Su·gar-bush. 1818. **1.** A grove or plantation of sugar-maples 1823. **2.** [Cape Du. *suikerbos*.] The S. African shrub *Protea mellifera* 1818.

Sugar-candy (ʃu:gəɹkæ·ndi). late ME. [ad. F. *sucre candi*, repr. Arab. *sukkar* SUGAR + *qandī* of sugar, f. *qand* sugar, a. Pers. *kand* = Skr. *khaṇḍa* sugar in pieces, orig. piece, fragment, f. root *khaṇd* to break.] **1.** Sugar clarified and crystallized by slow evaporation. **2.** *fig.* Something sweet, pleasant, or delicious 1591. **b.** *attrib.* or as *adj.* Sugared, honeyed, deliciously sweet 1575.

1. *Brown s.*, that obtained at the first crystallization. *White s.*, that obtained by re-boiling the former and allowing it to crystallize. Hence **Su·gar-ca·ndied** *a.* coated with or as with (fine white) sugar; also *fig.* (now usu. with pun on *candia*).

Su·gar-cane. 1568. [f. SUGAR *sb.* + CANE *sb.*[1]] A tall stout perennial grass, *Saccharum officinarum*, cultivated in tropical and subtropical countries, and forming the chief source of manufactured sugar.

Sugared (ʃu·gəɹd), *ppl. a.* late ME. [f. SUGAR *sb.* or *v.* + -ED.] **1.** Containing or impregnated with sugar; sweetened with sugar. **b.** Sugar-coated; candied, 'crystallized' 1855. **2.** *fig.* Full of sweetness; honeyed, luscious, delicious. late ME.

1. Wine Sugred inebriateth lesse, than Wine Pure BACON. **2.** This world of sugred lies 1633. Kisses, Tempting,..sugred, lingring. 1658.

Sugaring (ʃu·gəriŋ), *vbl. sb.* 1740. [f. SUGAR *v.* + -ING[1].] **1.** Sugary or sweet matter; sweetening. Also, the adding of sugar. **2.** *U.S.* The manufacture of sugar from the maple. Also *s. off* (see SUGAR *v.* 3). 1836. **3.** (See SUGAR *v.* 1 b.) 1857.

Su·gar-loaf. late ME. [f. SUGAR *sb.* + LOAF *sb.*[1] 3. **1.** A moulded conical mass of hard refined sugar (now rarely made). **2.** *transf.* A thing having the shape of a sugar-loaf. **a.** Usu. *s.-hat*: A conical hat, pointed, rounded or flat at the top, worn during the Tudor and Stuart periods and after the French Revolution 1607. **b.** A high conical hill. Also *s. mountain.* 1634. **c.** A kind of cabbage 1766. Hence **Su·gar-loafed** *a.* shaped like a s.

Su·gar-ma·ple. 1753. The N. Amer. tree *Acer saccharinum*, which yields maple-sugar.

Su·gar-plum. 1608. [f. SUGAR *sb.* + PLUM *sb.*] **1.** A small round or oval sweetmeat, made of boiled sugar and variously flavoured and coloured; a comfit 1668. **2.** *fig.* Something very pleasing or agreeable, esp. when given as a sop or bribe 1608. Hence **Su·gar-plum** *v. trans.* to reward or pacify with sweetmeats; hence, to pet, cosset.

Sugar-sop (ʃu·gəɹsǫp). 1581. [f. SUGAR *sb.* + SOP *sb.*] †**1.** *pl.* A dish composed of steeped slices of bread, sweetened and sometimes spiced -1776. **2.** The W. Indian Sweet-sop, *Anona squamosa* 1847.

Sugary (ʃu·gəri), *sb.* 1696. [for *sugarery, f. SUGAR *sb.*; see -ERY and cf. F. *sucrerie*.] A sugar-manufactory. *Obs.* exc. as in b. **b.** *U.S.* and *Canada.* A place where maple-juice is collected and boiled for the purpose of making sugar; a sugar-camp 1840.

Sugary (ʃu·gəri), *a.* 1591. [f. SUGAR *sb.* + -Y[1].] **1.** Full of, containing, or impregnated with sugar; pertaining to or resembling (that of) sugar; sweet, sweetened 1597. **2.** *fig.* Deliciously or alluringly sweet; honeyed; deceitfully or flatteringly pleasant; also, excessively or offensively sweet 1591.

2. A s. epistle BECKFORD. Hence **Su·gariness.**

Sugescent (si̯udʒe·sĕnt), *a. rare.* 1802. [f. L. *sugere* to suck + -ESCENT.] Misused for: Pertaining to or adapted for sucking.

Suggest (sŏdʒe·st), *v.* 1526. [f. L. *suggest-, suggerere*, f. *sug-* = SUB- 2 + *gerere* to bear, carry, bring.] **1.** *trans.* To cause to be present to the mind as an object of thought, an idea to be acted upon, a question or problem to be solved; in early use said *esp.* of insinuating or prompting to evil. In extended application, to propose as an explanation or solution, as a course of action, as a person or thing suitable for a purpose, or the like. **b.** Said of the conscience, feelings, etc.; hence, of external things, to prompt the execution of, provide a motive for 1583. **c.** Const. clause or inf.: To put forward the notion, opinion, or proposition (*that*, etc.) 1526. **d.** To utter as a suggestion 1837. **e.** *refl.* Of an idea, proposition, etc.: To present itself to the mind 1801. †**2.** To prompt (a person) to evil; to tempt *to* or *to do* something; to seduce or tempt away -1643. †**b.** To insinuate into (a person's mind) the (false) idea *that*, etc. -1689. **3.** To give a hint or inkling of, without plain or direct expression or explanation 1697. **4.** To call up the thought of by association or natural connexion of ideas 1709. **b.** To give the impression of the existence or presence of 1816. **5.** *Law.* To put forward in a 'suggestion' 1719. **6.** In hypnotism, to influence by suggestion 1895. **7.** *absol.* or *intr.* †To prompt or tempt to evil; to make or offer a suggestion 1599.

1. Why dost thou then s. to me distrust? MILT. It is difficult to s. a remedy 1901. **b.** Prudence suggested the necessity of a temporary retreat GIBBON. **2.** *Two Gent.* III. i. 34. **b.** We must s. the People, in what hatred He still hath held them SHAKS. **3.** It [*sc.* a statue] suggests far more than it shows HAWTHORNE. **4.** A certain kind of sound suggests immediately to the mind, a coach passing in the street 1764. **7.** When diuels will the blackest sinnes put on, They do s. at first with heauenly shewes SHAKS. Hence **Sugge·ster,** †one who imputes crime to, or brings a charge against, another; one who suggests or prompts. **Sugge·stingly** *adv.*

Suggestible (sŏdʒe·stĭb'l), *a.* 1890. [f. prec. + -IBLE.] **1.** Capable of being influenced by (hypnotic) suggestion. **2.** That can be suggested 1905. Hence **Suggestibi·lity.**

Suggestion (sŏdʒe·styən, -tʃən). ME. [a. AF., OF. *suggestioun*, ad. L. *suggestio, -onem*, f. *suggerere* to SUGGEST.] †**1.** Prompting or incitement to evil; an instance of this, a temptation of the evil one -1667. **2.** The action of prompting one to a particular action or course of action; the putting into the mind of an idea, an object of thought, a plan, or the like; an instance of this, an idea or thought suggested, a proposal. late ME. **b.** *Hypnotism.* The insinuation of a belief or impulse into the mind of a subject by words, gestures, or the like; the impulse or idea thus suggested 1887. †**3.** The act of making a false or suborned statement or supplying underhand information; an instance of this, a false representation or charge. Often *false s.* -1592. **4.** *Law.* An information not upon oath 1485. **5.** The process by which an idea brings to the mind another idea by association or natural connexion 1605. **6.** An indication of the presence or existence (*of* something); a hint, an inkling 1863.

1. The first sort by thir own s. fell, Self-tempted, self-deprav'd MILT. **2.** Believe not these suggestions which proceed From anguish of the mind MILT. At the s. of friends a subscription was raised 1842. **b.** Several cases of cure by s. 1887. **4.** *S. upon record*, an information drawn in writing showing cause for a prohibition to a suit. **6.** A faint s. of weariness struggling with habitual patience GEO. ELIOT.

Sugge·stionism. 1892. [f. prec. + -ISM.] The doctrine or practice of hypnotic suggestion. Hence **Sugge·stionist,** one who advocates or practises suggestion; one who treats disease by suggestion.

Suggestive (sŏdʒe·stiv), *a.* 1631. [ad. L. **suggestivus*, f. *suggest-* SUGGEST *v.*; see -IVE.] **1.** Calculated or fitted to suggest thoughts, ideas, a course of action, etc.; conveying a suggestion or hint; implying something that is not directly expressed. **b.** *euphem.* Apt to suggest something indecent 1889. **2.** Of a method, plan, etc.: That suggests itself 1806. **3.** Pertaining to hypnotic suggestion 1903.

1. Some thoughtful and s. chapters by M. de Remusat 1856. A very s. thinker 1857. Much that is s. of inquiry 1880. Hence **Sugge·stive-ly** *adv.*, **-ness. Suggesti·vity** (*rare*).

†**Sugge·stor.** 1591. [f. SUGGEST *v.* + -OR.] = SUGGESTER -1818.

‖ **Suggestum** (sŏdʒe·stŏm). *Pl.* **-a** (**-ums**). 1705. [L., f. *suggest-, suggerere* to SUGGEST.] A platform, stage, tribune.

Sugillate, suggillate (si̯ū·dʒilĕit, sʊ·dʒ-), *v.* Now *rare* or *Obs.* 1623. [f. L. *sugillat-, sugg-*, pa. ppl. stem of *sugillare*, of doubtful etym.] *trans.* To beat black and blue, bruise. Chiefly *Med.* in *pa. pple.*, marked with livid spots or patches, bruised. So **Sug(g)illa·tion,** †beating black and blue; *Med.* a livid or black-and-blue mark; a bruise; ecchymosis.

Suicidal (si̯ūisəi·dăl), *a.* 1777. [f. SUICIDE *sb.*[2] + -AL 1.] **1.** Of, pertaining to, or involving suicide or self-slaughter; (of persons) having a tendency to suicide 1837. **2.** *fig.* Leading to or involving self-destruction; destructive or fatal to those engaged 1777. Hence **Suici·dally** *adv.*

Suicide (si̯ū·isəid), *sb.*[1] 1728. [ad. mod. L. *suicida*, f. *sui* of oneself + *-cida* -CIDE 1.] One who dies by his own hand; one who commits self-murder. Also, one who attempts or has a tendency to commit suicide. Also *attrib.* or as *adj.* (= suicidal).

Suicide (si̯ū·isəid), *sb.*[2] 1651. [ad. mod.L. *suicidium*, f. *sui* of oneself + *-cidium* -CIDE 2.] The or an act of taking one's own life, self-murder. Phr. *to commit s.*

fig. The central tragedy of all the world, the s. of Greece RUSKIN. Hence **Su·icide** *v. intr.* and *refl.* to commit s.; *trans.* (*euphem.*) to do to death.

†**Suici·dical,** *a. rare.* 1755. [f. prec. + -ICAL.] = SUICIDAL -1835.

Suicidism (si̯ū·isəidiz'm). *rare.* 1807. [f. SUICIDE *sb.*[2] + -ISM.] The doctrine or practice of suicide.

‖ **Sui generis** (si̯ū·əi dʒe·nĕris). 1787. [L.] *lit.* Of one or its own kind; peculiar. †Also illiterately as *sb.*, a thing apart, an isolated specimen.

‖ **Sui juris** (si̯ū·əi dʒūə·ris). 1614. [L., = of one's own right.] **a.** *Anc. Roman Law.* Of the status of one who was not subject to the *patria potestas.* **b.** *Mod. Law.* Of full age and capacity, legally competent to manage one's own affairs 1675. **c.** *transf.* One's own master 1655.

Suilline (si̯ū·ilәin), *a.* and *sb.* 1880. [ad. med.L. *suillinus*, f. *suillus* (f. *sus, su-* swine) + -INE.] Pertaining to, an animal of, the family *Suidæ* or swine.

Suine (si̯ū·in). 1881. [f. L. *sus, su-* swine + -INE[5].] A fatty substance made from pig's lard, used as a butter-substitute.

Suing (si̯ū·iŋ), *vbl. sb.* ME. [f. SUE *v.* + -ING[1].] †**1.** The following of a person or thing; the pursuance of a course of action; the carrying out or execution of something -1465. **2.** 'Pursuing' at law; legal prosecution or suit; application for a writ. Also *s. forth.* 1440. **3.** The action of a suitor; paying court; entreaty, supplication 1591.

Suing (si̯ū·iŋ), *ppl. a.* late ME. [f. SUE *v.* + -ING[2].] **1.** That sues. **2.** In *absol.* or *advb.* const.: (*a*) In succession, one after another; (*b*) afterwards, after. late ME. Hence †**Su·ingly** *adv.* consequently; in due sequence; hence, subsequently, later; in succession.

Suint (swint). 1791. [ad. F., f. *suer* to sweat, with an indeterminate suffix.] The natural greasy substance in the wool of sheep, consisting of fatty matter combined with potash salts: called also *yolk.*

Suiogothic (swīogǫ·þik), *a.* and *sb.* 1759. [ad. mod.L. *Suiogothicus*, serving as adj. to *Suiones Gothique*, which was used to denote the *Sviar* (*Svear*) Swedes, and *Götar* (*Göthar*), older *Gautar*, the inhabitants of Götland (the southern portion of Sweden).] Swedish; the (Old and Middle) Swedish language.

‖ **Suisse** (swis, süis). 1837. [F., = Swiss.] The porter of a large house; the beadle of a church (in France).

Suit (si̯ūt), *sb.* ME. [a. AF. *siwte, siute, sute, suite* = OF. *sieute* :—pop.L. **sequita*, f. **sequere* to follow, SUE.] **I.** *Feudal Law.* **1. a.** In full, *s. of court*: Attendance by a tenant at the court of his lord. **b.** In full, *s. real* (*royal, regal*): Attendance of a person at the sheriff's court or tourn, attendance at the court-leet. **c.** An instance of this. late ME. **2.** *S. and service*: attendance at court and personal service due from a tenant to his lord; hence used as a formula in describing certain forms of tenure. Also *homage and s.* late ME. **3.** The resort of tenants to a certain mill to have their corn ground; the obligation of such resort. *Hist.* 1450. †**4.** A due paid in lieu of attendance at the court of a lord -1660.

1. Phr. *To do, give, owe s.* **2.** *fig.* I, being a cadet of my house, owed s. and service to him who was its head DE QUINCEY.

II. Pursuit; prosecution, legal process. †**1.** Pursuit, chase; also, a pursuit -1772. †**2.** The pursuit *of* an object or quest -1596. **3.** The action of suing in a court of law; legal prosecution; hence, †litigation 1477. †**4.** The prosecution *of* a cause; also, the suing for a writ -1607. **5.** A process instituted in a court of justice for the recovery or protection of a right, the enforcement of a claim, or the redress of a wrong; a prosecution before a legal tribunal. late ME. **b.** More fully, *s. in law* = LAWSUIT. Similarly *s. in chancery, equity.* 1530. **6.** The action or an act of suing, supplicating, or petitioning; (*a*) petition, supplication, or entreaty; *esp.* a petition made to a prince or other high personage. Now *poet.* 1449. †**b.** *To make one's s.*: to supplicate, petition, sue -1738. **7.** Wooing or courting of a woman; solicitation for a woman's hand. Also, an instance of this, a courtship. 1590.

3. Whose suite is he arrested at? SHAKS. **5.** Ordinary private law..upon which nine-tenths of the suits between man and man are founded 1888. **6.** The King sees me, and faine would heare my sute KYD. **7.** Doubtless, that agreeable figure of his must have help'd his s. surprizingly SHERIDAN.

†**III.** Livery, garb; sort, class. **1.** A livery or uniform; also, in wider sense, a dress, garb -1633. **b.** *Out of suits with*: out of favour with. SHAKS. **2.** Kind, sort, class -1642.

IV. Following, train, suite. A company of followers; a train, retinue, SUITE. Also, a company of disciples. Now *arch.* or *dial.* (repl. by *suite*). ME. **b.** The witnesses or followers of a plaintiff in an action at law. Now *Hist.* 1647.

V. Set, series. **1.** A number of objects of the same kind or pattern intended to be used together or forming a definite set or series, e. g. the whole of the sails required for a ship or for a set of spars; a suite of rooms. late ME. **2.** A set of garments or habiliments intended to be worn together at the same time. **a.** of church vestments 1495. **b.** of mens' or boys' outer garments; in full, *s. of apparel, of clothes.* late ME. **c.** of women's attire; in earlier use, an entire set of garments for wear at one time; in recent use, a costume (i. e. coat and skirt) 1761. **d.** of armour 1821. **e.** *transf., fig.*, and *allus.* 1593. **3.** Any of the four sets (spades, clubs, hearts, diamonds) of which a pack of playing-cards consists. Also, the whole number of cards belonging to such a set held in a player's hand at one time 1529.

1. A s. of Ribbands ADDISON. A whole s. of drawing-rooms DICKENS. **2. a.** One priestly cope, with the whole suite EVELYN. **b.** His light travelling s. 1892. **e.** The redbreast's sober s. 1804. If honour be your clothing, the s. will last a life-time 1858. *Birthday suit* (joc.), the bare skin. **3.** I purpose agayne to deale vnto you an other card, almost of the same sute LATIMER. Phr. *To follow s.* (†*in s.*), to play a card of the same s. as the leading card; hence often *fig.*, to do the same thing as somebody (or something) else. *One's strong s.*, one's forte.

VI. Sequence; agreement. †**1.** A succession, sequence (*rare*) -1625. **2.** *In s. with*: in agreement or harmony with. *Of a s. with*: of a piece with. 1797.

attrib. and *Comb.*: †**s.-broker,** one who made a business of procuring a favourable hearing for suits; **-case,** a small rigid portmanteau orig. designed to contain a s. of clothes; **-duty,** obligation to give s. at a mill; **-service** *Feudal Law*, service rendered by attendance at a lord's court.

b. In Bridge, where *suit* is contrasted with 'no trumps' (see No *a.* II. 3), as *s.-bid, -call*, etc.

Suit (sᶦū̆t), *v.* 1450. [f. prec.] †1. *intr.* To 'do suit' to a court; hence, to have recourse *to* -1540. †2. To prefer a suit; to sue *to* a person *for* something -1719. †3. To pay court *to* a woman -1749. †4. To arrange in a set, sequence, or series; to set in due order, sort out -1695. 5. *trans.* To provide with a suit of clothes; to clothe, attire, dress. Chiefly *pass. arch.* 1577. 6. To make appropriate or agreeable *to*; to adapt or accommodate in style, manner, or proportion *to*; to render suitable. Freq. in *pass.* 1596. 7. To provide, furnish. Chiefly *pass.* (or *refl.*), to be provided (or provide oneself) *with* something desired and in such a manner as to please one 1607. 8. To be agreeable or convenient to (a person, his inclinations etc.); to fall in with the views or wishes of 1578. 9. To be fitted for, adapted to, be suitable for, answer the requirements of 1603. b. To be good for, 'agree with'; *esp.* to be favourable to the health of (a person) 1814. c. To be becoming to 1819. 10. *intr.* To be suitable, fitting, or convenient 1821. 11. *To s. with*: to agree, harmonize, or fit in with; to be suitable to. *Obs.* or *arch.* 1605.

5. How odly he is suited, I thinke he bought his doublet in Italie SHAKS. 6. Sute the Action to the Word, the Word to the Action SHAKS. 7. I hope you are suited, my dear DICKENS. 8. That sort of promise which a man keeps when the thing suits his inclination 1779. 9. The Sofa suits The gouty limb COWPER. His own explanation did not s. all phenomena JOWETT. 10. Say Saturday; if that does not s. there will be time to tell me MRS. CARLYLE.

Suitable (sᶦū̆·tăb'l), *a.* (*adv.*) 1582. [f. prec. + -ABLE, after *agreeable.*] †1. Of furniture, dress, features, etc.: Conforming or agreeing in shape, colour, pattern, or style; matching, to match -1710. †2. Of persons, actions, qualities, conditions, institutions: Conforming or agreeing in nature, condition, or action; accordant; corresponding; analogous; *occas.* congenial -1748. †b. Of two or more things: That are in agreement or accord -1684. 3. That is fitted for, adapted or appropriate to a person's character, condition, needs, etc., a purpose, object, occasion, or the like. Const. *to, for.* 1607. †4. as *adv.* = Suitably *to* -1796.

3. Senseless fears not sutable to the occasion 1653. There are 750,000 in Ireland who could earn 2s. a week..if they had sutable employment 1672. The most s. season for transplanting the roots 1812. Hence **Suitabi·lity, Sui·tableness. Sui·tably** *adv.*

Suite (swīt). 1673. [a. F.; see SUIT *sb.*] 1. A train of followers, attendants, or servants; a retinue. 2. A succession or series; now chiefly said of series of specimens 1722. b. A number of rooms together forming a set used by a person, a family or company of persons 1716. c. A set of furniture of uniform pattern 1851. d. *Mus.* †(*a*) A set or series of lessons, etc.; (*b*) A series of dance tunes arranged for one or more instruments and composed in the same key or related keys 1801. 3. A sequel, result (*rare*) 1800. 4. ‖En s. (añ sṻit). a. In agreement or harmony (*with*) 1797. b. Of rooms: In a series leading from one to the other 1818.

2. d. (*c*) A collection of pieces or songs by one composer on one main theme to be performed in sequence at one time 1902.

Suited (sᶦū̆·tėd), *ppl. a.* 1632. [f. SUIT *sb.* or *v.* + -ED.] With qualifying word: Wearing a suit or attire of a specified kind.

Till civil-suited Morn appeer MILT.

Suiting (sᶦū̆·tiŋ), *vbl. sb.* 1561. [f. SUIT *v.* + -ING [1].] †1. The action of suing for something; suing out a writ; petitioning; paying court to a woman -1690. 2. The fitting or adaptation of one thing *to* another 1707. 3. *concr.* Trade name for: Material for making suits of clothes; usu. *pl.* 1883.

Suitor (sᶦū̆·təɹ), *sb.* late ME. [a. AF. *seutor, suitour*, ad. late L. *secutor, -orem* (f. *secut-, sequi* to follow) with assimilation to *suite* SUIT *sb.*] †1. One of a retinue or suite; hence, an adherent, follower, disciple -1830. 2. One who owed suit (see SUIT *sb.* I. 1) to a court, and in that capacity acted as assessor or elector. Now only *Hist.* late ME. 3. One who sues or petitions; a petitioner, suppliant. *arch.* late ME. 4. A petitioner or plaintiff in a suit 1503. 5. One who seeks a woman in marriage; a wooer 1586.

3. That you would..be a suter for him unto the heavenly powers GASCOIGNE. 5. She was rich —..of course she had suitors 1870. Hence **Sui·torship.**

Suitor (sᶦū̆·təɹ), *v.* Now chiefly *dial.* 1668. [f. prec.] 1. *trans.* To court, woo 1672. 2. *intr.* To be a suitor or wooer (*to*) 1668.

2. Counts a many, and Dukes a few, A suitoring came to my father's Hall BARHAM.

Suitress (sᶦū̆·trės). *rare.* 1714. [f. SUITOR *sb.* + -ESS [1].] A female suitor.

†‖**Suivante** (sṻivānt). 1698. [F., f. *suivre* to follow.] A confidential maid -1812.

‖ **Sula** (siū̆·lă). 1678. [mod.L., a. ON. *súla.*] Applied by Hoier and others to a supposed variety of sea-fowl; in mod. *Ornith.* a genus of gannets (family *Sulidæ*).

Sulcal (sʊ·lkăl), *a.* 1889. [f. SULCUS + -AL 1.] *Anat.* Belonging to or connected with a sulcus.

Sulcate (sʊ·lkeᶦt), *a.* 1760. [ad. L. *sulcatus, sulcare*; see next.] *Nat. Hist.* Marked with (parallel) furrows or grooves. So **Su·lcated** *ppl. a.* 1694.

†**Sulcate,** *v.* 1577. [f. L. *sulcat-, sulcare*, f. SULCUS.] *trans.* To plough (*esp.* the seas) -1656.

Sulcation (sʊlkēᶦ·ʃən). *rare.* 1658. [f. L. *sulcare* SULCATE *v.*; see -ATION.] 1. Furrowing, grooving. 2. A sulcus or set of sulci 1852.

Sulca·to-, used as comb. form of L. *sulcatus* SULCATE *a.* in the sense 'sulcate and ...', as *s.-costate* adj.

Sulciform (sʊ·lsifǭɹm), *a.* 1822. [See next and -FORM.] Having the form of a sulcus.

‖ **Sulcus** (sʊ·lkŏs). *Pl.* **sulci** (sʊ·lsəi). 1662. [L.] 1. a. A groove made with an engraving tool. b. A trench. c. A hollow or depression in the land. *rare.* 2. *Anat.* A groove or furrow in a body, organ, or tissue 1744. b. *spec.* A fissure between two convolutions of the brain 1833. 3. *Bot.* The lamella in some fungi 1856.

Suling (su·liŋ). *Hist.* [OE. *swulung, sulung*, prob. f. **swul(h)ian*, **sul(h)ian*, f. **swulh, sulh* plough.] In Kent, the fiscal unit.

Sulk (sʊlk), *sb.* 1804. [f. SULK *v.*[2]] 1. *pl.* A state of ill-humour or resentment marked by obstinate silence or aloofness from society. Often with *the* and in phr. *in the sulks.* b. *sing.* A fit of sulking; the action of sulking 1837. 2. A person who sulks (*rare*) 1883.

1. b. Mrs. Cadurcis remained alone in a savage s. 1837.

†**Sulk,** *v.*[1] *rare.* 1579. [ad. L. *sulcare* to plough, furrow, f. *sulcus* furrow.] *trans.* To plough (the seas). Also *intr.* -1682.

Sulk (sʊlk), *v.*[2] 1781. [Origin obsc.] *intr.* To keep aloof from others in moody silence; to indulge in sullen ill-humour; to be sulky.

He sulked with his old landlady for thrusting gentle advice and warning on him READE. Hence **Su·lker,** one who sulks.

Sulky (sʊ·lki), *sb.* 1756. [subst. use of next.] 1. A light two-wheeled carriage or chaise (occas. without a body), seated for one person: now used chiefly in America for trials of speed between trotting-horses. (So called because it admits only one person.) 2. *attrib.* passing into *adj.*, applied to (*a*) a set of articles for the use of a single person, (*b*) an agricultural implement having a seat for the driver (*U.S.*) 1786.

Sulky (sʊ·lki), *a.* 1744. [app. f. SULK *v.*[2]] 1. Of persons and their actions: Silently and obstinately ill-humoured; showing a tendency to keep aloof from others and repel their advances by refusing to speak or act. Also of animals; *spec.* of a fish that remains in hiding and motionless when hooked. 2. Of the weather, etc.: Gloomy, dismal. Of things, with respect to their growth, progress, or movement: Sluggish. Also, *dial.* difficult to work. 1817. Here **Su·lkily** *adv.*

Sullage (sʊ·lėdʒ). 1553. [Origin obsc.] 1. Filth, refuse, *esp.* such as is carried off by drains from a house, farmyard, or the like; sewage. †2. *fig.* Filth, defilement, pollution -1697. 3. The silt washed down and deposited by a stream or flood 1691. 4. *Founding.* Metal scoria or slag 1843.

2. The lightest act of dalliance leaves somthing of stain and s. behind it 1673.

Comb.: **s.-pipe,** a drain-pipe.

Sullen (sʊ·lən), *a., adv.,* and *sb.* 1573. [Later form of ME. *soleine*, ad. OF. *solain* lonely f. (ult.) L. *solus* alone.] A. *adj.* 1. Of persons, their attributes, aspect, actions: Characterized by, or indicative of, gloomy ill-humour or moody silence. b. *transf.* Of animals and inanimate things: Obstinate, refractory; stubborn, unyielding 1577. †c. *fig.* Baleful, malignant -1703. †2. Solemn, serious -1719. 3. Of immaterial things, actions, conditions: Gloomy, dismal, melancholy; sometimes with the notion of 'passing heavily, moving sluggishly' 1593. b. Of a sound or an object producing a sound: Of a deep, dull, or mournful tone. Chiefly *poet.* 1592. 4. Of sombre hue; of a dull colour; hence, of gloomy or dismal aspect 1586. 5. Of water, etc.: Flowing sluggishly. *poet.* 1622.

1. The answer of James was a cold and s. reprimand MACAULAY. b. As s. as a beast new-caged TENNYSON. 2. Such s. Planets at my Birth did shine, They threaten every Fortune mixt with mine DRYDEN. 3. The s. passage of thy weary steppes SHAKS. A bleak, s. day 1864. b. I hear the far-off Curfeu sound .. Swinging slow with s. roar MILT. 4. Like bright Mettall on a s. ground SHAKS. The sullen-purple moor TENNYSON. 5. S. Mole that runneth underneath MILT.

B. *adv.* = Sullenly (*rare*) 1718. C. *sb.* (in *pl.*, usu. *the sullens*; rarely *sing.*) A state of gloomy ill-humour; sullenness, sulks. *arch.* 1580.

Phr. *In the sullens, sick of the sullens.* Hence **Su·llen** *v.* (*rare*) *trans.* to make s. or sluggish. **Su·llen-ly** *adv.*, **-ness.**

Sulliage (sʊ·liedʒ). 1667. variant of SULLAGE, infl. by SULLY *v.*

Su·llow. Chiefly *w.* and *s.w. dial.* [OE. *sulh*, cogn. w. L. *sulcus* furrow.] A plough.

†**Su·lly,** *sb.* 1602. [f. next.] An act of sullying or polluting; a stain, blemish -1762.

Little Spots and Sullies in its Reputation ADDISON.

Sully (sʊ·li), *v.* 1591. [app. ad. F. *souiller*; see SOIL *v.*] 1. *trans.* To pollute, defile; to soil, stain, tarnish (in material sense now *rare* or *poet.*). Often in pa. pple. †2. *intr.* To become soiled or tarnished -1670.

1. The roofe and sides are..sullied..with the smoke of torches 1615. The purity of his virtue was sullied by excessive vanity GIBBON. 2. Looke you Francis, your white Canuas doublet will sulley SHAKS.

Sulph- (sʊlf) *Chem.*, var. of SULPHO- before a vowel, as in *sulphamide, -anilic* (*-ate*), *-antimonic* (*-ate*), *-arsenic* (*-ate*), *-iodide.*

Su·lphacid. 1859. [See SULPH-.] = SULPHO-ACID.

Sulphate (sʊ·lfeᶦt, -ĕt), *sb.* 1790. [ad. F., ad. mod.L. *sulphatum* (sc. *acidum* ACID), f. SULPHUR; see -ATE [1] 1 c.] *Chem.* 1. A salt of sulphuric acid: usu. with term indicating the base, as *s. of ammonia.* 2. *ellipt.* = Sodium sulphate 1900. Hence **Su·lphate** *v. intr.* to become sulphated. **Su·lphating** *vbl. sb.* the formation of a sulphate, *esp.* the deposit of lead sulphate on the plates of a battery.

Sulphated (sʊ·lfeᶦtėd), *ppl. a.* 1802. [f. mod.L. *sulphatus*; see SULPHUR, -ATE [1] 1 c.] Combined or impregnated with sulphur or sulphuric acid; charged with or containing sulphates.

Sulphato- (sʊlfēᶦ·to). *Chem.*, bef. a vowel sometimes **sulphat-** (sʊ·lfĕt), a prefix in the name of a compound denoting that it contains a sulphate as an ingredient, as *s.-carbonate.*

Sulphide (sʊ·lfəid). 1836. [f. SULPHUR + -IDE.] *Chem.* 1. A compound of sulphur with another element (usu. denoted by a qualifying term). b. *Hydrogen s.*, sulphuretted hydrogen, H_2S. 1849. 2. *attrib.*, chiefly with ref. to the treatment of metallic sulphides in manufacturing processes 1893.

Sulphinate (sʊ·lfinĕt). 1877. [f. SULPHINIC + -ATE [4].] *Chem.* A salt of sulphinic acid.

Sulphindigotic (sʊlfindigǫ·tik), *a.* 1857. [SULPH-.] *Chem.* In *s. acid*: an acid formed by the action of sulphuric acid on indigo. Hence **Sulphi·ndigotate,** a salt of s. acid.

Sulphine (sʊ·lfəin). 1880. [f. SULPH- + -INE [5].] *Chem.* Any of a group of compounds containing sulphur united to hydrocarbon radicals; also, the hypothetical radical SH_3 from which these are derived.

Sulphinic (sʊlfi·nik), *a.* 1877. [f. prec. + -IC.] *Chem.* Applied to acids containing the group SO.OH united to carbon, obtained by reducing the chlorides of the sulphonic acids.

Sulphion (sʊ·lfi͡ǫn). 1868. [f. SULPH- + ION.] *Chem.* The hypothetical radical consisting of one equivalent of sulphur and four of oxygen (SO_4).

Sulphite (sʊ·lfəit). 1790. [ad. F., arbitrary alteration of *sulphate*; see -ITE [1] 4 b.] *Chem.* 1. A salt of sulphurous acid: usu. with a qualifying term indicating the base. 2. *attrib.*, chiefly with ref. to the use of sulphite of soda or of lime in certain processes 1892.

Sulpho- (sʊ·lfo), bef. a vowel also SULPH- used as comb. form of SULPHUR, in names of chemical compounds containing sulphur, or (in mod. use) produced by the substitution of sulphur for oxygen (etc.) in a compound; now largely superseded by THIO-.

Su·lpho-a:cid. 1857. [f. prec. + ACID.] *Chem.* **a.** An acid obtained from another acid by substituting sulphur for oxygen; as SULPHOCYANIC acid, CNHS, from cyanic acid, CNHO, now called THIO-ACID. **b.** An acid which contains the group SO_2.OH united to carbon.

Sulphocyanic (sʊ·lfosəi,æ·nik), *a.* 1819. [f. SULPHO- + CYANIC.] *Chem.* Designating the sulpho-acid related to cyanic acid, occurring in cruciferous plants and in human saliva, and obtainable as a colourless liquid; now THIOCYANIC. Hence **Sulphocy·anate, -cy·anide** (in *Photogr.* short for ammonium sulphocyanide).

Sulphocyanogen(sʊ·lfosəi,æ·nǒdʒĕn). 1841. [f. SULPHO- + CYANOGEN.] *Chem.* A compound of sulphur and cyanogen $(CN)_2S$, obtained as a yellow amorphous powder.

Sulphonal (sʊ·lfŏnăl). 1889. [ad. G. *sulfonal*, f. *sulfon* SULPHONE.] *Chem.* Diethylsulphone-dimethyl-methane, a white crystalline substance, used as a hypnotic.

Sulphone (sʊ·lfo͡un). 1873. [ad. G. *sulfon*, f. *sulfur*; see -ONE a.] *Chem.* Any of a group of compounds containing the radical SO_2 united to two hydrocarbon radicals.

Sulphonic (sʊlfǫ·nik), *a.* 1873. [f. prec. + -IC.] *Chem.* Containing the radical SO_2.OH (called the *s. group* or *radical*). Hence **Su·lphonate.**

Sulphopurpuric (sʊ·lfopɒɪpiū̆·rik), *a.* 1838. [ad. F. *sulfo-purpurique*; see SULPHO- and PURPURIC.] *Chem.* Applied to an acid obtained by the action of sulphuric acid on indigo. Hence **Sulphopu·rpurate.**

Sulpho-salt (sʊ·lfosǫlt). 1833. [f. SULPHO- + SALT *sb.*[1] 5.] *Chem.* A salt of a sulpho-acid.

Sulphovinic (sʊlfovi·nik), *a.* 1826. [ad. F. *sulfovinique*, f. *sulfo-* SULPHO- + *vin* wine.] *Chem.* *S. acid*: an acid produced by the action of sulphuric acid on alcohol or spirit of wine; ethyl hydrogen sulphate or ethyl sulphuric acid. Hence **Sulphovinate** (-vəi·nět).

Sulphur (sʊ·lfəɪ), *sb.* late ME. [a. AF. *sulf(e)re*, OF. *soufre*:—L. *sulfur(em)*, *sulphur(em)*.] I. 1. A greenish-yellow non-metallic substance, found abundantly in volcanic regions, and occurring free in nature as a brittle crystalline solid, and widely distributed in combination with metals and other substances. In pop. and commercial language it is otherwise known as BRIMSTONE. In *Chem.*, one of the non-metallic elements: atomic weight 32, symbol S.

Sulphur exists in two distinct crystalline forms and in an amorphous form. It is manufactured largely from native sulphides of copper and iron; when refined and cast into moulds, it is the *roll* or *stick s.* of commerce. It is highly inflammable, and is used in the manufacture of matches, gunpowder, and sulphuric acid, for vulcanizing rubber, in bleaching, and as a disinfectant.

In popular belief sulphur has been associated with the fires of hell, with devils, and with thunder and lightning.

b. In a refined state, e.g. as flowers of sulphur, it is used medicinally as a laxative, a resolvent, and a sudorific, and as an ingredient of various ointments, esp. for skin diseases. ME. †**c.** *pl.* Masses or deposits of native sulphur –1771. 2. *Alch.* One of the supposed ultimate elements of all material substances. late ME. †3. A compound of sulphur; *esp.* a sulphide –1853. 4. †**a.** Applied to thunder and lightning, a discharge of gunpowder, etc. –1616. **b.** Applied pop. to minerals containing sulphur or supposed to be sulphurous 1799. **c.** *Vegetable s.*: see VEGETABLE *a.* 1855. 5. *ellipt.* = *sulphur butterfly* 1832. 6. *colloq.* or *slang.* Pungent talk, 'sulphurous' language 1897.

1. Thunder hath s. in it COWLEY. A fiery Deluge, fed With ever-burning S. unconsum'd MILT. *Virgin s.*, native s. in the form of transparent amber-coloured crystals. *Volcanic s.*, native s. in opaque, lemon-yellow, crystalline masses. *S. of ivy*, corruption of SULPHUR VIVUM. 4. **a.** The Gods throw stones of sulpher on me SHAKS.

Comb.: **s. acid,** an old name for sulphides of electronegative metals, as arsenic, antimony; **s. alcohol,** a compound of the nature of an alcohol in which s. replaces oxygen; **s. bath,** †(*a*) a sulphur spring; (*b*) a bath to which flowers of s. have been added, used in the treatment of skin diseases; **-cast** = *s. impression*; **s. ether,** a compound analogous to ether in which s. replaces oxygen; **-impression,** an impression taken of a seal, medallion, etc. in a composition consisting of s. and wax; **-match,** a lucifer match tipped with s.; **-ore,** an ore which yields s., e.g. iron pyrites; **s. salt,** an old name for a salt produced by the combination of a 's. acid' with another metallic base; **-spring,** a spring containing compounds of s. or impregnated with sulphurous gases; **-tree,** a hard-wooded tree, *Morinda lucida*, found in West Central Africa and used for building purposes; **-weed** = SULPHURWORT; **-work(s,** a s. manufactory; **-yellow,** (of) the pale-yellow colour characteristic of s.

II. *attrib.* passing into *adj.* = Of the colour of sulphur, sulphur-yellow, as in *s. butterfly, pearl; s.-breasted, -crested*; **s.-bottom** (in full *s.-bottom whale*), a rorqual of the Pacific Ocean, *Balænoptera sulphurea*, having yellow underparts; also **s.-whale.**

Sulphur (sʊ·lfəɪ), *v.* 1759. [f. prec.] *trans.* To fumigate with burning sulphur; to sprinkle (plants) with flowers of sulphur to prevent mould or the like; also, to put (wine) into casks that have been fumigated with sulphur to prevent fermentation.

Sulphurate (sʊ·lfiŭre͡ɪt), *v. rare.* 1757. [f. SULPHUR + -ATE [3].] *trans.* To combine with, or convert into, sulphur; to impregnate with, or subject to the action of, sulphur. Hence **Su·lphurator,** an apparatus for sprinkling plants with flowers of sulphur, for fumigating with sulphur, or the like.

Sulphurated (sʊ·lfiŭre͡ɪtėd), *ppl. a.* 1747. [f. late L. *sulphuratus* + -ED [1].] Chiefly *Chem.* Combined or impregnated with sulphur: applied chiefly to sulphides. (Survives chiefly in terms of the Materia Medica.)

Sulphuration (sʊlfiŭrē͡ɪ·ʃən). Now *rare* or *Obs.* 1713. [f. SULPHUR *v.*; see -ATION.] 1. Anointing with sulphur (*rare*). 2. Fumigation with sulphur 1791. 3. Combination with sulphur 1796. 4. Vulcanization 1853.

†**Sulphure·ity.** 1610. [ad. mod.L. *sulphureitas*, f. L. *sulphureus*; see -ITY.] Sulphureous quality or nature –1676.

Sulphureo- (sʊlfiū̆·rĭo), used as comb. form of L. *sulphureus* in the sense of 'sulphureous and...'.

Sulphureous (sʊlfiū̆·rĭəs), *a.* 1552. [f. L. *sulphureus*, f. *sulphur* SULPHUR; see -EOUS.] 1. Of or pertaining to sulphur; full of, containing, or consisting of sulphur 1626. †**b.** *Old Path.* Consisting of 'sulphur' as one of the principles of matter; (of disease) arising from 'sulphurous' matter –1702. 2. Derived or emanating from sulphur; hence, having the qualities associated with (burning) sulphur 1552. 3. *allus.* and *fig.* †Hellish, satanic; full of the 'sulphur' of hell 1664. 4. Sulphur-coloured, sulphur-yellow. Also, of the bluish colour of the flame with which sulphur burns. 1656.

1. The patients lie up to their chins in hot s. water 1792. 2. A s. smell ensues GOLDSM. Hence **Sulphu·reous-ly** *adv.*, **-ness.**

Sulphuret (sʊ·lfiŭret). 1790. [ad. mod.L. *sulphuretum*; see SULPHUR *sb.* and -URET.] *Chem.* = SULPHIDE. (Now only in the Materia Medica and in Mining.)

Sulphuretted (sʊ·lfiŭretėd), *a.* 1805. [f. prec. + -ED [2].] *Chem.* Combined chemically with sulphur; impregnated with sulphur.

S. hydrogen, hydrogen sulphide, H_2S, a colourless gas with a very offensive odour, prepared by the action of diluted hydrochloric or sulphuric acid upon iron (ferrous) sulphide.

Sulphuric (sʊlfiū̆·rik), *a.* 1790. [ad. F. *sulfurique*; see SULPHUR *sb.* and -IC 1.] 1. *Chem.* *S. acid*, a highly corrosive oily fluid (hydrogen sulphate, H_2SO_4), also called *oil of vitriol*, in its pure state a dense liquid without colour or smell. **b.** Related to or derived from sulphuric acid 1815. †2. Consisting of or containing sulphur –1811.

1. *Anhydrous s. acid*, sulphur trioxide. *Fuming s. acid* a mixture of sulphuric acid and sulphur trioxide. **b.** *S. anhydride*, sulphur trioxide. *S. ether*, ethylic or vinic ether, a compound formed by the action of sulphuric acid upon spirits of wine. *S. oxide*, sulphur trioxide.

Sulphuring (sʊ·lfəriŋ), *vbl. sb.* 1800. [f. SULPHUR *sb.* or *v.* + -ING [1].] 1. Exposure to the fumes arising from burning sulphur, to produce whiteness in fabrics, to prevent fermentation in casks, to disinfect, etc. 2. The sprinkling of plants with flowers of sulphur to prevent or destroy mildew 1891.

†**Sulphu·rious,** *a.* 1471. [ad. OF. *sulphurieux*; see SULPHUR *sb.* and -IOUS.] = SULPHUREOUS, SULPHUROUS –1727.

Sulphurize (sʊ·lfiŭrəiz), *v.* 1794. [a. F. *sulfuriser*; see SULPHUR *sb.* and -IZE.] 1. *trans.* To cause to combine chemically with or to be impregnated by sulphur; to convert into a sulphur compound. 2. To treat or dress with sulphur; to vulcanize (rubber) 1846. 3. To fumigate with burning sulphur 1856. Hence **Su:lphuriza·tion.**

Sulphurous (sʊ·lfiŭrəs, *in Chem. use* sʊlfiū̆·rəs), *a.* 1530. [ad. L. *sulphurosus*, or f. SULPHUR *sb.* + -OUS.] 1. = SULPHUREOUS 1. 2. = SULPHUREOUS 2. 1607. **b.** Applied to thunder and lightning (*poet.*). Also *occas.* volcanic. 1603. **c.** Of or belonging to (the smoke of) gunpowder 1620. 3 *allus.* and *fig.* **a.** Pertaining to sulphur or brimstone as an adjunct of hell; hellish, satanic. Also, pertaining to or dealing with hell-fire. 1602. **b.** Fiery, heated 1611. **c.** Of language, expression: Characterized by heat; in recent use, blasphemous, profane 1616. 4. = SULPHUREOUS 4. Also *advb.* 1837. 5. *Chem.* Designating compounds in which sulphur is present in a larger proportion than in sulphuric compounds 1790.

2. **b.** Cracks Of s. roaring SHAKS. 3. **a.** There's hell, there's darkenes, there is the s. pit SHAKS. **b.** Duc de Rohan rose, in a s. frame of mind CARLYLE. **c.** He used..s. words, and the very biggest D's, I was assured 1897. 4. Burning sulphurous-blue..it still shines CARLYLE. 5. *S. acid*: (*a*) more fully, *s. acid gas*, an old name for sulphur dioxide; (*b*) the acid (H_2SO_3) resulting from the combination of sulphur dioxide with water. *S. oxide* or *anhydride*, sulphur dioxide, SO_2, a transparent colourless gas with a pungent and suffocating smell, obtained by burning sulphur in dry air or oxygen. Hence **Su·lphurously** *adv.*

‖ **Sulphur vivum** (sʊ·lfəɪ vəi·vɒm). 1651. [L., = living sulphur.] Native or virgin sulphur; also in a fused, partly purified form.

Sulphurwort (sʊ·lfəɪwɒ̄ɪt). 1578. [f. SULPHUR *sb.* + WORT [1].] An umbelliferous plant, *Peucedanum officinale*, having pale yellow flowers; hog's fennel.

Sulphury (sʊ·lfəri), *a.* 1580. [f. SULPHUR *sb.* + -Y [1].] 1. = SULPHUROUS 1, 2, 2 b, c, 3 a, b. 2. = SULPHUREOUS 4. 1900.

Sulphuryl (sʊ·lfiŭril). 1867. [f. SULPHUR *sb.* + -YL.] *Chem.* The radical SO_2.

Sulphydrate (sʊlf(h)əi·dre͡ɪt). 1852. [f. SULPH- + HYDRATE *sb.*] *Chem.* A salt of sulphydric acid or hydrogen sulphide; a compound of a metallic atom or radical with the group SH; a hydrosulphide.

Sulphydric (sʊlf(h)əi·drik), *a.* 1838. [f. SULPH- + HYDRIC.] *Chem.* = SULPHURETTED. *S. acid* (*gas*), sulphuretted hydrogen.

Sulpician (sʊlpi·ʃiăn), *sb.* (*a.*) 1786. [ad. F. *sulpicien*, f. (*St.*) *Sulpice.*] *Eccl.* One of a congregation of secular priests founded in Paris in 1642 by the Abbé Olier, priest of the parish of St. Sulpice, mainly for the training of candidates for holy orders; as *adj.*, belonging to this congregation.

Sultan (sʊ·ltăn), *sb.* 1555. [a. F., or ad. med.L. *sultanus*, ad. Arab. *sulṭān* king, sovereign, queen, power, dominion.] 1. The sovereign or chief ruler of a Mohammedan country; in recent times *spec.* the sovereign of Turkey. Also formerly, a prince or king's son, a high officer. 2. An absolute ruler; *gen.* a despot, tyrant 1648. 3. (orig. †*sultan('s) flower.*) Either of two species of sweet-scented annuals, brought orig. from the East, usu. dist. as the purple or white sweet sultan, *Centaurea* (*Amberboa*) *moschata*, and the yellow sweet sultan, *C.* (*A.*) *suaveolens* 1629. 4. A small white-crested species of domestic fowl, orig. brought from Turkey 1855. Hence **Sultan, Su·ltanize,** *vbs. intr.* to rule as a s. or despot. **Su·ltanry** (*rare*) = SULTANATE 2. **Su·ltanship,** (*a*) = SULTANATE 2; (*b*) the personality of a s.

Sultana (sɒltā·nă). 1585. [a. It. (Sp., Pg.), fem. of *sultano* SULTAN.] 1. The wife (or a concubine) of a sultan; also, the queen-mother or some other woman of a sultan's family. 2. A mistress, concubine 1702. 3. Any bird belonging to either of the genera *Porphyrio* and *Ionornis*; the purple gallinule or porphyrio 1837. 4. In full *s. raisin*: A kind of small seedless raisin produced in the neighbourhood of Smyrna 1841.

Sultanate (sɒ·ltănĕ'ᵗt). 1879. [f. SULTAN *sb.* + -ATE [1].] 1. A state or country subject to a sultan; the territory ruled over by a sultan. 2. The office or power of a sultan 1884.

†Sultane. 1612. [ad. F., fem. of *sultan* SULTAN.] 1. = SULTANA 1 -1694. 2. = SULTANIN -1764. 3. A rich gown trimmed with buttons and loops, fashionable in the late seventeenth and the eighteenth c. -1798.

Sultaness (sɒ·ltănės). Now *rare.* 1611. [f. SULTAN *sb.* + -ESS [1].] = SULTANA 1.

Sultanic (sɒltæ·nik), *a.* 1827. [f. SULTAN *sb.* + -IC.] Of, belonging to, or characteristic of a sultan; hence, despotic, tyrannical.

†Su·ltanin. 1612. [ad. It. *sultanino*, or F. *sultanin*, ad. Arab. *sulṭānī* SULTANY.] A former Turkish gold coin valued at 8*s.* -1749.

†Sultany. 1612. [ad. Arab. *sulṭānī* adj. imperial, sb. kingdom, sultanin, f. *sulṭān* SULTAN.] 1. = SULTANATE. -1855. 2. = prec. -1674.

Sultry (sɒ·ltri), *a.* 1594. [f. †*sulter* vb., perh. for *swulter*, cogn. w. SWELTER + -Y [1].] 1. Of the weather, the atmosphere, etc.: Oppressively hot and moist; sweltering. b. Of places, seasons of the year, etc.: Characterized by such weather 1620. c. Of the sun, etc.: Producing oppressive heat. *poet.* 1697. 2. *fig.* and *allus.* a. Chiefly *poet.* (*a*) Associated with oppressive heat; hot with toil 1637. (*b*) Hot with anger or lust 1671. b. *colloq.* or *slang.* (*a*) 'Spicy', 'smutty' 1887. (*b*) Of language: Lurid, 'sulphurous' 1891. (*c*) 'Hot', 'warm', lively 1899.

1. The spring, Whom Sommers pride (with sultrie heate) pursues KYD. b. When weary reapers quit the s. field POPE. c. The s. Sirius burns the thirsty plains POPE. 2. a. (*a*) What time the Gray-fly winds her s. horn MILT. (*b*) Stalking..in a sultrie chafe MILT. Hence **Su·ltri-ly** *adv.*, **-ness.**

Sum (sɒm), *sb.* ME. [a. AF., OF. *summe*, *somme* :—L. *summa* fem. (sc. *res, pars*) of *summus* highest.] 1. A quantity or amount of money. a. *s. of money, gold, silver, †pence*, etc. b. *absol.* = 'sum of money'. late ME. c. A quantity of money *of* a specified amount. late ME. †d. *transf.* A quantity *of* goods regarded as worth so much -1872. †2. A number, company, or body (*of* people); a host, band -1601. †3. *Arith.* A number; *occas.* a whole number as dist. from a fraction -1709. 4. The total number (*of* individual persons or things capable of numeration). Now only as transf. use of sense 6. late ME. 5. The total amount or quantity, the totality, aggregate, or whole (*of* something immaterial) ME. 6. *Math.* The number, quantity, or magnitude resulting from the addition of two or more numbers, quantities, or magnitudes. late ME. 7. A series of numbers to be added or cast up 1579. 8. An arithmetical problem in the solution of which some particular rule is applied; also, such a problem worked out. *colloq.* 1803. 9. That which a statement, discourse, writing, or a system of laws, etc. amounts to, or is in essence; a summary, epitome. *Obs.* or *arch.* late ME. †b. = SUMMA 2. -1770. †10. The upshot, issue, conclusion -1670. 11. The ultimate end or goal; the highest attainable point. *Obs.* or *arch.* ME.

1. He supply'd her..with a convenient Summ of Money 1718. b. *Principal s.*: see PRINCIPAL *a.* II. 1. 4. 'Now', cried I, 'the s. of my miseries is made up' GOLDSM. 5. The stretching of a span, buckles in his summe of age SHAKS. 7. They might cast the s. without pen, or counters 1579. 8. A common multiplication or division s. 1862. 9. Tell us the s., the circumstance defer MILT. 11. Thus I have..brought My Storie to the s. of earthly bliss Which I enjoy MILT.

Phr. *In s.* [F. *en somme*, L. *in summa.*] a. (Expressed) in a few words, briefly or summarily. Now *arch.* and *rare.* b. Used *absol.* as an illative phr.: To conclude in few words; to sum up; in brief, in short. *S. and substance*, the essence (*of* anything); the gist or pith (*of* a matter). *The s. of things* [tr. L. *summa rerum*], the highest public interest the public good, the common weal; also, the totality of being, the universe.

Sum (sɒm), *v.* ME. [a. OF. *sommer*, *summer*, or ad. med.L. *summare*, f. *summa* SUM *sb.*] 1. *trans.* To find the sum or total number or amount of; to add *together*; to reckon or count up; to cast up (a column of figures, an account). Now *rare.* b. To bring *up* to a certain total (*rare*) 1597. c. *Math.* To find the sum of (a series); in the calculus of finite differences, to find the aggregate of the successive values of a function 1776. d. *intr.* To do sums in arithmetic 1825. e. *trans.* In transf. and fig. uses: To reckon, count, or total *up* 1597. 2. To collect into or embrace in a small compass; also with *up.* Chiefly *pass.* 1606. 3. To give the substance of in a few words or a brief statement; to summarize, epitomize. Said also of the statement made, etc. (Usu. with *up.*) 1621. 4. *To s. up*: (of the judge in a trial) to recapitulate (the evidence) to the jury before they retire to consider their verdict, giving an exposition of points of law when necessary. Often *absol.* 1700. b. To form an estimate of, summarize the qualities or character of 1889. †5. To bring to completion or perfection; also with *up* -1667.

1. b. The howre doth rather summe vp the moments then deuide the daye BACON. e. 2 *Hen. IV*, I. i. 167. 2. She..in her looks summs all Delight MILT. 3. Go to the Ant, thou Sluggard; (says the Wise-man) which in Few Words Summs up the Moral of This Fable 1692. 4. The judge summed up dead against the claim 1884. 5. Creatures animate with gradual life Of Growth, Sense, Reason, all summ'd up in Man MILT.

Sumach, sumac (siū·mæk, ʃū·mæk), *sb.* ME. [a. OF., or med.L. *sumac(h*, a. Arab. *summāq.*] 1. A preparation of the dried and chopped leaves and shoots of plants of the genus *Rhus*, esp. *R. Coriaria*, much used in tanning, also for dyeing and staining leather black, and medicinally as an astringent. b. The leaves of the sumach used as a substitute for tobacco 1823. 2. Any of the shrubs or small trees of the genus *Rhus*, esp. *R. Coriaria*, indigenous in southern Europe, which is the chief source of the material used in tanning, and *R. vernicifera* (lacquer tree), Japan or varnish sumach 1548. Hence **Sumac(h)** *v. trans.* to tan with s.

Sumatran (s'umā·trăn), *a.* and *sb.* 1688. [f. *Sumatra*, a large island in the Malay Archipelago + -AN.] A. *adj.* Of or pertaining to the island of Sumatra or its inhabitants or language 1783. B. *sb.* A native or inhabitant of the island of Sumatra; also, the Sumatran language 1688.

Sumbul (sɒ·mbɒl, su·mbul). 1790. [a. F., a. Arab. *sunbul.*] Applied to the roots of certain plants (and to the plants themselves) which are used medicinally; *esp.* (*a*) the spikenard, *Nardostachys Jatamansi*, (*b*) the musk-root, *Ferula* (*Euryangium*) *Sumbul*, (*c*) valerian.

‖**Sumen** (s'ū·men). 1662. [L., f. *sugere* to suck.] A sow's udder, the dugs of a sow; formerly *Anat.*, the hypogastrium. †Also *transf.*, the fat or rich portion of a thing.

Sumerian (s'umīº·riăn), *a.* and *sb.* 1875. [ad. F. *sumérien*, f. *Sumer.*] A. *adj.* Pertaining to Sumer or Sumir, one of the districts of ancient Babylonia, or to its population. B. *sb.* 1. A non-Semitic inhabitant of Sumer 1878. 2. The language spoken by the inhabitants of Sumer 1887.

Sumless (sɒ·mlės), *a.* Chiefly *poet.* 1599. [f. SUM *sb.* + -LESS.] Without number; that cannot be 'summed' or counted; incalculable.

As rich with prayse As is the Owse and bottome of the Sea With sunken Wrack, and sum-lesse Treasuries SHAKS.

‖**Summa** (sɒ·mă). 1442. [L.; see SUM *sb.*] †1. A sum-total -1784. 2. A summary treatise; e.g. the *Summa Theologiæ* of St. Thomas Aquinas 1725. 3. Phr. **S. rerum** (rīº·rɒm) [L. *rerum* of things or affairs]: the highest public interest 1715.

Summarist (sɒ·mărist). 1873. [f. as next + -IST.] One who compiles a summary.

Summarize (sɒ·mărəiz), *v.* 1871. [f. next + -IZE.] *trans.* To make (or constitute) a summary of; to sum up; to state briefly or succinctly. Hence **Su:mmariza·tion** 1865.

Summary (sɒ·mări), *sb.* 1509. [ad. L. *summarium*, neut. sing. of *summarius* (see next).] 1. A summary account or statement. †2. The highest point or summit; also, the ultimate outcome. CARLYLE.

Summary (sɒ·mări), *a.* late ME. [ad. L. *summarius*, f. *summa* SUM *sb.*; see -ARY [1].] 1. Of a statement or account: Containing or comprising the chief points or the sum and substance of a matter; compendious (now usu. with implication of brevity). b. *transf.* Characterized by or involving conciseness and brevity 1582. 2. *Law.* Applied to the proceedings in a court of law carried out rapidly by the omission of certain formalities required by the common law. Similarly of a court-martial 1765. 3. Performed or effected by a short method; done without delay 1713. †4. Highest, supreme (*rare*) -1733.

1. A s. and general view of the Vices and Follies reigning in his time DRYDEN. 2. *S. jurisdiction*, the determination of cases expeditiously without reference to the ordinary requirements of the common law. 3. It put into their heads the idea of s. vengeance 1833. Hence **Su·mmarily** *adv.* **Su·mmariness.**

Summation (sɒmē¹·ʃən). 1760. [ad. mod. L. *summationem*, f. med.L. *summare* to SUM.] 1. *Math.* The process of finding the sum of a series. 2. The adding up of numbers, quantities, etc.; an addition sum 1816. b. The accumulation of a number of stimuli applied to a muscle 1877. 3. The computation of the aggregate value of conditions, qualities, etc.; summing-up 1836. 4. The aggregate or sum-total; the resultant or product 1840.

3. Such is Mr. Wyndham's s. of Scott 1908. Hence **Summa·tional** *a.* produced by s. or addition.

Summed (sɒmd), *ppl. a.* late ME. [In branch I, f. OF. *som(m)é*, pa. pple. of *sommer* to sum, complete, ad. med.L. *summare.* In branch II, f. SUM *v.* + -ED [1].] †I. 1. Of a stag: Having a complement of antlers. Said also of the antlers. Often *full s.* -1637. 2. Of a hawk: Having the feathers full grown. Said also of the plumage. Often *full s.* Also *fig.* = equipped -1688.

2. Like a young Eagle summ'd..Disdaines a shoale of Dawes 1649. A full sumd or consumate Orator 1600.

II. Collected into one sum, forming a sum-total. Also with *up.* 1607.

Summer (sɒ·məɹ), *sb.*[1] [OE. *sumor* = OFris. *sumur, -er*, MLG., MDu. *somer* (Du. *zomer*), OHG. *sumar* (G. *sommer*), ON. *sumar*. Cognates are Skr. *samā* half-year, year, Zend *hama* in summer, OIr. *sam*, W. *haf* summer.]

1. The second and warmest season of the year, coming between spring and autumn; reckoned astronomically from the summer solstice (21 June) to the autumnal equinox (22 or 23 Sept.); in pop. use comprising in the northern hemisphere the period from mid-May to mid-August; also often, *esp.* in contradistinction to *winter*, the warmer half of the year. (Often with initial capital.) b. Applied, with qualification, to a period of fine dry weather in late autumn; see ALL-HALLOW(S 1, INDIAN SUMMER, MARTIN [2] 3; *St. Luke's* (*little*) *s.*, such a period occurring about St. Luke's Day, 18 Oct. c. *transf.* Summer weather; summery or warm weather ME. d. *fig.* and *allus.* 1535. 2. In *pl.* with numeral, put for 'year'. Now only *poet.* or in speaking of a young person's age. late ME. 3. *attrib.* passing into *adj.* a. = Of or pertaining to summer, characteristic of summer; suitable or appropriate to summer; existing, appearing, performed, etc. in summer ME. b. So *summer's* (now chiefly with *morning, evening, night*; cf. SUMMER'S DAY). late ME. c. Applied to crops, etc. that ripen in summer; also *spec.* in pop. names of early-ripening apples and pears. late ME. d. *fig.* with ref. to prosperous, pleasant, or genial conditions 1592.

1. When S. brings the lily and the rose MORRIS.

You will find me there all s. 1885. Phr. *s. and winter, winter and s.*, all the year round. **c.** There eternal S. dwels MILT. **d.** For now the wine made s. in his veins TENNYSON. **2.** Summers three times eight save one She had told MILT. **3. a.** An odorous Chaplet of sweet Sommer buds SHAKS. S. Quarters 1708. S. holidays LAMB. **b.** Their's is but a summer's song COWPER. **d.** If't be S. Newes, Smile too't before SHAKS.

Comb.: **s. catarrh** = HAY-FEVER; **s. cholera** = CHOLERA 2; **s. complaint** *U.S.*, s. diarrhœa of children; also, infantile cholera and dysentery; **-field,** *(a)* a field with the s. crop; *(b) dial.* a s.-fallow; **-heat,** the heat of s.; *spec.* an arbitrary maximum s. temperature commonly marked on thermometers; **s. lightning,** sheet lightning without audible thunder, often seen in hot weather; also *allus.* and *attrib.*; **s. parlour** *Obs.* or *arch.*, an apartment for s. use; **s. rash,** prickly heat, *Lichen tropicus*; **s. school,** a course of instruction and study in a subject or curriculum of subjects held during some part of the summer at a chosen centre. **-weight** *a.*, adapted in weight and texture to summer wear.

b. In names of animals and plants which are active or flourish in summer (often rendering L. *æstivus, æstivalis* as a specific name): **s. cypress** = BELVEDERE 2; **s. duck,** a N. Amer. duck, *Æx sponsa*, the wood-duck; **s. snipe,** the common sandpiper, *Tringoides hypoleucus*; **s. tanager,** the rose tanager, *Pyranga æstiva*, which summers in N. America; **s. teal,** the garganey; **s. yellowbird,** a N. Amer. wood-warbler, *Dendrœca æstiva*.

Summer (sʊ·məɹ), *sb.*[2] ME. [a. AF. *sumer, somer*, = OF. *somier* pack-horse, beam:—pop. L. *saumarius*, f. *sagma* packsaddle, a. Gr. σάγμα.] †**I.** A pack-horse –1470. **II. a.** *gen.* A main beam in a structure. *Sc.* –1715. **b.** A horizontal bearing beam in a building; *spec.* the main beam supporting the girders or joists of a floor (or *occas.* the rafters of a roof). When on the face of a building it is prop. called BREAST-SUMMER. ME.

attrib.: **s.-beam, -tree** = sense II. b.

Summer (sʊ·məɹ), *sb.*[3] 1611. [f. SUM *v.* + -ER[1].] One who sums or adds; *colloq.* or *dial.* one who does sums, an arithmetician.

Summer (sʊ·məɹ), *v.* 1440. [f. SUMMER *sb.*[1]] **1.** *intr.* To pass or spend the summer, to dwell or reside during the summer (now chiefly *Sc.* and *U.S.*); (of cattle, etc.) to be pastured in summer. **2.** *trans.* To keep or maintain during summer; *esp.* to provide pasture for (cattle, etc.); said of the land or the grazier 1599. **3.** To make summer-like, balmy, or genial 1863.

1. He is summering at Castellamare 1842. **2.** Dartmoor summers an immense number of sheep 1810.

Phr. *To s. and winter. intr.* **a.** To spend the whole year; *transf.* to remain or continue permanently. **b.** *trans.* To maintain one's attitude to or relations with at all seasons; to associate with, be faithful to, or adhere to constantly.

Su·mmer-bird. 1560. **1.** A bird that makes its appearance in summer; a summer migrant 1597. †**2.** With allusion to the cuckoo as the 'summer bird': A cuckold 1560.

Summer-cloud. (Also **summer's cloud.**) 1605. A cloud such as is seen on a summer's day, *esp.* one that is fleeting or does not spoil the fine weather. Also *allus.*

Can such things..ouercôme vs like a Summers Clowd, Without our speciall wonder? SHAKS.

Su·mmer-fa·llow, *sb.* 1733. [See FALLOW *sb.* 2.] A lying or laying fallow during the summer; also, land that lies fallow during the summer. **b.** as *adj.* Lying fallow during the summer 1801. So **Su·mmer-fa·llow** *v. trans.* to lay (land) fallow during summer 1669.

Su·mmer-house. ME. **1.** A summer residence in the country. Now *rare.* **2.** A structure in a garden or park, usu. of very simple and often rustic character, designed to provide a cool shady place in the heat of summer 1440.

Summering (sʊ·məriŋ), *vbl. sb.* 1703. [app. f. SUMMER *sb.*[2] + -ING[1].] *Arch.* **a.** *collect.* The beds of the stones or bricks of an arch considered with ref. to their direction. **b.** The radial direction of the joints of an arch. **c.** The degree of curvature of an arch.

Summerish (sʊ·məriʃ), *a.* 1726. [f. SUMMER *sb.*[1] + -ISH[1].] Somewhat summer-like.

Summer-like (sʊ·məɹləik), *a.* 1530. [f. SUMMER *sb.*[1] + -LIKE.] Like, or like that of, summer; summery.

Summerly (sʊ·məɹli), *a.* [OE. *sumerlic*; see SUMMER *sb.*[1] and -LY[1].] †**1.** Of or pertaining to summer; taking place in summer –1771. **2.** Having the qualities of summer; summer-like, summery ME.

Summer's day. ME. A day in summer; often put typically for a very long day.

A proper man as one shall see in a summers day SHAKS. To lament his fate In amorous dittyes all a Summers day MILT. Phr. *Some summer's day*, 'one of these fine days'.

Summer solstice. 1549. The time at which the sun reaches the summer tropic, *i. e.* in the northern hemisphere, the tropic of Cancer, in the southern, the tropic of Capricorn.

Su·mmer-tide. Now chiefly *poet.* ME. = SUMMER-TIME 1.

Su·mmer-time. late ME. **1.** The season of summer; the time that summer lasts. **2.** (as two words) The standard time (in advance of ordinary time) adopted in some countries during the summer months 1916.

Summery (sʊ·məri), *a.* 1824. [f. SUMMER *sb.*[1] + -Y[1].] Resembling or pertaining to summer; summer-like. Hence **Su·mmeriness.**

Summist (sʊ·mist). 1545. [ad. med.L. *summista*, f. *summa* SUM *sb.* + *-ista* -IST.] The author of a summa of religious doctrine, etc., e.g. St. Thomas Aquinas, author of *Summa theologiæ*; often used *gen.* of the schoolmen. †**b.** An epitomizer; *transf.* an epitome –1734.

Summit (sʊ·mit). 1470. [a. OF. *sommette, somete*, also *somet, sumet*, dim. of *som, sum*:—L. *summum*, neut. sing. of *summus* (see SUM *sb.*).] **1.** The topmost part, top; the vertex, apex. **b.** *Geom.* A point of a polyhedron where three or more faces meet, forming a solid angle 1805. **2.** The topmost point or ridge of a mountain or hill. Also, the highest elevation of a road, railway, or canal. 1481. **3.** *fig.* The highest point or degree; the acme 1711.

1. Vpon the somette or toppe of the tour, he maad an ymage of copre CAXTON. **2.** Ætna's smoking s. GRAY. **3.** If love be the s. of all virtue, humility is the foundation PUSEY.

attrib.: **s. angle** = *s. quoin*; **s. level,** *(a)* the highest level reached by a canal, watercourse, railway, or the like; *(b)* a level place in a railway or stretch of water in a canal, with descending planes on either side; **s. quoin,** the solid angle at a s. of a polyhedron. Hence **Su·mmitless** *a.* having no s.

†**Su·mmity.** *Obs.* or *arch.* late ME. [a. OF. *sommet(t)e, summite* (mod.F. *sommité*), ad. late L. *summitas, -atem*, f. *summus* highest (see SUM *sb.*).] = prec. –1862. **b.** A person or thing that is at the head of a body, series, etc. –1685.

†**Su·mmon,** *sb.* ME. [f. next.] = SUMMONS –1800.

Summon (sʊ·mən), *v.* ME. [a. AF., OF. *sumun-, somun-, somon-*, pres. stem of *somondre, semondre*:—pop.L. **summonēre* for *summonēre*, f. *sub-* + *monere* to warn.] **1.** *trans.* To call together by authority for action or deliberation. **b.** To call (a peer) to parliament by writ of summons; hence, to call to a peerage. late ME. **2.** To cite by authority to attend at a place named, *esp.* to appear before a court or judge to answer a charge or to give evidence; to issue a summons against ME. **3.** *gen.* To require the presence or attendance of; to bid (a person) to approach by a call, ringing a bell, knocking, or the like; with adv., to call (to a person) to go in a specified direction. late ME. **4.** *fig.* with immaterial or inanimate subject: To call, bid come or go. Often with adv. 1549. **5.** To call upon (a person) *to do* something. late ME. **b.** To call upon *to surrender* 1471. †**6.** To give warning or notice of, proclaim, call –1611. **7.** Often with *up*: To call (a faculty, etc.) to one's aid; to call up (one's courage, energy) 1582. **8.** To call *into* existence; to call forth 1742.

1. The Grand Master had summoned a chapter SCOTT. **2.** A witness who will not come of himself may be summoned JOWETT. **3.** They were soon summoned to table 1885. **4.** *absol.* Hearke how these Instruments s. to supper SHAKS. **5.** Cole-black clouds ..Do s. vs to part SHAKS. **b.** He first summoned the garrison GOLDSM. **6.** *Wint. T.* II. iii. 202. **7.** He summoned all his fortitude 1802. Hence **Su·mmonable** *a.* that can be or is liable to be summoned.

Summoner (sʊ·mənəɹ). ME. [a. AF. *sumenour*:—med.L. *summonitorem*, agent-n. f. *summonere.*] **1.** A petty officer who cites and warns persons to appear in court. Now *Hist.* **2.** One who summons another to a place. Often *fig.* of immaterial or inanimate agents. 1580. **3.** One who takes out a summons 1865.

Summons (sʊ·mənz), *sb.* ME. [a. AF., OF. *sumunse, somo(u)nse*:—pop. L. **summonsa* (for *summonita*), pa. pple. fem. (used subst.) of *summonere* to SUMMON.] **1.** An authoritative call to attend at a specified place for a specified purpose. **b.** The royal act of calling to the national council or parliament the bishops, earls, and barons by special writ, and the knights and freeholders by a general writ addressed to the sheriffs; hence *spec.* the call to a barony ME. **2.** A call or citation by authority to appear before a court or judicial officer; also (in full *writ of s.*), the writ by which the citation is made ME. **3.** *gen.* A peremptory or urgent call or command; a summoning sound, knock, or the like 1567. **4.** *Mil.* The act of summoning a place to surrender. Also, now only, with inf. 1617.

1. He obeyed the summons with the respect of a faithful subject GIBBON. **b.** The Parliament met according to s. upon the 13th of April in the year 1640 CLARENDON. **2.** Every action in the High Court shall be commenced by a writ of summons 1875. **3.** The Duke of Norfolke..Stayes but the s. of the Appealants Trumpet SHAKS. **4.** Vpon our s. of the Towne, after martiall manner 1617.

Summons (sʊ·mənz), *v.* 1658. [f. prec.] **1.** *trans.* = SUMMON *v.* 1–5b. Now *rare.* **2.** To cite before a court or a judge or magistrate; to take out a summons against 1780.

‖**Summum bonum** (sʊ·mŏm bōᵘ·nŏm). *Pl.* su·mma bo·na. 1563. [L. (Cicero).] The chief or supreme good: properly a term of *Ethics*; often *transf.* and in trivial or joc. use.

‖**Summum genus** (sʊ·mŏm dʒī·nŏs). *Pl.* su·mma ge·nera. 1592. [L.] The highest or most comprehensive division in a classification; in *Logic*, a genus that is not considered as a species of a higher genus.

‖**Summum jus** (sʊ·mŏm dʒʊs). 1588. [L.] The utmost rigour of the law, extreme severity.

Sumner[1] (sʊ·mnəɹ). late ME. [a. AF. *sum(e)nour*, f. *sumen-, sumon-*; see SUMMON *v.* and -ER[1].] One who is employed to summon persons to appear in court; *esp.* a summoning officer in an ecclesiastical court. Now surviving in the Isle of Man.

Sumner[2] (sʊ·mnəɹ). 1881. *Naut.* The name of T. H. *Sumner*, American sea-captain, designating a method of determining one's position on the earth's surface, and the line (*S. line*) which is used in the calculations.

I worked a S., or position by double altitude 1925.

Sump (sʊmp), *sb.* late ME. [a. (M)LG. *sump* (*sumpt*) or MDu. *somp, sump*, or ad. G. *sumpf* marsh, etc.; f. **swump-*, related by ablaut to **swamp-* (see SWAMP *sb.*).] **1.** A marsh, swamp, morass; (now *dial.*) a dirty pool or puddle. **2.** A pit or well for collecting water or other fluid; *spec.* a cesspool; a pond or well from which sea-water is collected for salt-manufacture 1680. **b.** *Mining.* A pit or well sunk at the bottom of an engine shaft to collect the water of the mine 1653. **3.** *Metall.* A pit of stone or metal at a furnace to collect the metal at the first fusion 1674.

attrib.: **s.-fuse,** a waterproof fuse used for blasting under water; **-man,** a pitman's assistant, one who attends to the machinery in an engine-shaft. Hence **Sump** *v. intr.* to dig a s. or (small or temporary) shaft.

Sumph (sʊmf). *Sc.* and *n. dial.* 1719. [Origin unkn.] A simpleton, blockhead. Also, a surly or sullen man.

Sumpitan (sʊ·mpităn). 1634. [a. Malay *sumpitan*, f. *sumpit* blowpipe.] A blow-gun made by the Malays from a hollowed cane, from which poisoned arrows are shot.

‖**Sumpsimus** (sʊ·mpsimŏs). 1545. [L., 1st pers. pl. perf. ind. of *sumere* to take.] A correct expression taking the place of an incorrect but popular one (*mumpsimus*).

Sumpter (sʊ·mᵖtəɹ). *arch.* ME. [a. OF. *som(m)etier*:—pop. L. **sagmatarius*, f. *sagmat-, sagma*, a. Gr. σάγμα; see -ER[2].] †**1.** The driver of a pack-horse –1601. **2.** A pack or baggage horse; a beast of burden 1570. †**3.** A pack, saddle-bag –1681. **4.** *attrib.* (often = *pack-*). late ME.

4. The s.-mule, in harness'd pride SMOLLETT.

Sumption (sʊ·mᵖʃən). 1440. [ad. L. *sumptio, -onem*, f. *sumpt-, sumere* to take.] †**1.** The reception (of the Sacrament, of Christ in the Sacrament) –1664. **2.** †**a.** The taking of a thing as true without proof; hence, an assumption, premiss. **b.** The major premiss of a syllogism 1572.

Sumptuary (sɒ·mᵖtiu,ări), *a.* 1600. [ad. L. *sumptuarius*, f. *sumptus*, f. *sumpt-*, *sumere* to consume.] Pertaining to or regulating expenditure.

S. law, a law regulating expenditure, esp. with a view to restraining excess in food, equipage, etc.

Sumptuosity (sɒmᵖtiu,ǫ·sĭti). 1559. [ad. late L. *sumptuositas*, f. *sumptuosus* SUMPTUOUS.] Lavishness or extravagance of expenditure; magnificence or luxuriousness of living, equipment, decoration, or the like. **b.** An instance of this; a sumptuous thing 1601.

b. To speak of his sumptuosities, of his largesses 1601.

Sumptuous (sɒ·mᵖtiu,əs), *a.* 1485. [a. OF. *somptueux*, *sumptueux*, ad. L. *sumptuosus*, f. *sumptus* expense, f. *sumpt-*, *sumere* to take, consume, spend.] **1.** Of buildings, apparel, repasts, and the like: Made or produced at great cost; costly and (hence) magnificent in workmanship, construction, decoration, etc. **b.** of conditions, functions, etc. 1590. **c.** Of natural objects: Splendid or magnificent in appearance 1594. †**2.** Of charges, expenses, etc.: Involving a great outlay of money -1616. †**3** Of persons, etc.: Spending largely; (hence) magnificent in equipment or way of living -1781.

1. Thir s. gluttonies, and gorgeous feasts MILT. A fine Lady dressed in the most s. Habit STEELE. **b.** Dressed in the most s. mode of the Court 1841. She spoke and turn'd her s. head TENNYSON. **3.** The bishops..were s. in their fare and apparell HOBBES. Hence **Su·mptuous-ly** *adv.*, **-ness.**

Sum-total (sɒ·m,tōᵘ·tăl). *Pl.* **sum-totals, sums-total.** late ME. [ad. med.L. *summa totalis*; see SUM *sb.* and TOTAL *a.*] The aggregate of all the items in an account; the total amount (of things capable of numeration). **b.** *gen.* The aggregate or totality *of* 1660.

Sun (sɒn), *sb.* [Com. Teut.: OE. *sunne* :—OTeut. **sunnōn-*, *-on-*, f. Indo-Eur. **sun-*, *s(u)wen-*, whence also Zend (gen.) *χvəng* sun, Gr. *ἥν-οψ* glittering.] **1.** The brightest (as seen from the earth) of the heavenly bodies, the luminary or orb of day; the central body of the solar system, around which the earth and other planets revolve, being kept in their orbits by its attraction and supplied with light and heat by its radiation; in the Ptolemaic system reckoned as a planet, in modern astronomy as one of the stars. **b.** OE. *sunne* being fem., the fem. pronoun was used until the 16th c. in referring to the sun; since then the masc. has been commonly used; the neuter is somewhat less frequent. **c.** As an object of worship in various religions, and thus (and hence generally) personified as a male being, sometimes identified with various gods, esp. Apollo; also in classical mythology said to be drawn in a chariot ME. **d.** As a type of brightness or clearness OE. **2.** With qualifying word, or in *pl.*, with ref. to its position in the sky (or occas. the zodiac), or its aspect or visibility at a particular time or times. late ME. **b.** With ref. to the heat produced by the sun; hence (poet.) = climate, clime. late ME. **3.** *fig.* In allusion to the splendour of the sun or to its being a source of light and heat OE. **4.** The direct rays of the sun; sunlight; sunshine OE. **5.** With qualification or in phr. **a.** Sunrise or sunset as determining the period of a day. *Obs.* or *arch.* late ME. **b.** A (particular) day, as being determined by the rising of the sun. *poet.* or *rhet.* 1606. **c.** The time of the sun's apparent revolution in the zodiac, a year. *poet.* 1742. **6.** *gen.* A luminary; *esp.* a star as the centre of a system of worlds. late ME. **7.** An appearance in the sky like a sun; a mock-sun, parhelion. late ME. **8.** A figure or image of, or an ornament or vessel made to resemble, the sun (*e.g.* a monstrance with rays); *Her.* a representation of the sun, surrounded with rays and usu. charged with the features of a human face; also freq. as the sign of an inn; hence, the name of an inn or a room in an inn 1450. †**9. a.** *Her.* In blazoning by the names of heavenly bodies, the name of the tincture Or. **b.** *Alch.* Gold. -1651.

1. Lett nott the sonne goo doune apon youre wrathe TINDALE *Eph.* iv. 26. Phrases, etc. *Under* (or *beneath*) *the s.*, on earth, in the world. (*As..*) *as the s. shines on* = as lives or exists; used in commendatory phrases. *On which the s. never sets*, applied formerly to the Spanish dominions, now to the British Empire. *With the s.*, from left to right; similarly *against the s.* (Chiefly *Naut.*) *To take the s.*, to make an observation of the meridian altitude of the sun. Provb. phrases. *To make hay while the s. shines*: see HAY *sb.*[1] **b.** For yet the S. Was not; shee in a cloudie Tabernacle Sojourn'd the while MILT. **c.** Who knows not Circe The daughter of the S.? MILT. A Persian, humble servant of the s. COWPER. **2.** A glen which sloped towards the southern s. KINGSLEY. **b.** Underneath another s. TENNYSON. **3.** The Sunne of Rome is set SHAKS. The Lord God is a sunne and shield *Ps.* lxxxiv. 11. *S. of righteousness*, a title of Jesus Christ (after *Malachi* iv. 2). **4.** Where the reaper..in the s. all morning binds the sheaves M. ARNOLD. Phr. *One's place in the s.*, an individual share in those things to which all have a right; hence, a position giving scope for the development of personal or national life. **5. b.** By the fift houre of the Sunne SHAKS. **6.** The Moone moues lowest, siluer Sunne of Night 1623.

attrib. and *Comb.*, as *s.-worship*, *-worshipper*; **s.-bath**, an exposure to the direct rays of the s., esp. as a method of medical treatment; basking in the s.; hence **-bathe** *v. intr.*, **-bather**; **-blink**, a gleam of sunshine; **-bonnet**, a light bonnet with a projection in front and a cape behind to protect the head and neck from the s.; **-bow**, an arch of prismatic colours like a rainbow, formed by refraction of sunlight in spray or vapour; **-burner**, a circular group of gas-burners with reflectors, placed near the ceiling of a large room; **-crack** *Geol.*, a crack produced by the heat of the s. during the consolidation of a rock; **-disk, -disc**, the disk of the s., or a figure or image of this, esp. in religious symbolism; **-dog**, a mock sun, parhelion; **-flag**, the Japanese flag, bearing an image of the s.; **-glade**, a beam or track of sunlight, *esp.* the track of reflected sunlight on water; **-glass**, (*a*) a lens for concentrating the rays of the sun, a burning-glass; (*b*) a screen of coloured glass attached to a sextant for moderating the light of the s.; **-glow**, (*a*) a glow or glare of sunlight; (*b*) a hazy diffused light seen around the s., due to fine solid particles in the atmosphere, as after a volcanic eruption; **-hat**, a broad-brimmed hat worn in hot climates to protect the head from the s.; so **-helmet**; **-myth**, a myth relating to the s., a solar myth; **-picture**, a picture made by means of sunlight, a photograph; **-proof** *a.*, through which the sunlight cannot penetrate; unaffected by the rays of the s.; **-signalling, -telegraphy**, = HELIOGRAPHY 4; **-trap**, a place adapted for catching sunshine; **-wheel**, (*a*) the wheel around which a planet-wheel turns (see *Sun-and-planet wheels*); (*b*) a figure resembling a wheel, with radiating arms or spokes. **b.** In names of plants and animals; **s.-animalcule**, a microscopic protozoan of the group *Heliozoa*, esp. the common species *Actinophrys sol*, of a spherical form with numerous long, slender, straight, radiating filaments; **-bear**, a small Malayan species of bear (*Helarctos malayanus*), the *bruang*, having close black fur and a white patch on the breast; also, the Tibetan bear (*Ursus thibetanus*); **-beetle**, any one of various scarabæid beetles of the sub-family *Cetoniinæ*, which appear in sunshine; **-bittern**, a S. Amer. bird, *Eurypyga ehlias*, with brilliantly coloured plumage, also called *peacock-bittern*; **-drop(s**, any of the species of *Œnothera* (evening primrose) which open in sunlight; **-gem**, a brilliantly coloured Brazilian species of humming-bird, *Heliactin cornutus*; **-grebe** = SUNBIRD 1 c; **-squall, -squawl** *U.S.*, a jelly-fish; **-star, -starfish**, a starfish having numerous rays, as those of the genus *Solaster*; **-trout**, *local U.S.*, the squeteague. **c. Sun-and-planet wheels**, a form of gearing (invented by James Watt) consisting of a central wheel or *s.-wheel* and an outer wheel or *planet-wheel* (of which there may be more than one) geared together so that the axis of the latter moves round that of the former like a planet round the sun; also extended to other forms of gearing on a similar principle.

Sun, *v.* 1519. [f. prec.] **1.** *trans.* To place in or expose to the sun; to subject to the action of the sun's rays; to warm, dry, etc. in sunshine. **2.** *refl.* To expose oneself to or bask in the sun 1610. **3.** *intr.* To shine as or like the sun (*rare*) 1611. **4.** *trans.* To shine upon or illumine as or like the sun. Chiefly *poet.* 1637.

1. *fig.* I sunn'd my heart in beauty's eyes BYRON. **2.** He suns himself there after his breakfast when the day is suitable THACKERAY. **3.** Shine out, little head, sunning over with curls, To the flowers, and be their sun TENNYSON. **4.** A glade Far, far within, sunned only at noonday 1820.

Su·n-baked, *a.* 1628. **1.** Baked by exposure to the sun, as bricks, pottery, etc. 1700. **2.** Excessively heated by the sun; parched or hardened by the heat of the sun 1628.

Sunbeam (sɒ·nbīm). [OE. *sun(n)bēam*, also (late) *sunne-bēam*; see SUN *sb.* and BEAM *sb.*] **1.** A beam of sunlight. **2.** Used as a literal rendering of a native word applied to a radiant-coloured humming-bird 1613.

1. The gay motes that people the Sun Beams MILT.

Su·nbird, su·n-bird. 1776. **1. a.** Any bird of the passerine family *Nectariniidæ*, which comprises small birds with brilliant and variegated plumage, found in tropical and subtropical regions of Africa, Asia, and Australia; also applied to similar birds of other families. **b.** The sun-bittern, *Eurypyga helias* 1825. **c.** Any bird of the family *Heliornithidæ*, comprising swimming birds found in tropical America, Africa, and Asia 1872. **2.** (With hyphen.) **a.** A bird sacred to the sun or connected with sun-worship. **b.** A mythical 'bird of the sun', or the sun regarded as a bird. 1871.

Su·n-bright, *a.* Chiefly *poet.* 1579. [OE. *sunbeorht* occurs in sense 2.] **1.** Bright as the sun; supremely bright. **2.** Bright with sunshine; illumined by the sun 1744.

1. Th' Apostat in his S. Chariot sate MILT.

Sunburn (sɒ·nbɒɹn), *sb.* 1652. [f. next.] The condition of being sunburnt; discoloration or superficial inflammation of the skin caused by exposure to the sun; the brown colour or tan thus produced.

Su·nburn, *v.* 1530. [Back-formation from SUNBURNT.] **1.** *trans.* To 'burn', scorch, or discolour (usu. the skin) by exposure to the sun; to affect with sunburn; to tan. **2.** *intr.* for *pass.* To be discoloured or tanned by exposure to the sun; also of a plant 1832.

1. The scorching rays had sun-burnt his face 1805. So **Su·nbu·rning**, sunburn 1530.

Su·nburnt, su·nburned, *a.* late ME. [f. SUN *sb.* + *burnt*, *burned*, pa. pple. of BURN *v.*[1]] **1.** Discoloured, tanned, or superficially inflamed by exposure to sunshine; chiefly of the skin or complexion. **b.** *transf.* Of a brown colour, as if sunburnt 1893. **2.** Scorched, parched, or dried up by the heat of the sun, as land or vegetation 1586. **3.** = SUN-BAKED 1. 1634.

Su·nburst. 1816. [See BURST *sb.* 3.] **1.** A burst of sunlight; a sudden shining of the sun from behind a cloud. **2.** A firework, a piece of jewellery, etc., constructed so as to imitate the sun with its rays 1902.

Sundae (sɒ·ndeⁱ). orig. *U.S.* 1904. [Said to be altered spelling of SUNDAY, in *Sunday ice cream*, an ice cream left over from Sunday and on sale later.] A portion of ice-cream with syrup, fruit, nuts, etc.

Sunday (sɒ·ndeⁱ, -di). [OE. *sunnandæg*; tr. L. *dies solis* = Gr. *ἡμέρα ἡλίου* 'day of the sun'. (Now with initial capital.)] **1.** The first day of the week, observed by Christians as a day of rest and worship, in commemoration of Christ's resurrection; the Lord's Day. **b.** With specific epithet, as *Advent*, *Midlent*, *Mothering*, *Trinity* ME. **2.** *Saint S.*, a rendering of *Sanctus Dominicus* = St. Dominic, due to confusion with *dies Dominica* = Sunday. *local.* 1490.

1. Phr. (colloq.). *When two Sundays come together* (*meet*), never. *A month of Sundays*, a very long time. So *A week of Sundays*.

attrib. and *Comb.*, as *S. book*, *clothes*, *dinner*, *paper*; **S. best**, one's best attire, usu. worn on S. **S. letter**, the dominical letter.

Su·nday-school. 1783. A school in which instruction is given on Sunday; *esp.* such a school for children held in connexion with a parish or congregation; such schools are now intended only for religious instruction, but orig. instruction in secular subjects was also given.

Sunder (sɒ·ndəɹ), *a.* ME. [In A, compounds formed after OE. compounds in *sundor-* = separate, peculiar, private; in B, derived from ME. *o(n)sunder*, OE. *onsundran* ASUNDER, by substitution of *in* for *on*, *o*, *a*.] †**A.** *adj.* **1.** In compounds, as *sunderred*, private advice, etc. ME. only. **2.** Separate; various, sundry. -late ME. **B. In sunder** = ASUNDER *adv.* Now *poet.* or *rhet.* ME.

Sunder (sɒ·ndəɹ), *v.* Now *poet.* or *rhet.* [Late OE. *syndrian*, *sundrian*, for earlier *āsyndrian*, *āsundrian* (see ASUNDER *v.*), *ge-*, *on-*, *tō-sundrian*; f. prec.] **1.** *trans.* To dissolve connexion between two or more persons or things; to separate or part one *from* another. **2.** To divide into two or more parts; to split, break up, cleave ME. **3.** To keep apart, separate by an intervening space or barrier, *from* something. *rare.* (Chiefly *pass.*) 1606. **4.** *intr.* To become separated or severed *from* something; *esp.* of a number of persons, to part ME. **5.** To be torn, break, or split in pieces. late ME.

1. When both the Chiefs are sund'red from the Fight DRYDEN. 3. No space of Earth shall s. our two hates SHAKS. 5. Euen as a splitted Barke, so s. we SHAKS.

Sundew (sʊ·ndiū). 1578. [ad. early mod. Du. *son-, sundauw*, = G. *sonnentau*, tr. L. *ros solis*.] Any plant of the genus *Drosera*, which comprises small herbs growing in bogs, having leaves covered with glandular hairs secreting viscid drops which glitter in the sun like dew; esp. *D. rotundifolia* (round-leaved or common s.).

Su·n-dial. 1599. [f. SUN *sb.* + DIAL *sb.*] A contrivance for showing the time of day by means of a shadow cast by the sun upon a surface marked with a diagram indicating the hours. (Earlier called simply *dial.*)

Sundown, sun-down (sʊ·ndaun). 1620. [perh. a shortening of *sun-go-down.*] 1. The going down of the sun; the time when the sun goes down; also, the glow of sunset; the west. Chiefly *U.S.* and *Eng.* and *Colonial dial.*; occas. *poet.* or *rhet.* 2. A hat with a wide brim. *U.S.* 1888.

Su·ndow:ner *Austral. & U.S. colloq.*, a tramp who makes a practice of arriving at a station about sundown under the pretence of seeking work, so as to obtain food and a night's lodging; also (*S. Africa*) a glass of spirit drunk at sunset. **Su·ndowning,** the practice of a sundowner.

Sun-dried (sʊ·nˌdrəid), *a.* 1600. [f. SUN *sb.* + *dried*, pa. pple. of DRY *v.*] 1. Dried by exposure to the sun, as clay, bricks, articles of food, etc. 2. Dried up or parched by the sun, as vegetation, etc. 1638.

2. As Fire the Sun-dri'd Stubble burnes 1638.

Sundries (sʊ·ndriz), *sb. pl.* 1815. [pl. of SUNDRY *a.* used subst.; cf. ODDS.] Small articles of a miscellaneous kind; *esp.* small items lumped together in an account as not needing individual mention.

Sundry (sʊ·ndri), *a.* [OE. *syndrig* separate, special, private, exceptional; f. *sunder* SUNDER *a.*; see -Y[1].] 1. Having an existence, position, or status apart; separate, distinct. *Obs.* exc. *dial.* †2. Belonging or assigned distributively to certain individuals; distinct or different for each respectively –1738. †3. Individually separate. Usu. with pl. sb. or sing. sb. in pl. sense: Various, (many) different. –1754. †4. Different, other. (Const. *from.*) –1668. b. Consisting of miscellaneous items 1790. 5. As an indefinite numeral: A number of, several. (The prevailing use.) late ME. b. *ellipt.* and (chiefly *Sc.*) *absol.* 1470.

2. Experience finds That s. Women are of s. Minds DRYDEN. 4. b. Yield, including s. revenue, £4,855. 1913. 5. The scripture moueth vs in sondrye places, to acknowledge and confesse our manyfolde synnes and wyckednesse *Bk. Com. Prayer.*

Phr. *All and s.*, every individual, every single; now only *absol.* = everybody of all classes, one and all. (orig. and chiefly Sc. = L. *omnes et singuli.*)

Sun-dry (sʊ·ndrəi), *v.* Chiefly in **sun-dried, sun-drying.** 1695. [Back-formation from SUN-DRIED.] To dry in the sun, *trans.* and *intr.*

Su·n-fish, *sb.* 1629. A name for various fishes, of rounded form or brilliant appearance, or that bask in the sun.

a. Any fish of the genus *Mola* (also called *Orthagoriscus* or *Cephalus*), comprising large fishes of singularly rounded and ungainly form, found in various seas. b. Any one of the various species of *Lepomis*, *Pomotis*, and related genera, small freshwater fishes abundant in N. America. c. A name for the basking shark. d. The OPAH, *Lampris luna.* e. A local name for fishes of the genus *Silene* = MOON-FISH. Hence **Su·nfish** *v.* (*U.S. colloq.*) *intr.* to act like a s., *spec.* of a bucking horse, bringing first one shoulder down almost to the ground and then the other.

Su·nflower. 1562. [tr. mod.L. *flos solis.*] †1. The heliotrope (*Heliotropium*). b. Used vaguely of any flower that turns so as to follow the sun; cf. HELIOTROPE 1. 1652. 2. Any species of the composite genus *Helianthus*, chiefly natives of N. America, having conspicuous yellow flower-heads with disk and ray suggesting a figure of the sun; esp. *H. annuus*, a tall-growing plant commonly cultivated for its very large showy flowers 1597. b. Applied (usu. with defining word) to various other composite plants with radiant yellow flower-heads 1731. 3. Applied to various plants whose flowers open only in sunshine or in daylight; as the pimpernel, the star-of-Bethlehem 1670.

Sung (sʊŋ), *ppl. a.* 1526. [pa. pple. of SING *v.*] Uttered in musical tones (*Liturg.* as dist. from being said without note).

‖**Sungar, sangar** (sʊ·ŋgəɪ). 1841. [Pashtō *sangar* = Panjābī *sañghar.*] A breastwork of stone.

Su·n-god. 1592. The sun regarded or personified as a god; a god identified or specially associated with the sun.

Sunk (sʊŋk), *ppl. a.* late ME. [pa. pple. of SINK *v.* (In present usage this form of the pa. pple. in adj. use tends to be restricted to senses implying deliberate human agency; e.g. *s. fence.*)] 1. = SUNKEN 2. Now *rare.* 2. Lowered in character, intensity, value, etc. Now *rare* or *Obs.* 1680. 3. = SUNKEN 1. 1799. 4. In mod. techn. use, applied to a surface or area lowered, or to an object let in, so as to lie below the general surface, or to work of which depression of level is a principal feature; as *s. carving, cistern, panel*, etc. 1762.

4. *S. fence* = HA-HA *sb.*[2] 1733.

Sunken (sʊ·ŋk'n), *ppl. a.* late ME. [pa. pple. of SINK *v.* See note on prec.] 1. That has sunk in water; submerged in, or situated beneath the surface of, water or other liquid. 2. Of the eyes, cheeks, etc.: Abnormally depressed or hollow; fallen in 1600. 3. That has sunk below the usual or general level; subsided 1832. 4. In tech. use: prec. 4. 1808.

4. *S. battery* (Mil.), a battery in which the platform is sunk below the level of the ground.

Sunless (sʊ·nlės), *a.* 1589. [f. SUN *sb.* + -LESS.] Destitute of the sun or of the sun's rays; dark or dull through absence of sunlight.

Sunlight (sʊ·nləit). ME. [f. SUN *sb.* + LIGHT *sb.*] 1. The light of the sun. 2. (prop. with hyphen.) = SUN-*burner* 1862.

Artificial s. = artificial sun-rays (SUN-RAY 2).

Sunlike (sʊ·nləik), *a.* and *adv.* 1596. [f. SUN *sb.* + -LIKE.] A. *adj.* Like or resembling the sun, or that of the sun; *esp.* very bright or resplendent.

Princes couched under the glow Of s. gems SHELLEY.

B. *adv.* Like or in the manner of the sun 1819.

That eternal honour which should live S., above the reek of mortal fame SHELLEY.

Sunlit (sʊ·nlit), *ppl. a.* 1822. [f. as prec. + LIT *ppl. a.*] Lighted or illumined by the sun.

‖**Sunn** (sʊn). *Indian.* 1774. [a. Urdū, Hindī *san* (Skr. *çāṇā* hempen).] A branching leguminous shrub, *Crotalarea juncea*, widely cultivated in Southern Asia for its fibre; also, the fibre used for rope, cordage, sacking, etc.

‖**Sunna** (sʊ·nă). 1728. [a. Arab. *sunnah* (*sunnat*) form, way, course, rule.] The body of traditional sayings and customs attributed to Mohammed and supplementing the Koran.

‖**Sunni** (sʊ·nī). 1626. [a. Arab. *sunnī* lawful, f. SUNNA.] *collect.* The orthodox Mohammedans, who accept the Sunna as of equal authority with the Koran. Also *sing.* a Sunnite.

‖**Sunnite** (sʊ·nəit). 1718. [f. SUNNA or SUNNI + -ITE[1].] A Mohammedan who accepts the orthodox tradition as well as the Koran.

‖**Sunnud** (sʊ·nʊd). *Indian.* Also **sanad.** 1759. [Urdū = Arab. *sanad* signature, deed.] A deed of grant; a charter, patent, warrant.

Sunny (sʊ·ni), *a.* ME. [f. SUN *sb.* + -Y[1].] 1. Characterized by or full of sunshine; in or during which the sun shines; esp. of a day, weather, or the like. 2. Exposed to, illumined or warmed by, the rays of the sun; on which the sun shines 1567. 3. Pertaining to the sun; solar (*rare*); of or proceeding from the sun 1579. 4. Resembling the sun in colour or brightness; appearing as if illumined by the sun; (of the hair) bright yellow or golden 1596. 5. *fig.* Bright, cheerful, joyous; expressing or awakening gladness or happiness 1545.

1. Far more welcome..Then s. daies to naked Sauages 1592. 2. Cleer Spring, or shadie Grove, or Sunnie Hill MILT. *S. side*, the best, most desirable, side *of* anything, esp. in phr. like *on the s. side of thirty, forty*, etc., = younger than.. 3. A tall stag.. lay..panting in the s. ray POPE. 4. Her s. locks Hang on her temples like a golden fleece SHAKS. 5. A sunnie looke of his SHAKS. Hence **Su·nnily** *adv.* **Su·nniness.**

‖**Sunnyasee** (sʊnyā·sī). *Indian.* 1613. [a. Urdū, Hindī *sannyāsī*, = Skr. *saṃnyāsin* laying aside, abandoning, ascetic, f. *saṃ* together + *ni* down + *as* to know.] A Brahman in the fourth stage of his life; a wandering fakir or religious mendicant.

Su·n-ray. 1829. 1. A ray from the sun; a sunbeam. Chiefly *poet.* or *rhet.* 2. *pl.* (Also *artificial sun-rays*) Ultra-violet rays used therapeutically as a substitute for sunlight 1928.

Sunrise (sʊ·nrəiz). 1440. [app. evolved from clauses such as *forto* (= until), *tofore*, or *before the sun rise*, where *rise* is a verb in the subj. Cf. SUNSET, SUNSHINE.] The rising, or apparent ascent above the horizon, of the sun at the beginning of the day; the time when the sun rises, the opening of day. Also, the display of light or colour in the sky at this time.

The gates I enter'd with S. MILT. *fig.* The first dawn of the arts, which preceded their..s. SCOTT.

Su·nri:sing. Now *rare* or *arch.* ME. [Cf. F. *soleil levant.*] = prec. b. *transf.* The east.

Sunset (sʊ·nset). late ME. [app. f. SUN *sb.* + SET *sb.*[1] (cf. next), but perh. like SUNRISE.] 1. The setting, or apparent descent below the horizon, of the sun at the end of the day; the time when the sun sets, the close of day. Also, the glow of light or display of colour in the sky when the sun sets. 2. *fig.* Decline or close, *esp.* of a period of prosperity or the like 1613.

1. In the evenyng after soone sette 1542. 2. The s. of life CAMPBELL.

attrib.: s. gun, a gun fired at s.

Sunsetting (sʊ·nse:tiŋ). Now *rare* or *arch.* 1440. [Cf. F. *soleil couchant.*] 1. = prec. 1. 2. *transf.* The west 1601.

Sunshade (sʊ·nʃēid). 1851. [See SHADE *sb.*] 1. An awning over the outside of a window, to keep the sunlight off. 2. A parasol; now usu. applied to the larger kinds 1852. 3. A device used with a telescope, etc. to diminish the intensity of sunlight 1894.

Sunshine (sʊ·nʃəin). [ME. *sunnesin*; see SUNRISE for probable origin; but cf. G. *sonnenschein*, etc.] 1. The shining of the sun; direct sunlight uninterrupted by cloud. †b. with *a* and *pl.* A burst or spell of sunshine –1747. 2. *fig.* a. A source of happiness or prosperity 1595. b. A favourable or gracious influence 1596. c. A condition or atmosphere of happiness or prosperity 1593. d. Sunny disposition 1742. 3. *transf.* Light or brightness resembling or suggesting that of the sun 1588. 4. *attrib.* passing into *adj.* 1579. b. With reference to a (saloon) motor car with a top which can be opened to admit sunshine 1929.

1. There was a long fight between mist and s. TYNDALL. Phr. *To have been in the s.* (slang), to be drunk. 2. a. Mamma's little s. 1901. b. That man that sits within a Monarches heart, And ripens in the Sunneshine of his fauor SHAKS. c. In the meantime all was s. with Vivian Grey DISRAELI. d. The s. of Goldsmith's nature would break out W. IRVING. 3. Vouchsafe to shew the s. of your face SHAKS. 4. Her sunshine face 1594. On a S. Holy-day MILT. My s.-friends have turned their backs on me 1876.

Sunshiny (sʊ·nʃəi:ni), *a.* 1590. [f. prec. + -Y[1].] = SUNNY *a.* 1, 2, 4, 5.

The..glorious light of her sunshyny face SPENSER. In warm, sun-shiny weather 1713. A s. landscape 1803. His..daughter—a s. young lady of eighteen 1857.

Su·n-spot. 1818. 1. *Path.* A spot or marking on the skin caused by exposure to the sun. 2. *Astr.* A spot or patch on the disk of the sun, appearing dark by contrast with the brighter general surface, and constituted by a cavity in the photosphere filled with cooler vapours 1868.

Su·nstone, su·n-stone. 1677. 1. A name given to amber, because the Heliades or daughters of the sun, according to a Greek myth, were changed into poplars and wept amber 1849. 2. *Min.* a. A name for several varieties of feldspar, showing red or golden-yellow reflexions from minute embedded crystals of mica, oxide of iron, etc. b. = CAT'S-EYE 2. 1677.

Su·nstroke. 1851. [For the earlier 'stroke of the sun', tr. F. *coup de soleil.*] Collapse or prostration, with or without fever, caused by exposure to excessive heat of the sun. So **Su·nstri:cken** *ppl. a.* 1844.

Su·nstruck, *pa. pple.* 1839. [f. SUN *sb.* + STRUCK, after prec.] Affected with sunstroke.

‖**Sunt** (sʊnt). 1820. [Arab.] A species of acacia of northern Africa, or its wood.

Sun-up, sunup (sʊ·nʊp). *local*, chiefly *U.S.* 1847. [f. SUN *sb.* + UP *adv.*, after SUNDOWN.] Sunrise.

Sunward (sʊ·nwǫ̈ɹd), *adv.* and *a.* 1611. [f. SUN *sb.* + -WARD.] A. *adv.* Toward the sun; in the direction of the sun. B. *adj.* Directed toward the sun; moving or facing in the direction of the sun 1769. So **Su·nwards** *adv.* 1574.

Sunwise (sʊ·nwəiz), *adv.* (*a.*) 1865. [f. SUN *sb.* + -WISE.] In the direction of the apparent daily movement of the sun, i.e. (in the northern hemisphere) from left to right; 'with the sun'.

Sup (sʊp), *sb.* Now *dial.* 1570. [f. next.] A small quantity of liquid such as can be taken into the mouth at one time; a mouthful; a sip.

Phr. (*A*) *bit* (later *bite*) *and* (*a*) *s.*, a little food and drink.

Sup (sʊp), *v.*[1] Pa. t. and pa. pple. **supped.** [OE. *sūpan*, **suppan*, **sūpian*, f. Teut. root **sūp-* (cf. SOP *sb.*, *v.*).] **1.** *trans.* To take (liquid) into the mouth in small quantities (as opp. to a draught). Now chiefly *Sc.* and *n. dial.*; often *spec.* to take (liquid food) with a spoon. **b.** To drink *up* or *off*, esp. by mouthfuls or spoonfuls. late ME. **2.** *intr.* To take a sip or sips; to take drink by mouthfuls or spoonfuls. Now chiefly *Sc.* and *n. dial.* OE. **3.** *fig.* To have experience of; to taste; esp. *to s. sorrow* (cf. L. *haurire dolorem.*) OE.

1. He began to s. his porridge 1889. **2.** Might I of Iove's nectar s. B. JONS. **3.** I'll make you one Days. Sorrow for this SWIFT.

Sup (sʊp), *v.*[2] ME. [a. OF. *soper*, *super*, *souper*; origin obsc.] **1.** *intr.* To eat one's supper; to take supper. **2.** *fig.* (or in fig. context) and *allus.* late ME. **3.** *trans.* **a.** *Falconry* and *Venery.* To give the last feed of the day to (a hawk, horse, or hound) 1575. †**b.** Of food: To furnish a supper for (*rare*) –1653. **c.** To give a supper to, entertain at supper 1619.

1. I kept him to sup, sleep..and breakfast here this morning H. WALPOLE. **2.** *Macb.* v. v. 13. People had supped full of horrors 1873. Phr. †*To s. with our Saviour, with Jesus Christ, to s. in heaven* or *hell*, etc., said of persons who have died or are about to die; You shall s. with Jesu Christ to night SHAKS. **3. c.** They will breakfast you, they will s. you 1865.

‖ **Supari** (sʊpā·rī). *Indian.* 1638. [Hindī *supārī* betel nut.] The areca palm; also, the areca nut which is chewed with the leaves of the betel palm.

Supawn (sʊpǭ·n). *U.S.* 1793. [Natick *saupáun* softened, f. *saupáe*, *sabáe* it is softened.] A kind of porridge made of maize flour boiled in water until it thickens.

Supe (siūp). *slang.* 1824. Short for SUPER *sb.*

Supellectile (siupĕle·ktəil, -til), *a.* and *sb.* 1597. [ad. L. *supellectilis*, prob. f. *super* SUPER- I. 1 + *lectus* couch; see -ILE.] A. *adj.* Pertaining to or of the nature of household furniture; *transf.* ornamental 1615. B. *sb.* Furniture; scientific apparatus or equipment 1597.

‖ **Supellex** (siupe·leks). *rare.* 1553. [L.] *lit.* Household furniture; *fig.* the equipment or apparatus for an experiment or operation.

Super (siū·pəɹ), *sb.* 1626. †**1.** [Short for INSUPER.] Something 'standing in super'; a balance remaining over –1642. **2.** *Theatr.* Short for SUPERNUMERARY. Also *gen.* 1853. **3.** = *super-hive* (see SUPER- I. 3); a box containing a certain number of sections of honey 1855. **4.** = SUPERINTENDENT 1870.

Super (siū·pəɹ), *a.* *Trade colloq.* 1833. [Short for various adj. compounds of SUPER-.] **1.** = SUPERFICIAL *a.* 2. (Usu. following the *sb.*) **2.** = SUPERFINE 3. 1842.

1. The price..is 3d. per foot s. 1881. **2.** A roll of cloth which he said was extra s. DICKENS.

Super- (siū·pəɹ, -ər), *prefix*, repr. L. *super-* = the adv. and prep. *super* above, on the top (of), beyond, besides, in addition, used in composition with various meanings.

I. Over, above, at the top (of); on, upon. **1.** Forming adjs. in which *super-* is in prepositional relation to the sb. implied in the second element. **a.** Compounds of a general character, and miscellaneous scientific and technical terms. **Su:peraeˑrial**, situated above the air or atmosphere. **Su:percretaˑceous** *Geol.*, lying above the Cretaceous series. **Super·liˑneal, ·liˑnear**, written above the line. **Su:permariˑne**, occurring, performed or moving above or upon the surface of the sea; hence *ellipt.* as sb., a supermarine aeroplane. **b.** *Anat.* and *Zool.* = Situated above, or on the dorsal side of, the part or organ denoted by the second element, as in *su:peracroˑmial*, *superceˑntral* (the centre sulcus of the brain), *super·oˑrbital* (also as *sb.*) **c.** *Bot.* in same sense as b (varying with SUPRA-), as *superaˑxillary*; also *superaˑrctic*, etc. **d.** Forming sbs. denoting something placed over or upon that which is denoted by the radical element as in SUPERALTAR, SUPERFRONTAL.

2. With advb. force, = Above, over, on, *occas.* from above (in material or non-material sense), prefixed to vbs., pples., adjs., and nouns of action or state, as in SUPERFLUOUS, SUPERSCRIPTION, SUPERSTRUCTURE. **Su·pernaˑtant** *a.*, swimming above, floating on the surface. †**Superseˑminate** *v. trans.* to sow on the top of something previously sown. ‖**Su·perstraˑtum**, an overlying or superficial stratum. **Su·pervolute** *a. Bot.* applied to convolute leaves one of which envelops another in the bud, or to vernation in which this occurs. (*a*) Forming intr. vbs. and other parts of speech of cognate meaning. **Super·creˑscent** *a.*, growing over or on the top of something; so **Supercreˑscence**, a parasitic growth. **Su·perjaˑcent** *a.*, lying above or over something else; superincumbent. **Supersaˑliency**, the leaping of the male for the act of copulation; so **Supersaˑlient** *a.* (*b*) Forming trans. vbs. and related words of cognate meaning. **Su·percolumniaˑtion**, the erection of one order of columns upon another. **Su·perindue·** *v.*, to put on as a garment, esp. over another. **Su·perinspeˑct** *v.*, to inspect as a superior official, to oversee (now *rare* or *Obs.*). **b.** with intr. vbs. and their derivatives: = Above (in *fig.* sense); in a higher condition, relation, etc.; nonce-words, as *su·per-exiˑst* vb., *-exiˑstent* adj.

3. Prefixed to descriptive sbs. with adj. force = Placed or situated above, over, or upon something; forming the upper part of (that which is denoted by the second element); higher, upper. **Su·percharge**, *Her.* a charge borne upon another charge (*rare*). **Su·perhive**, a removable upper compartment of a beehive. †**Su·per-plant**, a plant growing upon another plant; a parasite or epiphyte. **Su·pertunic**, *Antiq.* an outer tunic; *spec.* the vestment worn above the dalmatic by a sovereign at his coronation. **b.** *Anat.* (*a*) Designating the upper of two parts or members; superior; e.g. *supermaxilla*, the upper maxilla or jaw. (*b*) Designating a part overlapping another, or formed by such overlapping; e.g. *su·perfissure*, *supersulcus*. **c.** *Anat.* Forming adjs. (with *super-* in adj. relation to the sb. or subst. phr. implied in the second element): (*a*) derivs. from sbs. in b, as *su·permaxiˑllary* (= pertaining to the upper jaw); (*b*) situated in, or forming, the upper part of, e.g. *su·percerebeˑllar*, *-cerebral*, *-temporal*.[2]

II. Above (in various fig. senses); higher in rank, quality, amount, or degree. **1. a.** Prefixed to adjs.: Above or beyond, more or higher than, above the range, scope, capacity, etc. of (what is denoted or expressed by the radical part); e.g. *su·perangeˑlic* (= beyond that of an angel), *-essential* (= SUPERSUBSTANTIAL 2), *-intellectual*, *-organic*, *-physical*, *-rational*, *-regal*, *-secular*, *-sensible*, *-sensuous*, *-superlative*, *-temporal*[1]. (*b*) In corresponding advs., as *superaˑdequately*. **b.** Prefixed to sbs., forming adjs. in the same sense as above; e.g. *su·pergraduate*, *-standard*.

2. Prefixed to sbs., forming sbs. denoting something above, beyond, greater or higher than what is expressed by the radical part. **a.** *gen.*, as *su·per-Erastian*, †*-essence*, *-septuagenarian*. **b.** *Mus.* Designating a note next above some principal note, as SUPERTONIC. **Superdo·minant** the SUBMEDIANT, the sixth of the scale. **c.** *Nat. Hist.* In classification, denoting a group or division next higher than, or including a number of, those denoted by the radical part, as *su·per-family*, *-order*, *-species*, *-suborder*. So **Su·permo·lecule** *Chem.* a complex molecule formed by the combination of molecules of different substances. **d.** *Geom.* In geometry of more than three dimensions, designating a locus or figure having one more dimension than that denoted by the simple word; e.g. *su·per-cube*, *-curve*, *-line*. **e.** Prefixed to the name of a person, forming a vb. in the sense to outdo (the person named) in his characteristic quality or action; as *supercæsar* (rare).

3. Prefixed to sbs. with adj. force: Higher in rank, quality, degree, or amount; of a higher kind or nature; superior. **a.** With names of officials or persons in authority; e.g. *su·per-arbiter*, *-sovereign*; also in the names of the corresponding offices or functions, as *su·per-sovereignty*. **b.** With nouns of action or condition, etc.; e.g. *su·per-agency*, *-comprehension*, *-good*, *-organism*. **c.** In recent formations after SUPERMAN, used to designate a person, animal, or thing which typifies the highest point of development or evolution of its class; e.g. *su·per-brute*, *-critic*, *-film*. **Su·per-Dreaˑdnought**, an all-big-gun ship with an armament superior to that of the Dreadnought class. **d.** *Mus.* = Next higher in pitch: in *su·peroctave*.

4. Beyond in time, later. †**Superlaˑst** *v.*, *trans.* to last beyond, outlast. **b.** With prepositional force: see SUPERANNUATE.

5. Before in time, prior to. **Superlapsaˑrian** *sb.* and *a.* = SUPRALAPSARIAN. †**Supervive** *v.* = SURVIVE.

III. In or to the highest or a very high degree; hence, in excess of what is usual, or of what ought to be; superabundant(ly); excessive(ly). **1. a.** Prefixed in advb. relation to adjs.: Exceedingly, very highly, extremely, supremely, extraordinarily; over-. **Super·eˑxtra**, applied to commodities esp. to a style of bookbinding, of the very best quality. **Super-faˑtted, -faˑtty**, (of soap), containing an excess of fat, i.e. more than can combine with the alkali. **-regeˑnerative** *a. Wireless*, pertaining to regenerative reception in which the oscillations generated in the receiver are interrupted at a frequency above the range of inaudibility. **Supervacaˑneous** (now *rare* or *Obs.*), superfluous, redundant. (*b*) In corresponding advs., as *super-infinitely*. **b.** Prefixed to vbs. or pples. (with derivs.), in same senses as in a; e.g. *su·peraccuˑmulate* (= to accumulate beyond measure), *-exceed*, *-excel*, *-extol*, *-reward* vbs.; *su·peraciˑdulated* (= acidulated to excess), *-civilized*, *-elated*, *-peopled* pples. and ppl. adjs.

2. Prefixed with adj. force to abstract sbs.: Very great, or too great; surpassing; excessive, extreme; e.g. *su·peractiˑvity*, *-conformity*, *-infirmity*; hence occas. agent-nouns, as *su·per-confoˑrmist*, *-individualist*. **Su·per-regeneraˑtion** (cf. *super-regenerative* above). **b.** (Chiefly *Phys.* and *Path.*) Denoting processes or conditions in excess of the normal; e.g. *su·peralkaliˑnity*, *-irritation*, *-secretion*.

3. In prepositional relation with the radical element, as in SUPERNUMERARY.

4. *Chem.* †**a.** Prefixed to vbs., pa. pples., and cognate nouns of action, denoting a high proportion of the ingredient indicated by the radical element; e.g. *su·percaˑrbonate* vb., *-carburetted*, *-oxygenated* pa. pples., *-oxygenation*. **b.** In names of compounds, indicating that the ingredient denoted by the radical is in the highest proportion; e.g. *superoxide* (= PEROXIDE). Now surviving in the names of salts used in manufactures or the arts, e.g. SUPERPHOSPHATE.

IV. Expressing addition. **1.** In advb. or adj. relation to a vb., sb., or adj.: Over and above, in addition, additional(ly), as in SUPERADD, SUPEREROGATE. **Supercaˑlender** *v. trans.*, to subject (paper) to additional calendering, so as to produce a highly glazed surface; hence **Supercaˑlender** *sb.*, a roller used for supercalendering. **Supereleva·tion**, the (amount of) elevation of the outer above the inner rail at a curve on a railway, or of one side of a road above the other. **Su·per(in)feudaˑtion**, creation of a new feudal estate out of one already established. †**Super·impreˑgnate** *v. trans.* to impregnate or imbue in addition; hence **Superimpregnaˑtion**. †**Super·infuˑse** *v. trans.* to infuse in addition. **Superi·nstitute** *v. trans.* to institute to a benefice over the head of another (now *rare* or *Obs.*). †**Superluˑcrate** *v. trans.*, to gain in addition, make a profit of (so much). **Su·per-tax** *sb.*, an additional duty of income tax levied upon incomes above a certain value; hence as *vb.*

†**2.** *Math.* In adjs. denoting ratios expressible by unity (or some other integer) with some number of aliquot parts over; as in late L. *superdimidius* (sc. *numerus* number) 'that is a half more', i.e. $1\frac{1}{2}$, denoting a ratio of 3 : 2, *supertertius* 'that is a third more', i.e. $1\frac{1}{3}$ = 4 : 3, etc.

3. Upon something of the same kind, in a secondary relation; secondary, secondarily; e.g. *supercommentary* (= a commentary on a commentary), *-parasite*, *-reformation*, etc.

Superable (siū·pərăb'l), *a.* 1629. [ad. L. *superabilis*, f. *superare*; see -ABLE.] Capable of being overcome or vanquished; surmountable; opp. to *insuperable*.

Antipathies are generally s. by a single effort JOHNSON. Hence **Su:perabiˑlity, Su·perableness; Su·perably** *adv.*

Superabound (siū:pərăbau·nd), *v.* 1447. [ad. late L. *superabundare*; see SUPER- III. 1 b and ABOUND *v.*] **1.** *intr.* To abound beyond something else; to be more abundant (with allusion to *Rom.* v. 20.) **2.** To abound excessively; to be very or too abundant 1520.

2. Cony Ile..also superabounds with Seales 1638.

Superabundance (siū:pərăbʊ·ndăns). late ME. [ad. late L. *superabundantia*; see prec. and -ANCE.] **1.** The quality of being superabundant; the fact or condition of superabounding; excessive abundance or plentifulness; redundance. **2.** That which superabounds; a superabundant quantity or amount; a surplus (*of* something). late ME. So **-abuˑndancy.**

Superabundant (siū:pərăbʊ·ndănt), *a.* late ME. [ad. late L. *superabundant-*, *superabundare* to SUPERABOUND; see -ANT.] **1.** Abounding above something else, or above measure; enough and to spare; exceedingly abundant or plentiful. Now *rare.* **2.** Abounding above what is fitting or needful; exceeding the normal or required amount; more than sufficient (in a bad sense). late ME.

2. A s. population 1835. Hence **Su:perabuˑndantly** *adv.*

Su·per-acid, *a.* 1808. [SUPER- III. 4 b.] 1. *Chem. S. salt* = SUPERSALT. 2. Excessively acid 1901. Hence **Su·peraci·dity,** excessive acidity.

Superadd (siūpəræ·d), *v.* 1458. [ad. L. *superaddere*; see SUPER- IV. 1 and ADD *v.*] 1. *trans.* To add over and above; to add *to* what has been added; to put as a further addition. Often a mere strengthening of *add*: To add besides; 'to join any thing extrinsick' (J.) b. *absol.* To make a further addition *to* 1660. 2. *spec.* To add as a further statement; to say, state, or mention in addition 1640.

1. A French war is added to the American; and there is all the reason in the world to expect a Spanish war to be superadded to the French BURKE. 2. I s. a few essentials more COWPER.

Superaddition (siūpərădi·ʃən). 1609. [f. prec. after *addition.*] 1. The action (or an act) of superadding, or the condition of being superadded; further addition. Often a mere strengthening of *addition*. 2. Something superadded; a further addition 1649.

2. A s. to, not a constituent of, man's moral existence 1866. So **Su·peraddi·tional** *a.*

Superaltar (siū·pərǭltəɹ). late ME. [ad. med.L. *superaltare*; see SUPER- I. 1 d and ALTAR.] *Eccl.* 1. A portable consecrated stone slab for use upon an unconsecrated altar, a table, etc. 2. A structure erected above an altar (at the back); a. a reredos; b. a retable or gradine 1848.

†**Superannated,** *pa. pple.* and *ppl. a.* 1605. [f. med.L. *superannatus*, f. *super annum* beyond a year; see SUPER- II. 4 b and -ATE.[2]] Superannuated –1654.

Supera·nnuate, *a.* and *sb.* Now *rare*. 1647. [ad. mod.L. **superannuatus*, altered f. *superannatus* (see prec.).] A. *adj.* = SUPERANNUATED. B. *sb.* A superannuated person 1822.

Superannuate (siūpəræ·niueit), *v.* 1649. [Back-formation from next.] †1. *trans.* To render antiquated or obsolete: said of the lapse of time, etc. –1865. 2. To dismiss or discharge from office on account of age; *esp.* to cause to retire from service on a pension; to pension off 1692. 3. *pass.* and *intr.* To become too old for a position; to reach the age at which one leaves a school, retires from an office, etc. 1814.

Superannuated (siūpəræ·niueitėd), *pa. pple.* and *ppl. a.* 1633. [f. mod.L. **superannuatus*, altered f. med.L. *superannatus* SUPERANNATED, after L. *annuus.*] 1. Of persons (or animals): Disqualified or incapacitated by age; old and infirm 1639. b. *transf.* Of personal actions or attributes 1707. 2. Of things: Impaired by age, worn out; antiquated, obsolete, out of date 1633. b. *loosely.* That has lasted a very long time; inveterate; very old (*rare*) 1644. 3. Discharged from service on a pension after attaining a certain age. Also said of the pension. 1740.

1. A s. cock whose muscles were impenetrable to the teeth 1819. b. Her s. Charms 1707. 2. Thy threadbare Cassock and s. Beaver 1689. 3. A s. lieutenant on half-pay SMOLLETT.

Superannuation (siūpəræniuēi·ʃən). 1658. [f. SUPERANNUATE *v.* or prec.; see -ATION.] 1. The condition of being superannuated; impairment of the powers or faculties by old age; senile infirmity or decay. *Obs.* or *rare*. 1755.† b. The condition of being out of date (*rare*) –1845. 2. The action of superannuating an official; also, the allowance or pension granted to one who is discharged on account of age 1704. b. At certain schools, the attainment of the specified age at which a boy is required to leave 1831. 3. *attrib.* as *s. allowance, scheme* 1817.

1. The mere doating of s. 1782. b. A monk he seemed by..the s. of his knowledge DE QUINCEY.

Superb (siupə·ɹb), *a.* 1549. [ad. L. *superbus* proud, magnificent.] 1. Of buildings, monuments, and the like: Of noble and magnificent proportions or aspect. 2. Grandly and sumptuously equipped, arrayed, or decorated 1700. b. in specific appellations of many gorgeously coloured birds, plants, etc. 1760. 3. Of conditions, language, thought, etc.: Grand, stately, majestic 1784. 4. Expressing emphatic approval: Very fine; splendid; magnificent 1729.

1. The s. chapell of Ferdinand I. EVELYN. 2. Saw the s. funerall of the Protector EVELYN. b. **S. bird of paradise,** *Lophorina* (*Paradisea*) *superba*, a species of which the male is violet-black with green iridescence, having a gorget of metallic green feathers, and an erectile hood or mantle of velvet-black plumes on the shoulders. *S. lily*, a plant of the genus *Gloriosa* (*Methonica*), esp. *G. superba*. *S. warbler*, the blue wren of Australia, *Malurus cyaneus*. 4. The dinner was sumptuous, the wines s. DISRAELI. Hence **Superb·ly** *adv.*, **-ness** (*rare*).

†**Supe·rbious,** *a. rare*. 1510. [a. OF. *superbieus*, or ad. med.L. **superbiosus*, f. *superbia* pride, f. *superbus* SUPERB.] 1. Proud, overbearing, insolent –1700. 2. Stately, grand, superb –1714. So †**Supe·rbous** *a.* (*rare*) –1709.

Supercargo (siūpəɹkā·ɹgo). 1697. [Alteration of SUPRACARGO by prefix-substitution.] An officer on board a merchant ship whose business it is to superintend the cargo and the commercial transactions of the voyage. †Also formerly, an agent who superintended a merchant's business in a foreign country.

Supercelestial (siūːpəɹsǐle·stiăl), *a.* 1559. [f. late L. *supercælestis* = Gr. ὑπερουράνιος; see SUPER- I. 1 a, II. 1 a, and CELESTIAL.] 1. That is above the heavens; situated or existing above the firmament. 2. More than heavenly; of a nature or character higher than celestial 1561.

Su·percharged, *pa. pple.* and *ppl. a.* 1876. [SUPER- III. 1 b.] Charged to excess; overcharged; *spec.* of an internal combustion engine, having air forced into the carburettor by means of a fan or other device. So **Su·percharger,** a device for supercharging an engine; an engine, car, etc., fitted with such a device.

Superchery (siupə̄·ɹtʃəri). *Obs.* exc. in F. form **supercherie** (süpęrʃəri). 1598. [a. F. *supercherie*, ad. It. *superchieria*, f. *superchio* superfluous, excessive :—pop. L. **superculus*, f. *super* over, above.] †1. An attack made upon one at a disadvantage; (a piece of) foul play –1656. 2. Trickery. Also with *a* and *pl.* 1650.

Superciliary (siūpəɹsi·liări), *a.* and *sb.* 1732. [ad. mod.L. *superciliaris*, f. *supercilium* SUPERCILIUM; see -ARY[2].] Of or pertaining to the eyebrow, or to the region of the eyebrow; supra-orbital. b. Situated over the eye; also *transf.* having a marking over the eye 1872.

S. arch or *ridge*, a prominence of the frontal bone, over the eye, produced by the development of the frontal sinuses.

B. *sb.* A superciliary ridge or marking 1864.

Supercilious (siūpəɹsi·liəs), *a.* 1529. [ad. late L. *superciliosus*, f. *supercilium*; see -OUS.] 1. Haughtily contemptuous in character or demeanour; having or marked by an air of contemptuous superiority or disdain. †2. 'Dictatorial, arbitrary, despotic, overbearing' (J.); exacting in judgement, censorious –1791.

Hence **Superci·lious·ly** *adv.*, **-ness.**

‖**Supercilium** (siūpəɹsi·liŏm). *Pl.* **-ia** (-iă). 1563. [L., = eyebrow; ridge, summit.] 1. The eyebrow. *Obs.* exc. *Anat.* 1672. b. *Zool.* A superciliary streak or marking 1817. 2. *Arch.* †a. A narrow fillet above the cymatium of a cornice. b. A fillet above and below the scotia of an Attic base. c. The lintel of a door-case, 1563. 3. *Anat.* The lip or margin of a bony cavity, esp. of the acetabulum 1706.

Su·perconscious, *a.* 1884. [SUPER- II. 1 a; after *subconscious.*] That is above or beyond human consciousness. **Superco·nsciousness.**

Su·percool, *v.* 1907. [SUPER- III. 1 b.] *trans.* To cool (a liquid) below the freezing-point without solidification.

Supere·minence. 1616. [ad. late L. *supereminentia*, f. *supereminent-*; see next and -ENCE.] The quality or fact of being supereminent; supreme or special eminence; *rarely* in physical sense, supreme height or loftiness. So **Supere·minency** (now *rare* or *Obs.*) 1585.

Supereminent (siūpəre·minĕnt), *a.* 1555. [ad. L. *supereminent-, -ens*, *supereminere* to rise above, f. *super-*, SUPER- I. 2 + *eminere*; see EMINENT and cf. SUPER- III. 1 a.] 1. Lofty above the rest; supremely or specially high. Now *rare*. 2. Exalted above others in rank or dignity; supremely exalted 1583. 3. Distinguished *above* others in character or attainment; conspicuous *for* some quality 1599. 4. Of qualities, conditions, etc.: Specially or supremely remarkable in degree 1581.

1. A single s. tower 1892. 3. Som were s. for holines, and high virtues 1651. 4. Thy s. gifts 1592. Hence **Supere·minently** *adv.*

Supererogant (siūpəre·rŏgănt), *a. rare*. 1737. [ad. late L. *supererogans, -ant-*, *supererogare.*] = SUPEREROGATORY.

†**Supere·rogate,** *v.* 1582. [f. L. *supererogat-*, *supererogare*, f. *super-* SUPER- IV. 1 + *erogare* to pay out.] 1. *trans.* To pay over and above; to spend in addition. Also *absol. rare.* –1613. 2. *intr.* To do more than is commanded or required; *spec.* to perform a work of SUPEREROGATION –1727. b. To make up by excess of merit *for* the failing of another –1649.

2. We cannot..haue any perfection in this life, much lesse s. BURTON. b. The fervencie of one man in prayer cannot s. for the coldness of another MILT.

Supererogation (siūːpərerŏgēi·ʃən). 1526. [ad. late L. *supererogatio*, f. *supererogare*; see prec.] The action (or an act) of 'supererogating'; chiefly in phr. *work(s of s.* a. *R.C. Theol.* The performance of good works beyond what God commands or requires, which are held to constitute a store of merit which the Church may dispense to others to make up for their deficiencies. b. *transf.* and *gen.* Performance of more than duty or circumstances require; doing more than is needed 1592.

b. An Act of so great S., as singing without a Voice STEELE.

Supererogative (siūːpərǐrǫ·gătiv), *a. rare*. 1599. [f. late L. *supererogat-* (see SUPEREROGATE) + -IVE.] = next.

Supererogatory (siūːpərǐrǫ·gătŏri, siūːpəre·rŏgătŏri), *a.* (*sb.*) 1593. [ad. schol. L. *supererogatorius*, f. *supererogat-* SUPEREROGATE; see -ORY[2].] Characterized by, or having the nature of, supererogation; going beyond what is commanded or required; *loosely*, superfluous. †B. *sb.* A work of supererogation. RICHARDSON. Hence **Su·perero·gatorily** *adv.*

Su·perexa·lt, *v.* 1609. [ad. late L. *superexaltare*; see SUPER- III. 1 b and EXALT *v.*] 1. *trans.* To exalt or raise to a higher, or to the highest, position or rank; to exalt supremely 1625. 2. To extol or magnify exceedingly (*rare*) 1609. So **Su·perexalta·tion.**

Supere·xcellence. 1652. [f. next; see -ENCE.] The quality or condition of being superexcellent; superior or supreme excellence. So **Supere·xcellency** (now *rare*) 1587.

Supere·xcellent, *a.* 1561. [ad. late L. *superexcellent-, -ens*; see SUPER- III. 1 a and EXCELLENT.] That superexcels; excellent in a high degree; very or supremely excellent. Hence **Supere·xcellently** *adv.*

Superfetation (siū pəɹfītēi·ʃən). Also **-fœt-.** 1603. [ad. late or mod.L. *superfetatio*, f. *superfetare* to SUPERFETE.] 1. *Phys.* A second conception occurring after (esp. some time after) a prior one and before the delivery; the formation of a second fœtus in a uterus already pregnant; occurring normally in some animals, and believed by some to occur exceptionally in women. b. *Bot.* In early use, applied to processes supposed to be analogous to superfetation in animals, e.g. the growth of a parasite, etc.; in mod. use, the fertilization of the same ovule by two different kinds of pollen 1626. 2. *fig.* Additional production; the growth or accretion of one *upon* another; also, an instance of this 1641.

1. The hare is often troubled with s. 1661. 2. Layers of dust have accumulated (a superfœtation of dirt!) upon the old layers LAMB. Mark the s. of omens—omen supervening upon omen, augury engrafted upon augury DE QUINCEY.

†**Superfete,** *v.* 1645. [ad. L. *superfetare*, f. *super-* SUPER- IV. 1 + *fetus* FŒTUS.] *intr.* and *trans.* To conceive by superfetation –1654.

†**Superfice.** late ME. [a. OF., or ad. L. SUPERFICIES.] = SUPERFICIES 1, 2 –1823.

Superficial (siūpəɹfi·făl), *a.* (*sb.*) late ME. [ad. late L. *superficialis*, f. SUPERFICIES; see -AL.] A. *adj.* 1. Of or pertaining to the surface; that is, lies, or is found at or on the surface; constituting the surface, outermost part, or crust. b. Of actions or conditions: Taking place or existing at or on the surface 1815. c. *Anat.* Situated just beneath the skin; subcutaneous 1804. 2. Of or pertaining to a superficies; relating to or involving two dimensions; *esp.* relating to extent of surface. (Dist. from *linear* and *solid.*) *S. measure,* square measure. 1571. 3. Appearing 'on the surface'; external, outward 1561. 4. That is only on or near the surface; affecting only the surface; not deep 1594. 5. Concerned only with what is on the surface, and is therefore apparent or obvious; not deep, profound, or thorough; shallow 1533. b. *transf.* of persons, in respect of their actions, attainments, or character 1603. 6. Of conditions, qualities, actions, occupations: Not involving a profound or serious issue; of insignificant import or influence 1530. 7. That has only the outward appearance of being what is denoted by the sb.; only apparent, not real or genuine 1623.

1. The rise in the temperature of the s. blood HUXLEY. c. The s. veins appear remarkably large ABERNETHY. 2. *S. foot, yard,* etc., a rectangular space measuring a foot, yard, etc. each way, or a space of whatever shape containing the same amount of area; a square foot, etc. 3. There is a s. appearance of equity in this tax BURKE. 4. Small and superficiall Wounds 1676. 5. To vindicate our author's judgment from being s. DRYDEN. Men of s. understanding, and ludicrous fancy BOSWELL. The accounts..are s., confused and inexplicable 1777. b. A very superficiall, ignorant, vnweighing fellow SHAKS. 6. Empty noise And s. pastimes WORDSW. 7. The old quarrel has at least a s. reconcilement JOWETT.

B. *absol.* or as *sb.* 1. With *the*: That which is superficial (in any sense) 1579. 2. With *the*: Those who are superficial 1701. 3. *pl.* Superficial characteristics or qualities 1832.

3. Excepting in the merest superficials, there is a far greater variety in women than in men 1897. Hence **Superfi·cial·ly** *adv.*, **-ness.**

Superfi·cialism. 1839. [f. prec. + -ISM.] Superficial character, superficiality. So **Superfi·cialist,** one whose knowledge, observation, or treatment is superficial 1652.

Superficiality (s'ūpəɹfiʃiæ·lĭti). 1530. [f. as prec. + -ITY.] The quality or state of being superficial; also, an instance of this.

Superfi·cialize, *v.* 1593. [f. as prec. + -IZE.] †1. *trans.* To make a surface of (paint or colour); also *transf.* to paint (the cheeks). *rare.* –1633. 2. *intr.* To treat a subject or do something superficially 1656. 3. *trans.* To render superficial 1828.

3. It is a necessary consequence of the advance of education that every subject becomes vulgarized and superficialised 1863.

†Superficie. 1545. [ad. L. *superficies.*] = next –1726.

Superficies (s'ūpəɹfi·ʃiīz, U.S. also s'ūpəɹfi·ʃīz). *Pl.* **superficies.** 1530. [a. L., f. *super-* SUPER- I. 3 + *facies* FACE *sb.*] 1. *Geom.* A magnitude of two dimensions, having only length and breadth; that which forms the boundary or one of the boundaries of a solid, or separates one part of space from another; a surface. 2. The outer surface of a body, which is apparent to the eye, or is immediately adjacent to the air or to another body 1577. 3. That which constitutes the outermost part of a body; the surface layer. Now *rare.* 1603. b. *Rom.* and *Civil Law.* A building or other thing in or on the surface of a piece of land, which is by art or nature so closely connected with as to form part of it; the right possessed by a person over any such building or other thing in or on the surface of another's land 1850. 4. Superficial area or extent 1656. 5. †a. The 'surface' (of something immaterial, *esp.* of the mind or soul) –1700. †b. The outward form or aspect –1781. c. That which is merely superficial 1589.

3. To render the S. of the Earth loose 1707. 4. The whole s. of the parish contains 21 square miles 1798.

Superfine (s'ū·pəɹfəin, s'ūpəɹfəi·n), *a.* (*sb.*) 1575. [ad. med.L. **superfinus*; see SUPER- III. 1 a and FINE *a.*] A. *adj.* 1. Excessively refined, nice, fastidious, or elegant; over-refined, over-nice. †2. Consisting of very fine particles or threads. Also, of a file with extremely fine teeth. 1656. 3. Of manufactured goods: Extremely fine in quality; of the very best kind; (of liquids) the purest or clearest 1682. 4. Superlatively fine or excellent 1850. B. *sb. pl.* Goods of superfine quality 1812.

A. 1. S. distinctions of the Schools LOCKE. 3. The wax was s., its hue vermilion BYRON. 4. My eyes have not been in s. order 1850. Hence **Su·perfine·ly** *adv.*, **-ness** (*rare*).

Superfluent (s'ūpɔ̄·ɹfluĕnt), *a. rare.* 1440. [ad. L. *superfluent-, -ens, superfluere,* f. *super-* SUPER- I. 2 + *fluere* to flow.] 1. = SUPERFLUOUS. 2. Flowing or floating above. *Obs.* or *arch. rare.* 1440. 3. Superabundant 1711. So **Superfluence** (s'ūpɔ̄·ɹfluĕns). *arch. rare.* Superabundance.

Superfluity (s'ūpəɹflū·ĭti). late ME. [a. OF. *superfluite,* ad. med.L. *superfluitas,* f. *superfluus* SUPERFLUOUS; see -ITY.] The quality of being, or something that is, superfluous. 1. Superabundant supply, superabundance; the condition of there being (or of one's having) more than enough; an instance of this. 2. The condition or fact of being more abundant or copious than is necessary; excessive quantity or number; *esp.* excess in diet or dress. late ME. 3. A thing or part that is in excess of what is necessary, or that can be dispensed with. Chiefly *pl.* late ME. †4. Immoderate indulgence or expenditure; an instance of this –1801.

1. Her girlhood with its..s. of sisters GEO. ELIOT. 2. Thus the act of fertilization is completed, and there is no s. in the means employed DARWIN. 3. When we are in want of necessaries we must part with all superfluities ADAM SMITH.

Superfluous (s'ūpɔ̄·ɹfluəs), *a.* late ME. [f. L. *superfluus,* f. *superfluere,* f. *super-* SUPER- I. 2 + *fluere* to flow; see -OUS.] 1. That exceeds what is sufficient; of which there is more than enough; excessively abundant or numerous. 2. That is not needed or required; needless, uncalled-for 1450. b. *transf.* Of a person: Doing more than is necessary (*rare*) 1596. †3. Exceeding what is right, desirable, normal, or usual; immoderate, inordinate –1613. †4. Having, consuming, or expending more than enough; superabundantly supplied; extravagant in expenditure –1711.

1. Divesting myself of all s. clothes TYNDALL. 2. This warning was not s. 1898. b. 1 *Hen. IV,* I. ii. 12. 3. Purchas'd At a s. rate SHAKS. 4. *Lear* II. iv. 268. Hence **Supe·rfluous·ly** *adv.*, **-ness.**

Su·perflux. 1605. [ad. med. L. *superfluxus,* f. *superfluere*; see prec.] 1. A superfluity or surplus. 2. An overflowing, or excessive flow, of water or other liquid 1760.

Superfrontal (s'ū·pəɹfrɒntăl). 1858. [ad. med.L. *superfrontale*; see FRONTAL *sb.*] 1. [SUPER- I. 3.] A covering of silk or stuff hanging over the upper edge of an altar frontal. 2. [SUPER- I. 1 d.] A dossal 1887.

Superfuse (s'ūpəɹfiū·z), *v.* 1657. [f. L. *superfus-, superfundere*; see SUPER- I. 2 and FUSE *v.*] 1. *trans.* To pour over or *on* something. 2. To sprinkle or affuse; to suffuse in baptism 1657. 3. To cool (a liquid) below its melting-point without causing it to solidify; to supercool, overcool, undercool 1902.

Superfu·sion. 1657. [ad. late L. *superfusio.*] The action or result of superfusing.

Su·perheat, *v.* 1859. [f. SUPER- III. 1 b.] *trans.* To heat to a very high temperature; *esp.* to raise the normal temperature of (steam). Hence **Su·perheat** *sb.* the state of being superheated; the excess of temperature of a vapour above its temperature of saturation. **Su·perhea:ter,** an apparatus for superheating steam.

Superheterodyne (s'ūpəɹhe·tĕrŏdəin). 1922. [f. SUPER(SONIC + HETERODYNE.] *Wireless.* In full *superheterodyne receiver*: A receiving-set producing oscillations differing in frequency from those of the transmitting station and utilizing supersonic beat-notes thus produced. Often abbrev. **Superhe·t.**

Superhuman (s'ūpəɹhiū·măn), *a.* 1633. [ad. med.L. *superhumanus*; see SUPER- II. 1 and HUMAN *a.*] a. Of a quality, act, etc.: Higher than that of man; beyond the capacity or power of man. b. Of a person or being: Higher than man; having a nature above that of man 1824. c. In rhet. or hyperbolical use: Higher or greater than that of any ordinary man; beyond the average human capacity, stature, etc. 1822.

a. S. agencies and powers 1896. b. Christ is a s. person 1866. c. The s. yells which he uttered SCOTT. Hence **Su·perhuma·nity,** the character or quality of being s. **Superhu·manize** *v. trans.* to make, or represent as, s. **Superhu·manly** *adv.*

Superhu·meral. 1606. [ad. late L. *superhumerale,* neut. sing. (sc. *vestimentum*) of *superhumeralis*; see SUPER- I. 1 a and HUMERAL.] An ecclesiastical vestment worn over the shoulders, as the Jewish ephod, or an amice or pallium; *fig.* a burden carried on the shoulders.

Su:perimpo·se, *v.* 1794. [f. SUPER- I. 2 + IMPOSE *v.*, after next.] 1. *trans.* To impose or place (one object) *on* or *upon* another; to lay above or on the top; *spec.* in *Geol.* in ref. to stratification (always in pa. pple.) 2. *fig.* To cause to follow *upon* something else and to exist side by side with it 1855.

1. Four buried forests superimposed one upon the other 1863.

Su:perimposi·tion. 1684. [f. SUPER- I. 2 + IMPOSITION, after L. *superimponere.*] The action of superimposing, or state of being superimposed; superposition.

Su:perincu·mbent, *a.* 1664. [ad. L. *superincumbentem, superincumbere*; see SUPER- I. 2 and INCUMBENT.] Lying or resting upon, or situated on the top of, something else; overlying. (Chiefly in scientific use.) b. Situated or suspended above; overhanging 1835. c. Of pressure: Exerted from above 1854.

fig. A Power Girt round with weakness;—it can scarce uplift The weight of the s. hour SHELLEY. Hence **Su:perincu·mbence, -ency.** *rare.*

Su:perindu·ce, *v.* 1555. [ad. late L. *superinducere,* f. *super-* SUPER- I. 2, IV. 1 + *inducere* to INDUCE.] 1. *trans.* To bring (a person) into some position in addition to, or so as to displace, one who already occupies it. *Obs.* or *arch.* 2. To bring in over and above, or 'on the top of' something already present; to introduce in addition (esp. something extraneous) 1605. 3. To bring or cause to come *upon* a person or thing; to bring on, induce; *esp.* to induce (a disease, etc.) in addition to one already existing 1615. 4. In physical sense: To bring, draw, deposit, etc. *over* or *upon* a thing as a covering or addition 1660.

1. It was plain adultery to s. any other wife, his former living 1555. 2. Their improvement cannot come from themselves, but must be superinduced from without MILL. 4. To s. a Doctoral hood over a Friers Coul FULLER. Hence **Su:perindu·cement,** the action or an act of superinducing; something superinduced.

Superintend (s'ū:pərinte·nd), *v.* 1615. [ad. eccl. L. *superintendere*; see SUPER- I. 2 and INTEND *v.*] *trans.* To have or exercise the charge or direction of (operations or affairs); to look after, oversee, supervise the working or management of (an institution, etc.). b. To exercise supervision over (a person) 1776. c. *intr.* with †*over,* or *absol.* 1663.

The King will appoint Commissioners in the nature of a Council, who may s. the works of this nature, and regulate what concerns the colonies BACON.

Su:perinte·ndence. 1603. [f. as next; see -ENCE.] The function or occupation of a superintendent; the action or work of superintending.

Su:perinte·ndency. 1598. [ad. med.L. *superintendentia,* f. *superintendent-, -ens* SUPERINTENDENT; see -ENCY.] 1. The office or position of a superintendent; superintendence. 2. A district (*spec.* in the Lutheran Church, a collection of parishes) under the charge of a superintendent; in China, one of the administrative divisions of the country 1762.

1. The S. of Providence STEELE.

Superintendent (s'ū:pərinte·ndĕnt), *sb.* and *a.* 1554. [ad. eccl. L. *superintendent-, -ens, superintendere* to SUPERINTEND.] A. *sb.* One who superintends. 1. An officer or official who has the chief charge, oversight, control, or direction of some business, institution, or works; an overseer. Also *transf.* and *gen.* 1575. 2. *Eccl.* a. As tr. Gr. ἐπίσκοπος 'overseer' (see BISHOP) of the N.T.; used controversially instead of 'bishop' by extreme Protestant reformers of the 16th c., and subsequently by Papists with ref. to bishops of the Church of England. *Obs.* exc. *Hist.* 1554. b. *spec.* among the Lutherans, a minister who has control of the churches and pastors of a particular district 1560. c. In the Church of Scotland, a minister chosen to preside over a district and to ordain. *Hist.* 1561. d. The name given by John Wesley to men whom he ordained to act as bishops in the U.S.; now, among the Wesleyan Methodists, the presiding minister of a circuit 1784.

1. The Super-intendent over all the other Civil and Criminal Ministers 1653.

B. *sb.* Superintending; exercising superintendence or oversight; holding the position of a superintendent. Now (in English use) chiefly in designations of officials. 1597.

The s. visiting officer of the London wards 1913. Hence **Su·perinte·ndentship.**

Superior (s'ŭpīᵊ·riəɹ), *a.* and *sb.* late ME. [a. OF., ad. L. *superior, -orem,* compar. of *superus* that is above, f. *super* above.] **A.** *adj.* **1.** Higher in local position; situated above or further up than something else; upper; †heavenly, celestial. Now chiefly in techn. use. **b.** *predic.,* quasi-adv.: In or into a higher position; higher; upward. *poet.* 1718. **2.** Higher in rank or dignity; more exalted in social or official status 1485. **3.** Higher in ideal or abstract rank, or in a scale or series; of a higher nature or character. Sometimes, supernatural, superhuman. 1533. **b.** *Logic.* Having greater extension 1843. **4.** Higher in degree, amount, quality, importance, or other respect; of greater value or consideration 1579. **5.** Const. *to* (†occas. *with, than*). **a.** Higher in status or quality than; hence, greater or better than; †formerly also *advb.* = more or better than, above, beyond 1526. **b.** Too great or strong to be overcome or affected by; above the influence or reach of 1647. **c.** Transcending, on a higher plane than 1841. **6.** Characteristic of one who is superior (in senses 2, 3); also, from sense 5 b, 'free from emotion or concern; unconquered; unaffected' (J.). *poet.* or *rhet.* 1667. **b.** Applied ironically to persons of lofty, supercilious, or dictatorial manner or behaviour (or to their actions, etc.) 1864. **c.** *advb.* In a superior style; with a superior air 1716. **7.** In a positive or absolute sense (admitting comparison with *more* and *most*): Supereminent in degree, amount, or (most commonly) quality; surpassing the generality of its class or kind 1777. **8.** *Astr.* **a.** Applied to those planets whose orbits lie outside that of the earth (orig., according to the Ptolemaic astronomy, as having their spheres above that of the sun). **b.** *S. meridian*: that part of the celestial meridian which lies above the pole: so *s. passage* (of the meridian), etc. 1583. **9.** *Bot.* Growing above some other part or organ: said of the ovary when situated above or free from the (*inferior*) calyx, and of the calyx when adherent to the sides of the (*inferior*) ovary so that the calyx-lobes are above the ovary 1785. **10.** *Anat.* and *Zool.* Applied to parts or organs situated above, or in a higher position than, others of the same kind (dist. as *inferior*), or above the usual or normal position 1733. **11.** *Printing.* Applied to small letters or figures, or other characters, made to range above the line, at or near the top of the ordinary letters 1683.

1. The superiour or high India 1553. The s...portions of the earth's crust 1838. **2.** He says he obeyed s. orders CARLYLE. *Father* or *Mother S.* = B. 2. **3.** Conscience..supposes some s. law informing men to do, or not do a thing 1660. **4.** She escaped by s. sailing 1798. **5. a.** He was..s. in numbers to the enemy 1907. **b.** To that foible even she was not s. SCOTT. **6.** Here passion first I felt,..in all enjoyments else Superiour and unmov'd MILT. **b.** The 's.' person who posed as an authority on matters of culture 1897. **7.** What a woman she was—what a s. creature! THACKERAY.

B. *sb.* **1.** A person of higher rank or dignity; one who is above others in social or official station; *esp.* a superior officer or official 1483. **2.** The head of a community of religious (a monastery, nunnery, convent, abbey, etc.); also, the head of a religious order or congregation, or of a department of it 1497. **3.** *Feudal Law.* One who (or the successor of one who) has granted an estate of heritable property to another (termed the *vassal*) on condition of the annual payment of a certain sum or the performance of certain services 1538. **4.** A person, or (less commonly) a thing, of higher quality or value than another; one that excels another in some respect 1634. **5.** *Printing.* A superior letter or figure 1726.

1. The Rebukes and Censures of Superiours 1659. In respectable conformity to the commands of my ecclesiastical superiors 1817. **2.** The S. of the Passionist Monks 1844. **3.** *Subject s.,* a s. who holds as subject of a sovereign. **4.** No one is the s. of the invincible Socrates in argument JOWETT. Hence **Supe·rior·ess,** a female s. a mother s. **Supe·riorly** *adv.* in a s. place, degree, or manner.

Superiority (s'ŭpīᵊriǫ·rīti). 1495. [a. OF. *superiorite,* ad. med.L. *superioritas*; see prec. and -ITY.] The quality or condition of being superior; also, an instance of this.

They lost their s. in Greece by the ill-fought battle of Leuctra 1770. All nobility in its beginnings was somebody's natural s. EMERSON.

Superlative (s'ŭpɔ̄·ɹlătiv), *a.* and *sb.* late ME. [a. OF. *superlatif, -ive,* ad. late L. *superlativus,* f. *superlatus* (used as pa. pple. of *superferre,*) f. *super-* SUPER- II + *lat-,* pa. ppl. stem of *tollere* to take away.] **A.** *adj.* **1.** *Gram.* Applied to that inflexional form of an adj. or adv. used in comparing a number of things, to express the highest degree of the quality or attribute denoted by the simple word, as *sweet-est, tru-est, often-est* (or to the periphrasis used in the same sense, as *most sweet, most true, most often*); the adj. or adv. is then said to be in the *s. degree.* Freq. used *allus.* **b.** Exaggerative, hyperbolical 1588. **2.** Raised above or surpassing all others; extremely high, great, or excellent; supereminent, supreme. late ME.

2. Gowere and chaucere,..Superlatiue as poetis laureate 1423. Queene Elizabeth,..worthy of s. praise HOLLAND.

B. *sb.* **1.** *Gram.* The superlative degree; an adjective or adverb in the superlative degree. (Also, by extension, any word denoting the highest degree of some quality.) 1530. **b.** *transf.* An exaggerated or hyperbolical expression; usu. *pl.,* exaggerated language or phraseology 1597. **2.** A person or thing surpassing all others of the class or kind; the highest example (*of* a quality). Now *rare,* and with allusion to sense 1. 1600. **3.** The highest or utmost degree of something; the acme 1583.

1. *fig.* Virginity you say is delightful, yet matrimony more pleasant: Virginity you put in the positiue, but matrimonie in the superlatiue GREENE. **b.** He thought and felt in superlatives 1896. Hence **Supe·rlative-ly** *adv.,* **-ness.**

Superlunary (s'ŭpəɹl'ū·nări), *a.* 1614. [f. L. *super-* SUPER- I. 1 + *luna* + -ARY, after *sublunary.*] Situated above or beyond the moon; belonging to a higher world, celestial; *fig.* extravagant: the opposite of *sublunary.* So **Superlu·nar** *a.* 1742.

Superman (s'ū·pəɹmæn). 1903. [f. SUPER- II. 3 + MAN *sb.,* tr. by G. B. Shaw of G. *übermensch* (Nietzsche).] An ideal superior man conceived by F. W. Nietzsche (German philosopher, 1844–1900) as being evolved from the normal human type. Also *transf.* and *allus.*

Like Nietzsche, the modern German believes that the world must be ruled by a super-man, and that he is the super-man 1912.

Supermu·ndane, *a.* 1677. [ad. med.L. *supermundanus,* f. *super-* SUPER- I. 1 + *mundus*; cf. MUNDANE.] Elevated in nature or character above what pertains to the earth or world; belonging to a region above the world.

‖ **Supernaculum** (s'ŭpəɹnæ·kiŭlŏm), *adv.* and *sb. slang.* 1592. [mod.L. tr. G. *auf den nagel* on to the nail, in phr. *auf den nagel trinken* to drink off liquor to the last drop.] **A.** *adv.* Used in ref. to the practice of turning up the emptied cup or glass on one's left thumbnail, to show that all the liquor has been drunk; hence, to the last drop, to the bottom.

He drank thy health five times, *s.* DRYDEN.

B. *sb.* **1.** A liquor to be drunk to the last drop; a wine of the highest quality; hence, anything excellent of its kind 1704. **2.** A draught that empties the cup to the last drop; also, a full cup, a bumper 1827. Hence **Superna·cular** *a.* (of drink) excellent.

Supernal (s'ŭpɔ̄·ɹnăl), *a.* (*sb.*) 1483. [a. OF., ad. med.L. **supernalis,* f. *supernus,* f. *super* above, see -AL.] **A.** *adj.* **1.** That is above or on high; existing or dwelling in the heavens 1485. **2.** Belonging to the realm or state above this world or this present life; pertaining to a higher state of existence; coming from above 1483. **3. a.** Situated in, or belonging to, the sky or upper regions; celestial, heavenly. *Obs.* or *arch.* 1503. **b.** Situated above or at the top, upper; above ground; lofty in position (*rare*) 1599. **4.** High in rank or dignity, exalted 1549. **5.** Supremely great or excellent, 'divine' 1818. **B.** *sb.* A supernal being (*rare*) 1755.

A. 1. That s. Judge that stirs good thoughts SHAKS. **2.** Errands of s. Grace MILT. **4.** He hath put downe the mightie ones From their supernall seate 1549. Hence **Supe·rnally** *adv.*

Supernatural (s'ŭpəɹnæ·tiŭrăl, -tʃərăl), *a.* (*sb.*) 1526. [ad med.L. *supernaturalis,* f. *super-* SUPER- II. 1 a + *natura*; see -AL.] **A.** *adj.* **1.** That is above nature; transcending the powers or the ordinary course of nature. **b.** *transf.* Relating to, dealing with, or characterized by what is above nature 1569. **2.** More than the natural or ordinary; abnormal, extraordinary. *Obs.* or *arch.* 1533.

1. Inspiration..termed s. properly, in Contradistinction to all Knowledge resulting from the common Laws of Nature 1749. The pestilences which desolated nations were deemed s. 1865. **b.** Lady Hester Stanhope's conversation on s. topics KINGLAKE. **2.** Suddenly animated with s. strength 1797.

B. *absol.* or *sb.* **1.** *absol.* with *the.* That which is supernatural 1830. **2.** *sb. pl.* Supernatural things 1587. **3.** A supernatural being 1729.

1. The introduction of the s. and marvellous SCOTT. Hence **Su·pernatura·lity,** the quality of being s.; something that is s., a s. object, occurrence, etc. **Superna·tural-ly** *adv.,* **-ness.**

Superna·turalism. 1799. [f. prec. + -ISM.] **1.** Supernatural character or quality; a system or collection of supernatural agencies, events, etc. Rarely in *pl.* **2.** Belief in the supernatural; a theory or doctrine which admits or asserts the reality of supernatural beings, powers, events, etc. 1809. So **Superna·turalist,** an adherent of s. 1650. **Su·pernaturali·stic** *a.* holding the belief of a supernaturalist; of or belonging to supernaturalists; pertaining to or involving s.

Superna·turalize, *v.* 1643. [f. as prec. + -IZE.] *trans.* To make supernatural; to impart or attribute a supernatural character to.

Supernature (s'ū·pəɹnē̆ⁱtiŭɹ, -tʃəɹ). 1844. [f. SUPER- + NATURE, after *supernatural.*] A supernatural realm or system of things; something supernatural.

Superno·rmal, *a.* 1868. [SUPER- II. 1 a.] **1.** Exceeding that which is normal. **2.** Applied to phenomena of an extraordinary kind, involving a higher law or principle than those ordinarily occurring, but not necessarily supernatural 1885. Hence **Superno·rmally** *adv.*

Supernumerary (s'ŭpəɹniū·mĕrări), *a.* and *sb.* 1605. [ad. late L. *supernumerarius* applied to soldiers added to a legion after it is complete, f. *super numerum*; see SUPER- III. 3 and -ARY[1].] **A.** *adj.* **1.** That is beyond or in excess of the usual, proper, regular, stated, or prescribed number or †quantity; additional, extra, left over. Now *rare* in gen. sense. **b.** *spec.* Applied to an official, officer, or employee not formally belonging to the regular body or staff, but associated with it to assist in case of need or emergency 1624. **c.** *Bot.* and *Zool.* Applied to structures or organs occurring (either in individuals or in types) in addition to the normal ones 1733. **2.** That is beyond the number needed or desired; superfluous, unnecessary. Now *rare.* 1640.

1. I have had s. Copies wrought off HEARNE. **b.** To be a s. Usher in his Schoole 1683.

B. *sb.* A supernumerary person or thing; *esp.* a supernumerary official or employee 1639. **b.** On board ship, a sailor, or one of a body of sailors, over and above the ship's complement 1666. **c.** An additional officer attached to a body of men in the army or navy for some special purpose 1796. **d.** A retired Wesleyan minister 1791. **e.** *Theatr.* A person employed in addition to the regular company, who appears on the stage but does not speak. Colloq. abbrev. *super* (see SUPER *sb.* 2). 1836.

b. The whole crew with our black supernumeraries 1833.

Supero- (s'ū·pĕrŏ), mod. comb. form of L. *superus* that is above, upper (see SUPERIOR), in terms of anatomy and zoology, designating parts situated above or on the upper side. **a.** in adjs., as **Supero-ante·rior** *a.,* situated above and in front; **Supero-exte·rnal** *a.,* situated above and on the outside. **b.** in derived advs., as *supero-externally, -posteriorly.*

Su:perocci·pital, *a.* and *sb.* 1854. [SUPER- I. 1 b.] *Anat.* and *Zool.* **A.** *adj.* Situated at the upper part of the occiput or back of the head. **B.** *sb.* The s. bone, an element of the skull usu. forming part of the occipital bone, but in some lower vertebrates constituting a distinct bone.

Supero·rdinate, *a.* (*sb.*) 1620. [f. SUPER- II, after *subordinate*.] A. *adj.* Superior in rank: opp. to SUBORDINATE. Now only in *Logic*. B. *sb.* One who is superior in rank 1802.

Su·perordina·tion. 1655. [ad. eccl. L. *superordinatio, -onem* choice of a bishop's successor, f. *superordinare*; see SUPER- IV. 1 and ORDINATION.] 1. Ordination of a person, while another still holds an office, to succeed him in that office when it shall become vacant. 2. *Logic.* The action of superordinating or condition of being superordinated; superordinate position or relation 1864.

†**Su·perparti·cular,** *a.* (*sb.*) 1557. [ad. late L. *superparticularis*; see SUPER- IV. 2 and PARTICULAR.] *Arith.* Applied to a ratio in which the antecedent contains the consequent once with one aliquot part over (e.g. $1\frac{1}{2}$, $1\frac{1}{3}$, $1\frac{1}{4}$ times), i.e. the ratio of any number to the next below it ($\frac{3}{2}$, $\frac{4}{3}$, $\frac{5}{4}$). Also *sb.*, a superparticular ratio. -1842.

†**Superpa·rtient,** *a.* (*sb.*) 1557. [ad. late L. *superpartientem, -ens*, f. *super-* SUPER- IV. 2 + *partiens, partiri* to divide.] *Arith.* Applied to a ratio in which the antecedent contains the consequent once with any number (greater than one) of aliquot parts over. Also *sb.*, a superpartient ratio. -1788.

Superpho·sphate. 1797. [SUPER- III. 4 b.] 1. *Chem.* A phosphate containing an excess of phosphoric acid; an acid phosphate. 2. In full *s. of lime*: an impure superphosphate of lime prepared by treating bones, coprolites, etc. with sulphuric acid, and used as a manure 1843.

†**Su·perplus.** Chiefly *Sc.* 1561. [a. med.L.; see SUPER- IV. 1 and PLUS.] = SURPLUS -1825. So †**Superplusage,** surplusage 1450.

Superpose (s¹ūpəɪpōu·z), *v.* 1823. [ad. F. *superposer*, f. *super-* SUPER- I. 2 + *poser* to POSE, after L. *superponere* (see next).] 1. *trans.* To place above or upon something else. Usu. in *pa. pple.*; often loosely of two or more things in a vertical series (= placed one above or upon another). 2. *Physics*, etc. To bring into the same position so as to coincide; to cause to occupy or coexist in the same space without destroying one another, as two or more sets of physical conditions (e.g. light-rays, etc.), or one such in relation to another 1831. b. *Geom.* To transfer (one magnitude) ideally to the space occupied by another, esp. so as to show that they coincide 1870.

1. *fig.* Bursting through the network superpos'd By selfish occupation M. ARNOLD.

Superposition (s¹ū:pəɪpŏzi·ʃən). 1656. [ad. F., ad. late L. *superpositio, -onem*, f. *superponere*, f. *super-* SUPER- I. 2, IV. 1 + *ponere* to place (see POSITION).] 1. *gen.* The placing of one thing on or above another; an instance of this 1828. 2. *Geom.* The action of ideally transferring one figure into the position occupied by another, esp. so as to show that they coincide 1656. b. *Physics*, etc. The action of causing two or more sets of physical conditions or phenomena (e.g. undulations) to coincide, or coexist in the same place; the fact of such coincidence or coexistence 1830. 3. *Geol.* The deposition of one stratum upon another, or the condition of being so deposited 1799. 4. *Bot.* The relative position of leaves, etc., on an axis, when situated directly above one another, not alternating 1880.

Superre·alism. 1935. = SURREALISM.

Su·per-roy·al, *a.* 1612. [SUPER- II. 1.] 1. That is above royal or kingly rank; higher than royal (*rare*). 2. Designating a size of paper next above that called *royal* (ROYAL *a.* II. 4), measuring about 19–21 by 27–28 inches 1681.

1. The Popes superroiall power 1612.

Supersalt (s¹ū·pəɪsǭlt). 1806. [f. SUPER- III. 4 b + SALT *sb.*¹] *Chem.* A salt containing an excess of the acid over the base.

Supersa·turate, *v.* 1788. [f. SUPER- III. 1 b; after F. *sursaturer*.] *trans.* To saturate to excess; to add more of some other substance to (a given substance) than is sufficient to saturate it: chiefly in *Chem.* and *Physics*. Hence **Su·persatura·tion,** the action of supersaturating or condition of being supersaturated.

Superscribe (s¹ūpəɪskrəi·b, s¹ū·pəɪskrəib), *v.* 1598. [ad. late L. *superscribere*, f. *super-* SUPER- I. 2 + *scribere*.] 1. *trans.* To inscribe or mark *with* writing on the surface or upper part; to write upon; to put an inscription on or over 1605. 2. *spec.* To write a name, address, or direction on the outside or cover of; to address (a letter, etc.) *to* a person. *arch.* 1598. b. To write (a name or address) upon a letter 1728. 3. To write one's name at the head of a document 1611. 4. To write (a letter or word) above another, or above the line of writing 1776.

1. He received a Message..superscribed *With Speed* STEELE. 2. An envelope, superscribed *To Mr. Skinner, Merchant* MACAULAY.

Superscript (s¹ū·pəɪskript), *sb.* and *a.* 1588. [ad. late L. *superscriptus, superscribere*; see prec. and cf. SCRIPT.] †A. *sb.* = next 3. SHAKS. B. *adj.* Written above a letter, or above the line of writing: opp. to SUBSCRIPT B. 1861.

A. *L.L.L.* IV. ii. 135.

Superscription (s¹ūpəɪskri·pʃən). late ME. [a. OF. or ad. late L. *superscriptio, -onem*, f. *superscribere* to SUPERSCRIBE.] That which is superscribed. 1. A piece of writing or an inscription upon or above something. *arch.* (after Matt. xxii. 20, etc.). 2. *spec.* A piece of writing at the head or beginning of a document; a heading. late ME. 3. The address or direction on a letter. *Obs.* or *arch.* 1518. 4. A name signed; a signature. *Obs.* or *arch. rare.* 1681.

1. *fig.* I learn..How counterfeit a coin they are who friends Bear in their S. MILT. 2. *S.*, the sign ℞ before a prescription 1901.

Supersede (s¹ūpəɪsī·d), *v.* 1527. [a. OF. *superceder*, later *-seder*, ad. L. *supersedere* to sit above, etc., f. SUPER- I, II + *sedere* to SIT.] †1. *trans.* To desist from, discontinue (a procedure, an attempt, etc.); not to proceed with -1750. †b. *intr.* To desist, forbear, refrain -1850. †2. To refrain from (discourse, disquisition); to omit to mention, refrain from mentioning -1689. †3. To put a stop to (legal proceedings, etc.); to stop, stay -1838. b. *Law.* To discharge by a writ of supersedeas 1817. †4. To render superfluous or unnecessary -1797. 5. To make of no effect; to render void, nugatory, or useless; to annul; to override. Now *rare* or *Obs.* 1654. 6. *pass.* To be set aside as useless or obsolete; to be replaced *by* something regarded as superior 1642. 7. To take the place of (something set aside or abandoned); to succeed to the place occupied by; to serve, be adopted or accepted instead of 1660. 8. To supply the place of (a person deprived of or removed from an office or position) *by* another; also, to promote another over the head of; *pass.* to be removed from office to make way for another 1710. b. To supply the place of (a thing) 1861. 9. Of a person: To take the place of (some one removed from an office, or †promoted); to succeed and supplant (a person) in a position of any kind 1777.

5. The Norman invader superseded Anglo-Saxon institutions 1863. 6. When this work must be superseded by a more perfect history 1838. 7. Oxen were superseding horses in farm-work 1866. 9. Captain Maling takes his passage to s. Captain Nisbet in the Bonne Citoyenne NELSON.

‖**Supersedeas** (s¹ūpəɪsī·dǐæs). late ME. [L., = you shall desist (see prec.).] 1. *Law.* A writ commanding the stay of legal proceedings which ought otherwise to have proceeded, or suspending the powers of an officer: so called from the occurrence of the word in the writ. More fully *writ of s.* †2. *fig.* Something which stops, stays, or checks -1737.

2. A Supersedias for her loue was euery new-come frend 1592.

‖**Supersedere** (s¹ū:pəɪsīdī³rī). *Sc. Law.* 1547. [L. (see SUPERSEDE).] A judicial order or a private agreement granting protection to a debtor.

Supersedure (-sī·diŭɪ). *U.S.* 1788. [f. SUPERSEDE + -URE.] = SUPERSESSION.

Superse·nsual, *a.* 1683. [SUPER- II. 1 a.] That is above or beyond (the power of) the senses, or higher than what is perceived by the senses; also, relating to such things as transcend sense; often = spiritual. Also *absol.* with *the*.

Superse·rviceable, *a.* 1605. [SUPER- III. 1 a.] More serviceable than is required or fitting; officious. SHAKS.

Supersession (s¹ūpəɪse·ʃən). 1656. [ad. med.L. *supersessio*.] The action of superseding or condition of being superseded.

Supersonic (s¹ūpəɪsǫ·nik), *a.* 1919. [f. SUPER- II. 1 a + L. *sonus* SOUND *sb.* + -IC.] 1. Of or pertaining to sound-waves of such a high frequency as to be inaudible. 2. Exceeding the speed of sound in the medium concerned 1945.

Superstition (s¹ūpəɪsti·ʃən). late ME. [a. OF., or ad. L. *superstitio, -onem*, f. *superstare* to stand upon or over, f. *super-* SUPER- I. 2 + *stare* to stand.] 1. Unreasoning awe or fear of something unknown, mysterious, or imaginary, esp. in connexion with religion; religious belief or practice founded upon fear or ignorance 1538. b. An irrational religious belief or practice; a tenet, scruple, habit, etc. founded on fear or ignorance. late ME. 2. An irrational religious system; a false, pagan, or idolatrous religion. Now *rare* or *Obs.* 1526. b. A religious ceremony or observance of a pagan or idolatrous character. Now *rare* or *Obs.* 1529. 3. *transf.* (from 1). Irrational or unfounded belief in general; an unreasonable or groundless notion 1794.

1. S. is, when things are either abhord or obserued, with a zealous or fearefull, but erroneous relation to God HOOKER. b. When they began to say, that..all wine was an abomination, they pass'd into a direct s. JER. TAYLOR. 2. The Turks received the Mahometane s. 1603. 3. Of the political superstitions,..none is so universally diffused as the notion that majorities are omnipotent SPENCER.

Superstitious (s¹ūpəɪsti·ʃəs), *a.* late ME. [a. OF. *superstitieux*, ad. L. *superstitiosus*, f. *superstitio* SUPERSTITION.] 1. Of the nature of, involving, or characterized by superstition. 2. Subject or addicted to superstition; believing or practising superstitions 1526. †b. Idolatrously or extravagantly devoted -1704. †3. Over-scrupulous; punctilious; extremely careful or particular -1816. 4. Used in or regarded with superstition; venerated, observed, or believed in, in the way of superstition. Now *rare* or *Obs.* 1566. †b. Magical; credited with supernatural efficacy -1651. †5. Extraordinary; excessive; superfluous -1640.

1. Their S. Belief, of Ghosts, Spirits, Dæmons, Devils, Fayries, and Hob-goblins 1678. *S. uses* (Law), 'where lands, tenements, or goods, are given for the maintenance of persons to pray for the souls of dead men in purgatory, or to maintain perpetual obits, lamps, etc.' 2. It seem'd..to a S. eye the haunt Of Wood-Gods and Wood-Nymphs MILT. b. *Hen. VIII*, III. i. 131. 5. They..have such a s. conceit of their owne merit and temper [etc.] 1638. Hence **Supersti·tiously** *adv.*, **-ness.**

Superstruct (s¹ū·pəɪstrɒkt), *v.* Now *rare* or *Obs.* 1642. [f. L. *superstruct-, superstruere*, f. *super-* SUPER- I. 2 + *struere* to build.] To build upon something else; to construct upon a foundation; to erect as a superstructure. Usu. *fig.* or in fig. context. Also *absol.*

Those..on whose approbation his esteem of himself was superstructed JOHNSON.

Superstructive (s¹ūpəɪstrɒ·ktiv), *a.* (*sb.*) Now *rare.* 1625. [f. L. *superstruct-*; see prec. and -IVE.] A. *adj.* Belonging to the superstructure; opp. to *fundamental* 1642. †B. *sb.* Something belonging to or constituting the superstructure -1644. So †**Superstru·ctor,** one who builds a superstructure.

Superstructure (s¹ū·pəɪstrɒktiŭɪ, -tʃəɪ). 1641. [f. SUPER- I. 3 + STRUCTURE.] 1. A building considered in relation to its foundation; an upper part of a building, erected upon a lower supporting part; any material structure resting on something else as a foundation 1645. 2. *fig.* An immaterial structure, as of thought, action, etc., figured as being built upon something else as a foundation 1641.

1. In som Places, as in Amsterdam, the Foundation costs more than the S. 1645.

Supersubstantial (s¹ū:pəɪsŏbstæ·nʃăl), *a.* 1534. [ad. late L. *supersubstantialis*, f. *super-* SUPER- II. 1 a + *substantia* SUBSTANCE: see -AL 1.] 1. In allusion to late L. *supersubstantialis* in the Vulgate version of Matt. vi. 11 (tr. Gr. ἐπιούσιος, which is now usu. held to mean 'pertaining to the coming day'). Above or transcending material substance; spiritual: esp. in ref. to the eucharistic bread. 2. Above or transcending all substance or being: chiefly of God 1534. So Su·persubsta·ntiate *v.* [after *transubstantiate*] *trans.* to make s.

Superterranean (s'ū:pəɹtĕrē'·nĭăn), *a.* (*sb.*) 1691. [f. mod.L. **superterraneus*, f. *super-* SUPER- I. 1 a + *terra* earth; see -AN.] That is or dwells above, or on the surface of, the earth; above-ground: opp. to *subterranean*. Also *sb.*, a dweller above ground or on the earth.

Numerous chambers both s. and subterranean 1816. So **Su·perterra·neous** *a.* 1671.

Superterrene (s'ū:pəɹterī·n), *a.* 1709. [ad. late L. *superterrenus*; see SUPER- I. 1 a and TERRENE.] 1. = prec. 2. = next 1. 1755.

Superterrestrial (s'ū:pəɹtère·striăl), *a.* 1727. [See SUPER- I. 1 a and TERRESTRIAL.] 1. Existing, or belonging to a region, above the earth. 2. = SUPERTERRANEAN 1875.

Su·pertonic. 1806. [SUPER- II. 2 b.] *Mus.* The note next above the tonic; the second of the scale. Also *attrib.* applied to a chord having this note for its root.

Supervene (s'ūpəɹvī·n), *v.* 1647. [ad. L. *supervenire*, f. *super-* SUPER- IV. 1 + *venire* to come.] 1. *intr.* To come on or occur as something additional or extraneous; to come directly or shortly after something else, either as a consequence of it or in contrast with it; to follow closely upon some other occurrence or condition. †2. *trans.* To come directly or soon after, to follow closely; occas. to come after so as to take the place of, to supersede –1810.

1. Upon a sudden supervened the death of the king 1647. Typhus supervening on a gunshot wound 1870.

Supervenience (s'ūpəɹvī·niĕns). *rare.* 1644. [f. next; see -ENCE.] The fact of being supervenient, or of supervening; supervention.

Supervenient (s'ūpəɹvī·niĕnt), *a.* 1594. [ad. L. *supervenient-*, *-ens*, *supervenire* to SUPERVENE.] Supervening; coming on something as an extraneous addition; coming on after (and in connexion or contrast with) something else; occurring subsequently.

Some s. cause of discord may overpower this original amity JOHNSON.

Supervention (s'ūpəɹve·nʃən). 1649. [ad. late L. *superventio*, *-onem*, f. *supervenire* to SUPERVENE.] The action or fact of supervening; coming on in addition; subsequent occurrence.

Supervisal (s'ū·pəɹvəizăl). Now *rare.* 1652. [f. med.L. *supervis-*, *supervidere*, f. *super-* SUPER- I. 2 + *videre*.] = SUPERVISION.

Supervise (s'ū·pəɹvəiz), *v.* 1588. [f. med. L. *supervis-*, *supervidere*; see prec.] †1. *trans.* To look over, survey, inspect; to read through, peruse –1711. †b. *spec.* To read through for correction; to revise –1751. 2. To oversee, have the oversight of, superintend the execution or performance of (a thing), the movements or work of (a person) 1645. †**Supervise** *sb.* SHAKS.

Supervision (s'ūpəɹvi·ʒən). 1640. [ad. med.L. *supervisio*, *-onem*, f. *supervidere*.] The action or function of supervising; oversight, superintendence.

Supervisor (s'ū·pəɹvəizəɹ). 1454. [ad. med.L., f. *supervis-*, *supervidere*; see -OR.] One who supervises. 1. A person who exercises general direction or control over a business, a body of workmen, etc.; one who inspects and directs the work of others. †b. = OVERSEER *sb.* 1 b. –1767. c. An inspector of highways; now only *U.S.* a road-master on a railway 1555. †2. An onlooker, spectator, observer –1610. 3. One who reads over, esp. for the purpose of correction; a reviser. Now *rare* or *Obs.* 1624.

1. d. In some of the United States, an elected official charged with the administration of a township or other county subdivision 1882. e. *U.S.* One who supervises the courses and the teachers in a school. Hence **Su·pervisorship,** the office or function of a s.

Supervisory (s'ūpəɹvəi·zŏri), *a.* 1847. [f. L. *supervis-* SUPERVISE + -ORY [2].] Having the function of supervising; of, pertaining to, or exercising supervision.

Supinate (s'ū·pineit), *v.* 1831. [f. L. *supinat-*, *supinare*, f. *supinus* SUPINE *a.*] *Physiol. trans.* To turn (the hand or fore limb) so that the back of it is downward or backward; to turn (the leg) outwards. Opp. to PRONATE *v.*

Supination (s'ūpinē'·ʃən). 1666. [ad. L. *supinatio*, *-onem*, f. *supinare*; see prec. and -ATION.] *Physiol.* The action of turning the hand or fore limb so that the back of it is downward or backward; the position of a limb so turned. (Opp. to PRONATION.)

Supinator (s'ū·pinē'tŏɹ). 1615. [mod.L., f. *supinat-*, *supinare* to SUPINATE; see -OR.] *Anat.* A muscle by which supination is effected or assisted; *spec.* one of two muscles of the fore-arm or fore limb, *s. radii brevis* and *s. radii longus*.

Supine (s'ū·pəin), *sb.* 1522. [ad. L. *supinum*, neut. sing. (sc. *verbum*) of *supinus* (see next), tr. Gr. ὕπτιος passive.] *Gram.* In Latin grammar, applied to forms of a verbal noun, the one an accus. sing. ending in *-tum* or *-sum*, used with vbs. of motion and called the *first* or †*former s.*, the other a locative sing ending in *-tu* or *-su*, used with adjs. and called the *second* or †*latter s.* (The term is applied by some grammarians to the English infinitive with *to*, as in OE. *tó sceāwienne*, mod. Eng. *to show*.)

Supine (s'ūpəi·n, s'ū·pəin), *a.* 1500. [ad. L. *supinus*, f. Italic **sup-*, root of *super* above, *superus* higher; see -INE [1].] 1. Lying on one's back, lying with the face or front upwards. Also said of the position. b. Of the hand or arm: With the palm upward; supinated 1668. c. Of a part of the body: Situated so as to be upward; upper, superior 1661. d. *transf.* Sloping or inclining backwards. *poet.* 1697. 2. *fig.* Morally or mentally inactive, inert, or indolent 1603. b. Not active; passive 1843.

1. They buried their dead on their backs, or in a s. position SIR T. BROWNE. d. If the Vine On rising Ground be plac'd, or Hills s. DRYDEN. 2. The s. slaves Of blind authority SHELLEY. The listless and s. life which he had been leading THACKERAY. Hence **Supine·ly** *adv.*, **-ness.**

†**Supi·nity.** 1548. [ad. L. *supinitas*, f. *supinus* SUPINE *a.*; see -ITY.] 1. Supine behaviour or state of mind; inertness –1750. 2. Posture with the face upward (*rare*) –1755.

‖ **Suppedaneum** (svpĭdē'·nĭŏm). 1863. [Late L., f. *sup-* = SUB- + *ped-*, *pes* foot.] A support for the feet of a crucified person, projecting from the vertical shaft of the cross. So †**Suppeda·neous** *a. rare.* 1646–1711.

†**Suppe·ditate,** *v.* 1535. [f. L. *suppeditat-*, *suppeditare*.] *trans.* To furnish, supply –1754.

Suppeditation (svpeditē'·ʃən). Now *rare* or *Obs.* 1605. [ad. L. *suppeditatio*, *-onem*.] The action of supplying what is needful; supply.

Supper (sv·pəɹ), *sb.* ME. [a. OF. *soper*, *super*, *souper*, subst. use of *souper* SUP *v.*[2]] 1. The last meal of the day; (contextually) the hour at which this is taken, supper-time. (Formerly, the last of the three meals of the day (breakfast, dinner, and supper); now, the last substantial meal of the day when dinner is taken in the middle of the day, or a late meal following an early evening dinner.) Often without article, demonstrative, possessive, or the like, esp. when governed by a prep. (*to have s.*; *at, to, for, after s.*). 2. *spec.* a. *The Last S.*: the last meal taken by Jesus Christ with the Apostles before his crucifixion, at which he instituted the Eucharist ME. b. *The Lord's S.*, *the Dominical S.*, *the S.*: the Eucharist or Holy Communion 1533.

attrib. and *Comb.*, as *s.-dance*, *-dish*, *-table*, *-things*; **s.-party,** a party assembled at s., a social gathering of this kind; **-quadrille,** the quadrille danced just before s.; **-room,** a room in which s. is served; **-time,** the time at which s. is (normally) taken.

Su·pper, *v.* 1622. [f. prec.] 1. *trans.* a. To provide with supper; to entertain at supper. b. To give (horses, cattle, etc.) their evening feed and bed them down for the night. Chiefly *Sc.* and *n. dial.* 1816. 2. *intr.* To take one's supper; to sup 1691.

1. We intend to dinner him and s. him round, and by degrees make him our own 1715.

Supperless (sv·pəɹlĕs), *a.* 1515. [-LESS.] Without supper.

They'le..send him supperlesse to bed B. JONS.

Supping (sv·piŋ), *vbl. sb.*[1] late ME. [f. SUP *v.*[1] + -ING [1].] 1. The action of SUP *v.*[1]; drinking by spoonfuls or mouthfuls. 2. Chiefly *pl.* Food (*sing.* a food) that can be supped; *esp.* broth. Now *dial.* late ME.

Supping (sv·piŋ), *vbl. sb.*[2] late ME. [f. SUP *v.*[2] + -ING [1].] The action of taking supper.

Supplant (sŏplɑ·nt), *v.* ME. [a. OF. *supplanter*, or ad. L. *supplantare* to trip up, f. *sup-* = SUB- 25 + *planta* sole of the foot.] †1. *trans.* To trip up, cause to stumble or fall by tripping –1667. †2. *fig.* To cause to fall from a position of power, superiority, or virtue; to cause the downfall of, bring low –1780. 3. To dispossess and take the place of (another), esp. by treacherous or dishonourable means ME. †4. To take up by the roots; to root out, uproot (a plant, or something likened thereto) –1644. 5. To remove from its position, get rid of, oust; occas. to replace or supersede *by* something else. Now *rare.* 1576. 6. Chiefly of things: To take the place of, supersede 1671.

1. His Armes clung to his Ribs, his Leggs entwining Each other, till supplanted down he fell A monstrous Serpent MILT. 3. He most unworthily supplanted and turned out the worthy Curate..out of his own cure of souls 1731. 5. S. the Alpes, and lay them smooth and plaine DRAYTON. 6. These pantomimes will very soon s. all poetry 1789. Hence **Supplanter** ME.

Supplantation (svplɑntē'·ʃən). late ME. [a. OF., ad. late L. *supplantatio*, *-onem*, f. *supplantare* to SUPPLANT.] 1. The dispossession or displacement of a person in a position, esp. by dishonourable means. 2. The supersession or displacement *of* one thing *by* another 1608.

Supple (sv·p'l), *a.* ME. [a. OF. :—L. *supplicem*, *supplex* 'bending under', hence, submissive, suppliant, f. *sup-* SUB- 2 + *plic-*, root of *plicare* to fold.] †1. Not rigid; soft, tender. –late ME. 2. That is easily bent or folded without breaking or cracking; pliant, flexible, late ME. b. *fig.* Adaptable; elastic 1781. 3. Of the body, limbs, etc.: Capable of bending easily; moving easily or nimbly 1530. b. *transf.* of movements, etc.: Characterized by flexibility of body or limb 1592. 4. *fig.* Yielding readily to persuasion or influence; compliant ME. 5. Compliant or accommodating from selfish motives; artfully or servilely complaisant or obsequious 1607. b. *transf.* Characterized by ingratiating or fawning complaisance 1633.

2. Whipping the stream with his s. fly-rod 1872. Rubbed in..in sufficient quantity to keep the skin s. and unctuous 1899. b. His s. address and determination saved Rome from a revolution 1879. 3. Limbs so s.; will so stubborn! RICHARDSON. *S. knee*, in ref. to insincere or obsequious obeisance; Will ye submit your necks, and chuse to bend The s. knee? MILT. b. Keep a..s. position of the body 1809. 4. Let me be soft and s. to thy will G. HERBERT. 5. A s. and flattering courtier EVELYN. b. We Britons slight Those s. arts which foreigners delight 1690. Hence **Su·pple·ly** *adv.*, **-ness.**

Supple (sv·p'l), *v.* late ME. [f. prec., after OF. *asoplir* (mod.F. *assouplir*).] 1. *trans.* To soften, mollify (the heart or mind); to make compliant or complaisant. *Obs.* or *arch.* b. *intr.* and *refl.* To be submissive or compliant *to*. *Obs.* or *arch.* 1440. 2. To make (skin, leather, and the like) supple, pliant, or flexible 1530. †3. To reduce the hardness of, to soften. Also *absol.* –1728. †4. To soften or mollify (a wound, swelling, etc.) by applying an unguent, a fomentation, etc.; to anoint with oil –1688. 5. To make (the limbs, the body, the person) supple or capable of bending easily; *spec.* of the training of saddle-horses 1570. 6. *gen.* To make pliant, flexible, or smooth; also, to tone down, modify 1530.

1. Suppled with Sicknesse, he confessed his Fault FULLER. 2. Hard new boots not yet suppled by use 1915. 5. In order to s. the recruit,..he will be practised in the..movements 1847. 6. To set free, to s. and to train the faculties LOWELL.

Su·pple-jack. 1725. [f. SUPPLE *a.* + JACK *sb.*[1]] 1. A name for various climbing and twining shrubs with tough pliable stems found in tropical and subtropical forests; applied in the West Indies to various sapindaceous plants, as species of *Paullinia* and *Serjania*; in Central America, to the rhamnaceous *Berchemia volubilis*, and to a species of *Zizyphus*; and elsewhere to plants of similar habit. b. The stems of these plants as a material 1804. 2. A walking-stick or cane made of the stem of one of these plants; a tough pliant stick 1748. 3. A toy representing the human figure, the limbs of which are manipulated by a string (*U.S.*) 1829.

Supplement (sv·plĭmĕnt), *sb.* late ME. [ad. L. *supplementum*, f. *supplere* SUPPLY *v.*] 1. Something added to supply a deficiency; an auxiliary means, an aid; occas. of a person. (Now *rare* in general sense.) **b.** A part added to complete a literary work or any written account or document; *spec.* a part of a periodical publication issued as an addition to the regular numbers and containing some special item or items 1568. **c.** *Math.* (*a*) *S. of an arc* or *angle*, the amount by which an arc is less than a semicircle, or an angle less than two right angles. (*b*) An additional term introduced in certain cases in an equation or expression (abbrev. *Supp.*). 1570. †**2.** The action of supplying what is wanting; the making good *of* a deficiency or shortcoming -1660. **b.** Sc. Law. *Oath in s.*, a suppletory oath 1672. †**3.** The reinforcement *of* troops; chiefly *concr.* (*sing.* and *pl.*), reinforcement(s) -1665. †**4.** The action of supplying or providing; that which is supplied; supply, provision -1658.

Supplement (sɒ·plĭmĕnt, sɒplĭme·nt), *v.* 1829. [f. prec.] *trans.* To furnish a supplement to, supply the deficiency in; also, to supply (a deficiency).

The two sets of dissimilar conditions s. and throw light upon each other 1868.

Supplemental (sɒplĭme·ntăl), *a.* (*sb.*) 1605. [f. as prec. + -AL.] **A.** *adj.* = next A. Const. *to, of.* **b.** *Math.* 1798. **B.** *sb.* A supplementary fact, etc. (*rare*) 1670.

A. Womens Supplimentall Art, does but the rather bewray Natures Defects 1629. *S. air*, the air that remains in the lungs after an ordinary expiration. **b.** *S. angle*, either (in relation to the other) of two angles which are together equal to two right angles. *S. arc*, either of two arcs which are together equal to a semicircle. *S. chord*, the chord of a supplemental arc. Hence **Suppleme·ntally** *adv.*

Supplementary (sɒplĭme·ntări), *a.* (*sb.*) 1667. [f. as prec. + -ARY [1].] **A.** *adj.* Of the nature of, forming, or serving as, a supplement. Const. *to.* Often in techn. uses. **B.** *sb.* A supplementary person or thing 1812.

A. To this Claim..was added a s. paper containing a list of grievances MACAULAY. Hence **Suppleme·ntarily** *adv.*

Supplementation (sɒ:plĭmentē[i]·ʃən). 1854. [f. SUPPLEMENT *v.* + -ATION.] The action of supplementing; also, an instance of this, a supplementary addition.

Suppletion (sɒ̆plī·ʃən). *rare.* ME. [a. OF., ad. L. **suppletio*, n. of action f. *supplere* to SUPPLY.] The action or an act of supplying; something supplied.

Suppletive (sɒ̆plī·tiv), *a. rare.* 1816. [ad. med.L. *suppletivus*, f. *supplet-*, *supplere*.] Having the attribute of supplying deficiencies.

Suppletory (sɒ·plĭtŏri), *a.* and *sb.* 1628. [ad. late L. *suppletorius*, f. *supplet-*; see prec. and -ORY [2].] **A.** *adj.* Supplementary. Const. *to, of.* Now *rare.* **b.** Law. *S. oath*, an oath (given by a party in his own favour) admitted to supply a deficiency in legal evidence 1726. †**B.** *sb.* A supplement -1707.

The rite of confirmation..is an admirable s. of an early Baptisme JER. TAYLOR.

Supplial (sɒ̆plai·ăl). Now *rare.* 1752. [f. SUPPLY *v.* + -AL 2.] The act of supplying.

The..s. of all the wants of life 1819.

Suppliance [1] (sɒ̆plai·ăns). Now *rare.* 1598. [f. as prec. + -ANCE.] = SUPPLY *sb.*

Suppliance [2] (sɒ·pliăns). *rare. poet.* 1611. [f. SUPPLIANT *a.*[1]; see -ANCE.] The action of a suppliant; supplication. So **Su·ppliancy.**

Suppliant (sɒ·pliănt), *sb.* and *a.*[1] Now *poet.* or *rhet.* late ME. [a. F., pr. pple. of *supplier* :—L. *supplicare* SUPPLICATE *v.*] **A.** *sb.* One who supplicates; a humble petitioner.

Thy s. I beg, and clasp thy knees MILT.

B. *adj.* Supplicating, humbly petitioning 1586. **b.** *transf.* Expressing or involving supplication 1667.

The Rich grow s., and the Poor grow proud DRYDEN. **b.** To bow and sue for grace With s. knee MILT. Hence **Su·ppliantly** *adv.*

†**Suppli·ant,** *a.*[2] 1611. [f. SUPPLY *v.* + -ANT.] Supplementary. SHAKS.

Supplicant (sɒ·plikănt), *sb.* and *a.* Now *rare* exc. *arch.* 1597. [ad. L. *supplicantem*, *-ans, supplicare.*] **A.** *sb.* = SUPPLIANT *sb.* **b.** *spec.* One who supplicates for a degree; see SUPPLICATE *v.* 3. 1649.

The..supplicants, who repair to the churches 1834.

B. *adj.* = SUPPLIANT *a.*[1] 1597. Hence **Su·pplicantly** *adv.*

‖ **Supplicat** (sɒ·plikæt). 1660. [L., = he supplicates.] A supplication, petition; *spec.* (now only) in English universities, a formal petition for a degree or for incorporation.

Supplicate (sɒ·plikeɪt), *v.* late ME. [f. L. *supplicat-*, *supplicare*, f. *sup-* = SUB- 2 + *plic-*, root of *plicare* to bend.] **1.** *intr.* To beg, or entreat humbly; to present a humble petition. **2.** *trans.* To petition humbly 1642. **3.** *spec. intr.* In Oxford University, to present a formal petition for a degree or for incorporation 1691.

1. O holy Mary..s. for the devout Female Sex 1771. **2.** The Church..did s. protection from the temporall powers 1660. Shall I brook to be supplicated? TENNYSON. So **Su·pplicator,** one who supplicates; a su pliant, petitioner. **Su·pplicatingly** *adv.*

Supplication (sɒplikē[i]·ʃən). late ME. [a. OF., ad. L. *supplicatio-, -onem*, f. *supplicare.*] The action, or an act, of supplicating; humble or earnest petition or entreaty. **b.** A written or formal petition. *Obs.* exc. *Hist.* late ME. **c.** (A) humble prayer addressed to God (or a deity); chiefly pl., *spec.* the petitions for special blessings in litanies 1490. **d.** *Rom. Antiq.* A religious solemnity decreed on the occasion of some important public event, esp. in thanksgiving for victory 1606. **e.** *spec.* In Oxford University, a formal petition for a degree or for incorporation 1691.

Supplicatory (sɒ·plikĕtŏri), *a.* 1450. [ad. med.L. *supplicatorius*; see -ORY [2].] Expressing, consisting of, or containing supplication.

‖ **Supplicavit** (sɒplikē[i]·vit). 1507. [L., = he has supplicated.] *Law.* A writ formerly issuing out of the King's Bench or the Court of Chancery for taking surety of the peace against a person: so called from the first word in the writ.

Supplier (sɒ̆plai·əɹ). 1607. [f. SUPPLY *v.* + -ER [1].] One who (or that which) supplies.

Supply (sɒ̆plai·), *sb.* late ME. [f. next.] **I.** The action of supplying, or condition of being supplied. †**1.** Assistance, succour, support, relief -1697. **2.** The act of making up a deficiency, or of fulfilling a want or demand 1500. †**3.** The act of supplying something needed -1673. **b.** Now only in ref. to persons: The act, or position, of supplying a vacancy, or officiating temporarily instead of another, esp. as a minister or preacher; *on s.* = acting in such a capacity 1580. **4.** The provision or furnishing *of* a person, etc. with necessaries 1781. **II.** That which is supplied. †**1.** *collect. sing.* or *pl.* An additional body of persons, esp. reinforcements of troops -1750. **2.** One who supplies a vacancy or acts as substitute for another; *esp.* a minister or preacher who temporarily officiates in a vacant charge or pulpit 1584. **3.** A quantity or amount *of* something supplied or provided 1607. **4.** *absol.* (A) provision of funds or food; (a quantity of) money or provisions supplied or to be supplied: now chiefly *spec.* the food and stores necessary for an armed force 1611. **5.** *collect. sing.* or *pl.* A sum of money granted by a national legislature for expenses of government not provided for by the revenue 1626. **6.** *Pol. Econ.* The amount of any commodity produced and available for purchase: correl. to DEMAND *sb.* 4. 1776.

1. The Earle of Salisbury craueth s. SHAKS. **3.** The wine was passed, and a fresh supply ordered DICKENS. **4.** England..sent Money and other Supplies into Ireland 1687. **5.** The Commons declared..that redress of grievances must precede the grant of supplies GREEN. **6.** If the demand exceeds the s. the price will rise 1900.

Supply (sɒ̆plai·), *v.* late ME. [a. OF. *so(u)pleer*, later *supplier*, ad. L. *supplere*, f. *sup-* SUB- 25 + *-plere* to fill (*plenus* FULL).] †**1.** *trans.* To help, aid, assist; to succour, relieve; to support, maintain; *occas.* to deliver *from* -1750. †**2.** To furnish with (additional) troops; to reinforce. Also *absol.* -1825. **3.** †**a.** To supplement -1730. **b.** To add (something that is wanting) 1450. **4.** To make up for, make good, compensate for (a defect, loss, or void); to compensate for (the absence of something) by providing a substitute. late ME. **5.** To fulfil, satisfy (a need or want) by furnishing what is wanted 1567. **6.** To furnish, provide, afford (something needed, desired, or used): now usu. with impersonal subj. 1520. **7.** To furnish (a thing) *with* what is necessary or desirable; in early use, without const., to make provision for 1529. **b.** *transf.* To furnish with an occupant, tenant, or contents; to fill. *poet.* 1607. **c.** *Anat.* and *Phys.* Of a nerve or blood-vessel: To furnish with energy or nourishment (the part or organ to which it is distributed) 1843. **8.** To furnish or provide (a person) *with* something; in early use, without const., to satisfy the wants of, provide for; now usu., to furnish with regular supplies of a commodity 1567. **9.** To fill (another's place); *esp.* (now only) to occupy as a substitute. late ME. †**10.** To fulfil, discharge, perform (an office or function), *esp.* as a substitute for another -1748. **11.** To take the place of; to serve as, or furnish, a substitute for; to replace. Now *rare* or *Obs.* 1606. **12.** Of a cleric or minister: To occupy (a church, pulpit, etc.) as a substitute, or temporarily; to act as 'supply' for (another); also *absol.* 1719.

3. a. Nature is supplide in him by Art 1615. **b.** S. words that are wanting 1824. **4.** That which most supplied their want of experience 1600. **5.** Some private purse Supplies his need with an usurious loan COWPER. **6.** The fresco-paintings..of Crete have supplied the clearest proof of it 1910. **7.** She..With flow'r and fruit the wilderness supplies COWPER. **b.** *Timon* III. i. 18. **8.** Can Sir Reginald Glanville's memory..s. him with no probable cause? 1827. **11.** A comfortable heat..Which might s. the Sun MILT. **12.** To 's. the pulpits' of ministers who left home 1895. Hence †**Supply·ment** (*rare*), the act of supplying, or what is supplied -1611.

Support (sɒ̆pō[ə]·ɹt), *sb.* late ME. [f. next.] **I.** The action of supporting. **1.** The action, or an act, of preventing a person from giving way, backing him up, or taking his part; assistance, countenance, backing. **b.** Spiritual help; mental comfort 1500. **c.** Corroboration or substantiation (*of* a statement, principle, etc.); advocacy (*of* a proposal, motion, etc.) 1771. **d.** *Mil.* The action of supporting other troops. *In s.*: acting as a second line. 1805. **2.** The action of keeping from failing, exhaustion, or perishing; *esp.* the supplying *of* a living thing with what is necessary for subsistence; the maintenance *of* life 1686. **b.** The action of contributing to the success or maintaining the value of something 1912. **3.** The action or fact of holding up, keeping from falling, or bearing the weight of something; the condition of being so supported 1663.

1. Your gallant s. of me at the Battle of Copenhagen NELSON. **c.** The evidence to be called in s. of their statement 1891. **2.** Alone, it is insufficient for the s. of life 1857. A youth..found about the streets without visible means of s. 1915. **3.** Without any s. of columns EVELYN.

II. One who or that which supports. **1.** A supporter, 'prop', 'stay' 1594. **b.** *Mil.* (*pl.*) A supporting body of troops; the second line in a battle 1852. **2.** That which supports life; means of livelihood or subsistence 1599. **b.** One who or that which furnishes means of livelihood, or maintains a person or community 1745. **3.** Anything that holds up, or sustains the weight of, a body, or upon which it rests 1570.

1. High Ioue the heauens among (Their s. that suffer wrong) KYD. **2.** Liuelyhood and s. fit for their estates 1611. **b.** Her slender earnings were the sole s. of the family LAMB. **3.** A crucible,..with its cover and a s. FARADAY.

Support (sɒ̆pō[ə]·ɹt), *v.* late ME. [ad. (O)F. *supporter*, ad. L. *supportare* to convey, f. *sup-* = SUB- 25 + *portare* to carry.] **1.** *trans.* To endure without opposition or resistance; to bear with, put up with, tolerate. (In mod. use often a gallicism.) †**b.** To endure, undergo; to bear up against -1805. **2.** To strengthen the position of (a person or community) by one's assistance, countenance, or adherence; to stand by, back up. late ME. **b.** To uphold or maintain the validity or authority of (a thing); also, to give support to (a course of action) 1638. **3. a.** To back up in a statement or an opinion 1686. **b.** To furnish authority for or corroboration of (a statement, etc.); to bear out, substantiate 1761. **c.** To second or speak in favour of (a proposition, or one who makes a proposition); to maintain the truth of (an opinion, etc.) 1736. **4.** To provide for the maintenance of, bear the expense of. Now only with immaterial obj. late ME. **b.** *Law.* Of an estate: To be such as to provide for (a remainder) 1694. **5.** To furnish food or sustenance for; to supply with the necessaries of life. late ME. **b.** To sustain (the vital functions); also, to keep up the strength of (a sick person) 1704. **6.** To bear, hold, or prop up. late ME. †**b.** *refl.* To hold oneself up, keep an erect position –1727. †**c.** To give one's arm to (a lady); to take (a person) on one's arm –1816. **d.** To sustain (a weight of so much) 1726. **e.** *Her.* in *pass.* To be flanked by supporters 1562. **7.** To constitute the substratum of (a structure); to sustain in position above, have on it or at the top 1617. †**b.** *Metaph.* To be the subject or substratum of –1710. **8.** To keep (a person, his mind, etc.) from failing or giving way; to give courage, confidence, or power of endurance to. Also †*refl.* 1602. **9. a.** To maintain unimpaired, preserve from decay or depreciation 1515. **b.** To preserve from failure, contribute to the success of (an undertaking); also, to maintain (a price) 1779. **c.** To maintain in being or in action; to keep up, to provide the necessary matter for 1738. **d.** Of specie: To guarantee the convertibility of (a paper currency) 1868. **10.** To sustain (a character) in a dramatic performance; *gen.* to act or play (a part), bear (a character) 1709. **11.** To give assistance to in a battle, esp. by a second line of troops; to second (a leading actor); to assist as a subordinate in a contest, a musical performance, etc. 1848. **b.** To occupy a position by the side of, with the object of giving assistance or encouragement; hence, to assist by one's presence or attendance 1886.

1. These things his high spirit could not s. EVELYN. b. Prethee how does she s. this news? 1671. 2. He had no party in the country to s. him 1884. 3. b. The application was supported by an affidavit of the applicant 1885. c. Godolphin..had supported the Exclusion Bill MACAULAY. 4. This luxury was supported by a thriving trade MACAULAY. 5. The burden of supporting the poor ought to be sustained by all ranks 1801. 6. S. him by the arme SHAKS. 7. 'Andirons' in front to s. the logs of wood 1907. 9. a. To s. the ancient character of the corps 1802. b. Indian gold shares have been supported 1898. c. The conversation..was well supported till midnight 1785. 10. In order to s. the *rôle* which they unconsciously fall into 1888. 11. b. Mr. Gladstone was supported right and left by Lord Hartington and Sir William Harcourt 1886. Hence †**Suppo·rtment**, support.

Supportable (sŏpōᵊ·ɹtăb'l), *a.* 1577. [See prec. and -ABLE.] Capable of being supported; endurable; defensible. Hence **Supportabi·lity**, **Suppo·rtableness**. **Suppo·rtably** *adv.*

†**Suppo·rtance.** 1490. [f. SUPPORT *v.* + -ANCE.] = SUPPORT *sb.* in various senses –1830.

†**Supporta·tion.** late ME. [a. OF., ad. late L. *supportatio, -onem*, f. *supportare* to SUPPORT.] = SUPPORT *sb.* in various senses –1768.

Supporter (sŏpōᵊ·ɹtəɹ). late ME. [f. SUPPORT *v.* + -ER [1].] **1.** One who sides with, backs up, assists, or countenances a person, cause, etc. **2.** One who keeps a person or thing from failing, giving way, or perishing; a sustainer, maintainer 1475. **b.** *Chem.* A substance that maintains some process, esp. combustion 1806. **3.** = SUPPORT *sb.* II. 3. 1595. **b.** A leg. (Now only *joc.*) 1601. †**c.** A sepal –1712. **4.** *Her.* A figure of an animal, mythical creature, or human being, represented as holding up or standing beside the shield; each of two such figures, one on each side of the shield 1572. **5.** One who attends another for the purpose of giving physical or moral support; hence, an attendant, as in a procession 1586.

1. Staunch supporters of the Church 1836. 2. Loyalty..The great S. of his awful Throne DRYDEN. 3. A Building set upon Supporters 1707. c. The Sockets, and Supporters of Flowers, are Figured: As in the Five Brethren of the Rose BACON. 5. Ingratitude..sitting in its Throne, with Pride at its Right-hand, and Cruelty at its Left; worthy Supporters of..such a reigning Impiety 1675. **Suppo·rtress**, a female s.

Supportive (sŏpōᵊ·ɹtiv), *a. rare.* 1593. [f. SUPPORT *v.* + -IVE.] Having the quality of supporting; sustaining.

Suppo·rtless, *a.* 1643. [f. SUPPORT *sb.* + -LESS.] †**1.** That cannot be 'supported'; intolerable. MILT. **2.** Destitute of support, unsupported 1681.

Supposable (sŏpōu·zăb'l), *a.* 1643. [f. SUPPOSE *v.* + -ABLE.] Capable of being supposed; that may be thought to exist or to be true, or that can be assumed for the sake of argument; presumable, imaginable. Hence **Suppo·sably** *adv.* (chiefly *U.S.*), presumably.

Supposal (sŏpōu·zăl). late ME. [a. OF. *supposail(l)e*, f. *supposer* to SUPPOSE; see -AL.] †**1.** The action of supposing, supposition –1839. **2.** An act of supposing; something that is supposed; a supposition, hypothesis; an assumption, conjecture. Now *rare.* late ME. †**3.** A notion, opinion –1612. †**4.** A statement, allegation (as in a writ or indictment) –1651.

1. Phr. *Upon s.* (*of* or *that..*). *By, upon s.*, as is (or was) supposed, supposedly. 3. *Haml.* I. ii. 18.

Suppose (sŏpōu·z), *sb.* 1566. [f. next.] **1.** An act of supposing; a supposition, hypothesis, conjecture. Now always referring to a supposition expressed or expressible by means of the vb. 'suppose'. †**b.** *gen.* Supposition –1719. †**2.** (An) expectation –1606.

1. Fatted with Supposes of fine Hopes B. JONS.

Suppose (sŏpōu·z), *v.* ME. [a. OF. *sup(p)oser*, f. *sup-* = SUB- 2 + *poser* POSE *v.*[1], repr. L. *supposit- supponere.*] †**1.** *trans.* To hold as a belief or opinion; to believe as a fact; to think –1658. †**2.** To form an idea of, conceive, imagine; to apprehend, guess –1781. †**3.** To have in mind or as an object of thought or speculation; to think of, conceive, imagine, contextually, to suspect –1763. †**4.** To expect –1760. **5.** To assume (without ref. to truth or falsehood) as a basis of argument, or for the purpose of tracing the consequences; to frame as a hypothesis; to posit ME. **6.** Often in imper. or pres. pple. absol., introducing a hypothetical statement or case ME. **b.** In imper. parenthetically or ellipt.; often = 'as (for example)', 'say'. Now *rare* or *Obs.* 1577. **7.** *trans.* To infer hypothetically; to incline to think; sometimes implying mistaken belief 1601. **8.** To lay down or assume as true, take for granted. late ME. **b.** To presume the existence or presence of 1696. **9.** Of actions, conditions, facts: To involve as a ground or basis; to require as a condition; to imply, presuppose 1660. †**10.** To state, allege; esp. formally in an indictment –1651. †**11.** To substitute by artifice or fraud –1767. †**12.** To put or place under something; to append –1797.

1. Would you not s. Your bondage happy, to be made a Queene? SHAKS. 5. Which..might..do more harm than good in the case supposed SCOTT. 6. S. a man to have riches and honours 1678. S. you go to sleep, that you may get up in time enough 1844. Supposing them sculptors, will not the same rule hold? RUSKIN. b. A Person..breaks his Limbs, s. BUTLER. 7. Those foibles which are chiefly supposed proper to the female sex SCOTT. He fell and it is supposed was instantaneously killed 1885. 8. *pass.* (Not) to be expected *to do* or *be* so-and-so. He's not supposed to go into the kitchen (*mod.*). 9. Patience must s. pain JOHNSON. 11. Persons guilty of supposing children 1767. Hence **Suppo·sedly** (-ėdli) *adv.* in the way of supposition; as is (or was) supposed. †**Suppo·ser** (*rare*).

Supposition (sɒpŏzi·ʃən). 1449. [ad. L. *suppositio, -onem*, f. *supposit-, supponere.*] The action of supposing, or what is supposed. †**1.** *Scholastic Logic.* Something held to be true and taken as the basis of an argument –1590. **2.** The action of assuming, or, usu. that which is assumed (which may be either true or false), as a basis of argument or a premiss from which a conclusion is drawn 1596. **3.** A hypothetical inference, or the action of making such inferences; an uncertain (sometimes, by implication, a false or mistaken) belief 1596. †**b.** Used vaguely, with various shades of meaning: Idea, notion; imagination, fancy; *occas.* suspicion, expectation –1784. †**4.** Fraudulent substitution of another thing or person in place of the genuine one –1797. †**b.** Insertion of something not genuine in a writing; that which is so inserted (*rare*) –1662.

2. The s. that the defendant had broken the plaintiff's close 1887. 3. †*In s.*, in uncertainty, uncertain, doubtful; My meaning in saying he is a good man, is ..that he is sufficient, yet his meanes are in s. SHAKS. It is only said to be his [handwriting] by s. PEPYS. b. *Com. Err.* III. ii. 50. Hence **Supposi·tional** *a.* of the nature of or based on s.; hypothetical.

Suppositious (sɒpŏzi·ʃəs), *a.* Now *rare* or *Obs.* 1624. [Partly shortened or illiterate form of next, partly directly f. prec.] **1.** = next **1**, **2.** **2.** = SUPPOSITIONAL 1698.

Supposititious (sŏpǫziti·ʃəs), *a.* 1611. [f. L. *supposititius, -icius*, f. *supposit-, supponere*; see -ITIOUS.] **1.** Put by artifice in the place of another; fraudulently substituted for the genuine thing or person; hence, pretended (to be what it is not), spurious, counterfeit, false. **b.** *spec.* of a child, *esp.* one set up to displace the real heir or successor; sometimes used for 'illegitimate'; also said of the birth of such a child 1625. †**2.** Pretended or imagined to exist; feigned; fabulous; fancied, imaginary –1774. **3.** = next 1674.

2. I tearm the gold Mine he went to discover, an ayrie and s. Mine 1645. Hence **Supposi·ti·tious·ly** *adv.*, **-ness.**

Suppositive (sŏpǫ·zĭtiv), *a.* (*sb.*) 1605. [ad. late L. *suppositivus*, f. *supposit-, supponere.*] Of the nature of, implying, or grounded on supposition. **b.** *Gram.* Expressing a supposition; conditional; as *sb.* a conditional conjunction (*rare*) 1751. Hence **Suppo·sitive·ly** *adv.*

†**Suppo·sitor.** 1545. [Alteration of next after agent-nouns in -ER, -OR.] = next –1689.

Suppository (sŏpǫ·zitŏri), *sb.* late ME. [ad. late L. *suppositorium*, neut. sing., used subst., of *suppositorius* placed underneath or up, f. *supposit-, supponere.*] A plug of conical or cylindrical shape to be introduced into the rectum in order to stimulate the bowels to action (or to reduce hæmorrhoids), or into the vagina or urethra for various purposes.

Suppo·sitory, *a.* 1599. [ad. late L. *suppositorius* (see prec.).] †**1.** Used as, or pertaining to, a suppository –1607. **2.** = SUPPOSITIONAL. Now *rare.* 1644.

‖**Suppositum** (sŏpǫ·zitŏm). *Pl.* **supposita.** 1646. [Scholastic L., neut. sing., used subst., of *suppositus, supponere.*] †**1.** *Metaph.* A being that subsists by itself, an individual thing or person; occas., a being in relation to its attributes –1719. **2.** *Logic.* **a.** Something supposed or assumed, an assumption. **b.** *pl.* The things or objects denoted by a given term. 1833.

Suppost (sŏpōu·st). *Obs.* exc. *Hist.* 1490. [a. OF. *suppost*, ad. L. *suppositus, supponere.*] A subordinate; a supporter, follower, adherent.

Suppress (sŏpre·s), *v.* late ME. [f. L. *suppress-, supprimere*, f. *sup-* = SUB- 2 + *premere* to PRESS.] **1.** *trans.* To put down by force or authority; to quell; to vanquish, subdue. **b.** To withhold or withdraw from publication (a book or writing); to prevent or prohibit the circulation of 1560. **2.** To subdue (a feeling, thought, desire, habit) 1526. **3.** To keep secret; to refrain from disclosing or divulging; to refrain from mentioning or stating (either something that ought to be revealed, or that was formerly stated or included, or that may be understood from the context) 1533. **4.** To restrain from utterance or manifestation; not to express 1557. †**5.** To press down; to press or weigh upon –1620. †**6.** *fig.* To bring or keep low, into or in subjection; to weigh down –1649. **7.** To hinder from passage or discharge; to stop or arrest the flow of 1621.

1. To Discountenance, and S. all bold enquiries 1647. To blow up the houses to s. the fire 1679. A ..Meeting was suppress at Gallway 1699. Proclamations suppressing the National League 1887. b. Those books..cannot be suppress without the fall of learning MILT. 2. No cold repulses my desires suppress'd 1721. 3. What is told in the fullest..annals bears an infinitely small proportion to what is suppressed MACAULAY. 4. S. thy Sighs PRIOR. 7. Hæmorrhage, which..it was impossible to s. 1854. Hence **Suppre·ssor.**

Suppressal (sŏpre·săl). *rare.* 1651. [f. prec. + -AL.] = SUPPRESSION 1.

Suppressed (sŏpre·st), *ppl. a.* 1620. [f. as prec. + -ED [1].] In various senses of SUPPRESS *v.* **b.** *Bot.* Said of parts normally or typically present, but not found in the particular case in question 1849.

Suppressible (sŏpre·sĭb'l), *a.* 1837. [f. as prec. + -IBLE.] Capable of being suppressed.

Suppression (sŏpre·ʃən). 1528. [ad. L. *suppressio, -onem*, f. *suppress-, supprimere* to SUPPRESS.] **1.** The action of putting down, as by power or authority. **b.** Withholding or withdrawal from publication; prevention or prohibition of the circulation of a book or writing 1700. **2.** The action of keeping secret; refusal to disclose or reveal; also, the leaving of something unexpressed 1728. **3.** Restraint or stifling (of utterance or expression) 1706. 4. *Med.* and *Path.* Stoppage or arrest (of a discharge or secretion) 1601. 5. *Bot.* Absence or non-development of some part or organ normally or typically present 1845.

1. The s. of the last rebellion 1574. The S. of Play-houses 1737. The s. of the Society of Jesus 1784. 2. Unpardonable..suppressions of facts MACAULAY.

Suppressive (sŏpre·siv), *a.* 1778. [See SUPPRESS and -IVE.] Having the quality or effect of suppressing.

†**Supprise,** *v.* Chiefly *Sc.* late ME. [f. AF., OF. *supris-e*, var. of *sur-, sourpris-e* or *sous-pris-e*, pa. pple. of *surprendre* SURPRISE *v. sous-prendre.*] To surprise, esp. with violence.

Suppurate (sʊ·piŭreit), *v.* 1563. [f. L. *suppurat-, suppurare*, f. *sup-* = SUB- 2 + *pur-, pus* PUS.] †1. *trans.* To cause (a sore, etc.) to form or secrete pus; to bring to a head. Also *absol.* to induce suppuration. –1779. 2. *intr.* To form or secrete pus, come to a head 1656.

1. To s. and ripen impostumes 1600. 2. This Disease ..is generally fatal if it suppurates 1732.

Suppuration (sʊpiŭrē¹·ʃən). 1541. [ad. L. *suppuratio, -onem*, f. *suppurare* to SUPPURATE.] The process or condition of suppurating; the formation or secretion of pus; the coming to a head of a boil or other eruption.

Suppurative (sʊ·piŭrĕtiv), *a.* and *sb.* 1541. [ad. mod.L. *suppurativus*, f. *suppurat-* SUPPURATE *v.*; see -IVE.] A. *adj.* 1. Having the property of causing suppuration; inducing the formation of pus. 2. Attended or characterized by suppuration 1794. B. *sb.* A medicine or preparation which promotes suppuration 1568.

†**Supputa·tion.** late ME. [ad. L. *supputatio, -onem*, f. *supputare.*] The action, an act, or a method of calculating or computing; calculation, reckoning –1825. b. *transf.* Estimation –1677. So †**Su·pputate,** *v.* to calculate. 1559.

‖ **Supra** (s¹ū·pră), *adv.*, (*a.*), *prep.* 1440. [L. (see next).] A. *adv.* 1. Above; previously, before (in a book or writing). Also in L. phr. *ut supra* = as above. (abbrev. *sup.*) †2. In addition, further; more –1778. †B. *adj.* Additional, extra –1773. C. *prep.* in phr. *s. protest* [ad. It. *sopra protesto* 'upon protest']: see quot. and PROTEST *sb.* 2. 1809.

After a bill has been protested, it is sometimes accepted by a third party, for the purpose of saving the reputation of a drawer or of an endorser. Such an acceptance is called an acceptance 'Supra Protest'. 1809.

Supra- (s¹ū·pră), *prefix*, repr. L. *supra-* = *supra* (related to *super* and ult. to *sub*), adv. and prep., above, beyond, in addition (to), before in time. Its meanings in English are for the most part parallel to, but in much less vogue than those of SUPER-, except in certain scientific uses.

I. Over, above, higher than; (less commonly) on, upon: in a physical sense. 1. In prepositional relation to the sb. implied in, or constituting, the second element = SUPER I. 1. a. Miscellaneous adjs., chiefly scientific: = SUPER I. 1 a, c. **Supra·a·xillary,** *Bot.* arising above an axil, as a branch or bud. **Su·praco·ralline,** *Geol.* lying immediately above the Coralline Oolite. **Su·pracreta·ceous,** *Geol.* lying above the Cretaceous series, as the Tertiary and more recent formations. **Su·prafolia·ceous, Supra·fo·liar,** *Bot.* situated or arising above (or upon) a leaf. **Supragla·cial,** occurring upon the surface of ice, esp. of a glacier. **Su·pramari·ne,** situated or occurring above the sea. **Supra·me·dial,** lying above the middle (e. g. of a series of rocks). **Supra·tro·pical,** next 'above', i. e. higher in latitude than, the tropical. b. *Anat.* and *Zool.* Extensively used to form adjs. in the sense 'Situated above, or on the dorsal side of (occas. upon the upper surface of) the part or organ denoted by the second element'; = SUPER- I. 1 b. *Supra-acro·mial, -a·ngular* (the angular bone in some vertebrates), *-auri·cular, -bra·nchial, -ci·liary* (= SUPERCILIARY; as *sb.*, *spec.* any of the small scales attached to the eyelids in reptiles, below the supra-oculars), *-clavi·cular, -co·ndyloid* (= above a condyle or condyles of the humerus, etc.), *-co·stal, -cra·nial* (= on the upper surface of the cranium), *-do·rsal, -du·ral* (= above the dura mater), *-hepa·tic* (on the upper surface of the liver), *-neu·ral* (= above a neural axis), *-occi·pital, -o·cular* (= above the ocular region, *spec.* of the small scales in reptiles above the superciliaries; also *sb.*), *-œsopha·geal* (= on the dorsal side of the œsophagus, applied to a nervous ganglion in invertebrates), *-o·rbital* (= above the orbit of the eye; also as *sb.*), *-pe·dal* (= above the 'foot' of a mollusc), *-pu·bic, -ste·rnal, -te·mporal*¹, *-vagi·nal, -ventri·cular.* c. With sb., denoting a part situated above that denoted by the second element. **Supracla·vicle,** *Anat.* and *Zool.* a superior bone of the scapular arch in some fishes, above the clavicle.

2. In advb. relation to the second element: = SUPER- I. 2. **Su·prasori·ferous** *a.*, *Bot.* bearing sori on the upper surface.

3. In adjectival relation to the sb. constituting or implied in the second element: = SUPER- I. 3. a. *Anat.* and *Zool.* = Superior, upper; (a structure) situated above some other, or forming or belonging to the upper part of (that denoted by the second element): chiefly in mod.L. terms, as *supramamma.* **Supraco·mmissure,** a commissure of nerve-fibres above and in front of the pineal body. ‖**Suprasca·pula,** a bone (or cartilage) in the upper or anterior part of the scapular arch, in fishes, and in some batrachians and reptiles. b. *Anat* and *Zool.* Prefixed to adjs., or forming derivative adjs. from sbs. in a (sometimes used ellipt. as sbs.): = Pertaining to or situated on the upper..or the upper part of (what is expressed by the second element), as *suprala·bial* (the upper lip), *supramaxi·llary* (the upper jaw).

II. Above (in various fig. senses); higher in quality, amount, or degree. 1. a. Prefixed to adjs.: = SUPER- II. 1 a, as *supra-Chri·stian, -ra·tional, -temporal*². b. Prefixed to a sb., forming an adj., as *su·pra-state.* 2. Prefixed to a sb. = SUPER- II. 2; as *su·pra-entity.* 3. = Higher, superior, as *supra-consciousness, -world.* 4. Above in degree or amount, beyond, more than (what is expressed by the second element): as *su·pra-centena·rian, supra-o·ptimal.* 5. Before in time; = SUPER- II. 5, as in SUPRALAPSARIAN.

III. In the highest or to a very high degree; very highly, extremely = SUPER- III. 1 a, b, as *supra-censo·rious, -se·nsitive.*

IV. Expressing addition; involving addition or repetition. *Su·pra-compound* (= a compound of a compound, a compound of more than two elements). **Su·pradeco·mpound, Su·pradeco·mposite** *adjs.*, *Bot.* additionally decompound; triply or more than triply compound.

†**Supraca·rgo.** 1667. [ad. Sp. *sobrecargo* (f. *sobre* over + *cargo* CARGO).] = SUPERCARGO –1844.

Supralapsarian (s¹ū:prălæpsē·riăn), *sb.* and *a.* 1633. [f. mod.L. *supralapsarius*, f. *supra* SUPRA- II. 5 + L. *lapsus* LAPSE; see -IAN.] A. *sb.* A name applied to those Calvinists who held the view that, in the divine decrees, the predestination of some to eternal life and of others to eternal death was antecedent to the creation and the fall: opp. to INFRALAPSARIAN. B. *adj.* Of or pertaining to the Supralapsarians or their doctrine; that is a S. 1633. Hence **Su:pralapsa·rianism,** the doctrine of the Supralapsarians. So †**Suprala·psary** *sb.* and *a.*

Supraliminal (s¹ūprăli·minăl), *a.* 1892. [f. SUPRA- I. 1 a + L. *limin-*, LIMEN threshold; after *subliminal.*] *Psych.* Above the limen or threshold of sensation or consciousness; belonging to the ordinary or normal consciousness: opp. to SUBLIMINAL.

Supralunar (s¹ūprăl¹ū·năɹ), *a.* 1719. [See SUPRA- I. 1 a and LUNAR.] = next.

Supralunary (s¹ūprăl¹ū·nări), *a.* 1635. [See SUPRA- I. 1 a and LUNARY.] = SUPERLUNARY.

Supramundane (s¹ūprămʊ·ndein), *a.* 1662. [ad. mod.L. *supramundanus, f. *supra* SUPRA- I. 1 a, II. 1 a + *mundus* world.] = SUPERMUNDANE.

Supranatural (s¹ūprănæ·tiŭrăl, -tʃərăl), *a.* (*sb.*) *rare.* 1857. [See SUPRA- II. 1 a and NATURAL.] = SUPERNATURAL. So **Supra·na·turalism. Suprana·turalist, -istic** *a.* **Su·prana·ture.**

Suprarenal (s¹ūprărī·năl), *a.* (*sb.*) 1828. [ad. mod.L. *suprarenalis*; see SUPRA- I. 1 b and RENAL.] *Anat.* Situated above the kidney; applied to a pair of ductless glands (*s. bodies, capsules, corpuscles, glands*), one immediately above each kidney; also to other structures connected with these. b. *transf.* Of, pertaining to, or affecting the suprarenal capsules 1876. B. *sb.* A suprarenal capsule 1841.

‖**Suprasca·pular,** *a.* 1828. [ad. mod.L. *suprascapularis*; see SUPRA- I. 1 b, 3 b and SCAPULAR *a.*] *Anat.* and *Zool.* Situated above or upon the scapula; belonging to or connected with the upper or anterior part of the scapular arch, or the suprascapula.

Suprascript (s¹ū·prăskript), *a.* 1896. [ad. late L. *suprascriptus*, f. *supra* above + *scriptus* written.] = SUPERSCRIPT *a.*

Supraspinal (s¹ūprăspəi·năl), *a.* 1733. [ad. mod.L. *supraspinalis*; see SUPRA- I. 1 b and SPINAL.] *Anat.* Situated above or upon a (or the) spine. a. Situated above the spine of the scapula; opp. to *infraspinal.* b. = SUPRASPINOUS b. 1835.

‖ **Supraspinatus** (s¹ū:prăspəinē¹·tŏs). 1733. [mod.L., f. L. *supra* SUPRA- I. 1 b + *spina* SPINE; see -ATE².] *Anat.* A muscle arising from the supraspinal fossa of the scapula, and inserted into the greater tuberosity of the humerus, serving to raise and adduct the arm.

Supraspinous (s¹ūprăspəi·nəs) *a.* 1828. [ad. mod.L. *supraspinosus*, f. L. *supra* SUPRA- I. 1 b + *spina* SPINE.] Situated above or upon a spine. a. = SUPRASPINAL a. b. Situated above or upon the spinous processes of the vertebræ 1828.

†**Supravise,** *v. rare.* 1606. [f. med. or mod. L. *supravis-, supravidere*, f. *supra* SUPRA- I. 2 + *videre.*] *trans.* = SUPERVISE *v.* 2. Also *absol.* –1640. So †**Supravi·sion** = SUPERVISION 1 1642–67. †**Supravi·sor** 1566–1694.

Supremacy (s¹ŭpre·măsi). 1547. [f. SUPREME *a.* + -ACY 2.] 1. The condition of being supreme in authority, rank, or power; position of supreme or highest authority or power. 2. Supreme position in achievement, character, or estimation 1589.

1. Man disobeying..sinns Against the high Supremacie of Heav'n MILT. Possibly Rome had not then resolved to derive her S. from St. Peter 1714. Phr. *Act of S.* (or *S. Act*), any of the acts of Parliament in which is laid down the position of the sovereign (*royal* or *regal s.*) as supreme head on earth of the Church of England, or as supreme governor of England in spiritual and temporal matters. *Oath of* (*the King's*) *S.*, the oath in which this is acknowledged. 2. The naval s. of Athens over the rest of the Greek states 1872.

Supreme (s¹ŭprī·m), *a.* and *sb.* 1523. [ad. L. *supremus*, superl. of *superus* that is above, f. *super* above.] A. *adj.* 1. Highest (in literal sense), loftiest, topmost. Now only *poet.* 2. Highest in authority or rank; holding the highest place in authority, government, or power 1532. b. Said of the authority, command, etc. 1539. c. *transf.* and *fig.* 1656. 3. Of the highest quality, degree, or amount 1593. b. Of persons: Highest or greatest in character or achievement 1611. c. Of a point or period of time: Of highest or critical importance 1878. 4. *spec.* Applied to God (or his attributes), as the paramount ruler of the world, or the most exalted being or intelligence; also to the most exalted of heathen deities 1594. 5. Last, final, as belonging to the moment of death. Now only a gallicism. 1606.

1. Day set on Cambria's hills s. MACAULAY. 2. When we say that the legislature is s., we mean, that it is the highest power known to the constitution *Junius Lett.* c. The lower still I fall, onely Supream In miserie MILT. 3. They have..s. endurance in war and in labour EMERSON. b. The S. Quack CARLYLE. c. The s. moment of the battle 1883. 4. Human science is..adverse to the belief in a S. Intelligence 1854.

B. *sb.* †1. A person having supreme authority, rank, or power; sometimes = superior –1807. 2. The highest degree or amount *of* something 1760. 3. As a title of God (or an exalted deity). *The S.*: the Supreme Being, God. 1702.

2. A drainless shower Of light is poesy; 'tis the s. of power KEATS. Hence **Supre·me·ly** *adv.*, **-ness.**

Supremity (s¹ŭpre·miti). Now *rare.* 1538. [ad. late L. *supremitas, -tatem*, f. *supremus* SUPREME; see -ITY.] = SUPREMACY 1, 2.

Sur- (sŏɹ, sŏɪ), *prefix*, a. (O)F. *sur-* (repr. L. *super*), used in various senses of SUPER-, as in SURCHARGE, SURCOAT, SURNAME, SURPASS, SURVIVE. **Sura·ngular** *a.* = SUPRA-*angular.*

‖ **Sura**¹ (su·ra). *India.* 1598. [a. Skr. *surā* spirituous liquor, wine.] The fermented sap of various species of palm, as the wild date, the coco-nut, and the palmyra.

‖ **Sura**² (sū·ra). 1661. [a. Arab. *sūrah.*] A chapter or larger section of the Koran.

†**Suraddi·tion.** 1611. [See SUR- and ADDITION.] An additional name or title. SHAKS.

Surah (s¹ūə·ră). 1881. [perh. repr. a pronunc. of SURAT.] A soft twilled silk fabric used for women's dresses.

Sural (s¹ūə·răl), *a.* 1615. [ad. mod.L. *suralis*, f. *sura* calf of the leg.] *Anat.* Of or pertaining to the calf of the leg; esp. in *s. artery, vein.*

†**Su·rance.** ME. [a. OF. *surance*, f. *sur* SURE *a.*, after ASSURANCE.] = ASSURANCE –1603.

Surat (sĭuræ·t, sīū·ræt, su·ræt). 1643. Name of a town and district in the presidency of Bombay, India, used *attrib.* to designate (*a*) a kind of cotton produced in the neighbourhood, (*b*) coarse cotton goods, usu. uncoloured; also *ellipt.* and as *sb.* (with *pl.*) = *S. cotton*, etc.

Surbase (sɒ̄·ɪ,beᵗs). 1678. [f. SUR- + BASE *sb.*[1]] *Arch.* a. A border or moulding immediately above the base or lower panelling of a wainscotted room. b. A cornice or series of mouldings above the dado of a pedestal, podium, etc. 1815.

Surbased (sɒ̄ɪ,bē·st), *a.* 1763. [repr. F. *surbaissé*, f. *sur-* exceedingly = SUPER- III. 1 b + *baissé* lowered.] Arch. *S. arch*, an arch whose rise is less than half the span. So *s. dome*.

†**Surbate**, *v.* 1590. [Back-formation from †*surbated*, f. OF. *surbatu* (pa. pple. of *surbatre*, f. *sur-* exceedingly = SUPER- III. 1 b + *batre* to beat).] 1. *trans.* To bruise or make sore (the hoofs or feet) with excessive walking; to make (an animal or person) foot-sore –1707. 2. *intr.* for *pass.* To become foot-sore –1725.

†**Surbe·d**, *v.* 1677. [f. SUR- = 'up' + BED *sb.* II. 5 b.] *trans.* To set (a block of stone) edgeways; also, to set (coal) edgeways on a fire –1767.

Surcease (sɒ̄ɪ,sī·s), *sb. arch.* 1586. [f. next.] The action, or an act, of bringing or coming to an end; (a) cessation, stop; *esp.* (a) temporary cessation, suspension or intermission.

If th' Assassination Could trammell vp the Consequence, and catch With his s., Successe SHAKS. All the while he talked without s. LONGF.

Surcease (sɒ̄ɪ,sī·s), *v. arch.* late ME. [f. OF. *sursis*, pa. pple. of *surseoir* to refrain, delay, suspend:—L. *supersedere* to SUPERSEDE.] 1. *intr.* To leave off, stop, cease from some action (finally or temporarily). 2. To come to an end, be discontinued; to cease. late ME. 3. *trans.* To desist from, discontinue; to give up (a course of action, etc.); also, to refrain from 1464. †4. To put a stop to, bring to an end; to stay (legal proceedings) –1695.

1. The great Arch-Angel from his warlike toile Surceas'd MILT. 2. That the cause being taken away, the effect also might s. 1633. 3. [She] had surceased her tyranny 1897.

Surcharge (sɒ̄·ɪ,tʃāɪdʒ), *sb.* 1569. [f. next, or ad. F.; see SUR- and CHARGE *sb.*] 1. = OVERCHARGE *sb.* 2. 1601. b. *Equity.* The act of showing an omission in an account, or a statement showing this 1700. c. A charge made by an auditor upon a public official in respect of an amount improperly paid by him 1879. 2. *Law.* (tr. law-L. *superoneratio.*) The overstocking of a common or forest. *Obs.* exc. *Hist.* 1569. 3. = OVERCHARGE *sb.* 1. 1603. 4. The action of surcharging or condition of being surcharged; overloading 1625. 5. An additional mark printed on the face of a postage-stamp, esp. for the purpose of changing its face value 1881.

3. Any s. of punishment on persons adjudged to penance, so as to shorten their lives BLACKSTONE.

Surcharge (sɒ̄ɪ,tʃā·ɪdʒ), *v.* late ME. [a. OF. *surcharger*; see SUR- and CHARGE *v.*] 1. *trans.* To charge (a person) too much as a price or payment; to overburden with expense, exactions, etc.; to subject to an additional or extra charge or payment. b. *Equity.* To show an omission in (an account); *absol.* to show that the accounting party ought to have charged himself with more than he has 1754. c. To make a charge upon (a public official or body) in respect of an amount improperly paid by him; hence, to disallow (an item of expenditure in an account) 1885. 2. *Law.* To overstock (a common, etc.) by putting more cattle into it than the person has a right to do or than the pasture will sustain. Also *absol. Obs.* exc. *Hist.* 1480. 3. To put an additional or excessive (physical) burden or weight upon; to overload, weigh down 1582. b. With ref. to surfeit of food or drink 1603. c. To charge to excess *with* moisture, a substance in solution, or the like 1611. 4. In non-physical senses: To weigh down, overburden; to bear heavily upon 1581. b. To oppress or overwhelm (*with* emotion, sorrow, or suffering) 1566. c. *pass.* To have an excess of inhabitants, inmates, or members 1572. 5. To print an additional mark on the face of (a postage-stamp), esp. for the purpose of changing its value 1870.

1. c. If any item of expenditure is illegal it is liable to be surcharged by the auditor 1885. 3. Like a fair flower surcharg'd with dew MILT. 4. b. Till his spirit sank, Surcharged, within him WORDSW. Hence **Surcha·rger**, one who surcharges.

Surcingle (sɒ̄·ɪ,sing'l), *sb.* late ME. [a. OF. *sur-*, *so(u)rcengle*, *-sangle*; see SUR- and CINGLE.] 1. A girth for a horse or other animal; *esp.* a large girth passing over a sheet, pack, etc. and keeping it in place on the animal's back. 2. A girdle or belt which confines the cassock. Now *rare.* 1672.

† **Surcloy**, *v.* 1594. [f. SUR- + CLOY *v.*, after *surfeit.*] *trans.* To cloy excessively, surfeit –1620.

Surcoat (sɒ̄·ɪ,kōᵘt). ME. [a. OF. *sur-*, *sor-*, *sircot* (also *-cote*); see SUR- and COAT *sb.*] An outer coat or garment, commonly of rich material, worn by people of rank of both sexes; often worn by armed men over their armour, and having the heraldic arms depicted on it.

A long surcote of pers vpon he hade CHAUCER.

Surculose (sɒ̄·ɪkiŭlōᵘs), *a. rare.* 1845. [ad. L. *surculosus*, f. *surculus* twig; see -OSE.] *Bot.* Producing shoots or suckers.

Surd (sɒ̄ɪd), *a.* and *sb.* 1551. [ad. L. *surdus* deaf, silent, mute, (of sound, etc.) dull, indistinct. The mathematical sense 'irrational' arises from L. *surdus* being used to render Gr. ἄλογος (Euclid bk. x. Def.).] A. *adj.* 1. *Math.* Of a number or quantity (esp. a root): That cannot be expressed in finite terms of ordinary numbers or quantities: = IRRATIONAL A. 3. †2. Deaf (*rare*) –1819. 3. *fig.* †a. Insensate, unintelligent –1676. b. Irrational, stupid 1610. 4. *Phonetics.* Uttered without vibration of the vocal chords; voiceless, 'breathed': opp. to SONANT. Now *rare.* 1767.

2. Such a s. and Earless Generation of Men SIR T. BROWNE.

B. *sb.* 1. *Math.* A surd or irrational number or quantity, esp. root: see A. 1. 1557. 2. *Phonetics.* A speech-sound uttered without 'voice'; a 'breath' consonant: see A. 4. 1789. So **Surd** *v. trans.* to deaden or dull the sound of, as by a mute.

Surdity (sɒ̄·ɪdĭti). 1597. [ad. L. *surditas*, *-atem*, f. *surdus* SURD *a.*; see -ITY.] Deafness.

Sure (ʃūᵊɪ), *a.* and *adv.* ME. [a. OF. *sure*, *seure*:—L. *securus*, f. *se* without + *cura* care, CURE *sb.*[1]] A. *adj.* I. Safe, secure: = SECURE *a.* II. 1, 2, 3. –1718.

The Forrest is not three leagues off, If we recouer that, we are s. enough SHAKS. Phr. *To make* (a person or thing) *s.*, to get into one's possession or power, to secure, = *make s. of*; to put beyond the power of doing harm; (contextually) to kill.

II. Trustworthy, firm, steadfast. 1. That can be depended or relied on; trustworthy, reliable. Now *arch.* or *dial.* ME. b. Applied to agents or their actions, almost = Steady, steadfast, unfaltering 1450. 2. Of material objects (in early use esp. of weapons or armour): Not liable to break or give way, sound, 'trusty'; not liable to be displaced, firm, firmly fixed, immovable. *arch.* late ME. 3. Firmly established or settled; steadfast, stable; not liable to be destroyed or overthrown. *arch.* late ME. †b. Of possessions, etc.: That may be counted on to be received or held –1670. †4. a. Engaged to be married, betrothed, affianced (*to make s.*, to betroth); also, joined in wedlock, married –1665. †b. Engaged or bound by allegiance or devotion (*to* a person or party). –1715.

1. b. My Promise, Lord, is ever s. 1696. 2. He hath made the rounde worlde so s., that it can not be moued COVERDALE *Ps.* xcii[i]. 1. 3. In s. and certayne hope of resurreccion to eternall lyfe *Bk. Com. Prayer.* b. If I thought this would be s. money 1669. *To make s.*: to secure *to* or settle upon a person. 4. a. *Merry W.* v. v. 237. b. *To make s.*, to bind by allegiance, or secure the allegiance of.

III. Subjectively certain; certain in mind; having no doubt; assured, confident. Also, convinced, morally certain. ME.

He..gues'd that it was she, But being mask'd, he was not s. of it SHAKS. Phr. *I'm s. I don't know*, etc. (giving asseverative force to a statement). *Well, I'm s.!* used as an exclam. of surprise. *To be s.* = as one may be sure; for a certainty, certainly, undoubtedly, of course; now colloq. and often concessive = it must be admitted, indeed; also absol. *Well, to be s.!* as an exclam. of surprise.

IV. Objectively certain. 1. a. That one may count on as about to be; certain to come or happen 1565. b. That one may rely on as true; indisputable. Now *rare.* 1470. c. *For s.*: as or for a certainty, undoubtedly. Now *colloq.* 1586. 2. a. Of methods or means: That may be relied on to attain its end or produce the desired or stated result; unfailing, unerring 1530. b. Of signs or signals: Producing or leading to certainty; infallible 1559.

1. a. Luck's a chance, but trouble's s. HOUSMAN. Phr. *S. thing* (orig. *U.S.*): a certainty; often as an ejaculation of strong assent = Yes, indeed! b. He haid suire knawledg quhair the king was 1578. c. *P.R.* II. 35. 2. Phr. *S. card*: see CARD *sb.*[2] 1. *S.-fire* adj., certain to come off, unfailing (*U.S.*).

V. Senses combining III and IV. 1. With *of*: Certain to receive, get, attain, find, have, or keep. Also with gerund, as *s. of getting* = certain to get. ME. 2. With inf. (act. or pass.): Certain to do or to be something. late ME.

1. We are s. of Sea there DE FOE. 2. The..oration ..was s. to be full of pungent criticism 1885.

Phrases. *To make s.* (intr. or with clause). a. *absol.*, or with *of* followed by a noun of action: To make something certain as an end or result; to preclude risk of failure. (*b*) with *of* followed by a sb.: To act so as to be certain of getting or winning. b. With clause or *of*: To make something certain as a fact; to preclude risk of error; to ascertain. (*b*) *loosely.* To feel certain, be convinced. *Be s.* (*to do* something, or *that*.., also mod. colloq. *and*) = take care, don't fail (only in imper. or inf.).

B. *adv.* 1. Securely, safely. *Obs.* or *arch.* late ME. 2. Certainly, with certainty; without risk of failure. Now *dial.* = 'for certain, without fail'. late ME. 3. Qualifying a statement: Assuredly, undoubtedly. Now *poet.*, exc. *dial.* (Irish) and *U.S.* late ME. b. With weakened emphasis, (*a*) concessive = One must admit, admittedly, of course, (*b*) used to guard against overstatement = At any rate, to say the least, or (*c*) = SURELY *adv.* II. b. Now *dial.* 1552. c. Used to emphasize *yes* or *no*; also alone = Certainly. *dial.* 1813. 4. a. In similative phr. (*as*) *s. as* (*death*, '*eggs is eggs*', *fate*, *a gun*, etc.). late ME. b. In phr. *s. enough*: without doubt 1545.

1. 1 *Hen. VI*, v. i. 16. 2. I'll pay you the five dollars a week then, s. 1902. 3. That name speaks pardon, s. KINGSLEY. b. S. no clergyman ever offered so much out of his own purse for the sake of any religion POPE. S. it cannot be! GOLDSM. 4. a. As s. as the year came round 1833. b. The number came up s. enough THACKERAY. Hence **Su·reness**, the quality or condition of being s.

Sure-footed (stress variable), *a.* 1633. [SURE *a.* II. 1 b.] 1. Sure of foot; not liable to slip, stumble, or fall 1707. 2. *fig.* Not liable to make a 'slip' or error; unerring 1633.

Surely (ʃūᵊ·ɪli), *adv.* ME. [f. SURE *a.* + -LY[2].] I. 1. Without danger, risk of injury, loss, or displacement; securely, safely; firmly. *arch.* †b. Steadfastly –1612. 2. With certainty, assurance, or confidence; for certain. *arch.* late ME. 3. Without risk of failure; infallibly. Now chiefly in *slowly but s.* late ME.

1. The Indian must be..s. tied to a post by his hands 1648. b. *Tam. Shr.* IV. ii. 36. 2. As if they s. knew their sovran Lord was by MILT.

II. Certainly, assuredly, undoubtedly. Often as a mere intensive: Truly, verily, indeed ME. b. Used to express a strong belief in the statement, or as implying a readiness to maintain it against imaginary or possible denial: = as may be confidently supposed; as must be the case; may not one be sure that...? 1588.

Alas! they seem but too s. to be here SCOTT. b. This incident is s. an essential part of the story 1870.

†**Su·resby, su·reby.** 1553. [f. SURE *a.* + -BY 2.] An appellation for a person (and hence for a thing) that is 'sure' or may be depended upon –1675.

Surety (ʃūᵊ·ɪti), *sb.* ME. [a. OF. *surte*, *seurte*:—L. *securitatem*, f. *securus* SURE *a.*; see -TY[1].] I. Condition of being (or something that is) sure. †1. Safety, security *from* danger, an enemy, etc. –1620. 2. Accuracy; sureness (*rare*). late ME. 3. †a. = SECURITY I. 3 –1598. b. Certain knowledge. *arch.* 1509. 4. †a. Certainty of an end or result aimed at

-1607. †b. Certainty of a fact or event -1604. c. A certainty, fact. *arch.* 1460.

2. He handled French..with neatness of movement and s. of touch 1892. 4. c. Phr. *For* or *of a s.* = for certain (*arch.*).

II. Means of being sure. 1. A formal engagement entered into; a pledge, bond, guarantee, or security given for the fulfilment of an undertaking. Now superseded by SECURITY. ME. 2. *gen.* Ground of certainty or safety, guarantee. Now *rare.* late ME. 3. A person who undertakes some specific responsibility on behalf of another who remains primarily liable; one who makes himself liable for the default or miscarriage of another, or for the performance of some act on his part (e.g. payment of a debt, appearance in court for trial, etc.); a bail. late ME. b. A sponsor at baptism. *arch.* 1548. c. *fig.* Applied to Christ (after Heb. vii. 22) 1557.

3. When a man becomes s., let him give the security in a distinct form JOWETT. Phr. †*To call to s.*; She call'd the Saints to suretie That [etc.] SHAKS. c. Soon after He that was our S. died COWPER. Hence †**Surety** *v. trans.*, to be s. for. **Su·retyship,** the position or function of a s.

Su:rexcita·tion (sǖr-). 1873. [ad. F.; see SUR- and EXCITATION.] Excessive excitation.

Surf (sǖɹf). 1685. [prob. of Indian origin; cf. obs. *suff*, of the same meaning.] 1. The swell of the sea which breaks upon a shore, esp. a shallow shore. (Now usu. with implication of sense 2.) 2. The mass or line of white foamy water caused by the sea breaking upon a shore or a rock 1757. Hence **Surf** *v.*, to go surf-riding 1917.

Comb.: **s.-bathing,** bathing in the surf, usu. with a board; **-bird,** a small plover-like bird, *Aphriza virgata*, found on the Pacific coast of America; **-board,** a long narrow board on which one rides over a heavy s. to shore; **-boat,** a boat specially constructed for passing through s.; **-clam,** a large clam, esp. *Mactra* (or *Spisula*) *solidissima*, found on the Atlantic coast of the United States; **-coot, -duck,** a N. Amer. species of sea-duck of the genus *Œdemia*, esp. *O. perspicillata*, found sometimes in Great Britain; **-fish,** any one of the numerous species of the family *Embiotocidæ*, abundant on the coast of California; **-man** *U.S.*, a member of the crew of a surf-boat; **-riding,** riding on a s.-board as a sport; **-scoter** = *s.-duck*; **-smelt,** a species of smelt, *Hypomesus olidus*, found on the Pacific coast of the United States; **-whiting,** the silver whiting, *Menticirrus littoralis.*

Surface (sǖ·ɹfės, -ės), *sb.* 1611. [ad. F., f. *sur-* SUR- + *face* FACE *sb.*, after L. *superficies.*] 1. The outermost boundary (or one of the boundaries) of any material body, immediately adjacent to the air or empty space, or to another body. b. *fig.*, usu. denoting that part or aspect of anything which presents itself to a slight or casual mental view; outward appearance; often in such phrases as *on the s.* = superficial(ly) 1725. 2. *Geom.* A magnitude or continuous extent having only two dimensions (length and breadth, without thickness), such as constitutes the boundary of a material body or that between two adjacent portions of space; a superficies 1658. 3. The outermost part of a material body, considered with respect to its form, texture, or extent; *esp.* in art or manufacture, an exterior of a particular form or 'finish' 1698. b. *spec.* The upper boundary or top of ground or soil, exposed to the air (in *Mining*, as dist. from underground workings and shafts); the outer (according to ancient ideas, the upper) boundary of the earth 1612. c. The upper boundary or top of a body of water or other liquid 1625. d. The outside of an animal or plant body, or of any part of it; also, the inner boundary of a hollow or tubular part 1748. 4. An extent or area of material considered as a subject for operations 1662. 5. Superficial area or extent 1640.

1. An optical prism..is a solid having two plane surfaces 1831. c. The wing of a flying machine, whether plane or curved 1903. 3. b. The aged Earth agast.. Shall from the surface to the center shake MILT. c. The smiling s. of the deep COWPER. d. Diseases affecting internal surfaces 1822. 4. To calculate the area of the frictional surfaces 1867.

attrib. and *Comb.*: **s.-car** *U.S.*, a tram-car running on a track level with the s. of the ground, as dist. from an elevated or underground track; **s. condensation,** condensation of steam by a *s.-condenser*; **-condenser,** in a steam-engine, a condenser in which exhaust-steam is condensed by contact with cold metallic surfaces; **-contact,** (*a*) contact of surfaces; (*b*) applied *attrib.* to a system of electric traction in which the current is conveyed to the cars through conductors on the s. of the roadway; **-damage,** damage done to the s. of the ground by mining operations; *pl.* compensation payable for this; **-gauge,** an implement for testing the accuracy of plane surfaces; **-grub,** the larva of various moths, which live just beneath the s. of the soil; a CUTWORM; **-integral** *Math.*, an integral taken over the whole area of a s.; **-plate,** (*a*) a plate or flat bar of iron fixed on the upper s. of a rail on a railway; (*b*) an iron plate for testing the accuracy of a flat s.; **-printing,** printing from a raised s. (as dist. from an incised plate); **s. process,** a process of s.-printing; **-road** *U.S.*, a railway on the s. of the ground, as dist. from an elevated or underground railway; **-tension** *Physics*, the tension of the s.-film of a liquid, due to the cohesion of its particles; **-water,** (*a*) water that collects on the s. of the ground; (*b*) the s. layer of a body of water. b. quasi-*adj.* Pertaining to, existing or occurring on, a surface; acting upon or against a s.; *fig.* superficial.

Surface (sǖ·ɹfės, -ės), *v.* 1778. [f. prec.] 1. *trans.* To give a (particular kind of, esp. a smooth or even) surface to; to cover the surface of (*with* something). 2. *intr.* To mine near the surface 1860. Hence **Su·rfacer.**

Surfaceman (sǖ·ɹfėsmæ̆n, -ės-). 1878. A miner or other labourer who works at the surface, or in the open air; on a railway, a workman who keeps the permanent way in repair.

Surfeit (sǖ·ɹfėt), *sb.* ME. [a. AF., OF. *surfait* excess, surplus:—pop. L. **superfactum*, f. **superficere*, f. *super-* SUPER- III. b + *facere.*] 1. Excess, superfluity; excessive amount or supply *of* something. 2. (An) excessive indulgence, (an) excess. (Now only as fig. use of 3, 3 b.) late ME. 3. Excessive taking *of* food or drink; gluttonous indulgence in eating and drinking ME. b. An excessive indulgence in food or drink that overloads the stomach and disorders the system. late ME. †c. The excessive amount eaten -1700. 4. Sickness or derangement of the system arising from excessive eating or drinking 1513. 5. Disgust arising from excess; nausea, satiety 1644. 6. *Mining* = CHOKE-*damp* 1708.

1. A s. of the precious metals 1847. 3. Fasting is only to avoid surfeit 1684. b. It's possible to have a s. of water as well as wine 1649. 4. He died of a s. caused by intemperance GOLDSM. 5. Phr. *To* (*a*) *s.*, to satiety, *ad nauseam*; He enjoys to a s. these bounties of nature 1855.

Su·rfeit, *a. arch.* 1699. [app. contr. from *surfeited.*] Satiated, surfeited.

Surfeit (sǖ·ɹfėt), *v.* late ME. [f. SURFEIT *sb.*] 1. *trans.* To feed to excess or satiety; to sicken or disorder by overfeeding. Also *absol.* 2. *fig.* or *gen.* To fill or supply to excess; to oppress or disgust with over-abundance of something 1592. 3. *intr.* To eat or drink to excess *of.* (In early use including sensual indulgence in general.) late ME. b. *fig.* To indulge in something to excess; to take one's fill, 'feast', 'revel'. Now *rare* or *Obs.* 1586. 4. To fall sick in consequence of excess. Now *rare* or *Obs.* 1585. b. *fig.* or *gen.* To become disgusted or nauseated by excess of something; to grow sick *of.* Now *rare* or *Obs.* 1605.

1. Pork must be well done, or it is apt to s. MRS. GLASSE. 2. He is weary and surfeited of business PEPYS. 3. Ev'n the wholesomest Meats may be surfeited on BOYLE. b. *Twel. N.* I. i. 2. 4. They are as sicke that surfet with too much, as they that starue with nothing SHAKS. b. So early dost thou s. with the wealth CARY. Hence **Su·rfeiter,** one who surfeits, a glutton.

Surfuse (sɒɹ,fiū·z), *v.* 1883. [f. SUR- + FUSE *v.*] *Physics.* = SUPERFUSE 3. Hence **Surfu·sion** = SUPERFUSION 2.

Surfy (sǖ·ɹfi), *a.* 1814. [f. SURF + -Y [1].] Abounding in, consisting of, or resembling surf.

The countless ranks of s. breakers RUSKIN.

Surge (sǖɹdʒ), *sb.* 1490. [Origin obsc. First used as tr. OF. *sourgeon*, f. *sourge-*, pres. stem of *sourdre*:—L. *surgere* to rise. In senses 3, 4, f. SURGE *v.*] †1. a. A fountain, stream -1567. †b. The source of a river or other water -1588. 2. A high rolling swell of water, esp. on the sea; a large, heavy, or violent wave; a billow 1530. b. Such waves or billows collectively; the rising or driving swell of the sea 1567. c. *fig.* in ref. to feelings, actions, etc.: Impetuous onset or agitated movement 1520. d. *transf.* in ref. to fire, wind, sound, etc.; also to 'rolling' hills or the like 1667. 3. *Naut.*, etc. The slipping back of a rope or chain wound round a capstan, etc.; more gen., a sudden jerk or strain 1748. 4. *Naut.* The part of a capstan or windlass upon which the rope surges 1664.

2. The mountain-billows..s. above s., Burst into chaos with tremendous roar THOMSON. b. Some boats were overset by the S. of the Sea 1702. d. The surges of the warm south-west LOWELL. Hence **Su·rgeful** *a. poet.* (*rare*). **Su·rgeless** *a.* (*rare*).

Surge (sǖɹdʒ), *v.* 1511. [Partly a. OF. *sourge-* (see prec.), or a. early mod.F. *sorgir*, ad. L. *surgere* to rise; partly f. prec. sb.] 1. *intr.* To rise and fall or toss on the waves; to ride (at anchor, or along over the waves). †2. To rise, spring, issue, as a stream from its source, or from underground -1661. 3. To rise in great waves or billows, as the sea; to swell or heave with great force, as a large wave; to move tempestuously 1566. b. *transf.*, of a crowd of people, etc., and *fig.* (chiefly *s. up*), of feelings, thoughts, etc. 4. *trans.* To cause to move in, or as in, swelling waves or billows; to drive with waves 1607. 5. *Naut.* a. *intr.* To slip back accidentally, as a rope or chain round a capstan, windlass, etc.; to slip round without moving onwards, as a wheel 1625. b. *trans.* To let go or slacken suddenly (a rope wound round a capstan, etc.); also with the capstan, etc. as obj. Also *absol.* 1769. c. *intr.* Of a ship: To sweep, pull, or jerk in a certain direction 1839.

1. The..lighter..made faste to the shippe surging at an anker in the Thames 1611. 3. The waues of the sea..surged tempestuouslye 1586. b. From below there surged up the buzz of voices 1891. 5. b. It's blowing the devil himself, and I am afraid to s. 1853.

Surgent (sǖ·ɹdʒĕnt), *a.* 1592. [ad. L. *surgens, -entem*, pr. pple. of *surgere* SURGE *v.*] Rising or swelling in waves, or as a flood or spring; surging.

Surgeon (sǖ·ɹdʒən). ME. [a. AF. *surgien*, contr. f. OF. *serurgien, cirurgien* CHIRURGEON.] 1. One who practises the art of healing by manual operation; a practitioner who treats wounds, fractures, deformities, or disorders by surgical means. Formerly often a medical man, doctor, now *spec.* one who holds a licence or diploma from the Royal College of Surgeons or any other body, legally qualifying him to practise in surgery. b. A medical officer in the army or navy (on board ship = 'ship's doctor') 1591. 2. = *s.-bird, -fish* 1855.

1. b. *S.-general*: see GENERAL *a.*

Comb.: **s.-bird,** the jacana; **-fish,** a fish of the genus *Acanthurus* (cf. DOCTOR *sb.*); **surgeon's knot,** a knot in which the thread is passed twice through the same loop. Hence **Su·rgeoncy,** the office or position of a s. †**Su·rgeonry,** surgery.

Surgery (sǖ·ɹdʒəri). ME. [ad. OF. *surgerie*, contr. f. *ser-, cirurgerie* CHIRURGERY.] 1. The art or practice of treating injuries, deformities, and other disorders by manual operation or instrumental appliances; surgical treatment. 2. The room or office, often in a general practitioner's house, where patients are seen and medicine dispensed 1846.

Surgical (sǖ·ɹdʒikăl), *a.* 1770. [Alteration of CHIRURGICAL after SURGEON, SURGERY.] Pertaining to, dealing with, or employed in surgery or the surgeon's art. b. *Path.* Resulting from surgical treatment 1859.

S. scissors are of many forms 1846. b. Not unfrequently followed by S. fever 1859. Hence **Su·rgically** *adv.*

Surgy (sǖ·ɹdʒi), *a.* 1582. [f. SURGE *sb.* + -Y [1].] Full of or abounding in surge; pertaining to or characteristic of surge; billowy, tempestuous.

The s. murmurs of the lonely sea KEATS.

Suricate (siū̆ə·rikeit). 1781. [a. F. *surikate*, perh. of native African origin.] An animal of the genus *Suricata*, esp. *S. zenik* or *S. tetradactyla*, a viverrine burrowing carnivore of Cape Colony; the meerkat or zenick.

Surinam (siū̆ərinæ·m), name of the country in S. America also called Dutch Guiana; used *attrib.* in specific names of animals, plants, and products, as *S. bunting, grass, medlar*, etc.; S. toad (also *S. water toad*), a large flat toad, the PIPA.

Surly (sǖ·ɹli), *a.* 1572. [Altered spelling of obs. *sirly*, f. SIR *sb.* + -LY [1].] †1. Masterful, imperious; haughty, arrogant, supercilious

-1726. †b. as *adv.* -1693. 2. Churlishly ill-humoured; rude and cross; 'gloomily morose' (J.) 1670. 3. *fig.* †'Imperious', stern and rough; (of soil, etc.) obstinate, refractory, intractable; (of weather, etc.) rough and gloomy, threatening and dismal 1600.

1. Be opposite with a kinsman, s. with seruants SHAKS. b. *Jul. C.* I. iii. 21. 2. Nor s. porter stands in guilty state GOLDSM. A s., grumbling manner DICKENS. 3. In a s. Season EVELYN. Before the s. Clod resists the rake DRYDEN. Hence **Su·rlily** *adv.* **Su·rliness.**

‖ **Surma, soorma** (sūᵊ·ɹmă). *India.* 1819. [Urdū.] A black powder consisting of sulphide of antimony or of lead, used by Indian women for staining the eyebrows and eyelids.

Surmark, var. SIRMARK.

Surmaster (sɔ̄·ɹmāːstəɹ). 1512. [f. SUR- + MASTER *sb.*[1]] The title of the second master at St. Paul's School, London.

Surmisable (sɒɹməi·săb'l), *a.* 1817. [f. SURMISE *v.* + -ABLE.] That may be surmised; conjecturable, supposable.

Surmisal (sɒɹməi·zăl). Now *rare.* 1641. [f. as prec. + -AL.] = next.

Surmise (sɒɹməi·z, sɔ̄·ɹməiz), *sb.* 1451. [a. AF., OF., f. *surmettre*; see next.] †1. *Law.* A formal allegation or information; *spec.* in *Eccl. Law*, the allegation in the libel -1713. †2. An allegation, charge, imputation; *esp.* a false, unfounded, or unproved charge or allegation -1660. 3. (A) suspicion. *Obs.* or merged in 4. -1837. 4. An idea formed in the mind (and, often, expressed) that something may be true, but without certainty, and on very slight evidence, or with no evidence 1594. b. *gen.* 1590. †5. The formation of an idea in the mind; conception, imagination -1637.

4. Surmises and Sleight probabilities will not serue HOOKER. b. This is sure, the rest — s. BROWNING. 5. For so to interpose a little ease, Let our frail thoughts dally with false s. MILT.

Surmise (sɒɹməi·z), *v.* late ME. [f. AF., OF. *surmise*, pa. pple. of *surmettre* to accuse.] †1. *trans.* To put upon some one as a charge or accusation; to charge *on* or *upon*, allege *against* a person; *spec.* in *Law*, to submit as a charge or information, allege formally -1623. †2. To devise, plan, contrive, *esp.* falsely or maliciously -1632. †3. To suppose, imagine (*that* a thing is so); to expect -1725. †b. To conceive, imagine. Also *absol.* -1602. 4. To form a notion that the thing in question may be so, on slight grounds or without proof; to infer conjecturally. Also *absol.* or *intr.* 1700.

4. Whatever the Jewish nation might s. or know concerning a future life 1835. Can I know, who but s.? BROWNING. Hence **Surmi·ser.**

Surmount (sɔ̄ɹmau·nt), *v.* late ME. [a. AF., OF. *surmunter, so(u)rmonter*, ad. med.L. *supermontare*; see SUR-, SUPER I. 2 and MOUNT *v.*] †1. *trans.* To rise above, go beyond, surpass -1776. †b. = SURPASS *v.* 4. -1738. †2. *absol.* or *intr.* To be superior; to excel; to be greater or more numerous -1687. 3. *trans.* To prevail over, get the better of, overcome. late ME. 4. To mount, rise, or ascend above (also *fig.*); also, to surpass in height, overtop. Now *rare.* late ME. †5. *intr.* To mount, rise, ascend (above something); to extend in height; *fig.* to exalt oneself; to arise, spring up -1563. 6. *trans.* To mount upon, get on the top of; *usu.*, to mount and cross to the other side of, climb across, get over; *occas.* to round or weather (a cape); also, to extend over and across 1533. 7. To stand, lie, or be situated above; to rest on the top of; to top, crown; orig. in *Her.*, said of a crest, or of a charge represented as laid upon another so as to extend across and beyond it. Chiefly in pa. pple.: *surmounted by* = having above or on the top. 1610.

3. The attempts of the rival ministers to s. and supplant each other MACAULAY. 4. She the highest height in worth surmounts P. FLETCHER. 6. Simond surmounted the next ridge TYNDALL. 7. The huge square columns that supported the gate were surmounted by the family crest W. IRVING. Hence **Surmou·ntable** *a.* that may be surmounted. **Surmou·nter.**

Surmou·nted, *ppl. a.* 1728. [f. prec. + -ED[1].] *Arch.* Applied to an arch or vault whose rise is greater than half the span: opp. to SURBASED.

Surmullet (sɒɹmʊ·lėt). 1672. [ad. F. *surmulet.*] The red mullet; a name comprising species of *Mullus*, esp. *M. surmuletus*, the Striped S., highly prized as a food-fish, and *M. barbatus*, the Plain S., of a plain red.

Surname (sɔ̄·ɹneᶦm), *sb.* ME. [f. SUR- + NAME *sb.*, after AF., OF. *surnum, sornom.*] 1. A name, title, or epithet added to a person's name or names, esp. one derived from his birthplace or from some quality or achievement; e.g. William *Rufus. Obs.* or *arch.* †b. A second, or an alternative, name or title given to a person, place, edifice, etc. -1656. 2. The name which a person bears in common with the other members of his family, as dist. from his *Christian name*; a family name. late ME. b. *transf.*, esp. = COGNOMEN 1, e.g. Publius Cornelius *Scipio.* late ME.

Surname (sɔ̄·ɹneᶦm), *v.* 1512. [f. prec.] 1. *trans.* To give an additional name, title, or epithet to 1539. 2. To give such-and-such a surname to 1512.

1. Tamberlaine (sirnamed the Scourge of God) 1634. 2. Rockbeare..had..lords sirnamed thereof 1630.

Surnominal (sɒɹnǫ·minăl), *a.* 1875. [f. SURNAME *sb.*, after *name, nominal.*] Of or pertaining to surnames.

Surpass (sɔ̆ɹpɑ·s), *v.* 1555. [ad. F. *surpasser*, f. *sur-* = SUPER- I. 2 + *passer* to PASS.] 1. *trans.* To pass over, overstep (a limit); also, to go beyond (a certain period of time). *Obs.* or *arch.* †2. To surmount (*rare*) -1769. b. To extend above or beyond. Now *rare.* 1601. 3. To go beyond (another) in degree, amount, or quality; to be superior to, to excel 1555. b. To exceed (a specified measure, as weight, speed, etc.). *rare.* 1591. c. To do something that is more or better than (something done or existing) 1592. 4. To be beyond the range, reach, or capacity of; to be too much or too great for 1592.

1. Nor let the Sea S. his bounds MILT. 3. This would s. Common revenge MILT. c. When a Painter would surpasse the life SHAKS. 4. Thy strength they know surpassing human rate MILT. Hence **Surpa·ssable** *a.* capable of being surpassed, exceeded, or excelled.

Surpa·ssing, *ppl. a.* (*adv.*) 1580. [f. prec. + -ING[2].] That surpasses what is ordinary; greatly exceeding or excelling others; of very high degree. b. *adv.* Surpassingly 1598. Hence **Surpa·ssingly** *adv.* in a s. degree; exceedingly, pre-eminently; **-ness** (*rare*).

Surplice (sɔ̄·ɹplis). ME. [a. AF. *surpliz*, OF. *sourpeliz*, ad. med.L. *superpellicium, -eum* (sc. *vestimentum*), neut. of adj. f. *super-* SUPER- I. 1 a + *pellicia* fur garment (f. *pellis* skin).] A loose vestment of white linen having wide sleeves and, in its amplest form, reaching to the feet, worn (usu. over a cassock) by clerics, choristers, and others taking part in church services. (Formerly put on over the fur garments which used to be worn in church as a protection against the cold; hence the name.) b. *transf.* Applied to various ample or enveloping garments. late ME.

Comb.: **s.-fees,** the dues received by an incumbent for the performance of marriages, burials, and other ministerial offices. Hence **Su·rpliced** (-plist) *a.* wearing or vested in a s.

Surplus (sɔ̄·ɹplɒ̆s), *sb.* and *a.* *Pl.* **-uses.** late ME. [a. AF., OF., ad. med.L. *superplus*, f. *super-* SUPER- IV + *plus* more.] A. *sb.* 1. What remains over and above what has been taken or used; an amount remaining in excess. †Also, (a) superabundance. †2. What remains to make up a whole; the remainder, the rest -1759. B. *attrib.* or as *adj.* That is in excess of what is taken, used, or needed 1641.

They now exchange their s. peltry, for blankets, firearms, and brandy ADAM SMITH. The natural law gets rid of s. population 1879.

Surplusage (sɔ̄·ɹplɒ̆sėdʒ). late ME. [ad. med.L. *surplusagium*, f. *surplus*; see prec. and -AGE.] = prec. A. 1, 2. b. An excess or superabundance (*of* words); *spec.* in *Law*, a word, clause, or statement in an indictment or a plea which is not necessary to its adequacy.

Any..cause that generates a surplussage of blood 1607. b. Nor is it surplussage to reiterate the same thought or fact 1851.

Surprisal (sɔ̆ɹprəi·zăl). Now *rare* or *Obs.* 1591. [f. SURPRISE *v.* + -AL 2.] = next 1-4.

The surprizal of these three Cities, Glocester, Bathe, and Cirencester 1611. A sudden s. of the tide called the Eager, where he very narrowly escaped drowning 1647. I do desire some time to consider of it: for it is a great S. 1660.

Surprise (sɔ̆ɹprəi·z), *sb.* 1457. [a. AF., OF. *surprise*, pa. pple. fem., used subst., of *surprendre*; see next.] 1. *Mil.* The (or an) act of assailing or attacking unexpectedly or without warning, or of taking by this means; †formerly also in more general sense, seizure (of a person, a place, or spoil). 2. *gen.* The (or an) act of coming *upon* one unexpectedly, or of taking unawares; a sudden attack. Now *rare* or *Obs.* exc. as in b. 1598. b. *To take by s.*: to come upon unexpectedly, take unawares; hence, to astonish by unexpectedness 1691. †c. An attack of illness; a sudden access *of* emotion -1719. 3. Something that takes one by surprise; anything unexpected or astonishing 1592. b. *spec.* A fancy dish, or an ingredient of a dish, a present, or the like, designed to take one by surprise 1708. 4. The feeling or emotion excited by something unexpected, or for which one is unprepared; the feeling or mental state, akin to astonishment and wonder, caused by an unexpected occurrence or circumstance; †alarm, terror, or perplexity, caused by a sudden attack, calamity, or the like 1608.

1. The s. and combustion of Troy 1635. 2. This is no casual error, no lapse, no sudden s. BURKE. c. In the Heat and Surprize of Passion COLLIER. 3. Egypt ..is the land of surprises 1879. 4. *Per.* III. ii. 17. Circumstances which give a delightful Surprize to the Reader ADDISON.

Comb.: **s. packet,** a sealed packet with contents designed to surprise, sold at a trivial price; also *fig.*; **-party,** (*a*) a body of troops for an unexpected attack; (*b*) *U.S.* and *Colonial*, a party who meet by agreement at a friend's house without invitation, bringing provisions with them.

Surprise (sɔ̆ɹprəi·z), *v.* 1474. [f. AF., OF. *surprise*, pa. pple. of *surprendre*:—med. L. *superprendere*, **præhendere*; see SUR- and PREHEND. From the 14th to the 18th c. *supprise* was a frequent variant of this and prec.] †1. *trans.* To 'take hold of' or affect suddenly or unexpectedly -1720. 2. *Mil.*, etc. To assail or attack suddenly and without warning; †to take or capture in this way 1548. †b. *gen.* To capture, seize; to take possession of by force; to take prisoner -1799. 3. To come upon unexpectedly; to take unawares; to take or catch in the act; hence *fig.*, to find or discover (something) suddenly, to detect 1592. †4. To implicate or ensnare (a person) as by a sudden proposal or disclosure -1702. b. To lead unawares, betray *into* doing something not intended 1696. 5. To affect with the characteristic emotion caused by something unexpected; to excite wonder by being unlooked-for. Often *pass.*, const. *at* or inf.: colloq. *to be surprised*, to be scandalized or shocked. 1655.

1. All on a sudden miserable pain Surpris'd thee MILT. So..temperate, that I have heard he had never been surprised by excesse EVELYN. 2. Kerioth is taken, and the strong holds are surprised *Jer.* xlviii. 41. b. Is the Traitor Cade surpris'd? SHAKS. 3. High instincts before which our mortal Nature Did tremble like a guilty Thing surprised WORDSW. 4. b. If by chance he has been surprized into a short Nap at Sermon ADDISON. 5. I was exceedingly surpriz'd with the Print of a Man's naked Foot on the Shore DE FOE.

Surpri·sing, *ppl. a.* 1580. [-ING[2].] 1. That surprises or takes unawares 1645. 2. Causing surprise or wonder by its unexpectedness 1663. †b. Admirable -1831.

2. One of the lions leaped to a s. height EVELYN. b. The renowned, and surprizing, Archpoet Homer 1580. Hence **Surpri·sing·ly** *adv.*, **-ness.**

†**Su·rquidry, su·rquedry.** ME. [a. OF. *s(o)urcuiderie*, f. *s(o)urcuidier*:—pop. L. **supercogitare*, f. *super-* SUPER- + *cogitare* to COGITATE.] 1. Arrogance, haughty pride, presumption -1825. ¶2. Misused for: Excess, surfeit -1656. So †**Su·rquidy, -edy** -1819.

Surrealism (sɒri·ăliz'm). 1927. [ad. F. *surréalisme*: see SUR-.] A form of art in which an attempt is made to represent and interpret the phenomena of dreams and similar experiences. So **Surre·alist.**

Surrebutter (sɒrĭbɒ·təɹ). 1601. [f. SUR- + REBUTTER.] *Law.* In old common-law pleading, a plaintiff's reply to a defendant's rebutter. Also *transf.*, a further rejoinder. So

Surrebu·t *v. intr.* to reply to a rebutter; *trans.* to repel as by a s. **Surrebu·ttal.**

Surrejoin (sʊrĭdʒoi·n), *v.* 1594. [Back-formation f. next, after *rejoin.*] *Law. intr.* To reply, as a plaintiff, to the defendant's rejoinder; to make a surrejoinder.

Surrejoinder (sɒ̈rĭdʒoi·ndəɹ). 1542. [f. SUR- + REJOINDER.] *Law.* In old common-law pleading, a plaintiff's reply to the defendant's rejoinder. Also *transf.* an answer to a rejoinder or reply (in general).

Surrender (sɒ̈re·ndəɹ), *sb.* 1485. [a. AF., = OF. *surrendre*, inf. used as sb.; see next.] The action or an act of surrendering. **1.** *Law.* **a.** The giving up of an estate to the person who has it in reversion or remainder, so as to merge it in the larger estate; *spec.* the yielding up of a tenancy in a copyhold estate to the lord of the manor for a specified purpose; *transf.* a deed by which such surrender is made 1487. **b.** The giving up of letters patent granting an estate or office 1557. **c.** The giving up by a bankrupt of his property to his creditors or their assignees; also, his due appearance in the bankruptcy court for examination, as formerly required by the bankruptcy acts 1745. **d.** The abandonment of an insurance policy by the party assured on receiving part of the premiums 1755. **2.** The giving up of something (or of oneself) into the possession or power of another who has or is held to have a claim to it; *esp.* (*Mil.*, etc.) of combatants, a town, territory, etc. *to* an enemy or a superior. In wider sense: Giving up, resignation, abandonment. 1485.

1. a. I haue wastfully spente..the s. of my fathers landes 1583. d. *S. value*, the amount payable to an insured person on his surrendering his policy. 2. To speake..About s. vp of Aquitaine SHAKS. With eyes Of conjugal attraction unreprov'd, And meek s. MILT.

Surrender (sɒ̈re·ndəɹ), *v.* 1466. [a. AF., = OF. *surrendre*, f. *sur-* SUR- + *rendre* to RENDER.] **1.** *Law.* **a.** *trans.* To give up (an estate) to one who has it in reversion or remainder; *spec.* to give up (a copyhold estate) to the lord of the manor. Also *absol.* †**b.** To give up (letters patent, tithes) into the hands of the sovereign –1662. **c.** *refl.* or *intr.* of a bankrupt: To appear in the bankruptcy court for examination 1707. **d.** *trans.* Of a bail: To produce (the principal) in court at the appointed time. Also *intr.* or *refl.* of the principal, usu. in phr. *to s. to one's bail.* 1747. **2.** To give up (something) out of one's own possession or power into that of another who has or asserts a claim to it; to yield on demand or compulsion *esp.* (*Mil.*) to give up the possession of (a fortress, town, territory, etc.) to an enemy or assailant 1509. **b.** More widely: To give up, resign, abandon, esp. in favour of or for the sake of another 1509. **3.** *refl.* To give oneself up into the power of another, esp. as a prisoner 1585. **b.** *fig.* To give oneself up *to* some influence, course of action, etc.; to abandon oneself *to* 1713. **4.** *intr.* for *refl.* = 3; chiefly *Mil.* 1560.

2. One..More worthy this place then my selfe, to whom..I would s. it SHAKS. Luxembergh was surrendered to the French EVELYN. To s. up some of those great jurisdictions over the Highlands that were in his family BURNET. 3. b. We must s. ourselves..to our duties 1833. Hence **Surrenderee·** *Law*, the person to whom an estate, etc. is surrendered; correl. to *surrenderor.* **Surre·nderer**, one who surrenders. **Surre·nderor** *Law*, one who surrenders an estate, etc. to another; correl. to *surrenderee.*

Surrendry (sɒ̈re·ndri). Now *rare.* 1547. [f. SURRENDER; see -RY.] = SURRENDER *sb.*

Surreption[1] (sɒ̈re·pʃən). late ME. [ad. L. *surreptio, -onem*, f. *surripere* to seize or take away secretly, (in the Vulgate) to make false suggestions, f. *sur-* = SUB- 24 + *rapere* to seize.] †**1.** Suppression of truth or fact for the purpose of obtaining something, or the action of obtaining something in this way; more gen., fraudulent misrepresentation, or other underhand or stealthy proceeding –1720. **2.** The action of seizing or taking away by stealth; stealing, theft. Now *rare* or *Obs.* 1603.

1. Fame by s. got May stead us for the time, but lasteth not B. JONS. 2. Four soldiers..whose express office was to prevent the s. of the body 1860. *By s.*, by stealth, stealthily.

†**Surreption**[2]. 1502. [ad. patristic L. **surreptio, -onem*, f. *surrepere*, f. *sur-* = SUB- 2, 24 + *repere* to creep.] An unperceived creeping or stealing upon one or into one's mind (of evil thoughts or suggestions); hence, a sudden or surprise attack (of temptation, sin) –1711.

Surreptitious (sʊrepti·ʃəs), *a.* 1443. [f. L. *surreptitius, -icius* = *subrepticius* SUBREPTITIOUS + -OUS.] **1.** Obtained by 'surreption', suppression of the truth, or fraudulent misrepresentation. **2.** Secret and unauthorized; clandestine 1645. **b.** Of a passage or writing: Spurious, forged. Of an edition or copy of a book: Pirated. 1615. **c.** *transf.* Acting by stealth or secretly; stealthy, crafty, sly 1615.

2. O ladies! how many of you have s. milliners' bills? THACKERAY. c. The old man's look..betraying his s. curiosity 1856. Hence **Surrepti·tious-ly** *adv.*, **-ness.**

Surrey (sʊ·ri). *U.S.* 1896. An American four-wheeled two-seated pleasure carriage, the seats being of similar design and facing forwards; a motor-carriage of similar structure.

Surrogate (sʊ·rŏgět), *sb.* (*a.*) 1603. [ad. L. *surrogatus*, assim. f. *subrogatus* SUBROGATE *pa. pple.*] **1.** A person appointed by authority to act in place of another; a deputy 1604. **b.** The deputy of an ecclesiastical judge, of a bishop or bishop's chancellor, esp. one who grants licences to marry without banns 1603. **c.** In New York and some other States: A judge having jurisdiction over the probate of wills and settlement of estates of deceased persons 1816. **2.** *fig.* and *gen.* A person or (usu.) a thing that acts for or takes the place of another; a substitute. Const. *for, of.* 1644. **B.** *attrib.* or *adj.* That is a surrogate; representative 1638. Hence **Su·rrogateship**, the office of a s.

Surrogate (sʊ·rŏgēˈt), *v.* Now *rare* or *Obs.* 1533. [f. L. *surrogat-*, *surrogare*, assim. f. *subrogare* to SUBROGATE.] *trans.* = SUBROGATE *v.* 1–3.

Surrogation (sʊrŏgēˈ·ʃən). Now *rare.* 1533. [ad. med.L. *surrogatio, -onem*, assim. f. *subrogatio* SUBROGATION.] **1.** Appointment of a person to some office in place of another. **2.** *gen.* Substitution 1638.

Surround (sɒ̈rau·nd), *sb.* 1837. [f. next.] **1.** An act of surrounding; *spec.* (*U.S.*) the process of hunting certain wild animals by surrounding them and driving them into a place from which they cannot escape. **2.** A border or edging of a particular material, surrounding the central piece, as of linoleum or felt round a carpet 1893.

Surround (sɒ̈rau·nd), *v.* 1444. [a. AF. *sur(o)under*, OF. *soronder*, *s(o)uronder* to overflow:—late L. *superundare*, f. *super-* SUPER- I. 2 + *undare* to rise in waves, f. *unda* wave.] †**I.** *trans.* To overflow, inundate, flood, submerge –1634. **b.** *intr.* To overflow –1599. **II. 1.** To enclose, encompass, or beset on all sides; to stand, lie, or be situated around; also, to form the entourage of; often *pass.* 1616. **b.** *Mil.* To enclose (a place, or a body of troops) on all sides so as to cut off communication or retreat; to invest 1649. **2.** To go or extend round (an object or body, a room, or the like); to encircle, as a frame, border, etc. 1688. †**3.** To go or travel around; *esp.* to circumnavigate –1825. **4.** To cause to be enclosed or encircled *with* something 1635.

1. If the planet Neptune..be surrounded by an atmosphere TYNDALL. b. Our men surrounded the swamp..and shot at the Indians 1649. 3. When I was driven out to Sea..in my Attempt to s. the Island DE FOE.

Surrounding (sɒ̈rau·ndiŋ), *vbl. sb.* 1449. [-ING[1].] **1.** The action of SURROUND *v. rare* or *Obs.* **2.** *pl.* Those things which surround a person or thing, or in the midst of which he or it (habitually) is; things around (collectively); environment 1861. **3.** A number of persons standing around; entourage 1877.

Surrou·nding, *ppl. a.* 1634. [-ING[2].] That is (or are) around; encompassing, circumjacent.

Surroyal (sɒ̈·roiăl). late ME. [f. SUR- + ROYAL *sb.* 3.] *Venery.* An upper or terminal branch of a stag's antler, above the 'royal'.

†**Sursolid**, *sb.* and *a.* 1557. [app. an etymologizing alteration of †*surdesolid*, ad. mod.L. *surdesolidus*, app. f. *surde* irrationally.] *Math.* **A.** *sb.* The fifth power of a number or quantity; also, an equation of the fifth degree –1817. **B.** *adj.* Of the fifth degree; that is a fifth power or root; involving the fifth power of a quantity –1706.

Surtax (sɒ̈·ɹtæks), *sb.* 1881. [ad. F. *surtaxe*; see SUR- and TAX *sb.*] An additional or extra tax on something already taxed. So **Surta·x** *v. trans.* to charge with a s.

Surtout (sʊɹtū·t, sʊɹtū·). 1686. [a. F., f. *sur* above + *tout* everything.] A man's great-coat or overcoat. (Applied *c* 1870 to a kind of single-breasted frock-coat with pockets cut diagonally in front.) †**b.** A hood (with a mantle), worn by women –1785.

‖**Surturbrand** (sɒ̈·ɹtʊɹbrænd). 1760. [a. G., ad. Icel. *surtarbrandr*, f. *Surtar*, gen. of *Surtr* (related to *svartr* SWART *a.*) name of a fire-giant + *brandr* BRAND *sb.*] A name for lignite as occurring in Iceland.

Surveillance (sʊɹvēˈ·lăns, -vēˈlyăns, ‖ sürvęyaṅs). 1802. [ad. F., f. *surveiller*; see next and -ANCE.] Watch or guard kept over a person, esp. over a suspected person, a prisoner, or the like; often, spying, supervision; less commonly, superintendence.

General Becker—the officer who was charged with the s. of Buonaparte 1815.

Surveillant (sʊɹvēˈ·lănt, -lyănt, ‖sürvęyaṅ), *sb.* 1819. [ad. F., f. *surveiller*, f. *sur-* above, over + *veiller* (:—L. *vigilare*) to watch.] One who exercises surveillance; a person who keeps watch over another or others; a superintendent, e. g. of a prison.

Survei·llant, *a. rare.* 1841. [ad. F. (see prec.).] Exercising surveillance.

Survey (sɒ̈·ɹvēˈ, sɒ̈ɹvēˈ·), *sb.* 1535. [f. next.] The action, or an act, of surveying; the object or result of this. **1.** The act of viewing, examining, or inspecting in detail, esp. for some specific purpose; usu. *spec.* a formal or official inspection of the particulars of something, e. g. of an estate, of a ship or its stores, etc. 1548. **b.** *transf.* A written statement or description embodying the result of such examination 1613. †**2.** Oversight, supervision, superintendence –1654. **3.** The, or an, act of looking at something as a whole, or from a commanding position; a general or comprehensive view or look 1589. **b.** *concr.* That which is thus viewed; a view, prospect, scene 1700. **4.** *fig.* A comprehensive mental view, or (usu.) literary examination, discussion, or description, *of* something 1568. **5.** The process (†or art) of surveying a tract of ground, coast-line, or any part of the earth's surface; the determination of its form, extent, and other particulars, so as to be able to delineate or describe it accurately and in detail; also, a plan or description thus obtained; a body of persons or a department engaged in such work 1610.

1. b. The Domesday S. 1876. 3. He..O'relooks the Neighbours with a wide s. DRYDEN. After a moment's s. of her face DICKENS. 4. A s. of the various possible modes of punishment BENTHAM. 5. *Ordnance S.*: see ORDNANCE 5.

Survey (sɒ̈ɹvēˈ·), *v.* 1467. [AF. *surveier*, *-veir*, = OF. *so(u)rv(e)eir* (pres. stem *sorvey-*):—med.L. *supervidere.*] **1.** *trans.* To examine and ascertain the condition, situation, or value of, formally or officially, e. g. the boundaries, tenure, value, etc. of an estate, a building or structure, accounts, or the like; more widely, to supervise. **2.** To determine the form, extent, and situation of the parts of (a tract of ground, or any portion of the earth's surface) by linear and angular measurements, so as to construct a map, plan, or detailed description of it. Also *absol.* 1550. **3.** To look carefully into or through; to view in detail; to examine, inspect, scrutinize; to explore (a country). Now *rare* or *Obs.* 1592. **4.** To look at from, or as from, a height or commanding position; to take a broad, general, or comprehensive view of; to view or examine in its whole extent; also *fig.* 1586. †**b.** To observe, perceive, see (*rare*) –1615.

1. The Persian Monarch, st., is reported..to be leaking slightly..She will be surveyed 1880. 2. I was out surveying the whole morning 1846. 3. To s. all my letters and actions..with a most rigid and censorious eye 1658. 4. *absol.* Round he surveys, and well might, where he stood So high above the circling Canopie Of Nights extended shade MILT. b. *Macb.*

I. ii. 31. Hence **Survey·able** *a.* (*rare*). **Survey·al** (*rare*), the act of surveying; survey.

Surveyance (sɒ̆ɹvē·ăns). *rare.* late ME. [a. OF. *surve(i)ance, f. *surveeir* to SURVEY.] Survey; superintendence, oversight; inspection.

Surveying (sɒ̆ɹvē·iŋ), *vbl. sb.* 1467. [f. SURVEY *v.* + -ING 1.] The action of SURVEY *v.* 1. The action of viewing or examining in detail (esp. officially). 2. The process or art of making surveys of land 1551. 3. *attrib.* Applied to instruments or appliances used for, and to ships employed in, surveying 1641.

Surveyor (sɒ̆ɹvē·əɹ). 1440. [a. AF., OF. *surve(i)our*, f. *surveeir* to SURVEY; see -OR.] One who surveys. 1. One who has the oversight or superintendence of a person or thing; an overseer, supervisor. 2. One who designs, and superintends the construction of, a building; a practical architect 1460. 3. One whose business it is to survey land, etc.; one who makes surveys, or practises surveying 1551. b. A name for certain caterpillars 1682. c. One whose business it is to inspect and examine land, houses, or other property and to calculate and report upon its actual or prospective value or productiveness for certain purposes 1795. 4. One who views or looks at something; a beholder (*rare*) 1558. b. *fig.* One who takes a mental view of something; an examiner, contemplator 1606. 5. S.-general: a principal or head surveyor; one who has the control of a body of surveyors, or the general oversight of some business. In *U.S.*, a government officer who supervises the surveys of public lands. 1515.

1. *S. of highways, of taxes; borough, district, forest, road, timber s.* 3. *Surveyor's chain* = Gunter's chain: see GUNTER 1. 4. b. To the s. of the history of humanity this is the interest which Pelagius possesses 1905. Hence **Survey·orship**, the office of s.

Surview (sɒ̆ɹviū·), *sb.* late ME. [a. AF., OF. *surveu(e*, f. *surveeir* to SURVEY.] †1. = SURVEY *sb.* 1, 2. -1475. 2. = SURVEY *sb.* 3, 4. Now *rare* or *arch.* 1576.

Surview (sɒ̆ɹviū·), *v.* 1567. [f. prec.] = SURVEY *v.* 4. Now *Obs.* or *arch.*

Survival (sɒ̆ɹvəi·văl). 1598. [f. SURVIVE *v.* + -AL 2.] 1. The continuing to live after some event (*spec.* of the soul after death); remaining alive, living on. 2. *transf.* Continuance after the end or cessation of something else; *spec.* continuance of a custom, observance, etc. after the circumstances in which it originated or which gave significance to it have passed away 1820. 3. (with *a* and *pl.*) Something that continues to exist after the cessation of something else, or of other things of the kind; a surviving remnant; *spec.* applied to a surviving custom, observance, belief, etc. 1716.

1. *S. of the fittest* (Biol.): a phrase used to describe the process of *natural selection* (see SELECTION 3), expressing the fact that those organisms which are best adapted to their environment continue to live and produce offspring, while those of the same or related species which are less adapted perish. Also *transf.* in trivial use. 2. The use of stone knives in certain ceremonies is evidently a case of s. 1870.

Survivance (sɒ̆ɹvəi·văns). 1623. [ad. early mod.F., f. *survivant*; see next and -ANCE.] 1. = prec. 1, 2. Now *rare.* 2. The succession to an estate, office, etc. of a survivor nominated before the death of the existing occupier or holder; the right of such succession in case of survival 1674.

2. His son had the s. of the Stadtholdership BURNET. So †**Survi·vancy.**

†**Survi·vant**, *a.* 1555. [ad. F. *survivant*, pr. pple. of *survivre.*] Surviving -1677.

Survive (sɒ̆ɹvəi·v), *v.* 1473. [a. AF. *survivre*, OF. *so(u)rvivre*:—late L. *supervivere*, f. *super-* SUPER- I. 2 + *vivere* to live.] 1. *intr.* To continue to live after the death of another, or after the end or cessation of some thing or condition or the occurrence of some event (expressed or implied); to remain alive, live on. b. *transf.* To continue to exist after some person, thing, or event; to last on 1593. c. *Law.* Of an estate, etc.: To pass *to* the survivor or survivors of two or more joint-tenants or persons who had a joint interest 1648. 2. *trans.* To continue to live after (a person, an event, point of time, etc.), outlive 1572. b. *transf.* To continue to exist after the death or cessation of (a person, condition, etc.); to outlast 1633.

1. There are vastly more creatures born than can ever s. 1894. b. Yea though I die the scandale will suruiue SHAKS. 2. And, for that dowrie, Ile assure her of Her widdow-hood, be it that she suruiue me, In all my Lands and Leases whatsoeuer SHAKS. If I s. my journey, you shall hear from me again 1717. b. The principal works that have survived him are his magnificent roads EMERSON. Hence **Survi·ver** = SURVIVOR. **Survi·ving** *ppl. a.* that survives.

Survivor (sɒ̆ɹvəi·vəɹ). 1503. [f. prec. + -OR.] 1. One who (or that which) survives or outlives another or others 1624. 2. *spec.* in *Law.* One of two or more designated persons, esp. joint-tenants or other persons having a joint interest, who outlives the other or others; a longer or the longest liver 1503.

1. Of the band of patriots..he was the sole s. 1874.

Survivorship (sɒ̆ɹvəi·vəɹʃip). 1625. [f. prec. + -SHIP.] 1. *Law*, etc. a. The condition of a survivor, or the fact of one person surviving another or others, considered in relation to some right or privilege depending on such survival or the period of it 1697. b. A right depending on survival; e.g. the right of the survivor or survivors of a number of joint-tenants or other persons having a joint interest, to take the whole on the death of the other or others 1625. 2. *gen.* The state or condition of being a survivor; survival 1709.

1. a. *Presumption of s.*, the presumption of the momentary or brief survival of one of a number of persons who have perished by the same calamity, as affecting rights of inheritance.

Surwan (sɒ̆·ɹwan). *India.* 1821. [a. Urdū = Pers. *sārbān*, f. *sār* camel + *-bān* keeper.] A camel-driver.

Susceptibility (sɒ̆septibi·liti). 1644. [f. next; see -ITY.] 1. The quality or condition of being susceptible; capability of receiving, being affected by, or undergoing something. Const. *of* (now rare) or *to.* 2. Without const. a. Capacity for feeling or emotion; disposition or tendency to be emotionally affected; sensibility 1753. Also *pl.* Capacities of emotion, esp. such as may be hurt or offended; sensitive feelings; sensibilities 1846. b. Capacity for receiving mental or moral impressions 1782. c. Capability of being, or disposition to be, physically affected (as a living body, or an inanimate thing); *spec.* the capacity of a substance (e.g. iron) for being magnetized, measured by the ratio of the magnetization to the magnetizing force 1816.

Susceptible (sɒ̆se·ptib'l), *a.* 1605. [ad. med.L. *susceptibilis*, f. *suscept-*; see next and -IBLE.] 1. Capable of taking, receiving, being affected by, or undergoing something. Const. *of* or *to.* 2. Without const. a. Capable of being affected by, or easily moved to, feeling; subject to emotional (or mental) impression; impressionable 1709. b. Subject to some physical affection, as infection, etc. 1875.

1. My little boy..is now s. of instruction EVELYN. Infinitely too s. of criticism 1814. Swift..was exceedingly s. of female influence 1876. S. to smallpox 1887. 2. The sanguine and s. people of France 1849. Hence **Susce·ptibleness** = SUSCEPTIBILITY. **Susce·ptibly** *adv.* in a s. manner.

Susception (sɒ̆se·pʃən). 1610. [ad. L. *susceptio, -onem*, f. *suscept-, suscipere*, f. *sus-* SUB- 25 + *capere* to take.] †1. The action of taking up, or taking upon oneself (in various senses): taking, assumption, reception, acceptance, undertaking -1738. †2. Susceptibility *of*; also *transf.* an attribute of which something is susceptible (*rare*) -1687. 3. The action or capacity of taking something into the mind, or what is so taken; passive mental reception (dist. from *perception*). *rare.* 1756.

Susceptive (sɒ̆se·ptiv), *a.* 1548. [ad. med.L. *susceptivus*, f. *suscept-, suscipere*; see prec. and -IVE.] 1. Having the quality of taking or receiving; in later use *esp.* = SUSCEPTIBLE 2 a. 2. With *of*: = SUSCEPTIBLE 1. 1637. Hence **Susce·ptiveness** = next.

Susceptivity (sɒsepti·viti). 1722. [f. prec. + -ITY.] The quality of being susceptive; susceptibility.

†**Susce·ptor.** 1655. [a. late L., f. *suscept-*; see SUSCEPTION and -OR.] A godfather or sponsor at baptism -1743.

Suscipient (sɒsi·piĕnt), *a.* and *sb.* Now *rare* or *Obs.* 1611. [ad. L. *suscipient-, -ens*, *suscipere*; see SUSCEPTION.] A. *adj.* Receiving, recipient 1649. B. *sb.* One who receives, a recipient (esp. of a sacrament) 1611.

Suscitate (sɒ·sitēit), *v.* Now *rare.* 1528. [f. L. *suscitat-, suscitare*, f. *sus-* = SUB- 25 + *citare* to excite (see CITE *v.*).] *trans.* To stir up, excite (rebellion, a feeling, etc.); to raise (a person) out of inactivity; †to quicken, vivify, animate.

Suscitation (sɒsitē·ʃən). Now *rare.* 1646. [ad. late L. *suscitatio, -onem*; see prec. and -ATION.] The action of suscitating or condition of being suscitated; stirring up excitement; quickening; incitement.

‖**Suslik** (sɒ·slik). 1774. [Russ.] A species of ground squirrel, *Spermophilus citillus* (or other related species), found in Europe and Asia.

Suspect (sɒ̆spe·kt), *sb.*[1] *Obs.* or *arch.* late ME. [ad. L. *suspectus*, in class. L. looking up, a height, esteem, respect, in med.L. suspicion, f. *suspect-, suspicere*; see SUSPECT *v.*] 1. = SUSPICION 1, 1 b. †2. = SUSPICION 3. -1620.

1. You..draw within the compasse of s. Th' vnuiolated honor of your wife SHAKS.

Suspect (sɒ·spekt, sɒ̆spe·kt), *a.* and *sb.*[2] ME. [ad. L. *suspectus, suspicere* (see next).] A. *adj.* Suspected; regarded with suspicion or distrust; that is an object of suspicion; in early use also, exciting or deserving suspicion, suspicious.

I see What I can do or offer is s. MILT. Phr. †*To have* or *hold* (a person or thing) *s.*, to be suspicious of, suspect.

B. *sb.* A suspected person; a suspicious character, esp. one under surveillance as such 1591.

Arrested as a s. under the Coercion Act 1881.

Suspect (sɒ̆spe·kt), *v.* 1483. [f. L. *suspect-, suspicere* to look up, look up to, admire, esteem, to suspect, f. *su(b)-* SUB- 24, 25 + *specere* to look, cogn. w. Skr. *spaç* to see.] 1. *trans.* To imagine something evil, wrong, or undesirable in (a person or thing) on slight or no evidence; to believe or fancy to be guilty or faulty, with insufficient proof or knowledge; to be suspicious of 1500. 2. To imagine or fancy something, esp. something wrong, about (a person or thing) with slight or no proof 1483. 3. To imagine or fancy (something) to be possible or likely; to have a faint notion or inkling of; to surmise 1549. 4. *absol.* or *intr.* To imagine something, esp. some evil, as possible or likely; to have or feel suspicion 1592. 5. *trans.* With ref. to a future possibility: To expect; *esp.* to expect with dread or apprehension. *Obs.* or merged in 3. 1509.

1. The people suspected the gentlemen, the gentlemen feared the people FROUDE. 2. I do s. this Trash To be a party in this Iniury SHAKS. At thirty man suspects himself a fool Knows it at forty YOUNG. Tell me, that you do not really s. me of any hand in her death 1802. 3. You do not..s. half enough the villany of others BURKE. I did not even s. how ill she would be 1866. 4. Too young and simple to s. or to doubt 1849. Hence **Suspe·ctable** *a.* that may or should be suspected; open to suspicion. **Suspe·cted** *ppl. a.*, -ly *adv.*, -ness. **Suspe·cter, Suspe·ctor.**

Suspectful (sɒ̆spe·ktfŭl), *a.* Now *rare* or *Obs.* 1586. [f. SUSPECT *sb.*[1] + -FUL.] = SUSPICIOUS 2.

Alwaies emulous and suspectfull of her 1640. Hence **Suspe·ctfulness**, proneness to suspicion.

†**Suspe·ction.** ME. [a. OF. *s(o)uspection*, ad. L. *suspectio, -onem.*] = SUSPICION -1728.

†**Suspe·ctless**, *a.* 1591. [f. SUSPECT *sb.*[1] + -LESS.] 1. Having no suspicion; unsuspecting -1756. 2. Not liable to suspicion; unsuspected -1637.

Suspend (sɒ̆spe·nd), *v.* ME. [a. OF. *sus-, sospendre* or ad. L. *suspendere*, f. *sus-* SUB- 25 + *pend-* to hang.] I. 1. *trans.* To debar, usu. for a time, from the exercise of a function or enjoyment of a privilege; *esp.* to deprive (temporarily) of one's office. 2. To put a stop to, usu. for a time; *esp.* to bring to a (temporary) stop; to intermit the use or exercise of, put in abeyance ME. b. *intr.* for *pass.* To come to a stop for the time, cease temporarily, intermit (*rare*) 1650. 3. *trans.* To put off to a later time or occasion; to defer, postpone. *Obs.* or merged in other senses. 1577. †b. Of an event, etc.: To defer or delay the accomplishment of -1807. 4. To keep (one's judgement) undetermined;

to refrain from forming (an opinion) or giving (assent) decisively 1553. †b. *absol.* To suspend one's judgement, to be in doubt; hence *occas.* to doubt; also, to apprehend, suspect –1749. †5. a. To keep in a state of mental fixity, attention, or contemplation; to rivet the attention of –1812. b. To keep in suspense, uncertainty, or indecision. *Obs.* or *dial.* 1603. 6. Sc. Law. *trans.* To defer, stay; *intr.* to present a bill of 'suspension' 1650. 7. *Mus.* To prolong (a note of a chord) into the following chord, thus deferring the progression of the part in which it occurs, usu. so as to produce a temporary discord 1853.

1. The king had been obliged to s. the sheriffs in several counties FROUDE. 2. All power of thinking is suspended during a swoon PRIESTLEY. In great danger it was the Senate's business to s. the constitution FROUDE. Phr. *To s. payment*, to cease paying debts or claims on account of financial inability; to become insolvent. 3. Britain will s. her blow till she can strike very hard 1793. 4. The publick voice suspends its decision JOHNSON. 5. a. The harmony..Suspended Hell, and took with ravishment The thronging audience MILT.

II. 1. *trans.* To hang, hang up, by attachment to a support above 1440. b. To attach so as to allow of movement about the point of attachment 1827. 2. *fig.* To cause to depend; *pass.* to depend *on.* Now *rare.* 1608. 3. a. To hold, or cause to be held up, without attachment 1646. b. To hold, or cause to be held, in suspension; to contain in the form of particles diffused through its substance, as a fluid medium; to cause to be so diffused (*in* the medium) 1737.

1. The chandeliers suspended from the roof were of silver 1867. b. An index suspended from a cross-bar 1871. 3. a. That in the Temple of Serapis there was an iron chariot suspended by Loadstones in the ayre SIR T. BROWNE. b. Gold and silver inks are writing fluids in which gold and silver,..are suspended in a state of fine division 1880. Hence **Suspe·nded** *ppl. a.*, as in *s. animation.*

Suspender (sŏspe·ndəɹ). 1524. [f. prec. + -ER [1].] 1. One who or that which suspends. 2. *Sc. Law.* One who presents a bill of suspension 1650. 3. That by which something is suspended; *esp.* one of a pair of straps passing over the shoulders to hold up the trousers: usu. in *pl.* Chiefly *U.S.* 1810. b. A device attached to the top of a stocking or sock to hold it in place 1895. 4. An apparatus or a natural structure supporting something suspended 1839.

Suspense (sŏspe·ns), *sb.* late ME. [a. AF., OF. *suspens* masc., or OF. *suspense* fem. deferring, delay, repr. med.L. *suspensum*, **suspensa*, neut. and fem. of *suspensus, suspendere* to SUSPEND.] †1. (Chiefly *Law.*) *In s.*, not being executed, fulfilled, rendered, paid, or the like; esp. *to put in s.*, to defer the execution, payment, etc. of –1818. †b. Hence *gen.* (*a*) = SUSPENSION 2 –1818. (*b*) Deferment, delay –1718. 2. The state of being suspended or kept undetermined (chiefly *to hold, keep in s.*); hence, the action of suspending one's judgement 1560. 3. A state of mental uncertainty, with expectation of or desire for decision, and usu. some apprehension or anxiety; the condition of waiting, esp. of being kept waiting, for an expected decision, assurance, or issue; less commonly, a state of uncertainty what to do, indecision; esp. in *to keep* (or *hold*) *in s.* 1440. b. Objectively, as an attribute of affairs, etc.: Doubtfulness, uncertainty, undecidedness 1513. c. *attrib.* in **s. account** (*Book-keeping*), an account in which items are temporarily entered until their proper place is determined 1882. 4. = SUSPENSION 7 (*rare*) 1752. †5. = SUSPENSION 8 (*rare*) –1727.

2. Suspence of judgement and exercise of charitie HOOKER. 3. S. in news is torture, speak them out MILT. b. In this s. of his affairs at Rome 1741. Hence **Suspe·nseful** *a.* full of s.

Suspe·nse, *a.* Now *rare* or *Obs.* 1440. [a. OF., or ad. L. *suspensus, suspendere* to SUSPEND.] 1. In a state of mental suspense; doubtful, uncertain. †2. Refraining from hasty decision or action; cautious, deliberate –1684. 3. Hung, hung up, hanging 1440.

1. Expectation held His look suspence, awaiting who appeer'd To second,..The perilous attempt MILT. Hence †**Suspe·nsely** *adv.* (*rare*) cautiously –1625.

Suspensible (sŏspe·nsĭb'l), *a. rare.* 1827. [f. L. *suspens-, suspendere*; see -IBLE.] Capable of being suspended. So **Suspensibi·lity**, capability of being suspended 1794.

Suspension (sŏspe·nʃən). 1528. [ad. late L. *suspensio, -onem*, f. as prec.] The action of suspending or condition of being suspended. 1. The action of debarring or state of being debarred, esp. for a time, *from* a function or privilege; temporary deprivation of one's office or position. 2. The action of stopping or condition of being stopped, esp. for a time; temporary cessation, intermission; temporary abrogation (of a law, rule) 1603. b. Stoppage of payment of debts or claims on account of financial inability or failure 1889. c. *Palæography.* A form of abbreviation consisting in representing a word by its first letter or letters accompanied by the contraction-mark; also, a word abbreviated in this way 1896. 3. The action of putting off to a later time; deferring, postponement 1645. 4. *Sc. Law.* The staying or postponement of the execution of a sentence pending its discussion in the Supreme Court; a judicial order or warrant for such postponement and discussion (in full, *letters of s.*) 1581. 5. The action of keeping any mental action in suspense or abeyance; usu. in phr., e. g. *s. of judgement, opinion* 1568. 6. The action of keeping or state of being kept in suspense (*spec.* in *Rhet.*); doubt, uncertainty (with expectation of decision or issue). Now *rare* or *Obs.* 1635. 7. *Mus.* The action of deferring the progression of a part in harmony by prolonging a note of a chord into the following chord, usu. producing a temporary discord; an instance of this, a discord so produced 1801. 8. The action of hanging something up; the condition of being hung, or of hanging from a support; *occas.* hanging as a form of capital punishment; *spec.* in *Med.* the treatment of disease by suspending the patient 1656. b. *concr.* A support on which something is hung 1833. c. Attachment such as to allow of movement about the point of attachment; 'hanging' as of a vehicle on straps, springs, etc. 1891. 9. The action of holding up or state of being held up without attachment 1646. 10. The condition of being suspended, as particles in a medium; *concr.* a collection of suspended particles. 1707.

1. During your S. you are a Sort of Prisoner at large and do no Duty 1760. 2. *S. of arms* or *hostilities*, an armistice.

Comb.: **s.-bridge**, a bridge in which the roadway is suspended from spans of ropes, chains, or wire cables attached to and extending between supports; **s.-chain**, each of the chains which support a s.-bridge or similar structure; **-pier**, a pier supported in the manner of a s.-bridge.

Suspensive (sŏspe·nsiv), *a.* 1575. [ad. med.L. *suspensivus*, f. *suspens-, suspendere* to SUSPEND; see -IVE.] †1. Liable to be suspended (from office) –1606. 2. Having the power or effect of suspending, deferring, or temporarily stopping the operation of something; involving such suspension 1623. 3. Inclined to suspend one's judgement; undecided in mind; of, pertaining to, characterized by, or in a state of suspense 1614. b. Of a word, phrase, etc.: Expressing or indicating suspense; keeping one in suspense 1711. 4. Characterized by physical suspension (*rare*) 1827.

2. The king..declared his preference of the s. veto 1822. S. Conditions are such as suspend the sale and stay the transfer till something be done 1826. 3. The passion for watching chances—the..s. poise of the mind GEO. ELIOT. Hence **Suspe·nsive-ly** *adv.*, **-ness.**

Suspensor (sŏspe·nsǫɹ). 1746. [a. med.L.; see SUSPENSE and -OR.] †1. *Surg.* a. A kind of catheter. b. A suspensory bandage. 1803. 2. *Bot.* The filament by which the embryo is suspended in the seed of phanerogams; also applied to a similar structure in some cryptogams 1832. 3. *gen.* That by which something is suspended 1874.

Suspensorial (sɒspensŏ·riăl), *a.* 1871. [f. next + -AL 1.] *Anat.* Pertaining to or of the nature of a suspensorium; suspensory.

‖ **Suspensorium** (sɒspensŏ·riŏm). 1758. [mod.L., neut. sing. of med.L. **suspensorius* SUSPENSORY.] 1. *Surg.* A suspensory bag, bandage, etc. 2. *Zool.* The bone, or series of bones, cartilages, etc., by which the lower jaw is suspended from the skull in vertebrates below mammals 1869.

Suspensory (sŏspe·nsŏri), *a.* and *sb.* 1541. [ad. med.L. **suspensorius*, f. L. *suspens-, suspendere*; see SUSPENSE and -ORY.] A. *adj.* I. 1. *Surg.* and *Anat.* Having the function of suspending, i. e. supporting something suspended. II. †1. Marked by or indicating mental suspense; doubtful, lacking certainty or assurance –1682. 2. = SUSPENSIVE 2. 1884.

2. A short s. period during which actions could be brought that [etc.] 1885.

B. *sb. Surg.* and *Anat.* A suspensory bandage, ligament, etc.; a suspensorium 1699.

Sus. per coll. 1560. Abbrev. of L. *suspendatur per collum* 'let him be hanged by the neck', in the entry of a capital sentence in the jailer's books; an entry of this against a person's name; hence as *adj.* = hanged. Hence **Suspercо·llate** *v.* (*joc. nonce-wd.*) to hang.

Suspicable (sɒ·spikăb'l), *a.* Now *rare* or *Obs.* 1614. [ad. late L. *suspicabilis*, f. *suspicari* to suspect, f. *su-* SUB- 24 + *spic-*, as in *suspicere* to SUSPECT.] 1. That may be suspected or mistrusted; open to suspicion. 2. That may be suspected to be so; appearing likely 1651.

2. It is a very s. business that he means no more than empty Space by it 1653.

Suspicion (sŏspi·ʃən). [ME. *suspecioun, -spic-*, a. AF. *suspecioun*, var. OF. *so(u)speçon* :—med.L. *suspectionem*; later infl. by L. *suspicio.*] 1. The action of suspecting; the feeling or state of mind of one who suspects; imagination or conjecture of the existence of something evil or wrong without proof; apprehension of guilt or fault on slight grounds or without clear evidence. b. An instance of this. late ME. †c. *transf.* A ground of suspicion; a suspicious circumstance –1687. 2. *gen.* Imagination *of* something (not necessarily evil) as possible or likely; a slight belief or idea of something, or *that* something is the case; a surmise; a faint notion, an inkling. late ME. †3. Surmise of something future; expectation; *esp.* expectation or apprehension of evil –1700. 4. A slight or faint trace, very small amount, 'hint', 'suggestion' (*of* something) 1809.

1. No one may be discovered to whom s. attaches SCOTT. Phr. *Upon* or *on s.*, on the basis of mere supposition (*of* evil or wrongdoing). *Above s.*, too good or worthy to be suspected of evil. b. Svspicions amongst Thoughts, are like Bats amongst Birds, they euer fly by Twilight BACON. c. *Rom. & Jul.* v. iii. 187. 2. This may beget a little s., that even animals depend not on the climate HUME. 4. A wall-eyed horse, with a s. of spavin 1871.

Suspicious (sŏspi·ʃəs), *a.* ME. [a. AF., OF. *suspecious, suspicious*, ad. L. *suspiciosus*, f. *suspicio* SUSPICION; see -OUS.] 1. Open to, deserving of, or exciting suspicion; that is or should be an object of suspicion; suspected, or to be suspected; of questionable character. †b. with dependent clause, inf., or *of* –1788. 2. Full of, inclined to, or feeling suspicion; disposed to suspect; suspecting; *esp.* disposed to suspect evil, mistrustful. late ME. b. *transf.* Expressing, indicating, or characterized by suspicion 1478.

1. Suspecious was the diffame of this man, Suspect his face, suspect his word also CHAUCER. b. The wife of Richard Cornish was found s. of incontinency 1765. 2. The world is suspitious, And men may think what we imagine not KYD. The king was all his life s. of superior people THACKERAY. b. S. and black ideas 1797. Hence **Suspi·cious-ly** *adv.*, **-ness.**

Suspiration (sɒspirēⁱ·ʃən). Now *rare.* 1485. [ad. L. *suspiratio, -onem*, f. *suspirare* to SUSPIRE.] 1. Sighing; a sigh. 2. (Deep) breathing; breath; a (deep) breath 1602.

2. Nor Customary suites of solemne Blacke, Nor windy s. of forc'd breath SHAKS.

†**Suspi·re**, *sb.* 1450. [a. OF. *s(o)uspir*, ad. L. *suspirium*, f. *suspirare.*] A sigh –1637.

Suspire (sŏspəi°·ɹ), *v.* Now chiefly *poet.* 1450. [ad. L. *suspirare*, f. *su-* SUB- 25 + *spirare* to breathe.] 1. *intr.* To sigh; *rare* in lit. sense; chiefly *fig.* to sigh *for*, yearn *after.* 2. *trans.* To utter with a sigh; to sigh forth. Also, to breathe out. 1549. 3. *intr.* To breathe 1595.

2. A bolt from heaven..suspiring flame BROWNING. 3. *John* III. iv. 80.

Suspirious (sŏspi·riəs), *a.* 1657. [ad. L. *suspiriosus*, f. *suspirium.*] 1. Breathing with difficulty or painfully; chiefly *Path.* 2. Full of sighs, sighing 1751.

Sussex (sɒ·sěks). 1704. The name (OE. *Sūþseaxe* 'South Saxons') of a maritime county in the south-east of England; used attrib. in designations of breeds of cattle, agricultural implements, etc. produced in or peculiar to the county.

†**Sustain**, *sb.* 1653. [f. next.] That which sustains; means of sustenance. MILT.

Sustain (sǫstēⁱ·n), *v.* ME. [a. AF., OF. *sustenir, so(u)stenir*, ad. L. *sustinere*, f. *sus-* SUB-25 + *tenere* to hold, keep.] †1. *trans.* To support the efforts, conduct, or cause of; to succour, support, back up –1802. b. Const. clause or (rarely) acc. and inf.: To support the contention, maintain (that...). Now *rare*. late ME. 2. To uphold the validity or rightfulness of; to support as valid, sound, correct, true, or just. late ME. 3. To keep (a person or community, the mind, spirit, etc.) from failing or giving way ME. 4. To keep in being; to cause to continue in a certain state; to keep or maintain at the proper level or standard; to preserve the status of ME. 5. To keep going, keep up (an action or process); to keep up without intermission; to carry on (a conflict, contest) ME. †6. To support life in; to provide for the life or bodily needs of; to furnish with the necessaries of life; to keep –1700. †b. To supply (a person's need). SHAKS. †7. To provide for the upkeep of (an institution, estate, etc.) –1592. 8. To endure without failing or giving way; to bear up against, withstand. Also †*intr.* ME. 9. To undergo, experience, have to submit to (evil, hardship, or damage; now chiefly with *injury, loss* as obj.); to have inflicted upon one, suffer the infliction of. late ME. b. To bear (a burden, charge). late ME. c. To support (a part or character); to play the part of 1560. †10. To reconcile oneself to doing, to bear to do, something; to tolerate that something should be done –1726. 11. To hold up, bear the weight of; to keep from falling by support from below; often simply, to carry, bear. Now *rare*. ME. b. To be the support of, as in a structure or building; to have resting upon it. late ME. c. To bear, support, withstand (a weight or pressure). late ME. †d. *refl.* and *intr.* To hold oneself upright; also, to be in or maintain a fixed position –1728. 12. To be adequate as a ground or basis for 1828.

1. All the Grenadiers of their army, well sustain'd by a good body of other foot 1711. 2. If..such objection be sustained 1855. 3. That hope alone sustains me 1662. 4. Two Chiefs..Each able to s. a Nations fate DRYDEN. 5. The arts by which he sustains the reader's interest JOWETT. 6. Whatever was created, needs To be sustaind and fed MILT. 8. Capable of sustaining a siege MACAULAY. 9. His Majesty had sustained a signal defeat abroad 1833. b. To s. burdens which would have crushed any other people 1833. 11. In time the sauuage Bull sustaines the yoake KYD. Sustained in the arms of two sisters of her Order 1850. b. Two exceeding great Lyons in red marble, that sustaine two goodly pillars CORYAT. c. The same pressure must s. the same weight 1800. 12. We go beyond what the evidence is able to s. 1866. Hence **Sustai·nable** *a.* †supportable; maintainable. **Sustai·ned** *ppl. a.*, -ly *adv.* **Sustai·ner**, one who or that which sustains. **Sustai·ningly** *adv.*

Sustainment (sǫstēⁱ·nmĕnt). 1450. [f. prec. + -MENT.] 1. Means of support. 2. The action of sustaining; *esp.* maintenance in being or activity, in a certain condition or at a certain level; sustentation 1568.

Sustenance (sɒ·stĭnăns). ME. [a. AF. *sustenaunce*, OF. *sostenance*, f. *sostenir* to SUSTAIN; see -ANCE.] 1. Means of living or subsistence; livelihood. 2. Means of sustaining life; food, victuals ME. b. *gen.* and *fig.* Nourishment 1489. 3. The action of sustaining life by food; the action of supporting with the means of subsistence; the fact or state of being so sustained. late ME. 4. Something that sustains, supports, or upholds; a means or source of support. late ME.

1. She..Gain'd for her own a scanty s. TENNYSON. 2. Water is one part, and that not the least of our S. 1691. b. Lying is thy s., thy food MILT. 3. The quantity..requisite for human s. 1842. 4. The s. of his discourse is Newes OVERBURY.

Sustenant (sɒ·stĭnănt), *a. rare.* 1874. [f. prec.; see -ANT.] Sustaining.

‖**Sustentaculum** (sɒstentæ·kiŭlŏm). *Pl.* -a. 1838. [L., f. *sustentare* SUSTENTATE; see -CULE.] *Anat.* A sustaining or supporting part or organ. Hence **Sustenta·cular** *a.* of the nature of, pertaining to, a s.; supporting.

Su·stentate, *v. Obs.* or *arch. rare.* 1564. [f. L. *sustentat-, sustentare*, f. *sustent-, sustinere* to SUSTAIN; see -ATE 3.] *trans.* To sustain.

Sustentation (sɒstĕntēⁱ·ʃən). late ME. [a. AF., OF. *sustentacion*, ad. L. *sustentatio, -onem*, f. *sustentare*; see prec.] †1. The action of bearing or enduring; endurance –1653. 2. The action of sustaining or the state of being sustained; upkeep, maintenance; support; nourishment. late ME. b. *Phys.* The action of those vital functions or processes (as digestion, etc.) which sustain the life and normal activity of an organism 1877. 3. *concr.* That which sustains life; sustenance, food, nourishment. Also applied to spiritual food. Now *rare*. 1537. 4. The action of holding up or keeping from falling; the condition of being so supported. †Also *concr.*, a support. Now *rare*. late ME.

attrib.: s. **fund**, a fund in the Free Church of Scotland and other bodies for providing adequate support for ministers.

Sustentative (sɒ·stĕntēⁱtiv, sǫste·ntătiv), *a.* 1640. [f. L. *sustentat-* SUSTENTATE; see -IVE.] 1. Having the quality of sustaining. 2. *Phys.* Pertaining to sustentation 1877.

Sustention (sǫste·nʃən). 1868. [f. after *detain, detention*, etc.] 1. The action of sustaining or keeping up a condition, etc.; the holding-on of a musical note. 2. The quality of being sustained in argument or style 1871.

2. A paragraph of fine s. MORLEY.

Sustentive (sǫste·ntiv), *a. rare.* 1662. [f. L. *sustent-, sustinere* to SUSTAIN + -IVE.] Having the quality or property of sustaining.

‖**Susu** (sū·sū). 1801. [Bengali.] The Gangetic dolphin, *Platanista gangetica*.

Susurrant (siusɒ·rănt) *a.* 1791. [ad. L. *susurrant-, susurrare*, f. SUSURRUS.] Whispering, softly murmuring.

Susurration (siusɒrēⁱ·ʃən). late ME. [ad. L. *susurratio, -onem*, f. *susurrare*; see prec. and -ATION.] Whispering; *occas.* a whisper; in early use, malicious whispering, tattle. b. *transf.* A rustling murmur 1640.

b. No sound but the s. of the taller trees 1867.

Susu·rrous, *a. rare.* 1859. [f. L. SUSURRUS + -OUS.] Of the nature of a whisper.

‖**Susurrus** (siusɒ·rŏs). 1831. [L., = humming, muttering, whispering.] A low soft sound as of whispering or muttering; a whisper; a rustling.

The soft s. and sighs of the branches LONGF.

Sutile (siū·til, -əil), *a. rare.* 1682. [ad. L. *sutilis*, f. *sut-, suere* SEW *v.*1] Made or done by stitching or sewing.

Sutler (sɒ·tləɹ). 1590. [a. early mod.Du. *soeteler* small vendor, sutler, f. *soetelen* to befoul, to perform mean duties.] One who follows an army or lives in a garrison town and sells provisions to the soldiers. †b. *gen.* One who furnishes provisions –1793. Hence **Su·tlership**.

Sutlery (sɒ·tləri). 1606. [f. prec. + -Y 3.] 1. The occupation of a sutler; victualling. 2. A sutler's establishment 1636.

‖**Sutra** (sū·tră). 1801. [Skr. *sūtra* thread, string, (hence) rule, f. *siv* SEW *v.*1] In Skr. literature, a short mnemonic rule in grammar, law, or philosophy, requiring expansion by means of a commentary. Also applied to Buddhistic text-books.

Suttee (sɒtī·). 1786. [a. Skr. (Hindī, Urdū) *satī* faithful or virtuous wife, fem. of *sat* good, wise, lit. being, pr. pple. of *as* to be.] 1. A Hindu widow who immolates herself on the funeral pile with her husband's body. 2. The immolation of a Hindu widow in this way. Phr. *to do, perform s.* 1813. Hence **Suttee·ism**, the practice of s.

†**Suttle** (sɒ·t'l), *a.* 1596. [Old var. SUBTLE *a.* retained in techn. use.] *Comm.* Of weight, after tare, or tret, has been deducted –1812

Suttle (sɒ·t'l), *v. Obs.* or *arch.* 1648. [ad. early mod.Du. *soetelen*; see SUTLER.] *intr.* To carry on the business of a sutler. Hence **Su·ttling** *vbl. sb.* in *suttling-house*, a house where food and drink are supplied, esp. to soldiers.

Sutural (siū·tiŭrăl), *a.* 1819. [a. F., or mod.L. *suturalis*; see next and -AL 1.] Of, pertaining or related to, or situated in a suture. Hence **Su·turally** *adv.*

Suture (siū·tiūɹ, -tʃəɹ), *sb.* 1541. [ad. F., or L. *sutura*, f. *sut-, suere* SEW *v.*1; see -URE.] 1. *Surg.* The joining of the lips of a wound, or of the ends of a severed nerve or tendon, by stitches; also, an instance of this; a stitch used for this purpose. b. *gen.* Sewing, stitching; also, a stitch or seam; *fig.* union, now chiefly of the parts or sections of a literary composition, or a point at which it is made 1600. 2. *Anat.* The junction of two bones forming an immovable articulation; the line of such junction; *esp.* any of the serrated articulations of the skull 1578. 3. *Zool.* and *Bot.* The junction, or (more freq.) the line of junction, of contiguous parts, e.g. the line of closure of the valves of a shell, the conflux of the inner margins of elytra 1677. Hence **Su·ture** *v. trans.* to secure with a s. **Su·tured** *ppl. a.* sewn together.

Suzerain (siū·zĕrĕn), *sb.* (*a.*) 1807. [ad. F., app. f. *sus* above, up (:—L. *susum, sursum*), after *souverain*.] A feudal overlord. In recent use, a sovereign or a state having supremacy over another state which possesses its own ruler but cannot act as an independent power. b. *attrib.* or *adj.* as *s. lord, state*. So ‖**Su·zeraine**, a woman who is in the position of a s.

Suzerainty (siū·zĕrĕnti). 1823. [f. prec + -TY.] The position, rank, or power of a suzerain.

‖**Svarabhakti** (svarabʰa·kti). 1880. [Skr., lit. 'sound separation'.] *Philology*. The development of a glide vowel between two consonants, e.g. in OE. *buruh* for *burh*.

‖**Svelte** (svelt). 1817. [F.:—pop. L. **exvellitu-*, pa. pple. of **exvellere*, f. *ex* out + *vellere* to pluck.] Slim, slender, willowy.

Swab (swǫb), *sb.* 1659. [f. SWAB *v.*] 1. A mop made of rope-yarn, etc. used for cleaning and drying the deck, etc. on board ship. b. Anything used for mopping up; any mass or bundle of stuff that takes up moisture, or that, being soaked, is applied to a surface. Also *Med.* a specimen of a morbid secretion, etc., taken with a s. for bacteriological examination. 1787. c. A cylindrical brush or cleaner for cleaning out the bore of a firearm; a soft brush for wetting the mould in founding 1874. d. A naval officer's epaulette (*slang*) 1798. e. A piece of stuff that hangs loose, trails, etc. 1862. 2. †a. = SWABBER 1 1. b. A term of abuse or (now often mild) contempt. 1687.

Swab (swǫb), *v.* 1719. [Back-formation from next.] 1. *trans.* To apply a swab to; to cleanse or wipe with or as with a swab; to mop *up*. Also with *down*. 2. To mop *up* (liquid) with or as with a swab 1745. 3. To souse as with a mop 1762.

1. Swabbing the forward deck 1883.

Swabber 1 (swǫ·bəɹ). 1592. [a. early mod.Du. *zwabber*, f. *zwabben*, f. root **swab-* denoting backward-and-forward motion; see -ER 1.] 1. One of a ship's crew whose business it was to swab the decks, etc.; a petty officer who had charge of the cleaning of the decks. 2. One who behaves like a sailor of low rank; a low or unmannerly fellow: a term of contempt 1609. 3. A mop or swab 1607.

Swabber 2 (swǫ·bəɹ). *Obs.* exc. *Hist.* or *dial.* 1700. [perh. same wd. as prec.] Chiefly *pl.* Certain cards at the game of whist, which entitled the holder to part of the stakes.

Swabbers, the Ace of Hearts, Knave of Clubs, Ace and Duce of Trumps 1700. *Whisk and swabbers*, a form of whist in which these cards were so used.

Swabian (swēⁱ·biăn), *a.* and *sb.* Also **Suabian**. 1785. [f. *Suabia*, latinized f. G. *Schwaben* + -AN.] A. *adj.* Belonging or pertaining to, or native of Swabia (Schwaben), a former German duchy, now a province including Würtemberg and part of Bavaria. B. *sb.* 1. A native of Swabia 1845. 2. A variety of pigeon 1855.

Swad (swǫd), *sb.*1 Now *dial.* 1570. [perh. of Scand. origin; cf. Norw. dial. *svadde* big stout fellow.] 1. A country bumpkin; a loutish or clownish fellow: a common term of abuse. 2. A squat fat person 1606.

Swad (swǫd), *sb.*2 *dial.* 1600. [perh. related to SWATHE *sb.*2] The pod or husk of peas, beans, etc.

Swad (swǫd), *sb.*³ 1828. *U.S.* [Origin obsc.] A thick mass, clump, or bunch; hence, a great quantity (also *pl.*).

Swaddle (swǫ·d'l), *sb.* 1538. [f. next.] **1.** Swaddling-clothes. Now *U.S.* **2.** A bandage. *Obs.* or *arch.* 1569.

Swaddle (swǫ·d'l), *v.* 1491. [ME. *swaþel-* in *swaþelbond* swaddling-band, f. *swath-* (see SWATHE *sb.*²) + -LE.] **1.** *trans.* To bind (an infant) in swaddling-clothes. **b.** *fig.*, now esp. with ref. to the restriction of action of any kind 1539. **2.** To wrap round *with* bandages; to envelop with wrappings; to swathe, bandage 1522. †**3.** To beat soundly. *colloq.* –1822.

1. Ye shal fynde the babe swadled, and layed in a maunger COVERDALE *Luke* ii. 12. **2.** They immediately began to s. me up in my Night-Gown with long Pieces of Linnen ADDISON.

Swaddler (swǫ·dlər). 1747. [f. prec. + -ER¹.] *orig.* A nickname for a Methodist, esp. a Methodist preacher, in Ireland; now, for Protestants in general.

Swaddling (swǫ·dliŋ), *vbl. sb.* 1522. [f. as prec. + -ING¹.] **1.** The action of SWADDLE *v.* **2.** *pl.* (rarely *sing.*) Swaddling-clothes; also, a bandage 1623. †**3.** [After prec.] Methodism; hence, conduct supposed to be characteristic of Methodists –1772.

Swa·ddling, *ppl. a.* 1747. [f. SWADDLER; see -ING².] Of a Methodist character or practice; Protestant; †canting.

Swa·ddling-band, usu. pl. **-bands.** ME. [SWADDLING *vbl. sb.*, BAND *sb.*¹] = next.

Swa·ddling-clothes, *sb. pl.* 1535. [SWADDLING *vbl. sb.*] Clothes consisting of narrow lengths of bandage wrapped round a new-born infant's limbs to prevent free movement. Also *transf.* an infant's long-clothes. Now chiefly *fig.* or *allus.* in ref. to the earliest period of the existence of a person or thing, when movement or action is restricted.

Swa·ddling-clouts, *sb. pl.* 1530. [See SWADDLING *vbl. sb.* and CLOUT *sb.*] = prec.

‖**Swadeshi** (swadē·ʃi). *India.* 1905. [Bengali, lit. = own-country things, i.e. home industries.] The name of a movement in India, originating in Bengal, advocating the boycott of foreign goods. Hence **Swade·shism.**

Swag (swæg), *sb.* 1660. [f. next.] **1.** A swaying or lurching movement. **2.** A heavy fall or drop (*local*) 1700. **3.** A wreath or festoon of flowers, foliage, or fruit fastened up at both ends and hanging down in the middle, used as an ornament; also of a natural festoon 1794. **4.** A thief's plunder or booty; *gen.* a quantity of money or goods unlawfully acquired, gains dishonestly made (*slang*) 1812. **5.** *Austral.* The bundle of personal belongings carried by a traveller in the bush, a tramp, or a miner 1864.

Swag (swæg), *v.* Now chiefly *dial.* 1530. [Cf. Norw. dial. *svagga* and *svaga* to sway.] **1.** *intr.* To move unsteadily or heavily from side to side or up and down; to sway without control. **2.** To sink down; to hang loosely or heavily; to sag. Also with *down.* 1621. **3.** *trans.* To cause to sway uncertainly; to rock about; also, to cause to sink or sag 1530. **4.** [f. prec. 5.] *Austral.* **a.** intr. *To s. it*: to carry one's 'swag' or bundle of effects. **b.** *trans.* To pack up (one's effects) in a 'swag'. 1861.

1. I swagge, as a fatte persons belly swaggeth as he goth PALSGR. *transf.* The front of battle swagged to and fro 1887.

Swa·g be·lly, swag-belly. 1632. [f. prec. + BELLY *sb.*] **1.** (as two words) A pendulous abdomen. **b.** *Path.* A tumour or swelling of the abdomen 1857. **2.** (with hyphen or as one word) A person having a pendulous abdomen 1611. So **Swa·g-be·llied** *a.* having a pendulous paunch 1604.

Swage (swēⁱdʒ), *sb.* late ME. [a. OF. *souage, -aige.*] **1.** An ornamental grooving, moulding, border, or mount on a candlestick, basin, or other vessel. **b.** A circular or semi-circular depression or groove, as on an anvil 1680. **2.** A tool for bending cold metal (or moulding potter's clay) to the required shape; also, a die or stamp for shaping metal on an anvil, in a press, etc. 1812.

2. *attrib.* The holes in the s. block..are used after the manner of heading tools for large objects 1843.

Swage (swēⁱdʒ), *v.*¹ *Obs.* exc. *arch.* or *dial.* ME. [a. AF. *suag(i)er, swag(i)er*, :—pop. L. **suaviare*, f. L. *suavis* sweet.] = ASSUAGE *v.*

Swage (swēⁱdʒ), *v.*² 1831. [f. SWAGE *sb.*] *trans.* To shape or bend by means of a swage.

Swagger (swæ·gər), *sb.*¹ 1725. [f. SWAGGER *v.*] The action of swaggering; external conduct or personal behaviour marked by an air of superiority or defiant or insolent disregard of others. **b.** *transf.* Applied to a mental or intellectual attitude marked by the same characteristics 1819.

After much s., he asked the constable if he knew who he was? 1811.

Swagger (swæ·gər), *sb.*² *Austral.* 1855. [f. SWAG *v.* or *sb.* + -ER¹.] One who carries a swag.

Swagger (swæ·gər), *a. colloq.* or *slang.* 1879. [f. next.] Showily or ostentatiously equipped, etc.; smart or fashionable in style, manner, appearance, or behaviour; 'swell'.

Swagger (swæ·gər), *v.* 1590. [app. f. SWAG *v.* + -ER⁵.] **1.** *intr.* To behave with an air of superiority, in a blustering, insolent, or defiant manner; now *esp.* to walk or carry oneself as if among inferiors, with an obtrusively superior or insolent air. **b.** *spec.* To ta'k blusteringly; to hector; also, to grumble. Now only, to talk boastfully or braggingly. 1597. **c.** *trans.* To influence, force, or constrain by blustering or hectoring language 1605. **2.** *intr.* To sway, lurch 1724.

1. [He] swaggered about like an aide-de-camp at a review R. S. SURTEES. **b.** You may think I s., but as I hope to be saved it is true SHERIDAN. **c.** He would s. the boldest men into a dread of his power SWIFT. Hence **Swa·ggerer.**

Swagger-. 1887. The vb. SWAGGER used in comb.; **s.-cane, -stick** (*colloq.*), an officer's cane or stick; the short cane or stick carried by soldiers when walking out.

Swaggy (swæ·gi), *a. rare.* 1646. [f. SWAG *v.* + -Y¹.] Swagging, pendulous.

Swahili (swahī·li). 1814. [lit. = pertaining to the coasts, f. Arab. *sawāhil*, pl. of *sāhil* coast.] A Bantu people (or one of them) inhabiting Zanzibar and the adjacent coast; also, their language, Kiswahili. **b.** *attrib.* or as *adj.*

Swain (swēⁱn), *sb.* [Early ME. *swein*, a. ON. *sveinn* boy, servant, attendant.] †**1.** A young man attending on a knight; hence, a man of low degree. (Often coupled with *knight.*) –1572. †**2.** A male servant, serving-man; an attendant, follower –1579. †**3.** A man; a youth; a boy –1633. **4.** A country or farm labourer, *freq.* a shepherd; a countryman, rustic. *arch.* 1579. **5.** A country gallant or lover; hence *gen.* a lover, wooer, sweetheart, esp. in pastoral poetry 1585. ¶**6.** A freeholder within the forest 1615.

2. Hym boes serue hym selne that has na swayn CHAUCER. **4.** Those Swains with their Sheephooks in their hands 1663. **5.** Who is Siluia? what is she? That all our Swaines commend her? SHAKS. Hence **Swain** *v. intr.* (with *it*), to play the lover or wooer.

Swainish (swēⁱ·niʃ), *a.* 1642. [f. prec. + -ISH¹.] Resembling or characteristic of a swain or rustic; rustic, boorish.

An ungentle, and s. breast MILT. Hence **Swai·nishness.**

Swale (swēⁱl), *sb.*¹ *local.* ME. [perh. related to SWAG *v.*] Timber, planking.

Swale (swēⁱl), *sb.*² *local*; chiefly *East Anglian.* 1440. [prob. Scand.] Shade; a shady place; also, the cool, the cold.

Swale (swēⁱl), *sb.*³ *local.* 1584. [Origin unkn.] A hollow, low place; *esp. U.S.*, a moist or marshy depression in a tract of land, esp. in the midst of rolling prairie.

Swale, *v.*¹: see SWEAL *v.*

Swale (swēⁱl), *v.*² 1820. [prob. freq. f. SWAY *v.* + -LE.] *intr.* To move or sway up and down or from side to side.

Swallet (swǫ·lėt). *local.* (*s.w.*) 1668. [Obscure formation on SWALLOW *v.*] An underground stream of water such as breaks in upon miners at work. Also (in full *s. hole*), the opening through which a stream disappears underground.

‖**Swallo** (swǫ·lo). 1779. [a. Malay *suwāla.*] = SEA-SLUG 1, TREPANG.

Swallow (swǫ·lōᵘ), *sb.*¹ [Com. Teut.: OE. *swealwe* :—OTeut. **swalwōn-*.] **1.** A bird of the genus *Hirundo*, esp. *H. rustica*, a well-known migratory bird with long pointed wings and forked tail, having a swift curving flight and a twittering cry, building mud-nests on buildings, etc., and popularly regarded as a harbinger of summer. **b.** In allusion to the swift flight of the bird ME. **2.** In extended sense, any bird of the swallow kind, or of the family *Hirundinidæ*, e.g. a martin; often misapplied to the swifts, now reckoned as a distinct and unrelated family (*Cypselidæ*) 1758. **b.** With qualifying words, applied to various species of *Hirundinidæ* or *Cypselidæ*; also, to birds of other families resembling swallows 1552. **3.** †**a.** = SEA-SWALLOW **1.** **b.** A species of moth (*Leiocampa dictæa*). **c.** A variety of domestic pigeon. 1668.

1. Provb. *One s. does not make a summer.* (Cf. Gr. μία χελιδὼν ἔαρ οὐ ποιεῖ). **b.** True Hope is swift, and flyes with Swallowes wings SHAKS. **2. b.** **Cliff S.**, one of several species of the genus *Petrochelidon*, nesting in cliffs. **Window S.**, the house-martin.

attrib. and *Comb.*: **s.-dive,** a form of dive in which the arms are extended to simulate the outline of a gliding s.; so **s.-diving; -fish,** †(*a*) the flying fish; (*b*) the sapphirine gurnard; **-shrike,** a bird of the genus *Artamus* or family *Artamidæ*, found in India and Australia; **swallow's nest,** the nest of a swallow; *transf.* applied to a thing lodged at a height; *spec.* a battery of guns or company of shot placed on a height; **s.-warbler,** an Australian warbler (*Sylvia hirundinacea*), with plumage resembling that of a s.

Swallow (swǫ·lōᵘ), *sb.*² [Late OE. *geswelg*, **swelg*, *swelh* gulf, abyss, f. **swelg-*: *swalg-* (see SWALLOW *v.*).] **1.** A deep hole or opening in the earth; a pit, gulf, abyss. *Obs.* exc. as in b. **b.** *spec.* An opening or cavity, such as are common in limestone formations, through which a stream disappears underground; also called *s.-pit*, SWALLOW-HOLE, and locally SWALLET 1610. **2.** A depth or abyss of water; a yawning gulf; a whirlpool. *Obs.* or *arch.* OE. †**3.** *fig.* A gulf, abyss, sink (of evil) –1624. **4.** The throat, pharynx, or gullet, or these collectively; the gorge. late ME. **b.** *transf.* Capacity of swallowing; appetite for food or drink; voracity; also *fig.* appetite, relish, inclination 1592. **5.** *fig.* 1607. **6.** A single act of swallowing; a gulp 1822. **b.** A quantity (esp. of liquid) swallowed at once; a mouthful swallowed 1861. **7.** The space between the sheave and the shell in a pulley-block, through which the rope runs 1860.

4. b. 'Twill not down, sir! I have no s. for't MASSINGER. **5.** His Ungodly s., in gorging down the Estates of helpless Widows 1688. Even the largest minds have but narrow swallows LOCKE.

Swallow (swǫ·lōᵘ), *v.* [Com. Teut. orig. str. vb.: OE. *swelgan, swealh, swulgon, swolgen*; f. base **swelg-*: *swalg-*.] **1.** *trans.* To take into the stomach through the throat and gullet, as food or drink. In early use and still *poet.* also more gen. = to eat or drink up, devour. **b.** *absol.* or *intr.* To take food, drink, etc. into the stomach through the gullet; to perform the act of deglutition, as in an effort to suppress emotion 1700. **2.** *transf.* To take into itself (physically); to cause to disappear in its interior or depths; to engulf ME. **3.** *fig.* **a.** To make away with, destroy, consume, cause to vanish (as if by devouring or absorption into itself) ME. **b.** To cause to be 'lost' in something; to 'drown', 'absorb', engross, occupy wholly. (Now only with *up.*) ME. **c.** To take in eagerly, 'devour' (with one's ears or mind). late ME. **d.** To take for oneself, or into itself, as a territory or other possession; to absorb, appropriate 1637. **4.** To accept without opposition or protest; to take (an oath, etc.) without demur or lightly 1591. **b.** *esp.* To accept mentally without question or suspicion; to believe unquestioningly 1594. **5.** To put up with, submit to, take patiently (something injurious or irksome) 1611. **6.** To refrain from expressing or uttering; to keep down, repress. Also with *down.* 1642. **7.** To take back, retract, recant 1593.

1. [Salmons] s. the bait with the hook down into the stomach JOHNSON. **2.** The earthquake that swallowed man and beast 1905. **3.** Sloughs That s. common sense TENNYSON. **b.** The necessary Provision for Life swallows the greatest part of their Time LOCKE. **c.** *John* IV. ii. 195. **4.** The former laid a wager that there was no flattery so gross, but his friend would s.

H. WALPOLE. b. He that can s. the raining of Frogs 1691. 5. If I s. this wrong, let her thanke you 1611. 6. Hannibal swallowed his resentment 1878. 7. I have swallow'd my Words already; I have eaten them up 1703.

S. up. a. *lit.* To swallow completely or voraciously; to eat up, devour. b. *transf.* To engulf completely; to cause to disappear utterly in its depths. c. *fig.* To make away with or destroy completely; to cause to disappear utterly. d. To occupy entirely; engross. e. To take completely into itself, or for oneself; to appropriate, absorb. f. To pass over (a distance) rapidly. Hence **Swa·llower,** one who or that which swallows; also *fig.*

Swa·llow-hole. 1661. [f. SWALLOW *v.* or *sb.*[2] + HOLE *sb.*] = SWALLOW *sb.*[2] 1 b.

Swallow-tail, swallowtail (swǫ·lou,tēil). 1545. [f. SWALLOW *sb.*[1] + TAIL *sb.*] 1. A tail like that of a swallow; a forked tail 1703. 2. Applied to various animals having a forked tail. a. A swallow-tailed butterfly 1819. b. A humming-bird of the genus *Eupetomena* 1861. c. A swallow-tailed kite. 3. The white willow (*Salix alba*) 1626. 4. A broad or barbed arrow-head; an arrow with such a head 1545. 5. *Fortif.* An outwork characterized by two projections with a re-entrant angle between them, suggesting a swallow's tail 1688. 6. The cleft two-pointed end of a flag or pennon; also, a swallow-tailed flag 1697. b. The cleft tail-end of a vane 1843. 7. A swallow-tailed coat. *colloq.* 1835. b. The tail or skirt of such a coat (*rare*) 1894. 8. *attrib.* = SWALLOW-TAILED 1596.

7. The boys..exchanged their tweed coats for the regulation swallow-tails 1894.

Swallow-tailed (swǫ·lou,tēild), *a.* 1672. [f. prec. + -ED[2].] Having a tail like that of a swallow, or an end or part like a swallow's tail; also, of the form of a swallow's tail. I. Of natural objects. 1. In names of species or varieties of birds characterized by a long deeply forked tail, as **s. duck,** the long-tailed duck, *Harelda glacialis*; **s. gull,** a rare Amer. gull, *Creagrus furcatus*; **s. hawk, kite,** a widely distributed Amer. kite, *Elanoides forficatus*. 2. a. Having a pair of projecting parts suggesting a swallow's tail, as a seed. b. **S. willow** = prec. 3. 1712. 3. Having each of the hind wings prolonged into a 'tail', the two together suggesting the forked tail of a swallow, as the **s. butterfly** (*Papilio machaon* and other species of *Papilionidæ*) and the **s. moth** (*Urapteryx sambucaria*) 1743. II. Of artificial objects. 1. Of a flag or pennon: Having a cleft end with two tapering points 1697. 2. Dovetailed; also, having a cleft end 1726. 3. Of a coat: Having a pair of pointed or tapering skirts 1835.

Swallowwort (swǫ·louwɒɪt). 1548. [f. SWALLOW *sb.*[1] + WORT[1].] 1. The herb *Vincetoxicum officinale*; from the form of the pods, suggesting a swallow with outspread wings. 2. The Greater Celandine, *Chelidonium majus* 1578.

Swam, pa. t. and obs. pa. pple. of SWIM *v.*

‖ **Swami** (swā·mi). Also **-y.** 1773. [a. Hindi *swāmī* master, prince, a. Skr. *svāmin.*] 1. A Hindu idol. 2. A title for a Hindu religious teacher 1901. 3. *attrib.* **s.-house,** an idol temple or shrine 1778. b. Applied to jewellery ornamented with figures of Hindu deities 1880.

Swamp (swǫmp), *sb.* 1624. [usu. referred to the root which is the base of the several Germanic formations *swamp-, *swamb-, and *swamm-, with the meaning 'sponge' or 'fungus'.] A tract of low-lying ground in which water collects; a piece of wet spongy ground; a marsh or bog. Orig. and in early use only in the N. Amer. colonies, where it denoted a tract of rich soil having a growth of trees and other vegetation, but too moist for cultivation.

The Pontine Marshes, formerly the abode of thirty nations, are now a pestilential s. J. H. NEWMAN. *fig.* In this flat s. of convalescence, left by the ebb of sickness LAMB.

attrib. and *Comb.*: **s.-fever,** malarial fever prevalent in swampy regions; **-hook** (*U.S.*), a large hook used in swamping logs; **-ore** [G. *sumpferz*], bog iron ore. b. In names of animals (mostly birds) inhabiting swamps: **s. blackbird** = MARSH *blackbird*; **s. deer,** *Rucervus duvaucelli*, of India; **s. hare,** *Lepus aquaticus*, of the southern U.S., also called *water-rabbit*; **s. hen,** any of various rails, esp. of the genus *Porphyrio* **s. partridge,** the spruce partridge or Canada grouse; **s. pheasant,** *Centropus phasianus*, of Australia; **s. quail,** any species of the genus *Synœcus*, of Australia; **s. robin,** the cheewink or ground-robin, *Pipilo erythrophthalmus*, of N. America; **s. sparrow,** (*a*) a species of song-sparrow, *Melospiza palustris*, common in U.S. and Canada; (*b*) *Sphenœacus punctatus* of New Zealand, also called *fern-bird*. c. Denoting plants or vegetable products (chiefly of N. America) growing in swamps: **s.-cabbage** = SKUNK-CABBAGE; **s. gum,** various Australasian species of *Eucalyptus*; **s. honeysuckle,** *Rhododendron viscosum* (*Azalea viscosa*); **s. laurel,** the s. sassafras, *Magnolia glauca*; also *Kalmia glauca*; **s. maple,** the red maple, *Acer rubrum*; also several other species, as the silver maple, *A. dasycarpum*, the mountain maple, *A. spicatum*, and the allied *Negundo californicum*; **s. sassafras** = *s. laurel*; **s. willow,** the pussy willow, *Salix discolor*; **s. wood,** the N. Amer. leather-wood, *Dirca palustris*.

Swamp (swǫmp), *v.* 1688. [f. prec.] 1. *pass.* To be entangled or lost in a swamp. *N. Amer. Obs.* or *arch.* 2. orig. *pass.* To be submerged or inundated with water (or other liquid), as a boat, a piece of ground; hence *actively*, to submerge, inundate, or soak with water, etc. 1772. 3. *intr.* in passive sense: To be swamped or submerged; to fill with water and sink, as a boat 1795. 4. *fig.* (*trans.*) To plunge or sink as if in a swamp or in water; to overwhelm with difficulties, or esp. by superior numbers, so as to render inefficient 1818. b. To ruin financially 1864. 5. *U.S.* To make (a logging-road) in a forest or 'swamp' by felling trees, clearing away undergrowth, etc. Also, to haul (logs) to the skidways. 1857.

3. The boats swamped in the current—all were lost SCOTT. 4. The Whigs in 1718 sought to govern the country by 'swamping' the House of Commons DISRAELI. b. Mortgages enough to have swamped any man 1864.

Swa·mp-oak. 1683. 1. In N. America, any of several species of oak growing in swamps. 2. In Australia: Any of various species of *Casuarina*; cf. SHE-OAK 1837.

Swampy (swǫ·mpi), *a.* 1697. [f. SWAMP *sb.* + -Y[1].] Of the nature of a swamp; abounding in swamps; marshy, boggy. b. Of or pertaining to a swamp; found in swamps, as *s. iron ore* = BOG *iron ore*; proceeding from a swamp 1796. Hence **Swa·mpi·ly** *adv.*, **-ness.**

Swan (swǫn), *sb.* [Com. Teut.: OE. *swan*, *swǫn* :—OTeut. *swanoz.] 1. A large web-footed swimming-bird of the genus *Cygnus* or subfamily *Cygninæ* of the family *Anatidæ*, characterized by a long and gracefully curved neck and a majestic motion when swimming; esp. *C. olor*, *gibbus*, or *mansuetus*, with pure white plumage in the adult, black legs and feet, and a red bill surmounted by a black knob, named specifically the Domestic, Mute, or Tame Swan.

Other important species are **Black S.,** *Chenopsis atratus* of Australia, with plumage almost entirely black; **Black-necked S.,** *Cygnus* (*Sthenelides*) *nigricollis* or *melanocoryphus*, with black head and neck, and the rest of the plumage pure white; **Trumpeter S.** (see TRUMPETER); **Whistling S.,** (*a*) of Europe, *C.* (*O.*) *musicus* or *ferus*, also called Wild Swan, †Elk, or Whooper; (*b*) of N. America, *C.* (*O.*) *americanus* or *columbianus*.

b. In classical mythology, the swan was sacred to Apollo and to Venus (occas., as by Shaks., wrongly ascribed to Juno) 1592. 2. *fig.* or *allus.* a. Applied to persons or things, in ref. to the pure white plumage of the swan taken as a type of faultlessness or excellence; often in contrast to *crow* or *goose* ME. b. In allusions to the fabulous belief that the swan sings immediately or shortly before its death. late ME. c. Hence used for: A 'singer', bard, poet 1612. d. *Black s.*, provb. phr. for something extremely rare (or non-existent) 1579. 3. a. A figure of a swan, as in heraldry. late ME. b. *Astron.* The northern constellation *Cygnus* 1551.

2. a. *Rom. & Jul.* I. ii. 92. Provb. phr. *To think one's geese all swans*, to magnify the qualities of one's own possessions. b. *Oth.* V. ii. 247. Like some full-breasted s..fluting a wild carol ere her death TENNYSON. c. *The S. of Avon* = Shakspere. *The Mantuan S.* = Virgil.

Comb.: **s.-dive** *sb. U.S.*, = SWALLOW-*dive*; hence *s.-dive* vb. intr.; **-drop,** (*a*) the knob on a swan's bill; also *transf.*; (*b*) = *s.-shot*; **-quill,** a swan's feather, or a pen made of one; **swan's bath,** (*pseudo-arch.*) the water, the sea; **s.-shot,** a large size of shot, used for shooting swans; **-song,** a song like that fabled to be sung by a dying s.; the last work of a poet or musician, esp. one composed shortly before his death.

Swang, obs. pa. t. of SWING *v.*

Swanherd (swǫ·nhɜ̄ɪd). 1482. [f. SWAN *sb.* + HERD *sb.*[2]] One who tends swans; an official having charge of swans.

Swanimote (swǫ·nimout), **swainmote** (swēⁱ·nmout). *Obs.* exc. *Hist.* ME. [repr. OE. *swāngemōt, lit. meeting of swineherds, f. *swān* swineherd + *gemōt* MOOT *sb.* 2.] A forest assembly held three times a year in accordance with the Forest Charter of 1217, probably orig. to enable the forest officers to superintend the depasturing of pigs in the king's woods in the autumn and the clearance of the forest of cattle and sheep while the deer were fawning in the summer; later, applied vaguely or generically to courts of attachment, inquisitions, etc.

Swank (swæŋk), *sb. slang.* 1854. [See next.] Ostentatious or pretentious behaviour or talk; swagger; pretentiousness.

Swank (swæŋk), *v. slang.* 1809. [orig. a midl. and s.w. dial. wd.] 1. *intr.* To behave ostentatiously, to swagger; also, to pretend by one's behaviour to be something superior to what one is; *gen.* to make pretence. 2. To work hard, to 'swot' 1890.

Swa·nky, *a.* 1842. [f. SWANK *sb.* or *v.* + -Y[1].] Swaggering; pretentiously grand.

Swa·n-like, *a.* (*adv.*) 1591. [f. SWAN *sb.* + -LIKE.] A. *adj.* Like a swan or that of a swan. b. *esp.* in ref. to the fabled singing of the swan just before its death 1592. B. *adv.* Like or in the manner of a swan 1635.

A. b. If he loose, he makes a S. end, Fading in musique SHAKS.

Swa·n-mark. 1560. [MARK *sb.*[1] III. 2.] An official mark of ownership cut on the beak of a swan, on the occasion of SWAN-UPPING.

Swa·n-neck. Also **swan's neck.** 1686. 1. A neck like that of a swan; a long, slender (white) neck 1837. 2. Name for various structural parts or contrivances having a curved cylindrical form like a swan's neck 1686. 3. *attrib.* Of a curved form like a swan's neck 1844.

Swanner (swǫ·nəɪ). 1524. Clipped form of SWANHERD.

Swannery (swǫ·nəri). 1754. [f. as prec.; see -ERY.] A place where swans are kept and reared.

Swannish (swǫ·niʃ), *a. rare.* 1586. [f. SWAN *sb.* + -ISH.] Swan-like.

Swanny (swǫ·ni), *a.* 1567. [f. SWAN *sb.* + -Y[1].] 1. Full of or abounding in swans (*rare*). 2. Of, pertaining to, or resembling that of, a swan 1598.

2. The s. glossiness of a neck late so stately 1748.

‖ **Swan-pan** (swæ·n pæ·n). 1736. [Chinese, lit. reckoning-board.] The Chinese abacus.

Swan's down, swansdown (swǫ·nzdaun). 1606. [Cf. G. *schwanendaune.*] 1. The down or soft under-plumage of the swan, used for dress-trimmings, powder-puffs, etc. 2. a. A soft thick close woollen cloth. b. A thick cotton cloth with a nap on one side, also called *Canton* or *cotton flannel*. 1801.

Swanskin (swǫ·nskin). Also **swan's-skin.** 1610. [Cf. Sw. *svanskinn.*] 1. The skin of a swan (with the feathers on); *transf.* a soft or delicate skin. 2. A fine thick kind of flannel 1694. 3. *attrib.* Made or consisting of swan-skin 1610.

Swa·n-u·pping. 1810. The action or practice of 'upping' or taking up swans and marking them with nicks on the beak in token of being owned by the Crown or some corporation. So **Swa·n-u·pper,** an official who takes up and marks swans 1557.

Swap, swop (swǫp), *sb.* late ME. [f. next.] 1. An act of 'swapping' or striking; a stroke, blow. *Obs.* exc. *dial.* 2. An act, or the action, of 'swapping' or exchanging; (an) exchange. *slang* or *colloq.* 1625.

2. Phr. *To get* (or *have*) *the s.*, to be dismissed from employment (*slang*).

Swap, swop (swǫp), *v.* ME. [prob. echoic, signifying a smart resounding blow.] I. †1. *trans.* To strike, hit, smite -1582. b. To strike or smite *off*, *in two*, etc. *Obs.* exc. *arch.* ME. 2. *intr.* To strike, smite, deal a blow or blows. Now *rare* or *Obs.* late ME. 3. *trans.* To move (something) quickly or briskly, esp. so as to impinge on something else; to fling, cast, throw (*down*, etc.) forcibly; to bang (a door) *to. Obs.* exc. *dial.* ME. 4. *intr.* To move with haste or violence, esp. so as to strike or impinge upon something; to sink *into* a swoon. Now *rare* or *Obs.* late ME.

1. b. Who so wol nat sacrifise Swape of his heed CHAUCER. 4. With chilling fear, the Ladies swapped downe, In deadly sownd 1592.

II. †1. *trans.* To strike (a bargain) -1692. 2. To give or dispose of in exchange *for* something else; to exchange (a thing) *with* another person. Chiefly, now only, *slang* or *colloq.* 1594. b. *absol.* To exchange, make an exchange 1778. 3. *transf.* in various slang uses. a. To dismiss or be dismissed from employment. b. To cheat. c. To change one's clothes. 1862.

2. He bought and sold and swopped horses 1882. As they sat in the tavern, swapping stories 1891.

Swap, swop, *adv.* (*int.*) Now *dial.* 1672. [The stem of SWAP *v.*] At a blow; suddenly and forcibly.

‖**Swaraj** (swarā·dʒ). 1906. [Skr. = self-ruling.] Home rule or self-government as the aim of Indian nationals. Hence **Swara·jist,** an advocate of swaraj.

Sward (swǭɹd), *sb.* [OE. *sweard*, f. Teut. stem **sward-, swarð-*: *swarþ-* (SWARTH *sb.*[1]); ult. origin unkn.] 1. The skin of the body; *esp.* (now *dial.*) the rind of pork or bacon. 2. †a. Usu. with defining phr. *of the earth*, etc.: The surface or upper layer of ground usu. covered with herbage -1626. b. The surface of soil covered with grass or other herbage; turf, GREENSWARD 1508. (*b*) A growth of grass; a stretch of greensward 1733.

2. b. The grassy s. 1866. It has become the fashion ..to break up the s. of the downs 1879.

Comb.: **s.-cutter,** an implement for cutting a tough s. in preparation for ploughing.

Sward (swǭɹd), *v.* 1610. [f. prec.] 1. *intr.* To form a sward; to become covered with grassy turf. 2. *trans.* To cover with a sward; chiefly *pass.* to be covered with grass or herbage 1610. So **Swa·rded** *ppl. a.* covered with a sward or grassy turf; turfed 1513.

Swardy (swǭ·ɹdi), *a.* 1639. [f. SWARD *sb.* + -Y[1].] Covered with sward, swarded, turfy.

Sware, arch. pa. t. of SWEAR.

Swarf (swarf), *sb.*[1] *Sc.* 1470. [Cf. ON. *svarfa* to upset.] A swoon, a fainting-fit; a state of faintness or insensibility. So **Swarf** *v.* to faint, cause to faint 1513.

Swarf (swǭɹf, swāɹf), *sb.*[2] 1566. [repr. OE. *ʒeswearf, ʒesweorf, ʒeswyrf* filings, or a. ON. *svarf* file-dust.] The wet or greasy grit abraded from a grindstone or axle; the filings or shavings of iron or steel.

Swarm (swǭɹm), *sb.* [OE. *swearm* :— OTeut. **swarmoz*, of doubtful origin.] 1. A body of bees which at a particular season leave the hive or main stock, gather in a compact mass or cluster, and fly off together in search of a new dwelling-place, under the guidance of a queen, (or are transferred at once to a new hive). b. *allus.* of 1659. 2. A very large or dense body or collection; a crowd, throng, multitude. (Often *contempt.*) late ME.

1. A s. of bees in May Is worth a load of hay 1864. b. A new s. of Danes came over this year [875] HUME. 2. England in swarms did into Holland throng FULLER. A s. of fire-flies 1842. Swarms of dust 1890.

Comb.: **s.-cell** (*Biol.*) = *s.-spore*; **-movement,** the movement of s.-spores in 'swarming'; **-spore** (*Biol.*), (*a*) a motile spore in certain Algæ, Fungi, and Protozoa, a zoospore; (*b*) the free-swimming embryo or gemmule of freshwater sponges.

Swarm (swǭɹm), *v.*[1] late ME. [f. prec.] 1. *intr.* Of bees: To gather in a compact cluster and leave the hive in a body to found a new colony. Also with *off*. b. *allus.* 1609. c. *Biol.* Of certain spores or reproductive bodies: To escape from the parent organism in a swarm, with characteristic movement; to move or swim about in a swarm, as zoospores ('swarm-spores') do in the cell just before escaping, and in the water after escaping 1864. 2. To come together in a swarm or dense cloud; to crowd, throng; also, to go or move along in a crowd. late ME. 3. To occur or exist in swarms or multitudes; to be densely crowded; to be very numerous, abound excessively. (Often in reproach or contempt.) late ME. 4. *To s. with*: to be crowded or thronged with; to contain swarms or great numbers of. Now only in material sense. 1548. 5. *trans.* To fill or beset as, or with, a swarm; to crowd densely, throng. Chiefly *pass.* 1555.

1. Take heede to thy bees, that are readie to swarme 1573. 2. The crowd were swarming now..about the garden rails TENNYSON. The ideas swarming in men's minds JOWETT. 3. Native doctors s. in Mongolia 1883. 4. The river swarmed with alligators 1893. 5. Your house is so swarmed with rats 1810.

Swarm (swǭɹm), *v.*[2] 1550. [Origin obsc.] 1. *intr.* To climb *up* a pole, tree, or the like, by clasping it with the arms and legs alternately. b. *transf.* To climb a steep ascent or the like by clinging with the hands and knees, or in some way compared to this 1681. 2. *trans.* with the pole, etc. as obj. 1668.

1. b. People..swarming up a difficult ascent 1851.

Swart (swǭɹt), *a.* (*sb.*) Now only *rhet.*, *poet.*, or *dial.* [Com. Teut.: OE. *sweart*, f. root *swart-* 'dark'. Superseded in ordinary English use by *black*.] 1. Dark in colour; black or blackish; dusky, swarthy. b. *spec.* Of the skin or complexion, or of persons in respect of these. late ME. c. quasi-*adv.* qualifying an adj. of colour. late ME. 2. *transf.* Producing swarthiness of complexion 1637. b. Dressed in black 1688. 3. *fig.* a. 'Black', wicked, iniquitous. b. Baleful, malignant. OE.

1. Hitt shalle be swarte as any pyche 1430. b. Their countenance s. with the sunbeams SCOTT. c. Swart-green and gold BROWNING. 2. Ye valleys low ..On whose fresh lap the s. Star sparely looks MILT. Hence †**Swart** *v. trans.* and *intr.* to make or become s. **Swa·rt-ly** *adv.*, **-ness.**

Swa·rtback, swa·rthback. *local.* 1450. [ad. Icel. *svartbakur*; see prec. and BACK *sb.*[1]] The Great Black-backed Gull, *Larus marinus*.

Swarth (swǭɹþ), *sb.*[1] Now only *dial.* [OE. *swearþ*; see SWARD *sb.*] 1. Skin, rind; *fig.* the surface, outside. 2. Green turf, grass land, greensward. late ME.

2. Lanes, Of grassy s. close cropt by nibbling sheep COWPER.

Swarth (swǭɹþ), *sb.*[2] Now *dial.* 1552. [Altered f. SWATH.] = SWATH 3, 4 a, b.

Swarth, *a.* (*sb.*[3]) 1530. [Obsc. var. of SWART *a.*] Dusky, swarthy, black. B. *sb.* Swarthiness; dusky complexion or colour (*rare*) 1661. Hence **Swa·rth-ish** *a.*, **-ness.**

Swarthy (swǭ·ɹði, swǭ·ɹþi), *a.* 1577. [Obsc. var. of SWARTY.] Of a dark hue; black or blackish; dusky.

S. darknesse MARSTON. A s. Ethiope SHAKS. A queen, with s. cheeks and bold black eyes TENNYSON. Hence **Swa·rthily** *adv.* **Swa·rthiness.**

Swa·rtru·tter. *Obs.* exc. *Hist.* 1557. [a. early mod.Du.; see SWART *a.* and RUTTER.] One of a class of irregular troopers, with black dress and armour and blackened faces, who infested the Netherlands in the 16th and 17th centuries.

Swarty (swǭ·ɹti), *a.* Now *rare* or *Obs.* 1572. [f. SWART *a.* + -Y[1].] = SWARTHY *a.*

Swash (swǫʃ), *int.* or *adv.* and *sb.* Also **swosh.** 1528. [Echoic.] A. *int.* or *adv.* Expressive of the fall of a heavy body or blow: With a crash 1538. B. *sb.* I. 1. Pig-wash; also, wet refuse or filth 1528. 2. A body of water moving forcibly or dashing against something 1671. 3. Chiefly *U.S.* = SWATCH *sb.*[2] 1670. 4. A heavy blow, esp. of, or upon, some yielding substance; the sound of this 1789. 5. The action of water dashing or washing against the side of a cliff, ship, etc., or of waves against each other; the sound accompanying this 1847. 6. A watery condition of land; ground under water 1864. II. 1. A swaggerer; a swashbuckler; now *Sc.* an ostentatious person 1549. 2. Swagger; swashbuckling 1593.

attrib.: **s. channel, -way,** a channel across a bank, or among shoals'.

Swash, *a.*[1] 1599. [f. prec.] 1. Slashing with great force. 2. †a. Swashbuckling, swaggering. b. 'Swell', 'swagger', showy. *dial.* 1600.

Swash (swǫʃ), *a.*[2] 1680. [app. derived from †ASWASH *adv.* aslant.] 1. *Turning*, etc. Inclined obliquely to the axis of the work. 2. *Printing.* Applied to old-style capital letters having flourished strokes designed to fill up unsightly gaps between adjacent letters 1683.

Swash (swǫʃ), *v.* 1556. [Echoic.] 1. *trans.* To dash or cast violently 1577. 2. *intr.* To dash or move violently *about*; also occas. *refl.* 1583. 3. To make a noise as of swords clashing or of a sword beating on a shield; to fence with swords; to bluster with or as with weapons; to lash *out*; hence, to swagger 1556. 4. *trans.* To dash or splash (water) about; to dash water upon, souse with water or liquid; (of water) To beat with a splash against 1589. 5. *intr.* Of water or of an object in water: To dash with a splashing sound; to splash *about* 1836.

4. Men swishing and swashing and brooming about 1862. 5. The sea at the cliff foot—swashing ever louder and louder 1892.

Swashbuckler (swǫ·ʃbɒ:klǝɹ). 1560. [f. prec. + BUCKLER *sb.*[2]; hence *lit.* one who makes a noise by striking his own or his opponent's shield with his sword.] A swaggering bravo or ruffian; a noisy braggadocio.

attrib. The s. manners of the youth of fashion in the reign of Elizabeth 1816. Hence **Swa·shbu·ckling** *a.*

Swasher (swǫ·ʃǝɹ). 1589. [f. SWASH *v.* + -ER[1].] A swashbuckler; a blustering braggart or ruffian.

Swashing (swǫ·ʃiŋ), *ppl. a.* 1556. [f. SWASH *v.* + -ING[2].] 1. Swaggering; swashbuckling, dashing. 2. Applied to a particular slashing stroke in fencing; also of a weapon: Slashing with great force. Now only in reminiscences of Shaks. 1611. 3. Of water, etc.: Dashing and splashing 1620.

2. Gregorie, remember thy s. blowe SHAKS.

Swashy (swǫ·ʃi), *a.* 1796. [f. SWASH *sb.* or *v.* + -Y[1].] Sloppy, watery.

‖**Swastika** (swæ·stikă). 1871. [Skr. *svastika*, f. *svasti* well-being, luck, f. *sú* good + *asti* being (f. *as* to be).] A primitive symbol or ornament of the form of a cross with equal arms with a limb of the same length projecting at right angles from the end of each arm, all in the same direction and (usu.) clockwise.

Swat (swǫt), *sb. n. dial.* and *U.S.* 1800. [f. next.] A smart or violent blow.

Swat (swǫt), *v.* 1615. [n. dial. and U.S. var. of SQUAT *v.*] 1. *intr.* To sit down, squat. *north.* 2. *trans.* To hit with a smart slap or a violent blow. Now chiefly *U.S.* 1796.

Swatch (swǫtʃ), *sb.*[1] *Sc.* and *north.* 1512. [Origin unkn.] 1. †The 'foil' or 'counter-stock' of a tally; in Yorkshire, a tally attached to a piece of cloth before it is put with others into the dye-kettle. 2. A sample piece of cloth 1647. 3. *fig.* A sample, specimen 1697.

Swatch (swǫtʃ), *sb.*[2] *local.* 1626. [In local English use chiefly in Eastern counties.] A channel of water lying between sandbanks or between a sandbank and the shore.

Comb.: **swa·tchway** = SWASH-*way*.

Swath (swǭþ, swǫþ), **swathe,** *sb.*[1] (sweɪð). [OE. *swæþ, swaþu*, trace, track, f. Teut. root **swaþ-*, of unkn. meaning.] †1. Track, trace. *lit.* and *fig.* -ME. 2. The space covered by a sweep of the mower's scythe; the width of grass or corn so cut 1475. b. As a measure of grass land: A longitudinal division of a field. *local.* ME. c. A stroke of the scythe in reaping (*rare*) 1643. 3. A row or line of grass, corn, or other crop, as it falls or lies when mown or reaped; also *collect.*, a crop mown and lying on the ground ME. 4. *transf.* and *fig.* a. A broad track, belt, strip, or longitudinal extent of something 1605. b. Something compared to grass or corn falling before the scythe or sickle 1852.

2. The great mower Time, who cuts so broad a swathe THOREAU. 3. The grass had been cut, and left in swaths 1857. 4. a. *Swathe*, the entire length of a sea-wave 1867. b. We saw the dead lying in swathes as they had fallen 1895.

Comb.: **s.-balk,** a ridge of grass left unmown between the swaths, or between the sweeps of the scythe.

Swathe (sweɪð), *sb.*[2] [OE. **swæþ, swaþ-*, only in dat. pl. *swaþum*.] 1. A band of linen, woollen, or other material in which something is enveloped; a wrapping; sometimes, a single fold or winding of such; also *collect. sing.* †b. *sing.* and *pl.* An infant's swaddling-bands -1786. c. A surgical bandage 1615. 2. a. *transf.* A natural formation constituting a wrapping 1615. b. *fig.* Something that restricts or confines like a swaddling-band 1864.

1. Long Pieces of Linen folded about me till they

had wrapt me in above an hundred Yards of S. ADDISON. c. I turn'd a swath a little broader than the Patient's Hand once round him 1722. 2. a. Grey swathes of cloud still hung about the hills 1871. b. Within the swathes and fetters of civilisation 1906.

Swathe (swēⁱð), *v.* [Late OE. *swaþian*, f. *swaþ*; see prec.] **1.** *trans.* To envelop in a swathe or swathes; to wrap up, swaddle, bandage. **b.** Said of the swathe or wrapping 1856. **c.** To wrap round something, as or like a swathe or bandage 1656. **2.** *transf.* and *fig.* To enwrap, enfold; †to encircle so as to confine 1624.

1. From their Infancy their Feet are kept swathed up with bands 1697. 2. Who hath swathed in the great and proud Ocean, with a Girdle of Sand 1692.

Sway (swēⁱ), *sb.* late ME. [f. next.] †**1.** The motion of a rotating or revolving body –1610. **2.** The sweeping or swinging motion of a heavy body, a storm, etc.; the impetus or momentum of a body, etc. in motion. *Obs.* or *dial.* late ME. †**3.** Force or pressure bearing or inclining its object in one direction or another –1791. †**4.** Inclination or bias in a certain direction –1820. **5.** Prevailing, overpowering, or controlling influence 1510. **6.** Power of rule or command; sovereign power or authority; dominion, rule 1586. **b.** *contextually.* (*a*) Means of government. (*b*) Position of authority or power. 1645. †**7.** Manner of carrying oneself; deportment –1845. **8.** The action of moving backward and forward or from side to side 1846.

3. Expert When to advance, or stand, or turn the s. Of Battel MILT. 5. The girl had fallen under the s. of nuns and priests 1879. 6. The soul..originally govern'd the body with an absolute s. 1714.

Sway (swēⁱ), *v.* 1500. [app. ad. LG. *swâjen* to be moved hither and thither by the wind, Du. *zwaaien* to swing, wave, walk totteringly.] **1.** *intr.* To move or swing first to one side and then to the other, as a flexible or pivoted object. **b.** *fig.* To vacillate (*rare*) 1563. **2.** *trans.* To cause to move backward and forward or from side to side 1555. **3.** *intr.* To bend or move to one side, or downwards, as by excess of weight or pressure; to incline, lean, swerve 1577. †**b.** *transf.* To have a certain direction in movement; to move –1650. **4.** *trans.* To cause to incline or hang down on one side, as from excess of weight; *dial.* to weigh or press down; also, to cause to swerve 1570. **5.** To turn aside, divert (thoughts, feelings, etc.); to cause to swerve *from* a course of action 1596. †**b.** To influence in a specified direction –1807. †**6.** *intr.* To incline or be diverted in judgement or opinion –1659. **7.** *trans.* To wield as an emblem of sovereignty or authority; esp. in phr. *to s. the sceptre* 1575. **b.** *transf.* To wield (an instrument or implement). *poet.* (*rare.*) 1600. **8.** To rule, govern, as a sovereign. Chiefly *poet.* 1595. **b.** *transf.* To control, direct 1587. **9.** *intr.* To rule; to hold sway 1565. †**10.** To have a preponderating weight or influence, prevail –1768. **11.** *trans.* To cause (a person, his actions, conduct, or thoughts) to be directed one way or another; to have weight or influence with (a person) in his decisions, etc. 1593. **12.** To swing (a weapon or implement) about; *dial.* to swing (something) to and fro, or from one place to another. Also *intr.* to swing. 1590. **13.** *Naut.* (usu. with *up*). To hoist, raise (esp. a yard or topmast). Also *absol.* 1743.

1. The dreary estuary, where the slow tide sways backwards and forwards 1874. 2. He swayed himself backwards and forwards in his chair TROLLOPE. *fig.* He..swayes her conscience Which way he list 1650. 3. In these personal respects, the balance sways on our part BACON. b. 2 *Hen. IV*, IV. i. 24. 4. As Bowls run true, by being made Of purpose false, and to be sway'd 1678. 5. An huge advantage may s. him a little aside 1679. 6. *Hen. V*, I. i. 73. 7. b. This harp, which erst Saint Modan swayed SCOTT. 8. A gentle Nymph..That with moist curb sways the smooth Severn stream MILT. b. The will of man is by his reason sway'd SHAKS. 9. Lawless feasters in thy palace s. POPE. 11. Swayed in their opinions by men who..are incompetent judges GOLDSM.

Sway-, the vb.-stem or sb. used in comb.: **s.-beam**, an early name for the side-lever in a steam-engine; **-bracing**, diagonal bracing of a bridge, designed to prevent swaying; so **-brace** *sb.*; **-brace** *v.* to strengthen with a s.-brace.

Sway·-backed, *a.* 1680. [Of Scand. origin.] Of an animal, esp. a horse: Having a downward curvature of the spinal column; strained in the back, as by overwork.

†**Swayed**, *ppl. a.* 1577. [pa. pple. of SWAY *v.*] Of a horse: = prec. –1852.

Swaying (swēⁱ·iŋ), *vbl. sb.* 1598. [f. SWAY *v.* + -ING [1].] **1.** The action of SWAY *v.* 1665. **2.** *S. of* or *in the back*: the condition of being SWAY-BACKED 1598.

Sweal, swale [1] (swīl, swēⁱl). *v.* Now *dial.* [OE. *swǣlan* wk. trans. to burn, related to OE. *swelan* str. intr. to burn, f. Teut. root *swel- to be subjected to heat or slow burning.] **1.** *trans.* To consume with fire, burn; to set fire to (e.g. gorse, etc., soot in a chimney); to singe, scorch. **2.** *intr.* To burn with fire, or as a fire; to be consumed with fire; to be scorched; to be burning hot ME. **3.** Of a candle: To melt *away*; to gutter. Also said of the tallow or wax. Hence *fig.* to waste away. 1653. **4.** *trans.* To cause to waste away like a guttering candle. Chiefly *fig.* 1655.

Swear (swēᵊɹ), *sb.* Now *colloq.* 1643. [f. SWEAR *v.*] An act of swearing; an oath; a swear-word; a fit of swearing.

Swear (swēᵊɹ), *v.* Pa. t. **swore** (swōᵊɹ); pa. pple. **sworn** (swǭɹn). [Com. Teut. str. vb.; OE. *swęrian, swōr*, rarely *swerede, -swaren*, usu. *-sworen*:—OTeut. **swarjan*, f. *swar-*.] **I. 1.** *intr.* To make a solemn declaration or statement with an appeal to God or a superhuman being, or to some sacred object, in confirmation of what is said; to take an oath. **2.** To promise or undertake something by an oath; to take an oath by way of a solemn promise or undertaking, **a.** *intr.* OE. **b.** *trans.* with pron. as obj. ME. **3.** With certain sbs.: To promise or undertake on oath to observe or perform (something) ME. **4.** To affirm, assert, or declare something by an oath; to make an oath to the truth of a statement. **a.** *intr.*: *spec.* to give evidence on oath (*against* a person). Now *rare*. OE. **b.** with clause: often also, to affirm emphatically or confidently (without an oath) OE. **c.** *trans.* with pron. as obj. ME. **5.** *trans.* With certain sbs.: **a.** To take an oath as to the fact or truth of; to confirm (a statement) by oath. late ME. **b.** To proclaim or declare with an oath or solemn affirmation. late ME. **c.** To value on oath *at* so much 1854. **6.** To take or utter (an oath), either solemnly or profanely OE. †**7.** To use (a sacred name) in an oath; to invoke or appeal to (a deity, etc.) by an oath –1605. **8.** *intr.* To utter a form of oath lightly or irreverently, as a mere intensive, or as an expression of anger, vexation, or other strong feeling; to utter a profane oath, or use profane language habitually; more widely, to use bad language. late ME. **b.** To utter a harsh guttural sound, as an angry cat or other animal. *colloq.* 1700. **9.** *trans.* **a.** To bring or get into some specified condition or position by swearing 1588. **b.** To put *upon* or ascribe *to* a person in a sworn statement. *arch.* 1754.

1. Wee dare not sware least we sin against our God 1660. 2. a. God is said to s. when he binds himself absolutely to performance 1662. I have sworn to speak the truth only 1797. Rokeby sware, No rebel's son should wed his heir SCOTT. b. As I best koude I swore hir this CHAUCER. 3. Then sweare Allegeance to his Maiesty SHAKS. Thou ne're swore our covenant 1649. Repentance oft before I swore FITZGERALD. 4. Against themselves their Witnesses will S. DRYDEN. Phr. *To s. home, through a two-inch board*, denoting hard swearing. b. I dorste swere they weyeden ten pound CHAUCER. 5. a. He swore treason against his friend JOHNSON. b. Phr. *To s. the peace against*: see PEACE *sb.* 9. c. The gross personal estate is sworn at £37,405. 16. 10. 1896. 6. My lord swore one of his large oaths that he did not know..what she meant THACKERAY. 7. *Lear* I. i. 163. 8. Oft haue I seene the haughty Cardinall Sweare like a Ruffian SHAKS. 9. a. The miller swore himself as black as night that he stopt them SCOTT.

II. 1. orig. *pass.* To be bound by oath; hence *actively* to cause to take an oath; to bind by an oath; to put (a person) upon his oath; to administer an oath to OE. **2.** *spec.* To admit to an office or function by administering a formal oath ME.

1. Tender the oath: if he accepts it, s. him BENTHAM. He swore Harry to secrecy THACKERAY. Phr. *I dare be sworn, I'll be sworn*, expressing strong affirmation, properly implying readiness to take an oath upon the fact (*arch.*). 2. Richard..had been sworn of the Irish Privy Council 1855. The jury were sworn 1880.

S. at —. a. To imprecate evil upon by an oath; to address with profane imprecation; *gen.* to curse. **b.** *fig.* Of colours, etc.: To be violently incongruous or inharmonious with. *colloq.* **S. by —. a.** To appeal to (a divine being or sacred object, etc.) in swearing; to say 'by..' as a form of oath. **b.** To swear to or be sure of the existence of; in phr. *enough to s. by*, expressing a very slight amount. *colloq.* or *slang*. **c.** To accept as an infallible authority; to have absolute confidence in. *colloq.* **S. off —.** To abjure, forswear, renounce. *colloq.* or *slang*. **S. to —. a.** To promise or undertake with a solemn oath (an act or course of action). Now *rare*. **b.** To affirm with an oath; to express assurance of the truth of (a statement), or the identity of (a person or thing) by swearing. **S. away.** To take away by swearing; to give evidence on oath so as to destroy or cause the loss of. **S. in.** To admit or induct into an office by administering a prescribed oath. **S. off.** To abjure something, esp. intoxicating drink.

Swearer (swēᵊ·rəɹ). late ME. [f. prec. + -ER [1].] **1.** One who takes an oath; *spec.* one who takes or has taken an oath of allegiance. **2.** One who uses profane oaths; a person addicted to profane language. late ME. **3.** One who administers an oath to another (const. *of*) 1597.

1. *False s.*, one who swears falsely, or who breaks his oath; a perjurer.

Swearing (swēᵊ·riŋ), *vbl. sb.* ME. [f. SWEAR *v.* + -ING [1].] The action of SWEAR *v.* *False s.*, perjury. *Hard s.*: see HARD *a.* 18.

Swea·r-word. *colloq.* (orig. *U.S.*) 1883. [f. SWEAR *v.* + WORD *sb.*] A word used in profane swearing, a profane word.

Sweat (swet), *sb.* [ME. *swet, swete*, alteration of *swote*, after SWEAT *v.*] †**I.** The life-blood; in phr. *to tine, leave, lose, the s.*: to lose one's life-blood, die –1513. **II. 1.** Moisture excreted in the form of drops through the pores of the skin, usu. as a result of excessive heat or exertion, or of certain emotions; sensible perspiration. late ME. **2.** A condition or fit of sweating as a result of heat, exertion, or emotion; diaphoresis. late ME. †**b.** = SWEATING-SICKNESS. –1661. **3.** A fit of sweating caused for a specific purpose. **a.** as a form of medicinal treatment or to reduce one's weight 1632. **b.** A run given to a horse (often in a coat) as part of his training for a race 1705. **4.** *transf.* Something resembling sweat; drops of moisture exuded from or deposited on the surface of a body. late ME. **5.** A process of sweating or being sweated; exudation, evaporation, or deposit of moisture, fermentation, partial fusion, etc., as practised in various industries 1573.

1. Phr. *The s. of* (one's) *brow, face*, etc., expressing toil: after Gen. iii. 19. *Bloody s.*, (*a*) that of Jesus in the Garden of Gethsemane; see Luke xxii. 44; (*b*) *Path.*: see HÆMATIDROSIS. 2. *Cold s.*, sweating accompanied by a feeling of cold, esp. as induced by fear or the like. See also NIGHT-*sweat*.

III. 1. *fig.* Hard work; labour, toil; pains, trouble. Now *slang*. ME. **2.** A state of impatience, anxiety, or the like, such as induces sweat; a flurry, hurry, fume. Chiefly *Sc.* and *U.S.* 1715. **b.** *Old s.*, an old soldier (*slang*) 1919.

Comb.: **s.-band**, a band of leather or other substance forming a lining of a hat or cap for protection against s.; **-box**, (*a*) a narrow cell in which a prisoner is confined or interrogated (*slang*); (*b*) a box in which hides are sweated; (*c*) a large box in which figs are placed to undergo a 'sweat'; **-duct** *Anat.*, the duct of a s.-gland, by which the s. is conveyed to the surface of the skin; **-gland** *Anat.*, each of the numerous minute coiled tubular glands just beneath the skin which secrete s.; **-pore** *Anat.*, each of the pores of the skin formed by the opening of the s.-ducts.

Sweat (swet), *v.* Pa. t. †**sweat, sweated**; pa. pple. †**sweat, sweated.** [OE. *swǣtan*, f. *swāt* sweat. Avoided in refined speech in the ordinary physical senses.] **I. 1.** *intr.* To emit or excrete sweat through the pores of the skin; to perspire (sensibly). **2.** *trans.* To emit or exude through the pores of the skin, as or like sweat. Also with *out*. OE. **b.** *fig.* To give forth or get rid of as by sweating; *slang*, to spend, lay out (money) 1592. **3.** To cause to sweat; to put into a sweat 1621. **b.** To give (a horse) a run for exercise (*rare*) 1589.

1. I have toil'd, and till'd, and sweaten in the sun BYRON. 2. Thou, who..hast..sweat blood YOUNG. b. I could not sweate out from my hart that bitternes of sorrow 1610.

II. 1. *intr.* To exert oneself strongly; to work hard, toil, labour, drudge OE. **b.** *spec.* Formerly, in the tailoring trade, to work overtime at home 1851. 2. *trans.* a. To exact hard work from 1821. b. *spec.* To employ in hard or excessive work at very low wages, esp. under a system of sub-contract. Chiefly *pass.* 1879. 3. To work *out*; to work hard at; to get, make, or produce by severe labour (*rare*) 1589. b. *Naut.* To set or hoist (a sail, etc.) taut, so as to increase speed (also *intr.*); also with the ship as obj. 1890. 4. *intr.* To undergo severe affliction or punishment; to suffer severely. Often *to s. for it*, to suffer the penalty, 'get it hot'. Now *rare* or *Obs.* 1612. 5. To suffer perturbation of mind; to be vexed; to fume, rage. Now *rare* or *Obs.* late ME.

1. Lovers of money must s. or steal READE. 2. b. They declared that they were being 'sweated'—that the hunger for work induced men to accept starvation rates 1887. A low type of 'sweated' and overworked labour is employed 1889. 3. Leigh Hunt is sweating articles for his new Journal BYRON. 5. I s. to think of that Garret DRYDEN.

III. 1. *intr.* To exude, or to gather, moisture so that it appears in drops on the surface OE. b. *spec.* of products in store 1440. c. To exude nitroglycerine, as dynamite 1900. 2. *trans.* To emit (moisture, etc.) in drops or small particles like sweat; to exude, distil. Also with *out.* late ME. 3. *intr.* To ooze *out* like sweat; to exude. late ME. 4. *trans.* To cause to exude moisture; *spec.* to subject to a process of sweating 1686. 5. *slang.* To rob, 'fleece', 'bleed' 1847. 6. To lighten (a gold coin) by wearing away its substance by friction or attrition 1603. 7. To subject (metal) to partial fusion; to fasten by applying heat so as to produce partial fusion; *Metall.* to heat so as to melt and extract an easily fusible constituent 1884.

1. Stone or Wainscot that has been used to s. 1731. b. Salted hides..require..rather longer to s. 1852. 2. It is no little thing to make Mine eyes to s. compassion SHAKS. 8. *U.S. slang.* To use 'third-degree methods on (a prisoner).

Sweater (swe·təɹ). 1529. [f. prec. vb. + -ER 1.] 1. *lit.* One who sweats or perspires; *spec.* one who takes a 'sweating bath' 1562. 2. One who works hard, a toiler; †*spec.* a tailor who worked overtime at home for an employer 1529. 3. A sudorific, diaphoretic 1684. 4. One who exacts hard work at very low wages 1850. 5. One who 'sweats' gold coins 1868. 6. A woollen vest or jersey worn in rowing or other athletic exercise; also worn before or after exercise to prevent taking cold 1882.

Swea·t-house. 1750. 1. A hut or other structure in which hot-air or vapour baths are taken, among the N. Amer. Indians and other primitive tribes. 2. *Tanning.* A building in which hides are sweated 1891.

Sweating (swe·tiŋ), *vbl. sb.* ME. [f. SWEAT *v.* + -ING 1.] The action of SWEAT *v.* *attrib.* and *Comb.*: **s.-bath**, one used to induce sweating; **-house** = prec. 1; **-iron**, a piece of iron used to scrape off sweat, esp. from horses; **-room**, (*a*) a room in which persons are sweated, as in a Turkish bath; (*b*) a room in which cheeses are 'sweated' or deprived of superfluous moisture.

Swea·ting-si·ckness. 1502. A febrile disease characterized by profuse sweating, of which highly and rapidly fatal epidemics occurred in England in the 15th and 16th centuries. Now chiefly *Hist.* in ref. to these.

Sweaty (swe·ti), *a.* late ME. [f. SWEAT *sb.* + -Y 1.] 1. Causing sweat. a. Heating, excessively hot. b. Toilsome, laborious. 2. Covered with sweat; wet, moist, or stained with sweat 1590. †b. Of persons: Laborious, toiling –1667. 3. Consisting of sweat 1731.

1. The s. Forge PRIOR. A s. city BYRON. 2. S. hands 1759. b. A sweatie Reaper MILT. Hence **Swea·tily** *adv.* **Swea·tiness.**

Swede (swīd). 1614. [a. MLG., MDu. *Swede*, = HG. *Schwede* native of Sweden.] 1. A native of Sweden. 2. A Swedish ship (*rare*) 1799. 3. (= earlier *Swedish turnip.*) A large variety of turnip with yellow flesh, *Brassica campestris*, var. *Rutabaga*, introduced from Sweden in 1781–2. 1812.

Swedenborgian (swīd'nbǭ·ɹdʒiăn), *a.* and *sb.* 1802. [f. name of Emanuel *Swedenborg* or Svedberg (see below) + -IAN.] A. *adj.* Of or pertaining to Emanuel Swedenborg, a Swedish scientific and religious writer (1688–1772), or the body of followers of his religious teachings, organized in 1788 and styled by themselves 'The New Church'. B. *sb.* A follower of Swedenborg. Hence **Swedenbo·rgianism,** also *rarely* **Swe·denborgism.**

Swedish (swī·diʃ), *a.* and *sb.* 1605. [f. Sweden or SWEDE + -ISH 1, after G. *schwedisch*, etc.] A. *adj.* Of or belonging to Sweden or the Swedes 1632.

S. drill, gymnastics, movements, a system of muscular exercises as a form of hygienic or curative treatment. *S. turnip* = SWEDE 3.

B. *sb.* The language of Sweden 1605.

Sweeny (swī·ni). *U.S.* 1855. [prob. f. G. dial. *schweine* emaciation, atrophy.] Atrophy of the shoulder-muscles in the horse. Also *fig.* of the 'stiffness' of pride or self-conceit.

Sweep (swīp), *sb.* 1552. [Mainly f. SWEEP *v.*] I. The action of sweeping. 1. An act of sweeping or clearing up or (usu.) away; a clearance. b. An act of passing over an area in order to capture or destroy the occupants of it 1837. 2. The action of a person or animal moving along with a continuous motion, esp. with a magnificent or impressive air 1607. 3. The rapid or forcible and continuous movement of a body of water, wind, etc. 1708. b. Semi-*concr.* of a forcibly moving body of water 1815. 4. An action, or a process in expression, thought, etc., figured as movement of this kind 1662. 5. The action of driving or wielding a tool or weapon, swinging an arm, etc., so as to describe a circle or an arc 1725. 6. The action of moving in a continuous curve or a more or less circular path or track 1679. 7. *Astr.* A term used by Sir William Herschel to denote a method of surveying the heavens in sections; also, one of such sections of observation 1784. 8. An act of sweeping with a broom 1818. 9. The action of a garment, etc. brushing, or of the hand or an instrument passing in continuous movement, along or over a surface 1820. 10. *Cards.* a. In the game of casino, a pairing or combining all the cards on the board, resulting in the removal of all of them. b. In whist, the winning of all the tricks in a hand; a slam. 1814. 11. *Physics.* A process of settling, or tending to settle, into thermal equilibrium 1903.

1. Phr. *A general*, (now always) *a clean s.* 2. What a sweepe of vanitie comes this way SHAKS. 4. The first s. of royal fury being past CARLYLE. 5. The s. of scythe in morning dew TENNYSON. 9. A s. of lute-strings BROWNING.

II. Range, extent. 1. Compass, reach, or range of movement, esp. in a circular or curving course 1679. 2. Extent of ground, water, etc.; an extent, stretch, or expanse, such as can be taken in at one survey or is included in a wide-spreading curve 1767. 3. Extent or range of thought, observation, experience, influence, power, etc. 1781.

1. In our wake, and just outside the s. of our oars KANE. 2. Many a s. Of meadow 1842. A s. Of shops 1858. 3. The extensive s. of these four great principles 1855.

III. A curve or curved object, etc. 1. A curved line or form; a curve; also, curvature 1715. b. The continuously curved part of an arch 1685. 2. *concr.* a. A curved mass of building or masonry 1766. b. A semicircular plank fixed up under the beams near the fore-end of the tiller, which it supports; a similar support on which a gun travels 1756. c. A curved carriage drive leading to a house 1797. IV. That which is swept up. 1. *collect. sing.* or *pl.* The sweepings of gold and silver dust from the workshops of goldsmiths, silversmiths, etc. 1771. 2. = SWEEPSTAKE 3 b. 1849. 3. = ALMOND-FURNACE. 1706. V. Apparatus that sweeps or has a sweeping motion. 1. An apparatus for drawing water from a well, consisting of a long pole attached to an upright which serves as a fulcrum; hence, a pump-handle 1548. 2. A ballista. *Obs.* exc. *Her.* 1598. 3. Applied to various kinds of levers, or to a long bar which is swept round so as to turn a shaft 1657. 4. A sail of a windmill. Also *occas.* a paddle of a water-wheel 1639. 5. A long oar used to propel a ship, barge, etc. when becalmed, or to assist the work of steering 1800. 6. A length of cable used for sweeping the bottom of the sea, in mine-laying, etc. 1775. 7. An instrument used for drawing curves at a large radius; a beam-compass. Also, a profile tool for cutting mouldings in wood or metal in a lathe. 1680. 8. *Founding.* A movable templet used in loam-moulding, a striking-board 1864. VI. One who sweeps (and derived senses). 1. A chimney-sweeper 1812. b. *The Sweeps*: a nickname for the Rifle Brigade 1879. c. A disreputable person; a scamp, blackguard. *slang* and *dial.* 1853. 2. a. A crossing-sweeper. b. *U.S.* A servant who looks after university students' rooms. 1858.

1. Our faces..became almost as black as sweeps 1861.

Sweep (swīp), *v.* Pa. t. and pa. pple. **swept.** [ME. *swepe* (replacing ME. *swope*, OE. *swāpan*); of uncertain origin. See N.E.D.] I. 1. *trans.* To remove, clear *away*, *off* (etc.) with a broom or brush, or in a similar way by friction upon a surface; to brush away or off. 2. To cut *down* or *off* with a vigorous swinging stroke. Now *rare* or *Obs.* late ME. 3. To remove with a forcible continuous action; to brush *off*, *away*, *aside* 1577. 4. *transf.* and *fig.* To clear out, drive away, or carry off *from* a place or region, (as if) forcibly or by violence 1593. 5. Chiefly with *away*: To remove forcibly or as at one blow; do away with, destroy utterly 1560. 6. To carry or drive along with force; to carry *away* or *off* by driving before it, as a wind, tide, stream, etc. 1743. 7. To drive together or into a place by or as by sweeping; to gather or take *up*, esp. so as to allocate or consign to a place, object, or purpose ME. b. *fig.* To include in its scope; to extend to 1692. 8. To gather in or up, collect wholesale or at one stroke; esp. in phr. *to s. the stakes* (cf. SWEEPSTAKE) 1635. 9. To carry or trail along in a stately manner, as a flowing garment 1591. 10. To move or draw (something) over and in contact with a surface 1825. 11. To move (something) *round* with force and rapidity, or over a wide extent; to take *off* (one's hat) with a sweep of the arm 1845. 12. *intr.* and *trans.* To row, or to propel (a vessel), with sweeps or large oars. Also *intr.* of the vessel. *rare* or *Obs.* 1799.

1. I am sent with broome before, To sweep the dust behinde the doore SHAKS. 3. S. the chessmen off the board KINGSLEY. 4. A..storm..In its fury it had just swept away the pier at Ryde 1831. 5. Why are thy valiant men swept away? *Jer.* xlvi. 15. 6. The tide was sweeping us past 1840. 7. He is sure to s. fifty Pounds at least into his Pocket 1706. 8. Death's a devouring gamester, And sweepes up all SHIRLEY. 10. Again sweeping his fingers over the strings SCOTT. 11. He swept off his hat in continental style 1885.

II. 1. *trans.* To pass a broom or brush over the surface of (something) so as to clear it of any small loose or adhering particles; to cleanse with a brush or broom (as a floor of dust and small refuse, a path of dirt, snow, etc., or a chimney of soot). Also (rarely) said of the broom. ME. b. *absol.* or *intr.*; also said of the broom, esp. in prov. *New brooms s. clean* ME. 2. To pass over the surface of (something) in the manner of a broom or brush; to move over and in contact with; to brush 1500. 3. *transf.* and *fig.* To clear *of* something by vigorous action compared to that of a broom; *spec.* to clear (a place) *of* enemies or a mob by firing amongst them 1627. 4. To draw something, as a net or the bight of a rope, over the bottom of (a body of water) in search of something submerged; to drag. Also, to catch (something submerged) in this way. Also *intr.* to search *for* in this way. 1637. 5. To move swiftly and evenly or with continuous force over or along the surface of; in weakened sense, to pass over or across 1590. 6. To range over (a region of sea or land), esp. to destroy, ravage, or capture; to scour 1788. b. Of artillery: To have within range, to command (an extent of territory) 1748. 7. To pass the fingers over the strings of a musical instrument so as to cause it to sound. (With the strings, or the instrument, as obj.) Chiefly *poet.* 1637. b. *transf.* To produce (music) by such action *poet.* 1815. 8. To direct the eyes, or an optical instrument, to every part of (a region) in succession; to take a wide survey of. Also *absol.* or *intr.*; in *Astron.* to make systematic observations of a region of the heavens. 1727.

1. Be careful to have the used Chimneys sweep'd once a month 1775. 2. That garment is decently put on, Which does not s. the dust 1638. 3. *To s. the board*, see BOARD *sb.* II. 1. *To s. the deck* (or usu. *decks*), to clear the deck of a ship (as by artillery, or as a wave breaking over); also *fig.* 4. Earine was drown'd!

..Have you swept the river, say you, and not found her? B. JONS. 5. *To s. a constituency, the country*: to have an overwhelming majority of votes in it. 6. Their artillery swept the waters GIBBON. 7. Begin, and somewhat loudly s. the string MILT. 8. I swept with my telescope..the line of the horizon SMEATON.

III. Intr. senses denoting movement (esp. in a curve), and derived uses. 1. *intr.* To move with a strong or swift even motion; to move along over a surface or region, usu. rapidly, or with violence or destructive effect; sometimes, to come with a sudden attack, to swoop. late ME. 2. To move or walk in a stately manner, as with trailing garments; to move along majestically; 'to pass with pomp' (J.). Also with *it*. 1590. 3. To move along a surface or in the track of something like a trailing robe; to trail *after*; to brush *along* 1642. 4. To move continuously in a long stretch or over a wide extent, esp. *round* or in a curve 1725. 5. To extend continuously through a long stretch, or widely around; to present a surface of wide extent 1789. b. *trans.* with cogn. obj. To perform or execute (such a movement) 1848. 6. To describe, trace, mark out (a line, esp. a wide curve, or an area) 1664. 7. *Founding.* To form (a mould) with a sweep (SWEEP *sb.* V. 8) 1885.

1. That I, with wings as swift As meditation..May sweepe to my Reuenge SHAKS. There were light breezes sweeping up 1845. The plague swept over Europe 1889. 2. Sweepe on you fat and greazie Citizens SHAKS. 4. The first flight of the hawks, when they sweep so beautifully round the company SCOTT. 5. A road swept gently round the hill CLARE. b. Becky..swept the prettiest little curtsey ever seen THACKERAY. 6. They..found it much easier to s. circles than to design beauties RUSKIN.

Comb.: **s.-net**, a large net used in fishing, enclosing a wide space; a kind of seine; **-saw**, a saw adapted for cutting sweeps or curves; a bow-saw, turning-saw; **-seine** = *s.-net*.

Sweepage (swī·pėdʒ). 1628. [f. prec. + -AGE.] 'The Crop of Hay got in a Meadow' (1672); *gen.* what is mown.

Sweeper (swī·pəɹ). 1530. [f. SWEEP *v.* + -ER [1].] 1. *gen.* One who or that which sweeps. 2. A person employed in sweeping a room, chimneys, crossings, etc.; *spec.* in India, a person of the lowest caste 1657. 3. A mechanical apparatus for sweeping a floor, road, etc.; a sweeping-machine 1862.

Sweeping (swī·piŋ), *vbl. sb.* 1480. [-ING [1].] 1. The action of SWEEP *v.* a. Cleansing or removing, with or as with a broom or brush. b. Dragging for something under water; esp. in MINE-*s.* 1704. c. Movement over a surface or in an extended curve 1830. d. Rowing with sweeps 1831. 2. That which is swept up; matter, esp. dust or refuse, that is swept together or away 1480. b. *fig.* (*pl.*) Of persons or things: Rubbish, riff-raff 1641.

2. b. The sweepings of the gaols 1832.

Swee·ping, *ppl. a.* 1611. [-ING [2].] 1. That sweeps, in various senses; see SWEEP *v.* 2. Extending through a long stretch or wide space, esp. in a curve 1772. 3. *fig.* Having a wide scope; extensive, comprehensive; wholesale, indiscriminate 1771.

3. A s. measure of sanitary reform KINGSLEY. Hence **Swee·ping-ly** *adv.*, **-ness**.

Sweepstake (swī·pstēɪk), **sweepstakes** (-stēɪks). 1495. [f. SWEEP *v.* + STAKE *sb.*[2]] †1. One who 'sweeps', or takes the whole of, the stakes in a game, etc.; usu. *fig.* one who takes or appropriates everything -1687. (Occurs first as the name of one of the King's ships.) †2. The act of sweeping everything away; a clean sweep: usu. in phr. *to make s.*, *to play* (*at*) *s.* -1653. 3. orig. A prize won in a race or contest in which the whole of the stakes contributed by the competitors are taken by the winner or by a certain limited number of them; hence (now usu.) the race or contest itself 1773. b. A betting or gambling transaction in which each person contributes a stake, and the whole of the stakes are taken by one or divided among several under certain conditions 1862.

Sweepy (swī·pi), *a.* Chiefly *poet.* 1697. [f. SWEEP *sb.* or *v.* + -Y [1].] Characterized by sweeping movement or form; sweeping.

Hail furious flew and s. light'ning shone 1790.

Sweet (swīt), *sb.* ME. [SWEET *a.* used as sb.] 1. That which is sweet to the taste; something having a sweet taste. Chiefly *poet.* b. A sweet food or drink. late ME. c. *pl.* Syrup added to wine or other liquor to sweeten the taste; hence, wine or other liquor thus sweetened; applied *spec.* to British wines and cordials 1679. d. *spec.* A sweet dish forming a separate course at a meal. Usu. *pl.* 1834. e. A sweetmeat, esp. in lozenge or 'drop' form 1851. 2. Sweetness of taste; sweet taste (*rare*). late ME. 3. That which is pleasant to the mind or feelings; (a) pleasure, (a) delight; the pleasant part *of* something. In later use chiefly in *pl.* late ME. 4. A beloved person, darling, sweetheart ME. 5. Sweetness of smell, fragrance; *pl.* sweet odours, scents, or perfumes. *poet.* 1594. 6. *pl.* Substances having a sweet smell fragrant flowers or herbs; †scents, perfumes. Now *rare*. 1602.

1. A dram of s. is worth a pound of sowre SPENSER. 3. Must..Every s. warn ''Ware my bitter' BROWNING. 4. She is coming, my own, my s. TENNYSON. 5. He.. riots in the sweets of ev'ry breeze COWPER. 6. Sweets, to the s. SHAKS.

Sweet (swīt), *a.* and *adv.* [Com. Teut.: OE. *swēte*:—OTeut. **swōtja-*, **swōti-*, f. *swōt-*:—Indo-Eur. *swād-*, in Skr. *svādús* sweet, Gr. ἡδύς sweet, L. *suavis* sweet, etc.] A. *adj.* 1. Pleasing to the sense of taste; *spec.* having the characteristic flavour of sugar, honey, and many ripe fruits. Often opp. to *bitter* or *sour*. 2. Pleasing to the sense of smell; having a pleasant smell or odour; fragrant. Also said of the smell or odour. OE. †b. *spec.* Scented -1656. 3. Free from offensive taste or smell; not corrupt, putrid, sour, or stale; free from taint or noxious matter; in a sound and wholesome condition ME. †b. *spec.* Of water: Fresh, not salt. Also of butter: Fresh, not salted. -1796. c. Of milk: Fresh, not sour 1812. d. *Old Chem.* and *Metallurgy*. Free from corrosive salt, sulphur, acid, etc. 1666. 4. Pleasing to the ear; musical, melodious, harmonious: said of a sound, a voice, an instrument, a singer, a performer on an instrument OE. 5. Pleasing (in general); yielding pleasure or enjoyment; agreeable, delightful, charming. (Only literary in unemotional use.) OE. b. Ironically 1656. c. In colloq. use, an emotional epithet expressive of the speaker's personal feelings as to the attractiveness of the object 1779. 6. In extended use: Having an agreeable or benign quality, influence, operation, or effect. Chiefly techn. late ME. 7. *transf.* Fond of or inclined for sweet things, esp. in *s. tooth* 1591. 8. Dearly loved or prized, precious; beloved, dear OE. b. In forms of address, freq. affectionate, but also (now *arch.*) respectful or complimentary ME. c. *absol.* in affectionate address: Beloved, dear one ME. d. Dear to the person himself; usu. *sarcastically*: chiefly qualifying *self* or *will* 1621. 9. Having pleasant disposition and manners; amiable, kindly; gracious, benignant OE. 10. *To be s. on* (*upon*): †a. To treat caressingly -1754. b. To be enamoured of or smitten with (one of the opposite sex) 1740.

1. A sugred, sweet and most delitious tast 1596. After s. Meat comes sowr Sauce 1721. 2. S. muske roses SHAKS. S. after showers, ambrosial air TENNYSON. b. *Wint. T.* IV. iv. 253. 3. Preserving Fresh Water s., for the use of Seamen during long voyages 1791. b. Living in rivers and other s. waters 1661. 4. Like s. Bels iangled, out of tune, and harsh SHAKS. 5. S. are the vses of aduersitie SHAKS. Sweetest Shakespear fancies childe MILT. As s. an Autumn day As ever shone on Clyde CAMPBELL. c. Some s. thing in hats or handkerchiefs 1887. 6. Pleasaunt ground, sweete, blacke, rotten, and mellowed 1577. A s. ship in a seaway if one knew her idiosyncracies 1915. 8. Thy Life to me is s. SHAKS. b. O let me not be mad, not mad, s. Heauen SHAKS. c. Tell me not, s., I am unkind LOVELACE. d. *At one's own s. will*: just as one likes. 9. Preise ȝee his name, for swete is the Lord WYCLIF. *Ps.* xcix. [c.] 5. One of a s. nature, comely presence, courteous carriage FULLER. 10. b. I think he is s. upon your daughter DICKENS.

B. *adv.* Sweetly; so as to be sweet ME.

What early tongue so s. saluteth me? SHAKS. How s. the moonlight sleepes vpon this banke SHAKS. Then low and s. I whistled thrice TENNYSON.

Combs. and special collocations. 1. of the adj. a. with sbs.: **s.-cake**, a kind of cake having sugar as a principal ingredient; **-mart**, the pine-marten, as dist. from the FOUMART or polecat; **s. milk**, fresh milk having its natural s. flavour, as dist. from skimmed milk, or from 'sour milk', i. e. buttermilk; **s. oil**, any oil of pleasant or mild taste, *spec.* olive oil; **-stuff**, sweetmeats, sweets, confectionery; **s. tooth**, a taste or liking for s. things; **s. wine**, wine having a s. taste (as dist. from *dry* wine); wine in the manufacture of which 'sweets' or syrup is added. b. *spec.* in distinctive names of s.-scented or s.-flavoured species or varieties of plants, fruits, etc., as *s. almond*, *marjoram*, *potato*, *violet*; **s.-apple**, = SWEET-SOP; **s. bay**, (*a*) the bay laurel, *Laurus nobilis*; (*b*) in N. America applied to *Magnolia glauca*; also in comb. as **s. bay laurel** = (*a*); **s. bow** *U.S.* a variety of apple; **s. chestnut**, the common or Spanish chestnut, *Castanea vesca*, as dist. from the bitter inedible HORSE-CHESTNUT; **s.-corn** *U.S.*, a s.-flavoured variety of maize; **s. fern**, (*a*) locally in England, the s. cicely, *Myrrhis odorata* (family *Umbelliferæ*); in N. America, the shrub *Comptonia asplenifolia* (family *Myricaceæ*); **s. flag**, a rush-like plant, *Acorus calamus* (family *Araceæ* or *Orontiaceæ*), widely distributed in the North Temperate zone, growing in water and wet places, with an aromatic odour, and having a thick creeping rootstock of a pungent aromatic flavour; **-grass**, any kind of grass (or herb called 'grass') of a s. taste serving as fodder; **s. scabious**, *Scabiosa atropurpurea*; **s. sedge** = *s. flag*; **s. willow**, (*a*) *Salix pentandra*; (*b*) = SWEET-GALE.

2. Miscellaneous Combs., as *s.-tempered*, *-voiced* adjs: **s. and twenty**, a Shaks. phrase (see TWENTY A. 2) misunderstood later to mean 'a s. girl of twenty years old'; **-lipped**, **-lipt** *a.*, having s. lips; usu., speaking sweetly; **-mouthed** (-mauðd) *a.*, †(*a*) fond of s.-flavoured things, dainty; (*b*) speaking sweetly (usu. ironically); **-spoken** *a.*, speaking sweetly (cf. *plain-spoken*); **-toothed** (-tūþt) *a.*, having a s. tooth, fond of s. things. Hence **Swee·t-ly** *adv.*, **-ness**.

Sweet, *v.* Now *rare*. [f. prec.; in OE. *swētan*.] 1. *trans.* To make sweet, sweeten (*lit.* and *fig.*). 2. To affect in a sweet or pleasant way; to delight, gratify 1555.

Sweetbread (swī·tbred). (Also formerly as two words.) 1565. [app. f. SWEET *a.* + BREDE *sb.*[1]] The pancreas or the thymus gland of an animal, esp. as used for food (dist. respectively as *heart*, *stomach*, or *belly s.* and *throat*, *gullet*, or *neck s.*): esteemed a delicacy.

Swee·t-bri:er, -bri:ar. (Also as two words.) 1538. [See SWEET *a.* and BRIER *sb.*[1]] A species of rose, the Eglantine, *Rosa rubiginosa* (and some other species, as *R. micrantha*), having strong hooked prickles, pink single flowers, and small aromatic leaves; freq. cultivated in gardens.

Sweeten (swī·t'n), *v.* 1552. [f. SWEET *a.* + -EN [5].] 1. *trans.* a. To make sweet to the taste; *esp.* to add sugar or other sweet substance to (food or drink); also *absol.* b. To make sweet to the smell 1586. 2. To free from offensive taste or smell; to render fresh; to free from taint, purify, bring into a wholesome condition 1599. 3. To make sweet to the ear; to impart a pleasant sound to 1578. 4. To make pleasant or agreeable; sometimes, to make more pleasant 1586. 5. To make less unpleasant or painful; to alleviate, mitigate 1586. 6. With personal obj.: a. To produce a pleasant disposition in; to make gracious, mild, or kind; to refine 1561. b. To make things pleasant for, relieve, comfort, soothe, gratify. Now *rare* or *Obs.* 1647. c. To mollify, appease. Now *rare* or *Obs* 1657. 7. To persuade by flattery or gifts; to cajole; to take in; to bribe. Now only *slang* or *dial.* 1594. 8. *techn.* a. To cause to work smoothly or easily 1607. b. *Printing* and *Drawing*. To free from harshness, soften (a tint, line, etc.) 1688. c. To render (soil) mellow and fertile 1733. d. To neutralize (an acid) by means of an alkali 1681. 9. *slang.* a. *Cards.* To increase the stakes. b. To bid at an auction merely in order to raise the price. c. *Finance.* To increase the collateral of a loan by adding further securities. 1896. 10. *intr.* To become sweet (in various senses) 1626.

1. To get something to s. my husband's toddy with 1833. b. With fayrest Flowers..I'le s. thy sad graue SHAKS. 2. All the perfumes of Arabia will not s. this little hand SHAKS. Measures for airing and sweetning their Houses DE FOE. 3. Mine aduersary (who as the crafty fowler sweeteneth his voice to deceiue) 1578. 4. The Influence of Hope in general sweetens Life ADDISON. 5. To s. melancholy 1844. 6. To correct and s. the Tempers of Men 1706. 7. The talke..is.. that the Holland Embassador here do endeavour to s. us with fair words PEPYS. 8. b. Correggio has made his Memory immortal..by sweetning his Lights and Shadows, and melting them into each other so happily, that they are even imperceptible DRYDEN. 10. The soil laid in a heap to s. 1858. Hence **Swee·tener**, one who, or that which, sweetens; †one who softens, palliates, or extenuates; something that restores pleasant feeling; †*slang*, a decoy, cheat. **Swee·tening**

vbl. sb. the action of SWEETEN *v.*; that which sweetens. **Swee·tening** *ppl. a.* that sweetens.

Swee·t-field, -veld. 1785. [ad. Du. *zoetveld*, lit. sweet field.] In South Africa, land of good quality for food-plants.

Swee·t-gale. 1640. [See SWEET *a.* and GALE *sb.*[1]] The bog myrtle, *Myrica Gale.*

Sweetheart (swī·thāɹt), *sb.* ME. [See SWEET *a.* and HEART *sb.*] **1.** (prop. two words.) = darling: used chiefly in the vocative. †**2.** A paramour -1796. **3.** A person with whom one is in love 1576.

Swee·theart, *v.* 1798. [f. prec.] **1.** *trans.* To make a sweetheart of; to court, make love to 1804. **2.** *intr.* To be a sweetheart; to court a sweetheart, make love 1798. Hence **Swee·t-hea:rting** *vbl. sb.* and *ppl. a.*

Sweetie (swī·ti). orig. and chiefly *Sc.* 1721. [f. SWEET *a.* + -IE.] **1.** A sweetmeat, lollipop. Also, sweet cake or the like. **2.** A sweetheart.

Sweeting (swī·tiŋ). ME. [f. SWEET *a.* + -ING[3].] **1.** A 'sweet' or beloved person; dear one, darling, sweetheart. *arch.* **2.** Name for a sweet-flavoured variety of apple 1530.

1. How fares my Kate, what s. all a-mort? SHAKS.

Sweetish (swī·tiʃ), *a.* 1580. [-ISH[1].] Somewhat or slightly sweet. Hence **-ness.**

Sweetling (swī·tliŋ). *rare.* 1648. [-LING[1].] **1.** = SWEETING 1. **2.** A small sweet thing 1840.

Sweetmeat (swī·tmīt). ME. [See SWEET *a.* and MEAT *sb.*] **1.** *collect. pl.* (and †*sing.*) Sweet food, as sugared cakes, etc. (*obs.*); preserved or candied fruits, sugared nuts, etc.; also, globules, lozenges, 'drops', or 'sticks' made of sugar with fruit or other flavouring or filling; *sing.* one of these. **2.** A varnish used in the preparation of patent leather 1875.

Sweet pea. 1732. The common name of *Lathyrus odoratus*, a climbing annual leguminous plant, indigenous to Sicily, and cultivated in numerous varieties for its showy variously-coloured sweet-scented flowers; cf. next.

Sweet-scented (stress variable), *a.* 1591. Having a sweet scent; sweet-smelling, fragrant. **b.** *spec.* in names of species or varieties of plants having sweet-smelling flowers, leaves, etc. 1666.

b. *S.-s. pea*, an early name for the SWEET PEA.

Sweet singer. a. *Hist.* The phr. *sweet singer*, more fully *sweet singer of Israel* (app. with reminiscence of 2 Sam. xxiii. 1, where David is called 'the sweet psalmist of Israel'), designating a sect or sects which flourished in the latter years of the 17th c. 1680. **b.** A (religious) poet 1560.

Swee·t-sme:lling, *ppl. a.* ME. Smelling sweet; sweet-scented.

Swee·t-sop. 1696. [SOP *sb.*] The sweet fruit of a tree or shrub, *Anona squamosa*, allied to the SOUR-SOP, extensively cultivated in tropical countries. Also, the tree or shrub itself.

Sweet water, sweet-water. 1544. **1.** (as two words) Fresh water; *attrib.* (usu. with hyphen or as one word), living in or consisting of fresh water 1608. †**2.** (as two words, or with hyphen) A sweet-smelling liquid preparation; a liquid perfume or scent -1859. **3.** (with hyphen, or as one word) A variety of white grape, of specially sweet flavour 1786.

Sweetweed (swī·tˌwīd). 1760. Either of two scrophulariaceous plants of the West Indies and tropical America, *Capraria biflora*, and *Scoparia dulcis.*

Sweet-william (swīt wi·lyăm). 1562. **1.** A species of pink, *Dianthus barbatus*, cultivated in numerous varieties, bearing closely-clustered flowers of various shades of white and red, usu. variegated or parti-coloured. Also in wider use. **2.** †**a.** Applied to the tope or dog-fish 1730. **b.** A local name for the goldfinch 1848.

Sweetwood (swī·twud). 1607. Any of various trees and shrubs, chiefly lauraceous, of the West Indies and tropical America, some of which furnish valuable timber; also, the timber itself.

attrib.: **s. bark**, cascarilla bark.

Sweet-wort (swī·twɒɹt). 1567. [WORT[2].] A sweet-flavoured wort; *esp.* the infusion of malt, before the hops are added in the manufacture of beer.

Swell (swel), *sb.* ME. [In sense 1 prob. repr. OE. *geswell*; in the other senses f. SWELL *v.*] †**1.** A morbid swelling. ME. only. **2.** The condition of being swollen, distended, or increased in bulk; swelling or protuberant form, bulge; *concr.* a protuberant part, protuberance 1683. **3. a.** The rising or heaving of the sea or other body of water in a succession of long rolling waves, as after a storm; *concr.* such a wave, or, more usu., such waves collectively. (See also GROUNDSWELL.) 1606. †**b.** The rising of a river above its ordinary level -1812. **4.** A piece of land rising gradually and evenly above the general level; a hill, eminence, or upland with a smooth rounded outline and broad in proportion to its height; a rising ground 1764. **5.** Of sound, esp. musical sound: Gradual increase in loudness or force; hence, a sound or succession of sounds gradually increasing in volume 1803. **b.** *spec.* in *Mus.* A gradual increase of force (*crescendo*) followed by a gradual decrease (*diminuendo*), in singing or playing; hence, a character composed of the *crescendo* and *diminuendo* marks together, denoting this: < >. 1757. **6.** A contrivance for gradually varying the force of the tone in an organ or harmonium (also in the harpsichord and some early pianos), consisting of a shutter, a lid, or (now usu.) a series of slats like those of a Venetian blind, which can be opened or shut at pleasure by means of a pedal or (in the harmonium) a knee-lever. Also, short for *s.-box, s. keyboard, s. organ*, or *s. pedal* 1773. **7.** The action or condition of swelling, in fig. senses 1702. **8.** *colloq.*, orig. *slang.* A fashionably or stylishly dressed person; hence, a person of good social position, a highly distinguished person 1811. **b.** *transf.* (*colloq.*) One who is very clever or good *at* something 1816.

2. The s. or belly of the shaft 1726. His legs..had not..much more symmetry or s. than the lean Court sword which dangled by his side THACKERAY. 3. Their water-casks..rocking on the long swells of subsiding gales 1865. *fig.* Such ebbs of doubt, and swells of jealousy LANDOR. 4. An uninterrupted s. of moorland SCOTT. The swells and valleys of the veld 1908. 5. The choir's faint s., Came slowly down the wind SCOTT. 7. It Moderates the S. of Joy that I am in, to think of your Difficulties STEELE. The s. of insolence, the liveliness of levity JOHNSON. 8. I never was a gentleman—only a s. MARRYAT. 8. Russians are tremendous swells at palaver,..gammon you no end 1886.

attrib. (in sense 6) in names of apparatus connected with or actuating the s., as *s.-keyboard, -manual, pedal*; **s.-box**, the box or chamber, containing a set of pipes or reeds, which is opened and closed by the s. in an organ or harmonium; **-organ**, the set of pipes enclosed in the s.-box.

Swell, *a. colloq.* 1810. [attrib. use of prec. in sense 8.] That is, or has the character or style of, a 'swell'; befitting a 'swell'.

Two very s. coachmen 1826. You don't look as if you had such a s. time 1897. **S. mob**, a class of pickpockets who assume the dress and manners of respectable people in order to escape detection; hence **s.-mobsman**, a man belonging to the s. mob. *slang.*

Swell (swel), *v.* Pa. t. **swelled** (sweld); pa. pple. **swollen** (swōᵘ·l'n), **swelled.** [Com. Teut. str. vb.: OE. *swellan, sweall, swullon, -swollen*:—OTeut. **swellan.*] **1.** *intr.* To become larger in bulk, increase in size (by pressure from within, as by absorption of moisture, or of material in the process of growth, by inflation with air or gas, etc.); to become distended or filled out, *esp.* to undergo abnormal or morbid increase of size, be affected with tumour as the result of infection or injury. Also with *out, up.* **b.** Of a body of water: To rise above the ordinary level, as a river, or the tide; to rise in waves, as the sea in or after a storm; to rise to the brim, well up. late ME. **c.** Expressing form (not movement or action): To be distended or protuberant; to be larger, higher, or thicker at a certain part; to rise gradually and smoothly above the general level, as a hill 1679. **2.** *trans.* To make larger in bulk, increase the size of, cause to expand; to enlarge morbidly, affect with tumour. Also with *out, up.* late ME. **b.** To cause (the sea, a river) to rise in waves, or (more usu.) above the ordinary level 1605. **3.** In pa. pple., without implication of subject: Increased in bulk, dilated, distended; affected with morbid enlargement or tumour OE. **4.** *intr.* To become greater in amount, volume, degree, intensity, or force: now only in immaterial sense 1450. **5.** *trans.* To make greater in amount, degree, or intensity; to increase, add to. Also with *out, up.* 1599. **b.** To fill (a receptacle) to overflowing. *poet.* and *rare.* 1601. **c.** To magnify; to exalt. Now *rare* or *Obs.* 1600. **6.** *intr.* Of sound, esp. music: To increase in volume, become gradually louder or fuller; to come upon the ear with increasing clearness, or with alternate increase and diminution of force. Also of a musical instrument: To give forth a swelling sound or note. 1749. **b.** *trans.* To utter with increase of force, or with increasing volume of sound (*rare*) 1775. **7.** *fig. intr.* **a.** Of a feeling or emotion: To arise and grow in the mind with a sense as of distension or expansion. late ME. **b.** Of a person, the heart, etc.: To be affected with such an emotion; to be puffed up, become elated or arrogant. Const. *with.* late ME. **8.** *trans.* To affect with such an emotion; to puff up, inflate. (Also said of the emotion.) ME. **9.** *intr.* To show proud or angry feeling in one's action or speech; to behave proudly, arrogantly, or overbearingly; to be 'puffed up'; to look or talk big. *Obs.* or *arch.* ME. **10.** To behave pompously or pretentiously, swagger; to play the 'swell' 1795.

1. His knee swelled, and he walked with great difficulty TYNDALL. Every flower-bud swelleth R. BRIDGES. **b.** Do but behold the teares that s. in me SHAKS. **c.** A varied surface—where the ground swells, and falls 1791. 2. The Major,..swelling every already swollen vein in his head DICKENS. **b.** Bids the winde..s. the curled Waters 'boue the Maine SHAKS. The upland showers had swoln the rills SCOTT. 4. The ranks of the unemployed are..daily swelling 1895. 5. The presence of the monarch swelled the importance of the debate GIBBON. 6. Choral warblings round him s. GRAY. 7. **a.** Remembrance..Swells at my breast, and turns the past to pain GOLDSM. **b.** He swell'd to see Varus a suppliant growne 1627. 8. What other notions..could s. up Caligula to think himself a God? MILT. 9. Thy furious foes now s. And storm outrageously MILT.

Swell-, the verb-stem in comb.: **s.-fish,** a fish that inflates itself by swallowing air, also called *puffer* or *puff-fish*; **-front** *U.S.*, a bow-front of a house; *transf.* a house having such a front; **-head** *colloq.* = *swelled head* (see SWELLED b); also, a person affected with 'swelled head'; **-shark,** (*a*) a small shark, *Scyllium ventricosum*, of the Pacific coast of America; (*b*) a Californian shark, *Catulus uter*, which when caught inflates itself by swallowing air.

Swelldom (swe·ldəm). *colloq.* 1855. [f. SWELL *sb.* 8 + -DOM.] The realm or world of 'swells'; people of distinction of any kind.

Swelled (sweld), *ppl. a.* 1611. [Weak pa. pple. of SWELL *v.*; see -ED[1].] In senses of SWELL *v.*, *lit.* and *fig.*; *esp.* in sense 'morbidly enlarged, affected with tumour'. **b. S. head** (*fig.*): inordinate self-conceit, excessive pride or vanity (humorously regarded as a morbid affection). *colloq.* 1891.

Swelling (swe·liŋ), *vbl. sb.* late ME. [f. SWELL *v.* + -ING[1]. In OE. *swelling* (once).] **1.** The process of swelling, or condition of having swollen 1577. **2.** *concr.* A swollen part of something; a protuberance, prominence; *esp.* an abnormal or morbid enlargement in or upon any part or member; a tumour. late ME.

1. What wilt thou do in the s. of Iorden? *Bible* (Genev.) Jer. xii. 5. The s. of the buds, and the expansion of the leaves 1842. The proud s. of his heart SCOTT. 2. Swellings or Tumours in Horses, come by Heats, by hard Riding or by sore Labour 1704. *White s.*, a form of swelling without redness, *spec.* a tuberculous arthritis; strumous synovitis of a joint.

Swe·lling, *ppl. a.* OE. [f. as prec. + -ING[2].] That swells. Hence **Swe·llingly** *adv.*

Swellish (swe·liʃ), *a. colloq.* 1820. [f. SWELL *sb.* 8 + -ISH[1].] Stylish, dandified.

S'welp. 1899. Perversion of *so help*, in the oath 'so help me God'.

Swelt (swelt), *v.* Now *dial.* [Com. Teut. str. vb.: OE. *sweltan, swealt, swulton, -swolten.* The Teut. root **swelt-*: *swalt-*: *swult-* is perhaps a secondary formation on the root **swel-* to burn slowly.] **I.** *intr.* **1.** To die, perish. **2.** To be overcome, faint, swoon ME. **3.** To be faint with heat. late ME.

2. His olde wo þat made his herte to swelte CHAUCER.

II. *trans.* To overheat, broil, scorch; also in

fig. phr. *to s. one's heart*, to exert oneself to the utmost. Now *dial.* late ME.

Swelter (swe·ltəɹ), *v.* late ME. [f. root of SWELT *v.* + -ER 5.] 1. *intr.* To be oppressed with heat; to sweat profusely, languish, or faint with excessive heat. b. To move slowly or painfully (as if) oppressed with heat 1834. 2. *trans.* To oppress with heat; to cause to sweat, languish, or faint with oppressive heat. Chiefly *pass.* 1601. †3. *intr.* and *pass.* To be bathed *in* liquid; hence, to welter, wallow (*lit.* and *fig.*) –1865. 4. *trans.* with allusion to Shakspere's *sweltered venom* (see next, 1): To exude (venom); also *absol.*, and *intr.* for *pass.* 1834.

1. A fat official sweltering in his uniform under the burning sun 1880. b. The labouring ship sweltered about on the boiling sea 1834. 4. The fat seemed sweltering and full of poison L. HUNT.

Sweltered (swe·ltəɹd), *ppl. a.* 1605. [f. prec. + -ED 1.] 1. Exuded like sweat (as if) by heat. Only in *s. venom* in and after Shaks. 2. Bathed in, or oppressed with, great heat 1776.

1. Toad, that vnder cold stone..ha's..Sweltred Venom sleeping got SHAKS. 2. S. cattle COLERIDGE.

Sweltry (swe·ltri), *a.* Now *arch.* and *dial.* 1576. [f. SWELTER *v.* + -Y 1.] 1. Of heat, weather, etc.: Oppressively hot, sultry. 2. Oppressed or languishing with heat 1635.

Swept (swept), *ppl. a.* 1552. [pa. pple. of SWEEP *v.*] In senses of the verb; freq. as second element of compounds, as *wind-s.*

Swerve (swɜ̄ɹv), *sb.* 1741. [f. next.] An act of swerving, turning aside, or deviating from a course.

Swerve (swɜ̄ɹv), *v.* [Com. Teut. (orig.) str. vb.: ME. *swerve*, pa. t. *swarf* to turn aside, repr. OE. *sweorfan, swearf, sworfen* to file, scour. The original sense of the radical may be that of agitated, irregular, or deflected movement.] 1. *intr.* To turn aside; to deviate in movement from the straight or direct course ME. b. To turn in a specified direction; to be deflected (statically) 1600. 2. To turn away or be deflected from a (right) course of action, a line of conduct, an opinion, etc.; †to vacillate. late ME. †3. To give way; to sway, totter; *fig.* to shrink *from* action –1818. 4. To rove, stray. Also *fig.* to digress. 1543. †5. = SWARM *v.* 2 –1697. 6. *trans.* To cause to turn aside or deviate. late ME. b. *Cricket, Baseball*, etc. To cause a ball to deflect by imparting a spinning motion to it as it leaves the bowler or pitcher 1906.

1. His lab'ring team, that swerv'd not from the track COWPER. b. The road swerves to the left 1883. 2. Yet swarue not I from thy commaundementes COVERDALE *Ps.* cxviii[i]. 110. Honour that knows the path and will not s. WORDSW. The wealth around him never made Walpole s. from a rigid economy GREEN. 3. The battel swerv'd, with many an inrode gor'd MILT. 4. Al are swarued and clene gone out of the way 1543. 5. Nimbly up, from bough to bough I swerv'd DRYDEN. 6. My decided opinion..from which nothing shall s. me 1801. Hence **Swe·rveless**, unswerving.

Sweven (swe·v'n). *Obs.* exc. *arch.* [OE. *swef(e)n*:—OTeut. *swefno-:—Indo-Eur. *swepno-, f. *swep-* (cf. Gr. ὕπνος).] A dream, a vision.

Allas and konne ye been agast of sweuenys No thyng god woot, but vanitee in sweuene is CHAUCER.

Swift (swift), *sb.* 1530. [subst. use of next.] I. 1. The common newt or eft. Now only *dial.* b. A name for several swift-running small lizards, as the N. Amer. fence-lizard, *Sceloporus undulatus* 1530. 2. A bird of the family *Cypselidæ*, comprising many and widely distributed species, outwardly resembling swallows, and noted for their swiftness of flight; *esp.* the common swift, *Cypselus apus*, a summer visitant to the British Isles and Europe generally 1668. b. Name for a breed of domestic pigeons having some resemblance to swifts 1879. 3. Collector's name for moths of the genus *Hepialus* or family *Hepialidæ*, distinguished by their rapid flight 1819. II. 1. A light kind of reel, usu. of adjustable diameter, upon which a skein of silk, yarn, etc. is placed in order to be wound off 1564. b. A cylinder in a carding-machine 1853. †2. A rapid current; a rapid –1712. 3. The sail of a windmill. *dial.* 1763. 4. *Printers' slang.* A quick or expeditious type-setter 1841.

Swift, *a.* (*adv.*) [OE.:—prehistoric *swipt-, repr. Indo-Eur. root *(swoib-) sweib-, swib-: *(swoip-), sweip-, swip- to move in a sweeping manner with ppl. suffix *-to-*.] 1. 'Moving far in a short time' (J.); moving, or capable of moving, with great speed or velocity; rapid, fleet. b. Of movement, or action regarded as movement: Taking place or executed at high speed; rapid, quick OE. 2. Coming on, happening, or performed without delay; prompt, speedy OE. b. Acting, or disposed to act without delay; prompt, ready. Usu. const. *to* with inf. or sb. ME. 3. Done or finished within a short time; passing quickly, that is soon over, brief. Chiefly *poet.* ME.

1. A Swalwe s. of winge GOWER. The race is not to the s., nor the battel to the strong BIBLE (Geneva) *Eccl.* ix. 11. b. A s. but not very legible..penmanship CARLYLE. 2. Those proud Towrs to s. destruction doom'd MILT. b. Crafty of counsel, and s. of execution 1855. 3. My dayes are swifter then a weauers shuttle *Job* vii. 6.

B. *adv.* (Now chiefly *poet.*) Swiftly. late ME. Hence **Swi·ftly** *adv.*, **-ness**.

Swift, *v.* 1485. [Origin obsc.] *Naut. trans.* To tighten or make fast by means of a rope or ropes drawn taut.

Swiften (swi·ft'n), *v. rare.* 1638. [f. SWIFT *a.* + -EN 5.] 1. *trans.* To make swift or swifter. 2. *intr.* To become swift or swifter; *loosely*, to move swiftly, hasten, hurry 1839.

Swifter (swi·ftəɹ), *sb.* 1625. [See SWIFT *v.*] *Naut.* A rope used for swifting. a. One of a pair of shrouds, fixed above the other shrouds, for swifting or stiffening a mast. b. A rope passed through holes or notches in the outer ends of the capstan-bars and drawn taut. c. A rope passed around a boat or ship as a protection against strain or collision. Hence **Swi·fter** *v. trans.* to fasten a s. to, or tighten with a s.

Swi·ft-foot, *a.* and *sb.* 1594. A. *adj.* = SWIFT-FOOTED *a.* B. *sb.* A swift-footed person or animal, a fast runner; *spec.* = COURSER 3 1825.

Swift-footed (stress variable), *a.* 1600. Having swift feet; capable of running or going swiftly.

Swiftian (swi·ftiăn), *a.* 1762. [f. name of Jonathan *Swift* (1667–1745) + -IAN.] Pertaining to or characteristic of the satirist Swift or his works.

Swiftlet (swi·ftlėt). 1892. [f. SWIFT *sb.* + -LET.] A little or young swift; a small species of swift, as those of the genus *Collocalia*, which construct the edible birds' nests of China.

Swig (swig), *sb.* 1 *slang* or *colloq.* 1548. [Origin unkn.] †1. Drink, liquor –1635. b. Applied locally to special drinks 1827. 2. An act of 'swigging'; a deep or copious draught; a 'pull' 1621.

Swig, *sb.* 2 1807. [Cf. SWIG *v.* 2] *Naut.* 1. A tackle the falls of which are not parallel. 2. The act of 'swigging' at a rope 1904.

Swig, *v.* 1 *slang* or *colloq.* 1654. [app. f. SWIG *sb.* 1] *trans.* and *intr.* or *absol.* To drink in deep draughts; to drink eagerly or copiously.

I am..drinking as much tea..as I can s. RUSKIN.

Swig, *v.* 2 1663. [perh. related to SWAG, with general sense 'to cause to sway about, pull'.] 1. *trans.* To castrate (a ram) by tying the scrotum tightly with a string. 2. *Naut.* To pull at the bight of a rope which is fast at one end to a fixed object and at the other to a movable one; to pull (a sail, etc.) *up* in this manner 1794. 3. *intr.* To sway about, waver; to move with a swaying motion 1833.

Swill (swil), *sb.* 1553. [f. next.] I. Liquid or partly liquid food, chiefly kitchen refuse, given to swine; hog-wash, pig-wash. b. *transf.* A liquid or partly liquid mess, a slop 1665. 2. Copious or heavy drinking; liquor, esp. when drunk to excess; †a swig (of liquor) 1602.

Swill (swil), *v.* [OE. *swillan, swilian.*] 1. *trans.* To wash or rinse *out* (a vessel or cavity), or, now usu., to cause water to flow freely upon (a surface, floor, etc.) in order to cleanse it; formerly also, to wash, bathe, drench, soak. b. To stir (something) about in a vessel of liquid; to shake or stir (liquid) in a vessel by moving the vessel about 1580. c. To carry by a current of water, to wash down, against something, etc. Also, to pour or carry (liquid) freely down. 1598. 2. *intr.* To move or dash about, as liquid shaken in a vessel; to flow freely or forcibly; to flow or spread over a surface 1642. 3. To drink freely, greedily, or to excess, like hogs devouring 'swill' or 'wash'. *trans.* and *intr.* (*esp.* to tipple, booze). 1530. 4. *trans.* To cause to drink freely; to fill with drink; *refl.* to drink one's fill. Const. *with*, †*in.* 1548.

1. A galled Rocke..Swill'd with the wild and wastfull Ocean SHAKS. 2. The river went swishing, swilling past 1895. 3. Ye eat, and s., and sleep, and gourmandise SHERIDAN. 4. Till they can show there's something they love better than swilling themselves with ale GEO. ELIOT. Hence **Swi·ller**, one who swills. **Swi·lling** *vbl. sb.* the action of the vb.; *concr.* (usu. *pl.*) = SWILL *sb.* 1.

Swill-bowl (swi·lbōul). *Obs.* or *arch.* 1542. [f. prec. and BOWL *sb.* 1] One who habitually 'swills the bowl' or drinks to excess; a toper, drunkard.

Swill-tub (swi·ltʋb). 1575. [f. SWILL *sb.* 1 + TUB *sb.*] A tub for swill or hog-wash. Also *fig.* with allusion to heavy drinking.

Swim (swim), *sb.* 1547. [f. SWIM *v.*] †1. The clear part of a liquid which floats above the sediment –1676. †2. A smooth gliding movement of the body –1772. †3. The swimming-bladder or sound of a fish –1833. 4. A swimming motion; *colloq.* or *dial.* a swimming or dizzy sensation 1817. 5. An act of swimming 1805. 6. A part of a river or other piece of water much frequented by fish, or in which an angler fishes 1828. b. fig. phr. *In the s. with*: in the same company with, in league with 1885. 7. *fig.* The current of affairs or events, *esp.* the popular current in business, fashion, or opinion; chiefly in phr. *in* (*out of*) *the s.* 1869.

Swim (swim), *v.* Pa. t. **swam** (swæm); pa. pple. **swum** (swʋm). [Com. Teut. str. vb.: OE. *swimman*:—Indo-Eur. root *swem-.] I. *intr.* 1. To move along in or on water by movements of the limbs or other natural means of progression. 2. To float on the surface of any liquid; not to sink; to form the upper part of a mass of liquid. Sometimes, to rise and float on the surface. OE. b. To be supported in a fluid medium 1547. c. *fig.* 1547. 3. To move or float along on the surface of the water, as a ship. Now *poet.* OE. b. To be conveyed by a body floating on the water. late ME. 4. To move as water or other liquid, esp. over a surface; to flow. late ME. 5. To glide with a smooth or waving motion 1553. b. Of a plough (in full, *to s. fair*): To go steadily 1797. 6. To move, or appear to move, as if gliding or floating on water; *esp.* to move, glide, or be suspended in the air or ether, occas. by mechanical means 1661. b. Said of the apparent motion of objects before the eyes of a person whose sight is troubled or blurred 1678. 7. Of the head or brain: To be affected with dizziness; to have a giddy sensation. Also, of the head, *to s. round* = to be in a whirl. 1702. b. Of the eyes: To be troubled or blurred: with mixture of sense 9. 1817. 8. To float, be immersed or steeped, *in* a fluid 1450. b. *fig.* To be immersed or sunk *in* pleasure, grief, etc.; †to abound *in.* late ME. 9. To be covered or filled with fluid; to be drenched, overflowed, or flooded. Const. *with*, *in.* 1542. b. *fig.* To be full to overflowing *with* 1548.

1. Maoris and Kanakas can s., repeated the old man ..White men like you and me can only paddle. 1890. Phr. *To s. between two waters* (tr. F. prov. *nager entre deux eaux*), to steer between two extremes. *To s. with* or *down the stream* or *tide*, to act in conformity with prevailing opinion or tendency; so, *to s. against the stream.* 2. A boat, the only one that could s. 1798. Phr. *sink or s.* (occas. *s. or drown*), used *spec.* in ref. to the ordeal of suspected witches, hence *fig.* = 'whatever may happen'. 3. b. I will scarce thinke you haue swam in a Gundello SHAKS. 5. She..swam across the floor as though she scorned the drudgery of walking STEVENSON. 6. High up the vapours fold and s. TENNYSON. b. The arena swims around him—he is gone BYRON. 7. His brain swam with the thought 1851. 8. A cotton-wick swimming in oil 1775. b. At noon we s. in wine; at night, in tears 1644. 9. The marble floors of the Temple of Jerusalem swam in blood 1891.

II. *trans.* 1. To traverse or cover (a certain distance) by swimming. Also, to perform (a stroke or evolution) by swimming. OE. 2. To pass or cross by swimming; to move in, on, or over by swimming; to swim across 1591. 3. To cause (an animal) to swim, esp. across a river, etc. 1639. b. To cause (something) to pass over the surface of water; to float 1743. 4. To cause to float; to buoy up 1669. b. To put (a person suspected of witchcraft) to the ordeal of being immersed in water, the proof of innocence being that the person did not sink 1718. c. To furnish sufficient depth of water for (something) to swim or float in 1815.

1. He could not s. a stroke 1893. 2. You are ouer-bootes in loue, And yet you neuer swom the Hellespont SHAKS. 3. Sometimes swimming their horses, sometimes losing them and struggling for their own lives SCOTT. 4. Brine that will s. an egg 1842. c. Wide rivers..almost deep enough to s. a horse 1887.

Swi·m-bla·dder. 1837. [f. prec.] A fish's swimming-bladder.

Swimmer (swi·məɹ). late ME. [f. SWIM *v.* + -ER [1].] 1. A person (or animal) that swims in the water. 2. An animal that (habitually) swims; *spec.* a bird of the order *Natatores*, a swimming bird. late ME. 3. A swimming-organ of an animal 1816. 4. A thing which floats upon the surface of a liquid; *spec.* an angler's float 1609.

Swimmeret (swi·məret). 1840. [f. prec. + -ET.] An abdominal limb or appendage of a crustacean, adapted for swimming; a swimming-foot, pleopod.

Swimming (swi·miŋ), *vbl. sb.* late ME. [f. SWIM *v.* + -ING [1].] 1. The action of SWIM *v.* 2. A state of dizziness or giddiness 1530.

attrib. and *Comb.*, as *s.-bath*, *-pool*; **s.-bell**, a bell-shaped part or organ, as a nectocalyx, by which an animal propels itself through the water; **-bladder**, (*a*) the air-bladder of a fish, which enables it to keep its balance in swimming; (*b*) an inflated bladder to assist a person in swimming.

Swimming (swi·miŋ), *ppl. a.* OE. [f. SWIM *v.* + -ING [2].] 1. That swims. b. Of the eyes: Suffused with tears; watery 1729. 2. Affected with, or characterized by, dizziness or giddiness 1607. b. Of the eyes or sight (cf. L. *oculi natantes, lumina natantia*) 1697.

1. Poor Tom, that eates the s. Frog SHAKS. b. She rose, and fixt her s. eyes upon him TENNYSON. 2. b. No trembling of the hand, no error of the s. sight 1827. Hence **Swi·mmingly** *adv.* in a s. manner; smoothly and without impediment; with uninterrupted success or prosperity; with a smooth gliding movement. **Swi·mmingness** (*rare*), a misty appearance (of the eyes); smooth gliding movement.

Swimmy (swi·mi), *a.* 1836. [f. SWIM *v.* + -Y [1].] Inclined to dizziness or giddiness. Hence **Swi·mminess.**

Swindle (swi·nd'l), *sb.* 1852. [f. next.] 1. An act of swindling; a cheat, fraud, imposition. 2. Something that is not what it appears or is pretended to be; a 'fraud'. *colloq.* 1866.

Swindle, *v.* 1782. [Back-formation from next.] 1. *intr.* To act the swindler; to practise fraud, imposition, or mean artifice, esp. for the purpose of obtaining money. 2. *trans.* To cheat, defraud (a person) *out of* money or property 1803. 3. To get by swindling 1804.

2. Though she swindles Delphine out of her estate 1803. 3. Lamotte..had..swindled a sum of three-hundred livres from one of them CARLYLE.

Swindler (swi·ndləɹ). orig. *Cant.* 1775. [ad. G. *schwindler* giddy-minded person, extravagant projector, cheat, f. *schwindeln* to act thoughtlessly or extravagantly.] One who practises fraud, imposition, or mean artifice for purposes of gain; a cheat.

Dupes to the designing arts of the wretches distinguished by the name of Swindlers 1775. A s., living as he can SHELLEY.

Swine (swəin). *Pl.* **swine.** [Com. Teut.: OE. *swīn*:—OTeut. *_swīnom_, neut. of adj. formation with suffix *-īno-* (cf. L. *suinus*, and see -INE [1]) on the root of L. *sus*, Gr. ὗς, and SOW *sb.*] 1. An animal of the genus *Sus* or the family *Suidæ*, comprising bristle-bearing non-ruminant hoofed mammals, of which the full-grown male is called a *boar*, the full-grown female a *sow*; esp. the common species *Sus scrofa*, domesticated from early times by Gentile nations for its flesh, and regarded as a type of greediness and uncleanness. (Now only literary, dialectal, or as a generic term in zoology, etc., being superseded in common use by *pig* or *hog*.) 2. *fig.* Applied opprobriously to a sensual, degraded, or coarse person; also (in mod. use) as a mere term of contempt or abuse. late ME. 3. = *swine-fish* 1844.

1. Oh monstrous beast, how like a s. he lyes SHAKS. A herd of Swine MILT. 2. I shall be butchered to amuse these s. 1891.

Comb. (also with *swine's*): **s.-backed** (bækt) *a.*, having a back like that of a s.; *spec* in *Archery*, having a convexly curved outline (opp. to *saddle-backed*); **-eyes**, eyes like those of a s., which cannot be directed upwards; **s. fever**, a name for two infectious diseases of swine, *hog-cholera*, chiefly affecting the intestines, and *s.-plague*, chiefly affecting the lungs; **-fish**, the wolf-fish, *Anarrichas lupus*, so called from the movement of its snout; **-plague** (see *s. fever*); **swine's back**, a narrow hill-ridge (*local*); **-cress**, †(*a*) = *swine's-grass*; (*b*) the cruciferous plant *Senebiera Coronopus*; (*c*) ragwort (*local*); (*d*) nipplewort *Lapsana communis*; **-grass**, knotgrass, *Polygonum aviculare*; **swine's grease**, the fat of a s., lard (now *dial.*); **swine's thistle** = SOW-THISTLE 1 (*dial.*).

Swine-bread (swəi·nbred). 1591. [Cf. G. *schwein(s)brot*, mod.L. *panis porcinus*.] †1. The plant cyclamen –1648. †2. Truffles –1755. 3. The earth-nut or pig-nut (*local*) 1888.

Swine-cote. Now only *Hist.* or *dial.* late ME. [f. SWINE + COTE *sb.*[1]] A pigsty.

Swineherd (swəi·nhɜːd). Not in colloq. use. [Late OE. *swȳnhyrde*; see SWINE and HERD *sb.*[2]] A man who tends swine, esp. for hire.

Swine-pipe (swəi·npəip). 1668. [A book-name; origin unkn.] The redwing.

Swi·ne-pox. 1530. †1. Chicken-pox –1676. 2. An eruptive disease in swine 1704.

Swinery (swəi·nəri). 1778. [f. SWINE *sb.* + -ERY.] 1. A place where swine are kept; a piggery. 2. A swinish condition; swine collectively 1849.

Swine's feather. *Mil.* (now only *Hist.*) 1635. [ad. G. *schweinsfeder.*] A pointed stake or pike, used as a weapon of defence against cavalry, being either fixed in the ground as a palisade or carried in a musket-rest like a bayonet.

Swine-stone (swəi·nstōun). 1794. [ad. G. *schweinstein* (see SWINE and STONE *sb.*).] An early name for ANTHRACONITE.

Swine-sty (swəi·nstəi). Now chiefly *dial.* ME. [f. SWINE + STY *sb.*] A pigsty.

Swing (swiŋ), *sb.*[1] late ME. [In sense 1 app. repr. OE. *ȝeswing* in *hand-*, *sweordȝeswing* stroke with a weapon in fight, f. Teut. *_swingw-_ (see SWING *v.*). In sense 2, app. a substitute or var. of *swinge*. In other senses f. SWING *v.*] I. Abstract senses. †1. A stroke with a weapon. late ME. only. †2. *To bear the s.*: to have full sway or control. Also (*to have*) *s. and sway*. –1633. 3. The course of a career, practice, period of time, etc., esp. as marked by vigorous action of some kind. Now chiefly in phr. *in full s., in the full s. of..* 1570. †4. Impulse; inclination, tendency –1716. 5. Freedom of action, free scope 1584. 6. Forcible motion of a body swung or flung. *arch.* 1595. b. Continuous vigorous movement or progress 1856. c. *Full s.*: at full speed; with the utmost vigour or energy 1848. 7. The act of swinging or waving about a weapon or other body; a movement describing a curve, such as that made in flourishing a weapon, etc. 1635. 8. The act of swinging or oscillating, as a suspended body, or a body turning upon a fixed centre or axis; oscillation; also, the amount of oscillation, the arc or curve traced or moved through in this way. Also with adv., as *swing-to*. 1589. b. The distance which determines the diameter of the work that can be admitted by a lathe 1875. c. The leaning outward from the vehicle of the upper part of a wheel 1875. 9. Movement of the body or limbs in a manner suggesting the action of swinging 1730. 10. A steady vigorous rhythm or movement characterizing a verse or musical composition 1829.

3. It was still early..but the fishing was in full s. 1894. 5. The giving free s. to one's temper and instincts M. ARNOLD. 6. The Ramme that batters downe the wall, For the great s. and rudenesse of his poize [etc.] SHAKS. b. The..eight-oar coming with a steady s. up the last reach 1861. 7. Instantaneous photographs of first-class players taken when at the top of the s 1899. 8. Constant as the swings of a pendulum STEELE. The s. Of measured oars MORRIS. Phr. *On the s.*, oscillating. 9. An easy s. in my walk W. IRVING. 10. The 's.' and 'go'..of these popular religious ballads 1884.

II. Concrete senses. 1. A contrivance used for recreation, consisting of a seat which is suspended from above on ropes or rods and on which a person may sit and swing to and fro; also = *swing-boat*. (Allusive phr.: see ROUNDABOUT 4 b.) 1687. 2. The rope or chain attached to the tongue of a wagon, along which the horses between the leaders and the wheelers are attached, they being said to be *in the s.*; hence, the horses occupying that position (more fully, *s.-pair*, *-team*) 1891. b. The outriders who keep a moving herd of cattle in order. *U.S.* 1903.

Swing, *sb.*[2] Now *Hist.* 1830. Used, chiefly *attrib.*, to designate a system of intimidation practised in districts of the South of England in 1830–1, consisting in sending to farmers and landowners threatening letters over the signature of a fictitious Captain Swing, followed by the incendiary destruction of their ricks and other property.

Swing (swiŋ), *v.* Pa. t. **swung** (swʌŋ), *rarely* **swang** (swæŋ); pa. pple. **swung.** [OE. *swingan* (*swang, swungon, ȝeswungen*), f. Teut. *_swingw-_, older *swengw-*: *swangw-* (*swangwj-*), to be or to put in violent (circular or rotatory) motion.] †1. *trans.* To scourge, whip, flog, beat (a person); also, to strike with a weapon or the hand –1460. †2. To throw with force, fling, hurl –1495. †3. *intr.* To move or go impetuously; to rush; to fling oneself –1582. 4. *trans.* To draw *out* (a sword) with a vigorous movement (*obs.*); to flourish, brandish, wave *about*; in later use: to wield (a weapon or implement), or move (a body held or grasped) with an oscillating or rotatory movement. late ME. 5. *intr.* To move freely backwards and forwards, as a body suspended from a support above; to oscillate below a point of support, as a pendulum or the like 1545. b. Of a person: To move backwards and forwards through the air upon a suspended rope or on a swing, as a sport; to ride in a swing 1545. c. Of a (suspended) bell: To give forth a sound by swinging; to sound, ring *out* 1632. d. *fig.* To waver, vacillate 1833. e. *trans.* To mark or indicate by swinging; *to s. seconds*, to oscillate once in every second 1736. 6. *trans.* To cause to oscillate, as a body suspended from a support above; to move or sway (something) to and fro in this or a similar manner 1560. b. To cause (a person) to oscillate as in a swing; to give (one) a ride in a swing 1615. c. To lift and transport (something suspended) as with a crane; *transf.* to convey or transport from point to point 1856. d. *refl.* To hoist oneself up or transport oneself from point to point by grasping a support above. Also *intr.* 1899. 7. *intr.* To be suspended from a support above (without necessarily implying oscillation). a. *spec.* To be hanged. *slang* or *colloq.* 1542. b. *gen.* To be suspended, to hang; *transf.* to appear as if suspended 1641. 8. *trans.* To hang, suspend; *rarely*, to hang (a person). *slang* or *colloq.* 1528. 9. *intr.* To oscillate (without suspension); to move to and fro, or from side to side; to sway; to hover; *spec.* to sway the body backward and forward in rowing 1607. 10. To turn in alternate directions, or in either direction (usu. horizontally), around a fixed axis or point of support; *spec. Naut.* said of a vessel riding at a single anchor or moored by the head, and turning with the wind or tide 1769. b. To go along or round in a curve or with a sweeping motion; to wheel, sweep 1810. 11. *trans.* To cause to turn in alternate directions, or in either direction, on or as on an axis or pivot; to turn or cause to face in another direction 1768. b. *Naut.* To turn (a ship) to all points in succession, in order to ascertain the deviation of her magnetic compass 1859. c. To drive or cause to move in a curve; also, to make or execute by moving in a curve (in phr. *to s. a cast*, in hunting) 1854. 12. *intr.* To go along with undulating or swaying movement, or in a vigorous manner; to walk with swinging step 1854. 13. trans. *fig.* To direct or control the movement or action of; to sway, wield. *U.S.* 1889. 14. a. To fix (the work) on the centre or centres in a lathe. b. Of a lathe: To have a 'swing' or capacity of (so much). 1884.

4. He..swung his arms like the sails of a wind-mill SCOTT. 5. The shrill bell rings, the censer swings TENNYSON. c. Oft..I hear the far-off Curfeu sound, Over som wide-water'd shoar, Swinging slow with sullen roar MILT. d. He should endeavour..not to invest when the pendulum has swung upwards 1877. 6. Phr. *To s. a cat* (i. e. holding it by the tail); in *no room to s. a cat in* and similar expressions, said of a confined or narrow space. *To s. the lead*: to tell a 'tall' story; to make pretence. d. The Douglas swung himself into the saddle 1899. 7. a. They all lovingly swung together at Execution-Dock DE FOE. b. A lantern swung from the roof of the coach 1898. 9. A single hawk swung in the atmosphere above us TYNDALL. 10. While safely she at anchor swings 1812. 11. Swinging the parlour-door upon its hinge COWPER. c. He swings his team into the Avenue de l'Impératrice 1889. 12. The camels, swinging at a steady trot 1894. 13. He can s. the market so as to break a man 1908.

Swing- in comb. 1. In general attrib. or adj. use (mostly without hyphen, as a separate word), applied to a piece of mechanism, apparatus, or utensil suspended, hinged, or pivoted so as to be capable of oscillating or turning to and fro; sometimes var. of SWINGING *ppl. a.* 2. Special combs.: **s.-back**, the back of a photographic camera, carrying the sensitized plate, arranged so as to be 'swung' or turned on a hinge or pivot into any required position; **-beam**, a beam arranged to turn, or to enable something to turn, on a pivot or the like; **-bed**, a movable stool-bed in a gun-carriage; **-boat**, a boat-shaped swing used for amusement at fairs, etc.; **-bridge**, a form of drawbridge which turns horizontally on a pivot (either at one end or in the centre); **-cart**, a spring-cart; **-door**, a door constructed to swing to or shut of itself; **-front**, in a photographic camera (cf. *s.-back*); **-handle**, a handle turning on pivots; **-plough**, a plough without wheels; **-span** *U.S.* = *s.-bridge*; **-wheel**, the escape-wheel of a clock, which drives the pendulum; also, the balance-wheel of a watch.

Swinge (swindʒ), *sb.* *Obs.* exc. *dial.* 1531. [Related to SWINGE *v.*[1]] †1. Sway, power, rule, authority, influence -1636. †2. = SWING *sb.*[1] I. 5. -1687. †3. Impetus, impulse, driving power (of passion, will, etc.); inclination; drift, tendency -1804. †4. Impetus (of motion); impetuous or forcible sweeping or whirling movement -1696. 5. A leash for hounds 1661.

Swinge (swindʒ), *v.*[1] 1553. [Later form of ME. *swenge*:—OE. *swęngan* to shake, smite.] 1. *trans.* To beat, flog, whip, thrash. *arch.* or *dial.* †b. *fig.* To chastise, castigate; to pay out, serve out -1711. †2. To brandish, flourish; to lash (the tail, or something with the tail) -1629.

1. Saint George that swindg'd the Dragon SHAKS. I would so s. and leather my lambkin 1764. b. One Boyer, a French dog, has abused me..the Secretary promises me to s. him SWIFT. 2. Th' old Dragon under ground..Swindges the scaly Horrour of his foulded tail MILT.

Comb.: †**s.-buckler** = SWASHBUCKLER.

Swinge (swindʒ), *v.*[2] Now *dial.* and *U.S.* 1590. [app. alteration of SINGE.] *trans.* To singe, scorch.

Swing(e)ing (swi·ndʒiŋ), *ppl. a.* (*adv.*) 1590. [f. SWINGE *v.*[1]] 1. That swinges; scourging, flogging (*rare*) 1614. 2. Very forcible, large, or great; huge, immense. Now only *colloq.* or *slang*; mostly *arch.* or *dial.* 1590. b. as *adv.* Hugely, immensely 1690.

2. The jury gave swinging damages 1904. **Swi·ng(e)ing·ly** *adv.* (*colloq.* or *slang*).

Swinger[1] (swi·ndʒəɹ). 1583. [f. SWINGE *v.*[1] + -ER[1].] †1. One who acts vigorously or forcibly; a powerful fellow -1684. 2. Something forcible or effective; *esp.* something very big, a 'whopper'. *colloq.* or *slang*; now *rare* or *local.* 1599. †b. *spec.* A great or bold lie -1781. c. A forcible blow or stroke 1836.

Swinger[2] (swi·ŋəɹ). 1543. [f. SWING *v.* + -ER[1] 2.] One who or that which swings.

Swi·nging (-ŋ-), *ppl. a.* 1560. [f. SWING *v.* + -ING[2].] That swings.

Comb.: **s.-boom** *Naut.*, a boom swung or suspended over the ship's side, used to stretch the foot of a lower studding-sail, and (when at anchor) for a boat to ride by; **-bridge** = *swing-bridge*; **-tree** *dial.* = SWINGLE-TREE. Hence **Swi·ngingly** *adv.*

Swingle (swi·ŋg'l), *sb.* ME. [a. MDu. *swinghel* swingle for flax, corresp. in form to OE. *swingell*, *swingle* stroke or stripe with a rod, etc., f. SWING *v.* + -LE 1.] 1. A wooden instrument resembling a sword, used for beating and scraping flax or hemp so as to cleanse it of woody or coarse particles; also called *s.-hand*, *-staff*, or *-wand*, *swingling-bat*, *-knife*, or *-staff*. 2. The striking part or swipple of a flail (*local*). late ME. b. A weapon resembling a flail; a kind of cudgel 1818.

Swi·ngle, *v.*[1] ME. [a. MDu. *swinghelen*, f. *swinghel* SWINGLE *sb.*] *trans.* To beat and scrape (flax or hemp) with a swingle, in order to cleanse it of the coarser particles; to scutch.

Swi·ngle, *v.*[2] 1450. [freq. of SWING *v.*] †1. *trans.* To swing or flourish about. 2. *intr.* To swing; to hang, be suspended. *dial.* 1755.

Swingle- in comb.: **s.-bar** = SWINGLE-TREE 2; **-hand**, **-staff** = SWINGLE *sb.* 1; **-tail**, a species of shark = THRASHER[1] 2; **-wand** = SWINGLE *sb.* 1.

Swingletree (swi·ŋg'ltrī). 1462. [f. SWINGLE *sb.* + TREE *sb.*] 1. A board used in dressing flax or hemp. *Obs.* or *dial.* 2. In a plough, carriage, etc., a cross-bar, pivoted at the middle, to which the traces are fastened, giving freedom of movement to the shoulders of the horse or other draught animal 1483.

Swingling (swi·ŋgliŋ), *vbl. sb.* 1462. [f. SWINGLE *v.*[1] + -ING[1].] The process of dressing flax or hemp with a swingle; scutching.

attrib.: **s.-bat**, **-knife**, **-staff** = SWINGLE *sb.* 1; **-tow**, the coarse part of flax, separated by swingling.

Swing-swang (swi·ŋswæŋ). 1683. [Reduplicated f. SWING *v.* with change of vowel.] A swinging to and fro; a reciprocating movement; *occas.* see-saw.

Swing-tree (swi·ŋtrī). late ME. = SWINGLETREE 2.

Swinish (swəi·niʃ), *a.* ME. [f. SWINE *sb.* + -ISH[1].] 1. Having the character or disposition of a swine; hoggish, piggish; sensual, gluttonous; coarse, gross, or degraded in nature. b. Of actions, etc.: Characteristic of or befitting a swine; coarse, beastly. late ME. 2. Pertaining to or fit for swine 1592. 3. Having the nature of a swine; that is a swine; consisting of swine 1612. b. Resembling a swine or that of a swine, in aspect or other physical quality 1805.

1. Drunkards, s. Epicures, heretiques 1606. b. In S. sleepe SHAKS. 3. b. The s. outline of the porpoise 1889. Hence **Swi·nish·ly** *adv.*, **-ness.**

Swink (swiŋk), *sb.* *arch.* [OE. *swinc*, f. *swincan* SWINK *v.*] †1. Trouble, affliction (*rare*) -late ME. 2. Labour, toil ME.

Swink (swiŋk), *v.* *arch.* and *dial.* [OE. *swincan*, parallel formation to *swingan* SWING *v.*] 1. *intr.* To labour, toil; to exert oneself, take trouble. †2. *trans.* and *intr.* To drink deeply, tipple -1590.

1. For they doo swinke and sweate to feed the other SPENSER. Hence **Swi·nker**, *arch.* one who swinks.

Swinked, swinkt (swiŋkt, *also* swi·ŋkėd), *ppl. a.* *arch.* (after Milton). 1634. [f. prec. + -ED[1].] Wearied with toil; overworked.

What time..the swink't hedger at his Supper sate MILT.

Swipe (swəip), *sb.*[1] 1600. [app. local var. of *swape* sb. or SWEEP *sb.*] A contrivance of the form of a lever for raising a weight, *esp.* for raising water.

Swipe (swəip), *sb.*[2] 1807. [perh. local var. of SWEEP *sb.*] A heavy blow; *spec.* a driving stroke made with the full swing of the arms, in cricket or golf; *transf.* one who makes such a stroke. *colloq.* b. (*a*) = SWATH 3. 1869. (*b*) A streak or stripe produced as if by swiping 1890.

With the cricketers he was accounted a hard *s.*, an active *field*, and a stout bowler 1825.

Swipe (swəip), *v.* 1825. [app. partly local var. of SWEEP *v.*, partly f. prec.] 1. *trans.* and *intr.* To drink hastily and copiously; to drink at one gulp 1829. 2. *intr.* To strike *at* with the full swing of the arms; chiefly in cricket 1825. b. *trans.* To deal a swinging blow or hit at (esp. in cricket) 1881. 3. *intr.* and *trans.* = SWEEP *v.* II. 4. 1881. 4. *trans.* To steal, 'appropriate'; to loot. *U.S.* 1890.

2. Wilson was now as bold as a lion, swiping at every ball 1869. Hence **Swi·per.**

Swipes (swəips). *slang* or *colloq.* 1796. [perh. f. prec. 1.] Poor weak beer; small beer; hence, beer in general.

Swipple (swi·p'l). 1450. [prob. orig. f. *swēp-* SWEEP *v.* + instrumental suffix -ELS.] The part of a flail that strikes the grain in thrashing.

Swirl (swə̄ɹl), *sb.* late ME. [orig. Sc.; origin uncertain; cf. Norw. dial. *svirla*, Du. *zwirrelen* to whirl, G. dial. *schwirrlen* to totter.] 1. An eddy, a whirlpool; an eddying or whirling body of water, in later use also of cloud, dust, etc. 2. A whirling or eddying motion; a whirl, gyration 1818. 3. A twist or convolution; a curl of hair; a knot in the grain of wood 1786. b. A tress of hair or strip of material round the head or hat 1909.

1. Seen through clefts in grey swirls of rain-cloud RUSKIN.

Swirl (swə̄ɹl), *v.* 1513. [orig. Sc.; see prec.] 1. *trans.* To give a whirling or eddying motion to; to bring into some position by a whirling motion; to whirl, brandish. b. To give a twisted or convolute form to; also, to wrap round *with* something 1902. 2. *intr.* a. Of water or of objects borne on water: To move in or upon eddies or little whirlpools 1755. b. Of other objects: To move rapidly in eddies or in a whirling or circular course 1858. 3. Of the head, etc.: To swim; to be giddy 1818.

1. Some withered leaves were swirled round and round, as if by the wind 1818. 2. b. Starlings swirling from the hedge M. ARNOLD.

Swish (swiʃ), *int.* or *adv.* and *sb.*[1] 1820. [Echoic.] A. *int.* or *adv.* Expressive of the sound described in B. 1; with a swish 1837.

S. went the whip 1890.

B. 1. A hissing sound like that produced by a switch or similar slender object moved rapidly through the air or an object moving swiftly in contact with water; movement accompanied by such sound 1820. 2. A dash of water upon a surface 1851. 3. A cane or birch for flogging; also, a stroke with this 1860.

1. The s. of the angler's rod 1886.

C. *adj.* (*colloq.*) Smart, 'swell' 1879.

Swish (swiʃ), *sb.*[2] 1863. [perh. native name.] A native building mortar of W. Africa.

Swish (swiʃ), *v.* 1756. [Echoic.] 1. *intr.* To move with a swish; to make the sound expressed by 'swish'. 2. *trans.* To cause to move with a swish; *esp.* to whisk (the tail) about 1799. b. *intr.* (const. *with*) 1854. c. *trans.* To move or remove with (or as with) a swishing movement 1894. 3. *intr.* To jump a high hedge, brushing through the twigs at the top and making them bend 1825. 4. *trans.* To flog, esp. at school 1856.

1. The wheels swished through the pools 1877. 2. And backward and forward he swish'd his long tail As a Gentleman swishes his cane COLERIDGE. 4. As he wouldn't tell he must be swished 1872.

Swish-, the vb.-stem used attrib. or advb.: **s.-cane**, a light slender cane such as can be swished; **-tail**, †(*a*) *slang*, a pheasant; (*b*) a long flowing tail which can be swished about.

Swiss (swis), *sb.* and *a.* 1515. [ad. F. *Suisse*, ad. MHG. *Swiz.*] A. *sb.* 1. (Pl. *the Swiss*; †formerly *the Swisses.*) A native or an inhabitant of Switzerland. 2. The Swiss dialect of German or other language spoken by the Swiss (*rare*) 1846. B. *adj.* 1. Of, belonging to, or characteristic of the Swiss or Switzerland; native to, or coming from, Switzerland 1530. 2. In names of things, animals, etc. actually or reputedly coming from Switzerland; e. g. *S. cheese, lace, milk*, etc. 1700.

2. **S. guards**, mercenary soldiers from Switzerland used as a special body-guard by former sovereigns of France, and other monarchs; still employed at the Vatican. **S. roll**, a 'sweet' consisting of sponge cake rolled up with a layer of jam. **S. stone-pine**; see STONE-PINE. **S. sword**, a basket-hilted sword used in the 16th c. by S. foot-soldiers.

†**Swi·sser.** 1530. [ad. MHG. *Swycer*, *Schwyczer*, var. *Sweitzer* SWITZER, or f. F. *Suisse* SWISS + -ER[1].] A Swiss -1734.

Switch (switʃ), *sb.* 1592. [Early forms *swits*, *switz*; prob. ad. Flem. or LG. word represented by Hanoverian *swutsche* long thin stick, switch. In sense 5, f. SWITCH *v.*] 1. A slender tapering riding whip. 2. A thin flexible shoot cut from a tree 1610. 3. Name for various mechanical devices for altering the direction of something, making a connexion or disconnexion, or other purposes. a. On a railway: A movable rail or pair of rails pivoted at one end, forming part of the track at a junction with a branch line, etc., and used to deflect or shunt a train, car, etc from one line to another 1797. **b.** *Electr.* A lever, plug, or other device for making or breaking contact, or altering the connexions of a circuit. Also *loosely* = SWITCHBOARD. 1866. **4.** A long bunch or coil of hair, esp. of false hair worn by women to supplement the natural growth of hair 1878. **5.** An act of switching; a blow with a switch 1809.

1. To cut off the heads of some nettles..with his s. JANE AUSTEN. Phr. *S. and spurs* = at full speed, in hot haste. 5. b. *Bridge.* A change of call from one suit to another 1921.

Comb.: **s.-bar**, a bar connected with a s. (on a railway or electrical apparatus); **-grass**, the couch-grass; **-horn**, a stag's horn without branches; also, a stag having such horns; **-man**, a man who works a s. or set of switches on a railway; **-rail** = sense 3a; **-room**, a room containing the switches of an electrical system; **-tail** = SWISH-*tail*.

Switch, *v.* 1611. [f. prec.] **1.** *trans.* To strike, hit, beat, flog, or whip with or as with a switch. **b.** *intr.* or *absol.* To strike, deal a blow or blows, with or as with a switch 1612. **2.** *trans.* To drive with or as with a switch 1616. **3.** To flourish like a switch, to whisk, lash; to move (something) with a sudden jerk 1842. **4.** To cut off the switches or projecting twigs from; to trim (a tree, hedge, etc.) 1811. **5.** To turn (a railway train, car, etc.) on to another line by means of a switch; to shunt; also *intr.* for *pass.* **b.** *intr.* Of a railway line: To branch or turn *off* at a switch. *U.S.* 1875. **6.** *fig.* To turn *off*, divert. Chiefly *U.S.* 1860. **7.** *trans.* In electrical apparatus: To direct (a current) by means of a switch; to put *on* or *off*; to turn (an electric light) *on* or *off* 1881.

3. He..stood switching his riding-whip 1856. 6. The Colonel..switched the conversation off to the chances of the morrow 1897. b. *intr. Bridge.* To change to another suit in bidding 1921.

Switchback (swi·tʃbæk), *a.* and *sb.* 1887. [f. SWITCH *v.* 5 + BACK *adv.*] **A.** *adj.* **a.** Applied to a form of railway used on steep slopes, consisting of a zigzag series of lines connected by switches, at each of which the train or car is 'switched back' or reversed in direction. **b.** Applied to a railway consisting of steep alternate ascents and descents, on which the train or car runs partly or wholly by the force of gravity, the momentum of each descent carrying it up the succeeding ascent; *esp.* to such a railway constructed for amusement at a pleasure-resort, fair, etc. Hence *transf.* of a road having steep alternate ascents and descents. 1888. **B.** *sb.* A switchback railway (in either sense); also *transf.* and *fig.* 1887.

Switchboard (swi·tʃbōᵊɹd). 1884. [f. SWITCH *sb.* 3b + BOARD *sb.*] A board or frame bearing a set of switches for connecting and disconnecting the various circuits of an electrical system, as of a telegraph, telephone, etc.

Switchel (swi·tʃĕl). *U.S.* 1800. [Origin unkn.] A drink made of molasses and water, sometimes with vinegar, ginger, or rum added.

Switching (swi·tʃiŋ), *vbl. sb.* 1625. [-ING [1].] The action of SWITCH *v.*

Comb.: **s.-angle** *Gunnery*, the angle between the lines of fire of the directing gun when the latter is brought to bear on the left of the new target **-engine, -locomotive**, one used in or for shunting on a railway.

Switchy (swi·tʃi), *a. rare.* 1812. [f. SWITCH *sb.* + -Y [1].] Of the nature of or resembling a switch or slender rod; moving or bending like a switch.

Switzer (swi·tsəɹ). *arch.* 1577. [ad. MHG. *Switzer, Schwytzer*, or MDu. *Switser, Swytzer*; f. *Switz(en* Switzerland.] **1.** = SWISS *sb.* 1. **2.** *pl.* = *Swiss guards* (SWISS *a.* 2); rarely *sing.* 1591. **3.** *attrib.* or *adj.* = SWISS *a.* 1598.

Swive (swəiv), *v. Obs.* or *arch.* late ME. [app. repr., with a specialized meaning, the OE. str. vb. *swīfan* to move in a course, sweep.] **1.** *trans.* To have sexual connexion with (a female). **2.** *intr.* To copulate 1440.

Swivel (swi·v'l), *sb.* ME. [f. weak grade *swif-* of OE. *swīfan* (see prec.) + *-el* (see -LE).] **1.** A simple fastening or coupling device made so that the object fastened to it can turn freely upon it, or so that each half of the swivel itself can turn independently; *e.g.* a ring or staple turning on a pin or the like. **b.** *spec.* A pivoted rest for a gun, *esp.* on the gunwale of a boat, enabling it to turn horizontally in any required direction 1697. **2.** Short for *s.-gun* 1748. **3.** A kind of small shuttle used in ribbon-weaving, etc. 1894.

Comb.: **s.-bridge**, a swing-bridge; **-chair**, a chair the seat of which turns horizontally on a pivot; **s. eye** *colloq.* or *slang*, a squinting eye; an eye that rolls in its socket; hence **s.-eyed** *a.*, squint-eyed; **-gun**, a gun or cannon, usu. a small one, mounted on a s., so as to turn horizontally in any required direction; **-hook**, a hook fastened to something, *e.g.* a pulley-block, by means of a s.; **-shuttle** = sense 3.

Swi·vel, *v.* 1794. [f. prec.] **1.** *trans.* To turn (something) on or as on a swivel. **2.** *intr.* To turn or rotate as, or as on, a swivel 1846. **3.** *trans.* To furnish with a swivel; to fasten *to* something by means of a swivel 1870.

Swizzle (swi·z'l), *sb. slang* or *colloq.* 1813. [Origin unkn.; cf. SWITCHEL.] A name for various compounded intoxicating drinks; occas. vaguely used for intoxicating drink in general.

Comb.: **s.-stick**, a stick used for stirring drink into a froth.

Swi·zzle, *v. slang* or *colloq.* and *dial.* 1847. [f. prec.] **1.** *intr.* To drink to excess, tipple. **2.** *trans.* To stir with a swizzle-stick 1859.

Swollen (swōᵘ·l'n), *ppl. a.* ME. [str. pa. pple. of SWELL *v.*] **1.** Increased in bulk, as by internal pressure; distended; *esp.* morbidly enlarged, affected with tumour; also, of a distended form, bulging, protuberant. **b.** Increased in amount or degree 1631. **2.** *fig.* **a.** Said of a feeling or mental state such as causes a sense of distension or expansion, or of a person affected with such a feeling, etc.; *esp.* inflated with pride, puffed up. late ME. **b.** Of language: Turgid, inflated 1605.

1. Her s. eyes were much disfigured SPENSER. b. The s. shelves of our libraries 1921. 2. a. His s. heart almost bursting DICKENS. b. Swoln panegyrics COLERIDGE.

Swoon (swūn), *sb.* ME. [orig. in phr. *in swoune*, etc. (sense 1), alteration of *a swoun* ASWOON; otherwise f. SWOON *v.*]. **1.** The action of swooning or the condition of one who has swooned; syncope. **b.** A fainting fit. late ME. **†2.** A (deep or sound) sleep. SPENSER.

Swoon (swūn), *v.* [ME. *swoȝene, swowene*, prob. a back-formation from *swoȝning, swowening* SWOONING *vbl. sb.*] **1.** *intr.* To fall into a fainting-fit; to faint. **b.** *fig.* said of natural phenomena 1818. **2.** *pass.* To fall into a swoon; chiefly *pa. pple.* or *ppl. a.*: In a swoon 1450.

1. Many will s. when they do look on bloud SHAKS. b. All round the coast the languid air did s. TENNYSON. 2. She lies swooned on a paillasse CARLYLE.

Swooning (swū·niŋ), *vbl. sb.* [ME. *suowengue, swoȝning*, app. f. *iswowen, iswoȝen*, OE. *geswōgen* pa. pple. fainting, in a swoon.] **1.** fainting, syncope. **2.** A fainting-fit ME.

Swooning (swū·niŋ), *ppl. a.* 1646. [f. SWOON *v.* + -ING [2].] That swoons or faints; characterized by swooning. Hence **-ly** *adv.*

Swoop (swūp), *sb.* 1544. [f. next.] **†1.** A blow, stroke –1711. **2.** The act of swooping down; *esp.* the sudden pouncing of a bird of prey from a height upon its quarry 1605. **b.** A sudden descent, as by a body of troops, esp. *upon* something which it is intended to seize 1824.

2. Swift as the s. of the eagle 1847. Phr. *At one (fell*, etc.) *s.*, at one sudden descent, as of a bird of prey; hence, at a single blow or stroke. b. Influenza came down upon me with a s. HUXLEY.

Swoop (swūp), *v.* 1566. [app. a dial. development of OE. *swāpan* to sweep, f. Teut. root **swaip-*.] **†1.** *intr.* To move or walk in a stately manner as with trailing garments; to sweep along –1622. **†2.** *trans.* To sweep *up, away, off*, etc. –1888. **†3.** To pounce upon, as a bird of prey; to seize, catch up with a sweeping movement –1822. **4.** *intr.* To make a rapid sweeping descent through the air *upon* its prey, as a bird 1837. **5.** To come down *upon* suddenly with a sweeping movement, esp. with the intention of seizing, as a body of troops 1797.

2. A rich patrimonie..he swoopt away HOLLAND. 3. Till now at last you came to s. it all DRYDEN. 4. Sea-gulls were swooping down and around the tall masts 1873. 5. At other times a breeze would s. down upon us TYNDALL.

†Swoo·pstake, *sb.* and *adv.* 1600. [Altered f. SWEEPSTAKE after SWOOP *v.*] **A.** *sb.* = SWEEPSTAKE 2. **B.** *adv.* By sweeping all the stakes at once; hence, indiscriminately.

Sword (sǭɹd, sōᵊɹd), *sb.* [Com. Teut. (not in Gothic): OE. *sweord* :—OTeut. **swerdo*[m].] **1.** A weapon adapted for cutting and thrusting, consisting of a handle or *hilt* with a cross-guard, and a straight or curved blade with either one or two sharp edges (or sometimes with blunt edges) and a sharp point. **b.** As used on ceremonial occasions as a symbol of honour or authority (*s. of honour, of state*, etc.) late ME. **2.** *fig.* Something that wounds or kills, a cause of death or destruction, a destroying agency; also, something figured as a weapon of attack in spiritual warfare OE. **3.** *transf.* The use of the sword in warfare, massacre, etc.; hence, slaughter; warfare; military force or power; also, the military profession or class, the army OE. **4.** As the instrument or symbol of penal justice; hence, the authority of a ruler or magistrate to punish offenders; more generally, power of government, executive power, authority, jurisdiction; also, the office of an executive governor or magistrate. late ME. **5.** A material object resembling a sword. **a.** One of various mechanical devices in the form of a flat wooden blade, bar, or rod 1530. **b.** The sharp projecting jaw-bone of the sword-fish 1641. **c.** A sword-like ray or flash of light 1866.

1. Put vp thy swearde into hys sheath BIBLE (Great) *Matt.* xxvi. 52. Phr. *S.-in-hand*, armed with a s.; *fig.* militant. 2. This Auarice..hath bin The S. of our slaine Kings SHAKS. 3. It hath bin oft anough told him, that he hath no more autority over the s. then over the law MILT. Phr. *To put to the s.*, to kill or slaughter with the s. *The power of the s.* 4. This Power Coercive, or (as men use to call it) the S. of Justice HOBBES. 5. a. Swords are these parts of the loom that the lay is fixed to 1863.

attrib. and *Comb.*, as *s.-exercise, -hilt, -thrust*; **s.-and-buckler** *a.*, armed with or using a s. and buckler; pertaining to or performed with s. and buckler; †*fig.* bragging, blustering; **s.-arm**, the arm with which the s. is wielded, the right arm; also *rhet.* = military power or action; **-bayonet**, a form of bayonet which may be used as a s.; **-belt**, a belt by which the s. in its scabbard is suspended; **-bill**, a S. Amer. humming-bird, *Docimastes ensiferus*, with a very long bill; **-blade**, the blade of a s.; **-cane**, a hollow cane or walking-stick containing a steel blade, which may be drawn or shot out and used as a s.; **-dance**, a dance in which the performers go through some evolutions with swords, or in which a person dances among naked swords laid on the ground; so **-dancer, -dancing**; **-hand**, the hand with which the s. is wielded, the right hand; **-knot**, a ribbon or tassel tied to the hilt of a s.; **-law**, government by the power of the s. or by military force, martial law; **-leaved** *a.*, having s.-shaped or ensiform leaves; **-mat** *Naut.*, a piece of matting used to protect parts of the rigging, etc., so called from the wooden 'sword' with which the fabric is beaten close in weaving; so **-matting**; **-side**, the male line in descent; **-stick** = *s.-cane*; **-swallower**, one who entertains for money by swallowing or pretending to swallow swords; **-tail**, an animal of the group *Xiphosura*, comprising only the genus *Limulus*, a king-crab; **-taker**, one who 'takes the s.' (Matt. xxvi. 52) without authority or right, a lawless killer; **-whale**, the grampus, also called SWORDFISH. **b.** In names of plants having sword-shaped leaves or other parts, as **s.-flag**, the yellow water-flag, *Iris Pseudacorus*; **-flax**, a name for the New Zealand flax, *Phormium tenax*; **-lily**, the genus *Gladiolus*; **-rush, -sedge**, an Australian sedge, *Lepidosperma gladiatum*. Hence **Sword** *v.* (*rare*) *trans.* to arm or equip with a s.; to strike or kill with a s.; also *absol.* or *intr.*

Swo·rd-bea:rer. late ME. A person who bears a sword. **a.** *spec.* A municipal official who carries a sword of state before a magistrate on ceremonial occasions. **b.** A ruler or magistrate having authority to punish offenders (with allusion to Rom. xiii. 4) 1660. **c.** *gen.* One who carries or wears a sword 1530. **d.** One of an order of knights in Poland founded in 1204. 1656.

Sworded (sǭ·ɹdĕd, sōᵊ·ɹdĕd), *a.* OE. [f. SWORD *sb.* + -ED [2].] Equipped or armed with a sword. **b.** *trans.* Having some part resembling a sword 1681.

Sworder (sǭ·ɹdəɹ, sōᵊ·ɹdəɹ). 1593. [f. SWORD *sb.* + -ER [1], after L. *gladiator*.] **1.** One who kills another with a sword, an assassin, cut-throat; one who habitually fights with a sword; a gladiator. **2.** One skilled in the use of the sword; a swordsman 1814.

Swo·rdfish. late ME. [f. SWORD *sb.* + FISH *sb.*[1], after Gr. ξιφίας, L. *gladius*.] **1.** A large fish of the Atlantic, Mediterranean, and Pacific, *Xiphias gladius*, having the upper jaw prolonged into a sword-like weapon; the flesh is used for food. Also extended to other species of the genus *Xiphias* and related genera. **2.** The southern constellation Dorado or Xiphias 1771.

Swo·rd-grass. 1598. A name for several plants with sword-shaped leaves, as the sword-lily (*Gladiolus*), *Arenaria* (*Spergularia*) *segetalis*, *Melilotus segetalis* or *sulcata*, and various grasses or sedges, as the reed canary-grass (*Phalaris arundinacea*), *Arundo conspicua* of New Zealand, and *Cladium psittacorum* of Australia.

Swo·rding, *ppl. a. Obs.* or *arch.* 1611. [f. SWORDER; see -ING².] Martial, warlike.

Swordless (sǭ·ɹdlės, sǭᵊ·ɹd-), *a.* 1440. [f. SWORD *sb.* + -LESS.] Destitute of a sword; not having, carrying, or using a sword.

Swo·rdman. Now *rare* or *Obs. Pl.* **-men.** late ME. [f. SWORD *sb.* + MAN *sb.*] **1.** = SWORDSMAN 1. **b.** A soldier who fights with a sword; one of a body of troops armed with swords; hence, an armed follower. late ME. **2.** A man 'of the sword'; a warrior, military man, fighter, soldier 1601.

2. *All's Well* II. i. 62.

Swo·rd-play. [OE. *sweordplega*, f. SWORD *sb.* + PLAY *sb.*] †**a.** Fight, battle. OE. only. **b.** The action of plying or wielding a sword briskly, as in fencing; the art or practice of fencing 1647. **c.** *fig.* Spirited or skilful controversy or debate 1847. So **Swo·rd-play:er,** (*rare* or *Obs.*) one skilled in s.; chiefly, a gladiator; also, a fencer. late ME.

Swordsman (sǭ·ɹdz-, sǭᵊ·ɹdzmæ̆n). *Pl.* **-men.** 1680. [f. gen. of SWORD *sb.* + MAN *sb.*] **1.** A man who uses, or is skilled in the use of, a sword; *spec.* one skilled in fencing. **b.** = SWORDMAN 1 b. 1865. **2.** = SWORDMAN 2. 1701. Hence **Swo·rdsmanship,** the quality or art of a s.

Swore, pa. t. and obs. pa. pple. of SWEAR *v.*

Sworn (swǭɹn), *ppl. a.* ME. [Pa. pple. of SWEAR *v.*] **1.** That has taken or is bound by an oath. **b.** Thoroughly devoted or addicted to some course of action; resolute, out-and-out 1607. **2.** Appointed or admitted with a formal or prescribed oath to some office or function. late ME. **3.** Affirmed or promised by an oath; to which one is sworn 1818.

1. *S. brother*, either of two companions in arms who took an oath according to the rules of chivalry to share each other's good and bad fortunes; hence, a close or intimate friend or companion; so *s. friend*. *S. enemy, foe*, one who has vowed perpetual enmity against another; hence, a determined or irreconcilable enemy. 2. *S. man* (formerly as one word), a man bound by oath to the performance of a duty or office; hence, a man bound to strict service, a 'vassal'.

Swot, swat (swǫt), *sb. slang.* 1850. [dial. var. of SWEAT *sb.*] **1.** Work or study at school or college; in early use *spec.* mathematics. Hence *gen.* labour, toil. **2.** One who studies hard 1850. Hence **Swot, swat** *v.* (*slang*) *intr.* to work hard at one's studies; *trans.* to 'get *up*', 'mug *up*' (a subject). **Swo·tter.**

Swound (swaund), *sb.* Now *arch.* and *dial.* 1440. [Later form of *swoune* SWOON, with excrescent *d*.] A fainting-fit. So **Swound** *v. intr.* to swoon, faint.

†**Swounds,** *int.* 1589. Euphemistic abbrev. of *God's wounds* used in oaths and asseverations –1620.

-sy, hypocoristic dim. suffix added to (i) proper names, as *Betsy, Topsy*, also in the form *-cy*, as *Nancy*; (ii) common nouns, as *babsy, ducksy, mopsy.*

‖**Syagush** (syā·gūʃ). 1727. [Urdū = Pers. *siyāh gosh* black ear.] The caracal, a feline animal.

Sybarite (si·bărəit), *sb.* and *a.* 1598. [ad. L. *Sybarita*, ad. Gr. Συβαρίτης, f. Σύβαρις Sybaris.] **A.** *sb.* **1.** A native or citizen of Sybaris, an ancient Greek city of southern Italy, noted for its effeminacy and luxury. **2.** A person devoted to luxury or pleasure, an effeminate voluptuary or sensualist. (Now usu. spelt with small initial.) 1623.

2. The Lords of Lacedæmon were true soldiers, But ours are Sybarites BYRON. The very room for an artist and a s. 1863.

B. *adj.* = SYBARITIC *a.* 1599. Hence **Sy·baritism,** sybaritic habits or practices, effeminate voluptuousness.

Sybaritic (sibări·tik), *a.* 1619. [ad. late L. *Sybariticus*, ad. Gr. Συβαριτικός; see prec.] **1.** Of or pertaining to Sybaris or its inhabitants 1786. **2.** Effeminately luxurious 1619.

2. S. dinners WARBURTON. An atmosphere of s. enjoyment 1876. So **Sybari·tical** *a.* (now *rare*) 1617, **-ly** *adv.*

Sycamine (si·kămin, -əin). *arch.* 1526. [ad. Gr. συκάμινον mulberry, f. Heb. *shiqmah*, with assimilation to σῦκον fig.] The common black mulberry, *Morus nigra.*

Sycamore, sycomore (si·kămoᵊɹ, si·kǒmoᵊɹ). ME. [a. OF. *sic(h)amor*, mod.F. *sycomore*, ad. late L. *si-, sycomorus*, ad. Gr. συκόμορος, f. σῦκον fig + μόρον mulberry. The spelling *sycamore* is the more usual.] **1.** A species of fig-tree, *Ficus Sycomorus*, common in Egypt, Syria, and other countries, and having leaves somewhat resembling those of the mulberry. **2.** A large species of maple, *Acer Pseudo-platanus*, introduced into Britain from the Continent, and grown as a shady ornamental tree and for its wood 1588. **3.** In N. America, a plane or tree of the genus *Platanus*, esp. the buttonwood, *P. occidentalis* 1814. **4.** The wood or timber of the sycamore. late ME. **5.** Short for *s. moth* 1843.

Comb.: **s.-fig,** the fig-tree, *Ficus Sycomorus*, or its fruit; **s. maple** = sense 2; **s.-moth,** a noctuid moth, *Acronycta* (*Apatela*) *aceris*, the larva of which feeds on the s. (sense 2); **-tree** = sense 1, 2, 3.

Syce (səis). *India.* 1653. [Hind. = Arab. *sā'is*, f. *sūs* to tend a horse.] A groom; also, an attendant who follows on foot a mounted horseman or a carriage.

Sycee (səisī·). 1711. [Chinese *si* (pronounced in Canton *sai, sei*) *sz'* fine silk; 'so called because, if pure, it may be drawn out into fine threads.'] Fine uncoined silver in the form of lumps of various sizes, usu. having a banker's or assayer's seal stamped on them, used by the Chinese as a medium of exchange. Also *s. silver.*

Sychnocarpous (siknokā·ɹpəs), *a.* 1832. [f. Gr. συχνός many + καρπός fruit + -OUS.] *Bot.* Bearing fruit many times, as a perennial plant; polycarpous.

Sycoceric (sikose·rik, -sīᵊ·rik), *a.* 1860. [f. Gr. σῦκον fig + κηρός wax + -IC.] *Chem.* Of, pertaining to, or derived from the waxy resin of an Australian species of fig, *Ficus rubiginosa*; as in *s. acid*, a crystalline compound, $C_{18}H_{28}O_2$. So **Sycoce·ryl,** the hypothetical radical of the s. compounds.

‖**Syconium** (səikōᵘ·niǒm). 1856. [mod.L., f. Gr. σῦκον fig.] *Bot.* A multiple fruit developed from numerous flowers imbedded in a fleshy receptacle, as in the fig. So ‖**Syco·nus,** in same sense 1832.

Sycophancy (si·kǒfănsi). 1622. [ad. L. *sycophantia*, a. Gr. συκοφαντία, f. συκοφάντης SYCOPHANT.] The practice or quality of a sycophant. **1.** The trade or occupation of an informer; calumnious accusation, tale-bearing. Now only in *Gr. Hist.* **2.** Mean or servile flattery; the character of a mean or servile flatterer 1657.

2. The people, like the despot, is pursued with adulation and s. MILL.

Sycophant (si·kǒfănt), *sb.* (*a.*) 1548. [ad. L. *sycophanta*, ad. Gr. συκοφάντης, f. σῦκον fig + φαν-, root of φαίνειν to show. The origin of the Gr. word, lit. = 'fig-shower', is not known.] **1.** *Gr. Hist.* One of a class of informers in ancient Athens 1579. †**2.** *transf.* and *fig.* An informer, tale-bearer; a calumniator, slanderer –1697. **3.** A mean, servile, cringing, or abject flatterer; a parasite, toady 1575. †**4.** Vaguely used for: Impostor, deceiver –1728.

3. The young monarch was accompanied by a swarm of courtly sycophants 1843.

B. *attrib.* or *adj.* Sycophantic 1692. Hence †**Sy·cophant** *v. trans.* to act the s. towards; *intr.* to play the s. **Sy·cophantism,** = SYCOPHANCY 2.

Sycophantic (sikǒfæ·ntik), *a.* 1676. [ad. Gr. συκοφαντικός.] **a.** Having the character of, or characteristic of, a sycophant; meanly flattering; basely obsequious. **b.** Calumnious, slanderous.

a. Upon sycophantic knees they bowed before the conqueror 1854. So †**Sycopha·ntical** *a.* 1566, **-ly** *adv.* 1643.

Sycophantish (si·kǒfæntiʃ), *a.* 1840. [f. SYCOPHANT *sb.* + -ISH ¹.] Basely obsequious. Hence **Sy·cophantishly** *adv.*

Sy·cophantize, *v. rare.* 1605. [f. as prec. + -IZE.] *intr.* To deal in servile flattery.

‖**Sycosis** (səikōᵘ·sis). 1580. [mod.L., a. Gr. σύκωσις, f. σῦκον fig.] *Path.* **1.** Applied to various kinds of ulcer or morbid growth on the skin, resembling a fig. **2.** An eruptive disease characterized by inflammation of the hair-follicles, esp. of the beard 1822.

Syenite (səi·ěnəit). 1796. [ad. F. *syénite*, ad. L. *Syenites* (*lapis*), (stone) of Syene, f. *Syene*, Gr. Συήνη, a town of upper Egypt, the modern Assouan.] *Min.* A crystalline rock allied to granite, mainly composed of hornblende and feldspar, with or without quartz. Hence **Syeni·tic** *a.* of, pertaining to, composed of, allied to, or having the character of s.

Sy·llab(e. *Obs.* exc. *dial.* 1440. [a. OF. *sillabe*; see SYLLABLE *sb.*] = SYLLABLE *sb.*

‖**Syllabarium** (silăbēᵊ·riǒm). *Pl.* **-ia.** 1850. [mod.L., neut. of med.L. *syllabarius*, f. *syllaba* SYLLABLE.] = next.

Syllabary (si·lăbări). 1586. [ad. mod.L. SYLLABARIUM.] A collection, set, system, list, or table of syllables.

‖**Syllabatim** (silăbē̆ⁱ·tim), *adv. rare.* 1628. [L., f. *syllaba*, after *gradatim*.] By syllables; syllable by syllable.

Syllabation (silăbēⁱ·ʃən). *rare.* 1856. [f. L. *syllaba* + -ATION.] = SYLLABIFICATION.

Syllabic (silæ·bik), *a.* and *sb.* 1728. [ad. mod.L. *syllabicus*, ad. Gr. συλλαβικός, f. συλλαβή SYLLABLE *sb.*] **A.** *adj.* **1.** Of, pertaining or relating to, a syllable or syllables 1755. **b.** Forming or constituting a syllable 1728. **c.** Denoting a syllable; consisting of signs denoting syllables 1865. **2. a.** Applied to singing, or a tune, in which each syllable is sung to one note (i.e. with no slurs or runs) 1789. **b.** Pronounced syllable by syllable 1890.

1. In English pronunciation s. quantity is..imperfectly marked 1852. b. *S. augment*: see AUGMENT *sb.* c. A s. writing evidently of immense antiquity 1884. 2. b. His English was careful, select, s. 1890.

B. *sb.* (ellipt. use of the adj.) **1.** A syllabic sign; a character denoting a syllable 1880. **2.** A syllabic sound; a vocal sound capable by itself of forming a syllable, or constituting the essential element of a syllable 1890. So **Sylla·bical** *a.* (now *rare* or *Obs.*) 1530, **-ly** *adv.* **Sylla·bicness,** the quality of being s.

Syllabication (silæbikēⁱ·ʃən). 1631. [ad. med.L. *sill-, syllabicatio, -onem*, f. *syllabicare*, f. *syllaba* SYLLABLE.] = next. **b.** The action of making syllabic; pronunciation as a distinct syllable 1857.

Syllabification (silæ:bifikēⁱ·ʃən). 1838. [f. med.L. *syllabificare*, f. *syllaba*; see -FICATION.] Formation or construction of syllables; the action or method of dividing words into syllables.

What he said was unintelligible; but..the s. was distinct POE.

Syllabism (si·lăbiz'm). 1883. [f. L. *syllaba* + -ISM.] **a.** The use of syllabic characters. **b.** Division into syllables.

Syllabize (si·lăbəiz), *v.* 1656. [ad. med. L. *syllabizare*, ad. Gr. συλλαβίζειν, f. συλλαβή SYLLABLE *sb.*; see -IZE.] *trans.* To form or divide into syllables; to utter or articulate with distinct separation of syllables.

Syllable (si·lăb'l), *sb.* late ME. [a. AF. *sillable* (OF. *-abe*), ad. L. *syllaba*, a. Gr. συλλαβή, f. συλλαμβάνειν to take or put together, f. σύν SYN- + λαμβάνειν to take.] **1.** A vocal sound or set of sounds uttered with a single effort of articulation and forming a word or an element of a word; each of the elements of a spoken language comprising a sound of greater sonority (vowel or vowel-equivalent) with or without one or more sounds of less sonority (consonants or consonant-equivalents); also, a character or set of characters forming a corresponding element of written language. **b.** Used pregnantly of a word of one syllable, or in ref. to a part of a word, considered in relation to its significance. late ME. **2.** The least portion or detail of speech or writing (or of something expressed or expressible in speech or writing); the least mention, hint, or trace *of* something: esp. in neg. context. late ME.

1. Our English tong, hauing in vse chiefly, wordes of one s. ASCHAM. **b.** Those awful syllables, hell, death, and sin COWPER. **2.** To the last S. of Recorded time SHAKS. I know every s. of the matter GOLDSM.

Syllable (si·lăb'l), *v.* 1633. [f. prec.] *trans.* To utter or express in (or as in) syllables or articulate speech; to pronounce syllable by syllable; to utter articulately or distinctly; to articulate. **b.** To read (something) syllable by syllable; to read in detail or with close attention; to spell out (*rare*) 1728. **c.** To represent by syllables (*rare*) 1887.

Airy tongues, that s. mens names On Sands, and Shoars, and desert Wildernesses MILT.

Syllabus (si·lăbɒs). *Pl.* **syllabi** (si·lăbəi) or **syllabuses** (si·lăbɒsėz). 1656. [mod.L. *syllabus*, orig. misreading of a form of L. *sittyba*, Gr. σιττύβα title-slip or label. See N.E.D.] **1.** A concise statement or table of the heads of a discourse, the contents of a treatise, the subjects of a series of lectures, etc.; a compendium, abstract, summary, epitome. **2.** *R. C. Ch.* A summary statement of points decided and errors condemned by eccl. authority; *spec.* that annexed to the encyclical *Quanta cura* of Pope Pius IX, 8 Dec. 1864. 1876.

‖**Syllepsis** (silе·psis). *Pl.* **-es** (-īz). 1577. [a. late L., a. Gr. σύλληψις, f. σύν SYN- + λῆψις taking.] *Gram.* and *Rhet.* A figure by which a word or a particular form or inflexion of a word, is made to refer to two or more other words in the same sentence, while properly applying to or agreeing with only one of them (e.g. a masc. adj. qualifying two sbs., masc. and fem.; a sing. verb serving as predicate to two subjects, sing. and pl.), or applying to them in different senses (e.g. literal and metaphorical). Cf. ZEUGMA.

Sylleptic (silе·ptik), *a.* 1865. [ad. Gr. συλληπτικός, f. σύλληψις.] Pertaining to, of the nature of, or involving syllepsis. So **Sylle·ptical** *a.* 1846, **-ly** *adv.* 1802.

‖**Sylloge** (si·lŏdʒī). *rare.* 1686. [a. Gr. συλλογή, f. συλλέγειν to collect.] A collection; a summary.

Syllogism (si·lŏdʒiz'm). late ME. [a. OF. *silogisme*, or ad. L. *syllogismus*, Gr. συλλογισμός, f. συλλογίζεσθαι to SYLLOGIZE.] **1.** *Logic.* An argument expressed or claimed to be expressible in the form of two propositions called the premisses, containing a common or middle term, with a third proposition called the conclusion, resulting necessarily from the other two. Example: *Omne animal est substantia, omnis homo est animal*, ergo *omnis homo est substantia.* **b.** *transf.* and *allus.* An argument or something ironically or humorously regarded as such, *esp.* a specious or subtle argument or piece of reasoning; †in early use, a subtle or tricky speech; a poser; more widely, an artifice, trick. late ME. **2.** *gen.* The form of such arguments, or argumentation in that form; the form or instrument of reasoning from generals to particulars. Also, as a mental act: mediate inference or deduction. 1588.

Syllogist (si·lŏdʒist). 1799. [f. prec. or SYLLOGIZE; see -IST.] One who reasons by syllogisms; one versed in syllogism.

Syllogistic (silŏdʒi·stik), *a.* (*sb.*) 1669. [ad. L. *syllogisticus* or Gr. συλλογιστικός, f. συλλογίζεσθαι to SYLLOGIZE; see -ISTIC.] Of, pertaining to, of the nature of, or consisting of a syllogism or syllogisms. **B.** *sb.* Reasoning by syllogisms; that department of logic which deals with syllogisms. Also pl. (see -ICS). *rare.* 1833. So **Syllogi·stical** *a.* (now *rare*) syllogistic; also, addicted to reasoning by syllogisms 1529; **-ly** *adv.*

Syllogization (si:lŏdʒəizēi·ʃən). *rare.* 1660. [f. next + -ATION.] The action of syllogizing; syllogistic reasoning.

Syllogize (si·lŏdʒəiz), *v.* late ME. [a. OF. *sil(l)ogiser*, or ad. med.L. *syllogizare*, ad. Gr. συλλογίζεσθαι, f. σύν SYN- + λογίζεσθαι to reckon, infer, f. λόγος discourse, reason.] *intr.* To argue by syllogisms; to reason syllogistically; also *gen.* (Also with *it.*) **b.** *trans.* To deduce by syllogism. (Only in transl. and echoes of Dante *Paradiso* x. 138.) 1867.

To S. is to collect, that is, conclude, or from some certain Propositions to draw up the Summ of an Argument or Proof 1697. **b.** Those who, as Dante says, s. hateful truths LOWELL. Hence **Syllogi·zer.**

Sylph (silf). 1657. [ad. mod.L. (pl.) *sylphes*, G. *sylphen* (Paracelsus). Perh. an arbitrary coinage, blending *sylvestris* and *nympha.*] **1.** One of a race of beings or spirits supposed to inhabit the air (orig. in the system of Paracelsus). **b.** Applied to a slender graceful woman or girl 1838. **2.** Gould's name for various humming-birds with long forked tails 1861. Hence **Sy·lphic, Sy·lphish** *adjs.* pertaining to, resembling, of the nature of, or characteristic of a s.

Sylphid (si·lfid), *sb.* (*a.*) 1680. [ad. F. *sylphide*, f. *sylphe*; see prec. and -ID².] A little or young sylph. Also *attrib.* or as *adj.*

Ye Sylphs and Sylphids, to your chief give ear! POPE. If to S. Queen 'twere given, To show our earth the charms of Heaven SCOTT.

‖**Sylva, silva** (si·lvă). 1636. [L. *silva* a wood, woodland; commonly misspelt *sylva* in imitation of Gr. ὕλη.] **1. a.** A title for a treatise on forest trees, or a descriptive list or catalogue of trees 1664. **b.** The trees of a particular region or period collectively 1846. †**2.** A title for a collection of pieces, esp. of poems; also, a thesaurus of words or phrases –1787.

Sylvan, silvan (si·lvăn), *sb.* and *a.* 1565. [ad. F. *sylvain* or ad. L. *silvanus, sylvanus*, f. *silva, sylva*: see prec. and -AN.] **A.** *sb.* One who (or something that) inhabits a wood or forest; a being of the woods. **a.** *Mythol.* A deity or spirit of the woods. **b.** A forester; a rustic 1589. **c.** An animal, esp. a bird, living in or frequenting the woods 1612.

a. Goate-feete Syluans 1616. **b.** Her private orchards, wall'd on ev'ry side, To lawless sylvans all access deny'd POPE.

B. *adj.* **1.** Belonging, pertaining, or relating to, situated or performed in, associated with, or characteristic of, a wood or woods 1580. **2.** Consisting of or formed by woods or trees 1594. **3.** Furnished with, abounding in, or having as its chief feature, woods or trees; wooded, woody 1667.

1. May all the S. Deityes Bee still propitious to you COWLEY. **3.** O s. Wye! thou wanderer thro' the woods! WORDSW.

Sylvanite (si·lvănəit). 1796. [f. (*Tran*)*sylvania*, where found; see -ITE¹.] *Min.* **a.** Native tellurium, with slight admixture of gold, iron, etc. **b.** A telluride of gold and silver (sometimes also containing lead), occurring in crystals or masses of a steel-grey, silver-white, or yellow colour with metallic lustre. Hence **Sylvani·tic** *a.* containing s.

Sylvate, silvate (si·lvēɪt). 1836. [f. SYLVIC + -ATE¹ c.] *Chem.* A salt of sylvic acid.

Sylvatic, silvatic (silvæ·tik), *a. rare.* 1661. [ad. L. *silvaticus*, f. *silva* SYLVA; see -ATIC.] Belonging to or found in woods; of the nature of a wood or woodland; sylvan; †*transf.* rustic, boorish.

Sylvester (si·lvéstəɹ). 1838. [Proper name.] St. Sylvester's day, Dec. 31.

Sylvestrian, sil- (silve·striăn), *a.*¹ 1657. [f. L. *silvestris* + -AN.] Belonging to or found in woods; sylvan, rustic.

Sylve·strian, *a.*² and *sb.* 1693. [f. *Sylvester* (see below) + -IAN.] *Ch. Hist.* Belonging to, or a member of, an order of Benedictines founded by Sylvester Gozzolini in 1231.

Sylvian (si·lviăn), *a.*¹ 1871. [ad. F. *sylvien*, f. François de la Boë *Sylvius*, a Flemish anatomist (1614–1672).] *Anat.* Described by or named after the anatomist Sylvius: applied to certain structures in the brain.

Sylvian, *a.*² (*sb.*) 1891. [f. mod.L. *Sylvia*, f. L. *silva* a wood.] *Ornith.* Belonging to the genus *Sylvia* or family *Sylviidæ* of oscine passerine birds (the warblers). **B.** *sb.* A bird of this genus or family.

Sylvic, silvic (si·lvik), *a.* 1836. [ad. F. *sylvique*, f. L. *sylva, silva* a wood; see -IC 1 b.] Chem. *S. acid*: a colourless crystalline substance, isomeric with pinic acid, forming a constituent of colophony or turpentine-resin.

Sylvicoline (silvi·kŏləin), *a.* and *sb.* 1872. [ad. mod.L. *Sylvicolinæ*, f. *Sylvicola*, a former generic name, = L. *silvicola* inhabiting woods; see -INE¹.] *Ornith.* **A.** *adj.* Belonging to the *Sylvicolinæ*, a former division of the family then called *Sylvicolidæ* (now *Mniotiltidæ*), comprising the typical American warblers. **B.** *sb.* A bird of this division.

Sylviculture, silvi- (si·lvikɒltiŭr, -tʃəɹ). 1880. [ad. F., f. L. *sylva, silva* a wood + F. *culture* cultivation.] The cultivation of woods or forests; the growing and tending of trees as a department of forestry. Hence **Sylvicu·lturist,** a person engaged or skilled in s.

Sylvine (si·lvin). 1850. [a. F., from the old name of the salt, *sal digestivus Sylvii*; see -INE⁵.] *Min.* Native potassium chloride, occurring in some salt-mines and on Mount Vesuvius. Also called **Sy·lvite.**

Sym- (sim), *prefix*, repr. Gr. συμ-, assimilated form of συν- SYN-, before labials (β, μ, π, φ, ψ), hence in words of Gr. derivation in Latin and modern languages before *b, m, p.* **Symble·pharon,** *Path.* [Gr. βλέφαρον eyelid] adhesion of the eyelid to the eyeball. **Sympelmous** (simpe·lməs), *a.* [Gr. πέλμα sole of the foot] *Ornith.* having the tendons of the deep flexors of the toes united before separating to each of the four digits. **Sympetalous** (simpe·tăləs), *a. Bot.*, having the petals united; gamopetalous. **Symphyllous** (simfi·ləs), *a.* [Gr. φύλλον leaf] *Bot.* having the perianth-leaves united; gamophyllous. **Sympolar** (simpōu·lăɹ), *a. Geom.* reciprocally polar: said of a pair of polyhedra so related that every face of each corresponds to a summit of the other.

‖**Symbiosis** (simbiōu·sis, -bəi-). 1877. [mod.L., ad. Gr. συμβίωσις a living together, f. συμβιοῦν to live together, f. σύμβιος adj. living together, sb. companion, partner, f. σύν SYM- + βίος life.] *Biol.* Association of two different organisms (usu. two plants, or an animal and a plant) which live attached to each other, or one as a tenant of the other, and contribute to each other's support. Hence **Symbio·tic** *a. Biol.* associated or living in s.; relating to or involving s.; **-ly** *adv.*

Symbol (si·mbəl), *sb.*¹ 1490. [ad. late L. *symbolum*, a. Gr. σύμβολον mark, token, ticket, 'tessera', f. σύν SYM- + root of βολή, βόλος a throw.] **1.** A formal authoritative statement of the religious belief of the Christian church, or of a particular church or sect; a creed or confession of faith, *spec.* the Apostles' Creed. †**b.** *transf.* A brief or sententious statement; a formula, motto, maxim; *occas.* a summary, synopsis –1751. **2.** Something that stands for, represents, or denotes something else (not by exact resemblance, but by vague suggestion, or by some accidental or conventional relation); *esp.* a material object representing or taken to represent something immaterial or abstract 1590. **b.** An object representing something sacred; *spec.* (*absol.*) either of the elements in the eucharist, as representing the body and blood of Christ 1671. **c.** *Numism.* A small device on a coin, additional to and usu. independent of the main device or 'type' 1883. **d.** Symbols collectively; symbolism (*rare*) 1856. **3.** A written character or mark used to represent something; a letter, figure, or sign conventionally standing for some object, process, etc. 1620.

1. The credo and symbole of the fayth CAXTON. **b.** The celebrated s. of Pythagoras, ἀνεμῶν πνεόντων τὴν ἠχὼ προσκύνει; 'when the wind blows, worship its echo' JOHNSON. **2.** Salt as incorruptible, was the Simbole of friendship SIR T. BROWNE. The offering of incense is a natural s. of adoration 1865. **3.** *Symboles*, are Letters used for Numbers in Algebra 1700. Table of Symbols of the elementary bodies 1844. Hence **Sy·mbol** *v. trans.* = SYMBOLIZE II. 1.

†**Symbol,** *sb.*² 1627. [ad. L. *symbola*, a. Gr. συμβολή, f. συμβάλλειν to put together, f. σύν SYM- + βάλλειν to throw.] A contribution (properly to a feast or picnic); a share, portion.

The persons who are to be judged..shall all appear to receive ther S. JER. TAYLOR. Let me contribute my Symbole on this Subject FULLER.

Symbolic (simbǫ·lik), *a.* 1656. [ad. late L. *symbolicus*, a. Gr., f. σύμβολον SYMBOL *sb.*[1]; see -IC.] **1.** Having the character of a symbol or representative sign or mark; constituting or serving as a symbol (*of* something) 1680. **2.** Consisting of, denoted by, or involving the use of written symbols or significant characters; *spec.* in *Math.* 1656. **3.** Expressed, denoted, or conveyed by means of a symbol or set of symbols; concerning, involving, or depending upon representation by symbols; also, dealing with or using symbols 1684. **4.** Pertaining to or of the nature of a formal confession of faith 1867. So **Symbo·lical** *a.* 1607. **Symbolically** *adv.* 1603. **Symbo·licalness** 1633.

Symbolics (simbǫ·liks). 1657. [pl. of prec. used subst. (see -ICS, -IC 2).] †**1.** The use of written symbols, as in mathematics. HOBBES. **2.** The study of creeds and confessions of faith, as a branch of theology 1847.

Symbolism (si·mbǒliz'm). 1654. [f. SYMBOL *sb.*[1] + -ISM.] **1.** The practice of representing things by symbols, or of giving a symbolic character to objects or acts; the systematic use of symbols; hence, symbols collectively or generally. **b.** A symbolic meaning attributed to natural objects or facts 1835. **c.** The use of symbols in literature or art; *spec.* the principles or practice of the Symbolists 1866. **2.** The use, or a set or system, of written symbols 1864. **3.** = prec. 2. 1846.

1. Heraldry grew out of s. 1870. 2. I had..invented a short-hand s. for crystalline forms RUSKIN.

Symbolist (si·mbǒlist). 1585. [f. SYMBOL *sb.*[1] + -IST.] **1.** *Ch. Hist.* One who holds that the elements in the Eucharist are mere symbols of the body and blood of Christ. *Obs.* exc. *Hist.* **2.** One who uses symbols, or practises symbolism 1812. **b.** One who uses symbolism in art or literature: (*a*) A painter who aims at symbolizing ideas rather than representing the form or aspect of actual objects; *spec.* applied to a recent school of painters who use representations of objects and schemes of colour to suggest ideas or states of mind; (*b*) One of a recent school of French poets who aim at representing ideas and emotions by indirect suggestion rather than by direct expression, and attach a symbolic meaning to particular objects, words, sounds, etc. 1892. **3.** One versed in the study or interpretation of symbols or symbolism 1839. Hence **Symboli·stic, -al** *adjs.* pertaining to or characteristic of a s.; belonging to or characterized by symbolism; **-ly** *adv.*

Symbolization (si:mbǒləizē¹·ʃən). 1603. [ad. F., f. *symboliser* to SYMBOLIZE.] **1.** †**a.** The fact of 'symbolizing' in nature or quality; agreement or participation in qualities -1693. **b.** The action of 'symbolizing' in tenets or practice; conformity (*with*). Now *rare* or *Obs.* 1633. **2.** The action of symbolizing; representation by a symbol or symbols; *transf.* something in which this is exemplified; a symbol or symbolism 1603. **b.** Representation by written symbols; *transf.* a set of written symbols or characters 1842.

Symbolize (si·mbǒləiz), *v.* 1590. [ad. F. *symboliser*, ad. mod.L. *symbolizare*, f. *symbolum* SYMBOL *sb.*[1]; see -IZE.] **I.** †**1.** *intr.* To agree or harmonize in qualities or nature (or in some quality); *s. with*, to partake of the qualities or nature of; hence often = to be like, resemble -1816. †**b.** To combine, unite, as elements having qualities in common; to form a harmonious union or combination -1628. †**c.** *trans.* To mix, combine, unite (elements or substances) -1610. **2.** *intr.* To agree in belief or practice (esp. religious); to comply, conform. Now *rare* or *Obs.* 1605. **II. 1.** *trans.* **a.** To represent by a symbol or symbols. Also *absol.* 1606. **b.** To be a symbol of; to typify 1603. **2.** To make into or treat as a symbol; to regard as symbolic or emblematic (*rare*) 1646. **III.** To formulate or express in a creed or confession of faith 1895. Hence **Sy·mbolizer** (*rare*), one who or that which symbolizes.

Symbolography (simbǒlǫ·grăfi). 1865. [f. Gr. σύμβολον + -γραφία -GRAPHY.] Symbolic writing.

Symbology (simbǫ·lŏdʒi). 1840. [ad. mod.L. *symbologia*, shortened form of **symbolologia*, f. Gr. σύμβολον SYMBOL *sb.*[1]; see -LOGY.] The science or study of symbols; *loosely*, the use of symbols, or symbols collectively; symbolism. So **Symbolo·gical** *a.* **Symbo·logist** (*rare*).

Symbololatry (simbǒlǫ·lătri). 1828. [f. Gr. σύμβολον SYMBOL *sb.*[1] + λατρεία worship; see -LATRY.] Worship of or excessive veneration for symbols (in any sense).

‖ **Symmelia** (simī·liă). 1894. [mod.L., f. Gr. σύν SYM- + μέλος limb; see -IA [1].] *Path.* A form of monstrosity in which a pair of limbs, esp. the hinder limbs, are fused into one.

Symmetral (si·mĕtrăl), *a.* 1660. [f. Gr.-L. *symmetros* commensurate, proportionable (f. Gr. σύν SYM- + μέτρον measure) + -AL 1.] †**1.** *fig.* Commensurate wlth the Divine idea or pattern; agreeing with the word of God: applied to the early church or its times, etc. -1685. **2.** *Geom.* Related to or determining symmetry; about which a figure is symmetrical; as in *s. axis, plane* = axis or plane of symmetry 1878.

†**Symme·trian.** *rare.* 1586. [f. L. *symmetria* SYMMETRY + -AN.] An advocate of, or one studious of, symmetry -1623.

Symmetric (sime·trik), *a.* 1796. [f. SYMMETRY + -IC.] = next.

Symmetrical (sime·trikăl), *a.* 1751. [f. SYMMETRY + -ICAL, after *geometrical.*] Characterized by or exhibiting symmetry. **1.** Having the parts or elements regularly and harmoniously arranged; regular in form; well-proportioned; balanced. **2.** *Geom.*, etc. Said of a figure or body whose points or parts are equably distributed about a dividing line, plane, or point, i. e. arranged in pairs or sets so that those of each pair or set are at equal distances on opposite sides of such line, plane, or point; consisting of, or capable of being divided into, two or more exactly similar and equal parts. Also said of the form of such a figure or object, of its parts or their arrangement, or of any part in relation to the corresponding part 1794. **b.** *Alg.* and *Higher Math.* Applied to an expression, function, or equation whose value is never altered by interchanging the values of any two of the variables or unknown quantities 1816. **c.** *Photogr.* Applied to a lens of symmetrical form; also *ellipt.* as *sb.* = symmetrical lens 1890. **3. a.** *Bot.* Of a flower = ISOMEROUS 1. 1849. **b.** *Anat.* and *Zool.* Having similar or corresponding parts or organs on opposite sides of a dividing plane, or regularly arranged around an axis or centre; consisting of two or more similar or corresponding divisions. Also said of the parts. (*b*) *Path.* Of a disease: Affecting such corresponding parts or organs simultaneously. 1851.

1. The s. clauses of Pope's logical metre RUSKIN. 2. b. *S.* or *symmetric determinant*, a determinant in which the constituents in each row are the same respectively, and in the same order, as those in the corresponding column, and which is therefore symmetrical about its principal diagonal. Hence **Sym·me·trically** *adv.*, **-ness.**

Symmetrize (si·mĕtrəiz), *v.* 1786. [ad. F. *symétriser*, or f. SYMMETRY + -IZE.] †**1.** *intr.* To be symmetrical; to correspond symmetrically. H. WALPOLE. **2.** *trans.* To make symmetrical; to reduce to symmetry 1796.

Symmetrophobia (si:mĕtrofōu·biă). 1809. [irreg. f. next + -O- + -PHOBIA.] Dread or avoidance of symmetry, as shown or supposed to be shown in Egyptian temples, Japanese art, etc.

Symmetry (si·mĕtri). 1541. [a. F. †*symmetrie*, or ad. late L. *symmetria*, a. Gr. συμμετρία, f. σύμμετρος, f. σύν SYM- + μέτρον measure.] †**1.** Mutual relation of parts in respect of magnitude and position; relative measurement and arrangement of parts; proportion -1730. **2.** Due or just proportion; harmony of parts with each other and with the whole; fitting, regular, or balanced arrangement and relation of parts or elements; the condition or quality of being well-proportioned or well-balanced. In stricter use: Exact correspondence in size and position of opposite parts; equable distribution of parts about a dividing line or centre. (As an attribute either of the whole or of the parts composing it.) 1599. **3.** Various spec. and techn. uses. †**a.** *Physiol.* Harmonious working of the bodily functions, producing a healthy temperament or condition -1541. **b.** *Geom.*, etc. Exact correspondence in position of the several points or parts of a figure or body with ref. to a dividing line, plane, or point (or a number of lines or planes); arrangement of all the points of a figure or system in pairs (or sets) so that those of each pair (or set) are at equal distances or opposite sides of such line, plane, or point 1823. (*b*) *Alg.* and *Higher Math.* The fact of being symmetrical, as an expression or function: see SYMMETRICAL 2 b. 1888. **c.** *Anat.* and *Zool.* Arrangement of parts or organs in pairs or sets on opposite sides of a dividing plane, or around an axis or centre; repetition of similar corresponding parts in the two halves, or other number of divisions, of the body. (*b*) *Path.* Affection of such corresponding parts simultaneously by the same disease. 1849. **d.** *Bot.* Equality of the number of parts in the several whorls of the flower 1845.

1. True and native beauty consists in the just composure and symetrie of the parts of the body 1650. 3. b. *Axis of s., centre of s., plane of s.*, the line, point, or plane about which a figure or body is symmetrical, i. e. which bisects every straight line joining a pair of corresponding points of such figure or body.

Symmory (si·mŏri). 1847. [ad. Gr. συμμορία, f. σύμμορος sharing (*sc.* the burden of taxation), f. σύν SYM- + μορ- (= μέρος portion, share).] *Anc. Gr. Hist.* Each of the companies or fellowships, graded according to wealth, into which the citizens of Athens and other cities were divided for purposes of taxation.

Sympathetic (simpăþe·tik), *a.* (*sb.*) 1644. [ad. mod.L. *sympatheticus*, a. Gr. συμπαθητικός, f. συμπαθεῖν, after παθητικός PATHETIC.] **1.** Pertaining to, involving, depending on, acting or effected by 'sympathy', or a (real or supposed) affinity, correspondence, or occult influence. Now chiefly *Hist.* **b.** *Physiol.* and *Path.* Produced by 'sympathy' (see SYMPATHY 1 b): applied to a condition, action, or disorder induced in a person, or in an organ or part of the body, by a similar or corresponding one in another 1728. **c.** *Anat.* Designating one of the two great nerve-systems in vertebrates (the other being the *cerebro-spinal*), consisting of a double chain of ganglia, with connecting fibres, along the vertebral column, giving off branches and plexuses which supply the viscera and blood-vessels and maintain relations between their various activities; belonging to or forming part of this system. Also applied to a similar set of nerves supplying the viscera in some invertebrates. 1769. **d.** *Physics.* Used in ref. to sounds produced by responsive vibrations induced in one body by transmission of vibrations from another 1832. **2.** †Agreeing, harmonious, befitting, consonant, accordant (*obs.*); according with one's feelings or inclinations, congenial 1673. **3. a.** Feeling or susceptible of sympathy; sharing or affected by the feelings of another or others; sympathizing, compassionate 1718. **b.** Pertaining to, of the nature of, characterized by, arising from, or expressive of sympathy or fellow-feeling 1684.

1. *S. powder* = 'powder of sympathy': see SYMPATHY 1. *S. ink*, a name for various colourless liquid compositions used as ink, the writing with which remains invisible until the colour is developed by heat or some chemical reagent. 2. Now o'er the soothed accordant heart we feel A s. twilight slowly steal WORDSW. 3. a. An unusually tender and s. audience DICKENS. b. The head of the Coal Miners' Union is opposed to s. strikes 1901.

B. *sb.* **1.** *Anat.* Short for *s. nerve* or *system*: see 1 c above 1808. **2. a.** A person affected by 'sympathy' (SYMPATHY 1 b); one who is susceptible or sensitive to hypnotic or similar influence. **b.** A sympathizer (*rare*). 1888. So †**Sympathe·tical** *a.* 1639, **-ly** *adv.* 1621.

Sympathic (simpæ·þik), *a.* Now *rare* or *Obs.* 1659. [ad. F. *sympathique*, ad. mod.L. **sympathicus*, f. *sympathia* SYMPATHY; see -IC.] †**1.** = prec. A 1, 1 b, 2. -1684. **2.** = prec. 1 c. 1836.

Sympathist (si·mpăþist). *rare.* 1819. [f. SYMPATHY + -IST.] One who sympathizes, a sympathizer.

Sympathize (si·mpăþəiz), *v.* 1588. [a. F. *sympathiser*, f. *sympathie* SYMPATHY; see -IZE.] **1.** *intr.* To suffer with or like another; to be affected in consequence of the affection of some one or something else; to respond sympathetically to some influence; *spec.* in *Path.* to be or become disordered in consequence of the disorder of some other part. Const. *with.* 1597. †**2. a.** To have an affinity; to agree in nature, disposition, qualities, or fortunes; to be alike; with *with*, to be like, resemble –1668. †**b.** To agree, be in harmony, accord, harmonize *with* –1711. †**3.** *trans.* To agree with, correspond to, match –1606. †**b.** To represent or express by something corresponding or fitting; to apprehend mentally by the analogy of something else –1645. †**c.** To make up or compound of corresponding parts or elements; to form or contrive harmoniously or consistently –1606. **4.** *intr.* To feel sympathy; to have a fellow-feeling; to share the feelings of another or others; *spec.* to be affected with pity for the suffering or sorrow of another, to feel compassion. Const. *with* a person (or, in extended or *fig.* use, a thing), *in*, *with* (rarely †*at*) a feeling, experience, etc. 1605. **b.** *transf.* To express sympathy; to condole (*with* a person) 1748. **c.** In weakened sense: To agree or be disposed to agree in some opinion or way of thinking, to be of (about) the same mind *with* a person or party; also, with *in* or (now usu.) *with*, to approve or incline to approve, to regard with favour (a scheme, cause, etc.) 1828.

1. The mind will s. so much with the anguish and debility of the body, that it will be..too distracted to fix itself in meditation 1812. 2. a. *Hen. V*, III. vii. 158. b. Nature in aw to him Had doff't her gawdy trim, With her great Master so to s. MILT. 3. *Rich. II*, V. i. 46. b. Thou truly faire, wert truly simpathizde, In true plaine words, by thy true telling friend SHAKS. c. *L.L.L.* III. i. 52. 4. Friends and foes pittyed my case, sympathized with me 1685. c. Pope..sympathized with his schemes 1880. Hence **Sy·mpathizer**, one who or that which sympathizes.

Sympathy (si·mpăþi). 1579. [ad. late L. *sympathia*, a. Gr. συμπάθεια, f. συμπαθής, f. σύν SYM- + παθ-, root of πάθος suffering, πάσχειν to suffer.] **1.** A (real or supposed) affinity between certain things, by virtue of which they are similarly or correspondingly affected by the same influence, affect or influence one another (esp. in some occult way), or attract or tend towards each other. *Obs.* exc. *Hist.* 1586. **b.** *Physiol.* and *Path.* A relation between two bodily organs or parts (or between two persons) such that disorder, or any condition, of the one induces a corresponding condition in the other 1603. **2.** Agreement, accord, harmony, consonance, concord; agreement in qualities, likeness, conformity, correspondence. *Obs.* or merged in 3 a. 1579. **3. a.** Conformity of feelings, inclinations, or temperament, which makes persons agreeable to each other; community of feeling, harmony of disposition 1596. **b.** The quality or state of being affected by the condition of another with a feeling similar or corresponding to that of the other; the fact or capacity of entering into or sharing the feelings of another or others; fellow-feeling. Also, a feeling or frame of mind evoked by or responsive to some external influence. Const. *with* (a person, etc., or a feeling). 1662. **c.** *spec.* The quality or state of being thus affected by the suffering or sorrow of another; a feeling of compassion or commiseration 1600. **d.** In weakened sense: A favourable attitude of mind towards a cause, etc.; disposition to agree or approve 1823.

1. *Powder of s.* (*s.-powder*), a powder supposed to heal wounds by 'sympathy' on being applied to a handkerchief or garment stained with blood from the wound, or to the weapon with which the wound was inflicted; also called *sympathetic powder*. Phr. *In s. with* (Comm.), used in market reports in ref. to a rise or fall in the price of a commodity induced by a rise or fall in that of another. 2. There should be..simpathy in yeares, Manners, and Beauties: all which the Moore is defective in SHAKS. 3. a. They enjoy the s. of kindred souls 1876. b. With answering looks Of sympathie and love MILT. c. To awaken something of s. for the unfortunate natives BURKE. d. He had no s. with the anti-opium party 1893.

‖**Symphonia** (simfōᵘ·niă). 1579. [L., a. Gr. συμφωνία.] = SYMPHONY 2, 3, 5.

Symphonic (simfǫ·nik), *a.* (*sb.*) 1864. [f. SYMPHONY + -IC, after *harmonic.*] **1. a.** = HOMOPHONOUS 2. **b.** Applied to a shorthand sign denoting more than one sound. 1880. **2.** Harmonious (*rare*) 1864. **3.** *Mus.* Of, pertaining to, or having the form or character of a symphony. Also *transf.* in ref. to poetry. 1864.

3. *S. poem* (tr. G. *symphonische dichtung*), a descriptive orchestral composition of the character and dimensions of a symphony, but freer in form, founded on some special poetic theme or idea. So †**Sympho·nical** *a.* (*rare*) = sense 2. 1589–1650.

Symphonious (simfōᵘ·niəs), *a.* Only *literary.* 1652. [f. L. *symphonia* SYMPHONY + -OUS, after *harmonious.*] **1.** Full of or characterized by 'symphony' or harmony of sounds: = HARMONIOUS 2. **b.** *fig. or gen.* = HARMONIOUS 1. Const. *to, with.* 1742. **2.** Sounding together or in concert 1816.

1. The sound S. of ten thousand Harpes, that tun'd Angelic harmonies MILT. Hence **Sympho·niously** *adv.* harmoniously.

Symphonist (si·mfŏnist). 1789. [f. next or SYMPHONY + -IST.] A composer of symphonies.

Symphonize (si·mfŏnəiz), *v.* Now *rare* or *Obs.* 1491. [f. next; see -IZE.] **1.** *intr.* To sing or sound together, in concert, or in harmony. †**2.** To agree, be in accordance, harmonize (*with* something) –1712.

Symphony (si·mfŏni). ME. [a. OF. *simphonie*, ad. L. *symphonia*, a Gr. συμφωνία agreement or concord of sound, f. σύμφωνος, f. σύν SYM- + φωνή sound.] †**1.** Used vaguely, after late L. *symphonia*, as a name for different musical instruments –1602. **2.** Harmony of sound, esp. of musical sounds; concord, consonance. Also occas. of speech-sounds, as in verse. Now *rare* or *Obs.* 1440. **3.** Harmony (in general), agreement, accord, concord, congruity. Now *rare* or *Obs.* 1598. **4.** (transf. from 2.) Music in parts, sung or played by a number of performers with pleasing effect; concerted or harmonious music; a performance or strain of such music. Chiefly *poet.* or *rhet.* 1599. **b.** *fig.* A collection of utterances, or sounds of any kind, likened to concerted music; a 'chorus' (of praise, etc.) 1654. **c.** Applied to a collection or composition of various colours which harmonize, with pleasing or brilliant effect 1874. **5.** *Mus.* **a.** A passage for instruments alone (or, by extension, for a single instrument) occurring in a vocal composition as an introduction, interlude, or close to an accompaniment; also, a short instrumental movement occurring between vocal movements, as the 'Pastoral Symphony' in Handel's 'Messiah'; also formerly applied to a more extended instrumental piece, often in several movements, forming the overture to an opera or other vocal work of large dimensions 1661. **b.** An elaborate orchestral composition in three or more movements, orig. developed from the operatic overture (see prec. sense), similar in form to a sonata, but usu. of grander dimensions and broader style 1789.

1. With harpe and pype and symphonye CHAUCER. The strings of natures s. Are crackt MARSTON. 3. Their domestic s. was liable to furious flaws CARLYLE. 4. From afar I heard a suddain S. of War DRYDEN. c. Symphonies of colour, like Whistler's 1874. 5. a. Thir gold'n Harps they took,..and with Præamble sweet Of charming symphonie they introduce Thir sacred Song MILT.

Symphyo- (si·mfiŏ), before a vowel **symphy-**, used as comb. form of Gr. συμφυής growing or grown together.

Symphysial (simfi·ziăl), *a.* 1835. [f. SYMPHYSIS + -AL 1.] Of or pertaining to, situated at, or forming a symphysis. So **Symphy·sian** *a.*

Symphysio-, also **-eo-** (after Fr. *-éo-*, from stem συμφυσε- of Gr. σύμφυσις), comb. form of next. **Sy:mphysio·tomy** [Gr. -τομία cutting], the operation of cutting through the symphysis pubis to facilitate delivery.

Symphysis (si·mfisis). 1578. [mod.L., a. Gr. σύμφυσις a growing together, f. σύν SYM- + φύσις growth.] **1.** *Anat.* and *Zool.* The union of two bones or skeletal elements originally separate, either by fusion of the bony substance (*synostosis*) or by intervening cartilage (*synchondrosis*); the part or line of junction where this takes or has taken place: used esp. of such union of two similar bones on opposite sides of the body in the median line, as that of the pubic bones (*symphysis pubis*) or of the two halves of the lower jaw-bone (*s. mandibulæ* or *menti*). **2.** *Bot.* Coalescence or fusion of parts of a plant normally distinct 1866.

Symphytic (simfi·tik), *a. rare.* 1871. [ad. Gr. συμφυτικός, f. συμφύειν to make to grow together, f. σύν SYM- + φυ- to grow.] Formed by or involving coalescence or fusion of two parts or elements. Hence **Symphy·tically** *adv.* in the way of such coalescence or fusion; so **Sy·mphytism** (tendency to) such coalescence or fusion.

Sympiesometer (si:mpiesǫ·mĭtəı). 1817. [irreg. f. Gr. συμπίεσις compression (f. συμπιέζειν to compress, f. σύν SYM- + πιέζειν to press) + -OMETER.] A form of barometer in which the column of liquid in the tube has above it a body of confined air or other gas (instead of a vacuum), so that the pressure of the atmosphere acts against the weight of the liquid and the elastic pressure of the gas; a thermometer is attached for correction of the readings according to the expansion or contraction of the gas with changes of temperature.

Symplectic (simple·ktik), *a.* and *sb.* 1839. [ad. Gr. συμπλεκτικός, f. σύν SYM- + πλέκειν to twine, plait, weave; see -IC.] **A.** *adj.* Epithet of a bone of the suspensorium in the skull of fishes, between the hyomandibular and the quadrate bones. **B.** *sb.* The symplectic bone.

‖**Symploce** (si·mplŏsī). 1577. [Late L., a. Gr. συμπλοκή an interweaving, f. σύν SYM- + πλέκειν (see prec.).] *Rhet.* A figure consisting in the repetition of one word or phrase at the beginning, and of another at the end, of successive clauses or sentences; a combination of *anaphora* and *epistrophe*.

Sympode (si·mpoᵘd). 1880. *Bot.* Anglicized form of SYMPODIUM.

‖**Sympodia** (simpōᵘ·diă). 1848. [mod.L., f. Gr. συμποδ- with the feet together + -IA[1].] A malformation in which the legs or lower extremities are united.

Sympodial (simpōᵘ·diăl), *a.* 1875. [f. next.] **1.** *Bot.* Pertaining or relating to, of the nature of, or producing a sympodium. **2.** *Anat.* Affected with sympodia; having the lower extremities united 1902.

‖**Sympodium** (simpōᵘ·diŏm). *Pl.* **-ia.** 1862. [mod.L., f. Gr. σύν SYM- + ποδ- πούς foot.] *Bot.* An apparent axis or stem in a dichotomously branched plant, made up of the bases of successive branches so arranged as to resemble a simple or monopodial axis; a pseudaxis.

Symposiac (simpōᵘ·ziæk), *sb.* and *a.* 1603. [ad. late. L. *symposiacus* adj., in neut. pl. *symposiaca*, or Gr. συμποσιακός adj., f. συμπόσιον SYMPOSIUM; see -AC.] **A.** *sb.* A symposiac meeting or conversation, or an account of one; a symposium. Now *rare* or *Obs.* **B.** *adj.* Of, pertaining to, or suitable for a symposium; of the nature of a symposium; convivial 1642.

Symposiarch (simpōᵘ·ziaɹk). 1603. [ad. Gr. συμποσίαρχος, f. συμπόσιον SYMPOSIUM + ἀρχός ruler, chief.] The master, director, or president of a symposium; the leader of a convivial gathering.

Symposiast (simpōᵘ·ziæst). 1656. [ad. Gr. type *συμποσιαστής, f. συμποσιάζειν to drink together, f. συμπόσιον.] **1.** A member of a drinking party. **2.** One who contributes to a 'symposium' on some topic 1878.

Symposium (simpōᵘ·ziŏm). *Pl.* **-ia** (rarely **-iums**). 1586. [a. L. *symposium*, ad. Gr. συμπόσιον, f. συμπότης fellow-drinker, f. σύν SYM- + πότης drinker.] **1.** A drinking-party; a convivial meeting for drinking, conversation, and intellectual entertainment. **b.** An account of such a meeting or the conversation at it; *spec.* the title of one of Plato's dialogues 1586. **2.** *transf.* A meeting or conference for discussion of some subject; hence, a collection of opinions delivered, or a series of articles contributed, by a number of persons on some special topic 1784.

1. Our s. at the King's head broke up 1787.

Symptom (si·mptəm). [Late ME. *synthoma, sinthoma*, medieval ff. late L. *symptoma*, a. Gr. σύμπτωμα chance, accident, mischance, disease, f. συμπίπτειν to fall together, fall upon, happen to, f. σύν SYM- + πίπτειν to fall. In mod. use, ad. F. *symptome*, or directly ad. L. *symptoma*.] **1.** *Path.* A (bodily or mental) phenomenon, circumstance, or change of condition arising from and accompanying a disease or affection and constituting an indication or evidence of it; a characteristic sign *of* some particular disease. **2.** *gen.* A phenomenon or circumstance accompanying some condition, process, feeling, etc., and serving as evidence of it (orig. and prop. of something evil); a sign or indication *of* something 1611. **b.** With neg. expressed or implied: A slight, or the least, sign *of* something; a trace, vestige 1722.

1. His skin was hot, and his pulse strong. These symptoms could be attributed to..inflammation of the brain. ABERNETHY. *attrib.*: **s.-complex, -group,** a set of symptoms occurring together and characterizing or constituting a particular disease or affection. 2. Symptoms of discontent began to appear MACAULAY.

Symptomatic (simptǒmæ·tik), *a.* (*sb.*) 1698. [ad. F. *symptomatique* or late L. *symptomaticus*, f. *symptomat-, symptoma* SYMPTOM; see -IC.] **1.** *Path.* Of the nature of, or constituting, a symptom of disease; *spec.* applied to a secondary disease or morbid state arising from and accompanying a primary one (opp. to *idiopathic*). **2.** Relating to or concerned with symptoms 1767. **3.** *gen.* That is a symptom of something; characteristic and indicative *of* 1751.

1. S. of a weak state of stomach L. HUNT. 2. The mere s. practitioner 1843. 3. The s. smoke has puffed up from the social volcano 1847.

B. *sb.* in *pl.* **Symptoma·tics** = SYMPTOMATOLOGY 1748. So **Symptoma·tical** *a.* in senses 1, 3 (now *rare* or *Obs.*) 1586, **-ly** *adv.* 1615.

Symptomatize (si·mptǒmătəiz), *v.* 1794. [f. Gr. συμπτωματ-, σύμπτωμα SYMPTOM + -IZE.] *trans.* To be a symptom of; to characterize or indicate as a symptom.

Symptomatology (si:mptǒmătǫ·lŏdʒi). 1798. [ad. mod.L. *symptomatologia*; see SYMPTOM and -LOGY.] **1.** The study of symptoms; that branch of pathology which treats of the symptoms of disease; also, a discourse or treatise on symptoms 1804. **2.** *transf.* The symptoms of a disease collectively (as a subject of study) 1798.

Syn- (sin), *prefix*, latinized form of Gr. συν- (= σύν prep. with), together, similarly, alike, occurring in many modern scientific terms. (It undergoes assimilation before consonants: before *l* to *syl-*, before labials to SYM- (q.v.), before simple *s* to *sys-*; before *s* + consonant and *z* it is reduced to *sy-*.)

Syna·cmic [Gr. ἀκμή point] *a. Bot.* having the stamens and pistils ripening at the same time; so **Syna·cmy**, simultaneous ripening of the stamens and pistils of a flower. **Synanthe·reous,** *a.* (*rare*) *Bot.* belonging to the *Synantherex* (= *Compositæ*); having the anthers united. **Synanthe·sis,** *Bot.* simultaneous ripening of the stamens and pistils in a flower; hence **Synanthe·tic** (-þe·tik) *a.* **Syna·nthous,** *a. Bot.* (*a*) applied to plants whose leaves expand at the same time as the flowers; (*b*) characterized by synanthy. **Syna·nthy,** abnormal union or fusion of two or more flowers. **Syna·ptase** [Gr. συναπτός joined together] *Chem.* an albuminous ferment found in almonds and other oily seeds; also called *emulsin.* **Synapti·cula,** each of a number of transverse calcareous processes connecting the septa in certain corals. ||**Synarthro·sis** [Gr. ἄρθρωσις jointing] *Anat.* a form of articulation in which the bones are firmly fixed so as to be incapable of moving upon one another, as in the sutures of the skull; so **Synarthro·dial** *a.* **Sy·ncarp,** *Bot.* a multiple fruit, i.e. one arising from a number of carpels in one flower. **Synca·rpous,** *a.* consisting of united or adherent carpels. **Synchondro·sis** [Gr. χόνδρος cartilage] *Anat.* the junction of two bones by cartilage; the structure or part in which this takes place; hence **Synchondro·sial,** *a.* **Syncotyle·donous,** *a. Bot.* having the cotyledons united. **Syncrante·rian,** *a. Anat.* having the teeth in a continuous row, as certain snakes. ||**Syncytium** (-si·tiǒm, -si·ʃiǒm) [Gr. κύτος receptacle] *Biol.* (*a*) a single cell or protoplasmic mass containing several nuclei, formed by fusion of a number of cells without fusion of the nuclei, or by division of the nucleus without division of the cell-substance; (*b*) a structure composed of such cells forming the outermost fetal layer of the placenta; hence **Syncy·tial** *a.* **Synda·ctyl,** *a.* having some or all of the fingers or toes wholly or partly united, as certain mammals and birds; *sb.* a syndactyl animal. **Syndya·smian,** *a. Anthrop.* pertaining to or marked by sexual union without exclusive coition, or with temporary cohabitation. **Synechia** (sine·kiă), *Path.* an affection of the eye, consisting in adhesion of the iris to the cornea (*anterior s.*) or to the capsule of the lens (*posterior s.*). **Syne·nergy** (*rare*) = SYNERGY. ||**Syne·rgia,** (*a*) *Physiol.* = SYNERGY; (*b*) *Anthropol.* agreement in bodily movements or acts, as a hypothetical stage in the development of sympathy. ||**Syne·rgida,** *Bot.* either of two naked nucleated cells at the apex of the embryo-sac, regarded as co-operating with the oosphere in the production of the embryo. **Sy·ngamy,** (*a*) free interbreeding between organisms; (*b*) the fusion of two cells, or of their nuclei, in reproduction. **Sy·ngnathous,** *a. Zool.* belonging to the genus *Syngnathus* or sub-order *Syngnathi* of fishes, characterized by the jaws being united into a tubular snout. **Synneuro·sis** [Gr. νεῦρον sinew] *Anat.* connexion or articulation of bones by a ligament. **Sy·nocil,** *Zool.* a structure in certain sponges, supposed to be a sense-organ, perhaps analogous to the rods and cones of the retina of the eye. **Synse·palous** *a. Bot.* having the sepals united, gamosepalous. **Sy·ntheme,** *Math.* a system of groups of elements, each of the groups being formed of a certain number of elements, so that each occurs exactly a given number of times among all the groups. **Synthe·rmal,** *a.* having the same temperature; *sb.* an isotherm connecting places having the same temperature at the same moment of time. **Sy·ntype,** *Nat. Hist.* any one of the original set of specimens from which a species has been described and named.

Synæresis (sinī°·rĭsis). 1577. [Late L., a. Gr. συναίρεσις a taking or drawing together, contraction, f. σύν SYN- + αἱρεῖν to take.] *Gram.* Contraction, esp. of two vowels into a diphthong or a simple vowel.

||**Synæsthesia** (sinīzþī·ziă, -siă). *Pl.* **-æ** (-ī). 1891. [mod.L., f. Gr. σύν SYN- + stem αἰσθε- to feel, perceive, after *anæsthesia.*] *Psychol.* **a.** A sensation in one part of the body produced by a stimulus applied to another part. **b.** Agreement of the feelings or emotions of different individuals, as a stage in the development of sympathy. **c.** Production, from a sense-impression of one kind, of an associated mental image of a sense-impression of another kind.

Synagogal (si·năgǒugăl), *a.* 1682. [f. next + -AL 1.] Of, pertaining or relating to, or characteristic of a or the synagogue. So **Sinago·gical** *a.* 1621.

Synagogue (si·năgǫg). ME. [a. OF. *sinagoge*, or ad. late L. *synagoga*, a. Gr. συναγωγή meeting, assembly, f. συνάγειν, f. σύν SYN- + ἄγειν to lead, bring.] **1.** The regular assembly or congregation of the Jews for religious instruction and worship apart from the service of the temple, constituting, since the destruction of the temple, their sole form of public worship; hence, the religious organization of the Jews as typified by this, the Jewish communion. **2.** *transf.* in hostile controversial use, often in phr. *s. of Satan* (see Rev. ii. 9) 1464. **3.** A building or place of meeting for Jewish worship and religious instruction ME. †**b.** *transf.* A place of worship; a temple. In post-Reformation use applied disparagingly to abbeys, etc. –1655. **4.** *gen.* An assembly; chiefly as a literalism of biblical translation ME.

1. *The Great S.*, a Jewish council of 120 members, said to have been founded and presided over by Ezra after the return from the Babylonian captivity. 2. By the incitement..of that unchristian S. [*sc.* Scots Presbytery] at Belfast MILT.

Synallactic (sinĕlæ·ktik), *a. rare.* 1853. [ad. Gr. συναλλακτικός, f. συναλλάσσειν to exchange, bring into intercourse, reconcile, f. σύν SYN- + ἀλλάσσειν to exchange.] Reconciliatory.

Synallagmatic (sinælæ̆gmæ·tik), *a.* 1792. [ad. Gr. συναλλαγματικός, f. συνάλλαγμα covenant, contract, f. συναλλάσσειν; see prec.] Pertaining to or of the nature of a contract or mutual engagement; imposing mutual obligations; reciprocally binding; esp. in *Civil Law*, of a treaty or the like.

Synallaxine (sinæ̆læ·ksəin, -in), *a.* 1862. [ad. mod.L. *Synallaxinæ* pl., f. *Synallaxis*, name of the typical genus; see -INE [1].] *Ornith.* Belonging to the subfamily *Synallaxinæ* of dendrocolaptine birds, found in tropical America, in habits and appearance resembling tree creepers.

||**Synalœpha** (sinălī·fă), **-phe** (-fī). 1540. [Late L., a. Gr. συναλοιφή, f. συναλείφειν to smear or melt together, f. σύν SYN- + ἀλείφειν to anoint.] *Gram.* The coalescence or contraction of two syllables into one; *esp.* the coalescence (in verse) of two vowels at the end of one word and the beginning of the next, by obscuration of the former (or, *loosely*, by suppression of it, in which case more properly called *elision*).

||**Synangium** (sinæ·ndʒiǒm). *Pl.* **-ia.** 1875. [mod.L., f. Gr. σύν SYN- + ἀγγεῖον vessel.] **1.** *Anat.* and *Zool.* A collective or common blood-vessel from which several arteries branch; *spec.* the terminal part of the arterial trunk in the lower vertebrates. **2.** *Bot.* The oblong mass of coherent sporangia in ferns of the order *Marattiaceæ* 1881. Hence **Syna·ng·ial, -ic** *adjs.*

||**Synaphe** (si·năfī). 1801. [a. Gr. συναφή, f. σύν SYN- + ἅπτειν to fasten, fix.] *Anc. Gr. Mus.* The 'conjunction' of two tetrachords.

||**Synaphea** (sinăfī·ă). 1827. [Late L., ad. Gr. συνάφεια connexion.] *Anc. Pros.* Continuity of rhythm; maintenance of the same rhythm throughout, esp. in anapæstic verse.

Synapse (sinæ·ps). 1899. [ad. Gr. σύναψις; see next.] *Anat.* The junction, or structure at the junction, between two neurons or nerve-cells.

||**Synapsis** (sinæ·psis). *Pl.* **synapses** (-sīz). 1892. [mod.L., ad. Gr. σύναψις connexion, junction, f. σύν SYN- + ἅψις joining, f. ἅπτειν to join.] **1.** *Biol.* The condensation and fusion of the chromatin to one side of the nucleus, as a stage in the development of a fertilized cell. **2.** *Anat.* = prec. 1897. So **Syna·ptic** *a.*

Synarchy (si·naɹki). *rare.* 1732. [ad. Gr. συναρχία, f. συνάρχειν to rule jointly.] Joint rule or sovereignty; participation in government.

Synastry (sinæ·stri). Also in L. form **synastria.** 1657. [f. Gr. σύν SYN- + ἀστρ-, ἀστήρ star + -Y [3].] *Astrol.* Coincidence or agreement of the influences of the stars over the destinies of two persons.

||**Synaxarion, -ium** (sinæksē°·riǫn, -iǒm). *Pl.* **-ia.** 1850. [eccl. L., a. eccl. Gr. συναξάριον, f. σύναξις SYNAXIS.] *Gr. Ch.* An account of the life of a saint, read as a lesson in public worship; also, a collection of such accounts. So **Syna·xarist**, the compiler of a s.

||**Synaxis** (sinæ·ksis). *Pl.* **-es** (-īz). 1624. [eccl. L., a. eccl. Gr. σύναξις, f. συνάγειν to gather together.] *Eccl. Hist.* A meeting for worship, esp. for celebration of the Eucharist.

Syncategorem (sinkæ·tĭgǒrem). 1653. [ad. med.L. *syncategorema*, a. Gr. συγκατηγόρημα, f. συγκατηγορεῖν (in Logic) to predicate jointly.] *Logic.* A word which cannot be used by itself as a term, but only in conjunction with another word or words; e.g. a sign of quantity (as *all, some, no*), or an adverb, preposition, or conjunction.

Syncategorematic (sinkæ:tĭgǫrīmæ·tik), *a.* 1827. [ad. Gr. συγκατηγορηματικός, f. συγκατηγόρημα; see prec. and -IC.] *Logic.* Of the nature of a syncategorem; opp. to CATEGOREMATIC. So †**Syncategorema·tical** *a.* 1646–1701, †**-ly** *adv.* 1600.

||**Syncellus** (sinse·lǒs). *Pl.* **-i.** Also in anglicized form **syncel.** 1706. [med.L. *syncellus, sincellus*, lit. one who shares a cell with another, a. Byzantine Gr. σύγκελλος, hybrid f. Gr. σύν SYN- + *cella* CELL *sb.*] In the Eastern Church, orig. an ecclesiastic who lived continually with a prelate; later, a dignitary who was associated with a prelate and succeeded to his office.

Synchronal (si·ŋkrǒnăl), *a.* Now *rare* or *Obs.* 1660. [f. late L. *synchronus* SYNCHRONOUS + -AL 1.] = SYNCHRONOUS 1, 1 b, 2.

Synchronic (siŋkrǫ·nik), *a. rare.* 1833. [f. late L. *synchronus*; see prec. and -IC.] = SYNCHRONOUS 1, 1 b, 2.

Synchronical (siŋkrǫ·nikăl), *a.* Now *rare* or *Obs.* 1652. [f. as prec. + -ICAL.] = SYNCHRONOUS 1, 1 b, 2. Hence **Synchro·nically** *adv.*

Synchronism (si·ŋkrŏniz'm). 1588. [ad. mod.L. *synchronismus*, ad. Gr. *συγχρονισμός*, f. *σύγχρονος* SYNCHRONOUS.] **1.** The quality of being synchronous; coincidence or agreement in point of time; contemporary existence or occurrence. **b.** *Geom.* The property of being synchronous, as a curve; *spec.* of a circle, the property that chords starting from the same point of the circumference will be described in equal times by particles descending under the influence of gravity 1867. **2.** Arrangement or treatment of synchronous events, etc. together or in conjunction, as in a history; agreement in relation to the time of the events described 1612. **b.** (with *a* and *pl.*) A statement or argument that two or more events, etc. are synchronous; a parallel drawn between occurrences, etc. in respect of time; a description or account of different events belonging to the same period; a tabular arrangement of historical events or personages according to their dates 1593. **c.** (*a*) Treatment of details according to identity of period, as in architecture. (*b*) Representation of events of different times together, e.g. in the same picture. 1843. **3.** Recurrence at the same successive instants of time; the fact of keeping time, i.e. proceeding at the same rate and exactly together; coincidence of period, as of two sets of movements, vibrations, or alternations of electric current 1854. Hence **Sy·nchronist** (*rare*) a contemporary.

3. *spec.* of the audible and visible components in cinematography, etc.

Synchroni·stic, *a.* 1685. [f. prec.; see -ISTIC.] Belonging to synchronism; relating to or exhibiting the concurrence of events in time.

Synchronize (si·ŋkrŏnəiz), *v.* Also **-ise.** 1624. [f. as prec.; see -IZE.] **1.** *intr.* To occur at the same time; to be contemporary or simultaneous. Const. *with*. **b.** *trans.* To cause to be, or represent as, synchronous; to assign the same date to; to bring together events, etc. belonging to the same time. Also *absol.* 1806. **2.** *intr.* To occur at the same successive instants of time; to keep time *with*; to have coincident periods, as two sets of movements or vibrations 1867. **b.** *trans.* To cause to go at the same rate; *spec.* to cause (a timepiece) to indicate the same time as another 1879.

2. c. *Cinematogr.* To add (sound effects) in time and harmony with the action of a picture; to furnish (a picture) with such effects; also *intr.* of the audible and visible components. Hence **Sy·nchroniza·tion. Sy·nchronized** *ppl. a.*; spec. *s. gear-changing, -shifting*, a form of gear-changing in a motor vehicle by which both gears are brought to the same speed before the change is made. **Sy·nchronizing** *vbl. sb.* and *ppl. a.*, also, of gun-firing apparatus.

Synchrono·logy. 1736. [f. SYN- + CHRONOLOGY.] Combined or comparative chronology; arrangement of events according to dates, those of the same date being placed or treated together. Hence **Sy:nchronolo·gical** *a.*

Synchronous (si·ŋkrŏnəs), *a.* 1669. [f. late L. *synchronus*, a. Gr. *σύγχρονος*, f. *σύν* SYN- + *χρόνος* time; see -OUS.] **1.** Existing or happening at the same time; coincident in time; contemporary, simultaneous. **b.** *transf.* Relating to or treating of different events or things belonging to the same time or period; involving or indicating contemporaneous or simultaneous occurrence 1823. **c.** *S. curve* (Geom.), a curve which is the locus of the points reached at any instant by a number of particles descending from the same point down a family of curves under the action of gravity 1867. **2.** Recurring at the same successive instants of time; keeping time *with*; having coincident periods, as two sets of vibrations or the like 1677. **b.** *Electr.* applied to alternating currents having coincident periods; also, to a machine or motor working in time with the alternations of current 1901. Hence **Sy·nchronous-ly** *adv.*, **-ness.**

Sy·nchrony. 1848. [f. Gr. *σύγχρονος*; see prec. and -Y³.] = SYNCHRONISM 1, 2, 2 b.

‖**Synchysis** (si·ŋkisis). 1577. [Late L., a. Gr. *σύγχυσις*, f. *συγχεῖν* to mingle, confuse, f. *σύν* SYN- + *χεῖν* to pour.] **1.** *Gram.* and *Rhet.* A confused arrangement of words in a sentence, obscuring the meaning. **2.** *Path.* Softening or fluidity of the vitreous humour of the eye; called *sparkling s.* (*s. scintillans*) when minute flakes of cholesterin float in the humour, causing a sparkling appearance in the field of vision 1684.

Synclastic (sinklæ·stik), *a.* 1867. [f. Gr. *σύν* SYN- (alike) + *κλαστός* 'bent', f. *κλᾶν* to break.] *Geom.* Of a curved surface: Having the same kind of curvature (concave or convex) in all directions.

Synclinal (siŋkləi·năl, si·ŋklinăl), *a.* and *sb.* 1833. [f. Gr. *σύν* SYN- + *κλίνειν* to bend + -AL.] **A.** adj. *Geol.* Applied to a line or axis towards which strata dip or slope down in opposite directions; also said of the fold or bend in such strata, or of a valley, trough, or basin so formed. Opp. to ANTICLINAL. **b.** *transf.* and *gen.* Inclined or sloping towards each other, or characterized by such inclination 1880. **B.** *sb. Geol.* A s. line, fold, or depression 1855. Hence **Sy·ncline,** a s. fold or depression. **Syncli·nical** *a.* = SYNCLINAL A.

Syncopal (si·ŋkŏpăl), *a.* 1689. [ad. med. L. *syncopalis*, f. SYNCOPE.] *Path.* Of, pertaining to, or marked by syncope.

Syncopate (si·ŋkŏpeᵗt), *v.* 1605. [f. late L. *syncopat-*, *syncopare* to affect with syncope, f. SYNCOPE.] **1.** *Gram. trans.* To contract (a word) by omitting one or more syllables or letters in the middle; also *pass.*, to be produced by syncopation. **2.** *Mus.* **a.** *trans.* To begin (a note) on an unaccented part of a bar and sustain it into the accented part; to introduce syncopation into (a passage). Often in pa. pple. **b.** *intr.* To be marked by syncopation. 1667.

1. *Soldo* is syncopated for *solido* 1857.

Syncopation (siŋkŏpē·ʃən). 1532. [ad. med.L. *syncopatio, -onem*, f. *syncopare*; see prec.] **1.** *Gram.* Contraction of a word by omission of one or more syllables or letters in the middle; *transf.* a word so contracted (*rare*). **2.** *Mus.* The action of beginning a note on a normally unaccented part of the bar and sustaining it into the normally accented part, so as to produce the effect of shifting back or anticipating the accent; the shifting of accent so produced 1597.

‖**Syncope** (si·ŋkŏpi). late ME. [ad. late L., a. Gr. *συγκοπή*, f. *σύν* SYN- + *κοπ-* stem of *κόπτειν* to strike, beat, cut off, weary.] **1.** *Path.* Failure of the heart's action, resulting in loss of consciousness, and sometimes in death. **2.** *Gram.* = prec. 1. Now *rare.* 1530. †**3.** *Mus.* = prec. 2. –1795. **4.** A cutting short; abbreviation, contraction; sudden cessation or interruption (*rare*) 1658.

4. Revelry, and dance, and show, Suffer a s. and solemn pause COWPER. Hence **Sy·ncopist** (*nonce-wd.*), one who syncopates a word; *spec.* one who omits letters and supplies their places with dashes, etc. as in satirical writing ADDISON.

Syncretic (siŋkrī·tik, -kre·tik), *a.* (*sb.*) 1840. [f. next.] Characterized by syncretism; aiming at a union or reconciliation of diverse beliefs, practices, or systems. **B.** *sb.* = SYNCRETIST 1883.

Syncretism (si·ŋkrĭtiz'm). 1618. [ad. mod.L. *syncretismus*, a. Gr. *συγκρητισμός*, f. *συγκρητίζειν* to SYNCRETIZE.] Attempted union or reconciliation of diverse or opposite tenets or practices, esp. in philosophy or religion; *spec.* the system or principles of a school founded in the 17th c. by George Calixtus, who aimed at harmonizing the sects of Protestants and ultimately all Christian bodies. (Usu. derogatory.)

Syncretist (si·ŋkrĭtist). 1758. [f. prec.; see -IST.] One who practises or favours syncretism; *spec.* = CALIXTIN 2. Hence **Syncreti·stic** *a.* of or pertaining to syncretism or syncretists; characterized by syncretism.

Syncretize (si·ŋkrĭtəiz), *v.* 1675. [ad. mod.L. *syncretizare*, ad. Gr. *συγκρητίζειν* to combine, as two parties against a third (etym. unkn.).] **1.** *intr.* To practise syncretism; to attempt to combine different or opposing tenets or systems; †*loosely*, to agree, accord. **2.** *trans.* To combine, as different systems, etc. 1907.

Sy·ncro-mesh, abbrev. of *synchronized mesh*, used *attrib.* to designate a form of automatic gear-changing box.

Synderesis: see SYNTERESIS.

Syndesmo- (sinde·smo), bef. a vowel **syndesm-**, repr. Gr. *σύνδεσμος* a ligament. **Syndesmo·graphy,** description of the ligaments. **Syndesmo·logy,** that branch of anatomy which treats of the ligaments. **Syndesmo·sis,** the union of two bones by a ligament; hence **Syndesmo·tic** *a.* **Syndesmo·tomy,** dissection or surgical section of ligaments.

Syndetic (sinde·tik), *a.* 1621. [ad. Gr. *συνδετικός*, f. *συνδεῖν* to bind together.] Serving to unite or connect; connective, copulative. So **Synde·tical** *a.*, **-ly** *adv.*

Syndic (si·ndik). 1601. [ad. F., ad. late L. *syndicus* advocate or delegate representing a town, a. Gr. *σύνδικος* defendant's advocate, f. *σύν* SYN- + *δίκη* judgement.] **1.** An officer of government having different powers in different countries; a civil magistrate, or one of several such, entrusted with the affairs of a city or community; *spec.* each of the four chief magistrates of Geneva. **2.** One deputed to represent and transact the affairs of a corporation, e.g. a university; *spec.* in the University of Cambridge, applied to members of special committees of the senate, appointed by grace for specific duties 1607. †**3.** A censor of the actions of another –1658. **4.** *Gr. Hist.* The title of various officials at Athens and elsewhere 1682.

Syndical (si·ndikăl), *a.* 1864. [ad. F. *syndical*, f. *syndic* SYNDIC.] Only in *s. chamber* (occas. *union*) = F. *chambre syndicale*, a union of people engaged in a particular trade, for the protection of their interests; a trade-union.

Syndicalism (si·ndikăliz'm). 1907. [ad. F. *syndicalisme*, f. *syndical*; see prec. and -ISM.] A movement among industrial workers having as its object the transfer of the means of production and distribution from their present owners to unions of workers for the benefit of the workers, the method generally favoured for the accomplishment of this being the general strike. So **Sy·ndicalist,** an adherent of s.

Syndicate (si·ndikĕt), *sb.* 1624. [ad. F. *syndicat* office of syndic, body of syndics, †censure, ad. med.L. **syndicatus*, f. *syndicus* SYNDIC; see -ATE¹.] †**1.** The office, status, or jurisdiction of a syndic –1728. **2.** A council or body of syndics; also, a meeting of such a body 1624. **3.** A combination of capitalists or financiers entered into for the purpose of prosecuting a scheme requiring large resources of capital, esp. one having the object of obtaining control of the market in a particular commodity. Hence, more widely, a combination of persons formed for the promotion of an enterprise; *esp.* a combination for the acquisition of articles, etc. and their simultaneous publication in a number of periodicals; also, a combination of newspapers controlled by such a body 1865.

Syndicate (si·ndikeᵗt), *v.* 1610. [In sense 1, f. med.L. *syndicat-*, *syndicare*. In other senses, f. prec.] †**1.** *trans.* To judge, censure –1822. **2.** To control, manage, or effect by a syndicate; *esp.* to publish simultaneously in a number of newspapers 1882. **3.** To combine into a syndicate 1889.

2. Dr. Talmage syndicates his sermons, and they are published in Monday's newspapers in all quarters of America 1891.

Syndication (sindikēᵗ·ʃən). 1650. [In sense 1, ad. L. *syndicatio, -onem* examination. In sense 2, f. SYNDICATE *v.*; see -ATION.] †**1.** The action of judging. HOBBES. **2.** The action or process of forming a syndicate 1887.

‖**Syndrome** (si·ndrŏmi). 1541. [mod.L., a. Gr. *συνδρομή*, f. *σύν* SYN- + *δρομ-*: *δραμεῖν* to run.] **1.** *Path.* A concurrence of several symptoms in a disease; a set of such concurrent symptoms. †**2.** *transf.* or *gen.* A concurrence; a set of concurrent things (*rare*) –1661.

Syne (səin), *adv. Sc.* and *n. dial.* ME. [Contracted f. SITHEN.] **1.** = SINCE A. 1 (occas. strengthened by *after*.) **2.** At a later time, afterwards, subsequently; esp. in *soon or syne*, sooner or later. late ME. **3.** Since then. late ME. **4.** (So long) before now; ago 1573.

Synecdoche (sine·kdŏki). late ME. [a. late L., a. Gr. *συνεκδοχή*, f. *συνεκδέχεσθαι* lit. to take with something else, f. *σύν* SYN- + *ἐκδέχεσθαι* to take, take up.] *Gram.* and *Rhet.* A figure by which a more comprehensive term is used for a less comprehensive or *vice versa*;

as whole for part or part for whole, genus for species or species for genus, etc. Hence **Synec·do·chic, Synecdo·chical** *adjs.* involving s. or synecdochism. **Synecdo·chically** *adv.* by s.

Synecdochism (sine·kdǒkiz'm). 1854. [f. prec. + -ISM.] **a.** *Gram.* and *Rhet.* Synecdochical style; the use of synecdoche. **b.** *Ethnol.* Belief or practice in which a part of an object or person is taken as equivalent to the whole, so that anything done to, or by means of, the part is held to take effect upon, or have the effect of, the whole.

Synectic (sine·ktik), *a.* 1697. [ad. late L. *synecticus*, a. Gr. συνεκτικός, f. συνέχειν, f. συν- SYN- + ἔχειν to have, hold.] **a.** Of a cause: Producing its effect directly; immediate; *spec.* in *Old Med.* = CONTINENT *a.* 6. **b.** *Math.* Applied to certain continuous functions 1888.

Synedrian (sine·driăn), *sb.* and *a.* 1606. [f. next + -AN.] **A.** *sb.* A member of a synedrion. **B.** *adj.* Of or belonging to a synedrion.

‖**Synedrion** (sine·driǒn), **synedrium** (-ǒm). *Pl.* synedria. 1584. [mod.L., a. Gr. συνέδριον, f. σύνεδρος sitting with, f. σύν SYN- + ἕδρα seat.] A judicial or representative assembly, a council, consistory; *spec.* the Jewish SANHEDRIM.

‖**Syneidesis** (sinəidī·sis). 1620. [Scholastic L., a. Gr. συνείδησις, f. συνειδέναι.] *Theol.* That function or department of conscience which is concerned with passing judgement on acts already performed.

Synergetic (sinəɹdʒe·tik), *a. rare.* 1682. [ad. Gr. συνεργητικός, f. συνεργεῖν to work together, co-operate.] = next.

Synergic (sinɔ̄·ɹdʒik), *a.* 1859. [ad. mod.L. *synergicus*, f. Gr. συνεργός, -εργεῖν; see prec. and -IC.] *Physiol.* Working together, co-operating, as a group of muscles for the production of some movement; pertaining to or involving synergy.

Synergism (si·nəɹdʒiz'm). 1764. [ad. mod.L. *synergismus*, f. Gr. συνεργός, συνεργεῖν.] *Theol.* The doctrine that the human will co-operates with Divine grace in the work of regeneration.

Synergist (si·nəɹdʒist). 1657. [f. Gr. συνεργός + -IST.] **1.** *Theol.* One who holds the doctrine of synergism. **2.** *Med.* and *Physiol.* A medicine, etc., or a bodily organ (*e. g.* a muscle) that co-operates with another or others. Hence **Synergi·stic** *a. Theol.* of or pertaining to synergism or the synergists; (of a medicine, etc.) acting as a s.

Synergy (si·nəɹdʒi). 1847. [ad. mod.L. *Synergia.*] Combined or correlated action of a group of bodily organs (as nerve-centres, muscles, etc.); hence, of mental faculties, of remedies, etc.

‖**Syngenesia** (sindʒĭnī·ziă, -siă). 1753. [mod.L. f. Gr. σύν SYN- + γένεσις GENESIS; see -IA.] *Bot.* The nineteenth class in the Linnæan Sexual System, comprising plants having stamens coherent by the anthers, and flowers (florets) in close heads or *capitula*; corresponding to the family *Compositæ*. Hence **Syngene·sian** *a.* = next.

Syngenesious (sindʒĭnī·ʃəs, -ī·siəs), *a.* 1753. [f. prec. + -OUS.] *Bot.* **a.** Belonging to the class *Syngenesia*; having the stamens united by their anthers. **b.** Of the stamens: United by the anthers so as to form a tube, as in the *Syngenesia*; also said of the anthers.

Syngenesis (sindʒe·nĭsis). 1836. [mod.L.; see SYN- and GENESIS.] *Biol.* Formation of the germ in sexual reproduction by fusion of the male and female elements, so that the substance of the embryo is derived from both parents. Hence **Syngene·tic** *a.*

Syngraph (si·ŋgraf). Also in L. form. 1633. [ad. L. *syngrapha*, *-us*, ad. Gr. συγγραφή, σύγγραφος, f. συγγράφειν to compose in writing, draw up, f. σύν SYN- + γράφειν to write.] A written contract or bond signed by both or all the parties.

‖**Synizesis** (sinizī·sis). *Pl.* **-ses** (-sīz). 1820. [Late L., a. Gr. συνίζησις, f. συνιζάνειν to sink down, collapse, f. σύν SYN- + ἱζάνειν to seat, sit, settle down, f. ἵζειν to seat, sit.] **1.** *Gram.* and *Pros.* Fusion of two syllables into one by the coalescence of two adjacent vowels (or of a vowel and a diphthong) without the formation of a recognized diphthong 1846. **2.** *Path.* Closure of the pupil of the eye 1820.

‖**Synocha** (si·nǒkă). 1801. [med.L. fem. of SYNOCHUS.] *Path.* A continued or unintermitting fever (or a particular variety of this; cf. SYNOCHUS). Hence **Sy·nochal** *a.* of the nature of or pertaining to s. (or synochus) 1541.

‖**Synochus** (si·nǒkǒs). late ME. [med.L., a. Gr. σύνοχος, f. σύν SYN- + ὀχ-: ἔχειν to have, after συνέχειν to hold together, be continuous.] *Path.* = SYNOCHA (but often dist. as a different species).

Synod (si·nǒd). late ME. [ad. late L. *synodus*, a. Gr. σύνοδος, f. σύν SYN- + ὁδός way, travel.] **1.** *Eccl.* An assembly of the clergy of a particular church, nation, province, or diocese (sometimes with representatives of the laity) duly convened for discussing and deciding ecclesiastical affairs. †In early use freq. applied to general councils. **b.** In Presbyterian Churches: A body or assembly of ministers and other elders, constituting the ecclesiastical court next above the presbytery, and consisting of the members of, or of delegates from, the presbyteries within its bounds 1593. **2.** *gen.* and *transf.* An assembly, convention, or council of any kind 1578. †**3.** *Astrol.* A conjunction of two planets or heavenly bodies -1686.

2. Sir, we could not have had a better dinner, had there been a S. of Cooks JOHNSON.

Synodal (si·nǒdăl), *a.* and *sb.* 1450. [ad. late L. *synodalis*, f. *synodus* SYNOD; see -AL.] **A.** *adj.* **1.** Done or made by, or proceeding from a synod (†or general council). **2.** Of the nature of or constituted as a synod 1530. †**b.** *transf.* Connected with or related to church government by synodal assemblies, presbyterian -1640. **3.** Of, belonging to, or connected with, having or characterized by, a synod or visitation 1579.

1. The S. decrees of the Council of 214 Bishops at Carthage 1865.

B. *sb.* **1.** A synodal decision, constitution, or decree. *Obs.* exc. *Hist.* 1485. **2.** A payment made by the inferior clergy to the bishop, properly on the occasion of a synod, and hence at an episcopal or archidiaconal visitation 1534.

2. At Easter Visitation the Ministers pay their Pascal Rents, or Synodals 1667.

Synodic (sinǫ·dik), *a.* 1640. [ad. late L. *synodicus*, a. late Gr. συνοδικός (both in sense 2), f. σύνοδος SYNOD.] **1.** *Eccl.* = SYNODAL *a.* **2.** *Astron.* = next 2. 1654.

Synodical (sinǫ·dikăl), *a.* 1561. [f. as prec.; see -ICAL.] **1.** *Eccl.* = SYNODAL *a.* **2.** *Astron.* Pertaining to the conjunction of two heavenly bodies (see CONJUNCTION 3); said *esp.* of the revolution, or period of revolution, of a planet between two successive conjunctions with the sun, or of a satellite between two successive conjunctions with (or occultations or eclipses by) its primary planet 1669.

1. A Synodicall Epistle 1561. S. majorities 1866. 2. *S. month*, the synodic period of the moon, i. e. the time from new moon to new moon; a lunar month, lunation. Hence **Syno·dically** *adv.* by the action or authority of a synod; in synod, as a synod.

Synodist (si·nǒdist). 1626. [f. SYNOD + -IST.] †**1.** A member of a synod -1650. **2.** An adherent of a synod; used disparagingly of those who accepted the decrees of the Council of Chalcedon (*rare*) 1846.

Synœcious (sinī·ʃiəs), *a.* 1863. [f. SYN-, after DIŒCIOUS, etc.; cf. Gr. συνοικία community living together.] *Bot.* Having male and female flowers in the same flower-head, as some *Compositæ*, or male and female organs in the same receptacle, as some mosses.

Synœcism (sinī·siz'm). 1886. [ad. Gr. συνοικισμός, f. συνοικίζειν to cause to dwell with, to unite under one capital city, f. σύν SYN- + οἰκίζειν, f. οἶκος house.] *Gr. Antiq.* The union of several towns or villages into or under one capital city. So **Synœ·cize** *v. trans.* to unite into or under one capital city.

Synomosy (sinǭu·mǒsi). 1808. [ad. Gr. συνωμοσία to confederate, f. σύν SYN- + ὀμνύναι to swear.] *Gr. Antiq.* A political society of men leagued by oath.

Synonym (si·nǒnim). late ME. [ad. late L. *synonymum*, *-on*, a. Gr. συνώνυμον, neut. sing. used subst. of συνώνυμος, f. σύν SYN- + -ωνυμ- = ὄνομα NAME.] **1.** Strictly, a word having the same sense as another (in the same language); but more usu., either of any two or more words (in the same language) having the same general sense, but possessing each of them meanings which are not shared by the other or others, or having different shades of meaning appropriate to different contexts, e. g. *serpent, snake*; *ship, vessel*; *glad, happy*; *to kill, slay, slaughter.* **b.** spec. in *Nat. Hist.* A systematic name having the same, or nearly the same, application as another, esp. as another which has superseded it 1659. **c.** The equivalent of a word in another language 1594. **2.** By extension: A name or expression which involves or implies a meaning properly or literally expressed by some other, 'another name *for*' 1631. **3.** *transf.* Either of two or more things of like or identical nature but called by different names, e. g. corresponding geological formations in different regions 1839.

1. Change the structure of the sentence; substitute one synonyme for another; and the whole effect is destroyed MACAULAY. **b.** We cannot have too complete a catalogue of all the species..together with their synonyms 1833. **c.** Had *life* been used instead of its Latin s. *ens* 1804. 2. 'Hobbism became..the popular s. for irreligion and immorality GREEN.

Synonymic (sinǒni·mik), *a.* (*sb.*) 1816. [f. prec. + -IC.] Of, relating to, consisting of, or exhibiting synonyms. **B.** *sb.* The study of synonyms, as a department of grammar. Also **Synony·mics** 1857.

Synony·mical, *a. rare.* 1645. [f. as prec. + -ICAL.] †**1.** = SYNONYMOUS 1. -1690. **2.** = prec. 1806. Hence **Synony·mically** *adv.* as a synonym or synonyms 1599.

Synonymist (sinǫ·nimist). 1753. [f. as prec. + -IST.] One who treats of, or makes a list of, synonyms.

Synonymity (sinǒni·mĭti). 1875. [f. SYNONYMOUS; see -ITY.] The quality or fact of being synonymous, or having the same meaning 1880. **b.** *transf.* Identity of nature of things having different names 1875.

Synonymize (sinǫ·nimǝiz), *v. rare.* 1595. [f. late L. *synonymum* + -IZE.] **1.** *trans.* To give the synonyms of. **2.** *intr.* To use synonyms; to express the same meaning by different words 1700.

1. This worde *fortis* wee maye synnonomize after all these fashions, stoute, hardye, valiaunt, doughtye, Couragious, aduenturous, &c. 1595.

Synonymous (sinǫ·niməs), *a.* 1610. [f. med.L. *synonymus*, ad. Gr. συνώνυμος; see SYNONYM and -OUS.] **1.** Having the character of a synonym; equivalent in meaning: said of words or phrases denoting the same thing or idea. Const. *to*, (now usu. *with*). **b.** *transf.* Said of things of the same nature denoted by different names, i. e. by synonyms; thus = identical 1789. **2.** In extended sense, said of words or phrases which denote things that imply one another 1659. **3.** *loosely* = HOMONYMOUS 2. 1734.

1. Words are seldom exactly synonimous JOHNSON. To say that a person 'is down in the mouth' is s. with saying that he is out of spirits DARWIN. 2. The name of soldier was s. with that of marauder 1855. Hence **Syno·nymous-ly** *adv.*, **-ness.**

Synonymy (sinǫ·nimi). 1609. [ad. late L. *synonymia*, a. Gr. συνωνυμία, f. συνώνυμος SYNONYM.] †**1.** = SYNONYM 1. -1799. **2.** The use of synonyms or of words as synonyms; *spec.* a rhetorical figure by which synonyms are used for the sake of amplification 1657. **3.** The subject or study of synonyms; synonyms collectively; a set of synonyms 1683. **4.** The quality or fact of being synonymous; identity of meaning 1794.

Synopsis (sinǫ·psis). *Pl.* **synopses** (-sīz). 1611. [a. late L., a. Gr. σύνοψις general view, f. σύν SYN- + ὄψις view.] **1.** A brief or condensed statement presenting a combined or general view of something; a table, or set of paragraphs or headings, so arranged as to exhibit all the parts or divisions of a subject or work at one view; a conspectus. **2.** *Eastern Ch.*

A book of prayers for the use of the laity 1850.
1. He hath written a s. of the history of man 1611.

Synoptic (sinǫ·ptik), *a.* (*sb.*) 1763. [ad. mod.L. *synopticus*, ad. Gr. συνοπτικός, f. σύνοψις SYNOPSIS.] 1. Of a table, chart, etc.: Pertaining to or forming a synopsis; furnishing a general view of some subject. b. Of a mental act or faculty, conduct, etc.: Pertaining to, involving, or taking a combined or comprehensive view of something 1852. 2. Applied distinctively to the first three Gospels (viz. of Matthew, Mark, and Luke) as giving an account of the events from the same point of view or under the same general aspect. Also *transf.* pertaining or relating to these Gospels. 1841. b. as *sb.* Any one of the Synoptic Gospels (or of their writers). Usu. in *pl.* 1858. So **Syno·ptical** *a.* 1664, **-ly** *adv.* in the way of a synopsis.

Synoptist (sinǫ·ptist). 1860. [f. prec.; see -IST.] Any one of the writers of the Synoptic Gospels. (Usu. in *pl.*)

Synostose (si·nǫstōᵘz), *v.* 1878. [Back-formation from next.] *pass.* and *intr.* To be affected with synostosis; to be united by a growth of bone.

Synostosis (sinǫstōᵘ·sis). *Pl.* **-oses** (-ōᵘ·sīz). 1848. [Contracted from *synosteosis*.] *Anat.* and *Physiol.* Union or fusion of adjacent bones by growth of bony substance (either normal or abnormal). Hence **Synosto·tic** *a.*

‖**Synovia** (sinōᵘ·viă, səi-). 1661. [mod.L. *sinovia*, *synovia*, also *sinophia*, an invention, prob. arbitrary, of Paracelsus (died 1541), applied by him to the nutritive fluid peculiar to the several parts of the body, and also to the gout.] *Physiol.* The viscid albuminous fluid secreted in the interior of the joints, and in the sheaths of the tendons, and serving to lubricate them; also called *joint-oil* or *joint-water* 1726. †b. *Path.* A morbid condition or discharge of this fluid -1766.

Synovial (sinōᵘ·viăl, səi-) *a.* 1756. [f. prec. + -AL 1.] Pertaining to, consisting of, containing, or secreting synovia. b. *transf.* Occurring in or affecting a synovial membrane 1846.
The s. fluid is viscid, transparent, of a yellow or reddish colour, faintly saline 1846. Hence **Syno·vially** *adv.* by means of synovia, or of a joint containing synovia.

Synovitis (sinǒvəi·tis, səi-). 1835. [f. SYNOVIA + -ITIS.] *Path.* Inflammation of a synovial membrane.

Syntactic (sintæ·ktik), *a.* 1828. [ad. mod.L. *syntacticus*, ad. Gr. συντακτικός, f. συντάσσειν; see SYNTAX and -IC.] = next.

Synta·ctical, *a.* 1577. [See prec. and -ICAL.] Belonging or relating to grammatical syntax. Hence **Synta·ctically** *adv.* in relation to, or according to the rules of, syntax.

‖**Syntagma** (sintæ·gmă). *Pl.* **-ata** or **-as.** 1644. [mod.L., a. Gr. σύνταγμα, f. συντάσσειν (see SYNTAXIS).] 1. A regular or orderly collection of statements, propositions, doctrines, etc.; a systematically arranged treatise. 2. *Antiq.* a. A body of persons forming a division of the population of a country. b. A body of troops forming a division of a phalanx. 1813. 3. *Bot.* An aggregate of 'tagmata' 1885.

Syntax (si·ntæks). 1605. [ad. F. *syntaxe*, ad. late L. *syntaxis*, a. Gr. σύνταξις SYNTAXIS.] †1. Orderly or systematic arrangement of parts or elements; constitution (of body); a connected order or system of things -1696. 2. *Gram.* a. The arrangement of words (in their appropriate forms) by which their connexion and relation in a sentence are shown. Also, the constructional uses of a word or form or a class of words or forms, or those characteristic of a particular author. b. The department of grammar which deals with the established usages of grammatical construction and the rules deduced therefrom: dist. from *accidence*. 1613. c. Name of a class in certain English Roman Catholic schools and colleges, next below that called *Poetry* 1629.
1. Concerning the S. and disposition of studies, that men may know in what order..to reade BACON. 2. Neither Sense nor S. would allow of that Signification BENTLEY. Hence **Synta·xian**, a member of the Syntax class in a R. C. school.

†**Synta·xis.** 1540. [Late L., a. Gr. σύνταξις, f. συντάσσειν, f. σύν SYN- + τάσσειν (base *ταγ-) to arrange.] = prec. 2. -1749.

‖**Synteresis** (sintĭrī·sis). *Pl.* **-eses** (-ī·sīz). Also †**synderesis** (cf. F. *syndérèse*). 1594. [med.L., a. Gr. συντήρησις careful guarding or watching, preservation, 'scintilla conscientiæ' (Jerome), f. συντηρεῖν, f. σύν SYN- + τηρεῖν to guard, keep.] 1. *Theol.* That function or department of conscience which serves as a guide for conduct; conduct as directive of one's actions: dist. from SYNEIDESIS. Now *Hist.* 2. *Med.* Prophylactic or preventive treatment. (prob. only a book-term.) 1848.

Synthesis (si·nþĭsis). *Pl.* **-es** (-īz). 1611. [a. L., a. Gr. σύνθεσις composition, f. συντιθέναι to put together, f. σύν SYN- + τιθέναι to place.] 1. *Logic*, *Philos.*, etc. The action of proceeding in thought from causes to effects or from laws or principles to their consequences. (Opp. to ANALYSIS 8.) †2. *Gram.* A figure by which a sentence is constructed according to the sense, in violation of strict syntax -1704. 3. *Chem.* Formation of a compound by combination of its elements or constituents; esp. applied to artificial production in this way of organic compounds formerly obtained by extraction from natural products 1733. b. *Physics.* Production of white or other compound light by combination of its constituent colours, or of a complex musical sound by combination of its component simple tones 1869. 4. In the philosophy of Kant, the action of the understanding in combining and unifying the isolated data of sensation into a cognizable whole 1817. 5. In wider philosophical use and *gen.* The putting together of parts or elements so as to make up a complex whole; the combination of immaterial or abstract things, or of elements into an ideal or abstract whole. (Opp. to ANALYSIS 1.) Also, the state of being so put together. 1833. b. A body of things put together; a complex whole made up of a number of parts or elements united 1865. c. *Philol.* Synthetic formation or construction 1869. 6. *Rom. Antiq.* A loose flowing robe, white or bright-coloured, worn at meals and festivities 1606.
3. Alcohol can also be prepared from its elements by s. 1869. 4. Experience proves the possibility of the s. of the predicate 'heavy', with the subject 'body'; for these two notions, although neither is contained in the other, are nevertheless parts of a whole, or of experience 1839. 5. The happiest *s.* of the divine, the scholar, and the gentleman COLERIDGE.

Synthesist (si·nþĭsist). 1863. [f. next; see -IST.] One who uses synthesis, or proceeds by a synthetic method. (Opp. to ANALYST.)

Synthesize (si·nþĭsəiz), *v.* 1830. [f. SYNTHES(IS + -IZE.] *trans.* To make a synthesis of; to put together or combine into a complex whole; to make up by combination of parts or elements. Also *absol.* (Opp. to ANALYSE.) b. *Chem.* To produce (a compound, esp. an organic compound) by synthesis 1865.
b. The kidney is capable of synthesising complex organic substances 1897.

Synthetic (sinþe·tik), *a.* 1697. [ad. F. *synthétique*, or mod.L. *syntheticus*, ad. Gr. συνθετικός, f. συνθετός, συντιθέναι (see SYNTHESIS).] (In most senses opp. to ANALYTIC.) 1. *Logic*, *Philos.*, etc. Proceeding from causes or general principles to consequences or particular instances; deductive. 2. *Chem.* Pertaining to or involving synthesis; of organic compounds, produced by artificial synthesis 1753. 3. In the philosophy of Kant, (*a*) applied to judgements which add to the subject attributes not directly implied in it; (*b*) pertaining to the synthesis of the manifold 1819. 4. Of, pertaining to, consisting in, or involving synthesis, or combination of parts into a whole; constructive 1702. b. Concerned with or using synthesis 1864. 5. *Gram.* and *Philol.* Characterized by combination of simple words or elements into compound or complex words; expressing a complex notion by a single compounded or complex word instead of by a number of distinct words 1835. 6. *Biol.* Combining in one organism different characters which in the later course of evolution are specialized in different organisms; having a generalized or undifferentiated type of structure 1859. 2. b. Applied gen. to preparations simulating a natural product; hence, artificial 1916. 5. The s. character of ancient languages 1869. So **Synthe·tical** *a.* 1620, **-ly** *adv.*

Synthetism (si·nþĭtiz'm). 1832. [ad. mod.L. *synthetismus*, f. Gr. συνθετίζεσθαι to SYNTHETIZE.] A synthetic system or doctrine.

Synthetist (si·nþĭtist). 1848. [f. SYNTHETIC, SYNTHETIZE; see -IST.] = SYNTHESIST.

Synthetize (si·nþĭtəiz), *v.* 1828. [ad. Gr. συνθετίζεσθαι, f. συνθετός; see SYNTHETIC and -IZE.] *trans.* = SYNTHESIZE.

‖**Synthronus** (si·nþrǒnǒs). *Eccl.* 1861. [eccl. L. a. eccl. Gr. σύνθρονος.] The joint throne of the bishop and his presbyters.

Syntonic (sintǫ·nik), *a.* 1892. [f. Gr. σύν SYN- + τόνος TONE + -IC.] *Electr.* Denoting a system of wireless telegraphy in which the transmitting and receiving instruments are accurately 'tuned' or adjusted so that the latter responds only to vibrations of the frequency of those emitted by the former; also said of the instruments so 'tuned'. Hence **Synto·nically** *adv.*

Syntonin (si·ntǒnin). 1859. [f. Gr. σύντονος strained tight, f. σύν SYN- + τείνειν + -IN.] *Chem.* An acid albuminous substance found in muscular tissue, or produced from myosin by the action of acids.

Syntonize (si·ntǒnəiz), *v.* 1892. [f. SYNTONIC + -IZE.] *Electr. trans.* To make syntonic. Hence **Sy·ntonizer**, an apparatus for syntonizing.

Syntonous (si·ntǒnəs), *a.* 1789. [f. Gr. σύντονος; see SYNTONIN and -OUS.] *Mus.* An epithet for the ordinary form of diatonic scale (διάτονον σύντονον) in ancient Greek music, in which the tetrachord was divided into a semitone and two tones, the third note of it being thus tuned to a higher pitch than in the other scales; nearly corresponding to the modern diatonic scale.

Syntony (si·ntǒni). 1892. [f. SYNTONIC + -Y[3].] *Electr.* The condition of being syntonic.

Sypher (səi·fəɹ), *v.* 1841. [var. of CIPHER *v.*] *Carpentry.* To make a lap-joint by overlapping two bevelled or chamfered plank-edges, so as to leave a plane surface. So **S.-joint.**

Syphilide (si·filəid). 1879. [orig. in pl., ad. F. *syphilides*, f. SYPHILIS; see -ID[3].] *Path.* A generic term for any skin affection of a syphilitic nature.

Syphilis (si·filis). 1718. [mod.L. *syphilis* (*syphilid-*), orig. the title (in full, *Syphilis, sive Morbus Gallicus*) of a poem, published 1530, by Girolamo Fracastoro (1483-1553), a physician, astronomer and poet of Verona, but used also as the name of the disease in the poem itself; the name *Syphilis*, being formed on the analogy of *Æneis*, *Thebais*, etc., from that of a shepherd *Syphilus*, the first sufferer from the disease.] *Path.* A specific disease caused by *Treponema pallidum* (*Spirochæte pallida*) and communicated by sexual connexion or accidental contact (acquired form) or by infection of the child in utero (congenital form).
Three stages of the disease are distinguished, *primary*, *secondary*, and *tertiary s.*; the first characterized by chancre in the part affected, the second by affections of the skin and mucous membranes, the third involving the bones, muscles, and brain.

Syphilitic (sifili·tik), *a.* (*sb.*) 1786. [ad. mod.L. *syphiliticus*, f. SYPHILIS.] *Path.* Of, pertaining to, caused by, or affected with syphilis. B. *sb.* A person affected with syphilis 1881.

Syphilize (si·filəiz), *v.* 1854. [ad. F. *syphiliser*; see SYPHILIS and -IZE.] *Med.* and *Path. trans.* To inoculate with the virus of syphilis, as a means of cure or prevention; also, to infect with syphilis. Hence **Sy·philiza·tion.**

Syphilo- (si·filo), used as comb. form of SYPHILIS. **Sy·philoderm**, ‖**-derma** (pl. *-ata*) [Gr. δέρμα skin] = SYPHILIDE; hence **Syphilode·rmatous** *a.* **Syphilo·grapher**, a writer on syphilis; so **Syphilo·graphy**, the description of syphilis. **Syphilo·logist**, **-o·logy.**

Syphiloid (si·filoid), *a.* (*sb.*) 1813. [f. SYPHILIS + -OID.] *Path.* Resembling syphilis. **B.** *sb.* A s. disease or affection 1890.

Syphiloma (sifilōu·mă). *Pl.* **-ata.** 1864. [f. SYPHILIS + -OMA, as in *sarcoma.*] *Path.* A syphilitic tumour. Hence **Syphilo·matous** *a.*

Syphilosis (sifilōu·sis). 1898. [f. SYPHILIS + -OSIS.] *Path.* Syphilitic condition.

Syphon: see SIPHON.

Syracusan (səi·ərăkiū·zăn), *a.* and *sb.* 1576. [ad. L. *Syracusanus*, f. *Syracusæ*, Gk. Συράκουσαι Syracuse + -AN.] Of or belonging to (a native or inhabitant of) Syracuse, a city in Sicily. So †**Syracu·sian** *a.* and *sb.* -1796.

Syracuse (səi·ərăkiūz). 1768. [See prec.] A luscious red muscadine wine made in Italy.

Syriac (si·riæk), *a.* and *sb.* 1602. [ad. L. *Syriacus* = Gr. Συριακός, f. *Syria*, Συρία.] **A.** *adj.* Of or pertaining to Syria: only of or in ref. to the language; written in Syriac; writing, or versed, in Syriac.

A very curious old S. copy of the Four Gospels 1867.

B. *sb.* The ancient Semitic language of Syria; formerly, = ARAMAIC; now, the form of Aramaic used by Syrian Christians, in which the Peshito version of the Bible is written 1611. **b.** A or the Syriac version (of the Bible) 1644. Hence **Sy·riacism** (-ăsiz'm) = SYRIASM. **Sy·riacist** (-ăsist), a S. scholar.

Syrian (si·riăn), *sb.* and *a.* late ME. [a. OF. *sirien*, f. L. *Syrius* Syrian or *Syria*; see -AN.] **A.** *sb.* A native or inhabitant of Syria. **B.** *adj.* Of, belonging to, or characteristic of Syria or the Syrians 1537. Hence **Sy·rianism** = SYRIASM.

Syriarch (si·riaɹk). 1840. [ad. L. *Syriarcha, -archus*, a. Gr. Συριάρχης, f. Συρία Syria + -άρχης ruling, ἄρχειν to rule.] The director of public games in Syria under the Romans, who was at the same time the chief priest.

Syriasm (si·riæz'm). 1684. [f. SYRIAC, after Gr. *Συριάζειν, for Συρίζειν.] A phrase or construction characteristic of the Syriac language; a Syriac idiom or expression.

It hath..many Hebraisms and Syriasms 1684.

Syringa (siri·ŋgă). 1664. [mod.L., f. Gr. συριγγ-, σῦριγξ SYRINX. First applied to the mock-orange, from its stems being used for pipe-stems, later to the lilac.] Any of the shrubs of the genus *Philadelphus*, esp. *P. coronarius*, the mock-orange, having creamy-white strongly sweet-scented flowers, cultivated as an ornamental shrub.

Syringe (si·rindʒ), *sb.* late ME. [ad. med.L. *siringa, sirynga.* In the 16th c. assim. to the oblique cases of the class. form *syrinx*, pl. *syringes* (siri·ndʒīz), by being spelt with a final *e* and pronounced with (dʒ).] **1.** A small cylindrical instrument, in its commonest form consisting of a tube fitted with a piston, used to draw in a quantity of water or other liquid, and to eject it forcibly in a stream or jet for making injections, cleansing wounds, etc.; †also used as a catheter. **b.** A similar instrument used for various purposes, as exhausting or compressing air, squirting water over plants, etc. 1659. **2.** Applied to certain structures in insects 1826.

Syringe (si·rindʒ), *v.* 1610. [f. prec.] **1.** *trans.* To treat with a syringe; to inject or sprinkle fluid into or upon by means of a syringe. Also *absol.* **2.** *intr.* To inject (liquid) by means of a syringe 1653.

2. This Balsam..is to be syringed..into the Wound 1737.

Syringeal (siri·ndʒĭăl), *a.* 1872. [f. L. *syring-*, SYRINX + -AL 1.] *Ornith.* Of, pertaining to, or connected with the syrinx in birds.

Syringin (siri·ndʒin). 1843. [a. F. *syringine*, f. *Syringa*, generic name of the lilac; see -IN[1].] *Chem.* A white crystalline substance, $C_{17}H_{24}O_9$, obtained from the lilac, *Syringa vulgaris.*

Syringo- (siri·ŋgo), comb. form of Gr. σῦριγξ, συριγγ- SYRINX. ‖ **Syri·ngomye·lia**, ‖ **-my·elus** [Gr. μυελός marrow], dilatation of the central canal of the spinal cord, or formation of abnormal tubular cavities in its substance; so **Syri·ngomyeli·tis**, inflammation of the spinal cord producing syringomyelia.

Syri·ngotome [mod.L. *syringotomus*, Gr. -τομος cutting], an instrument for cutting a fistula; so **Syringo·tomy**, incision of a fistula.

Syrinx (si·riŋks). *Pl.* **syringes** (siri·ndʒīz), also **sy·rinxes.** 1606. [L., a. Gr. σῦριγξ pipe, tube, channel, fistula.] **1.** = PAN-PIPE. Also *attrib.* **2.** *Archæol. pl.* Narrow rock-cut channels or tunnels, esp. in the burial vaults of ancient Egypt 1678. **3.** *Ornith.* The organ of voice in birds, the lower larynx, at or near the junction of the trachea and bronchi 1872.

‖ **Syrma** (sō·ɹmă). 1753. [L., a. Gr. σύρμα, f. σύρειν to drag or trail along.] *Antiq.* A long trailing garment, as that worn by tragic actors.

‖ **Syrmæa** (səɹmī·ă). Also **surmaia, surmia.** 1833. [mod.L., a. Gr. συρμαία radish, purge, f. συρμός vomiting, purging, f. σύρειν to drag along, sweep away, purge.] *Antiq.* A cathartic said to have been used in some Egyptian forms of embalming.

Syro- (səiə·ro), ad. Gr. Συρο-, comb. form of Σύρος a Syrian, used with adjs. or sbs. denoting other peoples, countries, languages, etc., signifying 'Syrian or in a Syrian way', or 'Syrian and...', as *Syro-Arabian, -Galilæan, -Roman.*

Syrophœnician (səiə:rofĭni·ʃăn), *sb.* (*a.*) 1560. [f. L. *Syrophœnix, -ic-*, a. Gr. Συροφοίνιξ, -ικ-; see SYRO- and PHŒNICIAN.] A native or inhabitant of Syrophœnicia, a Roman province of Western Asia, including Phœnicia and the territories of Damascus and Palmyra. Also *adj.* belonging to this country or its inhabitants.

‖ **Syrphus** (sō·ɹfŏs). *Pl.* **syrphi** (sō·ɹfəi). 1834. [mod.L., ad. Gr. σύρφος gnat.] *Ent.* A fly of the genus *Syrphus*, typical of the *Syrphidæ*, a large and widely distributed family of two-winged flies, mostly bright-coloured, feeding on pollen and in the larval state often on plant-lice, etc. Hence **Sy·rphian, Sy·rphid** *adjs.* belonging to this family; also as *sbs.*

†**Syrt.** 1575. [ad. L. SYRTIS.] = SYRTIS. -1718.

Syrtic (sō·ɹtik), *a.* 1846. [ad. L. *syrticus*, f. *Syrtis*; see next and -IC.] Of, pertaining to, or of the nature of a quicksand.

‖ **Syrtis** (sō·ɹtis). *Pl.* **syrtes** (-īz). 1526. [L., a. Gr. Σύρτις, σύρτις, f. σύρειν to drag along, sweep away.] Proper name of two large quicksands (*S. major* and *minor*) off the northern coast of Africa; hence *gen.* a quicksand.

Quencht in a Boggie S., neither Sea, Nor good dry Land MILT.

Syrup (si·rəp), *sb.* late ME. [a. OF. *sirop, cyrop*; (ult.) f. Arab. *sharāb* wine or other beverage, syrup, *shurb* drink; see SHRUB[2], SHERBET.] **1.** A thick sweet liquid; esp. one consisting of a concentrated solution of sugar in water (or other medium, e.g. the juices of fruits). **a.** Such a liquid medicated, or used as a vehicle for medicines. **b.** As used in cookery, confectionery, etc. as a sweetener, preservative, or article of food; also *gen.* (often in ref. to its thick or viscid consistence). late ME. **c.** *spec.* (*a*) = MOLASSES. *local* (*U.S.*, etc.). (*b*) In sugar-manufacture, applied to various stages of the liquid. 1553. **d.** *transf.* A liquid of syrupy consistence 1838. **2.** With qualifying words, indicating the source, or the flavouring or medicinal ingredient, as *s. of almonds, of poppies, of squills, of violets*, etc.; **s. of sugar,** molasses. Also **golden s.,** syrup of a bright golden-yellow colour, drained off in the process of obtaining refined crystallized sugar.

1. **a.** Not Poppy, nor Mandragora, Nor all the drowsie Syrrups of the world SHAKS. **b.** Lucent syrops, tinct with cinnamon KEATS. *fig.* Words steep'd in syrop of Ambrosia 1600.

Sy·rup, *v.* 1619. [f. prec.] **1.** *trans.* To cover with or immerse in syrup. **2.** To make into or bring to the consistence of syrup 1847.

Syrupy (si·rəpi), *a.* 1707. [f. SYRUP *sb.* + -Y[1].] Partaking of the qualities of syrup; *esp.* having the viscid consistence of syrup.

‖ **Syssarcosis** (sisaɹkōu·sis). 1676. [mod. L., a. Gr. συσσάρκωσις, f. συσσαρκοῦν to unite by flesh, cover over with flesh, f. σύν SYN- + σάρξ flesh.] **1.** *Anat.* The union of bones by means of intervening muscle. **2.** *Path.* and *Surg.* The healing of a wound by granulation or the formation of new flesh 1753.

‖ **Syssitia** (sisi·ʃiă, -i·tiă). 1835. [a. Gr. συσσίτια, pl. of συσσίτιον common meal, f. σύν SYN- + σῖτος food.] **a.** Meals eaten together in public. **b.** The custom of eating the chief meal of the day at a public mess, as practised in Sparta and Crete. Also **Syssition** (-i·ʃiǫn, -i·tiǫn), a common meal, mess.

Systaltic (sistæ·ltik), *a.* 1676. [ad. late L. *systalticus*, a. Gr. συσταλτικός, f. σύν SYN- + σταλτός, vbl. adj. f. σταλ-: στέλλειν to place, put.] *Phys.* Contracting; of the nature of contraction; *spec.* applied to movement, as that of the heart, in which there is alternate contraction (*systole*) and dilatation (*diastole*).

†**Sy·stasis.** 1605. [med. or mod.L., ad. Gr. σύστασις composition, collection, union, alliance, f. σύν SYN- + στα- (see next).] **1.** The act, or the result, of setting or putting together; combination, synthesis -1710. **2.** A political union or confederation. BURKE.

Systatic (sistæ·tik), *a.* (*sb.*) 1640. [ad. med. and mod.L. *systaticus*, a. Gr. συστατικός commendatory, drawing together, compacting, f. σύν SYN- + στα- to place, after συνιστάναι to associate, put together, etc.] **1.** Pertaining to or involving 'systasis'; synthetic. *Obs.* or *rare.* **2.** *Path.* Involving several of the sensory powers simultaneously; *sb.* a disease which does this 1820.

System (si·stėm). 1619. [ad. late L. *systema* musical interval, in med. or mod.L. the universe, body of the articles of faith, a. Gr. σύστημα organized whole, etc., f. σύν SYN- + στα-, root of ἱστάναι to set up.] **I.** An organized or connected group of objects. **1.** A set or assemblage of things connected, associated, or interdependent, so as to form a complex unity; a whole composed of parts in orderly arrangement according to some scheme or plan; rarely applied to a simple or small assemblage of things (nearly = 'group' or 'set') 1638. **b.** *spec.* (with *this*, a possessive, or the like): The whole scheme of created things, the universe 1619. **2.** *Physics.* A group of bodies moving about one another in space under some particular dynamical law, as the law of gravitation; *spec.* in *Astron.* a group of heavenly bodies connected by their mutual attractive forces and moving in orbits about a centre or central body, as the *solar s.* (the sun with its attendant planets, etc.), the *s.* of a planet (the planet with its attendant satellites) 1690. **3. a.** *Biol.* A set of organs or parts in an animal body of the same or similar structure, or subserving the same function, as the *nervous, muscular, osseous*, etc. *systems*, the *digestive, reproductive*, etc. *systems*; also, each of the primary groups of tissues in the higher plants 1740. **b.** With *the* or possessive: The animal body as an organized whole; the organism in relation to its vital processes or functions. (Occas. including the mind.) 1764. **4.** In various scientific and technical uses: A group, set, or aggregate of things, natural or artificial, forming a connected or complex whole 1830. **5.** *Mus.* **a.** In ancient Greek music, A compound interval, i.e. one consisting of several degrees (opp. to DIASTEM); also, a scale or series of notes extending through such an interval, and serving as the basis of musical composition 1656. **b.** Applied to †a stave, or to a set of staves connected by a brace in a score of concerted music 1672. **6.** *Gr. Pros.* A group of connected verses or periods, esp. in anapæstic metres 1850.

1. The body is a s. or constitution: so is a tree: so is every machine 1729. The universe itself is a s. PALEY. 2. First satellite-systems, then planetary systems, then star-systems, then systems of star-systems 1870. 3. **b.** Introducing vaccine virus into the s. 1805. 4. A s. of telegraph wires 1855. The glacier s. of the region TYNDALL. Low pressure s. or cyclone 1893.

II. A set of principles, etc.; a scheme, method. **1.** The set of correlated principles, ideas, or statements belonging to some department of knowledge or belief; a department of knowledge or belief considered as an organized whole; a comprehensive body of doctrines, conclusions, speculations, or theses 1656. **b.**

spec. in *Astron.* A theory or hypothesis of the arrangement and relations of the heavenly bodies, by which their observed movements and phenomena are or have been explained 1678. †c. In weakened sense: A theory or hypothesis; also, theory (as opp. to practice). *colloq.* -1768. d. *transf.* A systematic treatise. *Obs.* exc. in titles of books. 1658. 2. An organized scheme or plan of action; an orderly or regular method of procedure. Now usu. with defining word or phrase. 1663. b. A formal, definite, or established scheme or method (of classification, notation, or the like) 1753. c. *Cryst.* Each of the six different general methods in which different minerals crystallize, constituting the six classes of crystalline forms 1820. 3. In the abstract (without *a* or *pl.*): Orderly arrangement or method; systematic form or order 1699.

1. The dry Systems of the Old Philosophers 1699. Morality is not a s. of truths, but a s. of rules 1845. b. The Copernican s. 1855. d. A S. of Magick; or, a History of the Black Art DE FOE. 2. Subsidising the denominational s. 1873. b. The s. of chemical notation now in use 1866. 3. There is more of s. in the Phædo than appears at first sight JOWETT.

Systematic (sistėmæ·tik), *a.* and *sb.* 1680. [ad. late L. *systematicus*, a. late Gr. συστηματικός (both relating to systems of metres), f. σύστημα SYSTEM.] A. *adj.* †1. = next 1 b. 2. = next 1. 1725. 3. Arranged or conducted according to a system, plan, or organized method; involving or observing a system; (of a person) acting according to system, regular, methodical 1790. b. Qualifying nouns of unfavourable meaning: Regularly organized (for an evil purpose), or carried on as a regular (and reprehensible) practice. Also said of the agent. 1803. 4. *Nat. Hist.*, etc. Pertaining to, following, or arranged according to a system of classification; classificatory. Also of a writer: Composing or adhering to a system of classification. 1796.

2. Now we deal much in Essays, and most unreasonably despise s. Learning 1725. S. books of morality 1821. 3. The systematick proceedings of a Roman senate BURKE. He is very s. with the luggage DICKENS. b. The s. intrigues of the Papal Court D'ISRAELI. Pope..was a s. appropriator..of other men's thoughts 1874. 4. Endeavouring to perfect s. botany 1829.

B. *sb.* 1. *Nat. Hist.*, etc. A systematist 1771. 2. *pl.* **Systematics**: the subject or study of systems, esp. of classification 1888.

Systema·tical, *a.* Now *rare* or *Obs.* 1661. [See prec. and -ICAL.] 1. Of a writing or treatise: Containing or setting forth a system or regular exposition of some subject. Of a subject or study: Set forth, or pursued, in the way of a system or regular scheme. Of a writer: Dealing with a subject in this way. b. Belonging to, or dealing in, a 'system' or theory; theoretical 1748. 2. *gen.* = prec. 3. 1692. b. = prec. 3 b. 1750. †3. Belonging to the system of the universe, or to the solar system; cosmical -1797. 4. *Nat. Hist.* = prec. 4. 1813. Hence **Systema·tically** *adv.*

Sy·stematism. *rare.* 1846. [f. SYSTEMATIZE *v.* + -ISM.] The practice of systematizing.

Sy·stematist. 1700. [f. Gr. σύστημα, -ατ- SYSTEM + -IST.] One who constructs, or adheres to, a system, esp. a system of classification in natural history; a classifying naturalist.

Systematize (si·stėmătəiz), *v.* 1764. [f. as prec. + -IZE.] *trans.* To arrange according to a system; to reduce to system. b. *absol.* or *intr.* To construct a system (e.g. of philosophy, classification, etc.) 1891.

His restless ambition..had systematised intrigue D'ISRAELI. Hence **Sy·stematiza·tion**, the action or process of systematizing; a systematic arrangement, statement, etc. **Sy·stemati·zer.**

Sy·stematy. 1912. [-Y³.] Systematic classification.

Systemic (siste·mik), *a.* 1803. [irreg. f. SYSTEM + -IC.] 1. *Physiol.* and *Path.* Belonging to, supplying, or affecting the system or body as a whole; orig. and esp. in ref. to the general circulation as dist. from that supplying the respiratory organs. b. Belonging to or affecting a particular system of bodily organs, esp. the nervous system or special parts of it 1887. 2. *gen.* Of or pertaining to a system (*rare*) 1850.

1. The S. Circulation..divisible into Arterial and Venous 1896. b. S. sclerosis of a small but defined tract of the spinal cord 1896.

Systemize (si·stėməiz), *v.* 1778. [irreg. f. SYSTEM + -IZE.] *trans.* = SYSTEMATIZE. Hence **Sy·stemiza·tion**, systematization. **Sy·stemizer**, a systematizer.

Systemless (si·stėmlės), *a.* 1851. [-LESS.] 1. Devoid of system or orderly arrangement; unsystematic. 2. *Biol.* Having no differentiated systems of organs; structureless 1862.

‖ **Systole** (si·stŏlī). 1577. [mod.L., ad. Gr. συστολή, f. Gr. σύν SYN- + στολ- (: στέλλειν to place), after συστέλλειν to contract.] 1. *Phys.* The regular contraction of the heart and arteries that drives the blood outward: opp. to DIASTOLE 1578. b. Applied to similar rhythmical contraction in other organs, as the lungs, the intestines, the pulsatile vesicles in protozoans, etc. 1578. 2. *Pros.* The shortening of a vowel or syllable which is long by nature or position 1577.

1. *fig.* A s. and *diastole* of the spiritual life 1899. So **Systo·lic** *a.* pertaining to or marked by s.

Systyle (si·stəil), *a.* and *sb.* 1704. [ad. Gr.-L. *systylos*, a. Gr. σύστυλος, f. σύν SYN- + στῦλος column, pillar.] *Arch.* A. *adj.* Applied to architecture in which the columns are close together, viz. at a distance from each other of twice their thickness. B. *sb.* a building characterized by such intercolumniation.

Systylous (si·stiləs), *a.* 1863. [f. mod.L. *systylus* (f. Gr. σύν SYN- + στῦλος column) + -OUS.] a. In mosses, having the lid permanently fixed to the columella. b. Having the styles united into a single column.

Syud, var. SAYYID.

Syzygetic (sizidʒe·tik), *a.* 1850. [Loosely f. SYZYGY + *-etic*.] *Math.* Of, pertaining to, or constituting a syzygy (sense 4).

Syzygial (sizi·dʒiăl), *a.* 1863. [f. late L. *syzygia* SYZYGY + -AL 1.] *Astron.* and *Zool.* Pertaining to a syzygy or syzygies; having the character of a syzygy (senses 1 b, 3).

Syzygy (si·zidʒi). 1656. [ad. late L. *syzygia*, a. Gr. συζυγία yoke, pair, etc. f. σύζυγος yoked, paired, f. σύν SYN- + ζυγ- (: ζευγνύναι to yoke).] 1. *Astron.* †a. Orig. = CONJUNCTION 3. -1704. b. Now extended to include both conjunction and opposition (OPPOSITION 3) of two heavenly bodies, or either of the points at which these take place, esp. in the case of the moon with the sun (new and full moon). 2. *Biol.* a. A suture or immovable union of two joints of a crinoid; also, the joints thus sutured. b. The conjunction of two organisms without loss of identity, as in the genus DIPLOZOON; a syzygium. 1873. 3. *Anc. Pros.* A dipody, or combination of two feet in one metre 1836. 4. *Math.* A group of rational integral functions so related that, on their being severally multiplied by other rational integral functions, the sum of the products vanishes identically; also, the relation between such functions 1850. 5. A pair of connected or correlative things; in Gnostic theology, a couple or pair of opposites, or of æons 1838.

T

T (tī), the twentieth letter of the English and the nineteenth of the ancient Roman alphabet, corresponding in form to the Greek T (*tau*) from the Phœnician (and ancient Semitic) + X X X (*tau*). It represents the point-breath-stop consonant of Bell's 'Visible Speech', or 'surd dental mute'; in English it is gingival or alveolar, not dental.

In mod. English, besides its proper sound as above described, *t* in the combinations *-tion*, *-tious*, *-tial*, *-tia*, *-tian*, *-tience*, *-tient*, after a vowel or any consonant except *s*, has the sound of *sh* (ʃ), in which the following *i* is absorbed, as in *nation* (nē·ʃən), *factious* (fæ·kʃəs), *partial* (pā·ɹʃăl), etc.; but in *-ia*, *-ian*, *i* is sometimes more or less preserved, esp. in proper names, as in *inertia*, *Portia*, etc. After *s* the original sound of *t* has remained, as in *bestial*, *Christian*. A modern change is the development in southern England of the sound (tʃ) from *t* followed by [*iu*], [*yu*] in such combinationsas *-tual*, *-tuous*, and esp. *-ture*, as in *nature* (nē·tiŭɹ, nē·tʃəɹ). In rapid speech *ti* after *s* usu. passes similarly into tʃ, as (kwe·stʃən) for (kwe·styən).

T between *s* and syllabic *l* or *n* (*en*), as in *bustle*, *castle*, *epistle*, *christen*, *fasten*, *hasten*, is now usu. mute; so between *s* and *m* in *Christmas*, and between *f* and syllabic *n* in *often*, *soften*.

TH is a consonantal digraph representing two simple sounds (þ, ð), for which the Roman alphabet has no simple symbols, and is thus phonetically a distinct letter (or two letters), inserted between TE- and TI-.

I. 1. The letter and its sound. The pl. is variously written t's, *t's*, *ts* (tīz). b. In phr. *to cross the t's*: to make the horizontal stroke of *t* (often omitted in hasty writing); *fig.* to be minutely exact or particular in one's account; to make the meaning more distinct; to particularize and emphasize the points. c. Phr. *To a T* (also *to a tee*): exactly, properly, to a nicety. 2. The shape of the letter; an object having the shape T. 3. *attrib.* (sometimes hyphened): Shaped like the letter T; having a cross piece at the top, as *T hinge*, *joint*. See also TEE *sb.*¹, TEE-*piece*, etc. b. *Special Combs.* (sometimes hyphened). **T branch**, in piping, a right-angled joint of a small pipe to a main; a T joint. **T cart**, an open phaeton, so called from its ground plan resembling the letter T. **T cloth**, a plain cotton cloth exported to India, China, Africa, etc., so called from the large letter T stamped on it. **T rail**, a railway metal or rail having a T section. **T square**, a square of the form of a T or rather ⊢ (with a long stem) used for drawing lines parallel, or at right angles, to each other. **TV**, television.

II. 1. Used to denote serial order; applied e.g. to the twentieth (or more usu. the nineteenth) of any series, to the nineteenth sheet of a book, etc. 2. A mediæval symbol for the numerical 160, and with a stroke over it (T̄) for 160,000. 3. *Abbreviations* for various proper names, as Thomas, Theresa, etc.; officially stamped on a letter, = *taxed*, i. e. postage to be paid; in *Music*, = tasto, tempo, tenor, tutti; in a ship's log-book, = thunder; in *Math.*, = time, terms; *t.b.(d.)* = torpedo boat (destroyer); *T.O.* = turn over; *T.U.C.* = Trade Union Congress. Also T.B., T.N.T.

T' ¹, ME. Shortened form of TO, before an infinitive beginning with a vowel, formerly in use, often combined with the following word, as *tabandon* to abandon.

T' ², north. dial. form of *the*, before a vowel or consonant.

't, shortened form of *it*, initially or finally, as in *'tis*, *'twas*; *do't*, *see't*, *on't*; formerly often written without apostrophe as one word; see IT.

Ta (tā), *int.* 1772. An infantile word expressing thanks.

Ta, obs. and dial. form of THE, THEE, THOU. **Ta, taa**, obs. ff. TAKE *v.*

Taal (tāl). *S. Afr.* 1896. [a. Du., 'language, speech' = OE. *talu* TALE.] *The t.*, Cape Dutch or Afrikaans, a variety of Dutch spoken in South Africa.

Tab (tæb) ¹. 1607. [Origin obsc.] I. 1. A short broad strap, flat loop, or the like, attached by one end to an object, or forming a projecting part by which a thing can be taken hold of, hung up, fastened, or pulled. b. *spec.* A shoe latchet, for fastening with a buckle, button, or thong. Chiefly *dial.* 1674. 2. As an ornament of dress: Each of the projecting square pieces formed by cutting out the lower edge of a jacket or other article of dress, or sewn on to its uncut edge, and usu. embellished with buttons, embroidery, etc. 1880. b. A similar piece sewn by its upper edge on the surface of dress, so as to hang loose; or c. in recent use, sewn on entirely, and variously adorned with buttons, beads, embroidery, etc. 1834. d. *Red t.*: a staff officer: so called from the 'red tab' on his uniform. 3. A tie-label, a luggage label 1904. II. *U.S. colloq.* A table, an account; a check; esp. in phr. *to keep (a) tab* 1889.

Tab ², colloq. shortening of CANTAB (a Cambridge man).

Tabac (tăbæ·k), *a.* 1894. [f. F., = TOBACCO.] Of a deep shade of brown; tobacco-coloured.

Tabacco, obs. f. TOBACCO.

‖ **Tabagie** (tabaʒī). 1819. [F., irreg. deriv.

of *tabac* tobacco.] A group of smokers who meet in club fashion; a 'tobacco-parliament'.

Tabanid (tæ·bănid), *a.* and *sb.* 1891. [f. L. *tabanus* gad-fly, horse-fly + -ID[3].] A. *adj.* Belonging to the family *Tabanidæ* of flies, of which *Tabanus* is the typical genus. B. *sb.* A fly of this family, a gad-fly.

Tabard (tæ·bă̆ɹd). ME. [a. OF. *tabart, tabar*; ult. derivation unkn.] †1. A garment of coarse material; a loose upper garment without sleeves; formerly worn out of doors by the lower classes, also by monks and foot-soldiers –1568. 2. A short surcoat open at the sides and having short sleeves, worn by a knight over his armour, and emblazoned on the front, back, and sleeves with his armorial bearings. Now *Hist.* 1450. 3. The official dress of a herald or pursuivant; a coat or jerkin having short sleeves, or none, and emblazoned with the arms of the sovereign 1598.

1. A Plowman..In a t. he rood vpon a Mere CHAUCER. Hence **Ta·barded** *a.* wearing a t.

Tabaret (tæ·bărėt). 1851. [mod. trade name, prob. f. TABBY.] A fabric of alternate satin and watered silk stripes used in upholstery.

Tabasco (tăbɑ·sko). 1898. [From *Tabasco*, name of a river and state of Mexico.] More fully *T. (pepper) sauce*: A very pungent sauce made from the pulp of the ripe fruit of a variety of *Capsicum annuum*. Also *fig.*, a story 'highly spiced'.

‖**Tabasheer** (tæbăʃīə·ɹ). 1598. [Arab., Pers., Urdū *tabāshīr* chalk, mortar.] A siliceous substance, white or translucent, occasionally formed in the joints of the bamboo; also called *bamboo salt*; used medicinally in the East.

‖**Tabatière** (tabatyēr). *rare.* 1823. [F., for *tabaquière*, f. *tabac* TOBACCO.] A snuff-box.

Tabby (tæ·bi), *sb.* and *a.* 1638. [In sense 1, a. F. *tabis*, earlier *atabis*, med.L. *attabi*, app. a. Arab. *'attābiy*, name of a quarter of Bagdad in which this stuff was manufactured, named after *'Attāb*, great-grandson of Omeyya. The connexion of the other senses is not clear. See N.E.D.] A. *sb.* 1. A general term for a silk taffeta, app. orig. striped, but afterwards applied also to silks of uniform colour waved or watered. b. Short for *t. gown* or *dress* 1727. 2. Short for *t. cat*: A cat having a striped or brindled coat 1774. b. Also, a she-cat: correl. to *tom-cat* 1826. 3. An old or elderly maiden lady: a dyslogistic appellation; sometimes applied to any spiteful or ill-natured female gossip or tattler 1748. 4. A collector's name for two pyralid moths, the T., *Aglossa pinguinalis*, and the Small T., *A. cuprealis*, both with fore wings greyish brown, clouded with a darker colour 1819. 5. A concrete formed of a mixture of lime with shells, gravel, or stones in equal proportions, which when dry becomes very hard. orig. *t. work.* 1802. B. *adj.* (The sb. used attrib.) 1. Made or consisting of tabby (see A. 1) 1638. 2. Of a brownish, tawny, or grey colour, marked with darker parallel stripes or streaks; brindled; primarily and esp. in **t. cat** or **t.-cat**, a cat of this coloration, or of any other colour similarly marked 1665.

A. 1. His lady in crimson t. HAWTHORNE. B. 2. Demurest of the t. kind GRAY. Hence **Ta·bbyhood**, the condition of being an old maid.

Tabby (tæ·bi), *v.* 1728. [f. prec.] 1. *trans.* To give a wavy appearance to (silk, etc.) by calendering. 2. To stripe or streak in parallel lines with darker markings. Usu. in pa. pple. **Ta·bbied.** 1860.

Tabefa·ction. *rare.* 1658. [f. late L. *tabefacere* TABEFY *v.*] The action or process of tabefying; the wasting away or consumption of the body.

Tabefy (tæ·bĭfəi), *v. rare.* 1656. [a. obs. F. *tabéfier*, ad. late L. *tabefacere*, to cause to waste (f. *tabere* to waste, melt + *facere*); see -FY.] 1. *trans.* To waste away, consume; to emaciate; †to melt down. 2. *intr.* To waste away gradually, become emaciated (*rare*) 1891.

‖**Tabe·lla.** *Pl.* -æ(*i*). 1693. [L., dim. of *tabula* TABLE.] *Pharm.* = TABLET 3.

Taberdar (tæ·bəɹdāɹ). 1648. [f. *taberd*, obs. f. TABARD.] *lit.* One who wears a tabard; a name formerly given to certain scholars of Queen's College, Oxford, from the gown they wore; still surviving in the name of some of the scholarships at that college and in *Taberdars' Room*, the junior common room.

Tabernacle (tæ·bəɹnæk'l), *sb.* ME. [a. F., ad. L. *tabernaculum*, dim. of *taberna* hut, booth.] 1. A temporary dwelling; usu. movable, constructed of branches, boards, or canvas; a hut, tent, booth. 2. *spec.* in *Jewish Hist.* The curtained tent, containing the Ark of the Covenant and other sacred appointments, which served as the portable sanctuary of the Israelites during their wandering in the wilderness and afterwards till the building of the Temple. Also called *t. of the congregation* (or *meeting*), *of testimony*, and *of witness.* ME. b. Transferred to the Jewish temple. late ME. 3. *fig.* In phraseology chiefly of biblical origin: A dwelling-place. a. *spec.* The dwelling-place of Jehovah, or of God ME. b. *gen.* A dwelling-place, a place of abode. late ME. c. Applied to the human body regarded as the temporary abode of the soul or of life. late ME. 4. A canopied niche or recess in a wall or pillar, to contain an image. late ME. 5. *Eccl.* An ornamented receptacle for the pyx containing the consecrated host reserved 1487. 6. A place of worship distinguished in some way from a church. a. A temporary place of worship; esp. applied to the structures temporarily used during the rebuilding of the churches destroyed by the Fire of London in 1666. 1693. b. A meeting-house or place of worship of Protestant Nonconformists, esp. when not of ecclesiastical architecture. (Now chiefly *contempt.*) 1768. c. *fig.* Applied to the 'edifice' which for the time enshrines the principles of a party 1902. 7. *Naut.* An elevated socket or step for the mast of a river-boat, or a post to which the mast is hinged, so that it may be lowered to pass bridges 1877.

1. *Feast of Tabernacles*, a Jewish festival, commemorating the dwelling of the Israelites in tents during their sojourn in the wilderness, held from the 15th to the 23rd of Tisri (October); it was also called the Feast of Ingathering, and was observed as a thanksgiving for the harvest. 2. b. At Salem is his t., & his dwellinge in Sion COVERDALE *Ps.* lxxv[i]. 3. b. And all The crowned Gods in their high tabernacles Sigh unawares TENNYSON. c. True image of the Father,..enshrin'd In fleshly T., and human form MILT. 6. b. Pewing which would disgrace a t. of the last century 1878.

attrib. and *Comb.*: **t. roof**, a roof which slopes at the ends, as well as the sides, to a central ridge shorter than the side-walls; **-work**, (*a*) the ornamental carved work or tracery usual in canopies over niches, stalls, or pulpits, and in the carved screens of churches; (*b*) architectural work in which tabernacles or canopied niches form the characteristic feature.

Ta·bernacle, *v.* 1653. [ad. med.L. *tabernaculare* (rendering Gr. σκηνοῦν in John i. 14), f. *tabernaculum* (see prec.).] 1. *intr.* To occupy a tabernacle, tent, or temporary dwelling, or one that can be shifted about; to dwell for a time, to sojourn: usu. *fig.*, said of the sojourning of Christ on earth or 'in the flesh', and of the indwelling of the Spirit of Christ; also of men as spiritual beings dwelling in the 'fleshly tabernacle' of the body. 2. *trans.* To place in a tabernacle; to enshrine 1822.

1. The Evangelist Saint John..saith, He tabernacled amongst us 1653.

Tabernacular (tæbəɹnæ·kiŭlăɹ), *a. rare.* 1678. [f. L. *tabernaculum*; see -AR[1].] Of or pertaining to a tabernacle. 1. Of the style or character of an architectural tabernacle; constructed or decorated with open-work and tracery. 2. Savouring of the language of a 'tabernacle' or conventicle. (*contempt.*) 1847.

2. The word 'shortcomings'..being horridly t. DE QUINCEY.

‖**Tabes** (tē̆i·bīz). 1651. [L., 'wasting away'.] 1. *Path.* Slow progressive emaciation of the body or its parts; consumption. 2. Decay of plants caused by disease or injury 1832.

Tabescent (tăbe·sėnt), *a.* 1890. [ad. L. *tabescentem, tabescere*, inceptive of *tabere* to waste away; see -ESCENT.] Wasting away. So **Tabe·scence**, emaciation 1890.

Tabetic (tăbe·tik), *a.* and *sb.* 1847. [irreg. f. L. *tabes, tabi-*, on false analogy of *diabetic*, etc.] A. *adj.* Of, pertaining to, or affected with tabes or emaciation. B. *sb.* One who suffers from tabes 1899.

Tabid (tæ·bid), *a.* Now *rare.* 1650. [ad. L. *tabidus* wasting, f. *tabere*; see -ID.] 1. *Path.* Affected with tabes; wasted by disease; consumptive; marcid 1651. †2. Corrupted, decomposed –1657. 3. Causing consumption, wasting, or decline 1671. 4. Of the nature of tabes; characterized by wasting away 1747.

1. Sinking..into a premature and t. old age 1822. Hence **Ta·bid-ly** *adv.*, **-ness.**

Tabific (tăbi·fik), *a. rare.* 1669. [ad. L. *tabificus*, f. TABES; see -FIC.] Causing tabes; consumptive, emaciating, wasting. So †**Tabi·fical** *a.* 1608–1657.

Tabinet (tæ·binėt). 1611. [app. arbitrarily f. TABBY.] A watered fabric of silk and wool resembling poplin: chiefly associated with Ireland.

Tablature (tæ·blătiŭɹ, -tʃəɹ). 1574. [app. a. F., f. L. *tabula* table; prob. in imitation of It. *tavolatura* 'any kind of Prick-song' (Florio), f. *tavolare* to board, plank, enclose with boards.] 1. *Mus.* An old name for musical notation in general, esp. for systems differing from the ordinary staff notation; *spec.* a peculiar form of notation used for the lute and other stringed instruments, in which the lines of the stave denoted the several strings, and letters or figures were placed upon them to indicate the points at which they were to be 'stopped' with the fingers; also, a similar notation for the flute, etc. *Obs.* exc. *Hist.* 2. A tabular formation or structure bearing an inscription or design; a tablet. *Obs.* or *arch.* 1606. †3. A painting; a picture –1767. †b. *collect.* Work consisting or of the nature of paintings or pictures –1819. c. *fig.* A 'picture' formed by description or in fancy; *pl.* the 'pictures' of memory, or the faculty of retaining these 1779.

1. Organ T. was a system of writing the notes without the stave by means of letters... Figured bass has also been called T. 1898. 3. c. Yielding a t. of benevolence and public spirit SHERIDAN.

Table (tē̆i·b'l), *sb.* [In OE. *tabule*, later also *tabele*, ad. L. *tabula*. In ME. *table*, a. F. *table*, ad. L. *tabula*, prob. from same root as *taberna* tavern.] I. A flat slab or board. 1. A flat and comparatively thin piece of wood, stone, metal, or other solid material (usu. shaped by art); a board, plate, slab, or tablet; also applied to natural formations, as the laminæ of a slaty rock. *Obs.* exc. in special applications. 2. *spec.* a. A tablet bearing or intended for an inscription or device: as the stone tablets on which the ten commandments were inscribed, a votive tablet, etc. *arch.* OE. †b. A writing-tablet. Often in phr. *a pair (of) tables.* –1656. c. *Anc. Hist.* pl. The tablets on which certain collections of ancient Greek and Roman laws were inscribed; hence the laws themselves; esp. *the Twelve Tables*, drawn up by the decemviri B.C. 451 and 450, embodying the most important rules of Roman Law, and forming the chief basis of subsequent legislation 1726. d. *First, second t.*: the two divisions of the decalogue, relating to religious and moral duties respectively, held to have occupied the two 'tables of stone' 1560. †3. A board or other flat surface on which a picture is painted; hence, the picture itself –1700. †4. The 'board' on which chess, draughts, or any similar game is played –1801. b. Each of the two folding leaves of a backgammon board (*inner* and *outer t.*); †hence in *pl.* (often *pair of tables*) a backgammon board. Also, the half of each leaf in relation to the player to whom it belongs. 1483.

1. The inner part of the temple is altogether plastered and couered with great tables of Porphyre 1585. 2. a. As stern as the statue of Moses breaking the tables 1849. 3. *fig.* Mine eye hath play'd the painter and hath steeld, Thy beauties forme in t. of my heart SHAKS. 4. b. Phr. *To turn the tables*, to reverse the relation between two persons or parties; to effect a complete reversal of the state of affairs (a metaphor from the notion of players reversing the position of the board so as to reverse their relative positions.)

II. A raised board at which persons may sit. 1. An article of furniture consisting of a flat top of wood, stone, or other solid material, supported on legs or on a central pillar, and used to place things on for various purposes, as for meals, for some work or occupation, or for ornament ME. 2. *spec.* An article of furniture as described in II. 1 upon which food is served, and at or around which persons sit at a meal. late ME. **b.** *transf.* Provision of food for meals; supply of food; fare; entertainment of a family or guests at table; eating, feasting. late ME. **3.** Usu. with defining word, as *the Lord's t., the holy t.*: (*a*) In a church, that upon which the elements are placed at the Communion; the communion table: esp. when the rite is not regarded as a sacrifice. (*b*) *transf.* The Communion. ME. **4.** *transf.* A company of persons at a table ME. **b.** The company at dinner or at a meal 1602. **c.** A 'board' of persons who normally transact their business at a table (in various special uses) 1606. **5.** A table on which some game of chance is played; a gaming-table; also, the company of players at such a table 1750.

1. Phr. *Upon the t.*, under consideration or discussion. *To lay on* or *upon the t.*, of a legislative or deliberative body, to leave (a report, a proposed measure, etc.) for the present, subject to its being considered or called up at any subsequent time; hence, sometimes, to defer its consideration indefinitely; so *to lie on the t.* **2.** Phr. *At t.*, at a meal or meals. *For* (*the*) *t.*, for eating at a meal, for food; The greening [of potatoes]..renders them unfit for t. 1855. **4. b.** Your flashes of Merriment that were wont to set the T. on a Rore SHAKS. **5.** The plan will be for two to bank against the t. DISRAELI.

III. An arrangement of numbers, words, or items of any kind, in a definite and compact form, so as to exhibit some set of facts, or relations in a distinct and comprehensive way, for convenience of study, reference, or calculation. Now chiefly applied to an arrangement in columns and lines occupying a single page or sheet, as the multiplication t., tables of weights and measures, insurance tables, TIME-TABLES, etc. Formerly sometimes merely: An orderly arrangement of particulars, a list. late ME. **†b.** *absol.* = *t. of contents* (CONTENT *sb.*[1] 1) –1824. **c.** *Tables*: the common arithmetical tables, esp. as learnt at school 1828. **IV.** Special and techn. senses (chiefly arising out of sense I. 1). **†1.** *pl.* **Tables,** formerly the ordinary name of BACKGAMMON; app. orig. the 'men' or pieces used in playing early forms of this game –1808. **2.** *Arch.* **a.** A general term for a horizontal projecting course or moulding, as a cornice; a string-course. late ME. **b.** A member consisting of a flat vertical surface, usu. of rectangular form, plain or ornamented, sunk in or projecting beyond the general surface of a wall, etc.; a panel 1678. **3.** A flat elevated tract of land; a table-land, plateau; a flat mountain-top; also *Geol.* applied to a horizontal stratum 1587. **4.** *Palmistry.* The quadrangular space between certain lines in the palm of the hand 1460. **5. a.** A large flat circular disk, plate, or sheet of crown-glass, being the form in which it is made 1688. **b.** A crystal of flattened or short prismatic form 1796. **6.** *Anat.* Each of the two dense bony layers of the skull, separated by the diploë 1612. **7.** A flat plate, board, or the like, forming part of a mechanism or apparatus 1677. **a.** In various manufactures, A flat metal plate (often movable or adjustable) for supporting something to be operated upon, etc.; the plate with a raised rim on which plate-glass is made 1727. **b.** In an organ: (*a*) The upper part of the sound-board, above the sound-board bars and grooves, perforated with holes for admitting air to the pipes. (*b*) The upper board of the bellows. 1852. **c.** *Shipbuilding.* = COAK *sb.* 1. 1890. **d.** *Plain t.* (surveying instrument): see PLANE-TABLE. **8. a.** The upper horizontal surface of a table diamond or a brilliant. **b.** Short for TABLE DIAMOND; also applied to other precious stones cut in a similar form. 1530.

3. The ascent to the Sugar-loafe and T. [= Table Mountain], two Hils so named 1634.

attrib. and *Comb.*: **t.-allowance,** an allowance of money for provisions; = *t.-money* (*a*); **-bell,** a small hand-bell placed upon the t. for summoning attendants; **-centre,** a piece of embroidery, decorated work, etc., for the centre of a table, sometimes placed over the table-cloth; **-cover,** a cloth of wool or other fabric used for covering a t. permanently or when not in use for meals; **-faced** *a.* = TABLE-CUT; **-glass,** (*a*) glass made in 'tables' (see sense IV. 5 a); (*b*) a glass (drinking-vessel) for use at t.; **-knife,** a knife used at t., esp. one of the shape or size used in cutting meat on the plate; **-lifting,** the lifting of a table by supposed spiritual agency; **-linen,** linen for use at t., as t.-cloths and t.-napkins; **-money,** (*a*) an extra allowance of money made to the higher officers in the British army and navy for t. expenses; (*b*) a charge made in some clubs for the use of the dining-room; also, an extra charge made in some restaurants; **-mountain,** a flat-topped mountain; *spec.* the name of the mountain which rises behind Capetown; **-napkin,** a napkin used at t. for wiping the fingers and lips; **-shore** *Naut.*, a low level shore; **-tennis** = PING-PONG; **-tilting, -tipping,** the tilting or tipping of a table by supposed spiritual agency; **-work** *Printing*, the setting up of tables (sense III), or of matter between column rules; *concr.* printed matter of this kind, as dist. from ordinary letter-press. Hence **Ta·ble-wise** *adv.* in the manner of a t.; *spec.* of the placing of the Holy Table with its length in the direction of the church or chancel (opp. to *altar-wise*).

Table, *v.* 1450. [f. prec.] **1.** *trans.* To enter in a table or list; to tabulate. Now *rare.* **2. a.** To entertain at table as a guest, or for payment; to provide with meals. Now *rare.* 1457. **b.** *intr.* (for *refl.*) To have a meal, to dine; to take one's meals habitually (at a specified place or with a specified person). Now *rare* or *Obs.* 1562. **3.** *trans.* To picture, depict, represent as in a picture. *Obs.* or *rare arch.* 1607. **4.** To place or lay upon a table. **a.** To lay (an appeal, proposal, etc.) on the table of a deliberative or legislative assembly; hence, to bring forward for discussion or consideration. In the *U.S. Congress*, to lay on the table as a way of postponing indefinitely; to shelve. 1718. **b.** To pay down (money); to throw down or play (a card) 1827. **5.** *Carpentry.* To join two pieces of timber firmly together by means of flat oblong projections (see TABLE *sb.* IV. 7 c) in each alternately, fitting into corresponding recesses in the other. Also *intr.* for *pass.* 1794. **6.** *Sail-making.* To make a broad hem or 'tabling' on the edge of (a sail), to strengthen it in that part which is sewed to the bolt-rope 1794.

2. They haue..ten pound a yeere..and t. themselues also of the same 1583. **b.** Comming to Ordinaries about the Exchange where Merchants do t. for the most part 1602. **3.** This last Powder Treason, fit to be tabled and pictured in the chambers of meditation, as another hell above the ground BACON.

‖**Tableau** (tæ·blo^u^, F. tablo). *Pl.* **tableaux**(-o^u^z, F. -o). 1699. [F., OF. *tablel*, dim. of *table*.] **1.** A picture; usu. *fig.* a picturesque or graphic description. **2.** A group of persons and accessories, producing a picturesque effect 1813. **b.** = *T. vivant* 1828. **c.** Used *ellipt.* to express the sudden creation of a striking or dramatic situation, a 'scene' which it is left to the hearer or reader to imagine 1885. **3.** A table, a schedule; an official list 1798.

2. **T. vivant** (tablo vivaṅ), pl. **tableaux vivants** (same pron.), lit. 'living picture': a representation of a personage, character, scene, incident, etc., or of a well-known painting or statue, by one person or a group of persons in suitable costumes and attitudes, silent and motionless.

Ta·ble-board. 1483. **†1.** = TABLE *sb.* I. 4. –1623. **2.** A board forming the top of a table; also a table (*obs.* or *dial.*) 1603. **3.** Board, i.e. meals, without lodging. *U.S.* 1884.

Ta·ble-book. 1596. **†1.** A book composed of tablets for memoranda; a pocket note-book or memorandum-book –1816. **2.** An ornamental book for a drawing-room table 1845.

Table-cloth (tē^i^·b'l,klǭþ; for pl. see CLOTH *sb.*). 1467. A cloth for covering a table. **a.** A cloth, usu. of linen, spread upon a table in preparation for a meal, and upon which the dishes, plates, etc. are placed. **b.** A cloth, usu. of woollen material and often of ornamental design, used to cover a table permanently or when not in use for meals 1610. **c.** Name for a cloud covering the flat top and hanging down over the edge of Table Mountain at the Cape of Good Hope 1836.

Ta·ble-cut, *a.* 1688. [f. TABLE *sb.*, used advb. + CUT *ppl. a.* or *sb.*[2]] Of a diamond, etc.: Cut in the form of a 'table'.

‖**Table d'hôte** (tab(lə),dōt). 1617. [F., = host's table.] A common table for guests at a hotel or eating-house; a public meal served there at a stated hour and at a fixed price; an ordinary. Also, in full *t. dinner, lunch*, a dinner or lunch (of several courses) served at a fixed price for the whole, whatever may be actually consumed.

Ta·ble di·amond. 1470. [f. TABLE *sb.* IV. 8 + DIAMOND.] A diamond cut with a table or large flat upper surface surrounded by small facets; esp. a thin diamond so cut having a flat under surface.

†Table·ity. 1542. [f. TABLE *sb.* + -ITY; tr. Erasmus's L. *menseitas* = Gr. τραπεζότης.] The abstract quality of a table –1702.

Ta·ble-land. 1697. [f. TABLE *sb.* + LAND *sb.*] An elevated region of land with a generally level surface, of large or considerable extent; a lofty plain; a plateau. **b.** Without *a* or *pl.*: Elevated level ground 1836.

The great irregular tableland of Dartmoor, over a thousand feet above the sea 1899.

Tablement (tē^i^·b'lmĕnt). ME. [f. TABLE *v.* + -MENT, after L. *tabulamentum.*] *Arch.* = TABLE *sb.* IV. 2 a; also, a foundation or basement.

Tabler (tē^i^·bləɹ). Now *rare.* 1598. [f. TABLE *v.* + -ER.] One who gets his meals at another's table for payment.

Ta·ble-ra:pping. 1858. The production of raps or knocking sounds on a table without apparent physical means; by spiritualists ascribed to the agency of departed spirits, and used as a supposed means of communication with them.

Table Round, = ROUND TABLE.

Ta·ble ru:by. 1529. A ruby cut with a large flat upper surface surrounded by small facets.

Ta·ble-spoon. 1763. A spoon (larger than a dessert-spoon) used for taking soup, and, in a larger size, for serving vegetables, puddings, etc. at table. Hence **Ta·blespoonful,** as much as a t. will hold.

Ta·ble-stone. 1840. *Archæol.* A flat stone supported by two or more upright stones; a cromlech or dolmen; also, the horizontal stone forming the top of this.

Tablet (tæ·blėt), *sb.* ME. [a. OF. *tablete*, F. *tablette*, dim. of *table* TABLE *sb.*; see -ET, -ETTE.] **1.** A small, flat, and comparatively thin piece of stone, metal, wood, ivory, or other hard material, artificially shaped for some purpose. **a.** A small slab of stone or metal bearing or intended to bear an inscription or carving, *esp.* one affixed to a wall as a memorial. **b.** A slab or panel, usually of wood, for a picture or inscription. Chiefly *arch.* or *Hist.* 1581. **c.** A small smooth inflexible or stiff sheet or leaf for writing upon; usu., one of a pair or set hinged or otherwise fastened together 1611. **†2.** An ornament of precious metal or jewellery of a flat form, worn about the person –1620. **3.** A small flat or compressed piece of some solid confection, drug, or the like; a lozenge of flattened (orig. rectangular) form; a flat cake of soap 1582. **4.** *Arch.* = TABLE *sb.* IV. 2 a, b. 1823.

1. **b.** *Votive t.*, an inscribed panel anciently hung in a temple in fulfilment of a vow, e.g. after deliverance from shipwreck or dangerous illness. **c.** I took out my tablets, and wrote down the address 1836.

Tablet (tæ·blėt), *v.* 1864. [f. prec.] *trans.* To furnish with a tablet (esp. one bearing an inscription); to affix a tablet to. **b.** To inscribe on a tablet 1878.

Table-talk (tē^i^·b'l,tǭk). 1569. Talk at table; familiar conversation at meals. (Now usu. applied to the social conversation of famous men or of intellectual circles, esp. as reproduced in literary form.) Hence **Ta·ble-talker,** one who converses at table; esp. a person of high conversational powers.

Ta·ble-tu:rning. 1853. The action of turning or moving a table without the use of any apparently adequate means, as by a number of persons placing their hands or fingers upon it; such movements being ascribed by some to spiritual agency. So **Ta·ble-tu:rner.**

Tableware (tē^i^·b'lwēᵊɹ). 1832. Ware for the service of the table; a collective term for the articles which are used at meals, as dishes, plates, knives, forks.

‖**Tablier** (tæ·blie, F. tabliye). 1474. [Fr.] **†1.** A chess-board. CAXTON. **2.** A part of a lady's dress resembling an apron; the front of a skirt cut or trimmed in the form of an apron 1835.

Tabling (tē^i^·bliŋ), *vbl. sb.* late ME. [f. TABLE *v.* and *sb.* + -ING[1].] **1.** The action of setting down or entering in a table; tabulation.

Now *rare*. 1450. †2. Playing at 'tables' or backgammon –1608. 3. The action of providing or fact of being provided with food; boarding, board. Now *rare* or *Obs.* 1553. 4. Material for table-cloths; table-linen 1640. 5. *Arch.* The making of a 'table' or horizontal projecting course; *concr.* such a course itself; *spec.* a coping. late ME. 6. *Carpentry* and *Shipbuilding.* See TABLE *v.* 5. 1794. 7. *Sailmaking.* A broad hem made at the edge of a sail to strengthen it 1769.

Tabloid (tæ·bloid). 1898. [A term registered in 1884 by Messrs. Burroughs, Wellcome & Co., as a trademark applied to chemical substances used in medicine and pharmacy, and afterwards for other goods; held by the Court of Appeal to be a 'fancy word' as applied to the goods for which it is registered, and legally restricted to the preparations of the firm named.] In fig., transf., and sometimes joc. use, chiefly *attrib.* or as *adj.*, with relation chiefly to the compressed or concentrated form of the drugs sold under the name.

The proprietor intends to give in t. form all the news printed by other journals 1902. b. A newspaper which gives its news in a concentrated form.

Taboo, tabu (tăbū·), *a.* and *sb.* 1777. [ad. Tongan *ta·bu.*] A. *adj.* (chiefly predic.). As orig. used in Polynesia, Melanesia, New Zealand, etc.: Set apart for or consecrated to a special use or purpose; restricted to the use of a god, a king, priests, or chiefs, while forbidden to general use; prohibited to a particular class (esp. to women), or to a particular person or persons; inviolable, sacred; forbidden, unlawful; also said of persons under a permanent or temporary prohibition from certain actions, from food, or from contact with others. Also *transf.* and *fig.*

transf. The mention of her neighbours is evidently t., since..she is in a state of affront with nine-tenths of them MISS MITFORD.

B. *sb.* 1. The putting of a person or thing under prohibition or interdict, perpetual or temporary; the fact or condition of being so placed; the prohibition or interdict itself. Also, the institution or practice by which such prohibitions are recognized and enforced. 1777. 2. *transf.* and *fig.* Prohibition or interdiction generally of the use or practice of anything, or of social intercourse; ostracism 1833.

1. Tabus connected with animals and plants are.. part of totemism 1905.

attrib. The t. custom, which is a prohibition with a curse 1897.

Taboo, tabu (tăbū·), *v.* 1777. [f. prec.] 1. *trans.* To put (a thing, place, action, word, or person) under a (literal) taboo; see prec. B. 1. 2. *transf.* and *fig.* a. To give a sacred or privileged character to (a thing), which restricts its use to certain persons, or debars it from ordinary use or treatment: †(*a*) to consecrate, set apart, render inviolable; (*b*) to forbid, prohibit *to* the unprivileged, or to particular persons 1825. b. To put (a person, thing, name, or subject) under a social ban; to ostracize, boycott 1791.

1. On the day of a chief's decease work is tabooed 1896. 2. a. That sacred enclosure of respectability was tabooed to us LOWELL. b. I found myself as strictly tabooed as if I had been a leper 1860.

Tabor, tabour (tē¹·bəɹ), *sb.* Now *rare.* ME. [a. OF. *tabur, tabour*, beside *tanbor, tamb(o)ur*; app. of Oriental origin; cf. Pers. *tabīrah*, and *tabūrāk*, both meaning 'drum', and Arab. *ṭanbūr* a kind of lute or lyre.] The earlier name of the drum; in later use, A small kind of drum, used chiefly as an accompaniment to the pipe or trumpet; a taborin or tabret. Now *Hist.*, *arch.*, or *poet.* b. *transf.* The drummer (with his drum). late ME.

Tabor, tabour (tē¹·bəɹ), *v.* Now *rare.* ME. [f. prec., or a. OF. *taborer.*] 1. *intr.* To perform upon or beat the tabor; to drum. b. *transf.* and *fig.* To beat as upon a tabor; to drum 1579. 2. *trans.* To beat (a tune, etc.). late ME. †3. To beat, thump (anything); to thrash –1655. Hence **Ta·borer**, one who tabors; a drummer.

†**Ta·borin.** 1500. [a. F. *tabourin*, f. *tabour* TABOR.] A kind of drum, less wide and longer than the tabor, and struck with one drumstick only, to accompany the sound of a flute which is played with the other hand –1765.

Tabouret (tæ·bŏret, *or as Fr.*). 1656. [a. F., (taburę), in sense 2; orig. a small tabor or drum, dim. of *tabour* TABOR.] †1. = TABRET –1885. 2. A low seat or stool, without back or arms, for one person; so called orig. from its shape 1656. 3. A frame for embroidery, a tambour-frame 1858.

2. In France the priviledge of the T. is of a stool for some particular Ladies to sit in the Queens presence 1656.

Tabret (tæ·brĕt). late ME. [f. TABOR *sb.* + -ET.] 1. A small tabor; a timbrel. *Hist.* or *arch.* 1464. †2. *transf.* A performer on a tabret –1634.

Tabu, var. f. TABOO.

‖**Tabula** (tæ·biŭlă). *Pl.* -æ(-*i*). 1845. [L., TABLE.] 1. An ancient writing-tablet; also *transf.* a body of laws inscribed on a tablet 1881. 2. *Eccl.* A wooden or metal frontal for an altar 1845. 3. *Palæont.* Name for the horizontal dissepiments in certain corals; cf. TABULATE *a.* 2. 1855.

T. rasa [L. = scraped tablet], a tablet from which the writing has been erased, and which is therefore ready to be written upon again, a blank tablet; usu. *fig.*

Tabular (tæ·biŭlăɹ), *a.* 1656. [ad. L. *tabularis* of or relating to a board or plate, f. *tabula.*] 1. Having the form of a 'table', tablet, or slab; flat and (usu.) comparatively thin; consisting of, or tending to split into, pieces of this form, as a rock; of a short prismatic form with flat base and top, as a crystal; flat-topped, as a hill. 2. a. Entered in, or calculated by means of, a table or tables, as a number or quantity 1710. b. Of the nature of, or pertaining to, a table, scheme, or synopsis; arranged in the form of a table; set down in a systematic form, as in rows and columns 1816. c. *Printing.* Applied to matter set up in the form of tables 1771.

1. *T. spar*, a name for WOLLASTONITE, as occurring in masses of t. structure, or rarely in t. crystals. 2. a. Uranus still deviates from his t. place 1837.

Ta·bularize, *v.* 1853. [f. TABULAR + -IZE.] *trans.* To put into a tabular form, to tabulate. Hence **Ta:bulariza·tion.**

Tabulary (tæ·biŭlări), *sb.* 1656. [ad. L. *tabularium*, f. *tabula*; see -ARIUM.] *Rom. Antiq.* A place where the public records were kept in ancient Rome; hence, in other places.

Ta·bulary, *a.* Now *rare.* 1594. [ad. L. *tabularis*, f. *tabula* table; see -ARY [2].] = TABULAR 2 a, b.

Tabulate (tæ·biŭlĕt), *a.* (*sb.*) 1826. [ad. L. *tabulatus*; see next.] 1. = TABULAR 1. 2. *Palæont.* Having *tabulæ* or horizontal dissepiments, as the corals of the group *Tabulata* 1862. †B. *sb.* = TABLET 3. SOUTHEY.

Tabulate (tæ·biŭleit), *v.* 1734. [f. late L. *tabulat-*, *tabulare*, f. *tabula* TABLE.] *trans.* To put into the form of a table, scheme, or synopsis; to arrange, summarize, or exhibit in a table; to draw up a table of. Hence **Ta·bulator**, one who tabulates; a machine or apparatus for this purpose; also, an attachment to a typewriter for typing columns of figures.

We may tabulate the Italic family as follows 1869.

Tabulated (tæ·biŭleitĕd), *ppl. a.* 1681. [In sense 1, f. TABULATE *a.* + -ED [1]; in 2, pa. pple. of prec.] 1. Shaped with or having a flat upper surface; flat-topped. Also, composed of thin parallel layers. 2. Arranged or exhibited in the form of a table, scheme, or synopsis 1802.

1. The zoned or t. form of the onyx 1794.

Tabulation (tæbiŭlē¹·ʃən). 1837. [f. TABULATE *v.*] 1. The action or process of tabulating; arrangement in the form of a table or orderly scheme. 2. *Arch.* Division into successive stages of height by 'tables' or horizontal mouldings, etc. 1886.

Tacamahac (tæ·kămăhæk), **tacamahaca** (tæ:kămăhă·kă). 1577. [ad. obs. Sp. *tacamahaca*, ad. Aztec *tecomahiyac.*] 1. An aromatic resin, used for incense, and formerly extensively in medicine. a. *orig.* That yielded by a Mexican tree, *Bursera* (*Elaphrium*) *tomentosa.* b. Extended in the West Indies and S. America to similar resins obtained from other species of *Bursera* and the allied genus *Protium*, and subsequently to resins imported from Madagascar, Bourbon, and the E. Indies, chiefly the product of species of *Calophyllum.* 2. The resin of the buds of the N. Amer. Balsam Poplar, *Populus balsamifera*; hence, the tree itself 1739.

‖**Tace** (tē¹·si). 1697. [L., imper. of *tacere.*] The Latin for 'Be silent'. *T. is Latin for a candle*, a humorously veiled hint to a person to keep silent about something.

‖**Tacet** (tē¹·set). 1724. [L., = 'is silent', f. *tacere.*] *Mus.* A direction that the voice or instrument is to be silent for a time.

Tache [1] (†tætʃ, ‖taʃ). [ME. *teche*, a. OF., (F. *tache*); origin unkn.] 1. A spot, blotch, blot. In mod. scientific use only as Fr. †2. *fig.* A moral spot or blemish; a fault or vice; a bad quality or habit; also, a physical blemish –1602. 3. A trait, a characteristic, good or bad. *Obs.* exc. *dial.* (tetʃ). late ME.

Tache [2], **tach** (tætʃ). Now *rare.* late ME. [a. OF. *tache* fibula, also a large nail. A doublet of TACK *sb.*[1]] 1. A contrivance for fastening two parts together; a fibula, a clasp, a buckle, a hook and eye, or the like; a hook for hanging anything on. *Obs.* or *arch.* †b. A band or strap that may be fastened round anything (*rare*) –1611. c. *fig.* A means of attachment, a bond of connexion 1701. 2. *techn.* A rest for the shank of a punch or drill. Now *dial.* 1683.

1. Thou shalt make fiftie taches of gold, and couple the curtaines together with the taches *Exod.* xxvi. 6.

Tache [3] (tætʃ). 1657. [app. a. obs. or dial. F. *tache*, *têche* plate of iron.] 1. *Sugar-boiling.* Each pan of the series through which the juice of the sugar-cane is passed in evaporating it; *esp.* the smallest and last of these, the *striking-t.* †2. Applied to the flat iron pan in which tea-leaves are dried –1802.

Tacheometer (tæki̯ǫ·mǐtəɹ). 1876. [a. F. *tachéomètre*, f. Gr. ταχε-, stem of ταχύς quick, swift, τάχος swiftness + -METER.] = TACHYMETER. Hence **Tacheome·tric** *a.* pertaining to a t. or tacheometry. **Tacheo·metry**, surveying by means of a t.

Tachometer (tækǫ·mǐtəɹ). 1810. [f. Gr. τάχος speed + -METER.] a. An instrument by which the velocity of machines is measured. b. An instrument for measuring the velocity of a moving body of water, a current-measurer. So **Tacho·metry**, the scientific use of a t.; the measurement of velocity.

Tachy- (tæ·ki), comb. form of Gr. ταχύς swift, in scientific terms.

Tachhy·drite, Tachy·drite [ad. G. *tachhydrit*, contr. for **tachyhydrit*, f. Gr. ὕδωρ water + -ITE [1]; from its property of deliquescing readily], *Min.* a chloride of calcium and magnesium found at Stassfurt in Prussian Saxony. ‖**Tachycardia** (-kā·ɹdiă) [Gr. καρδία heart], *Path.* abnormal rapidity of the heart's action. **Ta·chygen** [-GEN], *Biol.* the sudden appearance of an organ in evolution; the part so appearing; so **Tachyge·nesis** [GENESIS], acceleration in development by the shortening or suppression of intervening stages; **Tachyge·nic** *a.*, appearing or developing suddenly. **Tachyglo·ssal** *a.* [Gr. γλῶσσα tongue], *Zool.* of a tongue, capable of being quickly thrust forth and retracted, as that of the ant-eater; so **Tachyglo·ssate** *a.*, having a tachyglossal tongue; belonging to the *Tachyglossidæ*, a family of aculeate monotrematous mammals, of which the typical genus *Tachyglossus* contains the Echidna or porcupine anteater of Australia; **Tachyglo·ssid**, an animal of this family.

Tachygraph (tæ·kigrɑf). 1810. [a. F. *tachygraphe*, ad. Gr. ταχυγράφος a swift writer, f. ταχύς swift + -γράφος writing, writer.] One who practises tachygraphy; a stenographer; *spec.* one of the shorthand writers of the ancient Greeks and Romans.

Tachygraphic (tækigræ·fik), *a.* 1763. [f. as prec. + -IC.] Of or pertaining to tachygraphy or rapid writing; *spec.* applied to a cursive or running handwriting, as opp. to one having separate and fully-formed letters, also to writing with many contractions, ligatures, and compendia. So **Tachygra·phical** *a.*

Tachygraphy (tæki·grăfi). 1641. [f. Gr. ταχύς swift + -GRAPHY.] 'The art or practice of quick writing' (J.); variously applied to shorthand, and (in palæography) to cursive as dist. from angular letters, to the Egyptian hieratic writing, etc.

Tachylite, -lyte (tæ·kiləit). 1868. [ad. G. *tachylit*, f. Gr. ταχύς swift + λυτός soluble, in ref. to its easy fusibility.] *Min.* A black basaltic glass, formerly regarded as a homogeneous mineral.

Tachymeter (tæki·mɪtəɹ). 1860. [f. Gr. ταχύς + -METER.] Name of a surveying instrument, adapted to the rapid location of points on a survey. So **Tachy·metry**, the use of such an instrument.

Tacit (tæ·sit), *a.* 1604. [ad. L. *tacitus*, pa. pple. of *tacere* to be silent.] 1. Unspoken; silent, emitting no sound; noiseless, wordless 1605. b. Saying nothing; still, silent 1604. 2. Not openly expressed or stated, but implied; understood, inferred 1637.

1. A t. thankfulness in his looks W. IRVING. b. A t. spectator of events 1804. 2. A t. Consent LOCKE. Hence **Ta·cit-ly** *adv.*, **-ness** (*rare*).

Tacitean (tæsitī·ăn), *a.* 1890. [f. the name of the Roman historian *Tacitus* (*c* 54–117); see -AN.] Pertaining to Tacitus, or resembling his pregnant sententious style.

Taciturn (tæ·sitɒ̄ɹn), *a.* 1771. [ad. L. *taciturnus*, f. *tacitus* TACIT.] Characterized by silence or disinclination to conversation; reserved in speech; uncommunicative.

Godolphin, cautious and t., did his best to preserve neutrality MACAULAY. Hence **Ta·citurnly** *adv.*

Taciturnity (tæsitɒ̄·ɹnĭti). 1450. [a. F., or ad. L. *taciturnitas*, f. *taciturnus*; see prec. and -ITY.] Habitual silence or disinclination to conversation; reservedness in speech; a taciturn character or state.

My natural T. hindered me from shewing my self to the best Advantage ADDISON.

Tack (tæk), *sb.*[1] ME. [Doublet of TACHE[2]. The etymological history is obscure.] **I.** That which fastens or attaches, etc. 1. That which fastens one thing to another, or things together: applied to a fibula or clasp, a buckle, a nail, or the like. *Obs.* exc. as in 2 and 3. 2. *spec.* (perh. orig. short for *t.-nail.*) A small sharp-pointed nail of iron or brass, usu. with a flat and comparatively large head, used for fastening a light or thin object to something more solid, esp. in a slight or temporary manner, so as to admit of easy undoing 1574. 3. *techn.* a. *Gardening.* A fastening for shoots, etc., consisting of a strip or band secured at each end to a wall or the like. b. *Plumbing.* A strip of lead having one end soldered to a pipe, and the other fastened to a wall or support. 1545. 4. An act of tacking or fastening together, now esp. in a slight or temporary way; a stitch, *esp.* a long slight stitch used in fastening seams, etc., preparatory to the permanent sewing; a very slight fastening or tie, by which a thing is loosely held, as *hanging by a t.* 1705. b. Adhesiveness 1908.

2. *To come* (or *get*) *down to brass tacks*, to deal with actual facts; to come to the real business. 4. If dear mother will give us her blessing, the parson shall give us a t. VANBRUGH.

II. Nautical and derived senses. 1. A rope, wire, or chain and hook, used to secure to the ship's side the windward clews or corners of the courses (lower square sails) of a sailing ship when sailing close hauled on a wind; also, the rope, wire, or lashing used to secure amidships the windward lower end of a fore-and-aft sail 1481. b. The lower windward corner of a sail, to which the tack (rope or chain) is attached 1769. 2. An act of tacking (TACK *v.* II. 1); hence, the direction given to a ship's course by tacking; the course of a ship in relation to the direction of the wind and the position of her sails; a course or movement obliquely opposed to the direction of the wind; one of a consecutive series of such movements to one side and the other alternately made by a sailing vessel, in order to reach a point to windward 1614. b. *fig.* and *transf.* A zigzag course on land 1788. 3. *fig* A course or line of conduct or action; implying change or difference from some preceding or other course 1675.

1. *To bring, get, haul,* or *put the tacks aboard*, to haul the tacks into such a position as to trim the sails to the wind, to set sail. *To bring* or *have the starboard* or *port tacks aboard*, to set the sails to, or sail with, the wind on the side mentioned. 2. A ship is said to be *on the starboard* or *port t.* as the wind comes from starboard or port N.E.D. 3. The bill ..seemed to proceed upon the wrong t. 1901.

III. That which is tacked on or appended. 1. Something tacked on or attached as an addition or rider; an addendum, supplement, appendix; *spec.* in parliamentary usage, A clause relating to some extraneous matter, appended, in order to secure its passing, to a bill, esp. a bill of supply 1705. 2. *dial.* a. A hanging shelf 1446. b. *Coal-mining.* A temporary prop or scaffold 1849.

1. Some tacks had been made to money-bills in king Charles's time BURNET.

IV. As a quality. Hold; holding quality; adherence, endurance, stability, strength, substance, solidity. Now *dial.* late ME. b. Stickiness 1850.

There will neuer bee any holde or tacke in it 1583. Phr. †*To hold* (a person, etc.) *t.* (*to t.*), to be a match for; to hold at bay. †*To bear, hold t.*, to be strong or lasting; to hold out, endure, hold one's own.

Tack (tæk), *sb.*[2] Chiefly *Sc.* and *n. dial.* late ME. [f. *tac, tak*, TAKE *v.*] 1. Tenure or tenancy, of land, benefice, etc., *esp.* leasehold tenure, the period of tenure. 2. Pasture for cattle let on hire 1804. 3. A take of fish 1596.

Tack, *sb.*[3] *Obs.* or *dial.* late ME. [Origin obsc.] †1. A spot, a stain; a blemish –1603. 2. A smack, taste, or flavour (*of* something); *esp.* an alien, peculiar, or ill flavour 1602.

Tack, *sb.*[4] 1833. [Origin obsc.; perh. f. TACK *sb.*[1] IV.] Food-stuff; chiefly in HARD-TACK, ship's biscuit, SOFT-TACK; also *gen.* stuff, often in depreciatory sense.

Tack, *v.* late ME. [Cf. TACK *sb.*[1]] **I.** To attach. †1. *trans.* To attach, fasten (one thing to another, or things together). *Obs.* exc. as in 3. –1843. b. *transf.* and *fig.* To attach 1533. †c. To join in wedlock (*slang*) –1821. †2. To connect or join by an intervening part –1771. 3. To attach in a slight or temporary manner; *esp.* to attach with tacks (short nails or slight stitches), which can be easily taken out 1440. 4. To join together (events, accounts, etc.) so as to produce or show a connected whole; to bring into connexion. (Often implying arbitrary or artificial union.) 1683. 5. To attach or add as a supplement; to adjoin, append, annex; *spec.* in parliamentary usage: see TACK *sb.*[1] III. 1. 1683. 6. *Law.* To unite (a third or subsequent incumbrance) to the first, whereby it acquires priority over an intermediate mortgage 1728.

1. He dried and tacked together the Skins of Goats STEELE. c. We will employ this honest gentleman here, to t. our son and daughter together FIELDING. 3. They are lined with a layer of cotton-wool neatly tacked in 1896. 4. The Gentleman..tacks these two accounts together BENTLEY. 5. A strong party in the Commons..proposed to t. thé bill which the Peers had just rejected to the Land Tax Bill MACAULAY.

II. Nautical senses. 1. *intr.* To shift the tacks and brace the yards, and turn the ship's head to the wind, so that she shall sail at the same angle to the wind on the other side; to go about in this way; also *t. about.* Hence, to make a run or course obliquely against the wind; to proceed by a series of such courses; to beat to windward: often said of the ship itself. 1557. b. Said of the wind: To change its direction 1727. 2. a. *transf.* To make a turning or zigzag movement on land 1700. b. *fig.* To change one's attitude, opinion, or conduct; also, to proceed by indirect methods 1637. 3. *trans.* To alter the course of (a ship) by turning her with her head to the wind (sometimes said of the ship); opp. to WEAR *v.* Also, to work or navigate (a ship) against the wind by a series of tacks. 1637.

1. His Ketch Tackt to and fro, the scanty wind to snatch 1600. 2. b. He is not for a moment diverted, although he sometimes consents to t. STUBBS. 3. All hands were turned up to t. ship 1860. Hence **Ta·cking** *vbl. sb.* the action of the vb.; *concr.* = tacking threads.

Tacker (tæ·kəɹ). 1704. [f. prec. + -ER[1].] One who tacks; in various senses. a. *Eng. Hist.* One who favoured the tacking of other bills in parliament to money-bills, in order to secure their passage through the House of Lords. b. In various trades: One who tacks or fastens articles or parts of things; also, a machine for putting or driving in tacks 1727.

Tacket (tæ·kėt). Now *dial.* ME. [f. TACK *sb.*[1] + -ET.] A nail; in later use, a small nail, a tack; now in *Sc.* and *n. dial.*, a hob-nail for studding the soles of shoes.

Tackle (tæ·k'l), *sb.* ME. [a. MLG., LG. *takel*, f. MLG. *taken* to lay hold of, with instrumental suffix *-el*; see -LE 1.] 1. Apparatus, utensils, instruments, implements, appliances; equipment, furniture, gear. 2. The rigging of a ship; in later use *spec.* the running rigging or ropes used in working the sails, etc., with their pulleys; passing into sense 3 ME. b. Cordage; a rope used for any purpose 1529. 3. An arrangement consisting of a rope and pulley-block, or more usu. a combination of ropes and blocks, used to obtain a purchase in raising or shifting a heavy body 1539. b. A windlass and its appurtenances, used for hoisting ore, etc. 1874. †4. Implements of war, weapons; *esp.* arrows; also, a weapon, an arrow –1663. 5. Apparatus for fishing; fishing-tackle. late ME. 6. The equipment of a horse; harness 1683. 7. Victuals; food or drink; 'stuff' (*slang*) 1857. 8. [from the vb.] *Football*, etc. a. The or an act of tackling; see TACKLE *v.* 4. 1901. b. In Amer. football: Each of two players (right and left) stationed next to the end rusher or forward in the rush-line 1894.

1. George wanted the shaving t. 1889. 2. With all her bravery on, and t. trim, Sails fill'd, and streamers waving MILT. 4. This said, she to her T. fell, And on the Knight let fall a peal Of Blows so fierce 1663. *attrib.* and *Comb.*: **t.-block**, = BLOCK *sb.* 4; **-board**, a frame, placed at the end of a rope-walk, containing the whirls to which the yarns are attached to be twisted; **-fall**, the loose end of a t., to which the power is applied in hoisting; **†-house**, a building in which porters employed in loading and unloading ships kept their tackle.

Tackle (tæ·k'l), *v.* late ME. [f. prec.] †1. *trans.* To furnish (a ship) with tackle –1686. †b. To handle or work the tackle of (a ship) –1642. 2. To harness (a horse) for riding or draught. Also *absol.* with *up.* 1714. 3. *colloq.* a. To grip, lay hold of, take in hand, deal with; to fasten upon, encounter (a person or animal) physically 1828. b. To 'come to grips with', to enter into discussion or argument with; to attack; to approach or question on some subject 1840. c. To grapple with, to try to deal with (a task, a difficulty, etc.); to try to solve (a problem) 1847. d. To attack, to begin to eat (food) 1889. 4. a. *Football.* (*a*) In *Rugby*, To seize and stop (an opponent) when in possession of the ball; (*b*) In *Association*, To obstruct (an opponent) with the object of getting the ball away from him. b. *Hockey.* To attempt to take the ball from (an opponent) with the stick. Also *absol.* 1884.

2. I'll get a spare saddle and bridle, and will t. him 1890. 3. b. He too was tackled on the subject, but when he explained it..he found the electors..reasonable 1901. d. We tackled the cold beef for lunch 1889. Hence **Ta·ckler**, one who tackles.

†Ta·ckled, *ppl. a.* 1592. [f. TACKLE *sb.* + -ED.] Made of tackle or ropes. SHAKS.

Tackling (tæ·kliŋ), *vbl. sb.* ME. [f. TACKLE *v.* + -ING[1].] †1. *concr.* The rigging of a ship; the tackle –1769. †2. = TACKLE *sb.* 1. –1813. †b. A horse's harness –1787. †3. Arms, weapons, instruments –1679. †4. Fishing tackle –1727. 5. The action of TACKLE *v.* 1893.

5. The splendid t. of the Oxford men 1900.

Tacksman (tæ·ksmæ̆n). *Sc.* 1533. [f. *tack's*, poss. of TACK *sb.*[2] + MAN.] One who holds a tack or lease of land, coal-mines, fisheries, tithes, customs, etc.; esp. in the Highlands, a middleman who leases directly from the proprietor of the estate a large piece of land which he sublets in small farms.

Next in dignity to the laird is the T. JOHNSON.

Tacky (tæ·ki), *a.* 1788. [f. TACK *sb.*[1] + -Y[1].] Slightly sticky or adhesive: said of gum, glue, or varnish nearly dry.

Tacnode (tæ·knōud). 1852. [f. L. *tactus* touch + NODE.] *Geom.* A point at which two parts of the same curve have ordinary contact.

Tact (tækt). 1609. [ad. L. *tactus* touch, f. **tag-*, *tangere* to touch.] 1. The sense of touch 1651. b. *fig.* A keen faculty of perception or discrimination likened to the sense of touch 1797. 2. Ready and delicate sense of what is fitting and proper in dealing with others, so as to avoid giving offence or to win good will; the faculty of saying or doing the right thing at the right time 1804. **3.** *Mus.* A stroke in beating time 1609.

1. Sight is a very refined t. 1881. **b.** You..must needs have a better t. of what will offend that class of readers COLERIDGE. **2.** A most delicate task; requiring t. CARLYLE. That fine instinct in the management of men which is commonly called t. 1892. Hence **Ta·ctful** *a.* full of or endowed with t.; displaying or inspired by t.; **-ly** *adv.* **Ta·ctless** *a.* destitute of t.; awkward; **-ly** *adv.*, **-ness.**

Tactic (tæ·ktik), *sb.* 1638. [ad. mod.L. *tactica*, a. Gr. τακτική (sc. τέχνη) fem. of τακτικός TACTIC *a.*[1]] **1.** = TACTICS. †**2.** A tactician –1641.

Tactic (tæ·ktik), *a.*[1] 1604. [ad. mod.L. *tacticus*, a. Gr. τακτικός of arrangement or tactics, f. τακτός ordered, vbl. adj. of τάσσειν.] †**1.** = TACTICAL *a.* **1.** –1831. **2.** Of or pertaining to arrangement or order 1811.

Ta·ctic, *a.*[2] *rare.* 1625. [f. L. *tact-, tangere* to touch + -IC.] Of, belonging or relating to touch; tactual.

Tactical (tæ·ktikăl), *a.* 1570. [f. Gr. τακτικός (see TACTIC *a.*[1]) + -AL; see -ICAL.] **1.** Of or pertaining to (military or naval) tactics. **2.** Of or relating to arrangement, esp. the arrangement of procedure with a view to ends 1876. **3.** Of a person, his actions, etc.: Characterized by skilful tactics; skilful in devising means to ends 1883. Hence **Ta·ctically** *adv.*

Tactician (tækti·ʃăn). 1798. [f. as TACTIC *sb.* + -IAN.] One skilled in the science or art of tactics.

Tactics (tæ·ktiks), *sb. pl.* 1626. [pl. of TACTIC *sb.*, tr. mod.L. *tactica* pl., Gr. τὰ τακτικά, lit. 'matters pertaining to arrangement'; see -IC 2.] The art or science of deploying military or naval forces in order of battle, and of performing warlike evolutions and manœuvres.

fig. We have seen principles strangled by t. so often 1842.

Tactile (tæ·ktəil), *a.* 1615. [ad. L. *tactilis* tangible, f. *tact-, tangere* to touch.] **1.** Perceptible to the touch; tangible. **2.** Of or pertaining to touch; relating to the sense of touch 1657. **b.** Of organs: Endowed with the sense of touch 1768.

1. Certain visible and t. signs 1898. **2.** T. anæsthesia 1899. *T. values*: the quality of painting which represents the tangibility of objects. **b.** The t. papillæ of the fingers 1768. Hence **Tactility** (tækti·lĭti), t. quality or condition.

Taction (tæ·kʃən). 1623. [ad. L. *tactionem*, *tangere.*] The action of touching; contact.

Tactor (tæ·ktǫɹ). 1817. [a. L., f. *tangere.*] A feeler; an organ of touch.

Tactual (tæ·ktiuăl), *a.* 1642. [f. L. *tactus* touch + -AL 1; cf. *visual.*] Of or pertaining to touch; of the nature of or due to touch.

In the lowest organisms we have a kind of t. sense diffused over the entire body TYNDALL.

Tadpole[1] (tæ·dpoul). late ME. [f. ME. *tāde, tadde* TOAD + (app.) POLL *sb.*[1] head, round head.] **1.** The larva of a frog, toad, or other batrachian, from the time it leaves the egg until it loses its gills and tail. Chiefly applied in the early stage when the animal appears to consist simply of a round head with a tail. **2.** Sometimes applied to the tailed larva of a tunicate, the swimming tail of which is afterwards dropped or absorbed 1880. **3.** *U.S.* The Hooded Merganser, *Lophodytes cucullatus*, app. from the size of its head (*local*) 1891.

1. *transf. Tit. A.* IV. ii. 85.

Comb.: **t.-fish, -hake,** a ganoid fish of the North Atlantic, *Raniceps raninus.*

Tadpole[2]. 1844. In *T. and Taper*, names of two political schemers in Disraeli's *Coningsby*; hence allus., in the sense 'professional politicians, the hacks of a political party'.

Tael (tēl). 1588. [a. Pg., ad. Malay *tahil*, *tail* weight.] **1.** The trade name for the Chinese *liang* or 'ounce', a weight used in China and the East 1598. **2.** Hence, a money of account, orig. a tael (in weight) of standard silver, the value of which fluctuated with the price of the metal 1588.

Ta'en (tēn), contr. f. *taken*, pa. pple. of TAKE *v.*

‖**Tænia, tenia** (tī·niă). *Pl.* **-æ, -as.** 1563. [L., a. Gr. ταινία a band, fillet, ribbon.] **1.** *Archæol.* A headband, ribbon, or fillet 1800. **2.** *Arch.* In the Doric order, A band separating the architrave from the frieze 1563. **3.** *Surg.* A long narrow ribbon used as a ligature 1882. **4.** *Anat.* A ribbon-like structure; applied *esp.* to the bands of white nervous matter in the brain and the longitudinal muscles of the colon 1882. **5.** *Zool.* A tapeworm [so in L.]; *spec.* a genus of cestoid worms, including the common tapeworm 1706. Hence **Tænian** (tī·niăn) *a.* pertaining to tapeworms. **Tæ·niate** *a.* tænioid, tæniiform.

Tænii- (tī·ni,i), comb. form of L. *tænia* ribbon, often contracted to **tæni-.** **Tæ·ni(i)cide** [-CIDE[2]], a destroyer of tapeworms, a tænifuge. **Tæ·ni(i)form** *a.* [-FORM], having the form of a tape or ribbon, tænioid. **Tæ·nifuge** [-FUGE], *sb.* a substance used to expel tapeworms from the body; *adj.* expelling tapeworms.

Tænio- (tī·ni,o), comb. form of Gr. ταινία ribbon. **Tæ:nioglo·ssate** *a.* [Gr. γλῶσσα tongue], in Mollusca, having upon the lingual ribbon one median tooth between three admedian teeth on either side. **Tæ·niosome** [Gr. σῶμα body], one of the sub-order *Tæniosomi* of teleocephalous fishes, a ribbon-fish.

Tænioid (tī·ni,oid), *a.* 1836. [f. TÆNIA + -OID.] Of a ribbon-like shape; related to the tapeworms.

‖**Tæniola** (tīni·ŏlă). 1884. [mod.L., dim. of *tænia.*] *Zool.* One of the radial partitions in the body of some acalephans.

Tafferel (tæ·fĕrĕl, tæ·frĕl). 1622. [a. Du. *tafereel* panel, picture, dim. of *tafel* TABLE.] †**1.** A panel; *esp.* a carved panel –1632. **2.** *Naut.* The upper part of the flat portion of a ship's stern above the transom, usu. ornamented with carvings, etc. In later use including, and now applied to, the aftermost portion of the poop-rail, and spelt TAFFRAIL. 1704.

Taffeta, taffety (tæ·fĕtă, -ĕti), *sb.* and *a.* late ME. [a. OF. *taffetas, taphetas*, or med.L. *taffata*; ult. a. Pers. *tāftah*, (*a*) silken cloth, (*b*) linen clothing, subst. use of *tāftah*, pa. pple. of *tāftan* to shine, also, to twist, spin.] **A.** *sb.* A name applied at different times to different fabrics; in more recent times, a light thin silk or union stuff of decided brightness or lustre. Latterly misapplied to various mixtures of silk and wool, and even cotton and jute, thin fine woollen material, etc. **B.** *attrib.* or as *adj.* **1.** Of taffeta; of the nature of taffeta 1552. **2.** *fig.* Florid, bombastic; over-dressed; dainty, delicate, fastidious 1588.

2. Taffata phrases, silken tearmes precise SHAKS.

Taffrail (tæ·frĕl). 1814. [Altered form of TAFFEREL, due to false etym., the termination *-rel* being taken as RAIL *sb.*[2]] *Naut.* The aftermost portion of the poop-rail of a ship.

Taffy[1] (tæ·fi). 1817. [The earlier form of TOFFEE, now Sc., North Eng., and Amer.] **1.** = TOFFEE. **2.** *U.S. slang.* Crude or vulgar compliment or flattery; 'soft soap'; blarney 1879.

Taffy[2] (tæ·fi). 1682. [An ascribed Welsh pronunc. of *Davy* or *David*, in Welsh *Dafydd.*] A familiar nickname for a Welshman.

‖**Tafia** (tæ·fiă). 1777. [Given in 1722 as native name in West Indies; but *tāfīa* is also given in Malay dicts. as 'a spirit distilled from molasses'.] A rum-like spirituous liquor obtained from the lower grades of molasses, refuse brown sugar, etc.

Tag (tæg), *sb.*[1] late ME. [Origin obsc.] **1.** Orig., one of the narrow, often pointed, *laciniæ* or pendent pieces made by slashing the skirt of a garment; hence, any hanging ragged or torn piece; also, any end or rag of ribbon or the like. **2.** A small pendent piece or part hanging from, or attached more or less loosely to the main body of anything 1640. **3.** A point of metal or other hard substance at the end of a lace, string, strap, or the like, to facilitate its insertion through an eyelet-hole, when externally visible often made ornamental; an aglet 1570. **4.** An ornamental pendent; a tassel; a ribbon bearing a jewel, etc. 1570. **b.** *pl.* A footman's shoulder-knots 1837. **5.** The tip of the tail of an animal; the tail piece of an angler's fly 1681. **6.** The strip of parchment bearing the pendent seal of a deed 1688. **7.** A tab or tie-label attached by one end to a package, to luggage, etc.; also, a label pinned on as a badge, etc. Orig. and chiefly *U.S.* 1864. **8.** Something appended or added to a writing or speech, esp. by way of ornament or improvement, e.g. the moral of a fable, etc. 1734. **b.** A brief and usu. familiar quotation added for special effect; a much used or trite quotation 1702. **c.** The refrain or catch of a song or poem; the last words of a speech in a play, etc. 1793. †**9.** The rabble, the lowest class of people; *esp.* in collocation with *rag.* See also TAG-RAG. –1825. **10.** A disease in sheep; = *t.-sore* 1741.

8. b. The Latin t. holds: 'Quem Deus vult perdere, prius dementat' 1897. **9.** *T. and rag*, all the components of the rabble; all and any, every man Jack, everybody; Tom, Dick, and Harry.

attrib. and *Comb.*: **t.-belt,** = *t.-sore*; **t. day** *U.S.* = *flag-day* (FLAG *sb.*[4]); **-end,** = FAG-END; **-lock,** = DAG-LOCK; **-sore,** pustular excoriation of a sheep's tail set up by the irritation of diarrhœal flux; **-tail,** a worm with a yellow t. or tail.

Tag (tæg), *sb.*[2] 1738. [?] = TIG *sb.*

Tag, var. of TEG, a young sheep.

Tag (tæg), *v.*[1] late ME. [f. TAG *sb.*[1]] **1.** *trans.* To furnish or mark with or as with a tag (in various senses). **2.** To append as an addition or afterthought; to fasten, tack on, or add as a tag *to* something 1704. †**3.** To fasten or tack together; to join –1750. **b.** To join or string together (verses, rhymes) 1720. **4.** *intr.* To trail or drag behind; to follow closely, follow in one's train 1676. **5.** *trans.* To cut off tag-locks from (sheep) 1707.

1. Canning tags his speeches with poetry 1823. All my beard Was tagg'd with icy fringes in the moon TENNYSON. After inspection each animal will be tagged and described 1896. **3.** His clothes were tagg'd with thorns DRYDEN.

Tag, *v.*[2] 1891. [f. TAG *sb.*[2]] *trans.* = TIG *v.*

Tagalog (tăgā·lǫg). 1834. One of the Malayo-Polynesian languages.

Tagel (tē·gəl), *a.* Also **tegal, tagal.** 1905. [Place-name.] In *t. straw*, a soft fine straw for hats, etc. Also ellipt. as *sb.*

Tagger (tæ·gəɹ). 1648. [f. TAG *v.*[1] or *sb.*[1] + -ER[1].] **1.** One who tags. **2.** A device for tagging a sheep 1891. **3.** *pl.* Very thin sheet-iron, usu. coated with tin. (Also **taggar.**) [prob. so called from being used to make tags of laces.] 1834.

Taglet (tæ·glĕt). *rare.* 1578. [f. TAG *sb.*[1] + -LET.] A small tag; *spec.* **a.** A tendril; **b.** A catkin.

Taglioni (talyō·nī). *Hist.* 1832. [Named after a family of ballet-dancers of the early 19th c.] **1.** A dress skirt modelled on a ballet-dancer's skirt, fashionable *c* 1835. **2.** A kind of overcoat in use in the first half of the 19th c.

‖**Tagnicati** (tanʸīkā·tī). 1827. [a. Guarani and Sp. *tañicati.*] Native name of the White-lipped Peccary of Paraguay.

Tag-rag (tæ·g,ræg), *sb.*, *a.*, *adv.* 1582. [Orig. two words, = both *tag* and *rag*; cf. TAG *sb.*[1] 9.] **A.** *sb.* The rabble, the riff-raff; also (with *pl.*) a member of the rabble. Now *rare* exc. as in D. 1609. **b.** A ragged tag or appendage 1827. **B.** *adj.* †**a.** Of or belonging to the rabble. **b.** Consisting of tags and rags of dress, etc.; dressed in rags, ragged. 1601.

If the tag-ragge people did not clap him, and hisse him,..I am no true man SHAKS.

†**C.** *adv.* (for *tag and rag.*) All to tags and rags; also, pell-mell; one and all; promiscuously –1737. **D. Tag, rag, and bobtail** [see BOBTAIL *sb.* Now occas. tagrag and bobtail.] A contemptuous term for a number of persons of various sorts and conditions; all and sundry, esp. of the lower classes 1645.

‖**Tagua** (tæ·gwă). 1830. [Native name in Colombia.] The ivory-palm, *Phytelephas macrocarpa*, which produces the ivory-nut or corozo-nut.

‖**Taguan** (tæ·gwăn). 1807. [app. native name in the Philippines.] The Malayan Flying Squirrel, *Pteromys petaurista.*

‖**Tagus** (tē·gŏs). 1839. [Latinized f. Gr. ταγός ruler, leader, etc.] *Gr. Hist.* A commander, leader, ruler, chief; *spec.* the title of the chief of the confederation of Thessaly.

‖**Taha** (tā·hā). 1836. [Native name.] A S. African species of weaver-bird, *Euplectes taha* of Sir A. Smith, now *Pyromelana taha*, the male of which is chiefly yellow and black.

‖**Tahsildar** (tʊχsī·ldār). *India.* 1799. [Urdū, f. Arab., Pers. *taḥsīl* collection + Pers. *dār*, agential suffix.] The chief revenue-officer of a subdivision of a district under the Mogul rule; retained by the British; formerly sometimes applied to the cashier in a business house.

Tail (tēl), *sb.*[1] [Com. Teut.; OE. *tægel, tægl.*] **1.** The posterior extremity of an animal, in position opposite to the head, either forming a distinct flexible appendage to the trunk, or being the continuation of the trunk itself behind the anus. Also, a representation or figure of this part.

In most vertebrate animals, consisting of a number of gradually attenuated coccygeal vertebræ covered with flesh and integument; in quadrupeds often clothed with hair, in birds with feathers (see also PEACOCK'S TAIL), and in fishes bearing the caudal fin; in invertebrate animals, sometimes a distinct and well-marked member, at other times not distinctly marked off from the rest of the body.

b. The tail of a horse, of which one, two, or three were borne before a pasha as insignia of rank 1717. **2.** A thing, part, or appendage, resembling the tail of an animal in shape or position ME. **3.** The train or tail-like portion of a woman's dress (now *colloq.*); the pendent posterior part of a man's dress-coat or a peasant's long coat; the loose part of any coat below the waist; (often *pl.*) the bottom or lower edge of a skirt, etc., which reaches quite or nearly to the ground. Also *dial.* the skirt of a woman's dress; *tails*, skirts. ME. **4.** The lower or hinder extremity of anything; the part opposite to what is regarded as the head; the terminal or concluding part of anything. late ME. (Cf. CART-TAIL, PLOUGH-TAIL, etc.) **b.** The reverse side of a coin; esp. in *head(s or tail(s* 1684. **c.** *Surg.* Either end of an incision, which does not go through the whole thickness of the skin 1846. **5.** The lower and hinder part of the human body; the fundament, posteriors, buttocks, backside. Now *dial.* or *low colloq.* ME. **6.** A train or band of followers; a following; a retinue ME. **7.** (Also *pl.*) The inferior, less valuable, or refuse part of anything; foots, bottoms, dregs, sediment 1542. **8.** The inferior, least influential, or least skilful members of a body; e. g. of a profession, a political party, a cricket team, etc. 1604.

1. b. It was governed by beys, and pashas of two tails 1820. **2.** The cipher is turned into 9 by adding the t. 1599. The t. is..by no means an invariable appendage of comets HERSCHEL. Hair..plaited in long tails behind 1877. **3.** His friends at home..hadn't put him into tails 1857. **4.** The Tayles of Mills 1613. (Cf. TAIL-RACE.). At the t. of their conversation 1833. His place is at the t. of a procession 1858. At the plough's t. 1887. *T. of the eye*, the outer corner of the eye. *Out of, with the t. of the eye*, with a sidelong or furtive glance.

Phrases. *Head and (or, nor) t.*: see HEAD *sb.* *To twist the lion's t.*: see LION 1. *To put salt on the t.*: see SALT *sb.*[1] 1. *With the t. between the legs*, lit. of a dog or other beast; *fig.* with a cowed and dejected demeanour. *To turn t.* (orig. a term of falconry) to turn the back; hence, to run away, take to flight. *Tail(s) up*, (fig.) of persons, in good spirits.

Comb.: **t.-bandage**, a bandage divided into strips at the end; **-bay**, (*a*) the space between a girder and the wall; (*b*) in a canal-lock, the narrow water-space just below the lock, opening out into the lower pond; **-beam**, a beam that is tailed in, as to a wall; a t.-piece; **-coat**, a coat with tails, *esp.* a dress or swallow-tailed coat; **-coverts (-covers)**, *sb. pl. Ornith.* the feathers that cover the rectrices or quill-feathers of the t. in birds; divided into upper and lower, according to their position on the dorsal or ventral surface; **-joist**, a joist tailed into the wall, a t.-piece; **-lamp, -light**, the (usu. red) light or lights carried at the rear of a train, motor car, etc.; **-lock**, a lock at the exit or lower end of a dock; **-pin**, the centre in the tail-spindle of a lathe; **-rod**, a continuation of the piston-rod, which passes through the back cover of the cylinder, and serves to steady the piston and rod by giving the former a double bearing; **-spin** (cf. SPIN *sb.* 5); **-spindle**, the spindle in the t.-stock of a lathe; **-stock** = DEAD-HEAD 2; **-valve**, (*a*) the air-pump valve in some forms of condenser; (*b*) = SNIFTING-*valve*; **-water**, the water in a mill-race below the wheel, or in a canal or navigable channel below a lock.

Tail (tēl), *sb.*[2] ME. [a. OF. *taille* cut, cutting, division, etc., vbl. sb. f. *taillier* TAIL *v.*[2]] **I.** †**a.** The individual assessment of a subsidy or tallage levied by the king or lord; a tax, impost, due, duty, or payment levied –1645. ‖**b.** Now only as Fr., in form taille. A tax formerly levied upon the unprivileged classes in France 1533. **II.** *Law.* The limitation or destination of a freehold estate or fee to a person and the heirs of his body, or some particular class of such heirs, on the failure of whom it is to revert to the donor or his heir or assign. Hence phrase *in t.*, as *estate in t.*, *tenant in t.*, *heir in t.*, i. e. within or under the limitation in question. late ME.

T. general, limitation of an estate to a man and the heirs of his body lawfully begotten. *T. special*, limitation of an estate to a special class of heirs, e. g. to a man and his wife and the heirs of their bodies lawfully begotten. *T. male* (or *female*), limitation of an estate to male (or female) heirs.

†**III.** A tally; a score, an account; = TALLY *sb.*[1] 1, 2. –1677.

Tail (tēl), *a.* 1473. [a. AF. *taylé, tailé* = OF. *taillié, taillé*, pa. pple. of *taillier* to cut, shape.] Of a fee or freehold estate: Limited and regulated as to its tenure and inheritance by conditions fixed by the donor: thus dist. from *fee simple* or absolute ownership. See also FEE-TAIL.

Tail (tēl), *v.*[1] 1663. [f. TAIL *sb.*[1]] **I.** *trans.* **1.** To furnish with a tail or final appendage 1817. **2.** To grasp or drag by the tail 1663. **3.** To dock the tail of (a lamb, etc.); to cut or pull off that which is regarded as the tail, esp. of a plant or fruit 1794. **4.** To form the tail of (a procession, etc.); to terminate 1835. **5.** To join on behind, annex, subjoin *to* 1523. **6.** *Building.* To insert the tail or end of (a beam, stone, or brick) *into* a wall, etc.; to let in, dovetail 1823.

5. What is this but to t. one folly to another? 1685.

II. *intr.* **1.** Of a ship: To run *aground* stern foremost 1725. **2.** Of a moving body of men or animals: **a.** To lengthen out into a straggling line, as in racing, etc.; to drop behind, fall away 1781. **b.** To move or proceed in the form of a line or tail; to fall into a line or tail 1859. **3.** To take a position in which the tail or rear is directed away from the wind, current, etc. 1849. **4.** *Building.* Of a beam, stone, or brick: To have its end let into a wall, etc. 1842. **5.** Of a fish: To show its tail at the surface 1892.

1. The Formidable..tailed on the..mud 1799. **3.** Sea-weed always 'tails to' a steady or a constant wind 1860.

With advs. **T. away.** *intr.* To fall away in a tail or straggling line; to die away. **T. off (out). a.** *trans.* To taper off. **b.** *intr.* To fall away in a tail; to diminish and cease; to subside. **c.** To turn tail, go or run off; to withdraw. *colloq.* **d.** *trans.* To pass and leave behind (other competitors in a race, etc.). **T. on. a.** *trans.* To add on as an appendage. **b.** *intr.* To join on in the rear.

Tail (tēl), *v.*[2] [ME. *taille*, a. OF. *taillier*:—late pop. and med.L. *taliare, talliare*, f. *tal(l)ia*, cl. L. *talea* rod, twig, cutting.] †**I.** *trans.* To cut, esp. to a certain size or shape; to shape, fashion –1562. **II.** †**1.** To decide or determine in a specified way; to settle, arrange, or fix (a matter) –1473. **2.** *Law.* To limit (an estate of inheritance) to the donee and his heirs general or special; to grant in tail; to tie up by entail; to ENTAIL. late ME. †**III.** To impose a 'tail' or tax upon; to tax –1577. †**IV. 1.** To mark or record on a tally; to charge (a person) with a debt; *transf.* to mark –1655. **2.** *intr.* To deal by tally, or on credit –1570.

Tail-board (tē·lbōəɹd). 1805. [f. TAIL *sb.*[1] + BOARD *sb.*] The board at the hinder end of a cart, barrow, van, etc.; usu. one attached to the bottom by a hinge, for convenience in loading, etc.

Tailed (tēld), *a.* and *ppl. a.* ME. [f. TAIL *sb.*[1] and *v.*[1] + -ED.] **A.** *adj.* Having, or furnished with, a tail or tails; in *Zool.* and *Bot.* = CAUDATE. **B.** *ppl. a.* Deprived of the tail or tails 1550.

A. *T. rhyme* (rarely *tail-rhyme*), tr. F. *rime couée*, applied to a couplet, triplet, or stanza with a tail, tag, or additional short line, either unrhymed or rhyming with another tag further on.

Tail-end (tē·lˌe·nd). 1837. [f. TAIL *sb.*[1] + END *sb.*] The hindmost or lowest end of anything; that part which is opposite the head. **b.** *fig.*; *esp.* the concluding part of an action, period of time, etc. 1845.

Tailing (tē·liŋ), *vbl. sb.* 1495. [f. TAIL *v.*[1] + -ING [1].] **1.** The action of TAIL *v.*[1] 1703. **2.** *pl.* A name for the inferior qualities, leavings, or residue of any product; foots, bottoms 1764. **3.** The end or latter part 1646. **b.** *Arch.* The part of a projecting stone or brick inserted in a wall 1842. **4.** *attrib.* as *t.-rope* = TAIL-ROPE 1495.

‖**Taille** (tay). 1663. [F.] **1.** Cut, shape, form; shape of the bust from the shoulders to the waist; figure, build, make. In *Dress-making*, the waist or bodice of a gown; the style or fit of this. **2.** See TAIL *sb.*[2] I. b.

‖**Taille-douce** (taydus). 1650. [F., = soft cutting.] Engraving on a metal plate with a graver or burin, as dist. from work with the dry point, and from etching.

Tai·lless (tē·lˌlės), *a.* 1550. [f. TAIL *sb.*[1] + -LESS.] Having no tail; deprived of a tail.

Tailor (tē·ləɹ), *sb.* [ME., a. AF. *taillour* = OF. *tailleor, -eur*:—late L. or Com. Rom. *taliatorem* cutter, f. *taliare* to cut.] **1.** 'One whose business is to make clothes' (J.); a maker of the outer garments of men, also sometimes those of women, esp. riding-habits, walking costumes, etc. See also MERCHANT-TAILOR. **b.** *provb.* and *allus.*; often implying disparagement and ridicule 1605. **2.** A name given to several kinds of fish, as **a.** The t.-herring and the t.-shad. **b.** The Silversides. **c.** The Bleak. 1676. **3.** Short for TAILOR-BIRD 1848.

1. They all sit down cross-legg'd, as Taylors do 1704. **b.** They say it takes nine tailors to make a man—apparently, one is sufficient to ruin him SCOTT.

Comb.: **t.-herring, -shad**, a clupeoid fish, *Pomolobus mediocris*, of the Atlantic coast of N. America; **-warbler** = TAILOR-BIRD; **t.'s block, dummy**, a lay figure on which to fit or display clothes.

Tailor (tē·ləɹ), *v.* 1662. [f. prec.] **1.** *intr.* To do tailor's work; to make clothes; to follow the calling of a tailor. **2.** *trans.* To make or fashion (a garment, etc.) by tailor's work. Hence **Tailored** *ppl. a.*, tailor-made. 1856. **3.** To fit or furnish (a person) with clothes; to apparel, to dress 1832. **4.** To shoot at (birds) in a bungling manner, so as to miss or merely damage them (*slang*) 1889.

1. I set to work a Tayloring, or rather indeed a Botching DE FOE. **2.** A tailored suit of tabac brown 1908.

Tailor-bird (tē·ləɹbɜ̄ɹd). 1769. [f. TAILOR *sb.* + BIRD.] One of a number of species of Asiatic passerine singing birds, belonging to the genera *Orthotomus, Prinia, Sutoria*, etc., which stitch together the margins of leaves with cotton, etc., so as to form a cavity for their nest. Orig. applied to a particular species (*Motacilla sutoria* of Pennant, now variously called *Orthotomus sutorius, Sutoria longicauda*, or *S. sutoria*) of India and Ceylon.

Tailoress (tēi·lərės). 1654. [f. TAILOR *sb.* + -ESS.] A woman tailor.

Tailoring (tē·ləriŋ), *vbl. sb.* 1662. [f. TAILOR *v.* + -ING [1].] The action or business of a tailor; the making of garments. **b.** The production of the tailor; tailor's work 1850.

Tai·lor-ma·de, *a.* 1832. **1.** Made by a tailor; esp. said of women's garments of a heavier type, close-fitting and plain in style, prop. when made by a tailor (as dist. from a dressmaker); hence ellipt. as *sb.* 1873. **2. a.** *fig.* Made such by the tailor, i. e. by one's dress. **b.** *transf.* Dressed in tailor-made garments. 1832.

1. Braid is the favourite trimming for tailor-mades 1892. **2. b.** Some severely tailor-made ladies 1896.

Tail-piece (tē·lpīs). 1601. **1.** The piece of anything forming its tail or end, or tailed into it; the piece at the end. **2.** *Printing.* A small decorative engraving placed at the end of a book, chapter, etc. 1707.

Tail-race (tē·lrēs). 1776. [Cf. RACE *sb.*[1] III. 2 b.] The part of a mill-race below the wheel.

Tail-rope (tē·lrōup). ME. †**1.** That part of a horse's harness near the tail, as a breeching or crupper. –late ME. **2.** A rope forming or attached to the tail, or the hinder or lower end of anything; in various techn. applications 1495.

Tailye, tailzie, taillie (tē·lyi, tē·li). *Sc.* late ME. [(1) a. OF. *taille* TAIL *sb.*[2]; (2) a.

OF. *tailliee* sb. fem. from pa. pple. of *taliare* to cut.] †**1.** A cut or slice –1819. **2.** *Sc. Law.* = TAIL *sb.*[2] II, ENTAIL *sb.*[2] **1.** So Tailye *v.* *Sc.* = TAIL *v.*[2] II. 2.

Taint (tēⁱnt), *sb.* late ME. [Two words of distinct origin run together. See A and B.] **A.** [Aphetic f. ATTAINT *sb.*] †**1.** = ATTAINT *sb.* 1. –1611. **2.** = ATTAINT *sb.* 2. 1565. †**3.** = ATTAINT *sb.* 3. –1706. †**B.** [a. OF. *teint, taint*:—L. *tinctus*, and *teinte*:—late and med.L. *tincta*, f. *tinctus, tingere* to TINGE.] Colour, hue, tint; tinge; dye –1593. **C.** [Senses app. combining A and B.] **1.** A stain, a blemish; a sullying spot; a touch of discredit, dishonour, or disgrace; a slur 1601. **2.** A cause or condition of corruption or decay; an infection 1613. **b.** A trace or tinge of disease in a latent state 1615. †**3.** (Also **tant.**) Short for TAINT-WORM; also, a small red spider –1848.

1. Free from the foul T. of High Treason 1643. 2. A deep and general t. infected the morals of the most influential classes MACAULAY. b. Hereditary nervous t. 1899.

Taint (tēⁱnt), *v.* Pa. pple. **tainted**; also formerly †**taint.** late ME. [Two words of distinct origin. See A and B.] †**A.** [Aphetic f. ATTAINT *v.*] **1.** *trans.* = ATTAINT *v.* 2. –1603. **2.** = ATTAINT *v.* 1. –1590. **b.** To break (a lance, staff) in tilting, etc. –1624. †**B.** [a. F. *teinter*, f. *teint*, pa. pple. of *teindre*:—L. *tingere* to TINGE.] **1.** *trans.* To colour, dye, tinge –1725. **b.** To dip, bathe. MARLOWE. **2.** To apply tincture, balm, or ointment to (a wound, etc.) –1639. **C.** [Senses in which A and B appear to blend.] **1.** *trans.* To affect (esp. in a slight degree); to touch, tinge, imbue slightly (usu. *with* some bad or undesirable quality) 1591. †**2.** To affect injuriously; to hurt, injure, impair –1623. †**b.** To sully, stain (a person's honour) –1722. †**3.** To affect with weakness –1611. †**b.** *intr.* To lose vigour or courage; to become weak or faint; to fade, wither –1639. **4.** *trans.* To infect with pernicious, noxious, corrupting or deleterious qualities; to touch with putrefaction; to corrupt, contaminate, deprave 1573. **b.** *intr.* To become putrefied, corrupted, or rotten; to tarnish 1601.

1. Nowise tainted with enthusiasm HUME. 2. *Twel. N.* III. iv. 13. 3. Fear taints me worthily, Though firm I stand, and show it not CHAPMAN. b. *Macb.* v. iii. 3. 4. One..who tainted a great society by a bad example THACKERAY. b. Nay pursue him now, least the deuice take ayre, and t. SHAKS.

Tainted (tēⁱ·ntėd), *ppl. a.* 1577. [f. TAINT *v.* + -ED[1].] **1.** In the senses of TAINT *v.* **2.** Imbued with the scent of an animal (usu. a hunted animal). *Obs.* or *arch.* 1704.

1. *Tainted goods*, (in trade-unionism) goods that members of a union must not handle because non-union labour has been employed on them. 2. [The stag] A moment snuffed the t. gale SCOTT.

Taintless (tēⁱ·ntlės), *a.* Chiefly *poet.* 1590. [-LESS.] Free from taint or blemish; immaculate; clean, pure, innocent. Hence **Tai·ntlessly** *adv.* without taint.

Tainture (tēⁱ·ntiŭɹ). Now *rare.* 1593. [a. OF., ad. L. *tinctura* TINCTURE.] Tainting, staining, stain, defilement, infection.

Tai·nt-worm. *arch.* 1573. [f. TAINT *sb.* + WORM *sb.*] A worm or crawling larva supposed to infect cattle, etc.

As killing as the Canker to the Rose, Or T. to the weanling Herds that graze MILT.

‖**Tai-ping** (tai,piŋ). Also **Taë-ping.** 1860. [Chinese *T'ai-p'ing*, i.e. *t'ai* great, *p'ing* peace.] The name given to the adherents of a great rebellion which arose in Southern China in 1850, under the leadership of Hung-siu-tsuen, styled *T'ai-p'ing-wang*, Prince of great peace, who claimed a divine commission to overthrow the Manchu dynasty and establish one of native origin, to be called *T'ai-p'ing Chao* or Great Peace Dynasty.

Tais(c)h (taiʃ). *Gaelic Folklore.* [Gael.] A phantom, esp. of a person about to die.

Take (tēⁱk), *sb.* 1654. [f. next.] **1.** The act of taking or leasing (land); the land taken; a holding. *dial.* 1805. **2.** That which is taken or received in payment; *pl.* takings, receipts, proceeds 1654. **3.** An act of taking or capturing an animal, or (usu.) a number of animals (esp. fish) at one time; also, the quantity so caught; a catch 1753. **4.** An act of taking (in general) 1816. **5.** *Printing.* A portion of copy taken at one time to be set up in type 1864. **6.** *Cinematography.* A portion of a scene photographed at one time 1928.

Take (tēⁱk), *v.* Pa. t. **took** (tuk); pa. pple. taken (tēⁱ·k'n). [Late OE. *tacan, tóc*, **tacen*, a. ON. *taka, tók, tekinn.*] †**I.** To touch (*intr.* with *on*, also *trans.*) –ME. **II.** To seize, grip, catch, etc. **1.** *trans.* To lay hold upon, get into one's hands by force or artifice; to seize, capture, esp. in war; to make prisoner; hence, to get into one's power, to win by conquest (a fort, town, country). Also, to apprehend (a person charged with an offence), to arrest; to seize (property) by legal process, as by distraint, etc. **b.** To catch, capture (a wild beast, bird, fish, etc.); also of an animal, to seize or catch (prey). ME. **c.** In various games, as chess, cards, etc.: To capture (an adversary's piece, card, etc.) so as to put it out of play; also (*Cards*) to gain possession of (a trick). late ME. **d.** *Cricket.* To catch (the ball) off the bat so as to put the batsman 'out' (also with the batsman as obj.); of the bowler, To 'capture' (a wicket) by striking it with the ball or otherwise 1882. **2.** To lay hold of, grasp (with the hand, arms, etc.); to seize and hold ME. **3.** *intr.* Of a hook, a mechanical device, etc.: To catch, engage. late ME. **b.** *trans.* Of a mechanical appliance, etc.: To 'lay hold of'; to act upon by contact, adhesion, or the like 1659. **4.** *trans.* To strike, hit, impinge upon (a person, etc.), usu. *in, on* (*across, over*, etc.) some part. late ME. **b.** With double obj.; e. g. *to t.* (a person) *a blow* 1448. **5.** *absol.* or *intr.* Of a plant, seed, or graft: To 'get hold' of that on which it grows; to take root, 'strike', germinate, begin to grow 1440. **6.** *trans.* Of a disease, a pain, an injurious or destructive agency, etc.; also of a notion, fancy, feeling, etc.: To affect, seize, lay hold of, attack. Also in imprecations, as 'plague t. him'. ME. **b.** *pass.* with complemental adj., as *to be taken ill*, to be seized or struck with illness, etc. late ME. **c.** *intr.* for *pass.*, with *compl.*, as *to t. ill* = to be taken ill, to fall ill. *colloq.* and *dial.* 1674. **d.** *intr.* To catch, catch hold; *esp.* of fire, to seize upon combustible substances, to begin burning; also of a condition, humour, fancy, etc. Now *rare.* 1523. **7.** *trans.* To 'catch' or come upon (a person) *in* some action or situation; *fig.* to catch or detect *in* a fault or error 1577. **b.** To come upon suddenly, overtake, catch. *Obs.* or *arch.* exc. in certain phrases, as *t. by* SURPRISE, etc. 1533. **8.** To catch the fancy or affection of; to captivate, delight, charm; to 'fetch' 1605. **b.** *absol.* or *intr. To t.* = to take the fancy, gain acceptance; *esp.* to become popular 1635. **9.** *intr.* Of a plan, operation, etc.: To succeed, 'come off'. Now *rare.* 1622. **b.** Of a medicine, inoculation, etc.: To take hold, prove effective 1626.

1. I was taken into custody 1803. I took two guns and retook two 1854. Phr. *To t. by storm*: see STORM *sb.* II. c. The king takes the queen 1735. 2. I took her hand 1825. *To t. in one's arms*, to embrace. 4. T. him on the Costard, with the hiltes of thy Sword SHAKS. b. If he tooke you a box o' th' eare SHAKS. 6. Fire tooke the Temple 1604. I was going to be taken with a fit 1888. What in the name of wonder has taken the girl? 1892. c. Mr. William Pitt..took ill and died after Austerlitz 1903. d. The tinder was ready, and the spark took 1803. 7. The doctor was not easily taken off his guard 1885. 8. Such sweet neglect more taketh me, Than all th' adulteries of art B. JONS. He was much taken with my little Jeannie CARLYLE. b. The new melodrame..takes mightily 1817. 9. The design took and the Fellow got away 1701.

III. Weakened sense of 'seize', with elimination of the notion of force or art: the ordinary current sense. **1.** *trans.* To perform the voluntary physical act by which one gets (something) into one's hand or hold; to transfer to oneself by one's own physical act. (Now the main sense.) ME. **b.** with the instrumentality not expressed or considered ME. **2.** To receive into one's body by one's own act; to eat or drink, to swallow (food, drink, medicine, opium, etc.); to inhale (snuff, †tobacco-smoke, etc.) ME. **b.** To expose oneself to (air) so as to inhale it or get the physical benefit of it; chiefly in phr. *to t. the air*, to walk or ride out in the open air (now *rare* or *arch.*): see AIR *sb.* 4. So *to t. a bath*, to bathe. late ME. **c.** Phr. *Not to be taking any..*: not to be in the mood for, to be disinclined for. *slang.* 1900. **3.** To bring, receive, or adopt (a person) into some relation to oneself (e. g. into one's service, protection, tuition, care) ME. **b.** *spec.* in ref. to marriage or cohabitation; often in phr. *to t. to wife, in marriage* ME. **4.** To transfer by one's own direct act (a thing) into one's possession or keeping; to appropriate; to enter into possession or use of ME. **b.** *absol.* To take possession; *spec.* in *Law*, to enter into actual possession. late ME. **c.** To secure beforehand by payment or contract; e. g. *to t. a house*, etc., to engage (a house or other place) for the purpose of occupying it 1604. **d.** To get or procure regularly by payment (something offered to the public, as a periodical, a commodity) 1593. **5. a.** To assume (a form, nature, character, name, or other attribute); sometimes, to assume the part or character of ME. **b.** To assume, adopt (a symbol, a badge, or something connected with a function): in spec. phrases ME. **6.** To assume, charge oneself with, undertake (a function, responsibility, etc.) ME. **b.** To subject oneself to (an oath, vow, pledge, or the like) 1511. †**c.** *To t. it*: to affirm, asseverate. Const. *on* (one's death, honour). –1631. **7.** *To t. on* or *upon oneself.* **a.** To charge oneself with, undertake (an office, etc.); to make oneself responsible for ME. **b.** With *inf.*: To undertake; to presume (*to do* something) ME. †**c.** To affect, feign (*to do* something) –1606. †**d.** *absol.* or *intr.* To assume authority or importance; usu. in bad sense, = to take too much upon one, assume airs –1720. **8. a.** To undertake and perform, conduct, or discharge (a part, function, duty, service, or the like). late ME. **b.** Phr. *To t. pains, trouble*: to take upon oneself and exercise these activities and qualities; to exercise care and diligence ME. **9.** To adopt as one's own (a part or side in a contest, controversy, etc.); to range oneself on, ally oneself with (a side or party). late ME. **10.** To assume as if one's own, to appropriate or arrogate to oneself (credit, etc.); to assume as if granted, e.g. *to t. leave, liberty*, etc. 1525. **11.** *Gram.* Of a word, clause, or sentence: To have by right or usage, either as part of itself or with it in construction (a particular inflexion, accent, case, mood, etc.) as the proper one 1818.

1. Iesus then commeth, and taketh bread, and giueth them *John* xxi. 13. He could t. his hat and go 1833. b. T. a quart of shrimps 1771. 2. He died by taking poison 1875. 3. He took pupils to increase his income 1891. Colloq. phr. *To t. too much* (sc. drink). 5. a. France cannot t. the offensive, but she can paralyse Germany and Italy 1887. b. *To t. the crown, the throne*, to assume sovereignty. *To t. the ball* (at cricket), to assume the position of bowler. *To t. an oar*, to begin to row. See also HABIT *sb.* I. 2, SILK 2 b, VEIL *sb.* 6. Grenville refused to t. office without Fox 1890. b. She has taken the monastic Vow 1803. 7. b. I took upon me..to go to Leeds DE FOE. c. *Tr. & Cr.* I. ii. 153. d. Lord! to see how Duncomb do t. upon him is an eyesore PEPYS. 8. a. She would t. the grammar class at ten 1890. 10. We would t. leave to recommend..an alteration 1820. He took credit to himself that..her son remained stanch 1870.

IV. Pregnant senses related to III. **1.** To pick out from a number: either by chance, at random, or with intention; to select, choose ME. **2.** To adopt or choose in order to use in some way; to adopt in some capacity (*as, for*); hence, to employ for a purpose, to have recourse to (a means or method); to seize (an opportunity, etc.) ME. **b.** To use (one's hands, a tool, weapon, etc.) for doing something. *To t. a stick* (etc.) *to*, to use it to beat (a person, etc.). 1768. **c.** *esp.* To take into use or employment as a means of progression; to enter or mount (a vehicle, ship, horse, one's limbs, etc.) for a journey or voyage. Often without article, as *to t. boat, coach, ship*, etc. 1450. **3.** To gain the aid or help of (a place) by betaking oneself to it; to gain, reach, repair to, go into, enter (esp. for refuge or safety); to get into or on to ME. **b.** To adopt and enter upon (a road, way, path, course, etc.): sometimes with mixture of sense 'to choose, select' ME. **c.** *To t.* (*a place or person*) *in* (*on*) *one's way*, to touch at or visit in one's journey; to include in one's route 1622. **4.** To proceed or begin to deal with or treat in some way or do something to; hence, 'to take in hand', 'tackle', deal with, treat 1523. **b.** To proceed to deal with mentally; to consider; to reckon. So *to t. into* or *under consideration.* ME. **5.** To proceed to occupy, enter on the occupation of (a place or position) ME. **6.** To use, occupy, use up, consume (so much material, space, time, energy, activity, etc.). Sometimes nearly = 'need' or 'require'. Hence (*colloq.*) to require (a person or thing of so much capacity or ability) *to do* something 1578. †**7.** To begin or start afresh after leaving off, or after some one else; to resume. late ME. (superseded by *t. up* m).

1. Good Commanders in the Warres, must be taken, be they neuer so Ambitious BACON. 2. *To t.* ADVANTAGE, MEASURE, OCCASION: see the sbs. **c.** They ..took train to London 1892. 3. Vipers occasionally t. the water 1831. A harbour which may be easily taken and left in stormy weather 1880. **b.** The court..left the parties to t. their own course 1895. 4. To t. the Distemper in its first Stage 1737. Phr. *To take it easy*: see EASY B. *To t. in vain*: see VAIN A. **b.** He was a man, take him for all in all: I shall not look vpon his like againe SHAKS. 5. Phr. *To t. the* CHAIR, FLOOR, *to t.* PRECEDENCE: see the sbs. 6. Any ignoramus can construct a straight line, but it takes an engineer to make a curve 1890. Her Mamma took nines in gloves 1897. Phr. *To t. (one's) time*, to allow oneself ample time (to do something); hence (sarcastically), to be 'quite long enough', i.e. too long; to loiter.

V. To obtain from a source, to derive. **1.** To get, obtain, or derive by one's own act from some source (something material or non-material); to adopt, copy, 'borrow'; to take example of, 'get' or 'learn' *from* some one ME. **b.** *spec.* To obtain from its natural source (e.g. stone from a quarry); to get; to pluck, gather (plants, a crop). Now *rare.* 1477. **2.** To derive, draw (origin, name, character, or some attribute or quality) from some source ME. **3.** To get as a result or product by some special process, e.g. by inquiry, by measurement, scientific observation, etc. late ME. **4. a.** To obtain in writing, make (notes, a copy, etc.); to write down (spoken words), report in writing (a speech, etc.) 1591. **b.** To obtain by drawing, delineating, etc.; also *transf.*, to obtain or make a figure or picture of, to portray; now *esp.* to photograph. Also (*colloq.*) *intr.* for *pass.* (with adv.) of a person: To be a (good or bad) subject for photographing. 1538.

1. The proportions of the three Grecian orders were taken from the human body BERKELEY. 2. The Turks ..took their..taste for poetry from the Persians 1772. 3. He hastened down to the country to take the sense of his constituents 1817. Isn't it about time for taking the sun?..it is four days since we knew our position 1887. 4. **a.** Minutes of the meeting must be taken 1883. **b.** A limner, who..took likenesses for fifteen shillings a head GOLDSM. The photographers..say a woman 'takes' better standing 1889.

VI. To take something given or offered; to receive, accept, exact, etc. **1.** To receive, get (something given, bestowed, or administered); to have conferred upon one; to win, or receive as won (a prize, reward); to acquire (experience, etc.). Also *absol.* ME. **b.** To receive (something inflicted); to have (something) done to one; to suffer, undergo, submit to ME. **c.** To receive information of, to hear; in *imper.* often = 'let me tell you'. Somewhat *arch.* 1595. **2.** To enter into the enjoyment of (pleasure, recreation, rest, or the like) ME. **3.** To receive, as wages, etc., or by way of charge or exaction as a fine, tribute; sometimes with connotation 'accept' or 'charge, exact, demand' ME. **4.** To exact (satisfaction or reparation) for an offence; hence, to execute vengeance, revenge, etc.) ME. **5.** To receive, exact, or accept (a promise, oath, etc.); hence, to administer or witness (an oath) 1450. **6.** To receive (something offered); to receive willingly; to accept ME. **b.** Of a female animal: To admit (the male) 1577. **c.** Of fish: To seize (the bait). Also *absol.* 1863. **7.** To accept (a wager, or the person who offers it). So also in ref. to a proposal, etc. 1602. **8.** To accept and act upon (advice, a hint, warning, etc.) ME. **b.** To accept as true or correct. Also, to accept mistakenly as trustworthy ME. **9.** To accept with the mind or will in some specified way (*well, ill, in earnest*, etc.) ME. **b.** To be content with; to put up with, tolerate, 'stand' 1470. **10.** To face and attempt to get over, through, up, etc.; clear (an obstacle, as a fence, ditch, space, etc.); to mount (a slope), get round (a corner), clear (the points on a railway line), etc. 1579. **11. a.** To admit, let in 1674. **b.** To absorb or become impregnated with (something detrimental, as moisture); to be affected injuriously by; to contract (disease, infection, injury, etc.); to fall into (a fit or trance) ME. **c.** To absorb, become impregnated with (a dye, colour, quality, salt, etc.); to receive (an impression, a polish, or the like) 1592. **d.** *absol.* or *intr.* To become affected in the desired or required way 1599.

1. It is more blessyd to gyue than t. 1450. In the house where the Doctors, and other Graduates take their degrees 1617. **b.** He professed himself ready to t. his trial 1879. **c.** Then t. the worst in brief, Samson is dead MILT. 2. So perforce I took holiday 1897. 3. A thousand guilders! Come, t. fifty! BROWNING. 5. Commissioners to t. oaths and affidavits 1873. 6. T. no repulse, what euer she doth say SHAKS. **c.** Fish always t. best after rain 1889. 7. I'll t. ten to one on it 1850. Phr. *To t. one's death* (upon a thing), to stake one's life upon it. 8. They'l t. suggestion, as a Cat laps milke SHAKS. **b.** I would not t. this from report SHAKS. 9. Phr. *To t. to heart* (HEART *sb.* II. 7); *to t. in good* (etc.) *part* (PART *sb.*). **b.** I had the good sense to t. things as I found them 1809. He must t. the consequences 1896. 11. **b.** As men t. diseases, one of another SHAKS. **c.** It takes dyes admirably 1865. **d.** Vaccinated just six weeks ago-o! Took very finely! DICKENS.

VII. Senses related to VI, denoting intellectual action. **1.** To receive and hold with the intellect; to grasp mentally, apprehend, comprehend. (Now only in ref. to the meaning of words.) late ME. **b.** *transf.* To understand (a person, i.e. what he says) 1513. **2. a.** With *adv.* or *advb. phr.* To understand or apprehend in a specified way. Also with person as obj. ME. †**b.** With *simple compl.* To consider as, suppose to be -1709. **c.** With *dependent cl.*: To suppose, be of opinion, assume as a fact (*that*..). Usu. *take it.* late ME. **d.** With *inf.* To understand, suppose, imagine, assume (*to be* or *to do* something) 1548. **3.** *To t...for*: To suppose to be, consider as; often, to mistake for. late ME. **4.** To regard, hold, esteem (*as*); to reckon (*at* so much) 1531. **5.** To begin to have or be affected by (a feeling or state of mind); to conceive; hence, to experience (*delight, pleasure, pride*, etc.) ME. **6.** *trans.* To conceive and adopt with the will (a purpose, resolution, etc.), or with the intellect (an estimate, view, etc.); to form and hold in the mind ME. **b.** To conceive and exercise (*courage, heart, compassion, pity*, etc.); to form in the mind and exhibit in action ME. **c.** To exercise with the mind, in thought (*note, notice*, etc.), or with the mind and will, in action (*care*, etc.) ME.

1. An audience..quick to t. his points 1893. **b.** You t. me right, Eupolis BACON. 2. **a.** So was the law taken in Anno 4. H. 3. 1642. **b.** I t. myself obliged in Honour to go on STEELE. **c.** I t. it your owne busines calls on you SHAKS. 3. Do you t. me for a fool? 1889. Phr. *To t. for granted*: see GRANT *v.* 7. 5. Persons to whom I had taken so much Dislike 1773. Women do t. prejudices 1888. 6. **a.** We do not t. the alarmist view of our correspondent 1891. **b.** The Arabs would have taken fresh heart 1888.

VIII. Various senses, nearly = make, do, perform (some action). **1.** To perform, make, do (an act, action, movement, etc.). late ME. **2.** *To t. counsel*: to get advice, to consult, deliberate ME. †**3.** To arrange, agree upon (a truce, peace, league, etc.) -1656. **4.** *To t. adieu, farewell*: to bid farewell, say good-bye. Const. *of.* 1560. **5.** To lay hold of, raise, make (an objection, an exception, a distinction, etc.) 1542.

1. The salmon took a great leap 1889. *To t. one's departure*, to depart. 2. She took counsel with witches and magicians 1879. 3. Betwixt mine eye and heart a league is tooke SHAKS. 5. The distinction which they took was..ingenious 1849.

IX. Senses denoting movement or removal, and related senses. **1. a.** To carry, convey; to conduct, lead, escort (a person or animal). Also said of a vehicle, etc., and of a road, way, etc.; so of a journey, etc. ME. **b.** To carry or bear (a thing) with one; to carry to some place or person. late ME. **c.** *fig.* To induce (a person) to go; to be the cause of his going 1848. **2.** With *from, off* (hence sometimes *simply*): To carry away, to remove; to extract; to deprive or rid a person or thing of ME. **b.** *To t. the life of*: to deprive of life, to kill 1591. **c.** To remove by death 1552. **d.** To subtract, deduct 1611. **e.** *absol.* with *from*: To detract from, lessen 1625. **f.** *intr.* for *pass.* To be capable of being, or adapted to be, taken *off, out, to pieces*, etc.; to be removable, detachable, etc. 1669. **3.** *fig.* **a.** To carry, draw, or lead in thought, etc.; with *from, off*, to distract 1611. †**b.** *To t.* (a person) *with one*: to speak so that (he) can 'follow'; to be explicit -1695. **c.** To bring or convey to a higher or lower degree; to advance or put back 1589. †**4.** *trans.* To deliver, hand over; to give; to commit, entrust -1533. **5.** *refl.* To devote or give oneself up; to apply oneself *to* (some pursuit, action, or object) ME. **6.** *intr.* To apply oneself *to* a habitual action 1677. **7. a.** To make one's way, go, proceed ME. **b.** Of a road, a river, etc.: To proceed, go, run, strike off (in some direction). *Obs.* or *dial.* 1610. **c.** *refl.* In same sense as a; also to betake oneself *to* 1470.

1. I took my man Friday with me DE FOE. **b.** T. thy face hence SHAKS. **c.** What took you out so late? 1883. 2. The doing so would..t. the case from under the statute SCOTT. **d.** Twopence in the pound was taken off the tea duty 1890. **e.** It takes greatly from the pleasure 1891. 3. **a.** Your heart is full of something, that do 's t. Your minde from feasting SHAKS. **b.** *Rom. & Jul.* III. v. 142. **c.** Phr. *To t. down a peg*, see PEG *sb.*[1] 3. 5. Art thou a craftsman? t. thee to thine arte GASCOIGNE. 6. Their taking to smoke tobacco 1890. 7. **a.** I took across some fields 1801. **c.** I am to..t. myself elsewhere 1865.

Phrases. **I.** With special obj. **Take aim.** To direct a missile at something with intention to strike it; to aim. **T. alarm.** To accept and act upon a warning of danger; hence, to become alarmed. **T. charge. a.** To assume the care or custody *of*, make oneself responsible. **b.** To get out of control and act automatically. **T. fire. a.** *lit.* = *catch fire* (CATCH *v.* IX). **b.** *fig.* To become 'inflamed' or excited, 'fire up'. **T. hold. a.** = *catch* or *lay hold*: see HOLD *sb.*[1] 1. **b.** *fig.* To get a person or thing into its (or one's) 'hold' or power; of a feeling, a disease, etc.: to seize and affect forcibly and more or less permanently; of fire, to 'lay hold' *of* (something), begin to burn. Also, to seize (an opportunity). **T. horse. a.** To mount a horse (esp. for a journey). **b.** Of a mare: see HORSE *sb.* I. 1 b. **T. possession. a.** To enter into possession. With *of*: to take into one's possession, appropriate. **b.** *fig.* To begin to 'possess', dominate, or actuate. **II.** Intr. uses in idiomatic combination with preps. **T. after** —. To follow the example of; hence, to resemble (a parent, ancestor, superior, etc.) in nature, character, habits, appearance, or other quality. **T. to** —. **a.** To undertake, take in hand; to take charge of. *Obs.* exc. *dial.* **b.** To have recourse to (esp. some means of progression, as in *t. to the boats, one's heels*, etc.); also (now *dial.*) *to* some resource or means of subsistence). **c.** To betake oneself to (a place); to take refuge in; to enter. **d.** To adopt or take up as a practice, business, habit, or something habitual. **e.** To apply oneself (*well, kindly*); to adapt oneself. **f.** To take a liking to. **III.** In comb. with advs., forming the equivalent of compound verbs, chiefly trans. **T. aback**: see ABACK *adv.* 3. **T. away. a.** *trans.* To remove, withdraw, abstract; to remove by death; to subtract. **b.** *absol.* To clear the table after a meal. **c.** *absol.* To detract *from.* **T. back. a.** *trans.* To take possession of again, resume. **b.** To withdraw, retract, unsay (a statement, promise, etc.). **c.** To carry back in thought to a past time. **T. down. a.** *trans.* To remove from a higher to a lower, or from an upright to a prostrate, position; to lower; to carry down; to cut down, fell (a tree); to pull down (a house, etc.); to distribute (type). **b.** (*a*) To swallow; (*b*) in *Falconry*, to cause (a hawk) to fly down; (*c*) in school, to get above (another scholar) in class; so of a boat in a race, to get in front of (another boat); (*d*) to lead (a lady) down to dinner. **c.** *fig.* To humble, humiliate, abate the pride or arrogance of. **d.** To write down so as to use or preserve (what is said); to take a written report or notes of. **T. in. a.** *trans.* To take, draw, or receive into itself, or into something (see simple senses and IN *adv.*). **b.** To receive (money) in payment, etc.; to receive and undertake (work) to be done at home for pay. **c.** To subscribe for and receive regularly (a newspaper or periodical). **d.** To lead or conduct into a house, room, etc. *To t.* (a lady) *in to dinner.* **e.** To receive or admit as inmate or guest. **f.** To bring into smaller compass, draw in, reduce the extent of, contract, make smaller; to shorten, narrow, or tighten; to furl (a sail). *T. in a reef*, to roll or fold up a reef in a sail so as to shorten the sail. **g.** To enclose (a piece of land, etc.); to take into possession (a territory, a common), or into cultivation (a waste); to include; to annex. **h.** To admit into a number or list; to include, comprise, embrace. **i.** To receive into or grasp with the mind; to comprehend, realize; to learn; to conceive. **j.** To comprehend in one view; to perceive at a glance. **k.** To believe or accept unquestioningly. *colloq.* **l.** To deceive, trick, impose upon. *colloq.* **T. off. a.** *trans.* To remove from the position or condition of being *on* (see simple senses and OFF *adv.*). (*b*) *spec.* To divest oneself, or another, of, doff (a garment). (*c*) To remove or convey (a person) from on shore, from a rock, or from on board ship. **b.** *trans.* To drink to the bottom or at one draught; to 'toss off'. **c.** To lead away summarily; *refl.* to take one's departure, 'be off'. **d.** To lead away or draw off (in *fig.* sense); to divert, distract, dissuade. **e.** To dismiss; to withdraw (a coach, train, etc.) from running. **f.** To remove by death, kill, 'carry off', cut off: said of a person (esp. an assassin), of disease, devouring animals, etc. **g.** To remove (something imposed), esp. so as to relieve those subject to it. **h.** To remove or do away with (a quality, condition, etc.). **i.** (*a*) To make or obtain (an impression) from something; to print off. (*b*) To make (a figure of something); *transf.* to draw a likeness of, to portray. (*c*) To measure off; to mark the position of. **j.** To imitate or counterfeit, esp. by way of mockery; to mimic, caricature, burlesque. *colloq.* **k.** To close the stitches in knitting; to knit off. Also *absol.* **l.** *intr.* To abate, grow less; (of rain) to cease. **m.** To go off, start off, run away; to branch off from a main stream. (*b*) To start in jumping or rising from the ground, etc. (*c*) *Croquet.* To make a stroke from contact with another ball (cf. TAKE-OFF A. 4). **n.** *Aeronautics.* To start from rest, attain flying speed, and become air-borne. **T. on. a.** *trans.* See simple senses and ON *adv.* (*b*) To 'put on' (flesh, etc.). **b.** To assume, 'put on' (a form, quality, etc.): to assume, begin to perform (an action or function); to contract, 'catch'. **c.** To take (a person) into one's employment or upon one's staff; †to accept in marriage; to receive into fellowship. **d.** To undertake; to begin to handle or deal with, to 'tackle'. **e.** To undertake the management of (a farm, etc.), esp. in succession or continuance. **f.** *intr.* To 'go on' madly or excitedly; to be greatly agitated; to make a great fuss, outcry, or uproar; now *esp.* to distress oneself greatly. Now *colloq.* and *dial.* **g.** To take service or employment, to engage oneself; to enlist. **h.** To 'catch on', become popular. *colloq.* **T. out. a.** *trans.* See simple senses and OUT *adv.* (*b*) To remove, extract (a stain, etc.). **b.** To leave out, except, omit. **c.** To lead or carry out or forth. (*b*) Cricket. *To take out one's bat*: see CARRY *v.* III. **d.** To make a copy from an original; to copy (a writing, etc.); *esp.* to extract a passage from a writing or book. (*b*) To extract from data. **e.** To apply for and obtain (a licence, etc.) from the proper authority. **f.** To obtain, spend, the value of (something) *in* another form. **g.** *Bridge.* To remove (one's partner) from the suit he has called by a higher bid. **T. out of. a.** *trans.* See simple senses and OUT OF. **b.** To get, derive, or obtain from. **c.** To deprive a person or thing of (some quality, etc.); *spec.* to deprive of (energy or the like); usu. *to t. it out of*, to exhaust, fatigue (*colloq.*). **d.** To remove from the jurisdiction of; to prove not to come under (a statute). **e.** To take (something) from a person in compensation; *to t. it out of*, to exact satisfaction from (*colloq.*). **T. over. a.** To take by transfer from, or in succession to another. **b.** To carry or convey across, to transport. **T. up. a.** *trans.* To raise, lift; to pick up. Somewhat *arch.* (*b*) With special obj., implying a purpose of using in some way: as, *to t. up one's pen*, to proceed or begin to write; *to t. up a book* (i.e. with the purpose of reading); *to t. up the* (or *one's*) *cross*; *to take up* ARMS, *the* GLOVE, etc., see the sbs. (*c*) To take (a person) from the ground into a vehicle, or on horseback, etc. Said of a person, or of the carriage, horse, train, etc. Also *absol.* of a vehicle, a train, etc., to take up its occupants. **b.** To lead, conduct, convey, or carry (a person or thing), to a higher place or position. **c.** To pull up or in, so as to tighten or shorten; to make fast in this way, as a dropped stitch. (*b*) To tie up or constrict (a vein or artery); 'to fasten with a ligature passed under' (J.). **d.** To take into one's possession, possess oneself of; with various shades of meaning, as: to purchase wholesale, buy up; to get, receive, or exact in payment; to levy; to borrow (at interest); to hire. (*b*) To take (land) into occupation. (*c*) To accept or pay (a bill of exchange); to advance money on (a mortgage); to subscribe for (stocks, shares, a loan) at their original issue. **e.** To receive into its own substance or interstices; to absorb (a fluid); to dissolve (a solid). **f.** To accept. **g.** To take (a person) into one's protection, patronage, or other relation; to adopt as a *protégé* or associate; to begin to patronize. **†h.** To levy, raise, enlist (troops). **i.** To seize by legal authority, arrest, apprehend. **j.** *intr.* for *refl.* To check oneself, 'pull up'; to slacken one's pace; to reform. *Obs.* exc. *dial.* (*b*) Of weather: To improve, become fair. **k.** *trans.* To check (a person) in speaking; to interrupt sharply, esp. with an expression of dissent or disapproval; to rebuke, reprove, or reprimand sharply or severely. Also *to take up short*: see SHORT. **†l.** To oppose, encounter, cope with. **m.** To begin afresh (something left off, or begun by another); to resume. **n.** To adopt (a practice, notion, idea, purpose, etc.); to assume (an attitude, tone, etc.); to 'go in for' (a study, profession, business, etc.). (*b*) To take in hand, proceed to deal practically with (a matter, question, etc.); to interest oneself in, embrace (a cause). **†o.** To make up, settle (a dispute, quarrel, etc.). **p.** To proceed to occupy (a place or position, *lit.* or *fig.*); to station or place oneself in. †(*b*) *absol.* or *intr.* To lodge, 'put up'. **q.** *trans.* To occupy entirely; to fill up (space, time, etc.); to occupy exclusively; to obstruct. (*b*) To engage or occupy fully, engross (a person, his attention, mind, etc.). **r.** *intr.* *T. up with.* (*a*) To associate with (a person); to consort with (esp. with a view to marriage). (*b*) To adopt, espouse (esp. as a settled practice); to assent to, agree with. *arch.* †(*c*) To put up with, tolerate.

Take-, the vb.-stem in combs. and phrases used as sbs. or adjs.: **t.-down** *colloq.* = SET-DOWN 2; **t.-it-or-leave-it** *a.*, allowing acceptance or rejection; showing indifference; **t.-on**, a state of 'taking on' or mental agitation.

Take-in (tēⁱ·kˌin), *sb. colloq.* 1778. [The vbl. phr. *take in* used as sb. or adj.] The act of taking in; a cheat, swindle, deception; a thing or person that takes one in; a 'fraud'.

Take-off (tēⁱ·kˌǫf), *sb.* and *a.* 1826. [f. the vbl. phr. *take off.*] **A. 1.** A thing that 'takes off' or detracts from something; a drawback. **2.** An act of 'taking off' or mimicking; a mimic; a caricature. *colloq.* 1855. **3.** The act of 'taking off', or springing from the ground, etc.; usu. *transf.* a place or spot from which one takes or may take off 1869. **4.** *Croquet.* A stroke made from contact with another ball so as to send one's own ball nearly or quite in the direction of aim, the other ball being moved only slightly or not at all 1874. **5.** *Aeronautics.* See *take off* n. (TAKE *v.*) 1914. **B.** *attrib.* or *adj.* **1.** From which one 'takes off' or makes the spring in leaping, as *the t. line* 1889. **2.** Applied to a part of mechanism for taking something off 1896.

Taker (tēⁱ·kəɹ). late ME. [f. TAKE *v.* + -ER [1].] One who or that which takes; one who captures or seizes. **b.** One who takes possession, esp. of land; often with *first* or *next* 1766. **c.** One who accepts a bet 1810.

Take-up (tēⁱ·kˌʊp), *sb.* 1825. [f. the vbl. phr. *take up* (TAKE *v.*).] **1.** The act of 'taking up' the stuff so as to form 'gathers' in a dress; *concr.* one of such 'gathers'. Now *rare.* **2.** A contrivance for taking up; *spec.* a device in a sewing-machine for drawing up the thread so as to tighten the stitch 1877. **3.** In a loom or other machine, the process of winding up the stuff already woven or treated; *concr.* the part of the mechanism by which this is done 1877. **4.** The part between the smoke-box and the bottom of the funnel of a marine engine boiler 1838.

‖**Takin** (tā·kin). 1850. [Native name in Mishmi.] A horned ruminant (*Budorcas taxicolor*) of south-eastern Tibet on the northern frontier of Assam.

Taking (tēⁱ·kiŋ), *vbl. sb.* ME. [f. TAKE *v.* + -ING [1].] The action or condition expressed by TAKE *v.* **1.** Touching, touch. ME only. **2.** Capture, seizure (in warfare, etc.); apprehension, arrest; catching (of fish or other animals) ME. **†b.** A seizure or attack of disease, *esp.* a stroke of palsy or the like; also, malignant influence –1639. **3.** The physical act of possessing oneself of anything, of receiving, accepting, etc. ME. **†b.** Mental acceptance or reception; estimation –1639. **4. a.** Condition, plight (in unfavourable sense). *Obs.* exc. *Sc.* 1522. **b.** *spec.* A disturbed or agitated state of mind; excited condition, passion 1577. **5. a.** That which is received or gained; *esp.* in *pl.*, the receipts or earnings of merchants, tradesmen, or workmen 1632. **b.** That which is captured; *esp.* the fish or other animals caught at one time, a capture, a catch 1809. **c.** *Printing.* = TAKE *sb.* 5. 1808.

3. Their t. of notes at sermons 1660. The t. of the census 1896. **b.** Manifested in his sorrowful t. of her death 1639. 4. **a.** The poor boy was in a pitiful t. and pickle PEPYS. **b.** By this time your Mother is in a fine t. 1676.

Ta·king, *ppl. a.* 1483. [f. as prec. + -ING [2].] That takes; see the vb. **1.** Seizing, getting something into one's possession; rapacious (*rare*). **2.** That takes the fancy or affection; captivating, charming, attractive. Now *colloq.* 1605. **3.** †Blasting, pernicious; infectious, catching (*rare*) 1605.

2. Phillis has such a t. way, She charms my very soul PRIOR. 3. Strike her yong bones, You t. Ayres, with Lamenesse SHAKS. Hence **Ta·king·ly** *adv.*, **-ness.**

‖**Talapoin** (tæ·lăpoin). 1586. [ad. Pg. *talapão*, ad. Talaing (Old Peguan) *tala pôi* 'my lord', the title of a Buddhist monk.] **1.** A Buddhist monk or priest, properly of Pegu; extended by Europeans to those of Siam, Burma, and other Buddhist countries. **2.** *Zool.* (In full *t. monkey.*) A small W. African monkey, *Cercopithecus talapoin* 1774.

Talar (tē̆·lăɹ). 1738. [ad. L. *talaris*, f. *talus* ankle; see -AR.] A long garment or robe, reaching down to the ankles.

‖**Talaria** (tălēə·riă), *sb. pl.* 1593. [L., neut. pl. of *talaris*; see prec.] *Anc. Rom. Mythol.* Winged sandals or small wings attached to the ankles of some deities, esp. Mercury.

Talbot (tǭ·lbət). 1491. [Supposed to be derived from the ancient Eng. family name *Talbot.*] **1.** Name of a variety of hound, formerly used for tracking and hunting; a large white or light-coloured hound, having long hanging ears, heavy jaws, and great powers of scent 1562. **2.** A representation of a hound or hunting-dog; *esp.* in *Her.* that borne by the Talbot family 1491.

Talbotype (tǭ·lbŏtəip). Also **Talbot-type.** 1846. [f. W. H. F. *Talbot*, the inventor's name + TYPE *sb.*] = CALOTYPE; also, a picture produced by this process.

Talc (tælk), *sb.* 1601. [a. F., or ad. med.L. *talcum*, ad. Arab. *ṭalq*; prob. f. Pers. *talk.*] A name applied by the Arabs and mediæval writers to various transparent, translucent, or shining minerals, as talc proper, mica, selenite, etc. Now: **1.** In popular and commercial use, (loosely) applied to MICA or Muscovy glass. **b.** With *a* and *pl.* A plate of mica used as a microscopic slide 1761. **2.** *Min.* A hydrated silicate of magnesium, usu. consisting of broad flat laminæ or plates, white, apple-green, or yellow, having a greasy feel, and shining lustre, translucent, and in thin plates often transparent; it exists in three varieties—foliated, massive (*steatite* or *soapstone*), and indurated (*talc slate* or *schist*) 1610.

Comb.: **t. powder**, talcum powder; **t. schist**, **slate**, a schistose rock consisting largely of t. Hence **Talcky** (tæ·lki) *a.* pertaining to, of the nature of, or consisting of t. **Ta·lcoid** *a.* resembling t.; *sb.* a snow-white, broadly-foliated variety of t. **Ta·lcose** *a.* abounding in t. **Ta·lcous** *a.* of the nature of t.; talcose.

‖**Talcum** (tæ·lkŏm). 1558. [med.L.] = TALC. *T. powder*, powdered talc or French chalk for toilet use, usu. perfumed.

Tale (tēⁱl), *sb.* [OE. *talu* = Du. *taal* speech, G. *zahl* number:—OTeut. **talā*, f. stem of **taljan* to relate, reckon, TELL *v.*] **I. †1.** The action of telling, relating, or saying; discourse, conversation, talk –1592. **2.** That which one tells; the relation of a series of events; a narrative, statement, information OE. **b.** *pl.* Things told so as to violate confidence or secrecy; idle or mischievous gossip ME. **3.** A true or fictitious story or narrative; a literary composition cast in narrative form ME. **4.** A mere story as opp. to a narrative of fact; a fiction, an idle tale; a falsehood ME. **b.** A thing now existing only in story; a thing of the past 1780.

1. *Rom. & Jul.* II. iv. 99. 2. The t. of hym wente forth..in to al..Galilee WYCLIF. One t. is good, untill anothers told 1601. Phr. *Thereby hangs a t.* (and such phrases) = 'about that there is something to tell'. *In the same t.*, *in a* (= one) *t.*, in the same enumeration, statement, or category; hence, in agreement (*arch.*). **b.** Phr. *To tell* (*bring, carry*) *tales.* Dead men tell no tales 1838. *Tales out of school* (see SCHOOL *sb.*[1] 1 b). 3. Indeed Sir the best Tales in England are your Canterburie tales 1606. Hates the T. of Troy for Helen's sake GRAY. 4. There was more of t. than of truth in those things DE FOE. Phr. *A Canterbury t.*, *old wives' tales*, *travellers' tales*, *a t. of a tub* (see TUB), etc. **b.** No power..could have prevented a general conflagration; and at this day London would have been a t. BURKE.

II. 1. Numerical statement or reckoning; enumeration; number ME. **2.** The number all told; the complete sum, enumeration, or list ME. **†3.** An account, a reckoning of numbers –1807. **†4.** Reckoning of value; account, estimation –1496.

1. An exact t. of the dead bodies DE FOE. Phr. *By t.*, by number; as dist. from *by weight*, *by measure*; Where oysters are..sold by t. 1594. 2. Yet shal ye delyuer the hole t. of brycke BIBLE (Great) *Exod.* v. 18. 4. Phr. *To hold* (*make, give, tell*) *no t. of*, to hold of no account. Hence **Ta·leful** *a.* full of tales; talkative. THOMSON.

Tale (tēⁱl), *v.* Now *rare.* [OE. *talian* to reckon, impute, enumerate:—OTeut. **talōjan*,

f. stem *tal-*; see prec.] †1. *trans.* To account, reckon (something) to be (so and so). -late ME. 2. To count up; to deal *out* by number. Now *dial.* 1626. †3. *intr.* To discourse, talk, gossip; to tell (*of*); to tell tales -1500.

Talebearer (tēⁱ·l,bē͡ᵊ:rəɪ). 1478. [f. TALE *sb.* + BEARER.] One who officiously carries gossip or reports of private matters to gratify malice or idle curiosity. So **Ta·lebearing**, the carrying of malicious or injurious reports.

‖**Talegalla** (tælĭgæ·lă). 1842. [mod.L., f. Malagasy *talèva* the porphyrio and L. *gallus* cock.] *Ornith.* A genus of megapod birds inhabiting Australia and New Guinea. As English, chiefly applied to *T. lathami*, the Brush-turkey of Australia.

Talent (tæ·lĕnt), *sb.* [In OE. *talente, -an*, ad. L. *talenta*, pl. of *talentum*, ad. Gr. τάλαντον balance, weight, sum of money (f. vbl. root ταλ-, τλα- to bear).] **I.** A denomination of weight, used by the Assyrians, Babylonians, Greeks, Romans, and other ancient nations, varying greatly with time, people, and locality. **b.** The value of a talent weight (of gold, silver, etc.): a money of account OE. †**c.** *fig.* Treasure, riches, abundance -1635.

b. The Babylonian silver t. was equal to 3000 shekels; the Greek t. contained 60 minæ or 6000 silver drachmæ, and the value of the late Attic t. of silver, with pure silver at 4*s.* 9*d.* an oz. troy, has been estimated at £200. N.E.D.

II. †1. Inclination, propension, or disposition for anything; 'mind', 'will', wish, desire, appetite -1530. †2. An evil inclination, disposition, or passion; esp. and usu. anger -1695.

1. Grete t. and desyre..to knowe hym 1485. 2. One that had of a long time borne an ill T. towards the King BACON.

III. Mental endowment, natural ability. [From the parable of the talents, Matt. xxv. 14-30, etc.] 1. Power or ability of mind or body viewed as something divinely entrusted to a person for use and improvement. late ME. 2. A special natural ability or aptitude, usu. for something expressed or implied; a natural capacity for success in some department of mental or physical activity 1660. **b.** *pl.* Aptitudes or faculties of various kinds; mental powers of a superior order 1654. **c.** collect. *sing.* (without *a* or *pl.*). Mental power or ability; cleverness 1622. **d.** Talent as embodied in the talented; *occas.*, persons of ability collectively; rarely, as sing., a person of talent. By the sporting press, applied to backers of horses, as dist. from the bookmakers. 1856. †3. The characteristic disposition or aptitude of a person or animal -1774.

1. Though Nature weigh our talents, and dispense To every man his modicum of sense COWPER. 2. He is chiefly to be considered in his three different talents, as he was a critic, a satirist, and a writer of odes DRYDEN. b. The Duke of Buckingham, a man of talents and power GOLDSM. c. He was a person of no t. MORLEY. d. (*Administration of*) *All the Talents* (Eng. Hist.), an ironical appellation of the Ministry of Lord Grenville, 1806-7, implying that it combined in its members all the talents. 3. It is the t. of human nature to run from one extreme to another SWIFT. Hence **Ta·lent** *v.* (*rare*) *trans.* to endow with t. or talents; chiefly in *pa. pple.* (cf. next).

Talented (tæ·lĕntĕd), *a.* 1824. [f. prec. + -ED[2].] Endowed with talent or talents; possessing talent; gifted, clever, accomplished.

‖**Tales** (tēⁱ·līz). 1495. [L., pl. of *talis* such, in the phrase *tales de circumstantibus* 'such (or the like) persons from those standing about', occurring in the order for adding such persons to a jury.] *Law.* orig., in *pl.*, Persons taken from among those present in court or standing by, to serve on a jury in a case where the original panel has become deficient in number by challenge or other cause, these being persons *such* as those originally summoned; loosely applied in Eng. as a singular (*a tales*) to the supply of men (or even of one man) so provided. Also, contextually applied to the order or act of supplying such substitutes, as *to pray, grant, award a t.* Now restricted to such summoning of common jurors to serve on a special jury; orig., and still in U.S., in general use (including criminal jurisdiction).

Comb.: **t.-book**, the entry-book of persons summoned on a t. Hence **Talesman** (tēⁱ·līz-, tēⁱ·lzmæ̆n), a member of the t. impanelled to complete a jury.

Ta·le-te:ller. late ME. [f. TALE *sb.* + TELLER.] 1. A teller of tales or stories; a narrator. 2. A talebearer; a tell-tale. late ME.

Taliacotian (tæ:liăkō͡u·ʃiăn), *a.* 1656. [f. *Taliacotius*, latinized f. It. *Tagliacozzi* + -AN.] *Surg.* Of, pertaining to, or named after Tagliacozzi, a surgeon of Bologna (1546-99); esp. in *T. operation*, a plastic operation described by him for restoration of the nose by means of tissue taken from another part.

Talia·tion. *Obs.* exc. *Hist.* 1591. [f. L. *talis* such, the like, as if from a vb. **taliare*.] A return of like for like; retaliation; = TALION.

‖**Talio** (tēⁱ·lio). 1611. [L., f. *talis* such.] = next.

Talion (tæ·liən). late ME. [a. F., ad. L. *talionem*, nom. *talio*; see prec.] Retaliation; *esp.* in the Mosaic, Roman, and other systems of Law, the *lex talionis*, the principle of exacting compensation, 'eye for eye, tooth for tooth'; also, the infliction of the same penalty on the accuser who failed to prove his case as would have fallen upon the accused if found guilty.

‖**Talipes** (tæ·lipīz). 1857. [mod.L., f. L. *talus* ankle + *pes* foot.] 1. *Path.* Club-foot; clubfootedness. 2. *Zool.* A twisted disposition of the feet, occurring naturally in sloths 1891.

Talipot (tæ·lipǫt, -pət). 1681. [a. Sinh. *talapata*, Malayālam *tālipat*:—Skr. *tālapattra*, leaf of the *tāla* palmyra or fan-palm.] A South Indian fan-palm, *Corypha umbraculifera*, native in Ceylon and Malabar, noted for its great height, and its enormous fan-shaped leaves, which are much used as a material to write on.

†**Talisman**[1]. 1599. [= F. *talisman*, of uncertain history. See N.E.D.] A name formerly applied to a Turk learned in divinity and law, a Mullah; sometimes to a lower priest of Islam, a religious minister, a muezzin -1668.

Talisman[2] (tæ·lizmăn). 1638. [= F., Sp. *talisman*, It. *talismano*, ad. MGr. τέλεσμαν = Gr. τέλεσμα TELESM (whence Arab. *ṭilsam*, pl. *ṭilsamān*).] 1. A stone, ring, or other object engraven with figures or characters, to which are attributed the occult powers of the planetary influences and celestial configurations under which it was made; usu. worn as an amulet to avert evil from or bring fortune to the wearer; also, used medicinally to impart healing virtue; hence, any object held to be endowed with magic virtue; a charm. 2. *fig.* Anything that acts as a charm or by which extraordinary results are achieved 1784.

1. He had stolen from Henry..a T., which rendered its wearer invulnerable STUBBS. Hence **Talisma·nic, -al** *adjs.* of, pertaining to, or of the nature of a t., **-ly** *adv.*

Talk (tǭk), *sb.* 1475. [f. next.] The action or practice of talking. 1. Speech, discourse; *esp.* conversation (of a familiar kind). With *a* and *pl.* A conversation 1548. **b.** A short lecture 1900. 2. A more or less formal or public oral interchange of views, opinions, or propositions; a conference; an informal lecture. **b.** A palaver or pow-wow with savages; also, a verbal message to or from these. 1550. 3. Mention (of a subject); the making of statements and remarks; rumour, gossip, or an instance of this 1560. 4. The subject, theme, or occasion of topical conversation, esp. of current gossip or rumour 1624. 5. Utterance of words, speaking (to others), speech; also *contempt.*, empty words, verbiage 1539. **b.** Applied to writing of the nature of familiar or loose speech 1552.

1. We had t. enough, but no conversation; there was nothing discussed JOHNSON. 3. Great t. of a comet 1677. That would make a t. MRS. GASKELL. Phr. *The t. of the town.* 4. Just when these letters were the t. of all London MACAULAY. 5. Phr. *Tall t.*, speaking in a boastful or exaggerated fashion; see also SMALL TALK. **b.** Columns of..dangerous t. are appearing in most of our newspapers 1884.

Talk (tǭk), *v.* [ME. *talkien, talken*; a deriv. vb. from TALE *sb.* or TELL *v.* (**taljan*).] **I.** *intr.* 1. To convey or exchange ideas, information, etc. by means of speech, esp. the familiar speech of ordinary intercourse; to converse. **b.** To communicate by wireless signals 1912. 2. To exercise the faculty of speech; to speak, utter words, say things; often *contempt.*: to speak trivially, utter empty words, prate. late ME. **b.** To say something as a rumour or matter of gossip; hence, to indulge in idle or censorious gossip 1461. 3. To utter words, or the sound of words, unconsciously, mechanically, or imitatively, as *to t. in one's sleep, like a parrot*, etc. 1591. 4. *fig.* Of inanimate things: To make sounds or noises resembling or suggesting speech; to produce the effects of speech. 1793.

1. My mother and I talked at large on the subject 1819. Phr. *T. about..*, often used *colloq.* to contrast something already mentioned with something still more striking; T. about English people being fond of eating, that Canadian party beat all I had ever seen 1891. *T. of*, speak of, about, or in reference to (anything). *To t. of* (doing something), to speak somewhat vaguely, so as to suggest a notion, or express one's probable intention, of doing it. *Talking of..*, apropos of... 2. What canst thou talke..hast thou a tonge? SHAKS. A disposition to be talking for its own sake 1729. Phr. *To t. to*, to address words to; *colloq.* to rebuke, scold, reprimand. *To t. back*, to answer, esp. impertinently. **b.** They t. heere as if the King would goe a northerne progresse this summer 1669. Phr. *To t. big, tall*, etc., to talk boastfully, to indulge in inflated language. *To t. down* (*to* an audience), to adapt one's discourse to the assumed lower level of their intelligence. *To t. at*, to make remarks intended for some one but not directly addressed to him. **c.** *pregnantly*. To say something to the purpose 1840. 4. The ship was talking, as sailors say, loudly, treading the innumerable ripples with an incessant weltering splash STEVENSON.

II. *trans.* 1. To utter or speak in familiar language (words, a tale, etc.); to express in talk or speech (matter, opinions, etc.) ME. **b.** To use as a spoken language, to speak conversationally; as *to t. dialect, French, slang, Somerset.* 1859. 2. To discourse about. speak of, discuss. Now *colloq.* late ME. 3. To bring or drive (oneself or another) into some specified state by talking 1599.

1. **b.** *To t. Greek, Hebrew, Double-Dutch, gibberish*, etc., to use language unintelligible to the hearer. 2. Phr. *To t. shop*: see SHOP *sb.* 5. 3. They would talke themselves madde SHAKS. Phr. *To t.* (a person) *over* or *round*, to win over or bring into compliance by talking. *To t.* (a thing) *over*, *to t. over* (a matter), to discuss it in familiar conference or conversation. *To t. down*, to put down by talking; to out-talk. *To t. out*, to t. to the end of; to carry on the discussion of (a bill in Parliament, etc.) till the time for adjournment is reached, and so frustrate its progress by preventing its being put to the vote. *To t.* (a person) *into* or *out of*, to persuade into, or dissuade from (something) by talking. *To t. through one's hat*, to exaggerate or bluff or make wild statements (*slang*).

Talkative (tǭ·kătiv), *a.* late ME. [f. prec. + -ATIVE.] Given to talking; inclined to talk; chatty, loquacious; garrulous, 'full of prate' (J.). **b.** Said of personal qualities, etc. late ME.

b. Nothing is so t. as misfortune STEELE. Hence **Ta·lkative-ly** *adv.*, **-ness.**

Talkee-talkee (tǭ·ki,tǭ·ki). 1808. [A redupl. deriv. of TALK, with dimin. ending.] 1. The imperfect or broken English of some native races; *esp.* the lingua franca of negro slaves in the W. Indies. 2. Small-talk; chatter; continuous prattle; mere talk. *contempt.* 1812.

Talker (tǭ·kəɪ). late ME. [f. TALK *v.* + -ER[1].] One who talks or is given to talking; a speaker, a conversationalist; a talkative person.

Great Talkers should always be mistrusted 1701.

Talkie (tǭ·ki). 1928. [f. TALK(ING *picture* + -IE, -Y[6], after *movie*; cf. SPEAKIE.] A talking film or picture.

Talking (tǭ·kiŋ), *vbl. sb.* ME. [f. TALK *v.* + -ING[1].] The action of TALK *v.*

Words learn'd by rote a parrot may rehearse, But t. is not always to converse COWPER. *T. to*, a reprimand, an admonition (*colloq.*).

Talking (tǭ·kiŋ), *ppl. a.* 1562. [f. TALK *v.* + -ING[2].] That talks; loquacious.

The hawthorn bush, with seats beneath the shade, For t. age and whispering lovers made GOLDSM. *T. film, picture*, a cinematograph film accompanied by talking (and other sounds).

Talky (tǭ·ki), *a.* 1862. [f. TALK *sb.* + -Y[1].] Inclined to or abounding in talk; talkative, loquacious. Hence **Ta·lky-ta·lky** *a.* (cf. TALKEE-TALKEE) abounding in (mere) talk; not rising above the level of talk.

Tall (tǭl), *a.* ME. [Origin obsc.; prob. repr. OE. *ge-tæl* swift, prompt (with loss of prefix).] **I.** †1. Quick, prompt, ready, active (*rare*) -1542. †2. Meet, becoming, seemly -1440. †**b.** Comely, goodly, fair, handsome; elegant, fine -1656. †3. Good at arms; doughty, brave, bold, valiant -1825. †4. Phr. *t. of* (*his*) *hand*(*s*: sometimes, (cf. sense 1) ready, skilful with (his) hands; sometimes, (cf. sense 3) stout of arm, formidable with weapons -1632.

2. b. That such a base slave as he should be saluted by such a tall man as I am, from such a beautiful dame as you MARLOWE. 3. Now sirs, quite our selues like t. men and hardie UDALL

II. 1. Of a person: High of stature; of more than average height. Usu. appreciative. Also of animals, as a giraffe, stag, or the like. 1530. b. Having a specified or relative height; measuring in stature (so much): without implication of great height 1588. 2. Of things, as ships, trees, etc.: High, lofty; esp. of things high in proportion to their width, as *a t. chimney, mast*, etc. 1548. b. Of more than average length, measured from bottom to top 1608. 3. *fig.* †a. Lofty, grand, eminent -1827. b. High-flown, esp. in *t. talk* (TALK *sb.* 5). *colloq.* 1670. c. Exaggerated, highly coloured. *U.S. colloq.* 1846. d. Large, in amount; big. *slang* (*orig. U.S.*) 1842. †4. *fig.* Great, eminent (*at* something) -1662.

1. Fair Galatea,..T. as a Poplar, taper as the Bole DRYDEN. b. If a Man could make himself happy by imagining himself six Foot tall, tho' he was but three 1744. 2. A t. house in the city of Paris 1852. b. The faith they haue in Tennis and t. Stockings, Short blistred Breeches, and those types of Trauell SHAKS. *T. folio, t. copy* (of a book). *T. hat*, a man's silk hat with a high cylindrical crown. 3. c. 'T. stories' are the perquisite of every traveller 1897. d. It's a t. order, but it's worth trying 1893. Hence Ta·llness.

Tallage (tæ·lėdʒ), *sb.* ME. [a. OF. *taillage*, f. *tailler* TAIL *v.*² III; see -AGE.] orig., in *Eng. Hist.*, An arbitrary tax levied by Norman and early Angevin kings upon the towns and the demesne lands of the Crown; hence, a tax levied upon feudal dependants by their superiors; also, by extension, a municipal rate; a toll or customs duty; a grant, levy, imposition. Hence Ta·llage *v. trans.* to impose t. upon; to tax.

Tallboy (tǭ·lboi). 1676. [f. TALL *a.* + (app.) BOY.] 1. A tall-stemmed glass or goblet. Now *local.* 2. A tall chest of drawers (often raised on legs), usu. in two parts, one standing on the other; sometimes applied to a chest of drawers or a bureau standing on a dressing-table 1769. 3. A tall chimney-pot 1884.

Talliable (tæ·liăb'l), *a.* Now *Hist.* 1531. [a. OF. *taillable*, f. *tailler* TAIL *v.*² III.] Subject to tallage.

Talliate (tæ·li,eit), *v.* 1754. [f. med.L. *talliat-*, *talliare*; see TAIL *v.*²] *trans.* = TALLAGE *v.*

Ta·llier. Now only in Fr. form **tailleur** (taiyör). 1709. [f. F. *tailler* to deal (at cards).] *Cards.* In rouge-et-noir and similar card-games, the name of the dealer or banker.

Tallish (tǭ·liʃ), *a.* 1748. [f. TALL *a.* + -ISH ¹.] Inclining towards tallness; rather tall.

‖**Tallith** (tæ·liþ, ‖tal,lī·þ). 1613. [Rabbinical Heb. *tallīþ*, f. *ṭālal* to cover, shelter.] The garment or mantle (now often a scarf) worn by Jews at prayer.

Tallow (tæ·lōu), *sb.* [Late ME. *talȝ*, *talgh*, corresp. to MLG. *talg*, *talch*, M.Icel. *tólg*, *tólk*; ult. etym. unkn.] 1. The fat or adipose tissue of an animal, esp. that which yields the substance described in 2; suet. 2. A substance consisting of a somewhat hard animal fat (esp. that obtained from the parts about the kidneys of ruminating animals), separated from the membranes, etc., naturally mixed with it by melting and clarifying; used for making candles and soap, dressing leather, and other purposes. 3. Applied to various kinds of grease or greasy substances, e.g. those obtained from plants 1745.

attrib. and *Comb.*: t. **candle**, a candle made of t.; **-chandler**, one whose trade is to make or sell t. candles; **-chandlery**, the business of a t.-chandler; also, the place of work of a t.-chandler; **-tree**, any of various trees yielding substances resembling t.; *spec.* (*a*) *Stillingia sebifera*, a euphorbiaceous tree of China, also cultivated elsewhere for the fatty covering of its seeds; (*b*) *Pentadesma butyracea*, a guttiferous tree of Sierra Leone; (*c*) *Vateria indica* of Malabar; (*d*) *Eucalyptus microcorys* of Australia, called also **t.-wood.**

Ta·llow, *v.* ME. [f. prec.] 1. *trans.* To smear or anoint with tallow; to grease. †b. *intr.* (for *refl.*) -1720. 2. a. *intr.* Of cattle, etc.: To produce, or yield tallow 1722. b. *trans.* To cause (cattle, etc.) to form tallow; to fatten 1765.

2. b. The largest pasture..will neither skin nor t., or, in other words, is fit for nothing but young stock 1765.

Ta·llow-face. Now *rare* or *Obs.* 1592. A pale yellowish-white face; hence, a person having such a face.

Out you baggage, You tallow face SHAKS. So Ta·llow-faced *a.*

Tallowish (tæ·lōu,iʃ), *a.* 1552. [f. TALLOW *sb.* + -ISH ¹ 2.] Of the nature of or resembling tallow.

Tallowy (tæ·lōu,i), *a.* 1440. [f. as prec. + -Y ¹.] 1. Having the nature or properties of tallow; sebaceous. 2. Resembling tallow in colour or complexion 1832. 3. Of a beast: Abounding in tallow, fat 1495.

Tally (tæ·li), *sb.*¹ 1440. [In 15th c. *talye* = AF. *tallie* = Anglo-L. *talea*, *talia*, *tallia*, in same sense, L. *talea* cutting, rod, stick.] 1. A stick or rod of wood, usu. squared, marked on one side with notches representing the amount of a debt or payment. The rod being cleft lengthwise across the notches, the debtor and creditor each retained one of the halves, the tallying of which constituted legal proof of the debt, etc. b. Such a cloven rod, as the official receipt formerly given by the Exchequer for a tax, tallage, etc. paid, or in acknowledgement of a loan to the sovereign 1604. c. *transf.* Any tangible means of recording a payment or amount 1863. †2. The record of an amount due; a score or shot, an account -1833. 3. *fig.* (from 1 and 2). Reckoning, score, account. Now *rare.* 1614. 4. Each of the two corresponding halves or parts of anything; a thing, or part, that exactly fits or agrees with another thing or corresponding part, a counterpart; *fig.* an agreement, correspondence 1651. 5. A number, group, series, lot, tale; *esp.* a certain number or group (of things or persons) taken as the unit of computation 1674. b. The last of a specified number forming a unit of computation, on the completion of which the t.-man calls 'tally' and notes it down 1886. †6. A mark (such as the notch of a tally) representing a unit quantity, or a series or set of units -1807. 7. A distinguishing mark on a bale or case of merchandise, etc., corresponding to one in a list, for the purpose of comparison or identification; hence, a mark, label, ticket, or tab, used for this purpose, or to denote the weight and contents, etc.; a gardener's plant label 1860.

2. †*Upon* or *on t.*, on credit, 'on tick'. †*Petty t.* (Naut.), a petty account kept of a ship's provisions; hence *transf.* provisions. 4. So suited in their minds and persons That they were fram'd the tallies for each other DRYDEN. *To live* (*on*) *t.*, to cohabit without marriage (*slang*). 5. Used *spec.* in certain trades.

attrib. and *Comb.*, as *t.-book*, *-stick*, *-trade*; **t.-board**, a board on which an account is notched or chalked; **-clerk**, one who checks merchandise with a list in loading or discharging cargo; **-sheet**, a score-sheet, esp. (*U.S.*) in recording votes; **-stick**, a stick used as or like a t.

†**Tally**, *sb.*² 1706. [f. TALLY *v.*³] *Cards.* At faro, basset, etc., a deal -1760.

Tally (tæ·li), *v.*¹ 1440. [f. TALLY *sb.*¹] I. 1. *trans.* †To notch (a stick) so as to make it a tally; hence, to mark, score, set *down* or enter (a number, etc.) on or as on a tally; *transf.* to record, register. b. *spec.* To identify, count, and enter each bale, case, article, etc. of a cargo or lot of goods in loading or discharging 1812. c. To distinguish, mark, or identify (a bale of goods, etc.) by or as by a tally 1837. 2. To count or reckon *up*, to number. Now *rare*, 1542. †3. To deal on tally or credit; to open or have a credit account *with* any one -1724.

1. c. Leaving his people to mark and t. the bales MARRYAT. 2. They anchor'd at morning to t. their spoil 1885.

II. †1. *trans. fig.* To cause (things) to correspond or agree; to match; *pa. pple.* matched, suited, adapted -1812. 2. *intr.* To agree, as one half of a cloven tally with its fellow; to correspond or answer exactly; to accord, conform, fit. (The chief current sense.) 1705.

2. A Theory that does not exactly t. with fact 1738.

Ta·lly, *v.*² Now *rare.* 1450. [Origin obsc.] *Naut.* 1. *trans.* To haul taut (the fore or main lee-sheets). 2. *intr.* To catch hold or 'clap' *on* to a rope 1840.

†**Tally**, *v.*³ 1706. [ad. F. *tailler* TAIL *v.*²] *Cards. intr.* At faro, basset, etc., to be banker (i.e. to deal) -1748.

Tally (tǭ·l,li), *adv.* Now *rare* or *Obs.* ME. [f. TALL *a.* + -LY ².] In a tall manner. †1. In a seemly manner; elegantly; well, bravely -1450. 2. Highly, loftily 1611.

Tally-ho (tæ:li,hōu·), *int.* and *sb.* 1772. [app. an altered form of Fr. *taïaut*, *tayaut*, used in deer-hunting.] 1. The view-halloo raised by huntsmen on catching sight of the fox. used as *int.* and as *sb.* 1787. 2. orig., The proper name given to a fast day-coach between London and Birmingham, started in 1823; subsequently the name was appropriated by other fast coaches, and treated somewhat as a common noun. Also *t. coach.* 1831. b. *U.S.* A large four-in-hand coach or drag 1882.

Ta·lly-ho·, *v.* 1812. [f. prec.] 1. *trans.* To salute or make known the presence of (a fox) by the cry of 'tally-ho'. 2. *intr.* To cry 'tally-ho' or a similar call 1826.

Tallyman (tæ·limăn). 1654. [f. TALLY *sb.*¹ + MAN *sb.*] 1. One who carries on a tally-trade, or supplies goods on credit, to be paid for by instalments. 2. One who tallies, or keeps account of, anything; *spec.* a clerk who checks a cargo in loading or discharging 1888. 3. One who 'lives tally' with a woman. *slang.* 1890. So Ta·llywoman 1727.

Talma (tæ·lmă). *Pl.* -as. 1860. [Named after François Joseph *Talma*, French tragedian (1763-1826).] A cape or cloak worn by men, and also by women in the 19th c.

‖**Talmud** (tæ·lmŏd, talmū·d). 1532. [a. late Heb. *talmūd* instruction, f. *lāmad* to instruct, teach.] In the wide sense, The body of Jewish civil and ceremonial traditionary law, consisting of the MISHNAH or binding precepts of the elders, additional to and developed from the Pentateuch, and the later GEMARA or commentary upon these, forming a complement to the Mishnah. The term was orig. applied to the Gemara, of which two recensions exist, known respectively as the Jerusalem (or Palestinian) and the Babylonian T.; to the latter of which the name is in strictest use confined. Hence Talmu·dic, -al *adjs.* of or pertaining to the T.; contained in the T. Ta·lmudize *v.*

Talmudist (tæ·lmŏdist, talmū·dist). 1569. [f. prec. + -IST.] a. One of the authors of the Talmud. b. One who accepts the authority of the Talmud. c. A Talmudic scholar. Hence Talmudi·stic, -al *adjs.* = TALMUDICAL.

Talon (tæ·lən). late ME. [a. OF. :—Com. Rom. *talo, *talonem* heel, f. *talus* ankle.] I. †1. The 'heel' or hinder part of the foot of certain quadrupeds, as swine and deer, or of the hoof of a horse -1725. †b. The hallux of a bird -1577. 2. *pl.* The claws (or less usu. in *sing.* any claw) of a bird or beast. late ME. b. *spec.* The powerful claws of a bird of prey, or of a dragon, griffin, etc. late ME. c. Allusively applied to the grasping hands or fingers of human beings 1588. d. *fig.* 1586.

2. A kite..would have certainly carried me away in his talons SWIFT. d. That they may yet be able to save something from the talons of despotism BURKE.

II. 1. *transf.* A heel-like part or object. a. *Naut.* The curved back of a ship's rudder. *Obs.* or *arch.* 1485. b. *Arch.* An ogee moulding 1704. c. The projection on the bolt of a lock against which the key presses 1877. 2. *fig.* a. *Cards.* The remainder of the pack after the hands have been dealt 1891. b. *Comm.* The last portion of a sheet of coupons 1882.

‖**Talpa** (tæ·lpă). 1693. [L., mole.] 1. *Zool.* The genus typified by the common mole (*Talpa europæa*) 1706. 2. *Path.* An encysted cranial tumour; a wen 1693.

‖**Taluk, taluq** (tălu·k). *India.* 1799. [a. Urdū *ta'alluq* estate, f. Arab. *'alaqa* to adhere, be affixed.] *orig.* A hereditary estate belonging to a native proprietor; also, more usu., a subdivision of a *zillah* or district, comprising a number of villages placed for purposes of revenue under a native collector; a collectorate.

‖**Talukdar, taluqdar** (tălu·kdāɹ). *India.* 1798. [f. prec. + -*dār*, Pers. agential suffix.]

The holder of a taluk or hereditary estate, or the officer in charge of the district so called.

Talus[1] (tē̆ⁱ·lǒs, F. talü). 1645. [a. F. *talus*, †*talut*, ult. f. L. *talus* ankle (taken in sense of F. *talon* heel).] **1.** A slope; *spec.* in *Fortification*, the sloping side of a wall or earthwork, which gradually increases in thickness from above downwards. **2.** *Geol.* A sloping mass of detritus lying at the base of a cliff or the like, and consisting of material which has fallen from its face; also, the slope or inclination of the surface of such a mass 1830. **b.** *gen.* A mountain slope 1830.

‖**Talus**[2] (tē̆ⁱ·lǒs). *Pl.* **tali.** 1693. [L.] **1.** The ankle-bone or astragalus; also applied to an analogous part in birds and insects. **2.** *Path.* A variety of club-foot in which the toes are drawn up, the heel resting on the ground 1864. **3.** A nodular concretion somewhat resembling an astragalus bone 1728.

Ta·lwood. *Obs.* exc. *Hist.* ME. [Rendering of OF. *bois de tail*, f. *tail* cutting, cut.] Wood for fuel, usu. cut up to a prescribed size.

‖**Tamal** (tămā·l). Also *erron.* **tamale.** 1856. [Mexican Sp. *tamal*, pl. *tamales*.] A Mexican delicacy, made of crushed Indian corn, flavoured with pieces of meat or chicken, red pepper, etc., wrapped in corn-husks and baked.

‖**Tamandua** (tămæ·nduā). 1614. [Pg., a. Tupi *tamanduá*.] †**a.** orig., a name for the Brazilian Ant-eaters generally –1774. **b.** Now usu. restricted to the smaller *Tamandua tetradactyla* and its congeners 1834.

‖**Tamanoir** (tamanwār). 1849. [F., corrupt form of Carib *tamanoá*, = Tupi *tamanduá*; see prec.] The French name of the Great Ant-eater or Ant-bear, *Myrmecophaga jubata.*

Tamarack (tæ·mǎræk). 1841. [app. a native Indian name in Canada.] **a.** prop., The American Larch (*Larix americana*); also, the timber of this tree. **b.** Also, applied to the Black or Ridge-pole Pine (*Pinus murrayana*) of dry inland regions of western N. America, and app. sometimes to the Scrub Pine of the coast.

Tamarin (tæ·mǎrin). 1780. [a. F., a. native name in Carib dial. of Cayenne.] Any of several species of the genus *Midas* of S. Amer. marmosets or squirrel-monkeys.

Tamarind (tæ·mǎrind). 1533. [(ult.) ad. Arab. *tamr-hindī*, i.e. date of India.] **1.** The fruit of the tree *Tamarindus indica*, a brown pod containing one to twelve seeds embedded in a soft brown or reddish-black acid pulp, used medicinally, and in cookery as a relish, etc. In *Comm.*, *Med.*, etc. *tamarinds* is used for the pulp. **2.** A large tree, *Tamarindus indica*, of the family *Leguminosæ*, supposed to be a native of the E. Indies, but now cultivated in warm climates generally, bearing dark-green pinnate leaves and racemes of fragrant yellow flowers streaked with red, and producing the fruit described in 1, and a hard and heavy timber 1614. **3.** Applied to various trees (or their fruits) resembling the t. in some respect 1833.

3. Black, Black-crown, Brown, or **Velvet t.,** a small leguminous tree, *Codarium acutifolium* or *Dialium guineense.* **Wild t.,** applied to various leguminous trees or shrubs, as, in the W. Indies, *Pithecolobium filicifolium*; in Jamaica, *Acacia arborea*, etc.

attrib. and *Comb.*: **t.-fish,** a relish made from various kinds of Indian fish preserved with the acid pulp of the t. fruit; **-plum,** an E. Indian tree, *Dialium indicum*, or its fruit; **-tea, -water,** an infusion of tamarinds, used as a cooling drink.

Tamarisk (tæ·mǎrisk). late ME. [ad. late L. *tamariscus*, var. of *tamarix*, *-icem*; ult. source unkn.] A plant of the genus *Tamarix*, esp. *T. gallica*, the Common T. (called in L. *myrica*), a graceful evergreen shrub or small tree, with slender feathery branches and minute scale-like leaves, growing in sandy places in S. Europe and W. Asia, and now much planted by the sea-shore in the south of England. †**b.** A decoction of the leaves of this plant, formerly used in medicine –1718.

attrib. and *Comb.*; **t. salt,** salt found adhering to the trunk of *Tamarix orientalis* in edible quantity; **t. ware,** vessels or dishes of t. wood.

‖**Tamasha** (tămā·ʃă). *India.* 1872. [Urdū (Arab.), f. *masha(y)* to walk.] An entertainment, public function. **b.** A fuss, commotion 1882.

Tambour (tæ·mbuᵊɹ, -bəɹ), *sb.* 1484. [a. F.; see TABOR.] **1.** A drum; *spec.* the great or bass drum. ‖**b. T. de basque** [F.], a tambourine 1688. **2.** An instrument for recording pulsations, as in respiration 1877. **3.** (Also **tambor.**) A fish which makes a drumming noise, or which resembles a drum in form; as a fish of the genus *Pogonias*, a drum-fish; a globe-fish, swell-fish, or puffer 1854. **4.** A circular frame formed of one hoop fitting within another, in which silk, muslin, etc. is stretched for embroidering 1777. **b.** A species of embroidery in which patterns are worked with a needle of peculiar form on material stretched on such a frame; now superseded by pattern-weaving; in recent use = *t.-lace* 1813. **c.** A kind of fine gold or silver thread 1899. **5.** *Arch.* **a.** The core of a Corinthian or Composite capital. **b.** Any one of the courses forming the shaft of a cylindrical column. **c.** The wall of a circular building surrounded with columns. **d.** A round exterior building surrounding the base of a dome or cupola; also, the circular vertical part of a cupola. **e.** A projecting part of the wall of a tennis court. 1706. **6.** *Mil.* A small defensive work formed of palisades or earth, usu. in the form of a redan, to defend an entrance or passage 1834.

2. Each bag communicates by a separate air-tight tube with an air-tight t. on which a lever rests; so that any pressure on either bag is communicated to the cavity of its respective t., the lever of which is raised in proportion 1877.

attrib. and *Comb.*: **t.-frame,** = sense 4; **-lace,** a modern lace resembling t. (4 b), consisting of needle-work designs on machine-made net; **-needle,** the needle used in t.-work; **-stitch,** the loop-stitch used in t.-work; also, a stitch used in crochet.

Tambour (tæ·mbuᵊɹ, tæmbūᵊ·ɹ), *v.* 1774. [f. prec.] **1.** *trans.* To work or embroider in a tambour-frame; to ornament with tambour-work. **2.** *intr.* To work at a tambour-frame; to do tambour-work 1845.

‖**Tambourin** (F. tãnburæ̃, tæ·mburin). 1797. [F., dim. of *tambour* drum.] **1.** The long narrow drum or tabor used in Provence: see TABORIN 1833. **2.** A Provençal dance, orig. accompanied by the tambourin. **b.** Music for such a dance, in duple rhythm and quick time. 1797.

Tambourine (tæmbŭrī·n). 1579. [app. ad. F. *tambourin* (see prec.), used in the sense of F. *tambour de basque.*] **1.** A musical instrument consisting of a wooden hoop having skin or parchment stretched over one side, and pairs of small cymbals, called jingles, placed in slots round the circumference. It is played by shaking, striking with the knuckles, or drawing the fingers across the parchment. **2. T. pigeon** (also ellipt. *tambourine*): an African species of pigeon, so called from the resonance of its note 1891.

‖**Tambreet** (tæmbrī·t). 1840. [Mallangong lang. of New South Wales.] The Duckbilled Platypus.

Tame (tēⁱm), *a.* [OE. *tam* (*tǫm*) :—OTeut. **tamoz.* The Teut. stem *tam-* is cogn. w. that of L. *domare*, Gr. δαμᾶν to tame, subdue.] **1.** Of animals (rarely of men): Reclaimed from the wild state; brought under the control and care of man; domestic; domesticated. (Opp. to *wild.*) **b.** *joc.* Of a person: Domestic; kept for domestic or private use 1711. **2.** Applied to plants, also (in *U.S.*) to land: Cultivated, improved by culture; garden- as opp. to *wild.* late ME. **3.** Having the disposition or character of a domesticated animal; accustomed to man; not showing the natural shyness, fear of, or fierceness to man; also of persons, their disposition, etc.: made tractable, docile, or pliant OE. **4.** Subdued by taming; submissive; meek poor-spirited, pusillanimous; servile 1563. **5.** Lacking animation, force, or effectiveness; deficient in striking features; weak, spiritless, insipid, dull 1602. **b.** Of scenery: Wanting boldness; having no striking features 1807.

1. They have also t. Lions 1660. **2.** *fig.* His lordship sowed t. oats now after his wild ones THACKERAY. **3.** *T. cat*, one who is on the footing of a domestic cat; a person who is made a convenience by his friends. **4.** A t. surrender of their rights 1769. **5.** The t. correct paintings of the Flemish school GOLDSM. **b.** A broad expanse of t. arable country 1894. Hence **Ta·me·ly** *adv.*, **-ness.**

Tame (tēⁱm), *v.*[1] [ME. *tamen*, f. TAME *a.*] **1.** *trans.* To bring (a wild animal) under the control or into the service of man; to reclaim from the wild state; to domesticate. †**b.** To bring (a wild plant) under or into cultivation; to reclaim or improve (land) by cultivation –1746. **2.** To overcome the wildness or fierceness of (a man, animal, or thing); to subdue, subjugate, curb; to render gentle, tractable, or docile. late ME. **b.** *intr.* To become tame; to grow gentle, submissive, or sedate 1646. **3.** *trans.* To reduce the intensity of, tone *down*; to temper, soften, mellow; also, to render dull or uninteresting 1500.

1. To t. the vnicorne, and Lion wild SHAKS. **2.** She hoped she had tamed a high spirit or two in her day DICKENS. **3.** The first editors had tamed down some of the more startling statements 1847. Hence **Ta·meable, ta·mable** *a.* capable of being tamed. **Ta·meableness. Ta·meability** (ta·ma·).

Tame (tēⁱm), *v.*[2] Now *dial.* late ME. [Aphetic f. ATTAME, ENTAME *vbs.*] *trans.* To pierce, cut into (in fighting or carving); to cut or break into, so as to use. †**b.** To broach (a cask, bottle, etc.) –1681.

Tameless (tēⁱ·mlės), *a.* 1597. [f. TAME *v.*[1] + -LESS.] That has never been tamed; that cannot be tamed; untamed, untameable. Hence **Ta·melessness.**

Tamer (tēⁱ·məɹ). 1530. [f. TAME *v.*[1] + -ER [1].] One who or that which tames.

Tamil, Tamul (tæ·mĭl, -ŭl). 1734. [ad. *Tamir*, *Tamil*, native name of the people and language.] One of a race of people of the Dravidian stock, inhabiting the south-east of India and part of Ceylon. **b.** The language spoken by this people, the leading member of the Dravidian family. Also *attrib.* or as *adj.* Hence **Tami·lian (Tamu·lian)** *a.* Tamulic; *sb.* a member of the Tamil people. **Tamu·lic** *a.* pertaining to the Tamils or their language, Tamil.

Tammany (tæ·mǎni). 1683. The name of the central organization of the Democratic party in the City (formerly also in the State) of New York, located in *Tammany Hall*, in 14th Street, New York. In Eng. use associated with political and municipal corruption.

Tammy (tæ·mi), *sb.*[1] 1665. [Of uncertain origin; cf. F. *estame* worsted, *estamet* cloth-rash; also †*tamise* (perh. borrowed from Eng.) 'étoffe de laine lustrée'.] A fine worsted cloth of good quality, often with a glazed finish.

Ta·mmy, *sb.*[2] 1769. [app. a. F. *tamis* assim. to prec.] A strainer. Hence **Ta·mmy** *v. trans.* to strain through a t.

Tammy (tæ·mi), *sb.*[3] 1894. Short for *Tammy Shanter*, corruption of next.

Tam o' Shanter (tæməʃæ·nteɹ). 1840. [f. name of the hero of Burns's poem of that name.] In full *Tam o' Shanter bonnet, cap*: A soft woollen bonnet with flat circular crown, the circumference of which is about twice that of the head, formerly worn by Scottish ploughmen, etc.; introduced, in a modified form, *c* 1887, as a head-dress for girls and young women. Abbrev. *Tam*, TAMMY *sb.*[3]

Tamp (tæmp), *v.* 1819. [app. a 19th c. workmen's word; perh. a backformation from *tampin* (var. of TAMPION) taken as = *tamping.*] **1.** *trans. Mining.* **a.** To stop up (a bore-hole) with clay, sand, etc., rammed in upon the charge before firing the shot; also, to pack up (a gallery of a military mine) before firing it, in order to concentrate the effect. **b.** To ram home (the charge) in a bore-hole. Also *absol.* **2.** To ram down hard, so as to consolidate (earth, gravel, etc.); to pun; also, to pack (anything) round with earth so rammed down 1879.

2. The track is raised, the gravel tamped well under the ties, and the track is ready for use 1890. Hence **Ta·mper,** one who tamps a boring, etc.; also, a tamping-bar.

‖**Tampan** (tæ·mpæn). 1880. [perh. Sechuana name.] A S. African species of acarus remarkable for the venom of its bite.

Tamper (tæ·mpəɹ), *v.* 1567. [Before 1600 mostly spelt *temper*, and app. originating in TEMPER *v.*, as used in ref. to clay. *Tamper* was prob. a dial. or workmen's pronunciation.] †**I. a.** *intr.* To work in clay, etc. so as to mix it thoroughly. **b.** *trans.* To temper (clay). –1766. **II. 1.** *intr.* To work or busy oneself for some end; to machinate, scheme, plot. Const. *in* some practice, *for* something, *to do* something. 1596. **2.** To try to deal or enter into clandestine dealings *with*; often with connotation of improper interference with a person 1567. **3.** To have to do or interfere *with* improperly; to meddle *with* (a thing) 1601. **4.** To meddle or interfere *with* (a thing) so as to misuse, alter, corrupt, or pervert it 1593.

1. Others tamper'd For Fleetwood, Desborough, and Lambert 1678. The queen dowager tampered in this plot H. WALPOLE. 2. He was trafficking with her enemies and tampering with her friends 1852. 4. To have her up for tampering with the evidence DE FOE. Accused of..tampering with ballot boxes 1888. Hence **Ta·mperer,** one who tampers; a schemer, a meddler.

Tamping (tæ·mpiŋ), *vbl. sb.* 1828. [f. TAMP *v.* + -ING [1].] The action of TAMP *v.*; the plugging of a blast-hole above the charge; the packing of the part of a military mine nearest the charge with earth or other material. **b.** *concr.* The material used for this purpose 1828.

Comb.: **t.-bar, -iron,** = STEMMER; **-plug,** a plug or stopper used to block up a bore-hole.

Tampion, tompion (tæ·mpiən, tǫ·mp-). 1460. [a. F. *tampon*, nasalized var. of F. *tapon*, deriv. of *tape* plug.] †**1.** A plug for stopping an aperture –1882. †**2.** A disk-shaped or cylindrical piece of wood made to fit the bore of a muzzle-loading gun, and rammed home between the charge and the missile, to act as a wad –1828. **3.** A block of wood fitting into the muzzle of a gun, and serving to exclude rain, sea-water, etc. 1625. **4.** In the organ: A plug used to stop up the upper end of an organ-pipe 1864.

Tampon (tæ·mpǫ̈n), *sb.* 1860. [ad. F. *tampon*; etymologically a doublet of prec.] **1.** *Surg.* A plug or tent inserted tightly into a wound, orifice, etc., to arrest hæmorrhage, or used as a pessary. **2.** The dabber or inking ball used in lithography and copperplate printing. (So in Fr.) 1877. Hence **Ta·mpon** *v. trans. Surg.* to fill or stop (a wound, cavity, etc.) with a t.; to plug.

Tan (tæn), *sb.* (*a.*) 1604. [prob. a. F., = med.L. *tannum*, app. of Celtic origin; cf. Breton *tann* oak.] **I. 1.** The crushed bark of the oak or of other trees, an infusion of which is used in converting hides into leather. **b.** Spent bark from the tan-pits, used by gardeners, and for riding-courses, etc. 1739. **2.** The astringent principle contained in oak-bark, etc.; tannin; also, the solution of this, tan-liquor, 'ooze' 1800. **II. 1.** The brown colour of tan; tawny 1851. **b.** *esp.* The bronzed tint imparted to the skin by exposure to the sun or the weather 1827. **2.** *pl.* [ellipt. use of the adj.] Articles of dress, etc., of a tan colour; *esp.* tan shoes or boots 1902.

I. b. With the t. of a southern sun upon his face 1885.

attrib. and *Comb.*: **t.-bark,** = sense I. 1; **-bed,** a hot-bed made of spent t.; a bark-bed; **-ooze, -pickle,** the liquor of a t.-vat; **-ride,** a riding-track covered with t.; **-spud,** a curved chisel for peeling the bark from trees; **-stove,** a bark-stove; also, a hot-house with a bark-bed; **-vat,** the receptacle containing the 'ooze' in which the hides are laid in tanning.

B. *adj.* Of the colour of tan or of tanned leather; of a yellowish or reddish brown 1665.

Black and t. (see BLACK *a.*) Beautiful black and tan spaniels DISRAELI. *Black and Tans*: an armed force raised against the Sinn Feiners in 1921, so named from the mixture (black and khaki) of constabulary and military uniforms worn by them.

Tan (tæn), *v.* [Late OE. *tannian*, prob. f. med.L. *tannare* to tan, f. *tannum* TAN *sb.*] **1.** *trans.* To convert (skin or hide) into leather by steeping in an infusion of an astringent bark, as that of the oak, or by a similarly effective process. **b.** *transf.* To treat (fishing-nets, sails, etc.) with tanners' ooze or some preserving substance; also, to act upon as an astringent 1601. **c.** In the manufacture of artificial marble to steep (the composition) in a hardening and preservative preparation 1891. **2.** To make brown (the face or skin), esp. by exposure to the sun or weather; to embrown; hence, to make dark or tawny in colour 1530. **b.** *intr.* (for *refl.*) To become sunburnt or darkened by exposure 1530.

1. Phr. *To t.* (a person's) *hide*, also simply *to t.* (a person), to thrash soundly (*slang* or *colloq.*). 2. You shall tanne your selfe more upon the see than upon lande PALSGR. Often in pa. pple. **Tanned** (tænd).

Tan, *Math.* abbrev. of TANGENT B. 1.

‖**Tana** (tā·nă). *India.* 1803. [Hindī *thāna, thānā.*] A police station in India; formerly, a military station or fortified post. Hence ‖**Tanada·r,** an officer in charge of this 1802.

Tanager (tæ·nădʒəɹ). 1614. [ad. mod. L. *Tanagra*, for Tupi *tangara.*] *Ornith.* A bird of the genus *Tanagra* or family *Tanagridæ* of passerine birds, of Central and South America. Hence **Ta·nagrine** *a.* of or pertaining to tanagers; belonging to the family *Tanagridæ*, or subfamily *Tanagrinæ*. **Ta·nagroid (tangaroid)** *a.* resembling the tanagers.

Tanagra (tæ·nägrä). 1893. Applied to terra-cotta statuettes found in the neighbourhood of Tanagra in Bœotia.

Tandem (tæ·ndĕm), *sb.* and *adv.* 1785. [app. L. *tandem* at length (of time) used punningly.] **A.** *sb.* **1.** A two-wheeled vehicle drawn by two horses (or other beasts of draught) harnessed one before the other. **b.** *transf.* A pair of carriage-horses harnessed one before the other 1795. **2.** Short for *t. bicycle* (*tricycle*), *canoe, engine* 1884. **B.** *adv.* One behind the other, in single file; orig. of a team of two horses 1795.

A. 1. We shall..proceed in a t...to Inverary BYRON. B. Three logs chained t. constituted the load 1893.

attrib. and *Comb.*: **t. bicycle, (tricycle), canoe,** a bicycle (tricycle) or canoe for two persons, one seated behind the other; **t. engine,** a steam-engine with two cylinders one in front of the other, the two pistons working on a common piston-rod.

‖**Tandstickor** (tæ·nd,sti:kəɹ). 1884. [a. Swed. *tändstickor* matches.] In full *t. match*, a cheap kind of lucifer match imported from Sweden.

Tang (tæŋ), *sb.*[1] ME. [a. ON. *tange* point, spit of land, tang of a knife, etc.] **I. 1.** A projecting pointed part or instrument. **a.** The tongue of a serpent; the sting of an insect. Now *dial.* **b.** *dial.* A sharp point or spike; the pin of a buckle; one of the prongs or tines of a fork; a prong or tine of a stag's horn 1688. **2.** An extension of a metal tool or instrument, as a chisel, file, knife, axe, coulter, pike, scythe, sword, etc., by which it is secured to its handle or stock 1440. **3.** One of various fishes having spines, as the common t. (*Teuthis hepatus*), the blue t. (*T. cæruleus*), etc. 1734. **II. 1.** A penetrating taste or flavour; usu. an after-taste, or a disagreeable or alien taste from contact with something else 1440. **b.** A pungent odour, a penetrating scent 1858. **2.** A slight 'smack' *of* some quality, opinion, habit, form of speech, etc.; a 'suspicion', a suggestion; a trace, a touch *of* something 1593. **b.** Distinctive or characteristic flavour or quality 1868.

1. A strong t. of tallow or onion in your bread and butter 1806. 2. Some little t. of Gentry 1625. The language has a t. of Shakespear GRAY.

Tang (tæŋ), *sb.*[2] 1669. [Echoic.] The strong ringing note produced when a large bell or any sonorous body is suddenly struck with force, or a tense string is sharply plucked; often denoting a sound of a particular tone, esp. one of an unpleasant kind; a twang.

Tang (tæŋ), *sb.*[3] *dial.* 1547. [Of Norse origin; = Norw., Da., Færoese *tang* fucus, etc.] A collective name for large coarse seaweeds; tangle, sea-wrack; also called *sea-tang.*

Tang (tæŋ), *sb.*[4] Also **tangue.** 1891. [f. native name.] = TANREC.

Tang (tæŋ), *v.*[1] late ME. [f. TANG *sb.*[1]] **1.** *trans.* †To pierce, prick; to sting as a serpent or insect; also *absol.* Now *dial.* **2.** To furnish with a tang, spike, flange, etc. 1566. **3.** To affect with a tang or (unpleasant) taste 1686.

Tang (tæŋ), *v.*[2] 1556. [Mainly echoic.] **1.** *trans.* To strike (a bell or the like) so as to cause it to emit a sharp loud ringing note. **2.** To utter with a tang or ringing tone 1601. **3.** *intr.* To emit a sharp and loud ringing or clanging sound; to ring, clang 1686.

2. Let thy tongue t. arguments of state SHAKS. 3. The smallest urchin whose tongue could t., Shock'd the Dame with a volley of slang HOOD.

‖**Tanga** (tæ·ŋgă, ‖tǫ·ŋgă). *India.* 1598. [app. a. Pg. *tanga*, ad. *ṭaṅka* in various Indian vernaculars:—Skr. *ṭaṅka* a weight = 4 māshās (beans), a coin.] A name (orig. of a weight) given in India, Persia, and Turkestan to various coins (or moneys of account); still applied in certain places to a copper, in others to a silver coin.

‖**Tangalung** (tæ·ŋgălʊŋ). 1820. [Malay.] The civet cat of Sumatra and Java, *Viverra tangalunga*; the Sumatran civet.

Tangency (tæ·ndʒĕnsi). 1819. [f. L. *tangentem*; see -ENCY.] The quality or condition of being tangent; state of contact.

Tangent (tæ·ndʒĕnt), *a.* and *sb.* 1594. [ad. L. *tangens, tangentem*, pr. pple. of *tangere.*] **A.** *adj.* **1.** *Geom.* Of a line or surface in relation to another (curved) line or surface: Touching, i.e. meeting at a point and (ordinarily) not intersecting; in contact. **b.** *transf.* Said of the wheel of a bicycle or tricycle having the spokes tangent to the hub 1886. **2.** *fig.* 'Flying off at a tangent'; divergent, erratic 1787. **3.** *gen.* Touching, contiguous 1846.

1. All the vibrations t. to the little circle..are reflected perfectly polarized TYNDALL. 2. The voluble loquacity and t. style of reasoning of their new companion 1799.

B. *sb.* **1.** *Math.* (ellipt. for *t. line.*) **a.** *Trigonometry.* One of the three fundamental trigonometrical functions (cf. SECANT, SINE), orig. considered as functions of a circular arc, now usu. of an angle (viz. that subtended by such an arc at its centre); *orig.* The length of a straight line perpendicular to the radius touching one end of the arc and terminated by the *secant* drawn from the centre through the other end; in mod. use, the ratio of this line to the radius, or (equivalently, as a function of the angle) the ratio of the side of a right-angled triangle opposite the given angle (if acute) to that of the side opposite the other acute angle (the t. of an obtuse angle being numerically equal to that of its supplement, but of opposite sign). (Abbrev. *tan*) 1594. **b.** *Geom.* A straight line which touches a curve (or curved surface), i.e. meets it at a point and being produced does not (ordinarily) intersect it at that point 1655. **c.** In general use, chiefly *fig.* from b, esp. in phrases (*off*) *at, in, upon a t.*, i.e. off or away with sudden divergence, from the course or direction previously followed; abruptly from one course of action, subject, thought, etc., to another 1771. **2.** Short for *t. scale, galvanometer* 1861. **3.** A straight section of a railway track. *U.S. colloq.* 1895.

1. c. That manner which they have..of flying off in tangents when they are pressed BENTHAM.

Comb.: **t. backsight,** = *t. scale* (*a*); **galvanometer,** a galvanometer in which the t. of the angle of deflexion of the needle is proportional to the strength of the current passing through the coil; **t. scale,** (*a*) in *Gunnery*, a kind of breech-sight in which the heights of the steps or notches correspond to the tangents of the angle of elevation; (*b*) a graduated scale indicating the tangents of angles; **t. screw,** a screw working tangentially upon a toothed circle or arc so as to give it a slow motion for delicate measurements or adjustments; **t. sight,** = *t. scale* (*a*).

Tangential (tændʒe·nʃăl), *a.* (*sb.*) 1630. [f. L. **tangentia*, f. *tangentem* TANGENT; see -AL.] **1.** Of, pertaining to, or of the nature of, a tangent; identical with, or drawn at, a tangent to a curve or curved surface; acting along a tangent. **2.** *fig.* Going off suddenly 'at a tangent'; erratic; divergent; digressive 1867. **b.** That merely touches a subject or matter 1825.

2. A collection of mixed and t. information 1903. b. Emerson had only t. relations with the experiment 1885.

B. *sb.* Geom. *T. of a point* (in a curve of the third or higher order): the point at which a tangent at the given point meets the curve again 1858. Hence **Tange·ntially** *adv.*

Tangerine (tændʒĕrī·n), *a.* and *sb.* 1710. [f. *Tanger, Tangier* + -INE [1].] **A.** *adj.* Of or pertaining to, or native of Tangier, a seaport in Morocco, on the Strait of Gibraltar.

T. orange, a small flattened deep-coloured variety of orange from Tangier, *Citrus nobilis* var. *Tangeriana.*

B. *sb.* **1.** A native of Tangier 1860. **2.** A T. orange 1842. **b.** A deep orange colour 1899.

‖**Tanghin** (tæ·ŋgin). 1788. [a. F., ad. Malagasy *tangena, tangen'.*] **1.** A poison obtained from the kernels of *Tanghinia venenifera*, of the family *Apocynaceæ*, a shrub of Madagascar, the fruit of which is a large purplish drupe.

The kernels were formerly used by the natives to test the guilt of a suspected person. 2. The shrub itself: more prop. *tange·na* or *tangi·na* 1866.

Tangible (tæ·ndʒĭb'l), *a.* 1589. [a. L. *tangibilis*, f. *tangere* to touch; see -BLE.] 1. Capable of being touched; affecting the sense of touch; touchable. Hence, material, externally real, objective. 2. That may be discerned or discriminated by the sense of touch; as *a t. property* or *form* 1664. 3. *fig.* That can be laid hold of or grasped by the mind, or dealt with as a fact; that can be realized or shown to have substance 1709.

1. Not..much chance of winning t. rewards 1874. 3. T. ideas BERKELEY. Without any t. ground of complaint 1852. Hence **Tangibi·lity. Ta·ngibleness. Ta·ngibly** *adv.*

Tangle (tæ·ŋg'l), *sb.*[1] 1536. [= Norw. *taangel, tongul*, Færoese *tongul* the stalk of *Laminaria digitata*, app. deriv. of Icel. *þang* bladder-wrack.] 1. = TANG *sb.*[3] 2. *spec.* Either of two species of seaweed, *Laminaria* (*Fucus*) *digitata* and *L. saccharina*, having long leathery fronds which are edible, as is the young stalk 1724.

2. I never saw it cast ashore anything but dulse and t. SCOTT.

Comb.: **t. fish**, the needle-fish or pipe-fish, *Syngnathus acus*; **-picker**, a bird, the Turnstone (*Strepsilas interpres*).

Tangle (tæ·ŋg'l), *sb.*[2] 1615. [f. TANGLE *v.*] 1. A tangled condition, or *concr.* a tangled mass; a complication of threads, hairs, fibres, branches, boughs, or the like, confusedly intertwined, or of a single long thread, line, or rope, involved in coils, loops, and knots; a snarl, ravel, or complicated loose knot. Also *transf.* of streams, paths, etc. b. *spec.* A dredger for sweeping the sea-bed, consisting of a bar to which are attached a number of hempen 'mops', in the fibres of which the more delicate marine specimens are entangled 1883. 2. *fig.* A complicated and confused assemblage; a muddle, jumble, complication, puzzle; a confused network of opinions, facts, etc.; also, a perplexed state 1757.

1. The tangles of Neæra's hair MILT. This bow became covered with a tangle of creepers DARWIN. 2. The tangles of metaphysics 1858. He reduced into method and compass the..t. of facts and figures 1883.

Tangle, *sb.*[3] 1857. [perh. belonging to TANGLE *sb.*[1] or [2].] Applied to plants having long, winding, and often tangled stalks, as Water Milfoil and Pondweed; and to plants of tangled growth, as Blue Tangle(s, (U.S.) *Gaylussacia frondosa.*

Tangle (tæ·ŋg'l), *v.* ME. [app. a nasalized var. of obs. *tagle*, prob. of Scand. origin.] †1. *trans.* = ENTANGLE *v.* 2. Chiefly *refl.* and *pass.* –1671. 2. To involve in material things that surround or wind about, so as to hamper and obstruct; also, to cover or wreathe with intertwined growth or with something that obstructs 1506. 3. To catch and hold fast in or as in a net or snare; to entrap 1526. 4. To intertwist (threads, branches or the like) complicatedly or confusedly together; to intertwist the threads or parts of (a thing) in this way; to put or get (a long thread or a number of threads, etc.) into a tangle. Also *intr.* for *refl.* 1530.

1. Not willingly, but tangl'd in the fold Of dire necessity MILT. 2. A country tangled with rivers 1829. The hedges were tangled with wild rose bushes 1885. 3. Looke how a bird lyes tangled in a net SHAKS. 4. He had cut the knot which the Congress had only twisted and tangled MACAULAY. Hence **Ta·nglingly** *adv.*

Tanglefoot (tæ·ŋg'lfut), *a.* and *sb.* 1860. [f. prec. + FOOT *sb.*] A. *adj.* That tangles or entangles the foot. B. *sb.* That which tangles or entraps the foot; *spec. U.S. slang*, an intoxicating beverage, esp. whisky.

Tangly (tæ·ŋgli), *a.*[1] 1762. [f. TANGLE *sb.*[1] + -Y[1].] Strewn with, consisting of, or full of tangle.

Helpless, on the t. beach he lay 1762.

Ta·ngly, *a.*[2] 1813. [f. TANGLE *sb.*[2] + -Y[1].] Abounding in tangles; tangled.

The jungle's t. growth 1899.

Tango (tæ·ŋgoᵘ), *sb.* 1913. [Amer Sp., negro or native dance, music for this, (in Honduras) musical instrument of the tambourine kind.] A Spanish (or S. Amer.) dance adapted for the ballroom; the music for this. Hence **Ta·ngo** *v.* to dance the t.

Tangram (tæ·ŋgræm). 1864. [Origin obsc.] A Chinese geometrical puzzle consisting of a square dissected into five triangles, a square, and a rhomboid, which can be combined so as to make two equal squares, and also so as to form several hundred figures, having a rude resemblance to houses, boats, bottles, glasses, urns, birds, beasts, men, etc.

‖**Tania, tan(n)ier** (ta·nyă, tæ·nyəɹ). 1756. [a. Tupi *taña, taya*, Carib *taya.*] A species of *Caladium* or *Xanthosoma* (*X. sagittifolium*), of the family *Araceæ*, cultivated in Brazil, the West Indies, and tropical Africa, for its farinaceous tuberous root.

Tanist (tæ·nist). 1538. [ad. Ir. and Gael. *tánaiste* anything parallel or second to another, the next heir to an estate.] *Anc. Ir.* and *Gaelic Law.* The successor apparent to a Celtic chief, usu. the most vigorous adult of his kin, elected during the lifetime of the chief.

The T. he to great O'Neale SCOTT.

Tanistry (tæ·nistri). 1589. [f. prec. + -RY.] *Anc. Ir.* and *Gaelic Law.* A system of life-tenure among the ancient Irish and Gaels, whereby the succession to an estate or dignity was conferred by election upon the 'eldest and worthiest' among the surviving kinsmen of the deceased lord. †b. The office of a tanist. SCOTT.

Tank[1] (tæŋk). 1616. [In sense 1, perh. from an Indian vernacular; or f. Pg. *tanque* pond = Sp. *estanque*, F. *étang*:—L. *stagnum.*] 1. In India, a pool or lake, or an artificial reservoir or cistern, used for purposes of irrigation, and as a storage-place for drinking-water. b. A natural pool or pond; a 'stank'. *dial.* and *U.S.* 1678. 2. An artificial receptacle, usu. rectangular or cylindrical and often of plate-iron, used for storing liquids or gases 1690.

attrib. and *Comb.*: **t.-engine**, a railway engine which carries the fuel and water receptacles on its own framing and not in a separate tender; **-iron, -plate**, plate-iron of a thickness suitable for making tanks; **-steamer**, one fitted with a t. for carrying liquids, esp. mineral oils, in bulk; **-worm**, a nematoid worm inhabiting the mud of Indian tanks, and believed to be the young of the guinea worm.

Tank[2] (tæŋk). [Special use of TANK[1] adopted in December 1915 for the purpose of secrecy during manufacture.] A type of armoured car with caterpillar wheels, equipped with a crew and guns, for attacking an enemy in difficult country.

‖**Tanka** (tæ·ŋkă). Also **tankia, tanchia.** 1839. [f. Chinese *tan* lit. egg + Cantonese *ka*, in South Mandarin *kia*, North Mandarin *chia* family, people.] The boat-population of Canton, who live entirely on the boats by which they earn their living; they are descendants of some aboriginal tribe of which *Tan* was app. the name. *T. boat*, a boat of the kind in which these people live.

Ta·nkage (-èdʒ). 1866. [f. TANK *sb.*[1] + -AGE.] 1. Tanks collectively; a provision or system of storage-tanks, sometimes with special ref. to its capacity. 2. The act or process of storing liquid in tanks; the price charged for this 1891. 3. The residue from tanks in which fat, etc. has been rendered, used as a coarse food, and as manure 1886.

Tankard (tæ·ŋkăɹd). ME. [= MDu., Du. *tanckaert.* Ulterior history unkn.] †1. A large open tub-like vessel, usu. of wood hooped with iron, etc.; *spec.* such a vessel used for carrying water, etc. –1688. 2. A drinking-vessel, formerly made of wooden staves and hooped; now *esp.* a tall one-handled mug or jug, usu. of pewter, occas. with a lid, used chiefly for beer 1485. b. *transf.* in COOL *tankard* 1700.

2. Tankards foaming from the tap WORDSW.

Comb.: **t.-turnip**, a variety of turnip with a long tuber.

Tanker (tæ·ŋkəɹ). 1900. [f. TANK *sb.*[1] + -ER[1].] A tank-steamer. Also *t.-ship.*

Ta·nling. *rare.* 1611. [f. TAN *a.* + -LING.] One tanned by the sun's rays.

To be still hot Summers Tanlings, and The shrinking Slaues of Winter SHAKS.

Tannage (tæ·nèdʒ). 1662. [f. TAN *v.* + -AGE, or a. F.] The art or process of tanning; also *concr.* the produce of tanning.

Tannate (tæ·nět). 1802. [a. F., f. TANNIC + -ATE[4].] *Chem.* A salt of tannic acid.

Tanned: see TAN *v.*

Tanner[1] (tæ·nəɹ). [OE. *tannere* (rare) and OF. *tanere*, acc. *taneör, tanour*:—L. *tannator, -orem.*] One whose occupation is to tan hides.

Tanner[2] (tæ·nəɹ). *slang.* 1811. [Origin obsc.] A sixpence.

Tannery (tæ·nəri). late ME. [f. TANNER[1] + -Y[3].] 1. A place where tanning is carried on 1736. 2. The process or trade of tanning; tannage. late ME.

Tannic (tæ·nik), *a.* 1836. [f. next + -IC.] *Chem.* In *t. acid*: orig. applied to the tannin principle obtained from oak-galls, a white amorphous strongly astringent substance, $C_{14}H_{10}O_9$, now dist. from other forms of tannin as GALLOTANNIC *acid.* Now chiefly used in a general sense to include a great number of allied substances, which differ in the proportion of their elements.

Tannin (tæ·nin). 1802. [a. F. *tanin* 'le principe tannant', f. *tan* TAN *sb.* + -IN[1].] *Chem.* Any member of a group of astringent vegetable substances, the *tannins*, which possess the property of combining with animal hide and converting it into leather. (Cf. GALLOTANNIN.)

Tanno- (tæ·no). Combining base of *tannic, tannin*, as in **Tannocaffe·ic** *acid* = CAFFETANNIC ACID. **Tannoga·llic** *a.* = GALLOTANNIC.

‖**Tanrec, tenrec** (tæ·n-, te·nrek). 1729. [= F. *tanrec*, ad. Malagasy *tàndraka*, dial. form of *tràndraka*, the native name.] An insectivorous mammal, *Centetes ecaudatus*, allied to the hedgehog, and covered with spiny bristles intermixed with silky hairs; the Madagascar hedgehog. Also, any species of the genus *Centetes* or of the family *Centetidæ.*

Tansy (tæ·nzi). late ME. [a. OF. *tanesie*, mod.F. *tanaisie*, aphetic f. *athanasie*, ad. med. L. *athanasia* tansy, a. Gr. ἀθανασία immortality. Cf. EVERLASTING and F. *immortelle.*] 1. An erect herbaceous plant, *Tanacetum vulgare*, growing about two feet high, with deeply cut and divided leaves, and terminal corymbs of yellow rayless button-like flowers; all parts of the plant have a strong aromatic scent and bitter taste. 2. Applied to other plants, esp. the Silverweed or Goose-grass, *Potentilla anserina* (Wild, Dog's or Goose T.). late ME. 3. A pudding, omelet, or the like, flavoured with juice of tansy. (Said to have been eaten at Easter in memory of the 'bitter herbs' of the Passover.) *arch.* or *dial.* 1450.

3. Spent an houre or two..with her, and eat a t. PEPYS. Phr. †*Like a t.* [origin unkn.], properly, perfectly; perfect.

Tantalate (tæ·ntălět). 1849. [f. TANTAL(UM + -ATE[4].] *Chem.* A salt of tantalic acid.

Tantalic (tæntæ·lik), *a.* 1842. [f. TANTALUM + -IC.] *Chem.* Of or derived from tantalum; in names of chemical compounds in which tantalum is pentavalent, as *t. chloride*; *t. oxide, anhydride*, Ta_2O_5.

Tantalite (tæ·ntăləit). 1805. [ad. G. and Sw. *tantalit*, f. TANTALUM (of which it is a source); see -ITE[1].] *Min.* Native tantalate of iron or ferrous tantalate, found in black lustrous crystals.

Tantalize (tæ·ntăləiz), *v.* 1597. [f. TANTALUS + -IZE.] 1. *trans.* To subject to torment like that inflicted on Tantalus; to torment by the sight, show, or promise of a desired thing which is kept out of reach, or removed or withheld when on the point of being grasped. Also *absol.* b. *fig.* To tease or torture into an artificial form 1807. †2. *intr.* To act Tantalus; to suffer like Tantalus –1673.

1. Our Richard II. was starved at Pomfret Castle by being tantalized TRAPP. Hence **Ta·ntaliza·tion, Ta·ntalizer. Ta·ntalizingly** *adv.*

Tantalous (tæ·ntăləs), *a.* 1868. [f. next + -OUS.] *Chem.* Applied to compounds containing a greater proportion of tantalum than those called *tantalic*, as *t. oxide*, tantalum dioxide, TaO_2.

Tantalum (tæ·ntălŏm). 1809. [f. next, with the ending *-um* (more usu. *-ium*) appropriate to metallic elements. So called by Ekeberg, 'partly in allusion to its incapacity, when immersed in acid, to absorb any and be saturated'.] *Chem.* A rare metal, occurring in combination in various rare minerals, and in certain metallic ores; discovered in 1802 by Ekeberg in two minerals, which he named *tantalite* and *yttrotantalite*. It has been isolated as a solid of greyish-white colour and metallic lustre, and is used for the incandescent filament of electric lamps. Atomic weight 182; symbol Ta. Also *attrib.*, as *t. lamp*.

Tantalus (tæ·ntălŏs). late ME. [L., a. Gr. Τάνταλος.] 1. Name of a mythical king of Phrygia, son of Zeus and the nymph Pluto, condemned, for revealing the secrets of the gods, to stand in Tartarus up to his chin in water, which constantly receded as he stooped to drink; he had branches of fruit hanging above him which always evaded his grasp. Hence *allus.* 2. A stand containing (usu. three) decanters which, though apparently free, cannot be withdrawn until the grooved bar which engages the stoppers is raised 1898. 3. *Ornith.* A genus of storks, including *T. ibis*; the wood stork or wood ibis 1824.

1. It seems like our cup of T.: we are never to reach it KANE.

†**Ta·ntamount**, *sb.* 1637. [app. f. TANTAMOUNT *v.*] Something equivalent (*to*); an equivalent –1646.

Tantamount (tæ·ntămaunt), *a.* 1641. [app. from the sb.] As much; that amounts to as much, that comes to the same thing; of the same amount; equivalent. Usu. const. *to*.

They are t. to a plain acknowledgement 1659. A t. service should be given in exchange for them 1868.

†**Ta·ntamount**, *v.* 1628. [a. AF. *tant amunter*, or perh. ad. It. *tanto montare* to amount to as much.] 1. *intr.* To amount to as much, to come to the same thing; to be or become equivalent –1716. 2. *trans.* To amount or come up to (something); to equal –1683.

1. It ought to be pardoned specially, or by words which tant amount COKE.

Tantara (tæ·ntără, tæntā·ră), *int.* and *sb.* Also extended tantara·ra, etc. 1537. [Echoic.] A. *int.* Imitative of the sound of a flourish blown on a trumpet, or sometimes of a drum. B. *sb.* A fanfare, or flourish of trumpets; hence, any similar sound 1584.

‖**Tanti** (tæ·ntəi). 1590. [L., 'of so much (value)', gen. of *tantum*, neut. of *tantus* so great.] Of so much value, worth so much; worth while. †As an exclam.: So much *for*...!

Is it *t.* to kill yourself, in order to leave a vast deal of money to your heirs? WARBURTON.

Tantivy (tæ·ntivi, tænti·vi), *adv.*, *sb.*, *a.*, *int.* Now *rare* or *arch.* 1641. [Origin obsc.; perh. echoic, repr. the sound of a horse's feet.] †A. *adv.* At full gallop; headlong –1823.

Up at five a' Clock in the morning..And T. all the country over, where Hunting..or any Sport is to be made 1641.

B. *sb.* 1. (from the adv.) A rapid gallop; a ride at this pace 1658. 2. A nickname given to the post-Restoration High-Churchmen and Tories, esp. in the reigns of Charles II and James II. See N.E.D. 1680. 3. *erron.* applied to a blast or flourish on a horn 1785. C. *adj.* perh. orig. in *t. men* and the like, attrib. use of B. 1; afterwards often of B. 2. 1681.

C. Master Wildrake is one of the old school—one of the t. boys SCOTT.

D. *int.* An imitation of the sound of galloping or scudding feet; later (*erron.*) of the sound of a horn 1697. Hence †Tantivy *v.* (*rare*) *intr.* to ride full tilt, to hurry away.

‖**Tanto** (ta·ntǫ), *adv.* 1876. [It.:—L. *tantum* so much.] *Mus.* So, so much: as *allegro non tanto*, fast, but not too fast.

Tantony (tæ·ntəni). 1567. Shortened form of *St. Anthony*, chiefly used *attrib.*; *spec.* a. (in full *t. bell*) a hand-bell; a small church bell; b. (in full *t. pig*) [St. Anthony the hermit, usu. represented as accompanied by a pig, being the patron of swine-herds], the smallest pig of a litter 1659.

fig. Dangling after me every where, like a t. pig 1765.

‖**Tantra** (tæ·ntră). 1799. [Skr., loom, warp, hence groundwork, system, doctrine, etc., f. *tan* to stretch, extend.] One of a class of Hindu religious works in Sanskrit, of comparatively recent date, chiefly of magical and mystical nature; also, one of a class of Buddhist works of similar character. Hence **Ta·ntrism**, the doctrine of the Tantras. **Ta·ntrist**.

Tantrum (tæ·ntrŏm). *colloq.* 1748. [Origin unkn.] An outburst or display of petulance or ill-temper; a fit of passion. Mostly in *pl.*

Taoism (tā·oˌiz'm). 1839. [Cf. Chinese *tao* way, path, right way (of life), reason + -ISM.] A system of religion, founded on the doctrine set forth in the work *Tao tê king* 'Book of reason and virtue', attributed to the ancient Chinese philosopher Lao-tsze (or Lao-tzŭ), born 604 B.C. It ranks with Confucianism and Buddhism as one of the three religions of China. So **Ta·oist**; also *attrib.* or as *adj.*; hence **Taoi·stic** *a.*

‖**Taotai** (tā·otai). 1876. [Chinese *tao* circuit, division, *t'ai* eminence.] A provincial officer in a *tao*.

Tap (tæp), *sb.*[1] [Com. Teut.; OE. *tæppa* :—OTeut. **tappon-*, orig. a tapering cylindrical stick or peg (cf. *tap-root*).] 1. A cylindrical stick, long peg, or stopper, for closing or opening a hole bored in a vessel; hence, a hollow or tubular plug through which liquid may be drawn, having some device for shutting off or governing the flow; a cock, a 'faucet', esp. for turning on the water over a sink, bath, etc. 2. A tap-room or tap-house. *colloq.* 1725. 3. The liquor drawn from a particular tap; a particular species or quality of drink. Also *fig.* a particular strain or kind of anything. *colloq.* 1623. 4. *Mech.* A tool used for cutting the thread of an internal screw, consisting of a male screw of hardened steel, grooved lengthways to form cutting edges, and having a square head so that it may be turned by a wrench 1677. 5. An object having the shape of a slender tapering cylinder, as an icicle; *esp.* a t.-root 1658.

1. Phr. *On (in) t.*, on draught, ready for immediate consumption or use; *on t.* spec. of treasury bills, etc. obtainable when and as required at a fixed rate; so *t. rate*, etc.

attrib. and *Comb.*, as *t.-boy*, *-man*; **t.-bolt**, a threaded bolt which is screwed into a part, as dist. from one that penetrates it and receives a nut; **-cinder**, the slag or refuse produced in a puddling furnace; **-rivet**, **-screw**, = *t.-bolt*.

Tap (tæp), *sb.*[2] late ME. [f. TAP *v.*[2]; cf. F. *tape* slap.] 1. A single act of tapping; a light but audible blow or rap; the sound made by such a blow. 2. *pl.* (*U.S. Mil.*) A signal sounded on the drum or trumpet, fifteen minutes after the tattoo, at which all lights in the soldiers' quarters are to be extinguished. Sounded also over the grave of a soldier. 1862. 3. A piece of leather with which the worn-down heel or sole of a boot is 'tapped' (*U.S.*); a plate or piece of iron with which the heel is shielded 1688.

Tap-tap, a repeated t.; a series of taps; also *adv.* Comb. *t.-dancing*, exhibition dancing characterized by rhythmical tapping of the feet.

Tap (tæp), *v.*[1] [Com. Teut.; OE. *tæppian*, f. *tæppa* TAP *sb.*[1]] I. To open (a cask, reservoir). 1. *trans.* To furnish (a cask, etc.) with a tap or spout, in order to draw the liquor from it. 2. To pierce (a vessel, tree, etc.) so as to draw off its liquid contents; to broach; to draw liquid from (any reservoir); *slang*, to draw blood from the nose 1694. b. *spec.* in *Surg.* To pierce the body-wall of (a person) so as to draw off accumulated liquid; to drain (a cavity) of accumulated liquid 1655. c. To divert part of the current from (an electric wire or cable), esp. so as to intercept a telegraphic communication 1879. 3. *fig.* To open up (anything) so as to liberate or extract something from it; to open, penetrate, break into, begin to use 1575.

2. The season for tapping the [maple] trees is in March 1792.

II. To draw off (liquid, etc.). 1. To draw (liquor) from a tap; to draw and sell in small quantities. late ME. †b. *absol.* To draw liquor; to act as a tapster –1625. 2. To draw off (liquid) from any source 1597. †b. *intr. fig.* To spend or 'bleed' freely. *slang.* –1713.

1. b. *Merry W.* I. iii. 11. 2. *To tap one's claret*, to cause one's nose to bleed; He told Verdant, that his claret had been repeatedly tapped 1853.

III. 1. *Mech.* a. To furnish (a hole) with an internal screw-thread, or (any part) with a threaded hole 1808. b. To furnish with an external screw-thread; to convert (a bolt or rod) into a screw 1815. c. To cause to pass through or in by screwing 1869. 2. To deprive (a plant) of its tap-root 1792.

Tap (tæp), *v.*[2] [ME. *tappen*, of echoic origin.] 1. *trans.* To strike lightly, but clearly and audibly; rarely applied by meiosis to a sharp knock or rap. b. To strike (the foot, hand, etc.) lightly upon something 1500. 2. *intr.* and *absol.* To strike a light but distinct blow; to make a sound by so striking, e. g. on a drum; *esp.* to knock lightly *on* or *at* a door, etc. in order to attract attention. late ME. 3. *trans.* To add a thickness of leather to the sole or heel of (a shoe) in repairing. *dial.* and *U.S.* 1818.

1. He sate there tapping his boot with his cane THACKERAY. 2. She tapped gently at the door 1791.

‖**Tapa** (ta·pă). Also **tappa**. 1823. [Com. Polynesian *tapa*.] A kind of unwoven cloth made by the natives of Polynesia from the bark of the Paper Mulberry (*Broussonetia papyrifera*). Also *attrib.* as *t. cloth*, *mat*.

‖**Tapayaxin** (tæpăyæ·ksin). 1753. [Native Mexican.] The orbicular horned lizard, *Phrynosoma orbiculare*, incorrectly called the *Horned Frog* or *Toad*.

Tape (tēⁱp), *sb.* late ME. [Relation to OE. *tæppan* pl. 'tenia' uncertain.] 1. A narrow woven strip of stout linen, cotton, silk, etc. used as a string for tying garments, as binding, as measuring lines, etc. b. Without article, as name of the material. Also *fig.*: see RED-TAPE. 1537. c. A piece of tape suspended across the course at the finishing point in a race, or (formerly) between the goal-posts in Association football 1867. 2. A long, narrow, thin and flexible strip of metal or the like; *esp.* such a strip of steel used as a measuring line in surveying 1884. b. The paper strip or ribbon on which messages are printed in the receiving instrument of a recording telegraph system 1884. 3. *slang.* Spirituous liquor, esp. gin (*white t.*); brandy (*red t.*) 1725.

1. A black Box..tied about with a white T. 1690. b. *fig.* Twenty years gone in t. and circumlocution 1856. 2. Base measurement with steel tapes 1900. b. Now we watch the t., day by day, and hour by hour 1888.

attrib. and *Comb.*: **t.-fish**, a ribbon-fish; **-grass**, an aquatic herb, *Vallisneria spiralis*, with narrow grass-like leaves; **-line**, a line of t.; *spec.* a strip of linen or steel marked with subdivisions of the foot or metre, sometimes coiling in a cylindrical case with a winch or spring; **-machine**, the receiving instrument of a recording telegraph system, in which the message is printed on a paper t.; **-measure**, a measuring line of prepared t., marked with feet and inches, etc., esp. one of five or six feet long used by tailors, dress-makers, etc.; **-needle**, an eyed bodkin for inserting t.

Tape (tēⁱp), *v.* 1609. [f. prec.] I. *trans.* To attach a tape or tapes to; to tie *up*, fasten, bind, or wind with tape; *spec.* in *Bookbinding*, to join the sections of (a book) with tape. 2. *trans.* To measure with a tape-line 1886. 3. *intr.* To appear (of such a size) on measurement with a tape; to measure (so much) 1895.

2. fig. phr. (colloq.) *To have* (a person) *taped*: to have taken his measure, to have summed him up.

Taper (tēⁱ·pəɹ), *sb.*[1] [OE. *tapur*, *-or*, *-er*; not in cogn. langs.] *orig.* A wax candle, in early times used chiefly for devotional or penitential purposes; now *spec.* a long wick coated with wax for temporary use as a spill, etc. b. *fig.* Something that gives light or is figured as burning; in mod. use esp. a thing that gives a feeble light OE.

b. The Apostles, those holy Tapours of the..Church 1635. To husband out life's t. at the close GOLDSM.

Taper (tēⁱ·pəɹ), *sb.*[2] 1793. [f. the vb. or adj.] 1. Gradual diminution in width or thickness in an elongated object; *fig.* gradual decrease of action, power, capacity, etc. 2. Anything that gradually diminishes in size towards one extremity, as a tapered tube 1882.

Taper, *sb.*[3]: see TADPOLE[2].

Taper (tēⁱ·pəɹ), *a.* 1496. [f. TAPER *sb.*[1]] Diminishing gradually in breadth or thickness towards one extremity (orig., upward); tapering.

To the fine t. fingers' ends 1821. Hence Ta·perness.

Taper (tēⁱ·pəɹ), *v.* 1589. [f. TAPER *sb.*[1]] †**1.** *intr.* To rise or shoot up like a flame, spire, or pyramid; *fig.* to rise or mount up continuously in honour, dignity, rank, etc. –1887. **2.** To narrow or diminish gradually in breadth or thickness towards one end; to grow smaller by degrees in one direction. Also *fig.* 1610. **3.** *trans.* To reduce gradually in breadth or thickness in one direction; to make tapering 1675. Hence **Ta·pering** *ppl. a.*, **-ly** *adv.*

Tapered (tēⁱ·pəɹd), *a.* 1745. [f. TAPER *sb.*[1] + -ED[2].] Lighted by, or accompanied by the use of, tapers.

Tapered (tēⁱ·pəɹd), *ppl. a.* 1669. [f. prec. + -ED[1].] Made to taper; diminished in thickness or breadth by degrees; tapering, taper.

Tapestry (tæ·pėstri), *sb.* late ME. [Corruption of *tapesry*, *tapesserie*, or other form of TAPISSERY. (In Milton and Dryden a disyllable.)] A textile fabric decorated with ornamental designs or pictorial subjects, painted, embroidered, or woven in colours, used for wall hangings, curtains, etc.; esp., such a decorated fabric in which a weft containing ornamental designs in coloured wool or silk, gold or silver thread, etc., is worked with bobbins or broaches, and pressed close with a comb, on a warp of hemp or flax stretched in a frame. Often loosely applied to imitative textile fabrics.

Comb.: **t.-carpet**, a carpet resembling Brussels, but in which the warp-yarn forming the pile is coloured so as to produce the pattern when woven; **-moth**, a species of clothes-moth, as *Tinea tapetzella*; **-stitch**, used loosely for various stitches used in tapestry work; **-weaving**, the weaving of t.; the method of weaving by bobbin and comb, used in making t., as dist. from weaving in a loom with a shuttle; **-work**, tapestry.

Tapestry (tæ·pėstri), *v.* 1630. [f. prec.] **1.** *trans.* To cover, hang, or adorn with, or as with, tapestry. (Chiefly in *pass.*) **2.** To work or depict in tapestry 1814.

1. My walls..were tapestried with..lichen 1798.

Tapet. *Obs.* exc. *Hist.* [OE. *tęped*, later *tæpped*, *-et*, (ult.) ad. late L. *tapetum.*] A piece of figured cloth used as a hanging, table-cover, carpet, or the like.

‖**Tapeti** (tæ·pĕti). 1613. [Tupi.] The Brazilian rabbit, *Lepus brasiliensis.*

‖**Tapetum** (tăpī·tŏm). 1713. [Late and med.L., for L. *tapete* carpet.] **1.** *Comp. Anat.* An irregular sector of the choroid membrane in the eyes of certain animals (e.g. the cat), which shines owing to the absence of the black pigment. **2.** *Bot.* The layer of epithelial cells which lines the inner wall of the sporangium in ferns, etc., or of the pollen-sac in flowering-plants 1882.

Tapeworm (tēⁱ·pwɒɹm). 1752. [f. TAPE *sb.* + WORM *sb.*; from its flat ribbon-like form.] A cestoid worm (e.g. *Tænia solium*), which when adult infests the alimentary canal of vertebrates. **b.** *fig.* A parasite 1824.

Tap-hole (tæ·phōᵘl). 1594. [f. TAP *sb.*[1] + HOLE. *sb.*] **1.** The hole in a cask, vat, or the like, in which the tap is inserted. **2.** A small opening in a furnace, through which the metal, or slag, or both, may be run out 1825.

Ta·p-house. 1500. [f. TAP *sb.*[1] + HOUSE *sb.*[1]] A house where beer drawn from the tap is sold in small quantities; an ale-house; sometimes in connexion with a brewery. Also, the tap-room of an inn.

‖**Tapia** (tā·piă). 1748. [Sp., mud-wall.] Clay or mud puddled, rammed, dried, and used for walls.

Tapinocephalic, tapeino- (tăpəi:nǫ,sĭfæ·lik), *a.* 1878. [f. Gr. ταπεινός low + κεφαλή head + -IC; see CEPHALIC.] *Anthrop.* Of the nature of, or having, a low flattened skull.

Tapioca (tæpi,ōᵘ·kă). 1707. [a. Pg., Sp., F. *tapioca*, a. Tupi-Guarani *tipioca*; f. *tipi* residue, dregs + *og*, *ók* to squeeze out.] A starch used for food, the prepared flour of the roots of the CASSAVA plant.

Tapir (tēⁱ·pəɹ). 1774. [ad. Tupi *tapira* or *tapyra.*] An ungulate mammal of tropical America of the genus *Tapirus* or family *Tapiridæ*, somewhat resembling the swine (but more nearly related to the rhinoceros), having a short flexible proboscis.

orig. applied to the species *Tapirus americanus* of Brazil; thence extended to the two Central Amer. species, *T. Dowii* and *T. Bairdi* (also *Elasmognathus*), and the Malay t., *T.* (or *Rhinochærus*) *indicus*. Hence **Ta·pirine** *a.* of or pertaining to the tapirs. **Ta·piroid** *a.* allied to or resembling the tapirs.

Tapis (tæ·pis, ‖ta·pī), *sb.* 1494. [a. F.:—pop. L. **tappetium*, for late L. *tapetium* (*-ecium*), ad. Gr. ταπήτιον, dim. of τάπης tapestry.] †**a.** A cloth worked with artistic designs in colours, used as a curtain, table-cloth, carpet, or the like –1800. **b.** Phr. *On* (*upon*) *the t.* [from F. *sur le tapis*], 'on the table-cloth', under discussion or consideration 1690.

b. Several marriages are adjusted, and many others are on the t. 1782.

Tapis, tapish (tæ·pis, -iʃ), *v. Obs.* or *arch.* ME. [f. OF. (*se*) *tapir*, *tapiss-*; see -ISH.] To lie close to the ground, lie low so as to be hid; to lurk, skulk, lie hid. **b.** *trans.* (and *refl.*) To hide 1660.

Ta·pisser. *Obs.* exc. *Hist.* late ME. [a. AF. *tapicer* = OF. *tapicier*, mod.F. *tapissier.*] A maker or weaver of figured cloth or tapestry.

†**Ta·pissery.** late ME. [a. F. *tapisserie*, f. *tapissier*, or *tapisser* to cover with carpet, f. *tapis* TAPIS; see -ERY.] The early form of the word TAPESTRY.

Tap-lash (tæ·p,læʃ). Now *dial.* 1623. [f. TAP *sb.*[1] + LASH *v.*[1]] The 'lashings' or washings of casks or glasses; dregs or refuse of liquor; very weak or stale beer.

fig. This the T. of what he said MARVELL.

Tapotement (tăpōᵘ·tmĕnt). 1889. [a. F., f. *tapoter* to tap; see -MENT.] *Med.* Percussion, esp. as a part of the treatment in massage.

‖ **Tappen** (tæ·pĕn). 1865. [Sw. and Norw.] The plug by which the rectum of a bear is closed during hibernation.

Tapper (tæ·pəɹ). 1810. [f. TAP *v.*[2] + -ER[1].] **1.** One who taps or lightly strikes; a dialect name of the spotted woodpecker. **2.** That which taps or lightly strikes, as a hammer for striking a bell; *spec.* a key in an electric telegraph which is depressed to complete the circuit; in wireless telegraphy, a device for restoring the filings to their original condition 1876.

Tappet (tæ·pėt). 1745. [app. f. TAP *v.*[2] + -ET.] A projecting arm or part in a machine, which by the movement of the latter comes intermittently into contact with another part, so as to give or receive motion.

Tappit (tæ·pit), *ppl. a. Sc.* 1721. = TOPPED *ppl. a.*; *esp.* crested, tufted; chiefly in **t. hen, a.** a hen having a crest or topknot; hence **b.** a drinking-vessel having a lid with a knob; *spec.* one containing a Scotch quart.

Ta·p-room. 1807. [f. TAP *sb.*[1] + ROOM *sb.*] A room in a tavern, etc., in which liquors are kept on tap.

Tap-root (tæ·p,rūt). 1601. [f. TAP *sb.*[1] + ROOT *sb.*] A straight root, of circular section, thick at the top, and tapering to a point, growing directly downwards from the stem and forming the centre from which subsidiary rootlets spring.

Tapster (tæ·pstəɹ). [OE. *tæppastre*, fem. of *tæppere*, f. *tæppa* TAP *sb.*[1], *tæppian* TAP *v.*[1]; see -STER.] †**1.** *orig.* A woman who tapped or drew ale or other liquor for sale in an inn; a hostess –1568. **2.** A man who draws the beer, etc. for customers in a public house; the keeper of a tavern. late ME.

Ta·pstress. 1631. [f. prec. + -ESS; formed after *tapster* had ceased to be fem.] A female tapster.

Tar (tāɹ), *sb.* [OE. *teru*:—**terwo-*; generally taken to be a deriv. of OTeut. **trewo-*, OE. *treow* tree. Thus **terwo-* may have meant orig. 'the product (pitch) of certain kinds of trees'.] **1.** A thick, viscid, black or dark-coloured, inflammable liquid, obtained by the destructive distillation of wood, coal, or other organic substance; chemically, a mixture of hydrocarbons with resins, alcohols, and other compounds, having a heavy resinous or bituminous odour, and powerful antiseptic properties; much used for coating and preserving timber, cordage etc. See also COAL-TAR. **b.** *fig.* in ref. to extraction from a negro or dark-coloured ancestry (cf. TAR-BRUSH b) 1897. **2.** Applied, with distinctive epithets, to natural substances resembling tar, as petroleum or bitumen; see MINERAL *a.* 1747. **3.** A familiar appellation for a sailor: perh. abbrev. of TARPAULIN 1676.

Comb.: **t.-board**, a strong quality of millboard made from junk and old tarred rope; **-weed** *U.S.*, any plant of the genera *Madia*, *Hemizonia*, and *Grindelia*, from their viscidity and heavy scent **-wood**, resinous wood from which t. is obtained.

Tar (tāɹ), *v.*[1] ME. [f. OE. *teoru*, *teorw-* TAR *sb.*] *trans.* To smear or cover with tar. Also *absol.* **b.** To smear (a person's body) over with tar; esp. in phr. *to t. and feather*, to smear with tar and then cover with feathers: a punishment occas. inflicted by a mob (esp. in *U.S.*) on an unpopular or scandalous character 1769. **c.** To dirty or defile as with tar; esp. in phr. *tarred with the same stick* (or *brush*), stained with the same or similar faults or obnoxious qualities 1612.

Tar, †tarre, *v.*[2] *Obs.* or *arch.* [ME. *terren*, app. repr. OE. **tęrw*(*i*)*an*, collateral form of *tęrgan* to vex, irritate, provoke.] *trans.* To vex, irritate, provoke. Now only in *tar on*, to incite, hound on.

Pride alone Must tarre the Mastiffes on, as 'twere their bone SHAKS.

Taradiddle, tarradiddle (tæ·rădid'l). *colloq.* 1796. [Cf. DIDDLE *v.*[2]] A colloquial euphemism for a lie; a 'fib', trifling falsehood.

Tarantara: see TARATANTARA.

‖**Tarantas**(s (ta:rănta·s). 1850. [ad. Russ. *tarantasŭ.*] A four-wheeled Russian travelling-carriage without springs, on a long flexible wooden chassis.

‖**Tarantella** (tærănte·lă). 1782. [It., dim. formation from *Taranto* the town of *Tarentum* in southern Italy; pop. assoc. w. *tarantola*, *tarantula* the spider.] A rapid whirling South Italian dance popular with the peasantry since the 15th c., when it was supposed to be the sovereign remedy for tarantism. **b.** The music for such a dance, or a composition in its rhythm, formerly in quadruple, but now always in 6–8 time, with whirling triplets, and abrupt transitions from the major to the minor 1833.

Tarantism (tæ·răntiz'm). 1638. [ad. mod.L. *tarantismus* = It. *tarantismo*, from It. *Taranto* (see prec.), but pop. assoc. w. *tarantola* the tarantula spider.] A hysterical malady, characterized by an extreme impulse to dance, which prevailed as an epidemic in Apulia and adjacent parts of Italy from the 15th to the 17th c., popularly attributed to the bite or 'sting' of the tarantula.

Tarantula (tăræ·ntiŭlă). 1561. [a. med.L., It. *tarantola*, f. *Taranto*:—L. *Tarentum*, ad. Gr. Τάρας (Τάραντα).] **1.** A large wolf-spider of Southern Europe, *Lycosa tarantula* (formerly *Tarantula Apuliæ*), named from the town in the region where it is commonly found, whose bite is slightly poisonous, and was fabled to cause TARANTISM. **b.** Pop. applied to other noxious spiders, esp. to the great hairy spiders of the genus *Mygale*, natives of the warmer parts of America 1794. **2.** Contextually, the bite of the tarantula; hence, erroneously, = TARANTISM 1586. **3.** *fig.* from 1 and 2 1608.

3. Saw the sun ever such a swearing people? Have they been bit by a swearing t.? CARLYLE.

Comb.: **t.-hawk, -killer**, names in Texas for a kind of wasp, *Pepsis formosa*. Hence **Tara·ntulate** *v. trans.* to affect with tarantism.

Taratantara (tărătæ·ntără, -tæntā·ra). 1553. Also **tarantara**, etc. [Echoic.] A word imitating, and hence denoting, the sound of a trumpet or bugle.

Taraxacin (tăræ·ksăsin). 1858. [f. next + -IN[1].] *Chem.* A bitter crystalline substance obtained from the juice of dandelion-root.

‖**Taraxacum** (tăræ·ksăkŏm). 1706. [med.L. from Arabic, ult. Persian.] **a.** *Bot.* The genus of Composite plants including the dandelion (*T. Dens-leonis*, *T. officinale*, or *Leontodon Taraxacum*). **b.** *Pharm.* A drug prepared from the root of the dandelion, used as a tonic and in liver complaints.

Tar-barrel (tā·ɹ,bæ:rĕl). 1450. A barrel containing or that has contained tar: esp. as used for making a bonfire; formerly also in the carrying out of capital punishment by burning. †Also applied opprobriously to a person.

‖**Tarboosh** (taɹbū·ʃ). 1702. [a. Arab. *ṭarbūsh.*] A cap or cloth of felt (almost always red) with a tassel (usu. of blue silk) attached at the top, worn by Mohammedans either by itself or as part of the turban; the *fez* is the Turkish form.

Tar-brush (tā·ɹ,brɒʃ). 1711. A brush used for smearing anything with tar. **b.** *fig.* esp. in such phrases as *a dash* or *touch of the tar-brush*, i.e. of negro or Indian blood, showing itself in the complexion 1835.

Knight of the t., a sailor.

Tardigrade (tā·ɹdigrēⁱd), *a.* and *sb.* 1623. [a. F., or ad. L. *tardigradus* walking slowly, f. *tardus* + *-gradus.*] **A.** *adj.* **1.** Walking or going slowly; 'slow-going'. **2.** *Zool.* **a.** Belonging to the sub-order (*Tardigrada*) or family (*Bradypodidæ*) of edentate mammals, comprising the sloths 1799. **b.** Belonging to the group *Tardigrada* of Arachnida, comprising the minute aquatic animals called water-bears or bear-animalcules 1847. **B.** *sb.* **a.** An edentate mammal of the sub-order *Tardigrada*; a sloth 1827. **b.** An arachnid of the group *Tardigrada*; a water-bear 1860.

Tardigradous (taɹdi·grădəs), *a.* 1658. [f. L. *tardigradus* + -OUS; see prec.] = prec. A.

Tardity (tā·ɹdĭti). Now *rare.* 1450. [a. OF. *tardité*, ad. L. *tarditas*, f. *tardus* slow; see -ITY.] **1.** Slowness of movement or action. In later use, a techn. term of *Physics*, opp. to *velocity*. **2.** The fact of being late; lateness 1599.

Tardive (tā·ɹdiv), *a. rare.* 1597. [a. F. *tardif*, *-ive*; see TARDY.] Characterized by lateness; of late appearance or development.

Tardy (tā·ɹdi), *a.* (*adv.*) 1483. [a. F. *tardif*, *-ive*:—pop. L. **tardivus*, f. *tardus* slow; see -IVE.] **1.** Slow, in various senses. **a.** Slow in motion, action, or occurrence; of a slow nature, sluggish. **b.** Not acting, coming, or happening until after the proper, expected, or desired time; late, behindhand; delaying or delayed; dilatory; sometimes, delaying through unwillingness, reluctant, 'slow' (*to* some action, or *to do* something) 1667. †**2.** Phr. *To take* (also rarely, *catch, find*) a person *t.*: to overtake; to surprise; hence, to detect, 'catch' in a crime, fault, error, etc. –1690. †**b.** *ellipt.* for 'taken tardy': Detected in a fault, caught tripping –1706. **3.** quasi-*adv.* Behind time, late 1586.

1. a. Thus the firmest timber is of t. growth JOHNSON. **c.** *U.S.* Late for a meeting, assembly, class, school, or appointment 1638. **2.** *Rich. III*, IV. i. 52. **3.** Too swift arriues as tardie as too slow SHAKS. Hence **Ta·rdily** *adv.* **Ta·rdiness.**

†**Tardy**, *v.* 1611. [f. prec.] *trans.* To make tardy; to delay, keep back –1623.

Tare (tēᵊɹ), *sb.*[1] ME. [Origin obsc.] **1.** The seed of a vetch: usu. in ref. to its small size. **2.** A name given to some species of vetch. **a.** In early times, esp. to those occurring as weeds in cornfields. late ME. **b.** Now, in general agricultural use, applied to the cultivated vetch, *Vicia sativa*, grown as fodder 1482. **3.** *pl.* Used to render L. *zizania* (Vulg., *Matt.* xiii. 25) Gr. ζιζάνια, as name of an injurious weed among corn. *Obs.* exc. as a biblical use, and as in b. late ME. **b.** Hence in fig. and allusive uses 1711.

3. Declare vnto vs the parable of the tares of the field *Matt.* xiii. 36. **b.** The tares of sedition have been industriously sown among you KEN.

Tare (tēᵊɹ), *sb.*[2] 1486. [a. F., ad. Arab. *ṭarḥah* that which is thrown away, f. *ṭaraḥa* to reject.] The weight of the wrapping, receptacle, or conveyance containing goods, which is deducted from the gross in order to ascertain the net weight; hence, a deduction made from the gross weight to allow for this; also, the weight of a motor vehicle without its fuel and other equipment. **b.** *Chem.* The weight of a vessel in which a substance is weighed, or of another vessel equal to it, deducted in ascertaining the weight of the substance 1888. **c.** *T. and tret*: the two ordinary deductions in calculating the net weight of goods to be sold by retail: see TRET; also, the rule in arithmetic by which these are calculated 1670. Hence **Tare** *v. trans.* to ascertain, allow for, or indicate the t. of. **Tared** *ppl. a.* of which the t. or weight when empty has been ascertained.

‖**Tarfa** (tarfā·). 1858. [a. Arab. *ṭarfā.*] The tamarisk, *Tamarix gallica*, which exudes a gum called manna.

Targe (tāɹdʒ). Now *arch.* and *poet.* OE. [= OF. *targe*, ad. ON. *targa* shield, cogn. w. OHG. *zarga* edging, border.] A shield; *spec.* a light shield or buckler, borne esp. by footmen and archers.

Target (tā·ɹgėt), *sb.* late ME. [dim. of prec.] **1.** A light round shield or buckler; a small targe. Now chiefly *Hist.* **2.** orig., A shield-like structure, marked with concentric circles, set up to be aimed at in shooting practice; hence, any object used for the purpose 1757. **b.** Something aimed at or to be aimed at; *esp.* a person who is the object of general abuse, derision, or the like 1757. **c.** A shooting match; the score made at such a match 1825. **3.** Applied to various objects resembling a target or shield; *esp.* **a.** *Cookery.* The neck and breast of lamb as a joint; the fore-quarter without the shoulder 1756. **b.** The sliding sight on a levelling staff; a vane 1877. **c.** A disk-shaped signal on a railway switch, etc., indicating its position. *U.S.* 1884.

2. b. A t. for the abuse of the prejudiced, the ignorant and the profane 1889. **c.** The Artists' team have made a magnificent t. 1884. Hence **Ta·rget** *v. trans.* †to protect with or as with a t.; to use (a person) as a t.; *U.S.* to signal the position of (a railway switch, etc.) by means of a t. **Ta·rgeted** (tā·ɹgėtėd) *a.* furnished with a t. or shield, or with something resembling one.

Targeteer (tāɹgėtīᵊ·ɹ). *Obs.* exc. *Hist.* 1586. [prob. ad. It. *targhettiere*, f. *targhetta* target; see -EER.] A foot-soldier armed with a target; a peltast.

Targum (tā·ɹgɒ̆m, ‖targū·m). 1587. [a. Chaldee *targūm*; see DRAGOMAN.] Each of several Aramaic translations, interpretations, or paraphrases of the various divisions of the Old Testament, committed to writing from about A.D. 100 onwards. **Targumic** (taɹgū·mik), **-al** *adjs.* **Ta·rgumist**, one of the compilers of the Targums, one versed in the Targums. **Targumi·stic** *a.*

Tarheel (tā·ɹ,hīl). *U.S. colloq.* 1888. A native or inhabitant of N. Carolina, in allusion to tar as a principal product of that State.

Tariff (tæ·rif), *sb.* 1591. [ad. It. *tariffa*, ad. Arab. *taʿrīf* notification, explanation, etc., f. *ʿarafa* to notify, make known.] †**1.** An arithmetical table or statement; a table of multiplication, a ready reckoner, or the like –1770. **2.** An official list or schedule of customs duties to be imposed on imports and exports; a table or book of rates; any item of such a list, the impost (on any article); also the whole body or system of such duties as established in any country 1592. **3.** A classified list or scale of charges made in any private or public business; as, a hotel tariff, a railroad tariff. *U.S.* 1751.

2. A free-trade t. 1868. **3.** The t. of fares 1867. *Comb.* **t.-wall**, a rate of tariff duties which check imports. Hence **Ta·riff** *v. trans.* to subject to a t.-duty; to fix the price of (something) according to a t.

Ta·riff-refo:rm. 1891. *gen.* The reform of a tariff, or of existing tariff conditions; *spec.* in U.S. politics, a reform favouring a general reduction of import duties, and a movement away from Protection; in British politics since *c* 1903 (sometimes with caps. *Tariff Reform*), the extension of the tariff on imports, as opp. to 'Free Trade'. Hence **Ta·riff-refo:rmer.**

Taring (tēᵊ·riŋ). 1622. [f. TARE *sb.*[2] and *v.* + -ING[1].] The calculation and abatement of the tare on goods.

Tarlatan (tā·ɹlătăn). 1727. [a. F. *tarlatane*, dissimilated f. *tarnatane*; prob. of Indian origin.] A kind of thin open muslin, used esp. for ball-dresses.

Ta·r maca·dam. 1882. [f. TAR *sb.* + MACADAM *sb.*] A material for making roads, consisting of some kind of broken stone or ironstone slag in a matrix of tar alone, or of tar with some mixture of pitch or creosote. Hence **Ta·rmac**, the registered trade-mark of a kind of tar macadam consisting of iron slag impregnated with tar and creosote.

Tarn (tāɹn). [ME. *terne*, a. ON. **tarnu*, *tjorn*, *tjörn.*] A small mountain lake, having no significant tributaries. (orig. local northern Eng.)

That sable t., In whose black mirror you may spy The stars, while noon-tide lights the sky SCOTT.

Tarnal (tā·ɹnăl), *a.* (*adv.*) *slang*, chiefly *U.S.* 1790. Aphetic dial. pronunc. of *eternal*, vulg. used as an expression of execration, passing into a mere intensive.

Tarnation (taɹnēⁱ·ʃən), *sb.*, *a.*, *adv. slang*, chiefly *U.S.* 1784. Variant of *darnation*, DAMNATION 3; app. assoc. w. prec.

Tarnish (tā·ɹniʃ), *v.* 1598. [ad. F. *terniss-*, extended stem of *ternir*, f. *terne* dull, dark; of doubtful origin.] **1.** *trans.* To dull or dim the lustre of, to discolour (as a metallic surface by oxidation, etc.); to cause to fade; to spoil, wither. **b.** *fig.* To take away from the purity of, cast a stain upon; to sully, taint; to bring disgrace upon 1697. **2.** *intr.* To grow dull, dim, or discoloured; to fade, wither; *esp.* of metals, to lose external brightness or lustre. Also *fig.* 1676.

1. Her Clothes were very rich, but tarnished ADDISON. **b.** Unwilling that his reputation should be tarnished 1786. **2.** Till thy fresh glories, which now shine so bright, Grow stale, and t. with our daily sight DRYDEN. Hence **Ta·rnish** *sb.* the fact of tarnishing or condition of being tarnished; discoloration; also *concr.* the substance of such discoloration. **Ta·rnisher**, one who or that which tarnishes.

Taro (tā·ro, tæ·ro). 1779. [Native Polynesian name.] A food-plant, *Colocasia antiquorum*, family *Araceæ*, cultivated in many varieties in most tropical countries for its starchy root-stocks, or its succulent leaves or stems, which in a raw state are acrid, but lose their acridity by boiling.

‖**Tarot** (taro). Also **taroc.** 1598. [F., ad. It. **tarocco* (pl. *tarocchi*), of unkn. origin.] **a.** One of a set of playing-cards, first used in Italy in the 14th c. Also used in fortune-telling. **b.** *pl.* The game played with these.

‖**Tarpan** (tā·ɹpæ̆n). 1841. [Kirghiz Tatar name.] *Zool.* The wild horse of Tartary.

Tarpaulin (tā·ɹpǫlin, taɹpǭ·lin), *sb.* 1605. [perh. f. TAR *sb.* + PALL *sb.*[1] + -ING[1] 1 (as in *netting*, etc.).] **1.** A covering or sheet of canvas coated or impregnated with tar so as to make it waterproof, used to spread over anything to protect it from wet. Also without *a* or *pl.*, canvas so tarred. **b.** A sailor's hat made of tarpaulin 1841. **2.** *transf.* A nickname for a mariner or sailor, esp. a common sailor. Now *rare* or *arch.* (Cf. TAR *sb.* 3.) 1647. **b.** Formerly applied to a sea-bred superior officer (captain, etc.) as contrasted with the military officers often appointed to command men-of-war 1690.

2. Every tarpawling, if he gets but to be lieutenant of a press smack, is called captain DE FOE. **b.** Drake and his brother tarpaulins 1894. Hence **Tarpau·lin** *v. trans.* to cover with a t.

Tarpeian (taɹpī·ăn), *a.* 1607. [f. L. *Tarpeius.*] Denoting a rock-face on the Capitoline Hill at Rome over which persons convicted of treason to the state were thrown headlong.

Tarpon (tā·ɹpǫn). 1685. [So Du. *tarpoen*; origin unkn.] The Jew-fish, *Megalops atlanticus*, a giant representative of the herring tribe found in the warmer waters of the western Atlantic: see JEW-FISH and ELOPS.

Tarragon (tæ·răgən). 1538. [Given in 1538–48 as English for med.L. *tragonia* and *tarchon*, the latter repr. Byzantine Gr. ταρχών, repr. Arab. *ṭarkhōn*, a foreign word, perh. ad. Gr. δράκων (assoc. w. δρακόντιον dragonwort).] **1.** A composite plant, *Artemisia Dracunculus*, of the wormwood genus, a native of Southern Russia and Eastern Europe, the aromatic leaves of which are used to flavour salads, soups, etc **2.** *attrib.*, as **t. vinegar**, vinegar flavoured with the leaves or oil of t. 1855.

Tarragona (tærăgōᵘ·nă). 1885. [Name of a town in Spain.] A Spanish port-like wine.

Tarras (tæ·răs), *sb.* Now *rare* or *Obs.* 1612. [ad. early mod.Du. *tarasse*, *terras*, *tiras* (whence Du. *tras*, Ger. *trasz*), of Rom. origin; cf. TERRACE.] A kind of rock, allied in composition to pozzolana, consisting largely of comminuted pumice or other volcanic substance; it is found along the Rhine between Cologne and Mainz, and was formerly imported from Holland for making a mortar or hydraulic cement.

Hence, the mortar or cement made of this, used for pargeting, lining cisterns, etc.; also applied to other similar cements.

Tarras, *v.* Now *rare* or *Obs.* 1485. [orig. prob. f. F. *terracer, terrasser*; later, app. f. prec.] *trans.* To cover, coat, or lay with plaster; in later use, with tarras.

Tarriance (tæ·riăns). *arch.* 1460. [f. TARRY *v.* + -ANCE.] 1. The action of tarrying; delay, procrastination. 2. Temporary residence or continuance in a place; sojourn, abiding 1530. †3. Abiding in expectation; awaiting, waiting -1646.

1. I am impatient of my t. SHAKS.

Tarrier[1] (tæ·riəɹ). *arch.* late ME. [f. TARRY *v.* + -ER[1].] 1. One who tarries or delays; a lingerer; one who stays or remains. †2. A hinderer; an obstruction -1622.

Tarrier[2] (tæ·riəɹ). 1460. [a. OF. *tarere*, F. *tarière*:—late L. *taratrum*.] A boring instrument, an auger; now, an instrument for extracting a bung from a barrel.

Tarrier[3], obs. or vulgar f. TERRIER[2].

Tarrock (tæ·rɒk). 1674. [Origin obsc.] A name applied locally to various sea-birds: in the Shetland Islands, to the Arctic Tern; elsewhere to the Kittiwake, to the young of the Common Gull, and to the Common Guillemot.

Tarry (tæ·ri), *sb.* late ME. [f. TARRY *v.*] †1. The act of tarrying; spending or loss of time; delay, procrastination -1745. 2. Sojourn; a 'stay'. Now chiefly *U.S.* late ME.

Tarry (tā·ri), *a.* 1552. [f. TAR *sb.* + -Y[1].] 1. Consisting or composed of tar; of the nature of tar. b. Resembling tar; having the consistence, colour, or flavour of tar 1880. 2. Covered, smeared, soiled, or impregnated with tar; black as if smeared with tar 1585.

Comb.: **t.-breeks** (orig. *Sc.*), **-jacket, -John,** joc. nicknames for a sailor. Hence **Ta·rriness.**

Tarry (tæ·ri), *v.* Now chiefly *literary.* ME. [Origin obsc.] †1. *trans.* To delay, put off (a thing, an action); to protract, prolong -1583. †2. To delay, keep back (a person or agent) for a time; to keep waiting; to hold in check, impede, hinder -1609. 3. *intr.* To delay or be tardy in beginning or doing anything, esp. in coming or going; to wait before doing something; to linger, loiter ME. b. To linger in expectation of a person or occurrence, or until something is done or happens; to wait. late ME. †4. To remain, stay, continue -1814. b. To abide temporarily; to stay, remain, lodge (in a place). *arch.* exc. in *U.S.* late ME. 5. *trans.* To wait for, wait in expectation of; to await, expect; †to stay for (a meal). late ME.

2. Sir kyng, he sayd, tary me noo lenger for I may not tary MALORY. 3. Why tarie the wheeles of his charets? *Judg.* v. 28. b. Time and tide t. for no man SCOTT. 4. b. There they were to t. through Lent FREEMAN. 5. I pressed him..to t. your coming 1829. Phr. *To t.* a person's *leisure*: see LEISURE 3 (*arch.*).

Tarsal (tā·ɹsăl), *a.* and *sb.* 1817. [ad. mod. L. *tarsalis*, f. *tarsus* TARSUS; see -AL.] A. *adj.* 1. *Comp. Anat.* Of or pertaining to the tarsus of the ankle or foot. 2. Of or pertaining to the tarsi of the eyelids 1839. B. *sb.* Short for *t. bone, joint*, etc. 1881.

‖**Tarsia** (tā·ɹsiă). 1665. [It.] A kind of mosaic inlaid work in wood of various colours.

Tarsier (tā·ɹsiəɹ). 1774. [a. F., f. *tarse* TARSUS; so named from the structure of the foot.] *Zool.* A small lemuroid quadruped, *Tarsius spectrum*, of Sumatra, Borneo, Celebes, and the Philippines, called also malmag or spectre, related to the aye-aye of Madagascar.

The T...The bones of..the Tarsus, are..so very long, that from thence the animal has received its name GOLDSM.

Tarso- (tāɹso), bef. a vowel **tars-**, comb. form of Gr. ταρσός TARSUS, as in **Tarso·rrhaphy** [Gr. ῥαφή seam], plastic suture of the eyelid. **Tarso·tomy** [Gr. τομή cutting], the section or removal of the tarsal cartilages.

Tarso-metatarsal (tā:ɹso,metătā·ɹsăl), *a.* and *sb.* 1835. *Comp. Anat.* A. *adj.* a. Of or pertaining to the tarsus and the metatarsus, as 'the tarso-metatarsal ligaments'. b. Of or pertaining to a tarso-metatarsus. B. *sb.* Short for *t. bone* or *ligament.*

‖**Tarso-metatarsus** (tā:ɹso,metătā·ɹsɒs). 1854. *Comp. Anat.* The bone formed by ankylosis of the tarsus and the metatarsus in birds and early reptilian types.

‖**Tarsus** (tā·ɹsɒs). *Pl.* **-i** (əi). 1676. [mod.L., a. Gr. ταρσός the flat of the foot between the toes and the heel, the rim of the eyelid.] 1. The first or posterior part of the foot: a collective name for the seven small bones of the human ankle, arranged in two transverse series, the proximal or tibial, consisting of the astragalus and os calcis, and the distal, or metatarsal, consisting of the naviculare, the cuboides, and the three ossa cuneiformia; also, the corresponding part in mammalia generally, and in some reptiles and amphibia. b. In birds: The third segment of the leg, the shank: = TARSO-METATARSUS 1828. c. In insects and other arthropods, a series of small articulations forming the true foot; in spiders, the last joint, forming, with the preceding joint or metatarsus, the foot 1826. 2. The thin plate of condensed connective tissue found in each eyelid. Now *rare* or *Obs.* 1691.

Tart (tāɹt), *sb.*[1] late ME. [a. F. *tarte* an open tart, = med.L. *tarta*; of uncertain origin.] Name for various dishes consisting of a crust of baked pastry enclosing different ingredients: †a. Formerly with meat, fish, cheese, fruit, etc. b. In current use: (*a*) a flat, usu. small, piece of pastry, with no crust on the top, filled with fruit preserve or other sweet confection; (*b*) a covered fruit pie.

b. Her rejection of a nice little jam t...'she never touched *patisserie*' 1899.

Tart, *sb.*[2] *slang.* 1887. [Shortened f. SWEETHEART.] Applied (orig. endearingly) to a girl or woman (esp. one of immoral character).

Tart (tāɹt), *a.* [OE. *teart*; ult. etym. obsc.] †1. Of pain, punishment, suffering, law, etc.: Sharp, severe, painful, grievous -1605. 2. Sharp to the sense of taste; now *esp.* sour, acid, or acidulous. late ME. †b. Of the sense of taste: keen. B. JONS. †3. Sharp, keen (as an edge, point, weapon) -1600. 4. *fig.* Of words, speech, a speaker: Sharp in tone or tendency, biting, cutting, acrimonious, caustic 1601.

1. *Lear* IV. ii. 87. 2. Cherries..the juice of which was agreeably t. 1772. 4. Sometimes a t. Irony goes for Wit 1691. Entertaining the Company with t. ill-natured Observations ADDISON. Hence **Ta·rt-ly** *adv.*, **-ness.**

Tartan (tā·ɹtăn), *sb.*[1] orig. *Sc.* 1500. [Origin obsc.] A kind of woollen cloth woven in stripes of various colours crossing at right angles so as to form a regular pattern; worn chiefly by the Scottish Highlanders, each clan having usu. its distinctive pattern. Also, the pattern or design of such cloth. Also applied to silk and other fabrics having a similar pattern. b. *transf.* Applied to one who wears tartan; a Highlander; collectively, those who wear tartan; the body of Highlanders; the men of a Highland regiment 1817.

Shepherds' t., shepherds' plaid (see PLAID 1). Hence **Ta·rtan** *v. trans* to clothe or array in t.

Tartan, tartane (tā·ɹtăn, ‖tartan), *sb.*[2] 1621. [a. F. *tartane*, a. It., = Sp., Pg. *tartana*, perh. from Arab. *tarīdah*.] A small one-masted vessel with a large lateen sail and a foresail, used in the Mediterranean. So **Tarta·na** 1588.

‖**Tartan,** *sb.*[3] 1880. [Assyrian. See 2 Kings xviii. 17, Isa. xx. 1.] The ancient Assyrian commander-in-chief.

Tartar (tā·ɹtăɹ), *sb.*[1] late ME. [a. F. *tartre* = med.L. *tartarum*, med.Gr. τάρταρον; perh. of Arabic origin.] 1. *Chem.* Bitartrate of potash (acid potassium tartrate), present in grape juice, deposited in a crude form in the process of fermentation, and adhering to the sides of wine-casks in the form of a hard crust, also called *argal* or ARGOL, which when purified forms white crystals, which are *cream of t.* b. Hence, 'A generic name for salts of tartaric acid' (Watts). 2. *transf.* Any calcareous or other incrustation deposited from a liquid upon bodies in contact with it 1605. b. *spec.* A deposit of calcium phosphate from the saliva, which tends to harden and concrete upon the teeth 1806.

Cream of t.: see sense 1 and CREAM *sb.* **T. eme·tic,** common name in pharmacy of potassio-antimonious tartrate, $C_4H_4K(SbO)O_6 + \frac{1}{2}H_2O$, a poisonous substance, used in medicine to excite vomiting.

Tartar (tā·ɹtăɹ), *sb.*[2] (*a.*), **Tatar** (tā·tăɹ). late ME. [a. F. *Tartare*, or ad. med.L. *Tartarus*, pl. *Tartari*, ethnic name. The form *Tâtar* and its derivs. are now often used in ethnological works in sense 1.] 1. A native inhabitant of the region of Central Asia extending eastward from the Caspian Sea. First known in the West as applied to the mingled host of Mongols, Tartars, Turks, etc., which under the leadership of Jenghiz Khan (1202–1227) overran and devastated much of Asia and Eastern Europe; hence vaguely applied to the descendants of these now dwelling in Asia or Europe; more strictly and ethnologically, to any member of the Tâtar or Turkic branch of the Ural-Altaic or Turanian family, including the Turks, Cossacks, and Kirghiz Tartars. 2. *transf.* †a. A strolling vagabond, a thief, a beggar -1697. b. As an opprobrious appellation 1590. 3. *fig.* A savage; a person supposed to resemble a T. in disposition; a rough and violent or irritable and intractable person: when applied to a female, a vixen, a shrew, a termagant 1663. 4. The language of the Tartars 1884.

1. Looke how I goe, Swifter then arrow from the Tartars bowe SHAKS. 2. a. *Merry W.* IV. v. 21. b. *Mids N.* III. ii. 263. 3. The old man was a awful T. DICKENS. Phr. *To catch a T.*, to get hold of one who can neither be controlled nor got rid of.

B. *adj.* Of or pertaining to the Tartars, or their country. Also applied to plants, animals, etc., belonging to Tartary. 1731.

†**Ta·rtar,** *sb.*[3]: see TARTARUS.

Tartarated (tā·ɹtărēɪtėd), *a.* 1863. [f. TARTAR *sb.*[1] + -ATE + -ED.] *Chem.* Combined with tartar; as in *t. iron, soda.*

Tartarean (taɹtēᵊ·rĭăn), *a.* 1623. [f. L. *Tartareus* + -AN.] Of or belonging to the Tartarus of the ancients; hence, pertaining to hell or to purgatory; infernal.

Mixt with T. Sulphur, and strange fire MILT.

Tartareous (taɹtēᵊ·rĭəs), *a.*[1] 1625. [f. mod.L. *tartareus* + -OUS.] †1. *Path.* Of the nature of a tartar, or calcareous or earthy deposit; characterized by such deposits -1677. †2. Like tartar in consistence or formation; of the nature of a concretion or crust; gritty -1683. †3. *Chem.* Having the quality of tartar or argol; containing or derived from tartar -1822. 4. *Bot.* Of a crust-like structure like tartar: descriptive of certain lichens 1845.

†**Tarta·reous,** *a.*[2] 1619. [f. L. *tartareus* (f. TARTARUS) + -OUS.] Of or pertaining to Tartarus; infernal, hellish, very wicked -1667.

Tartarian (taɹtēᵊ·riăn), *sb.* and *a.*[1] late ME. [a. OF. *Tartarien*; later f. med.L. *Tartaria* TARTARY + -AN.] A. *sb.* = TARTAR *sb.*[2] 1, 2 a. B. *adj.* = TARTAR *a.* 1590. b. In names of things of actual or supposed Tartar origin; as *T. cherry, lamb* 1805.

Tarta·rian, *a.*[2] *rare.* 1864. [f. L. TARTARUS + -IAN.] = TARTAREAN *a.*

Tartaric (taɹtæ·rik), *a.*[1] 1790. [f. TARTAR *sb.*[1] + -IC.] *Chem.* Of the nature of, related to, or derived from tartar or argol.

T. acid, an organic acid, $C_4H_6O_6 = C_4H_2O_2 + (OH)_4$, or $CO_2H \cdot (CHOH)_2 \cdot CO_2H$, of which there are five isomeric forms, differing in their optical properties; spec. one of these (*dextrotartaric* acid), a colourless crystalline compound, occurring largely in the vegetable kingdom, esp. in unripe grapes, and as a potassium salt in argol or tartar of wine, from which it is commercially prepared.

Tartaric (taɹtæ·rik), *a.*[2] Also **Tataric.** 1811. [f. TARTAR *sb.*[2] + -IC.] Of, pertaining to, or connected with the Tartars or Tartary.

Tartarin (tā·ɹtărin, ‖tartaræṅ). 1903. Name of a bombastic character, 'Tartarin of Tarascon', created by A. Daudet; hence, used *allus.* as sb. or adj.

Tartarize (tā·ɹtărəiz), *v.*[1] 1706. [f. TARTAR *sb.*[1] + -IZE.] Chem. *trans.* To treat or impregnate with tartar; to rectify by means of the salt of tartar.

Ta·rtarize, *v.*[2] Also **Tatarize.** 1877. [f. TARTAR *sb.*[2] + -IZE.] *trans.* To convert or transform into a Tartar.

Tartarly (tā·ɹtăli), *a.* *nonce-wd.* 1821. [f. TARTAR *sb.*[2] + -LY[1].] Rough and fierce.

Who killed John Keats? 'I' says the Quarterly, So savage and T. BYRON.

†**Tartarous** (tā·ɹtărəs), *a.* 1605. [f. TARTAR *sb.*[1] + -OUS.] **1.** Of the nature of, consisting of, or containing tartar or argol –1768. **2.** *Path.* Said of indurations, inspissated fluids, phlegms, etc., attributed to the presence of tartar in the body –1744. **3.** Of the nature of or derived from tartar; *t. acid*, an earlier name of TARTARIC *acid* 1790.

‖**Tartarus** (tā·ɹtărŏs). 1586. [L., a. Gr. Τάρταρος.] The infernal regions of ancient Greek and Roman mythology, or the lowest part of them; hence sometimes used for: Hell. **b.** A place likened to Tartarus, in situation or character 1821. Also †**Tartar** 1500–1601.

b. She never emerged from the dismal T. of the kitchens, &c., to the upper air DE QUINCEY.

Tartary (tā·ɹtări). late ME. [a. F. *Tartarie*, ad. med.L. *Tartaria* land of the Tartars; assoc. w. TARTARUS.] **1.** The country of the Tartars; see TARTAR *sb.*[2] †**2.** Tartarus, as a region –1620.

‖**Tartine** (tartīn). 1826. [F., f. *tarte* TART *sb.*[1]] A slice of bread spread with butter or preserve.'

Tartish (tā·ɹtiʃ), *a.* 1712. [f. TART *a.* + -ISH [1].] Somewhat tart, slightly pungent or acid; also *fig.*

Tartlet (tā·ɹtlėt). late ME. [a. F. *tartelette*, dim. of *tarte* TART *sb.*[1]] A small tart.

Tartralic (taɹtræ·lik), *a.* 1857. [ad. F. *tartralique*, arbitrarily f. *tartrique*, to indicate derivation from tartaric acid; cf. TARTRELIC.] *Chem.* In *t. acid* (also called *ditartaric* or *isotartaric acid*), $C_8H_{10}O_{11}$, an amorphous deliquescent substance obtained by heating tartaric acid. Its salts are **Ta·rtralates.**

Tartramic (taɹtræ·mik), *a.* 1857. [f. TARTRO- + AMMONIUM + -IC.] *Chem.* In *t. acid*, $C_4H_7NO_5$, an amidated derivative of tartaric acid. Its salts are **Ta·rtramates.**

Ta·rtrami·de. 1868. [f. TARTRO- + AMIDE.] *Chem.* The amide of tartaric acid, $C_4H_4(NH_2)_2O_4$, a crystalline body produced by passing dry ammonia gas into an alcoholic solution of tartaric ether.

Tartrate (tā·ɹtrĕt). 1794. [a. F., f. *tartre* TARTAR *sb.*[1]; see -ATE [1].] *Chem.* A salt of tartaric acid. Hence **Ta·rtrated** *ppl. a.* made into a t.; tartarated.

Tartrelic (taɹtre·lik), *a.* 1838. [ad. F. *tartrélique*, arbitrarily formed, along with TARTRALIC, to indicate derivation from tartaric acid by further heating; the *a* and *e* indicating the order of production of these modifications.] *Chem.* In *t. acid*, soluble tartaric anhydride, $C_4H_4O_5$, obtained as a yellowish deliquescent mass by quickly heating small quantities of tartaric acid. Its salts are **Ta·rtrelates.**

Tartro-, bef. a vowel **tartr-** [f. F. *tartre* TARTAR *sb.*[1]], in names of chemical compounds containing or derived from tartaric acid; as **Ta·rtrazine** [AZO- + -INE [5]], a fast and brilliant dye-stuff of rich orange yellow; **Tartrethy·lic** *acid*, $C_6H_{10}O_6$; **Tartrovi·nic** *acid* = *tartrethylic acid.*

Tartronic (taɹtrǭ·nik), *a.* 1866. [ad. F. *tartronique*, arbitrarily f. *tartrique* (perh. with *ni-* of *nitro-*).] *Chem.* In *t. acid*, a dibasic acid, $C_3H_4O_5$, produced by the spontaneous decomposition of nitro-tartaric acid, crystallizing in large prisms. Its salts are **Ta·rtronates.**

‖**Tartuffe, Tartufe** (taɹtu·f, ‖tartüf). 1676. [F., name of the principal character (a religious hypocrite) in a comedy by Molière (1664); app. = OF. *tartuffe* truffle, as a concealed production.] A hypocritical pretender to religion, or, by extension, to excellence of any kind. Hence **Tartu·fferie, -ery**, the character or conduct of a T., hypocrisy. **Tartu·ffian, Tartu·f(f)ish** *adjs.* pertaining to or characteristic of a T.; hypocritical, pretentious.

Ta·r-wa·ter. 1740. [f. TAR *sb.* + WATER *sb.*] **1.** An infusion of tar in cold water, formerly in repute as a medicine. **2.** The ammoniacal water of gas-works 1858.

‖**Tasajo** (tasā·χo). 1783. [Sp.] Buffalo meat cut into strips and dried in the sun.

Tasimeter (tăsi·mĭtəɹ). 1878. [f. Gr. τάσις tension + -METER.] An electrical apparatus for measuring minute variations of temperature, length, moisture, etc. by means of changes in the electrical conductivity of carbon resulting from alterations of pressure caused by these variations.

Task (tɑsk), *sb.* ME. [a. ONF. *tasque* = OF. *tasche*, F. *tâche*; or ad. med.L. *tasca*, according to Diez, by metathesis for *taxa*, f. L. *taxare*.] †**1.** A fixed payment to a king, lord, or feudal superior; an impost, tax; tribute –1766. **2.** A piece of work imposed, exacted, or undertaken as a duty or the like; orig., a fixed or specified quantity of work imposed on or exacted from a person; later, the work appointed to one as a definite duty ME. **b.** *spec.* A portion of study imposed by a teacher; a lesson to be learned or prepared. Now *arch.* 1742. **3.** *gen.* Any piece of work that has to be done; something that one has to do (usu. involving labour or difficulty) 1593.

2. The silk-worm, after having spun her t., lays her eggs and dies ADDISON. She..appoints them a t. of needle-work JOHNSON. **3.** He had taken upon himself a t. beyond the ordinary strength of man FROUDE. Phr. *To take to t.*, to deal with in the way of fault-finding or censure, to call to account about a matter.

Task (tɑsk), *v.* 1483. [f. prec.] **I.** †**1.** *trans.* To impose a tax upon; to tax; to exact tribute from –1642. **2.** To force, put, or set (a person) to a task; to impose a task on; to assign a definite amount of work to 1530. **3.** *transf.* and *fig.* To occupy or engage fully or burdensomely; to put a strain upon; to put in a condition of stress or difficulty; to put to the proof 1598. **b.** *spec.* To test the soundness of (a ship's timbers, a plank, etc.) 1803.

2. But now to taske the tasker SHAKS. Man alone ..tasks creation to assist him in murdering his brother worm! W. IRVING. **3.** Some things of weight, That taske our thoughts SHAKS. You must not t. me too high RICHARDSON.

†**II.** To take to task; to reprove –1632.

Tasker (tɑ·skəɹ). late ME. [f. TASK *v.* (or *sb.*) + -ER [1].] †**1.** One who assesses or regulates a rate or price (e. g. of things brought to market, etc.) –1614. **2.** One who imposes or sets a task; a taskmaster 1588. **3.** One who works or is paid by the task or piece, as dist. from a day-labourer, etc. *dial.* 1621. **b.** *spec.* One who threshes corn with a flail, as TASK-WORK or piece-work. late ME.

Ta·skma·ster. 1530. [f. TASK *sb.* + MASTER *sb.*[1]] One whose office is to allot tasks and see to their performance; an overseer; a middleman; also *fig.* one who allots a duty, or imposes a heavy burden or labour.

All is, if I have grace to use it so, As ever in my great task Masters eye MILT. So **Ta·skmi·stress.**

Ta·sk-work. 1486. [f. TASK *sb.* + WORK *sb.*] **1.** Work performed as a task; forced labour; hence, burdensome or oppressive work 1582. **2.** Piece-work 1486.

Tasmanian (tæzmē¹·niăn, tæs-), *a.* Of or pertaining to Tasmania in Australasia. In names of animals, plants, etc., native to Tasmania, as *T. devil* (see DEVIL 7), *T.* WOLF.

Tass [1] (tɑs). Now *dial.* ME. [a. OF. *tas*, also *tasse*, = Pr. *tatz*; perh. of LG. origin.] A heap, pile, stack.

Tass [2] (tæs). Now chiefly *Sc.* 1483. [a. OF. *tasse* goblet, in mod.F. cup, app. a. Arab. *tass, tassah* basin, perh. ad. Pers. *tast* cup, goblet.] A cup or small goblet; the contents of this; a small draught of liquor.

Tasse (tæs). *Obs.* exc. *Hist.* 1548. [In sense = F. *tassette*, a small pocket or pouch, a steel plate to guard the thigh, dim. of *tasse.*] *pl.* A series of articulated splints or plates depending from the corslet, placed so that each slightly overlapped the one below it, forming a sort of kilt of armour to protect the thighs and the lower part of the trunk.

Tassel (tæ·s'l), *sb.*[1] ME. [a. OF. *tasel*, *tassel* clasp.] †**1.** A clasp or fibula by which the two sides of a cloak or the like are held together. late ME. **2.** A pendent ornament consisting of a bunch or thick fringe of threads or small cords hanging in a somewhat conical shape from a solid rounded knob or mould, or from a knot formed by their junction with a cord. Frequently attached to a curtain, cushion, cap, umbrella, etc., or forming the pull of a blind-cord or bell-cord. late ME. **3.** Anything resembling or suggesting a tassel; as a pendent catkin, blossom, or bud; *spec.* the staminate (terminal) inflorescence of the maize-plant (*U.S.*) 1646.

2. A knotted girdle, ending in tassels, encircled the loins 1849. **3.** The yellow tassels on the hazel MISS MITFORD.

Comb.: **t.-flower**, (*a*) a tassel-like flower; *spec.* the orange, scarlet, or yellowish blossom of *Emilia sagittata*, family *Compositæ*, or the plant itself; (*b*) a shrub or tree of the genus *Inga*; **-grass**, an aquatic herb, *Ruppia maritima*, of which the seed-vessels are borne on clusters of pedicels; **-hyacinth**, *Muscari comosum*, the stalk and flower of which resemble a t. Hence **Tassel(l)ed** (tæ·s'ld) *a.* 1611.

Tassel, torsel (tæ·s'l, tǭ·s'l, tǭ·ɹs'l), *sb.*[2] 1632. [a. OF., mod.F. *tasseau* = It. *tassello* a bit of stone or wood to stop a hole:—L. *taxillus* a small die.] *Arch.* A short board or 'templet' placed under the end of a beam or other timber where it rests on brickwork or stonework.

Tassel (tæ·s'l), *v.* late ME. [f. TASSEL *sb.*[1]] **1.** *trans.* To furnish or adorn with or as with a tassel or tassels. **2.** *intr.* Of maize and sugar-cane: To form 'tassels', i. e. to flower, bloom. Chiefly *U.S.* 1785.

Tassets (tæ·sėts), *sb. pl.* 1834. [ad. F. *tassette*; see TASSE.] = *tasses*; see TASSE. (Only in recent archæological or romantic use.)

Taste (tē¹st), *sb.*[1] ME. [a. OF. *tast* touching, touch, f. *taster* (mod.F. *tâter*) TASTE *v.*] **I.** †**1.** The sense of touch, feeling (with the hands, etc.); the act of touching, touch. late ME. †**2.** A trying; a trial, test –1633. **II.** †**1.** The act of tasting or perceiving the flavour of a thing with the organ of taste; the fact of being tasted –1766. **b.** *transf.* The means of tasting; hence, such a small quantity as admits of being tasted; a very small quantity (esp. of spirits), a sip 1530. **c.** *fig.* A slight experience, received or given; a slight show or sample *of* any condition or quality. late ME. **2.** The faculty or sense by which that particular quality of a thing described in 3 is discerned; one of the five bodily senses. late ME. **3.** That quality or property of a body or substance which is perceived when it is brought into contact with certain organs of the mouth, etc., esp. the tongue; savour, sapidity; the particular sensation excited by anything in this manner. late ME.

1. The Fruit Of that Forbidden Tree, whose mortal tast Brought Death into the World, and all our woe MILT. **2.** Second childishnesse, and meere obliuion, Sans teeth, sans eyes, sans t., sans euery thing SHAKS. **3.** Iron..has a styptic t., very sensible 1800. *fig* I haue..forgot the t. of Feares SHAKS. The poems leave a nasty t. in the mouth; the t. of a snarl and a sneer 1904.

III. †**1.** Mental perception of quality; judgement, discriminative faculty. *Obs.* exc. as in 3 below –1692. **2.** The fact or condition of liking or preferring something; inclination, liking *for*; †appreciation 1477. **3.** The sense of what is appropriate, harmonious, or beautiful; *esp.* discernment and appreciation of the beautiful in nature or art; *spec.* the faculty of perceiving and enjoying what is excellent in art, literature, and the like 1671. **b.** Style or manner exhibiting æsthetic discernment; good or bad æsthetic quality; the style or manner favoured in any age or country 1739.

2. Whoever hath a t. for true humour SWIFT. The other girl is more amusing, more to my t. LYTTON. **3.** No, no, hang him, he has no Taste CONGREVE. A fine Musical t. is soon dissatified with the Harmonica 1834. **b.** Nothing could be..'in better t.' DISRAELI. It was..built something in the Moorish t. 1843.

attrib. and *Comb.*: **t.-beaker, -bud, -bulb, -goblet**, one of the flask-shaped bodies in the epithelium of the tongue, believed to be organs of taste; †**-paper**, in the (old) Greats examination at Oxford, the paper in which passages were set from the classical authors for critical and exegetical treatment.

Taste (tē¹st), *sb.*[2] *U.S. local.* 1847. [Origin obsc.] A kind of narrow thin silk ribbon used for edge-binding: now commonly called taffeta-binding.

Taste (tē¹st), *v.* [ME. *tasten*, a. OF. *taster* to touch, feel:—Com. Rom. or late pop. L. **tastare*, app. f. **taxitare*, freq. of *taxare* to touch, feel, etc.; see TAX *v.*] **I.** †**1.** *trans.* To try, examine, or explore by touch; to feel; to handle –1648. †**2.** *trans.* To put to the proof;

to try, test -1670. b. spec. *Shipbuilding*. To chip (a plank or timber) with an adze for the purpose of finding any defects 1711. 3. *fig.* To have experience or knowledge of; to experience, feel; to have a slight experience of ME. †b. To have carnal knowledge of -1752.

3. You have tasted the Pleasures of the Town 1693. b. *Cymb.* II. iv. 57.

II. 1. *trans.* To perceive by the sense of taste; to perceive or experience the taste or flavour of ME. †b. *fig.* To perceive as by the sense of taste -1616. c. *absol.* or *intr.* To experience or distinguish flavours; to have or exercise the sense of taste. late ME. 2. *transf.* (*trans.*) To perceive by some other sense, esp. smell. Now only *poet.* or *dial.* 1656. 3. To try the flavour or quality of by the sense of taste; to put a small quantity of (something) into the mouth in order to ascertain the flavour, etc.; *spec.* to test the quality of by tasting, for trade purposes. Also *absol.* ME. b. *spec.* (*trans.*) To test or certify the wholesomeness of (food provided) by tasting it; also *absol.* to act as taster *to* a person 1595. c. *fig.* To make trial of as by the sense of taste; to try the quality of. Also *absol.* or *intr.* late ME. 4. To have or take a taste of (food or drink); to eat or drink a little; but often by meiosis, simply for 'eat' or 'drink'. Negatively, *not to t.* = not to eat or drink at all. ME. 5. To like the taste of (usu. *fig.*); to like, take pleasure in; formerly sometimes in neutral sense: to appreciate. Now *arch.* or *dial.* 1605. 6. *intr.* Of a substance: To have a taste of a specified or implied kind; to have a taste or flavour *of* 1552. b. *fig.* To partake of the nature, character, or quality *of*; to savour *of* 1599. 7. *trans.* To impart a taste or flavour to. Now *rare.* 1577.

1. This daye am I foure score yeare olde. How shulde I..taist what I eate or drynke? COVERDALE *2 Sam.* xix. 35. b. Nay, then I t. a Trick in 't B. JONS. c. O, you are sicke of selfe-loue, Maluolio, and t. with a distemper'd appetite SHAKS. 2. To t. the cold breath of the earliest morn KINGLAKE. 3. The ale teaster to teast the ale before they sell it 1604. b. How did he take it [poison]? Who did t. to him? SHAKS. c. O taist and se how frendly the Lorde is COVERDALE. *Ps.* xxxiii. 9. 4. I often..t. a cup of Ale there WALTON. 5. The King seemed to t. the Duke of Grafton, and commended his parts 1768. 6. Let him drink deeply..nor grumble if it tasteth of the cork 1871. b. The place, the air Tastes of the nearer north CLOUGH. 7. We will have a bunch of radish and salt to t. our wine B. JONS.

T. of: a. = II. 3. b. = II. 7. c. = I. 3.

Tasteable, tastable (tē¹·stăb'l), *a.* 1572. [f. TASTE *v.* + -ABLE.] 1. Capable of being tasted. †2. Pleasant to the taste -1791.

Tasteful (tē¹·stfŭl), *a.* 1611. [f. TASTE *sb.*¹ + -FUL.] †1. Having the capacity of tasting or trying. CRASHAW. 2. Having an agreeable taste; palatable, toothsome, tasty. Now *rare.* 1611. 3. Having or showing good taste, as a person; displaying good taste, as a work of art, etc. 1756.

2. T. food 1747. A t. dish 1887. 3. The t. pencil of Stothard 1816. The t. publisher of the 'Aldine Poets' 1849. Hence **Ta·steful-ly** *adv.*, **-ness.**

Tasteless (tē¹·stlės), *a.* 1591. [f. TASTE *sb.*¹ + -LESS.] 1. Destitute of the sense of taste; unable to taste. Also *fig.* Now *rare.* 2. Without taste or flavour; insipid 1611. 3. Devoid of good taste; of things, showing want of good taste 1676.

1. The t. palate of age 1820. 2. Very dry and t. food 1748. *fig.* A while on trivial things we held discourse, To me soon t. WORDSW. 3. The t. fashion of an artificial and decaying civilization KINGSLEY. Hence **Ta·steless-ly** *adv.*, **-ness.**

Taster¹ (tē¹·stəɹ). late ME. [orig. a. AF. *tastour* = OF. *tasteur*, f. OF. *taster*; later, f. TASTE *v.* + -ER¹.] 1. One who tastes, or tries the quality of a thing by tasting; *spec.* one whose office, business, or employment is to test by taste the quality of victuals sold to the public, as ales, wines, teas, etc. 1440. 2. A domestic officer whose duty it is to taste food and drink about to be served to his master, in order to ascertain their quality, or to detect poison. late ME. 3. An implement by which a small portion of anything is taken for tasting. a. A small shallow cup of silver, for tasting wines. late ME. b. An instrument by which a small portion is taken from the interior of a cheese; a skewer for testing the condition of hams 1784. 4. A small portion of food, etc., for a sample 1826.

2. Princes have their tasters before they eat, lest there should be poison in the dish 1662.

‖**Taster**² (ta·stəɹ). 1884. [G., feeler, antenna, f. *tasten* to feel, touch.] *Zool.* In certain Hydrozoa, A modified zooid situated on the polyp-stem, and somewhat resembling the polypites, but having no mouth; a hydrocyst or feeler.

Tasting (tē¹·stiŋ), *vbl. sb.* ME. [-ING¹.] 1. The action of the vb. TASTE; now, the action of TASTE *v.* II; †also formerly, the faculty or sense of taste, and the quality of a substance so apprehended. 2. quasi-*concr.* A small portion taken to try the taste; a taste (esp. of spirituous liquor) 1526.

Comb.: **t.-knife**, a cheese-taster.

Tasty (tē¹·sti), *a.* Now *colloq.* and *dial.* 1617. [f. TASTE *sb.*¹ + -Y.¹] 1. Pleasing to the taste; appetizing, savoury. 2. Tasteful, elegant. Now *rare.* 1762.

1. A t. bird, that pheasant 1795. 2. [The silk] is at once rich, t., and quite the thing GOLDSM. Hence **Ta·stily** *adv.* **Ta·stiness.**

Tat (tæt), *sb.*¹ *slang.* 1688. [Origin unkn.] *pl.* **Tats**: Dice; *esp.* false or loaded dice.

Tāt (tāt), *sb.*² *India.* Also **taut.** 1820. [Hindī *ṭāṭ*.] Coarse canvas made from various fibres, esp. jute, and used as sacking.

Tat, tatt (tæt), *sb.*³ *India.* 1840. Short for TATTOO *sb.*³, a native pony of India.

Tat, *sb.*⁴, in phr. *tit for tat*: see TIT.

Tat, *v.* Also **tatt.** 1842. [Origin unkn.] *intr.* To do tatting. *trans.* To make by tatting.

Ta-ta (tætā·), *int.* 1837. A nursery expression for 'Good-bye': also used playfully by adults.

Tatar: see TARTAR.²

‖**Tatou, tatu** (ta·tu). 1568. [Native name in Tupi.] An armadillo. b. In comb. with defining words, applied (in Tupi and Guarani) to various species, as **ta:touay·** (tatou-áiba), the wounded armadillo; **ta:touhou·**, **ta:toupe·ba**, = PEBA.

Tatter (tæ·təɹ), *sb.*¹ late ME. [Of Scand. origin; cf. ON. †*taturr* (later Icel. *tǫturr*, *töturr*), pl. *tötrar* tatters, rags.] 1. An irregularly torn piece, strip, or scrap of cloth or similar substance, hanging loose from the main body, esp. of a garment; more rarely applied to the separate pieces into which a thing is torn; a rag. In *pl.* often = tattered or ragged clothing; rags. †2. *transf.* A person wearing tattered or ragged clothes; a tatterdemalion -1637.

1. *fig.* To see a robustious Pery-wig-pated Fellow, teare a Passion to tatters, to verie ragges SHAKS.

Tatter, *sb.*² *rare.* 1881. [f. TAT *v.*] One who tats or does tatting.

Tatter (tæ·təɹ), *v.* late ME. [app. a back-formation from TATTERED.] *trans.* To tear or reduce to tatters; to make ragged; to tear in pieces. b. *intr.* To be or become tattered 1595. *fig.* A Nation so exhausted and tattered by divisions 1652.

Tatterdemalion, -demallion (tæ:tədĭmē¹·liən, -mæ·liən). 1608. [f. TATTER *sb.*¹, or more prob. TATTERED *a.*, + a factitious element suggesting a descriptive derivative.] A person in tattered clothing; a ragged or beggarly fellow; a ragamuffin. Also *attrib.* or as *adj.*

Tattered (tæ·təɹd), *a.*, *ppl. a.* late ME. [app. orig. f. TATTER *sb.*¹ + -ED².] †1. Having 'tatters', jags, or long pointed projections; denticulated; slashed or laciniated, as a garment -1501. 2. Torn or rent so as to hang in tatters; ragged 1596. 3. *transf.* Having tattered or ragged garments 1623. †4. Of a ship, building, or other solid structure: Dilapidated, battered, shattered -1798. †b. Of troops: Routed and broken up -1728.

2. Crowds of People in t. Garments ADDISON. 3. This is the man all t. and torn *Nursery Rhyme.* 4. [He] warns his t. fleet to follow home DRYDEN. I do not like ruined, t. cottages JANE AUSTEN.

Tatting (tæ·tiŋ). 1842. [Origin unkn.] A. *sb.* A kind of knotted lace, netted with a small flat shuttle-shaped instrument from stout sewing-thread; used for edging or trimming, etc. B. *vbl. sb.* The action or process of making this. Also *attrib.*, as *t.-cotton*, *-shuttle.*

Tattle (tæ·t'l), *sb.* 1529. [f. next.] The action of tattling; idle or frivolous talk; chatter, gossip. Also with *a* and *pl.* (now *rare*).

Like olde wiues tales, or tattles 1612. They..told the t. of the day SWIFT.

Tattle (tæ·t'l), *v.* 1481. [Ult. onomatopœic. Cf. MFlem. *tatelen*, LG. *tateln*, *täteln* to gabble, cackle.] †1. *intr.* To speak hesitatingly, falter, stammer; *esp.* to prattle as a young child. 2. To utter small talk; to talk idly or lightly; to chatter, babble; to chat, gossip 1547. 3. To talk without reticence so as to reveal private affairs. (Now usu. with mixture of sense 2.) 1581. 4. *trans.* To utter, say, or tell over in tattling. Now *rare.* 1588.

2. I must tell you, sir, you have tattled long enough DRYDEN. 3. She never tattled 1876.

Tattler (tæ·tləɹ). 1550. [f. TATTLE *v.* + -ER¹.] 1. One who tattles; an idle talker; a gossip; a telltale. †2. *slang.* A striking watch, a repeater; a watch in general -1844. 3. *Ornith.* Any of the sandpipers of the genus *Totanus* or subfamily *Totaninæ*; so called from their vociferous cry 1831.

Ta·ttling, *ppl. a.* 1576. [f. as prec. + -ING².] That tattles; chattering; gossiping; tale-telling. Hence **Ta·ttlingly** *adv.*

Tattoo (tætū·), *sb.*¹ 1644. [In 17th c. *taptoo*, a Du. *taptoe* in same sense; f. *tap* the tap (of a cask) + *toe* = *doe toe* 'shut'.] 1. *Mil.* A signal made, by beat of drum or bugle-call, in the evening, for soldiers to repair to their quarters in garrison or tents in camp. b. A military entertainment consisting of an elaboration of the tattoo by extra music and military exercises, usu. at night and by torch or other artificial light 1742. c. A drum-beat in general, as a means of raising an alarm, attracting attention, etc. 1688. 2. *transf.* A beating or pulsation as of a drum; the action of beating, thumping, or rapping continuously upon something 1755.

2. Beginning to play a rapid t. with her feet THACKERAY. Phr. *Devil's t.*, the action of idly tapping or drumming with the fingers, etc. upon a table or other object, in an irritating manner, or as a sign of vexation, impatience, or the like.

Tattoo (tætū·). *sb.*² 1777. [In 18th c. *tattaow*, *tattow* (tatau·), a. Polynesian *ta·tau*.] The act or practice of tattooing the skin (see the vb.); the mark or design made by tattooing.

Tattoo (tæ·tu), *sb.*³ *India.* 1629. [a. Hindī *ṭaṭṭū*.] A native-bred Indian pony.

Tattoo·, *v.*¹ 1780. [f. TATTOO *sb.*¹] 1. *trans.* To beat (a drum, etc.); to strike (something) with a succession of blows, to thump. 2. *intr.* To beat as upon a drum 1806.

Tattoo·, *v.*² 1769. [f. TATTOO *sb.*²] *trans.* To make permanent marks or designs upon the skin by puncturing it and inserting a pigment or pigments: practised by various tribes of low civilization, and by individuals in civilized communities. Hence **Tattoo·er.**

‖**Tatty** (tæ·ti), *sb. India.* 1792. [a. Hindī *ṭaṭṭī*.] A screen or mat, usu. made of the roots of the fragrant cuscus grass, which is placed in a frame so as to fill up the opening of a door or window, and kept wet, in order to cool and freshen the air of a room.

Tau (tǭ, tau). ME. [a. Gr. ταῦ, name of the letter **T** in the Greek alphabet; see T, the letter.] 1. The name of the letter T in the Greek, Hebrew, and ancient Semitic alphabets. Often in the sense 'last letter', as *tau* was orig. in Greek, and continued to be in Hebrew, etc. 2. A mark of the shape of the letter **T**, a St. Anthony's cross; a figure of this as a sacred symbol ME. 3. The Amer. toad-fish (*Batrachus tau*): so called from having markings resembling the letter **T**.

Comb.: **tau-cross** = sense 2.

‖**Taube** (tau·bə). 1913. [G., dove.] A type of German aeroplane.

Taught (tǭt), *ppl. a.* ME. Pa. t. and pa. pple. of TEACH *v.*

Taunt (tǭnt), *sb.* 1529. [Origin obsc.; perh. from F. *tant pour tant* tit for tat; hence, primarily, 'a return thrust, an effective rejoinder'.] †1. In phr. *t. for* (*pour*) *t.*, like for like, tit for tat, in reply or rejoinder -1620. (Also *tint for t.* 1620-1828.) †2. A smart or clever rejoinder; banter -1625. 3. An insulting or provoking gibe or sarcasm; a mocking or scornful reproach or challenge; a casting of something in any one's teeth 1529. †b. *transf.* An object of scornful gibes (*biblical*) –1611.

3. Haue I liu'd to stand at the t. of one that makes Fritters of English? SHAKS. With ireful taunts each other they oppose POPE. b. *Jer.* xxiv. 9.

Taunt (tǭnt), *a.* 1579. [Origin obsc.] *Naut.* Of masts: Excessively tall or lofty.

Taunt (tǭnt), *v.* 1513. [See TAUNT *sb.*] †1. *intr.* To make an effective rejoinder; to exchange banter –1548. †2. *trans.* To 'chaff', banter –1596. 3. To reproach (a person) *with* something in a sarcastic, scornful, or insulting way 1560. b. *intr.* To utter taunts or stinging reproaches 1560. 4. *trans.* To drive or get by taunting; to provoke 1813.

3. They taunted him with cowardice FROUDE. 4. Proscribed at home, And taunted to a wish to roam BYRON. Hence **Tau·nter.**

Tau·nting, *ppl. a.* 1548. [-ING [2].] That taunts or reproaches provokingly.

They accompanied their notice..with every kind of insolent and t. reflection BURKE. Hence **Tau·ntingly** *adv.*

Tauric (tǭ·rik), *a.* 1816. [f. Gr. ταῦρος or L. *taurus* + -IC.] Taurine.

Taurid (tǭ·rid). 1888. [f. TAURUS, after LEONID, PERSEID.] *Astron.* In *pl.* A system of meteors which appear to radiate from a point in the constellation Taurus about the 20th of November.

Tauriform (tǭ·rifǭɹm), *a.* 1721. [ad. L. *tauriformis*, f. *taurus*; see -FORM.] Having the form of a bull.

Taurine (tǭ·rəin), *sb.* 1842. [f. TAURO- in TAUROCHOLIC + -INE [5].] *Chem.* A neutral crystallizable substance, $C_2H_7NSO_3$, amido-ethyl-sulphonic acid, obtained in 1826 by L. Gmelin from ox-bile, and contained in the bile of most other animals, resulting from the transformation of taurocholic acid under the influence of acids and alkalies.

Taurine (tǭ·rəin), *a.* 1613. [ad. L. *taurinus*, f. *taurus*; see -INE [1].] Of, pertaining to, of the nature of, or resembling a bull.

Tauro-, repr. Gr. ταυρο-, comb. form of ταῦρος (= L. *taurus*) bull, occurring in a few words derived from Greek, and modern chemical terms.

Tauro·boly [L. *taurobolium*, f. Gr. ταυροβόλος] the sacrifice of bulls. **Taurocho·lic** *a.*, *Chem.* in *t. acid*, an acid ($C_{26}H_{45}NSO_7$) found in the bile of the ox and of most animals, mostly together with glycocholic acid. **Tau·rocol(l** [Gr. ταυρόκολλα], glue made from bulls' hides (*rare*). **Tauro·machy** [Gr. ταυρομαχία], the practice or custom of bull-fighting; with *a* and *pl.*, a bull-fight; so **Tauroma·chian,** *a.* of or pertaining to tauromachy.

‖ **Taurus** (tǭ·rɒs). late ME. [L.] *Astron.* a. The second of the zodiacal constellations, the Bull, in which are included the groups of the Pleiades and Hyades. b. Also, the second of the divisions or signs of the Zodiac, into which the sun enters on or near the 21st of April: orig. identical with the constellation. Symbol ♉.

Taurylic (tǭri·lik), *a.* 1868. [f. L. *taurus* + -YL + -IC.] *Chem.* In *t. acid*, a colourless oil (C_7H_8O) obtained together with phenol from human urine and that of cows and horses.

Taut, taught (tǭt), *a.* ME. [The same word as ME. *toȝt*, perh. an altered form of *tiȝt* TIGHT, under the influence of *toȝen* 'drawn', pa. pple. of TEE *v.*[1]] †1. Tense, as a surface; tight, distended –1612. 2. Tightly drawn, as by longitudinal tension; stiff, tense, not slack 1604. b. Tightly or trimly done up; put into good order. Of a person: Neat in appearance. 1870. c. *fig.* Of a person: Strict or severe as to duty 1833.

2. The hawser was as t. as a bowstring STEVENSON. b. A fair wind, and the ship t. and trim 1887. Hence **Tau·tly** *adv.* **Tau·tness.**

Tautegorical (tǭtĭgǫ·rikăl), *a.* *nonce-wd.* 1825. [f. TAUTO-, after ALLEGORICAL.] Expressing the same subject but with a difference; opp. to *metaphorical*, etc. COLERIDGE.

Tauten (tǭ·t'n), *v.* 1814. [f. TAUT *a.* + -EN [5].] *trans.* and *intr.* To make, or become, taut.

Tauto- (tǭto), bef. a vowel properly **taut-**, repr. Gr. ταυτο-, comb. form of ταὐτό, contr. of τὸ αὐτό the same; occurring in TAUTOLOGY, TAUTOMERISM, and their derivs.; also in various rare technical words.

Tauto‚ou·sian, -ious *adjs.* [f. eccl. Gr. ταὐτοούσιος, f. οὐσία essence], *Theol.* having absolutely the same essence. **Tauto·phony** [med. Gr. ταυτοφωνία, f. φωνή voice], repetition of the same (vocal) sound; so **Tautopho·nic, -al** *adjs.* repeating the same round. **Tautozo·nal** *a.*, *Cryst.* belonging to or situated in the same zone.

Tautochrone (tǭ·tŏkroun). 1774. [f. TAUTO- + Gr. χρόνος time.] *Math.* That curve upon which a particle moving under the action of gravity (or any given force) will reach the lowest (or some fixed) point in the same time, from whatever point it starts. So **Tauto·chronous** *a.* having the character of a t.; occupying the same time; isochronous.

Tautog (tǭtǫ·g). Also **tautaug.** 1643. [ad. Narragansett *taut-auog*, pl. of *taut*, name of the fish.] A labroid fish, *Tautoga americana* (*T. onitis*), also called *black-fish* or *oyster-fish*, abundant on the Atlantic coast of N. America, and esteemed for food.

Tautologic (tǭtolǫ·dʒik), *a.* *rare.* 1818. [f. Gr. ταὐτολογία TAUTOLOGY + -IC.] = next 1.

Tautological (tǭtolǫ·dʒikăl), *a.* 1620. [f. as prec. + -ICAL.] 1. Pertaining to, characterized by, involving, or using tautology; repeating the same word, or the same notion in different words. 2. Of an echo: Repeating a sound several times. Now *rare* or *Obs.* 1677. Hence **Tautolo·gically** *adv.*

Tautologize (tǭtǫ·lŏdʒəiz), *v.* 1607. [f. next + -IZE.] *intr.* To repeat the same thing in the same or different words; to use tautology. Hence **Tauto·logism,** the use or practice of tautology; an instance of this. **Tauto·logist,** one who practises tautology.

Tautologous (tǭtǫ·lŏgəs), *a.* 1714. [f. Gr. ταὐτολόγος (f. ταὐτό the same + -λογος saying) + -OUS.] = TAUTOLOGICAL 1.

Tautology (tǭtǫ·lŏdʒi). 1579. [ad. late L. *tautologia*, a. Gr. ταὐτολογία, f. ταὐτολόγος (see prec.).] a. A repetition of the same statement. b. The repetition (esp. in the immediate context) of the same word or phrase, or of the same idea or statement in other words: usu. as a fault of style. With *a* and *pl.*, an instance of this. c. Applied to the repetition of a statement as its own reason, or to the identification of cause and effect 1659. d. *transf.* A mere repetition of acts, incidents, or experiences 1650.

b. That villanous t. of lawyers, which is the scandal of our nation WESLEY. d. Our whole Life is but a nauseous T. 1687.

Tautomerism (tǭtǫ·mĕriz'm). 1885. [f. Gr. ταὐτο- TAUTO- + μέρος part, after ISOMERISM.] *Chem.* The property exhibited by certain organic compounds of behaving in different reactions as if they possessed two (or more) different constitutions, that is, as if the atoms of the same compound or group were arranged in two (or more) different ways, expressible by different structural formulæ (e.g. the group —CH:C(OH)—, or —CH_2.CO—, in ethyl aceto-acetate). So **Tau·tomer,** any one of the forms of a tautomeric compound in relation to another. **Tautomeric** (tǭtome·rik) *a.* pertaining to or exhibiting t.

Tavern (tæ·vəɹn). ME. [a. OF. *taverne* :—L. *taberna* hut, booth, etc., also a tavern or inn.] 1. In early use, a public house or tap-room where wine was retailed; a dram-shop; now = PUBLIC HOUSE 2 b. †2. A shop or workshop attached to, or (often) under, a dwelling-house. *dial.* –1703.

Taverner (tæ·vəɹnəɹ). ME. [a. AF., = OF. *tavernier*, f. *taverne* TAVERN.] 1. A tavern-keeper. *arch.* †2. One who frequents taverns; a tippler –1612.

†**Taw,** *sb.*[1] *rare.* 1562. [f. TAW *v.*] 1. Tawed leather; white leather. 2. A thong, whip. [app. the sing. of TAWS, TAWSE.] –1853.

Taw (tǭ), *sb.*[2] 1709. [Origin obsc.] A large fancy marble, often streaked or variegated, being that with which the player shoots. b. *transf.*, often *pl.* A game played with such marbles 1709. c. The line from which the players shoot in playing the game 1740.

Taw (tǭ), *v.* [OE. *tawian* :—OTeut. **tawōjan* (cf. Du. *touwen*; Goth *taujan* to make).] 1. *trans.* To prepare or dress (some raw material) for use, or for further manipulation; e.g. to soften (hides) by beating, to heckle (hemp), etc. 2. *spec.* To make (skins) into leather by steeping them in a solution of alum and salt; the product is white and pliant, and is known as *alum*, *white*, or *Hungarian leather* ME. †3. *fig.* To treat (a person) abusively or with contumely –1549. b. To flog. *Obs.* exc. *dial.* 1600.

Tawdry (tǭ·dri), *sb.* and *a.* 1612. [As sb., short for TAWDRY LACE; hence referring to the showy but cheap quality of these in the 17th c.] A. *sb.* †1. Short for next. DRAYTON. 2. Cheap and pretentious finery 1680.

1. Of which the Naïdes, and the blew Nereïdes make Them Taudries for their necks DRAYTON. 2. A poor bedizened creature, clad in t. 1867.

B. *adj.* 1. Of the nature of cheap finery; showy or gaudy without real value 1676. 2. *transf.* Of persons or their condition: Tawdrily dressed or decked out; cheaply adorned 1676. 3. *fig.* esp. of style, diction, etc.; hence of a speaker or writer: Pretentiously fine 1696.

1. The high altar is wretchedly t. 1859. 2. Taudry affected Rogues, well drest WYCHERLEY. 3. 'Tis but Taudry Talk, and next to very Trash PENN.

†**Tawdry lace.** 1548. [f. *t* (final letter of *Saint*) + *Audrey*.] orig. *St. Audrey's lace*, i.e. lace of St. Audrey or Etheldrida (patron saint of Ely): A silk 'lace' or necktie, much worn by women in the 16th and early 17th c.; sometimes taken as a type of female adornments –1750.

Taudrey Lace, so called from St. Audrey..who thought her self punished for wearing rich Necklaces of Jewels; and therefore women after that wore Necklaces of fine silk, called Taudrey laces BLOUNT.

Tawer (tǭ·əɹ). late ME. [f. TAW *v.*; see -ER [1].] One who taws or who prepares white leather.

Tawery (tǭ·əri). *rare.* 1830. [f. or as prec.] An establishment where skins are tawed.

Tawny (tǭ·ni), *a.* and *sb.* [Late ME. *tauny*, *tawne*, a. AF. *taune*, OF. *tané*, later *tanné*, 'foncé comme le tan', f. *tan* TAN *sb.*] Name of a colour consisting of brown with a preponderance of yellow or orange; but formerly applied also to other shades of brown. A. as *adj.* Having, or being of, this colour.

A lion's t. skin COWPER. A light and t. wine DICKENS.

B. as *sb.* 1. Tawny colour. In *Her.* = TENNE. late ME. †2. Cloth of a tawny colour –1587. 3. = TAWNY-MOOR. *arch.* 1660. Hence **Taw·niness,** t. quality or condition.

†**Taw·ny-moor.** 1603. [f. prec. + MOOR *sb.*[2]] A name given to the tawny or brown-skinned natives of foreign lands; prob. orig. to natives of northern Africa –1849.

Taws, tawse (tǭz), *sb.* Chiefly *Sc.* 1585. [app. pl. of TAW *sb.*[1] (but evidenced much earlier); occas. treated as a sing.] An instrument of family or school discipline, used in Scotch and some English schools, consisting of a leathern strap or thong, divided at the end into narrow strips.

A pedagogue called Fate; ..his fees are very high, and his tawse are rather heavy CARLYLE. Hence **Tawse** *v. trans.* to chastise with the t.

Tax (tæks), *sb.* ME. [app. f. next. In ME. *taxe* and *taske* TASK *sb.* were at first almost synonymous.] 1. A compulsory contribution to the support of government, levied on persons, property, income, commodities, transactions, etc., now at fixed rates, mostly proportional to the amount on which the contribution is levied. (In British practice few of the individual imposts are called by the name, the most notable being the INCOME TAX, LAND TAX, and PROPERTY TAX, also *dog-t.*, *match-t.*, *window-t.* In U.S. 'tax' is more generally applied to every federal, state, or local exaction of this kind). 2. *fig.* Something compared to a tax in its incidence, obligation, or burdensomeness; an oppressive or burdensome charge, obligation, or duty; a burden, strain, heavy demand 1628. †3. = TASK *sb.* I. 2, 2 b. (*rare*) –1564. †4. A charge, accusation; censure –1642.

1. A tax on German linen encourages home manufactures HUME. A t...is said to be *direct* when it is immediately taken from income or capital; and *indirect* when it is taken from them by making their owners pay for liberty to use certain articles, or to exercise certain privileges 1840. 2. The greatness of

the question..justifies even a heavier t. on the reader's attention 1862. *Comb.*, as *t.-collector.*

Tax (tæks), *v.* ME. [a. OF. *taxer* or ad. L. *taxare* to censure, charge; to rate, value, etc.; in med.L., also, to impose a tax.] **I. 1.** To determine the amount of (a tallage, fine, penalty, damages, etc.); to assess; rarely, to impose, levy (a tax); also, to settle the price or value of. *Obs.* exc. in *Law*, to assess (costs). †**2.** To impose, ordain, prescribe (a thing) *to* a person; also, to order (a person) *to* or *to do* something –1814. **3.** To impose a tax upon; to subject to taxation ME. **4.** *fig.* To burden; to make serious demands upon; to put a strain on 1672.

1. The costs to be taxed to the vttermost charge approved due 1592. 3. The King cannot t. any by way of Loans SIR E. COKE. The right of the people to be taxed entirely by their representatives 1857. 4. My ingenuity was often taxed for expedients KANE.

II. 1. To censure; to reprove, blame (a person, his action, etc.); to accuse, charge; to take to task, call to account; freq. const. *with.* 1569. †**2.** To call in question; to challenge, dispute (a statement, etc.) –1777.

1. None shall t. me with base Perjury DRYDEN. 2. Prone to taxe Gods wisedom, and call him to our barre 1642.

†**III.** Used in translations of the Bible as tr. Gr. ἀπογράφειν, to enter in a list, enrol –1611.

Taxable (tæ·ksăb'l), *a.* (*sb.*) 1474. [a. F., f. *taxer* to tax + -ABLE.] **A.** *adj.* †**1.** Liable to be assessed (*to* a tax, etc.); assessable –1569. **2.** Liable to be taxed; subject to a tax or duty 1583. †**3.** Liable to a charge or accusation; chargeable (*with* some fault); censurable, blamable –1792. **4.** *Law.* Of legal costs or fees: Liable to be taxed or reduced by the taxing-master 1828. **B.** *sb.* One who or that which is subject to taxation; *esp.* in *pl.* persons or things liable to a tax. orig. *U.S.* 1662.

2. To learn..the t. capacities of their farms COBBETT. Hence **Taxabi·lity, Ta·xableness**, t. quality or condition; liability to taxation. **Ta·xably** *adv.*

Taxaceous (tæksēⁱ·ʃəs), *a.* 1846. [f. mod. L. *Taxaceæ* (f. L. *taxus* yew); see -ACEOUS.] *Bot.* Belonging to the family *Taxaceæ*, including the yew.

Taxaspidean (tæksæ̆spi·diăn), *a.* 1899. [f. mod.L. *Taxaspidea* (f. Gr. τάξις arrangement + ἀσπίς shield) + -AN.] *Ornith.* Belonging to the division *Taxaspidea* of passerine birds, having the metatarsus regularly scutellated behind.

Taxation (tæksēⁱ·ʃən). ME. [a. AF. *taxacioun* = OF. *taxation*, ad. L. *taxationem*, f. *taxare.*] **1.** The fixing of the sum of an impost, damages, price, etc.; assessment, valuation. *Obs.* exc. *Hist.* **b.** *T. of costs*, the allowing or disallowing, by certain officials of courts of law, of the charges made by solicitors or other persons (e.g. arbitrators) subject to the jurisdiction of the court 1552. **2.** The imposition or levying of taxes (formerly including local rates); the action of taxing or the fact of being taxed; also *transf.* the revenue raised by taxes. With *a* and *pl.*, an instance of this. 1447. †**3.** Accusation; censure, reproof, blame –1653.

Taxative (tæ·ksătiv), *a. rare.* 1862. [ad. med. or mod.L. *taxativus*, f. ppl. stem of *taxare* to TAX; see -ATIVE.] Having the function of taxing; of or pertaining to taxation.

Taxator (tæksēⁱ·tǫɹ). *Hist.* late ME. [med. L., f. *tāxare* to TAX.] = TAXER.

†**Ta·x-cart.** orig. **taxed cart.** 1795. [f. TAX *sb.* or *taxed* pa. pple. of TAX *v.* + CART *sb.*] A two-wheeled (orig. springless) open cart drawn by one horse, and used mainly for agricultural or trade purposes, on which was charged only a reduced duty (afterwards taken off entirely) –1884.

Taxeopodous (tæksi,ǫ·pǒdəs), *a.* 1887. [irreg. f. Gr. τάξις (gen. τάξεως) arrangement + -ποδος footed (f. πούς foot) + -OUS.] *Zool.* Having each one of the carpal or tarsal bones of one row articulated with one of the other row; opp. to *diplarthrous.* So **Ta·xeopod** *a.* = *taxeopodous*; *sb.* a member of the division *Taxeopoda* of ungulate mammals, having this arrangement of the tarsal bones.

Taxer, taxor (tæ·ksəɹ, -ǫɹ). late ME. [a. AF. *taxour*, f. *taxer* to TAX; see -ER².] †**1.** An assessor –1695. **b.** *spec.* In the ancient universities, an officer (one of two) who fixed the rents of students' lodgings. At Cambridge, they also regulated the prices of commodities, kept the standard of weights and measures, and punished those who offended in these matters. Now *Hist.* 1532. **2.** One who levies a tax or taxes 1603.

Ta·x-ga:therer. *arch.* 1693. A collector of taxes.

Taxi (tæ·ksi), *sb.* 1907. Colloq. abbrev. of TAXIMETER; also of TAXI-CAB, -PLANE.

Comb. **t.-dance** *U.S.*, a dance at which a partner may be hired; so **t.-dancer.**

Taxi (tæ·ksi), *v.* 1914. [app. f. prec.] **1.** To travel by taxi-cab 1915. **2.** Of an aeroplane: To run along the ground before taking off or after alighting 1914.

Taxiarch (tæ·ksi,aɹk). 1808. [ad. Gr. ταξίαρχος, f. τάξις TAXIS + ἄρχειν to rule.] *Anc. Gr. Hist.* The commander of a taxis.

Taxi-cab, taxicab (tæ·ksi,kæb). 1907. [Short for TAXIMETER *cab*, and itself shortened to TAXI.] A cab for public hire, fitted with a taximeter; *esp.* a motor-cab so furnished.

Taxicorn (tæ·ksikǭɹn), *a.* and *sb.* 1842. [a. mod.L. *Taxicornes* pl., app. f. Gr. τάξις arrangement, a row or series + L. *cornu* horn.] *Ent.* **A.** *adj.* Having perfoliate antennæ, as the beetles of the obsolete family *Taxicornes.* **B.** *sb.* A beetle of this family.

Taxidermal (tæksidǭ·ɹmăl), *a.* 1877. [f. TAXIDERMY + -AL 1.] Of or pertaining to taxidermy. So **Taxide·rmic** *a.* 1847.

Taxidermy (tæ·ksidǝ:ɹmi). 1820. [mod. f. Gr. τάξις arrangement + δέρμα skin.] The art of preparing and preserving the skins of animals, and stuffing and mounting them so as to present the appearance, attitude, etc., of the living animal. Hence **Taxide·rmist**, one skilled in t.

Taximeter (tæksi·mītəɹ). 1898. [ad. F. *taximètre*, f. *taxe* tariff + *-mètre* -METER.] An automatic contrivance fitted on a cab, etc., to indicate to the passenger at any point the distance traversed and the fare due.

attrib., as *t.-cab, -driver.*

Taxin (tæ·ksin). 1907. [f. L. *taxus* yew + -IN¹.] *Chem.* 'A resinous substance obtained from the leaves of the yew-tree' (Watts). So **Ta·xine** (-əin), a poisonous alkaloid found in these leaves 1899.

Ta·xing, *vbl. sb.* late ME. [f. TAX *v.* + -ING¹.] The action of the vb. TAX.

Comb.: **t.-master**, an officer in a court of law who examines and allows or disallows items in a solicitor's bill of costs when disputed.

Taxinomy (tæksi·nǒmi). 1865. A more etymological form of TAXONOMY.

Ta·xiplane. 1920. [f. TAXI *sb.* + PLANE *sb.*³] A light aeroplane for public hire.

‖**Taxis** (tæ·ksis). 1758. [a. Gr. τάξις arrangement, f. τάσσειν to arrange.] **1.** *Surg.* A manipulative operation employed for replacing displaced parts, reducing hernia, etc. **2.** *Anc. Gr. Hist.* A company of soldiers, esp. foot-soldiers, variously answering in size to a modern company, battalion, regiment, or brigade 1850. **3.** *Biol.* The reaction of a free organism to external stimulus by movement in a particular direction 1904.

Taxless (tæ·kslės), *a.* 1615. [-LESS.] Free from taxes or taxation; untaxed.

Taxonomy (tæksǫ·nǒmi). 1828. [ad. F. *taxonomie*, irreg. f. Gr. τάξις TAXIS + -νομία distribution.] Classification, esp. in relation to its general laws or principles; that department of science, or of a particular science or subject, which consists in or relates to classification. So **Taxo·nomer**, a scientific classifier. **Taxono·mic, -al** *adjs.* classificatory. **Taxo·nomist** = *taxonomer.*

Ta·x(-)pay:er. 1816. One who pays a tax or the taxes generally; one who is liable to taxation; in U.S. including local rate-payers.

‖**Tayassu, tayaçu** (tā,yăsū·). 1698. [Tupi *tayaçu* = tania-eater, f. *taña, taja*, TANIA + *çu* to eat.] The Common or Collared Peccary, *Dicotyles torquatus* (*D. tajacu*).

‖**Tayra** (tai·rā). 1854. [Tupi *taira.*] Native name in Brazil of a mammal of the weasel family, *Galera barbara.*

‖**Tazza** (ta·ttsa). *Pl.* **tazze** (ta·ttsė). 1828. [It., app. a. Arab. *ṭass, ṭassah* basin; see TASS².] A shallow ornamental bowl or vase; prop., one supported on a foot.

T.B., colloq. abbrev. of TUBERCLE-*bacillus*, pop. of TUBERCULOSIS.

Tcheka, che(-)ka (tʃē·kă). 1921. [Russ., f. the names (*tche, ka*) of the initial letters of *tchrezvytchâinaya kommíssiya* extraordinary commission.] An organization set up in 1917 under the Soviet régime in Russia for the secret investigation of counter-revolution activities, superseded in 1922 by the OGPU.

Tchetvert (tʃe·tvəɹt). 1544. [Russ., = quarter.] A Russian measure of capacity for grain.

Tchick (tʃik), *sb.* 1823. A representation of the click made by pressing some part of the tongue against the palate and withdrawing it with suction; prop. the unilateral palatal click used to urge on a horse, etc. So **Tchick** *v.*

Tea (tī), *sb.* 1601. [prob. ad. Du. *thee* (from Malay) = F. *thé*, etc.; ad. Chinese, Amoy dial. *t'e* = Mandarin *ch'a* (whence Pg. *cha*, etc.). In English orig. pronounced (tē), and sometimes spelt *tay.*] **1.** The leaves of the tea-plant (see 3), usu. in a dried and prepared state for making the drink (see 2); first imported into Europe in the 17th c. 1655. **b.** With qualifying words, denoting various kinds 1704. **2.** A drink made by infusing these leaves in boiling water, having a somewhat bitter and aromatic flavour, and acting as a moderate stimulant; largely used as a beverage 1601. **3.** The plant from which tea is obtained, a shrub of the genus *Thea* (now often included in *Camellia*), family *Ternstrœmiaceæ*, with white flowers, and oval pointed slightly-toothed evergreen leaves; grown in China, Japan, India, and adjacent countries. (Now chiefly in comb., as *t.-leaf, -plant.*). 1663. **4.** A meal or social entertainment at which tea is served; *esp.* an ordinary afternoon or evening meal, at which the usual beverage is tea 1738. **5.** Used as a general name for infusions made in the same way as tea; mostly used medicinally; e.g. *camomile t., senna t.* 1665. **6.** With defining words, applied to various plants whose leaves, flowers, etc. are used in the same way as tea (also to the leaves, etc. themselves, or the drink infused from them) 1727.

1. A small parcel of most excellent t...to be sold.. the lowest price is 30s. a pound 1680. **b. Black t.** is exposed to the air for some time, so as to produce fermentation, before roasting. **Green t.** is roasted almost immediately after gathering, and often artificially coloured. 2. I did send for a cup of tee (a China drink) of which I never had drunk before PEPYS. Here, thou, great Anna! whom three realms obey, Dost sometimes counsel take—and sometimes Tea POPE. 4. The now universally-honoured institution of 'five o'clock tea' 1882. *High t., meat t.*: see HIGH *a.*, MEAT *sb.* 5. Valerian, or rosemary, t. 1783. Poppy t. 1893. 6. **Arabian t.**, *Catha edulis*, whose leaves furnish a stimulating beverage used in Arabia. **Australian t., Botany Bay t.**, an Australian species of sarsaparilla, *Smilax glycyphylla*, also called *sweet tea.* **Brazil** or **Brazilian t.**, *Stachytarpha jamaicensis.* **Labrador t.**, *Ledum latifolium* and *L. palustre.* **New Jersey t.**, *Ceanothus americanus.* **New Zealand t.**, *Leptospermum scoparium.* **Oswego t.**, a N. Amer. aromatic labiate, *Monarda didyma*, used as a tonic and stomachic. **Paraguay t.**, *Ilex paraguayensis*, used in S. America as a substitute for t. **Sweet t.** = *Botany Bay t.*

attrib. and *Comb.*: *t.-drinker, -duty, -planter, -shop*; **t.-basket**, a basket containing the requisites for afternoon t.; **-berry**, the Amer. wintergreen *Gaultheria procumbens*, also called *Canada t.* or *mountain t.*; also, the fruit of this; **-board** (now *local*), a t.-tray, esp. a wooden one; **-bug**, a destructive insect which infests tea-plants; **-caddy**, a small box formerly with divisions, for holding t.; **-cake**, a light kind of flat cake to be eaten at t.; **-canister** = *t.-caddy*; **-clam**, *U.S.* a very small clam; **-clipper**, a clipper or fast-sailing vessel formerly employed in the t.-trade; **-cloth**, a cloth used for wiping the utensils used for a meal after washing them; (*b*) *afternoon t.*, a small table-cloth used at afternoon t.; **-cosy**, a covering for a t.-pot to keep it hot; **-fight**, *colloq.* or *slang*, joc. name for a t.-party or t.-meeting; **-gown**, a special fashion of garment worn by girls and women at t.; **-house**, a refreshment-house where t. is served (esp. in China or Japan); **-kettle**, a kettle in which water may be boiled for making t.; **-meeting**, a public social meeting (usu. in connexion with a religious organization) at which t. is taken; **-room**, a room in which t. is served in a refreshment-house, etc.; notably, that of the British House of Commons, the scene of numerous informal meetings of members; **-scented** *a.*, having a scent like that of t. (applied to a variety of rose); **-service, -set,** a set of articles used in serving t. at table, comprising t.-pot, milk-jug, sugar-basin, cups and saucers, etc.; **-things** *sb. pl.* articles used in serving t.; **-time,** the time at which the meal called t. is usu. taken; **-urn,** an urn with a tap, placed upon a t.-table, to hold hot water for making t.

Tea, *v. colloq.* 1812. [f. prec.] I. *trans.* To supply or regale with tea; to give a tea to. 2. *intr.* To drink tea; *esp.* to have one's tea 1823.

Teach (tītʃ), *v.* Pa. t. and pa. pple. **taught** (tǭt). [OE. *tǽc(e)an* (*tǽhte, getǽht*):—OTeut. **taikjan*, from an ablaut series **teik-, taik-, tik-* to show, pre-Teut. **deig-, dig-*, also **deik-*, in Skr. *diç-*, Gr. δεικνύναι, δεῖγμα.] I. †1. *trans.* To show –1567. 2. *Ship-building.* (*absol.*) Of a line: To point in a particular direction 1850. II. To show by way of information or instruction. 1. *To t. a thing*: to impart or convey the knowledge of; to give instruction or lessons in (a subject); †to make known (a message) OE. 2. *To t. a person a thing, a thing to a person* (or *agent*): to communicate something to a person, by way of instruction; †to inform OE. b. To show or make known to a person (how to do something) OE. c. Used by way of threat: To let a person know the cost or penalty of something 1575. 3. *To t. a person* or *agent* (with personal object only): to impart knowledge to, give instruction to; to inform, instruct, educate, train, school. OE. *To t.* (*a*) *school* (now *dial.* and *U.S.*): to teach in a school 1590. 4. *absol.* or *intr.* To communicate knowledge; to act as a teacher OE.

1. He cam first hom..and þer taute he gramer 1451. 2. Thynges that I shal teche the LYDG. I am being taught French 1825. b. Education..means teaching children to be clean, active, honest, and useful RUSKIN. c. I'll t. you to be too clever, my lad 1889. 3. All Nations they shall t. MILT. †*To t. to*: to train to. 4. One that teacheth by publique Authority HOBBES.

Teachable (tī·tʃăb'l), *a.* 1483. [f. TEACH *v.* + -ABLE.] †1. Able to teach –1695. 2. Capable of being taught (as a person); docile 1483. 3. Capable of being taught (as a subject); that may be communicated or imparted by instruction 1669.

2. These old Greeks were t., and learnt from all the nations round KINGSLEY. 3. To teach you..everything that is t. RUSKIN. Hence **Teachabi·lity, Tea·chableness,** docility; †instructiveness; the quality of being communicable by instruction. **Tea·chably** *adv.*

Teacher (tī·tʃəɹ). ME. [f. as prec. + -ER[1].] One who or that which teaches or instructs; *spec.* one whose function is to give instruction, esp. in a school.

A t. of anatomy 1799. His daily teachers had been woods and rills,..The sleep that is among the lonely hills WORDSW. Hence **Tea·chership,** the office, function, or position of a t.

Tea·-chest. 1740. [f. TEA *sb.* + CHEST *sb.*[1]] †1. = *tea-caddy* –1850. 2. A large box or chest of cubical form, lined with sheet-lead, in which tea is packed for transport 1801.

Tea·ching, *vbl. sb.* ME. [f. TEACH *v.* + -ING[1].] The imparting of instruction; the occupation or function of a teacher. b. That which is taught; a thing taught, doctrine, instruction, precept ME.

Tea·-cup. 1700. A cup from which tea is drunk; usu. of small or moderate size, with a handle.

Phr. *A storm in a tea-cup*, a great commotion in a circumscribed circle, or about a small matter. Hence **Tea·cupful,** as much as a tea-cup will hold, a gill.

Tea·-garden. 1802. 1. An open-air enclosure, connected with a house of entertainment, where tea and other refreshments are served. 2. A plantation in which tea-plants are grown 1882.

Teague (tēg, tīg). *colloq. Obs.* or *arch.* 1661. [Anglicized spelling of the Irish name *Tadhg*, variously pronounced (tēg, tīg, taig).] A nickname for an Irishman.

Teak (tīk). 1698. [ad. Pg. *teca*, ad. Malayalam *tēkka*.] 1. A large E. Indian tree *Tectona grandis* (family *Verbenaceæ*), with opposite egg-shaped leaves and panicles of white flowers; more usu., its timber, a dark, heavy, oily wood of great strength and durability, used largely in the construction of ships and railway carriages, and for other purposes; distinctively called *Indian t.* 2. Applied, usu. with defining word to other trees which produce strong or durable timber, or otherwise resemble the Indian t. 1842.

2. **African T.,** *Oldfieldia africana* (family *Euphorbiaceæ*), or its wood, which is too heavy to be exclusively used in shipbuilding; **T. of New Zealand,** *Vitex littoralis*.

Teal (tīl). [ME. *tele* :—WGer. **taili-*.] 1. A small freshwater fowl, *Querquedula* or *Anas crecca*, or other species of the genus, the smallest of the ducks, widely distributed in Europe, Asia, and America; also locally applied to other genera of the *Anatidæ*. Also as collect. pl. b. The flesh of this bird as food 1475. 2. With distinctive prefixes, applied to various species of *Querquedula* and allied genera 1678.

2. **American** or **Green-winged T.,** *Q. carolinensis*; **Blue-winged T.** of N. and S. America, *Q. discors* or *cyanoptera*; **Garganey T.,** the GARGANEY, *Q. circia*; **Chinese T.,** the mandarin duck, *Aix galericulata*. Hence **Tea·lery,** a place where teal are kept and fattened.

Tea·-leaf. 1756. The leaf of the tea-plant; *esp.* in *pl.* the leaves after being infused to make the beverage.

Team (tīm), *sb.* [OE. *tēam* :—OTeut. **taumoz*, prob. from **taugmoz* the action of drawing, draught, from ablaut series **teuh-, tauh-, tuh-*, to draw, L. *ducere* to lead.] I. †a. Child-bearing –ME. b. A family or brood of young animals; now *dial.* applied to a litter of pigs, a brood of ducks OE.

b. We have a few teams of ducks, bred in the moors G. WHITE.

II. 1. A set of draught animals; two or more oxen, horses, dogs, etc. harnessed to draw together. (Pl., after a numeral, *team.*) OE. 2. a. *fig.* Applied to persons drawing together 1614. b. *transf.* A number of persons associated in some joint action; now *esp.* a definite number of persons forming a side in a match, e.g., in a football match or a 'tug-of-war' 1529. 3. Two or more beasts, or a single beast, along with the vehicle which they draw; a horse and cart, or waggon with two horses. Now *dial.* and *U.S.* 4. A flock of wild ducks or other birds flying in a line or string 1688.

3. He was returning..with a loaded t. 1798. b. *fig.* (*U.S.*) Usu. *a whole* (or *full*) *t.* 1833. 4. Like a long t. of snowy swans on high DRYDEN.

III. In Anglo-Saxon Law. a. In a suit for the recovery of goods alleged to have been stolen, the action or procedure by which the holder transferred or referred it back to a third person to defend the title to them; vouching to warranty. *Obs.* exc. *Hist.* b. The right or prerogative of jurisdiction in a suit of *tēam*, together with the fees and profits thence accruing; from the 11th c. usually included in charters granting land (in which it regularly followed *toll*, esp. in the formula *with sac and soc, toll and team, infangthief*, etc.).

Comb.: **t.-work,** (*a*) work done with a t. of beasts; (*b*) the combined action of a t. of players, etc.; (*c*) work done by a t. of operatives; (*d*) work done by persons working as a team, i.e. with concerted effort.

Team (tīm), *v.* 1552. [f. prec. II.] 1. *trans.* To harness (beasts) in a team; to yoke. 2. To transport by means of a team. b. *absol.* or *intr.* To drive a team. *U.S.* 1841. c. *fig.* (*U.S.*) *To t. up with*: to join forces with. 3. *trans.* To get (work) done by a team or teams of workmen; to let (work) to a contractor who employs teams of workmen. *U.S.* 1877.

Teamster (tī·mstəɹ). 1779. [f. TEAM *sb.* + -STER.] The driver or owner of a team.

Tea·-party. 1778. A party assembled to take tea together; a social entertainment at which tea is taken.

Boston t.: the revolutionary proceeding (1773) when tea was thrown overboard in Boston harbour as a protest against British taxation; hence, a lively proceeding.

Tea·-plant. 1727. = TEA *sb.* 3, 6.

Tea·-pot. 1705. A pot with a lid, spout, and handle, to contain an infusion of tea.

‖**Teapoy** (tī·poi). *India.* Also **tepoy.** 1828. [f. Hindī *tīn*, in comb. *tir-* three + Pers. *pāē, pāī* foot.] A small three-legged table or stand, or any tripod; (by erron. association with *tea*), such a table with a receptacle for tea.

Tear (tīəɹ), *sb.*[1] [OE. *tēar*, contr. from earlier **teahr, *teag(o)r*; cogn. w. Gr. δάκρυ, OL. *dacrima* (L. *lacrima*).] 1. A drop of the limpid fluid secreted by the lachrymal gland appearing in or flowing from the eye; chiefly as the result of emotion, esp. grief, but also of physical irritation or nervous stimulus: usu. in *pl.* b. As the visible feature of weeping: hence, put for this, or as the expression of grief or sorrow ME. 2. *transf.* and *fig.* A drop of any liquid; *spec.* a drop or bead of liquid spontaneously exuding OE. 3. *spec.* Applied to various gums that exude from plants in tear-shaped or globular beads, which then become solid or resinous OE. 4. Anything resembling or suggesting a tear; e. g. (*a*) a defect in glass caused by a small particle of vitrified clay; (*b*) a detonating bulb, or Prince Rupert's drop 1832.

1. There are also tears of joy 1855. b. He must not flote upon his watry bear..Without the meed of som melodious t. MILT. He gave to Mis'ry all he had, a t. GRAY. *In tears*, weeping, in sorrow or commiseration. 2. I would these dewy teares were from the ground SHAKS.

attrib. and *Comb.*, as *t.-drop*; **t.-bag,** (*a*) = *t.-pit*; (*b*) = *t.-gland*; **-bomb, -shell,** a bomb or shell charged with lachrymatory gas; **-gas,** lachrymatory gas; **-gland,** the lachrymal gland; **-mask,** a gas-mask; **-pit,** the lachrymal or sub-orbital sinus found in many species of deer, a fold or cavity beneath the inner corner of the eye, containing a thin waxy secretion.

Tear (tēəɹ), *sb.*[2] 1611. [f. TEAR *v.*] 1. An act of tearing or rending; the action of tearing; hence, damage caused by tearing (or similar violent action): also used *fig.* in ref. to body or mind 1666. 2. *concr.* A torn part or place; a rent or fissure 1611. 3. a. A rushing gallop or pace 1838. b. A spree. *U.S. slang.* 1869. c. A rage or passion; a violent flurry 1880.

1. Phr. *t. and wear, wear and t.*, including damage due to common use and ordinary wear; *fig.* The t. and wear of the campaign is telling severely on the ..Yeomanry 1901.

Tear (tēəɹ), *v.* Pa. t. **tore** (tōəɹ), *arch.* and *dial.* **tare** (tēəɹ). Pa. pple. **torn** (tǭɹn). [OE. *teran*, (*tær, tǽron, toren*). OTeut. **teran* was cogn. w. Gr. δέρειν to flay, Skr. *dar-* to burst.] I. 1. *trans.* To pull asunder by force (a body or substance, now esp. one of thin and flexible consistence, as cloth or paper), usu. so as to leave ragged or irregular edges; to rend. b. *transf.* To make a (hole, etc.) by tearing 1593. c. To shatter, split, rive (a hard solid body). Now *dial.* 1582. †d. Phr. *To t. a* (*the*) *cat*: to rant and bluster. SHAKS. 2. To wound or injure by rending; to lacerate OE. 3. In various *fig.* applications; *esp.* in later use, to split into parties or factions OE. b. Used of the effect of sounds, esp. loud or 'piercing' noises, on the air, etc. 1592. c. To harrow, wound (the heart, soul, feelings, etc.) 1666. 4. *To t.* (*out*) *the hair* in a frenzy of grief or anger: now a hyperbolical expression OE. 5. To pull, wrench, or drag by main force from its attachment or fixed place ME. b. *fig.* To take or remove by force or violence; to force; *refl.* to force oneself away 1574. 6. *intr.* To perform the act of tearing; to make a tear or rent 1526. 7. *intr.* (for *refl.* and *pass.*) To become torn or rent; *dial.* to burst asunder, split, snap 1526.

1. He hath torne my gowne a foote and more 1530. The unpopular minister of finance was torn in pieces by the mob 1841. Phr. (vulgar slang), *That's torn it*, that has spoilt or ruined everything. c. Their Fregates..were torne in pieces and sunke 1582. 2. Their defenceless Limbs the Brambles t. DRYDEN. 3. b. What noise or shout was that? it tore the Skie MILT. That man torn by domestic affliction 1859. 5. By tearing up the Trees by the Roots 1699. Ships from their Anchors torn ADDISON. b. At length he tore himself away 1797. 7. The Boards will T. or Shake, which is in vulgar English, Split or Crack 1703.

II. 1. *intr.* †To rant and bluster as a roisterer; †to vociferate; to 'go on' violently, to rave, to rage (*dial.*) 1601. 2. To move with violence or impetuosity; to rush or 'burst' impetuously or violently. *colloq.* 1599.

1. He goes through life, tearing, like a man possessed with a devil THACKERAY. 2. This river tore down the narrow valley with headlong violence 1894.

Tear-, the stem of TEAR *v.* in comb., as in **tear-away** *adj.*, characterized by impetuous speed, tearing; *sb.*, one who or that which 'tears' or rushes away, or acts with great impetuosity; **tear-off** *adj.*, adapted to be torn off; *sb.*, a sheet or slip of paper so attached as to be easily torn off; **tear-thumb**, two species of *Polygonum* the halberd-leaved tear-thumb, *P. arifolium*, and the arrow-leaved, *P. sagittatum*; so called from the hooded prickles on the petioles and angles of the stems.

Tear-bottle (tīᵊ·ɹ,bǫ:t'l). 1658. A bottle containing tears (cf. Ps. lvi. 8); *spec.* = LACHRYMATORY B. 1.

Tearer (tēᵊ·rəɹ). 1625. [f. TEAR *v.* + -ER¹.] 1. One who or that which tears or rends. 2. A person who tears or rushes along or about; a ranter, roisterer, swaggerer, bully 1625.

Tearful (tīᵊ·ɹfŭl), *a.* 1586. [f. TEAR *sb.*¹ + -FUL.] Full of tears; weeping; lachrymose. Sory and feareful, yea penitent and tearefull 1597. Hence **Tea·rful-ly** *adv.*, -**ness**.

Tearless (tīᵊ·ɹlės), *a.* 1603. [f. TEAR *sb.*¹ + -LESS.] Void of tears; shedding no tears, not weeping. Hence **Tea·rless-ly** *adv.*, -**ness**.

Tea·-rose. 1850. A variety (or group of varieties) of cultivated rose, derived from the species *Rosa indica*, var. *odorata*, having flowers of a pale yellow colour, with a delicate scent supposed to resemble that of tea. (Orig. *tea-scented rose.*) **b.** The colour of this rose 1884.

Teary (tīᵊ·ri), *a.* late ME. [f. TEAR *sb.*¹ + -Y¹.] 1. Full of or suffused with tears; tearful. Now *colloq.* 2. Of the nature of or consisting of tears (*rare*). late ME.

Tease, *sb.* 1693. [f. next.] 1. The action of teasing. 2. A person addicted to teasing. *colloq.* 1852.

Tease (tīz), *v.* [OE. *tǣsan* to tear or pull to pieces, tease (wool, etc.):—OTeut. **taisjan.*] 1. *trans.* To separate or pull asunder the fibres of; to comb or card (wool, flax, etc.) in preparation for spinning; to open *out* by pulling asunder; to shred. **b.** To comb the surface of cloth, after weaving, with teasels, which draw all the free hairs or fibres in one direction, so as to form a nap 1755. 2. To worry or irritate by persistent action which vexes or annoys; now *esp.* in lighter sense, to disturb by persistent petty annoyance, out of mere mischief or sport; to bother or plague in a petty way. Also *absol.* and *intr.* 1627.

1. To ply The sampler, and to teize the huswifes wooll MILT. 2. Harry ceased to t. and torment them with little tricks and devices of mischief 1881. *fig.* The earth..constantly teized more to furnish..luxuries..than..necessities GOLDSM.

Teasel, teazle (tī·z'l), *sb.* [OE. *tǣsel, tǣsl*:—OTeut. **taisilā*, f. **tais-* (OE. *tǣsan* to tease) with instr. suffix -*lā*.] 1. A plant of the genus *Dipsacus*, comprising herbs with prickly leaves and flower-heads; *esp.* **Fullers' T.**, *D. fullonum*, the heads of which have hooked prickles between the flowers, and are used for teasing cloth (see 2); **Wild T.**, *D. sylvestris*, having straight instead of hooked prickles. 2. The dried prickly flower-head or bur of the fullers' teasel (see 1), used for teasing or dressing cloth, so as to raise a nap on the surface. late ME. 3. *transf.* A mechanical substitute for the natural teasel in cloth-working 1835.

Comb.: **t.-frame**, a frame in which t. heads are fixed for dressing cloth (so **t.-board, -cylinder, -rod**). Hence **Tea·sel, tea·zle** *v. trans.* to raise a smooth nap on (cloth) with or as with teasels.

Teaseler (tī·z'ləɹ). late ME. [f. prec. + -ER¹.] 1. One whose occupation is to teasel cloth. 2. An implement for teaseling 1607.

Teaser (tī·zəɹ). late ME. [f. TEASE *v.* + -ER¹.] One who or that which teases, in various senses. **b.** Local name of several birds which chase gulls and force them to disgorge their prey, as the skua 1833. 2. Something that teases, or causes annoyance; something difficult to deal with, a 'poser'. *colloq.* 1759.

Tea·-spoon. 1686. A small spoon, usu. of silver or silvered metal, of a size suitable for stirring tea or other beverage in a cup. Hence **Tea·spoonful**, as much as a tea-spoon will hold; in medical prescriptions = 1 fluid-drachm.

Teat (tīt). [ME. *tete, tette*, a. OF. *tete*, later (and mod.) *tette*, replacing OE. *titt* (mod. dial. *tit*, dim. *tittie*) in the standard lang.] 1. The small protuberance at the tip of each breast or udder in female mammalia (except monotremes), upon which the ducts of the mammary gland open, and from which the milk is sucked by the young; the nipple. Formerly also applied to the whole breast or udder. Now usu. only of quadrupeds. †**b.** *fig.* A source of nourishment or supply -1675. 2. *transf.* A structure, natural or artificial, resembling a teat; a nipple 1587. Hence **Tea·ted** *a.* furnished with or having teats.

Tea·-ta:ble. 1688. [f. TEA *sb.* 4 + TABLE *sb.*] 1. A table at which tea is taken, or on which tea-things are placed for a meal. 2. *transf.* The company assembled at tea 1712. 3. *attrib.* chiefly in ref. to social gatherings 1700.

3. T. Talk—Such as mending of Fashions, spoiling Reputations, railing at absent Friends CONGREVE.

Tea-taster (tī·tē¹:stəɹ). 1858. One whose business is to test the quality of samples of tea by tasting them; a tea-expert. So **Tea·-ta:sting.**

Tea·-tray. 1773. [TRAY *sb.*¹] A tray for holding tea-things.

Tea·-tree. 1760. 1. *prop.* = TEA *sb.* 3. 2. *transf.* Applied in Australia, Tasmania, and New Zealand to various shrubs or trees of the myrtle family, of which the leaves have been used as a substitute for tea 1790.

Tec, 'tec (tek), *sb. slang.* 1888. Abbreviation for DETECTIVE.

Technic (te·knik), *a.* and *sb.* 1612. [ad. L. *technicus*, a. Gr. τεχνικός, f. τέχνη art, craft; see -IC.] **A.** *adj.* Pertaining to art, or to an art: = TECHNICAL. Now *rare.* **B.** *sb.* 1. A technical term, expression, point, or detail; a technicality. Chiefly *U.S. rare.* 1826. 2. Technical details or methods collectively; the technical department of a subject; *esp.* the formal and mechanical part of an art (now more commonly TECHNIQUE) 1855. **b.** Collective pl. **Technics** in same sense; also constr. as a sing. 1850. 3. = TECHNOLOGY 1. Usu. in pl. **Technics**. 1864.

2. Icelandic poetry..shows a powerful and developed t. M. ARNOLD. **b.** Literary technics, especially that of the novel, depends on reproducing experiments from life 1909.

Technical (te·knikăl), *a.* (*sb.*) 1617. [f. Gr. τεχνικός (see prec.) + -AL.] 1. Of a person: Skilled in or practically conversant with some particular art or subject (*rare*). 2. Belonging or relating to an art or arts; appropriate or peculiar to, or characteristic of, a particular art, science, profession, or occupation; also, of or pertaining to the mechanical arts and applied sciences generally, as in *t. education, t. school* 1727. **b.** *spec.* said of words, terms, phrases, etc., or of their senses or acceptations; as, the *t. terms* of logic; the *t. sense* of 'subject' in logic 1652. **c.** *transf.* Of an author, a treatise, etc.: Using technical terms; treating a subject technically 1779. **d.** That is such from the technical point of view 1860. **B.** *sb.* In *pl.* Technical terms or points; technicalities 1790.

2. *T. difficulty*, a difficulty arising in connexion with the method of procedure (esp. legal). **e.** Legally such, in the eyes of the law, as *t. assault* 1911. Hence **Te·chnicalism**, t. style, method, or treatment; addiction to technicalities. **Te·chnical-ly** *adv.*, -**ness**.

Technicality (teknikæ·līti). 1814. [f. prec. + -ITY.] 1. Technical quality or character; the use of technical terms or methods 1828. 2. A technical point, detail, term, or expression; something peculiar or specially belonging to the art or subject referred to. Usu. in *pl.* 1814.

2. To translate the technicalities of Kant into plain English 1874.

Technician (tekni·ʃăn). 1833. [f. TECHNIC + -IAN.] **a.** A person conversant with the technicalities of a particular subject. **b.** One skilled in the technique or mechanical part of an art, as music or painting.

Technicist (te·knisist). 1881. [f. as prec. + -IST.] = prec.; one who has technical knowledge.

Technico-, comb. element from Gr. τεχνικός (see TECHNIC). **Technico·logy**, = TECHNOLOGY 1, 2.

Technique (teknī·k). 1817. [a. F. (*la*) *technique*, sb. use of *technique* adj. TECHNIC.] Manner of artistic execution or performance in relation to formal or practical details (as dist. from general effect, expression, sentiment, etc.); the mechanical or formal part of an art, esp. of any of the fine arts; also, skill or ability in this department of one's art; mechanical skill in artistic work. (Usu. in ref. to painting or musical performance.)

A player may be perfect in t., and yet have neither soul nor intelligence GROVE.

Techno- (tekno), repr. Gr. τεχνο-, comb. τέχνη art: **Techno·cracy** (1932), an organization for the control of industrial resources by technologists; so **Te·chnocrat; Technocra·tic** *a.*

Technology (teknǫ·lŏdʒi). 1615. [ad. Gr. τεχνολογία, systematic treatment, f. τέχνη art, craft; see -LOGY.] 1. A discourse or treatise on an art or arts; the scientific study of the practical or industrial arts. **b.** *transf.* Practical arts collectively 1859. 2. The terminology of a particular art or subject; technical nomenclature 1658.

2. An engine, called, in the t. of that day, *fork* BENTHAM. So **Technolo·gical** *a.* pertaining or relating to t. **Techno·logist.**

Tecno- (also **tekno-**), repr. Gr. τεκνο-, comb. form of τέκνον child; used in Eng. in a few rare technical words, as **Tecnology** (teknǫ·lŏdʒi) [-LOGY], the scientific study of children.

Tectibranch (te·ktibræŋk), *a.* and *sb.* 1851. [f. L. *tectus* covered + *branchiæ* (Gr. βράγχια) gills.] *Zool.* **A.** *adj.* Belonging to the order or sub-order *Tectibranchiata* of gasteropod molluscs, comprising marine forms having the gills covered by the mantle, and small shells often concealed by this division. **B.** *sb.* A gasteropod belonging to this division. So **Tectibra·nchian** *a.* 1839. **Tectibra·nchiate** *a.* 1836.

Tectiform (te·ktifǭɹm), *a.* 1834. [ad. mod. L. *tectiformis*, f. *tectum* roof; see -FORM.] *Zool.* **a.** Roof-shaped; sloping downwards on each side from a central ridge. **b.** Serving as a covering or lid.

Tectology (tektǫ·lŏdʒi). 1883. [ad. G. *tektologie* (Haeckel), for **tektonologie*, f. Gr. τέκτων carpenter, builder; see -LOGY.] *Biol.* A sub-science of morphology, which regards the organism as composed of organic individuals of different orders; cf. PROMORPHOLOGY.

Tectonic (tektǫ·nik), *a.* 1656. [ad. late L. *tectonicus*, a. Gr. τεκτονικός pertaining to building, f. τέκτων, -ον- builder.] 1. Of or pertaining to building, or construction in general; constructional, constructive: used esp. in ref. to architecture and kindred arts. 2. *Geol.* Belonging to the actual structure of the earth's crust, or to general changes affecting it 1893. So **Tecto·nics** [= G. *tektonik*], the constructive arts in general.

Tectorial (tektōᵊ·riăl), *a.* 1890. [f. L. *tectorium* covering, a cover + -AL 1.] *Anat.* Covering like a roof: applied to a membrane in the internal ear.

‖**Tectrix** (te·ktriks). Usu. in pl. **tectrices** (tektrəi·sīz). 1874. [mod. L., fem. of L. *tector*, f. *tect-*, ppl. stem of *tegere* to cover; see -TRIX.] *Ornith.* = COVERT *sb.* 4. Hence **Tectri·cial** *a.* pertaining to the tectrices.

Ted (ted), *v.* late ME. [app. repr. an OE. **teddan*, cogn. w. Icel. *teðja*, pa. t. *tadda*, to dung, (prob.) to spread manure.] 1. *trans.* To spread out, scatter, or strew abroad (new-mown grass) for drying. Also *absol.* 2. *transf.* and *fig.* To scatter; to dissipate 1560.

1. The Grasse being cutte, must be well tedded and turned in the Sommer 1577. Hence **Te·dded** *ppl. a.* spread out for drying, as grass. **Te·dder**, one who teds new-mown grass; also, a machine for doing this.

Teddy-bear (te:dibēᵊ·ɹ). 1907. [*Teddy*, pet form of *Theodore*.] A stuffed figure of a bear in plush, used as a toy: called after Theodore Roosevelt (President of U.S.A. 1901–9). Also simply **Te·ddy.**

‖**Tedesco** (tede·sko), *a.* (*sb.*) *Pl.* **tedeschi** (-ki). 1814. [It., 'German'; ad. med. L. *theodiscus*; see DUTCH.] The Italian word for German; esp. used to express Teutonic influence as shown in some spheres of Italian art.

Te Deum (tī· dī·ŏm). OE. [From the opening words of the L. original, *Te Deum laudamus* 'Thee, God, we praise'.] An ancient Latin hymn of praise in the form of a psalm, sung as a thanksgiving on special occasions, as after a victory or deliverance; also regularly at Matins in the R. C. Ch., and (in an Eng. translation) at Morning Prayer in the Ch. of England. **b.** With *a* and *pl.* **(Te Deums),** in ref. to a recital of this, or (*allus.*) to any public utterance of praise to God; also, a service of (public) thanksgiving marked by the singing of this hymn 1679. **c.** A musical setting of this hymn 1864.

Tedious (tī·diəs), *a.* late ME. [ad. late L. *tædiosus*, f. *tædium* TEDIUM; see -OUS.] **1.** 'Wearisome by continuance' (J.); long and tiresome; *esp.* of a speech or narrative, hence of a speaker or writer: prolix, so as to cause weariness. †**b.** *joc.* Long (in time or extent) –1630. **2.** Wearisome in general; annoying, irksome, disagreeable, painful. *Obs.* exc. *dial.* 1454. **3.** Late, tardy, dilatory, slow. *Obs.* exc. *dial.* 1485.

1. Come: you are a t. foole: to the purpose SHAKS. 2. I may be t., but I will not be long TILLOTSON. Hence **Te·dious-ly** *adv.*, **-ness.**

Tedium (tī·diŏm). Also †**tædium.** 1662. [a. L. *tædium* weariness, disgust, f. *tædere* to weary.] The state or quality of being tedious; wearisomeness, tediousness, ennui.

The charge and t. of travelling 1662. When he remembered the tædium of his quarters SCOTT.

Tee (tī), *sb.*[1] 1610. **1.** The name of the letter T; also applied to objects having the form of this letter (T or ⊢). See also T (the letter) 2. **2.** *attrib.* Shaped like a T, having a cross-piece at the top or end, as *t.-joint, -piece, -square*; also, *t.-headed, -shaped* adjs. 1819.

Tee (tī), *sb.*[2] orig. *Sc.* 1673. [app. a shortened form of *teaz*, of unkn. origin.] *Golf.* The starting-place, usu. a little heap of sand, from which the ball is driven in beginning to play each hole.

Tee (tī), *sb.*[3] orig. *Sc.* 1789. [perh. orig. same word as TEE *sb.*[1]] *Curling*, etc. The mark, a cross made on the ice and surrounded by circles, at which the stones are aimed; applied also to the 'jack' at bowls, and the 'hob' at quoits.

‖**Tee** (tī), *sb.*[4] Also **htee.** 1800. [Burmese *h'ti* umbrella.] A metallic decoration, in the shape of an umbrella, usu. gilded and hung with bells, surmounting the topes and pagodas of Burma and adjacent countries.

†**Tee,** *v.*[1] [OE. *téon* (*téah, tugon, togen*), Com. Teut. str. vb., cogn. w. L. *ducere.*] *trans.* To draw, pull, drag, tug –1446. **b.** *intr.* To proceed, go –1450.

Tee (tī), *v.*[2] 1673. [f. TEE *sb.*[2]] *Golf.* **a.** *trans.* To place (a ball) on the tee. **b.** *intr.* with *off*: To play a ball from the tee. Hence **Tee·ing-ground,** a small patch of ground from which the ball is teed off.

Teem (tīm), *v.*[1] [OE. *tīeman* :—**taumjan*, f. OE. *téam* :—**taumoz*; see TEAM *sb.*] **1.** *trans.* To bring forth, produce, give birth to, bear (offspring). *Obs.* or *arch.* †**2.** *intr.* To bring forth young, bear or produce offspring; to be or become pregnant –1636. **3.** To be full, as if ready to give birth; to be prolific or fertile; to abound, swarm 1593.

1. Nothing teemes But hatefull Docks, rough Thistles, Keksyes, Burres SHAKS. 3. The house-tops teemed with people DICKENS. Hence **Tee·mful** *a.* prolific, productive, fruitful, teeming. †**Tee·mless** *a.* barren. DRYDEN.

Teem (tīm), *v.*[2] Now *dial.* and *techn.* [ME. *temen*, a. ON. *tæma* to empty :—**tōmjan*, f. *tómr* TOOM.] **1.** *trans.* **a.** To empty (a vessel, etc.); to discharge or remove the contents of; to empty (a wagon, etc.). **b.** To empty out, pour out 1482. **2.** *intr.* Of water, etc.: To pour, flow in a stream, flow copiously; of rain, to pour 1828.

1. b. You immediately t. out the remainder of the ale into the tankard SWIFT.

Teeming (tī·miŋ), *ppl. a.* 1535. [f. TEEM *v.*[1] + -ING[2].] **1.** That bears or breeds offspring; pregnant, gravid. *arch.* and *dial.* †**b.** Germinating, sprouting –1835. **2.** Fertile, prolific 1593. **b.** *transf.* Abounding; swarming; crowded 1715.

2. The t. Autumne big with ritch increase SHAKS. b. The t. streets of Jerusalem 1873. Hence **Tee·ming-ly** *adv.*, **-ness.**

Teen (tīn), *sb. arch.* [OE. *téona* hurt, trouble = OFris. *tiona, tiuna* injury, OS. *tiono* wrong, injury; also OE. *téon* damage, loss.] †**1.** Harm inflicted or suffered; injury, hurt, mischief; damage –1609. **2.** Irritation, annoyance; anger, rage; spite, ill-will, malice. *Obs.* exc. *Sc.* ME. **3.** Affliction, suffering, grief, woe. *arch.* ME.

3. Each howres ioy wrackt with a weeke of teene SHAKS.

Teen, *v.* *Obs.* or *dial.* [OE. *téonian*, f. *téon* TEEN *sb.*] **1.** *trans.* To vex, anger, enrage. **2.** To grieve, distress. *trans.* and *intr.* for *refl.* –1611.

-teen (tīn). [OE. *-*tīene, -týne, -téne*, ME. -*tēne.*] An inflected form of TEN, added to the numerals from *three* to *nine*, to form those from *thirteen* to *nineteen.* The stressing of these forms depends on their position in the sentence, e. g. *she is se·venteen years old*; *she is seventee·n*, *sweet seventee·n.* Hence **-teenth** (tīnþ), forming the ordinals of the cardinals in *-teen*, from *thirteenth* to *nineteenth.*

Teens (tīnz), *sb. pl.* 1673. [-TEEN treated as a separate word with pl. suffix.] The years of a person's life (rarely, of a thing's age) of which the numbers end in *-teen*, namely 13 to 19; chiefly in phr. *in one's t.*, *out of one's t.* Hence **Tee·n-a·ger,** a person in his or her teens.

Teeny (tī·ni), *a.*[1] *Obs.* exc. *dial.* 1594. [f. TEEN *sb.*] Characterized by 'teen'; malicious; peevish.

Tee·ny, *a.*[2] *dial.* and *colloq.* 1847. An emphasized form of TINY; esp. in childish use. Also in jingling comb. *teeny-weeny.*

Teer (tīəɹ), *v.* *dial.* and *techn.* late ME. [app. a. OF. *ter(r)er* to plaster, f. *ter(r)e* earth.] **1.** *trans.* To daub with earth, clay, or plaster. **2.** To spread (colour) 1839.

‖**Teetee**[1] (tī·tī). Also **titi.** 1832. [Native name in Tupi.] Any Brazilian monkey of the genus *Callithrix*; a sagoin.

Teetee[2] (tī·tī). Also **ti-ti.** 1882. [Maori name.] A name in New Zealand for the Diving Petrel (*Pelecanoides* or *Halodroma urinatrix*), and for allied species.

Teeter (tī·təɹ), *sb.* *dial.* and *U.S.* 1867. [f. next.] A see-saw; a see-sawing or swaying motion; the game of see-saw; also *fig.*, hesitation between two alternatives, vacillation.

Teeter (tī·təɹ), *v.* *dial.* and *U.S.* 1846. [var. of dial. *titter* to totter, move unsteadily.] **1.** *intr.* **a.** To see-saw. **b.** To move like a see-saw; to sway from side to side; to move unsteadily; *esp.* of a person or animal, to balance oneself unsteadily on alternate feet 1850. **2.** *trans.* To move (anything) with a see-saw motion; to tip up and down, to tilt 1874.

1. b. The peetweets..'teter' along its stony shores all summer THOREAU.

Teeth, pl. of TOOTH.

Teethe (tīð), *v.* late ME. [prob. repr. OE. **tēþan*, f. *tóþ* TOOTH.] **1.** *intr.* To develop or 'cut' teeth. (Now only in pr. pple. and vbl. sb.) **2.** *trans.* To furnish with teeth, to set teeth in. Chiefly *dial.* 1775.

Teething (tī·ðiŋ), *vbl. sb.* 1732. [f. TEETHE *v.* + -ING[1].] The action of TEETHE *v.*; the process of developing teeth, dentition; usu. applied to the cutting of the milk-teeth.

attrib. and *Comb.*, as *t.-rash*; **t. powder,** a medicinal powder given to children when teething.

Teetotal (tītōu·tăl), *a.* (*sb.*) 1834. [A reduplication or extension of the word TOTAL, app. first used (in sense 1) by a working-man, Richard Turner of Preston, in a speech advocating total abstinence from intoxicating liquors, in preference to abstinence from ardent spirits only.] **1.** Of or pertaining to total abstinence from alcoholic drinks; pledged to, or devoted to the furtherance of, total abstinence. **2.** *dial.* Absolute, complete, perfect, entire. (More emphatic than *total.*) 1840. **B.** *sb.* (The adj. used *absol.*; now *rare* or *dial.*) **a.** The total abstinence principle or pledge; teetotalism; a society for the promotion of total abstinence. **b.** A teetotaller (*rare*) 1834. Hence **Teeto·talism,** total abstinence from alcoholic liquors. **Teeto·tal(l)er,** a total abstainer.

Tee·to·tally, *adv.* *dial.* and *U.S.* 1832. [redupl. form of TOTALLY.] Entirely, wholly.

Teetotum (tītōu·tŏm). 1720. [Orig. *T totum*, formed by prefixing to L. *totum* 'all, the whole', its initial T, which stood for it on one of the sides of the toy (itself in earlier use called simply a *totum*).] **1.** A small four-sided disk or die having an initial letter inscribed on each of its sides, and a spindle passing down through it by which it could be twirled or spun with the fingers like a small top, the letter which lay uppermost, when it fell, deciding the fortune of the player; now, any light top spun with the fingers, used as a toy. **2.** A game of chance played with this device 1753.

1. The letters were orig. the initials of Latin words, viz. T *totum*, A *aufer*, D *depone*, N *nihil.* Later they were the initials of English words, T *take-all*, H *half*, N *nothing*, P *put down* (i. e. a stake equal to that you put down at first). *attrib.* His own t. brain is upset 1863.

‖**Teff** (tef). 1790. [Amharic *ṭēf.*] The principal cereal of Abyssinia, *Poa abyssinica.*

Teg (teg), **tag** (tæg). 1530. [perh. Scand.; cf. Sw. *tacka* a ewe.] **1.** A sheep in its second year, or from the time it is weaned till its first shearing; a yearling sheep. Formerly restricted to the female. 1537. **b.** *T. wool*, also ellipt. *teg* 1854. †**2.** A doe or female deer in its second year –1774.

1. b. T. wool is the wool of the first shearing when the sheep is little more than a year old 1854.

‖**Tegmen** (te·gmen). *Pl.* **tegmina.** 1817. [L., covering, f. *tegere* to cover.] A cover, covering, coating, integument. (Only in scientific use.) **a.** *Ent.* (*pl.*) The wing-covers, i. e. the fore wings when modified so as to serve as coverings for the hind wings; esp. those of orthopterous insects (corresp. to the *elytra* of beetles). **b.** *Bot.* The thin inner coat of a seed, immediately enveloping the nucleus; the *endopleura* 1857. **c.** *Ornith.* (*pl.*) = *Tectrices*: see TECTRIX 1891.

Tegmental (tegme·ntăl), *a.* 1890. [f. L. *tegmentum* + -AL 1.] Of or pertaining to the tegmentum.

‖**Tegmentum** (tegme·ntŏm). *Pl.* **-a.** 1832. [L.] **1.** *Bot.* Each of the scales forming the covering of a leaf-bud; a bud-scale. **2.** *Anat.* The upper and hinder portion of each of the *crura cerebri* 1879.

‖**Teguexin** (tegwe·ksin). 1879. [ad. Aztec *tecoixin, tecouixin* a lizard.] *Zool.* A large S. Amer. lizard of the genus *Teius*, esp. *T. teguexin.*

‖**Tegula** (te·giŭlă). *Pl.* **-æ** (*ī*). 1826. [L., a tile, f. *tegere* to cover.] *Ent.* **a.** A small scale-like structure covering the base of the fore wing in hymenopterous and other insects. **b.** Each of a pair of membranous scales (*prehalteres*) in front of the halteres in dipterous insects.

Tegular (te·giŭlăɹ), *a.* 1796. [f. as prec. + -AR.] **a.** Pertaining to or of the nature of a tile; composed of or arranged like tiles. **b.** *Ent.* Pertaining to or of the nature of a *tegula* 1891. So **Te·gularly** *adv.* in the manner of tiles; so as to overlap like tiles. **Te·gulated** *a.* (of armour) composed of overlapping plates.

Tegument (te·giŭmĕnt). 1440. [ad. L. *tegumentum* covering, f. *tegere* to cover; see -MENT.] Something that serves to cover; a covering, coating, envelope, investment, integument. **a.** *gen.* **b.** *Nat. Hist.* and *Anat.* The natural covering of the body, or of some part or organ, of an animal or plant; a skin, coat, shell, husk, or the like; *spec.* = TEGMEN a. Now *rare* or *Obs.*; mostly repl. by INTEGUMENT. 1646. Hence **Tegume·ntal** *a.* = next.

Tegumentary (tegiŭme·ntări), *a.* 1828. [f. prec. + -ARY[1].] Constituting, or serving as, a tegument; pertaining to or occurring in the tegument; integumentary.

Tehee (tīhī·), *int.* and *sb.* late ME. **A.** *int.* A representation of the sound of a light laugh, usu. derisive.

And all the Maids of Honour cry Te! He! 1773.

B. *sb.* A laugh of this kind; a titter, a giggle 1593. So **Tehee·** *v.* to utter *t.* in laughing; to titter, giggle ME.

‖**Teichopsia** (təikǫ·psiă). [mod.L., f. Gr. τεῖχος wall + -οψία sight.] *Path.* Half-blindness accompanied by an appearance as of the zigzag outline of battlements.

‖**Te igitur** (tī i·dʒitŏɹ). 1819. [L., = 'Thee therefore', the opening words of the prayer.] The first prayer in the Canon of the

Mass in the Roman and some other Latin liturgies.

Teil (tīl). Now *rare* or *Obs.* 1589. [Partly ad. L. *tilia* linden-tree; partly a. OF. *til, teil,* masc. forms collateral with *tille, teille,* ad. L. *tilia.*] The lime or linden-tree, *Tilia europæa.* Usu. *t.-tree.*

Teind (tīnd), (*a.*) *sb. Sc.* and *north.* [Early ME. *tende,* adj. and sb., collateral form of TENTH; cf. also TITHE.] **A.** *adj.* See TENTH A. 1, and 3. **B.** *sb.* †**1.** The tenth part (of anything); a tenth –1475. **2.** *spec.* = TITHE *sb.* 1; now, in Scotland, that portion of the estates of the laity which is liable to be assessed for the stipend of the clergy of the established church. Now chiefly in pl. ME. **b.** *transf.* The payment, institution or system of teinds 1817.

Teinoscope (tai·nǒskōup). 1822. [f. Gr. τείνειν to stretch, extend + -SCOPE.] An optical instrument in which prisms are so arranged and combined as to increase or diminish the apparent linear dimensions of objects, while the chromatic aberration of the light is corrected.

†**Teise,** *v.* Also **tease.** late ME. [Origin obsc.] *trans.* app. To drive (esp. a hunted beast); to chase; to urge on –1819.

They..did tease Their horses homeward, with convulsed spur KEATS. Hence †**Tei·ser,** one who rouses the game; *spec.* one of the first brace or leash of deerhounds let slip.

‖**Telæsthesia** (telĭsþī·ziă, -siă). 1882. [mod. L., f. Gr. τῆλε far off + αἴσθησις perception + -IA[1].] *Psychics.* Perception at a distance; direct sensation or perception of objects or conditions independently of the recognized channels of sense. So **Telæsthe·tic** *a.* having physical perception of things at a distance; of or belonging to t.

‖**Telamon** (te·lămǫn). *Pl.* **Telamones** (telămōu·nīz). 1706. [In pl. a. L. *telamones,* = Gr. τελαμῶνες, pl. of Τελαμών name of a hero in mythology.] *Arch.* A figure of a man used as a column to support an entablature or other structure.

‖**Telangiectasis** (tĭlændʒi,e·ktăsis). *Pl.* **-ses** (-sīz). 1831. [mod.L., f. Gr. τέλος end + ἀγγεῖον vessel + ἔκτασις extension, dilatation.] *Path.* Dilatation of the small blood-vessels, producing small red or purple tumours in the skin; one of such tumours. Also **Telangie·ctasy.** Hence **Telangiectatic** (-tæ·tik) *a.* pertaining to or resulting from t.

Telautograph (telǭ·tǒgrɑf). 1884. [f. Gr. τῆλε far off + AUTOGRAPH, after *telegraph.*] A telegraphic apparatus by which writing or drawing done at the transmitting end is reproduced in facsimile at the receiving end, by means of an electric current conveyed along a wire. Hence **Telautogra·phic** *a.* pertaining to the t. **Telauto·graphy,** the use of the t.

Tele- (te·lĭ) (bef. a vowel properly **tel-,** but more often in the full form), repr. Gr. τηλε-, comb. form of τῆλε far off.

Telacou·stic *a. Psychics,* pertaining to or involving the perception of a sound beyond or apart from the possibility of ordinary hearing. **Tele·gony,** [Gr. -γονια begetting] *Biol.* the (hypothetical) influence of a previous sire seen in the progeny of a subsequent sire from the same mother; hence **Telego·nic** *a.* **Tele·graphone,** a form of telephone in which the spoken message is recorded at the receiving end magnetically on an iron ribbon, so as to be capable of reproduction. ‖**Telekine·sis** [Gr. κίνησις motion] *Psychics,* movement of or in a body occurring at a distance from, and without material connexion with, the motive cause or agent. **Telelec·tric** *a.,* producing mechanical motions or effects at a distance by electrical means. **Telemecha·nics,** the art of transmitting power to a distance, esp. by etherial vibrations as in wireless telegraphy. **Te·lemo·tor,** an apparatus for transmitting motive power to a distance; *esp.* a device for steering a ship from some part distant from the tiller, by means of hydraulic or pneumatic pressure, etc. **Telepho·nograph,** an instrument consisting of a combination of telephone and phonograph, by which telephone messages can be recorded and subsequently reproduced; also (*U.S.*) = *telegraphone.* **Te·lergy** [after *energy*] *Psychics,* the supposed force operating in telepathy, regarded as correlated with the various forms of physical energy, or as directly affecting the brain or organism of the percipient. **Te·leseme** [Gr. σῆμα sign], an electric signalling apparatus used in hotels, etc., fitted with an indicator which shows the article or service required. **Te·letype,** a type-printing telegraph. **Telewriter** (te·lĭrəi·təɹ), an instrument which electrically reproduces in facsimile a written message.

‖**Teledu** (te·lĕdu). 1824. [Native name in Javanese.] A carnivorous animal of Java and Sumatra (*Mydaus meliceps*), allied to the skunk and of similar habits; also called *stinking badger* or *stinkard.*

‖**Telega** (telē·gă). 1558. [a. Russ. *teljĕga.*] A four-wheeled Russian cart, of rough construction, without springs.

Telegram (te·lĭgræm). 1852. [f. Gr. τῆλε TELE- + -GRAM.] A message sent by telegraph; a telegraphic dispatch or communication.

'A t.'—a new Yankee word for a telegraphic despatch 1857. Hence **Te·legramma·tic, Telegra·mmic** *adjs.* of or pertaining to telegrams; concise or condensed like a t. *rare.*

Telegraph (te·lĭgrɑf), *sb.* 1794. [a. F. *télégraphe,* f. Gr. τῆλε TELE- + -γραφος -GRAPH.] **1.** An apparatus for transmitting messages to a distance, usu. by signs of some kind. The name was first applied to that invented by Chappe in France in 1792, consisting of an upright post with movable arms, the signals being made by various positions of the arms according to a pre-arranged code. Hence applied to later devices operating by movable disks, shutters, etc., flashes of light, sounds of bells, horns, etc., or other means. (Now *rare* in this sense, such contrivances being usu. called *semaphores* or *signalling apparatus.*) **2.** In full, *electric* or *magnetic t.*: An apparatus consisting of a *transmitter,* a *receiver,* and a line or wire of any length connecting these, along which an electric current from a battery or other source passes, the circuit being made and broken by working the transmitter, so as to produce movements, as of a needle or pointer, in the receiver, which indicate letters, etc., either according to a code of signs, or by pointing to characters upon a dial; in some forms the receiver works so as to print or trace the message upon a prepared strip of paper. Also, an apparatus for wireless telegraphy. 1797. †**3.** A telegram –1862. **4.** In *Cricket,* A board upon which the number of runs obtained and wickets taken are exhibited during a match in large figures so as to be visible at a distance; a scoring-board. Also, a similar device used in other athletic sports. 1859. **5.** Used as individual name of a newspaper, a variety of plant, etc. 1794.

attrib. and *Comb.,* as *t. boy, cable* (CABLE *sb.* 3), *line, message, office, wire,* etc.; **t.-board** = sense 4; **t. form,** a paper printed with spaces in which the words of a telegram are to be written for dispatch; **-key,** a small lever or other device in a telegraphic transmitter, worked by the hand, for making and breaking the circuit; **-plant,** an E. Indian leguminous plant, *Desmodium gyrans,* remarkable for the spontaneous movements of its leaflets, suggesting signalling; also called *moving plant*; **-pole, -post,** one of a series of poles upon which a telegraph wire or wires are carried above the ground; **-register,** a telegraphic receiver, or part of one, which gives a permanent record of the messages received.

Telegraph (te·lĭgrɑf), *v.* 1805. [f. prec.] **1. a.** *intr.* To signal or communicate by telegraph; to send a telegram 1815. **b.** *trans.* To send, transmit, or announce (a message, news, etc.) by telegraph. In *Cricket,* etc., to exhibit (the score, etc.) on the telegraph-board. 1805. **c.** To send a message to (a person) by telegraph, summon by a telegram 1810. **2.** *fig.* **a.** *intr.* To make signs, signal (*to* a person). **b.** *trans.* To make (a signal), convey or announce by signs. **c.** To signal to (a person). Now *rare.* 1825.

Telegrapher (te·lĭgrɑfəɹ). 1795. [f. TELEGRAPH *sb.* or *v.* + -ER[1].] **1.** One who works a telegraph. (Now *rare* exc. in U.S.: the techn. term being *telegraphist.*) **2.** The sender of a telegram 1865.

Telegraphese (te:lĭgrɑfī·z). *colloq.* or *joc.* 1885. [f. TELEGRAPH *sb.* + -ESE.] **1.** The concise and elliptical style in which telegrams are worded. **2.** *joc.* An elaborate or inflated style, such as that of leading articles in the (London) *Daily Telegraph* newspaper 1885.

1. Electric T. is as short and spare as Daily T. is longwinded and redundant 1885.

Telegraphic (telĭgræ·fik), *a.* 1794. [f. as prec. + -IC.] **1.** Of, pertaining to, of the nature of, or connected with a telegraph; made, sent, or transmitted by telegraph. **2.** *fig.* †**a.** Making signals (as by glance or gesture); conveyed by a sign or signal. **b.** Resembling an (electric) telegraph; conveying impulses or intelligence as by electricity. **c.** Abbreviated or concise like a telegram. 1820.

1. Lord Nelson made the t. signal, 'England expects that every man will do his duty' 1805. As if on t. wires 1854. **2. c.** His speech as t. as though each word were paid for 1896.

Telegraphist (tĭ-, tele·grăfist, te·lĭgrɑfist). 1854. [f. as prec. + -IST.] A person employed, or skilled, in working a telegraph; a telegraph-operator.

Telegraphy (tĭle·g-, tele·grăfi, te·lĭgrɑfi). 1795. [f. TELE- + -GRAPHY.] The art or science of constructing or using telegraphs; the working of a telegraph or telegraphs. *Wireless t.*: see WIRELESS.

Telemark (te·lĕmaɹk). 1910. [Name of a district of Norway.] An expert swing turn in ski-ing, used in changing direction or stopping short.

Telemeter (tĭ-, tele·mĭtəɹ). Also **telometer.** 1860. [f. TELE-, TELO-[2] + -METER.] **1.** An instrument for ascertaining the distances of objects: applied to instruments of various kinds used in surveying, and in military operations. **2.** An apparatus for recording the readings of any physical instrument at a distance by means of an electric current 1891. Hence **Teleme·tric, -al** *adjs.*

Teleo-[1] (te·lĭ,o), bef. a vowel **tele-,** repr. Gr. τελεο- (τελειο-), comb. form of τέλεος, τέλειος perfect, complete, f. τέλος end. **Teleocephalous** (-se·făləs) [Gr. κεφαλή head] *a., Ichth.* belonging to the order *Teleocephali* of teleostean fishes, having the full number of bones in the skull; so **Teleoce·phal,** a teleocephalous fish. **Te·leosaur** (-sǭɹ) [Gr. σαῦρος lizard], *Palæont.* a crocodile of the extinct genus *Teleosaurus* or family *Teleosauridæ*; so **Teleosau·rian** *a.* belonging to this genus or family; *sb.* = *teleosaur.* ‖**Teleozoon** (-zōu·ǫn) [Gr. ζῷον animal], *Biol.* an animal of perfect or complete organization; one of the higher animals; hence **Teleozoic** (-zōu·ik) *a.,* pertaining to the teleozoa.

Teleo-[2], bef. a vowel **tele-,** comb. form repr. Gr. τέλος end (stem τελε-), as in TELEOLOGY and its derivs.; also in **Teleorga·nic** *a.,* serving the purposes of an organism; necessary to organic life.

Teleologic (teli,olǫ·dʒik), *a.* and *sb.* 1842. [f. as next + -IC.] **A.** *adj.* = next. **B.** *sb.* The science of final causes; that branch of knowledge which deals with ends or purposes 1865.

Teleological (teli,olǫ·dʒikăl), *a.* 1809. [f. TELEOLOGY + -ICAL.] Of, pertaining to, or involving teleology; relating to ends or final causes; dealing with design or purpose, esp. in natural phenomena. **Teleolo·gically** *adv.*

Teleologist (teli,ǫ·lŏdʒist). 1864. [f. as prec. + -IST.] A believer in or maintainer of the doctrine of teleology; one versed in this.

Teleology (teli,ǫ·lŏdʒi). 1740. [ad. mod. L. *teleologia,* f. Gr. τέλος end (see TELEO-[2]) + -λογια (see -LOGY).] The doctrine or study of ends or final causes, esp. as related to the evidences of design or purpose in nature; also *transf.* such design as exhibited in natural objects or phenomena.

Teleostean (teli,ǫ·stĭăn), *a.* and *sb.* 1859. [f. mod.L. *teleosteus* (f. Gr. τέλεος, -ειος TELEO-[1] + ὀστέον bone) + -AN.] *Ichth.* **A.** *adj.* Belonging to or characteristic of the order *Teleostei,* having the skeleton (usu.) completely ossified. **B.** *sb.* A fish of this order. So **Te·leost** *sb.* and *a.* **Teleo·steous** *a.* = t.

Teleostome (te·li,ǒstoum). 1896. [ad. mod.L. *teleostomus,* f. TELEO-[1] + Gr. στόμα mouth.] *Ichth.* A fish of the division *Teleostomi,* including the teleosts and ganoids (i. e. all the higher fishes), characterized by well-developed maxillary, dentary, and membrane bones.

Telepathy (tĭ-, tele·păþi, te·lĭpæþi). 1882. [f. TELE- + Gr. -πάθεια; see -PATHY.] *Psychics.* The communication of impressions from one mind to another, independently of the recognized channels of sense. So **Te·lepath, Tele·pathist,** an adept in, a subject of, or believer in t. Tele-pa·thic *a.* pertaining to, of the nature of, or effected by t.

Telephone (te·lĭfōun), *sb.* 1835. [f. Gr. τῆλε TELE- + φωνή voice, sound, -φωνος -voiced, -sounding.] **1.** An instrument, apparatus, or device for conveying sound to a distance. Now chiefly *Obs.* **2.** An apparatus for reproducing sound, esp. that of the voice, at a great distance, by means of electricity; consisting, like the electric telegraph, of transmitting and receiving instruments connected by a line or wire which conveys the electric current 1866.

1. *Lovers'* or *String T.*, a toy consisting of two stretched membranes or metal disks connected by a tense cord which mechanically transmits sound-waves from the one to the other. 2. The t. proper differs from other instruments of a like class, in that it reproduces instead of merely conveying vibrations 1884. (The first electrical telephone was described by P. Reis in 1861; the first of practical use was A. G. Bell's of 1876.) Phr. *On the t.*, connected with a system of telephonic intercommunication.

attrib. and *Comb.*, as *t. message, operator, receiver*; **t. exchange**, the office or central station of a local t. system, where the various lines are brought to a central switchboard, and communication between subscribers is effected; sometimes applied to the switchboard itself, as in an 'automatic exchange'; **t. girl**, a girl employed at the switchboard to connect the wires so as to put two persons into communication.

Telephone (te·lĭfōun), *v.* 1879. [f. prec.] **1. a.** *intr.* To convey sound to a distance by or as by a telephone; *esp.* to send a message or communicate by speaking through a telephone 1880. **b.** *trans.* To convey or announce by telephone 1879. **c.** To speak to or summon by telephone 1889. **2.** To furnish with telephones; to establish a system of telephones in (a place) 1901.

2. Estimates for telephoning London 1901. **c.** She telephoned you on the impulse of the moment 1894.

Telephonic (telĭfǫ·nik), *a.* 1834. [orig. f. Gr. τῆλε TELE- + φωνή voice + -IC; in later use, f. TELEPHONE + -IC.] Transmitting, or relating to the transmission of, sound to a distance; of, pertaining to, of the nature of, or conveyed by a telephone. Hence **Telepho·nically** *adv.* in the manner of or by means of a telephone.

Telephonist (tĭ-, tele·fŏnist, te·lĭfōunist). 1882. [f. TELEPHONE *sb.* + -IST.] A person employed in transmitting messages by telephone.

Telephony (tĭ-, tele·fŏni, te·lĭfōuni). 1835. [f. Gr. τῆλε TELE- + -φωνία -sounding.] †1. Name for a system of signalling by means of musical sounds, and for the practice of other early forms of telephone –1835. **2.** The art or science of constructing telephones; the working of a telephone or telephones. *Wireless t.*; see WIRELESS. 1876.

Telephote (te·lĭfōut), *sb.* 1880. [f. Gr. τῆλε TELE- + φῶς, φωτ- light.] A name employed or proposed for various devices or apparatus used or projected. **a.** A means of transmitting signals or messages from a distance by means of light. **b.** A device for the electric transmission of pictures, so that they are reproduced as pictures at a distance. **c.** An apparatus for photographing at a great distance; a telephotographic lens or camera. Hence **Te·lephote** *v. trans.* to transmit (an optical image) to a distance by means of electricity. **Telepho·tic** (-fǫ·tik) *a.* of or pertaining to a t., or to TELEPHOTY.

Telephoto. 1898. Abbrev. of TELEPHOTOGRAPHIC *a.*[2]

Telephotograph (telĭfōu·tŏgraf), *sb.*[1] 1881. [f. as TELEPHOTE *sb.* + -GRAPH.] A picture or image electrically reproduced at a distance; also, an apparatus for doing this. So **Te:lephotogra·phic** *a.*[1] **Te:lephoto·graphy**[1], = TELEPHOTY.

Telepho·tograph, *sb.*[2] 1900. [f. Gr. τῆλε TELE- + PHOTOGRAPH; a back-formation from next.] A photograph of a distant object taken with a telephotographic lens. So **Telepho·tograph** *v. trans.* to photograph with a telephotographic lens or apparatus. **Te:lephoto·graphy**[2], the art or practice of taking photographs of distant objects by a camera with a telephotographic lens.

Telephotographic (te:lĭfōuto,græ·fik), *a.*[2] 1892. [f. Gr. τῆλε TELE- + PHOTOGRAPHIC *a.*] Of, pertaining to, or used in the photographing of distant objects, within the field of sight but beyond the limits of distinct vision, esp. in *t. lens*, a lens or combination of lenses for this purpose.

Telephoty (te·lĭfōuti). 1908. [f. as TELEPHOTE + -Y[3].] The art or practice of reproducing pictures or views at a distance by means of the electric current; the theory and practice of the telephote.

Telescope (te·lĭskoup), *sb.* 1648. [ad. It. *telescopio* or mod.L. *telescopium*, f. Gr. τηλεσκόπος far-seeing, f. τῆλε TELE- + σκοπεῖν to look, -σκοπος -SCOPE.] An optical instrument for making distant objects appear nearer and larger, consisting of one or more tubes with an arrangement of lenses, or of one or more mirrors and lenses, by which the rays of light are collected and brought to a focus and the resulting image magnified. Telescopes are of two kinds: *refracting*, in which the image is produced by a lens (the object-glass), and *reflecting*, in which it is produced by a mirror or *speculum*; being magnified in each case by a lens or combination of lenses (the EYE-PIECE). The smaller hand-telescopes are always refracting, and consist of two or more tubes made to slide one within another for convenience of packing into a narrow compass and for adjusting the lenses as required for focusing the image. **b.** *Astr.* A constellation south of Sagittarius 1891.

1. By what strange Parallax or Optic skill Of vision multiplyed through air, or glass Of Telescope MILT.

Comb.: **t.-carp**, a monstrous variety of goldfish, having protruding eyes; **-driver**, a clockwork apparatus for driving an astronomical t. so as to follow the apparent movements of the heavenly bodies and thus keep the same object continually in the field of view; **-eye**, an eye which can be protruded and retracted like a t.-tube, as in gasteropod molluscs; **-fish** = *t. carp*; **-fly**, a fly of the genus *Diopsis*, having the eyes on long stalks; **-shell**, the long conical shell, with numerous whorls, of an Indian gasteropod (*Telescopium fuscum*); **-sight**, a small t. mounted as a sight upon a firearm or surveying instrument.

Telescope (te·lĭskoup), *v.* 1861. [f. prec.] **1. a.** *trans.* To force or drive one into another (or into something else) after the manner of the sliding-tubes of a hand-telescope: usu. said in ref. to railway carriages in a collision 1872. **b.** *intr.* To slide, run, or be driven one into another (or into something else); to have its parts made to slide in this manner; to collapse so that its parts fall into one another 1877. **2.** *trans.* To make into or use as a telescope 1861.

1. b. They telescoped like cars in railroad smashes O. W. HOLMES. 2. Looking through his telescoped hand 1861.

Telescopic (telĭskǫ·pik), *a.* 1705. [f. as prec. + -IC.] **1.** Of or pertaining to a telescope; of the nature of or consisting of a telescope, as *t. sight* = telescope-sight; done by means of a telescope, as *t. observations*. **2.** Seen by means of a telescope; *spec.* of a heavenly body, visible only through a telescope 1714. **3.** Having the property of a telescope; having the power of distant vision, far-seeing; contemplating something distant (*lit.* and *fig.*) 1781. **4.** Consisting of parts made to slide one within another like the tubes of a hand-telescope 1846.

1. The limits of t. vision have not been reached 1855. 2. These asteroids..are..entirely t. 1893. 3. These Saxons..have..the t. appreciation of distant gain EMERSON. So **Telesco·pical** *a.* (now *rare*), in senses 1 and 2. 1665. **Telesco·pically** *adv.*

Telescopist (tĭ-, tele·skŏpist, te·lĭskōupist). 1870. [f. TELESCOPE + -IST.] One skilled in using a telescope; one who makes telescopic observations.

Telescopy (tĭ-, tele·skŏpi, te·lĭskŏpi). *rare.* 1861. [f. as TELESCOPE + -Y[3].] The art or practice of using the telescope, or of making telescopes.

†**Te·lesm.** 1646. [ad. late Gr. τέλεσμα completion, f. τελεῖν to complete, fulfil, f. τέλος end.] = TALISMAN[2] 1. –1693. So **Telesma·tic** (*rare*), †**Telesma·tical** *adjs.* of or pertaining to a t.; talismanic; magical.

Telestich (tĭ-, tele·stik, te·lestik). 1637. [irreg. f. Gr. τελε, τέλος- end + στίχος a row, line of verse, after ACROSTIC.] A short poem (or other composition) in which the final letters of the lines, taken in order, spell a word or words.

Teleutospore (tĭ-, teliū·tŏspoᵊɪ). 1874. [f. Gr. τελευτή completion, end (f. τέλος) + SPORE.] *Bot.* A special form of spore, usu. produced at the end of the period of fructification, in parasitic fungi of the family *Uredineæ*. **Teleutospo·ric** *a.*

Television (te·lĭviʒən). 1909. [f. TELE- + VISION.] Vision of a distant (moving) object or scene electrically transmitted and reproduced; also, the process by which this is effected. Hence **Te·levise** *v. trans.*, to transmit by t. **Te·levisor**, a t. apparatus.

Telic (te·lik), *a.* 1846. [ad. Gr. τελικός final, f. τέλος.] **1.** *Gram.* Of a conjunction or clause: Expressing end or purpose. **2.** Directed or tending to a definite end; purposive 1889.

Telinga (tĕli·ŋgă), *sb.* and *a.* 1698. [Origin obsc.] **1.** The Telugu language. (As *sb.* or *a.*) **2.** One of the Telugu people 1800. †**b.** *spec.* A native Indian soldier disciplined and dressed in quasi-European fashion; a sepoy –1883.

Tell (tel), *sb.*[1] Now *dial.* 1742. [f. TELL *v.*] **1.** What one tells or has to tell; a tale, statement, account. **2.** A talk, conversation, gossip 1864.

1. I am at the end of my t. H. WALPOLE.

‖**Tell** (tel), *sb.*[2] Also **tel.** 1864. [a. Arab. *tall* a hillock.] Arab name for an artificial hillock or mound, usu. one covering the ruins of an ancient city.

Tell (tel), *v.* Pa.t. and pa. pple. **told** (tōuld). [OE. *tęllan, tealde, (ge)teald*:—OTeut. **taljan*, f. **talā*, OE. *talu* TALE *sb.*] **I.** To mention in order, narrate, make known. †**1.** *trans.* To recount, enumerate; to give a list of –1440. **2.** To give an account or narrative of (facts, actions, or events); to narrate, relate. Also *to t. over*. OE. **b.** *intr.* for *pass.* To sound (well, etc.) when told 1584. **3.** To make known by speech or writing; to communicate (information, facts, ideas, news, etc.); to state, announce, report, intimate ME. **b.** To declare, state formally or publicly; to announce, proclaim, publish ME. **4.** To utter (words); to say over, recite (a passage, composition, etc.); to say. Now *dial.* ME. **b.** To utter, speak, say (things). *rare.* late ME. **c.** To express in words (thoughts, things known). Now *rare.* ME. **5.** To disclose or reveal (something secret or private) late ME. **6.** To discern so as to be able to say with knowledge or certainty; hence, to distinguish, recognize, decide, determine 1687. **b.** Preceded by *can*: To be able to state; to know; to make out, understand. Usu. in neg. or interrog. sentences, as *Nobody can t.*, *Who can t.?* late ME. **7.** trans. *To t. a person*: To inform (a person) of something; to make aware, apprise, acquaint; to instruct ME. **8.** To assert positively to; to assure (a person). Often *parenthetically*. 1440. **9.** To order or direct (a person) *to do* something; to bid 1599. **10.** *intr.* To give an account, description, or report ME. **11.** *fig.* To give evidence, be an indication *of* 1798. **12.** To disclose something wished to be kept secret, to play the informer, tell tales, blab 1539.

2. Others of some note, As story tells, have trod this Wilderness MILT. 3. I'le t. you one piece of my mind 1673. Tell me not, in mournful numbers, Life is but an empty dream! LONGFELLOW. **b.** Phr. *T. it not in Gath* (from 2 *Sam.* i. 20), publish it not to the enemy, or to the Philistine, or to the world. 4. **b.** The lippes of the vnwyse wylbe tellynge foolish thinges COVERDALE *Ecclus.* xxi. 25. 5. She neuer told her loue SHAKS. *To t. tales*: see TALE *sb.* 2 b. 6. They can be told by their complexions, dress, manner, and..speech 1840. 7. He..tolde me of my fault 1573. Wherefore was I not told of all this? SCOTT. 8. I t. you, it got on my nerves 1905. 9. Tell the Sergeant to keep his eye open KIPLING. 10. He told of bloody fights CRABBE. 11. Blocks of basalt..telling of a still more ancient Moabite city 1873. 12. He didn't want to 't.' of Maggie GEO. ELIOT.

Phrases. *To t. a tale, a story*, to relate a story or narrative. *To t. a tale, t. its own tale*: to be significant of itself. *To t. the tale*, to pitch a yarn. *To t. one's tale*, to relate one's story; also, to say what one has to t., to deliver one's message. *To t. (the) truth*, to make a true statement; to state the fact or circumstance as it really is; also, used parenthetically to emphasize a statement. So *to t. a lie*, to make a wilfully false statement or report. *To hear t.*; usu.

const. *of*: see HEAR *v.* 2; now chiefly *dial.* and *colloq.* *Never t. me, don't t. me,* expressing incredulity or impatience. *I can t. you,* I can assure you. *I'll t. you what* = 'I'll t. you what it is', or 'I'll t. you something'. *To t. any one his own,* to t. him frankly of his faults. *To t.* (a person) *good-bye*: to say good-bye (*U.S.*). *To t. the world*: to announce openly (*U.S.*).

II. To mention numerically, to count, reckon. **1.** *trans.* To mention or name (the single members of a series or group) one by one, specifying them as *one, two, three,* etc.; hence, to enumerate, reckon in; to reckon up, count, number. Also *absol.* Now *arch.* or *dial.* OE. **b.** *spec.* To count (voters or votes). Also *absol.* *To t. noses*: To count heads; see NOSE *sb.* **2.** To count out (pieces of money) in payment; hence, to pay (money). *arch.* or *dial.* ME. **b.** To reckon up or calculate the total amount or value of (money or other things). *arch.* OE.

1. Phr. *To t. one's beads*: see BEAD *sb.* 2. †*To t. the clock,* to count the hours as shown by a clock; hence, to pass one's time idly. *To t.* (so many) *years,* to have lived (so many) years. *Obs.* or *arch.* *All told,* when all are counted; in all. **b.** The House was told by Mr. Speaker 1899. **2.** He told the money into my hand DE FOE. **b.** Those who weigh and t. over money MARVELL. As a miser tells his gold 1827.

With advs. **T. off. a.** To count off from the whole number or company; to separate, detach, esp. so many men for a particular duty; hence *gen.* to appoint to a particular task, object, position, or the like. **b.** To scold; to rebuke strongly (*slang*). **c.** *intr.* for *refl.* *Mil.* Of a rank or troop of men: To number themselves in succession. **T. out,** to separate by counting: to count out (*arch* or *dial.*).

III. To account, or estimate, qualitatively. †**1.** To account, esteem as being (something) –1430. **2.** *intr.* To count (for something); to have its effect, be effective, act or operate with effect; to make an impression 1797.

1. Wordly selynesse Which clerkes tellyn fals felicite CHAUCER. **2.** Every blow..tells 1797. Everything in the print, to use a vulgar expression, tells LAMB. It tells somewhat against his interpretation 1870. Hence **Te·llable** *a.* capable of being told or narrated; fit to be told; worth telling.

Tellen (te·lĕn). 1711. [ad L. *tellina,* a. Gr. τελλίνη.] A bivalve of the genus *Tellina* or family *Tellinidæ.*

Teller (te·ləɹ). ME. [f. TELL *v.* + -ER [1].] One who or that which tells, in various senses: *esp.* **a.** One who counts or keeps tally; now *esp.* one who counts money; *spec.* an officer in a bank who receives or pays money over the counter 1480. **b.** One of four officers of the Exchequer formerly charged with the receipt and payment of moneys 1488. **c.** In a deliberative assembly (esp. the House of Commons), A person (usu. one of two or more) who counts the votes on a division 1669. Hence **Te·llership,** the office or position of a t.

Telling (te·liŋ), *vbl. sb.* ME. [f. TELL *v.* + -ING.[1]] The action of TELL *v.*

Phr. That's (or *that would be*) *telling* (trivial colloq.), that would be to divulge something secret.

Te·lling, *ppl. a.* 1852. [-ING [2].] That tells; effective, forcible, striking.

A *t.* reply 1852. Drawn up with t. force 1870. Hence **Te·llingly** *adv.*

Tell-tale (te·l,tēl), *sb.* (*a.*) 1548. **1.** One who tells tales; one who idly or maliciously discloses private or secret matters; a tale-bearer, a tattler. Also *transf.* of things. **b.** A name of a species of Sandpiper (*spec.* in *U.S.*), so named from their loud cry 1824. **2.** *Mech.* A device for mechanically indicating or recording some fact or condition not otherwise apparent; an indicator, a gauge 1801. **3.** *attrib.* or as *adj.* **a.** That tells tales, that is a tell-tale. Now *rare* or *Obs.* in *lit.* sense. 1594. **b.** Applied to a thing: That betrays something meant to be kept secret 1577. **c.** That gives notice or warning of something 1867.

3. **a.** *Rich. III,* IV. iv. 149. **b.** These tell-tale articles must not remain here SCOTT. **c.** *T. clock,* a clock with an attachment of some kind requiring attention at certain intervals, by which the vigilance of a watchman may be checked. *T. compass,* a compass suspended overhead in the captain's cabin, enabling him to detect any deviation from the course.

†**Te·ll-truth.** 1558. **1.** One who or that which tells the truth –1810. **2.** The telling of the truth; candour (*rare*) –1734.

Te·llur-, tellu·ri-, *Chem.,* used as comb. forms of TELLURIUM; as in **Tellurhy·dric** *acid,* hydrogen telluride.

Tellurate (te·liŭrĕ't). 1826. [f. TELLUR- + -ATE [1] 1 c.] *Chem.* A salt of telluric acid.

Telluret (teliŭret). Now *rare.* 1842. [f. TELLURIUM; see -URET.] *Chem.* A compound of tellurium with hydrogen or a metal, as *t. of sodium,* $TeNa_2$: now usu. TELLURIDE.

Telluretted (te·liŭretĕd), *a.* Now *rare.* 1819. [f. as prec. + -ED.] *Chem.* Combined with tellurium, as in *telluretted hydrogen,* a gaseous compound of hydrogen and tellurium, TeH_2, formerly also called *hydrotelluric* or *tellurhydric acid,* and now *hydrogen telluride.*

Tellurian (teliūə·riăn), *a.* and *sb.* 1846. [f. L. *tellurem* the earth + -IAN.] **A.** *adj.* Of or pertaining to the earth; earthly, terrestrial. **B.** *sb.* An inhabitant of the earth 1847.

Telluric (teliūə·rik), *a.*[1] 1800. [f. TELLURIUM + -IC.] *Chem.* and *Min.* Derived from or containing tellurium. Applied to compounds in which tellurium is present in a smaller proportion than in tellurous compounds, as *t. acid,* H_2TeO_4. Also in *t. gold, silver, bismuth,* the tellurides of these metals occurring as native alloys.

Telluric (teliūə·rik), *a.*[2] 1836. [f. L. *tellurem* the earth + -IC.] Of or belonging to the earth, terrestrial; pertaining to the earth as a planet; of or arising from the earth or soil.

A 't. poison' is generated in it [the Campagna] by the energy of the soil 1884.

Telluride (te·liŭrəid). 1849. [f. TELLURIUM + -IDE.] *Chem.* A combination of tellurium with an electro-positive element (e.g. hydrogen or a metal), or with a radical; as *t. of hydrogen.*

T. of bismuth, telluric bismuth, tetradymite, or bornite. *T. of gold and silver* = SYLVANITE.

Tellurion (teliūə·riŏn). Also **tellurium.** 1831. [f. L. *tellus, tellurem* the earth.] An apparatus for showing the effect of the earth's motions and obliquity of axis in causing the alternations of day and night and the succession of the seasons; a simple kind of orrery.

Tellurism (te·liŭriz'm). 1843. [f. L. *tellurem* the earth + -ISM.] **1.** A magnetic influence or principle supposed by some to pervade all nature and to produce the phenomena of animal magnetism; also, the theory of animal magnetism based on this, propounded in 1822 by Kieser in Germany. **2.** Influence of the soil in producing disease 1890.

Tellurite (te·liŭrəit). 1799. [f. TELLURIUM -ITE [1] 2 b, 4 b.] **1.** *Min.* Native oxide of tellurium, found in minute whitish or yellow crystals; telluric ochre. **2.** *Chem.* A salt of tellurous acid 1847.

Tellurium (teliūə·riŏm). 1800. [mod.L., f. L. *tellus, tellurem* the earth + *-ium,* suffix of names of metals.] *Chem.* One of the rarer elements, a tin-white shining brittle substance, formerly from its outward characteristics classed among the metals, but chemically belonging to the same series as sulphur and selenium. It occurs native in rhombohedral crystals, isomorphous with those of antimony, arsenic, and bismuth. Symbol Te; atomic weight 128. **b.** *Graphic t.* = SYLVANITE.

Comb.: **t. glance** *Min.* nagyagite or black telluride of lead.

Tellurous (te·liŭrəs), *a.* 1842. [f. TELLURIUM + -OUS.] *Chem.* Characterized by or of the nature of tellurium; said of compounds containing a greater proportion of tellurium than those called *telluric*; as *t. acid,* H_2TeO_3.

‖**Tellus** (te·lŏs). late ME. [L.] In Roman mythology, the goddess of the earth; hence, the earth personified; the planet Earth, the terrestrial globe.

Telo- [1] (telo), comb. form repr. Gr. τέλος, τέλεος end; as in **Te·loblast** [Gr. βλαστός germ], each of a number of proliferating cells at one end of the embryo in segmented animals, as insects and annelids.

Telo- [2], repr. Gr. τηλο-, comb. form of τῆλε or τηλοῦ far off, occurring exceptionally instead of τηλε- (TELE-). See next and TELOTYPE.

Telodynamic (te:lodinæ·mik, -dəi-), *a.* Also teledynamic. 1870. [f. TELO- [2] + DYNAMIC.] Term applied to a cable transmitting mechanical power to a distance.

‖**Telos** (te·lǫs). 1904. [a. Gr. τέλος end.] End, purpose, ultimate object or aim.

Telotroch (te·lǫtrǫk). 1877. [f. TELO- [1] + Gr. τροχός wheel. Cf. mod.L. *Telotrocha* neut. pl., as name for larvæ having this structure.] *Zool.* A zone of cilia circling either or each end of the preoral (and perianal) segments of a free-swimming polychætus annelid larva. **b.** A larva of this kind. Hence **Telo·trochal, Telo·trochous** *adjs.* possessing a t. or telotrochs; of the nature of a t.

Telotype (te·lǫtəip). 1858. [f. TELO- [2] + TYPE.] An electric telegraph that automatically prints the messages as received; also, a telegram so printed.

Telpher (te·lfəɹ), *a.* and *sb.* 1884. [Syncopated form of *telepher* or *telephore,* f. Gr. τῆλε TELE- + -φορος bearing.] **A.** *adj.* or *attrib. sb.* Of or relating to a system of telpherage. **B.** *sb.* Any travelling unit on a telpher line; also, the plant and rolling stock of a system of telpherage.

a. *T. line, railway,* a light overhead line on which the haulage is worked by electric power; so *t. train.* Hence **Te·lpher** *v. trans.* to transport (goods, etc.) by means of telpherage.

Telpherage (te·lfəredʒ). 1883. [f. as prec. + -AGE.] Transport effected automatically by the aid of electricity.

Telson (te·lsən). 1855. [a. Gr. τέλσον a limit.] *Zool.* The last segment of the abdomen or its median axis in certain crustaceans and arachnidans, as the middle flipper of a lobster's tail-fin, the sting of the scorpion, etc.

‖ **Telugu, Teloogoo** (te·lugū), *sb., a.* 1789. [Native name of the language, and of a man of the race. Origin and deriv. unkn.] **1.** The name of a Dravidian language, spoken on the Coromandel coast of India, north of Madras 1813. **2.** One of the Dravidian people or race who speak this language 1789. **3.** *attrib.* or as *adj.* Of or pertaining to this language, people, or country 1888.

‖**Temenos** (te·menǫs). 1820. [a. Gr. τέμενος, f. τεμ-, stem of τέμνειν to cut off, sever.] *Gr. Antiq.* A piece of ground surrounding or adjacent to a temple; a sacred enclosure or precinct.

Temerarious (temĕrēə·riəs), *a.* Now only *literary.* 1532. [f. L. *temerarius* (f. *temere* blindly, rashly + *-arius*) + -OUS.] **1.** Characterized by temerity; reckless, heedless, rash. †**2.** Fortuitous, casual, haphazard –1775.

1. Your resolves are t. and presumptuous 1645. Hence **Temera·rious-ly** *adv.,* **-ness.**

Temerity (tĭme·rĭti). late ME. [ad. L. *temeritas, -tatem,* rashness, f. *temere* adv. by chance, blindly; see -ITY.] Excessive boldness, rashness; foolhardiness, recklessness; an instance of this.

Marlborough might have been made to repent his t. at Blenheim JOHNSON.

Temerous (te·mĕrəs), *a.* Now *rare.* 1461. [f. L. **temerosus* rash, f. *temere* adv.; see -OUS.] Rash, foolhardy. **Te·merous-ly** *adv.,* **-ness.**

Temp., abbrev. of L. *tempore,* in the time of.

Tempe (te·mpĭ). 1567. [a. L. *Tempe,* a. Gr. Τέμπη.] Proper name of a valley in Thessaly, watered by the Peneus, between Mounts Olympus and Ossa; used orig. in Latin literature as a general name for a beautiful valley; hence for any delightful rural spot.

The gay solitude of my own little T. 1770.

Temper (te·mpəɹ), *sb.* late ME. [f. next.] **I. 1.** The due or proportionate mixture or combination of elements or qualities; the condition or state resulting from such combination; proper or fit condition. Now *rare* or *Obs.* **2.** Proportionate arrangement of parts; regulation, adjustment; hence, mean or medium, a middle course; a compromise; a settlement. *arch.* 1523. **3.** Mental balance or composure, esp. under provocation of any kind; moderation in or command over the emotions, esp. anger; calmness, equanimity; now usu. in phr. *to keep* or *lose* (*one's*) *t., to be out of t.* 1603.

2. The king..compiled a new body of laws, in order to find a t. between both BURKE. **3.** I keep my T., and win their Money STEELE. It would put me out of t., which is a state of mind I can't endure DICKENS.

II. †**1.** = TEMPERAMENT II. –1759. †**b.** Of

things immaterial: Character, quality –1651. **2.** The particular degree of hardness and elasticity or resiliency imparted to steel by tempering 1470. †**3.** = CLIMATE *sb.* 3, TEMPERAMENT II. 2. –1705. †**4.** The relative condition of a body in respect of warmth or coldness –1884. †**5.** Bodily habit, constitution, or condition –1707. **6.** Mental constitution; habitual disposition 1595. **7.** Actual state of the mind or feelings; inclination, humour 1628. **8.** = *ill-temper*: Heat of mind or passion; explosive ill-humour 1828.

2. Between two blades, which beares the better t. SHAKS. *fig.* Intellectual implements of more ethereal t. 1866. **6.** The t. of the Puritan was eminently a t. of law GREEN. **7.** The Commons were in no t. to listen to such excuses MACAULAY. *Good t., ill t., bad t.* (cf. GOOD-TEMPERED, ILL-TEMPERED, *bad-tempered*). **8.** Johnson, when the first ebullition of t. had subsided, felt he had been unreasonably violent 1846. I can't tell you..what a t. I was in 1900.

III. Concr. senses. **a.** *Sugar-making.* A solution containing lime or some other alkaline substance serving to neutralize the acid in the raw cane-juice and clarify it 1657. **b.** An alloy of tin and copper 1875.

Comb.: **t.-screw**, a set-screw for adjustment; *esp.* in boring, a screw-connexion for automatically adjusting the drill as the boring proceeds.

Temper (te·mpəɹ), *v.* [OE. *temprian*, ad. L. *temperare*, reinforced by OF. *temprer.*] **I. 1.** *trans.* To bring (anything) to a proper or suitable condition, state, or quality, by mingling with something else; to qualify, alloy, or dilute by such mixture or combination. *arch.* **2.** To modify (some unsuitable or excessive state or quality, or some thing or person in respect of such), esp. by admixture of some other quality, etc.; to reduce to the suitable or desirable degree or condition free from excess in either direction; to moderate, mitigate, assuage, tone down OE. **3.** To mix, mingle, blend (ingredients) *together*, or (one ingredient) *with* another, in proper proportions. *arch.* late ME. **4.** To prepare by mingling; to make by due mixture or combination; to concoct, compound, make up, devise. *Obs.* or *arch.* late ME. †**5.** To restore the proper 'temper' or 'temperament' to; to cure, heal, refresh –1613. **6.** To bring into a suitable or desirable frame of mind; to dispose favourably; also, to appease, mollify, pacify. *Obs.* or *arch.* 1525.

1. As wine is tempered with water, so let discretion t. zeale 1591. **2.** T. sorow with mirth 1552. He.. who tempers judgment with mercy 1871. **3.** Whan metalles be well tempered togyther they wyll be all as one 1530. **4.** Lo, thus I tempre mi diete 1390. **6.** The Lady so well tempered and reconciled them both, that she forced them to join Hands STEELE.

II. 1. To keep, conduct, or manage in just measure; to regulate; to control, guide, govern, overrule. *Obs.* exc. *dial.* OE. **2.** To restrain within due limits, or within the bounds of moderation; in later use often simply, to restrain, check, curb. Also †*refl.* OE. **3.** To regulate suitably to need or requirement; to fit, adapt, conform, accommodate, make suitable. Const. *to.* Now *rare* or *Obs.* 1450.

1. Supremest Jove Tempers the fates of human race above POPE. **2.** I wish that not onely Kings, but all other Persons..would so t. themselves as to commit no wrong HOBBES. Cortes..was more solicitous to t. than to inflame their ardour 1777. **3.** They were indeed not temper'd to his temper MILT.

III. Techn. uses. **1.** To bring (clay, mortar, etc.) to a proper consistence for use by mixing and working it up *with* water, etc. ME. †**2.** To moisten (a substance, usu. medicinal or culinary ingredients in a comminuted state) so as to form a paste or mixture –1674. **b.** *spec.* in *Painting.* To prepare (colours) for use by mixing them with oil, etc. 1531. †**3.** *trans.* To soften (iron, wax, etc.) by heating; to melt. Also *intr.* for *pass.* –1597. **4.** To bring (steel) to a suitable degree of hardness and elasticity or resiliency by heating it to the required temperature and immersing it, while hot, in some liquid, usu. cold water. Also *intr.* for *pass.* late ME. †**5.** To tune, adjust the pitch of (a musical instrument) –1593. **b.** *spec.* To tune (a note or instrument) according to some temperament; see TEMPERAMENT III. 3. 1727. **6.** To bring into harmony, attune. *Obs.* or *arch.* late ME.

3. 2 *Hen. IV*, IV. iii. 140. **4.** They have a great advauntage in Spayne, to t. their blades well, bycause of the nature of their ryvers PALSGR. **6.** Mean while the Rural ditties were not mute, Temper'd to th'Oaten Flute MILT.

‖**Tempera** (te·mperă). 1832. [It., in phr. *pingere a tempera* to paint in distemper.] The method of painting in distemper: see DISTEMPER *sb.*[2]

Temperable (te·mpərăb'l), *a.* Now *rare.* late ME. [prob. ad. med.L. *temperabilis*; but perh. f. TEMPER *v.* + -ABLE.] †**a.** Of weather or climate: = TEMPERATE *a.* 3. †**b.** Of a person: = TEMPERATE *a.* 1. –1629. **c.** That may be tempered or made plastic 1841.

a. In somer he muste haue t. eir. late ME. **c.** The fusible, hard, and t. texture of metals EMERSON. Hence **Temperabi·lity.**

Temperality, joc. misused for *temper.* SHAKS.

Temperament (te·mpĕrămĕnt), *sb.* late ME. [ad. L. *temperamentum* due mixture, f. *temperare* to TEMPER; see -MENT.] **I.** †**1.** A moderate and proportionable mixture of elements in a compound; the condition in which elements are combined in their due proportions –1684. †**2.** Consistence, composition; mixture –1673. **II.** †**1.** In the natural philosophy of the Middle Ages: The combination of supposed qualities (*hot* or *cold*, *moist* or *dry*), in a certain proportion, determining the nature of a plant or other body; characteristic nature; known *spec.* as *universal t.* –1677. **2.** The condition of the weather or climate as resulting from the different combinations of the qualities, heat or cold, dryness or humidity; climate. *Obs.* or *arch.* 1610. †**3.** Condition with regard to warmth or coldness –1799. **4.** In mediæval physiology: The combination of the four cardinal humours (see HUMOUR *sb.* 2 b) of the body, by the relative proportion of which the physical and mental constitution were held to be determined; known *spec.* as *animal t.*; also, the bodily habit attributed to this, as a *sanguine, choleric, phlegmatic*, or *melancholic t.* (see the adjs.) 1628. **5.** Constitution or habit of mind, esp. as depending upon or connected with physical constitution; natural disposition 1821.

2. The t. of their seasons is such that they have no disease JOWETT. **4.** Our minds are perpetually.. wrought on by the Temperament of our Bodies DRYDEN. **5.** The man of sanguine t. 1868.

III. 1. Moderating, moderation; lightening, alleviation, mitigation; due regulation. *Obs.* or *arch.* 1475. **2.** The action of duly combining or adjusting different principles, claims, etc.; adjustment, compromise. *Obs.* or *arch.* 1660. **b.** A middle course or state; a medium, mean. *Obs.* or *arch.* 1604. **3.** *Mus.* The adjustment of the intervals of the scale (in the tuning of instruments of fixed intonation, as keyboard instruments), so as to adapt them to purposes of practical harmony: consisting in slight variations of the pitch of the notes from true or 'just' intonation, in order to make them available in different keys; a particular system of doing this. (Sometimes extended to any system of tuning.) 1727.

2. These admit no t. and no compromise BURKE. **b.** The causes..of this t.—this *mezzo termino*—this middle course BENTHAM. **3.** The chief temperaments ..are *mean-tone t.*..and *equal t.* (now almost universal), in which the octave is divided into twelve (theoretically) equal semitones, so that the variations of pitch are evenly distributed throughout all keys. N.E.D. Hence **T·emperament** *v. rare. trans.* to endow with a t.

Temperamental (te:mpĕrăme·ntăl), *a.* 1646. [f. prec. + -AL.] Of or relating to the temperament (chiefly in sense II. 5); in recent colloq. use, liable to or marked by variable or unaccountable moods. Hence **Temperame·ntally** *adv.*

Temperance (te·mpĕrăns). ME. [a. AF. *temperaunce*, ad. L. *temperantia* moderation, f. *temperantem*, *temperare* to TEMPER.] **I. 1.** The practice or habit of restraining oneself in provocation, passion, desire, etc.; rational self-restraint. (One of the four cardinal virtues.) **2.** *spec.* The avoidance of excess in eating and drinking; *esp.*, in later use, moderation in regard to intoxicants; sobriety. Now often applied to teetotalism. 1542. **b.** *attrib.* Pertaining to, practising, or advocating total abstinence, as *t. association, drink, movement, society, work*; **t. hotel, inn,** one where no intoxicants are provided 1836.

1. He..calmd his wrath with goodly t. SPENSER. The secret of t. lies not in the scanty supply, but in the strong self-restraint 1846. **2.** With a delicate frame..I have been enabled, by t., to do the work of a strong man COBDEN. Where I can enjoy a stiff glass of grog with my feet on the hobs, and with nobody to preach t. 1887.

II. †**1. a.** = TEMPERAMENT III. 1, 2. –1596. **b.** = TEMPERAMENT I. 1, 2. –1638. †**2.** Moderate temperature; freedom from the extremes of heat and cold; mildness of weather or climate; temperateness –1610.

1. b. But were all Men of my T., and Wisdom too, You should woo us COWLEY. **2.** It [the island] must needs be of..tender, and delicate t. SHAKS. So †**Te·mperancy,** = TEMPERANCE, in senses I. 1, 2, II. 1 b.

Temperate (te·mpĕrĕt), *a.* late ME. [ad. L. *temperatus*, *temperare* to TEMPER.] **1.** Of persons, their conduct, practices, etc.: Observing moderation, self-restrained, moderate. **2.** Of things, actions, qualities, conditions, etc.: Tempered; not excessive in degree; restrained; late ME. **3.** *spec.* Of the weather, season, climate, etc.: Moderate in respect of warmth: neither too hot nor too cold; of mild and equable temperature. late ME. **4.** Of monarchy or sovereignty, hence also of the sovereign: Restricted in extent of authority; not absolute; limited; constitutional. *Obs.* or *arch.* 1560.

1. This is a t. statement MILL. The t. life has gentle pains and pleasures JOWETT. That a young man of strictly t. habits should thus suddenly become a drunkard 1890. **2.** At the t. hour of nine, the bridal festivities closed 1855. **3.** So cleare the ayre, so t. the clime 1587. *T. zone*, each of the two zones or belts of the earth's surface lying between the torrid and frigid zones. **4.** That sober freedom out of which there springs Our loyal passion for our t. Kings TENNYSON. So †**Te·mperate** *v.* = TEMPER *v.* **Te·mperately** *adv.*, **-ness.**

Te·mperative, *a.* Now *rare* or *Obs.* late ME. [ad. late L. *temperativus*, f. *temperare* TEMPER *v.*; see -IVE.] Having the quality of tempering; alleviative, mitigating; tending to temperateness.

Temperature (te·mpĕrătiŭɹ, -tʃəɹ). 1531. [ad. L. *temperatura*, f. ppl. stem of *temperare*; see -URE.] †**1.** The action or process of tempering; mixing or combination (of elements) –1677. †**2.** The fact or state of being tempered or mixed, mixture; also, the condition resulting from the mixture or combination in various proportions of ingredients or elements; the composition, consistence, or complexion so produced –1826. †**3.** Due measure or proportion in action, thought, etc.; freedom from excess or violence; moderation –1659. †**b.** A mean between opposites; a middle course, a compromise –1712. †**4.** = TEMPERAMENT II. 1. –1616. †**5.** = TEMPERAMENT II. 4. –1837. †**b.** = TEMPERAMENT II. 5. –1768. †**6.** A tempered or temperate condition of the weather or climate; also, a (specified) condition of these –1727. **7.** The state of a substance or body with regard to sensible warmth or coldness, referred to some standard of comparison; *spec.* that quality or condition of a body which in degree varies directly with the amount of heat contained in the body, and inversely with its heat-capacity; usu. measured by means of a thermometer or similar instrument 1670. †**8.** The temper of steel –1630.

3. b. His Constitution is a just T. between Indolence on one hand and Violence on the other 1712. **5.** There is no t. so exactly regulated but that some humour is fatally predominant JOHNSON. **b.** As touching the manners of learned men..no doubt there be amongst them, as in other professions, of all temperatures BACON. **7.** A moderate Expence of Fire..serves to keep this large Room in a due T. STEELE. A comparison of the temperatures shown by the two thermometers HUXLEY. Phr. *To have a t.*, i. e. one higher than the normal, as in fever (*colloq.*).

Comb.: **t.-chart,** (*a*) a chart or card containing a *t.-curve* or its equivalent; (*b*) a chart of a region indicating temperatures at different points, as by isotherms; **-curve,** a curve showing variations of t., usu. in relation to equal periods of time, *esp.* in clinical use.

Tempered (te·mpəɹd), *a.* late ME. [f. TEMPER *v.* and *sb.* + -ED.] **1.** Brought to or having a proper or desired temper, quality, or consistence; hence, temperate. **b.** *Mus.* That has been tuned or adjusted in pitch according to some TEMPERAMENT (sense III. 3) 1727. **2.**

Constituted or endowed with a specified temper or disposition (in various senses of *temper*). late ME. **3.** Modified by the admixture or influence of some other element; moderated, toned-down; limited 1654.

1. A court, open to the t. aire 1577. An excellently t. complexion 1638. T. steel 1655. **2.** A quiet and equally t. people 1628. Children, sweetly t. like their mother 1760. Hard at bargaining..and cross-tempered 1901. **3.** A t. monarchy BURKE. The t. wisdom of the Queen 1828.

Temperer (te·mpərəɹ). 1617. [f. TEMPER *v.* + -ER[1].] One who or that which tempers; *esp.* in senses III. 1 and 4 of the vb.

Te·mpersome, *a.* orig. *dial.* 1875. [f. TEMPER *sb.*] Quick-tempered. **Te·mpersomeness.**

Tempest (te·mpėst), *sb.* ME. [a. OF. *tempeste* :—pop. L. **tempestam*, for cl. L. *tempestas, -atem* season, weather, storm, f. *tempus* time, season; also a. OF. *tempest* :—L. **tempestum.*] **1.** A violent storm of wind, usu. accompanied by a downfall of rain, hail, or snow, or by thunder. **b.** A thunder-storm (*dial.*) 1532. **2.** *transf.* and *fig.* A violent commotion or disturbance; a tumult, rush; agitation, perturbation ME. **3.** A tumultuous throng; †a crowded assembly; a rushing crowd 1746.

1. A Station safe for Ships, when Tempests roar DRYDEN. **2.** In the midst of all this t. the ministers.. seem much at their ease BURKE. **3.** There are also drum-major, rout, t., and hurricane, differing only in degrees of multitude and uproar SMOLLETT.

Tempest (te·mpėst), *v.* late ME. [ad. OF. *tempester*, f. *tempeste*; see prec.] **1.** *trans.* To affect by or as by a tempest; to throw into violent commotion, to agitate violently. **2.** *fig.* To disturb violently (a person, the mind). late ME. †**3.** *intr.* Of the wind, weather, etc., and *impers.*: To be tempestuous, to blow tempestuously; to rage, storm -1615.

1. Fish..Wallowing unweildie, enormous in thir Gate, T. the Ocean MILT.

Tempestive (tempe·stiv), *a. arch.* 1611. [ad. L. *tempestivus* timely; see TEMPEST *sb.* and -IVE.] Timely, seasonable.

The chearefull and tempestiue showres HEYWOOD. Hence **Tempe·stively** *adv.*

†**Tempesti·vity.** 1569. [ad. L. *tempestivitas*, f. *tempestivus*; see -ITY.] **1.** Seasonableness, timeliness -1656. **2.** A season, a time of a particular character -1683.

Te·mpest-to:ssed, -to:st, *a.* 1592. Tossed by, or as by, a tempest.

Tempestuous (tempe·stiŭəs), *a.* 1447. [ad. L. *tempestuosus.*] **1.** Of. pertaining to, involving, or resembling a tempest; subject to or characterized by tempests; stormy, very rough or violent 1509. **2.** *transf.* and *fig.* Characterized by violent agitation or commotion; turbulent; passionate; agitated as by a tempest 1447.

1. A very blustering and a t. day LAUD. **2.** A winning wave (deserving note) In the t. petticote HERRICK. Cecilia was still in this t. state MISS BURNEY. Hence **Tempe·stuous-ly** *adv.*, **-ness.**

Templar (te·mplăɹ), *sb.* ME. [a. AF. *templer*, OF. *templier* = med.L. *templarius*, f. *templum* TEMPLE *sb.*[1]; see -ER[2] 2, -AR[2].] **1.** A member of a military and religious order, consisting of knights (*Knights Templars, Knights* or *Poor Soldiers of the Temple*), chaplains, and men-at-arms, founded *c* 1118, chiefly for the protection of the Holy Sepulchre and of Christian pilgrims visiting the Holy Land; so called from their occupation of a building on or near the site of the Temple of Solomon at Jerusalem. They were suppressed in 1312. **2.** A barrister or other person who occupies chambers in the Inner or Middle Temple 1588. **3. a.** A member of an order of Freemasons calling themselves Knights Templars, extensively established in the United States 1859. **b.** Short for GOOD TEMPLAR -1874.

Templar (te·mplăɹ), *a.* 1728. [ad. late L. *templaris*, f. *templum* TEMPLE *sb.*[1]; see -AR[1].] Of, pertaining to, or characteristic of a (or the Jewish) temple.

Templary (te·mplări), *sb.* late ME. [ad. med.L. *templarius* TEMPLAR *sb.*; see -ARY[1].] †**1.** = TEMPLAR *sb.* 1. -1656. **2.** Templars collectively; *Hist.* the system or organization of the Templars; the Masonic and Temperance societies so called. 1661.

Template, var. of TEMPLET.

Temple (te·mp'l), *sb.*[1] [OE. *templ, tempel*, ad. L. *templum*, reinforced by F. *temple.*] **I. 1.** An edifice or place regarded primarily as the dwelling-place or 'house' of a deity or deities; hence, an edifice devoted to divine worship. **b.** *spec.* The sacred edifice at Jerusalem, the 'House of the Lord' and seat of the Jewish worship of Jehovah OE. **c.** *fig.* 1607. **2.** *transf.* A building dedicated to public Christian worship; a church; esp. applied to a large or grand edifice. late ME. **3.** *fig.* Any place regarded as occupied by the divine presence; *spec.* the person or body of a Christian (1 Cor. iii. 16) OE.

1. But he that is hyest of all dweleth not in temples made with hondes TINDALE *Acts* vii. 48. Tempilis & places of sacrifice to prophane Godis 1596. **c.** A t. of science now in ruins TYNDALL. **3.** Most sacrilegious Murther hath broke ope The Lords anoynted T., and stole thence The Life o' th' Building SHAKS.

II. †**1.** The head-quarters of the Knights Templars, on or contiguous to the site of the temple at Jerusalem; hence, the organization of the Templars -1656. **2.** *spec.* Name of two of the Inns of Court in London, known as the *Inner* and *Middle T.*, which stand on the site of the buildings once occupied by the Templars (of which the church alone remains) ME. **b.** Name of the place in Paris which formed the head-quarters of the Templars in Europe 1617.

Temple (te·mp'l), *sb.*[2] ME. [a. OF. :—pop. L. **tempula*, **templa*, app. for cl. L. *tempora*, pl. of *tempus* 'temple of the head'.] **1.** The flattened region on each side of the (human) forehead. (Chiefly in *pl.*) Also *transf.*, a corresponding part in lower animals. **2.** Each of the side-members or limbs of a pair of spectacles, which clasp the sides of the head of the wearer. *U.S.* 1877.

Temple (te·mp'l), *sb.*[3] 1483. [a. F., perh. orig. the same word as prec.] **1.** A contrivance for keeping cloth stretched to its proper width in the loom during the process of weaving. Usu. *pl.* **2.** = TEMPLET[1] 2 (*rare*) 1688.

Temple (te·mp'l), *v.* 1593. [f. TEMPLE *sb.*[1]] **1.** *trans.* To enclose in or as in a temple; to honour with a temple or temples, to build a temple to or for. **2.** To make or fashion into a temple 1839. †**3.** To dwell as in a temple. KEN.

1. The Heathen..Templed and adored this drunken god 1628. **2.** *ppl. a.* O'er which ye rise in templed majesty 1839.

Temple-bar. ME. [f. TEMPLE *sb.*[1] II. 2 (because of its proximity to the Temple buildings) + BAR *sb.*[1]] The name of the barrier or gateway closing the entrance into the City of London from the Strand; removed in 1878.

Templet[1] (te·mplėt). Also **template.** 1677. [Origin obsc.] **1.** *Building.* A horizontal piece of timber in a wall, or spanning a window or doorway, to take and distribute the pressure of a girder, or of joists or rafters; a plate. **2.** An instrument used as a gauge or guide in bringing any piece of work to the desired shape; usu. a flat piece of wood or metal having one edge shaped to correspond to the outline of the finished work; also, used as a tool in moulding, etc. 1819. **b.** A flat plate or strip perforated with holes used as a guide in marking out holes for riveting or drilling 1874.

Templet,[2] **-ette.** 1889. [Origin uncertain.] Each of the four-sided facets which surround and 'support' the table of a brilliant.

‖**Tempo** (te·mpo). *Pl.* **tempi** (te·mpi). 1724. [It., :—L. *tempus* time.] *Mus.* Relative speed or rate of movement; pace; time; *spec.* the proper or characteristic speed and rhythm of a dance or other tune (in phr. *t. di marcia, t. di minuetto*, etc.).

T. primo, first or former time; a direction to resume the original speed after an alteration of it. *T. rubato*, robbed or stolen time; i.e. time occasionally slackened or hastened for the purposes of expression.

Temporal (te·mpŏrăl), *a.*[1] and *sb.*[1] ME. [ad. L. *temporalis*, f. *tempus, tempor-* time; in B. 2, ad. eccl. L. *temporale.*] **A.** *adj.* **1.** Lasting or existing only for a time; passing, temporary. Now *rare* or merged in 2. late ME. **2.** Of or pertaining to time as the sphere of human life; terrestrial as opp. to heavenly; of man's present life; worldly, earthly. (Opp. to *eternal* or *spiritual.*) late ME. **3.** Secular as opp. to sacred; lay as dist. from clerical. Of law: civil or common as dist. from canon. Of rule, authority, or government: civil as dist. from ecclesiastical. (Opp. to *spiritual*) ME. **4. a.** *Gram.* and *Pros.* Relating to or depending on the quantity of syllables 1678. **b.** *Gram.* Of or pertaining to the tenses of a verb; of tense; also, expressing or denoting time, as an adv., a clause, etc. 1786. **5.** *gen.* Of, pertaining, or relating to time, the present time, or a particular time 1877.

1. For the things which are seene, are temporall, but the things which are not seene, are eternall 2 *Cor.* iv. 18. **2.** The Jews..expected..a t. prince 1772. **3.** His Scepter shewes the force of temporall power, The attribute to awe and Maiestie SHAKS. *Lords t.*: see LORD *sb.* 9. **4.** *T. augment* (Gr. Gram.): see AUGMENT *sb.* 2.

B. *sb.* **1. a.** That which is temporal; esp. in *pl.* Temporal things or matters. late ME. **b.** Temporal power, possession, or estate; TEMPORALITY; chiefly in *pl.* = temporalities 1450. **2.** (Also in L. form **Temporale** (tempŏrē^i·li, -ā·le).) That part of the breviary and the missal which contains the services in the order of the eccl. year, as dist. from those proper to saints' days. late ME.

1. b. The Pope commaundeth ouer the temporall of the Church called S. Peters patrimonie, as King 1594. Hence **Te·mporalism**, secularism, addiction to t. or mundane interests; also the principle of the t. power of the Pope. **Te·mporal-ly** *adv.*, **-ness** (*rare*).

Temporal (te·mpŏrăl), *a.*[2] and *sb.*[2] 1541. [ad. L. *temporalis*, f. *tempora* the temples; see TEMPLE *sb.*[2]] *Anat.* **A.** *adj.* Of, belonging to, or situated in the temples: esp. in names of structures, as *t. artery, bone, muscle, vein*, etc. 1597. **B.** *sb.* Ellipt. for *t. artery, bone, muscle*, etc.

A. *T. canals*, small passages for vessels and nerves through the malar bone to the t. surface; *t. fossa*, that in which the t. muscle originates.

Temporality (tempŏræ·lĭti). ME. [ad. late L. *temporalitas*, f. *temporalis* TEMPORAL *a.*[1]; see -ITY.] †**1.** = next 1. -1818. **b.** *pl.* Temporal or material possessions (esp. of the church or clergy) 1475. **2.** = next 2. 1456. **3.** The quality or condition of being t. or temporary; temporariness; relation to time 1634.

1. The Churches so great encrease of T. 1613.

Temporalty (te·mpŏrălti). *Obs.* or *arch.* late ME. [app. a. F. **temporelté*, f. OF. *temporel* TEMPORAL *a.*[1]; see -TY. Now TEMPORALITY.] **1.** Temporal or secular things, affairs, business; temporal authority. **b.** Chiefly *pl.* = prec. 1 b. late ME. **2.** The body of temporal persons or laymen, the laity; the temporal estate or estates of the realm, i.e. the temporal peers and the commons. late ME.

Temporaneous (tempŏrē^i·nĭəs), *a.* Now *rare* or *Obs.* 1656. [f. L. *temporaneus* timely (f. *tempus, tempor-* time) + -OUS.] †**1.** Lasting only for a time, temporary -1818. **2.** Pertaining or relating to time, temporal 1656. Hence **Tempora·neous-ly** *adv.*, **-ness.**

Temporary (te·mpŏrări), *a.* (*sb.*) 1547. [ad. L. *temporarius*, f. *tempus, tempor-* time; see -ARY.] **1.** Lasting for a limited time; existing or valid for a time (only); transient; made to supply a passing need. †**2.** = TEMPORAL *a.*[1] 2. -1751. †**3.** *Metaph.* Occurring or existing in time (not from eternity) -1701.

1. Inconveniences which they felt to be only t. J. H. NEWMAN. *T. star* (*Astron.*), a star which appears suddenly, shines for a time, and then disappears. *T. tooth.* a deciduous tooth, milk-tooth. **2.** *Meas. for M.* v. i. 145.

B. *sb.* †**1.** *pl.* Temporal goods -1665. **2.** A person employed or holding a post temporarily; a 'casual' 1848. Hence **Te·mporarily** *adv.* **Te·mporariness.**

†**Te·mporist.** 1596. [f. L. *tempus, tempor-* time + -IST.] A temporizer, a time-server -1666.

Why, turne a t., row with the tide, Pursew the cut, the fashion of the age MARSTON.

Temporiza·tion. 1763. [f. next + -ATION.] The action of temporizing; time-serving; procrastination; gaining of time.

Temporize (te·mpŏrəiz), *v.* 1555. [a. F. *temporiser* to pass one's time, wait one's time, = med.L. *temporizare* = *temporare* to delay, f. L. *tempus, tempor-* time; see -IZE.] **1.** *intr.* To adopt some course for the time or occasion; hence, to adapt oneself or conform to the time and circumstances. †2. *intr.* To let time pass, spend time, 'mark time'; to procrastinate; to delay or wait for a more favourable moment. *Obs.* exc. as in 3. –1696. 3. To act, parley, treat, deal (*with* a person, etc.) so as to gain time 1586. 4. To negotiate, to discuss terms; to arrange or make terms, or effect a compromise (*with* a person, etc., *between* persons or parties) 1579.

1. The pope..had privately advised Becket to avoid a quarrel with the king and to temporise FROUDE. 3. William was still temporizing with Stigand; the time for his degradation was not yet come FREEMAN. Hence **Te·mporizer**, one who temporizes. **Te·mporizingly**, in a way designed to gain time, in a temporizing manner.

Temporo- (te·mpŏrŏ), bef. a vowel occas. **tempor-**, used in *Anat.* as comb. form of L. *tempora* temples (of the head), forming adjs. in the sense 'pertaining to the temple or temples and (some other part)', as *t.-auricular, -facial, -malar, -mastoid, -maxillary.*

Tempt (tempt), *v.* ME. [a. OF. and AF. *tempter*:—L. *temptare, tentare* to handle, try, etc., from a root *tem-, temp-*.] I. To test, put to the test, try. †1. To try, make trial of, put to the test or proof. *Obs.* exc. as in 2. –1644. 2. To make trial of, put to the proof or test, in a way that involves risk or peril ME. †3. = ATTEMPT *v.* 1. –1538. b. *with simple obj.* To attempt, try 1697.

2. *To t. God*, to experiment presumptuously upon His power, forbearance, etc.; to try how far one can go with Him; hence sometimes to provoke, defy; so *to t. providence, fate, fortune*, etc. *To t.* (*the storm, flood, sea*, etc.), to risk the perils of (chiefly *poet.*) 3. b. Ere leave be giv'n to t. the nether skies DRYDEN.

II. To try to attract, allure, incite, induce. 1. *trans.* To try to attract, to entice (a person) to do evil; to allure or incite to evil with the prospect of some pleasure or advantage. Const. *to* something, *to do* something. Also *absol.* ME. b. To try to draw (a person) to contradict, confute, or commit himself. *arch.* late ME. 2. To attract or incite *to* some action or *to do* something; to allure, entice, invite, attract; to dispose, incline ME.

1. Idle men t. the devil to t. them 1869. b. Why tempte ye me? Brynge me a peny, that I maye se yt. TINDALE *Mark* xii. 15. 2. Unhappy land! whose blessings t. the sword COLLINS.

Temptable (te·mptăb'l), *a.* 1628. [f. prec. + -ABLE.] That may be tempted; liable or open to temptation. Hence **Temptabi·lity**, **Te·mptableness**, accessibility to temptation.

Temptation (temptēi·ʃən). ME. [a. OF. *temptaciun, tentation*, ad. L. *tempt-, tentationem*, f. *temptare, tentare* to TEMPT.] 1. The action of tempting or fact of being tempted, esp. to evil. b. With *a* and *pl.* An instance of this ME. c. *transf.* A thing that tempts; a cause or source of temptation 1596. 2. The action or process of testing or proving; trial, test. *Obs.* or *arch.* late ME.

1. Watche and praye that ye fall not into temptacion TINDALE *Matt.* xxvi. 41. *The T.*, that of Jesus in the wilderness (*Matt.* iv. etc.). c. Dare to be great, without a guilty crown; View it, and lay the bright t. down DRYDEN. Hence **Tempta·tious** *a.* full of t.; tempting.

Tempter (te·mptəɹ). [Late ME. *temptour* = obs. F. *tempteur*:—L. *temptatorem*, f. *temptare* to tempt.] One who or that which tempts or entices to evil; *the t.*, (*spec.*) the devil.

The T., or the Tempted, who sins most? SHAKS.

Te·mpting, *ppl. a.* 1546. [f. TEMPT *v.* + -ING[2].] 1. That entices to evil, or with evil design. 2. Seductive, attractive, alluring, inviting 1596.

2. 'Tis such a t. offer 1818. Hence **Te·mpting·ly** *adv.*, **-ness.**

Temptress (te·mptrĕs). 1594. [f. TEMPTER + -ESS.] A female tempter.

Temse (tems, temz), *sb.* Now *dial.* late ME. [OE. **tęmes* (in *tęmes-pile, tęmesian*), app. Com. WGer.] A sieve, esp. one used for bolting meal; a searce, a strainer. In mod. local use *esp.* a sieve used in brewing.

Comb.: t.-bread, -loaf, bread or a loaf made of finely sifted flour.

Temse (tems, temz), *v.* Now *dial.* [OE. *tęm(e)sian*; see prec.] *trans.* To sift or bolt (flour, etc.) with a temse. Hence **Temsed** *ppl. a.*; *temsed-bread* = *temse-bread* (see prec.).

Temulence (te·miŭlĕns). *rare.* 1803. [f. as next; see -ENCE.] = next.

Temulency (te·miŭlĕnsi). Now *rare.* 1623. [ad. post-cl. L. *temulentia* drunkenness, f. *temulentus*; see next and -ENCY.] Drunkenness, inebriety.

Temulent (te·miŭlĕnt), *a.* Now *rare.* 1628. [ad. L. *temulentus*, from root *tem-* in *temetum* intoxicating drink, after *violentus* from *vinum* wine.] Drunken, intoxicated; given to, characterized by, or proceeding from drunkenness; intoxicating.

Ten (ten), *a., sb.* (*adv.*). [Com. Teut.; OE. *tīen, -e*, Anglian *tēn, -e* (the inflected forms in *-e* were used when the numeral was used absol.):—OTeut. **teχan, -un*, repr. pre-Teut. **dekm*, L. *decem*, Gr. δέκα, Skr. *daça(n-.)*] The cardinal numeral next higher than nine; the number of the digits on both hands or feet, and hence the basis of the ordinary or decimal numeration. A. *adj.* 1. In concord with a sb. expressed. b. As multiple of another higher cardinal number, as in *ten hundred*, etc.; also in the ordinals of these, as *ten thousandth* OE. c. Used vaguely or hyperbolically, esp. in *t. times, tenfold*, etc. late ME. 2. Absolutely or with ellipsis of sb. OE.

1. Which rage of water lasted tenne dayes 1513. *The T. Commandments*, the Mosaic decalogue; *slang*, the t. fingers. *T. tribes*, the lost tribes of Israel; *joc.* the Jews, as money-lenders. b. The guarantee for the ten-million loan 1905. c. A Iewell in a t. times barr'd vp Chest SHAKS. 2. About t. at night 1843. Two girls of, perhaps, eight and t. 1891. A t.-and-sixpenny kettle 1908. Phr. *T. to one*, t. chances to one; odds of t. times the amount offered in a bet; hence, an expression of very strong probability. *Hart of t.*: see HART *sb.* *Upper t.* (= *upper t. thousand*): see UPPER *a.*

B. *sb.* (With pl. *tens*; and (less usu.) possessive *ten's*.) 1. The abstract number; a symbol or the figures representing this, 10, X. OE. b. In a number expressed in decimal notation, the digit expressing the number of tens, e.g. in 1837 the figure 3. 1542. c. A person or thing distinguished by the number ten, usu. as the tenth of a series. Also *number ten*. 1888. 2. A set of ten things or persons OE. 3. *Coal-mining.* A measure of coal, locally varying between 48 and 50 tons, being the unit of calculation on which the lessor's rent or royalty is based. *n. dial.* 1590. 4. A playing-card marked with ten pips 1593. 5. Short for (*a*) ten-oared boat; (*b*) ten-pound note or ten-dollar bill. 6. a. Short for *tenpenny nail* (i.e. costing 10*d.* a hundred); *double ten*, a nail costing the double of the tenpenny. 1572. b. A tallow candle weighing ten to a pound. 1802.

1. 12 tens, which do make 2 sixties 1594. 2. I..made them..captaines ouer tennes *Deut.* i. 15. *T. of rupees*, a unit of account in Indian money.

†C. *quasi-*adv. Ten times, tenfold. –late ME.

Comb.: t.-foot *a.*, measuring, or having, t. feet; *t.-foot coal*, in Yorkshire, a thick seam; **t.-hours act**, a law limiting the hours of work in factories; *spec.* the pop. name of the Act 10 & 11 Vict., c. 29; so, in the U.S.A., **t.-hour law**; **t. o'clock**, Amer. name for *Ornithogalum umbellatum*, the flowers of which open late in the morning; **-pointer**, a stag having antlers with t. points, a hart of t.; **-pound** *a.*, of or involving the amount or value of t. pounds; also, weighing t. pounds; spec. *t.-pound householder* = TEN-POUNDER 2 b; **-spot** (*U.S.*), a t.-dollar bill; also = TEN *sb.* 4 **-year** *a.*, of t. years' duration or standing.

Tenable (te·năb'l, †tī·n-), *a.* 1579. [a. F., f. *tenir* to hold + -ABLE.] 1. Capable of being held; that may be kept, kept in, kept back, retained, restrained, or held in control. Now *rare.* 1602. 2. That may be held against attack; that may be successfully defended 1579. 3. Capable of being held, occupied, possessed, or enjoyed 1840.

1. If you have hitherto concealed this sight Let it be t. in your silence still SHAKS. 2. The City being not t. ..it yeelded 1579. *fig.* The letter of their theories is no longer t. 1837. 3. Scholarships..t. for three years 1883. Hence **Tenabi·lity, Te·nableness**, the quality of being t.

Tenace (te·nēs). 1655. [ad. Sp. *tenaza* lit. 'pincers, tongs'.] *Whist.* The combination of two cards of any suit, consisting of the next higher and the next lower in value than the highest card held by the other side, esp. when this combination is held by the fourth player. Used esp. in phr. *to have the t.*, formerly *tenaces.*

Tenacious (tĭnēi·ʃəs), *a.* 1607. [f. L. *tenax, tenaci-* holding fast (f. *tenere* to hold) + -OUS; see -ACIOUS.] 1. a. Holding together, cohesive. b. Adhesive; viscous, glutinous; sticky 1641. 2. Holding fast or inclined to hold fast; clinging tightly 1656. 3. Keeping a firm hold; retentive *of* something 1645. 4. *fig.* Strongly retaining, holding persistently, or inclined to retain, preserve, or maintain (a principle, method, secret, etc.); of memory, retentive. Const. *of.* 1640. 5. Persistently continuing; resolute; perseveringly firm; obstinate, stubborn, pertinacious 1656. †6. *erron.* Persistently averse to any action –1811.

1. a. Gun-metal, or bronze, is a hard and t. alloy 1869. b. Female feet, Too weak to struggle with t. clay COWPER. 2. T. hooked prickles 1869. 4. T. of his Purpose once resolv'd 1708. 5. He is..quick in opposition, and t. in defence JOHNSON. Hence **Tena·cious·ly** *adv.*, **-ness.**

Tenacity (tĭnæ·sĭti). 1526. [ad. rare L. *tenacitas*, f. *tenax, tenaci-* tenacious; see -ACITY.] The quality or property of being tenacious. 1. Cohesiveness, toughness; viscosity, clamminess (of a liquid); also, adhesive quality, stickiness 1555. 2. The quality of retaining what is held, physically or mentally; firmness of hold or attachment; firmness of purpose, persistence, obstinacy 1526. b. Retentiveness (of memory) 1814. †3. Miserliness, niggardliness, parsimony –1706.

2. The t. of Prejudice and Prescription SIR T. BROWNE. The t. of the English bull-dog 1878.

Tenacle (te·năk'l). Now *rare.* late ME. [ad. L. *tenaculum* holder; see next.] †1. *pl.* Forceps, pincers, nippers –1597. 2. That by which a plant, a fruit, etc. is upheld or supported; in *pl.* the organs by which some climbing plants attach themselves 1500.

‖**Tenaculum** (tĭnæ·kiŭlŏm). *Pl.* **-ula.** 1693. [mod. uses of L. *tenaculum* holder, f. *tenere* to hold.] 1. *Surg.* A kind of forceps. b. See quot. 1842. 2. *Ent.* The abdominal process by which the springing organ is retained in the *Poduridæ* or spring-tails 1878.

1. b. *T.*, a surgical instrument, consisting of a fine sharp-pointed hook, by which the mouths of bleeding arteries are drawn out, so that in operations they may be secured by ligaments 1842.

‖**Tenaille** (tĭ-, tenēi·l). 1589. [F. :—L. *tenacula*, pl. of *tenaculum* holder; see prec.] †1. *pl.* Pincers, forceps –1727. 2. *Fortif.* A small low work, consisting of one or two re-entering angles (*single* or *double t.*), placed before the curtain between two bastions 1589.

‖**Tenaillon** (tĕnæ·liǫn). 1842. [F., f. *tenaille* (see prec.).] *Fortif.* A work sometimes placed before each of the faces of a ravelin, leaving the salient angle exposed.

Tenancy (te·nănsi). 1579. [f. TENANT *sb.*; see -ANCY.] 1. *Law.* A holding or possession of lands or tenements, by any title of ownership 1590. b. Occupancy of lands or tenements under a lease. Also, (contextually) the duration of a tenure; the period during which a tenement is held. 1598. 2. Occupation or enjoyment of or residence in any place position, or condition 1597. †3. That which is held by a tenant. a. A tenement. b. A post or office; occupation, employment. *rare.* –1670.

Tenant (te·nănt), *sb.* ME. [a. F., orig. pr. pple. of *tenir* :—L. *tenere* to hold.] 1. *Law.* One who holds or possesses lands or tenements by any kind of title. (In English Law implying a *lord*, of whom the tenant holds.) b. With qualifications indicating the species of tenure, the relation between lord and tenant, etc. ME. 2. One who holds a piece of land, a house, etc., by lease for a term of years or a set time. (Correl. of *landlord.*) late ME. 3. *transf.* and *fig.* One who or that which inhabits or occupies any place; a denizen, inhabitant, occupant, dweller. late ME. 4. *attrib.*, as *t.-farmer, occupier* 1710.

1. b. *Customary, kindly, mesne, several, sole t.*: see the adjs. *T. in capite, in chief, in common, by courtesy*, etc.: see these words. *T. to the præcipe*, a t. against whom the writ præcipe was brought, being one to whom an entailed estate had been granted in order that it might be alienated by a recovery. 3. That Frame [the gallows] outliues a thousand Tenants SHAKS. Sorrow..the t. of the soldier's bosom SCOTT. Tenants of our British waters 1879.

Hence **Te·nantless** *a.* without a t.; untenanted, empty.

Tenant (te·nănt), *v.* 1634. [f. prec.] **1.** *trans.* To hold as tenant, to be the tenant of (land, a house, etc.); *esp.* to occupy, inhabit. **2.** *intr.* To reside, dwell, live *in* (*rare*) 1650.

1. We bought the farm we tenanted TENNYSON. Hence **Te·nantable** *a.* capable of being tenanted; fit for occupation; **-ness.**

Te·nant at wi·ll. 1500. *Law.* A tenant who holds at the will or pleasure of the lessor.

Te·nant-right. 1527. The right that a person has as a tenant (of any kind). *spec.* **a.** The right of a customary tenant; **b.** the right of a tenant at will or for a term of years to compensation for unexhausted improvements; **c.** the right of a tenant at will to sell his interest and goodwill to the incoming tenant.

Tenantry (te·năntri). late ME. [f. TENANT *sb.* + -RY.] **1.** The state or condition of being a tenant; occupancy as a tenant; tenancy; tenantship. **2.** Land held of a superior; land let out to tenants; also, the profits of such land. late ME. **3.** *spec.* That part of a manor or estate under common or open-field husbandry occupied by tenants, as dist. from the lord's demesne. Hence, locally applied to the condition or system of tenancy under open-field husbandry. 1794. **4.** The body of tenants on an estate or estates 1628.

Tenantship (te·nănt,ʃip). 1883. [f. TENANT *sb.* + -SHIP.] The condition or position of a tenant; tenancy, occupancy.

Tench (tenʃ). late ME. [a. OF. *tenche*, mod.F. *tanche*:—late L. *tinca*.] A thick-bodied freshwater fish, *Tinca vulgaris*, allied to the carp, inhabiting still and deep waters; also, the flesh of this fish as food.

Tend (tend), *v.*[1] ME. [Aphetic f. ATTEND *v.*, *entend*, INTEND *v.*, F. *attendre*, *entendre*.] †**1.** *intr.* and *trans.* = ATTEND *v.* I. 1. –1816. **2.** To turn the mind, attention, or energies; to apply oneself. **a.** *intr.* with *to*, *unto*. To attend to, look after. *Obs.* exc. *dial.* ME. †**b.** To apply oneself *to do* something –1688. **c.** *trans.* To attend to, mind (a thing). Now *rare*. 1549. **3.** To apply oneself to the care and service of (a person); now *esp.* to watch over and wait upon (the sick or helpless) 1489. **b.** To have the care and oversight of (a flock, herd, etc.) 1515. **c.** To attend to (*esp.* a plant, etc.); to work or mind (a pump, a machine, etc.) 1631. **4.** To wait upon as attendant or servant; to attend on. Now *dial.* late ME. **b.** *intr.* with *on*, *upon*; *spec.* to wait at table 1593. **5.** *trans.* To give one's presence at (a meeting, ceremony, etc.). Now *dial.* and *U.S.* 1460. †**6.** To wait for, await –1818. †**b.** *absol.* or *intr.* To wait in expectation or readiness. SHAKS. (Cf. TENDANCE 3.)

1. Take in the toppe-sale: T. to th' Masters whistle SHAKS. 2. c. Tending the fire 1866. 3. Nurses to t. those that were sick DE FOE. b. So many Houres, must I t. my Flocke SHAKS. c. He.. tended the graves hewn in the living stone KINGSLEY. 4. Good Angels t. thee SHAKS. b. I t. on them, to fetch things for them DE FOE. 6. By all the stars That t. thy bidding KEATS.

Tend (tend), *v.*[2] ME. [a. F. *tendre*:—L. *tendere*.] **I.** To have a motion or disposition to move towards. **1.** *intr.* To direct one's course, make one's way, move or proceed towards something. **a.** Of persons or things. *Obs.* or *arch.* **b.** Of a road, course, journey, series of things 1574. **c.** To have a natural inclination to move (in some direction) 1641. **2.** *fig.* To have a disposition to advance, go on, come finally, or attain *to* (*unto*, *towards*) some point in time, degree, quality, state, or other non-material category; to be drawn *to* or *towards* in affection. late ME. **3.** To have a specified result, if allowed to act; to lead or conduce *to* some state or condition. Const. *to*, rarely *against*. 1560. **b.** To lead or conduce to some action 1565. **4.** *Naut.* Of a ship at anchor: To swing round with the turn of the tide or wind. Also *trans.* 1770.

1. a. Thither let us t. From off the tossing of these fiery waves MILT. c. As weighty bodies to the centre t. POPE. 2. It is to this point all their speeches, writings, and intrigues of all sorts, t. BURKE. 3. The labour of the righteous tendeth to life BIBLE (Genev.) *Prov.* x. 16. b. Acts tending to the conservation of the Peace HOBBES. To live in a society of equals tends..to make a man's spirits expand M. ARNOLD.

†**II.** *intr.* To extend, stretch, or reach (*to* a point, or in a particular direction) –1725.

The land tending to the west DE FOE.

†**III.** **1.** *trans.* To stretch, make tense or taut; to set (a trap, snare, etc.) –1834. **2.** To bend (one's steps) –1644. **3.** *trans.*, or *intr.* with *to*. To relate or refer to; to concern –1654.

†**Te·ndable,** *a.* 1450. [f. TEND *v.*[1] + -ABLE.] Ready to give attention; attentive –1654.

Tendance (te·ndăns). 1573. [Aphetic f. ATTENDANCE, or occas. f. TEND *v.*[1] + -ANCE.] **1.** The attending to or looking after anything; tending, attention, care. **2.** The bestowal of personal attention and care; ministration to the sick or weak 1578. **b.** Attendants collectively; train or retinue 1607. †**3.** Waiting in expectation. SPENSER.

1. Hops dried in loft, aske t. oft 1573. They at her coming sprung And toucht by her fair t. gladlier grew MILT.

Tendence (te·ndĕns). Now *rare* and *literary*. 1627. [ad. med.L. *tendentia*, f. L. *tendentem*, *tendere* TEND *v.*[2]; see -ENCE.] = next 1.

Tendency (te·ndĕnsi). 1628. [f. as prec.; see -ENCY.] **1.** The fact or quality of tending to something; constant disposition to move or act in some direction or toward some point, end, or purpose; leaning, inclination, bent, or bias toward some object, effect, or result. †**b.** A making toward something –1721. **c.** Drift, trend, or aim of a discourse; in recent use, conscious or designed purpose of a story, novel, or the like. (= G. *tendenz*.) 1732. **2.** *attrib.* *T. drama, novel, story*, one composed with an unexpressed but definite purpose. [After G.] 1838.

1. He seldom converses but with Men of his own T. 1680. A gouty t. 1806. c. The t. of all he said was to prove his own merits 1832.

Tendent (te·ndĕnt), *a.* Now *rare*. ME. [a. OF. *tendant*, *tendre* TEND *v.*[2]] Tending, having a tendency (*to* or *towards* some end). *Obs.* bef. 18th c.; revived late in 19th.

Tendential (tende·nʃăl), *a.* 1889. [f. as next + -AL.] Of the nature of, or characterized by having, a tendency; *spec.* = next.

Tendentious (tende·nʃəs), *a.* 1900. [As if f. med.L. *tendentia* TENDENCY + -OUS, after G. *tendenziös*.] Having a purposed tendency; composed or written with such a tendency.

A false and t. account of what had taken place 1909. Hence **Tende·ntious·ly** *adv.*, **-ness.**

Tender (te·ndəɹ), *sb.*[1] 1470. [f. TEND *v.*[1] + -ER[1], or aphet. f. ATTENDER.] **1.** †One who tends, or waits upon, another; an attendant, nurse, ministrant (*obs.*); a waiter; an assistant to a builder or other skilled workman (*dial.*). **2.** One who attends to, or has charge of, a machine, a business, etc., as *bar-tender* (a barman), *bridge-t.*, *machine-t.*; now esp. *U.S.* 1825. **3.** A ship or boat employed to attend a larger one. **a.** orig. A vessel commissioned to attend men-of-war, chiefly for supplying her with stores, conveying intelligence, dispatches, etc. Now, a vessel commissioned to act under the orders of another vessel. 1675. **b.** *gen.* A small steamer used to carry passengers, luggage, mails, goods, stores, etc., to or from a larger vessel 1853. **4.** A carriage specially constructed to carry fuel and water for a locomotive engine, to the rear of which it is attached 1825.

3. b. *fig.* Here she comes, i' faith, full sail, with..a shoal of fools for tenders CONGREVE.

Tender (te·ndəɹ), *sb.*[2] 1542. [f. TENDER *v.*[1]] An act of tendering. **1.** *Law.* A formal offer duly made by one party to another 1562. **b.** *spec.* An offer of money, or the like, in discharge of a debt or liability, *esp.* an offer which thus fulfils the terms of the law and of the liability 1542. **2.** *gen.* An offer of anything for acceptance 1577. **3.** *Comm.* An offer made in writing by one party to another (freq. to a public body) to execute, at an inclusive price or uniform rate, an order for the supply or purchase of goods, or for the execution of work, the details of which have been submitted by the second party 1666. **4.** (esp. *legal*, *lawful*, or *common t.*) Money or other things that may be legally tendered or offered in payment; currency prescribed by law as that in which payment may be made 1740.

1. *T. of issue*, a plea which in effect invites the adverse party to join issue upon it. 2. [He] made a t. of his sword and purse to the prince of Orange HUME. 3. The lowest t. was accepted 1882.

Tender (te·ndəɹ), *a.* and *sb.*[3] ME. [a. F. *tendre*:—L. *tenerum* (nom. *tener*) tender, delicate.] **A.** *adj.* **I.** **1.** Soft or delicate in texture or consistence; fragile; easily broken, divided, compressed, or injured; of food, easily masticated, succulent. †**2.** Frail, thin, fine, slender (*rare*) –1703.

1. The t. Grass, and budding Flower DRYDEN. Many t. and fragile shells 1832. *fig.* There is Nothing of so t. a Nature..as the Reputation..of Ladies 1709. *T. porcelain*: soft porcelain.

II. Transf. from I. **1.** Of weak or delicate constitution; unable or unaccustomed to endure hardship, fatigue, or the like; delicately reared, effeminate ME. **b.** Of animals or plants: Delicate, easily injured by severe weather or unfavourable conditions; needing protection 1573. **2.** Having the weakness and delicacy of youth; youthful, immature ME. **3.** In ref. to colour or light (rarely, sound): Of fine or delicate quality or nature; soft, subdued 1503. **4.** Of things immaterial, subjects, topics, etc.: Easy to be injured by tactless treatment; needing cautious or delicate handling; delicate, ticklish 1625.

1. A tendre womman and a delicate WYCLIF *Deut.* xxviii. 56. 2. Boys and girls of a t. age 1844. 3. The t. green of the young ferns 1894. 4. A topic too t. to be tampered with SCOTT.

III. Tender toward or in regard to others. **1.** Of an action or instrument: Not forcible or rough; gentle, soft; acting or touching gently ME. **2.** Of persons, their feelings, or the expression of these: Characterized by, exhibiting, or expressing delicacy of feeling or susceptibility to the gentle emotions; kind, loving, gentle, mild, affectionate ME. †**b.** *transf.* Tenderly loved; dear, beloved, precious –1611. **3.** *T. of* (*for*, *on behalf of*, etc.): Careful of the welfare of; considerate of, thoughtful for; fond of ME. **b.** Chary *of*; scrupulous, cautious, circumspect; reluctant. Const. *of*, *in*. 1651.

1. Her other t. hand his faire cheeke feeles SHAKS. 2. Call to remembrance, O Lorde, thy t. mercies & thy louing kindnesses COVERDALE *Ps.* xxiv. [xxv.] 6. *The t. passion* or *sentiment*, sexual love. 3. So t. is the legislature of his interest 1868. b. I confess, I am sorry to find him so t. of appearing PEPYS.

IV. Easily affected, sensitive. **1.** Sensitive to, or easily affected by, external physical forces or impressions. late ME. **b.** *spec.* Acutely sensitive to pain; painful when touched; easily hurt 1709. **c.** Of a ship: Leaning over too easily under sail-pressure; crank, not 'stiff' 1722. **2.** Susceptible to moral or spiritual influence; impressionable, sympathetic; sensitive to pious emotions 1586. **3.** Sensitive to injury; ready to take offence; 'touchy'. *Obs.* exc. as *fig.* from 1 b. 1635.

1. b. The tumor being hard, and very t. 1799. c. The ship..was leaky and t. DE FOE. 2. The form of words used, out of regard to t. consciences 1844. 3. I am choleric by my nature and t. by my temper FULLER.

†**B.** *sb.* [the adj. used absol.] **1.** Tender state or condition (*rare*) –1691. **2.** Tender feeling, tenderness (*rare*) –1742. †**3.** Tender consideration; care, regard, concern. SHAKS.

2. To disengage my heart from this furious t., which I have for him DRYDEN. 3. *Lear* I. iv. 230.

Comb.: chiefly parasynthetic adjs., as *t.-bodied*, *-minded*, *-natured*, etc.; **t.-dying** *a.*, dying young; **-foreheaded** *a.*, modest, ready to blush; †**-hefted** *a.*, set in a delicate 'haft' or bodily frame; hence, womanly, gentle; **-mouthed** *a.*, (*a*) of a horse: having a tender mouth, answering readily to the rein; †(*b*) dainty; (*c*) gentle in speaking. Hence **Te·nder-ly** *adv.*, **-ness.**

Tender (te·ndəɹ), *v.*[1] 1542. [a. AF. *tender*, F. *tendre* to hold out, offer:—L. *tendere* to stretch, hold forth.] **1.** *trans.* *Law.* To offer or advance (a plea, issue, averment, evidence) in due and formal terms; *spec.* to offer (money) in discharge of a debt or liability, esp. in exact fulfilment of the requirements of the law and of the obligation. **2.** *gen.* To present (anything) for approval and acceptance; to offer, proffer 1587. **3.** [from TENDER *sb.*[2] 3.] *intr.* To offer by tender *for* a proposed contract, etc. 1865.

2. Several Aldermen..tendered their resignations 1849. *To t. an oath*, to offer or present an oath *to* a

person, that he may take it; to put it *to* any one to take an oath.

Tender (te·ndəɹ), *v.*[2] *arch.* or *dial.* late ME. [f. TENDER *a.*] **1.** *trans.* To make tender. Now *dial.* and *techn.* **2.** To feel or act tenderly towards; to regard or treat with tenderness. late ME. **b.** To treat with proper regard 1490.

1. Deal with me, Omniscient Father! as thou judgest best And in thy season t. thou my heart LAMB. The fibre (of flax) tendered by excess of moisture 1880. 2. He advised me, as I tendered my own safety, to keep aloof from his house 1786.

Te·nder, *v.*[3] 1905. [f. TENDER *sb.*[1]] *trans.* To ship (mails, luggage) on board a tender.

Tenderfoot (te·ndəɹfut). orig. *U.S.* and *Colonial. Pl.* **-foots, -feet.** 1881. A name given, orig. in the ranching and mining regions of the U.S., to a newly-arrived immigrant, unused to the hardships of pioneer life; a greenhorn; hence, a raw inexperienced person. Also, in the Boy Scout movement, a newly-joined recruit, until he has won his first 'badge' and become a 'Second Class Scout'.

Tender-hearted (stress var.), *a.* 1539. [f. *tender heart* + -ED[2].] Having a tender heart; pitiful, compassionate; loving; impressionable. Hence **Te:nder-hea·rtedness.**

Tenderling (te·ndəɹliŋ). 1541. [-LING[1].] **1.** A delicate person or creature; *contempt.*, an effeminate person. Now *rare.* **2.** A person of tender years; a young child 1587. †**3.** *pl.* The soft tops of a deer's horns when they are coming through -1688.

Te·nderloin. *U.S.* 1828. [f. TENDER *a.* + LOIN *sb.*] **1.** The tenderest or most juicy part of the loin of beef, pork, etc., lying under the short ribs in the hind quarter, and consisting of the psoas muscle; the fillet or 'undercut' of a sirloin. **2.** *slang.* In full *t. district*: applied to the police district of New York (and some other cities) which includes the great mass of theatres, hotels, and places of amusement 1895.

Tendinous (te·ndinəs), *a.* 1658. [ad. F. *tendineux*, f. med. or mod.L. *tendo, tendinem* TENDON.] Of the nature of a tendon; consisting of tendons.

‖**Tendo** (te·ndo). 1874. [med. or mod.L.; see next.] *Anat.* = next: freq. in *t. Achillis* (see next), and **t.-synovitis,** inflammation of the synovial membrane of a tendon.

Tendon (te·ndən). 1541. [ad. med.L. *tendo, tendonem* and *tendinem*, app. ad. Gr. τένων, τενοντ- sinew, tendon, influenced by L. *tendere* to stretch.] A band or cord of dense fibrous tissue forming the termination of a muscle, by which it is attached to a bone or other part; a sinew: usu. applied to such when rounded or cord-like, broad flat tendons being called *fasciæ* and *aponeuroses*.

T. of Achilles (L. *tendo Achillis*), the t. of the heel, by which the muscles of the calf of the leg are attached to the heel. So named because, when dipped in the Styx as an infant, Achilles was held by the heel, which thereby escaped dipping and remained vulnerable.

Tendonous (te·ndŏnəs), *a.* 1597. [f. prec. + -OUS.] = TENDINOUS.

‖**Tendre** (tãndr). Now *rare.* 1673. [F., from *tendre* TENDER *a.*] A tender feeling or regard; a fondness, an affection; a tenderness.

A pretty maid, who had a *t.* for me SMOLLETT.

‖**Tendresse** (tãndrẹs). *Obs.* exc. as Fr. late ME. [F., f. *tendre* TENDER *a.*] = TENDERNESS.

Tendril (te·ndril). 1538. [Origin obsc.; app. from L. *tendere*, F. *tendre* to stretch.] A slender thread-like organ or appendage of a plant (consisting of a modified stem, branch, flower-stalk, leaf, or part of a leaf), often spiral in form, which stretches out and attaches itself to or twines round some other body so as to support the plant. (Dist. from a *twining stem* by not bearing leaves.)

transf. The glossy tendrils of his raven hair BYRON. *fig.* Inextricable seem to be the twinings and tendrils of this evil EMERSON. Hence **Te·ndrilled, -iled** (-ild) *a.* having a t. or tendrils.

Tendron (te·ndrən). late ME. [a. F., f. *tendre* TENDER *a.*] **1.** A young tender shoot or sprout of a plant; a bud. Now *rare.* **2.** *pl.* The cartilages of the ribs (*esp.* in *Cookery*, of a deer or calf). late ME.

‖**Tenebræ** (te·nĕbrī). *R. C. Ch.* 1525. [L., 'darkness'; in med.L. in the eccl. sense.] The name given to the office of matins and lauds of the following day, usu. sung in the afternoon or the evening of Wednesday, Thursday, and Friday in Holy Week, at which the candles lighted at the beginning of the service are extinguished one by one after each psalm, in memory of the darkness at the time of the Crucifixion.

Tene·bricose, *a. rare.* 1730. [ad. L. *tenebricosus*, f. *tenebricus* dark, gloomy; see -OSE.] Full of darkness; dark, obscure; gloomy.

Tenebrific (tenībri·fik), *a.* 1785. [f. L. *tenebræ* darkness; see -FIC.] Causing or producing darkness; obscuring.

Books done by pedants and t. persons under the name of men CARLYLE. *T. stars*, by whose influence night is brought on, and which do ray out darkness and obscurity upon the earth as the sun does light; also *fig.*

Tenebrious (tĕne·briəs), *a.* 1594. [app. altered f. TENEBROUS; not on L. analogies.] = TENEBROUS *a.*

Tenebrose (te·nībrōus), *a.* 1490. [ad. L. *tenebrosus*; see -OSE.] Dark. Also *fig.*, mentally or morally dark; gloomy, obscure. So **Tenebro·sity,** darkness, obscurity.

Tenebrous (te·nībrəs), *a.* late ME. [a. OF. *tenebrus*, ad. L. *tenebrosus.*] Full of darkness, dark. **b.** *fig.* Obscure, gloomy 1599.

The towering and t. boughs of the cypress LONGF. b. That t. philosophy 1849.

Tenement (te·nĭmĕnt). ME. [a. AF., ad. med.L. *tenementum*, f. L. *tenere* to hold + *-mentum* -MENT.] †**1.** The fact of holding as a possession; tenure -1651. **2.** Land or real property which is held of another by any tenure; a holding ME. **b.** *pl.* The technical expression for freehold interests in things immovable considered as subjects of property, they being not 'owned' but 'holden'; *esp.* in *lands and tenements*, i. e. lands and all other freehold interests ME. **3.** *gen.* A building or house to dwell in; a dwelling-place, a habitation, residence, abode. late ME. **b.** *transf.* and *fig.* An abode; a dwelling-place, esp. applied to the body as the abode of the soul; also, the abode of any animal 1592. **4.** *spec.* **a.** In England, a portion of a house, tenanted as a separate dwelling; a flat; a suite of apartments, or a single room so let or occupied 1593. **b.** In Scotland, a large house let in portions to a number of tenants, each portion being called a 'house' (HOUSE *sb.*[1] 1 b) 1693.

1. *Free t.* = FREEHOLD. 2. *T. at will*, a t. held at the will of the superior. 3. The dingy t. inhabited by Miss Tox DICKENS. b. That spirit—now struggling to quit its material t. C. BRONTË. 4. Almes-houses. . let out in Tenements 1593.

attrib. and *Comb.*: **t. house** (orig. U.S.), a house or edifice let out in flats or sets of apartments, or single rooms for separate tenants; **t. householder,** a tenant in a t. house. So **Teneme·ntal** *a.* of, pertaining to, or of the nature of a t.; let out to tenants. **Teneme·ntary** *a.*, (*a*) leased to tenants; (*b*) consisting of tenements or dwelling-houses.

‖**Tenendum** (tĭne·ndŏm). 1628. [L., = 'to be held'.] *Eng. Law.* That part of a deed which defines the tenure by which the things granted are to be held (cf. HABENDUM).

†**Tenent.** 1551. [a. L. *tenent* they hold.] = TENET -1722.

Being so fickle in their Tenents FULLER.

Teneral (te·nĕrăl), *a.* 1891. [f. L. *tener* tender + -AL.] *Ent.* Said of the imperfect imago of a neuropterous insect, when it has just emerged from the pupa state, and is still soft.

‖**Tenesmus** (tĭne·zmŏs). 1527. [med.L., = L. *tenesmos*, a. Gr. τεινεσμός, τηνεσμός straining, f. τείνειν to stretch, strain.] *Path.* A continual inclination to void the contents of the bowels or bladder, accompanied by straining, but with little or no discharge. Hence **Tene·smic** *a.* of, pertaining to, or of the nature of t.

Tenet (tī·net, te·net, -ĕt). 1619. [a. L. *tenet* he holds.] A doctrine, dogma, principle, or opinion, in religion, philosophy, politics, or the like, held by a school, sect, party, or person. **b.** *gen.* Any opinion held 1630.

The generall T., of all the Philosophers 1619. b. The Master of Benet Is of the like Tenet GRAY.

Tenfold (te·nfōuld), *a.* and *adv.* OE. [-FOLD.] **A.** *adj.* Ten times as great or as much; ten times increased or intensified; also *indefinitely*, many times as great. **b.** As predicate, passing into subst. use 1769.

1. Our t. griefe SHAKS. b. T. I'll give thee to preserve thy faith 1769.

B. *adv.* Ten times (in amount or degree) 1538.

False to himself, but ten-fold false to me! TENNYSON.

Tennantite (te·nǎntəit). 1839. [Named after Smithson *Tennant*; see -ITE[1].] *Min.* A sulph-arsenide of copper and iron, closely related to tetrahedrite.

Tenné, tenny (te·ni), *a.* and *sb.* 1562. [a. obs. F. *tenné*, var. of *tanné* TAWNY.] *Her.* 'Tawny' as a heraldic colour: variously described as 'orange-brown' or 'bright chestnut'; in engraving represented by diagonal lines from sinister to dexter, crossed by others, according to some authors, vertically, according to others, horizontally.

Tenner (te·nəɹ). *colloq.* 1861. [f. TEN + -ER[1].] A number or amount of ten; *spec.* A ten-pound note; in U.S. a ten-dollar bill.

Tennis (te·nis). [Late ME. *tene·tz*, later *tenne·s*, etc.; gen. held to be a. AF. *tenetz* = F. *tenez* take, receive, called by the server to his opponent.] **1.** A game in which a ball is struck with a racket and driven to and fro by two players in an enclosed oblong court. **2.** Short for LAWN-TENNIS, a game played with a ball and rackets on an unenclosed rectangular space on a smooth grass lawn, or a floor of hard gravel, cement, etc., called a court 1888.

attrib. and *Comb.*: *t.-flannels, -lawn, -racket*; **t. -arm, elbow, -knee,** an arm, elbow, or knee sprained in playing lawn-t.

Te·nnis-ball. 1450. The small ball used in tennis or lawn-tennis. Also *fig.*; *esp.* a thing or person that is tossed or bandied about like a t.

The very tennisse-ball, in some sort, of fortune 1610.

Te·nnis-court. 1564. **1.** The enclosed quadrangular area, or building, in which the game of tennis is played. **2.** The plot of ground prepared and marked out for lawn-tennis 1881.

Te·nnis-play. 1440. The game of tennis; playing at tennis. So **Te·nnis-play:er,** one who plays at tennis; now, usu., at lawn-tennis.

Tennysonian (tenisōu·niăn), *a.* and *sb.* 1853. [f. name of the poet Alfred (Lord) *Tennyson* (1809–1892) + -IAN.] **A.** *adj.* Of or pertaining to Tennyson, his works, or his style. **B.** *sb.* An admirer, imitator, disciple, or student of Tennyson 1883.

Teno-, comb. element, arbitrarily formed from Gr. τένων TENDON. **Teno·logy** [-LOGY], that part of anatomy which relates to the tendons. **Te:no-synovi·tis** [see SYNOVIA and -ITIS], inflammation of a tendon and its sheath.

Tenon (te·nən), *sb.* late ME. [a. F., f. *tenir* to hold + suffix *-on* (= L. *-onem*).] A projection fashioned on the end or side of a piece of wood or other material, to fit into a corresponding cavity or MORTISE in another piece, so as to form a close and secure joint.

Comb.: **t.-saw,** a fine saw for making tenons, etc., having a thin blade, a thick back, and small teeth very slightly 'set'.

Tenon (te·nən), *v.* 1596. [f. prec.] **1.** *trans.* To fix together with tenon and mortise. **2.** To furnish or fit with a tenon 1771. **b.** *intr.* To engage or fit in by or as by a tenon 1797.

Tenonian (tĕnōu·niăn), *a.* 1890. [f. name of J. R. *Tenon*, a French anatomist (1724–1816) + -IAN.] *Anat.* Discovered or described by Tenon; as in *T. fascia* or *capsule* (*Tenon's capsule*), a delicate band of fascia with involuntary muscle fibres disposed round the eyeball. So **Tenoni·tis** inflammation of Tenon's capsule.

Tenonto-. 1860. [f. Gr. τένων, τενοντ- tendon.] A formative in technical terms relating to the tendons, as **Tenonto·logy** = TENOLOGY.

Tenor (te·nəɹ), *sb.* (*a.*) ME. [a. OF.:— L. *tenorem* course, import (of a law, etc.), f. *tenere* to hold.] **I. 1.** The course of meaning which holds on through something written or spoken; the general sense or meaning of a document, speech, etc.; substance, purport, effect, drift. (In techn. legal use implying the actual wording of a document; dist. from *effect.*) **b.** *concr.* An exact copy of a document, a transcript. Now *techn.* 1450. **c.** The value of a bank note or bill as stated on it: in phr. *old t.*, *middle t.*, *new t.*, referring to the successive issues of paper currency in the colonies of Massachusetts and Rhode Island in the 18th c. *Hist.* 1740. **2.** †**a.** The action or fact of holding on or continuing; continuance, duration -1694. **b.** Continuous progress, course, movement (*of* action, etc.); way of proceeding, procedure. late ME. **c.** The length of time that a bill is drawn to run before presentation for payment 1866. **3.** Quality, character, nature; condition, state. *Obs.* exc. in non-physical sense: the way in which a thing continues; *esp.* habitual condition of mind. *rare.* 1530.

1. *Merch. V.* IV. i. 235. **2. b.** Along the cool sequester'd vale of life They kept the noiseless tenour of their way GRAY. **3.** The senses, strongly affected in some one manner, cannot quickly change their tenour BURKE.

II. *Mus.* **a.** The adult male voice intermediate between the bass and the counter-tenor or alto, usu. ranging from the octave below middle C to the A above it; also, the part sung by such a voice, being the next above the bass in vocal part-music. (So called app. because the melody or *canto fermo* was formerly allotted to this part.) late ME. **b.** A singer with a tenor voice; one who sings the tenor part 1475. **c.** = *T. bell*: see B. *Second t.*, the next bell to the tenor. 1541. **d.** A name for the tenor violin or VIOLA 1836. **B.** *attrib.* or *adj.* Applied to a voice, part, instrument, string, etc. of the pitch described in II above, or intermediate between bass and alto 1522.

T. bell, the largest bell of a peal or set. *T. clef*, the C clef when placed upon the fourth line of the stave. *T. violin* (†*viol*), the viola.

Tenotomy (tĕnǫ·tŏmi). 1842. [ad. F. *tenotomie*; see TENO- and -TOMY.] *Surg.* Cutting or division of a tendon; also *attrib.*, as *t. knife*. So **Te·notome**, a surgeon's slender knife for (subcutaneous) division of tendons.

Tenpence (te·npĕns). 1592. A sum of money equal to ten pennies; a foreign coin of about this value.

Tenpenny (te·npĕni), *a.* (*sb.*) late ME. Valued at, costing, or amounting to ten pence; sold at tenpence the piece, dozen, pound, quart, yard, etc.; also in contempt; cf. *twopenny*.

T. piece = B. 1. *T.-worth*, the amount of anything to be bought for tenpence. *T. nail*, orig. a nail sold at tenpence a hundred; now, vaguely, a nail of large size.

B. *sb.* **1.** A piece of money: = TENPENCE 1824. **2.** A tenpenny nail 1820.

Ten-pins (te·npinz), *sb. pl.* Chiefly *U.S.* 1807. A game in which ten pins or 'men' are set up to be bowled at; cf. NINEPINS. Also, the pins, and in sing. *tenpin*, one of these.

Ten-pounder (te·npau·ndəɹ). 1695. [f. *ten pound*(*s* + -ER [1].] **1. a.** A thing (e.g. a ball, a fish) weighing ten pounds; *spec.* a fish, *Elops saurus*, inhabiting the warmer parts of the Pacific and Atlantic Oceans. **b.** A cannon throwing a ten-pound shot. **2.** Something of the value of, or rated at, ten pounds. **a.** A ten-pound note. **b.** A voter in a borough who was enfranchised in virtue of occupying property of the annual value of ten pounds. 1755.

Tenrec: see TANREC.

Tense (tens), *sb.* ME. [a. OF. *tens*, mod.F. *temps*:—L. *tempus* time.] †**1.** Time -1509. **2.** *Gram.* Any one of the different forms or modifications (or word-groups) in the conjugation of a verb which indicate the different times (*past*, *present*, or *future*) at which the action or state denoted by it is viewed as happening or existing, and also (by extension) the different nature of such action or state, as continuing (*imperfect*) or completed (*perfect*); also *abstr.* that quality of a verb which depends on the expression of such differences. late ME.

Tense (tens), *a.* 1670. [ad. L. *tensus*, *tendere* to stretch.] **1.** Drawn tight, stretched taut; strained to stiffness; tight, rigid: chiefly of cords, fibres, membranes. Opp. to *lax*, *flaccid*. **b.** *Phonetics.* Pronounced with tense muscles 1908. **2.** *fig.* In a state of nervous or mental strain or tension; highly strung; excited, or excitable 1821.

1. The skin was t. 1676. **2.** Gwendolen..looked at her with t. expectancy, but was silent GEO. ELIOT.

Hence **Te·nse·ly** *adv.*, **-ness.** **Te·nsity**, t. condition 1658.

Te·nseless, *a.* 1886. [f. TENSE *sb.* + -LESS.] Having no tenses or distinctions of tense (*loosely*, not expressing time).

Te·nser, -or. *Hist.* [OF., f. *tenser* (med.L.) *tensare* to protect.] A denizen of a city or borough.

Tensible (te·nsĭb'l), *a.* 1626. [ad. mod.L. **tensibilis*, f. *tens-*, *tendere* to stretch.] = next 1. Hence **Tensibi·lity.**

Tensile (te·nsəil, -il), *a.* 1626. [ad. mod.L. *tensilis*, f. *tens-*, *tendere* to stretch; see -ILE.] **1.** Capable of being stretched; susceptible of extension; ductile. **2.** Of, of the nature of, or pertaining to tension; exercising or sustaining tension 1841.

2. A..t. strain 1841. A t. strength double that of good malleable iron 1868. Hence **Te·nsilely** *adv.* in relation to tension. **Tensi·lity.**

Tension (te·nʃən), *sb.* 1533. [prob. a F., ad. late L. *tensionem*, f. *tendere* to stretch.] The action of stretching or condition of being stretched. **1.** *Physiol.* and *Path.* The condition, in any part of the body, of being stretched or strained; a sensation indicating or suggesting this; a feeling of tightness. **b.** *Bot.* Applied to a strain or pressure in the cells or tissues of plants arising from changes taking place in the course of growth 1875. **2.** *fig.* A straining, or strained condition, of the mind, feelings, or nerves 1763. **3.** *Physics.* A constrained condition of the particles of a body when subjected to forces acting in opposite directions away from each other (usu. along the body's greatest length), thus tending to draw them apart, balanced by forces of cohesion holding them together; the force or combination of forces acting in this way, esp. as a measurable quantity. (The opposite of *compression* or *pressure.*) 1685. **b.** Inexactly used for the expansive force of a gas or vapour, properly called *pressure* 1678. **c.** *transf.* A device in a sewing-machine for regulating the tightness of the stitch. Also *t.-device.* 1877. **4.** *Electr.* The stress along lines of force in a dielectric. Formerly applied also to surface density of electric charge, and until about 1882 used vaguely as a synonym for potential, electromotive force, and mechanical force exerted by electricity: still so applied, in industrial and commercial use, in *high* and *low t.*; see sense 5. 1802. **5. High tension**, a high degree of tension (of any kind): **a.** *esp.* in *Electr.* a term for a high degree of electromotive force or difference of potential. So **Low t.** (See sense 4.) Chiefly *attrib.* as in *high* or *low t. system* (of electric lighting, etc.); also *high t.* or *low t. accumulator*, *battery*, *charge*, *current*, *fuse*, etc. 1889. **b.** Of the pulse 1898.

2. A t. of feeling which has had no parallel since the outbreak of the Crimean war 1885. **3. b.** The air ..has a certain degree of elasticity or t. FARADAY. Hence **Te·nsion** *v. trans.* to subject to t., tighten, make taut (hence **Te·nsioned** *ppl. a.*). **Te·nsional** *a.* of, pertaining to, of the nature of, or affected with t.

Tensive (te·nsiv), *a.* 1702. [a. F. *tensif*, *-ive*, f. L. *tens-*, *tendere* (see TENSE *a.* and -IVE). Cf. *intensive.*] Having the quality of stretching or straining; causing tension; in *Path.* applied to a sensation of tension or tightness in any part of the body.

‖**Tenson** (te·nsən, F. tãnsoṅ). 1840. [F., = Pr. *tenso* a poetical contest.] A contest in verse between rival troubadours; a piece of verse or song composed for or sung in such a contest.

Tensor (te·nsǫɹ, -əɹ). 1704. [a. mod.L., f. *tendere* to stretch.] **1.** *Anat.* (also *t. muscle*): A muscle that stretches or tightens some part. Opp. to *laxator*. **2.** *Math.* In Quaternions, a quantity expressing the ratio in which the length of a vector is increased 1853.

Tent (tent), *sb.*[1] ME. [a. OF. *tente*:—L. *tenta*, pl. of *tentum*, pa. pple. of *tendere* to stretch.] **1.** A portable shelter or dwelling of canvas (formerly of skins or cloth), supported by means of a pole or poles, and usu. extended and secured by ropes fastened to pegs which are driven into the ground; used by travellers, soldiers, nomads, and others; a pavilion. **2.** *transf.* Something likened to or resembling a tent; *spec.* **a.** in *Photogr.*, a curtained box serving as a portable dark-room; **b.** the silken web of a t.-caterpillar 1599. **3.** *fig.* An abode, residence, habitation, dwelling-place; esp. in phrases *to have*, *pitch one's tent*(*s*. late ME. **4.** *Sc.* (*Hist.*) A portable pulpit set up in the open air 1678.

1. To your tents, O Israel 1 *Kings* xii. 16. **3.** To dwell in the tentes of the vngodly COVERDALE *Ps.* lxxxiii[i]. 10.

Comb.: **t.-barge**, a barge having a t.-like canvas awning; **-bed**, (*a*) a camp bed; (*b*) a bed having an arched canopy and covered sides; **-caterpillar**, the gregarious larva of a N. Amer. bombycid moth, *Clisiocampa*, which spins a t.-like web; **-door**, the entrance or opening of a t.; **-fly**, see FLY *sb.*[2] 2 b; also, an exterior sheet stretched over the ridge-pole so as to cover the ordinary tent-roof with an air-space between; **-maker**, one who makes tents; **-pin** = TENT-PEG.

Tent (tent), *sb.*[2] Now *Sc.* and *n. dial.* ME. [Aphetic f. ATTENT, *entent* INTENT.] Attention, heed, care.

Phr. *Take t.*, to take heed, take care; with *to*, to pay attention to, take heed to.

Tent (tent), *sb.*[3] late ME. [a. F. *tente*, f. *tenter*:—L. *temptare*, *tentare*.] †**1.** A probe -1693. **2.** A roll or pledget, usu. of soft absorbent material, often medicated, formerly much used to search and cleanse a wound, or to keep open or distend a wound, sore, or natural orifice. late ME. †**3.** A paste which sets hard, used in setting precious stones -1656.

1. Modest Doubt is cal'd..the t. that searches To' th' bottome of the worst SHAKS.

Tent (tent), *sb.*[4] 1542. [ad. Sp. *tinto* dark-coloured:—L. *tinctus*, *tingere* to dye.] A Spanish wine of a deep red colour, and of low alcoholic content. Also *t. wine.* (Often used as a sacramental wine.)

Tent, *sb.*[5] 1548. [f. TENT *v.*[3]; or shortened from TENTER *sb.*[1]] A stretching frame for embroidery, etc.

Tent, *v.*[1] Now *Sc.* and *n. dial.* ME. [perh. short for *take tent*; see TENT *sb.*[2]] †**1.** *intr.* To give or pay attention to; to attend, take heed -1572. **b.** *trans.* To attend to, give heed to, take notice of (a person, his words, a matter) ME. **2.** To look after, attend to, tend (a person, flock, plant, machine, etc.). late ME. **3.** To take care to prevent or hinder (a person) *from* doing something 1781.

Tent (tent), *v.*[2] *arch.* 1597. [app. f. TENT *sb.*[3]] †**a.** *trans.* To probe. **b.** To treat by means of a tent; to apply a tent to (a wound, etc., also to a person); to plug with a tent.

I have a sword dares t. a wound as far As any SHIRLEY.

Tent (tent), *v.*[3] 1553. [f. TENT *sb.*[1]] **1.** *intr.* To abide or live in a tent; to encamp 1856. **b.** *fig.* To dwell temporarily; to tabernacle; of a thing, to have its seat, 'reside' 1607. **2.** *trans.* To cover or canopy as with a tent 1838. **3.** To accommodate, put up, or lodge in tents 1863. †**4.** To pitch or spread (a tent); to put up, as a tent or its canvas -1634.

1. b. The smiles of Knaues T. in my cheekes SHAKS. **3.** All officers are tented in the same manner as the men 1898.

Tentability (tentăbi·lĭti). *rare.* 1844. [f. L. **tentabilis*; see -BILITY.] = TEMPTABILITY.

Tentacle (te·ntăk'l). 1762. [ad. mod.L. TENTACULUM.] *Zool.* A slender flexible process in animals, esp. invertebrates, serving as an organ of touch or feeling. **b.** *Bot.* Applied to a sensitive filament, as the viscous gland-tipped leaf-hairs of the Sundew 1875.

fig. The tentacles of the all-devouring Republic [Rome] 1895.

Comb.: **t.-sheath**, the sheath-like structure surrounding the base of the tentacles of many molluscs. Hence **Te·ntacled** *a.* having tentacles. So **Tenta·cular** *a.* of, pertaining to, or of the nature of a t. or tentacles.

Tentaculate (tentæ·kiŭlĕt), *a.* (*sb.*) 1846. [f. mod.L. TENTACULUM + -ATE [2].] *Zool.* **1.** Furnished with tentacles or tentaculiform appendages; rarely = TENTACULIFORM; *spec.* of or pertaining to the *Tentaculata*, or stalked echinoderms; also *sb.* one of these, a pelmatozoan. So **Tenta·culated** *a.* (in sense 1). 1804.

Tentaculi- (tentæ·kiŭli). 1837. Combining form of mod.L. TENTACULUM, as in **Tenta·culi·ferous** *a.*, bearing tentacles: said of an animal or organ. **Tenta·culiform** *a.*, having the form or appearance of a tentacle.

Tentaculite (tentæ·kiŭlait). 1839. [ad. mod.L. *Tentaculites*; see TENTACULUM and -ITE [1] 2 a.] *Palæont.* A fossil mollusc of the genus *Tentaculites* or family *Tentaculitidæ* (thought by some to be allied to the pteropods) of which the conical usu. ringed shells abound in the Middle Devonian strata.

Tentaculocyst (tentæ·kiŭlo,si:st). 1880. [f. next + Gr. κύστις CYST.] *Zool.* One of the vesicular or cystic tentacles of a hydrozoan, representing a reduced and modified tentacle.

‖**Tentaculum** (tentæ·kiŭlŏm). *Pl.* **-a.** Also tentacule. 1752. [mod.L., f. *tentare* = *temptare* to feel, try; see -CULE.] = TENTACLE.

Tentage (te·ntėdʒ). 1603. [f. TENT *sb.*[1] + -AGE.] Equipment of tents, tent accommodation.

‖**Tentamen** (tentē·mĕn). *Pl.* **tentamina** (-æ·mină). 1673. [L., f. *tentare* to TEMPT.] An attempt, trial, experiment.

Tentation (tentē·ʃən). ME. [ad. L. *tentationem*, late f. *temptationem*.] †**1.** Early f. TEMPTATION -1818. **2.** *techn.* A mode of working or adjusting by trial or experiment 1877.

Tentative (te·ntătiv), *a.* and *sb.* 1588. [ad. med.L. *tentativus*, f. *tentat-*, *tentare* for *temptare* to TEMPT; see -IVE.] **A.** *adj.* Of the nature of an experiment, trial, or attempt; made or done provisionally as an experiment; experimental.

The interpretations must therefore be regarded as t. 1851.

B. *sb.* Something done as an experiment or trial; an essay, an attempt 1632.

Tentatives were made in both directions 1898. Hence **Te·ntative-ly** *adv.*, **-ness.**

Tented (te·ntėd), *a.* 1604. [f. TENT *sb.*[1] and *v.*[3]] **1.** Of a place: Covered with or full of tents. **2.** Formed or shaped like a tent 1747. **3.** Of persons: Lodged in, or furnished with, a tent or tents 1811.

1. The T. Field SHAKS. **3.** The t. Arabs 1811.

Tenter (te·ntəɹ), *sb.*[1] ME. [app. a. AF. or OF. *tentour, L. *tentorem stretcher, f. *tendere* to stretch; but neither the OF. nor the L. word is known in the sense 'tenter'.] **1.** A wooden framework on which cloth is stretched after being milled, so that it may set or dry evenly and without shrinking. Also in pl. †**2.** = TENTER-HOOK 1. -1849. †**3.** *fig.* esp. in phr.: *To be on* (*the*) *tenter*(*s*, i.e. in a position of strain, difficulty, or uneasiness; to be in a state of anxious suspense; now *rare* or *Obs.*, repl. by *on tenter-hooks* 1533.

Comb.: †**t.-ground,** ground occupied by tenters for stretching cloth, etc. †**-yard,** a yard or enclosure with tenters for stretching cloth, etc.

Tenter (te·ntəɹ), *sb.*[2] *dial.* 1828. [f. TENT *v.*[1] + -ER [1].] **1.** One who minds, or has charge of, anything requiring attention, as a machine, a flock, etc. **2.** An attendant on a skilled workman, who gives him unskilled help, supplies materials, etc. 1894.

Tenter (te·ntəɹ), *v.* late ME. [f. TENTER *sb.*[1]] **1.** *trans.* To stretch (cloth) on a tenter or tenters. †**2.** *fig.* To set on the tenter, or on tenter-hooks. Also, to injure or pain as by stretching; to rack, torture (the feelings, etc.) -1734. †**3.** *intr.* Of cloth: To admit of being stretched on the tenter. BACON.

3. Woollen cloth will t., linen scarcely BACON.

Tenter-hook (te·ntəɹ,huk). 1480. [f. as prec. + HOOK *sb.*] **1.** One of the hooks or bent nails by which the edges of the cloth are firmly held on a tenter; a hooked or right-angled nail or spike. **b.** *transf.* A hooked organ or part 1665. **2.** *fig.* That on which something is stretched or strained; something that causes suffering or painful suspense 1532.

2. Phr. *To be on* (*the*) *tenter-hooks*, i.e. in a state of painful suspense or impatience.

Tenth (tenþ), *a.* and *sb.* [OE. (WSax.) *tēoða* (early ME. *tēþe*); also early ME. *tenðe*, *tenþe*, f. *ten* with suffix -TH [2].] The ordinal numeral corresp. to the cardinal number TEN. **A.** *adj.* **1.** In concord with a sb. expressed or understood. **2.** The last of each row or series of ten; each or every tenth individual or part OE.

2. *T. wave*: every t. wave was formerly held to be larger than the nine preceding waves; hence *allus.* *T. part*, any one of the ten equal parts into which a whole may be divided.

B. *absol.* or *sb.* [orig. the adj. used ellipt. or absol., but from *c* 1200 treated as sb. with pl.] **1.** A tenth part *of* anything ME. **b.** *spec.* A tenth part of produce or profits, or of the estimated value of personal property, appropriated as a religious or ecclesiastical due, a royal subsidy, etc. 1474. **2.** *Mus.* A note ten diatonic degrees above or below a given note (both notes being counted); the interval between, or the consonance of, two notes ten diatonic degrees apart 1597. **3.** The tenth day of the month 1580.

1. b. In the eccl. use *spec.*, the tenth part of the annual profit of every living in the kingdom, originally paid to the pope, but now forming a part of the fund known as Queen Anne's Bounty.

Comb.: **tenthmetre,** a metre divided by the t. power of ten (= one ten-millionth of a millimetre); **tenth-rate** *a.*, of the tenth relative quality, very inferior. Hence **Tenth** *v. trans.* to decimate, to tithe (*rare*). **Te·nthly** *adv.* in the t. place.

‖**Tenthredo** (tenþrī·do). 1658. [Latinized form of Gr. τενθρηδών, -δον- a kind of wasp.] *Ent.* A saw-fly: in mod. scientific use, a genus of hymenopterous insects, typical of the family *Tenthredinidæ*, comprising the large saw-flies called hornet-flies.

‖**Tentorium** (tentō·riŏm). 1661. [L., f. *tendere*, *tent-* to stretch; see -ORIUM.] †**1.** A canopy. EVELYN. **2.** *Anat.* A membranous (sometimes ossified) partition between the cerebrum and cerebellum 1800. So **Tento·rial** *a.* *Anat.* of or pertaining to the t.

Te·nt-peg. 1869. One of the (usu. wooden) pegs, with a notch at the upper end, to which when stuck in the ground the ropes of a tent are fastened. Hence **Te·nt-pe·gging,** an Indian cavalry sport, in which the player, riding at full speed, tries to transfix and carry off, on the point of his lance, a tent-peg fixed in the ground.

Te·nt-stitch. 1639. [Origin of first element obsc.] A kind of embroidery or worsted-work stitch, in which the pattern is worked in series of parallel stitches arranged diagonally across the intersections of the threads.

Tentwort (te·ntwɒɹt). 1550. [perh. f. TAINT *sb.*] An old name for a small fern, *Asplenium Ruta-muraria.*

‖**Tenue** (tənü). 1892. [F., deportment, sb. use of fem. pa. pple. of *tenir.*] Carriage, bearing, deportment; also, costume, 'rig'.

Tenui- (teniu,i), comb. form of L. *tenuis* thin, narrow, slender, in scientific use as in **te:nuifo·lious** [L. *folium* leaf] *a.*, having narrow or thin leaves.

Tenu·ious, *a.* Now *rare.* 1495. [f. L. *tenuis* thin + -OUS.] Thin, attenuated.

Tenuiroster (te:niu,irɒ·stəɹ). 1837. [ad. F. *tenuirostre*, ad. mod.L. *tenuirostris*, f. *tenuis* thin + *rostrum* beak, bill.] *Ornith.* A member of the *Tenuirostres*, passerine or insessorial birds with slender bills; a slender-billed bird. So **Te:nuiro·stral** *a.* of or pertaining to the *Tenuirostres.*

‖**Tenuis** (te·niu,is). 1650. [L., = thin, slender, fine; used in early Gr. Grammars as tr. Gr. ψιλόν bare, smooth, applied by Aristotle to the consonants κ, τ, π, as opp. to the *aspiratæ* (in Gr. δασέα, pl. of δασύ rough, thick).] *Phonetics.* An unvoiced, voiceless, or breath stop.

Tenuity (tĕniū·iti). 1535. [ad. L. *tenuitas*, f. *tenuis* thin; see -ITY.] **1.** Thinness of form or size; slenderness 1578. **2.** Thinness of consistence; dilute or rarefied condition; rarity 1603. **b.** Faintness (of light); thinness (of voice) 1794. **3.** *fig.* Meagreness; slightness, slenderness, weakness, poverty 1535.

1. The t.—the thin part—behind, which a bull-dog ought to have JOHNSON. **2.** The t. and fineness of the mud 1802. **b.** A shrill, yet sweet, t. of voice 1858. **3.** The t. of the evidence 1867.

Tenuous (te·niu,əs), *a.* 1597. [Syncopated from L. *tenuis* thin + -OUS; the etymologically regular form being TENUIOUS, now rare.] **1.** Thin or slender in form; of small transverse measure or calibre; slim 1656. **2.** Thin in physical consistency; sparse; rare, rarefied, subtile; unsubstantial 1597. **3.** *fig.* Slender, of slight importance or significance; meagre, weak; flimsy, vague, unsubstantial 1817. Hence **Te·nuous-ly** *adv.*, **-ness.**

Tenure (te·niŭɹ). late ME. [a. AF., OF. *tenure*:—earlier OF. *teneüre*, in med.L. *tenitura*, *tenura*, f. *tenere* to hold; see -URE.] **1.** The action or fact of holding a tenement (esp. in *Eng. Law*) 1442. **b.** *gen.* and *fig.* The action or fact of holding anything material or non-material; hold upon something; maintaining a hold; occupation 1599. **2.** The condition of service, etc., under which a tenement is held of the superior; the title by which the property is held; the relations, rights, and duties of the tenant to the landlord. late ME. **b.** *transf.* Terms of holding; title; authority; hold over a person or thing; control 1871. **c.** *fig.* 1659. **3.** *concr.* A holding; = TENEMENT 2. Now *rare.* late ME.

1. We have not the mark system, but we have the principle of common t. STUBBS. **b.** Their salary cannot be altered during their t. of office 1844. **2.** Those, who by their military tenures were bound to perform forty days service in the field BLACKSTONE. *T. at will*: cf. TENANT AT WILL. **c.** The office of a favourite hath a very uncertain t. SWIFT. **3.** Greenwich-park.. is still a royal t. 1766.

Tenurial (teniūə·riăl), *a.* 1896. [f. med.L. *tenura* TENURE + -IAL.] Of, pertaining to, or of the nature of the tenure of land.

‖**Tenuto** (tenū·to), *a.* and *adv.* [It., = held.] *Mus.* Held, sustained: a direction to sustain a note its full length. Usu. abbrev. *ten.*

‖**Teocalli** (tī,okæ·li). 1578. [Mexican, f. *teotl* god + *calli* house.] A structure for purposes of worship among the ancient Mexicans and Central Americans, usu. a four-sided truncated pyramid built terrace-wise, and surmounted by a temple.

‖**Teosinte** (tī,osi·ntī). 1877. [ad. Mexican *teocintli*, app. f. *teotl* god + *cintli* dry ear or cob of maize.] An annual grass of Central America, *Euchlæna luxurians*, of large size, allied to maize; now widely cultivated as a fodder plant, occas. also as a cereal.

Tepee (tī·pi, tipī·). Also **teepee.** 1872. [Sioux or Dakota Indian *tī·pī* tent, house.] A tent or wigwam of the American Indians, formed of bark, mats, skins, or canvas stretched over a frame of poles converging to and fastened together at the top.

Tepefy (te·pĭfəi), *v.* Also **tepify.** 1656. [f. L. *tepefacere* to make tepid, f. *tepere* to be lukewarm; see -FY.] *trans.* and *intr.* To make or become tepid or moderately warm.

‖**Tephillim, -in** (tĭfi·llīm, -īn), *sb. pl.* 1613. [Rabbinical Heb. *t'phillīm*, heteroclite pl. of *t'phillāh* prayer.] A name for Jewish phylacteries, or for the texts inscribed on them.

Tephrite (te·frəit). 1879. [f. Gr. τεφρός ash-coloured (f. τέφρα ashes) + -ITE [1].] *Min.* Name given to a class of volcanic rocks related to the basalts. Hence **Tephri·tic** *a.* pertaining to or consisting of t.

Tephroite (te·fro,əit). 1850. [ad. G. *tephroit*, irreg. f. Gr. τεφρός; see prec. and -ITE [1].] *Min.* A silicate of manganese, occurring in crystalline masses of an ashy grey or reddish colour.

Tephromancy (te·fromænsi). 1652. [f. Gr. τέφρα ashes + -MANCY.] Divination by means of ashes.

Tepid (te·pid), *a.* late ME. [ad. L. *tepidus* lukewarm, f. *tepere* to be warm.] Moderately or slightly warm; lukewarm.

Let the Water stand in the Sun till it grow t. EVELYN. A t. assent H. SPENCER. Hence **Te·pid-ly** *adv.*, **-ness.**

‖**Tepidarium** (tepidē·riŏm). *Pl.* **-ia.** 1585. [L., f. *tepidus* TEPID; see -ARIUM.] The warm room in an ancient Roman bath, situated between the *frigidarium* and the *caldarium.*

Tepidity (tėpi·dĭti). 1656. [ad. late or med.L. *tepiditas*, f. *tepidus* TEPID.] The quality or condition of being tepid; moderate or slight warmth; lukewarmness.

Ter- (təɹ), the L. adv. *ter* 'thrice', in comb.

1. Prefixed to *adjs.*, in sense 'thrice, three times', as **ter-tri·nal** *a.*, consisting of three sets of three. **b.** Prefixed to *adjs.* and *sbs.*, as **ter-diu·rnal** *a.*, occurring or done thrice a day. **2.** *Chem.* With the names of classes of compounds, as *acetate*, *bromide*, expressing the presence of three atoms, molecules, or combining equivalents of the element or radical indicated by the rest of the word, as *nitrogen terchloride* NCl_3. Now mostly repl. by TRI- **b.** In other compounds, as **ter-equi·valent, te·rvalent** *a.* = TRIVALENT; **te·rvalence** = TRIVALENCE.

‖**Terai** (tĕrai·, -rəi·). 1899. [From *Terai* (Hindī *tarāī* moist (land), f. *tar* moist, damp), name of a belt of marshy and jungly land between the lower foothills of the Himalayas and the plains, where this form of hat was first worn by hunters and travellers.] A wide-brimmed felt hat with double crown and special ventilation, worn by white men generally in subtropical regions.

Teraphim (te·răfīm). late ME. [a. eccl. L. *theraphim* (Vulg.), Gr. θεραφίν (LXX), ad. Heb. *tĕrāphīm.*] A kind of idols or images, or an idol or image; app. *esp.* household gods; an object of reverence and means of divination among the ancient Hebrews and kindred peoples. As *pl.*, or as *sing.* with pl. *teraphims.* Also sing. *teraph*, pl. *teraphs.*

‖**Terata** (te·rătă), *sb. pl.* 1902. [mod.L., = Gr. τέρατα, pl. of τέρας marvel, prodigy, monster.] *Biol.* and *Path.* Monstrous formations or births.

Teratical (tĕræ·tikăl), *a. rare.* 1722. [f. Gr. τέρας, τερατ- (see prec.) + -IC + -AL I.] Relating to marvels or prodigies.

‖**Teratogenesis** (te:rătoˌdʒe·nĕsis). 1857. [mod.L., f. Gr. τέρας, τερατ- (see TERATA) + γένεσις GENESIS.] *Biol.* and *Path.* The production of monsters or misshapen organisms. So Teratogeny (-ǫ·dʒĕni) in same sense.

Teratoid (te·rătoid), *a.* 1876. [f. Gr. τέρας, τερατ- + -OID.] *Biol.* and *Path.* Having the appearance or character of a monster or monstrous formation; *t. tumour* = TERATOMA.

Teratological (te:rătǫlǫ·dʒikăl), *a.* 1857. [f. next + -IC + -AL I.] Of or pertaining to teratology; treating of monstrosities; involving monstrosity, monstrous.

Teratology (terătǫ·lŏdʒi). 1678. [f. Gr. τέρας, τερατ- + -LOGY.] **1.** A discourse or narrative concerning prodigies; a marvellous tale, or a collection of such tales. **2.** *Biol.* The study of monstrosities or abnormal formations in animals or plants 1842. Hence **Terato·logist.**

‖**Teratoma** (terătōᵘ·mă). *Pl.* **-omata** (-ōᵘ·mătă). 1890. [mod.L., f. Gr. τέρας, τερατ-, after *sarcoma*, etc.] *Path.* See quot.

T., a tumor composed of various tissues or systems of tissue, as bone, teeth, etc., which do not normally exist at the place where the tumor grows 1890.

Terbium (tɔ̄·ɹbiŏm). 1843. [mod.L., from *Yt|terby* in Sweden; cf. ERBIUM.] *Chem.* One of the rare metallic elements found (together with yttrium and erbium) in gadolinite and other minerals.

Terce, variant of TIERCE.

Tercel, tiercel (tɔ̄·ɹs'l, tīᵊ·ɹs'l). late ME. [a. OF. *tercel*:—pop. L. *tertiolus*, dim. from L. *tertius* third.] The male of any kind of hawk; in Falconry esp. of the peregrine falcon (TERCEL-GENTLE) and the goshawk.

Tercelet, tiercelet (tɔ̄·ɹslĕt, tīᵊ·ɹslĕt). late ME. [a. AF. *tercelet*, = F. *tiercelet* (dim. of OF. *tercel*).] = prec.

Tercel-ge·ntle. 1486. [f. TERCEL, after FALCON-GENTLE.] The male of the falcon.

fig. Hist Romeo hist, o for a falkners voyce, To lure this Tassel gentle back againe SHAKS.

Tercentenary (tɔ̄ɹse·ntĭnări, -sĕntī·nări), *a.* and *sb.* 1844. [f. TER- + CENTENARY.] **A.** *adj.* Of or belonging to the number of three hundred; usu., to a completed period of 300 years. **B.** *sb.* A duration of three hundred years; the three-hundredth anniversary of an event, or a celebration of it 1855.

Tercentennial (tɔ̄ɹˌsente·niăl), *a.* and *sb.* 1882. [f. TER- + CENTENNIAL.] **A.** *adj.* Of or belonging to a period of three hundred years; of or relating to the three-hundredth anniversary. **B.** *sb.* The three-hundredth anniversary of an event.

Terceroon (tɔ̄ɹsĕrū·n). *rare.* 1760. [a. Sp. **terceron*, f. *tercero* a third person, f. *tercio* third.] The offspring of a white person and a mulatto, being third in descent from a negro; = QUADROON 1 a.

Tercet (tɔ̄·ɹsĕt). 1598. [ad. It. *terzetto*, dim. of *terzo* (:—L. *tertius*) third + -*etto* -ET.] *Pros.* A set or group of three lines rhyming together, or bound by double or triple rhyme with the adjacent triplet or triplets; *spec.* **a.** each of the triplets of the Italian TERZA RIMA; **b.** each of the two triplets usu. forming the last six lines of a sonnet.

Tercine (tɔ̄·ɹsin). 1832. [= F. *tercine*, f. F. *tiers, tierce*, or L. *tertius* third; see -INE [1].] *Bot.* A third integument supposed by some to occur in certain ovules.

Tercio, tertio (tɔ̄·ɹsio, tɔ̄·ɹʃio). Now *Hist.* 1583. [a. Sp. :—L. *tertium.*] *orig.* A regiment of the Spanish infantry 16–17th c.; applied also to the Italian forces of that period; hence, a body of foot forming a main division of an army.

Terebene (te·rĕbīn). 1857. [f. TEREBINTH + -ENE.] *Chem.* **1.** Used by Deville (1840) for a liquid obtained by the action of sulphuric acid on pinene, now known to be a mixture of terpenes together with cymene: one of the drugs of the British Pharmacopœia; also *attrib.* as *t. soap* 1898. †**2.** Sometimes a synonym of TERPENE –1871.

Terebenthene (terĕbe·nþīn). 1857. [a. F. *térébenthène*, f. F. *térébenthine*, ad. L. *terebinthina (resina)*; with suffix -ENE as in BENZENE.] *Chem.* Berthelot's name for the TERPENE which forms the chief constituent of French turpentine-oil, obtained from *Pinus Pinaster* (*P. maritima*).

Terebic (tĕre·bik), *a.* 1857. [f. TEREBINTH + -IC.] *Chem.* Of, belonging to, or derived from turpentine, as in *t. acid*, $C_7H_{10}O_4$, a dibasic acid, a product of the action of nitric acid on turpentine-oil. Hence **Te·rebate,** a salt of t. acid.

Terebinth (te·rĕbinþ). late ME. [= OF. *therebint(e*, ad. L. *terebinthus*, a. Gr. τερέβινθος, prob. a foreign word.] **1.** A tree of moderate size, *Pistacia Terebinthus*, family *Anacardiaceæ*, the source of Chian turpentine; also called *turpentine tree.* †**2.** The resin of this tree; = TURPENTINE –1673.

‖**Terebinthina** (-i·nþină). 1693. [med.L., short for *terebinthina resina* terebinthine resin.] The pharmacopœial name of turpentine.

Terebinthinate (terĕbi·nþinĕt), *a.* and *sb.* 1680. [ad. med.L. *terebinthinatus*, f. *terebinthina* turpentine.] **A.** *adj.* Impregnated with turpentine; having the nature or quality of turpentine. **B.** *sb.* A terebinthine product; a medicinal preparation of turpentine 1750. So **Terebi·nthinate** *v. trans.* to impregnate with turpentine.

Terebinthine (terĕbi·nþin), *a.* and *sb.* 1513. [ad. L. *terebinthinus*, f. Gr. type *τερεβίνθινος, f. τερέβινθος terebinth; see -INE [1].] **A.** *adj.* **1.** Of, pertaining to, of the nature of, or allied to the terebinth 1550. **2.** Of, pertaining to, or consisting of turpentine; turpentiny 1656. †**B.** *sb.* (the adj. used ellipt.) **1.** The terebinth –1513. **2.** Turpentine –1725.

‖**Terebra** (te·rĭbră). 1611. [L., a borer.] †**1.** An instrument for boring; *Surg.*, a trephine, or the boring part of it; also, a miner's drill –1787. **2.** *Ent.* The modified ovipositor of certain female insects, esp. terebrant Hymenoptera, with which they puncture leaves, fruit, etc., in order to insert their eggs 1713.

Terebrant (te·rĭbrănt), *a.* 1826. [ad. L. *terebrantem, terebrare* to bore.] Boring, or having the function of boring; belonging to the division *Terebrantia* of hymenopterous insects, having a boring ovipositor.

Terebrate (te·rĭbreᵗt), *v.* Now *rare.* 1623. [f. L. *terebrat-, terebrare* to bore.] *trans.* To bore, pierce, perforate; to penetrate by boring.

Terebration (terĭbrēᵗ·ʃən). Now *rare* or *Obs.* late ME. [ad. late L. *terebrationem*, f. *terebrare* to bore.] The action of boring or perforating; †*spec.* in *Surg.* the operation of trephining.

‖**Terebratula** (terĭbræ·tiŭlă). *Pl.* **-æ** (-ī), or **-as** (-ăz). Also (after F.) **terebra·tule.** 1822. [mod.L., quasi-dim. of L. *terebratus*, pa. pple. of *terebrare* to bore.] *Zool.* and *Palæont.* A genus of brachiopods, mostly extinct: so called from the perforated beak of the ventral valve. Formerly used to include any (esp. fossil) members of the *Terebratulidæ* and related families; the lamp-shells. Hence **Terebra·tular** *a.* of or pertaining to a t. **Terebra·tuliform** *a.* having the form of a t.

Teredo (tĕrī·do). *Pl.* **teredines** (-ī·dinīz), **teredos** (tĕrī·doᵘz). late ME. [L., ad. Gr. τερηδών a wood-gnawing worm, f. τερ-, root of τείρειν to rub hard, wear away, bore.] **1.** *Zool.* A genus of lamellibranch boring molluscs; *esp.* the shipworm, *T. navalis*, well-known for its destruction of submerged timbers in ships, piers, seadikes, etc. by boring into the wood. **2.** *transf.* Any disease in plants produced by the boring of insects 1866.

Terentian (tĕre·nʃiăn), *a.* 1599. [ad. L. *Terentianus*, f. *Terentius* Terence.] Pertaining to, or in the style of, the ancient Roman dramatic poet Terence.

Terephthalic (terĕfþæ·lik), *a.* 1857. [f. TEREBIC *a.* + PHTHALIC *a.*] *Chem.* Derived from or containing terebic and phthalic acids, as in *t. acid* (also called *insolinic acid*), $C_8H_6O_4 = C_6H_4(CO_2H)_2$, a dibasic acid produced as a white tasteless crystalline powder, nearly insoluble in water, alcohol, and ether. Hence **Tere·phthalate,** a salt of this acid.

Terete (tĕrī·t), *a.* 1619. [ad. L. *teres, teretem* rounded (off).] Rounded, smooth and round; in *Nat. Hist.*, having a cylindrical or slightly tapering form, circular in cross-section, and a surface free from furrows or ridges. Hence **Tere·tish** *a.* somewhat t.

Tereti- (te·rĭti), comb. form of L. *teres, teret-* TERETE, as in **Te:reticau·date** *a.*, having a rounded tail, round-tailed.

Tereu (tĭrū·). 1576. A feigned note of the nightingale. (*Tereu*, vocative of Gr.-L. *Tereus*, husband of Philomela's sister Progne; see Ovid *Met.* VI. viii.)

Tergal (tɔ̄·ɹgăl), *a.* 1860. [f. L. *tergum* + -AL.] *Zool.* Belonging to the tergum; dorsal.

Tergeminate (təɹˌdʒe·minĕt), *a.* 1793. [f. L. *tergeminus* triple + -ATE [2].] *Bot.* Thrice-double; having three pairs of leaflets.

Tergite (tɔ̄·ɹdʒəit). 1885. [f. L. *tergum* back + -ITE [1] 3.] *Zool.* A back-plate, formed by the fusion of a pair of serial plates of one of the somites or segments of an arthropod or other articulated animal. Hence **Tergi·tic** *a.* of or pertaining to a t.

Tergiversate (tɔ̄·ɹdʒivəɹseᵗt, -vɔ̄:ɹseᵗt), *v.* 1654. [f. L. *tergiversat-, tergiversari* to turn one's back, shuffle, f. *tergum* the back + *vers-, vertere* to turn.] **1.** *intr.* To practise tergiversation; to turn renegade, apostatize; to shuffle, use subterfuge; †to act the recusant. **2.** *lit.* To turn the back (for flight or retreat) 1875.

Tergiversation (tɔ̄:ɹdʒivəɹsēᵗ·ʃən). 1570. [ad. L. *tergiversationem*; see prec. and -ATION.] **1.** The action of 'turning one's back on', i.e. forsaking, something in which one was previously engaged, interested or concerned; desertion or abandonment of a cause, party, etc.; apostasy, renegation. Also with *a* and *pl.*, an instance of this. 1583. **2.** Turning in a dishonourable manner from straightforward action or statement; shifting, shuffling, equivocation, prevarication. Also, an instance of this. 1570. **3.** The turning of the back for flight; flight, retreat (*lit.* and *fig.*). Now *rare* or *Obs.* 1652.

1. Their tergiuersation and backsliding from their duties 1583. **2.** The duplicity and t. of which he had been guilty SCOTT. His shifts and tergiversations G. MEREDITH.

Tergiversator (tɔ̄·ɹdʒivəɹsēᵗtəɹ). 1716. [f. TERGIVERSATE *v.*; see -OR.] One who tergiversates; a renegade; a shuffler.

Tergo- (tɔ̄ɹgo), comb. form repr. L. *tergum* the back, used instead of the regular *tergi-*, as in **Tergola·teral** *a. Zool.*, pertaining to the tergum and the lateral plates of the shell in cirripeds.

‖**Tergum** (tɔ̄·ɹgŏm). *Pl.* **terga.** 1826. The L. word for 'back' (synon. w. DORSUM). **a.** The back of an arthropod or other articulated animal; more usu. the upper plate of each somite or segment of such an animal: opp. to *sternum.* **b.** Each of the two upper plates of the shell in cirripeds.

Term (tɜ̄ɹm), *sb.* ME. [a. F. *terme*:—L. *terminum* limit, boundary.] **I.** A limit in space, duration, etc. **1.** That which limits the extent of anything; a limit, extremity, boundary, bound. Usu. in *pl.* Now *rare* or *arch.* late ME. **b.** Utmost or extreme limit, end. Now *rare* or *arch.* ME. **c.** That to which movement or action is directed or tends, as its object, end, or goal; (less commonly) that from which it begins, starting-point, origin. Now *rare* or *Obs.* late ME. **2.** *Astrol.* A certain portion of each sign of the zodiac, assigned to a particular planet. late ME.

1. Corruption is a Reciprocall to Generation: and they two, are as Natures two Terms or Boundaries BACON. **b.** He had now reached the t. of his prosperity GIBBON. **c.** Vehement actions without scope or t. M. ARNOLD.

II. A limit in time; a space of time. **1.** A definite point of time at which something is to be done, or which is the beginning or end of a period; a set or appointed time or date, esp. for payment of money due. *Obs.* or *arch*, exc. in spec. uses. ME. **b.** *spec.* Each of the days in the year fixed for payment of rent, wages, and other dues, beginning and end of tenancy, etc. late ME. **2.** *transf.* A portion of time having definite limits; a period, *esp.* a set or appointed period; the space of time through which something lasts or is intended to last; duration, length of time ME. **3.** *spec.* Each of the periods (usu. three or four in the year) appointed for the sitting of certain courts of law, or for instruction and study in a university or school. Opp. to *vacation*. 1454. **4.** *Law.* An estate or interest in land, etc. for a certain period; in full, *t. of* or *for years*. late ME. **5. a.** The completion of the period of pregnancy; the (normal) time of childbirth 1844. †**b.** *pl.* The menstrual periods; the menstrual discharge, menses –1714.

2. Seven years (the usual t. of transportation) BYRON. Phr. *For t. of* (*one's*) *life*; The husbande hath Estate in the speciall tayle, and the wife but for terme of lyfe 1544. 3. I am obliged to give up..the hope of coming to Oxford this t. M. ARNOLD. Phr. *In t.*, during the t. *To keep terms*: see KEEP *v.* 4. 4. Every estate which must expire at a period certain and prefixed..is an estate for years. And therefore this estate is frequently called a t. BLACKSTONE. *Outstanding t.*, *satisfied t.* when the purposes for which an estate was created were fulfilled (e. g. by the death of all beneficiaries) it was called a *satisfied t.*; but unless express provision had been made that it should then cease, it continued to exist for the period for which it was created, and was then known as an *outstanding* or *attendant t.*

III. Limiting conditions. **1.** *pl.* Conditions or stipulations limiting what is proposed to be granted or done. Rarely in *sing.* ME. **b.** *spec.* Stipulations for payment in return for goods or services; conditions with regard to price or wages; payment offered, or charges made 1670. **2.** *pl.* Standing, footing, mutual relation between two persons or parties 1543. †**3.** *pl.* Condition, state, situation, position, circumstances; (in Shaks.) vaguely or redundantly: relation, respect (rarely in *sing.*) –1656.

1. He was obliged..to offer terms of peace HUME. Phr. *On* or *upon terms*, (*a*) (advb.) on (such and such) conditions; also (without qualification) on certain conditions, conditionally; (*b*) (pred.) in treaty, negotiating. *To come to terms*, to agree upon conditions; so *to bring to terms*. *To keep terms*, to have or continue to have dealings *with*; also *fig.* to 'have to do *with*', be connected *with*. *To make terms* = *come to terms*. †*To stand on* or *upon terms*, to insist upon conditions; to stand upon one's rights or dignity. *Terms of reference*, the terms which define the scope of an inquiry. 2. Phr. *On terms*, on friendly terms, friendly, sociable; in sporting slang, on terms of equality, on an equal footing *with*. *On* (*upon*) *equal terms*, *good terms*, *speaking terms*, *visiting terms*, etc. 3. Be iudge..Whether I in any iust terme am Affin'd To loue the Moore? SHAKS.

IV. Uses leading up to the sense 'expression'. **1.** *Math.* (*a*) Each of the two quantities composing a ratio (antecedent and consequent), or a fraction (numerator and denominator). (*b*) Each of any number of quantities forming a series or progression. (*c*) Each of (two or more) quantities connected by the signs of addition (+) or subtraction (—) in an algebraical expression or equation. 1542. **b.** *In terms of*: (*Math.*) said of a series or expression stated in terms involving some particular quantity; hence *gen.*, by means of, or in reference to (some particular set of symbols, ideas, etc.); often used as if = in the phraseology of 1743. **c.** *transf.* A member or item of any series; each of the things constituting a series. Also more vaguely, an element of any complex whole. 1841. **2.** *Logic*, etc. Each of the two things or notions which are compared, or between which some relation is apprehended or stated, in an act of thought, or (more commonly) each of the words or phrases denoting these in a verbal statement; *spec.* the subject and predicate of a proposition; the *major*, *minor*, or *middle t.* of a syllogism, each of which occurs twice 1551. **3.** A word or phrase used in a definite or precise sense in some particular subject, as a science or art; a technical expression (more fully *t. of art*). late ME. **b.** More widely: Any word or group of words expressing a notion or conception, or denoting an object of thought; an expression (*for* something). Usu. with qualifying adj. or phr. (as *an abstract t.*, *a t. of reproach*). 1477. **4.** Only in *pl.* Words or expressions collectively or generally (usu. of a specified kind); manner of expressing oneself, way of speaking, language. late ME. †**b.** *In terms*: in so many words –1667.

1. *Lowest terms* (*Math.*), the form of a fraction when the numerator and denominator are the least possible, i. e. have no common factor; hence *fig.* the simplest condition of anything; usu. in phr. *to bring* or *reduce to its lowest terms*. 3. I ne kan no termes of Astrologye CHAUCER. The idea involved in the t. latent heat 1862. 4. She in milde termes beg'd my patience SHAKS. **b.** He says in terms that the match ..hath undone the nation PEPYS.

V. *Arch.* A statue or bust like those of the god TERMINUS, representing the upper part of the body, sometimes without the arms, and terminating below in a pillar or pedestal out of which it appears to spring; a terminal figure; the pillar or pedestal bearing such a figure 1604.

Term (tɜ̄ɹm), *v.* late ME. [In sense 1, prob. a. OF. *termer* to bring to an end; in sense 2, f. prec.] †**1.** *trans.* To bring to an end or conclusion; to terminate –1570. **2.** To express or denote by a term or terms; to name, denominate, designate. Now only with compl. 1560.

2. The brain, which we tearme the seat of reason SIR T. BROWNE.

Termagant (tɜ̄·ɹmăgănt), *sb.* (*a.*) [In early ME. *Tervagant*, OF. *Tervagan*, proper name in *Chanson de Roland*.] **1.** (With capital T.) An imaginary deity held in mediæval Christendom to be worshipped by Mohammedans: in the mystery plays representing a violent overbearing personage. **2.** A savage, violent, boisterous, overbearing, or quarrelsome person (or thing personified); a blusterer, bully. Now *rare* exc. as in b. 1500. **b.** *spec.* A woman of this character; a virago, shrew 1659. **3.** *attrib.* or *adj.* Having the character of a termagant 1596.

1. I could haue such a Fellow whipt for o'redoing T.: it out-Herod's Herod SHAKS. 2. Thys terryble termagaunt, thys Neroth, thys Pharao 1542. **b.** Yonder is Sarah Marlborough's palace, just as it stood when that t. occupied it THACKERAY. 3. The most t. spirit that ever animated a female breast 1761. Hence **Te·rmagancy**, t. quality, violence of temper or disposition. †**Te·rmagantly** *adv.*

Termer (tɜ̄·ɹməɹ). 1556. [f. TERM *sb.* + -ER[1].] **1.** One who resorted to London in term, either for business at a court of law, or for amusements, intrigues, or dishonest practices. Now *Hist.* †**2.** Obs. form of TERMOR 1631.

‖**Termes** (tɜ̄·ɹmīz). *Pl.* **termites** (tɜ̄·ɹmitīz). 1800. [mod.L., a. late L., 'wood-worm', f. root of L. *terere*, Gr. τείρειν to rub, bore.] = TERMITE.

Terminable (tɜ̄·ɹminăb'l), *a.* late ME. [f. TERMINE *v.* + -ABLE.] †**1.** That may be or is to be terminated, determined, or finally decided –1450. **2.** Capable of being or liable to be terminated; limitable, finite; not lasting or perpetual 1581.

2. *T. annuity*, an annuity which comes to an end after a definite term; see ANNUITY 3. *T. annuitant*, one who holds a t. annuity. Hence **Terminabi·lity**, **Te·rminableness**, the quality of being t. **Te·rminably** *adv.*

Terminal (tɜ̄·ɹminăl), *a.* and *sb.* 1744. [ad. L. *terminalis*, f. *terminus* end, boundary; see -AL.] **A.** *adj.* **1.** Belonging to or placed at the boundary of a region, as a landmark. **b.** Applied to a statue, bust, or figure terminating in and apparently springing from a pillar or pedestal; also to the pillar or pedestal itself 1857. **2.** Situated at or forming the end or extremity of something: chiefly in scientific use 1805. **b.** Situated at the end of a line of railway; forming, or belonging to, a railway terminus 1878. **3.** Occurring at the end of something (in time, or generally); forming the last member of a series; closing, concluding, final, ultimate 1831. **4.** Belonging to or lasting for a term or definite period; *esp.* pertaining to a university or law term; occurring every term or at fixed terms; termly 1827.

2. A prism with a six-sided t. pyramid 1869. *T. moraine* (Geol.), a moraine at the lower end of a glacier. **b.** T. stations 1878. 4. The t. examinations called 'Collections' 1885.

B. *sb.* **1.** A terminal part or structure, i. e. one situated at or forming the end, or an end, of something; *spec.* in *Electr.* each of the free ends of an open circuit (by connecting which the circuit is closed), or any structure forming such an end, as the carbons in an arc-light, or the clamping-screws in a voltaic battery by which it is connected with the wire that completes the circuit 1850. **2.** A final syllable, letter, or word; a termination 1831. **3.** *pl.* Charges made by a railway company for the use of a terminus or other station, and for services rendered in loading or unloading goods, etc., there 1878. **4.** A terminus; a terminal point of a railway, a place or town at which it has a terminus. *U.S.* 1888. Hence **Te·rminally** *adv.*

Terminant (tɜ̄·ɹminănt), *a.* (*sb.*) Now *rare* or *Obs.* 1589. [ad. L. *terminantem*, *terminare*.] **1.** Terminating, concluding, final. Also as *sb.* A final syllable, termination, terminal. †**2.** Determining, defining –1610.

Terminate (tɜ̄·ɹminĕt), *ppl. a.* late ME. [ad. L. *terminatus*, *terminare*; see next.] Terminated, in various senses; see the vb.

Terminate (tɜ̄·ɹmineᵗt), *v.* 1589. [f. L. *terminat-*, *terminare* to limit, end, f. *terminus* end, boundary.] **I.** *trans.* †**1.** To determine; to state definitely (*rare*) –1706. **2.** To direct (an action) to something as object or end 1599. †**b.** Of a thing: To be the object of (an action) –1704. **3.** To bring to an end, put an end to, cause to cease; to end (an action, condition, etc.) 1615. **b.** To come at the end of, form the conclusion of 1798. †**4.** To put a limit or limits to; to restrict, confine *to* (*in*) –1674. **5.** To bound or limit spatially; to be situated at the end of 1634. **6.** †**a.** To define (visual objects) –1762. **b.** To finish, complete (*rare*) 1825.

3. She had every hope that this..would t. every perplexity 1796. 5. On another side, the great deep terminates the view 1746. 6. **b.** During this interval of calm and prosperity, he terminated two figures of slaves..in an incomparable style of art 1857.

II. *intr.* **1.** To be directed to something as object or end 1699. **2.** To come to an end (in space); to end *at*, *in*, or *with* something 1644. **b.** Of a word: To end *in* (a letter or sound) 1824. **3.** To come to an end, so as to extend no further; to have its end or terminus *in* something 1613. **4.** To come to an end (in time); to end, cease, close 1815. **b.** To issue, result (*in* something) 1710.

1. My thoughts all t. in God 1856. 2. The spot where the present gulf terminates 1862. 4. The sweetest notes must t. and die WORDSW.

Termination (tɜ̄ɹminēⁱ·ʃən). 1450. [ad. L. *terminationem*, f. *terminare*.] **I.** †**1.** The action of determining; determination, decision –1660. **2.** The action of ending. †**a.** Bounding, limiting. **b.** Putting an end to; bringing to a close. 1604. **II.** The point or part in which anything ends. **1.** End (in time), cessation, close, conclusion 1500. **b.** Outcome, issue, result 1806. **2.** The ending of a word; the final syllable, letter, or group of letters; *spec.* in *Gram.* an (inflexional or derivative) ending, a suffix 1530. **3.** A limit, bound; an end, extremity 1755.

1. All human power has its t. sooner or later J. H. NEWMAN. **b.** Dissensions which could hardly have other than a hostile t. 1884. 3. To improve the t. of the line at the Liverpool end 1830. Hence **Termina·tional** *a.* of, pertaining to, or forming a t. or terminations; closing, final (chiefly *Gram.*)

Terminative (tɜ̄·ɹmineᵗtiv, -ĕtiv), *a.* late ME. [See TERMINATE *v.* and -ATIVE.] **1.** †Forming a boundary or limit, bounding; forming the termination or extremity of something.

†2. Constituting an end, final, ultimate -1701. 3. Bringing or coming to an end; finishing; conclusive 1680. Hence **Te·rminatively** *adv.*

Terminator (tɜ̄·ɹmineʹtəɹ). 1770. [a. late L.] 1. One who or that which terminates 1846. 2. *Astron.* The line of separation between the illuminated and unilluminated parts of the disk of the moon or a planet 1770.

Te·rminatory, *a. rare.* 1756. [See prec. and -ORY².] Forming the end or extremity; terminal.

†**Te·rmine,** *v.* ME. [a. F. *terminer*, ad. L. *terminare*.] = TERMINATE *v.* -1705.

Terminer, in *oyer and t.*: see OYER.

Terminism (tɜ̄·ɹminiz'm). 1882. [f. L. *terminus* end, limit + -ISM.] **a.** *Philos.* The doctrine that universals are mere terms or names: = NOMINALISM b. **b.** *Theol.* The doctrine (maintained by Reichenberg at Leipzig in the 17th c.) that God has appointed a definite term or limit in the life of each individual, after which the opportunity for salvation is lost. So **Te·rminist,** one who holds or maintains t. 1727.

Terminology (tɜ̄ɹminǫ·lŏdʒi). 1801. [f. L. *terminus*, in its med.L. sense 'term' + -LOGY, after G. *terminologie* (1786).] Etymologically, The doctrine or scientific study of terms; in use almost always, the system of terms belonging to any science or subject; technical terms collectively; nomenclature.

Kant, who..gave old ideas a novelty by giving them a new t. 1847. Every calling has its technical t. HUXLEY. Hence **Te·rminolo·gical** *a.* pertaining to t.; -**ly** *adv.* **Termino·logist,** one versed in t.

It could not..be classified as slavery..without some risk of terminological inexactitude W. S. CHURCHILL 1906.

Terminus (tɜ̄·ɹminɒ̆s). *Pl.* **termini** (-əi). 1555. [L., = end, limit, boundary, etc.] 1. *Anc. Rom. Myth.* (With initial capital.) The deity who presided over boundaries or landmarks 1600. 2. A statue or bust of, or resembling those of, the god Terminus; also, the pedestal of such a statue. Sometimes, a boundary post or stone. 1645. 3. The point to which motion or action tends, goal, end; occas., starting-point 1555. 4. A boundary, limit (*rare*) 1673. 5. The end of a line of railway; also, the station at the end; the place at which a tram-line, etc. ends 1836. **b.** *transf.* or *gen.* An end, extremity; the point at which something comes to an end 1855.

3. Phr. (orig. scholastic L.) *T. a quo* 'term from which'. *T. ad quem* 'term to which'. 5. b. The grey matter [of the brain] is a t.; to it the fibrous collections tend, or from it commence 1855.

Termite (tɜ̄·ɹməit). 1781. [ad. L. *termes, termitem*; see TERMES.] A pseudoneuropterous social insect of the genus *Termes* or family *Termitidæ*, chiefly tropical, and very destructive to timber; also called *white ant.*

Termless (tɜ̄·ɹmlės), *a.* 1586. [-LESS.] 1. Having no term or limit; boundless. †2. Inexpressible. SHAKS. 3. Unconditional 1902.

1. Infinite and t. complication of detail RUSKIN.

Termly (tɜ̄·ɹmli), *a.* Now *rare.* 1598. [f. TERM *sb.* + -LY¹; cf. *weekly*.] Occurring every term or at fixed terms; periodical; *esp.* paid or due every recurrent term or at fixed terms.

Te·rmly, *adv.* 1484. [f. as prec. + -LY².] Term by term; every term, or at fixed terms.

I would..put it in order for you t., or weekly, or daily SCOTT.

Termon (tɜ̄·ɹmən). 1533. [OIr.] *Irish Hist.* Land belonging to a religious house.

Termor (tɜ̄·ɹmǫ̆ɹ). ME. [a. AF. *termer*, f. *terme* TERM; see -ER².] *Law.* One who holds lands or tenements for a term of years, or for life; one who has a term (TERM II. 4).

Te·rm-time. late ME. The period during which the law-courts are in session; the period of study at a university or school.

Tern (tɜ̄ɹn), *sb.*¹ 1678. [Of Norse origin; cf. Da. *terne*, Sw. *tärna*, Norw. *terna* :—ON. *þerna*.] The common name of a group of seabirds of the genus *Sterna*, or sub-family *Sterninæ*, akin to the gulls, but having generally a more slender body, long pointed wings, and a forked tail; a sea swallow.

Tern (tɜ̄ɹn), *a.* and *sb.*² ME. [As adj., ad. L. *terni* three each. As *sb.*, app. a. F. *terne*.] †**A.** adj. *Bot.* Arranged in threes; ternate -1828. **B.** *sb.* A set of three; a trio, triplet. *spec.* †**a.** *pl.* A double three in dicing. **b.** In a lottery, three winning numbers drawn together; a prize gained by such a drawing. **c.** A group of three stanzas. ME.

1. c. This late Poem composed of two Terns and an Envoy FURNIVALL.

Ternary (tɜ̄·ɹnări), *a.* and *sb.* late ME. [ad. late L. *ternarius* consisting of three, f. *terni*, f. *ter* thrice; see -ARY¹.] **A.** *adj.* 1. Pertaining to, consisting of, compounded of, or characterized by a set (or sets) of three; three-fold, triple 1573. **b.** *Chem.* and *Min.* Compounded or consisting of three elements or constituents 1808. **c.** *Bot.* Arranged in threes around a common axis: usu. in ref. to the parts of a flower 1830. **d.** *Math.* Constructed on the number three as a base, as *t. scale* (of notation), etc.; involving three variables 1860. 2. Third in subordination, rank, or order 1826.

1. *T. system* (of classification), one in which each division is into three parts. **b.** *Perfect granite* is a t. compound of quartz, felspar, and di-axial mica, universally diffused 1851.

†**B.** *sb.* A set or group of three; a ternion, a trio -1781.

I conclude this T. of Worthies with Cato 1654.

Ternate (tɜ̄·ɹnĕt), *a.* 1760. [ad. mod.L. *ternatus*, in form pa. pple. of med.L. *ternare* to treble.] Produced or arranged in threes; *spec.* in *Bot.* applied to a compound leaf composed of three leaflets, or to leaves arranged in whorls of three; also to leaflets borne on secondary or tertiary similarly arranged petioles (*biternate, triternate*). Hence **Te·rnately** *adv.* in threes.

Tern(e)-plate (tɜ̄·ɹnplĕ̄t). 1858. [prob. f. F. *terne* dull, lacking brilliancy.] Thin sheet-iron coated with an alloy of lead and tin; an inferior kind of tin-plate; a sheet or plate of this.

Ternion (tɜ̄·ɹniǫ̆n). 1587. [ad. L. *ternionem* triad.] 1. A set of three (things or persons); a triad. 2. A quire of three sheets, each folded in two 1609.

Terpene (tɜ̄·ɹpīn). 1873. [f. *terp-* in *terpentin*, obs. f. TURPENTINE, with suffix -ENE.] *Chem.* A general name of hydrocarbons having the formula $C_{10}H_{16}$, many of which occur in the volatile oils of plants, chiefly of the coniferous and aurantiaceous families. (Sometimes used to include hydrocarbons of formula C_5H_8 and its polymers.) Hence **Terpeny·lic** in *terpenylic acid*, $C_8H_{12}O_4$, obtained by oxidizing a t. with chromic acid.

Terpin (tɜ̄·ɹpin). 1848. [f. as prec. + -IN¹.] *Chem.* A derivative of pinene and other terpenes, $C_{10}H_{18}(OH)_2$, of which two modifications are known, *cisterpin*, melting at 103° C., and *transterpin*, at 156° C. Hence **Te·rpineol** (in Pharmacy **Terpinol**), a colourless oil formed by dehydrating t.

‖**Terpsichore** (təɹpsi·kŏrī). 1711. [a. Gr. Τερψιχόρη 'dance-enjoying', f. τέρπειν to delight + χορός dance, CHORUS.] The Muse of dancing; hence, a female dancer; dancing as an art. Hence **Terpsichorean** (təɹpsikŏrī·an) *a.* of, pertaining to, or of the nature of dancing.

‖**Terra** (te·ră). 1871. L. (and It.) *terra* earth, used, with qualifying adjs., to form the names of medicinal and other earths, boles, and the like, as **t. alba,** pipe-clay; **t. cariosa,** tripoli or rotten-stone; **t. chia,** also *chia t.*, Chian earth, an astringent and cosmetic bole formerly obtained from the island of Chios; **t. merita** = TURMERIC; **t. ponderosa,** barium sulphate, heavy spar.

‖**Terra a terra.** Also (now always) ‖**terre à terre.** 1614. [It. *terra terra* level with the ground, infl. by F. *terre à terre*, Sp. *tierra à tierra*.] †1. An artificial gait formerly taught to horses, resembling a low curvet. 2. Applied to a kind of dance. Also *fig.* and *attrib.* Without elevation of style. 1727.

Terrace (te·rĕ̄s), *sb.* 1515. [a. F., rubble, platform, terrace :—L. **terracea*, fem. of **terraceus* adj., earthen, of the nature of earth, f. *terra*; cf. -ACEOUS.] 1. A raised level place for walking, with a vertical or sloping front or sides faced with masonry, turf, or the like, and sometimes having a balustrade; *esp.* a raised walk in a garden, or a level surface formed in front of a house on naturally sloping ground, or on the bank of a river 1575. †**b.** *Mil.* An earthwork thrown up by a besieging force -1816. 2. A natural formation of this character: **a.** a table-land; **b.** *spec.* in *Geol.*, a horizontal shelf or bench on the side of a hill, or sloping ground 1674. †3. A gallery, open on one or both sides; a colonnade, a portico; a balcony on the outside of a building; a raised platform or balcony in a theatre or the like -1703. 4. The flat roof of a house, resorted to for coolness in warm climates. Now *rare.* 5. A row of houses on a level above the general surface, or on the face of a rising ground; now *freq.*, a row of houses of uniform style on a site slightly, if at all, raised above the level of the roadway; more recently often used arbitrarily 1769. 6. A soft spot in marble, which is cleaned out and the cavity filled up with a paste 1877.

1. Gardens and marble terrases full of orange and cypress trees GRAY.

Comb.: **t.-cultivation,** the cultivation of hill-sides in terraces; **-epoch** (*Geol.*), the epoch during which the river-terraces of N. America were formed.

Terrace (te·rĕ̄s), *v.* 1615. [f. prec., or a. F. *terrasser*.] 1. *trans.* To form into a terrace or raised bank; to fashion or arrange in terraces 1650. †2. To furnish with a 'terrace' or balcony; to provide with a loggia or terrace-roof -1634. Hence **Te·rracing** *vbl. sb.*, also *concr.*

‖**Terra-cotta** (te:ră,kǫ·tă). 1722. [It., 'baked earth' :—L. *terra cocta*.] 1. A hard unglazed pottery of a fine quality, of which decorative tiles and bricks, architectural decorations, statuary, vases, and the like are made. **b.** With *a* and *pl.*: An object of art made of this substance 1810. 2. The colour of this pottery, a brownish red of various shades 1882.

1. The Romans have left us numerous examples in bronze and *terra cotta* 1867. **b.** Ancient Terracottas in the British Museum 1810.

†‖**Te·rra damna·ta.** 1633. [L., 'condemned earth'.] = CAPUT MORTUUM 2. -1710.

‖**Terræ filius** (te:rī fi·liŏs). *Pl.* **terræ filii** (fi·li,əi). 1621. [L.] 1. A person of obscure parentage. 2. Formerly, at the University of Oxford: An orator privileged to make humorous and satirical strictures in a speech at the public 'act' 1651.

‖**Terra firma** (te:ră fɜ̄·ɹmă). 1605. [L., 'firm land'.] †1. A mainland or continent, as dist. from portions of land partly or wholly isolated by water -1741. †2. *spec.* **a.** The territories on the Italian mainland which were subject to the state of Venice -1832. **b.** The northern coast-land of S. America (Colombia), as dist. from the West India Islands; also, in narrower sense, the Isthmus of Panama -1827. 3. The land as dist. from the sea; dry or firm land 1693. †4. *joc.* Landed estate; land -1728.

3. They again got footing on terra firma 1779.

Terrain (terē̆·n), *sb.* (*a.*) 1727. [a. F., :—pop. L. **terranum* = cl. L. *terrenum*.] †1. 'The Manage-Ground upon which the Horse makes his Pist or Tread' (Bailey). †**b.** Standing-ground, position. -1832. 2. A tract of country considered with regard to its natural features, configuration, etc.; in military use esp. as affecting its tactical advantages, fitness for manœuvring, etc.; also, an extent of ground, region, territory 1766. 3. *Geol.* (Usu. spelt terrane.) A connected series, group, or system of rocks or formations; a stratigraphical subdivision 1823. **B.** *adj.* Of the earth, terrene, terrestrial 1882.

‖**Terra incognita** (te:ră inkǫ·gnită). *Pl.* **terræ incognitæ.** 1616. [L., 'unknown land'.] An unknown or unexplored region. Often *fig.*

‖**Terra japonica** (te:ră dʒăpǫ·nikă). 1654. [mod.L., 'Japanese earth'.] = CATECHU.

Terramare (terămā·ɹ, -mē·ɹ). *Pl.* **-ares.** Also in It. form **terrama·ra,** pl. **terrema·re.** 1866. [a. F., ad. dial. It. *terramara*, for *terramarna*, f. *terra* earth + *marna* MARL.] An ammoniacal earth found in the valley of the Po, in Italy, and collected as a fertilizer; it occurs in flat mounds, identified as the sites of dwellings of a people of the later neolithic period. Hence *transf.* (*pl.*) The prehistoric settlements themselves.

Terraneous (terē̆·nĭəs), *a. rare.* 1711. [f. L. **terraneus*, f. *terra* earth; see -OUS.] Of or pertaining to the earth; terrestrial. **b.** *Bot.* Growing upon land 1882.

Terrapin (te·răpin). 1613. [Of Algonquin origin.] A name orig. given to one or more species of N. Amer. turtles; thence extended to many allied species of the turtle and tortoise family, *Testudineæ*, widely distributed over America, the East Indies, China, N. Africa, etc. In N. America, *spec.* the Diamond-backed or Saltmarsh terrapin, *Malaclemmys palustris*, famous for its delicate flesh. **b.** The flesh of this animal as food 1867.

Terraqueous (terē·kwi̦əs), *a.* 1658. [f. L. *terra* earth + AQUEOUS.] **1.** Consisting of, or formed of, land and water; usu. in *t. globe.* **2.** Living in land and water, as a plant; extending over land and water, as a journey 1694.

Terrar, terrer. *Obs.* exc. *Hist.* 1593. [ad. med.L. *terrarius*, f. *terrarius* adj., pertaining to land or lands.] An officer of a religious house, who was orig. estates bursar for farms and manors belonging to the house; but whose office by the 16th c. at Durham was mainly connected with the entertainment of strangers.

†‖ **Te·rra Sie·nna.** 1760. [ad. It. *terra di Siena* 'earth of Sienna'.] = SIENNA- 1844.

‖ **Terrazzo** (teræ·tso). 1902. [It., = terrace, balcony.] A proprietary name for a kind of flooring made of small chips of marble set irregularly in cement and polished. Chiefly *attrib.*

†‖ **Terre·lla.** 1613. [mod.L., dim. of *terra* earth; see -EL[2].] **1.** A little Earth; a small orb or planet -1682. **2.** A spherical loadstone or magnet -1837.

Terrene (těrī·n), *a.* ME. [ult. ad.L. *terrenus*, f. *terra* earth.] **1.** = TERRESTRIAL 1. **2.** Of the nature of earth (the substance); earthy 1601. **3.** Occurring on or inhabiting the land as opp. to water 1661. **4.** = TERRESTRIAL 2. 1635. **5.** *absol.* or as *sb.* **a.** The earth, the world. **b.** A land or territory. 1667.

1. Alacke our T. Moone is now Eclipst SHAKS. 5. Many a Province wide Tenfold the length of this t. MILT. Hence **Terre·ne·ly** *adv.*, **-ness** (*rare*).

‖ **Terreno** (terre·no). 1740. [= It. (*piano*) *terreno* :—L. *terrenum* TERRENE.] A ground-floor; also, a parlour.

Terreplein (tēə·ɹ‚plē̆ⁱn, ‖ tęr(ə)plæ̃n). 1591. [a. F., f. *terre* earth + *-plein* :—L. *plenus* full.] **1.** *orig.*, The talus or sloping bank of earth behind a wall or rampart; hence, the surface of a rampart behind the parapet; and strictly, the level space on which the guns are mounted, between the banquette and the inner talus. **2.** The level base (above, on, or below the natural surface of the ground) on which a battery is placed in field fortifications; sometimes, the natural surface of the ground 1669.

Terrestrial (tĕre·striăl, tė-), *a.* and *sb.* late ME. [f. L. *terrestris* (f. *terra*) + -AL.] **1.** Of or pertaining to this world, or to earth as opp. to heaven; earthly; worldly; mundane. **2.** Of, pertaining, or referring to the earth; often in *t. ball, globe, sphere*, the earth 1593. **b.** *spec. T. globe*, a globe with a map of the earth on its surface; *t. telescope*, one used for observing terrestrial objects 1559. †**3.** Of the nature or character of earth, esp. as being dry and solid or pulverulent; possessing earth-like properties or qualities; earthy -1756. **4.** Of or pertaining to the land of the world, as dist. from the water 1628. **5.** *Nat. Hist.* Occurring on, or inhabiting, land: **a.** *Zool.* Living on the land as dist. from the waters, or on the ground as dist. from the air 1638. **b.** *Bot.* Growing in the soil; dist. from *aquatic, marine, parasitic*, or *epiphytic* 1831.

1. The happiest lot of t. existence JOHNSON. 2. From vnder this Terrestriall Ball SHAKS. 4. The t. and naval battailes here graven EVELYN. 5. a. Fishes need lesse Refrigeration than Terrestriall Creatures 1638.

B. *sb.* (The adj. used absol.) **a.** A t. being; *esp.* a human being, a mortal 1598. **b.** The terrestrial world, the earth (*rare*) 1742. **c.** *pl.* Terrestrial animals, orders, or families 1842. Hence **Terre·strial-ly** *adv.*, **-ness** (*rare*).

†**Terre·strious,** *a.* 1600. [f. L. *terrestris* + -OUS.] **1.** Having the nature of earth, earthy -1741. **2.** Of or consisting of the land surface of the earth -1862. **3.** = prec. 5. SIR T. BROWNE.

Terret, -it (te·rėt, -it). late ME. [orig. *teret, tyret*, collateral form of *toret*, a. OF. *toret, touret*, dim. of OF. *tor, tour* TOUR.] A round or circular loop or ring; *spec.* a ring on a dog's collar; each of the two rings by which the leash is attached to the jesses of a hawk; in horse-harness: one of the two (brass) rings fixed upright on the pad, or saddle, and on the hames, through which the driving reins pass. Hence **Te·rreted** *a.* provided or fitted with a t.

Terre-tenant (tēə·ɹ‚te:nănt). late ME. [a. AF. *terre tenaunt* holding land.] *Law.* One who has the actual possession of land; the occupant of land.

‖ **Terre-verte** (tęr‚vęrt). 1658. [f. *terre verte* 'green earth'.] A soft green earth of varying composition used as a pigment; esp. = CELADONITE or *green earth*, a variety of glauconite.

Terrible (te·rĭb'l), *a.* (*sb.*) late ME. [a. F., ad. L. *terribilis*, f. *terrere* to frighten; see -BLE.] **1.** Exciting or fitted to excite terror; frightful, dreadful. **2.** Very violent, severe, painful, or bad; hence *colloq.* as a mere intensive: Very great, excessive 1596. **3.** quasi-*adv.* Terribly 1489. **B.** *sb.* A terrible thing or being; something that causes terror or dread. Usu. in *pl.* 1619.

A. 1. A foe more t. than the avalanches TYNDALL. 2. The t. Bill against Conventicles MARVELL. She 's a t. one to laugh DICKENS. 3. I was in a t. bad way 1877. B. Job calls it the king of terrors..or the most t. of terribles 1682. Hence **Te·rribleness. Te·rribly** *adv.* in a t. manner.

Terricole (te·rikoul), *a.* (*sb.*) 1882. [ad. L. *terricola* earth-dweller, f. *terra* + *colere* to inhabit.] **1.** *Bot.* Growing on the ground, as some lichens. **2.** *Zool.* Living on the ground or in the earth 1899. **B.** *sb.* An animal living on the ground, or burrowing in the earth; *spec.* a member of the *Terricolæ*, a group of annelids including the common earthworm 1896.

Terricolous (teri·kŏləs), *a.* 1835. [f. as prec. + -OUS.] *Zool.* Inhabiting the ground, not aquatic or aerial; living in the earth; *spec.* of or belonging to the *Terricolæ* or earthworms. So **Terri·coline** *a.*

Terrier[1] (te·riəɹ). Now only *Hist.* 1477. [a. OF. 'rent-roll', sb. use of *terrier* adj. :—med.L. *terrarius*, f. *terra*.] A register of landed property, formerly including lists of vassals and tenants, with particulars of their holdings, services, and rents; a rent-roll; in later use, a book in which the lands of a private person, or of a corporation civil or ecclesiastical, are described by their site, boundaries, acreage, etc. Also, an inventory of property or goods.

Terrier[2] (te·riəɹ). 1440. [a. F. (*chien*) *terrier* (also as sb.), = med.L. *terrarius*, f. *terra*.] **1.** A small, active, intelligent variety of dog which pursues its quarry (the fox, badger, etc.) into its burrow or earth; the numerous breeds are dist. into two classes, the *short-* or *smooth-haired*, as the fox-t., black and tan t., etc., and the *long-* or *rough-haired*, as the Scotch t., Skye t., etc. Formerly also *t. dog.* **2.** A punning appellation for a territorial 1908.

Terrific (těri·fik, tė-), *a.* 1667. [ad. L. *terrificus*, f. stem of *terrere* to frighten; see -FIC.] **1.** Causing terror, terrifying; fitted to terrify; dreadful, terrible, frightful. **2.** Applied intensively to anything very severe or excessive. *colloq.* 1809.

1. The Serpent..with brazen Eyes And hairie Main t. MILT. 2. The crowd was immense, and the applause t. 1855. So **Terri·fical** *a.* (*rare*), **-ly** *adv.* **Terri·fic-ly** *adv.*, **-ness.**

Terrify (te·rifəi), *v.* 1575. [ad. L. *terrificare* to frighten, f. *terrificus*; see -FY.] **1.** *trans.* To fill with terror; to frighten or alarm greatly. Also *absol.* 1578. **b.** To drive *from, out of, into*, etc. by terrifying 1575. **2.** To irritate, torment, harass, annoy, tease. Now only *dial.* 1641. †**3.** To make terrible. MILT.

1. Terrifi'd Hee fled, not hoping to escape, but shun The present MILT. b. It may t. her to death SCOTT. 3. If the law, instead of aggravating and terrifying sin, shall give out licence, it foils itself MILT.

Terrigenous (teri·dʒĭnəs), *a. rare.* 1684. [f. L. *terrigenus* earth-born + -OUS.] **1.** Produced or sprung from the earth; earth-born. **2.** *Geol.* Land-derived: applied to marine deposits derived from the neighbouring land 1882.

Terrine (těrī·n). 1706. [Original form of TUREEN.] **1.** = TUREEN. *arch.* exc. as Fr. ‖**2.** *Cookery.* A French dish of game, meat, poultry, etc., stewed in a covered earthenware vessel 1706. **3.** A small earthenware vessel containing a table delicacy for sale; this with its contents 1911.

Territorial (teritōə·riăl), *a.* (*sb.*) 1625. [ad. late L. *territorialis*, f. *territorium* TERRITORY.] **1.** Of, belonging or relating to, territory or land, or to the territory of any state, sovereign, or ruler 1768. **b.** Of or pertaining to landed property 1773. **c.** Owning or having an estate in land; landed 1832. **2.** Of or pertaining to a particular territory, district, or locality; local 1625. **3.** Of or belonging to one of the 'territories' of the United States 1812. **4.** *Mil. T. Army* or *Force*, the British Army of Home Defence instituted (on a territorial or local basis) in 1908. Also *Territorial* as *sb.* a member of the T. Army. 1907.

1. An actual Invasion of our t. rights WASHINGTON. b. The..t. revenue of India 1800. c. The t. aristocracy 1832. 2. The gods..were local and t. divinities PRIESTLEY. Hence **Territoria·lity**, t. quality, condition, position, or status. **Territo·rially** *adv.*

Territorialism (teritōə·riăliz'm). 1881. [f. prec. + -ISM.] A territorial system; landlordism; the organization of the Army on a t. or local basis; also applied, as tr. G. *Territorialsystem*, to a theory of church government which places the supreme authority in the civil power. So **Territo·rialist**, a member or representative of the class of landowners.

Territorialize (teritōə·riăləiz), *v.* 1818. [f. as prec. + -IZE.] *trans.* To make territorial; to place upon a territorial basis; to associate with or restrict to a particular territory or district.

Territory (te·ritŏri). late ME. [ad. L. *territorium* the land round a town, a domain, district, territory.] **1.** †**a.** The land or district lying round a city or town and under its jurisdiction. Chiefly as tr. L. *territorium*. -1651. **b.** The land or country belonging to or under the dominion of a ruler or state 1494. **c.** *transf.* Each half of a football ground considered as belonging to one of the teams: so in hockey, baseball, etc. 1896. **2.** A tract of land, or district of undefined boundaries; a region 1610. **3.** *fig.* The sphere, province or domain of a science, art, class, word, etc. 1640. **4.** In the U.S., One of certain regions in the West belonging to and under the government of the American Republic, and having some degree of self-government, but not yet admitted as a State into the Union 1799. **5.** orig. *U.S.* The district in which a commercial traveller operates. 1925.

1. As they governed the City of Rome, and Territories adjacent HOBBES. b. A small port, still within the Neapolitan territories 1799. 2. The most fertile territories of Anjou HOLLAND.

Terror (te·rəɹ). [Late ME. *terrour*, a. OF. (F. *terreur*) :—L. *terrorem*, *terror*, f. *terrere* to frighten; see -OR.] **1.** The state of being terrified or greatly frightened; intense fear, fright, or dread. Also, with *a* and *pl.*, an instance of this. **2.** *transf.* The action or quality of causing dread; terrific quality, terribleness; also *concr.* a thing or person that excites terror or awe; something terrifying, awe-inspiring; *trivially*, a 'trying', embarrassing, or unruly person 1528.

1. The terrors of death are fallen vpon me BIBLE (Genev.) *Ps.* lv. 4. 2. So spake the grieslie terrour MILT. Phr. *King of Terrors*, Death personified. *Reign of terror*, a state of things in which the general community live in dread of death or outrage; esp. in *French Hist.* the period of the First Revolution from about March 1793 to July 1794, called also *the T., the Red T.* Hence **Te·rrorless** *a.* devoid of t.; exciting no dread.

Terrorism (te·rŏriz'm). 1795. [a. F. *terrorisme*, f. L. *terror*; see -ISM.] A system of terror. **1.** Government by intimidation; the system of the 'Terror' (1793-4); see prec. **2.** *gen.* A policy intended to strike with terror those against whom it is adopted; the fact of terrorizing or condition of being terrorized 1798.

Terrorist (te·rŏrist). 1795. [a. F. *terroriste*, f. L. *terror* TERROR; see -IST.] 1. As a political term: a. Applied to the Jacobins and their agents and partisans in the French Revolution. b. Any one who attempts to further his views by a system of coercive intimidation; *spec.* applied to members of one of the extreme revolutionary societies in Russia 1866. 2. An alarmist, a scaremonger 1803.

1. Thousands of those Hell-hounds called Terrorists ..are let loose on the people BURKE. Hence **Terror·i·stic, -ical** *adjs.* characterized by or practising terrorism.

Terrorize (te·rŏrəiz), *v.* 1823. [f. TERROR + -IZE.] 1. *trans.* To fill or inspire with terror, reduce to a state of terror; *esp.* to coerce or deter by terror. 2. *intr.* To rule, or maintain power, by terrorism; to practise intimidation 1856.

1. Superstitions which yet more or less..terrorise the ignorant 1885.

Terry (te·ri), *sb.* and *a.* 1784. [Origin obsc.] A. *sb.* The loop raised in pile-weaving left uncut; also short for *t. fabric, t. velvet*, etc. B. *adj.* Of pile-fabrics: Looped, having the loops that form the pile left uncut, as *t. pile, t. velvet*. Also, Of or pertaining to such a fabric. 1835.

‖**Ter-sanctus** (tɜːɪsæ·ŋktɒ̆s). 1832. [L. *ter* thrice + *sanctus* holy.] The Latin title of the hymn in the Liturgy beginning 'With Angels and Archangels'.

Terse (tɜɪs), *a.* 1601. [ad. L. *tersus*, pa. pple. of *tergere* to wipe.] †1. Wiped, brushed; smoothed; clean-cut, sharp-cut; polished, burnished; neat, trim, spruce -1824. †2. *fig.* Polite, polished, refined, cultured: esp. in ref. to language -1774. 3. *spec.* Freed from verbal redundancy; neatly concise; compact and pithy in style or language 1777.

1. I am enamour'd of this street..'tis so polite and t. B. JONS. 2. Pure, t., elegant Latin 1695. 3. In eight t. lines has Phædrus told..A tale of goats 1777. Hence **Te·rse·ly** *adv.*, **-ness.**

Te·rtia. Now *Hist.* 1630. [app. altered f. TERCIO.] A division of infantry, a TERCIO.

Tertial (tɜ̄·ɪʃiăl), *a.* and *sb.* 1836. [f. L. *tertius* third + -AL.] *Ornith.* A. *adj.* Of or pertaining to the third rank or row of quill- or flight-feathers in the wing of a bird. B. *sb.* A flight-feather of the third row.

Tertian (tɜ̄·ɪʃăn), *a.* and *sb.* [Late ME. in *fever terciane*, or *terciane*, ad. L. *febris tertiana*, also *tertiana* sb., f. *tertius* third; see -AN.] A. *adj.* 1. *Path.* Of a fever or ague: Characterized by the occurrence of a paroxysm every third (i. e. every alternate) day. 2. *Mus.* Applied to the mean-tone temperament (in which the major thirds are perfectly in tune) 1875. 3. *T. father*: a Jesuit in the third period of his probation 1855. Also as *sb.* Hence **Te·rtianship.** B. *sb.* 1. Short for *t. ague* or *fever*. late ME. †2. A liquid measure for wine, oil, etc., the third of a tun, i. e. 84 wine gallons (= 70 imperial gallons); also, a large cask of this capacity; a puncheon -1749. 3. A mixture stop on an organ, consisting of a tierce and larigot combined 1876.

Tertiary (tɜ̄·ɪʃiări), *a.* and *sb.* 1550. [f. L. *tertiarius* of the third part or rank, f. *tertius*; see -ARY¹.] A. *adj.* 1. Of, in, or belonging to the third order, rank, degree, class, or category; third 1656. b. *Chem.* Applied to the substitution ammonias formed by the replacement of all three hydrogen atoms by an alcohol or acid radical 1857. 2. *Geol.* Forming a third series in point of origin or age. b. In mod. geology, Of or pertaining to the third series of stratified formations: now restricted to the strata from the Eocene to the Pliocene, both inclusive. Also called CAINOZOIC. 1794. 3. *Painting.* Applied to a colour formed by the mixture of two secondary colours 1848. 4. *Path.* Of or belonging to the third or last stage of syphilis 1875. 5. *R. C. Ch.* Of or belonging to the Third Order (i. e. an order of lay members not subject to the strict rule of the regulars, but retaining the secular life) in certain religious fraternities 1891. 6. *Ornith.* Applied to certain feathers of the wing 1858.

1. I venture to assume that you will admit duty as at least a secondary or t. motive RUSKIN.

B. *sb.* 1. *R. C. Ch.* A member of the Third Order of certain religious fraternities 1550. 2. *Geol.* A stratum or formation belonging to the Tertiary system 1851. 3. *Ornith.* (*pl.*) The quill- or flight-feathers that grow upon the humerus in the wing of a bird 1834. 4. *Path.* (*pl.*) Tertiary syphilitic symptoms 1897. 5. *Painting.* A tertiary colour 1854.

‖**Tertium quid** (tɜ̄·ɪʃiɒ̆m kwi·d). 1724. [L., app. rendering Gr. τρίτον τι 'some third thing'.] Something (indefinite or left undefined) related in some way to two (definite or known) things, but distinct from both.

‖**Tertius** (tɜ̄·ɪʃiɒ̆s). 1870. [L.] In some public schools, appended to a surname to designate the youngest (in age or standing) of three boys of that name.

‖**Teru-tero** (te·ru͡ₗte·ro). 1839. [From its noisy cry.] The Cayenne lapwing or spur-winged plover, *Vanellus cayennensis*.

‖**Terza rima** (te·rtsă rī·mă). 1819. [It., = 'third rhyme'.] An Italian form of iambic verse, consisting of sets of three lines, the middle line of each set rhyming with the first and last of the succeeding (*a b a, b c b, c d c*, etc.).

‖**Terzetto** (tertse·tto). *Pl.* **-i** (-ī). 1724. [It.; see TERCET.] *Mus.* A (small) trio, esp. vocal.

Tesla (te·slă). 1902. The name of Nikola *Tesla* (born 1857), American electrician, used attrib. to denote certain apparatus and phenomena.

Tessara- (te·sără), also **tessera-**, a. Gr. τέσσαρα, -ερα, neut. pl. and comb. form of τέσσαρες, -ερες four, as in **Te·ssaraglo·t** *a.*, in, of, or pertaining to four languages.

‖**Tessella** (tese·lă). *Pl.* **-æ**; rarely **-as.** 1693. [L., dim. of TESSERA.] A small tessera.

Tessellate (te·sĕleit), *v.* 1791. [f. ppl. stem of late or med.L. *tessellare*, f. L. *tessella* TESSELLA.] 1. *trans.* To make into a mosaic; to form a mosaic upon, adorn with mosaics; to construct (esp. a pavement) by combining variously coloured blocks so as to form a pattern. 2. To combine so as to form a mosaic; to fit into its place in a mosaic 1838.

1. The floor is tesselated with great elegance 1826.

Tessellated (te·sĕlēitĕd), *ppl. a.* 1695. [f. L. *tessellatus* or It. *tesselato*, with Eng. suffix.] 1. Composed of small blocks of variously coloured material arranged to form a pattern; formed of or ornamented with mosaic work 1712. 2. Combined or arranged so as to form a mosaic 1838. 3. *transf.* Consisting of or arranged in small cubes or squares; in *Bot.* and *Zool.* having colours or surface-divisions in regularly arranged squares or patches; chequered, reticulated 1695. Also **Te·ssellate** *a.* 1826.

1. The t. Pavement at Stansfield 1712. 3. Fruit..a fleshy t. berry 1829. *T. cells*, cells arranged in layers.

Tessellation (tesĕlē¹·ʃən). 1660. [f. TESSELLATE *v.*; see -ATION.] 1. The action or art of tessellating; tessellated condition; *concr.* a piece of tessellated work 1813. 2. An arrangement or close fitting together of minute parts or distinct colours 1660.

Te·ssellite. 1819. [f. TESSELLA + -ITE¹.] *Min.* A variety of apophyllite, exhibiting in polarized light a tessellated structure.

‖**Tessera** (te·sĕră). *Pl.* **-æ** (-ī). 1647. [L., f. Ionic Gr. τέσσερες, -ρα, = Attic τέσσαρες, -ρα FOUR.] 1. *Anc. Hist.* A small quadrilateral tablet of wood, bone, ivory, or the like, used for various purposes, as a token, tally, ticket, label, etc. 1656. b. *fig.* A distinguishing sign or token; a watchword, a password 1647. 2. *spec.* Each of the small square (usu. cubical) pieces of marble, glass, tile, etc. of which a mosaic pavement or the like is composed. Usu. in pl 1797. b. *transf.* Any of the quadrilateral divisions into which a surface is divided by intersecting lines 1873. c. *Zool.* Each of the plates of which the carapace of an armadillo is composed 1909. †**Tessera·ic** *a.* (*rare*) of, pertaining to, or composed of tesseræ; mosaic, tessellated.

Tesseral (te·sĕrăl), *a.* 1846. [f. prec. + -AL.] 1. Of, pertaining to, or resembling a tessera or tesseræ; composed of tesseræ. 2. *Cryst.* = ISOMETRIC 3, CUBIC *a.* 1 b. 1854. 3. *Math* Relating to the tesseræ of a spherical surface 1873.

Tessular (te·siŭlăɪ), *a.* 1796. [f. mod.L. **tessula*, irreg. dim. of TESSERA + -AR.] *Cryst.* = ISOMETRIC 3.

Test (test), *sb.*¹ late ME. [a. OF. *test* pot, mod.F. *têt* cupel, etc.:—L. *testum, testu*, collateral form of *testa* tile, earthen vessel, pot. In mod. use, treated mainly as n. of action from TEST *v.*²] 1. *orig.* The cupel used in treating gold or silver alloys or ore; now *esp.* the cupel, with the iron frame or basket which contains it, forming the movable hearth of a reverberatory furnace. 2. That by which the existence, quality, or genuineness of anything is or may be determined; 'means of trial' (J.) 1594. b. *Cricket.* Short for *t.-match* 1908. 3. That by which beliefs or opinions, esp. in religion, are tested or tried; *spec.* the oaths or declarations prescribed by the TEST ACT of 1673; also, either of the test acts 1665. 4. a. *Chem.* The action or process of examining a substance under known conditions in order to determine its identity or that of one of its constituents; also, a substance by means of which this may be done 1800. b. *Mech.*, etc. The action by which the physical properties of substances, materials, machines, etc. are tested, in order to determine their ability to satisfy particular requirements 1877. 5. *Microscopy.* A test object 1832. 6. An apparatus for determining the flash-point of hydrocarbon oils 1877.

1. Of oure siluer citrinacion..Oure yngottes testes and many mo CHAUCER. 2. Phr. *To bring* or *put to the t.*, *to bear* or *stand the t.*; It is not madnesse That I have vttered; bring me to the Test SHAKS. 3. The belief in tests ought to be as dead as the belief in witches 1906. Phr. *To take the t.*

Comb.: **t. case** (*Law*), a case the decision of which is taken as determining that of a number of others in which the same question of law is involved; **-frame,** the iron frame or basket in which a cupel is placed; **-furnace,** a reverberatory refining furnace in which silver-bearing alloys are treated; **-match** (*Cricket*), one of a series of matches played between representative teams to test the cricketing strength of the countries which they represent; **-meter,** a meter for testing the consumption of gas by burners; **t. object,** (*a*) a minute object used as a t. of the power of a microscope; (*b*) an object upon which a testing experiment is tried; **-paper,** (*a*) a paper impregnated with a chemical solution which changes colour in contact with certain other chemicals, and thus becomes a t. of the presence of the latter; (*b*) *U.S.* a document produced in court in determining a question of handwriting; (*c*) a paper set beforehand to try whether a student is fit and ready for an examination; **-roll,** the roll signed by a member of the House of Lords or Commons after having taken the oath or made the declaration required of him as such; **-type,** letters of graduated sizes used by opticians in testing sight.

Test (test), *sb.*² 1545. [ad. L. *testa*; see prec.] †1. A piece of earthenware, an earthenware vessel; a potsherd -1600. 2. *Zool.* The shell of certain invertebrates 1842.

Test (test), *v.*¹ 1582. [orig. a. OF. *tester* to bequeath, ad. L. *testari*, f. *testis* witness; but in 2 app. from TESTE 2.] 1. *intr.* To make a will. *Obs.* exc. *Sc.* 2. *trans. Eng. Law.* To date and sign the teste of a writ, etc. 1727.

Test (test), *v.*² 1603. [f. TEST *sb.*¹] 1. *trans.* To subject (gold or silver) to a process of separation and refining in a test or cupel; to assay. 2. To subject to a test of any kind; to try, put to the proof 1748. 3. *Chem.* To subject to a chemical test 1839.

2. Experience is the surest standard by which to t. the real tendency of the existing constitution WASHINGTON. They have not the means of testing the statements 1820.

‖**Testa** (te·stă). 1796. [L.] *Bot.* The skin or coating of a seed.

‖**Testacea** (testē¹·ʃiă), *sb. pl.* 1743. [L., neut. pl. of *testaceus* adj. consisting of *testæ*, i. e. tiles, shells, etc.; also, covered with a shell; see -ACEA.] †1. Testaceous substances, as limestone, chalk (*rare*). 2. *Zool.* A name for various groups of invertebrate animals having shells (excluding Crustacea); *spec.* in present use, (*a*) a suborder of pteropod molluscs including all having calcareous shells; (*b*) an order of Protozoa having shells, with apertures through which the pseudopodia are protrusible. 1816.

Testacean (testē¹·ʃiăn), *a.* and *sb.* 1842. [f. prec.; see -ACEAN.] A. *adj.* Of or pertaining to the TESTACEA; shell-bearing: chiefly applied to molluscs 1846. **B.** *sb.* A member of the testacea; a shell-bearing invertebrate, *esp.* a mollusc 1842.

Testaceo- (testē¹·ʃio), comb. form of L. *testaceus*, as in **Testaceo·graphy**, descriptive testaceology; **Testaceo·logy**, the zoology of the testaceous animals.

Testaceous (testē¹·ʃəs), *a.* 1646. [f. L. *testaceus*; see TEST *sb.*² and -ACEOUS.] †**1.** Made of baked clay; pertaining to or of the nature of earthenware or a potsherd (*rare*) –1675. **2.** Having a shell, esp. a hard, calcareous, unarticulated shell 1646. **3.** Of the nature or substance of shells; shelly; consisting of a shell or shelly material 1668. **4.** Of the colour of a tile, a flower-pot, unglazed pottery, etc.; dull red; in *Zool.* and *Bot.* applied to shades of brownish red, brownish yellow, and reddish brown 1688.

Te·st Act. 1708. [See TEST *sb.*¹ 3.] The name given in English History to various acts directed against Roman Catholics and Protestant Nonconformists; particularly, the act of 1673 (25 Chas. II. c. 2) by which the provisions of the Corporation Act of 1661 were extended to include all persons holding office under the Crown, and a declaration against transubstantiation was introduced. It was repealed 9 May, 1828.

Testacy (te·stăsi). 1864. [f. TESTATE *a.*, after INTESTACY.] *Law.* The state of being testate; the condition of leaving a valid will.

Testament (te·stămĕnt), *sb.* ME. [ad. L. *testamentum* will, also (in early Christian Latin) covenant, f. *testari*; see -MENT.] **I.** *Law.* A formal declaration, usu. in writing, of a person's wishes as to the disposal of his property after his death; a will. Formerly, properly applied to a disposition of personal as dist. from real property. Now *rare* (chiefly in phr. *last will and t.*). **b.** *transf.* and *fig.* late ME.

b. The Gospels are Christ's T.; and the Epistles are the Codicils annex'd JER. TAYLOR.

II. In Christian L. use of *testamentum*. **1.** In Holy Scripture, a covenant between God and man. *arch.* ME. **2.** Hence **a.** Each of the two main divisions of the Sacred Scriptures or Bible, the *Old* and the *New T.*, consisting of the books of the old or Mosaic and the new or Christian covenant or dispensation respectively ME. **b.** The New Testament as dist. from the Old; a copy of the New Testament; a volume containing this. Common in *Greek T.* 1500.

2. The coachman could..have taken his oath on the two Testaments DICKENS. **b.** Her little well-worn T. open on her knee 1888. Hence **Te·stament** *v. intr.* to make a will; *trans.* to leave by will, bequeath. **Testame·ntal** *a.* (now *rare*), of, pertaining to, or of the nature of a t.; **-ly** *adv.* by way of a t.

Testamentary (testăme·ntări), *a.* 1456. [ad. L. *testamentarius*, f. *testamentum*; see ARY¹.] **1.** Of, pertaining to, or having relation to a testament or will; of the nature of a will. **2.** Made or done by will; appointed by will 1547. **b.** Expressed or contained in a will 1762. **3.** Of or pertaining to the Old or New Testament 1849.

1. *T. capacity*, capacity to make a will. *T. estate*, estate subject to disposal by will. **2.** T. dispositions of land 1794. **b.** T. directions 1851.

†**Testamenta·tion.** 1765. [f. med.L. *testamentare* to give by testament.] The disposal of one's property by will. BURKE.

‖**Testamur** (testē¹·mɒ̈ɹ). 1840. [f. L. *testamur* 'we testify', as used in the document.] In University use: A certificate from the examiners that a candidate has satisfied them. Also, a certificate generally.

Testate (te·stĕt), *a.* and *sb.* 1475. [ad. L. *testatus*, *testari*.] **A.** *adj.* **1.** That has left a valid will at death. **2.** *transf.* Disposed of or settled by will 1792.

1. Persones dying T. and Intestate 1475. **2.** His succession was partly intestate, partly t. 1875.

B. *sb.* †**1.** A witness; also, testimony –1652. †**2.** = TESTE 2. –1641. **3.** One who at death has left a valid will 1864.

Testate (te·stēⁱt), *v.* *rare.* 1624. [f. L. *testat-*, *testari*; see -ATE ³.] **1.** *intr.* To testify, to attest. **2.** To make one's will 1892.

Testation (testē¹·ʃən). 1642. [ad. L. *testationem*; see TESTATE *a.*] †**1.** Attestation, testimony –1656. **2.** The disposal of property by will 1832.

Testator (testē¹·tɒ̈ɹ). 1447. [In sense 1, a. AF. *testatour*, ad. late L. *testatorem*. In 2, direct from L.] **1.** One who makes a will; one who has died leaving a will. †**2.** A witness –1698.

Testatrix (testē¹·triks). 1591. Pl. **-trixes** (triksēz), **-trices** (trisīz). [a. late L., fem. of *testator*.] A female testator.

‖**Testatum** (testē¹·tɒ̈m). 1607. [L., neut. pa. pple. of *testari* (*-are*) to attest, etc.] *Law.* †**1.** A writ formerly issued when a writ of capias was returned, the sheriff to whom it was first addressed testifying that the defendant was not to be found within his jurisdiction –1848. **2.** The witnessing-clause of a deed 1844.

Teste (te·stī). late ME. [a. L., abl. of *testis* witness.] **1.** The L. word *teste* in abl. absol. constr. with a pronoun (e.g. *meipso* myself) or name of a person, as used in the authenticating clause of a writ, etc.: hence, in non-legal use, = (So-and-so) being witness, on the authority or evidence of (So-and-so); also as *sb.* 1654. **2.** The final clause in a royal writ naming the person who authorizes the affixing of the king's seal. late ME. †**b.** Hence, more gen., a clause stating the name of a witness (as to a charter in writ-form) –1617.

1. Many..commanders 'Swore terribly (*t.* T. Shandy) in Flanders' BARHAM.

Tester¹ (te·stəɹ). late ME. [prob. from OF.; cf. *testre*, *testière*.] **1.** A canopy over a bed, supported on the posts of the bedstead or suspended from the ceiling; formerly also, a t.-bed's headboard and its fittings. **2.** *transf.* and *fig.* Something that overhangs; a shrine; a canopy carried over a dignitary; the sounding-board of a pulpit, etc. late ME. **3.** *attrib.*, as *t.-bed* 1622.

1. A bedstead gilt, with a testor and counterpoint, with curtains belonging to the same 1548. **2.** A night under the starry t. of the heavens 1830.

†**Te·ster².** Also ‖**testiere.** late ME. [a. OF. *testière*, f. OF. *teste* head.] A piece of armour for the head; a head-piece, a casque; also, a piece of armour for the head of a horse –1484.

Tester³ (te·stəɹ). *arch.* 1546 [app. the result of a series of corruptions or perversions of TESTON.] A name for the TESTON of Henry VIII, esp. as debased and depreciated; later a colloq. or slang term for a sixpence.

Tester⁴ (te·stəɹ). 1661. [f. TEST *v.*² or *sb.*¹; see -ER ¹.] One who tests or proves; a device for testing.

‖**Testicardines** (testikā·ɹdinīz), *sb. pl.* 1878. [mod.L., f. *testa* shell + *cardo*, *cardin-* hinge. *Zool.* A primary division of brachiopods having hinged shells; opp. to *Ecardines*. Hence **Testica·rdinate** *a.* having a hinged shell.

Testicle (te·stik'l). late ME. [ad. L. *testiculus*, dim. f. *testis* TESTIS ²; see -CULE.] Each of the two ellipsoid glandular bodies constituting the sperm-secreting organs in male mammals and usu. enclosed in a scrotum. **b.** Rarely applied to the corresponding organs in non-mammals 1713. †**c.** *transf.* The ovary in females –1691.

Testicular (testi·kiŭlăɹ), *a.* 1656. [f. L. *testiculus* TESTICLE; see -AR ¹.] **1.** Of or pertaining to, containing, or having the nature or function of a testicle or testicles. **2.** Resembling a testicle in form; testiculate 1769.

Testiculate (testi·kiŭlĕt), *a.* 1760. [ad. late L. *testiculatus*; see TESTICLE and -ATE ².] Formed like a testicle; also, applied to the twin tubers of certain species of Orchis. So **Testi·culated** *a.* 1725.

Testification (te:stifikē¹·ʃən). Now *rare.* 1450. [a. obs. F. *testificacion*, or ad. L. *testificationem*.] The action or an act of testifying; the testimony borne; a fact or object (as a document, etc.) serving as evidence or proof.

Testificator (te·stifikē¹tɔɹ). *rare.* 1730. [f. L. *testificari*; see -OR.] One who testifies or attests. So **Testifica·tory** *a.* of such a kind as to testify, or serve as evidence 1593.

Testifier (te·stifəi,əɹ). 1611. [f. TESTIFY *v.* + -ER ¹.] One who testifies; a witness.

Testify (te·stifəi), *v.* late ME. [ad. late or med.L. *testificare*, cl. L. *testificari* to bear witness, f. *testis* witness + *-ficus* making; see -FY.] **1.** *trans.* To bear witness to, or give proof of (a fact); to assert the truth of (a statement); to attest. Also *intr.* (usu. with *of*) and *absol.* **2.** *transf.* of things: **a.** *trans.* To serve as evidence of; to constitute proof or testimony of 1445. **b.** *intr.* and *absol.* 1596. **3.** *trans.* To profess belief in; to proclaim as something that one knows or believes. Chiefly *biblical.* 1526. **b.** *intr.* To bear testimony 1784. **4.** *intr.* and *trans.* = PROTEST *v.* 1. *Obs.* exc. in biblical use. 1526. **5.** *trans.* To give evidence of, display (desire, emotion, etc.). *Obs.* or *arch.* 1560.

1. We speake that we knowe, and t. that we have sene TINDALE *John* iii. 11. Those which take in hand to testifie of any matter whatsoever 1579. **2.** The brickes are aliue at this day to testifie it SHAKS. **3.** I testifie my sauioure openly COVERDALE 2 *Esdras* ii. 36. **4.** At length a Reverend Sire among them came..And testifi'd against thir wayes MILT. **5.** He was the only person..who testified any real concern FIELDING.

Testimonial (testimōu·niăl), *a.* and *sb.* late ME. [a. OF., ad. late L. *testimonialis*; f. L. *testimonium* TESTIMONY; see -AL.] **A.** *adj.* (now *arch.* or *techn.*) Of, pertaining to, or of the nature of testimony; serving as evidence; conducive to proof.

T. proof, proof by the testimony of a witness; parole evidence. †**Letter t.**, rarely **t. letter** (usu. pl. *letters testimonial(s)*, a letter testifying to the bona fides of the bearer; credentials.

B. *sb.* †**1.** = TESTIMONY *sb.* 1. –1707. †**2.** Something serving as proof or evidence; a token, record, manifestation –1803. †**3.** An affidavit, acknowledgement; a certificate; *spec.* an official warrant; a passport (as given to vagrants, labourers, discharged soldiers or sailors, etc.); a diploma; a credential or other authenticating document –1806. **4.** A writing testifying to one's qualifications and character, written usu. by a present or former employer, or by some responsible person who is competent to judge; a letter of recommendation of a person or thing 1571. **5.** A gift presented to some one by a number of persons as an expression of appreciation or acknowledgement of services or merit, or of admiration or respect 1838.

Testimonialize (testimōu·niăləiz), *v.* 1852. [f. prec. + -IZE.] *trans.* To furnish with a letter of recommendation; also, to present with a public testimonial.

‖**Testimonium** (testimōu·niɒ̈m). 1692. [L., f. *testis* a witness + *-monium*; see -MONY.] **1.** A letter of recommendation given to a candidate for holy orders testifying to his piety and learning; also = TESTAMUR. **2.** *Law.* That concluding part of a document, usu. commencing 'In witness whereof', which states the manner of its execution; also *t. clause* 1852.

Testimony (te·stiməni), *sb.* late ME. [ad. L. *testimonium*; see prec.] **1.** Personal or documentary evidence or attestation in support of a fact or statement; hence, any form of evidence or proof. **b.** Any object serving as proof or evidence 1597. †**2.** A written certificate, a testimonial –1657. **3.** In Scriptural language (chiefly in O.T.). **a.** *sing.* The Mosaic law or decalogue as inscribed on the two tables of stone. late ME. **b.** *pl.* The precepts (of God), the divine law 1535. **4.** Open attestation or acknowledgement; confession, profession. *Obs.* or *arch.* 1550. **b.** *spec.* An expression or declaration of disapproval or condemnation of error; a protestation 1582.

1. Where a mans T. is not to be credited, he is not bound to give it HOBBES. **3. a.** *The two tables of t.* (Ex. xxxi. 18); *Ark of (the) T.* = *Ark of the Covenant*, the chest containing the tables of the law and other sacred memorials; *tabernacle* or *tent of (the) t.*, the tabernacle containing the ark with its contents. **b.** So shall I kepe the testimonies of thy mouth COVERDALE *Ps.* cxviii. [cxix.] 88. **4.** Thou..for the testimonie of Truth hast born Universal reproach MILT. **b.** Shake of the dust from your feete for a testimonie to them N.T. (Rhem.) *Mark* vi. 11.

†**Te·stimony,** *v.* [ME. ad. ONF. *testimoiner*, ad. med.L. *testimoniare*, f. *testimonium*; later, f. prec.] **1.** *trans.* and *intr.* To bear witness, testify (to) –1642. **2.** *trans.* To test or prove by evidence. SHAKS.

†‖**Te·stis¹.** *Pl.* **testes** (te·stīz). 1483. The L. word for 'witness': from its legal use (cf. TESTE), occasional in Eng. context –1611.

‖ **Testis** [2] (te·stis). Chiefly in pl. **testes** (te·stīz). 1681. [L.; etym. uncertain.] *Anat.* 1. = TESTICLE 1704. †b. *transf.* The ovary in females -1841. 2. *transf. pl.* The posterior pair of the optic lobes or *corpora quadrigemina*, at the base of the brain in mammals 1681.

Teston, testoon (te·stən, testū·n). *Obs.* exc. *Hist.* 1543. [a. obs. F., = obs. It. *testone*, augm. of *testa* head; see -OON.] 1. *orig.* The French name of a silver coin first struck at Milan by Galeazzo Maria Sforza (1468–76), bearing a portrait or head of the duke. Applied later to equivalent silver coins without a portrait, both in Italy and France. 1545. 2. In England, a name first applied to the shilling of Henry VII, the first English coin bearing a true portrait; also to like coins of Henry VIII, and early pieces of Edward VI. It sank in value from 12 pence to 6*d.* and even lower, being of debased metal. 1543. †b. = TESTER [3] -1598. 3. The Portuguese silver *testão* or *tostão*; now = 100 reis, and worth about 2½*d.* 1598.

†**Te·stril.** [A dim. alteration of TESTER [3].] A sixpence. SHAKS.

Te·st-tube. 1846. [f. TEST *sb.*[1] + TUBE.] A cylinder of thin transparent glass closed at one end, used to hold liquids under test. Also *attrib.* as *t. culture.*

Testudinarious (testiūdineᵊ·riəs), *a.* 1826. [f. L. *testudo, testudinem* + -ARIOUS.] Having the character of a tortoise; marked or coloured like tortoise-shell.

Testudinate (testiū·dinět), *a.* (*sb.*) 1847. [ad. late L. *testudinatus*, f. as prec.; see -ATE [2] 2.] 1. Formed like a testudo; arched, vaulted. 2. Of or pertaining to tortoises 1850. B. *sb.* A tortoise 1880. So **Testu·dinated** *ppl. a.* = 1.

Testudineous (testiudi·niəs), *a.* 1652. [f. L. *testudineus*, f. TESTUDO; see -EOUS.] 1. Resembling the shell of a tortoise, or a testudo 1656. 2. Slow, dilatory, like the pace of a tortoise 1652.

Testudo (testiū·do). late ME. [a. L. *testudo* tortoise, etc., f. *testa* a pot, shell, etc.] 1. *Path.* = TALPA 2. 2. *Zool.* The typical genus of the tortoise family, *Testudinidæ*; a member of this genus 1520. 3. *Rom. Antiq.* a. An engine of war used by besiegers, consisting of a screen or shelter with a strong arched roof, moved on wheels up to the walls, which could then be attacked in safety 1609. b. A shelter formed by a body of troops locking their shields together above their heads 1680. 4. *Anc. Mus.* A lyre, said to have been made by Mercury of the shell of a tortoise 1702.

Testy (te·sti), *a.* late ME. [a. AF. *testif, -ive*, f. *teste* head; see -IVE.] †1. Of headstrong courage; impetuous; precipitate, rash; in later use, aggressive, contentious -1658. 2. Prone to be irritated by small checks and annoyances; resentful of contradiction or opposition; irascible, short-tempered, peevish, tetchy, 'crusty' 1526. b. Of words, actions, personal qualities, etc. 1538.

2. A chollericke and testie Consull HOLLAND. b. Must I stand and crouch Vnder your Testie Humour? SHAKS. Hence **Te·stily** *adv.* **Te·stiness.**

Tetanic (tītæ·nik), *a.* (*sb.*) 1727. [ad. L. *tetanicus*, a. Gr. τετανικός.] Of, pertaining to, or of the nature of tetanus; characterized by tetanus. Hence **Teta·nically** *adv.* by, or as by, tetanus.

Tetanine (te·tănin). 1857. [f. TETANUS + -INE [5].] †a. Strychnine. b. A ptomaine, $C_{13}H_{30}N_2O_4$, obtained from meat extract containing Rosenbach's microbe, the tetanus bacillus; occurring also in decaying corpses.

Tetanize (te·tănəiz), *v.* 1849. [f. TETANUS + -IZE.] *trans.* To produce tetanus or tetanic spasms in. Hence **Tetaniza·tion**, the production of tetanus or tetanic contraction in a muscle.

Tetano- (tetăno), comb. form of Gr. τέτανος TETANUS, as in **Tetano·lysin** [Gr. λύσις a loosening], a toxin produced by the tetanus bacillus; **Tetanomo·tor**, an instrument for producing muscular tetanus.

Tetanoid (te·tănoid), *a.* (*sb.*) 1856. [f. next + -OID.] Of the nature of, or resembling tetanus. B. *sb.* A tetanoid spasm or attack.

‖ **Tetanus** (te·tănŏs). late ME. [L., a. Gr. τέτανος muscular spasm, f. τείνειν to stretch.] 1. A disease characterized by tonic spasm and rigidity of some or all of the voluntary muscles, usu. occasioned by a wound or other injury. (Cf. LOCKJAW.) 2. *Physiol.* A condition of prolonged contraction produced by rapidly repeated stimuli 1877.

Tetany (te·tăni). 1890. [ad. F. *tétanie* intermittent tetanus, f. prec.] A tetanoid affection characterized by intermittent muscular spasms.

Tetarto- (tĭtā·ɹto), comb. form of Gr. τέταρτος fourth (cf. TETRA-), in terms belonging chiefly to crystallography; as **Teta:rtohe·dral** [Gr. ἕδρα base] *a.*, having one fourth of the number of faces required by the highest or holohedral degree of symmetry belonging to its system; hence **Teta:rtohe·drally** *adv.*, in a tetartohedral manner. **Teta:rtohe·drism**, the property or quality of crystallizing in tetartohedral forms.

Tetch (tetʃ). Now *dial.* 1642. [Origin obsc.] A fit of petulance or anger; a tantrum.

Tetchy, techy (te·tʃi), *a.* 1592. [Origin uncertain.] Easily irritated or made angry; quick to take offence; short-tempered; peevish, irritable; testy. b. Of qualities, actions, etc.: Characterized by or proceeding from irritability 1592. Hence **Te·tchily** *adv.* **Te·tchiness.**

‖ **Tête** (tēˈt, F. tęt). *Obs.* exc. *Hist.* 1756. [F.] A woman's head of hair, or wig, dressed high and elaborately ornamented, in the fashion of the second half of the 18th c.

‖ **Tête-à-tête** (tēˈ·tātēˈ·t, F. tętatęt), *adv.*, *sb.*, and *a.* 1697. [F., lit. 'head to head'.] A. *adv.* Together without the presence of a third person; in private; face to face 1700.

The General and I..moping together *t.* THACKERAY.

B. *sb.* (pl. *tête-à-têtes.*) 1. A private conversation or interview between two persons; also *concr.* a party of two 1697. 2. A form of sofa, of such a shape as to enable two persons to converse more or less face to face 1864. C. *adj.* (the sb. used *attrib.*) Pertaining to a *tête-à-tête*; consisting of or attended by two persons 1728.

A pretty cheerful *tête-à-tête* dinner 1728.

‖ **Tête-bêche** (tęt bęʃ). 1882. [Fr., f. *tête* head + *bêche*, reduced from *bechevet* lit. double bed-head.] *Philately.* A term used to describe the printing of postage or other stamps upside down or sideways with reference to one another.

Tether (te·ðəɹ), *sb.* late ME. [orig. a northern word; app. a. ON. *tjóðr* tether.] 1. A rope, cord, or other fastening by which a horse, goat, or other beast is tied to a stake or the like, so as to confine it to the spot. 2. *fig.* The cause or measure of one's limitation; the radius of one's field of action; scope, limit 1579. b. A bond or fetter 1609.

2. We soon find the shortness of our t. POPE. Phr. *The end* (*length*) *of one's t.*, the extreme limit of one's resources, endurance, etc. b. When weary of the matrimonial t. BYRON.

Tether (te·ðəɹ), *v.* 1470. [f. prec.] 1. *trans.* To make fast or confine with a tether 1483. 2. To fasten, make fast generally 1563. 3. *fig.* To fasten or bind by conditions or circumstances; to bind so as to detain 1470.

1. The lamb..by a slender cord was tethered to a stone WORDSW. 3. All my life tethered to the law 1879.

Tetra- (tetră), bef. a vowel **tetr-**, a. Gr. τετρα-, comb. form of τέτταρες, τέτταρα four.

1. *gen.* **Te·trabrach** (-bræk) [Gr. τετράβραχυς], *Anc. Pros.* a word or foot of four short syllables, as *facinora*; as a foot usu. called *proceleusmatic.* **Te·traca·rpellary** *a.*, *Bot.* of a compound fruit: having four carpels. **Tetracho·motous** *a.*, *Zool.* and *Bot.* ramifying into four branches or divisions; doubly dichotomous. **Tetracoccous** (-kǫ·kəs) [Gr. κόκκος berry] *a.*, *Bot.* having four cocci or carpels; also, applied to bacteria when in four segments. ‖ **Tetraco·lon**, *Gr. Pros.* a metrical period consisting of four cola or members. **Tetraco·ral**, one of the *Tetracoralla*, a division of corals (= *Rugosa*) in which the septa are in multiples of four. **Tetrada·ctyl(e** *a.*, having four fingers or toes; *sb.*, a four-toed animal, esp. a vertebrate. **Tetrade·capod** *a.*, having fourteen feet; belonging to the *Tetradecapoda*, an order of Crustaceans; *sb.*, a crustacean of this order. **Te·traglot** *a.*, speaking four languages; written or composed in four languages. **Tetrahexahe·dron**, *Geom.* a solid figure contained by twenty-four planes. **Tetrale·mma**, *Logic* a position presenting four alternatives. **Tetrano·mial** *a.*, *Math.* consisting of four (algebraic) terms; quadrinomial. **Tetrape·talous** *a.*, having four petals. **Tetraphy·llous** [Gr. φύλλον leaf] *a.*, *Bot.* having or consisting of four leaves; abbrev. *4-phyllous.* **Tetrapneumo·nian** *a.*, *Zool.* of or pertaining to the *Tetrapneumones*, a division of spiders with two pairs of lung-sacs; *sb.*, a spider of this division. **Tetrapneu·monous** *a.*, *Zool.* having four lungs or respiratory organs; applied to the *Tetrapneumones* (see prec.) and to the *Tetrapneumona*, a group of holothurians (sea-cucumbers). ‖ **Te·tra·polis**, a district of four cities; a state or political division consisting of four towns. **Te·traptote** [Gr. τετράπτωτος], *Gram.* a noun with (only) four cases. **Te·trarch** *a.*, *Bot.* proceeding from four distinct points of origin. **Tetrase·palous** *a.*, *Bot.* having four sepals. **Tetraspe·rmous** [Gr. σπέρμα seed] *a.*, *Bot.* having four seeds, or seeds in fours. **Tetrathe·cal** [Gr. θήκη case, cell] *a.*, *Bot.* four-celled, as an ovary. **Tetra·xial** *a.*, having four axes, as some sponge-spicules; so **Tetra·xile** *a.* in same sense.

2. *Chem.* In the names of compounds and derivatives with the general sense of 'four-', 'four times'. a. In sbs.: (*a*) Prefixed to names of binary compounds of elements or radicals, names of salts, etc., to signify four atoms, groups, or equivalents of the element or radical in question; as *tetrachlo·ride*, a compound of four atoms of chlorine with some other element or radical; so *tetrasu·lphide*, TETROXIDE, etc. (*b*) Prefixed to names of elements or radicals (or the combining forms, as *bromo-*, *nitro-*, etc.) entering into the name of a compound, to signify that four atoms or groups of the element or radical are substituted in the substance designated by the rest of the name, as *te:trabromobe·nzene*, $C_6H_2Br_4$, in which four of the hydrogen atoms of benzene, C_6H_6, are replaced by four bromine atoms. (*c*) In some words used irregularly, as *te:trasa·licylide* $C_{28}H_{18}O_9$. b. Prefixed to adjs., in the names of acids, alcohols, aldehydes, ethers, salts, etc.; as *tetraso·dic*, containing four sodium atoms. c. In vbs. and their pples. derived from sbs. as in a., as *tetrahy·drated* (containing 4 molecules of water), etc.

Tetrabasic (tetrăbēˈ·sik), *a.* 1863. [f. TETRA- + BASIC.] *Chem.* Of an acid: Containing four atoms of hydrogen replaceable by more electropositive elements or radicals. Of a salt: Derived from such an acid.

Tetrabranchiate (tetrăbræ·ŋkiět), *a.* and *sb.* 1835. [ad. mod.L. *tetrabranchiatum*, f. TETRA- + Gr. βράγχια gills + -ATE [2] 2.] *Zool.* A. *adj.* Belonging to the *Tetrabranchiata*, an order of cephalopods (mostly extinct) having four branchiæ or gills. B. *sb.* A cephalopod belonging to this order. So **Te·trabranch** *sb.* and *a.*

Tetrachord (te·trăkǭɹd). 1603. [ad. Gr. τετράχορδον (*sc.* ὄργανον), a Greek musical instrument, f. τετρα- TETRA- + χορδή string.] 1. An ancient musical instrument with four strings. 2. *Mus.* A scale-series of four notes, being the half of an octave. †b. The interval between the first and last notes of this series; a perfect fourth. 1603. Hence **Tetracho·rdal** *a.*

‖ **Tetractys** (tĭtræ·ktis). 1603. [a. Gr. τετρακτύς.] A set of four; the number four; *esp.* the Pythagorean name for the sum of the first four numbers (1 + 2 + 3 + 4 = 10) regarded as the source of all things.

Tetrad (te·træd). 1653. [ad. Gr. τετράς, τετραδ- a group of four, the number four.] 1. A sum, group, or set of four; four (things, etc.) regarded as a single object of thought. 2. a. *Chem.* An element, compound, or radical having a combining power of four units, i.e. of four atoms of hydrogen; a tetravalent element, etc. 1865. b. *Biol.* (*a*) A group of four cells, e.g. spores, pollen-grains. (*b*) A group of four chromosomes formed by the division of a single chromosome. (*c*) A quaternary unit of organization differentiated from a triad. 1876.

Te·tradeca:ne. 1877. [f. Gr. τετρα- four + δέκα ten + -ANE 2 b.] *Chem.* The saturated hydrocarbon or paraffin of the 14-carbon series, $C_{14}H_{30}$, = tetradecyl hydride; a waxy solid.

Tetradic (tĭtræ·dik), *a.* 1788. [f. TETRAD + -IC.] Of, pertaining to, or of the nature of a tetrad. b. *Chem.* That is a tetrad; tetravalent 1868. c. *Anc. Pros.* (*a*) Containing four different metres or rhythms. (*b*) Composed of groups of systems, each of which contains four unlike systems. 1891.

Tetradite (te·trădəit). 1727. [ad. late Gr. τετραδίτης, pl. -αι, f. τετράς, -αδ- TETRAD; see -ITE 1.] *pl.* The Manichees and others, who believed the Godhead to consist of four persons.

Tetradrachm (te·trădræm). 1579. [ad. Gr. τετράδραχμον; see TETRA- and DRACHM.] *Gr. Antiq.* A silver coin of ancient Greece, of the value of four drachms; see DRACHM 1. Hence **Tetradrachmal** (-dræ·kmăl) *a.* of or pertaining to a t.

Tetradymite (tĭtræ·dimait). 1850. [a. G. *tetradymit*, f. Gr. τετράδυμος fourfold + -ITE [1].] *Min.* Telluride of bismuth, found in pale steel-grey laminæ with a bright metallic lustre.

‖ **Tetradynamia** (te:trădinæ·miă, -dəi-). 1760. [mod.L., f. Gr. τετρα- TETRA- + δύναμις power, strength + -IA [1]; cf. DIDYNAMIA.] *Bot.* The fifteenth class in the Linnæan Sexual System comprising plants which bear hermaphrodite flowers with six stamens in pairs, four of which are longer than the others; corresponding to the family *Cruciferæ*. Hence **Tetradyna·mian** *a.* tetradynamous; *sb.* a plant of the class *Tetradynamia*. **Tetrady·namous** *a.* of or pertaining to this class; having four longer and two shorter stamens.

Tetragon (te·trăgǫn). 1626. [ad. Gr. τετράγωνον quadrangle; see TETRA- and -GON.] 1. *Geom.* A figure having four angles and four sides; a quadrangle considered as one of the polygons. *Regular t.*, a square. 1630. 2. A square fort; a quadrangular building or block of buildings 1669. 3. *Astrol.* The aspect of two planets when they are 90° distant from one another relatively to the earth; the square or quadrate aspect 1626.

Tetragonal (tĭtræ·gŏnăl), *a.* 1571. [f. prec. + -AL 1.] 1. Of or pertaining to a tetragon; having four angles; quadrangular. 2. *Bot.* and *Zool.* Quadrangular in section, like a 'square' rod; tetraquetrous 1753. 3. *Cryst.* Applied to a system of crystallization in which the three axes are at right angles, the two lateral axes being equal, and the vertical of a different length 1868. Hence **Tetra·gonal-ly** *adv.*, -ness.

Tetragonous (tĭtræ·gŏnəs), *a.* 1760. [f. as prec. + -OUS.] *Bot.* = prec. 2.

Tetragram (te·trăgræm). 1870. [ad. Gr. τὸ τετράγραμμον, the (word) of four letters, f. τετρα- TETRA- + γράμμα letter.] = next.

‖ **Tetragrammaton** (tetrăgræ·mătǫn). *Pl.* -ata. late ME. [a. Gr. (τὸ) τετραγράμματον the (word) of four letters, neut. of τετραγράμματος, adj. f. τετρα- TETRA- + γραμματ- letter.] A word of four letters; *spec.* the Hebrew word YHWH or JHVH (vocalized as YAHWEH, JAHVEH or JEHOVAH); often substituted for that word (regarded as ineffable), and treated as a mysterious symbol of the name of God; occas. used as a title of the Deity. b. *gen.* with *a* and *pl.* A word of four letters used as a symbol 1656.

‖ **Tetragynia** (tetrădʒi·niă), *a.* 1760. [mod. L., f. TETRA- + Gr. γυνή, taken in sense 'female organ, pistil'.] *Bot.* An order or division in many of the Linnæan classes of plants, comprising those having four pistils. Hence **Tetra·gy·nian, -ious, Tetra·gynous** *adjs.* belonging to this order of any class; having four pistils.

Tetrahedral (tetrăhī·drăl, -he·drăl), *a.* 1794. [f. late Gr. τετράεδρος (see TETRAHEDRON) + -AL.] 1. Having four sides (in addition to the base or ends); enclosed or contained laterally by four plane surfaces. 2. Of, pertaining to, or having the form of a tetrahedron; *spec.* in *Cryst.*, belonging to a division of the isometric system of which the regular tetrahedron is the characteristic form 1805.

1. *T. quoin, angle*, one bounded by four planes meeting at a common apex. So **Tetrahe·drally** *adv.* **Tetrahe·dric, -al** *adjs.* **Tetrahe·droid** *a.* resembling a tetrahedron.

Tetrahedrite (tetrăhī·drəit, -he·drəit). 1868. [ad. G. *tetraëdrit*, f. as prec. + -ITE [1].] *Min.* Native sulphide of antimony and copper, with various elements sometimes replacing one or other of these, often occurring in tetrahedral crystals.

Tetrahedron (tetrăhī·drǫn, -he·drǫn). *Pl.* -a or -ons. 1570. [ad. late Gr. τετράεδρον sb., prop. neut. of τετράεδρος four-sided, f. τετρα- four + ἕδρα base.] *Geom.* A solid figure contained by four plane triangular faces, a triangular pyramid; *spec.* the *regular t.*, the first of the five regular solids, contained by four equilateral triangles. Hence, any solid body, esp. a crystal, of this form.

Tetra-icosane (tetrăˌəi·kosēin). 1894. [f. Gr. τετρα- four + εἴκοσι twenty + -ANE 2 b.] *Chem.* The saturated hydrocarbon or paraffin of the 24-carbon series, $C_{24}H_{50} = CH_3(CH_2)_{22}CH_3$, a solid waxy substance.

Te:trakis-hexahe·dron. 1878. [f. Gr. τετράκις four times + HEXAHEDRON.] A solid figure contained by twenty-four equal triangular planes, having the appearance of a cube with a low pyramid raised on each of its six faces. (In *Cryst.* belonging to the isometric system.)

Tetralogy (tĭtræ·lŏdʒi). 1656. [ad. Gr. τετραλογία, f. *tetra-* TETRA- + -λογία -LOGY.] 1. *Gr. Antiq.* A series of four dramas, three tragic (the *trilogy*) and one satyric, exhibited at Athens at the festival of Dionysus. b. Hence, any series of four related dramatic or literary compositions 1742. 2. A set of four speeches 1661. Hence **Tetralo·gic** *a.*

Tetramerous (tĭtræ·mĕrəs), *a.* 1826. [f. mod.L. *tetramerus* (ad. Gr. τετραμερής four-parted) + -OUS.] Having, consisting of, or characterized by four parts. *spec.* a. *Bot.* Having the parts of the flower-whorl in series of four. (Often written *4-merous.*) b. *Ent.* Having the tarsi four-jointed, as the *Tetramera* among *Coleoptera*. c. Having four rays, as a star-fish. So **Tetra·meral** *a.* having parts in fours. **Tetra·merism**, t. condition.

Tetrameter (tĭtræ·mĭtəɹ). 1612. [ad. L. *tetrametrus*, a. Gr. τετράμετρος, f. τετρα- TETRA- + μέτρον measure.] *Pros.* A verse or period consisting of four measures. Also *attrib.* or as *adj.*

Tetramorph (te·trămǭɹf). 1848. [ad. Gr. τετράμορφον, prop. neut. adj. four-shaped, f. τετρα- four + μορφή form.] *Christian Art.* A composite figure combining the symbols of the four evangelists (derived from Rev. iv. 6–8 and Ezek. i. 5–10).

Tetramorphic (tetrămǭ·ɹfik), *a.* 1870. [f. as prec. + -IC.] a. *Nat. Hist.* Occurring in four different forms. b. Of or pertaining to a tetramorph.

‖ **Tetrandria** (tetræ·ndriă). 1760. [mod.L. (Linn.), f. Gr. τετρα- TETRA- + ἀνδρ-, stem of ἀνήρ man, male.] *Bot.* The fourth class in the Linnæan Sexual System comprising plants bearing hermaphrodite flowers with four equal stamens. Also an order in the classes Gynandria, Monœcia, and Diœcia, having four stamens. Hence **Tetra·ndrian** *a.* having four stamens. **Tetra·ndrious, Tetra·ndrous**, *adjs.* having four equal stamens; belonging to the class *T.*

Tetraonid (tĭtrē·onid), *a.* (*sb.*) 1847. [f. mod.L. *Tetraonidæ*, f. L. *tetrao* (*-onem*), a. Gr. τετράων, applied to the Black Grouse, etc.; see -ID [3].] *Ornith.* Pertaining to the family *Tetraonidæ* of gallinaceous birds, including the grouse and allied forms; also as *sb.* a member of this family. (The term has also been used more widely to include the partridges, quails, and other birds.)

‖ **Tetrapla** (te·trăplă). 1684. [a. Gr. τετραπλᾶ, neut. pl. of τετραπλοῦς fourfold, f. τετρα- TETRA- + -πλοος -fold.] A text consisting of four parallel versions, esp. that of the Old Testament made by Origen.

Tetrapod (te·trăpǫd), *a.* and *sb.* 1826. [ad. mod.L. *tetrapodus*, ad. Gr. τετράπους, τετραποδ- four-footed, f. τετρα- + πούς (ποδ-).] A. *adj.* Having four feet or four limbs; *spec.* in *Ent.*, belonging to the *Tetrapoda*, a division of butterflies having only four perfect legs, the anterior pair being unfitted for walking. B. *sb.* A four-footed animal; one of the *Tetrapoda*.

Tetrapody (tĭtræ·pŏdi). 1846. [ad. Gr. τετραποδία, f. τετραποδ-; see prec.] *Pros.* A group of four metrical feet; a verse of four feet. So **Tetrapo·dic** *a.*

Tetrapterous (tĭtræ·ptĕrəs), *a.* 1826. [f. mod.L. *tetrapterus* (a. Gr. τετράπτερος four-winged) + -OUS.] Having four wings; *spec.* in *Ent.* applied to four-winged flies; in *Bot.* having four wing-like appendages, as certain fruits. So **Tetra·pteran** *a.* tetrapterous; *sb.* a four-winged insect.

Tetrarch (te·t-, tī·traɹk). late ME. [ad. late L. *tetrarcha*, cl. L. *tetrarches*, a. Gr. τετράρχης, f. τετρα- four- TETRA- + -αρχης ruling, ruler.] 1. *Rom. Hist.* The ruler of one of four divisions of a country or province; applied later to subordinate rulers generally, esp. in Syria. 2. *transf.* and *fig.* a. A ruler of a fourth part, or of one of four parts, divisions, elements, etc.; also, a subordinate ruler generally 1610. b. One of four joint rulers or directors 1661. Hence **Te·trarchate**, the office or position of a t.

Tetrarchic (tĭtrā·ɹkik), *a.* 1818. [ad. Gr. τετραρχικός of a tetrarch; see -IC.] Of or pertaining to four rulers; pertaining to a tetrarch or to a tetrarchy. So **Tetra·rchical** *a.* (now *rare*) 1638.

Tetrarchy (te·traɹki). late ME. [ad. L. *tetrarchia*, a. Gr. τετραρχία, f. τετράρχης TETRARCH *sb.*] 1. The district, division, or part of a country or province ruled by a tetrarch; the government or jurisdiction of a tetrarch. 2. *transf.* and *fig.* A government by four persons jointly; a set of four tetrarchs or rulers; a country divided into four petty governments.

Tetraspore (te·trăˌspōəɹ). 1857. [f. TETRA- + SPORE.] *Bot.* A group (usu.) of four asexual spores, resulting from the division of a mother cell, in the *Florideæ*, a group of *Algæ*. Hence **Tetrasporic** (-spǫ·rik), **Tetrasporous** (tetrăˌspō·rəs, tĭtræ·spŏrəs) *adjs.* composed of or producing tetraspores.

Tetrastich (te·trăstik, tetræ·stik). 1580. [ad. L. *tetrastichon* (also used), a. Gr. τετράστιχον, neut. of τετράστιχος containing four rows, f. τετρα- TETRA- + στίχος row, line of verse.] *Pros.* A stanza of four lines.

Tetrastyle (te·trăstəil), *sb.* and *a.* 1704. [ad. L. *tetrastylos* adj., *tetrastylon* sb., a. Gr. τετράστυλος (neut. -ον) with four pillars, f. τετρα- TETRA- + στῦλος pillar.] *Arch.* A. *sb.* A structure having four pillars or columns; a group of four pillars. B. *adj.* Having or consisting of four columns 1837. Hence **Tetrastylic** (-sti·lik) *a.* = B.

Tetrasyllable (tetrăsi·lăb'l), *sb.* (*a.*) 1589. [f. TETRA- + SYLLABLE.] A. *sb.* A word of four syllables. B. *adj.* Tetrasyllabic. So **Tetrasylla·bic, -al** *adjs.* consisting of four syllables.

Tetrathionic (tetrăˌþəiˌǫ·nik), *a.* 1848. [f. TETRA- + Gr. θεῖον sulphur + -IC.] *Chem.* In *t. acid*, $H_2S_4O_6$, a colourless, inodorous, very acid liquid containing four atoms of sulphur in the molecule. Hence **Tetrathi·onate**, a salt of t. acid.

Tetratomic (tetrătǫ·mik), *a.* 1862. [f. TETR(A)- + ATOMIC.] *Chem.* Containing four atoms in the molecule.

Tetravalent (tĭtræ·vălĕnt, tetrăvē·lĕnt), *a.* 1868. [f. Gr. τετρα- TETRA- + L. *valentem*, *valere* to be worth.] *Chem.* Combining with four atoms of hydrogen or other monovalent element, or with four monovalent radicals, or capable of replacing four atoms of monovalent elements in a compound. Also called *quadrivalent*. So **Tetravalence**, quadrivalence.

Tetrazone (te·trăzōᵘn). 1895. [f. TETRA- + AZ(O- + -ONE.] *Chem.* Name of a class of basic compounds containing four nitrogen atoms, with the formula $R_2NN : NNR_2$, in which R is any monovalent group.

†**Te·tric**, *a.* 1533. [ad. L. *tætricus, tetricus*, f. *tæter* foul; see -IC.] = next –1811.

Tetrical (te·trikăl), *a.* *Obs.* or *arch.* 1529. [f. as prec. + -AL.] Austere, severe, harsh, bitter, morose.

Tetrobol (te·trǒbǫl). 1693. [ad. mod.L. *tetrobolum*, a. Gr. τετρώβολον a four-obolus piece, f. τετρα- four + ὀβολός OBOLUS.] A silver coin of ancient Greece of the value of four oboli.

‖ **Tetrodon** (te·trǒdǫn). 1774. [mod.L. (Linn.), f. Gr. τετρα- four + ὀδούς, ὀδοντ- tooth.]

Ichth. A genus of plectognathic fishes, typical of the family *Tetrodontidæ*, in which the jaws are divided longitudinally by a groove, giving the appearance of four large teeth; a fish of this family, a globe-fish. So Te·trodont *a.* having (apparently) four teeth; belonging to the *Tetrodontidæ*; *sb.* a t. or globe-fish.

Tetrous (te·trəs), *a.* Now *rare.* 1637. [f. L. *tæter* foul + -OUS.] Offensive, foul.

Tetroxide (tetrǫ·ksəid). 1866. [f. TETRA- 2 a + OXIDE.] *Chem.* A binary compound containing four atoms of oxygen; e. g. nitrogen tetroxide, NO_4.

Tetryl (te·tril). 1857. [f. TETR(A- 2 + -YL.] *Chem.* The monovalent radical of the tetracarbon series, C_4H_9, also called BUTYL; chiefly attrib. = *tetrylic.* Hence **Tetry·lic** *a.* of t., in *tetrylic acid*, etc.

Tetter (te·təɹ), *sb.* [OE. *teter*:—OTeut. **tetru-*, pre-Teut. **dedru-*, Skr. *dadru* a kind of cutaneous disease, f. *dṛ* to crack.] **1.** A general name for any pustular herpiform eruption of the skin, as eczema, herpes, impetigo, ringworm, etc. **2.** A cutaneous disease in animals, esp. horses 1552.

1. *Crusted, pustular, running t.*, impetigo. *Eating t.*, lupus. *Honeycomb t.*, favus. *Humid* or *moist t.*, eczema. *Scaly t.*, psoriasis. Hence †**Te·tter** *v. trans.* to affect with, or as with, a t. SHAKS.

Tetter-berry (te·təɹberi). 1597. The common Bryony, *Bryonia dioica*; also, its berry. Variously said to cure and to produce tetter.

Tetterous (te·tərəs), *a.* 1719. [f. TETTER *sb.* + -OUS.] Of the nature of, proceeding from, or causing tetter.

Tetterworm (te·təɹwɒɹm). 1622. A cutaneous affection; a form of ringworm.

Tetterwort (te·təɹwɒɹt). late ME. The common Celandine, *Chelidonium majus*: so named because supposed to cure tetters.

‖**Tettix** (te·tiks). 1775. [a. Gr. τέττιξ.] **1.** The cicada or tree-cricket, a homopterous winged insect. **2.** *Ent.* A genus of *Acridiidæ*, or short-horned grasshoppers, typical of the orthopterous subfamily *Tettiginæ* 1891. **3.** *Golden t.* (Gr. χρυσοῦς τέττιξ), an ornament worn in the hair by Athenians before Solon's time, as an emblem of their being aboriginal 1874.

Teuto- (tiū·to), bef. a vowel **Teut-**, comb. form irreg. f. TEUTON, TEUTONIC.

1. Combined with other ethnic sbs. or adjs. in the sense 'That is a Teuton, or Teutonic and..', as *Teut-Aryan, Teuto-Celt.* 2. Formative of derivatives, as **Teutoma·nia,** a mania for what is Teutonic or German; **Teu·tophile, -phil** *sb.*, a lover or friend of Germany and the Germans; also as *adj.*

Teuton (tiū·tǫn, -t'n). 1727. [ad. L. *Teutones, Teutoni* (rarely sing. *Teuton, -us*), ethnic name.] **1.** In *pl.* (usu. in L. form *Teutones*) applied to an ancient people of unknown race, said to have inhabited the Cimbric Chersonesus in Jutland *c* 320 B.C., who, in company with the Cimbri, in 113–101 B.C. devastated Gaul and threatened the Roman Republic. **2.** A German; in extended ethnic sense, a member of the races or peoples speaking a Germanic or Teutonic language; now often used like 'Saxon' in opposition to 'Celt', and in avoidance of 'German' in its modern political sense 1833.

Teutonic (tiutǫ·nik), *a.* and *sb.* 1605. [ad. L. *Teutonicus*, f. *Teutones.*] **A.** *adj.* **1.** Of or pertaining to the Teutons; German, esp. High German 1645. †**b.** Of or pertaining to the ancient Teutones –1741. **2.** Of or pertaining to the group of languages allied to German (including Gothic, Scandinavian, Low German, and English), forming one of the great branches of the Indo-European, Indo-Germanic, or Aryan family, and to the peoples or tribes speaking these languages; now often called *Germanic* 1605. **3. T. Knights, T. Order** (of Knights): A military order of German Knights, orig. enrolled *c* 1191 as the Teutonic Knights of St. Mary of Jerusalem, for service in the Holy Land 1617. **4. T. cross,** a cross potent, being the badge of the Teutonic Order 1882. **B.** *sb.* **1.** †The language of any Teutonic race, *spec.* the German language (*obs.*); now applied by philologists only to the common or primitive speech, which afterwards broke up into the languages named in A. 2; also known as *Germanic* 1605. †**2.** *pl.* = Teutonic Knights –1796. Hence **Teuto·nicism,** T. (i. e. German) character or practice; a Teutonic expression; a Teutonism.

Teutonism (tiū·tŏnizm). 1854. [f. TEUTON + -ISM.] **1.** An idiom or mode of expression peculiar to or characteristic of the Teutonic languages, esp. German; a Germanism 1889. **2.** Teutonic or German character, type, constitution, system, or spirit; German feeling and action 1854. So **Teu·tonist,** one versed in the history, etc., of the Teutonic race or languages; one whose writings have a Teutonic character or style.

Teutonize (tiū·tŏnəiz), *v.* 1845. [f. TEUTON + -IZE.] *trans.* To make or render Teutonic or German. **b.** *intr.* To conform to Teutonism 1882.

Tew (tiū), *sb.* *Obs.* exc. *dial.* 1440. [f. TEW *v.*] †**1.** The tawing of leather. **2.** Constant work and bustling; a state of worry or excitement. *dial.* and *U.S.* 1825.

Tew (tiū), *v.* *Obs.* exc. *dial.* ME. [In branch I, app. f. TAW *v.* Branch II may be from branch I.] **I. 1.** *trans.* = TAW *v.* 2. **2.** To work (anything) into proper consistency by beating, etc.; to temper (mortar) 1641. †**3.** = TAW *v.* 3, 3 b. –1670. **II. 1.** *trans.* To fatigue or tire with hard work. *dial.* 1825. **2.** *intr.* To work hard, to toil; to bustle about. Now *dial.* and *U.S.* 1787.

Tewhit, tewit (tī·hwit, tī·wit, tiū·it; also tyū·χit, tyʊ·χit, tiū·fit). Now *local.* 1450. [orig. echoic; see PEWIT.] The common Lapwing or Pewit, *Vanellus cristatus.*

†**Tewtaw,** *sb.* 1649. [Goes with next.] An implement for breaking hemp or flax –1727.

Tewtaw, *v.* 1601. [Origin obsc.; cf. TAW *v.*] *trans.* To beat or dress (hemp or flax); = TAW *v.* Now *dial.*

Texan (te·ksăn), *a.* and *sb.* 1860. [f. next + -AN.] Of or pertaining to the State of Texas; in some specific names of animals and plants.

Texas (te·ksăs). Name of one of the United States. **1.** *Western U.S.* The uppermost structure of a river-steamer, containing the pilot-house and officers' quarters 1872. **b.** The elevated gallery, resembling a louver or clear-story, in a grain-elevator 1909. **2.** In names of native Texan plants, animals, etc.: as *T. bead-tree, flax, snake-root* 1858.

Text (tekst), *sb.* late ME. [a. F. *texte*, ad. med.L. *textus* the Gospel, written character, L. *textus* style, tissue of a literary work, lit. that which is woven, web, texture, f. *text-, texere* to weave.] **1.** The wording of anything written or printed; the structure formed by the words in their order; the very words, phrases, and sentences as written. **b.** The wording adopted by an editor as (in his opinion) most nearly representing the author's original work; a book or edition containing this; also, with qualification, any form in which a writing exists or is current, as a *good, bad, corrupt t.* 1841. **2.** *esp.* The very words and sentences as originally written: **a.** in the original language, as opp. to a translation or rendering; **b.** in the original form and order, as dist. from a commentary, or from annotations. Hence, in later use, the body of any treatise, the authoritative or formal part, as dist. from notes, appendices, etc. late ME. **c.** That portion of the contents of a manuscript or printed book, or of a page, which constitutes the original matter, as dist. from the notes, etc. late ME. †**3.** *spec.* The very words and sentences of Holy Scripture; hence, the Scriptures themselves; also, any single book of the Scriptures –1668. **b.** A copy of the Scriptures, or of a book of the Scriptures; *spec.* a volume containing the Gospels. *Obs.* exc. *Hist.* late ME. **4.** A short passage from the Scriptures, esp. one quoted as authoritative, as a motto, to point a moral, or as the subject of an exposition or sermon. late ME. **b.** A short passage from some book or writer considered as authoritative; a received maxim or axiom; a proverb; an adage; in later use, esp. one used as a copy-book heading. Now *rare.* late ME. **c.** *fig.* The theme or subject on which any one speaks; the starting-point of a discussion 1605. **5.** Short for TEXT-HAND. See also CHURCH *t.*, GERMAN *t.* 1588.

1. Say, Stella, when you copy next, Will you keep strictly to the t.? SWIFT. **b.** The t. seems very corrupt FREEMAN. 2. **b.** Coke upon Littleton, where the comment is of equal authority with the t. FIELDING. 4. **b.** That t... That seith that hunters beth nat hooly men CHAUCER. **c.** No more; the t. is foolish SHAKS. 5. Faire as a t. B. in a Coppie booke SHAKS.

attrib. and *Comb.*: **t.-blindness,** word-blindness; **-cut, -engraving, -picture,** an illustration occupying a space in the t. of a book **-title,** a half-title, at the beginning of the t. of a book.

Text (tekst), *v.* Now *rare.* 1564. [f. prec.] †**1.** *trans.* To inscribe, write, or print in text-hand or in capital or large letters –1639. **b.** *intr.* To write in text-hand 1660. †**2. a.** To cite texts. **b.** *trans.* To cite a text at or against a person. –1615.

Text-book (te·kst,buk). 1779. A book used as a standard work for the study of a particular subject; a manual of instruction in a subject of study.

Te·xt-hand. 1542. A fine large hand in writing. *orig.* One of the larger and more formal hands in which the text of a book was often written, as dist. from the smaller and more cursive hand appropriate to the gloss, etc. **b.** In recent use, applied to a school-hand written in lines about half an inch wide.

Textile (te·kstəil, -il), *a.* and *sb.* 1626. [ad. L. *textilis* woven, *textile* (sc. *opus*) woven fabric, f. *text-, texere* to weave.] **A.** *adj.* **1.** That has been or may be woven 1656. **b.** *Nat. Hist.* Having markings resembling a woven surface; e. g. *t. snake* 1802. **2.** Of or connected with weaving 1844.

1. Cotton and wool and other t. materials 1868. **b.** *T. cone*, a species of cone-shell, *Conus textilis*, having markings resembling a woven surface.

B. *sb.* **1.** A woven fabric; any kind of cloth. (Usu. in *pl.*) 1626. **b.** *attrib.* (or as *adj.*) Of or pertaining to weaving or to woven fabrics 1844. **2.** Fibrous material, as flax, cotton, silk, etc., suitable for being spun and woven into yarn, cloth, etc. 1641.

†**Te·xt-le:tter.** 1511. [cf. TEXT-HAND.] A large or capital letter in handwriting –1706.

Textorial (tekstōə·riăl), *a.* 1774. [f. L. *textor, -orem* weaver, *textorius* pertaining to weaving + -AL.] Of or pertaining to weavers or weaving.

Textual (te·kstiu,ăl), *a.* [Late ME. *textuel*, app. a. AF., ad. L. type **textualis*, f. *textus*; see TEXT *sb.* and -AL; refash. later after L.] †**1.** Of a person: Well acquainted with 'texts' or authors; well-read; literally exact in giving the text –1613. **2.** Of, pertaining to, or contained in the (or a) text, esp. of the Scriptures 1470. **3.** Based on, following, or conforming to the text, esp. of the Scriptures 1614.

1. But as I seyde I am noght textueel CHAUCER. 2. The admitted principles of t. criticism 1859. His sagacity in t. emendations 1872. Hence **Te·xtually** *adv.* in or as regards the text; in the actual words of the text.

Textualism (te·kstiu,ăliz'm). 1863. [f. prec. + -ISM.] **1.** Strict adherence to the text, esp. of the Scriptures; the principles or method of a textualist. **2.** That department of scholarship which deals with the text of the Bible; textual criticism 1888.

Textualist (te·kstiu,ălist). 1629. [f. as prec. + -IST.] **a.** One learned in the text of the Bible. **b.** One who adheres strictly to, and bases his doctrine upon, the text of the Scriptures.

Textuary (te·kstiu,ări), *a.* and *sb.* 1608. [f. med.L. *textus* TEXT *sb.* + *-arius* -ARY [1].] **A.** *adj.* **1.** Of or belonging to the text; textual 1646. †**2.** That ranks as a text-book; regarded as an authority –1682.

1. The t. proofs of St. Peter's supremacy 1854.

B. *sb.* **1.** = prec. a; also, one ready at quoting texts 1608. †**2.** = prec. b. –1828.

†**Textuist.** 1631. [f. L. *textus* TEXT *sb.* + -IST.] A textual scholar –1700.

The crabbed textuists of his time MILT.

Textural (te·kstiŭrăl), *a.* 1835. [f. L. *textura* TEXTURE + -AL.] Of or belonging to texture. **b.** *Painting.* See TEXTURE *sb.* 6. 1859. Hence **Te·xturally** *adv.* in or as regards texture.

Texture (te·kstiŭɹ, -tʃəɹ), *sb.* 1447. [ad. L. *textura* a weaving; see TEXT *sb.* and -URE.] †1. The process or art of weaving -1726. 2. The produce of the weaver's art; a woven fabric; a web. *arch.* 1656. b. *transf.* Any natural structure having an appearance or consistence as if woven; a tissue; a web, e.g. of a spider 1578. 3. The character of a textile fabric, as to its being fine, close, coarse, ribbed, twilled, etc., resulting from the way in which it is woven 1685. 4. The constitution, structure, or substance of anything with regard to its constituents, formative elements or physical character 1660. 5. *fig.* Of immaterial things: Constitution; nature or quality, as resulting from composition. Of the mind: Disposition, as 'woven' of various qualities; temperament, character. 1611. 6. In the fine arts: The representation of the structure and minute moulding of a surface (esp. of the skin), as dist. from its colour 1859.

2. Others..far in the grassy dale..their humble t. weave THOMSON. 3. The t. that belongs to Linen BOYLE. 4. Thou know'st the T. of my Heart, My Reins, and every vital Part WESLEY. The loose t. of snow HUXLEY. 5. An argument..of so frail and brittle a t. BENTLEY. Hence †**Te·xture** *v. trans.* to construct by or as by weaving; to give a t. to.

‖**Textus** (te·kstɒ̆s). 1856. [L.] 1. = TEXT *sb.* 3 b. 1874. 2. *Textus receptus*, lit., received text; *spec.* the received text of the Greek New Testament 1856.

Text-writer (te·kstˌrəi:təɹ). 1463. †1. A professional writer of text-hand -1491. 2. *Law.* An author of a legal text-book 1845.

‖**Tezkere** (te·zkĕrĕ). 1612. [Turk. (Arab.).] A Turkish official memorandum or certificate.

Th, in words of Old English or Old Norse origin, and in words from Greek, is a consonantal digraph representing one or other of a pair of simple sounds, one voiceless, the other voiced, denoted in this dictionary by the OE. letters (þ) and (ð); the former, as in *thin, bath* (þin, baþ), being the breath dental spirant akin to *t*, and the latter, as in *then, bathe* (ðen, bēið), the voiced dental spirant akin to *d*.

Th-, th' (ME. þ-), a clipped form of some unstressed monosyllables, esp. when the following word begins with a vowel or *h*. 1. = THE OE. †2. = THOU -1594. †3. = THEY -1707.

1. To th' shore SHAKS.

-th, *suffix* [1], a formative of sbs. **a.** from vbs.; in some words, as *bath, birth, death*, OTeut., repr. the Indo-Eur. suffixes **-tos, -tâ, -tis, -tus*; in others, as *tilth*, going back to ON. or OE.; in others, as *growth, spilth, stealth*, of later analogical formation. **b.** from adjs. (rarely sbs.), repr. Indo-Eur. **-itâ*, OTeut. **-iþô*, OE. *-þu, -þo, -þ*, forming abstract nouns of state; as *filth, health, strength*, etc.; of later analogical formation, *breadth, sloth, wealth, width*. See also -T *suffix* [3] b.

-th, *suffix* [2], forming ordinal numbers; in mod. literary Eng. used with all simple numbers from *fourth* onward; repr. OE. *-þa, -þe*, or *-oþa, -oþe*, from an original Indo-Eur. **-tos* (cf. Gr. πέμπτος, L. *quintus*), understood to be identical with one of the suffixes of the superlative degree.

In compound numerals *-th* is added only to the last, as $\frac{1}{1345}$, the *one thousand three hundred and forty-fifth part*.

Thack (þæk), *sb.* Now *dial.* [Com. Teut.: OE. *þæc*:—OTeut. **þakom*, f. root *þek-* to cover, Indo-Eur. *teg-*, in L. *tegere* to cover, *toga* covering, gown, Gr. τέγος, στεγή roof, στέγειν to cover, etc. See THATCH *v.*] †1. The roof of a house or building -1526. 2. = THATCH *sb.* 1. OE.

Thack (þæk), *v.* Now *dial.* ME. [app. f. prec.] 1. *intr.* = THATCH *v.* 5. 2. *trans.* To cover (a roof) or roof (a house) with thatch, formerly also with lead, tiles, etc.; *spec.* to cover the top of a rick with straw or other material so laid as to carry off the rain 1440.

‖**Thakur, thakoor** (tʰā·kur). *India.* 1800. [a. Hindī *ṭhākur*, Skr. *ṭhā·kkura* a deity.] A word meaning Lord, used as a title and term of respect; also applied to a chief or noble, esp. of the Rajput race.

‖**Thalamencephalon** (þæ:lămense·fălɒn). 1875. [f. THALAM(O- + ENCEPHALON.] *Anat.* That part of the brain which develops from the posterior part of the anterior cerebral vesicle, and includes the optic thalami, optic nerves, and parts about the third ventricle. Also called *diencephalon, middle brain*, etc.

Thalamic (þălæ·mik, þæ·lămik), *a.* 1860. [ad. mod.L. *thalamicus*; see THALAMUS and -IC.] Of or pertaining to a thalamus; in *Anat.*, pertaining to the optic thalamus.

Thalamifloral (þæ:lămiflōᵊ·răl), *a.* 1857. [f. mod.L. *Thalamifloræ* (f. THALAMUS + L. *flos, flor-*) + -AL.] *Bot.* Belonging to the subclass *Thalamifloræ* of dicotyledons, in which the stamens are inserted on the thalamus or receptacle; hypogynous. So **Thalamiflo·rous** *a.*

Thalamo- (þæ·lămo), bef. a vowel **thalam-**, comb. form of Gr. θάλαμος THALAMUS, in some anatomical terms, as **Thalamocœle** (þæ·lămosīl) [Gr. κοιλία cavity, ventricle], the cavity of the thalamencephalon; the third ventricle of the brain.

‖**Thalamus** (þæ·lămɒ̆s). *Pl.* **-mi** (-məi). 1753. [L., a. Gr. θάλαμος an inner chamber.] 1. *Anat.* A part of the brain at which a nerve originates or appears to originate; *spec.* the OPTIC thalamus 1756. 2. *Bot.* **a.** The receptacle of a flower, on which the carpels are placed; the torus 1753. **b.** = THALLUS 1842. 3. *Archæol.* An inner or secret chamber 1850.

Thalassian (þălæ·siăn), *a.* and *sb.* 1850. [f. Gr. θαλάσσιος marine, f. θάλασσα sea + -AN.] **A.** *adj.* Of or pertaining to the sea, marine; *spec.* applied to the marine tortoises and turtles. **B.** *sb.* A marine tortoise or turtle 1850.

Thalassic (þălæ·sik), *a.* 1860. [ad. F. *thalassique*, f. Gr. θάλασσα sea; see -IC.] 1. Of or pertaining to the sea; marine. †In *Geol.* applied to strata supposed to be of marine formation. 2. Pertaining to the (smaller or inland) seas as dist. from the pelagic waters or oceans 1883.

Thalassi·nian, *a.* and *sb.* 1842. [f. mod. L. *Thalassina* + -IAN.] **A.** *adj.* Of or pertaining to the *Thalassinidæ*, a family of long-tailed decapod crustaceans, the scorpion-lobsters. **B.** *sb.* A crustacean of this family.

Thalass(o- (þălæ·s(o), **Thala·ssi(o-,** from Gr. θάλασσα sea, and θαλάσσιος marine, formative elements of learned words, as in **Thalassa·rctine** *a.*, *Zool.* of or pertaining to the Polar Bear, *Thalassarctos*. **Thala·ssio-, Thala·ssophyte,** a plant of the *Thalassiophyta*; a seaweed, a marine alga. Also (after Attic Gr. θάλαττα) **Thalatto-**.

Thalassocracy (þælæ̆sɒ·krăsi). 1846. [ad. Gr. θαλασσοκρατία; see prec. and -CRACY.] Mastery at sea, sovereignty of the sea. So **Thala·ssocrat,** one who has the mastery of the sea.

Thalassography (þælæ̆sɒ·grăfi). 1888. [f. THALASSO- + -GRAPHY.] The branch of physical geography which treats of the sea, its configuration and phenomena; oceanography.

‖**Thaler** (tā·ləɹ). 1787. [G.] A German silver coin; a dollar: see DOLLAR 1.

Thalerophagous (þælĕrɒ·făgəs), *a.* 1819. [f. Gr. θαλερός blooming, fresh + -φαγος eating + -OUS.] *Ent.* Feeding on fresh vegetable substances.

‖**Thalia** (þăləi·ă). 1656. [a. Gr. Θάλεια (blooming, f. θάλλειν to bloom).] 1. The eighth of the Muses, presiding over comedy and idyllic poetry; also, one of the three Graces, patroness of festive meetings. 2. *Bot.* A genus of aquatic herbaceous plants, family *Marantaceæ*, natives of tropical America 1756. 3. *Astron.* The twenty-third of the asteroids 1886.

Thaliacean (þæliˌēⁱ·ʃiăn), *a.* and *sb.* 1888. [f. mod.L. *Thaliacea* (f. *Thalia*) + -AN.] *Zool.* **A.** *adj.* Of or pertaining to the *Thaliacea*, an order of tunicates, including the *Salpidæ*, etc. **B.** *sb.* A member of this order.

Thalian (þăləi·ăn, þēⁱ·liăn), *a.* 1864. [f. THALIA + -AN.] Of or pertaining to Thalia as the muse of pastoral and comic poetry; hence, of the nature of comedy, comic.

Thallic (þæ·lik), *a.* 1868. [f. THALLIUM + -IC.] *Chem.* Of, pertaining to, or derived from thallium; *spec.* applied to compounds containing thallium in smaller proportion, relatively to oxygen, than *thallious* compounds. *T. oxide* = thallium trioxide, Tl_2O_3.

Thalline (þæ·ləin), *sb.* Also **-in.** 1885. [f. Gr. θάλλειν to flourish + -INE [5].] *Pharm.* A trade name for a colourless compound used as an antipyretic, obtained by the reduction of the corresponding chinoline derivative.

Thalline (þæ·ləin), *a.* 1856. [f. THALLUS + -INE [1].] *Bot.* Of or pertaining to a thallus.

Thallious (þæ·liəs), *a.* 1868. [f. next + -OUS.] *Chem.* Abounding in thallium; *spec.* containing thallium in greater proportion, relatively to oxygen, than *thallic* compounds.

Thallium (þæ·liɒ̆m). 1861. [f. Gr θαλλός green shoot (f. θάλλειν to bloom), from the brilliant green line distinguishing its spectrum + -IUM.] *Chem.* A rare metal, bluish white in colour with leaden lustre, extremely soft and almost devoid of tenacity or elasticity; occurring in small quantities in iron and copper pyrites. Atomic weight 204; symbol Tl.

Thallogen (þæ·lŏdʒen). 1846. [f. THALLUS + -GEN, after *exogen*, etc.] *Bot.* = THALLOPHYTE.

Thalloid (þæ·loid), *a.* 1857. [f. THALLUS + -OID.] *Bot.* Of the form of a thallus. So **Thalloi·dal** *a.*

Thallophyte (þæ·lŏfəit). 1854. [f. mod.L. *Thallophyta*, pl. f. Gr. θαλλός green twig + φυτόν plant.] *Bot.* A plant belonging to the lowest of the great groups in the vegetable kingdom, comprising those of which the vegetative body is a thallus, including Algæ, Fungi, and Lichens; a cellular cryptogam.

Thallous (þæ·ləs), *a.* 1888. [f. THALLIUM + -OUS.] *Chem.* = THALLIOUS.

‖**Thallus** (þæ·lɒ̆s). 1829. [L., a. Gr. θαλλός green shoot, f. θάλλειν to bloom.] *Bot.* A vegetable structure without vascular tissue, in which there is no differentiation into stem and leaves, and from which true roots are absent.

‖**T(h)alweg** (tā·lveg). 1862. [G., f. *t(h)al* valley + *weg* WAY *sb.*] *Physiog.* The line that follows the lowest part of a valley.

Thames (temz). [OE. *Temese*:—**Tamisa*, ad. L. *Tamesa, Tamesis*, ad. Brit. *Tamesa.*] The name of the river on which London is situated; also *attrib.* and *Comb.*

Phr. *To set the T. on fire*, to do something marvellous, to work wonders; usu. with neg. = to work no wonders, never to distinguish oneself.

‖**Thamin** (þămi·n). 1888. [Burmese *thă-min.*] A deer (*Cervus eldi*) of Burmah and Siam, resembling the swamp deer.

‖**Thammuz, Tammuz** (tæ·mūz). 1535. [Heb. *tammûz.*] The tenth month of the Jewish civil year, and the fourth of the sacred, containing twenty-nine days, and corresponding to parts of June and July. Also, the name of a Syrian deity, identified with the Phœnician *Adōn* or Adonis, whose annual festival began with the new moon of this month.

Than (ðăn, ðən; *when quoted alone called* ðæn), *conj.* [OE. *þanne, þonne, þænne*, also *þan, þon*; orig. the same word as THEN.] 1. The conjunctive particle used after a comparative adj. or adv. to introduce the second member of the comparison; the conjunction expressing the comparative of inequality. In use it is always stressless, usu. joined accentually to the prec. word, e.g. *more than, other than* (mōᵊ·ɹðən, ʌ·ðəɹðən). **b.** With a personal or relative pronoun in the objective case instead of the nominative (as if *than* were a prep.). Now considered incorrect, exc. with *whom.* 1560. **c.** Followed by *that*, or by *infin.* expressing a hypothetical result or consequence 1528. 2. *Than* is regularly used after *other, else*, and their compounds (*otherwise, elsewhere*, etc.) ME. **b.** Hence sometimes after adjs. or advbs. of similar meaning to 'other', as *different, diverse*, etc., and after Latin comparatives, as *inferior, junior*: usu. with clause following. (Now mostly avoided.) late ME. 3. Peculiar uses. **a.** = Except, besides, but. (perh. ellipsis for *other than, else than*, etc.) *Obs.* or *arch.* late ME. ¶ **b.** After *hardly, scarcely*: = When (by confusion with *no sooner than*) 1864.

1. He is more to be feared then all goddes COVER-

DALE *Ps.* xcv[i]. 4. I had rather dye t. once to open my mouth 1566. Water, colder t. Ice, and clearer than Christal ADDISON. 'Tis better to have loved and lost, T. never to have loved at all TENNYSON. b. Bëëlzebub..then whom, Satan except, none higher sat MILT. He was much older t. me 1792. c. The bed is shorter, then that a man can stretch himselfe on it *Isa.* xxviii. 20. He is more modest..t. to deny it CONGREVE. Mr. Creech..knew his business better t. to satisfy their curiosity 1779. 2. The acts or defaults of any person other t. himself 1896. 3. a. There is almost nothing left then a shadow thereof 1585.

Than, þan, obs. and dial. f. THEN.

Thanage (þē̆ˑnėdʒ). *Hist.* late ME. [= AF. *tha(y)nage*, f. THANE + -AGE.] The tenure by which lands were held by a thane; the land held by a thane, a thane-land; also, the rank, office, or jurisdiction of a thane.

Thanatism (þæˑnătiz'm). 1900. [f. Gr. θάνατος death + -ISM.] The belief or doctrine that at death the soul ceases to exist.

Thanato- (þæˑnăto), bef. a vowel **thanat-**, comb. form of Gr. θάνατος death, chiefly in scientific words. **Thanatoˑgraphy** (*nonce-wd.*) [after *biography*], an account of a person's death. ‖ **Thanatoˑpsis** [Gr. ὄψις sight], a contemplation of death.

Thanatology (þænătǫˑlŏdʒi). *rare.* 1842. [f. Gr. θάνατος death + -LOGY.] The scientific study of death, its causes and phenomena. So **Thanatoloˑgical** *a.* of or pertaining to t.

Thane (þēin). *Hist.* [OE. *þegn, þegen, þēn* :—OTeut. **þegnoz*, orig. child, boy, lad :—pre-Teut. **teknó-* (cf. Gr. τέκνον), f. root **tek-* : *tok-* to beget.] †1. A servant, minister, attendant; in OE. often applied to (Christ's) disciples –1591. †2. A military attendant, follower, or retainer; a soldier. OE. only. 3. One who in Anglo-Saxon times held land of the king or other superior by military service; orig. in the designation *cyninges þegn*, 'king's thane, military servant or attendant'; in later times simply *þegn*, as a term of rank, including several grades below that of an *ealdorman* or *eorl* (EARL *sb.* 2) and above that of the *ceorl* or ordinary freeman. (Superseded in the 12th c. by *baron* and *knight*.) OE. 4. In *Sc. Hist.* A person, ranking with the son of an earl, holding lands of the king; the chief of a clan, who became one of the king's barons. late ME. b. *transf.* to modern persons, in various senses; e.g. a Scottish lord 1750.

3. Ecgulf the kings horse-thane 1853. 4. By Sinells death, I know I am T. of Glamis, But how, of Cawdor? the T. of Cawdor liues SHAKS.

Comb.: t.-land, land held by a t., or by military tenure. Hence **Thaˑnedom**, the domain or jurisdiction of a Scottish t. **Thaˑnehood**, the condition or rank of a t. **Thaˑneship**, the position or office of a t.; esp. in the Sc. sense.

Thank (þæŋk), *sb.* [OE. *þanc, þonc* :—OTeut. **þankoz*, f. **þenk-, þank-, þunk-*: see THINK.] †1. = THOUGHT –ME. †2. Good will; graciousness, favour –1609. †3. Grateful thought, gratitude. Rarely in *pl.* –1677. 4. The expression of gratitude; the grateful acknowledgement of a benefit or favour. †a. in *sing.* –1642. b. in *pl.* †Formerly occas. const. as sing. ME.

4. a. Turning to god with lawde and thanke 1534. b. Else is his thanks too much SHAKS. Prayers precede, and Thanks succeed the benefit HOBBES. I return it to you with my sincere thanks 1805.

Phrases. *Thanks* (colloq.), = I give you my thanks, my thanks to you, or the like; also *many thanks, best thanks*. *Thanks to*, thanks be given to, or are due to; hence, owing to, as a result of (often ironical); so *no thanks to*, no credit to; not because or by reason of. *To give thanks*, to express gratitude; *spec.* = 'to give thanks to God'; now esp. of saying grace at a meal (*arch.*). *To return thanks*, to render thanks in return for a benefit or favour; now chiefly used of the formal or public expression of thanks, or of grace at a meal.

Thank (þæŋk), *v.* [OE. *þancian, þoncian* :—OTeut. **þankōjan*, f. **þankoz* THANK *sb.*] †1. *intr.* To give thanks. *Obs.* exc. as *absol.* of 2. –1500. 2. *trans.* To give thanks to; to express gratitude or obligation to. (orig. *intr.* with *dat.*) Occas. const. *that*. ME. b. Const. *for* a thing 1591. c. *fig.* To make a return to a person in evidence of obligation or gratitude 1821. d. In the future tense, used to express a request 1843. 3. With a thing as sole obj.: To return thanks for, express one's gratitude for (*rare*) 1470. 4. To give the thanks or credit *for* something to; to consider or hold responsible: esp. in ironical use, = to blame 1560.

2. Yes I t. God, I am as honest as any man liuing, that is an old man, and no honester then I SHAKS. Sir Harry, you may t. your stars that conducted you to me FIELDING. That he has subjects in Scotland, I think he may t. God and his sword SCOTT. The young prince kissed his hand and thanked him 1841. b. *T. you for nothing*, an ironical expression indicating that the speaker thinks he has been offered nothing worth thanks. 3. Charles forgot To t. his tale BYRON. 4. She might t. herself for what happened 1794. The defendant had only himself to t. for it 1885.

Thankee (þæˑŋki). 1824. Vulgar colloq. for *thank ye* THANK YOU.

Thankful (þæˑŋkfŭl), *a.* OE. [f. THANK *sb.* + -FUL.] 1. Feeling or expressing thanks or gratitude; grateful. †2. Worthy of thanks, gratitude, or credit; acceptable, grateful, agreeable –1611.

1. The thankfull songe of Anna COVERDALE 1 *Sam.* ii. Contents. Live ever in our t. hearts! DRYDEN. 2. His good successe shall be most thankeful to your trust 1611. Hence **Thaˑnkfulˑly** *adv.*, **-ness.**

Thaˑnkless, *a.* 1536. [f. THANK *sb.* + -LESS.] 1. Not moved by or expressing gratitude; unthankful, ungrateful. Also *fig.* of things: Making no return, unresponsive. 2. Of a task, or the like: Which brings no thanks; receiving or deserving no thanks 1547. 3. Unthanked (*rare*) 1638.

1. And strictly meditate The thankles Muse MILT. 2. A thancklesse office and displeasing SAVILE. 3. To ..send him thanklesse back againe 1638. Hence **Thaˑnklessˑly** *adv.*, **-ness.**

Thaˑnk-oˑffering. 1530. [f. THANK *sb.* + OFFERING *vbl. sb.*] In the Levitical law, An offering presented as an expression of gratitude to God; hence, an offering or gift made by way of thanks or acknowledgement.

Thaˑnksgiˑver. 1621. [f. as next + GIVER.] One who gives thanks.

Thanksgiving (stress var.). 1533. [f. *thanks*, pl. of THANK *sb.* + GIVING *vbl. sb.*] 1. The giving of thanks; the expression of thankfulness or gratitude; *esp.* the act of giving thanks to God. b. A public celebration, with religious services, held as a solemn acknowledgement of Divine favours; a day set apart for this purpose, *spec.* in *U.S.* Thanksgiving Day 1641. 2. An act or expression of thanks; *esp.* a form of words, a prayer or religious service used to render thanks for Divine benefits 1535.

1. For all the creatures of God are good, and nothing to be refused, yf it be receaued with thankesgeuynge BIBLE (Great) 1 *Tim.* iv. 4. 2. He hath put a new songe in my mouth, euen a thankesgeuynge vnto oure God COVERDALE *Ps.* xxxix. [xl.] 3. *General T.*, the first of the forms of t. in the Book of Common Prayer, that for the blessings of life in general.

attrib.: T. day, a day set apart for public t. for Divine goodness; *spec.* in the U.S., an annual religious and social festival, now appointed by proclamation and held on the last Thursday of November.

Thaˑnkwoˑrthy, *a.* late ME. Worthy of thanks; deserving gratitude or credit.

For it is thankeworthye yf a man for conscience towarde god endure grefe, sufferinge wrongfully TINDALE 1 *Pet.* ii. 19. Hence **Thaˑnkwoˑrthily** *adv.* **Thaˑnkwoˑrthiness.**

Thaˑnk you. late ME. [Aphetic for *I thank you*.] A phrase used in courteous acknowledgement of a favour or service. b. as *sb.* An utterance of this phrase 1887.

She..said something meant for 'No, thank you'; but of which nothing was to be heard but 'q' 1862. **Thank-you-ma'am** *U.S. colloq.*, a hollow or ridge in a road. See N.E.D.

‖ **Thar** (thār). 1833. [Native name.] *Zool.* 1. The native name in Nepal of a goat-antelope, *Nemorhædus bubalina*, belonging to the same genus as the Goral (*N. goral*). 2. Also applied to the TEHR, or Himalayan wild goat (*Hemitragus jemlaicus*) 1896.

Tharf, *a. dial.* [OE.] Unleavened; e.g. *t.-cake.*

Tharf, thar, *v. Obs.* exc. *Sc. dial.* [Com. Teut. pret.-pres. vb.; OE. **þurfan*, pres. *þearf, þurfon*, pa. *þorfte* :—OTeut. **þarf-, þurb-*.] 1. *intr.* To be under a necessity or obligation (*to do* something). 2. *impers.* It is needful ME.

Tharm (þāɹm). Now *dial.* [OE. *þarm, þearm* :—OTeut. **þarmoz*, f. Indo-Eur. ablaut series **ter-*: *tor-*: *tr-* to go through.] 1. An intestine; chiefly in *pl.* 2. An intestine as cleansed and prepared for some purpose. Also in *sing.*, as a substance or material; catgut for fiddle-strings, etc. 1671.

That (ðæt), *dem. pron.*, *adj.*, and *adv.* [In OE. *þæt*, nom. and acc. sing. neuter of the simple demonstrative pron. and adj. *se, séo, þæt*.] A. Demonstrative Pronoun. *Pl.* THOSE. I. As simple demonstrative pronoun. 1. Denoting a thing or person pointed out or present, or that has just been mentioned or considered. 2. Used emphatically, instead of repeating a previous word or phrase OE. 3. In opposition to *this*: esp. in phr. *this and* (*or*) *that* = one thing and (or) another OE. 4. As quasi-*sb.*, with pl. *thats* 1656.

1. The errur of Vibicus. And t. was this. 1579. The more fools they,—that 's all RUSKIN. 'Bless us', cried the Mayor, 'what 's t.?' BROWNING. Who 's t. laughing? THACKERAY. 2. The Moderator is full of Rhetorick and Oratory too, t. he is 1642. It was necessary..to act, and t. promptly 1833. 'They must be very curious creatures'. 'They are t.', said Humpty Dumpty. L. CARROLL.

Phrases. *T. is* (more fully *t. is to say*, †*to wit*, etc.), introducing (or more rarely following) an explanation of the preceding word, phrase, or statement (or a modifying correction of it). *That's*, colloq. used in actual or anticipatory commendation, e.g. *that's a good lad, that's a dear*. *That's right*: a formula of approval: vulgarly used for 'It is so'. *That's that*, that is the end of the matter. *All t.*, that and everything of the kind. *And all t.*, and so forth, *et cetera*. *Not so.. as all t.*, not so..as that amounts to; not quite so..as that. *For all t.*: see FOR VII. 4. *Like t.*, of that kind or in that manner. *After t.*, = after that time, or after that had happened. *At t.*: (*a*) immediately after that, upon that; (*b*) orig. *U.S. colloq.* or *slang*, even when that has been taken into consideration; estimated at that rate, at that standard, even in that capacity, in respect of that, too; 'into the bargain'. *By t.*, = by that time, or by the time that happened. *Upon t., with t.*, = as or immediately after that was said, done, etc. *Come out of t.!* (slang): clear out! *Take t.!* a phrase used in delivering a blow.

II. As antecedent pronoun. 1. As antecedent to a relative (pron. or adv.) expressed or understood. late ME. 2. With ellipsis of a following relative (subj. or obj. of the relative clause): = that person or thing (*sc.* 'that' or 'which'). Now only where *that* is demonstrative or emphatic, as in I. 1. 1598. 3. Followed by defining words (*of* or other prep. with a sb., or a pple. or other vbl. adj.) which serve to qualify or particularize *that* in the manner of a relative clause. late ME.

1. What the Mouth is, to an Animal; t. the Root is to a Plant 1674. Fine Art is t. in which the hand, the head, and the heart..go together RUSKIN. 2. Be t. thou know'st thou art, and then thou art As great as t. thou fear'st SHAKS. 3. So doth their Pearch exceed t. of other Countries 1602. T. in the mortar—you call it a gum? BROWNING.

B. Demonstrative Adjective. 1. The simple demonstrative used (as adj. in concord with a sb.), to indicate a thing or person either as being actually pointed out or present, or as having just been mentioned and being thus mentally pointed out ME. b. Indicating a person or thing assumed to be known, or to be known to be such as is stated. Often (esp. before a person's name) implying censure, dislike, or scorn; but sometimes commendation or admiration. ME. c. Used with a plural sb. or numeral, instead of *those*; now only with plurals treated as singulars (e.g. *means, pains*) or taken in a collective sense ME. 2. In opposition to *this*: prop. denoting the more distant of two things, but often vaguely indicating one thing as dist. from another ME. 3. In concord with a sb. which is the antecedent to a relative (expressed or understood). Often interchangeable with *the*, but usu. more emphatic. 1470. 4. Indicating quality or amount: Of that kind or degree; such, so great. Now chiefly *arch.* or *dial.* 1450. †5. As neut. sing. of the definite article. *Obs.* (exc. in *that ilk*: ILK *a.*[1]) –1576.

1. Almost a yard broad, and twice t. length WALTON. b. T. Drug-damn'd Italy SHAKS. I hate that Andrew Jones WORDSW. c. T. ill manners..I have been often guilty of SWIFT. 3. A manne may saye 'the man that we spake of was here', or 't. man that we spake of was here' 1532. 4. He blushed to t. degree that I felt quite shy 1865.

C. Demonstrative Adverb. To that extent or degree; so much, so; *esp.* with an adv. or adj. of quantity, e.g. *that far* (= as far as that), *that much, that high*: more definite than *so*, as indicating the precise amount. Now *dial.* and *U.S.* 1450.

I was on my guard for a blow, he was t. passionate DICKENS. I never liked anything t. long [=six weeks] MRS. STOWE.

That (ðăt, ðət), *relative pron.* OE. [An unstressed and phonetically weakened form of prec. used to subordinate one predication to another.] The general relative pronoun, referring to any antecedent, and used without inflexion irrespective of gender, number, and case. **I. 1.** Introducing a clause defining or restricting the antecedent, and thus completing its sense. (The ordinary use; referring to persons or things.) **b.** As obj. of a prep., which in this case stands at the end of the relative clause ME. **2.** Introducing a clause stating something additional about the antecedent (the sense of the principal clause being complete without the relative clause). Now only *poet.* or *rhet.*; usu. repl. by *who* (*whom*) of persons, and *which* of things. OE. **3.** As subj. or obj. of the relative clause, with ellipsis of the antecedent. **a.** Of things: = (the thing) that, that which, what. Now *arch.* and *poet.*; repl. by *what* in prose. OE. **b.** Of persons: = (the person) that, he (or him) that, one that; *pl.* (persons) that, they (them), or those who. Now only after *there are* and the like. ME.

1. O thou t. hearest prayer *Ps.* lxv. 2. This is about all t. he has to say JOWETT. **b.** The cuppe t. y shall drinke of TINDALE *Matt.* xx. 22. All the cities t. they came to *Judges* xx. 48. **2.** Smale foweles maken melodye, T. slepen al the nyght with open eye CHAUCER. **3. a.** I earne t. I eate: get t. I weare SHAKS. **b.** I am t. I am *Exod.* iii. 14.

II. In various special or elliptical constructions, in some of which *that* passes into a relative or conjunctive adverb. (Cf. THAT *conj.*) **1.** After *same*: occas. = *as* ME. **2.** Preceded by a descriptive noun or adj., in a parenthetic exclamatory clause (e.g. *fool t. he is*): = As B. VI. 3. late ME. **3.** In *not t. I know*, and similar expressions: = According to what, as far as 1460. **4.** After the word *time*, or any sb. meaning a point or space of time: At, in, or on which; when OE. **5.** Connecting two clauses loosely or anacoluthically, the relative or dependent clause being imperfect (the part omitted being suggested by the principal clause). Now considered illiterate. late ME. **6.** *That* followed by a poss. pron. corresp. to the antecedent (e.g. *you t. your, the man t. his*) is an ancient mode of expressing the genitive of the relative = *whose*. Now *dial.* 1456. ¶**7.** The relative is very frequently omitted by ellipsis ME.

1. They say Diana is the same t. the Moon is 1690. **2.** Stand still, true poet t. you are! I know you BROWNING. **3.** Nor was he there, t. I know of 1776. **4.** The night t. he went to the play 1802. **5.** Who riseth from a feast With that keene appetite t. he sits downe? SHAKS. **7.** I am monarch of all I survey COWPER. This is a spray the Bird clung to BROWNING.

That (ðăt, ðət), *conj.* OE. [Uses of THAT *dem.* or *rel. pron.* in which it becomes a mere relative or conjunctive particle; cf. THE particle.] **1.** Introducing a dependent substantive-clause, as subject, object, or other element of the principal clause, or as complement of a sb. or adj., or in apposition with a sb. therein. **b.** Introducing a clause in apposition to or exemplifying the statement in the principal clause: = in that, in the fact that. *Obs.* or *arch.* (now usu. expressed by *in* with gerund). OE. †**c.** Introducing a sb.-clause as obj. of a preceding preposition: = the fact that (*rare*) –1557. **d.** In periphrastic construction, following a clause of the form *it is* (*was*, etc.) + an adv. or advb. phr., to which emphasis is given by the periphrasis OE. **e.** Introducing an exclamatory clause expressing some emotion, usu. (now always) sorrow, indignation, or the like. (Now usu. with *should*.) OE. **2.** Introducing a clause expressing the cause, ground, or reason of what is stated in the principal clause ME. **b.** *Not that*.. (ellipt.): = 'I do not say this because..'; or 'It is not the fact that..'; or 'One must not suppose that..': see NOT *adv.* 1601. **3.** Introducing a clause expressing purpose, end, aim, or desire OE. **b.** In exclams. of desire or longing ME. **c.** Introducing a clause expressing a hypothetical desired result: with vb. in subjunctive 1601. **4.** Introducing a clause expressing the result or consequence of what is stated in the principal clause: with verb. usu. in indicative OE. **b.** Introducing a clause expressing a fact or a supposition as a consequence attributed to the cause indicated by the principal clause (usu. interrog.): sometimes nearly = in consequence of which; or = since, seeing that OE. **5.** With a negative in the dependent clause (the principal clause having also a negative expressed or implied): = But that, but. (Now expressed by *without* with gerund.) OE. **6.** Added to relatives or dependent interrogatives (*who, which, what, why*, etc.). *Obs.* or *arch.* OE. †**b.** *That* alone had formerly the force of 'when that', 'when', after *hardly, scarcely*, etc. –1780. **7.** Formerly added with conjunctive force to various words that are now commonly used conjunctively without it; e.g. *because, if, lest, only, the* adv., *though*, etc. *arch.* or *Obs.* ME. **8.** Used (like Fr. *que*) as a substitute instead of repeating a previous conjunction, or conjunctive adv. or phr. Now *rare* or *arch.* ME. ¶**9.** The conjunction *that* is very frequently omitted by ellipsis, esp. in sense **1.** ME.

1. This shall be the token, yᵗ I haue sent the COVERDALE *Exod.* iii. 12. The story is as certain as t. Dr. Dodd was hung COLERIDGE. **b.** Thou hast well done, t. thou art come *Acts* x. 33. **d.** It was because he failed to prove this t. his case broke down 1890. **e.** T. a brother should Be so perfidious SHAKS. **2.** I wondered t. there was none to vphold *Isa.* lxiii. 5. Neither should we censure Novalis t. he dries his tears CARLYLE. **b.** Where is she staying now? Not t. I care. T. HARDY. **3.** This is to Advertise all Persons, t. they do not lend her any Mony 1708. **b.** Oh t. those lips had language! COWPER. **c.** I would give all my goods that it had never happened 1861. **4.** He was a man of morals so bad t. his own relations shrank from him MACAULAY. A fire..scorch'd me t. I woke TENNYSON. **b.** Who is Silvia?..T. all our Swaines commend her? SHAKS. **5.** He never turned in his bed during that whole time t. she did not hear SOUTHEY. **6.** When t. the poore haue cry'de, Cæsar hath wept SHAKS. **b.** Until just t. we came CROMWELL. **8.** Although the rear was attacked..and t. 50 men..were captured SIR W. NAPIER. **9.** I think I do BUNYAN.

Thatch (þætʃ), *sb.* late ME. [A late collateral form of THACK *sb.*, conformed to next.] **1.** Material used in thatching; straw or the like with which roofs are covered; esp. that actually forming a roof, the thatching. **b.** *transf.* A thatched dwelling. Now *rare.* 1693. **2.** *fig.* Covering; often *joc.* the hair of the head 1633. **3.** Name in the West Indies for several species of palm, the leaves of which are used for thatching. Also *thatch-palm.* 1866.

Thatch (þætʃ), *v.* [Com. Teut; OE. *þecc(e)an* :—OTeut. **þakjan*, f. **þakom* THACK *sb.*] †**1.** *trans.* To cover. OE. only. **2.** *spec.* To cover or roof (a house) with straw, reeds, palm-leaves, heather, or the like, laid so as to protect from the weather; also, to cover the top of (a rick or wall) in a similar way. late ME. **3.** *fig.* To cover as with thatch 1589. **4.** Of a thing: To serve as a covering or roof to; to cover, to roof OE. **5.** *intr.* To do thatching; to thatch houses. late ME.

2. Many of the churches are thatched with heath 1774. Hence **Tha·tcher,** one who thatches.

Thatching (þæ·tʃiŋ), *vbl. sb.* late ME. [f. prec. + -ING¹.] The action of THATCH *v.*; also *concr.* = THATCH *sb.* **1.**

Thatness (ðæ·tnės). 1643. [f. THAT *dem. pron.* + -NESS.] *Philos.* The quality or condition of being 'that', i.e. of existing as a definite thing.

Thaumato- (þǭmăto), comb. form of Gr. θαῦμα, θαυματ- wonder, marvel. **Thaumato·latry** [-LATRY], excessive reverence for the miraculous or marvellous. **Thaumato·logy** [-LOGY], an account of miracles; the description or discussion of the miraculous.

Thaumatrope (þǭ·mătrōup). 1827. [irreg. f. Gr. θαῦμα (see prec.) + -τροπος turning.] A scientific toy illustrating the persistence of visual impressions, consisting of a card or disk with two different figures drawn upon the two sides, which are apparently combined into one when the disk is rotated rapidly.

Thaumaturge (þǭ·mătɒ̄ɹdʒ). 1715. [ad. med.L. *thaumaturgus* (also used), ad. Gr. θαυματουργός, f. θαυματ- wonder + -εργος working.] A worker of marvels or miracles; a wonder-worker.

Thaumaturgic (þǭmătɒ̄·ɹdʒik), *a.* and *sb.* 1680. [f. as prec. + -IC.] **A.** *adj.* **1.** That works, or has the power of working, miracles or marvels; wonder-working. **2.** Of, pertaining to, or involving thaumaturgy 1825. **B.** *sb. pl.* **Thaumatu·rgics**: feats of magic, conjuring tricks 1730. So **Thaumatu·rgical** *a.* 1621.

Thaumaturgist (þǭ·mătɒ̄ɹdʒist). 1829. [f. THAUMATURGY + -IST.] = THAUMATURGE.

Thaumaturgy (þǭ·mătɒ̄ɹdʒi). 1727. [ad. Gr. θαυματουργία, f. THAUMATO- + -εργος working; see -Y³.] The working of wonders; miracle-working; magic.

Thaw (þǭ), *sb.* late ME. [f. next.] **1.** The melting of ice and snow after a frost; the condition of the weather caused by the rise of temperature above the freezing point. **2.** *transf.* and *fig.* 1598.

1. The frost resolves into a trickling t. THOMSON. **2.** That t. Of rigid disapproval into dew Of sympathy BROWNING.

Thaw (þǭ), *v.* Pa. t. and pple. **thawed**; pa. pple. also †thawn. [OE. *þawian*, ME. *þawen*; ME. also *thowe*; cogn. w. OFris. **thâia* (:—**þawian*), OHG. *douwen*, ON. *þeyja*; ult. history unkn.] **1.** *trans.* To reduce (a frozen substance, as ice or snow) to a liquid state by raising its temperature above the freezing point; to melt (a frozen liquid). **b.** *fig.* 1591. **2.** *intr.* Of ice, snow, etc.: To pass from a frozen to a liquid or semi-liquid state; to melt under the influence of warmth; esp. by rise of temperature after frost ME. **b.** *transf.* and *fig.* 1602. **3.** *impers.* *It thaws*: said of the cessation of frost, when the ice, snow, etc. begin to melt ME. **4.** *trans.* To free from the physical effect of frost; to unfreeze 1596. **5.** *intr.* To become unfrozen; to become flexible or limp by rise of temperature 1596. **6.** *fig.* **a.** *trans.* To soften to sympathy or geniality 1582. **b.** *intr.* Of a person, his manner, etc.: To become softened; to throw off coldness and reserve 1598.

1. b. O, weep for Adonais! though our tears T. not the frost which binds so dear a head! SHELLEY. **2. b.** *Haml.* I. ii. 130. **4.** *Tam. Shr.* IV. i. 9. **6. a.** Tea even fails to t. completely their reserve 1883. **b.** Pride of rank..thawed into paternal love 1827.

Thawless (þǭ·lės), *a.* 1813. [f. THAW *sb.* or *v.* + -LESS.] That does not thaw; that never thaws.

Thawy (þǭ·i), *a.* 1728. [f. THAW *sb.* + -Y¹.] Characterized by thaw; of or pertaining to a thaw.

The (*bef. cons.* ðĕ, ðə; *bef. vowel* ði; *emphatic* ðī), *dem. adj.* ('*def. article*'). [Late OE. *þe*, substituted, under the influence of the oblique uses and *þæt* THAT, for OE. *se, séo*, nom. sing. masc. and fem. of the demonstr. pron. and adj., which is based on two Com. Teut. and Indo-Eur. items, *sa-, so-* and *te-, to-*, repr. by Skr. *sa, sā, tat*, Gr. ὁ, ἡ, τό, Goth. *sa, sô, þata*, OFris. *thi, thiu, that*, G. *der, die, das*, Du. *de, dat*, ON. *sá, sú, þat*, etc.] **I.** Referring to an individual object (or objects). *Marking an object as before mentioned or already known, or contextually particularized. **1.** The ordinary use. **2.** Used before a word denoting time, as *the time, day, hour, moment*: the time (etc.) in question, or under consideration; the time (now or then) present OE. **b.** Used before numerals denoting years. (Now only in ref. to certain historical events or in expressions denoting a particular decade of a century or of a person's life.) ME. **3.** Before the name of a unique object, or one of which there is only one at a time OE. **b.** With names of rivers; of mountains, groups of islands, or regions, in the plural; of places or mountains, in the sing., now only when felt to be descriptive, as *the Land's End, the High Street, the Matterhorn*, or when *the* has come down traditionally, as *the Lennox, the Merse*; exceptionally in *the Tyrol* OE. **c.** With names of natural phenomena, seasons, etc.; of the points of the compass, as *the north, the east* OE. **4.** With a class-name, to indicate the individual example most familiar to one, or with which one is primarily or locally concerned, e.g. *the King, the Lord Mayor, the Tower*; *the Gospel, the Epistle* (for the day) ME. **5.** Formerly with names of branches of learning, arts, crafts, games, and pursuits. Now chiefly *dial.* ME. **6.** With names of literary or musical compositions; also of newspapers and periodicals ME. **7.** Formerly with names of languages; now only in consciously elliptical phrases, as *from* *the German* (sc. *language* or *original*) 1593. 8. With names of diseases, ailments, etc. Now more often omitted. OE. 9. Elliptically with the names of ships, as *the* (*ship*) *Swiftsure*, and of taverns, as *the Mermaid* (*tavern*), theatres, and other well-known buildings 1450. 10. Before higher titles of rank, as *the King*, *Prince*, etc. (but not now when followed by the name, as *King George*, *Prince Edward*, etc.); also with some courtesy titles, as *the Right Honourable*, *the Reverend*, etc. ME. b. With the surnames of some Irish and Scottish chiefs of clans, as the O'Gorman Mahon, *the MacNab* 1561. c. Before names and titles of men; often in ME. a corruption of French *de*, as in *Robert the Bruce*, *the Mortimer*, etc. (*arch.*) ME. d. Before the names of well-known singers, actresses, etc., after French and Italian usage 1786. 11. *spec.* Used emphatically, in the sense of 'the pre-eminent', 'the typical', or 'the only.. worth mentioning'; *the* being usu. stressed in speech (ðī), and printed in italics 1824. 12. With any part of the body of a person previously named or indicated, instead of the possessive pronoun; as 'he took him by the hand', i. e. *his* hand. So with *heart*, *soul*, used *fig.*; also with parts of personal attire. ME. b. Used colloq. with names of relatives, as *the wife*, *the mater* = my (your) wife, mother 1838. 13. Used before names of weights and measures, in stating a rate: as (*so much*) *the pound*, etc. late ME.

1. What's the matter now? CONGREVE. *The one*, *the other*: see ONE, OTHER. 2. At the moment, the bell rang DICKENS. On the morrow 1866. b. Ye have heard of a year they call the Forty-five SCOTT. It was in the early eighties (*mod.*). 3. *The sun*, *the earth*, *the universe*, *the Almighty*, *the Saviour*, *the Bible*, *the Shah*, etc. b. *The Thames*, *the Alps*, *the Azores*, *the Indies*. c. *The spring*, *the day*, *the night*; *the wind*, *the cold*, etc. 5. The Mathematickes, and the Metaphysickes Fall to them SHAKS. What was the use of my getting you taught the dress-making? 1824. 6. The Edinburgh Review SCOTT. Plato, in the Timæus, gives the fullest account 1845. 8. I..fell.. ill of the measles 1671. 10. d. The Guiccioli was present BYRON. 11. His Commentary..is still *the* text-book on Corneille 1904.

**Marking an object not before mentioned, but now identified by a clause, phrase, or word. 14. Where the object is defined by a relative clause, *the* stands before the object OE. 15. Where the object is defined: a. by a following phrase with prep. (esp. *of*, repr. an OE. genitive) OE.; b. by an infinitive phrase with *to*. late ME. c. With an object particularized by a pple. 1658. 16. *The* stands before a sb. defined by another sb. (usu. a proper name) in apposition, as *the poet Virgil* OE. b. More usu. the proper name precedes, as *William the Conqueror* OE. 17. *The* is used with a sb. particularized or described by an adj. The adj. usu. precedes, but sometimes follows the sb.: in either case *the* stands first, as *the good man*, *the church militant*. OE. b. So with proper names of persons or places; e. g. *the judicious Hooker* OE. c. But when the adj. becomes a permanent epithet, *the* and the adj. usu. follow; e. g. *Alfred the Great*; so with ordinals following the names of sovereigns or popes, as *George the Fifth* OE. 18. *spec.* When a sb. is particularized by a superlative, or by an ordinal number, the latter is regularly preceded by *the* OE. b. *The* also stands before the same adjs. when used absolutely OE.

14. The light that never was, on sea or land WORDSW. 15. a. Like the poore Cat i' th' Addage SHAKS. b. The power To save th' Athenian Walls from ruine bare MILT. c. The privileges accorded..to the merchants of the Hanse Towns 1876. 18. This was the most vnkindest cut of all SHAKS. b. Your letter of Tuesday the 19th 1779.

II. Referring to a term used generically or universally. 1. Before the name of an animal, plant, or precious stone, used generically OE. b. *gen.*, with the name of anything used as the type of its class; e. g. with the names of musical instruments, tools, etc. c. Before *body*, *mind*, *soul*, or parts, functions, and attributes of these OE. d. With names of days of the week, as *on the Monday*, i. e. on Monday of any or every week, on Mondays generally ME. 2. Before a word of individual meaning used as the type of a class of persons OE. 3. With an adj. used absol., usu. denoting an abstract notion; e. g. *the beautiful*, that which is beautiful. late ME. 4. With a sb. in the plural, chiefly the name of a nation, class, or group of people, where *the* = 'those who are'; 'the.. taken as a whole'. Also with family surnames, as 'the *Joneses* are of Welsh origin'. ME. 5. Before an adj. or pple. having a plural reference (usu. of persons), as *the poor*, those who or such as are poor OE.

1. Burleigh..was of the willow, and not of the oak MACAULAY. It purrs like the Cat 1854. b. The pen is mightier than the sword 1839. c. [They] pall on the palate THACKERAY. 2. 'Tis the voice of the Sluggard WATTS. Phr. *To act*, *be*, *play the man*, *the soldier*, etc. = to sustain the character of a man, a soldier, etc; to do that which is manly, soldier-like, etc. 3. A nose inclining to the aquiline SMOLLETT. 4. The Tarquins were banished from Rome 1816. 5. How low, how little are the Proud, How indigent the Great! GRAY. Thou knowest what a thing is Poverty Among the fallen on evil days SHELLEY.

The (ðĕ, ðə), *adv.* [OE. *þē*, orig. locative or instrumental case of the demonstr. and rel. pron. *se*, *séo*, *þæt* (see prec.).] 1. Preceding an adj. or adv. in the compar. degree, the two words forming an advb. phrase modifying the predicate. (The radical meaning is 'in or by that', 'in or by so much'.) 2. *The.. the..*: by how much.. by so much; in what degree.. in that degree.. [= L. *quo.. eo..*, Gr. ὅσῳ.. τοσούτῳ..] denoting proportional dependence between the notions expressed by the two clauses, each having *the* + a comparative; one *the* being demonstrative, and the other relative in force OE.

1. Your fav'rite horse Will never look one hair the worse COWPER. And if others do not follow their example,—the more fools they RUSKIN. 2. The bells must be removed, and the sooner the better 1771. The less said the sooner mended KINGSLEY.

Theandric (þiˌæ·ndrik), *a.* 1612. [ad. eccl. Gr. θεανδρικός, f. θέανδρος god-man; see -IC.] Of or pertaining to both God and man; partaking of both the human and the divine.

Theanthropic (þīˌænþrǫ·pik), *a.* 1652. [f. eccl. Gr. θεάνθρωπος THEANTHROPOS + -IC.] Pertaining or relating to, having the nature of, both God and man; at once divine and human.

Theanthropism (þiˌæ·nþrǒpiz'm). 1817. [f. as prec. + -ISM.] 1. *Theol.* The doctrine of the union of the divine and human natures, or of the manifestation of God as man, in Christ. 2. *Mythol.* The attribution of human nature or character to the gods 1878. So **Thea·nthropist**, a believer in t. (also *attrib.* or as *adj.*).

†‖**Thea·nthropos.** 1635. [a. eccl. Gr. θεάνθρωπος god-man, f. θεός God + ἄνθρωπος man.] A title given to Jesus Christ as being both God and man -1730. Hence **Thea·nthropy** [ad. eccl. Gr. θεανθρωπία], the union of the divine and human natures (in Christ).

Thearchic (þiˌā·ɹkik), *a.* 1855. [See next and -IC.] Of or pertaining to thearchy.

Thearchy (þī·āɹki). 1643. [ad. eccl. Gr. θεαρχία, f. θεός God + -αρχια a ruling.] 1. The rule or government of God or of a god; a theocracy. 2. An order or system of deities 1839.

Theatine (þī·atəin), *sb.* (*a.*) 1581. [ad. mod.L. *Theatinus*, f. *Teate*, ancient name of *Chieti* in Italy; see -INE [1].] *R. C. Ch.* A member of a congregation of 'regular clerks' founded in 1524 by St. Cajetan in conjunction with John Peter Caraffa (till then Archbishop of Chieti, whence the name, and later Pope Paul IV); also, a corresponding congregation of nuns, founded *c* 1600. b. as *adj.* Of or pertaining to the Theatines 1693.

Theatral (þī·ătrăl), *a.* Now *rare.* 1594. [ad. L. *theatralis*, f. *theatrum*; see -AL.] Of, pertaining to, or connected with the theatre; theatrical; dramatic.

Theatre (þī·ătəɹ). Also *U.S.* **theater.** late ME. [ad. L. *theatrum*, a. Gr. θέατρον, a place for viewing, esp. a theatre, f. θεᾶσθαι to behold.] 1. *Gr.* and *Rom. Antiq.* A place constructed in the open air, for viewing dramatic plays or other spectacles. †b. An amphitheatre -1548. c. A natural formation or place suggesting such a structure 1652. 2. In mod. use, An edifice specially adapted to dramatic representations; a playhouse 1577. †3. *transf.* a. The stage or platform on which a play is acted -1774. b. A theatreful of spectators; the audience at a theatre 1602. c. Dramatic performances as a branch of art, or as an institution; the drama 1668. d. Dramatic works collectively 1640. 4. A temporary platform, dais, or other raised stage, for any public ceremony 1517. 5. A room or hall fitted with tiers of rising seats facing the platform, lecturer's table, etc. for lectures, scientific demonstrations, etc. 1613. 6. *fig.* Something represented as a theatre in relation to a course of action performed or a spectacle displayed 1581. b. A place where some action proceeds; the scene of action 1615. †7. A book giving a 'view' or 'conspectus' of some subject; a text-book -1704.

1. High towers, faire temples, goodly theaters SPENSER. c. In Jura is a far retiring t. of rising terraces RUSKIN. 2. *Patent t.*, a t. established or licensed by royal letters patent. *Picture t.*, a hall in which cinematographic pictures are exhibited. 3. c. *Good* (etc.) *t.*, used predic. of a play, scene, etc., of specified dramatic quality, or that produces a good (etc.) effect on the stage. 6. A t. on which he might display his great qualities 1769. b. The T. of a Civil War 1720. *Comb.*: **t.-goer**, one who frequents theatres; so **-going** *sb.* and *adj.*

Theatric (þiˌæ·trik), *a.* 1656. [ad. late L. *theatricus*, ad. Gr. θεατρικός, f. θέατρον THEATRE; see -IC.] 1. = next 1. 1706. b. Resembling a theatre or amphitheatre in shape or formation 1764. 2. Suggestive of the theatre; stagy 1656.

1. b. Its uplands sloping deck the mountain's side, Woods over woods in gay t. pride GOLDSM.

Theatrical (þiˌæ·trikăl), *a.* and *sb.* 1558. [f. as prec. + -AL.] A. *adj.* 1. Pertaining to or connected with the theatre, or with scenic representations. 2. That 'plays a part'; that simulates, or is simulated; artificial, affected, assumed 1649. 3. Extravagantly or irrelevantly histrionic; 'stagy'; showy, spectacular 1709.

1. He..joins a t. company 1905. 3. His T. Manner of making Love 1709.

B. *sb.* 1. *pl.* The performance of stage plays; dramatic performance by amateurs (*amateur theatricals*), occas. in a private house (*private theatricals*). Also *fig.* doings of a theatrical character; 'acting', pretence. 1657. 2. *pl.* Stage matters 1815. 3. A professional actor 1859. Hence **Thea·tricalism**, t. style or character; 'staginess'. **Thea·trica·lity**, theatricalness an instance of this. **Thea·trical·ly** *adv.*, **-ness.**

Theatricalize (þiˌæ·trikălǝiz), *v.* 1778. [f. prec. + -IZE.] 1. *trans.* To make or render theatrical. 2. *intr.* a. To act on the stage. b. To attend or frequent theatrical performances. 1794.

Theatro- (þī·ătro, þiˌæ·tro), comb. form of Gr. θέατρον THEATRE, as in **Theatro·cracy**, absolute power exercised by the ancient Athenian democracy, as exhibited at their assemblies in the theatre. **Thea·tropho·bia** [-PHOBIA], horror of theatres and theatre-going.

Theave, thaive (þīv, þāv). *local.* 1465. [Origin unkn.] A female sheep of a particular age; usu. applied to a ewe of the first or second year that has not yet borne a lamb.

Thebaic (þībē·ik), *a.*[1] 1687. [ad. L. *Thebaicus*, ad. Gr. Θηβαϊκός, f. Θῆβαι, Θήβη Thebes.] Of or pertaining to the ancient city of Thebes on the Nile, formerly a centre of Egyptian civilization; *spec.* noting the Sahidic version of the Bible.

T. marble, *stone*, the syenite of Thebes and Upper Egypt.

Theba·ic, *a.*[2] 1746. [f. as prec., in ref. to the fact that Egypt is a chief source of the opium of commerce.] *Pharm. Chem.* Of or derived from opium; *t. extract*, *tincture*, laudanum. So **Thebaïne** (þī·beˌīn, ǝin) [-INE [5]], a highly poisonous alkaloid, $C_{19}H_{21}NO_3$, obtained from opium.

Thebaïd (þī·beˌid), *a.* and *sb.* 1727. [ad. Gr. Θηβαΐς, -ιδ-, L. *Thebais*, *-id-*.] A. *adj.* Pertaining to Thebes; usu. B. *sb.* the territory belonging to (*a*) Egyptian, or (*b*) Bœotian Thebes; the name of certain poems, esp. that of Statius relating to Bœotian Thebes.

Theban (þī·băn), *a.* and *sb.* late ME. [ad. L. *Thebanus*, f. *Thebæ*, Gr. Θῆβαι Thebes.] A. *adj.* 1. Of or belonging to Thebes, capital of ancient Bœotia in Greece. **2.** = THEBAIC *a.*[1] 1645.

2. *T. drug*, opium or laudanum. *T. year*, the Egyptian year of 365¼ days.

B. *sb.* A native or inhabitant of Bœotian Thebes, a Bœotian. late ME.

Ile talke a word with this same lerned T. SHAKS.

||**Theca** (þī·kă). *Pl.* **thecæ** (þī·si). 1662. [L., ad. Gr. θήκη case.] **1.** A receptacle, a cell. **2.** *Bot.* A part of a plant serving as a receptacle; a sac, cell, or capsule; *spec.* (*a*) an anther cell, containing pollen; (*b*) a vessel containing spores in various cryptogamous plants, as the capsule of a moss, the sporangium of a fern, etc, 1676. **3.** *Zool.* and *Anat.* A case or sheath enclosing some organ or part: as (*a*) the horny case of an insect pupa; (*b*) the loose sheath investing the spinal cord; (*c*) a cup-like or tubular structure in corals, containing a polyp 1665. Hence **The·cal** *a.* of, pertaining to, or of the nature of a t. **The·cate** *a.* having a t., sheathed.

Theclan (þe·klăn), *a.* 1884. [f. mod.L. *Thecla*, generic name + -AN.] *Ent.* Belonging to the genus *Thecla* of butterflies, comprising the Hair-streaks.

Theco- (þī·ko), erron. **theca-**, comb. form of Gr. θήκη case, receptacle.

Thecoda·ctyle [Gr. δάκτυλος digit] *a.*, having thick toes whose transverse scales furnish a sheath for the claw, as in some lizards; *sb.* a gecko of this type; so **Thecoda·ctylous** *a.* **The·codont** [Gr. ὀδούς, ὀδοντ- tooth] *a.*, of or belonging to the *Thecodontes*, an extinct family of saurians having the teeth fixed in sockets in the jaw-bone; *sb.*, a saurian having this character. **The·cophore** [-PHORE], (*a*) a surface or receptacle bearing a theca or thecæ; (*b*) GYNOPHORE 1. **Theco·so·mate, The·cosoma·tous** [Gr. σῶμα body] *adjs.*, belonging to the *Thecosomata*, a group of pteropods having the body sheathed in a mantle-skirt. **The·co·spore**, a spore produced in a theca, an ascospore; hence **Theco·sporous** *a.*, having thecospores.

Thé dansant (*te* dañsañ). 1845. [F.] An afternoon dance at which tea is served.

Thee (ðī, ði, ðĭ), *pers. pron.* [(1) OE. acc. *ðec, ðeh*, later *ðē, þē*:—OTeut. **þeke*, pre-Teut. **tege*; cf. L. *te*, Gr. σέ, Doric τέ. (2) OE. dat. (later also acc.) *ðē, þē*:—OTeut. **þez*, pre-Teut. **tes*.] **1.** The objective case of the pronoun THOU, repr. the OE. accusative and dative. **2.** *Reflexive*: = thyself OE. **b.** After some intr. vbs. of motion and posture; esp. *sit* 1593. **3.** Used as *nom.*, instead of *thou*. (Often dial., and, in recent times, usu. by Quakers, esp. with vb. in 3rd pers. sing.) late ME. **4.** As *sb.* **a.** The person or 'self' of the individual addressed 1600. **b.** The word itself as used in addressing a person; esp. in phr. *thee and thou* 1694.

1. They haue not refused the, but me COVERDALE 1 *Sam.* viii. 7. I haue..Told thee no lyes, made thee no mistakings SHAKS. To thee I call MILT. 2. Get thee behinde me, Satan BIBLE (Genev.) *Matt.* xvi. 23. Thou wilt neuer get thee a husband, if thou be so shrewd of thy tongue SHAKS. b. Sit thee by our side SHAKS. 3. How agrees the Diuell and thee about thy Soule? SHAKS. Friend, thee isn't wanted here 1852. 4. a. That 's for thy selfe to breed an other thee SHAKS. b. The Thee and Thou of the Quakers LONGF.

†**Thee**, *v.*[1] [OE. *þīon, þēon*, contr. from **þīhan*:—OTeut. **þinχ-*, earlier **þenχ-* (**þanχ-*, **þung-*):—Indo-Eur. root *tenk*.] *intr.* To grow; to thrive, prosper (*arch.* in 16th c. use) –1573. **b.** In imprecations and asseverations –1800.

He can not t. SKELTON. b. Ful ill mought they both t. 1586.

Thee (ðī), *v.*[2] 1662. [f. THEE *pron.*] *trans.* and *intr.* (or *absol.*). To use the pronoun 'thee' to a person: see THOU *v.*

Though I Thee Thee and Thou Thee, I am no Quaker 1662.

Theft (þeft). [OE. (WS.) *þīefð, þȳfð*, non-WS. *þēofð*, later *þēoft*:—OTeut. **þeuþiþā*, f. **þeuƀo* THIEF + suffix *-iþa* = L. *-itatem*; see -TH[1] b, -T[3] b.] **1.** The action of a thief; the felonious taking away of the personal goods of another; larceny; also, with *a* and *pl.*, an instance of this. **2.** *concr.* That which is or has been stolen; the proceeds of thieving. Now *rare.* OE.

2. Yf the thefte be founde in his hande alyue..he shall restore double TINDALE *Exod.* xxii. 4.

Theft-boot, -bote. *Obs.* exc. *Hist.* ME. [orig. *thef-bote*, f. *thef* THIEF + *bote* BOOT *sb.*[1]] The taking of some payment from a thief to secure him from legal prosecution; either the receiving back by the owner of the stolen goods or of some compensation, or the taking of a bribe by a person who ought to have brought the thief to justice.

Thegn (þēⁱn). *Hist.* 1848. A form used by some recent historians to represent the OE. *þegn* THANE (sense 3), to distinguish the Anglo-Saxon from the Scottish use of THANE (sense 4), made familiar by Shakspere. Hence **The·gn-hood**, the condition or position of a t.; the order of thegns, thegns collectively.

Theine (þī·əin). 1838. [f. mod.L. *thea* TEA + -INE[5].] *Chem.* A vegetable alkaloid, orig. thought to be a principle peculiar to tea, but found to be identical with CAFFEINE.

Their (ðē³ɹ), *poss. pron.* and *a.* ME. [a. ON. *þeir(r)a*, genit. pl. of demonstrative *sá, sú, þat* (= OE. *se, séo, þæt*) the, used in ON. also as pl. of 3rd pers. pron.] **1.** Of, belonging or pertaining to them; also *refl.*, of or belonging to themselves. **b.** *obj. genit.* Of (for, to) them 1553. **c.** Coupled with genit. pl. of *all, bo, both*: †*t. aller, t. beyre, t. bother* (obs.); also *all t., t. both, both t., each of t.* (arch.): meaning 'of all of them, of both or each of them' ME. **2.** Used of a thing with which a number of persons have to do, or which is assumed to be the common possession of a class 1785. **3.** Often used in relation to a singular sb. or pronoun denoting a person, after *each, every, either, neither, no one, every one*, etc. Also so used instead of 'his or her', when the gender is inclusive or uncertain. (Regarded as ungrammatical.) ME. †**4.** After a sb. (usu. a proper name), instead of the genitive inflexion. –1681. **5.** As antecedent to a following relative. (Now usu. avoided.) 1574.

1. Vereley I saye vnto you they have there rewarde TINDALE *Matt.* vi. 5. b. Shall..quite from off the earth t. memory be raste? SPENSER. c. Saying thus in all t. hearings PUTTENHAM. 2. All those who love t. Devon 1905. 3. A person can't help t. birth THACKERAY. It's enough to drive anyone out of t. senses G. B. SHAW. 4. An answer to the parliament of England t. declaration 1642. 5. Under t. obedience whome God hath set ouer us 1579.

Theirs (ðē³ɹz), *poss. pron.* ME. [In form a double possessive, f. THEIR + *-es* (cf. *hers, ours*, etc.). Of northern origin.] The form of THEIR used when no sb. follows, i.e. either absol. or predic.: That or those belonging to them. **b.** *Of theirs.* late ME. †**c.** Used instead of THEIR (*rare*) –1774.

Their's not to make reply, Their's not to reason why, Their's but to do and die TENNYSON. b. An old acquaintance of t. 1831. c. Upon the importation ..into t. or our country MARVELL.

Theism[1] (þī·iz'm). 1678. [f. Gr. θεός god + -ISM.] **a.** *gen.* Belief in a deity or deities, as opp. to *atheism*. **b.** Belief in one god, as opp. to *polytheism* or *pantheism*. **c.** Belief in the existence of God, with denial of revelation: = DEISM. **d.** *esp.* Belief in one God as creator and supreme ruler of the universe, without denial of revelation; in this use dist. from *deism*.

Theism[2] (þī·iz'm). 1886. [f. mod.L. *thea* TEA + -ISM.] *Path.* A morbid condition characterized by headache, sleeplessness, and palpitation of the heart, caused by excessive tea-drinking.

Theist (þī·ist). 1662. [f. Gr. θεός god + -IST.] One who holds the doctrine of theism: in earlier use DEIST; in later use, esp. as dist. from this. Hence **Thei·stic, -al** *adjs.* of or pertaining to theists or theism; **-ly** *adv.*

Thelytokous (þili·tŏkəs), *a.* 1877. [f. Gr. θηλυτόκος bearing females + -OUS.] *Zool.* Producing only female offspring, as the parthenogenetic females of some species: opp. to *arrenotokous*. So **Thely·toky**, the production of females in parthenogenesis.

Them (ðem, ðĕm), *pers. pron.* [ME. *þeim, þeym*, a. ON. *þeim* to those, to them, dat. pl. of *sá, sú, þat*, pl. *þeir* THEY; properly a dat. form which was early used as a direct obj. The northern *tham(e* represents the equivalent OE. *þām, þǣm*. See N.E.D.] **I.** Personal pronoun. **1.** As pronoun of the third person plural, objective, direct and indirect (accus. and dat.) of THEY. Also as antecedent pron. followed by relative or prepositional phrase, and having then a demonstrative function, equivalent to *those* but less emphatic. **b.** Sometimes *indefinitely*, as obj. case of THEY I. 3. *colloq.* or *dial.* **2.** Often used for 'him or her', referring to a singular person whose sex is not stated, or to *anybody, nobody, somebody, whoever*, etc. 1742. (Cf. THEIR 3.) **3.** Used for the nominative *they*. **a.** As antecedent or demons. pron.: = THOSE. Now only *dial.* or *illiterate.* 1489. **b.** As pers. pron. after *than, as*, and in the predicate after the vb. *to be*. Common *colloq.*, but considered grammatically incorrect. 1654.

1. T. that honour me, I wil honour BIBLE (Genev.) 1 *Sam.* ii. 30. To show t. what they are to understand 1779. Too solemn for the comic touches in t. TENNYSON. 2. Nobody else..has so little to plague t. 1853. 3. b. It was not t. we wanted 1845.

II. As reflexive pron. = themselves.

They haue made t. a molten calfe COVERDALE *Exod.* xxxii. 8.

III. As demonstr. adj. = THOSE. Now only *dial.* or *illiterate* 1596.

It was a rare rise we got out of t. chaps THACKERAY. T. ribbons of yours cost a trifle, Kitty S. LOVER.

||**Thema** (þī·mă). *Pl.* **themata** (þī·mătă) *rare.* 1531. [See THEME.] = THEME *sb.* I, 4, 5.

Thematic (þĭmæ·tik), *a.* 1861. [ad. Gr. θεματικός, f. θέμα THEME; see -IC.] Of or pertaining to a theme or themes. **1.** Of or pertaining to a subject or topic of discourse or writing (*rare*) 1871. **2.** *Mus.* Of, pertaining to, or constituting themes or subjects (see THEME 4); relating to themes and their contrapuntal development 1867. **3.** *Gram.* Of or pertaining to the theme or stem-form of a word: see THEME 5. 1861.

2. *T. catalogue, index, summary*, one containing the opening themes or passages of musical pieces. 3. *T. vowel*, a vowel which comes between the root and the inflexion in a vb. or sb., as the o and ε in φέρ-ο-μεν, φέρ-ε-τε. So **Thema·tical** *a.*, **-ly** *adv.*

Theme (þīm), *sb.* [ME. *teme*, a. OF. **teme*; in *theme* conformed to L. *thema*, a. Gr. θέμα proposition, f. θε-, root of τιθέναι to put, set, place, lay down.] **1.** The subject of discourse, discussion, conversation, meditation, or composition; a topic. †**b.** *transf.* A subject treated by action (instead of by discourse, etc.); hence, matter, subject *of* or *for* specified action, feeling, etc. –1806. †**c.** *Logic.* That which is the subject of thought –1725. †**2.** *spec.* The text of a sermon; also, a proposition to be discussed –1618. **3.** An exercise written on a given subject, *esp.* a school essay. (The usual term in Jesuit schools.) 1545. **4.** *Mus.* The principal melody, plainsong, or *canto fermo* in a contrapuntal piece; hence, any one of the principal melodies or motives in a sonata, symphony, etc.; also, a simple tune on which variations are constructed 1674. **5.** *Philol.* The inflexional base or stem of a word, consisting of the 'root' with modification or addition; thus in Gr. λείπειν, the root is λιπ, the present theme or stem λειπ-; in τέκνον, the root is τεκ, the theme τεκνο- 1530. **6.** *Astrol.* The disposition of the heavenly bodies at a particular time, as at the moment of a person's birth 1652. **7.** *Anc. Hist.* Each of the twenty-nine provinces into which the Byzantine empire was divided 1788.

1. My t. is alwey oon and euere was Radix malorum est Cupiditas CHAUCER. His Highness's notorious treachery..the t. of all the public dispatches WELLINGTON. b. I must play my theame SHAKS. An infallible Theame of endlesse troubles SIR T. HERBERT. 3. The theam of a Grammar lad MILT. Hence **Theme** *v. trans.* to furnish with a t. or subject.

||**Themis** (þe·mis, þī·mis). 1656. [a. Gr. Θέμις.] **1.** Name of the ancient Greek goddess of law and justice; hence, Law or Justice personified. **2.** Name of the twenty-fourth of the asteroids 1886.

Themselves (ðĕmse·lvz), *pron. pl.* ME. [The original construction was nom., acc. *hī, héo selfe*, dat. *heom selfum*, whence ME. *hem-selve(n*. In 14th c. this was superseded in north. dial. by *þaim self(e, þaim selven. Themselfs, themselves* appears c 1500, and became the standard form c 1540.] **I.** Emphatic. = Those very persons or things. **1.** Standing in apposition with the pron. *they* (rarely *them*), or with a sb., or adj. used subst. **2.** Used alone for emphasis as a simple nominative. *arch.* ME. **b.**

To be t.: to be in their normal condition of mind, body, or behaviour 1698. **3.** As emphatic objective. Now chiefly as object of a preposition. late ME.

1. Music-paper (which they mostly ruled themselves) T. HARDY. **2.** To remember how t. sate in fear of their persons SWIFT. **3.** You are one of t., you know—Middlemas of that Ilk SCOTT.

II. Reflexive: = L. *sibi, se*; Fr. *se, soi*; G. *sich.* **1.** As direct obj. (acc.), indirect obj. (dat.), or object of a preposition ME. **2.** In concord with a sing. pron. or sb. denoting a person, in cases where the meaning implies more than one, as when the sb. is qualified by a distributive, or refers to either sex: = himself or herself 1464. (Cf. THEIR 3.)

1. They..made themselues aprons *Gen.* iii. 7. Not to make fools of t. 1779. **2.** Every one likes to keep it to t. as long as they can 1874.

III. From the 14th c. there has been a tendency to treat *self* as a sb. (= person, personality), and substitute *their* for *them.* (In literary Eng. this has place only where an adj. intervenes, as *their own, sweet, very selves.*)

Liking it well their selues ASCHAM. They theirselves stumbled and fell 1836.

Then (ðen), *adv.* (*conj., adj., sb.*) [OE. *þanne, þænne, þonne,* ME. *þenne, þan, þen*; advb. formations from the demons. root *þa-*; cf. THAT, THE. See also THAN *conj.*] **I.** Demonstrative adv. of time. **1.** At that time. Referring to a specified time, past or future: (opp. to NOW I. 1.) **b.** At the time defined by a relative or other clause (with vb. in pres. tense) ME. **2.** *Now and t.*, at one time and at another, at various times, at intervals, occasionally. *Now .. then ..*, at one time .. at another time. ME.

1. History, as it was t. written BUCKLE. Phr. *T. and there*, at that precise time and place; immediately and on the spot; also *there and t.* **b.** Yse which dissolueth, t. when it vanisheth away 1567. **2.** Restive, now sullen, t. in boisterous revolt 1894.

II. Of sequence in time, order, consequence, incidence, inference. **1.** At the moment immediately following the action, etc. just spoken of; upon that, thereupon, directly after that; also, next, after that, afterwards, subsequently (often in contrast to *first*) OE. **b.** In the next place, next (in a series of any kind, or esp. in order of narration); beyond that, more than that, in addition, besides ME. **2.** In that case; in those circumstances; if that be (or were) the fact; if so; when that happens. Often correl. to *if* or *when.* OE. **b.** *But t...*: but, that being so; but at the same time; but on the other hand, but: introducing a statement (rarely a phrase) in some way contrasted with or limiting the preceding 1445. **3.** (As a particle of inference, often unemphatic or enclitic.) That being the case; since that is so; on that account; therefore, consequently, as may be inferred; so. *Now t.*: see NOW II. b. OE.

1. First we Fast, and t. we Feast SELDEN. **b.** And t. she had such a fine head of hair C. BRONTE. **2.** Suppose you..had never a farthing but of your own getting; where would you be t.? MISS BURNEY. *What t.?* (ellipt.) what happens (or would happen) in that case? What of that? **b.** Pope knew next to no Greek, but t. he did not work upon the Greek text BIRRELL. **3.** Well t., take a good heart, and counterfeit to be a man SHAKS.

†III. As relative or conjunctive adv. of time: At the time that; when –1440.

IV. As *sb.* or *adj.* **1.** Preceded by a prep., as *by, since, till,* etc. (= by, etc. that time) ME. **2.** That time; the time referred to (esp. a past time): often contrasted with *now* 1549. **3. a.** In sense 1, followed by a pple. or adj. forming an adj. phrase, as *the t. existing system* = the system then existing 1653. **b.** *attrib.* or as *adj.* That existed or was so at that time; *the t. ruler* = the ruler that then was 1584.

1. Till t. who knew The force of those dire Arms? MILT. *By t. that*, by the time that; ellipt. *by t.* (as relative), by the time (*arch.* or *dial.*); By t. he had folded and addressed it, she returned READE. **2.** The tyme is tourned: t. was t., and now is now 1549.

Thenad (þe·n-, þī·næd), *adv.* 1803. [f. THENAR + *-ad*; see DEXTRAD *adv.*] *Anat.* Towards the thenal aspect.

Then-a-days (ðe·nādēⁱz), *adv. rare.* 1688. [f. THEN *adv.*, after *nowadays.*] In those days, at that (past) time.

Thenal (þī·năl), *a.* 1803. [f. next + -AL.] *Anat.* Of or pertaining to the thenar.

Thenar (þī·năı). 1672. [mod.L., a. Gr. θέναρ palm of the hand, sole or flat of the foot.] *Anat.* The ball of muscle at the base of the thumb; the palm of the hand; the sole of the foot. Also *attrib.* or as *adj.* 1857.

T. muscles, the muscles which form the *t. eminence*, the ball at the base of the thumb.

Thenardite (þenā·ıdəit, ten-). 1842. [f. name of L. J. *Thénard*, French chemist; see -ITE [1].] *Min.* Anhydrous sodium sulphate occurring in white or brown translucent crystals.

Thence (ðens), *adv.* [ME. *þannes, þennes,* f. THENNE *adv.*, with advb. genitive suffix *-es, -s.* Spelt *thence* to preserve the breath sound of *s* when final inflexional *s* became (z).] **1.** From that place; from there. (Now chiefly *literary.*) **b.** Preceded by redundant *from.* late ME. **2.** At a place distant or away from there; distant; absent. Now chiefly in stating distance. ME. **3.** From that time or date. Mostly with *from.* Now *rare* or *Obs.* late ME. **4.** From that, as a source, origin, or cause; from those premisses or data; therefrom. Also preceded by *from.* 1652.

1. If Sion hill Delight thee more..I t. Invoke thy aid MILT. **b.** Homeward from t. by easy stages GEO. ELIOT. **3.** From t. down to the present day 1751. **4.** It would t. follow, that [etc.] 1796.

Thenceforth (ðe·ns͵fōᵊɹþ, ðens͵fōᵊ·ɹþ), *adv.* late ME. [orig. two words.] **1.** From that time onward. Also with *from.* **2.** From that place or point onward (*rare*) 1449.

1. From thence forthe sought Pilate meanes to loose hym TINDALE *John.* xix. 12.

Thencefo·rward, *adv.* 1457. [orig. two words.] = prec. Also with *from.* So †**Thencefo·rwards** *adv.* –1727.

Thence-from, *adv. arch.* 1618. [Inversion of *from thence.*] From that place or source; thence.

†**Thenne, then**, *adv.* [OE. *þanon(e, þonan*, f. stem *þa-* of dem. THAT.] = THENCE –1450.

Theo- (þīo), or, bef. a vowel, **the-**, repr. Gr. θεο-, stem of θεός God; in many compounds adopted from, or formed on the analogy of, Greek, or from Greek (rarely Latin or other) elements.

Theoce·ntric *a.*, centring or centred in God; having God as its centre. **Theochri·stic** [Gr. θεόχριστος] *a.*, anointed by God. **The·o͵philoso·phic** *a.*, that applies philosophy to theology.

‖**Theobroma** (þīobrōᵘ·mă). 1760. [mod. L., f. Gr. θεός god + βρῶμα food.] *Bot.* A genus of low trees, of which one species, *T. Cacao*, a native of tropical America, is the source of cocoa and chocolate. Hence **Theobro·mic** *a. Chem.* in *theobromic acid*, $C_{64}H_{128}O_2$, obtained from cacao-butter. **Theobromine** (þīobrōᵘ·məin), a bitter volatile alkaloid, $C_7H_8N_4O_2$, resembling caffeine, contained in the seeds of the cacao tree.

Theocracy (þi͵ǫ·krăsi). 1622. [ad. Gr. θεοκρατία; see THEO- and -CRACY.] A form of government in which God (or a deity) is recognized as the king or immediate ruler, and his laws are taken as the statute-book of the kingdom, these laws being usu. administered by a priestly order as his ministers and agents; hence (loosely) a system of government by a sacerdotal order, claiming a divine commission; also, a state so governed: esp. applied to the commonwealth of Israel from the exodus to the election of Saul as king. **b.** *transf.* A priestly order or religious body exercising political or civil power 1825.

Theocrasy (þī·o͵krēⁱ:si, þi͵ǫ·krăsi). 1816. [ad. Gr. θεοκρασία, f. θεός god + κρᾶσις mingling; see -Y [3].] *Anc. Myth.* A mingling of various deities or divine attributes into one personality; also, a mixture of the worship of different deities.

Theocrat (þī·okræt). 1827. [f. next; see -CRAT.] **1.** One who rules in a theocracy as the representative of the Deity; a divine or deified ruler. **2.** An advocate of theocracy 1843.

Theocratic (þīokræ·tik), *a.* 1741. [f. Gr. θεοκρατία THEOCRACY + -IC.] Of, pertaining to, or of the nature of theocracy. So **Theocra·tical** *a.* 1690, -ly *adv.*

Theodicy (þi͵ǫ·disi). 1797. [ad. F. *Théodicée*, title of a work of Leibnitz (1710), f. Gr. θεός God + δίκη justice.] The, or a vindication of the divine attributes, esp. justice and holiness, in respect to the existence of evil; a writing, doctrine, or theory intended to 'justify the ways of God to men'.

Theodolite (þi͵ǫ·dŏləit). 1571. [Origin unkn.] A portable surveying instrument, orig. for measuring horizontal angles, and consisting essentially of a planisphere or horizontal graduated circular plate, with an alidad or index bearing sights; subsequently variously elaborated with a telescope instead of sights, a compass, level, vernier, micrometer, and other accessories, and now often with the addition of a vertical circle or arc for the measurement of angles of altitude or depression. Hence **Theodoli·tic** *a.* of, pertaining to, done, or made with a t.

Theodosian (þīŏdōᵘ·siăn, -dōᵘ·ʃiăn), *a.* and *sb.* 1765. [f. the name *Theodosius*; see -AN.] **A.** *adj.* Of or pertaining to one named Theodosius; *esp.* to the Roman emperor Theodosius II (A.D. 408–450).

T. code, a collection of laws made by direction of Theodosius II, and published A.D. 438.

B. *sb.* **1.** A follower of Theodosius, a rhetorician of Alexandria, who became (A.D. 535) the leader of a division of the Monophysites 1788. **2.** A member of a sect founded by Theodosius, a Russian monk 1860.

Theogony (þi͵ǫ·gŏni). 1612. [ad. Gr. θεογονία generation or birth of the gods, f. θεός + -γονία a begetting.] The generation of the gods; *esp.* an account or theory, or the belief or study, of the genealogy or birth of the deities of heathen mythology. Hence **Theogo·nic** *a.* of, pertaining to, of the nature of t. **Theo·gonist**, one who is versed in or treats of t. **Theo·gonism**, a system or theory of t.

Theolatry (þi͵ǫ·lătri). 1806. [ad. Gr. θεολατρεία; see -LATRY.] The worship of a deity or deities.

Theologal (þi͵ǫ·lŏgăl), *a.* and *sb.* 1484. [a. F. *théologal*, f. Gr.-L. *theologus* theologian; see -AL.] †**A.** *adj.* in *t. virtues*; see THEOLOGICAL *a.* 1. –1610. **B.** *sb. R.C.Ch.* A lecturer on theology and Holy Scripture attached to a cathedral or collegiate church. Also called *theologus* and, more usually, *canon theologian* 1638.

Theologaster (þi͵ǫlŏgæ·stəɹ). 1621. [a. mod.L. (Luther 1518), f. *theologus* theologian; see -ASTER.] A shallow or paltry theologian; a smatterer or pretender in theology.

Theologer (þi͵ǫ·lŏdʒəɹ). Now *rare.* 1588. [f. stem of Gr.-L. *theologus* + -ER [1]; see -LOGER.] = next (but now with less implication of scholarship). **a.** In ref. to Christianity or other monotheistic religions. **b.** In ref. to pagan religions 1609.

Theologian (þīŏlōᵘ·dʒiăn). 1483. [a. F. *théologien*, f. *théologie* or L. *theologia*; subseq. assim. to L. spelling; see -LOGIAN.] One who is versed in theology; *spec.* one who makes a study or profession of theology; a divine. **b.** = prec. b (*rare*) 1603. **c.** *Canon t.* (R. C. Ch.) = THEOLOGAL B. 1885.

The common gloss of Theologians MILTON.

Theologic (þīŏlǫ·dʒik), *a.* (*sb.*) 1477. [ad. F. *théologique*, ad. L. *theologicus*, a. Gr. θεολογικός, f. θεολογία THEOLOGY.] **1.** = next 2. †**2.** = next 1. –1637. †**B.** *absol.* as *sb.* (*pl.*) Theological matters. YOUNG.

Theological (þīŏlǫ·dʒikăl), *a.* (*sb.*) 1484. [ad. med.L. *theologicalis*, f. L. *theologicus* (see prec.) + *-alis* -AL; see -ICAL.] **1.** Of or pertaining to the word of God, i.e. the Bible; scriptural; in *t. virtues* [*virtutes theologicæ*], applied to faith, hope, and charity (1 Cor. xiii. 13), as dist. from the four *cardinal virtues* of Plato and the Stoics. **2.** Of, pertaining to, or of the nature of theology; treating of theology 1603.

2. The abolition of all t. tests 1904.

B. *sb.* †**1.** *pl.* The theological virtues –1600. †**2.** *pl.* Theological matters or principles –1774. **3.** A man trained at a theological college 1866. Hence **Theolo·gically** *adv.* in a t. manner; from a t. point of view; as regards theology.

Theologician (þiˌǫlǫdʒi·ʃăn). Now *rare.* 1560. [f. L. *theologicus* + -IAN; see -ICIAN.] = THEOLOGIAN.

Theologico- (þiǫlǫ·dʒiko), comb. form from Gr. θεολογικός THEOLOGICAL: 'theologically-, theological and..'; as in *t.-metaphysical.*

Theologism (þiˌǫ·lŏdʒiz'm). 1867. [f. next; see -ISM.] The action or product of theologizing; theological speculation or system: usu. in a derogatory sense.

Theologist (þiˌǫ·lŏdʒist). 1638. [ad. med. L. *theologista* (Luther), agent-n. f. *theologizare* THEOLOGIZE; see -IST.] A professed theologian. **a.** = THEOLOGER b. Now *rare.* **b.** = THEOLOGER a. 1641. **c.** In derogatory sense 1900.

Theologize (þiˌǫ·lŏdʒəiz), *v.* 1649. [In sense 1, ad. med. L. *theologizare*, f. *theologia*; see -IZE. In 2, perh. formed directly from *theology.*] **1.** *intr.* To play the theologian; to speculate in theology 1656. **2.** *trans.* To render theological; to conform to theology; to treat theologically 1649.

1. My Design, which is not to T. in Philosophy 1662. Hence **Theo·logizer**, a theologer.

Theologo- (þiˌǫ·lŏgo), comb. form repr. Gr. θεολόγος a theologian; as in **t.-inquisito·rial** *a.*, of or pertaining to a theological inquisitor.

Theologue (þī·ǒlǫg). late ME. [ad. L. *theologus*, a. Gr. θεολόγος, f. θεός GOD + λέγειν to discourse; see -LOGUE. Before the 17th c. only Sc.] **1.** = THEOLOGIAN. Now *rare.* **2.** [prob. after G. *theolog.*] A theological student. *U.S. colloq.* 1663.

Theology (þiˌǫ·lŏdʒi). late ME. [a. F. *théologie*, ad. L. *theologia*, a. Gr. θεολογία, f. θεολόγος; see prec. and -LOGY.] The study or science which treats of God, His nature and attributes, and His relations with man and the universe; 'the science of things divine' (Hooker); divinity. **b.** A particular theological system or theory 1669. **c.** Applied to pagan or non-Christian systems 1662.

Peter Lombard, the founder of systematic t. in the twelfth century 1837. *Dogmatic t.*, t. as authoritatively held and taught by the church; a scientific statement of Christian dogma. *Natural t.*, t. based upon reasoning from natural facts apart from revelation. *Pastoral t.*, that branch of t. which deals with religious truth in its relation to the spiritual needs of men, and the 'cure of souls'. **b.** Latest development of 'New T.' 1907.

Theomachy (þiˌǫ·măki). 1570. [ad. Gr. θεομαχία, f. θεός god + -μαχία fighting.] †**1.** A striving or warring against God; opposition to the will of God -1690. **2.** A battle or strife among the gods: esp. in ref. to that narrated in Homer's Iliad 1858. Hence **Theo·machist**, one who fights against God.

Theomancy (þī·omænsi). 1651. [ad. Gr. θεομαντεία spirit of prophecy, f. θεός + μαντεία; see -MANCY.] A kind of divination drawn from the responses of oracles or the predictions of sibyls and others supposed to be immediately inspired by some divinity.

Theomorphic (þiomǭ·ɪfik), *a.* 1870. [f. Gr. θεόμορφος of divine form (f. θεός + μόρφη) + -IC.] Having the form or likeness of God; of or pertaining to theomorphism. So **Theomo·rphism**, the doctrine that man has the form or likeness of God.

Theopaschite (þiopæ·skəit). 1585. [ad. eccl. L. *theopaschita*, ad. Gr. θεοπασχίτης, f. θεός god + πάσχειν to suffer; see -ITE[1] 1 a.] *Eccl. Hist.* A member of a Monophysite sect of the 6th c., who held that the divine nature of Christ suffered on the Cross.

Theopathetic (þioˌpăþe·tik), *a.* 1748. [f. next, after *pathetic.*] Of, pertaining to, or characterized by theopathy. So **Theopa·thic** *a.*

Theopathy (þiˌǫ·păþi). 1748. [f. THEO- + -PATHY.] Sympathetic passive feeling excited by the contemplation of God; susceptibility to this feeling; sensitiveness or responsiveness to divine influence; pious sentiment.

Theophany (þiˌǫ·făni). 1633. [ad. L. *theophania*, a. Gr. θεοφάνεια and θεοφάνια (neut. pl.), f. θεός + φαίνειν to show; see -PHANY.] A manifestation or appearance of God or a god to man.

Theophilanthropist (þī·oˌfilæ·nþrǒpist). 1797. [f. THEO- + PHILANTHROPIST, after F. *théophilanthrope*, erron. employed to express 'loving God and man'.] A member of a sect of Deists which appeared in France in 1796. So **The:ophila·nthropism** = next.

The:ophila·nthropy. 1798. [a. F. *théophilanthropie*, intended to express 'love to God and man'; cf. prec.] The deistic system of the theophilanthropists, based on a belief in the existence of God and in the immortality of the soul.

‖**Theophobia** (þioˌfōᵘ·biă). 1870. [f. THEO- + -PHOBIA.] Anxious fear of God; dread of divine anger. So **Theo·phobist**, one who is affected with t.

Theopneust (þī·opniūst), *a.* 1647. [ad. Gr. θεόπνευστος, f. θεός god + -πνευστος inspired, f. stem πνευ- of πνεῖν to breathe, blow.] Divinely inspired. So **Theopneu·stic** *a.* in same sense. **Theopneu·sty**, ‖**Theopneu·stia**, divine inspiration.

Theor (þī·ǫɪ). Also in L. form **theo·rus.** 1847. [ad. Gr. θεωρός spectator, envoy; see THEORY[2].] *Gr. Antiq.* An ambassador or envoy sent on behalf of a state, esp. to consult an oracle or perform a religious rite.

Theorbo (þiˌǭ·ɪbo). 1605. [ad. F. *téorbe, théorbe*, ad. It. *tiorba* 'a kind of musicall instrument used among countrie people' (Florio); origin unkn.] A large kind of lute with a double neck and two sets of tuning-pegs, the lower holding the melody strings and the upper the bass strings; much in vogue in the 17th c. Hence **Theo·rbist**, a player on the t.

Theorem (þī·ŏrĕm), *sb.* 1551. [ad. late L. *theorema*, a. Gr. θεώρημα, f. θεωρεῖν to look at, inspect. Perh. directly a. F. *théorème.*] A universal or general proposition or statement, not self-evident (thus dist. from an AXIOM), but demonstrable by argument (in the strict sense, by necessary reasoning); 'a demonstrable theoretical judgement'. **a.** In Mathematics and Physics; *spec.* in Geometry, a proposition embodying merely something to be proved, as dist. from a PROBLEM, which embodies something to be done. **b.** *gen.*, or in ref. to any particular science or technical subject 1597.

a. Geometrical theorems grew out of empirical methods H. SPENCER. **b.** The..peaceful Theoremes of..a holy Religion JER. TAYLOR. Hence **The·orem** *v. trans.* to express in or by means of a t.

Theorematic (þī:ŏrĕmæ·tik), *a.* 1656. [ad. Gr. θεωρηματικός, f. θεώρηματ- THEOREM + -ικος -IC.] Pertaining to, by means of, or of the nature of a theorem. So †**Theorema·tical** *a.*, -ly *adv.* †**Theore·mic** *a.*

Theoretic (þiŏre·tik), *a.* (*sb.*) 1656. [ad. late L. *theoreticus*, a. Gr. θεωρητικός, f. θεωρητός, f. θεωρεῖν to look at, inspect.] †**1.** Speculative -1706. **2.** (tr. Gr. θεωρητικός in Aristotle.) Contemplative, as opp. to active or practical (πρακτικός). *rare.* 1907. **3.** = THEORETICAL 2, 2 b. 1661. **b.** Of persons, their minds, etc.: Versed in or proceeding by the scientific theory of the subject: opp. to *empirical*; also, Given to theories; speculative; theorizing: sometimes opp. to *practical* 1727.

3. I soon reduced my T. Knowledge to Practice 1773. Plots which cannot be executed; which are mostly t. CARLYLE. **b.** Distinguished..as a t. and practical farmer GEO. ELIOT.

B. *sb.* Usu. *pl.* Theory (as opp. to *practic*, practice); theoretical matters 1656.

Theoretical (þiŏre·tikăl), *a.* (*sb.*) 1616. [f. as prec. + -AL; see -ICAL.] †**1.** Contemplative -1623. **2.** Of, pertaining or relating to theory; of the nature of or consisting in theory. Often opp. to *practical.* 1652. **b.** That is such according to theory; ideal, hypothetical 1826. **3. a.** Of the mind or intellectual faculties: Having the power of forming theories; speculative 1652. **b.** Of persons: Addicted to theory; constructing or dealing with theories; speculative 1840. **B.** *sb.* (*pl.*) Theoretical points or matters 1860.

2. These observations agree with the t. deductions 1860. **3. b.** Doubts have been thrown on this principle only by t. writers DARWIN. Hence **Theore·tically** *adv.*

‖**Theoria** (þiˌō·riă). *rare.* 1590. [a. Gr. θεωρία.] †**1.** Contemplation, survey. MARLOWE. **2.** The perception of beauty regarded as a moral faculty: dist. from *æsthesis*. RUSKIN.

Theoric (þī·ŏrik), *sb.* and *a.*[1] [Late ME. *theorique*, a. OF. *theorique*, prob. repr. a med.L. **theorica*, Gr. θεωρική.] **A.** *sb.* **1.** = THEORY[1] 3 b, c, 4: chiefly in sense 3 b. *Obs.* or *arch.* †**b.** *pl.* **Theorics**: theoretical statements or notions; theory -1661. †**2.** A mechanical device theoretically representing or explaining a natural phenomenon -1657. †**3.** A man devoted to contemplation or speculation; a member of a contemplative sect of Essenes -1798.

1. So that the Art and Practique part of Life, Must be the Mistresse to this Theorique SHAKS.

†**B.** *adj.* = THEORETICAL *a.* -1804. So †**Theo·rical** *a.*, -ly *adv.*

Theoric (þiˌǫ·rik), *a.*[2] 1727. [ad. Gr. θεωρικός pertaining to spectacles, f. θεωρία viewing.] *Gr. Antiq.* Pertaining to or connected with public spectacles, religious functions, and solemn embassies: applied esp. to a fund provided for these purposes from the public treasury at Athens.

Theorician (þīori·ʃăn). 1841. [f. (after F. *théoricien*) on THEORIC *sb.* + -IAN.] A holder of a theory; = THEORIST.

‖**Theoricon** (þiˌō·rikǫn). 1828. [a. Gr. θεωρικόν neut. of θεωρικός THEORIC *a.*[2]] *Gr. Antiq.* The theoric fund in ancient Athens.

Theorist (þī·ŏrist). 1594. [f. THEORY + -IST.] **1.** An adept in the theory (as dist. from the practice) of a subject. Often with mixture of sense 2. **2.** One who theorizes; a theoretical investigator or writer; one who holds or maintains a theory; occas., a framer or maintainer of a mere hypothesis or speculation 1646.

2. It [gravitation] is lately demonstrated..by that very excellent and divine t. Mr. Isaac Newton 1692.

Theorize (þī·ŏrəiz), *v.* 1638. [f. as prec. + -IZE.] **1.** *intr.* To form or construct theories. **2.** *trans.* To construct a theory of or about 1848. **b.** To suppose, or assume, in the way of theory 1838. **c.** To bring *into* or *out of* some condition theoretically 1843.

2. [Mechanics] theorizes the forces and motions of the masses; [Chemistry] the intimate structure of each 1848. Hence **The:oriza·tion**, the action of theorizing. **The·orizer**, one who theorizes.

Theory[1] (þī·ŏri). 1597. [ad. late L. *theoria*, a. Gr. θεωρία viewing, a sight, spectacle, abstr. sb. f. θεωρός (:—*θεαορός) spectator, f. stem θεα- of θεᾶσθαι.] †**1.** Mental view, contemplation -1710. **2.** A conception or mental scheme of something to be done, or of the method of doing it; a systematic statement of rules or principles to be followed 1597. **3.** A scheme or system of ideas or statements held as an explanation or account of a group of facts or phenomena; a hypothesis that has been confirmed or established by observation or experiment, and is propounded or accepted as accounting for the known facts; a statement of what are held to be the general laws, principles, or causes of something known or observed 1638. **b.** That department of an art or technical subject which consists in the knowledge or statement of the facts on which it depends, or of its principles or methods, as dist. from the *practice* of it 1613. **c.** A systematic statement of the general principles or laws of some branch of mathematics; a set of theorems forming a connected system: as *the t. of equations, of numbers* 1799. **4.** Without article: Systematic conception or statement of the principles of something; abstract knowledge, or the formulation of it: often used as implying more or less unsupported hypothesis: dist. from or opp. to *practice* 1624. **5.** In loose or general sense: A hypothesis proposed as an explanation; hence, a mere hypothesis, speculation, conjecture; an idea or set of ideas about something; an individual view or notion 1792.

1. Nor can I thinke I have the true T. of death when I contemplate a skull, or behold a Skeleton with those vulgar imaginations it casts upon us SIR T. BROWNE. 2. The t. of the old Government of India was one which could not be defended BRIGHT. 3. Were a t. open to no objection it would cease to be a t., and would become a law 1850. The Copernican t., which placed the sun in the centre of our system 1879. **b.** Logic being concerned with the t. of Rea-

soning 1827. 4. Theorie without Practice will serve but for little 1692. 5. Whether I am right in the t. or not,..the fact is as I state it BURKE.

Theory [2] (þī·ŏ°ri). 1842. [ad. Gr. θεωρία, in a specialized sense.] *Gr. Antiq.* A body of theors sent by a state to perform some religious rite or duty; a solemn legation.

Theosoph (þī·ŏsǫf). 1822. [= F. *théosophe*, ad. med.L. *theosophus*, a. late Gr. θεόσοφος, f. θεός God + σοφός wise.] One who pursues THEOSOPHY (sense 1).

Theosopher (þiˌǫ·sǒfəɹ). 1647. [f. THEOSOPHY + -ER [1].] = THEOSOPHIST. (Applied spec. to Jacob Boehme, 'the Teutonic T.', and his followers.)

Theosophic (þīosǫ·fik), *a.* 1649. [f. as prec. + -IC.] Of, pertaining to, or of the nature of theosophy; versed in theosophy. So **Theoso·phical** *a.* theosophic; also, of or belonging to THEOSOPHY (sense 2) 1642; **-ly** *adv.*

Theosophism (þiˌǫ·sǒfiz'm). 1791. [f. as THEOSOPH + -ISM.] The theory and practice of theosophy; theosophizing.

Theosophist (þiˌǫ·sǒfist). 1569. [f. as prec. + -IST.] 1. One who professes or believes in THEOSOPHY (in sense 1). a. With specific ref. to Boehme. b. *gen.* 1814. 2. A professor or adherent of THEOSOPHY (in sense 2); a member of the Theosophical Society; name of a magazine, the organ of that society 1881.

1. b. The t. is one who gives you a theory of God, or of the works of God, which has not reason, but an inspiration of his own for its basis 1856. Hence **Theosophi·stic, -al** *adjs.* of the nature of or pertaining to a t. or theosophy.

Theosophize (þiˌǫ·sǒfəiz), *v.* 1846. [f. as prec. + -IZE.] *intr.* To practise or pretend to theosophy; to reason or discourse theosophically.

Theosophy (þiˌǫ·sǒfi). 1650. [ad. med.L. *theosophia*, a. late Gr. θεοσοφία, f. θεόσοφος THEOSOPH.] 1. Any system of speculation which bases the knowledge of nature upon that of the divine nature: often with ref. to Boehme. 2. Applied to a system of recent origin, resembling the above in its claim to a knowledge of nature profounder than is obtained from empirical science, and contained in an esoteric tradition of which the doctrines of the various historical religions are held to be only the exoteric expression. Sometimes called Esoteric Buddhism. 1881.

1. The Ancient, reall Theosophie of the Hebrewes and Egyptians 1650. 2. T. has no code of morals, being itself the embodiment of the highest morality MRS. BESANT.

Theotechny (þī·otekni). 1858. [f. Gr. θεός god + τέχνη art.] The introduction of divine or supernatural beings in the construction of a drama or epic; such beings collectively.

‖**Theotokos** (þiˌǫ·tŏkǫs). 1874. [a. Gr. θεοτόκος adj. f. θεός God + -τοκος bringing forth, f. stem τεκ-, τοκ- of τίκτειν to bear.] A title of the Virgin Mary as 'Mother of God'; = DEIPARA.

Theow, thew [1]. Now only *Hist.* or *arch.* [OE. *þéow, þéow, þéo*, masc.:—OTeut. **þewoz*; beside OE. *þeow* fem.] A slave, bondman, thrall. Hence **The(o)w·dom**, slavery, bondage, thraldom (*Obs.* exc. *Hist.*).

-ther, *suffix*, repr. ult. Indo-Eur. compar. suffix *-tero-*, as in FURTHER; cf. AFTER.

‖**Therapeutæ** (þerăpiū·tī), *sb. pl.* 1681. [eccl. L., a. Gr. θεραπευταί servants, attendants.] A sect of Jewish mystics residing in Egypt in the first century A.D., described in a book attributed to Philo.

Therapeutic (þerăpiū·tik), *sb.* 1541. [In sense 1, ad. mod.L. *therapeutica*, a. Gr. θεραπευτική (sc. τέχνη) the art of healing, fem. sing. of θεραπευτικός; see next. In sense 2 absol. uses of the adj.] 1. That branch of medicine which is concerned with the remedial treatment of disease; the art of healing. Now usu. in pl. Therapeutics. 2. a. A curative agent. b. A medical man. 1842.

Therapeu·tic, *a.* 1646. [In sense 1, ad. mod.L. *therapeuticus*, a. Gr. θεραπευτικός, f. θεραπευτής, f. θεραπεύειν to treat medically, f. θέραψ, θεραπ- attendant. In sense 2, f. THERAPEUTÆ.] 1. Of or pertaining to the healing of disease. 2. Of or pertaining to the Therapeutæ 1681. So **Therapeu·tical** *a.* (in sense 1) 1605; **-ly** *adv.*

Therapeutist (þerăpiū·tist). 1816. [f. THERAPEUTIC *sb.* + -IST.] One skilled in therapeutics; a physician.

Therapy (þe·răpi). 1846. [ad. mod.L. *therapia*, a. Gr. θεραπεία healing.] The medical treatment of disease; curative medical treatment.

There (ðē°ɹ, *unstressed*, ðĕr, ðəɹ), *adv.* (*sb.*) OE. *þǽr, þér*; f. demons. stem *þa-*, pre-Teut. *to-* (see THE).] I. As demonstrative adv. 1. In or at that place; in the place (country, region, etc.) pointed to, indicated, or referred to, and away from the speaker; the opposite of *here*. 2. Appended, unstressed, to the name of a person or thing to whose presence attention is called: = who or that is there, whom or which you see there 1590. b. As a brusque mode of address to a person or persons in the place or direction indicated: = you (that are) there 1596. c. Emphatically appended to the demonstrative *that*. *dial.* and *vulgar*. 1742. 3. Pointing to something as present to the sight or perception, chiefly in *there is, there are*; also calling attention to something offered (often *absol.*) 1535. b. Pointing out a person or object with approval or commendation, or the contrary. Also in anticipatory commendation of the person addressed. 1595. 4. Used unemphatically to introduce a sentence or clause in which, for the sake of emphasis or preparing the hearer, the verb comes before its subject, as *t. comes a time when*, etc., *t. was heard a rumbling noise*, *breathes there the man..?* OE. b. esp. with the verb *to be* OE. c. (esp. with *to be*) as virtual antecedent of a rel. pron. (e.g. *there are who say..*) *arch.* late ME. 5. At that point or stage in action, proceeding, speech, or thought; formerly sometimes referring to what immediately precedes or follows: at that juncture; on that; on that occasion; then. late ME. 6. a. In that thing, matter, or business; in that fact or circumstance; in that respect, as to that. late ME. b. Referring to something said or done: In those words, in that act 1596. 7. Used interjectionally, usu. to point (in a tone of vexation, derision, satisfaction, etc.) to some fact, condition, or consummation, presented to the sight or mind 1535. 8. To that place: now taking in ordinary use the place of THITHER OE.

1. I have walked t., but have never walked thither COWPER. T. rolls the deep where grew the tree TENNYSON. 2. Hand me that book t., please (*mod.*). b. Silence t., hoe! 1596. Ball, you t. 1859. 3. T. is my hand, You shall be as a Father, to my Youth SHAKS. There's for you, dear Sir! 1742. T. was that lazy Mr. Lethbridge lounging in the doorway 1890. b. There's a Word for a Lady's Mouth! RICHARDSON. Have a cup of tea, there's a good soul DICKENS. There's glory for you! 'L. CARROLL'. 4. Lurk t. no hearts that throb with secret pain? BYRON. b. For many Miles about There's scarce a Bush SHAKS. c. T. was no knyȝt knewe from whens he came MALORY. 5. T. we are at this instant 1647. *And there('s) an end*, and that is the end of the matter; 'and that's all' (*Obs.* or *arch.*). 6. a. Thy Iuliet is aliue,..T. art thou happy SHAKS. T. is where the Japanese differ from us 1896. b. You have me t.! (*mod. colloq.*). 7. T.! I have put my foot in it! MRS. CARLYLE. 8. *T. and back*, to that place and back again. *To get t.* (colloq. or slang): see GET *v.* V. 1 b.

†II. As a relative or conjunctive adverb. 1. In, on, at, or into which place; = WHERE –1594. 2. In the very case or circumstances in which; where on the other hand, or on the contrary; whereas, while. -late ME.

1. It had been better for hym to haue taryed t. he was LD. BERNERS.

III. as *sb.* That place; the (or a) place yonder 1588.

He left. t. last night (*mod.*).

Phrases. *To be t.*, to be at or in the place in question; to be present or at hand. *To be all t.* (colloq.), to have all one's faculties or wits about one; to be smart or on the alert; hence, *not all t.* = not quite right in the head. *T. and then*, at that precise place and time; on the spot, forthwith. *Here and t., here, t., and everywhere, neither here nor t.*: see HERE *adv.* *T. or thereabouts*, primarily in the literal sense; hence also = that or very nearly that (amount); approximately. *T. he* (or *she*) *goes, t. you, they, go*, is primarily literal; but it also calls attention to the way in which a person goes on, acts, talks, etc., usu. expressing surprise or disapproval. *T. you are!* (colloq.) (*a*) = *t. you go!*; (*b*) = t. it is for you, t. you have it, the thing is done.

Thereabout (ðē°răbau·t, ðē°·răbaut), *adv.* [OE. *þǽr abútan*, two words; see THERE and ABOUT.] 1. = next 1. 2. a. About or somewhere near a specified time or date. b. About a stated number, quantity, size, space of time, etc.; very nearly so; approximately so. (Chiefly after *or*.) ME. 3. About, concerning, or with reference to that matter or business. Now *arch.* or *rare*. ME.

1. Quartered in the different villages t. 1864. 3. What wol ye dyne? I wol go ther-aboute. CHAUCER.

Thereabou·ts, *adv.* late ME. [f. prec. with advb. *-s*. Now more freq. than prec. in senses 1 and 2.] 1. About, or in the neighbourhood of, that place; in the district, region, etc., round about there. b. *fig.* About that; near to that state or action. *Obs.* or *rare*. 1606. 2. = prec. 2 a, b. late ME. †3. = prec. 3. –1657.

1. It is the best house t...in a broad street 1797. b. *Ant. & Cl.* III. x. 29. 2. In three hours, or t. DE FOE. From the year 1660 or t. HUXLEY.

Thereafter (ðe°ra·ftəɹ), *adv.* [OE. *þǽr æfter*, two words; see THERE and AFTER.] 1. After that in time, order, or sequence; subsequently; afterwards. (Now somewhat formal.) †2. Conformably thereto, accordingly –1727.

2. †*T. as*, according as; That, Madam, is t. as they be GAY. †*To be t.*, to be conformable or agreeable thereto. So **Therea·fterward** (*rare*) = sense 1.

Thereagainst (ðē°răge·nst, -ăgē^i·nst), *adv.* Now *arch.* late ME. [f. THERE + *againes*, AGAINST *prep.*] 1. Against or in opposition to that. †2. As a set-off thereto; contrariwise; on the other side –1558. 3. In pressure or impact against that 1863.

1. Remedy provided there-against by an Act of Parliament 1647.

Thereanent (ðē°răne·nt), *adv.* Orig. and chiefly *Sc.* and *north.* ME. [orig. two words, THERE and ANENT *prep.*] About, concerning, or in reference to that matter, business, etc.; relating thereto.

Thereat (ðe°ræ·t), *adv.* Now *formal* or *arch.* [OE. *þǽræt*, two words; see THERE and AT.] 1. At the place, meeting, etc. mentioned; there. b. Expressing attachment to a thing 1566. 2. On the occasion or occurrence of that, thereupon, because of that ME.

1. Many there be which goo yn there att TINDALE *Matt.* vii. 13. 2. T. the feend his gnashing teeth did grate SPENSER.

Therebesi·de, *adv.* Now only *arch.* and *poet.* ME. [orig. two words; see THERE and BESIDE *prep.*] By the side of that; next to that; near by.

Thereby (ðē°ɹbəi·, ðē°·ɹbəi), *adv.* [OE. *þǽrbī*, f. *þǽr* THERE + *bī* BY *prep.*] 1. By that; by means of, or because of, that; through that. 2. Beside, adjacent to, or near that. Now *arch.* and *dial.* ME. †3. Besides, together with, or in addition to that –1500. 4. *Sc.* In ref. to a number or quantity Very nearly so 1557. 5. *T. hangs a tale*: see TALE *sb.* 2.

1. For fear of having my attention distracted..and of my t. losing my bearings 1896. 2. The twelve fountaines of Elim, and the seventy Palmes that grew t. 1641.

Therefore (ðē°·ɹfǫɹ), **therefor** (ðe°ɹfǭ·ɹ), *adv.* (*sb.*) [Early ME. *þerfore, þerefore*, f. OE. *þǽr-, þér-* THERE + *fore*, OE. and early ME. collateral form of *for*; see FORE *adv.* and *prep.*] I. (Now stressed ðē°ɹfǭ·ɹ, and usu. spelt *therefor* for distinction from II.) *formal* or *arch.* For that (thing, act, etc.); for that, for it. b. By reason of that; for that reason, on that account ME.

The love I had therefor MORRIS. b. They would all be..healthier men therefor HAWTHORNE.

II. (Now always spelt *therefore*, and stressed ðē°·ɹfǫɹ.) In consequence of that; that being so; as a result or inference from what has been stated; consequently. Formerly sometimes unemphatic = THEN II. 3. late ME.

Things obscure are not t. sacred BERKELEY.

B. as *sb.* The word 'therefore' as marking a conclusion; an expressed conclusion or inference 1641.

Let him first answer our *Therefores*, and wee will quickly answer his *Wherefores* 1641.

Therefrom (ðeəɹfrǫ·m), *adv. arch.* or *formal.* ME. [orig. two words.] From that; from that place; away from there.

They took their name t. 1728.

Therein (ðeəri·n), *adv.* Now *formal, arch.*, or *dial.* [OE. *þærin*, f. *þær* THERE + IN *prep.*] **1.** In that place or (material) thing. **b.** In or during that time 1539. **2.** In that affair or matter; in that thing, circumstance, or particular ME. **3.** Into that place or (material) thing ME. **4. T. a·fter, t. befo·re, t. u·nder,** = after, before, below in that document, statute, etc. (Usu. written as single words.) 1818.

1. The compasse of the worlde, and all yᵗ dwell therin COVERDALE *Ps.* xxiv. 2. **3.** Smell to a Spunge dipt there-in WESLEY.

Thereinto (ðeəri·ntu), *adv. arch.* ME. [f. THERE + INTO.] **1.** Into that place, matter, condition, etc. †**2.** = prec. 2. –1676.

1. Let not them..enter t. *Luke* xxi. 21.

Thereness (ðēə·ɹnės). *rare.* 1674. [f. THERE + -NESS.] The quality or condition of being there; existence in a defined place. (Usu. opp. to *hereness.*)

Thereof (ðēərǫv, *stress variable*; ðēərǫ·f). Now *formal* or *arch.* [OE. *þær of*; see THERE and OF.] **1.** Of that or it. **b.** = *of it*, as obj. gen. ME. **c.** = *of it, its*, as possess. gen. late ME. **2.** From or out of that as source or origin ME.

1. Men makes þeroff gude glasse 1400. **b.** Disburse the summe, on the receit t. SHAKS. **c.** The chariot of Israel, and the horsemen t. 2 *Kings* ii. 12. **2.** Much more good t. shall spring MILT.

Thereon (ðeərǫ·n, ðēə·rǫn), *adv.* Now *formal* or *arch.* [OE. *þæron*, f. *þær* THERE + ON *prep.*] **1.** Of position: On or upon that or it. **2.** Of motion or direction: On or upon that or it; onto that ME. **3.** = THEREUPON 2. ME.

1. If t. you relye. I'll take my leaue. SHAKS. To confer with him t. 1786. **2.** His hands t. to lay 1887. **3.** I care not greatly what succeed t. 1618.

Thereout (ðeərau·t), *adv.* [OE. *þærūt(e*; see THERE and OUT.] **1.** Outside of that place, etc.; without. Now *rare.* **2.** Out of doors; in the open. Now *Sc.* ME. **3.** From or out of that (it, them), as source or origin; thence. *arch.* late ME.

3. As oft as he drank t. 1871.

Thereover (ðeərōu·vəɹ), *adv. arch.* [OE. *þærofer*; see THERE and OVER *prep.*] **1.** Over or above that, in position (or in transit; also in charge, rank, number, or amount). **2.** *fig.* In reference to that (which is under consideration or observation, or is the object of occupation, discourse, or attention) 1535.

1. In a dark blue kirtle was he clad, And a grey cloak t. MORRIS. **2.** I..came oft in parell of death therouer, tyll I was delyuered from it COVERDALE *Ecclus.* xxxiv. 12.

Therethrough (ðeəɹþrū·), *adv. arch.* [Early ME. *þer þurh*; see THERE and THROUGH *prep.*] **1.** Of place: Through that, it, or them. **2.** By means, or by reason, of that; thereby ME.

1. To make t. a navigable passage 1594. **2.** Winning renown and fame t. 1894.

Thereto (ðeəɹtū·, ðēə·ɹtu), *adv.* Now *formal* or *arch.* [OE. *þær tó, þærtó*; see THERE and TO *prep.*] **1.** To that place, thing, affair, etc. **2.** (Belonging, pertinent, suitable, needful) to that matter or thing; (according) therewith; for that matter, purpose, etc. OE. **3.** In addition to that; besides, also, moreover. Now *arch.* and *poet.* OE.

1. He maketh it a grauen image, and falleth downe t. *Isa.* xliv. 15. **2.** Nothing more is needful t. 1748. **3.** Hir mouth ful smal, and ther to softe and reed CHAUCER.

Theretofore (ðēə·ɹtufōəɹ), *adv.* Now *formal.* [ME. *þer tofore*; see THERE and TOFORE *adv.*] Before that time; previously to that.

Thereunder (ðeərv·ndəɹ), *adv.* Now *formal.* [OE. *þærunder*; see THERE and UNDER *prep.*] **1.** Under that or it; below or beneath that. **2.** Under that title, heading, etc.; under the provisions, or by the authority, of that 1617.

2. Royalties paid t. were to be paid to the publishers 1908.

Thereunto (ðēərvntū·, ðeərv·ntu), *adv. arch.* [ME., f. THERE + UNTO *prep.*] **1.** Unto or to that place; unto that thing, matter, subject, etc. †**2.** = THERETO 3. –1678.

Thereupon (ðēərvpǫ·n, ðēə·rvpǫn), *adv.* [In ME. two (or three) words.] **1.** Upon that or it (of position or motion). *arch.* or *formal.* **2.** Upon that (in time or order); on that being done or said; (directly) after that ME. **b.** On that ground; in consequence of that. *arch.* 1534. **3.** On that subject or matter; with reference to that (it, them). *arch.* or *formal.* late ME.

1. The Goods and Merchandizes laden t. 1716. **2.** For the purposes of the argument and the decision following t. 1891. **b.** *Com. Err.* v. i. 388.

Therewith (ðeəɹwi·ð, ðeəɹwi·þ), *adv.* Now *formal* or *arch.* [OE. *þær wiþ, þærwið*, f. *þær* THERE + *wið* WITH *prep.*] **1.** With that (or those) as accompaniment, adjunct, etc.; together or in company with that. **b.** In addition to that; besides ME. **c.** With that (word, act, or occurrence); that being said or done; thereat, thereupon, forthwith. late ME. **2.** With that as instrument; by means of that ME. **b.** With that as cause or occasion; on account of or because of that; in consequence of that 1440.

1. Every person connected t. 1886. **b.** Pagett, M.P., was a liar, and a fluent liar t. KIPLING. **2.** If you bathe the affected Part t. 1725. **b.** T. affrayd I ranne away SPENSER.

Therewithal (ðēəɹwiðǫ·l), *adv. arch.* ME. [Orig. two words, THERE and WITHAL *adv.*] **1.** = prec. 1, 1 b. **2.** = prec. 1 c. ME. †**3.** = prec. 2. –1656.

1. Giue her that Ring, and therewithall This letter SHAKS. **2.** And t. to cover his intent A cause he found into the Town to go WORDSW.

Therewithin (ðēəɹwiði·n), *adv. arch.* [Early ME. *þer wiþinnen, wiþinne.*] Within or into that place; within there.

Theriac (þīə·riæk), *sb.* (*a.*) *arch.* 1440. [a. late L. *theriaca, theriace* (med.L. *theriacum*), a. Gr. θηριακή (ἀντίδοσις), θηριακὸν (φάρμακον), fem. and neut. of θηριακός pertaining to wild beasts or poisonous reptiles, f. θηρίον, dim of θήρ.] An antidote to poison, esp. to the bite of a venomous serpent. **B.** *adj.* Theriacal 1440. Hence **Theriacal** (þirəi·ǎkǎl) *a.* pertaining to or of the nature of t.; antidotal.

Thericlean (þeriklī·ǎn), *a.* 1692. [f. L. *Thericleus*, a. Gr. Θηρίκλειος made by Thericles, a famous Corinthian potter; see -AN.] Of Thericles; of the form or kind made by Thericles, as a cup.

Therio- (þīəriǫ), bef. a vowel **theri-** (þīəri), repr. Gr. θηριο-, comb. form of θηρίον, dim. of θήρ wild beast.

The·riodont [Gr. ὀδούς, ὀδοντ- tooth], a fossil reptile with teeth of a mammalian type, *spec.* one of the order *Theriodontia*; also *attrib.* or as *adj.* †**Therio·lo·gic, †-al** *adjs. rare*, zoological. **Therio·tomy** [Gr. τομή cutting], the dissection or anatomy of wild beasts; zootomy.

Theriomorphic (þīəriǫ,mǭ·ɹfik), *a.* 1882. [f. THERIO- + Gr. μορφή form + -IC.] Having the form of a beast; also *transf.* of or pertaining to a deity worshipped in the form of a beast.

Therm[1] (þɔ̄ɹm). *arch.* 1549. [a. F. *therme* in pl., or ad. L. *thermæ*, a. Gr. θέρμαι hot baths, pl. of θέρμη heat.] A public bath or bathing establishment.

Therm[2] (þɔ̄ɹm). 1888. [f. Gr. θερμός hot, θέρμη heat.] *Physics.* A unit of heat: the quantity of heat required to raise the temperature of one gramme of water at its maximum density one degree centigrade. Also, a unit of heat adopted as a basis of the charge for the use of gas; = one hundred thousand British thermal units (see THERMAL *a.* 2).

‖**Thermæ** (þɔ̄·ɹmī), *sb. pl.* 1600. [L.; see THERM[1].] *Class. Antiq.* One of the public bathing establishments of the ancient Romans and Greeks.

Thermal (þɔ̄·ɹmǎl), *a.* 1756. [f. Gr. θέρμη heat + -AL.] **1.** Of, pertaining to, or of the nature of *thermæ* or hot springs; of a spring, etc., (naturally) hot or warm; also, having hot springs. **2.** Of or pertaining to heat; determined, measured, or operated by heat 1837. **3.** *fig.* Heated with passion; erotic, passionate, impassioned 1866.

1. The t. waters of Bath or Buxton 1800. **2.** *T. unit*, a unit of heat; the *British t. unit* (abbrev. *B.Th.U.*) is the amount of heat required to raise the temperature of a pound of water at its maximum density through one degree Fahrenheit. **3.** A t. school of poetry 1866. Hence **The·rmally** *adv.*

Thermantidote (þəɹmæ·ntidǒut). 1840. [f. Gr. θέρμη heat + ANTIDOTE.] An antidote to heat; *spec.* a rotating fan fitted in a window-opening and encased in wet tatties, used in India to drive in a current of cooled air.

Thermic (þɔ̄·ɹmik), *a.* 1846. [f. Gr. θέρμη heat + -IC.] = THERMAL 2.

T. balance = BOLOMETER. *T. fever*, fever resulting from external heat, e.g. heat-stroke, insolation.

Thermidor (þɔ̄ɹmidǭ·ɹ, ‖ tęrmidor). 1827. [F., f. Gr. θέρμη heat + δῶρον gift.] The eleventh month of the French revolutionary calendar, extending (in 1794) from July 19 to August 17.

Thermidorian (þɔ̄ɹmidǭə·riǎn), *sb.* and *a.* 1827. [a. F. *thermidorien*, f. prec. + *-ien* -IAN.] **A.** *sb. Fr. Hist.* One of those who took part in the overthrow of Robespierre on the 9th Thermidor (27 July) 1794. **B.** *adj.* Of or pertaining to Thermidor or to the Thermidorians 1891.

Thermion (þəɹməi·ǒn) 1920. [f. Gr. θερμός hot, θέρμη heat + ION.] An electrically charged particle emitted by an incandescent substance. Hence **Thermio·nic** *a.* freq. in *thermionic valve.* **Thermio·nically** *adv.*

Thermite (þɔ̄·ɹməit). 1900. [ad. G. *thermit*, f. Gr. θέρμη heat, θερμός hot + *-it* -ITE[1].] A mixture of finely divided aluminium and oxide of iron or other metal, which produces on combustion a very high temperature (*c* 3000° C.). Used as a composition for incendiary bombs.

Thermo- (þɔ̄·ɹmǫ), bef. a vowel also **therm-**, repr. Gr. θερμο-, comb. form of θερμός hot, θέρμη heat (in some recent formations used as an abbreviation of THERMO-ELECTRIC).

Thermoba·rograph, an instrument which simultaneously records temperature and atmospheric pressure. **Thermobaro·meter**, a barometric instrument graduated for giving altitudes by the boiling point of water. **Thermo·ba·ttery**, short for *thermo-electric battery.* **Thermo·cau·tery**, any form of actual cautery; *spec.* a hollow platinum cautery in which heat is maintained by means of benzine or gasolene vapour. **The·rmocurrent**, the electric current produced in a thermo-electric battery. **The·rmo-electro·meter**, an instrument for measuring the heating power of an electric current, or for determining the strength of a current by the heat produced. **Thermoge·nesis**, generation of heat. **Thermokinema·tics**, the theory of the motion of heat. **Thermola·bile** *a.* liable to destruction at moderately high temperatures, as certain toxins and serums: opp. to *thermostable.* **Thermo-magne·tic** *a.*, pertaining to or of the nature of thermo-magnetism. **Thermo-ma·gnetism**, magnetism caused or modified by the action of heat. **Thermo-mo·tive** *a.*, of, pertaining to, or caused by heat applied to produce motion. **Thermo-mu·ltiplier**, early name for a THERMOPILE. **The·rmophil, -phile** *a.* requiring a high temperature for development, as certain bacteria; *sb.* a thermophil organism. **The·rmophone**, an apparatus in which sonorous vibrations of a diaphragm are produced by heat-rays. **The·rmoscope**, an instrument for indicating changes of temperature; hence **Thermosco·pic** *a.* **Thermosta·ble** *a.* retaining its character or active quality at moderately high temperatures: opp. to *thermolabile.* **Thermosysta·ltic** *a.*, of or pertaining to systaltic motion due to heat. **Thermote·lephone**, a thermo-electric telephone. **Thermote·nsion**, tension or strain applied to material at a specified temperature to increase or test its tensile power. **Thermotro·pic** *a. Bot.* turning or bending under the influence of heat. **Thermo·tropism**, *Bot.* the property possessed by growing plant-organs of turning or bending towards or away from the sun or other source of heat. **Thermo-volta·ic** *a.* of or pertaining to the thermal effects of voltaic electricity, or to heat and voltaic electricity.

Thermoche·mistry. 1844. [f. THERMO- + CHEMISTRY.] That branch of chemical science which deals with the quantities of heat evolved or absorbed when substances undergo chemical change or enter into solution. Also sometimes used to include all relations of heat to substances, such as conductivity, specific heat, etc. So **Thermoche·mic, -al** *adjs.* of or pertaining to t.; **-ly** *adv.* by means of or with reference to t.

Thermochrosy (þɔ̄·ɹmǫkrǒusi, þəɹmǫ·krǒsi). 1847. [f. THERMO- + Gr. χρῶσις colouring.] The 'coloration' of heat-rays; the property possessed by radiant heat of being composed of waves of different lengths and degrees of refrangibility (thus corresponding to the different colours of light rays). So **Thermochro·ic** *a.* of or pertaining to t.

The:rmodyna·mic, *a.* 1849. [f. THERMO- + DYNAMIC.] Of or relating to thermodynamics; operating or operated by the transformation of heat into motive power. So **Thermodyna·mical** *a.*, **-ly** *adv.*

The:rmodyna·mics, *sb. pl.* 1854. [f. as prec. + DYNAMICS.] The theory of the relations between heat and mechanical energy, and of the conversion of either into the other.

The:rmo-ele·ctric, *a.* 1823. [f. THERMO- + ELECTRIC.] **1.** Of or pertaining to thermo-electricity; characterized or operated by an electric current produced by difference of temperature. **2.** Of or pertaining to heat and electricity; *t. alarm* or *call*, a device in which a rise or fall in temperature to a prearranged point closes an electric circuit so as to cause a bell to ring 1877.

1. A current of electricity will continue to flow so long as a difference of temperature is maintained between the junction and the extremities. This current is named a t. current, and the two metals form what is known as a t. pair; a combination of these pairs forms the t. pile or battery. 1876. So **Thermo-ele·ctrical** *a.*, **-ly** *adv.*

The:rmo-ele:ctri·city. 1823. [f. THERMO- + ELECTRICITY.] Electricity generated in a body by difference of temperature in its parts. Also, that branch of electrical science which treats of currents produced by means of heat.

Thermogram (þɔ̄·ɹmǒgræm). 1883. [f. THERMO- + -GRAM.] = next 2.

Thermograph (þɔ̄·ɹmǒgrɑf). 1840. [f. as prec. + -GRAPH.] **1.** A figure or tracing produced by the action of heat, esp. of the heat-rays of the spectrum upon a prepared surface. **2.** A graphic record of variations of temperature 1843. **3.** A self-registering thermometer 1881.

Thermography (þəɹmǫ·grăfi). 1840. [f. as prec. + -GRAPHY.] Any process of writing or drawing effected or developed by the influence of heat.

Thermology (þəɹmǫ·lǒdʒi). 1840. [ad. F. *thermologie*; see THERMO- and -LOGY.] The science of heat; that department of physics which treats of heat. Hence **Thermolo·gical** *a.*

Thermolysis (þəɹmǫ·lisis). 1875. [f. THERMO- + Gr. λύσις loosing, etc., after Ger. *thermolyse*.] **1.** *Chem.* The separation of a compound into its elements by the action of heat; decomposition or dissociation by heat. **2.** *Physiol.* The dissipation or dispersion of heat from the body 1896. Hence **Thermoly·tic** *a.* pertaining to or producing t.; *sb.* a thermolytic agent or substance. **The·rmolyse** *v. trans.* to subject to t.; to decompose by the action of heat.

Thermometer (þəɹmǫ·mĭtəɹ). 1633. [f. Gr. θέρμη heat, θερμός hot + μέτρον measure; see -METER.] An instrument for measuring temperature by means of a substance whose expansion and contraction under different degrees of cold and heat are capable of accurate measurement.

Air-, Clinical, Differential, Register t., etc.: see the first elements. *Metallic* (or *bimetallic*) *t.*, a t. which indicates temperature by differential expansion and contraction of composite metal bars.

Thermometric (þɔ̄ɹmome·trik), *a.* 1784. [f. prec. + -IC.] = next.

Thermometrical (þɔ̄ɹmome·trikăl), *a.* 1664. [f. as prec. + -AL.] Of or pertaining to the thermometer or its use; made with or involving the use of the thermometer. Hence **Thermome·trically** *adv.* according to or by means of the thermometer or its indications.

Thermometrograph (þɔ̄ɹmome·trǒgrɑf). 1837. [f. THERMOMETER + -GRAPH.] A self-registering thermometer.

Thermometry (þəɹmǫ·mĕtri). 1669. [f. as prec.; see -METRY.] The department of science which deals with the construction of thermometers; the scientific use of the thermometer; the measurement of temperature.

Thermopile (þɔ̄·ɹmǒpəil). 1849. [f. THERMO- + PILE *sb.*[3]] A thermo-electric battery, used in connexion with a galvanometer for measuring minute quantities of radiant heat.

Thermos (þɔ̄·ɹmǫs). 1907. [a. Gr. θερμός warm, hot.] A registered trade term noting a flask, bottle, or the like capable of being kept hot by the device (invented by Sir James Dewar) of surrounding the interior vessel with a vacuum jacket to prevent the conduction of heat.

Thermostat (þɔ̄·ɹmǒstæt). 1831. [f. THERMO- + Gr. στατός standing; cf. HELIOSTAT.] An automatic apparatus for regulating temperature; *esp.* a device in which the expansive force of metals or gas acts directly upon the source of heat, ventilation, or the like, or controls them indirectly by opening and closing an electric circuit. **b.** An apparatus which gives notice of undue increase of temperature; an automatic fire-alarm 1881. So **Thermosta·tic** *a.* of, pertaining to, or of the nature of a t. **Thermosta·tically** *adv.* by means of a t.

‖**Thermotaxis** (þɔ̄·ɹmǒtæksis). 1891. [mod. L., f. THERMO- + Gr. τάξις arrangement.] **1.** *Physiol.* That function of the nervous system on which the normal temperature of the body depends; the regulation of the bodily heat. **2.** *Biol.* Movement or stimulation in a living body caused by heat 1900. Hence **Thermota·ctic, -ta·xic** *adjs.* of or pertaining to t. 1877.

Thermotic (þəɹmǫ·tik), *a.* 1837. [f. Gr. θερμωτικός warming, calorific.] Of or pertaining to heat; *esp.* relating to thermotics. So **Thermo·tical** *a.*, **-ly** *adv.* **Thermo·tics** *sb. pl.* the science of heat, thermology.

Thero- (þīᵊro), repr. Gr. θηρο-, comb. form of θήρ wild beast, as in THEROPODOUS, etc.

Theroid (þīᵊ·roid), *a.* 1867. [f. Gr. θήρ (see prec.) + -OID.] Like or having the form of a brute; of bestial nature or character.

Theromorph (þīᵊ·rǫmǭɹf). 1887. [f. mod. L. *Theromorpha* neut. pl., f. Gr. θηρο- THERO- + μορφή form.] *Palæont.* A reptile of the extinct order *Theromorpha*, of Permian and Trias age, having certain mammalian characters.

Theropodous (þirǫ·pǒdəs), *a.* 1889. [f. mod.L. *Theropoda* neut. pl. (f. Gr. θηρο- THERO- + -πούς, ποδ- foot) + -OUS.] *Palæont.* Of or belonging to the *Theropoda*, an order of carnivorous dinosaurs having feet like those of mammals. So **Theropod** (þīᵊ·rǫpǫd) *a.* theropodous; *sb.* a dinosaur of this order.

Thersitical (þəɹsi·tikăl), *a.* *rare.* 1650. [f. Gr. Θερσίτης Thersites ('the Audacious'), an ill-tongued Greek at the siege of Troy + -ICAL.] Like Thersites in language or address; abusive, reviling, scurrilous.

‖**Thesaurus** (þǐsǭ·rǒs). *Pl.* **-i.** 1736. [L., a. Gr. θησαυρός store, treasure, storehouse.] **1.** *Archæol.* A treasury, as of a temple, etc. 1823. **2.** A 'treasury' or 'storehouse' of knowledge, as a dictionary, encyclopædia, or the like 1736.

These (ðīz), *dem. pron.* and *adj.* (*pl.*). [OE. *þás*, pl. of *þes, þéos, þis* THIS, ME. *þōs*, mod. THOSE, became ultimately the plural of THAT *a.* and *pron.*, its place as plural of *this* being taken first by *þes, þis*, and later by extended forms with the ending *-e* (on the analogy of *al, alle, sum, sume,*) *þese, þise*, which are the immediate antecedents of the present form.] The pl. of THIS *pron.* and *adj.*, often in explicit or implied opposition to THOSE.

I haue ywedded bee Thise Monthes two CHAUCER. When those went, t. went. and when those stood, t. stood *Ezek.* i. 21. T. are the wordes of S. Paule 1581. T. are diuels SHAKS. I'l give you another dish of fish one of t. dayes WALTON. Then was he glad, and that for t. reasons: First [etc.] BUNYAN. Some place the bliss in action, some in ease, Those call it Pleasure, and Contentment t. POPE. Though wedded we have been T. twice ten tedious years COOPER.

Thesis (þī·sis, þe·sis). *Pl.* **theses** (þī·sīz). late ME. [a. Gr. θέσις putting, placing, a proposition, affirmation, f. root θε- of τιθέναι to put, place.] **I.** In *Prosody*, etc.: opp. to ARSIS. **1.** orig. and properly, according to ancient writers, The setting down of the foot, or lowering of the hand in beating time, and hence (as marked by this) the stress or *ictus*; the stressed syllable of a foot in verse; a stressed note in music 1864. **2.** By later Latin writers used for the lowering of the voice on an unstressed syllable; hence in prevalent acceptation: The unaccented or weak part of a foot in verse (classical or modern), or an unaccented note in music. late ME. ‖**3.** *Mus. Per arsin et thesin* (= 'by raising and lowering'): used of a fugue, canon, etc. in which the subject or melody is inverted, so that the rising parts correspond to the falling ones in the original subject and *vice versa*: = *by inversion* 1597. **II.** In *Logic, Rhetoric*, etc. **1.** A proposition laid down or stated, esp. as a theme to be discussed and proved, or to be maintained against attack (in *Logic* sometimes as dist. from HYPOTHESIS 2, in *Rhetoric* from ANTITHESIS 2); a statement, assertion, tenet 1579. **b.** *spec.* dist. from HYPOTHESIS 1. 1620. **c.** A theme for a school exercise, composition, or essay 1774. **2.** A dissertation to maintain and prove a thesis; esp. one written or delivered by a candidate for a university degree 1653.

2. Scott's t. was, in fact, on the Title of the Pandects, 'Concerning the disposal of the dead bodies of criminals' LOCKHART.

Thesmothete (þe·zmoþīt, -þet). Also in Gr. form **thesmothetes** (þezmǫ·þĕtīz), pl. **-thetæ.** 1603. [ad. Gr. θεσμοθέτης, pl. -θέται, f. θεσμός law + -θετης.] Each of the six inferior archons in ancient Athens, who were judges and lawgivers; *transf.* one who lays down the law.

Thespian (þe·spiăn), *a.* and *sb.* 1599. [f. Gr. proper name Θέσπις + -AN.] **A.** *adj.* Of or pertaining to Thespis, the traditional father of Greek tragedy (6th c. B.C.); hence, of or pertaining to tragedy, or the dramatic art; tragic, dramatic. **B.** *sb.* A tragedian; an actor or actress 1827.

Theta (þī·tă). 1603. [a. Gr. θῆτα.] The eighth letter of the Greek alphabet, Θ, θ TH. (In ancient Greece, on the ballots used in voting upon a sentence of life or death, θ stood for θάνατος death; hence *allus.*)

attrib. and *Comb.*: **t.-function**, *Math.* (*a*) the sum of a series from $n = -\infty$ to $n = +\infty$ of terms denoted by $\exp(n^2a + 2na)$; also extended to a similar function of several variables; (*b*) a function occurring in probabilities, expressed by the integral $\int e^{-2} dt$.

Thete (þīt). 1652. [ad. Gr. θής, θητ-.] *Gr. Antiq.* In ancient Athens, by the constitution of Solon, a free man of the lowest class, whose property in land was assessed at less than 150 medimni.

Thetic (þe·tik), *a.* 1678. [ad. Gr. θετικός, f. θετός placed, f. root θε- to place (cf. THESIS).] **1.** Characterized by laying down or setting forth; involving positive statement. **2.** *Pros.* That bears the thesis; stressed 1815.

Thetical (þe·tikăl), *a.* 1653. [f. as prec. + -AL; see -ICAL.] Of the nature of or involving direct or positive statement; laid down positively or absolutely; dogmatic; arbitrary. Hence **The·tically** *adv.*

Thetis (þe·tis). late ME. [a. Gr. Θέτις, proper name.] **1.** *Gr.* and *Rom. Myth.* One of the Nereids or sea-nymphs, the mother of Achilles; *poet.*, the sea personified. **2.** *Astron.* Name of the seventeenth asteroid 1886.

Theurgy (þī·ɒɹdʒi). 1569. [ad. L. *theurgia*, a. Gr. θεουργία sorcery, f. θεός god + -εργος working.] **1.** A system of magic, orig. practised by the Egyptian Platonists, to procure communication with beneficent spirits, and by their aid produce miraculous effects; in later times distinguished as 'white magic' from GOETY or 'black magic.' **2.** The operation of a divine or supernatural agency in human affairs; the effects produced among men by direct divine or spiritual action 1858.

1. There is yet another art, which is called Theurgie; wherein they worke by good angels 1584. Hence **Theu·rgic, -al** *adjs.* of or pertaining to t.; **-ly** *adv.* **The·urgist,** one who practises or believes in t.; a magician.

Thew *sb.*[1], see THEOW.

Thew (þiū), *sb.*[2] [OE. *þéaw* = OS. *thau* usage, custom, habit, OHG. *thau* (*dau*) discipline; ult. etym. unkn.] †**1.** A custom, usage; *pl.* ordinances -1624. †**2.** A custom or habit of an individual; hence, a characteristic, attribute, trait -1805. †**b.** A good quality or habit; a virtue; courteous or gracious action -1575. **3.** *pl.* Physical good qualities, features, or personal endowments. †**a.** *gen.* -1567. **b.** The bodily powers or forces of a man (L. *vires*), might, strength, vigour; in Shaks., bodily proportions, lineaments, or parts, as indicating physical strength; in mod. use after Scott, muscular development, associated with *sinews*, and hence materialized as if = muscles or tendons 1566.

2. Forsoth yuele spechis corumpen (or distroyen) goode thewis (or vertues) WYCLIF 1 *Cor.* xv. 33. 3. b. Romans now Haue Thewes, and Limbes, like to their Ancestors SHAKS. Hence **Thew·y** *a.* muscular, brawny.

†**Thew,** *v.* ME. [app. f. OE. *þéaw* THEW *sb.*[2]] *trans.* To instruct in morals or manners; to discipline, train, instruct, chastise -1625.

Thewed (þiūd), *ppl. a.* ME. [orig. f. prec., but app. often treated as if f. THEW *sb.*[2] + -ED[2].] †1. Trained, instructed in morals or manners; having qualities or manners (of a specified kind) -1596. 2. Having thews or muscles (of a specified kind) 1864.

1. Men..full of vicis, ryotous and evil thewit 1456.

They (ðē¹), *pers. pron.* [Early ME. *þei*, a. ON. *þeir*, nom. pl. masc. of *sá, sú, þat*; corresp. to OE. *þá*, ME. *þā, þō* THO), which in ON. filled the place of the lost pl. of the 3rd pers. pron.] I. 1. As pron. of the 3rd pers. pl., nom. case; the pl. of *he, she,* or *it*: The persons or things in question, or last mentioned. 2. Often used in ref. to a sing. noun made universal by *every, any, no,* etc., or applicable to either sex (= 'he or she') 1526. 3. As indef. pron.: People in general; any persons, not including the speaker; people. Often in phr. *t. say* = people say, it is said. late ME.

1. They're Rogues, as sure as Light 's in Heaven 1707. 2. If a person is born of a..gloomy temper.. t. cannot help it CHESTERF. 3. To strange sores strangely t. straine the cure SHAKS.

II. 1. As demonstr. pron., chiefly as antecedent: = THOSE I. 2, 4. Somewhat *arch.* late ME. 2. As demonstr. adj. = THOSE II. 2, 4; but often in weaker sense, = THE (*pl.*). Now *dial.* ME.

1. The simple plan, That t. should take, who have the power, And t. should keep who can WORDSW.

‖**Thiasus** (þəi·ăsŏs). 1850. [L., a. Gr.] An assembly celebrating a festival of one of the gods.

Thick (þik), *a.* (*sb.*) [OE. *þicce*:—OTeut. **þik(k)uz*, fem. **þik(k)wī-*; ult. etym. unkn.] I. 1. Having relatively great extension between the opposite surfaces or sides; of comparatively large measurement through. Opp. to *thin*; distinct from *long* and *broad*. †b. Extending far down from the surface; deep -1693. c. Of a person or animal: Thickset, stout, burly. *Obs.* exc. *dial.* ME. 2. Used to express the third dimension of a solid, which has a direction at right angles at once to the length and the breadth: Having a (specified) thickness. (Sometimes = *deep*, but not now said of a body of water or other fluid.) In this sense not opp. to *thin*. OE. 3. *fig.* Excessive in some disagreeable quality; too much to manage or to stand; *spec.* too gross or indelicate. *slang.* 1884.

1. My litle fynger shall be thicker then my fathers loynes COVERDALE 1 *Kings* xii. 10. The Grapes..have a t. skin 1687. T. lips 1809. (*To give one*) *a t. ear*, an ear swollen from a blow; hence freq. in threats (*vulg. slang*). *T. 'un*, a sovereign (*vulg. slang*). b. A t. Frost would kill the Roots, as well as the Head EVELYN. c. Vp on a thikke palfrey..Sit Dido CHAUCER. 2. Let her paint an inch thicke, to this fauour she must come SHAKS. 3. It 's a bit t...when a man of my position is passed over for a beginner like young Merrick 1907.

II. In general sense of *dense*. 1. Closely occupied, filled, or set with objects or individuals; crowded. Of hair: Bushy, luxuriant. OE. b. Often const. *with*. Also *transf.* Thickly covered (as in *t. with dust*). late ME. 2. Of the individual things collectively: Densely arranged, crowded; hence, numerous, abundant, plentiful. (Usu. *predic.*) OE. †b. Of actions: Occurring in quick succession; rapid, frequent -1665. 3. Having great or considerable density; dense, viscid; stiff. (Said of liquids and easily liquefiable solids.) OE. b. Of air: Foul from admixture of fumes, vapours, etc.; stuffy, close; also, dense, not rare or thin. Now *rare* or *Obs.* ME. 4. Of mist, fog, smoke, etc.: Having the component particles densely aggregated, so as to intercept or hinder vision. Hence of the weather, etc.: Characterized by mist or haze; foggy, misty. OE. b. *transf.*, esp. of darkness: Difficult to penetrate; dense, deep, profound OE.

1. T. as the galaxy with stars is sown DRYDEN. A t. Forest ADDISON. Walls and towers..t. with defenders FREEMAN. 2. His Legions..T. as autumnal leaves that strow the brooks In Vallombrosa MILT. b. He furnaces The thicke sighes from him SHAKS. 3. Make the Grewell thicke, and slab SHAKS. It should solidify into a t. jelly 1893. *fig.* The people muddied, Thicke and vnwholsome in their thoughts SHAKS. 4. The fogge..was so thicke, that we could not see two ships length before us 1654. b. Come t. Night, And pall thee in the dunnest smoake of Hell SHAKS.

III. *transf.* 1. Of the voice, etc.: Not clear; hoarse; husky; indistinct, inarticulate; also, of low pitch; deep; guttural; throaty. late ME. 2. a. Of or in ref. to hearing: Dull of perception; not quick or acute. Also of sight. Now *dial.* 1526. b. Of mental faculties or actions, or of persons: Slow of apprehension; dense, crass, thick-headed; stupid, obtuse. Now *dial.* 1597.

1. A t. confused cluttering Voice 1748. 2. a. Their eares wexe thycke of hearinge TINDALE *Acts* xxviii. 27. b. SHAKS. 2 *Hen. IV*, II. iv. 262.

IV. (*fig.* from II. 2.) Close in confidence and association; intimate, familiar 1756.

Colloq. phr. *As t. as glue, as peas in a shell, as (two) thieves, as three in a bed.*

Comb.: **t. ear**, a swollen or thickened external ear resulting from a blow or blows; **t. register,** the lowest register of the voice.

B. *absol.* use of *adj.*, passing into *sb.*: That which (rarely, one who) is thick, in any sense. I. Only in *sing.* 1. The most densely occupied or crowded part (*of* a wood, an assemblage, etc.) ME. b. *fig.* The position, time, stage, or state in which activity is most intense; the midst, the height (of an action). Always *in the t. of* 1681. 2. The thick part of a limb or of the body. late ME. 3. So **thi·ckest**: the thickest part 1470.

1. In the t. of the dust and smoke presently entered his men 1610. b. We are now in the t. of a Cabinet crisis 1885. 3. The t. of the fight 1868.

II. *sb.* with *pl.* 1. = THICKET. Now *rare.* OE. 2. *School slang.* A thick-headed or stupid person 1857.

1. Among the bushy thickes of bryar SURREY.

Thick (þik), *adv.* [OE. *þicce* = OS. *thikko*, OHG. *diccho*; see prec.] In a thick manner, thickly. 1. So as to be thick; to a great depth. 2. In a thick, dense, or crowded state; closely, densely, compactly; in crowds or throngs; numerously, abundantly OE. 3. In close or rapid succession; frequently; quickly; fast. Often *t. and fast.* OE. 4. With confused articulation; with a husky or hoarse voice 1556. 5. With density or thick consistence; densely 1711.

1. The snow...lay t. upon the glacier TYNDALL. Phr. *To lay it on t.*, (*fig.*) to do something with vehemence or excess. 2. Doubts came t. upon him 1855. 4. 2 *Hen. IV*, II. iii. 24.

Phr. **T. and threefold,** *advb.* (*sb., adj.*) *phr.* a. In large numbers; in quick succession; with rapid iteration. *arch.* and *dial.* †b. With vehemence. †c. as *adj.* Abundant and frequent.

Thick (þik), *v.* Now *rare* or *Obs.* [OE. *þiccian*, f. *þicce* THICK *a.*] 1. *trans.* To make dense in consistence. *arch.* †2. To make (cloth, etc.) close in texture by fulling -1719. 3. *intr.* To become thick, in various senses. Now *dial.* or *arch.* OE.

Thick and thin, thi·ck-and-thi·n, *phr.* late ME. A. as *sb.* 1. Phr. *Through thick and thin*: through everything that is in the way; without regard to or in spite of obstacles or difficulties (app. orig. with ref. to 'thicket and thin wood'.) 2. Adherence to some course, principle, or party, under all circumstances. b. *attrib.* or *adj.* (usu. hyphened): That adheres in all circumstances; constant, unwavering 1884.

1. And tag and rag through thick and thin came running DRAYTON. A thorough-paced liar, that will swear through thick and thin DRYDEN. 2. The hidebound partisans of thick and thin 1884. b. A.. thick-and-thin admirer 1886.

B. as *adj.* 1. *Naut.* Of a tackle-block: Having one sheave larger than the other 1815. 2. See A. 2 b.

Thicken (þi·k'n), *v.* late ME. [f. THICK *a.* + -EN[5].] To make or become thick or thicker. 1. *trans.* To make dense in consistence; to coagulate, inspissate. b. *intr.* To increase in density or consistence; also, to become turbid, cloudy, indistinct, etc. 1598. 2. To become dark, obscure, or opaque; of the weather, to become misty 1605. †3. *trans.* To make close or dense in disposition of parts or in texture -1812. 4. *intr.* To become crowded, numerous, or frequent; to gather thickly 1726. 5. a. *trans.* To increase the substance between opposite surfaces of; to make thicker in measure; *fig.* to make more substantial; to confirm 1604. b. *intr.* To become thicker in measurement 1763. 6. To become more complex or intricate (esp. said of a plot); to increase in intensity 1671.

1. Oatmeal was used scantily, but generally for thickening soup 1866. b. *fig.* There comes a time when..the speech thickens 1888. 2. Light thickens,.. Good things of Day begin to droope, and drowse SHAKS. I'll face this Storm that thickens in the Wind DRYDEN. 4. The crowd every instant thickening 1789. 5. a. This may helpe to t. other proofes, That do demonstrate thinly SHAKS. b. Ice in the river thickening 1805. 6. Ay, now the Plot thickens very much upon us 1671. Hence **Thi·ckener,** that which (or one who) thickens; in *Dyeing*, a substance used to increase the consistence of the colours or mordants.

Thickening (þi·k'niŋ), *vbl. sb.* 1580. [f. prec. + -ING[1].] The action of THICKEN *v.*; *concr.* the result of this; a thickened substance or part. b. = THICKENER 1839.

Thicket (þi·kėt). [OE. *þiccet*, f. *þicce* thick + *-et*, denominative suffix.] A dense growth of shrubs, underwood, and small trees; a place where low trees or bushes grow thickly together.

They sang like nightingales among the thickets 1855. *fig.* A t. of ever-growing problems 1866.

Thi·ck-head. 1837. One who or that which has a thick head. 1. One who is dull of intellect; a blockhead. Also *attrib.* or *adj.* 1871. 2. Any bird of the sub-family *Pachycephalinæ*, the Thick-headed Shrikes of the Australian region 1837.

Thick-headed (stress var.), *a.* 1707. [Parasynthetic f. prec. + -ED[2].] Having a thick head; *fig.* dull of intellect; slow-witted, obtuse. Hence **Thickhea·dedness.**

Thickish (þi·kiʃ), *a.* 1545. [f. THICK *a.* + -ISH[1].] Somewhat thick.

Thick-knee (þi·kₗnī). Also **thicknee.** 1816. Any bird of the genus *Œdicnemus*, esp. the Stone Curlew, *Œ. scolopax*; so called from the enlargement of the tibio-tarsal joint. So **Thi·ck-knee:d** *a.* having thick knees 1776.

Thick-leaved (-līvd), **-leafed** (-līft), *a.* 1582. a. Having or covered with dense foliage; thickly set with leaves. b. Having thick fleshy leaves 1707.

Thick-lipped (stress var.), *a.* Having thick or full lips. So **Thi·ck-lips,** one who has thick lips; a contemptuous appellation for a negro.

Thickly (þi·kli), *adv.* late ME. [f. THICK *a.* + -LY[2].] In a thick manner; so as to be thick, in various senses.

Thickness. [OE. *þicness*, f. THICK *a.* + -NESS.] 1. The quality or condition of being thick. 2. That which is thick or has thickness; the part (of anything which is thick; the space between opposite surfaces (e. g. a wall); a layer OE. Hence **Thi·cknessing** *vbl. sb.* the action of reducing (boards, etc.) to a given thickness.

Thick-set, *a.* and *sb.* late ME. [f. THICK *adv.* + *set*, pa. pple. of SET *v.*] A. *adj.* (Stress variable.) 1. Composed of individuals or parts arranged in close order; thickly studded or planted (*with* something). 2. Set or placed close together; closely arranged 1570. 3. Having a dense or close-grained nap 1709. 4. Of close compact build; *esp.* short and strongly made; square-built; stocky 1724.

1. T. with trees, a venerable wood DRYDEN. A t. underwood of bristling hair DRYDEN. 2. A..fence.. with t. stakes 1848. 4. He was short and t. 1830.

B. *sb.* (þi·kₗset). 1. A thicket; a thick-set plantation 1766. 2. A stout twilled cotton cloth with a short very close nap; a kind of fustian; also, a garment of this. Now *rare* or *Obs.* 1756.

†**Thick-sighted,** *a.* 1592. Not seeing clearly; having obscure or dim vision -1863.

Thickskin (þi·kₗskin). 1582. One who has a thick skin; a person dull or slow of feeling.

Thick-skinned (stress var.), *a.* 1545. 1. Having a thick skin. 2. *fig.* Dull of sensation or feeling; obtuse, stolid; now *esp.* not sensitive to criticism or rebuff; the opposite of *thin-skinned* 1602.

2. He would be t. if he stands the clamour SCOTT.

Thick-skulled (stress var.), *a.* 1653. Having a thick skull; hence *fig.* = THICK-HEADED. So **Thi·ck-skull,** a thick-skulled person.

Thick-sown (stress variable), *a.* 1683. Sown thickly.
Metaphors are not so thick sown in Milton ADDISON.

Thick-witted (stress var.), *a.* 1634. Having 'thick' wits; dull of intellect, stupid.

Thief (þīf). *Pl.* **thieves** (þīvz). [Com. Teut.; OE. *þēof*:—OTeut. **þeuboz* (G. *dieb*).] **1.** One who takes portable property from another without the knowledge or consent of the latter, converting it to his own use; one who steals. **a.** *spec.* One who does this by stealth, esp. from the person; one who commits theft or larceny. **b.** One who robs with violence; a robber, freebooter, pirate, etc.; now *rare* exc. as a general designation of one who obtains goods by fraudulent means, over-reaching, deceit, etc. OE. **c.** *fig.* That which steals or furtively takes away 1742. **2.** As a general term of reproach or opprobrium: Evil man, villain, scoundrel. *dial.* ME. **3.** A horse that does not run up to form in a race. *slang.* 1896. **4.** 'An excrescence in the snuff of a candle' (J.) which causes it to gutter and waste 1628.
1. A theef of venyson..Kan kepe a Forest best of any man CHAUCER. Provb. When theeues fall out, trewe men come to their goode 1562. Set a t. to take a t. 1670. A sort of honour may be found..even among thieves BENTHAM. **b.** The Story of Ali Baba, and the Forty Thieves 1712. *Border thieves*, the freebooters of the Scottish Border. **c.** Procrastination is the t. of time YOUNG.
attrib. and *Comb.*: **t.-catcher,** (*a*) = THIEF-TAKER; (*b*) a device used formerly in apprehending thieves; †**-leader,** a t.-taker; **-tube,** a tube for withdrawing liquids from casks, etc. Also with *thieves'*, as **thieves' Latin,** cant used by thieves; **thieves' vinegar,** an infusion of rosemary tops, sage leaves, etc., in vinegar, formerly esteemed as an antidote against the plague.

Thie·f-ta:ker. 1535. One who detects and captures a thief; *spec.* one of a company who undertook the detection and arrest of thieves.

Thieve (þīv), *v.* [OE. *þēofian*, f. *þēof* THIEF.] **1.** *intr.* To act as a thief, commit theft, steal. **2.** *trans.* To steal (a thing) 1695.

Thievery (þī·vəri). 1568. [f. THIEF, *thiev-*, or THIEVE *v.* + -ERY.] **1.** The committing or practice of theft; stealing. With *a* and *pl.*, an act of thieving. **2.** The result or produce of thieving; stolen property 1583.
1. They were whipped so for picking pockets, and other petty thieveries DE FOE. **2.** *Tr. & Cr.* IV. ii. 45.

Thievish (þī·viʃ), *a.* 1450. [f. THIEF, *thiev-* + -ISH[1].] †**1.** Infested or frequented by thieves -1632. **2.** Inclined or given to thieving; dishonest 1538. **3.** Of, pertaining to, or characteristic of a thief or thieves; thief-like; furtive, stealthy 1450.
1. Or walke in theeuish waies SHAKS. **2.** Their Magistrates are corrupt, their people t. 1748. **3.** Times theeuish progresse to eternitie SHAKS. Hence **Thie·vish-ly** *adv.*, **-ness.**

Thigh (þəi). [Com. Teut.: OE. *þēoh*:— OTeut. **þeuhom*, from Indo-Eur. **teuk-*.] **1.** The upper part of the leg, from the hip to the knee (in man). **2.** In lower vertebrate animals, The part of the hind leg which is homologous with the human thigh, or which is regarded as corresponding to it in position or shape; in certain quadrupeds, as the horse, applied to the tibia; in birds to the tarsus; hence in insects, etc., the third section of the leg ME.
Comb.: **t.-bone,** the bone of the t., the femur; **-boot,** a boot with uppers reaching to the t.; **-piece,** a piece of armour for the t.

Thight, early and dial. f. TIGHT.

Thigmo-, used as comb. f. Gr. θίγμα touch, as in *thigmota·xis, thigmo·tropism.*

Thilk (ðilk), *dem. adj.* and *pron. arch.* or *dial.* [ME. *þilke*, f. *þe* THE + *ilca*, *-e* ILK, meaning 'that' or 'the same'.] **A.** *adj.* The very (thing, person, etc.) mentioned or indicated; the same; that; this. **B.** *pron.* That (or this) person or thing ME.

Thill[1] (þil). ME. [Origin obsc.] The pole or shaft by which a wagon, cart, or other vehicle is attached to the animal drawing it, *esp.* one of the pair of shafts between which a single draught animal is placed.

Thill[2] (þil). ME. [Local; origin unkn.] The thin stratum of fire-clay, etc. usu. underlying a coal-seam; under-clay; the floor or bottom of a seam of coal.

Thiller (þi·lər). 1552. [f. THILL[1] + -ER[1].] = next.

Thill-horse (þi·lhǭɪs). ME. [f. THILL[1] + HORSE.] The shaft-horse or wheeler in a team.

Thimble (þi·mb'l), *sb.* [OE. *þȳmel*, f. *þūma* THUMB + *-el* -LE, suffix forming names of instruments.] †**1.** A fingerstall. OE. only. **2.** A bell-shaped sheath of metal, etc. (formerly of leather) worn on the end of the finger to push the needle in sewing. late ME. **b.** A thimble or similar article as used by a thimblerigger 1716. **3.** *Naut.* A broad ring of metal, having a concave outer surface, around which the end of a rope is spliced, so that the thimble forms an eye to the rope 1711. **4.** *techn.* **a.** *Mech.* A ring, tube, or similar part, e. g. a sleeve, bushing, ferrule, etc. 1789. **b.** The outer casing of a rifle-ball 1860. **5.** Applied (usu. in *pl.*) to certain flowers and plants, or parts of them, e.g. (*a*) the Foxglove, also known as *Fairy* or *Witches' Thimbles*; (*b*) the Sea Campion; (*c*) the Harebell; (*d*) the cup of an acorn 1873.
attrib. and *Comb.*: **t.-berry (t. blackberry),** the black raspberry of America, *Rubus occidentalis*, so called from the shape of its receptacle; **-eye,** (*a*) *Naut.* an eye in a plate through which a rope is rove without a sheave; (*b*) a fish, the Chub Mackerel, *Scomber colias*; **-plating,** the formation of a cylindrical boiler-shell or a flue by successive slightly overlapping rings of plate; **-weed,** any plant of the genus *Rudbeckia*, so called from the shape of its receptacle. Hence **Thi·mble** *v. intr.* to use a t., to sew.

Thimbleful (þi·mb'lful). 1607. [f. prec. + -FUL.] As much as a thimble will hold; hence, a small quantity; a dram.
Cordials were..on special occasions dealt out in thimblefuls 1889.

Thimblerig (þi·mb'lrig), *sb.* 1825. [f. THIMBLE *sb.* + RIG *sb.*[3] 2; *lit.* 'thimble-trick'.] A swindling game usu. played with three thimbles and a pea which is ostensibly placed under one of them; the sharper then challenging the bystanders to guess under which thimble the pea has been placed, and to bet on their choice. Hence **Thi·mblerig** *v. intr.* to practise the cheat of the t.; *fig.* to cheat in a juggling manner; *trans.* to manipulate (a thing or matter) in this manner. **Thi·mblerigging** *vbl. sb.* and *ppl. a.*

Thimblerigger (þi·mb'lri:gər). 1831. [f. prec. + -ER[1].] A professional sharper who cheats by thimblerigging; also *transf.*

Thin (þin), *a.* (*sb.*) and *adv.* [OE. *þynne.* OTeut. **þunnuz* is Indo-Eur. **tnús* (cf. Skr. *tanús*, Gr. τανυ- long-, L. *tenuis*).] **A.** *adj.* **I.** Having relatively little extension between opposite surfaces; of little thickness or depth. **b.** Of small cross-section in proportion to length; slender, tenuous, attenuated. late ME. **c.** *spec.* Having little flesh; lean, spare. Also of ears of corn. OE. **d.** Penetrable by light or vision; *fig.* easily 'seen through', transparent, flimsy, as a pretext or excuse 1613.
1. Thyn skynne 1530. **b.** A very t. wire 1885. **c.** Seuen kyne,..thynne, euell fauoured, and leenfleshed COVERDALE *Gen.* xli. 3. **d.** Under a t. disguise of name 1851. A t. veil of fog TYNDALL.

II. 1. Consisting of or characterized by individual constituents or parts placed at relatively large intervals; not thick, dense, or bushy. Opp. to THICK *a.* II. 1. OE. †**b.** Of the members of a collective group or class: Not numerous or abundant; scarce, rare, few, scanty -1725. †**c.** Of a place: Sparsely occupied or peopled; with *of*, sparsely furnished or supplied with; thinly occupied or attended by -1800. **d.** Of an assembly or body of people: Scantily furnished with members; thinly attended; not full 1637. **2.** Of a liquid or pasty substance: Of slight density or consistence; fluid; of air or vapour, not dense; rare, tenuous, subtile. Opp. to THICK *a.* II. 3. OE. **b.** *transf.* and *fig.* Wanting body or substance; unsubstantial; intangible 1610. **c.** Wanting depth or intensity; faint, weak, dim, pale 1649. **d.** Of sound: Wanting fullness, volume, or depth; weak and high pitched; shrill and feeble 1660. **3.** *fig.* Deficient in substance or quality; poor; unsubstantial; feeble; slight; scanty; not full or rich ME. **b.** *spec.* Of liquor: Without body; weak 1440.
1. [Lord Mountjoy's] haire was..thinne on his head 1617. **c.** The town being t., I am less pestered with company SWIFT. **d.** There I found but a t. congregation already PEPYS. **2.** Chalk, ground up with a little water into a t. paste 1850. **b.** These our actors..were all Spirits, and Are melted into Ayre, into t. Ayre SHAKS. **d.** I hear the groans of ghosts; T., hollow sounds DRYDEN. **3.** Yet was her wit but t. 1580. A t. and slender pittance SHAKS. A t. Diet 1707. Slang phr. *A thin time*, an uncomfortable or distasteful experience. **b.** To forsweare thinne Potations, and to addict themselues to Sack SHAKS.

B. *absol.* as *sb.*: mostly ellipt. or nonce-uses. *T. and thick*: see THICK AND THIN. ME. **C.** *adv.* **1.** With little thickness or depth; with thin clothing. †*To go t.*: to be thinly clad. ME. **2.** Sparsely; not closely or thickly. late ME.
2. To sow something thinner than ordinary 1707.
Comb.: **t. coal,** coal found in shallow beds or seams; **t. miner,** a miner who gets coal from thin seams; **t. seam,** applied to coal seams less than 3 feet in thickness; **-sown** *a.*, sown or planted thinly; **-spun** *a.*, spun thinly; drawn out in spinning to a slender thread. Hence **Thi·n-ly** *adv.*, **-ness.**

Thin (þin), *v.* [OE. *þynnian*, f. *þynne* THIN *a.*] **1.** *trans.* To make thin; to reduce in thickness or depth; to spread or draw *out* in a thin layer or thread. **2.** *intr.* To become thin or thinner; to decrease in thickness or depth 1804. **b.** *spec.* To lose flesh; to become spare or lean 1870. **3.** *trans.* To render less crowded or close by removing individuals; hence, to reduce in number 1440. **4.** *intr.* Of a place: To become less full or crowded; of a crowd: to become less numerous 1779. **5.** *trans.* To dilute OE. **6.** *intr.* To become less dense or consistent; to grow fluid, tenuous, or rare 1834.
1. *To t. off, down*, to diminish gradually to vanishing point. **2.** *To t. out* (*off, away*), to become gradually thinner until it disappears, as a layer or stratum. **3.** To t. our population 1832. T. out superfluous shoots 1850. A head already thinned of hair 1905. **4.** The town begins to t., though Parliament is still sitting 1779. Hence **Thi·nner,** one who or that which thins; *spec.* a preparation for thinning paint.

Thine (ðəin), *poss. pron.* [OE. *þīn*, used as genitive case of *þū* THOU, and as possessive adj.:—OTeut. **þīno-*, deriv. of stem *þe-*; see also THEE.] †**I.** Genitive case of THOU: = of thee -1500. **II.** The possess. adj. or pron. of the second person sing.: Belonging to thee. **1.** *attrib.* Now *arch.* or *poet.* bef. a vowel or *h*, or when following the sb.; otherwise superseded by THY. OE. **2.** *predic.* OE. **3.** *ellipt.* = THY with a sb. to be supplied from the previous context. late ME. **4.** *absol.* **a.** That which is thine; thy property OE. **b.** *pl.* Those who are thine; thy people, family, or kindred OE. **c.** *Of thine*: that is (or are) thine; belonging to thee. late ME.
I. *Maugre t.*, in spite of thee. **II. 1.** Drink to me only with t. eyes B. JONS. **2.** For thyne is the kyngedome and the power, and the glorye TINDALE *Matt.* vi. 13. **3.** *S.* Tastes are different, you know... *E.* That 's true; but thine's a devilish odd one. CHESTERF. **4. a.** Myne and Thyne (the seedes of all Myscheefe) 1555. **b.** Lasting shame On thee and thine..I will inflict SHAKS.

Thing (þiŋ), *sb.*[1] [Com. Teut.; OE. *þing.*] **I.** †**1.** A meeting, assembly, *esp.* a deliberative or judicial assembly. OE. only. †**2.** A matter brought before a court of law; a legal process; a charge brought, a suit or cause pleaded before a court -1548. **3.** That with which one is concerned (in action, speech, or thought); *pl.* affairs, concerns, matters OE. **4.** That which is done or to be done; a doing, act, deed, transaction; an event, occurrence, incident; a fact, circumstance, experience OE. **5.** That which is said; a saying, utterance, expression, statement; with various connotations ME. **b.** That which is thought; an opinion, a notion, an idea 1765. †**6.** Used *absol.*, also *a t.*, in indefinite sense: = anything, something -1678.
3. You shall heare how things goe SHAKS. Things changed greatly in the course of a year 1867. **4.** The great t. was to get there 1902. (*The*) *first t.* (advb.), as that which is first done or to be done; in the first place, firstly. So (*the*) *next t.*, next; (*the*) *last t.*, in the last place, lastly; He often goes round the last t. ..to make sure that all is right 1871. **5.** I never heard a better T. SWIFT. The people who went about saying things 1859. **b.** Putting things in the poor girl's head 1885. **6.** Shall I tell you a t.? SHAKS.

II. An entity of any kind. **1.** That which exists individually (in the most general sense, in fact or in idea); that which is or may be in any way an object of perception, knowledge, or thought; a being, an entity. **a.** In unemphatic use OE. **b.** Applied to an attribute, quality, or property of an actual being or entity; hence sometimes = point, respect OE. **c.** Used indefinitely: a something, a somewhat 1602. **d.** In emphatic use: That which has separate or individual existence 1817. **2.** *spec.* That which is signified as dist. from a word, symbol, or idea by which it is represented; the actual being or entity as opp. to a symbol of it 1450. **b.** *esp.* A being without life or consciousness; an inanimate object 1689. **3.** Applied (usu. with qualifying word) to a living being or creature; occas. to a plant OE. **4.** Applied to a person, now only in contempt, reproach, pity, or affection; formerly also in commendation or honour ME. **5.** A material object, a body; a being or entity consisting of matter, or occupying space OE. **b.** A material substance (usu. of a specified kind); stuff, material; in mod. use chiefly applied to substances used as food, drink, or medicine OE. **6. a.** A piece of property, an individual possession; usu. in *pl.*, possessions, belongings, goods; *esp.* (*colloq.*), those which one has or carries with one at the time, e.g. on a journey ME. **b.** *spec.* (*pl.*) Articles of apparel; clothes, garments; *esp.* such as women put on to go out in, in addition to the indoor dress. *colloq.* 1634. **c.** *pl.* Implements or equipment for some special use; utensils. Chiefly *colloq.* 1698. **7.** An individual work of literature or art, a composition; a writing, piece of music, etc. late ME.

1. a. To compare Great things with small MILT. A man of parts is one t., and a pedant another BERKELEY. A t. of beauty is a joy for ever KEATS. The latest t. in tattooing GEO. ELIOT. b. I side in all things with the mob BERKELEY. Ignorance is an odious t. 1838. c. No Bird, but an invisible t., A voice, a mystery WORDSW. d. True words are things BYRON. 2. The supposition that things are distinct from ideas takes away all real truth BERKELEY. b. Consideration of persons, things, times and places DICKENS. 3. I wish no living t. to suffer pain SHELLEY. 4. At a Play..looking..at a young t. in a Box before us STEELE. To accept the sovereignty of a t. like Henry of Valois MOTLEY. 5. Things perceivable by touch BERKELEY. Callest thou that t. a leg? TENNYSON. 6. a. Busie in packing vp his things against his departure 1603. b. Take off your things—and we will order..tea 1833. c. The breakfast things 1844. 7. I have a t. in prose, begun above twenty-eight years ago, and almost finished SWIFT.

Phrases, etc. *..and things* (colloq., unstressed), and other things of the same kind; and the like, *et cetera*. *For one t.*, as one point to be noted; in the first place; so *for another t.* *To make a good t. of*, to turn to profit, make gain out of. *No great things* (used predic.), nothing great, nothing much (*colloq.* or *dial.*). *T. in itself* (tr. G. *ding an sich*, Kant), *Metaph.* a thing regarded apart from its attributes; a noumenon. *To know a t. or two*: see KNOW *v.* IV. 4; so *to learn, to show* (a person) *a t. or two*. *To be up to a t. or two* = to know a thing or two. **The t.** (colloq., emphatic). a. the correct thing; what is proper, befitting, or fashionable; also of a person, in good condition or 'form', 'up to the mark', fit (physically or otherwise); b. the special, important, or notable point; *esp.* what is specially required. *Any t., every t., no t., some t.* (in which *thing* is an unemphatic stressless use of sense II. 1 or II. 5), are now written each as one word (see ANYTHING, EVERYTHING, NOTHING, SOMETHING).

Thing (þiŋ), *sb.*[2] 1840. [a. ON. *þing* (mod. Scand. *ting*); the same word as prec., but taken independently from ONorse.] In Scandinavian countries (or settlements, as in parts of England before the Conquest): A public meeting or assembly; *esp.* a legislative council, a parliament; a court of law. (Usu. with capital T.)

Thingman (þi·ŋmæn). *Pl.* **-men.** 1870. [ad. ON. *þingmaðr*, in pl. *þingmenn*.] A member of a Scandinavian Thing; *spec.* = HOUSE-CARL.

Thingum (þi·ŋəm). *colloq.* *Obs.* exc. *dial.* 1680. [f. THING *sb.*[1], with meaningless suffix.] = THINGUMMY. So **Thingumajig** (þi·ŋəmădʒig) 1876.

Thingumbob (þi·ŋəmbǫb). Also **thingume-, thingummybob.** *colloq.* 1751. [Arbitrary extension of prec.] = next.

Thingummy (þi·ŋəmi). *colloq.* 1796. [f. THINGUM.] Used to indicate vaguely a thing (or person) of which the speaker cannot at the moment recall the name, or which he is at a loss or does not care to specify precisely; a 'what-you-may-call-it'.

Think (þiŋk), *sb.* *dial.* or *colloq.* 1834. [f. THINK *v.*[2]] **1.** An act of (continued) thinking; a meditation. **2.** What one thinks about something; an opinion 1835.

†**Think**, *v.*[1] *Obs.* exc. in METHINKS. [OE. *þync(e)an, þúhte, geþúht* :—OTeut. *þunkjan, *þunχt- to seem, appear. In ME., owing to the fact that both *þync-* and *þenc-* gave ME. *þink-*, and both *þúht* and *þóht* appeared in ME. as *þouȝt, thought*, the forms of this vb. and of THINK *v.*[2] became coincident.] *intr.* To seem, to appear -1635.

Think (þiŋk), *v.*[2] Pa. t. and pa. pple. **thought** (þǭt). [OE. *þenc(e)an, þóhte, (ge)þóht*. In form, a factitive verb f. *þank-, str. grade of ablaut series *þink-, þank-, þunk-. Cf. pre-Teut. *tong- of L. *tongere* to ascertain.] **I.** To conceive in the mind, exercise the mind. **1.** *trans.* To form in the mind, conceive; to have in the mind as a notion, an idea, etc.; to do in the way of mental action. †**2.** (with simple obj.) To meditate on, ponder over, consider -1605. **b.** with indirect question as obj. OE. **c.** To have one's thoughts full of, imbued with, or influenced by; to think in terms of 1821. **3.** *intr.* To exercise the mind, esp. the understanding, in any active way; to form connected ideas of any kind; to meditate, cogitate OE. **4.** To form or have an idea of (a thing, action, or circumstance, real or imaginary) in one's mind; to imagine, conceive, fancy, picture. **a.** *trans.*; also *absol.* in colloq. phrases *only t.! you can't t.!* ME. **b.** *intr.* with *of* (*on* obs. or arch.), in same sense ME. **c.** *trans.* with simple obj. To picture in one's mind, apprehend clearly, cognize (with or without direct perception) 1864.

1. To thinke so base a thought SHAKS. I thought, He will surely come out to me 2 *Kings* v. 11. *To t. scorn* (*of* or *to do* something), to scorn (*arch.*); *to t. shame*, to be ashamed (now *dial.*). 2. b. A-thinking what he should do 1778. c. Unless thou hast been drinking beer and thinking beer KINGSLEY. 3. Who now thought of nothing but the pursuite of vanity EVELYN. Those who t. must govern those that toil GOLDSM. *T. aloud*, to express one's thoughts by audible speech as they pass through the mind. 4. a. Thinke but this..That you haue but slumbred heere SHAKS. b. T. of me ever being rich! 1861. c. We t. the ocean as a whole by multiplying mentally the impression we get at any moment when at sea 1890.

II. To call to mind, take into consideration. **1. a.** *trans.* To call to mind; to consider, reflect upon; to recollect, remember, bear in mind OE. **b.** *intr.* To consider the matter; to reflect OE. **c.** *intr.* with *of* (arch. *on, upon*), or *inf.*: To call to mind, remember, bethink oneself (of), hit upon mentally ME. **2.** *intr.* with *of*, arch. *on* (*upon*): To take into consideration, have regard to, consider. ME. **3.** To bethink oneself of something in the way of a plan or purpose; to contrive, devise, plan, plot. **a.** *trans.* ME. **b.** *intr.* with *of* (*on, upon*, obs. or arch.) 1598. **4.** To conceive or entertain the notion of doing something; to intend, mean, 'have a mind', 'have thoughts (of)'. **a.** *trans.* OE. **b.** *intr.* with *of* 1698. **c.** *spec.* with *of*: To consider (a person) in view of some vacancy, or *esp.* of marriage; to cherish the notion or intention of marrying 1670.

1. a. I am afraid, to thinke what I haue done SHAKS. b. Pause here, and t. COWPER. c. The most conuenient place, that I can thinke of..is Black-Fryers SHAKS. *To t. better of*: see BETTER *adv.* 2. Nothing was thought of, but how to save ourselves, and the little goods we had JOHNSON. 3. b. His Majesty..hath thought of a way 1630. 4. a. Peace is despaird, For who can t. Submission? MILT. He..thought he would send for his mother; and then he thought he would not T. HARDY. b. Each thought of taking to himself a wife CRABBE. c. I trust to your prudence, not to t. of Flora..; for you can't..marry a girl with so small a fortune MAR. EDGEWORTH.

III. To be of opinion, deem, judge, etc. **1.** *trans.* with *obj. cl.*, or parenthetic: To be of opinion, hold the opinion, believe, deem, judge, apprehend, consider; usu., to regard it as likely, to have the idea, to suppose; in ref. to a future event, to expect OE. **b.** *intr.* To hold the opinion (indicated by context) ME. **2.** *trans.* with complement: To believe, consider, or suppose (to be..); to look upon as ME. **3.** *intr.* To have a (good, bad, or other) opinion with regard to a person or thing; to value or esteem something (highly or otherwise). late ME. **4.** To believe possible or likely; to suspect; to expect, anticipate. **a.** *trans.* with simple obj. late ME. **b.** with *inf.* To expect. late ME. **c.** *intr.* with *of*, †*on* (*upon*), †*to*: To suspect; to expect, look for 1483. **d.** with *for*, after *as* or *than*, and with the prep. at the end of the clause: To expect, suppose 1530. **5.** *trans.* To judge or consider to exist; to believe in the existence of (*rare*) 1532.

1. Who would haue thought that our Uncle of Englande would haue made warre on vs? HALL. I t. that I understand him JOWETT. *Who do you t.? What do you t.?* (colloq.) phrases used, esp. parenthetically, to introduce a surprising statement. *I don't t.* (slang), used after an ironical statement, to indicate that the reverse is intended; 'You're a amiably-disposed young man, sir, I don't t.', resumed Mr. Weller DICKENS. b. He said he spake as he thought 1560. *To t. so*, to be of that opinion. *To t. with*, to be of the same opinion as. 2. May I be bold To thinke these spirits? SHAKS. The little narrative which I thought proper to put forth in October SCOTT. *T.* (*it*) *long*, to grow weary with waiting; to be impatient; to long, yearn (*Obs.* exc. *dial.*). †*T.* (*it*) *much*, to think it a great or serious matter; to object, grudge; to be shy, hesitate; to be surprised, wonder (*that*..). 3. I thinke nobly of the soule SHAKS. I didn't t. much of her 1813. Phr. *T. nothing of*, (*a*) to set no value upon, esteem as worthless; (*b*) to make light of, make no difficulty or scruple about. 4. a. He, thinking no harm, agreed DE FOE. b. I thought to have seen you ere this SOUTHEY. d. Oh sir, the conceit is deeper than you t. for SHAKS. 5. Unless there be who t. not God at all MILT.

Phr. **T. out** (*a*) to find out, devise, or elaborate by thinking, to construct intellectually; (*b*) to solve by a process of thought; (*c*) to think to the end, complete or finish in thought. **T.** (a thing) **over**, to give continued thought to (it) with the view of coming to a decision.

Thinkable (þi·ŋkăb'l), *a.* 1854. [f. prec. + -ABLE. Cf. *unthinkable* (1430).] **1.** Capable of being thought; such as one can form a notion or idea of; cogitable. **2.** Conceivable or imaginable as an existing fact 1865.

Thinker (þi·ŋkəɹ). 1440. [f. as prec. + -ER[1].] One who thinks. **a.** *gen.* A person or being engaged in thinking, or having the power to think. **b.** with qualifying adj.: One who thinks in the way expressed by the adj. 1698. **c.** *spec.* One who has special or well-trained powers of thought, esp. abstract thought; also, a person who devotes himself to thinking, as dist. from action or practical affairs 1830.

Thinking (þi·ŋkiŋ), *vbl. sb.* ME. [f. THINK *v.*[2] + -ING[1].] The action of THINK *v.*[2] **1.** Thought, cogitation, meditation, mental action or activity, etc. **b.** *pl.* Thoughts; meditations. late ME. **2.** The holding of an opinion or opinions; judging, mental viewing; opinion, judgement, belief; colloq. phr. *to my t.* = in my opinion. late ME.

1. Plain living and high t. are no more WORDSW. b. I am wrap'd in dismall thinkings SHAKS. 2. I heare a Bird so sing, Whose Musicke (to my t.) pleas'd the King SHAKS.

attrib. and *Comb.*: **t.-cap** (see CAP *sb.*[1]); **t. part** (*Theatr. colloq.*), a part in which the actor has no words to speak.

Thi·nking, *ppl. a.* 1678. [f. as prec. + -ING[2].] **1.** That thinks; cogitative. **2.** Given to thinking; having special or well-trained powers of thought; thoughtful, reflective, intellectual 1681.

1. What was the proper Employment of a t. Being? 1709.

Thi·nk-so. *dial.* 1666. [The phr. (*I*) *think so* used as a sb.] A mere opinion.

How if all our Faith, and Christ, and Scriptures should be but a Think-so too? BUNYAN.

Thinnish (þi·niʃ), *a.* 1545. [f. THIN *a.* + -ISH[1].] Somewhat thin; tending to thinness.

Thin-skinned (-skind; stress variable), *a.* 1598. **1.** Having a thin skin or rind. **2.** *fig.* Sensitive to criticism, ridicule, or abuse; easily hurt or offended; touchy 1680.

Thio- (þəi,o), also bef. a vowel **thi-**, repr. Gr. θεῖον sulphur; a formative element in names of substances containing or connected with sulphur.

1. *Chem.* In names of compounds containing sulphur = *sulpho-*. **Thia·ldine** [ALD(EHYDE + INE[5]], a crystalline substance, $NH:2(CHCH_3.S):CHCH_3$, produced by passing hydrogen sulphide into a solu-

tion of aldehyde ammonia. **Thi·alol** [AL(COHOL + -OL 3], diethyl disulphide ($(C_2H_5)_2S_2$, a colourless oily compound, having an odour like garlic. **Thi·enyl**, the radical C_4H_3S contained in *thiophene*, C_4H_4S. **Thi·o-acid**, an acid in which oxygen is replaced by sulphur. **Thioca·rbonate**, a salt of thiocarbonic acid. **Thiocarbo·nic** *a.*, in *t. acid*: in derivatives, as *mono-, di-, tri-thiocarbonic acid*: the last, H_2CS_3, is a dark yellow strongly smelling oil, very easily decomposed by heating into CS_2 and H_2S. **Thiocy·anate**, a salt of thiocyanic acid. **Thiocya·nic** *a.*, in *t. acid*, N ⋮ C.SH = cyanic acid, N ⋮ C.OH, in which oxygen is replaced by sulphur; a liquid with a penetrating odour. **Thiona·phthene**, a colourless crystalline compound, C_8H_6S, consisting of benzene, C_6H_6, of which two atoms of H are replaced by CH:CH.S. **Thionic** (þəi·ǫnik) *a.*, in *t. acids*, group name for the acids represented by the formula $H_2S_nO_6$. **Thi·onine**, a brownish-black dye, $SC_{12}H_9N_3$, crystallizing in plates, called *phenylene violet* or *Lauth's violet*, and largely used to stain microscopic objects. **Thi·onyl** [-YL], the radical $(SO)''$. **Thi·ophene**, C_4H_4S, a colourless liquid with an odour like benzene, occurring in benzene from coal-tar to the extent of about 0·5 per cent.; hence **Thiophe·nic** *a.*, in *t. acid*, $C_4H_3S.CO_2H$, derived from thiophene. **Thiophe·nol**, a colourless liquid, C_6H_5SH (= PHENOL with S in place of O), with the odour of garlic. **Thiosu·lphate**, a salt of thiosulphuric acid; formerly called *hyposulphite*. **Thi·osulphu·ric** *a.*, in *t. acid*, $H_2S_2O_3$, an acid, the salts of which are applied in bleaching and photography; it is sulphuric acid, H_2SO_4, in which one atom of oxygen is replaced by sulphur; formerly called *hyposulphurous* acid. **Thioto·luene** [TOLUENE] = *methylthiophene*, $C_4H_3(CH_3)S$, a colourless oily compound, found as an impurity in crude toluene. **Thioxene** (þəi|ǫ·ksīn) = *dimethylthiophene*, $C_4H_2(CH_3)_2S$, found as an impurity in xylene.

2. In pharmaceutical and other terms, as **Thi·ocamph** [CAMPH(OR], a fluid disinfectant, used for fumigation, formed by the action of sulphur dioxide on camphor. **Thi·oform** [after *chloroform*], trade-name of a basic bismuth di-thiosalicylate, as an antiseptic for wounds.

Thiol- (þəi·ǫ̆l). 1899. [arbitrarily f. THIO-.] *Chem.* A name for the group SH in combination, analogous to hydroxyl, OH.

Thion- (þəi·ǫ̆n). 1899. [a. Gr. θεῖον sulphur; cf. THIO-.] *Chem.* A name for sulphur taking the place of oxygen in a compound and joined by two bonds to carbon. (Certain words beginning with *thion-* do not conform to this system; see THIONIC, etc.)

Third (þ̄ɔ̄ɹd), *a.* (*adv.*), *sb.* [Com. Teut. and Indo-Eur. OE. *þridda, -e, þird(d)a, -e* :— OTeut. **þriđjó* :—Indo-Eur. **tritjós*; cf. Gr. τρίτος; L. *tertius*, Skr. *tṛtīyas*.] **A.** *adj.* **1.** The ordinal numeral corresponding to the cardinal three: last of three; that comes next after the second. **b.** *Gram.* In *t. person*: see PERSON *sb.* VI. Also in *t. declension, conjugation*, and in names of tenses, as *t. future* 1530. **2.** Additional to and distinct from two others already known or mentioned. *T. person* (in Law) = THIRD PARTY. ME. **3.** *T. part* = B. 1. ME. **4.** The last of each successive group of three; one in every three, i. e. one third of the whole. late ME.

1. The thryde day of Marche 1497. Pope Innocent the thred 1550. 'Hush! thou knave!' said a t. SCOTT. 3. The t. part of the sea became blood *Rev.* viii. 8. 4. *T. penny*, one third of the whole sum.

Comb.: **t. best**, that is next inferior to the SECOND BEST; **t. degree**, *U.S.* applied to severe and prolonged cross-questioning of a suspected person by the police; [Wigmore] An American authority declared that an officer of the law administers the first degree when he makes the arrest, the second when the prisoner is taken to a place of confinement, and the t. when he is taken to private quarters and interrogated; **t. estate**, the Commons; **t. floor**, (*a*) in England, the floor or story of a building separated by two from the ground floor; (*b*) *Sc.*, *U.S.*, etc., the t. story, counting the ground floor as the first; **t. hour**, (*a*) among the Jews, the t. of the twelve equal divisions of time between morning and evening; the hour between 8 and 9 a.m.; (*b*) the hour of TERCE; **t. order**: see TERTIARY A. 5; **t. rail**, in some systems of electric railways, an additional rail which conveys the current.

B. *sb.* **1.** A third part (A. 3) *of* anything; any one of three equal parts into which a whole may be divided. late ME. **2.** *Law.* (Mostly *pl.*) The third of the personal property of a deceased husband allowed to his widow. Also, the third of his real property to which the widow might be legally entitled for her life (*obs.* exc. *Hist.*). late ME. †**3.** A third of the proceeds of captures, or of certain fines, forfeitures, etc., of which two thirds were due to the king -1627. **4.** *Mus.* A note three diatonic degrees above or below a given note (both notes being reckoned); also (usu.) the interval between this and the given note, equivalent either to two tones (*major t.*), or to one tone and one diatonic semitone (*minor t.*); also, the harmonic combination of two such notes 1597. **5.** *Comm. pl.* Goods of the third degree of quality 1823. **6.** Ellipt. uses of the adj. passing into sb.: **a.** for third person (in Grammar); third day (of the month); third chapter (of a book of the Bible); third year (of a reign); third class (in an examination list) 1530. **b.** *T. of exchange*: the last of a set of three bills of exchange of even tenor and date.

4. We shall have the word In a minor t. There is none but the cuckoo knows BROWNING. *Diminished t.*, an interval equal to two diatonic semitones, being less by a chromatic semitone than a minor third. 6. a. On Sunday the 3d of May. He only got a third in Modern Greats (*mod.*). Hence **Third** *v. trans.* to divide into three equal parts. **Thi·rdly** *adv.* in the t. place.

Thi·rdborough, thri·dborrow. *Obs.* exc. *Hist.* 1475. [prob. a ME. corruption of *fridborgh* :—OE. *friðborg* peace-pledge, peace-surety; see FRITHBORH, FRANK-PLEDGE.] Formerly, The head man of a frithborh or frank-pledge; hence, the conservator of peace or peace-officer of a tithing, the petty constable of a township or manor.

Third class, third-class (stress var.), *phr.* (*sb.* and *a.*) 1839. **1.** *sb.* The class next below the second; esp. of railway carriages; also in an examination list; hence, a place in the third class in an examination 1845. **2.** *attrib.* or *adj.* Of or belonging to the class next below the second 1839. **3.** quasi-*adv.* By a third-class conveyance 1864.

3. Natives almost invariably travel third-class 1864.

Third hand, third-hand. 1553. **1.** In advb. phr. *at* (†*the*) *third hand*: from a second middleman or intermediary; at the second remove from the original source. **2.** *attrib.* or as *adj.* Obtained, copied, or imitated from a second-hand source 1599.

Thi·rd pa·rty. 1818. A party or person besides the two primarily concerned, as in a law case or the like. Also *attrib.*, as in *third-party insurance, risk*, etc.

Third-rate, *a.* and *sb.* 1649. [See RATE *sb.*[1]] **A.** *adj.* †**1.** Of the third 'rate' (esp. of ships) -1693. **2.** Of the third class in point of quality; usu. *depreciative*, of decidedly poor or inferior quality 1838.

2. An actor of t. parts THIRLWALL.

B. *sb. Naut.* A war-vessel of the third rate 1666.

A Third Rate of 62 Guns 1695. Hence **Third-rater.**

Thirdsman (þ̄ɔ̄·ɹdzmæ̆n). 1818. A third person or party; *esp.* one called in as an intermediary, mediator, or arbiter.

Thirl (þ̄ɔ̄ɹl), *sb.* Now *dial.* [OE. *þȳrel*, f. *þurh* THROUGH + -EL[1].] **1.** A hole, bore, perforation; an aperture. **b.** A nostril ME. **2.** An opening in a wall or the like. Also *fig.* OE.

Thirl (þ̄ɔ̄ɹl), *v. Obs.* exc. *dial.* and *local.* [OE. *þyrlian*, f. *þȳr(e)l* THIRL *sb.*] **1.** *trans.* To pierce, to run through or into (a body) as a sharp-pointed instrument does; to pierce (anything) with such an instrument; to perforate. **2.** *spec. Coal-mining.* To cut through (a wall of coal, etc.). Also *absol.* or *intr.* 1686. †**3.** *intr.* or *absol.* To pierce, penetrate (as a sharp instrument). Also *fig.* -1600.

Thirlage (þ̄ɔ̄·ɹlėdʒ). *Sc.* 1513. [A metathetic var. of †*thirlage* (f. *thirl*, var. THRALL *sb.*).] †**1.** Thraldom, bondage, servitude -1609. **2.** *Sc. Law.* A condition of servitude or state of obligation, in which the tenants of certain lands, or dwellers in certain districts are bound to restrict their custom to a particular mill, forge, or the like. In later times, spec. the obligation to grind their corn at a particular mill (orig. that of the lord or his assignee), and pay the recognized consideration (multure), or at least to pay the dues in lieu thereof. 1681. **b.** The multure exacted under this system 1799.

Thirst (þ̄ɔ̄ɹst), *sb.* [OE. *þurst* :—OTeut. **þurstuz*. Cf. L. *torrere* to dry, Skr. *tṛš* to thirst.] **1.** The uneasy or painful sensation caused by want of drink; also, the physical condition resulting from this want. **2.** *fig.* A vehement desire (*of* (arch.), *for*, *after* something, *to do* something) ME.

1. Þey deyde for hunger & þirst R. BRUNNE. The long t. of Tantalus allay GRAY. 2. Not in t. for Reuenge SHAKS. T. for money 1849. Hence **Thi·rstless** *a.* having no thirst; not thirsty.

Thirst (þ̄ɔ̄ɹst), *v.* [OE. *þyrstan*, f. *þurst* THIRST *sb.*] †**1.** *impers.*, as in *me thirsteth*, I am thirsty -1440. **2.** *intr.* To feel or suffer thirst; to be thirsty. Also *transf.*, e.g. of parched ground or plants. Somewhat *arch.* OE. **3.** *fig.* To have a longing, craving, or strong desire. Const. in OE. with gen., = of; later *after*, *for* something, *to do* something. OE. †**4.** *trans.* To desire vehemently; to long for -1718.

1. So thursted hym, that he Was wel ny lorn CHAUCER. 2. Ho, euery one that thirsteth, come ye to the waters *Isa.* lv. 1. 3. It is not necessary to teach men to t. after power BURKE. 4. Wicked men, that thursted the blud of all the senate Q. ELIZ. Hence **Thi·rster**, one who thirsts.

Thirsty (þ̄ɔ̄·ɹsti), *a.* [OE. *þurstig, þyrstig*, f. *þurst* THIRST *sb.* + *-ig* -Y[1].] **1.** Having the sensation of thirst; feeling desire or craving for drink. **b.** *transf.* Of earth or plants: Greatly wanting moisture; dry, parched, arid. late ME. **2.** *fig.* Having or characterized by a vehement desire or craving; eager, greedy OE. **3.** *transf.* That causes thirst. Now *colloq.* 1599.

1. The Fountain being..very inviting to the t. Passenger 1703. b. The country was parched and t. 1878. 2. Refreshing to the t. curiosity of the traveller LAMB. 3. A t. walk up and down terrible bad roads 1897. Hence **Thi·rstily** *adv.* **Thi·rstiness.**

Thirteen (þ̄ɔ̄ɹtī·n, þ̄ɔ̄·ɹtīn). [OE. *þréotiene, -téne*, f. *þréo* THREE + *tiene, téne*: see -TEEN.] The cardinal number composed of ten and three, represented by the symbols 13 or XIII. **A.** *adj.* **1.** In concord with a sb. expressed. Often *absol.* (with sb. implied in context) OE. †**2.** As ordinal: Thirteenth -1641.

1. Thirtine yeares past 1561. If t. sit down to sup, And thou first have risen up, Goodman, turn thy money! 1865. 2. He..died the t. of November, Anno 1142 KNOLLES.

B. *sb.* (With pl. *thirteens*.) **1.** The abstract number; a symbol or the figures representing this. late ME. **b.** A thing distinguished by the number thirteen, as an article of a certain size so called 1799. †**2.** An Irish silver shilling, as being worth thirteen pence of Irish copper currency -1830.

1. To shame the superstitious public out of their dread of the number 13. 1905. 2. Oft was his pocket without a t. 1810.

Thirteener (þ̄ɔ̄ɹtī·nəɹ). 1762. [f. prec. + -ER[1].] **1.** = prec. B. 2. **2. a.** *Cricket.* A hit for thirteen runs. **b.** The thirteenth of a series. 1891.

Thirteenth (þ̄ɔ̄ɹtī·nþ, þ̄ɔ̄·ɹtīnþ), *a.* and *sb.* [In OE. *þrie-, þréotéoþa*, etc. Northern ME. had *þrett-, þrittend(e* from ON. *þrettánde*. Hence *a* 1400 *þrett-, þrittenþ(e*, and by metathesis *ther-, thyr- thirtenth*, and in 16th c. *thirteenth*, as if f. *thirteen* + -TH[2].] **A.** *adj.* The ordinal numeral belonging to the cardinal thirteen; the last of thirteen; that comes next after the twelfth.

The literature of the t. century 1878.

B. *sb.* **1.** A thirteenth part 1611. **b.** *Eng. Hist.* A thirteenth part of the value of movables, or of the rent of the year, formerly granted or levied as a tax 1893. **2.** *Mus.* A note thirteen diatonic degrees above or below a given note (both notes being counted); the interval between, or consonance of, two notes thirteen diatonic degrees apart; a chord containing this interval 1597. Hence **Thirtee·nthly** *adv.* in the thirteenth place.

Thirtieth (þ̄ɔ̄·ɹti,ėþ), *a.* and *sb.* [OE. *þritigoða, -e*, f. *þritig* + *-oþa, -oþe* -TH[2].] **A.** *adj.* The ordinal numeral belonging to the cardinal thirty; the last of thirty.

B. *sb.* A thirtieth part; in *Eng. Hist.* a thirtieth part of movable goods payable as an aid 1800.

Thirty (þ̄ɔ̄·ɹti), *a.* and *sb.* [OE. *þritig*, f. *þri* THREE + *-tig* -TY.] The cardinal number equal to three tens, represented by the symbols 30, or XXX, xxx. **A.** *adj.* **1.** In concord with a sb. expressed or implied. **2.** *spec.* (*ellipt.*) **a.** The age of thirty; thirty years (of age, old, etc.). So *thirty-one*, etc. OE. **b.** In stating the time of day, thirty minutes; as in *six-thirty* = 6.30 o'clock, half-past six; also *attrib.* as *the*

6.30 *train* 1870. †3. As ordinal = THIRTIETH –1609.

1. Thirty per cent. interest 1837. *The T. (Tyrants)*, the t. magistrates imposed by Sparta upon Athens at the end of the Peloponnesian War (403 B.C.). *The T. Years' War*, the religious wars of 1618–48 fought chiefly on German soil. 3. Ere the t. day of the next month 1594.

B. *sb.* 1. The abstract number; also, a symbol representing this. So *thirty-one*, etc. OE. 2. *The thirties*: the years of which the numbers begin with 30. 1880. 3. *Thirty* and its compounds in elliptical uses 1802.

2. Some time in the early thirties 1892. 3. *T.-two*, a t.-two-pound gun; a flower-pot of which there are 32 in a 'cast'; see also THIRTYTWOMO.

Thirtytwomo (-tū·mo). 1771. [English reading of the symbol 32mo or XXXIImo, for L. (*in*) *tricesimo secundo*.] The size of a book, or of a leaf of a book, formed of sheets each folded five times, making thirty-two leaves; hence, a book of this size. Also **Thirty-twos**. So **Thirtysi·xmo** (**thirty-sixes**).

This (ðis), *dem. pron.* and *adj.* *Pl.* THESE. [orig. the sing. neuter, nom. and acc., now the sole sing. form of the OE. demonstrative *þes*, fem. *þéos*, neut. *þis*.] I. Demonstrative Pronoun. 1. Indicating a thing or person near or present (actually in space or time, or ideally in thought); *spec.* as being nearer than some other (hence opp. to *that*). Of a person, now indicating a person actually present, and always as subj. of the vb. *to be* with the person as predicate. b. After various preps. (*after, before, by, ere*, etc.), = 'this time' OE. c. After a prep., or as obj. of a verb, = 'this place'. Now (in colloq. use) more usu. *here*. 1460. 2. In contrast to *that*: now almost always of things ME. b. *spec.* (after L. idiom.) The latter; in contrast to *that* = the former 1440. c. With *That*, as quasi-proper names (with capital), indefinitely denoting one person and another 1824.

1. O Stephano, ha'st any more of t.? SHAKS. T. is the wood they live in FLETCHER. T., t. is she To whom our vows and wishes bend MILT. Yet all of us hold this for true, No faith is to the Wicked due 1664. They said t. as a jeer to the Jews 1693. b. By t. the sun is setting KEATS. c. You filthy beast, get out of t. W. S. GILBERT. 2. T. is not fair; nor profitable that; Nor t'other Question proper for Debate DRYDEN. *T. and (or) that* = one thing (or person) and (or) another. b. Warm water.. mixed with hot and cold, will lessen the heat in that, and the cold in t. BERKELEY. c. Miss That or This, or Lady T'other BYRON.

Phrases. *For all t.*, notwithstanding this. *Like t.*: of this kind; in this manner, thus. *T., that, and the other*: everything conceivable.

II. Demonstrative Adjective. 1. Used in concord with a sb., to indicate a thing or person present or near (actually or in thought), esp. one just mentioned OE. b. Referring to something which is mentioned immediately after OE. c. In phrases denoting or referring to the present state or stage of existence; esp. *t. life*, THIS WORLD OE. d. Referring to something as known, talked about, or inferred; esp. to something now in vogue or recently introduced 1533. e. Used before a date, esp. (now only) in legal or formal documents 1503. f. Used instead of THESE in concord with a plural sb. or numeral; esp. (now only) with a plural treated as a singular (e.g. *means, odds*), or with a numeral expression denoting a period of time taken as a whole. late ME. 2. In contrast to *that*; prop. denoting the nearer of two things, but often vaguely indicating one thing as distinct from another, esp. in phr. *this and (or) that..* = one and (or) another 1460.

1. I have t. moment heard that Sheridan is returned 1772. *T. morning, t. afternoon, t. evening* now always mean the morning (etc.) of to-day. b. T. additional list..is larger than I expected THORESBY. c. For t. corruptible must putt on incorruptibilite TINDALE 1 *Cor.* xv. 53. d. Oh t. learning, what a thing it is SHAKS. e. Given under my hand, this 20th September, 1648 CROMWELL. f. Within t. three houres will faire Iuliet wake SHAKS. The silence has kept my own heart heavy t. many a day RUSKIN. 2. T. way and that the impatient captives tend DRYDEN.

This (ðis), *adv.* late ME. [In I, prob. OE. *þýs, þis*, instrumental case of THIS *dem. pron.*; in II, app. advb. use of accus. sing. neut.] †I. In this way or manner; like this; thus –1592.

What am I that thou shouldst contemne me t.? SHAKS.

II. †a. To this extent or degree; as much as this; thus –1567. b. Qualifying an adj. or adv. of quantity, now chiefly in *t. much* 1460.

b. And t. far of the Iles called Hebrides 1596.

Thisness (ði·snės). 1643. [f. THIS + -NESS; tr. med. (scholastic) L. *hæcceitas*.] = HÆCCEITY.

Thistle (þi·s'l), *sb.* [OE. *þistil* :—OTeut. **þistiloz*, **þistila*.] 1. The common name of the prickly herbaceous plants of the composite genus *Carduus* and several closely allied genera (*Cnicus, Cirsium, Onopordum*, etc.), having the stems, leaves, and involucres thickly armed with prickles, the flower-heads usu. globular, and the flowers most commonly purple; many species are abundant as weeds. b. As the heraldic emblem of Scotland; also, a figure of a thistle as such 1488. c. As a part of the insignia of the *Order of the T.*, the distinctively Scottish order of knighthood; hence *transf.* the order itself, or membership in it 1687. d. *fig.* or in fig. context, with ref. to the thistle as a noxious or prickly weed 1563. †2. Applied (definitely) to other prickly plants, as artichoke, sea-holly (*Eryngium*), teasel, etc. –1578. 3. With qualifying words, applied to various species of *Carduus* and allied genera, and to prickly plants of other families 1578.

1. c. The Duke of Argyll..received his T. from Lord Palmerston 1898. d. He snatcheth at the t. of a project, which first pricks his hands, and then breaks FULLER. 3. **Bull t.**, a local (Ireland and U.S.) name for *Carduus lanceolatus*. **Canada t.** (*U.S.*), **Corn-t.**, **Creeping t.**, *Carduus arvensis*, a troublesome weed with creeping root-stocks. **Gentle t.**, *Carduus anglicus*. **Holy t.**, (*a*) *Centaurea benedicta* (*Cnicus benedictus*), with yellow flowers and weak prickles on the leaves, formerly in repute as an antidote; also called *blessed t.*; (*b*) erron. applied to *Carduus Marianus*, with white veins on the leaves; also called *Our Lady's t.* or *milk t.* **Russian t.** (*U.S.*), a species of saltwort, *Salsola Tragus*, with prickly stems, introduced from Russia and now abundant as a weed in S. Dakota and neighbouring States. **Scotch t.**, a name for the species supposed to be that figured as the emblem of Scotland, variously identified as the spear-t. (*Carduus lanceolatus*), the musk t. (*C. nutans*), the milk t. (*C. Marianus*), and the cotton-t. (*Onopordum Acanthium*). **Silver t.**, a name for the cotton-t. **Yellow t.**, (*a*) a species of thistle with pale-yellow or purple flowers (*Cnicus horridulus*), found in the eastern U.S.; (*b*) the prickly poppy (*Argemone mexicana*).

attrib. and *Comb.*: **t.-ball**, the globular head of feathery seeds of the t.; **-bird**, a bird that feeds on t.-seeds; *spec.* the American goldfinch, *Chrysomitris (Spinus) tristis*; **-butterfly**, the 'painted lady', *Vanessa (Pyrameis) cardui*, whose larva feeds on the t.; **-cock** (*dial.*), the corn bunting, *Emberiza miliaria*; **-crown, -dollar**, names of Scottish coins having a thistle on the reverse; **t. funnel**, a funnel having a large bulb between the conical flaring part and the tube, so as to suggest the form of a thistle-head upon its stalk; **t. noble**, a Scottish gold half-merk of James VI, bearing the figure of a t. on the reverse. Hence **Thi·stle** *v. trans.* to clear of thistles. **Thistled** (þi·s'ld) *a.* covered with thistles; adorned with figures of thistles.

Thistle-down (þi·s'l,daun). 1561. [f. prec. + DOWN *sb.*[2]] The down or pappus which crowns the 'seeds' or achenes of the thistle, and by means of which they are carried along by the wind: either collectively, or that of a single 'seed'. b. As a type of lightness, flimsiness, or instability; hence *fig.* 1868.

b. The t. of sentiment hung about me all the time 1868.

Thi·stle-finch. 1589. [f. as prec. + FINCH.] Any one of several species of finches which feed on the seeds of the thistle; *spec.* the goldfinch, *Carduelis elegans*.

†**Thi·stlewarp.** 1606. [f. as prec. + WARP *v.*] = prec. –1624.

Thistly (þi·s'li), *a.* 1598. [f. as prec. + -Y[1].] 1. Of the nature of or resembling a thistle; spiny, prickly; consisting of or constituted by thistles. 2. Full of, abounding or overgrown with thistles 1710.

1. *fig.* A world, so thorny,.. where none Finds happiness.. Without some t. sorrow at it's side COWPER. 2. The t. lawn THOMSON.

This world. OE. The present world; the present stage or state of existence, as dist. from another, esp. a future one.

They alle shalle neuer mete more in thys world MALORY. Hence **Thi·s-wo·rld·ly** *a.*, **-ness**

Thither (ði·ðəɹ), *adv.* (*a.*) [OE. *þider*, refashioning (after HITHER) of *þæder*, f. *þa-*, stem of THAT, THE + suffix denoting motion towards.] 1. To or towards that place (with verb of motion expressed or implied). (Now almost exclusively literary; usu. repl. by THERE.) b. *Hither and t.*: see HITHER *adv.* OE. †2. *transf.* To or towards that end, purpose, result, or action. SHAKS. B. *adj.* Lying on that side or in that direction, i.e. the side or direction away from *this*; the farther or more remote (of two things) 1830.

These all came in..on the t. side of innocence LAMB.

Thitherto (ðiðəɹtū·, ði·ðəɹtu), *adv.* 1449. [f. prec. + TO *prep.*; after *hitherto*.] 1. Up to that time; until then. Now *rare*. †2. To that condition, point, or result –1662.

Thitherward (ði·ðəɹwǭɹd), *adv.* (*a.*) *arch.* [OE. *þiderweard*; see THITHER and -WARD.] 1. Towards that place; in that direction; thither. †2. On the way thither; going thither –1634.

1. They shal aske the waye to Zion, with their faces thetherward BIBLE (Genev.) *Jer.* l. 5. So **Thi·ther·wards** *adv. arch.* (in sense 1).

‖**Thitsi, thitsee** (þi·tsī). *East Ind.* 1832. [Burmese *þitsi*, f. *þit* tree, wood + *asī*, in comb. *-sī* gum.] The 'black varnish tree', *Melanorrhœa usitatissima*, of the family *Anacardiaceæ*, Burma and Pegu; also, the varnish obtained from it.

†**Tho**, *dem. pron.* and *adj.* (*rel. pron.*), *pl.* [OE. *þá*, nom. and acc. pl. of *se, séo, þæt* THAT, THE.] I. Demonstrative pron. = THOSE I. (they, them) –1600. II. Demonstrative adj. 1. = THOSE II. –1553. 2. pl. of def. article THE –ME. III. Relative pron., pl. of THAT *rel. pron.* –late ME.

Tho, *adv.* (*conj.*) *Obs.* exc. *dial.* [OE. *þá*, = ON. *þá* then, when; orig. a case-form of the demonstrative stem *þa-* of THE, THAT; meaning 'that time', the sb. being omitted.] As dem. adv.: Then. a. At that time. †b. (Next) after that, upon that, thereupon –1642.

The queene..had herde ofte of Eneas er thoo CHAUCER. b. Vn-to this Angel spak the frere tho CHAUCER.

Tho, tho', abbrev. ff. THOUGH.

Thole (þōul, þaul), *sb.* [OE. *þol(l*, corresp. to ON. *þollr*, etc. Ulterior etym. unkn.] 1. A vertical pin or peg in the side of a boat against which in rowing the oar presses as the fulcrum of its action; *esp.* one of a pair between which the oar works; hence, a rowlock. 2. A pin or peg in general: *spec.* a. A pin by means of which the shafts are fastened to the carriage or axle of a cart, etc. b. The handle or 'nib' of a scythe-snathe (*local*) 1440.

Thole (þōul), *v.* Now *n. dial.* or *arch.* [OE. *þolian*, f. OTeut. stem **þul-* :—wk. grade of root* *tel-, tol-, tl-* to bear, suffer; cf. L. *tuli, tol-erare, toll-ere*, Gr. τλῆναι.] 1. *trans.* To be subjected or exposed to (something evil); to have to bear, suffer, endure, undergo. Also *absol.* 2. To submit with patience to; to bear or put up with, 'abide', tolerate. Also *absol.* OE. †3. To allow, suffer, permit –1721.

2. He that has a good crop may t. some thistles 1800.

Tho·le-pin. 1440. [f. THOLE *sb.* + PIN *sb.*] = THOLE *sb.*

‖**Tholus** (þōu·lǒs). *Pl.* **tholi** (-əi). Also in Gr. form **tholos** (þǫ·lǫs), *pl.* **tholoi** (-oi). 1644. [L., a. Gr. θόλος a round building with a conical or vaulted roof.] *Arch.* A circular domed building or structure; a dome, cupola; a lantern. b. *Gr. Antiq.* An excavated circular tomb of the Mycenæan age, domed and lined with masonry 1885.

Thomæan (tomī·ăn), *a.* and *sb.* 1727. [app. f. med.L. *Thomæus* (f. the name *Thomas*) + -AN.] A. *adj.* Of or pertaining to the Christian church traditionally said to have been founded by St. Thomas the Apostle, which has existed from early times on the Malabar coast. B. *sb.* A member of this church.

Thomas (tǫ·măs). OE. [a. L., Gr. Θωμᾶς.] 1. A Greek, Latin, and common Christian name: well known as that of the 'doubting apostle' (see John xx. 25), and hence used allus.; also used as a representative proper name for one of the populace taken at random.

Abbrev. TOM, TOMMY. **2.** Generic name for a footman or waiter 1846. **3. Thomas Atkins** (also *Thomas*): a familiar name for the typical private soldier in the British Army; arising out of the casual use of this name in the specimen forms of the official regulations. (Now more popularly TOMMY ATKINS or TOMMY.) 1815.

1. Doubting Thomases, who will only believe what they see 1883.

Thomism (tōu·miz'm). 1727. [f. prec. + -ISM.] *Theol.* The doctrines of Thomas Aquinas or of the Thomists.

Thomist (tōu·mist), *sb.* (*a.*) 1533. [ad. med.L. *Thomista* (Wyclif), f. *Thomas.*] *Eccl.* A follower of Thomas Aquinas (known as 'The Angelical Doctor'), a scholastic philosopher and theologian of the 13th c. Also *attrib.* or as *adj.* Hence **Thomi·stic, -al** *adjs.* of or pertaining to the Thomists or their doctrines.

Thomite (tōu·məit). *rare.* 1727. [f. THOMAS + -ITE [1].] = THOMÆAN *sb.*

Thomsenolite (tǫ·msĕnŏləit). 1868. [Named after Dr. Julius *Thomsen* of Copenhagen; see -LITE.] *Min.* Hydrous fluoride of aluminium, calcium, and sodium, found with pachnolite on the cryolite of Greenland.

Thomsen's (tǫ·msənz) **disease.** 1890. [Named after Dr. *Thomsen* of Schleswig-Holstein, who first described it.] *Path.* A peculiar congenital affection characterized by inability to relax the muscles immediately after contraction.

Thomsonian (tǫmsōu·niăn), *a.* (*sb.*) 1833. [f. the proper name *Thomson* + -IAN.] **1.** Of or pertaining to the system of medicine practised by Dr. Samuel Thomson, of Massachusetts (1769–1843). Also as *sb.*, one who follows this system. **2.** Of, pertaining to, or characteristic of the poet James Thomson, author of 'The Seasons' 1890. Hence **Thomso·nianism,** the T. medical system.

Thomsonite (tǫ·msənəit). 1820. [Named after Dr. Thomas *Thomson* (1773–1852), professor of chemistry at Glasgow; see -ITE [1].] *Min.* Hydrous silicate of aluminium, calcium, and sodium, found often in fibrous radiated masses, white to reddish-brown in colour; = COMPTONITE.

Thong (þǫŋ). [OE. *þwang, þwǫng,* f. ablaut-stem **þwing-, þwang-, þwung-* to restrain :—Indo-Eur. root **twenk-.*] A narrow strip of hide or leather, for use as a lace, cord, band, strap, or the like. **b.** Such a strip used as an instrument of flagellation; also as the lash of a whip; hence *spec.* a whip-lash of plaited hide 1592.

Thongs of raw hide 1867. **b.** Man's coltish disposition asks the t. COWPER.

Thong (þǫŋ), *v.* ME. [f. prec.] **1.** *trans.* To furnish with a thong; to fasten or secure with a thong or thongs; to bind with thongs. **2.** To flog or lash with a thong 1746.

Thooid (þōu·oid), *a.* (*sb.*) 1880. [f. Gr. θωός a beast of prey of the dog kind + -OID.] *Zool.* Resembling in form, or related to, the sub-genus *Thous*; in an extended sense applied to a division of the genus *Canis* including the wolf, dog, and jackal; as dist. from the alopecoid, typified by the fox. **B.** *sb.* A beast of this division.

Thor (þǭı). OE. [a. ON. *þórr* :—**þunroz* THUNDER.] The Scandinavian god of thunder, whose weapon was a hammer; his belt doubled his strength; hence in allusive use.

Thoraci- (þoræ·si), comb. form of L. *thorax, -acem,* in same sense as THORACO-; as in **Thora·ciform** *a.*, thorax-shaped.

Thoracic (þoræ·sik), *a.* (*sb.*) 1656. [ad. med.L. *thoracicus,* a. Gr. θωρακικός, f. θώραξ, θωρακ- THORAX; see -IC.] **1.** *Anat.* Of, pertaining to, or contained in the thorax; pectoral. **b.** Pertaining to, attached to, or forming part of the thorax (of an insect or crustacean) 1817. **2.** *Ichthyol.* Having the ventral fins situated directly beneath the pectoral; belonging to the *Thoracici*, the third order of fishes in the Linnæan system 1769. **3.** Having a thorax (as a distinguishing character); belonging to the *Thoracica*, a sub-order of cirripeds, in which the body consists of six thoracic segments, with a rudimentary abdomen 1891. **4.** As a specific distinction in *Nat. Hist.*: Having the thorax conspicuously marked or coloured 1812. **B.** *sb.* †**1.** A medicine acting on the thorax; a pectoral –1710. **2.** A thoracic fish: see 2 above 1828.

‖**Thoraco-** (þorē¹·ko), bef. a vowel **thorac-,** comb. form of Gr. θώραξ, θωρακ- THORAX.

Thoracente·sis, ‖**Thoracocentesis** (-sentī·sis) [Gr. κέντησις pricking], the perforation of the chest-wall to draw off morbid accumulations of fluid. **Thoracometer** (-kǫ·mītəı), an apparatus for measuring the movement of the chest-wall in respiration; a stethometer. **Thoraco·scopy,** the sounding or exploration of the chest. **Thoraco·stracous** [Gr. ὄστρακον hard shell] *a.*, of or pertaining to the *Thoracostraca*, a division of crustaceans, having a cephalothoracic shield and (usu.) stalked eyes. **Thoraco·tomy** [Gr. τομή cutting], incision into the thorax.

Thorax (þōə·ræks). *Pl.* **tho·raxes** (*rare*), or in L. form **thoraces** (þorē¹·sīz). late ME. [a. L., a. Gr. θώραξ breast-plate, also breast, chest.] **1.** *Anat.* and *Zool.* That part of the body of a mammal between the neck and the abdomen, comprising the cavity enclosed by the ribs, breast-bone, and dorsal vertebræ, and containing the chief organs of circulation and respiration; the chest; also, the corresponding part in the lower vertebrates, as birds, serpents, and fishes. **2.** *Zool.* The middle region of the body of an arthropod, between the head and the abdomen 1750. ‖**3.** *Gr. Antiq.* A cuirass, corselet 1842.

‖**Thoria** (þōə·riă). 1847. [f. as THORIUM + *-a*, after *alumina, silica,* etc.] *Chem.* An oxide of thorium, ThO_2, important in the manufacture of incandescent gas mantles.

Thorianite (þōə·riănəit). 1904. [f. **thorian* (f. THORIA) + -ITE [1].] The mineral consisting chiefly of the oxides of thorium, uranium, and other rare metals, found in the south-west of Ceylon in small brownish-black crystals having a resinous lustre; a variety of pitch-blende.

Thorite (þōə·rəit). 1832. [a. Sw. *thorit,* f. *Thor* + -ITE [1] 2 b.] *Min.* Hydrous silicate of thorium, occurring crystalline, massive, and compact, orange-yellow (ORANGITE) to brownish-black or black, with a vitreous or resinous lustre.

‖**Thorium** (þōə·riŏm). 1832. [f. THOR, the Norse deity + -IUM, to range with other names of metals.] *Chem.* A rare metallic element discovered by Berzelius in the mineral thorite, and subseq. found in small quantities in some other rare minerals. Symbol Th. (Now noted as one of the radio-active elements.)

Thorn (þǭın), *sb.* [OE. *þorn* :—OTeut. **þurnuz* :—Indo-Eur. **trnus.*] **I. 1.** A stiff, sharp-pointed, straight or curved woody process on the stem or other part of a plant; a spine, a prickle. **2.** *fig.* (or in fig. context): Anything that causes pain, grief, or trouble ME. **3.** A spine or spiny process in an animal ME.

1. Flours of all hue, and without T. the Rose MILT. 2. Phr. *A t. in the flesh* or *side,* a source of continual grief, trouble, or annoyance. (*To be, sit, stand, walk*) *upon thorns,* (to be, etc.) in a painful state of anxiety or suspense.

II. 1. A plant which bears thorns or prickles; a bramble or brier; a prickly bush, shrub, or tree; a thorn-tree or thorn-bush; esp. any species of the genus *Cratægus*; in England, *spec.* the Hawthorn or White-thorn (*C. Oxyacantha*) OE. **b.** (*without article*). Thorn bushes or branches collectively; also, the wood of a thorn-tree ME. **c.** *fig.* (occas. alluding to Matt. xiii. 7). ME. **2.** With qualifying words used to distinguish species and varieties of *Cratægus*, and to designate various other thorny plants. See BLACKTHORN, BOX-*t.*, WHITE-THORN, etc. 1731.

1. Do briers bringe forth figges, and thorns grapes? 1545. **b.** It pricks like thorne SHAKS. **c.** I fall upon the thorns of life! I bleed! SHELLEY.

III. The name of the Old English and Icelandic runic letter þ (= th); named, like other runes, from the word of which it was the initial OE.

attrib. and *Comb.*: **t.-bill,** a humming bird of the S. Amer. genus *Rhamphomicron*; **-bird,** a S. Amer. bird, *Anumbius acuticaudatus,* which builds a large domed nest of thorny twigs; **-devil,** an Australian lizard, = MOLOCH 2; **-head, -headed worm,** one of the *Acanthocephala,* intestinal parasitic worms having the proboscis furnished with hooks or spines; **-hopper,** a tree-hopper, *Thelia cratægi,* which frequents thorny shrubs; **-tail,** pop. name of the humming-birds of the S. Amer. genus *Gouldia,* distinguished by a long pointed tail.

Thorn (þǭın), *v.* Now *rare.* 1483. [f. prec.] **1.** *trans.* To make thorny, to furnish with thorns; *esp.* to protect (a newly planted quick-set hedge or the like) with dead thorn-bushes. **2.** To prick with or as with a thorn; to vex 1590.

2. I am the only rose of all the stock That never thorn'd him TENNYSON.

Tho·rn-a:pple. 1578. The common name of *Datura Stramonium,* of the family *Solanaceæ,* a coarse annual plant bearing large four-celled capsules covered with prickly spines; also, the capsule or fruit itself.

Thornback (þǭ·ınbæk). ME. **1.** The common ray or skate (*Raia clavata*) of British seas, distinguished by having several rows of short sharp spines arranged along the back and tail. **2.** Short for *t. crab* 1891. †**3.** An old maid (*slang*) –1709.

attrib.: **t. crab,** a species of spider-crab or sea-spider, *Maia squinado,* called also in U.S. king-crab; **t. ray** = sense 1.

Tho·rn-bush. ME. Any bush that bears thorns; e. g. a hawthorn, a bramble.

Tho·rn-hedge. 1560. A hedge of thorny shrubs; *spec.* a hedge composed of hawthorn 'sets'.

Thornless (þǭ·ınlės), *a.* 1776. [f. THORN *sb.* + -LESS.] Free from thorns; without a thorn.

One of those Whose love has prov'd a t. rose! 1803.

Tho·rn-tree. 1483. A tree having or bearing thorns; in Great Britain, usu. a hawthorn tree.

attrib.: **t. fly,** a March trout-fly.

Thorny (þǭ·ıni), *a.* [OE. *þornig,* f. THORN *sb.* + *-ig* -Y [1].] **1.** Abounding in, characterized by, or consisting of thorns or spines; spiny, prickly. **b.** Of an animal (or a part of one): Having thorn-like organs or appendages; spiny 1711. **2.** Overgrown with thorns or brambles OE. **3.** *fig.* Pricking or piercing to the mind; painful, distressing; harassing, vexatious, irritating ME. **b.** Full of points of contention or difficulty; delicate, ticklish 1653. **4.** In the names of species or varieties of plants, animals, or shells, characterized by having thorns or spines 1578.

1. Daphne roming through a thornie wood SHAKS. 2. *T. ground,* fig. after the parable of the sower, *Matt.* xiii. 7, etc. 3. The t. point Of bare distresse, hath tane from me the shew Of smooth ciuility SHAKS. **b.** I have finally arranged a t. transaction SCOTT. Hence **Tho·rnily** *adv.* **Tho·rniness.**

Thoro- (þōə·ro), comb. form of THORIUM, in names of compound salts, minerals, etc., e.g. **Thorogu·mmite** *Min.*, a hydrated thoro-silicate of uranium.

Thorough (þɒ·rŏ, þɒ·rə), *prep.* and *adv.* Chiefly *arch.* or *Obs.* [Later OE. *þuruh,* variant of *þurh* THROUGH.] **I.** *prep.* **1.** From side to side or end to end of. **2.** Along (to any distance) within. Without implication of traversing from end to end. OE. **3.** Over the whole extent of, in or to all parts of; throughout OE. **4.** From beginning to end of a space of time OE. **5.** Indicating intermediation, means, agency, instrumentality OE.

1. You ryde thorowe streetes, and townes 1540. 2. He wente þorow a foreste fowre longe myle 1430. 3. O'er hilly path and open Strath We'll wander Scotland t. WORDSW. 5. Not thorow thy swerde, ner thorow thy bowe COVERDALE *Josh.* xxiv. 12.

II. *adv.* (Now *arch* or *dial.*) **1.** = THROUGH *adv.* 1, 2. *arch.* OE. **2.** Qualifying pa. pple. or adj.; = THROUGH *adv.* 4 a. *Obs.* or *dial.* ME.

1. The future hides in it Gladness and sorrow; We press still thorow CARLYLE. 2. He had a t. good opinion of himself GOLDSM.

Thorough (þɒ·rŏ, þɒ·rə), *adj.* and *sb.* 1489. [attrib. use of prec. adv.] **A.** *adj.* **1.** Used chiefly with sbs. of action or position, being a kind of ellipt. use of the adv. = 'going, passing, or extending through'. *Obs.* exc. in special applications. **2. a.** Of an action, etc.: Carried out through the whole of something; thorough-going; fully executed; affecting every part or detail. Hence *gen.* That is fully what is expressed by the noun. 1489. **b.** of a person in ref. to his action or quality 1655.

2. a. A t. knowledge of the world GOLDSM. b. The ..most t. gentleman I ever saw LYTTON.

B. *sb.* [Ellipt. or absol. uses of THOROUGH *a.* or *adv.*] 1. Thorough-going action or policy: in *Eng. Hist.* (with capital T) applied to that of Strafford and Laud in the reign of Charles I, and sometimes to that of Cromwell as Lord Protector 1634. 2. *Agric.* A furrow; *water-t.*, a 'thorough' made for surface-draining; a water-furrow 1733.

1. And for the state, indeed, my lord, I am for T. LAUD.

Thorough- in combination.

1. With verbs, pples., or adjs.: **thoˑrough-bind** *v.*, *trans.* to bind or fasten (a wall, etc.) by a stone or iron, passing through from side to side; **-drain** *v.*, *trans.* to drain (a field) by means of water-thoroughs; **-felt** *pa. pple.*, felt throughout; **-ripe** (**throuˑgh-ripe**) *a.*, ripe throughout, thoroughly ripe. 2. With sbs. or derived adjs.: **thoˑrough-band** (**throuˑgh-band**), a stone, etc., extending through the breadth of a wall or dyke so as to bind the sides together; **-draught** (**throuˑgh-draught**), a draught or current of air passing through a room, etc.; **-edged** *a.*, thoroughly or perfectly edged; keen-edged; **-hearted** *a.*, whole-hearted; entirely devoted; **-winded** *a.* (of a horse) sound in 'wind'; not broken-winded.

Thoroughbass (þʊˑrǒbēˢs). 1662. [f. THOROUGH *prep.* or *adv.* + BASS *sb.*[5]] *Mus.* A bass part extending through a piece of music, and written by itself, with figures indicating the chords or harmonies to be played with it; a figured bass, *basso continuo*; *esp.* (formerly) an accompaniment thus written or played; hence *loosely*, an accompaniment in general. Also, the method of indicating harmonies by a figured bass, or the art of playing from it; *loosely*, the science of harmony in general. ¶b. *erron.* A loud or deep bass 1749.

Thoroughbrace (þʊˑrǒbrēˢs). *U.S.* 1837. [f. THOROUGH *prep.* or *adv.* + BRACE *sb.*[2]] Each of a pair of strong braces or bands of leather connecting the front and back C-springs and supporting the body of a coach or other vehicle. Hence **Thoˑroughbraced** *a.*

Thoroughbred (þʊˑrǒbred), *a.* (*sb.*) [f. THOROUGH *adv.* + BRED *ppl. a.*] 1. Thoroughly educated or accomplished; hence, complete, thorough, out-and-out. (Now regarded as *fig.* from 2.) 2. Of a horse: Of pure breed or stock; *spec.* applied to a race-horse whose pedigree for a given number of generations is recorded in the stud-book. Also of a dog, bull, etc. 1796. b. *transf.* Applied to human beings or their attributes, usu. implying grace, distinction, or the like 1820.

2. b. More thorough-bred or fairer fingers BYRON.

B. *sb.* 1. A thoroughbred animal, esp. a horse 1842. 2. *transf.* and *fig.* A well-born, well-bred, or thoroughly trained person. Also, a first-rate motor-car, bicycle, etc. 1894.

1. I can't afford a t., and hate a cock-tail THACKERAY.

Thoroughfare (þʊˑrǒfēˑɹ), *sb.* (*a.*) [In late ME. *thurghfare*, f. *þurh*, *þuruh* THROUGH + FARE *sb.*[1]] 1. A passage or way through. a. *gen.* †b. *spec.* A town through which traffic passes; a town on a highway or line of traffic –1829. c. A public way unobstructed and open at both ends; *esp.* a main road or street, a highway 1540. d. A piece of water, as a strait or river, affording passage for ships, etc.; an unobstructed channel 1699. 2. The action of going or passing through, or the condition of being passed through or traversed; passage. Now *rare* or *Obs.* 1667. 3. *attrib.* or *adj.* That is a t.; passed or travelled through by traffic; chiefly in *t. town* = sense 1 b. 1553.

1. a. This world nys but a thurghfare ful of wo, And we been pilgrymes, passynge to and fro CHAUCER. Phr. *No t.*, no public way through or right of way here. c. The Strand, that goodly thorow-fare betweene The Court and City 1658. 2. Ye..have..made one Realm Hell and this World, one Realm, one Continent Of easie thorough-fare MILT.

Thoroughgoing (þʊˑrǒgōᵘ:iŋ), *a.* 1819. [f. THOROUGH *adv.* + *going*, pr. pple. of Go *v.*] Going the full length; doing things thoroughly; acting with completeness; uncompromising, thorough, extreme, out-and-out. (Of persons, actions, etc.) Hence **Thoˑroughgoˑingly** *adv.*, **-ness**.

Thoˑrough-light. Now *rare* or *Obs.* 1605. a. *pl.* Windows on opposite sides of a room, so that the light passes right through 1625. b. *fig.* (*sing.* and *pl.*) in ref. to the 'light' of knowledge or discovery. So **Thoˑrough-lighted** *a.* having thorough-lights.

Thoroughly (þʊˑrǒli), *adv.* ME. [f. THOROUGH *adv.* or *adj.* + -LY[2].] †1. In a way that penetrates or goes through; right through, quite through (*rare*) –1703. 2. In a thorough manner or degree; in every part or detail; fully, completely, entirely, perfectly 1473.

Thoroughness (þʊˑrǒnės). 1843. [f. THOROUGH *a.* + -NESS.] The quality of being thorough or of doing things thoroughly; the condition of being done thoroughly; completeness.

Thorough-paced (þʊˑrǒ͵pēˢst), *a.* 1646. [f. THOROUGH *adv.* + PACED.] †1. *lit.* Of a horse: Thoroughly trained; having all his paces (*rare*) –1668. 2. *fig.* Thoroughly trained or accomplished, perfectly skilled or versed (*in* something); hence, thoroughgoing, complete, perfect, thorough 1646.

2. A thoro'-pac'd villain 1710. A hearty t. liar LAMB.

Thorough-pin (þʊˑrǒ͵pin). 1789. [f. THOROUGH- + PIN *sb.*[1]] *Farriery.* A swelling in the sheath of the tendon of the flexor perforans muscle in a horse's hock, appearing on both sides so as to suggest a pin passing through; also a similar swelling in the carpal joint of the fore-leg.

Thoˑrough-stitch, throuˑgh-stitch, *sb.*, *adv.* and *adj.* *Obs.* exc. *dial.* 1569. [f. THOROUGH *adv.* + STITCH *sb.*] †A. *sb.* A stitch drawn right through the stuff; hence *fig.* in ref. to thoroughness of action (*rare*) –1663. B. *adv.* Right through, through to the end; thoroughly; completely 1579.

Phr. *To go t.* (*with*), to perform something thoroughly, go through with; 'a tailor's expression for finishing any thing once begun'; The..Cheif Justice Jefferies..went thorough stitch in that tribunal EVELYN.

†C. *adj.* Thoroughgoing, out-and-out –1828.

Thoroughwax (þʊˑrǒwæks). 1548. [f. THOROUGH *prep.* and *adv.* + WAX *v.* to grow; from the branches appearing to grow through the leaves.] The umbelliferous herb *Bupleurum rotundifolium*, also called *hare's ear*, having roundish-oval perfoliate leaves, and small greenish-yellow flowers with conspicuous bracts.

Thoroughwort (þʊˑrǒwɒ̄ɹt). 1828. [f. THOROUGH *prep.* or *adv.* + WORT, after prec.] A N. Amer. composite plant, *Eupatorium perfoliatum*, having connate-perfoliate leaves and large corymbs of numerous white flowers; also called *boneset* or *crosswort*.

Thorp (þǭɹp). *arch.* and *Hist.* Also **thorpe.** [Com. Teut.; OE. and ME. *þrop* and *þorp* hamlet, village, farm, estate:—OTeut. **þorpom*. Ult. etym. obsc.] A hamlet, village, or small town; in ME. *esp.* an agricultural village. (A frequent second element in place-names in the forms *-thorpe*, *-thrup*, *-trup*, chiefly in the Danelaw district.)

Within a little thorpe I staid at last 1600. I hurry down..By twenty thorps, a little town, And half a hundred bridges TENNYSON.

‖**Thos** (þǒus). *Pl.* **thoes** (þǒuˑīz). 1601. [L., a. Gr. θώς, pl. θῶες, a beast of prey of the dog kind.] The Gr. and L. name of a beast of the canine group; probably a jackal of some species.

Those (ðǒuz), *dem. pron.* and *adj.* (*pl.*) [OE. *þás*, ME. *þǭs*, pl. of THIS, which during the ME. period became synonymous with *þā* THO, pl. of *that*, whence its current sense.] I. Demonstrative pronoun. †1. = THESE *pron.* –ME. 2. Pl. of THAT: indicating things or persons pointed to or already mentioned ME. b. Preceded by *and*, introducing an additional qualification of the things or persons mentioned in the previous clause 1545. 3. In opposition to *these*; sometimes *spec.* = 'the former'. Also in contrast to (*the*) *others*. 1611. 4. As antecedent pronoun, followed by a defining word or phrase ME. II. Demonstrative adjective. †1. Pl. of THIS II; = THESE *adj.* –ME. 2. Pl. of THAT I. 1, 1 b. ME. b. Used instead of *that* with a sing. noun of multitude (now only with collectives in pl. sense, as *clergy, horse, vermin*); and esp. with *kind, sort*, followed by *of* with pl. sb. 1560. 3. In opposition to *these*; pl. of THAT II. 2. 1641. 4. In concord with a noun which is the antecedent to a relative, or which is further defined by a participle ME. 5. = Such; pl. of THAT II. 4. Now *rare.* 1605.

2. Thy lips, t. kissing cherries SHAKS. Binde vp t. tresses SHAKS. A noted family in t. parts 1741. b. You, and t. poore number saued with you SHAKS. The little regard shown..to t. sort of things H. WALPOLE. 5. He spoke of you in t. terms that make me glad that I have met the son DISRAELI.

Thou (þau), *sb.* 1869. A colloq. and familiar abbrev. of *thousand*, esp. = a thousand pounds (sterling).

Thou (ðau), *pers. pron.*, *2nd sing. nom.* [Com. Teut. and Indo-Eur.; OE. *þū*:—OTeut. **þū*:—pre-Teut. **tū*: = L. *tu*, Gr. σύ, Doric τύ, Skr. *twa-m*. The oblique cases, and the possessive, are formed on a stem *þe-* = pre-Teut. *te-*; see THEE, THINE. The pl. YE, in OE. *gē*, is from a different root. The paradigm of *thou* in mod.Eng. is as follows:

	SINGULAR.	PLURAL.
Nom.	thou	ye, you.
Dat. Acc.	thee	you
Poss. Pron. { *absol.*	thine	yours
{ *adj.*	thy	your.]

1. The pronoun by which a person (or thing) is addressed, in the nom. (or voc.) sing.; the pronoun denoting the person or thing spoken to.

Thou and its cases *thee, thine, thy* were in OE. used in ordinary speech; in ME. they were gradually superseded by the pl. *ye, you, your, yours*, in addressing a superior, and (later) an equal, but were long retained in addressing an inferior. Long retained by Quakers in addressing a single person, though now less general. In general English used in addressing God or Christ, also in homiletic language, and in poetry, apostrophe, and elevated prose.

b. Used in apposition to and preceding a sb. in the vocative; in reproach or contempt often emphasized by being placed or repeated after the sb. OE. 2. as *sb.* a. The person or 'self' of the individual addressed 1693. b. The word itself; see also THEE *pron.* 4. 1655.

1. T., O God, art praysed in Sion COVERDALE *Ps.* lxiv. [lxv.] 1. Good t., saue mee a piece of Marchpane SHAKS. b. T. lyest, t. iesting Monkey t. SHAKS. 2. b. They also used the plain language of T. and Thee to a single person PENN.

Thou (ðau), *v.* 1440. [f. prec.] *trans.* and *intr.* To use the pronoun 'thou' to a person: familiarly, to an inferior, in contempt or insult, or as done on principle by Quakers.

She [a Quakeress] thou'd him [the king] all along PEPYS. In this country 'thouing' is a lost art 1883.

Though (ðǒᵘ), *adv.* and *conj.* [The OE. forms were *þéah*, *þéh*. The present form (which dates from *c* 1200) is from Norse, repr. ON. **þóh*, *þó*.] An adversative particle expressing that relation of two opposed facts or circumstances (actual or hypothetical) in which the one is inadequate to prevent the other, and therefore both concur, contrary to what might be expected. I. *adv.* For all that; in spite of that; nevertheless, howbeit, however, yet. Now *colloq.*

Your hands then mine, are quicker for a fray, My legs are longer t. to runne away SHAKS. It did its duty, t. BROWNING.

II. *conj.* (or *conjunctive adv.*) 1. Introducing a subordinate clause expressing a fact: Notwithstanding that; in spite of the fact that, although OE. b. With ellipsis of the subordinate clause 1592. 2. Introducing a subordinate clause expressing a supposition or possibility: Even if; even supposing that; granting that OE. b. With ellipsis (as in 1 b) 1591. 3. Introducing an additional statement restricting or modifying the preceding: And yet, but yet, but still, however ME. 4. †a. After neg. or interrog. phrases with *wonder, marvel, be sorry, care*, etc., where *if* or *that* is now substituted –1637. b. In phr. *as though*: as if; as would or might be the case if; so as to suggest the supposition that ME. 5. With special constructions (in sense 1, 2, or 3). †a. Followed by *that* –1711. b. Strengthened by *all*, following or preceding. *Obs.* exc. in comb. ALTHOUGH. Also by *even* preceding. ME.

1. The hone Gives edge to razors, t. itself has none 1746. The French..are very civil, thof I don't understand their lingo SMOLLETT. b. The base (t. bitter) disposition of Beatrice SHAKS. 2. T. he slaye me, yet wyll I put my trust in hym BIBLE (Great) *Job* xiii. 15. b. T. nere so blacke, say they haue Angells faces SHAKS. 4. a. He cares not t. the Church sinke 1637. b. I'faith, Ile eate nothing: I thanke you as much as

t. I did SHAKS. 5. a. *Lear* IV. vi. 219. b. Nor, even t. it be told to her, can she enter into it 1856.

Thought (þǭt), *sb.* [OE. *þoht*, shortened from **þóht* :—**þanχt-*, from stem of *þencan* THINK *v.*² + -T *suffix*³.] 1. The action or process of thinking; mental action or activity in general, esp. that of the intellect; exercise of the mental faculty; formation and arrangement of ideas in the mind. b. Thinking as a permanent characteristic or condition; the capacity of thinking; the thinking faculty OE. c. The product of mental action or effort; what one thinks; that which is in the mind ME. d. In a collective sense (with defining adj.): What is or has been thought by the thinkers of a specified class, time, or place 1853. 2. (with *a* and *pl.*) A single act or product of thinking; an item of mental activity; something that one thinks or has thought; a thing that is in the mind; an idea, notion OE. b. *spec.* An idea suggested or recalled to the mind; a reflection, a consideration ME. 3. In various specialized senses (from 1 and 2). a. Consideration, attention, heed, care, regard ME. b. Meditation, mental contemplation ME. c. Conception, imagination, fancy ME. d. The entertaining of some project in the mind; the idea or notion of doing something, as contemplated or entertained in the mind; hence, intention, purpose, design; *esp.* an imperfect or half-formed intention. Also in *pl.*, as *to have thoughts* (*of*). ME. e. Remembrance, 'mind'. *Obs.* or merged in general sense. ME. f. Mental anticipation, expectation ME. g. An opinion or judgement; a belief or supposition; what one thinks of or about a thing or person 1596. 4. Anxiety or distress of mind; solicitude; grief, care, vexation. *Obs.* exc. *dial.* ME. 5. A very small amount, a very little, a trifle. (Usu., now always, adverbial.) 1581.

1. Whether Brutes are capable of t.? 1704. b. Had he bin where he thought, By this had t. bin past SHAKS. c. Thus Bethel spoke, who always speaks his t. POPE. d. The leaders of scientific t. 1884. 2. Good Thoughts in Bad Times FULLER. One scarce can say..That he even gave it a t. BROWNING. Phr. *Second thoughts*, ideas occurring subsequently; later and maturer consideration; so *first thoughts*. b. *Rich. II*, v. v. 28. 3. a. Evil is wrought by want of T., As well as want of Heart! HOOD. Phr. *To take t.*, to consider, meditate (how to do something, etc.). b. She was lost in t. (*mod.*). c. O change beyond report, t., or belief! MILT. d. I do begin to haue bloody thoughts SHAKS. g. My first t. was, he lied in every word BROWNING. 4. Therfore take no t. saynge what shall we eate? TINDALE *Matt.* vi. 31. 5. I like the new tire..if the haire were a t. browner SHAKS.

attrib and *Comb.*: **t.-executing** *a.*, (*a*) in *Lear*, 'doing execution with the swiftness of t.'; (*b*) executing the t. or intention of a person; †**-sick** *a.*, sick with 't.' or thinking; **-transfer, -transference** (*Psychics*), transference or communication of t. from one mind to another apart from the ordinary channels of sense; telepathy; **-wave**, (*a*) *Psychics*, a 'wave' or undulation of a hypothetical medium of t.-transference; (*b*) a 'wave' or impulse of t. passing simultaneously through a crowd of persons or other living beings.

Thought (þǭt), pa. t. and pple. of THINK *v.*¹ and ².

Thoughted (þǭ·tėd), *a.* 1592. [f. THOUGHT *sb.* + -ED².] Having thoughts (of a specified kind).

Thoughtful (þǭ·tfŭl), *a.* ME. [f. THOUGHT *sb.* + -FUL.] 1. Full of or characterized by thought; meditative, contemplative; preoccupied in mind. Also *transf.* of personal attributes, actions, etc. b. Disposed to think about or consider matters; reflective; †heedful or mindful *of*. Also *transf.* Characterized by thought or reflection. ME. †2. Full of mental trouble; anxious; sorrowful; melancholy, moody –1744. 3. Showing thought or consideration for others; considerate 1851.

1. War, horrid war, your t. walks invades POPE. b. T. persons..had heard of these doings with uneasiness FROUDE. Not beyond the reach of t. enquiry 1884. 2. The merry soul is freer from intended mischief than the t. man 1627. Hence **Thou·ghtful-ly** *adv.*, **-ness.**

Thoughtless (þǭ·tlės), *a.* 1592. [f. as prec. + -LESS.] 1. Not taking thought; unreflecting, heedless, imprudent. b. With *of* or dependent clause: Not thinking; unmindful; heedless; unsuspecting. Now *rare.* 1615. †c. Free from care or anxiety –1789. d. Inconsiderate 1794. 2. Deficient in or lacking thought; not given to thinking; stupid; destitute of ideas. Now *rare.* 1682. †b. Of inanimate things: Devoid of thought –1705.

1. Youth may be alleged as an excuse for rashness and folly, as being naturally t. 1736. c. The t. day, the easy night GRAY. d. Little fly, Thy summer's play My t. hand Has brush'd away BLAKE. 2. An earnest thinker in a t. time 1879. Hence **Thou·ghtless-ly** *adv.*, **-ness.**

Thought-out (þǭtˌaut; stress variable), *ppl. a.* 1870. [pa. pple. of *think out* used as adj.] Elaborated, constructed, or arrived at by thinking or mental labour; thoroughly considered.

Thou·ght-rea:ding, *sb.* 1855. The reading of another person's thoughts; direct perception by one mind of what is passing in another, independent of ordinary means of expression or communication; a power alleged to be possessed by certain persons or by persons in certain psychic states. So **Thou·ght-rea:der. Thou·ght-rea:ding** *a.*

‖**Thous** (þōu·ŏs). 1839. [mod.L., a. Gr. θώς, θωός THOS.] *Zool.* A species or group of beasts of the extended genus *Canis*, canine beasts, natives of Africa and Asia; including *Thous* (or *Canis*) *anthus* (the North African Jackal), and *T. mesomelas, variegatus*, and *Senegalensis*, African jackals.

Thousand (þau·zănd), *sb.* and *a.* [OE. *þúsend*; generally held to be cogn. w. Lith. *túkstantis*, Russ. *tysjatʃa*, Pol. *tysiac*, Czech *tisic*, pointing to an orig. Slavo-Teut. **tūssontiā* or **tussntjā*, whence OTeut. **þūsundi*, prob. an indefinite term for a 'great multitude', used as the equivalent of Gr. χιλιάς and L. *mille.*] 1. The cardinal number equal to ten times one hundred: denoted by the symbols 1000 or M (for L. *mille*), formerly often by m̄ or ᵐ, as xxxᵐ. a. As sb. or quasi-sb., with pl. (*a*) In sing. Usu. *a t.*, emphatically or precisely *one t.* OE. (*b*) In pl. *thousands* OE. (*c*) After another numeral the sing. is now commonly used as a collective pl. OE. (*d*) As a sb. it takes after it *of*, repr. the OE. genitive pl. Now after a numeral only as a unit of quantity by which things are sold. OE. b. As adj. or quasi-adj., followed immediately by a pl. (or collective) noun OE. 2. Often used vaguely or hyperbolically for a large number OE. 3. Ellipt. uses. a. A thousand of some weight, measure, or quantity OE. b. A thousand pounds sterling 1547. †4. As ordinal: = THOUSANDTH –1680.

1. a. (*a*) A t. to one, they have..some gnawing care 1668. *One in a t.*, a paragon. (*b*) They amounted in all to some thousands 1771. (*d*) Thousands of arrobas were ..obtained 1880. b. So many t. Christians..murdered 1650. 2. You may do good to thousands 1779. 3. a. Instead of looking twenty, he looked a t. THACKERAY. The price of gas..was 3*s.* 9*d.* per t. 1901. b. A man of two t. a yeere B. JONS.

Thousandfold (þau·zăndfōuld), *a.*, *adv.*, and *sb.* [OE. *þúsendfeald*; see prec. and -FOLD.] A. *adj.* One thousand times as much or as many; consisting of a thousand parts; a thousand times repeated or multiplied. B. *adv.* A thousand times (in amount); a thousand times as much ME. C. *sb.* A thousand times the amount or number 1711.

Thousandth (þau·zăndþ), *a.* and *sb.* 1552. [f. THOUSAND + -TH.] The ordinal number belonging to the cardinal THOUSAND. A. *adj.* 1. Coming last in order of a thousand successive individuals. 2. *T. part*: one of a thousand equal parts into which anything may be divided 1561. B. *sb.* A thousandth part 1793.

Thraldom (þrǭ·ldəm). ME. [f. next + -DOM.] The state or condition of being a thrall; bondage, servitude; captivity.

In the midst of my thraldome in Turkie 1590. This t. to their pleasures YOUNG.

Thrall (þrǭl), *sb.* (*a.*) Now *arch.* or *Hist.* [OE. *þrǽl*, a. ON. *þrǽll*, perh. (ult.) f. OTeut. root *þreh-* to run.] 1. One who is in bondage to a lord or master; a villein, serf, bondman, slave; also, a servant, subject; *transf.* one whose liberty is forfeit; a captive, prisoner of war. b. *fig.* A slave (*to* something) OE. 2. The condition of a thrall; thraldom, bondage, servitude; captivity ME. †3. Oppression, trouble, distress –1829.

1. Outcast of Nature, Man! the wretched t. Of bitter-dropping sweat THOMSON. b. Slaues of drinke, and thralles of sleepe SHAKS. 2. To bring this noble Realme of England to thraule 1592.

B. *adj.* [The sb. used attrib.] 1. That is a thrall; subject, captive, enslaved, in bondage ME. †2. Belonging to or characteristic of thraldom; slave-like, slavish, servile –1535.

1. To be t. to no vice UDALL. We now are captives that made others t. HAYWOOD.

Thrall (þrǭl), *v. arch.* [Early ME. *þrallen*, f. prec.] *trans.* To bring into bondage or subjection; to deprive of liberty; to hold in thraldom, enthrall, enslave; to take or hold captive.

Thranite (þrēⁱ·nəit). 1842. [ad. Gr. θρανίτης, f. θρᾶνος bench.] *Gr. Antiq.* In the ancient trireme, a rower in one of the tiers, prob. the uppermost tier, which had the longest oars and hardest work.

Thrash, thresh (þræʃ, þreʃ), *v.* [Com. Teut.; OE. *þerscan* (*þærsc*, *þurscon*, *þorscen*) :—OTeut. **þresk-* :—Indo-Eur. **tresk-*. The historical form in Eng. is *thresh*; a dial. var. *thrash* is now the ordinary form, esp. in the sense 'to beat, flog, or belabour', while *thresh* is largely retained in ref. to corn.] I. To **thresh** or **thrash** corn, etc. and directly derived senses. 1. To separate by any mechanical means, e.g. rubbing, shaking, trampling, stamping, beating, or intermittent pressure, the grains of any cereal from the husks and straw; esp. by beating with a flail; now also by the action of revolving mechanism in a mill or machine. Also, to shake out or separate in the same way the seed of any plant. *trans.* and *absol.* or *intr.* 2. *fig.*: in earlier use sometimes with ref. to ancient modes of threshing ME. 3. *transf.* To beat or strike as with a flail. *trans.* and *intr.* 1573.

1. Afftir hervest..men thresshe shevys LYDG. First thrash the Corne, then after burne the straw SHAKS. 2. Phr. *To t. straw*, to work at what is unproductive or unprofitable. *To t. out* (*a subject*, etc.), to discuss (a matter) exhaustively; to get at the truth of (a question) by discussion or argument. 3. The angler goes on threshing the water 1867.

II. To beat a person, an army, etc. (Now commonly **thrash.**) 1. *trans.* To beat by way of punishment; to chastise by or as by beating; to flog, orig. with a stick, cudgel, whip, etc.; in mod. use also to pommel with the fists OE. 2. To beat completely or thoroughly; to overcome with severe loss in war or fighting, or *at* a game or contest 1606.

1. Take a good cudgel, and thrash him with it FIELDING. 2. The Colonel..has just been thrashing me at billiards 1890.

III. Transf. uses. (Usually **thrash.**) 1. *intr. Naut.* To force or work one's way against opposing wind, tide, etc. Also *trans.* with *way.* 1830. b. *trans.* To force (a ship) forward, esp. against contrary wind or sea 1886. 2. *intr.* To make wild movements like those of a flail or whip; to lash out; to throw oneself (or itself) to and fro with violence; to toss, plunge; of hair, branches, or anything free at one end: to flap, whip, lash 1850.

1. Hard labour to..thrash for an hour through blocks of ice before we could get out 1830. b. The screw began to thrash the ship along the Docks KIPLING. 2. [A whale] blindly thrashed and rolled about in great agony 1850.

Thrasher¹, **thresher** (þræ·ʃəɹ, þre·ʃəɹ). late ME. [f. prec. + -ER.¹] 1. One who or that which thrashes or threshes grain; a threshing-machine. (More usu. spelt *thresher.*) 2. A sea-fox or fox-shark, *Alopias vulpes*; so called from the very long upper division of the tail, with which it lashes an enemy. Also called *thresher-* or *thrasher-fish, -shark.* 1609. 3. One who thrashes or beats another 1907.

Comb.: **t.-whale**, a grampus or killer, as *Orca gladiator*.

Thrasher² (þræ·ʃəɹ). 1808. [perh. a survival of *thrusher, thresher*, an Eng. dial. name of the THRUSH (*Turdus musicus*).] A bird of the N. Amer. genus *Harporhynchus*, resembling the Song Thrush; esp. *H.* (*Turdus*) *fuscus*, the best known of the species, of the north-eastern U.S., called also *brown t.*, *brown thrush.*

Thra·shing-, thre·shing-floor. late ME. A prepared hard level surface on which corn is threshed.

Thra·shing-, thre·shing-machi·ne. 1797. A power-driven machine for separating grain or other seed from the straw or husk.

Thra·shing-, thre·shing-mill. 1797. A fixed threshing-machine; usually, one driven by water or wind power.

‖**Thraso** (þrē·so). *Pl.* **-os, -oes,** also as L., Thrasones (-ōu·nīz). 1576. [L., ad. Gr. Θράσων, name of a braggart soldier in Terence's *Eunuchus*, f. θρασύς bold, spirited.] A braggart, a boaster.

Thrasonic (þrĕsǫ·nik), *a.* 1657. [f. as next + -IC.] = next.

Thrasonical (þrĕsǫ·nikăl), *a.* 1564. [f. L. *Thrason-*, THRASO + -ICAL.] Resembling Thraso or his behaviour; given to or marked by boasting; bragging, boastful, vainglorious.

Cesars Thrasonicall bragge of I came, saw, and ouercame SHAKS. Hence **Thraso·nically** *adv.*

Thrave, threave (þrēⁱv, þrīv). Chiefly *Sc.* and *north.* OE. [Of Scand. origin.] **1.** Two shocks or stooks of corn (or pulse), gen. containing twelve sheaves each, but varying in different localities; hence used as a measure of straw, fodder, etc. **2.** *transf.* and *fig.* A large number; a company; a multitude, a 'heap', a 'lot'. late ME.

2. Gallants..[have] beene seene to flock here In threaues B. JONS. Tidings..of a thrave of Jews newly converted 1656.

Thread (þred), *sb.* [OE. *þrǣd* :—OTeut. **þrǣđuz*, f. **þrǣ-* to turn, twist, THROW.] **1.** A fine cord composed of the fibres or filaments of flax, cotton, wool, silk, etc. spun to a considerable length; *spec.* such a cord composed of two or more yarns, esp. of flax, twisted together; applied also to a similar product from glass, asbestos, a ductile metal, etc. **b.** The sacred thread with which Brahmins and Parsees are invested at initiation 1582. **2.** Each of the lengths of yarn which form the warp and woof of a woven fabric; hence, any one of these as an ultimate constituent of such a fabric, and thus of one's clothing; the least part of one's dress; esp. in the phr. *not a dry t. on one* ME. **b.** A lineal measure of yarn: the length of a coil of the reel, varying in amount according to the material, and also with the locality 1662. **c.** *fig.* A single element interwoven with others in any composite fabric, mental, moral, social, political, or the like 1836. **3.** Without *a*, as name of the substance of which the above-mentioned things are composed, or of these things taken in the mass; often with distinctive word, as *gold* or *silk t.*; sometimes *spec.* flaxen or linen thread as dist. from silk or cotton; in *pl.*, kinds of thread. late ME. †**b.** *fig.* The material or 'fibre' of which anything is composed; 'texture', quality, nature -1746. **4.** Something having the slenderness or fineness of a thread; e.g. a hair, a filament of a cobweb, etc. late ME. **b.** A 'string' of any viscid substance; a thin continuous stream of liquid, sand, etc.; a narrow strip of space; a fine line or streak of colour or light; a 'thin' continuity of sound 1593. **c.** A degree of stickiness reached in boiling clarified syrup for confectionery 1862. **5.** *transf.* The spiral ridge winding round the shank of a screw; also, each complete turn of this 1674.

1. From these little Threads..such strong Cables are form'd 1720. **2.** Till April's dead, change not a t. 1908. *T. and thrum*, each length of the warp-yarn, and the tuft where it is fastened to the loom; hence *fig.* the whole of anything; good and bad together. Also *threads and thrums*, ends of warp threads, miscellaneous scraps or waste fragments. **c.** The only threads of light in the dark web of his history are clerical and theurgic KINGSLEY. **3.** Linens and threads maintain the improvement lately reported 1887. **4. b.** The pale Aare..winds its white t. through the valley 1884.

II. 1. *fig.* Something figured as being spun or drawn out like a thread; esp. the continued course of life, represented in classical mythology as a thread which is spun and cut off by the Fates 1447. **2.** That which guides through a maze, perplexity, difficulty, or intricate investigation 1580. **3.** The sequence of events or ideas continuing through the whole course of anything; train of thought 1642. **4.** Some continuous feature which runs through the pattern of anything 1685. **5.** The central line of the current of a stream, esp. as a boundary line. [tr. L. *filum aquæ.*] 1691. **6.** That by which something is suspended, or upon which things hang OE. **7.** In ref. to other functions of a thread; esp. as a means of connecting or holding together 1818.

1. For my owne part, I would not..beginne againe the thred of my dayes SIR T. BROWNE. **3.** The matron ..then Resumed the thrid of her discourse again DRYDEN. **6.** Phr. *To hang by a t.*, to be in a precarious condition. **7.** She kept in her hands the t. of many a political intrigue SCOTT.

attrib. and *Comb.*: **t.-animalcule,** a vibrionine animalcule; **-cell,** (*a*) a stinging cell in cœlenterates; a nematocyst; (*b*) a spermatozoon; **-drawing,** the process of ornamenting a textile fabric by drawing out some of the threads so as to form a pattern; **-fin** = *thread-fish* (*a*); **-fish,** (*a*) a polynemoid fish; (*b*) the West Indian Cobbler-fish, *Blepharis crinitus*; (*c*) the cutlass-fish or silvery hair-tail, *Trichiurus lepturus*; **-gauge,** a gauge for ascertaining the number of turns to the inch in, or the accuracy of, a screw-t.; **-lace,** lace made with linen or cotton t., as dist. from silk lace; **-plant,** any plant from which fibre for t.-making is obtained; **t. rush,** *Juncus filiformis.*

Thread (þred), *v.* Also (now *arch.* and *dial.*) **thrid.** Pa. t. and pple. **threaded** (*arch.* and *dial.* **thrid, thridden**) late ME. [f. prec.] **1.** *trans.* To pass one end of a thread through the eye of (a needle) in order to use it in sewing; to furnish (a needle) with a thread. Also *transf.* and *fig.* **2.** To fix (anything) upon a string or wire that passes through it; *esp.* to string (a number of things) together on or as on a thread 1633. **3.** *fig.* To run or pass like a continuous thread through the whole length or course of; to pervade 1830. **4.** *trans.* To make one's way through (a narrow place, a forest, a crowd, or the like); to pass skilfully through the intricacies or difficulties of. Also to *t. one's way, course*, etc., also *intr.* 1593. **5.** *intr.* To creep, twine, wind 1611. **6.** *trans.* To interweave 1853. **b.** *pass.* To be penetrated, permeated, or interspersed as with threads 1861. **7.** To stretch threads across or over; to intersperse with threads so stretched 1884. **8.** To form a screw-thread on; to furnish (a bolt or the like) with a screw-thread 1858. **9.** *Cinematogr.* To feed (film) into a camera; to feed (a camera) with film 1917.

1. The Girl can scarce t. a Needle STEELE. **2.** Amber..beads..Threaded 1705. **3.** One spirit and purpose threads the whole, and gives a sort of unity 1871. **4.** See where he thrids the thickets FLETCHER. **6. b.** His tawny hair..began to be threaded with silver 1891. **8.** The extreme end is threaded for a nut 1888.

Threadbare (þre·dbēᵊɹ), *a.* late ME. [f. THREAD *sb.* + BARE *a.*] **1.** Of a garment, etc.: Having the nap worn off, leaving bare the threads of the warp and woof; worn to the thread; shabby; worn-out. **2.** *fig.* Resembling a threadbare garment; hence meagre, scanty, poor, beggarly; 'sorry'. late ME. **b.** *esp.* Having lost its influence, freshness, or force by much use; trite; commonplace, stale, hackneyed 1598. **3.** Of persons: Wearing threadbare clothes; shabby, seedy; down-at-heel, out-at-elbows. Now *rare* or *Obs.* 1577.

1. Thread-bare cote, and cobled shoes, hee ware SPENSER. Hence **Threa·dbareness.**

Threaden (þre·d'n), *a.* Now *arch.* or *dial.* late ME. [f. THREAD *sb.* + -EN [4].] Composed or made of thread; *spec.* made of linen thread.

Threader (þre·dəɹ). late ME. [f. THREAD *v.* + -ER [1].] One who or that which threads; *spec.* **a.** a person who keeps the shuttles threaded in weaving; **b.** a bodkin for threading tape or ribbon through interstices in a garment, etc.

Threa·d-nee·dle. Also **thread-the-needle,** etc. 1751. [f. THREAD *v.* + NEEDLE.] **1.** A children's game in which, all joining hands, the player at one end of the string passes between the last two at the other end, the rest following. **2. Thread the needle,** as *verb. phr.*: in dancing, denoting the movement in which the lady passes under her partner's arm, their hands being joined 1844.

Threa·dneedle Street. A street in the City of London, the locality of the Bank of England; phr. *the Old Lady of* (or *in*), *the Old Woman of T.S.*, the Bank, its business, etc. (1797).

Threa·d-pa:per. 1746. A strip of folded paper serving to hold skeins of thread in its divisions 1761. **b.** *fig.* A person of slender or thin figure; also *attrib.* 1746.

Threadworm (þre·dwɒɹm). 1802. A worm of thread-like form, as the GUINEA WORM, HAIR-WORM, etc.; *esp.* the pin-worm, *Oxyuris* (*Ascaris*) *vermicularis*, parasitic in the human rectum, chiefly in children.

Thready (þre·di), *a.* ME. [f. THREAD *sb.* + -Y [1].] †**1.** Full of or covered with thread (*rare*) -1757. **2.** Of thread-like texture; composed of fine fibres; stringy, fibrous. late ME. **b.** Of liquid: Forming strings; viscid, ropy 1733. **3.** Of the nature of, consisting of, or resembling a thread or a mass of loose threads; thread-like, hair-like; of a root: fibrous 1597. **4.** Of the pulse (see quot.) 1753. **5.** Of the voice, etc.: Dry and thin; wanting in fullness 1860.

4. The pulse becomes quick,..and so t., it is not like a pulse at all, but like a string vibrating just underneath the skin FLOR. NIGHTINGALE.

Threap (þrīp), *v.* Now *Sc.* and *n. dial.* [OE. *þrēapian*, of obsc. history.] **1.** *trans.* To rebuke, reprove, chide, scold, blame. **2.** *intr.* To contend in words; to inveigh *against*; to argue, dispute; to quarrel, bicker, disagree; to haggle ME. **3.** *trans.* (usu. with *obj. cl.*) To persist in asserting (something contradicted or doubted); to affirm positively or pertinaciously; to maintain obstinately or aggressively. late ME. Hence **Threap** *sb.* an act or the action of threaping.

Threat (þret), *sb.* [OE. *þrēat* :—OTeut. **þrautoz, -ā*, from ablaut series **þreut-, þraut-, þrut-*; cf. L. *trudere* to press, thrust.] †**I.** A throng, press, crowd, multitude of people; a troop, band, body of men -ME. **II.** †**1.** Painful pressure, oppression, compulsion; vexation, torment; affliction, distress, misery; danger, peril -1450. **2.** A denunciation to a person of ill to befall him; *esp.* a declaration of hostile determination or of loss, pain, punishment or damage to be inflicted in retribution for or conditionally upon some course; a menace. Also *fig.* an indication of impending evil. OE.

2. There is no terror Cassius in your threats SHAKS. Clouds full of the t. of rain 1884. Hence **Threa·tful** *a.* (*rare*) full of threats, threatening **-ly** *adv.*

Threat (þret), *v. arch.* and *dial.* [OE. *þrēatian*, f. *þrēat* THREAT *sb.* :—OTeut. **þrautōjan.*] †**1.** *trans.* To press, urge, try to force or induce; esp. by means of menaces -1638. **2.** = next 2. OE. **b.** *fig.* Said of things. late ME. **3.** = next 3. ME. **4.** *absol.* or *intr.* = next 5. ME.

2. Sufficient..to t. the British fleets and islands with the most imminent danger 1781. **b.** The fate which threats kingdoms 1832. **3.** If ancient fabrics nod and t. to fall DRYDEN. Does haughty Gaul invasion t.? BURNS. **4.** Whiles I t., he liues SHAKS.

Threaten (þre·t'n), *v.* [OE. *þrēatnian*, f. *þrēat* THREAT *sb.* + -EN [5] 2.] †**1.** = THREAT *v.* **1.** OE. only. **2.** To try to influence (a person) by menaces; to utter or hold out a threat against; to declare (usu. conditionally) one's intention of inflicting injury upon; to menace ME. **b.** *fig.* To be likely to injure; to be a source of danger to; to endanger actively 1638. **3.** To hold out or offer (some injury) by way of a threat; to declare one's intention of inflicting ME. **4.** *fig.* Of things, conditions: To give ominous indication of (impending evil); to presage, portend 1611. **b.** With infin.: To appear likely *to do* some evil 1780. **5.** *absol.* or *intr.* To utter or use threats; to declare one's intention of injuring or punishing in order to influence ME. **b.** *fig.* To portend evil 1610.

2. Threatning them with Punishment HOBBES. **b.** The wind..blew very hard, threatening us with a storm DE FOE. **3.** Threatning to murder all who should oppose them 1748. The party that has lost the election threatens a petition BURKE. **4.** The skies look grimly, and t. present blusters SHAKS. **b.** It threatens to be wet to night DICKENS. **5.** An eye like Mars, to t. or command SHAKS. **b.** Though the Seas t. they are mercifull SHAKS. Hence **Threa·tener,** one who threatens. **Threa·tening** *ppl. a.*, **-ly** *adv.*

Three (þrī), *a.* and *sb.* [Com. Teut. and Indo-Eur.; OE. *þrī* (*þrīe*), *þrīo, þrēo* :—OTeut. **þrīz* (:—**þrijiz*), **þrijā* :—Indo-Eur. **treies, *treja* (Gr. τρεῖς, τρία, L. *tres, tria*, W. *tri*).] The cardinal number next above two, represented by the symbols 3, III, or iii. **A.** *adj.* **1.** In concord with a sb. expressed. **b.** Standing alone as predicate, or in concord with and following a pronoun, or pronominal adj. OE. †**c.** Rarely used for THIRD -1598. **2.** Used vaguely for a small or trifling number 1534. **3.** Absol. or with ellipsis of sb. (most often *persons*). late ME.

1. Like Cerberus, t. Gentlemen at once SHERIDAN. *T. fourths*, t. out of four equal parts into which a whole is or may be divided; t. quarters; often *loosely*, the greater part, most *of*. b. I galloped, Dirck galloped, we galloped all t. BROWNING. c. *Merry W*. I. i. 142. 2. If they have but t. words of latin 1638. 3. Sold in pots at two-and-three, and three-and-nine THACKERAY. The chubby, dirty-faced child of t. 1909.

Special collocations; *The t. kings, magi*, or *wise men* (MAGUS 2, WISE MAN 3); *the t. Persons* (PERSON *sb*. V. a); *the t. R's* (R II. 2 b); *t. sheets in the wind* (SHEET *sb*.[2] 1). *T. vowels* (slang), an I.O.U.

B. *sb*. (With pl. *threes*.) 1. The abstract number ME. b. The figure (3) denoting this number 1895. 2. A group or set of three things or persons. *spec*. a. A card, a domino, or the side of a die marked with three pips or spots. b. *Cricket*. A hit for which three runs are obtained. 1540. c. In military drill, when each three men form a unit for the purpose of wheeling 1796. 3. a. *ellipt*. for *t. parts* or *divisions*; as *to divide* (a thing) *in(to) t*. ME. b. With omission of *hours* (of the day): *t. o'-clock*, also simply *t*.; *half-past t*.; *t. fifteen*, 3.15 = a quarter past three 1460.

1. By Ioue, I alwaies tooke t. threes for nine SHAKS.

In phrases and specific uses. *T. in One* = the Trinity, the Triune God (also *One in T*., and simply *T*.). *T. to one*, three chances to one. *T. times t*., i. e. cheers. *Rule of T*.: see RULE *sb*. II. 2. *Threes*, short for three per cent stock, or THREE PER CENTS; for three-quarter-backs (in Football); for three-pennyworth (of liquor).

Comb. (unlimited in number). a. Adjs. formed of *three* and a sb. meaning 'of, pertaining to, consisting of, containing, measuring, etc. three of the things named', as *t.-act, -bushel, -cylinder, -fathom, -mile, -row, -volume*, etc. b. Parasynthetic adjs. in -ED[2], = 'having or characterized by three of the things named', as *t.-aisled, -angled, -handed, -storied, syllabled*, etc.; spec. in bot. and zool. adjs., as *t.-capsuled, -celled, -nerved*, etc. c. Parasynthetic sbs. in *-er* [see -ER[1] 1], as *t.-miler, -tonner, -wheeler*, etc.

Special combs. and collocations: **t.-bottle** *a*., applied to one who can drink t. bottles of wine at a sitting; **-card** *a*., pertaining to or played with t. cards, as *t.-card trick*, a trick of race-course sharpers, also known as *find the lady*, in which a queen and two other cards are spread out face downwards, and bystanders invited to bet which is the queen; **-coat** *a*., requiring t. coats, as work in plastering and painting; **-colour** *a*., designating a photomechanical process of printing in which a coloured picture or letterpress is produced by the superposition of the three primary colours or their complementaries; also applied to a process of colour-photography; **-eight** (usu. $\frac{3}{8}$) *Mus*., denoting a 'time' or rhythm with t. quavers in a bar; **t. estates** (see ESTATE *sb*.); **-field** *a*., applied to a method of agriculture in which t. fields are worked on a t.-course system of two crops and a fallow; **-four** (usu. $\frac{3}{4}$) *Mus*., denoting a 'time' or rhythm with t. crotchets in a bar; **-line, -lined** *a*., having, consisting of, or marked with t. lines; in *Printing*, extended through t. lines, as a large capital letter; **-ply** *a*., in *t.-ply wood*, also *absol*.: see PLYWOOD; **-pounder**, a thing weighing t. pounds: a gun firing a t.-pound ball; **-throw** *a*., having t. throws (see THROW *sb*.[2]), as a *t.-throw crank*; hence, having such a crank, as *t.-throw pump* or *-engine*, one worked by a t.-throw crank-shaft; **-two** (usually $\frac{3}{2}$) *Mus*., denoting a 'time' or rhythm with three minims in a bar; **-wire** *a*., applied to a system of distributing electric power, involving t. mains and two dynamos, the two outer mains being joined to the free terminals of the dynamos, and the central main to a conductor joining the two.

Three-corner, *a*. 1548 = next, 1.

Three-cornered (þrīˌkǭ·ɪnəd; stress var.), *a*. late ME. 1. Having three corners or angles; triangular. b. *transf*. Applied to a constituency represented by three members 1882. c. Applied to a contest, discussion, or the like, between three persons 1891. 2. a. Of a horse: Awkwardly shaped. *colloq*. 1861. b. *fig*. Awkward, cross-grained, peevish 1850.

1. The old t. hat 1855. c. A t. fight 1894. 2. b. A t., impracticable fellow GEO. ELIOT.

Three-·de·cker. 1795. [See DECKER[2].] 1. A three-decked ship; formerly *spec*. a line-of-battle ship carrying guns on three decks. b. *fig*. Applied to a thing (or person) of great size or importance 1835. 2. *transf*. Something consisting of three ranges or divisions; as, a three-volume novel, etc. 1874.

Some great t. of orthodoxy 1886.

Three-·fa·rthings. 1561. In the literal sense: see FARTHING. Also, money of the value of three farthings; hence the name of a silver coin of that value issued by Queen Elizabeth. Hence **Three-fa·rthing** *a*. of the value of three farthings; hence, paltry, insignificant.

Threefold (þrī·fōuld), *a*. (*adv*.) [OE. *þri-feald, þrȳfeald*; see THREE and -FOLD.] **A.** *adj*. 1. Consisting of three combined in one, or one thrice repeated; comprising three kinds, parts, divisions, or branches; triple. 2. Three times as great or as numerous ME.

1. His popish pride, and threefald crowne 1600.

B. *adv*. 1. In a threefold manner, triply; in or into three parts (now *rare*) OE. 2. Three times, thrice (in amount); three times or thrice as much. late ME.

Three-·foot, *a*. 1590. †a. Having three feet. b. Measuring three feet in length, breadth, or other dimension. So **Three-·foo·ted** *a*. (in sense a).

Three-halfpence (þrīhē̆ˑpĕns). 1483. Money of the value of three halfpennies, or a penny and a halfpenny ($1\frac{1}{2}d$.); a silver coin of this value issued by Queen Elizabeth; also a silver coin of William IV and Victoria, issued for use in Ceylon.

Three-halfpenny (-hē̆ˑpĕni), *a*. (*sb*.) 1552. That is worth, or costs, three-halfpence; often a depreciatory epithet of anything held in small esteem: paltry, contemptible. Also *sb*. a three-halfpenny piece. Hence **Three-half-pennyworth**, usu. contr. **-ha'porth** (hēˑpəɪþ).

Three-·inch, *a*. 1596. Measuring three inches in length, thickness, etc.

Three-·legged (legd, le·gėd), *a*. 1596. Having three legs, as *a t. stool*.

T. race, a race run by couples, the right leg of one person being bound to the left leg of the other.

Three-·man, *a*. late ME. Requiring three men; managed, worked, or performed by three men; esp. in *three-man('s) song, glee*, a trio for male voices.

If I do, fillop me with a three-man-Beetle SHAKS.

Three-·mast, *a*. 1775. Having three masts. So **Three-·ma·sted** *a*. **Three-·ma·ster**, a three-masted ship.

Three-·pair, *a*. 1788. In full, *three pair of stairs*. Of or belonging to the third floor, as *three-pair room, back*, etc.

Three-·part, *a*. (*adv*.) 1840. Containing, consisting of, having, or involving three parts 1854. b. *adv*. (in comb.) = next 1840. So **Three-parted** *a*. tripartite 1553.

Three parts. 1711. Three out of four equal parts, three quarters. Hence as *advb. phr*., To the extent of three quarters; well-nigh, almost.

Threepence (þri·pĕns, þre·pĕns, þrʊ·p-). 1589. [f. THREE + PENCE.] 1. A sum of money equal in value to three pennies 1605. 2. A silver coin of this value; a threepenny piece 1589.

Threepenny (þri·pĕni, þre·pĕni, þrʊ·p-), *a*. (*sb*.) late ME. 1. Of the value or price of threepence. b. Costing or involving an outlay of threepence 1698. c. *transf*. Of or pertaining to threepence or to something worth threepence; able or willing to pay threepence 1630. 2. *fig*. Of little worth; trifling, paltry, cheap, worthless 1613.

1. *T. bit, piece* = prec. 2, also *fig*. something very small. b. I play but t. ombre SWIFT. 2. That threepenny baggage, Mistress Nelly SCOTT. So **Threepennyworth** (þrī·pe·niwǝ̄ɪþ), contr. **three-penn'orth** (-pə·nəɪþ), the quantity that is worth, or costs, threepence.

Three· per ce·nt, *adj*. and *sb. phr*. 1753. **A.** as *adj*. a. Yielding three per cent. interest. b. Containing three parts in every hundred.

b. A three-per-cent solution of carbolic acid 1880.

B. as *sb*. (*absol*. use of A. a.) In pl. **three per ce·nts**, the Government securities of Great Britain, consolidated in 1751 into a single stock paying 3 per cent. interest (reduced in 1888 to $2\frac{3}{4}$ per cent., and in 1903 to $2\frac{1}{2}$ per cent., so that the name ceased to be applicable) 1794.

Three-·pi·le, *a*. (*sb*.) 1607. [See PILE *sb*.[4]] Applied to velvet in which the loops of the pile-warp (which constitutes the nap) are formed by three threads, producing a pile of treble thickness; so of carpets; also *absol*. or as *sb*. = t. velvet.

I haue seru'd Prince Florizell, and in my time wore three pile SHAKS. Carpets of t. 1844.

Three-·piled (-pəild), *a*. 1588. [f. prec. + -ED[2].] 1. = prec. 1603. †2. *fig*. Of the highest quality, refined, exquisite; also, of very great degree, excessive, extreme, intense –1690.

1. *Meas. for M*. I. ii. 35. 2. Taffata phrases, silken tearmes precise, Three-pil'd Hyperboles SHAKS.

Three-qua·rter, -qua·rters, *sb*., *adj*., and *advb. phr*. 1470. **A.** as *sb*. 1. *Three quarters*, three of the four equal parts into which anything is or may be divided; *loosely*, the greater part of anything. 2. *Three-quarter* (pl. *-quarters*), in *Football*, short for *three-quarter back* 1889. **B.** as *adj*. *Three-quarter* (rarely *-quarters*). Amounting to three quarters of the whole; three-fourths of the ordinary; also vaguely 1677. b. *spec*. Of portraits, etc. (*a*) orig. applied to a canvas 30 inches by 25 (about three-fourths of the area of a kitcat, 36 in. by 28). (*b*) Now usu. applied to a portrait showing three-fourths of the figure (in full *three-quarter(s length)*); also, to a lady's coat of similar length. (*c*) *Three-quarter-face* (esp. in *Photogr*.), the aspect intermediate between full face and profile. 1712. c. *ellipt*. Measuring or relating to three quarters (of a yard) in Cloth Measure, or three fourths of any quantity indicated by context; *spec*. of a coal seam, three quarters of a yard thick 1708. **C.** as *adv*. To the extent of three quarters 1584.

Comb.: **three-quarter back**, in *Rugby Football*, etc., one of two, three, or four players stationed between the half-backs and the full-backs; **three-quarter binding**, a style of bookbinding having more leather than half-binding; **three-quarters face**, *Mil*. three quarters of a full 'face' or turn.

Threescore (þrī·skōəɪ, þrī·skōə·ɪ), *a*. (*sb*.) *arch*. late ME. [SCORE *sb*.] Three times twenty; sixty. (Formerly sometimes written in Roman numerals iij^{xx}.) b. *absol*. with ellipsis of *years*, in ref. to age 1605.

b. T. and ten I can remember well SHAKS.

Three-sided (stress var.), *a*. 1601. Trilateral; *fig*. having three parts or aspects.

T. stem.. having three plane sides 1793. One of those t. tables 1878.

Threesome (þrī·sǝ̆m), *sb*. and *a*. Chiefly *Sc*. late ME. [f. THREE + -SOME[2].] **A.** *sb*. Three persons together, three forming a company. b. *Golf*. A game in which one person plays against two opponents 1899. **B.** *adj*. Consisting or composed of three; performed by three together 1839.

Three-·square, *a*. Now *dial*. or *techn*. 1440. [f. THREE, after *four-square*.] Having three equal sides; equilaterally triangular. Also *fig*. threefold, triple.

Take a triangular file, t. file it is called 1873.

Three-·way, *a*. 1587. Having, or connected with, three ways, roads, or channels; situated where three ways meet.

Three-·years, -year, *a*. 1617. 1. Of or pertaining to, or lasting for, three years; of the age of three years 1665. 2. **Three-·year-o·ld**, of the age of three years; *spec*. of horses; also, of three years' standing. Also *absol*. or as *sb*.; also *attrib*. 1617.

Thremmatology (þremătǫ·lŏdʒi). 1888. [f. Gr. θρέμμα, -ατ- nursling + -LOGY.] *Biol*. That part of biology which treats of the propagation or breeding of domestic animals and plants.

Threne (þrīn). Now *rare* or *Obs*. late ME. [ad. Gr. θρῆνος funeral lament.] A song of lamentation; a dirge, threnody; formerly *spec*. (in *pl*.) the Lamentations of Jeremiah. So **Threne·tic, -al** *adjs*. pertaining to a threnody; mournful.

Threnode (þrī·nōud). 1858. [Alteration of next, after *ode*.] = next.

Threnody (þre·nŏdi, þrī·n-). 1634. [ad. Gr. θρηνῳδία dirge, f. θρῆνος THRENE + ᾠδή song.] A song of lamentation; *spec*. a lament for the dead, a dirge. So **Threno·dial, -o·dian, -o·dic** *adjs*. of or pertaining to a t.; mournful. **Thre·nodist**, one who composes or utters a t.

‖**Threnos** (þrī·nǫs). 1601. [a. Gr. θρῆνος, L. *threnus*.] = THRENE, THRENODY.

Thresh *v*., see THRASH *v*.

Threshold (þre·ʃould). [OE. *þerscold, -wold, þerxold*, etc.] 1. The piece of timber or stone which lies below the bottom of a door, and has to be crossed in entering a house; the sill of a doorway; hence, the entrance to a house or building. ¶b. (*erron*.) The upper horizontal part of a door-case; the lintel (*rare*) 1821. 2. *transf*. and *fig*. a. Border, limit (of a region); the line which one crosses in entering OE. b.

In ref. to entrance, the beginning of a state or action, outset, opening 1586.

2. a. On what is known as 'the t. of England', the Sussex coast 1899. The t. of consciousness 1886.

Threw (þrū), pa. t. of THROW *v.*

Thrice (þrəis), *adv.* [ME. *þriȝes*, *þriës*, *þryës*, f. *þrië*, *þryë* three times + *-s* of advb. gen., after ME. *anes*, *ones* ONCE, *twies* TWICE.] 1. Three times (in succession); on three successive occasions. 2. Three times as much (in number, amount, or value). Often vaguely or hyperbolically: Many times (as much) ME. 3. Combined with any adj., used vaguely (as in 2): Very, highly, greatly (L. *ter*) 1579.

1. Before the cocke crowe twise, thou shalt deny me thrise *Mark* xiv. 30. A Spoonful or two of Canary Wine twice or t. a day 1732. 2. T. two hundred warriors GRAY. 3. T. happy Iles MILT.

Thridace (þri·dǽs). 1831. [ad. mod.L. *thridacium*, f. θρίδαξ lettuce.] *Pharm.* The inspissated juice of lettuce, used as a sedative; = LACTUCARIUM.

Thrift (þrift), *sb.* ME. [f. THRIVE *v.* + -T *suffix*³ a.] †1. The fact or condition of thriving; prosperity, success, good luck -1679. b. Means of thriving; industry, labour; profitable occupation. Now *dial.* 1580. c. Prosperous growth, physical thriving. (*rare*) ME. 2. Savings, earnings, gains, profit; acquired wealth, estate, or substance (*arch.*) ME. 3. Economical management, economy; frugality, saving; †*euphem.* parsimony, niggardliness 1553. 4. A name given to various plants. a. The plant *Armeria maritima* (*vulgaris*), a sea-shore and alpine plant bearing rose-pink, white, or purple flowers on naked stems growing from a tuft of grass-like radical leaves; also called *sea-pink*, *sea gillyflower*, *sea-grass*, and *ladies' cushion* 1592. b. Hence, extended to other species of *Armeria*; also to plants of allied genera, or similar habit, as Lavender T., *Statice Limonium*, etc. 1776.

1. b. With her distaff..and her spindle..she plied..the old fashioned Scottish t. SCOTT. 2. He that drinks, or spends his t. at dice 1605. 3. These people are well given to t. and good husbandry 1600. Hence **Thrift** *v. trans.* to save thriftily, to economize.

Thriftily (þri·ftili), *adv.* late ME. [f. THRIFTY + -LY².] †1. In a becoming or seemly manner, properly; handsomely; hence, thoroughly, well -1638. 2. Frugally, carefully 1581. 3. Thrivingly; vigorously 1865.

1. She toke here leue at hem ful þryftyly CHAUCER. 2. They could neither order a household t., nor cut out a gown 1883.

Thriftiness (þri·ftinės). 1530. [f. as prec. + -NESS.] The state or quality of being thrifty.

Thriftless (þri·ftlės), *a.* late ME. [f. THRIFT + -LESS.] †1. Not thriving -1693. 2. Unprofitable, worthless, useless. Now *rare*. 1568. 3. Devoid of thrift; wasteful, improvident, spendthrift 1576. Hence **Thri·ftless-ly** *adv.*, -**ness**.

Thrifty (þri·fti), *a.* ME. [f. THRIFT *sb.* + -Y¹.] 1. Characterized by success or prosperity; thriving, prosperous; fortunate. †2. Of a person: Worthy, worshipful, respectable -1596. 3. Thriving physically; growing with vigour; in good or healthy condition; flourishing 1440. 4. Characterized by thrift or frugality; economical; provident 1526. †b. Well-husbanded. SHAKS.

1. The family generally has been getting t. in the world 1860. 2. The þriftieste and oon þe beste knyght That yn his tyme was CHAUCER. 3. A small but t. specimen of the Sequoia, or California tree 1862. 4. I told my wife she had been too t., for I found she had starved herself and her daughter SWIFT.

Thrill (þril), *sb.* 1680. [f. next.] I. A subtle nervous tremor caused by intense emotion or excitement (as pleasure, fear, etc.), producing a slight shudder or tingling through the body; a penetrating influx of feeling or emotion. b. Thrilling property (of a play, novel, narrative, speech, etc.); sensational quality; *transf.* (*slang*), a literary work having this quality, a 'thriller' 1886. 2. The vibrating or quivering of anything tangible or visible; acute tremulousness, as of a sound; a vibration, throbbing, tremor 1817. b. *Phys.* and *Path.* A vibratory movement, resonance, or murmur, felt or heard in auscultation 1822.

1. Those communications..shot cold thrills through his frame 1799. 2. The harplike t. of the breeze 1865. The electric nerve, whose instantaneous t. Makes next-door gossips of the antipodes LOWELL.

Thrill (þril), *v.* ME. [Metathetic form of THIRL *v.*] I. Of the action of material bodies. †1. *trans.* To bore, pierce, penetrate. Also *intr.* with *through*. -1661. †2. To cause (a lance, dart, etc.) to pass; to dart, hurl (a piercing weapon) -1646. II. Of the action of non-material forces. †1. *fig.* To pierce, penetrate (as a sound, or an emotion) -1642. 2. *trans.* To affect or move with a sudden wave of emotion 1605. b. *intr.* To produce a thrill, as an emotion, or anything causing emotion; to pass with a thrill *through* 1592. c. To feel, or be moved by, a thrill of emotion 1595. 3. To move tremulously or with vibration; to quiver, vibrate. (Said esp. of sound or light.) 1776. b. *trans.* To send forth tremulously 1647. c. To cause to quiver; to throw into vibration 1800.

1. Such sound..the Airy region thrilling MILT. 2. A kind of pleasing dread thrilled her bosom MRS. RADCLIFFE. b. I haue a faint cold feare thrills through my veines SHAKS. c. Till the blood thrilled in his veins 1825. 3. The great valley of purple heath thrilling silently in the sun T. HARDY.

†**Thrillant**, *a. rare.* 1590. [irreg. f. THRILL *v.* + -ANT¹.] = THRILLING *ppl. a.* 1.

Thriller (þri·ləɹ). 1889. [f. THRILL *v.* + -ER¹.] One who or that which thrills; *spec.* (*slang* or *colloq.*) a sensational play or story (cf. SHOCKER).

Thrilling (þri·liŋ), *ppl.a.* 1579. [f. THRILL *v.* + -ING².] That thrills. †1. Penetrating, piercing -1718. b. Piercing or penetrating, as cold 1603. 2. Producing a sudden wave of excitement or emotion; piercing the feelings 1761. 3. Quivering, vibrating 1850.

1. b. To recide In t. Region of thicke-ribbed Ice SHAKS. 2. The t. verse that wakes the Dead GRAY. Hence **Thri·lling-ly** *adv.*, -**ness**.

Thri·msa, thry·msa. *Hist.* [OE. *þrimsa*, *þrymsa*, gen. pl. of *trimes*, *trymes*, ad. L. *tremis* the third part of an aureus; also a weight, a drachma.] The OE *trimes* or *trims*, a coin (or money of account) representing the Roman *tremis*, of uncertain value; also, as a weight, a drachma.

‖**Thrips** (þrips). Often erron. taken as pl., with a false sing. **thrip.** 1795. [L. *thrips* (Pliny), a. Gr. θρίψ, pl. θρῖπες a wood-worm.] *Ent.* The typical genus of the *Thripsidæ* or *Thripidæ*, the sole family of the order *Thysanoptera*, comprising minute insects with four fringed wings, many of which are injurious to various plants; an insect of this genus or family.

Thrive (þrəiv), *v.* Pa. t. **throve** (þrōᵘv), **thrived** (þrəivd); pa. pple. **thriven** (þri·v'n), **thrived.** [ME. *þrive*, ad. ON. *þrífask* refl., to thrive.] 1. *intr.* To grow or develop well and vigorously; to flourish, prosper. 2. Of a person or community: To prosper, increase in wealth, be successful or fortunate ME. b. Of a thing: To be successful, turn out well 1587.

1. The young Prince continued there about twelve months, thriving apace 1697. *fig.* Thought thrives on conflict 1907. 2. As I intend to thriue in this new World SHAKS. b. God is iust, iniustice will not t. 1587. Hence **Thri·veless** *a.* (*poet.*) not thriving; unsuccessful, profitless. **Thri·ver** (now *rare*), one who or that which thrives.

Thriving (þrəi·viŋ), *ppl. a.* late ME. [f. prec. + -ING².] That thrives. †1. Excelling, excellent, worthy -1470. 2. Growing vigorously, flourishing 1645. 3. Prosperous, doing well in business; successful, fortunate 1607. Hence **Thri·ving-ly** *adv.*, -**ness** (*rare*).

Throat (þrōᵘt), *sb.* [OE. *þrote*, *-u*; app. from OTeut. **þrut-* (cf. OE. *prútian* to swell).] I. The part of the body. 1. The front of the neck beneath the chin and above the collar-bones, containing the passages from the mouth and nose to the lungs and stomach. Also, the corresponding or analogous parts in vertebrates generally, and occas. the analogous part in insects, etc. 2. The passage in the anterior part of the neck, leading from the mouth and nose to the gullet and windpipe; also, either of these passages considered separately OE. 3. This part with its passages, considered in various capacities, e.g. as the entrance to the stomach, as containing the vocal organs, as a vital part, etc. ME. †4. *fig.* The devouring capacity of any destructive agency, as death, war, etc. (*rare*) -1746.

1. Her t. is well turned but seems to me somewhat thin 1878. 2. Thou..choakst their throts with dust MARSTON. To clear the t. 1769. 3. *To pour* (*send*) *down the t.*, to waste or squander (property or money) in eating and drinking. *To cram, ram, thrust down one's t.*, to force (an opinion or the like) upon one's acceptance. *To jump down one's throat*, to interrupt one in his speech sharply or roughly. *At the top of one's t.*, at the top of one's voice. (*To give*, etc. *one the lie*) *in one's t.*, regarded as the place of issue, to which the assertion is thrown back; also, with merely intensive force, *to lie in one's t.*, to lie foully or infamously. *To cut one's* (*own*) *t.*, to commit suicide by this method; hence, to adopt a self-destructive policy. *To cut one another's throats*, to engage in ruinous competition (*mod. colloq.*). 4. He fights, Seeking for Richmond in the t. of death SHAKS.

II. *transf.* 1. A narrow passage, esp. in or near the entrance of something; a narrow part in a passage 1584. 2. *spec.* in technical use. a. *Arch.*, *Building*, etc. (*a*) The neck of an outwork. (*b*) The part in a chimney, furnace, or furnace-arch immediately above the fire-place, which narrows down to the neck or 'gathering'. (*c*) A groove on the underside of a coping or projecting moulding to keep the drip from reaching the wall. 1663. b. *Shipbuilding* and *Naut.* (*a*) The hollow of the bend of a knee-timber. (*b*) The outside curve of the jaws of a gaff; hence, the forward upper corner of a fore-and-aft sail. (*c*) The amidships part of a floor-timber. (*d*) The curve of the flukes of an anchor where they join the shank. 1711. 3. *Bot.* The throat-like opening of a gamopetalous corolla at which the tube and the petals unite 1847.

1. The..t. of Vesuvius EMERSON. Lang's Nek, the t. of the passage into the Transvaal 1899.

attrib. and *Comb.*: **t.-band**, *Saddlery* = THROAT-LATCH; **-deafness**, deafness caused by a diseased condition of the t.; **-halyards**, the ropes employed to hoist up a gaff; **-pipe**, the windpipe; also, the steam supply pipe in a steam-engine; **-register**, the lowest register of the voice.

Throat (þrōᵘt), *v.* 1611. [f. prec.] †1. *trans.* To utter in or from one's throat; to speak in a guttural tone (*rare*) -1622. 2. *Building.* To furnish with a throat; to groove or channel. (Chiefly in *pa. pple.* and *vbl. sb.*) 1823. Hence **Throa·ting** *vbl. sb.*; *Building.* The cutting of a 'throat'; *concr.* the groove or channel thus cut.

Throat-latch, throat-lash. 1794. [f. THROAT *sb.* + LATCH *sb.*¹, LASH *sb.*² 1.] *Saddlery.* A strap passing under the horse's throat which helps to keep the bridle in position.

Throatwort (þrōᵘ·twɒɹt). 1578. [f. as prec. + WORT.] The Nettle-leaved Bell-flower (*Campanula Trachelium*), so called because formerly considered to cure diseases of the throat; also extended to other species, and locally applied to the Foxglove, Figwort, and American Button Snake-root.

Throaty (þrōᵘ·ti), *a.* 1645. [f. as prec. + -Y¹.] 1. Of vocal sounds, or of the voice: Guttural; hoarse. 2. Of an animal: Having the skin about the throat loose and pendulous; having a prominent throat or capacious swallow 1778.

1. A wonderful mixture of the t. and the nasal 1876. Hence **Throa·tily** *adv.* **Throa·tiness.**

Throb (þrǫb), *sb.* 1579. [f. next.] An act of throbbing; a violent beat or pulsation of the heart or an artery. b. Applied to a (normal) pulsation 1653. c. *transf.* and *fig.* 1626.

The feverish t. of his pulsation was diminished SCOTT. c. Every t. of the locomotive 1892. Hence **Thro·bless** *a.*

Throb (þrǫb), *v.* late ME. [app. echoic.] 1. *intr.* Of the heart, etc.: To beat strongly, esp. as the result of emotion or excitement; to palpitate. b. To beat as the heart does normally; to pulsate (*rare*) 1725. c. *transf.* Said of the emotion or the like which affects the heart 1591. d. *transf.* Of a person, a body of people, etc.: To feel or exhibit emotion; to quiver 1841. 2. *gen.* To be moved or move rhythmically; to pulsate, vibrate, beat 1847. b. Said esp. of a steamship with ref. to the beat of the engine 1864. 3. *trans.* To cause to throb or beat violently (*rare*) 1606.

1. Your hearts will t. and weepe to hear him speake SHAKS. His temples throbbed—his head rang 1825. c. The simple affections of human nature throbbing under the ermine W. IRVING. 2. The very air..

Throbbed with sweet scent MORRIS. Hence **Thro·bbingly** *adv.*

Throe (þrōu), *sb.* [A late alteration of †*throw(e* (of uncertain origin and history, but prob. rel. to THROW *v.* I. 1).] **1.** A violent spasm or pang, such as convulses the body, limbs, or face. Also, a spasm of feeling; a paroxysm; agony of mind; anguish. **b.** *spec.* The pain and struggle of childbirth; *pl.* labour-pangs ME. **c.** The agony of death; the death-struggle, death-throe ME. **2.** *transf.* and *fig.* A violent convulsion or struggle preceding or accompanying the 'bringing forth' of something 1698.

Throe, *v. rare.* 1610. [f. prec.] †**1.** *trans.* To cause to suffer throes; to agonize as in childbirth; to torture (*rare*) –1683. **2.** *intr.* To suffer throes; to agonize; to 'labour' 1618.

Thro·gmorton Street. A street in the City of London, the locality of the Stock Exchange; hence the Stock Exchange, its operations, etc. (1900).

Thrombin (þrǫ·mbin). 1898. [f. Gr. θρόμβος THROMBUS + -IN.] *Phys. Chem.* The substance which by interaction with fibrinogen gives rise to fibrin, and is hence the immediate cause of the clotting of shed blood.

Thrombo- (þrǫ·mbo), bef. a vowel **thromb-**, comb. form of Gr. θρόμβος THROMBUS, as in **Thro·mbo-arteri·tis,** arterial inflammation producing thrombosis, etc.

‖**Thrombosis** (þrǫmbōu·sis). 1706. [mod. L., a. Gr. θρόμβωσις curdling, f. θρομβοῦσθαι, f. θρόμβος THROMBUS; see -OSIS.] †A coagulation or curdling (*rare*); *spec. Path.* a local coagulation of the blood in any part of the vascular system during life, the formation of a thrombus. Hence **Thrombo·tic** *a.* of, pertaining to, of the nature of, or caused by t.

‖**Thrombus** (þrǫ·mbŏs). 1693. [mod.L., a. Gr. θρόμβος lump, piece, clot of blood, curd of milk.] †**a.** A small tumour occasioned by the escape of blood from a vein into the adjacent cellular tissue, and its coagulation there. **b.** A fibrinous clot which forms in a blood-vessel and obstructs the circulation.

Throne (þrōun), *sb.* ME. [a. OF. *trone*, ad. L. *thronus*, a. Gr. θρόνος an elevated seat.] **1.** The seat of state of a potentate or dignitary; *esp.* the seat occupied by a sovereign on state occasions; now a more or less ornate chair, with a footstool, usu. placed on a dais and standing under a canopy. **b.** *Eccl.* (*a*) The seat occupied by a pope or a bishop on ceremonial occasions. late ME. (*b*) The rest on which the monstrance stands during the exposition of the Host. **c.** A seat provided by portrait-painters for their sitters 1838. **2.** As the seat of a deity, esp. of God or Christ ME. **3.** *fig.* A seat or position of dominion or supremacy 1548. **4.** *transf.* The position, office, or dignity of a sovereign; sovereign power or authority, dominion ME. **5.** *transf.* Put for: The occupant of the throne; the sovereign 1762. **6.** (With capital T.) *pl.* In mediæval angelology, The third of the nine orders of angels ME.

1. See where Salomon is set In royal throan DRAYTON. 2. *The t. of grace* or *the t.*, the mercy-seat, the place where God is conceived as seated to answer prayer. 3. The t. which Newton was destined to ascend 1855. 4. To wade through slaughter to a t. GRAY. *T. and altar*, the civil and ecclesiastical systems as established. 6. Thrones, Dominations, Princedoms, Vertues, Powers MILT. Hence **Thro·neless** *a.* without a t.; deposed from a t.

Throne (þrōun), *v.* late ME. [f. prec.] **1.** *trans.* = ENTHRONE. **2.** *intr.* To be enthroned; to sit on or as on a throne; to sit in state 1607.

1. The seate Where loue is thron'd SHAKS. The Pope..Thrones and Unthrones Kings MILT. 2. He wants nothing of a God but Eternity, and a Heauen to T. in SHAKS.

Throng (þrǫŋ), *sb.* [ME. *þrang, þrong*, prob. shortened f. OE. *geþrang* throng, crowd, deriv. from vbl. ablaut series **þring-, þrang-, þrung-*.] **I.** Oppression; distress, straits; trouble, woe, affliction; danger. Now *dial.* (*rare*). **II. 1.** Pressing or crowding of people; an act of thronging or crowding; crowded condition ME. **2.** *concr.* A crowded mass of persons actually (or in idea) assembled together; a crowd ME. **b.** A great number of things crowded together; a multitude 1549. **3.** Pressure, or a pressing amount, *of* work or business. Now *dial.* 1642.

1. Went the summons forth Into all quarters, and the t. began COWPER. 2. The streets were filled with throngs of people DICKENS. 3. This t. of Businesse CHAS. I.

Throng (þrǫŋ), *a.* (*adv.*) Now *Sc.* (in thrang) and *n. dial.* [Late ME. *þrang, þrong*, from same root as prec.] **1.** Pressed or massed closely together as a crowd; crowded; †dense, close, thick. **2.** Crowded with people, etc., thronged 1660. **3.** Of times, seasons, places, etc.: Into which much is crowded; full of work; busy 1568. **4.** Of a person or persons: Closely engaged in work or business; pressed; busy 1623. **B.** *adv.* Earnestly; busily. late ME.

1. A t. congregation 1743. As t. as three in a bed 1770. 4. When we're t., I help Hester 1863. As t. as Throp's wife (*local prov.*).

Throng (þrǫŋ), *v.* [ME. *þrange, þronge*, from same root as prec.] †**1.** *trans.* To press or compress violently; to squeeze, crush –1825. †**2.** *intr.* To push or force one's way; to press –1625. **3.** To assemble in a crowd or group; to crowd; also, to go in large numbers 1550. **4.** *trans.* To crowd round and press upon; to press upon as in a crowd, to jostle 1534. **5.** To bring or drive into a crowd, or into one place; to collect closely, to crowd. Chiefly in *pa. pple.* 1578. **6.** To fill or occupy (a place) *with* a large number of things or persons, or a quantity of something; to crowd, cram, stuff 1607. **b.** Of a multitude of persons or things: To occupy completely, fill, crowd (a place, etc.) 1819. **c.** *pa. pple.* Occupied by a crowd or multitude; crowded, crammed.

3. Childe Harold saw them..Thronging to war BYRON. *fig.* I hear the Echoes through the mountains t. WORDSW. 4. Moche people followed him, and thronged him TINDALE *Mark* v. 24. 6. Thronging the Seas with spawn innumerable MILT. c. The streets were thronged 1894.

Thropple, thrapple (þrǫ·p'l, þra·p'l). *Sc.* and *n. dial.* ME. [Origin obsc.] The throat; now *esp.* the windpipe or gullet.

Throstle (þrǫ·s'l). [OE. *þrostle*, f. root of OTeut. **þrastuz* (ON. *þrǫstr*), commonly referred to Indo-Eur. **trozdu-s*, whence L. *turdus* thrush.] **1.** A thrush; *esp.* the song-thrush or mavis, *Turdus musicus.* Now only *literary* and *dial.* **2.** A spinning-machine for cotton, wool, etc., a modification of that orig. called a *water-frame*; differing from a *mule* in having a continuous action, the processes of drawing, twisting, and winding being carried on simultaneously 1825.

Thro·stle-cock. ME. The male throstle or song-thrush; *dial.* the male missel-thrush.

Throttle (þrǫ·t'l), *sb.* 1547. [History obsc.] **1.** The throat. Now chiefly *dial.* **b.** The larynx. Now *rare.* 1615. **2.** Short for *t.-valve*; also a similar valve in a motor engine 1877.

attrib. and *Comb.*: **t.-lever,** a lever for opening or closing a t. or t.-valve; **-valve** (prob. from the vb.), a valve for regulating the supply of steam, esp. to the cylinder of a steam-engine.

Throttle (þrǫ·t'l), *v.* [Late ME. *throtel, -il*, perh. f. THROAT + -LE *suffix* [3].] **1.** *trans.* To stop the breath of by compressing the throat, to strangle; to kill in this way; *loosely*, to stop the breath of in any way, to choke, suffocate. **b.** *transf.* To compress by fastening something round 1863. **2. a.** To check or break off (utterance) as if choking 1582. **b.** *fig.* To stop forcibly the utterance of (a person or thing) 1641. **3.** *intr.* To undergo suffocation; to choke 1566. **4.** *trans.* To check or stop the flow of (a fluid in a tube, etc.) esp. by means of a valve, or by compression; to regulate the supply of steam or gas to (an engine) in this way 1875.

1. Then t. thy self with an Ell of strong Tape SWIFT. 2. I haue seene them shiuer and looke pale..T. their practiz'd accent in their feares SHAKS. b. And thus you t. your selfe with your owne Similies MILT.

Through (þrū), *a.* 1523. [attrib. use of THROUGH *adv.*] That passes, extends, or affords passage through something. **b.** That goes, extends, or conveys through the whole of a long distance or journey without interruption, or without change; as a *t. train, passenger, fare, ticket, traffic* 1845.

Through (þrū, þru), *prep.* and *adv.* Also **thro', thro.** [OE. *þurh*, a Com. WGermanic prep. and adv.] **A.** *prep.* The preposition expressing the relation of transition or direction within something from one limit of it to the other; primarily in ref. to motion in space. **1.** From one end, side, or surface to the other or opposite end, side, or surface of (a body or a space) by passing within it; usu. implying into, at one end, side, etc. and out of at the other. **b.** Denoting transmission of light, or of sight, by an aperture or a transparent medium ME. **c.** In ref. to a (more distant or fainter) sound heard simultaneously with another which does not 'drown' it or prevent it from reaching the ear 1819. **d.** With pl. (or collective) sb., expressing passage between or among things so as to penetrate the whole mass or body of them 1535. **2.** Of motion or direction within the limits of; along within OE. **3.** Over or about the whole extent of, all over a (surface); so as to traverse or penetrate every part or district of; in or to all parts of; throughout; everywhere in OE. **4.** During the whole of (a period of time, or an action, etc., with ref. to the time it occupies from beginning to end) OE. **5.** From beginning to end of; in or along the whole length or course of (an action, an experience, a piece of work, etc.; also of a discourse, a book, etc.) 1449. **b.** with emphasis on the intervening or intermediate stage or condition 1671. **c.** with emphasis laid upon the completion: To the end of 1628. **6.** Indicating a point or position ultimately reached. (Usu. in predicate, after verb *to be.*) 1791. **7.** Indicating medium, means, agency, or instrument: By means of; by the action of, by (*obs.* or *arch.*). Now *spec.* by the instrumentality of OE. **8.** Indicating cause, reason, or motive: In consequence of, by reason of, on account of, owing to OE.

1. George..was lying..dead, with a bullet t. his heart THACKERAY. *To speak t. the throat, the nose*, etc. *T. one's hands, t. a machine*, etc., referring to something being handled, manufactured, subjected to some process, or dealt with in any way. *To pay t. the nose*: see NOSE *sb.* *T. thick and thin*: see THICK AND THIN. *T. and t.*, repeatedly through; right through; entirely through. b. Thurgh a wyndow..He cast his eye vpon Emelya CHAUCER. c. Thy voice is heard thro' rolling drums TENNYSON. d. Bounding t. the trees 1890. 2. The Night-Hag..riding t. the Air MILT. 3. We will make thee famous t. the World SHAKS. 4. T. the length of times he stands disgraced SHAKS. It will be like this all the night t. 1873. 5. I had..put my horse t. all his paces GOLDSM. b. The..crisis t. which the world was to pass 1881. c. Seven children, who came all very well t. the smallpox 1744. 6. I am half t. the poem SOUTHEY. 7. The..Society..seeks to do t. him what it cannot otherwise do 1883. 8. If he t. frailty err MILT.

B. *adv.* **1.** From end to end, side to side, or surface to surface (of a body or space) by passing or extending within; so as to penetrate OE. **b.** In ref. to travel or conveyance: Along the whole distance; all the way; to the end of the journey; to the destination 1617. **c.** In ref. to size: As measured from side to side; in diameter 1687. **2.** From beginning to end (of a time, course of action, life, trial, book, etc.; to the end or purposed accomplishment ME. **3.** Predicatively, after the verb *to be*, indicating a position, point, or condition ultimately arrived at 1481. **4.** Qualifying adjs. and pa. pples.: Throughout: hence, entirely, completely, thoroughly. †**a.** Standing before a pple. or adj. –1901. **b.** Now regularly after the adj. or pple., and only in ref. to physical condition 1766.

1. Huon..strake hym with his spere clene throwe 1533. b. The great bulk of our luggage had been registered t. to Paris 1858. 2. Who now reads Bolingbroke? Who ever read him t.? BURKE. 3. [He] did not arrive till the speech was half t. 1896. *To be t. with*, to have finished or completed; to have done with; also, to have arranged matters with (a person) (now *dial.*). *To be t.*: to have finished (*U.S.*). 4. a. Once t.-hot long in cooling FULLER. b. It is of no use to put up your umbrella when you are wet t. 1825.

Phr. *T. and t.*, with repeated or complete penetration; completely from beginning to end; right through; entirely through; also, in all points or respects; thoroughly, wholly, out and out.

Through-, in combination.

1. Combinations of THROUGH *prep.* or *adv.* with verbs (pples., vbl. sbs.), or adjs. Chiefly *Obs.* †**Through-old** *a.*, extremely old; antiquated. †**Through-pierce**

v., *trans.* to pierce through, transfix. †**Through-swim** *v.*, *trans.* to swim through. **2.** Combinations with sbs. **Throu·gh-bo·lt**, a bolt passing through the objects fastened by it, and secured at each end. †**Through-co·ld**, a penetrating or deep-seated cold or chill. **Throu·gh-jo·int**, a joint passing through the thickness of something. **Throu·gh-tang**, a method of hafting knives, forks, etc. by inserting the tang in a hole drilled right through the handle and riveting it at the end.

Throughly (þrū·li), *adv. arch.* 1440. [f. THROUGH *adv.* or *adj.* + -LY[2].] **1.** Fully, completely, perfectly. **2.** Through the whole thickness, substance, or extent; through, all through, quite through. *poet.* 1541. †**b.** Through, from beginning to end; for the whole length or time; all through -1692.

1. T. equipped from Head to Foot STEELE. 2. When tis t. tosted..they eat it SIR T. HERBERT. b. Take this book; peruse it t. MARLOWE.

Throughout (þru,au·t), *prep.*, *adv.*, *adj.* [In OE. two words, *þurh* THROUGH, *ūt* OUT, later as one word or hyphened.] **A.** *prep.* †**1.** = THROUGH *prep.* 1; 2. -1629. **2.** Through the whole of (a space, region, etc.); in or to every part of; everywhere in ME. **b.** Through or during the whole of (a period of time or course of action); from beginning to end of 1540.

2. In euery parish t. the Realme STUBBES. b. T. my command in the Levant seas NELSON.

B. *adv.* †**1.** Right through, quite through -1660. **2.** Through the whole of a body, region, etc.; in or to every part, everywhere ME. **b.** Through the whole of a time or course of action; at every moment or point; all through 1766.

1. I never read a Romancy Book t. in all my life D'CHESS NEWCASTLE. 2. A furde gowne lyned with foxe thorow-oute 1544. b. Act on these Principles t. 1766.

†**C.** *adj.* Thorough, out-and-out -1670.

Such t. saints 1670.

Throu·gh-pa·ssage. 1566. A passage through; a thoroughfare.

Through-stone[1] (þrʋ·χʷstoun, þrʋ·f-). Now only *Sc.* and *n. dial.* ME. [f. OE. *þrūh*, a tube, chest, trough + STONE *sb.*] A horizontal gravestone or slab over a tomb.

Through-stone[2] (þrū,stoun), **thorough-stone** (þʋ·rŏ,stoun). 1805. [f. THROUGH *prep.* + STONE *sb.*] *Building.* A stone placed so as to extend through the thickness of a wall; a bond-stone.

Throu·gh-toll. 1567. [See TOLL *sb.*[1]] A toll or duty levied on persons, animals, or goods passing through certain places, esp. through a town or territory. Also, a toll which passes one through two or more turnpike gates.

Throve, pa. t. of THRIVE *v.*

†**Throw**, *sb.*[1] [OE. *þrág*, *þráh*.] **1.** The time at which anything happens; an occasion -1513. **2.** An instant, a moment -1590.

2. Downe himselfe he layd Upon the grassy ground to sleepe a t. SPENSER.

Throw (þrōu), *sb.*[2] 1530. [f. THROW *v.*] **I.** A twist, a turn. **1.** *Sc.*, in form **thraw**. An act of twisting or turning; the fact or condition of being twisted; a wrench, crook, warp; also, the act of turning a key or the like 1585. **2.** *Mech.* The action or motion of a slide-valve, or of a crank, eccentric, or cam; also, the extent of this measured on a straight line passing through the centre of motion; also, a crank-arm; a crank 1829. **3.** A machine by which a rotary motion is given to an object while being shaped; a lathe, esp. one worked by hand 1657.

1. Deil be wi' me if I do not give your craig [neck] a thraw SCOTT.

II. 1. An act of throwing a missile, etc.; a forcible propulsion from, or as from, the hand or arm; a cast 1530. **2.** The distance to which anything may or is to be thrown; often qualified, as a *stone's t.* 1582. **3.** *spec.* **a.** A cast at dice; the number cast 1577. **b.** A cast of a net, a fishing-line, etc. 1548. **c.** *Wrestling.* The throwing down of an opponent which finishes a bout or round 1819. **4.** *Geol.* and *Mining.* A dislocation in a vein or stratum, in which the part on one side of the fracture is displaced up or down; also, the amount of vertical displacement so caused 1796. **5.** A sudden angular movement of a galvanometer needle.

1. *To have a t. at* (*fig.*), to attack, have an attempt at; to have a 'fling' at. He hewd, and lasht, and foynd, and thundred blowes..Ne plate, ne male, could ward so mighty throwes SPENSER. 3. *fig.* This able general, who never risques his fortune on a single t., began to think of a retreat 1759.

Throw, *sb.*[3], earlier form of THROE *sb.*

Throw (þrōu), *v.* Pa. t. **threw** (þrū); pa. pple. **thrown** (þrōun). Also *Sc.* **thraw**; pa. pple. **thrawn.** [OE. *þráwan* (*þréow*, *þráwen*):—OTeut. root **þræ-*:—pre-Teut. *trē-*, *ter-* to turn (in Gr. and L., to bore).] **I.** To twist, to turn, and derived uses. **1.** *trans.* To twist, to wring; to turn to one side; to twist about, twine, wreathe; to turn (a key or the like); in OE., to torture on the rack. Now *Sc.* and *n. dial.* **2.** *intr.* To turn, twist, curl, twine, writhe; of a moored boat, to swing, sway. Chiefly *Sc.* OE. **3.** *trans.* To form or fashion by means of a rotary or twisting motion. **a.** To turn (wood, etc.) in a lathe; to shape (pottery) on a potter's lathe or 'throwing-wheel'. Now *techn.* or *dial.* 1440. **b.** *Silk-manuf.* To prepare and twist (raw silk) into thread; *spec.* to form into thread by twisting two or more threads or 'singles' in the direction opposite to that of their component filaments 1455.

2. The empty boat thrawed i' the wind, Against the postern tied ROSSETTI. 3. a. Balls thrown in a lathe JOHNSON. b. Silk is still 'thrown' at Derby 1897.

II. To project or propel through the air, and connected uses. **1.** *trans.* To project (anything) with a force of the nature of a jerk, from the hand or arm, so that it passes through the air or free space; to cast, hurl, fling; *spec.* to cast by a sudden jerk or straightening of the arm, esp. at the level of or over the shoulder (as dist. from *bowl*, *pitch*, *toss*) ME. **b.** *absol.* To hurl a missile, a weapon, etc. ME. **2.** *refl.* To fling or cast oneself; to precipitate oneself ME. **3.** *trans.* To cast (dice) from the dice-box; to make (a cast) at dice; also *absol.* or *intr.* to cast or throw dice; to play at dice 1587. **b.** To play (a card) out of one's hand; *esp.* to discard 1748. **c.** To cast (a vote) 1844. **4.** To hurl, project, shoot, as a missile engine does; also of a person using such an engine. Often *absol.* late ME. **5.** To put forth with a throwing action (a fishing net, line, or bait); to cast, make a cast with. Also *absol.* 1841. **6.** Of the sea or wind: To drive or cast with violence (on rocks or a coast); to cast away, wreck 1659. **7.** To project (a ray, beam, light) *on*, *upon*, *over*, etc.; to emit (light); to project, cast (a shadow) 1598. **8.** To direct (words, an utterance) *towards*, etc., esp. in hostility or contempt; to hurl, cast; to cause (sound, or *fig.* a gesture) to pass or travel; to waft (a kiss), to cast (a nod) 1580. **9.** *To t. one's eye* or *eyes*, *a glance*, *a look*, to turn or direct one's gaze, to look; *esp.* to look hastily, rapidly or cursorily; to glance 1590. **10.** To perform, execute (a somersault or a leap, in which the body is thrown with force); also *to t. a fit*, to have a fit (*U.S. slang*) 1826.

1. When a man throweth his goods into the Sea for feare the ship should sink HOBBES. 2. He threw himself upon his horse LEVER. Phr. *To t. oneself upon*, to attack with violence or vigour; to fall upon. 3. That great day..on which a man is to t. his last cast for an eternity of joys JER. TAYLOR. 5. Violet..learnt to t. a fly 1889. 6. A billow..threw me..on dry land BURTON. 7. Phr. *To t.* (*a*) *light on*, to contribute to the elucidation of, to make clearer or plainer. *To t. a shadow, cloud, gloom, lustre, over*: see the sbs. 8. Not a word? *Ros.* Not one to t. at a dog. SHAKS. Throwing a kiss towards the boy SCOTT.

III. Pregnant uses. **1.** *trans.* To cause to fall to the ground; to cast down, knock down, prostrate, lay low; *spec.* in *Wrestling*, to bring (one's opponent) to the ground ME. **b.** *fig.* or in fig. context: To defeat in a contest; also, to be the cause of defeat to; to give or gain the verdict against in an action at law (*U.S.*) 1850. **2.** To cause forcibly (a tree or structure) to fall; to bring, knock, break, or cut down; to fell 1568. **3.** Of a horse, etc.: To cause (the rider) to fall off; to unseat, shake off; also in passive *to be thrown* (from a horse or vehicle) 1531. **4.** Of a snake, a bird, etc.: To cast (the skin); to moult (feathers). Of a horse: To cast or lose (a shoe). 1590. **5.** Of domestic animals: To produce as offspring; to give birth to, to drop. Also *absol.*, *to t. true*, to produce offspring true to the parent type. 1845. **6.** Of a fountain or pump: To eject or project (water); to discharge; also *absol.* 1644. **7.** Of a horse: *To t. the feet*, to lift them well in moving 1827.

1. b. The sceptic cannot t. his opponent if his own feet are in the air 1909. 3. The untutored jade Threw me, and kicked me MASSINGER. 4. There the snake throwes her enammel'd skinne SHAKS. 5. You cannot possibly tell what sort of foal your mare may t. 1845. 6. The pumps..t. daily 60,000 to 70,000 gallons 1864.

IV. *fig.* and *transf.* **1.** *trans.* To cause to pass, go, or come into some place or position by some action likened to throwing; to put or place with haste, suddenness, or force; e. g. to put (a garment) *on* or *off* hurriedly, hastily, or carelessly. late ME. **b.** In fig. uses of various phrases 1611. **c.** With immaterial object (e. g. blame, influence, power, obstacles, etc.) 1620. **d.** To put *into* as an addition; to add, incorporate 1676. **2.** *spec.* **a.** *To throw into prison*, etc. to imprison roughly or forcibly 1560. **b.** Troops, succour, supplies, etc. are said to be *thrown* into a besieged place, or a strategic position. Also *refl.* 1617. **c.** A bridge or arch is said to be *thrown* from one side to another of, or *over*, a river, passage, or space 1751. **3.** To cause to fall, pass, or come into or out of some condition or relation (or place or thing implying this); properly, with the connotation of abruptness, suddenness, or force; to cast, force, drive, plunge, thrust. Usu. with *prep.* 1560. **b.** To put deftly into a particular form or shape; to express in a specified form (in speech or writing); to convert, change, or translate *into* some other form, or another language 1723.

1. Her arms Round Ellen's neck she threw COLERIDGE. T. the rifle smartly to the front of the right shoulder 1859. b. Phr. *To t. a veil over. To t. good money after bad*, to incur a further loss in trying to make good a previous one. *To t. oneself* or *be thrown at* or *at the head of* (a man), of a woman, to put herself or be put designedly in the way of, so as to invite the attention of. *To t. oneself into the arms of*, to become the wife or mistress of. d. The saddle being thrown into the bargain 1862. 3. The fatigues I had undergone threw me into a fever GOLDSMITH. Easily thrown off its balance SCOTT. Phr. *To t. open* (*apart*, *asunder*), to set open (separate, break asunder) with a sudden or energetic impulse; hence *fig.* to make publicly accessible or available. *To t. open one's doors to*, to receive as a guest. *To t. oneself on* or *upon*, to have urgent recourse to (some one) for succour, etc.; to commit oneself entirely to; also, *pass.*, to be made or become dependent upon. *To t. oneself into*, to engage in with zeal or earnestness; so *to t. one's soul, heart, spirit, energy, efforts*, etc., *into* a thing or action. b. Two dress boxes..were thrown into one 1824. Cædmon..throws Scripture into metrical paraphrase 1893.

With adverbs. **T. about. a.** *trans.* See simple senses and ABOUT. **b.** *Naut. absol.* or *intr.* To turn about at once; to go about, put about. **T. aside. a.** *trans.* See simple senses and ASIDE. **b.** *spec.* To cast aside, out of use, or as useless; *fig.* to discard, cease to use. **T. away. a.** *trans.* To cast away out of one's hands or possession as useless or unneeded. **b.** To spend or use without adequate return; to squander, waste; to bestow upon an unworthy object; also, to neglect to take advantage of (an opportunity, etc.); *spec.* at *Cards*, to play (a losing card) when one cannot follow suit, to discard. **c.** refl. *To t. oneself away*: chiefly said of a woman in ref. to an unsuitable marriage. **T. back. a.** *trans.* See simple senses and BACK *adv.* **b.** To put back in time or condition; to delay, make late; to retard or check in expected or desired progress. **c.** With *upon*: to compel to fall back upon. **d.** *intr.* To revert to an ancestral type or character not present in recent generations, to exhibit atavism (*colloq.*). **e.** *intr.* To go back in date *to*. †**T. by.** *trans.* To put aside with decision; discard. **T. down. a.** *trans.* See simple senses and DOWN *adv.* **b.** Expressing a symbolic action; as *to t. down one's arms*, to surrender; *to t. down one's brief* (of a barrister), to decline to go on with a case; *to t. down one's tools*, (of a workman) to 'strike'. **c.** To cause to fall; to demolish (a building, etc.). **d.** To deposit or cause to be deposited from solution; to precipitate. **e.** *fig.* To put down with force; to lower in rank or station; to degrade; also, to bring to nought. **T. in. a.** *trans.* See simple senses and IN. **b.** To put in as a supplement or addition; to add esp. to a bargain. **c.** To introduce, insert, or interject in the course or process of something; *esp.* to interpose or contribute (a remark). **d.** In techn. uses (often *absol.*). (*a*) *Fishing.* To make a cast. (*b*) *Hunting.* To start (hounds) upon the scent. (*c*) *Wrestling* and *Pugilism.* To toss one's hat into the ring as a challenge or acceptance; hence *fig.* to become a candidate, put in *for*. (*d*) *Football* and *Cricket.* cf. *throw-in* sb. (THROW- 2). **e.** *To t. in one's lot with*, to enter into association with, so as to share the fortunes of. **f.** *To t. in one's hand*, in Poker, etc., to give up one's cards without betting, or without finishing the game; hence *fig.* **T. off. a.** *trans.* See simple senses and OFF. **b.** To rid oneself by force from, shake off (a yoke, restraint, burden, etc.); also, to cast off, disown (an associate). **c.** To cast off, put off energetically (something put on or assumed, as a garment); to divest oneself of (a quality, illness, habit, feeling, etc.); to lay aside quickly or decisively; to discard. **d.** To shake off (a pursuer or competitor in a race); also, to put off the scent. **e.** *Hunting.* To free from the leashes, to start (hounds) in the chase; to let fly (a hawk, etc.). Now esp. *absol.* or *intr.*, of foxhunters or hounds: To begin hunting; hence *fig.* to begin. **f.** To eject, emit, give off, esp. from the body or system; *esp.* to expel or discharge (waste or morbid products). **g.** To produce and send forth (as offspring or the like); *esp.* of a hive of bees: to send forth (a swarm). **h.** To produce with speed and facility (a literary or artistic work or sketch). **i.** *Printing.* To print off. **T. on. a.** *trans.* See simple senses and On. **b.** To put on (apparel) hastily or carelessly; the opposite of *throw off.* **c.** To put (hounds) on the scent. **T. out. a.** *trans.* See simple senses and Out; *spec.* of frost, etc.: to force (young plants) out of the ground. **b.** To eject, expel, turn out. **c.** *transf.* and *fig.* To put forth vigorously from within; to emit, radiate (heat or light); to exude; to produce, be the source of; to send out, put forth (buds, shoots, etc.). **d.** To cause to project, protrude, stretch out, or extend. **e.** To cause to 'stand out'. **f.** *Mil.* To send out (skirmishers, etc.) to a distance from the main body. **g.** To put forward tentatively, give (a hint or suggestion); also with obj. clause, to suggest. **h.** To dismiss from acceptance, use, or consideration; to reject; to leave out of a reckoning; in *Écarté*, to discard. **i.** Of a legislative assembly or a grand jury: To reject (a bill, etc.). **j.** *Sporting.* To put out of place or order by leaving behind in a chase or race; to distance, outpace. **k.** = Put *out.* **l.** *Cricket.* Of a fieldsman: To put (the batsman) 'out' by throwing the ball so as to hit his wicket. **m.** *intr.* for *refl.* To move outwards from a centre; to strike out with hands or feet; to let oneself go; to push out (as a root). **n.** *intr.* or *absol.* Of a printing machine: To fail to register. **T. over. a.** See simple senses and Over. **b.** To throw overboard (in *fig.* sense); to cast off (a lover, associate, or ally); to abandon. **T. together. a.** *trans.* See simple senses and Together. **b.** To put together hastily or roughly. (Said *esp.* in relation to literary work.) **c.** To bring (persons) casually into contact or association. **T. up. a.** *trans.* See simple senses and Up. **b.** To discharge by vomiting; to vomit. **c.** To raise (the hands, eyes, etc.) quickly or suddenly; *spec.* in *T. up your hands*, as a command to surrender. *To t. up the sponge*: see Sponge *sb.* I. 1. **d.** To cast up (a heap or earthwork) with or as with the spade; to construct hastily. **e.** To render prominent or distinct; to cause to 'stand out'. **f.** *Naut. To t.* (a ship) *up in* (*into, on*) *the wind*, to turn the vessel into the wind till she points almost directly to windward; also *absol.* said of the navigator. **g.** To cease definitely to do, use, or practise; to relinquish, abandon, quit, give up (a project, associate, etc.); orig. in the phr. *to t. up the game* or *one's cards*, i.e. to place one's cards face upwards on the table on withdrawing from the game. **h.** Of hounds: To lift the head from the ground, the scent having been lost.

Throw- in Comb. [Throw *sb.*[2] or stem of Throw *v.*, in comb. with sbs. or advbs., forming sbs. or adjs.]

1. In comb. with sbs. **a. t.-crank,** a crank which converts rotary into reciprocating motion; **-disk, -lever,** a disk-crank or a lever having a specified or adjustable throw; **-lathe,** a lathe driven by hand; **-wheel,** the driving-wheel of a throw or lathe. **b. t.-line,** a fishing-line thrown out by hand, a handline.

2. In comb. with advbs., forming sbs. expressing the action of the corresponding vbl. phrases; as *t.-in, -up* (an act of throwing in or up); **t.-in,** in Football, an act of throwing the ball into play again after it has crossed one of the touch-lines; in Cricket, an act of throwing in the ball from the field to the wicket-keeper or bowler; **-out,** an act of throwing-out, or a thing thrown out; anything discarded or rejected.

Throw·-back. 1856. [f. phr. *to throw back.*] An act of throwing back; a check, reverse; *spec.* reversion to an earlier ancestral type or character; an example of this.

Throw·-crook. *Sc.* and *n. dial.* **thraw·-crook.** 1568. [f. Throw *v.* + Crook *sb.*] A hooked implement for 'throwing' or twisting coarse rope from hay, straw, or hair.

Thrower (þrōu·ər). 1450. [f. Throw *v.* + -er [1].] One who throws, in various senses. *spec.* **a.** One who shapes pottery on a potter's wheel or throw; a potter 1604. †**b.** One who twists filaments of silk into silk thread; a throwster -1688.

Throwing (þrōu·iŋ), *vbl. sb.* ME. [f. as prec. + -ing [1].] The action of Throw *v.*

attrib. and *Comb.*: **t.-balls,** the S. Amer. Bolas; **-iron,** a knife-like missile used by some African savages; **-mill,** (*a*) a building in which silk-throwing is carried on; (*b*) a machine for twisting raw silk into thread; **-wheel,** a potter's wheel.

Throw·ing-stick. 1770. **a.** A short wooden implement by which a dart or spear is thrown, in order to give increased velocity to it. **b.** A short club used as a missile.

Thrown (þrōun), *ppl. a.* 1463. [Pa. pple. of Throw *v.*] **I. 1. a.** Turned on a lathe, as woodwork. Now *dial.* **b.** Shaped on the potter's wheel 1483. **2.** Of silk: Twisted into thread 1463.

2. *T. silk*, silk thread consisting of two or more singles twisted together. *T. singles*, silk thread consisting of a single strand of raw silk which has been cleaned, wound, and twisted.

II. Cast, pitched, hurled; unseated from a horse 1833.

Throw·-off. 1859. [f. the vbl. phr. *to throw off.*] **a.** *Fox-hunting.* The throwing-off of the hounds, the start of a hunt; by extension, of a race; hence, a start generally. **b.** A mechanism by which some part of a machine is disconnected, or its action suspended. **c.** That which is thrown off; something produced or given off, an offshoot.

Throw·-over. 1819. [f. the vbl. phr. *to throw over.*] The act or result of throwing over; also, *concr.*, a wrap to throw over the shoulders; a loose outer garment.

Throwster (þrōu·stər). 1455. [f. Throw *v.* + -ster.] One who twists silk fibres into raw silk or raw silk into thread, a silk-throwster; orig. a woman who did this.

Throw·-stick. 1837. [f. Throw *v.* + Stick *sb.*] **a.** An ancient kind of boomerang. **b.** = Throwing-stick a.

Thrum (þrvm), *sb.*[1] [OE. *þrum* (in comb.), ME. *thrum, throm*; f. OTeut. ablaut-stem *þrum-, þram- :—Indo-Eur. *trmo-; cf. L. *terminus*, Gr. τέρμα end.] **1.** *Weaving.* Each of the ends of the warp-threads left unwoven and remaining attached to the loom when the web is cut off; usu. in *pl.* (also *collect. sing.*) the row or fringe of such threads. late ME. **2.** A short piece of waste thread or yarn (including the unwoven ends of the warp); *pl.* or *collect. sing.* odds and ends of thread; also, a tuft, tassel, or fringe of threads at the edge of a piece of cloth, etc. ME. **b.** *Naut.* (*pl.*, also *collect. sing.*) Short pieces of coarse woollen or hempen yarn, used for mops, etc. 1466. **c.** *fig.*: *pl.* (or *collect. sing.*) Odds and ends, scraps 1648. †**3.** Applied to various structures in plants or animals resembling small threads, or a tuft of these -1812. †**4.** Applied joc. or contemptuously to a person -1727.

attrib. and *Comb.*: †**t.-cap,** a cap made of thrums; *transf.* a person wearing a t. cap; **-eyed** (-əid) *a.*, applied by florists to the short-styled form of a flower (esp. of the genus *Primula*), which shows the boss of 'thrums' or anthers at the top of the corolla-tube (opp. to Pin-eyed); so **t. eye;** †**-stone,** a name for asbestos, as being a fibrous mineral.

Thrum (þrvm), *sb.*[2] 1553. [Echoic.] A word representing various sounds, esp. those produced by 'thrumming' a guitar or similar instrument; also *dial.* the purring of a cat.

Thrum, *v.*[1] 1525. [f. Thrum *sb.*[1]] *trans.* To furnish or adorn with thrums or ends of thread (or something similar); to cover with thrums or small tufts, raise a pile upon (cloth); to make shaggy. Now *dial.* †**b.** *transf.* and *fig.* To fringe or clothe -1630. **c.** *Naut.* To sew or fasten bunches of rope-yarn over (a mat or sail) so as to produce a shaggy surface, suitable to prevent chafing or stop a leak 1711.

b. A craggy Rocks steep-hanging boss (Thrumm'd half with Ivie, half with crisped Moss) Sylvester.

Thrum, *v.*[2] 1592. [Echoic.] **I. a.** *intr.* To play on a stringed instrument, as a guitar, harp, etc. by plucking the strings; to play on any stringed instrument in an idle, mechanical, or unskilful way; to strum. **b.** *trans.* To play (a stringed instrument, or a tune on it) idly, monotonously, or unskilfully; to strum upon; also, to pluck, twang (a string) 1625. **2.** *intr.* To sound as an instrument or string when thrummed; to sound monotonously; to hum 1763. †**3. a.** *trans.* To recite or tell in a 'singsong' or monotonous way; also, to hum over (a melody) 1710. **b.** *intr.* To speak or read monotonously; to 'drone', mumble 1774. **4.** To strike something with the fingers as if playing on a musical instrument; to drum upon (a table, etc.) **a.** *trans.* 1750. **b.** *intr.* with *on* or *upon* 1820.

3. b. Boswell..has thrummed upon this topic till it is threadbare Scott. **4. b.** The squire was thrumming on the back of his chair 1865.

Thrummy (þrv·mi), *a.* Now *rare.* 1597. [f. Thrum *sb.*[1] + -y [1].] Consisting of, characterized by, or resembling thrums; covered with thrums; shaggy, downy, velvety. Formerly of flowers with conspicuous anthers, of fibrous roots, etc.

Thrumwort (þrv·mˌwɒɹt). 1829. [f. as prec. + Wort [1].] A name for plants having parts resembling thrums. **a.** The water-plantain, *Alisma Plantago*; also, the allied star-fruit, *Actinocarpus Damasonium.* **b.** 'Love-lies-bleeding', *Amarantus caudatus.*

Thrush [1] (þrvʃ). [OE. *þrysce* :—OTeut. **þruskjôn.*] Historically, a name of two British and general European birds; (1) that also called *Throstle* and *Mavis*, distinctively Song-thrush (*Turdus musicus*); (2) the Mistletoe thrush, Mistle- or Missel-thrush, (*T. viscivorus*) a larger and less musical species. Thence extended (with qualifications) by ornithologists to other species of the genus *Turdus*, or more widely, to all members of the family *Turdidæ.* **b.** With qualifying words applied to various species of the genus *Turdus* or family *Turdidæ*; also, popularly, to numerous species of other families (starlings, warblers, shrikes, etc.) more or less resembling the true thrushes.

b. Migratory t., the American robin. **New York t.,** an American water-t., *Seiurus nævius.* **Pacific t.,** a Polynesian bird, *Lalage pacifica.* **Shrike-t.:** see Shrike. **Wilson's t.,** the Veery of N. America. See also Ant-thrush, Ground-thrush, Hermit-thrush, etc.

Comb.: **t.-nightingale,** a nightingale (*Daulias philomela*) with a slightly speckled breast, found in central and eastern Europe; **-tit,** a book-name for birds of the genus *Cochoa* (or *Xanthogenys*) inhabiting the Himalayas, China, and Java.

Thrush [2] (þrvʃ). 1665. [Origin obsc.] **1.** A disease, chiefly of infants, characterized by white vesicular specks on the inside of the mouth and throat, and on the lips and tongue, caused by a parasitic fungus; scientifically called *aphtha* or *parasitic stomatitis.* **2.** In the horse, an inflammation of the lower surface of the frog of the hoof, accompanied with a fetid discharge 1753.

1. He hath a fever, a t. and a hickup Pepys.

Comb.: **t.-fungus,** the parasitic fungus *Saccharomyces albicans*, which causes thrush (sense 1).

Thrust (þrvst), *sb.* 1513. [f. next.] **I.** †**1.** An act of pressing or pressure; chiefly *fig.* 'pinch', hardship -1670. †**2.** Pressure or pushing of a crowd, jostling, crowding; a crowd, throng, 'press' -1620. **3.** *Mech.*, etc. A pushing force exerted by one part of a structure, etc. upon another contiguous part; *spec.* (*a*) *Arch.*, etc. Such a force exerted laterally by an arch or other part of a building or structure against an abutment or support; (*b*) the driving force exerted by a paddle or propeller-shaft in a ship or aeroplane; (*c*) *Mining*, the breaking down or the slow descent of the roof of a gangway; (*d*) *Geol.* a compressive strain in the earth's crust. 1708. **b.** Short for *t.-bearing* 1875. **II. 1.** An act or the action of thrusting (in sense I. 1 of the vb.); a forcible push or pushing 1823. **2.** An act of thrusting (in sense II. 1 of the vb.); a lunge or stab made with a weapon 1586. **b.** *transf.* and *fig.* 1668.

1. The t. of the descending glacier Tyndall. **2.** While we were enterchanging thrusts and blowes Shaks. Phr. *Cut and t.*: Cut *sb.*[2]; *t. and parry* (*lit.* and *fig.*).

Comb.: †**t.-bearer, t.-bearing,** a bearing designed to receive a t. in machinery; *spec.* the bearing in which revolves the foremost length of propeller-shafting in a screw steamer, its function being to transmit the t. of the shaft to the hull of the ship; **-fault** *Geol.* = Overfault; **-plane** *Geol.* the plane of dislocation in an overfault, along which the dislocated strata have been driven; **-shaft,** a propeller-shaft.

Thrust (þrvst), *v.* Pa. t. and pa. pple. **thrust.** [Early ME. *þrusten* (*ü*), *þrysten*, a. ON. *þrýsta* to thrust, press, compress, force.] **I. 1.** *trans.* To exert the force of impact upon or against (a body) so as to move it away; to push, shove, drive. Now chiefly *literary.* **b.** *transf.* and *fig.* Applied to action of any kind having an effect analogous to that of physical pushing or moving ME. **c.** *absol.* or *intr.* To push against something; to make a thrust ME. **2.** To push or force one's way, as through a crowd; to crowd *in*; to press onwards or into a place, etc. ME. **3.** *trans.* To press, compress, squeeze. *Obs.* exc. in spec. ref. to cheese-making. late ME.

1. T. him downe stayres SHAKS. b. Thrusting aside all authority but that of Reason 1854. c. They thrust at me, that I might fall COVERDALE *Ps.* cxvii[i]. 13. 2. She thrust in between them SCOTT.

II. †1. To strike with a pushing action; to stab or pierce *with* a pointed instrument -1770. b. *intr.* To make a thrust, stab, or lunge with a pointed weapon; *spec.* in *Fencing* 1596. 2. *trans.* To cause (anything, esp. something grasped in the hand) to enter, pierce, or penetrate something or place by or as by pushing; to put, drive, or force into some place or position ME. b. To put forth, extend (a limb or member) into some place or in some direction; to put forth as in the process of growth (a root, branch, or connected part) so as to project. late ME. c. *transf.* and *fig.* 1588.

1. b. These foure..thrust at me; I..tooke all their seuen points in my target SHAKS. 2. You should have..thrust The dagger thro' her side TENNYSON. b. I perceived him t. his tongue in his cheek SMOLLETT. c. Thrusting this report Into his eares SHAKS.

III. 1. *fig.* To put a person forcibly *into* some condition or course of action (usu. against his own will). late ME. b. To put (something) improperly *into* some position; esp. in phr. *t. in*, to interpolate 1574. 2. To put (a person) forcibly *into* some position (against the will of others concerned); to intrude (some one) *upon* (a person or persons) 1559. b. *refl.* To intrude oneself *into* any position, condition or circumstances, or *upon* another person; to push oneself forward 1530. c. To press, force, or impose the acceptance of something (*upon* some one) 1593.

1. I will not willfully t. myself in danger 1639. 2. Stephen Langhton, thrust into the archebisshoppricke of Canterbury by the pope 1559. b. They would t. themselves into my company 1797. c. Some are born great, some atcheeue greatnesse, and some haue greatnesse thrust vppon em SHAKS.

Thruster (þrʊ·stəɹ). 1597. [f. prec. + -ER 1.] 1. One who or that which thrusts. 2. *Hunting slang.* One who thrusts himself forward in the field, or rides too close to the hounds 1886.

Thru·sting, *vbl. sb.* late ME. [f. as prec. + -ING 1.] 1. The action of THRUST *v.* 2. *concr.* in pl. *thrustings* = *thrutchings*, whey which is squeezed out while the cheese is under pressure 1794.

Comb.: t.-screw, a screw by which a press, esp. a cheese-press, is actuated and regulated.

Thrutch (þrʊtʃ), *v.* Now *dial.* [OE. *þryc-c(e)an* :—WGer. **þrukkjan*, f. **þrukki-*, whence G. *drucken* to press.] 1. *trans.* To press, squeeze, crush; to crowd, throng; *fig.* to oppress. b. *spec.* To press (cheese) 1688. 2. To thrust, push ME. 3. *intr.* To push or press into a place; to jostle 1837.

Thud (þʊd), *sb.* orig. *Sc.* or *n. dial.* 1513. [Cf. next.] 1. A blast of wind or tempest; a gust; a squall. *Sc.* 2. A heavy blow; a thump with the fist. Also *fig.* a severe affliction, a 'blow'. *Sc.* and *n. dial.* 1787. 3. A dull heavy sound without resonance, such as is produced when a heavy stone strikes the ground. 1825. b. As interj. or adv.: With a thud 1880.

2. The heavy t. of the steam-hammer 1878.

Thud (þʊd), *v.* orig. *Sc.* 1513. [app. echoic; cf. prec.] 1. *intr.* To come with a blast or gust, as the wind; sometimes including the notion of sound. *Sc.* 2. To produce a thud or dull heavy sound; to fall or impinge with a thud; also said of the body or surface struck 1796.

2. A bullet thudded into the wall above me 1908.

Thug (þʊg), *sb.* 1810. [a. Hindī *ṭhag*, Marathī *ṭhag*, *ṭhak* cheat, swindler.] (With capital T.) One of an association of professional robbers and murderers in India, who strangled their victims. b. *transf.* A cutthroat, ruffian, rough. Now *U.S.* 1839. Hence Thug *v. trans.* to assassinate by thuggee. Thu·ggery, Thu·gism = next.

Thuggee (þʊgī·). 1837. [a. Hindī *ṭhagī*, abstr. sb. f. *ṭhag* THUG.] The system of robbery and murder practised by the Thugs.

‖**Thuja** (þiū·dʒă). 1760. [mod.L. (Linn.); see THUYA.] The more common English form of the name of trees or shrubs of the botanical genus now called THUYA, also of the wood of *T. occidentalis*, and of drugs derived from it.

Oil of t., an essential oil obtained by distilling the ends of the branches and leaves of *T. occidentalis* with water.

‖**Thule** (þiū·lī). OE. [L., = Gr. Θούλη (Θύλη), proper name of unkn. origin.] The ancient Gr. and L. name for a land six days' sail north of Britain, which Polybius supposed to be the most northerly region of the world. (Variously identified with the Shetland Islands (so app. in Pliny and Tacitus), Iceland, the northern point of Denmark, or some point on the coast of Norway). b. *transf.* As the type of the extreme limit of travel and discovery, chiefly in the phr. *ultima Thule* (farthest Thule); hence *fig.* the highest or uttermost point or degree attained or attainable; the acme 1771.

Thumb (þʊm), *sb.* [OE. *þūma* :—OTeut. **þūmon-*, pre-Teut. **tūmon-* the stout or thick (finger), f. root *tū-* to swell; cf. Skr. *tumrá* fat, L. *tumere* to swell.] 1. The short thick inner digit of the human hand, opposable to the fingers, and distinguished from them by having only two phalanges; hence, *gen.*, the inner digit of a limb when opposable to and set apart from the other digits (as in the *Quadrumana* and opossums). †b. The great toe -1643. c. In the lower animals generally: The inmost digit of the fore-foot; in a bird, the first digit of the wing, bearing the bastard-wing or alula; also, the hind toe, inner hind toe, or hallux 1607. 2. *transf.* The part of a glove or mitten which covers the thumb 1888. 3. A part or thing analogous to or in some way resembling a thumb 1745. 4. As a measure: The breadth of the thumb, taken as equal to an inch 1622.

1. 'Twixt his Finger and his Thumbe, he held A Pouncet-box SHAKS. 3. 'Tot', a small mug, that held a quartern, also called a t. 1901.

Phrases. *T. of gold*, *a golden t.*, *miller's t.*, in ref. either to the alleged dishonesty of millers or the lucrativeness of their trade. *One's fingers all thumbs* (etc.), said of a person who is clumsy or wanting in dexterity. *To bite one's thumbs*, as an indication of anger or vexation; *to bite the t. at*, as an insult: see BITE *v.* *Under the t. of*, entirely at the disposal or direction of, completely subservient to. *To turn up (down) the thumb(s*, in ref. to the use of the t. by the spectators in the ancient amphitheatre, to indicate approbation or the opposite. *(Put your) thumbs up!* (mod. slang), be cheerful, 'keep smiling'.

Comb.: t.-bird, a local name for the Goldcrest; -index, a reference-index consisting of grooves cut in the front edges of the leaves, or formerly of projecting tabs, or margins so cut as to show initial letters or titles, so that any division may be turned to by placing the t. or finger on the proper initial, etc.; -latch, a door-latch which is operated by pressing with the thumb; -nut, a nut for a screw, having wings to grasp between the thumb and fingers in turning it; -pot, a flower-pot of the smallest size; -print, an impression made with the inner surface of the top joint of the t.; -rule = RULE OF THUMB; -tack, a tack with a broad head, which may be pushed in with the t.

Thumb (þʊm), *v.* 1593. [f. prec.] 1. *trans.* To feel with or as with the thumb; to handle 1623. 2. To play (a wind instrument, an air) with or as with the thumbs; to perform or manipulate clumsily. Also *intr.* with *it*, 1593. 3. To soil or wear (esp. a book) with the thumbs in using or handling; hence, to read much or often 1644. 4. a. To press, smooth, clean, spread, or smear with the thumb. b. To cover (the touchhole of a cannon) with the thumb 1768.

2. One winds a Horn..Another thumbs it on a Tabor COTTON. 3. These early editions were thumbed out of existence ARBER. 4. a. To t. down the tobacco in his pipe 1904.

Thumbed (þʊmd), *a.* 1529. [f. THUMB *sb.* and *v.* + -ED.] 1. *adj.* Provided with or having thumbs (of a certain kind); chiefly in comb. 2. *ppl. a.* Of a book or the like: Having the pages soiled or worn by the thumbs of readers; showing signs of much use 1800.

Thumbikins, thumbkins (þʊ·mikinz, þʊ·mkinz). *sb. pl.* *Sc.* 1684. [f. THUMB *sb.* + -(*i*)KIN dim. suffix.] = THUMB-SCREW 2.

Thumbless (þʊ·mles), *a.* 1720. [-LESS.] Having no thumb or thumbs; destitute or deprived of thumbs; *spec.* applied to the African *Colobus* and to the Amer. Spider-monkeys (*Ateles*) in which the thumb is rudimentary or functionless.

Thu·mb-mark, *sb.* 1845. A mark made with the thumb, esp. on the page of a book in turning the leaves; also, such a mark made with the inked thumb for identification of a person. Hence Thu·mb-mark *v. trans.* to mark with the thumb.

Thu·mb-nail. 1604. 1. The nail of the thumb. Often *allus.* 2. *transf.* A drawing or sketch of the size of the thumb-nail; hence *fig.* a description on a small scale; a brief word-picture. Chiefly *attrib.*, as *t. sketch*. 1900.

1. The whole code..may be written on the t. 1841.

Thu·mb-ring. 1596. a. A ring formerly worn on the thumb. b. A ring for the thumb on the guard of a sword or dagger 1891.

Thu·mb-rope. Now *dial.* 1601. A rope made by twisting hay or straw on the thumb.

Thu·mb-screw, thu·mbscrew, *sb.* 1794. [f. THUMB *sb.* + SCREW *sb.*] 1. A screw with a flattened or winged head, for turning with the thumb and fingers; a butterfly screw; also, a small clamp adjusted by such a screw. 2. An instrument of torture by which one or both thumbs were compressed; also called 'the screws' 1817. Hence Thu·mb-screw, thu·mb-screw *v. trans.* to torture by screwing the thumbs; to torture with or as with thumb-screws.

Thu·mb-stall. 1589. [STALL *sb.*[1] 6.] a. A shoemaker's or sailmaker's thimble. b. A sheath worn on the thumb to protect it when injured 1654.

‖**Thummim** (þʊ·mim). 1539. [a. Heb. *tum-mim*, *thummim*, pl. of *tōm* completeness, integrity.] Used in the collocation *Urim and T.*, rarely *T. and Urim*; see URIM.

Thump (þʊmp), *sb.* 1552. [Goes with next.] 1. 'A hard heavy dead dull blow with something blunt' (J.), as with a club or the fist; also, the heavy sound of such a blow (not so dull as a *thud*). b. Repeated, expressing a series of thumps 1850. c. *advb.* With a thump 1704. 2. *spec.* a. A knocking or pounding of machinery arising from slackness at a joint where there is reciprocal motion. b. *pl.* A beating of the chest in the horse due to spasmodic contractions of the diaphragm, analogous to the hiccup in man. 1903.

1. Down with a t. he falls upon his face HOBBES. b. The t.-t. and shriek-shriek Of the train BROWNING.

Thump (þʊmp), *v.* 1537. [Echoic.] 1. *trans.* To strike or beat heavily, as with the fist, a club, or any blunt instrument, producing a dead, dull, somewhat hard sound; also, to hammer, pound, knock forcibly. b. Of the feet, etc.: To beat or strike (the ground, etc.) heavily and noisily; also of a body: to impinge upon with a thump; to strike violently 1582. 2. *fig.* To 'beat' (in a fight), to drub, lick, thrash severely. *colloq.* 1594. 3. *intr.* To strike or beat with force or violence, with an abrupt dull noise 1565. b. To walk with heavy sounding steps; also, of a thing, to move with thumps or noisy jolts 1604. c. Of the heart, etc.: To beat violently or audibly 1784.

1. The sturdy Pavior thumps the ground GAY. *To t. a cushion, the pulpit*, etc., said of a preacher who uses violent gestures. 2. These bastard Britaines, whom our Fathers Haue in their owne Land beaten, bobb'd, and thump'd SHAKS. 3. I heard the boat thumping under the main channels MARRYAT. c. How my heart thumps 1880.

Thumper (þʊ·mpəɹ). 1537. [f. prec. + -ER 1.] 1. One who or that which thumps. 2. Anything 'thumping' or strikingly big of its kind; *esp.* a 'thumping' lie, a 'whopper', 'whacker'. *colloq.* 1660.

Thu·mping, *ppl. a.* 1576. [f. as prec. + -ING 2.] 1. That thumps; beating, banging, throbbing 1581. 2. *fig.* Exceptionally large or heavy; 'whacking', 'whopping'. *colloq.* 1576.

Thunder (þʊ·ndəɹ), *sb.* [OE. *þunor*, ME. *þoner*, etc. (later *þonder*, etc. with epenthetic *d*) :—OTeut. **þonaroz*, f. Indo-Eur. ablaut series **ten-*, *ton-*, *tn-* to stretch, resound, whence L. *tonare* to thunder.] 1. The loud noise accompanying a flash of lightning (apparently following it, being heard after it at an interval depending on distance), varying from a sharp report or crash to a prolonged roll or reverberation. Also, the meteorological condition or action from which the loud noise proceeds. b. Regarded as the destructive agent producing the effects usu. attributed to the lightning; (with *a* and *pl.*) a thunderstroke or 'thunderbolt'. Now only *poet.* or *rhet.* (exc. *fig.*). OE. **c.** (with *a* and *pl.*) A peal of thunder, a thunder-clap. Now only *poet.* or *rhet.* OE. **d.** (with *a* and *pl.*) A thunderstorm. *Obs.* exc. *dial.* ME. **2.** *transf.* Any loud deep rumbling or resounding noise. (Also with *a* and *pl.*) 1590. **3.** *fig.* **a.** Threatening, terrifying, or strongly impressive utterance; awful denunciation, menace, censure, or invective; vehement or powerful eloquence. (*sing.* and *pl.*) late ME. **b.** In phrases denoting great force or energy 1535. **4.** *slang* or *colloq.* Used vaguely in exclams., intensive phrases, etc. 1709.

1. A drumme..That shall..mocke the deepe mouth'd T. SHAKS. **b.** Let thy blowes..Fall like amazing t. on the Caske Of thy amaz'd pernicious enemy SHAKS. **c.** Low thunders bring the mellow rain TENNYSON. **2.** The t. of my Cannon shall be heard SHAKS. Thunders of applause 1807. The t. of surf on the shore 1887. **3.** Phr. *To steal (a person's) t.*, to use his weapons or equipment so as to reduce or annul the effect of his words or actions (see N.E.D., Suppl.).

Comb.: **t.-bird,** (*a*) a species of Australian shrike or thickhead (*Pachycephala gutturalis*); (*b*) a mythical bird thought by some savage tribes to cause t.; **-dint** (*arch.*), a t.-stroke; **-drop,** one of the large scattered drops of rain which fall at the beginning of a t.-shower; **-fish,** (*a*) a siluroid fish of African rivers, *Malapterurus electricus*, capable of inflicting electric shocks; (*b*) a European cyprinoid fish, *Misgurnus fossilis*, which burrows in mud, and comes to the surface before bad weather; also called *weather-fish*; **-hammer,** pop. name for a celt or other prehistoric implement; **-head,** a rounded mass of cumulus cloud seen near the horizon projecting above the general body of cloud, and portending a t.-storm; **-pumper,** (*a*) the Amer. bittern, also called *pump-t.*; (*b*) the Amer. fish *Haplodinotus grunniens*, also called *fresh-water drum, croaker*, or *sheepshead*; in both cases from the sounds they emit; **-shower,** a shower of rain accompanied by t. and lightning, or one of similar violence; **-snake,** (*a*) a snake of the genus *Ophibolus*, (*b*) the common little worm-snake, *Carphiophis amœna*, of the U.S.; **-tube** = FULGURITE 1.

Thunder (þʊ·ndəɹ), *v.* [OE. *þunrian*, in 13th c. *þondren*, f. *þunor* THUNDER *sb.*] **1.** *intr.* **a.** Impersonally: *it thunders*, thunder sounds, there is thunder. **b.** With subject (the or a deity, heaven, the clouds, the sky, etc.): To cause or give forth thunder; to sound with thunder OE. **c.** *trans.* To deal *out* or inflict by thunder; to strike *down* by thunder; to utter in thunder. *arch. rare.* 1579. **2.** *transf. intr.* To make a loud resounding noise like thunder; to sound very loudly; to roar. Occas. connoting violent movement: To rush or fall with great noise and commotion. late ME. **b.** *trans.* To deal or inflict, drive or impel, sound or give forth, strike, attack, or bombard, put *down* or overwhelm, etc. with a loud noise or other action like thunder 1590. **3.** *fig.* **a.** *intr.* To speak in the way of vehement threatening or reproof; to 'fulminate', to inveigh powerfully *against*; occas., to speak bombastically, or with powerful eloquence. Also simply, to shout loudly, to vociferate. ME. **b.** *trans.* To utter or publish in the way of terrible threatening, denunciation, or invective; also, to shout out, roar. late ME.

1. b. He would not flatter..Ioue, for's power to T. SHAKS. **2.** The great artillary began to t. from either side 1568. Avalanches thundered incessantly from the Aiguille Verte TYNDALL. **3. a.** The Ministers..thundered against these, and other wicked Practices DE FOE. **b.** Fearful echoes t. in mine ears, 'Faustus, thou art damned!' MARLOWE.

Thu·nder and li·ghtning. 1460. **1.** *lit.* **2.** *fig.* Denunciation, invective 1638. **3.** *transf.* †**a.** Applied to a cloth, app. of glaring colours, worn in 18th c. 1766. **b.** *attrib.* Applied to articles of apparel of a 'loud' or 'flashy' style, or combining two strongly contrasted colours 1837.

3. b. A tall fellow, in thunder-and-lightning waistcoat HUGHES.

Thu·nder-bea·rer. 1605. The bearer of thunder or of thunderbolts, i.e. Jupiter.

Thu·nder-blast. Chiefly *poet.* ME. **a.** A peal or clap of thunder. **b.** A stroke of 'thunder'. So **Thu·nder-bla·sted** *a.* blasted with 'thunder', struck by lightning.

Thunderbolt (þʊ·ndəɹbōult). 1440. **1.** A supposed bolt (BOLT *sb.*[1]) or dart formerly (and still vulgarly) believed to be the destructive agent in a lightning-flash when it 'strikes' anything; *Myth.* an attribute of Jove, Thor, or other deity. **b.** An imaginary or conventional representation of the above as an emblem of a deity, a heraldic bearing, etc. 1727. **2.** *fig.* Something very destructive, terrible, or startling 1559. **b.** Applied to a person noted for violent or destructive action 1593. **3.** Locally applied to: **a.** a belemnite or other fossil cephalopod; **b.** a flint celt or similar prehistoric implement; **c.** a mass or nodule of iron pyrites occurring in chalk 1618. **d.** *erron.* Applied to a meteoric stone or meteorite 1802.

2. This information was a t. to her 1787. **b.** Prince Edward the t. of warre in his time 1599.

attrib.: **t. beetle,** a species of beetle, *Arkopalus fulminans*, with dark wing-cases crossed with zigzag grey lines.

Thu·nder-clap. late ME. [f. THUNDER *sb.* + CLAP *sb.*[1]] A clap or loud crash of thunder; formerly also, a thunderstroke. **b.** *transf.* of other loud noises 1610. **c.** *fig.* A sudden startling or terrifying occurrence, act, utterance, or piece of news 1610.

This Answer was like a T. 1686. **b.** Thunder-claps of Applause ADDISON.

Thu·nder-cloud. 1697. A storm-cloud charged with electricity, that sends forth thunder and lightning.

Thunderer (þʊ·ndərəɹ). late ME. [f. THUNDER *v.* + -ER [1].] One who or that which thunders. **1.** He who thunders or causes thunder: applied to God, or to a deity, as Jupiter or Thor. **2.** *fig.* A resistless warrior; a powerful declaimer, an utterer of violent invective, or the like; *spec.* as a sobriquet of the London *Times* newspaper 1586.

Thu·nder-gust. Chiefly *U.S.* 1748. [GUST *sb.*[1]] A strong gust of wind accompanying a thunder-storm.

Thundering (þʊ·ndəriŋ), *vbl. sb.* OE. [f. THUNDER *v.* + -ING [1].] The action of the vb. THUNDER. **1.** *lit.*; also in *pl.*: = THUNDER *sb.* 1, 1 c (now *rare* or *arch.*). **2.** *transf.* = THUNDER *sb.* 2. 1560. **3.** *fig.* = THUNDER *sb.* 3. 1564.

Thu·ndering, *ppl. a.* (*adv.*) 1530. [f. as prec. + -ING [2].] That thunders. **b.** Very energetic or forcible; freq. as a mere intensive: Very great or big, 'tremendous', 'terrific' *colloq.* or *slang.* 1618. **c.** as *adv.* Excessively, immensely, 'tremendously'. *colloq.* or *slang.* 1852.

The double, double, double beat of the thundring Drum DRYDEN. T. letters came from the Parliament, with great menaces what they would do CLARENDON. **b.** Such a t. lie 1900. Hence **Thu·nderingly** *adv.*

Thunderous (þʊ·ndərəs), *a.* 1582. [f. THUNDER *sb.* + -OUS.] **1.** Full of or charged with thunder; of or pertaining to thunder; thundery. **2.** Resembling thunder in its loudness 1606. **3.** *fig.* Suggestive of thunder; of threatening aspect, or charged with latent energy, like a thunder-cloud; violent, destructive, or terrifying like thunder 1844.

1. Notus and Afer black with thundrous Clouds MILT. **3.** Homer, with the broad suspense Of t. brows MRS. BROWNING. Hence **Thu·nderous-ly** *adv.*, **-ness.**

Thunder-stone (þʊ·ndəɹ,stōun). 1598. **1.** = THUNDERBOLT 1. *arch.* **2.** = THUNDERBOLT 3. 1681.

1. I..Haue bar'd my Bosome to the Thunder-stone SHAKS.

Thu·nder-storm. 1598. A storm of thunder and lightning, usu. accompanied with heavy rain.

Thunderstricken (þʊ·ndəɹ,stri:k'n), *a.* 1586. [f. THUNDER *sb.* + STRICKEN.] = THUNDERSTRUCK 1, 2.

Thunderstrike (þʊ·ndəɹ,strəik), *v.* Pa. t. and pple. **thunderstruck.** 1613. [prob. a back-formation from prec., that being taken as a pa. pple.] **1.** *trans.* (*lit.*) To strike with 'thunder' or lightning. **2.** *fig.* To strike as with 'thunder'. **a.** To strike with amazement. *Obs.* exc. as in *thunderstricken, thunderstruck.* 1613. **b.** To inflict severe or terrible vengeance, reproof, or the like, upon 1638.

2. b. He had..thunder struck him, with a storme of mighty words SIR T. HERBERT.

Thunderstroke (þʊ·ndəɹ,strōuk). 1600. A stroke of 'thunder'; the impact of a lightning flash.

They fell together..as by a Thunder-stroke SHAKS.

Thunderstruck (þʊ·ndəɹ,strʊk), *ppl. a.* 1613. [orig. a later equivalent of *thunder-stricken.*] **1.** *lit.* Struck by lightning. Now *rare* or *Obs.* 1638. **2.** *fig.* Struck with amazement, terror, or the like 1613.

2. Thunder-struck with this unexpected answer 1687.

Thundery (þʊ·ndəri), *a.* 1598. [f. THUNDER *sb.* + -Y [1].] **1.** Of or pertaining to thunder; characterized by or betokening thunder. **2.** *fig.* Threatening an explosion of anger or passion; gloomy, frowning 1824.

1. In sultry, thundry weather 1774. **2.** That t. countenance of yours CARLYLE.

Thurible (þiū°·rib'l). 1440. [ad. L. *turibulum, thuribulum* censer, f. *tus, thus, thur-* incense; see THUS *sb.*] A vessel in which incense is burnt in religious ceremonies; a censer. (Now usu. a metal vase with pierced cover, containing combustible material to burn the gums used as incense, which is swung in the hand or suspended by chains.)

Thurifer (þiū°·rifəɹ). 1853. [a. mod.L., 'incense-bearer', f. *thur-* THUS *sb.* + *-fer* bearing.] An acolyte who carries the thurible. So **Thuri·ferous** *a.* that produces frankincense.

Thurification (þiū°:rifikē·ʃən). 1496. [f. eccl. L. *thurificare* to THURIFY; see -FICATION.] The action of thurifying; the burning or offering of, or perfuming with incense.

Thurify (þiū°·rifəi), *v.* late ME. [a. F. *thurifier*, ad. eccl. L. *thurificare*, f. *thur-* THUS *sb.* + *-ficare* -FY.] †**1.** *intr.* = CENSE *v.*[1] 2 (*rare*) –1460. **2.** *trans.* To perfume with incense; to burn incense before, offer incense to 1570.

Thuringite (þiuri·ndʒəit, -i·ŋgəit). 1844. [ad. G. *thuringit*, f. *Thuringia*, where found.] *Min.* A hydrous silicate of aluminium and iron, occurring as an aggregation of minute dark-green scales.

Thursday (þʊ·ɹzdei, -di). [OE. *þunres-, þur(e)sdæg*, 'day of Thunor or Thor', infl. by ON. *þórsdagr*; so (M)Du. *Donderdag*, G. *Donnerstag*; Teut. rendering of late L. *dies Jovis* (It. *giovedì*, F. *jeudi*) day of Jupiter.] **1.** The fifth day of the week. **2. Holy Thursday. a.** Thursday in Rogation Week, Ascension Day ME. **b.** Maundy Thursday, Sheer Thursday 1645.

Thus (þʊs, þūs), *sb.* late ME. [Late L., = cl. L. *tus, tur-*.] Frankincense. **a.** Olibanum. **b.** Resin obtained from the spruce-fir, and from various species of pine.

Thus (ðʊs), *adv.* Now chiefly *literary* or *formal.* [OE. *þus* = OS. *thus*, MDu., Du. *dus*, app. f. the (demonstrative) stem of THAT or THIS, but the pre-Teut. hist. is obsc.] **1.** In this way, like this. **b.** Ellipt. for *thus says* or *said* (referring to either a preceding or a subsequent speech). *poet.* or *arch.* 1568. **2.** In accordance with this; accordingly, and so; consequently; therefore ME. **3.** Qualifying an adj. or adv.: To this extent, number, or degree; as..as this; esp. *thus far*, to this point; *thus much*, as much as this OE.

1. T. the Hogen-Dutchman got Money 1689. After tea..she began t. GOLDSM. **b.** Cassandra t.; and t. the Paphian maid: Your gen'rous love [etc.] 1757. **c.** *U.S.* = So; esp. in *thus and so*, var. of *so and so* (cf. SO-AND-SO C. 2) 1873. **3.** But t. moche dar I sayn CHAUCER. T. farre..Our bending Author hath pursu'd the Story SHAKS.

Thusness (ðʊ·snės). *colloq.* 1867. [f. THUS + -NESS.] The condition of being thus. Chiefly *joc.* So **Thu·sly** *adv.*

What is the reason of this t.? 'A. WARD.'

Thuswise (ðʊ·swəiz), *adv.* ME. [f. THUS + *-wise* (WISE *sb.*[1] II).] = THUS.

‖**Thuya** (þiū·yă). 1707. [An irregular repr. of Gr. θυία, more correctly θύα, name of an African tree (*Thuja articulata* Linn., now *Callitris quadrivalvis*).] *Bot.* Name of a genus of coniferous trees, consisting of about ten species, of which the N. Amer. *T. occidentalis* and the Chinese *T. orientalis* are commonly cultivated under the name Arbor Vitæ. Also *attrib.*, as *thuya-wood.*

Thwack (þwæk), *sb.* 1587. [f. next.] A vigorous stroke with a stick or the like; a whack.

But Talgol first with hardy T. Twice bruis'd his head, and twice his back BUTLER.

Thwack (þwæk), *v.* 1530. [app. echoic.] **1.** *trans.* To beat or strike vigorously, as with a stick; to bang, thrash, whack. **2.** To drive or force by or as by thwacking; to knock (*down, in, out*, etc.) 1566. **3. a.** To clap; to clap *together*, to pack or crowd together (things or persons); to clap *down* 1589. †**b.** To pack or crowd (a thing or place) -1698.

1. Take all my cushions down and t. them soundly MIDDLETON. *fig.* Here's he that was wont to thwacke our Generall, Caius Martius SHAKS. **2.** Wee'l t. him hence with Distaffes SHAKS.

Thwait(e (þwēⁱt). *dial.* 1628. [a. ON. *þveit, þveiti* piece of land, paddock, lit. cutting, cut-piece, f. **þvíta* = OE. *þwitan* to cut, cut off.] A piece of ground; *esp.* one cleared from forest or reclaimed from waste. Now *rare* or *Obs.* as a separate word. (Entering into numerous place-names, as *Applethwaite, Crosthwaite, Seathwaite*, etc.)

Thwart (þwǭɹt), *sb.*[1] Now *rare*. 1611. [f. THWART *v.*] An act or instance of thwarting; a check, hindrance, obstruction, frustration.

Thwart (þwǭɹt), *sb.*[2] 1736. [app. a sb. use of THWART *adv.* and *adj.*, having ref. to the position of the rowing seats *athwart* or across the boat.] A seat across a boat, on which the rower sits; a rower's bench.

Thwart (þwǭɹt), *adv., prep.*, and *adj.* [Early ME. *þwert*, a. ON. *þvert* adv., across, athwart, orig. neut. of the ON. adj. *þverr* transverse, cross, shortened from *þwerh, þweorh* crooked, cross, perverse :—OTeut. **þwerh-* :— **þwerhw-* :—Indo-Eur. **twerkw-*, whence L. *torquere* to twist, etc.] **A.** *adv.* †**1.** Across or transversely to the length, direction, or course of anything; athwart -1664. **2.** From one side to the other of anything (with motion implied); across. *arch.* 1511. †**3.** *T. of.* **a.** *Naut.* Opposite to, over against (a place on the coast) -1670. †**b.** Transversely to, across the direction of. MILT.

3. a. Being t. of the Shoals of Brazil 1670.

B. *prep.* **1.** From side to side of, across. *arch.* or *poet.* 1470. **2.** = Across the course or direction of. *T. the hawse*, across the stem of a ship. Chiefly *Naut.* 1495. †**3.** Across the course of, so as to obstruct. MILT. **C.** *adj.* **1.** Lying, extending, or passing across; transverse, cross. late ME. **2.** *fig.* **a.** Of persons or their attributes: Disposed to resist, oppose, or obstruct; cross-grained; perverse, froward, obstinate, stubborn, awkward ME. **b.** Of things: Adverse, unfavourable, untoward, unpropitious; esp. applied (with mixture of literal sense) to a wind or current: cross 1610. †**3.** Opposed, contrary (*to*) -1624.

1. The Diagonal or T.-walk 1712. **2. a.** Ignorance makes them churlish, t., and mutinous BACON. **b.** A t. sea-wind full of rain and foam SWINBURNE. Hence **Thwa·rt-ly** *adv.*, †**-ness.**

Thwart (þwǭɹt), *v.* late ME. [f. prec. adv.] **I. 1.** *trans.* To pass or extend across from side to side of; to traverse, cross; also, to cross the direction of, to run at an angle to. *Obs.* or *arch.* **b.** *intr.* To pass or extend across, to cross. *Obs.* or *arch.* 1552. †**c.** *trans.* To cross the path of; to meet -1812. †**d.** *Naut.* Of a ship, etc.: To get athwart so as to be foul of. Also *intr.* -1813. †**2.** To lay (a thing) athwart or across; to place crosswise; to set or put (things) across each other -1632. **3.** To cross *with* a line, streak, band, etc. (Only in pa. pple.) *Obs.* or *arch.* 1610. **b.** To cross-plough; also, to cut crosswise 1847. **4.** To obstruct (a road, course, or passage) with something placed across; to block. *Obs.* exc. *fig.* 1630.

1. The current thwarts the course of a ship 1769. **3.** I saw Vesuvius..thwarted by a golden cloud 1861.

II. 1. To act or operate in opposition to; to oppose, hinder. Also *absol.* Now *rare*. ME. **b.** *intr.* To speak or act in contradiction or opposition; to be adverse or at variance; to conflict. Const. *with*. Now *rare* or *Obs.* late ME. **2.** *trans.* To oppose successfully; to prevent (a person, etc.) from accomplishing a purpose; to prevent the accomplishment of (a purpose); to foil, frustrate, balk, defeat 1581.

1. General laws, however well set and constituted, often t. and cross one another PALEY. **2.** Thus are all our best plans thwarted WELLINGTON. The party which had long thwarted him had been beaten down MACAULAY. Hence **Thwa·rter**, one who or that which thwarts. **Thwa·rtingly** *adv.*

Thwart-ship, thwartship (þwǭ·ɹt,ʃip), *a.* and *adv.* 1829. [f. THWART *prep.* + SHIP *sb.*] *Naut.* **A.** *adj.* Placed or fixed across the ship's length. **B.** *adv.* (þwǭ·ɹt,ʃi·p). From side to side of the ship; across the length of the ship 1882. So **Thwa·rt-shi·ps** *adv.* 1625.

Thwartwise (þwǭ·ɹtwəiz), *adv.* and *a.* 1589. [f. THWART *a.*] **A.** *adv.* Crosswise, transversely. **B.** *adj.* Situated or extending transversely; cross, transverse 1890.

Thy (ðəi), *poss. adj.* [Early ME. *þī*, reduced form of *þīn* THINE, used in ME. bef. consonants exc. *h*.] Of or belonging to thee, that thou hast.

Turn, Fortune, turn t. wheel and lower the proud TENNYSON.

Thyestean (þəi,estī·ăn, þəi,e·stiăn), *a.* 1667. [f. L. *Thyesteus*, ad. Gr. Θυέστειος (f. Θυέστης, prop. name) + -AN.] Of or belonging to Thyestes, in ancient Gr. legend brother of Atreus, who at a banquet made him eat of the flesh of his own two sons; hence *allus.*

Thyiad (þəi·i,æd), **Thyad** (þəi·æd). 1846. [a. Gr. θυιάς, stem θυιαδ- (pl. -άδες) a frenzied woman; prop. adj. fem. from verbal root θυι-, Æolic form of θυ- to rush, rage.] A Bacchante.

Thyine (þəi·in), *a.* ME. [ad. L. *thyinus*, a. Gr. θύϊνος of the tree θύα THUYA.] Epithet of a tree and its wood, mentioned in Rev. xviii. 12; supposed to be the African coniferous tree *Callitris quadrivalvis*, which yields gum sandarac.

Thylacine (þəi·lăsəin). 1838. [a. F., in mod.L. *Thylacinus*, f. Gr. θύλακος pouch + (app.) L. suffix *-inus* -INE [1].] The native Tasmanian 'wolf' or 'zebra-wolf', *Thylacinus cynocephalus*, the largest of existing carnivorous marsupials (now very scarce).

Thyme (təim). late ME. [a. F. *thym*, ad. L. *thymum*, a Gr. θύμον (θύμος), f. θύειν to burn sacrifice.] **1.** A plant of the genus *Thymus*, family *Labiatæ*, comprising shrubby herbs with fragrant aromatic leaves, found chiefly in the Mediterranean region; esp. *T. vulgaris* (Garden T.), cultivated as a pot-herb, and *T. Serpyllum* (Wild T.), occurring on dry banks and pastures in Britain and throughout Europe. **b.** With qualifying words, denoting various species or varieties. Also applied to plants of other genera, as BASIL *t.*, CAT- *thyme*, HORSE-*thyme* 1558. **2.** *Oil of t.*: a fragrant volatile oil obtained from the common thyme, used as an antiseptic 1753.

1. I knowe a banke where the wilde time blowes SHAKS. Desert Caves, With wilde T. and the Gadding Vine o'regrown MILT. **b. Creeping t., mother of t., running t.** = *wild t.*; **lemon t.**, a cultivated variety of *T. Serpyllum*, having a scent like that of lemons.

‖**Thymele** (þi·mĭlī). 1753. [a. Gr. θυμέλη altar, f. θύειν to sacrifice.] *Gr. Antiq.* The altar of Dionysus in the centre of the orchestra in an ancient Greek theatre.

Thymene (þəi·mīn). 1857. [f. THYME + -ENE.] *Chem.* A clear oily hydrocarbon, $C_{10}H_{16}$, of the terpene group, contained in the oil of thyme.

Thymic (þəi·mik), *a.*[1] 1656. [f. Gr. θύμος THYMUS + -IC.] **1.** *Anat.* and *Path.* Of, pertaining to, or connected with the thymus gland. **2.** *Phy. Chem.* In *t. acid*, $C_{16}H_{25}N_3P_2O_{12}$, a colourless acid obtained from the thymus gland. Its salts are **Thymates** (þəi·mēⁱts). 1894.

Thymic (þəi-, təi·mik), *a.*[2] 1868. [f. Gr. θύμον THYME + -IC.] *Chem.* Of, pertaining to, or derived from thyme; in *t. acid* = THYMOL.

Thymin (þəi·min). 1894. [f. THYMIC *a.*[1] + -IN [1].] *Chem.* A colourless crystalline alloxur base, $C_5H_6N_2O_2$, obtained by the action of dilute sulphuric acid on thymic acid.

Thymo-, comb. form from Gr. θύμον THYME, as in **Thy·moform** *Pharm.*, a yellowish antiseptic powder prepared from formaldehyde and thymol.

Thymol (þəi·mǫl). 1857. [f. Gr. θύμον THYME + -OL.] *Chem.* The phenol of cymene, $C_{10}H_{13}.OH$, obtained from oil of thyme, also from the volatile oil of horse-mint, crystallizing in transparent rhomboidal plates; a powerful antiseptic.

‖**Thymus** (þəi·mǒs). *Pl.* **thymi** (þəi·məi). 1693. [mod.L., a. Gr. θύμος a warty excrescence; also the thymus gland (Galen).] *Anat.* A glandular body (one of the so-called 'ductless glands') situated near the base of the neck in vertebrate animals; in man usu. disappearing after the period of childhood. **b.** Now usu. *t. gland* (rarely *body*) 1776.

Thymy (təi·mi), *a.* 1727. [f. THYME + -Y [1].] **1.** Abounding in or overgrown with thyme. **2.** Pertaining to or of the nature of thyme; *esp.* having the scent of thyme 1747.

1. Lingering about the t. promontories TENNYSON. **2.** The t. sweetness of the fell breeze 1880.

Thyro- (þəiᵊ·ro), also (more correctly but less commonly) **thyreo-** (þəiᵊ·rio), used as comb. form of THYROID, in ref. to the thyroid cartilage or the thyroid gland.

1. In ref. to the thyroid cartilage. **Thyro-aryte·noid** (ærĭtī·noid) *a.*, pertaining to or connecting the thyroid and arytenoid cartilages of the larynx. **Thy·ro-hyal** (həi·ăl) *a.* = next; usu. as *sb.* applied to the greater cornu of the hyoid bone in mammals, or to each of the long horns of the same bone in birds. **Thyro·hyoid** (həi·oid) *a.*, pertaining to or connecting the thyroid cartilage and the hyoid bone; *sb.* = thyrohyoid muscle. **Thyro·tomy** (also **thyreo-**) [Gr. τομή cutting], incision or division of the thyroid cartilage.

2. In ref. to the thyroid gland. (Often **thyreo-**.) **Thyro-antito·xin**, an antitoxin developed in thyroid poisoning; trade-name of a thyroid preparation used as a therapeutic. **Thy·rocele**, a tumour of the thyroid gland; goitre. **Thyrothe·rapy**, treatment of disease by a preparation of the thyroid glands of sheep.

Thyroid (þəiᵊ·roid), *a.* (*sb.*) 1726. [Etymologically *thyreoid*, ad. Gr. θυρεοειδής shield-shaped, f. θυρεός oblong shield + -ειδης; see -OID.] Having the form of a shield, shield-shaped. *Anat.* **a.** *T. cartilage*: the largest of the cartilages of the larynx, consisting of two broad quadrilateral plates united in front at an angle, forming the projection in front of the throat known (in men) as 'Adam's apple'; within the angle are attached the vocal chords. **b.** *T. gland* (also called *t. body*): one of the so-called 'ductless glands', a very vascular body adjacent to the larynx and upper part of the trachea in vertebrates 1726. **c.** Applied to various structures connected with the thyroid cartilage or gland, as the *t. arteries, nerves, veins*, etc. 1831. **d.** *T. foramen, membrane*: names for the obturator foramen and membrane of the hip-bone, from their shield-like shape 1890. **B.** as *sb.* **1.** Short for *t. cartilage* 1840. **2.** Short for *t. gland*; also for *t. extract* or *product* 1849. So **Thyroi·dal, Thyroi·deal, Thyroi·dean,** *adjs.* pertaining to the thyroid cartilage or gland. **Thyro·xin**, a product secreted by the thyroid gland.

Thyrse (þɔ̄rs). 1603. [a. F., ad. L. *thyrsus*, a. Gr. θύρσος stalk or stem of a plant, the Bacchic staff.] **1.** *Gr.* and *Rom. Antiq.* = THYRSUS **1. 2.** †**a.** A stem or shoot of a plant. **b.** *Bot.* = THYRSUS **2.** 1658.

Thyrsoid (þɔ̄·ɹsoid), *a.* 1829. [f. THYRSUS + -OID.] *Bot.* Of the form of, or resembling, a thyrsus or contracted panicle. So **Thyrsoi·dal** *a.*

‖**Thyrsus** (þɔ̄·ɹsǒs). *Pl.* **thyrsi** (þɔ̄·ɹsəi). 1591. [L., a. Gr. θύρσος THYRSE.] **1.** *Gr.* and *Rom. Antiq.* A staff or spear tipped with an ornament like a pine-cone, and sometimes wreathed with ivy or wine branches; borne by Dionysus (Bacchus) and his votaries. **2.** *Bot.*, etc. A form of inflorescence: a contracted kind of panicle, esp. one in which the primary branching is centripetal (racemose) and the secondary centrifugal (cymose), as in lilac and horse-chestnut 1744.

Thysanopter (þisæ̆nǫ·ptəɹ). 1864. [ad. mod.L. *Thysanoptera*, f. Gr. θύσανος tassel, fringe + πτερόν wing.] *Ent.* An insect of the order *Thysanoptera*, comprising *Thrips* and allied genera, characterized by long fringes on the wings. So **Thysano·pteran** *a.* = *thysano-*

pterous; *sb.* = *thysanopter.* **Thysano·pterous** *a.* belonging to the order *Thysanoptera.*

Thysanuran (þisăniū·răn), *a.* and *sb.* 1835. [f. mod.L. *Thysanura* (f. Gr. θύσανος + οὐρά tail) + -AN.] *Ent.* **A.** *adj.* Belonging to the *Thysanura*, a wingless order of insects, comprising springtails, bristletails, etc., having filamentous appendages at the posterior end of the body. **B.** *sb.* An insect of this order. So **Thysanu·rous** *a.* belonging to or having the characters of the *Thysanura.*

Thyself (ðəise·lf), *pron.* (In OE. *þē* 'thee' followed by the adj. *self.* From 13th c., *þi, þy, thy*, poss. adj., took the place of the pers. pron. *thee*; *self* being treated as a sb.] **I.** Emphatic uses. **1.** Accompanying the subject-pronoun *thou* (or, after a vb. in the imperative, without *thou*). **2.** By ellipsis of *thou*, used as a simple subject (with vb. usu. in 2nd person; occas. in 3rd, *self* being treated as a sb.) ME. **b.** Used as predicate, or after *as* or *than* 1535. **3.** Used instead of *thee* as object of a vb. or prep. late ME.

1. Then get thee gone, and digge my graue thy selfe SHAKS. 2. T. hast called me by my name WESLEY. b. Thou art Dromio, thou art my man, thou art thy selfe SHAKS. 3. He, whom next thy selfe Of all the world I lou'd SHAKS.

II. Reflexive uses. As direct or indirect object of a vb., or in dependence on a prep. (orig. only emphatic reflective; later in general use, taking the place of *thee* reflexive, which is more decidedly archaic.) OE.

Learn Solons saying, 'Mortall know thy selfe' 1616.

Tiar (təi·ăɹ). Chiefly *poet.* 1513. [Anglicized f. next.] **1.** = next 1. **2.** = next 2. 1616. **3.** = next 4. 1660.

Tiara (tiˌā·ră, *U.S.* təiˌē̆ə·ră). 1555. [a. L., a. Gr. τιάρα, τιάρας; origin unkn.] **1.** The raised head-dress or high-peaked cap worn by the Persians and some other eastern peoples, varying in shape according to the rank of the wearer; a kind of turban. **2.** A high ovate-cylindrical or dome-shaped diadem worn by the Pope, surmounted by the orb and cross of sovereignty, and encircled with three crowns symbolic of triple dignity, and usu. richly wrought with jewels; often called the *triple t.* or *triple crown.* Hence *transf.* the position or dignity of pope; the papacy. 1645. **3.** The head-dress of the Jewish High Priest 1868. **4.** An ornamental frontal, coronet, or head-band. (In mod. use, a jewelled or profusely decorated ornament worn by women above the forehead.) 1718. **5.** *Zool.* A mitre shell, or a genus of mitre-shells 1835.

4. *fig.* She [Venice] looks a sea Cybele..with her t. of proud towers BYRON. Hence **Tia·raed, -ra'd** (-ăd) *ppl. a.* adorned with a t.

†**Tib** (tib). 1533. [perh. the same as *Tib*, pet form of *Isabel.*] Formerly, a typical name for a woman of the lower classes, as in *T. and Tom.* Also, a girl or lass, a sweetheart, a mistress; *dyslogistically*, a strumpet, -1700.

Comb.: **t.-cat**, *dial.*, a female cat.

Tibet, Thibet (tibe·t). 1827. Name of a country in central Asia; used *attrib.* of wool obtained thence, or of cloth or garments made from this. *absol.* Tibet cloth, or a gown or shawl made of it. Hence **Tibetan** (tibe·tăn) *a.* of, belonging to, or characteristic of T.

‖**Tibia** (ti·biă) *Pl.* **-æ** (*i*). 1548. [L., shin-bone, pipe or flute.] **1.** *Anat.* and *Zool.* The inner and usu. larger of the two bones (*tibia* and *fibula*) of the lower leg, from the knee to the ankle; the shin-bone. **b.** *Ent.* The fourth of the five joints of the leg of an insect, that between the femur and the tarsus 1815. **2.** *Antiq.* An ancient (single or double) flute or flageolet 1705.

Tibial (ti·biăl), *a.* (*sb.*) 1599. [ad. L. *tibialis*; see prec. and -AL.] **1.** *Anat.* and *Zool.* Of or pertaining to the tibia. Also as *sb.*, ellipt. for *t. artery, muscle*, etc. **2.** Of or pertaining to a tibia or ancient flute 1656.

Tibio- (tibio), used as comb. form of TIBIA, as in **Tibiota·rsal** *a.*, of or pertaining to the tibia and the tarsus; pertaining to the tibiotarsus; **Tibiota·rsus**, *Ornith.* the tibia of a bird's leg with the condyles formed by its fusion with the proximal bones of the tarsus.

Tiburtine (təi·bɒɹtəin), *a.* 1440. [ad. L. *Tiburtinus*, f. *Tiburs, Tiburtem*, adj., of Tibur.] Of or pertaining to the region or district of Tibur (now Tivoli) in ancient Latium. *T. stone* = TRAVERTINE.

Tic (tik). 1800. [a. F. Origin uncertain.] **1.** A disease or affection characterized by spasmodic twitching of certain muscles, esp. of the face; nearly always short for *tic douloureux*: see 2. 1822. **2.** *Tic douloureux* (dulurö) [F., = painful twitching], severe facial neuralgia with twitching of the facial muscles 1800.

‖**Tical** (*in Siam* tikā·l. *in Burma* ti·k'l). 1662. [repr., through Pg. *tical*, the Indian *ṭaṅkā*, also *ṭakā.*] A term in use by foreign traders in Siam and Burma, applied to a silver coin and its weight, repr. roughly the Indian rupee (orig. the same as the *ṭaṅkā*), which has varied in value from 2*s.* 6*d.* to 1*s.* 2*d.*

‖**Ticca** (ti·kă, tī·kă). *India.* 1827. [ad. Hindi *ṭhīkā* or *ṭhikah* hire, fare, fixed price (Yule).] *attrib.* Engaged on contract, hired; esp. in *t. gharry*, hired carriage.

Tice (təis), *sb.* 1874. [f. next.] An act of enticing, an enticement; *spec.* a stroke at croquet, or 'ball' (bowled) at cricket, which tempts or entices the opponent to take aim.

Tice (təis), *v.* *Obs.* exc. *dial.* ME. [aphet. form of *atise* ATTICE or ENTICE.] *trans.* To entice; to induce or attract by the offer of pleasure or advantage. Also *absol.*

Tichorhine (təi·kərəin), *a.* Also **-orrhine, -orine.** 1851. [ad. mod.L. *tichorrhinus*, f. Gr. τεῖχος wall + ῥίς (ῥιν-) nose.] *Palæont.* Having an ossified nasal septum; the English form of the specific name of the Woolly Rhinoceros.

Tick (tik), *sb.*[1] [OE. **tica*, ME. *teke, tyke, tycke, tick.*; ult. etym. obsc.] **1.** The common name for several kinds of mites or acarids, esp. of the genus *Ixodes* or family *Ixodidæ*, which infest the hair or fur of various animals, as dogs, cattle, etc., and attach themselves to the skin as temporary parasites; also, for the similarly parasitic dipterous insects of the families *Hippoboscidæ* (bird-ticks, horse-ticks, sheep-ticks) and *Nycteribiidæ* (bat-ticks). **2.** Short for *t.-bean* 1765.

Comb.: **t.-bean**, a small-seeded variety of the common bean, *Vicia Faba*, so called from the resemblance of the seed to a dog-t.; **-bird**, any bird, e.g. the African *Buphaga* (rhinoceros-bird), which feeds on the ticks that infest large quadrupeds; **-fly**, any of the dipterous insects called ticks (see 1); **-seed**, name for various plants having seeds resembling ticks; **-trefoil**, a plant of the genus *Desmodium*, so named from the joints of the pods adhering like ticks to the fur of animals.

Tick (tik), *sb.*[2] 1466. [Ult. ad. L. *teca, theca*, a. Gr. θήκη case.] The case or cover containing feathers, flocks, or the like, forming a mattress or pillow; also, applied to the strong hard linen or cotton material used for making such cases.

Tick (tik), *sb.*[3] 1440. [perh. onomatopœic; cf. Du. *tik* pat, touch, tick, *tikken* to pat, tick, LG. *tikk* a touch, etc.] **1.** A light but distinct touch; a pat, a tap. *Obs.* exc. *dial.* **b.** = TIG *sb.*[1] 2. (*rare*) 1622. **2.** A quick light dry sound, distinct but not loud; *esp.* the sound produced by the alternate check and release of the train in the escapement of a watch or clock; also the similar sound made by the death-watch beetle 1680. **b.** A beat of the heart or of the pulse 1823. **3.** A small dot or dash (often formed by two strokes at an acute angle) made with a pen or pencil, to draw attention to something or to mark a name, figure, etc., in a list as having been noted or checked 1844. **4.** *transf.* (from 2). The time between two ticks of the clock; a moment, second, instant. *colloq.* 1879.

4. It's all right. Can explain in two ticks 1904.

Tick, *sb.*[4] *colloq.* or *slang.* 1642. [app. abbrev. of TICKET in the phr. *on the ticket.*] **1.** Phr. *On* or *upon* (†*the*) *t.*, on credit, on trust; *to go on t.* (also *go t.*), *run on, upon t.*, to buy on credit, run into debt. **2.** Hence, credit, trust; reputation of solvency and probity 1668. **3.** A debit account; a score, reckoning 1681.

1. This villainous habit of living upon t. STEVENSON. 3. He..had a long t. at the tavern 1755.

Tick (tik), *v.*[1] 1546. [f. TICK *sb.*[3]] **1.** *intr.* To touch or tap a thing or person lightly. *Obs.* exc. *dial.* **2.** Of a clock, watch, etc.: To make the light quick sound described under TICK *sb.*[3] 2. 1721. **b.** *trans.* With complement: To wear *away* or *out*, bring to an end, in ticking; to throw *off* or deliver by ticking 1870. **3.** To mark (a name, an item in a list, etc.) with a tick; to mark *off* with a tick, as noted, passed, or done with 1861. **b.** *slang. To t. off*, to reprimand, scold, 'tell off' 1919.

1. Stand not ticking and toying at the braunches.. but strike at the roote LATIMER. 3. I compared each with the bill, and ticked it off DICKENS.

Tick (tik), *v.*[2] *colloq.* or *slang.* 1648. [f. TICK *sb.*[4]] **1.** *intr.* To 'go on tick' (see TICK *sb.*[4] 1); to deal with a tradesman, or the like on credit; to run into debt. **b.** *trans.* To leave (an amount) owing to be entered to one's debit 1674. **2.** *intr.* To give credit 1712. **b.** *trans.* To give (a person) credit 1842.

Ticken (ti·k'n). 1701. Local f. TICKING.

Ticker (ti·kəɹ). 1828. [f. TICK *v.*[1] + -ER [1].] Something that ticks. **a.** The pendulum or escapement of a clock or watch; also (*slang*) a watch. **b.** A telegraphic recording instrument, a tape-machine; a stock-indicator 1883.

Ticket (ti·kėt), *sb.* 1528. [In 16th c. *tiket*, aphet. f. **etiket*, a. obs. F. *etiquet*, or the parallel F. *étiquette*:—OF. *estiquet(te*, f. *estiquer* to stick, fix, from Teut.; ad. OLG. *stekan* to stick, fix.] †**1.** A short written notice or document; a memorandum, a note, a billet. *Obs.* exc. as in b, c. -1760. **b.** *spec.* A written tender for ore, made by the smelter (*local*) 1778. **c.** *Stock Exch.* see quot. 1882. **2.** A written notice for public information; formerly, a notice posted in a public place, a placard; now *esp.* a slip of cardboard, etc. attached to an object and bearing its name, description, price, or the like; a label, show-card 1567. **3.** A visiting-card. Now *Obs.* or *dial.*; also *Anglo-Ind.* 1673. †**4.** A certificate or voucher; a warrant, licence, permit -1675. **5.** A slip, usu. of paper or cardboard, bearing the evidence of the holder's title to some service or privilege, to which it admits him; as a *railway, tram* or *bus t., lottery-t., member's t., luncheon-t., soup-t.*, etc. 1673. **6.** A pay-warrant; *esp.* a discharge warrant in which the amount of pay due to a soldier or sailor is certified 1596. **b.** Short for TICKET OF LEAVE 1904. †**7.** An I O U; a promise to pay; a note or memorandum of money or goods received on credit; a debit account, a score; hence phr. *on, upon* (*the*) *t.*, on credit, on TICK -1656. **8.** In U.S. politics, the list of candidates for election nominated or put forward by a party or faction 1711. **9.** *slang.* **a.** The correct thing; what is wanted, expected, or fashionable; esp. in phr. *that's the t.* 1838. **b.** The program or plan of action; that which is to be done; the thing on hand 1842.

1. c. *T. Day*, The day for the passing of tickets between brokers and jobbers, by means of which they learn the amount of stocks and shares they have respectively to deliver or receive on the day following 1882. 2. The t. in the window which announced 'Apartments to Let' THACKERAY. 5. *fig.* Your Approbation is the T. by which they gain Admittance into your Paper STEELE. 8. According to circumstances a man is said to vote the *straight t.*, i. e. the t. containing the 'regular nomination' of his party without change; a *scratch t*, a t. from which the names of one or more of the candidates are erased; a *split t.*, a t. representing different divisions of his party; or a *mixed t.*, a t. in which the nominations of different parties are blended into one 1859.

Comb.: **t.-day** (see quot., sense 1 c); **-porter**, a member of a body of porters in the City of London who were licensed by the Corporation (now *Hist.*).

Ticket (ti·kėt), *v.* 1611. [f. prec.] **1.** *trans.* To attach a ticket to; to distinguish by means of a ticket; to label. Chiefly in *pa. pple.* **b.** *fig.* To describe or mark as by a ticket; to designate, set down (*as* so and so) 1654. **2.** To furnish with a ticket; to 'book'; also *absol.*, to issue tickets. *U.S.* 1842. **3.** *intr.* To make a tender *for* tin or copper ore by means of a 'ticket' or written tender (*local*) 1778.

1. Pictures which are sold during the exhibition will be ticketed as such 1810. 2. We were 'ticketed through to the depot LONGF.

Ticket of leave. 1732. A ticket or document giving leave or permission; an order, a permit (*rare*). Now, 'an order of licence' giving a convict his liberty under certain restrictions before his sentence has expired. Also *attrib.*, as *ticket-of-leave man*, etc.

Ticking (ti·kiŋ). 1649. [f. TICK *sb.*^{2} + -ING^{1}.] The material of which bed-ticks are made; see TICK *sb.*^{2}

Tickle (ti·k'l), *sb.*^{1} 1770. [Origin obsc.] A name given on the coasts of Newfoundland and Labrador to a narrow difficult strait or passage.

Tickle (ti·k'l), *sb.*^{2} 1801. [f. TICKLE *v.*] An act of tickling; a touch that tickles; a tickling sensation; a tickled or pleasantly excited feeling.

Tickle (ti·k'l), *a.* (*adv.*) late ME. [Related to next.] †1. Easily affected in any way; not firm or steadfast; loose; also, susceptible to tickling –1563. **2.** Not to be depended upon; uncertain; unreliable; changeable, capricious, fickle. Now *dial.* late ME. **3.** In unstable equilibrium, easily upset or overthrown, insecure, tottering, crazy; also, easily set in motion; nicely poised; delicate, sensitive. Now *dial.* 1515. **b.** *transf.* Of a place, condition, etc.: Insecure; precarious; risky. *Obs.* or *arch.* 1579. **4.** = TICKLISH *a.* 5. Now *dial.* 1569. **b.** Fastidious, dainty, squeamish; easily upset or disordered. Now *dial.* 1456. **c.** Difficult to deal with 1570. **d.** Of an animal: Easily scared; shy, wild. *dial.* 1876.

2. This world is now ful tikel sikerly CHAUCER. 3. *T. of the sear*: see SEAR *sb.* b. Footing..still more t., and unsafe COTTON. 4. Tell wit how much it wrangles In t. points of niceness RALEIGH. Hence †**Ti·ckle-ly** *adv.* (*rare*), **-ness.**

Tickle (ti·k'l), *v.* ME. [Origin obsc.] **I.** *intr.* †1. To be affected or excited by a pleasantly tingling or thrilling sensation: said of the heart, lungs, blood, 'spirits', etc., also of the person –1647. **2.** To tingle; to itch; also *fig.* (*dial.*) to have an uneasy desire (usu. *to do* something); to be eager. Now *rare.* 1542.

1. Oh, how my lungs do t.! ha, ha, ha! FLETCHER. 2. Whose eares euer tickled to heare newes 1557.

II. *trans.* (= L. *titillare*). **1.** Said of a thing, or impersonally with *it*: To excite agreeably (a person, his ears, palate, etc.); to please, gratify. late ME. **2.** To touch or stroke lightly with or as with the finger-tips, a straw, a feather, a hair, or the like; to irritate lightly, so as to cause a peculiar uneasy sensation. Also *absol.* 1450. **b.** To touch or poke (a person) lightly in a sensitive part so as to excite spasmodic laughter. Also *absol.* 1530. **c.** Applied to a method of catching trout or other fish: see TICKLING *vbl. sb.* b. Often *allus.* 1601. **3.** *fig.* To excite amusement in; to divert; often in the phr. *to t. the fancy.* Also *absol.* 1688. **4.** To touch (a stringed instrument, etc.) lightly; to stir (a fire, etc.) slightly 1589. **b.** *iron.* To beat, chastise 1592. †**5.** To excite, affect, move; also, to vex, irritate, provoke –1698. †**b.** To arouse by or as by tickling; to stir up, incite, provoke; to prompt or impel *to do* something –1592. **c.** With *up*: To stir up, arouse by tickling, excite to action 1567. **d.** To get or move (a thing) *into* or *out of* some place, position, or state, by action likened to tickling 1677.

1. Elements that..tickled..curiosity GEO. ELIOT. Phr. *To t. to death*, to divert greatly. 2. If my haire do but t. me, I must scratch SHAKS. b. If you t. vs, doe we not laugh? SHAKS. Phr. *To t. (a person's) palm*, to tip him. c. *Twel. N.* II. v. 26. 4. To t. a Cittern, or have a sweete stroke on the Lute NASHE. b. These little rogues..should be well tickled with the birch 1800. 5. Shee's tickled now, her Fume needs no spurres SHAKS.

Comb.: †**t.-brain**, potent liquor; hence *transf.* one who supplies it; †**-toby**, a birch, rod, switch.

Ticklenburgs (ti·klənbɒ̄ɪgz), *sb. pl.* 1696. [f. *Tecklenburg*, Westphalia, noted for its manufactures of linen.] A coarse mixed linen fabric made for the West India market.

Tickler (ti·klər). 1680. [f. TICKLE *v.* + -ER^{1}.] One who or that which tickles, in various senses. **1.** One who tickles by touching or stroking lightly 1715. **2.** Something that tickles or is used for tickling; e. g. an instrument for extracting bungs from casks; a rod or birch used in castigation; a slender steel rod used for stirring the fire; an implement for tickling a person, with the purpose of irritating or teasing; (*U.S.*) a book in which a register of notes or debts is kept for reference 1680. **3.** *U.S.* A large Amer. longicorn beetle, *Monohammus titillator*, with very long antennæ 1841.

Tickling (ti·kliŋ), *vbl. sb.* late ME. [f. TICKLE *v.* + -ING^{1}.] The action or condition denoted by TICKLE *v.*; slight nervous irritation akin to itching; uneasy desire, hankering, craving; pleasing excitement, gratification; etc. **b.** *spec.* The taking of trout, etc., by the method described in the quot. 1616.

Women haue in them selues a t. and studie of vaine glorie KNOX. He had some t. in his throat 1898. b. Groping for trout (or tickling) — is tracing it to the stone it lies under, then rubbing it gently beneath, which causes the fish to gradually move backwards into the hand, till the fingers suddenly close in the gills JEFFERIES.

Ticklish (ti·kliʃ), *a.* 1581. [f. TICKLE *a.* or *v.* + -ISH^{1}.] **1.** Easily tickled; sensitive to tickling 1598. **2.** Unstably balanced or poised; easily upset; unsteady; of a boat, easily capsized 1601. **3.** *fig.* Easily upset in temper; apt to be offended, sensitive, touchy 1581. **4.** Unstable, unsteady, unsettled, uncertain, fickle 1606. **5.** Needing cautious handling or action; delicate, precarious, risky, hazardous 1591. **6.** quasi-*adv.* Ticklishly. Now *rare.* 1661.

1. Some part of the skin is..thin, as in the..soales of the feete, which is the reason that there men are t. 1615. 2. So t. are the scales of victory, a very mote will turn them FULLER. 3. You are t. on such points BYRON. 4. But foreign friendship is t., temporary, and lasteth no longer than it is advantaged with mutual interest FULLER. 5. A very t. predicament 1809. Hence **Ti·cklish-ly** *adv.*, **-ness.**

Tickly (ti·kli), *a.* 1530. [f. TICKLE *a.* + -Y^{1}.] Ticklish.

Tick-tack (ti·kˌtæ·k). 1549. [Echoic.] **1.** An imitation of a reduplicated or alternating ticking sound, esp. that made by a clock; also that of the firing of small artillery. (Used as *adv.* or *int.*, and hence as *sb.* to denote the sound.) **b.** (usu. in Fr. form *tic-tac.*) In auscultation, the sound of the heart-beat 1853. †**2.** An old variety of backgammon, played on a board with holes along the edge, in which pegs were placed for scoring. (Also called TRIC-TRAC.) –1740. **3.** A system of signalling used by bookmakers, hence the men who practise this 1899. **4. Tick-tack-toe,** a children's game played with a pencil on a slate 1884. Hence **Tick-tack** *v.* to signal (cf. 3 above).

Tick-tick (ti·kˌti·k). 1774. An imitation of the ticking of a clock or watch, or a similar sound; hence, a child's name for a clock or watch. Also **Ti·ck-to·ck** 1848.

‖**Tic-polonga** (tikˌpǫlǫ·ŋgā). 1825. [ad. Sinhalese *tit-polongā*, f. *tita*, in comb. *tit-* speck, freckle, spot, mark + *polongā* viper. *Tik* spot, freckle, etc. has app. been substituted for *tit-*.] *Zool.* A venomous snake of India and Ceylon; the chain viper or necklace-snake, *Daboia Russellii.*

Tidal (təi·dăl), *a.* 1807. [f. TIDE *sb.* II. + -AL.] **1.** Of, pertaining to, or affected by tides; ebbing and flowing periodically. **b.** *T. wave*: the high water wave caused by the movement of the tide; *erron.* an exceptionally large ocean wave caused by an earthquake or other local commotion 1830. (*b*) *fig.* A great progressive movement or manifestation of feeling, opinion, or the like 1884. (*c*) *Physiol.* The main or primary height of flow in a beat of the pulse 1896. **2.** *transf.* and *fig.* That 'ebbs and flows'; periodic, intermittent; alternating, varying 1872. **3.** Dependent upon or regulated by the state of the tide or time of high water 1858.

1. *T. river*, a river which is affected by the tides for some distance from its mouth; Up to Teddington.. the Thames is a t. river HUXLEY. 2. *T. air* (*Physiol.*), the air passing in and out of the lungs at each ordinary respiration. 3. *T. basin, harbour*, a basin or harbour which is accessible or navigable only at high tide. *T. boat, steamer*, a vessel the sailings of which depend on the time of the tide. *T. train*, a train running in connexion with a t. steamer. Hence **Ti·dally** *adv.* in a t. manner; by or in respect of the tides.

Tiddle (ti·d'l), *v.* *Obs.* exc. *dial.* or *slang.* 1560. [Origin obsc.] **1.** *trans.* To fondle or indulge to excess; to tend carefully, nurse, cherish. **2.** *intr.* To potter, trifle, 'fiddle'; to fidget, fuss 1747.

Ti·ddler. 1885. [Origin obsc.] Nursery name for a small minnow or a stickleback.

Tiddlywink (ti·dliwiŋk). 1870. [Origin obsc.] **a.** A game played with dominoes. **b.** *pl.* A game in which small counters are caused to spring from the table into a receptacle, by pressing upon their edges with larger counters.

Tide (təid), *sb.* [OE. *tīd* :—OTeut. **tīdiz*, referred by some to a root **tī-* to extend.] **I.** Time. †**1.** A portion, extent, or space of time; an age, a season, a while –1871. **2.** A point in the duration of the day, month, or year, of human life, or of other period. *arch.* or *poet.* OE. **b.** A suitable, favourable, or proper time or occasion; opportunity. *arch.* OE. **3.** Any definite time in the course of the day; *Obs.* exc. as EVENTIDE, NOON-TIDE OE. **b.** A more or less definite point or season in the course of the year, of life, etc.; as *New-Year's tide*, SPRING-TIDE, etc. *arch.* or *poet.* OE. **4.** An anniversary or festival of the church. See EASTER-TIDE, LAMMAS-TIDE, WHITSUNTIDE, etc. OE.

2. He, who, from ill death Saved me that t. MORRIS. 3. b. High over all the yellowing Autumn-tide TENNYSON. 4. What hath this day deseru'd..That it..should be set Among the high tides in the Kalendar? SHAKS.

II. Tide of the sea. [prob. ad. MLG. *getīde.*] **1.** The flowing or swelling of the sea, or its alternate rising and falling, twice in each lunar day, due to the attraction of the moon and, in a less degree, of the sun; the alternate inflow and outflow produced by this on a coast, the flood and ebb. late ME. **b.** *transf.* A recurrent flow, alternate rise and fall or increase and decrease, other than of the sea 1604. **2.** The space of time between two successive points of high water, or between low water and high water, in the sea; also, that portion of this time during which the height of the water ('state of the tide') allows of work being done, as in *tide's work.* So, in *Mining* a period of twelve hours. 1495. **3.** *fig.* Applied to that which is like the tide of the sea in some way; as in ebbing or flowing, rising or falling, or 'turning' at a certain time. late ME. **4.** *spec.* = FLOOD-TIDE. Also *fig.* 1570. **5.** *transf.* A body of flowing water or other liquid; a stream, a current. *poet.* and *rhet.* 1585. **b.** *transf.* and *fig.* 1601. **6.** The water of the sea; the sea (esp. when the tide is flowing). *poet.* 1791.

1. Both winde and t. stayes for this Gentleman SHAKS. Phr. **Cross t.**, a tide running across the direction of another; **high t.**, (*a*) = HIGH WATER; (*b*) = SPRING TIDE; **low t.** = LOW WATER; **leeward, neap, windward t.**: see the defining words; also FLOOD-TIDE, SPRING-TIDE. b. Swayed by the sweeping of the tides of air 1856. 2. *Tide's work*, the amount of progress a ship has made during a favourable t. Also, a period of necessary labour on a ship during the ebbing and slack water of a t. 1867. 3. *Jul. C.* IV. iii. 218. From that moment the t. of battle turned MACAULAY. 4. I haue important businesse The t. whereof is now SHAKS. 5. Deep in the roaring t. he plung'd GRAY. b. Thou art the Ruines of the Noblest man That euer liued in the T. of Times SHAKS. b. Bounding o'er yon blue t. BYRON.

Phrases. †*T. and (or) time* (also *time and t.*), an alliterative reduplication, in which the two words were more or less synonyms, or = time and (or) season. *Time and t. wait for no man* (here *tide* orig. meant 'time', but from the 16th c. has usually meant the tide of the sea). (*In*) *double tides*, perh. = as if taking advantage of both the tides in one day; esp. *to work double tides*, to work as hard as possible.

Comb.: **t.-boat**, a boat or small vessel which travels with or by means of the t.; **-gate**, a gate through which the water passes into a dock or the like at flood t., and by which it is retained during the ebb; **-lock**, a double lock between tidal water and a canal or the like; a guard-lock; **-river**, a tidal river; **-rode** *a.*, *Naut.* (for *tide-ridden*), swung by the tide, as a ship at anchor; opp. to *wind-rode*; **-surveyor**, a customs official who supervised the t.-waiters; **-table**, a table, or tabular list showing the times of high water at a place or places during some period; **-wave**, the undulation which passes over the surface of the ocean, and causes high or low tide as its highest or lowest point reaches any place; **-work**, work which can be carried on only during hours when the tide is low, or that is paid for by the tide.

Tide (təid), *v.*^{1} [OE. *tīdan* (oftener *getīdan*) to happen, come about, f. *tīd* TIDE *sb.*] *intr.* To happen, befall. Often impersonal. *arch.*

Tide (təid), *v.*^{2} 1593. [f. TIDE *sb.* II.] **I.** *trans.* **a.** To carry, as the tide does 1640. **b.** To enable (a person) to surmount (a difficulty) as on a swelling tide 1860. **2.** *intr.* To flow or surge, as does the tide; to flow to and fro; sometimes = 'flow' as opp. to 'ebb' 1593. **3.** To float or drift on the tide; *spec. Naut.* to navigate a ship by taking advantage of favouring tides, and anchoring when the tide turns;

usu. with adv. of direction. Often *to t. it.* 1627. **b.** *fig.* To pass or be carried as on the tide; to drift 1835. **4.** *intr. fig. To t. over*: To get over or surmount (a difficulty, etc.) as if by rising on the flowing tide, or by taking advantage of a favourable tide 1659.

1. The Relicks of the Wrack..are tided back By the wild Waves, and rudely thrown ashore DRYDEN. 2. The seas, Whose equal valour neither ebbs nor tides 1661. 3. Hither there tided The loose-limbed Briton 1896. 4. For the moment the difficulty is tided over 1884.

Tideless (təi·dlės), *a.* 1779. [f. TIDE *sb.* + -LESS.] Having no tide; unaffected by tides; not washed or covered by a tide.

The waters of the t. Mediterranean 1886. Hence **Ti·delessness.**

Tideling, -lynge, var. TIDLING.

Ti·de-mark. 1799. The mark left or reached by the tide at high or (rarely) low water; by extension, the mark left by a river-flood. Also, a post or the like set up to mark the rise or fall of, or the point reached by the tide.

Ti·de-mill. 1796. **1.** A mill driven by the flux and reflux of the tide acting on a water-wheel. **2.** A mill for clearing lands from tide-water 1828.

Ti·de-rip. 1830. [RIP *sb.*³ 1.] **1.** A commotion of the sea caused by opposing currents, or by a rapid current passing over an uneven bottom. **2.** A tidal wave or current 1903.

Tidesman (təi·dzmæn). 1667. †**1.** = TIDE-WAITER 1. -1809. **2.** One whose work depends on the tide 1882.

Ti·de-wai:ter. 1699. **1.** A customs officer who awaited the arrival of ships (formerly coming in with the tide), and boarded them to prevent the evasion of custom-house regulations. Now *Hist.* **2.** *fig.* One who waits for a favourable season 1841.

Ti·de-wa:ter. 1799. **1.** Water brought by the flood-tide. **2.** *U.S.* Water affected by the ordinary ebb and flow of the tide; tidal water 1789. **b.** *attrib.* as *t.-w. country* 1829.

Tideway (təi·d,wei). 1627. A channel in which a tidal current runs; also, the tidal part of a river; *transf.* a strong current running in such a channel.

Ti·dily, *adv.* ME. [-LY ².] In a tidy manner. So **Ti·diness,** the quality of being tidy.

Tiding (təi·diŋ); pl. **tidings** (təi·diŋz). [Late OE. *tīdung*, early ME. *tiding*, as if f. OE. *tīdan* to happen, befall + -ING ¹; but prob. ad. ON. *tíðendi, -indi* events, occurrences, the reports of these, f. *tíðr* occurring + *-endi, -indi* nominal suffix.] **1.** Something that happens; an event, incident, occurrence. *Obs.* or *arch.* **2.** The announcement of an event or occurrence; a piece of news (*obs.* or *arch.*); usu. in pl. *tidings*, reports, news, intelligence, information OE.

1. How that this blisful tidyng is bifalle CHAUCER. 2. To me þis is a Ioyfull tydyng 1485. Her Son.. left at Jordan, tydings of him none MILT. The tidings was world-old, or older CARLYLE.

Tidling (ti·dliŋ). Now *dial.* (**tiddling**). 1520. [?f. TIDDLE *v.* 1: see -LING ¹.] A child or animal reared with special care; a pampered pet.

Tidy (təi·di), *a.* (*sb.*, *adv.*) [ME., f. *tīd* TIDE + -Y ¹.] †**1.** Timely, seasonable, opportune; in season -1721. **2.** In good condition, or of good appearance; fair, well-favoured; fat, plump, healthy. Now *dial.* ME. **3.** As an indefinite epithet of admiration or commendation. †**a.** Good, excellent, satisfactory, useful -1625. **b.** Fairly satisfactory, 'pretty good'; decent; 'nice' (*colloq.*) 1844. **c.** Considerable (in amount or degree); 'pretty big'. *colloq.* 1838. **4. a.** Of persons: Orderly in habits, or in personal appearance; disposed to keep things neat and in order 1706. **b.** Of things, esp. of a house, room, receptacle, etc.: Neatly arranged; orderly, neat, trim 1828.

2. Thou whorson little tydie Bartholmew Bore-pigge SHAKS. A t. girl 1881. 3. b. He was a t. chap, though queer 1899. c. They do swear a t. bit 1903. c. *A t. penny* = 'a pretty penny' (PRETTY *a.* 5). 4. a. A t. Servant 1706. The tidiest woman in the world 1849.

B. *sb.* **a.** A pinafore or overall. *dial.* 1825. **b.** *U.S.* An ornamental loose covering for the back of a chair or the like; an antimacassar 1850. **c.** A bag in which to keep scraps, odds and ends, etc.; a work-bag, toilet-tidy, hair-tidy 1828. **C.** *adv.* Tidily; pretty well; nicely, finely; also *iron.*, *dial.*, or *vulgar.* 1824.

Ti·dy, *v.* Chiefly *colloq.* 1821. [f. TIDY *a.*] *trans.* To make tidy or orderly; to arrange neatly; *refl.* to put one's hair, dress, etc. in order; to make oneself neat. Often with *up*. Also *absol.* **b.** To stow *away* or clear *up* for the sake of tidiness 1867.

b. It..had been 'tidied up' by one of those..housemaids who are the bane of every busy man 1884.

Tie (təi), *sb.* [OE. *teáh, téag* :—OTeut. **taugō, -ā*, f. second grade of the vb. stem **teuh-, tauh-, tuh-*: see TEE *v.*¹] **1.** That with which anything is tied; *esp.* an ornamental knot or bow of ribbon, etc. **2.** *Naut.* **a.** A rope or chain by which a yard is suspended 1465. **b.** A mooring-bridle 1867. †**3.** A knot of hair; a pig-tail; also short for TIE-WIG -1817. **4.** A neck-tie, a cravat. Also, a woman's fur necklet. 1761. **5.** A kind of low shoe fastened with a tie or lace 1826. **6.** *gen.* Something that connects or unites two or more things in some way; a link 1711. **b.** *Mus.* A curved line placed over or under two notes of the same pitch, to indicate that the sound is to be sustained (not repeated) 1656. **7.** *Arch.*, etc. A beam or rod used to 'tie' or bind together two parts of a building or other structure by counteracting a tensile strain which tends to draw them apart 1793. **b.** *U.S.* A (transverse) railway sleeper 1857. **8.** *fig.* Something that ties or binds in an abstract or fig. sense 1555. **9.** The fact or method of tying; the condition of being tied, bound, or united 1718. **10.** Equality between two or more competitors or the sides in a match or contest; a match in which this occurs, a drawn match; a dead heat. Hence, *to play off, shoot off*, etc. *a tie*, to determine a tie by playing another match 1680. Hence **b.** A deciding match played after a draw; also, a match played between the victors in previous matches or heats 1895.

1. Great formal wigs, with a t. behind DICKENS. 4. He'll come down to dinner in a flannel shirt and no t. 1895. 8. They haue charitie in such sure t. that they cannot lose it LATIMER. I was..under tye of Secrecy 1641. Bound..by..the Ties of Moral Duty 1754. The ties of a common blood, and a common speech 1874. 10. b. *Cup.-t.*, a match between two sides in a knock-out competition for a cup.

Tie (təi), *v.* Infl. **tied, tying.** [OE. *tīgan* :—**tēagjan* to bind, f. *téag* TIE *sb.*] **1.** *trans.* To bind, fasten, make fast (one thing to another, or two or more things together) with a cord, rope, band, or the like, drawn together and knotted; to confine (a person or animal) by fastening to something. **b.** To draw together the parts of (a single thing) with a knotted cord or the like; to fasten (a part of dress, etc.) in this way, esp. with strings already attached to it (as a bonnet, a shoe); also, to draw together (a cord or the like) into a knot, esp. for the purpose of fastening something. late ME. **c.** *Surg.* To bind and constrict (an artery or vein) with a ligature, so as to prevent the flow of blood through it 1597. **d.** To make or form by tying (a knot, etc.) 1647. **2.** To fasten together, connect, join (material things) in any way; *spec.* in *Arch.* to connect and make fast by a rod or beam, or by other means 1585. **b.** To check the free movement or working of 1597. **c.** *Mus.* To connect (notes) by a tie or ligature 1597. **d.** *U.S.* To furnish (a railway line) with 'ties' or sleepers 1883. **3.** *fig.* To join closely or firmly; *esp.* to unite in marriage (now *dial.*) OE. **b.** *intr.* for *refl.* To attach oneself *to*. *U.S. colloq.* 1879. **4.** To bind, oblige, restrain, constrain *to* (also *from*) some course of action, etc.; to limit, confine, restrict ME. **b.** To bind, oblige (*to do* something): usu. in *pass.* Now only *dial.* 1596. †**c.** To bring into bondage -1613. **d.** To bind by favour or service rendered: usu. in *pass.* 1576. **e.** To restrict (a dealer or firm) to a particular source for articles sold; only in *pa. pple.*, usu. applied to a public house so restricted as to liquor 1817. †**5.** *fig.* To confirm, ratify; to 'knit', 'cement' -1697. **6.** *intr.* To be equal (*with*) in a contest, etc. 1680.

1. Such bells were also tyed to Hawks 1816. Phr. *Ride and t.*: see RIDE *v.* Phr. *To t. the hands of*, to deprive of freedom of action. *Tied to* a woman's *apron-strings*: see APRON-STRING. b. They tye their Garments about with a Girdle 1662. d. *To t. the knot*, to perform the ceremony of marriage. 3. How could you think of tying yourself to such a family? DE FOE. 4. Phr. *To be tied to* (or *for*) *time*, to be limited to a certain time for doing something. b. *Tam. Shr.* I. i. 217. c. *Hen. VIII*, IV. ii. 36. d. *Cymb.* I. vi. 23.

With advbs. **Tie down. a.** To fasten down or confine by tying. **b.** *fig.* To confine stringently (*to* some thing or action). **T. up. a.** *trans.* To fasten (a thing) with a cord or band tied round it; to bind up, wrap up. **b.** To tie (a person or animal) to some fixed object or in some confined space, so as to prevent from escaping. **c.** *fig.* To bind, restrain, or confine strictly; to oblige to act in a particular way. **d.** To moor (a ship or boat); also *absol.* or *intr.* for *pass.* **e.** *fig.* To invest or place (money or property) in such a way as to prevent it from being spent or alienated. **f.** To join in marriage (*colloq.* or *slang*). **g.** To associate oneself *with* (orig. *U.S.*).

Tie- in comb. [f. TIE *sb.* or *v.*]

1. attrib. or obj. combs. of TIE *sb.*; **tie-block** *Naut.*, the block on the yard through which the tie passes (see TIE *sb.* 2 a); **-maker**; **-pin**, a pin., usu. ornamental, worn in a neck-tie; **-shooting**, the shooting off of a tie (TIE *sb.* 10) in rifle practice.

2. *Comb.* with sbs., in which the first element may be either TIE *sb.* or *v.*: **tie·-bar**, a bar which ties or acts as a tie, in a building, etc.; **-beam**, a horizontal beam which acts as a tie; **-bolt** *sb.*, a bolt which ties together the component parts of a structure; hence as *vb.*; †**-dog**, a dog kept tied or chained up, either to guard a house, or because of its fierceness; **-knot**, a knot with which something is tied; **-post**, a post to which a horse, etc. may be tied; **-rod**, a long tie-bolt or iron rod which acts as a tie in a building, etc.; **-string**, a string for tying something, e. g. a bonnet or other part of costume; **-vote**, a vote resulting in a tie, the numbers on each side being equal.

Tier (tīᵊɹ). 1569. [orig. *tire*, a. F. *tire*, f. *tirer* to draw, elongate.] **1.** A row, rank, range, course; usu. one of a series of rows placed one above another, or rising each above the preceding one. **b.** A row of guns or gun-ports in a man-of-war or a fort 1573. **c.** A rank of pipes in an organ controlled by one stop 1828. **d.** *transf.* and *fig.* Rank, grade; stratum 1590. **2.** *Naut.* **a.** A row of ships moored or anchored at a particular place; hence, an anchorage or mooring-place where ships lie in rows or columns 1732. **b.** A large rack, in which the cables, anchor gear, runners and tackles, etc. are stowed 1797.

1. e. *U.S.* A range of counties, etc. 1693.

Tier (təi·əɹ). Also **tyer.** 1633. [f. TIE *v.* + -ER ¹.] **1.** One who ties; *spec.* a person employed to tie something. Also *t. up.* **2.** Something that ties or is used for tying; a band 1844. **3.** *U.S.* A pinafore or apron covering the whole front of the dress 1846.

Tierce (tīᵊɹs). [a. OF. *terce, tierce*, fem. of *tiers, tierz* :—L. *tertius* third.] †**1.** A third part -1651. **2.** *Eccl.* **a.** The third hour of the canonical day, ending at 9 a.m.; also, the period from 9 a.m. till noon. *Obs.* exc. *Hist.* late ME. **b.** (Now usu. spelt **terce.**) The office said at this hour. late ME. **3.** An old measure of capacity equivalent to one third of a pipe (usu. 42 gallons old wine measure); also, a cask or vessel holding this quantity, usu. of wine, but also of various kinds of provisions or other goods; also, such a cask with its contents 1531. **4.** One of the positions in fencing; the third of the eight parries in sword-play, or the corresponding thrust 1692. **5.** In piquet and other card games, a sequence of three cards in any suit 1659. **6.** *Mus.* **a.** The interval of a third; the note at this interval above a given note. Now *rare* or *Obs.* **b.** The note two octaves and a major third (= a major 17th) above a fundamental note; hence, a mutation stop in an organ giving tones at this interval above the normal pitch 1696. **7.** *Her.* The division of a shield by lines into three equal parts: see next 1847.

5. *T. major*, the highest three cards of a suit; *t. minor*, the lowest three, i. e. seven, eight, and nine; *t. to a king, queen*, etc., a t. of which the king, queen, etc. is the highest.

‖**Tiercé** (tyęrse, tīᵊ·ɹse), *a.* 1725. [F., f. *tiercer* to divide into three parts.] *Her.* Said of a field divided *en tierce*, i. e. into three equal parts all of different tinctures. Also anglicized as Tierced (tīᵊɹst).

Tierceron (tīᵊ·ɹsěrǫn). 1842. [a. F., f. *tiers, tierce* third + *-on* (see -OON), with intercalated *-er-*.] *Arch.* A subordinate arch springing from the point of intersection of two main arches of a vault.

‖**Tierras** (tye·ras), *sb. pl. U.S.* 1874. [Sp., pl. of *tierra* earth :—L. *terra*.] *Mining.* Pulverulent ore, *spec.* of quicksilver, mingled with sand and earthy matter; in Mexico, inferior pulverulent ores generally.

‖**Tiers état** (tyęrzeta). 1783. [Fr., = third estate; see TIERCE and ESTATE *sb.*] A third estate or class; *esp.* the third estate, the body of commons or their representatives in the French National Assembly before the Revolution; occas. also, the corresponding body in other countries.

Tie·-wig. 1713. [Cf. TIE- 2.] A wig having the hair gathered together behind and tied with a knot of ribbon. Now *arch.*

Tiff (tif), *sb.*[1] *colloq.* or *slang.* Now *rare* or *Obs.* 1635. [Origin obsc.] **1.** Liquor, *esp.* poor, weak, or 'small' liquor, 'tipple'. **2.** A sip or little drink of punch or other diluted liquor 1727.

Tiff (tif), *sb.*[2] *colloq.* 1727. [Origin obsc.] **1.** A slight outburst or fit of temper, pettishness, or ill-humour. Now *rare.* **2.** A slight or petty quarrel; a 'breeze'; occas. applied to a more serious quarrel 1754.

†**Tiff,** *v.*[1] ME. [a. OF. *tifer, tiffer* to adorn.] *trans.* To attire, deck out, 'tittivate' (one's person, hair, etc.). Also *absol.* or *intr.* -1768.

Tiff, *v.*[2] *colloq.* or *slang.* Now *rare* or *Obs.* 1769. [f. TIFF *sb.*[1]] *trans.* To drink; *esp.* to drink slowly or in small portions, to sip.

Tiff, *v.*[3] 1727. [f. TIFF *sb.*[2]] *intr.* To be in a tiff or pet; to have a tiff, or petty quarrel.

Tiff, *v.*[4] *India.* 1803. [app. back-formation from or abbrev. of *tiffing* TIFFIN.] *intr.* = TIFFIN *v.*

Tiffany (ti·făni). ME. [a. OF. *tifinie, tiphanie* :—L. *theophania* THEOPHANY, applied to the EPIPHANY. Sense 2 is found only in English, and the origin of this sense is obsc.] †**1.** The festival of the Epiphany or Twelfth Day (Jan. 6) -1633. **2.** A kind of thin transparent silk; also, a transparent gauze muslin, cobweb lawn 1601. **b.** An article made of tiffany, as a head-dress, a sieve, etc. 1606. **c.** *attrib.* or as *adj.* Made of tiffany; *fig.* 'transparent', flimsy 1608.

2. Their sleeves..shewing their naked armes, thro' false sleeves of t. EVELYN.

Tiffin (ti·fin), *sb. India.* †Also **tiffing.** 1785. [app. f. *tiffing*, f. TIFF *v.*[2] to take a little drink or sip; specialized in Anglo-Ind. use.] In India and neighbouring eastern countries: A light midday meal; luncheon. Hence **Ti·ffin** *v. intr.* to take t., to lunch.

Tift. *dial.* 1751. [app. var. of TIFF *sb.*[2]] = TIFF *sb.*[2]

Tig (tig), *sb.* 1721. [f. next.] **1.** A touch, usu. a light but significant touch, a tap or pat. **2.** A children's game, in which one of the players pursues the others until he overtakes and touches or 'tigs' one 1816.

Tig (tig), *v.* 1821. [History obsc.; cf. TICK *v.*[1]] *trans.* To touch in the game of tig. Also *absol.*

‖**Tige** (tīʒ). 1664. [F., 'stalk' :—L. *tibia* shank, pipe.] The shaft of a column; also *transf.*; in *Bot.* a stem.

Tigelle (tiʒe·l). Also **tigel,** and in L. form **tigella.** 1860. [F., dim. of *tige.*] *Bot.* The embryonic axis or primitive stem, which bears the cotyledons; the caulicle or radicle. Sometimes applied to the plumule. Hence **Tigellate** (ti·dʒelĕt) *a.* having a t.

Tiger (təi·gəɪ). [ME. a. OF. *tigre*, ad. L. *tigrem, tigris*, a. Gr. τίγρις, app. an oriental word.] **1.** A large carnivorous quadruped, *Panthera tigris*, one of the two largest living felines, a cat-like maneless animal, in colour tawny yellow with blackish transverse stripes and white belly; widely distributed in Asia, and proverbial for its ferocity and cunning. **2.** Applied to other animals of the same genus, as in America to the Jaguar, *Felis onca*, and the Puma or Cougar, *F. concolor* (rare); and esp. in S. Africa, to the Leopard or Panther, *F. pardus* 1604. **b.** esp. with qualifications 1774. **c.** Applied to other than feline beasts 1832. **3.** The figure or representation of a tiger, *esp.* one used as a badge or crest; hence, pop. applied to an organization or society having this badge; also, a member of such a society; *spec.* (*Tammany T.*), the Tammany organization (*U.S.*) 1475. **4.** *transf.* and *fig.* Applied to one who or that which in some way resembles or suggests a tiger 1500. **5.** A smartly-liveried boy acting as groom or footman; less strictly, an outdoor boy-servant. *slang. Hist.* 1817. †**6.** A vulgarly or obtrusively overdressed person; also, a hanger-on, parasite; a roué, rake, swell-mobsman. *slang.* -1849. **7.** *U.S. slang.* A shriek or howl (often the word 'tiger') terminating a prolonged and enthusiastic cheer 1856. **8.** Short for *t.-moth, -shark*, etc. 1797.

1. Tiger, tiger, burning bright, In the forests of the night BLAKE. *Bengal t., Royal t.*, the tiger of Bengal, where it attains its typical development. 2. b. †*American t.*, †*Mexican t.*, the jaguar; *clouded t., marbled t., tortoiseshell t.*, species of TIGER-CAT. c. *Tasmanian* or *native t.*, the striped wolf or zebra-wolf of Tasmania. *Sabre-toothed t.*, see SABRE *sb.* 3. The 17th [foot]..the Bengal Tigers, from their badge—a t. 1874. 4. The blood-thirsty tygers of the French revolution 1806. 'The tigers of the sea' [sharks] 1885. 6. That man is a t...a low man THACKERAY. 7. The scamp ..proposes three cheers and a t. for Mr. Gordon 1869.

Comb.: **t.-beetle,** any species of the family *Cicindelidæ*, characterized by variegated colouring, activity, and voracity; **-bird,** (*a*) a S. Amer. scansorial barbet; (*b*) = *t.-bittern*; **-bittern,** a S. Amer. bittern of the genus *Tigrosoma*, with striped plumage; **-eye** = *tiger's eye*; **-flower,** any plant or species of *Tigridia*, a genus of tropical Amer. bulbous plants bearing large purple, yellow, or white spotted flowers; esp. *T. Pavonia* with brilliant orange blooms; **-foot** = *tiger's foot*; **-grass (palm),** a dwarf fan-palm, *Nannorhops* (*Chamærops*) *Ritchieana*, of Western India and Persia; **-lily,** a tall garden lily, *Lilium tigrinum*, with bell-like orange flowers marked with black or purplish spots; **-moth,** a moth of the family *Arctiidæ*, esp. the British species *Arctia caja*, a large scarlet and brown moth spotted and streaked with white; **-shark,** any of various voracious sharks, as *Galeocerdo maculatus* of warm seas, *Stegostoma tigrinum* of the Indian Ocean; in New Zealand, the Porbeagle, *Lamna cornubica*; **-ware,** an old English stoneware with a spotted glaze; **-wolf,** (*a*) the Spotted Hyena (*Hyæna crocuta*); (*b*) the striped wolf or zebra-wolf of Tasmania; **-wood,** a streaked black and brown cabinet-maker's wood; also, a variety of citron-wood.

b. *Comb.* with *tiger's*: **tiger's eye,** a yellowish brown quartz with brilliant lustre, used as a gem; **tiger's-foot,** a convolvulaceous plant, *Ipomœa Pestigridis*, common in India, with hairy palmate leaves; **tiger's horn, tiger's tooth,** old names for species of *Strombus* or wing-shell; **tiger's mouth,** a local name for the Snapdragon, Foxglove, and various species of Toad-flax.

Ti·ger-cat. 1699. Any of the feline beasts of moderate or small size which resemble the tiger in their markings or otherwise; including the Margay, Ocelot, Serval, etc. **b.** In Australasia applied to two carnivorous marsupials, *Dasyurus viverrinus* and *D. maculatus* 1832.

Tigerish (təi·gəriʃ), *a.* 1573. [f. TIGER + -ISH[1].] **1.** Like, or like that of, a tiger; *esp.* cruel, bloodthirsty, fierce, relentless. †**b.** Loud, flashy (*slang*) -1853. **2.** Abounding in or infested with tigers 1819. Hence **Ti·gerish·ly** *adv.*, **-ness.**

Tight (təit), *a.* (*adv.*) late ME. [app. altered f. earlier *thight* (now dial.), a. early ON. **þéhtr* tight, close in texture.] †**1.** Dense, as a wood or thicket. late ME. only. †**b.** Close or compact in texture or consistency; dense, solid (*rare*) -1797. **2.** Of such close texture or construction as to be impervious to a fluid, etc. 1501. **b.** *esp.* Of a ship: Water-tight; not leaky 1568. **c.** *transf.* and *fig.* 1661. **3.** *fig.* of a person, expressing somewhat indefinite commendation: Competent, able, skilful; smart; lively, vigorous; also in ironical use. *Obs.* exc. *dial.* 1598. **4.** Neat in appearance; trim, tidy, smart; also, well-made, shapely. *arch.* or *dial.* 1697. **b.** Of things: Neatly constructed or arranged; tidy, snug, compact. Now *dial.* 1720. **5.** Firmly fixed or bound in its place; also *fig.* faithful, constant. Now *rare.* 1513. **6.** Drawn or stretched so as to be tense; not loose or slack; taut 1576. **b.** *fig.* Strict, stringent; severe 1872. **7.** Drunk; tipsy (*slang*) 1853. **8.** Of a garment, etc.: Fitting closely; often = *too t.*, closely fitting because not large enough 1779. **9.** Difficult to deal with or manage; hard, severe, 'tough', 'stiff'; esp. in phr. a *t. place, corner, squeeze*, etc. (*colloq.*) 1764. **10.** *colloq.* or *techn.* **a.** Said of a contest in which the combatants are evenly matched; close; so of a bargain: with little margin of profit. *orig. U.S.* 1828. **b.** Of a person: Close-fisted. **c.** *Finance.* Of money: Difficult to obtain except on high terms; also *transf.* of the money-market when money is scarce. 1828. **11. a.** Closely packed 1856. **b.** Of language: Terse, concise, condensed 1870. **c.** *Art slang.* Lacking freedom or breadth of treatment; restricted 1891. **12.** The adj. used absol. (See also TIGHTS.) *Rugby Football.* = SCRIMMAGE *sb.* 3. *rare.* 1904. †**13.** Formerly appended to *ton, pipe, hogshead*, etc. as measures of capacity, orig. and esp. in stating the number of tons burden (*i. e.* the tonnage) of a ship -1603.

2. A t. house, warm apparel, and wholesome food BERKELEY. *Air-, water-, -wind-tight*, etc., the first element denoting that which the vessel keeps in or out. c. O, 'tis a snug little island! A right little, t. little island! DIBDIN. 3. *Ant. & Cl.* IV. iv. 16. 4. A t. clever wench 1712. 6. The belt..was..drawn t. 1885. 8. *A t. fit*, a garment, etc. which fits tightly; hence *transf.* (*colloq.*). 10. c. Money was 'tight' being the text of all he said 1868.

B. *adv.* (The adj. used advb.) **1.** Soundly, roundly. Now *dial.* and *U.S.* 1790. **2.** Firmly, closely, securely; so as not to allow any movement 1680. **3.** With close constriction or pressure; closely, tensely 1818.

2. Phr. *To sit t.*, to maintain one's position firmly in reference to something; also, to sit close, to remain under cover (*colloq.*); No money is forthcoming, and banks sit t. 1898.

Comb.: **t. barrel** or **cask,** a barrel for liquids; also called *wet barrel* or *cask* so **t. cooper,** a cooper who makes casks for liquids; **-fisted** *a.*, parsimonious, close-fisted.

Tighten (təi·t'n), *v.* 1725. [f. TIGHT *a.* + -EN[5].] **1.** *trans.* To draw tight or tighter; to make taut or tense, to draw close; hence, to fix tightly, to make strict or rigid; to secure. **2.** *intr.* To grow tight or tense; to be stretched tight or drawn close 1846.

1. What reins were tightened in despair SCOTT. *To t. one's belt*: orig. as a device to mitigate the pangs of hunger; *fig.* to reduce one's consumption of food or one's expenditure. 2. As the market tightens..the rate of discount rises 1868. Hence **Ti·ghtener,** one who or that which tightens.

Tight-laced (-lēst; stress var.), *a.* 1741. That is laced tightly; wearing stays tightly laced; constricted or compressed by tight-lacing. **b.** *fig.* Strict in the observance of rules or usages of morality or propriety. (Usu. dyslogistic.) So **Ti·ght-la·cing** *vbl. sb.* the action or process of lacing tightly; *spec.* the practice of wearing tightly-laced stays in order to reduce or preserve the form of the waist.

Tightly (təi·tli), *adv.* 1598. [f. TIGHT *a.* + -LY[2].] In a tight manner. **1.** Soundly, properly, well; stoutly, vigorously. Now *dial.* **2.** With constriction, tension, or compression; closely; strictly 1758. **3.** Firmly, securely 1866. **4.** Neatly, tidily, smartly (*rare*) 1825. So **Ti·ghtness,** the quality or condition of being tight.

Tight rope, ti·ght-rope. 1801. A tightly stretched rope, wire, or wire cable, on which rope-dancers and acrobats perform feats of equilibristic skill. Also *attrib.* as *t. dancer.*

Tights (təits), *sb. pl.* 1833. [ellipt. use of TIGHT *a.*] **a.** Tight-fitting breeches, worn by men in the 18th and early 19th c. and still forming part of court dress. **b.** Garments of thin elastic material, fitting tight to the skin, worn by dancers, acrobats, and others to facilitate their movements or display the form. Sometimes covering the whole body, but usu. the legs only. 1836.

Tiglic (ti·glik), *a.* 1875. [f. mod.L. *Tiglium*, specific name of the croton oil plant, *Croton Tiglium*.] *Chem.* Contained in or derived from croton oil; *t. acid*, a colourless crystalline compound, crystallizing in triclinic plates or rods, obtained from croton and other oils. So **Ti·glate,** a salt of this acid.

Tigress (təi·grės). 1611. [f. TIGER + -ESS, after F. *tigresse.*] **1.** A female tiger. **2.** *fig.* A fierce, cruel, or tiger-like woman 1700.

Tigrine (təi·grəin), *a.* 1656. [ad. L. *tigrinus*; see -INE[1].] Of, pertaining to, or resembling a tiger, esp. in marking or colouring; in specific names of animals tr. L. *tigrinus.*

Carpet, diamond, and t. snakes 1908. So **Ti·groid** *a.* 1901.

Tigurine (ti·giurəin), *a.* and *sb.* 1651. [ad. L. *Tigurinus* in *Tigurinus pagus*, a district of ancient Helvetia.] A. *adj.* Of or pertaining to Zürich; hence = ZWINGLIAN. B. *sb.* A Zwinglian.

‖**Til**[1] (til). *India.* 1840. [Hindi.] The plant *Sesamum indicum*; esp. in *t.-seed* (*oil*).

‖**Til**[2]. 1858. [Native name in Madeira; perh. a use of Pg. *til* linden.] A lauraceous tree, *Oreodaphne fetens*, of the Canary Islands and Madeira; also its wood, which has a fetid smell. Chiefly *attrib.*, as *t.-tree*, *-wood*.

Tilbury (ti·lbŏri). 1796. [f. *Tilbury*, name of the inventor.] A light open two-wheeled carriage, fashionable in the first half of the 19th c.

‖**Tilde** (ti·ldĕ). 1864. [Sp., metathetic form of *tidlo, ad. L. *titulus* TITLE.] The diacritic mark ~ placed in Spanish above the letter *n* to indicate the *mouillé* or palatalized sound (nʸ), as in *señor* (senʸor).

Tile (təil), *sb.* [OE. *tigule, tigele*:—WGer. **tegala*, ad. L. *tegula*, f. *tegere* to cover.] 1. A thin slab of burnt clay; usu. unglazed and flat or curved for covering the roofs of buildings, flat for lining ovens, etc.; flat, usu. glazed and often ornamented when used to pave floors or line walls, fireplaces, etc.; of semi-cylindrical, tunnel or tube shape when used for purposes of drainage. b. *Metall.* A small flat piece of baked earth or earthenware used to cover vessels in which metals are fused 1741. 2. The material of which tiles or bricks consist, burnt clay; tiles collectively (in early use const. as pl.) ME. 3. *slang.* A hat 1823.

1. The house..is couered with Tiles of siluer PURCHAS. The better houses..have red tiles upon the roofs 1840. The fireplace..paved with quaint Dutch tiles DICKENS. Phr. *To have a t. loose*, to be slightly crazy or not quite right in the head (*slang*). 3. Afore the brim went, it was a very handsome t. DICKENS.

attrib. and *Comb.*: t.-drain *sb.*, a drain constructed of tiles; so t.-drain *v. trans.*, to drain (a field, etc.) by means of tiles; -earth, a kind of clay adapted for making tiles; -kiln, a kiln in which tiles are baked; -ore, an earthy variety of cuprite or copper ore, usu. of a reddish colour; -pipe, a hollow cylindrical t. for drainage; -red *a.* and *sb.*, (of) a red colour like that of tiles; -tea, an inferior kind of brick-tea; -yard, a yard or enclosure where tiles are made.

Tile (təil), *v.* late ME. [f. prec; in sense 2, back-formation from TILER 2.] 1. *trans.* To cover with tiles; to overlay (a floor or roof) or line (a wall, fire-place, etc.) with tiles. b. *transf.* and *fig.* 1512. 2. *Freemasonry.* (Usu. with spelling tyle.) To protect (a lodge or meeting) from interruption or intrusion, so as to keep its proceedings secret, by posting a tyler at the door. Also *transf.* to bind (a person) to secrecy; to keep (any meeting or proceeding) strictly secret. 1762.

1. b. God..hath..tyled one favour upon another 1641. 2. Come, come, Snob my boy, we are all tiled, you know THACKERAY. Hence Tiled (təild) *a.*

Ti·le-fish. 1881. [Suggested by the termination of the generic name *Lophalotilus*.] The fish *Lophalotilus chamæleonticeps*, found in abundance in 1879 off the coast of New England, and valued as food; supposed to be extinct from 1882 till 1892, since which year its numbers have again increased.

Ti·le-pin. ME. A 'pin' or peg of hard wood used to fasten the tiles to the laths of a roof.

Tiler (təi·ləɹ). ME. [f. TILE *sb.* and *v.* + -ER[1].] 1. One who covers the roofs of buildings with tiles, a tile-layer; also formerly, a tile-maker. 2. *Freemasonry.* (Usually tyler.) The door-keeper who keeps the uninitiated from intruding upon the secrecy of the lodge or meeting 1742.

Tilery (təi·ləri). 1846. [f. TILE *sb.*, TILER; see -ERY.] A place where tiles are made; a tile-field or -kiln.

Tilestone (təi·lˌstōᵘn). [OE. *tigelstān*, f. *tigele* TILE *sb.* + *stān* STONE *sb.*] †1. = TILE *sb.* 1, 2. –1681. 2. *Geol.* Any laminated flagstone, splitting into layers thicker than *slate*, suitable for roofing-tiles; *spec.* a group of sandstones forming the transition beds between the Silurian and Devonian systems 1668.

Tiliaceous (tiliˌēⁱ·ʃəs), *a.* 1891. [f. L. *tiliaceus* (f. *tilia* lime-tree) + -OUS.] *Bot.* Belonging to the family *Tiliaceæ*, typified by the genus *Tilia*, the lime or linden tree.

Tiling (təi·liŋ), *vbl. sb.* 1440. [f. TILE *v.* and *sb.* + -ING[1].] 1. The action of TILE *v.*; the covering (of a roof, etc.) with or as with tiles. b. *Freemasonry.* (Usually tyling.) The proper guarding of a lodge 1888. 2. *concr.* Work consisting of tiles; the tiles forming the covering of a roof, floor, etc., collectively 1526.

Till (til), *sb.*[1] 1452. [Origin obsc.] †1. A small box, casket, or closed compartment, contained within or forming part of a larger box, chest, or cabinet; sometimes one that could be lifted out, sometimes a drawer in a cabinet or chest of drawers; used for keeping valuables, etc., more safely –1737. 2. *spec.* A drawer, money-box, etc. in a shop or bank, in which cash for daily transactions is temporarily kept 1698.

Comb.: t.-alarm, a device by which a bell is automatically rung when the till is opened.

Till, *sb.*[2] orig. and chiefly *Sc.* 1672. [Origin unkn.] 1. A stiff clay, more or less impervious to water, usu. occurring in unstratified deposits, and forming an ungenial subsoil 1765. b. In the majority of cases this clay belongs to the Glacial or Drift period, and in geological use 'till' has the specific sense 'boulder clay' 1842. 2. Hard or soft shale; app. = THILL[2], *dial.* 1672.

Till, *sb.*[3] *Printing.* 1611. In early hand-presses, a board or shelf through which the sleeve and spindle pass.

Till (til), *v.*[1] [OE. *tilian* to strive, acquire:—OTeut. **tilôjan*, **tilējan*, f. **tilom*; see TILL *prep.*] I. †1. *intr.* To labour, work –ME. 2. *trans.* To bestow labour and attention, such as ploughing, harrowing, manuring, etc., upon (land) so as to fit it for raising crops; to cultivate. Also *absol.* ME. b. *spec.* To plough (land). Also *absol.* late ME. 3. *fig.* To cultivate (the mind, a 'field' of knowledge, a virtue, etc.). late ME.

2. The prisoners were forced to t. the enemy's land 1835. b. They drained, they tilled, they planted 1850.

II. 1. *trans.* To spread (a net), set (a trap or snare). Also, to set in any position. Now *s. w. dial.* Also *absol.* ME. †2. To pitch (a tent) –1628.

Till (til), *v.*[2] 1841. [f. TILL *sb.*[1]] *trans.* To put (money) into a till.

Till (til), *prep.*, *conj.* [ONorth. *til*, a. ON. *til*; prob. orig. a sb. **til* = OE. *till* fixed point, station; hence const. with genitive; prop. 'with the limit or goal of (the place or time named)'. Characteristically northern in ref. to place or purpose; in ref. to time now often repl. by UNTIL.] A. *prep.* I. Local and datival. Now *n. dial.* and *Sc.*, where normally used instead of *to* before a vowel or *h*. 1. = To *prep.* 2. Expressing the indirect object or dative relation OE. II. Of time: Onward to (a specified time); until ME. b. After a neg., denoting the continuance of the negative condition up to the time indicated (and implying its cessation then); thus nearly = *before* 1590.

Fight t. the last gaspe SHAKS. 'Till then farewel 1746. b. [He] begged of me not to go on shore t. day DE FOE.

III. = *To* with inf. Now only *Sc* ME.

B. *conj.* (orig. the prep. governing the dem. pron. *that*, in apposition with the following clause). 1. To the time that; up to (the point) when; until OE. b. So long or so far that; so that at length ME. †2. During the time that; so long as; while –1604.

1. I shall count the hours t. I return 1796. We shall never prosper..t. the system is wholly changed 1832. b. Blow t. thou burst thy winde SHAKS.

Tillable (ti·lăb'l), *a.* 1573. [f. TILL *v.*[1] + -ABLE.] Capable of being tilled or cultivated usu., capable of being ploughed, arable.

Tillage (ti·lėdʒ). 1488. [f. TILL *v.*[1] + -AGE.] 1. The act, operation, or art of tilling or cultivating land so as to fit it for raising crops; agriculture, husbandry 1538. b. The state or condition of being tilled or cultivated 1488. c. *fig.* The culture of the mind or spirit 1555. 2. *concr.* Tilled or ploughed land; land under crops as dist. from pasturage; the crops growing on tilled land 1543.

‖**Tillandsia** (tilæ·ndziă). 1759. [mod.L., named after Elias *Tillands*, a Swedish botanist.] *Bot.* A large genus of herbaceous plants of the pine-apple family (*Bromeliaceæ*), found in tropical and subtropical America and the West Indies, chiefly epiphytic on trees.

Tiller (tiləɹ), *sb.*[1] Now *literary* or *arch.* [ME. *tiliere*, repl. OE. *tilia*, f. *tilian* TILL *v.*[1] + *-ere* -ER[1]; subseq. spelt after the vb.] One who tills the soil; a husbandman, cultivator; a farmer or farm labourer.

Ti·ller, *sb.*[2] late ME. [a. OF. *telier, tellier*, in sense 1; orig. a weaver's beam, med.L. *telarium*, f. L. *tela* web.] †1. *Archery*, etc.: In a cross-bow: The wooden beam which is grooved for reception of the arrow, or drilled for the bolt or quarrel –1618. †b. *transf.* A bow fitted with a tiller –1688. 2. *Naut.* A horizontal bar or beam attached to the rudder-head, acting as a lever by means of which the rudder is moved in the act of steering 1625.

Comb.: t.-head, the extremity of the t. to which are secured the two ends of the t.-rope or -chain; -rope, (*a*) the rope (now usu. a chain) connecting the t.-head with the drum or barrel of a ship's steering-gear; (*b*) a rope leading from the t.-head to each side of the deck, to assist in steering in rough weather; -steerage, -steering, the arrangement for steering a motor-car by means of a lever (as dist. from wheel-steerage).

Ti·ller, *sb.*[3] Now *dial.* [app. repr. OE. *telgor, tealgor, telgra*, extended f. *telga* branch, bough, twig.] †1. (In OE.) A plant, a shoot, a twig; *esp.* a shoot or sucker from the root. 2. A young tree, a sapling; *esp.* a stock-shoot, rising from the stock or stool of a felled tree 1664. 3. One of the lateral shoots from the base of the stalk of corn or grass or other herbaceous plant 1733.

Tiller (ti·ləɹ), *v.* 1677. [f. prec.] *intr.* Of corn or other plants: To produce 'tillers' or side shoots from the root or base of the stem; also said of the shoots thus arising.

Tillet (ti·lėt), **tillot** (ti·lət). 1466. [app. ad. OF. *tellette*, collateral form of *teilete, toilete*, a wrapper of cloth; see also TOILET.] A kind of coarse cloth, used for wrapping up textile fabrics and (formerly) garments; also for making awnings. b. A bag of thin glazed muslin, used as a covering for dress-goods 1871.

Tilly (ti·li). 1712. [app. a. F. *tilli*, ad. med.L. *tiglium*.] In *t.-seed*, the seed of a species of *Croton* (formerly called *C. Pavana*, now identified with *C. Tiglium*), which yields croton oil.

Tilly-vally, *int.* *Obs.* or *arch.* 1529. [Origin unkn.] An exclam. of impatience: Nonsense! Fiddlesticks!

Tilt (tilt), *sb.*[1] 1440. [Collateral form of ME. *tild*, perh. influenced by *tent*.] 1. A covering of coarse cloth; an awning; a booth, tent, or tabernacle. 2. *spec.* An awning over a boat 1611. 3. An awning or cover for a cart or wagon, usu. of canvas or tarpaulin 1620. 4. In Labrador and Newfoundland: a fisherman's or wood-cutter's hut 1895.

Comb.: t.-bonnet, a woman's or girl's bonnet in the form of a wagon-tilt; -roof, a round-topped roof, shaped like a t. or wagon-cover.

Tilt (tilt), *sb.*[2] 1510. [In branch I, of doubtful origin; perh. a use of prec. In branch II, f. TILT *v.*[1]] I. 1. The barrier which separated the combatants in a tilt (sense 2). Hence, a tilting ground or yard; the lists. 2. A combat for exercise or sport between two armed men on horseback with lances, riding on opposite sides of a barrier and scoring by attaints and lances broken; also, the exercise of riding with a lance or the like at a mark, as the quintain 1511. b. *transf.* and *fig.* An encounter, a combat; a debate 1567. c. A thrust of a weapon, as at a tilt. Now only *fig.* 1716.

1. *To run at (the) t.* = TILT *v.*[2] III. 1. 2. *Full t.* (advb. phr.), at full speed and with direct thrust; with the utmost adverse force or impetus.

II. 1. The act of tilting or the fact or condition of being tilted; inclination upward or downward 1562. b. *Geol.* An abrupt upheaval of strata to a considerable angle from the horizontal. c. *gen.* A slope, or sloping portion, of the surface of the ground. 1859. 2. Short for TILT-HAMMER 1831.

1. Phr. *On* or *upon the t.*, in a tilted position, like a cask or vessel raised on one end or side when nearly empty.

III. The Stilt or Long-legged Plover of North America 1831.

attrib. and *Comb.*: **t.-cart**, a cart of which the body can be tilted so as to empty out the contents; **-mill**, (*a*) the machinery for working a t.-hammer; (*b*) a building in which a t.-hammer is worked.

Tilt (tilt), *v.*[1] [Late ME. *tilten*, repr. an OE. **tyltan* for **tieltan* :—**taltjan*, f. OE. *tealt* unsteady, shaky. Branch III is from TILT *sb.*[2] I. 1; in branch IV, from TILT-HAMMER.] **I.** †**1.** *trans.* To cause to fall; to thrust, push, throw down or over; to overturn, upset -1587. **2.** *intr.* To move unsteadily up and down; *esp.* of waves or a ship at sea, to pitch 1590.

2. The floating Vessel..with beaked prow Rode tilting o're the Waves MILT.

II. *trans.* To cause to lean abruptly from the vertical or incline abruptly from the horizontal; to slope, slant; *to t. up.* to raise one end or side above the other, to tip up 1594. **b.** *intr.* To move into a slanted position or direction; to incline, slope, slant, heel over, tip *up* 1626. **c.** *trans.* To pour or empty out (the contents of a vessel), or cause them to flow to one side, by tilting the vessel 1613.

His helmet tilted well to the rear to screen his neck 1908. **c.** To tumble out their sentences as they would t. stones from a cart 1865.

III. [orig. for *run at tilt*: see prec. I. 1.] **1.** *intr.* To engage in a 'tilt' 1595. **b.** *transf.* and *fig.* To engage in a contest; to combat, encounter, contend (*with*); to strike or thrust *at* with a weapon, to charge or impinge *against* 1588. **2.** *trans.* **a.** To poise (the lance) for a thrust 1708. **b.** To tilt at; to rush at, charge; to drive or thrust by tilting 1796.

1. He ran at the ring, and tilted with the Lord Montjoy 1622. **b.** He Tilts With Peircing steele at bold Mercutio's breast SHAKS.

IV. To forge or work with a tilt-hammer 1825.

Tilt (tilt), *v.*[2] 1499. [f. TILT *sb.*[1]] *trans.* To cover with a tilt or awning. (Chiefly in *pa. pple.*)

Ti·lt-boat. 1463. [f. TILT *sb.*[1] (or short for *tilted*) + BOAT *sb.*] A large rowing boat having a tilt or awning, formerly used on the Thames, esp. as a passenger boat between London and Gravesend.

Tilter (ti·ltəɹ), *sb.* 1611. [f. TILT *v.*[1] + -ER[1].] **1.** One who tilts or jousts; a combatant in a tilt. †**b.** A rapier or sword. *slang.* -1713. **2.** One who or that which tilts, inclines, or slopes (something) up or down; *spec.* an apparatus for tilting a cask so as to empty it without stirring up the dregs 1630. **3.** One who works with a tilt-hammer 1829.

1. *fig.* I was always a t. at windmills 1898.

Tilth (tilþ). [OE. *tilþ*, *tilþe*, f. OE. *tilian* TILL *v.*[1] + -TH *suffix*[1].] †**1.** Labour, work, or effort directed to useful or profitable ends. OE. only. **2.** *esp.* Labour or work in the cultivation of the soil; tillage, agricultural work, husbandry OE. **b.** *fig.* The cultivation of knowledge, religion, the mind. *arch.* ME. **c.** (with *pl.*) An act of tilling; a ploughing, harrowing, or other agricultural operation 1565. **d.** The condition of being under tillage; hence (good or bad) condition (of land under tillage) 1488. †**3.** *transf.* Crop, harvest -1781. **4.** Land under cultivation, as dist. from pasture, forest, or waste land; tilled or arable land; a piece of tilled land, a ploughed field. late ME. **b.** The prepared surface soil; the crumb, or depth of soil dug or cultivated 1743.

2. After four year's t., lay down your land 1660. **4.** Vineyard and t., Green meadow-ground, and many-coloured woods WORDSW.

Ti·lt-ha·mmer. 1773. [f. TILT *sb.*[2] or *v.*[1]] A heavy hammer used in forging, fixed on a pivot and acted upon by a cam-wheel or an eccentric, which alternately tilts it up and allows it to drop.

Tilting (ti·ltiŋ), *vbl. sb.* 1610. [f. TILT *v.*[1] + -ING[1].] **1.** The action of TILT *v.*[1]; justing. **b.** With *a* and *pl.* A tilt. Now *rare* or *Obs.* 1618. **2.** Inclination from the vertical or horizontal 1658. **3.** Working with a tilt-hammer 1839.

attrib. and *Comb.*: **t.-helm, -helmet**, a large heavy helmet worn over the ordinary one in tilting, completely covering head and face, with slits for breathing and vision; **-mill** = *tilt-mill*; **-yard** = TILT-YARD.

Ti·lt-up, *sb.* and *a.* 1848. [f. phr. *to tilt up.*] **A.** *sb.* Something that tilts up; *spec.* the American sandpiper (*U.S.*) **B.** *adj.* That tilts up 1891.

Tilt-yard (ti·lt,yāɹd). 1528. [f. TILT *sb.*[2] + YARD.] A yard or enclosed space for tilts and tournaments; a (permanent) tilting-ground.

‖**Timar** (tīmā·r). 1601. *Hist.* [Pers. (and Turk.) *tīmār* attendance, watching.] Formerly, in the feudal system of Turkey, a fief held by military service.

Timariot (timā·riǫt). 1601. [a. F., ad. It. *timariotto*, f. *tīmār* TIMAR + -OT[2].] The holder of a timar.

Timbal, tymbal (ti·mbăl). Now *Hist.* or *arch.* 1680. [= mod.F. *timbale*, substituted for, and app. altered from, earlier F. *attabale*, ATABAL.] A kettledrum.

Timbale (tæñbal). 1854. [F.; see prec.] **1.** *Ent.* A membrane (resembling a drum-head) in certain insects, as the cicada, by means of which a shrill chirping sound is produced. **2.** *Cookery.* A dish made of finely minced meat, fish, or other ingredients, cooked in a crust of paste or in a mould; so called from its shape 1880.

Timber (ti·mbəɹ), *sb.*[1] [OE. :—OTeut. **timrom* :—**temrom* :—Indo-Eur. **demrom*, f. ablaut series **dem-*, *dom-*, *dm-*, to build; cf. Gr. δέμειν, δόμος, L. *domus.*] †**1.** A building, edifice, house. OE. only. †**2.** Building material generally; the matter or substance of which anything is built up or composed; matter, material, stuff -1840. **3.** *spec.* Wood used for the building of houses, ships, etc., or for the use of the carpenter, joiner, or other artisan; wood in general as a material OE. **b.** Wood as a substance. Now *dial.* 1530. **4.** Applied to the wood of growing trees capable of being used for structural purposes; hence collectively to the trees themselves; *standing t.*, trees, woods. Rarely in *pl.* OE. **b.** *spec.* in *English Law*, Trees growing upon land, and forming part of the freehold inheritance; embracing usu. the oak, ash, and elm, of the age of twenty years and more; in particular districts, by local custom, including other trees 1766. **5.** *transf.* Applied to any object familiar to the speaker, composed wholly or chiefly of wood, as a ship; the stocks (*slang*); wooden gates and fences (*Hunting slang*); a wicket (*Cricket slang*). late ME. **6.** A single beam or piece of wood forming or capable of forming part of any structure. Also collectively in *pl.* **a.** *gen.* 1555. **b.** *pl. spec. Naut.* The pieces of wood composing the ribs, bends, or frames of a ship's hull 1748. **7.** *fig.* Bodily structure, frame, build; also in later use, the 'stuff' of which a person is made 1612. **8.** *attrib.* or *adj.* Made or consisting of wood; wooden 1529.

2. Such disposicions are..the fittest tymber to make great Pollitiques of BACON. **3.** Thir Boats of T. without any Iron in them MILT. **4.** A forest of grand t. 1880. **b.** By the custom of the county of Buckingham beech trees are t. 1891. **6. b.** Her timbers yet are sound COWPER. *My timbers! Shiver my timbers!* meaningless exclams. (*Naut. slang*).

Comb.: **t.-beetle**, any beetle which, in the larval or the perfect state, is destructive to t.; **-doodle** *U.S. local*, the Amer. woodcock, *Philohela minor*; *slang*, spirituous liquor; **-grouse** *U.S.*, any species of grouse frequenting woodlands; **-head** *Naut.*, the head or end of any t.; *spec.* such an end rising above the deck and serving as a bollard; **-hitch** *sb.*, a knot used in attaching a rope to a log or spar for hoisting or towing it; hence **-hitch** *v.*, *trans.* to make fast with a t.-hitch; **-jumper** *Hunting slang*, a horse good at jumping over gates and fences; **-mare**, a kind of wooden horse on which offending soldiers and others were made to ride as a punishment; **-sow**, a wood-louse or sow-bug, *Oniscus*; **-toe** *slang*, a wooden leg; hence **-toe, -toes**, a wooden-legged man; so **-toed** *a.*; **-worm**, a 'worm' or larva injurious to t.

Timber (ti·mbəɹ), *sb.*[2] ME. [In OF. *timbre*, med.L. *timbrium*, *timbria.*] A definite quantity of furs, a package containing 40 skins (i.e. half-skins, 20 pair) of ermine, sable, marten, and the like. (After a numeral commonly *timber*, less usu. *timbers.*)

Timber (ti·mbəɹ), *v.* [OE. *timbran* and *timbrian* :—OTeut. **timrjan*, f. **timr-* TIMBER *sb.*[1]] **1.** *trans.* To build, construct, make (as a house, ship, etc.); *spec.* (in later use) to build or construct of wood. *Obs.* or *arch.* **b.** *absol.*; *spec.* of a bird, to build (*sc.* its nest) OE. †**2.** To construct, frame, effect, do, form, cause, bring about, bring into existence or operation (any action, condition, etc.) -1646. **3.** To furnish with timber; to put in or apply timber to support the roof of a mine, the sides of a shaft, etc. 1548.

2. Heads that were never timber'd for it SIR T. BROWNE. **3.** The new shaft..has been sunk, timbered, and centred to a depth of 260 feet 1872.

Timbered (ti·mbəɹd), *ppl. a.* late ME. [f. TIMBER *sb.*[1] and *v.* + -ED.] **1.** Constructed of timber; built or made of wood; wooden. **2.** †**a.** Of a thing: Having a structure (of a specified kind); constructed, framed, built, made -1771. **b.** Of a person or animal: Having (such and such) a bodily structure or constitution 1581. **3.** Furnished with growing trees; wooded 1701.

A low t. House 1699. **2. a.** *Haml.* IV. vii. 22. **b.** A fine straite timber'd man and a brave soldier 1622. **3.** A very ill-t. estate FIELDING.

Timbering (ti·mbəriŋ), *vbl. sb.* ME. [f. TIMBER *v.* + -ING[1].] **1.** The action of TIMBER *v.* **2.** *concr.* Building material (esp. of wood); timber-work; *spec.* in *Mining*, the timber used to support the sides of a shaft or the roof of a working 1486.

Timberling (ti·mbəɹliŋ). 1787. [f. TIMBER *sb.*[1] + -LING.] A young timber-tree; a sapling.

Timberman (ti·mbəɹmæ̆n). late ME. [f. TIMBER *sb.*[1] + MAN *sb.*] †**1.** A man who supplies or deals in timber -1656. **b.** A man employed in handling timber 1890. **2.** A man employed in timbering the shafts or roofs of a mine, the sides of a trench, or any other excavation 1849.

Ti·mber-tree. 1505. A tree yielding timber fit for building or construction.

Ti·mber-wood. Now *rare.* 1483. = TIMBER *sb.*[1] 3.

Ti·mber-work. late ME. **1.** Work executed in timber; the wooden part of any structure. **2.** *pl.* An establishment where timber is prepared or worked up 1875.

Ti·mber-yard. 1482. An open yard or place where timber is stacked or stored.

†**Ti·mbre**, *sb.*[1] ME. [a. OF., :—late pop.L. **timbano*, for L. *tympanum*, a. Gr. τύμπανον timbrel, kettledrum.] = TIMBREL *sb.* -1516.

Timbre, tymber (ti·mbəɹ), *sb.*[2] *Obs.* exc. *Hist.* late ME. [a. F., the same wd. as in prec., in transf. sense.] The crest of a helmet; hence, the crest or exterior additions placed over the shield in heraldic arms. Hence **Ti·mbre** *v. trans.* to furnish or adorn with a crest; to surmount as a crest.

‖**Timbre** (tæñbr), *sb.*[3] 1849. [a. mod.F., from the transf. sense of 'bell', 'small bell', from which also the sense of prec. arose.] The character or quality of a musical or vocal sound (distinct from its pitch and intensity) depending upon the particular voice or instrument producing it; caused by the proportion in which the fundamental tone is combined with the harmonics or overtones (= G. *klangfarbe*).

Timbrel (ti·mbrĕl), *sb.* Now chiefly *biblical.* 1500. [app. a dim. of TIMBRE *sb.*[1]; see -EL.] A musical instrument of percussion; a tambourine or the like that could be held up in the hand.

Miriam the prophetisse..toke a tymbrell in hir hande, and all the women folowed out after her with timbrels in a daunse COVERDALE *Exod.* xv. 20. Hence **Ti·mbrel** *v. intr.* to play upon a t.; *trans.* to accompany with a t.

Time (təim), *sb.* [OE. *tīma* :—OTeut. **tīmon-*, app. f. a root **tī-* to stretch, extend + abstr. suffix *-mon-*, *-man-*.] **I.** A space or extent of time. **1.** A limited stretch or space of continued existence, as the interval between two successive events or acts, or the period through which an action, condition, or state continues; as *a long t.*, *a short t.*, *some t.*, *for a t.* **2.** A particular period indicated or characterized in some way OE. **3.** A period in the existence or history of the world; an age, an era. In later use more indefinite, esp. in *pl.* OE. **4.** With possessive or *of*: The period contemporary with the life, occupancy, or activity of some one; (his) age, era, or generation.

Often *pl.* OE. **5.** A period considered with ref. to its prevailing conditions; the general state of affairs at a particular period. Chiefly *pl.* 1484. **b.** *pl.* Used as the name of a newspaper 1788. **6.** A period considered with ref. to one's personal experience; hence, an experience of a specified nature lasting some time 1529. **7.** Period of duration; prescribed or allotted term. **a.** Period of existence or action; period of one's life OE. **b.** *spec.* (*a*) The period of gestation OE. (*b*) (One's) term of apprenticeship 1645. (*c*) The duration of a term of imprisonment; usu. in phr. *to do t.* (slang) 1865. (*d*) The prescribed duration of the interval between two rounds in boxing, or the like, or the moment at which this begins or ends; also *ellipt.* as the signal to begin or end a bout, as in *to call t.* 1812. **8.** The length of time sufficient, necessary, or desirable for some purpose; also, time available for employment; leisure or spare time ME. **b.** The (shortest) period in which a given course of action is completed 1894. **9.** *spec.* The amount of time worked under a specific contract; hence, in workmen's speech, pay equivalent to the period worked 1795. **10.** *Anc. Prosody.* A unit or group of units in metrical measurement 1589. **11.** *Mil.* The rate of marching, calculated on the number of paces taken per minute 1802. **12.** *Mus.* **a.** †The duration of the breve in relation to the semibreve; hence, the rhythm or measure of a piece of music, now marked by division of the music into bars, and usu. denoted by a fraction expressing the number of aliquot parts of a semibreve in each bar (*t.-signature*). 1531. **b.** The rate at which a piece is performed; hence, the characteristic tempo, rhythm, form, and style of a particular class of compositions, usu. in comb. as *dance-t.*, *march-t.* 1887.

1. *In no t.*, *in less than no t.* (colloq.), immediately, very quickly or soon; In less than no t. you shall hear JOWETT. *Absolute t.*, t. considered in itself without ref. to that portion of duration to which it belongs. 2. You can fool all the people some of the t., and some of the people all the t., but you cannot fool all the people all the t. (*attributed to President Lincoln*). *At* or *for the t.*, *for the t. being*, during the period under consideration. 3. A superstition of these modern times 1884. *Time(s past, past time(s*; *old, olden*, or *ancient time(s*, etc. *Time(s to come*, *times to be* (arch.), future time; esp. future ages, the future. *The t.* (*the times*), the age now or then present. 4. The spacious times of great Elizabeth TENNYSON. 5. When times grew cold and unbelieving J. H. NEWMAN. Colloq. phrases. *As times go*, as things go in these times. *Behind the times*, behind the modes or methods of these times. 6. I went and had as good a t. as heart could wish PEPYS. Phr. (*To have*) *a* (*good, bad*, etc.) *t.* (*of it*). *To have the t. of one's life*, i. e. the best one has ever had. 7. a. One man in his t. playes many parts SHAKS. It will last my t. CARLYLE. 8. Pray take your own t. 1796. 9. Phr. *T. and lime*, in the shipbuilding trade, applied to a contract to build at cost plus an agreed percentage. 11. See also QUICK TIME. 12. a. *In t.*, *out of t.*, in or out of correct rhythm. *To beat t.*: see BEAT *v.*[1] II. 9.

II. Time when: a point of time; a space of time treated without ref. to its duration. **1.** A point in the course of time or of a period. In mod.Eng. *What is the t.?* i.e. the hour and minute as shown by the clock. (*At*) *what t.*, = when, at the time that: see WHAT *a.* ME. **b.** A point or fixed part of the year, a season; also, of a day, as *t. of day*, *t. of night*, *dinner-t.*, *bed-t.* OE. **2.** A point in duration marking or marked by some event or condition; a point of time at which something happens; an occasion OE. **3.** Appointed, due, or proper time OE. **b.** Qualified by poss. pron., as *his*, *her*, *its*; often ellipt. for *t. of death*, *of childbirth*, etc.; *before* (*his*, etc.), *t.*, prematurely OE. **4.** A or the favourable, convenient, or fitting point of time for doing something; the right moment; opportunity. (Often with *his*, *her*, etc.) OE. **5.** Any one of the occasions on which something is done or happens. Often qualified by a numeral. ME. **6.** Preceded by a cardinal numeral and followed by a number or expression of quantity: used to express the multiplication of the number, etc. late ME. **b.** Also followed by an adj. or adv. in the comparative degree, or in the positive by *as* with an adj. or adv., expressing comparison 1551. **7.** *pl.* orig. The fixed hours of the day at which an omnibus started from its various stations; hence, the established business enterprise of running an omnibus on a given route at such times, and the 'goodwill' thus created by the owners of public service vehicles over particular routes as a recognized vendible asset 1863.

1. To knowe..euery tyme of the nyht by the sterres fixe CHAUCER. b. Fleeting showers..unseasonable at the t. of year 1825. 2. This..trick escaped detection at the t. 1845. Phr. *At no t.*, on no occasion. *Once upon a t.*: at a certain (undefined) period. *At one t.*: = ONCE 4. 3. It was tyme to go to bed CAXTON. *No t. for*: not a fitting occasion for. b. Y[e] Quene..was with childe, and nere her t. 1560. 4. When he sawe his tyme, he cryed his worde & token 1533. It is the T. to buy STEELE. The devil bides his t. 1722. 5. He did it fifty times, at the very least LANDOR. Phr. *At a t.*, *at one t.*, *at the same t.*, at once, simultaneously. *Many a t.*, *many times*, ellipt. *times*, also *times without* or *out of number*, *many a t. and oft* (*often*), on many occasions, in many instances; often, frequently. 6. Four times fifty living men COLERIDGE. b. Men who had ten or twenty times less to remember GLADSTONE.

III. *gen.* **1.** Indefinite continuous duration regarded as that in which the sequence of events takes place. late ME. **2.** Personified as an aged man, bald, but having a forelock, and carrying a scythe and an hour-glass 1509. **3.** In restricted sense, duration conceived as beginning and ending with the present life or material universe; finite duration as dist. from eternity. late ME. **4.** A system of measuring or reckoning the passage of time 1706.

1. Remember that t. is money B. FRANKLIN. Add event to event, still T. is recognised as stretching forth, and still there is room for more 1854. 2. *To take T. by the forelock*, to seize one's opportunity, to act promptly. 3. All t. compared with eternitie is but short t., yea indeed as no t. 1635. 4. Common watches and clocks, are made to show the hour of mean t. 1834.

Phrases. **1. Time of day. a.** The hour as shown by the clock; hence, a point or stage in any course or period (somewhat *colloq.*). **b.** In salutations, as *to give one*, or *pass*, *the t. of day* (now *dial.* and *colloq.*), to greet, salute, exchange salutations. **c.** *colloq.* or *slang.* The state of the case; (to know) 'what's what'; also, the right way of doing anything; the latest dodge. **T. out of mind,** from a time or during a period beyond human memory; so *t.* (also *for*, *from t.*) *immemorial.* **T. and tide,** an alliterative reduplication; now only or mainly in proverbial phrases, as *t. and tide wait* (or *stay*) *for no man.* **T. after t.,** repeatedly. **Time and again,** with frequent recurrence; repeatedly, very often. **T. enough,** soon enough, in time, sufficiently early.

2. Against t., in competition with the passage of time; so as to finish one's task before the expiry of a certain period. **At time(s,** at one time and another, at various times, occasionally. **b.** (*At*) *one t. with* (*and*) *another*, during various detached periods, on various occasions. **c.** *At the same t.*, during the same period, at the same moment, not before or after. Also, used in introducing a reservation, explanation, or contrast, = 'while saying this, nevertheless, however, yet, still'. **Between times,** in the intervals between other actions; between-whiles. **From t. to t. a.** At more or less regular intervals; now and again, occasionally. **†b.** Continuously, at all times. **In t. a.** In the course of time, sooner or later. **b.** Soon or early enough, not too late. **c.** *In good t.* (*a*) After the lapse of a suitable interval; in due course; at a proper time. (*b*) Soon or early; quickly. †(*c*) As an expression of ironical acquiescence, incredulity, or the like: To be sure! indeed! very well! (Cf. F. *à la bonne heure.*) **On t.,** punctually; also *pred.* punctual. Chiefly *U.S. colloq.* **Out of t. a.** *adv. phr.* After the prescribed period has elapsed; too late. **b.** *adj. phr.* Unseasonable. **With t.,** with the lapse of time, in the course of time.

3. (The) t. was (hath been, shall be), inversion of *there was* (etc.) *a time* (*when*). **To keep t.: a.** *Mus.* To mark the rhythm by movements of the hands or baton; to beat time; also, of a performer, to adhere to the correct rhythm and rate of the music, to keep pace *with* a measure or another performer, etc. **b.** Of a timepiece: To register the passage of time correctly.

Comb.: **t.-bill,** (*a*) a t.-table of trains, etc.; (*b*) a record kept by the guard of a train of the t. it leaves each station; **-book,** (*a*) a book in which an entry is made of the t. worked by employees; (*b*) = *t.-bill* (*a*); **-card,** a card on which a record is kept of t. worked; **-clock,** a clock which records the t. at which a workman arrives or departs, or punches a t.-card; **-course** *Naut.*, a ship's run, as in a fog, calculated by the vessel's speed, the t. occupied, and the direction; **-detector,** a clock (stationary at a point) or watch (carried by the watchman) having additional mechanism, operated by the watchman, to show the times at which he was at certain points of his round; also called *t.-watch*; **-expired** *a.*, whose term of engagement has expired; **-exposure** *Photogr.*, exposure for a regulated time, as dist. from instantaneous exposure; **-lag,** the length of t. separating two correlated physical phenomena; **-lock,** a lock with clock-work attachment which prevents its being unlocked until a set t.; **-sheet,** a t.-table (on a sheet); the paper on which are entered the names of workmen and the hours worked by them; **-shutter** *Photogr.*, a shutter for t.-exposures; **-signal,** a visible or audible signal made at an observatory, etc., to announce the exact t.; **-signature** *Mus.*, a sign placed at the beginning of a piece of music, or where the t. changes, to show the measure or rhythm; **-value** *Mus.*, the relative duration of a note; **-watch** = *t.-detector*; **-work,** work paid for on the basis of the t. occupied; dist. from *piece-work.*

Time (təim), *v.* Pa. t. and pa. pple. **timed** (təimd). late ME. [f. prec.] **1.** *trans.* To appoint or arrange the time of (an action or event); to choose the moment for. Usu. (in context) to do (a thing) at the right time; 'to adapt to the time' (J.). **b.** To arrange the time of arrival of (a train, etc.); hence, to regulate the rate of travelling of; also, to calculate the pace and moment of impact of (a ball or moving body) 1861. **c.** To adjust (a clock, etc.) to keep accurate time 1825. **2.** To mark the rhythm or measure of, as in music; to sing or play (an air or instrument) in (good or bad) time 1500. **b.** To set the time of; to cause to coincide in time with something 1655. **c.** *intr.* To keep time *to*; to sound or move in unison or harmony *with* 1850. **3.** To fix the duration of; to assign the metrical quantity of (a syllable) or the duration of (a note); also, to regulate the action of (a mechanism, etc.) as to duration 1589. **4.** To ascertain or note the time at which (something) is done or happens; to note the time occupied by (a person) or the duration of (an action, etc.) 1670. **5.** *Mech.* To adjust the parts of (a mechanism) so that a succession of movements or operations takes place at the required intervals and in the desired sequence 1895.

1. There is surely no greater Wisedome, then well to t. the Beginnings, and Onsets of Things BACON. b. The Royal train was timed to reach Leamington at 1.17 p.m. 1861. 2. He was a thing of Blood, whose euery motion Was tim'd with dying Cryes SHAKS. b. Old Epopeus..Who overlook'd the oars, and tim'd the stroke ADDISON. c. Beat, happy stars, timing with things below TENNYSON. 3. Phr. †*To t. it out* to procrastinate, delay, spin out the time (*rare*). 4. Slowly as he read, it was over in twelve minutes, for I timed him 1859. Hence **Timed** *ppl. a.* esp. in comb., as *well-timed.*

Ti·me-ball. 1858. A ball moving on a vertical rod or pole, placed in some prominent position, for the purpose of indicating mean time, which it does by dropping at a certain moment each day from the top to the bottom of the rod.

Ti·me-ba·rgain. 1775. A contract for the sale or purchase of goods or stock at a stipulated price on a certain future day; in Stock Exchange parlance, a transaction in which one accepts the liability to profit or lose by the amount of the difference between the prices of the stock involved on the day of dealing and on the settling-day.

Timeful (təi·mfŭl), *a. rare.* ME. [f. TIME *sb.* + -FUL.] Seasonable, due. Hence **Ti·mefully** *adv.* with timely action CARLYLE.

Ti·me-ho·noured, *a.* 1593. Honoured or made honourable by length of time; respected on account of long existence or old establishment.

Old Iohn of Gaunt, time-honoured Lancaster SHAKS.

Ti·me-kee·per, timekeeper. 1686. **1.** An instrument for registering the passage of time; a timepiece; formerly, a chronometer. **2.** One who notes, measures, or records time; *spec.* **a.** one who is employed in keeping account of workmen's hours of labour; **b.** one who beats time in music; **c.** one who marks the time occupied by a race, the rounds in a pugilistic encounter, etc. 1795. **3.** A person or thing that keeps (good or bad) time 1899.

Timeless (təi·mlės), *a.* (*adv.*) 1560. [-LESS.] **1.** That is out of its proper time; untimely; ill-timed. Chiefly *poet.*, now *arch.* or *Obs.* **b.** as *adv.* Out of due time 1586. **2.** Not subject to time; not affected by the lapse of time; eternal. Chiefly *poet.* and *rhet.* 1628. **3.** *Gram.* Not expressing time or a temporal aspect.

1. Let earth and heaven his t. death deplore MARLOWE. 2. When worlds..headlong rush To t. night, and chaos, whence they rose YOUNG. Hence **Ti·melessly** *adv.* out of due time (*arch.* or *Obs.*); without

reference to time, independently of the passage of time.

‖**Timelia** (təimī·liă). 1896. [Altered from *Timalia*, said to be from an E. Ind. name.] *Ornith.* A genus of East Indian oscine birds, the type of which is *T. pileata*, a small bird found from Nepāl to Cochin China and Java. Hence Time·lian *a.* Timeliine (təimī·li,əin) *a.* allied, or assumed to be allied, to *T.*

Ti·me-li:mit. 1880. A limit in time, or to the duration of some action or condition; also, a limit to the duration of a licence or privilege.

Timeliness (təi·mlinės). 1599. [f. next + -NESS.] The quality of being timely; †early maturity (*rare*); seasonableness, suitableness to the time.

Timely (təi·mli), *a.* ME. [f. TIME *sb.* + -LY[1].] 1. Occurring or appearing in good time; early. Now *rare* or *Obs.* late ME. 2. Seasonable, opportune, well-timed ME.

2. Now Gilpin had a pleasant wit, And loved a t. joke COWPER.

Timely (təi·mli), *adv.* [Late OE. *tīmlīce*, f. *tīma* TIME *sb.* + -LY[2].] 1. Early, betimes; soon, quickly. Now *arch.* or *poet.* 2. †Soon enough, in time; hence, in due season seasonably; opportunely as regards time ME. 3. Usu. hyphened to an adj. or pple. when used attrib. 1593.

1. The Spring visiteth not these quarters so t., as the Eastern parts 1602. 2. All requisite materials t. provided 1715. 3. Our t.-repented and often-forsaken habits of sin JER. TAYLOR.

Timenoguy (ti·mənǫgi). *Naut.* 1794. [app. f. †*timon* rudder + GUY *sb.*[1]] A rope passing from the fore-rigging to the anchor-stock to prevent the fouling of the fore-sheet.

Timeous, timous (təi·məs), *a.* (*adv.*) Chiefly *Sc.* 1470. [f. TIME *sb.* + -OUS. Occas. pronounced (təi·mĭəs) or (ti·myəs), from the spelling.] 1. = TIMELY *a.* 1. b. as *adv.* Early, betimes. Now *dial.* 1578. 2. = TIMELY *a.* 2. 1626. Hence Ti·meously *adv.* in a t. manner.

Timepiece (təi·m,pīs). 1765. [PIECE *sb.* II. 8 ('pieces made at Augsburgh, that moved by the help of Clock-work', 1698).] An instrument for measuring and registering the passage of time.

Timer (təi·məɹ). 1841. [f. TIME *sb.* and *v.* + -ER[1].] 1. One who appoints the time for an action, event, etc. 2. a. A (good or bad) time-keeper. b. One who times clocks, etc. c. = TIME-KEEPER 2 c. 1884. 3. In comb., as FULL-TIMER, HALF-TIMER, etc.; **fast t.**, one who or that which completes a race, etc. in fast time 1891.

Ti·me-se:rver. 1584. [f. phr. *to serve the time*; see SERVE *v.*] One who adapts his conduct to the time or season; usu., one who on grounds of self-interest shapes his conduct in conformity to the views that are in favour at the time; a 'trimmer'.

Ti·me-se:rving, *vbl. sb.* 1621. [See prec.] The action or conduct of a time-server; 'trimming'.

Ti·me-se:rving, *ppl. a.* 1630. Characterized by interested compliance; 'trimming', temporizing.

Ti·me-spi:rit. 1831. [tr. G. *zeitgeist.*] The spirit of the time, the genius of the age.

Ti·me-ta:ble. 1838. A tabular list or schedule of the times at which successive things are to be done or happen, or of the times occupied in the parts of some process. *spec.* a. A printed table or book of tables showing the times of arrival and departure of railway trains at and from the stations; also, a similar table of times of arrival and departure of steam-boats, etc. b. A chart used in railway traffic offices, showing by means of cross lines, in one direction representing hours and minutes and in the other miles, the position of the various trains at any given moment. c. A table showing how the time of a school, etc., for any day, or for a week, is allotted to classes and subjects.

a. Bradshaw's Railway Time Tables 1839.

Ti·me-worn, *a.* 1729. Worn by process of time; impaired by age.

Timid (ti·mid), *a.* 1549. [ad. L. *timidus*, f. *timere.*] Subject to fear; easily frightened; wanting boldness or courage; fearful, timorous. b. Characterized by or indicating fear 1741.

Poor is the triumph o'er the t. hare THOMSON. b. Carry to him thy t. counsels GRAY. **Ti·mid-ly** *adv.*, **-ness** (*rare*).

Timidity (timi·dĭti). 1598. [ad. L. *timiditas*, f. *timidus* TIMID; see -ITY.] The quality of being timid; fearfulness.

Timist (təi·mist). 1613. [-IST.] †1. A time-server –1658. 2. One who keeps correct time in music 1765. 3. *Cricket.* One who times the ball (well or badly) 1893.

Timocracy (təimǫ·krăsi). 1586. [a. OF. *tymocracie*, mod.F. *timocratie*, ad. med.L. *timocratia*, a. Gr. τιμοκρατία, f. τιμή honour (Plato), value or valuation (Aristotle) + -κρατια; see -CRACY.] 1. In the Aristotelian sense: A polity with a property qualification for the ruling class. 2. In the Platonic sense: A polity (like that of Sparta) in which love of honour is said to be the dominant motive with the rulers 1656. Hence **Timocra·tic, -al** *adjs.*

Timon (təi·mǫ̆n). 1588. [Gr. Τίμων, personal name.] The name of a noted misanthrope of Athens, the hero of Shakspere's *Timon of Athens*; hence, one like Timon, a misanthrope.

Timoneer (təimŏnīə·ɹ). *rare.* 1762. [a. F. *timonier*, f. *timon* helm :—L. *temonem* beam, pole; see -EER.] A helmsman, steersman.

Timorous (ti·mŏrəs), *a.* 1450. [= OF. *temeros, -ous*, later *timoreus, timoreux*, f. L. *timorem* fear.] 1. Full of or affected by fear (either for the time or habitually); fearful. b. Indicating or proceeding from fear; characterized by timidity 1581. †2. Causing fear or dread; dreadful, terrible –1632.

1. Timerous of death 1613. Animals of the hare kind..are inoffensive and t. GOLDSM. b. This t. policy 1838. Hence **Ti·morous-ly** *adv.*, **-ness.**

Timorsome (ti·məɹsǒm), *a.* Now *dial.* 1599. [app. f. *timorous*, with substitution of *-some* suffix for *-ous.*] Subject to or characterized by fear; timorous, timid.

Timothy (ti·mŏþi). 1747. Short for next. Also *attrib.* as *t. field, hay.*

Ti·mothy grass. 1736. [Said to be f. name of *Timothy* Hanson, who was the first to cultivate it as an agricultural plant.] A name (orig. Amer.) for Meadow Cat's-tail Grass, *Phleum pratense*, a native British grass, introduced into cultivation under this name in the N. Amer. colonies in the 18th c.

†Timwhi·sky. 1764. [See WHISKY *sb.*[2]; first element obsc.] A kind of high light carriage, seated for one or two, drawn by a single horse or by two horses driven 'tandem'; a gig; a whisky –1837

Tin (tin), *sb.* [OE. *tin* :—OTeut. **tinom*; not known outside Teut.] 1. A well-known metal, nearly approaching silver in whiteness and lustre, highly malleable, and taking a high polish; used in the manufacture of articles of block tin, in the formation of alloys, as bronze, pewter, etc., and, on account of its resistance to oxidation, for making tin-plate and lining culinary and other iron vessels. As a chemical element, symbol Sn (*stannum*), atomic weight 119. b. With defining attribute 1610. 2. A vessel made of tin, or more usu. of tinned iron; *spec.* a vessel in which meat, fish, fruit, etc., is hermetically sealed for preservation; locally, a small cylindrical drinking vessel or mug with a handle 1821. b. Tin-plate as the material of such vessels 1879. 3. *slang.* Money, cash 1836.

1. b. **Bar-t.** = *block t.*; **black t.**, t. ore (the dioxide, SnO_2) prepared for smelting; **block t.**, metallic t. refined and cast into blocks; **grain t.**, a very pure t. obtained by fusing stream t. in a blast furnace supplied with charcoal and breaking it into small pieces; **phosphor t.**, an artificial compound of t. and phosphorus; **stream t.**, t. ore washed from the sand or gravel in which it occurs; **white t.**, refined metallic t.

attrib. and *Comb.*: as *t. box, -mine, -ore, -whistle, -works*; also *fig.* with ref. to t. as a base metal; also, made of corrugated iron; **t.-bath**, the mass of melted t. in a t.-furnace; **-can** = sense 2, **t. hat** (*Mil. slang*), a shrapnel helmet; *to put the t. hat on*, to 'finish', 'put the lid on'; **t. god** *fig.*, a base or unworthy object of veneration; **-liquor**, a solution of t. in strong acid mixed with common salt, used as a mordant in dyeing; **-mordant**, a mordant consisting of a solution of t. in acid. as *t.-liquor*; **-opener**, an instrument for opening soldered tins; **-pyrites**, a sulphide of t.; **-stuff**, a miner's name for tin ore.

Tin (tin), *v.* late ME. [f. prec.] 1. *trans.* To cover with a thin deposit of tin; to coat or plate with tin. 2. In soldering iron, brass, etc.: To perform the preliminary processes of heating the surfaces and covering them with a thin coating of the solder 1873. 3. To put up or seal (provisions) in a tin for preservation; to can 1887.

‖**Tinamou** (ti·nămū). 1783. [a. F., a. *tinamu*, native name in Galibi.] A bird of the genus *Tinamus* or family *Tinamidæ* of dromæognathous birds, having an external resemblance to partridges or quails.

Tincal (ti·ŋkăl), **tincar** (ti·ŋkăɹ). 1635. [In form *tincal*, a. Malay *tingkal* :—Skr. *ṭankaṇa*; in Pers., Arab., Urdū *tankār, tinkār* whence the form *tincar.* Cf. ALTINCAR.] Crude borax, found in lake-deposits in Tibet, Persia, and other Asiatic countries.

Tinchel (ti·nχ^y̆ĕl, ti·ŋkĕl). *Sc.* 1549. [ad. Gael. *timchioll* (tʃi·mχ^y̆ŏl) circuit, compass, round.] In Scotland, a wide circle of hunters driving together a number of deer by gradually closing in on them.

Tinct (tiŋkt), *sb.* Now *poet.* 1471. [ad. L. *tinctus* a dyeing, f. *tingere* to stain.] 1. = TINCTURE *sb.* 1, 2, 4. 1602. †2. *Alch.* A transmuting elixir –1606.

1. White and Azure lac'd With Blew of Heauens owne t. SHAKS. 2. *Ant. & Cl.* I. v. 37.

Tinct, *ppl. a. poet.* 1579. [ad. L. *tinctus, tingere.*] Coloured, tinted; dyed, tinged; imbued. Const. as *pa. pple.*

Lucent syrops, t. with cinnamon KEATS.

†Tinct, *v.* 1594. [f. L. *tinct-, tingere* to dye, colour.] 1. *trans.* To colour; to dye; to tinge, tint –1686. 2. *transf.* and *fig.* = TINCTURE *v.* 2 a, b. –1734. 3. *Alch.* To subject to a transmuting elixir –1655.

Tinctorial (tiŋktō°·riăl), *a.* 1655. [f. L. *tinctorius* (f. *tinctorem* dyer) + -AL.] Of, pertaining to, or used in dyeing; yielding or using dye or colouring matter. Hence **Tincto·rially** *adv.*

Tincture (ti·ŋktiŭɹ, -tʃəɹ), *sb.* late ME. [ad. L. *tinctura* a dyeing, tinging, f. *tinct-, tingere*; see -URE.] †1. A dye, pigment; *spec.* a dye used as a cosmetic –1825. 2. Hue, colour; a tinge, tint. Now *rare.* 1477. b. *Her.* Inclusive term for the metals, colours, and furs used in coats of arms, etc. 1610. †3. The action of dyeing, staining, or colouring –1681. †b. *fig.* A stain, blemish –1658. †4. *fig.* An imparted quality likened to a colour or dye; a specious or 'colourable' appearance; a tinge –1806. †5. A physical quality (other than colour) communicated to something; *esp.* a taste or flavour, a taint –1727. b. A slight infusion (*of* some element, quality, etc.); a tinge, shade, flavour, trace; a smattering (*of* knowledge, etc.) 1612. †6. *Alch.* A supposed spiritual principle or immaterial substance whose character or quality may be infused into material things, which are then said to be tinctured; the quintessence, spirit, or soul of a thing. *Universal t.*, the Elixir. –1693. †b. An active principle, of a physical nature, emanating or derivable from any body or substance; a liquid or volatile principle –1677. 7. *Chem.* and *Pharm.* †a. The (supposed) essential principle of any substance obtained in solution. Also, the extraction of this essential principle. 1610. b. *Mod. Pharmacy.* A solution, usu. in a menstruum of alcohol, of some principle used in medicine, chiefly vegetable, as t. of opium (laudanum), but occas. animal, as t. of cantharides, or mineral, as t. of ferric chloride 1648.

More particularly called an *alcoholic tincture.* But the menstruum may also be sulphuric ether or spirit of ammonia (both mainly alcohol), which give *ethereal* and *ammoniated* tinctures respectively when wine is used they are called *medicated wines.*

2. 'Tis not..The t. of a skin, that I admire ADDISON. b. *Tinctures*, in Heraldry are of three descriptions: metals, colours, and furs. The former are or, argent; the second gules, azure, sable, vert, purpure, sanguine, and tenny. The chief furs are ermine and vair; but there are several varieties of both, distinguished by different names. 1842. 4. The Saxon language received little or no t. from the Welsh BURKE. 5. b.

This, perhaps, cannot be called Affectation; but it has some T. of it STEELE.

Ti·ncture, *v.* 1616. [f. prec.] **1.** *trans.* To impart a tincture or dye to; to dye; to colour, tinge, imbue. (Chiefly in pa. pple.) **2.** *transf.* and *fig.* To imbue or impregnate with a quality; to communicate some quality to; to affect, tinge, taint. (Chiefly in pa. pple., const. *with*.) †**a.** with a physical quality, as smell or taste –1820. **b.** with a mental or moral quality or character 1636.

1. Cheekes tinctured with Vermillion SIR T. HERBERT. 2. b. His Conversation was tinctured throughout with the Ancient Mythology 1718.

Tind (tind), *v.* *Obs.* exc. *dial.* [Early ME. *tende(n* represented an OE. **tęndan*, corresp. to Goth. *tandjan*, Da. *tænde*, Sw. *tända*; causative of **tindan* str. vb. (ablaut series **tind-*, *tand-*, *tund-*) to be on fire, burn, glow. Early ME. *tiende*, *tinde*, now *tind*, *tīnd* (təind), is prob. a parallel formation, repr. an OE. **tyndan*.] **1.** *trans.* To set fire to, light, kindle (a fire, torch, flame.). **2.** *intr.* To catch fire, kindle, become ignited, begin to burn ME. **3.** *fig. trans.* To inflame, excite, arouse, inspire ME.

1. As one candle tindeth a thousand 1663. 2. Wash your hands, or else the fire Will not teend to your desire HERRICK. 3. Shop-consciences,.. Preach'd up, and ready tined for a rebellion DRYDEN.

‖**Tindal** (ti·ndăl). *India.* 1698. [ad. Malayālam *tanḍal*, Telugu *tanḍelu*, also Hindūstānī *tanḍēl* chief or head man of a body of men.] **1.** A native petty officer of lascars, on board ship, or in the ordnance department; also, the foreman of a gang of labourers on public works (Yule); a boatswain; a foreman. **2.** A personal attendant 1859.

Tinder (ti·ndəɹ). [OE. *tynder* and *tyndre*, f. OTeut. **tund-*, wk. grade of **tind-* to kindle; see TIND *v.*] Any dry inflammable substance that readily takes fire from a spark and burns or smoulders; esp. that prepared from partially charred linen and from species of *Polyporus* or corkwood fungus (AGARIC 1), formerly in common use to catch the spark struck from a flint with a steel, as the means of kindling a fire or 'striking' a light.

attrib. and *Comb.*: **t.-box**, a box containing t. (also usu. the flint and steel with which the spark was struck); **-fungus**, a fungus from which t. is made, as **t.-polypore**, *Polyporus fomentarius*.

Tindery (ti·ndəri), *a.* 1754. [f. prec. + -Y[1].] Of the nature of or resembling tinder, tinder-like also *fig.* 'inflammable', passionate.

Tine (təin), *sb.*[1] [OE. *tind*:—OTeut. **tindiz*.] **1.** Each of a series of projecting sharp points on some weapon or implement, as a harrow, fork, etc.; a prong, spike, tooth. **2.** Each of the pointed branches of a deer's horn. late ME.

†**Tine**, *sb.*[2] (Only in and after Spenser.) 1590. [By-form of TEEN *sb.*[1], perh. from Norse.] Affliction, trouble, sorrow –1610.

To seek her out with labor and long tyne SPENSER.

†**Tine**, *a.* and *sb.*[3] late ME. [Origin dubious.] **A.** *adj.* = TINY *a.* –1605.

A ioynt of Mutton, and any pretty little t. Kickshawes SHAKS.

B. *sb.* or quasi-*sb.* A very little space, time, or amount; a very little; 'a bit' –1556.

Tine, tyne (təin), *v.*[1] *Obs.* exc. *dial.* [OE. *tȳnan*:—OTeut. **tūnjan*, f. **tūno-* enclosure, TOWN.] **1.** *trans.* To close, shut (a door, gate, or window; a house, one's mouth, eyes, etc.). Also with *to* adv. and *absol.* **2. a.** To enclose or shut (a thing) up *in* something. late ME. **b.** To fence, hedge in OE.

Tine, tyne (təin), *v.*[2] Now *n. dial.* and *Sc.* Pa. t. and pa. pple. **tint** (tint). ME. [a. ON. *týna*, f. *tjón* loss, damage.] = LOSE *v.*[1]

Tine, var. of TIND *v.*

‖**Tinea** (ti·nĭă). late ME. [L., a gnawing worm, a moth, bookworm.] **1.** *Path.* Technical name of the disease RINGWORM. **2.** *Ent.* A genus of small moths (*Microlepidoptera*), including *T. tapetzella* and *T. pellionella*, and *T. destructor*, the larvæ of which are very destructive to cloth, feathers, soft paper, stuffed birds, etc. In earlier times the word was applied to other destructive insects and worms. Hence **Ti·nean**, **Ti·neid** *a.* of or belonging to the genus *T.* or family *Tineidæ*; *sb.* a member of this genus or family.

Tined (təind), *a.* late ME. [f. TINE *sb.*[1] + -ED.] Furnished with or having tines.

Tinfoil (ti·nfoil), *sb.* late ME. [f. TIN *sb.* + FOIL *sb.*[1]] Tin hammered or rolled into a thin sheet; also, a sheet of the same rubbed with quicksilver, used for backing mirrors and precious stones; a similar sheet of an alloy of tin and lead, used as a wrapping to protect comfits, etc., from moisture or air. Hence **Ti·nfoil** *v. trans.* to cover or coat with t.; **Ti·nfoiled** *ppl. a.* esp. *fig.*

Ting (tiŋ), *sb.* 1602. [f. next.] The sound emitted by a small bell, or other resonant body, as the result of a single stroke. Also *advb.*, or without grammatical construction, esp. when repeated. **b.** *T.-a-ling*, *t.-a-ring*, the sound of the ringing of a small bell, or the like 1833. Also **Ting-tang** 1680.

The sharp t. of a hand-bell 1895. b. Ting-a-ling. Telephone again. 1906.

Ting (tiŋ), *v.* 1495. [Echoic.] **1.** *trans.* To cause (a small bell or the like) to emit a ringing note. **2.** *intr.* Of a bell, a metal or glass vessel, or the like: To emit a high-pitched ringing note when struck, to ring 1562. **3.** To make a ringing sound *with* a bell, etc. 1605.

Tinge (tin^dʒ), *sb.* 1752. [f. TINGE *v.*] **1.** A slight shade of colouring, *esp.* one modifying a tint or colour. **2.** *fig.* A modifying infusion or intermixture; a touch or flavour of some quality 1797.

2. His political opinions had a t. of Whiggism MACAULAY.

Tinge (tin^dʒ), *v.* 1477. [ad. L. *tingere* to dye.] **1.** *trans.* To impart a trace or slight shade of some colour to; to tint; to modify the tint or colour of (const. *with*). Also *absol.* **b.** *transf.* To impart a slight taste or smell to; to affect slightly by admixture 1690. **2.** *intr.* To become modified in colour; to take a (specified or implied) tinge 1662. **3.** *fig.* To qualify, modify, or slightly vary the tone of 1674.

3. This grief tinged the whole of Mr. Croker's subsequent life 1884.

Tingent (ti·ndʒĕnt), *a.* Now *rare* or *Obs.* 1650. [ad. L. *tingentem*, *tingere*.] That tinges or colours, colouring, dyeing.

Tin-glass. Now *rare.* 1478. [f. TIN *sb.* + GLASS.] An old name for: Bismuth.

Tingle (ti·ŋg'l), *sb.* 1700. [f. next.] An instance, act, or condition of tingling. Also advb. or without constr.

The t. of the morning air 1908.

Tingle (ti·ŋg'l), *v.* late ME. [app. a modification of TINKLE *v.*[1]] **I. 1.** *intr.* Said of the ears: To be affected with a ringing or thrilling sensation at the hearing of anything. **b.** Said also of the cheeks under the influence of shame, indignation, etc. 1555. **2.** Of other parts of the body: To be thrilled by a peculiar stinging or smarting sensation, physical or emotional; to smart, thrill, vibrate; also *fig.* of inanimate things, companies of persons, etc. late ME. **b.** Predicated of that which causes the sensation: To thrill, vibrate; to pass with a thrill 1819. **3.** *trans.* To cause to tingle; to sting, excite, stimulate 1572. **b.** *absol.* or *intr.* 1872.

1. Least I cause good and learned mens eares to t. at his leud and vnseemely rimes HAKLUYT. 2. Wounds t. most when they are about to heal THACKERAY. b. The lust of battle tingling in him from head to heel KINGSLEY. 3. The cold, inconsiderate of persons, tingles your blood EMERSON.

II. 1. *intr.* To make a continued light ringing sound. Now *rare.* late ME. **2.** *trans.* To cause (a bell) to ring lightly; to ring (a bell, a chime, etc.). Now *rare.* 1649. Hence **Ti·ngler**, something that causes tingling, as a blow; a 'stinger'. **Ti·nglingly** *adv.*

Tink (tiŋk), *int.* and *sb.* 1609. [Echoic.] A representation of the abrupt sound made by striking resonant metal with something hard and light; often reduplicated; also with such variations as *t.-tank*, *t.-a-t.*, etc. Hence as *sb.* a single sound of this kind; also *fig.* in ref. to rime or verse.

Tink (tiŋk), *v.*[1] Now *rare* or *Obs.* late ME. [Echoic.] **1.** *intr.* To emit a metallic sound with very short resonance, e.g. as is done by a cracked bell, but occas. used as = TINKLE, to chink, clink. **2.** Of a person: To make such a sound by striking upon metal or other resonant substance 1533. **3.** *trans.* To cause to emit an abrupt metallic sound 1495.

1. Prov. *As the fool thinketh, the bell tinketh*, i.e. to the fool the bell seems to say what he wants it to say; in ref. to a superstitious notion that the tinkling of a bell sometimes gives an oracular monition or answer.

Tink, *v.*[2] Now *rare* or *Obs.* ME. [perh. a back-formation from *tinker*.] *trans.* To mend, solder, rivet (rarely, to make) pots and pans, as a tinker.

Tinker (ti·ŋkəɹ), *sb.* ME. [Goes with prec.] **1.** A craftsman (usu. itinerant) who mends pots, kettles, and other metal household utensils. **b.** In Scotland and north of Ireland, a gipsy. Also applied to itinerant beggars, traders, and performers generally. 1561. **c.** A clumsy or inefficient mender; a botcher; also *fig.* In U.S. also applied to a 'jack-of-all-trades'. 1644. **2.** [f. next.] An act or bout of tinkering; *fig.* a bungling or unskilful attempt at mending something 1857. **3.** Local name for: **a.** The skate. **b.** The stickleback. **c.** *U.S.* A small or young mackerel. **d.** The guillemot 1836. (Cf. TINKERSHERE.) **4.** *Ordnance.* A small mortar fixed on the end of a staff, and fired by a trigger and lanyard. *U.S.* 1877.

1. Phr. *Not to care*, or *be worth*, *a tinker's curse* or *damn*, an intensification of 'not to care a curse or damn', with ref. to the reputed addiction of tinkers to profane swearing.

Tinker (ti·ŋkəɹ), *v.* 1592. [f. prec.] **1.** *intr.* To work as a tinker; to mend metal utensils (and hence *gen.* any material objects), esp. in a clumsy or bungling way. **b.** *fig.* To work at something (immaterial) clumsily or imperfectly; also, to occupy oneself about something in a trifling or aimless way; to potter 1658. **2.** *trans.* To mend as a tinker; to patch *up* 1753.

1. b. The public were tired of government which merely tinkered at legislation 1880. 2. *fig.* Men are prone to be tinkering the work of their own hands LOWELL.

†**Ti·nkerly**, *a.* 1586. [f. TINKER *sb.* + -LY[1].] Having the character of a tinker or of tinker's work; clumsy, bungling, unskilful; of poor quality; mean, low, disreputable –1681.

Tinkershere, -shire (ti·ŋkəɹʃiəɹ). *local.* 1799. [f. TINKER *sb.*; second element obsc.] The common guillemot; the black guillemot.

Tin-kettle. 1775. A kettle of tinned iron. (Often *fig.* with allusion to its being fastened to a dog's tail to tease and frighten it, or to the noise made by beating it.)

Tinkle (ti·ŋk'l), *sb.* 1682. [f. next.] The act or action of tinkling; a sharp light ringing sound, such as that made by a small bell, etc. 1804. **b.** *fig.* in ref. to speech or verse 1725. **c.** Reduplicated, expressing repetition of such sounds; also as *adv.* 1682.

Of ice and glass the t., Pellucid, silver-shrill HENLEY.

Tinkle (ti·ŋk'l), *v.*[1] late ME. [app. a freq. of TINK *v.* (see -LE 3).] **I.** *intr.* Of the ears: = TINGLE *v.* 1. Now *rare.*

His Ears tinckled, and his Colour fled DRYDEN.

II. 1. To give forth a series of short light sharp ringing sounds. Said of bells, musical instruments, and other resonant objects. late ME. **b.** To flow or move with a tinkling sound 1822. **c.** *transf.* To rime or jingle 1626. **2.** Of a person: To produce such a sound 1750. **b.** *fig.* To utter empty sounds or senseless words, talk idly, prate 1641. **3.** *trans.* **a.** To make known, call attention to, or express by tinkling (*lit.* or *fig.*) 1562. **b.** To affect, attract, or summon by tinkling 1582. **4.** To cause (something) to tinkle or make a short light ringing sound 1582.

1. A sheepbell tinkles on the heath 1819. b. A small rill tinkled along close by W. IRVING. 2. We are but crackt cimbals, we do but tinckle, we know nothing MILTON.

†**Tinkle**, *v.*[2] 1599. [f. next.] = TINKER *v.* 1 –1630.

Tinkler (ti·ŋkləɹ). *Sc.* and *dial.* ME. [app. f. TINKER, with different suffix.] A tinker, a worker in metal; in Scotland, etc., usu. a gipsy, or other itinerant mender of pots, pans, and metal-work.

Tinkling (ti·ŋkliŋ), *vbl. sb.* 1495. [-ING[1].] **1.** The action of TINKLE *v.*[1] **2.** Short for *tinkling grackle*; see next. 1847.

1. Drowsy tinklings lull the distant folds GRAY.

Tinkling (ti·ŋkliŋ), *ppl. a.* 1440. [f. TINKLE *v.*[1] + -ING[2].] That tinkles. **b.** *T. grackle*, also simply *tinkling*: a bird, a species of grackle (*Quiscalus crassirostris*) found in Jamaica; so called from its note 1847. Hence Ti·nklingly *adv.*

Tinkly (ti·ŋkli), *a.* 1892. [f. TINKLE *v.*[1] or *sb.* + -Y.[1]] Characterized by tinkling.
The t. piano 1894.

Tinman (ti·nmæ̆n). 1611. [f. TIN *sb.* + MAN *sb.*] A man who works in or with tin; a tinsmith. In Cornwall, a man employed in dressing tin ore.

Tinned (tind), *ppl. a.* late ME. [f. TIN *sb.* or *v.* + -ED.] **1.** Coated or plated with tin. **2.** Preserved in air-tight tins; canned 1879.
3. Of music: Produced by mechanical means, as in a cinema 1929.

Tinner (ti·nəɹ). 1512. [f. TIN *sb.* or *v.* + -ER[1].] **1.** A tin-miner. **2.** One who works in tin; a tin-plater, tinman, tinsmith 1611. **3.** One who tins meat, fruit, etc.; a canner 1906.

Tinnery (ti·nəri). 1769. [f. prec. + -Y[3].] Tin-mining; *pl.* tin-mines or tin-works.

Tinning (ti·niŋ), *vbl. sb.* 1440. [f. TIN *v.* or *sb.* + -ING[1].] **1.** Coating, lining, or plating with tin; working at tin-ware. **b.** *concr.* A tin coating or lining 1761. **2.** The putting up and sealing of meat, fish, fruit, etc., in tins for preservation 1903. **3.** Tin-mining 1855.

‖**Tinnitus** (tinəi·tŏs). 1843. [L., f. *tinnire* to ring, tinkle.] *Med.* A sensation of ringing in the ears.

Tinny (ti·ni), *a.* 1552. [f. TIN *sb.* + -Y[1].] **1.** Consisting of, abounding in, or yielding tin; formerly also, of tin, made of tin. **2.** Like or resembling tin or that of tin; *esp.* of sounds; in *Painting*, hard, crude, metallic 1877. **3.** *slang.* Having plenty of 'tin'; wealthy 1871.
1. Dart, nigh chockt with sands of t. mines SPENSER. 2. The old t.-sounding spinnet 1904.

Tinoceratid (təinose·rătid), *a.* and *sb.* 1889. [irreg. f. Gr. τείνειν to stretch, as if = stretching out + κέρας, κερατ- horn + -ID.] *Palæont.* **A.** *adj.* Of, pertaining to, or having the characters of the *Tinoceras*, a very large fossil mammal. **B.** *sb.* A fossil of this genus 1891.

Tin-plate. 1677. Sheet-iron or, in recent use, often sheet-steel, coated with tin; a plate of this. So Ti·n-pla·ted *ppl. a.* Ti·n-pla·ter.

Tin-pot (ti·nˌpǫ·t, ti·npǫt). 1772. **1.** (as two words) A pot made of tin or tin-plate. **2.** The pot of molten tin into which the sheet of iron is dipped in the manufacture of tin-plate 1839. **3.** *attrib.* Resembling or suggesting a tin pot in quality or sound; hence *contempt.*, of inferior quality, shabby, poor, cheap 1865.
3. Miserable t. politicians 1897.

Tinsel (ti·nsĕl, -s'l), *sb.* and *a.* 1502. [f. OF. *estincelle*:—pop.L. **stincilla* for *scintilla* spark.] **1.** *adj.* passing into *sb.* used *attrib.* Of satin, etc.: Made to sparkle or glitter by the interweaving of gold or silver thread, by brocading with such thread, or by overlaying with a thin coating of gold or silver. †**2.** A kind of cloth or tissue; tinselled cloth; a rich material of silk or wool interwoven with gold or silver thread; occas., a thin net or gauze thus made; later, a cheap imitation of this -1755. **3.** Very thin plates or sheets, spangles, strips, or threads, orig. of gold or silver, later of copper, brass, etc., used chiefly for ornament; now esp. for cheap and showy ornamentation, gaudy stage costumes, and the like 1593. **4.** *fig.* Anything showy or attractive with little or no intrinsic worth 1660. **5.** *attrib.* passing into *adj.* †Glittering, splendid. Chiefly in disparagement: Showy with little real worth; cheaply gaudy, tawdry 1595.
3. As twinckling starres, the tinsell of the night 1593. 4. That poverty of ideas which had been hitherto concealed under the t. of politeness JOHNSON. 5. Neither their t. wit, nor superficial learning will hold them up then 1680.

Ti·nsel, *v.* 1594. [f. prec.] **1.** *trans.* To make glittering with gold or silver (or imitations thereof) interwoven, brocaded, or laid on. **2.** To give a speciously attractive or showy appearance to; to cover the defects of with or as with tinsel 1748. Hence Ti·nselled *ppl. a.* = prec. **1**; also, embellished with gold or silver leaf.

Tinselly (ti·nsĕli), *a.* 1811. [f. as prec. + -Y[1].] Of the nature of, characterized by, or abounding in tinsel; hence, cheaply splendid or sparkling, 'pinchbeck'.

Tinsmith (ti·nˌsmiþ). 1858. [f. TIN + SMITH.] A worker in tin; a maker of tin utensils; a whitesmith.

Ti·n-stone. 1602. The most commonly occurring form of tin ore; cassiterite, native tin dioxide (peroxide).

Tint (tint), *sb.* 1717. [app. altered from TINCT, perh. infl. by It. *tinta.*] **1.** A colour, hue, usu. slight or delicate; a tinge; *esp.* one of the several lighter or deeper shades or varieties, or degrees of intensity, of the same colour. **b.** *fig.*; *esp.* Quality, kind; a slight imparted or modifying character 1760. **2.** *spec.* **a.** *Painting.* A grade of colour; *spec.* a mixture of a colour with white 1753. **b.** *Engraving.* The effect produced by a series of fine parallel lines more or less closely drawn so as to produce an even and uniform shading 1880.
1. Autumn tints of brown and gold 1878. **b.** Our inborn spirits have a t. of thee BYRON.
Comb.: **t.-block**, a block of wood or metal hatched with fine parallel lines suitable for printing tints; **-tool**, an implement used for hatching a t.-block.

Tint (tint), *v.* 1791. [f. prec.] *trans.* To impart a tint to; to colour, esp. slightly or with delicate shades; to tinge. Also *absol.* **b.** *intr.* for *pass.* To become tinted or coloured 1892.

Tint, pa. pple. of TINE *v.*[2]

Ti·n-tack. 1840. [TACK *sb.*[1]] A tack, or short light iron nail, coated with tin.
Phr. *To come down to tin-tacks*: cf. TACK *sb.*[1] I. 2.

Tintamarre (tintămā·r) Now *rare.* 1567. [a. F.; origin obsc.] A confused noise, uproar, clamour, racket, hubbub, clatter.

†**Tint for tant,** = *tit for tat* (TIT *sb.*[1]). 1620–1828.

Tintinnabulant (tintinæ·biŭlănt), *a.* 1812. [f. as next + -ANT[1].] Ringing or tinkling as a small bell; jingling. (This and the allied words are all pedantic.)

Tintinnabular (tintinæ·biŭlăɹ), *a.* 1767. [f. L. *tintinnabulum* bell + -AR.] = next.

Tintinnabulary (tintinæ·biŭlări), *a.* 1787. [f. as prec. + -ARY[1].] Of or pertaining to bells or bell-ringing; of the nature of a bell; characterized by bell-ringing.

Tintinnabulation (ti:ntinæbiŭlēi·ʃən). 1831. [f. as prec.; see -ATION.] Bell-ringing; the sound or music so produced.

Tintinnabulous (tintinæ·biŭləs), *a.* 1791. [f. as prec.; see -OUS.] Characterized by or pertaining to bell-ringing.

‖**Tintinnabulum** (tintinæ·biŭlŏm). *Pl.* **-a.** 1597. [L., bell, f. *tintinnare* to ring + *-bulum*, suffix of instrument.] A small tinkling bell.

Tintometer (tintǫ·mĭtəɹ). 1889. [f. TINT *sb.* + -OMETER.] An apparatus for the exact determination of colour.

Tin-type (ti·nˌtəip). 1875. [f. TIN *sb.* + TYPE.] *Photogr.* A photograph taken as a positive on a thin tin plate.

Tiny (təi·ni), *a.* (*sb.*) 1598. [app. f. TINE *a.* and *sb.* + -Y[1].] Very small, little, or slight; minute.
This Cupid was a little tyny, Cogging, Lying, Peevish Nynny.
B. as *sb.* A tiny one, a very small child, an infant. Usu. in pl. *tinies.* 1863.

-tion, a compound suffix, repr. (orig. through F. *-tion*) L. *-tio, -tionem*, which consists of the suffix *-io, -ionem* added to the *-t-* of a L. ppl. stem, as in *rela-t-ion, deten-t-ion, op-t-ion.* The etymological meaning was primarily 'the state or condition of being (what the pa. pple. imports)'. But already in L. *-tio* was used for action or process, and also concretely or quasi-concretely, as in *dictio, natio, oratio.* In Eng. the most usual sense is that of a noun of action, = ING[1].

-tious, compound suffix, repr. L. *-t-iosus*, which consists of *-iosus* -IOUS, added to the *-t-* of a L. ppl. stem. It thus serves to form adjs. belonging to sbs. in *-tion*, as in *ambition, ambitious, caution, cautious*, etc.

Tip (tip), *sb.*[1] late ME. [Origin uncertain; prob. a. MLG. MDu. *tip* (cf. G. *zipfel*).] **1.** The slender extremity or top of a thing; *esp.* the pointed or rounded end of anything long and slender; the top, summit, apex, very end 1440. †**b.** *fig.* Utmost point; highest point -1626. **2.** A small piece of metal, leather, etc., attached or fitted on to something so as to form a serviceable end; as a ferrule, the leather pad on the point of a billiard-cue, a protecting cap or plate for the toe of a shoe, etc. 1440. **b.** *Costume.* The end of a tail of fur, or of a feather, as used in trimming, etc. 1681. **c.** *Angling.* The topmost joint of a fishing-rod 1891. **d.** *Hat-making.* The upper part of the crown of a hat; a stiff lining pasted in this part 1864. **3.** A thin flat brush of camel's or squirrel's hair (orig. the tip of a squirrel's tail), used for laying gold-leaf, as in bookbinding 1815.
1. The Pole-star..in the t. of the little Beares taile 1634. The t. of a root DARWIN.
Phrases. *From t. to toe*, from head to foot. *On* (or *at*) *the t. of one's tongue*, on the point of being, or ready to be, uttered. So *at the tips of one's fingers*, ready to be performed or executed.

Tip, *sb.*[2] 1466. [app. f. TIP *v.*[1]] An act of tipping; a light but distinct impact, blow, stroke, or hit; a noiseless tap; a significant touch.

Tip, *sb.*[3] 1755. [f. TIP *v.*[4]] A small present of money given to an inferior; a gratuity, a douceur. Also *attrib.*
A schoolboy's t. THACKERAY. The porter will expect a t. (*mod.*).

Tip, *sb.*[4] *colloq.* or *slang.* 1845. [perh. from TIP *v.*[1], or from TIP *v.*[4] in the phr. *to tip* (any one) *a wink.*] A piece of useful private or special information communicated by an expert; a friendly hint; *spec.* 'an advice concerning betting or a Stock-Exchange speculation intended to benefit the recipient'; also, a hint as to points thought likely to come up in an examination; hence *transf.* a 'wrinkle', 'dodge'.
Phr. *The straight t.*, orig. a t. coming direct from the owner or trainer of a horse; now often, a direct hint on any subject. *To miss one's t.*, to fail in one's aim or object.

Tip, *sb.*[5] 1673. [f. TIP *v.*[2]] †**I.** *Skittles.* The knocking over of a pin by another which falls or rolls against it -1819. **II. 1.** An act of tipping up or tilting, or the fact of being tilted; inclination 1849. **2.** A place or erection where wagons or trucks of coal, etc. are tipped and their contents discharged into the hold of a vessel, or into a cart, etc. **b.** A wagon or truck from which coal, etc. is tipped. 1862. **3. a.** The mound or mass of rubbish, etc. that is tipped. **b.** A dumping-ground. 1863.

Tip, *v.*[1] 1567. [Cf. mod.G. *tippen*, Sw. *tippa*; origin obsc.] **1.** *trans.* To strike or hit smartly but lightly; to tap noiselessly. **b.** *Cricket.* To hit (a ball) with the edge of the bat so that it glances off. **2.** *intr.* To step lightly; to trip, to walk mincingly, or on tiptoe 1819.
1. [He] felt himself suddenly tipped on the shoulder THACKERAY. **b.** *T.-and-run*, a form of cricket in which the batsman is obliged to run if he touches the ball with the bat.

Tip, *v.*[2] late ME. [Origin obsc.] **I.** *trans.* **1.** To overthrow, knock, or cast down, cause to fall or tumble; to overturn, upset; to throw down by effort or accidentally. **b.** *Skittles.* Applied to various modes of knocking down a pin 1679. **2.** To raise, push, or move into a slanting or sloping position; to incline, tilt. Often with *up.* 1624. **3.** To empty out (a wagon, cart, or the like, or its contents) by tilting it up; to dump 1838.
1. I tipp'd my nag over a broken place in the wall 1791. 2. Phr. *To t. the scales*: to turn the scale; also *fig.* 3. A piece of land..used for the purpose of tipping rubbish 1910.
II. *intr.* **1.** To fall by overbalancing; to tumble or topple over 1530. **2.** To assume a slanting or sloping position; to incline, tilt; now *esp.* of a cart, a plank, etc. (usu. with *up*), to tilt up at one end and down at the other 1666. **3.** *To t. off*, also simply *to t.*, or *t.* (*over*) *the perch*: to die. *slang* or *dial.* 1700.
1. Over tips table, candle, and cloth and all 1890. Hence Ti·pper[1], a workman engaged in tipping; a device for tipping.

Tip, *v.*[3] late ME. [f. TIP *sb.*[1]] *trans.* To furnish with a tip; to put a tip on, or put something on at the tip (const. *with*); to form the tip of, or adorn at the tip. Usu. in pa. pple.

Flowers..white tipped with green 1776.

Tip, *v.*4 1610. [orig. Rogues' Cant; origin obsc.] **1.** *trans.* (*Rogues' Cant*, and *slang.*) To give; to hand, pass; to let one have; to present or exhibit the character of: usu. with dat. of person. **2.** *colloq.* (orig. *slang*). To give a gratuity to (an inferior), esp. a servant or employee of another; also to a child or schoolboy 1706. **b.** *absol.* To give a tip or tips 1727.

1. 'T. me your fin, my heart of oak', said Joe 1884. Come, t. me a shilling 1884. 2. T'wou'd have paid The reck'ning clean, and tipp'd the maid 1747. You ..used to t. me when I was a boy at school THACKERAY. Phr. *To t. the* (or *a*) *wink*, to give (a person) a private signal or warning.

Tip, *v.*5 *colloq.* 1883. [f. TIP *sb.*4] **1.** *trans.* To give a 'tip' or piece of private information about. **2.** To give a 'tip' to; to furnish (a person) with private information as to the chances of some event 1891. **3.** *intr.* To furnish 'tips'; to carry on the business of a tipster 1903.

1. Florio Rubattino..has been 'tipped' by some of the papers for this race 1897.

Tip-, the stem of TIP *v.*2 (or TIP *sb.*5), in comb., as in *t.-cart*, *-truck*, *-wagon*, etc., vehicles constructed to tip or tilt for the purpose of emptying out the contents; also **t.-head**, the top of the slope over which material or rubbish is tipped; **-horse**, the horse which runs out the wagons to the tip-head.

Tip-cat. 1676. [f. TIP *v.*2 + CAT *sb.*1 II. 5.] **1.** A short piece of wood tapering at both ends, used in the game described in 2. **2.** A game in which the tip-cat (see 1) is struck or 'tipped' at one end with a stick so as to spring up, and then knocked to a distance by the same player 1801.

†**Tipe, type.** 1530. [Origin obsc.] **1.** A small cupola or dome –1708. **2.** *fig.* The summit, acme, or highest point (*of* honour, dignity, etc.) –1603.

Ti·p-it, ti·ppit. 1889. [f. phr. *to tip it.*] A game of chance in which an object hidden in a player's hand is to be detected.

Tipper 2 (ti·pəɹ). 1844. [From name of Thomas *Tipper* (d. 1785), who first brewed it.] A kind of ale brewed in Sussex.

Tippet (ti·pėt). ME. [Origin obsc.] **1.** **a.** A long narrow slip of cloth or hanging part of dress, formerly worn, either attached to and forming part of the hood, head-dress, or sleeve, or loose, as a scarf or the like. *Obs.* exc. *Hist.* **b.** A garment, usu. of fur or wool, covering the shoulders, or the neck and shoulders; a cape or short cloak 1481. **c.** *Eccl.* A band of silk or other material worn round the neck, with the two ends pendent from the shoulders in front 1530. **d.** = CAMAIL 1 (*rare*). late ME. †**2.** *joc.* A hangman's rope: usu. *Tyburn t.* –1823. **3.** An organ or formation in animals resembling or suggesting a tippet; in birds, dogs, etc. = RUFF *sb.*2 3. 1815. **4.** *Angling.* **a.** A length of twisted hair or gut forming part of a fishing-line. *Sc.* **b.** Part of an artificial fly. 1825.

1. Phr. †*To turn* (*one's*) *t.*, to change one's course or behaviour completely; in bad sense, to act the turncoat or renegade. b. She had furry articles for winter wear, as tippets, boas, and muffs DICKENS.

attrib. and *Comb.*: **t. cuckoo, grouse,** names for species of these birds having a t. or ruff; **-grebe,** a species of grebe, of which the skin, with the feathers on, is used for tippets.

Ti·pping, *vbl. sb.* 1819. [f. TIP *v.*1 + -ING 1.] The action of TIP *v.*1 *spec.* **b.** *Mus.* The action of striking the tongue against the palate: = TONGUING 1898.

Tipple (ti·p'l), *sb.*1 *colloq.* or *slang.* 1581. [f. TIPPLE *v.*1] Drink; *esp.* strong drink.

Ti·pple, *sb.*2 *U.S.* 1886. [f. TIPPLE *v.*2] = TIP *sb.*5 2.

Tipple (ti·p'l), *v.*1 1500. [Related to Norw. dial. *tipla* 'to drip slowly', also 'to drink in small quantities', 'tipple'.] †**1.** **a.** *trans.* To sell (ale or other strong drink) by retail. **b.** *absol.* or *intr.* To carry on the trade of a 'tippler'; to sell from the tap. –1662. **2.** *intr.* To drink of intoxicating liquor: in earlier use, to drink freely or hard; to booze; now *esp.*, to indulge habitually to some excess in taking strong drink 1560. **b.** *trans.* To drink (intoxicating liquor), esp. to take (drink) constantly in small quantities 1581. **c.** *transf.* and *poet.* To drink, sip. *intr.* and *trans.* Now *rare* or *Obs.* 1648. †**3.** *trans.* To intoxicate, make drunk –1648.

2. I wondered to see how the ladies did t. PEPYS. c. Fishes that t. in the deep Know no such liberty LOVELACE. 3. Opium,..which tipples, intoxicates and duls them PURCHAS.

Ti·pple, *v.*2 *dial.* 1847. [frequent. of TIP *v.*2] **1.** *intr.* To tumble or topple over. **2.** *trans.* To throw, pitch 1887. Hence **Ti·ppler** 1, a tipping contrivance; a tumbler pigeon 1831.

Tippler 2 (ti·pləɹ). late ME. [In form and sense agent-n. from TIPPLE *v.*1, but known 150 years earlier.] †**1.** A tapster; a tavern-keeper –1642. **2.** One who tipples; a habitual drinker of intoxicating liquor (implying some excess, but usu. short of positive drunkenness) 1580.

Ti·ppling-house. *Obs.* exc. *Hist.* 1547. [f. *tippling*, vbl. sb. f. TIPPLE *v.*1 + HOUSE *sb.*] A house where intoxicating liquor is sold and drunk; an ale-house, a tavern.

Tippy (ti·pi), *a.* 1892. [f. TIP *sb.*1 + -Y 1.] Of tea: Containing a large proportion of the 'tips' or leaf-buds of the shoot.

Tipsify (ti·psifəi), *v.* 1830. [f. TIPSY *a.* + -FY.] *trans.* To make tipsy; to intoxicate.

Tipstaff (ti·pˌstɑf). *Pl.* **-staffs** (-stɑfs), or **-staves** (stēivz). 1541. [contr. of *tipped* or *tipt staff.*] †**1.** A staff with a tip or cap of metal, carried as a badge by certain officials –1695. **2.** An official carrying a tipped staff; *spec.* **a.** A sheriff's officer, bailiff, constable; **b.** A court crier or usher. *arch.* 1570.

Tipster (ti·pstəɹ). 1862. [f. TIP *sb.*4 + -STER.] A man who makes a business of furnishing 'tips' or confidential information as to the probable chances of an event on which betting depends, esp. in horse-racing. **b.** *transf.* One who furnishes 'tips' in general 1884.

Tipsy (ti·psi), *a.* 1577. [app. f. TIP *v.*2] Affected with liquor so as to be unable to walk or stand steadily; partly intoxicated: often *euphem.* for: Intoxicated, drunk. **b.** *transf.* Characterized or accompanied by intoxication; arising from or causing tipsiness 1634. **c.** *fig.* Unsteady as if from drink; inclined to tip or tilt 1754.

The riot of the tipsie Bachanals SHAKS. b. Tipsie dance, and Jollity MILT. c. He was t. poor man with his joy RICHARDSON. Hence **Ti·psily** *adv.* **Ti·psiness.**

Ti·psy-cake. 1806. A cake saturated with wine or spirit, stuck with almonds, and served with custard.

Ti·p-ti·lted, *a.* 1872. [f. TIP *sb.*1 + pa. pple. of TILT *v.*1 II.] Having the tip 'tilted', i.e. turned up.

Her slender nose T. like the petal of a flower TENNYSON.

Tiptoe, tip-toe (ti·pˌtōu), *sb. adv., a.* late ME. [f. TIP *sb.*1 + TOE *sb.*] **1.** *pl.* The tips of the toes. **b.** *fig.*: usu. with ref. to expectation or eagerness (formerly to pretension or haughtiness) 1579. **2.** *sing.* The tips of the toes collectively; almost always in phr. *on* or *upon tiptoe* 1440.

1. To go soft and faire on his tippetoes 1573. b. All stood on the tiptoes of expectation FULLER. 2. Standing on tiptoe, [he] looked into one of the windows 1833. *fig.* Your eyes should sparkle joy, Your bosome rise on t. at this news MARSTON.

B. *adv.* Short for *on* or *a-tiptoe* 1592.

Iocond day Stands tipto on the mistie Mountaines tops SHAKS.

C. *adj.* Standing or walking, or characterized by standing or walking, on tiptoe 1744. **b.** *transf.* and *fig.* in various senses: e. g. straining upwards, ambitious; eagerly expectant; tripping dancing; silent, stealthy 1593.

b. How tiptoe Night holds back her dark-grey hood KEATS.

Ti·ptoe, *v.* 1661. [f. prec.] **1.** *intr.* To raise oneself or stand on tiptoe. **2.** To go or walk on tiptoe; to step or trip lightly 1748.

Tip-top, *sb., a., adv. colloq.* 1702. [f. TIP *sb.*1 + TOP.] **A.** *sb.* **1.** The very top; the highest point or part. **2.** *fig.* **a.** Highest pitch or degree; extreme height; acme 1702. †**b.** *sing.* and *pl.* People of the highest quality or rank (collectively); 'swells' –1849.

2. b. We go here to the best houses, the tiptops, I tell you THACKERAY.

B. *adj.* Situated at the very top; very highest; almost always *fig.* first-rate, superlatively good; of persons, belonging to the highest rank or class 1722.

A t. price 1825. The t. nobility THACKERAY.

C. *adv.* In the highest degree, superlatively, extremely well 1888.

‖**Tipula** (ti·piŭlă). *Pl.* **tipulæ** (-lī). 1752. [L. *tippula* water-spider, water-bug.] *Ent.* A genus of dipterous insects, typical of the family *Tipulidæ* or crane-flies. Hence **Ti·pulary** *a.* belonging or allied to the genus *T.* or family *Tipulidæ.*

Ti·p-up, *sb.* and *a.* 1848. [f. phr. *tip up*; TIP *v.*2] **A.** *sb.* A name for the Amer. sandpiper. **B.** *adj.* Constructed to tip or tilt up, as a receptacle, for the purpose of emptying out its contents, a seat (in a theatre, etc.) when not occupied 1884.

Tirade (ti-, təirē·d). 1801. [a. F., ad. It. *tirata* volley, etc., f. pa. pple. of *tirare* to draw, shoot; see -ADE.] **1.** A volley of words; a long and vehement speech on some subject; a declamation; a protracted harangue, *esp.* of denunciation, abuse, or invective. **2.** *spec.* A passage or section of verse, of varying length, treating of a single theme or idea 1878.

1. The King..had..to impose silence on the tirades which were delivered from the University pulpit GREEN.

‖**Tirailleur** (tirα·lyör). 1796. [F., f. *tirailler* to shoot in independent firing, f. *tirer* to draw, shoot.] One of a body of skirmishers employed in the wars of the French Revolution (1792); a skirmisher, a sharp-shooter; a soldier (usu. of infantry) trained for independent action.

Tire (təiəɹ), *sb.*1 ME. [aphet. f. *atir* ATTIRE *sb.*] †**1.** Apparatus, equipment, accoutrement –1705. **2.** Dress, apparel, raiment. *arch.* ME. **3.** *spec.* A woman's head-dress; occas. perh. confused with TIAR, tiara. *arch.* late ME. **4.** A pinafore or apron to protect the dress; also written *tier. U.S.* 1846.

1. *Per.* III. ii. 22. 2. You in Grecian tires are painted new SHAKS. 3. And on her head she wore a tyre of gold SPENSER.

attrib. and *Comb.* (*Obs.* or *arch.*): **t.-glass,** a toilet-glass **-room,** a dressing-room, tiring-room.

Tire (təiəɹ), *sb.*2 See also TYRE. 1485. [prob. the same word as prec.] †**1.** *collect. sing.* The curved pieces of iron plate, called strakes or streaks, placed end to end or overlapping, with which cart and carriage wheels were formerly shod –1827. **2.** A rim of metal encompassing the wheel of a vehicle, consisting of a hoop of iron or steel 1782. **b.** An endless cushion of rubber, solid, hollow, or tubular, fitted (usu. in combination with an inner tube filled with compressed air) on the rim of a bicycle, tricycle, motor-car, etc., wheel. In this sense now usu. spelt *tyre* in Great Britain, *tire* in America. 1877.

2. b. Rubber tires, in place of iron ones, appeared in 1868. 1910.

†**Tire,** *sb.*3 1575. [ad. F. *tir*, f. *tirer* to draw, shoot.] The simultaneous discharge of a battery of ordnance; a volley or broadside –1687.

In posture to displode thir second t. Of Thunder MILT.

Tire (təiəɹ), *v.*1 [OE. *tiorian*, *tēorian*. Not known in cogn. langs.; origin and history unkn.] **I.** *intr.* †**1.** To fail, cease (as a supply, etc.); to give out –ME. **2.** To become weak or exhausted from exertion; to become fatigued OE. **3.** To have one's appreciation, power of attention, or patience exhausted by excess; to become or be weary or sick *of*, to 'have enough' *of* 1500.

2. A merry heart goes all the day, Your sad tyres in a Mile-a SHAKS. 3. Unwearied himself, he supposed his readers could never t. GOLDSM.

II. *trans.* **1.** To wear down or exhaust the strength of by exertion; to fatigue, weary. Also *absol.* OE. **2.** To weary or exhaust the patience, interest, or appreciation of (a person, etc.) by long continuance, sameness, or want of interest; to satiate, make sick of something; to bore. Also *absol.* 1500. **b.** *fig.* To exhaust (another's patience, bounty, efforts, etc.); †to wear out, spend (time) 1589.

1. The same work tires, but different works relieve BERKELEY. 2. I hope I have not tired your Lordship

with my long tale GOLDSM. **b.** Till tiring all his Arts, he turns agen To his true Shape DRYDEN.

Phr. *To t. out, t. to death*, to tire to utter exhaustion (*colloq.*). *To t. down*, to exhaust (a hunted animal) by persistent pursuit.

Tire (təiəɹ), *v.*[2] *arch.* ME. [a. F. *tirer* :— Com. Rom. **tirare* to draw, etc.; origin obsc.] †**I.** *intr.* and *trans.* To draw, pull, tug –1580. **II.** *Falconry. intr.* Of a hawk: To pull or tear with the beak at a tough morsel given to it that it may exercise itself in this way; also, to tear flesh in feeding, as a bird of prey. *arch.* or *Obs.* ME. †**b.** *fig.* To prey *upon* –1624. **c.** To exercise oneself *upon* SHAKS.

b. The grief that tires upon thine inward soul 1594. **c.** *Timon* III. vi. 4.

Tire (təiəɹ), *v.*[3] ME. [Aphetic f. ATTIRE *v.*[1]] **1.** *trans.* †**a.** To attire, clothe duly, dress, adorn –1706. **b.** To dress (the hair or head), esp. with a tire or head-dress. *arch.* 1539. **2.** To plaster or decorate (a building). Now *dial.* late ME.

1. b. Iezabel..starched her face, and tired her heed BIBLE (Great) 2 *Kings* ix. 30.

Tire (təiəɹ), *v.*[4] 1891. [f. TIRE *sb.*[2]] *trans.* To furnish with a tire or tires.

Tired (təiəɹd), *ppl. a.* late ME. [f. TIRE *v.*[1] + -ED[1].] **1.** Fatigued, wearied; also, sick or weary *of*, impatient *with* (something); *slang*, habitually disinclined to exertion, incorrigibly lazy. **2.** *transf.* and *fig.* Exhausted, worked out, used up 1548. Hence **Ti·red-ly** *adv.*, **-ness.**

1. *T. Tim*, usu. associated with *Weary Willie*, both being taken as symbolical names of men who are disinclined to work. *To make* (a person) *t.* (U.S. slang), to annoy and bore 1896.

Tireless (təiə·ɹlės), *a.* 1591. [f. TIRE *v.*[1] + -LESS.] Untiring, indefatigable. Hence **Ti·reless-ly** *adv.*, **-ness.**

†**Tireling** (təiə·ɹliŋ), *sb.* (*a.*) 1590. [app. f. TIRE *v.*[1] + -LING; cf. *hireling*.] A tired person or animal; only *attrib.* or as *adj.* –1613.

Tiresome (təiə·ɹsŏm), *a.* 1500. [f. TIRE *v.*[1] + -SOME.] **1.** Having the property of tiring by continuance, sameness, or lack of interest; wearisome, tedious. **b.** *loosely.* Troublesome, disagreeable, unpleasant; annoying, vexatious. *colloq.* 1798. †**2.** Causing physical fatigue. (Now merged in **1.**) –1728.

1. It is slow, t. work 1854. **b.** A t. fidgety schoolboy as a travelling companion 1898. Hence **Ti·resome-ly** *adv.*, **-ness.**

Ti·re-wo:man. 1615. [f. TIRE *sb.*[1] + WOMAN.] A woman who assists at a lady's toilet; a lady's maid (*arch.*); †also, a dress-maker, costumier.

To Mrs. Grotier's, the Queen's t., for a pair of locks for my wife PEPYS.

Tiring (təiə·riŋ), *vbl. sb.* 1552. [f. TIRE *v.*[3] + -ING[1].] The action of TIRE *v.*[3]; also *concr.* attire, apparel, head-dress (*arch.*).

Comb.: **t.-house** = next; **-woman,** a lady's maid (*Obs.* or *arch.*).

Tiring-irons (təiə·riŋ,əiəɹnz), *sb. pl.* 1601. Also †**tarr(y)ing-.** [TIRE *v.*[1], TARRY *v.*] A ring-puzzle.

Tiring-room (təiə·riŋ,rūm). 1623. [f. prec. + ROOM.] A dressing-room (*arch.*); *spec.* the dressing-room of a theatre.

Tiro, tyro (təiə·ro). *Pl.* **-oes, -os** (-*oz*). 1611. [a. L. *tiro*, pl. *tirones* (in med.L. often spelt *tyro, tyrones*) a young soldier, a recruit, a beginner. Commonly spelt *tyro.*] A beginner or learner in anything; one who is learning or who has mastered the rudiments only of any branch of knowledge; a novice.

The management of tiroes of eighteen Is difficult COWPER.

‖**Tirocinium** (təirosi·niŏm). Also (less correctly) **tyro-.** 1651. [L., first military service on campaign, young troops, f. TIRO + -*cinium.*] **a.** First experience of or training in anything; apprenticeship, pupilage, novitiate; hence, inexperience, rawness. **b.** *concr.* A band of novices or recruits.

Tironian (təirōu·niăn), *a.* 1828. [ad. L. *Tironianus*, in *notæ Tironianæ* Tironian notes.] Of or pertaining to Tiro, the freedman of Cicero: *T. notes*, a system of shorthand in use in ancient Rome, said to have been invented or introduced by Tiro.

Tirra-lirra (ti·ră,li·ră). 1611. [Echoic.] A representation of the note of the skylark, or of a similar sound uttered as an exclam. of delight or gaiety, or as a refrain.

The Larke, that tirra-Lyra chaunts SHAKS.

Tirrit (ti·rit). *rare.* 1597. [perh. illiterate for *terror.*] A fit of fear or temper; an 'upset'.

‖**Tirshatha** (tiɹʃă·þă). late ME. [Heb., a. OPers. *tarsāta* his reverence.] The title of an ancient Persian viceroy or prefect: applied in O.T. to Nehemiah.

'Tis (tiz), aphetic abbrev. of *it is*, now *poet.* or *arch.* exc. in *'tisn't.*

‖**Tishri** (ti·ʃri), **Tisri** (ti·zri). 1833. [ad. late Heb. *tishrī*, f. Aramaic *shᵉrā* to begin.] The first month of the Jewish civil year, or the seventh of the ecclesiastical, corresponding to parts of September and October.

Tisic, -ical, obs. and dial. ff. PHTHISIC, -AL.

Tissue (ti·ʃu, ti·siu), *sb.* late ME. [a. OF. *tissu*, from pa. pple. of obs. F. *tître*, OF. *tistre* :—L. *texere* to weave.] **1. a.** A rich kind of cloth, often interwoven with gold and silver. *Obs.* exc. *Hist.* **b.** Now applied to various rich or fine stuffs of delicate or gauzy texture 1730. †**2.** A band or girdle of rich stuff –1603. **3.** Any woven stuff or fabric 1565. **4.** *fig.* Something likened to a woven fabric; a 'fabric', 'network', 'web' (*of* things abstract, usu. of a bad kind, as absurdities, lies, etc.). Also the structure or contexture of such a 'fabric'. 1711. **5.** *Biol.* The substance, structure, or texture of which an animal or plant body, or any part or organ of it, is composed; *esp.* any one of the various structures, each consisting of an aggregation of similar cells or modifications of cells, which make up the organism 1831. **6.** Short for TISSUE-PAPER 1780. **7.** *Photogr.* Paper made in strips coated with a film of gelatine containing a pigment, used in carbon printing 1873.

1. The quene..clothed in a riche mantell of t. GRAFTON. **3.** They..weave with bloody hands the t. of thy line GRAY. **4.** The t. of misrepresentations..woven round us 1820. **5.** The chief forms of t. in the higher animals are the *epithelial* (incl. *glandular*), *connective* (incl. *cartilaginous* and *osseous*), *muscular*, and *nervous* tissues. In the higher plants there are three systems of tissues, the *epidermal, fundamental*, and *fibro-vascular.* N.E.D.

Tissue, *v.* Now *rare.* 1483. [f. prec.] *trans.* To make into a tissue, to weave; *spec.* to weave with gold or silver threads, to work or form in tissue; to adorn or cover with tissue.

The Charriot was covered with cloth of Gold tissued upon Blew BACON.

Tissued (ti·ʃiud, ti·siud), *ppl. a.* 1584. [f. F. *tissu*, pa. pple. (see TISSUE *sb.*) + -ED.] Woven, *spec.* woven with gold or silver thread (cf. F. *or tissu*).

Ti·ssue-pa:per. 1777. A very thin soft gauze-like unsized paper, used for wrapping delicate articles, for covering illustrations in books, as copying-paper, etc.

Tit, *sb.*[1] 1556. [Goes w. TIT *v.*] **1.** In phr. **tit for tat.** One blow or stroke in return for another; retaliation. **2.** *dial.* A light stroke or tap; a slap 1808.

Tit, *sb.*[2] 1548. [app. of onomatopœic origin, as a term for a small animal or object.] **I. 1.** A small horse; later often applied in depreciation or meiosis to any horse; a nag. Now *rare.* †**b.** *fig.* of a person, etc. –1734. **2.** A girl or young woman. Usu. in depreciation: a hussy, a minx. (Now *low slang.*) 1599. **II.** Used in comb. in the names of various small birds as TITLARK, TITMOUSE, TOMTIT, etc. Used alone, as a shortened form of TITMOUSE, applied to: **a.** any bird of the genus *Parus*, and, more widely, any member of the family *Paridæ*; **b.** with qualification, to certain birds of other families, as the *Bearded t.* 1706.

attrib. and *Comb.*: **t.-babbler,** one of several species of hill-tits, esp. *Trichostoma rostratum*; **-pipit,** the TITLARK or meadow pipit, *Anthus pratensis*; **-warbler,** a bird of the sub-family *Parinæ.*

Tit, *sb.*[3] *dial.* and *vulgar.* [OE. *titt.*] = TEAT.

Tit, *v.* Now *dial.* 1589. [Goes with TIT *sb.*[1]] *trans.* and *intr.* To strike or tap lightly.

Titan (təi·tăn). late ME. [a. L., name of the elder brother of Kronos; also in poetry, the Sun-god; a. Gr. Τιτάν, in pl. Τιτᾶνες.] **1.** Used (chiefly in poetry) as a name for the Sun-god, the grandson of Titan, or for the sun personified. **2. a.** *Gr. Myth.* In *sing.* The ancestor of the Titans, the elder brother of Kronos. In *pl.* a family of giants, the children of Uranus (Heaven) and Gæa (Earth), who contended for the sovereignty of heaven, and were overthrown by Zeus 1667. **b.** *transf.* and *allus.* 1828. **c.** Applied descriptively to machines of great size and power; e.g. a dredger, crane, etc. 1876. **3.** *Astron.* Name of the sixth and largest of Saturn's eight satellites 1868. **4.** *attrib.* or as *adj.*; *transf.* titanic, gigantic 1697.

1. Let T. rise as early as he dare SHAKS. **2. a.** T. Heav'ns first born With his enormous brood MILT. **b.** *Weary T.*, Atlas, who held up the world on his shoulders; *fig.* a state or empire that has heavy responsibilities; The weary T. need not complain too much 1903. **4.** The T. obelisk of the Matterhorn TYNDALL. So **Titane·sque** *a.* colossal, gigantic. **Ti·taness,** a female T.; a giantess. **Tita·nian** *a.* Titanic.

Titanate (təi·tănėt). 1839. [f. TITANIC *a.*[2] + -ATE[4].] *Chem.* A salt of titanic acid.

Titanic (təitæ·nik), *a.*[1] 1656. [ad. Gr. τιτανικός, f. Τιτᾶνες; see TITAN and -IC.] †**1.** Of or pertaining to the sun (*rare*) –1658. **2.** Pertaining to, resembling, or characteristic of the Titans of mythology; gigantic, colossal; also, of the nature or character of the Titans 1709.

2. The figure of Napoleon was **t.** CARLYLE. So †**Tita·nical** *a.* (in sense 2).

Tita·nic, *a.*[2] 1826. [f. TITANIUM + -IC b.] Of, pertaining to, or derived from titanium; in *Chem.* applied to compounds in which titanium has its higher valency as *t. oxide* (*t. acid*), a white tasteless powder, TiO_2. In *Min.*, *t. iron-ore* = ILMENITE; *t. schorl* = RUTILE.

Titaniferous (təităni·fĕrəs), *a.* 1828. [f. TITANIUM + -IFEROUS.] Containing or yielding titanium.

Titanism (təi·tăniz'm). 1867. [a. F. *titanisme*; see TITAN and -ISM.] The character of a Titan. **a.** Revolt against the order of the universe. **b.** Titanic force or power.

Titanite (təi·tăneit). 1858. [ad. G. *titanit*, f. TITANIUM + -*it* -ITE[1].] *Min.* A metal composed chiefly of calcium titano-silicate, $CaO.TiO_2.SiO_2$; also called *sphene.*

Titanium (təitē^i·niŏm). 1796. [f. Gr. Τιτᾶνες the Titans + -IUM.] *Chem.* One of the rare metals, never found free in nature, but obtainable as an iron-grey powder with a metallic lustre. It belongs to the same group as zirconium, cerium, and thorium. Symbol Ti; atomic weight 48.1.

Titano-[1], a. Gr. τιτανο-, comb. form of Τιτάν TITAN, as in **Titano·machy** [-MACHY], the warfare of the Titans. ‖**Tita:no-, ti:tano,the·rium** [mod.L. f. Gr. θηρίον beast], also anglicized **ti·tanothe:re,** an extinct genus of ungulates from the Tertiary formation, resembling gigantic rhinoceroses.

Titano-[2] (təi·tăno), comb. form of TITANIUM (and TITANITE), used in the names of chemical and mineral compounds, as *t.-cyanide, -ferrite, -fluorite, -silicate.*

Titanous (təi·tănəs), *a.* 1866. [f. TITANIUM + -OUS.] *Chem.* Containing titanium, spec. in its lower valency, as *t. oxide*, sesquioxide of titanium, Ti_2O_3; contrasted with TITANIC *a.*[2]

Tit-bit (ti·t,bi·t), **tid-bit** (ti·d,bi·t). 1640. [In 17th c. *tyd bit, tid-bit*, perh. f. dial. *tid* adj. + BIT *sb.*[2]; later mainly *tit-bit.*] A small and delicate or appetizing piece of food; a toothsome morsel. **b.** *fig.*; *spec.* a brief and isolated interesting item of news or information; hence in *pl.*, name of a periodical consisting of such items 1798.

Tithable (təi·ðăb'l) *a.* 1440. [f. TITHE *v.* + -ABLE.] **1.** Of produce: Subject to the payment of tithes. **2.** Liable to pay tithes (*rare*) 1722.

Tithe (təið), *a.* and *sb.* [Early ME. *tiȝ(e)þe*, later ME. *tiþe, tyþe*:—OE. *teogoþa, tēoþa* TENTH.] **A.** *adj.* Tenth.

One good woman in ten Madam..Weed finde no fault with the t. woman SHAKS.

B. *sb.* Absolute use of the adj. **1.** The tenth part of the annual produce of agriculture, etc., being a due or payment (orig. in kind) for the support of the priesthood, religious establishments, etc.; *spec.* applied to that ordained by the Mosaic law, and to that introduced in conformity therewith in England and other Christian lands ME. **b.** chiefly in *pl.*, including the various amounts thus due or received ME. **2.** Any levy, tax, or tribute of one tenth 1600. **3.** A tenth part (of anything); now chiefly hyperbolical: a very small part 1494.

1. Half the cultivated land of Great Britain is unaffected by t. 1845. *Great t.*, the chief predial tithes, as corn, hay, wood, and fruit. *Mixed t.*: (partly personal, partly predial). *Personal t.*, t. of the produce of labour or occupation. *Predial t.*: see PREDIAL *a. Rectorial t.*, tithes pertaining to the rector of the parish, the great tithes. *Small t.*, such predial tithes as are not great tithes, together with the personal and mixed tithes. *Vicarial t.*, tithes pertaining to the vicar of the parish; the small tithes. 2. The admirals took t. on every ship and cargo seized at sea 1871. 3. I cannot tell you a t. of what he said 1872.

attrib. and *Comb.*: **t.-barn**, a barn for holding the parson's t.-corn; **-man**, a collector of tithes (now only *Hist.*); **-pig**, a pig due or taken as t.; **-proctor**, an agent employed to collect a parson's tithes, or one who farmed the t.

Tithe (təið), *v.* [OE. *teogoþian*, etc., f. *teogoþa*, *tēoþa* TITHE *sb.*] *gen.* To take the tenth of, to decimate. **1.** *trans.* To grant or pay one tenth of (one's goods, earnings, etc.), esp. to the support of the church; to pay tithes on. †**2.** *intr.* To pay tithe; to pay the tenth, esp. to the church –1606. **3.** *trans.* To impose the payment of a tenth upon (a person, etc.); to exact tithe from. late ME. **b.** To exact or collect one tenth from (goods or produce) by way of tithe; to take tithe of (goods) 1591. †**4. a.** *trans.* To take every tenth thing or person from (the whole number); to take one tenth (of the whole); to divide into tenths –1641. †**b.** *spec.* To reduce (a multitude) to one tenth of its numbers by keeping only every tenth man alive (always with ref. to the sacking of Canterbury by the Danes in 1011) –1670.

1. *To t. mint (and anise) and cummin* (*Matt.* xxiii. 23), to be conspicuously scrupulous in minutiæ while neglecting important matters of duty. 4. b. The multitude are tith'd, and every tenth only spar'd MILT.

Tither (təi·ðəɹ). late ME. [f. TITHE *v.* + -ER[1].] **a.** One who pays tithes. Now *rare.* **b.** An exactor or receiver of tithes; also, a supporter of the system of ecclesiastical tithes 1591.

Tithing (təi·ðiŋ). [OE. *tēoþung*, f. *tēoþa* TITHE *sb.* or *tēoþian* TITHE *v.*; see -ING[1, 3].] **1.** = TITHE *sb.* 1. †**2.** A tenth part of anything –1609. **3.** A company *orig.* of ten householders in the system of FRANKPLEDGE; now only as a rural division (orig. regarded as one tenth of a hundred) to which this system gave its name OE.

Tithingman[1] (təi·ðiŋmæn). OE. [f. prec. + MAN *sb.*] **a.** Anciently, The chief man of a tithing, a headborough; in later use, a parish peace-officer, or petty constable. Now *Hist.* **b.** In Maryland and New England: A former elective officer of a township, whose functions were derived from those of the English tithingman; in particular he was charged with the prevention of disorderly conduct, and, in New England in later times, chiefly with enforcing the observance of the Sabbath and of order during divine service. Now *Hist.* 1638.

Ti·thing-man[2]. 1625. [f. *tithing* vbl. sb., f. TITHE *v.*] A collector of tithes; a tithe-proctor.

Titian (ti·ʃăn). 1824. [The name *Titian*, Fr. and Eng. for Tiziano Vecellio, Venetian painter (died 1576).] With capital T: A picture by Titian. Also *attrib.* or *adj.* denoting a 'bright golden auburn' colour of the hair favoured by Titian in his pictures; also more loosely as an appreciative word for 'red'. Hence **Titia·nic** *a.* of or belonging to T. **Titiane·sque** *a.* in the stye of T.

Titillate (ti·tilēᵗt), *v.* 1620. [f. L. *titillat-*, *titillare* to tickle.] **1.** *trans.* = TICKLE *v.* 3. **2.** = TICKLE *v.* 4. Also *absol.* 1837.

1. Not to t. his palate but to keep up his character for hospitality MACAULAY.

Titillation (titilēⁱ·ʃən). late ME. [ad. L. *titillationem*; see prec.] **1.** Excitation or stimulation of the mind or senses; *esp.* pleasing excitement, gratification. **2.** A sensation of being tickled; a tingling, an itching 1621. **3.** The action of tickling, or touching lightly so as to tickle 1623. †**4.** *transf.* A means of titillating –1610.

1. Thrills and titillations from games of hazard T. HARDY. 3. Laughter provok'd by T., grows an excessive Pain SHAFTESB.

Titivate, tittivate (ti·tivēᵗt), *v. colloq.* 1805. [In early examples *tidi-* or *tiddivate*, perh. f. TIDY, after *cultivate.*] *trans.* To make small alterations or additions to one's toilet, etc. so as to add to one's attractions; to make smart or spruce; to put the finishing touches to. Also with *off*, *up*. Also *intr.* for *refl.* Hence **Titi-, tittiva·tion.**

Titlark (ti·t,lāɹk). 1668. [f. TIT *sb.*[2] + LARK *sb.*[1]] A bird of the genus *Anthus* or some allied genus, resembling a lark; a pipit; *esp.* in England, the meadow pipit, *A. pratensis*; in U.S., *A. ludovicianus* (American t.).

Title (təi·t'l), *sb.* [ME. a. OF., ad. L. *titulus* superscription, title.] †**1.** An inscription placed on or over an object, giving its name or describing it; a legend –1645. **2.** The descriptive heading of each section or subdivision of a book (now only in law-books); the formal heading of a legal document ME. **3.** The name of a book, poem, or other (written) composition; an inscription at the beginning of a book, describing or indicating its subject, contents, or nature, and usu. giving also the name of the author, compiler, or editor, and of the publisher, and the place and date of publication; also = TITLE-PAGE. Also, the designation of a picture or statue. ME. **b.** *Bookbinding.* The label or panel on the back of a book giving a brief title (*binder's t.*) 1891. **4.** A descriptive or distinctive appellation; a name, denomination, style. late ME. **5.** An appellation attaching to an individual or family in virtue of rank, function, office, or attainment, or the possession of or association with certain lands, etc.; *esp.* an appellation of honour pertaining to a person of high rank; also *transf.* (colloq.) a person of title 1590. **6.** That which justifies or substantiates a claim; a ground of right; hence, an alleged or recognized right. Const. with *inf.*, or *to*, *in*, or *of* the thing claimed. ME. **7.** *spec. Law.* Legal right to the possession of property (esp. real property); the evidence of such right; title-deeds. late ME. †**b.** An assertion of right; a claim –1701. **8.** *Eccl.* A certificate of presentment to a benefice, or a guarantee of support, required (in ordinary cases) by the bishop from a candidate for ordination. late ME. **9.** *Eccl.* Each of the principal or parish churches in Rome, the incumbents of which are cardinal priests; a cardinal church 1460. **10.** *Assaying*, etc. The expression in carats of the degree of purity of gold (= F. *titre*) 1873.

1. An aulter..with this t. ther by: Vnto the Lorde COVERDALE *Isa.* xix. 19. 3. The fifth t. of the fifth book *De Magistris* 1581. 5. From the death of this young Earle of Warwicke this t. lay asleepe 1610. A gay young Gentleman, who has lately succeeded to a T. and an Estate STEELE. If you retain any Curate, to whom you did not give a T. for Orders 1720.

attrib. and *Comb.*: **t.-part**, **-rôle**, the part in a play, etc., from which the t. of the piece is taken; **-sheet**, the first sheet of a book, one page of which bears the t.

Title (təi·t'l), *v.* ME. [f. prec.] **I.** †**1.** *trans.* To write, set down, or arrange under titles or headings; to make a list of; to set down in writing –1552. **2.** To furnish with a (specified) title; also, to inscribe the title on (a book or the like); to write the headings to or in (a manuscript book or account). late ME. †**3.** To dedicate (by name); to assign, ascribe –1584. †**4.** To inscribe as a title, attach as a label –1642.

2. In the Order of the Day these questions now appear numbered and titled 1894. 4. By the intrapping autority of great names titl'd to false opinions MILT.

II. To designate by a certain name, indication of relationship, character, office, etc.; to term style, name, call 1590. **b.** To endow or dignify with a title of rank; to speak of by a title of dignity 1746.

That sober Race of Men, whose lives Religious titl'd them the Sons of God MILT.

Titled (təi·t'ld), *ppl. a.* 1746. [f. prec. + -ED[1].] Having or furnished with a title, esp. a title of rank.

A younger scion of a t. family 1909.

Title-deed (təi·t'l,dīd). 1768. A deed or document containing or constituting evidence of ownership. (Most common in *pl.*)

Titleless (təi·t'l,lės), *a.* late ME. [f. TITLE *sb.* + -LESS.] Having no title, destitute of a title; untitled.

Ti·tle-page. 1613. The page at (or near) the beginning of a book which bears the title.

The world 's all t., there 's no contents YOUNG.

Titler (təi·tləɹ). 1594. [app. f. TITLE *sb.* + -ER[1].] †**1.** One who claims or asserts a legal title–1634. **2.** Trade name for a truncated cone of refined sugar 1858.

Titling (ti·tliŋ). ME. [f. TIT *sb.*[2] + -LING.] †**1.** A small size of stockfish –1858. **2. a.** The hedge-sparrow. Now only *Sc.* and *n. dial.* **b.** = TITLARK. **c.** = TITMOUSE (*rare*) 1549.

2. He had frequently .. watched young cuckoos while being fed by titlings (*Anthus pratensis*) 1882.

Titmouse (ti·t,maus). *Pl.* **titmice** (-məis). [ME. *titmose*, f. TIT *sb.*[2] + *mose* (OE. *māse*) titmouse. In the 16th c. *-mose*, was interpreted as *mouse.*] **1.** A bird of the genus *Parus* or family *Paridæ*, comprising numerous species of small active birds. (Now commonly shortened to *tit.*) **2.** With qualification, denoting various species of *Parus* or of the family *Paridæ* 1609. **3.** *fig.* A small, petty, or insignificant person or thing 1596.

2. **Blue t.**, *P. cæruleus*; **coal t.**, *P. ater*; **crested t.**, *Parus* (*Lophophanes*) *cristatus*, or any species of the subgenus *Lophophanes*; **great t.**, *P. major*, also called OX-EYE; **long-tailed t.**, *Acredula caudata*; **marsh t.**, *P. palustris.*

Titrate (ti·trēᵗt), *v.* 1870. [f. F. *titrer*, f. *titre* title, qualification, fineness of alloyed gold or silver, etc.; see -ATE[3].] *Chem. trans.* To ascertain the amount of a constituent in (a mixture, or (less usu.) a compound) by volumetric analysis; i.e. by adding to a solution thereof of known proportion, a suitable reagent of known strength, until a point is reached at which reaction occurs or ceases. So **Ti·trated** *ppl. a.* (= F. *titré*) of a solution, having a known strength, and thus being suitable for use in titration.

Titration (titrēⁱ·ʃən). 1864. [f. prec.; see -ATION.] The action or process of titrating; volumetric analysis.

‖**Titre, titer** (tī·təɹ). 1839. [a. F.; see TITRATE.] The fineness of gold or silver; *Chem.* the strength of a solution as determined by titration.

Titrimetry (titri·mĕtri). 1891. [f. F. *titre*; see TITRATE *v.* and -METRY.] *Chem.* = TITRATION.

Titter (ti·təɹ), *sb.* 1728. [f. next.] The act of tittering; a stifled laugh, a giggle.

A continual t. among the young ladies MME D'ARBLAY.

Titter (ti·təɹ), *v.*[1] 1619. [app. echoic.] *intr.* To laugh in a suppressed or covert way (often as a result of nervousness, or in affectation or ridicule); to giggle. **b.** *trans.* To utter or say with suppressed laughter 1787.

Upon which Mrs. Nickleby tittered, and Sir Mulberry laughed, and Pyke and Pluck roared DICKENS.

Titter (ti·təɹ), *v.*[2] Now *dial.* [Late ME. *titer*, = ON. *titra* to shake, shiver:—OTeut. *titrōjan. Cf. TEETER.] **1.** *intr.* To move unsteadily, totter, reel, sway to and fro. **2.** To see-saw 1825.

Titter-totter (ti·təɹ,tǫ·təɹ), *sb.* (*adv.*) Now *dial.* 1530. [Reduplication from stem of prec. or TOTTER *v.*] **A.** *sb.* = SEE-SAW. **B.** *adv.* Totteringly; *fig.* hesitatingly, waveringly 1725. Hence **Ti·tter-to·tter** *v. intr.* to see-saw.

Tittle (ti·t'l), *sb.* [Late ME. *titel*, *-il*, orig. the same word as TITLE.] **1.** A small stroke or point in writing or printing. **a.** orig. tr. L. *apex*, applied to any minute point or part of a letter, also to the mark over a long vowel, as *ā*, later to a line indicating an abbreviation, etc. By extension, any stroke or tick with a pen. **b.** The dot over the letter *i*; a punctuation mark; a diacritic point over a letter; any Hebrew or Arabic vowel-point or accent; also, a pip on dice 1538. **2.** *fig.* The smallest or a very small part of something; a minute amount. Often in phr. *jot or t.*; see JOT *sb.*[1] late ME.

2. I owe much more to his father's memory than ever I can pay a t. of SCOTT. Phr. *To a t.*, with minute exactness, to a T.

Tittle (ti·t'l), *v.* Now *dial.* or *colloq.* late ME. [app. onomatopœic.] *intr.* and *trans.* To speak in a whisper or in a low voice, to whisper; also, to tell or utter by way of tattle or gossip.

Tittlebat (ti·t'lbæt). Also **-back.** 1820. A variant of STICKLEBACK, of childish origin.

Tittle-tattle (ti·t'l,tæ·t'l), *sb.* 1529. [A reduplicated compound of TATTLE *sb.*] 1. Talk, chatter, prattle; *esp.* petty gossip. †2. A habitual tattler, one given up to gossip; esp. a woman so addicted -1710. 3. *attrib.* or as *adj.* Characterized by or addicted to tattling; gossiping 1719.

3. Bath is as t. a town as Lynn MME D'ARBLAY. So **Ti·ttle-ta·ttle** *v. intr.* to chatter, talk idly; to gossip. **Ti·ttle-ta·ttling** *vbl. sb.* and *ppl. a.*

Tittup (ti·tǒp), *sb.* Chiefly *dial.* 1703. [app. echoic, from the sound of the horse's feet.] 1. A horse's canter; a hand-gallop; also, a curvet. 2. An impudent or forward woman or girl; a hussy, minx 1762.

Tittup (ti·tǒp), *v.* 1785. [Goes with prec.] *intr.* To walk or go with an up-and-down movement; to walk in an affected manner; to mince or prance in one's gait; of a horse or other animal, to canter, gallop easily; also, to prance; hence of a rider, or one driving a vehicle. b. *Naut. slang.* To toss for drinks.

Tittupy (ti·tǒpi), *a. colloq.* 1798. [f. TITTUP *sb.* or *v.* + -Y.[1]] Apt to tittup or tip up; unsteady, shaky.

Ti·tty. 1746. A dial. and nursery dim. of TEAT, the breast, esp. the mother's breast.

Titubancy (ti·tiǔbănsi). *rare.* 1800. [ad. rare late L. *titubantia*, f. *titubare* to TITUBATE.] The condition of being titubant; unsteadiness, tipsiness. (This and allied words all more or less affected.)

Titubant (ti·tiǔbănt), *a. rare.* 1724. [ad. L. *titubantem*; see prec.] Staggering, reeling, unsteady; *transf.* and *fig.* stammering; tipsy; hesitating, wavering.

Titubate (ti·tiǔbe't), *v. rare.* 1575. [f. L. *titubat-*, *titubare.*] 1. *intr.* To stagger, reel, totter, stumble; to rock, roll. 2. *fig.* To stammer 1623.

Titubation (titiǔbē·ʃən). *rare.* 1641. [ad. L. *titubationem.*] The action of titubating; staggering, reeling, tottering; unsteadiness in gait or carriage, *spec.* in *Path.*; *fig.* faltering, perplexity, embarrassment.

Titular (ti·tiǔlăɹ), *a.* and *sb.* 1591. [ad. L. **titularis*, f. *titulus* TITLE; see -AR [1].] A. *adj.* 1. That exists or is such only in title or name, as dist. from *real* or *actual*; nominal, so-styled 1611. 2. Of, pertaining to, consisting of, or denoted by a title of dignity; also, having a title of rank, titled; bearing, or conferring, the appropriate title 1611. 3. Of or pertaining to a title or name; of the nature of or constituting a title. *T. character*, title-rôle. 1656. 4. From whom or which a title or name is taken; *spec.* noting the parish churches of Rome from which the titles of the cardinals are derived; hence *transf.* of a cardinal 1664.

1. Her mother the t. queen of Naples and Jerusalem H. WALPOLE. *T. bishop*, in R. C. Ch., a bishop deriving his title from an ancient see lost (esp. by Mohammedan conquest) to the control of the Roman pontificate.

B. *sb.* 1. One who holds a title to an office, benefice, or possession, irrespective of the functions, duties, or rights attaching to it; *spec.* a cleric who bears a title whether he performs the duties or not; esp. short for *t. bishop* 1620. b. *transf.* One who has a title or appellation of some kind 1824. 2. A titled person 1757. Hence **Titula·rity** (*rare*), the quality or state of being t., or merely t. **Ti·tularly** *adv.* in respect of title, name, or style; *esp.* in name only, nominally.

Titulary (ti·tiǔlări), *a.* (*sb.*) Now *rare.* 1603. [f. L. *titulus* TITLE + -ARY[1].] = prec., in various senses.

Titule (ti·tiul), *v.* 1569. [f. L. *titulare* to TITLE.] Occasional var. of TITLE *v.*, esp. in pa. pple. or ppl. adj. **Ti·tuled.**

†**Tityre-tu** (ti·tire,tiū·). 1623. [The first two words of Virgil's first eclogue.] One of an association of well-to-do roughs who infested London streets in the 17th c.

Tiver (ti·vəɹ), *sb. dial.* 1792. [mod., app. repr. OE. *téafor*, glossing 'minium' (red lead).] A red colouring matter, used esp. for marking sheep. Hence **Ti·ver** *v. dial. trans.* to mark or colour with t.

Tivy (ti·vi), *int.* and *v. rare.* 1669. [See TANTIVY.] = TANTIVY *int.* and *v.* 1.

‖**Tiza** (tī·ză). 1865. [a. Quichua (Peruvian) *t'isa* to card wool; from its fibrous appearance.] *Min.* Ulexite or hayesine.

Tizzy (ti·zi). *slang.* 1804. [Origin obsc.] A sixpenny-piece.

‖**Tmesis** (tmī·sis). 1577. [a. Gr. τμῆσις a cutting.] *Gram.* and *Rhet.* The separation of the elements of a compound word by the interposition of another word or words.

T.N.T. (tī·,en,tī·). = TRINITROTOLUENE, -TOLUOL.

To (tū, *tu*, tu, tŭ, tə), *prep.*, *conj.*, *adv.* [OE. *tō*:—OTeut. **tô* adv., beside which OTeut. had **ti.*; pre-Teut. **dō*, **de* (OSl. and OIr. *do*, Lith. *da-* prefix, Gr. -δε, L. *-do* suffix).] A. *prep.* I. Expressing a spatial or local relation. 1. Expressing motion directed towards and reaching. (The opposite of FROM.) b. In fig. expressions of motion; the following sb. denoting (*a*) a state or condition attained, or (*b*) a thing or person reached by some action figured as movement OE. c. Elliptical uses. (*a*) with ellipsis of *go* or other verb of motion, esp. in commands, or (*arch.*) after an auxiliary verb. late ME. (*b*) = Gone to; in going to, on the way to. (Chiefly *dial.*) 1451. (*c*) after a sb. implying or suggesting motion: = That goes, or takes one, or causes one to go, to OE. 2. Expressing direction: In the direction of, towards OE. b. In expressing the position of something lying in a specified direction OE. c. In fig. expressions of direction (inclination, tendency, etc.). Also *fig.* from b, in phr. *to the bad*, *to the good* (= on the wrong, or right, side of the account), *to the fore*; in *to the contrary* with both senses (2 and 2 b). ME. 3. Indicating the limit of a movement or extension in space: As far as (to) OE. b. After expressions of distance, indicating the remote limit OE. 4. Expressing simple position: At, in (a place, also *fig.* a condition, etc.). Now only *dial.* and *U.S. colloq.* OE. 5. Expressing the relation of contact or the like. a. Into (or in) contact with; on, against OE. b. By, beside. Also *fig.* or with additional implication, as in *to one's face, teeth*, etc. = in presence and defiance of. OE.

1. When the poore man might turne out a cow, or two..to the commons 1583. b. When he came to the crown LAUD. To reclaim a lost child to virtue GOLDSM. c. (*a*) To youre tentes, O Israel! BIBLE (Great) 1 *Kings* xii. 16. (*b*) For now the sonne is to his rest 1500. (*c*) The path of duty was the way to glory TENNYSON. 2. As pilot..That to a stedfast starre his course hath bent SPENSER. b. Cannon to right of them, Cannon to left of them TENNYSON. 3. Wet to the skin 1873. 5. a. Applying plenty of yellow soap to the towel DICKENS. c. Phr. *To hand*: see HAND *sb.*

II. Expressing a relation in time. 1. Indicating a final limit in time, or the end of a period: Till, until; often correl. to *from* OE. b. (So long) before (a definite future time); *esp.* in stating the time of day: (so many minutes) before (an hour). Opp. to *past.* OE. c. *from* .. *to*, with repeated sb. of time, denoting regular recurrence; as *from day to day*, etc. OE. 2. Indicating the precise time at which something is to be done, or at which one is to arrive: At and not after (an appointed time), precisely or punctually at or on 1722.

1. The business hours..were from ten to six DICKENS. b. It was exactly a quarter to four o'clock 1843. We shall be late..it's..ten *to* now 1852. 2. Unable to pay their hearth money to the day MACAULAY.

III. Expressing the relation of purpose, destination, result, effect, resulting condition or status. 1. Indicating aim, purpose, intention, or design: For; for the purpose of; with the view or end of; in order to. (Now often repl. by *for.*) OE. b. *spec.* Towards or for the making of; as a contributory element or constituent of 1450. 2. Indicating destination, or an appointed or expected end or event ME. 3. Indicating result, effect, or consequence: So as to produce, cause, or result in OE. 4. Indicating a state or condition resulting from some process: So as to become OE. b. Indicating resulting position, status, or capacity: For, as, by way of, in the capacity of. *Obs.* or *arch.* exc. in certain phrases, as *to take to wife, to call to witness*, etc. OE. 5. a. Indicating the object of inclination, desire, or need: For. Also (after *to drink*, etc.), as an expression of desire for (one's health, success, etc.). ME. b. Indicating the object of a right or claim ME.

1. He was bred up to Joynery 1683. We were out..to breakfast 1838. The captain..came to our rescue 1843. b. Whole gardens of roses go to one drop of the attar 1890. *That's all there is to it* (colloq. phr., orig. U.S.), there is no more to add or to do. 2. Born to bitter Fate DRYDEN. He was..sentenced to transportation 1887. 3. To his..astonishment 1802. 4. Forester..took the flowers..and pulled them to pieces 1802. b. Who had Canace to wife? MILT. 5. a. Instead of marrying Torfrida..I have more mind to her niece KINGSLEY.. b. This lease..is a document of title to land 1890.

IV. Followed by a word or phrase expressing a limit in extent, amount, or degree. 1. Indicating a limit or point attained in degree or amount, or in division or analysis: As far as; to the point of; down to (an ultimate element or item), as in phr. *to a hair, to the last man, to a man* (including every man, without exception); within (a limit of variation or error), as *to an inch, to a day* OE. b. Indicating the final point or second limit of a series, or of the extent of a variable quantity or quality; correl. to *from* 1699. 2. Indicating the full extent, degree, or amount: So as to reach, complete, or constitute OE. b. So far or so much as to cause ME. c. Before a sb. expressing the amount, extent, space, etc. to which something is restricted 1518.

1. He was generally punctual to a minute 1779. b. Every style from early Norman to late perpendicular 1891. 2. Phr. *To a certainty, to a degree, to* (*that*, etc.) *extent, to a fault, to the full*, etc. b. The schoolroom was hot to suffocation 1890. c. To cut down the widow's absolute interest to a life estate 1885.

V. Indicating addition, attachment, accompaniment, appurtenance, possession. 1. In addition to, besides, with OE. b. To the accompaniment of; as an accompaniment to 1561. 2. After words denoting attachment or adherence; hence, occas. = Attached, fastened, or joined to OE. 3. After *belong* and similar verbs; also after *be* with the sense of *belong*; also after a sb., in the sense 'appertaining or belonging to'; sometimes = 'of' or the possessive case of the sb. OE.

1. He can't have cream to his tea RUSKIN. b. Phr *To ride to hounds*: see HOUND *sb.*[1] 2. 2. Sincerely attached to the Established Church MACAULAY. 3. Clerk to an attorney DE FOE. Without clothing to his back, or shoes to his feet 1840.

VI. Expressing relation to a standard or to a stated term or point. 1. Expressing comparison: In comparison with, as compared with OE. 2. a. Connecting the names of two things compared or opposed to each other in respect of amount or value: Against, as against 1530. b. Connecting two expressions of number or quantity which correspond to each other, or of which one constitutes the amount or value of the other: In; making up. (*To the* = in every.) OE. †c. Introducing an expression denoting price or cost: For, at. *Obs.* (exc. as coinciding with b). -1862. 3. Expressing agreement or adaptation: In accordance with, according to, after, by OE. 4. After words expressing comparison, proportion, correspondence, agreement or disagreement, and the like ME. 5. Expressing relation: In respect of, concerning, about, of, as to. Now only in special collocations. ME. 6. Expressing relative position; esp. *Geom.* 1570.

1. The men are noodles to her 1863. 2. a. Their enemies..wer foure to one HALL. b. He..made vs pay..one shilling to the pound SHAKS. Thirteen to the dozen 1801. 3. Temple is not a man to our taste MACAULAY. They were to all appearances distinct bills 1885. *To my knowledge*, qualifying a positive statement = 'as I actually know'; qualifying a negative statement = 'as far as I know'. 4. I can finde out no rime to Ladie but babie, an innocent rime SHAKS. 5. What will Doris say to it? 1884. Asking questions intended to show the untrustworthy character of a witness, or..'cross-examining to credit' 1892. 6. Unable to see how they lie to each other 1848.

VII. Expressing relations in which the sense of direction tends to blend with that of the dative. 1. After words denoting application, attention, or the like, indicating the object of this. Also (*arch.* or *rhet.*) with ellipsis of *go*, *betake oneself*, etc. (in imper., or after an auxiliary). ME. **2.** Expressing impact or attack: At, against, upon ME. **b.** After words denoting opposition or hostility: Against; towards (*obs.* or *arch.*). late ME. **3.** Indicating the object of speech, address, or the like OE. **b.** In honour of; for the worship of; in salutation of and expression of good wishes for (as *to drink to*). late ME. **4.** Expressing response or the like (of a voluntary agent); e.g. reply (*to* a statement, question, etc.) obedience (*to* a command, etc.) ME. **b.** Expressing reaction or responsive action (of an involuntary or inanimate agent). *poet.* 1682. **5.** Expressing exposure (of a thing *to* some physical agent). *rare.* 1460.

1. I'll to my own Art WALTON. Come, lads, all hands to work! 1843. 2. His father's unmerciful use of the whip to him 1882. 3. Hail to thee, blithe Spirit! SHELLEY. b. An auter, in which was writun, To the vnknowun God WYCLIF *Acts* xvii. 23. Drink to me, only with thine eyes B. JONSON. 4. Disobedience to his orders 1766. b. Little waves..sparkling to the moonbeams SCOTT. 5. That tower of strength Which stood four-square to all the winds that blew TENNYSON.

VIII. Supplying the place of the dative in various other languages and in the earlier stages of English itself. **1.** Introducing the recipient of anything given, or the person or thing upon whom or which an event acts or operates ME. **2.** For; for the use or benefit of; for (some one) to deal with (esp. after *leave* vb.); at the disposal of ME. **b.** Indicating the person or thing towards which an action, feeling, etc., is directed; esp. as the object of conduct, behaviour, or demeanour OE. **3.** Used in the syntactical constr. of many intr. verbs, as *yield, trust, allude*, etc. (See the verbs themselves.) ME. **b.** After, *testify, witness, confess, swear*, etc.: In support of; in assertion or acknowledgement of 1630. **4.** In the syntactical const. of many trans. verbs, introducing the indirect or dative object. (See the verbs themselves.) ME. **5.** Expressing the relation of an adj. (or derived adv. or sb.) to a sb. denoting a person or thing to which its application is directed or limited OE. **b.** After pa. pples. of verbs of perception (now only with *known, unknown*; nearly = by) ME.

1. Having a Son born to him ADDISON. Phr. *To be* (something) *to*, to be (something) in the eyes, view, apprehension, or opinion of; also, to be of importance or concern to. *What is that to you?* How does that concern you? 2. The rest is left to the imagination DRYDEN. Phr. *To oneself* (as pred.), to or at one's own disposal, free from the approaches or action of others; I'll first assay To get the Persian kingdom to myself MARLOWE. b. Bacchus is a friend to Love 1758. Phr. *To you*, an elliptical formula of courtesy, = 'my service to you'. 3. b. That is a fact to which I can speak 1776. 4. We fought them and put them to the run PEPYS. 5. This..is new to me 1777. True to nature 1843. Comte..lays himself specially open to attack 1886. Alive to the value of his wares 1887.

B. To before an infinitive (or gerund). **I.** with infinitive in advb. relation. **Indicating purpose or intention.* **1. a.** Dependent on a vb., *to* with inf. = *in order to* OE. **b.** Dependent on an adj.; indicating the purpose or function to which the adj. refers OE. **c.** Dependent on a sb.; the inf. expressing the use or function of that which is denoted by the sb. OE. (*b*) After *time, room*, etc.: equivalent to *for* with gerund, or = at or in which (one) can or should.. ME. **2.** In absol. or independent construction, usu. introductory or parenthetic ME.

1. I gave a soldier five dollars to carry them news DE FOE. Fools, who came to scoff, remained to pray GOLDSM. c. A light to lighten the gentyls TINDALE *Luke* ii. 32. (*b*) The time to learn is when you're young 1887. 2. But to return to our Subject ADDISON.

** *Indicating objectivity.* **3.** Dependent on various verbs chiefly trans., pass., or refl.: indicating an action, etc. to which that of the principal verb is in some way directed. (See also the verbs themselves.) OE. **b.** In obsolete, arch., or dial. uses; now replaced by various prepositions with the gerund, or by other constructions 1525. **4.** Dependent on various adjs. (also pples. and adjectival or predicative phrases): usu. indicating the application of the adj., etc. OE. **b.** With inf. passive. *arch.* 1460. **5.** Dependent on various abstract sbs.: usu. indicating object or application; also (after *favour, honour, pleasure*, etc.) indicating an action which is the substance or form of that which is denoted by the sb., i. e. in which it consists; often replaceable by *of* with gerund OE.

3. I strive to be concise 1746. b. Abstaining to write to her G. MEREDITH. 4. Careless their merits or their faults to scan GOLDSM. At liberty to enforce her claims 1838. b. The fittest to be chosen EVELYN. 5. I had the Honour to be a Member of it SWIFT. As though in act to spring 1842. *Going to*: see GO *v.* V.

*** *Indicating appointment or destination.* **6.** Indicating destiny, or (expected or actual) event or outcome. late ME.

When we two parted..To sever for years BYRON.

**** *Indicating result or consequence.* **7.** Expressing result or consequence (potential or actual); esp. after *so* or *such* (now always with *as* before *to* = *that* with finite vb.), or *enough* ME. **b.** After *too*, with neg. implication (*too.. to..* = *so.. as not to*, or *so.. that.. not..*) ME.

The man is become as one of us, to know good & euill *Gen.* ii. 22. b. Too proud to care from whence I came TENNYSON.

***** *Indicating occasion or condition.* **8.** Indicating occasion (passing into ground, reason, or cause): = *at, in, on, for, of, by*, etc. with gerund, or *because* with finite vb. late ME. **9.** With inf. after an adj. or (predicate) sb., in passive sense, the main sb. of the principal clause being the implied object of the inf., or of a preposition following OE. **10.** With inf. expressing a fact or supposition which forms the ground of the statement in the principal clause, or is considered in connexion with it ME. †**b.** With inf. equivalent to a conditional clause with indef. subject (= *if one were to..*) –1611.

8. I blusht to heare his monstrous deuices SHAKS. 9. A flour, þat es fayre to se HAMPOLE. 10. Thou art a rustic to call me so ADDISON. b. To keepe them here, they would but stinke SHAKS.

II. With infinitive in adjectival relation. **1.** With inf. in adjectival relation to a sb.; either as predicate after the vb. *to be*, or immediately qualifying the sb. **a.** Expressing intention or appointment, and hence simply futurity (thus equivalent to a future pple.) OE. **b.** Expressing duty, obligation, or necessity OE. **c.** Expressing possibility or potential action OE. **d.** Expressing quality or character: = such as to.., such as would... late ME. **2.** With inf. equivalent to a relative clause with indicative; chiefly after *first, last*, or the like; as *the first to come* = 'the first in coming', 'the first who comes *or* came' 1535.

1. a. The best is yet to be BROWNING. This house to let or for sale (*mod.*) b. Unprofitable questions are to be avoided 1560. They had no time to lose 1794. What, then, are you to do? 1887. c. There was no man to saye hym naye 1533. Not a sound was to be heard 1818. The gates are mine to open, As the gates are mine to close KIPLING. d. A sight to gladden Heav'n! THOMSON. 2. Not an eye that sees you, but is a Physician to comment on your Malady SHAKS.

III. With infinitive in substantival relation. Equivalent to a noun or gerund; *to* being ult. reduced to a mere 'sign' of the inf. without any meaning of its own. **1. a.** with inf. as subj., or as obj. with complement, introduced by *it* or an impersonal vb. OE. **b.** with inf. as direct subj. or predicate, or in apposition with a sb. or pron., or after *than* ME. **2.** with inf. as direct obj. of a trans. vb. OE. **b.** rarely as object of another preposition, instead of the vbl. sb. or gerund 1485.

1. a. God hath pronounc't it death to taste that Tree MILT. b. Talking is not always to converse COWPER. 2. I love not to be idle B. JONS. b. Not to affirm is a very different thing from to deny 1879.

IV. With infinitive equivalent to a finite vb. or clause. **1.** With inf. as complement to a sb. or pron., forming a compound obj. or sb. phrase, corresponding to the 'accusative and infinitive' construction in Latin and Greek OE. **2.** With inf. after a dependent interrogative or relative; equivalent to a clause with *may, should*, etc. ME. **b.** In absolute or independent const. after an interrogative, forming an elliptical question 1713. **3.** In absolute or independent constr., with subject expressed (in nom.) or omitted: in exclams. expressing astonishment, indignation, sorrow, or (after *O* or other interj.) longing 1450. †**4.** With inf. immediately following the subject, in vivid narrative, equivalent to a past tense indic.; almost always with *go* and vbs. of like meaning –1668.

1. Shee will..cause thy throate to be cut CORYAT. b. The Houyhnhnms..could hardly believe me to be a right Yahoo SWIFT. 2. He..wyst not what to do MALORY. b. But..how to hinder vexatious prosecutions? J. H. NEWMAN. 3. My owne flesh and blood to rebell SHAKS. Oh, to be in England! BROWNING. 4. I..away home..and there to read again and sup with Gibson PEPYS.

V. Peculiar constructions. †**1.** *To* was formerly often used with the second of two infinitives when the first was without it –1803. **2.** Occasionally an adv. or advb. phr. (formerly sometimes an object or predicate) is inserted between *to* and the infinitive, forming the construction now usu. (but loosely) called 'split infinitive' ME. **3.** Used absol. at the end of a clause, with ellipsis of the inf. *rare* bef. 19th c.; now a frequent colloquialism. ME.

1. *Merry W.* IV. iv. 57. 2. Milton was too busy to much miss his wife JOHNSON. This answer seemed to seriously offend him 1805. 3. I kept on..I had to 1883.

†**C. To** *conj.* **a.** To the time that; till, until –1575. **b.** followed by *that* –1626.

D. To (tū) *adv.* †**1.** Expressing motion resulting in arrival: To a place, etc. implied or indicated by the context –1450. **2.** Expressing direction: Towards a thing or person implied; after *end, head*, etc., forming advb. phrases 1889. **b.** In conjunction with other advs. of direction: In one direction (as contrasted with the opposite one). Now only in TO AND FRO. late ME. **3.** Expressing contact: So as to come close against something; *esp.* with vbs. forming phrases denoting shutting or closing. Now *arch.* and *colloq.* ME. **4.** Expressing attachment, application, or addition; also predic., *spec.* of a horse: = harnessed to a vehicle. Now *dial.* or *colloq.* late ME. **b.** In the senses 'in addition, besides, also', and 'in excess', now written TOO. **5.** Expressing attention or application; after vbs., as *fall, go, set.* †Also *absol.* (with ellipsis of vb. in imper.). ME. **6.** Used idiomatically with many vbs., as *bring, come, go, lay, lie*, etc.: see the vbs. **7. To and again. a.** = TO AND FRO A. 1. *Obs.* exc. *dial.* 1627. †**b.** For and against a question –1666. †**c.** Again and again –1666.

2. Three young owls with their feathers turned wrong end to 1889. b. *Ant. & Cl.* I. iv. 46. 3. She..clapte the wyndow to CHAUCER. 4. Can Honour set too a legge? SHAKS. 5. To Achilles, to Aiax, to SHAKS. 7. c. Sent him to and again to get me 1000 *l.* PEPYS.

To-, *prefix* 1, the prep. and adv. To used in combination with vbs., sbs., adjs., and advs. in the sense of motion, direction, or addition to, or as the mark of the infinitive.

To-, *prefix* 2. *Obs.* exc. in rare *arch.* or *dial.* use. [OE. *to-*, ME. *to-* (*te-*), substituted for, WGer. **ti-*:—OTeut. **tiz-* (OHG. *zi-, ze-, zir-, zar*, G. *zer-*) = L. *dis-*, a particle expressing separation, 'asunder, apart, in pieces'.] **1.** With separative force: Asunder, apart, to or in pieces; also, away, about, abroad, here and there. **2.** Used as a mere intensive: Completely, entirely, soundly, greatly, severely, etc. **3.** Hence **all to-, all to, all-to,** †**alto,** employed in middle and early modern Eng. as an intensive to any vb.

Toad (tōud), *sb.* [OE. *tādige*, of unkn. origin.] **1.** A tailless amphibian of the genus *Bufo*; primarily the common European species *B. vulgaris*; thence extended to many foreign species of the genus or of the family *Bufonidæ*. **b.** As a type of anything hateful or loathsome 1548. **c.** *fig.* and *prov.* 1649. **2.** Applied to allied animals, as *Surinam t.* = PIPA; *midwife, obstetrical t.*, the nurse-frog: see OBSTETRICAL 1757. **3.** Applied opprobriously to human beings and animals 1568. **4.** = TOADY *sb.* 2. 1831. **5.** Cookery. *Toad in a hole*: meat (usu. sausage-meat) baked in a batter pudding 1787.

1. The t., ougly and venemous SHAKS. Him there they found Squat like a T., close at the eare of Eve MILT. *Running t.*, the natterjack. b. *Tr. & Cr.* II. iii. 170. c. *To eat* (*any one's*) *toads*, to toady. *T. under a harrow*, a simile for a person under constant persecution or oppression. 3. What a miserable poor t. is a husband, whose misfortunes not even death can relieve! 1771.

Comb.: **t.-cheese**, a poisonous fungus; **-head**, the Amer. golden plover (*local U.S.*); **-lizard** (*a*) the horned t.; (*b*) the labyrinthodon; **-pipe**, any one of various species of *Equisetum*; **-rush**, *Juncus bufonius*; **toad's mouth**, the snapdragon, *Antirrhinum majus*; **-snatcher**, the reed-bunting; **-spit, -spittle** = CUCKOO-SPIT 2 1. Hence **Toad** *v. trans.* to act as a toady to; to toady; also *intr.* **Toa·dish** *a. rare*, of the nature of a t.; like a t. **Toa·dlet, Toa·dling,** a young or little t.

Toad-eat (tōu·d,īt), *v. rare.* 1766. [Back-formation from next.] *trans.* To flatter, fawn upon (a person); to toady. Also *intr.* So **Toa·d-ea:ting** *vbl. sb.* and *ppl. a.*

Toad-eater (tōu·d,ī:təɹ). 1629. **1.** One who eats toads; *orig.* the attendant of a charlatan, employed to eat toads (held to be poisonous) to enable his master to exhibit his skill in expelling poison. **2.** *fig.* A fawning flatterer, parasite, sycophant 1742. **b.** A humble friend or dependant; *spec.* a female companion or attendant. *contempt.* Now *rare.* 1744.

2. Lord Edgcumbe's [place]..is destined to Harry Vane, Pulteney's toad-eater H. WALPOLE.

Toad-fish (tōu·d,fiʃ). 1612. A name applied, from their appearance, to several fishes; *esp.* **a.** A swell-fish, or puffer, spec. *Tetrodon turgidus.* **b.** The sea-devil, fishing frog, angler, or wide-gab, *Lophius piscatorius.* **c.** *American t.,* the oyster-fish, *Batrachus tau,* of the Atlantic coast of U.S.A.

Toad-flax (tōu·d,flæks). 1578. [From the flax-like appearance of the foliage.] The European plant *Linaria vulgaris*; hence extended as a generic name to other species of *Linaria.*

Toadstone[1] (tōu·dstoun). 1558. [tr. Gr. and L. *batrachites,* or med.L. *bufonites.*] Formerly, any of various stones likened to a toad in colour or shape, or supposed to be produced by a toad; often worn as jewels or amulets, or set in rings. The most valued kind was fabled to be found in the head of the toad; cf. *A. Y. L.* II. i. 13.

Toadstone[2] (tōu·dstoun). *local.* 1784. [perh. corruption of G. *todtes gestein* dead rock.] A name given by the Derbyshire lead-miners to an igneous rock, occurring as irregular sheets of contemporaneous lava, interstratified with, or in connexion with the metalliferous mountain limestone.

Toadstool (tōu·dstūl). late ME. A fungus having a round disk-like top and a slender stalk, a mushroom. **b.** Popularly restricted to poisonous or inedible fungi, as distinct from edible 'mushrooms' 1607.

Toady (tōu·di), *sb.* 1826. [f. TOADEATER + -Y[6].] A servile dependant or parasite; = TOADEATER 2, 2 b.

Toady (tōu·di), *a. rare.* 1628. [f. TOAD *sb.* + -Y[1].] **1.** Toad-like, repulsive. **2.** Infested with toads 1882.

Toady (tōu·di), *v.* 1827. [f. TOADY *sb.*] **1.** *trans.* To play the toady to; to flatter or attend to with servility from interested motives. **2.** *intr.* To play the servile dependant; to pay deference from interested motives 1861.

Toadyism (tōu·di,iz'm). 1840. [f. TOADY *sb.* + -ISM.] The action or behaviour of a parasite or sycophant; mean and interested servility.

To and fro (tūənᵈfrōu·), *phr.* ME. [TO, FRO *advs.* and *preps.*] **A.** *adv.* **1.** Successively to and from some place, etc.; hence more vaguely: In opposite or different directions alternately; from side to side; backwards and forwards; hither and thither; up and down. †**2.** In places lying in opposite or different directions; here and there –1697. †**3.** To or on opposite sides alternately; for and against a question; pro and con –1690.

1. Idle children, wandering to and fro CRABBE. 3. Thus shall they be too and fro, doubtfull and ambiguous in all thir doings MILT.

B. *prep.* To and from (a place); alternately to and from each of (two places): the latter now commonly expressed by *between.* Now *rare.* 1574. **C.** *sb.* (now with hyphens; but pl. *tos and fros*). **1.** Alternating or reciprocating movement; the action of walking or passing to and fro 1847. **2.** *fig.* Alternation generally; vacillation 1553.

1. Watching the to-and-fro of a shuttle 1906.

D. *adj.* (usu. with hyphens). Executed, as movement, in opposite directions alternately; alternating, reciprocating; characterized by, or characterizing, such movement; passing to and fro 1839.

The regular to-and-fro motion of the water in its estuary HUXLEY.

E. as *vb. phr.* (only in pres. pple. and vbl. sb.) **a.** *intr.* To pass to and fro, to go hither and thither 1847. **b.** *trans.* To lead to and fro 1852.

a. There were clerks to-ing and fro-ing 1872.

Toarcian (to,ā·ɹsiăn), *a.* (*sb.*) 1885. [ad. F. *Toarcien,* f. L. *Toarcium* (F. *Thouars*), in western France.] *Geol.* Applied to a series of strata corresponding in position to the Upper Lias of England, which are extensively developed in Central and Southern France.

Toast (tōust), *sb.*[1] late ME. [f. TOAST *v.*[1]] **1.** (with *a* and *pl.*) A slice or piece of bread browned at the fire: often put in wine, water, or other beverage. Now *rare* or *Obs.* exc. as in b. **b.** As the type of what is hot or dry. late ME. **2.** As a substance (without *a* or *pl.*): Bread so browned by fire 1730. †**3.** *fig.* (usu. *old t.*) One who drinks to excess, a soaker, a boon companion; a brisk old fellow fond of his glass. *slang.* –1709.

1. b. It keeps this end of the valley as warm as a t. STEVENSON. 2. *Ale and t., t. and ale, t. and water. On t.,* served up on a slice of toast; fig. *to have* (a person) *on t.,* to have at one's mercy (*slang*).

Comb.: **t.-rack,** a contrivance for holding toast, keeping each piece on edge and separate; **-water,** water in which toasted bread has been steeped, used as a drink for invalids, etc.

Toast, *sb.*[2] 1674. [A fig. application of prec., the name of a lady being supposed to flavour a bumper like a spiced toast in the drink.] **1.** A lady who is named as the person to whom a company is requested to drink; often one who is the reigning belle of the season. Now only *Hist.* **2.** Any person, male or female, whose health is proposed and drunk to; also any event, institution, or sentiment, in memory or in honour of which a company is requested to drink; also, the call or act of proposing such a health 1746.

1. The present beauty,..a Mrs. Musters,..the reigning t. of the season MME D'ARBLAY. 2. He then gave as a t., 'Success to Scotland, and its worthy inhabitants' 1831.

Comb.: **t.-master,** one who at a public dinner or the like is appointed to propose or announce the toasts.

Toast (tōust), *v.*[1] late ME. [ad. OF. *toster* to roast or grill :—pop. L. **tostare,* f. *tost-, torrere* to parch.] **1.** *trans.* To burn as the sun does, to parch; to heat thoroughly; now *spec.* as in technical operations. **b.** *intr.* for *refl.* To warm oneself thoroughly 1614. **2.** To brown (bread, cheese, etc.) by exposure to the heat of a fire. late ME. **b.** *transf.* To warm (one's feet or toes) at a fire 1860. Hence **Toa·sting** *vbl. sb.*; **toa·sting-fork,** a fork used for toasting bread, etc.; *fig.* a rapier or sword.

Toast, *v.*[2] 1700. [f. TOAST *sb.*[2]] **1.** *intr.* To name a person to whose health or in whose honour, or a thing or sentiment to the success of which or in honour of which, the company is requested to drink; to propose or drink a toast. Const. *to.* **2.** *trans.* To name when a toast is drunk; to drink in honour of (a person or thing) 1700.

2. Times without number did he t. 'The Liberty of the Press' 1836.

Toaster (tōu·stəɹ). 1582. [f. TOAST *v.*[1] + -ER[1].] **1.** One who toasts anything by the fire. **2.** A toasting-fork, *joc.* a rapier or similar weapon 1695. **b.** A kind of cheese, bread, etc., that toasts (well or otherwise) 1845.

Tobacco (tŏbæ·ko). 1577. Also (orig.) †**tabaco,** †**tabacco.** [Altered from Sp. *tabaco,* according to Oviedo the native name of the tube or pipe through which the Indians inhaled the smoke; but according to Las Casas, 1552, applied to a tubular roll of leaves used by the Indians like a rude cigar. Taken by the Spaniards as the name of the herb or leaf, in which sense it passed into the other European langs.] **1.** The leaves of the tobacco-plant dried and variously prepared, forming a narcotic and sedative substance widely used for smoking, also for chewing, or in the form of SNUFF, and to a slight extent in medicine 1588. **2.** The plant whose leaves are so used: Any one of various species of *Nicotiana* (family *Solanaceæ*), esp. *N. Tabacum,* a native of tropical America, or *N. rustica* (*green* or *wild t.*), now widely cultivated 1577. **b.** With defining words, applied to plants of other genera, as **Indian t.,** (*a*) *Lobelia inflata* of N. America, used medicinally; (*b*) Indian hemp, *Cannabis indica*; **mountain t.,** *Arnica montana*; wild t. = *Indian t.* (*a*) 1597.

Comb., as *t.-ash, -jar, -smoke*: **t.-cutter,** (*a*), a person employed in cutting t.; (*b*) a machine or knife for this purpose; **t. heart,** *Path.,* a heart functionally disordered by excessive use of t., characterized by a rapid and irregular pulse; **-man,** a tobacconist (now *rare* or *Obs.*); **-pouch,** a pouch for carrying t. for smoking or chewing; **-stopper,** a contrivance for pressing down the t. in the bowl of a pipe while smoking; **-worm,** the larva of a sphinx-moth, *Protoparce carolina,* which feeds on the leaves of the t.-plant.

Toba·cco-box. 1599. **1.** A box for holding tobacco, *esp.* a small flat box to be carried in the pocket. **2.** Local name for two N. Amer. fishes, from their flattened shape: (*a*) a species of skate or ray, *Raia erinacea*; (*b*) the common sunfish, *Pomotis gibbosus* 1891.

Tobacconist (tŏbæ·kŏnist). 1599. [f. TOBACCO + -IST, with inserted *-n-.*] †**1.** A person addicted to the use of tobacco –1757. **2.** A dealer in, or manufacturer of, tobacco 1657.

Toba·cco-pipe. 1596. **1.** A pipe for smoking tobacco, consisting of a bowl in which the tobacco is placed and ignited, with a slender tube through which the smoke of it is drawn into the mouth. **2.** *U.S.* Local name for a parasitic plant, also called *Indian pipe* 1845.

1. *King's* (*Queen's*) *tobacco-pipe*: see PIPE *sb.*[1] III. *Comb.*: **t. clay** = PIPE-CLAY.

Toba·cco-plant. 1761. = TOBACCO 2. b. A name for species of *Nicotiana* 1884.

Tobe (tōub). 1835. [Arab.] A length of cotton cloth used as a garment.

To-be (tŭ,bī·), *a.* and *sb.* 1600. [inf. of vb. BE.] That, that which, is to be; future.

Tobin's tube. Also **Tobin tube.** 1884. A device for admitting fresh air into a room in an upward direction, invented by Martin Tobin of Leeds in 1873.

Toboggan (tŏbɒ·găn). 1829. [Adaptation of a Canadian Indian name of a sleigh or sledge.] **1.** orig., A light sledge consisting of a thin strip of wood turned up in front, used by the Canadian Indians for transport over snow; now, a similar vehicle, sometimes with low runners, used in the sport of coasting (esp. down prepared slopes of snow or ice). **2.** [f. next.] The sport of tobogganing 1879.

Tobo·ggan, *v.* 1856. [f. prec.] *intr.* To ride on a toboggan or sleigh; *esp.* to 'coast' or slide down a snowy (or other) slope on a toboggan. Hence **Tobo·gganer, Tobo·gganist.**

†**To-brea·k,** *v.* [OE. *tobrecan,* f. TO-[2] + *brecan* to BREAK.] **1.** *trans.* To break to pieces; to shatter, rupture; to break down, demolish –1688. **2.** *intr.* To break into pieces; to burst asunder; to be ruptured, shattered, or fractured –1520.

1. This was it, that all to-brake his heart BUNYAN.

Toby (tōu·bi). 1681. [Familiar form of Christian name *Tobias.*] **1.** The posteriors, the buttocks. **2.** (With capital T.) A jug or mug in the form of a stout old man in a long and full skirted coat and a three-cornered hat (18th c. costume). Also *attrib.* as *T. jug.* 1840. **3.** The name of the trained dog introduced (in the first half of the 19th c.) into the Punch and Judy show 1840.

3. *T. collar, frill*: a turndown pleated frill like that of dog Toby.

‖**Toccata** (tokkā·tă). 1724. [It., lit. a touching, f. *toccare* to touch.] *Mus.* A composition for a keyboard instrument, intended to exhibit the touch and technique of the performer, and having the air of an improvisation; in later times loosely applied.

Toc H (tɒk ēⁱtʃ). [Telephonist's letter T + H, the initials of Talbot House, Poperinghe, founded 1915 in memory of Gilbert Talbot (killed July 1915).] A society for the maintenance of comradeship since the war of 1914–18.

Tocher (tɒ·χəɹ). *Sc.* and *n. dial.* 1485. [a. Ir. and OGael. *tochar.*] The marriage portion which a wife brings to her husband; dowry, *dot.*

‖**Toco**[1] (tōu·kŏ). 1781. [Native name in Guiana.] *Ornith.* The typical species of TOUCAN, *Rhamphastos toco,* a native of Guiana.

Toco[2] (tōu·ko). *slang.* Also **toko.** 1823. [Origin obsc.] Chastisement, corporal punishment.

Toco- (tǫko), comb. form of Gr. *τόκος* offspring, as in **Toco·logist**, one versed in tocology; **Toco·logy**, the science of parturition or of midwifery, obstetrics.

Tocsin (tǫ·ksin). 1586. [a. F., OF. *toquassen*; ad. Prov. *tocasenh*, f. *tocar* to TOUCH + *senh* 'appel de la cloche':—L. *signum* sign, in later L. also a bell.] **1.** A signal, esp. an alarm-signal, sounded by ringing a bell or bells: used orig. and esp. in ref. to France. **2.** *transf.* A bell used to sound an alarm 1842.

1. The t...is pealing madly from all steeples CARLYLE. 2. The great bell of St. Paul's was the t. which summoned the citizens to arms 1868.

Tod (tǫd), *sb.*¹ *Sc.* and *n. dial.* ME. [Origin unkn.] **1.** A fox. **2.** *fig.* A person likened to a fox; a crafty person 1500. †**3.** *ellipt.* Fox-skin –1564.

2. Take care of the old t.; he means mischief STEVENSON.

Tod (tǫd), *sb.*² late ME. [app. the same word as mod. EFris. *todde* bundle, pack, small load (of hay, straw, turf, etc.).] **1.** A weight used in the wool trade, usu. 28 pounds or 2 stone, but varying locally. **b.** A load, either generally, or of a definite weight 1479. **2.** A bushy mass (esp. of ivy; also *ivy-tod*: see IVY) 1553.

Tod (tǫd), *v. dial.* Now *rare* or *Obs.* 1611. [f. prec.] *intr.* Of (so many) sheep or fleeces: To produce a tod of wool; *to t. threes* (etc.), to produce a tod from every three (etc.) sheep; hence, To obtain a tod of wool from a specified number of sheep.

To-day (tŭdēⁱ·), *adv.* and *sb.* [OE. *tó dæg*, To *prep.* A. II. 2 + DAY.] **A.** *adv.* **1.** On this very day. **2.** *transf.* At the present time, in the present age; in these times; nowadays ME.

1. To day they chas'd the Boar OTWAY.

B. *sb.* **1.** This day; also, any day considered as present 1535. **2.** *transf.* This present time or age 1848.

2. The fad of today is the orthodoxy of tomorrow 1910.

Toddle (tǫ·d'l), *sb.* 1825. [f. next.] **1.** An act or the action of toddling; *transf.* a leisurely walk, a stroll. **2.** (Also **toddles.**) A toddling child 1825.

Toddle (tǫ·d'l), *v.* 1600. [orig. *todle*, Sc. and north. Eng.; origin obsc.] *intr.* To walk or run with short unsteady steps, as a child just beginning to walk, an aged or invalid person. **b.** Hence, To walk or move with short easy steps; to saunter, stroll; by meiosis, simply = walk, go 1724.

When his strength enabled him to t. abroad THACKERAY. Hence **To·ddler**, one who toddles; *esp.* a toddling child.

Toddy (tǫ·di). 1609. [ad. Hind. *tāṛī* (with cerebral *r*, approaching Eng. *d*), f. Hind. *tār* palm-tree:—Skr. *tāla* palmyra.] **1.** The sap obtained from the incised spathes of various species of palm, esp. *Caryota urens*, the wild date, the coco-nut, and the palmyra, used as a beverage in tropical countries; also, the intoxicating liquor produced by its fermentation. **2.** A beverage composed of whisky or other spirituous liquor with hot water and sugar 1786.

Comb.: **t.-bird**, any of various E. Indian birds, as *Ploceus baya*, which feed on the sap of palms; **-cat** = *palm-cat* a.; **-palm**, any palm that yields t.; spec. *Caryota urens*, and the wild date-tree of India, *Phœnix sylvestris*.

To do, to-do: see DO *v.* IV. 2.

Tody (tōᵘ·di). 1773. [ad. F. *todier*, ad. L. *todus*, name of some small bird.] *Ornith.* Any member or species of the genus *Todus* or family *Todidæ* of small insectivorous birds, resembling and allied to the kingfisher; of which four species are found in the Greater Antilles.

Toe (tōᵘ), *sb.* [OE. *tá*, pl. *tán*, ME. *tō*, pl. *tōn*, *tōs*:—OTeut. **taih(w)ōn*.] **1.** Each of the five digits of the human foot. **2.** Each of the digits of the foot of a beast or bird. late ME. **b.** The front part of the hoof (or shoe) of a horse 1566. **3.** *transf.* The part of a shoe or stocking which covers the toes; the hood or cap for the toe sometimes attached to a stirrup; a toe-piece 1600. **4.** A part resembling a toe or the toes, in shape or position; (usu.) the lower extremity or projection of anything; a point, tip; often identical with *foot*. **a.** *gen.* 1440. **b.** The lower extremity of a spindle or screw, as in a press: the projection on a lock-bolt or the like, against which the key or a cam presses 1677. **c.** The lower extremity of a gun-stock, rafter, organ-pipe, etc. 1860. **d.** The thin end of a hammer-head, the peen; the tip of the 'head' of a golf or hockey club 1873.

1. *Big* or *great t.*, the thick inner toe; *little t.*, the short outer toe. *fig.* What do you thinke? You, the great T. of this Assembly? SHAKS. 3. Place thy foot on the t. of my boot SCOTT.

Phrases (chiefly *colloq.* and *slang*). *T. and heel*, (*a*) a style of dancing, in which the toe and heel tap rhythmically on the ground; also *attrib.*; (*b*) a manner of walking in which the heel of one foot and the toe of the other are always upon the ground together. *To kiss the pope's t.*: to kiss the golden cross of the sandal on the pope's right foot, as a mark of respect: the customary salutation of those (excepting sovereigns) to whom audience is granted. *To step* or *tread on the toes of*; also *fig.* to give offence to, to vex. *To turn one's toes up*, to die.

Comb.: **t.-ball**, the thickened fleshy pad under the t.; **-cap**, a cap of leather covering the t. of a boot or shoe; **-clip**, (*a*) an attachment to a bicycle-pedal in which the t. of the shoe is placed to prevent the foot slipping; (*b*) a tip turned up at the t. of a horse-shoe, to keep the shoe in position; **-crack** *Farriery*, a sand-crack in the front of the hoof; **-dancer**, one who dances on the extreme tips of the toes; **-hardy**, a half-round hardy or cold-chisel; **-hold**, in *Wrestling*, a hold in which the t. is seized and the leg forced backwards; **-nail** *sb.*, the nail of a t.; **-nail** *v.*, to fasten with toed nails: see TOED 2; **-step** *Mech.*, the socket in which the end of a spindle works.

Toe (tōᵘ), *v.* 1607. [f. prec.] **1.** *trans.* To furnish with a toe or toes; to make or put a new toe on (a stocking, etc.). **2.** To touch or reach with the toes 1833. **3. a.** To kick with the toe. **b.** *Golf.* To strike (a ball) with the tip of the club. 1865. **4.** *intr.* To move the toe, to tap rhythmically with the toe in dancing; *to t. and heel* (*it*), to dance 1828. **5.** *trans. Carpentry.* To secure or join together by nails driven obliquely: see TOED 2. 1877.

2. Phr. *To t. a* or *the line, mark, scratch, crack*: to stand with the tips of one's toes exactly touching a line; to stand in a row; hence *fig.* to present oneself in readiness for a race, contest, or undertaking; also, to conform to the defined standard or platform of a party.

Toed (tōᵘd), *ppl. a.* 1611. [f. TOE *sb.* and *v.* + -ED.] **1.** Having a toe or toes, as *three-t.*, *black-t.* Of a stocking, Having separate divisions for the toes; of a clog, or the like, Having a (leather) toe-piece. **2.** *Carpentry.* Secured or joined by nails driven obliquely; also of a nail, driven obliquely 1877.

To-fall (tū·fǫl). *Sc.* and *n. dial.* late ME. [f. To *prep.* + FALL *v.* or *sb.*] **1.** A lean-to; a penthouse; a shed. **2.** The act of falling to; *t. of the day* or *night*, the close of day 1749.

Toff (tǫf). *vulgar.* 1851. [perh. perversion of TUFT.] One who is stylishly dressed or who has a smart appearance; a swell; hence, one of the well-to-do, a 'nob'. **b.** Sometimes applied in compliment to a person who behaves 'handsomely'; a 'gent' 1898.

Toffee, toffy (tǫ·fi). 1825. [Origin obsc.] A sweetmeat made from sugar or treacle, butter, and sometimes a little flour, boiled together; often mixed with bruised nuts, as *almond* or *walnut t.* Also, with *a* and *pl.*: A piece of toffee.

Not for t. (vulgar phr.): not under any circumstances. *Not to be able to do* a thing *for t.* (slang): to be incompetent at it.

†**Tofo·re**, *prep.*, *adv.*, and *conj.* [OE. *tóforan*, f. To *prep.* + *foran* adv., deriv. of OTeut. **fora* fore, for.] = BEFORE, in various senses.

Toft (tǫft). [Late OE., a. ON. *topt*, *tupt*, later *toft*, *tuft*:—OTeut. **tumf(e)t-*, with which cf. Gr. *δάπεδον* (:—**dmpedom*) level surface, lit. 'site for building'.] **1.** *orig.* A homestead, the site of a house and its outbuildings; a house site. Often in *t. and croft*, the whole holding, consisting of the homestead and attached piece of arable land. **2.** Apparently including the croft, or applied to a field or piece of land larger than the site of a house 1440. **3.** An eminence, knoll, or hillock in a flat region. Now *local.* late ME.

3. I sauh a Tour on A T...; A Deop Dale bi-neoþe LANGL.

Comb.: **toftman**, the owner and occupier of a t.

Tog (tǫg), *sb.*; usu. *pl.* **togs.** *slang* or *colloq.* 1798. [app. a shortening of TOGEMAN(S, TOGMAN.] **1.** *Cant.* and *slang.* A coat; any outer garment. **2.** *pl.* Clothes. *slang* and *joc. colloq.* 1809.

2. *Long togs* (Naut.), landsmen's clothes.

Tog, *v.* 1793. [Occurs chiefly as *togged* (tǫgd), prob. orig. from prec.] *trans.* To clothe, to dress: often with *up*. Also *intr.* for *refl.*

‖**Toga** (tōᵘ·gă). 1600. [L., = cloak or mantle, f. ablaut-stem of *tegere* to cover.] *Rom. Antiq.* The outer garment of a Roman citizen in time of peace, consisting of a single piece of stuff, long, broad, and flowing, without sleeves or armholes, and covering the whole body with the exception of the right arm. **b.** *transf.* and *fig.* A robe of office; a professional gown, a cloak, a 'mantle'; a dress coat 1738.

T. prætexta, a toga with a broad purple border worn by children, magistrates, persons engaged in sacred rites, and later by emperors. *T. virilis*, the toga of manhood, assumed by boys at puberty. Hence **To·gaed, to·ga'd** (tōᵘ·găd): clad in a t.; togated.

Togate (tōᵘ·gĕⁱt), *a.* 1851. [ad. L. *togatus*; see -ATE ².] = TOGAED.

Togated (tōᵘ·gĕⁱtĕd), *a.* 1634. [f. as prec. + -ED.] **1.** Clad in a toga; wearing the toga; hence, associated with the idea of peace, peaceful. **2.** Of words: Latinized; stately, majestic 1868.

2. Such t. words as 'The multitudinous sea incarnadine' 1868.

†**To·ged**, *a.* 1604. [f. as next + -ED ².] Clad in a toga, togated; hence, robed –1862.

†**To·geman(s, to·gman.** *Vagabonds' Cant. rare.* 1567. [app. f. F. *toge* or L. *toga* + the cant suffix *-man(s*, as in *darkmans* night, etc.] A cloak or loose coat –1785.

Together (tŭge·ðəɹ), *adv.* (*prep.*) [OE. *tógædere*, *tógadore*, f. To prep. + *gædre*:—**gaduri*, orig. locative or instr. of **gador*, *-ur*, OE. *geador* 'together', whence also *gaderian* to GATHER.] **1.** Into one gathering, company, mass, or body. **b.** Of two persons or things: Into companionship, union, proximity, contact, or collision OE. **2.** In one assembly, company, or body; in one place ME. **b.** Of two persons or things: In each other's company; in union or contact ME. **c.** In ideal combination; considered collectively 1796. **3.** In ref. to a single thing. **a.** With union or combination of parts or elements; into or in a condition of unity; so as to form a connected whole ME. **b.** After *fold*, *roll*, etc.: Of different parts (sides, ends, etc.): Into or in contact or junction, so as to form a compact body 1480. **4.** At the same time, at once, simultaneously ME. **5.** Without intermission, continuously, consecutively, uninterruptedly, 'running', 'on end'. (Usu. in ref. to time.) ME. **6.** In concert or co-operation; unitedly; conjointly ME. **7.** In the way of, into, or in mutual action; with or against each other; mutually, reciprocally ME. **b.** After *multiply*: By or into one another 1709. **c.** After *belong*: To one another; hence, to one or the same whole, company, or set 1897. **8. Together with**: Along with; in combination with, in addition to, or with the addition of; in company or co-operation with; at the same time as 1478.

1. My next care was to get t. the wrecks of my fortune GOLDSM. b. Two flints struck t. yielded fire 1894. 2. b. You and I have eaten a great deal of salt t. 1645. 3. a. While society holds t. 1832. 5. He ..never slept twice t. in the same apartment 1840. 6. The contract and the label t. constituted a written warranty 1891. 7. I could perceive..my wife and daughters in close conference t. GOLDSM.

†**B.** *prep.* Along with, in addition to, with the addition of, with (*rare*) –1657.

Togger (tǫ·gəɹ). *slang.* 1897. [Perversion of TORPID.] A boat rowing in the Oxford college races called 'Torpids'; *pl.* the Torpids.

Toggery (tǫ·gəri). *slang* or *colloq.* 1812. [f. TOG *sb.* + -ERY.] **1.** Garments; clothes collectively. **b.** *esp.* Professional or official dress 1826. **2.** The trappings of a horse 1877.

1. b. *Long t.* = long togs.

Toggle (tǫ·g'l), *sb.* 1769. [orig. naut.; closely related to TAGGLE *v.* and TANGLE.] **1.** *Naut.* A short pin passing through a loop or the eye of a rope, or a link of a chain, or through a bolt, to keep it in place, or for the attachment of another line. **2.** *transf.* **a.** A cross-piece attached to the end of a line or chain (e. g. a watch-chain), or fixed in a belt or strap for attaching a weapon, etc. by a loop or ring; also, a cross-piece put through a loop to effect compression by twisting. **b.** A movable pivoted cross-piece serving as a barb in a harpoon. **c.** *Mech.* A toggle-joint. 1873.

Comb.: **t.-bolt**, a bolt having a hole through the head to receive a t.; **-harpoon, -iron**, a harpoon with a pivoted t. instead of barbs; **-joint**, a joint consisting of two pieces hinged endwise, operated by applying pressure at the elbow. Hence **To·ggle** *v. trans.* to secure or make fast by means of a t. or toggles; to furnish with a t. or toggles.

Togue (tōᵘg). 1877. [Adaptation of Indian name.] The great lake trout (*Salvelinus namaycush*) of N. America; also called *lunge* or *longe* and *namaycush*.

‖**Tohu-bohu** (tō·hū,bō·hū). 1619. [a. Heb. *thōhū wa-bhōhū* 'emptiness and desolation', in Gen. i. 2, rendered in Bible of 1611 'without form and void'. So Fr.] That which is empty and formless; chaos; utter confusion.

Tohunga (tohū·ŋgă). 1872. A Maori priest or doctor.

Toil (toil), *sb.*[1] ME. [a. AF., dispute, contention, forensic strife = OF. *tooil, toeil* bloody mêlée, trouble, f. *tooillier* TOIL *v.*[1]] **1.** †Verbal contention, argument; also, battle, strife, mêlée, turmoil (*arch.* or merged in 2). **2.** With *a* and *pl.* A struggle, a 'fight' (with difficulties); hence, a spell of severe labour; a laborious task or operation 1576. **3.** Without *a* or *pl.* Severe labour; hard and continuous work or exertion which taxes the bodily or mental powers 1594.

1. To toils of battle bred POPE. 2. I doo not loue so to make a toyle of a pleasure 1603. 3. The t. of man is irksome to him, and he earns his subsistance with pain GOLDSM.

Toil (toil), *sb.*[2] 1529. [a. OF. *teile, toile*:—L. *tela* web; F. pl. *toiles* large pieces of cloth made into toils, nets, etc.] **1.** A net or nets set so as to enclose a space into which the quarry is driven, or within which the game is known to be. In later use usu. *pl.* †**2.** A trap or snare for wild beasts (*rare*) –1727. **3.** *fig.* or in fig. context (*sing.* and *pl.*) 1548.

1. He drives into a T. the foaming Boar COWLEY. The Toiles are already set round a large Lake 1707. 3. Extol not Riches then, the toyl of Fools MILT.

Toil (toil), *v.*[1] ME. [a. AF. *toiler* to strive, dispute = OF. *toeillier, tooillier*, mod. F. *touillier* to soil, stir up, agitate.] †**I. 1.** *intr.* To dispute, argue; also, to contend in battle; to fight, struggle. –late ME. **2.** *trans.* To pull, drag, tug about –1440. **II. 1.** *intr.* To struggle for some object, or for a living; to labour arduously. late ME. **b.** *fig.* To struggle mentally 1788. **c.** *intr.* With advb. extension: To move or advance toilsomely or with struggling and labour 1781. **2.** *trans.* To bring into some condition or position, or to procure, by toil; *t. out*, to accomplish by toil 1667. **3.** To subject to toil; to weary, tire, fatigue, esp. with work. *arch.* and *dial.* 1549.

1. For worldlie wealth, men can t. and moil all the week long 1654. **c.** The women and children weeping, famished, and toiling through the mud up to their knees MACAULAY. **2.** I Toild out my uncouth passage MILT. **3.** *T. out*, to tire out or exhaust with toil; The army was toiled out with cruell tempests HOLLAND.

Toil (toil), *v.*[2] 1592. [f. TOIL *sb.*[2]] *trans.* To trap or enclose in a toil; to drive (game) into a toil; *fig.* to entangle; *dial.* to set (a trap).

‖**Toile** (twal). 1858. [F., linen cloth, canvas:—L. *tela* web.] A dress material: linen cloth or a mixture of silk and linen.

Toiler (toi·lər). 1549. [f. TOIL *v.*[1] + -ER[1].] One who toils, a hard worker.

Toilet (toi·lĕt). Also †**toilette, toy-.** 1540. [a. F. *toilette*, dim. of *toile* cloth.] †**1.** A piece of stuff used as a wrapper for clothes –1611. †**b.** A towel or cloth thrown over the shoulders during hairdressing –1687. **2.** A cloth cover for a dressing-table; now usu. called a *t.-cover* 1682. **3.** *collective.* The articles required or used in dressing; the furniture of the toilet-table; †a case containing these 1662. †**4.** The table on which these articles are placed; a toilet-table –1838. **5.** The action or process of dressing 1681. **b.** The reception of visitors by a lady during the concluding stages of her toilet; very fashionable in the 18th c. Now *Hist.* 1703. **6.** Manner or style of dressing; dress, costume, 'get-up'; also, a dress or costume, a gown 1821. **7.** A dressing-room; in *U.S. esp.*, a dressing-room furnished with bathing facilities; also, a bathroom, a lavatory 1819. **8.** *transf.* from 5. **a.** *Surg.* The cleansing of a part after an operation 1879. **b.** The cleaning up of a street, a ship, etc. 1901. **c.** Preparation for execution (in Fr. form *toilette*) 1885.

5. The long labours of the T. cease POPE. 6. Lady Dudley's black toilette was much admired 1883.

Comb.: **t.-case**, a dressing-case; **-cloth, -cover**, a cloth for the t.-table; **-glass**, a looking-glass for dressing; **-paper**, soft paper prepared for shaving, hair-curling, use in lavatories, etc.; **-room**, a dressing-room; in *U.S. spec.* a lavatory or bath-room; **-table**, a dressing-table furnished with the utensils and materials of the t.; **-vinegar**, aromatic vinegar used as an emollient. Hence **Toi·leted** *ppl. a.*, dressed, 'got up'.

Toilful (toi·lfŭl), *a.* 1596. [f. TOIL *sb.*[1]] **1.** Characterized by toiling; labouring; hard-working. **2.** Of an action, condition, etc.: = TOILSOME 1. 1614.

1. The fruitful lawns confess his t. care 1789. 2. Long trauell, tyrings, and toylefull labours 1621. Hence **Toi·lfully** *adv.*

Toi·linet, -ette, toilene·tte. 1799. [app. f. F. *toile* linen, after *satinet, -ette*, etc.] A kind of fine woollen cloth; used formerly for waistcoats of grooms, huntsmen, etc.; see also quot.

Toilinet, a kind of German quilting; silk and cotton warp with woollen weft 1858.

Toilless (toi·l,lĕs), *a.* 1606. [f. TOIL *sb.*[1] + -LESS.] Without toil. †**a.** Entailing no toil. **b.** That is or acts without labour or exertion.

Toilsome (toi·lsŏm), *a.* 1581. [f. TOIL *sb.*[1] + -SOME.] **1.** Of actions, conditions, etc.: Characterized by or involving toil; laborious, tiring. **b.** Of concrete things: Entailing toil 1609. **2.** Of an agent = TOILFUL 1. 1655. †**3.** Caused by toil. SPENSER.

1. What can be toilsom in these pleasant Walkes? MILT. **b.** The t. oar COWPER. 3. Toylsom sweat SPENSER. Hence **Toi·lsome-ly** *adv.*, **-ness.**

Toil-worn (toi·lwō̆ɹn), *a.* 1751. [f. TOIL *sb.*[1] + WORN *ppl. a.*] Worn by toil; showing marks of toil.

Toise (toiz), *sb.* 1598. [a. F.:—OF. *teise* = It. *tesa*:—late L. *tesa, tensa* (sc. *brachia*) 'the outstretched arms', taken as a fem. sing.] A French lineal measure of 6 French feet, roughly = 1·949 metres, or 6⅜ English feet. Chiefly in military use. So **Toise** *v.* (*rare*) *trans.* to measure with the eye, to eye from head to foot.

‖**Toison d'or** (twazoṅdōr). 1623. [F., = fleece of gold.] **a.** The golden fleece; see GOLDEN *a.* 1. **b.** *Her.* The figure of this, giving name to an order of knighthood (see FLEECE *sb.* 1 b), and afterwards borne by certain families.

Tokay[1] (tokē[i]·). 1710. [Name of a town in Upper Hungary.] A rich sweet wine of aromatic flavour, made near Tokay in Hungary. (Also *T. wine.*) **b.** *T. grape*, the variety of grape from which this wine is made 1896.

‖**Tokay**[2] (tōᵘ·kē). 1753. [a. Malay *tōkē.*] A species of gecko, or lizard of the family *Geckonidæ*, app. *G. verticillatus*, of Burma, Siam, and the Malay region.

Token (tōᵘ·kĕn), *sb.* [OE. *tácen, tácn*:—OTeut. **taiknom*, cogn. w. **taikjan*, OE. *tǽcean* TEACH *v.*] **1.** Something that serves to indicate a fact, event, object, feeling, etc.; a sign, a symbol. **2.** A sign or mark indicating some quality, or distinguishing one object from others; a characteristic mark OE. **b.** A spot on the body indicating disease, esp. the plague. Now *rare* or *Obs.* 1603. **3.** Something serving as proof of a fact or statement; an evidence OE. **4.** In biblical use: An act serving to demonstrate divine power or authority. *Obs.* or *arch.* OE. **5.** A sign or presage of something to come; an omen, portent, prodigy. *Obs.* (exc. as included in 1). OE. **6.** A signal given; a sign to attract attention or give notice. Now *rare* or *Obs.* OE. **7.** A sign arranged or given to indicate a person; a word or material object employed to authenticate a person, message, or communication; a mark giving security to those who possess it; a password. late ME. **8.** Something given as an expression of affection, or to be kept as a memorial; a keepsake. late ME. **9.** A stamped piece of lead or other metal given (orig. after confession) as a voucher of fitness to be admitted to the communion: in recent times used in Scotland in connexion with the Presbyterian Communion service, but now usually represented by a 'communion card' 1534. **10.** A stamped piece of metal, issued as a medium of exchange by a private person or company, who engage to take it back at its nominal value, giving goods or legal currency for it 1598. **11.** *Printing.* A measure or quantity of press-work; a certain number of sheets of paper (usu. 250 pulls on a hand-press) passed through the press 1683.

1. Charlemayne..kyssyd Huon in t. of peace 1533. 2. The tokens on his helmet tell The Bruce SCOTT. 3. These..were brought as tokens of peace and amity COOK. 4. They also that dwell in the vttermost parts are afraid at thy tokens *Ps.* lxv. 8. 10. Buy a tokens worth of great pinnes B. JONS.

Phrases. *By the same t., by this* (or *that*) *t.*, (*a*) in the 15th c. app.: on the same ground; for the same reason; in the same way; (*b*) since 1600 (= F. *à telles enseignes que*), 'the proof of this being that'; introducing a corroborating circumstance, often weakened down to a mere associated fact that helps the memory or is recalled to mind by the main fact (*arch.* or *dial.*). *More by t.*, still more, the more so (*dial.*).

Comb.: **t. coin, coinage, currency**: see TOKEN-MONEY; **-payment**, payment of small proportion of sum due as indication that a debt is not repudiated; **-sheet**, *Printing*, the last sheet of each t. (see 11), turned down to facilitate counting the whole number.

Token (tōᵘ·kĕn), *v.* Now *rare.* [OE. *tácnian*:—OTeut. **taiknōjan*, f. **taiknom* TOKEN *sb.*] **1.** *trans.* To be a token or sign of; to signify. **2.** To typify, symbolize OE.

To·ken-mo·ney. 1546. **a.** *Eccl.* The payment made or contribution given (by way of Easter Offering) by persons on receiving their token that they were duly prepared to make their Easter communion. **b.** Private tokens issued by a trader or company to serve as a fractional currency and temporary medium of exchange between trader and customer 1890. **c.** State coinage of money not having the intrinsic value for which it is current, but bearing a fixed value relative to gold coin, for which it is exchangeable 1889.

Toko: see TOCO[2].

‖**Tola** (tōᵘ·lă). *India.* 1614. [Hindī *tola*:—Skr. *tulā* balance, scale, weight, f. *tul* to weigh.] An E. Indian weight, since 1833, in the British dominions fixed at 180 grains (the weight of the rupee); a coin of this weight.

Tolbooth, toll-booth (tōᵘ·lbūð, -būþ, tǫ·lbūþ). Chiefly *Sc.* ME. [f. TOLL *sb.*[1] + BOOTH, *lit.* the booth, stall, or shed of the tax-collector.] †**1.** A booth, stall, or office at which tolls, duties, or customs are collected; a custom-house –1756. **2.** A town hall or guildhall. (Often comprehending senses 1 and 3.) 1440. **3.** A town prison, a jail. (Formerly usu. consisting of cells under the town hall.) 1470.

1. He seiȝ a man sittynge in a tolbothe, Matheu by name WYCLIF *Matt.* ix. 9.

Told (tōᵘld), *ppl. a. rare.* ME. [pa. pple. of TELL *v.*] Related, narrated, recounted; counted, reckoned; †esteemed. Chiefly in comb., as *oft-t., twice-t.*

Tol de rol. 1765. A song refrain.

Toledo (tolī·do). 1598. [Name of a city in Spain, long famous for its finely tempered sword-blades.] Short for *T. blade* or *sword*: A sword or sword-blade made at Toledo, or of the kind made there.

Tolerable (tǫ·lĕrăb'l), *a.* (*adv.*) late ME. [a. F. *tolérable*, ad. L. *tolerabilis* that may be borne, that can bear or endure, f. *tolerare*; see -ABLE.] **1.** Capable of being borne or endured; supportable; bearable. **2.** Such as to be tolerated, allowed, or countenanced; sufferable, allowable. Now *rare.* 1531. **3.** Moderate in degree, quality, or character; mediocre, passable; now *esp.* moderately good, fairly good or agreeable, not bad 1548. **4.** as *adv.* **a.** Tolerably 1673. **b.** *pred.* In fair health. *colloq.* 1847.

1. He did not know how to maintain himself and his Family in any t. sort 1704. 3. Found a t. road 1835. He had eaten a very t. lunch 1866. 4. **b.** We're t., sir, I thank you C. BRONTË. Hence **To·lerabi·lity, To·lerableness. To·lerably** *adv.*

Tolerance (tǫ·lĕrăns). late ME. [a. F. *tolérance*, ad. rare L. *tolerantia*, f. *tolerare* to

TOLERATE; see -ANCE.] †1. The action or practice of enduring or sustaining pain or hardship; the power or capacity of enduring; endurance -1814. b. *Phys.* The power, constitutional or acquired, of enduring large doses of active drugs, or of resisting the action of poison, etc. 1875. 2. The action or practice of tolerating; toleration; the disposition to be patient with the opinions or practices of others; forbearance; catholicity of spirit 1765. 3. *techn.* a. *Coining.* The small margin within which coins, when minted, are allowed to deviate from the standard fineness and weight; also called *allowance* 1868. b. *Mech.* An allowable amount of variation in the dimensions of a machine or part 1909.

1. Diogenes, one terrible frosty Morning, came into the Market-place; And stood Naked shaking to show his T. BACON. So **To·lerancy** (*rare*), the quality or habit of being tolerant.

Tolerant (tǫ·lĕrănt), *a.* (*sb.*) 1780. [a. F. *tolérant*, ad. L. *tolerantem*, *tolerare.*] A. *adj.* Disposed or inclined to tolerate or bear with something; practising or favouring toleration 1784. b. *transf.* Of a thing: Capable of bearing or sustaining. Const. *of.* 1864. c. *Phys.* Able to endure the action of a drug, an irritant, etc., without being affected; capable of resisting. Const. *of.* 1879. B. *sb.* (sb. use of the adj.; so in Fr.) One who tolerates opinions or practices different from his own; one free from bigotry 1780.

A. b. How far the Articles were t. of a Catholic, or even of a Roman interpretation J. H. NEWMAN. Hence **To·lerantly** *adv.*

Tolerate (tǫ·lĕreᶦt), *v.* 1531. [f. F. *tolérer*, ad. L. *tolerare*; see -ATE [3].] †1. *trans.* To endure, sustain (pain or hardship) -1616. b. *Phys.* To endure with impunity the action of (a poison or strong drug) 1895. 2. To allow to exist or to be done or practised without authoritative interference or molestation; also *gen.* to allow, permit 1533. 3. To bear without repugnance; to allow intellectually, or in taste, sentiment, or principle; to put up with 1646.

2. England..was in no humour to t. treason FROUDE. 3. By discipline of Time made wise, We learn to t. the infirmities And faults of others WORDSW.

Toleration (tǫlĕrēᶦ·ʃən). 1517. [a. F. *tolération*, ad. rare L. *tolerationem*, f. *tolerare.*] †1. The action of sustaining or enduring; endurance (of evil, suffering, etc.) -1623. b. *Phys.* = TOLERANCE 1 b (*rare*) 1877. †2. The action of allowing; permission granted by authority, licence -1727. 3. The action or practice of tolerating or allowing what is not actually approved; forbearance, sufferance 1582. 4. *spec.* Allowance (with or without limitations), by the ruling power, of the exercise of religion otherwise than in the form officially established or recognized 1609. b. *Act of T.*, *T. Act*, an act or statute granting such toleration; esp. in *Eng. Hist.* Act 1 Will. & Mary (1689) cap. 18, by which freedom of religious worship was granted, on certain conditions, to Dissenting Protestants 1692. 5. *Coining.* = TOLERANCE 3 a. 1887. Hence **Tolera·tionism**, toleration of religious differences as a principle or system. **Tolera·tionist**, one who advocates or supports t.

Toll (tōᵘl), *sb.*[1] [OE. *toll*, usu. referred to late pop. L. *to·loneum* for L. *telonium*, a. Gr. τελώνιον place of custom, toll-house, f. τελώνης farmer of taxes, τέλος toll, tax, duty.] 1. orig., A general term for (*a*) a definite payment exacted by a king, ruler, or lord, or by the state or the local authority, by virtue of sovereignty or lordship, or in return for protection (*Obs.* exc. *Hist.*); more especially, (*b*) for permission to pass somewhere, do some act, or perform some function; or (*c*) as a share of the money passing, or profit accruing, in a transaction; a tax, tribute, impost, custom, duty. b. In the obsolete law phrase *sac and sóc, t. and team*, etc.: The right to 'toll' included (among others) in the grant of a manor by the crown OE. 2. *spec. uses.* a. A proportion of the grain or flour taken by the miller in payment for grinding. *Obs.* or *rare dial.* late ME. b. A charge for the privilege of bringing goods for sale to a market or fair, or of setting up a stall ME. c. A charge for the right of passage along a road (at a turnpike or toll-gate: now abolished in Great Britain), along a river or channel, over a bridge or ferry 1477. d. A charge for the right of landing or shipping goods at a port; formerly also, a customs duty. *Obs.* exc. *Hist.* 1680. e. A charge made for transport of goods, esp. by railway or canal. (Arising out of c.) 1889. f. *fig.* (Cf. *tribute*, similarly used.) late ME. g. with defining words: **through t.** (also *t. through*, *thorough*), **t. traverse, turn t.** (also *t. turn*): see quots. 1567.

1. The Graunte of the Tolle of oure Towne of Knyghton 1485. Phr. *To take t. of.* b. *T.* is sometimes the right to take toll, sometimes the right to be free of toll; but often it is merely the right to tallage one's villeins POLLOCK & MAITLAND. 2. f. Nott's gallant division..paid its t. of killed and wounded 1909. g. *Through tolle*, is where a Towne prescribes to haue tol for euery beast that goeth through their Towne. *Tolle trauers*, that is where one claimeth to haue a halfepeny, or such like toll of euery beast that is driuen ouer his ground. 1567. *Toll-turn*, which is Toll paid at the return of Beasts from Fair or Market, though they were not sold BLOUNT. h. A short-distance telephone trunk-call: freq. *attrib.* 1927.

Comb.: **t.-bar**, a barrier (usu. a gate) across a road or bridge, where t. is taken; **-bridge**, a bridge at which t. is charged for passage; **-corn**, corn retained by a miller as t.; **-farmer**, one who farms the t. at a certain place; **-road**, a turnpike road (*Sc.* and *U.S.*).

Toll (tōᵘl), *sb.*[2] 1452. [f. TOLL *v.*[2]] The act of tolling a bell, or the sound made by a bell when tolled; (with *pl.*) a single stroke made in tolling, or the sound made by such stroke.

Toll, tole (tōᵘl), *v.*[1] Now *dial.* and *U.S.* [ME. *tollen, tullen*:—OE. **tollian*, **tullian* :—**tullōjan.*] 1. *trans.* To attract, entice, allure, decoy. 2. *spec. U.S.* To lure or decoy (wild animals) for the purpose of capture. Also *absol.* or *intr.* 1858. †3. To pull, drag, draw physically -1654.

1. Whatever you observe him to be more frighted at..be sure to tole him on to by..Degrees LOCKE.

Toll (tōᵘl), *v.*[2] 1452. [prob. orig. a particular use of prec. 3.] 1. *trans.* To cause (a great bell) to sound by pulling the rope, esp. in order to give an alarm or signal; to ring (a great bell). *arch.* or *rhet.* 1494. 2. *spec.* To cause (a large or deep-toned bell) to give forth a sound repeated at regular intervals by pulling the rope so that the bell swings through a short arc (in contrast to *ringing* it in full swing), or by striking it with a hammer or the like, or pulling the clapper; esp. for summoning a congregation to church, and b. (now) on the occasion of a death (the passing-bell) or funeral. Also *absol.* or *intr.* 1526. 3. Said of a bell (also of the ringer): To sound (esp. a knell, etc.) by ringing as in sense 2; also of a clock, to strike (the hour) in a deep tone with slow measured strokes 1452. 4. *intr.* Of a bell: To give forth sounds of this character by being tolled. Also said of a clock striking the hour on a deep-toned bell. 1551. b. *transf.* and *fig.* To make a sound like the tolling of a bell 1747. 5. *trans.* To announce (a death, etc.) by tolling; to toll for (a dying or dead person) 1597. 6. To summon or dismiss by tolling 1611.

1. Let the Bell of the Church of S. German be touled 1684. 2. A large bell may be tolled easily by one man, if it is properly hung 1868. b. T. for the brave! The brave that are no more! COWPER. 3. Slow tolls the village-clock the drowsy hour 1771. 4. If I heard the Bell Toull for some that were dead BUNYAN. b. Sullen tolls the far-off river's flow 1849. 5. Groning like a bell, That towles departing soules MARSTON.

Toll (tōᵘl), *v.*[3] Now *rare.* ME. [f. TOLL *sb.*[1]] 1. *intr.* To take or collect toll; to exact or levy toll. 2. *trans.* To take toll of (something); to exact a part of by way of toll. late ME. b. To charge (a person, etc.) with a toll, impose a toll upon 1583. c. To take or gather (something) as toll 1597. †3. *intr.* To pay toll; *to t. for* (*spec.*), to enter (a horse, etc.) for sale in the toll-book of a market -1664.

1. No Italian priest Shall tythe or t. in our dominions SHAKS. 2. c. Like the bee toling from euery flower The vertuous Sweetes SHAKS.

Toll (tōᵘl), *v.*[4] 1467. [a. AF. *toller, toler, touller*, ad. L. *tollere* to take away.] *Law. trans.* To take away, bar, defeat, annul. *To t. an entry*, to take away the right of, or bar entry.

Tollage (tōᵘ·lėdʒ). 1494. [perh. f. TOLL *v.*[3] + -AGE; confounded with TALLAGE *sb.*] 1. = TOLL *sb.*[1] †2. = TALLAGE *sb.* -1634.

†**To·ll-book.** 1596. [TOLL *sb.*[1]] A book containing a register of beasts or goods to be sold at a market or fair, and the tolls payable for them; also, a tax-collector's register or assessment-book -1679.

To·ll-dish. 1550. [TOLL *sb.*[1]] A dish or bowl of stated dimensions for measuring the toll of grain at a mill; a multure-dish.

Tollent (tǫ·lĕnt), *a. rare.* 1837. [ad. L. *tollentem*, *tollere.*] *Logic.* That 'takes away' or negatives; opp. to PONENT.

Toller [1] (tōᵘ·ləɹ). Now *rare.* [OE. *tollere*, f. TOLL *sb.*[1] + -ER [1].] One who takes toll, a toll-collector.

Toller [2], **toler** (tōᵘ·ləɹ). 1440. [f. TOLL *v.*[1] + -ER [1].] †1. One who 'tolls', entices, or instigates. 2. A decoy; *spec.* a dog of a small breed used in decoying ducks. *U.S.* 1874.

Toller [3] (tōᵘ·ləɹ). 1562. [f. TOLL *v.*[2] + -ER [1].] One who tolls a bell.

To·ll-free, *a.* OE. Exempt from payment of toll.

To·ll-ga:therer. Now *rare.* late ME. [f. TOLL *sb.*[1] + GATHERER.] A tax-gatherer.

To·ll-house. 1440. [f. TOLL *sb.*[1] + HOUSE.] A house or building at which tolls or dues are collected. 1. = TOLBOOTH 1 (*obs.*) or 2 (now *local*). 2. A house by a toll-gate or toll-bridge, occupied by the toll-taker 1763.

Tollman (tōᵘ·lmăen). *Pl.* **-men.** 1743. [f. TOLL *sb.*[1]] A man who collects tolls; the keeper of a toll-gate.

Tol-lol (tǫ:l,lǫ·l), *a. slang.* 1797. [f. the first syllable of TOLERABLE, with rhyming extension.] Tolerable, passable, 'middling'.

Tolsel (tōᵘ·lsĕl). Also **tolzey.** *local.* ME. [f. TOLL *sb.*[1] + *seld* booth, or *sale* hall.] = TOLBOOTH 2.

Tolstoyan (tǫ·lstoi,ăn), *a.* and *sb.* Also **Tolstoian.** 1894. [f. proper name *Tolstoi* + -AN.] Of or pertaining to, a follower of, Count Leo N. Tolstoi a famous Russian writer and social reformer (1828–1910).

Tolt (tōᵘlt). 1607. [a. AF. *tolte, toulte* = med.L. *tolta*, f. L. *tollere* to take up, raise, lift.] *Old Law.* A writ by which a cause was removed from a court-baron to the county court.

Tolu (tolʼū·, tōᵘ·lʼu). 1671. [f. *Tolu* (now *Santiago de Tolu*) in the United States of Colombia, whence obtained.] In **T. balsam, balsam of T.**: A balsam obtained by incision from the bark of the **T.-tree,** *Myrospermum* (*Myroxylon*) *toluiferum*, a leguminous tree of tropical S. America; used in medicine and perfumery.

Tolu-, the prec. word as a formative element in chemical terms. **To·luate**, a salt of toluic acid, as toluate of calcium, $C_{16}H_{14}Ca''O_4$. **Toluene** (tōᵘ·liu,īn), [so named because first obtained by the dry distillation of tolu balsam.] C_7H_8 = Benzylic hydride, $C_7H_7.H$, a colourless very mobile strongly refracting liquid, with a smell like benzene and a burning taste. **Toluic** (tōᵘliu·ik) *a.* [*toluene* + -IC], in *toluic* or *toluylic acid*, $C_8H_8O_2$, an aromatic acid, homologous with benzoic acid, prepared from toluene, cymene, or xylene. **To·luides**, compounds homologous with the anilides, derived from toluidine salts by abstraction of water, e.g., *aceto-toluide.* **Tolu·idine**, also called *amidoto·luene*, and formerly *toluylia*, $C_7H_7(NH_2)$, a crystalline base, produced by the action of sulphydric acid on nitrotoluene, solidifying in snow-white crystals, which gradually turn brown on contact with the air. **To·luol**, earlier name of *toluene.* **Toluo·xyl**, C_8H_7O, the radical of toluic acid and its derivatives. **Tolu·ric** *a.*, in *toluric acid*, $C_{10}H_{11}NO_3$, also called *toluglycic acid*, homologous with hippuric acid, produced in the passage of toluic acid through the animal body; its salts are **Tolu·rates.** **Toluyl** (tōᵘ·liu,il -əil), the radical, C_8H_9; hence **To·luylene** = STILBENE; **Toluy·lic** *a.*, of or belonging to toluyl.

†**Toluta·tion.** *rare.* 1646. [f. stem of L. *tolutim* adv. 'at a trot' + -ATION.] *prop.* Trotting; but used by Sir T. Browne and others for 'ambling'; in later use only a humorous pedantry -1803.

Tolyl (tǫ·lil, -əil). *Chem.* 1868. [f. TOLU + -YL.] A hypothetical monatomic radical, C_7H_7.

Tolypeutine (tǫlipiū·tǝin), *a.* and *sb.* 1885. [f. mod.L. *Tolypeutes* + -INE [1].] *Zool.* **A.** *adj.* Belonging to the genus *Tolypeutes* of armadillos. **B.** *sb.* An armadillo of this genus.

Tom (tǫm). late ME. **1.** (With capital T.) A familiar shortening of the Christian name *Thomas*; often a generic name for any male representative of the common people; esp. in *T., Dick,* and *Harry*, any men taken at random from the common run; *Blind T.*, blindman's-buff. †**b.** = *T. o' Bedlam* –1683. **2.** As the name of some exceptionally large bells, esp. in *great, mighty T., T. of Lincoln, T. of Christ Church, of Oxford*, etc. 1630. **3. a.** (usu. *long t.*) A long trough formerly used in gold-washing 1855. **b.** *Long T.*: a long gun; *esp.* a naval gun mounted amidships, as dist. from the shorter guns of the broadside 1867. **4.** *Old T.*: gin (*slang*) 1823. **5.** The male of various beasts and birds; perh. first for a male cat 1791.

Phrases: **T. tower**, a tower in which a great bell hangs; *spec.* at Oxford, the western tower of Christ Church. (*b*) As the first element in a personal name, allus.: **T. Farthing**, a fool, simpleton; **T. Tyler, Tiler**, any ordinary man; also, a hen-pecked husband. (*c*) Followed by another word, forming a *quasi*-proper name or nickname: **T. Long**, one who takes a long time in coming, or in finishing his tale; **T. o' Bedlam**, a madman; a deranged person discharged from Bedlam and licensed to beg.

Tomahawk (tǫ·măhǭk), *sb.* 1634. [a. Renâpe (N. Amer. Indian of Virginia) *tämähāk*, apocopated form of *tämähākan*, 'what is used for cutting', from *tämähāken* 'he uses for cutting', from *tämäham* 'he cuts'.] The axe of the N. Amer. Indians, used as a weapon of war and the chase, and also as a tool and agricultural implement; in Eng. use usu. applied to it as the war-axe. **b.** erron. applied to a war-club or knobkerry 1674. **c.** *transf.* Applied to similar weapons used by savages elsewhere; also *Naut.* a pole-axe used by sailors; in Australia, the usual word for *hatchet* 1670.

fig. That age of fierce and savage controversy, of the t. and scalping-knife 1836.

Phrases. *To bury* or *lay aside the t.*, to lay down one's arms, to cease from hostilities. *To dig up, raise,* or *take up the t.*, to commence hostilities.

Tomahawk (tǫ·măhǭk), *v.* 1755. [f. prec.] **1.** *trans.* To strike, cut, or kill with a tomahawk. **2.** *Australia.* To cut (a sheep) in shearing it 1859.

1. *fig.* The book which Thackeray tomahawked 1895.

‖**Tomalley** (tǫmæ·li, tǫmæ·li). 1666. [Said to be a Carib word.] The fat or 'liver' of the N. Amer. lobster, which becomes green when cooked, and is then known as *t. sauce*.

‖**Toman** [1] (tomā·n, tu·măn, tɒ·măn). 1566. [a. Pers. *tūmān, tumān, tuman*, a Yuzbeg Tartar word, lit. 'ten thousand'.] **1.** Formerly among the Mongols, Tartars, etc., and thence in Persia and Turkey: The sum of ten thousand; also, a military division consisting of 10,000 men. Now *rare.* 1599. **2.** A Persian gold coin, nominally worth 10 silver krans or 10,000 dinars; formerly a money of account, which was constantly depreciated in value 1566.

‖**Toman** [2] (tǫ·măn). 1811. [Gaelic, dim. of *tom* hill.] A hillock; a mound of earth. Often applied to mounds representing ancient glacial moraines, found in the heads of valleys in the Highlands.

Tom and Jerry. 1828. Names of the two chief characters in Egan's *Life in London*, 1821, and its continuation, 1828: whence in various allus. and attrib. uses, esp. as name of a kind of highly-spiced punch (U.S.); and *attrib.* in *Tom and Jerry shop*, a low beer-house.

Tomato (tǒmā·to, U.S. -ēi·to). 1604. [In 17th c. *tomate*, a. F. *tomate*, or Sp. and Pg. *tomate*, ad. Mexican *tomatl*.] The glossy fleshy fruit of a solanaceous plant (*Solanum Lycopersicum* or *Lycopersicum esculentum*), a native of tropical America, now widely cultivated. It varies when ripe from red to yellow in colour, and greatly in size and shape, the common form being irregularly spheroidal. Formerly called *love-apple*, from supposed aphrodisiac qualities. Also, the plant, an annual with a weak trailing or climbing stem, irregularly pinnate leaves, and yellow flowers resembling those of the potato.

attrib. and *Comb.*, as *t.-ketchup, sauce*; **t. hawk-moth** or **sphinx**, an American sphingid moth, *Protoparce celeus*; **-worm**, the caterpillar of this, which feeds on t. leaves.

Tomb (tūm), *sb.* [Early ME. *toumbe, tumbe*, a. AF. *tumbe*, OF. *tombe*:—late L. *tumba*, ad. Gr. τύμβος sepulchral mound.] **1.** A place of burial; an excavation in earth or rock for the reception of a dead body, a grave. Also, a chamber or vault formed wholly or partly in the earth, and, in early times, a tumulus or mound raised over the body. **b.** *transf.* and *fig.* 1812. **2.** A monument erected to enclose or cover the body and preserve the memory of the dead; a sepulchral structure raised above the earth. Hence sometimes a cenotaph. Also formerly, a tombstone erected over a grave. ME. **3.** Regarded as the final resting-place of every one; hence occas. used for the state of death 1559. **4.** *R.C.Ch.* A cavity in an altar, where relics are deposited 1886.

1. A t...which was..believed to contain his bones 1838. **b.** The t. of thy dead self SHELLEY. **2.** To make a Toombe ouer his wiues Graue 1657. **3.** Charity, that glows beyond the t. GRAY.

Tomb (tūm), *v.* Now *rare.* ME. [f. prec.] **1.** *trans.* To deposit (a body) in the tomb; to bury, inter, entomb. **2.** To enclose or contain as a tomb; to serve as a tomb for 1586.

1. In the Atlantic's bed Tombed ten leagues deep 1899. **2.** The Stone that tombs the Two SIDNEY.

Tombac (tǫ·mbæ̆k). 1602. [a. F., a. Malay *tambâga* copper.] An alloy of copper and zinc, in various proportions, containing from 82 to 99 per cent. of copper. Used in the East for gongs or bells; in Europe, under various names, as Prince's metal, Mannheim gold, etc., as a material for cheap jewellery.

To·mb-bat. 1883. A bat of the genus *Taphozous*, family *Emballonuridæ*, which frequent tombs as their dwelling-places.

Tombless (tū·mlės), *a.* 1594. Having no tomb, destitute of a grave; unburied.

Tombola (tǫ·mbǒlă). 1880. [a. F., or It., f. *tombolare* to turn a somersault, tumble.] A kind of lottery resembling lotto.

Tomboy (tǫ·mboi). 1553. [f. TOM *sb.* + BOY *sb.*] †**1.** A rude, boisterous, or forward boy –1599. †**2.** A bold or immodest woman –1700. **3.** A girl who behaves like a spirited or boisterous boy; a wild romping girl 1592.

Tombstone, tomb-stone (tū·mstoun). 1565. A horizontal stone covering a grave; in early use, the cover of a stone coffin, or the stone coffin itself. **b.** A stone or monument of any kind placed over a grave to preserve the memory of the dead; a gravestone; including a headstone. Also *fig.* 1611.

To·m ca·t. 1809. [TOM 5.] A male cat.

Tom-cod (tǫ·mˌkǫ·d). 1795. Name for several small fishes. In U.S.: **a.** The frost-fish; also, loosely, one of various small fishes confused with this. **b.** In California, the Jack-fish (*Sebastodes paucispinis*), a rock-fish. **c.** = KINGFISH d. In Great Britain: **d.** A young codfish.

Tome (tōum). 1519. [app. a F., ad. L. *tomus*, a. Gr. τόμος volume, section of a book, f. τομ-: τέμ-νειν to cut.] †**1.** Each of the separate volumes which compose a literary work or book; rarely, one of the largest parts or sections of a single volume –1731. **2.** A book, a volume; now usu. suggesting a large, heavy, old-fashioned book 1573. **3.** A papal letter or epistle. *Hist.* 1788.

-tome [1] (tōum), terminal element (= F. *-tome*) repr. Gr. -τόμον, neut. of -τόμος -cutting, in designations of instruments used in the surgical operation expressed by the corresp. word in -TOMY.

-tome [2], terminal element repr. Gr. τομή a cutting, with the meaning 'section', 'segment'.

Tomentose (tōume·ntōus), *a.* 1698. [ad. mod.L. *tomentosus*, f. L. *tomentum* stuffing for cushions + -OSE.] **1.** *Bot.* Closely covered with down or short hairs; pubescent, downy. **2.** *Ent.* and *Anat.* Flocculent, flossy, woolly 1826. So **Tome·ntous** *a.*

‖**Tomentum** (tome·ntǒm). 1699. [L.; see prec.] **1.** *Bot.* The soft down or pubescence growing on the stems, leaves, or seeds of certain plants. **2.** *Anat.* A downy covering or investment; *spec.* the flocculent inner surface of the pia mater 1811.

To·m-foo·l. ME. [f. TOM + FOOL *sb.* [1]] **a.** As quasi-proper name, *Tom Fool*: a half-witted man. **b.** One who enacts the part of a fool in the drama, etc.; a buffoon; *spec.* a buffoon who accompanies morris-dancers; also, a butt, laughing-stock 1650. **c.** A foolish or stupid person. (More emphatic than *fool.*) 1721. **d.** *attrib.* (in senses b and c) 1819.

More folks know Tom Fool, than Tom Fool knows 1865. **d.** You may..wear whatever tomfool costume you like to assume 1879. Hence **Tomfoo·lery**, the action or behaviour of a t.; foolish action; silly trifling; an instance of this.

‖**Tomin** (tomī·n). 1600. [Sp.] A Spanish measure of weight for silver, = 9·26 grains; also, **b.** in Spain and Sp. America, the name of various small silver coins.

‖**Tomium** (tōu·miǒm). *Pl.* **tomia** (-iă). 1834. [mod.L., f. Gr. τομός cutting + L. *-ium*.] *Ornith.* Each of the cutting edges of a bird's bill. Hence **To·mial** *a.* of or pertaining to the tomia or to a t.

Tommy (tǫ·mi). 1783. [dim. or pet form of TOM.] **1.** With capital T: Familiar form of *Thomas*. **b.** A simpleton. *dial.* 1829. **c.** Short for *T. Atkins* 1893. **2.** A soldiers' name for the brown bread formerly supplied as rations (also *brown t.*); with *a* and *pl.*, a loaf of bread (*dial.*); among workmen, Food, provisions generally, *esp.* those carried with them to work each day 1783. **b.** Goods; *esp.* provisions supplied to workmen under the truck system; also, short for *t.-shop*, and for the truck system 1830.

1. c. A group of Tommies in uniform 1907. **2.** Soft T., or white T.; bread is so called by sailors, to distinguish it from biscuit GROSE.

attrib. and *Comb.*: **T. Atkins**, familiar form of *Thomas Atkins*, as a name for the typical private soldier; see THOMAS 3; hence, *transf.* a private in any army; **T. Dod(d**, the 'odd man' in odd-man-out; **t.-ro·t**, nonsense, bosh, twaddle; **-shop**, a store (esp. one run by the employer) at which vouchers given to employees instead of money wages may be exchanged for goods.

Tom-noddy (tǫmˌnǫ·di). 1702. [f. TOM + NODDY *sb.* [1]] **1.** *local.* The Puffin (*Fratercula arctica*). **2.** A foolish or stupid person 1828.

To-morn (tŭmǫ·ɹn), *adv.* and *sb.* Now *dial.* or *arch.* [OE. *to morg(en)ne*, f. To *prep.* II. 2 + OE. *morgenne*, dative of *morgen* MORN.] **A.** *adv.* = next A. Revived as poetical archaism *c* 1850. **B.** *sb.* = next B. 1. ME.

To-morrow (tŭmǫ·rou), *adv.* and *sb.* [ME. from *to morgen, to morwen* (see prec. and MORROW).] **A.** *adv.* For or on the day after to-day; for or on the morrow.

Euery day in the weeke it was sayde, he departeth to morwe GRAFTON.

B. *sb.* **1.** The day after this day; the next succeeding day; the morrow. late ME. **2.** *attrib.* with times of the day: *to-morrow morning, afternoon*, etc. The comb. is used both as *sb.* and as *adv.* ME.

1. One to-day is worth two to-morrows FRANKLIN. Phr. *To-morrow come never*, a day that will never arrive; 'on the Greek Kalends'.

†**Tompion** (tǫ·mpiǝn). 1727. [f. name of Thomas *Tompion*, a noted watchmaker in the reign of Queen Anne.] A watch made by Tompion or of the same type –1871.

Tompion, variant of TAMPION.

Tom Thumb. 1579. [In ref. to diminutive stature.] **1.** A dwarf or pigmy of popular tradition, whose history was common as a chapbook; hence, a name for a dwarf or diminutive male person; also *contempt.* a petty or insignificant person, a pigmy holder of a high position. **2.** *attrib.* Applied to dwarf varieties of animals or plants; also, *ellipt.* or *absol.* as *sb.* **a.** A kind of dwarf oyster. **b.** A dwarf variety of cabbage, lettuce, or other vegetable, of antirrhinum, nasturtium, or other flower. 1876.

Tom Tiddler's ground. Also *dial.* 1823. Name of a children's game, in which one of the players is 'Tom Tiddler', his territory being marked by a line drawn on the ground; over this the other players run, crying 'We're on Tom Tiddler's ground, picking up gold and silver'. **b.** *transf.* Any place where money, etc., is 'picked up' or acquired readily; also, a 'debatable territory, a no man's land between two states' 1848.

Tom-tit, tomtit (tǫmˌtiˑt). 1709. [See TIT *sb.*[2]] A common name of the Blue Titmouse (*Parus cæruleus*); also *locally* of the Coal Titmouse (*P. ater*), and the American *P. atricapillus*; incorrectly of other small birds, as the Wren, and the Tree-creeper. **b.** *transf.* applied to a little man or boy 1741.

Tom-tom (tǫˑmˌtǫm), *sb.* 1693. [a. Hind. *tam-tam*; echoic.] **1.** A native E. Indian drum; extended also to the drums of barbarous peoples generally. **2.** The beating of a drum; an imitation of the sound of this 1898.

To·m-tom, *v.* 1857. [Partly f. prec., partly echoic.] **a.** *intr.* To beat a tom-tom or drum; to drum. **b.** *trans.* To call attention to by beating a tom-tom. **c.** To perform on a tom-tom or drum; *transf.* to play in a monotonous way, to strum.

-tomy, a. Gr. -τομια, often through mod.L. *-tomia*, used to form abstract sbs. from adjs. in -τομος cutting; f. ablaut-series τεμ-, τομ-, τμ-, in τέμνειν to cut, τομή, τμῆσις cutting.

Ton[1] (tɒn). late ME. [In origin the same word as TUN. Differentiated from *tun c* 1688 in the senses hereunder.] †**1.** A large wine-vessel, a cask; hence, a measure of capacity used for wine; now spelt TUN. **2.** A unit used in measuring the carrying capacity or burden of a ship, the amount of cargo, freight, etc. Orig. the space occupied by a tun cask of wine. Now, for the purposes of registered tonnage, the space of 100 cubic feet. For purposes of freight, usu. the space of 40 cubic feet, unless that bulk would weigh more than 20 cwt., in which case freight is charged by weight. late ME. **3.** A measure of capacity: **a.** for timber; usu. = 40 cubic feet (or for hewn timber, 50) 1521. **b.** for various solid commodities, as stone, gravel, lime, plaster, wheat, cheese, etc. late ME. **4.** A measure of weight, now generally 20 cwt.; in Great Britain legally 2240 lbs.; in U.S. and some of the colonies, for most purposes 2000 lbs. *Metric t.* (F. *tonne*) = 1000 kilogrammes (2204·6 lbs. avoirdupois). 1485. **b.** *colloq.* A very large amount. Mostly in *pl.* 1895.

3. A pound of goold is worth a tunne of leade 1588. 4. b. 'Is there any culture at Chicago?'..'You bet your sweet life!..Tons of it. 1895.

attrib. and *Comb.*: **t.-fathom,** the equivalent of the work done in raising a t. through the depth of a fathom, as in the shaft of a mine; **-mile,** the same in carrying a t. the distance of a mile, as by a railway-train; **-mileage,** amount of or reckoning in ton-miles, or charge per ton-mile; **t. tight:** see TIGHT *a.* 14.

‖**Ton**[2] (toṅ, †tǫn). Now *rare.* 1769. [F., :—L. *tonus* TONE.] The fashion, the vogue, the mode; fashionable air or style. **b.** *transf.* People of fashion; the fashionable world 1815.

None of the London whips of any degree of t. wear wigs now SHERIDAN.

Tonal (tōᵘ·năl), *a.* 1776. [ad. med.L. *tonalis*, f. *tonus* TONE; see -AL.] **1.** *Mus.* †**a.** Pertaining to the eccl. modes. **b.** Applied to a fugue or a sequence, in which the repetitions of the subject in different positions are all in the same key, and therefore vary in their intervals 1869. **2.** Of, pertaining to, or relating to the tone or tones. Of speech or a language: expressing difference of meaning by variation of tone 1866. Hence **To·nally** *adv.* in respect of tone.

Tonality (tonæ·lĭti). 1838. [f. TONAL *a.* + -ITY.] Tonal quality. **1.** *Mus.* The relation, or sum of relations, between the tones or notes of a scale or musical system; *spec.* in modern music, = KEY *sb.* II. 5 c; hence *transf.* a particular scale or system of tones; in modern music = KEY *sb.* II. 5 b. **2.** *Painting.* The quality of a painting in respect of tone; the general tone or colour-scheme of a picture 1866.

To-name (tū·nēᵊm). Now *dial.* [OE. *tó-nama*, f. TO-[1] + NAME *sb.*] A name or epithet added to an original name; a cognomen, surname, nickname; now in *Sc.* a name added to distinguish one individual from another having the same Christian name and surname.

‖**Tondo** (to·ndo). *Pl.* **tondi** (to·ndi). 1890. [It., 'a round, circle, compass'; shortened from *rotondo* round.] An easel painting of circular form; also, a carving in relief within a circular space.

Tone (tōᵘn), *sb.* ME. [Partly a. OF. *ton* :—L. *tonum*, acc. of *tonus*; and partly directly f. L. *tonus*, a. Gr. τόνος, f. strong grade of vbl. ablaut series τεν-, τον-, τα-, in τείνειν to stretch.] **I. 1.** A musical or vocal sound considered with ref. to its quality, as acute or grave, sweet or harsh, loud or soft, clear or dull. **b.** (without *a* or *pl.*) Quality of sound 1663. **2.** *Mus.* and *Acoustics.* A sound of definite pitch and character produced by regular vibration of a sounding body; a musical note. late ME. †**b.** (without *a* or *pl.*) Pitch of a musical note; correct pitch, 'tune' -1704. **3.** *Mus.* In plainsong, any of the nine psalm-tunes (including the *peregrine t.*), each of which has a particular 'intonation' and 'mediation' and a number of different 'endings'; commonly called *Gregorian tones* 1776. **4.** *Mus.* One of the larger intervals between successive notes of the diatonic scale; a major second; sometimes called *whole t.*, as opp. to *semitone* 1609. **5.** A particular quality, pitch, modulation, or inflexion of the voice expressing or indicating affirmation, interrogation, hesitation, decision, or some feeling or emotion; vocal expression 1610. **b.** The distinctive quality of voice in the pronunciation of words, peculiar to an individual, locality, or nation; an 'accent' 1680. **c.** Intonation; †*esp.* a special, affected, or artificial intonation in speaking 1687. **d.** *transf.* A particular style in discourse or writing, which expresses the person's sentiment or reveals his character 1765. **6.** *Phonetics.* **a.** A word-accent; a rising, falling, or compound inflexion, by which words otherwise of the same sound are distinguished, as in ancient Greek, modern Chinese, and other languages 1763. **b.** The stress accent (F. *accent tonique*) on a syllable of a word; the stressed or accented syllable 1874.

1. Harmonie Divine So smooths her charming tones, that Gods own ear Listens delighted MILT. 2. *Difference-t.* (or *differential t.*), *summation-t.* (or *summational t.*), the secondary or resultant tones produced when two notes of different pitch are sounded together with sufficient force, having rates of vibration equal respectively to the difference and the sum of those of the primary tones. *Fundamental, partial,* (etc.) *t.*: see the adjs. 5. She asked in a t. of displeasure, who was there? 1796. b. The t. and accent remained broadly Scotch LOCKHART. d. His book..is bright and joyous in t. 1866.

II. 1. *Physiol.* The degree of firmness or tension proper to the organs or tissues of the body in a strong and healthy condition 1069. †**2.** A state or temper of mind; mood, disposition -1820. **3.** A special or characteristic style or tendency of thought, feeling, action, etc.; *esp.* the character of the prevailing state of morals or manners in a society or community 1635.

1. Of sovereign efficacy in restoring debilitated stomachs to their proper t. 1780. 2. A philosophical t., or temper 1744. A healthful t. of mind and spirits W. IRVING. 3. The t. of the market is..dull 1884.

III. The prevailing effect of the combination of light and shade, and of the general scheme of colouring, in a painting, building, etc. 1816. **b.** A quality of colour; a tint; *spec.* the degree of luminosity of a colour; shade 1821.

attrib. and *Comb.*: **t.-arm,** the tubular arm connecting the sound-box of a gramophone to the horn; **-colour** (after G. *tonfarbe*), timbre; **-painting,** the employment of tone and esp. tone-colours in creating musical effects; so **-painter**; **-picture,** a musical composition, usu. for orchestra, characterized by pictorial suggestion; **-poem** [G. *tondichtung*], (*a*) an orchestral composition illustrating or translating a poetic idea; (*b*) a painting in which the tones are harmonized poetically; so **-poet, -poetry; -syllable,** the stressed syllable.

Tone (tōᵘn), *v.* ME. [f. prec.] **I.** †**1.** *trans. Mus.* To sound with the proper tone or musical quality -1570. **2.** *intr.* To issue forth in musical tones (*rare*) 1447. **3.** *trans.* To utter with a musical sound, or in a special or affected tone; to intone 1660.

II. To alter or modify the tone or general colouring of; to give the desired tone to; *spec.* to cover (a painting) with oil or varnish so as to soften the colouring; to alter the tint of (a photograph) in the process of finishing it. Also *absol.* 1859. **b.** *intr.* To receive or assume a tone, tint, or shade of colour; *esp.* in *Photogr.* 1868. **c.** To harmonize *with* in colouring 1880.

III. *trans.* To impart a tone to (in various senses of the sb.); to modify, regulate, or adjust the tone or quality of; to give physical or mental tone to, to brace 1811. **b.** *T. down,* to lower the tone, quality, or character of; to soften. *T. up,* to raise or improve the tone of, to give a higher or stronger tone to. 1860. **c.** *intr.* for *pass. T. down,* to become lowered, weakened, or softened in tone; *t. up,* to rise or improve in tone 1850.

Your mind is properly toned by these influences 1871. b. Some remedy that will tone-up the nervous system 1896. c. Public excitement with respect to Russia has considerably toned down 1885.

Toned (tōᵘnd), *ppl. a.* and *adj.* 1460. **A.** *ppl. a.* [f. prec. + -ED[1].] **1. a.** Sounded with the proper, or a specified, tone. **b.** Of body or mind: Brought into tone; braced, strung 1742. **2.** Slightly or finely coloured or shaded; tinted 1864. **b.** *Photogr.* Treated with chemicals so as to acquire the desired tone or shade of colour 1861.

1. b. A human being whose mind was quite as firmly toned at eighty as at forty MACAULAY. 2. *T. paper,* paper which is not quite white, but cream-coloured or slightly buff.

B. *adj.* [f. TONE *sb.* + -ED[2].] In comb.: Having a tone (in various senses) of a specified kind or quality; e.g. *deep-, high-, low-t.* 1790.

Toneless (tōᵘ·nlės), *a.* 1773. [f. TONE *sb.* + -LESS.] Destitute of tone, in various senses. Hence **To·neless·ly** *adv.*, **-ness.**

Tong (tǫŋ). 1918. [Chinese *t'ang* hall, meeting-place.] A Chinese secret society.

Murder by order of a t. 1928.

‖**Tonga**[1] (tǫ·ŋgă). *India.* 1874. [a. Hindī *tāngā.*] A light and small two-wheeled carriage or cart used in India.

‖**Tonga**[2] (tǫ·ŋgă). 1880. [Arbitrary.] A drug extracted from the root of the Fijian plant *Epipremnum pinnatum,* used by the natives of Fiji as a remedy for neuralgia; also known in England and America.

Tongrian (tǫ·ŋgriăn), *a.* 1883. [f. *Tongres,* in Belgium, where developed + -IAN.] *Geol.* Name for marine strata of the Lower Oligocene of Belgium.

Tongs (tǫŋz), *sb. pl.* [OE. *tang, tange* :—OTeut. **tangô-* :—Indo-Eur. **dankâ-*, referred to the root **dak-, dank-* to bite (Skr. *damç, daç,* Gr. δάκνειν).] An implement consisting of two limbs or 'legs' connected by a hinge, pivot, or spring, by means of which their lower ends are brought together, so as to grasp and take up objects which it is impossible or inconvenient to lift with the hand. Used formerly in sing., now always in pl. with pl. or (chiefly Sc.) sing. concord. *Pair of t.* is used when qualification by a numeral or an indef. article is necessary. **b.** Used in burlesque music 1590. **c.** Often short for *curling-t., sugar-t.,* etc. 1713. **d.** In various transf. and techn. applications. late ME.

Phr. *Not to touch with a pair of t.,* expressing repugnance to have anything to do with. b. I haue a reasonable good eare in musicke. Let us haue the tongs and the bones. SHAKS.

Tongue (tɒŋ), *sb.* [OE. *tunge* :—OTeut. **tungôn-*, generally held to be cogn. w. L. *lingua,* for older **dingua.*] **I. 1.** An organ, possessed by man and most vertebrates, occupying the floor of the mouth, and attached at its base to the hyoid bone; often protrusible and freely movable. In its development in man and the higher mammals, it is tapering, blunt-tipped, muscular, soft and fleshy, important in taking in and swallowing food, also as the principal organ of taste, and in man of articulate speech. **b.** In ref. to invertebrate animals, applied to organs or parts of the mouth having some analogy to the tongue of vertebrates 1753. **c.** Erron. regarded as the 'stinging organ' 1581. **2.** A figure or representation of this organ ME. **3.** The tongue of an animal as an article of food; *esp.* an OX-TONGUE or NEAT'S TONGUE. late ME.

1. I had rather haue this t. cut from my mouth SHAKS. Phr. *To put one's t. out,* to protrude the tongue either for medical inspection or as a grimace. c. *Much Ado* v. i. 90. 2. And tungis dyuersely partid as fyer apperiden to hem WYCLIF *Acts* ii. 3. The classical 'egg and t.' and 't. and dart' patterns 1886.

II. In ref. to speech. **1.** Considered as the principal organ of speech; hence, the faculty of speech; voice, speech; words, language OE. **2.** The action of speaking; speech, talking, utterance, voice; also, what is spoken or uttered; words, talk, discourse OE. **b.** Speech as dist. from or contrasted with thought, action, or fact. late ME. †**c.** A 'voice', vote, suffrage. SHAKS. †**d.** Eulogy, fame. FLETCHER. **3.** Manner of speaking or talking, with regard to the sense or import of what is said, the mode of expression or form of words used, or the sound of the voice 1460. **4.** Of a dog. **a.** In phrases: *To give t., to throw (its) t.*, prop. of a hound: to give forth its voice when on the scent or in sight of the quarry. Also *transf.* of persons. 1737. **b.** Hence, the hunting-cry or 'music' of a hound in pursuit of game 1787. **5.** The speech or language of a people or race; also, that of a particular class or locality OE. **b.** *The tongues*, foreign languages; often *spec.* the classical or learned languages 1535. **c.** The knowledge or use of a language; esp. in phrases *gift of tongues, to speak with a t. (tongues)*, in ref. to the Pentecostal miracle and the miraculous gift in the early Church 1526. **6.** *transf.* in biblical use: A people or nation having a language of their own. Usu. in pl.: *all tongues*, people of every tongue. late ME.

1. This our life..Findes tongues in trees, bookes in the running brookes SHAKS. I would..give him a lick with the rough side of my t. SCOTT. Vather'll.. call ee everything he can lay his t. to 1899. Phr. *To hold one's t.*, to refrain from speech, keep silence, say nothing. *To put*, or *speak with, one's t. in one's cheek*, to speak insincerely. So, *to stick* (or *thrust*) *one's t. in one's cheek*, as a gesture of contemptuous or sly humour. *To keep a civil t. in one's head*, to avoid rudeness. *To have lost one's t.*, to be too bashful or sulky to speak; Have you lost your t.. Jack? DICKENS. So *to find one's t.*, to speak after a period of shyness or sullenness. 5. To speak all Tongues, and do all Miracles MILT. 6. I wil come to gather all people and tonges COVERDALE *Isa.* lxvi. 18.

III. Anything that resembles or suggests the human or animal tongue by its shape, position, function, or use; a tapering, projecting, or elongated object or part, esp. when mobile, or attached at one end or side. **1.** Any tongue-like part or organ of the human or animal body. †*T. of the throat*, the uvula. late ME. **2.** (Cf. *t.-fish.*) A young or small-sized sole 1825. **3.** A tongue-like projecting piece of anything. **a.** A narrow strip of land, running into the sea, or between two branches of a river, or two other lands; also, a narrow inlet of water running into the land, etc. 1566. **b.** A narrow and deep part of the current of a river, running smoothly and rapidly between rocks 1891. **c.** A tapering jet of flame 1797. **4.** *techn.* **a.** The pin of a buckle or brooch ME. **b.** The pointer of a balance; also of a dial. late ME. **c.** = REED II. 3 a, c. 1551. **d.** The clapper of a bell; hence, the pistil or a stamen of a bell-flower 1577. **e.** The pole of a wagon or other vehicle 1591. **f.** A projecting tenon along the edge of a board, to be inserted into a groove or mortise in the edge of another board; in *Mech.* a projecting flange, rib, or strip for any purpose 1842. **g.** A short piece of rope spliced into the upper part of the standing backstays, etc. 1815. **h.** The wedge-shaped or tapered end of a scion in grafting 1832. **i.** The tapered end of a pole, etc., by which it is fixed in a socket 1815. **j.** A projecting piece of leather or the like forming a tab or flap; the strip of thin leather closing the opening in a laced or buttoned shoe or boot 1597. **k.** The movable tapered piece of rail in a railway switch 1841.

Comb.: **t.-bird**, local name of the wryneck, from its long retractile t.; **-bit**, a bridle bit having a plate attached so as to prevent the horse from putting his t. over the mouthpiece; **-bone**, the hyoid bone; **-fence**, argument, debate; **-fish**, the sole; **-grafting**, whip or splice grafting, in which a thin wedge-shaped t. of the scion is fitted into a cleft in the stock; **-pipe**, a reed-pipe in an organ or similar instrument; **-shaped**, *a.* shaped like a t.; linguiform; **-shell**, a brachiopod of the family *Lingulidæ*; **-test**, a test of the existence or strength of an electric current by applying the t. to a break in the circuit; **-twister**, something said to twist the t.; *spec.* a sequence of words, often alliterative, difficult to articulate quickly; **-worm**, (*a*) a pentastom; (*b*) the 'worm' of the t. in dogs; = LYTTA.

Tongue (tɒŋ), *v.* late ME. [f. prec.] **1.** *trans.* To assail with words; to reproach, scold; to discuss or talk about injuriously. **2.** *intr.* To use the tongue, talk, speak; *esp.* to talk volubly, to prate 1624. **b.** Of a hound: To give tongue 1832. **3.** *trans.* To utter or turn *over* with the tongue; to say 1611. **4.** To touch with the tongue 1687. **5.** *intr.* To project as a protruding tongue (of ice); to throw out tongues (of flame) 1814. **6.** *trans.* To furnish with a tongue (*lit.* or *fig.*) **a.** To give a speaking tongue or utterance to 1602. **b.** (*a*) To cut a tongue on (a plank, etc.). (*b*) To slit or shape a tongue in (a plant-stem or shoot) for grafting or layering 1733. **c.** To join or fit together by means of a tongue and groove or tongue and socket 1823.

1. *Meas. for M.* IV. iv. 28. 3. 'Tis still a Dreame; or else such stuffe as Madmen T., and braine not SHAKS.

Tongued (tɒŋd), *a.* (*ppl. a.*) late ME. [f. TONGUE *sb.* or *v.* + -ED.] Having or furnished with a tongue or tongues (in various senses).

Nosd like a Goose, and toungd like a woman 1611. Reeded and t. instruments 1854. Grooved and T. Flooring Boards 1884.

Tongueless (tɒ·ŋlės), *a.* late ME. [See -LESS.] **1.** Having no tongue, without a tongue. **2.** Without the faculty of voice or speech, dumb, mute; also, without speaking, speechless, silent 1447. **b.** Said of things 1593. †**3.** Not spoken of. SHAKS.

2. b. Euen from the toonglesse cauernes of the earth SHAKS. 3. One good deed, dying tonguelesse, Slaughters a thousand, wayting vpon that SHAKS.

Tonguelet (tɒ·ŋlėt). 1840. [f. TONGUE *sb.* + -LET.] A little tongue or tongue-like object; *spec.* **a.** = LIGULA 1 b.; **b.** = *tongue-worm* (*a*).

Tongue-tie (tɒ·ŋtəi), *sb.* 1641. [f. TONGUE *sb.* + TIE *sb.*] That which ties the tongue, or restrains speech; also, the condition of being tongue-tied (*lit.* and *fig.*).

Tongue-tie, abnormal shortness of the frænum linguæ, or adhesion of the tongue to the floor of the mouth 1890.

Tongue-tie (tɒ·ŋtəi), *v.* 1555. [prob. a back-formation from next.] *trans.* To tie or confine the tongue of; to restrain or debar from speaking; to render speechless.

Tongue-tied (tɒ·ŋtəid), *ppl. a.* 1529. [f. TONGUE *sb.* + TIED *ppl. a.*] Tied as to or in the tongue. **1.** Having the frænum of the tongue too short, so that its movement is impeded or confined; incapable of distinct utterance from this cause; also, unable to speak, dumb (*poet.*) 1530. **2.** *fig.* Restrained or debarred from speaking or free expression from any cause; dumb, silent; also, reticent, reserved 1529.

2. Criticks be tongue-ti'd, stand, admire 1640.

Tonguey (tɒ·ŋi), *a.* late ME. [f. TONGUE *sb.* + -Y[1].] **1.** Full of 'tongue' or talk; loquacious (now *U.S.* and *dial.*); of hounds, 'giving tongue'. **2.** Of the nature of the tongue; produced or modified by the tongue; lingual 1859.

1. A very t. Yankee lawyer 1836.

Tonguing (tɒ·ŋiŋ), *vbl. sb.* 1682. [f. TONGUE *v.* + -ING[1].] The action of TONGUE *v.*; *spec.* in playing the flute and other wind instruments: the use of the tongue to produce certain effects.

Tonic (tǫ·nik), *a.* and *sb.* 1649. [ad. Gr. τονικός of or for stretching, f. τόνος TONE *sb.*] **A.** *adj.* **1.** *Phys.* and *Path.* Pertaining to, consisting in, or producing tension; *esp.* in relation to the muscles. **b.** Pertaining to, or maintaining, the tone or normal healthy condition of the tissues or organs 1684. **2.** *Med.*, etc. Having the property of increasing or restoring the tone or healthy condition and activity of the system or organs; strengthening, invigorating, bracing 1756. **3.** *Mus.* Formerly applied to the key-note of a composition (*t. note*), now called simply *tonic* (see B. 2); now, Pertaining to or founded upon the tonic or key-note 1760. **4.** Pertaining or relating to tone or accent in speech; indicating the tone or accent of spoken words or syllables; characterized by distinctions of tone or accent 1859.

1. *T. contraction*, continuous muscular contraction without relaxation. *T. convulsion* or *spasm*, one characterized by such contraction (opp. to CLONIC). 2. T. bitters 1800. 3. *T. chord*, a chord having the tonic for its root. *T. pedal*, the tonic sustained as a PEDAL. *T. sol-fa*, a system of teaching music, esp. vocal music, in which the seven notes of the ordinary major scale in any key are sung to syllables written *doh, ray, me, fah, soh, la, te* (modification of the older *do, re, mi, fa, sol, la, si*), and indicated in the notation by the initials d, r, m, etc.; *doh* always denoting the tonic or key-note, and the remaining syllables indicating the relation to it of the other notes of the scale. 4. *T. accent* (= F. *accent tonique*), the stress-accent of a word.

B. *sb.* **1.** *Med.* A tonic medicine, application, or agent 1799. **b.** *fig.* A bracing influence 1840. **2.** *Mus.* = KEY-NOTE 1. 1806.

1. b. The t. of a wholesome pride CLOUGH. 2. *T. major* or *minor*, that key (major or minor) which has the same key-note as a given key (minor or major). Hence **To·nic** *v. trans.* to act as a t. upon, to 'brace up'; to administer a t. to. So †**To·nical** *a.* in senses 1, 1 b, 4; **-ally** *adv.*

Tonicity (toni·sĭti). 1824. [f. prec. + -ITY.] Tonic quality or condition; the property of possessing tone; the normal state of elastic tension of living muscles, arteries, etc., by which the tone of the organs is maintained. **b.** Of spasm: see TONIC *a.* 1. 1897.

To-night (tŭnəi·t), *adv.* and *sb.* [OE. *tō niht*, TO *prep.* II. 2 + NIGHT.] **A.** *adv.* **1.** On this very night (i.e. the night now present) ME. **b.** On any night (as contrasted with the next day) 1500. **2.** On the night following this day OE. **3.** Last night. *Obs.* exc. *dial.* ME.

1. T. I saw the sun set TENNYSON. 2. Duncan comes here to Night SHAKS. 3. I dreampt a dreame to night SHAKS.

B. *sb.* This night, or the night after this day ME.

Tonish, tonnish (tǫ·niʃ), *a.* Now *rare.* 1778. [f. TON[2] + -ISH[1].] Having 'ton'; fashionable, modish, stylish.

Tonite (tōu·nəit). 1881. [f. L. *tonare* to thunder + -ITE.] A high explosive composed of pulverized gun-cotton impregnated with barium nitrate; cotton powder.

Tonitrual (toni·tru̥ăl), *a. rare.* 1693. [ad. rare L. *tonitrualis*, f. *tonitrus* thunder.] Pertaining to, or loaded with, thunder. So **Toni·truous** *a.* thundery (*lit.* and *fig.*).

Tonk (tǫŋk), *v.* 1910. [Echoic.] *trans.* To strike vigorously. So **Tonk** *sb.*

‖**Tonka** (tǫ·ŋkă). 1796. [Negro name in Guiana of the bean.] **1. Tonka bean**: the black, fragrant, almond-shaped seed of a large leguminous tree, *Dipterix odorata*, of Brazil, Guiana, and adjacent regions, used for scenting snuff, and as an ingredient in perfumes. Also the tree itself. **2. Tonka-bean** (or *Tonga-bean*) **wood**, the wood of *Alyxia buxifolia*, a Tasmanian evergreen shrub, also called *Tonquin Bean-tree*; scentwood 1862.

Tonnage (tɒ·nėdʒ), *sb.* Also **tunnage.** late ME. [In sense 1, a. OF., f. *tonne* TUN; see -AGE; in other senses, f. TON *sb.*[1] + -AGE.] **I.** Charge, duty, or payment of so much per ton or tun. **1.** *Eng. Hist.* A tax or duty formerly levied upon wine imported in tuns or casks, at the rate of so much for every tun. Commonly in association with *poundage.* †**2.** A charge for the hire of a ship of so much a ton (of her burden) per week or month –1587. **3.** A charge or payment per ton on cargo or freight; e.g. that payable at any port or wharf, or on a canal 1617. **II.** Carrying capacity, weight, etc., in tons. **1.** The carrying capacity of a ship expressed in tons of 100 cubic feet (see TON[1] 2) 1718. **2.** *transf.* Ships collectively, shipping (in relation to their carrying capacity, or together with the merchandise carried by them) 1633. **3. a.** Weight in tons (*rare*) 1793. **b.** Weight of (iron or other heavy merchandise) in the market 1898. **4.** Mode of reckoning the ton of cargo for freightage 1913.

1. *Under-deck t.* the cubic content of the space under the t.-deck; this with the addition of the contents of all enclosed spaces above this deck gives the *gross t.*; the deduction from the latter of the space occupied by the quarters of the crew, and that taken up in a steamer by the engines, boilers, etc., gives the *register t.*, for which vessels are registered, and on which the assessment of dues and charges on shipping is based. *Dead-weight t.* (or *carrying capacity*), occas. applied to the number of tons of 20 cwt. that a ship will carry laden to her load-line. *Displacement t.*, the number of tons of water displaced by a ship when thus loaded, used in England in stating the tonnage of men-of-war since *c* 1870. 2. If the additional T. does not arrive tomorrow, I shall settle to leave behind the veteran battalion or the 36th WELLINGTON.

attrib. and *Comb.*: **t.-deck**, in a ship, the second deck from below in all vessels of two or more decks;

the only deck in a vessel of one deck; **t.-displacement** = displacement t. Hence **To·nnage** *v. trans.* to impose t. upon; to have a t. of (so much).

‖**Tonneau** (tǫ·nōᵘ). 1901. [F., spec. application of *tonneau* cask, tun.] Name for the rounded rear body of a motor-car (orig. with the door at the back).

Tonner (tɒ·nəɹ). 1883. [f. Ton¹ + -er¹.] In comb. with prefixed numeral: A vessel of (so many) tons burden.

Tono- (tǫnǫ), repr. Gr. τονο-, comb. form of τόνος stretching, tension, Tone, as in **To·nograph** [-graph], a recording tonometer. **To·nophant** [Gr. -φάντης one who shows], a device whereby acoustic vibrations are rendered visible.

Tonometer (tonǫ·mǐtəɹ). 1725. [f. Tono- + -meter.] **1.** *Mus.* An instrument for determining the pitch of tones; *spec.* a tuning-fork, or a graduated set of tuning-forks, for determining the exact number of vibrations per second which produce a given tone. **2.** An instrument for measuring (*a*) tension of the eyeball in glaucoma 1876, (*b*) intravascular blood-pressure 1898, (*c*) strains within a liquid 1909. Hence **Tonome·tric** *a.* of or pertaining to tonometry. **Tono·metry**, the using of a t.; measurement of vibrations of sound or of tension.

Tonsil (tǫ·nsĭl), usu. in pl. **tonsils** (tǫ·nsĭlz). 1601. [ad. L. *tonsillæ* (pl.).] **1.** Each of two oval lymphoid glands situated one on each side of the fauces between the anterior and posterior arches. **2.** Each of the two lobes of the cerebellum; also called *amygdala* 1891.

†**To·nsile**, *a.* 1664. [ad. L. *tonsilis*, f. *tons-*, *tondere* to shear; see -ile.] That may be clipped or shorn -1878.

Tonsillar (tǫ·nsilăɹ), *a.* 1831. [ad. med. or mod. L. *tonsillaris*, f. *tonsillæ*; see Tonsil and -ar.] Of or pertaining to the tonsils; affected by the tonsils, as a *t. voice*. So **To·nsillary** *a.*

Tonsillectomy (tǫnsil,e·ktŏmi). 1901. [f. as next + Gr. ἐκτομή excision + -y³.] Surgical excision of the tonsils. So **Tonsille·ctome** (see -tome ¹).

Tonsillitis (tǫnsiləi·tis). 1801. [f. L. *tonsilla* + -itis.] *Path.* Inflammation of the tonsils. Hence **Tonsilli·tic** *a.* affected with t.

Tonsillo·tomy. 1881. [irreg. f. as prec. + -tomy.] = Tonsillectomy. **Tonsi·llotome**.

Tonsor (tǫ·nsǫɹ). 1656. [a. L., f. *tondere* to shear.] A barber.

Tonsorial (tǫnsōᵊ·riăl), *a.* 1813. [f. L. *tonsorius* + -al.] Of or pertaining to a barber or his work; often used joc., as a 't. artist'.

Tonsure (tǫ·nʃəɹ, tǫ·nsiŭɹ), *sb.* late ME. [a. F., or ad. L. *tonsura*, f. *tondere, tonsum*.] **1.** *gen.* The action or process of clipping the hair or shaving the head; the state of being shorn. **2.** *spec.* The shaving of the head or part of it as a religious practice or rite, esp. as a preparation to entering the priesthood or a monastic order. late ME. **b.** The part of a priest's or monk's head left bare by shaving the hair. late ME. †**3.** The clipping (*a*) of coin; (*b*) of shrubs or hedges (*rare*) -1691. Hence **To·nsure** *v. trans.* to clip or shave the hair of; to confer the ecclesiastical t. upon.

Tonsured (tǫ·nʃəɹd, tǫ·nsiŭɹd), *ppl. a.* 1706. [f. Tonsure *v.* + -ed¹.] **1.** That has received tonsure; hence, in orders. **b.** *fig.* Bald or partially bald 1855. **2.** Clipped, as a yew or box (*rare*) 1837.

1. The cowled and t. Middle Age M. Arnold.

Tontine (tǫntī·n), *sb.* (*a.*) 1765. [a. F., f. name of Lorenzo *Tonti*, a Neapolitan banker, who initiated the scheme in France *c* 1653.] A financial scheme by which the subscribers to a loan or common fund receive each an annuity during his life, which increases as their number is diminished by death, till the last survivor enjoys the whole income; also applied to the share or right of each survivor.

This gentlewoman had ventured 300 livres in each T.; and in the last year of her life she had for her annuity..about 3600 *l.* a year 1791.

B. *adj.* (or *attrib.* use of the sb.) Of, pertaining to, or of the nature of a tontine 1824.

‖**Tonus** (tōᵘ·nɒs). 1876. [L., a. Gr. τόνος Tone.] *Physiol.* and *Path.* **1.** The condition or state of muscular tone; tonicity. **2.** A tonic spasm 1891.

†**To·ny**, *sb. slang.* 1654. [A particular application of *Tony*, short for *Antony*.] A foolish person; a simpleton -1784.

Tony (tōᵘ·ni), *a.* orig. *U.S.* and *Colonial. colloq.* 1886. [f. Tone *sb.* + -y¹.] High-toned, stylish; 'swell'.

Too (tū), *adv.* OE. [Stressed form of To *prep.*, which in the 16th c. began to be spelt *too*.] **1.** In addition; furthermore, besides, also. (Not now used, exc. in U.S., at the beginning of a clause.) **2.** In excess; more than enough; overmuch, superfluously, superabundantly OE. **3.** As a mere intensive: Excessively, extremely, exceedingly, very. (Now chiefly an emotional colloquialism.) ME. **4.** Reduplicated for emphasis: *too too* 1489. **b.** as *adj.* Excessive, extreme; extremely good, highly exquisite. (*affected.*) 1891.

1. Prettie and wittie; wilde, and yet t. gentle Shaks. 2. One that lou'd not wisely, but t. well Shaks. Men of Letters know t. much to make good Husbands Steele. At best a blunderer and t. probably a traitor Macaulay. 3. 'We shall see you at dinner perhaps' ..'I shall be too happy', replied Noel 1825. 4. Oh that this t. t. solid Flesh would melt Shaks. b. My frocks are too too! 1893.

Special collocations. *T. much* (as predicate), more than can be endured, intolerable; also *t. much of a good thing*. *T. much for*, more than a match for; so *t. many for*, *t. hard for*, etc. (chiefly *colloq.*). *But t...*, *only t.*: here *t.* is app. = 'more than is desirable', or 'more than is or might be expected', while *but* or *only* app. emphasizes the exclusion of any different quality or state of things such as might be desired or expected. *Only t.* in recent use, is often a mere intensive, = 'extremely'. *None too*..is used by meiosis for 'not quite..enough', 'somewhat insufficiently'. *Quite t...*: see Quite 4.

Tool (tūl), *sb.* [OE. *tōl* = ON. *tól* n. pl.:— OTeut. **tōwlom*, **tōlom*, f. **tōw-* to prepare, make + agent-suffix *-lom* -el¹.] **1.** 'Any instrument of manual operation' (J.); a mechanical implement for working upon something, as by cutting, striking, rubbing, or other process, in any manual art or industry; usu., one held in and operated directly by the hand, but including also certain simple machines, as the lathe. See also Edge-tool. **b.** A weapon of war, *esp.* a sword. *arch.* late ME. **c.** *spec.* in techn. use: (*a*) *Bookbinding.* A small stamp or roller used for impressing an ornamental design upon leather book-covers 1727. (*b*) A large kind of chisel 1815. (*c*) A generic name for any kind of paint-brush used by house-painters or decorators 1859. **2.** *fig.* Anything used in the manner of a tool; a means of effecting something; an instrument OE. **b.** A bodily organ; *spec.* the male generative organ. Now *arch* or *slang.* 1553. **3.** *fig.* A person who is, or allows himself to be, made a mere instrument by another; a cat's-paw 1663. **b.** (esp. qualified by *poor* or the like.) An unskilful workman; a shiftless person. *slang* or *dial.* 1700. **4.** *Bookbinding.* (*transf.* from 1 c (*a*).) A tooled design on a book-cover 1881.

1. b. Draw thy toole, here comes of the house of Mountagues Shaks. 2. They..make use of Similitudes..and other tooles of Oratory Hobbes. 3. The sheriffs were the tools of the government Macaulay.

Comb.: **t.-box**, *spec.* the steel box in which the cutting t. of a planing or other machine is clamped; **-post**, an upright piece in the t.-rest of a lathe, with a slot and a screw for holding the cutting-t.; **-rest**, a part of a lathe serving to support a hand-t., or to hold a mechanical t. in place; **-stock** = *t.-post*.

Tool, *v.* 1812. [f. prec.] **1.** *trans.* To work or shape with a tool; *spec.* to smooth the surface of a building stone with the chisels called 'tools' 1815. **b.** *Bookbinding.* To impress an ornamental design upon the binding of (a book) with a special tool 1836. **c.** *intr.* To work with a tool or tools 1890. **2.** *slang.* **a.** *trans.* To drive (a team of horses, a vehicle, or a person in a vehicle); of a horse, to draw (a person) in a vehicle 1812. **b.** *intr.* To drive, to travel in a horse-drawn vehicle; also said of the vehicle or team; hence, to travel, go *along* 1839.

1. Aluminium..is ductile, but difficult to t. 1895. 2. a. He could t. a coach Lytton. b. Went to Ascot ..and we 'tooled' down in very good style 1893.

Tooled (tūld), *ppl. a.* 1815. [f. prec. + -ed¹.] Worked or shaped with a t.; *spec.* in *Bookbinding*.

Tooling (tū·liŋ), *vbl. sb.* 1815. [f. as prec. + -ing¹.] The action of Tool *v.*; *spec.* **a.** The dressing of stone with a broad chisel. **b.** *Bookbinding.* The impressing of ornamental designs upon the covers of books by means of heated tools or stamps; also applied to the designs so formed: either with gilding (*gold-* or *gilt-t.*) or without it (*blind-t.*) 1821.

Toom (tūm; in mod. Sc. tŏm, tüm), *a.* Now only *Sc.* and *n. dial.* [OE. *tōm*:—OTeut. **tômoz* or **tômuz*; ult. origin unkn. Hence Teem *v.*²] Empty (*lit.* and *fig.*); destitute (*of* something).

Toom, *v.* *Sc.* and *n. dial.* 1500. [f. prec.] **1.** *trans.* To empty (a vessel, etc.); *esp.* to drink off the contents of. **2.** To empty out (water, the contents of a vessel, etc.) 1535.

‖**Toon, tun** (tūn). *India.* 1810. [a. Hindī *tun*, *tūn*, Skr. *tunna*.] An E. Indian tree, *Cedrela Toona*, which yields a timber resembling mahogany but softer and lighter; the wood of this tree, also called *Indian mahogany*.

Toon, obs. f. Tone, Tun; dial. f. Town.

Toot (tūt), *sb.* 1461. [f. Toot *v.*²] An act of tooting; a note or short blast of a horn, trumpet, etc.

Toot (tūt), *v.*¹ Now *dial.* [OE. *tōtian*.] **1.** *intr.* To protrude, stick *out*, 'peep *out*', so as to be seen. **2.** *intr.* To peep, peer, look out; to gaze ME. **b.** To pry. late ME.

2. b. With bowe and bolts..For birds in bushes tooting Spenser.

Toot (tūt), *v.*² 1510. [Cf. MLG., LG. *tûten*, also Ger. *tuten*, Du. *tuyten*, *toeten* to blow a horn; perh. orig. echoic.] **I.** *intr.* **1.** To sound or blow a horn or the like 1549. **2.** Of a wind-instrument: To give forth its characteristic sound; to sound 1510. **3.** Of an animal: To make a sound likened to that of a horn, etc.; to trumpet as an elephant, bray as an ass; *spec.* of grouse, to 'call' 1817.

1. Tooting with their Trumpets, and beating with their Drums 1698. 3. The storm-cock touts on his towering pine Hogg.

II. *trans.* **1.** To cause (a horn, etc.) to sound by blowing it. Also *transf.* of an animal. 1682. **2.** To sound (notes, a tune, etc.) on a horn, pipe, or the like 1614. **3.** To call out aloud, to shout (something) 1582.

2. With eight Trumpeters tooting the Dead March in Saul Barham. Hence **Too·ter**, one who or that which toots.

Tooth (tūþ), *sb.* *Pl.* **teeth** (tīþ). [Com. Teut. and Indo-Eur.; OE. *tōþ*:—OTeut. **tanþ*- beside **tunþ*-:—Indo-Eur. **dent*-, *dont*-, *dnt*-, whence Skr. *dan*, *danta*, Gr. ὀδούς (ὀδόντος), L. *dens* (*dentis*), OIr. *dét*, W. *dant*.] **1.** *pl.* The hard processes within the mouth, attached in a row to each jaw in most vertebrates except birds, having points, edges, or grinding surfaces, and serving primarily for the biting, tearing, or trituration of solid food, and secondarily as weapons of attack or defence, and for other purposes; in *sing.* each of these individually. Also applied to similar analogous structures occurring in the mouth or alimentary canal in some invertebrates. **b.** *spec.* An elephant's tusk (projecting upper incisor tooth), as a source of ivory OE. **c.** In expressions referring to speech (now esp. biting or angry speech) ME. **2.** *fig.* or in fig. expressions: **a.** referring to eating, esp. to the sense of taste; hence often = taste, liking. late ME. **b.** referring to biting or gnawing 1546.

1. She has not a T. in her Head Steele. 2. a. What a t. for fruit has a monkey! 1851. b. It is impossible to auoide the teethe of malicious enuy 1546.

II. *transf.* A projecting part or point resembling an animal's tooth; esp. one of a row or series of such. **a.** As an artificial structure, in an implement, machine, etc.; e.g. one of the pointed projections of a comb, saw, file, rake, harrow, fork, etc.; a prong, tine; a cog 1523. **b.** As a natural structure, in animals, plants, etc.; e.g. the odontoid process of the axis vertebra; each of a row of small projections on the edge of one valve of the shell in some bivalve molluscs; each of the pointed processes on the margin of leaves or other parts in many plants, or of those forming the peristome of the capsule in mosses; also, gen., a projecting point of rock, etc. 1694. **c.** *pl.* The lower zone of facets in a rose-diamond 1877. **d.** *pl. fig.* A ship's guns. *Naut. slang.* 1810.

d. They were..large schooners..showing a very good set of teeth MARRYAT.

Phrases. **In the teeth, in** (one's) **teeth. a.** *In the teeth of*, in direct opposition to, so as to face or confront. **b.** *In the teeth of*, in defiance of, in spite of. **c.** *In the teeth of*, in the presence of, in the face of; threateningly confronted by. **d.** *To cast* (a thing) *in* a person's *teeth*, *to throw in* a person's *teeth*, to reproach, upbraid, or censure with; to bring up in reproach against; also in similar phrases expressing reproachful or defiant utterance. **In spite of** (*despite, maugre*, etc.) one's **teeth**: notwithstanding one's opposition; in spite of one, in defiance of one. Now *rare* exc. *dial.* **To the teeth. a.** So as to be completely equipped; very fully or completely: in *armed to the teeth*. **b.** *To* (one's) *teeth, to the teeth of*, intensive of 'to one's face'; directly and openly; defiantly. **Tooth and nail** (orig. *with tooth and nail*), advb. phr. *lit.* With the use of one's teeth and nails as weapons; by biting and scratching: almost always *fig.*, vigorously, fiercely, with one's utmost efforts, with all one's might. **From the teeth forward(s or outward(s** (also *simply* **from one's teeth**), in profession but not in reality (opp. to *from the heart*). **To set one's teeth,** to press or clench one's teeth firmly together from indignation or fixed resolution; hence *fig.* and *allus.* **To show one's teeth,** *lit.* to uncover the teeth by withdrawing the lips from them: see SHOW *v.* II. 6. **b.** *Long in the t.*, old (orig. of horses, from recession of gums with age) 1852 (THACKERAY).

attrib. and *Comb.*: **t.-back,** a moth of the family *Notodontidæ*, or its larva, which has a t.-like prominence on the back; **-bone,** (*a*) = DENTINE; (*b*) the bony substance or 'cement' of the teeth; **-comb,** a small-t. comb; **-coralline** = SERTULARIA; **-ivory** = DENTINE; **-mark,** a mark made by a t. in biting; **t. ornament,** *Arch.* a kind of ornament or moulding suggesting a t. or teeth; **-paste,** a paste used for cleaning the teeth; **-powder,** a powder used for cleaning the teeth, a dentifrice; **-rail,** a tramway rail having teeth or cogs; **-rash,** an eruptive disease incident to infants when teething; **-sac,** a sac or hollow structure of connective tissue, within which a tooth is developed; **-wheel,** a toothed wheel, cog-wheel.

Tooth (tūþ), *v.* late ME. [f. prec.] †**1.** *intr.* To develop, grow, or 'cut' teeth; to teethe –1796. **2.** *trans.* To supply or furnish with teeth; to fit or fix teeth into; to cut teeth in or upon; to indent 1483. **3.** To exercise the teeth upon; to bite, gnaw 1579. **4.** To fit or fix into something by projections like teeth, or in the manner of teeth. **a.** *trans.* 1672. **b.** *intr.* for *pass.* To interlock 1703.

2. I toothed two Pieces of Brass..to fit each other 1745.

Toothache (tū·þ,ēⁱk). late ME. [TOOTH *sb.*, ACHE *sb.*] An ache or continuous pain in a tooth or the teeth. (As a malady, commonly *the tooth ache* down to 19th c.)

Comb.: **t.-grass,** a N. Amer. grass (*Ctenium americanum*) having a very pungent taste; **-tree,** (*a*) name for N. Amer. species of *Xanthoxylon*, having pungent aromatic fruit, esp. *X. fraxineum*, also called *prickly ash*; (*b*) the similar N. Amer. *Aralia spinosa*, also called *angelica-tree*.

Tooth-billed (tū·þ,bild), *a.* 1862. *Ornith.* Having one or more tooth-like projections on the edge of the bill; dentirostral or serratirostral. So **Too·thbill,** the t. pigeon.

Too·th-brush. 1651. A small brush with a long handle, used for cleansing the teeth. **b.** *attrib.* **t. moustache,** a short bristly moustache 1904.

Too·th-drawer. late ME. **1.** One who 'draws' or extracts teeth; a dentist. Now *contemptuous.* †**2.** A dentist's instrument for extracting teeth –1694.

Toothed (tūþt, *poet.* tū·þėd), *a.* ME. [f. TOOTH *sb.* or *v.* + -ED.] **1.** *lit.* Having teeth; having teeth of a specified kind. †**b.** *fig.* 'Biting', pungent, corrosive –1675. **2.** Having natural projections or processes like teeth; dentate, indented; jagged: *esp.* of leaves or other parts of plants; also of the bill of birds, the margin of shells, etc. late ME. **3.** Made or fitted artificially with teeth or tooth-like projections; *spec.* of a wheel, cogged. late ME.

2. *T. vertebra*, the axis vertebra, from its tooth or odontoid process. **3.** *T. ornament* (Arch.) = *tooth-ornament.*

Toothful (tū·þful), *sb.* 1774. [f. TOOTH *sb.* + -FUL 2.] *lit.* As much as would fill a tooth; a small mouthful, esp. of liquor.

Toothful (tū·þful), *a.* 1591. [f. TOOTH *sb.* + -FUL 1.] **1.** Full of teeth; having many teeth (*rare*). †**2.** = TOOTHSOME –1622.

Toothing (tū·þiŋ), *vbl. sb.* 1440. [f. TOOTH *sb.* or *v.* + -ING¹.] **1.** = TEETHING *vbl. sb.* **1.** *Obs.* or *rare.* **2.** A structure or formation consisting of teeth or tooth-like projections; such teeth collectively; dentation, serration 1611. **b.** *spec.* in *Building.* Bricks or stones left projecting from a wall to form a bond for additional work to be built on; the bond or attachment thus formed; the construction of this 1672. **3.** The process of forming teeth or serrations; the furnishing (of a saw, etc.) with teeth 1833.

Comb.: **t.-plane,** a plane having the iron almost upright, with a serrated edge, used to score and roughen a surface.

Toothless (tū·þlės), *a.* late ME. [-LESS.] Having no teeth; destitute of teeth. **1. a.** That is naturally without teeth. **b.** That has not yet cut its teeth. **c.** Having lost the teeth, as from age. **2.** *transf.* Destitute of tooth-like formations or projections; not jagged or serrated 1812. **3.** *fig.* Destitute of keenness or 'edge'; not biting or corrosive 1592.

Toothpick (tū·þpik). 1488. [See PICK *sb.*¹ II. 3.] **1.** An instrument for picking the teeth: usu. a pointed quill or small piece of wood. **2.** *pl.* Splinters, small elongated fragments, 'matchwood'; in hyperbolical phr. *smashed* (etc.) *into toothpicks* 1839. **3.** *U.S. slang.* A bowie-knife; also *Arkansas t.* 1867. **4.** A very narrow pointed boat. *slang.* 1897.

Too·th-shell. 1711. The long tubular shell, in shape like a tooth or tusk, of any gasteropod mollusc of *Dentalium* or other allied genus; also, the mollusc itself.

Toothsome (tū·þsŏm), *a.* 1551. [-SOME¹.] **1.** Pleasant to the taste, savoury, palatable. **2.** Having a 'dainty tooth' 1837.

1. The Patattoes, which they eate as a delicate and t. meate 1604. Hence **Too·thsome-ly** *adv.*, **-ness.**

Toothwort (tū·þwɒɹt). 1597. [f. TOOTH *sb.* + WORT¹.] **1.** *Lathræa squamaria* (family *Orobanchaceæ*), a leafless fleshy herb, parasitic on the roots of hazel and other trees, having tooth-like scales upon the root-stock. **2.** A plant of the cruciferous genus *Dentaria*, characterized by tooth-like projections upon the creeping root-stock; *esp.* the British species *D. bulbifera*, occurring locally in woods 1668.

Toothy (tū·þi), *a.* 1530. [f. TOOTH *sb.* + -Y¹.] **1.** Having numerous, large, or prominent teeth. **2.** Furnished with or full of teeth or tooth-like projections; toothed 1611. **3.** *fig.* 'Biting', ill-natured, peevish. *n. dial.* and *Sc.* 1691.

3. T. critics by the score BURNS.

Too·thy-peg. 1828. [f. TOOTH *sb.* + PEG *sb.*¹ Cf. local *toossie-*, *tushypeg* (f. *tush* tooth).] Nursery name for a tooth.

Tootle (tū·t'l), *sb.* 1852. [f. next.] **1.** An act or the action of tootling or sounding a horn or similar wind-instrument. **2.** Speech or writing of more sound than sense; twaddle 1883. So **Too·tle-te-too·tle,** a piece of continuous tootling.

Tootle (tū·t'l), *v.* 1820. [frequent f. TOOT *v.*² + -LE 4.] *intr.* To toot continuously; to produce a succession of modulated notes on a wind-instrument 1842. **b.** Of birds: To make a similar noise 1820. **c.** *fig.* To write twaddle or mere verbiage 1883.

Tootling on the sentimental flute STEVENSON.

Too-too (tū,tū·), *v.* 1828. [Echoic; usu. depreciatory.] *intr.* To make an instrumental or vocal sound resembling these syllables.

The singers..begin too-tooing most dismally DICKENS.

Tootsy, tootsy-wootsy (tu·tsi, wu·tsi). *colloq.* 1854. [Fanciful substitution for *foot.*] A playful or endearing name for a child's or a woman's small foot.

Top (tǫp), *sb.*¹ [Com. WGer. and Norse; OE. *top* :—OTeut. **tuppoz* (G. *zopf*).] **I.** A tuft, crest, or bush of hair, etc. **1.** The hair on the summit or crown of the head; the hair of the head. *Obs.* exc. *Sc.* **2.** A tuft or handful of hair, wool, fibre, etc.; *esp.* the portion of flax or tow put on the distaff. Now only *Sc.* and *n. dial.* ME. **b.** *spec.* A bundle of combed wool prepared for spinning. Chiefly *pl.* (also *collect. sing.*). 1637.

1. Let's take the instant by the forward t.: For we are old SHAKS.

II. The highest or uppermost part. **1.** The highest point or part of anything; the highest place or limit *of* something OE. **b.** That part of anything portable which, when it is in use, occupies the highest place; e.g. the t. of a page, map, etc. 1593. **c.** The higher end of anything on a slope; also, that end of anything which is conventionally considered the higher, as of a room or dining-table; the end of a billiard-table opposite the baulk 1624. **2.** The uppermost division of the body; the head; *esp.* the crown of the head ME. **3.** Usu. *pl.* The part of a plant growing above ground as dist. from the root; esp. of a vegetable grown for the 'root', as *turnip-tops* 1523. **4.** *pl.* (also *collect. sing.*) The smaller branches and twigs of trees as dist. from the timber 1485. **5.** The extremity of a growing part; hence the narrower end (of anything tapering), the point, tip 1538.

1. From Sinai's t. Jehovah gave the law COWPER. *To go over the t.*, to scale the parapet of a trench, for an attack or raid. **c.** In the omnibus to the t. of Sloane Street 1849. **2.** Soft hoa, what truncke is heere? Without his t.? SHAKS. **4.** In a sale of standing timber trees they are advertised with their 'lop, t., and bark' 1858. **5.** *T. and butt* (Shipbuilding), a method of working long tapering planks together in pairs with the t. of one to the butt of another, so as to maintain a constant width.

III. A piece or part placed upon or fitted to anything, and forming its upper part or covering. **1.** A platform near the head of each of the lower masts of a ship. In a modern warship, an armoured platform on a short mast, for machine-guns, signalling, etc.; more fully *fighting t.*, *military t.* In a sailing ship, a framework and platform serving to extend the rigging, and for convenience in making sail. late ME. **b.** *Naut.* Short for *topsail* 1513. **c.** *T. and topgallant*, short for *topsail and topgallant sail*; hence *fig.*; as *advb.* with all sail set, in full array or career 1593. **2.** The uppermost part of the leg of a high boot or riding-boot, *spec.* when widened out or turned over; now, a broad band of material (simulating the turned-over part), white, light-coloured, or brown. Also *pl.* short for TOP-BOOTS. 1629. **b.** The gauntlet part of a glove; the turned-down top part of men's hose 1819. **3.** In various techn. uses, e.g. the stopper of a scent-bottle or the like; the part of an earring worn in the lobe of the ear; the hood or cover of a carriage 1453. **b.** Short for *t.-button* 1852.

IV. *fig.* and *transf.* The part of anything which has the first place in time, order, or precedence. **1.** Of time: The earliest part of a period 1440. **2.** The highest or chief position, place, or rank; the head, forefront; now esp. in *the t. of the tree* (fig.) 1627. **b.** One who or that which occupies the highest or chief position; the head (of a clan, family, etc.) 1612. **3.** The highest pitch or degree; the height, summit, zenith, pinnacle 1552. **b.** The most perfect example or type of something 1593. **c.** *Motoring slang.* The top or highest gear; usu. *on* (*the*) *t.* 1906. **4.** The highest point reached in a progression or series; the culminating point 1670. **5.** The best or choicest part; the cream, flower, pick. Now esp. in *the t. of the morning*, as an Irish morning greeting. 1663.

3. By how much from the t. of wondrous glory,..To lowest pitch of abject fortune thou art fall'n MILT. Phr. *The t. of one's bent* (see BENT *sb.*²); *the t. of one's voice.* **b.** If he, which is the t. of Iudgement, should But iudge you, as you are SHAKS. **4.** Phr. *The t. of the tide. The t. of the market*, the moment at which prices are highest. **5.** A 't. of the basket' young lady 1894.

V. Forward spin imparted to a ball by the mode of its impulsion or delivery (in billiards, by striking it above the centre; hence in cricket and tennis) 1901.

VI. *attrib.* passing into *adj.* **1.** Having a top, as *t.-buggy*, *-wagon*, *ship* 1686. **2.** Of or pertaining to the top; upper, uppermost. Now usu. written separate as *adj.* 1593. **3.** Forming the top, or the exterior surface or layer; upper, outer. Now usu. separate. 1603. **4.** First in rank, order, or quality 1647. **5.** Highest (in degree), greatest (in amount); very high, very great; also in weakened sense, first-rate, tip-top, excellent 1714.

2. There were two doors on the t. landing 1888. **3.** A foot-and-a-half of blackish t.-soil 1904. **4.** The t. wits of the Court SWIFT. **5.** His common trot is just a match for your t. speed 1806.

Phrases. **At t., on t.** (see prec. senses); *fig.* supreme, dominant; **on** or **upon** (*the*) **t. of,** above, upon, close upon, following upon. **T...bottom.** a. *T. to bottom*, so that the highest part becomes the lowest; with complete inversion. b. *From t. to bottom* = *from t. to toe*. **T...tail.** a. *T. and tail.* (*a*) The whole, every part. (*b*) The long and short of it, the substance, upshot. (*c*) *advb.* From head to foot; all over. b. *T. or tail*, (in neg. statements), any part; anything definite or intelligible; head or tail. c. *From t. to tail* = a (*c*); also *fig.* wholly, absolutely. **T...toe.** *From t. to toe*, from head to foot, in every part.

Comb.: **t.-button**, †(*a*) a metal button of which the t. or face is gilt or silvered; (*b*) an ornamental knob on the top of a mast; **-card** *Spinning*, a flat strip of wood covered with hooked teeth set over the drum of a carding-engine; **-coat**, overcoat, great-coat, outer-coat; hence **-coated** *a.*; **t. dog**, *lit.* the dog uppermost or 'on top' in a fight; *fig.* the victorious or dominant party; **t. drawer**, the uppermost drawer of a chest, etc.; *to come out of the t. drawer*, to be well bred; **-gear**, (*a*) the rigging, sails, and spars of a ship; (*b*) (without hyphen) in power transmission, the alternative gearing which produces the highest speed in proportion to that of the motor; **-heat** *Hortic.*, heat generated in a frame or greenhouse; **-hole**, **t. notch**, the highest hole or notch; *fig.* the highest point attainable; also *attrib.* first-rate, 'tip-top' (*slang*); hence **t.-notcher**; **t. note**, the highest note in a singer's compass; **-proud** *a.*, proud to the highest degree; **t. sergeant** (*U.S. colloq.*), the first sergeant; **t. story**, the uppermost story of a house; *fig.* the head as the seat of intellect; **-tool**, any smith's tool which is held upon the work while being struck, as dist. from a *bottom-tool*, which is socketed in the anvil; **-weight**, the heaviest weight carried by a horse in a race; *transf.* a horse carrying this weight.

b. From sense III. 1; (*top* being also short for *topsail* or *topmast*): **t.-block**, a large block suspended below the cap of the lower mast, used in hoisting or lowering topmasts; **-chain**, a chain used to sling the yards in action, in case the ropes by which they are hung should be shot away; **-lantern**, **-light**, a signal-light carried in the top of a vessel; **-rope**, a rope used for hoisting or lowering topmasts; *to sway* (erron. *swing*) *on all top-ropes*, to go to great lengths; **-tackle**, a tackle used in raising or lowering topmasts.

Top (tǫp), *sb.*[2] [Late OE. *top*; cf. *top*, used in parts of Holland, etc., MDu. *dop(pe*, OHG. *topfo*, *topf*, MHG. *topfe*, *topf*, G. dial. *topf*.] 1. A toy of various shapes (cylindrical, obconic, etc.), but always of a circular section, with a point on which it is made to spin, usu. by the sudden pulling of a string wound round it; the common *whip-* or *whipping-top* is kept spinning by lashing it with a whip. b. As the type of a sound sleeper, in ref. to the apparent stillness of a spinning top when its axis of rotation is vertical 1616. 2. A marine gasteropod having a short conical shell; any species of the genus *Trochus* or family *Trochidæ*; a top-shell. In earliest use, *sea t.* 1682. 3. *Rope-making.* (Also *laying-t.*) A conical piece of wood, with three or four grooves for the strands 1794.

1. *Parish t.*, *town t.*, a large t. kept for public use, which two players or parties whipped in opposite directions. b. Phr. *To sleep like* (*as sound* or *as fast as*) *a t.* *Old t.* (slang), old fellow, old girl.

Comb.: **t.-shell** = sense 2.

Top (tǫp), *v.*[1] ME. [f. Top *sb.*[1]] **I.** To deprive of the top. †1. *trans.* To cut *off* (the hair of the head), poll (the head), crop (a person) –1632. 2. To cut off the top of (a growing tree, a plant, or the like); to poll or pollard (a tree); to cut or break off the head, flower, or ear of (a plant), the withered calyx from (a gooseberry or other fruit); often in phr. *to t. and lop*, *t. and tail* 1509. †3. To snuff (a candle) –1840.

2. *fig.* Topping rank desires which vain exceed 1633.

II. To put a top on or form a top to. 1. To furnish with a top; to cover or surmount, crown, cap (*with*) 1581. 2. To complete by putting the top on, or forming the top of (a stack, etc.); often *to t. up*; hence (*colloq.*) to finish *off*, round *off*, crown 1504. b. *absol.* or *intr.* To finish *up* or *off* (*with* something). *colloq.* 1836. 3. *trans.* a. *Dyeing.* To give a final bath of colour to; to finish *off* (a dyeing process) with a certain dye. b. To top-dress (land). c. To stain the tips of the hair of (fur). 1856. †4. To 'cover', copulate with (*rare*) –1633.

2. *To t. up* (Electr.): to maintain the acid level in an accumulator, by adding distilled water. b. Then you..find the inmates of another room topping off with chocolate or coffee 1870. Everything went wrong.., and to t. up with I got the fever badly 1885. 4. *Oth.* III. iii. 396.

III. To exceed or come up to in height. 1. *trans.* To exceed in height; to overtop; also, to exceed in weight, amount, number, etc. 1582. b. To surpass, excel, outdo; to cap 1586. 2. To rise above; to mount beyond the level of 1773. b. To get or leap over the top of 1735. 3. To ascend to the top of 1600. 4. *Theatr. To t. one's part*, to play one's part to its utmost possibilities; also, to transcend the character assigned to one; *transf.* to sustain (a character) with success 1672. 5. To be at the top of, constitute the top of 1615. b. To get the better of 1633.

1. She was so tall that she topped her father..by a head 1887. b. Topping all others in boasting Shaks. 3. Wind about, till thou have topp'd the Hill Denham. 5. The decent church that topt the neighbouring hill Goldsm. In character as in intellect Bacon tops the list 1861.

Phrases. *To t. a ball* (Golf), to hit the ball above its centre; so *to t. one's drive*. *To t. a saw* (*U.S.*), to fix a stiffening piece or a gauge for limiting the depth of the cut.

Top (tǫp), *v.*[2] 1549. [perh. a special application of prec.] I. *Naut.* 1. *trans.* To tip *up* or slant (a yard) by tilting up one arm and depressing the other. 2. *intr.* To assume a slanting position, tip *up*, tilt *up* 1860. II. †1. *intr.* = Topple *v.* 1. –1620. 2. *trans.* = Topple *v.* 3. *Obs.* exc. *dial.* 1662.

Toparch (tǫ·paɹk). 1640. [ad. Gr. τοπάρχης, f. τόπος place + -αρχης ruler.] The ruler or prince of a small district, city, or petty state; a petty 'king'. So **Topa·rchical** *a.* of or pertaining to a t. or toparchy.

Toparchy (tǫ·paɹki). 1601. [ad. L. *toparchia* (also used), a. Gr. τοπαρχία, f. τοπάρχης Toparch.] The small district or territory under the rule of a toparch.

Topass (tōu·pǎs). *India.* 1680. [a. Pg. *topaz*, app. ad. *tōpāshī*, Malayālam form of Hindī *dōbāshī* man of two languages, interpreter.] A dark-skinned half-breed of Portuguese descent; often applied to a soldier, or a ship's scavenger or bath-attendant, who is of this class.

Topaz (tōu·pæz). [ME. a. OF. *topaze*, *topace*, *-ase*, ad. L. *topazus*, a. Gr. τόπαζος.] 1. a. The name given by the Greeks and Romans to the *yellow* or *oriental t.*, a yellow sapphire or corundum; by Pliny also to the modern chrysolite. b. In mod. use (*true* or *occidental t.*), a fluosilicate of aluminium, transparent and lustrous, yellow, white, pale blue, or pale green, found in Brazil, Mexico, Saxony, Scotland, the Ural Mountains, etc. 2. *Her.* In blazoning by precious stones, the tincture Or 1562.

1. *False t.*, a transparent pale yellow variety of quartz. *Pink t.*, pink or rose-coloured t., artificially produced by exposing the yellow Brazilian stone to strong heat.

Comb.: **t. humming-bird**, two S. Amer. species of humming-bird of brilliant colours, *Topaza pella* and *T. pyra*.

Topazolite (topæ·zoləit). 1819. [f. Gr. τόπαζος Topaz + λίθος stone; see -lite.] *Min.* A variety of garnet resembling topaz in colour.

Top-boot (tǫ·pˌbū·t). 1813. [f. Top *sb.*[1] + Boot *sb.*[3]] 1. *prop.* A high boot, having a top of white, light-coloured, or brown leather or the like (Top *sb.*[1] III. 2); now worn by hunting men, jockeys, grooms, and coachmen. Usu. in *pl.* 2. Improperly applied to any long or high boots which partly cover the leg 1891.

†**Top-castle.** ME. An embattled platform at the head of a ship's masts, from which missiles were discharged –1688.

To·p-dre:ss, *v.* 1733. [f. Top *sb.*[1] + Dress *v.*] *trans.* To manure on the surface, as land, grass, or any crop. Also *absol.*

To·p-dre:ssing, *vbl. sb.* 1764. [f. as prec.] The application of manure to the surface of the soil; *concr.* the manure or fertilizer so applied. Also *transf.* and *fig.*

Tope (tōup), *sb.*[1] 1686. [perh. Cornish name.] A small species of shark, *Galeus galeorhinus* or *G. canis*, native to British seas, esp. off the coast of Cornwall. Called also *dog-fish*, *penny-dog*, *miller's-dog*. b. The Australasian species, *Galeus australis* 1898.

Tope (tōup), *sb.*[2] 1813. A local name for the wren.

‖**Tope** (tōup), *sb.*[3] *India.* 1698. [ad. Tamil *tōppu*, Telegu *tōpu*.] A clump, grove, or plantation of trees; in Upper India, chiefly of fruit-trees; *esp.* a mango grove or orchard.

‖**Tope** (tōup), *sb.*[4] *India.* 1815. [a. Hind. (Panjābī) *tōp*, held to be:—Prākrit or Pālī *thūpo*:—Skr. *stūpa*.] In India and south-eastern Asia: An ancient structure, in the form of a dome or tumulus of masonry, for the preservation of relics or in commemoration of some fact; usu. of Buddhist or Jain origin.

Tope, *v.* Now only *literary* or *arch.* 1654. [Origin obsc.] 1. *trans.* To drink, *esp.* to drink copiously and habitually. 2. *intr.* To drink largely or in large draughts 1667.

2. I'll T. with you, I'll Sing with you, I'll Dance with you Dryden.

†**Tope**, *int.* 1651. [app. a. F. *top*, *tope*, *tôpe*, ellipt. for *je tope* I accept the wager; orig. a word of dice-play; = It. *toppa* 'done!' Used also in drinking.] An exclam. used in drinking; app. = I pledge you –1664.

Toper (tōu·pəɹ). Now chiefly *literary*. 1673. [f. Tope *v.* + -er [1].] One who topes or drinks a great deal; a hard drinker; a drunkard.

Top-full (tǫ·pfu·l), *a.* Now *rare.* 1553. [f. Top *sb.*[1] + Full *a.*] Full to the top; brimfull. †b. *transf.* Said of that which fills (to the top): Brimming (*rare*) –1608.

A huge great purse top full of gold 1617. *fig.* Topfull of busines as I am 1648.

Topgallant (tǫpgæ·lănt, təgæ·lănt), *sb.* and *a.* 1514. [f. Top *sb.*[1] III. 1 + Gallant *a.*, as making a gallant show in comparison with the lower tops.] **A.** *sb.* †1. *Naut.* A 'top' at the head of the topmast, and thus in a loftier position than the original top-castle or top 1590. 2. *pl.* Short for *t. sails*, the sails above the topsail and topgallant 1599. 3. a. *transf.* (from 1 and 2) The most elevated (*lit.* or *fig.*) part or member *of* anything 1581. b. *fig.* The highest point or pitch; summit 1592.

2. She had..got up..jury-masts, with topgallants for topsails Marryat. 3. b. Which to the high top gallant of my ioy, Must be my conuoy in the secret night Shaks.

B. *attrib.* or *adj.* 1. Of, pertaining to, or having the position of topgallant 1514. 2. Allowing topgallant sails to be used, as *t. weather* 1697. 3. *fig.* Lofty, grand, topping 1613.

1. *T. mast*, *sail*, *yard*, the mast, sail, or yard above the topmast and topsail; the third mast, sail, or yard above the deck. 2. The wind..blew what seamen call a top-gallant breeze 1806.

Toph(e (tǫuf). Now *rare.* 1552. [ad. L. Tophus.] 1. usu. *toph stone*: = Tophus 1. 2. *Path.* = Tophus 2. 1584.

Tophaceous (tofēi·ʃəs), *a.* 1672. [ad. L. *tof-*, *tophaceus*, f. Tophus; see -aceous.] 1. Of the nature of tophus; sandy, gritty; rough, stony. 2. *Path.* Gritty or calcareous, as the matter deposited in gout 1687.

To·p-ha·mper. 1791. [f. Top *sb.*[1] + Hamper *sb.*[2]] *Naut.* Weight or encumbrance aloft; orig. said of the upper masts, sails, and rigging of a ship; later, also, weight or encumbrance on the deck, as in a steamer, ironclad, etc.

To·p-ha·t. *colloq.* 1881. A man's silk or beaver hat with high cylindrical crown; a tall or high hat.

Top-heavy (stress var.), *a.* 1533. Disproportionately heavy at the top; having the upper part so heavy as to overbalance the lower; hence, unstable and inclined to topple. b. Said of an intoxicated person: Tipsy 1687.

Tophet (tōu·fĕt). late ME. [a. Heb. *topheth*; etym. uncertain.] 1. *orig.* Proper name of a place near Gehenna or the Valley of the Son or Children of Hinnom, south of Jerusalem, where the Jews made human sacrifices to strange gods (Jer. xix. 4). Later, it was used as a place for the deposit of refuse, and became symbolic of the torments of hell. 2. The place of punishment for the wicked after death; hell, Gehenna. late ME. 3. *fig.* A place, state, condition, or company likened to hell 1618.

1. [Moloch] made his Grove The pleasant valley of Hinnom, Tophet thence And black Gehenna call'd, the Type of Hell Milt. 2. *Isa.* xxx. 33.

†**To·phous**, *a.* 1634. [ad. rare L. *toph-*, *tofosus*, f. next; see -ous.] Of the nature of a stony or calcareous concretion –1756.

‖**Tophus** (tōu·fəs). *Pl.* ‖**tophi** (əi). 1555. [a. L. *tophus*, better *tofus*, a general name for loose porous stones of various kinds, whence It. *tufo*, F. *tuf*; see also TUFF, TUFA.] 1. A soft porous stone, arenaceous, calcareous, or volcanic; *esp.* a stony substance deposited by calcareous springs. 2. *Path.* A concretion which forms on the surface of the joints, the teeth, the pinna of the ear, etc. in gout; a gouty deposit; also gravel, or a stone or calculus, formed within the body 1607.

Comb.: t.-stone = TRAVERTINE.

‖**Topi, topee** (to̤pī·). *India.* 1826. [a. Hindī *ṭopī* hat.] Orig. applied by Indian natives to the European hat; now *spec.* in Anglo-Indian, as a name for the *sola topi*, sola hat or helmet: see SOLA *sb.*

Topiarian (tōupiˌēᵊ·riăn), *a.* 1694. [f. L. *topiarius*; see -AN.] = TOPIARY.

‖**Topiarius** (tōupiˌēᵊ·riŏs). 1706. [L. adj. 'of or belonging to ornamental gardening'; sb. 'an ornamental gardener'; f. L. *topia*, a. Gr. τόπια, pl. of τόπιον, dim. of τόπος place.] One skilled in fanciful landscape-gardening.

Topiary (tōu·piări), *a.* (*sb.*) 1592. [ad. rare L. *topiarius*; see prec.] *Gardening.* Consisting in clipping and trimming shrubs, etc. into ornamental or fantastic shapes. **B.** *sb.* The topiary art 1908.

Topic (tǫ·pik), *a.* and *sb.* 1568. [As adj., ad. Gr. τοπικός of or pertaining to τόπος a place, local, or concerning τόποι commonplaces; see -IC. As *sb.*, ad. L. *topica*, a. Gr., in τὰ τοπικά, title of a work of Aristotle, lit. matters concerning τόποι.] †**A.** *adj.* 1. Pertaining to or of the nature of a 'commonplace' (COMMONPLACE A. 1) or general maxim –1653. b. Containing 'commonplaces'; *t. folio*, a commonplace-book –1644. 2. Of or pertaining to a particular place or locality; local –1793. b. *Med.* Of or pertaining to a particular part of the body; designed for external local application –1671.

B. 1. *pl.* As title of the treatise of Aristotle, or as name for a work of the same nature, or for a set of general rules or maxims 1568. †2. A kind or class of considerations suitable to the purpose of a rhetorician or disputant, passing into the sense 'consideration', 'argument' –1840. †b. A head under which arguments or subjects may be arranged –1806. 3. The subject of a discourse, argument, or literary composition; a theme; also, a subject of admiration, animadversion, satire, mockery, or other treatment 1720. †4. *Med.* An external remedy locally applied, as a plaster or blister –1758.

1. These Topics or Loci, were no other than general ideas applicable to a great many different subjects, which the Orator was directed to consult, in order to find out materials for his Speech 1783. 2. These strong topics, in favour of the house of Lancaster, were opposed by arguments no less convincing on the side of the house of York HUME. 3. He had exhausted every t. of conversation 1797.

Topical (tǫ·pikăl), *a.* 1588. [f. as prec. + -AL.] 1. Of or pertaining to a place or locality; local. b. *Med.* That belongs or is applied to a particular part of the body 1608. †2. Pertaining to a topic or general maxim; hence, not demonstrative but merely probable –1710. 3. Of or pertaining to a general heading, a topic or subject of discourse, composition, etc. 1856. b. Of or pertaining to the topics of the day; containing local or temporary allusions 1873.

1. Their truth is not t. and transitory, but of universal acceptation 1870. 2. This Argument is..but Topicall and probable 1624. 3. b. A great many 't.' allusions to events of the hour, and rough political hits 1881. As *sb.*, a film dealing with t. events. **To·pically** *adv.* in a t. manner; in reference to topics.

Topknot (tǫ·pˌnǫt). 1686. [f. TOP *sb.*¹ + KNOT *sb.*¹] 1. a. A knot or bow of ribbon worn on the top of the head by ladies towards the end of the 17th and in the 18th century; later, a bow of ribbon worn in a lace cap. b. A tuft of hair on the top or crown of the head of a person or animal; also, a plume or crest of feathers or filaments on the head of a bird 1700. c. The head. *slang.* 1869. 2. *transf.* a. One who wears a topknot 1697. b. One of several species of small European flatfish, with a tapering filament on the head 1832. Hence **To·pknotted** *a.* having a t.

Topless (tǫ·plės), *a.* 1589. [f. TOP *sb.*¹ + -LESS.] 1. Having no top (*rare*) 1596. 2. *fig.* Seeming to have no top or summit; immensely or immeasurably high; unbounded 1589.

2. The glister of the Sunne vpon the toplesse Promontorie of Sicilia GREENE. My toplesse villany 1602.

Topman (tǫ·pmæ̆n). 1513. [f. TOP *sb.*¹ + MAN *sb.*] †1. A ship with a top on its mast –1577. 2. *Naut.* A seaman stationed in one of the tops, to attend to the upper sails, or in a fighting ship as a marksman 1748. 3. a. The upper man in a saw-pit 1678. b. A miner or pitman working at the top of the shaft 1890.

Topmast (tǫ·pˌmast, -məst). 1485. A smaller mast fixed on the top of a lower mast; *spec.* the second section of a mast above the deck, which was formerly the uppermost mast, but is now surmounted by the topgallant mast.

Topmost (tǫ·pmoᵘst, -mŏst), *a.* 1697. [f. TOP *sb.*¹ + -MOST.] Uppermost, highest. Also *absol.*, highest part.

The..spear..shore away the t. of his crest MORRIS.

Topo-, bef. a vowel **top-**, a. Gr. τοπο-, comb. f. τόπος place, as in τοπο-γράφος (see next).

Topographer (tǒpǫ·grăfəɹ). 1603. [f. Gr. τοπογράφος + -ER ¹.] One who is skilled in topography; one who describes or delineates a particular locality.

Topographic (tǫpǒgræ·fik), *a.* 1632. [ad. Gr. τοπογραφικός, f. stem of τοπογραφία TOPOGRAPHY: see -IC.] = next.

Topographical (tǫpǒgræ·fikăl), *a.* 1570. [f. as prec. + -ICAL.] Of, pertaining to, or dealing with topography. Hence **Topogra·phically** *adv.*

Topo·graphize, *v.* 1810. [f. as. TOPOGRAPHER + -IZE.] a. *trans.* To describe or treat topographically. b. *intr.* To make topographical researches.

Topography (tǒpǫ·grăfi). late ME. [ad. late L. *topographia*, ad. Gr. τοπογραφία, f. τοπογράφος; see above and -GRAPHY.] 1. The science or practice of describing a particular place, city, town, manor, parish, or tract of land; the accurate and detailed delineation and description of any locality 1549. b. A detailed description or delineation of the features of a locality. late ME. c. Localization, local distribution; the study of this 1658. 2. The features of a region or locality collectively 1847.

2. *fig.* I am not so well acquainted with the t. of the mind 1764.

Topology (tǒpǫ·lǒdʒi). 1659. [f. TOPO- + -LOGY.] 1. †a. The department of botany which treats of the localities where plants are found. 2. The scientific study of a particular locality 1850.

2. The comparatively new study of topology, the science by which, from the consideration of geographical facts about a locality, one can draw deductions as to its history 1905.

Toponymy (tǒpǫ·nĭmi). 1876. [f. TOPO- + Gr. -ωνυμια, f. ὄνομα name.] The place-names of a country or district as a subject of study. Also **Topony·mic, -ical** *adjs.*

Topped (tǫpt), *ppl. a.* 1459. [f. TOP *sb.*¹, *v.*¹ + -ED.] 1. Having or furnished with a top or tops. 2. Having the top removed; of a tree: polled, pollarded 1712.

Topper (tǫ·pəɹ). Chiefly *slang* or *low colloq.* 1709. [f. TOP *sb.*¹ + -ER ¹.] 1. A 'top' thing or person; the best or one of the best of the kind. *colloq.* 2. A top-hat, a tall hat. *slang* and *colloq.* 1820. 3. *pl.* The largest and finest fruit (orig. esp. strawberries) displayed at the top of a punnet, package, or pile. *slang.* 1839.

To·p-piece. 1682. The piece that forms or is at the top of anything; *spec.* †a. The *chef-d'œuvre*, masterpiece. BUNYAN. b. The head. *colloq.* 1838. c. *Shoe-making.* The piece put on and nailed down to the lifts of the heels 1911.

To·pping, *vbl. sb.* ¹ late ME. [f. TOP *v.*¹ + -ING ¹.] 1. The action of TOP *v.*¹ in various senses 1504. 2. A distinct part or appendage which forms a top to anything, a crest; as a forelock of the hair, the crest of a bird; also *joc.* the head. late ME. 3. That which is put on the top of anything to complete it; a top layer 1839. 4. *pl.* a. Cuttings from the tops of trees; also, the tops of hemp removed in hatchelling. b. The second skimmings of milk. *dial.* c. The best bran. *dial.* 1531.

To·pping, *vbl. sb.*² 1743. [f. TOP *v.*² + -ING ¹.] The action of TOP *v.*²

T.-lift (Naut.), each of a pair of lifts by which a yard may be topped.

To·pping, *ppl. a.* 1681. [f. TOP *v.*¹ + -ING ².] That tops, in various senses of TOP *v.*¹ †1. *lit.* That exceeds in height; very high (*rare*) –1705. 2. *fig.* Very high or superior in position, rank, estimation, etc.; chief, principal; pre-eminent, distinguished; overhanging; 'towering' 1674. 3. Of high quality; very fine, excellent; tip-top, first-rate. *colloq.* and *slang.* 1822. 4. Domineering; confident, boastful. *U.S.* 1885.

2. Some of the t. Sinners of the World 1716. 3. We came on at a t. pace 1841. Hence **To·pping·ly** *adv.* (*slang.* or *dial.*), **-ness.**

Topple (tǫ·p'l), *v.* 1590. [f. TOP *v.*¹ + -LE 3.] 1. *intr.* To fall top foremost, or as if top-heavy; to fall headlong, tumble or pitch over. 2. To lean over unsteadily, as if on the point of falling; to overhang threateningly 1827. 3. *trans.* To cause to tumble over or fall headlong; to thrust over, overturn, throw down 1596. 4. To cause to tip or tilt so as to be in danger of being upset (*rare*) 1656.

1. Though castles t. on their Warders heads SHAKS. 2. Masses of granite..toppling above the terminal face of the glacier TYNDALL. 3. They t. over the biggest trees in this way 1907.

Topsail (tǫ·psē̆l, tǫ·ps'l). late ME. [f. TOP *sb.*¹ III. 1 + SAIL *sb.*] A sail set above the lower course, orig. the uppermost sail. In a square-rigged vessel, orig. a single square sail set next above the lower sail or yard; now, in larger ships, divided into an *upper* and a *lower t.* (*double topsails*). In a fore-and-aft rig, a square or triangular sail set above the gaff.

fig. You may tell Your Pope, that..I shall not strike a t. for the breath Of all his maledictions! SOUTHEY.

To·p-saw·yer. 1823. a. The sawyer who works the upper handle of a pit-saw. Hence, b. *fig.* One who holds a superior position; the best man 1826. c. *loosely.* A first-rate hand at something; a distinguished person 1823.

Topside (tǫ·psəid), *sb.* (*adv.*) 1677. [f. TOP *sb.*¹ + SIDE *sb.*¹] a. *gen.* The upper side of anything. b. *Shipbuilding.* The upper part of a ship's side 1815. c. *Butchering.* The outer side of a round of beef, cut from the haunch between the 'leg' and the 'aitch-bone'; the bottom of this is the 'silver-side' 1898. **B.** *adv.* On the top. Also *fig.* (*colloq.*) 1873.

To·psman. *dial.* and *slang.* 1825. [f. *top's*, genitive of TOP *sb.*¹ + MAN *sb.*] 1. *Sc.* and *n. dial.* A head man, bailiff, or principal servant; *esp.* the chief drover in charge of a herd of cattle on the road. 2. *slang.* A hangman 1825.

To·p-stone. 1658. A stone which is placed upon or forms the top of something; a cap-stone: chiefly *fig.* Also, the upper end-stone or jewel in a chronometer.

To·psy-tu·rn, *v.* Now *rare.* 1573. [f. *topsy* as in next + TURN *v.*] *trans.* To turn topsy-turvy, turn upside down; *fig.* to throw into confusion.

Topsy-turvy (tǫ·psiˌtv̄·ɹvi), *adv.* (*a.*, *sb.*, and *v.*) 1528. [The first element is almost certainly *top* (or *tops*), and prob. the second is related to *terve* vb. to turn, turn over, overturn (cf. prec.); for the terminal elements *-sy* and *-y* cf. ARSY-VERSY.] With the top where the bottom should be; in or into an inverted position; upside down, bottom upwards.

A chaos of carts, overthrown and jumbled together, lay t. at the bottom of a..hill DICKENS. *fig.* I found nature turned topsy-turvey, women changed into men, and men into women ADDISON.

B. *adj.* Turned upside down; inverted, reversed; *fig.* utterly confused or disorderly 1618.

A very t. way of reasoning 1887.

C. *sb.* The act of turning or fact of being turned upside down; state of utter confusion or disorder 1655. **D.** as *vb. trans.* To turn topsy-turvy or upside down; to invert; *fig.* to reverse; to throw into utter confusion 1626.

My poor mind is all topsy-turvied RICHARDSON.

To·p-ti·mber. 1626. *Shipbuilding.* One of the uppermost timbers in the side of a ship, one of the timbers forming the topside.

Toque (tōuk, ‖tok). 1505. [a. F., app. the same word as It. *tocca* cap, etc. Ult. origin unkn.] **1. a.** A kind of small cap or bonnet worn by men and women in various countries. **b.** A kind of bonnet, cap, or, as now worn by women, a small hat without a brim, or with a very small or closely turned-up brim 1817. **2.** *T. monkey*, also simply *t.*: the bonnet-monkey or bonnet-macaque, *Macacus pileatus*, a native of Ceylon 1840.

Tor (tǭɹ). OE. [prob. cogn. w. Gael. *tòrr* hill of an abrupt or conical form, lofty hill, eminence, mound grave, heap of ruins, primarily heap, pile.] **1.** A high rock; a pile of rocks, *gen.* on the top of a hill; a rocky peak; a hill. **2.** *attrib.* **T. ouzel**, local name of the ring ouzel, *Turdus torquatus* 1770.

1. Mount St. Michaells a Steepe and most craggie torr 1610.

‖**Torah** (tōᵒ·rā). 1577. [Heb. *tōrāh* direction, instruction, doctrine, law.] The teaching or instruction, and judicial decisions, given by the ancient Hebrew priests as a revelation of the divine will; the Mosaic or Jewish law; hence, a name for the five books of the law, the Pentateuch.

Torbanite (tǭ·ɹbănəit). 1858. [f. *Torbane* Hill in Linlithgowshire, where found; see -ITE [1].] *Min.* A deep brown shale, allied to cannel coal, valuable for the production of petroleum and gas.

Torbernite (tǭ·ɹbəɹnəit). 1852. [ad. G. *torbernit*, f. *Torbernus*, latinized form of the name of the chemist *Torber* Bergmann. See -ITE [1].] *Min.* A native phosphate of uranium and copper, found in bright green tubular crystals; also called *copper-uranite*.

Torch (tǭɹtʃ), *sb.* ME. [a. OF. *torche*, app. :—late pop. L. **torca*, from stem *tork-* of *torquere* to twist.] **1.** A light to be carried in the hand or upon a pole or the like, consisting of a stick of resinous wood, or of twisted hemp or the like soaked with tallow, resin, or other inflammable substance. In church use, a large candle for carrying. **b.** *fig.* or *allus.* Something figured as a source of illumination, enlightenment, or guidance, or of heat or 'conflagration' 1621. **2.** *transf.* **a.** A spike composed of spikelets; also *fig.* said of a red or flame-coloured flower 1578. **b.** (Usu. in *pl.* **Torches.**) The Great Mullein, *Verbascum Thapsus* (or other species): from its tall spike of yellow flowers 1552.

1. *Electric t.*, a contrivance consisting essentially of an electric lamp enclosed in a portable case containing a battery. **b.** The t. of Greek learning and civilisation was to be extinguished 1878. *To hand on the t.*, to preserve the knowledge of a subject.

attrib. and *Comb.*: **t.-fishing**, fishing by t.-light at night; **-lily**, the liliaceous genus *Tritoma*, having spikes of bright scarlet flowers; also called 'red-hot poker'; **-race** = LAMPADEDROMY; **-thistle**, a name for a columnar cactus of the genus *Cereus*. Hence **Torch** *v. trans.* to furnish, or light, with a t. or torches. †**To·rcher**, = next SHAKS.

To·rch-bea:rer. 1538. One who carries a torch.

To·rch-light. late ME. The light of a torch; illumination by a torch or torches. **b.** The time when torches are lighted; dusk 1656. **c.** *attrib.* Performed or carried on by torch-light 1876.

c. In the evening, a t. procession 1876.

‖**Torchon** (torʃoṅ). 1879. [F., duster, dish-cloth; f. *torcher* to wipe.] Used *attrib.* in **t. board**, a board covered with *t. paper*, used in water-colour drawing; **t. lace** (also abbrev. *torchon*, pl. *-ons*), a coarse bobbin lace, of loose texture; **t. paper**, a kind of paper with a rough surface, used for water-colour drawing, etc.

To·rch-wood. 1601. **1.** Resinous wood of which torches are made. **2. a.** A tree of the genus *Amyris*, family *Rutaceæ*, having resinous wood, as *A. sylvatica* and *A. balsamifera*. **b.** A W. Indian shrub, *Casearia* (*Thiodia*) *serrata*. **c.** A species of cactus, *Cereus heptagonus*.

‖**Torcular** (tǭ·ɹkiulăɹ). 1621. [L., a press for wine or oil.] **1.** *Anat.* (in full *t. Herophili*) = †*Press of Herophilus*: a depression in the occipital bone at the confluence of a number of venous sinuses. **2.** *Surg.* A tourniquet 1727. So **To·rcular** *a.* pertaining to the *t. Herophili*.

Tore (tōᵒɹ), *sb.* 1664. [a. F., ad. L. *torus*.] = TORUS 1, 4.

Tore: see TEAR *v.*

Toreador (tǫriădōᵒ·ɹ). 1618. [Sp., f. *torear* to fight bulls, f. *toro* (:—L. *tauru-s*) bull.] A Spanish (usu. mounted) bull-fighter.

†**To-re·nd**, *v.* [OE. *tórendan*: see TO-2, REND *v.*] *trans.* To rend in pieces –1631.

‖**Torero** (torē·ro). 1728. [Sp.] A (Spanish) bull-fighter (on foot).

Toreutic (torū·tik), *a.* and *sb.* 1837. [ad. Gr. τορευτικός, f. τορεύειν to work in relief, etc.] **A.** *adj.* Of or pertaining to toreutics; chiefly in phr. *t. art* = toreutics; also, of figures, etc., executed according to the toreutic art; of an artist, working in toreutics. **B.** *sb.* [tr. Gr. τορευτική (sc. τέχνη).] Chiefly in pl. **Toreutics**: The art of chasing, carving, and embossing, esp. metal.

‖**Torgoch** (tǭ·ɹgǫχ). Also †**torcoch.** 1611. [Welsh, f. *tor* belly + *coch* red.] The red-bellied char, found in the Welsh lakes.

Toric (tōᵒ·rik), *a.* 1900. [f. TOR-US + -IC.] Of or pertaining to a torus (see TORUS 4).

T. lens, a spectacle lens having for one of its surfaces a segment of an equilateral zone of a torus. Also *ellipt.* as *sb.*

Torment (tǭ·ɹmĕnt), *sb.* [ME. a. OF. *torment*, *tourment* :—L. *tormentum*, f. *torquere* to twist. In sense 5, a. F. *tourmente*, from L. *tormenta* neut. pl.] †**1.** An engine of war worked by torsion, for hurling stones, darts, etc. –1531. **2.** An instrument of torture; hence, the infliction of torture by such an instrument; torture inflicted or suffered ME. **b.** *spec.* The punishment of hell 1852. **3.** A state of great suffering, bodily or mental; agony; severe pain felt or endured ME. **4.** An action, circumstance, or condition which causes extreme pain or suffering of body or mind; a source of pain, trouble, or anguish, or in weakened sense, of worry or annoyance 1599. **b.** Applied to a person who causes trouble 1784. **5.** A violent storm; a tempest, tornado. *Obs.* exc. in F. form *tourmente*. ME.

2. It was a t. To lay upon the damn'd SHAKS. 3. That doubleth al my t. and my wo CHAUCER. 4. Why, death 's the end of evils, and a rest Rather than t. B. JONS. The conviction that he had made himself absurd..was his t. 1825.

Torment (tǫɹme·nt), *v.* ME. [a. OF. *torment*-, *tourmenter*, f. *tor*-, *tourment*.] **1.** *trans.* To put to torment or torture; to inflict torture upon. **2.** To afflict or vex with great suffering or misery, physical or mental; to pain, distress, plague ME. **b.** To tease or worry excessively; to trouble, 'plague' 1718. **3.** To throw into agitation; to toss, disturb, shake up, or stir physically. *Obs.* exc. as a Gallicism. 1491. **b.** *fig.* To twist, distort (sense, style, etc.) 1647.

1. For what offences..men are to be Eternally tormented HOBBES. 2. **b.** We are tormenting our brains with some scheme of politics 1718. 3. That warr.. soaring on main wing Tormented all the Air MILT.

Tormentil (tǭ·ɹmĕntil). late ME. [= F. *tormentille*, ad. med.L. *tormentilla*, in form dim. of *tormentum* TORMENT *sb.* Reason of name obscure.] A low-growing rosaceous herb, *Potentilla Tormentilla* (*T. repens*), of trailing habit, common on heaths and dry pastures, and having strongly astringent roots; in use from early times in medicine, and in tanning. Also called *septfoil*.

Torme·nting, *ppl. a.* 1575. [f. TORMENT *v.* + -ING [2].] That torments, in various senses.

Sight hateful, sight t.! MILT. Hence **Torme·nting·ly** *adv.*, **-ness.**

Tormentor (tǫɹme·ntǫɹ). [ME. a. AF. *torment(e)our* :—L. **tormentatorem*, f. *tormentare*.] **1.** An officer who inflicts torture or cruelty; an official torturer; an executioner. **2.** One who or that which persistently inflicts intense pain, suffering, vexation, or annoyance 1553. **3.** An instrument that torments in some way, as a wheel-harrow for breaking up stiff soil; *pl.* riding spurs (*slang*), etc. 1609.

2. These words heereafter, thy tormentors bee SHAKS.

Tormentress (tǫɹme·ntrĕs). late ME. [a. AF. *tormenteresse*, fem. of *tormentour*.] A female tormentor.

To·rmentry. Now *rare.* late ME. [a. OF. *tourmenterie*, f. *tormentour*; see -RY.] †**1.** The infliction or suffering of torture or torment, as by executioners or fiends –1534. **2.** Tormenting feeling; severe suffering, pain, or vexation. Now *rare.* late ME.

‖**Tormina** (tǭ·ɹminǎ), *sb. pl.* 1656. [L., gripes, pl. of **tormen*, f. *torquere* to twist.] *Path.* Acute griping or wringing pains in the bowels; gripes. Hence **To·rminal**, †**To·rminous** *adjs.* of the nature of or characterized by t.

Torn (tǭɹn), pa. pple. of TEAR *v.*[1]

‖**Tornada** (tǫɹnā·dă). 1823. [Prov., f. pa. pple. of *tornar* to turn.] An envoy of three lines, in which the verse-endings of the preceding stanzas recur.

Tornado (tǫɹnē·do). 1556. [In Hakluyt and his contemporaries, *ternado* perh. orig. a blundered spelling of Sp. *tronada* thunder-storm (f. *tronar* to thunder), referred later, in the form *tornado*, to Sp. *tornar* to turn, return.] **1.** A term applied by 16th c. navigators to violent thunder-storms of the tropical Atlantic, with torrential rain, and often with sudden and violent gusts of wind. Now *rare.* **2.** A very violent storm affecting a limited area, in which the wind is constantly changing its direction or rotating; a whirling wind, whirlwind; loosely, any very violent storm of wind, a hurricane 1626.

2. *fig.* One of Turner's magnificent tornadoes of colour THACKERAY. On this passage followed a great t. of cheering 1849. Hence **Tornadic** (tǫɹnæ·dik) *a.* of, pertaining to, or of the nature of a t.

‖**Tornaria** (tǫɹnē·riă). 1888. [mod.L., f. Gr. τόρνος or L. *tornus* a turner's wheel, in ref. to the shape of the larva.] *Zool.* The larval form of species of the Sea-acorn, *Balanoglossus.*

‖**Tornus** (tǭ·ɹnŏs). *Pl.* **-i** (-əi). 1897. [L., a. Gr. τόρνος tool for rounding (see TURN).] *Ent.* The inner or anal angle of the wing of an insect, esp. of the secondary wing of a tineid moth. Hence **To·rnal** *a.* of or pertaining to the t.

Torose (torōᵘ·s), *a.* 1760. [ad. L. *torosus*, f. *torus* bulge, brawn; see -OSE.] *Nat. Hist.* Bulging, swollen, protuberant: said of an approximately cylindrical body swollen here and there. So **To·rous** *a.* 1657.

Torpedinous (tǫɹpi·dinəs), *a.* *rare* or *Obs.* 1774. [f. L. *torpedinem*, TORPEDO + -OUS.] Having the quality of a torpedo; benumbing, paralysing; also, of or pertaining to the torpedo or electric ray.

Fishy were his eyes; t. was his manner DE QUINCEY.

Torpedo (tǫɹpī·do), *sb.* *Pl.* **-oes.** 1520. [a. L., stiffness, numbness, also the cramp-fish or electric ray, f. *torpere* to be stiff or numb.] **1.** A flat fish of the genus *Torpedo* or family *Torpedinidæ*, having an almost circular body with tapering tail, and characterized by the faculty of emitting electric discharges; the electric ray; also called *cramp-fish*, *cramp-ray*, *numb-fish*. **b.** *fig.* One who or that which has a benumbing influence 1590. **2.** *orig.* A case charged with gunpowder designed to explode under water after a given interval so as to destroy any vessel in its immediate vicinity; later also, a self-propelled submarine missile, usu. cigar-shaped, carrying an explosive which is fired by impact with its objective 1775. **b.** A type of car-body shaped like a torpedo 1909.

The original torpedo was a towed or drifting submarine mine, still used to defend channels, harbours, and the like (*drifting* or *moored t.*); it was towed at an angle by means of a spar extending at right angles (*otter* or *towing t.*), or carried on a ram or projecting pole (*boom-*, *outrigger-*, *spar-t.*).

3. a. *Mil.* A shell furnished with a percussion or friction device buried in the ground, which explodes when the ground above the device is trodden upon; a petard. *U.S.* **b.** A toy which explodes when thrown on a hard surface. **c.** A cartridge exploded in an oil-well to cause a renewal or increase of the flow. *U.S.* **d.** = FOG-SIGNAL 2 (*U.S.*). **e.** *Aerial t.*, a torpedo discharged from aircraft 1786.

attrib. and *Comb.*: **t.-anchor**, an anchor for mooring a stationary t.; **-beard**, a pointed beard; **-body**, a motor-car body tapered at the ends; **-boom**, a spar bearing a t. on its upper end, the lower end swivelled and anchored to the bottom of the channel; **t. destroyer**, a torpedo-boat destroyer (officially called simply 'a destroyer'); **t. gun** = *t.-tube*; **-net**, a steel-wire netting suspended round a ship on projecting booms as a protection against torpedoes; **-ram**, a ram provided with t.-tubes; **-spar**, a spar rigged to a t. boat, to which a t. is attached; **-tube**, a kind of gun from which torpedoes are discharged by compressed air or gunpowder.

Torpe·do, *v.* 1873. [f. prec.] **1.** *trans.* To destroy or damage by means of a torpedo; to attack with a torpedo 1879. **b.** To lay (a channel, etc.) with torpedoes or submarine mines; to defend with torpedoes 1877. **2.** To explode a 'torpedo' at the bottom of (an oil-well) to increase the flow by shattering the rock or clearing the passage. Also *intr. U.S.* 1873.

Torpe·do boat. 1810. A vessel carrying one or more torpedoes; now, a small, fast warship from which torpedoes are discharged.

Comb. **torpedo-boat catcher, torpedo-boat destroyer** (abbrev. *t.b.d.*), two types of small fast war-ships, orig. designed to prevent torpedo-boats from operating against a fleet.

Torpid (tǭ·ɹpid), *a.* (*sb.*) 1613. [ad. L. *torpidus* benumbed, f. *torpere.*] **1.** Benumbed; deprived or devoid of the power of motion or feeling; dormant. **b.** *Path.* Sluggish in action or function 1807. **2.** *fig.* Wanting in animation or vigour; inactive; slow, sluggish; dull; stupefied; apathetic 1656.

1. Some animals became t. in winter, others were t. in summer EMERSON. **b.** Tendency to t. liver 1899. 2. It is a man's own fault..if his mind grows t. in old age JOHNSON.

B. *sb.* At Oxford: usu. *pl.* The races rowed in Lent term in eight-oared clinker-built open boats; orig. designating the boats; later also the crews 1838. Hence **To·rpid·ly** *adv.*, **-ness.**

Torpidity (tǫɹpi·dĭti). 1614. [f. prec. + -ITY.] The condition or quality of being torpid; torpor, sluggishness, numbness.

Torpitude (tǭ·ɹpitiūd). Now *rare.* 1713. [irreg. for **torpetude*, f. L. *torpere* + -TUDE.] = prec.

Torpor (tǭ·ɹpǒɹ). 1607. [a. L., f. *torpere.*] Torpid condition or quality. **a.** Absence or suspension of motive power, activity, or feeling; †inertia; suspended animation or development; *Path.* morbid inertia or insensibility, stupor 1626. **b.** *transf.* Intellectual or spiritual lethargy; apathy; dullness; indifference 1607.

b. A universal t. of the mental faculties 1789.

Torporific (tǭɹpǒri·fik), *a.* (*sb.*) 1769. [f. L. *torporem* + -FIC.] Causing torpor; also *fig.* stupefying, deadening. **b.** *absol.* as *sb.* Something causing torpor 1840.

Torquate (tǭ·ɹkwe'it), *a.* 1661. [ad. L. *torquatus* wearing a TORQUES; see -ATE [2].] *Zool.* Having a ring-like marking, formed by hairs or feathers of special colour or texture, round the neck; collared.

To·rquated, *a.* 1623. [f. as prec. + -ED [1].] **1.** Wearing a torque. **2.** Formed as or like a torque; twisted from a narrow strip or band 1851. **3.** *Zool.* = prec. 1891.

Torque [1], **torc** (tǭɹk). 1834. [ad. L. *torques* TORQUES.] A collar, necklace, bracelet, or similar ornament, consisting of a twisted narrow band or strip, usu. of precious metal, worn especially by the ancient Gauls and Britons.

Torque [2] (tǭɹk). 1884. [f. L. *torquere* to twist.] *Physics.* The twisting or rotary force in a piece of mechanism (as a measurable quantity); the moment of a system of forces producing rotation. **b.** *attrib.*, as *t. rod, tube.*

Torqued (tǭɹkt), *a.* 1572. [After obs. F. *torqué, torquer*, ad. L. *torquere*; see -ED.] **1.** Twisted, convoluted; formed like a torque 1577. **2.** *Her.* Twisted or bent into a double curve like the letter S: said of a serpent or dolphin used as a bearing 1572.

‖**Torques** (tǭ·ɹkwīz). 1693. [L., f. *torquere.*] **1.** = TORQUE [1]. **2.** *Zool.* A collar or ring-like marking round the neck of an animal, formed by hair, feathers, etc. of special colour or texture 1891.

Torrefaction (tǫrĭfæ·kʃən). 1612. [f. L. *torrefacere* to TORREFY; see -TION.] The process of drying or roasting by fire; the state or condition of being roasted.

Torrefy (tǫ·rĭfəi), *v.* 1601. [a. F. *torréfier*, ad. L. *torrefacere* to dry by heat, f. *torrere* to dry, parch, roast + *facere*; see -FY.] **1.** *trans.* To roast, scorch, or dry by fire. **b.** To deprive of all moisture by heating, as a chemical or drug 1601. **c.** *Metall.* To roast, as ores, in order to deprive of sulphur, arsenic, or other volatile substance 1686. **2.** *intr.* To become reduced to a cinder or ash 1615.

Torrent (tǫ·rĕnt), *sb.* (*a.*) 1601. [a. F., ad. L. *torrentem* burning, boiling, rushing, f. *torrere* to scorch, burn; also as sb. a torrent.] **1.** A stream of water flowing with great swiftness and impetuosity, whether from the steepness of its course, or from being temporarily flooded; more esp. applied (as in F.) to a mountain stream which at times is swollen and at other times more or less dry. **2. a.** *fig.* A violent or tumultuous flow or 'stream', e.g. of words, feelings, opposition, etc. 1647. **b.** *transf.* A forcible stream, e.g. of lava, loose stones, wind, light; also, a violent downpour of rain 1781.

1. The dry beds of mountain torrents, which had lived too fierce a life to let it be a long one HAWTHORNE. **2. a.** A t. of abuse 1784. **b.** A soaking t. of rain 1806.

B. *adj.* Rushing like a torrent 1667.

A t. mountain-brook TENNYSON.

Torrential (tǫre·nʃăl), *a.* 1849. [f. L. *torrentem* + -IAL.] **1.** Of, pertaining to, or of the nature of a torrent; produced by the action of a torrent 1861. **2.** Like a torrent in rapidity or violence; rushing; falling in torrents, as rain 1849. **b.** *fig.* As copious or impetuous as a torrent 1877.

2. To the intense heat, .. has succeeded t. rain 1865.

Torricellian (tǫritʃe·liăn, tǫrise·liăn), *a.* 1660. [f. name of *Torricelli*, an Italian physicist (1608–1647) + -AN.] Of or belonging to Torricelli.

T. experiment, that by which, in 1643, Torricelli proved that the column of mercury in a closed tube inverted in a vessel of mercury is supported by the pressure of the atmosphere on the mercury in the vessel, and that the height of the column corresponds exactly to the atmospheric pressure. *T. tube*, early name for the tube of the mercurial barometer. *T. vacuum*, the vacuum above the mercurial column in the barometer, produced by filling the tube with mercury and then inverting it in a cup of mercury.

Torrid (tǫ·rid), *a.* 1586. [ad. L. *torridus*, f. *torrere* to dry with heat; see -ID.] **1.** Scorched, burned, exposed to great heat; also, intensely hot, burning, scorching 1611. **b.** *esp.* in *t. zone*, the region of the earth between the tropics 1586. **2.** *fig.* **a.** In ref. to the 'heat' of persecution 1635. **b.** Hot in temper or passion; ardent, zealous 1646.

1. A t. and scorched earth PURCHAS. **2. a.** In Maryes t. dayes.., when Cruelty was witty 1635. **b.** Temper'd 'twixt cold despair and t. joy CRASHAW. Hence **To·rrid·ly** *adv.*, **-ness. Torri·dity,** the state, condition, or quality of being t.

Torse [1] (tǭɹs). 1572. [a. obs. F. *torse* a wreath, f. stem *tors-* for L. *tort-* from *torquere* to twist.] *Her.* The twisted band or wreath by which the crest is joined to the helmet.

Torse [2] (tǭɹs). 1622. [a. F., ad. It. *torso.*] = TORSO.

Torse [3] (tǭɹs). 1863. [f. med.L. *torsus*, *-um*, for L. *tortus* twisted.] *Geom.* A developable surface; a surface generated by a moving straight line which at every instant is turning, in some plane or other through it, about some point or other in its length. Hence **To·rsal** *a.* of or pertaining to a t.

Torsibi·lity. 1864. [f. **torsible* (f. L. *tors-*, for *tort-*, *torquere*) + -ITY.] Capability of being twisted; esp. in ref. to degree or amount.

Torsile (tǭ·ɹsəil, -il), *a.* 1882. [f. L. *tors-* (see prec.) + -IL, -ILE.] Of the nature of torsion.

Torsion (tǭ·ɹʃən). late ME. [a. F., ad. late L. *torsionem*, by-form of *tortionem*, f. L. *torquere* to twist, wring.] **1.** The action of twisting, or turning a body spirally by the operation of contrary forces acting at right angles to its axis; also, the twisted condition produced by this action; twist 1543. **b.** A twisting of the body or a part of it (*rare*) 1660. **c.** *Surg.* The twisting of the cut end of an artery to stop hæmorrhage 1835. †**2.** *Path.* A wringing or griping of the bowels; tormina –1689.

1. *Angle of t.*, (*a*) the angle through which one end of a rod or other body is twisted while the other end is held fast; (*b*) *Geom.* the infinitesimal angle between two consecutive osculating planes of a tortuous curve. *Balance of t.* = t.-balance.

attrib. and *Comb.*: **t.-balance,** an instrument for measuring minute horizontal forces, consisting of a wire or filament having a horizontal arm to the end of which the force is applied so as to make it revolve and twist the wire, etc., through an angle proportional to the twisting moment of the force; **-curve,** a curve caused by t. Hence **To·rsional** *a.* of, pertaining or relating to, caused by or resulting from t.; **-ly** *adv.*

Torsk (tǭɹsk). 1680. [a. Norw. *torsk, tosk*, Sw., Da. *torsk*:—ON. *þorskr, þoskr*; prob. f. root of ON. *þurr* dry.] A gadoid fish, *Brosmius brosme*, much used for food in the dried form of *stockfish.*

Torso (tǭ·ɹsǫ). *Pl.* **torsos.** 1797. [a. It., stalk, stump, trunk of a statue:—L. *thyrsus* stalk, stem (of a plant), a. Gr. θύρσος THYRSUS.] **1.** *Sculpture.* The trunk of a statue, without or considered independently of head and limbs; also, the trunk of the human body. **2.** *fig.* Something left mutilated or unfinished 1852.

1. The T. of the Belvedere, a colossal fragment of Herculean stature 1875. Clad only in a waist-cloth, his t. was fully revealed 1899.

Tort (tǭɹt). ME. [a. OF., = med.L. *tortum*, subst. use of L. *tortus*, *-um* twisted, wrung.] †**1.** Injury, wrong –1748. **2.** *Eng. Law.* The breach of a duty imposed by law, whereby some person acquires a right of action for damages 1586.

1. No wild beasts should do them any torte SPENSER.

‖**Torta** (tǭ·ɹtă). 1839. [Sp., :—late L. *torta* cake.] *Mining.* One of the large flat circular heaps or 'cakes' of ore spread upon the floor or *patio* in the Mexican amalgamation process.

‖**Torteau** (tortō). *Pl.* **torteaux** (tortōuz, Fr. -ō). 1486. [a. F. *tourteau* large round cake or flat bannock of bread, etc., deriv. of *tourte*:—late L. *torta.*] **1.** *Her.* A roundle gules; the specific name of a small red circular figure charged upon a shield, supposed to represent a cake of bread. †**2.** A flat cake, a pancake. PURCHAS.

Tortfeasor (tǭ·ɹt,fī·zǫɹ). 1659. [a. OF. *tort-fesor, -faiseur*, etc., f. *tort* wrong, evil + *-fesor, faiseur* doer.] *Law.* One who is guilty of a tort; a wrong-doer, trespasser.

‖**Torticollis** (tǭɹtikǫ·lis). 1811. [mod.L., f. L. *tortus* crooked, twisted + *collum* neck.] *Path.* A rheumatic or other affection of the muscles of the neck, in which it is so twisted as to keep the head turned to one side; wry-neck.

Tortile (tǭ·ɹtəil, -il), *a. rare.* 1658. [ad. L. *tortilis*, f. *tort-*, *torquere*; see -IL, -ILE.] Twisted, coiled; winding; capable of being twisted. Hence **Torti·lity,** the quality of being t.

‖**Tortilla** (tortī·lʸa). 1699. [Sp. dim. of *torta* cake; see TORTA.] In Mexico, A thin round cake made of maize-flour, baked on a flat plate of iron, earthenware, etc. and eaten hot.

Tortious (tǭ·ɹʃəs), *a.* late ME. [a. Anglo-F. *torcious*, f. stem of *torcion, tortion*:—L. *tortionem* torment; see -IOUS. Later assoc. w. TORT *sb.*] †**1.** Wrongful, injurious, hurtful; illegal –1742. **2.** *Law.* Pertaining to or of the nature of a tort 1544.

1. A torcious vsurper HALL. Hence **To·rtiously** *adv.*

Tortive (tǭ·ɹtiv), *a. rare.* 1606. [ad. L. *tortivus*, f. *tort-*, *torquere*; see -IVE.] Twisting, twisted, tortuous.

Tortoise (tǭ·ɹtəs). [ult. from late pop. L. (and Romanic) *tortuca* (presumably f. L. *tortus* twisted, with ref. to the crooked feet of the S. European species), whence F. *tortue*, Sp. *tortuga*. The Engl. forms (late ME. onwards) have been various, *tortuce, -use* from L., *tortu(e* from Fr., superseded by *torteise, -esse* (16th–17th c.), and finally by the present form, which dates from the 16th c.] **1.** A four-footed reptile of the order *Chelonia*, in which the trunk is enclosed between a carapace and plastron, formed by the dorsal vertebræ, ribs, and sternum; the skin being covered with large horny plates, commonly called the shell.

The *Chelonia* are usually divided into Land tortoises (*Testudinidæ*), Marsh-tortoises (*Emydæ*), River-tortoises (*Trionycidæ*), and Marine tortoises (*Chelonidæ*). The last are now commonly distinguished as *turtles.* By some zoologists the name 'tortoise' is confined to the terrestrial genus *Testudo* and its immediate congeners; see also TERRAPIN.

b. A figure or image of a tortoise 1648. **c.** Taken as a type of slowness of motion; hence, applied to a very slow person or thing 1825.

2. = TESTUDO 3 a, b. 1569. 3. Short for TORTOISE-SHELL. Usu. *attrib.* or as *adj.* 1654.

2. His soldiers, protected from missiles by moveable penthouses (called Tortoises) GROTE. 3. A Gold Snuff-box,..the bottom T. 1702.

attrib. and *Comb.*: **t.-beetle**, a leaf-beetle of the family *Cassididæ*, from the resemblance of the wing-cases and prothorax to the carapace of a t.; **-lyre**, a lyre made of a t.-shell; **-plant**, a S. African plant, *Testudinaria elephantipes*, allied to the yam, having a large fleshy root-stock growing above ground, the surface of which becomes deeply cracked so as to suggest the carapace of a t.

Tortoise-shell (tǭ·ɹtəs,ʃəːl, *usually* tǭ·ɹtəʃel). 1601. 1. The shell, esp. the upper shell or carapace, of a tortoise, consisting of horny scales covering the dermal skeleton. b. As a material (without *a* or *pl.*): The shell of certain tortoises, esp. that of the hawk's-bill turtle, *Chelone imbricata*, which is semi-transparent, with a mottled or clouded coloration, and is much used in ornamental work, as inlaying, etc. 1632. †2. Short for (*a*) *t. cat*, (*b*) *t. butterfly* 1840. 3. *attrib.* or as *adj.* a. Made of tortoise-shell 1651. b. Having the colouring or appearance of tortoise-shell; mottled or variegated with black, red, and yellow, etc. 1782. c. Producing tortoise-shell 1886.

3. b. **T. butterfly**, one of several butterflies, esp. the European *Vanessa urticæ* and *V. polychlorus*, and the Amer. *Aglais milberti*; **t. cat**, a domestic cat of this colour. c. **T. turtle**, the hawk's-bill turtle, or other species from which t. is obtained.

Tortricid (tǭ·ɹtrisid), *a.* and *sb.* 1889. [f. mod.L. *Tortricidæ* pl., f. TORTRIX; see -ID [3].] a. *Ent. adj.* Belonging to the family *Tortricidæ* of *Lepidoptera*, comprising the leaf-roller moths, typified by the genus *Tortrix*; *sb.* a moth of this family. b. *Zool. adj.* Belonging to the family *Tortricidæ* of snakes, typified by the genus *Tortrix* or *Ilysia*; *sb.* a snake of this family.

‖**Tortrix** (tǭ·ɹtriks). *Pl.* **tortrices** (-əi·sīz). 1797. [mod.L.] 1. *Ent.* A genus of moths, typical of the family *Tortricidæ* (see prec. a); a moth of this genus or family, a leaf-roller moth. 2. *Zool.* A genus of snakes, also called *Ilysia*, including the coral-snake of Guiana, *T.* (*I.*) *scytale* 1843.

Tortuosity (tǭtiu,ǫ·sĭti). 1603. [ad. L. *tortuositas*, f. *tortuosus*; see -ITY.] The quality or condition of being tortuous; twistedness, crookedness, sinuosity; an instance of this.

Tortuous (tǭ·ɹtiu,əs), *a.* late ME. [a. AF., = 14th c. F. *tortueux*, ad. L. *tortuosus*, f. *tortus* a twisting, f. *tort-*, *torquere*.] 1. Full of twists, turns, or bends; winding, crooked, sinuous. b. *Geom.* Applied to a curve of which no two successive portions are in the same plane 1867. 2. *fig.* Not direct or straightforward; devious, circuitous, crooked: esp. in a moral sense 1682.

1. We found the river-course very t. DARWIN. 2. A more t. way of trying to get possession of goods he had never heard of 1911. Hence **To·rtuous·ly** *adv.*, **-ness.**

Torturable (tǭ·ɹtiŭrăb'l, -tʃər-), *a. rare.* 1655. [f. TORTURE *v.* + -ABLE.] Capable of being tortured.

Torture (tǭ·ɹtiŭɹ, -tʃəɹ), *sb.* 1540. [a. F., ad. L. *tortura*, f. *torquere*, *tort-* to twist, torment.] 1. The infliction of excruciating pain, as practised by cruel tyrants, savages, brigands, etc., in hatred or revenge, or as a means of extortion, etc.; spec. *judicial t.*, inflicted by a judicial or quasi-judicial authority, for the purpose of forcing an accused or suspected person to confess, or an unwilling witness to give evidence or information; a form of this (often in *pl.*) 1551. †b. *transf.* An instrument or means of torture –1722. 2. Severe or excruciating pain or suffering (of body or mind); anguish, agony, torment; the infliction of such 1540. b. *transf.* A cause of severe pain or anguish 1612. 3. *transf.* and *fig.* Severe pressure; violent perversion or 'wresting'; violent action or operation; severe testing or examination 1605.

1. *To put to (the) t.*, to inflict t. upon, to torture. 2. The tortures of suspense 1797. b. An ugly picture was t. to his cultivated eye 1873. 3. Much so-called wit..is nothing more than the systematic t. of words 1887.

To·rture, *v.* 1588. [f. prec.] I. *trans.* To inflict torture upon; *spec.* to subject to judicial torture; to put to the torture 1593. 2. To inflict severe pain or suffering upon; to torment; to distress or afflict grievously; also, to puzzle or perplex greatly. Also *absol.* to cause extreme pain. 1588. 3. *fig.* a. To act upon violently in some way, so as to strain, twist, distort, etc. 1626. b. To 'twist' (language, etc.) from the proper meaning or form; to distort 1648. 4. To extract by torture; to extort (*rare*) 1687.

1. Slowly tortured to death by the Turks 1847. 2. Jeffreys was..tortured by a cruel internal malady MACAULAY. 3. The Bow tortureth the String continually, and thereby holdeth it in a Continuall Trepidation BACON. b. To t. Scripture for the defending of his errors 1648. Hence **To·rturer**, one who or that which inflicts or causes torture; a tormentor; *spec.* one who executes judicial torture. **To·rturingly** *adv.*

Torturous (tǭ·ɹtiŭrəs, -tʃər-), *a.* 1495. [a. AF., = OF. *tortureus*, *-eux*, f. L. *tortura*; see -OUS.] Full of, involving, or causing torture.

The torterous inventions of hard snaffles 1618.

‖**Torula** (tǫ·rulă). *Pl.* **-æ** (-ī). 1833. [mod.L. dim. (with change of gender) of TORUS (sense 3).] *Biol.* lit. A small rounded swelling or bulge. a. Each of the small rounded cells of various fungi or microbes, as the yeast-plant, etc.; also, a chain of such cells. b. (With capital.) A genus of fungi, chiefly fermentative. Hence **To·ruliform** *a.* having the form of a t. or chain of rounded cells, moniliform. **To·rulose** (1806), **To·rulous** (1752) *adjs.* (*Nat. Hist.*) having at intervals small rounded swollen parts, as a stem, pod, tube, antenna.

‖**Torus** (tō°·rŏs). *Pl.* **tori** (tō°·rəi). 1563. [L., swelling, bulge, knot, etc.; in *Arch.* a round moulding.] 1. *Arch.* A large convex moulding, of semicircular or similar section, used esp. at the base of a column. 2. *Bot.* The swollen summit of the flower-stalk, which supports the floral organs 1829. 3. a. *Zool.* A protuberant part or organ, as the ventral parapodia in some annelids. b. *Anat.* A smooth rounded ridge or elongated protuberance, as of a muscle; *spec.* the *tuber cinereum* of the brain. 1877. 4. *Geom.* A surface or solid generated by the revolution of a circle or other conic about any axis; e.g. a solid ring of circular or elliptic section 1870.

Torve (tǭɹv), *a. rare.* 1650. [ad. L. *torvus* grim.] Stern in aspect; grim, fierce-looking. So **To·rvid, To·rvous** *adjs.* in same sense. **To·rvity**, grimness.

Tory (tō°·ri), *sb.* and *a.* 1646. [Anglicized spelling of Irish **tóraidhe*, *-aighe* (tōriye) pursuer, f. *tóir* to pursue.] A. *sb.* 1. In the 17th c., one of the dispossessed Irish, who became outlaws, subsisting by plundering and killing the English settlers and soldiers; a bog-trotter, a rapparee; later, often applied to any Irish Papist or Royalist in arms. *Obs.* exc. *Hist.* 2. With capital T: A nickname given 1679–80 by the Exclusionists to those who opposed the exclusion of James, Duke of York (a Roman Catholic) from the succession to the Crown 1681. 3. Hence, from 1689, the name of one of the two great parliamentary and political parties in England, and (at length) in Great Britain. (The party sprang from the 17th c. Royalists and Cavaliers, and its members at first were more or less identical with the Anti-Exclusionists or 'Tories' in sense 2.) Opp. orig. and during the 18th c. to WHIG; later to LIBERAL, RADICAL, or LABOUR; superseded officially *c* 1830 by CONSERVATIVE, which was partly eclipsed by UNIONIST after 1886; retained colloq. and in hostile use. N.E.D. 4. *U.S. Hist.* A member of the British party during the Revolutionary period; a loyal colonist 1775. 5. *transf.* Applied to any one in foreign countries or former ages holding views analogous to those of the English Tories; also, one who is by temperament or sentiment inclined to conservative principles 1797. B. *adj.* 1. That is a Tory; of, pertaining to, or characteristic of a Tory or Tories; consisting of or constituted by Tories; also, having the principles or aims of a Tory; supported or recognized by the Tory party; Conservative 1682. 2. In extended or transf. senses: see A. 5. 1832.

1. We drank 'Church and King' after dinner with true T. cordiality BOSWELL. 2. The still orthodox and t. view found in the Old Testament 1899.

Comb.: **T. Democracy**, combination of Toryism with democracy; democracy under T. leadership; new or democratic Toryism; progressive Conservatism; so **T. democrat**, one who professes T. democracy. Hence **To·ryish** *a.*

Toryism (tō°·ri,iz'm). 1682. [f. prec. + -ISM.] The principles, practices, and methods of Tories.

‖**Tosca** (tǫ·skă). 1818. [Sp., fem. of *tosco* coarse.] A soft dark-brown limestone occurring embedded and sometimes stratified in the surface formation of the Pampas.

Tosh. *slang.* 1892. [perh. back-formation from next.] Bosh, nonsense, twaddle.

Tosher (tǫ·ʃəɹ). *Undergraduates' slang.* 1889. [joc. deformation of *unattached* + -ER [6].] An unattached or non-collegiate student at a university having residential colleges.

Toss (tǫs), *sb.* 1634. [f. next.] An act of tossing. 1. A pitching up and down or to and fro. †2. A state of agitation or commotion –1837. 3. An act of casting, pitching, throwing, or hurling; a throw, a pitch 1660. 4. A sudden jerk; *esp.* a quick upward or backward movement of the head 1676. 5. An act of tossing a coin; a decision arrived at thus 1798. *T. and catch* (U.S.) = PITCH-AND-TOSS 1904. 6. The throwing off of homing pigeons in a trial of their flight and homing powers 1897.

2. Lord! what a tosse I was for some time in PEPYS. 3. *Full t.*, in *Cricket*, the delivery of a ball which does not touch the ground in its flight between the wickets. b. A throw from a horse 1917; phr. *to take a t.* (lit. and fig.). 4. She throws up her Head with a scornful T. 1718.

Comb.: **t.-up**, the throwing up of a coin to arrive at a decision; *fig.* an even chance (*colloq.*).

Toss (tǫs), *v.* Pa. t. and pa. pple. **tossed** (tǫst), also **tost.** 1506. [Origin unkn.] I. *trans.* 1. To throw, pitch, or fling about, here and there, or to and fro: expressing the action of wind or wave, or the light, careless, or disdainful action of a person, on something easily moved. 2. To shake, shake up, stir up 1557. 3. *fig.* To disturb or agitate; to disorder, disquiet 1526.

1. The shippe was in the middes of the see, and was toost with waves TINDALE *Matt.* xiv. 24. *fig.* Here, there, by various fortune tost GAY. 3. Thus was I tost..With strugling doubts 1632.

II. *intr.* †1. To be in mental agitation or distraction; to be disquieted in mind or circumstances –1582. 2. a. for *refl.* To fling or jerk oneself about; to move about restlessly 1560. b. for *pass.* To be flung or rocked about; to be kept in motion; to be agitated 1582.

2. a. Wretch, that long has tost On the thorny bed of Pain GRAY. b. A fleet of merchantmen tossing on the waves MACAULAY.

III. *trans.* 1. To throw, cast, pitch, fling, hurl (without any notion of agitation) 1570. b. *absol.* To fling oneself (like a body tossed) 1728. 2. *esp.* Of two players: To throw, or impel by hitting (a ball, etc.) to and fro between them. Often *fig.* or in fig. context. 1514. b. *fig. spec.* To bandy (a subject or question) from one side to the other in debate; to discuss; to make the subject of talk 1540. 3. To throw up, throw into the air; *esp.* to throw (a coin, etc.) up, to see how it falls; = *toss up*. Also *absol.* 1526. 4. To throw or jerk up suddenly without letting go 1590. †b. To drink out of (a cup, etc.), tilting it up; hence, to empty by drinking; = *toss off* –1708. 5. To lift, jerk, or throw up (the head, etc.) with a sudden, impatient, or spirited movement 1591.

1. The governor's daughter..tossed a note to him over the wall 1718. b. She tossed out of the room THACKERAY. 2. Phr. *To t. from pillar to post* (PILLAR *sb.*). b. If we were to t. the matter about..for twenty days, we could only end as we began BURKE. 3. Phr. *To t. in a blanket*, to throw (a person) upward repeatedly from a blanket held slackly at each corner. *To t. a pancake*, to throw it up so that it falls back into the pan with the other side up. 4. Phr. *To t. oars*, 'to throw them up out of the rowlocks, and raise them perpendicularly an-end' (Adm. Smyth).

With advs. **T. off.** a. To drink off with energetic action. b. To dispose of in an off-hand manner. **T. up.** a. See prec. senses and UP. b. *absol.* To t. a coin, etc., in the air to wager on which side it will fall, or to determine a question by this. †c. To prepare, serve up, hastily. Hence **To·sser**, one who or that which tosses.

Tosspot (tǫ·spǫt). 1568. [f. phr. *to toss a pot*, TOSS *v.* III. 4 b.] One accustomed to toss off his pot; a heavy drinker; a toper.

Tost, var. Tossed, pa. t. and pa. pple. of Toss *v.*, also *ppl. a.* Still freq. in poetry and combs. as *tempest-t.*

Tosticate (tǫ·stikeˈt), *v.* Now *dial.* 1650. Usu. in pa. pple. *tosticated*, app. orig. for *intoxicated*, but later also assoc. w. *tossed, tost*, and used as = tossed about, distracted.

I have been so tosticated about since my last Swift.

Tot (tǫt), *sb.*[1] 1690. [Short for *total* or L. *totum*.] The total of an addition; hence, an addition sum; also (*t.-up*), adding up, totalling.

Tot, *sb.*[2] *colloq.* or *local.* 1725. [Origin obsc.] **1.** A very small or tiny child. **2.** A very small drinking-vessel; a child's mug. Chiefly *dial.* 1828. **3.** A minute quantity, esp. of drink; a dram; also, anything very small 1828.

Tot (tǫt), *v. colloq.* 1760. [f. Tot *sb.*[1]] *trans.* To add *together* and bring out the total of; to sum *up*. **b.** *intr. To t. up*: to amount, 'come' (*to*) 1882.

b. Three stalls a week t. up frightfully in a year 1892.

Total (tōᵘ·tăl), *a.* and *sb.* late ME. [a. F., ad. schol. L. *totalis*, f. L. *totus* entire; see -al.] **A.** *adj.* **1.** Of, pertaining to, or relating to the whole of something. Now *rare* exc. in *t. eclipse*, an eclipse of the sun or moon in which the whole of the disk is obscured. **2.** Constituting or comprising a whole; whole, entire. late ME. **3.** Complete in extent or degree; absolute, utter 1647.

2. Its t. revenue does not pay its expenses 1833. 3 A t. absence of self-respect 1838. *T. abstinence, spec.* entire abstinence from alcoholic drinks; so *t. abstainer*.

B. *sb.* (the adj. used absol.) The aggregate; the whole sum or amount; a whole 1557. Hence **To·tally** *adv.*

Total (tōᵘ·tăl), *v.* 1716. [f. prec.] **1. a.** *trans.* To reach the total of, amount to 1859. **b.** *intr.* To amount *to*, mount *up to* 1880. **2.** *trans.* To bring to a total, add up, complete 1716.

Totality (totæ·lĭti). 1598. [ad. schol. L. *totalitas*, f. *totalis* Total.] **1.** The quality of being total; entirety 1627. **b.** *Astron.* Total obscuration of the sun or moon in an eclipse; the moment of occurrence or time of duration of this 1842. **2.** That which is total; a whole; the total number or amount 1598.

Hence **Totalita·rian** *a. Civics*, of or pertaining to a polity which permits no rival loyalties or parties.

Totaliza·tion. 1888. [f. Totalize *v.*; see -ation.] The action or process of totalizing, or the condition of being totalized; calculation of the total.

Totalizator (tōᵘ·tăləizeˈ:təɹ). 1879. [ad. F. *totalisateur*, agent-n. f. *totaliser*.] A machine or apparatus for registering and showing the total of operations, measurements, etc.; *spec.* an apparatus for registering and indicating the number of tickets sold to betters on each horse in a race.

Totalize (tōᵘ·tăləiz), *v.* 1818. [f. Total *a.* + -ize.] *trans.* To make total; to combine into a total or aggregate.

‖**Totara** (tōᵘ·tără, totā·ră). 1832. [Maori.] A large New Zealand coniferous tree, *Podocarpus Totara*, producing light, durable, tough timber of a dark red colour, highly valued for building, piles, cabinet work, etc.

Tote (tōᵘt), *sb.* 1771. **I.** [Short for *total*.] The total amount, number, or sum. Chiefly in pleonastic phr. *the whole t.* Now *dial.* **2.** Abbreviation of *total abstainer* (*dial.* or low *colloq.*) 1870; and (orig. *Australian*) of Totalizator *colloq.*) 1891. attrib. *tote club, -house.*

Tote (tōᵘt), *v. U.S. colloq.* 1676. [Origin obsc.] *trans.* To carry as a burden or load; also, to transport, esp. supplies to, or timber, etc. from, a logging-camp or the like.

At Baltimore I made a stay of two days, during which I was toted about town W. Irving.

†**To-tea·r,** *v.* [OE. *to-teran*, f. To-[2] + *teran* Tear *v.*] *trans.* To tear to pieces -1605.

Totem (tōᵘ·tĕm). 1760. [From Odjibewa, or some kindred Algonkin dialect.] Among the Amer. Indians: The hereditary mark, emblem, or badge of a tribe, clan, or group of Indians, consisting of a figure or representation of some animal, less commonly a plant or other natural object, after which the group is named; also applied to the animal or natural object itself, sometimes considered to be ancestrally or fraternally related to the clan. **b.** By anthropologists the name has been extended to refer to other savage peoples or tribes, which (though they may not use totem marks) are similarly divided into groups or clans named after animals, etc. 1874.

Twelve of these placed their totems opposite my signature; each t. consisting of the rude representation of a bear, a deer, an otter, a rat, or some other wild animal 1887.

Comb.: **t.-exogamy,** the custom of marrying only one of a different t. or totem-clan; **-pole, -post,** a post carved and painted with totem figures, erected by the Indians of the north-west of North America in front of their houses. Hence **Tote·mic** *a.* of, pertaining to, or of the nature of a t. or totems; characterized by or having totems.

Totemism (tōᵘ·tĕmiz'm). 1791. [f. prec. + -ism.] The use of totems, with the clan division, and the social, marriage, and religious customs connected with it.

To·temist. 1881. [f. as prec. + -ist.] **1.** One who belongs to a totem clan, or has a totem. **2.** One who is versed in the history of totemism 1897. So **Totemi·stic** *a.* of, pertaining to, or characterized by totemism.

Tother (tʌ·ðəɹ), *pron.* and *a.* Also **t'other.** Now *dial.* [ME. *þe toþer*, for earlier *þet oþer, þat oþer* the other, *þet, þat* being orig. neut. of the def. art.] **A.** *pron.* or *adj.* used absol. **1.** The other (of two). †**2.** The second (of two or more) -1450. **3.** *pl.* (†*the tother, tothers* rare): The others, the rest ME.

1. Thei crieden the t. to the t. Wyclif *Isa.* vi. 3. You cannot tell one from t. 1870. ¶ *To tell t. from which* (= to distinguish between a number of things), joc. phr in gen. colloq. use.

B. as *adj.* preceding a sb. **1.** The other (of two) ME. †**b.** After a possessive: Other -1721. **2.** The second, another, one more. *Obs.* exc. *Sc.* 1600. **3.** (*The*) *t.* (*day*, etc.), the other (day, night, etc.); a few (days, etc.) ago 1575.

‖**Toties quoties** (tōᵘ·ʃiīz kwōᵘ·ʃiīz), *adv.* Also **totiens quotiens.** 1525. [L. 'so often as often'.] As often as something happens or occasion demands; repeatedly.

Totipalmate (tōᵘtipæ·lmeˈt), *a.* (*sb.*) 1872. [f. L. *toti-*, *totus* whole + Palmate *a.*] *Ornith.* Wholly webbed; having all the toes connected by membrane which reaches to the extremities; steganopodous. **B.** *sb.* A totipalmate bird. Hence **To:tipalma·tion,** the condition of being t.

Totipotent (toti·pǫtĕnt), *a.* 1901. [f. L. *toti-* (see prec.) + Potent *a.*] *Biol.* Capable of developing into or generating a complete organism: said of a cell.

‖**Toto** (tōᵘ tǫ), abl. sing. masc. and neut. of L. *totus* all, whole, entire (cf. In toto): occurring in a few phrases, as **Toto cælo** (tōᵘ·to sī·lo), 'by the whole heaven', by as much as the distance between the poles, diametrically.

Toto-, used as comb. form of L. *totus* whole, in certain cases, instead of *toti-* (see -o-), forming compound adjs., **a.** in sense 'wholly' (see -o- 1), as **to:to-conge·nital, to:to-mu·te; b.** in sense 'total and..' (see -o- 2), as **To:to-pa·rtial** *Logic*, of a proposition: of which one term is universal and the other particular; so **To:to-to·tal,** having both terms universal.

Totter (tǫ·təɹ), *sb.* 1747. [f. Totter *v.*] The action, or an act, of tottering; wavering, oscillation; an unsteady or shaky movement or gait as of one ready to fall.

I..had his bend in my shoulders, and his t. in my gait Johnson.

Comb.: **t.-grass,** quaking-grass, *Briza media.*

Totter (tǫ·təɹ), *v.* ME. [perh. from Norse: cf. Norw. dial. *tutra, totra* to quiver, shake, Sw. dial. *tuttra.*] †**1.** *intr.* To swing to and fro, esp. at the end of a rope; *fig.* to waver, vacillate -1633. **2.** To rock or shake to and fro on its base, as if about to overbalance or collapse. late ME. **3.** To walk or move with unsteady steps; to go shakily or feebly; to toddle; also, to walk with difficulty; to reel, stagger 1602. †**4.** *trans.* To cause to shake to and fro, to rock; to render unstable -1693.

1. *All's Well* I. iii. 129. 2. Troy nods from high, and totters to her fall Dryden. *fig.* If th' other two be brain'd like vs, the State totters Shaks. 3. He totterd from the reeling decke Marston. Hence **To·tterer. To·tteringly** *adv.*

Tottery (tǫ·təri), *a.* 1861. [f. prec. + -y[1].] Given to tottering; shaky; unsteady.

Totty (tǫ·ti), *a.* Now *dial.* late ME. [app. f. *tot-* as in *totter* + -y[1].] Unsteady, shaky, tottery (physically or mentally); dizzy, dazed; tipsy, fuddled.

Myn heed is toty of my swynk to nyght Chaucer.

Toucan (tu̇kā·n, tū·kăn). 1568. [= F. *toucan*, Sp. *tucan*, a. Brazilian, Tupi *tucana*, Guarani *tucà, tucãn*, the native name, prob. from its cry or call.] **1.** A Neotropical bird of the genus *Rhamphastos* or the family *Rhamphastidæ*, inhabiting the tropical parts of South America, etc. They are noted for the enormous size of the beak and their striking colouring. The species orig. so named was app. *R. toco.* **b.** Misapplied to other birds; esp. in the East Indies to species of Hornbill (*Buceros*) 1816. **2.** *Astron.* Name of a southern constellation 1669. Hence **Toucanet** (tū·kăneˈt), any of the smaller kinds of t.

Touch (tʌtʃ). *sb.* ME. [orig. a. OF. *touche*, f. *toucher* to Touch. In some later uses, f. Touch *v.*] **I. 1.** The action or an act of touching; exercise of the faculty of feeling upon a material object. **b.** *euphem.* Sexual contact ME. **c.** *Med.* Examination by feeling, esp. of a cavity of the body; palpation 1805. **d.** *Mil.* Contact between the elbows of a rank of soldiers 1877. **e.** A children's game, in which one player touches another, who then chases and tries to touch any of the other players; in full *t.-and-run* 1815. **2.** The act, fact, or state of touching or being touched; contact. late ME. **b.** A small quantity of some substance brought into contact with a surface so as to leave its mark or effect; a dash, as of paint; a mark or stain so produced 1581. **3.** That sense by which a material object is perceived by means of the contact with it of some part of the body; the most general of the bodily senses, diffused through all parts of the skin, but (in man) specially developed in the tips of the fingers and the lips. late ME. **b.** The sensation caused by touching something (considered as an attribute of the thing); tactile quality, feel 1674. **4.** A hit, knock, stroke, blow; *esp.* a very slight blow or stroke ME. **b.** *fig.* A 'hit', stroke (of wit, satire, etc.); a 'knock', a 'blow' 1522.

1. He toucheth the face and breast with cold touches Purchas. A submissive t. to his cap 1898. Phr. *Within* or *in t.*, near enough to touch or be touched; within reach (*of*); accessible. b. *Meas. for M.* v. i. 141. 2. The t. of the cold water made a prettie kinde of shrugging come ouer her bodie Sidney. b. Phr. *A t. of the tar-brush*, a small amount of negro blood. 3. By t. the first pure qualities we learn Which quicken all things, hot, cold, moist, and dry 1599. b. A Country Lip may have the Velvet t. Dryden. 4. b. To whom soon mov'd with t. of blame thus Eve Milt.

II. Technical and allied senses. **1.** The action or process of testing the quality of gold or silver by rubbing it upon a touchstone. late ME. **b.** An official mark or stamp upon gold or silver indicating that it has been tested, and is of standard fineness; also, a die, punch, or stamp for impressing this. Also, an official mark stamped upon pewter. late ME. **c.** The quality or fineness of gold or silver (or other metal) as tested with the touchstone and indicated by the official mark ME. **d.** *fig.* Quality, kind, sort, 'stamp'. late ME. †**2.** Short for *touchstone* (see Touchstone 2) 1485. **3.** *fig.* An act of, or thing that serves for, testing; a test, trial, proof; a criterion, 'touchstone'. Now chiefly in phr. *to put to the t.* 1581. **4.** *Mus.* The act or manner of touching or handling a musical instrument, so as to bring out its tones; now *esp.* the manner of striking or pressing the keys of a keyboard instrument so as to produce special varieties of tone or effect. Hence *transf.* (chiefly *poet.*) a note or brief strain of instrumental music. late ME. **b.** As an attribute of the performer: capacity, skill, or style of playing 1601. **c.** As an attribute of a keyboard instrument, referring to the manner in which its keys and action respond to the touch of the player 1884. **5.** *Bell-ringing.* Any series of changes less than a peal 1872. **6.** An act of touching a surface with the proper tool in painting, writing, carving, etc.; a stroke or dash of a brush, chisel, or the like; a slight act or effort added in doing or completing a piece of work of any kind 1607. **b.** Artistic skill or faculty; style or quality of artistic work; method of handling, execution 1815. **7.** *Magnetism.* The action or process of magnetizing a steel bar or needle by contact with one or more magnets 1705. **8.** *Football.* The act (in the Rugby game) of touching the ground with the ball behind the goal, usu. the opponents' goal; *transf.* (esp. in phr. *in* or *into t.*), that part of the ground outside the bounding lines of the field of play (*t.-lines* and *goal-lines*); *t.-in-goal*, that part of this behind the goal-line 1864.

1. Good metall bides the t. that trieth out the gold 1587. **d.** My Friends of Noble t. SHAKS. 2. Gates all like Masonrie, of White and Blacke, Like Touche and White Merbell HALL. 4. Orpheus Lute,..Whose golden t. could soften steele and stones SHAKS. 6. It [a picture] tutors Nature, Artificiall strife Liues in these toutches, liuelier then life SHAKS.

III. *fig.* **1.** The act of touching or fact of being touched (in *fig.* senses of the vb.) 1586. **b.** *spec.*, An impression upon the mind or soul; a feeling, sense (*of* some emotion, etc.) 1586. **2.** A faculty or capacity of the mind analogous or likened to the sense of touch; mental or moral perception or feeling 1656. **3.** A stroke of action, an act; a brief turn or 'go' *at* some occupation; †in early use, a sly, mean, or deceitful trick. Now *rare.* 1481. **4.** An act of touching upon or mentioning something; a mention, slight notice, hint. Now *rare* or *Obs.* late ME. †**b.** The fact or quality of touching, affecting, concerning, or relating to something. BACON. †**5.** The quality or fact of affecting injuriously; reproach, blemish, stain, taint –1616. **6.** A distinguishing quality, characteristic, trait 1539. **7.** 'A small quantity intermingled' (J.); a trace, spice, smack 1594. **b.** *spec.* A slight affection or attack *of* illness or disease; a twinge 1662. **8.** *slang.* or *colloq.* An article or 'affair' that will touch or move purchasers to the extent of a certain price 1712.

1. Free From all t. of age 1586. Phr. *In* or *out of t. with, to keep* or *lose t. with*: To bring religion into t. with conduct 1887. **b.** Didst thou but know the inly t. of Loue SHAKS. 2. An accuracy and delicacy of intellectual t. 1872. 4. **b.** Speech of t. toward others, should bee sparingly vsed BACON. 6. One t. of nature makes the whole world kin: That all with one consent praise new borne gaudes SHAKS. But cared greatly to..keep the Nelson t. 1897. 7. Madam, I haue a t. of your condition, That cannot brooke the accent of reproofe SHAKS. **b.** A t. of sore throat 1890. 8. At night went to the Ball at the Angel. A guinea t. 1720.

IV. Concrete senses. **1.** Short for TOUCH-POWDER, TOUCHWOOD, or the like. *Obs.* exc. *dial.* 1541. **2.** *Shipbuilding.* In a plank tapering both ways, the projecting angle at the broadest part (near one end if worked top-and-butt, in the middle if worked anchor-stock fashion); also, each of the angles of the stern-timbers at the counters 1711.

Phrases. †*To keep t.* **a.** To keep covenant, act faithfully; so *to break t.* **b.** To keep up communication, keep in touch *with*. *Rum t.*: an odd or queer fellow or affair (*slang*). *In* or *out of t. with*: see III. 1. *In* or *within t.*: see I. 1. *To put to the t.*: see II. 3.

Touch (tɒtʃ), *v.* [ME. a. OF. *tochier, tuchier*, mod.F. *toucher* = Sp. and Pg. *tocar*, It. *toccare*. The Romanic *toccare* is prob. an onomatopœic formation from the syllable *toc* imitating a knock.] **I. 1.** *trans.* To put the hand or finger or some other part of the body upon, or into contact with (something) so as to feel it; 'to exercise the sense of feeling upon' (Phillips, 1696). Also with the hand, etc., as subject, and in other constrs.; rarely *absol.* **2.** *spec.* **a.** To have sexual contact with. *trans.* or †*intr.* with *to*. *Obs.* exc. as in II. 1. ME. **b.** To lay the hand upon (a diseased person) for the cure of the 'king's evil' or scrofula, as formerly practised by French and English sovereigns. Also *absol.* 1606. **c.** *Med.* To examine by touch or feeling. Also *absol.* 1734. **d.** To bring by touching *into* some condition 1813. **e.** *Football.* = T. down 1864. **f.** *absol.* or *intr.* Of soldiers in the rank: To close up until the elbows are in contact 1803. **3.** *trans.* To come into or be in contact with. Also *intr.* or *absol.* ME. **4.** To adjoin, border on; to skirt. late ME. **b.** *Geom.* Of a line (straight or curved) or a surface: To meet (another line or surface) at a point so that when produced it does not (ordinarily) intersect or 'cut' it at that point; to be tangent to. Also *absol.* or *intr.* in reciprocal sense. 1570. **5.** To strike or hit lightly (esp. with the spur, or in *Fencing*) ME. **6.** To affect physically in some way by contact. **a.** To make an impression upon; to stain, scratch, abrade, corrode, decompose, etc. 1440. **b.** To magnetize by contact or rubbing with a magnet. Now *rare* or *Obs.* 1627. **c.** To apply some substance lightly to (a part of the body, etc.) by contact, esp. for medicinal purposes; const. *with* 1602. **7.** To affect injuriously in some physical way, (e.g. by fire or frost), esp. in a slight degree. (Usu. in *pa. pple.*) 1595. **8.** To test the fineness of (gold or silver) by rubbing it upon a touchstone 1548. **b.** To mark (metal) with an official stamp, after it has been tested. late ME. **9.** To strike the strings, keys, etc. of (a musical instrument) so as to make it sound; to play on, esp. to play a few notes on; to sound (a horn, a bell) 1470. **b.** *transf.* To produce (musical sounds) by 'touching' an instrument; to play (an air) 1823. **10.** In drawing, painting, etc.: To mark, draw, delineate (a detail of the work) by touching the surface with the pencil, brush, etc.; also, to modify or alter by such touches. Hence *transf.* in literary composition. 1675. **b.** *fig.* To mark slightly or superficially *with* some colour or aspect: chiefly in *pa. pple.* 1600. **11.** *intr.* Of a ship or those on board: To arrive and make a short stay in passing at a port or place on the way. Also *transf.* of a traveller. Usu. with *at*. 1517. **b.** *trans.* with the port or place as obj.: To land upon; to visit in passing 1593.

1. Jesus sayde vnto her: touche me not TINDALE *John* xx. 17. Him thus intent Ithuriel with his Spear Touch'd lightly MILT. T. a match to it, and you will presently have a fire 1897. 2. **b.** His Majestie began first to t. for the evil, according to costome EVELYN. 3. Loose shingle..falls upon the ice where it touches the rocks TYNDALL. *absol.* Those spheres..T., mingle, are transfigured SHELLEY. 6. **a.** The Aqua Regalis, which dissolves Gold, will not t. Silver 1725. **c.** Phr. *To t. the gums* (Med.), to induce salivation, as by the use of mercury. 7. A horse which was touched in the wind 1772. The plants that were touched with frost 1884. 8. They haue all bin touch'd, and found Base-Mettle SHAKS. 9. Timotheus..With flying fingers touched the lyre DRYDEN. **b.** [He] touched a light and lively air on the flageolet SCOTT. 10. The lines, tho' touch'd but faintly, are drawn right POPE. **b.** The rock on the woody promontory..is touched with rose-colour 1847. 11. We touched at Panaria 1828. **b.** Shall we t. the continent? JOHNSON.

II. 1. To handle or have to do with in any or the slightest degree; to 'lay a finger on'. (Usu. with neg.) late ME. **b.** *spec.* To lay hands on or meddle with so as to harm; to injure, hurt, in any or the least degree ME. **c.** To take (food or drink); usu. (with neg.), not to take any at all. late ME. **2.** *trans.* To get or go as far as; to reach, attain (*lit.* and *fig.*); *fig.* to attain equality with, compare with. late ME. **3.** *intr.* with *at, to, on, upon* (also *absol.*): To approach closely; to verge upon 1451. **b.** *Naut.* (*trans.*) To keep as close to (the wind) as the vessel will sail. Also *absol.* 1568. **4.** *trans.* To take in the hand, take, receive, draw (money) = F. *toucher de l'argent*; sometimes, to get by underhand means. Also *absol.* Now chiefly *slang* or *colloq.* 1654. **5.** To 'come down upon' (a person) *for* money, to succeed in getting money from. *colloq.* 1760.

1. I had never touched a card RUSKIN. **b.** The Lion will not t. the true Prince SHAKS. **c.** I never t. a drop GOLDSM. 2. I haue touch'd the highest point of all my Greatnesse SHAKS. *fig.* Is there one of you that could t. him? DICKENS. 3. During the course of a political life just touching to its close BURKE. 4. The..matrimonial arrangement is concluded (the agent touching his percentage) THACKERAY. 5. I could t. Dad for a few hundreds 1809.

III. †**1.** *trans.* To succeed in getting at, 'hit'; to guess or state correctly –1797. **2.** To treat of, mention; now always, to mention briefly, casually, or in passing; to allude to. Now *rare* or *arch.* late ME. **b.** *intr.*, usu. with *on, upon*, etc., in same sense ME. **3.** *trans.* To say something apt or telling about, esp. in censure. Also *to t. to the quick.* 1529. **4.** To pertain or relate to; to be the business of; to concern. *Obs.* or *arch.* ME. **b.** To have affinity with. *Obs.* or *arch.* 1611. **5.** To be a matter of moment to; to affect, make a difference to 1470. †**6.** To strike, impress (the senses, or organs of sense) –1667. **7.** To affect mentally or morally, to imbue *with* some quality; in bad sense, to infect, taint. Also predicated of the quality. Usu. in *pa. pple.* ME. **b.** *pass.* To be deranged mentally in a slight degree; in *pa. pple.* slightly insane or crazy, 'cracked' 1704. **8.** To affect *with* some feeling or emotion; *spec.* to affect with tender feeling, as pity or gratitude ME. **b.** To influence, move (in mind or will) 1570. **9.** To hurt or wound in mind or feelings, as if by touching a sore or tender part; to irritate, sting, nettle. Often in *fig.* phrases, as *t. to the quick.* 1589.

1. There you toucht the life of our designe SHAKS. 2. **b.** He touches on the same difficulties and he gives no answer to them JOWETT. 3. Ev'n those you t. not, hate you POPE. 4. This..touches us not as Liberals or Conservatives, but as citizens 1883. 5. His Curses and his blessings T. me alike: th' are breath I not beleeue in SHAKS. 7. High nature amorous of the good, But touch'd with no ascetic gloom TENNYSON. **b.** You see master 's a little—touched, that 's all VANBRUGH. 8. I can't say how much the thought of that fidelity has touched me THACKERAY. 9. It touched.. scores of labourers on the raw 1898.

Phrases. *To t. and go*, to touch for an instant and immediately go away or pass on; to deal with momentarily or slightly. *To t. one's cap, hat*, to raise the hand to the cap or hat and touch it in token of salutation; const. *to*. *To t. wood*, in folk-lore or *quasi*-superstitious use: to t. wood as a charm to avert apprehended misfortune, esp. that apt to follow untimely boasting or self-gratulation.

With adverbs. **Touch down.** *Rugby Football. trans.* To t. the ground with (the ball) behind the goal, usu. that of the opponents; also *absol.* **T. in.** *trans.* In drawing, etc.: To insert (a detail) by touching with the pencil, brush, etc. **T. off.** *trans.* **a.** To represent exactly, to 'hit off'. **b.** To fire off (a cannon, etc.), orig. by putting a match to the touch-hole. **c.** To break off a telephone interview. **T. up. a.** *trans.* To improve, finish, or modify, by adding touches or light strokes. **b.** To stimulate by striking lightly or sharply, as with a whip.

Touch- *sb.* or *vb.* in comb.

1. a. t.-judge, in *Rugby Football*, an umpire who marks when and where the ball goes 'into touch'; **-needle**, a slender bar or rod of gold or silver, one of a set of different standards of fineness, used in conjunction with a touchstone for testing the fineness of gold or silver; **-plate**, one of a set of plates bearing the 'touches' or official marks of the company of pewterers; **-watch**, a watch so contrived that the time by it can be ascertained by touch, e.g. in the dark. **b.** Connected with the notion of ready ignition; cf. TOUCH-POWDER; **t.-pan**, the pan of an old-fashioned gun, into which the touch-powder was put; **-string**, string steeped in nitre used as a fuse.

2. t.-back (*Rugby Football*), the act of touching the ground with the ball on or behind the player's own goal-line after it has been driven there by the opposing side; **-down** (*Rugby Football*), the act of touching the ground with the ball behind the goal-line, usu. that of the opposing side; *safety touch-down*, the same done behind the player's own goal-line after it has been driven there by his own side, in order to prevent the opposing side from making a touch-down; **-up**, an act of touching up; a stroke added by way of improvement or finish; also, a slight reminder.

Touchable (tɒ·tʃăb'l), *a.* late ME. [f. TOUCH *v.* + -ABLE.] Capable of being touched. Hence **Tou·chableness.**

Tou·ch and go·, *sb.* and *adj. phr.* (Also with hyphens.) 1655. [The vbl. phr. *touch and go* used as sb. or adj.] **A.** *sb.* **1.** The act of touching for an instant and quitting immediately; something done quickly or instantaneously. **2.** A risky, precarious, or ticklish case or state of things (such that a mere touch may cause disaster); a narrow escape, 'near shave' 1815.

2. Though it was touch and go she managed to retain her seat 1887.

B. *adj.* **1.** Involving or characterized by rapid, slight, or superficial execution; sketchy; casual; instantaneous; expeditious 1812. **2.** Risky, of the nature of a narrow escape 1856.

1. 'Touch-and-go' sketches 1891.

Tou·ch-box. *Obs.* exc. *Hist.* 1549. [for *touch-powder box*; see TOUCH-POWDER.] A box for 'touch-powder' or priming-powder, formerly forming part of a musketeer's equipment.

Touched (tɒtʃt), *ppl. a.* late ME. [f. TOUCH *v.* + -ED[1].] In various senses of TOUCH *v.*

T. proof, a 'proof' from an engraved or etched plate approaching completion, submitted to the artist of the picture copied, for his approval or criticism.

Toucher (tɒ·tʃəɹ). late ME. [f. as prec. + -ER[1].] One who or that which touches, in senses of the vb.; *esp.* in *Bowls*, a bowl which touches the jack. b. *colloq.* or *slang.* (*a*) A case of close contact, an exact fit. (*b*) A very near approach; in phr. *as near as a t.*, very nearly, all but. 1828.

Tou·ch-hole. 1501. [f. TOUCH- + HOLE.] A small tubular hole in the breech of a fire-arm, through which the charge is ignited; the vent.

Touching (tʊ·tʃiŋ), *vbl. sb.* ME. [f. TOUCH *v.* + -ING [1].] The action of TOUCH *v.* 1. The action, or an act, of feeling something with the hand, etc.; the fact or state of being contiguous; touch, contact; a touch; *spec.* for the 'king's evil'. 2. In various *fig.* senses: Mention, treatment or discussion; affecting or injuring, etc. late ME.

Tou·ching, *ppl. a.* 1508. [f. as prec. + -ING [2].] That touches: esp. *fig.* that touches the feelings or emotions; such as to excite tender feeling or sympathy; affecting, pathetic.

O insupportable, and t. losse! SHAKS. A t. faith in the efficacy of acts of parliament 1870. Hence **Tou·ching-ly** *adv.*, **-ness.**

Tou·ching, *prep.* Now somewhat *arch.* ME. [The pres. pple. of TOUCH *v.* used prepositionally; prob. after F. *touchant.*] 1. Where *touching* is in concord with a prec. sb. or pron., and may be rendered 'that refers or relates to'. (Cf. CONCERNING *prep.* 1.) 2. Without concord: In reference or relation to; as to, respecting, regarding; in the way of mentioning or treating of; concerning, about. late ME. 3. Preceded by *as.* late ME.

1. A late Request..t. the Care of a young Daughter STEELE. 2. T. the bargain, your..mother was a little too calm DICKENS. 3. As t. the Guls or Sea-cobs, they build in rockes 1601.

Tou·ch-line. 1551. [f. TOUCH- + LINE *sb.*[2]] †1. *Geom.* A tangent -1675. 2. (*touch line.*) A line in a diagram representing the touch of the counter of a ship 1797. 3. *Football*, etc. The boundary line on each side of the field of play, extending from goal-line to goal-line 1868.

Tou·ch-me-no:t, *sb.* (*a.*) 1597. [phrase used as sb.; transl. of NOLI-ME-TANGERE.] 1. Name for two different kinds of plants with seed-vessels which burst at a touch. †a. The Squirting Cucumber -1760. b. The Yellow Balsam (*Impatiens Noli-tangere*), or other species of *Impatiens* 1659. 2. *gen.* A person or thing that must not be touched 1893. b. *attrib.* or as *adj.* 1852.

2. b. The saucy little beauty carried her head with a toss..and assumed a t. air THACKERAY.

Tou·ch-pa:per. 1750. [TOUCH- 1 b.] Paper steeped in nitre so as to burn slowly on being touched by a spark, used for firing gunpowder, etc.

Tou·ch-piece. 1844. [f. TOUCH- + PIECE *sb.*] 1. A coin or medal given by the sovereign to each person touched for the 'king's evil'. 2. A piece of mechanism operated by a touch 1897.

†Tou·ch-pow:der. 1497. [app. the earliest of a series of compounds (see TOUCH- 1 b) in which *touch-* signifies the ready setting fire to something; app. f. OF. *tochier* (*le feu*), *touchier* to set fire; prob. repr. an OF. **poudre-à-toucher* (*le feu*).] A fine kind of gunpowder placed in the pan over the touch-hole in an old-fashioned fire-arm; priming powder.

Touchstone (tʊ·tʃ,stoun). 1481. [f. TOUCH- 1 + STONE.] 1. A smooth, fine-grained, black or dark-coloured variety of quartz or jasper (also called BASANITE), used for testing the quality of gold and silver alloys by the colour of the streak produced by rubbing them upon it; a piece of such stone used for this purpose 1530. b. *fig.* That which serves to test or try the genuineness or value of anything; a test, criterion 1533. 2. Applied to other stones of similar texture and colour, as black marble or basalt 1481.

1. b. Time..is the only true t. of merit 1720.

Touchwood (tʊ·tʃ,wud). 1579. [f. TOUCH- 1 b + WOOD *sb.*] Wood or anything of woody nature, in such a state as to catch fire readily, and which can be used as tinder. a. The soft white substance into which wood is converted by the action of certain fungi, esp. of *Polyporus squamosus*, and which has the property of burning for many hours when once ignited, and is occas. self-luminous. b. A name given to various fungi, esp. two species of *Polyporus* (*P.* or *Fomes fomentarius* and *P.* or *F. igniarius*), or to the tinder called 'amadou' made from them 1598. c. *fig.* Said of a thing or person that easily 'takes fire'; *esp.* an irascible or passionate person, one easily incensed. Now *rare.* 1617.

Touchy (tʊ·tʃi), *a.* 1605. [f. TOUCH *sb.* or *v.* + -Y [1]; in sense 1 perh. an alteration of TETCHY.] 1. Easily moved to anger; apt to take offence on slight cause; irascible, irritable, testy, tetchy. 2. Sensitive to touch; physically irritable 1618. b. Easily ignited 1660. 3. Ticklish, risky; not to be touched without danger 1620.

1. She was most t. upon the subject of age 1843. Hence **Tou·chily** *adv.* **Tou·chiness.**

Tough (tʊf), *a.* (*sb.*) [OE. *tôh* :—OTeut. **tanχuz*, f. **tanχ-*, var. **tang-*, whence OE. *ge-tenge* near, close.] 1. Of close tenacious substance or texture; not easily broken, divided, or disintegrated; not fragile, brittle, or tender; of food, difficult to masticate. 2. Of viscous consistence or nature; sticky, adhesive, tenacious; glutinous OE. 3. *fig.* Stiff, severe, violent; of a contest, etc.: stoutly maintained, strenuous, vigorous and stubborn ME. 4. Capable of great physical endurance; hardy, stout, sturdy ME. 5. Having great intellectual or moral endurance; difficult to influence, affect, or impress; firm, persistent; also, stubborn, hardened. late ME. 6. Difficult to do, perform, or deal with 1619. b. Taxing credulity or comprehension 1820. 7. *U.S.* Of criminal or vicious propensities; also, rowdy, disorderly 1884.

1. The pure parts of metals are of themselves very flexible and tuff 1665. The 'cold fowl' was..as t. as leather 1843. 2. T. viscid saliva 1789. 3. A t. breeze from the westward 1865. 4. That was what t. old Sir Evan Dhu used to say SCOTT. 5. A man of ripe yeares, but..t. in opinion 1603. 6. A t. job SCOTT. b. Tell us t. yarns, and then swear they are true BARHAM.

B. *sb. U.S.* A street ruffian 1866.

Comb.: **t.-cake, -pitch,** refined or commercial copper. Hence **Tou·gh-ly** *adv.*, **-ness.**

Toughen (tʊ·f'n), *v.* 1582. [f. prec. + -EN [5].] *trans.* and *intr.* To make or become tough.

Toughish (tʊ·fiʃ), *a.* 1776. [f. as prec. + -ISH [1].] Somewhat tough.

Toupee (tū·pi). Now *rare.* 1727. [app. ad. F. *toupet*; see next.] A curl or artificial lock of hair on the top of the head, esp. as a crowning feature of a periwig; a periwig in which the front hair was combed up, over a pad, into such a top-knot; also, the natural hair dressed in this mode; a patch of false hair or a small wig to cover a bald place 1731. †b. One who wears a toupee; a beau -1747.

‖**Toupet** (tū·pe, F. tupę). 1728. [a. F., tuft of hair, dim. of OF. *toup*, tuft of hair, etc.; ad. LG. **topp-* top, tuft, summit.] 1. = prec. 2. †The forelock of a horse, etc.; a thick head of hair 1797. 3. *attrib.*, as **t.-titmouse,** the Crested Titmouse 1731.

Tour (tūəɹ), *sb.* [ME., a. F. *tour*, OF. *tor*, back-formation from nom. *tors* :—L. *tornus*, a. Gr. τόρνος a tool for describing a circle, etc. In some senses perh. f. F. *tourner* to turn.] I. 1. One's turn or order (to do something); also, a spell of work or duty; a shift. In later use *Mil.* †2. A turning round, revolution (*rare*) -1719. 3. A going or travelling from place to place, a round; an excursion or journey including the visiting of a number of places in a circuit or sequence 1643. b. *transf.* and *fig.* A round 1704. †c. A short outing; also, the route taken; in 17th c., in London, the drive round Hyde Park -1773. d. The circuit *of* an island, etc.; a round 1719. 4. A crescent front of false hair. *Obs.* exc. *Hist.* 1674.

2. He made so many Tours..and led us by such winding Ways DE FOE. 3. *The* (*grand*) *t.*: see GRAND TOUR. *On t.*, touring: see TOUR *v.* 2. c. Mr. Povy and I in his coach to Hyde Parke, being the first day of the t. there PEPYS.

II. Fig. uses (mostly from French). †1. A shift, expedient -1699. †2. A 'turn' given to a phrase or sentence, etc. -1751. †3. Manner of presenting or exhibiting anything -1734. †4. Range, scope -1737. †5. A round, a course (of engagements, etc.). STEELE. 6. One of the several trills, variations, or changes in the song of a trained canary 1906.

Tour (tūəɹ), *v.* 1746. [f. prec.] †1. *intr.* To 'take a turn' in or about a place, esp. riding or driving -1760. 2. *intr.* To make a tour or circuitous journey, in which many places are visited, for recreation or business; *spec.* of an actor, a theatrical company, or the like: to go 'on tour', to travel from town to town fulfilling engagements 1789. 3. *trans.* To make the tour or round of (a country or district) 1885. 4. *spec. Theatr.* To take (a play or entertainment) on tour; to tour with 1897.

3. Mr. R. is this week touring his constituency 1898. 4. The American drama..now being toured in the provinces 1897. Hence **Tou·rer** one who tours; a touring-car. **Tou·ring** *vbl. sb.* (*attrib.* in *touring-car*).

‖**Touraco** (tūə·răko). 1743. [= F. *touraco*; native name in W. Africa of *Turacus persa.*] Any bird of the family *Musophagidæ* (plantain-eaters), natives of southern, western, and central Africa, and esp. of the genus *Turacus*, large birds with brilliant purple, green, and crimson plumage and prominent crest (hence formerly called *crown-birds*); also of the genus *Schizorrhis*, with plumage of a plainer character.

Tourbillion (tuəɹbi·lyən), ‖**tourbillon** (turbīlyoṅ). 1477. [a. F. *tourbillon* whirlwind, app. an irregular deriv. of L. *turbo, -inem* 'whirlwind'.] 1. A whirlwind; a whirling storm. Now *rare* or *Obs.* 2. *transf.* A whirling mass or system; a vortex; a whirl. *Obs.* exc. as F. 1712. 3. A kind of firework which spins as it rises, describing a spiral 1765.

2. The *t.* of Ranelagh surrounds you H. WALPOLE.

‖**Tour de force** (turdəfors). 1805. [F. *tour* turn, feat, *de* of, *force* strength.] A feat of strength, power, or skill.

Tourism (tūə·riz'm). 1811. [f. TOUR *sb.* + -ISM.] The theory and practice of touring; travelling for pleasure.

Tourist (tūə·rist). 1800. [f. TOUR *sb.* + -IST.] One who makes a tour or tours; *esp.* one who does this for recreation; one who travels for pleasure or culture, visiting a number of places for their objects of interest, scenery, or the like. Also *attrib.*, as *t. agency, ticket*; **t.-car,** a railway carriage with special accommodation for tourists.

Tourmaline (tūə·ɹmălin, *-in*). 1759. [= F. *tourmaline*, G. *turmalin*; ult. f. Sinhalese *tòramalli* a general name for the cornelian.] *Min.* A brittle pyro-electric mineral, occurring in crystals, also massive, compact, and columnar, orig. obtained from Ceylon; a complex silicoborate with a vitreous lustre, usu. black or blackish and opaque (SCHORL), but also blue (INDICOLITE), red (RUBELLITE), green, or colourless, and in various rich transparent or semi-transparent shades, known as *precious t.*, and much used as a gem. b. With *a* and *pl.* A specimen or gem of this mineral; also, a transparent plate of tourmaline cut parallel to the vertical crystal axis, used in polariscopes, etc.

Tourmente (turmāṅt). 1847. See TORMENT *sb.* 5.

Tourn (tūəɹn). late ME. [a. AF., f. *tourner* to turn, go round.] *Eng. Hist.* The tour, turn, or circuit formerly made by the sheriff of a county twice in the year, in which he presided at the hundred-court in each hundred of the county; the great court leet of the county, held on these occasions: it was a court of record.

Tournament (tūə·ɹnăment). ME. [a. OF. *torneiement, to(u)rnoiement*, etc., f. *tourneier, -oier* TOURNEY *v.*; see -MENT.] 1. *orig.* A martial sport or exercise of the middle ages, in which two parties of combatants, mounted and in armour, fought with blunted weapons for the prize of valour; later, a meeting at an appointed time and place for knightly sports and exercises. 2. *fig.* An encounter or trial of strength 1638. 3. *transf.* A contest in any game of skill in which a number of competitors play a series of selective games, e.g. a *chess* or *lawn tennis t.* 1761.

1. After they be-gonne a turnemente, and departed hem in two partyes 1450.

Tourney (tūə·ɹni, tʊ·ɹni), *sb.* [ME. a. OF. *tornei, tornai, tournay*, F. *tournoi*, vbl. sb. f. *torneier* TOURNEY *v.*] = prec. 1.

1. ..hauntyd the iustes & tornoys 1533. Great Bards ..have sung, Of Turneys and of Trophies hung MILT.

Tourney (tūə·ɹni, tɔ̄·ɹni), *v.* [ME. a. OF. *to(u)rneier*:—Rom. **tornidiare*, **tornizare*, f. *torno*, L. *tornus* sb. or *tornare* vb.; see TURN *sb.* and *v.*] *intr.* To take part in a tourney; to contend or engage in a tournament.

They justyd and turneyd there 1435. Hence **Tou·rneyer,** one who engages in a tourney.

Tourniquet (tūə·ɹniket, ‖turnike). 1695. [a. F., deriv. of *tourner* to TURN.] 1. A surgical instrument, consisting essentially of a bandage, a pad, and a screw, for stopping or checking by compression the flow of blood through an artery; also, a bandage tightened by twisting a rigid bar put through it. 2. A turnstile (*rare*) 1706.

‖**Tournois** (turnwa), *a.* (*sb.*) *Hist.* ME. [F. :—L. *Turonensis* of Tours, *Turones*, a city of France.] Of or pertaining to Tours: esp. said of the money coined at Tours, one-fifth less in value than that struck at Paris 1475. **B.** *sb.* Money or a coin of Tours ME.

‖**Tournure** (turnūr). 1748. [Fr. :—late pop. L. **tornatura*, f. *tornare* to TURN.] 1. (Graceful) manner or bearing; cultivated address. 2. The turning of a phrase (*rare*) 1816. 3. Contour, shape (of a limb, etc.) 1841. 4. A pad formerly worn round the waist or hips to give shapeliness to a woman's figure; also = BUSTLE *sb.*[2] 1874.

Touse (tauz, taus), *sb. dial.* 1795. [f. next.] Horse-play; a 'row', commotion; a fuss.

Touse (tauz), *v.* Now *rare*. 1509. [The compounds with *be-* and *to-* are found from *c* 1300:—OE. **tūsian*:—OTeut. vb. stem **tūs-*, closely allied in sense to *tais-*, whence TEASE.] 1. *trans.* To pull roughly about; to handle roughly; of a dog: to tear at, worry. †**b.** To pull out of joint, to rack. SHAKS. 2. To disorder, dishevel (the hair, dress, etc.); to tumble, rumple (bed-clothes, sheets, etc.) 1598. 3. *fig.* To abuse or maltreat in some way. Now *rare* or *Obs.* 1530. †4. To tease (wool) –1706. †5. *intr.* To touse each other, tussle –1681.

1. As a Beare, whom angry curres have touzd SPENSER. 3. Fortune, the World that towzes to and fro DRAYTON.

Tou·sle, tou·zle (see next), *sb.* 1738. [f. next.] 1. A struggle, a tussle. *Sc.* 2. A tousled mass or mop (of hair) 1880.

Tousle, touzle (tau·z'l, *Sc.* tū·z'l), *v.* 1440. [Iterative of TOUSE *v.*; see -LE 3. Cf. TUSSLE.] 1. To pull about roughly; to handle (esp. a woman) rudely or indelicately; to disorder, dishevel (the hair, clothes, etc.). 2. *intr.* To toss oneself about; also, to rout, rummage 1852. Hence **Tou·sled** *ppl. a.*

‖**Tous-les-mois** (tulẹmwa). 1839. [F., = 'all the months, every month'; but prob. a popular perversion of *toloman*, the name in the French Antilles.] The name in St. Kitts, etc., of species of *Canna*, esp. *C. edulis*, and of the starch obtained from its root-stocks.

Tousy, towsy (tau·zi, tū·zi), *a.* Chiefly *Sc.* and *n. dial.* 1786. [f. TOUSE *v.* + -Y [1].] Dishevelled, unkempt, tousled; shaggy, rough.

Tout (taut), *sb.*[1] 1718. [f. TOUT *v.*] 1. A thieves' scout. *slang.* 2. One who solicits custom 1853. 3. (More fully *racing t.*) One who surreptitiously watches the trials of race-horses, so as to gain information for betting purposes 1865.

Tout (tū), *sb.*[2] 1678. [perh. F. *tout* all.] A specially successful result in certain games.

Tout (taut), *v.* [ME. *tuten*, pointing to an OE. **tūtian*, synonymous with OE. *tōtian* TOOT *v.*[1], and OE. *tȳtan*:—**tūtjan*.] †1. *intr.* To peep, peer, look out; to gaze –1676. **b.** To keep a sharp look-out. *Thieves' cant.* 1700. 2. *trans.* To watch, spy on. *slang.* 1700. **b.** To watch furtively or spy upon (a race-horse or its trainer) with a view to using or disposing of the information for betting purposes 1812. 3. *intr.* To solicit custom, employment, etc. importunately; also, *Colonial* and *U.S.*, to canvass for votes 1731. Also *trans.* with the person or thing as object 1928.

‖**Tout court** (tu kūr). [F. = quite short.] Without further addition or explanation.

Tout ensemble: see ENSEMBLE B.

Touter (tau·təɹ). 1754. [f. TOUT *v.* + -ER [1].] = TOUT *sb.*[1]

Tow (tōu), *sb.*[1] late ME. [perh. related to ON. *tó* uncleansed wool or flax; doubtfully conn. w. OE. **tow-* spinning, weaving, and obs. Du. *touwen* to knit, to weave.] †1. *app.* The unworked stem or fibre of flax, before it is heckled. late ME. only. 2. The fibre of flax, hemp, or jute prepared for spinning by some process of scutching. late ME. 3. More strictly, the shorter fibres of flax or hemp, which are separated by heckling from the fine and long-stapled, called *line* 1530. 4. *attrib.* 1601.

Tow (tōu), *sb.*[2] 1600. [f. TOW *v.*[1]] 1. A rope used for towing, a tow-line. 2. The action of towing or fact of being towed 1622. 3. A vessel taken in tow; also, a string of barges, boats, etc., being towed 1805. **b.** A vessel that tows; a tug 1874.

2. Phr. *In t.*, in the condition of being towed (*of* or *by* the towing vessel). *To take in t.* (said of a ship, etc.), to begin and continue to tow, to tow; *fig.* to take under one's guidance or patronage; to take charge of.

Comb.: **t.-boat**, a boat used in towing; *spec.* a tug; **-post**, a towing-post.

Tow (tōu), *v.*[1] [OE. *togian*, ME. *toȝen towen*:—OTeut. **togōjan*, f. **tog-*, wk. grade of ablaut series **teuh-*, *tauh-*, *tug-* (*tog-*) to draw; see TEE *v.*[1]] †1. *trans.* To draw by force; to pull, drag –1583. 2. *spec.* To draw or drag (a vessel, etc.) on the water by a rope. late ME. 3. To drag by or as by a line. *joc.* 1663. 4. *intr.* or *absol.* To proceed by towing or being towed 1612.

3. A mounted Mexican towing a bull 1883.

Tow (tōu), *v.*[2] 1615. [f. TOW *sb.*[1]] *trans.* To comb or card flax; also, to reduce to the state of tow or fibre.

Towage (tōu·ėdʒ). ME. [In mod. use, f. TOW *v.*[1]] 1. The charge or payment for towing a vessel 1562. 2. The action or process of towing or being towed ME.

Towan (tau·ăn). *Cornw.* 1803. [Cornish.] A coast sand-hill.

Toward (tōu·(w)əɹd), *a.* and *adv.* [OE. *tōweard* adj., f. *tó* To *prep.* + *-weard* -WARD.] **A.** *adj.* †1. That is to come, coming, future –1613. †2. Approaching, imminent, impending –1586. **b.** *pred.* Now *rare* or *Obs.* OE. **c.** In progress, going on; being done 1838. 3. Of young persons: Promising, 'hopeful', forward; making good progress; disposed, willing or apt to learn; docile. *Obs.* or *arch.* ME. 4. Willing, compliant, obliging, docile. *Obs.* or *arch.* 1440. **b.** Of things: Favourable, propitious; the opposite of *untoward* (rare) 1850.

2. b. There is sure another flood t., and these couples are comming to the Arke SHAKS. 3. There was neuer mother had a towarder son HEYWOOD. 4. b. A t. breeze GLADSTONE.

B. *adv.* 1. In a direction toward oneself, or toward something aimed at. *Obs.* or *arch.* ME. 2. Onward (in a course), forward. late ME.

Toward (tǔwǭ·ɹd, tōu·ərd, tōəɹd), *prep.* [OE. *tōweard*, f. *tó* To *prep.* + *-weard* -WARD; orig. the uninflected form or sing. neut. of TOWARD *a.*] 1. Of motion (or action figured as motion): In the direction of; so as to approach (but not necessarily reach). †**b.** With implication of reaching; to –1611. 2. Of position: In the direction of; on the side next to; facing ME. 3. In the direction of (in *fig.* senses) ME. 4. Of time: So as to approach; at the approach of, shortly before, near. late ME. 5. Nearly as much as, nearly 1449. 6. In the way of a contribution to; as a help to; for 1468.

1. I presse t. the marke *Phil.* iii. 14. b. Pilgrimes were they alle That t. Caunterbury wolden ryde CHAUCER. 2. Under Suth-rey t. the South lieth.. Suth-sex HOLLAND. 3. This is the way in which I act t. my own children 1867. 4. At dates well t. the middle of this century 1876. 5. They rise..t. a hundred feet above the plain 1879. 6. Here is two and eightpence halfpenny t. your loss SWIFT. A fund.. t. the expenses of removing paupers by emigration SOUTHEY.

Towardly (tōu·(w)əɹdli, tō·əɹd-), *a. arch.* 1520. [f. TOWARD *a.* + -LY [1].] 1. Likely to lead to a desired result; propitious; favourable; seasonable, befitting. 2. = TOWARD *a.* 3. 1528. 3. Well-disposed, dutiful, tractable 1513. **b.** Favourably disposed, friendly, affable 1550.

1. He must choose a t. hour 1884. 2. He was my Pupil at Oxford, and a very t. one 1627. 3. b. England proved not yet so t. as he expected CLARENDON. **To·wardliness** (now *dial.* or *arch.*). So **To·wardly** *adv.* in a toward or t. manner.

Towardness (tōu·(w)əɹdnės, tō·əɹd-). Now *Obs.* or *arch.* 1461. [f. as prec. + -NESS.] The quality or condition of being 'toward'.

Towards (tǔwǭ·ɹdz, tōu·əɹdz, tōəɹdz), *prep.* and *adv.* [OE. *tōweardes*, f. *tōweard* TOWARD *a.* + -s.] **A.** *prep.* = TOWARD *prep.* **B.** *adv.* or predicative *adj.* †1. In preparation, at hand, imminent –1697. 2. In the direction of some person or thing indicated by the context. *Obs.* or *arch.* 1590.

Towel (tau·ěl), *sb.* [ME. *towaille*, *-aile*, etc., a. OF. *toaille*, mod.F. *touaille* (in med.L. *toacula*, etc., from the mod. langs.) a. WGer. **þwahljō*, OHG. *dwahilla*, *-ila* cloth for washing or wiping, f. OHG. *dwahan*, *twahan* (OE. *þwēan* to wash).] 1. A cloth for wiping something dry, esp. for wiping the hands, face, or person after washing or bathing. Also formerly a table-napkin or other cloth used at meals. **b.** Phr *To throw* (or *toss*) *in the t.*: cf. SPONGE *sb.*[1] I. 1. Phr. †2. *Eccl.* Applied to an altar-cloth; also, a communion-cloth –1737. 3. slang. *Oaken t.*, a stick, cudgel; *lead t.*, a bullet 1709.

1. *Bath-*, *face-*, *glass-t.*

Comb.: **t.-horse**, a wooden frame on which towels are hung; **-roller**, a horizontal roller on which an 'endless' t. (*roller-* or *round-t.*) is hung.

Tow·el, *v.* 1705. [f. prec.] 1. *trans.* To apply a towel to; to rub or dry with a towel 1836. **b.** *intr.* with *at* 1861. 2. *slang.* To beat, cudgel, thrash 1705.

Towelling, toweling (tau·ělin). 1583. [f. TOWEL *sb.* and *v.* + -ING [1].] 1. Material for or of towels. 2. Rubbing with, or application of, a towel 1859. 3. *slang.* A drubbing, thrashing 1851.

Tower (tauəɹ, tau·əɹ), *sb.*[1] [In OE. *torr*, ad L. *turris*; in late OE. and early ME. *tūr*, later *tour*, a. OF. *tor*, *tur*, F. *tour*:—L. *turrem turris*.] **I.** 1. A building lofty in proportion to the size of its base, either isolated, or forming part of a castle, church, or other edifice, or of the walls of a town. 2. Such a structure used as a stronghold, fortress, or prison, or built primarily for purposes of defence. (In this sense often used to include the whole stronghold of which the tower was the nucleus.) ME. 3. *fig.* ME. 4. *transf.* A lofty pile or material mass ME. 5. The gun-turret on an ironclad 1889. 6. Applied to things having the form of, or likened to a tower. †**a.** *Chess.* The castle or rook –1649. **b.** A very high head-dress worn by women in the reigns of William III and Anne. *Hist.* 1612. **c.** Applied to various technical structures and devices, now only descriptively 1662. **d.** *U.S.* A railway signal-box 1904.

1. *Bell-*, *church-*, *watch-*, *water-t.* *Round t.*: see ROUND *a.* *T. of silence*, the structure on which the Parsees expose their dead. 2. The Bastile is but another word for a t. STERNE. *T. of London*, also called *His Majesty's T.*, and often simply *The T.*, is the entire fortress surrounding the original *White T.* of William Rufus. 3. He is my goodnes and my fortres, my t. and my deliuerer BIBLE (Genev.) *Ps.* cxliv. 2.

II. a. Lofty flight; soaring 1486. **b.** The vertical ascent of a wounded bird 1890.

Phr. *T. and town* (also *town and t.*), an alliterative phrase for the inhabited places of a country or region generally.

Comb.: **t.-cress**, the cruciferous plant *Arabis turrita*; **t. hill**, a hill near or on which a t. is built; *spec.* (with caps.) the rising ground by the T. of London; **-man** *U.S.*, a railway signalman; **-stamp**, the official mark on gold and silver articles; hall-mark.

Tower (tōu·əɹ), *sb.*[2] 1611. [f. TOW *v.*[1] + -ER [1].] One who tows or draws with a rope; *esp.* one who tows a boat on a river or canal.

Tower (tauəɹ, tau·əɹ), *v.* 1582. [f. TOWER *sb.*[1]] 1. **a.** *intr.* To rise to a great height like a tower; to rise aloft, stand high. **b.** *fig.* Usu. const. *above*. 1776. 2. *trans.* To raise or uplift to a height; to exalt 1596. 3. *intr.* **a.** *Hawking.* To mount up, as a hawk, so as to be able to swoop down on the quarry 1593. **b.** To soar aloft, as a bird 1647. **c.** To rise vertically, as a bird when wounded 1812. †4. *fig.* To rise on high, to soar –1748. †5. *trans.* To soar aloft in or into; to rise to –1667.

1. a. On th' other side an high rocke toured still SPENSER. b. Does not Gray's poetry, sir, t. above the

common mark? BOSWELL. 2. Where hills tower'd high their crowns CLARE. 3. a. My Lord Protectours Hawkes do towre so well SHAKS. b. The Eagle had cast its Feathers, and could towre no more 1647 5. Yet oft they..towre The mid Aereal Skie MILT.

Towered (tau·əɹd), *a.* late ME. [f. TOWER *sb.*¹ and *v.* + -ED.] 1. Having a tower or towers, adorned or defended by towers; raised or rising on high like a tower. †2. Immured in a tower -1750.

1. Towred Cities please us then MILT.

Tow·ering, *ppl. a.* 1598. [f. TOWER *v.* + -ING².] 1. That towers, in various senses. 2. Rising to a high pitch of violence or intensity 1602.

1. The towring Ash is fairest in the Woods DRYDEN. A man..of t. ambition 1840. 2. The brauery of his griefe did put me Into a Towring passion SHAKS. Hence Tow·eringly *adv.*

Tower mustard. 1597. [So named from its habit of growth.] A cruciferous plant *Turritis glabra*, found on banks and cliffs. b. Sometimes applied to *Arabis turrita*, the *tower-cress* 1760.

Tower pound. Also †pound Tower. 1469. [So called from the standard pound which was kept in the Tower of London.] A pound weight of 5400 grains (= 11¼ Troy ounces), which was the legal mint pound of England prior to the adoption of the Troy pound of 5760 grains in 1526. So **Tower weight**, weight expressed in terms of the Tower pound.

Towery (tau^ə·ri), *a.* 1611. [f. TOWER *sb.*¹ + -Y¹.] 1. Having towers; adorned or defended with towers. 2. Rising to a lofty height; tower-like; also *fig.* aspiring; exalted 1731.

1. Windsor's tow'ry pride POPE. 2. T. trees 1870.

Towhee (tau·hī, tau·ī). *U.S.* 1730. ['From one of its notes' (Newton).] The ground-robin or CHEEWINK of N. America.

Towing (tōu·iŋ), *vbl. sb.* 1494. [f. TOW *v.*¹ + -ING¹.] The action of TOW *v.*¹

attrib.: **t.-lights** *sb. pl.* white lights carried one above another by a vessel which has another or others in tow; **-path** = TOW-PATH; **-post**, a post to make a tow-rope fast to.

Tow-line (tōu·ləin). 1719. [f. TOW *v.*¹ or *sb.*² + LINE *sb.*²] A line, rope, or hawser by which anything is towed; *spec.* in *Whaling*, the whale-line.

Town (taun), *sb.* [OE. *tūn*:—OTeut. **tūnoz* (cf. G. *zaun* hedge), cogn. w. Celtic *dūn*- fortified place.] †1. An enclosed place or piece of ground, an enclosure; a field, garden, yard, court. -late ME. †b. *spec.* The enclosed land surrounding or belonging to a single dwelling; a farm with its farmhouse; a manor; the enclosed land of a village community; sometimes also = parish, when this was coextensive with a manor -1785. 2. The house or group of houses or buildings upon this enclosed land; the farmstead or homestead on a farm or holding. Now esp. *Sc.* OE. 3. A (small) group of dwellings or buildings; a village or hamlet with little or no local organization. (Often = L. *vicus*.) Now *dial.* OE. 4. Now commonly designating an assemblage of buildings, public and private, larger than a village, and having more complete and independent local government; applied not only to a 'borough', and a 'city', but also to an 'urban district', and sometimes also to small inhabited places below the rank of an 'urban district' ME. b. Without article, after preps. and verbs, as *in*, *out of*, *to t.*, *to leave t.*, etc.: i.e. the particular town under consideration, or that with which one has to do; the chief town of the district or province, the capital; in England since *c* 1700 *spec.* said of London ME. c. With def. art., opp. to *the country*. late ME. d. In ME., and later in ballad poetry, etc., often added after the name of a town, in apposition. *arch.* ME. 5. As a collective sing. a. The community of a town in its corporate capacity; the corporation; b. The townspeople; c. *spec.* The fashionable society of London (or other leading city thought of); 'society'. *arch.* ME. d. *absol.* at Oxford and Cambridge: The body of citizens or townsmen as dist. from members of the university; esp. in phr. *t. and gown* 1647. 6. *U.S.* A geographical division for local or state government. a. A township; also, its inhabitants. (Esp. in the New England States.) b. A municipal corporation, having its own geographical boundaries (as dist. from a.). 1808. 7. *transf.* An assemblage of burrows of prairie-dogs, nests of penguins, etc. 1808.

2. Waverley learned..from this colloquy that in Scotland a single house was called a *town* SCOTT. 4. b. When he is in T., he lives in Soho-Square STEELE. c. You say I love the t. 1712. Land in the town seems to be let by the grain as if it was radium 1909. d. A trainband captain eke was he Of famous London t. COWPER. 5. a. I find all the t. almost going out of t. PEPYS.

Phrases. *To come to t.*, to make one's appearance, arrive, come in. *Man about t.*, one who is in the round of social functions, fashionable dissipations, etc. in 'town'. *Man* or *woman* (*girl*) *of the t.*, one belonging to the shady or 'fast' side of t. life. *On the t.*, (*a*) in the swing of fashionable life (*b*) getting a living by prostitution, thieving, or the like; cf. *on the streets*; (*c*) chargeable to the parish (*dial.*); so *to come upon the t.*

attrib. and *Comb.*: **t.-bull**, a bull formerly kept in turn by the cow-keepers of a village; hence *fig.* of a man; **-council**, the elective, deliberative, and administrative body of a t.; hence **t.-councillor**; **-crier**, a public crier; **-cross**, the market cross of a t.; **-ditch** (now *Hist.*) the ditch or moat surrounding a walled t.; **-dweller**, one who dwells in a t., a townsman; **-living**, town-life; also, an eccl. benefice in a t.; **-mouse**, *fig.* a dweller in a t., esp. as unfamiliar with country life (in allusion to Æsop's fable); **-reeve** (now *Hist.*), the bailiff or steward of a *tūn*. b. Combs. with *town's*: **townsfolk** = TOWNSPEOPLE; **†town's husband**, a borough official having charge of the accounts, etc.; **townswoman**, a woman inhabitant of the t.; with possessive, a woman of the same t.

Town, *v. rare.* (Only in *pa. pple.* **Towned.**) 1585. [f. prec.] *trans.* a. To furnish with towns. b. To make into a town.

Town-clerk. ME. The clerk or secretary to the corporation of a town, who has charge of the records, correspondence, and legal business, the conduct of municipal elections, etc.

†Tow·n-cress. [OE. *tūncressa*, f. *tūn* garden, TOWN + CRESS.] Garden cress (*Lepidium sativum*).

Townee (tauni·). 1897. [f. TOWN *sb.* + -EE.] A townsman, esp. as dist. from a member of the university.

Town-end. Now *dial.* Also **town's end.** late ME. The end of the main street of a town or village; one of the extremities of a town.

Tow-net (tōu·net). 1816. [f. TOW *sb.*² or *v.*¹ + NET *sb.*¹] A drag-net or dredge used for the collection of natural specimens.

Town hall. 1481. A large hall used for the transaction of the public business of a town, the holding of a court of justice, assemblies, entertainments, etc.; the great hall of the town-house; now commonly applied to the whole building.

Town-house, town house. 1530. 1. A municipal building containing the public offices, court-house, and town hall; now usu. called TOWN HALL. b. *U.S.* (*a*) An almshouse, workhouse. (*b*) A town prison. 1889. 2. (**Town house.**) A house in a town; a residence in town, as dist. from a country house 1825.

Townish (tau·niʃ), *a.* late ME. [f. TOWN *sb.* + -ISH¹.] †1. Of or pertaining to a town; urban -1674. 2. Pertaining to or characteristic of the town or town life, esp. as dist. from the country; having the manners or habits of town-dwellers 1500.

Townlet (tau·nlėt). 1552. [f. as prec. + -LET.] A tiny or diminutive town.

Townly (tau·nli), *a.* 1749. [-LY¹.] = TOWNISH 2.

Town-made (stress var.), *a.* 1809. Made or manufactured in a town; spec. in the town of the district. Also as *sb.*

Town-major. *Obs.* or *Hist.* 1676. a. The major of a town-guard, as formerly in Edinburgh. b. The chief executive officer in a garrison-town or fortress 1702. c. Applied vaguely to the chief magistrate or administrative officer of a foreign town 1748.

Town-meeting. 1636. A general assembly of the inhabitants of a town; *spec.* in *U.S.* a legal meeting of the qualified voters of a 'town' for the transaction of public business, having certain powers of local government.

To·wn-pla:nning. 1906. The preparation and construction of plans in accordance with which the growth and extension of a town is to be regulated, so as to make the most of the natural advantages of the site, and to secure the most advantageous conditions of housing and traffic, etc.

Township (tau·nʃip). [OE. *tūnscipe*, f. *tūn* TOWN + *-scipe* -SHIP.] †1. In OE., The inhabitants or population of a *tūn* or village collectively. 2. The inhabitants of a particular manor, parish, or division of a hundred, as a community, or in their corporate capacity. Now chiefly *Hist.* 1444. b. Applied to the manor, parish, etc. itself, as a territorial division. Now chiefly *Hist.* late ME. c. *spec.* Each of the local divisions of, or districts comprised in, a large original parish, each containing a village or small town, usu. having its own church 1540. 3. *transf.* Often rendering L. *pagus*, Gr. δῆμος, and thus applied to independent or self-governing towns of ancient Greece, Italy, and other lands, etc. 1602. 4. *Sc.* A farm held in joint tenancy 1813. 5. *U.S.* and *Canada.* A division of a county having certain corporate powers of local administration (in the newer states, a division six miles square, and so called even when still unsettled); the same that in New England is called a town 1685. 6. In Australia, A site laid out prospectively for a town 1802. 7. By some 19th c. historical writers, adopted to designate what they consider to have been the simplest form of local or social organization in primitive OE. times 1832.

Townsman (tau·nzmæ̆n). OE. [f. *town's*, genitive of TOWN + MAN *sb.*] †1. OE. (*tūnesman*). One who lives in a *tūn*; a villager, a villein. 2. A man who lives in a town or city; a citizen. late ME. b. A man of one's own or the same town; a fellow-townsman ME. c. An ordinary citizen or resident of a university town as dist. from a GOWNSMAN (3c) 1768. 3. *New England.* = SELECTMAN 1656.

Townspeople (tau·nz,pī:p'l). 1648. [f. as prec.] People or inhabitants of a town or towns; townsmen and townswomen; townsfolk. (Usu. const. as *pl.*)

Town-talk. 1654. The common talk or gossip of the people of a town; the subject or matter of such talk.

Townward (tau·nwǒɹd), *adv.* (*a.*) late ME. [f. TOWN *sb.* + -WARD.] Towards or in the direction of the town. **B.** *adj.* Going or directed toward the town 1806.

The t. drift of the people 1893. So **Tow·nwards** *adv.*

Tow-path (tōu·paþ). 1846. [f. TOW *v.*¹ + PATH.] A path by the side of a canal or navigable river for use in towing.

Tow-rope (tōu·rōup). ME. [f. TOW *v.*¹ + ROPE *sb.*¹] A rope (hawser, cable, or the like) used in towing.

Tow-row (tau·rau), *sb.* and *a.* 1709. [Redupl. form of ROW *sb.*²; orig. *dial.*] **A.** *sb.* An uproar, hubbub, din 1877. †**B.** *adj.* Intoxicated.

Towser (tau·zəɹ). 1678. [f. TOUSE *v.* + -ER¹.] (With capital T.) A common name for a large dog, such as was used to bait bears or bulls; also *transf.* of a person.

Towy (tōu·i), *a.* 1601. [f. TOW *sb.*¹ + -Y¹.] Like or of the nature of tow.

Tox-¹, comb. form, repr. TOXI- or TOXO-² bef. a vowel.

‖**Toxæmia** (tǫksī·miă), [Gr. αἷμα blood, after *anæmia*, etc.], a morbid condition of the blood caused by a toxin; blood-poisoning; hence **Toxæmic** (-ī·mik) *a.*, pertaining to or affected with toxæmia. **Toxanæmia** (-ănī·miă), anæmia caused by the action of a poison, usu. a ptomaine.

Tox-²: see TOXO-¹.

Toxi- (tǫksi), comb. form arbitrarily repr. TOXIC or TOXIN, as in **Toxidermic** (-dō·ɹmik) *a.* [Gr δέρμα skin], pertaining to skin-disease produced by a poison. ‖**Toxipho·bia** [-PHOBIA] fear of being poisoned, as a form of insanity or monomania.

Toxic (tǫ·ksik), *a.* (*sb.*) 1664. [f. med.L. *toxicus* poisoned, imbued with poison, adj. of which the neut. *toxicum* was already in cl. L. = poison, a. Gr. τοξικόν φάρμακον poison for smearing arrows (τοξικός orig. meaning 'of or pertaining to the bow', τόξον).] 1. Of the nature of a poison; poisonous. 2. Caused or produced by a poison; due to poisoning 1872. B. *sb.* A toxic substance, a poison 1890.

1. The introduction into the torrent of the circulation of t. substances 1876. 2. T. Insanity 1874. So **To·xical** *a.* of t. nature or character 1607.

Toxicant (tǫ·ksikănt), *a.* and *sb.* *rare.* 1882. [f. pr. pple. of med.L. *toxicare* to poison; see -ANT.] A. *adj.* Acting as a poison; poisonous, toxic 1891. B. *sb.* A poisonous substance, a poison 1882.

Toxication (tǫksikēi·ʃən). 1821. [f. med. L. *toxicare*, f. *toxicus* TOXIC.] Poisoning: esp. by toxic substances produced by disease-germs.

Toxicity (tǫksi·sĭti). 1881. [f. TOXIC + -ITY.] Toxic or poisonous quality, esp. in relation to its degree or strength.

Toxico- (tǫ·ksiko), bef. a vowel **toxic-**, repr. Gr. τοξικόν in sense 'poison' (see TOXIC), but mostly used as comb. form of TOXIC, as in ‖**Toxicoderma** (-dō·ımă), **-dermati·tis**, **-dermi·tis** [Gr. δέρμα skin; see -ITIS], inflammation of the skin caused by an irritant poison. ‖**Toxicoma·nia** [MANIA], a morbid craving for poisons. **Toxicopho·bia** = *toxiphobia*.

Toxicology (tǫksikǫ·lŏdʒi). 1799. [ad. F. *toxicologie*, f. Gr. τοξικόν (see TOXIC) + -LOGY.] The science of poisons; that department of pathology or medicine which deals with the nature and effects of poisons. So **To:xicolo·gical** *a.* belonging or relating to t. (sometimes erron. used for *toxical*). **To:xicolo·gically** *adv.* in relation to t. **Toxico·logist**, a person versed in t.

‖**Toxicosis** (tǫksikōu·sis). *Pl.* **-oses** (-ōu·sīz). 1857. [mod.L., f. as prec. + -OSIS.] *Path.* A disease or morbid condition produced by the action of a poison.

To·xifer. 1853. [ad. mod.L. *Toxifera*, f. Gr. τόξα arrows + L. *-fer* bearing.] *Zool.* A mollusc of the sub-order *Toxifera*.

Toxin (tǫ·ksin). 1886. [f. TOXIC + -IN[1].] A specific poison, usu. of an albuminous nature, esp. one produced by a microbe, which causes a particular disease when present in the system of a human or animal body.

Toxo-[1] (tǫksǫ), bef. a vowel **tox-**, comb. form repr. Gr. τόξον bow, in TOXODON, TOXOPHILITE, etc.

Toxo-[2], used as comb. form of TOXIN (cf. TOXI-) or instead of TOXICO-, as in **To·xophil** (-fil) *a.* [Gr. -φιλος loving], having affinity for a toxin. **To·xophore** (-fōəɹ), **Toxophoric** (-fǫ·rik), **Toxophorous** (-ǫ·fŏrəs) *adjs.* [Gr. -φορος bearing, carrying], poison-bearing; applied to a particular group of atoms in the molecule of a toxin to which its toxic properties are due.

Toxodon (tǫ·ksŏdǫn). 1837. [mod.L., f. Gr. τόξον bow + ὀδούς, ὀδοντ- tooth.] *Palæont.* A genus of large extinct quadrupeds, having strongly curved molar teeth, whose remains are found in Pleistocene deposits in S. America. Hence **To·xodont** *adj.* belonging to or having the characters of the order *Toxodonta*, typified by this genus; *sb.* a quadruped of this order.

Toxoglossate (tǫksǫglǫ·seit), *a.* 1853. [f. mod.L. *Toxoglossa*, f. Gr. τόξα arrows, darts + γλῶσσα tongue; see -ATE[2] 2.] *Zool.* Having the characters of the *Toxoglossa* of Troschel, a group of gasteropod molluscs; the same as Gray's *Toxifera*.

Toxophilite (tǫksǫ·filəit). 1794. [app. f. *Toxophilus*, title of Ascham's book (1545) intended to mean 'lover of the bow' (f. Gr. τόξον bow + φίλος) + -ITE[1]; *quasi* 'a follower of Toxophilus'.] A lover or devotee of archery, an archer 1812. b. *attrib.* Of or pertaining to archers or archery 1794. Hence **Toxo·phily**, the practice of, or addiction to, archery.

Toy (toi), *sb.* 1500. [Origin obsc.; prob. LG.] I. Abstract senses. †1. Amorous sport, dallying, toying; with *pl.*, an act or piece of this, a light caress –1707. †2. A sportive or frisky movement; an antic, a trick –1777. 3. A fantastic or trifling speech or piece of writing; a foolish or idle tale; a jest, joke, pun; a light or facetious composition. *arch.* 1542. †4. A whim, crotchet, caprice –1699. †b. *spec.* A foolish or unreasoning aversion; esp. in phr. *to take (a) t. at* something –1697.

1. So said he, and forbore not glance or t. Of amorous intent, well understood Of Eve MILT. 3. I neuer may beleeue These anticke fables, nor these Fairy toyes SHAKS.

II. Concrete senses. 1. *gen.* A thing of little or no value or importance, a trifle; a foolish or senseless affair, a piece of nonsense; *pl.* trumpery, rubbish 1530. 2. A plaything for children or others; also, something contrived for amusement rather than for practical use (esp. in phr. *a mere t.*) 1586. 3. A small article of little intrinsic value; a knick-knack, trinket, gewgaw; hence applied to anything small, flimsy, or inferior of its kind (now chiefly *attrib.*) 1596 4. *fig.* Applied to a person 1598. 5. Applied to a diminutive breed or variety of animals 1877. 6. *Sc.* A close cap or head-dress, of linen or wool, with flaps coming down to the shoulders, formerly worn by women of the lower classes in Scotland. Now *rare* or *Obs.* 1724. 7. *attrib.*: a. That is a toy (in sense II. 2); applied to small models or imitations of ordinary objects used as playthings, as *t. cannon, train*, etc. 1836. b. *transf.* and *fig.* Applied to things of diminutive size, flimsy construction, or petty character 1821. c. Applied to an animal, esp. a dog of a diminutive breed or variety, kept as a pet 1863.

1. From this instant, There's nothing serious in Mortalitie: All is but Toyes SHAKS. 2. Lead soldiers, dolls, all toys..are in the same category 1881. 3. A conspicuous t. of a church 1888. 4. Elues, list your names: Silence, you aiery toyes SHAKS. A Russian ..being a mere t. in the hands of the commonest policeman 1883. Hence **Toy·ful** *a.*; amusing (now *rare* or *Obs.*).

Toy, *v.* 1529. [Goes with TOY *sb.*] 1. *intr.* To act idly; to trifle, 'play' (*with* a person or thing). 2. To sport amorously; to dally, flirt. Usu. const. *with*. 1550. 3. To play, sport; to frisk about 1530.

2. To t., to wanton, dallie, smile, and iest SHAKS. *fig.* He had..toyed a little with the muses 1842. 3. *T. with*, to play with (a material object), to handle or finger idly; hence, to work idly or carelessly with or at. Hence **Toy·er**, one who toys; a trifler.

To-year (tŭ,yīə·ɹ), *adv.* Now *dial.* ME. [f. To *prep.* A. II. 2 + YEAR; cf. *to-day*, etc.] This year.

Toy·ing, *ppl. a.* 1566. [f. TOY *v.* + -ING[2].] That toys; *esp.* amorously sportive. Hence **Toy·ingly** *adv.*

Toyish (toi·iʃ), *a.* Now *rare.* 1563. [f. TOY *sb.* + -ISH[1].] Having the character of a toy, or addicted to toys. 1. Trifling; foolish, nonsensical 1574. †2. Sportive, frisky, skittish; amorously sportive, wanton –1680. 3. Of the nature of, or fit for, a plaything; of a sportive character, as a writing 1699. Hence **Toy·ish-ly** *adv.*, **-ness.**

Toyman (toi·mæ̆n). 1707. [f. TOY *sb.* + MAN *sb.*] A man who sells toys, or who keeps a toy-shop.

Toy·-shop. 1693. 1. A shop for the sale of trinkets, knick-knacks, or small ornamental articles. *arch.* 2. A shop for the sale of toys or playthings 1818.

†**Toy·some**, *a.* *rare.* 1638. [f. TOY *sb.* + -SOME.] Full of 'toys', or having the character of a 'toy'; fantastic; playful; amorously sportive –1754.

Toze, tose (tōuz), *v.*[1] *Obs.* exc. *dial.* [ME. *tosen* :—OE. **tǽsian*, f. vbl. root *tǽs-* :—OTeut. *tais-*, whence also OE. *tǽsan* to TEASE.] *trans.* = TEASE *v.* 1. Also *fig.*

Toze (tōuz), *v.*[2] 1758. [Possibly same word as prec.] *Tin-mining. (trans.)* To separate tin ore from the gangue or rough ore by stirring the slimes in a kieve, and allowing the heavier particles to settle.

‖**Trabea** (trēi·bĭă). *Pl.* **-eæ** (-ĭ,ī). 1600. [L.] *Rom. Antiq.* A toga ornamented with horizontal purple stripes, worn as a state robe by kings, consuls, and other men of rank in ancient Rome.

Trabeate (trēi·bĭeit), *a.* 1890. [irreg. f. L. *trabs, trabem* beam + -ATE[2].] *Arch.* = next.

Trabeated (trēi·bĭ,ĕitĕd), *a.* 1843. [f. as prec. + -ED[1].] *Arch.* Constructed with beams; having beams or long squared stones as lintels and entablatures, instead of using the arch; covered with a beam or entablature, as a doorway.

Trabeation (trēibĭ,ēi·ʃən). 1563. [irreg. f. L. *trabs, trabem* beam; see -ATION.] *Arch.* †a. An entablature. b. Trabeated structure.

‖**Trabecula** (trăbe·kiŭlă). *Pl.* **-æ** (-ī). 1886. [L., dim. of *trabs* beam.] A structure in an animal or plant resembling a small beam or bar. So **Trabe·cular** *a.* pertaining to or of the nature of a t.; composed of or furnished with trabeculæ 1822. **Trabe·culate** (1866), **-ated** (1876) *adjs.* furnished with or having trabeculæ.

Trabuch (trăbu·k). *Obs.* or *arch.* 1482. [a. OF. *trabuc*, f. *tra-, très-* (:—L. *trans-*, expressing displacement) + OF. *buc* trunk (of the body) bulk, a. WGer. **bûh-*, Ger. *bauch* belly.] A mediæval engine of war for throwing great stones against walls, etc.

‖**Tracasserie** (trakasrī). 1656. [F., f. *tracasser* to bustle, worry oneself; see -ERY.] A state of disturbance or annoyance; a turmoil, bother, fuss; a petty quarrel. (Chiefly in *pl.*)

Trace (trēis), *sb.*[1] ME. [a. F., f. OF. *tracier*, F. *tracer* to TRACE *v.*] †1. The way or path which anything takes; course, road –1768. †2. A line, file, or train of persons –1598. †3. *pl.* The series or line of footprints left by an animal; hence in *sing.* a footprint –1706. 4. The track made by the passage of any person or thing, whether beaten by feet or indicated in any other way. late ME. b. *spec.* A beaten path through a wild or unenclosed region, made by the passage of men or beasts; a track, a trail. *U.S.* 1807. 5. *pl.* Vestiges or marks remaining and indicating the former presence, existence, or action of something; *sing.* a vestige, an indication. late ME. b. An indication of the presence of a minute amount of some constituent in a compound; a quantity so minute as to be inferred but not actually measured; esp. in *Chem.*; *transf.* a very little 1827. 6. *fig.* A non-material indication or evidence of the presence or existence of something, or of a former event or condition; a sign, mark 1656. 7. A line or figure drawn; a tracing, drawing, or sketch; the traced record of a self-recording instrument; in *Fortif.* the ground-plan of a work 1744. 8. *Geom.* a. The track described by a moving point, line, or surface. b. The intersection of a line or surface with a surface; *spec.* the intersection of a plane with one of the co-ordinate planes, or with one of the planes of projection. 1834.

4. Phr. *On one's trace(s*, in pursuit of one. 5. My niece..saw the traces of the ditch at once SCOTT. b. Traces of oxalic acid can be detected 1838. 6. The shady empire shall retain no t. Of war or blood, but in the sylvan chase POPE.

Trace (trēis), *sb.*[2] [ME. *trays*, a. OF. *traiz, trais*, pl. of *trait*; = It. *tratto*, L. *tractus* draught, f. *trahere* to draw. Orig. treated as collect. pl. and at length as a sing. with a new pl. *trasys, traces.*] †1. as *pl.* The pair of ropes, chains, or (now usu.) leather straps by which the collar of a draught-animal is connected with the splinter-bar or swingletree. (Usu. *collective.*) –1807. 2. as *sing.* Each of the individual ropes or leather straps mentioned above; in *pl.* = sense 1. late ME. Also *attrib.*, as *t-horse.*

2. Phr. (*fig.*) *Into the traces*, into regular work; He was too fond of my genius to force it into the traces 1824. *To kick over the traces*: see KICK *v.*[1] 1.

Trace (trēis), *v.* [ME. *tracen*, a. OF. *tracier*, F. *tracer* = It. *tracciare* :—pop. L. or Com. Rom. **tractiare*, f. L. *tractus* track, course.] †I. 1. *intr.* To take one's course, make one's way; to proceed, pass, go, travel, tread –1793. 2. To pace or step in dancing; to dance –1808. 3. *trans.* To tread (a path, way, street, etc.) –1794. 4. To travel or range over; to traverse –1807.

3. The passage..commonly called the dolorous way, ..traced with the blessed feet of our Saviour FULLER.

II. 1. To follow the footprints or traces of; *esp.* to track by the footprints; also with the traces as object; hence, to pursue, to dog 1440. 2. *fig.* To follow the course, development, or history of. Also with the course, etc. as object. 1654. b. *intr.* for *pass.* To go *back* in time, to date *back* 1886. 3. *trans.* To make out and follow the course or line of 1703. b. To make out, decipher (worn or obscure writing) 1761. **4.** To ascertain by investigation; to search out 1642. **b.** To find traces of 1697.

1. It is forbydden to t. hares in snowe tyme 1530. 2. No libel on the government had ever been traced to a Quaker MACAULAY. 3. The form of the ancient manor house may still be traced 1907. b. Thrice he traced the runic rhyme GRAY. 4. Tracing a connection..where in reality none exists 1869. b. He observes no Method that I can t. DRYDEN.

III. 1. *trans.* To mark, make marks upon; *esp.* to ornament with lines, figures, or characters. late ME. **2.** To make a plan, diagram, or chart of (something existing or to be constructed); to mark out the course of (a road, etc.) on, or by means of, a plan or map; to set out (the lines of a work or road) on the ground itself. Also *fig.* to devise (a plan of action), map out (a policy). late ME. **3.** To draw; to draw an outline or figure of; also, to put down in writing, to pen. late ME. **b.** To copy (a drawing, plan, etc.) by following the lines of the original drawing on a transparent sheet placed upon it; to make a tracing of 1762.

1. The deep-set windows, stain'd and traced TENNYSON. 2. The castle [in Milan], by which the citadel of Antwerp was traced 1645.

Traceable (trēⁱ·săb'l), *a.* 1748. [f. prec. + -ABLE.] Capable of being traced. Hence **Traceabi·lity, Tra·ceableness. Tra·ceably** *adv.*

Traceless (trēⁱ·slės), *a.* 1651. [f. TRACE *sb.*[1] + -LESS.] Leaving no trace or track; that cannot be traced; of a surface, that shows no traces or lines.

Tracer (trēⁱ·səɹ). 1552. [f. TRACE *v.* + -ER [1].] One who or that which traces. **1.** One who follows the track of anything; one who tracks, investigates, or searches out. **2.** A thing used for tracing; *spec.* in *Anat.* a slender probe used in tracing the course of a nerve or vessel 1882. **3.** *gen.* Something which traces lines or makes tracings, in various spec. uses 1790. **4.** = *t. bullet, shell*; also, the smoke emitted 1910.

attrib.: **t. bullet**, etc., a bullet, etc., whose trajectory is made visible by smoke or a luminous glow.

Tracery (trēⁱ·səri). 1464. [app. an Eng. formation f. TRACE *v.* or TRACER; see -ERY.] †**1.** A place for tracing or drawing (*rare*). **2.** *Arch.* The term given to the intersecting ribwork in the upper part of a Gothic window, formed by the elaboration of the mullion, and to the interlaced work of a vault, and that on walls, in panels, and in tabernacle work or screens 1699. **3.** *trans.* and *fig.* Any delicate interweaving of lines or threads, as in embroidery, carving, etc.; also, an interlacing of boughs or foliage; network, open-work 1827.

‖**Trachea** (trēⁱ·kiă, trăkī·ă). *Pl.* **-eæ.** late ME. [med.L., = late L. *trachia*, a. Gr. τραχεῖα (fem. of τραχύς rough), short for ἀρτηρία τραχεῖα 'rough artery'.] **1.** *Anat.* and *Zool.* **a.** The musculo-membranous tube extending from the larynx to the bronchi, and surrounded by gristly (or in birds often bony) rings, which conveys the air to the lungs in air-breathing vertebrates; the windpipe. **b.** Each of the tubes which constitute the respiratory organ in insects and other arthropods 1826. **2.** *Bot.* One of the ducts or vessels in the woody tissue of plants, formed from the coalescence of series of cells by disappearance of the partitions between them, formerly supposed to serve for the passage of air; a wood-vessel 1744. So **Tracheal** (trēⁱ·kiăl, trăkī·ăl) *a.* pertaining to or of the nature of a t.; connected with, composed of, tracheæ. **Trachean** (trēⁱ·kiăn, trăkī·ăn) *a. Zool.* pertaining to or of the nature of a t.; having tracheæ; *sb.* a tracheate arachnid.

Tracheary (trēⁱ·kiări), *a.* (*sb.*) 1835. [ad. mod.L. *trachearius.*] **1.** *Zool.* Belonging to the order *Trachearia* of arachnids. **2.** *Bot.* Of the nature of, or composed of, tracheæ; esp. applied to tissue containing both tracheæ and tracheides 1885. **B.** *sb.* A tracheate arachnid 1835.

Tracheate (trēⁱ·kiˌeⁱt), *a.* (*sb.*) 1877. [ad. mod.L. *Tracheata*, f. *trachea*; see -ATE [2] 2.] *Zool.* Furnished with or having tracheæ, as an arthropod; belonging to the group *Tracheata*, in some classifications comprising the insects, myriapods, arachnids, and the genus *Peripatus*, or *spec.* to the order *Tracheata* or *Trachearia* of arachnids, which breathe by tracheæ alone. **B.** *sb.* A tracheate arthropod. So **Tra·cheated** *a.*

Tracheide (trēⁱ·ki-, trăkī·ˌəid). 1875. [a. G. *tracheïde*, f. TRACHEA + -IDE, -ID [2].] *Bot.* A vascular cell, with pitted lignified wall, which serves for the conduction of water; a vascular wood-cell. Hence **Tracheidal** *a.* pertaining to or of the nature of a t.

‖**Tracheitis** (trēⁱkiˌəi·tis, træk-). 1859. [mod.L., f. TRACHEA + -ITIS.] *Path.* Inflammation of the trachea.

Trachelate (træ·kĭleⁱt), *a.* 1826. [ad. mod.L. *trachelatus*, f. Gr. τράχηλος neck; see -ATE [2].] *Entom.* Having a neck, or a constriction like a neck: said of the prosternum in certain hymenopterous insects. So **Tracheliate** (trăkī·liˌeⁱt) *a.* belonging to the division *Trachelia* or *Trachelida* of beetles, which have a necklike constriction behind the eyes. **Trachelidan** (trăke·lidăn) *a.* = *tracheliate*; *sb.* a member of the *Trachelida.*

Trachelo- (trăkī·lo), comb. form repr. Gr. τράχηλος neck.

Trache·lobra·nchiate *a.*, *Zool.* having branchia or gills on the neck, as the division *Trachelobranchia* of gasteropod molluscs. **Trachelo·rrhaphy** [Gr. ῥαφή sewing], *Surg.* repair or suture of a laceration of the neck of the womb. **Trachelo·tomy** [Gr. τομή cutting], *Surg.* amputation of the neck of the womb.

‖**Trachenchyma** (trăke·ŋkimă). 1848. [f. TRACHEA + Gr. ἔγχυμα infusion, after PARENCHYMA.] *Bot.* Tracheary tissue.

Tracheo- (trēⁱ·kio, trăkī·o), used as comb. form of TRACHEA.

‖**Tracheobranchia** (-bræ·ŋkiă), pl. **-æ**, a respiratory organ in certain insect larvæ, combining the characters of a trachea and a branchia or gill. **Tracheobronchial** (-brǫ·ŋkiăl) *a.*, pertaining to the trachea and the bronchi; also as *sb.* a tracheobronchial muscle (in birds). **Trache·ocele** (-sīl) [Gr. κήλη tumour], a tumour in or upon the trachea; also loosely applied to goitre. **Trache·ophone** (-fōun) [Gr. φωνή voice], *sb.* a member of the *Tracheophonæ* or *Tracheophones*, a group of S. American passerine birds, having the syrinx or vocal organ situated wholly or chiefly in the trachea; *adj.* belonging to this group. **Tracheo·scopy** [Gr. -σκοπία, f. σκοπεῖν to view], inspection of the trachea, as with a laryngoscope.

Tracheotomy (trēⁱkiˌǫ·tŏmi, træ·k-). 1726. [f. TRACHEO- + -TOMY.] *Surg.* Incision of the trachea or windpipe.

Trachinoid (træ·kinoid), *a.* and *sb.* 1889. [f. mod.L. *Trachinus*, the typical genus + -OID; f. med.L. *trachina*, local name of a fish.] **A.** *adj.* Resembling, allied to, or having the characters of, the *Trachinidæ* or weevers, a family of spiny-finned fishes. **B.** *sb.* A fish of this family.

‖**Trachoma** (trăkōu·mă). 1693. [mod.L., a. Gr. τράχωμα roughness, f. τραχύς rough.] *Path.* An infectious disease of the eyes, characterized by roughness or granulation of the inner surface of the eyelids, often supervening upon purulent ophthalmia; also called *granular lids.* **b.** Also, an affection of the larynx characterized by nodular swellings on the vocal chords.

Trachomedusan (trēⁱ:komĭdiū·săn), *a.* and *sb.* 1907. [f. mod.L. *Trachomedusæ*, pl., f. *tracho-*, var. of TRACHY- + MEDUSA; see -AN.] *Zool.* **A.** *adj.* Belonging to the sub-order *Trachomedusæ* of the order *Trachymedusæ* of craspedote Hydrozoa. **B.** *sb.* A hydrozoan of this sub-order.

Trachy- (trēⁱki, træki-), combining form repr. Gr. τραχύς rough.

Trachyca·rpous [Gr. καρπός fruit] *a.*, *Bot.* rough-fruited. **Tra·chymedu·san**, *Zool.*, *a.* belonging to the family *Trachymedusæ* of Craspedote Hydrozoa; *sb.* a hydrozoan of this family. **Trachyspe·rmous** [Gr. σπέρμα seed] *a.*, *Bot.* rough-seeded. **b.** *Min.* In names of rocks, taken as comb. form of TRACHYTE, and denoting an igneous rock or lava intermediate between trachyte and that denoted by the second element, as **trachyba·salt**, etc.

Trachyte (trēⁱ·kəit, træ·kəit). 1821. [a. F., f. Gr. τραχύς rough.] *Geol.* and *Min.* A group of volcanic rocks, having a characteristically rough or gritty surface. Now confined to rocks mainly consisting of sanidine (or glassy orthoclase) felspar. Hence **Trachy·tic** *a.* consisting or of the nature of t.; containing or abounding in trachyte. **Tra·chytoid** *a.* resembling or allied to trachyte.

Tracing (trēⁱ·siŋ), *vbl. sb.* 1440. [f. TRACE *v.*[1] + -ING [1].] **1.** The following of traces, tracking, *esp.* **2.** Drawing, delineating, marking out; the copying of a drawing, etc., by means of a transparent sheet placed over it 1440. **b.** *concr.* That which is produced by tracing or drawing; a drawing; *spec.* a copy made by tracing; also, the record of a self-registering instrument 1811.

Comb.: **t.-cloth, -linen**, smooth transparent linen sized on one side, used for making tracings; **-paper**, (*a*) transparent paper for copying drawings, etc. by tracing; (*b*) lithographic transfer paper; **-wheel**, a toothed wheel or roulette for marking out patterns.

Track (træk), *sb.* 1470. [a. OF. *trac, traq*, F. *trac*, of uncertain origin. Cf. MLG. and Du. *treck, trek* draught, drawing, line drawn, etc., f. *trecken, trekken* to draw, etc.] **I. 1.** The mark or series of marks left by the passage of anything; a trail; a wheel-rut; the wake of a ship; a series of footprints; the scent followed by hounds; *spec.* in *Geol.* a series of fossilized footprints of an animal. **b.** *Zool.* The sole of the foot, esp. in birds 1891. †**2.** *fig.* = TRACE *sb.*[1] 5, 6. –1694. **3.** A way made or beaten by the feet of men or animals; a path; a rough unmade road 1643. **4.** A line of travel, passage, or motion; the actual course or route followed 1570. **b.** The course of a nerve or blood-vessel, or the like; the course of a wound 1807. **5.** *fig.* **a.** A course of action or conduct; a method of proceeding. *The beaten t.*, the ordinary (*quasi* well-worn) way. 1638. **b.** A train or sequence of events, thoughts, etc. 1681. **6.** A path made or laid down for a special purpose; *spec.* **a.** (now *U.S.*) A continuous line of a pair of rails and the space between them, on which railway vehicles travel. *Off the t.*, off the line, derailed; also *fig.* 1805. **b.** A course prepared or laid out for racing, or the like 1887. **c.** Each of the bands of a caterpillar tractor 1927. **7.** [f. TRACK *v.*[1]] The action of tracking; the pursuit of a criminal or fugitive 1542.

1. They came on the trakkys of there enmyes 1500. The tracks of snails and slugs DICKENS. 3. An Indian t., newly made 1675. The road was only a slight t. upon the grass 1791. 4. Far from t. of men MILT.

Phrases. *In one's tracks* (U.S.), on the spot where one is at the moment; instantly, immediately. *On the t.* (*of*), in pursuit of; also, having a trace of or clue to. *To cover* (*up*) *a person's tracks*, to conceal or screen his motions or measures. *To make tracks* (*for*), to make off, to make *for*; to go off quickly (orig. *U.S.*). *To keep t.*, to follow or grasp the course, progress, or sequence *of*; so *to lose t. of.*

II. [Used by confusion for TRACT *sb.*[3]] An extent of land; also, a space of time, a period; also, †a sequence or succession of actions or events 1687.

attrib. and *Comb.*: **t.-brake**, a railway brake which acts by pressure directly against the rail; **-clearer**, a cross-bar carried immediately in front of the wheels of a locomotive or tram-car to push obstructions off the rails; also, a cow-catcher or snow-sweeper fixed in front of a locomotive; **-mile**, a mile of 't.' or single line; hence **-mileage**; **-scale**, a weigh-bridge for railway vehicles.

Track, *v.*[1] 1565. [f. prec.] **1.** *trans.* To follow up the track of; to pursue by or as by the track left. **b.** To find out and follow (a track, trail) 1681. **c.** *intr.* Of the wheels of a vehicle: To run in the same track; of a gear-wheel, To be in alinement (*with* another wheel). **2.** *trans.* To mark out, trace (a path); to indicate the path or course of; *esp.* to mark out (a path) by repeatedly traversing it; to mark (a way) with tracks; to tread, beat 1589. **b.** To lay a track on or for (a railway); to furnish with a line of rails. Only in compounds, as *to double-t., single-t. U.S.* 1874. **3.** *intr.* To follow a track or path; to make one's way, pass, go, travel. Now *U.S. slang.* 1590. **b.** *Path.* To make a track for itself; to find its way 1903.

1. The first point was to t. the lion to his covert 1834. 2. The way was smooth and well tracked 1815.

Track, *v.*[2] 1727. [app. ad. Du. *trekken* to draw, pull, etc. (see TREK), assimilated in form to prec.] *trans.* To tow (a vessel), esp. from the bank or tow-path. Also *absol.* **b.** *intr.* To proceed by towing. Said of a boat or of those in it. 1854.

Track-, stem of TRACK *v.*², in comb., as *t.-barge*, *-boat*, *-road*.

Trackage¹ (træ·kėdʒ). 1820. [f. TRACK *v.*² + -AGE.] The action or process of tracking or towing, or fact of being tracked; towage, haulage.

Tra·ckage². *U.S.* 1884. [f. TRACK *sb.* 6 a + -AGE.] The tracks or lines of a railway system collectively. Also *attrib.* **t. charge**, charge made for the use of a railway line by another company.

Tracker¹ (træ·kəɹ). 1617. [f. TRACK *v.*¹ + -ER¹.] One who or that which tracks; one skilled in following a track or trail.

Black t., an Australian native employed by the government to track criminals.

Tra·cker². 1791. [f. TRACK *v.*²; cf. Du. *trekker*.] 1. One who tracks or tows a vessel; a tower; also, a tugboat. 2. *Organ-building.* A strip or rod of wood forming part of the connexion between the key and the pallet, and exerting a pulling action 1843.

Trackless (træ·klės), *a.* 1656. [f. TRACK *sb.* + -LESS.] Without a track or path; pathless; untrodden. **b.** Leaving no track or trace 1695. **c.** Not running on a track or line of rails, while propelled by electric power from overhead conductors 1909.

The recesses of a t. wilderness. Hence **Tra·cklessly** *adv.*, **-ness.**

Trackway (træ·kwēɪ). 1818. [f. TRACK *sb.* + WAY.] A path beaten by the feet of passers, a track; also, an ancient British roadway, a ridgeway.

Tract (trækt), *sb.*¹ late ME. [app. abbrev. of L. *tractatus* TRACTATE; not in any other lang.] †1. Literary treatment or discussion (*rare*) –1659. 2. A book or written work treating of some particular topic; a treatise; a written or printed discourse or dissertation. Now *rare* in *gen.* sense. **b.** A division of a book or literary work treating of a separate subject or branch (*rare*) 1662. 3. In later use: A short pamphlet on some religious, political, or other topic, suitable for distribution or for purposes of propaganda 1806.

3. Am I really as dull as a t., my dear? G. MEREDITH. *Tracts for the Times*, a series of pamphlets on theological and ecclesiastical topics (known also as the *Oxford Tracts*), started by J. H. Newman, and published at Oxford 1833–41, on the doctrines of which the Tractarian movement was based.

Tract, *sb.*² late ME. [ad. med.L. TRACTUS.] *Liturg.* An anthem consisting of verses of Scripture, usu. from the Psalms, sung instead of the Alleluia in the Mass from Septuagesima till Easter Eve.

Tract (trækt), *sb.*³ 1486. [ad. L. *tractus* drawing, etc., f. ppl. stem of *trahere* to draw, drag.] I. †1. The drawing out, duration, process, or lapse *of time*; the course *of time* –1734. †**b.** Protraction (of time), delay –1600. **c.** An extent of time, a period 1494. 2. The continuance or continued duration *of* some action or state; the course or continuity *of* a narrative, etc.; a continued series. Now *rare* or *Obs.* 1581. 3. A stretch or extent *of* territory, etc.; a space or expanse of land (more rarely, of water, air, etc.); a region, district 1553. **b.** *Nat. Hist.*, etc. A region or area of some natural structure, as a mineral formation, or the body of an animal or plant 1811.

1. We conclude this art..to be very ancient, and derived to us by long t. of time 1658. **c.** A long t. of serene weather 1799. 3. This vast t. of land DE FOE. A t. of water..which..boiled white all over 1886.

†II. The action of drawing or pulling; attraction (*rare*) –1620. †III. = F. *trait* (see TRAIT). A lineament, a feature –1775. IV. Senses coinciding with those of TRACK and TRACE. Now chiefly *rare* or *Obs.*, being in the main superseded by these words. 1. = TRACK *sb.* I. 3, 4. 1555. 2. *fig.* = TRACK *sb.* I. 5. 1566. 3. = TRACE *sb.*¹ 3, 4. 1547.

1. In the t. of the Manila ship 1726. 2. Any particular thought which breaks in upon the regular t. or chain of ideas HUME. 3. But flies an Eagle flight ..Leauing no T. behinde SHAKS.

†**Tract**, *v.*¹ 1508. [ad. L. *tractare* to handle, etc., freq. of *trahere* to draw.] 1. *trans.* To negotiate. 2. To deal with in speech or writing; to discuss or discourse (*trans.*, or *intr.* with *of*) –1637.

†**Tract**, *v.*² 1523. [f. L. *tract-*, *trahere* to draw.] I. 1. *trans.* To draw, pull along, haul, tow –1769. 2. To lengthen out, prolong, protract (time); to spend or waste in delay; to delay, put off –1647. 3. *fig.* To draw on, draw out; to induce 1615. II. 1. = TRACE *v.* I. 3. –1613. 2. = TRACE *v.* II. 1. –1654.

Tractable (træ·ktăb'l), *a.* 1502. [ad. L. *tractabilis*, f. *tractare* TRACT *v.*¹] 1. That can be easily managed; docile, compliant, governable. **b.** Const. *to* with sb. or inf. 1509. 2. Of things (usu. concrete): Easy to deal with, handle, or work; manageable 1555. †3. That can be handled; palpable, tangible –1694.

1. A large wolf-dog,..as t. as he was strong and bold SCOTT. Hence **Tractabi·lity, Tra·ctableness. Tra·ctably** *adv.*

Tractarian (træktē·riăn), *sb.* and *a.* 1824. [f. TRACT *sb.*¹ + *-arian*, after *trinitarian*, etc.] A. *sb.* 1. A writer, publisher, or distributor of tracts (*nonce-uses*). 2. A member of that school of High Churchmen which maintains the doctrines and practices set forth in 'Tracts for the Times' (see TRACT *sb.*¹ 3) 1839. B. *adj.* Of or belonging to the Tractarians 1840. 2. Distributing tracts (*nonce-us*) 1885. Hence **Tracta·rianism**, the tenets or principles of the Tractarians, the T. system; adherence to or maintenance of this.

Tractate (træ·ktēɪt). 1474. [ad. L. *tractatus*, f. *tractare*; see TRACT *v.*¹] 1. A book or literary work treating of a particular subject; a treatise. †2. Negotiation, dealing, transaction –1630.

1. In the Rabbinic t. on the Samaritans 1883.

†**Tracta·tor.** 1638. [a. L.; see TRACT *v.*¹ and -OR 2 c.] One who treats of a subject; the writer of a tractate –1725. **b.** *spec.* Any one of the writers of 'Tracts for the Times' –1844.

Tractile (træ·ktəil, -il), *a. rare.* 1626. [ad. late L. *tractilis*, f. *tract-*, *trahere* to draw; see -ILE.] †1. Capable of being drawn out to a thread. BACON. 2. That may be drawn, as money from a bank 1892. Hence **Tracti·lity**, the quality of being t.

Traction (træ·kʃən). 1615. [ad. med.L. *tractionem*, f. *trahere*, *tractum* to draw.] 1. The action of drawing or pulling; draught; opp. to *pulsion* or pushing, and (in *Dynamics*) to *pressure* 1656. **b.** *Phys.* and *Path.* A drawing or pulling of a part or organ (in an animal or plant) by some vital process, as the contraction of a muscle, etc. 1615. **c.** A drawing or pulling movement used in massage, etc. 1841. **d.** *fig.* Drawing, attraction, attractive power 1649. 2. *spec.* The drawing of vehicles or loads along a road or track; esp. in ref. to the power by which this is done 1822. 3. Short for *force of t.* (as a measurable quantity); the amount of rolling friction (also *t. of adhesion*) as measuring this 1825.

1. *Force of t.*, the force exerted in or required for t. *Line of t.*, the line along which this force acts. *Angle of t.*, the angle between the line of t. and the surface along which the body is drawn. **b.** There was..a slight..t. of face to the right side when the patient laughed 1876. **d.** He feels the resistless t. of fate 1883. 2. The three stages are horse-t., steam t., and electric t. 1902.

Comb.: **t.-wheel**, a driving-wheel.

Tra·ction-e·ngine. 1859. A steam-engine used for drawing heavy loads along an ordinary road; also, a similar engine used in agricultural work.

†**Tra·ctism.** 1834. [f. TRACT *sb.*¹ + -ISM.] = TRACTARIANISM –1844.

Tractive (træ·ktiv), *a.* 1615. [f. L. *tract-*, *trahere* + -IVE.] Having the property of drawing or pulling; used for traction.

Tractor (træ·ktǫɹ, -əɹ). 1798. [Late or med.L., f. L. *trahere*, *tractum*; see -OR.] 1. *pl.* (in full (*Perkins's*) *metallic tractors*): A device consisting of a pair of pointed rods of different metals, as brass and steel, which were believed to relieve rheumatic or other pain by being drawn or rubbed over the skin: see PERKINISM. *Obs.* exc. *Hist.* 2. One who or that which draws or pulls something; *esp.* a traction-engine 1856. 3. An aeroplane with one or more propellers or screws in front: opp. to *pusher*. Also *t.-aeroplane* 1912. Hence **Tractora·tion**, the use of metallic tractors (see 1).

Tractory (træ·ktŏri), *a.* and *sb. rare.* 1684. [ad. L. *tractorius* of or for drawing, f. *tract-*, *trahere*; see -ORY.] †A. *adj.* Serving for traction; tractive. B. *sb. Geom.* = next 1820.

‖**Tractrix** (træ·ktriks). *Pl.* **tra·ctrices** (-isīz). 1727. [mod.L., fem. of *tractor*.] *Geom.* A curve such that the intercept on the tangent between its point of contact and a fixed straight line is constant; so called as being traced by the centre of gyration of a rigid rod of which one end is moved along the fixed straight line. Also, one of a class of curves similarly traced, e. g. by movement along a fixed curve.

‖**Tractus** (træ·ktɒs). 1450. [med.L., sc. *cantus*, lit. drawn-out song; see TRACT *sb.*³] = TRACT *sb.*²

Tradable (trēɪ·dăb'l), *a.* Also **tradeable.** 1599. [f. TRADE *sb.* or *v.* + -ABLE.] That may be dealt with in the way of trade; marketable.

Trade (trēɪd), *sb.* ME. [a. MLG. *trade* track :—OS. *trada* footstep, track, f. WGer. ablaut-series **tred-*, *trad-* to TREAD.] I. †1. A course, way, path –1564. †2. The track or trail of a man or beast; footprints –1596. 3. Course, way, or manner of life; course of action; mode of procedure, method. *Obs.* or *dial.* 1456. **b.** A regular or habitual course of action. *Obs.* exc. *dial.* 1586. 4. The practice of some occupation, business, or profession habitually carried on, esp. when practised as a means of livelihood or gain; a calling; now usu. applied to a mercantile occupation and to a skilled handicraft, as dist. from a profession, and *spec.* restricted to a skilled handicraft, as dist. from a professional or mercantile occupation on the one hand, and from unskilled labour on the other 1546. **b.** Anything practised for a livelihood 1650. 5. *The t.*: those concerned in the particular business or industry in question; *spec.* the publishers and booksellers; now more commonly, those engaged in the liquor trade 1697.

1. A postern..there was, A common t. to passe through Priams house SURREY. *fig. Hen. VIII*, v. i. 36. 2. As Shepheardes curre, that..Hath tracted forth some salvage beastes t. SPENSER. 3. Teache a childe in the t. of his way, and when he is olde, he shal not departe from it BIBLE (Genev.) *Prov.* xxii. 6. **b.** Thy sinn's not accidentall, but a T. SHAKS. Phr. †*To blow t.*, of the wind, to blow in a regular or habitual course, or constantly in the same direction (cf. TRADE-WIND). 4. A Potter, Sir, he was by t. WORDSW. His being in t. was an obstacle 1813. *The t.* (Navy colloq.), the submarine service 1916.

II. 1. **a.** *lit.* Passage to and fro; coming and going; resort. Now *dial.* 1591. †**b.** *fig.* Intercourse, 'commerce', dealings –1708. 2. Passage or resort for the purpose of commerce; hence, the buying and selling or exchange of commodities for profit; commerce, traffic, trading 1555. 3. With *a* and *pl.* An act of trading, a transaction, a bargain; *spec.* in politics, a 'deal' or 'job'. orig. *U.S. slang.* 1829. †4. A fleet of trading ships under convoy –1803. 5. Stuff, goods, materials, commodities; now *dial.*, usu. = rubbish, trash 1645. 6. Commodities for use in bartering with savages; also, native produce for barter 1847. 7. Abbrev. of TRADE-WIND; chiefly in *pl.* 1796.

1. **a.** He be buryed in the Kings high-way, Some way of common T., where Subjects feet May howrely trample on their Soueraignes Head SHAKS. **b.** Haue you any further T. with vs? SHAKS. 2. The balance of t...is the difference between the aggregate amount of a nation's exports or imports, or the balance of the particular account of the nation's trade with another nation 1835. 4. This squadron,..and the t. under their convoy,..tided it down the Channel 1748.

Comb.: **t. allowance**, a wholesale discount, allowed to dealers or retailers on articles to be sold again; **t. board**, a council regulating conditions of employment in certain trades; **t. dollar**, a dollar issued by the U.S.A. for Asiatic t.; **-name**, (*a*) a descriptive or fancy name used to designate some proprietary article of t.; (*b*) the name by which an article or substance is known to the trade; (*c*) the name or style under which a business is carried on; **t. price**, the price at which the wholesale dealer sells to the retailer; **-route**, a route followed by traders or caravans, or by trading-ships; **-sale**, an auction held by and for a particular t.; **t. school**, a school in which handicrafts are taught; **-show**, the performance of a cinematograph picture for 'exhibitors'; hence **-show** *v. trans.* Hence **Tra·deful** *a.* full of t.; †full of traffic. **Tra·deless** *a.* without a t.; destitute of t. or commerce.

Trade (trēɪd), *v.* 1548. [f. prec.] †1. *trans.* To tread (a path); to traverse (the sea);

fig. to go through, lead (one's life) –1649. †2. *intr.* To tread, step, walk, go in a course –1651. †3. *trans.* To follow (a course) habitually; to practise –1631. †4. To familiarize with the use, practice, or knowledge of something; to accustom *to* or *to do* something; to school, exercise –1652. 5. *intr.* †a. To have dealings; to treat, negotiate (*with* a person) –1676. b. To occupy oneself *in* something; to deal, have dealings *in*. *Obs.* exc. as *fig.* from 6 b. 1606. 6. a. To resort *to* a place for purposes of trade 1570. Hence, b. to engage in or carry on trade (*with* a person, *in* a commodity) 1570. c. With sinister implication: To traffic *in* something which should not be bought or sold 1663. d. *To t. on* or *upon*: to make use of for one's own ends; to take advantage of by 1884. †7. *trans.* To frequent for purposes of trade –1707. 8. †To employ (money) in trade (*rare*); to make (anything) the subject of trade, to trade in; to acquire or dispose of (also *to t. off*) by barter (*U.S.*); to buy and sell, to barter, to exchange 1628.

2. By the labour of trading from one place to another HOBBES. 4. Being..traded in wel doing, from the cradle 1603. 5. a. How did you dare To T. and Trafficke with Macbeth, In Riddles, and Affaires of death SHAKS. b. Musicke, moody foode of vs that t. in Loue SHAKS. 6. a. They traded with profit only to China 1844. b. I used..to t. in salt 1776. d. They..still t. on the fears and fancies of their fellows 1885. 8. *To t. in* (U.S.), to give used articles in part payment for new ones 1927.

†Traded (trēⁱ·dėd), *ppl. a.* and *a.* 1548. [f. TRADE *v.* and *sb.* + -ED.] 1. Of a road: Much used or trodden; frequented; also *gen.* habitually used –1631. 2. Versed, practised; experienced; conversant –1654. 3. Of a place: Frequented for the purpose of trading. (Usu. with *well*, etc.) –1707. 4. Having a trade (of such a kind) –1656.

†Tra·de-fa:llen, *a.* 1596. Fallen or broken in trade, bankrupt –1632.

Trade-mark (trēⁱ·dmāɹk), *sb.* 1838. [f. TRADE *sb.* + MARK *sb.*[1]] A mark (now, one secured by legal registration) used by a manufacturer or trader to distinguish his goods from similar wares of other firms. b. *fig.* A distinctive mark or token 1873. Hence **Tra·de-mark** *v. trans.* to affix or imprint a t. upon.

Trader (trēⁱ·dəɹ). 1585. [f. TRADE *v.* + -ER [1].] 1. One whose business is trade or commerce, or who is engaged in trading; a dealer or trafficker. b. A vessel engaged in trading 1712. †2. One who is occupied or concerned *in* something; a dealer –1800.

1. Great traders, with merchandise & ready monie 1585. 2. The nonconformists were great traders in Scripture 1673.

‖Tradescantia (trædėskæ·ntiă). 1766. [mod.L., f. name of John *Tradescant* (the elder), a 17th c. naturalist + -IA [1].] *Bot.* An Amer. genus of perennial herbs of the family *Commelynaceæ*; spiderwort.

Tradesfolk (trēⁱ·dzfoᵘk). 1760. [f. as next + FOLK.] People in trade; tradespeople. a. Artisans; b. Shopkeepers.

Tradesman (trēⁱ·dzmăn). *Pl.* **-men.** 1597. [f. *trade's*, gen. of TRADE + MAN *sb.*] 1. One who is skilled in and follows one of the industrial arts; an artisan, a craftsman. Now *Sc.*, *local Eng.*, *U.S.*, and *Colonial*. 2. One who is engaged in trade or the sale of commodities; *esp.* a shopkeeper 1601.

Tra·despeo:ple. 1728. [f. as prec. + PEOPLE *sb.*] People engaged in trade; tradesmen, and their families and employees.

Tra·deswo:man. *Pl.* **-women.** 1707. [f. as prec. + WOMAN.] A woman engaged in trade, or in a particular trade or calling.

Trade-u·nion, trades-u·nion. 1831. [f. TRADE or pl. *trades* + UNION.] An association of the workers in any trade or in allied trades for the protection and furtherance of their interests in regard to wages, hours, and conditions of labour, and for the provision, from their common funds, of pecuniary assistance to the members during strikes, sickness, unemployment, old age, etc. Hence **Trade-, trades-u·nionism**, the system, principles, or practice of trade-unions. **Trade-, trades-u·nionist**, a member of a t.

Tra·de-wind. 1650. [f. TRADE *sb.* + WIND *sb.* App. originating in the phr. *to blow trade*; see TRADE *sb.* I. 3 b. Often shortened in naut. use to *trade*, pl. *the trades*.] †1. Any wind that 'blows trade', i.e. in a constant course or way; a wind that blows steadily in the same direction –1807. †2. Applied to the seasonal winds of the Indian Ocean; = MONSOON 1, 2. –1840. 3. Now *spec.* The wind that blows constantly towards the equator from about the thirtieth parallels, north and south; its main direction in the northern hemisphere being from the north-east, and in the southern hemisphere from the south-east 1712.

3. The heat of the torrid zone and its velocity of rotation produce the trade winds which blow constantly in the same directions in the same latitudes on the great oceans 1867.

attrib.: **t. cloud**, the cumulus which collects in the t. region in the day-time.

Trading (trēⁱ·diŋ), *vbl. sb.* 1590. [f. TRADE *v.* + -ING [1].] The action of TRADE *v.*; *esp.* the carrying on of trade; buying and selling; commerce, trade, traffic. b. *attrib.*, esp. in sense 'frequented for, employed in, made or done for trading', as *t. craft, house, post, station, vessel, voyage*, etc. 1590; **t. stamp** (*U.S.*), a coupon given as a voucher by a trader to a customer.

Tra·ding, *ppl. a.* 1690. [f. TRADE *v.* + -ING [2].] That trades; *esp.* engaged in trade, commercial. †b. That trades in or makes a trade of something (e.g. a public office) –1839.

b. The common herd of t. politicians 1839.

Tradition (trădi·ʃən), *sb.* late ME. [a. OF. *tradicion*, ad. L. *traditio*, f. *tradere* to hand over, f. *tra-* = *trans-* + *do* I place, give.] 1. The action of handing over (something material) to another; delivery, transfer. (Chiefly in *Law*.) 1540. †2. A giving up, surrender; betrayal –1653. b. *spec.* in *Ch. Hist.* Surrender of sacred books in times of persecution 1840. 3. Delivery, *esp.* oral delivery, of information or instruction. Now *rare*. 1500. b. *T. of the Creed* (Ch. Hist.): oral instruction upon the Creed given to catechumens 1888. 4. The act of transmitting or handing down or fact of being handed down, from one to another, or from generation to generation; transmission of statements, beliefs, rules, customs, or the like, esp. by word of mouth, or by practice without writing. Chiefly in phr. *by t.* 1591. 5. a. That which is thus handed down; a statement, belief, or practice transmitted (esp. orally) from generation to generation. late ME. b. More vaguely: A long established and generally accepted custom, or method of procedure, having almost the force of a law; an immemorial usage 1593. 6. *spec.* (*Theol.* and *Eccl.*) a. Among the Jews, Any one, or the whole, of an unwritten code of regulations, etc. held to have been received from Moses, and handed down orally from generation to generation and embodied in the MISHNAH. late ME. b. In the Christian Church, Any one, or the whole, of a body of teachings transmitted orally from generation to generation since early times; held by Roman Catholics to comprise teaching derived from Christ and the apostles, together with that subsequently communicated to the church by the Holy Spirit, and to be of equal authority with Scripture. Also, (as in 4) the transmission of such teaching. 1551. c. Among Mohammedans, An account of sayings and doings of Mohammed transmitted at first orally, and afterwards recorded; esp. = SUNNA 1718.

1. A deed takes effect only from this t. or delivery BLACKSTONE. 4. Old songs delivered to them, by t., from their fathers 1591. Wolves, so says t., first took gold to Delphi 1863. 5. a. The traditions associated with these..monuments 1851. b. The t. is that a President may be re-elected once and once only 1882. 6. a. But whi breken ȝe Goddis maundement, for ȝoure veyn tradicioun? WYCLIF. b. The Sunday, or the Lord's-Day, which we observe by Apostolical T. instead of the Sabbath 1737.

Comb.: **T. Sunday** (*Ch. Hist.*), a name for Palm Sunday, as the day of 't. of the creed' (see 3 b) in some churches.

Tradition, *v. rare.* 1640. [f. prec.] *trans.* To transmit by tradition, relate as a tradition.

Traditional (trădi·ʃənăl), *a.* 1594. [f. as prec. + -AL.] 1. Belonging to, consisting in, or of the nature of tradition; handed down by or derived from tradition 1600. b. That is such according to tradition 1856. †2. Observant of, bound by tradition (*rare*) –1644.

1. The t. records of the respectable and ingenious Mrs. Grant of Laggan SCOTT. b. The heirlooms of a t. past 1874. 2. *Rich. III*, III. i. 45. Hence **Tradi·tionally** *adv.*

Tradi·tionalism. 1860. [f. prec. + -ISM.] 1. A system of philosophy which arose in the Roman Church *c* 1840, according to which all human knowledge is derived by traditional instruction from an original divine revelation 1885. 2. Adherence to traditional doctrine or theory; maintenance of, or submission to, the authority of tradition; excessive reverence for tradition: esp. in matters of religion 1860. So **Tradi·tionalist**, an adherent of t.; one who upholds the authority of tradition.

Traditionary (trădi·ʃənări), *a.* (*sb.*) 1613. [f. TRADITION + -ARY [1].] 1. = TRADITIONAL *a.* 1, 1 b. 1661. †2. = TRADITIONAL *a.* 2. –1666.

1. The Corrupted Remains of some t. Revelation 1748.

B. *sb.* One who maintains or accepts the authority of tradition; a traditionalist (*rare*) 1727.

Traditioner (trădi·ʃənəɹ). *rare.* 1646. [f. as prec. + -ER [1].] = next.

Traditionist (trădi·ʃənist). 1666. [f. as prec. + -IST.] 1. One who accepts, adheres to, or maintains the authority of tradition. 2. One who gives vogue to, hands on, or records a tradition 1759.

Traditive (træ·ditiv), *a.* Now *rare.* 1611. [app. ad. obs. F. *traditif, -ive* traditional, f. L. *traditus, tradere* to deliver; see -IVE.] Characterized by, belonging to, or being transmitted by, tradition; traditional.

The question lay between t. and private interpretation KEBLE.

Traditor (træ·ditǫɹ). late ME. [a. L., f. *tradere*.] †1. A betrayer, traitor. *Obs.* in general sense. –1711. 2. *Ch. Hist.* One of those early Christians who, in the great persecution under Diocletian, in order to save their own lives, delivered up their sacred books, vessels, etc., or betrayed their fellow-Christians 1597.

Traduce (trădiū·s), *v.* 1533. [ad. L. *traducere* to lead across, etc.; also, to lead along as a spectacle, to bring into disgrace; f. *trans* across + *ducere* to lead.] †1. *trans.* To convey from one place to another; to transport –1678. †b. To translate, render; to alter, modify, reduce –1850. †c. To transfer from one use, sense, ownership, or employment to another –1640. †2. To transmit, esp. by generation –1733. †b. *transf.* To propagate –1711. †c. To derive, deduce, obtain *from* a source –1709. 3. To speak evil of, esp. (now always) falsely or maliciously; to defame, malign, slander, calumniate, misrepresent 1586. †b. To expose (to contempt); to dishonour, disgrace (*rare*) –1661. †4. To falsify, misrepresent, pervert –1674.

1. b. Milton has been traduced into French and overturned into Dutch SOUTHEY. 2. Vertue is not traduced in propagation, nor learning bequeathed by our will, to our heires 1606. 3. The man that dares t., because he can With safety to himself, is not a man COWPER. b. By their own ignoble actions they t., that is, disgrace their ancestors 1661. 4. Who taking Texts..traduced the Sense thereof 1648. Hence **Tradu·cement**, the, or an, action of traducing; defamation, calumny, slander. **Tradu·cingly** *adv.*

Traducer (trădiū·səɹ). 1614. [f. prec. + -ER [1].] One who traduces; a slanderer, calumniator.

Traducian (trădiū·siăn, -diū·ʃiăn), *sb.* and *a.* 1727. [ad. late L. *traducianus*, deriv. of *tradux, -ducem* a layer or shoot for propagation, etc.] A. *sb.* (*a*) One who holds that the soul of a child, like the body, is propagated by or inherited from the parents. (*b*) *less commonly*, One who holds the doctrine of the transmission of original sin from parent to child. B. *adj.* Applied to such doctrine or theory. Hence **Tradu·cianism**, the doctrine of the Traducians.

Traduction (trădv·kʃən). 1501. [a. OF., or ad. L. *traductionem*.] †1. Conveyance from one place to another; transportation, transference –1677. †2. Translation into another language; *concr.* a translation –1823. 3. Transmission by generation to offspring or posterity; propagation; derivation from ancestry, descent. Now *rare* or *Obs.* 1593. †b. *gen.* Transmission;

derivation; handing down, tradition -1827. †c. *transf.* Something transmitted or derived -1794. 4. The action of traducing or defaming; calumny, slander (*rare*) 1656. 5. *Logic.* Transference or transition from one classification or order of reasoning to another 1847.

1. T. of the Brutes into America from the known World 1677. 3. A great question,..touching the t. of the soule 1617. b. Arts have their successive invention and perfection and t. from one People to another 1677. 4. I left t. to its perjuries 1881.

Traductive (trădʊ·ktiv), *a.* 1657. [f. L. *traduct-*, *traducere* + -IVE.] 1. Having the property of being 'traduced' or transmitted; hereditary; derivative. Now *rare* or *Obs.* 2. *Logic.* Involving 'traduction' 1847.

Traffic (træ·fik), *sb.* 1506. [a. F. *trafique*, mod.F. *trafic*, ad. It. *traffico*, f. *trafficare* to TRAFFIC; perh. f. *tra* :—L. *trans* + *-ficare* = L. *facere* to do, make; cf. L. *transigere.*] 1. The transportation of merchandise for the purpose of trade; hence, trade between distant or distinct communities; commerce. 2. In wider sense: The buying and selling or exchange of goods for profit; bargaining; trade. Also with *a* and *pl.* 1568. b. With evil connotation: Dealing or bargaining in something which should not be made the subject of trade 1663. 3. *fig.* Intercourse, communication; dealings, business. Now *rare.* 1548. †4. *transf.* Saleable commodities. Also *pl.* in same sense. -1778. 5. The passing to and fro of persons, or of vehicles or vessels, along a road, railway, canal, or other route of transport 1825. b. The amount of business done by a railway, etc., in the transport of passengers and goods; the account of or revenue from this 1858.

1. It was not in the Way to or from any Part of the World, where the English had any Traffick DE FOE. 2. Engaged in a low clandestine traffick, prohibited by the laws of the Country BURKE. 3. The two hours' t. of our stage SHAKS. 4. You'll see a draggled damsel, here and there From Billingsgate her fishy t. bear GAY. 5. We have long since agreed to call street movement 't.' 1894. b. This week's batch of Home Railway traffics 1905.

attrib. and *Comb.*: as *t. signal*; **t. density,** the number of passengers and of tons of freight carried over any section of a railway or highway in a given period; **t.-taker,** a railway official whose business is to compile t. returns. Hence **Tra·fficless** *a.* devoid of t.

Traffic (træ·fik), *v.* Infl. **trafficked** (-ikt), **trafficking.** 1542. [ad. OF. *trafiquer*, F. *trafiquer* = It. *trafficare*; see prec.] I. *intr.* 1. To carry on trade, to trade, to buy and sell; to have commercial dealings *with* any one; to deal *for* a commodity. Occas., To resort *to* a place for the purpose of trade. b. In a disparaging sense, or said of dealing considered improper 1657. †2. *fig.* To be concerned, to busy or exercise oneself (*in* some matter) -1882. b. To deal, intrigue, conspire (*with* some one, *in*, *for*, or *to do* something); to practise 1567.

1. He was..A thriving man, and trafficked on the seas WORDSW. b. Beautiful and dissolute females.. trafficking in their charms 1854. 2. On no pretence I trafick in any tainting politique 1721. b. He was trafficking with her enemies and tampering with her friends 1852.

II. *trans.* †1. To frequent for the purpose of trading; to carry on trade in (a place) -1611. b. To pass to and fro upon (a road, etc.); to traverse 1825. 2. To carry on a trade in, to buy and sell; to deal in; often with sinister implication. Now *rare.* 1597.

2. The honour of the proud house of Este was being basely trafficked away 1879.

Trafficable (træ·fikăb'l), *a.* 1649. [f. prec. + -ABLE.] 1. That may be bought or sold; marketable. 2. Suitable for passage to and fro 1890.

Trafficker (træ·fikəɹ). 1570. [f. TRAFFIC *v.* + -ER[1].] 1. One who is engaged in traffic or trade; a trader, merchant, dealer 1580. b. With opprobrious force 1785. 2. A go-between, a negotiator; an intriguer; a schemer 1570.

1. b. Some fell traficker in slaves 1785. 2. The whole clan of old Jacobite spies and traffickers STEVENSON.

Tragacanth (træ·găkænþ). 1573. [a. F. *tragacante*, ad. L. *tragacantha*, a. Gr. τραγάκανθα goat's-thorn, tragacanth-shrub, f. τράγος he-goat + ἄκανθα thorn.] 1. A 'gum' or mucilaginous substance obtained from several species of *Astragalus*, by natural exudation or incision, in the form of whitish strings or flakes, only partially soluble in water. Used in medicine (chiefly as a vehicle for drugs) and in the industrial arts. Commonly called *gum t.* †2. Any one of several low-growing spiny leguminous shrubs of the genus *Astragalus*, found in Persia, etc., which yield gum t. (*rare*) -1741. Hence **Tragaca·nthin** (also contr. **traga·nthin**), *Chem.* = BASSORIN.

Tragedian (trădʒī·diăn). [Late ME., prob. a. OF. *tragediane*, mod.F. *tragédien*, f. *tragédie* TRAGEDY; see -AN.] 1. A tragic poet or author. 2. A tragic actor 1592. †3. *fig.* The victim, or inflicter, of a tragic fate -1635.

1. Under this curled marble..Sleepe rare T. Shakespeare, sleepe alone DONNE. 2. The well-lung'd Tragedians Rage DRYDEN.

‖**Tragédienne** (traʒedyęn). 1851. [F., fem. of *tragédien* TRAGEDIAN.] A female tragedian; a tragic actress.

†**Trage·dious,** *a.* 1494. [f. L. *tragœdia* TRAGEDY + -OUS.] Full of, or having the character of, tragedy; calamitous, tragic -1691.

Tragedize (træ·dʒĭdəiz), *v.* 1593. [f. TRAGEDY + -IZE.] 1. *trans.* To act or perform as a tragedy; *fig.* to do or carry on tragically. 2. *intr.* To perform as a tragedian; *fig.* to act or speak in tragic style 1756. 3. *trans.* To dramatize in tragic form 1811.

Tragedy (træ·dʒĭdi). [Late ME. *tra-*, *tregedie*, a. OF. *tragedie*, *tregedie*, ad. L. *tragœdia*, a. Gr. τραγῳδία, perh. (obscurely) f. τράγος goat + ᾠδή ODE.] 1. A play or other literary work of a serious or sorrowful character, with a fatal or disastrous conclusion: opp. to COMEDY 1. †a. In mediæval use: A tale or narrative poem of this character -1593. b. Applied to ancient Greek and Latin works, the earlier (Dorian) being lyric songs, the later (Attic and Latin) dramatic pieces. late ME. c. Applied to a modern stage-play 1538. 2. That branch of dramatic art which treats of sorrowful or terrible events, in a serious and dignified style: opp. to COMEDY 2. late ME. 3. *fig.* An unhappy or fatal event or series of events in real life; a dreadful calamity or disaster 1509. †b. A doleful or dreadful tale -1664. †c. With *of* or possessive: Sad story, unhappy fate; *esp.* sorrowful end, violent death -1738.

1. a. Tragedye is to seyn, a dite of a prosperite for a tyme þat endith in wrecchydnesse CHAUCER. c. Five of his sixteen plays are tragedies, that is, are concluded in death 1838. 2. Som time let Gorgeous T. In Scepter'd Pall com sweeping by MILT. *attrib.* She bowed me out of the room like a t. queen THACKERAY. 3. c. Thou..shalt look on and see The Wicked's dismal T. WESLEY.

Tragelaph (træ·gĭlæf). Also in L. form **tragelaphus** (trăge·lăfʊs), pl. -i. late ME. [ad. L. *tragelaphus*, a. Gr. τραγέλαφος, f. τράγος he-goat + ἔλαφος deer.] 1. (tr. Gr. τραγέλαφος.) a. A name for some foreign species of capriform antelope or other horned beast, vaguely known to the ancients. b. *Myth.* A fabulous or fictitious beast compounded of a goat and a stag; hence *allus.* 1644. 2. *Zool.* Any antelope of the modern genus *Tragelaphus*, as the S. African boschbok, *T. sylvaticus.* 1888. So **Trage·laphine** *a.* belonging to the group *Tragelaphinæ* of antelopes, typified by the genus *Tragelaphus*; *sb.* an antelope of this group.

Tragi- (trædʒi), comb. form repr. TRAGIC, in a few nonce-words on the model of TRAGI-COMEDY, as *tragi-farce.*

Tragic (træ·dʒik), *a.* and *sb.* 1545. [ad. L. *tragicus*, a. Gr. τραγικός of or pertaining to tragedy, f. τράγος goat; see -IC.] A. *adj.* 1. Of, pertaining, or proper to tragedy as a branch of the drama; composing, or acting in, tragedy; opp. to COMIC *a.* 1. b. Befitting, or having the style of, tragedy 1684. 2. Resembling tragedy in respect of its matter; relating to or expressing fatal or dreadful events; sad, gloomy 1593. 3. Resembling the action or conclusion of a tragedy; characterized by or involving 'tragedy' in real life; calamitous, disastrous, terrible, fatal 1545.

1. Yclad in costly garments fit for tragicke Stage SPENSER. b. Never any exprest a more lofty and Tragick height 1684. 2. The t. story that you are well acquainted with 1718. 3. Swift..is the most t. figure in our literature 1876.

B. *sb.* 1. = TRAGEDIAN 1, 2. 1587. †2. A tragic poem or drama -1750. †3. quasi-*sb.* *The t.*: that which is t.; the tragic side of the drama, or of life; tragic style or manner 1872. So **Tra·gical** *a.* 1489; hence **-ally** *adv.*, **-ness.**

Tragi-comedy (trædʒi,kǫ·mĭdi). 1579. [a. F. *tragi-comédie*, ad. late L. *tragicomœdia*, syncopated from *tragico-comœdia*; f. L. *tragicus* tragic + *comœdia* comedy.] 1. A play (or, *rarely*, a story) combining the qualities of a tragedy and a comedy, or containing both tragic and comic elements; occas. *spec.* a play mainly of tragic character, but with a happy ending 1581. 2. *fig.* A combination of pathetic and humorous elements in real life 1579.

1. The noble tragicomedy of Measure for Measure MACAULAY. 2. This t., called life 1649. Hence **Tra:gi-come·dian**, an actor who performs in t.

Tragi-comic (træ:dʒi,kǫ·mik), *a.* 1683. [f. TRAGI- + COMIC.] Having the character of a tragi-comedy; combining tragic with comic elements. So **Tra:gi-co·mical** *a.* 1567, **-ly** *adv.* Also **Tra:gi-co:mi-pa·storal** *a.* (*nonce-wd.*), combining the qualities of tragi-comedy and pastoral.

Tragopan (træ·gopæn). 1831. [a. L., a. Gr. τραγόπαν a reputed bird of Ethiopia; f. τράγος goat + Πάν Pan.] *Ornith.* A pheasant of the genus *Ceriornis* (formerly *T.*), having a pair of erectile fleshy horns on the head.

‖**Tragus** (trē¹·gʊs). *Pl.* **tragi** (-dʒəi). 1693. [Late L., from *tragus*, a. Gr. τράγος he-goat, so named on account of the bunch of hairs which it bears.] *Anat.* A prominence at the entrance of the external ear, in front of and partly closing the orifice, and in men usu. bearing a tuft of hairs.

Trail (trēl), *sb.*[1] late ME. [app. f. TRAIL *v.*] I. Something that trails or hangs trailing. 1. A long-trailing or loose-hanging slender mass of hair, fibres, or the like; 'any thing drawn to length' (J.) 1844. 2. A trailing ornament in the form of a wreath or spray of leaves or tendrils; a wreathed or foliated ornament. late ME. b. A trailing tendril or branch 1598.

1. A t. of golden hair MRS. BROWNING. 2. b. Trails of tangled eglantine 1861.

II. Something trailed or made by trailing. †1. A sledge [= L. *tragula*] -1600. 2. A dragnet [= L. *tragula*] 1711. 3. The hinder end of the stock of a gun-carriage, which rests or slides on the ground when the gun is unlimbered 1768. 4. Anything drawn behind as an appendage; a train 1621. 5. A mark left where something has been trailed or has passed along; a trace, track 1610. b. *spec.* in astronomical photography, The trace produced by the motion of the image of a star across the plate during exposure 1889. 6. *spec.* The track or other indication, as scent, left by a person or animal, esp. as followed by a huntsman or hound, or by any pursuer 1590. 7. A path or track worn by the passage of persons travelling in a wild or uninhabited region. (Chiefly in U.S. and Canada.) 1807. 8. *Geol.* A name for certain mixed glacial or other deposits resting upon older formations 1866.

4. Seeming Stars..shooting through the Darkness.. with..long Trails of Light DRYDEN. 5. But the t. of the serpent is over them all MOORE. 6. How cheerfully on the false Traile they cry SHAKS. 7. Indian Paths—which were narrow trails worn by the feet in marching single file 1875.

III. Action of trailing. 1. The action of dragging oneself or something along, or of creeping or crawling (*rare*) 1547. 2. The action of hunting by the trail; chase by the track or scent 1669. 3. *Mil.* The act of trailing a rifle, or the position of it when trailed 1833. 4. An act of drawing out, enticing, befooling (*rare*) 1847.

Comb.: **t.-board,** a carved piece in a ship, reaching from the main stem to the figure, or to the brackets; **-net** = sense II. 2.

†**Trail,** *sb.*[2] [Late ME. *treylle*, *trayle*, app. a. OF. *treille*, *traille*:—L. *trichila*, later also *tricla*, bower, arbour, summer-house.] 1. A trellis for training climbing plants upon -1727. 2. A lattice; a grating; a grill -1552.

†**Trail,** *sb.*[3] 1764. [Aphetic f. ENTRAIL.] Entrails, intestines, collectively; *esp.* those of certain birds, as woodcock and snipe, and fishes,

as red mullet, which are cooked and eaten with the rest of the flesh -1846.

Trail (trēˑl), *v.* [ME. *trail(l)e*, app. a. ONF. *trailler* to haul or tow (a boat) :—Com. Rom. **tragulare* to drag, f. L. *tragula* drag-net, sledge, f. **tragere, trahere* to draw.] **I.** *trans.* **1.** To draw behind one; to drag along upon the ground or other surface (esp. something hanging loosely, as a long garment); also, to drag (a person) roughly, to hale; to haul. late ME. **b.** To carry or convey by drawing or dragging, as in a vehicle or ship. late ME. **c.** To draw (the body or limbs) along wearily or with difficulty in walking, etc., esp. from disablement or exhaustion. Also *refl.* 1562. **2.** *Mil.* orig. To carry (a pike, etc.) in the right hand in an oblique position with the head forward and the butt nearly touching the ground; later *spec.* to carry (a lance or rifle) in a horizontal position in the right hand with the arm fully extended downward. Phr. †*To t. a pike*, to serve as a soldier. 1549. **3.** *fig.* or in fig. context 1604. **b.** To draw as by persuasion or art; to draw on; hence *colloq.* 'to quiz, befool' 1717.

1. They shall not t. me through thir streets Like a wild Beast MILT. What boots..That long behind he trails his pompous robe? POPE. b. The yacht is not big enough to convey all the tables and chairs and conveniences that he trails along with him H. WALPOLE. c. He trailed himself, a broken-hearted man, to Falkland Palace 1908. 2. How proud..should I be To t. a pike under your brave command FLETCHER & MASSINGER. 3. Not in utter nakedness, But trailing clouds of glory do we come From God WORDSW. b. I..perceived she was (what is vernacularly termed) trailing Mrs. Dent; that is, playing on her ignorance C. BRONTE.

II. *intr.* **1.** (*intr.* for *pass.*) To hang down so as to drag along the ground or other surface; to be drawn loosely behind (by a person, animal, or thing in motion) ME. **2.** To hang down or float loosely from its attachment, as dress, hair, etc.; of a plant: to grow decumbently and stragglingly to a considerable length, so as to rest upon the ground or other support; to 'creep'. late ME. **3.** To drag one's limbs, walk slowly or wearily as if dragged along; to move or go in extended order; to creep, crawl, as a serpent or other reptile 1608. **b.** Of inanimate things: To move along slowly; to form a trail 1470. **4.** To extend in a straggling line, to straggle 1600.

1. The sound Of silken dresses trailing o'er the ground MORRIS. 2. In open sunny situations it grows trailing,..but in woods it is upright 1776. 3. The camels that trailed away from the city 1905.

III. **1.** *trans.* To decorate or cover *with* a trailing pattern or ornament. late ME. **2.** To follow the trail of, to track 1590. **3.** To mark out (a trail or track) 1586. **4.** *intr.* To follow the trail of game 1741.

2. The ranchman is away..trailing horse thieves 1910.

IV. *intr.* To fish by trailing a bait from a moving boat 1857.

Trailer (trēˑləɹ). 1590. [f. prec. + -ER¹.] **1.** One who, or that which trails. **2.** *spec.* **a.** A rail or road car designed to be drawn along by a motor vehicle. **b.** A small carriage, usu. a light chair on wheels, drawn along by a bicycle or tricycle. 1890. **c.** The rear-wheel of a front-driven bicycle, or one of the rear wheels of a locomotive, as opp. to the *driver* or driving-wheel 1884.

Trailing (trēˑliŋ), *ppl. a.* ME. [f. as prec. + -ING².] **1.** That trails (almost always in *intr.* sense). **2.** techn. *T. wheel*, a wheel to which the motive force is not directly applied (opp. to *driving-wheel*), as one of the hinder wheels of a locomotive. Also applied to parts connected with this, as *t. axle, spring* 1849. **b.** *T. points*, points directed away from an oncoming railway train (opp. to *facing points*) 1889. Hence **Traiˑlingly** *adv.*

Train (trēⁱn), *sb.*¹ ME. [repr. two French sbs., *traine* fem., and *train* masc., both f. *trainer* TRAIN *v.*] **I.** †**1.** Tarrying, delay -1553. †**2.** Course or manner of running (of a horse); a course of riding -1677. **II.** That which drags or trails, or is trailed. **1.** An elongated part of a robe or skirt trailing behind on the ground 1440. **b.** The tail or tail-feathers of a bird, esp. when long and trailing, as in the peacock; in *Falconry*, the technical name for the tail of a hawk 1579. **c.** The tail of a comet; a luminous trail, such as that following a meteor 1602. **2.** *poet.* Applied to the current of a river, etc., also to the elongated body of a serpent 1667. †**3.** Something dragged along the ground to make a scent or trail; a drag; also pieces of carrion, etc. laid in a line or trail for luring certain wild beasts, as wolves, foxes, etc. into a trap -1727.

1. A Baronesse may haue no trayne borne; but haueing a goune with a trayne, she ought to beare it her selfe 1600. They..pinned up each other's trains for the dance J. AUSTEN. b. A splendid goshawk,.. with a..queenly t. 1852. 2. Within those banks, where Rivers now Stream, and perpetual draw thir humid traine MILT.

III. **1.** A number of persons following or attending on some one, usu. a person of rank; a retinue, suite 1440. **b.** *Mil.* The artillery and other apparatus for battle or siege, with the vehicles conveying them, and the men in attendance, following an army 1523. **2.** *fig.* A set of attendant things, circumstances, or conditions; a series of consequences. Often in phr. *in the t. of*, as a sequel to. 1570. **3.** A body of persons, animals, vehicles, etc., travelling together in order, esp. in a long line or procession; *fig.* (chiefly *poet.*) a set or class of persons 1489. **4.** A series or course of actions, events, etc. 1530. **b.** Proper sequence, order, or arrangement for some result; connected order 1528. **5.** A line of gunpowder or other combustible substance laid so as to convey fire to a mine or charge for the purpose of exploding it 1548. **6.** An extended series of material objects or the like; a row, rank 1610. **7.** A set of connected parts of mechanism which actuate one another in series 1797. **8.** (orig. *t. of carriages*, etc.) A number of railway carriages, vans, or trucks coupled together (usu. including the locomotive by which they are drawn) 1824.

1. A t. of listeners followed him JOWETT. 2. This vice draweth after it a t. of evils BERKELEY. 3. The best Hawks..fly in Trains like Wild Geese 1698. 4. He that leads of life an uncorrupted traine SIDNEY. A t. of Ideas, which constantly succeed one another in his Understanding LOCKE. Long..trains of reasoning 1764. b. Putting matters in t. for the election 1885. 5. *fig.* He..had already laid his t...for revolt GROTE. 8. A t. left Warsaw early in the morning 1885. Comb. (*U.S.*) *t.-man, -master, -porter.*

IV. Applied to various material objects that are dragged. **a.** The trail of a gun-carriage 1769. **b.** A rough kind of sledge or sleigh used in Canada for transport 1835. †**c.** A drag-net, a seine -1609.

attrib. and *Comb.*: **t.-bearer**, an attendant who carries the t. of a sovereign or other person; **-ferry**, a ferry for conveying trains across a piece of water from one railway to another; **-mile**, each mile of the aggregate distance run by all the trains on a railway in a given period, as a unit in estimating amount of traffic, working expenses, etc.; so *t.-mileage*; **-net** = sense IV. c; **-rope, -tackle**, a tackle hooked to the trail of a gun-carriage on board ship; **-sickness**, sickness or nausea induced by travelling in a t.; **-stop**, an automatic apparatus, in connexion with a railway signal, for stopping a t.; **-way**, (*a*) a temporary line of rails for the conveyance of small loads; (*b*) a platform hinged to a wharf, with a line of rails upon which railway cars or trucks may run to and from a ferry-boat (*U.S.*).

†**Train**, *sb.*² late ME. [a. OF. *traïne* guile f. OF. *traïr* (F. *trahir*) to betray.] **1.** Treachery, guile, deceit, trickery -1600. **b.** With *a* and *pl.* A trick, stratagem, artifice, wile -1767. **2.** A trap or snare for catching wild animals. (In phr. *to lay a t.*, assoc. with or merged in senses of TRAIN *sb.*¹) -1697. **3.** A lure, bait, decoy -1602.

1. b. *Macb.* IV. iii. 118. 2. Caught in the T. which thou thyself hast laid DRYDEN.

†**Train**, *sb.*³ 1497. [orig. *trane*, a. (M)LG. *trân*, MDu. *traen*, Du. *traan* (perh. the word meaning 'tear', 'drop').] = TRAIN-OIL -1802. Hence †**Traiˑny** *a.* having the quality of train-oil. GAY.

Train, *v.* [Late ME. a. OF. *traïner*, *trahiner*; app. a deriv. of L. *trahere* to draw, drag.] **I.** **1.** *trans.* To draw or pull along after one; to drag, haul, trail. *Obs.* or *arch.* 1450. **b.** *intr.* (for *pass.*) Of a garment: To hang down, esp. so as to drag or trail. Now *rare.* 1590. †**2.** *fig.* (*trans.*) To draw out, protract, spin out. Also *intr.* -1652. †**3.** To lead, conduct, bring -1642.

1. Behold..the Foe Approaching..; in hollow Cube Training his devilish Enginrie MILT.

II. *fig.* To draw by art or inducement; to draw *on*; to allure, entice, decoy; to lead astray, take in. *arch.* late ME. †**b.** To draw by persuasion; to persuade, convert -1612.

Being trained into a well-laid ambush 1781.

III. **1.** To treat so as to bring to the proper or desired form; *spec.* in *Gardening*, to manage (a plant or branch) so as to cause it to grow in some desired form or direction, esp. against a wall, or upon a trellis or the like 1440. **2.** **a.** To instruct and discipline generally; to educate, rear, bring up 1542. **b.** To instruct and discipline in or for some particular art, profession, occupation, or practice; to exercise, practise, drill. Const. *in, to, for.* 1555. **c.** To discipline and instruct (an animal) so as to make it obedient to orders, or capable of performing tricks; to prepare a race-horse for its work 1609. **d.** To bring by diet and exercise to the required state of physical efficiency for a race or other athletic feat 1835. **3.** *intr.* for *pass.* To undergo or follow a course of instruction and discipline 1605.

1. The vines are trained and supported by poles 1792. 2. a. Traine vp a childe in the way he should goe *Prov.* xxii. 6. b. Bandsmen..fully trained to the use of the rifle 1859. c. The present Robert Sherwood, who now trains at Newmarket 1894. 3. Phr. *T. on*, to improve by training; †*t. off*, to lose one's vigour or skill as by over-training; *t. down*, to reduce one's weight by training; *t. with* (fig., U.S. colloq.), to associate with, ally oneself with.

IV. **1.** *trans. Mining.* To trace (a vein, etc.) 1710. **2.** To direct, point, or aim (a cannon or other fire-arm, or *transf.* a photographic camera); to bring by horizontal movement to bear (*on, upon*, the thing aimed at) 1841. **3.** To convey by a railway train (*rare*) 1886. **b.** *intr.* To go by train, travel by railway 1888. Hence **Traiˑnable** *a.* capable of being trained; educable.

Traiˑnband, train-band. Now *Hist.* 1630. [Clipped f. *trained band.*] A trained company of citizen soldiery, organized in London and other parts in the 16th, 17th, and 18th centuries.

The Country Captains of the Train-bands were.. very unskilful..in the use of their Armes 1654. *attrib.* A train-band captain eke was he Of famous London town COWPER.

‖**Traineau** (trēⁱnōᵘ, ‖trɛno). 1715. [F., f. *traîner* TRAIN *v.*] A sledge, sleigh; esp. one drawn by one or more horses over snow or ice.

Trained (trēⁱnd, *poet.* trēⁱnėd), *ppl. a.* 1570. [f. TRAIN *v.* + -ED¹.] In the senses of TRAIN *v.* **b.** *spec.* Subjected to military discipline and instruction, drilled; esp. in *t. band* = TRAIN-BAND (now *Hist.*).

Trainer (trēⁱnəɹ). 1581. [f. TRAIN *v.* + -ER¹.] One who trains; an instructor; *spec.* †(*a*) one who trains or drills soldiers, a drill-sergeant; (*b*) one who trains persons or animals for some athletic performance, as a race; *spec.* one who trains race-horses 1598. **b.** A member of a train-band, esp. when assembled for 'training' or drill; a militiaman. (In later use *U.S.*) 1581.

Training (trēⁱniŋ), *vbl. sb.* 1440. [f. TRAIN *v.* + -ING¹.] The action of TRAIN *v.*; *spec.* Military drill; *esp.* in former use, a public meeting or muster at a stated time for drill of militia and volunteer forces; now much used for the periodical camp work of the Territorials.

Phr. *In t.*, in a state of athletic 'fitness' induced by training; so *out of t.*

attrib. and *Comb.*: **t.-college**, a college for training persons for some particular profession; *spec.* a college for training teachers; **-day**, a day devoted to training; *spec.* in former use, a stated or legally appointed day for the drilling of militia and volunteer forces; **-ship, -vessel**, a ship on which boys are trained for naval service.

Trainless (trēⁱnlės), *a.* 1859. [f. TRAIN *sb.*¹ + -LESS.] **1.** Devoid of a train (as a robe, a meteor, etc.) 1868. **2.** Devoid of (railway) trains 1859.

Traiˑn oiˑl, traiˑn-oil. 1553. [f. TRAIN *sb.*³ + OIL *sb.*] Oil obtained by boiling from the blubber of whales, esp. of the right whale; also, formerly, that obtained from seals, and from various fishes.

Traipse: see TRAPES.

Trait (trē¹, *U.S.* trē¹t). 1477. [a. F. :— L. *tractus* drawing, draught. In *U.S.* (trē¹t) is the established pronunciation; in England (trē¹) is prevalent.] †1. 'Shot' of any kind, missiles; *orig.* arrows. CAXTON. 2. A stroke made with pen or pencil; a short line; a touch (in a picture) 1589. 3. A line or lineament of the face; a feature 1773. 4. A distinguishing quality; a characteristic 1752. b. A 'touch' *of* some quality. Now *rare.* 1815. †5. A stroke or flash of wit, sarcasm, or pleasantry –1859.

3. Her face is somewhat altered. The traits have become more delicate. SHELLEY. 4. Who have no national t. about them but their language W. IRVING.

‖**Traiteur** (tretör). 1751. [F., f. *traiter* to treat, to supply with food for money.] A keeper of an eating-house (in France, Italy, etc.) who supplies or sends out meals to order.

Traitor (trē¹·tər). ME. [a. OF. *traitre* :— pop. L. *tradi·tor* for L. *tra·ditor* traitor, betrayer.] 1. One who betrays any person that trusts him, or any duty entrusted to him; a betrayer. In early use often, and still traditionally, applied to Judas Iscariot. 2. *spec.* One who is false to his allegiance to his sovereign or to the government of his country; one adjudged guilty of treason or of any crime so regarded ME. 3. *attrib.* or as *adj.* That is a traitor, traitorous ME.

2. Vnlesse I proue false t. to my selfe SHAKS. He is a t., and betray'd the state BYRON. *Traitor's Gate*, the river gate of the Tower of London by which traitors, and state prisoners generally, were committed to the Tower.

†**Trai·torly**, *a.* 1586. [f. prec. + -LY¹.] = prec. –1668.

Traitorous (trē¹·tərəs), *a.* late ME. [app. ad. OF. *traitreus, -eux*, f. *traitre* TRAITOR.] Having the character of, or characteristic of, a traitor; treacherous; perfidious.

A t. Crew of villanous Phanaticks 1683. Hence **Trai·torous-ly** *adv.*, **-ness.**

Traitress (trē¹·três), **trai·toress.** late ME. [a. OF. *traitresse*, fem. of *traitre* TRAITOR; see -ESS. In form *traitoress* f. TRAITOR + -ESS.] A female traitor; a traitorous or treacherous woman (or being personified as a woman).

Traject (træ·dʒekt), *sb.* 1552. [ad. L. *trajectus* a passing over, place for crossing, f. *trajicere* to throw across, f. *trans* + *jacere.*] 1. A way or place of crossing over; *esp.* a ferry. 2. The action or an act of crossing over water, land, a chasm, etc.; passage 1774.

Traject (trădʒe·kt), *v.* 1624. [f. L. *traject-*, *trajicere*; see prec.] †1. *trans.* To pass across (a river, sea, etc.). Also *intr.* –1711. 2. To carry or convey across or over; to transport. †a. (something material) –1684. b. To transmit (light, shadow, or colour) 1657. c. To transmit (thought, words, etc.) 1711.

2. b. A Prism, by which the trajected Light might be refracted either upwards or sideways NEWTON.

Trajection (trădʒe·kʃən). 1594. [ad. L. *trajectionem* f. *trajicere.*] 1. The action of trajecting or fact of being trajected; a throwing or carrying across; passage through 1633. †2. A perception transmitted to the mind; an impression, a mental image –1646. 3. Transposition; metathesis 1612.

Trajectory (træ·dʒektəri, trădʒe·ktəri). 1668. [ad. med.L. *trajectorius* pertaining to trajection, f. L. *traject-* TRAJECT *v.*; see -ORY.] A. *adj. Physics.* Of or pertaining to that which is thrown or hurled through the air or space. B. *sb.* 1. *Physics.* The path of any body moving under the action of given forces; *esp.* the curve described by a projectile in its flight through the air 1696. 2. *Geom.* A curve or surface passing through a given set of points, or intersecting each of a given series of curves or surfaces according to a given law, e.g. at a constant angle 1795.

‖**Trajet** (F. traʒe, træ·dʒet). 1741. [a. F. :— L. *trajectus* TRAJECT *sb.*] A crossing, passage.

Tra-la, Tra-la-la (trălā·, trălălā·), *int.* 1823. Phrase expressive of joy or gaiety, sometimes used as a refrain; also used to symbolize the flourish of a horn, etc.

The flowers that bloom in the spring tra-la, Have nothing to do with the case W. S. GILBERT.

Tralatitious (trælăti·ʃəs), *a.* 1645. [f. L. *tralaticius* (f. *tralat-*, *transferre* + *-icius* -ITIOUS¹).] 1. Characterized by transference; *esp.* of words or phrases, metaphorical, figurative. 2. Handed down from generation to generation; traditional; also, repeated by one from another, as a statement 1795.

1. A secondary and t. Association 1748. Hence **Tralati·tiously** *adv.* metaphorically.

†**Trali·neate**, *v. rare.* 1700. [f. It. *tralignare*, repr. L. **tra(ns)lineare*, f. TRANS- + *linea* LINE *sb.*²; see -ATE³.] *intr.* To go out of the direct line; to deviate –1745.

†**Tralu·cency.** 1599. [f. as next; see -ENCY.] = TRANSLUCENCY –1649.

†**Tralu·cent**, *a.* 1592. [ad. L. *tralucentem*, *tralucere* to shine across or through.] = TRANSLUCENT –1664.

Tram, *sb.*¹ 1679. [a. F. *trame*, OF. *traime*, *treme* :— L. *trama* woof.] Woof or weft; *spec.* silk thread consisting of two or more single strands loosely twisted together; used for the weft or cross threads of the best silk goods. Also *t. silk.*

Tram (træm), *sb.*² 1500. [app. the same word as LG. *traam* balk, beam, e.g. of a wheelbarrow. EFris., MLG *trām, trame.*] 1. Each of the two shafts of a cart or wagon, a hand-barrow, or a wheelbarrow. *Sc.* 2. *Coal-mining.* A quadrilateral frame or skeleton truck on which the corves were formerly carried; now in some colliery districts applied to the small iron truck which supplies the place of the earlier 'tram' and corve 1516. 3. A continuous line or track of timber beams or 'rails', or later of stone blocks or slabs, a parallel pair of which lines formed a tramway, orig. in or from a mine. Hence, each 'rail' of a tramroad of an early type, or of a tramway or railway. 1826. 4. A road laid with such wooden planks or rails, or with parallel rows of stone slabs or of iron plates or 'rails'; a tram-road of an early type 1850. 5. (Short for *tram-car.*) A passenger car on a street tramway; a tram-car 1879.

5. The discordant clanging of the gongs of electric trams 1902.

attrib. and *Comb.*, as *t.-conductor*, *-driver*, *-ticket*; **t.-man**, a man employed on a tramway, esp. a t.-conductor or driver.

Tram (træm), *v.* 1826. [f. prec.] 1. *intr.* To travel by a tramway or on a tram-car. *colloq.* 2. trans. *Mining.* To convey (coal, ore, etc.) by a tram or trams 1874. b. To push (a tram, etc.) to and from the shaft in a mine 1883.

Tram-car (træ·m,kāɹ). 1873. [f. TRAM *sb.*² 3 + CAR.] A public car or carriage running on a tramway for the conveyance of passengers; also simply *tram.*

Tra·m-line. 1886. [f. TRAM *sb.*² 4 or 5 + LINE *sb.*²] A tramway; also, a tram-rail.

Trammel (træ·mĕl), *sb.* late ME. [In sense 1, a. OF. *tramail* a fishing- or fowling-net with three layers of meshes :—late pop. L. **tramaculum*, generally explained as f. L. *tri-* three + *macula* mesh. The history of the other senses is obscure.] 1. In full *t.-net*: A long narrow fishing-net, set vertically with floats and sinkers; consisting of two 'walls' of large-meshed netting, between which is a net of fine mesh, loosely hung. b. A fowling-net 1530. †2. A hobble to prevent a horse from straying or kicking; also, a contrivance for teaching a horse to amble –1766. 3. *transf.* and *fig.* Anything that confines, restrains, fetters, or shackles. Chiefly *pl.* 1653. 4. *Mech.* An instrument for describing ellipses, consisting of a cross with two grooves at right angles, in which slide pins carrying a beam or ruler with a pencil; also applied to the *beam-compass.* Also *pl.* 1725. 5. A series of rings or links, or other device, to bear a crook at different heights over the fire. Now *local Eng.* and *U.S.* 1537. †6. *pl.* The plaits, braids, or tresses of a woman's hair –1673.

3. She, for the most part, refused to bind herself by conventional trammels 1889.

Tra·mmel, *v.* 1588. [f. prec.] 1. *intr.* To use a trammel-net; *trans.* to take (fish or birds) with a trammel-net. †2. *trans.* To fasten together (the legs of a horse) with trammels –1639. 3. *fig.* To entangle or fasten *up* as in a trammel 1605. 4. *fig.* To put restraint upon, hamper, impede, confine 1727.

3. If th' Assassination Could trammell vp the Consequence, and catch.. Successe SHAKS. Hence **Tra·mmeller**, one who or that which trammels.

Tra·mmel-net. 1516. [f. TRAMMEL *sb.* + NET *sb.*¹] = TRAMMEL *sb.* 1, 1 b.

Trammer (træ·məɹ). 1839. [f. TRAM *sb.*² or *v.*] 1. *Coal-mining*, etc. A man or boy who removes the trams of coal, etc. from the workings; a putter. 2. One who is employed on a tramway; also, a horse used to draw a tram-car 1889.

Tramontane (trămǫ·ntē¹n, træmǫntē¹·n), *a.* and *sb.* late ME. [ad. It. *tramontana* north wind, pole-star, *tramontani* 'those folkes that dwell beyond the mountaines' (Florio) :—L. *transmontanus*, f. *trans* across, beyond + *mons* mountain.] A. *adj.* 1. Dwelling or situated beyond, or pertaining to the far side of, the mountains (orig. and in ref. to Italy, the Alps); hence, foreign 1596. b. With the connotation 'uncouth, unpolished, barbarous'. Now *rare.* 1739. 2. Of the wind: Coming across or from beyond the mountains; *spec* in ref. to Italy, blowing from beyond the Alps 1705.

1. A t. ecclesiastic 1884.

B. *sb.* †1. The north pole-star: orig. so called in Italy and Provence, because visible beyond the Alps –1633. 2. In the Mediterranean and esp. in Italy, The north wind, as coming from beyond the Alps; hence *gen.*, a cold wind from a mountain range. (Now usu. in It. form *tramontana.*) 1615. 3. One who dwells beyond the mountains: orig. applied in Italy to foreigners beyond the Alps; also by these to the Italians; hence, a stranger, a foreigner; an outsider, barbarian 1593.

3. Yet was it a great labour for a Tramountain to climb over the Alps to S. Peters Chair FULLER.

Tramp (træmp), *sb.* 1664. [f. next.] 1. An act of tramping; a heavy or forcible tread; a stamp 1808. 2. The measured and continuous tread of a body of persons or animals; hence, the sound of heavy footfalls 1817. 3. A bout of tramping on foot; a trudge; a walking excursion. *colloq.* 1786. 4. A person on the tramp; one who travels from place to place on foot, esp. in search of employment, as a vagrant 1664. 5. In full. *ocean t.*: A cargo vessel, esp. a steamship, which takes cargoes wherever obtainable and for any port 1880. 6. a. A plate of iron worn under the hollow of the boot to protect it in digging; also, the part of the spade, etc., which is pressed upon by the foot 1825. b. A piece of spiked iron fastened to the sole of the shoe to give a firm foothold on the ice 1830.

3. Phr. *On (the) t.*, on one's way from place to place on foot, esp. in search of employment, or wandering as a vagrant.

Tramp (træmp), *v.* [Late ME. *trampen* :— OTeut. **tramp-*, related to **tremp-*, nasalized form of OTeut. **trep-*, **trap-*, whence G. *treppen* steps, stairs.] 1. *intr.* To tread or walk with a firm, heavy, resonant step; to stamp. 2. = TRAMPLE *v.* 3. 1596. 3. *trans.* To press or compress by treading; to tread or trample upon 1533. b. *refl.* Of a horse: To injure itself by setting one foot on another 1844. 4. *intr.* To walk; *esp.* to walk steadily or heavily; to trudge; to go on a walking expedition. *colloq.* 1643. b. To go about or travel as a tramp. *colloq.* 1891. 5. *trans.* To walk through or over with heavy or weary tread; to traverse on foot, *spec.* as a tramp 1774. 6. *intr.* To make a voyage on a tramp steamer; also *trans.* to run (a tramp steamer). *colloq.* 1899. 7. The vb.-stem used *advb.* 1796.

4. b. I'd rather have tramped it than gone in for any top-hatted occupation 1909. 5. He tramped the island in pursuit of his calling 1894. Hence **Tramping-card**, a certificate issued to a member of a trade organization, entitling him to maintenance while tramping in search of employment.

Tramper (træ·mpəɹ). 1725. [f. prec. + -ER¹.] 1. One who or that which tramps. 2. A person who tramps or travels on foot, a pedestrian; *spec.* a tramp, a vagrant 1760.

Trample (træ·mp'l), *sb.* 1604. [f. the vb.] An act or the action of trampling.

Trample (træ·mp'l), *v.* [Late ME. *trampelen*, in form a freq. of TRAMP *v.* (see -LE 3).] 1. *intr.* To tread or walk heavily; to stamp. †2. = TRAMP *v.* 4 (*rare*) –1631. 3. With *on*, *upon*, *over.* a. *lit.* To tread repeatedly upon with heavy or crushing steps 1577. b. *fig.* To treat with contempt; to domineer over 1646. 4. *trans.* To tread heavily and (esp.) injuriously upon; to crush, break down or destroy by heavy treading; also *to t. down, t. under foot* 1530.

3. An elephant trampling upon a snake 1879. b. Wit tramples upon rules JOHNSON. 4. Neither cast yee your pearles before swine: lest they t. them vnder their feet *Matt.* vii. 6. *fig.* Thus they t. all Learning under foot 1675. Hence **Tra·mpler,** one who tramples.

Tram-road (træ·m,rōᵘd). 1800. [f. TRAM *sb.*² + ROAD.] a. In mining districts, a road having 'trams' (see TRAM *sb.*² 3) laid in parallel lines, to form wheel-tracks for the easier transport of minerals in 'trams' or wagons; hence, *gen.*, a track thus made for vehicles. b. A special track or narrow railroad for wagons or cars, as dist. from a *tramway* laid down for tram-cars on an ordinary road or street.

Tramway (træ·mwēⁱ). 1825. [f. TRAM *sb.*² + WAY.] 1. = prec. b. Now *spec.* A track with rails flush with the road surface, laid in a street or road, on which tram-cars are run, for the conveyance of passengers 1860. 2. *transf.* A cable or system of cables on which suspended cars can travel. *U.S.* 1872.

Trance (trɑns), *sb.* late ME. [a. OF. *transe* passage, etc., f. *transir*, ad. L. *transire* to pass over, cross, f. *trans* across + *ire* to go.] †1. A state of extreme apprehension or dread; a state of doubt or suspense –1577. 2. An unconscious or insensible condition; a swoon, a faint; in mod. use, a state characterized by a more or less prolonged suspension of consciousness and inertness to stimulus; a cataleptic or hypnotic condition. late ME. 3. An intermediate state between sleeping and waking; a stunned or dazed state. late ME. b. A state of mental abstraction from external things; absorption, exaltation, ecstasy. late ME.

2. Most of the night he had lien in a t. 1617. 3. All thys I saw as I lay in a traunce 1420. b. As, in a kind of holy t., She hung above those fragrant treasures MOORE.

Trance (trɑns), *v.* ME. [In sense 1, a. OF. *transir* to pass away, to die; in sense 2, f. prec.] †1. *intr.* a. To pass away, to die. b. To swoon, faint. c. To be in great dread, doubt, or suspense. –1632. 2. *trans.* To throw into a trance or a similar state; †to stupefy; to entrance, enrapture. Chiefly *poet.* 1597.

2. I trod as one tranced in some rapturous vision SHELLEY. *fig.* When thickest dark did t. the sky TENNYSON.

‖**Tranché** (trɑ̃ʃe), *a.* 1661. [F.] *Her.* Party per bend.

†**Tra·ngam.** 1658. [Origin unkn.] An odd or intricate contrivance of some kind; a knick-knack, a puzzle: used with contempt. –1820.

Tranquil (træ·ŋkwil), *a.* 1604. [ad. L. *tranquillus.*] Free from agitation or disturbance; calm, serene, placid, quiet, peaceful. b. Of things or actions: Steady, regular, even 1769.

Farewell the Tranquill minde; farewell Content SHAKS. The treasures of this t. scene CRABBE. b. The heating power of the t. flame FARADAY. So **Tranqui·llity** [a. F. *tranquillité* (12th c.)], the quality or state of being t.; serenity, calmness. late ME. **Tra·nquil-ly** *adv.*, **-ness.**

Tranquillize (træ·ŋkwiləiz), *v.* 1623. [f. TRANQUIL *a.* + -IZE.] *trans.* and *intr.* To make or become tranquil or quiet.

It tranquillises the mind as well as the body 1835. Hence **Tra·nquilliza·tion. Tra·nquillizer.**

‖**Tranquillo** (traŋkwi·llo), *adv.* 1854. [It.] *Mus.* In a tranquil style or tempo.

Trans- (trans, tranz), *prefix.* The Latin preposition *trans* across, to or on the farther side of, beyond, over; also used in comb. In English *trans-* occurs in compounds representing those already used in Latin, and in others formed analogously from L. elements, or in which the second element is an English or other non-Latin word.

1. With the sense 'across, through, over, to or on the other side of, beyond, outside of, from one place, person, thing, or state to another': in vbs. and their derivative sbs. and adjs. representing L. compounds, or formed on L. elements; e.g. *transcribe, transcript, transport, transportation.* 2. In vbs., etc. formed on Eng. vbs., adjs., or sbs., as *transfashion, tranship, trans-shape.* 3. in adjs. and their derivs., repr. L. adjs. or formed on L. words, as *transmarine, transmural*, also on Eng. sbs. or adjs., as *trans-border, -frontier, -oceanic.* Special groups are: 4. in adjs. with the sense 'beyond, surpassing, transcending', as *transhuman, -material.* 5. in adjs., scientific terms (chiefly anatomical), with the sense 'through, across' (the thing denoted by the sb. implied), as *transfrontal, -ocular, -uterine.* 6. in sbs. with the sense 'transverse', as *trans-muscle, trans-stroke* (rare). 7. in geographical adjs. (unlimited in number), formed on the names of rivers, seas, mountains, territories, etc., with the sense 'situated or lying beyond or on the other side of', as TRANSATLANTIC, TRANS-PACIFIC. 8. in geographical adjs., formed as in 7, with the sense 'passing across, crossing', as in *trans-African, -Andean, Balkan, -Manchurian, -Siberian.*

Transaccidentation (trans,æ:ksidentēⁱ·ʃən, -z-). 1581. [ad. schol.L. *transaccidentatio* (Duns Scotus); after *transubstantiatio.*] A transmutation of the accidents of the bread and wine in the Eucharist, as dist. from *transubstantiation*, in which the substance alone is changed.

Transact (tranzæ·kt, trans-), *v.* 1584. [f. L. *transact-, transigere* to drive through, accomplish, f. TRANS- + *agere* to drive, do, act.] 1. *intr.* To carry through negotiations; to have dealings, do business; to treat; also, to manage or settle affairs. Now *rare.* b. *fig.* (usu. *dyslogistic.*) To have to do, to compromise 1888. 2. *trans.* To carry through, perform (an action, etc.); to manage (an affair); now *esp.* to carry on, do (business) 1635. 3. To deal in or with; to traffic in, negotiate about; to handle, treat; to discuss. *arch.* 1654. †4. To transfer –1889.

1. b. In his criticism..he seems to us a little to 't.' with cant 1890. 2. A country fully stocked in proportion to all the business it had to t. ADAM SMITH.

Transaction (tranzæ·kʃən, trans-). 1460. [ad. L. *transactionem*, f. *transigere*; see prec.] 1. *Roman* and *Civil Law.* The adjustment of a dispute between parties by mutual concession; compromise; hence *gen.* an arrangement, an agreement, a covenant. Now *Hist.* exc. as in 3 b. 2. The action of transacting or fact of being transacted 1655. 3. That which is or has been transacted; a piece of business; in *pl.* doings, proceedings, dealings 1647. b. *Theol.* In ref. to the Atonement, 'transaction' has senses ranging from 1 to 3. (In sense 1 chiefly in deprecation.) 1861. †4. The action of passing or making over a thing from one person, thing, or state to another –1691. 5. *pl.* The record of its proceedings published by a learned society. Rarely in *sing.* 1665.

3. Discoursing of the Court of France, and the transactions there CLARENDON. Hence **Transa·ctional** *a.*, -ly *adv.*

Transactor (tranzæ·ktəɹ, trans-). 1611. [a. L., f. *transigere.*] One who transacts; a negotiator or intermediary; a manager, conductor, doer.

Transalpine (trans,æ·lpəin, -z-), *a.* (*sb.*) 1590. [ad. L. *transalpinus*, f. *trans-* TRANS- + *alpinus* Alpine, f. *Alpes* the Alps.] 1. That is situated beyond the Alps: a. orig. beyond the Alps from Rome or Italy, i.e. north of the Alps; also, belonging to a region beyond the Alps; also †*transf.* rude, uncultured. b. Beyond the Alps from England, or from Europe generally; Italian 1624. c. Of or pertaining to the party in the Roman Church opposed to the Ultramontanes 1794. 2. (Passing) across the Alps (*rare*) 1654. B. *sb.* A native or inhabitant of a country beyond or across the Alps (*rare*) 1617.

1. The first t. garden of this kind arose at Leyden 1837. 2. In his Trans-Alpine Expedition 1654.

Tra·ns,anima·tion. Now *rare.* 1574. [ad. med.L. *transanimationem*, f. TRANS- + *anima* soul; see -TION.] = METEMPSYCHOSIS.

Tra·nsatla·ntic (trɑns,-, tranz,-), *a.* (*sb.*) 1779. [f. TRANS- + ATLANTIC.] 1. Passing or extending across the Atlantic Ocean. 2. Situated or resident in, or pertaining to a region beyond the Atlantic; chiefly in European use: = American 1782. B. *sb.* (the adj. used absol.): One who or that which is across the Atlantic; *spec.* an American; also short for 't. steamer' 1826.

Trans-bo·rder, *a.* 1897. [f. TRANS- 3 + BORDER *sb.*] Lying or living beyond a (or the) border; occupying territory outside the border.

Transcalent (trans,kēⁱ·lĕnt, trɑ·ns,kălĕnt), *a.* 1834. [f. TRANS- + L. *calentem*, *calere* to be hot, glow.] Having the property of freely transmitting radiant heat; diathermanous. Hence **Tra·ns,calency,** the property of being t.

Transcend (transe·nd), *v.* ME. [ad. L. *tran(s)scendere* to climb over or beyond, f. TRANS- + *scandere* to climb.] †1. *trans.* To pass over or go beyond (a physical obstacle or limit); to climb or get over the top of (a wall, mountain, etc.) –1695. 2. To pass or extend beyond or above (a non-physical limit); to go beyond the limits of (something immaterial); to exceed ME. b. *Theol.* To be above and independent of: esp. said of the Deity in relation to the universe 1898. 3. To rise above, surpass, excel, exceed. late ME. †4. *intr.* To ascend, go up, rise –1613. 5. To be transcendent; to excel. *arch.* 1635.

1. Nimble Wings which can T. the Polar Height 1695. 2. Unable as we are to t. consciousness H. SPENCER. 3. Electro-magnets far t. permanent magnets in power 1866.

Transcendence (transe·ndĕns). 1601. [ad. med.L. *transcendentia*, f. L. *transcendentem* TRANSCENDENT; see -ENCE.] 1. The action or fact of transcending, surmounting, or rising above; also, the condition or quality of being transcendent. b. *spec.* Of the Deity: The attribute of being above and independent of the universe; dist. from *immanence* 1848. †2. Exaggeration, hyperbole (*rare*) –1645.

2. This would have done better in Poesy: where Transcendences are more allowed BACON.

Transcendency (transe·ndĕnsi). 1615. [f. as prec.; see -ENCY.] The condition or quality of being transcendent; excess; surpassing excellency; with *pl.* a transcendent quality. b. The fact of transcending; an instance of this 1907.

Transcendent (transe·ndĕnt), *a.* and *sb.* 1581. [ad. L. *transcendentem*, *transcendere* to TRANSCEND.] A. *adj.* 1. Surpassing or excelling others of its kind; pre-eminent; extraordinary. Also, loosely, Eminently great or good. 1598. †2. Of an idea or conception: Transcending comprehension; hence, obscure or abstruse –1646. 3. *Philos.* a. Applied by the Schoolmen to predicates which were considered to transcend the Aristotelian categories or predicaments 1706. b. By Kant applied to that which transcends his own list of categories; hence, not an object of possible experience 1803. 4. *Theol.* Of the Deity: In His being, exalted above and distinct from the universe; dist. from *immanent* 1877.

1. That t. Apostle Saint Paul MILT. Such t. goodness of heart RICHARDSON.

B. *sb.* [the adj. used *absol.*] 1. *Philos.* †a. A predicate that transcends, or cannot be classed under, any of the Aristotelian categories or predicaments –1697. b. *transf.* A person or thing that transcends classification 1591. c. In Kantian philosophy: That which is beyond the bounds of human cognition and thought 1810. †2. One who or that which transcends the ordinary rank of persons or things –1679. 3. *Math.* A transcendental expression or function; see next 4. 1809. Hence **Transce·ndent-ly** *adv.*, **-ness** (*rare*).

Transcendental (transende·ntăl), *a.* (*sb.*) 1668. [ad. med. *transcendentalis*, f. as prec. + -AL.] 1. = prec. A. 1. 1701. 2. *Philos.* a. *orig.* in Aristotelian philosophy: Transcending or extending beyond the bounds of any single category. In 17th c. often synonymous with *metaphysical.* 1668. b. In Kant (1724–1804): Not derived from experience, but concerned with the presuppositions of experience; *a priori*; critical 1798. c. Used of any philosophy which resembles Kant's in being based upon the recognition of an *a priori* element in experience 1829. d. By Schelling 't. philosophy' was used for the philosophy of mind as dist. from that of nature 1903. 3. Hence, a. Beyond the limits of ordinary experience, extraordinary 1831. b. Super-rational, superhuman, supernatural 1826. c. *Vaguely*, Abstract, metaphysical, *a priori* 1835. d. Applied to the movement of thought in New England of which Emerson was the principal figure 1844. 4. *Math.* Not capable of being produced by (a finite number of) the ordinary algebraical operations of addition, multiplication, involution, or their inverse operations; expressible in terms of the variable only in the form of an infinite series 1706. **B.** *sb.* [the adj. used *absol.*] A transcendental term, conception, or quantity 1668.

3. a. Very frightful it is when a Nation..becomes t. CARLYLE. c. An unmeaning and t. conception JOWETT. 4. The..t. functions,..sin x, cos x, &c.,.. e^x, and log x 1882. Hence **Transcende·ntal·ly** *adv.*, **-ness** (*rare*).

Transcendentalism (transende·ntăliz'm). 1803. [f. prec. + -ISM.] 1. Transcendental philosophy; a system of this; applied to that taught by Kant and others; also, to the idealism of Schelling. b. The religio-philosophical teaching of the New England school of thought represented by Emerson and others 1842. 2. Exalted character, thought, or language; also, that which is extravagant, vague, or visionary in philosophy or language; idealism 1831. So **Transcende·ntalist**, an adherent of some form of t.

Transcendentalize (transende·ntălaiz), *v.* 1846. [f. as prec. + -IZE.] *trans.* a. To render transcendent. b. To idealize.

Transcension (transe·nʃən). *rare.* 1611. [ad. med.L. *transcensionem.*] A passing beyond or above; transcendence.

Trans,colora·tion, -coloura·tion. Now *rare* or *Obs.* 1664. [f. TRANS- + COLORATION.] The action or process of transcolouring; change of colour.

†Trans,co·lour, *v. rare.* 1664. [f. TRANS- + COLOUR *v.*] *trans.* To change the colour of; to cause to change colour -1837.

Tra·ns-contine·ntal, *a.* 1869. [f. TRANS- 3 + CONTINENTAL.] That extends or passes across a continent.

Tran,scri·bble, *v. rare.* 1750. [f. TRANS- + SCRIBBLE *v.*, after next.] *trans.* To transcribe carelessly. So **Transcri·bbler** 1746.

Transcribe (trăn,skrai·b), *v.* 1552. [ad.L. *transcribere.*] 1. *trans.* To make a copy of (something) in writing; to copy out from an original; to write (a copy). Also *absol.* b. Less exactly: To copy or reproduce the matter or statements of (a writing or book) without regard to the wording. Now *rare.* 1633. 2. To write out in other characters, to transliterate; to write out (a shorthand account) in ordinary 'long-hand'; formerly also, to translate 1639. b. *Mus.* To adapt (a composition) for a voice or instrument other than that for which it was originally written 1891. †3. *fig.* To copy or imitate (a person, his qualities, etc.); to reproduce -1729. †4. To ascribe *to* another by transference -1651. 5. *Rom. Law.* To transfer *to* another 1880.

1. The primitive Christians were careful to t. copies of the gospels BERKELEY. b. A few plain, easy rules. Chiefly transcribed from Dr. Cheyne. WESLEY. 2. The Agamemnon of Æschylus transcribed by Robert Browning 1877. Hence **Tran,scri·ber.**

Transcript (tra·n,skript). ME. [a. OF. *transcrit*:—L. *transcriptum, transcribere.*] 1. A written copy; also *transf.* a printed reproduction of this; *spec.* in *Law*, a copy of a legal record. 2. *transf.* and *fig.* A copy, reproduction; a rendering 1646.

1. A t. of which lettre hereaftur ensueth 1481. 2. Let our lives be a true t. of our Sermons 1657.

Transcription (tran,skri·pʃən). 1598. [ad. L. *transcriptionem*, or a. F.] 1. The action or process of transcribing or copying. 2. A transcript; a copy 1650. 3. *Mus.* The arrangement, or (less properly) modification, of a composition for some voice or instrument other than that for which it was originally written; a transcribed piece 1864. 4. *Rom. Law.* A transfer, assignment (of a debt or obligation) 1677.

1. The error was committed in the t. of the copy from Ptolomies library 1610.

Transcriptive (tran,skri·ptiv), *a.* 1646. [f. L. *transcript-, transcribere* + -IVE.] 1. Having the quality or habit of transcribing; given to transcription. 2. *Rom. Law.* Transferring obligation 1875. Hence **Tran,scri·ptively** *adv.*

†Trans,cu·rsion. 1624. [ad. late L. *transcursionem*, f. *transcurrere* to run across.] The action of running or passing across or through; transition, penetration; also, a journey or passage through a country, etc. -1665.

Transdialect (transdai·ălekt, -z-), *v. rare.* 1698. [f. TRANS- + DIALECT.] *trans.* To translate from one dialect into another.

Transduction (trans,dʊ·kʃən). *rare.* 1656. [ad. L. *tra(ns)ductionem, tra(ns)ducere*; see TRADUCE.] The action of leading or bringing across.

Transect (transe·kt), *v.* 1634. [f. TRAN(S- + *sect-, secare* to cut.] *trans.* To cut across; in *Anat.* to dissect transversely. So **Transe·ction**, the action of transecting; a transverse section.

Transelement (tranz,e·liment), *v.* 1567. [ad. med.L. *transelementare*, f. TRANS- + L. *elementum.*] *trans.* To change or transmute the elements of. So **Trans,e·lementa·tion**, the action or process of changing the elements of something 1550.

Transept (tra·nsept). 1538. [ad. med. or mod.(Anglo-)L. **transseptum*, f. TRANS- + SEPTUM hedge, enclosure, f. *sæpire.*] The transverse part of a cruciform church considered apart from the nave; also, each of the two arms of this (the *north* and *south transepts*).

Transfashion (transfæ·ʃən), *v.* 1601. [TRANS- 2.] *trans.* To change the fashion of, to transform.

Transfer (tra·nsfəɹ), *sb.* 1674. [f. next.] 1. *Law.* Conveyance from one person to another of property, *spec.* of shares or stock. 2. *gen.* The act of transferring or fact of being transferred; conveyance or removal from one place, person, etc. to another; transmission; transference 1785. 3. A thing (*rarely*, a person) that is transferred; *spec.* writing, drawing, or a design, transferred or to be transferred in reverse, from one surface to another, as by copying-ink, or by pressure in lithography, photography, etc. 1839. 4. A means or place of transfer. Chiefly U.S. *spec.* a. *U.S. Post Office.* A telegraphic money-order. b. On a railway, etc.: (*a*) A siding connecting tracks at a crossing or on different levels; (*b*) a t.-ticket; (*c*) the conveyance of passengers and luggage from one railway station to another, when these are not contiguous (attrib. *t.-man, -porter*) 1891.

2. b. The transference of a worker or player from one sphere to another; also, one transferred (attrib. *t. fee, money*) 1911.

attrib. and *Comb.*: **t.-book**, a register of transfers of property, esp. that of its shares or stock, kept by a joint-stock company; **-day**, at the Bank of England, a day for the register of transfers of bank-stock; **-ink**, ink used in lithography; **-paper**, paper used in making transfers in lithography, etc.; **-printing**, a process by which designs are printed on fictile, etc. ware; **-table** (*U.S.*), a railway traverse-table; **-ticket**, a ticket entitling a passenger to change from a conveyance to one on another line or route without re-booking or further payment.

Transfer (transfɔ̄·ɹ), *v.* Infl. **transferred, -ing.** late ME. [a. F. *transférer* or L. *transferre*, f. TRANS- + *ferre* to bear, carry.] 1. *trans.* To convey or take from one place, person, etc. to another; to transmit, transport; to give or hand over from one to another. b. *intr.* for *refl.* or *pass.* 1646. 2. *Law.* To convey or make over (title, right, or property) by deed or legal process 1598. 3. To convey (a drawing or design) from one surface to another, esp. to a lithographic stone 1839.

1. For transferring £5690 Reduced Stock into the Four per Cents 1809. b. He transferred later to the 19th Hussars 1901. 2. A grant only transfers what the grantor may lawfully give 1818. Hence **Transfe·rrer**, one who or that which transfers.

Transferable (tra·nsfĕrăb'l, transfɔ̄·răb'l), *a.* 1646. [f. prec. + -ABLE.] Capable of being transferred or legally made over to another; *spec.* of bills, drafts, cheques, etc.: Assignable in the course of business from one person to another. Hence **Tra·nsferabi·lity**, the quality of being t.

Transferee (transfĕrī·). 1736. [f. as prec. + -EE.] 1. One to whom a transfer is made. 2. One who is transferred or removed 1892.

Transference (tra·nsfĕrĕns). 1760. [ad. L. type **transferentia*, f. *transferentem, transferre* to transfer; see -ENCE.] The action or process of transferring; transfer. b. *Psycho-analysis.* [tr. G. *übertragung.*] Direction of feelings and desires toward a new object 1916.

Transferor (tra·nsfĕrǭɹ, -ǒɹ). 1875. [f. TRANSFER *v.* or *sb.* + -OR.] One who makes a transfer or conveyance of property, etc.

Transfe·rrable, *a.* Also **-ible.** 1660. [f. TRANSFER *v.* + -ABLE.] = TRANSFERABLE.

Transfigurate (transfi·giŭrĕit), *v.* Now *rare.* late ME. [f. L. *transfigurat-, transfigurare.*] *trans.* = TRANSFIGURE.

High heaven is there Transfused, transfigurated BYRON.

Transfiguration (transfigiŭrē·ʃən, -figər-, tranz-). late ME. [ad. L. *transfigurationem*, f. *transfigurare* (see next).] 1. The action of transfiguring or state of being transfigured; metamorphosis 1548. 2. The change in the appearance of Jesus Christ on the mountain (Matt. xvii. 2; Mark ix. 2, 3). late ME. b. *Eccl.* The church festival commemorating this event, observed on the 6th of August. 1460. c. A picture of this event 1712.

Transfigure (transfi·giŭɹ, -fi·gəɹ, -z-), *v.* ME. [ad. L. *transfigurare* to change the shape of (f. TRANS- + *figura*); or a. F. *transfigurer.*] 1. *trans.* To alter the figure or appearance of; to transform. 2. *trans. fig.* (in allusion to the Transfiguration of Christ): To elevate, glorify, idealize, spiritualize. late ME.

1. They saw Jesus transfigured in a radiance of glory 1911. 2. His morality is transfigured into Religion 1841.

Transfission (transfi·ʃən). 1891. [f. TRANS- 1 or 6 + FISSION 2.] *Biol.* The transverse splitting of a cell or organism as a mode of reproduction.

Transfix (transfi·ks), *v.* 1590. [f. L. *transfix-, transfigere*, f. TRANS- + *figere* to FIX.] *trans.* To pierce through with, or impale upon, a sharp-pointed instrument (also said of the instrument); to fix or fasten by piercing.

fig. His heart transfixt With anguish COWPER.

Transfixion (transfi·kʃən). 1609. [f. as prec.] The action of transfixing or state of being transfixed. b. *Surg.* The process of piercing the limb transversely, and cutting from within outward, in amputation 1872.

Transfluent (tra·nsflu,ĕnt), *a. rare.* 1828. [ad. L. *transfluentem.*] Flowing across or through; in *Her.* said of a stream represented as flowing through a bridge.

Transfluvial (transflū·viăl), *a.* 1806. [ad. post-cl. L. *transfluvialis*, f. TRANS- + *fluvius* river; see -AL.] Situated or dwelling across or beyond a river.

Transform (transfǭ·ɹm), *v.* ME. [ad. L. *transformare*, f. TRANS- + *formare* to form, f. *forma.*] 1. *trans.* To change the form of; to metamorphose. b. *transf.* To change in character or condition; to alter in function or nature 1556. c. *Math.* To alter (a figure, expression, etc.) to another differing in form, but equal in quantity or value 1743. d. *Physics.* To change (one form of energy) into another 1871. e. *Electr.* To change a current in potential or in type 1883. 2. *intr.* To undergo a change in form or nature; to change. Now *rare.* 1597.

1. To Samarcand..we owe the art of transforming linen into paper J. H. NEWMAN. b. He transformed an undisciplined body of peasantry into a regular army of soldiers 1796. 2. Then did this iolly feast, to fast transforme 1597. Hence **Transfo·rmable** *a.* capable of transformation.

Transformation (transfǫɹmē·ʃən). late ME. [ad. late L. *transformationem*; see prec.] 1. The action of changing in form, shape, or appearance; metamorphosis. †b. A changed form; a person or thing transformed. SHAKS. c. *Theatr.* More fully *t. scene*: A mechanical disclosing scene in a pantomime; *spec.* the scene in which the principal performers were transformed in view of the audience into the players of the ensuing harlequinade 1859. 2. *transf.* A complete change in character, condition, etc. 1581. 3. a. *Zool.* Change of form in animal life; metamorphosis 1638. b. *Physiol.* and *Path.* Change of form or substance in an organ, tissue, vital fluid, etc. 1834. c. *Math.* Change of form without alteration of quantity or value; substitution of one geometrical figure for another of equal magnitude but different form 1571. d. *Physics.* Change of form of a substance from solid to liquid, from liquid or solid to gaseous, or the reverse; *Chem.* change of chemical composition, as by replacement of one constituent of a compound by another 1857. e. Change of energy from one form into another

1877. f. *Electr.* Change of a current into one of different potential, or different type, or both, as by a transformer 1884. 4. An artificial head of hair worn by women 1901.

Transformative (transfǭ·ɹmătiv), *a.* 1671. [ad. med.L. *transformativus*, f. *transformare* to TRANSFORM; see -ATIVE.] Having the faculty of transforming; fitted or tending to transform.

Transfo·rmer. 1601. [f. TRANSFORM *v.* + -ER [1].] 1. One who or that which transforms. 2. *Electr.* An apparatus for transforming electric energy; now *spec.* a static apparatus for transforming alternating currents, and consisting essentially of two coils of wire wound round an iron core 1883. *Rotary t.*, also called *dynamotor*.

Transformism (transfǭ·ɹmiz'm). 1878. [a. F. *transformisme*; see -ISM.] 1. *Biol.* The hypothesis that existing species are the product of the gradual transformation of other forms of living beings (*loosely*, such transformation itself); any form of the doctrine of evolution of species. 2. The doctrine of gradual evolution of moral and social relations; *loosely*, such evolution itself 1885. Hence **Transfo·rmist.**

†**Transfreta·tion.** 1612. [ad. late L. *transfretationem*, f. L. *transfretare*, f. TRANS- + *fretum* strait.] The action of crossing or passing over a strait, channel, or narrow sea -1782.

Transfro·ntal, *a.* 1889. [TRANS- 5.] *Anat.* Crossing the forehead or the frontal lobe of the brain.

Trans-fro·ntier, *a.* 1877. [TRANS- 3.] Lying, living or done beyond the frontier of a country.

Transfuse (transfiū·z), *v.* late ME. [f. L. *transfus-*, *transfundere*, f. TRANS- + *fundere* to pour.] 1. *trans.* To pour (a liquid) from one vessel or receptacle into another 1601. 2. *transf.* and *fig.* To cause to 'flow' from one to another; to diffuse into or through something; to cause to permeate; to instil. late ME. 3. *Med.*, etc. To transfer (the blood of a person or animal) into the veins of another 1666. b. To treat (a person) with transfusion of blood (or of some solution) 1897.

2. The sole way of transfusing the principles of Christianity into men 1618. It's..Influence is transfus'd thro' several..Channels 1709. So **Transfu·sible** *a.* (*rare*) capable of being transfused.

Transfusion (transfiū·ʒən). 1578. [ad. L. *transfusionem*.] 1. The action of pouring a liquid from one vessel into another; also *fig.* transference; translation. 2. *Med.*, etc. The process of transferring the blood of a person or animal into the veins of another; the injection of blood or other fluid into the veins 1643.

1. I grant that something must be lost in all t., that is, in all translations DRYDEN.

Transfusive (transfiū·siv), *a.* 1677. [f. L. *transfus-*, ppl. stem (see TRANSFUSE) + -IVE.] Having the quality of or a tendency to transfusion.

†**Tra·nsgress,** *sb. rare.* 1578. [ad. L. *transgressus*, f. *transgredi*; see next.] Transgression, trespass -1839.

Transgress (transgre·s, -z-), *v.* 1526. [app. a. F. *transgresser*, f. L. *transgress-*, *transgredi*, f. *trans* across + *gradi* to step.] 1. *trans.* To go beyond the limits prescribed by (a law, command, etc.); to break, violate, infringe, trespass against. b. *absol.* or *intr.* (const. *against*): To trespass, offend, sin 1526. †c. *trans.* To offend against (a person); to disobey (*rare*) -1625. 2. To go or pass beyond (any limit or bounds) 1619.

1. So they transgresse & breke the commaundement of god 1526. b. I would not marry her, though she were indowed with all that Adam had left him before he transgrest SHAKS. c. I never Blasphemed 'em, uncle, nor transgrest my parents FLETCHER. 2. Hard mouthed coursers..Apt to run riot, and t. the goal DRYDEN.

Transgression (transgre·ʃən, -z-). late ME. [app. a. F., ad. L. *transgressionem*, f. *transgredi* to TRANSGRESS.] 1. The action of transgressing or passing beyond the bounds of legality or right; a violation of law, duty, or command; disobedience, trespass, sin. b. The action of passing over or beyond (due bounds) 1623. 2. *Geol.* The spread of the sea over the land along a subsiding shore-line, producing an overlap by deposition of new strata upon old 1882.

1. Heauen lay not my t. to my charge SHAKS. Punishments ordained beforehand for their t. HOBBES. Hence **Transgre·ssional** *a.* of or pertaining to t.; of the nature of a t.

Transgressive (transgre·siv, -z-), *a.* 1646. [f. L. *transgress-* (see TRANSGRESS) + -IVE.] 1. Having the character or quality of transgressing; sinful; passing beyond some limit (*rare*). 2. *Geol.* Overlapping; cf. TRANSGRESSION 2. 1854.

1. Adam..from the t. infirmities of himselfe might have erred alone, as well as the Angels before him SIR T. BROWNE. Hence **Transgre·ssively** *adv.*

Transgressor (transgre·səɹ, -z-). late ME. [a. AF. *transgressour*, a. late L. *transgressorem*, f. L. *transgredi* to TRANSGRESS.] One who transgresses; a law-breaker; a sinner.

To committe the transgressours..to the next Gaole 1463. A t. of the laws 1875.

Tranship (tranʃi·p), *less commonly* **transship** (transʃi·p), *v.* 1792. [f. TRANS- + SHIP *v.*] 1. *trans.* To transfer from one ship (or *transf.* from one railway train or other conveyance) to another. Also *absol.* 2. *intr.* Of a passenger: To change from one ship or other conveyance to another 1879. **Trans(·)shi·pment.**

Transhuman (transhiū·măn, -z-), *a.* 1812. [f. TRANS- 4 + HUMAN; after It. *trasumanar* in Dante.] Beyond the human; superhuman. So **Transhu·manize** *v. trans.* to make t. **Transhumana·tion.**

Transhumance (transhiū·măns). 1911. [a. Fr. (ult. f. L. *trans* across + *humus* ground).] The seasonal moving of live stock to regions of different climate. **Transhu·mant** *a.*, **-hu·me** *v.*

Transience (tra·nsiĕns, -z-; tra·nʃĕns, -ʒ-). 1745. [f. as TRANSIENT; see -ENCE.] 1. The action or fact of being transient, transiency. 2. = TRANSCENDENCE 1 b. 1882.

Transiency (cf. prec.). 1652. [See -ENCY.] 1. The quality or condition of being transient; transitoriness. 2. A transient thing or being 1866.

Transient (tra·nsiĕnt, -z-), *a.* (*sb.*) 1607. [f. L. *transiens*, *transire*, f. *trans* across + *ire* to go.] 1. Passing by or away with time; not durable or permanent; temporary, transitory; *esp.* passing away quickly or soon, brief, momentary, fleeting. 2. Passing out or operating beyond itself; transitive; opp. to *immanent*. (Often spelt *transeunt*.) 1613. 3. Passing or flowing through; passing from one thing or person to another. Now *rare*. 1619. 4. Passing through a place without staying in it, or staying only for a short time; *spec.* (*U.S. colloq.*) applied to a guest at a hotel, etc. 1685.

1. b. *U.S.* Of a newspaper advertisement: appearing only once 1857. 4. Love, hitherto a t. guest SWIFT. *transf.* of a hotel.

B. *sb.* 1. A transient thing or being 1652. 2. *U.S. colloq.* A person who passes through a place, or stays in it only for a short time; *spec.* a 'transient guest' at a hotel or boarding-house 1880. Hence **Tra·nsient-ly** *adv.*, **-ness.**

Transilience (transi·liĕns). *rare.* 1657. [f. as next; see -ENCE.] A leaping from one thing to another, an abrupt transition; *spec.* in *Min.* abrupt transition of one mineral or rock into another.

Transilient (transi·liĕnt), *a.* 1811. [ad. L. *tran(s)silientem*, *tran(s)silire* to leap across, etc., f. *trans* + *salire* to leap.] Leaping or passing from one thing or condition to another; in *Min.* said of one rock substance passing abruptly into another.

Transilluminate (transˌiliū·mineˈt, -z-), *v.* 1900. [f. TRANS- + ILLUMINATE *v.*] *trans.* To cause light to pass through; *spec.* in *Med.* to throw a strong light through (an organ or part) to discover the presence or cause of disease. So **Transillumina·tion** 1890.

‖**Transire** (transˌəi·rĭ, -z-). 1599. [L., 'to go across', f. *trans* + *ire*.] *Law.* A warrant issued by the custom-house, permitting the passage of merchandise.

Transit (tra·nsit, -z-), *sb.* 1440. [ad. L. *transitus*, f. *transire*; see prec.] 1. The action or fact of passing across or through; passage or journey from one place or point to another. b. The passage or carriage of persons or goods from one place to another 1800. 2. *fig.* A passing across; a transition or change; *esp.* the passage from this life to the next by death 1657. 3. *Astrol.* The passage of a planet across some special point or region of the zodiac 1671. 4. *Astron.* a. The passage of an inferior planet (Mercury or Venus) across the sun's disk, or of a satellite or its shadow across the disk of a planet 1669. b. The passage of a star or other celestial body across the meridian at its culmination 1812. c. Short for *t.-circle*, *-compass*, *-instrument*, *-theodolite* 1793.

1. Sometimes..the t. from Nantes to Orleans takes two months! 1833. Phr. *In t.* b. The means of t. are so bad, that much good corn is left to rot upon the ground 1870.

attrib. and *Comb.*: **t.-circle**, an astronomical instrument consisting of a telescope carrying a large graduated circle, by which the right ascension and declination of a star may be determined by observation of it in t.; a meridian-circle; **-compass**, an instrument, resembling a theodolite, used in surveying for the measurement of horizontal angles; **-duty**, a duty paid on goods passing through a country; **-instrument**, an astronomical telescope mounted on a fixed east-and-west axis, by which the time of the passage of a celestial body across the meridian may be determined; usu. applied to one without a circle; **-theodolite**, = *t.-compass*; **-trade**, trade arising out of the passage of foreign goods through a country.

Transit (tra·nsit, -z-), *v.* 1440. [f. L. *transit-*, *transire*; see prec.] 1. *intr.* To pass through or over; to pass away. 2. *trans.* *Astrol.* To pass across (a sign, 'house', or special point of the zodiac). Also *absol.* or *intr.* 1647. 3. *Astron.* To pass across (the disk of a celestial body, the meridian of a place, or the field of view of a telescope). Also *absol.* or *intr.* 1686.

Transition (transi·ʒən, -si·ʃən, -zi·ʃən). 1551. [ad. L. *transitionem*, f. *transire*, *transit-* (see prec.).] 1. A passing or passage from one condition, action, or (rarely) place, to another; change. 2. Passage in thought, speech, or writing from one subject to another 1592. 3. *Mus.* The passing from one key to another, modulation; *spec.* a passing or brief modulation; also, modulation into a remote key 1877. 4. The passage from an earlier to a later stage of development or formation. a. *Geol.* Formerly *spec.* applied *attrib.* to certain early stratified rocks believed to contain the oldest remains of living organisms; now classified as Silurian 1813. b. *Arch.* Change from an earlier style to a later; a style of mixed character 1835. c. *Philol.* The historical passage of language from one well-defined stage to another; hence, applied to the interval occupied by this, and to the transitional form of the language during this interval 1873.

1. A quick t. from poverty to abundance can seldom be made with safety JOHNSON. 2. Heer the Archangel paus'd..Then with t. sweet new Speech resumes MILT. Hence **Transi·tional** *a.* of or pertaining to t.; characterized by or involving t.; intermediate; **-ly** *adv.* **Transi·tionary** *a.* transitional.

Transitive (tra·nsitiv, -z-), *a.* (*sb.*) 1560. [ad. late L. *transitivus*, f. *transit-* (see TRANSIT) + *-ivus* -IVE.] †1. Transient, transitory (*rare*) -1845. 2. *Gram.* Of verbs and their construction: Expressing an action which passes over to an object; taking a direct object to complete the sense 1571. b. as *sb.* A transitive verb 1612. 3. *Philos.* Passing out of itself; passing over to or affecting something else; operating beyond itself; opp. to *immanent* 1613. 4. Characterized by or involving transition, in various senses. Now *rare* or *Obs.* 1660.

3. Cold is Active and T. into Bodies Adjacent, as well as Heat BACON. Hence **Tra·nsitive·ly** *adv.*, **-ness.**

Transitory (tra·nsitəri, -z-), *a.* late ME. [ad. F. *transitoire*, ad. post-Aug. L. *transitorius* having or allowing a passage through, in Christian L. transient, f. *transit-*; see TRANSIT *v.* and -ORY [2].] 1. Having the quality of passing away; fleeting, momentary, brief; transient. 2. *Law.* *T. action*, an action in which the venue might be laid in any county 1665. †3. (app.) Trifling, of little moment. DRYDEN.

1. This world is not but a vayn thinge and transitoire CAXTON. Hence **Tra·nsitorily** *adv.* **Tra·nsitoriness.**

Translatable (transˌlē·tăb'l), *a.* 1745. [f. TRANSLATE *v.* + -ABLE.] Capable of being translated.

Translate (trɑns,lēⁱ·t), *v.* Pa. t. and pple. **translated.** ME. [prob. first used in *translat(e* pa. pple., ad. L. *translatus*, pa. pple. of *transferre* to TRANSFER.] I. *trans.* To bear, convey, or remove from one person, place or condition to another; to transfer, transport; *spec.* to remove a bishop from one see to another, or a bishop's seat from one place to another; also, to remove the body or relics of a saint (or a hero) from one place of interment or repose to another. **b.** To carry or convey to heaven without death; also, in later use, said of the death of the righteous. late ME. **c.** *Med.* To remove the seat of (a disease) from one person, or part of the body, to another. Now *rare* or *Obs.* 1732. **d.** *Physics.* To move (a body) from one place or point to another without rotation.

Hys body was translat to Rome 1517. Morley, made at first bishop of Worcester, and soon after.. translated to Winchester BURNET. **b.** Bi feith Enok is translatid, that he schulde not se deeth; and he was not founden, for the Lord translatide him WYCLIF *Heb.* xi. 5.

II. 1. To turn from one language into another; 'to change into another language retaining the sense' (J.); to render; also, to paraphrase ME. **b.** *absol.* To practise translation; also *intr.* for *pass.*, of a language, speech, or writing: To bear or admit of translation 1440. **2.** *fig.* To interpret, explain; also, to express (one thing) in terms of another 1598.

1. It was translated out of latyn in to frenshe 1477. **b.** Sometimes Johnson translated aloud MACAULAY. **2.** There's matters in these sighes..These profound heaues You must t. SHAKS.

III. 1. To change in form, appearance, or substance; to transmute; to transform. late ME. **2.** To re-transmit (a telegraphic message) by means of an automatic repeater 1855. **3.** To transport with the strength of some feeling, to enrapture, entrance. *arch.* 1643.

1. Nabuchadnezar was really translated into a beast BURTON. **3.** Their souls, with devotion translated LONGF.

Translating (trɑns,lēⁱ·tiŋ), *vbl. sb.* 1460. [f. prec. + -ING[1].] The action of TRANSLATE *v.* *attrib.*: **t.-relay** (*Telegr.*): see RELAY *sb.* 4.; **-roller, -screw** (*Mech.*), a screw which moves a part of a mechanism in relation to the other parts; **-station** (*Telegr.*) a station at which an automatic repeater is introduced.

Translation (trɑns,lēⁱ·ʃən). ME. [a. OF., or ad. L. *translationem*, f. *translat-*, *transferre* to TRANSFER.] I. Transference; removal or conveyance from one person, place, or condition to another. **b.** Removal from earth to heaven, *orig.* without death, as the translation of Enoch; but in later use also said *fig.* of the death of the righteous. late ME. **c.** *Med.* Transference of a disease from one person or part of the body to another. Now *rare* or *Obs.* 1665. **d.** *Physics.* Transference of a body, or form of energy, from one point of space to another 1715.

The Feast of the T. of Saint Eadward 1869. *T. of a feast* (Eccl.), its transference from the usual date to another, to avoid its clashing with another (movable) feast of superior rank. **b.** The news of dear Mr. Polhill's sudden t. 1760. **d.** *Motion* or *movement of t.*, onward movement without (or considered apart from) rotation.

II. 1. The action or process of turning from one language into another; also, the product of this; a version in a different language ME. **b.** *transf.* and *fig.* The expression or rendering of something in another medium or form 1588. **2.** Transformation, alteration, change; changing or adapting to another use; renovation. late ME.

1. Nor ought a genius less than his that writ, Attempt t. DENHAM. **b.** His translations on copper, to compare them with..verbal translations..display much of the elegance of Pope 1812.

III. 1. *Law.* A transfer of property; *spec.* alteration of a bequest by transferring the legacy to another person 1590. **2.** In long distance telegraphy, the automatic re-transmission of a message by means of a relay 1866.

1. All Contract is mutuall t., or change of Right HOBBES.

attrib.: **t.-wave**, an ocean wave with a propelling or forward impulse; a forced wave. Hence **Transla·tional** *a.* of or pertaining to t. in *Physics*, consisting in onward motion, as dist. from rotation, vibration, oscillation, etc.

Translative (trɑns,lēⁱ·tiv, trɑ·ns,lătiv), *a.* 1589. [ad. L. *translativus* (see TRANSLATE and -IVE).] †1. Involving transference of meaning. PUTTENHAM. **2.** Involving transference from one place to another; in *Physics*, of the nature of onward movement without rotation or reciprocation 1682. **3.** Relating to translation 1748. **4.** *Law.* Expressing or constituting transference of property, etc. 1875.

Translator (trɑns,lēⁱ·təɹ). ME. [a. OF., or L.; see TRANSLATE and -OR.] One who (rarely, that which) translates. **1.** The author of a translation. **b.** One who renders a painting by engraving, or the like 1855. **2.** One who transforms, changes, or alters; *spec.* a cobbler who renovates old shoes 1594. †**3.** One who transfers or transports -1633. **4.** An automatic repeater in long-distance telegraphy 1855.

1. The symple..translatore of this litel book 1413. Mr. Cary, the t. of Dante 1837. Hence **Transla·torship**, the function of a t. **Transla·tory** *a.* of or pertaining to (physical) translation. **Transla·tress, -trix**, a female t.

Transliterate (trɑns,li·tĕreⁱt, -z-). *v.* 1861. [f. TRANS- 1 + L. *littera* + -ATE[3].] *trans.* To replace (letters or characters of one language) by those of another used to represent the same sounds; to write (a word, etc.) in the characters of another alphabet.

Transliteration (trɑns,litĕrēⁱ·ʃən, -z-). 1861. [f. as prec. + -ATION.] The action or process of transliterating; the rendering of the letters or characters of one alphabet in those of another; *concr.* a word or character thus rendered.

Translocation (trɑns,lokēⁱ·ʃən). 1624. [f. TRANS- + LOCATION.] Removal from one place to another; displacement; dislocation; †transmigration. **b.** *Vegetable Phys.* The transference of reserve material from one part to another. 1900. So **Tra·nslocate** *v. trans.* to remove from one place to another; to displace (*rare*).

Translucence (trɑns,l'ū·sĕns, -z-). 1755. [f. as next; see -ENCE.] **1.** The action or fact of shining through 1826. **2.** = next 1755.

Translucency (trɑns,l'ū·sĕnsi, -z-). 1630. [f. next; see -ENCY.] The quality or condition of being translucent; partial transparency.

Translucent (trɑns,l'ū·sĕnt, -z-), *a.* 1596. [f. L. *translucentem*, *-lucere* to shine through.] †1. That shines through; emitting penetrating rays -1791. **2.** Through which light passes; transparent 1607. **b.** Now, allowing the passage of light, yet diffusing it so as not to render bodies lying beyond clearly visible; semi-transparent 1784.

2. Sabrina fair..sitting Under the glassie, cool, t. wave MILT. **b.** A pane of thin t. horn COWPER. Hence **Trans,lu·cently** *adv.*

Translucid (trɑns,l'ū·sid), *a.* 1626. [ad. L. *translucidus* translucent; see prec. and -ID.] = prec. 2, 2 b.

Translunary (trɑns,l'ū·nări, -z-), *a.* 1627. [f. TRANS- 3 + L. *luna* moon, after *lunary*.] Lying beyond or above the moon: the opposite of *sublunary*; chiefly *fig.*, etherial, insubstantial, visionary.

Neat Marlow bathed in the Thespian springs Had in him those braue t. things DRAYTON.

Trans,ma·ke, *v.* 1844. [f. TRANS- 2 + MAKE *v.*, rendering Gr. μεταποιεῖν.] *trans.* To make into something different.

Transmarine (trɑns,mărī·n, -z-), *a.* 1583. [ad. L. *transmarinus*, f. *trans* + *mare* sea, after MARINE.] **1.** Born, existing, situated, or found on the other side of the sea; over-sea. **2.** Crossing or extending across the sea 1860.

1. An aliaunt, or a t. straunger 1583. The King's other T. Dominions 1700. **2.** Long t. migrations 1860.

Transmeridional (trɑns,mĕri·diŏnăl), *a.* 1883. [TRANS- 3.] Crossing or traversing the meridian lines; running east and west.

Transmew, transmue (trɑns,miū·), *v.* *Obs.* or *arch.* late ME. [a. F. *transmuer*:—L. *transmutare* to TRANSMUTE.] = TRANSMUTE 1.

Transmigrant (trɑ·ns,migrănt, -z-), *a.* and *sb.* 1622. [f. L. *transmigrant-*, *transmigrare*; see next.] **A.** *adj.* That transmigrates (*rare*) 1654. **B.** *sb.* †1. *orig.* One who leaves his own land and dwells in another. BACON. **2.** A person passing through a country or place on his way from the country from which he is an emigrant to that in which he will be an immigrant 1894.

Transmigrate (trɑ·ns,məigreⁱt, -migreⁱt, -z-), *v.* late ME. [f. L. *transmigrat-*, *transmigrare*, f. TRANS- + *migrare* to MIGRATE.] **1.** *intr.* To remove or pass from one place to another; *esp.* of persons, or a tribe; to migrate 1611. **b.** *trans.* in causal sense: To transfer. late ME. **2.** *intr. spec.* Of the soul: To pass after death into another body 1606. **b.** *trans.* To cause to pass 1559.

2. I think my soul would transmigrat into some tree, when she bids this body farewell 1645. Hence **Tra·nsmigrator**, one who or that which transmigrates.

Transmigration (trɑns,məigrēⁱ·ʃən, -mi-, -z-). ME. [ad. late L. *transmigrationem*, f. *transmigrare*; see prec.] †1. The removal of the Jews into captivity at Babylon; sometimes used for the Captivity -1609. **2.** Passage or removal from one place to another, esp. from one country to another. late ME. †**3.** Transition from one state or condition to another; *esp.* passage from this life, by death; also *absol.* death -1675. **4.** *spec.* Passage of the soul at death into another body; metempsychosis 1594.

4. Imagining as did Pythagoras, the t. of mens soules into other creatures 1634.

Transmigratory (trɑns,məi·grătəri, -z-), *a.* 1816. [f. TRANSMIGRATE + -ORY[2].] Having the quality of transmigrating; of or pertaining to transmigration.

Transmissible (trɑns,mi·sĭb'l, -z-), *a.* 1644. [f. L. *transmiss-*, *transmittere* to TRANSMIT + -IBLE.] Capable of being transmitted. Hence **Trans,missibi·lity**, t. quality.

Transmission (trɑns,mi·ʃən, -z-). 1611. [ad. L. *transmissionem*.] The action of transmitting or fact of being transmitted; conveyance from one person or place to another; transference. **b.** *Physics.* Conveyance or passage through a medium, as of light, heat, sound, etc. 1704. **c.** *Biol.* The transmitting of the peculiar nature, or of some character, of an organism to its descendants 1871. **d.** *Mech.* Transference of motive force from one place to another; *concr.* a device for effecting this 1906.

Alphabetical writing made..the t. of events more easy and certain JOHNSON. **b.** *spec.* in *Wireless*.

Transmissive (trɑns,mi·siv, -z-), *a.* 1649. [f. L. *transmiss-* + -IVE.] **1.** Having the quality or action of transmitting. **2.** Having the quality of being transmitted 1700.

2. The Sire [may] inculcate to his Son T. Lessons of the King's Renown PRIOR.

Transmit (trɑns,mi·t, -z-), *v.* late ME. [ad. L. *transmittere*, f. *trans* + *mittere* to send.] **1.** *trans.* To cause (a thing) to pass, go, or be conveyed to another person, place, or thing; to send across an intervening space; to convey, transfer. **2.** *fig.* To convey or communicate (usu. something immaterial) *to* another or others; to pass on, esp. by inheritance or heredity; to hand down 1629. **3.** *Physics* and *Mech.* To cause (light, heat, sound, etc.) to pass through a medium; also, of a medium, to allow (light, etc.) to pass through; to conduct. Also, to convey (force or movement) from one part of a body, or of mechanism, to another. 1664.

1. Hasten in my rents and debts, and t. them with all possible speed PENN. **2.** His Apostles..transmitted the same Spirit by Imposition of hands HOBBES. **3.** *spec.* in *Wireless*. Hence **Trans,mi·ttable, -ible** *a.* (*rare*) transmissible.

Transmittal (trɑns,mi·tăl). *rare.* 1724. [f. prec. + -AL.] The action of transmitting; transmission.

Transmitter (trɑns,mi·təɹ, -z-). 1727. [f. as prec. + -ER[1].] One who or that which transmits. **b.** *spec.* That part of a telegraphic or telephonic apparatus by means of which messages are transmitted or dispatched; a transmitting instrument; opp. to RECEIVER 6. 1876.

b. Also, the transmitting apparatus used in wireless telegraphy 1898.

Transmogrify (trɑns,mǫ·grifəi, -z-), *v.* Chiefly *joc.* 1656. [Origin obsc.] *trans.* To alter or change in form or appearance; to transform (utterly, grotesquely, or strangely). Hence **Transmo·grifica·tion**, (strange or grotesque) transformation.

Transmontane (trɑns,mǫ·nteⁱn, -mǫntēⁱ·n), *a.* 1727. [ad. L. *transmontanus*; see

TRAMONTANE.] 1. = TRAMONTANE A. 1. b. In ref. to mountains other than the Alps, e.g. the Grampians in Scotland, the Rocky Mountains in N. America 1884.

Transmundane (trans,mʊ·ndeɪn), *a.* 1777. [f. TRANS- 3 + L. *mundus* world.] That is or lies beyond the world.

Transmutable (trans,miū·tăb'l, -z-), *a.* 1460. [ad. med.L. *transmutabilis*, f. L. *transmutare* to TRANSMUTE.] Capable of being transmuted or changed into something else. †b. Liable to change, mutable –1509. Hence **Transmutabi·lity**, t. quality. **Transmu·tably** *adv.*

Transmutation (trans,miutē·ʃən, -z-). late ME. [a. F., or ad. late L. *transmutationem*.] 1. Change of condition; mutation. *Obs.* or *arch.* 2. Change of one thing into another; alteration, transformation. Also with *a* and *pl.* an instance of this. late ME. 3. *spec.* a. *Alch.* The (supposed or alleged) conversion of one element or substance into another, esp. of a baser metal into gold or silver 1478. b. *Law.* Transfer: usu. *t. of possession*, transfer or change of ownership 1488. c. *Biol.* Conversion or transformation of one species into another; *spec.* applied to the form of evolution or development propounded by Lamarck (1815–1822) 1626. †d. *Math.* = TRANSFORMATION 3 c –1743.

2. The supposed change of Worms into Flies is no real t. 1692. Hence **Trans,muta·tionist**, one who believes in or advocates a theory of t., e.g. in sense 3 c.

Transmutative (trans,miū·tătiv, -z-), *a.* 1611. [ad. med.L. *transmutativus*, f. L. *transmutat-*, *transmutare*; see -IVE.] Having the quality of transmuting; tending to transmute.

Transmute (trans,miū·t, -z-), *v.* late ME. [ad. L. *transmutare*, f. TRANS- + *mutare* to change.] 1. *trans.* To alter or change in nature, properties, appearance, or form; to transform, convert, turn. b. *Alch.* To change (one substance) into another, esp. a baser metal into gold or silver. Also *absol.* †2. To remove from one place to another (*rare*) –1817.

1. To t. its energy..into vibratory motion TYNDALL. 2. I was transmuted to Dublin, to be..lodged in Kilmainham MAR. EDGEWORTH. Hence **Transmu·ter**.

Trans,na·ture, *v.* Now *rare.* 1567. [f. TRANS- 2 + NATURE *sb.*] *trans.* To change the nature of.

Trans,no·rmal, *a.* 1860. [f. TRANS- 4 + NORMAL *a.*] Beyond or above the normal.

Trans-oceanic (tranz,ōuʃi,æ·nik, -s-), *a.* 1827. [f. TRANS- + OCEANIC.] 1. Existing or situated beyond the ocean; *transf.* pertaining to a region beyond the ocean. 2. Passing or extending across the ocean 1868.

1. A t. world 1899.

Transom (træ·nsəm). [Late ME., app. a corruption of L. *transtrum*, f. *trans* or the root *tra-* across + instr. *-trum* = Gr. *-τρον*.] 1. In building, etc.: A cross-beam or cross-piece, esp. one spanning an opening to carry a superstructure; a lintel 1487. b. A beam resting across a saw-pit to support the log. *dial.* 1885. 2. A horizontal bar of wood or stone across a mullioned window 1502. b. Short for *t. window*: A window divided by a transom; also, a small window above the lintel of a door. *U.S. colloq.* 1844. 3. *techn.* †a. The vane of a cross-staff –1696. †b. The transverse member in a cross –1864. c. A cross-piece connecting the cheeks of a gun-carriage 1688. d. *pl.* On a railway: Cross-timbers laid between (or, formerly, beneath) longitudinal sleepers 1838. e. The seat of a throne; also, a couch or seat built at the side of a cabin or state-room on board ship 1883. 4. *Shipbuilding.* †A cross-beam in the frame of a ship; *spec.* each of several transverse beams bolted to the stern-post, which support the ends of the decks and determine the breadth of the stern at the buttocks 1545.

attrib. and *Comb.*: **t.-bar**, the cross-bar over a door having a fan-light above it (*U.S.*); **-knee** (*Shipbuilding*), each of the curved timbers or angle-irons by which the transoms are fastened to the stern-timbers; **-window** = 2 b. Hence **Tra·nsomed** (-səmd) *a.* divided by or having a t. or transoms.

Tra·ns-Paci·fic, *a.* 1891. [TRANS- 7, 8.] a. Across or crossing the Pacific Ocean. b. On the other side of the Pacific.

Transpadane (tra·ns,pădēɪn), *a.* (*sb.*) 1617. [ad. L. *transpadanus*, f. *trans* across + *padanus* of the river Po.] That is beyond the river Po (from Rome); opp. to *cis-padane*. B. *sb.* One living north of the Po.

Transparence (trans,pē·rĕns). *rare.* 1594. [f. as next; see -ENCE.] = next 1.

Transparency (trans,pē·rĕnsi, -pæ·rĕnsi). 1591. [ad. med.L. *transparentia*, f. *transparentem*; see next and -ENCY.] 1. The quality or condition of being transparent; diaphaneity, pellucidity 1615. 2. That which is transparent 1591. b. *spec.* A picture, print, inscription, or device on some translucent substance, made visible by means of a light behind 1807. c. A photograph or picture on glass or other transparent substance, intended to be seen by transmitted light 1874. 3. A burlesque translation of the German title of address *Durchlaucht* 1844.

Transparent (trans,pē·rĕnt, -pæ·rĕnt), *a.* (*sb.*) late ME. [ad. med.L. *transparentem*, *transparere*, f. TRANS- + *parere* to appear.] 1. Having the property of transmitting light, so as to render bodies lying beyond completely visible; that can be seen through. †b. Penetrating, as light –1593. †c. Admitting the passage of light through interstices (*rare*) –1693. 2. *fig.* a. Open, candid, ingenuous 1590. b. Easily seen through, recognized, or detected; manifest, obvious 1592.

1. The Firmament, expanse of liquid, pure, T., Elemental Air MILT. b. Like to the glorious Sunnes transparant Beames SHAKS. 2. a. An ingenuous, t. life HARDY. b. A t. fallacy 1638. The t. sincerity of his purpose 1879. Hence **Trans,pa·rent-ly** *adv.*, -ness (*rare*).

†**Trans,pa·ss**, *v. rare.* 1592. [= obs. F. *transpasser*, f. TRANS- + F. *passer* to pass.] 1. *intr.* To pass away, depart, die. DANIEL. 2. To pass across or through; also *trans.* to pass beyond (a boundary or limit) –1646.

Transpeciate (tran,spī·ʃi,eɪt), *v.* Now *rare.* 1643. [f. TRANS- + L. *species* look, form, kind + -ATE [3].] *trans.* To change into a different form or species; to transform.

Transpicuous (tran,spi·kiu,əs), *a.* 1638. [f. med. or mod.L. *transpicuus*, f. L. *transpicere*, f. TRANS- + *specere* to look.] That can be seen through; pervious to vision. b. *fig.* Of language, etc.: Plain, clear in meaning; also *gen.* easily detected, manifest 1877.

Transpierce (trans,pī·ɹs), *v.* 1594. [a. F. *transpercer*, f. TRANS- + *percer* to pierce.] 1. *trans.* To pierce through from side to side (with the agent or the instrument as subject). Also *transf.* and *fig.* 2. To pass through, to penetrate 1604.

Transpirable (tran,spəi·răb'l), *a.* 1578. [ad. med. or mod.L. *transpirabilis*, or a. F.; see TRANSPIRE and -ABLE.] Admitting of transpiration; capable of being breathed through.

Transpiration (tran,spirē·ʃən). 1551. [ad. med. or mod L. *transpirationem*, f. *transpirare* to TRANSPIRE.] The action or process of transpiring. 1. Exhalation through the skin or surface of the body; formerly, also, evaporation. Also *concr.* matter transpired. 1562. 2. *Bot.* The exhalation of watery vapour from the surface of the leaves and other parts of plants, in connexion with the passage of water or sap through the tissues 1551. 3. *Physics.* The passage of a gas or liquid under pressure through a capillary tube or porous substance 1867. 4. The action or fact of something transpiring or becoming indirectly known (*rare*) 1802.

Transpire (tran,spəi·ɹ), *v.* 1597. [ad. med. or mod.L. **tran(s)spirare* (f. TRANS- + *spirare* to breathe), or a. F. *transpirer*.] 1. *trans.* To emit or cause to pass in the state of vapour through the walls or surface of a body; also, to exhale (an odour); to breathe forth (vapour or fire). b. To cause (a gas or liquid) to pass through the pores or walls of a vessel 1864. 2. *intr.* Of a body: †To emit vapour or perfume; of the animal body (or a person): to give off moisture through the skin (*obs.* exc. as tr. F. *transpirer*); now only of plants: to give off watery vapour from the surface of leaves, etc. 1648. 3. Of a volatile substance: To pass out as vapour through pores, to exhale; of a liquid: to escape by evaporation 1643. 4. *fig.* 'To escape from secrecy to notice' (J.); to 'leak out' 1741. ¶b. Misused for: To occur, happen. *orig. U.S.* 1804.

4. Yesterday's quarrel may t. 1741. b. An event.. which we believe transpired eighteen hundred years ago 1841.

Transplace (trans,plē·s), *v. rare.* 1615. [f. TRANS- + PLACE *v.*] *trans.* To change the place of, transpose; to oust from its position in favour of something else.

Transplant (tra·ns,plant), *sb.* 1756. [f. next.] That which is transplanted; *spec.* in forestry, a seedling transplanted once or several times.

Transplant (trans,pla·nt), *v.* 1440. [ad. post-cl. L. *transplantare*, f. TRANS- + *plantare* to PLANT.] 1. *trans.* To remove (a plant) from one place or soil and plant it in another. 2. To remove from one place to another; to transport; *esp.* to bring (people, a colony, etc.) from one country to settle in another 1555. 3. *Surg.* To transfer (an organ or portion of tissue) from one part of the body, or from one person or animal, to another 1786. 4. *intr.* (for *pass.*) To bear transplanting 1796.

2. The policy of transplanting nations..was adopted, as a regular part of Assyrian, Babylonian, and Persian policy PUSEY. Hence **Transpla·nter**, one who transplants; an implement or contrivance for transplanting.

Transplantation (trans,plantē·ʃən). 1601. [f. prec.] 1. The action of transplanting, in senses of the verb. 2. *Surg.* The operation of transferring an organ or a portion of tissue from one part of the body, or from one person or animal, to another 1813. 3. That which has been transplanted; a transplanted company or body. *rare.* 1641.

1. The T. of the Plague from Turkey to Holland 1720.

Tran,sple·ndent, *a. rare.* 1541. [f. TRANS- 1 + L. *splendentem*, *splendere*.] Brilliantly translucent; resplendent in the highest degree. Hence **Tran,sple·ndently** *adv.*

Transpontine (trans,pǫ·ntəin), *a.* 1844. [f. TRANS- 3 + L. *pons*, *pontem* bridge + -INE [1].] That is across or over a bridge; *spec.* on the other side of the bridges in London, i.e. south of the Thames; *transf.* (from the style of drama in vogue in the 19th c. at the 'Surrey-side' theatres), melodramatic, sensational.

Transport (tra·ns,poɹt), *sb.* 1456. [f. next.] 1. The action of transporting; conveyance 1611. †b. Transfer or conveyance of property –1682. 2. The state of being 'carried out of oneself'; vehement emotion (now usu. of a pleasurable kind); rapture, ecstasy. Also with *a* and *pl.*, an instance of this. 1658. 3. A means of transportation or conveyance; orig. a vessel employed in transporting soldiers, military stores, or convicts; later also, the horses, wagons, etc. employed in transporting the ammunition and supplies of an army 1694. †4. A person sentenced to transportation. –1851.

1. The Bill against t. of golde and sylver 1621. 2. An unheard-of T. of Fury 1686. The letter was received with transports of joy BURNET. Moderate your transports DICKENS. 3. The Dee was crowded with men of war and transports 1855.

Comb.: **t.-buoy**, a buoy used for the mooring and warping of vessels; **-rider** (*S. Afr.*), a goods carrier; **-ship**, **-vessel**: see 4.

Transport (trans,pō·ɹt), *v.* late ME. [ad. F. *transporter*, or L. *transportare*, f. *trans* + *portare* to carry.] 1. *trans.* To carry, convey, or remove from one person or place to another; to convey across 1483. b. *fig.* late ME. †c. To remove from this world to the next. SHAKS. 2. *Sc. Ch.* To translate (a minister); to remove (the site of a church) 1637. 3. To carry away or convey into banishment, as a criminal or a slave; to deport 1666. 4. *fig.* To 'carry away' with the strength of some emotion; to cause to be beside oneself, to enrapture 1509.

1. Mules to t. his Provisions and Ammunition STEELE. c. *Meas. for M.* IV. iii. 72. 4. Transported with celestiall desyre Of those faire formes SPENSER. Seest thou what rage Transports our adversarie? MILT. Hence **Transpo·rtable** *a.* capable of being transported; involving or liable to transportation. **Trans,portabi·lity**, **Trans,po·rtableness**, transportable quality. **Transpo·rtal**, **Transpo·rtance**, transport, conveyance. †**Transpo·rtment**, transportation (*rare*); vehement emotion, rapture, ecstasy.

Transportation (transˌpoɹtēⁱ·ʃən). 1540. [f. prec. + -ATION.] 1. The action or process of transporting; conveyance (of things or persons) from one place to another. (After 1660 gradually repl. by *transport*.) b. *Geol.* The movement of land-waste by rivers, ocean-currents, glaciers, winds, etc. 1830. 2. *spec.* Removal or banishment, as of a criminal to a penal settlement; deportation 1669. 3. *transf.* Means of transport or conveyance. *U.S.* 1861. b. A ticket or pass for travelling by a public conveyance. *U.S.* 1909. †4. Transport (of feeling), rapture, ecstasy -1690.

1. The t. of the troops was going..on PRESCOTT. 2. Were you sentenc'd to T.? GAY.

Transported (transˌpōᵊ·ɹtėd), *ppl. a.* 1600. [f. TRANSPORT *v.* + -ED[1].] 1. Conveyed from one place to another 1693. b. Compulsorily carried to a distant country 1728. 2. 'Carried away' by excitement or vehement emotion; excited beyond self-control; enraptured 1600. Hence **Transpo·rted-ly** *adv.*, **-ness.**

Transporter (transˌpōᵊ·ɹtəɹ). 1535. [f. as prec. + -ER[1].] 1. One who transports. 2. Any carrying apparatus; *esp.* a device for transporting coal from a quay or from one vessel to another 1893.

2. *T.-bridge*, a bridge over a navigable waterway, high enough not to interfere with navigation, carrying a suspended platform or car which travels from bank to bank and conveys the traffic.

Transposable (transˌpōᵘ·zăb'l), *a.* 1879. [f. TRANSPOSE *v.* + -ABLE.] Capable of being transposed; interchangeable.

Transposal (transˌpōᵘ·zăl). *rare.* 1695. [f. as prec. + -AL.] Transposition.

Transpose (transˌpōᵘ·z), *v.* late ME. [a. F. *transposer*, f. TRANS- + *poser* to place.] †1. *trans.* To transform, transmute, convert -1605. †2. To change the purport, application, or use of; in bad sense, to corrupt, pervert, misapply -1644. 3. To remove from one place or time to another; to transfer, shift (*lit.* and *fig.*; now *rare* exc. as in 4) 1510. 4. To alter the order of (a set or series of things), or the position of (a thing) in a series; to interchange; *esp.* to alter the order of letters in a word or of words in a sentence 1538. b. *Algebra.* To transfer (a quantity) from one side of an equation to the other, with change of sign 1810. 5. *Mus.* To alter the key of; to put into a different key 1609.

1. That which you are, my thoughts cannot t.; Angels are bright still, though the brightest fell SHAKS. Hence **Transˌpo·ser**, one who transposes.

Transposition (transˌpŏzi·ʃən). 1538. [prob. a. F., or ad. med.L. *transpositionem*, f. L. *transponere* (f. TRANS- + *ponere* to place); but assoc. in Eng. w. prec.] 1. *gen.* Removal from one position to another; transference. 2. Alteration of order, or interchange of position, esp. of letters in a word, or words in a sentence; the result of such action; a word or sentence transposed 1582. 3. *Mus.* a. Alteration of key; also *transf.* a transposed piece. †b. Inversion of parts in counterpoint. 1609. 4. *Algebra.* Transference of a quantity from one side of an equation (or one member of a proportion) to the other 1664. 5. *Anat.* Abnormal position of the organs of the body; heterotaxy 1857.

2. For in an Anagram Iskariott is, By letters t., Traitor kis 1630. So **Transˌpo·sitive** *a.*, characterized by or given to t.

Transprose (transˌprōᵘ·z), *v.* 1671. [f. TRANS- 2 + PROSE *sb.*] *trans.* To turn into prose; to render in prose. (Chiefly *joc.*)

Transrhenane (transrī·neⁱn), *a.* 1727. [ad. L. *transrhenanus*, f. *trans* across + *Rhenus* the Rhine.] That is across or beyond the Rhine; hence, German as opp. to Roman or to French.

Trans-shape (transˌʃēⁱ·p), †**transha·pe**, *v.* Now *rare. arch.* 1575. [f. TRANS- + SHAPE *v.*] *trans.* To alter the shape or form of; to transform.

†**Trans-shi·ft**, *v.* [TRANS- 2.] *trans.* and *intr.* To shift across or away. HERRICK.

Trans-subje·ctive, *a.* 1887. [TRANS- 4.] That transcends or is beyond subjective or individual experience as such.

Transubstantial (tranˌsŏbstæ·nʃăl), *a.* 1567. [f. TRANS- 1 + L. *substantialis*, f. *substantia* SUBSTANCE.] a. Changed or changeable from one substance into another; of or pertaining to transubstantiation. b. Made of something beyond substance; non-material, incorporeal.

Transubstantiate (tranˌsŏbstæ·nʃiˌeⁱt), *v.* 1533. [f. ppl. stem of med.L. *tran(s)substantiare*, f. TRANS- + *substantia* SUBSTANCE. App. first used in pa. pple.] *trans.* To change from one substance into another; to transform, transmute. Also *absol.* 1584. b. *spec.* in *Theol.*: see next 2. 1533.

The Philosophers stone..which would..t., other Metals into..Gold and Silver 1670. So **Tranˌsubsta·ntiate** *ppl. a.* transubstantiated 1450.

Transubstantiation (tra:nˌsŏbstænʃiˌēⁱ·ʃən, -stænsiˌēⁱ·ʃən). late ME. [ad. med.L. *tran(s)substantiatio*, f. *tran(s)substantiare*; see prec.] 1. The changing of one substance into another. 2. The conversion in the Eucharist of the whole substance of the bread into the body and of the wine into the blood of Christ, only the appearances (and other 'accidents') of bread and wine remaining: according to the doctrine of the Roman Catholic Church 1533.

Transudation (tranˌsiudēⁱ·ʃən). 1612. [ad. mod.L. *tran(s)sudatio*, f. *trans* across + *sudatio* a sweating.] The action or process of transuding. b. *concr.* Something which is transuded 1650.

Tranˌsu·datory, *a.* 1752. [See next and -ORY[2].] Having the quality of transuding; characterized by transudation.

Transude (tranˌsiū·d), *v.* 1664. [ad. mod. L. *tran(s)sudare*, f. TRANS- + *sudare* to sweat.] a. *intr.* To ooze through or out like sweat; to exude through pores (in the human body or anything permeable). b. *trans.* To ooze through (something) like sweat 1781. c. To cause (something) to ooze through 1861.

Transume (tranˌsiū·m), *v.* *Obs.* exc. *Hist.* 1482. [ad. L. *tran(s)sumere*, f. TRANS- + *sumere* to take.] 1. *trans.* To make an official copy of a (legal) document. †2. To take over; to transfer, transport -1656. †3. To transmute (*into* something else) -1652.

Transumpt (tranˌsʋ·mᵖt). 1480. [ad. med. L. *tran(s)sumptum*, f. ppl. stem of L. *tran(s)sumere*; see prec.] A copy, transcript; *spec.* a copy of a record, deed, or other legal document; an exemplification.

†**Tranˌsu·mption.** late ME. [ad. late L. *tran(s)sumptionem*; see TRANSUME.] 1. Transcription, copying; a passage copied from any author; a quotation -1716. 2. Transference or translation to another part or place -1684. 3. *Rhet.* Transfer of terms; metaphor -1677.

Tranˌsu·mptive, *a.* *Obs.* or *arch.* 1597. [ad. L. *transumptivus*, f. *transumpt-*, *transumere* to TRANSUME + *-ivus* -IVE.] Characterized by transumption; metaphorical.

Transvaal (tra·nzvāˑl, -s-). [f. TRANS- 7 + *Vaal*, a tributary of the Orange River in S. Africa.] A former S. African republic, now a state of the Union of S. Africa, lying north of the Orange Free State, from which it is separated by the River Vaal.

Transvase (transvēⁱ·s), *v.* *rare.* 1839. [a. F. *transvaser*, f. TRANS- + L. *vas* vessel.] *trans.* To pour out of one vessel into another.

Transversal (tranzvō·ɹsăl, -s-), *a.* and *sb.* 1440. [ad. med.L. *transversalis*; see TRANSVERSE and -AL.] A. *adj.* 1. = next A. 1. †2. *Genealogy.* Collateral -1594. B. *sb.* †1. Something transversal, a transverse line; *fig.* a deviation, digression (*rare*) -1620. 2. *Geom.* A line intersecting two or more lines, or a system of lines 1881. 3. *Roulette.* A bet placed at the end of any three numbers taking them horizontally 1895. Hence **Transve·rsally** *adv.*

Transverse (tranzvō·ɹs, tra·nzvəɹs, -s-), *a.* (*sb.*, *adv.*) 1596. [ad. L. *transversus* turned or directed across, pa. pple. of *transvertere* TRANSVERT *v.*] A. *adj.* 1. Lying across; situated or lying crosswise or athwart; *esp.* situated or extending across the length of something, *spec.* at right angles 1621. †2. Of kindred: Collateral, as between brothers, cousins-german, etc. (*rare*) -1660.

1. A kettle slung Between two poles upon a stick t. COWPER. **T. axis**, (*a*) an axis transverse to the main axis, as in a crystal; (*b*) *Geom.* the axis passing through the foci of a conic section (in an ellipse, the major axis); **t. muscle**, *Anat.* any one of various muscles extending across other parts; **t. process**, a lateral process of a vertebra; **t. suture**, the suture between the frontal and facial bones.

B. *sb.* [The adj. used *absol.*] 1. Something that is transverse; e.g. the transverse axis of a conic section, a transverse muscle, etc. 1633. †2. *By t.* [L. *per transversum*], crosswise; athwart. SPENSER. C. *adv.* In a transverse direction or position; transversely, across, athwart. Now *rare* or *poet.* 1660.

These two proportiond ill drove me t. MILT. Hence **Transve·rsely** *adv.*

Transverse (transvō·ɹs, -z-), *v.*[1] Now *rare.* late ME. [a. OF. *transverser* = med.L. *transversare* to cross, f. L. *transvers-*, *transvertere* TRANSVERT *v.*] 1. *trans.* To pass or lie athwart or across; to cross, traverse (*rare*). 2. To turn upside down or backwards; to overturn, turn topsy-turvy. Now *rare* or *Obs.* 1520. b. To convert into something different 1687.

Transve·rse, *v.*[2] 1672. [f. TRANS- 2 + VERSE *sb.* (orig. as a pun on prec.).] *trans.* To turn into verse; to translate or render in verse. Hence **Transve·rsion**[2], a turning into verse; *concr.* a metrical version of something.

Transversion[1] (transvō·ɹʃən, -z-). *rare.* 1656. [f. L. *transvers-*, *transvertere*.] The action of turning across or athwart; intersection; a turning into something else; transposition.

†**Transve·rt**, *v.* late ME. [ad. L. *transvertere*, f. TRANS- + *vertere* to turn.] *trans.* To turn across or athwart; to turn *into* something else, transform, convert; to turn about, reverse, overturn -1660.

Tranter (tra·ntəɹ). Now *dial.* ME. [app. syncopated from *traventer*, in med. (Anglo-) L. *travetarius*, perh. a corruption of L. **tra(ns)vectarius*, f. *transvehere* to transport.] In various local uses: chiefly, a man who does jobs with his horse and cart. Hence **Trant** *v.* to follow the occupation of a tranter 1597.

Trap (træp), *sb.*[1] [Late (and rare) OE. *treppe*, *træppe*, ME. *trappe*, *trapp*; cf. rare MDu. *trappe* trap, gin, snare, mod.WFlem. *traap*, *trape*; also med.L. *trap(p)a*.] 1. A contrivance set for catching game or noxious animals; a gin, snare, pitfall. b. *transf.* and *fig.* ME. c. Popularly applied to a police arrangement for the timing of motorists over a measured distance, in order to secure the conviction of such as exceed the legal speed-limit. Also *police-*, *speed-t.* 1906. 2. A movable covering of a pit, or of an opening in a floor, designed to fall when stepped upon; hence applied to any similar door flush with the surface in a floor, ceiling, roof, the top of a cab, or the like ME. 3. The pivoted wooden instrument with which the ball is thrown up in the game of TRAP-BALL; hence, the game itself 1591. 4. A device for suddenly releasing or throwing into the air an object to be shot at, as a clay pigeon 1812. 5. *colloq.* or *slang.* Deceitful practice; trickery; fraud 1681. 6. *slang.* One whose business is to 'trap' or catch offenders; a thief-taker; a detective or policeman; a sheriff's officer 1705. 7. *colloq.* A small carriage on springs; usu., a two-wheeled spring carriage, a gig 1806. 8. A device for preventing the upward escape of noxious gases from a pipe, as a double curve in or U-shaped section of the pipe, in which water stands 1833. b. Applied to various contrivances for preventing the passage of steam, water, silt, etc. Also, a ventilation door in a mine. 1877. 9. A recess in the butt of a musket or rifle in which accessories are carried 1844.

1. See also MAN-TRAP, MOUSE-TRAP, RAT-TRAP, etc. b. Let her lay traps for admiration 1765. 4. b. In greyhound racing, a compartment in which a greyhound is placed and from which it is released at the start of a race 1928. 5. *To understand t.*, to know one's own interest; *to be up to t.*, to be knowing or cunning.

attrib. and *Comb.*: **t.-bat**, a bat used in playing t. or t.-ball; also, the game itself; **-creel**, a basket used for catching lobsters, etc.; **-drummer**, one who plays a drum and other instruments at once; **-hole**, a hole closed by a t.-door; also (*pl.*) pits dug in the ground to serve as obstacles to an enemy, *trous-de-loup*; **-nest**, a nesting-box which a hen can get into but cannot leave until released; **-net**, a large net with a device for trapping fish; **-point**, on railways, a safety-point which prevents an unauthorized movement of a train or vehicle from a siding on to the main line by derailing it; **-shooting,** the sport of shooting clay pigeons, glass balls, etc., released from a spring t.; **-tree,** the jack-tree, *Artocarpus integrifolia*, which provides gum for bird-lime.

Trap, *sb.*[2] 1794. [a. Swed. *trapp*, so named from the stair-like appearance often presented by the rock, f. *trappa* stair.] *Min.* A dark-coloured igneous rock more or less columnar in structure: now extended to include all igneous rocks which are neither granitic nor of recent volcanic formation. Also *attrib.*, as *t.-rock, -shale.*

Trap, *v.*[1] [ME. *trappen*:—OE. **træppan* in *betræppan*, f. *træp* TRAP *sb.*[1]] **I.** *trans.* **1.** To catch in or as in a trap, entrap, ensnare. **2.** To furnish with traps; to set (a place) with a trap or traps 1841. **3.** To furnish (a drain, etc.) with a trap or traps 1862. **4.** Chiefly *Mech.* To stop and hold or retain by a trap or contrivance for the purpose; to separate or remove by a trap.

1. *fig.* With ambush'd arms I trapp'd the foe DRYDEN. 2. The right of hunting and trapping the streams and lakes 1841.

II. *intr.* **1.** To practise catching wild animals in traps for their furs; also *gen.* to set traps for game 1807. **2.** To use, handle, or work a trap or traps 1842.

1. I should like to come and t. on these waters all winter 1835.

Trap, *v.*[2] ME. [f. †*trap*, altered form of F. *drap* cloth, covering.] *trans.* To adorn (a horse, mule, etc.) with trappings; to caparison.

fig. A Prophecy so trapped with the ornaments of speech 1641.

Trap-ball (træ·pˌbǭl). 1658. [f. TRAP *sb.*[1] + BALL *sb.*[1]] A game in which a ball, placed upon one end (slightly hollowed) of a trap (TRAP *sb.*[1] 3), is thrown into the air by the batsman striking the other end with his bat, with which he then hits the ball away.

Trap-cut. 1850. [app. f. Du. *trap* step, stair + CUT *sb.*] A mode of cutting gems with the facets in parallel planes round the centre of the stone; also *step-cut, degree-cut.*

Trap-door (træ·pˌdōᵊɹ, træ·pˌdōᵊɹ). late ME. [TRAP *sb.*[1]] A door, either sliding or moving on hinges, and flush with the surface, in a floor, roof, or ceiling, or in the stage of a theatre. **b.** *Mining.* A door in a level for directing the ventilating current; a weather-door 1851. **c.** An L-shaped tear in cloth, etc.

Comb.: **t. spider,** one of a group of large spiders, which make a nest in the shape of a tube with a hinged lid which opens and shuts like a t.

Trapes, traipse (trēⁱps), *sb.* 1676. [Goes with next.] **1.** An opprobrious name for a slovenly woman or girl; 'a dangling slattern'. *dial.* **2.** An act or course of 'trapesing'; a tiresome or disagreeable tramp. *colloq.* 1862.

Trapes, traipse (trēⁱps), *v. colloq.* and *dial.* 1593. [Origin unkn.; related to obs. *trape*. In many dialects a disyllable.] **1.** *intr.* To walk in a trailing or untidy way; to walk with the dress trailing or bedraggled; to walk about aimlessly or needlessly (usu. said of a woman or child.) **2.** *trans.* To walk or tramp over; to tread, tramp (the fields, streets, etc.) 1885.

Trapeze (trăpī·z). 1861. [a. F. *trapèze*, ad. L. TRAPEZIUM.] A gymnastic apparatus, consisting of a horizontal cross-bar suspended by two ropes in the manner of a swing.

Trapeziform (trăpī·zifǭɹm), *a.* 1776. [f. next + -(I)FORM.] Having the form of a trapezium.

Trapezium (trăpī·ziŏm). *Pl.* **-ia, -iums.** 1570. [a. mod.L., ad. Gr. τραπέζιον, dim. of τράπεζα table.] **1.** *Geom.* Any four-sided plane rectilineal figure that is not a parallelogram; any irregular quadrilateral. (The Euclidean sense.) **b.** *spec.* A quadrilateral having only one pair of its opposite sides parallel 1570. **c.** = TRAPEZOID A. 1 a. Now *rare.* 1795. **2.** *Anat.* **a.** A bone of the wrist, articulating with the metacarpal bone of the thumb (so called from its shape); also, the corresponding bone in the lower animals. Also *t. bone.* 1840. **b.** (in full, *t. cerebri.*) A band of nerve-fibres in the *pons Varolii* of the brain 1890. **3.** = TRAPEZE (*rare*) 1856.

‖**Trapezius** (trăpī·ziŏs). *Pl.* **-ii** (-iˌəi). 1704. [mod.L. *trapezius* (*musculus*), f. *trapezium*; see prec.] *Anat.* Each of a pair of large flat triangular muscles (together forming the figure of a trapezium) extending over the back of the neck and adjacent parts. Also *t. muscle.*

Trapezohedron (træ:pĭzohī·drŏn, -he·drŏn). *Pl.* **-hedra, -hedrons.** 1816. [f. *trapezo-*, as comb. form of TRAPEZIUM, after *tetrahedron*, etc.] *Geom.* and *Cryst.* A solid figure whose faces are trapeziums or trapezoids; as the icositetrahedron or deltohedron, with 24 faces, etc. Hence **Tra:pezohe·dral** *a.* pertaining to or of the form of a t.

Trapezoid (træ·pĭzoid, trăpī·zoˌid), *sb.* and *a.* 1706. [ad. mod.L. *trapezoïdes*, a. late Gr., f. τράπεζα table; see -OID.] **A.** *sb.* **1.** *Geom.* **a.** A quadrilateral figure no two of whose sides are parallel. **b.** *occas.* = TRAPEZIUM 1 b. *rare* or *Obs.* 1795. **2.** *Anat.* A bone of the wrist, the second of the distal row of the carpus: so called from its shape 1831. **B.** *adj.* = next 1819. **b.** Anat. *T. body* = TRAPEZIUM 2 b. *T. bone* = A. 2. *T. ligament*, the CORACO-CLAVICULAR ligament. 1890.

Trapezoidal (træpĭzoi·dăl), *a.* 1796. [f. prec. + -AL.] Having the form of a trapezoid; irregularly quadrilateral. **b.** Having trapezoidal faces; trapezohedral 1796.

Trapfall (træ·pfǭl). 1596. [f. TRAP *sb.*[1] + FALL *sb.*[2]] A trap consisting of a trap-door or covering over a pit or cellar arranged so as to give way beneath the feet.

‖**Trapiche** (trapī·tʃe). 1648. [Amer. Sp.] A mill for grinding sugar-cane or ore.

Trappean (træ·piăn), *a.* 1813. [f. TRAP *sb.*[2] + *-ean* (L. *-eus* + -AN).] *Min.* Pertaining to, of the nature of, or consisting of trap-rock.

Tra·pper[1]. *Obs.* exc. *Hist.* ME. [ad. OF. **trapeüre* (cf. med.L. *trappatura*), **drapeüre, drapure.*] A covering put over a beast of burden, made of metal or leather for defence or of cloth for shelter and adornment.

Trapper[2] (træ·pəɹ). 1768. [f. TRAP *v.*[1] and *sb.*[1]] **1.** One who sets traps or snares; *spec.* one engaged in trapping wild animals for their furs. **2.** A boy stationed to open and shut a trap-door for the passage of trams in a coal-mine 1815. **3.** One who manages a trap in trap-shooting 1892.

Trapping (træ·piŋ), *vbl. sb.* Chiefly in pl. **trappings.** late ME. [See TRAP *v.*[2] and -ING[1].] A cloth or covering spread over the harness or saddle of a horse or other beast of burden; a caparison. **b.** *transf.* 'Ornaments; dress; embellishments; external, superficial, and trifling decoration' (J.) 1596.

The embroidered trappings of the elephants 1817. b. These, but the Trappings, and the Suites of woe SHAKS. He needs no Trappings of fictitious Fame DRYDEN.

Trappist (træ·pist) *sb.* (*a.*) 1814. [ad. F. *trappiste*, from *La Trappe*, name of the convent.] A monk of the branch of the Cistercian order observing the reformed rule established in 1664 by De Rancé, abbot of La Trappe, in Normandy. **b.** *attrib.* or as *adj.* Of or pertaining to this branch of the Cistercian order 1836.

Trappose (træ·pōᵘs), *a.* 1796. [f. TRAP *sb.*[2] + -OSE.] *Min.* Of, pertaining to, or of the nature of trap or trap-rock; trappean.

Traps (træps), *sb. pl. colloq.* 1813. [app. shortened from *trappings.*] Portable articles for dress, furniture, or use; personal effects; baggage; belongings.

Tra·pˌstick. 1591. [f. TRAP *sb.*[1] + STICK *sb.*] A stick used in the game of trap or trap-ball.

Trash (træʃ), *sb.*[1] 1518. [Origin obsc.] **1.** That which is broken, snapped, or lopped off anything in preparing it for use; e.g. twigs, splinters, 'cuttings from a hedge, small wood from a copse', straw, rags; refuse 1555. **b.** Broken ice mixed with water 1856. **2.** *spec.* The refuse of sugar-canes after the juice has been expressed; cane-trash; also, the dried leaves and tops of the canes, stripped off while still growing, to allow them to ripen; field-trash 1707. **3.** Worthless stuff; dross; rubbish 1518. **b.** Worthless notions, talk, or writing; nonsense; 'rubbish', 'stuff' 1542. †**c.** Contemptuously applied to money or cash; 'dross'. *slang.* –1809. **4.** A worthless or disreputable person; now usu., such persons collectively 1604.

3. Who steales my purse, steales t. SHAKS. b. Those Theological Disputations..leven pure Doctrin with scholastical T. MILT. 4. I do suspect this T. To be a party in this Iniurie SHAKS. *White t.*, the poor white population in the southern U.S.

Comb.: **t.-ice** = sense 1 b.

Trash, *sb.*[2] Now *dial.* 1611. [Goes with next.] In full *t.-cord*: a cord used to check dogs in breaking or training them; a leash.

Trash (træʃ), *v.*[1] 1610. [Origin obsc.] †**1.** *trans.* To check (a hound) by a cord or leash; hence *gen.* to hold back, retard, encumber, hinder –1837. **2.** *West. U.S.* To efface 1859.

1. Who t' aduance, and who To t. for ouertopping SHAKS.

Trash, *v.*[2] *Obs.* exc. *dial.* 1607. [app. f. Norse; cf. Sw. *traska*, Norw. *traske.*] **1.** *intr.* To walk or run with exertion and fatigue, esp. through mud or mire. **2.** *trans.* To fatigue (with walking, running, etc.); to wear out 1650.

Trash, *v.*[3] 1793. [f. TRASH *sb.*[1]] **1.** *trans.* To free from trash or refuse; *spec.* to strip the outer leaves from (growing sugar-canes) so that they may ripen more quickly. **2.** To treat as trash; hence, to discard as worthless 1909.

Trashy (træ·ʃi), *a.* 1620. [f. TRASH *sb.*[1] + -Y[1].] Of the nature of trash; rubbishy; worthless. Hence **Tra·shily** *adv.* **Tra·shiness.**

Trass (tras). 1796. [a. Du. *tras*, earlier *terras, tiras.*] = TARRAS.

‖**Trattoria** (tratorī·a). 1832. [It.] In Italy, an eating-house and cook-shop.

Traulism (trǭ·liz'm). *rare.* Also in L. form **traulismus.** 1678. [ad. Gr. τραυλισμός, f. τραυλίζειν to lisp.] A stammering, stuttering.

‖**Trauma** (trǭ·mă). 1693. Pl. **traumata** (trǭ·mătă), also **traumas.** [a. Gr. τραῦμα wound.] *Path.* A wound, or external bodily injury in general; also, the condition caused by this; traumatism. **b.** *Psychoanalysis.* A disturbing experience which affects the mind or nerves of a person so as to induce hysteria or 'psychic' conditions; a mental shock 1916.

Traumatic (trǫmæ·tik), *a.* 1656. [ad. late L. *traumaticus*, ad. Gr. τραυματικός, f. τραῦμα, -ματ- wound.] Of, pertaining to, or caused by a wound, injury, or shock.

Traumatism (trǭ·mătiz'm). 1857. [f. Gr. τραῦμα, -ματ- wound + -ISM.] *Path.* The morbid condition of the system due to a trauma.

Traumato- (trǭmătǫ), repr. Gr. τραυματο-, comb. f. τραῦμα wound, as in **Traumato·logy,** the scientific description of wounds.

Travail (træ·vēⁱl), *sb.* ME. [a. OF., f. *travailler* TRAVAIL *v.*] **1.** Bodily or mental labour or toil, esp. of a painful or oppressive nature; exertion; trouble; hardship; suffering. *arch.* †**2.** With *a* and *pl.* A work, a task; *pl.* labours –1724. †**3.** The outcome of toil or labour; a (finished) 'work'; *esp.* a literary work –1624. **4.** The labour and pain of child-birth. Now freq. *fig.* ME. **5.** Journeying, a journey. Now differentiated under the spelling TRAVEL, q. v.

1. Faint and sick with travaile and fear JER. TAYLOR. 4. Phr. *In t.*; A woman, when shee is in trauaile, hath sorrow, because her houre is come *John* xvi. 21.

Travail (træ·vēⁱl), *v.* [ME. *travaille(n, -vaylle, -vaile*, etc., a. OF. *travaill(i)er*, app. repr. a late pop. L. or Com. Rom. **trepaliare*, f. *trepalium* an instrument of torture (prob. f. L. *tres, tria* three + *palus* stake).] **1.** *trans.* To torment, distress, afflict, trouble; to weary, tire. *Obs.* or *arch.* †**b.** To put to work, cause to work; to exert, employ –1630. **2.** *intr.* (for *refl.*). To exert oneself, labour, toil, work hard. *arch.* ME. **3.** Of a woman: To suffer the pains of child-birth; to be in labour ME. †**4.** To journey, etc.: see TRAVEL *v.*

1. They were wery and sore traueyled by the waye which was longe CAXTON. 2. Trauell not too much to be rich 1612. 3. Flowres which only Dame Nature trauels with 1634.

Tra·vailous, *a. Obs.* or *arch.* ME. [a. OF. *travaillos, travailleus*, f. *travail* TRAVAIL *sb.*; see -OUS.] Full of or characterized by 'travail' or hard labour; toilsome; wearisome.

Trave. *Obs.* exc. *dial.* late ME. [In sense 1, a. OF. *trave* beam:—L. *trabem, trabs* beam. With sense 2 cf. F. *entrave.*] 1. A (timber or wooden) beam. 2. A frame or enclosure of bars in which a restive horse is placed to be shod. late ME.

Travel (træ·vĕl, -v'l), *sb.* ME. [orig. the same word as TRAVAIL *sb.*] †1. = TRAVAIL *sb.* 2. The action of travelling or journeying. late ME. b. With *a* and *pl.* An act of travelling; a journey. Now only *pl.*, exc. *dial.* 1559. c. *pl.* (*ellipt.*) 'Account of occurrences and observations of a journey into foreign parts' (J.) 1706. d. *transf.* Passage of anything in its course or path, or over a distance 1742. 3. A single movement of some part of mechanism, as a piston, etc.; also, the distance through which it moves 1841. 4. Capacity or force of movement 1816.

2. The wayes are everywhere unsafe for travell 1650. b. His travels ended at his country seat DRYDEN.

Comb., as *travel-stained, -worn* adjs.

Travel (træ·vĕl, -v'l), *v.* ME. [orig. the same word as TRAVAIL *v.* Derivs., as *travelled, -er, -ing*, etc. are usu. spelt with *ll* in Great Britain, with single *l* in America.] †1. = TRAVAIL *v.* 2. *intr.* To make a journey; to go from one place to another; to journey ME. b. To journey from place to place as a commercial traveller. Const. *in* a commodity. 1830. c. Of an animal: To walk or run; *spec.* of deer, to move on while browsing 1877. 3. *transf.* To move, go; to pass from one point or place to another; *esp.* in mod. scientific use, to pass, be transmitted 1662. b. *fig.* of some action figured as movement 1600. c. Of a piece of mechanism: To move, or be capable of movement, along a fixed course 1815. d. *colloq.* To bear transportation 1852. e. To move on, esp. with speed. *colloq.* or *slang.* 1884. 4. *trans.* (or with advb. accus.) To journey through (a country, district, space, etc.); to traverse (a road, etc.); to follow (a course or path) ME. b. To traverse, cover (a specified distance) 1660. 5. To cause to journey, to drive or lead from one place to another 1598.

2. To preserue all that trauayle by lande or by water *Bk. Com. Prayer.* b. Mr. Bingle travelled in whisky 1906. 3. Thy thunders t. over earth and seas COWPER. Phr. *To t. out of the record*: see RECORD *sb.* II. 1. 4. The senior judge . who actually travels that circuit 1885. Phr. †*To t. the road*, to practise highway robbery. b. Their number is..greater than that of the miles you t. 1804. 5. It would be advisable..not..to t. any stock at present 1891.

Travelled (træ·vĕld), *ppl. a.* Also (chiefly *U.S.*) traveled. late ME. [f. prec. + -ED[1].] 1. That has travelled, esp. to distant countries; experienced in travel. Also with adv. as *far-t.* 2. *Geol.* Of blocks, boulders, etc.: Transported to a distance from their original site, as by glacial action; erratic 1830. 3. Of a road, etc.: Frequented by travellers 1882.

1. A well trauelled knight and well knowen LD. BERNERS.

Traveller (træ·vĕlər). Also (chiefly *U.S.*) traveler. late ME. [f. TRAVEL *v.* + -ER[2].] One who or that which travels. 1. One who is travelling from place to place, or along a road or path; one who is on a journey; a wayfarer; a passenger. b. = TRAMP *sb.*[1] 4. Now *dial.* 1763. 2. *spec.* One who travels abroad; one who journeys or has journeyed through foreign countries or strange places 1556. 3. *spec.* (in full, *commercial t.*): An agent employed by a commercial firm to travel from place to place showing samples of goods and soliciting custom 1800. 4. a. A horse, a vehicle, etc., that travels or goes along (fast, well, etc.). b. Applied to birds making a long flight, or migrating. 1660. 5. A piece of mechanism constructed to 'travel', run, or slide along a support; as a travelling crane, etc. 1842. b. *Naut.* An iron ring or thimble running freely on a rope, rod, or spar 1762. c. In ring-spinning, a metal ring or loop used to guide the yarn in winding it on the spindle 1853. d. *Angling.* A tackle which permits the bait to travel or move down the swim 1867.

Comb. with *traveller's*: **traveller's joy**, the wild shrub *Clematis Vitalba*, from its trailing over and adorning hedges by the wayside; **traveller's palm, tree**, names for certain trees which yield water or sap sought after by travellers to allay thirst, as *Ravenala madagascariensis*, a palm-like tree of Madagascar whose hollow leaf-sheaths contain a store of water.

Tra·velling, *vbl. sb.* Also (chiefly *U.S.*) traveling. late ME. [-ING[1].] The action of TRAVEL *v.*

attrib., as *t. clock, expenses*; **t.-carriage**, a strong carriage used for t. before railways were introduced; **t. fellowship, scholarship**, one given to enable the holder to travel for purposes of study or research.

Travelogue (træ·vĕlǫg). 1903. [f. TRAVEL *sb.*, after *monologue*, etc.] A lecture or talk on travel, often illustrated pictorially.

Traversable (træ·vəɹsăb'l), *a.* 1534. [f. TRAVERSE *v.* + -ABLE.] 1. Capable of being traversed or crossed 1656. 2. *Law.* Capable of being traversed or formally denied 1534.

1. Roads..t. at all seasons 1859.

Traverse (træ·vəɹs), *sb.* ME. [repr. two OF. sbs., *travers*:—pop. L. **traversum*, for L. *transversum* TRANSVERSE *a.*, and *traverse*, chiefly from *traverser* TRAVERSE *v.*] I. The action of TRAVERSE *v.* in a local sense. 1. = PASSAGE 4. *Obs.* exc. *Hist.* 2. The action of traversing, passing across, or going through (a region, etc.); passage, crossing: orig. from side to side 1599. 3. *Surveying.* A single line of survey carried across a region or through a narrow strip of country, by measuring the lengths and azimuths of a connected series of straight lines. Also, a tract of country so surveyed. 1881. †4. *Fencing.* The action or an act of traversing –1706. 5. *Mountaineering.* An act of traversing or making one's way in a horizontal direction across the face of a mountain or rock; also *concr.* a place where a traverse is made 1893.

5. Three o'clock found us still working westwards on the t. 1897.

II. 1. Something that crosses, thwarts, or obstructs; opposition; an obstacle; a mishap; *pl.* crosses. Now *rare.* late ME. 2. *Law.* The traversing or formal denial in pleading of some matter of fact alleged by the other side; also, a plea consisting of this. late ME. †3. A dispute, controversy –1651. III. 1. A passage by which one may traverse or cross; a way, pass; a crossing 1678. 2. *Naut.* The zigzag track of a vessel sailing against the wind; with *a* and *pl.*, each of the runs made by a ship in tacking 1594. b. *transf.* Each lap, length, or *pli* of a zigzag ascending road 1731.

2. b. We mounted by a military road cut in traverses JOHNSON.

IV. 1. A curtain or screen placed crosswise, or drawn across a room, hall, or theatre; also, a partition of wood, a screen of lattice-work, or the like. *Obs.* exc. *Hist.* late ME. 2. A small compartment shut off or enclosed by a curtain or screen in a church, house, etc.; a closet. *arch.* 1494. †3. A bar or barrier across anything –1759. 4. *Fortif.* A barrier or barricade thrown across an approach, the line of fire, etc. as a defence; *spec.* (*pl.*) parapets of earth raised at intervals across the terreplein of a rampart or the covered way of a fortress, to prevent its being enfiladed 1599. 5. A natural structure forming a transverse partition, as the diaphragm; anything lying transversely or across 1604. 6. Anything laid or fixed athwart or across; a cross-piece; a cross-beam in a timber roof; a rung of a ladder; etc. 1708.

attrib. and *Comb.*: **t.-board, travis-board,** *Naut.* a circular board marked with the points of the compass, and having holes and pegs by which to indicate the course of the ship; **-circle**, a circular or segmental track on which a gun-carriage is turned to point the gun in any required direction; **-drill**, a drill in which the boring tool has at the required depth a lateral motion; also, a drill in which the drill-stock is adjustable laterally on the bed; **t. jury**, a jury empanelled to adjudicate on an appeal from another jury; **-map**, a rough map, the main points on which have been determined by traversing.

Traverse (træ·vəɹs), *a. rare.* late ME. [a. OF. *travers*:—late pop. L. and med.L. *traversus*:—L. *transversus* TRANSVERSE *a.*] 1. Lying, passing, or extending across; cross, transverse. †2. Slanting; oblique –1649.

1. The t. part of the Cross 1703. The explosions at the Waltham Cordite Factory..the strong t. walls being blown to pieces 1894.

Traverse (træ·vəɹs), *v.* ME. [a. F. *traverser* to cross, f. *travers* TRAVERSE *sb.* or *a.*] I. To run across or through; to cross. 1. *trans.* †a. To run (something) through *with* a weapon; to pierce, stab. b. To pass through as a weapon, to penetrate, pierce. Now *rare.* late ME. c. To cross (a thing) with a line, stripe, bar, barrier, or anything that intersects. In *pass.*, To be crossed *with* lines, etc. Now *rare.* late ME. 2. To cross (a mountain, river, sea) in travelling; now *esp.* to pass or journey across, over, or through; to pass through (a region) from side to side, or from end to end; also, to pass through (a space or solid body), as rays of light, etc. 1489. b. To trace (a geometrical figure, or part of one) continuously without lifting the pen or pencil. Also *intr.* or *absol.* 1905. 3. *fig.*, etc. To 'go through' (life, time, or anything figured as an extended space or region); to read through or consider thoroughly (a subject, treatise, etc.) 1477. 4. Of a thing: To lie, be situated, extend, stretch, or 'run' across (something); to cross, intersect 1481. 5. To go to and fro over or along; to cross and recross 1590. 6. *Surveying.* To make or execute a traverse (TRAVERSE *sb.* I. 3) of (a region); to delimit (an area) by thus determining the position of points on its boundaries; to trace the course of (a road, river, etc.) in this way 1874.

1. c. They traversed the streets with barricadoes 1748. 2. What Experience Vlisses got by trauersing strange Countries GREENE. 3. It was in the years which we are traversing that England became firmly Protestant GREEN. 4. Deeply worn footpaths..traversing the country W. IRVING. 5. Phr. *To t. one's ground*, to move from side to side, in fencing or fighting.

II. To turn, move, or bring (a thing) across. 1. *trans.* To alter the position of (a gun, etc.) laterally, so as to take aim. Also *absol.* 1628. b. *intr.* To carry a gun so that it points at the head or body of another sportsman 1886. †2. To turn away, to divert; *fig.* to pervert (*rare*) –1689. III. To direct oneself or act against. 1. *trans.* To act against, go counter to; to cross, thwart, oppose. late ME. 2. *Law.* To contradict formally (a matter of fact alleged in the previous pleading); to deny at law. Also *absol.* ME. †3. To dispute; to discuss –1599.

1. He resolved to t. this new project ARBUTHNOT. 2. Phr. *To t. an indictment*, to deny or take issue upon an indictment. *To t. an office*, to deny or impeach the validity of an inquest of office.

IV. *intr.* 1. To move, pass, or go across; to cross, cross over; (of a ship) to tack. late ME. 2. To move from side to side; to dodge. *Obs.* or *arch.* 1470. 3. To run freely in its proper socket, ring, channel, or course (as a rope); to turn or move freely on a traverse-circle (as a gun); to turn about on a pivot (as the needle of the compass) 1829. 4. a. *Falconry.* To move from side to side, to wriggle, as a hawk. b. *Manège.* To advance obliquely, as a horse. 1486. 5. To advance or ascend in a zigzag line 1773. 6. *Mountaineering.* To make one's way in a horizontal or transverse direction across the face of a mountain or rock 1893.

1. *fig.* His thoughts tossed and traversed like the inconstant clouds 1824. 2. To see thee fight, to see thee foigne, to see thee trauerse SHAKS.

Traverser (træ·vəɹsəɹ). 1613. [f. prec. + -ER[1].] 1. A person or thing that crosses or passes over. 2. *Law.* One who traverses a plea 1812. 3. On a railway: A platform, moving laterally on wheels, by which trucks or carriages may be shifted from one set of rails to another parallel to it 1851.

Tra·verse-ta:ble. 1669. [f. TRAVERSE *sb.*] 1. *Naut.* A table from which the difference of latitude and departure corresponding to any given course and distance may be ascertained. 2. On a railway: = prec. 3. *U.S.* 1864.

Travertine, -in (træ·vəɹtin). 1797. [ad. It. *travertino*, older *tivertino*:—L. *tiburtinus* TIBURTINE.] A white or light-coloured concretionary limestone, usu. hard and semi-crystalline, deposited from water holding lime in solution; also called *t. stone*; quarried in Italy for building.

Travesty (træ·vĕsti), *ppl. a.* and *sb.* 1662. [orig. a. F. *travesti*, pa. pple. of (*se*) *travestir*, ad. It. *travestire* to disguise, f. *tra-* = TRANS- + *vestire*:—L. *vestire* to clothe.] A. *ppl. a.* Dressed so as to be made ridiculous; burlesqued. (Const. as pa. pple.) *Obs.* or only as F. B. *sb.* 1. A burlesque or ludicrous imitation of a serious work; literary composition of this kind; hence, a grotesque or debased image or likeness 1674. **2.** In etym. sense: An alteration of dress or appearance; a disguise (*rare*) 1732.

1. It..has sometimes the effect of a ludicrous travesti of the Odyssey 1789. 2. My design was to have travelled..*incognito*...But all my art and travestie was vain. 1732.

Travesty (træ·vĕsti), *v.* 1673. [First used in the pa. pple. *travestied*, f. prec.] **1.** *trans.* To alter in dress or appearance; to disguise by such alteration 1686. **2.** To turn into ridicule by grotesque parody or imitation; to caricature, burlesque 1673.

1. Old Naturalism thus travestied under the name of Religion 1754. 2. The comic poets..travestied known characters so as to make them hardly recognisable 1874.

Travis: see TRAVERSE *sb.*

Trawl (trǭl), *sb.* 1759. [Origin obsc.] **1.** A strong net or bag dragged along the bottom of fishing-banks; a drag-net; esp. that now often dist. as the *beam-t.*, a triangular purse-shaped net, the mouth of which is kept open by a beam supported on two upright iron frames (the *t.-heads*). **2.** *U.S.* A buoyed line used in sea-fishing, having numerous short lines with baited hooks attached at intervals; a trawl-line 1864.

attrib. and *Comb.*: **t.-beam**, the beam which holds open the mouth of a t.-net; **-head**, see sense 1; **-warp**, the warp or rope of a t.-net.

Trawl (trǭl), *v.* 1561. [Goes with prec.; cf. MDu. *traghelen* to drag, f. *traghel.*] **1.** *intr.* To fish with a net the edge of which is dragged along the bottom of the sea to catch the fish living there, esp. flat-fish; to fish with a trawl-net or in a trawler. **2.** To drag a seine-net behind and about a shoal of herring, etc., in order to drive, enclose, and catch them. (Also *trans.* with the net as obj.) 1864. **3.** *trans.* To catch or take with a trawl or trawl-net 1864.

Trawler (trǭ·ləɹ). 1599. [f. TRAWL *v.* + -ER[1].] **1.** One who trawls. **2.** A vessel employed in fishing with a trawl-net; often more explicitly *steam-t.* 1847.

Traw·l-net. 1696. [f. TRAWL *sb.* or *v.* + NET *sb.*[1]] **1.** = TRAWL *sb.* 1. **2.** *Sc.* and *U.S.* Applied (erron.) to a kind of seine-net used to surround and enclose shoals of herring and other fish 1855.

Tray (trēⁱ), *sb.*[1] [OE. *trĕg*:—OTeut. *trau-jom.] **1.** A utensil of the form of a flat board with a raised rim, or of a shallow box without a lid, made of wood, metal, or other material, of various sizes and shapes; now used for carrying plates, dishes, cards, etc., for containing and exhibiting small articles, as jewellery, etc., and for various other purposes, as in mining, photography, chemistry, etc. **2.** Part of the life-guard used on tram-cars, etc., a flat grid on which obstructions are picked up 1910.

Comb.: **t.-cloth**, a cloth or napkin placed upon a tray on which dishes, etc. are carried. Hence **Tray·ful**, as much as a t. will hold.

Tray, *sb.*[2] 1812. [Same word as TREY, re-spelt after BAY *sb.*[6]] *Venery.* The third branch of a stag's horn.

†**Trea·cher.** ME. [a. OF. *trecheor*, *tricheor*, f. *trechier*, *tricher* to cheat, trick.] A deceiver, cheat; *occas.* a traitor –1767.

Those same treachours vile SPENSER.

Treacherous (tre·tʃərəs), *a.* ME. [a. OF. *trecher-*, *tricheros*, *-eus*, f. *trecheur*, *tricheur* TREACHER; see -OUS.] **1.** Of persons, etc.: Characterized by treachery; deceiving, perfidious, false; disloyal, traitorous. **2.** *fig.* Of things: Deceptive, untrustworthy, unreliable; of ground, ice, etc., unstable, insecure 1573.

1. A t., thievish, murderous cannibal 1897. 2. I haue ..One o' the treacherou'st memories, I doe thinke, Of all mankind B. JONS. Hence **Trea·cherous-ly** *adv.*, **-ness.**

Treachery (tre·tʃəri). ME. [a. OF. *trecherie*, *tricherie*, f. *tricher* to cheat + *-erie* -ERY.] Deceit, cheating, perfidy; violation of faith or betrayal of trust; perfidious conduct. **b.** *esp.* The deception or perfidy of a traitor; treason against a sovereign, lord, or master ME. **c.** With *a* and *pl.* An instance of this; an act of perfidy or treason ME.

But Talus usde..To keepe a nightly watch for dread of t. SPENSER. b. Iudas and his trecheri ME.

Treacle (trī·k'l), *sb.* [ME. *tryacle*, *triacle*, a. OF. *triacle*: = Pr. *triacla*, It. *triaca*, pop. forms for Pr. *tiriaca*, It. *teriaca*, repr. pop. L. **triaca* for *theriaca*:—Gr. θηριακή antidote against a venomous bite.] **I.** †**1.** *Old Pharm.* A medicinal compound, orig. a kind of salve, formerly in repute as an alexipharmic against, and an antidote to, venomous bites, poisons generally, and malignant diseases –1804. †**b.** *transf.* A sovereign remedy –1727. †**2.** *fig.* ME.

1. The chief Use of Vipers is for the making of T. 1693. 2. With the sovran t. of sound doctrine..to fortifie their hearts MILT.

II. The uncrystallized syrup produced in the process of refining sugar 1694. **b.** An inspissated saccharine juice obtained from various trees and plants 1731. **c.** *fig.* Something cloyingly sweet; *esp.* extravagant laudation, blandishment 1771.

attrib. and *Comb.*: **T. Bible**, a collector's name for any English version or edition of the Bible having 'triacle' or 'treacle' where others have 'balm', as in Jer. viii. 22, etc.; **t.-mustard**, the plant *Thlaspi arvense*, so-called on account of its supposed medicinal virtue; by later writers applied to *Clypeola Jonthlaspi*, also to *Erysimum cheiranthoides*; **-posset**, a hot drink made of cider or milk and treacle; **-vinegar**, **-water**, a cordial distilled with a spirituous menstruum from Venice treacle and various drugs and simples. Hence **Trea·cly** *a.*, resembling t. in quality or appearance; *fig.* cloyingly sweet; honeyed.

Treacle (trī·k'l), *v.* 1838. [f. prec.] *trans.* To smear or spread with treacle; to dose with (brimstone and) treacle. **b.** To catch (moths) by attracting them with treacle or the like spread on trees. Also *intr.* 1905.

Tread (tred), *sb.* [Early ME. *trede*, f. stem of OE. *tredan* to TREAD.] **I. 1.** A footprint (*rare*). †**2.** A line of footsteps; the track or trail of a man or animal –1820. †**3.** A trodden or beaten way, a path, a track. *Obs.* exc. **b.** *fig.* path or way (of life or action). late ME. **4.** The action or an act of treading or trampling; a step. late ME. **b.** Manner of treading; hence, style of walking 1609. **c.** *transf.* The sensation produced by treading upon something (considered as an attribute of the thing). *rare.* 1819.

1. An Otter's T. is almost like that of a Badger 1727. 3. b. Conditions which determine the t. and destiny of nations BUCKLE. 4. That incessant t. of feet wearing the rough stones smooth DICKENS. b. She had the t. of an Empress 1881. c. A sloping green of mossy t. KEATS.

II. 1. a. *Farriery.* A bruise or wound of the coronet of a horse's foot, caused by setting one foot upon the other, or by over-reaching 1661. **b.** An act of treadling or pedalling a machine 1680. **2. a.** The action of the male bird in coition 1674. **b.** The cicatricula or chalaza 1593. **3.** The horizontal upper surface of a step in a stair; also, the width of this from front to back; also, each of the rungs of a ladder 1712. **4.** *Fortif.* A terrace at the back of a parapet, on which the defenders stand to fire over the parapet 1834. **5.** *techn.*, as a wheel track, a rut (*dial.*); the flat under side of the foot or of a shoe, the sole; the transverse distance between the two wheels of a cart or other vehicle; the outer surface of a wheel, tire, or sledge runner; the rail surface on which the wheel bears, etc. 1735.

Tread (tred), *v.* Pa. t. **trod** (trǫd), *arch.* trode (trōᵘd). Pa. pple. **trodden** (trǫ·d'n), **trod** (trǫd). [Com. Teut. str. vb.; OE. *tredan*:—OTeut. **tređ-* (G. *treten*, etc.).] **1.** *trans.* To step upon; to pace or walk on (the ground, etc.); to walk in (a place); hence, to go about in (a place, etc.). **2.** To step or walk upon or along; to follow, pursue (a path, track, or road) OE. **3.** *intr.* To walk, go, pace; to set down the feet in walking; to step. Also said of the foot. OE. **4.** To step *on*; to put the foot down *upon*, esp. so as to press upon. late ME. **5.** *trans.* †**a.** To step or walk with pressure on (something) esp. so as to crush, beat down, injure or destroy it; to trample –1712. **b.** With advb. extension ME. **c.** *fig.* To crush, to oppress; to treat with contemptuous cruelty 1526. **6.** *intr.* To trample *on* or *upon* OE. **7.** *trans.* To press (something) downwards with the foot or feet in treadling or pedalling 1680. **8.** Of the male bird: To copulate with (the hen) ME. **b.** *absol.* Of birds: To copulate 1486. **9.** *trans.* To thresh (corn) by trampling it on a threshing-floor: said of the oxen, etc., or of one using them; also with *out*. **b.** To press out the juice of (grapes) by trampling them in a vat. **c.** To tramp (clothes) in washing. late ME. **10.** To make or form by the action of the feet in walking; *esp.* to beat *out* (a path or track). late ME. **11.** *Horticulture.* To beat down and consolidate (soil) by treading; also with plants, etc., as object 1440. **12.** *intr.* Of land (*t. loose*, hence ellipt. *t.*): To yield or give to the tread. *dial.* 1847. **13.** *trans.* With advs.: To get or put into or out of some position or condition by treading; *esp.* to put *out* (fire) by treading 1542.

1. 'Tis joy enough..to t. the grass of England once again WORDSW. *To t. the stage* (*the boards*), to act upon the stage, to follow the profession of an actor. *To t. this earth, shoe-leather*, to be alive, to live; A better man never trod shoe-leather 1828. *To t. the deck*, to be on board ship, be a sailor. *To t. the ground*, to walk; Methought she trod the ground with greater grace DRYDEN. 2. The downward track he treads DRYDEN. *To t. a measure*, to go through a dance in a rhythmic or stately manner (*arch.* and *poet.*). 3. As proper men as euer trod vpon Neats Leather SHAKS. fig. phr. *To t. on air*, to walk buoyantly or jubilantly. 4. The poore Beetles that we treade upon SHAKS. Phr. *To t. on any one's heel* or *toes* (also *fig.*): see the sbs. 5. b. *To t. down*, *under foot*, *to pieces*, etc. 6. T. upon his neck, And treble all his father's slaveries MARLOWE. 7. Phr. *To t. water*, in swimming, to move the feet as in walking upstairs, keeping the body erect, and the head above water. 9. b. Who wine desires, let him the ripe grapes t. 1871. c. The clothes that they trod in the wash-tub CLOUGH. 10. Paths trodden by the footsteps of ages FROUDE. 13. The flame of civil war ..was trodden out before it had time to spread MACAULAY. Phr. *To t. one's shoe awry*, to fall from chastity. Hence **Trea·der**, one who or that which treads.

Treadle (tre·d'l), *sb.* OE. [f. prec. + -LE 1.] †**1.** A step or stair (*rare*) –1878. **2.** A lever worked by the foot in machines and mechanical contrivances, usu. to produce reciprocating or rotary motion. late ME. **b.** A pedal of a bicycle or the like 1887. **3.** = TREAD *sb.* II. 2 b. Now *dial.* 1658.

Treadle (tre·d'l), *v.* 1891. [f. prec.] **1.** *intr.* To work a treadle; to move the feet as if doing this; also, of a cyclist: to make one's way by pedalling one's cycle: also *trans.* with *way*. **2.** *trans.* To operate (a machine) by working a treadle 1906.

Treadmill (tre·dmil). 1822. [f. TREAD *v.* + MILL *sb.*[1]] A horizontal cylinder made to revolve by the weight of persons treading on boards arranged as equidistant steps around its periphery. Formerly in use as an instrument of prison discipline.

A kind of mental tread-mill, where you are perpetually climbing, but can never rise an inch SCOTT.

Trea·d-wheel. 1573. [f. TREAD *v.* + WHEEL *sb.*] A wheel rotated by the treading of persons or animals to give motion to machinery, to raise water, etc.; *esp.* a wheel turned by the weight of a person or animal walking on the inside of its periphery; also = prec.

†**Treague.** *rare.* 1590. [ad. med.L. *tregua*, ad. Goth. *triggwa* treaty, f. *triggws* true, sure.] A truce –1660.

Treason (trī·z'n). ME. [a. AF. *tresun*, *treysoun*, = OF. *traïson*, mod.F. *trahison*:—L. *traditionem*, f. *tradere* to deliver up, betray.] **1.** The action of betraying; betrayal of the trust undertaken by or reposed in any one; breach of faith, treachery. **2.** *Law.* **a.** *High t.* or *treason* proper: Violation by a subject of his allegiance to his sovereign or to the state.

Defined 1350-51 by Act 25 Edw. III, Stat. 5, c. 2, as compassing or imagining the king's death, or that of his wife or eldest son, violating the wife of the king or of the heir apparent, or the king's eldest daughter being unmarried, levying war in the king's dominions, adhering to the king's enemies in his dominions, or aiding them in or out of the realm, or killing the chancellor or the judges in the execution of their offices. In 1795 the offence was extended to actual or contemplated use of force to make the king change his counsels, or to intimidate either or both of the Houses of Parliament.

b. *Petit* or *petty t.*, treason against a subject; *spec.* the murder of one to whom the murderer owes allegiance, as of a master by his servant, a husband by his wife, etc. Now only *Hist.* 1496. **c.** *Constructive t.*, action which though not actually or overtly coming under any of the acts specified in the Statute of Treason, was declared by law to be treason and punishable as such. *Misprision of t.*: see MISPRISION [1] 1.

1714. †3. With *a* and *pl.* An act of treason; also, a species of treason -1708.

1. Whas mouth is ful of weriynge & bitternes & treson HAMPOLE. 2. a. Tell Bullingbroke..That euery stride he makes vpon my Land, Is dangerous Treason SHAKS. T. doth never prosper, what 's the reason? For if it prosper, none dare call it T. 1612. b. Joseph Armstrong was tried for petty t., in poisoning his master's lady 1777.

Comb.: **t.-fe·lony**, an offence, formerly included among acts of t., which by subsequent legislation has been removed from these, and is not punishable with death.

Treasonable (trī·z'năb'l), *a.* late ME. [f. prec. + -ABLE.] Of the nature of treason; characteristic of or involving treason; perfidious, treacherous. orig. *Sc.*

The t. packet had been found in his bosom MACAULAY. Hence **Trea·sonableness. Trea·sonably** *adv.*

Treasonous (trī·z'nəs), *a.* 1450. [f. as prec. + -OUS.] Full of or abounding in treason; treasonable.

To prohibit such and such pieces, that were blasphemous, libellous or t. 1784. Hence **Trea·sonably** *adv.*

Treasure (tre·ʒŭı), *sb.* [Early ME. *tresor*, a. OF. *tresor*:—popular L. **tresaurus* for L. *thesaurus*, a. Gr. θησαυρός treasure.] 1. Wealth stored or accumulated, esp. in the form of precious metals; gold or silver coin; hence *gen.*, money, riches, wealth. Usually without article or pl. b. *pl.* in same sense ME. †c. A store or stock *of* anything valuable (*rare*) -1707. 2. *transf.* and *fig.* Anything valued and preserved as precious; also of a person, a 'jewel', 'gem'. *colloq.* ME. †3. A treasury; a treasure-house, a treasure-chest (*rare*) -1596.

1. Where a mans threasure ys there is his hart 1597. b. The last coin out of all their treasures RUSKIN. 2. My..nurse, a t. and the most respectable of dames 1810. The fine house and its treasures 1907.

Comb.: †**t.-city**, a city in which supplies were stored.

Trea·sure, *v.* late ME. [f. prec.] 1. *trans.* To put away or lay aside (anything of value) for preservation, security, or future use; to hoard or store up. Often *to t. up.* 2. *fig.* To keep in store, lay up (e.g. in the mind, in memory). late ME. †3. To furnish with treasures; to enrich (*rare*) -1630. 4. To hold or keep as precious; to cherish, prize 1907.

1. Wher ben the princes..that siluer tresoren and gold? *Baruch* iii. 16. 3. T. thou some place, With beauties treasure SHAKS. 4. Treasured as his most precious possessions 1907.

Trea·sure-hou:se. 1475. A house, building, or chamber in which treasure is kept; a treasury.

fig. The t. of literature 1895.

Treasurer (tre·ʒŭrəı). [ME. *treso(u)rer*, a. ONF., AF. *tresorer* = OF. *tresorier*, f. *tresor* TREASURE; see -ER [2].] 1. One who has officially the charge of treasure; orig., a person entrusted with the receipt, care, and disbursement of the revenues of a king, noble, or other dignitary of a state, city, or church; now, one who is responsible for the funds of a public body, or of any corporation, association, society, or club. b. *U.S.* An officer of the Treasury Department, who receives and keeps the moneys, disbursing them only upon warrants drawn by the Secretary of the Treasury; also, an officer having the same function in each State 1790. 2. *fig.* One who or that which is entrusted with the keeping of anything precious or valuable ME. 3. [f. TREASURE *v.* + -ER [1].] One who treasures or hoards up; a preserver, keeper *of* something precious 1597.

1. *Lord High T. of England, of Great Britain*, also called *T.*, *Lord T.*, *High T.*, *T. of the Exchequer*, formerly, the third great officer of the Crown, controlling the revenues of the sovereign (the duties of the office are now discharged by five Lords of the Treasury). Hence **Trea·surership**, the office of t.

Treasuress (tre·ʒŭrės). Now *rare.* 1450. [orig. *tresoresse* for *tresoreresse*, f. *tresorer* TREASURER; see -ESS.] A female treasurer.

Treasure-trove (tre:ʒŭı,trōᵘ·v). 1550. [orig. two words, in AF. *tresor trové* = L. *thesaurus inventus.*] *lit.* 'Treasure found', i.e. anything of the nature of treasure which any one finds; *spec.* in *Eng. Law*: Treasure (gold or silver, money, plate, or bullion) found hidden in the ground or other place, the owner of which is unknown.

Treasury (tre·ʒŭri). [ME. a. OF. *tresorie*, f. *tresor* TREASURE + -*ie* -Y [3].] 1. A room or building in which precious or valuable objects are preserved, *esp.* a place or receptacle for money or valuables (now *Hist.*); *transf.* the funds or revenue of a state or of a public or private corporation. 2. *fig.* A repository of 'treasures'; a thesaurus. late ME. 3. The department of State which controls the collection, management, and expenditure of the public revenue; *spec.* that of the United Kingdom. (This department is now managed by a T. Board of Commissioners, the First Lord of the T. (usu., the Prime Minister), the Chancellor of the Exchequer, and junior Lords not more than five in number, who act as party whips. The actual head of the department is the Chancellor of the Exchequer. late ME. b. The building where the Treasury Commissioners transact business; formerly also *T. Office* 1706. 4. *Theatr. slang.* The weekly payment of a company of actors 1885. †5. = TREASURE *sb.* 1 -1672.

2. The Golden T. of English Songs PALGRAVE. 5. As he, who hauing found great T. DANIEL.

Comb.: **t.-bench**, the front bench on the right hand of the Speaker in the House of Commons, occupied by the Leader of the House (usu. the First Lord of the T.), and other members of the Government; **-bill**, an instrument of credit, usu. drawn for 3 or 6 months, issued by authority of Parliament to the highest bidder, when money is temporarily needed by the Commissioners of the T.; **-bond**, an exchequer bond; **t. lord**, one of the commissioners of the T.; **t. department**, in the U.S. government, the finance department under the Secretary of the T.; **t. minute**, an administrative regulation for any department under the T.; **-note**, (*a*) *U.S.*, a demand note issued by the T. Department, receivable as legal tender for all debts; (*b*) English paper money used as currency, esp. a £1 or 10s. note; **-warrant**, a warrant or voucher issued by the T. for any sum disbursed by the exchequer.

Treat (trīt), *sb.* late ME. [f. next.] †1. The action or an act of treating, or discussing terms; parley; agreement; treaty -1645. †2. = TREATMENT 1; an instance of this -1711. 3. *concr.* An entertainment *of* food and drink, esp. one given without expense to the recipient. *Obs.* or merged in b. 1651. b. Hence, an entertainment of any kind given gratuitously, esp. to children 1683. c. The action of treating or entertaining; one's part or turn to treat; an invitation to eat or drink 1690. 4. Something highly enjoyable; a great pleasure, delight, or gratification. *colloq.* 1805.

1. [He] Bad that same boaster..bide him batteill without further t. SPENSER. 3. A very handsome table, covered with a cold t. of roasted mutton and beef DE FOE. Phr. *To stand t.*: see STAND *v.* IV. 7.

Treat (trīt), *v.* ME. [a. OF. *tretier*, *traitier*:—L. *tractare* to drag, frequent. of *trahere* to draw.] 1. a. *intr.* To deal or carry on negotiations (*with* another) with a view to settling terms; to bargain, negotiate. †b. *trans.* To negotiate, plan -1715. 2. a. *intr.* To deal with some matter in speech or writing; to discourse. Const. *of*, formerly *on*, *upon*. late ME. b. *trans.* To deal with (a subject) in speech or writing; to discuss. In mod. use often: To deal with in the way of literary art. ME. 3. To deal with, behave or act towards (a person, animal, etc.) in some specified way; to 'use' (well, ill, etc.). late ME. b. To consider or regard in a particular aspect and deal with accordingly. (Often with *as.*) 1456. 4. To entertain, esp. with food and drink; to regale, feast, esp. at one's own expense, by way of kindness or compliment, or *spec.* of bribery, as at an election 1500. b. *absol.* or *intr.* To stand treat 1710. 5. *trans.* To deal with in the way of art; to handle or represent artistically 1695. 6. a. To deal with or operate upon (a disease or affection, a part of the body, or a person) in order to relieve or cure 1781. b. To subject to chemical or other physical action; to act upon *with* some agent 1816.

1. a. The governor beat a parley, desiring to t. 1647. b. He was treating a marriage with the archduchess BURNET. 2. a. Certain writings of our divines that t. of grace BERKELEY. b. Questions which shall be treated under their proper heads TYNDALL. 3. That Mahometan Custom..of treating Women as if they had no Souls STEELE. b. The clergy are often treated as obstacles to the diffusion of knowledge 1868. 4. Rebecca..ordered a bottle of sherry and a bread cake ..to t. the enemy's lawyers THACKERAY. *To t.* (a person, etc.) *to*, to entertain with (food or drink, or any enjoyment or gratification); Dick had treated himself to two ices and a strawberry squash 1897. 5. Familiar subjects..treated with great lustre and fullness of colouring H. WALPOLE. 6. b. Potato-starch when treated with sulphuric acid becomes sugar 1845.

Treatable (trī·tăb'l), *a.* [ME. *tretable*, a. F. *traitable*:—L. *tractabilem* TRACTABLE. In some senses f. TREAT *v.* + -ABLE.] 1. Easily handled or dealt with; tractable, docile; open to appeal or argument, affable. *Obs.* or *arch.* †b. Of or in ref. to actions, etc.: Gentle, easy, deliberate, not violent -1690. †c. Of utterance: Deliberate; distinct -1641. 2. Capable of being or proper to be treated or dealt with 1570.

1. b. In France, and the Low Countries..the Heats or the Colds, and Changes of Seasons, are less t. than they are with us 1690. c. [The parson's] voyce is humble, his words t. and slow G. HERBERT. Hence **Trea·tably** *adv.*

Treater (trī·təı). 1489. [In sense 1, a. OF. *traiteor*, *traiteur* ambassador; in other senses, f. TREAT *v.* + -ER [1].] One who treats. 1. One who negotiates terms of settlement; a negotiator. 2. One who treats of or writes upon a subject 1594. 3. One who gives a treat, or stands treat; an entertainer 1692.

Treatise (trī·tiz, -is). ME. [a. AF. *tretiz*, repr. an OF. **treiteïz*, f. *traitier*, F. *traiter* TREAT *v.*] 1. A book or writing which treats of some particular subject; now always, one containing a methodical discussion or exposition of the principles of the subject; formerly occas., a literary work in general. †b. A story, tale, narrative (spoken or written) -1605. †2. Negotiation, discussion of terms; arrangement of terms -1641.

1. I remember 'tis a letter, noe t., I have in hand 1633. b. The time ha's beene..my Fell of haire Would at a dismall T. rowze, and stirre SHAKS. Hence †**Trea·tiser**, the writer of a t.

Treatment (trī·tmĕnt). 1560. [f. TREAT *v.* + -MENT.] 1. Conduct, behaviour; action or behaviour towards a person, etc.; usage. 2. = TREAT *sb.* 3. *Obs.* exc. *dial.* 1656. 3. Management in the application of remedies; medical or surgical application or service 1744. 4. Subjection to the action of a chemical agent 1828. 5. Action or manner of dealing with something in literature or art; literary or artistic handling esp. in ref. to style 1856.

Treaty (trī·ti). [ME. *trete(e*, a. AF. *treté*, OF. *trait(i)é*, ppl. sb. of *trait(i)er* TREAT *v.*, and :—L. *tractatum* TRACTATE.] †1. a. The treatment of a subject in speech or writing; (literary) treatment; discussion -1663. b. A treatise, a dissertation; in early use, a story, narrative -1715. 2. The treating of matters with a view to settlement; discussion of terms, conference, negotiation. Now *rare* or *Obs.* exc. in phr. *in t.* late ME. 3. †a. A settlement arrived at by treating or negotiation; an agreement, covenant, compact, contract. *Obs.* exc. as in b. -1753. b. *spec.* A contract between states, relating to peace, truce, alliance, commerce, or other international relation; also, the document embodying such contract. late ME. †4. Entreaty, persuasion, request -1649. †5. Treatment, usage; behaviour (*rare*) -1654.

1. b. Sir Kenelme Digby in his excellent T. of bodies SIR T. BROWNE. 2. It appears he is in t. for a place in the North 1881. 3. b. A peace was concluded..being in effect rather a bargain than a t. BACON. 4. *Ant. & Cl.* III. xi. 62.

attrib. and *Comb.*: **t. coast, shore**, a coast on or along which some foreign nation has certain rights guaranteed by t.; **t.-port**, a port opened to foreign commerce by a t.

Treble (tre·b'l), *sb.* ME. [a. OF., sb. use of TREBLE *a.*] I. 1. Anything threefold; a sum or quantity three times as great as another. late ME. 2. *techn.* and *ellipt.* a. A triple barrier; an obstacle consisting of three successive fences 1569. b. *Paper-making*, etc. A frame on which hand-made paper or printed sheets are hung to dry 1727. c. A kind of step-dance; the measure or music for this. *dial.* 1805. d. *Whist.* A game (at short whist) in which one side scores five and the other none, counting three points to the winners 1870. e. A method of crocheting in which three loops of thread are carried on the hook 1882.

1. Forfeiture..of the t. of his seid wages 1463.

II. 1. *Mus.* The highest part in harmonized musical composition; the soprano part ME.

2. A treble voice; also, a singer having a treble voice; one who sings the treble part 1475. **b.** *transf.* A high-pitched or shrill voice, sound, or note 1600. **3.** The string of treble pitch in a musical instrument; also, the chanter of a bagpipe 1562. **b.** = *t. bell* (see next A. 2 b.) 1598.

2. b. His bigge manly voice, Turning againe toward childish trebble, pipes And whistles SHAKS.

Treble (tre·b'l), *a.* and *adv.* ME. [a. OF. :—pop. L. *triplus* for L. *triplex.*] **A.** *adj.* **1.** = TRIPLE *a.* **1.** late ME. **b.** Of threefold character or application; existing or occurring in three ways or relations; of three kinds. late ME. **c.** Three times as much or as many; triple. late ME. **2.** *Mus.* Of, pertaining to, or suited to the highest part in harmonized musical composition 1440. **b.** Hence in the names of musical instruments (or strings) of the highest pitch 1530. **c.** High-pitched; shrill 1562.

1. Thro' t. Plates it went Of solid Brass DRYDEN. b. A t. difficulty SCOTT. 2. *T. voice,* a soprano voice. *T. clef,* the G clef when placed (as usually) upon the second line of the stave. b. *T. bell,* the smallest bell of a peal.

B. *adv.* **1.** In three ranks or rows, threefold; to three times the extent; three times over; trebly ME. **2.** In a high-pitched tone 1811.

Treble (tre·b'l), *v.* ME. [f. prec.] **1.** *trans.* To make three times as many or as great; to multiply by three. **b.** To be three times as many or as much as 1615. **2.** *intr.* (for *refl.*) To grow to three times the number, amount, or size; to become threefold 1625.

1. Double sixe thousand, and then t. that SHAKS. b. A body of the Carlists..whose numbers more than trebled his own BORROW. 2. The circulation doubled, trebled, quadrupled 1882.

Trebly (tre·bli), *adv.* 1590. [f. TREBLE *a.* + -LY [2].] In a threefold degree or manner; triply.

Trebuchet (tre·bŭʃet, ‖ trebüʃe). ME. [In I, a. OF. *trebuchet,* also *trebuket,* etc., mod.F. *trébuchet* trap, balance, f. OF. *tre-, tres-, trabucher* to overturn, overthrow, stumble, fall. In II, an application, in England, of med.L. *trebuchetum* to the device known as the cucking-stool.] **I. 1.** A mediæval military engine for casting heavy missiles. *Hist.* **2.** A small delicately poised balance or pair of scales: an assay balance; a tilting scale 1550. **II.** = CUCKING-STOOL 1640.

‖**Trecento** (tre͵tʃe·nto). 1841. [It., lit. 'three hundred', short for *mil trecento* 1300; cf. CINQUECENTO, SEICENTO.] The fourteenth century considered as a period of Italian art, architecture, etc. Hence **Trece·ntist,** ‖**Trecenti·sta** (It., pl. **-isti**), an Italian author, artist, etc., of the 14th c.

Treddle (tre·d'l). Now *dial.* [OE. *tyrdel,* dim. of *tord* TURD.] A pellet of sheep's or goat's dung.

Treddle, var. of TREADLE.

Tredrille, tredille (tredri·l, -di·l). 1764. [f. QUADRILLE, with *tre-* three for *qua(d)-.*] A card-game played by three persons, usu. with thirty cards.

Tree (trī), *sb.* [OE. *trēow,* = OS. *treo,* ON. *trē* :—OTeut. *trewo-, cogn. w. Skr. *dru* tree, *dāru* wood, Gr. δρῦς oak, δόρυ spear, Russ. *drevo* tree, W. *derwen* oak.] **1.** A perennial plant having a self-supporting woody main stem or *trunk* (which usu. develops woody branches at some distance from the ground), and growing to a considerable height and size. **b.** Extended to bushes or shrubs of erect growth and having a single stem; and even some perennial herbaceous plants which grow to a great height, as the banana and plantain ME. **2.** The substance of the trunk and boughs of a tree; wood; timber. *Obs.* or *arch.* OE. **3.** A piece of wood; a stem or branch of a tree, or a portion of one, usu. (now always) shaped for some purpose; a pole, post, stake, beam, wooden bar, etc.; *esp.* (now only) one forming part of some structure; usu. in comb., as AXLE-TREE, CROSS-TREE, †*door-tree,* ROOF-TREE, SWINGLETREE OE. **4. a.** The cross on which Christ was crucified. *arch.* and *poet.* OE. **b.** A gallows. Also *Tyburn t.* late ME. **5.** The wooden shaft of a spear, handle of an implement, etc.; hence, a spear, lance. Now *dial.* late ME. †**b.** A wooden structure; applied *poet.* or *rhet.* to a ship –1594. **c.** = SADDLE-TREE 1535. **d.** = BOOT-*tree.* late ME. **6.** Something resembling a tree with its branches: **a.** A diagram or table of a family, indicating its original ancestor as the root, and the various branches of descendants; in full *family* or *genealogical t.*; (*b*) *Porphyrian t.* (Logic): see PORPHYRIAN ME. **b.** Any structure or figure, natural or artificial, of branched form 1706.

1. *fig.* The Royall T. hath left vs Royall Fruit SHAKS. 2. At Aberladie he shall light With hempen halters and hors of t. 1500. 4. a. He..suffride oure synnes in his body on the t. WYCLIF 1 *Pet.* ii. 24. b. Though it was thy luck to cheat the fatal t. 1704. 6. a. Two genealogic trees H. WALPOLE.

Phrases. *At the top of the t.,* in the highest position. *Up a t.* (*colloq.,* orig. *U.S.*), debarred from escape, like a hunted animal driven to take refuge in a t.; entrapped; in a difficulty or 'fix'. *To bark up the wrong t.* (orig. *U.S.*), to make a mistake in one's object of pursuit. *T. of heaven* = AILANTO. *T. of Jesse*: see JESSE. *T. of knowledge,* (*a*) = next; (*b*) knowledge in general, or in all its 'branches'. *T. of the knowledge of good and evil*: see Gen. ii. 9, etc. *T. of liberty,* a tree (or a pole) planted in celebration of a revolution or victory securing liberty (chiefly in ref. to the French Revolution). *T. of life,* (*a*) see Gen. ii. 9, etc.; (*b*) = ARBOR VITÆ 1; (*c*) *Phys.* = ARBOR VITÆ 2.

Comb.: **a.** in names of plants, usu. denoting species or varieties that grow to the stature or in the form of a t., as *t. cabbage,* or those that grow on trees, as *t. orchis*; **t.-clover,** *Melilotus alba*; **t. cotton,** *Gossypium arboreum*; **t. sorrel,** *Rumex lunaria.* **b.** In names of animals frequenting trees, as *t.-beetle, -kangaroo, -pipit*; **t.-bear** (*U.S. local*), the racoon; **-bug,** any one of various hemipterous insects which feed upon the juices of trees and shrubs; **-cat,** (*a*) a viverrine animal of the genus *Paradoxurus,* a palm-cat; (*b*) = *t.-fox*; **-crab,** a species of land-crab, *Birgus latro,* also called *palm-crab*; **-cricket,** a cricket of the genus *Œcanthus*; **-crow,** any one of various Oriental birds intermediate between crows and jays, as the genera *Crypsirhina, Dendrocitta,* etc.; **-dove,** any one of numerous arboreal species of pigeon of India, Australia, etc., belonging or allied to the genus *Macropygia*; **-duck,** a duck of the genus *Dendrocygna* or an allied genus; **-fox,** *Mustela pennanti,* also called *t.-cat*; **-frog,** any frog of arboreal habits; **-hopper,** any one of various homopterous insects which live on trees; sometimes *spec.* the cicada; **-lizard,** a lizard of the group *Dendrosaura*; **-lobster** = *t.-crab*; **-louse,** an aphis, a plant-louse; **-mouse,** any species of mouse of arboreal habits; **-oyster,** an oyster found upon the roots of the mangrove; **-pie,** a t.-crow of the genus *Dendrocitta,* found in India, China, and neighbouring countries; **-pigeon,** any one of various arboreal pigeons inhabiting Asia, Africa, and Australia; **-porcupine,** any porcupine of the subfamily *Sphingurinæ,* inhabiting America and the West Indies, living in trees, and having prehensile tails; **-rat,** an arboreal rodent, as those of the West Indian genera *Capromys* and *Plagiodon*; **-serpent, -snake,** any snake of arboreal habits, as those of the families *Dendrophidæ* and *Dipsadidæ*; **-tiger,** a name for the leopard; **-warbler,** a bird of the genus *Hypolais.*

c. Other Combs.: **t.-calf** *Bookbinding,* calf stained with acids in conventional imitation of the branches of a t.; **-coffin,** a prehistoric coffin made of a hollow t.-trunk; **-line,** the line or level on a mountain above which no trees grow (cf. *snow-line*); **-marble, marbling** *Bookbinding,* marbling or staining in a tree-like branching pattern (cf. *t.-calf*); **-nymph,** a nymph supposed to inhabit a t.; **-wool,** a woolly substance obtained from a t., as pine-wool.

Tree, *v.* 1650. [f. prec.] †**1.** *intr.* with *it*: To grow into a tree. FULLER. **2.** *trans.* To drive into or up a tree; to cause to take refuge in a tree, as a hunted animal. Also *fig.* to put into a difficulty or 'fix'. 1700. **3.** *intr.* To climb up or perch upon a tree; *esp.* to take refuge in a tree from a hunter or pursuer 1700. **4.** *techn.* **a.** *trans.* To furnish with an (axle-)tree. **b.** To stretch or shape upon a tree, as a boot or saddle. 1765.

3. Then the hunter must t. for his life 1902.

Tree·-cree:per. 1814. **1.** Any of various birds which creep on the trunks and branches of trees; *esp.* the common European *Certhia familiaris,* or other species of the family *Certhiidæ.* **2.** A plant that creeps or climbs upon trees; *spec.* the African rubber-plant, *Landolphia florida* 1887.

Tree·-fern. 1846. A fern with an upright stem, growing to the size and form of a tree; as those of the genera *Cyathea* and *Alsophila,* found in tropical regions, and in Australia and New Zealand.

Tree·-goose. *Obs.* exc. *Hist.* 1597. The barnacle-goose, formerly believed to be produced from a tree in the form of the barnacle (cirriped).

Treeless (trī·lės), *a.* 1814. [f. TREE *sb.* + -LESS.] Destitute of trees. Hence **Tree·lessness.**

Tree·-moss. 1611. **a.** Any moss or moss-like plant that grows on trees; applied esp. to certain lichens. **b.** A moss-like plant of branched form like a miniature tree, as club-moss (*Lycopodium*).

Treen (trī·ĕn, trīn), *a.* *Obs.* exc. *dial.* [OE. *trēowen,* f. *trēow* TREE + -EN [4].] **1.** Made of 'tree'; wooden. †**2.** Of or belonging to, obtained or made from, a tree or trees –1670.

2. These T. Liquors; Especially, that of the Date EVELYN.

Treenail, trenail (trī·nēl, tre·n'l), *sb.* ME. [f. TREE *sb.* + NAIL *sb.*] A cylindrical pin of hard wood used in fastening timbers together, esp. in shipbuilding and other work where the materials are exposed to the action of water. Hence **Tree·-nail** *v. trans.* to fasten or secure (timbers) with treenails (chiefly in *pa. pple.*).

Tree·-spa:rrow. 1770. **a.** *Passer montanus,* a species of sparrow, widely distributed in Europe and Asia, and found locally in Britain. **b.** *Spizella monticola,* a bird (not of the sparrow family) common in N. America.

Tree·-toad. 1778. Any toad of arboreal habits, esp. those of the family *Hylidæ,* found chiefly in tropical America: often erron. called *t.-frogs.*

Tree·-top, tree top. 1530. The top of a tree; the uppermost branches of a tree.

Nursery rhyme. Hush-a-by, baby, On the t.

Trefa (trē·fă). 1851. Also **trifa** (trəi·fă). [Heb., lit. that which is torn.] Flesh meat forbidden to Jews because improperly killed.

Trefle (tre·f'l). 1510. [a. F. *trèfle* :—pop. L. *trifolum for cl. L. *trifolium.*] †**1.** = TREFOIL **1.** –1527. **2.** *Mil.* A mine having three chambers 1756. **3.** = TREFOIL **2.** 1877.

‖**Treflé, treflee** (trefle·, -ī·), *a.* 1725. [F. *tréflé,* f. *trèfle* TREFOIL.] *Her.* Adorned with trefoils, either along one edge or at the end of each arm (of a cross).

Trefoil (trī·foil, tre·foil), *sb.* (*a.*) late ME. [ad. L. *trifolium* or AF. *trifoil*; f. L. *tri-* three + *folium* leaf.] **1.** A plant of the genus *Trifolium,* having triple or trifoliate leaves; a clover: commonly applied to varieties other (esp. smaller) than those cultivated under the name of 'clover'; often to *T. minus,* and also to *Medicago lupulina.* **b.** With defining words, applied to particular species of *Trifolium* or to plants of other genera having triple leaves (see e.g. BIRD'S-FOOT, HOP *sb.*[1], etc.) 1548. **2.** An ornamental figure representing or resembling a trifoliate leaf; *spec.* in *Arch.* an ornament with an opening divided by cusps so as to present or suggest the figure of a three-lobed leaf. late ME. **b.** *Her.* A bearing conventionally representing a clover-leaf with its stalk 1562. **3.** *fig.* A set of three closely united 1826. **4.** as *adj.* Three-leaved; having the figure of a trefoil or clover-leaf furnished with such figures 1752. Hence **Tre·foiled** *a.* **a.** (chiefly *Arch.*) ornamented with a t. or trefoils; formed as a t. (sense 2); **b.** trifoliate; *transf.* three-lobed.

Tre·getour. *arch.* ME. [a. OF. *tre(s)geteo(u)r* juggler, f. *tre(s)geter* to cast across or to and fro :—L. *tra(ns)jectare, f. TRANS- + *jactare* to throw.] One who works magic or plays tricks by sleight of hand; a conjurer, juggler; hence, a trickster, a deceiver.

Trehala (trīhā·lă). Also **tricala.** 1862. [ad. Turk. *tīqālah,* native name.] The substance of the cocoons of a coleopterous insect, *Larinus maculatus,* found in Asia Minor; also called *t.-manna, Turkish* or *Syrian manna.* Hence **Trehalose** (trī·hălōus, trīhā·lōus), *Chem.* a white crystalline sugar, $C_{12}H_{22}O_{11} \cdot 2H_2O$, obtained from t.

Treillage (trē·lėdʒ, ‖trę·yāʒ). 1698. [a. F., f. *treille* TRAIL *sb.*[2] + *-age* -AGE.] **1.** Lattice-work; a framework upon which vines or ornamental plants are trained; a trellis. **2.** A lattice or grill in a room 1836.

1. A walk under a t. of vines GREVILLE.

Trek (trek), *sb. S. Africa.* 1849. [a. Cape Du., = Du. *trek* draw, pull, march, f. *trekken*, TREK *v.*] In travelling by ox-wagon, a stage of a journey between one stopping-place and the next; hence, a journey made in this way; also, travel by ox-wagon. **b.** An organized migration or expedition by ox-wagon 1890.

b. There has been a Boer t. into German South-west Africa 1901. **c.** Comb. as *t. Boer, sheep.*

Trek (trek), *v. S. Africa.* 1850. [a. Du. *trekken* to draw, pull, march, travel.] **1.** *intr.* To make a journey by ox-wagon; hence, to travel, migrate; also, to go, proceed; to go away, depart (*slang*). Also *transf.* of wild animals. **2.** *trans.* To draw or drag (a vehicle): said of oxen, etc. Also *absol.* 1863.

1. The wagons had been quietly treking along over an immense open country 1863. Hence **Tre·kker**, one who treks.

‖ **Trekschuit, treck-** (tre·kskoit, Du. -sχüt). 1696. [Du., f. *trek* or *trek-* vb.-stem of *trekken* + *schuit* boat, barge :—OTeut. **skûtô.*] A canal- or river-boat drawn by horses, carrying passengers and goods, as in common use in Holland; a track-boat.

Trellis (tre·lis), *sb.* [Late ME. a. OF. *treliz, -is, trelice* :—late pop. L. *trilicius*, f. L. *trilix, -licem*, f. *tri-* three + *licium* a thread of the warp; said of strong woven fabrics.] **1.** A structure of light bars of wood or metal crossing each other at intervals and fastened where they cross, having open square or diamond-shaped spaces between; a window, gate, screen, etc. so constructed; a lattice; a grating. Now *rare*. **b.** *Her.* The figure of a trellis used as a charge 1823. **2.** A similar framework used as a support upon which fruit-trees or climbing plants are trained 1513.

Trellis (tre·lis), *v.* late ME. [Almost always in pa. pple. *trellised* (tre·list), f. prec. + -ED.] **1.** *trans.* To furnish with a trellis; to enclose in a trellis or grating. **2.** To train (a plant) upon a trellis; to support on or as on a trellis 1818.

2. The vines..are trellissed upon..stakes SHELLEY.

Trellised (tre·list), *ppl. a.* 1472. [f. TRELLIS *sb.* or *v.* + -ED.] **1.** Furnished with a trellis or trellis-work; formed of trellis-work; trained upon a trellis. **2.** Shaped or arranged like a trellis; having a pattern or markings resembling a trellis 1664.

1. Trelliced vines SOUTHEY. The t. walls covered with honeysuckle and wild roses 1844.

Tre·llis-work. 1712. [f. TRELLIS *sb.* + WORK.] = TRELLIS *sb.* 1. Also anything resembling this in structure or pattern.

Trematode (tre·mătǒud), *a.* and *sb.* 1836. [ad. mod.L. *Trematoda* neut. pl., a. Gr. τρηματώδης perforated, f. τρῆμα hole, orifice.] *Zool.* **A.** *adj.* Belonging to the class or order *Trematoda* or *Trematoidea* of parasitic worms, found in the bodies of various animals, having a flattish or cylindrical form, with skin often perforated by pores, and usu. furnished with adhesive suckers. **B.** *sb.* A trematode worm 1876. So **Tre·matoid** *a.* and *sb.*

Tremble (tre·mb'l), *sb.* 1609. [f. next.] **1.** An act or the action of trembling; a fit or state of trembling; a tremor; a vibration. **b.** Tremulousness or unsteadiness (of the voice) caused by emotion 1779. **2.** *pl. The trembles*: Any disease or condition characterized by an involuntary shaking, as ague or palsy (esp. in sheep); the tremor due to delirium tremens, etc.; the 'shakes' 1812.

1. Phr. (*All*) *in, all of a t., on the t.* (colloq.), trembling, esp. with agitation or excitement.

Tremble (tre·mb'l), *v.* ME. [a. F. *trembler* :—pop. and med.L. *tremulare*, f. L. *tremulus*, f. *tremere* to tremble, quake, shake.] **1.** *intr.* Of persons (less commonly of animals), or of the body or a limb: To shake involuntarily as with fear, cold, or weakness; to quake, quiver, shiver. **b.** *fig.* and *rhet.* To be affected with dread or apprehension, or with any feeling that is accompanied by trembling. late ME. **2.** Of things: To be affected with vibratory motion; to shake, quake, quiver. late ME. **b.** Said of the tremulous or vibratory motion or effect of light, sound, speech, etc. late ME. **c.** *fig.* 1819. **3.** *trans.* To cause to tremble or shake 1591. **4.** *intr.* To pass tremulously. Chiefly *poet.* 1730.

1. I t. as doth a leef vpon a tree 1413. He trembled with anxiety 1797. **b.** The Grand Signior, with all his absolute power, trembles at a janissary's frown 1717. **2.** A little Harebell trembling in the breeze 1908. **b.** Tell how the Moon-beam trembling falls POPE. **c.** The liberties of Scotland..were trembling in the balance BUCKLE. **3.** Thou art as a dove Trembling its closed eyes KEATS. **4.** A tear-drop trembled from its source TENNYSON.

Tremblement (tre·mb'lmĕnt). 1677. [a. F., f. *trembler*; see -MENT.] **1.** The action or condition of trembling (*lit.* and *fig.*); also, an instance of this, a tremor. **2.** A cause of trembling; a terror (*rare*) 1677.

Trembler (tre·mblər). 1552. [f. TREMBLE *v.* + -ER [1].] **1.** One who trembles, esp. with fear; a timorous or terrified person. **2.** = QUAKER. *Obs.* or *Hist.* 1689. **3.** *Electr.* A vibrating spring blade which alternately makes and breaks the circuit in an induction coil 1877.

attrib.: **t.-bell**, an electric bell rung by a hammer attached to a t.

Tre·mbling, *ppl. a.* late ME. [f. as prec. + -ING [2].] That trembles. **b.** *transf.* Characterized or accompanied by trembling. late ME.

Comb.: **t. bog**, bog-land formed over water or soft mud, which shakes at every tread, a quaking bog; **-grass**, quaking-grass (*Briza media*); **t. palsy**, paralysis characterized by trembling of the extremities or of the head; **-poplar**, the Aspen, *Populus tremula*. Hence **Tre·mblingly** *adv.*

Trembly (tre·mbli), *a. colloq.* 1848. [f. TREMBLE *v.* or *sb.* + -Y [1].] Full of trembling; tremulous.

‖ **Tremella** (trĭme·lă). 1760. [mod.L., dim. from *tremulus, tremula.*] *Bot.* A genus of amorphous hymenomycetous fungi consisting of tremulous gelatinous substance, typical of the family *Tremellaceæ* or *Tremellineæ*, most species of which grow on decayed wood, but some on the ground. Hence **Tre·mellose** *a.* *Bot.*, shaking, like *T.*, tremulous.

Tremendous (trĭme·ndəs), *a.* 1632. [f. L. *tremendus*, gerundive of *tremere* to tremble, tremble at; see -OUS.] **1.** Such as to excite trembling, or awe; 'dreadful; horrible; astonishingly terrible' (J.). **2.** Hyperbolically, or as a mere intensive: Such as to excite wonder on account of its magnitude or violence; extraordinarily great; immense. *colloq.* 1812. **b.** Extraordinary in respect of some quality indicated in the context (*slang*) 1831.

1. Not blaspheming the t. name of God EVELYN. **2.** They..drive at a t. pace 1845. He..determined to smother his feelings in a t. dinner 1882. Hence **Treme·ndous-ly** *adv.*, **-ness.**

Tremogram (tre·mǒgræm). 1899. [f. Gr. τρέμειν to tremble + -GRAM.] A tracing recording involuntary muscular motion. So **Tre·mograph** (-GRAPH), an instrument for recording such motion.

‖ **Tremolando** (tremǒla·ndǒ), *a.* (*adv.*, *sb.*) Also **tremulando.** 1852. [It., pr. pple. of *tremolare* to shake, etc.] *Mus.* **A.** *adj.* (or *attrib.*) Tremulous, shaking. **B.** *adv.* In a tremulous or quivering manner; with a tremolo. **C.** *ellipt.* as *sb.* = TREMOLO 1, 2.

Tremolite (tre·mǒləit). 1799. [f. *Tremola*, in Switzerland, where found + -ITE [1].] *Min.* A white or grey (sometimes transparent) variety of AMPHIBOLE, occurring in fibrous masses or thin-bladed crystals. Also called *grammatite.*

‖ **Tremolo** (tre·mǒlo). 1801. [It.:—L. *tremulus.*] *Mus.* **1.** A tremulous or vibrating effect produced on certain musical instruments or in the human voice in singing, esp. to express intensity of emotion; cf. VIBRATO. **2.** A mechanical contrivance in an organ by which such an effect is produced. Also *t. stop.* 1867.

Tremor (tre·mǫı, trī·mǫı). [Late ME. *tremour*, a. OF. *tremor, -our* fear, terror :—L. *tremor, -orem*, f. *tremere* to tremble.] †**1.** Terror –1490. **2.** Involuntary agitation of the body or limbs, resulting from physical infirmity or from fear or other strong emotion; trembling 1615. **b.** With *a* and *pl.* A fit of trembling 1616. **c.** *fig.* A nervous thrill caused by emotion or excitement; also, a state of tremulous agitation or excitement 1754. **3.** A vibration, shaking, quivering, caused by some external impulse 1635. **4.** A tremble or quaver in the voice; a tremulous note or sound 1797.

2. c. He went about all day in a t. of delight DICKENS. **3.** The peculiar t. of a cotton-factory 1853. *Earth-t.*, an earthquake. Hence **Tre·mor** *v.*

Tremulant (tre·miŭlănt), *a.* and *sb.* 1837. [ad. L. *tremulantem*, *tremulare* to TREMBLE.] **A.** *adj.* Tremulous; trembling. **B.** *sb.* *Mus.* = TREMOLO 2. 1862.

Tremulous (tre·miŭləs), *a.* 1611. [f. L. *tremulus* (f. *tremere* to tremble) + -OUS.] **1.** Of persons, their limbs, etc.: Characterized or affected by trembling or quivering; hence, fearful, timorous. Also said of writing, a line, or the like, done by a tremulous hand; hence, finely wavy. **2.** Of things: Characterized by trembling or vibration 1616. **b.** Ready to vibrate in response *to* some influence 1794.

1. His voice unstrung Grew t. COWPER. **2.** The t. ripple on the surface of the sea 1860. Hence **Tre·mulous-ly** *adv.*, **-ness.**

Trenail: see TREENAIL.

Trench (tren[t]ʃ), *sb.* late ME. [a OF. *trenche*, later OF. and mod.F. *tranche* an act of cutting, cut, gash, etc.; f. OF. *trenchier*, F. *trancher* TRENCH *v.*] †**1.** A path or track cut through a wood or forest; an alley; a hollow walk –1575. **2.** A long and narrow hollow cut out of the ground; a cutting; a ditch, fosse; a deep furrow 1489. **3.** *Mil.* An excavation of this kind, the earth from which is thrown up in front as a parapet, serving either to cover or to oppose the advance of a besieging force, or to give cover to fighting or supporting forces, etc. Chiefly in *pl.* 1500. **4.** Something resembling a trench. **a.** A cut, scar, or deep wrinkle in the face 1588. **b.** *Anat.* and *Zool.* A cavity, pit, fossa 1615.

1. And in a t. forth in the park gooth she CHAUCER. **3.** There are trenches too In which to stand all night to the knees in water In gallants breeds the tooth-ache MASSINGER. Phr. *To open trenches*, to break ground for the purpose of making approaches towards a besieged place. *To mount, relieve the trenches*, to occupy them, relieve those who have been on duty there. **4. a.** Witnesse these Trenches made by griefe and care SHAKS.

Comb. as *t.-warfare*, etc.: **t.-cavalier** *Mil.*, a high parapet constructed by besiegers upon the glacis to command and enfilade the covered way of the fortress; **-coat**, a short rain-coat such as may be worn in trenches; **-feet**, a gangrenous disease of the feet caused by much standing in water; **-mortar**, a mortar used in trenches for throwing heavy charges of high explosive a short distance.

Trench (trenʃ), *v.* 1483. [a. OF. *trenchier*, F. *trancher* to cut, app. repr. pop. L. **trincare*, altered from L. *truncare* to cut or lop off, f. *truncus* the trunk of a tree.] **I.** To cut, make a cutting. **1.** *trans.* To cut; to divide by cutting, slice, cut in pieces; to cut off, cut into; to cut *one's way*. Also *absol.* †**b.** To cut *in(to)* a surface –1665. †**c.** To make (a cut, gash, wound) *in(to)* something –1610. **2.** To cut or make a cutting through a ridge or raised surface 1601. **b.** *fig.* (with the surface furrowed or cut as obj.) 1624.

1. b. This weake impresse of Loue, is as a figure Trenched in ice SHAKS. **c.** The wide wound, that the boare had trencht In his soft flanke SHAKS. **2.** The ridge is deeply trenched with gullies and narrow glens 1865.

II. From TRENCH *sb.* **1.** To cut a trench or trenches in (the ground) 1530. **b.** *spec.* in *Agric.* and *Hortic.*: To make a series of trenches in digging or ploughing (a piece of ground), so as to bring the lower soil to the surface. Also *absol.* 1573. **c.** *intr.* or *absol.* To dig a trench or trenches 1786. **2.** *trans.* To furnish with, set, or place in a trench 1596. **3.** *Mil.* To surround or fortify with a trench; to cast a trench *about*, *around* (an army, town, etc.); to entrench 1548.

1. b. Thy garden plot latelie well trenched and muckt TUSSER. Phr. *To t. up*, to lay (land) in trenches and ridges alternately. **c.** T. deeply..and as early in the winter as possible 1882. **3.** The place which they had trenched, dytched, and fortefied with ordenaunce HALL.

III. †**1.** *intr.* *To t. to* (*unto*): To extend in effect to; to extend so as to affect or touch –1633. †**b.** To extend or stretch (*rare*) –1775. **2.** †**a.** *To t. into* (*unto*): To 'cut' into, to enter into so as to affect or concern intimately –1641. **b.** *To t. on* or *upon*: To encroach (however slightly) *on* or *upon* a region which is the domain of another 1622. c. in vaguer use: To come in thought, speech, or action close *upon* (something); hence, to have a bearing *upon* or reference to (something) 1635.

2. b. To t. on the liberty of individuals 1799. c. He did t. a little too neare upon an untruth 1639. Some unlucky jest, trenching on treason 1841.

Trenchancy (tre·nʃănsi). 1866. [f. next; see -ANCY.] The quality of being trenchant.

Trenchant (tre·nʃănt), *a.* [a. OF., pr. pple. of †*trenchier, trancher* TRENCH *v.*; see -ANT.] 1. Cutting, adapted for cutting; sharp. *arch.* and *poet.* b. *Zool.* Of a tooth, bill, etc.: Having a cutting edge; sectorial 1831. c. *transf., fig.,* or *allus.* 1603. 2. *fig.* esp. of language: Incisive; vigorous and clear; effective, energetic ME. 3. *transf.* and *fig.* Clear-cut; distinct 1849.

1. The t. Blade, Toledo trusty 1663. 2. Their Swords Were sharp and trencheant, not their Words 1663. 3. The line of demarcation is seemingly most sharp and t. 1873. Hence **Tre·nchantly** *adv.*, **-ness.**

Trencher[1] (tre·nʃəɹ). ME. [a. AF. *trenchour* = OF. *trencheoir*, f. †*trenchier, trancher* TRENCH *v.*, with suffix *-oir*, repr. L. *-atorium.*] †I. A cutting or slicing instrument; a knife –1553. II. 1. A flat piece of wood, square or circular, on which meat was served and cut up; a plate or platter. *arch.* and *Hist.* ME. 2. A trencher and that which it bears; a supply of food. *arch.* 1576. 3. *transf.* A flat board, circular or otherwise 1511. 4. *spec.* = TRENCHER-CAP 1834.

1. The first dinner which she ate on wooden trenchers delighted her MAR. EDGEWORTH. 2. Phr. *To lick the t.*, to toady; to play the parasite. 4. The girl students..in their red gowns and trenchers adorned with a red tassel 1906.

Trencher[2] (tre·nʃəɹ). 1871. [f. TRENCH *v.* + -ER[1].] One who cuts or digs trenches; one who trenches ground.

Tre·ncher-cap. 1721. [f. TRENCHER[1] + CAP *sb.*[1]] A popular name for the academic or college cap, in shape thought to resemble an inverted trencher with a basin upon it; a MORTAR-BOARD.

Tre·ncher-man. 1586. [f. TRENCHER[1] + MAN *sb.*[1]] †1. A cook or caterer. SIDNEY. 2. A feeder; an eater; usu. qualified, as *good, stout, valiant*, etc., one who has a hearty appetite 1590. 3. One who frequents a patron's table; a dependent, hanger-on 1599.

Trenchmore (tre·nʃmōəɹ), *sb.* 1551. [Origin obsc.] An old English country dance of a lively or boisterous nature; also, the air to which it was danced.

Ile make him daunce a trenchmoor to my sword 1611. Hence **Tre·nchmore** *v. intr.* to dance the t.

Trench-plough, -plow (tre·nʃ,plau), *v.* 1731. [f. TRENCH *sb.* or *v.* + PLOUGH *v.*] *trans.* and *intr.* To plough to the depth of two furrows, bringing the lower soil to the surface. Hence **Tre·nch-plough** *sb.* a plough designed or adjusted for trench-ploughing.

Trend (trend), *sb.* 1777. [f. next.] I. *Naut.* a. That part of the shank of an anchor where it thickens towards the crown 1794. b. The angle between the direction of the anchor-cable and that of the ship's keel 1879. 2. The way something trends or bends away; the general direction which a stream, coast, mountain-range, etc., tends to take 1777. b. *fig.* The general course, tendency, or drift (of action, thought, etc.) 1884.

2. The t. and character of the marine currents 1854. b. The general t. of affairs in Munster 1912.

Trend, *v.* Pa. t. and pa. pple. **trended.** [ME. *trenden*, OE. *trendan* (rare) :—OTeut. **trandjan*, f. **trend-, trand-, trund-* (see TRENDLE, TRINDLE, TRUNDLE).] †1. *intr.* To turn round, revolve, rotate, roll; also *fig.* –1654. †2. *trans.* To cause (a thing) to turn round; to turn or roll (anything); *fig.* to revolve in one's mind –1616. b. To wind (wool, partly cleaned) into tops for spinning (*dial.*) 1777. †3. *intr.* To skirt, coast (*about, along*) –1622. †b. More vaguely: To turn or direct one's course –1846. 4. To turn off in a specified direction; to run, stretch, incline, bend (in some direction) 1598. b. *fig.* To have a general tendency (as a discussion, events, etc.) 1863.

2. Not farre beneath i'th valley as she trends Her siluer streame 1613. 3. b. The religion of blood, like the beasts of prey, will continue to t. northward LANDOR. 4. Their path lay along the coast trending round to the west 1876.

Trendle (tre·nd'l). [OE. *trendel* circle, ring, etc. :—OTeut. **trendilo-*, f. root of TREND *v.*] †1. A circle, a ring, a coronet; a circular disk, orb; a ball, globe. –late ME. 2. A wheel. *Obs.* exc. *dial.* ME. 3. A bundle of (partly cleaned) wool 'trended'. *dial.* 1493.

Trental (tre·ntăl). ME. [ad. med. (eccl.) L. *trentale*. f. pop. L. **trenta*, **trinta* (:—L. *triginta*) + *-alis, -ale* -AL.] 1. A set of thirty requiem masses, said on the same day or on different days; also, the payment made for this. *arch.* and *Hist.* †b. *loosely.* An elegy or dirge. HERRICK. 2. Used as = MONTH'S MIND, the commemoration service on the thirtieth day after burial. *arch.* 1659.

1. Obits, Trentals, and Services for the Dead 1694.

‖**Trente et quarante** (trāntekarānt). 1671. [F. = thirty and forty.] Another name for the game of *rouge-et-noir* (in which thirty and forty are respectively winning and losing numbers).

Trentine (tre·ntəin), *a.* 1601. [f. *Trent*, a city of the Tyrol + -INE[1].] = TRIDENTINE.

Trenton (tre·ntən). 1854. *Geol.* (*attrib.*, or *ellipt.* as *sb.*) Applied to a limestone formation exemplified at Trenton Falls, New York, and hence to the series of Lower Silurian rocks to which it belongs.

Trepan (trĭpæ·n), *sb.*[1] late ME. [a. F. *trépan*, ad. med.L. *trepanum*, ad. Gr. τρύπανον a borer.] 1. A surgical instrument in the form of a crown-saw, for cutting out small pieces of bone, esp. from the skull. †2. A military engine formerly used in sieges –1610. 3. A boring instrument for sinking shafts. (Usu. as F., *trépan.*) 1877.

Trepan, trapan (trĕ-, trăpæ·n), *sb.*[2] *Obs.* or *arch.* 1641. [Orig. *trapan*, prob. formed in some way from TRAP *sb.*[1] or *v.*[1] Prob. a term of thieves' or rogues' slang.] 1. A person who entraps or decoys others into actions or positions which may be to his advantage and to their ruin or loss. 2. [f. TREPAN *v.*[2]] The action of entrapping; a stratagem, trick; a trap or snare 1665.

1. He was a Rogue, and a manifest T. of the Earl's NORTH. 2. There being a Snare, and a Trapan almost in every Word we hear 1671.

Trepa·n, *v.*[1] ME. [f. TREPAN *sb.*[1] or F. *trépaner.*] *trans.* To operate upon with a trepan; to saw through with a trepan, as a bone of the skull. Also *absol.*

Trepan, trapan (trĕ-, trăpæ·n), *v.*[2] *Obs.* or *arch.* 1656. [f. TREPAN *sb.*[2]] *trans.* To catch in a trap; to entrap, ensnare, beguile. b. To lure, inveigle (*into* or *to* a place, course of action, etc., *to do* something, etc.) 1661. c. To cheat or beguile *out of* (a thing); to swindle 1662.

To lie upon the catch to t. his neighbour 1745. c. Ten of those Rogues had trapann'd him out of 500. Crowns 1662. Hence **Trepa·nner** = TREPAN *sb.*[2] 1.

‖**Trepang** (trĭpæ·ŋ). 1783. [Malay *trīpang.*] A marine animal, an echinoderm (*Holothuria edulis*), called also *sea-cucumber, sea-slug, sea-swallow*, or *bêche-de-mer*, eaten as a luxury by the Chinese.

Trephine (trĭfəi·n, -fī·n), *sb.* 1628. [orig. *trafine*, f. L. *tres fines* three ends, app. formed after TREPAN *sb.*[1]] An improved form of trepan, with a tranverse handle, and a removable or adjustable sharp steel centre-pin which is fixed upon the bone to steady the movement in operating. Hence **Trephi·ne** *v. trans.* to operate upon with a t. **Trephina·tion.**

Trepid (tre·pid), *a.* *rare.* 1650. [ad. L. *trepidus.*] Trembling; agitated; fearful.

Trepidate (tre·pidĕit), *v.* *rare.* 1623. [f. ppl. stem of L. *trepidare* to hurry, bustle, be agitated or alarmed.] *intr.* To tremble with fear or agitation; also simply, †To shake.

Trepidation (trepidē¹·ʃən). 1605. [ad. L. *trepidationem*, f. *trepidare*; see prec.] 1. Tremulous agitation; confused hurry or alarm; confusion; flurry; perturbation 1607. 2. Tremulous, vibratory, or reciprocating movement; vibration; oscillation, rocking; an instance of this; also, tremor, as in paralytic affections 1605. 3. *Astron.* A libration of the eighth (or ninth) sphere, added *c* 950 to the system of Ptolemy, in order to account for certain phenomena, esp. precession, really due to motion of the earth's axis 1631.

1. They did their work at leisure..without t., as men lawfully employed JOHNSON. 2. Earth-quakes and trepidations of the earth 1696.

Trepidity (trĕpi·dĭti). 1721. [f. L. *trepidus* TREPID + -ITY.] Agitation, alarm, fearfulness.

Tresai·el, tresay·le. *Obs.* exc. *Hist.* 1491. [AF., formed after BESAIEL; cf. F. *trisaïeul*, f. *tri-* TRI- + *aïeul* grandfather.] A grandfather's grandfather; a great-great-grandfather.

Trespass (tre·spăs), *sb.* [ME. *trespas*, a. OF., f. *trespasser* TRESPASS *v.*] 1. A transgression; a breach of law or duty; an offence, sin, wrong; a fault. 2. *Law.* Any violation or transgression of the law; *spec.* one not amounting to treason, felony, or misprision of either ME. 3. *Law. spec.* Any actionable wrong committed against the person or property of another; also short for *action of t.* ME. 4. A passing beyond some limit (*rare*) 1650. 5. An encroachment, intrusion *on* or *upon* 1769.

1. And ye wyll not forgeve men there trespases, no more shall youre father forgeve your treaspases TINDALE *Matt.* vi. 12. 3. *T. to land*, a wrongful entry upon the lands of another, with damage (however inconsiderable) to his real property. *T. on the case*, a form of action now obsolete in which the damage complained of is a result not immediate, but consequential of an unlawful act; so called from the L. name of the writs (*brevia de transgressione super casum*) under which it was brought; also the name of the writ itself. 5. One t. more I must make on your patience GLADSTONE.

Tre·spass, *v.* ME. [f. prec.; or a. OF. *trespasser* to pass beyond or across, mod.F. *trépasser* to pass away, to die, med.L. *transpassare* to pass beyond, f. L. *trans* (F. *très*) + *passare* to PASS.] 1. *intr.* To commit a transgression or offence; to offend; to sin. †2. *trans.* a. To transgress, violate (a law, etc.) –1613. †b. To offend against, wrong, violate (a person) –1556. 3. *Law. intr.* To commit a trespass (see TRESPASS *sb.* 2); *spec.* to enter unlawfully on the land of another, or on that which is the property or right of another. Const. *on, upon.* 1455. 4. *fig.* To make an improper or uninvited inroad on (a person's time, attention, patience, etc.); to intrude *on* or *upon* the rights or domain of; to encroach on, infringe 1652.

1. He trespasses against his duty who sleeps upon his watch BURKE. 2. a. She had trespaced his commaundement CAXTON. 4. I am afraid that I have trespassed a little upon the patience of the Reader 1652.

Trespasser (tre·spăsəɹ). [Late ME., a. AF. *trespassour* = OF. *trespasseor*, f. *trespasser* to TRESPASS.] 1. A law-breaker; a wrong-doer, sinner, offender. 2. *Law.* One who commits a trespass; *esp.* one who trespasses on the lands of another 1455.

Tress (tres), *sb.* ME. [a. F. *tresse*, OF. *tresce* :—late L. or Rom. **tricia*, **trecia.*] A plait or braid of the hair of the head, usu. of a woman. b. (By extension) A long lock of hair (esp. that of a woman); mostly in pl. *tresses* ME. c. *transf.* and *fig.* Applied to long leafy shoots or tendrils, rays of the sun, etc. late ME.

Their beautiful hair [was] divided into many tresses, hanging on their shoulders 1717. b. Rose-checkt Adonis with his amber tresses 1595. c. Luxuriant tresses of maiden-hair fern 1875. Hence **Tre·ssful** *a.* full of or fully furnished with tresses.

Tress, *v.* Now *rare* exc. in *pa. pple.* [Late ME. a. F. *tresser*; goes with prec.] *trans.* To arrange (hair) in tresses or (threads, etc.) in braids.

-tress, ending of feminines of agent-nouns in *-ter, -tor*, etc., usu. short for *-ter-ess, -tor-ess*, see -ESS[1].

Tressed (trest, *poet.* tre·sĕd), *ppl. a.* and *a.* ME. [f. TRESS *sb.* and *v.* + -ED.] 1. Of the hair: Arranged in tresses; braided. late ME. 2. Having or furnished with tresses; often in comb., as *gold-t.*, etc. ME.

Tressure (tre·siŭɹ, tre·ʃŭɹ). [ME. *tressour*, repr. OF. *tressure, -eure*, f. *tresse* TRESS.] †1. A ribbon or band worn round the head; a net with which a woman's tresses are confined; a head-dress –1483. **2.** *Her.* A diminutive of the orle (ORLE 1 a), consisting of a narrow band of one-quarter the width of the bordure 1440. **3.** *Numism.* An ornamental enclosure, circular or of several arches, containing the type or distinctive device, found on many gold and silver coins of former centuries 1745.

Tressy (tre·si), *a.* 1614. [f. TRESS *sb.* + -Y[1].] Resembling, characterized by, or adorned with tresses.

Trestle (tre·s'l). [ME. *trestel*, a. OF. *trestel* transom, beam:—popular L. **transtellum*, dim. of *transtrum* beam; see -LE[2].] **1.** A support for something, consisting of a short horizontal beam or bar with diverging legs, usu. two at each end; *esp.* one of a pair or set used to support a board so as to form a table. **2.** *Her.* A low stool or bench used as a bearing: usu. represented with three legs 1610. **3.** *spec.* **a.** A framework consisting of upright (or more or less inclined) pieces with diagonal braces, used to support a bridge or other elevated structure 1796. **b.** One of the timber props or shores used to support a ship while being built 1860. **c.** = TRESTLE-TREE. **4.** *transf.* and *fig.*: esp. (*pl.*) applied to the legs 1610.

Comb.: **t.-bed**, a movable bed supported upon trestles, as used in a hospital tent, etc.; **-board**, a board laid upon trestles to form a table **-bridge**, a bridge supported upon trestles or trestlework **-table**, a table made of a board or boards laid upon trestles; **trestlework**, a framework composed of a series of trestles fastened together, for supporting a bridge or viaduct, esp. on a railway.

Trestle-tree. 1652. [f. TRESTLE + TREE *sb.* 3.] *Naut. pl.* Two strong pieces of timber fixed horizontally fore-and-aft on opposite sides of a mast-head, to support the cross-trees, the top, and the fid of the mast above.

Tret (tret). *Obs.* exc. *Hist.* 1500. [Origin and history obscure.] *Comm.* An allowance of 4 lb. in 104 lb. (= $\frac{1}{26}$) on goods sold by weight after the deduction for tare.

Trews (trūz), *sb. pl.* 1568. [ad. Ir. *trius*, Gael. *triubhas*, ad. Eng. TROUSE sing. (with pl. *trouses*), but treated as a pl.] Close-fitting trousers, or breeches combined with stockings, formerly worn by Irishmen and Scottish Highlanders, and still by certain Scottish regiments.

Trey (trēi). late ME. [a. OF. and AF. *treis*, *trei* :—L. *tres* three.] **1.** The three at dice or cards. **2.** *slang.* The number three; a set of three; a threepenny piece 1896.

Comb.: **t.-ace**, a throw that turns up trey with one die and ace with the other; so **t.-deuce.**.

Tri- (trəi, *occas.* tri), *prefix*, a. L. *tri-*, Gr. τρι-, comb. form of *tres*, τρεῖς three, τρίς thrice.

I. Forming adjs. (and derived sbs. and advbs.) with the senses: **1.** Having, characterized by, or consisting (*rarely*, belonging or relating to) three (of the things denoted by the second element). **a.** In comb. with adjs. derived from sbs., or with sbs. without adjectival termination. **Triade·lphous**, *Bot.* of stamens: united by the filaments into three bundles; of a plant: having such stamens. **Triarti·culate**, three-jointed. **Tribra·cteate**, *Bot.* having three bracts. **Trico·ccous**, *Bot.* composed of three *cocci* or carpels; of a plant: having fruit of this kind. **Tri:consona·ntal**, consisting of or containing three consonants: said chiefly of radical words of the Semitic langs. **Trico·rporal, -co·rporate**, three-bodied. **Tricro·tic** [after DICROTIC], *Physiol.* of the pulse, etc.: having or showing three undulations for each beat of the heart. **Trida·ctyl**, having three fingers or toes. **Tride·ntate**, *Bot.* and *Zool.* having three teeth or tooth-like processes. **Tridime·nsional**, having or exhibiting three dimensions, as a solid body. **Trifo·liolate**, *Bot.* consisting of three leaflets, or having leaves of this form. **Trifu·rcate**, divided into three branches like the prongs of a fork. **Trili·neal**, *Geom.* = TRILINEAR. **Trili·ngual**, speaking or using, written or expressed in, or relating to three languages. **Trilo·bate**, *Nat. Hist.* three-lobed. **Trilo·cular**, *Nat. Hist.* having three cells or compartments. **Trima·cular**, having or marked with three spots. **Trine·rvate**, *Nat. Hist.* having three nerves or veins. **Trino·ctial**, belonging to or lasting three nights. **Trino·dal**, having three nodes. **Trino·minal**, having three names. **Tri·ode**, of a thermionic valve, having three electrodes; also *absol.* as *sb.* **Tri·part** (*rare*), **-parted** = TRIPARTITE. **Tripedal** (stress var.), three-footed. **Tripe·talous**, *Bot.* having, or consisting of, three petals. **Triphy·llous**, *Bot.* three-leaved; *spec.* of a calyx or corolla, trisepalous or tripetalous. **Trirecta·ngular**, having three right angles, as a spherical triangle. **Trise·palous**, *Bot.* having or consisting of three sepals. **Trise·rial**, **Trise·riate**, arranged in three series or rows. **Trispe·rmous** [Gr. σπέρμα seed], *Bot.* containing three seeds. **Tristi·chous**, *Bot.* arranged in, or characterized by, three rows or ranks. **Tristigma·tic**, **Tristi·gmatose**, *Bot.* having three stigmas. **Trisu·lcate**, *Bot.* marked with three grooves; *Zool.* divided into three digits. **Tritube·rculate**, *Comp. Anat.* having three tubercles, as a tooth. **Tri·valve**, *Nat. Hist.* having three valves. **b.** With Eng. sbs. (without adj. ending); chiefly nonce-wds. as *tri-church*, *-party*, *-phase*. **c.** Occas with sb. + -ED[2]; as *tri-bladed*, *-cornered*, *-faced*, etc.

2. Triply; three times; in three ways, directions, etc. **Tricli·nic**, *Cryst.* applied to that system of crystalline forms in which the three axes are unequal and obliquely inclined; belonging to this system. **Tricu·rvate**, 'curved in three directions, as a sponge-spicule.' **Trifa·cial**, *Anat.* applied to the fifth pair of cranial nerves, which divide into three branches supplying the face and some adjacent parts. **Triqua·drifid**, *Bot.* having three lobes each deeply divided into four segments. **Triqui·nate**, *Bot.* having three lobes each divided into five. **Trira·diate**, radiating in three ways from a central point. **Trite·rnate**, *Bot.* thrice ternate. **b.** *spec.* in *Cryst.* denoting forms having three ranges of facets, the number in each range being expressed by the second element; as **tri-octrahe·dral** (8); also **tri-rhomboi·dal**, having eighteen faces occupying the positions of those of three different rhomboids.

3. In comb. with an adj. (usu. in *-ly*) derived from a sb. denoting a period of time: Comprising three —, lasting three —, occurring or appearing every three (days, etc.); also (*loosely*) occurring three times (a day, etc.); those in -LY are also used as advbs. = every three (days, etc.); as *tridai·ly*, *triwee·kly*, etc.

II. Forming sbs. with the senses: **a.** Something consisting of or equivalent to three (of the things denoted by the second element); a triple —. **Tri·phony**, in early medieval music, diaphony for three voices. **b.** Something having, or related in some way to, three (of the things denoted or indicated by the second element). **Tri·phylite** [Gr. φυλή tribe], *Min.* a compound phosphate of iron, manganese, and lithium. **Tri·plane**, an aeroplane with three supporting planes. **Tri·pody**, *Pros.* a group or verse of three feet. **Tri·sacramenta·rian**, one who recognizes three and only three sacraments. **Tri·theism**, belief in three gods; *esp.* the doctrine that the three persons of the Trinity are three distinct gods; hence **Tri·theist, Tri·theite.** **Tri·tone**, *Mus.* an interval consisting of three whole tones; an augmented fourth. **Tri·valve**, a shell having three valves. **c.** Something (denoted by the second element) having three of some characteristic part, or related to three things. **Tri·car** (**-machine, -motor-car**), a motor-car with three wheels; a motor-tricycle with a seat for a person or a carrier for luggage in front. **Tri·coaster**, a combination of a three-speed gear with a 'coaster' brake on a cycle. **Tripy·ramid**, *Cryst.* a triangular pyramid, as a form in certain calcareous spars.

III. In Chemical nomenclature, in the names of compounds and derivatives, with general sense 'three', 'three times'. **a.** Prefixed to names of compounds of elements, radicals, or groups, names of salts, etc., to signify three atoms, groups, or equivalents of these elements or radicals in combination with another element or radical; e. g. **trichlo·ride**, a compound of three atoms of chlorine with another element or radical, as *arsenic trichloride*. So **tria·mide, -a·mine, -glyceride, -oxide, -saccharide, -silicate, -sulphate, -sulphide**, etc. Also in names of compound ethers or esters of glycerin with acids, as in **triolein, -palmitin, -stearin**, etc. **b.** Prefixed to adjs., or to sbs. used attrib., in the names or descriptions of acids, alcohols, compound ethers or esters, oxides, salts, etc.; e. g. *trisodic* or *trisodium*, (a salt) containing 3 atoms of sodium; *triethylic* or *triethyl* (a compound) containing 3 ethyl groups; so *trithionic*, etc. **c.** Prefixed to the names of elements or radicals, or their combining forms (as *azo-*, *bromo-*, etc.) entering into the name of a compound, to signify that three atoms or groups of the element or radical are present, or are substituted for hydrogen, in the substance designated by the rest of the name; so **triphen-, triphenyl-**, etc. **d.** In vbs. and their pples. derived from sbs. as in a, as *tribrominated*, *trichlorinated*, in which three hydrogen atoms have been replaced by atoms of bromine or chlorine; *trihydrated*, containing three molecules of water.

IV. Forming vbs. (and derivs.) as TRISECT, -SECTION.

Triable (trəi·ăb'l), *a.* late ME. [a. AF., f. as TRY *v.* + -ABLE.] **1.** *Law.* Capable of being tried in a court of law; liable to judicial trial. **2.** That may be ascertained, tested, or proved 1612.

2. In our..first Experiment, and..others tryable in our Engine BOYLE.

Triacontad (trəi,ăkǫ·ntæd). 1621. [ad. Gr. τριακοντάς, -αδ-, f. τριάκοντα thirty.] The number thirty, or a set of thirty. So **Triacontahedral** (-hī·drăl, -he·drăl) [Gr. ἕδρα base, side] *a.* contained by thirty faces, esp. by thirty rhombs, as a crystal. **Triaconter** (trəi·ăkǫntəɹ) [ad. Gr. τριακοντήρης], an ancient Greek galley with thirty oars.

Triad (trəi·æd). 1546. [f. L. *triad-*, stem of *trias*, a. Gr. τριάς, τριαδ-, a group of three.] **1.** A group or set of three (persons, things, words, attributes, etc.); three collectively or in connexion. **b.** The number three (in Pythagorean philosophy) 1660. **2.** *spec.* **a.** Applied to the Trinity 1661. **b.** A group of three associated or correlated deities, beings, or powers 1746. **c.** In Welsh literature: A form of composition characterized by an arrangement of subjects or statements in groups of three 1819. **d.** *Mus.* A chord of three notes, consisting of a given note with the third and fifth above it; e. g. a common chord (without the octave) 1801. **e.** *Chem.* A trivalent element or radical 1865. **f.** *Math.* (*a*) A set of three things, esp. in *Geom.* of three points. (*b*) In Quaternions, An indeterminate product of three vectors. 1850.

1. Three triads of Lancet windows 1898. Hence **Tria·dic** *a.* of, pertaining to, or constituting a t., consisting of triads; so **Tria·dical** *a.*, **-ly** *adv.*

Triage (trəi·ėdʒ). 1727. [a. F., f. *trier* TRY *v.*; see -AGE.] The action of assorting according to quality. Also *attrib.*; hence *concr.* coffee beans of the third or lowest quality.

Triakis- (trəi·ăkis), repr. Gr. τριάκις thrice, as in **Tri:akis,o:ctahe·dron** (pl. **-hedra**), *Geom.* and *Cryst.* a solid derived from the octahedron by erecting a triangular pyramid on each face, thus multiplying the original number of faces by three.

Trial (trəi·ăl), *sb.* 1526. [a. AF. *trial*, *triel*, f. *trier* to TRY; see -AL.] The action or fact of trying or being tried, in various senses of TRY *v.* **1.** *Law.* The examination and determination of a cause by a judicial tribunal 1577. **b.** The determination of a person's guilt or innocence, or the righteousness of his cause, by a combat between the accuser and accused (*t. by battle*, *by* (*single*) *combat*, *by wager of battle*, *by the sword*); see also *t. by* ORDEAL 1593. **2.** The action of testing or putting to the proof the fitness, truth, strength, or other quality of anything; test, probation 1526. **b.** The fact or condition of being tried by suffering or temptation; probation 1550. **3.** Action, method, or treatment adopted in order to ascertain the result; experiment 1570. **4.** A testing of qualifications, attainments, or progress; examination 1672. **5.** An attempt to do something; an endeavour, effort 1614. **6.** That which puts one to the test; *esp.* a painful test of one's endurance, patience, or faith; hence, affliction, trouble, misfortune 1754. **7.** Something that serves as a sample or proof of a manufacture or material, the skill of an operator, etc.; *spec.* in *Pottery manuf.* a piece of clay or the like by which the progress of the firing process may be judged; a trial-piece 1608.

1. Phr. *To bring* (a person or cause) *to t.*; *to put* (a person) *on his t.*, *to stand* (*one's*) *t.*, etc.; also *t. by jury*, etc. **2.** The triall of mettall by fire 1604. **b.** That which purifies us is triall MILT. **3.** *Rule of t.* and *error*: see POSITION *sb.* 3. **5.** I proposed to make a t. for landing if the weather should suit SMEATON. **6.** All people have their trials DICKENS.

Phrases. *On t.* (sense 2) on the basis or condition of being tried, as *to take* a person or thing *on t.*, to take subject to the condition of being satisfactory when tried. *To be on* (*his*, *her*, or *its*) *t.* (2, 4), to be in a state of probation until it is seen how he or it will succeed or work.

Comb.: **t. balance**, in book-keeping by double entry, an addition of the whole of the entries on each side of the ledger, when the sum of the debits ought to balance the sum of the credits; **t. eight**, *Boat-racing*, an eight-oared boat's provisional crew, from among whom some members of the final eight may be chosen; **-list**, the register of causes or prisoners to be tried; **-piece**, something made or taken as a specimen; *spec.* a coin or the like struck as a test of the die, or as a specimen of the design; **t. proof**, a proof taken from a plate during the process of engraving to show its state; **t. square** = try-square; **-trip**, a trip taken to test the speed, etc. of a vessel, etc.

Tri·al, *a.* 1886. [f. L. *tri-* + -AL, after *dual.*] *Gram.* = TRINAL *a.* 2.

Triality (trəi,æ·lĭti). *rare.* 1529. [f. as prec. after *duality*, *plurality*.] †**1.** The holding of three benefices at once –1637. **2.** The condition or quality of being threefold 1872.

Trialogue (trəi·ălǫg). 1532. [ad. med.L. *trialogus*, formed by substituting *tri-* for *di-* in *dialogus* DIALOGUE, being mistaken for DI-[2] = two.] A dialogue between three persons.

‖**Triandria** (trəi,æ·ndriă). 1748. [mod.L., f. *triandrus*, f. Gr. τρεῖς three + ἀνήρ, ἀνδρ- man, taken as = stamen; see -ANDROUS.] *Bot.* The third class in the Linnæan Sexual System, comprising plants having hermaphrodite flowers with three stamens not cohering; also, an order in some classes, comprising plants having three stamens. So **Tria·ndrian, Tria·ndrious,** and (usu.) **Tria·ndrous** *adjs.* having three stamens; belonging to the *T.*

Triangle (trəi·æŋg'l). late ME. [a. F., or ad. L. *triangulum*, sb. neut. from *triangulus* adj. three-cornered, f. *tri-* TRI- + *angulus* ANGLE.] **1.** *Geom.*, etc. A figure (usu. a plane rectilineal figure) having three angles and three sides. **b.** A figure of this form used symbolically (e. g. an equilateral triangle as a symbol of the Trinity), or in magic or necromancy 1584. **c.** *fig.* A group or set of three, a triad 1621. **2.** Something having the form of a triangle; any three-cornered body, object, or space 1618. **b.** *Astron.* The constellation *Triangulum*, north of *Aries*, characterized by three stars in the positions of the angular points of an isosceles triangle 1551. **c.** A musical instrument of percussion, consisting of a steel rod bent into a triangular form, but open at one corner; it is struck with a small straight steel rod. Also, the player of this. 1801. **d.** *Mil.* (usu. *pl.*) A tripod, originally formed of three halberds stuck in the ground and joined at the top, to which soldiers were formerly bound to be flogged; a structure resembling this 1847. **e.** A drawing-instrument in the form of a right-angled triangle of wood, vulcanite, etc.; a set square 1877.

1. *Circular t.*, a plane triangle formed by three intersecting circular arcs. *Spherical t.*, a triangle formed by three arcs upon the surface of a sphere; see SPHERICAL. *T. of forces*, the theorem in statics that if three forces in one plane, acting at one point, be in equilibrium, three straight lines in that plane parallel to their directions will form a triangle whose sides are proportional to their magnitudes. **c.** Mrs. Dudeney's novel..deals with the eternal t., which, in this case, consists of two men and one woman 1907.

†**Triangled,** *a.* 1486. [f. prec. + -ED.] Three-cornered, triangular -1828.

Triangular (trəi,æ·ŋgiŭlăɹ), *a.* 1541. [ad. late L. *triangularis*; see TRIANGLE and -AR [1].] **1.** Having, or arranged in, the form of a triangle; contained by three sides and angles; three-cornered, three-sided. **b.** Having three edges, as a prism or pyramid; trihedral, triquetrous 1644. **c.** Contained by triangles, as a solid figure (*rare*) 1805. **2.** Pertaining or relating to a triangle 1701. **3.** *fig.* Relating to or taking place between three persons or parties, three-sided; also, constituting a triad, threefold, triple 1812.

2. *T. compasses*, a kind of compasses with three legs, used for taking off triangles. *T. numbers*, the first series of POLYGONAL numbers (1, 3, 6, 10, 15, 21, etc.) obtained by continued summation of the natural numbers 1, 2, 3, 4, 5, 6, etc. So **Triangula·rity,** the quality of being t. **Tria·ngularly** *adv.*

Triangulate (trəi,æ·ŋgiŭlēt), *a.* 1610. [ad. med.L. *triangulatus* triangular, f. L. *triangulum* TRIANGLE; see -ATE [2].] Chiefly *Nat. Hist.* **1.** Having three angles, triangular. 1611. **2.** Made up or composed of triangles 1610. **3.** Having triangular markings 1891.

Triangulate (trəi,æ·ŋgiŭlēⁱt), *v.* 1833. [f. L. *triangulum* + -ATE [3].] **1.** *trans. Surveying* (also *transf.*, as in *Astron.*). To measure and map out (a region or territory) by tracing a series or network of triangles from a base-line and measuring their sides and angles; to determine (e.g. a distance or altitude) in this way. Also *absol.* **b.** *gen.* To mark out into triangles 1853. **2.** To divide or convert into triangles 1864.

Triangulation (trəi,æŋgiŭlēⁱ·ʃən). 1818. [ad. med.L. *triangulationem*, f. as prec.: see -ATION.] The action or process of triangulating. **1.** The tracing and measurement of a series or network of triangles in order to survey and map out a territory or region. **2.** Division of a rectilinear figure into triangles 1891.

Triarch (trəi·aɹk). 1886. [f. TRI- + *-arch* in *tetrarch*.] The ruler of one of three divisions of a country or territory.

Triarchy (trəi·aɹki). 1601. [f. TRI- + Gr. -αρχια government, or ad. Gr. τριαρχία triumvirate.] **1.** The government or jurisdiction of a triarch; one of three divisions of a country ruled by triarchs. **2.** Government by three rulers or powers jointly; a triumvirate 1656. **3.** A group of three districts or divisions each under its own ruler 1660.

Trias (trəi·æ̆s). 1610. [a. late L., a. Gr. τριάς the number three.] **1.** The number three; a set of three, a triad. **2.** *Geol.* Name for the series of strata lying immediately beneath the Jurassic and above the Permian; so called because divisible, where typically developed (as in Germany), into three groups (*Keuper, Muschelkalk*, and *Bunter Sandstein*) 1841.

Triassic (trəi,æ·sik), *a.* 1841. [f. prec. + -IC.] *Geol.* Of or belonging to the Trias; *T. system* = TRIAS 2.

Triatic (trəi,æ·tik), *a.* 1841. [app. f. TRI- three.] *Naut.* In *t. stay*: 'a rope secured at each end to the heads of the fore and main masts, with thimbles spliced into its bight, to hook the stay tackles to' (Dana).

Triatomic (trəi,ătǫ·mik), *a.* 1862. [f. TRI- + ATOM + -IC.] *Chem.* **a.** Having three atoms in the molecule. †**b.** = TRIVALENT. **c.** Containing three hydroxyl groups (OH).

Tribade (tri·băd, ‖tribad). 1601. [a. F., or ad. L. *tribas, -ad-*, Gr. τριβάς, τριβαδ-, f. τρίβειν to rub.] A woman who practises unnatural vice with other women. Hence **Tri·badism.**

Tribal (trəi·băl), *a.* 1632. [f. L. *tribus* TRIBE + -AL.] Of or pertaining to a tribe or tribes; characteristic of a tribe. Hence **Tri·bally** *adv.*

Tribalism (trəi·băliz'm). 1886. [f. prec. + -ISM.] The condition of existing as a separate tribe or tribes; tribal system, organization, or relations.

Tribasic (trəibēⁱ·sik), *a.* 1837. [f. Gr. τρι- TRI- + βάσις base + -IC.] *Chem.* Of an acid: Having the property of exchanging three atoms of hydrogen for three of potassium or sodium, and thus forming a salt. Of a salt: Containing three molecules of the basic oxide.

Tribble, obs. var. TREBLE.

Tribe (trəib), *sb.* [ME. *tribu*, a. OF. *tribu*, a. L. *tribus* (origin obsc.), which is prob. the immediate source of the Eng. *tribe* (late ME).] **1.** A group of persons forming a community and claiming descent from a common ancestor; *spec.* each of the twelve divisions of the people of Israel, claiming descent from the twelve sons of Jacob. **b.** A particular race of recognized ancestry; a family. late ME. **2.** *Rom. Hist.* One of the traditional three political divisions or patrician orders of ancient Rome in early times; later, one of the 30 political divisions of the Roman people instituted by Servius Tullius, and in B.C. 241 increased to 35. 1533. **b.** *Grecian Hist.* Rendering Gr. φυλή 1697. **c.** A division of some other nation or people 1693. **3.** A race of people; now applied esp. to a primary aggregate of people in a primitive or barbarous condition, under a headman or chief 1596. **4.** A class of persons; a fraternity, set, lot. Now often *contempt.* 1600. **5. a.** *Nat. Hist.* A group, usu. forming a subdivision of an order, and containing a number of genera; sometimes used as superior and sometimes as inferior to a family; also, loosely, any group or series of animals 1640. **b.** A class, group, sort, or kind of things 1731. **6.** A number or company of persons or animals; a 'troop'; in *pl.*, large numbers, flocks 1711.

1. The dukes were euer of the trybe of Iuda CAXTON. An Ebrew, as I guess, and of our T. MILT. **3.** Territory..occupied by numerous and warlike tribes of Indians 1823. **4.** The t. of vulgar politicians are the lowest of our species BURKE. *T. of Ben*, a name applied to themselves by literary associates and disciples of Ben Jonson in his later life. **6.** There were tribes of children in most of the cottages 1833. Hence **Tribe,** *v.* (*rare*), *trans.* to classify in tribes; also, to place in the same t. *with*. **Tri·beship,** the condition or position of being a t.; the members of a t. collectively, or their territory.

Tribesman (trəi·bzmæ̆n). 1798. [f. *tribe's*, genitive of TRIBE + MAN *sb.*] **a.** A member of a tribe. Chiefly *pl.* **b.** With possessive, a man of one's own tribe.

Triblet (tri·blĕt). 1611. [= F. *triboulet*, of unkn. origin.] A cylindrical rod or mandrel for forging rings, nuts, tubes, etc., or for drawing lead-pipe. Also *attrib.*: *t. tubes*, thin tubes which slide one upon the other, as in a telescope.

Tribometer (trəibǫ·mǐtəɹ). 1774. [ad. F. *tribomètre*, f. Gr. τρίβος rubbing + *-mètre* -METER.] An instrument for estimating sliding friction.

Tribrach (trəi·bræk, tri·-). 1589. [ad. L. *tribrachys*, a. Gr. τρίβραχυς, f. TRI- + βραχύς short.] *Prosody.* A metrical foot consisting of three short syllables. Hence **Tribra·chic** *a.* consisting of three short syllables; also, composed of tribrachs.

Tribrom-, tribromo- (trəi,brōᵘ·m(o). 1852. [f. TRI- III. c + BROM(O-.] *Chem.* A formative signifying that three atoms of bromine are substituted for hydrogen in the substance designated by the rest of the name.

Tribual (trəi·biuăl), *a.* 1650. [f. L. *tribus* TRIBE + -AL.] Of, belonging or pertaining to a tribe; tribal.

Tribulate (tri·biŭlēⁱt), *v.* 1637. [f. L. *tribulat-, tribulare*, or perh. f. next.] *trans.* To afflict; to oppress; to trouble greatly.

Tribulation (tribiŭlēⁱ·ʃən). *arch.* ME. [a. OF. *tribulacion*, ad. Chr.L. *tribulationem*, f. L. *tribulare*, f. *tribulum* a threshing-sledge, app. f. *tri-*, var. stem of *terere, trivi, tritum* to rub, grind + *-bulum* forming names of instruments.] **1.** A condition of great affliction, oppression, or misery; 'persecution; distress; vexation; disturbance of life' (J.). **b.** With *a* and *pl.* An affliction ME. †**2.** The condition of being held in pawn (*slang*) -1764.

1. Tri'd in sharp t., and refin'd By Faith and faithful works MILT.

†‖**Tribu·na.** 1644. [It., f. L. *tribunus* TRIBUNE *sb.*[1]] An octagonal saloon in the Galleria degli Uffizi at Florence containing many famous paintings and statues -1757.

Tribunal (trəi-, tribiū·năl), *sb.* (*a.*) 1526. [ad. L. *tribunal, -ale* tribunal, judgement seat, f. *tribunus* TRIBUNE *sb.*[1]; see -AL.] **1.** *orig.* A raised semicircular or square platform in a Roman basilica, on which the seats of the magistrates were placed; a dais; a raised throne or chair of state; a judgement seat (also *fig.*). **2.** A court of justice; a judicial assembly 1590. **b.** *fig.* Place of judgement or decision; judicial authority 1635. **c.** In the war of 1914–18, a local board set up to hear claims for exemption from military service 1916. †**3.** = TRIBUNE [2] 1, 2. -1797.

1. Those around the t. cried out against him 1833. **2. b.** Go up, my soul, into the t. of thy conscience QUARLES. The t. of public opinion BENTHAM. *The t. of penance*, = the confessional.

B. *attrib.* or as *adj.* Pertaining to, of the nature of, or authorized by a tribunal 1554.

Tribunate (tri·biunĕt). 1546. [ad. L. *tribunatus*, f. *tribunus* TRIBUNE *sb.*[1]; see -ATE [1].] **1.** The office of tribune; tribuneship; government by tribunes. **2.** *Fr. Hist.* A representative body of legislators established under the constitution of the year 8 of the Revolutionary Calendar (1800–1). 1827.

Tribune[1] (tri·biun, trəi·-). late ME. [ad. L. *tribunus*, lit. 'head of a tribe', f. *tribus* TRIBE.] **1.** A title designating one of several officers in the Roman administration: *spec.* **a.** *T. of the people* (L. *tribunus plebis*), one of two (later five, then ten) officers appointed to protect the interests and rights of the plebeians from the patricians. **b.** *Military t.* (L. *tribunus militaris*), one of six officers of a legion, each being in command for two months of the year. **2.** *transf.* and *fig.* An officer holding some position analogous to that of a Roman tribune; a judge; a popular leader, a demagogue 1587. Hence **Tri·buneship,** the office of a t.; the term of this office.

Tribune[2] (tri·biun, trəi·-). 1645. [a. F., ad. It. and med.L. *tribuna*.] **1.** = TRIBUNA. **2.** The semicircular or polygonal apse of a basilica or basilican church, usu. domed or vaulted 1771. 3. A raised platform or dais; a rostrum; a pulpit; the throne or stall of a bishop 1762. 4. A raised and seated area or gallery, esp. in a church; also applied to stands at continental race meetings 1865.

Tribunitial, -icial (tribiuni·ʃăl), *a.* 1598. [f. L. *tribunicius* + -AL.] = next a.

Tribunitian, -ician (tribiuni·ʃăn), *a.* 1533. [f. as prec. + -AN.] Of, belonging or pertaining to a Roman tribune, or the office of tribune. b. *transf.* and *fig.* Having the power of veto like the Roman tribunes; popularly appointed; demagogic; factious 1637.

b. The t. fury of ecclesiastical demagogues 1854.

Tributary (tri·biŭtări), *a.* and *sb.* late ME. [ad. L. *tributarius*; see next and -ARY[1].] A. *adj.* 1. Paying tribute; subject to imposts. 2. *transf.* and *fig.* Furnishing subsidiary supplies or aid; auxiliary, contributory; also said of a stream or river which flows into another 1611. 3. Of the nature of tribute; contributory 1588.

1. At those dayes a great parte of yᵉ worlde was trybutary to Rome 1494. 2. For me your t. stores combine GOLDSM. The rivers t. to the Thames HUXLEY. 3. Loe at this Tombe my tributarie teares, I render SHAKS.

B. *sb.* (The adj. used *absol.*) 1. One who pays tribute. late ME. 2. *transf.* and *fig.* One who or that which furnishes subsidiary supplies or aid; *spec.* a stream flowing into a larger stream or lake 1836.

2. What sedged brooks are Thames's tributaries M. ARNOLD.

Tribute (tri·biut), *sb.* ME. [ad. L. *tributum*, neut. of *tributus*, *tribuere* to assign, give, pay.] 1. A tax or impost paid by one prince or state to another in acknowledgement of submission or as the price of peace, security, and protection; rent or homage paid in money or an equivalent by a subject to his sovereign or a vassal to his lord. b. Hence contextually, The obligation or necessity of paying this; the condition of being tributary, as *to lay a t. on.* late ME. 2. *transf.* and *fig.* Something paid or contributed as by a subordinate to a superior; an offering or gift rendered as a duty, or as an acknowledgement of affection or esteem 1585. 3. In *Mining.* a. The proportion of the value of the ore raised, paid by the miners to the owners or lessors of the land or their representatives 1778. b. The proportion of ore raised or its value, paid to the miners by the owners of the mine or land, in payment of their labour 1832.

1. A large portion of the t. was paid in money GIBBON. b. *Under t.*, under obligation to pay t. 2. Some frail memorial..Implores the passing t. of a sigh GRAY. 3. Phr. *To work on t.*, or *on the t. system*, to work on the plan of paying or receiving certain proportions of the produce.

Comb.: t.-money, money paid as t. Hence **Tribute**, *v.* †*intr.* to yield t.; †*trans.* to pay as t.; *Mining, trans.* and *intr.* to work on t.

Trice (trəis), *sb.* 1440. [Found first in phrase *at a t.*, app. orig. 'at one pull', *trice* being vbl. sb. from TRICE *v.*; hence 'at once, immediately', whence later the simple sb. comes to be equal to 'instant, moment'.] 1. †a. *At a t.*, lit. at a single pluck or pull; hence, in an instant –1635. b. *In a t.* in same sense 1508. †2. One single attempt or act; the time taken for this; an instant or moment –1668.

Trice (trəis), *v.* late ME. [a. MDu. *trîsen*, Du. *trijsen* to hoist. History obsc.] †1. *trans.* To pull; to pluck, snatch; rarely, to carry off (as plunder) –1618. 2. To pull or haul with a rope; *spec.* (*Naut.*) usu. with *up*, to haul or hoist up and secure with a rope or lashing, to lash up. late ME.

-trice, *suffix*, a. F. *-trice*, ad. L. *-trix*, *-tricem*, or It. *-trice*; in Latin forming feminines to agent-nouns in *-tor*. In modern Eng. -TRIX from the L. nominative is preferred.

Tricenary (trəisī·nări), *a.* and *sb.* 1482. [ad. L. *tricenarius* of, pertaining to, or consisting of thirty, f. *triceni* thirty each.] A. *adj.* Of or pertaining to thirty; containing, or lasting, thirty days. Now *rare* or *Obs.* 1655. B. *sb.* *R. C. Ch.* A series of masses said on thirty consecutive days 1482.

Tricentenary (trəise·ntĭnări, -sĕntī·nări), *a.* and *sb.* 1846. [f. TRI- + CENTENARY.] = TERCENTENARY.

Triceps (trəi·seps), *a.* and *sb.* 1704. [a. L., f. TRI- + *-ceps*, deriv. form of *caput* head.] *Anat.* A. *adj.* Of a muscle: Having three heads or points of origin. B. *sb.* A triceps muscle; *spec.* that of the thigh (*t. extensor cruris*) and that of the upper arm (*t. extensor cubiti*).

Trichi (tri·tʃi). *colloq.* or *slang.* 1877. Short for TRICHINOPOLI (cigar).

Trichiasis (triki,ǣ·sis, trikəi·ăsis). 1661. [Late L., a. Gr. τριχίασις, f. τριχιᾶν to be hairy.] *Path.* a. Introversion of the eye-lashes. b. A disease in which small filamentous bodies are passed in the urine. c. A disease of the breasts in suckling women, in which the nipples crack into fine fissures.

‖**Trichina** (tri·kină, trikəi·nă). *Pl.* -æ. 1835. [mod.L., f. Gr. τρίχινος adj. 'of hair', f. θρίξ, τριχ- hair.] *Zool.* A genus of minute parasitic nematoid worms; *esp.* the species *T. spiralis*, which infests man and various animals, the adult inhabiting the intestinal tract, and the larvæ migrating to and becoming encysted in the muscular tissue, causing TRICHINOSIS. Hence **Tri·chinal** *a.* of or pertaining to the t. ‖**Trichini·asis** = TRICHINOSIS. **Tri·chinize** *v. trans.* to infect with trichinæ. **Tri·chinous** *a.* infested with trichinæ; affected with, or of the nature of, trichinosis.

Trichinopoli (tritʃinǫ·pǫli). Also **-poly.** 1863. Name of a district and city in the Madras presidency; used *attrib.*, as *T. cigar*; also *absol.* a T. cigar.

Trichinosis (trikinōᵘ·sis). 1866. [mod.L., f. *trichina* + -OSIS.] *Path.* A disease caused by the introduction of trichinæ into the alimentary canal, and the migration of their larvæ into the muscular tissue; characterized by digestive disturbance, slight fever, swelling, pain, and lameness in the muscles, etc.

Trichite (tri·kəit, trəi·-). 1868. [f. Gr. θρίξ, τριχ- hair + -ITE[1]; in 1, a. G. *trichit.*] 1. *Min.* A name for very minute dark-coloured hair-like bodies occurring in the substance of some vitreous rocks. 2. *Zool.* A name for extremely fine siliceous fibres occurring in certain sponge-spicules, or for such spicules themselves 1887. Hence **Trichi·tic** *a.*

Trichiurid (triki,yūᵊ·rid). 1819. [f. mod.L. *Trichiuridæ*, f. *Trichiurus*, prop. *Trichurus*, generic name, f. Gr. θρίξ, τριχ-hair + οὐρά tail.] *Ichthyol.* A fish of the family *Trichiuridæ*, typified by the genus *Trichiurus*, characterized by a ribbon-like body and a long filament at the end of the tail. So **Trichi,u·riform, Trichi,u·roid** *adjs.* having the form of the fishes of this genus or family.

Trichlor-, trichloro- (trəi,klōᵊ·rǫ). 1845. [f. TRI- III. c + CHLOR(O-.)] *Chem.* A formative expressing the substitution of three atoms of chlorine for hydrogen, as in *trichlorobenzene*, $C_6H_3Cl_3$.

Tricho- (trikǫ, trəikǫ), bef. a vowel **trich-** (trik, trəik), ad. Gr. τριχο-, τριχ-, comb. stem of θρίξ hair.

‖ **Trichobranchia** (trikǫbræ·ŋkiă), -æ, *Zool.* name for the gills, set with filaments, of certain decapod crustaceans; hence **Trichobra·nchial, Trichobra·nchiate** *adjs.* **Tri·chocyst** (-sist), *Zool.* one of a number of minute rod-like bodies, each containing a coiled protrusible filament, found in the cuticle of many *Infusoria*, resembling the thread-cells of cœlenterates; hence **Trichocy·stic** *a.* **Trichogyne** (-dʒəin) [Gr. γυνή], *Bot.* a hair-like process forming the receptive part of the female reproductive organ or procarp in certain algæ and fungi; hence **Trichogy·nial** (-dʒi·niăl), **Trichogynic** (-dʒi·nik) *adjs.* **Tricho·logy,** the study of the structure, functions, and diseases of the hair. ‖ **Trichomanes** (trikǫ·mănīz), *Bot.* a genus of ferns having filamentous outgrowths from the margins of the fronds; the bristle-ferns. **Tri·chophore** (-fōᵊɹ) [see -PHORE], (*a*) *Bot.* the structure which bears the trichogyne in florideous algæ; (*b*) *Zool.* one of several projections of the integument in certain annelids, from which spring bundles of setæ or bristles; **Trichophoric** (-fǫ·rik) *a.*, pertaining to or of the nature of a trichophore. **Tri·chophyte** [Gr. φυτόν], a genus of minute fungi, parasitic on the skin; esp. the species *Trichophyton tonsurans*, which produces ringworm. **Tricho·pter** [Gr. πτερόν wing], *Ent.* a member of the group *Trichoptera* of neuropterous insects, characterized by specially hairy wings; a caddis-fly; so **Tricho·pteran** *a.* = *trichopterous*; *sb.* = *trichopter*; **Tricho·pterous** *a.*, belonging to or having the characters of the *Trichoptera*, hairy-winged.

‖**Trichoma** (trikōᵘ·mă). 1799. [mod.L., a. Gr. τρίχωμα; see next.] 1. *Path.* A disease of the hair; = PLICA 1. 2. *Bot.* Each of the filaments composing the thallus in algæ of the order *Nostochineæ* 1866.

Trichome (tri·-, trəi·kōᵘm). 1875. [ad. Gr. τρίχωμα a growth of hair, f. τριχοῦν to cover with hair.] *Bot.* Any outgrowth of the epidermis or superficial tissue of a plant, as hairs, scales, prickles, etc.

Trichord (trəi·kǭɹd), *sb.* and *a.* 1776. [ad. Gr. τρίχορδος, f. τρι- TRI- + χορδή string.] A. *sb.* A musical instrument; of three strings; a three-stringed lyre or lute. B. *adj.* Having three strings to each note: applied to a pianoforte in which most of the keys have three strings each.

Trichotomize (tri-, trəikǫ·tŏməiz), *v.* 1651. [f. as next + -IZE.] *trans.* To divide into three parts; to arrange or classify in three divisions, or in groups of three.

Trichotomous (tri-, trəikǫ·tŏməs), *a.* 1800. [f. Gr. τρίχα triply + -τομος cut + -OUS.] 1. *Bot.* Dividing into three branches. 2. Making three divisions, classes, or categories; involving or of the nature of trichotomy 1855.

Trichotomy (tri-, trəikǫ·tŏmi). 1610. [f. as prec. + Gr. -τομία -TOMY.] Division into three; arrangement or classification in three divisions, classes, or categories.

Trichroic (trəikrōᵘ·ik), *a.* 1881. [f. Gr. τρίχροος, τρίχρους three-coloured + -IC.] Having or showing three colours; *spec.* of crystals, exhibiting three different colours when viewed in three different directions.

Trichroism (trəi·kro,iz'm). 1847. [f. as prec. + -ISM.] The property of being trichroic; *spec.* in *Cryst.*: see prec.

Trichromatic (trəi,kromæ·tik), *a.* 1891. [f. TRI- + χρωματικός CHROMATIC.] Having, showing, or pertaining to three colours; trichroic; *spec.* in *Optics*, having or relating to the three fundamental colour-sensations (red, green, violet) of normal vision. Applied also to lithographic printing in three colours. So **Trichro·matism. Trichro·mic** *a.* 1881.

Trick (trik), *sb.* late ME. [In sense 1, a. OF. dial. *trique*, cognate with *trikier* (mod.F. *tricher*), = Prov. *trichar*, It. *triccare*, perh. f. a late L. or Com. Rom. **triccare*, for *tricare*, *tricari* to trifle, play tricks, f. *tricæ* toys, trifles. Both sb. and vb. show developments of meaning unkn. in Fr.] I. 1. A crafty or fraudulent device of a mean or base kind; an artifice to deceive; a stratagem, ruse, wile. b. An illusory or deceptive appearance; a semblance, sham. *arch.* or *Obs.* 1592. 2. A freakish or mischievous act; a roguish prank; a frolic; a hoax, practical joke 1590. b. A capricious, foolish, or stupid act. Usu. *contempt.* or *depreciative.* 1591. 3. A clever or adroit expedient, device, or contrivance; a 'dexterous artifice' (J.); a 'dodge' 1573. 4. The art, knack, or faculty of doing something successfully 1611. 5. A feat of dexterity or skill, intended to surprise or amuse; a piece of jugglery or legerdemain 1606. 6. *concr.* A trifling ornament or toy; a trinket, bauble, knick-knack; hence *pl.*, small and trifling articles; 'traps'. *U.S.* 1553.

1. He was again at his old tricks FREEMAN. Phr. *To play one a t.*, *play* or *put a t.* or *tricks upon*: see PLAY *v.* I. 9, PUT *v.*[1] III. 13. 2. Fortune has played me such a cruel t. this day MRS. CARLYLE. b. It were but a fool's t. to die for conscience CARLYLE. 3. Rhetorical tricks HUME. The novelist..knows the tricks of his trade 1896. 5. You have more Tricks than a Dancing Bear SWIFT.

II. 1. A particular habit, way, or mode of acting. (Usu., a bad or unpleasant habit.) 1576. 2. a. A habit or fashion of dress. *arch.* 1543. b. A characteristic expression (of the face or voice) 1595. c. The mode of working a piece of mechanism, etc.; the system upon which a thing is constructed 1663. 3. *Naut.* The time allotted to a man on duty at the helm; a turn; *esp.* in *to take* or *stand one's t.* (*at the wheel*, etc.) 1669.

1. The t. of laughing frivolously is by all means to be avoided 1754. 2. b. The tricke of that voyce, I do well remember SHAKS.

III. *Her.* A sketch in pen and ink of a coat of arms. *In t.*, sketched in pen and ink. 1572. **IV.** *Card-playing.* The cards (usu. four) played, and won or 'taken' in one round, collectively; hence, *to take a* or *the t.* *Odd t.*: see ODD *a.* 1 1599.

Phrases. *A t. worth two of that*, a much better plan or expedient. *To do the t.*, to do what is wanted. *attrib.* and *Comb.* (chiefly in sense I. 5): Of, pertaining to, or in the nature of a t. or tricks, skilled in or trained to perform tricks, as *t.-cycling, -cyclist, -riding, -writing*, etc.

Trick, *v.* 1500. [app. f. prec. Branches II and III may be of different origin.] **I. 1.** *trans.* To deceive by a trick; to cheat 1595. **b.** *absol.* or *intr.* To practise trickery; to cheat 1700. **2.** To get or effect by trickery (*rare*) 1662. **3.** *intr.* To play tricks or trifle *with* 1881.

1. To t. a gauger was thought an excellent joke MAR. EDGEWORTH. 2. The trick..of a tricked marriage is common in Congreve 1895.

II. 1. *trans.* To dress; to deck, prank; to adorn (usu. with the notion of artifice) 1500. **b.** *transf.* To dress *up*, to prepare (food). *rare.* 1824. †**2.** To adjust, arrange, trim –1810.

1. Till civil-suited Morn appeer, Not trickt and frounc't..But Cherchef't in a comly Cloud MILT. She was well tutored and tricked off for the occasion 1821.

III. To sketch or draw in outline; *spec.* in *Her.*, to draw (a coat of arms) in outline, the tinctures being denoted by initial letters (*o, a, s*, etc.) or by signs. Also with *out.* 1545.

The..shields of arms recorded in the MS. are.. 'tricked',..thus necessitating a description of the bearings 1859.

†**Trick,** *a.* and *adv.* 1542. [Cf. TRIG *a.* Origin obsc.] **A.** *adj.* **1.** Smart, clever, nimble, 'neat' (*rare*) –1593. **2.** Trim, neat, handsome; smart, 'fine' –1630.

2. A neighbour mine..That maried had a tricke and bonny lasse SIDNEY.

B. *adv.* **1.** Cleverly, 'neatly', 'finely' –1584. **2.** Neatly, smartly, elegantly, 'trigly' –1658.

2. Unless you coy it t. and trim 1594.

Tri·cker. 1629. Early and dial. form of TRIGGER [1].

Trickery (tri·kəri). 1800. [f. TRICK *sb.* + -ERY.] The practice of tricks; deceitful conduct or practice; deception, artifice; imposture.

Trickish (tri·kiʃ), *a.* 1705. [f. TRICK *sb.* + -ISH [1].] **1.** Given to tricks or trickery; rather tricky, crafty, or cunning. **2.** = TRICKY 2. 1900. Hence **Tri·ckish-ly** *adv.*, **-ness.**

Trickle (tri·k'l), *sb.* 1580. [f. next.] A falling or flowing drop; a tear; a small quantity of liquid; a small fitful stream.

Trickle (tri·k'l), *v.*[1] late ME. [perh. orig. *strikle* as in Chaucer *Prioress' T.* 222 (Lansdowne MS.), a frequent. of ME. *striken* STRIKE *v.*] **1.** *intr.* To flow or fall in successive drops. Also, to flow in a very scanty and halting stream. **b.** *transf.* and *fig.* 1628. **2.** To emit falling or flowing drops; to drip or run (*with* tears, blood, etc.); to shed tears. late ME. **3.** *trans.* To give forth in successive drops or a thin fitful stream; also, to cause to trickle 1602.

1. Hise salte teeris trikled doun as reyn CHAUCER. A small glacier trickles into the desolate valley 1871. **b.** Fluent nonsense trickles from his tongue POPE. **2.** Mine eye trickleth downe and ceaseth not *Lam.* iii. 49. *Comb.*: **t.-charger**, a device for charging a low-tension accumulator from a supply of alternating high-tension current.

Tri·ckle, *v.*[2] orig. *dial.* 1825. [app. orig. East Anglian var. of TRUCKLE *v.*; in *Golf*, usu. assoc. w. prec.] *trans.* To trundle, to bowl. In *Golf*, to cause (the ball) to roll very slowly and gently. Also *intr.* of the ball.

Trickment (tri·kmĕnt). *rare.* 1619. [f. TRICK *v.* + -MENT.] Decoration, adornment.

Trickster (tri·kstəɹ). 1711. [f. TRICK *sb.* or *v.* + -STER.] One who practises trickery; a rogue, cheat, knave.

Tricksy (tri·ksi), *a.* 1552. [app. f. *tricks*, pl. of TRICK *sb.* + -Y [1].] **1.** Artfully trimmed or decked; spruce, fine, smart. **2.** Full of or given to tricks or pranks 1596. **3.** Full of tricks or deception; crafty, cunning, cheating 1766. **4.** = TRICKY *a.* 2. 1835.

3. T. trout 1856. 4. Kidderminster is a t. borough 1862. Hence **Tri·cksily** *adv.* **Tri·cksiness.**

Tricky (tri·ki), *a.* 1786. [f. TRICK *sb.* + -Y [1].] **1.** Given to or characterized by trickery. **b.** Skilled in performing clever tricks 1887. **2.** Having the deceptive character of a trick; needing cautious action or handling; risky, catchy, ticklish (*colloq.*) 1887.

2. Revolvers are t. things for young hands to deal with KIPLING. Hence **Tri·ckily** *adv.* **Tri·ckiness.**

‖**Triclinium** (trəikli·niŏm, tri,kləi·niŏm). *Pl.* -ia. 1646. [L., a Gr. τρικλίνιον, dim. of τρίκλινος, f. κλίνη couch, bed.] *Rom. Antiq.* A couch, running round three sides of a table, on which to recline at meals; also, a room for eating in; a dining-room. Hence **Tricli·nial** *a.* pertaining to a t.

Tricolour, tricolor (trəi·kɒləɹ), *a.* and *sb.* 1798. [ad. late L. *tricolor, -orem*, and F. *tricolore.*] **A.** *adj.* Having three colours; three-coloured 1815. **B.** *sb.* A tricolour flag, cockade, etc.; *esp.* the national flag of France adopted at the Revolution, consisting of equal vertical stripes of blue, white, and red 1798. So **Tri·coloured, -colored** *a.* (often with hyphen) 1795.

Tricorn (trəi·kǭɹn, tri·-), *a.* and *sb.* Also (as Fr.) tricorne. 1760. [ad. F. *tricorne* or L. *tricornis*, f. *tri-* TRI- + L. *cornu* horn.] **A.** *adj.* Having three horns or horn-like projections; *spec.* applied to a cocked hat with the brim turned up on three sides 1844. **B.** *sb.* **1.** An (imaginary) creature with three horns 1760. **2.** A tricorn hat 1876.

Tri·cosane, tri-i·cosane. 1894. [f. Gr. τρία three + εἴκοσι twenty + -ANE.] *Chem.* A hydrocarbon belonging to the paraffin series, containing 23 atoms of carbon.

‖**Tricot** (trī·ko). 1872. [F., f. *tricoter* to knit; etym. unkn.] Knitting; knitted work or fabric; a woollen fabric, knitted by hand, or by machinery in imitation of hand-knitting.

Tric-trac (tri·k,træ·k). Also **trick-track.** 1687. [a. F.; so called from the clicking sound made by the pieces in playing the game.] An old variety of backgammon.

Tricuspid (trəikɒ·spid), *a.* (*sb.*) 1670. [ad. L. *tricuspis, -pidem*, f. *tri-* TRI- + *cuspis* point.] Having three cusps or points. Also *absol.* or as *sb.*; hence *attrib.*

T. valve or **valves** (*Anat.*), the valve consisting of three triangular segments (or, as otherwise regarded, the set of three triangular valves) which guards the opening from the right auricle into the right ventricle of the heart. **Tricu·spidal, Tricu·spidate** *adjs.*

Tricycle (trəi·sik'l), *sb.* 1868. [a. F., f. TRI- + Gr. κύκλος circle, wheel.] A velocipede with three wheels (now usu. one in front and one on each side behind) driven by treadles actuated by the feet, or (*motor t.*) by a small motor attachment. Hence **Tri·cycle** *v. intr.* to ride a t.

‖**Tridacna** (trəi-, tridæ·knă). 1776. [mod. L., f. Gr. τρίδακνος eaten at three bites, f. τρι- TRI- + δάκνειν to bite.] *Zool.* A genus of bivalve molluscs, including the *T. gigas* or Giant Clam, the largest bivalve shell known.

Tridecane (trəi·dĕkēⁱn). 1894. [f. Gr. τρία three + δέκα ten + -ANE.] *Chem.* A colourless liquid hydrocarbon of the paraffin series, containing 13 atoms of carbon. So **Tridecyl** (trəi·dĕsil) [-YL], the radical ($C_{13}H_{27}$) contained in t.

Trident (trəi·dĕnt), *sb.* (*a.*) 1599. [ad. L. *tridens, tridentem*, f. *tri-* three + *dens, dentem* tooth.] **1.** An instrument or weapon with three prongs. **a.** *esp.* A three-pronged fish-spear or sceptre as the attribute of the sea-god Poseidon or Neptune, also figured as borne by Britannia. **b.** A three-pronged spear used by the *retiarius* in ancient Roman gladiatorial combats (*rare*) 1693. **c.** *transf.* and *fig.* 1638. **2.** *Geom.* A plane cubic curve of a form suggesting a three-pronged weapon; also *t. curve* 1710. **3.** as *adj.* Having three prongs or forks; tridental 1589. Hence **Tride·ntal** *a.* three-pronged, trifurcate. **Tri·dented** *a.* having a t.

Tridentine (tri·dĕntəin, trəide·ntəin), *a.* and *sb.* 1561. [ad. med.L. *Tridentinus*, f. *Tridentum* TRENT.] **A.** *adj.* Of or pertaining to the city of Trent in Tyrol, or to the Council of the Roman Catholic Ch. held there (1545–63). **B.** *sb.* One who accepts and conforms to the decrees of the Council of Trent 1836.

Triduan (trəi·diu,ăn), *a.* 1597. [ad. L. *triduanus*, f. *triduum*; see -AN.] Lasting for three days; also, occurring every third day.

‖**Triduo** (trī·duo). 1848. [It. and Sp.:—L. *triduum.*] *Eccl.* = next.

‖**Triduum** (trəi·diu,ŏm). 1883. [L., prop. neut. of **triduus* adj. (sc. *spatium*), f. *tri-* TRI- + *dies* day.] A period of three days; *esp.* of religious observance.

Tridymite (tri·dimait). 1868. [ad. G. *tridymit*, f. Gr. τρίδυμος threefold, f. TRI- + -δυμος; its compound forms consisting of three individual crystals.] *Min.* A crystallized form of silica, occurring in small hexagonal tables, found in trachyte and other igneous rocks.

Tried (trəid), *ppl. a.* ME. [f. TRY *v.* + -ED [1].] †**1.** Separated from the dross or refuse; of fat: rendered, clarified; of flour, etc.: sifted, bolted, fine. –1639. **2.** Proved or tested by experience or examination. late ME.

2. Public men of t. abilities 1841.

Triennial (trəi,e·niăl), *a.* and *sb.* 1620. [f. L. *triennis* of three years (f. *tri-* TRI- + *annus*) + -AL.] **A.** *adj.* **1.** Existing or lasting for three years; changed every three years 1640. **2.** Recurring every three years 1620. **B.** *sb.* **1.** A period of three years 1661. **2.** An event recurring every three years; *spec.* the visitation of his diocese by a bishop every three years 1640.

A. 1. *T. Act.*, an act of 1640, limiting the duration of parliament in England to three years. 2. There was a t. change of officers 1872. Hence **Tri,e·nnially** *adv.* every three years; once in three years.

‖**Triennium** (trəi,e·niŏm). 1847. [L., prop. neut. of **triennius* adj. (sc. *spatium*), f. *tri-* TRI- + *annus* year.] A space or period of three years.

‖**Triens** (trəi·enz). *Pl.* **trientes** (trəi,e·ntīz). 1601. [L., = third part.] The third part of anything; *spec.* in *Rom. Antiq.* a copper coin worth one-third of the as; also, in later times, a gold coin, one-third of the aureus.

Trier (trəi·əɹ). ME. [f. TRY *v.* + -ER [1].] **1.** One who examines judicially; a judge. **2.** *pl.* Two persons appointed by a court of law to determine whether a challenge made to the panel of jurors, or to any of them, is well founded 1511. **3.** *Hist. pl.* A committee appointed by the King to determine to which court petitions should be referred, and, if necessary, to report them to the parliament 1844. **4.** *pl.* Members of the House of Lords sitting as a jury at the trial of a peer for treason or felony. In full, *lords triers.* 1539. **5.** One who or that which tests or proves something; a prover; a tester or test 1483. **6.** One who tries or attempts to do something; one who persists in trying *colloq.* 1891. **7.** Something devised to test or try quality; something trying or difficult 1797.

Trierarch (trəi·ĕrāɹk). 1656. [ad. L. *trierarchus*, Gr. τριήραρχος, -αρχης, f. τριήρης trireme + -αρχος ruling, ruler.] *Gr. Hist.* **a.** The commander of a trireme. **b.** A citizen who, singly or in conjunction with others, was charged with the duty of fitting out a trireme or galley for the public service. So **Tri·erarchal** *a.*

Trierarchy (trəi·ĕrāɹki). 1837. [ad. Gr. τριηραρχία, f. τριήραρχος TRIERARCH.] The position or office of a trierarch. **b.** The trierarchs collectively 1882.

Trieteric (trəi,ĭte·rik), *a.* and *sb.* 1592. [ad. Gr. τριετηρικός, L. *trietericus*, f. τριετηρίς a festival celebrated every third, i. e. alternate, year, f. τρι- three + ἔτος year.] **A.** *adj.* Taking place every alternate year, as the festivals of Bacchus and other divinities 1656. **B.** *sb.* (also *pl.*) A festival, esp. of Bacchus, celebrated every alternate year 1592.

Triethyl (trəi,ī·þəil, -e·þil). 1858. [f. TRI- III + ETHYL.] *Chem.* A formative denoting the presence of three ethyl groups, C_2H_5, in a compound. **b.** *spec.* denoting the substitution of three ethyl groups for three hydrogen atoms in the substance designated by the rest of the name.

Trifarious (trəifēᵊ·riəs), *a. rare.* 1656. [f. L. *trifarius* + -OUS.] **1.** Of three sorts; facing three ways. **2.** *Bot.* Arranged in three rows 1846.

Trifid (trəi·fid), *a.* 1628. [ad. L. *trifidus*, f. *tri-* TRI- + *fid-*, stem of *findere* to split.] Split into three by deep clefts or notches; *esp.* in *Bot.* and *Zool.* **b.** *gen.* Tripartite (*rare*) 1871.

Trifle (trəi·fl), *sb.* [ME. *trufle*, etc., a. OF. *trufle*, *truffle*, parallel forms of *trufe*, *truffe*, trickery, deception; of unkn. origin.] †**1.** A false or idle tale, told (*a*) to deceive, cheat, or befool, (*b*) to divert; a lying story, a fiction; a jest or joke; a foolish, trivial, or nonsensical saying –1681. **2.** Hence, a matter of little value or importance; 'a thing of no moment' (J.); a trivial, paltry, or insignificant affair ME. †**b.** *transf.* A trifler –1716. **3.** *concr.* A small article of little intrinsic value; a toy, trinket, bauble. late ME. **4.** A literary work, piece of music, etc., light or trivial in style; a bagatelle. Often used in meiosis. 1579. **5.** A small sum of money, or a sum treated as of no moment; a slight 'consideration' 1595. **b.** An insignificant quantity or amount 1722. **c.** *A t.* (advb.): To a trifling extent; a little; somewhat, rather 1859. **6.** A light confection of sponge-cake or the like (freq. flavoured with wine or spirit), served with custard, whipped cream, etc. 1781. **7.** A kind of pewter of medium hardness; in *pl.* also, articles made of this 1610.

2. Trifles light as ayre, Are to the iealious, confirmations strong As proofes of holy Writ SHAKS. He 's a mighty exact Man about Trifles 1706. **4.** Poems to Stella, and trifles to Dr. Sheridan, fill up a great part of that period 1751. **5. c.** Jehu is a t. below middle height 1887.

Trifle (trəi·f'l), *v.* [ME. a. OF. *truffler*, *truiffler*, parallel form of *truffer*, *trufer* to make sport of, deceive, laugh at.] †**1.** *trans.* To cheat, delude, befool; to mock (*rare*) –1533. †**2.** *intr.* To say what is untrue, to jest in order to cheat, mock, amuse, or make sport –1602. **b.** *T. with*: To treat with a lack of seriousness or respect; to 'play' or dally with 1523. **3.** *intr.* To toy, play (*with* a material object); to fiddle, fidget *with* 1460. **4.** To dally, loiter; to waste time. late ME. †**5.** *trans.* To waste (time). *Obs.* exc. as in b. –1742. **b.** esp. with *away* 1532. †**6.** To make a trifle of. SHAKS. **7.** *intr.* To act (or speak) idly or frivolously, esp. in serious circumstances 1736.

2. b. He shall not t. with your affections 1852. **2.** O'er cold coffee t. with the spoon POPE. **5.** We t. time, I pray thee pursue sentence SHAKS. **b.** Come Lords we t. time away SHAKS. **6.** *Macb.* II. iv. 4. Hence **Tri·fler**, one who trifles; one who is not serious or earnest in what he does.

Trifling (trəi·fliŋ), *vbl. sb.* late ME. [-ING [1].] The action of TRIFLE *v.*

Agreeable t. or *badinage* CHESTERF. The solemn t. of the schools KINGSLEY.

Tri·fling, *ppl. a.* late ME. [-ING [2].] †**1.** Cheating, false, feigning –1560. **2.** Behaving idly or frivolously; frivolous; foolish 1535. **3.** Of little moment or value; trumpery; insignificant, petty 1538.

3. The worke of 10 years study for a t. reward EVELYN. Hence **Tri·fling-ly** *adv.*, **-ness.**

Trifoliate (trəifōu·liĕt), *a.* 1753. [f. TRI- + L. *foliatus* leaved.] Three-leaved; *esp.* in *Bot.* consisting of three leaflets, as a compound leaf; also of a plant, having such leaves; *transf.* having the form of such a leaf. Also **Trifo·liated** *a.* *Bot.* = prec.; *Arch.* having or consisting of trefoils 1698.

‖**Trifolium** (trifōu·liŏm, trəi-). 1625. [L., f. *tri-* TRI- + *folium.*] *Bot.* A large genus of leguminous plants with trifoliate leaves, and flowers mostly in close heads; including many valuable fodder-plants, known as *clovers* or *trefoils*; *spec.* in recent agricultural use, applied to the genus *T. incarnatum.*

‖**Triforium** (trəifōə·riŏm). *Pl.* **-ia.** 1703. [med.(Anglo-)L.; etym. unkn.] *Arch.* A gallery or arcade in the wall over the arches at the sides of the nave and choir, and sometimes of the transepts, in some large churches: orig. applied to that in Canterbury Cathedral; in the 19th c. extended as a general term.

Triform (trəi·fɒɹm), *a.* 1450. [ad. L. *triformis*, f. *tri-* + *forma* FORM.] **1.** Having a triple form; combining three different forms; formed in three parts. **2.** Existing or appearing in three different forms 1623.

2. The neighbouring Moon..With borrowd light her countenance t. Hence fills and empties MILT. So **Tri·formity** (*rare*), the quality of being t.

Trig (trig), *sb.*[1] 1647. [Goes w. TRIG *v.*[1]] A wedge or block placed under a wheel or cask to prevent it from rolling; hence *gen.*, a brake.

Trig (trig), *a.* (*sb.*[2]) ME., orig. *north.* and *Sc.* [a. ON. *tryggr* = Goth. *triggws* TRUE.] **1.** True, faithful, trusty. Now only *n. dial.* **2.** Trim or tight in person, shape, or appearance; of a place: neat, tidy. Chiefly *Sc.* and *dial.* 1513. **b.** Trim or neat in dress; spruce, smart 1725. **3.** Strong, sound, well; also, firm, steady 1704. **4.** Prim, precise, exact; cut and dried, smug (*rare*) 1793. †**B.** *sb.* A dandy, a coxcomb. B. JONS.

2. b. She really looked very smart and t. and jaunty 1893. **4.** Our system of t. and prig theology 1872. Hence **Tri·g-ly** *adv.*, **-ness.**

Trig, *v.*[1] 1591. [Origin obsc.; perh. ad. ON. *tryggja* to make firm or secure, f. *tryggr* firm, sure, true: see prec.] **1.** *trans.* To make firm or fast; to prevent from moving; *esp.* to apply a wedge, block, etc. to (a wheel). **2.** To wedge up; to prop (*up*) 1711.

Trig, *v.*[2] Now *dial.* 1660. [f. TRIG *a.*] **1.** *trans.* To make trig or trim; now often, to dress smartly: freq. with *out.* 1696. **2.** To fill full, to stuff, cram 1660.

Trigamous (tri·gæməs), *a.* 1842. [f. Gr. τρίγαμος thrice married (f. τρι- + -γάμος wedding) + -OUS.] **1.** Characterized by, involving, or living in trigamy 1886. **2.** *Bot.* Having male, female, and hermaphrodite flowers in the same head 1842.

Trigamy (tri·gămi). 1615. [ad. late L. *trigamia*, a. (eccl.) Gr. τριγαμία, f. τρίγαμος (see prec.).] **1.** *Eccl. Law.* Marriage for the third time after the death of former wives or husbands. *Obs.* or *arch.* **2.** The state of having three wives or husbands at the same time; the crime of contracting a third marriage while two previous spouses are alive 1634. So **Tri·gamist.**

Trigeminal (trəiˌdʒe·minăl), *a.* (*sb.*) 1830. [f. L. *trigeminus* born three at a birth + -OUS.] *Anat.* Applied to the fifth pair of cranial nerves, from their dividing into three branches; also *absol.* as *sb.* **b.** Pertaining to, occurring in, or affecting the t. nerve 1874.

‖**Trigeminus** (trəiˌdʒe·minŏs). 1706. [L., f. TRI- + L. *geminus* born at the same birth.] †**1.** The complexus muscle. **2.** The trigeminal nerve 1875.

Trigesimal (trəiˌdʒe·simăl), *a. rare.* 1637. [f. L. *trigesimus* thirtieth + -AL.] †**a.** Thirtieth. **b.** *loosely.* Consisting of thirty.

Trigger[1] (tri·gəɹ). 1621. [orig. *tricker*, ad. Du. *trekker* a trigger, f. *trekken* to pull.] **1.** A movable catch or lever the pulling or pressing of which releases a detent or spring, and sets some force or mechanism in action, e.g. springs a trap. **2.** *spec.* A small steel catch which on being 'drawn', 'pulled', or pressed by the finger, releases the hammer of a gunlock 1622.

Comb.: **t. finger**, the forefinger of the right hand, with which the t. is pulled; **-fish**, a fish of the genus *Balistes*; so named from the trigger-like second spine of the dorsal-fin. **b.** Also freq. *fig.* 'operating like a t.', as *t. action*, *question.*

Trigger[2] (tri·gəɹ). 1591. [f. TRIG *v.*[1] + -ER [1].] **1.** A device or appliance to retard or stop the motion of a vehicle descending a slope. Now *dial.* **2.** *Ship-building.* A support holding the dog-shore in position; also *transf.* the dog-shore itself 1867.

Trigintal (trəiˌdʒi·ntăl). Now only *Hist.* 1491. [ad. med.L. *trigintale*, f. L. *triginta*; see -AL.] = TRENTAL.

Triglyph (trəi·glif). 1563. [ad. L. *triglyphus*, a. Gr. τρίγλυφος thrice-grooved, f. τρι- TRI- + γλυφή carving.] *Arch.* A member or ornament in the Doric order, consisting of a block or tablet with three vertical grooves or glyphs (strictly, two whole grooves, and a half-groove on each side), repeated at regular intervals along the frieze, usu. one over each column, and one in two between every two columns. Hence **Trigly·phic, -al** *adjs.* pertaining to or of the nature of a t.

Trigon (trəi·gɒn). 1563. [ad. L. *trigonum*, ad. Gr. τρίγωνον triangle, neut. of τρίγωνος, f. τρι- TRI- + -γωνος -angled, -cornered.] **1.** A figure having three angles and three sides; a triangle. **2.** *Astrol.* **a.** A set of three signs of the zodiac, distant 120° from each other, as if at the angles of an equilateral triangle. **b.** = TRINE *sb.* 2. 1563. **3.** An ancient lyre or harp of triangular form 1727. **4.** An ancient game at ball, played by three persons 1842.

Trigonal (tri·gŏnăl), *a.* 1570. [ad. L. *trigonalis*; see prec. and -AL.] **1.** Of, pertaining, or relating to a trigon or triangle; triangular. **b.** *Geom.* and *Cryst.* Applied to a solid figure with triangular faces, or having some other relation to a triangle. Also, having a relation to three angles. 1878. **2.** Triangular in section, triquetrous: now *esp.* in *Zool.* and *Bot.* 1571.

Trigone (trigōu·n, trəi·gōun). 1835. [a. F., ad. L. *trigonum* TRIGON.] *Anat.* The triangular area at the base of the urinary bladder, between the openings of the ureters and urethra.

Trigono- (tri·gŏno, trigōu·no), comb. form repr. Gr. τρίγωνος adj. three-cornered, etc., neut. τρίγωνον as sb. a triangle; as in **Trigonocerous** (-ǫ·sĕrəs) *a.* [Gr. κέρας horn], *Zool.* having horns of triangular section.

Trigonometric (tri:gŏnoˌme·trik), *a.* 1811. [f. TRIGONOMETRY + -IC.] = next.

Trigonometrical (tri:gŏnoˌme·trikăl), *a.* 1666. [f. as prec. + -AL.] Of, pertaining to, or performed by trigonometry.

T. functions, those functions of an angle, or of an abstract quantity, used in trigonometry, viz. the sine, tangent, secant, etc. *T. survey*, a survey of a country or region performed by triangulation and t. calculation. Hence **Tri·gonome·trically** *adv.*

Trigonometry (trigŏnǫ·mĕtri). 1614. [ad. mod.L. *trigonometria*, f. Gr. τρίγωνον triangle + -μετρία measurement.] That branch of mathematics which deals with the measurement of the sides and angles of triangles, particularly with certain functions of their angles, or of angles in general (the SINE, COSINE, TANGENT, COTANGENT, SECANT, and COSECANT), and hence with these functions as applied to abstract quantities; thus including the theory of triangles, of angles, and of (elementary) singly periodic functions. Hence **Trigono·meter**, a person versed in t.

‖**Trigonon** (trigōu·nɒn). 1727. [a. Gr. τρίγωνον.] *Antiq.* = TRIGON 3.

Trigonous (tri·gŏnəs), *a.* 1821. [f. Gr. τρίγωνος + -OUS.] *Nat. Hist.* = TRIGONAL 2.

Trigram (trəi·græm). 1606. [f. Gr. τρι- TRI- + γράμμα, -ατ- line, letter, or γραμμή stroke, line.] **a.** An inscription of three letters; also = TRIGRAPH. **b.** A figure or character formed of three strokes. **c.** *Geom.* A set of three lines; *spec.* the figure formed by three straight lines in one plane not intersecting in the same point. So **Trigramma·tic, Trigra·mmic** *adjs.* consisting of three letters or sets of letters. **Trigra·mmatism** = TRILITERALISM.

Trigraph (trəi·graf). 1836. [f. Gr. τρι- TRI- + γραφή writing, drawing.] A combination of three letters denoting a simple sound, as *eau* in F. *beau*, *sch* in G. *schaf.*

‖**Trigynia** (trəiˌdʒi·niă). 1760. [mod.L. (Linn.), f. TRI- + Gr. γυνή woman, taken as = female organ, pistil.] *Bot.* An order in many classes of the Linnæan system, comprising plants having three pistils. Hence **Tri·gyn**, a plant of the order *T.* **Trigy·nian, Trigy·nious** *adjs.* of or belonging to the order *T.* **Trigynous** (tri·dʒinəs) *a.* having three pistils.

Trihedral (trəihī·drăl, -he·drăl), *a.* (*sb.*) Also **triedral.** 1789. [f. Gr. τρι- TRI- + ἕδρα base + -AL.] *Geom.*, etc. Of a solid figure or body: Having three sides or faces (in addition to the base or ends); triangular in section.

T. angle or *quoin*, a solid angle formed by three surfaces meeting at a point.

B. *sb.* *Geom.* A trihedral figure 1909. Also **Trihe·dron.** 1828.

Trike (trəik). Colloq. abbrev. of TRICYCLE.

Trilateral (trəilæ·tĕrăl), *a.* and *sb.* 1660. [f. L. *trilaterus* three-sided + -AL.] **A.** *adj.* Contained by three sides; three-sided. **B.** *sb.* A triangle 1766. **Trila·teral-ly** *adv.*, **-ness.**

Trilby (tri·lbi). 1895. [Name of the heroine of a novel (1893) of the same name by G. du Maurier.] (Usu. *attrib.*) Applied to various articles resembling those used or worn in the dramatized version of the novel; esp. **a** kind of soft felt hat worn by men; also *pl.* (*slang*) the feet (in allusion to the heroine's bare feet).

Trilemma (trəile·mă). 1672. [f. after DILEMMA; see TRI-.] A situation, or (in *Logic*) a syllogism, of the nature of a DILEMMA, but involving three alternatives instead of two.

Trilinear (trəili·niăɹ), *a.* 1715. [f. TRI- + L. *linearis* LINEAR, f. *linea* line.] *Geom.* Of, contained by, or having some relation to, three lines.

T. co-ordinates, a system of co-ordinates determining a point in a plane by its distances, measured in three fixed directions, from three fixed straight lines forming a triangle.

Triliteral (trəili·tĕrăl), *a.* (*sb.*) 1751. [f. TRI- + L. *littera* + -AL.] Consisting of three letters. **B.** *sb.* A triliteral word or root 1828. Hence **Trili·teralism**, the use of t. roots, as in Semitic languages. **Trilitera·lity, Trili·teralness**, t. character. **Trili·terally** *adv.*

Trilith (trəi·liþ). Also in Gr. form **trilithon** (trəi·liþǫn). 1740. [ad. Gr. τρίλιθον, neut. of τρίλιθος adj., of three stones, f. τρι- TRI- + λίθος stone.] A prehistoric structure or monument consisting of three large stones, two upright and one resting upon them as a lintel. Hence **Trili·thic** *a.* pertaining to or of the nature of a t.

Trill (tril), *sb.* 1649. [Goes with TRILL *v.*[3]; ad. It. *trillo*, beside *triglio*, 'a quiver or warble in singing' (Florio).] **1.** *Mus.* **a.** A tremulous utterance of a note or notes as a 'grace'. **b.** A rapid alternation of two notes a degree apart; a shake. **2.** *transf.* A tremulous high-pitched sound or succession of notes, esp. in the singing of birds 1704. **3.** *Phonetics.* The pronunciation of a consonant, esp. *r*, with vibration of the tongue or other part of the vocal organs; a consonant so pronounced 1848.

Trill (tril), *v.*[1] Now *dial.* or *arch.* [ME. *trille*; cf. Sw. and Norw. *trilla*, Da. *trilde*, *trille* to roll, trundle, wheel.] **1.** *trans.* To turn (a thing) round, to cause to revolve, rotate; to roll, bowl, trundle. †**2.** *intr.* Of a wheel, ball, etc.: To revolve, spin, roll, trundle -1681.

Trill, *v.*[2] *arch.* ME. [perh. developed from prec.] **1.** *intr.* Of tears, water, a stream: To roll, to flow in a slender stream, the particles of water being in constant revolution; to purl. **2.** *trans.* To cause to flow in this way 1485.

1. With many a teere trilling on my cheeke CHAUCER. A little dell, through which trilled a small rivulet SCOTT.

Trill, *v.*[3] 1666. [ad. It. *trillare*, cogn. w. *triglio*, *trillo* TRILL *sb.*] **1.** *intr.* To sing with vibratory effect; to sing a trill or shake, to 'shake'; of a voice, etc.: To sound with tremulous vibration. **2.** *trans.* To utter or sing (a note, tune, etc.) with tremulous vibration of sound 1701. **b.** To cause (an instrument or the voice) to vibrate with a tremulous sound 1848. **3.** To pronounce (a consonant, esp. *r*) with a vibration of the tongue (or other vocal organ) and the corresponding auditory effect 1848.

1. My wife..proud that she shall come to t., and.. I think she will PEPYS. 2. The sober suited songstress trills her lay THOMSON.

Trilling (tri·liŋ). 1846. [= Da., Sw. *trilling*, Du. *drieling*; see TRI- and -LING.] One of a set of three. **a.** One of three children born at the same birth; a triplet. **b.** *Min.* A crystal composed of three individuals.

Trillion (tri·lyən). 1690. [= F., It. *trillione*, from the stem of *million* with substitution of *tri-*; cf. *billion*.] The third power of a million; a million billions, i.e. millions of millions. (In France and local U.S., a thousand 'billions', i.e. an English billion; see BILLION.)

‖**Trillium** (tri·liŏm). 1760. [mod.L. (Linn.), in allusion to the triple leaves.] *Bot.* A genus of perennial endogenous herbs (family *Trilliaceæ*) bearing a whorl of three thin short-stalked or stalkless leaves at the summit of a simple stem, with a solitary flower in the middle. In America also called *wake-robin*. Also, a plant of this genus.

‖**Trillo** (tri·llo). 1651. [It.] = TRILL *sb.*

Trilobite (trəi·lobəit, tri·-). 1832. [ad. mod.L. *Trilobites*, f. Gr. τρι- TRI- + λοβός lobe + -ITE[1].] *Palæont.* A member of a large group of extinct arthropodous animals, characterized by a three-lobed body; allied to the extinct Eurypterids and the existing King-crabs (*Limulus*); their remains are found abundantly in Palæozoic rocks, esp. the Silurian. Hence **Trilobi·tic** *a.* pertaining to, of the nature of, or containing trilobites.

Trilogy (tri·lŏdʒi). 1661. [ad. Gr. τριλογία, f. τρι- TRI- + λόγος; see -LOGY.] **1.** *Gr. Antiq.* A series of three tragedies (orig. connected in subject) performed at Athens at the festival of Dionysus 1836. **2.** Any series or group of three related dramatic or other literary works 1661. **3.** *transf.* and *fig.* A group of three related utterances, subjects, etc. 1835.

1. All the plays of Æschylus, and the Henry VI of Shakespeare, are examples of a t. 1842. Hence **Trilo·gic, -al** *adjs.* of or pertaining to a t.

Trim (trim), *sb.* 1590. [f. TRIM *v.*] **I.** *Naut.* **1.** The state of being trimmed or prepared for sailing; esp. the condition of being 'fully rigged and ready to sail'. **2. a.** The most advantageous set of a ship in the water on her fore and aft line. **b.** Adjustment of the sails with ref. to the direction of the wind and the ship's course. **c.** The condition of being properly balanced. **d.** The difference between the draught forward and the draught aft 1614. **e.** In vague use, the general appearance or look of a ship 1757.

2. e. In gallant t. the gilded Vessel goes GRAY.

II. 1. Adornment, array; equipment, outfit; dress: usu. in ref. to style or appearance; hence occas. nearly = guise, aspect 1596. **b.** The act of trimming or condition of being trimmed 1608. **2.** Condition, state, or order, esp. for work or action of any kind 1628. **3.** The nature, character, or manner of a person or thing; his or its 'way' 1706.

1. Bucklaw, in bridegroom t. SCOTT. *fig.* The Paint, and T. of Retorick 1650. **c.** *U.S.* The lighter woodwork of a building, esp. around openings 1884. 2. Phr. *In t., into t.*, in or into proper condition or order.

Trim, *a.* (*adv.*) 1503. [Hist. obsc.] **1.** In good condition or order; well prepared, furnished, or equipped; fit, proper, suitable; hence, sound, good, fine, beautiful. (Often a vague term of approval.) *arch.* **2.** Neatly or smartly made, prepared, or arranged; elegantly or finely dressed or 'got up'; having a neat, spruce, or tidy appearance or effect 1521. †**3.** In ironical use; cf. 'fine', 'nice', 'pretty', in similar use -1680. **B.** *adv.* Trimly 1529.

1. 'Twas t. sport for them that had the doing of it SHAKS. The ship was t. BYRON. 2. Laurel hedges, but not so t. as ours BERKELEY. A t. and quiet girl came tripping to the door 1888. 3. News quoth a? T. News truly. OTWAY. Hence **Tri·m·ly** *adv.*, **-ness.**

Trim (trim), *v.* [OE. *trymman, trymian*:—**trumjan* to make firm or strong, f. OE. *trum* firm, strong, steadfast, stable. Not found between OE. and the 16th c.] †**I.** (Only OE.) *trans.* To make firm or strong; to give as security; to arm or array (a force); to settle, arrange; to encourage, comfort, exhort. **II.** †**1.** To put into proper condition for some purpose or use; to prepare; to dress -1725. **2.** To fit out (a ship, etc.) for sea. *arch.* 1513. †**3.** To repair, restore, put right (something broken, worn or decayed) -1687. **4.** *spec.* To put (a lamp, fire, etc.) into proper order for burning, by removing any deposit or ash, and adding fresh fuel; also, to cleanse or cut level (a wick); by extension, to renew the burned-out carbons or electrodes of (an arc lamp) 1557. †**5.** To equip, supply -1667. **6.** To array, dress; to adorn, dress *up* 1516. **7.** *spec.* To decorate (a hat, garment, etc.) with ribbons, laces, embroideries, or the like; also, of a thing, to form the trimming of 1547. **8.** To dress (the hair or beard); to clip (the hair), or to clip the hair of (a person); also, to dub (a cock) 1530. **9.** *fig.* To beat, thrash, trounce; also, to reprimand, scold 1518. **10.** To cut off the excrescences or irregularities of; to reduce to a regular shape by doing this. Also with the part removed as object. Also with *up*. 1594. **11.** *Carpentry.* To bring (a piece of timber, etc.) to the required shape 1679. **12.** *Naut.* To distribute the load of (a ship or boat) so that she floats on an even keel 1580. **b.** *intr.* of a ship or boat 1861. **c.** *transf.* (*trans.*) To adjust (the balance) so as to equalize it 1817. **13.** *Naut.* To adjust (the sails or yards) with reference to the direction of the wind and the course of the ship 1624. Also *Aeronautics.* **b.** *absol.* or *intr.* 1697. **c.** *transf.* and *fig.* (*trans.*) To turn, adjust, adapt 1779. **14.** To stow or arrange (coal or cargo) in the hold of a ship, or carry it to the hatches when discharging; also, to shift (coal) in a ship's hold, etc.; also, to arrange (coal) as it is loaded on a truck 1797. **15.** *intr.* (Also with *it*.) To modify one's attitude in order to stand well with opposite parties; also, to accommodate oneself to the mood of the times 1685. **b.** *trans.* To modify according to expediency 1885.

1. *Rich. II*, III. iv. 56. 4. Then all those virgins arose, & trymmed their lampes N.T. (Genev.) *Matt.* xxv. 7. 8. **b.** *fig.* To cheat (a person) out of money; to fleece (*slang*) 1600. 9. None of your jaw, you swab.. else I shall t. your lac'd jacket for you SMOLLETT. 10. No inclination..to t. the roadside hedges 1885. 11. Phr. *To t. in*, to fit or frame (one piece) to or into another. 13. The..dexterous pilot..will t. his sails to every variation of wind 1836. 15. Trimming it between God and the Devil 1685.

Trimelli·tic, *a.* 1872. [f. TRI- III + MELLITIC.] *Chem.* In *t. acid*, unsymmetrical benzene-tricarboxylic acid, obtained by the oxidation of colophony by means of nitric acid. (Named by Baeyer, 1870.)

Trimerous (tri·mĕrəs, trəi·-), *a.* 1826. [f. mod.L. *trimerus* (ad. Gr. τριμερής, f. τρι- TRI- + μέρος part) + -OUS.] Having, consisting of, or characterized by three parts: *spec.* **a.** *Bot.* Having the parts of the flower, or the leaves, in series or whorls of three. **b.** *Ent.* Consisting of three segments or joints. So **Trimeran** (tri·mĕrăn) *a.* *Ent.* belonging to the division *Trimera* of beetles, or of hymenopterous insects, characterized by t. tarsi; *sb.* an insect of either of these divisions.

Trimesic (trəimī·sik), *a.* 1889. [f. TRI- III + MES(ITYLENE + -IC.] *Chem.* In *t. acid*, $C_6H_3(CO_2H)_3$, symmetrical benzene-tricarboxylic acid. (So named by Fittig, 1867, when he obtained it from mesitylenic acid, and found it to be tribasic.)

Trimester (trəime·stəɹ). 1821. [ad. F. *trimestre* sb., ad. L. *trimestris* adj., f. TRI- + *mensis* month.] A period or term of three months.

Trimestrial (trəime·striăl), *a.* (*sb.*) 1693. [f. L. *trimestris* (see prec.) + -AL.] Consisting of or containing three months; occurring or appearing every three months. **b.** as *sb.* A quarterly publication.

Trimeter (tri·mĭtəɹ, trəi·-), *sb.* and *a.* 1567. [ad. L. *trimetrus* adj. and sb., a. Gr. τρίμετρος adj., f. τρι- TRI- + μέτρον METRE.] **A.** *sb.* A verse of three measures; i.e. in trochaics, iambics, or anapæstics, of three dipodies (= six feet); in other rhythms, of three feet. **B.** *adj.* Of a verse: Consisting of three measures 1706.

Trimethyl (trəimī·þəil, -me·þil). 1857. [f. TRI- III + METHYL.] *Chem.* **a.** A formative denoting the presence of three methyl groups, CH_3, in a compound. **b.** *spec.* denoting the substitution of 3 methyl groups for 3 hydrogen atoms in the substance denoted by the rest of the name. Hence **Trimethy·lic** *a.*

Trimetric (trəime·trik), *a.* 1837. [f. TRI- + Gr. μέτρον measure (or, in sense 2, f. as TRIMETER) + -IC.] **1.** *Cryst.* = ORTHORHOMBIC. **2.** *Pros.* Consisting of three measures 1889.

Trimmer (tri·məɹ). 1555. [f. TRIM *v.* + -ER[1].] **1.** One who trims, in the senses of the verb. **2.** One who or that which cuts, clips, prunes, etc.; *spec.* an implement or machine for trimming edges in industrial processes 1583. **3.** *Arch.* A short beam framed across an opening (as a stair-well or hearth) to carry the ends of those joists which cannot be extended across the opening 1654. **4.** One who trims between opposing parties in politics, etc.; hence, one who inclines to each of two opposite sides as interest dictates 1682. **5.** One who or that which trims or trounces; a stiff competitor, fighter, letter, bout, run, blow, etc. *colloq.* 1776. **6.** One whose business is to stow the cargo or coal in loading a ship; also, a mechanical contrivance for doing this; also, one who arranges the coal in loading trucks 1836. **7.** *Angling.*

(*a*) A float, to which a line, with baited hook, is attached, used for taking pike; (*b*) a bank-runner, for the same purpose 1799.

4. One of the trimmers who went to church and chapel both T. HARDY. 5. Mr. H. was clean bowled by a t. from Barnes 1882.

Trimming (tri·miŋ), *vbl. sb.* 1518. [-ING [1].] 1. The action of TRIM *v.* 1519. b. *pl.* Pieces cut off in trimming 1805. 2. *concr.* Adornment, array; *esp.* a. Any ornamental addition to the bare fabric of a dress, etc. Chiefly *pl.* 1625. b. *pl.* Accessories, usual accompaniments; e.g. to a joint of meat, etc. 1612. 3. A beating; a drubbing; a sharp censure 1518.

2. b. A boiled leg of mutton with the usual trimmings DICKENS. 3. He deserves a good t. for it 1787.

Comb.: **t.-joist**, a joist into which the end of a trimmer (sense 3) is fitted; **-tank**, a water-tank in the bow or stern of a ship which is filled or emptied as the trim of the ship demands.

Tri·mming, *ppl. a.* 1559. [f. TRIM *v.* + -ING [2].] That trims, in various senses of the verb; *colloq.* or *slang*, 'stunning', 'rattling', excellent. Hence **Tri·mmingly** *adv.*

Trimorphic (trəimǭ·ɹfik), *a.* 1866. [f. Gr. τρίμορφος (f. τρι- TRI- + μορφή form) + -IC.] Having, or existing in, three forms, as a plant, animal, or crystalline substance. So **Tri·morph**, *Cryst.* a t. substance, or each of its three different forms. **Trimo·rphism**, t. condition, occurrence in three different forms (of a plant, animal, or crystalline substance) 1860. **Trimo·rphous** *a.* = *trimorphic.*

Trinacrian (trəinǣ·kriăn), *a.* 1640. [f. L. *Trinacria* Sicily, a. Gr. Τρινακρία, taken as f. τρι- TRI- + ἄκρα point, cape; but orig. Θρινακίη, f. θρῖναξ trident.] Of Sicily, Sicilian; hence, three-pointed.

Trinal (trəi·năl), *a.* 1590. [ad. late L. *trinalis*, f. L. *trinus*, pl. *trini* three each, threefold; see -AL.] 1. Threefold; triple; trine. 2. *Gram.* Applied to a 'number' or inflected form expressing three 1853.

1. Wherwith he wont at Heav'ns high Councel-Table, To sit the midst of T. Unity MILT.

Trinary (trəi·nări), *a. rare.* 1474. [ad. late L. *trinarius* of three kinds.] Consisting or composed of a set of three; threefold; triple.

Trindle (tri·nd'l), *sb.* [Early ME. *trindel*, a parallel form to TRENDLE.] 1. A wheel; *esp.* a 'trundle' or lantern-wheel in a mill; also, the wheel of a wheelbarrow. *Obs.* exc. *dial.* †2. Something of rounded form, as a pellet of sheep's or goat's dung –1660. 3. *Bookbinding.* Each of several flat pieces of thin wood or metal, shaped like toy horse-shoe magnets, by which (in pairs) the stitched, glued, and rounded back of a book is held flat while the front edge is ploughed 1818.

Tri·ndle, *v. Obs.* or *dial.* OE. [A parallel form to TRENDLE.] †1. *trans.* To make round, to round. OE. only. 2. To cause (a wheel, etc.) to revolve; to cause to roll along a surface; to trundle 1595. 3. *intr.* To revolve or turn round; to roll along a surface. late ME.

Trine (trəin), *a.* and *sb.* late ME. [a. F. *trin, trine* :—L. *trinus* threefold, f. *tres, tria* three.] A. *adj.* 1. Threefold; triple. 2. *Astrol.* Denoting the 'aspect' of two heavenly bodies which are a third part of the zodiac, i.e. 120°, distant from each other. Also, connected with or relating to a trine aspect. Also *fig.*: Favourable, benign. 1477.

1. *T. immersion*, the immersion of a person three times in baptism, in the name of the three Persons of the Trinity.

B. *sb.* 1. A group of three; a triad 1552. b. *spec.* The Trinity 1568. 2. *Astrol.* A trine aspect. Phr. *in t.* 1581. 3. *pl.* Three children (or young) at a birth; triplets 1628.

1. O furyes! O Vindictive tryne 1614. b. Eternal One, Almighty T.! KEBLE. 2. Fortunate aspects of T. and Sextile 1614. Hence **Trine** *v. (rare) trans.* to put or join in a t. aspect; to make a t. or triad of.

Tringle (tri·ŋg'l). 1696. [a. F.] a. *Arch.* A small square moulding or ornament. b. A curtain-rod, or any long slender rod.

‖ **Trinidado** (trinidā·do). *Obs.* or *arch.* 1599. [Sp. adj. f. *Trinidad.*] A kind of tobacco from Trinidad.

Trinitarian (trinitē·ə·riăn), *a.* and *sb.* 1628. [f. 16th c. L. *trinitarius* (f. *trinitas* TRINITY) + -AN.] A. *adj.* (In senses 1, 2 with capital T.) 1. *Ch. Hist.* Belonging to the order of the Holy Trinity. 2. *Theol.* Relating to the Trinity; holding the doctrine of the Trinity (opp. to *Unitarian*) 1656. 3. Forming a trinity; triple, threefold 1812. B. *sb.* (With capital T.) 1. A member of the religious order of the Holy Trinity; = MATHURIN 1628. 2. *Theol.* One who holds the doctrine of the Trinity of the Godhead; a believer in the Trinity 1706. Hence **Trinita·rianism**, Trinitarian belief.

Trinitrate (trəi͵nəi·trēt). 1868. [f. TRI- III + NITRATE.] *Chem.* A compound formed from three molecules of nitric acid, HNO_3, by the replacement of the three hydrogen atoms by a trivalent element or radical.

Trini·trin. 1866. [f. TRI- III + NITR(IC + -IN [1].] *Chem.* = NITROGLYCERINE.

Trinitro- (trəinəi·tro), bef. a vowel **trinitr-**, 1851. [f. TRI- + NITRO-.] *Chem.* a. A formative denoting that three nitro-groups, NO_2, have replaced three hydrogen atoms in the substance designated by the rest of the name, the nitrogen atoms being directly joined to carbon atoms; e.g. **trinitro·phenol** or picric acid, $C_6H_2(NO_2)_3(OH)$; **trinitro·to·luene, -to·luol** (abbrev. *trotyl*, and T.N.T.), a high explosive (1916). b. In earlier nomenclature, *trinitro-* included cases in which the nitrogen atoms of the NO_2 groups were attached by oxygen atoms to the carbon atoms of the substance designated by the rest of the name; such compounds are now called TRINITRATES, e.g. **trinitro-ce·llulose**, gun-cotton.

Trinity (tri·nĭti). ME. [a. OF. *trinite* :—L. *trinitatem, trinitas* triad, trio, f. *trinus* TRINE.] 1. The state of being threefold, threefoldness, threeness. a. *gen.* late ME. b. *spec.* In theological use: applied to the existence of one God in three persons. (In early use esp. in phr. 'God in t.', i.e. in threeness.) ME. 2. The Father, Son, and Holy Spirit as constituting one God; the triune God. (Now always with capital T.) ME. b. *ellipt.* The festival of the Holy Trinity; Trinity Sunday ME. 3. Any combination or set of three (persons, things, principles, etc.) forming a unity, or closely connected; a triad, trio 1542.

attrib.: **T. House**, shortened title of a guild or fraternity having the charge of pilots, lighthouses, buoys, etc.; hence *T. Brethren, high-water mark, pilot*, etc.; **T. Sunday**, the Sunday next after Whit-Sunday, observed as a festival in honour of the T.; **T. term**, the fourth of the terms or sessions of the High Court of Justice in England; since 1873 called officially *T. Sittings*, and now beginning on the Tuesday following T. Sunday; also, one of the university terms.

Trinket (tri·ŋkĕt), *sb.* 1533. [Origin obsc.] †1. Any small article forming part of an outfit; usu. *pl.* paraphernalia, accoutrements, 'traps'. –1787. 2. A small ornament, usu. an article of jewellery for personal adornment 1533. †3. *fig.* Applied esp. to the decorations of worship, and to religious rites, beliefs, etc. –1655.

2. Trinkets, of which the girl was very fond SWIFT. Hence **Tri·nketry**, trinkets collectively; articles of personal decoration viewed as trinkets or toys.

†**Tri·nket**, *v.* Chiefly *Sc.* 1647. [Origin unkn.] *intr.* To intrigue *with*; to act in an underhand way, prevaricate –1821. Hence †**Tri·nketer**, a secret trafficker; an intriguer.

Trinomial (trəinōu·miăl), *a.* and *sb.* 1674. [Formed with TRI- after BINOMIAL.] A. *adj.* 1. *Math.* Consisting of three terms, as an algebraical expression 1704. 2. *Nat. Hist.* Consisting of three terms, viz. genus, species, and subspecies or variety, instead of the first two only; involving or characterized by three terms, as a system of nomenclature 1865. B. *sb.* 1. *Math.* An expression consisting of three terms connected by + or –. 1674. 2. *Nat. Hist.* The name of a subspecies or variety when composed of three terms (the names of the genus, species, and subspecies or variety) 1884.

Trio (trī·o, trəi·o). 1724. [a. F., a. It., f. *tre* three, formed in imitation of *duo.*] 1. *Mus.* A composition for three voices or instruments; also, a company of three performers singing or playing such a composition. b. Name for a second or subordinate division of a minuet or other dance movement, or of a scherzo or march; commonly in a different style (and occas., key) from the main part, which is repeated after it 1840. 2. A group or set of three 1777. b. At piquet, a combination of three aces, kings, queens, or knaves in one hand 1891.

2. The t. of Kentucky hunters, Robinson, Rezner, and Hoback W. IRVING.

Triobol (trəi·obǫl, trəi͵ǭ·bǫl). Also **triobolus.** 1837. [ad. Gr. τριώβολον, f. τρι- TRI- + ὀβολός OBOL.] An ancient Greek coin of the value of three obols, or half a drachma. So †**Trio·bolar**, †**Trio·bolary** *adjs. lit.* worth three obols; *fig.* of little value, paltry, mean.

Trioctile (trəi͵ǫ·ktəil). 1727. [f. TRI- + L. *octo* eight, after *quartile*, etc.] *Astrol.* = *sesquiquadrate* (SESQUI- I c).

Triode (trəi·oud). 1919. [f. TRI- + ELECTR)ODE.] *Wireless Telegr.* In full *triode valve*: Trade-name of a three-electrode valve.

‖ **Triœcia** (trəi͵ī·ʃiă). 1760. [mod.L. (Linn.), f. Gr. τρι- TRI- + οἶκος house; cf. DIŒCIA, etc.] *Bot.* The third order in the Linnæan class *Polygamia*, comprising plants having male, female, and hermaphrodite flowers on different individuals. Hence **Triœcious** (-ī·ʃəs), **Tri͵oi·cous** *adjs.* belonging to this order, or having the flowers thus distributed.

Triolet (trəi·ǫlĕt, trī·). 1651. [a. F., dim. of *trio.*] *Prosody.* A stanza of eight lines, constructed on two rhymes, in which the first line is repeated as the fourth and seventh, and the second as the eighth.

Trional (trəi·ǫnăl). 1889. [f. TRI- + *-onal* of *sulphonal.*] *Pharm.* Trade-name of a synthetic narcotic drug resembling sulphonal.

‖ **Triones** (trəi͵ǭu·nīz), *sb. pl.* 1594. [L., ploughing-oxen, also as here.] *Astron.* The seven principal stars in *Ursa Major.*

Trionyx (trəi·ǫniks, trəi͵ǭu·niks). 1835. [mod.L., f. Gr. τρι- TRI- + ὄνυξ nail.] *Zool.* A genus of chelonian reptiles, so called because only three of the five toes have nails. So **Trio·nychoid** *a.* belonging to the suborder *Trionychoidea* of *Chelonia*, typified by the genus *T.* of soft-shelled turtles; *sb.* a turtle of this suborder.

Trioxide (trəi͵ǫ·ksəid). 1868. [f. TRI- III + OXIDE.] *Chem.* A compound of three atoms of oxygen with an element or radical.

Trip (trip), *sb.*[1] late ME. [f. TRIP *v.*] I. 1. The action or an act of tripping; a light lively movement of the feet; tripping gait or tread; the sound of this 1600. 2. A short voyage or journey, a 'run'; *esp.* each of a series of journeys or runs over a particular route. App. orig. a sailor's term, but very soon extended to a journey on land. 1691. b. A short journey (by sea or land) for pleasure or health; later, often applied to such a journey whatever its length. Also, applied to a passage by rail provided at a fare lower than the usual; a *cheap t.*, an excursion; occas. short for 'party of trippers' or 'trip-train' 1749. 3. *Naut.* A single board or reach in tacking; a tack 1700.

1. Yonder comes Dalinda; I know her by her t. DRYDEN. 2. It will be what mariners call a *t.* to England RICHARDSON. The 'bus-driver..is paid by 't.', and anxious to get his trips done 1906.

II. 1. 'A stroke or catch by which the wrestler supplants his antagonist' (J.); a sudden catching of a person's foot with one's own so as to cause him to stumble or fall. late ME. 2. A stumble or mis-step causing one to lose one's equilibrium 1681. 3. A mistake, blunder, fault; a slip, lapse; a false step; a slip of the tongue 1548.

1. The Groom..watches with a T. his Foe to foil DRYDEN. *fig.* Or will not else thy craft so quickely grow, That thine owne t. shall be thine ouerthrow? SHAKS. 2. The poor Animal being now almost tired, made a second T. STEELE. 3. A t. in one point would have spoiled all 1773.

III. *Mech.* A contrivance that trips; a projecting part of some mechanism which comes into momentary contact with another part so as to cause or check some movement 1906.

attrib. and *Comb.*: **t. system**, a system of payment by the t. or journey; **-train**, a mineral train which is intended to make a certain number of trips, out and home, in the day; also, an excursion train.

Trip, *sb.*[2] ME. [etym. obsc.] †1. A troop or company of men –1578. 2. a. A small flock (of goats, sheep, hares, etc.). *Obs.* exc. *local.* ME. b. A small flock of wild-fowl 1805.

Trip (trip), *v.* late ME. [a. OF. *treper, triper, tripper*; = Pr. *trepar* to hop, spring; of Lower Frankish origin; cf. MDu., L.G. *trippen*.] **I. 1.** *intr.* To move lightly and nimbly on the feet; to skip, caper; to dance. *arch.* **b.** *intr.* with *it* 1579. **2.** *trans.* To perform (a dance) with a light lively step (*rare*) 1627. **b.** To tread lightly and nimbly, dance upon 1749. **3.** *intr.* To go, walk, skip, or run with a light and lively motion; to move with a quick light tread; also with *it.* late ME. **4.** *trans.* To cause to trip or go nimbly 1598. **5.** *intr.* To make a trip or short excursion. Also with *it.* 1664.

1. b. Com, and t. it as ye go On the light fantastick toe MILT. 2. b. The sportive graces t. the green SHENSTONE. 3. T. and goe, my sweete, deliuer this Paper into the hand of the King SHAKS. 5. I shall t. to Paris in about a fortnight H. WALPOLE.

II. 1. *trans.* To cause to stumble or fall by suddenly arresting or catching the foot; 'to throw by striking the feet from the ground by a sudden motion; to strike the feet from under the body' (J.). Also with *up.* Often with the heels, foot, etc. as object. late ME. **b.** *fig.* or in *fig.* context 1548. **2.** To overthrow by catching in a fault or blunder; to detect in an inconsistency or inaccuracy 1557. **3.** *intr.* To strike the foot against something, so as to hop, stagger, or fall; to stumble *over* an obstacle; to make a false step 1440. **b.** Said of the tongue: To stumble in articulation; to falter in speaking 1526. **4.** *intr.* To fall into an error; to make a mistake or false step; to commit a fault, inconsistency, or inaccuracy 1509.

1. Tho other following tript vp his heeles GREENE. b. To t. the course of Law, and blunt the Sword That guards the peace SHAKS. 2. *Cymb.* v. v. 35. 3. I tripped over my sword, and nearly fell on my nose MARRYAT. b. Drinking..till his Tongue trips LOCKE. 4. After many endeavours to catch me tripping in some part of my story SWIFT. Jenny had tript in her time TENNYSON.

III. 1. *Naut. trans.* To loose (an anchor) from its bed and raise it clear of the bottom by a cable or a buoy rope. Also *intr.* for *pass.* 1748. **2.** To tilt; *spec. Naut.* to give (a yard) the necessary cant in sending it down; also, to lift (an upper mast) in order that it may be lowered 1840. **3.** *intr.* To tilt or tip up 1869. **4.** *trans.* To release (a catch, etc.) by contact with a projection; to operate in this way 1897.

Tri·-pack. 1911. [f. TRI- II + PACK *sb.*[1]] In colour photography, a pack of three sensitive films.

Tripartite (trəi,pā·ɹtəit, tri·paɹtəit), *a.* late ME. [ad. L. *tripartitus*, f. *tri-* three + *partitus, partiri* to divide.] **1.** Divided into or composed of three parts or kinds; threefold, triple. **b.** Involving, or of the nature of, division into three parts 1576. **2.** Made in three corresponding parts or copies, as an indenture drawn up between three parties, each of whom preserves one of the copies 1442. **3.** Engaged in by or concluded between three parties 1497. **4.** *Her.* **a.** = TIERCÉ. **b.** Applied to a cross or saltire when each of its members consists of three narrow bands with spaces between. 1796. **5.** Consisting of three parts or divisions 1658. **b.** *Bot. spec.* of a leaf, etc., divided into three segments nearly to the base. (Abbrev. *3-partite.*) 1753.

1. b. A t. division of that vast country BURKE. 3. The t. treaty which..exists among three of the leading powers of the world 1857. Hence **Tripartitely** *adv.*

Tripartition (trəipaɹti·ʃən). 1652. [f. L. *tripartitus*; see prec. and -TION.] Division into three parts; partition among three.

Tripe (trəip). ME. [a. OF. *tripe, trippe* entrails of an animal, mod.F. *tripe*; origin unkn.] **1.** The first or second stomach of a ruminant, esp. of the ox, prepared as food. Now usu. *collect. sing.* **2.** The intestines, bowels, guts, as members of the body; hence, the paunch or belly including them. *arch.* or *low.* Commonly in *pl.* 1470. **b.** Applied *contempt.* to a person 1595. **3.** *transf.* and *fig.* Now freq.: Nonsensical rubbish, trash (*slang*) 1676.

1. *Plain t.*, the first stomach, paunch, or rumen; *honeycomb t.*, the second, or reticulum. 2. b. Saist thou me so, thou T., thou hated scorne? 1595. 3. A song..that would be worth a shopful of such 't.' 1895.

‖**Tripe de roche** (trīp də roʃ). 1809. [F., 'rock tripe', from the appearance of the thallus.] A name orig. given in Canada to various edible lichens of the genera *Gyrophora* and *Umbilicaria*, which afford a slightly nutritious but bitter and purgative food.

Tri-personal (trəi,pə̄·ɹsənăl), *a.* 1641. [f. TRI- + L. *persona* PERSON + -AL.] *Theol.* Consisting of or existing in three persons: said of the Godhead; also, relating to the three persons of the Godhead. Hence **Tripe·rsonalist**, one who holds the doctrine of three persons in the Godhead. **Tri:persona·lity**, the condition of being t., existence in three persons.

Tripetalous (trəi,pe·tăləs), *a.* 1830. [f. TRI- + L. *petalum* PETAL + -OUS.] *Bot.* Having, or consisting of, three petals. So **Tripe·taloid** *a.* (of a six-parted perianth) having three of the segments petaloid.

Tri·p-ha·mmer. 1809. [f. TRIP *sb.*[1] or *v.* + HAMMER.] A massive machine-hammer operated by a tripping device, as a wheel with projecting teeth, a cam, or the like, by which it is raised and then allowed to drop.

Triphane (trəi·fēⁱn). 1816. [a. F., f. Gr. τριφανής appearing threefold; so called from exhibiting three lustrous cleavages.] *Min.* = SPODUMENE.

Triphthong (tri·fþǫŋ). 1599. [f. TRI-, after DIPHTHONG.] A combination of three vowel sounds in one syllable; also, loosely, a combination of three vowel characters, a TRIGRAPH. Hence **Triphtho·ngal** *a.*

Tri·plane. 1912. See TRI- II.

Triple (tri·p'l), *sb.* late ME. [sb. use of next.] **1.** A triple quantity, sum, or number; thrice as much or as many. **2.** †**a.** *Mus.* Triple measure or rhythm 1597. **b.** A triple star 1890. **c.** A magic lantern having three optical tubes combined in one 1892. **3.** *Bell-ringing.* A peal rung on seven bells with the tenor, i.e. the eighth, behind; the bells interchanging in three sets of two 1798.

Triple (tri·p'l), *a.* (*adv.*) 1550. [a. F., or ad. L. *triplus*, a. Gr. τριπλοῦς, = L. *triplex* threefold.] **1.** = TREBLE *a.* 1. 1551. **2.** = TREBLE *a.* 1 b. 1567. **3.** Three times as much or as many; multiplied by three 1550. †**4.** That is one of three; third. SHAKS.

1. A t. thorn beneath the buds 1776. T. rows of chains 1874. 2. A t. vse of fasting 1587. 4. *All's Well* II. i. 111.

Special collocations. *T. alliance*, an alliance of three states or powers, e.g. that of Germany, Austria-Hungary, and Italy in 1883; also *transf.* *T. crown*, a threefold crown; *spec.* the papal tiara; also, a heraldic bearing representing this. *T. entente* (Fr.), an understanding as to political action between three powers. *T. line, plane* (*Geom.*), a line or plane formed by the coincidence of three lines or planes. *T. point* (*Geom.*) a point common to three branches of a curve, or at which the curve has three tangents. *T. ratio*, the ratio of three to one. *T. rhythm* (*Mus.*), a threefold rhythm consisting of one heavy and two light accents or beats. *T. salt* (*Chem.*), a salt containing three different bases. *T. star*, a treble star. *T. time* (*Mus.*), a rhythm of three beats in the bar.

Comb.: **t.-expansion** (see EXPANSION 7); **-screw**, having three screw-propellers; **t. tree**, (*Cant*, now *Hist.* or *arch.*) a gallows (in ref. to its three parts).

B. *adv.* To three times the extent or amount; in a threefold manner 1606. **Tri·ply** *adv.*

Triple (tri·p'l), *v.* late ME. [ad. med.L. *triplare.*] **1.** *trans.* To make three times as great or as many; to multiply by three; to treble. **b.** *spec.* in *Mech.* To alter (a steam-engine) from single or double expansion to the triple-expansion type; also, to fit (a vessel, etc.) with triple-expansion engines 1891. **2.** *intr.* To grow to three times the former number or amount 1799.

1. The export of foreign commodities was tripled 1858.

Triplet (tri·plėt). 1656. [f. TRIPLE, after DOUBLET.] **1.** A set of three; three persons or things combined or united 1733. **2.** *spec.* **a.** Three successive lines of verse, esp. when rhyming together and of the same length 1656. **b.** *pl.* Three children at a birth; *sing.* one of three at a birth 1787. **c.** *Mus.* A group of three notes to be played in the time of two of the same time-value 1801. **d.** *Arch.* A window of three lights 1849. **e.** *Naut.* Three links between the cable and the anchor-ring 1891.

Triplex (trəi·-, tri·pleks), *a.* (*sb.*) 1601. [a. L., f. *tri-* three + *plic-* to fold.] Triple, threefold. Also *absol.* as *sb.*

Triplicate (tri·plikėt), *a.* and *sb.* late ME. [ad. L. *triplicatus, triplicare.*] **A.** *adj.* Threefold, triple; forming three exactly corresponding copies; consisting of or related to three corresponding parts.

T. bills of loading 1756. *T. proportion, ratio*, the proportion or ratio of cubes (third powers) in relation to that of the radical quantities.

B. *sb.* One of three things exactly alike, *esp.* one of three copies of a document; *pl.* three things exactly alike 1762.

In t., in three exactly corresponding copies or transcripts.

Triplicate (tri·plikeⁱt), *v.* 1623. [f. L. *triplicat-, triplicare*, f. *triplex* triple.] **1.** *trans.* To multiply by three; to increase threefold; to triple. **2.** To make or provide in triplicate; to repeat a second time 1639.

Triplication (triplikēⁱ·ʃən). 1577. [a. F., ad. L. *triplicationem.*] **1.** The action or process of making threefold, or multiplying by three; also, the result of this 1610. **2.** *Civil* and *Canon Law.* The plaintiff's reply to the defendant's duplication, corresponding to the surrejoinder at common law 1577. So **Tri·plicature.**

‖**Triplice** (trīplī·tʃe). 1896. [It. 'triple'.] The Triple Alliance between Germany, Austria, and Italy, formed 1882–3 against Russia and France.

Triplicity (tripli·siti). late ME. [ad. late L. *triplicitatem*, f. L. *triplex* TRIPLEX; see -ITY.] **1.** The quality or condition of being triple; threefold character or existence; tripleness 1555. **2.** A triad, trio, triplet 1585. **3.** *spec.* in *Astrol.* = TRIGON 2 a. late ME.

2. Many an Angels voice Singing before th' eternall majesty, In their trinall triplicities on hye SPENSER.

Triplite (tri·pləit). 1850. [ad. G. *triplit*, f. Gr. τριπλοῦς threefold.] *Min.* A phosphate of iron and manganese, with cleavage in three directions mutually at right angles.

Triplo- (triplo), bef. a vowel **tripl-**, comb. form repr. Gr. τριπλόος, τριπλοῦς threefold, triple; as in **Triploblastic** (-blæ·stik) [Gr. βλαστός germ] *a.*, *Biol*, having three germinal layers in the embryo; belonging to the division *Triploblastica*, a synonym of CŒLOMATA.

Tri·p-madam. 1693. [a. F. *tripe-madame*, app. an alteration of *trique-madame.*] = PRICK-MADAM.

Tripod (trəi·pǫd, tri·pǫd), *sb.* and *a.* 1611. [ad. L. *tripus, -pod-*, a. Gr. τρίπους, -ποδ-, f. τρι- three + πούς foot.] **A.** *sb.* **1.** *Gr.* and *Rom. Antiq.* A three-legged vessel; a pot or cauldron resting on three legs. **2.** *spec.* A vessel of this kind at the shrine of Apollo at Delphi, on which the priestess seated herself to deliver oracles. Hence *allus.* the Delphic oracle; any oracle or oracular seat. 1603. **3.** A seat, table, stool, etc., with three legs 1656. **4.** A three-legged support of any kind; *esp.* a frame or stand with three (diverging) legs for supporting a camera, compass, or other apparatus 1825. **B.** *adj.* Having or resting upon three feet or legs; of the form of a tripod 1715. So **Tripodal** (tri·pŏdăl), **Tripo·dial**, **Tripo·dian** *adjs.* three-footed, three-legged; *Anat.* having three rays or processes, as a bone.

Tripoli (tri·pŏli). 1601. [= F., f. *Tripoli*, a region in N. Africa or town in Syria, where found.] A fine earth used as a polishing-powder, consisting mainly of decomposed siliceous matter; called also *infusorial earth* or *rottenstone.* Hence **Tri·poline** *a.* of or pertaining to t.

Tripos (trəi·pǫs). 1589. [app. irreg. alteration of L. *tripus* TRIPOD, after Gr. words in *-os.*] †**1.** = TRIPOD A. 1, 3, 4. –1827. †**b.** *spec.* = TRIPOD 2. –1780. **2.** *Cambridge University.* Formerly: **a.** A bachelor of arts appointed to dispute, in a humorous or satirical style, with the candidates for degrees at 'Commencement': so called from the three-legged stool on which he sat. **b.** A set of humorous verses, orig. composed by the 'Tripos', and (till 1894) published at Commencement after his office was abolished (in full *t. verses*). **c.** The list of candidates qualified for the honour degree in mathematics, orig. printed on the back of the paper containing these verses (in full, *t. list*).

1659. **d.** Hence, in current use: *orig.* The final honours examination for the B.A. degree in mathematics, consisting of two parts (formerly *first* and *second t.*, now the *Mathematical T.*, Parts I and II); later extended to the subsequently founded final honours examinations in other subjects (*Classical T.*, etc.) 1842.

attrib.: **t. list,** the list of successful candidates in a t.; **t. paper,** any one of the papers of questions set in a t. (examination); **t. speech,** the humorous or satirical speech delivered by the 'Tripos'; **t. verses** (see 2 b).

Trippant (tri·pănt), *a.* 1658. [a. OF., pres. pple. of *tripper* to TRIP.] *Her.* = TRIPPING *ppl. a.* 3.

Tripper (tri·pəɹ). late ME. [f. TRIP *v.* + -ER¹.] One who or that which trips. **1.** One who dances; one who moves with light sprightly steps. **2.** One who or that which causes to stumble 1605. **3.** One who goes on a 'trip'; an excursionist. *colloq.* 1813. (So **Tri·ppist** 1792.)

3. The modern t. leaves only desolation and dirty paper behind him 1899. *Cheap t.*, one who travels by a cheap trip. Hence **Tri·ppery** *a.*

Tripping (tri·piŋ), *vbl. sb.* 1591. [f. TRIP *v.* + -ING¹.] The action of TRIP *v.*

attrib. and *Comb.*: **t.-line** (*Naut.*), a light line for tilting the yards; also, a line for manipulating a drogue.

Tri·pping, *ppl. a.* 1562. [f. as prec. + -ING².] **1.** Moving quickly and lightly; light-footed; nimble 1567. **2.** Stumbling, erring, sinning 1577. **3.** *Her.* Of a buck, stag, etc.: walking, and looking toward the dexter side, with three paws on the ground and one fore-paw raised; the same as *passant* of other animals 1562. Hence **Tri·ppingly** *adv.*

Triptote (tri·ptōut), *sb.* and *a.* 1612. [ad. L. *triptota* pl., a. Gr. τρίπτωτα, pl. neut. of τρίπτωτος with three case-endings, f. τρι- TRI- + πτωτός falling (πτῶσις case).] **A.** *sb.* A noun (or other word) used in three cases only. **B.** *adj.* Having only three cases 1886.

Triptych (tri·ptik). 1731. [f. TRI- after DIPTYCH.] **1. a.** *Antiq.* A set of three writing-tablets hinged or tied together. **b.** A card made to fold in three divisions. **2.** A picture or carving (or set of three such) in three compartments side by side, hinged so that the lateral ones fold over the central one; chiefly used as an altar-piece 1849.

Tripudiary (trəipiū·diări), *a. rare.* 1646. [f. L. *tripudium*; see next and -ARY¹.] **1.** *Rom. Antiq.* Denoting a species of divination (called *tripudium*) from the behaviour of birds, esp. of the sacred chickens, when fed. **2.** Of or pertaining to dancing (*affected*) 1819.

1. The conclusions of Southsayers in their Auguriall, and T. divinations SIR T. BROWNE.

Tripudiate (trəipiū·diˌeit), *v.* Now *rare* and *affected.* 1623. [f. L. *tripudiat-*, *tripudiare*, f. *tripudium* a beating the ground with the feet, a leaping or dancing, a religious dance (prob. f. *tri-* three + *pod-*).] **1.** *intr.* To dance for joy, or with excitement; to exult. **2.** To jump (*on* or *upon*) in contempt or triumph 1888. So **Tripu·diant** *a.* dancing; *fig.* exultant. **Tripudia·tion,** the action of dancing or leaping; exultation.

‖**Triquetra** (trəikwe·tră, -kwī·tră). 1586. [L., fem. of *triquetrus*.] †**a.** A triangle. **b.** A triangular ornament, formed of three interlaced arcs or lobes.

Triquetral (trəikwe·trăl, -kwī·trăl), *a.* 1646. [f. L. *triquetrus* + -AL.] = next.

Triquetrous (trəikwe·trəs), *a.* 1658. [f. L. *triquetrus* three-cornered, triangular + -OUS.] Three-sided, triangular; in *Nat. Hist.* of triangular cross-section, three-edged, trihedral, triangularly prismatic or pyramidal.

Trireme (trəi·rīm), *sb.* and *a.* 1601. [ad. L. *triremis*, f. *tri-* three + *remus* oar.] **A.** *sb.* An ancient galley (orig. Greek, subseq. also Roman) with three ranks of oars one above another, used chiefly as a ship of war. **B.** *adj.* Having three ranks of oars 1697.

‖**Trisagion** (trisæ·giǫn, -ǣ·giǫn). Also in L. form **trisagium.** late ME. [a. Gr. (τὸ) τρισάγιον, neut. of τρισάγιος thrice holy, f. τρίς thrice + ἅγιος holy.] An ancient hymn, used esp. in the Oriental Churches, beginning with a threefold invocation of God as holy. Also loosely applied to the TERSANCTUS.

Trisect (trəise·kt), *v.* 1672. [f. TRI- + L. *sect-*, *secare* to cut, after BISECT.] *trans.* To divide into three equal parts (esp. in *Geom.*); sometimes *gen.* to divide into three parts. So **Trise·ction,** the action of trisecting; division into three (equal) parts 1664.

Triskele (tri·skīl). 1857. [f. Gr. τρι- TRI- + σκέλος leg.] A symbolic figure consisting of three legs radiating from a common centre.

‖**Trismus** (tri·zmŏs). 1693. [mod.L., ad. Gr. τρισμός = τριγμός scream, also a grinding, rasping.] *Path.* Lock-jaw. (Rarely extended to tetanus in general.)

Trisoctahedron (tri·sˌǫktăhī·drǫn, -he·drǫn). 1847. [f. Gr. τρίς thrice + OCTAHEDRON.] *Geom.* and *Cryst.* A solid figure having 24 faces, every three of which correspond to one face of an octahedron: either with triangular faces (= *triakisoctahedron*), or with trapezoidal faces (= *deltohedron, icositetrahedron,* or *trapezohedron*). So **Tri·stetrahe·dron.**

Trist, *a. Obs.* or *arch.*; in ordinary use now only as Fr. ‖**triste** (trīst). ME. [a. F. *triste*, ad. L. *tristis*.] **1.** Sad, sorrowful; melancholy; lamentable. **2.** Dull, depressing, dreary (only as Fr.) 1756.

Tristesse. Now only as Fr. (trīstẹs). [Late ME. a. OF. *tristesce*, *-tece*, F. *tristesse* :— L. *tristitia* sadness, f. *tristis*.] Sadness, grief, melancholy.

Tristful (tri·stfŭl), *a. arch.* 1491. [f. TRIST *a.* + -FUL 1.] Full of sadness; sad, sorrowful; dreary, dismal. Hence **Tri·stfully** *adv.*

Tristich (tri·stik). 1813. [f. TRI-, after DISTICH.] *Pros.* A group of three lines of verse; a stanza of three lines.

Trisyllabic (trəi-, trisilæ·bik), *a.* 1637. [a. F. *trissyllabique*, f. L. *trisyllabus*, a. Gr. τρισύλλαβος, f. τρι- three + συλλαβή syllable; see -IC.] Consisting of or involving three syllables. So **Trisylla·bical** *a.*, **-ly** *adv.*

Trisyllable (tri-, trəisi·lăb'l), *sb.* (*a.*) 1589. [f. TRI- + SYLLABLE.] A word, or a metrical foot, of three syllables. **B.** as *adj.* = prec. 1766.

Tritagonist (trəitæ·gŏnist). 1890. [ad. Gr. τριταγωνιστής, f. τρίτος third + ἀγωνιστής combatant, actor.] The third actor in a Greek tragedy.

Trite (trəit), *a.* 1548. [ad. L. *tritus*, pa. pple. of *terere* to rub.] **1.** Worn out by constant use or repetition; devoid of freshness or novelty; hackneyed, commonplace, stale. **2.** Well worn; worn out by rubbing; frayed; (of a road or path) beaten, frequented 1599.

1. A t. observation 1762. **2.** Specimens of..bronze coinage..mostly t. and faceless 1855. Hence **Tri·tely** *adv.*, **-ness.**

Trithing (trəi·ðiŋ), **thrithing** (þrəi·ðiŋ). [Late OE. **þriðiŋ*, **þriding*, ad. ON. *þriðjungr* 'thirding', third part.] = RIDING *sb.* Now only *Hist.*

Tritical (tri·tikăl), *a.* 1709. [f. TRITE *a.*, with play on *critical*.] Of a trite or commonplace character. Hence **Tri·tical-ly** *adv.*, **-ness.** So **Tri·ticism** (after *criticism*).

Triticin (tri·tisin). 1838. [f. L. *triticum* wheat + -IN¹.] *Chem.* †**1.** Name given to the gluten of wheat by Hermbstaedt; also applied to a substance obtained from potato starch –1860. **2.** A carbohydrate obtained from the roots of couch-grass, *Triticum repens* 1874.

Trito- (trit*o*, trəit*o*), bef. a vowel **trit-,** comb. form repr. Gr. τρίτος third, occurring in technical terms (usu. corresp. to terms in PROTO- and DEUTERO-); as in **Trito·vum,** a third stage of an ovum, succeeding the deutovum. **Tritozooid** (-zōu·oid), a tertiary zooid, produced from a deuterozooid.

Triton (trəi·tən). 1584. [a. L. *Triton*, Gr. Τρίτων.] **1.** *Gr.* and *Rom. Myth.* Proper name of a sea-deity, son of Poseidon and Amphitrite, or of Neptune and Salacia, or otherwise of Nereus; also, one of a race of inferior sea-deities, or imaginary sea-monsters, of semi-human form. **b.** A figure of a Triton in painting, sculpture, etc.; in *Her.* represented as a bearded man with the hind quarters of a fish, and usu. holding a trident and a shell-trumpet 1601. **c.** *fig.* and *allus.*: esp. applied to a seaman, waterman, or the like. *T. of* or *among the minnows*: see MINNOW. 1589. **2.** *Zool.* **a.** A genus of marine gastropods with trumpet-shaped shells; an animal, or shell, of this genus, or of the family *Tritonidæ*. Also called *Triton's shell.* 1777. **b.** An extensive genus (now divided) of newts; an animal of this genus or group 1839.

1. So might I..hear old T. blow his wreathèd horn WORDSW. **c.** From their Lowzy Benches up started such a noizy multitude of old grizly Tritons 1704.

Triturate (tri·tiŭreit), *v.* 1755. [f. late L. *triturat-*, *triturare* to thresh, f. L. *tritura* TRITURE.] *trans.* To reduce to fine particles or powder by rubbing, bruising, pounding, crushing, or grinding; to comminute, pulverize; also, to mix (solids, or a solid and a liquid) in this way. So **Tritura·tion,** the action or process of triturating; a mass produced, or medicine prepared, by trituration 1646.

†**Tri·ture.** 1657. [ad. L. *tritura*, f. *trit-*, *terere* to rub.] Pounding or grinding; comminution; trituration –1790.

Triumph (trəi·ŏmf), *sb.* [Late ME. a. OF. *triumphe*, F. *triomphe*, ad. L. *triumphus*; cf. Gr. θρίαμβος hymn to Bacchus.] **1.** *Rom. Hist.* The entrance of a victorious commander with his army and spoils in solemn procession into Rome, permission for which was granted by the senate in honour of an important achievement in war. **2.** *transf.* The action or fact of triumphing; victory, conquest, or the glory of this; also, a triumphal feat, signal achievement. late ME. †**b.** *transf.* The subject of triumph. MILT. †**3.** Pomp; splendour; glory; magnificence –1718. †**4.** A public festivity; a spectacle or pageant; *esp.* a tournament –1825. **5.** The exultation of victory or success; elation; rapturous delight 1582. **b.** *In t.*, triumphant; triumphantly 1593. †**6.** A triumphal arch (*rare*) –1658. †**7.** *Cards.* **a.** = TRUMP *sb.*² **1.** –1606. †**b.** = TRUMP *sb.*² 1 b. –1626.

1. *transf.* That my sad looke, Should grace the T. of great Bullingbrooke SHAKS. **2.** It was the t. of civilization over brute force 1853. A dress is a t. of ugliness (*mod.*). **4.** What newes from Oxford? Hold those Iusts & Triumphs? SHAKS.

Triumph (trəi·ŏmf), *v.* 1483. [a. OF. *triumpher*, *triompher*, ad. L. *triumphare*, f. *triumphus*.] **1.** *intr.* To celebrate a Roman triumph 1530. **2.** To be victorious; to prevail; to gain the mastery 1508. †**b.** *trans.* To triumph over; to conquer –1667. **c.** To live in pomp or splendour –1568. **3.** *intr.* To be elated at another's defeat, discomfiture, etc.; 'to insult upon an advantage gained' (J.); hence, to rejoice, be elated or glad; to glory 1535. †**4.** *intr. Cards.* To trump (*rare*) –1626.

1. He triumphed for his victories over the great Mithridates GIBBON. **2.** He shall ascend With victory, triumphing through the aire Over his foes and thine MILT. **b.** We, that..were born Free, equal lords of the triumphed world, And knew no masters, but affections B. JONS. **3.** France, t. in thy glorious Prophetesse SHAKS. *fig.* The blood of twentie thousand men Did t. in my face SHAKS. Hence **Tri·umpher. Tri·umphing** *ppl. a.* that triumphs; **-ly** *adv.* (now *rare*).

Triumphal (trəiˌŏ·mfăl), *a.* (*sb.*) late ME. [ad. L. *triumphalis*, f. *triumphus* TRIUMPH; see -AL.] **1.** Of, pertaining to, or of the nature of a triumph; celebrating or commemorating a triumph or victory. †**2.** Victorious, triumphant –1618.

1. A t. ode in honour of Hercules 1835. *T. arch*, an arch erected in commemoration of a victory. *T. chaplet, garland, wreath*, the laurel wreath worn by the victor at a Roman triumph.

B. *sb.* †**1.** An ode of triumph or victory; a pæan –1589. †**2.** A token of triumph. MILT.

Triumphant (trəiˌŏ·mfănt), *a.* 1494. [ad. L. *triumphantem*, *triumphare* to TRIUMPH; see -ANT.] **1.** Celebrating a triumph or victory; of, pertaining to, of the nature of, or befitting a triumph. Now *rare.* 1531. **2.** That has achieved victory or success; conquering; victorious 1494. †**b.** *transf.* Of or gained by conquest. SHAKS. †**3.** Splendid; glorious; magnificent; noble; notable –1696. **4.** Exulting or rejoicing for or as for victory; triumphing; exultant 1594.

1. Like Captiues bound to a T. Carre SHAKS. **2.**

There is no reconciling.. Goodness with t. evil BROWNING. *Church T.*: see CHURCH 4. 3. She 's a most t. Lady, if report be square to her SHAKS. 4. The t. cries of an immense multitude 1907. Hence **Triu·mphancy**, the state or quality of being t. **Triu·mphantly** *adv.*

Triumvir (trəi,ɒ·mvəɪ). *Pl.* **-virs** (vəɪz), or in L. form **-viri** (-virəi). 1579. [a. L., back-formation from *trium virorum*, gen. pl. of *tres viri* three men.] *Rom. Hist.* One of three magistrates or public officers forming a committee charged with one of the departments of the administration; also, a member of the coalition of Pompey, Cæsar, and Crassus, B.C. 60 (first triumvirate), or of the administration of Cæsar, Antony, and Lepidus, B.C. 43 (second triumvirate). **b.** *transf.* and *fig. pl.* Three persons (or things) associated in power or authority 1619. So **Triu·mviral** *a.* of or pertaining to a t. or a triumvirate 1579.

Triumvirate (trəi,ɒ·mvirět). 1584. [ad. L. *triumviratus*, f. *triumvir*; see -ATE [1].] **1.** *Rom. Hist.* The position, office, or function of the triumviri, or of a triumvir; an association of three magistrates for joint administration 1601. **2.** By extension: Any association of three joint rulers or powers 1584. **3.** Less exactly, A group or set of three persons (*rarely* things); *esp.* three persons of authority or distinction in any sphere 1654.

3. This plaguy t.! A parson, a milliner, and a mantua-maker! RICHARDSON.

†**Triu·mviry.** 1588. [perh. for L. *triumviri*, pl. of TRIUMVIR.] = prec. –1656.

Triunal (trəi,yū·năl), *a. poet. rare.* 1711. [f. as next + -AL.] = next.

Triune (trəi·yūn, *occas.* trəiyū·n), *a.* (*sb.*) 1605. [f. TRI- + L. *unus* one.] Three in one; constituting a trinity in unity. **a.** of the Godhead 1635. **b.** *gen.* 1705. **B.** *sb.* A being that is three in one; a group of three things united; a trinity in unity 1605.

Triunity (trəi,yū·nĭti). 1621. [f. prec. + -ITY, or f. TRI- + UNITY.] **1.** The state or attribute of being three in one 1653. **2.** A set or group of three constituting a unity; the Godhead conceived as three persons 1621.

Trivalent (trəi·vēlěnt, tri·v-), *a.* 1868. [f. TRI- + VALENT.] *Chem.* Having the combining power of three atoms of hydrogen or other univalent element; combining with three atoms of a univalent element or radical. Hence **Triva·lence, Triva·lency.**

Trivet (tri·vėt). [ME. *trefet*, app. repr. L. *tripedem, tripes* three-footed, f. *tri-* + *pes, ped-* foot.] A three-footed stand or support. Now *rare* exc. *spec.* A stand for a pot, kettle, or other vessel placed over a fire for cooking or heating something; orig. and properly standing on three feet; now often with projections by which it may be secured on the top bar of a grate. late ME.

Phr. *As right as a t.*, thoroughly or perfectly right (in ref. to a trivet's always standing firm on its three feet).

Trivial (tri·viăl), *a.* (*sb.*) late ME. [ad. L. *trivialis*, f. TRIVIUM.] **I. 1.** Belonging to the trivium of mediæval university studies. †**2.** Threefold, triple. late ME. only. **II. 1.** Such as may be met with anywhere; common, everyday, familiar, trite. Now *rare.* 1589. **2.** Of small account, paltry, poor; trifling, inconsiderable, unimportant 1593. **3.** *Nat. Hist.* Applied to names of animals and plants: **a.** to a Latin name added to the generic name to distinguish the species: = SPECIFIC A. 5. 1759. **b.** Popular, vernacular, vulgar 1815.

1. The t. round, the common task KEBLE. 2. The offence..could..be passed by as altogether t. FREEMAN. 3. b. The t. name for the whole family of terns ..is 'sea-swallow' 1901.

B. *sb.* **1.** *pl.* The three subjects of study constituting the trivium. Now only *Hist.* 1481. **2.** A trivial matter; a triviality, a trifle. Usu. *pl.* 1715. Hence **Tri·vialism** (*rare*) t. character; a triviality. **Tri·vialize** *v. trans.* to make t. **Tri·vial-ly** *adv.*, **-ness** (now *rare*).

Triviality (triviæ·lĭti). 1598. [f. L. **trivialitatem*, f. *trivialis* TRIVIAL; see -ITY.] **1.** The quality of being trivial; commonplace or trifling character. **2.** With *a* or (commonly) in *pl.*: Something trivial; a trivial matter, remark, etc.; a trifle 1611.

2. I..find little but repetitions and trivialities 1664.

‖**Trivium** (tri·viŏm). 1804. [L. (f. *tri-* TRI- + *via* way), a place where three ways meet.] **1.** In the Middle Ages, the lower division of the seven liberal arts, comprising grammar, rhetoric, and logic. **2.** *Zool.* The three anterior ambulacra of an echinoderm 1870.

-trix, *suffix*, ending of L. feminine agent-nouns (with stems in *-tric-*, acc. *-tricem*, whence F. *-trice*: see -TRICE), corresp. to masculines in *-tor*, as *venatrix* huntress, etc. Used chiefly in legal terms, as ADMINISTRATRIX, EXECUTRIX, TESTATRIX, etc. In Geometry, words in *-trix* denote straight lines (*linea* being understood), as BISECTRIX, etc.; more rarely curves or surfaces, as INDICATRIX, TRACTRIX. The commoner suffix in Eng. is -TRESS; see also -TRICE.

Troat (trōᵘt), *v.* 1611. [Cf. OF. *trout*, also *trut*, an interjection for urging on hunting dogs, asses, or sheep.] *Venery. intr.* To cry or bellow: said of a buck at rutting time.

Trocar (trōᵘ·kaɪ). 1706. [ad. F. *troquart*, *trois-quarts*, *trocart*, f. *trois* three + *carre* side, face of an instrument; so called from its triangular form.] A surgical instrument consisting of a perforator or stylet enclosed in a metal tube or cannula, used for withdrawing fluid from a cavity, as in dropsy, etc.

Trochaic (trokē¹·ik), *a.* and *sb.* 1589. [a. F. *trochaïque*, or ad. L. *trochaicus*, ad. Gr. τροχαϊκός, f. τροχαῖος TROCHEE.] *Pros.* **A.** *adj.* **1.** Of a verse, rhythm, etc.: Consisting of, characterized by, or based on trochees. **2.** Of a foot, etc.: Of the nature of a trochee 1756.

2. *T. spondee*, a spondee having the accent or *ictus* upon the first syllable.

B. *sb.* A trochaic verse or foot 1693.

Trochal (trǫ·kăl, trōᵘ·kăl), *a.* 1841. [f. Gr. τροχός wheel + -AL.] *Zool.* Resembling a wheel; rotiform.

Trochanter (trokæ·ntəɪ). 1615. [a. F., a. Gr. τροχαντήρ, f. τρέχειν to run.] *Anat.* and *Zool.* **1.** A protuberance or process in the upper part of the thigh-bone, serving for the attachment of certain muscles; usu., as in man, two in number, the *great t.* (*t. major*), and the *lesser t.* (*t. minor*). **2.** *Ent.* The second joint of an insect's leg, next to the coxa 1816. Hence **Trochanteric** (-te·rik) *a.* pertaining to a t.

Troche (trōᵘtʃ, trōᵘʃ, trōᵘk). 1597. [An altered f. TROCHISK; sometimes written *trochee* (trōᵘ·kī).] *Pharm.* = TROCHISK.

Trochee (trōᵘ·kī). 1589. [ad. L. *trochæus* (also used), ad. Gr. τροχαῖος, prop. adj. (*sc.* πούς foot) running, tripping, f. τρόχος, f. τρέχειν to run.] *Pros.* A metrical foot consisting of a long followed by a short syllable; in accentual verse, of an accented followed by an unaccented syllable.

Trochilic (troki·lik), *a.* and *sb. rare.* 1570. [f. Gr. τροχίλος, taken in sense of τροχός wheel + -IC.] **A.** *adj.* Of or pertaining to rotary motion; relating to wheels 1605. **B.** *sb.* The science or art of rotary motion 1570. Also **trochilics.**

Trochilidine (troki·lidəin), *a.* 1861. [f. mod.L. *Trochilidæ* (f. TROCHILUS [1]) + -INE [1].] *Ornith.* Belonging to or characteristic of the family *Trochilidæ* or humming-birds.

‖**Trochilus** [1] (trǫ·kilŏs). 1579. [L., a. Gr. τροχίλος, f. τρέχειν to run.] *Ornith.* **1.** A small Egyptian bird (not certainly identified) said by the ancients to pick the teeth of the crocodile. **2.** A Linnæan genus of Amer. birds, orig. including all the then known humming-birds: now greatly restricted 1752.

‖**Tro·chilus** [2]. 1563. [L., app. the same word as prec.] *Arch.* A concave moulding: esp. in classical architecture.

†**Tro·chisk.** late ME. [a. F. *trochisque*, ad. L. *trochiscus*, a. Gr. τροχίσκος, dim. of τροχός wheel.] A medicated tablet or disk; a (round or ovate) pastille or lozenge –1748.

Trochite (trǫ·kəit, trōᵘ·kəit). Now *rare* or *Obs.* 1676. [ad. mod.L. *trochites*, f. Gr. τροχός wheel; see -ITE [1].] *Palæont.* = ENTROCHITE. Hence **Trochitic** (troki·tik) *a.*

‖**Trochlea** (trǫ·kliă). 1693. [L.; cf. Gr. τροχιλία sheaf of a pulley.] *Anat.* A pulley-like structure or arrangement of parts, with a smooth surface upon which some other part, as a bone or tendon, slides; *spec.* (*a*) the surface of the inner condyle of the humerus at the elbow-joint, with which the ulna articulates; (*b*) the cartilaginous loop through which the superior oblique muscle of the eye passes.

Trochlear (trǫ·kliăɪ), *a.* 1681. [ad. mod.L. *trochlearis*, f. TROCHLEA; see -AR.] **1.** *Anat.* Belonging to or connected with a trochlea, as a muscle, nerve, etc.; forming a trochlea, as a surface of a bone, etc. **2.** *Bot.* Pulley-shaped, as the embryo of *Commelynaceæ* 1830.

1. *T. muscle*, the superior oblique muscle of the eye. *T. nerve*, each of the fourth pair of cranial nerves, the motor nerves for the t. muscles.

Trocho- (trǫko), bef. a vowel **troch-** (trǫk), comb. form repr. Gr. τροχός wheel, disk; as in **Tro·chosphere**, a larval form constituting a stage in the development of most molluscs and of certain worms, esp. marine annelids, characterized by a spheroidal body with a ring of cilia.

Trochoid (trǫ·koid, trōᵘ·koid), *sb.* and *a.* 1704. [ad. Gr. τροχοειδής round like a wheel, f. τροχός wheel + εἶδος; see -OID.] **A.** *sb.* **1.** *Geom.* A curve traced by a point on or connected with a rolling circle; *orig.* = CYCLOID 1; now usu. restricted to the *curtate* and *prolate cycloids* traced respectively by points within and without the circle; also extended to the HYPOTROCHOID and the EPITROCHOID 1704. **2.** *Zool.* A gasteropod of the family *Trochidæ*; a top-shell 1839. **B.** *adj.* **1.** *Geom.* = next 1 (*rare*) 1882. **2.** *Conch.* Top-shaped, conical with flat base, as the shells of the genus *Trochus* or family *Trochidæ*; *Zool.* belonging to the family *Trochidæ* 1859. **3.** *Anat.* Applied to a pivot-joint, in which one bone turns upon another with a rotary motion 1857.

Trochoidal (trokoi·dăl), *a.* 1799. [f. prec. + -AL.] **1.** *Geom.* Having the form or nature of a trochoid; pertaining or relating to trochoids. **2.** *Conch.* = prec. B. 2 (*rare*) 1891. **3.** *Anat.* = prec. B. 3 (*rare*) 1882.

‖**Trochus** (trōᵘ·kŏs, trǫ·kŏs). *Pl.* **trochi** (-kəi), also **trochuses.** 1706. [L., a Gr. τροχός, f. τρέχειν to run.] **1.** *Gr.* and *Rom. Antiq.* A wheel or hoop, used in athletic exercises or as a plaything. **2.** *Zool.* **a.** A genus of gasteropod molluscs, having a top-shaped or conical shell; the type of the family *Trochidæ* or top-shells 1753. **b.** The internal ring of cilia in the trochal organ of a rotifer 1888.

Trod (trǫd), *sb.* Now *dial.* [OE., = ON. *troð* treading, trampling, f. ON. *troða* (cf. Goth. *trudan* to tread, ablaut var. of WGer. **tredan* to tread).] †**1.** Tread, footprint, track, trace –1563. **2.** A trodden way; a footpath, path, way. *dial.* 1570.

2. Thus in the middle t. I safely went 1642.

Trod (trǫd), *ppl. a.* 1632. Shortened from TRODDEN: chiefly as second element of combs.

Trod (trǫd), pa. t. and pple. of TREAD *v.*

Trodden (trǫ·d'n), *ppl. a.* 1545. [Late ME. *troden*, repl. OE. and ME *treden*, pa. pple. of TREAD *v.*] That has been walked, stepped, or trampled upon.

Troglodyte (trǫ·g-, trōᵘ·glŏdəit), *sb.* (*a.*) 1555. [ad. L. *troglodyta*, ad. Gr. τρωγλοδύτης, f. τρώγλη hole + δύειν to get or go into.] **1.** One of various races or tribes of men (chiefly ancient or prehistoric) inhabiting caves or dens (natural or artificial); a cave-dweller, cave-man. **2.** Applied to: †**a.** A bird of the genus *Troglodytes*; a wren (*rare*). **b.** An anthropoid ape of the genus *Troglodytes*, as a gorilla or chimpanzee. 1706. **3.** *fig.* A person who lives in seclusion; one unacquainted with the ways of the world; a 'hermit'. Also, a dweller in a hovel or slum. 1854. **4.** *attrib.* or *adj.* That is a t.; of or belonging to a t. or troglodytes 1704.

1. They were Troglodites, and had no dwelling but in the hollowes of the rocks 1642. 3. A belief worthy only of troglodytes inaccessible to Imperial..thought 1905. Hence **Tro·glody·tal** *a.*

Troglodytic (trǫg-, trōᵘglodi·tik), *a.* 1585. [ad. L. *troglodyticus*, a. Gr. τρωγλοδυτικός.] **1.** Inhabited or frequented by troglodytes; pertaining to or characteristic of a troglodyte. **2.** Having the habits of a troglodyte; cave-dwelling 1676. 3. Resembling a troglodyte; of a degraded type; also *fig.* not interested in or conversant with affairs 1871.

3. A respectable t. peer 1910. So **Troglody·tical** *a.*

Trogon (trōu·gǫn). 1792. [mod.L., Gr. τρώγων, pr. pple. of τρώγειν to gnaw.] *Ornith.* A bird of the genus *Trogon* or family *Trogonidæ*, widely distributed in tropical and subtropical regions, esp. in the New World, and characterized by soft plumage of varied and usu. brilliant colouring.

Troic (trōu·ik), *a.* 1831. [ad. Gr. τρωικός, f. Τρώς, name of the mythical founder of Troy.] Pertaining or relating to ancient Troy; Trojan.

‖ **Troika** (troi·kă). 1842. [Russ.] A Russian vehicle drawn by three horses abreast.

Troilite (trōu·iləit). 1868. [f. the name of Dominico *Troili*, who described a meteorite containing this mineral which fell in 1766; see -ITE [1].] *Min.* A sulphide of iron found in meteorites.

Trojan (trōu·dʒăn), *a.* and *sb.* ME. [orig. *Troyan, Troian* (troi·ăn); ad. L. *Troianus*, f. *Troia* Troy.] **A.** *adj.* Of or pertaining to ancient Troy or its inhabitants. late ME. **B.** *sb.* **1.** An inhabitant or native of Troy ME. **2.** *colloq.* **a.** A merry or roystering fellow; a boon companion; a person of dissolute life; also (in later use only), a good fellow (often with *true* or *trusty*) 1600. **b.** A brave or plucky fellow; a person of great energy or endurance: usu. in phr. *like a T.* 1846.

2. a. He was a kinde good fellow, a true Troyan 1600. b. Working like a T. 1846.

Troll (trōul), *sb.*[1] 1663. [f. TROLL *v.*] **1.** The act of trolling; a going or moving round; routine or repetition 1705. **2.** A song the parts of which are sung in succession; a round, a catch 1820. **3.** *Angling.* The method of trolling in fishing for pike, etc. 1681. **4.** = TROLLEY *sb.* 1. *local.* 1663.

2. It is sad..to miss..the joyous t. of his ballads 1856.

Troll (trōul), *sb.*[2] 1616. [a. ON. and Swed. *troll*, Da. *trold.*] In Scandinavian mythology, One of a race of supernatural beings formerly conceived as giants, now, in Denmark and Sweden, as dwarfs or imps, supposed to inhabit caves or subterranean dwellings.

Troll (trōul), *v. arch.* and *dial.* late ME. [Origin obsc.; cf. OF. *troller* to quest; also F. *trôler* to run about, ramble, G. *trollen* to roll.] **I.** †**1.** *intr.* To ramble, saunter, stroll –1691. **2.** *trans.* To move (a ball, bowl, etc.) by or as by rolling; to roll, bowl, trundle; to roll (the eyes); to throw (dice). late ME. **3.** *intr.* To roll; also, to turn round and round; to spin, whirl 1581.

2. Shee trowled her angry eyes on euery side 1628. 3. To t. it in a Coach and Six SWIFT.

II. *intr.* To move nimbly, as the tongue in speaking; to wag. Also said of a person. *Obs.* or *arch.* 1616. †**b.** *trans.* To move (the tongue) volubly –1747.

b. To sing, to dance, To dress, and troule the Tongue, and roule the Eye MILT.

†**III. 1.** To cause to pass from one to another; esp. in phr. *to t. the bowl* –1600. **2.** *intr.* Of the vessel or its contents: To circulate, be passed round –1808. **3.** To come *in* abundantly; to 'roll' in –1689.

1. Trowl the bowl, the jolly nut-brown bowl DEKKER.

IV. 1. *trans.* To sing (something) in the manner of a round or catch; to sing in a full rolling voice; to chant merrily 1575. **b.** *intr.* To sing in this way; to carol, warble 1879. **2.** Of bells: To give forth a recurring cadence of full, mellow tones; of a song: to be uttered in a full, rolling, or jovial voice; *transf.* of a tune: to 'run in one's head' 1607. **3.** *trans.* To utter nimbly or rapidly; to recite in a full rolling voice. Also *intr.* of speech. 1625.

1. Will you troule the Catch You taught me but whileare? SHAKS. 2. I have had..a Tune trouling in my Head DRYDEN.

V. *Angling. intr.* To angle with a running line; also (*trans.*) to fish (water) in this way. *spec.* **a.** to fish for pike by working a dead bait by a sink-and-draw motion; **b.** to angle with a spinning bait; **c.** *U.S.* and *Sc.* to trail a baited line behind a boat 1606.

The peasant..With patient angle trolls the finny deep GOLDSM. Hence **Tro·ller.**

Trolley, trolly (trǫ·li). Also **trawley.** 1823. [perh. from TROLL *v.*] **1.** Locally applied to a low cart of various kinds, e.g. a costermonger's cart. **2.** A low truck without sides or ends, esp. one with flanged wheels for running on a railway, etc. 1858. **3.** A grooved metallic pulley which travels along, and receives current from, an overhead electric wire, the current being then conveyed by a *t.-pole* or other conductor to a motor, usu. that of a car on a street railroad; also called *t.-wheel.* Also applied to any pulley running along an overhead track. 1891. **b.** *U.S.* Short for *t. car* 1891.

Comb.: **t.-car** (*U.S.*), an electric car driven by means of a t.; **-pole**, a hinged pole on an electric car, supporting the t. and conveying the current from the overhead wire; **-wire**, an overhead electric wire supplying current to the trolleys of electric cars.

† **Tro·ll-ma:dam.** 1572. [app. an alteration of F. *trou-madame* (f. *trou* hole) by association with TROLL *v.*] A game played by ladies, resembling bagatelle –1819.

Trollop (trǫ·ləp). 1615. [perh. conn. w. TROLL *v.*] An untidy or slovenly woman; a slattern, slut; also, occas., a trull.

Hence **Tro·llop** *v.*, to act in a slovenly way.

Trolly (trǫ·li). 1700. [Cf. Flem. *tralje, traalje* trellis, lattice, mesh.] A kind of lace having the pattern outlined with a thick thread.

Tro·mbash. 1867. A Sudanese boomerang.

Trombone (trǫmbōu·n, trǫ·mbōun). 1724. [ad. It. *trombone*, augm. of *tromba* trumpet.] **1.** *Mus.* A large loud-toned brass instrument of the trumpet kind, consisting of a long tube bent twice upon itself, and ending in a bell mouth; the U-shaped bend nearer the mouthpiece is of double telescoping tubes, sliding upon one another, so that the length of the sounding tube may be adjusted to produce the desired note. (It is also made with valves and pistons instead of the slide.) **b.** One who plays this instrument 1848. ‖ **2.** (trombo·ne), pl. **tromboni** (-ni). = BLUNDERBUSS 1. 1754. **Trombo·nist** = 1 b.

Tromometer (tromǫ·mitəɪ). 1878. [f. Gr. τρόμος trembling + -METER.] An instrument for measuring or detecting faint earth-tremors. Hence **Tromome·tric, -al** *adjs.* **Tromo·metry,** the scientific use of the t.

‖ **Trompe** (trōnp). 1828. [F.] An apparatus for producing a blast, in which water falling in a pipe carries air into a receiver, where it is compressed, and thence led to the blast-pipe.

Tron (trǫn). *Hist.* Chiefly *Sc.* 1449. [a. OF. *trone* :—L. *trutina*, a. Gr. τρυτάνη balance.] A public weighing apparatus in a city or (burgh) town; also, the post of this used as a pillory; a market-place.

Trona (trōu·nă). 1799. [a. Swed., app. f. Arab. *ṭrōn*, apocopate f. *natrūn* NATRON, ad. Gr. νίτρον soda.] *Min.* Native hydrous sodium carbonate, found in N. Africa and America.

Tronage (trōu·nėdʒ). ME. [a. AF. *tronage*, f. OF. *trone*; see -AGE.] The weighing of merchandise at the tron or public weighing machine; a charge or toll upon goods so weighed; the right of levying such charge.

Trone, obs. f. THRONE.

‖ **Tronk** (trǫŋk). 1693. [Cape Du., ad. Pg. *tronco* trunk, stock (of a tree), etc.] A prison.

Troolie (trū·li). 1769. [Tupi *tururi.*] The leaf of the bussu palm. Also *t. hut.*

Troop (trūp), *sb.* 1545. [a. OF. *trope*, F. *troupe* :—late L. *troppus* flock; ult. origin unkn.] **1. a.** A body of soldiers. **b.** A number of persons (or things) collected together; a party, company, band 1584. **c.** Of animals: A herd, flock, swarm 1587. **d.** Used to indicate a great number; a 'lot'; esp. in *pl.* 'flocks', 'swarms' 1590. †**e.** = TROUPE –1835. **2.** *pl.* Armed forces collectively 1598. **3.** *Mil. spec.* A subdivision of a cavalry regiment commanded by a captain, corresp. to a *company* of foot and a *battery* of artillery 1590. **b.** The command of a troop 1813. **c.** A company of boy scouts 1908. **4.** *Mil.* A signal on the drum for troops to assemble in readiness to march; the assembly 1672.

1. a. Amid the thickest troupes of his enemies in the battaile of Agincourt HOLLAND. b. At a little Distance..a T. of Gipsies ADDISON. d. Honor, Loue, Obedience, Troopes of Friends SHAKS. 2. The courage displayed by our troops COBDEN.

attrib. and *Comb.*: **t.-bird** (*U.S.*), a troopial; **-boot** (*U.S.*), a cavalry boot; **-fowl** (*U.S.*), a scaup-duck; **-horse**, a cavalry horse.

Troop (trūp), *v.* 1565. [f. prec.] **1.** *intr.* To gather in a company; to come together; to flock, assemble. **2.** †**a.** *trans.* To assemble (individuals) into a troop or company –1620. **b.** *intr.* To associate *with* 1592. **3.** To walk, go, pass; *colloq.* (with *off, away,* etc.) to go away, 'be off', 'pack' 1590. **4.** To march in rank; to walk or pass in order. Now *colloq.* 1592. **5.** To come or go in great numbers; to flock (*in, out*) 1610. **6.** *trans.* (*Mil.*, from prec. 4) *To t. the colour* (or *colours*): to perform that portion of the ceremonial known as mounting guard in which the colour is received 1803. **7.** To transport (troops) 1882.

1. As Armies at the call Of Trumpet..T. to thir Standard MILT. 2. b. So shewes a Snowy Doue trooping with Crowes SHAKS. 4. Ye verger troops before ye Deane 1682. 5. The flocking shadows pale T. to th' infernall jail MILT.

Trooper (trū·pəɪ). 1640. [f. TROOP *sb.* + -ER [1].] **1.** A soldier in a troop of cavalry. **2.** A horse ridden by a trooper; a troop-horse 1640. **3.** In Australia: A mounted policeman 1858. **4.** A troop-ship 1872.

1. Phr. *To lie, swear, like a t.*

Troopial, troupial (trū·piăl). 1825. [ad. F. *troupiale*, f. *troupe* troop, from its living in flocks.] Any of various species of birds of the Amer. family *Icteridæ*; *esp.* the icteric oriole.

Troostite (trū·stəit). 1835. [f. name of Prof. G. *Troost* of Nashville, Tennessee; see -ITE [1].] **1.** *Min.* A variety of WILLEMITE, with admixture of iron and manganese, occurring in reddish hexagonal crystals. **2.** *Metall.* A transitional constituent of steel 1902.

Tropæolin (tropī·ŏlin). 1880. [f. next + -IN [1]; from the resemblance of the colour to that of the flowers of some species of *Tropæolum.*] Any of several orange dyes, of complex composition, belonging to the class of sulphonic acids.

‖ **Tropæolum** (tropī·ŏlŏm). *Pl.* **-a, -ums.** 1785. [mod.L., f. Gr. τρόπαιον trophy; so called from the resemblance of the leaf to a shield and the flower to a helmet.] *Bot.* A S. Amer. genus of herbs (family *Tropæolaceæ* or *Geraniaceæ*), mostly of trailing or climbing habit, with irregular spurred flowers, usu. deep orange or yellow.

Trope (trōup). 1533. [ad. L. *tropus* figure of speech, ad. Gr. τρόπος turn, f. τρέπειν.] **1.** *Rhet.* A figure of speech which consists in the use of a word or phrase in a sense other than that which is proper to it; also, in casual use, a figure of speech; figurative language. †**2.** In Gregorian Music, a short distinctive cadence at the close of a melody –1626. **3.** In the Western Church, a phrase, sentence, or verse introduced as an embellishment into part of the text of the mass or of the breviary office that is sung by the choir 1846. **4.** *Geom.* The reciprocal of a node on a curve or surface 1869.

1. [American] rhetoric is Rhodian rather than Attic, overloaded with tropes and figures BRYCE. Hence **Tro·pal** *a.* (*Geom.*) pertaining to or constituting a t.

‖ **Trophi** (trōu·fəi), *sb. pl.* 1826. [mod.L., pl. of *trophus*, a. Gr. τροφός feeder, f. τρέφειν.] *Zool.* A collective name for the mouth-parts in insects, as organs for seizing and preparing the food. Also applied to the parts of the pharynx in rotifers, having a similar function.

Trophic (trǫ·fik), *a.* 1873. [ad. Gr. τροφικός, f. τροφή nourishment; see -IC.] *Biol.* Of or pertaining to nutrition; *spec.* of certain nerves and nerve-centres, Concerned with or regulating the nutrition of the tissues. So **Tro·phical** *a.* 1857, **-ly** *adv.*

Trophied (trōu·fid), *a.* 1622. [f. TROPHY *sb.* or *v.* + -ED.] Adorned with a trophy or trophies.

Thro' t. tombs of heroes and of kings 1798.

Tropho- (trǫ·fo), comb. form repr. Gr. τροφή nourishment, f. τρέφειν to nourish; as in **Tro·phoblast,** a layer of cells external to the embryo, and supplying it with nourishment; also applied to the morbid growth in cancer. ‖ **Tro:phoneuro·sis,** any functional disorder due to derangement of the trophic action of the nerves. **Tro·phosome** [Gr. σῶμα body], the aggregate of nutritive zooids of a hydrozoan (dist. from *gonosome*).

Trophonian (trofōu·niăn), *a.* 1792. [f. L. *Trophonius*, Gr. Τροφώνιος, proper name + -AN.] Pertaining to Trophonius, the mythical builder of the original temple of Apollo at Delphi, who after his death was worshipped as a god, and had an oracle in a cave in Bœotia, which was said to affect those who entered it with such awe that they never smiled again: hence *allus.*

Trophy (trōu·fi), *sb.* 1513. [a. F. *trophée*, ad. post-cl. L. *trophæum*, cl. L. *tropæum*, ad. Gr. τρόπαιον, neut. of τροπαῖος, f. τροπή turning, putting to flight, defeat.] **1.** *Gr.* and *Rom. Antiq.* A structure erected (orig. on the field of battle, later in any public place) as a memorial of a victory in war, consisting of arms or other spoils taken from the enemy, hung upon a tree, pillar, etc. and dedicated to some divinity. Hence applied to similar monuments or memorials in later times. 1550. **b.** *transf.* A painted or carved figure of such a memorial; by extension, an ornamental or symbolic group of any objects, or a representation of such a group in decorative art 1634. **2. a.** *transf.* Anything taken in war, or in hunting, etc.; a spoil or prize, esp. if kept or displayed as a memorial 1513. **b.** *fig.* Anything serving as a token or evidence of victory, valour, skill, power, etc.; a monument, memorial 1569.

1. Around the posts hung helmets, darts, and spears, And captive chariots, axes, shields, and bars, And broken beaks of ships, the trophies of their wars DRYDEN. 2. a. A defeat and a wound were the only trophies of his expedition GIBBON. b. The triumphs and trophies of intellect 1871.

Comb.: **t.-money, -tax** *Hist.*, a tax formerly levied on householders in each county, for incidental expenses connected with the militia. Hence **Tro·phy** *v. trans.* (chiefly *pass.*) †to transform into a t. (*rare*); to bestow a t. upon; to adorn with a t. or trophies.

Tropic (trǫ·pik), *sb.* and *a.*[1] late ME. [ad. L. *tropicus*, a. Gr. τροπικός pertaining to the 'turning' of the sun at the solstice, tropical, f. τροπή turning.] **A.** *sb.* **1.** *Astr.* †**a.** Each of the two solstitial points, the most northerly and southerly points of the ecliptic, at which the sun reaches its greatest distance north or south of the equator, and 'turns' or begins to move towards it again; also (*loosely*), each of the two signs (Cancer and Capricorn) at the beginning of which these points occur –1662. **b.** Each of two circles of the celestial sphere (*t. of* CANCER and *t. of* CAPRICORN), parallel to the equinoctial or celestial equator, and distant about 23° 28′ north and south of it, touching the ecliptic at the solstitial points 1503. **c.** *fig.* Turning-point; limit, boundary 1639. **2.** *Geog.* Each of two parallels of latitude on the earth's surface (corresp. to the celestial circles, 1 b, and called likewise *t. of Cancer* and *t. of Capricorn*), distant about 23° 28′ north and south of the equator, being the boundaries of the torrid zone 1527. **b.** *pl.* With *the*: The region between (and about) these parallels; the torrid zone and parts immediately adjacent 1837.

2. b. The tropics are one vast garden EMERSON.

B. *adj.* **1.** *Astr.* = TROPICAL *a.* **1.** Now *rare* or *Obs.* 1551. **2.** *Geog.* = TROPICAL *a.* **2.** 1799. **3.** T. bird, any bird of the family *Phaethontidæ*, comprising sea-birds resembling terns, widely found in tropical regions, and characterized by webbed feet, rapid flight, and varied coloration. **b.** *T. grape*, the gulf-weed 1850.

2. The rapid t. vegetation has reclaimed its old domains KINGSLEY.

Tro·pic, *a.*[2] 1881. [Arbitrarily f. ATROPIC; cf. TROPINE.] *Chem.* In *t. acid*, an acid forming a constituent of atropine.

Tropical (trǫ·pikăl), *a.* 1527. [f. as TROPIC *a.*[1] + -AL.] **1.** *Astr.* Pertaining or relating to the tropics, or either tropic (in sense A. 1 a or b). **2.** *Geog.* Pertaining to, occurring in, or inhabiting the tropics; belonging to the torrid zone 1698. **b.** *Path.* Applied to diseases to which one is liable in tropical regions 1828. **c.** *fig.* Very hot, ardent, or luxuriant 1834. **3.** Pertaining to, involving, or of the nature of a trope or tropes; metaphorical, figurative 1567.

1. *T. year*, the interval between two successive passages of the sun through the same 'tropic' or solstitial point (or, equivalently, through the same equinoctial point); the natural year of the seasons as reckoned from one solstice or equinox to the next. So *t. month*, the time taken by the moon in passing from either tropic (or either equinoctial point) to the same again. 2. T. fruits 1700. The face of the desert ..is scorched by the direct and intense rays of a t. sun GIBBON. b. T. Liver 1893. c. Home he came.. in a hissing hot fit of t. rage 1834. 3. A strict and literall acception of a loose and tropicall expression SIR T. BROWNE.

Tropically (trǫ·pikăli), *adv.* 1564. [f. as prec. + -LY [2].] **1.** Metaphorically. **2.** With tropical heat, luxuriance, or violence 1852.

1. The Mouse-Trap: Marry how? T. *Ham.* III. ii. 247. 2. The rain..continues, although not quite so t. 1886.

Tropicopolitan (trǫ:piko,pǫ·lităn), *a.* 1878. [f. TROPIC, after COSMOPOLITAN.] *Nat. Hist.* Belonging to or inhabiting the whole of the tropics, or tropical regions generally.

Tropidine (trǫ·pidīn, -əin). 1883. [Arbitrarily f. TROPINE.] *Chem.* A colourless oily alkaloid obtained from tropine by the action of acids. So **Tropi·lidine**, a liquid hydrocarbon, C_7H_8, obtained by the dry distillation of tropine with quicklime.

Tropine (trōu·pīn, -əin). 1881. [Arbitrarily f. ATROPINE.] *Chem.* An alkaloid forming a constituent of atropine.

Tropism (trǫ·piz'm). 1899. [The second element of HELIOTROPISM, etc.] *Biol.* The turning of an organism, or part of one, in a particular direction in response to some special external stimulus.

Tropo-, comb. form repr. Gr. τρόπος turning, etc. (see TROPE); as in **Tropometer** (tropǫ·mītəɹ) [-METER], an instrument for measuring the angle of turning or torsion of some part of the body, as the eye-ball or a long bone.

Tropologic (trǫpolǫ·dʒik), *a.* late ME. [ad. late L. *tropologicus* = late Gr. τροπολογικός, f. τρόπος TROPE; see -IC.] = next.

Tropological (trǫpolǫ·dʒikăl), *a.* 1528. [f. as prec. + -AL.] Belonging to or involving tropology. **1.** Metaphorical, figurative 1555. **2.** Applied to a secondary sense or interpretation of Scripture, relating or applied to conduct or morals 1528. Hence **Tropolo·gically** *adv.*

Tropology (tropǫ·lŏdʒi). 1519. [ad. late L. *tropologia*, a. late Gr. τροπολογία, f. τρόπος trope; see -LOGY.] **1.** 'A speaking by tropes'; the use of metaphor in speech or writing. **2.** A moral discourse; a secondary sense or interpretation of Scripture relating to morals 1583. **3.** A treatise on tropes or figures of speech 1667.

Tropopause (trǫ·pǫpǭz). 1919. [f. as next + PAUSE *sb.*] The (imaginary) boundary between the troposphere and the stratosphere.

Troposphere (trǫ·pǫsfiəɹ). 1914. [f. TROPO- + SPHERE *sb.*] The lower stratum of the atmosphere, lying below the stratosphere, to which convective disturbances are confined.

Trot (trǫt), *sb.*[1] ME. [a. F., f. *trotter* to TROT.] **I. 1.** A gait of a quadruped, orig. of a horse, between walking and running, in which the legs move in diagonal pairs almost together; hence applied to a similar gait of a man (or other biped) between a walk and a run. **b.** The sound of a horse, etc. trotting 1858. **2.** A trotting-race (*rare*) 1891. **3.** A toddling child; also, a small or young animal. *colloq.* 1854. **4.** *U.S. slang.* = CRIB *sb.* 17. 1891.

II. *Fishing.* (perh. a different word.) A long-line lightly anchored or buoyed, with baited hooks hung by short lines a few feet apart; a trawl-line; also, each of the short lines attached to this 1858. Hence **Trot** *v.*[2] 1864.

Trot (trǫt), *sb.*[2] ME. [?] An old woman; usu. disparaging: an old beldame, a hag.

Trot (trǫt), *v.*[1] [Late ME. a. OF. *troter*, F. *trotter*.] **1.** *intr.* Of a horse, etc.: To go at the gait called the trot. Also said of a person. **b.** *transf.* Of a rider, etc., or of a vehicle. late ME. **2.** To go or move quickly; to bustle; to run. Now *colloq.*, implying short, quick motion in a limited area. late ME. †**3.** *trans.* **a.** To trot upon (something). *rare.* **b.** To go through at a trot. **c.** To traverse (a path) as if by trotting (*rare*). –1638. **4.** To cause to trot; to lead or ride at the trot 1592. **b.** To conduct or escort (a person) *to* or *round* a place 1888. **c.** To jog a child on one's knee; to 'give a ride to' 1853.

1. b. I will t. to morrow a mile SHAKS. *transf.* We college poets t...on very easy nags THACKERAY. 2. Wante makes the olde wyfe t. 1581. 3. a. My horse.. boundes from the Earth..he trots the ayre SHAKS. 4. To trott the horses up and downe 1628. Phr. *To t. out*, to lead out and show off the paces of (a horse); hence *fig.* to bring forward (a person, an opinion, etc.) for or as for inspection or approval; to exhibit, show off (*colloq.*).

Troth (trōuþ, trǫþ), *sb. arch.* [Early ME. *trowþe*, *trouþe*, for OE. *trēowþ* TRUTH.] **I. 1.** Faithfulness, good faith, honesty, loyalty. **2.** One's plighted word; the act of pledging one's faith, a promise, covenant. Chiefly in phr. *to plight one's troth*, to pledge one's faith; *spec.* to engage oneself to marry. ME.

1. I shall sweare that I will..true faith and t. beare to our soveraigne lord the king 1620. 2. And therto I plight thee my trouth *Bk. Com. Prayer, Matrimony. By* (rarely *upon*) *my t.*, a form of asseveration.

II. Truth, in various senses –1663. **b.** *In t.* (arch.), †*of* (*a*) *t.*: truly, verily, indeed. late ME. **c.** Also *ellipt.* or as *int.* arch. 1603. Hence **Tro·thless** *a.* perfidious, disloyal.

Troth, *v. Obs.* or *arch.* late ME. [f. prec., or aphetic f. BETROTH *v.*] *trans.* To plight one's troth to; to engage in a contract, esp. of marriage.

Troth-plight (trōu·þ,pləit), *sb. arch.* 1513. [f. TROTH *sb.* + PLIGHT *sb.*[1], *v.*[1]] The act of plighting troth, or troth plighted; a solemn engagement, esp. of marriage; betrothal.

Tro·th-plight, *pa. pple.* and *ppl. a. arch.* ME. [f. as prec. + *plight*, pa. pple. of PLIGHT *v.*[1]] Engaged by a 'troth' or covenant, esp. of marriage; betrothed.

Tro·th-plight, *v. arch.* 1440. [f. as prec. + PLIGHT *v.*[1]] *trans.* = TROTH *v.*

Trotter (trǫ·təɹ). late ME. [f. TROT *v.* + -ER [1].] **1.** A horse, etc. which trots; *spec.* a horse especially bred and trained to the trot. **2.** One who moves or goes about briskly and constantly 1562. **3.** Usu. *pl.* The feet of a quadruped, esp. those of sheep and pigs as used for food; also *joc.*, the feet of a human being 1522.

‖**Trottoir** (trotwār). 1804. [F., f. *trotter* to TROT + *-oir*, L. *-orium*.] A paved footway on each side of a street; a pavement.

Trotyl (trōu·til). 1918. [f. *trot* of *trinitrotoluol* + -YL.] Trinitrotoluol.

Troubadour (trū·bădūəɹ, -dōəɹ). 1727. [a. F., ad. Prov. *trobador*, f. *trobar*, F. *trouver* to find, invent, compose in verse.] One of a class of lyric poets, living in southern France, eastern Spain, and northern Italy, from the 11th to the 13th cc., who sang in Provençal (*langue d'oc*), chiefly of chivalry and gallantry, sometimes including wandering minstrels and jongleurs. **b.** *transf.* One who composes or sings verses or ballads 1826.

Trouble (trʋ·b'l), *sb.* [ME. a. OF. *truble*, *turble*, F. *trouble*, f. *tourbler*, *troubler* to TROUBLE.] **1.** Disturbance of mind or feelings; worry, vexation; affliction; grief; perplexity; distress. Now often also in lighter use. **b.** With *a* and *pl.*: An instance of this; a misfortune, calamity; a distressing circumstance, occurrence, or experience 1515. **c.** *transf.* A thing or person that gives trouble; a cause or occasion of affliction or distress 1591. **2.** Public disturbance, disorder, or confusion; with *a* and *pl.*, an instance of this. late ME. **3.** Pains or exertion; care, toil, labour. Phr. *To put to, to take* (*the*) *t.* 1577. **4. a.** A disease, ailment; a morbid affection 1726. **b.** A woman's travail. (Also of an animal.) *dial.* or *euphem.* 1825. **5.** *euphem.*, *colloq.*, etc. **a.** Unpleasant relations with the authorities, esp. such as involve arrest, imprisonment, or punishment 1560. **b.** Said of the condition of an unmarried woman with child 1891. **6.** *Mining.* A dislocation in a stratum; a fault (usu. small) 1672. **b.** Faulty working of apparatus or machinery 1889.

1. In the tyme of my t. I call vpon the COVERDALE *Ps.* lxxxv[i]. 7. To prevent t. in case of a breakdown on the mains 1910. b. To take Armes against a Sea of troubles SHAKS. 2. It maketh troble and rebellion in the realme LATIMER.

Trouble (trɒ·b'l), *v.* [ME. a. OF. *trubler, trobler*, etc., F. *troubler* :—late L. **turbulare*, f. **turbulus*, for cl. L. *turbidus* TURBID.] **I. 1.** *trans.* To disturb, agitate, ruffle (water, air, etc.); to make turbid, dim, or cloudy. Now *rare* or *arch.* **2.** To disturb, derange; to interrupt; to hinder, mar. *Obs.* or *arch.* ME.

1. Like a fountaine troubled, Muddie, ill seeming, thicke SHAKS. 2. T. not the peace SHAKS.

II. 1. To put into a state of (mental) agitation or disquiet; to disturb, distress, perplex ME. **2.** To injure; to molest, oppress. late ME. **b.** Of disease or ailment: To afflict; sometimes in weakened sense, to affect. late ME. **3.** To vex, annoy; to tease, plague, worry, pester, bother 1538. **b.** In lighter sense: To put to inconvenience, incommode; 'to give occasion of labour to: a word of civility or slight regard' (J.) 1516. **c.** With *for*: To pester with requests, importune; hence, in a formula of polite request: to give (a person) the trouble of passing or handing something 1516. **d.** *refl.* To take the trouble, exert oneself (*to do* something) 1500. **e.** *intr.* for *refl.* = d. (*colloq.*) 1880.

1. Now my soule is troublid WYCLIF *John* xii. 27. 2. b. Being troubled with a raging tooth, I could not sleepe SHAKS. 3. Take the Boy to you: he so troubles me, 'Tis past enduring SHAKS. b. Let me t. you with one more question JOWETT. c. The new pupil who 'troubled' Mr. Pecksniff for the loaf DICKENS. d. He had never troubled himself..to understand the question 1845. e. Do not t. to bring back the boat 1884. **Trou·bler**, one who or that which troubles; a disturber; an oppressor.

Troublesome (trɒ·b'lsɒm), *a.* 1548. [f. TROUBLE *sb.* + -SOME [1].] Full of, characterized by, or causing trouble.

Thys t. world *Bk. Com. Prayer.* Ile rather be vnmannerly, then t. SHAKS. The process is t. and dangerous 1836. Hence **Trou·blesome-ly** *adv.*, **-ness.**

Troublous (trɒ·bləs), *a.* Now only *literary* or *arch.* 1449. [a. OF. *troubleus, -eux, torbleus*, f. *trouble* TROUBLE; see -OUS.] **1.** Characterized by trouble, agitation, or disturbance; disordered, unsettled, confused. **b.** Causing disturbance; turbulent; restless, unquiet 1450. **2.** Causing trouble or grief; grievous; vexatious, troublesome 1463.

1. There are long t. periods, before matters come to a settlement CARLYLE. b. A sedicious fellow, and a t. preacher LATIMER. Hence **Trou·blous-ly** *adv.*, **-ness.**

‖**Trou-de-loup** (trudlu). 1789. [F., lit. 'wolf-hole, wolf-pit'.] *Mil.* In field fortification, a conical pit with a pointed stake fixed vertically in the centre, rows of which are dug before a work to hinder an enemy's approach. Usu. *pl.* **trous-de-loup** (trudlu).

Trough (trǭf, trǫf), *sb.* [Com. Teut.: OE. *troȝ* :—OTeut. **trugoz* :—Indo-Eur. **drukos*, deriv. of *dru* TREE.] **1.** A narrow open box-like vessel, made of wood, stone, metal, or earthenware, to contain liquid; *esp.* a drinking-vessel for domestic animals; also, a tank or vat used for washing, kneading, brewing, and various other purposes. (Often with prefix, as *drinking-, hog-, horse-, kneading-t.*) **b.** A small vessel of similar shape used in chemistry, photography, etc. 1819. **2.** *spec.* **a.** An oblong vessel containing the water in which a grindstone runs 1725. **b.** An oblong box with divisions serving as the cells of a voltaic battery; also short for *t.-battery* 1806. **c.** *Mining.* An oblong tank in which ores are washed; a rocker or buddle 1877. **d.** *Typog.* A metal-lined box in which stones, etc. are washed 1891. **†3.** A small primitive boat -1633. **4.** A channel, pipe, or trunk for conveying water; a conduit; a gutter fixed under the eaves of a building. late ME. **5.** A hollow or valley resembling a trough; *spec.* in *Geol.* a basin-shaped depression (longer than broad) 1513. **b.** *Meteorol.* A line or elongated region of lower barometric pressure between two regions of higher pressure 1882.

5. The whole valley, or strath, or t. of the Clyde 1819. *T. of the sea*, the hollow on the surface between two waves.

attrib. and *Comb.*: **t. girder**, an iron girder shaped like a t.; **t. gutter**, a box-like channel for drainage; a rain-water pipe of this form; **t. shell**, a mollusc of the family *Mactridæ*. Hence **Trough** *v. trans.* (*a*) *Geol.* to form into a t. or into the shape of a t. (*b*) To treat in some way in a t.; to stain or mould in a t.

Trounce (trauns), *v.* 1551. [Origin obsc.] †**1.** *trans.* To trouble, afflict, distress; to discomfit, harass -1655. **2.** To beat, thrash, belabour, cudgel; to flog 1568. **3.** To punish; also, to get the better of, defeat 1657. **b.** To indict, to sue at law. Now *dial.* 1638. **4.** To censure; to scold severely 1607.

2. Flattered with the hopes of seeing a bailiff trounced SMOLLETT. Hence **Trou·ncer**, one who trounces; *spec.* an odd man (see ODD A. II. 4 d).

‖**Troupe** (trūp). 1825. [Fr., = TROOP.] A company of dancers, players, or the like. Hence Troupe *v.* Trou·per.

Trouse (trūz, trauz). Now *Hist.* and *arch.* 1578. [app. from Ir. (and Sc. Gael.) *triubhas*, orig. pronounced *trīvăs* or *trīwăs*, in mod. Ir. pronunc. *trūs* (see TREWS). Ult. etym. obsc.] **1.** A close-fitting article of attire for the buttocks and thighs (divided below), to the lower extremities of which stockings were attached; *spec.* = TREWS. In later use, drawers or knee-breeches. †**2.** *pl.* = TROUSERS 2. -1820.

Trousers (trau·zəɹz), *sb. pl.* 1599. [Extended form of prec; perh. after DRAWERS.] †**1.** = prec. 1. -1834. **2.** A loose-fitting garment of cloth worn by men, covering the loins and legs to the ankles. (Also *a pair of t.*) 1681. **b.** The loose bag-like drawers or pantaloons worn by both sexes in Mohammedan countries 1775. **c.** Pantalettes 1821. **3.** In *sing.* form **trouser**, in various senses 1609. **b.** A single leg of a pair of trousers 1893.

Comb. (with *trouser-*): **trouser-press**, a contrivance for pressing the legs of t. so as to produce a crease; **trouser-stretcher**, a device for stretching t. so as to take out any 'bagginess'. Hence **Trou·ser** *v. slang, trans.* to put (money etc.) into the trouser-pocket, to pocket.

‖**Trousseau** (truso). ME. [F., dim. f. *trousse* TRUSS *sb.*] **1.** †**a.** A bundle. **b.** A bunch of keys. *rare.* (perh. only as Fr.) 1847. **2.** A bride's outfit of clothes, house-linen, etc. Also *attrib.* 1833.

Trout (traut). [OE. *truht*, ad. late L. *tructus, tructa, trutta*, etc. = Gr. τρώκτης, f. τρώγειν to gnaw.] **1.** A well-known freshwater fish of the genus *Salmo*, esp. *S. fario*, the common trout; it has numerous spots of red and black on its sides and head, and is greatly valued as a sporting fish and on account of its edible quality. **b.** *collect. sing.* 1602. **2.** Used as a name of various fish (chiefly *Salmonidæ*) resembling the trout in appearance or habits. Now *local.* 1604. **3.** With defining prefix, as the name of various species of the genus *Salmo* (or of the allied genus *Salvelinus*), and occas. of other genera 1661.

3. **Bastard t.** (*U.S.*), the squeteague, *Cynoscion nothus*; **brook t.**, *Salmo fario*; in *U.S.*, *S. fontinalis*, or *S. irideus*, the rainbow t.; **brown t.**, *S. fario*; **grey t.**, *Salmo trutta*; in *U.S.* the squeteague; **lake t.**, *S. ferox* (the great lake t.); in *U.S.* *S. confinis* (the N. Amer. lake t.), inhabiting the deepest waters of the Great Lakes; **rainbow t.**, *S. irideus*, a Californian species, now introduced in British t.-streams; **red-bellied t.**, the char, *S. salvelinus*; also *S.* or *Fario erythrogaster*, of the lakes of New York State and Pennsylvania; **rock t.**, *Chirus constellatus.*

attrib. and *Comb.*, as *t.-brook, -fishing, -preserve, -stream*; **t.-fly**, (*a*) the may-fly; (*b*) an artificial fly for t.-fishing; **-perch**, the black bass (*local U.S.*); also, a trout-like fish (*Percopsis guttatus*) of the rivers and Great Lakes of U.S., having the mouth and scales like those of a perch. Hence **Trou·ting**, t.-fishing. **Trou·tlet, Trou·tling**, a little or tiny t. **Trou·ty** *a.* full of, abounding in, or containing t.

‖**Trouvaille** (truvaʹy). 1842. [F., f. *trouver* to find.] A lucky find; a windfall.

‖**Trouvère** (truvę̄r), **trouveur** (truvö̆r). 1795. [OF. *trovere, -eur, truveur*, F. *trouvère, trouveur*, f. *trouver*.] One of a school of poets who flourished in Northern France from the 11th to the 14th c., whose works are chiefly epic in character. Cf. TROUBADOUR.

Trove: see TREASURE-TROVE. Also short for *treasure-trove*, in sense 'a valuable find' 1888.

Trover (trō̆u·vəɹ). 1594. [sb. use of OF. *trover*, F. *trouver* to find.] *Law.* The act of finding and assuming possession of any personal property; hence (in full, *action of t.*), an action at law to recover the value of personal property illegally converted by another to his own use.

Trow (trōu, *locally* trōu, trau), *sb. local.* ME. [dial. var. of TROUGH 3.] A name for various kinds of boats or barges; *spec.* **a.** in the south of Scotland and north of England, a double canoe or boat used in spearing salmon by torchlight (also *pl.* const. as *sing.*); now *rare* or *Obs.*; **b.** on the south coast of England, a small flat-bottomed boat used in herring-fishing.

Trow (trōu, trau), *v. arch.* [(1) OE. *trūwian*, f. *trūwa* faith, belief = OTeut. **trūwian*, from base *trŭ-*; (2) OE. *trēowan, trēowian*, from *trēowe* faith, belief.] †**1.** *trans.* (orig. *intr.* with *dat.*). To trust, have confidence in, believe (a person or thing) -1829. **2.** *intr.* To believe *in* or *on*; to have confidence *in*; to trust *to*. *Obs.* or *rare arch.* OE. **3.** *trans.* To believe (a statement, etc.); to accept as true or trustworthy ME. **4.** with *obj. cl.* To believe, think, be of opinion, suppose, imagine; sometimes, to feel sure, be assured OE. **b.** Parenthetically or at the end of a sentence (often merely expletive), as *I t.* (in assertions) = 'I suppose, I ween'; †also rarely in questions (where the sense is not clear) ME. †**c.** Also simply *t.* (ellipt. for *I t.* or *t. you*) -1741.

3. Speake lesse then thou knowest,..Learne more then thou trowest SHAKS. 4. Can anything be more clearly proved..? I t. not. 1872. b. Who 's there, I troa? SHAKS. c. And haue you euer seene her, t.? 1620.

Trowel (trau·ĕl), *sb.* [ME. *truel*, a. OF. *truele*, F. *truelle*, ad. vulgar or late L. *truella*, for L. *trulla*, dim. of *trua* stirring-spoon, skimmer, ladle.] A flat-bladed tool of metal or wood, with a short handle; used by masons, bricklayers, and others, for spreading, moulding, or smoothing mortar, cement, and the like. **b.** A culinary ladle or slice of this shape 1773. **c.** A tool of this kind used in gardening, having a hollow, scoop-like, semi-cylindrical blade 1796.

To lay it on with a t., to express a thing coarsely or bluntly; now *spec.* to flatter excessively or grossly. *Comb.*: **t.-bayonet**, a bayonet resembling a mason's trowel, which may be used as a light entrenchment tool, or, when detached from the rifle, as a hatchet. Hence **Trow·elful**, as much as can be taken up on a t.

Trowel (trau·ĕl), *v.* 1670. [f. prec.] **1.** *trans.* To spread, smooth, or dress (a surface) with or as with a trowel; to form or mould with a trowel. **2.** To put, place, or move (something) with or as with a trowel; to lay on with a trowel, i. e. thickly or clumsily; often *fig.* of flattery or laudation 1772.

Troy [1] (troi). 1520. Name of an ancient city in Asia Minor, besieged and taken by the Greeks; in comb. **Troy-fair, Troy-town**, *fig.* a scene of disorder or confusion (now *dial.*).

Troy [2] (troi). late ME. [app. named from a weight used at the fair of Troyes in France.] *T. weight*, also ellipt. *T.*: The standard system of weights used for the precious metals and precious stones; formerly also for bread. (The pound t. contains 5760 grains, and is divided into 12 ounces.) **b.** *fig.* in allusion to the pound troy being less than the pound avoidupois 1599.

b. There was Cressid was T. weight, and Nell was avoirdupois 1599.

Trs., abbrev. of *transpose* (Typog.), *trustees.*

Tru·ancy. 1784. [f. next + -CY.] The action of playing truant; truant conduct or practice.

Truant (trū·ănt), *sb.* (*a.*) [ME. a. OF. *truant*, F. *truand*; prob. from a Celtic source.] †**1.** One who begs without justification; a sturdy beggar; a vagabond; an idle rogue or knave. (Often a mere term of abuse.) -1656. **2.** A lazy, idle person; *esp.* a boy who absents himself from school without leave; hence *fig.*, one who wanders from an appointed place or neglects his duty or business 1449.

1. Hang him t., there's no true drop of bloud in him to be truly toucht with loue SHAKS. 2. I haue a T. beene to Chiualry SHAKS. Phr. *To play t.*

B. *adj.* **1.** That is a truant, or plays truant; idle, lazy, loitering, *esp.* of a boy, staying from school without leave; hence, wandering, straying 1550. **b.** Marked by truancy or idleness; befitting a truant or idler 1602. †**2.** Trivial, trite; idle, vain (*rare*) -1682.

1. b. But what in faith make you from Wittemberge? *Hor.* A t. disposition, good my Lord. SHAKS. Hence **Tru·antly** *adv.* (now *rare*). **Tru·antry**, truancy. †**Tru·antship** (*rare*), truancy; also as a mock title.

Tru·ant, *v.* late ME. [f. prec.] †**1.** *intr.* To play the vagabond or rogue -1440. **2.**

To idle, play truant (esp. from school); to wander, stray 1580. †3. *trans.* To waste or idle away (time); to spend in truanting -1708.

2. I must..truly study man, (A booke in which I yet have truanted) HEYWOOD. 3. I dare not be the author Of truanting the time FORD.

Truce (trūs), *sb.* [Represents pl. *trewes, triewes* of ME. *trewe, triewe*:—OE. *trēow* (fem. pl. *trēwa*, used in the sense of the sing.) truth or fidelity to a promise, good faith, promise:—WGer. **trewwa*; cf. Goth. *triggwa* covenant (whence Romanic *tregua*, F. *trève*) and OE. *trūwa*, ON. *trúa*; see TRUE *a.*] 1. A suspension of hostilities for a specified period between armies at war; a temporary peace or cessation from arms; an armistice; also, an agreement or treaty effecting this. b. Loosely or vaguely: Cessation or absence of hostilities (without limitation of time); peace. late ME. 2. Hence, Respite or intermission (more loosely, freedom or liberty) from something irksome, painful, or oppressive 1567. b. In interjectional phr. (*a*) *t. with*, now usu. (*a*) *t. to*, enough of, have done with 1700.

1. A t. which in the following November became a permanent peace STUBBS. *fig.* The Seas and Windes (old Wranglers) tooke a T. SHAKS. *T. of God*, a suspension of hostilities between armies, or of private feuds, ordered by the Church during certain days and seasons in mediæval times; hence *allus.* and *fig.* 2. Where he may..find T. to his restless thoughts MILT. b. A t. to this light conversation 1835. Hence **Truce** *v.* (now *rare*) *intr.* to make a t.; *trans.* to bring to an end by or as by means of a t. **Tru·celess** *a.* that is without t.; unceasing in hostility.

†Truchman. 1485. [ad. med.L. *turchemannus*, F. *trucheman*, ad. Arab. *turjamān* DRAGOMAN.] An interpreter.

fig. He is a Truch-Man, that interprets between learned Writers and gentle Readers 1680.

Trucial (trū·ʃăl), *a.* 1876. [f. TRUCE *sb.* + -IAL, app. after *fiducial*.] Of or pertaining to the maritime truce which regulated the relations of certain Arab Sheikhs to one another and to the British government: applied to (*a*) the sheikhs of the territories lying west of the Oman peninsula or the Arab littoral of the Persian Gulf, (*b*) the territories themselves.

Truck (trɒk), *sb.*[1] 1553. [a. AF. *truke*, OF. *troque*, †*troq*, *troc*, f. *troquer* TRUCK *v.*[1]] 1. The action or practice of trucking; trading by exchange of commodities; barter. b. with *a* and *pl.* A traffic, trade; an act of trading, a bargain or deal 1638. 2. The payment of wages otherwise than in money; the system or practice of such payment, the *t. system*; occas., goods supplied in lieu of wages 1743. 3. 'Traffic', intercourse, communication, dealings 1625. †4. Commodities for barter -1770. b. Small articles of a miscellaneous character; sundries; odds and ends; trash, rubbish. (Rarely *pl.*) 1785. c. *U.S.* Market-garden produce; hence, culinary vegetables 1784.

4. b. I can't smoke the t. the steward sells KIPLING. *attrib.* and *Comb.*, as *t.-farm, -farmer, -garden, -produce*; **t.-shop, store,** a shop at which vouchers given instead of wages may be exchanged for goods, a tommy-shop; **-system,** the system of paying wages in vouchers for goods instead of in money.

Truck (trɒk), *sb.*[2] 1611. [app. deriv. of L. *trochus* = Gr. τροχός TROCHUS; or short for TRUCKLE.] 1. A small solid wooden wheel or roller; *spec. Naut.* one of those on which the carriages of ships' guns were formerly mounted. 2. *Naut.* A circular or square cap of wood fixed on the head of a mast or flagstaff, usu. with small holes or sheaves for halliards 1626. b. One of the small wooden blocks through which the rope of a parrel is threaded to prevent its being frayed against the mast. c. A similar block lashed to the shrouds to form a guide or fair-leader for running rigging. 1625. 3. A wheeled vehicle for carrying heavy weights. a. A strong flat open trolley for carrying blocks of stone or the like; a lorry. b. A light two-wheeled hand-cart. c. An open railway wagon. d. = BOGIE 2. e. A low barrow of various types, with one to four wheels, as that used on railway platforms for moving luggage, etc. f. A small barrow, with two stout low wheels and a projecting plate or lip in front, used for moving sacks, etc. 1774.

3. f. Porters are hurrying to and fro with luggage on trucks 1866.

Truck (trɒk), *v.*[1] [ME. *trukie*, a. F. *troquer* to truck, barter, exchange, in med.L. *trocare*, of unkn. origin.] 1. *trans.* To give in exchange *for* something else; to exchange (one thing) *for* another; also, to exchange (a thing) *with* a person (also *absol.*). 2. To exchange (commodities) for profit; to barter 1440. 3. To barter away (what should be sacred or precious) *for* something unworthy 1649. 4. *intr.* To trade by exchange of commodities; to barter 1594. 5. *fig.* or in fig. context: To bargain or deal *for* a commodity *with* a person; to negotiate; also, to have dealings *in*, to trade; esp. of dealings of an underhand or improper character: to traffic 1615. b. To have dealings or intercourse, be on familiar terms *with*. Now *dial.* 1622. 6. *trans.* To pay (an employee) otherwise than in money; to pay or deal with on the truck-system (with the implication of profiting by the transaction). Also *intr.* 1871.

1. To t. the Latine for any other vulgar Language, is but an ill barter 1645. 3. Liberty 's too often truck'd for Gold DE FOE. 4. Chinese..tobacco, for which they t. with the Russians 1854. 6. The very paupers used to be 'trucked', the inspectors..gave the paupers their relief in kind 1871. Hence †**Tru·ckage,**[1] the action of trucking; exchange, barter. MILT. **Tru·cker,** *spec.* (*U.S.*) one who grows 'truck' or garden produce for market; so **Tru·cking** *vbl. sb.*

Truck, *v.*[2] 1809. [f. TRUCK *sb.*[2]] *trans.* To put on or into a truck; to convey by means of a truck or trucks. Hence **Tru·ckage,**[2] conveyance by truck or trucks, or the cost of this; also, supply of trucks collectively.

Truckle (trɒ·k'l), *sb.* late ME. [= AF. *trocle, trokle*, ad. L. *trochlea* = Gr. τροχιλία, τροχιλέα sheaf of a pulley, TROCHLEA.] 1. A small wheel with a groove in its circumference round which a cord passes; a pulley, a sheave. 2. A small roller or wheel placed under or attached to a heavy object to facilitate moving it; a castor on a piece of furniture. Now *dial.* 1459. 3. Short for TRUCKLE-BED 1637. 4. A low-wheeled car; a truck. Chiefly *Irish.* 1689.

Truckle (trɒ·k'l), *v.* 1613. [f. *truckle* in TRUCKLE-BED.] †1. *intr.* To sleep in a truckle-bed -1674. 2. *fig.* †a. To be subservient, to submit, to give precedence *to* -1738. b. To submit from an unworthy motive; to act with servility 1680. c. To submit or give way timidly 1837. †3. To move on truckles or castors -1796.

2. a. Publick good is made to t. to private gain 1704. b. Too proud to t. to a Superior 1789. Hence **Truckler** (trɒ·klər), one who truckles (in sense 2 b of the vb.).

Tru·ckle-bed. 1459. [TRUCKLE *sb.* 2.] A low bed running on truckles or castors, usu. pushed beneath a high or 'standing' bed when not in use. So **T. bedstead.**

Truculence (trɒ·k-, trū·kiŭlĕns). 1727. [ad. L. *truculentia*, f. *truculentus* TRUCULENT.] The condition or quality of being truculent; fierceness, savageness. So **Tru·culency** 1569.

Truculent (trɒ·kiŭlĕnt, trū·k-), *a.* 1540. [ad. L. *truculentus*, f. *truc-, trux* fierce, savage.] 1. Characterized by or exhibiting ferocity or cruelty; fierce, cruel, savage, barbarous. b. Of speech or writing: Violent; rude; scathing; savage; harsh 1850. ¶2. (In catachrestic use, assoc. w. TRUCK *sb.*[1], *v.*[1], TRUCKLE *v.*) Mean, base, mercenary 1825.

1. b. Voltaire is never either gross or t. MORLEY. 2. A t. exchange not only of truth, but of sincerity, for money BENTHAM. Hence **Tru·culent-ly** *adv.*, **-ness.**

Trudge (trɒdʒ), *sb.* 1748. [f. next.] †1. A person who trudges; a trudger -1775. 2. An act of trudging; a 'tramp' 1835.

Trudge (trɒdʒ), *v.* 1547. [Origin obsc.] 1. *intr.* To walk laboriously, wearily, or without spirit, but steadily and persistently; 'to jog on; to march heavily on' (J.). b. *spec.* To go away, be off, depart 1547. 2. *trans.* To perform (a journey) or travel over (a distance) by trudging; to tramp 1635.

1. From house to house he trudges in the snow, visiting poor widows 1856. b. 'Tis time for me to t. 1623. Hence **Tru·dger,** one who trudges.

Trudgen (trɒ·dʒən). Also *erron.* **trudgeon.** 1893. [f. proper name *Trudgen*.] In full *t. stroke*: applied to a kind of hand-over-hand or double over-arm breast-stroke in swimming, with leg action resembling that of walking.

John Trudgen..in 1863..went to Buenos Ayres, While there he learnt 'to trudge' from the natives 1904.

True (trū), *a.* (*sb., adv.*) [OE. *trēowe*, WS. *triewe*, whence ME. *trew(e*, by the side of which were types repr. by *trow* and *truwe*; deriv. of *trēow*, *trūw* faith, good faith, covenant: see TRUCE.] 1. Of persons: Steadfast in adherence *to* a commander or friend, *to* a principle or cause, *to* one's promises, faith, etc.; firm in allegiance; faithful, loyal, constant, trusty. Somewhat *arch.* b. *transf.* Of personal attributes or actions. Somewhat *arch.* OE. c. *fig.* of things: Reliable; constant ME. 2. Honest, honourable, upright, virtuous, trustworthy (*arch.*); free from deceit, sincere, truthful; of actions, feelings, etc.: sincere, unfeigned OE. 3. Of a statement or belief: Consistent with fact; agreeing with reality; representing the thing as it is ME. b. *transf.* Speaking truly, telling the truth; trustworthy in statement; veracious, truthful ME. 4. Agreeing with a standard, pattern, or rule; exact, accurate, precise; correct, right 1550. b. In more general sense: Of the right kind, such as it should be, proper ME. c. That is rightly or lawfully such; rightful, legitimate. late ME. d. Accurately placed, fitted, or shaped; exact in position or form, as an instrument, etc. 1474. e. *T. to*: consistent with, exactly agreeing with 'faithful to' 1735. f. Conformable to reality, natural 1870. g. Remaining constant to type 1839. 5. Real, genuine; properly so called; not counterfeit, spurious, or imaginary; also, approaching or conforming to the ideal character of such. late ME. b. In scientific use: Conformable to the type, or to the accepted idea or character of the genus, class, or kind; properly or strictly so called 1578. c. *True bill*, (in *Law*) a bill of indictment found by a Grand Jury to be supported by sufficient evidence to justify the hearing of a case. Hence *allus.* a true statement or charge (*true* being loosely taken in sense 3). 1591.

1. Ye haue done as a trew subjet ought to do to his lorde 1533. T...to the cause of civil freedom 1855. c. T. as the Needle to the Pole 1733. 2. Good Men and t. for a Petty Jury 1710. 3. The truer opinion 1608. It is t., we were all but young in the War DE FOE. *To come t.*, to be verified or realized in actual experience, be fulfilled. b. This way the noise was, if mine ear be t. MILT. 4. Apelles drew A Circle regularly t. PRIOR. b. Facts thus placed in their t. bearings 1911. d. Of the ground: Free from unevenness, level and smooth 1851. e. Be t. to your time in the morning DICKENS. f. I do not object to fiction provided it be t. 1894. g. This breed is very t. DARWIN. 5. The time of t. noon 1854. b. T. nerve tumours are exceedingly rare 1899.

B. *sb.* (the adj. used absol.) †1. Nickname for a member of the Protestant or Whig party in the 17th c. NORTH. 2. *The t.*: That which is true; truth, reality 1812. 3. Accurate position or adjustment; in phr. *out of (the) t.* 1890. C. *adv.* = TRULY 1-4. ME. b. In accordance with the ancestral type; without variation; in phr. *to breed t.* 1859. Hence **True·ness.**

True, *v.* 1841. [f. prec.] *trans.* To make true, as a piece of mechanism; to place, adjust, or shape accurately; to make accurately or perfectly straight, level, round, smooth, sharp, etc. as required. Hence **Tru·er,** also *truer-up.*

True·-born, *a.* 1591. Born of a true or pure stock; legitimately born; having the sterling qualities associated with such descent.

Though banish'd, yet a true-borne Englishman SHAKS.

True·-bred, *a.* 1596. a. Bred of a true or pure stock; of the true breed; thoroughbred. b. Having or manifesting true breeding or education.

True-hearted (stress var.), *a.* 1471. Having a true heart; faithful, loyal; honest, sincere. Hence **True:hea·rtedness.**

True-love (trū·lɒv). ME. [TRUE *a.*, LOVE *sb.*] 1. A faithful lover; one whose love is pledged; a sweetheart, beloved. late ME. †2. An ornament or symbol of true love; a TRUE-LOVE KNOT -1575. 3. Herb Paris (*Paris quadrifolia*), the whorl of four leaves with the single flower or berry in the midst suggesting the figure of a true-love knot. late ME.

1. My true-love hath my heart, and I haue his SIDNEY. 3. Vnder his tonge a trewe loue he beer For therby wende he to ben gracious CHAUCER.

True-love knot, true lover's knot. 1495. A kind of knot, of an ornamental form (usu. either a double-looped bow, or a knot formed of two loops intertwined), used as a symbol of true love; a figure of this. Also *fig.* or *allus.*

Truepenny (trū·peni). *arch.* 1519. A trusty person; an honest fellow (compared to a coin of genuine metal); *adj.* genuine. *colloq.*

Art thou there t.? SHAKS.

Truffle (trʊ·f'l, trū·f'l). 1591. [app. a deriv. of F. *trufe, truffe*; etym. obsc.] Any one of various underground fungi of the family *Tuberaceæ*; *spec.* an edible fungus of the genus *Tuber*, a native of Central and Southern Europe, esteemed as a delicacy; esp. *T. æstivum*, or *cibarium*, the Common (English) Truffle, and *T. melanosporum*, the French Truffle, which have a black, warty exterior, and more or less resemble a potato in shape.

attrib. and *Comb.*: **t.-dog, -pig,** a dog or pig trained to discover truffles; **-worm,** the larva of an insect infesting the t. Hence **Truffled** (trʊ·f'ld) *a.* cooked, garnished, or stuffed with truffles.

Trug[1] (trʊg). *local.* 1580. [? Dial. var. TROUGH.] **1.** A wooden milk pan. **2.** A shallow oblong basket made of wood strips, chiefly used for carrying fruit, vegetables, etc. 1862.

Trug[2]. *Obs.* exc. *dial.* 1592. [perh. ad. It. *trucca* a trull; perh. cogn. w. TRUCK *sb.*[1]] A prostitute. †**b.** A catamite (*rare*) –1630.

Truism (trū·iz'm). 1708. [f. TRUE *a.* + -ISM.] A self-evident truth, esp. one of slight importance; a statement so obviously true as not to require discussion.

The fear of t. in our modern writers 1861. Hence **Trui·stic, -al** *adjs.* having the character of a t.; trivially self-evident.

Trull (trʊl). 1519. [= G. *trulle* (Swiss *trolle*, Swabian *trull*).] **1.** A low prostitute or concubine; a drab, strumpet, trollop. †**2.** A girl, lass, wench (*rare*) –1600.

Truly (trū·li), *adv.* [OE. *trēowlīce*, ME. *treulich*, etc., f. *trēow, treu* TRUE; see -LY[2].] **1.** Faithfully, loyally, steadfastly. *arch.* †**2.** Honestly, honourably, uprightly –1558. **3.** In accordance with the fact; truthfully; correctly (in ref. to a statement) ME. **4.** In accordance with a rule or standard; exactly, accurately, precisely, correctly. late ME. **b.** Rightly; as it ought to be, properly; often in phr. *well and t.* late ME. **c.** In accordance with nature; naturally 1600. **d.** Without cross-breeding; also, without variation from the ancestral type 1854. **5.** Genuinely, really, actually, in fact, in reality; sincerely, unfeignedly. late ME. **b.** Used to emphasize a statement: Indeed, forsooth, verily ME. **c.** In phr. *yours truly*, one of the more formal of the phrases used in subscribing a letter; hence joc. = 'myself' 1788.

1. *Cymb.* III. v. 110. **3.** Tell me truely how thou lik'st her SHAKS. **b.** His innocent Babe t. begotten SHAKS. **5.** A Mind t. virtuous STEELE. **b.** A wide freedom, t.! RUSKIN. **c.** Give the young one a glass, ..and score it up to yours t. THACKERAY.

Trump (trʊmp), *sb.*[1] *arch.* and *poet.* [ME. a. F. *trompe*; ult. etym. uncertain.] **1.** = TRUMPET *sb.* **1.** **2.** *fig.* One who or that which proclaims, celebrates, or summons loudly like a trumpet; esp. in *t. of fame* and the like. 1531.

1. In the laste trumpe; forsoth the trumpe schal synge WYCLIF. 1 *Cor.* xv. 52. **2.** Say we sound The t. of liberty GRAY.

Trump (trʊmp), *sb.*[2] 1529. [Corruption of TRIUMPH *sb.*] **1.** A playing-card of that suit which for the time being ranks above the other three, so that any one such card can 'take' any card of another suit; *spec.* the card, usu. that last turned up by the dealer, determining this suit; also, *pl.*, the suit thus determined. †**b.** An obsolete card-game, known also as ruff –1798. **c.** An act of trumping (*rare*) 1853. **2.** *fig.* and in fig. context 1595. **3.** *colloq.* A first-rate fellow; a 'brick' 1819.

2. *To turn up trumps*, to turn out well or successfully. *To put* (a person) *to his t.* or *trumps*, to oblige a card-player to play out his trumps; *fig.* 'to put to the last expedient' (J.). **3.** You're a t. DICKENS.

Trump (trʊmp), *v.*[1] Now *rare* or *Obs.* [ME. a. OF. *tromper*, f. *trompe* TRUMP *sb.*[1]] **1.** *intr.* To blow or sound a trumpet. Also with *up.* **2.** *trans.* To proclaim, celebrate, or extol by, or as by, the sound of a trumpet. late ME.

Trump, *v.*[2] 1553. [f. TRUMP *sb.*[2]] **I. 1.** *Cards.* **a.** *trans.* To put a trump upon; to take with a trump 1598. **b.** *absol.* or *intr.* To play a trump 1680. **2.** *fig.* or in fig. context: now usu., to beat, to 'cap' 1586.

1. To T. a Card early in the Deal 1778. **2.** I trumped her old-world stories..with the latest..intelligence THACKERAY.

II. *T. up* (trans.). †**a.** To bring up, allege –1772. **c.** To get up or devise in an unscrupulous way; to forge, fabricate, invent 1695.

Trumpery (trʊ·mpəri), *sb.* (*a.*) 1456. [a. F. *tromperie*, f. *tromper* to deceive, cheat.] †**1.** Deceit, fraud, imposture, trickery –1847. **2.** 'Something of less value than it seems'; hence, 'something of no value; trifles' (J.); trash, rubbish 1456.

2. I haue sold all my Tromperie: not a counterfeit Stone, not a Ribbon, Glasse, Pomander, Browch..to keepe my Pack from fasting SHAKS. Embryos, and Idiots, Eremits and Friers White, Black and Grey, with all thir trumperie MILT. All the metaphysical t. of the schools DE FOE.

B. *attrib.* or *adj.* Of little or no value; paltry, insignificant; worthless, trashy 1576.

It seems a t. quarrel 1869.

Trumpet (trʊ·mpėt), *sb.* ME. [a. F. *trompette*, dim. f. *trompe* TRUMP *sb.*[1]] **1.** A musical wind-instrument (or one of a class of such) of bright, powerful, and penetrating tone, used from ancient times, esp. for military or other signals, and in modern times also in the orchestra; it consists of a cylindrical or conical tube, usu. of metal, straight or curved (or bent upon itself), with a cup-shaped mouthpiece and a flaring bell. (In modern forms of the instrument additional tones are obtained by means of slides, crooks, valves, or keys.) **2.** Something of the nature of or resembling a trumpet 1659. **b.** = EAR-T., SPEAKING-T. 1696. **3.** *fig.* A means or agent (real or imaginary) which proclaims, celebrates, or gives warning of something 1447. **4.** *transf.* A trumpeter. late ME. **b.** *fig.* = TRUMPETER 2. 1549. **5.** A sound like that of a trumpet; the loud cry of certain animals, esp. the elephant 1850. **6.** Something shaped like a trumpet 1668.

1. The general's t. gave the signal of departure GIBBON. *Feast of Trumpets*, a Jewish festival observed at the beginning of the month Tisri, blowing of trumpets being a prominent part of the solemnities. **2.** *Trumpet, Tromba*, a striking reed stop of clear penetrating tone 1876. *T. marine, marine t.* [tr. It. *tromba marina*, F. *trompette marine*], a large obsolete musical instrument of the viol kind, played with a bow, and having a single thick string passing over a bridge fastened at one end only, the other vibrating against the body, and producing a tone like that of a trumpet. **3.** The decree of Wormes was the trompet of this warre 1560. Phr. *To blow one's own t.*, to sound one's own praises, boast, brag. **4. b.** So hence: be thou the t. of our wrath SHAKS. **6.** The white and rosy trumpets of the bindweed 1883.

attrib. and *Comb.*: **t. animalcule,** an infusorian of the genus *Stentor* or family *Stentoridæ*, so called from its shape; **-call,** a call or summons sounded on the t.; **-conch** = *-shell*; **t. daffodil,** a variety of daffodil with a conspicuous 'trumpet' or tubular *corona*; **-fish,** any of various fishes with long tubular snout, *esp.* the bellows-fish or sea-snipe (*Centriscus scolopax*) and the tobacco-pipe fish (*Fistularia*); **-flower,** any of various plants with large or showy t.-shaped flowers, esp. of the genus *Tecoma* and *Bignonia*, also species of *Catalpa, Brunfelsia*, etc.; **-lily,** the white arum-lily; also some species of *Lilium*; **-major,** the chief trumpeter of a band or regiment; **-shaped** *a.*, *spec.* in *Nat. Hist.* tubular with one end dilated; **-shell,** a shell of the genus *Triton* or family *Tritonidæ*, or any other shell which can be blown like a t.; **-tongued** *a.*, 'having a tongue vociferous as a trumpet' (J.); loud-voiced; **-tree,** a W. Indian and S. Amer. tree *Cecropia peltata*, with hollow stem and branches which are used for wind-instruments; **-weed,** (*a*) = SEA-*trumpet*; (*b*) a N. Amer. species of hemp-agrimony, *Eupatorium purpureum*, with hollow stems which children blow through like trumpets; (*c*) a N. Amer. species of lettuce, *Lactuca canadensis.*

Tru·mpet, *v.* 1530. [f. prec.] **1.** *intr.* To blow or sound a trumpet. **b.** To emit a sound like that of a trumpet; esp. in ref. to the cry of an elephant when enraged or excited 1828. **2.** *trans.* **a.** To sound on a trumpet; to utter with a sound like that of a trumpet 1729. **b.** *fig.* To announce or publish as by sound of trumpet; to noise abroad 1604. **c.** To summon or denounce formally or to drive away, by sound of a trumpet 1680.

1. b. Anopheles, a mosquito that does not t. 1900. **2. b.** They trumpeted the story all over the town H. WALPOLE. **c.** They drummed and trumpeted the wretches out of their Hall BURKE.

Trumpeter (trʊ·mpėtəɹ). 1497. [f. TRUMPET *sb.* or *v.* + -ER[1], or a. F. *trompeteur.*] **1.** One who sounds or plays upon a trumpet; *spec.* a soldier in a cavalry regiment who gives signals with a trumpet. **2.** *fig.* One who gives the signal for, proclaims, or extols something as by sound of trumpet 1581. **3.** *T's. muscle*, †also simply *t.* = BUCCINATOR 1615. **4.** Any of various birds, from their loud note suggesting the sound of a trumpet. **a.** A variety of domestic pigeon 1725. **b.** Any species of the S. Amer. genus *Psophia* or family *Psophiidæ*, allied to the Cranes 1747. **c.** = *t.-swan* 1891. **5.** Any species of the genus *Latris*, comprising large food-fishes of Australia, Tasmania, and New Zealand; so called from the sound they utter when taken out of water 1834.

1. A t. was sent to summon the place MACAULAY. **2.** Subordinate instruments and trumpeters of sedition BURKE.

attrib.: **t. hornbill,** an African bird of the genus *Bycanistes*; **t. swan,** a large N. Amer. species of swan, *Cygnus* (*Olor*) *buccinator.*

Truncal (trʊ·ŋkăl), *a.* 1847. [f. L. *truncus* TRUNK + -AL.] Pertaining to, or of the nature of, a trunk; situated in or affecting the trunk.

Truncate (trʊ·ŋkeᶦt), *a.* 1716. [ad. L. *truncatus*; see next.] = TRUNCATED 2. So **Tru·ncately** *adv.* 1579.

Truncate (trʊ·ŋkeᶦt), *v.* 1486. [f. L. *truncat-, truncare*, f. *truncus* TRUNK.] *trans.* To shorten or diminish by cutting off a part; to cut short; to maim, mutilate. **b.** In scientific and technical use; *spec.* in *Cryst.* to 'cut off' or replace (an edge or solid angle) by a plane face, esp. so as to make equal angles with the adjacent faces. Chiefly in *pa. pple.* 1758. Hence **Truncature** (trʊ·ŋkătiŭɹ) = TRUNCATION 2.

Truncated (trʊ·ŋkeᶦtėd), *ppl. a.* and *a.* 1486. [f. L. *truncatus, truncare* (see prec.) + -ED[1] 2, or f. prec. + -ED[1].] Cut short (actually or apparently); having a part cut off, or of such a form as if a part were cut off. **1.** *Her.* Of a cross or tree: Having the arms or boughs cut off; couped. Now *rare* or *Obs.* **2.** In scientific or techn. use. (Const. as *adj.* preceding, or as *pa. pple.* following, the noun.) **a.** *Geom.*, etc. Of a figure: Having one end cut off by a transverse line or plane; *esp.* of a cone or pyramid: Having the vertex cut off by a plane section, esp. one parallel to the base 1704. **b.** *Cryst.* and *Solid Geom.* Of an edge or solid angle: Cut off or replaced by a plane face; also said of a solid figure having its edges or angles thus cut off 1796. **c.** *Nat. Hist.* Appearing as if the tip or end were cut off transversely; terminating in a flat or broad edge or surface instead of a point 1752. **d.** So in *Arch., Geol.*, etc. 1723. **3.** Maimed, mutilated 1731.

2. a. T. Pyramid or Cone 1704. **3.** *fig.* A t. and most imperfect friendship 1890.

Truncation (trʊŋkēᶦ·ʃən). 1579. [ad. late L. *truncationem.*] **1.** The action of truncating; cutting short; maiming, mutilation. **2.** In scientific and techn. use: The process of truncating, or condition of being truncated; *spec.* in *Cryst.* replacement of an edge or solid angle by a plane face, esp. one equally inclined to the adjacent faces 1796. **b.** *transf.* The part or place where something is truncated 1805.

Truncheon (trʊ·nʃən), *sb.* [ME. a. OF. *trunçun, tronchon*, F. *tronçon* a piece cut or broken off, f. late L. **truncionem*, f. L. *truncus.*] **1.** A piece broken or cut off, a fragment. *Obs.* or *arch.* **b.** *spec.* A fragment of a spear or lance. *Obs.* or *arch.* ME. **c.** The shaft of a spear. *Obs.* or *arch.* ME. **2.** A short thick staff; a club, a cudgel. *Obs.* or *arch.* exc. as in 3. ME. **3.** A staff carried as a symbol of office, command, or authority; a marshal's baton; now most freq., the short staff or club with which a police constable is armed 1573. **4.** A length cut from a plant, esp. one used for grafting or planting; a stout cutting. Now *rare.* 1572.

1. A huge t. of wreck half buried in the sands STEVENSON. **3.** Stones were thrown on the one side and truncheons used on the other 1880. Hence **Tru·ncheon** *v. trans.* to beat with a t. **Truncheoned** (trʊ·nʃənd) *a.* furnished or armed with a t. **Tru·ncheoner,** one who bears a t.

‖**Truncus** (trɒ·ŋkɒ̆s). 1693. [L.] **a.** *Anat.* The trunk or main stem of a vessel or nerve. **b.** *Zool.* The trunk or body of an animal, without the head, limbs, and tail; *Ent.* the thorax. **c.** *Bot.* The trunk or stem of a tree.

Trundle (trɒ·nd'l), *sb.* 1564. [Parallel form to TRENDLE, TRINDLE *sbs.*] **1.** A small wheel, roller, or revolving disk; *esp.* the wheel of a castor. **b.** In the draw-stop action of an organ, a roller by the rotation of which a slider is drawn or replaced 1876. **2.** A lantern-wheel (see LANTERN). Also, each of the staves of this device. 1611. †**3.** A low truck or carriage on small wheels –1766. **4.** An act of trundling 1675.

attrib. and *Comb.*: **t.-head,** (*a*) each of the disks of a trundle (sense 2); (*b*) *Naut.* 'the lower drum-head of a capstern, when it is double, and worked on one shaft both on an upper and lower deck' SMYTH.

Tru·ndle, *v.* 1598. [Parallel form to TRENDLE, TRINDLE *vbs.*] **1. a.** *trans.* To cause to roll along upon a surface, as a ball, hoop, etc.; to roll, bowl. **b.** *intr.* To move along on a surface by revolving; to roll 1629. **c.** *Cricket.* (*trans.* or *absol.*) To bowl. *colloq.* 1882. **2.** *trans.* To cause to rotate; to twirl, spin, whirl; *spec.* to twirl (a mop) so as to free it from water 1756. **3.** *intr.* To move or run on a wheel or wheels 1688. **b.** *trans.* To draw or push along on a wheel or wheels, as a wheelbarrow, vehicle, etc. 1825. **4.** To convey in a wheeled vehicle, to wheel 1773. **b.** *intr.* To go in a wheeled vehicle, on a bicycle, etc. 1840. **5.** *fig.* To go, walk, or run easily or rapidly; to go away, 'be off'; also, to walk unsteadily or with a rolling gait 1680. **b.** *trans.* To carry or send off, turn out, dismiss 1794.

3. Such are termed Truckle beds, because they t. under other beds 1688. **b.** Trundling a wheelbarrow full of sand 1862. **5. b.** The women..always contrived to t. me out of favour before the honeymoon was over SCOTT. Hence **Tru·ndler.**

Tru·ndle-bed. Now *rare.* 1542. [TRUNDLE *sb.* 1.] = TRUCKLE-BED.

Tru·ndle-tail. *Obs.* or *arch.* 1486. **1.** A dog with a curly tail; a low-bred dog, a cur. Also *attrib.* †**2.** (as two words) A curly tail (of a dog). *rare.* 1625.

Trunk (trɒŋk), *sb.* 1440. [a. F. *tronc*, ad. L. *truncum*, acc. of *truncus*. In branch III app. assoc. w. TRUMP *sb.*[1]] **I.** The main part of something. **1.** The main stem of a tree, as distinct from the roots and branches; the bole or stock 1490. **b.** *transf.* The shaft of a column; also, the dado or die of a pedestal 1563. **2.** The human body, or that of an animal, without the head, or esp. without the head and limbs, or considered apart from these; in *Ent.* the thorax 1494. †**3.** A dead body, a corpse; also, the body considered apart from the soul or life –1709. **4.** *Anat.* The main body or line of a blood-vessel, nerve, etc., as distinct from its branches; also *transf.* the main line of a river, railway, telegraph or telephone, road or canal system 1615. **b.** *pl.* Short for Grand Trunk Railway of Canada, or its stock 1892.

1. With Trunks of Elms and Oaks the Hearth they load DRYDEN. **2.** 2 *Hen VI*, IV. x. 90. **3.** *Lear* I. i. 180.

II. A chest, box, case, etc. (supposed to have been orig. made out of a tree-trunk). †**1.** A chest, coffer, box. *Obs.* in *gen.* sense. –1726. **2.** A box, usu. lined with paper or linen and with a rounded top, for carrying clothes and other personal necessaries esp. when travelling; orig. covered with leather, now often of fibre, painted metal, etc. 1609. **3.** A perforated floating box in which live fish are kept 1440. **b.** An open box or case (containing from 80 to 90 lb.) in which fresh fish are sold wholesale 1883. **4.** *Mining.* A long shallow trough in which lead or tin ore is dressed 1653. **5.** A box-like passage for light, water, etc., usu. made of boards; a shaft, conduit; a chute. Now chiefly *techn.* 1610. **b.** In a steam-engine, a tubular piston-rod large enough to allow of the lateral movement of the connecting-rod when jointed directly to the piston 1859. **c.** *Naut.* A water-tight shaft passing through the decks of a vessel, for loading, coaling, etc. 1862. **d.** *Salt-making.* A box-like cover placed over an evaporating-pan 1885.

2. We were forced to send for a smith, to break open her t. PEPYS. Have your trunks packed 1859.

III. A pipe or tube. †**1.** A pipe used as a speaking-tube or ear-trumpet –1704. †**2.** A blow-gun, a pea-shooter –1801. **3.** The elongated proboscis of the elephant; also *transf.* the prolonged flexible snout of the tapir, etc. 1565. **b.** The proboscis of some molluscs; also the proboscis of various insects. Now *rare* or *Obs.* 1661. †**3.** *pl.* Also *small trunks*: = TROLL-MADAM –1854. **IV.** *pl.* †**a.** = TRUNK-HOSE –1672. **b.** Short breeches of silk or other thin material; in theatrical use, often worn over tights 1825. **c.** *U.S.* Short tight-fitting drawers worn by swimmers and athletes 1883.

attrib. and *Comb.*: (sense I. 4) *t. line, road*; **t.-call,** a call from one telephone exchange to another; **-engine,** an engine having a tubular piston-rod; see sense II. 5 b; **t. main,** a large pipe for the conveyance of water, etc. under pressure, as dist. from the reticulation of smaller mains fed therefrom; **-nail,** a short nail with broad convex brass head used for ornamenting trunks, etc.; †**-work,** secret or clandestine action, as by means of a t. Hence **Trunk** *v. trans. Mining,* to dress (lead or tin ore) by agitating it in water; to cover or enclose as with a casing. **Tru·nkful,** as much or as many as a t. will hold.

Tru·nk-bree:ches, *sb. pl.* Now only *Hist.* 1662. = TRUNK-HOSE.

Trunked (trɒŋkt), *a.* 1640. [f. TRUNK *sb.* + -ED[2].] **1.** Having a trunk, as a tree; usu. in comb., as *straight-t.*, etc. **b.** *Her.* Having the trunk of a tincture different from the rest of the tree 1678. **2.** Having a trunk or proboscis 1794.

Tru·nk-fish. 1804. Any fish of the genus *Ostracion* or family *Ostraciontidæ*, inhabiting tropical seas, and having the body of angular cross-section and covered with bony hexagonal plates; a coffer-fish.

Tru·nk-hose. Now only *Hist.* 1637. [f. TRUNK *sb.* (or obs. *trunk* vb. to truncate) + HOSE.] Full bag-like breeches covering the hips and upper thighs, and sometimes stuffed with wool or the like; worn in the 16th and early 17th c. **b.** *attrib.*, in sense 'wearing trunk-hose'; hence, old-fashioned, out-of-date 1643.

Tru·nk-ma:ker. 1704. One whose business is the making of trunks; often with allusion to the use of the sheets of unsaleable books for trunk-linings.

Trunnion (trɒ·nyən). Chiefly in *pl.* 1625. [ad. F. *trognon* core of fruit, stump, trunk of a tree; origin unkn.] Each of a pair of opposite gudgeons on the sides of a cannon, upon which it is pivoted upon its carriage. (Disused in large modern guns.) **b.** Each of any similar pair of opposite pins or pivots on which anything is supported; *spec.* in the oscillating steam-engine, a hollow gudgeon on each side of the cylinder, upon which it is pivoted, and through which steam passes into and out of the cylinder; also, a single projecting pivot 1727.

attrib. and *Comb.*: **t.-box,** a metal case fixed over the t. to prevent the gun leaving the carriage; **-carriage,** the top carriage of a mortar; **-plate,** an iron plate on the cheek of a wooden gun-carriage, on which the t. plays; also, a strengthening shoulder reinforcing the t.; **-ring,** the raised band or moulding encircling a cannon a little in front of the trunnions.

Trusion (trū·ʒən). Now *rare* or *Obs.* 1604. [ad. med.L. *trusionem*, f. *trus-*, *trudere* to push, thrust.] **1.** *Law.* = INTRUSION 2. **2.** The action of pushing or thrusting 1656.

Truss (trɒs), *sb.* ME. [a. F. *trousse*, app. vbl. sb. from *trousser* to TRUSS.] **1.** A bundle, pack. Now chiefly *techn.* **b.** *spec.* A bundle of hay or straw; in techn. use, of a definite weight, varying at different times and places. (Now generally, in England, of old hay, 56 lbs.; of new hay, 60 lbs.; of straw 36 lbs.) 1483. **2.** *Naut.* A tackle by which the centre of the yard was hauled back and secured to the mast; in mod. use extended to an iron fitting consisting of a ring encircling the mast, with a gooseneck by which the yard is secured ME. †**3. a.** A close-fitting body-garment or jacket formerly worn by men and women –1612. †**b.** *pl.* = TROUSE[2] –1631. **4.** A surgical appliance serving for support in cases of rupture, etc., now usu. consisting of a pad with a belt or spring to produce equable pressure on the part 1543. **5.** *Gardening.* A compact cluster of flowers growing on one stalk 1688. **6.** *Building,* etc. A framework of timber or iron, or both, so constructed as to form a firm support for a superincumbent weight, as that of a roof or bridge 1654. **b.** *Arch.* A projection from the face of a wall, often serving to support a cornice, etc.; a kind of large corbel or modillion 1519. **c.** *Ship-building.* Any one of the diagonal shores crossing each other and resting against the abutments 1860.

1. Undir his heed no pilowe was, But in the stede a trusse of gras 1400. **3. a.** Puts off his Palmer's weede vnto his trusse, which bore The staines of ancient Armes DRAYTON.

Comb.: **t.-beam,** a beam forming part of a t.; also, a beam or iron frame used as a beam, strengthened with a tie-rod or struts, so as to form a t.; **-rod,** a tie-rod forming part of a t.

†**Truss,** *a.* 1674. [attrib. use of prec. in similative sense.] Of a thick rounded form, like a bundle or parcel; tight, compact –1825.

Truss (trɒs), *v.* ME. [ad. F. *trousser*, in OF. also *trusser*, etc.; origin obsc.] **1.** *trans.* To tie in a bundle, or stow away closely in a receptacle; to bundle, pack. Also with *up.* Now *rare* or *Obs.* **b.** *Naut.* To furl (a sail). Also *absol.* late ME. **2.** To make fast to something with or as with a cord, band, or the like; to bind, tie, fasten. Now *rare.* ME. **b.** *spec.* To tie the 'points' or laces with which the hose were fastened to the doublet. *Obs.* exc. *Hist.* 1460. **3.** To confine or enclose (the body, or some part of it) by something fastened closely round; to bind or tie up; to gird; to fasten up (the hair) with ribbon, pins, combs, etc.; to adjust and draw close the garments of (a person); hence contemptuously in ref. to dress. Also with *up.* Now *rare* or *Obs.* ME. **4.** To fasten *up* on a gallows or cross; to 'string up'. *arch.* 1536. **5.** To fasten the wings or legs of (a fowl, etc.) to the body with skewers or otherwise, in preparation for cooking 1450. **6.** Of a bird of prey: To seize or clutch (the prey) in its talons; *spec.* to seize (the quarry) in the air and carry it off. *arch.* (and *Her.*) 1567. **7.** To compress the staves of (a cask) into the required shape and position by means of a *trussing-hoop* 1535. **8.** *Building,* etc. To support or strengthen with a truss 1823.

1. But hood..wered he noon, For it was trussed vp in his walet CHAUCER. **6.** So—at last he has trussed his Quarry DRYDEN. Hence **Tru·ssing** *vbl. sb.* the action of the vb.; *concr.* the timber or other material forming a truss; a work or structure consisting of trusses; also *attrib.* adapted or used for trussing or adapted for being trussed, as *t.-hoop, -needle, -rope,* etc.

Trust (trɒst), *sb.* [Early ME. *trost(e, truste,* a. ON. *traust*; see next.] **1.** Confidence in or reliance on some quality or attribute of a person or thing, or the truth of a statement. **b.** *transf.* with possessive: That in which one's confidence is put; an object of trust 1526. **2.** Confident expectation of something; hope. late ME. **3.** = CREDIT *sb.* 9 a. Chiefly in phrases *on, upon t.* 1573. **4.** The quality of being trustworthy; fidelity; loyalty, trustiness. Now *rare.* 1470. **5. a.** The condition of having confidence reposed in one, or of being entrusted *with* something 1548. **b.** The obligation or responsibility imposed on one in whom confidence is placed or authority is vested, or who has given an undertaking of fidelity 1535. **c.** The condition of that which is entrusted to some one. Only in phr. *in t.* late ME. **d.** (with *pl.*) A duty or office, also a thing or person, entrusted to one 1643. **6.** *Law.* The confidence reposed in a person in whom the legal ownership of property is vested to hold or use for the benefit of another; hence, an estate committed to the charge of trustees; also *transf.* a trustee; a body of persons appointed as trustees 1442. **7.** *Commerce.* A body of producers or traders in some class of business, organized to reduce or defeat competition, lessen expenses, and control production and distribution for their common advantage; *spec.* such a combination of companies, with a central governing body of trustees which holds a majority or the whole of the stock of each of the combining firms, thus controlling each 1887.

1. To see and know and feel that our t. was not vain 1729. Phr. *To take on* or *upon t.*, to accept without investigation or evidence. **2.** His t. was with th' Eternal to be deem'd Equal in strength MILT. **3.** My master lived on t. at an ale-house JOHNSON. **5. a.** As we were allowed of God to bee put in t. with the Gospel 1 *Thess.* ii. 4. **b.** A breach of t. 1907. **c.** A gift to a college, in t. for another charitable object

1827. 7. A distiller's 'trust' 1887. A t. is defined.. as a combination to destroy competition and to restrain trade G. B. SHAW.

Comb.: **t.-certificate** (in full *t.-share certificate*) a negotiable certificate issued by the controlling board of a t. (sense 7), which entitles the holder to all dividends declared upon the surrendered shares which it represents, but gives him no voting power; **t. company**, a company formed (orig. in *U.S.*) for the purpose of exercising the functions of a trustee, with which other financial activities were later combined; **t. deed,** a deed of conveyance by which a t. (sense 6) is created, and its conditions set out; **t. house**, a public house or hotel owned and managed by a trust company, instead of by brewers or private individuals; **-investment,** the investment of t.-money; also trustee stock.

† **Trust,** *a.* ME. [Early ME. *trust, trost,* a. ON. *traustr.*] **1.** Confident, safe, secure. –late ME. **2.** Faithful, trusty; reliable –1440.

Trust (trɒst), *v.* ME. [app. f. TRUST *sb.* and *a.*, after ON. *treysta*, whence ME. *traiste* (also *treste, triste*).] **1.** *intr.* To have faith or confidence; to place reliance; to confide. Const. *in, to* (†*of, on, upon*). **2.** *trans.* To have faith or confidence in; to rely or depend upon. late ME. **b.** Imperative, used sarcastically or ironically to express one's assurance that a person will or will not do something. *colloq.* 1834. **3.** To have faith or confidence *that* something desired is, or will be, the case; also const. with *infin.* or *for*; to hope 1482. **4.** To give credence to (a statement); to rely upon the veracity or evidence of (a person, etc.). late ME. **5.** To commit the safety of (something) with confidence *to* a place, etc., *to* or *with* a person; to entrust; to place or allow (a person or thing) to be *in* a place or condition, or *to do* some action, with expectation of safety, or without fear of the consequences ME. **6.** To invest *with* a charge; to confide or entrust something to the care or disposal of 1548. **7.** To give (a person) credit *for* goods supplied; †to supply *with* goods on credit 1530.

1. Each had to t. to himself TYNDALL. 2. I cannot t. other people, without perpetual looking after them RUSKIN. b. T. a religious old maid for scenting out love! 1902. 3. I t. that these things are wholly repugnant to my nature BURKE. 4. T. me I am vnused to these deuices 1586. 5. My ventures are not in one bottome trusted SHAKS. He trusted the event to valour and to fortune GIBBON. 6. I will rather t. a Fleming with my butter..then my wife with her selfe SHAKS. 7. Without money the stubborn townspeople will not t. them for the worth of a penny CROMWELL. Hence **Tru·sting** *ppl. a.* that trusts; **-ly** *adv.*, **-ness.**

Trustee (trɒstī·), *sb.* 1647. [f. TRUST *v.* + -EE[1].] **1.** One who is trusted, or to whom something is entrusted (*rare*). *Obs.* or merged in 3. **2.** *Law. spec.* One to whom property is entrusted to be administered for the benefit of another; often *loosely*, one of a number of persons appointed to manage the affairs of an institution 1653. **b.** In *U.S.* by extension, One in whose hands the property of a debtor is attached in a *t. process* 1794. **3.** *transf.* One who is held responsible for the preservation and administration of anything 1655.

Comb.: **t. process,** in *U.S.*, a judicial process by which the goods, effects, and credits (but not the real estate) of a debtor may be attached while in the hands of a third person; in Eng. Law called *foreign attachment*; **t. security, t. stock,** a high-class stock in which trust-funds are or may legally be invested.

Trustee (trɒstī·), *v.* 1818. [f. prec.] **1. a.** *trans.* To place (a person or his property) in the hands of a trustee or trustees. **b.** *intr.* To act as a trustee. **2.** *U.S.* **a.** To appoint (a person) trustee in the *trustee process* (see prec.), in order to restrain a debtor from collecting moneys due to him. **b.** To attach (effects of a debtor) in the hands of a third person. 1883.

Trusteeship (trɒstī·ʃip). 1730. [f. TRUSTEE + -SHIP.] The office or function of a trustee; also, a body of trustees.

Truster (trɒ·stəɹ). 1537. [f. TRUST *v.* + -ER[1].] One who trusts, confides, or relies; one who believes or credits; one who gives credit, a creditor.

Trustful (trɒ·stfŭl), *a.* 1580. [-FUL 1.] †**1.** Trustworthy, trusty, faithful –1674. **2.** Full of or exercising trust; trusting, confiding 1832. Hence **Tru·stful-ly** *adv.*, **-ness.**

Trustify (trɒ·stifəi), *v.* 1902. *Commerce.* [f. TRUST *sb.* + -(I)FY.] *trans.* To convert into a trust. Hence **Tru:stifica·tion.**

Trustless (trɒ·stlės), *a.* 1530. [f. TRUST *sb.* + -LESS.] **1.** Not to be trusted; unreliable, treacherous, untrustworthy. **2.** Having no trust or confidence; unbelieving, distrustful 1598. Hence **Tru·stlessness.**

Trustworthy (trɒ·st,wɒ̄:rði), *a.* 1808. [f. TRUST *sb.* + WORTHY *a.*] Worthy of trust; reliable. Hence **Tru·stwo:rthily** *adv.* **Tru·stwo:rthiness.**

Trusty (trɒ·sti), *a.* (*sb.*) ME. [f. TRUST *sb.* + -Y[1].] **1.** Characterized by trust; having faith, confidence, or assurance; trustful, confident. Now *rare.* **2.** Characterized by faithfulness or reliability; that may be relied upon; trustworthy. (Privy Councillors are in letters addressed by the sovereign as Right t. and well-beloved.) ME. **b.** *transf.* and *fig.* of things 1596.

2. Our right t. and welbeloved George baron Keith 1803. b. His trustie sword, the servant of his might SPENSER.

B. *sb.* One who (or that which) is trusty; *spec.* in *U.S.*, a well-conducted convict to whom special privileges are granted 1573. Hence **Tru·stily** *adv.* **Tru·stiness.**

Truth (trūþ). [OE. *trīewþ, trȳwþ, trēowþ*, ME. *trewþe, treuþ(e*, f. OE. *trīewe, trēowe* TRUE; see -TH[1].] **I.** The quality of being true (and allied senses). **1.** The character of being, or disposition to be, true to a person, principle, cause, etc.; fidelity, loyalty, constancy, steadfast allegiance. Now *rare* or *arch.* †**2.** = TROTH 2. –1650. **3.** Disposition to speak or act truly or without deceit; truthfulness, veracity, sincerity; formerly sometimes in wider sense: Honesty, uprightness, righteousness, virtue, integrity ME.

1. Alas! they had been friends in youth: But whispering tongues can poison t. COLERIDGE. 3. Loue is all t., lust full of forged lies SHAKS.

II. 1. Conformity with fact; agreement with reality; accuracy, correctness (of statement or thought) 1570. **b.** Agreement with the thing represented, in art or literature; the quality of being 'true to life'. Also, in *Arch.*, absence of deceit, pretence, or counterfeit, e. g. of imitation of stone in paint or plaster 1828. **2.** Agreement with a standard or rule; accuracy, correctness; *spec.* accuracy of position or adjustment; often in phr. *out of t.* 1669. **3.** Genuineness, reality, actual existence 1599.

1. There is some t. in what you say 1849. 2. Otherwise the door, when put together, will be out of t. 1825. 3. On to dawn, when dreams Begin to feel the t. and stir of day TENNYSON.

III. Something that is true. **1.** True statement or account; that which is in accordance with the fact. late ME. **b.** *loosely.* Mental apprehension of truth; knowledge 1644. **2.** True religious belief or doctrine; orthodoxy. Often with *the*, esp. in Quaker language. late ME. **b.** Conduct in accordance with the divine standard. late ME. **3.** That which is true (in a general or abstract sense); reality; *spec.* in religious use, spiritual reality as the subject of revelation or object of faith. late ME. **b.** Personified; *spec.* each of the two goddesses of truth in ancient Egyptian mythology. late ME. **4.** The fact or facts; the actual state of the case; the matter or circumstance as it really is ME. **b.** The real thing, as dist. from an imitation; the genuine article; the reality corresponding to a type or symbol, the antitype. Now *rare* or *Obs.* 1531. **5.** With *a* and *pl.* A true statement or proposition; a point of true belief, a true doctrine; a fixed or established principle; a verified fact; a reality. late ME.

1. The t. you speake doth lacke some gentlenesse SHAKS. T. is always strange; Stranger than fiction BYRON. Phr. *To say, speak,* or *tell the t.* (also *arch.* without *the*), to speak truly, to report the matter as it really is. Prov. *Tell* (*speak*) *the t. and shame the devil*: see SHAME *v.* 2. Them who kept thy t. so pure of old When all our Fathers worship't Stocks and Stones MILT. The Friend was declaring the T., when the Priest..came in 1710. b. He that doth the trueth commeth to the light TINDALE *John* iii. 21. 3. T. has no greater enemy than its unwise defenders 1855. b. So T. be in the field, we do injuriously by licencing and prohibiting to misdoubt her strength MILT. 4. We judge the Distances to be less than the T. 1748. 5. Leave your friend to learn unpleasant truths from his enemies 1858.

Phrases. *In t., of a t.* (arch.), in fact, as a fact; really, indeed: mostly used to strengthen or emphasize a statement. *Truth!* either as an expression of assent, or as intensive (= *in t.*). *arch.* Hence **Tru·th-less** *a.* destitute of t.; faithless (*obs.* or *arch.*); untrue, false, mendacious. **Tru·thy** *a.* (*rare* or *dial.*) truthful, true.

Truthful (trū·þfŭl), *a.* 1596. [f. TRUTH *sb.* + -FUL.] **1.** Of statements, etc.: Full of truth; sincere. (Now only as *transf.* from 2.) **2.** Of persons (or their attributes): Disposed to tell, or habitually telling, the truth; veracious. Also *fig.*: Not deceptive. 1787. **3.** Of ideas, artistic representation, etc. Characterized by truth; corresponding with fact or reality; true, accurate, exact 1859.

2. A singularly t. person 1866. 3. A..t. portrait 1871. Hence **Tru·thful-ly** *adv.*, **-ness.**

Try (trəi), *sb.* 1475. [f. TRY *v.*] **1.** An act of trying; an experiment (*rare*), attempt, effort (chiefly *colloq.*); †a trial, test 1556. **b.** *Rugby Football.* The right of attempting to kick a goal, obtained by carrying the ball behind the opponent's goal-line and touching it on the ground; the points scored when the try is not 'converted' into a goal 1845. †**2.** A sieve or sifting screen –1804.

1. Then this breaking of his, Ha's beene but a T. for his Friends? SHAKS. I should have had a t. at it 1832. †*At try*: see A-TRY.

†**Try, trie,** *a.* [ME. *trie*, prob. a. OF. *trié*, pa. pple. of *trier* to pick out, cull, select.] **1.** Choice, excellent, good –1596. **2.** *Joinery.* Quite true, correctly wrought –1678.

1. Those hands of gold..those feete of silver trye SPENSER.

Try (trəi), *v.* Pa. t. and pple. **tried.** ME. [a. OF. *trier*, = Pr. *triar*, also med.L. *triare* to sift or pick out; origin unkn.] **1.** *trans.* To separate (one thing) from another or others; to set apart; to distinguish. Often with *out.* *Obs.* or *arch.* †**2.** To separate the good part of a thing from the rest, esp. by sifting or straining; hence, to sift or strain. Usu. with *out.* –1790. †**3.** *spec.* To separate (metal) from the ore or dross by melting; to refine, purify by fire; also, to remove (the dross or impurity) from metal by fire. Usu. with *out.* –1686. **4.** To extract (oil) from blubber or fat by heat; to melt down (blubber, etc.) to obtain the oil; to render; also, to extract (wax) from a honeycomb. Usu. with *out.* 1582. †**5.** To ascertain, find *out* (something doubtful, obscure, or secret) by search or examination –1761. **b.** To ascertain the truth or right of (a matter, a quarrel, etc.) by test or endeavour; with *out*, to thrash or fight out; to determine 1542. **6.** *Law.* To examine and determine (a cause or question) judicially; to determine the guilt or otherwise of (an accused person) by consideration of the evidence; to judge. Also *fig.* ME. **7.** To put to the proof, test, prove. late ME. **8.** *Joinery.* To bring (a piece of timber) to a perfectly flat surface by repeatedly testing it and planing off the projecting parts; to plane with the trying-plane; also, to test the straightness or correspondence of (a planed surface, adjoining surfaces); also *intr.* (of a surface) to prove accurate or straight when tested 1593. **9.** *T. on*: to test the fit or style of (a garment) by putting it on. Also *absol.* 1693. **10.** To subject to a severe test or strain; to put to straits, afflict 1539. **11.** To test the effect or operation of; to experiment with 1545. **b.** To experiment upon (*with* something); to test the effect of something upon 1784. **12.** To endeavour to ascertain by experiment or effort; to attempt to find out; sometimes nearly = sense 11. 1573. **13.** To show or find to be so by test or experience. Now *rare* or *Obs.* late ME. †**14.** To undergo, go through –1738. **15.** To test one's ability to deal with (something); to venture upon, to essay. *To t. over*, to go through (a performance, etc.) experimentally. ME. **16.** *intr.* To make an effort, endeavour, attempt. (With *inf.* or *absol.*) 1638. **b.** Followed by *and* and a co-ordinated verb (instead of *to* with inf.) expressing the action attempted. *colloq.* 1686. **c.** *intr.* and *trans.* To search a place in order to find something, esp. game, or its scent. *colloq.* 1810. †**17.** *Naut. intr.* Of a vessel: To lie to –1867.

3. I..will..trye them, like as golde is tryed COVERDALE *Zech.* xiii. 9. 5. b. He was enforced by them to t. it out in battel with them 1654. c. *To t. out* (orig. *U.S.*), to test the possibilities, etc. (of a thing); to test (a person). 7. The friends thou hast, and their

adoption tride, Grapple them to thy Soule, with hoopes of Steele SHAKS. *To t. a door, window,* etc., to ascertain by attempting to open it whether it is fastened or locked. **11.** *To t. an experiment*, to make an experiment; to do something in order to see what will come of it, or whether it produces the expected result. *To t. (one's) hand*, to attempt to do something for the first time; to test one's ability or aptitude *at* something. **c.** To test the effect of (a thing) *on* (a person, thing, etc.). *To t. it on the dog*: to experiment so that any harm will fall only upon an inferior person or thing; to test (a theatrical production) by provincial performance (orig. *U.S.*). **12.** *Tam. Shr.* I. ii. 17. They think they are *trying their luck*, as the phrase is 1838. **13.** He hath still beene tried a holy man SHAKS. **15.** Phr. *T. it on*, (*slang*) to attempt an imposition; *spec.* in *Thieves' Cant*, to live by thieving; also, to attempt something knowing that one is likely to be unsuccessful. **16.** You will have to t. and t. again 1847. *T. for*, to attempt to obtain or find (an object), or to reach (a place). *T. at*, to make an attempt upon; to attempt to do or accomplish. **c.** Phr. *T. back* (intr.), to go back (*lit.* or *fig.*) so as to cover ground afresh where something has previously been missed.

Try-, the vb. -stem in comb., as in **t.-cock,** = gauge-cock; **-pit,** a testing pit for trying new engines; **-square,** a carpenter's square for laying off short perpendiculars; also with advs. as **t.-on,** (*a*) (*slang*) an attempt, *esp.* an attempt at imposition or deceit; also *transf.* the subject of an attempt; (*b*) the act of trying on a garment; **-out,** a selective trial (*U.S. slang* or *colloq.*); also, a test of efficiency, fitness, etc.

‖ **Trygon** (trəi·gǫn). 1749. [L., a. Gr. τρυγών dove, also the fish.] A fish with a sharp spine in its tail, a sting-ray.

Trying (trəi·iŋ), *vbl. sb.* 1440. [f. TRY *v.* + -ING [1].] The action of TRY *v.*

attrib.: **t.-plane,** a long heavy plane used after the jack-plane for the accurate squaring of timber.

Trying (trəi·iŋ), *ppl. a.* 1577. [f. TRY *v.* + -ING [2].] That tries. **1.** That tests severely; that is a trial; that tries one's endurance or patience 1718. **2.** Attempting, endeavouring (*rare*) 1577.

1. The month of May is..a 't.' month HONE. Hence **Try·ing·ly** *adv.*, **-ness.**

‖ **Tryma** (trəi·mă). 1857. [mod.L., ad. Gr. τρῦμα or τρύμη hole, f. τρύειν to rub down, wear out.] *Bot.* A fruit resembling a drupe, but formed from an originally compound ovary, and having an ultimately dehiscent fleshy or fibrous exocarp, as the walnut and coco-nut.

‖ **Trypanosoma** (tri:pănoˌsōu·mă). 1880. [mod.L., f. Gr. τρύπανον borer + σῶμα body.] *Zool.* A genus of flagellate infusorian protozoa, species of which are parasitic in the blood of man and other animals, causing specific diseases, such as sleeping-sickness; an infusorian of this genus.

Trypsin (tri·psin). 1876. [perh. f. Gr. τρύειν to rub down, digest + *-psin* of PEPSIN.] *Physiol. Chem.* The chief digestive ferment of the pancreatic juice, which converts proteins into peptones. Hence **Trypsi·nogen** (-dʒən) [-GEN 1], a granular substance occurring in the pancreas, from which t. is formed.

Tryptic (tri·ptik), *a.* 1888. [f. prec. after *pepsin, peptic.*] Pertaining to or of the nature of trypsin. So **Tryptone** (tri·ptoun) a peptone formed by the action of trypsin upon a protein.

Trysail (trəi·sēl, trəi·s'l). 1769. [f. TRY *sb.* + SAIL.] *Naut.* A small fore-and-aft sail, set with a gaff, and sometimes with a boom, on the fore- or mainmast, or on a small supplementary mast abaft either of these.

Tryst (trist, trəist), *sb.* Chiefly *Sc.* bef. 19th c. late ME. [orig. the same word as ME. †*triste* trust.] **1.** A mutual appointment, agreement, covenant. Now *rare* or *Obs.* exc. as in **2.** **2.** *spec.* An appointment or engagement to meet at a specified time and place. late ME. **3.** = RENDEZVOUS 4. late ME.

2. Phr. *To make t.*; *to hold, keep t.*; *to break t.* *To bide t.*, to wait at the appointed place for the person with whom the appointment is made; 'You walk late, sir', said I...'I byde tryste', was the reply. SCOTT.

Tryst (trist, trəist), *v.* orig. and chiefly *Sc.* late ME. [f. prec.] **1.** *intr.* To make an agreement *to do* something, *with* a person; *esp.* to fix time and place of meeting *with* some one. **2.** *trans.* To engage (a person) to meet one at a given time and place; to appoint or agree to meet 1643. **3.** *intr.* To keep tryst; to meet at the appointed time and place 1842. Hence **Try·ster. Try·sting** *vbl. sb.*, *attrib.* in *t. day*, etc.

Tsar (tsāɹ, zāɹ). 1670. [Russ.] See CZAR.

Tsetse (tse·tsi). 1849. [Sechwana (i. e. Bechuana language) '*tsetse*.'] In full *t.-fly*: A dipterous insect (*Glossina morsitans*, of the family *Tabanidæ*), abundant in parts of tropical and southern Africa; its bite is often fatal to horses and other domestic animals. Also applied to other species of *Glossina*.

T square: see T 3 b.

‖ **Tuan** [1] (tū·ăn). 1846. Australian name for the Flying Squirrel.

‖ **Tuan** [2] (tuā·n). 1895. [Malay 'lord, master'.] Respectful form of address for a European.

‖ **Tuatara** (tūatā·ra). 1890. [Maori, f. *tua* on the back + *tara* spine.] A large lizard, *Sphenodon punctatum*, having a dorsal row of yellow spines; formerly common in N. Zealand.

‖ **Tuath** (tū·ăh). *Irish Hist.* 1873. [Ir. *túath* people.] A 'tribe' or 'people' in Ireland; hence, the territory occupied by a tuath.

Tub (tɒb), *sb.* [Com. West Ger.: late ME. *tubbe.*] **1.** An open wooden vessel, wide in proportion to its height, usu. formed of staves and hoops, of cylindrical or slightly concave form, with a flat bottom. †**b.** A sweating-tub formerly used in the treatment of venereal disease; hence, the use of this –1688. **2.** A bathing-tub, bath-tub (of any shape); *colloq.* or *joc.* a bath; hence, the action or practice of taking a bath, esp. on rising 1849. **3.** Applied to a slow clumsy ship, esp. one which is too broad in proportion to its length; often *joc.* or *contempt.*; also, a short, broad boat; *spec.* a stout roomy boat used for rowing practice, as dist. from a racing-boat 1618. **4.** Applied *contempt.* or *joc.* to a pulpit, esp. of a nonconformist preacher 1643. **5.** *Coal-mining.* Orig. a mining bucket, now specially applied to the open-topped box of wood or iron, mounted on wheels, in which coal is brought from the face to the surface 1851. **b.** The lining of a pit-shaft 1839.

1. b. *Meas. for M.* III. ii. 60.

Provb. phrases. †*A tale of a t.*, an apocryphal tale; a 'cock and bull' story. (*To throw out*) *a t. to the whale*, to create a diversion, esp. in order to escape a threatened danger. *Every t. must stand on its own bottom*: cf. BOTTOM *sb.* 9.

attrib. and *Comb.*: **t.-butter,** butter packed in tubs for keeping or export; †**-fast,** abstinence during treatment in the sweating-tub; **-frock,** a dress of washing material; **-gig,** (*a*) a governess car; (*b*) = **t.-pair,** a pair-oared practice boat; **-wheel,** (*a*) the wheel of a colliery 'tub'; (*b*) a horizontal water-wheel with spiral floats.

Tub (tɒb), *v.* 1610. [f. prec.] **1.** *trans.* To bathe or wash in a tub or bath. *colloq.* **b.** *intr.* To wash oneself in a tub or bath; to take a tub or bath, esp. on rising. *colloq.* 1867. **2.** *trans.* To line (a pit-shaft) with a water-tight casing of timber, masonry, or iron; to dam *back* (water) in a shaft or tunnel in this way; to shut *off* (watery strata or seams) from the shaft with tubbing 1812. **3.** To put or pack in a tub; to plant in a tub 1828. **4.** *trans.* and *intr.* To coach (oarsmen) in a 'tub'; to practise rowing in a 'tub'. *Rowing slang.* 1882.

1. b. Gentlemen who didn't t. of a morning 1867. **4.** An hour and a half was then spent in tubbing the men 1883.

‖ **Tuba** [1] (tiū·bă). 1852. [L. and It. *tuba.*] **1.** (*pl.* tubæ.) The straight bronze war-trumpet of the ancient Romans 1882. **2.** *Mus.* (*pl.* **tubas.**) A bass wind-instrument of the sax-horn family; a sax-tuba or bombardon; also, one who plays this instrument 1852. **b.** An 8-foot high-pressure reed-stop in an organ 1876.

‖ **Tuba** [2] (tū·ba). 1817. [Arab. *ṭūbah.*] A mythical tree growing in the Mohammedan paradise.

Tubal (tiū·băl), *a.* 1735. [f. L. *tubus* TUBE + -AL.] **1.** Of, pertaining to, or of the nature of a tube; consisting of tubes; tubular (*rare*). **2.** *Anat.* and *Path.* Pertaining to, occurring in, or affecting the Fallopian tube, as *t. dropsy*, the bronchial tubes, as *t. cough*, or the renal tubules, as *t. nephritis* 1822.

Tubbing (tɒ·biŋ), *vbl. sb.* 1657. [f. TUB *v.* (or *sb.*) + -ING [1].] **1.** The action of TUB *v.* **2.** The lining of a pit-shaft or tunnel with a watertight casing; *concr.* the casing of timber, masonry, or metal sections used for this 1839. **3.** Rowing or training in a 'tub' 1884.

Tubby (tɒ·bi), *a.* 1806. [f. TUB *sb.* + -Y [1].] **1.** Tub-shaped, tub-like; of rounded outline, and stout or broad in proportion to the length; of a person, corpulent 1835. **2.** Sounding like a tub when struck; dull or wooden in sound. (Said of stringed instruments.) 1806. Hence **Tu·bbiness.**

Tube (tiūb), *sb.* 1651. [a. F., ad. L. *tubus.*] **I. 1.** A hollow body, usu. cylindrical, and long in proportion to its diameter, of wood, metal, glass, etc., used to convey or contain a liquid, or for other purposes; a pipe 1658. **b.** = TUBING, material of a tubular form 1823. **2.** In specific applications usu. indicated by context; *esp.* = TEST-TUBE 1800. **3.** An optical instrument of tubular form, *esp.* a telescope; more fully *optic t.* Now *arch.* 1651. †**4.** A cannon; also, a rifle or hand-gun. *poet.* –1816. **b.** A small pipe introduced through the vent, formerly used in firing cannon; a *friction-t.*, *quill-t.*, or *priming-t.* 1797. **c.** The inner cylinder of a built-up gun, upon which the outer case is shrunk 1895. **5.** A musical wind-instrument, a pipe. *poet. rare.* 1820. **6. a.** A pneumatic dispatch-tube 1860. **b.** The cylindrical tunnel in which an underground electric railway runs; also short for *t.-railway* (*colloq.*) 1900. **7.** *Physics.* A tubular figure conceived as being formed by lines of force or action passing through every point of a closed curve 1878.

2. Collapsible tin tubes for artists' colours 1877. Owing to the depth of the wound two drainage tubes were introduced 1902. *Wireless* (*U.S.*) A valve. **6. b.** *Twopenny T.*: see TWOPENNY.

II. 1. *Anat.* and *Zool.* A hollow cylindrical vessel or organ in the animal body; a canal, duct, passage, or pipe; often preceded by a defining word, as *Eustachian, Fallopian, intestinal t.*, etc.; see the qualifying words 1661. **b.** One of the siphons of a mollusc 1839. **2.** A hollow cylindrical channel in a plant; *spec.* in *Bot.* the lower united portion of a gamopetalous corolla or gamosepalous calyx; also, a united circle of stamens 1704. **3.** Applied to other tubular or cylindrical objects or formations of natural origin 1831.

Comb.: **t.-case,** in a steam-engine, the chamber containing the tubes of a surface-condenser; **-colour,** paint packed in a collapsible t.; **-condenser,** in a steam-engine, a condenser in which the cooling surface consists of tubes; **-coral,** organ-pipe coral, or its polyp; **-culture,** culture of a microbe in a test-t.; **-foot,** one of the numerous ambulacral tubes of an echinoderm; **-medusa,** a siphonophore; **-nosed** *a.*, tubinarial; **-plate,** the plate in which the ends of the boiler-tubes are set; **-shell,** a bivalve mollusc of the family *Tubicolæ* or *Gastrochænidæ*, distinguished by having a shelly t. enclosing the siphons, in addition to the ordinary valves of the shell; **-spinner, -weaver,** a spider which spins a tubular nest or lair; **-worm,** a tubicolous worm; a pipe-worm; **-wrench,** a wrench for gripping pipes or tubes.

Tube, *v.* 1828. [f. prec.; cf. F. *tuber.*] **1.** *trans.* To furnish or fit with a tube or tubes; to insert a tube in. **2.** To pass through or enclose in a tube 1863. **3.** *intr.* To travel by tube railway; also, *to t. it* (*colloq.*) 1902. Hence **Tubed** *ppl. a. spec.* of a horse: having a tube introduced into the throat to enable it to breathe easily.

Tuber (tiū·bəɹ). 1668. [a. L., hump, swelling.] **1.** *Bot.* An underground structure consisting of a solid thickened rounded outgrowth of a stem or rhizome, bearing 'eyes' or buds from which new plants may arise; a familiar example is the potato. Also applied to other underground structures resembling this but of different origin. ‖**b.** A genus of underground discomycetous fungi, comprising the truffles 1704. **2. a.** *Path.* A morbid swelling, as of a gland, etc. 1706. **b.** *Anat.* A tuberosity 1741. **3.** *gen.* A protuberance (*rare*) 1888.

Tubercle (tiū·bəɹk'l). 1578. [ad. L. *tuberculum*, dim. of *tuber* TUBER.] **1.** *Anat.* and *Zool.* A small rounded projection or protuberance, as on a bone, or on the surface of the body in various animals. **2.** *Path.* A small firm rounded swelling or nodule on the surface of the body or in a part or organ; *spec.* a mass of granulation-cells characteristic of *tuberculosis*; *transf.* tuberculosis 1661. **3.** *Bot.* **a.** A small tuber, or a root-growth resembling a tuber, as in many orchids. b. A small wart-like swelling or protuberance on a plant. 1727.

Comb.: t.-bacillus, the species of bacillus which causes tuberculosis. Hence **Tubercled** (tiū·bəɹk'ld) *a. Nat. Hist.* and *Path.* furnished or affected with tubercules; tuberculate.

Tubercular (tiubə̄·ɹkiŭlăɹ), *a.* 1799. [ad. mod.L. *tubercularis*, f. L. *tuberculum* TUBERCLE + -AR.] 1. *Nat. Hist.*, etc. a. Of the nature or form of a tubercle; consisting of or constituting a tubercle. b. Having or covered with tubercles, tuberculate. 1817. 2. *Path.* Of, pertaining to, caused or characterized by, or affected with tubercles 1799. b. *spec.* In ref. to tuberculosis or the tubercle-bacillus; now techn. replaced by TUBERCULOUS 1799. Hence **Tube·rcularize** *v. trans.* to make t.; to infect with tubercles, *spec.* with tuberculosis. **Tube:rculariza·tion.**

Tuberculate (tiubə̄·ɹkiŭlĕt), *a.* 1785. [ad. mod.L. *tuberculatus*, f. L. *tuberculum* TUBERCLE; see -ATE [2].] *Nat. Hist.* and *Path.* Furnished or affected with tubercles; tubercled. So **Tube·rculated** *a.* 1771.

Tuberculation (tiubə̄ɹkiŭlē·ʃən). 1835. [f. L. *tuberculum* TUBERCLE + -ATION.] 1. *Nat. Hist.* Formation of tubercles; *concr.* a growth or set of tubercles. 2. *Path.* Formation of tubercles as a sympton of disease; tubercular or tuberculous affection 1861.

Tubercule (tiū·bəɹkiul). 1678. [a. F., ad. L. *tuberculum.*] = TUBERCLE.

Tuberculin (tiubə̄·ɹkiŭlin), *a.* 1891. [f. L. *tuberculum* TUBERCLE + -IN [1].] *Med.* A liquid prepared from cultures of tubercle-bacillus, used by hypodermic injection as a remedy, or (now esp.) as a test, for tuberculosis.

Tuberculize (tiubə̄·ɹkiŭləiz), *v.* 1847. [f. as prec. + -IZE.] *trans.* and *intr.* To affect or infect with tubercle or tuberculosis; to become tuberculous. Hence **Tube:rculiza·tion** 1843.

Tuberculo- (tiubə̄·ɹkiŭlo), comb. form of L. *tuberculum* TUBERCLE, prop. used advb.; also attrib. or objectively, in several technical terms, chiefly of pathology and medicine: **Tube:rculo-fi·broid** *a.*, 'characterized by tubercle that has undergone a fibroid degeneration'. **Tube:rculopho·bia**, morbid dread of tuberculosis.

Tuberculose (tiubə̄·ɹkiŭlōus), *a.* 1752. [See TUBERCLE and -OSE.] = TUBERCULATE.

‖**Tuberculosis** (tiubə̄ɹkiŭlōu·sis). 1860. [mod.L., f. L. *tuberculum* TUBERCLE; see -OSIS.] *Path.* orig. Any disease characterized by the formation of tubercles; now *spec.* restricted to disease caused by the tubercle-bacillus in any of the bodily tissues; examples are pulmonary consumption or phthisis (t. of the lungs), and scrofula (t. of the lymphatic glands).

Tuberculous (tiubə̄·ɹkiŭləs), *a.* 1747. [f. as prec.; see -OUS.] 1. *Path.* Pertaining to or produced by tubercles; consisting or of the nature of tubercles; affected with tubercles. b. Since the discovery of the tubercle-bacillus in 1882, usu. *spec.* in ref. to the tubercle-bacillus or to tuberculosis, and thus techn. dist. from *tubercular* in the general sense 1891. 2. *Nat. Hist.* Full of or covered with tubercles; tuberculate, tubercular. (Now disused.) 1828.

Tuberiferous (tiūbəri·fĕrəs), *a.* 1846. [f. L. *tuber* TUBER + -I)FEROUS.] *Bot.* Producing or bearing tubers.

Tuberiform (tiū·bərifǭɹm), *a.* 1822. [See TUBER and -FORM.] *Nat. Hist.* and *Path.* Having the form of a tuber; also characterized, as a disease, by growths of this form.

Tuberose (tiū·bəɹōus, often *erron.* tiū·bˌrōuz), *sb.* 1664. [ad. L. *tuberosa*, specific name of the plant, fem. of *tuberosus* (see next); corrupted by pop. etym. into a disyllable, as if f. *tube* + *rose.*] A liliaceous plant, *Polianthes tuberosa*, with creamy white, funnel-shaped, very fragrant flowers, and a tuberous root.

Tuberose (tiū·bərōus), *a.* 1704. [ad. L. *tuberosus*, f. *tuber* TUBER; see -OSE [1].] = TUBEROUS.

Tuberosity (tiūbərǫ·sĭti). 1541. [a. F. *tuberosité*, f. late L. *tuberositas*, f. *tuberosus* + -ITY.] 1. The quality or condition of being tuberous; bulging; gibbosity. Now *rare* or *Obs.* 2. *concr.* A tuberous formation or part; a swelling, protuberance 1611.

Tuberous (tiū·bərəs), *a.* 1650. [ad. F. *tubéreux, -euse*, ad. L. *tuberosus*, f. *tuber*; see -OUS.] 1. *Anat., Zool.*, etc. Of the form of, or constituting, a tuber or rounded projection; covered with such projections; knobbed, knobby. Now *rare.* 2. *Path.* Affected with tubers or morbid swellings; of the nature of such a swelling; characterized, as a disease, by such swellings 1656. 3. *Bot.* a. Of the nature of a tuber 1668. b. Of a plant: Producing or bearing tubers 1664. Hence **Tu·berous-ly** *adv.*, **-ness.**

Tubful (tɒ·bful). 1788. [f. TUB *sb.* + -FUL.] As much as a tub will hold.

Tubi- (tiūbi), comb. form of L. *tubus* TUBE; as in **Tubicolar** (tiubi·kŏlăɹ), **Tubicolous** (tiubi·kŏləs) *adjs.* [mod.L. *tubicola*, f. *colere* to cultivate, inhabit], inhabiting a tube; applied to annelids and rotifers that secrete tubular cases, spiders that spin tubular webs, and molluscs with shelly tubes; so **Tubicole** (tiū·bikōul) *a.* = prec.; *sb.* a tubicolar annelid or mollusc. **Tu·bicorn** [L. *cornu* horn], *sb.* a hollow-horned ruminant; *adj.* hollow-horned, as a ruminant; also **Tubico·rnous** *a.* **Tu·biform**, *a.* having the form of a tube; tube-shaped, tubular. **Tubinarial** (-nēə·riăl), **Tubinarine** (-nēə·rəin) [L. *naris* nostril], *adjs.* belonging to the order *Tubinares* of water-birds, comprising the albatrosses and petrels, having nostrils of tubular form. **Tu·bipore** (-pōəɹ), *sb.* a member of the genus *Tubipora*, family *Tubiporidæ*, or order *Tubiporaceæ*, of alcyonarians (the organ-pipe corals), in which each polyp has a tubular corallet opening by a pore; *adj.* belonging to or having the characters of this genus, family, or order; so **Tubi·porite** [-ITE [1] 2 a], a fossil tubipore. **Tu·bivalve**, *sb.* a bivalve mollusc having a shelly tube in addition to the valves of the shell; a tube-shell; *adj.* having such a tube.

Tubing (tiū·biŋ), *vbl. sb.* 1845. [f. TUBE *v.* or *sb.* + -ING [1].] The action of furnishing with a tube or tubes; also *concr.* tubes collectively, or as a material; a length or piece of tube.

Tubman, tub-man (tɒ·bmæ̆n). 1642. [f. TUB *sb.* + MAN *sb.*] †1. = TUB-PREACHER -1651. 2. A barrister in the Court of Exchequer whose place was beside the tub used as a measure of capacity in excise cases; the position conferred the right of precedence in motions, except over the 'postman' and in Crown business. *Obs.* exc. *Hist.* 1768.

Tubo- (tiūbo), used in certain cases as comb. form of L. *tubus* TUBE, instead of TUBI-.

Tu·b-prea:cher. *contempt.* 1643. [See TUB *sb.* 4.] One who preaches from a 'tub'; a dissenting preacher or minister.

Tu·b-thu:mper. *contempt.* 1662. [TUB *sb.* 4.] A speaker or preacher who for emphasis thumps the pulpit; a violent or declamatory preacher or orator; a ranter.

Tubular (tiū·biŭlăɹ), *a.* 1673. [f. L. *tubulus* small tube + -AR.] 1. Tube-shaped; constituting or consisting of a tube; cylindrical, hollow, and open at one or both ends. b. *Bot.*: *esp.* applied to a flower or floret consisting mainly of a tube, with small or inconspicuous limb 1776. 2. Constructed with or consisting of a number of tubes; as a *t. boiler* 1804. 3. *Phys.* and *Path.* Applied to a high-pitched respiratory murmur, like the sound made by blowing through a tube, heard normally over the trachea and bronchial tubes, and in diseased conditions over the lung 1834.

1. *T. bridge*, a bridge formed of a great tube or hollow beam, usu. of wrought iron, through which the road or railway passes. Hence **Tu·bularly** *adv.*

Tubularian (tiūbiŭlē·riăn), *a.* and *sb.* 1859. [f. mod.L. *Tubularia* (f. *tubulus*) + -AN.] *Zool.* A. *adj.* Belonging to the Linnæan genus *Tubularia*, the group *Tubulariæ*, or the family *Tubulariidæ*, of gymnoblastic Hydrozoa, in which the polyps are of tubular form, protected by a perisarc, with naked hydranths. B. *sb.* A tubularian hydroid.

Tubulate (tiū·biŭlĕt), *a.* 1753. [ad. L. *tubulatus*, f. *tubulus* TUBULE; see -ATE [2].] *Nat. Hist.* Formed into or like a tube; tubular.

Tubulated (tiū·biŭleˈtĕd), *a.* 1663. [f. L. *tubulatus* TUBULATE *a.* + -ED [1].] 1. Furnished with a tube; *esp.* of a retort or receiver: Having a short tube with a stopper (*tubulature* or *tubulure*), through which substances can be introduced. 2. Formed into, or like, a tube; longitudinally perforated; tubular 1713. So **Tubula·tion**, the process of making or becoming tubular. **Tu·bulature** [see -URE]: = TUBULURE.

Tubule (tiū·biul). 1677. [ad. L. *tubulus*, dim. of *tubus* TUBE.] A small tube; a minute tubular structure in an animal or plant body, as the *Malpighian* or *uriniferous tubules* of the kidney, etc.

Tubuli- (tiū·biŭli), comb. form of mod.L. *tubulus* TUBULE, as in **Tu:bulide·ntate** [L. *dentatus* toothed], *a. Zool.* belonging to the *Tubulidentata*, a group of edentates having compound teeth traversed by parallel vertical tubules. **Tubuli·ferous**, *a. Nat. Hist.* bearing tubules; *spec.* having a tubular ovipositor, as the females of certain insects. **Tu·bulifo:rm**, *a.* having the form of a tubule, tubular. **Tu·bulipo:re** [L. *porus* PORE], *Zool.* a polyzoan of the genus *Tubulipora* or family *Tubuliporidæ*, having tubular calcareous calicles.

Tubulose (tiū·biŭlōus), *a.* Now *rare.* 1713. [ad. mod.L. *tubulosus*, f. L. *tubulus* TUBULE.] = next 1. Now *rare.*

Tubulous (tiū·biŭləs), *a.* 1664. [ad. mod.L. *tubulosus.*] 1. = TUBULAR 1. 2. Containing or composed of tubes 1864. b. Of a steam-boiler: Having either fire-tubes or water-tubes 1860.

Tubulure (tiū·biŭliŭɹ). 1800. [a. F., f. L. *tubulus* TUBULE; see -URE.] A short tube, or projecting opening for the insertion of a tube, in a retort or receiver.

‖**Tubulus** (tiū·biŭlŏs). *Pl.* **-i** (-əi). 1826. [dim. of L. *tubus* TUBE.] = TUBULE; in *Ent.* a tubular ovipositor.

Tuchun (tū·tʃʊn). 1920. [Chinese]. The military governor of a province in China. Hence **Tu·chunate. Tu·chunism.**

Tuck (tɒk), *sb.* [1] late ME. [f. TUCK *v.* [1]] 1. A fold or pleat in drapery; now *spec.* a flattened fold (or one of several parallel folds) in a garment, secured by stitching, either to shorten the garment or for ornamentation. 2. The gathering of the ends of the bottom planks of a ship under the stern; that part of the hull where the bottom planks are collected and terminated by the *t.-rail* 1625. 3. *Fishing.* Short for TUCK-NET. 1602. 4. The thrusting in of the ends or edges of anything so as to secure them in position. Also with *in.* 1852. 5. *slang.* Usu. *t.-in* (also *t.-out*): A hearty meal; esp. in school use, a feast of delicacies 1823. b. Food, eatables; *esp.* delicacies, as sweet-stuff, pastry, jam, etc. (*school slang*) 1857.

Phr. *Nip and t.*: see NIP *sb.* [1] 4.

attrib. and *Comb.*: t.-boat, in seine-fishing, a boat which carries the t.-net; -rail, the rail which forms a rabbet for the purpose of caulking the butt ends of the planks of the bottom; -seine = TUCK-NET.

Tuck (tɒk), *sb.* [2] *arch.* and *dial.* Chiefly *Sc.* 1500. [f. TUCK *v.* [2]; cf. It. *tocco* stroke, knock, f. *toccare* to touch, strike.] A blow, a stroke, a tap; esp. in *t. of drum.*

Tuck (tɒk), *sb.* [3] *arch.* 1508. [app. ad. F. *estoc* in same sense, ad. G. *stock* stick.] A slender, pointed, straight, thrusting sword; a rapier.

Tuck (tɒk), *v.* [1] [OE. *tūcian*; cf. MLG. *tucken, tocken* to draw, pull sharply or forcibly, mod.G. *zucken* to jerk, tuck, tug.] †1. *trans.* To punish; to ill-treat, torment -ME. †b. *fig.* To reprove, check, rebuke, reproach -1651. 2. To dress or finish (cloth) after it comes from the weaver, esp. to stretch on tenters; also *intr.* to work as a tucker. Now *local.* late ME. 3. *Fishing.* To take the fish from (the seine) by means of a *tuck-net*; also with the fish as object 1786. 4. To pull or gather up in a fold or folds; *esp.* to gird up (a garment, etc.). Usu. const. *up.* 1440. b. To put a tuck or tucks in 1626. 5. To pull or gather up and confine the loose garments of; to gird (a person) *up.* Chiefly in *pa. pple.* Now *rare.* late ME. b. *fig.* To cramp or hamper by lack of space, time, or means 1886. 6. To thrust or put away (an object) into a close place where it is snugly held or concealed 1587. 7. To thrust in the edge or end of (anything pendent or loose) so as to retain or confine it; now *esp.* to turn in the edges of (bed-coverings or the like) under the bed or its occupant. With advs., esp. *in, up.* 1635. **b.** With the person as obj. 1692. **c.** *intr.* To draw together, contract, pucker 1797. **8.** *slang.* **a.** *trans.* To 'put away' (food or drink) 1784. **b.** *intr.* To feed heartily or greedily; esp. with *in, into* 1810. **9.** *slang.* To hang (a criminal); usu. with *up* 1700.

4. He tucked up his sleeves and squared his elbows DICKENS. 6. He tucked his wife's arm under his own 1874. 7. A nymph that can t. my bed-clothes up THACKERAY. 8. b. There is Rasherwell 'tucking' away in the coffee-room THACKERAY.

Tuck (tɒk), *v.*[2] Now *dial.* Chiefly *Sc.* late ME. [a. ONF. *toker, toquer, touker* to touch, strike, northern form of *toucher* to TOUCH.] *trans.* and *intr.* To touch (*rare*); to beat the drum; also *intr.* of a drum: To sound.

Tuckahoe (tɒ·kăhō). *U.S.* 1612. [ad. Powhatan or Virginian (N. Amer. Indian) *tockawhoughe.*] A name applied by N. Amer. Indians (esp. of Virginia) to edible roots of various plants. Now app. restricted to an underground tuber-like production (*Pachyma Cocos* or *Lycoperdon solidum*), prob. the sclerotium of some fungus, parasitic on tree-roots in the southern parts of North America, the affinities of which are uncertain. Also called *Indian bread, Indian loaf, Indian head,* and *t. truffle.*

Tucker (tɒ·kəɹ), *sb.* late ME. [f. TUCK *v.*[1] + -ER [1].] **1.** A fuller; a cloth-finisher. *Obs.* exc. *dial.* **2.** A piece of lace or the like, worn by women within or around the top of the bodice in the 17–18th c.; a frill of lace worn round the neck 1688. **3.** One who makes or 'runs' tucks; the device in a sewing-machine which does this 1905. **4.** *Australian slang.* The daily supply of food of a gold-digger or station-hand; rations, meals; also, food generally, victuals 1858.

2. *Best bib and t.*: see BIB *sb.*[1] 4. *To earn or make one's t.*, to earn merely enough to pay for one's keep.

Tucker (tɒ·kəɹ), *v.* *New England. colloq.* 1840. [f. TUCK *v.*[1]] *trans.* To tire, to weary; usu. *t. out*; esp. in pa. pple. *tuckered out,* worn out, exhausted.

Tucket (tɒ·kėt). *arch.* 1593. [conn. w. TUCK *sb.*[2]] A flourish on a trumpet; a signal for marching used by cavalry troops.

Tu·ck-net. 1520. [f. TUCK *v.*[1]] A smaller net used within the great seine to gather and bring the fish to the surface.

Tu·ck-shop. *slang.* 1857. [f. TUCK *sb.*[1]] A pastry-cook's shop for the sale of pastry, sweets, fruit, and the like, chiefly to schoolboys.

‖**Tucum** (tū·kɒm). 1810. [ad. Tupi *tucumá.*] Any of several Brazilian palms, esp. *Astrocaryum vulgare,* from the young leaves of which the natives obtain a fibre which they make into cordage, nets, hats, etc.; also, the fibre itself.

‖**Tucuma** (tū·kumă). 1824. [Tupi.] A Brazilian palm, *Astrocaryum Tucuma,* which produces a fleshy fruit used by the natives as food, and a fibre like that of tucum.

‖**Tucutucu** (tū·kuˌtū·ku). 1833. [Native name, imitating the sound made by the animal when in its burrow.] A rat-like burrowing rodent of the genus *Ctenomys,* esp. *C. magellanica* and *C. brasiliensis*; found in Patagonia and La Plata. Also, the sound made by this animal.

-tude (tiud), *suffix,* repr. L. *-tudo, -tudinem* (F. *-tude*), a suffix of abstract nouns, chiefly from adjs., as *altitudo* height, f. *altus* high, etc., less commonly from pa. pples., as *consuetudo* custom, f. *consuetus,* or verb-stems, as *valetudo,* f. *valere*; occurring in words derived directly from L., as *altitude,* etc., or through Fr., as *consuetude, solitude,* etc., or formed (in F. or Eng.) on L. analogies, as *decrepitude, exactitude.*

Tudor (tiū·dǫɹ), *a.* 1779. [attrib. use of the Welsh surname (*Tewdwr*).] **1.** Belonging to the line of English sovereigns (from Henry VII to Elizabeth) descended from Owen Tudor, who married Catherine, the widowed queen of Henry V. **2.** Applied to the style of architecture (the latest form of Perpendicular) which prevailed in England during the reigns of the Tudors; belonging to or characteristic of this 1815.

2. *T. flower,* an upright stalked trefoil ornament used in long rows on cornices, etc., in T. architecture. *T. rose,* a conventional figure of a rose adopted as a badge by Henry VII, occurring in decoration of the T. period; in *Her.* figured as a combination of a red and a white rose.

Tuedian (twī·diăn), *a.* 1856. [med.L. *Tueda* the river Tweed.] *Geol.* Applied to the lowest beds of the Carboniferous.

Tuesday (tiū·zdeⁱ, -di). [OE. *Tīwesdæg* (rendering L. *dies Martis*), f. genitive of *Tīw,* name of a Teutonic deity, identified with the Roman Mars. *Tīw* :—OTeut. **Tīwoz,* cogn. with L. *deus* god, Gr. genit. Διός of Zeus (cf. Skr. *dyāus*).] The third day of the week.

Tufa (tū·fă, tiū·fă). Also **tufo.** 1770. [a. It. *tufa, tufo*:—L. *tofus, tophus* TOPHUS; cf. TUFF.] *Geol.* A generic name for porous stones, formed of pulverulent matter consolidated and often stratified. *spec.* **a.** *Calcareous t.*: a porous or vesicular carbonate of lime, generally deposited near the sources and along the courses of calcareous springs 1811. **b.** *Volcanic t.*: see next 1 b. 1770. Hence **Tufaceous** (-ēⁱ·ʃəs) *a.* having the nature or texture of t.; consisting of t.

Tuff (tɒf). 1569. [ad. 16th c. F. *tufe, tuffe, tuf,* ad. It. *tufo*:—L. *tofus* TOPHUS.] *Geol.* = prec. (But there is a recent tendency to restrict *tuff* to 'volcanic t.'.) **a.** *Calcareous* (or *calc*) *t.*: see prec. a. **b.** *Volcanic t.,* a tuff produced by the consolidation of volcanic ashes and other erupted material 1815. Hence **Tuffa·ceous** *a.* having the properties of or composed of volcanic t.

Tuft (tɒft), *sb.* late ME. [Origin obsc.; perh. repr. F. *touffe.* The final *t* is an Eng. addition; cf. *cliff, clift, draff, draft,* etc.] **1.** A bunch (natural or artificial) of small things, usu. soft and flexible, as hairs, feathers, etc., fixed or attached at the base. **b.** *Bot.,* etc. A cluster of short-stalked leaves or flowers growing from a common point, of stems growing from a common root, etc.; an umbel or fascicle; also, a clump of small herbs growing closely together 1523. **2.** A small tufted patch of hair on the head or chin; a lock; an imperial 1601. **3.** A clump of trees or bushes 1555. **4.** *Anat.* A small cluster or plexus of capillary blood-vessels; a glomerule 1841. **5.** *Hist.* An ornamental tassel on a cap; *spec.* the gold tassel formerly worn by titled undergraduates at Oxford and Cambridge 1670. **b.** *transf.* in *Univ. slang,* One who wore a tuft; a titled undergraduate 1755.

1. b. A t. of deep purple, the beautiful Alpine saxifrage 1853. 2. On his Chin 2 thin forked Tuffs 1711. 3. Behind the t. of Pines I met them SHAKS.

Tuft, *v.* 1535. [f. prec.] **1.** *trans.* To furnish with a tuft or tufts. **2.** *intr.* To form a tuft or tufts; to grow in tufts 1598. **3.** *trans.* To beat (a covert) in stag-hunting. Also *absol.* 1590. **b.** To dislodge (the game) by 'tufting' 1640.

Tuftaffeta, -taffety (tɒfˌtæ·fĕtă, -tæ·fĕti). *Obs.* or *arch.* 1572. [f. *tuff,* TUFT *sb.* + TAFFETA, TAFFETY.] **1.** A kind of taffeta with a pile or nap arranged in tufts. **2.** *attrib.* **a.** Made of tuftaffeta 1587. **b.** Clothed in tuftaffeta; luxuriously dressed 1598.

2. a. I'll help to fit her With a tuft-taffeta cloak B. JONS.

Tufted (tɒ·ftėd), *a.* 1606. [f. TUFT *sb.* and *v.* + -ED.] **1.** Having or adorned with a tuft or tufts. **2.** Formed into or forming a tuft; growing in a tuft or tufts; clustered 1632. **3.** *Nat. Hist.* **a.** *Bot.* Bearing flowers in tufts or fascicles. **b.** *Bot.* and *Zool.* Growing in tufts, cæspitose. 1629. **c.** Of a bird: Having a tuft of feathers upon the head; crested: *esp.* in *Ornith.* as the epithet of a particular species 1768.

1. Tall rocks and t. knolls SCOTT. 2. Towers and Battlements..Boosom'd high in t. Trees MILT. 3. T. Loosestrife 1857. c. The t. plover [will] pipe along the fallow lea TENNYSON.

Tufter (tɒ·ftəɹ). 1856. [f. TUFT *v.* 3 + -ER [1].] *Stag-hunting.* A hound trained to drive the deer out of cover.

Tu·ft-hu·nter. 1755. [f. TUFT *sb.* + HUNTER.] One who meanly or obsequiously courts the acquaintance of persons of rank and title (orig. at the universities: see TUFT *sb.* 5, 5 b); a toady, sycophant. So **Tu·ft-hu·nting** *sb.* and *a.*

Tufty (tɒ·fti), *a.* 1611. [f. TUFT *sb.* + -Y [1].] **1.** Full of or abounding in tufts; covered or adorned with tufts 1612. **2.** Forming a tuft or tufts; consisting of or growing in tufts 1611.

1. Vallies..Deckt with t. woods 1638. 2. An humble dale, Where t. daizies nod at every gale 1613.

Tug (tɒg), *sb.* late ME. [f. next.] **1.** An act or the action of tugging; a forcible pull; a severe strain or drag 1500. **2.** A hard try; a struggle; a 'go' 1673. **3.** A strenuous contest between two forces or persons 1660. **4.** In harness; **a.** (Chiefly *pl.*) A pair of short chains attached to the hames, by which the collar is connected with the shafts. **b.** A trace. **c.** A short strap sewn on various parts of the harness and serving to keep it in position. **d.** A metal stud or pin on the shaft to prevent it running too far through the loops of the back-strap. Also *locally* applied to other parts of harness. late ME. **e.** *Mining.* The iron hoop of a corf or hoisting bucket 1858. **5.** A small, stoutly-built, powerful steamer used to tow other vessels; a tug-boat 1817.

1. Downward by the feet he drew The trembling dastard: at the t. he falls DRYDEN. 3. *T. of war*: (*a*) the decisive contest; the real struggle or tussle; (*b*) an athletic contest between two teams who haul at the opposite ends of a rope, each trying to drag the other over a line marked between them.

Tug (tɒg), *v.* [Early ME. *toggen,* intensive from weak grade of **teuhan, tauh, tuȝum,* OE. *tēon, tēah, tugon, togen*; see TEE *v.*[1]] **1.** *intr.* To contend, strive in opposition. Now *rare.* **2.** To toil, labour, struggle; to go toilsomely 1619. **b.** *trans.* To lug, drag. *colloq.* 1710. **3.** To pull at with force; to strain or haul at ME. †**b.** To pull about roughly; to maul –1611. **4.** To move by pulling forcibly; to drag, haul ME. **5.** *intr.* To pull with great effort or force; to drag, haul. Often with *at.* ME. **6.** *trans.* To tow by means of a steam-tug 1839.

1. Let us tugge, till one the mastrie winne 1598. 2. All for which you tugge thus diligently, shall perish 1634. 3. Those two massie Pillars..He tugg'd, he shook, till down they came MILT. Each oar was tugged by five or six slaves MACAULAY. b. *Macb.* III. i. 112. 4. Haled and tugged from place to place 1526. 5. *fig.* How many recollections tugged at his heart as he went on! 1833. Phr. *To t. at the* (*an*) *oar*: to row as a galley-slave; hence *fig.* to toil unremittingly; to do the drudgery. Hence **Tu·gger,** one who tugs. **Tu·ggingly** *adv.*

‖**Tui** (tū·i). 1835. [Maori.] = PARSON-BIRD 1.

Tuille, tuile (twīl). late ME. [a. OF. *tuile* :—L. *tegula* TILE, plaque.] In mediæval armour, one of two or more plates of steel hanging below or forming the lowest part of the tasses, and covering the front of the thighs.

Tuism (tiū·iz'm). *rare.* 1796. [f. L. *tu* thou + -ISM, after *egoism.*] A form of expression involving the use of the pronoun *thou,* or implying reference to a second person; also, in *Ethics,* primary regard to the interests of another person or persons; in *Philos.,* the doctrine that all thought is addressed to a second person, or to one's future self as a second person. Hence **Tui·stic** *a.* of the nature of t.

Tuition (tiuˌi·ʃən). late ME. [a. AF., obs. F. *tuition,* ad. L. *tuitio* guard, guardianship, f. *tueri* to look to, look after.] †**1.** The action of looking after or taking care of, or condition of being taken care of; protection, defence, custody, care, tutelage –1790. †**b.** *spec.* Guardianship –1690. **2.** The action or business of teaching a pupil or pupils, esp. in private; tutorial instruction 1582.

1. For the tuicion and defence of this owr Realme 1462. 2. T. on the violin and clavier 1845. Hence **Tui·tional, Tui·tionary** *adjs.* pertaining or relating to t.

Tula (tū·lă). 1839. In full *t. metal*: Niello made at Tula in Russia.

‖**Tule** (tū·le). *U.S.* Also **tula.** 1850. [ad. Aztec *tullin,* the final *n* being dropped by the Spaniards as in *Guatemala,* etc.] Either of two species of bulrush (*Scirpus lacustris* var. *occidentalis,* and *S. Tatora*) abundant in low lands along riversides in California; hence, a thicket of this, or a flat tract of land on which it grows.

Tulip (tiū·lip). 1578. [Formerly *tulipa, tulippa,* also *tulipant, -pan* = F. *tulipan, tulipe,* from *tul(i)band,* vulgar Turk. pronunc. of Pers.

dulband 'turban', which the expanded flower of the tulip is thought to resemble.] 1. A bulbous plant of the liliaceous genus *Tulipa* esp. the species *T. gesneriana*, introduced from Turkey into western Europe in the 16th c., blooming in spring, with broad bell-shaped or cup-shaped, usu. erect, showy flowers, of various colours and markings; also, the flower itself. b. Applied, with defining word, to species of this, and various plants or flowers more or less resembling it; also to the flowers of the TULIP-TREE 1759. 2. *fig.* A showy person or thing, or one greatly admired 1647. 3. A tulip-like object: a bishop's mitre; a bell-shaped outward swell in the muzzle of a gun, now generally disused 1879.

1. The bloud-red T. with a yellow bottome 1633. 2. Morgiana was a t. among women, and the t. fanciers all came flocking round her THACKERAY.

Comb.: **t.-grass,** any of several S. African poisonous herbs of the genus *Homeria*; **-root,** (*a*) the root or bulb of a t.; (*b*) a disease of oats, characterized by a swelling at the base of the stem, caused by a minute nematoid worm; **-shell,** (*a*) a bivalve of the genus *Tellina*; (*b*) any gasteropod of the family *Fasciolariadæ*, as *Fasciolaria tulipa*.

Tu·lip-tree. 1705. **a.** A large N. Amer. tree, *Liriodendron Tulipifera* (family *Magnoliaceæ*), bearing flowers resembling large tulips, of a greenish colour variegated with yellow and orange; also called *tulip poplar, saddle-tree* (from the shape of its truncated leaves), and *whitewood*. b. Applied to other trees with tulip-like flowers, as species of *Magnolia*, and the mountain mahoe (*Paritium elatum* or *Hibiscus elatus*, family *Malvaceæ*) of the West Indies 1751.

Tu·lip-wood. 1843. **a.** The wood of the tulip-tree (see prec. a), a light ornamental wood used by cabinet-makers, etc. b. Any of various coloured and striped woods, or the trees producing them, as *Physocalymma floribundum* of Brazil, and species of *Owenia* and *Harpullia*, of Australia.

‖**Tulle** (tiul, tul, Fr. tül). 1818. [F., f. name of the town of *Tulle*, where the fabric was first manufactured.] A fine silk bobbin-net used for women's dresses, veils, hats, etc.

Tulle, obs. f. TOLL *v.*[1]

Tullibee (tʊ·libī). Also **tulibbi.** 1888. [ad. N. Amer. Indian *too-nie-bee.*] A species of whitefish (*Coregonus tullibee*) found in the Great Lakes of N. America.

‖**Tulsi** (tū·lsi). *India.* 1698. [Hindī.] A species of basil sacred to Vishnu.

‖**Tulwar** (tʊ·lwār). Also **tal-.** 1834. [Hindī *talwār* (also *tarwār*).] An (Indian) sabre.

Tum (tʊm), *sb.* and *v.* 1830. [Echoic. Cf. TUM-TUM *sb.*[1]] An imitation of the sound made by plucking a tense string, striking a drum, or the like. As *v. trans.* and *intr.*, to produce this sound.

Tumble (tʊ·mb'l), *sb.* 1634. [f. next.] 1. An act of acrobatic tumbling (*rare*) 1824. 2. An accidental fall; also *fig.*, a fall, downfall 1716. 3. Tumbled condition; disorder, confusion; a confused heap 1634.

2. A t. in the deeper snow 1860. *fig.* The..Baronet had a bloody T. 1728.

Tumble (tʊ·mb'l), *v.* [ME. *tumbel*, frequent or dim. of OE. *tumbian* = OLG. *tumben* (whence F. *tomber*), ON. *tumba.*] I. 1. *intr.* †To dance with posturing, balancing, contortions, and the like; to perform as an acrobat; *esp.* to execute leaps, springs, somersaults, etc. 2. To roll about on the ground, or in the water or air; to wallow; also, to throw oneself about in a restless way on a bed or couch; to toss. late ME. b. *spec.* of a pigeon: To throw itself over backwards during its flight; in gunnery, of a projectile, to turn end over end in its flight 1698.

1. A man who is paid for tumbling upon his hands JOHNSON. 2. I saw the Porpas how he bounst and tumbled SHAKS. b. Pigeons tumbling in the Air 1698.

II. 1. To fall; *esp.* to fall in a helpless way, as from stumbling or violence; to be precipitated, fall headlong ME. b. To fall prone, fall to the ground; freq. const. *down, over.* Also, to stumble by tripping *over* an object. ME. c. Of a building, etc.: To collapse. late ME. d. *Commercial slang.* To fall rapidly in value, amount, or price 1886. 2. *trans.* To cause to fall suddenly or violently; to throw or cast down. late ME. 3. To cause to fall in a confused heap; to throw *down, in, out,* etc. without order or regularity; to jumble *together* 1562. 4. To propel or drive headlong or with a falling, stumbling, or rolling movement; to precipitate; to toss, pitch, bundle 1509. 5. *intr.* To move or pass with a motion as if falling or stumbling; to proceed hastily; to bowl, bundle, roll, rush. Now *colloq.* 1590. 6. *trans.* To turn over as in examination or search. Now *rare.* 1597. 7. To handle roughly or indelicately; to disorder, rumple; to disarrange by tossing 1602. 8. *intr. fig.* or in fig. context; *esp.* To come by chance, stumble, blunder *into, on, upon* 1565. b. *fig.* const. *to*: To understand something not clearly expressed; to apprehend a hidden design or signal. *slang.* 1851.

1. One of the gang tumbled off of his mule 1687. c. Obelisks have their term, and Pyramids will t. SIR T. BROWNE. 2. Vnruly Winde..which..tombles downe Steeples, and mosse-growne Towers SHAKS. T. her out at window 1623. 4. To be tossed and tumbled about like a football SMOLLETT. 5. T. into bed and go to sleep LEVER. 7. *Haml.* IV. v. 62. 8. b. I didn't t. to this for a long time 1889.

III. *intr.* Of the sides of a ship: To incline or slope inwards, to contract above the point of extreme breadth; to batter. Usu. *t. home.* Opp. to FLARE *v.* 3. 1687.

Tumble-, the vb.-stem in combination:

1. With sbs.: **t.-bug, -dung,** *U.S.* a scarabæid beetle which rolls up balls of dung, in which it deposits its eggs and in which the larvæ go through their transformations; a dung-beetle; **-weed,** *U.S.* any of various plants which form a globular bush which in late summer is broken off and rolled about by the wind; a rolling weed. 2. with advs.: **t. home,** in a ship, the inward inclination of the upper part of a ship's sides; opp. to FLARE *sb.*[1] 4.

Tu·mble-down, *a.* 1818. [The phr. *tumble down* used attrib.] That is in a tumbling condition; dilapidated, ruinous.

Tumbler (tʊ·mbləɹ). ME. [f. TUMBLE *v.* + -ER [1].] 1. One who performs feats of agility and strength, somersaults, leaps, and gymnastics; an acrobat. 2. A dog like a small greyhound, formerly used to catch rabbits; a lurcher: so called from its action in taking its quarry. *Obs.* exc. *Hist.* 1519. 3. A variety of domestic pigeon characterized by the habit or faculty of turning over and over backwards during its flight 1678. 4. One who tumbles or falls 1904. 5. A drinking cup, orig. having a rounded or pointed bottom, so that it could not be set down until emptied; often of silver or gold; now, a tapering cylindrical or barrel-shaped glass cup without a handle or foot, having a heavy flat bottom 1664. b. A tumblerful 1831. 6. = TUMBREL 2, 2 b. *slang* and *dial.* 1673. 7. *U.S.* = TUMBLE-*dung.* 1807. 8. In mechanical applications. a. In a gun-lock, a pivoted plate through which the mainspring acts on the hammer and in the notches of which the sear engages 1624. b. In a lock: †A pivoted piece through which the pressure of a spring was transmitted to the tail of the bolt, tending to keep it pushed forwards; now, a pivoted piece kept in position by a spring, with projections which drop into notches in the bolt and hold it until lifted by the proper key 1677.

attrib. and *Comb.*, as *t. lock, pigeon, screw*; **t. switch,** an electric switch operated by pushing over a small spring t. or thumb-piece. Hence **Tu·mblerful,** the quantity that fills a t.

Tumbling (tʊ·mbliŋ), *vbl. sb.* late ME. [f. TUMBLE *v.* + -ING [1].] The action of TUMBLE *v.* b. *T. home* = TUMBLE *home.* 1664.

Tumbling-. The vbl. sb. and ppl. adj. in combs. and special collocations: **t.-barrel** = *t.-box*; **-bay,** an outfall from a river, canal, or reservoir; a weir; also, the pool into which the water falls from this; **-box,** a rotating drum in which small articles (usu. of metal) are cleaned and polished by attrition; also used in dissolving and mixing paints, varnishes, etc.

Tumbrel, tumbril (tʊ·mbrĕl, -ĭl). 1440. [ad. med.L. *tumb(e)rellum, -ellus*, OF. *tumb-, tomberel*, mod.F. *tombereau* a tipcart for carting and shooting dung, sand, stones, etc., f. *tomber* to let fall, tumble out.] 1. An instrument of punishment; from 16th c. usu. identified with CUCKING-STOOL 1494. 2. A cart so constructed that the body tilts backward so as to empty out the load; *esp.* a dung-cart 1440. †b. app. *transf.* to a lumbering cart -1800. †3. *transf.* A flat-bottomed boat or barge -1676. 4. *Mil.* A two-wheeled covered cart which carries ammunition, tools, or sometimes money for an army 1715.

Tumefaction (tiūmĭfæ·kʃən). 1597. [a. F., f. L. *tumefacere* to tumefy; see -TION.] 1. The action or process of tumefying or state of being tumefied; swollen condition. 2. *concr.* A swollen part; a swelling, a tumour 1802.

Tumefy (tiū·mĭfəi), *v.* 1597. [= F. *tuméfier*, ad. L. **tumeficare*, f. *tumere* to swell; see -FY.] 1. *trans.* To cause to swell; to swell, make tumid. 2. *intr.* To swell, swell up, become tumid 1615.

1. *fig.* To swell, t., stiffen, not the diction only, but the tenor of the thought DE QUINCEY.

Tumescence (tiume·sĕns). 1859. [f. next.] A becoming tumid, swelling up; a tendency to tumidity; also *concr.* a tumid part, a swelling.

Tumescent (tiume·sĕnt), *a.* 1882. [f. L. *tumescentem, tumescere*, inceptive of *tumere* to swell.] Becoming tumid, swelling; somewhat tumid.

Tumid (tiū·mid), *a.* 1541. [ad. L. *tumidus*, f. *tumere* to swell; see -ID [1].] 1. Swollen; characterized by swelling. b. Morbidly affected with swelling, as a part of the body. c. Of a swollen or protuberant form; swelling, bulging. In later use chiefly *Nat. Hist.* 1621. 2. *fig.* esp. of language or literary style: 'Swelling', inflated, turgid, bombastic 1648. b. 'Big', pregnant, teeming (*rare*) 1840.

1. My thighs grow very t. JOHNSON. 2. Turgid ode and t. stanza BYRON. Hence **Tumi·dity,** the quality or condition of being t.; swollenness. **Tu·midly** *adv.*, **-ness.**

Tummy (tʊ·mi), *colloq.* (orig. infantile) alteration of STOMACH; also *attrib.*, in *t.-ache.*

Tumorous (tiū·mŏrəs), *a.* 1547. [ad. L. *tumorosus*, f. *tumor* TUMOUR.] †1. Swollen, protuberant, bulging, tumid. *Obs.* exc. as in b. -1678. b. Pertaining to or of the nature of a (morbid) tumour; affected with tumours 1863. †2. *fig.* Vainglorious, puffed up, haughty; also, = TUMID 2. -1676.

Tumour, tumor (tiū·məɹ). 1541. [a. L. *tumor, -orem*, f. *tumere* to swell.] †1. The action or an act of swelling; swollen condition -1693. 2. *concr.* A part rising above or projecting beyond the general level or surface; a swollen part or object; a swelling. Now *rare* or *Obs.* exc. as in 3. 1601. 3. An abnormal or morbid swelling or enlargement in any part of the body of an animal or plant; an excrescence; a tumefaction 1597. b. *spec.* A permanent circumscribed morbid swelling, consisting in a new growth of tissue, without inflammation 1804. †4. *fig.* 'Swelling' of passion, pride, or the like -1778. †b. Turgidity of language, style, or deportment; bombast -1840.

4. The tumour of insolence, or petulance of contempt JOHNSON.

Tump (tʊmp), *sb. local.* 1589. [Chiefly a western and w. midl. word; origin unkn.] 1. A hillock, mound; a mole-hill, or ant-hill; a barrow, tumulus. 2. A clump of trees, shrubs, or grass 1802.

Tump, *v.*[1] *local.* 1721. [f. prec.] To make a 'tump' or mound about the root of a tree.

Tump, *v.*[2] *U.S.* 1855. [Origin obsc.] *trans.* To drag or carry by means of a tump-line.

Tu·mp-line. *local U.S.* 1860. [Origin obsc.] A strap placed across the forehead to assist in carrying a pack on the back.

Tum-tum (tʊ·mˌtʊ·m), *sb.*[1] and *adv.* Also in extended forms, as **tum-ti-tum.** 1859. [Reduplication of TUM.] An imitation of the sound of a stringed instrument or instruments, esp. when monotonously played; strumming; a monotonous air. So **Tum-tum** *v. intr.* to play monotonously; to strum.

Tum-tum, *sb.*[2] *India.* 1863. [Origin unkn.] A dog-cart.

Tum-tu·m, *sb.*[3] *colloq.* Reduplicated f. *tum* in TUMMY.

Tumular (tiū·miŭlăɹ), *a.* 1828. [f. L. *tumulus* (see TUMULUS) + -AR [1].] Pertaining to or consisting of a mound or tumulus.

Tumulate (tiū·miŭleᵗt), *v. rare.* 1623. [f. ppl. stem of L. *tumulare* to bury, f. *tumulus*; see -ATE [3].] *trans.* To bury, entomb.

Tumult (tiū·mɒlt), *sb.* late ME. [ad. L. *tumultus*, f. *tumere* to swell.] **1.** Commotion of a multitude, usu. with confused speech or uproar; public disturbance; disorderly or riotous proceeding. **b.** (with *pl.*) An instance of this; a popular commotion or disturbance 1560. **2.** *gen.* Commotion, agitation, disturbance; disorderly or noisy movement or action. Also *pl.* 1580. **3.** *fig.* Great disturbance or agitation of mind or feeling; confused and violent emotion 1663.

1. When the loud T. speaks the Battel nigh PRIOR. **b.** The late tumults in Belgia EVELYN. **2.** It Thunders and Lightens..What tumult's in the Heauens? SHAKS. **3.** A t. of grief and indignation 1844.

Tu·mult, *v.* 1570. [f. prec.] †**1.** *intr.* To make a tumult, commotion, or disturbance; to riot -1864. **2.** *trans.* To put into tumult; to agitate violently 1819.

1. Why do the Gentiles t.? MILT. Hence †**Tu·multer**, one who stirs up a tumult; a rioter.

Tumultuary (tiumɒ·ltiu͵ări), *a.* (*sb.*) 1590. [ad. L. *tumultuarius*, f. *tumultus* TUMULT; see -ARY [1].] **1.** Of troops: Gathered hastily and promiscuously, without order or system; irregular, undisciplined. Also of warfare, etc. carried on by such troops, or in an irregular way. **2.** Hurriedly done; disorderly, confused; haphazard, unsystematic 1609. †**b.** Of a person: Acting, speaking, or writing hastily and at random -1648. **3.** Disposed to, marked by, or of the nature of tumult; tumultuous, turbulent 1650. **B.** *sb.* in *pl.* Tumultuary forces 1654.

1. A tumultuarie armie in great hast levied..out of all quarters HOLLAND. **2.** Ashamed of their t. injustice 1879. **3.** The t. disorders of our passions 1661. Hence **Tumu·ltuarily** *adv.* **Tumu·ltuariness.**

Tumultuate (tiumɒ·ltiu͵eᵗt), *v.* Now *rare.* 1611. [f. ppl. stem of L. *tumultuari*; see -ATE [3].] **1.** *intr.* To stir up a tumult; to become or be tumultuous, turbulent, agitated, or restless. **2.** *trans.* To excite to tumult; to disorder or disturb violently 1616.

1. Noise of Winds, that..t. 1671. So **Tumultua·tion** (now *rare*), the action of making a tumult; a condition of tumult; commotion.

Tumultuous (tiumɒ·ltiu͵əs), *a.* 1548. [ad. OF. *tumultuous*, F. *tumultueux*, ad. L. *tumultuosus*, f. *tumultus* TUMULT; see -OUS.] **1.** Full of tumult or commotion; disorderly and noisy; turbulent. **2.** Making a tumult or commotion; turbulent; riotous 1576. **3.** Of physical actions or agents: Marked by disorderly commotion; confusedly agitated 1667. **4.** *fig.* of, or in ref. to, emotion or thought 1667.

1. The t. advance of the conquering army 1840. **2.** His house was beset by a t. crowd 1868. **3.** A roaring and t. river 1856. **4.** A t. dream 1822. Hence **Tumu·ltuous·ly** *adv.*, **-ness.**

‖**Tumulus** (tiū·miŭlɒs). *Pl.* **-li** (-ləi). 1686. [L., deriv. of root *tum-* of *tumere* to swell, *tumor.*] An ancient sepulchral mound, a barrow.

Tun (tɒn), *sb.* [OE. *tunne*, ME. *tunne*, later *tonne*; cogn. w. MDu. *tonne*, OHG. *tunna*, ON. *tunna*; also med.L. *tunna*, OF. *tonne*. Origin uncertain.] **1.** A large cask or barrel, usu. for liquids, esp. wine, ale, or beer, or for various provisions. Now less common than *cask.* †**b.** A large vessel in general; a tub or vat; a chest -1601. **c.** *Brewing.* A mashing-vat (*mash-t.*) or fermenting-vat (*gyle-t.*) 1713. **2.** A cask of definite capacity; hence, a measure of capacity for wine and other liquids (formerly also for other commodities), usu. equivalent to 2 pipes or 4 hogsheads, containing 252 old wine-gallons. late ME. **3.** A measure of capacity or weight: see TON [1] 3, 4. **4.** *Conch.* = *t.-shell* 1837.

1. A vast T. (as big as that at Heidelberg) EVELYN. *fig.* A fat old Man; a Tunne of Man is thy Companion SHAKS.

Comb.: **t.-shell**, *Conch.* a shell of the genus *Dolium.*

Tun, *v.* late ME. [f. prec.] **1.** *trans.* To put into or store in a tun or tuns. Also *absol.* †**2.** To fill as, or like, a cask -1664.

1. *fig.* He used to t. down beer..during dinner 1841.

‖**Tuna** [1] (tū·na). 1555. [Haytian, through Sp.] = INDIAN FIG 1, PRICKLY PEAR; esp. *Opuntia Tuna*, a tall-growing species found in Central America and the West Indies.

‖**Tuna** [2] (tū·na). 1900. [Sp. Amer.; perh. related to L. *thunnus, tunnus* tunny.] Name in California for the tunny.

Tunable, tuneable (tiū·năb'l), *a. arch.* 1500. [f. TUNE *sb.* or *v.* + -ABLE.] Tuneful, musical, harmonious, sweet-sounding.

The tunable voyces of men LODGE. *M.N.D.* IV. i. 130. *fig.* This counsel, harsh at first, grew tunable in the ears of the Hospitallers FULLER. Hence **Tu·n(e)ableness. Tu·n(e)ably** *adv.*

‖**Tunal** (tunā·l). 1613. [Sp., f. TUNA [1] + *-al* (cf. CHAPARRAL).] A grove or thicket of tunas.

Tun-bellied (tɒ·n͵be:lid), *a.* 1550. Having a belly rounded like a tun; pot-bellied.

Tund (tɒnd), *v.* 1871. [ad. L. *tundere.*] **1.** *Winchester School slang. trans.* To beat with a stick, esp. an ash rod, by way of punishment. **2.** *gen.* To beat, thump (*trans.* and *intr.*) 1885.

Tun-dish, tundish (tɒ·n͵diʃ). Now *local.* late ME. [f. TUN *sb.* + DISH *sb.*] A wooden dish or shallow vessel with a tube at the bottom fitting into the bung-hole of a tun or cask, forming a kind of funnel used in brewing; hence *gen.* = FUNNEL *sb.*[1] 1.

‖**Tundra** (tu·ndră, tɒ·n-). 1841. [Lapp.] One of the vast, nearly level, treeless regions which make up the greater part of the north of Russia, resembling the *steppes*, but with arctic climate and vegetation. Also applied to similar regions in Siberia and Alaska.

Tune (tiūn), *sb.* late ME. [app. an unexplained alteration of TONE *sb.*] †**1.** = TONE *sb.* I. 1. -1849. **2.** A rhythmical succession of musical tones produced by (or composed for) an instrument or voice; an air, melody (with or without the harmony which accompanies it). late ME. **b.** *spec.* A musical setting of a hymn or psalm, usu. in four-part harmony, intended for use in public worship; a hymn-tune 1450. **3.** The state of being in the proper pitch; correct intonation in singing, or in instrumental music; agreement in pitch, unison, or harmony (*with* something); mostly in phr. *in* or *out of t.* 1440. **b.** *transf.* Harmony or accordance in respect of vibrations other than those of sound; *spec.* between the receiver and transmitter in wireless telegraphy or telephony 1909. †**4.** Style, manner, or 'tone' (of discourse or writing) -1610. **b.** *To change one's t., sing another t.* (etc.); *fig.* to change one's tone, speak in a different strain 1524. **5.** *fig.* Frame of mind, temper, mood, disposition, humour 1599.

1. Melodious discord, heauenly t. harsh sounding SHAKS. **2.** Best sing it to the t. of *Light o' Loue* SHAKS. *Prov.* He who pays the piper, calls the t. *The t. the* (*old*) *cow died of*, joc. applied to a grotesque or unmusical succession of sounds, or a tedious ill-played piece of music. **3.** My voice is harsh here, not in t. TENNYSON. *In t., out of t.* (fig.), in or out of order or proper condition; in or out of harmony *with* some person or thing. **4.** I must nedes now..write unto you in an other t. CROMWELL. **5.** This is the tone and t. of men in distress 1647.

Phrases. *To the t. of* (*fig.* from 2): †**a.** According to the gist of, in accordance with. **b.** To the amount or sum of. So *to some t.*, to a considerable extent.

Tune, *v.* 1500. [f. prec.] **1.** *trans.* To adjust the tones of (a musical instrument, etc.) to a standard of pitch; to bring into condition for producing the required sounds correctly; to put in tune. Also *absol.* 1505. **b.** To adapt (the voice, song, etc.) to a particular tone, or to the expression of a particular feeling or subject; to modify or modulate the tones of, according to the purpose in view 1596. **c.** *transf.* To adapt, put in accordance, or make responsive, in respect of some physical quality or condition 1887. **d.** *Wireless.* To adjust to a desired frequency. (See also *t. in* below.) **2.** *fig.* To 'put in tune' (with various shades of meaning) 1530. **3.** *intr.* To give forth a musical sound; to sound; to sing 1500. **4.** *trans.* To utter or express (something) musically, to sing; to celebrate in music. *poet.* or *arch.* 1593. †**b.** To set or start the tune for (a hymn, etc. in public worship), as a precentor -1895. **5.** To produce music from, to play upon (an instrument, esp. the lyre). *poet.* 1701.

1. Letts t. our instruments 1597. **b.** For now to sorrow must I t. my song MILT. **2.** All his life was religiously tuned FULLER. The most effective way..of tuning public opinion 1868. **3.** Last week..I heard a blackbird tuning 1906. **4.** To Bacchus..let us t. our Lays DRYDEN. **5.** When Orpheus tun'd his lyre ..Rivers forgot to run, and winds to blow ADDISON.

With advs. **T. in.** *trans.* To adjust (a wireless receiver) to receive a message, etc.; to adjust a receiver to the 'wave-length' of (a wireless station, etc.); also *absol.*; so **T. off, out. T. up. a.** *trans.* and *intr.* To raise one's voice, to sing out. **b.** *trans.* To bring (an instrument) up to the proper pitch, to put in tune; also *absol.* **c.** To put (a machine, a racing vessel, etc.) into the most efficient working order.

Tuneful (tiū·nfŭl), *a.* 1591. [f. TUNE *sb.* + -FUL.] **1.** Full of 'tune' or musical sound; musical, sweet-sounding 1598. **2.** Producing or yielding musical sounds; performing or skilled in music; musical (as a person, instrument, etc.) 1591. **3.** Relating or adapted to music 1697.

1. In tunefull numbers keeping musicks time MARSTON. **2.** Chaunt of t. Birds MILT. **3.** Milton's t. ear 1842. Hence **Tu·neful·ly** *adv.*, **-ness.**

Tuneless (tiū·nlės), *a.* 1594. [f. as prec. + -LESS.] **1.** Having no sweetness of tone; untuneful, unmusical, unmelodious. **2.** Giving no 'tune' or sound; songless; silent 1728.

1. My tuneless harp SPENSER. **2.** The heroic lay is t. now BYRON. Hence **Tu·neless·ly** *adv.*, **-ness.**

Tuner (tiū·nəɹ). 1580. [f. TUNE *v.* + -ER [1].] One who or that which tunes; *spec.* one whose occupation is to tune pianos or organs. **b.** *Electr.* An instrument for tuning an electric circuit. **c.** *Wireless.* The part of a receiving set consisting of the circuit or circuits used to tune in.

Tung-oil, -tree: see WOOD-OIL (*c*).

Tungstate (tɒ·ŋsteᵗt). 1800. [f. TUNGSTIC + -ATE [4].] *Chem.* A salt of tungstic acid.

Tungsten (tɒ·ŋstėn). 1770. [a. Sw., f. *tung* heavy + *sten* stone.] †**1.** *Min.* = SCHEELITE, native calcium tungstate -1822. **2.** *Chem.* A heavy, steel-grey, ductile, very infusible metal, contained in the above mineral and in wolfram and other minerals; used for wire in incandescent electric lamps. Symbol W (= *wolframium*); atomic weight 184.

Tungstic (tɒ·ŋstik), *a.* 1796. [f. prec. + -IC 1 b.] *Chem.* Pertaining to or formed from tungsten; applied to compounds in which tungsten combines as a hexad, as *t. oxide*, WO_3, etc.; also to minerals containing tungsten, as *t. ochre*, native tungstic oxide, called also **Tu·ngstite.**

Tungstous (tɒ·ŋstəs), *a.* 1860. [f. as prec. + -OUS c.] *Chem.* Applied to compounds in which tungsten combines as a tetrad, as *t. chloride*, WCl_4, *t. oxide*, WO_2.

Tunhoof (tɒ·nhūf). Now *dial.* [OE. *tunhōfe*, f. TUN *sb.* + *hōfe*: cf. ALE-HOOF.] The herb Ground Ivy (*Nepeta Glechoma*).

Tunic (tiū·nik). OE. [ad. L. *tunica*, and later a. (O)F. *tunique.*] **1.** A garment resembling a shirt, worn by both sexes among the Greeks and Romans; in OE. and mediæval times, a body-garment over which a loose mantle or cloak was worn. **2.** *Eccl.* = TUNICLE 2. *Hist.* 1696. **3.** In modern costume. **a.** A close, usu. plain, body-coat; now *spec.* that forming part of the uniform of soldiers and policemen 1667. **b.** A garment worn by women, consisting of a bodice and an upper skirt, belted or drawn in at (or fitted to) the waist, worn over and displaying a longer skirt. Also, a kind of belted frock or smock worn by children and by women at games 1762. **4.** *transf.* **a.** *Anat.* A membranous sheath lining an organ of the body 1661. **b.** The integument of a part or organ in a plant; *spec.* in *Bot.* any loose membranous skin not formed from the epidermis; also, each layer or coating of a tunicate bulb 1760.

3. **a.** Put on my new tunique of velvett; which is very plain, but good PEPYS. **4. b.** The tunics of the onion 1832.

Tunicary (tiū·nikări), *a.* and *sb.* 1835. [f. L. *tunica* TUNIC + -ARY [1].] **A.** *adj.* Of or pertaining to a tunic or membrane 1900. **B.** *sb.* *Zool.* A member of the *Tunicata*; a tunicated mollusc 1835.

‖**Tunicata** (tiūnikēⁱ·tă), *sb. pl.* 1828. [mod. L., neut. pl. of *tunicatus* (sc. *animalia*) TUNICATE.] *Zool.* A division of animals, now regarded as a sub-phylum of the *Chordata*; also called *Urochorda*: see next, B.

Tunicate (tiū·nikeᵗt), *a.* and *sb.* 1760. [ad. L. *tunicatus*, *tunicare* to clothe with a tunic or covering, f. *tunica* TUNIC.] **A.** *adj.* Having or enclosed in a tunic or covering; *spec. Bot.* having or consisting of a series of concentric layers, as a bulb; *Ent.* sheathed in or issuing from one another, as the joints of antennæ; *Zool.* having a tunic or mantle; belonging to the *Tunicata*. **B.** *sb.* One of a class of marine animals, formerly regarded as molluscs, but now classified as a degenerate branch of *Chordata*, comprising the ascidians and allied forms, characterized by a pouch-like body enclosed in a tough leathery integument, with a single or double aperture through which the water enters and leaves the pharynx 1848.

Tunicated (tiū·nikeˡtėd), *a.* 1744. [f. as prec. + -ED[1].] = prec. A.

Tunicin (tiū·nisin). 1862. [f. TUNIC + -IN[1].] *Chem.* A kind of animal cellulose, or chitin, occurring in the mantles of tunicates.

Tunicle (tiū·nik'l). late ME. [ad. L. *tunicula*, dim. of *tunica* TUNIC.] †1. A small tunic; also *fig.* a wrapping, covering, integument -1744. 2. *Eccl.* A vestment resembling the dalmatic, worn by a subdeacon over the alb (and also by bishops between the alb and the dalmatic) at a solemn celebration of the Eucharist. late ME. 3. = TUNIC 4 a, b. *Obs.* (or *rare arch.*) late ME.

3. The stomach had a very thick inward t. 1725.

Tuning (tiū·niŋ), *vbl. sb.* 1554. [f. TUNE *v.* + -ING[1].] The action of TUNE *v.*

attrib. and *Comb.*: **t.-crook**, (*a*) an implement used in tuning the reed-pipes of an organ; (*b*) in brass wind-instruments = CROOK *sb.* 5; **-hammer**, a tuning-key for a piano, prop. one with a double head like that of a hammer, used for driving in the wrest-pins when new strings are fitted in; **-peg**, **-pin**, one of the pegs round which the strings of a stringed instrument are passed, and by turning which they are tuned; **-slide**, a slide in a metal wind-instrument, used to bring it into tune with other instruments in an orchestra. Also in *Wireless*, as *t. coil, condenser, inductance.*

Tu·ning-fork. 1799. 1. A small steel instrument (invented in 1711) consisting of a stem with two stout flat prongs which on being caused to vibrate produce a definite musical note of constant pitch. 2. An instrument used for turning the pins in tuning a pianoforte 1877.

Tunnel (tɒ·nĕl), *sb.* 1440. [a. OF. *tonel*, F. *tonneau* tun, cask, and *tonnelle* arbour, semicircular vault, bird-snare, derivs. of *tonne* TUN *sb.*] 1. A net for catching partridges or waterfowl, having a pipe-like passage with a wide opening, and narrowing towards the end; a t.-net. Now *rare* or *Obs.* †2. The shaft or flue of a chimney -1818. b. A pipe or tube in general. Now *rare*. 1545. 3. A funnel. *Obs.* exc. *dial.* 1529. 4. A subterranean passage; a road-way excavated under ground, esp. under a hill or mountain, or beneath the bed of a river: now most commonly on a railway; also, on a canal, in a mine, etc. 1782. b. *transf.* The burrow of an animal 1873. c. A canal in an animal body resembling a tunnel, as that of the organ of Corti in the internal ear 1882. d. A working-hole in the wall of a glass-furnace 1839.

2. The Chimney is just under the window and the Tunnells runnes upon each side 1710. 4. The vein has been attacked by various tunnels and shafts 1872.

attrib. and *Comb.*: **t.-head**, (*a*) the top of a shaft- or blast-furnace; (*b*) the point to which the construction of a t. has progressed; **-hole**, the throat of a blast-furnace; **-kiln**, a lime-kiln in which coal is burnt, as dist. from a flame-kiln in which wood or peat is used; **-net** = sense 1; also, a similar net for fishing; **-pit**, **-shaft**, a shaft sunk to the level of a t.

Tu·nnel, *v.* 1687. [f. prec.] 1. *trans.* To catch (partridges) with a tunnel-net. Also *absol.* 2. *intr.* To make a tunnel; to excavate a passage under ground, or through some body or substance 1795. b. *trans.* To excavate, as a tunnel; to make (one's way) by boring or excavating 1856. c. To make a tunnel through 1865.

2. As some great earth-monster, Johnson tunnels under ground, and heaves out rocks and tons of soil 1839. c. You have tunnelled the cliffs of Lucerne by Tell's chapel RUSKIN. Hence **Tunnel(l)ed** (tɒ·nĕld) *ppl. a.* **Tu·nnel(l)er.**

Tunny (tɒ·ni). 1480. [Obscurely ad. F. *thon*, ad. Pr. *ton*, or It. *tonno*, L. *thunnus, thynnus*, ad. Gr. *θύννος*.] A scombroid fish of the genus *Orcynus*, esp. the common tunny, *O. thynnus*, which has been fished from ancient times in the Mediterranean and Atlantic; it is one of the largest of food-fishes.

Tunu (tū·nu). 1883. [Carib.] The Central Amer. tree *Castilloa Tunu*, yielding *t. gum.*

Tup (tɒp), *sb.* ME. [Origin unkn.; chiefly Sc. and north.] 1. A male sheep; a ram. b. *transf.* Applied to a person 1652. c. *transf.* The head of a forge-hammer or steam-hammer 1873.

Tup (tɒp), *v.* 1549. [f. prec.] 1. *trans.* Of the ram: To copulate with (the ewe); also *transf.* 1604. 2. *intr.* a. Of the ewe: To admit the ram. b. Of the ram: To copulate. Also *transf.* 1549.

‖**Tupaia** (tupai·ă). 1820. [mod.L., ad. Malay *tūpai* squirrel.] *Zool.* An animal of the genus of insectivorous mammals, typical of the family *Tupaiidæ*, including the Banxring, *T. peguana*, of Burma and Pegu, and the Tana T., *T. tana*, of Borneo, etc.

‖**Tupelo** (tū·pėlo). 1730. [N. Amer. Ind.] Native name of trees of the N. Amer. genus *Nyssa* (family *Alangiaceæ* or *Nyssaceæ*), large trees growing in swamps or on river banks in the southern States; esp. *N. villosa* or *multiflora* (also called Black or Sour Gum, and Pepperidge), and the large t. or t. gum (*N. uniflora*), which produces a light tough timber.

‖**Tupi** (tū·pī). 1882. A native language widely spoken in Brazil.

Tuque (tiūk, tūk). *Canadian.* 1871. [a. Canadian F., = F. *toque* TOQUE.] A knitted stocking-cap tapered and closed at both ends, one end being tucked into the other to form the cap; formerly the characteristic winter head-dress of the Canadian 'habitant'.

‖**Tu quoque** (tiū,kwōᵘ·kwī). 1671. [L., lit. 'thou also', = Eng. slang 'you're another!'] An argument which consists in retorting a charge upon one's accuser. Also *attrib.*

The t. rejoinder, 'Physician, heal thyself' 1874. I leave myself open to a *t.*, I know 1903.

Turacin (tiūᵊ·răsin). 1868. [f. mod.L. *Turacus* TOURACO + -IN[1].] *Chem.* A crimson animal pigment, found in the wing-feathers of several species of birds of the genera *Turacus, Gallirex*, and *Musophaga*; closely allied to hæmoglobin, but free from iron, and containing over 7 per cent. of copper.

Turacoverdin (tiūᵊ:răko,vɔ̄·ɹdin). 1885. [f. as prec.] *Chem.* A green colouring-matter occurring in the feathers of some touracos.

Turanian (tiurēˡ·niăn), *sb.* and *a.* 1777. [f. Pers. *Turān*, name of the realm beyond the Oxus, used by Firdusi *c* 1000 in opposition to *Irān* or Persia.] **A.** *sb.* 1. A member of any of the races speaking the 'Turanian' or Ural-Altaic languages. 2. The so-called Turanian languages collectively 1908. **B.** *adj.* 1. Applied loosely to a group or supposed 'family' of languages, orig. applied to all or nearly all of Asiatic origin that are neither Aryan or Semitic; in later use nearly = URAL[1]-*Altaic* 1854. 2. Applied to the peoples speaking these languages 1859.

Turban (tɒ̄·ɹbăn), *sb.* 1561. [Formerly also **tuliban, turbant, -band**; altered forms of Pers. *dulband* or *dōlband*, in vulgar Turkish pronounced *tulbant, tul(i)pant, toli-*. The change of *tul-* to *tur-* may have taken place in S.W., or in Portuguese India. Cf. TULIP.] 1. A head-dress of Moslem origin worn by men of Eastern nations, consisting of a cap round which is wound a long piece of linen, cotton, or silk. b. As the symbol of Mohammedanism, or of those who profess it 1610. c. A figure of a turban, e.g. on Moslem funeral monuments. Also in *Her.* 1687. d. *transf.* and *fig.* Applied to a head-dress, or a head of hair, likened to a turban 1609. 2. A head-dress made to resemble or suggest the Oriental turban, worn by ladies during the late 18th and the early 19th c., and temporarily revived in 1908. 1776. 3. A bright-coloured cloth worn as a head-dress by negroes (esp. women) in the West Indies and Southern U.S. 1839. 4. A small brimless hat, or round cap with closely turned up brim, worn, chiefly by women and children, since about 1850. 1862. 5. a. The spire or whorl of a twisted univalve shell (*rare*). b. A mollusc of the genus *Turbo*. 1681. 6. *Zool.* Any of certain species of echinoderms, esp. the genus *Cidaris* 1713.

1. b. Though turbans now pollute Sophia's shrine BYRON. 2. Went to the Opera: wore my tissue t. 1823.

attrib. and *Comb.*: **t.-shell**, = 5 b, 6; **-squash**, a variety of squash or pumpkin in which the fleshy receptacle does not extend over the ovary, which therefore protrudes so as to resemble a t.; **-stone**, a Moslem tombstone, a pillar having at the head the carved representation of a t. Hence **Tu·rban** *v. trans.* to envelop as or with a t.; also, to wind a cloth round (a cap).

Turbaned (tɒ̄·ɹbănd), *a.* 1591. [f. TURBAN *sb.* + -ED[2].] Wearing a turban. b. Of a Moslem tombstone: Surmounted by a carved turban 1835.

A malignant, and a Turbond-Turke SHAKS.

Turbary (tɒ̄·ɹbări). late ME. [a. AF. *turberie*, a, OF. *turb-, torb-, tourberie*, med.L. *turbaria*, f. OF. *tourbe*, med.L. *turba*, ad. LG. *turf* (-*v*-) TURF.] 1. Land, or a piece of land, where turf or peat may be dug for fuel; a peat-bog or peat-moss. 2. *Law.* In full *common of t.*: The right to cut turf or peat for fuel on a common or on another person's land 1567.

Turbellarian (tɒ̄ɹbelēᵊ·riăn), *a.* and *sb.* 1879. [f. mod.L. *Turbellaria*, neut. pl. (f. L. *turbella*, dim. of *turba* crowd) + -AN.] *Zool.* **A.** *adj.* Of or belonging to the *Turbellaria*, a class of worms inhabiting fresh or salt water or damp earth, having the body covered with vibratile cilia producing minute whirls in the water. **B.** *sb.* A worm of this class; a whirl-worm 1883.

Turbid (tɒ̄·ɹbid), *a.* 1626. [ad. L. *turbidus* full of confusion, troubled, muddy, etc., f. *turba* crowd, disturbance.] 1. Of liquid: Thick or opaque with suspended matter; not clear; cloudy, muddy. b. Of air, smoke, clouds, etc.: Thick, dense; dark 1705. 2. *fig.* Characterized by or producing confusion or obscurity of thought, feeling, etc.; mentally confused, perplexed, muddled; disturbed, troubled 1645.

1. The Lees doe make the Liquour turbide BACON. b. T. streaming Clouds Of Smoak sulphureous 1705. 2. The t. utterances and twisted language of Carlyle 1896. So **Turbi·dity, Tu·rbidness,** t. quality or condition. **Tu·rbidly** *adv.*

Turbinal (tɒ̄·ɹbinăl), *a.* and *sb.* 1584. [f. L. *turbo, turbinem* + -AL.] **A.** *adj.* Turbinated, top-shaped; in *Anat.* = TURBINATE *a.* **B.** *sb. Anat.* A turbinal or turbinate bone; the ethmo-, the maxillo-, or the spheno-turbinal 1848.

Turbinate (tɒ̄·ɹbinĕt), *a.* and *sb.* 1661. [ad. L. *turbinatus*, f. *turbo, turbin-*; see -ATE[2].] **A.** *adj. Nat. Hist.* Resembling a spinning-top in shape; of a mollusc, having a spiral shell; *Bot.* inversely conical; having a narrow tapering base and broad rounded apex; *Anat.* applied to the scroll-like spongy bones of the nasal fossæ in the higher vertebrates. **B.** *sb.* a. A turbinate shell. b. A turbinate bone. 1802.

Turbinated (tɒ̄·ɹbineˡtėd), *a.* 1615. [f. as prec. *a.* + -ED[1].] 1. = prec. A. †2. Of motion: Like that of a top; rotary, whirling -1692.

Turbination (tɒ̄ɹbinēˡ·ʃən). 1623. [ad. L. *turbinationem.*] 1. †The action of making top-shaped; top-like or turbinate form; formation of a whorl. †2. The action of spinning or whirling round like a top -1680.

Turbine (tɒ̄·ɹbin, -əin). 1842. [a. F., ad. L. *turbinem*, TURBO.] 1. Applied orig. to a wheel revolving on a vertical axis, and driven by a column of water falling into its interior, and escaping by pipes or apertures, so arranged as to press by reaction on the periphery of the wheel, and cause it to revolve in the direction opposite to that of the escaping water. Now applied to any kind of machine in which this principle is used or developed. 2. More fully *steam-t.*: A steam motor in which rotatory motion is produced by steam impinging directly upon a series of vanes upon the circumference of a revolving cylinder or disk (or, in some types, acting and reacting alternately on moving and stationary elements) 1900. c. A centrifugal separator used in sugar manufacture 1873.

attrib. and *Comb.*, as *t. boat, destroyer, steamer, yacht*, etc., one driven by a steam t.; **t.-alternator, -generator** (see TURBO-) **-pump**, a t. water wheel used to raise water by being driven by external power in the direction opposite to that in which it turns when used as a motor.

Turbiniform (tɜːbiˑnifǭɹm), *a.* 1826. [ad. med.L. *turbiniformis*, f. L. *turbin-*, TURBO: see -FORM.] *Nat. Hist.* Top-shaped, turbinate; also, having the form of the genus *Turbo* of gasteropods; turbinoid, spiral.

Turbinite (tɜ̄ˑɹbinəit). 1828. [ad. mod.L. *turbinites*; see TURBO and -ITE [1].] *Zool.* A fossil turbinate shell.

Turbinoid (tɜ̄ˑɹbinoid), *a.* 1861. [f. L. *turbinem*, TURBO + -OID.] *Zool.* Resembling the genus *Turbo* or family *Turbinidæ* of gasteropod molluscs.

Turbit (tɜ̄ˑɹbit). 1688. [app. f. L. *turbo* top, from its figure.] A small fancy variety of the domestic pigeon, dist. by its stout rounded build, a short beak, the ruffle or frill on its neck and breast, and a small crest.

Turbo (tɜ̄ˑɹbo). 1661. [a. L., whirlwind, spinning-top, etc.] ‖1. (mod.L., pl. *turbines* (-nīz).) A genus of gasteropod molluscs, typical of the family *Turbinidæ*, having a regularly turbinate or whorled shell, with a rounded aperture and a calcareous operculum; also loosely, any member of the *Turbinidæ*; any turbinate or wreathed shell. 2. *Mech.* = TURBINE. *colloq.* 1904.

Turbo- (tɜ̄ˑɹbo), used as combining form of TURBINE, in compounds forming the names of machines driven by and directly coupled to a turbine, or which are themselves turbines; as *t.-alternator, -dynamo, -generator*, etc.

Turbot (tɜ̄ˑɹbət). ME. [a. OF. *tourbout, torbout*, AF. *turbut*, MDu. *turbot, terbot, tarbot*; perh. a deriv. of L. *turbo* top, with ref. to its shape.] 1. A large flat fish (*Rhombus maximus* or *Psetta maxima*), having a wide scaleless body covered with conical bony tubercles, with the eyes normally on the left side, found on the European coasts and much esteemed as food. 2. Applied to other fish more or less resembling the turbot. a. The halibut *Sc.* and *north.* b. In U.S., any of various large flat fishes, as the diamond flounder of California (*Hypopsetta guttulata*), or the spotted flounder of the Pacific coast (*Bothus maculatus*). c. Locally, any of various species of *Balistes*, the file-fishes and trigger-fishes. 1555.

Turbulence (tɜ̄ˑɹbiŭlĕns). 1490. [ad. L. *turbulentia*, f. *turbulentus* TURBULENT; see -ENCE.] The state or quality of being turbulent; violent commotion, agitation, or disturbance; disorderly character or conduct; with *a* and *pl.*, an instance of this. b. Of natural conditions: Stormy or tempestuous state or action. c. The spirally curved path given to the gas entering the cylinders under pressure in supercharged internal-combustion engines 1928.

The t. of ecclesiastical politics NEWMAN.

Tuˑrbulency. Now *rare.* 1607. [See -ENCY.] Turbulent state, disturbed condition.

Turbulent (tɜ̄ˑɹbiŭlĕnt), *a.* 1538. [ad. L. *turbulentus*, f. *turba* crowd, *turbare* to disturb.] 1. Of persons, etc.: Causing disturbance or commotion; inclined to disorder; tumultuous; unruly; violent. †b. Of things: Having a disturbing effect -1671. c. Violent in action or effect (*rare*) 1656. 2. Characterized by violent disturbance or commotion; violently disturbed; disorderly, troubled 1573. 3. *Meteorol.* and *Aviation.* Of wind: Characterized by eddies 1907.

1. These t. and stormy assaultes of the wicked COVERDALE. b. Whose heads that t. liquor fills with fumes MILT. 2. T'as been a t. and stormie night SHAKS. Thir inward State of Mind, calme Region once And full of Peace, now tost and t. MILT. The City of London lately so t. MACAULAY. Hence **Tuˑrbulent-ly** *adv.*, **-ness** (*rare*).

†**Turcism** (tɜ̄ˑɹsiz'm). 1566. [f. med.L. *Turcus* TURK + -ISM.] The religion or system of the Turks; Mohammedanism -1721. b. Turkish principles or practice -1705.

Turco (tɜ̄ˑɹko). 1839. [a. Sp., Pg., and It. *turco* TURK.] 1. A Chilian bird, *Hylactes megapodius.* 2. One of a body of native Algerian light infantry in the French Army; a Zouave soldier 1860.

Turco-, Turko- (tɜ̄ˑɹko), comb. form repr. med.L. *Turcus* or TURK; as in *T.-Bulgarian*; also **Turcomaˑnia,** a rage for Turkish manners or customs; excessive favour for Turkish policy; **Tuˑrcophil, -e** *a.*, tending to favour Turkey or the Turks; also *sb.*

Turcoman (tɜ̄ˑɹkomæ̆n). 1600. [a. Pers. *turkumān*, f. TURK + *mān-dan* to resemble; applied to the Turkish nomads.] 1. A member of a branch of the Turkish race, consisting of a number of tribes inhabiting the region lying east of the Caspian Sea and about the Sea of Aral, formerly known as Turkestan and parts of Persia and Afghanistan. 2. A Turcoman horse 1831. 3. *attrib.* or as *adj.* Of or pertaining to the Turcoman people, their language, or the region they inhabit 1613.

3. *T. carpet* or *rug*, a soft rich-coloured carpet made by the Turcomans.

Turd (tɜ̄ɹd). Not now in polite use. [OE. *tord*; prob. :—Indo-Eur. **drtó-*, pa. pple. of **der-* to tear, split.] A lump or piece of excrement; also, excrement, ordure.

Turdiform (tɜ̄ˑɹdifǭɹm), *a.* 1874. [ad. mod.L. *turdiformis*, f. L. *turdus* thrush; see -FORM.] *Ornith.* Having the form or appearance of a thrush; thrush-like.

Tureen (tiurīˑn, tərīˑn). 1706. [a. F. *terrine*, OF. *therine*, fem. of OF. *terrin* of earth, earthen :—pop. L. **terrinus*, f. *terra.*] A deep earthenware or plated vessel (often oval) with a lid, from which soup is served. Also, a smaller vessel of similar shape for sauce or gravy.

Turf (tɜ̄ɹf), *sb. Pl.* **turves, turfs.** [Com. Teut.; OE. *turf* :—OTeut. **turƀ-* :—Indo-Eur. **drbh-* (Skr. *darbhá* tuft of grass).] 1. A slab pared from the surface of the soil with the grass and herbage growing on it; a sod of grass, with the roots and earth adhering. b. *collect.* as a substance or material. *arch.* 1565. 2. *collect. sing.* The covering of grass and other plants, with its matted roots, forming the surface of grass land; the greensward; growing grass OE. 3. A slab or block of peat dug for use as fuel ME. b. *collect.* as a substance; peat 1510. 4. *The turf* (often with capital T): the grassy track or course over which horse-racing takes place; hence, the institution, action, or practice of horse-racing; the racing world 1755.

1. A bench of turues fressh and grene CHAUCER. 2. The Shepheard.. Who you saw sitting by me on the Turph SHAKS. 3. b. Abundance of turfe.. for fewell 1610. 4. If you are a true sportsman and have the honour of the t. at heart 1755.

Comb.: **t.-ant**, a small yellow European ant (*Formica flava*, or *Lasius flavus*), living in dry heathy t.; **-drain**, a drain in which the channel is covered by turves placed over it; a sod-drain; **-man**, a devotee of the t., a racing man; **-spade**, a spade for cutting t. or peats; also, a turfing-iron; **-worm**, the sod-worm. Hence **Tuˑrfen** *a.* made or covered with t.; turfy. **Tuˑrfite**, a devotee of the t., a racing-man. **Tuˑrfless** *a.* devoid of t., bare.

Turf, *v.* ME. [f. prec.] 1. *trans.* To cover with turf; to lay with turf. b. *transf.* To place or lay under the turf; to cover with turf, or as turf does; to bury; also *intr.* with *it*, to die and be buried 1628. 2. To dig up or excavate for turf or peat 1780. 3. *intr.* To get turf or peat for fuel. *dial.* 1876.

1. b. That you may not think I have turfed it, to speak in the New market phrase.. I send you this letter COWPER.

Turfing (tɜ̄ˑɹfiŋ), *vbl. sb.* 1649. [f. TURF *v.* or *sb.* + -ING [1].] The action of TURF *v.*

attrib.: **t.-iron**, a tool for raising turf; **-spade**, a peat-spade.

Turfy (tɜ̄ˑɹfi), *a.* 1552. [f. TURF *sb.* + -Y [1].] 1. Covered with or consisting of turf; grassy; turfen. 2. Of the nature of or abounding in turf or peat; peaty 1660. 3. Pertaining to or characteristic of the turf; suggestive of horse-racing; horsy 1844.

1. Thy Turphie-Mountaines, where liue nibling Sheepe SHAKS. Hence **Tuˑrfiness.**

Turgent (tɜ̄ˑɹdʒĕnt), *a.* Now *rare* or *Obs.* 1440. [ad. L. *turgentem*, *turgere* to swell out; see -ENT.] 1. Physically swelling or swollen; distended, turgid. 2. *fig.* Swollen or inflated with pride or conceit; bumptious; also, using inflated language 1621.

2. Puffed vp with t. titles BURTON. Hence **Tuˑrgency** (now *rare* or *Obs.*).

Turgescence (tɜɹdʒeˑsĕns). 1631. [ad. med. or mod.L. *turgescentia*; see next and -ENCE.] 1. The action or condition of swelling up; the fact or state of being swollen. 2. *fig.* a. Progressive swelling or increase. b. Inflation, pomposity, bombast. 1806.

Turgescency (tɜɹdʒeˑsĕnsi). 1666. [ad. med. or mod.L. *turgescentia*, f. *turgescentem*, *turgescere*, inceptive of *turgere*; see TURGENT and -ENCY.] The quality or state of being turgescent; swelling or swollen condition.

Turgescent (tɜɹdʒeˑsĕnt), *a.* 1727. [ad. L. *turgescentem*; see prec. and -ENT.] Becoming swollen; swelling, growing bigger.

Turgid (tɜ̄ˑɹdʒid), *a.* 1620. [ad. L. *turgidus*, f. *turgere* to swell; see -ID [1].] 1. Swollen, distended, puffed out. 2. *fig.* in ref. to language: Inflated, grandiloquent, pompous, bombastic 1725.

1. Proud and t. buds 1669. Bladders.. t. with Sap 1674. 2. Their t. and loquacious rhetoric GIBBON. Hence **Tuˑrgid-ly** *adv.*, **-ness.**

Turgidity (tɜɹdʒiˑdĭti). 1732. [f. L. *turgidus* (see prec.) + -ITY.] 1. The state of being turgid or swollen. 2. Inflation of language; grandiloquence, pomposity, bombast; also with *a* and *pl.* an example of this 1756.

2. T., and a false grandeur of diction WARTON.

Turion (tiūᵊriǭn). 1725. [= F., ad. L. *turio*, pl. **turiones,** formerly also in Eng. use.] *Bot.* A young shoot rising from the ground, produced from a subterranean bud.

Turk [1] (tɜ̄ɹk). ME. [= F. *Turc*, med.L. *Turcus*, Byz. Gr. Τοῦρκος, Pers. (and Arab.) *turk.* A national name of unkn. origin.] 1. *Ethnology.* Pl. *Turks.* A numerous and widely spread family of the human race, occupying from prehistoric times large parts of Central Asia, and speaking a language belonging to the TURKIC branch of the Ural-Altaic linguistic family 1500. 2. *Politics.* A member of the dominant race of the Ottoman empire; in earlier times, a Seljúk; since 1300, an Osmanli or Ottoman. Sometimes, any subject of the Grand Turk or Turkish Sultan; but usu. restricted to Mohammedans. Pl. *The Turks*, the Ottomans, the Turkish people. ME. b. *The T.*: the Turks; the Turkish power; also, the Turkish Sultan. 1482. c. *The Grand* or *Great T.*, the Ottoman Sultan 1482. 3. Often used as = Moslem or Mohammedan 1548. 4. *transf.* Applied to any one having qualities attributed to the Turks; a cruel, savage, rigorous, or tyrannical man 1536. 5. *attrib.* or as *adj.* = TURKISH. late ME.

2. *Young Turk*: a member of a twentieth-century political group of Ottomans having for its object the rejuvenation of the Turkish Empire. 3. He is a Christian at Rome, a Heathen at Japan, and a T. at Constantinople 1697. Phr. *To turn T., become T.*; If the reste of my Fortunes turne Turke with me SHAKS. 4. The man who has been a T. all his life lives long to plague all about him 1875. *Young* or *little T.*: an unmanageable or violent child or youth.

Turk [2]. 1712. [ad. F. *turc*; origin and history uncertain.] The larva of an insect noted for the destruction of pear-trees by mining under their bark.

Turkey [1] (tɜ̄ˑɹki). ME. [= F. *Turquie*, med.L. *Turchia, Turquia*, f. *Turc, Turcus* TURK [1].] 1. The land of the Turks, 'Turkey in Asia' and 'Turkey in Europe'; formerly occas. Turkestan or Tartary. †2. Short for: a. TURKEY STONE. -1680. b. *T. leather* -1835.

Comb.: **T. corn**, an old name for Indian corn; **T. leather,** leather tawed with oil, the hair side not being removed until after the tawing; **T. oak,** the mossy-cup oak of southern Europe, *Quercus cerris*; **T. rhubarb**, medicinal RHUBARB (1); **T. wheat,** maize, called also †*Guinea corn* and *Indian corn.*

Turkey [2] (tɜ̄ˑɹki). 1555. [Short for TURKEY-COCK, -HEN, app. applied orig. to the Guinea-fowl, a native of Africa.] †1. The Guinea-fowl -1655. 2. A well-known large gallinaceous bird of the Linnæan genus *Meleagris*, the species of which are all American; esp. *M. gallopavo*, which was found domesticated in Mexico at the discovery of that country in 1518, and is now valued as a table-fowl in all civilized lands 1555. b. *Wild t.*, the wild original of the domestic fowl 1613. c. The flesh of this bird, esp. the domestic turkey, as food 1573. 3. Applied with qualification to other birds: A local name of the Bustard; now usu. applied to the Australian Bustard, also called *Native, Plain*, or *Wild T.* (*Eupodotis*

(*Otis*) *australis*); also in Australia, the *Brush-* or Wattled T.; etc. 1848.

2. c. Cold t. and ham, or roast chicken 1886.

attrib. and *Comb.*; **t.-beard,** also **turkey's beard,** a N. Amer. liliaceous herb, *Xerophyllum asphodeloides*, having a tuft of wiry root-leaves, and an erect stem with a raceme of white flowers; **-berry,** (*a*) *Solanum mammosum* and *S. torvum* of the West Indies; (*b*) the fruit of a W. Indian tree, *Cordia Collococca* (*t.-berry tree*); **-buzzard,** an Amer. carrion vulture, *Cathartes aura*, so called from its bare reddish head and neck and dark plumage; in W. Africa, the Vulturine Pie, *Picathartes gymnocephalus*; **-trot,** a kind of ball-room dance introduced from U.S. *c* 1912; **-vulture** = *t.-buzzard*.

Tu·rkey ca·rpet. 1546. [f. TURKEY 1 + CARPET.] A carpet made in or imported from Turkey, or of a style in imitation of this; woven in one piece of richly-coloured wools, and having a deep pile, cut so as to resemble velvet.

Turkey-cock (tǭ·ɹki kǫ:k). 1541. [f. TURKEY 1 + COCK *sb.*1 In the 16th c. synonymous with *Guinea-cock* or *Guinea-fowl*, the Amer. bird being at first identified with or treated as a species of this.] †1. The male of the Guinea-fowl, *Numida meleagris* –1601. 2. The male of the turkey 1578.

2. *fig. Twel. N.* II. v. 36.

Tu·rkey-hen. 1552. [Cf. prec.] †1. The guinea-hen –1601. 2. The female of the turkey 1555.

Turkey red. 1789. [TURKEY 1.] A brilliant and permanent red colour produced on cotton goods, essentially a madder red in combination with oil or fat, with an aluminous mordant. Also called *Adrianople* or *Levant red*. b. Cotton cloth of this colour 1880.

Turkey stone. 1607. [TURKEY 1.] 1. = TURQUOISE. 2. A hard, fine-grained, siliceous rock imported from the Levant for whetstones; novaculite; a whetstone made of this 1816.

Turki (tu·rkī), *a.* (*sb.*) 1782. [a. Pers. *turkī*, deriv. of TURK.] Turkish; belonging to the typical Turkic languages, *East* and *West T.*, and to the peoples speaking them. B. *sb.* A member of the Turkish race; also, a Turkish horse.

Turkic (tǭ·ɹkik), *a.* 1859. [f. TURK 1 + -IC.] Applied to one of the branches of the Ural-Altaic or Turanian family of languages, comprising Eastern Turki or Uigur, West Turki or Seljúk and Osmanli, Kazan Tartar, Kirghiz, Nogai, Yakut, etc., the languages of the Turks (in the wide sense); also applied to the peoples using these.

Turkish (tǭ·ɹkiʃ), *a.* (*sb.*) 1545. [f. TURK 1 + -ISH 1.] Of, pertaining or belonging to the Turks or to Turkey; now commonly = Ottoman. b. Resembling the Turks or their character; cruel, savage, barbarous 1600.

Collocations. **T. bath,** a hot steam bath introduced from the East, inducing copious perspiration, followed by soaping, washing, shampooing, massage, and cooling. **T. delight,** a sweetmeat of T. origin usu. made of jelly of tough consistence and sugar-coated; **T. music,** the noisy percussion instruments in an orchestra; **T. towel,** a cotton towel having a long nap, cut or uncut; hence **T. towelling.**

B. *sb.* 1. The Turkish or Turk's language 1718. 2. *ellipt.* for *T. delight*, *T. tobacco* (colloq.) 1898. Hence **Tu·rkish-ly** *adv.*, **-ness.**

Turkism (tǭ·ɹkiz'm). 1595. [f. TURK 1 + -ISM.] = TURCISM.

Turkize (tǭ·ɹkəiz), *v.* 1599. [f. TURK 1 + -IZE.] 1. *trans.* To render Turkish. 2. *intr.* To play the Turk; †to tyrannize *over* 1599.

Turk's cap. 1597. [TURK 1.] †1. Early name for the tulip –1629. 2. The Martagon lily; also *Turk's-cap lily* 1672. 3. The Melon-thistle, *Cactus Melocactus*; also †*Turk's head* 1829.

Turk's head. 1725. [TURK 1.] †1. = prec. 3. –1760. 2. *Naut.* An ornamental knot resembling a turban 1833. 3. A round long-handled broom or brush; = POPE'S HEAD 2. 1859.

Turm (tǭɹm). 1483. [a. OF. *turme*, *torme*, ad. L. *turma* troop, squadron.] A body or band of people, *esp.* a troop of horsemen; *spec.* a troop of thirty or thirty-two horsemen.

Legions and Cohorts, turmes of horse and wings MILT.

Turmeric (tǭ·ɹmərik), *sb.* (*a.*) 1538. [Origin obsc. In the early forms *tarmaret*, *tormarith*, perh. repr. F. *terre merite* and med. or mod.L. *terra merita* deserving or deserved earth.] 1. The aromatic and pungent root-stock of an E. Indian plant (see 2); the powder made from this, the chief ingredient in curry powder, used also as a dye, as a chemical test, and in the East as a condiment, as well as medicinally. 2. The plant *Curcuma longa*, family *Zingiberaceæ* 1601.

attrib. and *Comb.*: **t.-oil** = TURMEROL; **t. paper,** unsized paper tinged with a solution of t., used as a test for alkalis.

B. *adj. Chem.* Obtained from t.; in *t. acid*, an acid, $C_{11}H_{14}O_2$, formed by the oxidation of turmerol.

Turmerol (tǭ·ɹmərǫl). 1890. [f. prec. + -OL 3.] *Chem.* An aromatic volatile oil obtained from turmeric.

Turmoil (tǭ·ɹmoil), *sb.* 1526. [f. next.] A state of agitation or commotion; disturbance, tumult; trouble, disquiet. †b. Harassing labour, toil (*rare*) –1591.

b. And there Ile rest, as after much turmoile, A blessed soule doth in Elizium SHAKS.

Turmoil (tǭ·ɹmoil), *v.* 1511. [Origin unkn.] 1. *trans.* To agitate, disquiet, disturb; to trouble, worry, torment. Now somewhat *rare*. b. To disorder or distress physically. *arch.* 1542. †2. *intr.* To be or live in turmoil, agitation, or commotion –1681. 3. *intr.* To toil, drudge. Now *dial.* 1548.

1. I was so turmoyled in the contre where I was that I coude no lenger there dwell TINDALE.

Turn (tǭɹn), *sb.* ME. [Partly a. AF. **torn*, *turn*, *tourn*, = OF. *tor*, *tour*, F. *tour* :—L. *tornus*, a. Gr. τόρνος turning-lathe; partly f. TURN *v.*] I. Rotation, and connected senses. 1. The action of turning about an axis or centre, as a wheel; rotation, revolution. Now *rare*. 2. An act of turning; a movement of rotation (complete or partial); *esp.* a single revolution, as of a wheel 1481. 3. = GID 1. 1523. 4. A movement round something, a twist; *spec. Naut.* an act of passing a rope once round a mast or other object 1743. 5. *Mus.* A melodic ornament consisting of a group of three (four, or five) notes, viz. the principal note (*on* which it is performed) and the notes one degree above and below it 1801. 6. The condition of being or direction in which something is twisted or convoluted; hence, a portion of something of a convoluted or twisted form, corresponding to one whole revolution; a (single) coil or twist 1669. 7. A lathe; now only applied to a watch-maker's lathe, also called a *pair of turns* 1483.

1. Fortune's-wheel..is always..upon the T. 1680. 2. In a few turns of the hands of the..clock RUSKIN. Phr. (*Roasted*, *done*, etc.) *to a t.*, i. e. precisely right: orig. in ref. to the turns of the spit. *T. of the scale*(*s*, the slight advantage given to the buyer by which the article sold overbalances the weight and brings down the scale-pan; hence, a very little (just enough to *turn the scale*).

II. Change of direction or course, etc. 1. An act of turning or facing another way; a change of direction or posture. late ME. b. 'A step off the ladder at the gallows' (J.); hanging. Now *rare* or *Obs.* 1631. c. Change of position (by a rotatory movement) of something inanimate, as a die when thrown 1801. 2. *Printing.* A reversal of type in composing 1888. 3. An act (or, rarely, the action) of turning aside from one's course; deflexion, deviation; a roundabout course, a detour ME. 4. A place or point at which a road, river, or the like turns, or turns off; a bend, curve, or angle. late ME. 5. The act of turning so as to face about or go in the opposite direction; reversal of position or course; turning back. Also *fig.*, esp. in *t. of the tide*, etc. 1669. 6. *Coursing.* The act of suddenly turning, as of a hare when closely pursued, and making off more or less in the opposite direction, or at a considerable angle from the direction of pursuit. Usu. in phr. *to give the hare* (etc.) *a t.*, said of the hound. 1575. †7. A journey, tour, course –1734. b. A sheriff's tour or court; see TOURN. 8. An act of walking or pacing around or about a limited area; a short walk (or ride) forth and back, esp. by a different route; a stroll 1591.

1. She..made a sudden t. As if to speak TENNYSON. c. Stake their liberty upon the t. of the dice 1801. 3. The river nobly..flows..And all its thousand turns disclose Some fresher beauty BYRON. 5. Phr. *At every t.*, usu. *fig.* at every change of circumstance; hence, on every occasion, constantly. Phr. *On the t.*, in or close upon the act of turning, at the turning-point. 7. His design to take a t. into England H. WALPOLE. 8. A turne or two Ile walke To still my beating minde SHAKS. I took several Turns about my Chamber STEELE.

III. Change in general. 1. The action, or an act, of turning or changing; change, alteration (*rare* exc. as in 2.) 1597. 2. *spec.* A change in affairs, conditions, or circumstances; vicissitude; revolution; *esp.* a change for better or worse, or the like, at a crisis; hence, sometimes, the time at which such a change takes place 1607. 3. A momentary shock caused by sudden alarm, fright, or the like. *colloq.* 1846.

1. The t. of the leaf was very brilliant 1901. Phr. *On the t.*, turning sour, as food; of the weather or the season, changing. 2. Some t. this sickness yet might take TENNYSON. Phr. *T. of life*: = *change of life* (CHANGE *sb.* 3). 3. It was only a dream..But it gave me a terrible t. 1886.

IV. Senses denoting actions of various kinds. †1. A movement, device, or trick, by which a wrestler attempts to throw his antagonist; = F. *tour* –1562. †2. A subtle device of any kind; a trick, wile, artifice, stratagem –1735. 3. An act of good or ill will, or that does good or harm to another; usu. qualified, as *good t.*, a benefit, etc. ME. 4. A stroke or spell of work; a task, job. *north.* and *Sc. Obs.* exc. in *hand's t.* late ME. 5. A spell or bout of action, a 'go'; *spec.* a spell of wrestling; hence, a contest. late ME. b. An attack of illness, faintness, or the like; also, a fit of passion or excitement 1775. †6. An event, circumstance, trap. *Obs.* or merged in other senses. –1719.

2. A variety of artifices and turns H. WALPOLE. 3. One good t. deserves another 1654. 5. b. Some wild t. of anger TENNYSON.

V. Occasion, etc. 1. (Each or any one's) recurring occasion of action, etc. in a series of acts done, or to be done, by (or to) a number in rotation. late ME. 2. *spec.* a. A shift 1793. b. *Theatr.* A public appearance on the stage, preceding or following others; an item in a variety entertainment; also *transf.* applied to the performer 1890. 3. Requirement, need, exigency; purpose, use, convenience. *arch.* (Chiefly in special phrases.) 1573.

1. Phr. *By turns*, one after another in regular succession. *In t.*, *in turns*, each in due succession. *In one's t.*, in one's due order in the series; so *out of one's t.*, out of one's due order in the series. *T. about*, *t. and t. about*: *advb.* in t., by turns, alternately; *adj.* performed in t., mutual, reciprocal (*rare*); *sb.* the action of doing something in t. 3. You will answer my t...as well as another 1881. Phr. *To serve one's t.*, to answer one's purpose or requirement; to suit, answer, serve, avail, 'do'. So *To serve the t.* *To serve one's* (*one's own*, or *a*) *t.* (said of a person): to compass one's own purpose, consult one's own need.

VI. 1. Style, character, quality; *esp.* style of language, arrangement of words in a sentence 1601. 2. (with *a* and *pl.*) A modification of phraseology for a particular effect, or as a grace or embellishment; a special point or detail of style or expression 1693. 3. Form, make, mould, cast (of a material object). Now *rare* or *Obs.* 1702. 4. Natural inclination, disposition, bent; aptitude, capacity *for* something 1702. †b. A characteristic –1764. 5. Direction, tendency, drift, trend 1704. 6. A change from the original intention; a particular construction or interpretation put upon something: usu. with *give* 1710.

1. Her T. of Wit was gentle, polite, and insinuating 1718. 2. His felicitous turns of expression 1868. 3. The T. of his Neck and Arms ADDISON. 4. Mr. Ledbury was of an enquiring t. of mind 1844. Persons of a dyspeptic t. 1871. Phr. *T. of speed*, capacity for speed, ability to run or go fast. 5. I discovered what gave my thoughts a new t. 1845. 6. Do not give so cruel a t. to my silence FIELDING.

VII. Techn. senses. 1. A measure of various commodities, as of haddocks, wood, fur-skins, etc. 1674. 2. *Comm.* (in full, *t. of the market*): A change in price, or the difference between the buying and selling prices, of a stock or commodity; the profit made by this 1882.

Turn (tǭɹn), *v.* [OE. *tyrnan* and *turnian*, both ad. L. *tornare* to turn in a lathe, round off, f. *tornus* lathe = Gr. τόρνος compasses.] I. To rotate or revolve, and derived senses. 1. *trans.*

To cause to move round on an axis or about a centre; to cause to rotate or revolve, as a wheel. **b.** To cause to move round, or (usu.) partly round, in this way, esp. for opening or closing something: as a key, tap, door-handle, screw, etc. ME. **c.** To perform by revolving, as a somersault 1860. **2.** *intr.* To move round on an axis or about a centre; to move partly round in this way OE. **b.** *fig.* To revolve (as time, etc.). In later use said chiefly of the head or brain: To reel, swim, be in a whirl. OE. **3.** *To t. on* or *upon* (fig.): **a.** To hinge upon, depend on, have as the centre or pivot of movement or action 1661. **b.** To have as its subject, be about, relate to; usu. said of conversation or debate 1711.

1. Waters turning busy mills COWPER. b. The lamp was turned very low 1880. 2. As the dore turneth vpon his henges BIBLE (Genev.) *Prov.* xxvi. 14. A little boy..turning head over heels MME D'ARBLAY. b. I looked at the handbill and my head turned 1892. 3. a. Great Events often t. upon very small Circumstances SWIFT. b. The debate..did not t. upon any ..practical proposition 1884.

II. To form or shape by rotation, etc. **1.** *trans.* To shape, esp. into a rounded form, by cutting with a chisel or similar tool while rotating in a lathe; to form, work, or make by means of a lathe. Also *absol.* to work with a lathe. ME. **b.** *Building.* To form, construct, build (an arched or vaulted structure) 1703. **c.** *Cookery.* To pare off the rind or peel of (an orange, lemon, etc.) round and round in a long narrow thin strip; to stone (an olive) in this way 1706. **d.** *Knitting* and *Lace-making.* To make in a curved form 1882. **2.** *fig.* To shape, form, or fashion artistically or gracefully 1616. †**b.** *pa. pple.* Of a person (or the mind, etc.): Naturally adapted, fitted, or 'cut out' for some pursuit -1728.

1. Such as turne wooden vessels 1600. d. She..appeared to be in a perpetual state of turning the heel of a stocking 1902. 2. Some studied compliments.. finely turned BOSWELL. The hand long, delicate, and well turned 1847. b. By nature turn'd to play the rake SWIFT.

III. To change or reverse position. **1.** *intr.* To move or shift (by a rotary motion, or through an angle) so as to change one's posture or position; *esp.* to shift the body (as on an axis) from side to side; to twist or writhe about OE. **b.** Said of the scale or beam of a balance, or of the balance itself: To move up or down from the horizontal position 1596. **2.** *trans.* To alter the position or posture of (an object) by moving it through an angle; to move (a thing or person) into a different posture. late ME. **3.** *fig.* To revolve in the mind 1725. **4.** To give a curved or crooked form to; to bend or twist; to form by bending ME. **b.** *spec.* To bend back (the edge of a sharp instrument) so as to make it useless for cutting; to blunt in this way 1568. **c.** *intr.* for *pass.* To assume a curved form, to bend; to become blunted by bending 1579. **5.** *trans.* To reverse the position or posture of; to move into the contrary position, so that the upper side becomes the under, or the front the back ME. **6.** *spec.* **a.** To reverse (a leaf of a book) in order to read (or write) on the other side or on the next leaf; to do this with the leaves of (a book) in succession so as to read or search through ME. **b.** To reverse the position of the turf, or of the soil, in ploughing or digging, so as to bring the under parts to the surface. Also *absol.* 1477. **c.** To reverse (a garment, etc.) so that the inner side becomes the outer; hence, to alter or remake by putting the inner side outward 1483. **7.** To cause (the stomach) to reject or revolt against food 1622. **b.** *intr.* Of the stomach: To be affected with nausea 1719.

1. Phr. *To make* (a person) *t. in his grave*: see GRAVE *sb.*[1] 1. b. If the scale doe turne But in the estimation of a hayre SHAKS. 3. T. these things in your mind 1825. 4. His mustaches were turned and curled SCOTT. Phr. *To t.* (a person) *round one's* (*little*) *finger*, to be able to do what one likes with him. b. *fig.* A difficulty sufficient to t. the edge of the finest wit 1714. 5. Her..fine legerdemain in turning pancakes RUSKIN. *To t. turtle*; see TURTLE *sb.*[2] 1. 6. b. The first sod of the..Railway was turned on Tuesday 1892. c. A way of turning an old frock 1893. 7. This filthy simile..Quite turns my stomach POPE. b. Their stomachs turned at this sight DE FOE.

IV. To change or reverse course. **1.** *trans.* To alter the course of; to divert, deflect ME. **b.** To check the course of; to cause to go aside or retreat; to throw off, keep out (wet) 1620. **2.** *fig.* To divert or deflect from a course of action, purpose, thought, etc.; to alter the course of (something immaterial) ME. **3.** 'To keep passing in a course of exchange or traffick' (J.); to cause (money or commodities) to circulate 1605. **4.** *intr.* To change one's course so as to go in a different direction; to deviate ME. **b.** *Naut.* To beat to windward; to tack 1569. **c.** Of the wind: To shift 1610. **d.** Of a road, path, line, etc.: To change direction; also, to branch off from the main road or line 1535. **5.** *trans.* To go or pass round (a corner, etc.) 1687. **b.** *Mil.* To get round (an enemy's position, etc.) 1845. **6.** To pass, get beyond (a particular age, time or amount) 1789. **b.** *pa. pple.* (in active sense): Having passed (a particular age or time); more than, past 1700. **7.** To reverse the course of; to cause to go in the opposite direction ME. **8.** *intr.* To reverse one's, or its course; to begin to go, or to tend, in the opposite direction ME. †**9.** *intr.* and *trans.* To give or send back; to return -1637.

1. They turn'd the winding rivulet's course CLARE. b. Horatius Right deftly turned the blow MACAULAY. 2. She turn'd the talk DRYDEN. 3. Phr. *To t. the penny, to t. an honest penny*: see PENNY III, HONEST *a.* 4 b. 4. e. *Cricket.* Of a ball: To break 1911. 5. Before Gama had turned the Cape MACAULAY. 6. It had turned a quarter past one 1893. b. I'm nineteen ..and you are turned twenty 1890. 7. Phr. *To t. the dice, t. the tide*, to reverse the luck, the progress of circumstances. 8. Stocks fell..the exchange turned, money became scarce DISRAELI. 9. Ere from this warre thou turne a Conqueror SHAKS.

V. 1. a. *trans.* To change the direction of; to direct another way, or different ways alternately (esp. the eyes or face) ME. **b.** *refl.* = c. *arch.* ME. **c.** *intr.* To face about ME. **2. a.** *trans.* To direct, present, point (towards or away from some specified person or thing, or in some specified direction) ME. **b.** *refl.* = c. *arch.* late ME. **c.** *intr.* To direct oneself; to face (with implied change of direction) ME. **3. a.** *trans.* To set going in a particular direction; to bend the course of ME. **b.** *refl.* = c. *arch.* ME. **c.** *intr.* To direct one's course; to set oneself to go in a particular direction: usu. with implied change of course ME. **4.** *trans.* To cause or command to go away from a place or one's presence; *esp.* to send or order away 1526. **b.** *spec.* To drive or put forth (beasts) to pasture 1602. **c.** To put, cast, or convey into a receptacle or the like; now esp. by inverting the containing vessel, or diverting into a new channel 1594. **5.** *fig.* *trans.* To direct or set (thought, desire, speech, action, etc.) towards (or away from) something. Usu. const. *to*, rarely *on, upon*. ME. **b.** To cause or induce (a person, etc.) to take a particular course; to direct the course of (events, etc.) *arch.* late ME. **6.** *refl.* = 7, 7 b, c. Now *rare* or *arch.* ME. **7.** *intr.* To direct one's mind, desire, or will to or from some person, thing, or action ME. **b.** *spec.* To direct one's attention *to* a different subject. late ME. **c.** To direct one's attention *to* something practically; to apply oneself *to* an occupation or pursuit 1667. **d.** *To t. to*: to refer to, look up, consult (a book, list, etc.) 1631. **e.** To have recourse *to* (a person, etc.); to appeal *to* for help or support 1821. †**8.** *trans.* To convert; less commonly in bad sense, to pervert. *Obs.* or merged in other senses. ME. **9.** *intr.* To adopt a different (esp. the true) religion, or a godly life; to be converted ME. **b.** To go over to another side or party; to revolt, desert. Const *to*. *Obs.* or *arch.* ME. **10.** *trans.* To direct or bring to bear in the way of (active) opposition; to retort or cause to recoil *upon*; to proceed to use *against* ME. **b.** To direct *against* in feeling; to imbue with hatred or dislike 1831. **11.** *intr.* To recoil *upon*; to have an adverse tendency or result. Now *rare* or *Obs.* or merged in next. late ME. **12.** To change one's position in order to attack or resist some one; to take up an attitude of opposition; with *on* or *upon*, to assail suddenly or violently (in act or word); with *against*, usu. implying a change from previous friendliness ME. **13.** *trans.* To apply *to* some use or purpose; to make use of, employ ME. **b.** To set (a person) to some work or employment 1781.

1. b. Turne thee Benuolio, looke vpon thy death SHAKS. c. *Right t.! Left t.!*, as military words of command = turn (through a right angle), to the right, to the left. (*Right*) *about t.!* = turn (by a movement to the right) so as to face in the opposite direction. 2. a. A soured man prefers to t. his worst side outwards 1880. c. Where'er she turns the Graces homage pay GRAY. Phr. *Not to know which way to t.*, etc., not to know what course to take, what to do. 3. c. Thither their footsteps t. 1893. 4. You will not..t. me from your door MISS BURNEY. b. The privilege of turning stock into the park 1847. 5. We..turned our attention to poor Tom. STEVENSON. b. Great Apollo Turne all to th' best SHAKS. 6. Turne the vnto me, and haue mercy vpon me *Bible* (Great) *Ps.* xxv. 16. 7. Where'er I roam..My heart untravell'd fondly turns to thee GOLDSM. c. He turned next to log-splitting 1891. 9. So would they say to all Protestants..T., or burn 1679. 10. To wrest his weapon out of his hands, and turne it upon himselfe 1641. b. The hearts of the poor were turned in bitterness against the rich 1831. 12. His adulators of yesterday are prepared to t. and rend him 1892. 13. Virgil, turning his pen to the advantage of his country BACON.

VI. To change, alter. **1.** *trans.* To change, transmute; to alter, make different, or substitute something else (of the same kind) for. Now *rare* or *Obs.* ME. **2.** *intr.* To undergo change or alteration; to change (*rare*) ME. **3.** *trans.* with *into* or *to*: To change, transform, or convert into ME. **b.** *transf.* To exchange for; also, to substitute something else for 1449. **4.** *intr.* with *into* or *to*: To change into; to become ME. **5.** with *compl.* To change so as to be, to become ME. **6.** *trans.* with *compl.* (usu. *adj.*) To change so as to make . . .; to make (so) by alteration; to render 1607. **7.** With *into* or *to*: To make the subject of (praise, mockery, etc.) late ME. **8.** *intr.* with *to*: To lead to as a consequence; to result in, bring about. *Obs.* or merged in other senses. ME. †**b.** *To t.* (a person) *to* (something): to result in or bring about for the person; to put him to (trouble, etc.); to be for (his advantage, etc.) -1610. **9.** *trans.* To translate or paraphrase; to render. Also *absol.* ME. **b.** To alter the phrasing of (a sentence); to give another turn to 1593. **10.** To disturb or overthrow the mental balance of; to make mad or crazy, to distract, dement, infatuate ME. **b.** *intr.* for *pass.* of the head (*rare*) 1852. **11.** *trans.* To make sour, taint (milk, etc.) 1548. **b.** *intr.* To become sour or tainted 1577. **12.** To change colour, become of a different colour (as ripening fruit, fading leaves, etc.) 1578. **b.** *trans.* To change the colour of 1791.

1. *Merch. V*, III. ii. 249. 2. Things change their titles, as our manners t. POPE. 3. May not honey's self be turn'd to gall? GRAY. b. [They] turned their little stock into Cash 1855. 4. These rocks, by custom, t. to beds of down GOLDSM. 5. Vnlesse the diuell himselfe turne Iew SHAKS. Cygnets from Gray turne White BACON. 7. Phr. *To t.* (a thing) *into ridicule* (see RIDICULE *sb.*[1]). 8. b. All the trouble thou hast turn'd me to SHAKS. 9. In 1648 he turned nine psalms, and..in 1653, 'did into verse' eight more 1879. 10. The Prince's head was a little turned 1683. 12. When her hair had begun to t. 1888.

Phrases. **Turn the** (or **one's**) **back,** to turn away, go away; *t. the back upon*, to depart from, abandon. **T. the balance or beam,** = *t. the scale.* **T. bridle,** to turn one's horse and ride back; to retreat, as a rider. **T. one's coat,** to change one's principles or party (see COAT *sb.*). **T.** (**one's**) **colour,** to change colour; of a person, to become pale or red in the face (now *rare*). **T. a deaf ear,** to refuse to listen. **T. edge**: see III. 4 b. **Turn..flank,** *Mil.* to get round an enemy's flank, so as to make an attack in flank or rear; hence *fig.* to 'get round', circumvent, or outwit a person. **T. one's hand. a.** To make an attack *upon* (*arch.*). **b.** with *to*: To apply oneself to, set to work at, take up as an occupation. †**T. head,** to turn and face an enemy; to show a bold opposing front; opp. to *t. tail.* **T. the scale,** to cause one scale of a balance to descend: said of an additional weight, usu. a slight or just sufficient one; hence *fig.* to preponderate so as to determine the success or superiority of one of two opposing parties. **b.** with *at*, To weigh slightly more than. **T. tail. a.** (orig. in *Falconry*) To turn the back and flee; to run away. **b.** with *on* or *upon*: To abandon, forsake. **T. loose.** *trans.* To set free (an animal) and allow to go loose; *transf.* and *fig.* to leave to oneself or one's own devices. **T. to account.** †**a.** *intr.* To be profitable, to 'pay'. **b.** *trans.* To employ profitably. **T. to bay,** to turn and defend oneself as a hunted animal at bay; also *fig.* †**T. and wind. a.** *intr.* and *refl.* To turn this way and that; to go or move in a winding course. **b.** *trans.* To turn this way and that, as a rider his horse; *fig.* to do what one will with.

With advbs. **T. about.** (See simple senses and ABOUT *adv.*) †**a.** *intr.* To move circularly on an axis; to rotate, revolve. **b.** To t. so as to face or go in the opposite direction. Now *rare*. †**c.** *trans.* To cause to rotate or revolve. **d.** To put into a different or the opposite position (by a rotary motion). Now *rare* or *Obs.* **e.** To turn this way and that; to move or push about; also *fig.* = *t. over.* **T. again.** (See simple senses and AGAIN *adv.*) *intr.* †To face round the other way, return, go back. **T. aside:** see simple senses and ASIDE *adv.* **T. away.** (See simple senses and AWAY *adv.*) **a.** *trans.* To avert (one's face, etc.). **b.** *fig.* To divert; to avert (calamity, etc.). **c.** To send away, dismiss; *spec.* to dismiss from service. **d.** *intr.* To turn so as to face away from some person or thing; to avert one's face. **e.** To leave the straight course, deviate; to be averted. *Obs.* or *arch.* **T. back.** (See simple senses and BACK *adv.*) **a.** *trans.* To reverse the course of, drive back, cause to retreat. †**b.** To send or give back, return. **c.** To reverse the direction of; to direct backwards. **d.** To fold or double back or over (part of a garment, etc.). **e.** *intr.* To turn and go back. †**f.** To come or go back. **T. down.** (See simple senses and DOWN *adv.*) **a.** *trans.* To fold or double down; to bend downwards. **b.** To turn upside down; to turn (a card) face downwards. **c.** To put down, send to a lower position (as in a class at school). **d.** *slang.* orig. *U.S.* To rebuke, snub; to reject. **e.** *Sporting,* etc. To put (game, etc.) in a place to stock it. **f.** To lower (a lamp, gas, etc.) by turning the wick, tap, or stop-cock. **g.** *intr.* To turn aside and go down. **h.** To bend downwards. **T. in.** (See simple senses and IN *adv.*) **a.** *trans.* To send, drive, put, or take in. **b.** *Agric.* To dig or plough (weeds, stubble, manure) into the ground. Also with the ground as obj. **c.** To bend or fold inwards. **d.** To cause to point or face inwards. **e.** To hand in, bring in, deliver (*U.S.*). **f.** *intr.* To turn aside and go in (to a place, house, room, etc.). **g.** (orig *Naut.*) To go to bed. *colloq.* **h.** To have an inward direction, point inwards. **T. off.** (See simple senses and OFF *adv.*) **a.** *trans.* To dismiss, send away; *spec.* to discharge from service or employment. **b.** To hang (on a gallows); orig. *to t. off the ladder.* Now *rare* or *Obs.* **c.** *joc.* (perh. *fig.* from prec.) To marry, join in marriage. **d.** To deflect, divert. **e.** *spec.* To divert attention from, or alter the effect of (a remark, etc.). **f.** To stop the flow of (water, gas, etc.) by turning a tap or the like, or by closing a sluice; to shut off; to turn out (a light). Also with the tap, etc. as obj. **g.** To complete and get off one's hands; to produce (with skill or facility). **h.** *intr.* To deviate from the direct road; also *transf.* of a road or path, to branch off. **i.** To fall in quality, 'go off'; to wither and fall off; also, of food, etc., to become sour or bad. **T. on. a.** *trans.* To induce a flow of (water, steam, gas, etc.) by turning a tap or stop-cock, or by opening a sluice; also with the tap, etc. as obj.; also *intr.* for *pass.* **b.** To set (a person) *to do* something. *colloq.* **T. out.** (See simple senses and OUT *adv.*) **a.** *trans.* To cause to go or come out; to expel; also, to fetch or summon out. **b.** To drive or put out (beasts) to pasture or to the open, or (pheasants, etc.) into a covert. **c.** To dismiss or eject from office or employment. **d.** To put (things) out of a house, room, or receptacle; to empty out by sloping or inverting the containing vessel. **e.** (*transf.* from d.) To clear (a receptacle or room) of its contents; to empty (usu. for the sake of examining or re-arranging the contents). **f.** To put out (a lamp, gas) by turning a tap or the like. **g.** To finish making and get off one's hands; to produce (usu. implying rapidity, facility, or skill). **h.** To equip, 'rig out', 'get up'. **i.** To alter the position of so as to bring it to the outside. **j.** To direct or cause to point outwards. **k.** *intr.* To turn aside and go out; to 'clear out'; to go forth, sally forth (usu. with the notion of some compelling force, or of leaving a place of safety or comfort for one of danger or discomfort). **l.** To get out of bed. *colloq.* **m.** To leave one's abode and betake oneself to some outside occupation. **n.** To abandon one's work; to go out on strike. **o.** To bend or be directed outwards. **p.** (*a*) To result, eventuate. (*b*) with *compl.* To come to be, become ultimately (and so be found or known to be). (*c*) To prove *to be* (without implication of becoming). **T. out of.** (See simple senses and OUT OF.) **a.** *trans.* To drive, send, or put out of (a place) or dismiss from a position or office) forcibly or premptorily; to expel or eject from. **b.** *intr.* To get out of, leave, quit. **T. over.** (See simple senses and OVER *adv.*) **a.** *trans.* To turn (something) from its position on to one side, or from one side to the other, or upside down; to invert, reverse; to overturn, upset. **b.** To reverse (a leaf, or the successive leaves, of a book) in order to read (or write) on further; to read or search through (a book) by doing this. **c.** To reverse or shift (soil, hay, etc.) so as to expose the under parts, or different parts successively. **d.** To reverse and shift successively (papers or other articles lying flat in a heap) for the purpose of examining those that are beneath. **e.** *fig.* To agitate or revolve *in the mind,* consider and reconsider. **f.** To turn off the ladder in hanging. **g.** To transfer, hand over, make over, deliver, commit (*to*); *spec.* to transfer (an apprentice) to another master, (a sailor) to another ship. **h.** *Comm.* To pass or hand over in the way of exchange; to employ in business; to sell or dispose of goods to the amount of (a specified sum). **i.** *intr.* To turn on to one side, or from one side to the other, or upside down; to reverse itself; to capsize; to roll about. **T. round.** (See simple senses and ROUND *adv.*) **a.** *intr.* To move round on an axis or centre; to rotate, revolve. Also *fig.* of the brain or head. **b.** To turn so as to face in the opposite direction; to face about; to turn from one side to the other. **c.** *fig.* To change to the opposite opinion, state of mind, etc.; *esp.* to change from a friendly to a hostile attitude; with *on* or *upon,* to assail suddenly. **d.** *trans.* To cause to revolve or rotate; also, to cause to face in all directions successively. **e.** To reverse (*lit.* and *fig.*). **f.** To cause to face in a different direction. Also *fig.* to induce (a person) to take an opposite course or view. **T. to. a.** *intr.* To apply oneself to some task or occupation; to set to work. **b.** *trans.* To set (a person) to work. **T. up.** (See simple senses and UP *adv.*) **a.** *trans.* To direct or bend upwards. **b.** esp. in phr. *to t. up one's nose* (as an expression of contempt): usu. *fig.* **c.** To turn upside down, invert (now esp. in order to examine what is beneath). **d.** To fold over (a garment or part of one) so as to shorten it; also *transf.* with the person as obj. **e.** In *pa. pple.* of a garment: Having the border turned or folded over (and covered *with* some ornamental material). **f.** To turn (soil, etc.) so as to bring up the under parts to the surface; to dig or plough up; also, to bring to the surface (something buried) by digging, etc. **g.** To turn (a card) face upwards; *esp.* to do this in dealing to determine the trump suit. **h.** To find in a book, a set of papers, etc. some passage or document; to look up, refer to. (With the book, etc., or the passage, as obj.) **i.** To lay (a person or animal) on the back; hence, to kill. **j.** *To t. up one's heels* (or *toes*), to die; *to t. up* (a person's) *heels,* to lay low, kill. **k.** To turn the stomach of; also *fig.* **l.** To turn the regulator or tap of (a lamp or gas-jet) so as to raise the wick or increase the flow of gas, and thus make it burn more brightly. **m.** *Naut.* To cause to appear above the horizon, come in sight of. **n.** *Naut.* To summon (the crew) on deck. **o.** *intr.* To bend or point upwards. **p.** *Naut.* To beat up to windward; to tack. Also with *it.* **q.** To make its (or one's) appearance; to present (itself or oneself) casually or unexpectedly; to occur, appear, be discovered or encountered. **r.** with *compl.* To appear or present itself in a specified character, to be found to be. †**s.** *trans.* and *intr.* (for *refl.*): app. to prostitute; to prostitute oneself.

Turn-, the vb.-stem in comb. with a sb., adv., or adj., forming sbs. and adjs., in the sense 'that turns or is turned', 'for turning', in various uses of the vb.

T.-bridge, a bridge turning horizontally on a pivot; **-broach** = TURNSPIT 2, 3; **-plate,** †(*a*) a curved plate-rail; (*b*) = TURN-TABLE 1; **-rail** = TURN-TABLE 1; also, a point or switch for directing railway vehicles from one line to another; **-screw,** a screw-driver; **-stone,** a limicoline bird, *Strepsilas interpres,* which turns over stones to get at the crustacea and other small animals to be found under them; also, a wrench; **-to,** a tussle, a set-to.

Turnback (tɒ·ɹnbæk), *sb.* and *a.* 1847. [f. the vbl. phr. *turn back.*] One who or that which turns back or is turned back. **A.** *sb.* **a.** One who faintheartedly retreats, or gives up. **b.** That part of anything which is folded back. **B.** *attrib.* or *adj.* That is folded back.

Tu·rn-bu:ckle. 1703. [f. TURN *v.* + BUCKLE *sb.*] **1.** A catch or fastening for window casements, shutters, etc., consisting of a thin flat bar pivoted so that it falls by its weight into a slit or groove. **2.** A coupling with internal screw threads for connecting metal rods lengthwise or for regulating their length or tension; *transf.* a device for coupling electric wires 1877.

Turncoat (tɒ·ɹnkout), *sb.* and *a.* 1557. [f. TURN *v.* + COAT *sb.*, lit. one who turns his coat.] **A.** *sb.* One who changes his principles or party; a renegade; an apostate. †**b.** *transf.* applied to anything that changes in appearance or colour –1608. **B.** *adj.* Of, pertaining to, or that is a turncoat 1571.

A. Wine is a turne-coate (first a friend, then an enemy) 1632.

Tu·rncock. 1702. [f. TURN *v.* + COCK *sb.*[1]] †**1.** A stop-cock of which the plug is turned to open or close it –1755. **2.** A waterworks official who turns on the water from the mains to supply-pipes, etc. 1711.

Tu·rn-down, *a.* and *sb.* 1840. [f. the vbl. phr. *turn down.*] **A.** *adj.* **1.** That turns down or may be turned down, esp. said of a collar worn with the upper part turned down over the neck-band; *t. bed,* a folding bed. **2.** *Electr.* Designating an incandescent lamp of which one small filament only is used when little light is wanted 1911. **B.** *sb.* **1.** The turned-down part of anything; also, something worn turned down; *spec.* a turn-down collar 1849. **2.** *slang.* Rejection (cf. *turn down* d, TURN *v.*) 1902.

Turner (tɒ·ɹnəɹ). ME. [a. OF. *tornere* :— L. *tornator,* and *torneor,* F. *tourneur* :— L. *tornatorem,* agent-n. f. *tornare* to turn in a lathe; in later senses f. TURN *v.* + -ER[1]] **1.** One who turns or fashions objects of wood, metal, bone, etc. on a lathe. **b.** A potter, *esp.* one who finishes and smooths the ware before it is fired 1601. **2.** In general senses: see TURN *v.* 1440. †**3.** A variety of fancy pigeon –1735. **4.** [a. G. *turner,* f. *turnen* to perform gymnastic exercises.] A member of one of the gymnastic societies instituted in Germany by F. L. Jahn (1778–1852) 1860.

Turneresque (-e·sk), *a.* 1851. [f. name of J. M. W. *Turner* (1775–1851), landscape painter + -ESQUE.] Resembling in some respect the pictures of Turner.

The T. splendour of sunset in a great city 1877.

Turnerite (tɒ·ɹnərəit). 1823. [f. name of C. H. *Turner* + -ITE[1].] *Min.* A variety of monazite, occurring in yellow or brown crystals.

Turnery (tɒ·ɹnəri). 1644. [f. TURNER + -Y[3].] **1.** The art of the turner; the fashioning of objects or designs by means of a lathe 1662. **2.** *collect.* Turner's work; turnery ware 1644. **3.** A turner's workshop 1863.

2. [Some old chairs] the backs, arms, and legs loaded with t. H. WALPOLE.

Turning (tɒ·ɹniŋ), *vbl. sb.* ME. [f. TURN *v.* + -ING[1].] The action of TURN *v.* in various senses (also concretely). **1.** Movement about an axis or centre; rotation, revolution. late ME. **2.** The action of shaping or working something on a lathe; the art of shaping things by means of a lathe; the work of a turner 1440. **b.** *pl.* (*concr.*) Chips or shavings *of* some substance produced by turning in a lathe 1800. **3.** *fig.* Shaping, moulding, fashioning (of literary work, etc.) 1586. **4.** The action, or an act, of changing posture or direction by moving as on a pivot; movement so as to face or point in a different, or in some particular, direction ME. **b.** The practice of gymnastics according to the system of F. L. Jahn: cf. TURNER 4. 1888. **5.** Reversal, inversion 1536. **6.** The action of bending or folding over, or condition of being folded over; a fold 1631. **7.** A change in the direction of movement or course; deflexion, deviation; winding, tortuous course. late ME. **8.** A place or point where a road, path, etc. turns, or turns off. late ME. **9.** Reversal of movement or course 1440. **10.** *fig.* Conversion; perversion; desertion to another side. *arch.* ME. **11.** Change; vicissitude; alteration 1548.

3. Skill in the t. of phrases LONGF. 8. Turne vpon your right hand at the next t., but at the next t. of all on your left SHAKS. 9. I abhor even the shadow of changing or t. with the tide SCOTT.

attrib. and *Comb.*: **t. engine,** (*a*) a lathe; (*b*) a small engine for turning over a large one slowly for inspection or adjustment.

Tu·rning, *ppl. a.* 1450. [f. as prec. + -ING[2].] That turns, in various senses of the vb. *Comb.*: **t. bridge,** = *turn-bridge* (see TURN-); †**-stile,** = TURNSTILE; **-table,** = TURN-TABLE.

Tu·rning-point. 1851. [f. TURNING *vbl. sb.* + POINT *sb.*] **1.** *lit.* A point at which something turns, or changes its direction of motion 1856. **2.** *fig.* A point at which a decisive change of any kind takes place; a critical point, crisis 1851.

Turnip (tɒ·ɹnip), *sb.* 1533. [Earlier *turnepe, turnep*; the second element being NEEP, OE. *næp,* ad. L. *napus*; first element uncertain; perh. F. *tour* or Eng. TURN.] **1.** The fleshy, globular or spheroidal root of a biennial cruciferous plant, *Brassica Rapa,* var. *depressa,* cultivated from ancient times as a culinary vegetable, and for feeding sheep and cattle; also, the plant itself, of which the young shoots (*t.-tops*) are freq. boiled as greens. **2.** Applied to other species or varieties of *Brassica*; as **French t.** (*a*) the rape *B. Napus* (or *campestris*); (*b*) a variety of *B. Napus* extensively cultivated in France and Germany, and used to flavour soups; **Swedish t.,** *B. campestris Rutabaga*; 1548. **3.** Slang term for an old-fashioned thick silver watch 1840.

Comb.: **t.-aphid, -aphis,** the plant-louse of the t., *Aphis rapæ*; **-beetle, -flea** (also **t. flea beetle**), a minute shiny black leaping **beetle,** *Haltica nemorum,* which feeds on the young **leaves** of the t. and other crucifers; its larva mines in the **full**-grown leaf; **-fly,** (*a*) = *t.-flea*; (*b*) the t.-sawfly, *Athalia centifoliæ,* the larva of which feeds on t.-leaves; (*c*) a dipterous insect, *Anthomyia radicum,* whose larva lives in the root of the t.; **-lantern**, the hollowed rind of a t. employed as a lantern; **-shell**, a shell of the family *Turbinellidæ*, esp. of the genus *Rapa*; **-top** (usu. *pl.*), the sprouting leaves of the second year's growth of the t., used as a vegetable.

‖**Turnix** (tə̄·ɹniks). 1819. [mod.L., app. shortened from L. *coturnix* quail.] *Ornith.* A genus of quail-like birds (also called *Hemipodius*); the bush-quails.

Turnkey (tə̄·ɹnkī). 1654. [f. TURN *v.* + KEY *sb.*[1]] 1. One who has charge of the keys of a prison; a jailer, *esp.* a subordinate. 2. A tooth-key, formerly used in dentistry; a tooth-wrest 1877.

Turn-out (tə̄·ɹnˌaut), *sb.* (*a.*) 1688. [f. the vbl. phr. *turn out.*] 1. A turning out or getting out (of bed, etc.); hence, a call to duty, esp. during one's period of rest; *spec. Mil.* a signal to rise (now *rare* or *obs.*). 2. A strike 1806. 3. Those who turn out or assemble for any purpose; an assemblage, muster; also, a turning out or assembling of persons 1816. 4. A loop-line or siding in a railway or tramway; also, in a narrow road, a part wider than the rest, or a short side road, to enable vehicles to pass each other; a similar place in a canal 1824. 5. A turning or clearing out; a clearance 1856. 6. The manner in which anything is turned out or equipped; 'get-up'; also *concr.* equipment, outfit, array 1812. 7. A driving equipage 1817. 8. The quantity of anything turned out in an industry, etc.; the total product; output 1879. B. *attrib.* or as *adj.* That turns out, or is turned out, in various senses 1899.

1. The bugles were sounding the t. THACKERAY. 5. A t. of the den HUGHES. 7. A special prize..for the best t. of donkey and barrow 1895.

Turn-over (tə̄·ɹnˌōᵘːvəɹ), *sb.* and *a.* 1611. [f. the vbl. phr. *turn over.*] 1. The action of turning over; *spec.* in *Polit. slang*, a transference of votes from one party to another 1660. 2. An apprentice whose indentures are transferred to another master on the retirement or failure of his original one; also, the action or process of turning over an apprentice. Now *dial.* 1631. 3. Any part or thing which is turned or folded over; e.g. the flap of an envelope, etc. 1611. b. An article that begins in the last column of a newspaper page and continues overleaf 1842. 4. A kind of tart in which fruit or jam is laid on one half of the rolled out paste, and has the other half turned over it 1798. 5. The total amount of business done in a given time; also, the amount of goods produced and disposed of by a manufacturer; also, the 'turning over' of the capital involved in a business; also, the net profit derived from a business in a given time 1879. B. *adj.* That turns or is turned over, as *t. collar, majority* 1849.

Turnpike (tə̄·ɹnpəik). late ME. [f. TURN- + PIKE *sb.*[1]] 1. *Hist.* A spiked barrier fixed in or across a road or passage, as a defence against sudden attack, esp. of men on horseback. †2. A turnstile -1755. †3. A barrier across a water-course or stream; a water-gate; also, a lock on a navigable stream -1751. 4. A barrier placed across a road to stop passage till the toll is paid; a toll-gate. Now chiefly *Hist.* 1678. 5. *ellipt.* for TURNPIKE ROAD 1748. 6. *Sc.* A spiral or winding stair 1501.

2. I moue vpon my axell, like a turne-pike B. JONS.

Tu·rnpike road. 1745. A road on which turnpikes are or were erected for the collection of tolls; hence, a main road or highway, formerly maintained by a toll levied on cattle and wheeled vehicles.

Turn-sick (tə̄·ɹnsik), *a.* and *sb.* *Obs.* exc. *dial.* 1440. [f. TURN *v.* + SICK *a.*] †A. *adj.* Affected with vertigo; giddy; dizzy -1664. B. *sb.* †1. Vertigo; also, staggers in the horse -1592. 2. The gid or sturdy in sheep. *dial.* 1834.

Turnsole (tə̄·ɹnsōᵘl). late ME. [a. F. *tournesol*, prob. ad. older Prov. *tournasol*, f. Romanic *tornare* to TURN + L. *sol* the sun.] 1. A violet-blue or purple colouring matter, obtained from the plant *Crozophora tinctoria*. b. *transf.* = LITMUS 1839. 2. A plant of which the flowers or leaves turn so as to follow the sun. a. An annual euphorbiaceous plant, *Crozophora tinctoria*, cultivated in the south of France for its colouring juice (see 1) 1578. b. The plant *Heliotropium europæum* 1578. c. Formerly applied to the Sunflower; also to the Sun-spurge or Wartwort, *Euphorbia helioscopia* 1725.

Turnspit (tə̄·ɹnspit). 1576. [f. TURN *v.* + SPIT *sb*[1].] 1. A dog kept to turn the roasting-spit by running within a kind of tread-wheel connected with it; a *t. dog.* 2. A boy or man whose office was to turn the spit. Also as a term of contempt. 1607. 3. A roasting-jack (*rare*) 1606.

Turnstile (tə̄·ɹnstəil). 1643. [f. TURN *v.* + STILE *sb.*[1]] A gateway formed of four radiating arms of timber or iron at right angles to each other, revolving horizontally on a fixed vertical post, set up in a passage or entrance, orig. to exclude any but foot-passengers, now often to prevent the passage of more than one person at a time at a place where fees, fares, or tickets are collected.

Turn-table (tə̄·ɹntēⁱb'l). 1835. [f. TURN *v.* + TABLE *sb.*] 1. On a railway: A revolving platform turning on a central pivot, laid with rails connecting with adjacent tracks, for turning railway vehicles; a turn-plate. 2. A revolving platform, table, stand, or disk of various kinds; e.g. for carrying heavy guns in fixed armoured redoubts or barbettes, etc., or for carrying the record disk in a gramophone 1865.

Turn-up (tə̄·ɹnˌɒp), *sb.* and *a.* 1685. [f. the vbl. phr. *turn up.*] 1. The turned up part of anything, esp. of a garment 1688. b. *pl.* The turned-up part at the bottom of trouser-legs. 2. The turning up of a particular card or die in games of chance; the card or die turned up; hence *fig.*, a mere chance, a 'toss-up'; a result which is purely a matter of chance 1810. 3. A boxing contest; hence, *loosely*, a set-to, esp. with the fists; also, a tussle; a disturbance, row 1810. B. *attrib.* or *adj.* That is turned up, or turns up, in various senses 1685.

Turnwrest (tə̄·ɹnrest), *a.* (*sb.*) 1653. [f. TURN- + WREST *sb.*[2]] *T. plough*, a plough in which the mould-board may be shifted from one side to the other at the end of each furrow, so that the furrow-slice is always thrown the same way; a one-way plough. (In the 18th c. freq. called the *Kentish plough.*) b. *ellipt.* as *sb.* 1778.

Turonian (tiurōᵘ·niăn), *a.* 1850. [= F. *turonien*, f. L. *Turones*, a people of ancient Gaul, whence Tours on the Loire took its name; see -IAN.] *Geol.* Denoting a subdivision of the Cretaceous or Chalk period and series of strata, answering to the 'Lower White Chalk without flints' of English geologists.

Turpentine (tə̄·ɹpĕntəin), *sb.* late ME. [In 14–15th c. *terebentyne, terbentyne*, a. OF. *terebentine*, ad. L. *terbentina* or *terebenthina* (*resina*); see TEREBENTHINA, -INE.] 1. A term applied orig. (as in Gr. and L.) to the semifluid resin of the terebinth tree, *Pistacia Terebinthus* (Chian or Cyprian t.); now chiefly to the various oleoresins which exude from coniferous trees, consisting of more or less viscid solutions of resin in a volatile oil. b. With qualification, indicating different varieties 1577. c. *pl.* Varieties of turpentine 1605. d. = *Oil of t.* (see 3) 1876. 2. †a. The fruit of the terebinth tree. b. A terebinth tree. Also, any tree that yields turpentine, as the larch. 1562. 3. In full: **Oil of t.** (also vulgarly known as *spirit of t.*), a volatile oil, contained in the wood, bark, leaves, etc. of coniferous trees, and usu. prepared by distilling crude turpentine. There are many varieties according to the source, which, though all having the same formula, $C_{10}H_{16}$, vary in their physical, and, more especially, in their optical properties. 1597.

Comb.: **t. moth**, a leaf-roller moth of the genus *Retinia*, of which the larvæ bore into the twigs of conifers; **t. oil** = *oil of t.*; **T. State** (U.S.), North Carolina, so called from the quantity of t. obtained from its pine forests; **t. tree**, *orig.* the Terebinth, *Pistacia Terebinthus* (see 1); any tree yielding t., esp. species of pine and fir, as the Larch, which yields Venice t. Hence **Tu·rpentine** *v.* to treat, rub, or smear with t. or t. oil.

Turpeth, turbith (tə̄·ɹpĕþ, -biþ). [Late ME. *turbit*, a. OF. *turbit, -ith, turpet*, ad. Pers. and Arab. *turbid, -bed.*] 1. A cathartic drug prepared from the root of East Indian jalap, *Ipomœa Turpethum*, an Indian and Australian plant; also, the plant itself, or its root. 2. *T. mineral*, basic sulphate of mercury ($HgSO_4 \cdot 2HgO$), obtained as a lemon-yellow powder from the normal sulphate by washing with hot water 1616.

Turpinite (tə̄·ɹpinəit). 1895. [a. F., f. *Turpin*, name of the inventor + -ITE [1].] An explosive, used in making shells.

Turpitude (tə̄·ɹpitiūd). 1490. [a. F., or ad. L. *turpitudo*, f. *turpis* base; see -TUDE.] Base or shameful character; vileness; depravity, wickedness. b. With *a* and *pl.* An instance of this 1597.

Turps (tə̄ɹps). 1823. *colloq.* = TURPENTINE 3.

Turquoise (tə̄·ɹkoiz, tə̄·ɹkwoiz, tə̄·ɹkwāz, *arch.* tə̄ɹkī·z, tə̄·ɹkiz), *sb.* (*a.*) late ME. [In 15–16th c. *turkeis, -keys*, a. OF. *turqueise, -quaise*, later *turquoise*, fem. adj. Turkish, in full *pierre turquoise* 'Turkish stone'. So named as coming from Turkestan, where first found, or through the Turkish dominions.] 1. A precious stone found in Persia (the *true* or *Oriental t.*), much prized as a gem, of a sky-blue to apple-green colour, almost opaque or sometimes translucent, consisting of hydrous phosphate of aluminium. b. In *collect. sing.*, esp. as a substance 1607. 2. More fully t. stone. Now *rare.* 1556. 3. As name for a colour (short for *t. blue*) 1853. 4. Lapidaries' name for odontolite 1796. B. as *adj.* Of the colour of the turquoise; turquoise-blue 1573.

1. The azurn sheen Of Turkis blew and Emrauld green MILT. 3. The..t. of the heavens 1876.

Turret (tɒ·rĕt), *sb.* [ME. *turet, toret, tourette*, a. OF. *torete, tourete*, later *tourette*, dim. of *tur, tor, tour* TOWER:—L. *turris.*] 1. A small or subordinate tower, usu. one forming part of a larger structure; *esp.* a rounded addition to an angle of a building, sometimes commencing at some height above the ground, and freq. containing a spiral staircase. 2. *Mil.* A low flat armour-plated tower, commonly cylindrical or conical, on a ship of war or a fort, made to contain a gun and gunners, and usu. to revolve horizontally 1862. 3. *U.S.* A raised central portion in the roof of a railway passenger carriage 1875. 4. An attachment to a lathe, drill, etc., consisting of a round or polygonal block with sockets for various dies or cutting tools, and capable of being rotated, so as to present the required tool to the work 1875.

1. He perceived the turrets of an ancient chateau rising out of the trees W. IRVING.

attrib. and *Comb.*: **t. deck**, an upper deck of a cargo steamer to which the sides of the vessel curve upward convexly from the main deck; **t. head** = sense 4; **-lathe**, a lathe fitted with a t.; **-ship**, a ship of war with a t. Hence **Tu·rret** *v. trans.* to fortify, or adorn with or as with a t. or turrets; usu. in *pa. pple.*

Turreted (tɒ·rĕtĕd), *a.* 1550. [f. prec.] 1. Furnished with or having a turret or turrets. 2. Furnished with something resembling a turret 1610. b. *spec.* = TURRITED 1826.

2. Turretted ships 1837. Head of Kybele.., wearing t. crown 1872.

Turriculated (tɒri·kiŭlēⁱtĕd), *ppl. a.* 1822. [f. L. *turricula* (dim. of *turris* tower) + -ATE + -ED.] Furnished with a turret or turrets, turreted: *spec.* in *Conch.* = TURRITED. Also **Turri·culate** *a.*

Turrilite (tɒ·riləit). 1828. [ad. mod.L. *Turrilites*, f. L. *turris* tower + Gr. λίθος stone; see -LITE.] *Palæont.* A fossil cephalopod belonging or related to the genus *Turrilites*, allied to the ammonites, but having a long spiral (turreted) shell, found in the Cretaceous formations.

Turrited (tɒ·rəitĕd), *a.* 1758. [f. L. *turritus* towered (f. *turris* tower) + -ED.] = TURRETED 2: *spec.* of a shell, having a long spire resembling a tower or turret. Also **Tu·rrite** *a.*

Turritellid (tɒrite·lid). 1860. [ad. mod.L. *Turritellidæ* pl., f. *Turritella* (Lamarck), name of the typical genus, f. *turris* tower; see -ID [3].] *Zool.* A gasteropod of the family *Turritellidæ*, characterized by long turreted shells with spiral striations; a screw-shell. So **Turrite·lloid** *a.*

resembling a screw-shell; having the characters of the *Turritellidæ*.

Turtle[1] (tɜ̄·ɹt'l). Now *rare* or *arch.* [OE. *turtla, turtle*, either dim. or dissimilated form of L. *turtur* TURTUR.] **1.** = TURTLE-DOVE 1. **b.** *Greenland t., Sea-turtle*, the Black Guillemot 1678. **2.** *fig.* Applied to a person, as a term of endearment, etc., or esp. to lovers or married folk, in allusion to the turtle-dove's affection for its mate. late ME.

Turtle[2] (tɜ̄·ɹt'l). 1657. [app. a corruption, by English sailors, of the earlier *tortue* (see TORTOISE), assim. to prec.] **1.** Any species of marine tortoise; also extended to various other tortoises. (Pl. *turtles*, collectively usu. *turtle*.) **b.** The flesh of various species of turtle used as food; also short for *t.-soup*. (See also MOCK TURTLE.) 1755. **2.** *Typog.* A curved bed in which types or stereotypes are secured, and which is mounted on one of the cylinders of a rotary printing-press: so called from a fancied resemblance of the bed to the back of a turtle 1860.

1. Alligator-t., the snapping-t., also called *alligator-tortoise*; **chicken-t.**, *Chrysemys reticulata*, also called *chicken-tortoise*; **green t.**, various species of *Chelonia*, having green shells, as *C. midas* of the West Indies and *C. virgata* of the Pacific, both much esteemed as food. Phr. *To turn t.*: **a.** *lit.* to catch t. by throwing them on their backs; **b.** *fig.* to turn over, capsize, be upset.

attrib. and *Comb.*, as *t.-catcher, -fishing, -soup*; **t. cowry**, a large species of cowry, *Cypræa testudinaria*; **-grass**, either of two marine plants with long narrow grass-like leaves: (*a*) *Thalassia testudinum*, of the W. Indies, etc.; (*b*) the grass-wrack, *Zostera marina*; **-head**, a N. Amer. scrophulariaceous plant, *Chelone glabra*, so called from the shape of the flower; **-shell**, (*a*) the shell of a t.; the material of this, tortoise-shell; (*b*) = *t.-cowry*. Hence **Tu·rtler**, a person, or a vessel, engaged in turtling; a t.-catcher. **Tu·rtling**, the action of 'fishing' for or catching t.

Tu·rtle-back. 1881. [f. prec.] **1.** An arched structure over the deck of a steamer at the bow, and often also at the stern, to protect it from damage by a heavy sea. **2.** *Archæol.* A roughly chipped stone implement, having one or both faces slightly convex 1890. Hence **Tu·rtle-ba·cked** *a.* having a back like a turtle's; furnished with a t. (sense 1).

Turtle-dove (tɜ̄·ɹt'l,dɒv). ME. [f. TURTLE *sb.*[1] + DOVE.] **1.** A dove of the genus *Turtur*, esp. the common European species *T. communis*, noted for its graceful form, harmonious colouring, and affection for its mate. **2.** *fig.* applied to a person 1535.

2. My darling and my harts desyre, my onely Turtle Doue 1575.

†Turtur. [In OE. direct from L. In ME. partly a. OF. *turtre, tortre*, mod.F. *tourtre*; repr. L. *turturem, turtur*, app. an echoic name.] = TURTLE *sb.*[1] –1649.

Tuscan (tɒ·skăn), *a.* and *sb.* late ME. [= F. *Tuscan, -ane*, It. *Toscano, -a*, ad. late L. *Tuscanus, -a*, belonging to the *Tusci* or *Thusci*, a race of ancient Italy (called also *Etrusci* Etruscans), pl. of *Tuscus* adj. and sb., an ethnic name.] **A.** *adj.* **a.** = ETRUSCAN *a.* 1513. **b.** Of or pertaining to Tuscany, formerly a grand duchy, having Florence as its capital; now a part of the kingdom of Italy 1588. **c.** *Arch.* Applied to the simplest and rudest of the five classical orders of architecture; allied to the Doric, but devoid of all ornament; belonging to this order, as *a T. pillar* 1563. **d.** Applied to a method of plaiting the fine wheaten straw grown in Tuscany for hats, etc.; also to the golden yellow colour of this 1834. **B.** *sb.* **a.** = ETRUSCAN *sb.* late ME. **b.** A native or inhabitant of Tuscany 1633. **c.** The language of Tuscany, regarded as the classical form of Italian 1568.

Tush (tɒʃ), *sb.*[1] [ME. *tus(s)ch, tos(s)ch*, repr. OE. *tusc* TUSK *sb.*] **1.** = TUSK *sb.* **1.** Now chiefly *arch.* or *dial.* **b.** *spec.* A canine tooth, esp. of a horse 1607. **c.** A stunted tusk in some Indian elephants 1859. **2.** In a plough: = FIN *sb.* 3 b. *Obs.* exc. *dial.* 1649.

Tush (tɒʃ), *int.* (*sb.*[2]) *arch.* 1440. [A natural utterance.] An exclam. of impatient contempt or disparagement.

T., said Obstinate, away with your book BUNYAN.

B. *sb.* as a name for this utterance 1600. Hence **Tush** *v. intr.* to say 't.!', to scoff or express impatience *at*. **Tu·shery**, R. L. Stevenson's name for a style of romance characterized by excessive use of affected archaisms such as 't.!'.

Tusk (tɒsk), *sb.* [OE. *tux* (whence by metathesis ME. *tusk, tosk*), var. of the rare OE. *tusc* (whence TUSH *sb.*[1]).] **1.** A long pointed tooth; *esp.* a (canine or incisor) tooth specially developed so as to project beyond the mouth, as in the elephant, wild boar, etc. **b.** Applied *spec.* to the permanent canine teeth of the horse. More usu. called *tush*. 1808. **2.** A projecting part or object resembling the tusk of an animal, as (*Carpentry*), a bevel or sloping shoulder on a tenon, for additional strength 1679.

Comb.: **t.-shell** = TOOTH-SHELL; **t. tenon**, a tenon made with a t.

Tusk, *v.* 1614. [f. TUSK *sb.*] **1.** *intr.* **†a.** app., To show the teeth. B. JONS. **b.** To use, or thrust with, the tusks; of a horse, to pull roughly with the teeth *at* 1825. **2.** *trans.* To root or dig *up*, or to tear *off* with the tusks; to wound with the tusk 1629.

Tusker (tɒ·skəɹ). 1859. [f. TUSK *sb.* + -ER[1].] A beast having tusks, esp. an elephant or wild boar.

Tusky (tɒ·ski), *a.* 1620. [f. as prec. + -Y[1].] Characterized by tusks; tusked: chiefly as a poetic epithet of the wild boar.

On Mountain tops to chace the t. Boar DRYDEN.

Tusseh, -er: see TUSSORE.

Tussive (tɒ·siv), *a.* 1857. [f. L. *tussis* cough + -IVE.] Pertaining to or caused by cough.

Tussle (tɒ·s'l), *sb.* 1629. [f. TUSSLE *v.*] A vigorous or disorderly conflict; a severe struggle, a hard contest; a scuffle. **b.** fig.; *esp.* a sharp and determined contention or dispute 1857.

b. The t. of life 1883.

Tussle (tɒ·s'l), *v.* 1470. [orig. app. Sc. and north.: prob. dim. or frequent. of TOUSE *v.* Cf. TOUSLE.] **1.** *trans.* To push or pull about roughly, to hustle; to engage in a tussle with. Now *rare*. **2.** *intr.* To struggle or contend in a vigorous and determined way; to wrestle confusedly; to scuffle 1638. **b.** in *fig.* use 1862.

Tussock (tɒ·sək). 1550. [perh. altered form of obs. *tusk* tuft, assim. to diminutives in -OCK.] **1.** A tuft or bunch of hair. Now *rare*. **2.** A tuft, clump, or matted growth, forming a small hillock, of grass, sedge, or the like 1607. **3.** Short for *t.-moth* or *caterpillar* 1819. **4.** Short for TUSSOCK-GRASS. Also in *pl.* 1832.

1. Bushy tussocks of grey eyebrow 1893.

Comb.: **t.-caterpillar**, the larva of the **t.-moth**, any of various kinds of moth, as those of the genus *Orgyia*, the larvæ of which have long tufts of hairs. Hence **Tu·ssocky** *a.* abounding in or forming tussocks.

Tu·ssock-grass. 1842. **1.** Any of several grasses of the Southern Hemisphere; esp. (*a*) *Poa flabellata* (formerly *Dactylis cæspitosa*), a tall-growing valuable grass of the Falkland Islands and Patagonia; (*b*) various New Zealand species of *Arundo* and *Poa*. **2.** The tufted hair-grass, *Aira cæspitosa*, or other native grass growing in tussocks 1860.

Tussore (tɒsōᵊɹ, tɒ·soəɹ). Formerly **tusser** (tɒ·səɹ); also **tusseh, tussah.** 1619. [ad. Hindī (and Urdū) *tasar*:—Skr. *tasara* shuttle, 'perhaps from the form of the cocoon' (Yule & Burnell).] **1.** In full *t. silk*: A coarse brown silk (furnished by *Antheræa mylitta* and other species of silkworm) made in and imported from India. Also *ellipt.* a dress made of this. **2.** = *t.-worm* 1796.

Comb.: **t.-moth**, any moth of which the larva (*t.-worm*) yields t.; **t.-(silk)worm**, any silkworm yielding t.; the larva of a tusser-moth.

Tut (tɒt), *sb.*[1] 1553. [Origin unkn.] **1.** *western dial.* A small seat or hassock made of straw; a cushion or hassock for kneeling upon. **†2.** The orb borne as an emblem of sovereignty (*rare*) –1706.

Tut (tɒt), *sb.*[2] *local.* 1702. [Origin unkn.] Originally in Cornish tin-mines, and in s.w. agricultural areas, now also in Derbyshire lead-mining: in the phr. *upon t.* (also *by the t.*), and *attrib.* as *t.-work, -workman*: denoting a system of payment by measurement or by the piece, adopted in paying for work which brings no immediate returns; hence, work of this character; dead-work.

Tut (tɒt), *int.* (*sb.*[3]). 1529. [A natural utterance.] An ejaculation (often reduplicated) expressing impatience, dissatisfaction, or contempt. **B.** *sb.* The (or an) utterance of this exclam. 1676.

I come..once more, to ask pardon...T., boy, a trifle GOLDSM. Hence **Tut** *v. intr.* to utter the exclam. 'tut'.

Tutania (tiutēⁱ·niă). 1790. [f. *Tutin*, name of the maker or inventor.] An earlier name for Britannia-metal.

Tutelage (tiū·tĭlėdʒ). 1605. [f. L. *tutela* guardianship (f. *tut-, tueri* to watch) + -AGE.] **1.** The office or function of a guardian; protection, care, guardianship; governorship of a ward. **b.** Instruction, tuition 1857. **2.** The condition of being under protection or guardianship 1650.

1. Under the t. of a patron saint 1879. **b.** Under the t. of several different masters 1863.

Tutelar (tiū·tĭlăɹ), *a.* and *sb.* 1600. [ad. L. *tutelaris*, f. *tutela*; see prec. and -AR[1].] **A.** *adj.* = next A. **B.** *sb.* A tutelary deity, angel, or saint 1603.

Tutelary (tiū·tĭlări), *a.* and *sb.* 1611. [ad. L. *tutelarius* guardian, f. as prec.; see -ARY[1].] **A.** *adj.* **1.** Of supernatural powers: Having the position of protector, guardian, or patron; *esp.* protecting or watching over a particular person, place, or thing. **2.** *transf.* Of or pertaining to protection or a protector or guardian 1651.

1. The patron and t. genius of liberty 1806. **2.** Great acts of t. friendship GLADSTONE.

B. *sb.* = prec. B. 1652.

Tutenag (tiū·tĕnæg). 1622. [a. Marāṭhī *tuttināg*, app. derived from Skr. *tuttha-* blue vitriol, sulphate of copper + *nāga* tin or lead.] A whitish alloy of copper, zinc, and nickel, with a little iron, silver, or arsenic, resembling German silver; also used loosely in the Indian trade for zinc.

Tutiorist (tiū·ʃiŏrist). 1845. [f. L. *tutior* safer + -IST.] One who holds that in cases of conscience the course of greater moral safety should be chosen.

Tutor (tiū·təɹ), *sb.* late ME. [a. OF., AF. *tutour*, or a. L. *tutor* watcher, f. *tueri* to watch, guard.] **†1.** A guardian; a protector, defender –1602. **2.** One who has the custody of a ward; a guardian. **†a.** *gen.* –1690. **b.** *spec.* in *Rom.* and *Sc. Law*: The guardian and representative, and administrator of the estate, of a person legally incapable, failing the father. late ME. **3.** One employed in the supervision and instruction of a youth in a private household. Also, one engaged to travel abroad with one or more pupils, a *travelling* or *foreign t.* late ME. **4.** In the Universities of Oxford, Cambridge, and Dublin: A graduate (most often a fellow of a college), to whom the special supervision of an undergraduate (called his pupil) is assigned 1610. **b.** In U.S. universities and colleges: A teacher subordinate to a professor 1828.

4. *Private t.* (at the Eng. Universities), a person engaged by students to assist them in their studies and preparation for the examinations, but not appointed or recognized by their University or College; also, a person who makes it his business to 'coach' students for professional examinations apart from the universities.

Tu·tor, *v.* 1592. [f. prec.] **1.** *trans.* To act the part of a tutor towards; to give special or individual instruction to; to teach, instruct (*in* a subject). Also *absol.* **2.** To instruct under discipline; to subject to discipline, control, or correction; to school; also to admonish or reprove 1592. **3.** To tell (a person) what to do or say; often in sinister sense: to sophisticate or tamper with (a witness or his evidence) 1757. **4.** *intr.* (*U.S.*) To study under a tutor 1921.

2. The World however it may be taught will not be tutor'd SHAFTESB.

Tutorage (tiū·tərėdʒ). 1617. [f. as prec. + -AGE.] **1.** The office, authority, or action of a tutor or guardian; tutorship, guardianship, custody; tutorial control, direction, or supervision; instruction. **b.** *spec.* at a university; also, the charge for or cost of this 1638. **c.** A tutorship 1796. **†2.** = TUTELAGE 2. –1768.

Tu·toress. 1614. [See -ESS.] **a.** An instructress. **b.** A female guardian 1759.

Tutorial (tiutōᵊ·riăl), *a.* (*sb.*) 1742. [f. L. *tutorius* (f. *tutor* TUTOR) + -AL.] Of or pertaining to a tutor. 1. *Rom.* and *Sc. Law.* Of or pertaining to a legal guardian. 2. Of or pertaining to a teacher or instructor; *esp.* pertaining to a college tutor 1822. B. *sb.* [app. short for *t. hour.*] A period of individual instruction given by a college tutor 1923. Hence Tuto·rially *adv.*

Tutorize (tiū·tərəiz), *v.* 1611. [f. TUTOR *sb.* + -IZE.] a. *intr.* To act as a tutor. (Also with *it.*) b. *trans.* To be tutor to; to instruct as a tutor.

Tutorly (tiū·təɹli), *a. rare.* 1611. [f. as prec. + -LY^{1}.] Like a tutor; dictatorial, pedagogic.

Tutorship (tiū·təɹʃip). 1559. [f. as prec. + -SHIP.] †1. The office of guardian or protector; guardianship -1665. 2. The position or office of an instructor or teacher 1581.

Tutory (tiū·təri). late ME. [f. as prec.; see -ORY^{1}.] 1. Guardianship, charge, protection; *spec.* the custody of a ward. *Obs.* exc. in *Law.* †2. Tuition (*rare*) -1764.

‖**Tutoy·er**, *v.* 1697. [a. and ad. F. *tutoyer* (tütwaye), f. the second person sing. pron. *tu, toi.*] *trans.* To use the sing. pron. *tu, toi, te* ('thou' and 'thee') to; to treat as an intimate; to address with familiarity, or as an inferior in rank or order. Also *intr.*

Tutress (tiū·três). 1599. [ad. OF. *tutresse, tuteresse*, or f. L. *tutrix* by change of ending.] = TUTORESS.

†**Tutrix** (tiū·triks). 1515. [a. L. *tutrix*, fem. of *tutor* TUTOR.] = TUTORESS -1703.

Tutsan (tʊ·tsăn). late ME. [app. of F. or AF. origin.] A name applied to various plants on account of their healing virtues; formerly to Agnus Castus; now, in Eng., to a shrubby species of St. John's-wort, *Hypericum Androsæmum*, with strongly aromatic foliage and berry-like fruit; formerly esteemed as a vulnerary.

‖**Tutti** (tu·ttī). 1724. [It., = 'all'; pl. of *tutto* :—Rom. *tottus for L. *totus.*] *Mus.* In concerted music, a direction that all the performers are to take part; also, a passage or movement rendered by all the performers together.

Tutty (tʊ·ti). late ME. [a. F. *tutie*, a. Arab. *tūtiyā* oxide of zinc (perh. Pers.).] A crude oxide of zinc found adhering in grey or brownish flakes to the flues of furnaces in which brass is melted; also occurring in some countries as a native mineral; formerly used medically, and now as a polishing powder.

‖**Tutulus** (tiū·tiŭlŏs). *Rom. Antiq.* [L.] A head-dress worn by the flamen and his wife.

Tu-whit, tu-whoo (tuʰwi·t tuʰwū·), *int.* (*sb.*) 1588. [Imitative.] An imitation of the call of an owl. B. *sb.* The utterance of this cry; the hoot of an owl 1830.

Then nightly sings the staring Owle Tu-whit to-who. A merrie note. SHAKS.

Tu-whoo (tuʰwū·), *int.* (*sb.*) 1797. = prec. Hence Tu-whoo· *v. intr.*

Tuxedo (tʊksī·do). 1899. [Name of a club at T. Park, New York.] A dinner jacket.

Tuyere (twīᵊɹ, twəiᵊɹ, ‖tüiyę̄r, tüyę̄r). 1781. [Modern spelling of earlier *tewire* (whence *tew-iron*), *twire, twear*, a. OF. *toiere, tuyere*, mod.F. *tuyère.*] The nozzle through which the blast is forced into a forge or furnace.

Comb.: t. arch, in a blast furnace, an arch through which a t. is admitted.

Tuza (tū·ză). 1787. [a. Sp., ad. Mexican *tuçan* or *tozan*, native name.] A Mexican pocket-gopher or pouched rat.

Tw-, obs. and dial. var. QU-.

Twaddell (twǫ·d'l). 1860. [Short for *Twaddell's hydrometer*, from the inventor's name.] A form of hydrometer or hydrometric scale in which 200 degrees correspond to a unit of specific gravity, that of distilled water being denoted by zero.

Twaddle (twǫ·d'l), *sb.* (*a.*) 1782. [Origin obsc.] 1. Senseless, silly, or trifling talk or writing; empty verbiage; prosy nonsense. †2. A twaddler -1838. 3. *attrib.* or as *adj.* Of the nature of twaddle 1830.

1. No need to talk a lot of t. and nonsense to a woman with brains 1878. Hence Twa·ddly *a.*

Twa·ddle, *v.* 1825. [f. prec.] 1. *intr.* To utter twaddle; to talk or write in a silly, empty, or trashy style. 2. *trans.* To utter as twaddle, or in a trashy and prosy way 1837. So Twa·ddler, one who twaddles; one who talks or writes twaddle 1787.

Twain (twēⁱn), *numeral* and *sb. arch.* [OE. *twēgen*, nom. and accus. masc. of the numeral *twā* TWO.] = Two. A. *adj.* In concord with a sb., etc. 2. Absolutely with ellipsis of sb., or following a pron. or pronominal adj. OE. 3. a. Separate, parted asunder; disunited, estranged, at variance. (Only *predic.*) 1472. b. Double, twofold (*rare*). late ME.

1. The bottles t... Were shatter'd at a blow COWPER. 2. To tarry a day or t. SCOTT. Phr. *In t.*, in two, asunder. 3. a. Thou and I long since are t. MILT.

B. *sb.* †1. The abstract number two -1483. 2. A group of two; a pair, couple 1607. 3. *pl.* Twins. *dial.* 1580.

2. To blesse this twaine, that they may prosperous be SHAKS.

Twain, *v. Obs.* or *arch.* late ME. [f. prec.] *trans.* To part or divide in twain; to put apart, separate. late ME.

Twait(e (twēⁱt). *local.* 1613. [Origin unkn.] A European species of shad, *Alosa finta.*

Twang (twæŋ), *sb.*^{1} 1553. [Echoic.] 1. A vocal imitation of the resonant sound produced when a tense string is sharply plucked or suddenly released; used as interj. or advb. b. A sound of the above character; also, any sharp ringing sound resembling this 1565. c. *transf.* and *fig.* Ringing sound or tone 1646. 2. a. Nasal intonation; now esp. as characterizing an individual, a country, or locality. More fully *nasal t.* 1661. b. A distinctive manner of pronunciation or intonation; esp. one associated with a particular district or locality 1697. 3. *transf.* A ringing or resounding blow (*rare*) 1712. 4. *transf.* A sharp pluck or twitch; a tweak; also, the effect of this; a twinge, a sharp pang. Now *dial.* 1720.

1. b. The t. of a bow-string 1853. 2. a. Odious as the nasal t. Heard at conventicle COWPER. The true Kentucky t. through the nose 1839. b. A grating voice that had an Irish t. THACKERAY.

Twang, *sb.*^{2} 1611. [Alteration of TANG *sb.*^{1}; but often assoc. w. prec.] 1. A penetrating or persistent taste, flavour, or odour, usu. disagreeable. 2. *fig.* A 'smack', touch, tinge; a taint 1633.

Twang, *v.* 1542. [Echoic.] I. Of sound. 1. *intr.* To give forth a ringing note, as a tense string when plucked. Said also of the sound produced. 1567. 2. *trans.* To cause to make a ringing note, as by plucking or twitching a tense string or strings of a bow or of a musical instrument; hence, to play on (an instrument). 1579. 3. *intr.* To produce a ringing note by or as by plucking a string or stringed instrument; hence (in depreciative sense) to play *on* a stringed instrument 1594. 4. *trans.* To play (a melody or the like) on a stringed instrument; to sound forth on a twanging instrument. Also said of the instrument or its strings. 1542. †5. *trans.* To utter with a sharp ringing tone. SHAKS. 6. *intr.* To speak with a nasal intonation or twang. Also *trans.* with *nose* as obj. (*rare*) 1615. b. *trans.* To utter or pronounce with a nasal or other twang 1748.

1. This said, the bow-string twangs 1621. 2. Musicians came and twanged guitars to her THACKERAY. 4. She twanged off a rattling piece of Liszt THACKERAY.

II. Of the action (without special ref. to the sound). 1. *trans.* To pull or pluck (the string of a bow) so as to shoot 1600. 2. To discharge (an arrow) with a twang of the bow-string; to let fly (an arrow) 1751. b. *intr.* Of an arrow: To leave the bow-string with a twang 1795.

1. He..Twanged the string, out flew the quarell long 1600. 2. b. When twanged an arrow from Love's mystic string COLERIDGE.

Twangle (twæ·ŋg'l), *sb.* 1812. [Cf. next.] A twangling sound; a continuous or repeated resonant sound, usu. lighter or thinner than a twang; a jingle.

Twangle (twæ·ŋg'l), *v.* 1558. [dim. and frequent. of TWANG *v.* (see -LE).] 1. *intr.* Of a stringed instrument or one who plays it: To twang lightly and continuously or frequently; to jingle. 2. *trans.* To twang (a stringed instrument) lightly; to play upon in a petty or trifling manner. Also, to play (a melody) in this way. 1607.

Twankay (twæ·ŋke). 1840. [ad. Chinese *Tong* (or *Taung*) *-ké* (or *-kei*), dial. form of *Tun-ki* or *Tun-chi*, name of two streams (and a town) in An-hui and Chi-kiang, China.] A variety of green tea (in full *T. tea*), properly that from one of the places so called, but also applied to blends of this with other growths.

'twas (twǫz, twəz), abbrev. of *it was*, now poet. or arch., and dial.

Tway (twēⁱ), *numeral a.* Now *rare arch.* [Apocopate form, orig. Northumb. and Anglian, of OE. *twēgen* TWAIN.] = Two.

Twayblade (twēⁱ·blēⁱd). 1578. [f. prec. + BLADE leaf.] a. An orchidaceous plant of the genus *Listera*, characterized by two nearly opposite broad leaves springing from the stem; esp. the Common T., *L. ovata*, and Mountain or Heart-leaved T., *L. cordata*. b. Applied to N. Amer. species of the orchidaceous genus *Liparis*, with two leaves springing from the root.

Tweak (twīk), *sb.* 1609. [f. next.] 1. An act of tweaking; a sharp wringing pull; a twitch, a pluck. †2. *fig.* In phr. *in a t.*, in a state of excitement or agitation, in a 'taking' -1841.

Tweak (twīk), *v.* 1601. [Origin obsc.] *trans.* To seize and pull sharply with a twisting movement; to twitch, wring, pluck; *esp.* to pull (a person) *by* the nose (or a person's nose) as a mark of contempt or insult.

Twee (twī), *a. colloq.* 1905. [For *tweet*, minced pronunc. of *sweet.*] 'Sweet', dainty, chic.

Tweed (twīd). 1847. [A trade name originating in a misreading of *tweel*, Sc. form of TWILL, helped by association with the river *Tweed.*] A twilled woollen cloth of somewhat rough surface, orig. and still chiefly made in the south of Scotland (usu. of two or more colours combined in the same yarn); inferior kinds are made of wool with a mixture of shoddy or cotton. In *pl.*, cloths or garments of this kind. Hence Twee·dy *a.*

attrib. A young gentleman in t. suit and wideawake 1864.

Tweedle (twī·d'l), *v.* 1684. [app. echoic.] 1. *intr.* Of a musical instrument or one who plays it: To produce a succession of shrill modulated sounds; also, to play triflingly or carelessly *upon* an instrument. 2. *trans.* To entice by or as by music; to wheedle, cajole 1719.

2. A fiddler brought in with him a body of lusty young fellows, whom he had tweedled into the service ADDISON.

Tweedle- (twī·d'l), the stem of TWEEDLE *v.*, used in comb. to denote the action of the vb., or a high-pitched musical sound; chiefly in the humorous phrase Tweedledu·m and tweedledee·, used orig. in ref. to two rival musicians; hence b. *fig.* usu. in phr. *tweedledee and tweedledum*, two things or parties the difference between which is held to be insignificant 1851. Tweedle-dee· *v. intr.*, to play or sing in a high-pitched tone; also, to play idly; to tweedle.

'Tween, †tween (twīn), *prep.* ME. Aphetic form of ATWEEN, BETWEEN.

'Tween-decks (twī·nˌdeks). 1816. The usual sailors' abbrev. of BETWEEN-DECKS.

Tweeny (twī·ni). 1888. [f. 'TWEEN + -Y^{6}.] A maid-servant who assists both the cook and the housemaid; a between-maid. b. A small cigar.

Tweet (twīt), *sb.* and *int.* 1845. [Echoic.] An imitation of the sound made by a small bird. Also reduplicated. Hence Tweet *v. trans.* and *intr.* to twitter.

†**Tweeze**. 1622. [Aphetic f. *etweese* = *etuys, etuis*, pl. of ETUI.] A case of small instruments, an etui; also *pl.*, instruments kept or carried in a small case. Occas. *a pair* (= set) *of tweezes.* -1681.

Twee·zer, *sb.* 1654. [f. prec. Also, in mod. use, back-formation from TWEEZERS.] †1. A case of small instruments; an etui, a tweezer-case -1746. 2. = TWEEZERS 2; also *attrib.* formed like tweezers 1904.

Twee·zer, *v.* 1806. [f. TWEEZERS.] *intr.* To use tweezers; *trans.* to pull out with tweezers.

Twee·zer-case. 1686. [f. TWEEZER(S) + CASE *sb.*[2]] A case in which tweezers and other small instruments are carried; an etui or 'tweeze'.

Tweezers (twī·zəɹz), *sb. pl.* 1654. [Modified form of *tweezes*, pl. of TWEEZE, after *scissors.*] Also *a pair of t.* †1. A set or case of small instruments (*rare*) –1742. 2. Small pincers or nippers (orig. as included in the contents of an etui) used for plucking out hairs from the face or for grasping minute objects 1654.

1. Bought me a pair of t., cost me 14/- PEPYS.

Twelfth (twelfþ), *a.* and *sb.* [OE. *twelfta*, f. *twelf* TWELVE; see -TH [2].] **A.** *adj.* 1. The ordinal numeral corresponding to the cardinal TWELVE; the last of twelve; that comes next after the eleventh. **a.** In concord with a sb., expressed or understood; also with ellipsis of *day* (of the month), or *chapter* (of a book of Scripture). **b.** *spec.* The 12th of August, on which grouse-shooting legally begins 1868. 2. *T. part*, any one of twelve equal parts of a whole 1590. **B.** *sb.* 1. A twelfth part 1557. 2. *Mus.* A note twelve diatonic degrees above or below a given note (both notes being counted); the octave of a fifth; hence (usu.) the interval between two such notes 1597.

Twe·lfth-cake. 1774. [Short for *Twelfth-night* or *Twelfth-tide cake.*] A large cake used at the festivities of Twelfth-night, usu. frosted and otherwise ornamented, and with a bean or coin introduced to determine the 'king' or 'queen' of the feast.

Twe·lfth-day. OE. The twelfth day after Christmas; the sixth of January, on which the festival of the Epiphany is celebrated; formerly observed as the closing day of the Christmas festivities.

Twe·lfth-night. OE. The night of the twelfth day after Christmas (6 January) marked by merrymaking (cf. TWELFTH-CAKE and prec.).

†Twe·lfthtide. 1530. [See TIDE *sb.*] The season including Twelfth-night and Twelfth-day; the season of Epiphany –1687.

Twelve (twelv), *numeral a.* and *sb.* [Com. Teut.: OE. *twelf*:—OTeut. **twaliƀi-*, deriv. of *twa* two + *liƀ-*, prob. conn. w. OTeut. **liƀan* to LEAVE, thus denoting 'two left or remaining over (ten)'; cf. ELEVEN. The present form is due to an inflected ME. *twelvë*; cf. FIVE.] The cardinal number composed of ten and two; represented by the symbols 12 or XII. **A.** *adj.* 1. In concord with a sb. expressed. **b.** As multiplier before a higher numeral (*hundred, thousand*, etc.). ME. 2. *absol.* with ellipsis of sb., preceded by a pronoun or demonstrative, or as predicate OE. *spec.* **b.** with ellipsis of *hours* (of the day); also *t. o'clock* 1482. **c.** with ellipsis of *years* (of age) 1607. **d.** *The t.* (spec.): applied to various bodies of twelve men having some special office, as the twelve apostles, etc.; also, the books of the twelve 'minor prophets' in the Old Testament OE. 3. Used for the ordinal TWELFTH. *Obs.* (exc. after the sb. in *page t.*, *chapter t.*, etc.), late ME.

1. b. *T. score*, t. twenties, two hundred and forty. 2. b. Phr. *To strike t. the first time* (or *all at once*), *fig.* to display all one's capacities in one's first performance. c. At t. he was a..quiet boy BYRON.

B. *sb.* (with pl. *twelves*). 1. The abstract number. late ME. 2. A set or group of twelve persons or things; *esp.* a company of twelve players forming a 'side' at some game 1573. 3. **a.** A thing or person distinguished by the number twelve; also *number t.* (see NUMBER *sb.* 4). **b.** A shoe, glove, etc. of size twelve. 1607. 4. A thing characterized in some way by the number twelve; e.g. a t.-pounder gun, a candle weighing t. to the pound 1804. 5. (Always in *pl.*) **a.** A sheet of a book folded into twelve leaves (usu. in phr. *in twelves*) 1670. **b.** A book (or books) of which each sheet is folded into twelve leaves 1683.

4. A Ship Privateer, carrying sixteen twelves and sixes 1804. 5. b. Shelves..charged with octavos and twelves COWPER.

Comb.: **t. bore** *a.* (of a gun) having a bore corresponding to the diameter of spherical bullets of twelve to the pound; *sb.* a t.-bore gun; **-eight** (usu. $\frac{12}{8}$), *Mus.*, applied to a 'time' with t. quavers in a bar; **-pounder**, a cannon which discharges shot weighing t. pounds.

Twelvefold (twe·lvfōᵘld), *a.* and *adv.* 1557. [f. TWELVE + -FOLD.] **A.** *adj.* **a.** Twelve times as great or as much. **b.** Composed of twelve parts or divisions. **B.** *adv.* Twelve times in amount 1660.

Twelvemo (twe·lvmo). 1819. English reading of the abbreviation 12mo or XIImo for DUODECIMO.

Twelvemonth (twe·lvmɒnþ). [f. OE. *twelf* TWELVE + *mónaþ* pl., MONTH.] 1. A period of twelve months; a year. 2. *Twelvemonth('s mind*: a commemoration of a deceased person by celebration of masses, etc. a year after (or annually on the anniversary of) the day of his death or funeral. *Obs.* exc. *Hist.* late ME.

In phr., as *That day t., Michaelmas was a t., Easter come t.*: = a year before or after. Hence **Twe·lvemonthly** *adv.* every twelve months, annually.

Twelvepence (twe·lvpĕns). late ME. **a.** A sum of money equal to twelve pennies. Now *rare*. †**b.** A coin of this value, a shilling. Formerly abbrev. xijd.

Twelvepenny (twe·lvpĕni), *a.* Now *rare*. 1594. 1. Of the value of, or amounting to, twelvepence. 2. Costing or priced at twelvepence 1609. 3. That may be hired for twelvepence; paying, or receiving, twelvepence 1614.

Twentieth (twe·ntiĕþ), *a.* and *sb.* [OE. *twentigoða*, f. *twentig* TWENTY + *-oða* (see -TH [2]); becoming in ME. *twentiþe, -ythe*, from 16th c. *twentieth.*] **A.** *adj.* 1. The ordinal numeral corresponding to the cardinal TWENTY; last of twenty; next after the nineteenth. 2. *T. part*: any one of twenty equal parts into which a whole may be divided ME. **B.** *sb.* A twentieth part ME.

Twenty (twe·nti), *numeral a.* and *sb.* [OE. *twentig*, f. *twen-* two + *-tig* (see -TY [2]).] The cardinal number equal to twice ten: represented by the symbols 20 or XX (formerly occas. xx^{ti} = L. *viginti*). **A.** *adj.* 1. In concord with a sb. expressed (or in OE. in pl. form with implied sb.). **b.** Combined with the numerals below ten to express the numbers between twenty and thirty OE. **c.** As multiplier before a numeral, as *t. thousand*, etc. (often hyperbolically) OE. **d.** Used vaguely or hyperbolically for a large number 1470. 2. With ellipsis of sb. OE. **b.** *spec.* with ellipsis of *years* (of age); so *t.-one*, etc. 1773. 3. Used for the ordinal TWENTIETH. Now only after a sb. as in *chapter t.* OE.

2. His thermometer..registered t. below zero 1902. Phr. *T. to one*, twenty chances to one; an expression of strong probability.

B. *sb.* (with pl. *twenties*). 1. The abstract number 20; a symbol representing this. late ME. **b.** A person or thing distinguished by this number 1888. 2. A group or set of twenty persons or things 1637. **b.** Something equivalent to twenty of some unit, e.g. a t.-pound bank-note 1850. **c.** A sheet (of a book) folded into twenty leaves (4 × 5), or each leaf of such a sheet 1771. 3. Something characterized in some way by the number twenty 1842. 4. *pl.* The numbers from 20 to 29; the years in a century or of one's life, or the degrees of any scale (e.g. of a thermometer) so numbered 1874.

1. Five Twenties make a Hundred WATTS. 4. In their twenties girls feel differently from what they do in their teens 1874.

Twenty-fi·ve. 1877. *Rugby Football*, etc. The line drawn across the ground twenty-five yards from each goal; also, the space enclosed by this, and (in hockey) a bully on the twenty-five line.

Twentyfold (twe·ntifōᵘld), *a.* and *adv.* 1610. [f. TWENTY + -FOLD.] **A.** *adj.* Twenty times as many or as great; multiplied by twenty; twenty times repeated. **B.** *adv.* Twenty times (in amount); twenty times as much 1872.

Twenty-fou·r. 1673. A sheet folded into 24 leaves; a book in which the sheets are thus folded. (Always in *pl.*; usu. in phr. *in twenty-fours.*)

Twentyfou·rmo. 1841. [English reading of 24mo or xxivmo, used as abbrev. of L. *vicesimo quarto*, after 12mo = *duodecimo.*] The size of a book in which each sheet is folded into 24 leaves. So **Twe·ntymo** [= 20mo or xxmo, for L. *vicesimo*], the size of a book in which each sheet is folded into 20 leaves.

'twere (twēəɹ, twəɹ). 1605. Abbreviation of *it were*, now poet. or arch.; see IT.

Twi-, twy- (twəi), *prefix.* [OE. *twi-*; cogn. w. Skr. *dvi-*, Gr. δι- L. *bi-*, etc., from root related to Skr. *dwau, dwē*, Gr. δύο, L. *duo* Two.] In OE. the regular comb. form expressing *two*, sometimes *twice*.

Twibill, twybill (twəi·bil). *arch.* [OE. *twibil(l* and *twibile*, f. TWI- + BILL *sb.*[1] and *sb.*[2]] †1. A kind of axe with two cutting edges; formerly used for cutting mortises –1686. 2. A mattock; also, a similar tool used in mining. Now *local.* 1440. **b.** A reaping-hook used in cutting beans and peas; a pea-hook. *dial.* 1763. 3. A double-bladed battle-axe or bill. *poet.* 1558.

Twice (twəis), *adv.* (*sb., a.*) [Late OE. *twiges*, f. *twige* TWIE + advb. genitive ending *-es.*] 1. Two (successive) times; on two occasions. **b.** Contextually: A second time; for the second time ME. 2. Expressing multiplication by two: Two times in number, amount, or value; doubly ME. 3. quasi-*sb.*, preceded by a prep. or demonstrative: Two times 1494. 4. quasi-*adj.* Performed, occurring, given, etc. twice; doing something (implied by the sb.) twice 1577.

1. Wouldst thou haue a Serpent sting thee t.? SHAKS. *Once or t., t. or thrice*, a few times. **b.** They say, an old man is t. a childe SHAKS. *To think t.*, to consider a matter a second time (before deciding or acting). 2. Two is t. one 1875. 3. I have written this at t. H. WALPOLE. 4. His t. Imprisonment in the Tower 1683.

Comb. with pples., forming compound adjs., as *t.-baked, -boiled, -married*; **t.-laid**, of rope, made from the yarns of old rope; **-told**, counted or reckoned t.; t. as much as; narrated or related t.

Twi·ce-born, *a.* late ME. 1. Born twice; esp. as an epithet of Bacchus (also *absol.*). 2. An epithet of the three higher castes of Hindus. Also *absol.* 1794. 3. *Theol.* That has experienced the second birth; born again, regenerate. Also *absol.* 1849.

Twiddle (twi·d'l), *sb.* 1774. [f. next.] An act of twiddling; a twirl or twist; also, a twirled mark or sign.

Twiddle (twi·d'l), *v.* 1540. [app. onomatopœic.] 1. *intr.* To be busy about trifles; to trifle; also *to t. with* or *at* = sense 2. 2. *trans.* To turn (anything) about, esp. with the fingers; to twirl; to play with idly or absently 1676. 3. *intr.* To move in a twirling manner; to turn about in a light or trifling way 1812.

2. Phr. *To t. one's thumbs*, or *fingers*, to keep turning them idly around each other; *fig.* to have nothing to do.

†Twie, twye, *adv.* [OE. *twiga*, f. stem *twi-* TWI-.] = TWICE –1450.

†Twifa·llow, twy-, *v.* 1557. [f. TWI- + FALLOW *v.*[2]] *trans.* To fallow twice; to fallow a second time; to plough up (land) a second time in the course of its lying fallow –1733.

Twifold, twyfold (twəi·fōᵘld), *a.* and *adv. arch.* [OE. *twifeald, twyfeald*; see TWI- and -FOLD.] **A.** *adj.* 1. Twofold, double. †2. *fig.* **a.** Double-dealing, deceitful, insincere. **b.** Double-minded, irresolute. –ME.

1. Within those orbs the twyfold being shone CARY.

†**B.** *adv.* In two parts or divisions; (folded) double; doubly (*rare*) –1619.

Twig (twig), *sb.*[1] [Northern OE. *twigge*, obscurely related to OE. *twig*, later also *twi*; all app. variant formations from the stem TWI-.] 1. A slender shoot issuing from a branch or stem. 2. *spec.* Short for LIME-TWIG (*obs.*); also, in *pl.*, the twigs forming a birch-rod 1601. 3. transf. *Anat.* A small ramification of a blood-vessel or nerve 1683.

1. Just as the T. is bent, the Tree's inclin'd POPE.

Comb.: **t.-beetle, -borer** (*U.S.*), any of various small beetles which bore into the twigs of trees; **-girdler** (*U.S.*), an Amer. beetle, *Oncideres cingulatus*, which deposits its eggs in the tips of twigs, which it then girdles below the eggs; **t. insect**, the stick-insect or 'walking-stick'; **-rush**, a tall marsh-plant, *Cladium Mariscus*, family *Cyperaceæ*, having very long narrow rigid leaves.

Twig, *sb.*[2] *slang.* Now *rare* or *Obs.* 1811. [Origin unkn.] Style, fashion; also, condi tion, state, fettle; esp. in the phrases *in* (*prime good*) *t.*

Twig, *v.*[1] *Obs.* or *dial.* 1550. [f. TWIG *sb.*[1]] *trans.* To beat with or as with a twig; *fig.* to reprove.

Twig, *v.*[2] *slang.* or *colloq.* 1764. [Origin obsc.] 1. *trans.* a. To watch; to look at; to inspect. b. To become aware of by seeing; to perceive, catch sight of; to recognize 1796. 2. *fig.* To understand, comprehend. Also *intr.* 1815.

1. 'T. the old connoisseur', said the squire to the knight SCOTT. b. I twigged the tigress creeping away in front of us 1879. 2. I twigged what you were after, and kept him up in talk SURTEES.

Twiggen (twi·g'n), *a. arch.* 1549. [f. TWIG *sb.*[1] + -EN.] a. Made of twigs or wickerwork; also, having a wickerwork covering. b. Arising from burning twigs or brushwood.

Twiggy (twi·gi), *a.* 1562. [f. TWIG *sb.*[1] + -Y[1].] 1. Like a twig; slender, as a shoot or branch. 2. Full of or abounding in twigs; bushy, shrubby 1600.

2. Masses of t. growth at the bottom 1882.

Twilight (twai·lait). [Late ME., f. TWI- + LIGHT *sb.* The exact force of *twi-* here is doubtful; cf. MHG. *zwischenliecht* 'tweenlight'.] 1. The light diffused by the reflection of the sun's rays from the atmosphere before sunrise, and after sunset; the period during which this prevails between daylight and darkness 1440. b. *spec.* Most commonly applied to the evening twilight, from sunset to dark night. late ME. c. Morning twilight, which lasts from daybreak to sunrise 1440. 2. *transf.* A dim light resembling twilight; partial illumination 1667. 3. *fig.* An intermediate condition or period; a condition before or after full development 1600. 4. *attrib.* or as *adj.* a. Of, pertaining to, or resembling twilight; seen or done in the twilight 1633. b. *fig.* Having an intermediate character 1730. c. Lighted as by twilight; dim, obscure, shadowy; also *fig.* of early times 1629. d. *fig.* Of the nature of or pertaining to imperfect mental light 1677.

1. b. Now came still Eevning on, and T. gray Had in her sober Liverie all things clad MILT. 2. As when the Sun..In dim Eclips disastrous t. sheds MILT. 3. *T. of the gods* [tr. Icel. *ragna rökkr*, altered from *ragna rök* history or judgement of the gods], in Scandinavian mythology, the destruction of the gods and of the world in conflict with the powers of evil. 4. When the lingering t. hour was past BYRON. c. Arched walks of t. groves MILT. d. A doubtful, uncertain, and t. sort of rationality SCOTT. e. **T. sleep** [tr. G. *dämmerschlaf*], a method of making childbirth painless by inducing a comatose condition in the mother. So **Twi·lit** *ppl. a.* lit by or as by t. 1869.

Twill (twil), **tweel** (twīl), *sb.* ME. [north. and Sc. forms of ME. *twīle* TWILLY *sb.*[1]] A woven fabric characterized by parallel diagonal ridges or ribs, produced by causing the weft threads to pass over one and under two or more threads of the warp, instead of over and under in regular succession, as in plain weaving. b. The, or a, method or process of weaving this fabric; also, the ribbed appearance or diagonal pattern of the material so woven 1779.

Twill (twil), **tweel** (twīl), *v.* 1808. [f. prec.] *trans.* To weave so as to produce diagonal ridges on the surface of the cloth.

†Twi·lly, *a.* and *sb.*[1] [OE. *twili*, formed after L. *bilix* from *twi-* TWI-.] A. *adj.* Twilled. B. *sb.* A twilled cloth –1714.

Twilly (twi·li), *sb.*[2] Also **twilley.** 1858. [Altered f. *willy* WILLOW.] A willowing machine; also called *t. devil* (see DEVIL *sb.* 8). Hence **Twi·lly** *v. trans.* to willow.

Twin (twin), *a.* and *sb.* [OE. *twinn* adj. (rare), f. the stem TWI-.] A. *adj.* †1. Consisting of two; double. –late ME. 2. (attrib. use of B. 1.) Born at the same birth, as two children or animals, or one of such 1590. 3. Forming a pair or couple; two closely associated, connected, or related, and (usu.) alike or equal 1591. b. Composed of, or having, two similar and equal (or closely connected or related) parts or constituents 1585. c. *Nat. Hist.* Geminate 1812. 4. Forming one of a pair or couple; closely associated with or related to another 1605.

2. He, and I, And the t. Dromio SHAKS. 3. T. truths COLERIDGE. b. *T. crystal.* = B. 3 b. 4. Yesterday's face t. image of to-day COWPER.

B. *sb.* 1. *pl.* Two children or young brought forth at one birth ME. b. *sing.* One of two children or young brought forth at a birth; with possessive or *of* = twin brother or sister 1440. c. *Astron.* (pl.) The zodiacal constellation and sign GEMINI. late ME. 2. *fig.* a. *pl.* Two persons or things intimately associated, connected, or related; two forming a pair or couple 1589. b. *sing.* One of two thus related; now usu. with *of, to*, or possessive: a fellow, counterpart 1540. 3. A pair of twin children or young; also *fig.* or *gen.* a pair, couple, brace. *Obs.* exc. *dial.* 1569. b. *Cryst.* A composite crystal consisting of two (usu. equal and similar) crystals united in reversed positions with respect to each other, either by juxtaposition, embedding, or interpenetration 1845.

2. a. Two were never found Twins at all points COWPER. b. All who joy would win Must share it—Happiness was born a t. BYRON.

Comb.: **t.-axis** *Cryst.*, the axis of twinning in a t. crystal, i.e. the line about which either of the constituent crystals would have to revolve to come into the position of the other; **-birth**, the birth of twins; a pair born or produced as twins, or one of such in relation to the other (usu. *fig.*); **-law** *Cryst.*, the law or principle of twinning of a t. crystal; **-plane** *Cryst.*, a plane perpendicular to the t.-axis of a t. crystal; **-screw**, *a.* having twin screws; *spec.* of a steamer, having two screw propellers on separate shafts, which turn in opposite directions so as to counteract the tendency to lateral vibration; also *ellipt.* as *sb.* a t.-screw steamer.

Twin, *v.*[1] *Obs.* exc. *Sc.* [ME. *twinnen*, f. prec.] 1. *trans.* To put asunder (*prop.* two things or persons, or one *from* the other); to separate, disjoin, disunite, sunder, sever, part, divide; *fig.* to distinguish. 2. *intr.* To go asunder; to separate, part ME.

2. We twa will never t. 1790.

Twin, *v.*[2] late ME. [f. TWIN *a.* and *sb.*] 1. *intr.* To bring forth two children or young at a birth; to bear twins 1573. b. *trans.* To conceive or bring forth as twins, or as a twin *with* another 1607. c. *intr.* in passive sense: To be born at the same time *with.* Now *rare* or *Obs.* 1604. 2. *trans.* To couple, join, unite, combine (two things or persons) closely or intimately, late ME. b. *intr.* To be coupled; to join, combine, unite (*rare*) 1621. c. *Cryst.* (*trans.*) To unite (two crystals) according to some definite law so as to form a twin crystal. Only in passive, and in vbl. sb. 1845. 3. To be, or furnish, a 'twin' or counterpart to; to match, parallel 1605.

1. Two more ewes have twinned HARDY. c. *Oth.* II. iii. 212. 2. Still we moved Together, twinn'd as horse's ear and eye TENNYSON.

Twin-born, *a.* 1599. Born a twin or twins; born at the same birth, as two, or one of two.

Latona's twin-born progenie MILT.

Twin-brother. (Also as two words.) 1598. [TWIN *a.* 2.] A brother born at the same birth, as one of twins.

fig. Sleep, Death's twin-brother TENNYSON.

Twine (twain), *sb.* (*a.*) [OE. *twin*, ult. from the stem of TWI-.] 1. Thread or string composed of two or more yarns or strands twisted together; now *spec.* string or strong thread, made of hemp, cotton, or other fibre, used for sewing coarse materials, tying packages, netting, and the like; with *a* and *pl.* a piece or kind of this. 2. A twined or twisted object or part. a. A twining stem or spray of a plant 1579. b. A fold; a coil; a convolution 1600. c. A tangle, knot 1865. 3. The action or an act of twining. Now *rare* or *Obs.* 1602.

1. *fig.* Destiny..Spinn's all their fortunes in a silken t. DRYDEN. 2. b. Typhon huge ending in snaky t. MILT.

Twine (twain), *v.*[1] [ME. *twīnen*, related to TWINE *sb.*] I. *trans.* 1. To twist (two or more strands or filaments) together so as to form a thread or cord; to twist (one thread, etc.) *with* another; to form (thread or cord) by twisting or spinning; to spin (yarn, etc.) into thread or cord; also *gen.* to combine or make compact by twisting. b. *transf.* To form by interlacing; to weave, to wreathe 1612. c. *transf.* To interlace, entwine 1679. 2. To cause (one thing) to encircle or embrace another; to twist, wreathe, clasp, or wrap (a thing) *about* or *around* another 1585. 3. To enfold, wreathe, or encircle (one thing) *with* another; also of a plant, wreath, etc.: to encircle, enwrap 1602.

1. We'll t. a double strong halter for the Captain KINGSLEY. *fig.* Our fortunes Were twyn'd together 1612. 2. Let me t. Mine armes about that body SHAKS. 3. Let wreaths of triumph now my temples t. POPE.

II. *intr.* 1. To wind or twist (*about, over*, or *round* something): almost always of a plant: to grow in a twisting or spiral manner. late ME. 2. To extend or proceed in a winding manner; to bend, incline circuitously; to wind about, meander; of a serpent, etc., to crawl sinuously 1553. 3. To contort the body; to writhe, wriggle, squirm. Now *dial.* 1666.

1. Amidst thy Laurels let this Ivy t. DRYDEN. 2. The little brown river..twined to the sea 1902. Hence **Twi·ner**, one who or that which twines; a plant of twining habit.

Twine, *v.*[2] *Sc.* 1621. [Later form of TWIN *v.*[1]] *intr.* and *trans.* = TWIN *v.*[1]

Twinge (twinᵈʒ), *sb.* 1548. [f. next.] †1. An act of tweaking or pinching; a tweak or pinch –1692. 2. A sharp pinching or wringing pain; often, a momentary local pain; esp. applied to that of gout and rheumatism 1608. 3. *fig.* A sharp mental pain; a pang of shame, remorse, sorrow, or the like; a prick of conscience 1622.

1. For the twindge by th' nose, 'Tis certainly unsightly 1625. 2. The gout..gave him such severe twinges 1863. 3. It cost the Vicar some twinges of conscience HUGHES.

Twinge (twinᵈʒ), *v.* [OE. *twengan*; etym. obsc.] 1. *trans.* To pinch, wring, tweak, twitch. Also *intr.* *Obs.* exc. *dial.* 2. †To cause to smart or tingle, to irritate; to affect (the body or mind) with a twinge or sharp pain; to prick (the conscience) 1647. b. *intr.* To experience a twinge or smart 1640.

1. Twindging him by th' Ears or Nose 1678. 2. Nothing did t. my Conscience like this BUNYAN.

Twingle-twangle (twi·ŋg'l‚twæ·ŋg'l). 1634. [Reduplication of TWANGLE.] A representation of the sound of the harp, or other such instrument.

Twining (twai·niŋ), *ppl. a.* 1593. [f. TWINE *v.*[1] + -ING[2].] That twines, in various senses; *spec.* of a plant growing spirally round a support.

Twink (twiŋk), *sb.* late ME. [f. next.] A winking of the eye; *transf.* the time taken by this; a twinkling; now always in phr. *in a t.*

Twink (twiŋk), *v.* [Late ME. *twinken*, repr. the simple stem from which TWINKLE *v.* is formed.] †1. *intr.* To wink, to blink –1681. 2. To twinkle, sparkle 1637.

Twinkle (twi·ŋk'l), *sb.* 1548. [f. next.] 1. A winking of the eye; a wink, blink; also, a momentary glance. b. *transf.* A twitch, flicker, quiver 1733. 2. = TWINKLING *vbl. sb.* 3; now only in phr. *in a t., in the t. of an eye* 1592. 3. A sparkle, a scintillation; also, a faint or momentary gleam, a glimmer 1663.

1. Suddenly, with twincle of her eye, The Damzell broke his misintended dart SPENSER. 3. He had a roguish t. in his eye THOMSON.

Twinkle (twi·ŋk'l), *v.* [OE. *twinclian*, frequent. of **twincan*; see TWINK *v.*, -LE.] 1. *intr.* To shine with rapidly intermittent light; to sparkle; to glitter; †to shine dimly, to flicker. b. *trans.* To emit (radiance, flashes, or beams) rapidly and intermittently; to communicate (a message or signal) in this way 1547. c. *poet.* To guide or light *to* some place by twinkling 1690. 2. *intr.* To close and open the eye or eyes quickly; to make a signal by this means; to wink, blink; also said of the eye or eyes. *Obs.* or *arch.* ME. b. *trans.* With the eyes, eyelids, etc. as obj. 1591. 3. *intr.* To move to and fro, or in and out, with rapid alternation; to appear and disappear in quick succession; to flutter, flit, flicker 1616.

1. Hise eyen twynkled..As doon the sterres in the frosty nyght CHAUCER. b. The challenge-word..was twinkled..by the luminous dots and dashes from her masthead 1899. 2. The old Justice twinkles, hems, coughs, and chuckles 1784. 3. The open space..twinkles, is alive With heads WORDSW.

Twinkler (twi·ŋklǝɹ). 1591. [f. TWINKLE *v.* + -ER[1].] Anything which emits intermittent, transient, or faint radiance; sometimes applied to eyes.

Such tiny twinklers as the planet orbs SHELLEY.

Twinkling (twi·ŋkliŋ), *vbl. sb.* ME. [f. TWINKLE *v.* + -ING[1].] The action of the vb.

TWINKLE. 1. The action of shining with tremulous or faint radiance; scintillation. late ME. 2. The action or an act of winking; nictitation. *Obs.* exc. as in 3. ME. 3. The time taken in winking the eye; a moment, an instant ME.

1. The t. of the starres is the vibration or trembling of their light 1635. 3. Phr. *In the t. of an eye*, in an instant; In a moment, in the t. of an eye, at the last trump;..the dead shall be raised incorruptible 1 *Cor.* xv. 52. *In a t.*; I'll..be with you again in a t. DRYDEN.

Twinned (twind, *poet.* twi·nėd), *ppl. a.* 1607. [f. TWIN *sb.* or *v.*² + -ED.] 1. Born two at one birth; twin. 2. Intimately joined or united, as two things; coupled (usu. also implying close similarity) 1611. b. *Cryst.* United, as two crystals, or consisting of two crystals united, so as to form a 'twin' 1879.

Twi·nning, *vbl. sb.* 1573. [f. TWIN *v.*² + -ING¹.] The action of TWIN *v.*²

attrib.: **t.-axis, -law, -plane,** *Cryst.* = *twin-axis, -law, -plane.*

Twinship (twi·nʃip). 1674. [f. TWIN *a.* or *sb.* + -SHIP.] The condition of being twin, or a twin; the relation of a twin or twins.

Twin-sister. (Also as two words.) 1707. [TWIN *a.* 2.] A sister born at the same birth, as one of twins.

Twire (twəiᵊɹ), *v.* *arch.* and *dial.* 1568. [Origin obsc.; cf. MHG. *zwieren.*] 1. *intr.* To look narrowly or covertly; to peer; to peep. Also *fig.* of a light, etc. †2. *intr.* To wink. HOLLAND. Hence †**Twire** *sb.* (*rare*) a glance, a leer (*slang*).

Twirl (twɔ̄ɹl), *sb.* 1598. [f. next.] The action or an act of twirling, or the condition of being twirled; a rapid whirling or spinning; a twist; a spin; a whirl. b. Anything that twirls or is twirled; †a winch; each of the whorls of a shell; a curved line 1688. Hence **Twi·rly** *a.* full of or characterized by twirls or curves.

Twirl (twɔ̄ɹl), *v.* 1598. [Origin obsc.; perh. imitative, after *whirl.*] 1. *intr.* To rotate rapidly, to spin; to be whirled round or about; also *fig.* of the mind or head: to be in a whirl. 2. *trans.* To cause to rotate or spin; to turn (an object) round rapidly; to turn about with the fingers; to twiddle idly or playfully 1623. b. To turn (one's fingers or thumbs) rapidly about one another 1777. 3. To twist spirally (threads, etc.); now *esp.* to twist (the moustache) 1614. 4. To whirl. Now *rare.* 1646. 5. *intr.* To twine, coil, curl (*rare*) 1706.

1. The [compass] needle..sometimes twirling swiftly round TYNDALL. 2. When..dexterous Damsels twirle the sprinkling Mop GAY. b. Phr. *To t. one's thumbs*, as an idle occupation when one has nothing to do. 3. He twirled his long moustache 1894. 5. The monster's hideous tail..writhing and twirling THACKERAY.

Twist (twist), *sb.* ME. [Related to TWIST *v.*] I. A divided object or part. †1. The flat part of a hinge, fastened on a door or gate, and turning on a hook or pintle fixed in the post -1805. †2. A twig; a branch -1622. 3. The part of anything at which it divides or branches; *spec.* the junction of the thighs, the fork; now (exc. *arch.*) only that of sheep and cattle. late ME. II. The twisting of threads into a cord, etc. 1. Thread or cord composed of two or more fibres or filaments of hemp, silk, wool, cotton, or the like, wound round one another 1555. b. *spec.* (*a*) in *Cotton-spinning*, warp yarn, which is more twisted in spinning, and stronger than weft; (*b*) fine silk thread used by tailors, hatters, etc. With *pl.*, a kind of this. 1805. 2. A cord, thread, or the like, formed by twisting, spinning, or plaiting; also, a conical bag or wrapper made by twisting a piece of paper, etc., a 'screw' 1598. b. *Naut.* Each of the strands of which a rope consists 1635. †3. *fig.* The course of life figured as a thread -1638. 4. A beverage consisting of a mixture of two liquors or ingredients, as tea and coffee, gin and brandy, etc. *slang.* 1700. 5. Tobacco made into a thick cord; a piece or 'length' of this 1791. 6. A loaf made of one or more twisted rolls of dough; a small twisted roll of bread 1845.

3. Cruell Atropos..cutting the t. in twaine SPENSER. 5. The prize..was..a t. of tobacco 1808. 6. Dainty new bread, crusty twists, cool fresh butter DICKENS.

III. Senses denoting chiefly the action of the verb. 1. An act or the action of turning on or as on an axis; a turn; a twirl; the condition of being twisted or turned in this way; rotary motion, spin 1576. 2. a. In *Tennis, Cricket, Billiards*, etc.: Lateral spin imparted to a ball in striking or delivery, causing it to diverge on rebounding; 'screw'; a stroke by which such spin is given; the action or knack of giving this spin to a ball; also, a ball having such spin 1699. b. *Physics.* Movement parallel to, combined with rotation about, an axis (as in the motion of a screw); also, the velocity of such movement (= *t.-velocity*) 1891. 3. The amount or direction of twisting given to the strands of a rope (*rare*); also, the twisting given to yarn in spinning 1712. 4. The condition of being twisted spirally; the amount or degree of this; *spec.* the angle of torsion; also, a spirally twisted object or figure; a spiral line or pattern; *spec.* the rifling in the bore of a gun, etc. 1711. b. *Dynamics.* Twisting strain or force; torque 1891. 5. a. A twisting or screwing of the body or features; a contortion or screw 1865. b. A strain or wrench (of a limb or joint) 1865. 6. A hearty appetite. *slang.* 1785. 7. An irregular bend; a crook, a kink; also, a tangle 1776. 8. A turning aside, a deviation; also *fig.* a change of circumstances, vicissitude; also, a point or place at which a road alters its direction; a bend, turn 1798. 9. *fig.* a. An eccentric or perverted inclination or attitude; *esp.* a peculiar mental turn or bent; an intellectual or moral bias or obliquity; a craze, whim, crotchet 1811. b. A wresting, perversion, distortion 1862.

4. *spec.* A spiral ornament in the stem of a wine-glass 1897. 7. Phr. *A t. in one's tongue*, inability to articulate clearly. 8. Phr. *Twists and turns*, intricate windings, ins and outs; The twists and turns of the law 1875. 9. a. He has a t., or, as the Scotch say, a 'craze' on the subject of dress 1813. b. The most curious t. of meaning 1875.

Comb.: **t. barrel,** a gun-barrel formed of a spirally twisted strip or strips of iron; **-drill,** one having a twisted body like that of an auger; **-yarn** = sense II. 1 b (*a*).

Twist (twist), *v.* ME. [Evidently a deriv. from the stem TWI-, denoting either division in two, or combination of two into one.] I. To divide, separate. †1. *intr.* To divide into branches; to branch (*rare*). -late ME. 2. *trans.* To prune, clip. *Obs.* or *dial.* 1483. II. To combine, unite, etc. 1. *trans.* To combine two or more yarns or fibres of (any suitable material) into a thread or cord by spinning; to form (a thread or cord) by spinning the yarns or strands. Also *absol.* 1471. 2. To join or unite by twining or interlacing; to twine *together*; to entwine (one thing) *with* another; to intertwine, interweave 1563. 3. *fig.* To unite, combine, connect, associate intimately, like strands in a cord 1573. 4. To wind or coil (a thread or the like) *on* or *round* something; to attach in this way; to encircle (an object) *with* or as with a thread, etc.; to entwine *in* something else 1582. 5. *intr.* and *refl.* To pass or move in a tortuous manner; to coil or twine *about* or *round*; to penetrate *into* something with a tortuous movement or action 1635.

1. Tow-lines..they supplied by twisting a strong tough kind of flag or rush DE FOE. *fig.* He a rope of sand could t. As tough as learned Sorbonist 1663. 2. A Pillar made of three brazen Serpents twisted together 1687. 3. Our Monarch's Fate Was twist in his 1646. 4. A few wild flowers were twisted in her fine hair 1820. 5. The weeds..have twisted themselves into its crannies RUSKIN.

III. To wring, wrench. †1. *trans.* To compress with a turning movement; to wring; also *fig.* to torment, harass. late ME. only. 2. To wring out of place or shape, or so as to change the shape; *esp.* to force (a limb, etc.) round so as to sprain it; to wrench 1530. 3. To turn awry; to screw up or contract (the features, etc.); to contort, distort 1789. b. *fig.* To wrest the form or meaning of; to pervert; to distort; to force a meaning from 1821. 4. To force *down*, pull *off* or *out* with a turning strain; to wrench or wring *off*, etc. 1784. 5. To form into a spiral; to bend, curve, or coil spirally; to screw *up*. Also *intr.* for *refl.* or *pass.* 1744. 6. *intr.* and *trans.* To eat heartily; also *to t. (food) down. slang.* 1694.

3. b. Twisting my opinions into accordance with a party 1883. 5. Phr. *To t.* (a person) *round one's finger*, to have completely under one's influence; so *to turn, t., and wind* (a person). b. *Insurance.* (*U.S.*) To induce (a person) to drop a policy in one company and take out a new one in another 1906.

IV. To rotate, etc. 1. *trans.* To cause to rotate as on an axis; to turn (anything) round so as to alter its position or aspect 1789. b. *Cricket.* In bowling, to give a lateral spin to (the ball), so that it 'breaks' or turns aside on rebounding 1833. 2. *intr.* To rotate, revolve; also, to turn so as to face another way 1680. 3. To turn aside and proceed in a new direction; *spec.* of a ball (at cricket, etc.): to turn aside or 'break' on rebounding; also, to proceed with frequent turns; to follow a circuitous route; to wind, meander 1833.

3. He..twisted from side to side 1863.

Twi·sted, *ppl. a.* 1548. [f. prec. + -ED¹.] 1. Consisting of two or more threads, strands, or the like twined together; formed into a cord by being intertwined with another or others; made of spun or doubled thread, or by spinning; also *transf.* wreathed, plaited, interwoven. 2. Wrung out of shape; distorted; contorted; turned or bent awry; *spec.* in *Bot.* = CONTORTED 2; crooked, tortuous, winding; turned or wrung spirally, of coiled or screw-like form, spiral or helical; also, involved, tangled, confused 1725.

Special collocations: **t. bit,** a bit of which the mouthpiece consists of a square bar spirally twisted; **t. drill** = *twist-drill.*

Twister (twi·stəɹ), *sb.* 1579. [f. as prec. + -ER¹.] 1. A girder 1875. 2. One who (or that which) spins thread, cord, or the like; *spec.* one whose occupation is to twist together the ends of the yarns of the new warp to those of that already woven 1579. b. A mechanical device for spinning yarns, etc. 1703. 3. One who or that which turns about, turns from side to side, rotates, etc. a. One who turns this way and that; *fig.* one who shuffles or cheats 1834. b. *Cricket*, etc. A delivery in which the ball twists or 'breaks'; a break 1857. 4. One who curves, bends, or rolls something 1879. 5. That which (or one who) wrings or causes contortion; esp. *fig.* something that confounds, nonplusses, or 'doubles up'; a 'staggerer' (*slang*) 1873.

Twisty (twi·sti), *a.* 1857. [f. TWIST *sb.* or *v.* + -Y¹.] Full of twists or turns; also *fig.* dishonest, not straightforward.

Twit (twit), *sb.* 1528. [f. next.] An act of twitting; a (light) censure or reproach; a taunt.

Twit (twit), *v.* 1530. [orig. *twite*, aphet. f. ATWITE.] 1. *trans.* To blame, find fault with, censure, reproach, upbraid (a person), esp. in a light or annoying way; to cast an imputation upon; to taunt. 2. To condemn as a fault, blame, reprove, rebuke (an act, etc.); to cavil at, disparage. Now *rare.* 1571.

1. My friend..now twitting me with all his kindness, ..discarded me for ever FIELDING.

Twitch (twitʃ), *sb.*¹ 1523. [f. TWITCH *v.*¹] 1. An act of twitching; a sudden sharp pull or tug; a jerk; a pluck; a snatch. 2. A sharp pain; a pinch, pang, twinge. Freq. of mental pain. 1532. 3. A noose or loop; *spec.* a noose which may be tightened by twisting the stick to the end of which it is attached, used to compress the lip or muzzle of a horse to restrain him during a painful operation 1623. 4. *Mining.* A place in, or part of, a vein where it is compressed and narrowed 1653. 5. A quick, involuntary, usu. slight movement of a muscle, etc., esp. of nervous origin; a convulsive or spasmodic jerk or quiver 1718.

2. My conscience..beginning to give some twitches LAMB. 5. That side of his face was affected with a nervous t. 1897.

Twitch (twitʃ), *sb.*² 1595. [Altered f. QUITCH.] Couch-grass, *Triticum repens.*

Comb.: **t.-grass,** (*a*) *Triticum repens*; (*b*) a species of fox-tail grass, *Alopecurus agrestis.*

Twitch, *v.*¹ [ME. *twicchen*, prob. repr. an OE. **twiccan*, related to *twiccian* to twitch.] 1. *trans.* To give a sudden abrupt pull at; to pluck; to jerk. 2. *intr.* To pull or pluck sharply or forcibly (*at* something); to tug ME. 3. *trans.* To pull, draw, or take suddenly or with a jerk; to pluck, snatch ME. 4. To pinch and pull at with or as with pincers or the like; to nip; to hurt or pain, as by doing this. late ME. 5. *intr. Mining.* Of a vein of ore: To contract; with *out*, to come to an end; also *trans.* of the containing rock: to converge upon and contract or close (a vein of ore) 1709. 6. *trans.* To draw tight by means of a cord or the like; to tie, fasten, secure tightly or firmly. Also with the cord as obj. Now *dial.* 1615. 7. *intr.* To proceed in a jerking or irregular way (*obs. rare*); now always in ref. to involuntary bodily movements: to move in a jerky, spasmodic, or convulsive manner; to jerk, jump, start 1592.

1. She..twitch'd her fragrant robe COWPER. 2. It seemed as if a legion of imps were twitching at him W. IRVING. 7. I tried to keep my countenance,..but it would not do. My muscles began to t. W. IRVING.

Twitch (twitʃ), *v.*[2] *dial.* 1795. [f. TWITCH *sb.*[2]] *intr.* To gather and destroy twitch or couch-grass; also *trans.* to clean (land) from twitch.

Twite (twəit). 1562. [Imitative, from the note of the bird.] A species of linnet, *Linota flavirostris* or *L. montium* found in hilly and moorland districts in the northern parts of Britain and in Scandinavia, and elsewhere as a winter visitant; also **t.-finch.**

Twitter (twi·təɹ), *sb.* 1678. [f. TWITTER *v.*] 1. A condition of twittering or tremulous excitement; a state of agitation; a flutter; a tremble. Now chiefly *dial.* 2. An act or the action of twittering, as a bird; light tremulous chirping. Also *transf.* a sound resembling this. 1842.

1. In a t. of indignation THACKERAY. 2. The hesitating t. of sleepy birds 1849.

Twitter (twi·təɹ), *v.* late ME. [Imitative.] 1. *intr.* Of a bird: To utter a succession of light tremulous notes; to chirp continuously with a tremulous effect. b. *transf.* Of a person: To sing or chatter after the above manner 1829. 2. *trans.* Of a bird: To utter or express by twittering. late ME. b. *transf.* Of a person 1864. 3. *intr.* To move tremulously, tremble, shake, shiver; *esp.* to tremble with excitement, eagerness, fear, etc.; to be in a flutter. Now *dial.* 1616.

1. The swallow twittring from the straw-built shed GRAY. 2. The Squallid owle Twitters a midnight note 1645. 3. I was..twittering with cold STEVENSON. Hence **Twi·tterer.** **Twi·ttering** *vbl. sb.* the light tremulous chirping of a bird or birds; a sound resembling or likened to this.

'Twixt, †twixt (twikst), *prep.* ME. Aphetic form of ATWIXT, BETWIXT.

Two (tū), *numeral a., sb.* (*adv.*) [OE. *twá* fem. and neut., *tú* neut., of the numeral of which the masc. *twēgen* survives as TWAIN and TWAY. The word is common to all the Indo-European langs., as Skr. *dwau* masc., *dwē* fem. and neut., Gr. δύο, L. *duo*, OIr. *dá*.] The cardinal number next after one; one added to one; denoted by the symbols 2 or II. A. *adj.* 1. In concord with a sb. expressed. b. As ordinal: = SECOND *a.* Now only after the sb. (also *number t.*) 1586. 2. *absol.* with ellipsis of sb., or after a pronoun or demonstrative, or as predicate OE. b. *spec.* with ellipsis of *hours* or *years* (of age) 1485. 3. Forming compound numerals OE. 4. In pregnant sense: = Two different, two distinct 1570. †b. *predic.*: At variance -1738. 5. *A ... or t.*: an indefinite small number of... So *two or three.* ME.

1. To conquer Sin and Death the t. grand foes MILT. The t. best ships in the navy 1805. Phr. *T. parts*, t. out of three equal parts, t. thirds. Chiefly *Sc.* b. Column t. 1824. 2. The Ministry carried it t. to one 1779. Phr. *In t.*, into or in t. pieces or parts. *T. and t., t. by t.*, in groups or sets of t.; t. at a time; by twos. b. The minster-clock has just struck t. WORDSW. 3. *T.-and-thirty*, now usu. *thirty-t.*; *a hundred and t. T.-thirds*; also *attrib.* as a *t.-thirds majority*. *Comb.* A t.-hundred-pound buck 1897. 4. To say and to do are t. things 1570. *To be in t. minds* see MIND *sb.* II. 3.

B. *sb.* 1. The abstract number equal to one and one 1697. b. The figure (2) denoting this number 1877. c. A person or thing denoted by this number. Also *number t.* 1890. 2. A group or set of two persons or things; a pair, couple. Usu. in *pl.* 1585. b. A card or domino, or the side of a die, marked with two pips or spots 1500. c. In military drill, a set of two men forming a unit in wheeling 1796. d. *Cricket.* A hit for which two runs are scored 1881. e. *In t. twos*: in a very short time. *slang* or *colloq.* 1838. †C. *adv.* = TWICE 2. -1420.

1. Phr. *To put t. and t. together*, to consider several facts together and draw an inference. *T. and t. make four*, used as a typically obvious or undeniable statement. *T. of a trade*, two rival experts. c. Smith who rowed t. in the last University race 1890. 2. The people dispersed in twos and threes 1902. e. The business was over in t. twos 1882.

Comb. a. Adjs. formed of *two* with a sb. in sense 'of, pertaining to, consisting of, having, containing, measuring, etc. two of the things named', as *t.-bushel, -cylinder, -hour, -ounce, -party, -phase, -ply, -story, -syllable.* b. Parasynthetic adjs. formed on similar collocations, usu. with -ED[2], in sense 'having or characterized by two of the things named', as *t.-arched, -coloured, -handled, -storied, -toed*; also *t.-dimensional, -monthly.* c. Parasynthetic sbs. in -ER[1], as *t.-master* (a t.-masted vessel), *-pounder.* d. In sense 'in two, doubly', as *t.-cleft, -ploughed*, etc. e. Special combs.: **t.-bill** = TWIBILL; **-bottle** *a.*, applied to one who can drink t. bottles of wine at a sitting; **-ended** *a.*, having t. ends, *spec.* with different properties, as a magnet; **-eyed** *a.*, having t. eyes; involving or adapted for the use of both eyes; **-field** *a.*, denoting a system of agriculture in which t. fields are cropped and fallowed alternately; **-four,** (usu. $\frac{2}{4}$) *Mus.*, denoting a 'time' or rhythm with t. crotchets in a bar; **-lipped** (-lipt) *a.*, having t. lips; *esp.* in *Bot.* of a corolla, calyx, etc.; bilabiate; **-monthly** *a.*, occurring every t. months; **-oar,** a t.-oared boat; **-pair** *a.* (in full *t.-pair-of-stairs*), situated above t. 'pairs' or flights of stairs, i.e. on the second floor; also *ellipt.* as *sb.* (*sc.* room); **-shear,** *a.* of a sheep, that has been shorn twice; *sb.* a t.-shear sheep; **-step,** a round dance characterized by sliding steps in duple rhythm; also, the music for this; **-throw** *a.*, having t. throws, as a crank (see CRANK *sb.*[1]); **-tongued** *a.*, having t. tongues; *fig.* double-tongued, deceitful.

Two·-de·cker. 1790. [f. TWO + DECK *sb.* + -ER[1].] 1. A two-decked ship or boat; formerly *spec.* a line-of-battle ship carrying guns on two decks. 2. *transf.* and *fig.* Something consisting of two ranges or divisions, as a tram-car with seats on the roof and an additional roof over them 1884.

Two-edged (-edʒd, *poet.* -edʒėd), *a.* 1526. [Cf. OE. *twiecge, -ecgede.*] Having two edges; esp. of a sword, axe, etc., having two cutting edges, one on each side of the blade. Also *fig.* of a remark, etc.

Alashtar..wielded a t. sword 1850.

Two-faced (-fēˑst; stress var.), *a.* 1619. = DOUBLE-FACED *a.*

Twofold (tūˑfōuld), *a., adv.* ME. [app. orig. a refash. of TWIFOLD, after TWO.] A. *adj.* †1. Double (in *fig.* sense); double-minded, wavering. ME. only. 2. Consisting of two combined; composed of two parts or elements; existing in two relations or manners; of two kinds; double, dual 1559. 3. Double in amount; twice as great 1812. 4. Of yarn: Consisting of two strands twisted into one 1880.

2. A t. victorie HOLLAND. Two t. blocks NELSON.

B. *adv.* 1. In two folds; so as to be folded or doubled. Chiefly *Sc.* of persons. late ME. 2. To twice the amount, doubly 1526.

Two-foot (tūˑfut), *a.* 1620. 1. †a. Two-footed. b. Performed with both feet (*rare*). 2. Measuring two feet; two feet long, wide, or thick 1664.

2. *T. rule*, a measuring rule two feet long.

Two-footed (stress var.), *a.* late ME. Having two feet; biped; two-legged; standing on two feet.

Two·-hand, *a.* late ME. = next 1.

Two-handed (stress var.), *a.* ME. 1. Wielded with both hands, as a sword, etc.; involving the use of both hands. 2. Wielded or worked by the hands of two persons, as a saw; engaged in by two persons, as a card-game, etc. 1657. 3. Big, bulky, strapping. *colloq.* Now *rare* or *Obs.* 1687. 4. Having two hands 1847. 5. Ambidextrous; handy, efficient 1861.

1. That t. engine..Stands ready to smite MILT. 3. A huge two-handed lubber 1687.

Two-headed (stress var.), *a.* 1596. 1. Having, or represented with, two heads. 2. *fig.* Having or governed by two chiefs or rulers 1885.

1. By two-headed Ianus SHAKS.

Two-leaved (līvd), *a.* 1610. Having or consisting of two leaves. a. Having two hinged or folding parts, as a door, table, etc. b. Having two foliage-leaves or two petals or sepals; having leaves growing in pairs 1688.

Two-legged (legd, leˑgėd), *a.* 1561. Having two legs; usu. as an epithet suggestive of a human being having the qualities of the animal named.

The neighbours hens y[u] takest, and playes the two legged fox 1575.

Twoness (tūˑnės). 1648. [f. TWO + -NESS.] The fact or condition of being two; duality, doubleness.

Two·-part, *a.* 1854. Containing, consisting of, having, or involving two parts; composed in two parts, as a piece of music, or for two actors, as a play. So **Two·parted** *a.* divided into two parts, bipartite.

Twopence (tʊ·pĕns). 1450. A sum of money equal to two pennies 1477. 2. An English silver coin of the value of two pennies; = *half*-GROAT (since 1662 coined only as Maundy money). b. A copper coin of this value issued in the reign of George III. 1450. 3. As type of a very small amount; now esp. in phr. (*not*) *to care t.* 1691.

Twopenny (tʊ·pĕni), *a.* and *sb.* 1532. A. *adj.* 1. Of the value of, amounting to, or costing twopence. b. Involving an outlay of twopence; for the use of or admission to which there is a charge of twopence 1599. 2. *fig.* Of very little value; paltry, trumpery, trifling, worthless 1560.

1. *T. ale*, a quality of ale orig. sold at twopence per quart 1710. b. *T. tube*, former pop. name for the Central London Railway, opened in 1900, on which the fare was orig. twopence for any distance. 2. This woman, with her t. gentility THACKERAY.

B. *sb.* (the adj. used ellipt.) 1. Short for *t. ale* 1711. 2. A form of address to a child or young or small person 1844. 3. *colloq.* (with poss. adj.) One's head 1859. So **T.-halfpenny** (tʊ·pĕniˌhēˑpĕni) *a.* of the value of two pennies and a halfpenny; usu. *fig.* as an epithet of disparagement. **T.-pe·nnyworth,** as much as is worth or costs two pence; *fig.* a small amount.

Two-pile (tūˑpəil), *a.* 1611. Applied to velvet in which the loops of the pile-warp are formed by two threads, producing a pile of double thickness. Also **Two-piled** *a.*

Two-seater (tūˑsīˑtəɹ). 1906. [See TWO *Comb.* c.] A motor car or aeroplane having seats for two persons.

Two-sided, *a.* 1863. Having two sides, bilateral; *fig.* having two parts or aspects.

Twosome (tūˑsəm). Chiefly *Sc.* [f. TWO + -SOME[2].] Two persons together.

Two-way (stress var.), *a.* 1571. 1. Having, or connected with, two ways, roads, or channels; situated where two ways meet. 2. *Math.* Extending in two directions or dimensions, or having two modes of variation 1891.

1. *T. switch*, one by which electric current may be switched on or off from either of two points.

Two·-year-old, *a.* and *sb.* 1594. A. *adj.* Of the age of two years. Chiefly of animals, *esp.* colts 1601. B. *sb.* An animal (*esp.* a colt) or child of two years of age 1594.

-ty, *suffix*[1], denoting quality or condition, repr. ME. *-tie, -tee, -te*, from OF. *-te* (mod.F. *-té*), earlier *-tet* (*-ted*):—L. *-itatem*, nom. *-itas.* Such L. types as *bonitatem, feritatem*, were in OF. normally reduced to two syllables (*bontet, fertet*) by elision of the *-i-* between the two stresses, so that *-tet*, later *-te*, became the regular form of the suffix. From the types *lealte, realte*, the ending *-alte* (mod.F. *-auté*) was in OF. extended to formations from different stems, and many words of this form (ult. written with *-alty*) established themselves in English, as *admiralty, casualty, commonalty, mayoralty*, etc. Although occurring in a large number of words the suffix has been very little used as a formative element in English; *shrievalty, sheriffalty* are among the very small number of words from English stems with this suffix. Such words as *faculty, honesty, modesty* represent Latin formations in which *-tas* is directly added to a consonantal stem. The AF. form *-teth* survives in Sc. *bountith, poortith.*

-ty, *suffix*[2], denoting 'ten', forming the second element of the decade numerals from 20 to 90, as *twenty, thirty* (OE. *twentig, þrítig*), etc. OE. *-tig* corresponds to OFris. *-tich*, OS. *-tig*, OHG. *-zug* (G. *-zig*), and is the same as

ON. *tigr* and Goth. *tigus*, which were independent words.

Tyburn (təi·bə̆ɹn). late ME. The place of public execution for Middlesex until 1783, situated at the junction of the present Oxford Street, Bayswater Road, and Edgware Road.

attrib. †**T. ticket**, a certificate granted to one who secured the conviction of a felon, exempting the holder from all parochial duties in the parish where the offence was committed. **T. tree**, the gallows.

transf. Executed at T. near York, Colonel John Morrice 1736.

Tychonian (təikōu·niăn), *a.* and *sb.* 1647. [f. mod.L. *Tychon-*, stem of *Tycho*, latinized form of Da. *Tyge* + -IAN.] **A.** *adj.* = next 1710. **B.** *sb.* A disciple or adherent of Tycho Brahe or of his system of astronomy (*rare*) 1647.

Tychonic (təikǫ·nik), *a.* 1670. [f. as prec. + -IC.] Of or pertaining to the Danish astronomer Tycho Brahe (died 1601), or to his system of astronomy.

‖**Tycoon** (təikū·n). 1861. [ad. Jap. *taikun* great lord or prince, f. Chinese *ta* great + *kiun* prince.] The title by which the shogun of Japan was described to foreigners. **b.** *U.S.* A 'big bug'.

Tyg, tig (tig). 1855. [Origin unkn.] A drinking-cup with two or more handles, attributed to the 17th and 18th c.

Tying (təi·iŋ), *vbl. sb.* 1480. [f. TIE *v.* + -ING[1].] **1.** The action of TIE *v.* †**2.** *concr.* Something used for tying; a tie –1844.

Tyke (təik). Chiefly *Sc.* and *n. dial.* late ME. [a. ON. *tīk* bitch.] **1.** A dog; usu. in depreciation, a low-bred, or coarse dog, a cur, a mongrel. **2.** *transf.* A low-bred, lazy, mean, surly, or ill-mannered fellow; a boor. late ME. **3.** A nickname for a Yorkshireman; in full *Yorkshire t.* 1700.

1. Toby was the most utterly shabby, vulgar, mean-looking cur I ever beheld—in one word, a t. 1861. **3.** Give a t. a bridle and he'll soon have a horse 1820.

Tylo- (təilo), bef. a vowel or *h* **tyl-** (til), comb. form repr. Gr. τύλος knob or τύλη callus, cushion, used in a few terms of zoology; as in **Ty·lopod** [Gr. πούς, ποδ- foot], *a.* having pads on the digits instead of hoofs; belonging to the *Tylopoda*, a group of ruminants comprising the camels and llamas (synonymous with *Camelidæ*); *sb.* a member of the *Tylopoda*; so **Tylo·podous** *a.*

‖**Tylosis** (təilōu·sis). 1876. [mod.L., in sense 1 ad. Gr. τύλωσις, f. τύλος or τύλη; see TYLO- and -OSIS.] **1.** *Path.* **a.** An inflammatory disease of the eyelids, characterized by thickening and hardening of their edges. **b.** Callosity 1890. ¶**2.** *Bot.* An intrusive growth of the wall of a cell into the cavity of a vessel in woody tissue 1876. Hence **Tylo·tic** *a. Path.* of, pertaining to, or affected with t.

Tylote (tai·lout), *sb.* (*a.*) Also in L. form **tylo·tus.** 1887. [ad. Gr. τυλωτός knobbed, f. τυλοῦν to make knobby, f. τύλος knob.] *Zool.* A sponge-spicule of the form of a cylindrical rod with a knob at each end; also *attrib.* or *adj.*

Tymp (timp). 1645. [app. abbrev. of TYMPAN.] **1.** The mouth of the hearth of a blast-furnace through which the molten metal descends; formed by an arch of masonry (*t.-arch*), or a block of stone or iron (*t.-stone, t.-plate*), or by two of these together. **2.** *Coal mining.* A horizontal piece of timber for supporting the roof; also called *bar, cap,* or *lid* 1883.

Tympan (ti·mpăn). OE. [ad. L. *tympanum* TYMPANUM, or a. OF. *tympan, timpan* (mod.F. *tympan*).] **1.** A drum or similar instrument, as a timbrel or tambourine. *arch.* **b.** [Ir. *tiompan.*] An ancient Irish stringed instrument played with a bow. late ME. †**2.** = TYMPANUM 2. –1706. **3.** An appliance in a printing-press, interposed between the platen or impression-cylinder and the sheet to be printed, in order to soften and equalize the pressure; in a hand press consisting of two frames (*outer* and *inner t.*) with sheets of parchment or strong linen stretched upon them, and enclosing a packing either of blanket, rubber, etc., or sheets of paper, cloth, or other harder material, according to the nature of the work to be printed 1580. **4.** *Arch.* = TYMPANUM 3. 1704. **5.** A tense membrane or thin plate in any mechanical apparatus, e.g. in a phonograph 1883.

attrib.: **t.-sheet,** a sheet of paper, etc., laid on or fixed in the t., orig. as a guide for placing the sheets to be printed.

Tympanal (ti·mpănăl), *a.* (*sb.*) 1822. [f. TYMPANUM + -AL.] *Anat.* and *Zool.* = next 1. **b.** *sb.* A tympanal or tympanic bone 1875.

Tympanic (timpæ·nik), *a.* (*sb.*) 1808. [f. as prec. + -IC.] **1.** *Anat.* and *Zool.* Of, pertaining to, or connected with the tympanum, or drum of the ear; of the nature of a tympanum. **2.** Pertaining to or resembling a drum; in *Path.* tympanitic 1891. **3.** *Arch.* Pertaining to a tympanum 1909.

1. T. bone, in mammals, a bone of annular or tubular form supporting the tympanic membrane and surrounding the external auditory meatus (in the adult forming part of the temporal bone); in lower vertebrates, one of several bones variously supposed to be homologous with this.

B. as *sb.* Short for *t. bone* 1851.

Tympaniform (ti·mpăni-, timpæ·nifǫɹm], *a.* 1854. [ad. F. *tympaniforme*, f. TYMPANUM + *-forme* -FORM.] *Nat. Hist.* Having the form of a drum, or (usu.) of a drum-head; stretched like a drum-head: *spec.* applied to certain membranes in the bronchi of birds.

Tympanist (ti·mpănist). 1611. [ad. F. *tympaniste*, L. *tympanista*, Gr. τυμπανιστής, or f. *timpan* TYMPAN + -IST.] One who beats or plays upon a drum, a drummer.

‖**Tympanites** (timpănəi·tīz). late ME. [Late L., a. Gr. τυμπανίτης, f. τύμπανον TYMPANUM.] *Path.* Distention of the abdomen by gas or air in the intestine, the peritoneal cavity, or the uterus.

Tympanitic (timpăni·tik), *a.* 1834. [ad. L. *tympaniticus*, f. *tympanites*; see prec. and -IC.] Pertaining to, characteristic of, or affected with tympanites; also, hollow-sounding.

‖**Tympanitis** (timpănəi·tis). 1797. [In sense 1, an alteration of TYMPANITES. In sense 2, f. TYMPANUM + -ITIS.] **1.** = TYMPANITES. **2.** Inflammation of the lining membrane of the tympanum 1857.

Tympano- (timpăno), bef. a vowel occas. **tympan-**, comb. form repr. Gr. τύμπανον or L. TYMPANUM; as in **Tympane·ctomy** [Gr. ἐκτομή], excision of the tympanic membrane. **Ty:mpanohy·al** *a.*, pertaining to the tympanum and the hyoid arch; epithet of a small bone or cartilage at the base of the styloid process, which in early life becomes fused with the temporal bone; *sb.* = t. bone or cartilage.

‖**Tympanum** (ti·mpănə̆m). *Pl.* **tympana.** 1619. [L., drum, etc., a. Gr. τύμπανον, f. root of τύπτειν to strike.] **1.** A drum or similar instrument, as a tambourine or timbrel; also, the stretched membrane of a drum, a drum-head 1675. **2.** *Anat.* The drum of the ear; the middle ear separated from the outer ear by the tympanic membrane. Also often applied to the tympanic membrane simply. 1619. **b.** *Ornith.* (*a*) Each of the two inflatable air-sacs at the sides of the neck in certain birds, as grouse. (*b*) Applied to the bony labyrinth at the base of the trachea in certain species of duck, having resonant membranes in its walls. 1873. **3.** *Arch.* **a.** The die or cubical portion of a pedestal. **b.** The vertical recessed face of a pediment, often adorned with sculpture. 1658. **4.** *Mech.* A kind of wheel (orig. drum-shaped) with curved radial partitions, used for raising water 1875.

Tympany (ti·mpăni). 1528. [ad. med.L. *tympanias*, a. Gr. τυμπανίας, f. τύμπανον TYMPANUM.] **1.** = TYMPANITES; also sometimes used for a tumour or morbid swelling of any kind. Now *rare* or *arch.* †**b.** *transf.* or *allus.*, esp. in ref. to pregnancy –1711. **2.** *fig.* A swelling, as of pride, arrogance, self-conceit, etc., figured as a disease; a condition of being inflated or puffed up; an excess *of* something figured as a swelling; inflated style, turgidity, bombast. Now *rare* or *Obs.* 1581. **3.** = TYMPANUM 1. *Obs.* or *arch.* 1535.

1. b. A mere t...raised by a cushion DRYDEN. **2.** Puffed up with this Timpany of self conceit BURTON. Dr. Johnson..he charges..with a plethoric and tautologic t. of sentence 1828.

Tyne, obs. f. TIN, TIND, TINE.

Tynwald (ti·nwǫ̆ld, təi·n-). late ME. [ad. early ON. **þingwall-*, stem of ON. *þingvǫllr*, *þing* THING *sb.*[2] + *vǫllr* field, level ground.] (Also *T. Court.*) In the Isle of Man, an annual convention attended by the governor (representing the sovereign), a council acting as the upper house, and the House of Keys, at which the laws which have been enacted are proclaimed to the people.

Typal (təi·păl), *a.* 1853. [f. TYPE *sb.* + -AL.] **1.** Of the nature of, serving as, or answering to a type, pattern, or specimen; representative; typical. **2.** Of or pertaining to printing type; typographical 1882.

Type (təip), *sb.* 1470. [ad. F. *type* or L. *typus*, a. Gr. τύπος impression, etc., f. τύπτειν to beat, strike.] **1.** That by which something is symbolized or figured; a symbol, emblem; *spec.* in *Theol.* a person, object, or event of Old Testament history, prefiguring some person or thing revealed in the new dispensation; correl. to *antitype.* †**2.** A figure or picture of something; a representation; an image or imitation (*rare*) –1774. **b.** *Numism.* The figure on either side of a coin or medal 1785. **3.** A distinguishing mark or sign; a stamp (*rare*) 1593. **4.** *Path.* The characteristic form of a fever; *esp.* the character of an intermittent fever as determined by its period. *Obs.* or merged in 5. 1601. **5.** The general form, structure, or character distinguishing a particular kind, group, or class of beings or objects; hence *transf.* a pattern or model after which something is made 1843. **b.** *Ch. Hist.* [Gr. τύπος τῆς πίστεως type of the faith.] An edict of the Emperor Constans II, promulgated A.D. 648, prohibiting further discussion of the Monothelite controversy 1727. **6.** A kind, class, or order as dist. by a particular character 1854. **7.** *transf.* A person or thing that exhibits the characteristic qualities of a class; a typical example or instance 1842. **b.** *spec.* A person or thing that exemplifies the ideal qualities or characteristics *of* a kind or order; a perfect example or specimen *of* something; a model, pattern, exemplar 1847. **8.** *techn.* **a.** *Nat. Hist.*, etc. A certain general plan of structure characterizing a group of animals, plants, etc.; hence *transf.* a group or division of animals, etc., having a common form or structure 1850. **b.** *Nat. Hist.* A species or genus which most perfectly exhibits the essential characters of its family or group, and from which the family or group is (usu.) named; an individual embodying all the distinctive characters of a species, etc. 1840. **c.** *Chem.* A simple compound taken as representing the structure of more complex compounds 1852. **d.** *Math.* A succession of symbols susceptible of + and – signs 1891. **9.** A small rectangular block, usu. of metal or wood, having on its upper end a raised letter, figure, or other character, for use in printing 1713. **b.** *sing.* Types collectively; letter. *In t.*, set up ready for printing. 1778. **c.** *transf.* A printed character or characters, or an imitation of these 1784.

1. *In (the) t.*, in symbolic representation; He offered wine not water in the t...of his bloud JER. TAYLOR. **3.** Thy Father beares the t. of the King of Naples SHAKS. Tennis and tall Stockings, Short blistred Breeches, and those types of Trauell SHAKS. **5.** The t. upon which the whole was constructed 1857. **6.** The instruction in both is of the same t. 1879. **7.** Sir Roger de Coverley is a character, as well as a t. RUSKIN. **b.** Plato is the very t. of soaring philosophy J. H. NEWMAN. **8. a.** So careful of the t. she seems, So careless of the single life TENNYSON. **9.** Musical types had..been invented by an Italian 1880. **b.** This story goes straightway into t. DICKENS. **c.** To see small objects distinctly..such as..a small t. 1831.

attrib. and *Comb.*: **t.-bar,** (*a*) a line of t. cast in a solid bar, as by the linotype; (*b*) in a typewriter, each of the bars carrying the letters or characters; **-carriage,** in a printing-machine, a frame carrying the form; **-cutter,** one who engraves the dies or punches from which types are cast; **-cylinder,** the cylinder on which the types or plates are fastened in a rotary press; **-letter,** each of the types or letters of a typewriter; **-metal,** an alloy of lead and antimony, sometimes with tin or bismuth, of which printing types are cast; **-script,** typewritten matter or copy; also *attrib.*; **-setter,** a compositor; also, a composing-machine; so **-setting,** *sb.* and *a.*; **-theory,** *Chem.* the theory of the derivation of compounds from types by substitution; **-wheel,** a wheel with raised characters on its periphery, as in the printing telegraph and in some typewriters.

Type (təip), *v.* 1596. [f. prec.] **1.** *trans.* **a.** *Theol.* To prefigure or foreshadow as a type;

to represent in prophetic similitude. **b.** = TYPIFY 1. 1836. **2.** = TYPIFY 2. (*rare*) 1627. **3.** To print (*rare*) 1736. **4.** *trans.* and *intr.* To typewrite 1888. **5.** *Med.* To determine the compatibility of the blood of the donor for transfusion to that of the receptor 1927.

1. b. All nature typeth Thee and Thine 1839.

-type (təip), *suffix*, repr. F. *-type*, L. *-typus*, Gr. -τυπος, f. root of τύπτειν to beat, strike; as in *antitype, archetype, prototype*; also, with the sense 'type, block, or plate for printing from', in *electrotype, stereotype*; and with the sense 'impression or picture', also 'process of reproduction' as in *autotype, collotype, platinotype*.

Typewrite (təi·prəit), *v.* 1887. [Back-formation from next.] *trans.* To print by means of a typewriter; to type; also *intr.* to practise typewriting. So **Ty·pewri·ting** *vbl. sb.* and *ppl. a.* 1881. **Ty·pewritten** *ppl. a.*

Typewriter (təi·pˌrəi:tə). 1875. [f. TYPE *sb.* + WRITER.] **1.** A writing-machine having types for the letters of the alphabet, figures, and punctuation-marks, so arranged on separate rods (or on the periphery of a wheel) that as each key of the machine is depressed the corresponding character is imprinted in line on a moving sheet. **2.** One who does typewriting; a TYPIST 1884.

‖**Typhlitis** (tifləi·tis). 1857. [mod.L., f. Gr. τυφλόν the cæcum or blind gut (neut. of τυφλός blind) + -ITIS.] *Path.* Inflammation of the cæcum, cæcitis (often including *appendicitis*). Hence **Typhlitic** (tifli·tik) *a.*

Typhlo- (tiflo), bef. a vowel regularly **typhl-**, ad. Gr. τυφλο-, comb. form of τυφλός blind; occurring in a few recent pathological and surgical terms relating to the cæcum (Gr. τυφλόν; see prec.).

Typhlosole (ti·flosōul). Also **-solis.** 1859. [irreg. f. Gr. τυφλός blind + σωλήν channel, pipe.] *Zool.* A ridge or fold extending along the inner wall of the intestine and partly dividing the cavity of it, in various animals, as lampreys and certain ascidians, molluscs, and worms.

Typho- (təi·fo), ad. Gr. τυφο-, comb. form of τῦφος (see TYPHUS); used as comb. form of TYPHUS or TYPHOID, in recent terms of pathology, etc.; as **Typhomala·rial** *a.*, applied to a fever exhibiting both typhoid and malarial symptoms, or to typhoid fever with malarial complications, or of malarial origin. **Typho·to·xin**, a poisonous ptomaine obtained from cultures of the bacillus of typhoid fever.

Typhœan (təifī·ăn), *a.* [prop. *Typhoëan* (təifoī·ăn), f. *Typhoeus*, Gr. Τυφωεύς, name of a giant of Greek mythology.] Belonging to or characteristic of Typhoeus. MILT.

Typhoid (təi·foid), *a.* (*sb.*) 1800. [f. TYPHUS + -OID.] *Path.* **1.** Resembling or characteristic of typhus; applied to a class of febrile diseases exhibiting symptoms similar to those of typhus, or to such symptoms themselves, esp. to a state of delirious stupor occurring in certain fevers. **2.** *T. fever*: a specific eruptive fever (formerly supposed to be a variety of typhus), characterized by intestinal inflammation and ulceration; also called *enteric fever* 1845. **b.** Of, pertaining to, characteristic of, or affected with typhoid fever 1871. **B.** *sb.* Short for *t. fever* 1861. **b.** A case of typhoid; a patient suffering from typhoid (*colloq.*) 1890. Hence **Typhoi·dal** *a.* pertaining to, characteristic of, resembling, or having the character of t. fever.

Typhomania (təifomē·niă). 1693. [mod. L., ad. Gr. τυφωμανία, f. τῦφος TYPHUS + μανία MANIA; by mod. writers taken as f. TYPHUS (in the mod. sense) + MANIA.] *Path.* Delirium accompanied with stupor, occurring in typhus and other fevers.

Typhon[1] (təi·fǫn). 1592. [a. L., a. Gr. Τυφῶν, name of a giant; also, a tempestuous wind (see next), and applied to a comet or meteor.] The name of a giant or monster of ancient Greek mythology (according to Hesiod, the son of Typhoeus, and father of the Winds; later identified with Typhoeus), fabled to have been buried under Mount Etna, and represented as having a hundred heads and breathing out flames; also used as a name for the Egyptian evil divinity Set. Hence *allus.* Hence **Typho·nian** *a.* pertaining to or connected with T. or Set.

Ty·phon[2]. Now *rare* or *Obs.* 1555. [ad. Gr. τυφῶν; see prec. In later use partly suggested by TYPHOON.] A whirlwind, cyclone, tornado; a violent storm of wind, a hurricane.

Typhonic (təifǫ·nik), *a.* 1865. [ad. Gr. τυφωνικός, f. Τυφῶν; see TYPHON[1] and -IC.] **1.** Having the character of a whirlwind or tornado; tempestuous. **2.** = TYPHONIAN 1874.

Typhoon (təifū·n). 1588. [In sense a, a. Urdū *ṭūfān*, referred to Arab. *ṭāfa* to turn round, but possibly a. Gr. τυφῶν TYPHON[2]; in sense b, repr. Chinese *tai fung*, common dial. forms of *ta* big and *fêng* wind.] **a.** A violent storm or tempest occurring in India. **b.** A violent cyclonic storm or hurricane occurring in the China seas and adjacent regions, chiefly during the period from July to October.

Typhous (təi·fəs), *a.* 1805. [f. TYPHUS + -OUS.] *Path.* Pertaining to or having the character of typhus.

Typhus (təi·fɒs). 1643. [Late L. in sense 1, and mod.L. in sense 2, ad. Gr. τῦφος smoke, vapour, conceit, stupor, f. τύφειν to smoke, smoulder.] †**1.** Pride, haughtiness, conceit. **2.** *Path.* An acute infectious fever, characterized by great prostration and a petechial eruption, and occurring chiefly in crowded tenements, etc. Also *t. fever.* 1785.

Typic (ti·pik), *a.* 1601. [a. F. *typique*, ad. L. *typicus*, a. Gr. τυπικός typical, f. τύπος TYPE; see -IC.] **1.** = next 1. 1610. †**2.** Of a fever: Conforming to a particular type; intermittent; periodic –1857.

Typical (ti·pikăl), *a.* 1612. [ad. med.L. *typicalis*, f. L. *typicus* TYPIC; see -AL.] **1.** Of the nature of, or serving as, a type or emblem; pertaining or relating to a type or types; symbolical, emblematic. **2.** Having the qualities of a type or specimen; serving as a representative specimen of a class or kind 1860. **b.** *Nat. Hist.* That is the type of the genus, family, etc. 1847. **3.** Of or pertaining to a type or representative specimen; distinctive, characteristic 1850. **4.** Of or pertaining to printers' type; typographical. Now *rare* or *Obs.* 1770.

1. He renewed the custome of expounding Scripture in a typicall way 1661. 2. Horace is a t. Roman of the intellectual sort 1881. Hence **Typica·lity. Ty·pical-ly** *adv.*, **-ness.**

Typification (ti:pifikē·ʃən). 1811. [f. next; see -FICATION.] The action of typifying; representation by a type or symbol; also, that which typifies; an exemplification.

Typify (ti·pifəi), *v.* 1634. [f. L. *typus* TYPE *sb.*; see -FY.] **1.** *trans.* To represent or express by a type or symbol; to serve as a type, figure, or emblem of; to symbolize; to prefigure. **2.** To serve as the typical specimen of (a class, family, etc.); to exhibit the essential characters of; to exemplify 1854.

1. Glorie by the wreath is typifide 1634.

Typist (təi·pist). 1843. [f. TYPE *sb.* + -IST.] **1.** One who uses type; a printer, a compositor (*rare*). **2.** = TYPEWRITER 2. 1885.

Typo (təipo), *sb.* (*a.*) *slang.* 1816. [Short for *typographer* or *typographic.*] A typographer, a printer; *spec.* a compositor. **b.** *attrib.* or as *adj.* = TYPOGRAPHIC 1891.

Typo- (təi·po, ti·po), bef. a vowel **typ-**, comb. form repr. Gr. τύπος TYPE *sb.*; as in **Typonym** (təi·pŏnim), *Nat. Hist.* a name based on a type or specimen; hence **Typonymal** (-ǫ·nimăl), **Typonymic** (-ŏni·mik), *adjs.*

Typograph (təi·p-, ti·pŏgraf). 1737. [a. F. *typographe*, ad. med. L. *typographus*, f. Gr. τύπος + -γραφος.] **1.** A typographer or typographist. **2.** A writing-machine for the blind in which pressure upon raised types causes the corresponding letters to be printed 1820.

Typographer (təip-, tipǫ·grăfəɪ). 1643. [f. med.L. *typographus* (see prec.) + -ER[1].] One who is skilled in typography; a printer.

Typographic (təip-, tipŏgræ·fik), *a.* 1778. [ad. med.L. *typographicus*, f. *typographus* + -IC.] Of or pertaining to printing, typographical.

Typographical (təip-, tipŏgræ·fikăl), *a.* 1593. [f. as prec. + -AL; see -ICAL.] **1.** Of or pertaining to typography or printing; connected or dealing with printing. **b.** Produced or expressed by typography or in print; printed 1803. †**2.** Emblematic; figurative. JOHNSON. Hence **Typogra·phically** *adv.*

Typo·graphist. *rare.* 1890. [f. as TYPOGRAPHER + -IST.] One versed in the history or art of printing; a student of typography.

Typography (təip-, tipǫ·grăfi). 1641. [a. F. *typographie*, ad. mod.L. *typographia*. f. Gr. τύμος type + -γραφία writing; see TYPO- and -GRAPHY.] **1.** The art or practice of printing. **2.** The action or process of printing; *esp.* the setting and arrangement of types and printing from them; hence, the arrangement and appearance of printed matter 1697. **b.** *transf.* Printed matter; letterpress MILT.

Typology (təipǫ·lŏdʒi). 1845. [f. Gr. τύπος; see -LOGY.] **1.** The study of symbolic representation, *esp.* of the origin and meaning of Scripture types; also, *transf.* symbolic significance, representation, or treatment; symbolism. **2.** The study of or a discourse on printing types or printing 1882. **3.** *Archæol.* [after G.] The classification of remains and specimens according to the type they exhibit and its evolution, etc. 1886. So **Typolo·gic, -al** *adjs.*, **-ally** *adv.* **Typo·logist**, a student of t.

Tyranness (təiᵊ·rănės). 1590. [f. L. *tyrannus* TYRANT + -ESS.] A female tyrant.

Tyrannic (ti-, təiræ·nik), *a.* 1491. [ad. L. *tyrannicus*, a. Gr. τυραννικός, f. τύραννος TYRANT.] = next.

Tyrannical (ti-, təiræ·nikăl), *a.* 1560. [f. as prec. + -AL.] **1.** Of, pertaining to, or befitting an absolute ruler or his government; arbitrary, despotic. **2. a.** Of the nature or character of a tyrant; acting or operating in an oppressive, cruel, or unjustly severe manner 1538. **b.** Of, pertaining to, or befitting a tyrant; severely oppressive; despotically harsh or cruel 1579.

1. A t. dynasty 1838. 2. a. A dark and t. superstition MORLEY. Hence **Tyra·nnical-ly** *adv.*, **-ness.**

Tyrannicide[1] (ti-, təiræ·nisəid). 1657. [a. F., ad. L. *tyrannicida*, f. *tyrannus* TYRANT; see -CIDE[1].] One who kills a tyrant.

Tyra·nnicide[2]. 1650. [a. F., ad. L. *tyrannicidium*; see prec. and -CIDE[2].] The killing of a tyrant. Hence **Tyra·nnici·dal** *a.* pertaining or relating to, disposed or inclined to, t.

Tyrannize (ti·ranəiz), *v.* 1494. [a. F. *tyranniser*, f. *tyran* TYRANT; cf. late L. *tyrannizare*, Gr. τυραννίζειν.] **1. a.** *intr.* To be a despot or absolute ruler; to exercise absolute rule. Const. *over.* 1590. †**b.** *trans.* To rule over or dominate with absolute power –1795. **2.** *intr.* To reign tyrannically; to rule despotically or oppressively 1494. **3.** To act tyrannically, play the tyrant; to exercise power or control oppressively or cruelly 1529. **b.** *fig.* of things 1588. **4.** *trans.* To rule or govern tyrannically; to treat tyrannically, play the tyrant to or over. Now *rare.* 1533. **b.** *fig.* of things 1588. †**5.** To render tyrannical. MILT.

1. Polycrates, who..tyrannized in Samos HOBBES. 2. Oppressing and tyrannizing ouer her Maiesties subiects 1588. 3. The great were not allowed to t. over the poor 1846. b. The influences which t. over human passions and opinions 1805. 4. Had..rather sit still, and let his Country be tyrannized MILT. b. Poverty, which doth so t., crucifie, and generally depresse vs BURTON. Hence **Ty·rannizer,** one who or that which tyrannizes.

Tyrannous (ti·rănəs), *a.* 1491. [f. L. *tyrannus* TYRANT + -OUS.] **1.** Characterized by or inclined to tyranny; ruling or acting tyrannically; despotic. **2.** *transf.* Of the nature of or involving tyranny; oppressive, unjustly severe or cruel 1556.

1. The t. handes of any earthly Pharao 1577. *fig.* Yeeld vp (O Loue) thy Crowne To t. Hate SHAKS. Hence **Ty·rannous-ly** *adv.*, **-ness.**

Tyranny (ti·răni). late ME. [a. F. *tyrannie*, a. med.L. *tyrannia*, f. L. *tyrannus*, Gr. τύραννος TYRANT; cf. Gr. τυραννία (rare).] **1.** The government of a tyrant or absolute ruler; the position or rule of a tyrant. **b.** *gen.* Absolute sovereignty 1651. **c.** With *a* and *pl.* A state ruled by a tyrant or absolute prince; an absolute or despotic government 1605. **2.** The action or government of a tyrannical ruler; oppressive or unjustly severe government. late

ME. **3.** Arbitrary or oppressive exercise of power; unjustly severe use of one's authority; harsh, severe, or unmerciful action; with *a* and *pl.*, an instance of this. late ME. **b.** Violent or lawless action. *Obs.* or *arch.* 1475.

1. Pisistratus began to affect the T. of that city 1727. **c.** In most of the cities there were erected Tyrannies HOBBES. 2. Parliament T. began to succeed Church T. DE FOE. 3. 'Tis t. to trample on him that prostrates himself FULLER.

Tyrant (təi·rănt), *sb.* ME. [a. OF. (mod.F. *tyran*), a. L. *tyrannus*, Gr. τύραννος.] **1.** One who seizes upon the sovereign power in a state without legal right; an absolute ruler; a usurper. (Chiefly in ref. to ancient rulers.) †**2.** A ruler, governor, prince –1737. **3.** A king or ruler who exercises his power in an oppressive, unjust, or cruel manner; a despot ME. **4.** One who treats those under his control tyrannically ME. †**b.** By extension: Any one who acts in a cruel, violent, or wicked manner; a ruffian, desperado; a villain. Hence as a term of reproach. –1578. **c.** *fig.* Anything of which the action is likened to that of a tyrannical ruler 1508. **5.** *Ornith.* Any bird of the family *Tyrannidæ*; *esp.* any of several species of the genus *Tyrannus*, noted for attacking and driving off any other bird approaching its nesting place. Also called *t.-bird, t.-flycatcher.* 1730. **6.** *attrib.* or as *adj.* That is a tyrant, tyrannical, tyrannous; also, characteristic of a tyrant ME.

1. A tyraunt þat was kyng of sysile CHAUCER. 3. Do not tyrants..Think men were born for slaves to kings? GAY. 4. A plague vpon the T. that I serue SHAKS. **b.** I was a blasphemar, and a persecuter, and a tyraunt TINDALE 1 *Tim.* i. 13. **c.** Public opinion, the greatest t. of these times 1847. 6. When t. custom had not shackled man THOMSON.

Comb.: **t.-bird**: see sense 5; **-flycatcher, -shrike,** species of *Tyrannus*, resembling, and formerly confused with, the *Muscicapidæ* and *Laniidæ*. Hence **Ty·rant** *v. intr.* to play the t., to tyrannize (also with *it*).

‖ **Tyre,**[1] **tyer** (təiᵊr). *India.* 1613. [ad. Tamil *tayir.*] Name in India for curdled milk and cream beginning to turn sour.

Tyre [2] (təiᵊɹ). Also *U.S.* **tire.** 1796. [var. of TIRE *sb.*[2]] **1.** The iron or steel rim of a wheel, *esp.* the steel rim of the driving wheel of a locomotive. **2.** A rubber cushion around the wheel of a bicycle, motor-car, etc. 1875. Hence **Tyred** *ppl. a.* furnished with a t. or tyres: chiefly in compounds.

Tyrian (ti·riăn), *a.* and *sb.* 1513. [f. L. *Tyrius* (f. *Tyrus* Tyre) + -AN.] **A.** *adj.* Of or belonging to, native of, or made in Tyre, an ancient Phœnician city on the Mediterranean, the centre of an extensive commerce. **b.** *spec.* in ref. to the dye anciently made at Tyre from molluscs: see PURPLE B. 1. 1616. **B.** *sb.* A native or inhabitant of Tyre 1513.

b. Another finds the way to dye in Grain, And make Calabrian Wool receive the T. Stain DRYDEN.

Tyro: see TIRO.

Tyrolean (tirōᵘ·liăn) *a.* and *sb.* 1809. [f. *Tyrol* + -EAN.] **A.** *adj.* Belonging to Tyrol (often called 'the Tyrol'), a province of Austria-Hungary 1859. **B.** *sb.* A native or inhabitant of Tyrol 1809. So **Tyrolese** (-ī·z) *a.* and *sb.*

Tyrolite (ti·rǒləit). 1854. [ad. G. *tirolit*, f. *Tyrol*, where found; see -ITE [1].] *Min.* Hydrous arsenate of copper, found usually in reniform masses of pale green colour.

Tyrosine (təiᵊ·rosīn). 1857. [irreg. f. Gr. τυρός cheese + -INE [5].] *Chem.* A white crystalline substance ($C_9H_{11}NO_3$) produced by the decomposition of proteins.

‖ **Tyrotoxicon** (təiᵊrotǫ·ksikǫn). 1886. [mod. L., f. Gr. τυρός cheese + τοξικόν poison.] *Chem.* A poisonous ptomaine (diazobenzene hydroxide, $C_6H_5N.N.OH$), produced by a microbe in stale cheese and milk; cheese-poison. Also **Tyrotoxin.**

Tyrrhene (ti·rīn, tirī·n), *a.* and *sb.* late ME. [ad. L. *Tyrrhenus* of or pertaining to the *Tyrrheni* or Etruscans.] = next.

Coasting the T. shore MILT.

Tyrrhenian (tirī·niăn), *a.* and *sb.* 1660. [f. L. *Tyrrhenus* (see prec.) or *Tyrrhenia* Etruria.] **A.** *adj.* Of or pertaining to the Tyrrheni or their country; Etruscan, Etrurian. **B.** *sb.* One of the Tyrrheni; an Etruscan. **A.** *T. Sea*, the sea lying between the mainland of Italy and the islands of Corsica, Sardinia, and Sicily.

Tyrtæan (təɹtī·ăn), *a.* 1879. [f. proper name *Tyrtæus*, Gr. Τυρταῖος + -AN.] Pertaining to or in the style of Tyrtæus, a Greek poet of the 7th century B.C., who composed martial songs for the Spartans; martial, warlike.

Tysonite (təi·sənəit). 1880. [f. name of S. T. *Tyson* + -ITE [1].] *Min.* A rare native fluoride of the cerium metals.

Tzar, etc.: see CZAR, TSAR.

‖ **Tzigane** (tsigā·n), *sb.* and *a.* 1885. [a. F. *tzigane*, f. Magyar *cigány*, *czigány* (tsigā·ni).] **A.** *sb.* A Hungarian gipsy 1887. **B.** *adj.* That is a Tzigane; pertaining to or consisting of Tziganes 1885.

U

U (yū), the twenty-first letter of the modern English, and the twentieth of the ancient Roman alphabet, is a differentiated form of the letter V. Latin MSS. written in capitals have V only, modified in uncial, half-uncial, and minuscule MSS. into U. In Anglo-Saxon MSS. U was regularly employed as a minuscule to denote the vowel *u*, the corresponding capital being either V or U. In ME. after continental usage, the two symbols *u* and *v* were employed without distinction in value, but with preferences (1) for *v* as initial letter and *u* elsewhere (*vnder, vain,* but *full, euer*), and (2) for *v* where it made for clearness, e. g. next to *n* or *m* (*lvne, mvse*). During the 16th century, continental printers began to distinguish *u* as the vowel symbol, and *v* as the consonantal: and by 1630 this distinction was established in English also. V remained the capital symbol for both vowel and consonant rather longer, but during the 17th century was replaced in the vowel function first by U, and later by U. From about 1700, the vowel has been denoted by U, u, and the consonant by V, v. Dictionaries and alphabetical lists continued, into the 19th century, to give the items beginning with *u* and *v* as a single series, *va-* being followed by *vb-* (= *ub-*), etc.; this practice is still continued in some book-catalogues.

The vowel sounds of *u* in OE. were two, resembling those now heard (short) in *pull* and *bush*, and (long) in *rude* and *brute*. In ME. the short sound was still represented by *u*, but the long by the new symbol *ou* adopted from French, while *u* had acquired (in addition to its old short sound in native words) the short and long sounds of French *u* (*ü, ǖ*) in words introduced from Latin and French. In mod.Eng. the *ŭ* of OE. and ME. has become normally (*v*), written *u* or *o*, as in *dumb, sun, thus, some, love*, but retains its old sound universally in a few words, as *bull, bush, put*, etc., and locally in a much larger number. The OE. *ū* (ME. *ou*) has become the diphthong (au), written *ow* or *ou*, as in *town, thou*; but the ME. *ū* from French and Latin has become the diphthong (iū, iūᵊ), written *u, ue, u..e*, as in *huge, due, cure*, with reduction to (*ū*, ūᵊ), after *s* (= ʃ, ʒ), *j*, and *r*, as in *sure, jury, brute*, and optionally after *l*, as in *lute, lure*, and more widely in American usage. (A further development of (ūᵊ) to (ōᵊ) before (r), (ɹ) is characteristic of the pronunciation of some speakers.) In combination with other vowels, *u* is employed in the groups *au* (ǭ), *eu* (iū), *ou* (with varying value as in *foul, soul, four, young, route*), *ue* and *ui* (iū, ū) as in *hue, true, nuisance, fruit.* Between *g* and a vowel, and in final *-que*, *u* is often silent, as in *guard, guide, plague, grotesque*: it has the value of (w) after *q* in other positions and in some words after *s* and *g* (*queen, persuade, anguish*). The pronunciation of the name of the letter has changed from (*ū*) to (iū) in accordance with the change in the sound which it represents in words of French or Latin origin.

I. 1. The letter or its name. **b.** = YOU *pron.* in IOU. **2.** With ref. to the shape of the (capital) letter, esp. *attrib.* or *Comb.*, as *U-like, U bolt, U-magnet.* **b.** Something shaped like the letter U. **3.** Used to denote serial order. **II. 1.** Abbrevs.: U = Uranium; U.C. = upcast shaft; U.K. = United Kingdom; U.P. = United Presbyterian; U.S., U.S.A. = United States (of America); U.S.S.R. = Union of Soviet Socialist Republics. **2.** *slang.* U.P., the spelling pronunciation of UP *adv.* (*adv.*[2] II. 3 c), as in *it is all U.P.*

Uberous (yū·bĕrəs), *a.* Now *rare.* 1524. [f. L. *uber* rich, fruitful + -OUS.] **1.** Of animals or the breasts: Abounding in milk 1624. †**2.** Of places: Fertile –1651. **3.** Abundant, copious 1633.

Uberty (yū·bəɹti). Now *rare.* late ME. [a. OF. *uberté*, or ad. L *ubertas*, f. *uber*: see prec. and -TY.] Rich growth, fertility; copiousness.

Ubication (yūbikē·ʃən). 1644. [ad. mod.L. **ubicatio*, f. **ubicare* (Sp. *ubicarse* to be located), f. L. *ubi* where.] The being in or occupying a certain place; location.

Ubiety (yubəi·ėti). 1674. [ad. mod.L. *ubietas*, f. L. *ubi* where.] Condition in respect of place or location; local relationship.

Ubiquarian (yūbikwēᵊ·riăn). 1737. [f. L *ubique* everywhere.] **A.** *sb.* †**1.** *pl.* A society or club existing in the 18th cent. –1761. **2.** A person who goes everywhere (*rare*) 1767. **B.** *adj.* = UBIQUITOUS 1762.

Ubiquitarian (yubikwitēᵊ·riăn). 1640. [See next and -IAN.] **A.** *sb.* Chiefly in *pl.*: One of those Lutherans who held that Christ's body was everywhere present at all times 1651. **B.** *adj.* **1.** Of, pertaining to, or holding this doctrine 1640. **2.** = UBIQUITOUS (*rare*) 1641. Hence **Ubiquita·rianism** = UBIQUITISM.

Ubiquitary (yubi·kwitări), *sb.* and *a.* 1585. [ad. mod.L. *ubiquitarius*, f. L. *ubique* everywhere.] **A.** *sb.* **1.** A person or thing that is or can be everywhere at once. Now *rare.* 1587. †**2.** = UBIQUITARIAN *sb.* –1709.

1. A Nymph..all motion, an ubiquitarie, Shee is euerywhere B. JONS.

B. *adj.* †**1.** = UBIQUITARIAN *a.* 1. –1603. **2.** = UBIQUITOUS. Now *rare.* 1609.

2. The u. Assistance of the Deity is celebrated by.. the Psalmist STEELE. A few, such as the Dandelion and the Daisy, may be said to be almost u. 1853.

Ubiquitism (yubi·kwitiz'm). 1617. [f. prec.: see -ISM.] The doctrine of the omnipresence of Christ's body.

Ubiquitous (yubi·kwitəs), *a.* 1837. [f. as UBIQUITARY + -OUS.] **1.** Everywhere pervasively present, as God, an influence 1760. **b.** With joc. exaggeration, esp. of persons: 'Turning up' everywhere 1752. **2.** Universally or widely distributed as a class or its members 1840.

1. Heathendom was as a beleaguered city, mastered by an u. Presence PUSEY. **b.** Here as he lay nursing himself, u. Mr. Holt reappeared THACKERAY. Hence **Ubi·quitously** *adv.*, **Ubi·quitousness.**

Ubiquity (yubi·kwiti). 1576. [ad. mod.L. *ubiquitas*, f. L. *ubique* everywhere; see -ITY.] **1.** *Theol.* The omnipresence of Christ or of his body as maintained by the Ubiquitarians. **2.** The capacity of being everywhere at the same time: **a.** In general use 1597. **b.** as an attribute of God. (Variously taken as synonymous with or distinct from *omnipresence*). 1607. **c.** As expressing the Sovereign's relation to his Courts of law 1765.

1. Out of which vbiquitie of his body they gather the presence thereof with that sanctified bread and wine HOOKER. 2. **a.** The attention and activity which Quentin bestowed..had in it something that gave him the appearance of u. SCOTT. **b.** By God's Omnipresence, or U., we must be understood to mean that his Power and Knowledge extend to all Places 1748. Most Christians do not believe in the omnipresence of God; they only believe in His u. 1855. **c.** The legal u. of the king. His majesty, in the eye of the law, is always present in all his courts. BLACKSTONE.

U-boat (yū·bōᵘt). 1916. [ad. G. *U-boot*, abbrev. of *unterseeboot* 'under-sea boat'.] A German submarine.

Udal (yū·dăl). 1500. [Orkney and Shetland form of ODAL.] **1.** The old native form of freehold tenure in Orkney and Shetland 1588. **b.** Land so held 1750. **2.** *attrib.* Held or holding by, or based on, this tenure 1500.

2. There are three kinds of tenure of lands in Scotland...Thirdly, the U., being a right compleat without writing. 1793. Hence **U·daller,** a tenant of land by udal right. **U·dally** *adv.*

Udder (v·dəɹ). [OE. *ūder*:—OTeut. **ūðr-* = Gr. οὖθαρ, Skr. *ūdhar*, L. *uber.* In Eng. the original long vowel has been regularly shortened before the cons. group *-dr-*.] **1.** The pendulous baggy organ, with two or more nipples, by which the milk is secreted in some female animals OE. **b.** This part of an animal as an article of food 1474. **2.** *poet.* (in *pl.*). A dug or teat (*rare*) 1582.

1. Milk pressed from the swelling u. by the gentle hand of the beauteous milk-maid JOHNSON. b. Mr. Creed and I to the Leg in King Street, where he and I, and my Will had a good u. to dinner PEPYS. 2. A Lyonesse, with vdders all drawne drie SHAKS. Hence **U·ddered** *a.*

Udometer (yudǫ·mĭtəɹ). 1825. [ad. F. *udomètre*, f. L. *udus* wet; see -METER.] A rain-gauge.

†**Uds**, var. of ODS. 1586. Common in trivial oaths in the 17th cent. –1854.

Saint. Uds Niggers, but I will... *Wood.* Uds Niggers, I confess, is a very dreadful Oath DRYDEN.

Ufer (yū·fəɹ). 1754. [a. Du. *juffer* spar; see YUFFROUW.] A fir pole or piece of timber from 4 to 7 in. thick and from 20 to 40 ft. long.

Ugglesome (ʋ·g'lsǒm), *a.* Now *rare.* 1561. [app. f. obs. *uggle* ugly + -SOME [1].] Fearful, horrible, gruesome.

Ugh (uʰ, ʋʰ), *int.* and *sb.* 1765. [Imitative.] **1.** A representation of the sound of a cough; the sound itself. **2.** An interjection of disgust 1837.

1. The usurer..concluded his speech with a dry 'ugh, ugh' SCOTT. 2. It may have been a water-rat I speared, But, ugh! it sounded like a baby's shriek BROWNING.

Uglification (ʋ:glifikē¹·ʃən). 1820. [f. next; see -FICATION.] **1.** The action or process of uglifying. **2.** That which uglifies 1890.

Uglify (ʋ·glifəi), *v.* 1576. [f. UGLY *a.* + -FY.] *trans.* To make ugly.

The Covenanters had uglified it with pews and a gallery, and whitewash HAWTHORNE.

Ugliness (ʋ·glinės). ME. [f. UGLY + -NESS.] †**1.** Horror, dread, loathing. –late ME. **2.** The state of being ugly to look at; horrible, repulsive, unpleasing appearance ME. **b.** An ugly thing or feature 1856. **3.** Moral repulsiveness 1601.

2. The Egyptians..were..punished..with the number and vglines of them [frogs] 1608. A thing whose face, through u., frights children MIDDLETON. 3. The Bible tells the shameful history in all its naked u. 1869.

Ugly (ʋ·gli), *a.* (*adv.*, *sb.*) [ME., a. ON. *uggligr* to be dreaded, f. *ugga* to dread.] **A.** *adj.* **1.** Frightful or horrible, esp. through deformity or squalor. (Now merged in sense 3.) †**2.** Of events, times, sounds: Terrible –1725. **3.** Repulsive to the eye; unpleasant to look at; unsightly ME. **b.** *fig.* Repulsive to the imagination, unpleasant to contemplate 1440. **4.** Morally repulsive; base, degraded, vile ME. **5.** Of rank smell or taste; noisome. Now *rare.* late ME. **6.** Repugnant to refined taste; objectionable, disagreeable 1621. **7.** Troublesome, ominous, dangerous; suggestive of trouble or danger 1645. **b.** Of weather, sky, etc.: Stormy, threatening 1744. **c.** *U. customer*, a person formidable to attack or deal with 1811. **8.** Ill-tempered 1687. **9.** Comb., as *u.-faced*, *-looking*, *tempered* adjs.

1. Fayne would I die, but darksome vgly Death With-holds his darte 1594. 2. Great numbers came down to the shore, staring at us, and making confused u. noises DE FOE. 3. I cannot tell by what Logick we call a Toad, a Beare, or an Elephant, u. SIR T. BROWNE. You would be less zealous were the Queen old and u. 1742. The house itself was an u. residence TROLLOPE. *U. duckling*: (in allusion to the cygnet in a brood of ducks), a person of unpromising appearance or quality who ultimately proves handsome or successful. b. Amazement is the uggli'st shape of fear DAVENANT. 4. Tokens that God was grievously offended with such u. deeds 1650. 5. Stinking things have filthy and u. Vapors 1668. 6. The one person who comes out of that strife with an u. stain upon his shield..was the Prime Minister 1888. 7. I had an u. giddy fit last night in my chamber SWIFT. A long preface..is an u. symptom and always forebodes great sterility COWPER. The Under-Secretary for Foreign Affairs..admitted some u. facts 1890. b. With an u. black sky above, and an angry sea beneath KINGLAKE. c. You will find me, my young sir, an U. Customer! DICKENS. 8. He turned upon her with his ugliest look DICKENS. The clever promptitude with which they manage the brutes who look at all u. 1896.

B. *adv.* Terribly; uglily; †illtemperedly. Now *rare.* late ME.

With that he looked u. upon them BUNYAN.

C. *sb.* **1.** An ugly person, animal, etc. Chiefly in *beauties and uglies.* 1755. **2.** A kind of shade projecting from a lady's hat or bonnet 1850.

2. The broad eaves project so far over that they remind you almost of a lady's 'u.' 1856. Hence **U·glily** *adv.* in an u. manner. **U·gly** *v. trans.* to uglify.

Ugrian (ū·griăn, yū·g-), *a.* and *sb.* 1841. [f. *Ugri*, the Russian name of an Asiatic race dwelling east of the Urals.] **A.** *adj.* Also **U·gric** (see -IC) 1884. Of or belonging to a division of Ural-Altaic peoples including the Finns and Magyars. **B.** *sb.* **1.** A member of the Ugrian stock 1841. **2.** The Ugrian language 1862.

Ugsome (ʋ·gsǒm), *a.* Chiefly *north.* and *Sc.* late ME. [f. ME. *ug* to fear, a. ON. *ugga* to fear + -SOME [1].] Horrible, loathsome. (The modern literary use is perhaps due to Scott.)

Such an euyl fauoured face, such an vgsome countenaunce LATIMER. Hence **U·gsomely** *adv. rare.* **U·gsomeness.**

‖ **Uhlan** (ū·lăn, yū·lăn). 1753. [a. F., G., a. Polish (*h*)*ulan*, ad. Turk. *oghlān* son, youth, servant.] A type of cavalryman or lancer, orig. in the Polish and latterly in the German armies.

‖ **Uigur** (wī·guɹ). Also **Ouigour.** 1785. [East Turk. *uighur*, f. *ui* to follow + *-gur* adj. suffix.] **A.** *sb.* **1.** A Turk of the eastern branch prominent in Central Asia from the 8th to the 12th cent. 1785. **2.** The language of the Uigurs 1843. **B.** *adj.* Of or pertaining to the Uigurs 1844. So **Uigu·rean, -ian, -ic** *adjs.* 1773.

‖ **Uitlander** (oi·t-, ū·tlǎndəɹ). 1892. [(Cape) Du., f. *uit* out + *land* land.] = OUTLANDER b.

‖ **Ukase** (yukē¹·s). Also **ukaz.** 1729. [ad. Russ. *ukazŭ*, f. *ukazati* to direct.] **1.** An edict of the Russian emperor as government. **2.** *transf.* Any arbitrary order 1818.

Ukrainian (yukrē¹·niăn). 1816. [f. *Ukraine*, a southern district of Russia, ad. Russ. *Ukraina* border, f. *u-* at + *krai* edge.] **A.** *adj.* Of the Ukraine. **B.** *sb.* **1.** A native of the Ukraine 1823. **2.** The Ukrainian Slavonic dialect 1886.

Ukulele (yūkŭlē¹·li). 1900. Also **uke-.** [Hawaiian.] A four-stringed Hawaiian guitar.

-ular, *suffix*, repr. L. *-ularis* (see -ULE, -AR [1]) in adjs. formed from sbs. in *-ulus*, *-ula*, *-ulum.* Of Eng. adjs. in *-ular* some, as *angular*, are adaptations of L., med.L., or mod.L. forms, while others, as *auricular*, are formed directly on L. sbs. When both the simple noun and the dim. exist as *gland* and *glandule*, the adj. in *-ular* is usu. associated with the former (*glandular* = of the glands).

Ulcer (ʋ·lsəɹ), *sb.* late ME. [ad. L. *ulcer-*, *ulcus* neut. (related to Gr. ἕλκος).] **1.** *Path.* An erosive solution of continuity in any external or internal surface of the body, forming a purulent open sore. **b.** Used in sing. as a generic term 1623. **2.** *fig.* A corroding or corrupting influence; a moral plague-spot 1592. Hence **U·lcer** *v.* (now *rare*), to ulcerate (*trans.* and *absol.*) 1590. **U·lcered** *ppl. a.* = ULCERATED *ppl. a.* 1575.

Ulcerate (ʋ·lsərē¹t), *v.* late ME. [f. L. *ulcerat-*, ppl. stem of *ulcerare*, f. *ulcer-* ULCER; see -ATE [3].] **1.** *intr.* To form an ulcer or ulcers; to fester. **2.** *trans.* To cause ulcers in or on 1550. **3.** *fig.* To irritate or poison like an ulcer 1647. Hence **U·lcerated** *ppl. a.*, converted into, afflicted with, or characterized by an ulcer or ulcers 1547.

Ulceration (ʋlsərē¹·ʃən). late ME. [ad. L. *ulceration-*, *-tio*, f. *ulcerare*; see prec.] *Path.* **1.** The formation of ulcers; the being or becoming ulcerated; an ulcerated condition. **2.** An ulcer or group of ulcers 1580.

Ulcerative (ʋ·lsərē¹tiv, -ătiv), *a.* 1575. [ad. med.L. *ulcerativus*; see ULCERATE *v.* and -IVE.] **1.** Causing ulceration. **2.** Of the nature of ulceration 1800. **3.** Accompanied by ulceration 1813. **4.** Caused by ulceration 1876.

Ulcerous (ʋ·lsərəs), *a.* 1577. [ad. L. *ulcerosus*, f. *ulcer-*, ULCER.] **1.** Of the nature of an ulcer. **2.** Exhibiting ulceration 1599. **3.** Due to ulcers 1641.

-ule, *suffix*, repr. L. dim. endings *-ulus*, *-ula*, *-ulum* (e. g. *globulus*, *glandula*, *granulum*). Of current words, some correspond to L. forms, as *capsule*, *nodule*, *pustule*, others are of modern formation, as *anguillule.* Some words that appeared temporarily with this ending, as *scrupule*, have given way again to earlier forms of Fr. origin in *-le*; and others, as *formule*, to the original L. form in *-ula.*

‖ **Ulema** (ūlĕmā·, ū·lĕmă, yulī·mă). 1688. [a. Arab. *ʿulemā*, pl. of *ʿālim* learned, f. *ʿalama* to know.] **1.** as *pl.* Those Mohammedans whose special training qualifies them as authorities on law and religion: *spec.* the body of Mohammedan doctors headed by the Sheik-ul-islam. **2.** as *sing.* A Mohammedan doctor or divine 1843.

-ulent, *suffix*, repr. L. adj. suffix *-ulentus*, meaning 'full of . . .', as *fraudulentus.* Many such L. adjs. have been adopted in Eng., and a few, as *flatulent*, are from mod.L. formations. *Violent*, *pestilent*, and a few others, show variant forms in *-olentus*, *-ilentus.*

‖ **Ulex** (yū·leks). 1753. [mod.L., a. L. = shrub resembling rosemary.] *Bot.* A genus of thorny papilionaceous shrubs of the family *Leguminosæ*; a plant of this genus, esp. *U. europæus*, the gorse.

Ulexine (yū·leksīn). 1887. [f. prec. + -INE.] *Chem.* An alkaloid prepared from gorse seed.

Ulexite (yū·leksəit). 1867. [f. *Ulex*, personal name + -ITE [1].] *Min.* Native borate of lime and soda.

‖ **Ulicon**, var. of OOLAKAN.

Uliginous (yuli·dʒinəs), *a.* 1576. [ad. L. *uliginosus*, f. *uligin-*, *-igo* moisture; see -OUS.] **1.** Of a watery or oozy nature. **2.** Of places, or soil: Waterlogged, swampy 1610. So **Uli·ginal** *a.*, *Bot.* growing in wet ground 1863. **Uli·ginose** *a.*, swampy (*rare*) 1440; also *Bot.* = ULIGINAL 1866.

Ullage (ʋ·lėdʒ), *sb.* 1444. [ad. AF. *ulliage*, OF. *ouillage*, f. *ouiller* to fill up (a barrel).] **1.** The amount by which a cask or bottle falls short of being full. **b.** *On u.*, (in a cask, etc.) not completely full 1863. **2.** The amount of liquor (also *wet u.*) in a vessel that is not full 1832. **b.** *slang.* The liquor left in used wine-glasses or casks 1874. **3.** *transf.* **a.** The drainings of moist matter 1824. **b.** Waste metal cut away by the graving tool 1860. **c.** *Naut.* Off-scourings, worthless human or other material 1901. **4.** *attrib.*, as *u. cask* 1743.

1. I held the bottle up to the candle to ascertain the u. MARRYAT. b. It is injurious to Rhenish wine to be left on u. 1863.

U·llage, *v.* 1749. [f. prec.] **1.** *trans.* To calculate the ullage in (a cask). **2. a.** To draw a little from 1881. **b.** To fill up the ullage in 1888. Hence **Ullaged** (ʋ·lėdʒd) *ppl. a.* (of a cask or bottle) short of contents 1549; (of wine) damaged by being on ullage 1907; (*transf.* of any goods) inferior, refuse 1892. **U·llager**, a gauger of ullage 1885.

Ullmannite (ʋ·lmănəit). 1839. [f. name of J. C. *Ullmann* + -ITE [1].] *Min.* †**1.** Phosphate of manganese and iron. **2.** Sulphantimonide of nickel 1868.

Ulmate (ʋ·lmēt). 1836. [f. ULMIC; see -ATE.] *Chem.* A salt of ulmic acid.

Ulmic (ʋ·lmik), *a.* 1831. [f. L. *ulmus* elm, after next.] *Chem.* in *U. acid*: = ULMIN.

Ulmin (ʋ·lmin). 1813. [f. L. *ulmus* elm + -IN.] *Chem.* **1.** An exudation from the inner bark of the elm and some other trees; this as a distinct chemical principle. **2.** A dark-coloured product of the decay of wood or vegetable matter, or of the action of certain chemical agents on sugar, etc. 1843.

‖ **Ulna** (ʋ·lnă). 1541. [L., related to Gr. ὠλένη and OE. *eln* ELL [1].] *Anat.* **1.** The large inner bone of the fore-arm. **2.** The corresponding bone of a quadruped's foreleg and of a bird's wing 1831. Hence **U·lnad** *adv.* towards the ulnar aspect (cf. DEXTRAD) 1803.

U·lnage, var. of ALNAGE. Hence **U·lnager.**

Ulnar (ʋ·lnăɹ), *a.* and *sb.* 1741. [f. ULNA + -AR.] *Anat.* **A.** *adj.* **1.** Of the ulna. **B.** *sb.* The ulnar nerve 1899. So **Ulno-**, comb. form, as in *ulno-carpal.*

-ulose, *suffix*, repr. L. adj. suffix *-ulosus* (see -ULE, -OSE) formed on sbs. in *-ulus*, *-ula*, *-ulum.* Some of the Eng. words are adaptations of L. adjs., as *calculose*: others, as *globulose*, are analogical formations. Forms in *-ulose* from the same stem as others in *-ulous* are usu. either older forms now displaced by commoner *-ulous*, or later forms differentiated for special senses.

Ulotrichous (yulǫ·trikəs), *a.* Also **oulo-**. 1857. [f. mod.L. *Ulotrichi*, f. Gr. οὖλος crisp + -τριχος -haired, f. τριχ-, θρίξ hair.] *Anthrop.* Of the *Ulotrichi*, a division of mankind comprising the crisp-haired races. So **Ulo·trichan,** a u. person 1888.

-ulous, *suffix*, repr. both L. *-ulosus* (see -ULOSE), as in *fabulous, populous*, and L. *-ulus* adj., as in *garrulous, tremulous*.

Ulster (ʋ·lstəɹ). [The name of an Irish province, occurring in ME. as *Ulster, Ulvester* (= AF. *Ulvestre*), corresp. to ON. *Ulaztir, Ulaðstir*, f. Irish *Ulaidh* men of Ulster, with an obscure suffix (cf. *Leinster, Munster*).] **1.** *pl.* Ulstermen (as troops). *rare.* 1649. **2.** The Irish king-of-arms 1552. **3.** A long loose rough overcoat, often with a waist-belt 1878.

attrib.: *U. tenant-right, U. custom*, those securing to a tenant certain rights of occupancy, disposal, or compensation, in regard to land held by him. **U·lster-man,** a native or inhabitant of Ulster. Hence (from sense 3): **U·lstered** *a.* wearing an u. **Ulstere·tte,** a small or light u. **U·lstering,** cloth for the making of ulsters.

Ult., abbrev. of ULTIMO. 1750.

I have read yours of the 30th ult. with great pleasure 1750.

Ulterior (ʋltīᵊ·riəɹ), *a.* 1646. [a. L., further, comp. adj. (cf. *ultra, ultro* advs.).] **1.** Lying beyond what is immediate or present, coming at a later stage, further, future. **b.** *spec.* Beyond what is avowed or evident; kept in the background 1735. **2.** More remote in position 1721.

1. The request was only preparatory to u. measures FROUDE. **b.** There is no reason for suspecting him of u. designs 1856. **2.** Those u. regions which are beyond the limits of our astronomy 1817. Hence **Ulterio·rity,** an u. matter. **Ulte·riorly** *adv.*, at or to a further stage.

Ultimacy (ʋ·ltimăsi). 1842. [f. next; see -ACY.] The quality or state of being ultimate.

Ultimate (ʋ·ltimĕt), *a.* (*sb.*). 1654. [ad. late L. *ultimatus*, pa. pple. of *ultimare* to be at the end, f. *ultimus* last.] **A.** *adj.* **1.** Beyond which nothing is contemplated or intended. **2.** That concludes a process, course of action or series 1660. **b.** No longer alterable, definitive 1687. **c.** Precluding appeal or escape, decisive 1755. **d.** Beyond which there is no advance or progress 1794. **3.** Beyond which no advance can be made by investigation or analysis; fundamental, elemental 1659. **b.** Math. *U. ratio*, the final limiting ratio between two variable quantities which simultaneously approach definite fixed values or limits 1729. **4.** Forming a result or conclusion of a character different from the starting-point or present state; eventual 1777. **5.** Of a syllable or accent: Final; falling on the last syllable of a word 1837.

1. To be idle is the u. purpose of the busy JOHNSON. **2.** No man ever knew..what will be the u. result.. of any given line of conduct RUSKIN. **b.** I consented to wait till then for their u. decision 1803. **c.** The u. check to population appears then to be a want of food MALTHUS. **d.** The creatures [larvae] before us were not in their u. state, but were the produce of the bee-fly 1794. **3.** There are u. truths, far above human ken 1808. The u. particles of matter TYNDALL. **4.** The quiet of the town is purchased by the ruin of the country, and the u. wretchedness of both BURKE.

B. *sb.* **1.** The final point or result; the end; the last step 1681. **2.** A final or fundamental fact or principle 1709.

1. Having now obtain'd the u. of his Desires 1728. **2.** We come down then finally to Force, as the u. of ultimates H. SPENCER.

Ultimate (ʋ·ltimeⁱt), *v.*[1] 1834. [f. prec. or L. *ultimat-*, *ultimare*.] **1.** *trans.* To bring to completion 1849. **2.** *intr.* To result finally; to end (*in* something) 1834.

1. It is the soundness of the bones that ultimates itself in a peach-bloom complexion EMERSON. **2.** Unless the meditation ultimates in useful work 1868.

U·ltimate, *v.*[2] *rare.* 1892. [Back-formation from ULTIMATUM.] *trans.* = ULTIMATUM *v.*

Ultimately (ʋ·ltimĕtli), *adv.* 1660. [f. ULTIMATE *a.* + -LY [2].] **1.** In the last resort; fundamentally. **2.** In the end; at the last 1755. **3.** Conclusively, definitively 1785.

1. All government is u. and essentially absolute JOHNSON. **2.** I doubted not that I should u. succeed MRS. SHELLEY. So **U·ltimateness,** finality.

Ultima Thule. See THULE.

Ultimation (ʋltimēⁱ·ʃən). 1791. [f. as ULTIMATE *v.*[1]; see -ATION.] The action or process of bringing to an ultimate result; a final issue or development.

Ultimatum (ʋltimēⁱ·tǒm), *sb.* *Pl.* **-ata** (-ēⁱ·tă). 1731. [ad. late L., neut. sing. of *ultimatus*; see ULTIMATE *v.*[1]] **1.** Terms presented by one State to another as its last word, to be complied with on pain of a diplomatic rupture or war. **b.** *transf.* A final stipulation or offer 1733. **2.** The extreme limit; an ultimate aim 1748. †**3.** *slang.* The buttocks -1825. **4.** Something unanalysable or fundamental 1858. **5.** The most distant point (to be) reached 1862.

1. b. The official shrugged his shoulders and signified that his u. had been pronounced TROLLOPE. **2.** To be married was still the u. of her wishes 1802. **4.** Certain *ultimata* of belief not to be disturbed in ordinary conversation O. W. HOLMES. **5.** Almost to the coast of the Baltic; their u. there a place called Köslin CARLYLE. Hence **Ultima·tum** *v. trans.* to present with an u.

‖**Ultimo** (ʋ·ltimo), *adv.* 1582. [L. (sc. *die* or *mense*), abl. sing. masc. of *ultimus* last.] †**1.** On the last day (of a specified month) -1682. **2.** Of last month. (Abbrev. ULT. and ULTO.). 1616.

2. Your letter of the 31st u. WASHINGTON.

Ultimoge·niture. 1882. [f. L. *ultimus* last; after PRIMOGENITURE.] Inheritance by the youngest of a family, as in borough-english.

†**Ulto.,** abbrev. of ULTIMO 2. -1847.

Ultonian (ʋltōᵘ·niăn), *a.* and *sb.* 1766. [f. med.L. *Ultonia* Ulster, f. *Ult-*, stem of OIr. *Ulaidh*; see ULSTER.] (A native or inhabitant) of Ulster.

Ultra (ʋ·ltră), *a.* (*sb.*). 1817. [Independent use of ULTRA-; orig. as an abbrev. of F. *ultra-royaliste*.] **A.** *adj.* **1.** Ultra-royalist. **2.** Holding extreme views 1820. **3.** Excessive 1818. **4.** Expressive of extreme views 1827. **5.** Adapted for very minute measurements, etc., as *u.-microscope* 1910.

3. A little wearied by..the u. zeal of his countrymen W. IRVING.

B. *sb.* **1.** A (French) ultra-royalist 1817. **2.** An extremist, esp. in politics or religion 1826. **3.** One who goes to the extreme of fashion 1819.

‖**Ultra** (ʋ·ltră), *prep.* 1793. [L., = beyond.] **1.** *U. vires* (vəiᵊ·rīz), beyond the powers or legal authority (*of* a person, etc.; also with ellipsis of *for*). **2.** Lying beyond (*rare*) 1883.

1. It was not *ultra vires* the directors to advance money 1884.

Ultra- (ʋ·ltră), *prefix*, repr. L. *ultra* beyond, so used in late and med.L. (see ULTRAMARINE, ULTRAMONTANE, ULTRAMUNDANE). Senses 1 and 2 below answer to these types; sense 3 apparently originated in the F. *ultra-révolutionnaire* and *ultra-royaliste*, and has become prolific in English and other European languages.

1. Lying on the other side of or beyond in space. In adjs., as *ultra-Gangetic, -terrestrial, -zodiacal.* **b.** *U.-red, -violet*, applied to rays lying beyond the two ends of the visible spectrum. *U.-v. rays* are used in therapeutics and photography. **2.** Exceeding or surpassing the limits of the class denoted by the simple adj., as *ultra-microscopic* too small to be microscopic, *ultra-human* beyond what is human. **b.** Exceeding in respect of number or quantity, as *ultra-centenarian* living to over a hundred. **3.** Showing the highest degree of the quality denoted by the simple adj., as *ultra-fashionable, ultra-orthodox, ultra-dolichocephalic.* **b.** Similarly in advs., as *ultra-politely.* **c.** Similarly in sbs., mostly subst. uses of, or derivatives of, adjs., as *ultra-Christian, -papist; -discipline.*

U:ltracrepidarian (-krepidēᵊ·riăn), *a.* and *sb.* 1819. [f. the L. phr. (*ne sutor*) *ultra crepidam* (let the cobbler not go) beyond his last.] **A.** *adj.* Going beyond one's province. **B.** *sb.* A person who does this, esp. an ignorant or presumptuous critic 1825. Hence **Ultracrepida·rianism, Ultracrepida·tion, -cre·pidizing.**

Ultrafidian (-fi·diăn), *a.* 1825. [f. the L. phr. *ultra fidem* beyond faith.] Going beyond mere faith; blindly credulous.

Ultraism (ʋ·ltră,iz'm). 1821. [f. ULTRA *a.* + -ISM.] The fact or condition of being an extremist; extreme opinions. **b.** With *pl.* Any such opinion 1824. So **U·ltraist. Ultrai·stic** *a.*

Ultramarine (ʋltrămărī·n), *a.* and *sb.* 1598. [ad. med.L. *ultramarinus*, f. L. *ultra* beyond + *mare* sea.] **A.** *adj.* **1.** Situated beyond the sea. Now *rare.* 1652. **2.** From beyond the sea, foreign 1656. **3.** *U. blue* (or *colour*): **a.** A pigment of various shades of blue, named with ref. to the foreign origin of lapis lazuli, from which it was orig. obtained 1686. **b.** A blue colour like that of this pigment 1781. **4.** Of a special deep-blue colour 1783.

1. He tells them that the loss of her u. dominions lessens her expences BURKE.

B. *sb.* **1.** = A. 3. 1598. **b.** With distinguishing words, as *Dutch, yellow, green, German, artificial, u.* 1728. **2.** = A. 3 b. 1695.

Ultramontane (ʋltrămǫ·nteⁱn). 1592. [ad. med.L. *ultramontanus*, f. L. *ultra* beyond + *mont-*, *mons* mountain.] **A.** *sb.* **1.** *Eccl. Hist.* **a.** A representative of the Roman Catholic Church north of the Alps as opposed to the ecclesiastics in Italy. Now *rare.* **b.** = ULTRAMONTANIST (named from the point of view of countries north of the Alps) 1873. **2.** An inhabitant or native of a country north of the Alps 1618. **B.** *adj.* **1. a.** Of a country north of the Alps 1618. **b.** Of the Italian party in the Roman Church; zealous for papal authority 1728. **2.** *gen.* (From) beyond the mountains 1786.

Ultramontanism (ʋltrămǫ·ntăniz'm). 1827. [ad. F. *ultramontanisme*; see prec. and -ISM.] The principles and practice of the ultramontane party in the Roman Church; the doctrine of absolute papal supremacy. So **Ultramo·ntanist,** a supporter of the absolute supremacy of the Pope 1826.

Ultramundane (ʋltrămʋ·ndeⁱn), *a.* 1656. [ad. late L. *ultramundanus*, f. *ultra* beyond + *mundus* the world.] Beyond the world; of or pertaining to things beyond the limits of the solar system.

Ultroneous (ʋltrōᵘ·nīəs), *a.* 1637. [f. L. *ultroneus*, f. *ultro* of one's own accord.] Done, etc. of one's own accord; voluntary. **b.** *Sc. Law.* Of a witness: Not cited, but proffering testimony 1824. So **Ultro·neous-ly** *adv.* 1627, **-ness** (*rare*) 1623.

Ululate (ʋ·liuleⁱt, yū·l-), *v.* 1623. [f. L. *ululat-*, ppl. stem of *ululare*, of imitative origin.] *intr.* To howl, wail, lament loudly.

Troopes of Jackalls..all the while ululating 1638. The widow so often interrupted the service to u. 1893. So **U·lulant** *a.* howling; of, with or like howling. **Ulula·tion,** a wailing or howling 1599. **U·lulatory** *a.* ululant.

‖**Ulva** (ʋ·lvă). *Pl.* **-væ** (vī). 1706. [L., = sedge.] *Bot.* An alga, the typical genus of the *Ulvaceæ*; the laver or sea lettuce.

Ulyssean (yuli·sĭăn, yūlisī·ăn), *a.* 1639. [f. L. *Ulysses*, ad. Gr. Ὀδυσσεύς king of Ithaca and hero of the Odyssey.] Of or connected with Ulysses; *spec.* resembling him in craft or deceit, or in extensive wanderings.

Modern Greeks are U. in this respect, never telling straightforward truth, when deceit will answer the purpose 1850.

Um, 'um, var. of 'EM *pron.*, them. Now *dial.* 1606.

Um ('m), *int.* 1672. [Imitative.] = HUM *int.*

†**Um-, umb-, umbe-,** *prefixes* in many ME. verbs with the meaning 'around' 'about', as *umstand* to stand round, guard, *umb(e)set* to beset, surround, *umbego* to go round, encircle, UMBETHINK. *Um-* is a reduced form of *umb-*. *Umb-* was ad. ON. *umb-*, corresponding to OE. *ymb-*, *ymbe-* prefix, *ymbe* prep. *Umbe-* partly repr. OE. *ymbe-* is partly an extension of *umb-*, and partly a combination of *um-* with BE-. G. *um*, Gr. ἀμφί, and L. *ambi-*, are cognate.

Umbel (ʋ·mbĕl). 1597. [ad. L. *umbella* sunshade, dim. of *umbra* shadow.] **1.** *Bot.* An inflorescence borne on pedicels of nearly equal length springing from a common centre. **2.** *Zool.* An umbelliform arrangement of parts 1870.

1. The white umbels of the hemlocks lining the bushy hedgerows GEO. ELIOT. Hence **U·mbelled** *a.* *Bot.* umbellate. **Umbe·lliform** *a.*

‖**Umbella** (ʋmbe·lă). *Pl.* **-læ** (lī). 1699. [L.; see prec.] **1.** *Bot.* An umbel. **2.** *Zool.* A more or less convex disk supporting the tentacula in Medusæ 1834.

Umbellate (ʋ·mbĕlĕt), *a.* 1760. [ad. mod. L. *umbellatus*, f. L. *umbella*; see -ATE [2].] **1.** *Bot.* **a.** Of flowers: Forming an umbel or umbels. b. Of plants: Having such flowers 1785. 2. *Zool.* Having or forming an umbel 1870. So **U·mbellated** *ppl. a.* (in botanical senses) 1676. **U·mbellately** *adv.*

Umbellifer (ʊmbe·lifəɹ). 1718. [mod.L.; see UMBELLIFEROUS.] *Bot.* An umbelliferous plant.

Umbelliferone (ʊmbĕli·fĕroun). 1868. [f. prec. + -ONE.] *Chem.* A colourless, tasteless, crystalline substance obtained from mezereon bark, and, by distillation, from various umbellifers.

Umbelliferous (ʊmbĕli·fĕrəs), *a.* 1662. [f. mod.L. *umbellifer*; see UMBELLA and -FEROUS.] 1. *Bot.* Bearing umbellate flowers; of the family *Umbelliferæ*. 2. Produced by umbelliferous plants 1753.

Umbellule (ʊmbe·lyul). 1793. [ad. mod. L. *umbellula*, f. UMBELLA; see -ULE.] *Bot.* A partial or secondary umbel.

U·mber, *sb.*[1] ME. [a. OF. *umbre* or ad. L. *umbra* shade.] 1. Shade. Now *dial.* †b. The shadow of the pointer on a sun-dial –1400. †2. *Under the u. of*, on pretence of –1518. †3. A visor; = UMBRERE. –1616.

1. *fig.* Vnder the vmbre and shadowe of the noble protection of our moost dradde souerayn CAXTON.

Umber (ʊ·mbəɹ), *sb.*[2] 1496. [a. OF. *umbre*, or ad. L. *umbra* UMBRA [2].] = GRAYLING.

U·mber, *sb.*[3] 1568. [ad. F. (*terre d'*)*ombre* or It. (*terra di*) *ombra*, either = L. *umbra* UMBER *sb.*[1] or from L. *Umbra*, fem. of *Umber* Umbrian (cf. *Umbrica creta*, Pliny).] 1. A brown earth used as a pigment, or its colour. b. *Burnt u.*, a special preparation of the pigment, redder in colour 1650. 2. Any of various moths 1832. 3. *attrib.* or *adj.* U.-coloured 1802.

1. Ile put my selfe in poore and meane attire, And with a kinde of vmber smirch my face SHAKS. b. To crumble burnt u. with a dry brush for foliage and foreground RUSKIN. 3. The black woods—black, or with a faint u. shadow running through them 1866. Hence **U·mbery** *a.* umber-coloured, dark brown.

U·mber, *v.* 1610. [f. UMBER *sb.*[3]] *trans.* To stain or paint with umber; to colour dark brown. So **U·mbered** *ppl. a.* 1599.

Umbethi·nk, un-, *v. Obs.* exc. *dial.* ME. [See UM- and BETHINK.] †1. *trans.* To think about, consider –1501. 2. *refl.* To bethink oneself ME.

2. They'll prize what I leave 'em if I could only onbethink me what they would like MRS. GASKELL.

Umbilic (ʊmbi·lik). 1607. [ad. L. UMBILICUS, related to Gr. ὀμφαλός; see NAVEL.] †1. The centre –1638. 2. *Geom.* A point on a (curved) surface at which all the curvatures are equal 1843.

Umbilical (ʊmbi·likăl, ʊmbilǝi·kăl), *a.* 1541. [ad. med.L. *umbilicalis*, f. *umbilicus*; see prec.] 1. *Anat., Path., Med.* Of, affecting, proceeding from, or applied to the navel. b. Of descent: By the female side, uterine 1888. 2. *U. cord*: a. The flexible string attaching the fœtus to the placenta 1753. b. *Bot.* The peduncle attaching a seed to the placenta 1731. 3. *Conch.* That has, or forms, an umbilicus 1755. 4. *Geom.* Of or forming an umbilicus 1728. 5. Occupying a central position 1742.

1. The bloodvessels that go to the placenta..are plainly seen issuing from the navel (being therefore called the u. vessels) GOLDSMITH. 2. a. *fig.* He could never break the u. cord which held him to nature EMERSON. 5. The Chapter-house is large, supported, as to its arched Roof, by one u. pillar 1742. Hence **Umbi·lically** *adv.*

Umbi·licar, *a.* 1843. [f. UMBILICUS + -AR.] *Geom.* Of or belonging to the umbilicus.

Umbilicate (ʊmbi·likĕt), *a.* 1698. [ad. L. *umbilicatus*, f. UMBILICUS.] Navel-shaped; having a navel-like depression. So **Umbi·licated** *a.* 1698.

Umbilication (ʊmbilikēⁱ·ʃən). [f. next + -ATION.] *Path.* A central depression at the top of a pock or other vesicle; the condition of being so depressed.

Umbilicus (ʊmbilǝi·kŏs, -bi·likŏs). *Pl.* -ici (-ǝi·sǝi, -isǝi). 1704. [L.; see UMBILIC.] 1. *Anat.* The navel 1799. b. *Bot.* The part of a seed by which it is attached to the placenta 1837. c. *transf.* The central point 1897. 2. *Geom.* †a. A focus –1728. b. A point in a surface through which all its lines of curvature pass 1841. 3. A navel-shaped depression. (Chiefly *Bot., Ent., Zool.*, etc.) 1809.

1. c. Killare.., formerly regarded as the u. of Ireland 1897. 2. b. To determine the number of umbilici on a surface of the nth degree 1863. 3. The u. is small or obsolete in the typical nautili 1851.

Umbles (ʊ·mb'lz). late ME. [var. of NUMBLES.] 1. The edible inward parts of an animal, usu. of a deer. 2. attrib. in *umble-pie* (cf. HUMBLE PIE) 1663.

1. Fine, daintie, and tender bodies, as..Umbles, Chickens, Calves feete, or any other good thing 1616. 2. Mrs. Turner..did bring us an umble pie hot out of her oven PEPYS.

‖**Umbo** (ʊ·mbo). *Pl.* **umbones** (ʊmbōu·nīz), umbos. 1721. [L., = shield-boss, knob.] 1. The boss in or near the centre of a shield, sometimes pointed. 2. A round or conical projection from a surface 1753. b. *Conch., Ent.*, etc. Applied to protuberant parts or prominences 1822. 3. *Path.* A central patch in the affected area in skin diseases 1822. 4. *Anat.* The deepest point in the concavity of the tympanic membrane of the ear 1877. So **Umbonal** (ʊ·mbonăl) *a.* of, situated near, or forming an u. **U·mbonate** *a.* having an u. (chiefly *Bot.*).

‖**Umbra**[1] (ʊ·mbră). *Pl.* **-bræ** (-brī). 1599. [L.; see UMBER *sb.*[1]] 1. The shade, ghost, or spirit of one dead. 2. An uninvited guest accompanying an invited one 1696. 3. *Astr.* a. The earth's or moon's shadow in an eclipse; now *spec.* the complete shadow as dist. from the penumbra 1661. b. In sun-spots: The darker part (formerly called *nucleus*) as opposed to the lighter penumbra (formerly *umbra*) 1788. 4. *Alg.* A symbol that must be paired with another to denote a quantity 1851.

1. The *umbræ* or ghosts of some three or four playes, departed a dozen yeeres since B. JONS. 2. Most of the guests their umbra's brought 1724.

‖**U·mbra**[2]. *rare.* 1610. [L., perh. same word as prec.] 1. The grayling. 2. A sciænoid fish of the genus *Umbrina* 1753.

Umbrage (ʊ·mbrėdʒ), *sb.* late ME. Also †om-. [a. OF. *umbrage, ombrage*:—L. *umbraticum, -us*, f. *umbra* shadow.] †1. Shade, shadow –1763. 2. *spec.* The shade of trees; the foliage affording it 1540. 3. A shadowy appearance, semblance, hint, or trace (usu. *of*). Now *rare.* 1604. †4. A suspicion or doubt; an inkling *of* something; a ground for suspicion –1772. †5. Shelter, protection –1776. †6. A pretext; a false show –1735. †7. *To be* or *stand in u.*, to be in disfavour –1649. 8. Displeasure, offence, resentment; esp. in *to give u.* (*to*), *take u.* (*at*) 1620.

1. The Sun setting that Evening without any cloudy u. 1655. [To] live..under the Badge and U. of Ignominy and Shame 1727. 2. Where highest Woods impenetrable To Starr or Sun-light, spread thir u. broad MILT. By flowering u. shaded THOMSON. At the foot of some tree of friendly u. C. BRONTË. *fig.* The light of law was for a time obscured by the thick u. of novel facts TYNDALL. 3. To avoid even the umbrages of suspicion 1668. Jöys angelical..are all but a manifold u. of the one joy of God 1856. 4. I say iust feare,..not out of vmbrages, light iealousnesse, apprehensions a farre off, but out of cleare foresight of imminent danger BACON. But there is not the least u. for such a conjecture to be found in the scripture 1737. 5. Having the u. of the Editor's character to screen myself behind RICHARDSON. 6. Truth will appear from under all the false glosses and umbrages that men may draw over it 1693. To form a Party, and maintain a Struggle for personal Power, under the Pretence and U. of Principle BOLINGBROKE. 7. He knew Sir James stood in some u. with the King DRUMM. OF HAWTH. 8. Fearing the captain and his lady would take u., and leave his carriage SMOLLETT. Unless my pacific disposition was displeasing, nothing else could have given u. WASHINGTON.

U·mbrage, *v.* 1647. [f. prec., or ad. F. *ombrag(i)er*, †*umbrag(i)er*, f. *ombrage*; see prec.] 1. *trans.* To shade; also *fig.* to put in the shade. 2. To offend, displease (*rare*) 1894.

1. A ridge or hillock heavily umbraged with the rounded foliage of evergreen oaks 1888. 2. May I help myself to wine without umbraging you STEVENSON.

Umbrageous (ʊmbrēⁱ·dʒəs), *a.* 1587. [ad. F. *ombrageux*, f. *ombrage* UMBRAGE; or directly f. UMBRAGE *sb.* + -OUS] 1. Shady; giving or abounding in shade. b. Of shade: Caused by thick foliage 1830. 2. Of persons or disposition: Suspicious, jealous; apt to take offence 1601. †3. Obscure, dubious –1651.

1. Where the grove with leaves u. bends POPE. The u. loveliness of the surrounding country SHELLEY. 2. The people are idle, haughty, u., fiery, quarrelsome 1874. 3. We blesse God for the light they had, though u. and clouded 1651. Hence **Umbra·geous-ly** *adv.*, **-ness.**

Umbral (ʊ·mbrăl), *a.* 1851. [f. UMBRA[1] + -AL.] 1. *Alg.* Based on or consisting of umbræ. 2. *Astr.* Of the umbra of sun-spots or eclipses 1867. Hence **U·mbrally** *adv.*

Umbrated (ʊ·mbrēⁱtėd), *a.* 1486. [f. ppl. stem of L. *umbrare* (f. *umbra* UMBRA[1]) + -ED.] *Her.* Drawn merely in outline so that the field shows through.

Umbratic (ʊmbræ·tik), *a. rare.* 1677. [ad. L. *umbraticus*, f. *umbra* shade.] 1. = next 2. 2. = UMBRATILE *a.* 1. 1839.

†**Umbra·tical**, *a.* 1633. [f. as prec. + -AL.] 1. = next, A. 1. –1656. 2. That serves as a shadow or imperfect representation of something –1683. 3. Glozing, deceptive –1662.

Umbratile (ʊ·mbrătǝil, -til), *a.* (*sb.*). 1592 [ad. L. *umbratilis* keeping in the shade, f. *umbra* shade.] A. *adj.* 1. Secluded, in retirement, within doors; academic or recluse; not public or practical. 2. Of or like a shadow or shadows 1632. b. Shadowy, unsubstantial, unreal. Now *rare* or *Obs.* 1647. 3. Giving shade 1659.

1. A time of peace and security tends to foster an u. and academic science 1845. 3. His hat was u., as of the Pilgrim Fathers BLACKMORE.

B. *sb.* One who spends his time in the shade 1888.

Many thus are umbratiles in the booths, and give themselves almost to a perpetual slumber DOUGHTY.

Umbre (ʊ·mbəɹ). Also **umber.** 1773. [ad. L. *umbra* or F. *ombre* shade.] An African bird (*Scopus umbretta*) with deep-brown plumage; the hammer-head or African crow.

Umbrella (ʊmbre·lă). 1609. [ad. It. *ombrella*, f. *ombra*:—L. *umbra* shade.] 1. A large sunshade or parasol 1610. b. As an Oriental or African symbol of dignity 1653. 2. A similar defence against rain, now usu. of silk, alpaca, etc., fastened on slender ribs which are attached radially to a stick and can be readily raised so as to form a circular arched canopy 1634. †3. *fig.* A means of shelter or protection; a screen or disguise –1734. 4. Anything serving as protection from the sun, rain, etc. 1654. 5. An umbrella-shaped structure 1680. b. *Bot.* A part of a plant resembling an umbrella 1658. c. *Zool.* The gelatinous disk or bell-shaped structure of a jelly-fish 1834. d. *Conch.* A gasteropod of the genus *Umbrella*; the part of the shell resembling an open umbrella 1841.

1. The street was in a blaze with scarlet umbrellas 1860. 2. She always carried her stout little u. 1882.

attrib. and *Comb.*, as *u.-case, frame, -stand*; in plant-names, denoting u.-shaped, as *u.-acacia, -pine*; in names of birds, etc., as *u.-ant, -bird, -shell*; also, **u. roof,** one arched like an umbrella; **u. sail,** a kind that can be quickly set or furled; **-tree,** the *Magnolia tripetala* and other American magnolias, also various other trees of u.-like growth of leaves. Hence **Umbrellaed, -la'd** (-e·lăd) *ppl. a.* **Umbre·llaless** *a.* **Umbre·lla-like** *a.*

†**U·mbrere.** late ME. [app. a. AF. **umbrere*, f. *umbre* shade.] The visor of a helmet –1655.

Umbre·tte. 1884. [ad. mod.L. *umbretta* or F. *ombrette.*] = UMBRE.

Umbrian (ʊ·mbriăn), *a.* and *sb.* 1601. [f. L. *Umbr-, Umber* or *Umbria* + -(I)AN.] A. *adj.* 1. Of ancient Umbria, its people or language. 2. Of mediæval or modern Umbria. *U. School*, the fifteenth-century school of painting developed in Umbria. 1841. B. *sb.* 1. An inhabitant of Umbria, a province of central Italy; *esp.* one of the Italic race anciently inhabiting this district 1601. 2. The language of ancient Umbria 1858.

Umbriferous (ʊmbri·fĕrəs), *a.* 1616. [f. L. *umbrifer* (f. *umbra* shade) + -OUS.] Giving shade; umbrageous.

Umbril (ʊ·mbril). *Hist.* 1470. [Earlier *umbrel*, a. OF. *ombrel* shade.] A visor.

‖**Umbrina** (ʊmbrǝi·nă). 1834. [mod.L., a. Sp., It. *umbrina*, f. *umbra* UMBER *sb.*[2]] *Zool.* A fish of the genus *Umbrina*, chiefly found in warm seas.

Umbro- (ʊ·mbro), used as comb. f. L. *Umbr-, Umber* Umbrian.

Umbrose (vmbrōᵘ·s), *a.* *rare.* late ME. [ad. L. *umbrosus*, f. *umbra* shade.] Shady, giving shade; †dusky.

Umbrous (v·mbrəs), *a.* 1480. [ad. F. *ombreux*, or as prec.] In the shade; shady, shadowed.

Umiak, umyak, var. ff. OOMIAK.

‖**Umlaut** (u·mlaut). 1852. [G., f. *um* about + *laut* sound.] *Philol.* A change in the sound of a vowel produced by partial assimilation to an adjacent sound (usu. that of a vowel or semivowel in the following syllable); = MUTATION 3. Hence **U·mlauted** *a.* modified by u.

Umph (mh), *int.* (*sb.*, *v.*). 1568. [Imitative.] = HUMPH.

Umpirage (v·mpəirėdʒ). 1490. [f. next + -AGE.] The act of umpiring; the office or power of an umpire; arbitration.

Submission of the suit to arbitration or u. shall be made a rule BLACKSTONE.

Umpire (v·mpəiəɪ), *sb.* late ME. [Later form of late ME. †*noumpere*, a. OF. *nonper*, f. *non-* NON- + *per*, *pair* PEER by transference of the *n-* to the indefinite article, as in *adder*, *apron*.] **1.** One who decides between contending parties, and whose decision is to be accepted as final; an arbitrator. **b.** *transf.* Something that serves to decide a matter 1583. **2.** *Law.* A third person appointed to decide between arbitrators who cannot agree 1464. **3.** In games a person appointed to see that rules are kept and to decide all doubtful points. (Cf. REFEREE *sb.* 3.) 1714.

1. The Lords in Parliament tooke an Oath to be indifferent umpiers betweene the Bishop and Duke 1641. **b.** The judgment, u. in the strife That grace and nature have to wage through life COWPER. **2.** If they [*sc.* the arbitrators] do not agree, it is usual to add, that another person be called in as u. BLACKSTONE. **3.** [Football], Mr. Walker officiated as referee, and Messrs. Davies and Bryan as umpires 1884. Hence **U·mpireship**, the office of u. 1565. **U·mpiress**, a female u.

U·mpire, *v.* 1592. [f. prec.] †**1.** *trans.* To appoint (a person to an office) in virtue of being 'umpire'. BACON. †**b.** To act as umpire between (persons) –1657. **2.** To settle (a matter) as umpire 1611. **b.** *transf.* Of things 1609. **3.** *spec.* To supervise (games, etc.) as umpire 1861. **4.** *intr.* To act as umpire. Also const. *between*. 1613. Hence **U·mpiring** *vbl. sb.* the action of acting as an u., esp. in games.

Umpty (v·mᵖti). orig. *Army slang.* 1917. [Signallers' slang for 'dash', used in reading morse.] An indefinite (fairly large) number. Hence **Umptee·n** (also *umteen*) [see -TEEN], any (considerable) number. So **Um(p)tee·nth** *a.* **U·mptieth** *a.*

[Cf. A charming Miss of -teen summers 1887.]

Umquhile, umwhile (v·mhwəil), *adv.* and *a.* In later use *Sc.* Now *Obs.* or *arch.* ME. [repr. OE. *ymb hwīle*, with substitution of UM- for *ymb*.] **A.** *adv.* †**1.** At times, sometimes –1568. **2.** At some previous time, formerly. late ME. †**3.** At some later time, by-and-by –1513.

1. Vmquhill in plesure and prosperitie, Vmquhill in pane and greit penuritie 1535. **2.** I, Henrie Stewart, vmquhile of Scotland King 1567.

B. *adj.* Former, late. **a.** Of persons; *esp.* = now deceased. late ME. **b.** Of things (*rare*) 1548.

a. The estate which devolved on this unhappy woman by a settlement of her umwhile husband SCOTT. **b.** I saw my u. house existing as a bit of dingy wall 1854.

Un, 'un [1], *pers. pron.*, later dial. f. acc. HIN, HINE him.

Un, 'un [2], dial. f. ONE *pron.* VI. 1, 2.

Un-, *prefix* [1], expressing negation, repr. OS., OHG., Goth. *un-*, ON. *ú-*, *ó-*, OE. *un-*, corresp. to OIr. *in-*, *an-*, L. *in-* (see IN-), Gr. ἀν-, ἀ- (see A-, AN-), Skr. *an-*, *a-*, Indo-Eur. **n̥*, ablaut-variant of *ne* not. The prefix has been very extensively used in English as in other Germanic langs., and is now (as compared with IN-) the one which can be used with the greatest freedom in new formations.

The form of the prefix indicates that it was orig. unstressed, and normally it is still so. There is a tendency, however, to give stress to it in rare or casual formations, and esp. when the negation or contrast implied is emphasized.

The following sections enumerate the usual types of current formations. Since the actual number of compounds of *un-* is very great and their possible number indefinite, many unimportant and self-explanatory ones are omitted from the series of Main words, and others are entered in their alphabetical places, but, instead of a definition, are furnished with a reference to the section of this article under which the particular type of formation is explained; such words will usu. have appended to them the earliest (or latest, if the word is obsolete) known date of their use, or the name of the first author known to have used them.

1. *Un-* is freely prefixed to adjectives of all kinds, except where a Latin form in *in-* (*il-*, *im-*, etc.) has established itself by general preference. The two forms may, however, co-exist, and occas. a new formation with *un-* has been introduced when that with *in-* has acquired a connotation which it is sought to avoid. The form with *un-* is then purely negative, while the other may have rather a positive than a negative implication, e.g. *unmoral*, *immoral*. There is considerable restriction in the use of *un-* with short simple adjs. of native origin, the negative of these being naturally supplied by another simple word of an opposite signification; thus such forms as *unbroad*, *undeep*, *unglad*, *unfew*, *ungood*, *unstrong*, *unwhole* are now rarely found; on the other hand, derivative forms in *-able*, *-al*, *-ant*, *-ar*, *-ary*, *-ent*, *-ful*, *-ic(al*, *-ish*, *-ive*, *-like*, *-ly*, *-ous*, *-y*, etc., are too numerous to be recorded. (The unusual types *uncome-at-able* (1694), *unget-at-able* (1862) are later in date than the corresponding positive forms.) **2.** The prefixing of *un-* to pa. pples., common in OE. and revived in ME., was subsequently extended until it became the commonest of all uses of the prefix. **b.** Participial formations (and adjs. in *-able*) with *un-* frequently have an attached absol. prep. (usu. hyphened) as in *uncalled-for*, *unheard-of*, *unlivable-with*, *unwished-for*. Where ambiguity is not anticipated, the prep. may be dropped, as *unrepented* for *unrepented-of*. **3.** Adj. forms. in *-ed*, derived from sbs., as *unbearded*, *unbodied*. The usual sense is 'not provided or furnished with', but occas. 'not effected by', 'not treated with'. Many such compounds may be alternatively analysed as f. *un* + pa. pple. of the related vb., e.g. *uncarpeted*, *unfeathered*. **4.** The use of *un-* with pres. pples. is now frequent, and has given rise to a large number of permanent words, such as *unbecoming*, *unbending*, *unchanging*, *unfailing*, *unseeing*, *untiring*, *unwilling*. **5.** In OE. advb. formations in *-līce* were frequent. Few of them survived in ME., but additions were gradually made, and the use of *un-* with *-ly* later became common. In such formations either the suffix *-ly* is added to an existing word compounded with *un-*, or *un-* is prefixed to an already existing adv. in *-ly*. This distinction is occas. significant: e.g. *unprofessionally* formed from *unprofessional* means 'in a manner contrary to professional rules or etiquette'; formed from *professionally*, it means 'not in a professional manner or capacity'. **6.** The OE. use of *un-* with sbs. survived in ME., and many new formations of this type were then and subseq. introduced; these have been mainly words of abstract meaning, as *unchastity*, *unreality*, *unsociability*. In these the formation may not be ascertainable; e.g. *unchastity* may be f. *un-* + *chastity*, or f. *unchaste* + *-ity*. **b.** The prefixing of *un-* to nouns used attrib. is rare, and usu. joc.; e.g. *uncountry gentleman* (Byron). **7.** Verbs with prefixed *un-* have never been very numerous, and are now rare. **8.** In OE. there are a few instances of *un-* with vbl. sbs. in *-ung*; none of these survive in ME., and new forms in *-ing* are rare.

Un-, *prefix* [2], expressing reversal or deprivation, repr. OE. *un-*, *on-*, = OS. *ant-*, OHG. *ant-*, *int-*, Goth. *and-*, orig. identical with AND-.

1. In OE. most of the forms with *un-* have for their second part a simple vb., as *unbindan*, *undon*, and the prefix denotes a reversal of the action of the verb. Additions to this type of formation have been freely made at all subsequent periods. **2.** A small number of OE. verbs in *un-* imply removal or deprivation; the type remains rare in ME., but at a later date it became more frequent and is now common. **b.** In some vbs. *un-* implies freeing or releasing from something. This type has also become common in later use. **3.** The use of *un-* to denote the removal or extraction of a person or thing from a place or receptacle, as in *unbody*, *unearth*, *unhouse*, occurs in the 14th c., and becomes prominent at the beginning of the 17th. In some instances the sense passes into that of releasing from confinement, as in *uncage*, or of revealing to others, as in *unbosom*. **4.** From the 16th century formations in which *un-* expresses the fact or process of depriving a person or thing of a certain quality or property become frequent. **a.** When the formation has an adj. base, the adj. may be used in its simple form, with the suffix *-en*. **b.** Sbs. are similarly employed without ending. **c.** From sbs. (rarely from adjs.) there are numerous formations in *-(i)fy*, and from both sbs. and adjs. in *-ize*. Other endings, as *-ate*, are less frequent. **5.** The OE. vbs. in *un-* are almost always trans., and this is still the prevailing use. Intr. uses of some common words are found in ME., and later the usage increases to some extent, but is chiefly confined to words having some currency. **6.** Vbl. sbs., ppl. adjs., and agent-nouns from vbs. in *un-* begin to appear in the 14th c., and later become common. **7.** The redundant use of *un-* is rare, but occurs in OE. *unlīesan* and ME. *unloose*, which still survives. Later instances are *unbare*, *unsolve*, *unstrip*.

Una (yū·nă). 1878. [Name of the first boat of the kind brought from America to England in 1853.] A catboat. Also *attrib.*

Unaba·shable *a.* [UN-[1] 2] 1848. **Unaba·shed** *ppl. a.* [UN-[1] 2] 1571, **-ly** *adv.* **Unaba·ted** *ppl. a.* [UN-[1] 2] 1611, **-ly** *adv.* **Unaba·ting** *ppl. a.* [UN-[1] 4] 1768, **-ly** *adv.* **Unabbre·viated** *ppl. a.* [UN-[1] 2] 1805. **Unabi·ding** *ppl. a.* [UN-[1] 4] late ME., **-ly** *adv.*

Unable (vnē·b'l), *a.* late ME. [f. UN-[1] 1 + ABLE *a.*, after F. *inhabile* or L. *inhabilis*.] **1.** Not able *to* do something specified (chiefly of persons). **b.** Const. *for* or *to* (with sbs.) 1456. **2.** Unequal to the task or need, incompetent, inefficient. Somewhat *arch.* late ME. **3.** Physically weak, feeble. Now *Sc.* 1577.

1. b. Agrippa they accounted . . vnable for so great a charge 1598. **2.** No hopes of succour from such u. protectors GOLDSM. **3.** As little and as vnable as a child BURTON. Hence **Una·bly** *adv.* (now *rare* or *Obs.*).

Unabri·dged, *ppl. a.* 1599. [UN-[1] 2.] Not abridged; now usu. of literary works.

Una·brogated *ppl. a.* [UN-[1] 2] 1535. **Unabso·lved** *ppl. a.* [UN-[1] 2] 1611. **Unabso·rbed** *ppl. a.* [UN-[1] 2] 1766. **Unabsu·rd** *a.* [UN-[1] 1] 1742.

Unabu·sed, *ppl. a.* 1661. [UN-[1] 2.] **1.** Not deceived or misled. **2.** Not misused or wrongly employed 1864.

2. Human greatness is, when u., a majestic sight PUSEY.

Unacade·mic *a.* [UN-[1] 1] 1844. **Unacade·mical** *a.* [UN-[1] 1] 1840. **Unacce·nted** *ppl. a.* [UN-[1] 2] 1598. **Unacce·ntuated** *ppl. a.* [UN-[1] 2] 1716. **Unacce·ptable** *a.* [UN-[1] 1] 1483, **-ness.** **Unacce·ptably** *adv.* **Unacce·ptance** [UN-[1] 6] 1865. **Unacce·pted** *ppl. a.* [UN-[1] 2] 1612. **Unacce·ssory** *a.* [UN-[1] 1] 1660. **Unaccli·mated** *ppl. a.* [UN-[1] 2] 1846. **Unaccli·matized** *ppl. a.* [UN-[1] 2] 1863. **Unacco·mmodated** *ppl. a.* [UN-[1] 2] 1605. **Unacco·mmodating** *ppl. a.* [UN-[1] 4] 1790.

Unacco·mpanied, *ppl. a.* 1545. [UN-[1] 2.] **1.** Not accompanied or attended (*by* or *with*). **2.** *Mus.* With no instrumental accompaniment 1818.

Unacco·mplished, *ppl. a.* 1525. [UN-[1] 2.] **1.** Not achieved; not completed. **2.** Lacking accomplishments 1729.

1. All th' unaccomplisht works of Natures hand, Abortive, monstrous, or unkindly mixt MILT. So **Unacco·mplishment** MILT.

Unacco·rded, *a.* 1645. [UN-[1] 2.] Not agreed upon; not bestowed.

Unaccou·ntable, *a.* and *sb.* 1643. [UN-[1] 1.] **A.** *adj.* **1.** Impossible or difficult to account for; inexplicable, puzzling; of a strange or puzzling disposition. **2.** Not liable to be called to account; irresponsible 1649. **B.** *sb.* An unaccountable person, thing, or event 1748.

1. The u. and secret reasons of disaffection between man and wife MILTON. With the Character of an odd u. Fellow ADDISON. **2.** The Acknowledgment of his Supream and U. Power 1695. Hence **Unaccounta·bility.** **Unaccou·ntableness.** **Unaccou·ntably** *adv.*

Unaccou·nted, *ppl. a.* 1799. [UN-[1] 2, 2 b.] Not accounted *for*; of which no account is given.

Unaccre·dited *ppl. a.* [UN-[1] 2] 1828. **Unaccu·rsed, -st,** *ppl. a.* [UN-[1] 2] 1674. **Unaccu·sable** *a.* [UN-[1] 1] 1582, **-bly** *adv.* **Unaccu·sed** *ppl. a.* [UN-[1] 2] 1508.

Unaccu·stomed, *ppl. a.* 1526. [UN-[1] 2.] **1.** Not customary, unfamiliar, unusual. **2.** Not used *to* something, not wont *to* do something 1611. **b.** *attrib.* or *absol.*, without const. 1653.

1. The strange room and its u. objects DICKENS. **2. b.** Phlebotomy . . may prove dangerous to the u. 1653. Hence **Unaccu·stomedness.**

Unachie·vable *a.* [UN-[1] 1] 1657. **Unachie·ved** *ppl. a.* [UN-[1] 2] 1603. **Una·ching** *ppl. a.* [UN-[1] 4] SHAKS. **Unacknow·ledged** *ppl. a.* [UN-[1] 2] 1583. **Unacknow·ledging** *ppl.*

a. [UN-¹ 4] 1611. Unacquai·nt *a. Sc.* [UN-¹ 1] 1587. Unacquai·ntance [UN-¹ 6] 1598.

Unacquai·nted, *ppl. a.* 1529. [UN-¹ 2.] †1. Not personally known (to one) -1607. b. Of things: Unfamiliar, unknown, strange -1672. 2. Not acquainted *with* (= ignorant of) something 1563. †b. Const. *in, of, to* -1805. c. Inexperienced, ignorant 1581. 3. Not acquainted *with* another person; not mutually acquainted, not known to each other 1633.

2. b. Being very u. in the style and form of dedications SWIFT. Hence **Unacquai·ntedness.**

Unacqui·red, *ppl. a.* 1653. [UN-¹ 2.] 1. Not acquired; unattained (*rare*). 2. Not obtained from without; innate, native 1793.

Una·ctable, *a.* 1810. [UN-¹ 1.] That cannot be acted; unsuitable for dramatic representation.

Una·cted, *ppl. a.* 1593. [UN-¹ 2.] 1. Not carried out in action; not done. 2. *Unacted* (*up*)*on*: not affected or influenced 1794. 3. Of a play, etc.: Not performed on the stage.

1. A thought vnacted SHAKS. My sons lament..U. crimes, and follies not their own 1706. U. desires 1789. U. upon by any extraneous influence 1825.

†**Una·ctive** *a.* [UN-¹ 1] -1777, -ly *adv.* -1693, -ness, -1683. †**Unacti·vity** [UN-¹ 6] -1740. **Una·ctuated** *ppl. a.* [UN-¹ 2] 1661. **Unadaptabi·lity** [UN-¹ 6] 1829. **Unada·ptable** *a.* [UN-¹ 1] 1882. **Unada·pted** *ppl. a.* [UN-¹ 2] 1805. **Unaddi·cted** *ppl. a.* [UN-¹ 2] 1583. **Unaddre·ssed** *ppl. a.* [UN-¹ 2] 1885.

Unade·pt, *sb.* and *a.* 1742. [UN-¹ 6, 1.] (One who is) not (an) adept.

Unadjou·rned *ppl. a.* [UN-¹ 2] 1648. **Unadju·sted** *ppl. a.* [UN-¹ 2] JOHNSON. **Unadmi·nistered** *ppl. a.* [UN-¹ 2] 1590. **Unadmi·red** *ppl. a.* [UN-¹ 2] 1707. **Unadmi·ring** *ppl. a.* [UN-¹ 4] CARLYLE, -ly *adv.* **Unadmi·tted** *ppl. a.* [UN-¹ 2] 1616. **Unadmo·nished** *ppl. a.* [UN-¹ 2] 1591. **Unado·pted** *ppl. a.* [UN-¹ 2] MILT. **Unado·rned** *ppl. a.* [UN-¹ 2] MILT., -ly *adv.*, -ness. **Unadu·lterate** *ppl. a.* [UN-¹ 2] 1664, -ly *adv.* **Unadu·lterated** *ppl. a.* [UN-¹ 2] ADDISON, -ly *adv.* **Unadva·nced** *ppl. a.* [UN-¹ 2] late ME. **Unadve·nturous** *a.* [UN-¹ 1] MILT., -ly *adv.*, -ness.

Una·dvertised, *ppl. a.* 1450. [UN-¹ 2.] †1. Not warned or made aware; not informed *of* -1652. 2. Not announced or made known 1864.

Unadvi·sable, *a.* 1673. [UN-¹ 1.] 1. That cannot or will not be advised. 2. Inexpedient, inadvisable 1758. Hence **Unadvi·sably** *adv.*

Unadvi·sed, *ppl. a.* late ME. [UN-¹ 2.] 1. Of acts, words, etc.: Done or spoken, without due consideration; rash. 2. Of persons, disposition, etc.: Indiscreet, thoughtless, hasty. late ME. b. Not having consulted *with* another; not having been consulted *with* 1579. 3. Lacking advice or advisers 1851.

1. An unskilful or u. treatment 1833. 2. b. While the Parlament of England sate unadvis'd with MILT. Hence **Unadvi·sed-ly** *adv.* ME., -ness.

Unæsthe·tic *a.* [UN-¹ 1] 1832. **Unafea·r(e)d,** *a. arch.* [UN-¹ 2] 1550. **Una·ffable** *a.* [UN-¹ 1] 1603.

Unaffe·cted, *ppl. a.* 1586. [UN-¹ 2.] 1. Not simulated; genuine, sincere 1592. b. Of persons, speech, bearing, etc.: Free from affectation; simple, natural; not artificial or pretentious 1598. c. Sincere, honest (in some respect) 1796. 2. Not influenced or moved; untouched 1586. b. Not attacked by disease or illness 1797. 3. Not acted upon or altered *by* some agent or influence 1830.

1. A Chearfulness, the constant Companion of u. Virtue STEELE. b. The letters..lively, entertaining, and u. SCOTT. c. An u. admirer 1796. 2. It is impossible any reader, however stoical, can remain u. 1803. Hence **Unaffe·cted-ly** *adv.*, -ness.

Unaffe·cting *ppl. a.* [UN-¹ 4] 1602. **Unaffe·ctionate** *a.* [UN-¹ 1] 1588, -ly *adv.* **Unaffi·liated** *ppl. a.* [UN-¹ 2] 1849. **Unaffli·cted** *ppl. a.* [UN-¹ 2] 1599. **Unaffri·ghted** *ppl. a.* [UN-¹ 2] MARLOWE, -ly *adv.* **Unaffro·nted** *ppl. a.* [UN-¹ 2] 1753. **Unafrai·d** *a.* [UN-¹ 1] late ME. **Una·geing** *ppl. a.* [UN-¹ 4] 1860. **Una·gitated** *ppl. a.* [UN-¹ 2] 1638, -ly *adv.*

Unagree·able, *a.* Now *rare.* late ME. [UN-¹ 1]. 1. Not agreeable or pleasing; not to one's liking; disagreeable. †2. Unconformable *to*; incongruous *with* -1702.

1. Mr. M. was not u., though nothing seemed to go right with him JANE AUSTEN. 2. Adventrous work, yet to thy power and mine Not u. MILTON. Hence **Unagree·ably** *adv.*

Unagree·d *ppl. a.* [UN-¹ 2] 1525. **Unai·dable** *a.* [UN-¹ 1] SHAKS. **Unai·ded** *ppl. a.* [UN-¹ 2] MILT. **Unai·med** *ppl. a.* [UN-¹ 2] 1648. **Unai·red** *ppl. a.* [UN-¹ 2] 1616.

Unal (yū·năl), *a. rare.* 1883. [f. L. *unus* one + -AL.] Based on unity; single; that is one only.

Unala·rmed *ppl. a.* [UN-¹ 2] 1756. **Unala·rming** *a.* [UN-¹ 4] 1760. **Una·lienable** *a.* [UN-¹ 1] 1611, -bly *adv.* **Una·lienated** *ppl. a.* [UN-¹ 2] 1798.

Unalist (yū·nălist). *rare.* 1743. [f. UNAL *a.* + -IST; cf. *pluralist.*] A holder of only one benefice.

Unali·ve *a.* [UN-¹ 1] 1828. **Unallay·ed** *ppl. a.* [UN-¹ 2] 1519. **Unalle·viated** *ppl. a.* [UN-¹ 2] 1750. **Unalli·able** *a.* [UN-¹ 1] 1740.

Unallie·d, *ppl. a.* 1663. [UN-¹ 2.] 1. Not allied or related (*to*). 2. Having no ally or allies 1797.

Unallow·able *a.* [UN-¹ 1] 1560. **Unallow·ed** *ppl. a.* [UN-¹ 2] 1632. **Unalloy·ed** *ppl. a.* [UN-¹ 2] 1672. **Unallu·ring** *a.* [UN-¹ 4] 1775.

Una·lphabeted, *ppl. a.* 1799. [UN-¹ 2; after L. *analphabetus* ANALPHABET.] Not knowing the alphabet, illiterate.

Unalterabi·lity [UN-¹ 6] 1847. **Una·lterable** *a.* [UN-¹ 1] 1611. **Una·lterably** *adv.* 1643. **Una·ltered** *ppl. a.* [UN-¹ 2] 1551. **Unama·zed** *ppl. a.* [UN-¹ 2] 1598. **Unambi·guous** *a.* [UN-¹ 1] CHESTERF., -ly *adv.* **Unambi·tion** [UN-¹ 6] 1781.

Unambi·tious, *a.* 1621. [UN-¹ 1.] Not ambitious or aspiring; devoid of ambition.

Those who..pass their days in u. indolence BOSWELL. The calm delights Of u. piety WORDSW. Hence **Unambi·tiously** *adv.*, -ness.

Uname·nable *a.* [UN-¹ 1] 1771. **Uname·ndable** *a.* [UN-¹ 1] 1450. **Uname·nded** *ppl. a.* [UN-¹ 2] WYCLIF. **Un-Ame·rican** *a.* [UN-¹ 1] 1818. **Unamiabi·lity** [UN-¹ 6] 1829. **Una·miable** *a.* [UN-¹ 1] 1480, -ness, -bly *adv.* **Unamu·sed** *ppl. a.* [UN-¹ 2] YOUNG. **Unamu·sing** *a.* [UN-¹ 4] 1799, -ly *adv.* **Unanalo·gical,** *a.* [UN-¹ 1] 1755. **Unana·logous** *a.* [UN-¹ 1] 1782. **Una·nalysable** *a.* [UN-¹ 1] 1829. **Una·nalysed** *ppl. a.* [UN-¹ 2] 1668. **Unanaly·tical** *a.* [UN-¹ 1] MILL. **Una·nchor** *v.* [UN-² 2 b] 1648. **Una·nchored** *ppl. a.* [UN-¹ 2] 1651.

Unane·led, *ppl. a. arch.* 1602. [UN-¹ 2.] Not having received extreme unction.

Vnhouzzled, disappointed, vnnaneld SHAKS.

Unanimate (yunæ·nimeɪt), *v.* 1702. [f. L. *unanimis* UNANIMOUS + -ATE ³.] *trans.* To cause to be unanimous.

Unanimated (ʌnæ·nimeɪtėd), *a.* 1697. [UN-¹ 2.] 1. Not possessing life. 2. Not lively, dull 1734. 3. Not inspired *by* something 1856.

Unanimist (yunæ·nimist). 1921. [ad. F. *-iste*, f. *unanime* UNANIMOUS.] Applied to a school of French poets.

Unanimity (yunăni·mĭti). late ME. [ad. OF. *unanimite*, ad. L. *unanimitas*, f. *unanimis*, *-us*, f. *unus* one + *animus* mind.] The state or quality of being unanimous; agreement in opinion or purpose.

Unanimous (yunæ·nĭməs), *a.* 1624. [f. L. *unanimis, -us*; see prec.] 1. Of one mind, or opinion; agreed. b. Like-minded, of the same opinion. *arch.* 1637. 2. Expressing or based on general agreement or consent 1675.

1. b. Let not thine u. friend..know what thou dost 1637. Hence **Una·nimously** *adv.*

Unannea·led *ppl. a.* [UN-¹ 2] 1745. **Una·nnotated** *ppl. a.* [UN-¹ 2] 1859. **Unannou·nced** *ppl. a.* [UN-¹ 2] SCOTT. **Unannoy·ed** *ppl. a.* [UN-¹ 2] 1470. **Unanoi·nted** *a.* [UN-¹ 2] LOVELACE.

Una·nswerable, *a.* 1611. [UN-¹ 1]. †1. Not corresponding or analogous (*to*) -1674. 2. Admitting of no answer; irrefutable; insoluble 1613. 3. Unable to answer *for*; irresponsible 1884.

2. A new and u. proof BERKELEY. Embarrassing, u. questions 1894. 3. He committed the offence.. whilst..u. for his acts 1884. Hence **Una·nswerableness**, -ly *adv.*

Una·nswered *ppl. a.* [UN-¹ 2] late ME. **Unanta·gonized** *ppl. a.* [UN-¹ 2] 1862. **Unanti·cipated** *ppl. a.* [UN-¹ 2] 1779. **Una·nxious** *a.* [UN-¹ 1] 1742, -ly *adv.* **Unapologe·tic** *a.* [UN-¹ 1] 1834. **Unaposto·lic, -al** *adjs.* [UN-¹ 1] 1675, -ly *adv.* **Unappa·lled** *ppl. a.* [UN-¹ 2] 1578. †**Unappa·rel** *v. trans.* [UN-² 2] -1614. **Unappa·relled** *ppl. a.* [UN-¹ 2] BACON. **Unappa·rent** *a.* [UN-¹ 1] 1554.

Unappea·lable, *a.* 1635. [UN-¹ 1.] That cannot be appealed against (or *from*).

Unappea·ling, *ppl. a.* [UN-¹ 4] 1716. **Unappea·sable** *a.* [UN-¹ 1] 1561, -ness, -bly *adv.* **Unappea·sed** *ppl. a.* [UN-¹ 2] SHAKS. **Una·ppetizing** *ppl. a.* [UN-¹ 4] 1884. **Unapplau·ded** *ppl. a.* [UN-¹ 2] 1739. **Unapplie·d** *ppl. a.* [UN-¹ 2] 1540. **Unappoi·nted** *ppl. a.* [UN-¹ 2] 1560. **Unappre·ciated** *ppl. a.* [UN-¹ 2] 1828. **Unappre·ciative** *a.* [UN-¹ 1] 1857. **Unapprehe·nded** *ppl. a.* [UN-¹ 2] 1597. **Unapprehe·nding** *ppl. a.* [UN-¹ 4] 1794.

Unapprehe·nsive *a.* 1624. [UN-¹ 1.] 1. Not apprehensive or quick to understand, unintelligent. 2. Not afraid or anxious; not fearful *of* 1666.

1. As infants gaze at the objects which meet their eyes, in a vague u. way J. H. NEWMAN. Hence **Unapprehe·nsiveness.**

Unapproa·chable, *a.* (and *sb.*) 1581. [UN-¹ 1.] 1. Inaccessible. 2. Permitting no intimacy or confidence 1848. 3. Beyond rivalry; matchless 1831. B. as *sb.* One who or that which cannot be approached or equalled 1800.

1. All alone..in a place of almost u. seclusion SCOTT. 2. Mr. Dombey is u. by anyone DICKENS. 3. Paintings..unapproached and u. in their excellence 1856. Hence **Unapproachabi·lity. Unapproa·chableness. Unapproa·chably** *adv.*

Unappro·priate, *ppl. a.* 1767. [UN-¹ 2.] 1. Not appropriated or assigned. 2. = INAPPROPRIATE *a.* 1818.

Unappro·priated *ppl. a.* [UN-¹ 2] 1756. **Unappro·ved** *ppl. a.* [UN-¹ 2] SHAKS. **Unappro·ving** *a.* [UN-¹ 4] 1787, -ly *adv.*

Una·pt, *a.* late ME. [UN-¹ 1.] †1. Unfitted *to* do something -1736. 2. Unsuited *for* some use or purpose 1513. 3. Lacking the required qualities: †a. of persons -1680; b. of things 1588. 4. Of language, etc.: Inappropriate, ill chosen 1553. 5. Not readily tending or likely *to* do something 1587. b. Without const.: Unready, backward 1849.

1. Was neuere man ne woman yet bygete That was vnapt to suffren loues hete CHAUCER. A plot of ground u. to receive good seed 1610. 2. Such beasts..being vncleane, and vnapt for food 1608. Princes, when.. they grow u. for affairs 1648. 3. b. The u. and violent nature of the remedies 1842. 4. Your comparison is not u., sir GEO. ELIOT. 5. A mind which was u. to apprehend danger SCOTT. b. These u. scholars MILL. Hence **Una·pt-ly** *adv.*, -ness.

Una·rch *v.* [UN-² 1] 1598. **Una·rched** *a.* [UN-¹ 3] 1658.

Unarchite·ctural, *a.* 1849. [UN-¹ 1.] 1. Not in accordance with the principles of architecture. 2. Not skilled in architecture 1884.

Una·rguable *a.* [UN-¹ 1] 1881. **Una·rgued** *ppl. a.* [UN-¹ 2] B. JONS. **Unargume·ntative** *a.* [UN-¹ 1] 1722, -ly *adv.*

Una·rm, *v.* ME. [UN-² 2.] 1. *trans.* To relieve (a person) of armour; to free or strip (oneself) of armour. Also *absol.* †2. To deprive of armour or arms; to disarm -1654.

1. Vnarme, vnarme, and doe not fight to day SHAKS. 2. To u. his people of weapons, money, and all means, whereby they may resist his power RALEIGH.

Una·rmed, *ppl. a.* ME. [UN-¹ 2.] Having no armour or weapons. b. Of animals, plants, etc.: Not furnished with horns, teeth, prickles, thorns, etc. late ME c. Of things: Not provided with anything that protects, assists, or strengthens 1693.

Una·rmoured *ppl. a.* [UN-¹ 2] 1869. **Unarrai·gned** *ppl. a.* [UN-¹ 2] 1595. **Unarra·nged** *ppl. a.* [UN-¹ 2] BOSWELL. **Unarray·ed** *ppl. a.* [UN-¹ 2] ME. **Unarre·sted** *ppl. a.* [UN-¹ 2] late ME. **Unarri·ved** *ppl. a.* [UN-¹ 2] 1626.

Una·rtful, *a.* 1669. [UN-¹ 1.] 1. Free from artifice; artless; not artificial. 2. Lacking technical skill; inartistic 1675. Hence **Una·rtfully** *adv.*

Unarti·culated, *ppl. a.* 1700. [UN-1 2.] **1.** Not articulated or distinct. **2.** Not jointed or fitted together 1861.

1. That u. language, which was before the written tongue LAMB. 2. U. human bones 1894.

Unartifi·cial, *a.* 1591. [UN-1 1.] **1.** Lacking skill; inartistic. Now *rare* or *Obs.* **2.** Natural; not artificial. Now *rare.* 1603.

1. My verse is vnartificiall, the stile rude, the phrase barbarous 1591. 2. With an undisguised and u. goodness 1656. Hence **Unartifici·ally** *adv.*

Unarti·stic *a.* [UN-1 1] 1854. **Unasce·nded** *ppl. a.* [UN-1 2] SHELLEY. **Unascertai·ned** *ppl. a.* [UN-1 2] 1628.

Unasha·med, *ppl. a.* 1600. [UN-1 2.] Not ashamed. Hence **-ly, -ness.**

Una·sked, *ppl. a.* ME. [UN-1 2.] **1.** Uninvited; without being asked. **2.** Not asked *for*; not made the subject of a request 1456.

2. He delivered his u. opinion SCOTT. An u.-for concession T. HARDY.

Una·spirated *ppl. a.* [UN-1 2] 1793. **Unaspi·ring** *ppl. a.* [UN-1 4] 1729, **-ness** 1681. **Unassai·lable** *a.* [UN-1 1] 1596, **-ness, -bly** *adv.* **Unassai·led** *ppl. a.* [UN-1 2] 1586. **Unassay·ed** *ppl. a.* [UN-1 2] CHAUCER. **Unasse·rtive** *a.* [UN-1 1] DICKENS. **Unassi·gned** *ppl. a.* [UN-1 2] ME. **Unassi·milated** *ppl. a.* [UN-1 2] 1748. **Unassua·ged** *ppl. a.* [UN-1 2] 1654.

Unassi·sted, *ppl. a.* 1614. [UN-1 2]. Not helped. **b.** *spec.* Of the eye or sight: Unaided, naked 1661.

Unassu·ming, *ppl. a.* 1726. [UN-1 4.] Free from self-assertion; unpretentious.

A very u. young woman DICKENS. The u. things that hold A silent station in this beauteous world WORDSW. Hence **Unassu·ming-ly** *adv.*, **-ness.**

Unassu·red, *ppl. a.* late ME. [UN-1 2.] **1.** Not assured or safe; insecure. **2.** Not sure *of* something 1529. **3.** Not self-possessed; diffident 1627.

2. When men are by any accident u. they have slept, [dreams] seem to be real Visions HOBBES.

Unato·nable, *a.* 1645. [UN-1 1.] †**1.** Unaccordable. MILT. **2.** Irreconcilable 1683. **3.** That cannot be atoned for; inexpiable 1689.

1. Untunable or unattonable matrimony MILT.

Unatta·ched, *ppl. a.* (*sb.*) 1498. [UN-1 2.] †**1.** Not taken into custody –1639. **2.** Not attached or united (*to* something) 1821. **3.** Not belonging to a particular body, institution, sphere of work, etc. **a.** Of military officers: Not attached to a particular regiment or company 1796. **b.** Of clergy: Not attached to a particular diocese or parish 1865. **c.** Of students: Not attached to any college. Also as *sb.*, an u. student. 1870. **4.** Not engaged or married 1874.

Unatta·ckable *a.* [UN-1 1] 1805, **-bly** *adv.* **Unatta·cked** *ppl. a.* [UN-1 2] 1663.

Unattai·nable, *a.* and *sb.* 1661. [UN-1 1.] **A.** *adj.* That cannot be attained 1662. **B.** *sb.* **1.** An unattainable thing (*rare*) 1661. **2.** With *the*: That which is not attainable 1857. Hence **Unattai·nableness; -ably** *adv.*

Unattai·nted, *ppl. a.* 1592. [UN-1 2.] **1.** Unstained; free from blemish. **2.** Not attainted in law 1794.

1. The u. Honour of English Knighthood MILTON.

Unatte·mpted *ppl. a.* [UN-1 2] 1548.

Unatte·nded, *ppl. a.* 1603. [UN-1 2.] **1.** Not having attendants; unaccompanied. **b.** Of horses, vehicles, etc.: With no one in charge 1796. **2.** Not followed *by* or associated *with* some thing, circumstance, etc. 1687. **3.** Not attended *to*, disregarded 1729.

2. Night came, but u. with repose DRYDEN.

Unatte·nding *ppl. a.* [UN-1 4] MILT. **Unatte·sted** *ppl. a.* [UN-1 2] 1665. **Unatti·red** *ppl. a.* [UN-1 2] late ME. **Unattra·cted** *ppl. a.* [UN-1 2] 1727. **Unattra·ctive** *a.* [UN-1 1] SHELLEY, **-ly** *adv.*, **-ness.**

‖**Unau** (yū·nǫ). 1774. [Brazilian of the Island of Maranhão.] *Zool.* The S. Amer. two-toed sloth, *Cholopus didactylus.*

Unaugme·nted, *ppl. a.* 1555. [UN-1 2.] Not augmented or increased; *spec.* of Greek verbs.

†**Unauspi·cious** [UN-1 1] –1768. **Unauthe·ntic** *a.* [UN-1 1] 1631. **Unauthe·nticated** *ppl. a.* [UN-1 2] 1787. **Unautho·ritative** *a.* [UN-1 1] 1644, **-ly** *adv.* **Unau·thorized** *ppl. a.* [UN-1 2] 1596.

Unavai·lable, *a.* 1549. [UN-1 1.] **1.** Of no avail; ineffectual. **2.** Not available; incapable of being used 1855.

1. U. lamentations 1850. Hence **Unavaila·bility. Unavai·lableness. Unavai·lably** *adv.*

Unavai·ling *ppl. a.* [UN-1 4] 1670, **-ly** *adv.* **Unave·nged** *ppl. a.* [UN-1 2] 1481. **Unave·rted** *ppl. a.* [UN-1 2] 1753.

‖**Una voce** (yū·nei vōu·si). 1567. [L., 'with one voice'.] Unanimously.

Unavoi·dable *a.* [UN-1 1] 1577, **-ness, -bly** *adv.* **Unavoi·ded** *ppl. a.* [UN-1 2] 1565. **Unavow·ed** *ppl. a.* [UN-1 2] BURKE, **-ly** *adv.* **Unawa·kened** *ppl. a.* [UN-1 2] 1705, **-ness.**

Unaware (vnăwēə·ɪ), *adv.* and *a.* 1592. [UN-1 1.] **A.** *adv.* **1.** = next 1. **2.** = next 2. 1667. **3.** In phr. *at u.* = sense 1 and 2. 1598. **B.** *adj.* **1.** Not aware (*of*); not cognizant; ignorant, 1704. **2.** Blind to consequences; reckless (*rare*) 1817.

A. 1. As one that u. Hath dropp'd a precious jewel SHAKS. 2. Long have I sought for rest, and, u., Behold I find it! KEATS. 3. A Serpent shoots his Sting at u. DRYDEN. B. 2. I grew desperate and u. SHELLEY. Hence **Unawa·reness.**

Unawares (vnăwēə·ɪz), *adv.* 1535. [f. as prec. + -S.] **1.** Without being aware, unconsciously, inadvertently. **b.** Without being noticed 1667. **c.** *Unawares to*, without the knowledge of, unperceived by 1548. **2.** Without warning; unexpectedly 1535. **3.** *At unawares* = sense 1, 1 b, 2.

1. I have u. run into this long account BERKELEY. b. Age steals upon Us u. PRIOR. c. U. to myself, I had moved onward RICHARDSON. 2. The King..came u. upon the Lady FREEMAN. Phr. *To take, catch..u.*

Unaw·ed *ppl. a.* [UN-1 2] DRYDEN. **Una·zotized** *ppl. a.* [UN-1 2] 1828.

Unba·cked, *a.* 1592. [UN-1 2.] **1.** Of horses: Unmounted, untrained. **2.** Not backed or supported; not endorsed 1609. **b.** *Betting.* Having no backers 1883. **3.** Without a back or backing 1861.

Unba·g, *v.* 1611. [UN-2 3.] *trans.* To take or let (esp. a fox) out of a bag.

Unba·ked (vnbēi·kt), *ppl. a.* 1563. [UN-1 2.] **1.** Of tiles, etc.: Not baked in a kiln. **2.** Of food: Not prepared by baking 1577. †**3.** *fig.* Unfinished; immature –1635.

3. All the vnbak'd and dowy youth of a nation SHAKS.

Unba·lance *sb.* [UN-1 6] 1887. **Unba·lance** *v.* [UN-2 1] 1586.

Unba·lanced, *ppl. a.* 1650. [UN-1 2.] **1.** Of persons, the mind, judgement, etc.: Lacking equipoise; not balanced. **b.** Thrown out of balance; not balanced or equably poised 1732. **c.** Having no counterpoise; not offset *by* something 1818. **2.** Of an account: Not balanced 1828.

1. Interference with the old order was so far-reaching, that the minds of all were quite u. 1886. b. I was several times u., and on the very point of being hurled backward 1835. c. Valour u. by the observance of propriety 1879.

Unba·le *v.* [UN-2 3] 1752. **Unba·llast** *v.* [UN-2 2] 1684.

Unba·llasted, *ppl. a.* 1644. [UN-1 2.] **1.** Of vessels; Having no ballast 1657. **b.** *fig.* Not steadied by principles or solid qualities 1644. **2.** Of a railway line: Not filled in with ballast 1887.

1. b. To be tost and turmoild with their u. wits in fathomles and unquiet deeps of controversie MILTON.

Unba·ndage *v.* [UN-2 2] 1840. **Unba·nded** *ppl. a.* [UN-1 2] 1570. **Unba·nished** *ppl. a.* [UN-1 2] 1533. **Unba·nk** *v.* [UN-2 2] 1842. **Unbapti·ze** *v.* [UN-2 1] 1611. **Unbapti·zed** *ppl. a.* [UN-1 2] late ME. **Unba·r** *v.* [UN-2 1, 5] late ME. **Unba·rbarize** *v.* [UN-2 4 c] 1648.

Unba·rbed, *ppl. a.*1 1565. [UN-1 2.] Unarmed; not caparisoned.

Unba·rbed, *ppl. a.*2 1844. [UN-1 3.] Not furnished with a barb or barbs.

Unba·rded, *ppl. a.* 1598. [UN-1 2.] = UNBARBED *ppl. a.*1

Unba·re *v.* [UN-2 7] 1530. **Unba·rked** *ppl. a.* [UN-1 2] 1839.

Unba·rred, *ppl. a.* 1550. [UN-1 2.] **1.** Of harbours: Not obstructed with a bar 1550. **2.** Not secured or blocked with a bar or bars 1603. **3.** *Law.* Not excluded 1818. **4.** Of music: Not divided into bars 1879.

Unba·rrel *v.* [UN-2 3] 1611. **Unbarrica·de** *v.* [UN-2 2] 1623.

Unba·shful *a.* [UN-1 1] 1563, **-lly** *adv.* **Unba·stardized** *ppl. a.* [UN-1 2] H. WALPOLE.

Unba·ted, *ppl. a.* 1596. [UN-1 2.] **1.** Not abated, undiminished. *arch.* †**2.** Not bated or blunted –1815.

1. With u. zeal SCOTT. 2. You may choose A Sword vnbaited, and in a passe of practice, Requit him for your Father SHAKS.

Unbe·, *v.*1 *rare.* late ME. [UN-1 7.] *intr.* To be non-existent.

Unbe·, *v.*2 1624. [UN-2 2.] *trans.* To make non-existent.

God..could as easily..unbee them as conquer them 1646.

Unbea·rable, *a.* [UN-1 1.] 1449. Unendurable, intolerable. Hence **-ness, -bly** *adv.*

Unbea·rded, *ppl. a.* 1560. [UN-1 3.] **1.** Of persons: **a.** Having no beard. **b.** Not yet bearded, youthful. **2.** Of plants: Awnless 1688.

Unbea·ten, *ppl. a.* ME. [UN-1 2.] **1.** Not beaten or struck. **b.** Not pounded 1607. **2.** Not beaten or trodden down; unfrequented 1617. **3.** Undefeated 1757.

2. Some new u. passage to the sky SWIFT.

Unbeau·teous *a.* [UN-1 1] 1660. **Unbeautiful** *a.* [UN-1 1] 1495. **Unbeau·tify** *v.* [UN-2 4 c] 1570.

Unbeco·me, *v.* 1628. [UN-1 7.] *trans.* To be unbecoming to.

Unbeco·ming, *ppl. a.* 1598. [UN-1 4.] Not becoming; unsuitable; improper. **a.** Without const. **b.** Governing a sb. 1658. **c.** Const. *of.* 1741.

a. A grave irony which is not u. MACAULAY. b. Behaviour, so u. a Christian FIELDING. c. What was not u. of a child would be disgraceful to a youth CHESTERF. Hence **Unbeco·mingly** *adv.*, **-ness.**

Unbe·d *v.* [UN-2 3] 1611. **Unbe·dded** *ppl. a.* [UN-1 2] 1842. **Unbefi·tting** *ppl. a.* [UN-1 4] SHAKS., **-ly** *adv.*, **-ness.** **Unbefrie·nded** *ppl. a.* [UN-1 2] 1628. **Unbege·t** *v.* [UN-2 1] 1625. **Unbe·gged** *ppl. a.* [UN-1 2] 1579. **Unbegi·nning** *ppl. a.* [UN-1 4] 1591.

Unbego·tten, *ppl. a.* 1532. [UN-1 2.] **1.** Not yet begotten. **2.** Not begotten, self-existent 1561. Hence **Unbego·ttenly** *adv.*, **-ness.**

Unbegu·n, *ppl. a.* OE. [UN-1 2.] **1.** That had no beginning; ever existent. **2.** Not yet begun 1562.

1. The myhti god, which unbegunne Stant of himself GOWER.

Unbehe·ld *ppl. a.* [UN-1 2] MILT. **Unbeho·ldable** *a.* [UN-1 1] PUSEY.

Unbeho·lden, *ppl. a.* 1674. [UN-1 2.] **1.** Under no obligation (*to* a person). Now *dial.* **2.** Unseen *poet.* 1820.

2. A glow-worm golden..Scattering u. Its aëreal hue SHELLEY.

Unbeknow·n, *ppl. a.* 1636. [UN-1 2.] **1.** *advb.* or *absol.* *Unbeknown to*, without the knowledge of. **2.** Unknown 1824.

1. *ellipt.* My love rose up so early And stole out u. HOUSMAN.

Unbeknow·nst, *adv. vulgar* and *dial.* 1854. [f. prec.] = prec. 1.

Unbelie·f. ME. [UN-1 6.] Absence or lack of belief; disbelief; incredulity.

Unbelie·vable *a.* [UN-1 1] 1548, **-ness, -bly** *adv.* **Unbelie·ve** *v.*1 [UN-1 7] 1547. **Unbelie·ve** *v.*2 [UN-2 2] 1605. **Unbelie·ved** *ppl. a.* [UN-1 2] ME.

Unbelie·ver. 1526. [UN-1 6.] One who does not believe; *spec.* one who does not accept a particular (esp. the Christian) religious belief; an infidel. So **Unbelie·ving** *ppl. a.* [UN-1 4] late ME.

Unbelo·ved *ppl. a.* [UN-1 2] 1597. **Unbe·lt** *v.* [UN-2 2, 3] 1483. **Unbe·lted** *ppl. a.* [UN-1 2] BYRON.

Unbe·nd, *v.* ME. [UN-2 1, 5.] **1.** *trans.* To relax (a bow) from tension; to unstring. †**b.** *fig.* To slacken, weaken 1605. **2.** To give relaxation or rest to (the mind, etc.) 1594. **3.** *Naut.* To unfasten, untie (a cable, line, sail) 1627. **4.** To relax the tension or severity of (the brow, face, etc.) 1718. **5.** To straighten from a bent position 1663. **6.** *intr.* To free oneself from constraint, seriousness, or ceremony;

to become genial or allow oneself to relax 1746. **b.** Of the features: To relax 1818. **7.** To become straight or less bent or curved 1815.

1. b. You doe vnbend your Noble strength, to thinke So braine-sickly of things SHAKS. **2.** The Mind never unbends itself so agreeably as in the Conversation of a well chosen Friend ADDISON. **6.** In private company though he never forgot his rank, he could u. 1869.

Unbe·nding, *ppl. a.* 1688. [UN-1 4.] **1.** Inflexible, unyielding, obstinate. **2.** Rigid; not bending or curving; *esp.* of persons, remaining erect, not stooping 1709. Hence **Unbe·ndingly** *adv.*, **-ness.**

Unbe·neficed *ppl. a.* [UN-1 2] 1623. **Unbenefi·cial** *a.* [UN-1 1] 1626. **Unbe·nefited** *ppl. a.* [UN-1 2] POPE. **Unbeni·gn** *a.* [UN-1 1] CROMWELL, **-ly** *adv.* **Unbe·nt** *ppl. a.* [UN-1 2] 1483. **Unbenu·mb** *v.* [UN-2 1] 1598. **Unbequea·thed** *ppl. a.* [UN-1 2] 1483. **Unbere·ft** *ppl. a.* [UN-1 2] 1621.

Unbesee·m, *v.* 1657. [UN-1 7]. **1.** *trans.* To be unseemly for or discreditable to (a person). **2.** To fail in, fall short of 1812.

2. Nor u. the promise of thy spring BYRON.

Unbesee·ming *a.* [UN-1 4] 1583, **-ly** *adv.*, **-ness.** **Unbesou·ght** *ppl. a.* [UN-1 2] MILT. †**Unbespea·k** *v.* [UN-2 1] –1743. **Unbespo·ken** *ppl. a.* [UN-1 2] 1681. **Unbestow·ed** *ppl. a.* [UN-1 2] 1534.

Unbethou·ght, *ppl. a.* 1558. [UN-1 2.] **1.** Unpremeditated, unintentional. Also as *adv.* **2.** Unthought of, unrealized 1855.

Unbetray·ed *ppl. a.* [UN-1 2] 1595. **Unbetro·thed** *ppl. a.* [UN-1 2] 1577. **Unbe·tterable** *a.* [UN-1 1] 1806. **Unbe·ttered** *ppl. a.* [UN-1 2] 1628. **Unbewai·led** *ppl. a.* [UN-1 2] 1586. **Unbewi·ldered** *ppl. a.* [UN-1 2] WORDSW. **Unbewi·tch** *v.* [UN-2 1] 1584. **Unbi·as** *v.* [UN-2 1] SWIFT.

Unbias(s)ed (ʊnbəi·ăst), *a.* 1607. [UN-1 2.] **1.** Of bowls, etc.: Having no bias. **2.** *fig.* Impartial, not prejudiced; not unduly influenced *by* something 1647.

2. All..which a man without authority can give,—his u. opinion BURKE. U. by mob clamour BROUGHAM. Hence **Unbi·as(s)edly** *adv.*, **-ness.**

Unbi·blical *a.* [UN-1 1] PUSEY. **Unbi·d** *ppl. a.* (*arch.*) [UN-1 2] late ME. **Unbi·ddable** *a.* [UN-1 1] 1825.

Unbi·dden, *ppl. a.* OE. [UN-1 2.] Not asked or invited; not commanded or directed.

An u. Crew Of graceless guests DRYDEN. Adown his cheek A tear u. stole POPE.

Unbi·nd, *v.* [OE. *unbindan*, f. UN-2 + BIND *v.*] **1.** *trans.* To free from a band, bond or tie. **b.** *transf.* To loosen, open up or out, set free, etc. 1577. **c.** To take the bandage off (a limb or wound) 1639. **2.** To set free from bonds; to restore to personal liberty in this way OE. **3.** To untie, undo (a bond, cord, etc.) OE. **b.** *fig.* To dissolve, undo, destroy ME.

3. Then let..death u. my chain 1843. **b.** No force, no fortune, shall my vows u. DRYDEN.

Unbi·shop *v.* [UN-2 2, 4 b] 1598. **Unbi·shoped** *ppl. a.*2 [UN-2 6] 1563.

Unbi·shoped, *ppl. a.*1 OE. [UN-1 2.] **1.** Not having been confirmed. *arch.* **2.** Not consecrated as a bishop 1601.

Unbi·t, *v.* 1565. [UN-2 2 b.] *trans.* To free (a horse) from the bit. Also *absol.*

Unbi·tted, *ppl. a.* 1586. [UN-1 2.] Having no bit; unbridled, unrestrained.

fig. Our carnall Stings, or vnbitted Lusts SHAKS.

Unbla·cked *ppl. a.* [UN-1 2] 1836. **Unbla·ckened** *ppl. a.* [UN-1 2] 1864. **Unbla·m(e)able** *a.* [UN-1 1] 1531, **-ness, -bly** *adv.* **Unbla·med** *ppl. a.* [UN-1 2] late ME. **Unbla·nched** *ppl. a.* [UN-1 2] late ME. **Unbla·sted** *ppl. a.* [UN-1 2] 1589. **Unblea·ched** *a.* [UN-1 2] 1531.

Unble·mished, *ppl. a.* late ME. [UN-1 2.] **1.** Free from moral blemish or stain. **2.** Free from material blemish. Now *rare.* 1450.

1. His Spouse is chaste, vnblemisht with a spot QUARLES. All the authority which belongs to u. integrity MACAULAY. **2.** The religious houses only being spared, and left vnblemished HAKLUYT.

Unble·nched *ppl. a.* [UN-1 2] MILT. **Unble·nded** *ppl. a.* [UN-1 2] ME. **Unble·ss** *v.* [UN-2 1] SHAKS.

Unble·ssed, unble·st, *ppl. a.* ME. [UN-1 2.] **1.** Not formally blessed. **b.** Deprived of, excluded from, left without, a blessing or benediction 1590. **2.** Ill-fated, unfortunate, miserable ME. **3.** Unhallowed; evil, wicked. late ME. **4.** Not favoured or made happy *with* or *by* something 1743.

1. b. And there his corps, unbless'd, is hanging still DRYDEN. **2.** What matters, if unblest in love, How long or short my life will prove? PRIOR. **3.** Such resting found the sole Of unblest feet MILT. Hence **Unble·ssedness.**

Unbli·ghted *ppl. a.* [UN-1 2] COWPER. **Unbli·nd** *v.* [UN-2 1] 1590. **Unbli·nded** *ppl. a.* [UN-1 2] 1611. **Unbli·ndfold** *v.* [UN-2 2] late ME. **Unbli·nking** *a.* [UN-1 1], **-ly** *adv.* 1867. **Unbli·ssful** *a.* [UN-1 1] ME. †**Unbli·the** *a.* [UN-1] –1535. **Unblo·ck** *v.* [UN-2 1] 1611.

Unbloo·died, *ppl. a.* [UN-1 2.] Not stained with blood. SHAKS.

Unbloo·dy, *a.* 1544. [UN-1 1.] **1.** Not attended with (much or any) bloodshed. **2.** Not involving the shedding of blood 1548. **b.** Theol. *Unbloody sacrifice, offering, sacrament,* the Eucharist 1548. **3.** Not stained with blood 1590. **4.** Not bloodthirsty 1665.

3. *U. grave,* that of one who has not died by bloodshed. Hence **Unbloo·dily** *adv.*

Unblo·tted *ppl. a.* [UN-1 2] 1548.

Unblo·wn, *ppl. a.*1 1638. [UN-1 1.] **1.** Not blown by the wind. Also with advs. *away, out.* **2.** Not sounded 1815.

2. The lances unlifted, the trumpet u. BYRON.

Unblow·n, *ppl. a.*2 1587. [UN-1 2.] Of flowers: Not yet open; in the bud.

fig. Ah my tender babes! My vnblowne flowers SHAKS.

Unblu·nted *ppl. a.* [UN-1 2] 1656. **Unblu·rred** *ppl. a.* [UN-1 2] 1809.

Unblu·shing, *ppl. a.* 1595. [UN-1 4.] **1.** Not blushing. **2.** Shameless, unabashed 1736.

2. Strenuous and u. servility MACAULAY. Hence **Unblu·shing·ly** *adv.*, **-ness.**

Unboa·stful *a.* [UN-1 1] 1727. **Unboa·sting** *ppl. a.* [UN-1 4] 1802.

Unbo·died, *a.* and *ppl. a.* 1513. [UN-1 3.] **1.** Separated from the body; ghostly; not invested with a body. **2.** Incorporeal; not in material form 1606. **3.** Not having a definite form 1630.

1. Lastly his vn-bodied Soule departs 1589. **2.** Art naked, abstract and u. CUDWORTH. Like an u. joy SHELLEY. **3.** I skirmish with u. air DAVENANT.

Unbo·dily *a.* (now *rare*) [UN-1 1] late ME. **Unbo·dy** *v.* [UN-2 5] 1548. **Unboi·led** *ppl. a.* [UN-1 2] 1611. †**Unbo·ld** *a.* [UN-1 1] –1825.

Unbo·lt, *v.* 1470. [UN-2 5 and 1.] **1.** *intr.* Of a door: To have the bolt withdrawn. **2.** *trans.* To unfasten by withdrawing a bolt or bolts 1598.

Unbo·lted, *ppl. a.*1 1580. [UN-1 2, UN-2 6.] **1.** Not fastened with a bolt; released by withdrawal of a bolt. **2.** Not held together with a bolt or bolts 1793.

Unbo·lted, *ppl. a.*2 1598. [UN-1 2. See BOLT *v.*1] Not sifted.

Unbo·ne *v.* [UN-2 2 b] 1570. **Unbo·ned** *ppl. a.* [UN-1 2] 1611.

Unbo·nnet, *v.* 1810. [UN-2 2, 5.] **1.** *intr.* To remove the bonnet. **b.** *esp.* To do this as a mark of respect. Also *refl.* 1821. **2.** *trans.* To remove the bonnet from 1828.

1. b. Rise, u. yourself, and be silent SCOTT.

Unbo·nneted, *ppl. a.* 1604. [UN-1 2.] Not wearing a bonnet; having the head uncovered; *spec.* as a mark of respect. **b.** Of the head: Not covered by a bonnet 1820.

Unboo·ked, *ppl. a.* 1586. [UN-1 2.] **a.** Not registered. **b.** Not pre-engaged by booking. **c.** Not book-learned.

c. The u. freshness of the Scottish peasant 1870.

Unboo·kish *a.* [UN-1 1] SHAKS. **Unboo·t** *v.* [UN-2 2, 5] 1598. **Unbo·red** *ppl. a.* [UN-2 2] 1598. **Unbo·rn** *ppl. a.* [UN-1 2] OE. **Unbo·rrowed** *ppl. a.* [UN-1 2] 1638.

Unbo·som, *v.* 1588. [UN-2 3.] **1.** *trans.* To let out from the heart; to give vent to; to reveal, make no further secret of. **b.** *refl.* and *absol.* To disclose one's thoughts, secrets, etc. 1628. **2.** To display to the view 1610.

1. I have longed a great while to u. my sorrows DE FOE. **b.** To u. himself of whom his great secret THACKERAY. The last person to whom he could u. MEREDITH. **2.** Fair-handed Spring unbosoms every grace THOMSON.

†**Unbo·ttom,** *v.* 1598. [UN-2 2.] *trans.* To deprive of a bottom or foundation; to unsettle. Hence **Unbo·ttomed** *ppl. a.*2

Unbo·ttomed, *ppl. a.*1 1615. [UN-1 2.] **1.** Bottomless; unfathomable. **2.** Unfounded; not founded *on* or *in* something 1640.

2. Whether there be no Love u. on Self-love? 1675.

Unbou·ght *ppl. a.* [UN-1 2] OE.

Unbou·nd, *ppl. a.* OE. [UN-1 2.] **1.** Not bound or tied up; loose. **b.** Not under obligation; unconstrained. late ME. **2.** Not secured with a band or border of some strong material 1531. **3.** Of books: Having no binding 1541.

1. b. To constrain Thy u. spirit into bonds again COWPER.

Unbou·nded, *ppl. a.* 1598. [UN-1 2.] **1.** Not bounded or limited in extent or amount. **2.** Recognizing no limit; passing all bounds; uncontrolled 1608.

1. The wild u. hills we ranged SCOTT. Her..u. courage and energy 1897. **2.** U. expectations 1854. Hence **Unbou·nded·ly** *adv.*, **-ness.**

Unbow·elled *a.* [UN-1 3] 1592. **Unbo·x** *v.* [UN-2 3] 1611.

Unbra·ce, *v.* late ME. [UN-2 1.] **1.** *trans.* or *refl.* To free from bands or braces forming part of clothing or armour. Also *absol. arch.* **2.** *trans.* To undo, loosen (a band, grasp, etc.) *arch.* 1475. **b.** To loosen or detach by the undoing or removal of braces or bands. *arch.* 1593. **c.** To relax the tension of (a drum) 1593. †**3.** To carve (a mallard or duck) –1804. **4.** To make slack, enfeeble 1711. **b.** *absol.* To become slack, lose firmness 1693.

4. Laughter..slackens and unbraces the Mind ADDISON. So **Unbra·ced** *ppl. a.* 1510. [UN-1 2.]

Unbra·nched *a.* [UN-1 3] 1665. **Unbra·nching** *a.* [UN-1 4] GOLDSM. **Unbra·nded** *ppl. a.* [UN-1 2] MILT. **Unbrea·kable** *a.* [UN-1 1] 1480. **Unbrea·kfasted** *a.* [UN-1 3] 1646. **Unbrea·thable** *a.* [UN-1 1] 1846.

Unbrea·thed, *a.* 1590. [UN-1 2, 2 b, 3.] †**1.** Having had no training; unpractised –1644. **2. a.** Not having recovered breath 1692. **b.** Not out of breath 1901. **3.** Not breathed 1884. **b.** Not breathed *upon* 1817. **4.** Not uttered or whispered 1827.

1. A fugitive and cloister'd vertue, unexercis'd and unbreath'd MILTON.

Unbre·d, *ppl. a.* 1600. [UN-1 2.] †**1.** Unborn. SHAKS. **2.** Deficient in breeding; unmannerly, ill-bred 1622. **3.** Not trained *in* or *to* some occupation 1683.

Unbree·ch, *v.* 1548. [UN-2 2.] **1.** *trans.* To remove the breech or breeching from (a cannon). **2.** To strip of breeches 1598.

Unbree·ched, *a.* 1611. [UN-1 3.] Not (yet) dressed in breeches.

Unbrew·ed *ppl. a.* [UN-1 2] 1725. **Unbri·bable** *a.* [UN-1 1] 1661. **Unbri·bed** *ppl. a.* [UN-1 2] 1607. **Unbri·ck** *v.* [UN-2 2] 1598. **Unbri·cked** *ppl. a.* [UN-1 2] 1814. **Unbri·dged** *ppl. a.* [UN-1 2] WORDSW. **Unbri·dle** *v.* [UN-2 2 b] late ME.

Unbri·dled, *ppl. a.* late ME. [UN-1 2.] **1.** *fig.* Ungoverned; subject to no restraint; headstrong. **2.** Not furnished with a bridle 1553.

1. The unbridl'd impudence of this loose rayler MILT. Lands deluged by u. floods WORDSW. The u. rule of the multitude 1888. Hence **Unbri·dled·ly** *adv.*, **-ness** (*rare*).

Unbrie·fed *ppl. a.* [UN-1 2] 1889. **Un-Bri·tish** *a.* [UN-1 1] 1746. **Unbroa·ched** *ppl. a.* [UN-1 2] 1689.

Unbro·ken, *ppl. a.* ME. [UN-1 2.] **1.** Not broken or infringed; unviolated, inviolate. **2.** Not fractured; intact, whole 1495. **3.** Not humbled or subdued; not impaired 1513. **4.** Of horses, etc.: Not broken in; untrained 1538. **5.** Uninterrupted, continuous 1561. **b.** Const. *by.* 1743. **6.** Of ground: Not broken by ploughing or digging 1579. **7.** Of troops: Not thrown into disorder 1721.

1. Who first broke peace in Heav'n and Faith, till then Unbrok'n MILT. **2.** *fig.* My fortune, which is u. RICHARDSON. **5.** It required an u. attention BURKE. **7.** To charge large masses of u. infantry 1898. So **Unbro·ke** *ppl. a.* **Unbro·ken·ly** *adv.*, **-ness.**

Unbro·ther *v.* [UN-2 4 b] 1634. **Unbro·therly** *a.* [UN-1 1] 1586. **Unbrou·ght** *ppl. a.* [UN-1 2, 2 b] TINDALE. **Unbrui·sed** *ppl. a.* [UN-1 2] 1440. **Unbru·shed** *ppl. a.* [UN-1 2] 1640.

Unbu·ckle, *v.* late ME. [Un-^{2} 2 b.] **1.** *trans.* To undo the buckle of (a shoe, belt, etc.); to unfasten or set free in this way. **2.** *absol.* To undo the buckle or buckles of a belt, garment, etc. 1611. **b.** To unbend, become less stiff 1886.

1. A miser, who will not u. his purse to bestow a farthing SCOTT. 2. U., Calladine, the day is hott DAVENANT. b. Even the captain..would sometimes u. a bit, and tell me of the fine countries he had visited STEVENSON.

Unbu·ckled *ppl. a.* [Un-^{1} 2, Un-^{2} 6] 1489. **Unbu·dded** *ppl. a.* [Un-^{1} 2] KEATS. **Unbui·ld** *v.* [Un-^{2} 1] SHAKS.

Unbui·lt, *ppl. a.* 1455. [Un-^{1} 2, 2 b.] **1.** Not (yet) built. **b.** Not made by building 1882. **2.** Not built *on* or *upon*; not occupied with buildings 1631.

Unbu·lky *a.* [Un-^{1} 1] 1678. **Unbu·ndle** *v.* [Un-^{2} 1] 1606. **Unbu·ng** *v.* [Un-^{2} 1] 1611.

Unbu·rden, unbu·rthen, *v.* 1538. [Un-^{2} 2 b.] **1.** *trans.* To free from a burden. Chiefly *fig.*, to relieve (a person, the mind, etc.) by the removal or disclosure of something. Freq. const. *of*. **b.** *refl.* 1589. **2.** To cast off the burden of; esp. *fig.*, to disclose, reveal, confess 1593.

1. I may perhappes devise some way to be unburdened of my life 1568. We desire to unburthen the Consciences of men of needless..Ceremonies CHAS. I. 2. In unburdening to a friend the sins and sorrows of one's life 1876. So **Unbu·rdened** *ppl. a.* [Un-^{1} 2] 1548.

Unbu·ried *ppl. a.* [Un-^{1} 2] OE. **Unbu·rnished** *ppl. a.* [Un-^{1} 2] 1691.

Unbu·rnt, unbu·rned, *ppl. a.* ME. [Un-^{1} 2.] **1.** Not consumed by fire. **2.** Not subjected to the action of fire: *esp.* of bricks, clay, lime, etc. 1626.

Unbu·rst *ppl. a.* [Un-^{1} 2] 1782. **Unbu·ry** *v.* [Un-^{2} 1] late ME. **Unbu·sied** *ppl. a.* (now *rare*) [Un-^{1} 2] 1570. **Unbu·sinesslike** *a.* [Un-^{1} 1] SCOTT. **Unbu·sy** *a.* [Un-^{1} 1] 1731. **Unbu·ttered** *ppl. a.* [Un-^{1} 2] 1584.

Unbu·tton, *v.* ME. [Un-^{2} 1.] *trans.* To unfasten (buttons); to undo the buttons of (a garment). Also with personal obj. **b.** *absol.* To undo one's buttons; to loosen one's clothing 1605; *fig.* (*colloq.*) to be free and easy.

Thou art so fat-witted with drinking of olde Sacke, and vnbuttoning thee after Supper SHAKS. *fig.* Unbuttoning my bosom and showing him all the profitable secrets I had learnt GALT. b. Gluttony stuffs till it pants, and unbuttons and stuffs again 1760.

Unbu·ttoned *ppl. a.* [Un-^{1} 2] 1563. **Unca·ge** *v.* [Un-^{2} 3] 1620. **Unca·ged** *ppl. a.* [Un-^{1} 2] POPE. **Unca·lcined** *ppl. a.* [Un-^{1} 2] 1601. **Unca·lculated** *ppl. a.* [Un-^{1} 2] 1828. **Unca·lculating** *a.* [Un-^{1} 4] 1832, -**ly** *adv.* **Unca·lendared** *ppl. a.* [Un-^{2} 6, Un-^{1} 2] 1654.

Unca·lled, *ppl. a.* late ME. [Un-^{1} 2, 2 b.] **1.** Not summoned; uninvited. **b.** *transf.* Of things 1586. **2.** Not called to salvation; not of the elect 1561. **3.** *Uncalled-for*, rarely *uncalled*: Not called for; not asked for or requested; unnecessary, intrusive 1610. **4.** Of capital: Not called up 1882.

1. b. Sudden tears u. spring up 1839. 2. Either to conuert those that are vncalled, or to builde vp those which are conuerted 1619. 3. This arbitrary, impolitic, and u.-for measure 1817.

Unca·lm *v.* [Un-^{2} 4] 1655. **Unca·mbered** *ppl. a.* [Un-^{1} 2] 1881. **Unca·ncelled** *ppl. a.* [Un-^{1} 2] 1557. **Unca·ndid** *a.* [Un-^{1} 1] 1639, -**ly** *adv.*, -**ness**. **Unca·ndour** [Un-^{1} 6] 1879.

Uncanny (ʋnkæ·ni), *a.* orig. *Sc.* and *north.* 1596. [Un-^{1} 1.] **1.** †Mischievous; careless; †unreliable. *dial.* **2.** Untrustworthy or inspiring uneasiness by reason of a supernatural element; uncomfortably, strange or unfamiliar; mysteriously suggestive of evil or danger 1773. **3.** Dangerous, unsafe *dial.* 1785.

2. A slate quarry under the cliff—a scene of u. grandeur 1882. Hence **Unca·nnily** *adv.* **Unca·nniness.**

Uncano·nical, *a.* 1632. [Un-^{1} 1.] **1.** Not in accordance with ecclesiastical canons. **b.** Unclerical; ill suited to the clergy 1747. **2.** Not included in the canon of Scripture 1835.

1. b. Begirt..with a most u. buff-belt SCOTT. Hence **Uncano·nically** *adv.*

Unca·nonize *v.* [Un-^{2} 4 c] 1607. **Unca·nonized** *ppl. a.* [Un-^{1} 2] 1548. **Unca·p** *v.* [Un-^{2} 2] 1566. †**Unca·pable** *a.* [Un-^{1} 1] -1805. **Uncapa·cious** *a.* [Un-^{1} 1] 1635. **Unca·pped** *ppl. a.* [Un-^{1} 2] 1548. **Uncapsi·zable** *a.* [Un-^{1} 1] 1883. **Unca·ptived** *ppl. a.* (*arch.*) [Un-^{1} 2] 1601. **Unca·rdinal** *v.* [Un-^{2} 4 b] 1642.

Unca·red-for, *a.* 1597. [Un-^{1} 2 b.] Not looked after or tended; neglected.

Unca·reful, *a.* 1533. [Un-^{1} 1.] **1.** Deficient in care; careless. **2.** Not taking thought *of* or *for* 1559. **3.** Free from care; untroubled 1643.

1. An vncarefull Magistrate 1604. 2. Such [Gods] as are u. of us 1662. 3. One of the..most u. interludes of my life HAWTHORNE. Hence **Unca·reful·ly** *adv.*, †-**ness**.

Unca·ring *ppl. a.* [Un-^{1} 4] 1786. **Unca·rpeted** *a.* [Un-^{1} 3] 1816. **Unca·rried** *ppl. a.* [Un-^{1} 2] 1584. **Unca·rt** *v.* [Un-^{2} 3] 1641. **Unca·rved** *a.* [Un-^{1} 2] 1592.

Unca·se, *v.* 1575. [Un-^{2} 2, 3.] **1.** *trans.* †**a.** To flay -1712. **b.** To strip, undress (a person). *arch.* 1576. **c.** *absol.* To put off a garment or garments. *arch.* 1588. **2.** To lay bare, expose, bring to light. *arch.* 1587. **3.** To take out of a case, sheath, etc. 1589.

1. a. Cambyses once uncased a corrupt judge, and made a cushion of his skin 1658. c. Do you not see Pompey is vncasing for the combat? SHAKS. 2. His hypocrisie shall be uncased 1627.

Unca·shed *ppl. a.* [Un-^{1} 2] 1896. **Unca·st** *ppl. a.* [Un-^{1} 2] late ME. **Unca·stigated** *ppl. a.* [Un-^{1} 2] 1657. **Unca·stle** *v.* [Un-^{2} 3] 1611.

Unca·strated, *ppl. a.* 1725. [Un-^{1} 2.] **1.** Not gelded. **2.** Of books, etc.: Not expurgated; unmutilated 1737.

Unca·talogued *ppl. a.* [Un-^{1} 2] NEWMAN.

Unca·techized, *a.* 1619. [Un-^{1} 2.] Not formally instructed or examined in religion.

Unca·tholic, *a.* and *sb.* 1601. [Un-^{1} 1, 6.] **A.** *adj.* Not catholic or universal; also *spec.*, not Roman Catholic. **B.** *sb.* One who is not a Catholic 1865.

Unca·ught *ppl. a.* [Un-^{1} 2] ME. **Unca·ulked** *ppl. a.* [Un-^{1} 2] 1748. **Uncau·sed** *ppl. a.* [Un-^{1} 2] 1628. **Uncea·sing** *ppl. a.* [Un-^{1} 4] late ME., -**ly**, *adv.*, -**ness**. **Uncei·led** *ppl. a.* [Un-^{1} 2] CRABBE. **Unce·lebrated** *ppl. a.* [Un-^{1} 2] MILT. **Uncele·stial** *a.* [Un-^{1} 1] 1661. **Unceme·nted** *ppl. a.* [Un-^{1} 2] 1717. **Unce·nsored** *ppl. a.* [Un-^{1} 2] 1890. **Uncenso·rious** *a.* [Un-^{1} 1] 1711. **Unce·nsurable** *a.* [Un-^{1} 1] 1643. **Unce·nsured** *ppl. a.* [Un-^{1} 2] 1574. **Unce·ntre** *v.* [Un-^{2} 3] 1625. **Unce·ntred** *ppl. a.* [Un-^{1} 2] 1652.

Unceremo·nious, *a.* 1598. [Un-^{1} 1.] Characterized by lack of ceremony or formality; acting without ceremony. Hence **Uncere·mo·niously** *adv.*, -**ness**.

Unce·rtain, *a.* ME. [Un-^{1} 1.] **1.** Not fixed in point of time or occurrence; not determinate in amount, number, or extent. **2.** Not sure to happen; contingent ME. **b.** Liable to change or accident; mutable 1477. **3.** About which one cannot be certain or assured; not indubitable ME. **b.** Of doubtful issue or tendency. late ME. **4.** Not certainly known; doubtful, dubious ME. **b.** Ambiguous; of doubtful meaning. late ME. **c.** Unspecified; of doubtful identity 1617. **d.** Not clearly defined or outlined 1638. **5.** Not certain to remain in one state or condition; unsteady, variable, fitful; capricious 1591. **6.** Feeling no certainty; not assured *of* something. late ME. **b.** Const. *how, what, whether*, etc. 1526. **c.** Undecided; not directed to a definite end. late ME. So **Unce·rtainly** *adv.*

Unce·rtainty. late ME. [Un-^{1} 6.] **1.** The quality of being uncertain in respect of duration, continuance, occurrence, etc. **b.** With *a* and *pl.* Something of which the occurrence, issue, etc., is uncertain 1619. **2.** The state of not being definitely known or perfectly clear; vagueness, doubtfulness. late ME. **b.** Something not definitely known or knowable; a doubtful point. late ME. **3.** The state or character of being uncertain in mind; hesitation, irresolution 1548.

2. Phr. (Law) *Bad* or *void for u.*

Uncerti·ficated *ppl. a.* [Un-^{1} 2] DICKENS. **Unce·rtified** *ppl. a.* [Un-^{1} 2] 1535. **Unchai·n** *v.* [Un-^{2} 2.] 1582. **Unchai·ned** *ppl. a.* [Un-^{1} 2] 1660. **Uncha·llenged** *ppl. a.* [Un-^{1} 2] 1639.

Uncha·ncy, *a.* Chiefly *Sc.* 1533. [Un-^{1} 1.] **1.** Ill-omened, ill-fated, unfortunate. **b.** Inopportune, ill timed 1860. **2.** Formidable; not safe to meddle with 1786.

1. The lordis thocht that Johne was ane u. name to be ane king 1536. 2. A stalwart u. customer, who will not be gainsaid 1833.

Uncha·ngeable *a.* [Un-^{1} 1] ME., -**ness**, -**bly** *adv.* **Uncha·nged**, *ppl. a.* [Un-^{1} 2] late ME. **Uncha·nging** *a.* [Un-^{1} 4] SHAKS., -**ly** *adv.*, -**ness**. **Uncha·nnelled** (*ppl.*) *a.* [Un-^{1} 2, 3] 1600. **Uncha·peroned** *ppl. a.* [Un-^{1} 2] 1858.

Uncha·ractered, *ppl. a.* 1633. [Un-^{1} 2.] **1.** *Phonetics.* Of a sound: Not represented by a letter or sign. **2.** Lacking moral character 1841.

Uncharacteri·stic *a.* [Un-^{1} 1] 1753, -**ally** *adv.*

Uncha·rge, *v.* Now *rare*. ME. [Un-^{2} 1.] †**1.** *trans.* To free from a burden -1430. **b.** To acquit of guilt. SHAKS. **2.** To unload (a vessel). *arch.* ME. **3.** To remove the charge from (a gun) 1687.

1. b. Euen his Mother shall vncharge the practice, And call it accident SHAKS.

Uncha·rged, *ppl. a.* 1475. [Un-^{1} 2.] **1.** Not burdened (*with* something). **b.** Not formally accused 1900. **2.** Unassailed 1607. **3.** *Her.* Not furnished with a charge 1610. **4.** Not loaded with powder and shot 1719. **b.** Not charged with electricity 1815. **5.** Not subjected to a financial charge 1894.

Uncha·riot *v.* [Un-^{2} 3] POPE. **Uncha·ritable** *a.* [Un-^{1} 1] 1456, -**ness**, -**bly** *adv.* **Uncha·rity** [Un-^{1} 6] 1548.

Uncha·rm, *v.* 1575. [Un-^{2} 1.] **1.** *trans.* To deprive (a charm) of magical powers. **2.** To deliver from a spell or from enchantment. Also *absol.* 1621. **b.** To deprive of charm or fascination 1835.

2. That Harp, whose Charms uncharm'd the brest Of troubled Saul 1638.

Uncha·rmed *ppl. a.* [Un-^{1} 2] SHAKS. **Uncha·rnel** *v.* [Un-^{2} 3] 1805.

Uncha·rted, *ppl. a.* 1895. [Un-^{1} 2.] Not marked on a chart or map.

Uncha·rtered, *ppl. a.* 1805. [Un-^{1} 2.] **1.** *fig.* Not authorized as by a charter; irregular. **2.** Having no charter 1818.

1. Me this u. freedom tires WORDSW.

Uncha·ry *a.* [Un-^{1} 1] SHAKS. **Uncha·ste** *a.* [Un-^{1} 1] late ME., -**ly** *adv.*, -**ness**. **Uncha·stened** *ppl. a.* [Un-^{1} 2] MILT. **Unchasti·sed** *ppl. a.* [Un-^{1} 2] late ME. **Uncha·stity** [Un-^{1} 6] late ME. **Unchea·ted** *ppl. a.* [Un-^{1} 2] 1746. **Unche·cked** *ppl. a.* [Un-^{1} 2] 1469. **Unchee·red** *ppl. a.* [Un-^{1} 2] WORDSW. **Unchee·rful** *a.* [Un-^{1} 1] late ME., -**ly** *adv.*, -**ness**. **Unchee·ry** *a.* [Un-^{1} 1] STERNE. **Unche·quered** *ppl. a.* [Un-^{1} 2] 1796. **Unche·rished** *ppl. a.* [Un-^{1} 2] late ME. **Unchew·ed** *ppl. a.* [Un-^{1} 2] 1643. **Unchi·d** *ppl. a.* [Un-^{1} 2] 1860. **Unchi·dden** *ppl. a.* [Un-^{1} 2] 1472.

Unchi·ld, *v.* 1605. [Un-^{2} 2, 4 b.] **1.** *trans.* To deprive of children, make childless. **2.** To deprive of the status of a child or of the qualities peculiar to childhood 1615. Hence **Unchi·lded** *ppl. a.*

Unchi·ldlike *a.* [Un-^{1} 1] DICKENS. **Unchi·lled** *ppl. a.* [Un-^{1} 2] 1794. **Unchi·pped** *ppl. a.* [Un-^{1} 2] HERRICK. **Unchi·selled** *ppl. a.* [Un-^{1} 2] 1772. **Unchi·valrous** *a.* [Un-^{1} 1] 1846, -**ly** *adv.* **Uncho·ke** *v.* [Un-^{2} 1] 1588. **Uncho·ked** *ppl. a.* [Un-^{1} 2] 1833. **Uncho·sen** *ppl. a.* [Un-^{1} 2] 1529.

Unchri·sten, *v.* 1598. [Un-^{2} 1.] **1.** *trans.* To undo the christening of; to deprive of the baptismal name. †**2.** To deprive of the character or status of a Christian -1718.

Unchri·stened, *ppl. a.* ME. [Un-^{1} 2.] **1.** Not converted to Christianity, unbaptized, pagan. **b.** Of children: Never or not yet christened 1725. **2.** Unnamed 1832.

1. The Moores..beyng infideles and vnchristened people HALL.

Unchri·stian, *a.* 1555. [Un-^{1} 1, 6.] **1.** Not professing the Christian faith; devoid of Christian principles or feeling. **b.** Not Christian; of non-Christians 1816. **2.** Unbefitting a Christian; at variance with Christian principles 1581. **b.** *colloq.* Shocking to any decent person; outrageous 1630.

2. Disciples that obstinately continue in an u. life

Hobbes. b. The unchristianest, beastliest liquor I ever tasted Trelawny.

†**Unchri·stian**, *v.* 1633. [Un-2 4 a.] *trans.* = Unchristen *v.* 2. -1712.

Unchristia·nity [Un-1 6] 1652. **Unchri·stianize** *v.* [Un-2 4 c] 1714. **Unchri·stianlike** *a.* [Un-1 1] 1610. **Unchri·stianly** *adv.* [Un-1 5] 1547. **Unchro·nicled** *ppl. a.* [Un-1 2] 1598.

Unchronolo·gical, *a.* 1763. [Un-1 1.] 1. Not chronological; not in accordance with chronology; not chronologically arranged. 2. Unskilled in chronology 1817. Hence **Unchronolo·gically** *adv.*

Unchu·rch, *v.* 1620. [Un-2 2, 3, 4 b.] 1. *trans.* To deprive of church membership, excommunicate. 2. To exclude (a church, communion, sect) from participation in the Church (or some branch of it); to divest of the character of a church; to deprive of the possession of a church 1633.

Unchu·rched, *ppl. a.* 1681. [Un-1 2, Un-2 6.] 1. Excommunicated 1727. b. Deprived of the status of a church 1681. 2. Having, belonging to, no church 1870. 3. Of women: Not churched after childbirth 1727.

‖**Uncia** (*v*·nʃiă). *Pl.* -iæ (i,ī). 1834. [L., a twelfth part (of a pound or foot). Cf. Inch, Ounce.] A Roman copper coin, one-twelfth of the as in value.

Uncial (*v*·nʃiăl), *a.* and *sb.* 1650. [ad. L. *uncialis*, f. Uncia.] A. *adj.* 1. Pertaining to, connected with, an inch or an ounce. b. Duodecimal; divided into twelve equal parts 1842. 2. Of letters, writing: Having the large rounded forms (not joined to each other) used in early Latin and Greek manuscripts; also, more loosely, of large size, capital; hence written, cut, etc., in such characters 1712.

B. *sb.* 1. An uncial letter; (loosely) a capital letter 1775. b. Uncial writing 1883. 2. A manuscript written in uncial characters 1881. Hence **U·ncialize** *v. trans.* to convert into or write in u. characters. **U·ncially** *adv.*

Unciform (*v*·nsifǭɹm), *a.* and *sb.* 1733. [ad. mod.L. *unciformis*, f. L. *uncus* hook.] *Anat.* A. *adj.* Hook-shaped; esp. *u. bone, process.* B. *sb.* The u. bone of the wrist 1840.

Uncinate (*v*·nsinēt), *a.* and *sb.* 1760. [ad. L. *uncinatus*, f. Uncinus.] *Anat., Bot., Zool.* A. *adj.* Hooked; having hooks. B. *sb.* An u. process 1891. So **U·ncinated** *ppl. a.* 1752.

‖**Uncinus** (*v*nsəi·nǒs). *Pl.* -ni (-nəi). 1851. [L., f. *uncus* hook.] *Zool.* A hook-shaped part or process; esp. one of the hook-like teeth of molluscs.

Unci·rcumcised, *ppl. a.* late ME. [Un-1 2.] 1. Not circumcised. b. Not Hebrew, gentile. 2. *fig.* Not spiritually chastened or purified. late ME. So U:ncircumci·sion 1526.

Unci·rcumscribed *ppl. a.* [Un-1 2] 1610. **Unci·rcumspect** *a.* [Un-1 1] 1502, -ly *adv.* **Uncircumspe·ction** [Un-1 6] 1598. **Uncircumsta·ntial** *a.* [Un-1 1] 1646. **Unci·ted** *ppl. a.* [Un-1 2] 1581.

Unci·vil, *a.* 1553. [Un-1 1.] 1. Uncivilized; barbarous; unrefined. 2. Not courteous, impolite; unmannerly 1591. 3. Indecorous, improper 1586. 4. Contrary to civil well-being 1597.

1. Bad and unciuill Husbandry 1632. Men cannot enjoy the rights of an u. and of a civil state together Burke. 2. Ruffian: let goe that rude vnciuill touch Shaks. 3. Her faire haire..so covered her nakedness, that no part of her body was u. to sight 1611. 4. Our home-bred and inbred distractions and uncivill-civill warres 1642. Hence **Unci·villy** *adv.*

Uncivi·lity (now *rare*) [Un-1 6] 1598. **Unci·vilize** *v.* [Un-2 4 c] 1603. **Unci·vilized** *ppl. a.* [Un-1 2] 1607, -ness. **Uncla·d** *ppl. a.* [Un-1 2] late ME. **Unclai·med** *ppl. a.* [Un-1 2] Shaks. **Uncla·mp** *v.* [Un-2 1] 1809. **Uncla·rified** *ppl. a.* [Un-1 2] 1591.

Uncla·sp, *v.* 1530. [Un-2 1, 5.] 1. *trans.* To unfasten the clasp(s) of. †b. *fig.* To open up, display -1637. 2. To loosen the grasp or hold of 1627. b. *intr.* To relax a grip or grasp 1608. 3. *trans.* To release from a clasp or grip 1885.

1. b. In her bosome Ile unclaspe my heart Shaks. 2. b. I feel my feeble hands u. Longf.

Uncla·sped *ppl. a.* [Un-1 2] 1609. **Uncla·ss** *v.* [Un-2 4 b] 1873. **Uncla·ssed** *ppl. a.* [Un-1 2] 1820. **Uncla·ssical** *a.* [Un-1 2] 1725, -ally *adv.* **Uncla·ssifiable** *a.* [Un-1 1] 1849. **Uncla·ssified** *ppl. a.* [Un-1 2] 1865.

Uncle (*v*·ŋk'l), *sb.* ME. [a. AF. *uncle*, OF. *uncle, oncle* :—L. *avunculus* mother's brother.] 1. One's father's or mother's brother; also, an aunt's husband. b. *U.-in-law*, the husband of one's aunt 1561. c. *Welsh u.*, the first cousin of a parent 1747. d. *Dutch u.*: in phr. *To talk to* (a person) *like a Dutch u.*, to give him advice in a kindly, heavy manner 1838. 2. Used in addressing or designating one's uncle. late ME. b. *local* and *U.S.* Used as a form of address to an older or elderly man 1793. c. *Uncle Sam* (prob. a jocular expansion of *U.S.*), a personification of the United States of America 1813. d. Title of contributors to journals who write articles, etc. for young people, and of wireless broadcasters who entertain children 1880. 3. *slang.* A pawnbroker: usu. with possessive 1756.

2. c. Uncle Sam is rather despotic as to the disposal of my time Hawthorne. Hence **U·ncle** *v. trans.* to address (a person) as u. Shaks. **U·ncleship.**

Unclad (*v*nklæ·d), arch. pa. t. and pa. pple. of Unclothe, and partly of †*unclead* (cf. Clead *v.*) 1483.

Godiva..Unclad herself in haste Tennyson.

Unclea·n, *a.* [OE. *unclǣne*; see Un-1 1.] 1. Morally impure; unchaste; foul, obscene. b. *U. spirit*, a devil, esp. regarded as possessing or inhabiting a person OE. 2. Ceremonially impure; not to be used as food; not to be touched OE. b. Of fish: Out of season; in unwholesome condition 1861. 3. Not physically clean; dirty, foul ME. b. Of the tongue: Furred 1800.

2. Meats by the Law u. Milton. The Gentiles were no longer common or u. J. H. Newman. Hence **Unclea·n-ly** *adv.*, -ness.

Uncleanly (*v*nkle·nli), *a.* [OE. *unclǣnlic*; see Un-1 1.] 1. Morally or spiritually impure. 2. Lacking in physical cleanness; dirty. late ME.

2. Who is there so u...as to wash his feet in the water used by another? 1756.

Unclea·nsed *ppl. a.* [Un-1 2] OE. **Unclea·r** *a.* [Un-1 1] late ME., -ly *adv.*, -ness.

Unclea·red, *ppl. a.* 1637. [Un-1 2.] 1. Not cleared off or settled. 2. Of land, etc.: Not cleared of trees 1772. 3. Not freed from the imputation of guilt 1724. 4. Not cleared *up*; not explained 1802. 5. Of liquids: Not made clear 1837.

Uncle·nch *v.* [Un-2 1] ME. **Uncle·rical** *a.* [Un-1 1] 1762. **Uncle·rkly** *a.* [Un-1 1] 1875. **Uncle·ver** *a.* [Un-1 1] 1870, -ly *adv.*, -ness.

Unclew·, unclue·, *v.* 1607. [Un-2 1.] 1. *trans.* To unwind, undo; *fig.* to ruin. 2. To let down the clews of (a sail) 1855.

1. If I should pay you for 't as 'tis extold, It would vnclew me quite Shaks. Dædalus himself The cheats and windings of the dome unclewed 1855.

Uncli·mbable *a.* [Un-1 1] 1533. **Uncli·mbed** *ppl. a.* [Un-1 2] 1800. **Uncli·nch** *v.* [Un-2 1] 1598. **Uncli·ng** *v.* (*rare*) [Un-2 1, 5] 1645. **Uncli·pped, -cli·pt** *ppl. a.* [Un-1 2] late ME.

Uncloa·k, *v.* 1598. [Un-2 2.] 1. *trans.* To divest of a cloak. Usu. *refl.* or *absol.* 2. *fig.* To expose, lay bare 1659. So **Uncloa·ked** *ppl. a.* 1540.

Unclo·g *v.* [Un-2 2 b] 1607. **Unclo·gged** *ppl. a.* [Un-1 2] 1563. **Uncloi·ster** *v.* [Un-2 3] 1611. **Uncloi·stered** *ppl. a.* [Un-1 2] 1627.

Unclo·se, *v.* late ME. [Un-2 1, 5.] 1. *trans.* To cause to open. b. *fig.* To disclose, reveal. late ME. 2. *intr.* To become open. late ME.

1. Unwilling I my lips u. Gray. b. The briddes song I shal to the vnclose 1446. 2. Take roses that bigynneth forto vnclose 1440. Hence **Unclo·sing** *ppl. a.* that unclose(s).

Unclo·sed *ppl. a.* [Un-1 2] late ME.

Unclo·the, *v.* ME. [Un-2 2.] 1. *trans.* To undress (a person); to divest of clothing. Also *refl.* 2. To strip of leaves or vegetation 1547. 3. To remove a cloth or cloths from 1607.

1. *fig.* The Seleusians affirmed that He unclothed himself of His Humanity 1671. So **Unclo·thed** *ppl. a.*

Unclou·d, *v.* 1594. [Un-2 2 b.] 1. *trans.* To free from clouds 1598. 2. *fig.* To free from gloom or obscurity 1594. 3. *absol.* To become clear 1874.

Unclou·ded *ppl. a.* [Un-1 2] 1595. **Unclo·ven** *ppl. a.* [Un-1 2] 1620. **Uncloy·ed** *ppl. a.* [Un-1 2] 1562. **Uncloy·ing** *ppl. a.* [Un-1 4] 1768. **Unclu·bbable** *a.* [Un-1 1] Johnson. **Unclu·tch** *v.* [Un-2 1] 1667.

Unco (*v*·ŋkǒ), *a.*, *adv.*, and *sb.* *Sc.* and *n. dial.* late ME. [Clipped f. Uncouth *a.*] A. *adj.* 1. Unknown, strange; unusual. b. Weird, uncanny 1828. 2. Notable, great 1724.

1. Taken with an uncow disease, like unto convulsion fits 1683. It was an u. thing to bid a mother leave her ain house Scott. b. It was an u. place by night Stevenson. 2. She thinks an u. heep o' Mr. Ochtertyre 1869.

B. *adv.* Extremely, very 1724. b. *The u. guid*, rigidly moral and religious people 1786.

Whyles twalpennie-worth o' nappy Can mak the bodies u. happy Burns.

C. *sb.* 1. A strange thing or tale; a piece of news. Usu. *pl.* 1785. 2. A stranger 1800.

1. Each tells the uncos that he sees or hears Burns.

Uncoa·gulated *ppl. a.* [Un-1 2] 1770. **Uncoa·ted** *ppl. a.* [Un-1 2] 1663. **Unco·ck** *v.* [Un-2 1] 1598. **Unco·cked** *ppl. a.* [Un-1 2] 1721. **Unco·dified** *ppl. a.* [Un-1 2] 1867. **Uncoe·rced** *ppl. a.* [Un-1 2] 1791. **Unco·ffined** *ppl. a.* [Un-1 2] 1648. **Unco·gnizable** *a.* [Un-1 1] 1720. **Uncogno·scible** *a.* [Un-1 1] 1810. **Uncoi·f** *v.* (*arch.*) [Un-2 1] 1598. **Uncoi·fed** *ppl. a.* (*arch.*) [Un-1 2] 1611. **Uncoi·l** *v.* [Un-2 1] 1713. **Uncoi·ned** *ppl. a.* [Un-1 2] late ME. **Uncolla·ted** *ppl. a.* [Un-1 2] 1787. **Uncolle·cted** *ppl. a.* [Un-1 2] 1611. **Uncollo·quial** *a.* [Un-1 1] 1840.

Unco·loured, *ppl. a.* 1538. [Un-1 2.] 1. Having no colour. 2. Not invested with any specious or deceptive appearance or quality; not coloured *by* something 1585.

2. In naked simplicitie, in trueth vncoloured 1585.

Unco·mbated *ppl. a.* [Un-1 2] Lovelace. **Unco·mbed** *ppl. a.* [Un-1 2] 1561. **Uncombi·ne** *v.* [Un-2 1] 1595. **Uncombi·ned** *ppl. a.* [Un-1 2] 1611. **Uncombi·ning** *ppl. a.* [Un-1 4] Milt.

Uncome-at-able (*v*nk*v*mæ·tăb'l), *a.* 1694. [Un-1 1.] Unattainable; inaccessible.

My Honour is infallible and uncomatible Congreve.

Unco·mely, *a.* ME. [Un-1 1.] 1. Offending against propriety or decency; unbecoming, not seemly. Now *rare.* 2. Not pleasing to look upon; lacking beauty. late ME.

1. All such reasons are u. and unchristian to be objected 1622. 2. Your aspect is Dusky, but not u. Byron. Hence **Unco·meliness.**

Unco·mfortable, *a.* 1592. [Un-1 1.] 1. Causing or involving discomfort or uneasiness; deficient in provision for comfort; comfortless. †2. Inconsolable -1667. 3. Feeling discomfort 1796.

1. These five troublesome, u. years 1653. Most u. ruffians to meet in an unfriendly way 1873. Hence **Unco·mfortableness. Unco·mfortably** *adv.*

Unco·mforted *ppl. a.* [Un-1 2] 1583. **Uncomma·nded** *ppl. a.* [Un-1 2] late ME. **Uncomme·ndable** *a.* [Un-1 1] 1509, -bly *adv.* **Uncomme·nded** *ppl. a.* [Un-1 2] 1570. **Uncomme·rcial** *a.* [Un-1 1] 1768. **Uncommi·ssioned** *ppl. a.* [Un-1 2] 1659.

Uncommi·tted, *ppl. a.* late ME. [Un-1 2.] 1. Not entrusted to an agent. 2. Not committed or perpetrated 1598. 3. Not referred to a committee 1807. 4. Not committed to a course of action 1814.

Unco·mmon, *a.* 1548. [Un-1 1.] †1. Not held in common. Udall. 2. Of rare occurrence, unusual 1611. 3. Unusual in amount, degree, or quality; remarkable, exceptional 1700. 4. As *adv.* Very, remarkably. *colloq.* or *dial.* 1784. Hence **Unco·mmon-ly** *adv.*, -ness.

Uncommu·nicable *a.* [Un-1 1] late ME., -bly *adv.* **Uncommu·nicated** *ppl. a.* [Un-1 2] 1597. **Uncommu·nicating** *ppl. a.* [Un-1 4] 1650. **Uncommu·nicative** *a.* [Un-1 1] 1691, -ness. **Uncompa·cted** *ppl. a.* [Un-1 2] 1661.

Unco·mpanied, *ppl. a. arch.* 1547. [Un-1 2.] Unaccompanied.

Uncompa·nionable *a.* [Un-1 1] 1748. **Uncompa·nioned** *ppl. a.* [Un-1 2.] 1608. **Unco·mpassed** *a.* [Un-1 3] 1827, *ppl. a.* [Un-1 2] 1577. **Uncompa·ssionate** *a.* [Un-1 1] Shaks., -ly *adv.*, -ness. **Uncompe·lled** *ppl. a.* [Un-1 2] 1470. **Unco·mpensated** *ppl. a.* [Un-1 2] Burke. **Uncomplai·ning** *ppl. a.* [Un-1 4] 1744, -ly *adv.*, -ness. **Unco·mplaisant** *a.* [Un-1 1] 1693. **Uncomple·ted** *ppl. a.* [Un-1 2]

1513. Uncompli·ant *a.* [UN-¹ 1] 1659. Unco·mplicated *ppl. a.* [UN-¹ 2] 1792. Uncomplime·ntary *a.* [UN-¹ 1] 1846. Uncomply·ing *ppl. a.* [UN-¹ 4] MILT.

Uncompo·sed, *ppl. a.* 1570. [UN-¹ 2.] 1. Not composite; single. Now *rare.* 2. Not put together in proper form 1598. 3. Not reduced to an orderly or tranquil state; disordered, excited 1601. b. Unregulated, disorderly 1631. 4. Not brought into a state of concord 1650.

2. In playne and vncomposed wordes 1610. 3. b. The u. gestures of the drunkard 1649. 4. No jars undecided, no differences u. 1651.

Uncompou·nded *ppl. a.* [UN-¹ 2] 1587, -ly *adv.*, -ness. Uncomprehe·nded *ppl. a.* [UN-¹ 2] 1598. Uncomprehe·nding *ppl. a.* [UN-¹ 4] 1838, -ly *adv.*

U:ncomprehe·nsive, *a.* 1606. [UN-¹ 1.] †1. Incomprehensible. SHAKS. †2. Lacking in comprehension -1667. 3. Not comprehensive or inclusive 1862.

Unco·mpromising, *ppl. a.* 1828. [UN-¹ 4.] Not willing or seeking to compromise; unyielding, inflexible; downright; stubborn.

The most honest, fearless, and u. republican of his time MACAULAY. An u. square house 1889. Hence **Unco·mpromising-ly** *adv.*, -ness.

Unconcea·lable *a.* [UN-¹ 1] WORDSW. Unconcea·led *ppl. a.* [UN-¹ 2] 1839. Unconcei·vable *a.* (now *rare*) [UN-¹ 1] 1611, -bly *adv.* Unconcei·ved *ppl. a.* [UN-¹ 2] late ME.

Unconcei·ving, *ppl. a.* Now *rare.* 1593. [UN-¹ 4.] Slow-witted, dull.

Unconce·rn. 1711. [UN-¹ 6.] Lack of concern, anxiety, or solicitude; indifference, equanimity.

Doing all things with a graceful U. STEELE.

Unconce·rned, *ppl. a.* 1635. [UN-¹ 2.] 1. Devoid of concern or interest; unmoved, indifferent. 2. Not affected by concern or anxiety; undisturbed 1660. 3. Indifferent between two parties; impartial 1664. 4. Not concerned or involved, having no part, *in* something 1647. Hence **Unconce·rned-ly** *adv.*, -ness.

Unconce·rning, *ppl. a.* Now *rare.* 1612. [UN-¹ 4.] Of no concern to one; immaterial, irrelevant. †b. Const. *to* or with obj. -1667.

Idly casting her eyes as upon some u. pageant LAMB. b. A Subject so u. my own quality 1647.

Unconce·rnment [UN-¹ 6] 1660. Unconce·rted *ppl. a.* [UN-¹ 2] 1594. Unconclu·ded *ppl. a.* [UN-¹ 2] 1564. Unconco·cted *ppl. a.* [UN-¹ 2] 1611. Uncondem·ned *ppl. a.* [UN-¹ 2] 1526. Unconde·nsed *ppl. a.* [UN-¹ 2] 1711.

Uncondi·tional, *a.* 1666. [UN-¹ 1.] Not limited by or subject to conditions or stipulations; absolute. Hence **Uncondi·tional-ly** *adv.*, -ness.

Uncondi·tioned, *ppl. a.* 1631. [UN-¹ 2.] 1. = prec. 2. Not dependent upon, or determined by, an antecedent condition 1829. 3. *absol.* That which is not subject to the conditions of finite existence and cognition 1829.

2. I have termed this..group of reflexes *conditioned reflexes* to distinguish them from the inborn or *u. reflexes* 1927.

Unconfe·ssed, *ppl. a.* 1500. [UN-¹ 2.] 1. Not confessed or avowed. b. Of persons: Not self-avowed 1742. 2. Not having confessed; unshriven 1607.

1. It was love mutual—u., but ardent 1863. b. Like princes unconfest in foreign courts YOUNG.

Unco·nfident *a.* [UN-¹ 1] 1652. Unconfide·ntial *a.* [UN-¹ 1] 1772. Unconfi·nable *a.* [UN-¹ 1] SHAKS. Unconfi·ne *v.* [UN-² 2 b] 1651. Unconfi·ned *ppl. a.* [UN-¹ 2] 1607, -ly *adv.*, -ness. Unconfi·rmed *ppl. a.* [UN-¹ 2] 1565.

†Unconfo·rm, *a.* 1653. [UN-¹ 1.] 1. Not corresponding *to* -1667. 2. Nonconformist -1676.

1. He sees, Not u. to other shining Globes, Earth MILT.

Unconfo·rmable, *a.* 1594. [UN-¹ 1.] 1. Not conformable or correspondent *to* something. 2. *spec.* Not conforming to the usages of the Church of England, esp. as prescribed by the Act of Uniformity of 1662. 1611. 3. *Geol.* Not having the same direction or plane of stratification 1813. So **Unconformabi·lity.** **Unconfo·rmably** *adv.* **Unconfo·rmed** *ppl. a.* †nonconformist; *Geol.* = sense 3. **Unconfo·rmity,** lack of conformity (*to* something); *Geol.* the fact of being u.

Unconfou·nded *ppl. a.* [UN-¹ 2] 1577. Unconfro·nted *ppl. a.* [UN-¹ 2] 1656. Unconfu·sed *ppl. a.* [UN-¹ 2] 1609, -ly *adv.* Unconfu·table *a.* [UN-¹ 1] 1643. Unconfu·ted *ppl. a.* [UN-¹ 2] 1600. Uncongea·l *v.* [UN-² 1] 1593. Uncongea·led *ppl. a.* [UN-¹ 2] 1646.

Uncongenial, *a.* 1788. [UN-¹ 1.] 1. Not congenial or kindred; unsympathetic 1813. 2. Unsuited to the nature of the thing under consideration 1788. 3. Not to one's taste; unattractive or repellent *to* 1799.

2. In England,..where..its growth is impeded by an u. climate 1788. So **Uncongenia·lity.**

Unconje·cturable *a.* [UN-¹ 1] 1806. Unco·njugal *a.* [UN-¹ 1] MILT.

Unconne·cted, *ppl. a.* 1736. [UN-¹ 2.] 1. Not connected or associated *with* something. 2. Characterized by want of connexion; not in order or sequence; disconnected 1762. 3. Not having personal connexions; socially unallied 1802. Hence **Unconne·cted-ly** *adv.*, -ness.

Unconne·xion [UN-¹ 6] 1756.

Unco·nquerable, *a.* 1598. [UN-¹ 1.] 1. That cannot be overcome by conquest or force of arms; *fig.* of the mind, etc. 2. Incapable of being brought under control 1642.

1. The u. Will MILT. 2. The u. fertility of the soil GIBBON. His u. thirst of vengeance 1828.

Unco·nquered *ppl. a.* [UN-¹ 2] 1549. Unconscie·ntious *a.* [UN-¹ 1] BOSWELL, -ly *adv.*, -ness.

Unco·nscionable, *a.* (*adv.*) 1565. [UN-¹ 1.] 1. Having no conscience; unscrupulous; monstrously extortionate, harsh, etc. 1570. b. As an intensive 1597. 2. Of actions, etc.: Showing no regard for conscience; irreconcilable with what is right or reasonable 1565. b. Excessive, immoderate, inordinate 1586. c. As an intensive: Egregious, arrant 1593. 3. As *adv.* Unconscionably 1596.

1. *absol.* The u. will know no other law, but their profit, their pleasure 1623. 2. b. He had been, he said, a most u. time dying MACAULAY. Hence **Unco·nscionably** *adv.* in an u. manner; to an u. extent or degree.

Unco·nscious, *a.* 1712. [UN-¹ 1.] 1. Unaware (*of*); not realizing the existence, occurrence, etc., of something. 2. Not endowed with the faculty of consciousness 1712. b. Temporarily insensible 1860. c. Not present to or affecting the conscious mind; of the mind: of which the workings are not present to consciousness 1909. Also as *sb.* in *the u.* 1920. 3. Of qualities: Of which the possessor is unaware 1800. 4. Done, used, etc., without conscious action 1820.

1. He was u. of exercising any ascendancy KINGLAKE. The u. model, i.e., one taken unawares with a detective camera 1889. 2. Brute, u. matter 1744. b. The patient..was u. 1890. 3. [She] rode..with an u. grace 1890. 4. It is wrong to punish an u. act 1866. Hence **Unco·nscious-ly** *adv.*, -ness.

Unco·nsecrate *v.* [UN-² 1] 1598. Unco·nsecrate *ppl. a.* [UN-¹ 2] 1529. Unco·nsecrated *ppl. a.* [UN-¹ 2] 1579. Unconseque·ntial *a.* [UN-¹ 1] 1769. Unconsi·dered *ppl. a.* [UN-¹ 2] 1587. Unconsi·dering *ppl. a.* (now *rare*) [UN-¹ 4] 1660. Unconso·led *ppl. a.* [UN-¹ 2] 1814. Unconso·lidated *ppl. a.* [UN-¹ 2] 1802. Unco·nsonant *a.* [UN-¹ 1] 1535. Unconspi·cuous *a.* [UN-¹ 1] 1802. †Unco·nstant *a.* [UN-¹ 1] -1757.

U:nconstitu·tional, *a.* 1765. [UN-¹ 1.] Infringing the political constitution; contrary to the recognized principles of the state. Hence **Unconstitu·tionally** *adv.* **Unconstitutiona·lity.**

Unconstrai·ned, *ppl. a.* late ME. [UN-¹ 2.] 1. Not acting under constraint or compulsion. 2. Not done, made, etc., under compulsion; spontaneous 1535. 3. Free from constraint or embarrassment; natural 1704. 4. Not subject to restraint; unrestrained 1796. Hence **Unconstrai·nedly** *adv.*

Unconstrai·nt [UN-¹ 6] 1711. Unconsu·lted *ppl. a.* [UN-¹ 2] 1567. Unconsu·mable *a.* [UN-¹ 1] 1571. Unconsu·med *ppl. a.* [UN-¹ 2] 1549.

Unconsu·ming, *ppl. a.* [UN-¹ 4.] 1628. 1. That does not waste away or suffer diminution. 2. Of fire, etc.: That does not consume 1836.

2. God of the u. fire, On Horeb seen of old KEBLE.

Unconsu·mmate 1609, Unco·nsummated 1813, *ppl. adjs.* [UN-¹ 2.] Unconta·minate 1675, Unconta·minated 1611, *ppl. adjs.* [UN-¹ 2.] Unconte·mned *ppl. a.* [UN-¹ 2] SHAKS. Unco·ntemplated *ppl. a.* [UN-¹ 2] 1709. Unconte·nted *ppl. a.* [UN-¹ 2] 1568. Unconte·ntious *a.* [UN-¹ 1] 1828. Unconte·stable *a.* [UN-¹ 1] 1681. Unconte·sted *ppl. a.* [UN-¹ 2] 1678, -ly *adv.* Uncontra·cted *ppl. a.* [UN-¹ 2] 1527. Uncontradi·cted *ppl. a.* [UN-¹ 2] 1606.

Uncontro·llable, *a.* 1577. [UN-¹ 1.] †1. Irrefutable -1738. 2. Not subject to control from a higher authority; absolute 1593. 3. That cannot be controlled or restrained 1648.

1. Those, who think it an u. maxim, that power is always safer lodged in many hands than in one SWIFT. 2. His sentence in matters of Law and Religion is u. 1630. 3. His..fierce and uncontroulable temper RICHARDSON. Hence **Uncontro·llableness.** **Uncontro·llably** *adv.*

Uncontro·lled, *ppl. a.* 1513. [UN-¹ 2.] 1. Not restrained or subjected to control; ungoverned. †2. Not tested by comparison with facts -1584. †3. Undisputed -1731. Hence **Uncontro·lledly** *adv.*

Uncontrove·rsial *a.* [UN-¹ 1] 1861. Uncontrove·rtible *a.* [UN-¹ 1] 1664, -bly *adv.*

Unconve·ntional, *a.* 1839. [UN-¹ 1.] Disregarding or not according with convention. Hence **Unconventiona·lity.** **Unconve·ntional-ly** *adv.*, -ness.

Unconve·rsable, -ible, *a.* [UN-¹ 1] 1593. Unco·nversant *a.* [UN-¹ 1] 1674. Unconve·rt *v.* [UN-² 1] 1825. Unconve·rted *ppl. a.* [UN-¹ 2] 1648. Unconve·rtible *a.* [UN-¹ 1] 1695. Unconvi·cted *ppl. a.* [UN-¹ 2] 1675.

Unconvi·nced, *ppl. a.* 1643. [UN-¹ 2.] †1. Not disproved or refuted MILT. 2. Not convinced or persuaded 1675.

Unconvi·ncing *ppl. a.* [UN-¹ 4] MILT., -ly *adv.* Uncoo·ked *ppl. a.* [UN-¹ 2] 1846. Uncoo·led *ppl. a.* [UN-¹ 2] 1513. Unco·ordinated *ppl. a.* [UN-¹ 2] 1892. Unco·rd *v.* [UN-² 2 b] late ME. Unco·rdial *a.* [UN-¹ 1] 1470, -ly *adv.* Unco·rk *v.* [UN-² 1] POPE. Unco·rked *ppl. a.* [UN-¹ 2] 1791. Uncorre·cted *ppl. a.* [UN-¹ 2] late ME. Uncorru·pt *a.* [UN-¹ 1] late ME., -ly *adv.*, -ness. Uncorru·pted *ppl. a.* [UN-¹ 2] late ME., -ly *adv.*, -ness. Uncorru·ptible *a.* (now *rare*) [UN-¹ 1] late ME. Uncorru·ption [UN-¹ 6] late ME. Unco·rseted *ppl. a.* [UN-¹ 2] 1856. Unco·stly *a.* [UN-¹ 1] 1638. Uncou·nselled *ppl. a.* [UN-¹ 2] late ME.

Uncou·ntable, *a.* 1582. [UN-¹ 1.] 1. Too numerous to be counted. b. Of the pulse, etc.: Too rapid to be counted 1823. 2. Beyond estimating; immense 1858.

Uncou·nted *ppl. a.* [UN-¹ 2] 1500. Uncou·nterfeit *a.* [UN-¹ 1] 1542. Uncou·nterfeited *ppl. a.* [UN-¹ 2] 1571.

Uncou·ple, *v.* ME. [UN-² 2 b.] 1. *trans.* To release (dogs) from being fastened together in couples; to set free for the chase. b. *absol.* late ME. 2. *trans.* To disconnect, detach, sever 1533.

1. b. My Loue shall heare the musicke of my hounds. Vncouple in the Westerne valley. SHAKS.

Uncou·rsed, *a.* 1825. [UN-¹ 3.] Of masonry: Not laid or set in courses.

Uncou·rted *ppl. a.* [UN-¹ 2] 1595. Uncou·rteous *a.* [UN-¹ 1] ME., -ly *adv.*, -ness. Unco·urtly *a.* [UN-¹ 1] 1598, -liness.

Uncouth (vnkū·þ), *a.* and *sb.* [OE. *uncūþ*, f. UN-¹ + *cūþ* COUTH *a.* See also UNCO.] A. *adj.* †1. Unknown; uncertainly known -1650. 2. With which one is not acquainted; unfamiliar, unaccustomed. *arch.* OE. 3. Of an unknown or unfamiliar character; unusual, strange. Now *rare.* OE. †4. Unseemly, shocking, repellent -1797. 5. Of places: Unfrequented, desolate, wild 1542. b. Of life, surroundings, etc.: Unattractive, unpleasant, comfortless. *Obs.* or *arch.* 1611. 6. Of strange appearance; *spec.* awkward or clumsy in shape or bearing 1513. b. Uncultured; of rough or uneasy manners 1732. c. Of language, style, etc.: Awkward; pedantic; unpolished 1694.

2. The..stranger in an u. country 1632. 3. It is no u. thing To see fresh buildings from old ruines spring B. JONSON. 4. Þis unkouþe discencioun þat is bitwixe þes popes WYCLIF. 5. b. 'Tis so u. Living i' th' country, now I'm us'd to th' city MIDDLETON. 6. c.

The scholastic and u. words homogeneity, proportionateness COLERIDGE.
B. *sb.* †1. A stranger. -late ME. 2. *pl.* News. Now *dial.* 1529. Hence Uncou·th·ly *adv.*, -ness.

Unco·venanted, *ppl. a.* 1648. [UN-1 2.] 1. Not promised or secured by (*spec.* a Divine) covenant. 2. Not sanctioned by, not in accordance with, a covenant 1727. 3. Not bound by a covenant 1790. b. Not having subscribed the Covenant 1818.
1. I will cast me on his free u. mercy 1806. 3. b. To disclaim all allegiance to an u. Sovereign MACAULAY.

Unco·ver, *v.* ME. [UN-2 1, 3, 5.] 1. *trans. fig.* To disclose, make known. 2. To lay open by removing some covering. late ME. b. To strip of clothing; to expose unclothed or unveiled 1530. 3. To bare (the head) as a mark of respect or courtesy 1530. b. *absol.* 1627. 4. *Mil.* To expose, leave unprotected (troops, positions, etc.), by the moving or manœuvring of men 1796.
3. b. The House of Commons which uncovered and stood up to receive him MACAULAY.

Unco·vered, *ppl. a.* late ME. [UN-1 2.] 1. Not roofed or closed in overhead. 2. Unclothed, naked. late ME. b. Bare-headed 1570. c. Of women: Unveiled 1585. 3. Left open or exposed; not covered *by* or *with* something 1530. 4. Not protected or screened 1795. 5. Not covered by insurance 1892.

Unco·veted *ppl. a.* [UN-1 2] 1760. Unco·vetous *a.* [UN-1 1] 1500. Uncow·l *v.* [UN-2 2] 1611. Uncra·cked *ppl. a.* [UN-1 2] 1581. Uncra·mped *ppl. a.* [UN-1 2] 1797. †Uncra·nnied *ppl. a.* [UN-1 2] -1649. Uncrea·te *ppl. a.* [UN-1 2] 1548. Uncrea·te *v.* [UN-2 1] 1633.

Uncrea·ted, *ppl. a.* 1548. [UN-1 2.] 1. Not brought into existence by a special act of creation; existent without being created. 2. Not created 1607. Hence Uncrea·tedness.

†Uncre·dible *a.* [UN-1 1] -1680. Uncre·ditable *a.* [UN-1 1] 1643. Uncre·dited *ppl. a.* [UN-1 2] 1586. Uncre·sted *ppl. a.* [UN-1 2] 1611. Uncri·ppled *ppl. a.* [UN-1 2] 1800.

Uncri·tical, *a.* 1659. [UN-1 1.] 1. Lacking in judgement or discrimination; not addicted to criticism. 2. Not in accordance with critical canons or methods 1846.
1. An u. retailer of anecdotes 1854. *absol.* The u. who believe all they see in print 1874. 2. It is u. to judge an age by its greatest men 1874. Hence Uncri·tically *adv.*

Uncri·ticized *ppl. a.* [UN-1 2] 1846.

Uncro·pped, *ppl. a.* 1601. [UN-1 2.] 1. Of flowers, etc. Not cropped, e.g. by cattle. Also *fig.* Not deflowered, virgin. 2. Not docked or cut short 1802. 3. Left fallow 1857.

Uncro·ss *v.* [UN-2 1] 1599. Uncro·ssed *ppl. a.* [UN-1 2] 1560. Uncrow·ded *ppl. a.* [UN-1 2] 1701. Uncrow·n *v.* [UN-2 2] ME. Uncrow·ned *ppl. a.* [UN-1 2] 1634. Uncru·mple *v.* [UN-2 1] 1611. Uncru·mpled *ppl. a.* [UN-1 2] 1854. Uncru·shable *a.* [UN-1 1] 1873. Uncru·shed *ppl. a.* [UN-1 2] 1626. Uncry·stallizable *a.* [UN-1 1] 1791. Uncry·stallized *ppl. a.* [UN-1 2] 1759.

Unction (*v*·ŋkʃən). late ME. [ad. L. *unctionem*, f. *ung(u)ere, unct-* to smear.] 1. The action of anointing with oil as a religious rite or symbol. b. *Extreme unction*: see EXTREME *a.* 3. 1513. 2. The action of anointing as a symbol of investing with an office, esp. that of kingship. late ME. 3. *fig.* a. Of the Holy Ghost: chiefly in renderings and echoes of 1 John ii. 20 and of the hymn *Veni, Creator Spiritus* 8. late ME. b. Deep spiritual feeling, or the manifestation of this in speech; a manner suggestive of religious earnestness 1692. c. *transf.* A manner, etc., showing appreciation or enjoyment of a subject or situation; gusto 1815. 4. The action of anointing or rubbing with ointment or oil 1580. 5. An unguent or ointment 1580. b. *fig.* A soothing influence or reflection 1602.
1. Vnctions, sacrafices, and rites Ceremoniall 1500. 2. Leo III gave Alfred the royal u. HUME. 3. Thy blessed vnction from aboue 1627. b. There is a great decay of devotional u. COLERIDGE. c. He delivered the haughty speech...with u. C. BRONTË. 5. I bought an Vnction of a Mountebanke SHAKS. b. Lay not a flattering Vnction to your soule, That..my madnesse speakes SHAKS. Hence U·nctional *a.* full of spiritual u.

†U·nctious, *a.* 1477. [f. L. *unctum* ointment.] = UNCTUOUS *a.* 1. -1764.

Unctuosity (*v*ŋktiu*ǫ*·sĭti). late ME. [a. OF. *unctuosite* or ad. med.L. *unctuositas*, f. *unctuosus* UNCTUOUS; see -ITY.] Unctuousness; oiliness, greasiness.

Unctuous (*v*·ŋktiuəs), *a.* late ME. [ad. med.L. *unctuosus*, f. L. *unctum*, f. *unct-*, *unguere.*] 1. Of the nature or quality of an unguent or ointment; oily, greasy. b. Of meat: Greasy, fat, rich. *arch.* 1495. c. Characterized by the presence of oil or fat 1641. 2. Of ground or soil: Soft and adhesive, rich 1555. 3. Of vapours, etc.: Laden with oily matter; of the nature of oil or grease 1606. 4. Having an oily or greasy feel or appearance. Also of feel, touch, etc. 1668. 5. Characterized by spiritual unction (now *esp.* of an assumed or superficial kind); complacently agreeable or self-satisfied 1742.
1. Gummes..and other vnctuous frutes and trees 1555. c. Their u. and epicurean paunches MILT. 4. Oak, now black with time and u. with kitchen smoke HAWTHORNE. 5. Laying an u. emphasis upon the words DICKENS. Hence U·nctuous·ly *adv.*, -ness.

Uncu·lled *ppl. a.* [UN-1 2] MILTON. †Uncu·lpable *a.* [UN-1 1] -1748. Uncu·ltivable *a.* [UN-1 1] 1663. Uncu·ltivate *ppl. a.* (*arch.*) [UN-1 2] 1659.

Uncu·ltivated, *ppl. a.* 1646. [UN-1 2.] 1. *fig.* Not improved by education or training; uncultured. 2. Untilled 1683. b. Of plants: Wild, not cultivated 1697. 3. Not attended to or practised; not properly trained or developed 1684.
1. Such, the furniture of the u. soul! 1746. 3. Swift indeed has left..no branch of satyr u. 1751.

Uncultiva·tion [UN-1 6] 1796. Uncu·lture [UN-1 6] 1624.

Uncu·ltured, *ppl. a.* 1555. [UN-1 2.] 1. = UNCULTIVATED 2, 2 b. 2. *fig.* Unrefined; lacking culture 1777.
2. A rough soldier, u. as Marius and hardly less cruel 1878.

Uncu·nning *a.* (*arch.*) [UN-1 4] ME., -ly *adv.*, -ness. †Uncu·rable *a.* [UN-1 1] -1676. Uncu·rb *v.* [UN-2 2 b] 1580. Uncu·rbable [UN-1 1] SHAKS. Uncu·rbed *ppl. a.* [UN-1 2] 1599. Uncu·rdled *ppl. a.* [UN-1 2] 1823. Uncu·red *ppl. a.* [UN-1 2] 1548.

Uncu·rious, *a.* 1570. [UN-1 1.] 1. = INCURIOUS *a.* I. 2. Now *rare*, exc. as in 2. 2. = INCURIOUS *a.* II. 2. 1684. So Uncu·riously *adv.* 1490.

Uncu·rl *v.* [UN-2 1, 5] SHAKS. Uncu·rled *ppl. a.* [UN-1 2] 1596. Uncu·rling *ppl. a.* [UN-1 4] 1728. Uncu·rrent *a.* [UN-1 1] SHAKS. Uncu·rse *v.* [UN-2 1] SHAKS. Uncu·rsed, -st *ppl. a.* [UN-1 2] 1628. Uncurtai·led *ppl. a.* [UN-1 2] 1741. Uncu·rtain *v.* [UN-2 2] 1628. Uncu·rtained *ppl. a.* [UN-1 2] 1804.

‖**Uncus** (*v*·ŋkǝs). *Pl.* **unci** (*v*·nsəi). 1826. [L., hook.] *Zool.*, etc. A hook or hook-like process.

Uncu·shioned *ppl. a.* [UN-1 2] 1873. Uncu·stomary *a.* [UN-1 1] 1650.

Uncu·stomed, *ppl. a.* late ME. [UN-1 2.] 1. On which no custom or duty has been paid. 2. Unaccustomed *to* something. *arch.* 1520. 3. Not customary; unusual. *Obs.* or *arch.* 1552.

Uncu·t, *ppl. a.* late ME. [UN-1 2.] 1. Not cut, gashed, or wounded with a sharp-edged instrument. 2. That has not been subjected to cutting; not mown, lopped, etc. 1548. 3. Not fashioned or shaped by cutting 1596. 4. Of books: a. Not having the leaves cut open: now styled *unopened* 1828. b. Having the margins not cut down 1809. 5. Of plays, etc.: Not curtailed, without excisions 1896.

Unda·m *v.* [UN-2 1] DRYDEN. Unda·maged *ppl. a.* [UN-1 2] 1648. Unda·mned *ppl. a.* [UN-1 2] late ME. Unda·mped *ppl. a.* [UN-1 2] 1742. Unda·ngerous *a.* [UN-1 1] 1727. Unda·ring *ppl. a.* [UN-1 4] 1611. Unda·rkened *ppl. a.* [UN-1 2] 1742. Unda·rned *ppl. a.* [UN-1 2] 1797. Unda·shed *ppl. a.* [UN-1 2] 1601.

Undated (*v*·ndĕ¹tĕd), *a.* Now *rare* or *Obs.* 1486. [f. med.L. *undatus*, f. L. *unda* wave.] 1. *Her.* = UNDEE *a.* 2. *Ornith.*, *Bot.* Having wavy markings 1783.

Unda·ted, *ppl. a.* 1570. [UN-1 2.] 1. Not furnished or marked with a date; of uncertain or unstated date. 2. Having no fixed date or limit; unending 1624. 3. Marked by no striking events 1878.
3. The dull u. life of a sleepy country town 1878.

Undau·nted, *ppl. a.* late ME. [UN-1 2.] †1. Not broken in; untamed; unbridled, unrestrained -1683. 2. Undismayed, intrepid 1587. Hence Undau·nted·ly *adv.*, -ness.

Unda·zed *ppl. a.* [UN-1 2] 1757. Unda·zzled *ppl. a.* [UN-1 2] MILTON. Unda·zzling *ppl. a.* [UN-1 4] 1601. Undea·dened *ppl. a.* [UN-1 2] 1813.

Undea·dly, *a.* [OE. *undēadlic, undēaþlic*; f. UN-1 1.] †1. Not subject to death; immortal -1612. 2. Not causing death. CHAPMAN.

†Undea·f *v.* [UN-2 4 a] SHAKS. Undea·lt *ppl. a.* [UN-1 2] ME. Undea·r *a.* (*rare*) [UN-1 1] OE. Undeba·rred *ppl. a.* [UN-1 2] 1595. Undeba·sed *ppl. a.* [UN-1 2] 1753. Undeba·ted *ppl. a.* [UN-1 2] 1620. Undecay·able *a.* [UN-1 1] 1534. Undecay·ed *ppl. a.* [UN-1 2] 1513. Undecay·ing *ppl. a.* [UN-1 4] 1599.

Undecei·vable, *a.* 1534. [UN-1 1.] †1. Incapable of deceiving; undeceptive -1669. 2. Incapable of being deceived 1608.
1. Sure & vndeceiuable tokens 1534. Hence Undecei·vableness. Undecei·vably *adv.*

Undecei·ve, *v.* 1598. [UN-2 1.] *trans.* To free (a person) from deception or mistake; to deliver from an erroneous idea. Also const. *of* (an error, etc.) Hence Undecei·ver. Undecei·ving *vbl. sb.*

Undecei·ved *ppl. a.* [UN-1 2] late ME. Undecei·ving *ppl. a.* [UN-1 4] 1586. Unde·cency (now *rare* or *Obs.*) [UN-1 6] 1589.

†Unde·cent, *a.* (now *dial.*) [UN-1 1] 1546, †-ly *adv.* -1716.

Undece·ption. 1694. [UN-2 6.] The action of undeceiving or the fact of being undeceived.

Undeci·ded, *ppl. a.* and *sb.* 1540. [UN-1 2.] A. *ppl. a.* 1. That has not been decided; awaiting decision. b. Of action, opinion, etc.: Lacking in decision or definiteness 1828. c. *Coursing.* Resulting in no decision 1839. 2. Irresolute, hesitating 1779. B. *sb. Coursing.* An indecisive course 1876. Hence Undeci·dedly *adv.*

Unde·cimal, *a.* 1804. [f. L. *undecim* eleven.] Characterized by the number eleven.

Undeci·pher, *v.* 1654. [UN-2 7.] *trans.* a. To decipher. b. To make undecipherable.

Undeci·pherable *a.* [UN-1 1] WALPOLE. Undeci·phered *ppl. a.* [UN-1 2] 1668. Undeci·sive *a.* [UN-1 1] 1661, -ly *adv.*, -ness. Unde·ck *v.* (*rare*) [UN-2 1] SHAKS.

Unde·cked, *ppl. a.* 1570. [UN-1 2.] 1. Not decked or adorned. 2. Not furnished with a deck or decks 1769.
1. Eve Undeckt, save with her self MILTON. 2. Columbus found the New World in an u. boat EMERSON.

Undecla·red *ppl. a.* [UN-1 2] 1526. Undecli·nable *a.* [UN-1 1] 1530. Undecli·ned *ppl. a.* [UN-1 2] 1509. Undecompou·nded *ppl. a.* [UN-1 2] 1795. Unde·corated *ppl. a.* [UN-1 2] 1763. Unde·dicated *ppl. a.* [UN-1 2] 1661.

Undee, undé(e (*v*·ndē), *a.* 1513. [a. OF. *unde, -ee*, f. L. *unda* wave.] *Her.* Having the form of waves; wavy.

†Undee·ded *a.* [UN-1 3] SHAKS. Undee·med *ppl. a.* [UN-1 2] ME.

Undefa·ced *ppl. a.* [UN-1 2] late ME. Undefa·med *ppl. a.* [UN-1 2] 1450. Undefea·t·able *a.* [UN-1 1] 1640. Undefea·ted *ppl. a.* [UN-1 2] SHELLEY, -ly *adv.*

Undefe·nded, *ppl. a.* late ME. [UN-1 2.] †1. Not forbidden -1598. 2. Unprotected 1564. 3. *Law.* a. Not assisted by legal defence 1607. b. Against which no defence is raised 1898.
3. a. The accused is u. 1900. b. The u. petition.. for a divorce 1898.

Undefie·d *ppl. a.* [UN-1 2] SPENSER. Undefi·led *ppl. a.* [UN-1 2] late ME., Dan Chaucer, well of English vndefyled (SPENSER), -ly *adv.*, -ness. Undefi·nable *a.* [UN-1 1] LOCKE, -ness, -bly *adv.* Undefi·ned *ppl. a.* [UN-1 2] 1611, -ly *adv.*, -ness. Undeflow·ered *ppl. a.* [UN-1 2] 1533. Undefo·rmed *ppl. a.* [UN-1 2] 1672. Undege·nerate *a.* [UN-1 1] 1743. Undegra·ded *ppl. a.* [UN-1 2] 1821. Unde·ify *v.* [UN-2 4 c.] 1637. Undeje·cted *ppl. a.* [UN-1 2] 1613. Undelay·ed *ppl. a.* [UN-^{1} 2] late ME. Undelay·ing *ppl. a.* [UN-^{1} 4] 1791. Undeli·berate *a.* [UN-^{1} 1] 1550. Undeli·ght [UN-^{1} 6] SHELLEY. Undeli·ghted *ppl. a.* [UN-^{1} 2] MILT. Undeli·ghtful *a.* [UN-^{1} 1] 1585, -ly *adv.*, -ness. Undeli·vered *ppl. a.* [UN-^{1} 2] 1472. Undelu·ded *ppl. a.* [UN-^{1} 2] 1746. Unde·lved *ppl. a.* [UN-^{1} 2] 1602. Undema·nded *ppl. a.* [UN-^{1} 2] 1513. U:ndemocra·tic *a.* [UN-^{1} 1] 1839, -ally *adv.* Undemo·lished *ppl. a.* [UN-^{1} 2] 1571. Unde·monstrated *ppl. a.* [UN-^{1} 2] 1648.

Undemo·nstrative, *a.* 1846. [UN-^{1} 1.] Not given to or characterized by outward expression (of the feelings, etc.). Hence **Undemo·nstrative·ly** *adv.*, -ness.

Undeni·able, *a.* 1547. [UN-^{1} 1.] 1. That cannot be denied or refuted; indisputable. b. Of witnesses: Irrefragable 1619. 2. That cannot be refused; admitting or accepting no denial 1549. 3. Not open to objection; unexceptional 1793.

1. b. The testimony of many u. Witnesses 1663. 2. U. visitors 1839. 3. The grapes and green figs are u. 1884. Hence **Undeni·ably** *adv.*

U:ndenomina·tional, *a.* 1871. [UN-^{1} 1.] Not confined to any particular religious denomination (freq. with ref. to religious instruction in elementary schools).

Undepe·nding, *ppl. a.* Now *rare.* 1649. [UN-^{1} 4.] †1. Not depending *from* or *on* something. MILT. 2. Independent 1649.

Undeplo·red *ppl. a.* [UN-^{1} 2] 1611. Undepra·ved *ppl. a.* [UN-^{1} 2] 1646. Undepre·ssed *ppl. a.* [UN-^{1} 2] 1697. Undepri·ved *ppl. a.* [UN-^{1} 2] 1564.

Under (ʌ·ndəɹ), *sb. rare.* 1600. [f. UNDER *adv.* and UNDER- *prefix*^{1}.] 1. A state of inferiority. In phr. *to be at a great u.* Now *dial.* 2. *pl.* Under-clothes 1731.

Under (ʌ·ndəɹ), *a.* ME. [f. UNDER- *prefix*^{1}, detached from compounds on the analogy of OVER *a.*] 1. Situated lower; lying beneath or at a lower level. 2. Lying under (so as to be covered) 1547. b. Facing downwards 1731. 3. Of sound: Low, subdued 1806. 4. Subordinate; of lower rank or position 1580. 5. Below the proper standard, amount, etc.; insufficient 1673.

1. The Morne..Gaue light to all, As well to gods, as men of th' vnder globe CHAPMAN. Now gnaw'd his u., now his upper lip TENNYSON. 2. b. The upper and u. Surfaces of the two Leaves 1731. 3. Those self-solacing, those under, notes Trilled by the red-breast WORDSW. 4. For the u. characters, gather them from Homer and Virgil POPE. 5. 'Tis best to begin rather with an u. than over Dose 1737.

Under (ʌ·ndəɹ), *prep.* [Com. Teut.: OE. *under* = OS. *undar*, OHG. *untar*, ON. *undir*, Goth. *undar*; cf. Skr. *ádharas* lower, L. *infra* below.] I. In senses denoting position beneath or below something, so as to have it above or overhead, or to be covered by it. 1. With ref. to: a. The heavens or heavenly bodies. b. Particular heavenly regions, esp. as indicating terrestrial locality. late ME. c. The stars as having influence on persons 1583. 2. With ref. to the surface of the earth or water OE. 3. With words denoting natural or artificial structures or means of shelter; freq. = beneath the cover or shelter of OE. 4. *gen.* OE. b. Denoting the relationship of a horse to the rider or a ship to a person on board OE. c. = At a point just below (a part of the body) ME. d. Denoting position between the arm, etc., and the body. late ME. 5. Denoting the relationship of persons. a. To a head-covering OE. b. To something raised or carried above the head, as a standard; often as indicating military service, nationality etc. OE. c. *Naut.* Of ships, with ref. to the sails, etc. OE. 6. With ref. to something which covers, clothes, envelops, or conceals OE. b. Denoting the relationship of land to crops grown or animals reared, on it 1569. 7. Denoting position at the bottom or foot of something, or beside it but at a lower level OE. 8. With verbs of motion, impulsion, etc., denoting change of place to a position below or beneath something OE.

1. a. The greatest rascal u. the canopy of heaven GOLDSM. b. Vnder the very pole lyeth a black and high rocke 1611. c. Ah lucklesse babe, borne vnder cruell starre SPENSER. 3. *fig.* I love to shelter my self u. the Examples of Great Men 1711. 4. b. My Lord Galway had his Horse shot u. him STEELE. c. I had thought t' haue yerk'd him here vnder the Ribbes SHAKS. d. And now he her away with him did beare Vnder his arme SPENSER. 5. a. There may be..more pride and hypocrisy u. a close plain bonnet than u. a veil of silk 1846. b. A small frigate-built vessel, u. Spanish Colours DE FOE. c. Drove 24 hours u. bare poles 1780. 6. Send your letters to him, u. cover, directed to Mr. Alderman Lee FRANKLIN. b. The marshes which were formerly u. grass 1795. 7. The castle,..vnder which lieth a vallie very fertile 1585. 8. Various active substances may be introduced u. the cuticle 1806.

II. In senses denoting subordination or subjection. 1. With ref. to a person acting in a certain capacity, considered in relation to one of superior status or in authority or command OE. b. With ref. to derivative rights or claims 1818. c. Passing into the sense of 'in the time or period of' (a ruler, a dispensation, a state of affairs) OE. 2. With abstract or other sbs. denoting authority or control, direction, care, examination, restraint, etc. OE. b. With words denoting a compact, obligation, etc.: Subject to, bound, or constrained (legally or morally) by 1456. 3. With ref. to what is heavy, oppressive, or restrictive, as a burden, penalty, or disadvantage ME. b. With ref. to mental impressions: Possessed, swayed or affected by 1667. c. *ellipt.* = Under the influence of 1884.

1. The pope is the vycar generall vnder god 1531. I was commander of the ship, and had about fifty Yahoos u. me SWIFT. I made some progress in Ethics u. Professor John Bruce SCOTT. He..had fought bravely u. Monmouth MACAULAY. b. The acts or defaults of any person other than himself and those claiming u. him 1896. c. There were as many persons put to death for religious opinions u. the mild Elizabeth as u. the bloody Mary 1807. Under the reign of his present Majesty 1807. 2. Laws u. which we were born DRYDEN. But no laurels are to be won by sitting patiently u. the knife of a surgeon COWPER. Sent u. a strong guard to the tower DICKENS. U. the editorship of Mr. Charles Burney 1885. The subject u. discussion has nothing to do with chemicals 1892. b. As he was also u. a promise to the church of Philippi to see them PALEY. 3. U. Pain of never having an Husband STEELE. The glass vessels intended to retain gases u. pressure FARADAY. Wade was writing u. the dread of the halter MACAULAY. b. Are you u. the impression that they will be better cared for.. here? 1875. c. Treated..u. chloroform 1892.

III. In senses implying covering or inclusion. 1. Presented or observed in a certain form or aspect OE. b. With words implying a specious or deceptive appearance 1607. c. Beneath the form, guise, or concealment of ME. 2. Denoting inclusion in a group, category, class, etc. OE. b. Denoting occurrence in a particular section of a book, etc. 1589. 3. With words denoting protection, care, or benevolent interest OE. 4. Denoting a state or condition (freq. one imposed by implied circumstances) ME. 5. Denoting participation in the authoritative or confirmatory effect of a seal, signature, etc.: Authorized, warranted, or attested by ME. b. Implying a statement or suggestion as to the authorship of a work 1662. c. = In accordance with (some regulative power or principle) 1779.

1. When the Author represents any Passion, Appetite, Virtue or Vice, u. a Visible Shape ADDISON. *U. the name of*, = by the name of; The Egyptians..had ..even deified her u. the name of Isis BERKELEY. c. Extreme vanity sometimes hides u. the garb of ultra modesty 1854. 2. They shall speak without Oath unless the Fact be u. Felony 1676. b. The day of the present voyage u. which these remarks are introduced 1823. 3. Vnder safe conduct of the Dolphins seale 1596. 4. U. the ballot it is as easy to vote as to pay a morning call 1884. Phr. *U. the circumstances.* 5. A warrante vnder the kinges Maiesties owne handes 1551. b. Our hero..inserted his compositions, u. a fictitious signature, in his master's newspaper MAR. EDGEWORTH. c. U. this edict..more than fifty thousand human beings..were deliberately murdered FROUDE.

IV. In senses denoting inferiority or deficiency. 1. Below in dignity, rank, worth OE. 2. Less, below, in number or amount. late ME. b. Below (a specified age) late ME. c. At or for a less cost than. late ME. d. In less time than 1632. e. With less than; of less size, etc. than 1570. f. *ellipt.*: *and u.*, *or u.*, placed after statements of size, price, etc. 1482. 3. Below (a certain standard) 1615. b. *U. age*, below the (legal) age of majority 1590. c. *U.* (one's) *breath*, in a whisper 1832.

1. No person, u. a diviner, can..conduct a correspondence at such arm's length LAMB. 2. Repeated accounts make them u. five thousand H. WALPOLE. b. Then was Augustus u. nineteen years old 1692. c. They be sold far u. the Price that they be worth 1496. d. Neither can any be made u. three weeks' time 1639. e. To sink every Spanish ship u. 100 tons 1883. f. As many as were two yere old and vnder TINDALE *Matt.* ii. 16. 3. So many Nets and Fish, that are u. the Statute size WALTON. b. Three sonnes he dying left, all vnder age SPENSER. c. 'Oh hang!' she added,..u. her breath 1898.

Under (ʌ·ndəɹ), *adv.* [OE.; see prec.] 1. Below, beneath. b. With verbs of motion OE. c. Lower down on a page, etc. Chiefly in comb., as *u.-mentioned*, late ME. d. Of the sun, etc.: Below the horizon, set 1489. e. Under water, submerged 1830. f. *Down under*, in the Antipodes 1899. 2. In or into a position or state of subjection or submission ME. b. *Go u.* See GO *v.* VII. 3. *From u.*, from below 1535. 4. Less in amount, etc.; lower in price 1574.

1. Helped..with blessinges of ye depe y^t lyeth vnder COVERDALE *Gen.* xlix. 25. b. Let them..put no fyre vnder 1539. Pass your knife u. 1846. d. The sun was u. MEREDITH. 2. Love, which doth many a wonder And many a wys man hath put u. GOWER. But I keepe vnder my body, and bring it into subiection 1 *Cor.* ix. 27. The fire was got u. 1791.

Under- (ʌ·ndəɹ), *prefix*^{1}, repr. OE. *under-*: combining form of UNDER *adv.* and *prep.*; cf. OVER-. In OE. the prefix is common with verbs, less so with nouns, and rare with adjectives. Many of the OE. compounds are translations of Latin words in *sub-*, e.g. *underberan* = supportare, *undercuman* = subvenire. In most of its uses, *under-* may be freely employed to form new compounds, the meaning of which is usu. obvious.

I. Denoting local position. 1. With vbs. and parts of vbs. a. Denoting action (or continuance of a state) carried on under or beneath something, as in *under-build, -drain, -gird, -tie*, etc. **Underhanging**, *vbl. sb.* protrusion (of the lower jaw). **Underjawed**, *ppl. a.* underhung. **Underla·p**, *v. trans.* to extend some way beneath. **Undersi·gn**, *v. trans.* to sign one's name below (a writing). **Undertrea·d** *v. trans.* to tread underfoot; to subdue, subjugate. b. Denoting the action of moving so as to be or get or place oneself under something, as *undercreep, -fall, -flow, -run.* c. Rarely, the sense of 'from below' is found, as in *underpeep, -peer.* d. A noun of action with *under-* may have the same form as the verb, as *undercut, -hang, -run -thrust.*

2. With nouns. a. In names of garments worn under articles of clothing (common after the 16th century), as *under-bodice*, -PETTICOAT, *-robe*, -SKIRT, *-sleeve*, -VEST. b. Denoting that the thing specified is either placed below something else, or is the lower in position of two similar things. When pairs of things are contrasted *under-* becomes equivalent to *lower* (as *over-* to *upper*), and readily assumes an adjectival function. **U·nderboard**, the lower of two boards forming an organ bellows or wind-chest. **U·nderbough**, one of the lower branches of a tree. **U·nderfall**, a foot-hill slope. **U·nder-frame**, the substructure of a railway carriage, forming the frame on which the body rests. **U·nderlayer**, a lower layer, substratum. **U·nder-lid**, the lower lid of the eye; a lid placed under another. **U·ndersoil**, subsoil. **U·nder-su·rface**, the lower surface of something. c. Denoting position below a surface or covering, or at a depth. **U·nder-colour**, the colour under the surface-colour (as in fur, feathers, etc.). **U·nder-down**, the down below the outer feathers of birds. **U·nder-drain**, an underground drain. **U·nder-drift**, an undercurrent. **U·nderflow** *sb.*, an undercurrent. **Understra·tum**, an underlying layer or stratum. **U·nderswell**, a swell below the surface, an undercurrent. d. Denoting something which is either covered (completely or partially) by, or is subordinate to, something of the same kind, as UNDERGROWTH, UNDERWOOD. **U·nderscrub**, undergrowth, brushwood. e. With the sense of 'situated on the underside', as *underfeathering, -colouring.*

II. Denoting inferiority in rank or importance. 1. a. With designations of persons, esp. of subordinate officers, officials, or servants, as *under-actor, -agent, -bailiff, -butler, -captain, -chamberlain, -clerk, -cook, -gaoler, -gardener, -god, -housemaid, -keeper, labourer, -manager, -officer, -ranger, -servant, -sexton, -shepherd, -sheriff, -steward, -teacher, -tenant, -tutor, -vassal, -warden, -workman.* **U·nderlooker, -viewer**, *Mining*, a subordinate to the manager, who superintends the miners and workings; a subordinate overseer. b. With other nouns, in the sense of 'subordinate, subsidiary, minor', as *under-agency, -cause, -lease, -service.* **U·nder-school**, a (or the) lower or junior school.

2. With vbs., denoting reduction to (or acceptance of) an inferior or subordinate standing, as UNDERSTUDY *v.*

III. *fig.* 1. With vbs. a. In OE., various secondary meanings of *under-* are represented by such verbs as *underfōn* to receive, *understandan* to UNDERSTAND; several of these survive in ME., and a few more are added, as *undertake.* In later examples, the sense is usu. that of (secret) investigation, as *undersearch, -watch*, or of unobserved action, as †*underhear*. **b.** From the end of the 16th c. *under-* is used with vbs. in the sense of 'at a lower rate than another person', as *underbid, -buy, -quote, -sell*. **c.** occas., = 'to a point or degree below what is normal or customary', as in *undercooled*. **d.** Very rarely, subordinate action is implied, as in **Underlea·se** *v. trans.* to sublet.

2. With nouns, denoting actions, etc., which lie or are kept beneath the surface or in the background. **U·nderlook** *sb.* a covert look or glance. **U·nderplay** *sb.* an underlying or hidden motion or action. **U·ndersense,** an underlying sense (of something). **U·nderthought,** a hidden thought, reservation, *arrière-pensée*. **b.** With words denoting sound of a subdued or subordinate character, esp. when produced or perceived at the same time as a louder or more distinct sound, as UNDERTONE. **U·ndernote,** a subdued note; an undertone or suggestion.

IV. Denoting insufficiency or defect. **a.** With verbal forms. Denoting, freq. by contrast with OVER- II. 6, that the action falls below the usual or proper standard, and thus = 'at too low a rate', 'too low', 'too little', 'insufficiently'; as in *underburn, -colour-ed, -dose* v., *-horsed, -masted*, †*-matched, -measure, -officered, -paid, -pay, -peopled, -play, -praise, -prize, -reckon, -roast, -staff, -staffed, -stock, -stocked, -witted*, etc. **Underbi·ll** *v. trans.* (*U.S.*), to enter (goods) at less than the actual amount or value. **Under-expo·se** *v. intr.* and *trans.*, *Photogr.* to give too little exposure to; so **Under-exposed** *ppl. a.* **Underhi·ve** *v. trans.* to place (bees) in too small a hive. **Underli·mbed** *ppl. a.* having legs too slender in proportion to the body. **Underma·tch** *v. trans.* to unite or bestow in marriage below the proper rank or condition. **Underpri·nt** *v. trans.* to print (an engraving or photograph) with insufficient depth or distinctness. **Undershoo·t** *v. trans.* and *intr.* to shoot short (of) or too low (for). **Undertru·mp** *v. trans.* and *intr.* to follow (one's partner) in trumping, but with a lower card. **b.** With nouns, in the sense of 'insufficient, deficient, defective', contrasted with OVER- II. 8; as in *underbidder*, -ESTIMATE, *-exposure, -match* sb., *-price* sb., *-production, -wit*. **c.** With adjs., as opp. to OVER- II. 7, rare except when directly suggested by the latter, as in *underhonest* (SHAKS.; in contrast to *overproud*), *under-ripe, -scrupulous*.

Under- *prefix*[2], originating in the coalescence of UNDER *prep.* with a following noun, the compound being then usu. employed as an adj. or adv., as UNDERFOOT, -GROUND, -HAND. In attrib. use these compounds have the stress on the prefix. **U·nder-sea,** *a.* situated or lying below the sea or the surface of the sea; intended for use below the surface of the sea. **Undersea·,** *adv.* below the sea or its surface. **U·nder-size,** *a.* below the proper or ordinary size. **U·nderturf,** *a.* of earth or soil, situated or found below the turf.

Undera·ct, *v.* 1623. [UNDER-[1] IV. a.] To perform inadequately; *spec.* to act (a theatrical part) insufficiently.

U·nder-action. 1697. [UNDER-[1] II. 1 b, IV. b.] **1.** Subordinate or subsidiary action as in the plot of a play. **2.** Insufficient or defective action 1887.

U·nder-age, *a.* and *sb.* 1594. [See UNDER *prep.* IV. 3 b, and UNDER-[2].] **A.** *adj.* Not of full age; immature; in one's minority.

As if I were some u. heiress T. HARDY.

†**B.** *sb.* The time during which a person is under age; minority –1649.

The underage and weaknesse of his succeeding sonne 1641.

U·nder-arm, *a.* 1816. [UNDER-[2].] **1.** *Cricket.* = UNDERHAND *a.* Also in *Lawn Tennis*. **2.** *Swimming.* Of a side-stroke: In which the arm is not lifted above the water 1905.

U·nderback. 1635. [f. UNDER-[1] I. 2 b.] *Brewing.* A vessel placed below the mash-tub to receive the raw wort from this.

Underbea·r, *v.* Now *rare.* [OE. *underberan*; see UNDER-[1] I. 1 a and BEAR *v.*] **1.** *trans.* To sustain, endure. **2.** To support, bear up. late ME.

1. Leaue those woes alone, which I alone Am bound to vnder-beare SHAKS. **2.** To help to u. with grave advice The weighty beam whereon the state depends 1595.

Underbea·rer. Now *dial.* and *U.S.* 1700. [UNDER-[1] I. 1 a.] A coffin-bearer at a funeral.

Underbi·d, *v.* 1593. [UNDER-[1] III. 1 b, IV. a.] †**1.** *trans.* To undervalue or value at a lower rate –1645. **2.** *intr.* To make too low an offer 1611. **3.** *trans.* To supplant by making a lower or better offer 1677. **4.** *Bridge.* To bid less on (a hand) than its strength warrants 1908.

†**U·nderboard,** *adv.* 1548. [UNDER-[2].] **1.** Under the table –1642. **2.** Clandestinely, underhand; not openly or honestly –1703.

1. Till they have drunk themselves underboord 1642.

U·nder-body. 1621. [UNDER-[1] I. 2 a, b.] †**1.** The lower part of a woman's dress. **b.** *U.S.* A corset-cover. **2.** The underside of an animal's body 1879. **3. a.** *Naut.* The part of a ship's hull which is below the waterline 1895. **b.** The under part of the body of a vehicle 1904.

U·nder-breath, *sb., a.,* and *adv.* 1844 [UNDER- III. 2 b.] **A.** *sb.* A whisper or low tone. **b.** Whispered rumour 1880. **B.** *adj.* Whispered 1853. **C.** *adv.* In a whisper 1865.

Underbre·d, *ppl. a.* (*sb.*). 1650. [UNDER-[1] IV. a.] **A.** *ppl. a.* **1.** Of persons or their conduct: Of inferior breeding; wanting in refinement; vulgar. **2.** Of animals: Of inferior strain, not pure bred 1890.

1. An under-bred, fine-spoken fellow was he GOLDSM.

B. *sb.* An underbred animal (esp. a horse) 1880. So **U·nderbreeding** *vbl. sb.*

U·nderbrush. orig. *U.S.* 1813. [UNDER-[1] I. 2 c.] The shrubs or undergrowth of a forest.

A tall grove of oaks, firm under foot and clear of u. STEVENSON. Hence **U·nderbrush** *v. trans.* to clear of u. So **U·nderbush** *sb.* and *v.*

U·nder-carriage. 1794. [UNDER-[1] I. 2 b.] = UNDER-BODY 1 b. The lower framework of a vehicle which supports the superstructure.

U·nder-chap. 1607. [UNDER-[1] I. 2 b.] The lower jaw.

The stork..produces no other noise than the clacking of its under chap against the upper GOLDSM.

Undercha·rge, *v.* 1611. [UNDER-[1] IV. a.] **1.** *trans.* To charge (a person, etc.) too little; to make an inadequate charge for (a thing). Also *absol.* **2.** To charge (a gun, a receptacle) insufficiently 1794. So **U·ndercharge** *sb.*

Undercla·d, *ppl. a.* 1622. [UNDER-[1] IV. a.] Insufficiently clad.

U·nderclay. 1661. [UNDER-[1] I. 2 b.] A bed of clay beneath a seam of coal or other stratum.

U·ndercliff. 1829. [UNDER-[1] I. 2 b.] **1.** A terrace or lower cliff formed from landslips. Also *attrib.* **2.** = prec. 1883.

U·nderclothe, *v.* 1857. [Back-formation from UNDERCLOTHING.] *trans.* To provide with underclothing.

Underclo·thed, *ppl. a.* 1890. [UNDER-[1] IV. a.] Insufficiently clothed.

U·nderclothing. 1835. [UNDER-[1] I. 2 b.] Clothing worn below the upper or outer garments of ordinary indoor dress. So **U·nderclothes** 1884.

U·ndercoat. 1648. [UNDER-[1] I. 2 a, c.] **1.** A coat worn beneath another. †**2.** A petticoat –1759. **3.** The under layer of hair or down in some long-haired animals 1840.

Underconstumble, var. UNDERCUMSTUMBLE.

Undercoo·led, *ppl. a.* 1902. [UNDER-[1] III. 1 c.] Of a liquid: Brought below the normal freezing-point without crystallization.

U·nder-covert. 1805. [UNDER-[1] I. 2 b, c.] **1.** A covert of undergrowth. **2.** *Ornith.* One of the small close feathers on the underside of the wing or tail 1817.

Undercree·p, *v. Obs.* exc. *dial.* late ME. [UNDER-[1] I. 1 b, III. 1 b.] **1.** *intr.* To creep in (stealthily). **2.** *trans.* To creep under (something) 1440. **b.** *fig.* To subvert secretly; to outdo by craft or stealth 1592.

2. When we that stately wall had undercrept 1642. **b.** Now, for the price, others under-creep us, and so forestall our markets 1623.

U·ndercroft. late ME. [UNDER- I. 2 b + CROFT *sb.*[2]] A crypt; an underground vault.

The monkes..buried it [*sc.* the body] immediately in the vndercraft 1601.

Undercumsta·nd, -cumstu·mble, -constu·mble, *v. dial.* and *joc. colloq.* 1824. Jocular alterations of UNDERSTAND.

U·ndercurrent, *sb.* and *a.* 1683. [UNDER-[1] I. 2 b or c.] **1.** A current flowing beneath the upper current, or below the surface. **b.** *fig.* An activity, force, tendency, etc., of a suppressed or underlying character 1817. **2.** *attrib.* or as *adj.* That runs or flows out of sight; concealed; suppressed 1855.

1. Part of this air then returns as an u. HUXLEY. **b.** A continuous under-current of feeling COLERIDGE. **2.** Blest, but for some dark u. woe TENNYSON.

U·ndercut, *sb.* 1859. [UNDER-[1] I. 2 b, 1 a, d.] **1.** The under-side of a sirloin of beef. **2.** *U.S.* A cut made in the trunk of a tree on the side towards which it is intended to fall 1883.

Undercu·t, *v.* late ME. [UNDER-[1] I. 1 a, III. 1 b.] †**1.** *trans.* To cut down. **2.** To cut (away) below or beneath 1598. **b.** *spec.* in carving 1874. **c.** *Golf.* To strike (a ball) below the centre 1891. **3.** To supplant by working for lower wages or by underselling 1884.

2. To u. the Turf 1725. Cliffs..are often undercut by streams 1881. **b.** He has undercut his Madonna's profile..too delicately for time to spare RUSKIN. **3.** We do not want the Post Office to 'undercut' private agencies at the expense of the..taxpayer 1884. Hence **U·ndercut** *ppl. a.* **U·ndercutter,** an undercutting tool. **U·ndercutting** *vbl. sb.*

U·nder-deck. 1826. [UNDER-[1] I. 2 b.] The lower deck of a vessel.

U·nder-dip, *a.* 1839. [UNDER-[1] I. 2 c.] *Mining.* Lying lower than the bottom of the engine-pit.

Underdo·, *v.* 1611. [UNDER-[1] IV. a.] **1.** *intr.* To do less than is requisite or necessary. **2.** *trans.* To do or perform insufficiently or imperfectly 1716. **b.** *spec.* To cook insufficiently 1864.

1. He must neither ouerdoe nor vnderdoe, lest he utterly undoe 1622.

U·nderdog. orig. *U.S.* 1887. [UNDER-[1] I. 2 b.] The beaten dog in a fight; hence *fig.* the worsted party; an oppressed or (socially) inferior person.

Underdone (stress var.), *ppl. a.* 1683. [UNDER-[1] IV. a.] Of meat: Insufficiently cooked; partly raw. Also *transf.*

Underdraw·, *v.* 1799. [UNDER-[1] I. 1 a, IV. a.] **1.** *trans.* To underline. **2.** To cover (the inside of a roof, the under side of a floor) with boards or with lath and plaster 1843. **3.** To depict inadequately 1865.

2. The interior of it has been..made warmer by underdrawing the roof WORDSW.

U·nderdress, *sb.* 1785. [UNDER-[1] I. 2 a.] **1.** Underclothing. **2.** A dress or gown worn beneath another, or part of a dress simulating this 1861.

Underdre·ss, *v.* 1908. [UNDER-[1] IV. a.] *intr.* To dress too plainly. So **Underdressed** (stress var.) *ppl. a.* 1784.

U·nder-earth, *sb.* 1765. [UNDER-[2].] **1.** Subsoil. **2.** The regions below the earth 1878.

U·nder-earth, *a.* 1592. [UNDER-[2].] Subterranean.

Under-e·stimate, *v.* 1812. [UNDER-[1] IV. a.] **1.** *trans.* To estimate at too low a quantity. **2.** To rate too low; undervalue 1850. So **U·nderestimate** *sb.*

1. Neither does St. Paul ignore nor u. the value..of good works FARRAR.

Underfed (stress var.), *ppl. a.* 1835. [UNDER-[1] IV. a.] Insufficiently fed or nourished. So **Underfee·d** *v.*

†**Underfo,** *v.* Pa. t. **-feng, -fang, -fong.** Pa. pple. **-fangen, -fongen.** [OE. *underfōn*: see UNDER-[1] and FANG *v.*[1]] = next –1513.

†**Underfo·ng, -fa·ng,** *v.* ME. [UNDER-[1] III. 1 a. Cf. prec.] **1.** *trans.* To receive, accept; come to have or possess –1579. **2.** To undertake –1525. **3.** To seduce, entrap –1614.

2. To u. this labour they him prey LYDG. **3.** And some by sleight he eke doth vnderfong SPENSER.

U·nderfoot, *a.* Now *rare.* 1594. [attrib. use of next.] **1.** Lying under the foot or feet 1596. **2.** Abject, downtrodden 1594.

2. The most dejected, most u. and downe-trodden Vassals of Perdition MILT.

Under foot, underfoo·t, *adv.* Also **under-feet.** ME. [UNDER *prep.*] **1.** Beneath the foot or feet; on the ground; esp. with *tread, trample.* **b.** *Naut.* See FOOT *sb.* (Phrases). **2.** *fig.* In(to) a state of subjection or inferiority ME. †**3.** Below the real or current value –1654.

1. As a dead coarse that is troden vnder fete 1539. Katerine, that Cap of yours becomes you not, Off with that bable, throw it vnder foote SHAKS. Underfoot the Violet, Crocus, and Hyacinth with rich inlay Broiderd the ground MILT. **2.** Tho was the vertu sett above And vice was put under fote GOWER. **3.** When men did let their Land underfoot, the Tenants would fight for their Landlords SELDEN.

U·nder-frame. 1855. [UNDER-[1] I. 2 b.] The substructure of a railway carriage.

U·nder-ga·rment. 1530. [UNDER-[1] I. 2 a.] An article of underclothing.

U·nder-glaze, *a.* (*sb.*). 1882. [UNDER-[2].] 1. *U. painting*, the painting on pottery before the glaze is applied 1883. b. *absol.* as *sb.* 1882. 2. Of colours: Used in, adapted for, such painting 1883.

Undergo (vndəɪgōu·), *v.* [Late OE. *undergán*; f. UNDER-[1] I. 1 b + *gán* GO *v.*] †1. *trans.* To undermine; to defraud; to get the better of –1642. †2. To go or pass under –1627. 3. To be subject to, to serve (*rare*) 1586. 4. To bear, suffer, go through (pain, danger, etc.) ME. †b. To sustain (a burden) –1656. 5. To submit, or be subjected, to (a law, inspection, etc.); to experience ME. b. To come or fall under, to experience; to have imposed on one 1599. c. To experience, pass through (a change) 1634. †d. To partake of, enjoy. SHAKS. 6. To undertake. Now *rare.* 1601. †b. To discharge (an office) etc. –1726.

1. Þou hast me gyled and vndur-gone 1380. Affraid lest thou shouldest u. thy selfe in purchasing the pearle 1642. 2. Better my shoulders underwent the earth, than thy decease CHAPMAN. 3. So have you made our language u. you BROWNING. 4. Much danger do I vndergo for thee SHAKS. His fine spirit was broken by the anxieties he had undergone 1832. 5. In watir baptized he alle þo þat wolde bapteme vndir go 1425. Several clauses again underwent examination 1844. b. Every year thousands u. this operation LADY M. W. MONTAGU. c. She reviv'd And underwent a quick immortal change MILT. 6. I haue mou'd already Some certaine of the Noblest minded Romans To vnder-goe, with me, an Enterprize SHAKS. b. [He is] a very young man to u. that place PEPYS.

Undergraduate (vndəɪgræ·diu,ĕt), *sb.* and *a.* 1630. Also colloq. abbrev. **Undergra·d.** [UNDER-[2].] A. *sb.* 1. A university student who has not yet taken a degree. 2. *fig.* One imperfectly instructed or inexpert (*in* something) 1659.

2. Here the under graduates in iniquity commence their career with deer stealing 1795.

B. *adj.* †1. Of inferior importance –1659. 2. Of undergraduate status; of or belonging to an undergraduate; characteristic of undergraduates 1685.

2. In my u. days 1889. Hence **U·ndergraduette**, a woman undergraduate (*slang.* or *colloq.*) 1920.

U·nderground, *a.* (*sb.*). 1590. [f. next.] A. *adj.* 1. Found, living, situated, acting, occurring, used, etc., below the surface of the ground 1610. b. *U. railway*, a railway running under the surface of the ground, esp. one beneath a city 1834. 2. *fig.* Hidden, secret; not public, avoiding notice 1677.

1. Some Jerusalem or under-ground artichokes SOUTHEY. *fig.* The stream of London charity flows in a channel..noiseless and u. DE QUINCEY. b. *U.S.* (Also *u. line*) The secret system by which slaves were enabled to escape to the Free States and Canada 1852. 2. Brougham..has been for some time in u. communication with Carlton House 1820.

B. *sb.* 1. The region below the earth; the lower regions 1590. b. An underground space or passage 1594. 2. Subsoil 1812. b. Ground lying at a lower level or beneath trees 1842. 3. An underground railway 1887.

Undergrou·nd, *adv.* 1571. [UNDER-[2].] 1. Below the surface of the ground. 2. *fig.* In secrecy; in a hidden or obscure manner 1632.

1. Tisiphone, let loose from under Ground DRYDEN. He..wished that lady..u. rather than there THACKERAY. 2. But in Philosophical Disputes, 'tis not allowable to work u. SHAFTESB.

U·ndergrowth. 1600. [UNDER-[1] I. 2 b, IV. b.] 1. A growth of plants or shrubs under trees; brushwood. b. The shorter stems of flax and other plants 1765. 2. A growth of (shorter and finer) hair or wool underlying the outer fur or fleece 1641. 3. The condition of being undergrown or undersized 1891.

1. This intricate wild wilderness of trees..and u. of odorous plants SHELLEY.

U·nderhand, *a.* (*sb.*). 1592. [f. next.] 1. Of a swimming stroke: Made with the hand below the surface of the water 1705. b. *Cricket.* Of bowling: With the hand under the ball and lower than the shoulder or (formerly) the elbow 1850. c. Of a bowler: Bowling thus 1848. 2. Secret, surreptitious. Also *absol.* 1592. b. Of persons: Not straightforward 1842. 3. Not open or obvious; unobtrusive 1600. B. *sb.* An underhand ball; underhand bowling 1866.

2. Several indirect and u. Practices ADDISON. b. I am often accused of being u. and uncandid J. H. NEWMAN. 3. I..haue by vnder-hand meanes laboured to disswade him from it SHAKS.

Underha·nd, *adv.* OE. [UNDER-[2].] †1. In (or into) subjection; in (one's) possession or power; in hand, under attention or execution –1693. 2. *Cricket.* With underhand action (see prec. 1 b) 1828. 3. In secret; covertly, stealthily. Now *arch.* 1538.

3. He does it under hand, out of a reseru'd disposition to doe thee good without ostentation 1611. The rest being put to the sword, saue those that were vnderhand saued by the Sidonians 1615.

Underhanded (stress var.), *adv.* and *a.* 1822. [f. UNDERHAND *a.*] A. *adv.* = prec. 2, 3. B. *adj.* 1. = UNDERHAND *a.* 2, 2 b. 1853. 2. Short of 'hands'; undermanned 1834. Hence **Underha·ndedly** *adv.*, **-ness.**

Underhung (stress var.), *ppl. a.* 1683. [UNDER-[1] I. 1 a.] 1. Having the lower jaw projecting beyond the upper, or coming unusually far forward. b. Projecting beyond the upper jaw 1809. 2. *Mech.* Suspended on an underlying support; *spec.* of a sliding-door moving on a rail placed below it 1855.

1. He..must lament his being very much underhung JANE AUSTEN.

Underi·vative *a.* [UN-[1] 1] 1656. **Underi·ved** *ppl. a.* [UN-[1] 2] 1630.

U·nder-jaw. 1687. [UNDER-[1] I. 2 b.] The lower jaw or mandible.

U·nder-king. OE. [UNDER-[1] II. 1 a.] A prince or ruler subordinate to a chief king.

Each having its own Ealdorman or Under-King, though united under one supreme chief FREEMAN. So **U·nder-ki·ngdom** 1581.

Underlaid (stress var.), *ppl. a.* ME. [UNDER-[1] I. 1 a.] 1. Laid under or below. 2. Supported or strengthened from below 1530. b. Supplied underneath *with* or *by* (something) 1658. 3. *Printing.* Of type, etc.: Raised by means of an underlay 1771.

2. That mans faith is well u., that upholds it selfe by the Omnipotency of God 1618. b. The Floor of the Vault was all loose, and u. with several Springs 1712.

U·nderlay, *sb.* 1612. [UNDER-[1] I. 1 d.] 1. a. A piece added to the sole of a shoe. b. = EKE *sb.* 2 b. 1641. c. A wedge or piece inserted as a prop or support, esp. so as to make one part level with another 1683. d. *Printing.* A piece of paper or cardboard placed under type, plates, etc. to raise them to the required level 1683. e. Felt, etc. laid under a carpet or mattress. 2. *Mining.* = DIP *sb.* 5. 1831.

Underlay·, *v.* [OE. *underlecgan*; see UNDER-[1] I. 1 a and LAY *v.*] 1. *trans.* To support by placing something beneath. Const. *with.* †b. To sole or patch the soles of (shoes) 1530. c. *Printing.* To adjust (type, etc.) with an underlay (see prec. 1 d) 1683. 2. To put (something) beneath OE. 3. = UNDERLIE *v.* 3. 1591. 4. intr. *Mining.* To slope, incline from the perpendicular 1728.

1. If the Board be too thin, they u. that Board upon every Joyst with a Chip 1679. b. *fig.* Our souls have trode awry in all mens sight, We'll u. 'em till they go upright 1622. 4. It occurs reposing on granite, and underlaying basalt 1799.

U·nderleaf. 1707. [UNDER-[1] I. 1 b.] 1. A variety of cider apple. 2. The under surface of a leaf 1873.

Underle·t, *v.* 1677. [UNDER-[1] III. 1 c, d.] 1. *trans.* To let at an amount or rental less than the true value. 2. To let to a subtenant; to sublet 1819.

1. The land indeed had been greatly underlet 1874.

U·nderlie, *sb.* 1778. [UNDER-[1] I. 1 d.] *Mining.* = UNDERLAY *sb.* 2.

Underlie·, *v.* [OE. *underlicgan*; see UNDER-[1] I. 1 a + LIE *v.*[1]] †1. *trans.* To be ruled by, to be subject or subordinate to (a person or thing) –1594. 2. To submit to; to undergo; to have imposed on one: a. a penalty, accusation, etc., OE.; b. *Sc.* the law 1453. 3. To lie under; esp. *Geol.* of strata 1600. b. *fig.* To form a basis or foundation to; to exist beneath the surface-aspect of 1856. †4. *intr.* To be buried –1739. 5. *Mining.* = UNDERLAY *v.* 4. 1778.

1. Obeye ȝe to ȝoure prouostis, or prelatis, and vndir-ligge to hem WYCLIF *Heb.* xiii. 17. 2. [He] shall incur and underly the pain and punishment of death 1678. b. To underly the law for the said slauchter 1507. 3. These deep-seated igneous formations must u. all the strata containing organic remains 1830. b. The charm which underlies the facts of rustic life SYMONDS. 4. Here underlyes William Plowden 1739. 5. The vein underlies west 10 degrees from the vertical 1899.

U·nderlife. 1847. [UNDER-[1] I. 2 c.] A life beneath the surface.

U·nderline, *sb.* [UNDER-[1] I. 2 b, c.] 1. The line of the lower part of the body (of an animal). 2. A line drawn under written or printed words. b. *pl.* Ruled guiding lines placed under paper that is being written on. 1888.

Underli·ne, *v.*[1] 1545. [UNDER-[1] I. 1 a.] *trans.* To furnish with an underlining; to form an underlining to.

Underli·ne, *v.*[2] 1531. [UNDER-[1] I. 1 a.] *trans.* To mark (words, etc.) with a line or lines drawn underneath for emphasis, as a direction to italicize, etc. b. *fig.* To emphasize, esp. in utterance 1880.

U·nderlinen. 1862. [UNDER-[1] I. 2 a.] Underclothing of linen (or similar) material.

U·nderling, *sb.* (*a.*). [Early ME., f. UNDER *adv.* 2 + -LING.] A. *sb.* 1. One who is subordinate or subject to another; in later use *esp.* a lower official, an understrapper. b. A weakly plant, animal, or child. Now *dial.* 1688. 2. *predic.*, passing into adj. Subject, subordinate (*to*). late ME. b. So in attrib. use 1615.

1. My lord..I am ȝoure knyght and ȝoure vndirlyng 1400. He undoubtedly felt..an impatience of fools and underlings EMERSON. 2. Lilis..would not be vnderling, and Adam would not endure her his equall PURCHAS. b. The u. Pedlars amongst the Presbyterians may write what they please 1693.

B. *adj.* 1. Undersized, small, weak 1722. 2. Low-growing 1830. 3. Unimportant 1804.

2. A most troublesome u. weed 1830. 3. While they can employ me more to their own advantage in little u. works SOUTHEY.

U·nderlining, *sb.* 1580. [UNDER-[1] I. 2 c.] The inner lining of a garment, etc.; a lining under the brim.

Underli·ning, *vbl. sb.* 1864. [f. UNDERLINE *v.*[2]] The action of the vb. UNDERLINE; a line or lines drawn beneath words, etc.

U·nderlip. 1669. [UNDER-[1] I. 2 b. Cf. G. *unterlippe.*] The lower lip of a person, animal, or insect.

U·nderlying, *ppl. a.* 1611. [f. UNDERLIE *v.*] Lying under or beneath.

The stones That name the under-lying dead TENNYSON. The identity of phraseology does but serve to bring into prominence the u. differences 1882.

Undermanned (stress var.), *ppl. a.* 1867. [UNDER-[1] IV. a.] Not furnished with a sufficient number of men; short-handed.

U·ndermaster. late ME. [UNDER-[1] II. 1 a.] A subordinate instructor; esp. an assistant teacher in a school.

Under-mentioned (stress var.), *ppl. a.* 1640. [UNDER *adv.* 2 b.] Named or noted below or in a place beneath.

Undermi·ne, *v.* Also †**undermind(e.** ME. [f. UNDER-[1] I. 1 a + MINE *v.*] 1. *trans.* To excavate beneath, to make a passage or mine under (a wall, etc.), esp. as a military operation; to sap. b. *absol.* To make mines. late ME. c. *fig.* late ME. 2. a. Of water: To work under and wash away (ground, etc.). late ME. b. Of animals: To burrow under or in; to make insecure through burrowing; to make (a passage) by burrowing 1526. c. *Path.* To erode below the surface 1879. 3. *fig.* To work secretly against (a person); to overthrow or supplant by underhand means. late ME. 4. To win over, pervert, by subtle means 1457. 5. To weaken, injure, destroy or ruin, insidiously 1569. b. To sap (the health or constitution) by degrees 1812.

1. The wal of Babilon..with vndermyning shal be vndermyned WYCLIF *Jer.* li. 58. c. As yet, the house is not fallen; but it is completely undermined BURKE. 2. a. A strong heady streame, undermining great hygh bankes 1562. b. There was a Towne in Spayne vndermined with Connyes LYLY. 3. He maye well be called Iacob, for he hath vndermined me now two tymes COVERDALE *Gen.* xxvii. 36. He.. with slie shiftes and wiles did vnderminde All noble Knights SPENSER. 4. She undermin'd my Soul With Tears DRYDEN. 5. Goe not aboute to vndermine my life

SIR T. MORE. A dangerous sort of men that would u. received principles BERKELEY. b. But years advancing undermined his health CRABBE. Hence **Undermi·ning** *vbl. sb.* and *ppl. a.* **Undermi·ningly** *adv.*

U·ndermost, *a.* 1555. [UNDER *adv.* + -MOST.] 1. *adj.* Holding the lowest place or position. 2. *predic.* In the lowest or lower place or position 1617.

1. The fall is greater from the first to the second, then from the second to the vndermost SIDNEY. 2. The assailant..flung himself above the struggling Saracen, and..kept him u. SCOTT.

Undern (ʊ·ndəɹn). *Obs.* exc. *arch.* and *dial.* [Com. Teut.; OE. *undern*, OFris. *unden*, OS. *undorn*, OHG. *untarn*, ON. *undorn*, Goth. *undaurn-* (the relationships of the stems are doubtful).] †1. The third hour of the day; about 9 a.m.; in eccl. use = tierce -1500. †2. The sixth hour; midday -1493. 3. The afternoon or evening. Now *dial.* 1470. 4. *dial.* A light or intermediate meal esp. one taken in the afternoon 1691. †5. *attrib.* in *u. tide, time.*

1. Whanne it is the thridde our of the day, or vndirne WYCLIF *Acts* ii. 15. 2. Sothli the our was, as the sixte, or vndurn WYCLIF *John* iv. 6. 3. *The Aunder*, or as they pronounce it in Cheshire, Oneder; the afternoon RAY. 4. *Oanders*, the afternoon meal, often sent out in harvest time to the labourers in the fields 1887.

Undernamed (stress var.), *ppl. a.* 1599. [UNDER *adv.* 2 b.] Named or specified below.

Underneа·th, *prep., adv.,* and *sb.* [OE. *underneoðan*, f. UNDER *prep.* and *adv.* + *neoðan* beneath.] A. *prep.* 1. Beneath or below (in local position). b. *fig.* Under the form, cover, protection, authority, etc., of. late ME. 2. Under the power or control of. Now *arch.* late ME.

1. Vndernethe that castel they sawe a knyghte standynge MALORY. b. The truths which lay u. its false worship 1845. 2. A man u. many Passions, but above fear 1651.

B. *adv.* 1. Down below; at a lower level OE. b. Below or beneath other clothing. late ME. c. Lower down on a sheet of paper, etc. late ME. 2. On the under side 1776.

1. Lyke as they yt wrestleth be somtyme aboue, & somtyme vnderneath 1526. *fig.* If such a Union as this be not accepted on the Army's part, be confident there is a single Person u. MILT. b. He wore a suit of black armour..and u. a shirt of close mail 1856. 2. The leaves..not shining or hoary u. 1812.

C. *sb.* The under part or side 1676.

U·nderpart. 1662. [UNDER-¹ I. 2 b, II. 1 b.] 1. A lower part or portion. b. *pl.* The under-side of the body (of a bird or animal) 1783. 2. A minor role, esp. in a play; a subordinate actor 1679. 3. A subdivision 1711.

2. Making..even Jocasta but an u. to him DRYDEN. 3. Uniform Division into Parts and Under-Parts 1711.

U·nder-pe·tticoat: see UNDER-¹ I. 2 a.

Underpi·n, *v.* 1522. [UNDER-¹ I. 1 a.] 1. *trans.* To support, strengthen (a building, etc.) from beneath, *spec.* by laying a solid underground foundation or substituting stronger or more solid for weaker materials 1533. b. *fig.* To support, corroborate 1522. 2. To form a base or support to 1878.

1. We underpinned that West End of it, where we found that there was nothing supporting the upper Work, but the Bond of the Stones 1776. b. Was it unlawfull..to u. Episcopacy with some Texts of Scripture? 1646. Hence **Underpi·nning** *vbl. sb.* the action of the vb.; the materials or structure used for this; *fig.* a prop.

U·nderplay, *sb.* 1845. [UNDER-¹ II. 1 b. UNDER *adj.*] 1. An underlying action or motion. 2. *Cards.* The leading of a low card when a higher card is in the hand 1850.

U·nderplay, *v.* 1733. [UNDER *adv.*] 1. *refl.* To play below one's ability. 2. *intr.* To play a low card when holding a high one 1850.

U·nderplot. 1668. [UNDER-¹ II. 1 b, III. 2.] 1. A (dramatic or literary) plot subordinate to the main plot. 2. An underhand scheme or trick 1668.

1. I have laid my under-plot in low life SHERIDAN. 2. They still suspect an Under-Plot in every female Action ADDISON.

U·nderprop, *sb.* 1579. [UNDER-¹ I. 2 b.] A prop or support placed under a thing.

Underpro·p, *v.* 1513. [UNDER-¹ I. 1 a.] 1. *trans.* To support with or as with a prop or props 1532. 2. *fig.* To support; to maintain 1513. 3. To form a prop or support to (something) 1590.

1. This doctrine is a..Pillar, to under prop the Chamber in Hell, which they call Purgatory 1645. 2. He thought fit to u. it with his earthly God, the Leviathan WARBURTON. 3. Six columns..underpropt a rich Throne of the massive ore TENNYSON.

Underra·te, *v.* 1623. [UNDER-¹ IV. a.] †1. *trans.* To depreciate -1649. 2. To assess (for taxation) too low 1641. 3. To rate or estimate at too low a value or worth 1650. 4. To under-estimate in amount or extent 1691.

Underru·n, *v.* 1547. [UNDER-¹ I. 1 a, b.] 1. *trans.* To run, flow, or pass beneath 1594. 2. *Naut.* To overhaul or examine (a cable, etc.) on the under side, *spec.* by drawing a boat along under it 1547. b. To pull in (a net or trawl) in order to clear it of the catch and reset it 1883. 3. In pa. pple.: see quot. 1855.

1. The granite is under-run by schistose earth 1799. The principle..underran all these modifications 1882. 2. The harbour..is..very rocky, the bottom so much so as to make it necessary to under-run every cable 1798. b. Underrunning a trawl means pulling it in on one side of the dory, picking off the fish, rebaiting the hooks, and passing them back to the sea again KIPLING. 3. Cut away all hoof that is separated from the sensitive parts, or..'under-run' 1855.

U·nder-ru·nner. 1882. [UNDER- I. 1 b.] *Printing.* A side-note continued across the foot of the page.

Undersco·re, *v.* 1771. [UNDER- I. 1 d.] *trans.* To underline.

†**Underscri·ber.** 1681. [UNDER-¹ I. 1 b.] A subscriber to a document -1785.

U·nder-se·cretary. 1687. [UNDER-¹ II. 1 a.] An assistant secretary; esp. as the title of the official immediately subordinate to or ranking next in a department below a Secretary of State. Hence **U·nder-se·cretaryship.**

Underse·ll, *v.* 1622. [UNDER-¹ III. 1 b, IV. a.] 1. *trans.* To sell at a lower price than (another person). b. *transf.* (Said of the thing sold) 1757. 2. To sell at too low a price 1647.

2. The farmer for haste is forced to under-sell his corn 1662.

U·nderset, *sb.* 1747. [UNDER-¹ I. 2 b.] 1. *Mining.* A lower vein of ore. 2. An undercurrent running counter to the surface motion of water 1815.

Underse·t, *v.* ME. [UNDER-¹ I. 1 a.] 1. *trans.* To support or strengthen by something placed beneath; to prop up. b. To serve as a support to (*rare*) ME. 2. *fig.* To support, sustain, or strengthen. late ME. 3. To set or place under something ME. 4. To sublet 1804.

1. He shall prepare props..to vnder set his vines 1600. The Custom House, London, was underset some years ago, a new foundation having been made to it without the superstructure being disturbed 1842. 2. Yf oure soules be truely vnderset wyth sure hope TINDALE. 3. Iulian the Apostata did vnderset his shoulder, to shore vp the seruice of the false Gods 1587. 4. These middle-men will u. the land, and live in idleness MAR. EDGEWORTH. Hence **Underse·tter,** a supporter, a prop. **Underse·tting** *vbl. sb.*

U·nderse:ttle. *Obs.* exc. *Hist.* ME. [f. UNDER-¹ II. 1 a + *-set(t)le* = OE. *-setla*, f. *set-*, root of SIT *v.*] One who occupies a house (or part of one) held by another; a subtenant.

U·ndershirt. 1648. [UNDER-¹ I. 2 a.] A garment worn under a shirt; a vest.

Undersho·re, *v.* late ME. [UNDER-¹ I. 1 a.] 1. *trans.* To prop up; to strengthen with shores. 2. *fig.* To support, strengthen 1500.

1. To vnder-shore the ruinous walls 1608. 2. Yf ye wyll vnder-shore Hys croked old age 1500.

U·ndershot, (*ppl.*) *a.* (and *sb.*). 1510. [UNDER-¹ I. 1 a.] 1. Of a mill-wheel: Driven by water passing under the wheel; so of a mill. 2. = UNDERHUNG *ppl. a.* 1. 1881. B. *sb.* An undershot wheel or mill 1705.

U·ndershrub. 1598. [UNDER-¹ I. 2 d.] A low-growing shrub; *spec.* in *Bot.*, a plant with a shrubby base.

U·nderside. 1680. [UNDER-¹ I. 2 b.] The under or lower side or surface.

Undersigned, *ppl. a.* 1643. [Cf. SUBSIGN *v.*] Whose signature is below.

Under-sized (stress var.), *ppl. a.* 1706. [UNDER-¹ IV. a.] Below the proper or ordinary size.

U·nder-skirt. 1861. [UNDER-¹ I. 2 a.] 1. A skirt worn under another, a petticoat. 2. A foundation for the drapery of the skirt 1883.

U·ndersong. 1579. [UNDER-¹ III. 2 b.] 1. A subordinate song or strain, esp. one serving as an accompaniment or burden to another. Freq. *transf.* of natural sounds. 2. *fig.* An underlying meaning; an undertone 1631.

1. Who the Roundelay shoold singe And who againe the vndersong should beare DRAYTON. 2. If there is any fault in the Preface, it is not affectation, but an u. of disrespect to the public KEATS.

Understand (ʊndəɹstæ·nd), *v.* [OE. *understondan*, *-standan* = OFris. *understonda*; cf. MLG. *understân*, MHG. *understân*, *-stên*.] 1. *trans.* To comprehend; to apprehend the meaning or import of. b. To be expert with or at by practice 1533. c. To apprehend clearly the character or nature of (a person) 1587. †d. *refl.* To know one's place -1745. 2. To be able to interpret (a language, words, signs) OE. b. *To u. each other*, to be agreed or in collusion 1663. 3. To comprehend as a fact; to realize. Chiefly with clause as obj. OE. 4. To accept as true or existent; to regard as settled or implied without specific mention OE. b. To have knowledge of, to know or learn, by information received ME. c. To take or accept as a fact, without positive knowledge or certainty; to believe 1751. 5. To interpret or view in a certain way OE. b. To regard as denoted *by* (the expression used) ME. c. To regard (an expression, etc.) as used *of* or applied to 1549. 6. To supply mentally (something not expressly stated). Chiefly *Gram.* 1530. b. In pa. pple.: Implied, though not expressed 1580. 7. To stand under. late ME. 8. *intr.* To have comprehension or understanding (in general or in a particular manner) OE. b. Const. *about*, etc. OE. 9. In parenthetic use (chiefly *I u.*): To believe or assume, on account of information received or by inference ME.

1. The multytude of dyuerse ceremonyes..not being vnderstanded nor perceyued of the comen sorte 1523. Now clear I u. What oft my steddiest thoughts have searcht in vain MILT. One half of the world cannot u. the pleasures of the other JANE AUSTEN. b. He..understood a small Sword excellently well 1727. c. It is my misfortune to be little understood 1846. d. You doe not vnderstand your selfe so cleerely, As it behoues my Daughter, and your Honour SHAKS. 2. Now herkeneth, euery maner man That englissh understonde kan CHAUCER. b. 'You trust me', replied Leather..with a look as much as to say, 'we u. each other' SURTEES. 3. Howbeit they vnderstode not, that he spake of the father COVERDALE *John* viii. 27. This Œdipus, you must u...was son to a King of Thebes ADDISON. 4. Warr then, Warr Open or understood must be resolv'd MILT. b. When the colonell's wife understood her husband's bad accommodation 1664. c. The General, I u. by his last letter, is in town COWPER. 5. I shewed hym that it was not necessary, that the words shulde so be vnderstonde as they sownde 1533. b. We do not u. by this advancement, in general, the mere making of money RUSKIN. c. Which is true, if understood only of the Rivers of Italy ADDISON. 6. The Ancient Romans said *Saturam* understanding *Lancem* 1704. An exception in favour of the Nabob was, from standing usage, so much understood, that to express it had appeared altogether useless JAMES MILL. 7. Thy rude hand Would lift a shield, thou canst not vnder stand HEYWOOD. 8. They know not nor will u., In darkness they walk on MILT. b. You quite u. about that little matter of business being safe in my hands? 1860. 9. Hire fader was a man of grete powre, And kyng of aufrike as I vnderstonde 1440. Hence **Understa·ndable** *a.* **Understa·nder** (now *rare*).

Understanding (ʊndəɹstæ·ndiŋ), *vbl. sb.* OE. [f. prec. + -ING ¹.] 1. Ability to understand; intelligence, judgement. b. *Of u.*, intelligent, capable of judging with knowledge. late ME. c. With *the*: The faculty of comprehending and reasoning; the intellect. late ME. 2. The degree or quality of the intellectual faculty in a particular person or set of persons. late ME. †3. Meaning, signification -1728. 4. *A good u.*, amicable or friendly relations 1649. b. An agreement of an informal but more or less explicit nature 1812. 5. *slang. pl.* a. Boots, shoes 1822. b. Legs, feet 1828.

1. Vnderstanding is a power of the Soule, by which we perceiue, know, remember, and Iudge 1621. c. The U., like the Eye..takes no notice of it self LOCKE. 2. It gave him..a very mean opinion of our understandings SWIFT. 3. Single words haue their sence and vnderstanding altered 1589. 4. To cultivate a good u. between the two countries 1762. b. With this u. we parted for the night TYNDALL.

Understa·nding, *ppl. a.* ME. [f. as prec. + -ING 2.] Having knowledge and judgement; discerning, intelligent, sagacious.

Geue therfore vnto thy seruaunt an vnderstandyng hert BIBLE (Great) 1 *Kings* iii. 9. An elephant (an vnderstanding beast) SIR T. HERBERT. Aristotle.. was an u. fellow OTWAY. Hence **Understa·ndingly** *adv.*

Understa·te, *v.* 1824. [UNDER- IV. a.] *trans.* To fall below the truth in stating; to put too low. Also *absol.* So **Understa·tement** 1799.

U·nder-stew·ard. 1472. [UNDER-1 II.] Hence **U·nder-stew·ardship.**

Understoo·d, *ppl. a.* 1605. [f. UNDERSTAND *v.*] 1. Comprehended; known; appreciated, realized. 2. Agreed upon; assumed as known or fixed 1607. 3. *Gram.* Implied but not expressed 1848.

2. It was an u. thing that no one was to be ill or tired MRS. GASKELL.

U·nderstra:pper. 1704. [f. UNDER-1 II. 1 a + STRAP *v.*] A subordinate; an underling. So **U·nderstra:pping** *a.* of a subordinate or inferior character or standing.

Understu·dy, *v.* 1874. [UNDER-1 II. 2.] 1. *trans.* To study (a theatrical part) in readiness to take the place of a principal actor or actress if necessary. 2. To act as understudy to (an actor or actress) 1884. Hence **U·nderstu:dy** *sb.* one who understudies a part 1882.

Undertake (ɒndəɹtēi·k), *v.* ME. [f. UNDER-1 III. 1 a + TAKE *v.*, replacing OE. *underniman* (see NIM *v.*).] †1. *trans.* To overtake, seize -1470. †b. To rebuke -1691. †2. To receive, accept -1623. †b. To hear -1596. †c. To understand -1510. 3. To take upon oneself; to take in hand; freq. = to enter upon, begin ME. b. Const. *to* with inf. (Sometimes implying a solemn pledge or promise.) ME. c. To give a formal promise or pledge *that*; to venture to assert. late ME. d. *I (dare) u.*, added to a statement. late ME. 4. To take in charge, accept the charge of ME. b. To engage in combat with 1470. c. To take in hand to deal with (a person) 1601. †5. To pretend to, assume -1608. †6. *intr.* To enter upon, commit oneself to, an enterprise -1639. 7. To give a pledge or promise 1475. 8. To become surety or make oneself answerable *for* 1548.

1. So sire Tristram endured there grete payne, for sekenesse had vndertake hym MALORY. 2. b. Whose voice so soone as he did vndertake, Eftsoones he stood as still as any stake SPENSER. 3. He which þat no þyng vnder-taketh No þyng ne acheueth CHAUCER. [They] are readie to u. more than they are able to undergo 1654. b. I alone first undertook To wing the desolate Abyss MILT. c. He undertook to me, that the King should ask me no question BURNET. d. Wel coude he peynte, I vndirtake, That sich ymage coude make CHAUCER. You have gallants among you, I dare u., that have made the Virginia voyage SCOTT. 4. The Holy Ghost undertakes every man amongst us and would make every man fit for Gods service DONNE. b. Sir, he shall yeeld you all the honor of a competent aduersarie, if you please to vnder-take him B. JONSON. 5. You are like to Sir Vincentio. His name and credite shal you vndertake. SHAKS. 6. Hardy he was and wys to vndertake CHAUCER. 7. I, as I undertook,.. Have found him MILT. 8. She..undertook for her brother John's good behaviour ARBUTHNOT. Hence **Underta·kable** *a.* **Underta·ken** *ppl. a.*

Undertaker (ɒ·ndəɹtēikəɹ). late ME. [f. prec.] †1. A helper or protector -1645. †b. A surety -1706. †c. A baptismal sponsor -1697. 2. One who undertakes a task or enterprise. late ME. 3. *Hist.* a. One who undertook to hold crown lands in Ireland in the 16th and 17th centuries 1586. b. One of those who in the reigns of the first three Stuart kings of England undertook to influence the action of Parliament, esp. with regard to the voting of supplies 1620. c. One of those Lowland Scots who attempted to colonize the Island of Lewis in the late 16th c. 1819. 4. A contractor. Now *rare.* 1602. b. One who makes a business of carrying out the arrangements for funerals 1698. 5. One who embarks on or takes part in some business enterprise. Now *rare.* 1615. †b. One who undertakes the preparation of a literary work -1800. †c. A publisher -1823. †d. A dramatic producer or impresario -1740.

1. Columbus..repaires to some Christian Princes for his vndertakers SIR T. HERBERT. c. A venerable old Deacon who had been the U. for him at his Baptism 1673. 2. The Devil..Who was the first bold U. Of bearing Arms against his Maker 1680. 3. a. These lands in the counties of Cork and Kerry..were parcelled out among English undertakers at low rents HALLAM. 4. An Agreement is concluded with Undertakers for furnishing the Magazines..with Forage 1710. b. His appearance has a stronger effect on my spirits than an undertaker's shop GOLDSM. 5. The mine..yielded vast profit to the undertakers 1752. b. The u. himself will publish his proposals with all convenient speed SWIFT. d. No Company could flourish while the chief Actors and Undertakers were at variance CIBBER.

Underta·king, *vbl. sb.* late ME. [f. as prec. + -ING 1.] †1. Energy, enterprise (*rare*). 2. Something undertaken or attempted; an enterprise. late ME. b. The action of taking in hand 1600. c. *spec.* The business of a funeral undertaker 1850. 3. A pledge, promise; a guarantee. late ME.

2. The consequences, which would naturally attend such a rash u. CLARENDON. b. That which is required of each one towardes the vndertaking of this aduenture HAKLUYT. 3. Three hundred pounds a year, which he proposed to pay to her on an u. that she would never trouble him THACKERAY.

U·nderthings, *sb. pl.* 1864. [UNDER-1 I. 2 b.] Underclothing.

Under-time, var. UNDERN-*time.*

U·ndertone, *sb.* 1806. [UNDER- I. 2 c, III. 2, 2 b.] 1. A low or subdued tone: a. of utterance. b. of sound 1833. 2. *fig.* An underlying tone or undercurrent (*of* feeling, etc.) 1861. b. A subdued or underlying tone of colour 1891. c. The general basis of Exchange or market dealings in any stock or commodity 1897.

2. Throughout all these high reasonings..there runs an u. of controversy 1879. c. Maize has had a weak u. during the entire session 1902. Hence **U·ndertone** *v. trans.* to accompany as an u. **U·ndertoned** *ppl. a.*1 expressed in an u.

U:nderto·ned, *ppl. a.*2 1849. [UNDER-1 IV. a.] Defective in tone.

U·ndertow. 1817. [UNDER-1 I. 2 c.] A current below the surface of water, moving in a contrary direction to that of the surface current.

U·nder-trea·surer. 1447. [UNDER 1 II. 1 a.] A deputy treasurer; *spec.* the officer immediately subordinate to the Lord High Treasurer of England.

U:nderva·lue, *v.* 1596. [UNDER-1 IV. b.] †1. *trans.* To rate as inferior in value *to* -1612. 2. To rate at too low a monetary value 1599. b. To reduce or diminish in value 1622. 3. To estimate too low; to value or appreciate insufficiently; to depreciate 1611.

1. Or shall I thinke in Siluer she's immur'd Being ten times vndervalued to tride gold SHAKS. 2. b. The currency has been undervalued by the fraudulent issue 1866. 3. He who undervalues himself is justly undervalued by others HAZLITT. Hence **U·ndervaluation.** **U·nderva:lue** *sb.* **U·nderva·luer.**

U·ndervest. 1813. [UNDER-1 I. 2 a.] A vest worn underneath a shirt.

U·nderwa·ter, *sb.* 1637. [UNDER-1 I. 1 a, 2 a, b.] 1. Water below the surface of the ground. 2. Water entering a vessel from beneath 1645.

U·nderwa·ter, *a.* 1627. [attrib. use of phr. *under water.*] 1. Placed, situated, carried on, etc., under water. 2. *spec.* In ships: Situated below the water-line 1882.

U·nderwear. 1880. [UNDER-1 I. 2 a.] Underclothing.

U·nderweight. 1596. [UNDER-1 IV. b.] Insufficient weight; deficiency in weight.

U·nderwing. 1535. [UNDER-1 I. 2 b, UNDER-2.] 1. A wing placed under, or partly covered by, another. 2. Used *attrib.*, with adjs. of colour, in collectors' names of moths 1749. b. *ellipt.* an u. moth 1819.

2. The great yellow-u. moth 1749. b. The common yellow under-wings DARWIN.

U·nderwood. ME. [UNDER-1 I. 2 d.] 1. Small trees or shrubs growing beneath timber trees; brushwood. 2. With *a* and *pl.* A quantity or stretch, a special kind, of this 1541.

1. Thinke when an oake fals, vnderwood shrinkes downe, And yet may liue, though brusd 1596. *fig.* But these are the Under-Wood of Satire, rather than the Timber-Trees DRYDEN. 2. Our little habitation was..sheltered with a beautiful u. behind GOLDSM.

U·nderwork, *sb.* 1624. [UNDER-1 I. 2 c, III. 2, IV. b.] 1. A structure placed under or supporting something. 2. Subordinate or inferior work 1645. b. Underhand or secret work 1814.

Underwo·rk, *v.* 1595. [UNDER-1 III. 1 a, b, IV. a.] †1. *trans.* To work secretly against -1659. 2. To impose too little work on 1882. b. *intr.* To do too little work 1902. 3. *trans.* To work for less wages than (another) 1695.

U·nderworld. 1608. [UNDER-1 I. 2 b, 1 c.] 1. The sublunary or terrestrial world 1609. 2. The abode of the dead; the nether world 1608. b. Any subterranean region 1885. 3. The Antipodes; also, the part of the earth beyond the horizon 1847. 4. A sphere or region lying below the ordinary one 1859.

2. The western Hades, the u. of night and death 1871. b. The u. in the Potteries is honeycombed with coal mines 1885. 3. The first beam glittering on a sail, That brings our friends up from the u. TENNYSON.

U·nderwrite, *v.* late ME. [f. UNDER-1 I. 1 a, after L. *subscribere.*] 1. *trans.* To write (words, etc.) below something, esp. after other written matter. †b. To sign (one's name) to a document -1793. †2. To subscribe (a document) with one's name -1748. b. To subscribe (a policy of insurance) thereby accepting the risk of insurance 1622. c. *absol.* To carry on the business of insurance 1784. 3. To subscribe to (a decision, statement, etc.); to agree to or confirm by signature 1606. †4. To guarantee to contribute (a certain sum of money, etc.) -1705. b. To agree to take up, in a new company or new issue (a certain number of shares if not applied for by the public) 1889.

1. Each Subscriber should u. his Reason for the Place he allots his Candidate 1709. b. The Acceptant, when he accepts, must u. his Name 1682. 2. No importunity could prevail with him to u. this will 1655. b. Whosoever..hath underwritten any Policy of Insurance on the Ship Samuel 1703. 3. I could, with a safe conscience, u. all that he there relates 1853. 4. The Subscription-Money did not come in with the same readiness, with which it had been underwritten 1705. b. A promoter of a company who had agreed to u. 10,000 shares 1889. Hence **U·nderwriting** *vbl. sb.* the action of the vb.; the action or practice of (marine) insurance.

U·nderwri:ter. 1622. [f. prec.] 1. One who underwrites an insurance policy; *spec.* one who carries on an insurance business, esp. of shipping. 2. One who underwrites company shares 1889.

Underwri·tten, *ppl. a.* late ME. [UNDER-1 I. 1 a.] 1. Written (out), expressed in writing, below; following upon what is already written; specified or set down in writing below, etc. 2. Of persons: Whose names are written or signed below, etc. late ME.

Undescri·bable *a.* [UN-1 1] 1728.

Undescri·bed, *ppl. a.* 1575. [UN-1 2.] Not described. b. *Nat. Hist.* = NONDESCRIPT *a.* 1. 1680.

Undescrie·d *ppl. a.* [UN-1 2] 1595. **Undescri·ptive** *a.* [UN-1 1] 1744. **Undese·rve** *v.* [UN-1 7] 1621.

Undese·rved, *ppl. a.* late ME. [UN-1 2.] †1. Without having deserved it; undeserving -1593. 2. Not deserved, better or worse than has been deserved. late ME. Hence **Undese·rved·ly** *adv.*, **-ness.**

Undese·rver. Now *rare.* 1597. [UN-1 6.] One who is not deserving (*of* something); an unworthy person.

Undese·rving, *vbl. sb.* 1598. [UN-1 8.] Want of desert or merit.

Undese·rving, *ppl. a.* 1549. [UN-1 4.] 1. Lacking desert or merit, not deserving (something good). b. With direct object 1603. 2. Not deserving (bad fortune, etc.); guiltless, innocent 1586. †3. Undeserved, unmerited. SHAKS.

1. The vndeseruing rich man COVERDALE. Though u. of our Love 1748. b. Creatures u. respect 1860. 2. To destroy this sonne..u. destruction SIDNEY. If your hard decrees..Have doomed to death his u. head DRYDEN. Hence **Undese·rvingly** *adv.*

Undesi·gned, *ppl. a.* 1654. [UN-1 2.] Not resulting from design; unintentional. Hence **Undesi·gned·ly** *adv.*, **-ness.**

Undesi·gning, *ppl. a.* 1673. [UN-1 4.] 1. Not designing or planning (*rare*). 2. Having no ulterior or selfish designs; free from designing or underhand motives 1697.

Undesi·rable, *a.* and *sb.* 1667. [UN-1 1.] A. *adj.* Not to be desired; objectionable. B. *sb.* An undesirable person or thing 1883. Hence **Undesirabi·lity.** **Undesi·rableness, -bly** *adv.*

Undesi·red, *ppl. a.* 1470. [UN-1 2.] **1.** Not asked or requested; uninvited. Now *rare.* **2.** Not wished for; unwelcome 1599.

Undesi·ring *ppl. a.* [UN-1 4] DRYDEN. **Undesi·rous** *a.* [UN-1 1] 1654. **Undespai·ring** *ppl. a.* [UN-1 4] 1730. **Undestroy·ed** *ppl. a.* [UN-1 2] 1450. **Undete·cted** *ppl. a.* [UN-1 2] 1593. **Undete·riorated** *ppl. a.* [UN-1 2] 1856. **Undete·rminable** *a.* [UN-1 1] 1581. **Undete·rminate** *a.* (now *rare*) [UN-1 1] 1603, **-ly** *adv.*, **-ness.**

Undete·rmined, *ppl. a.* 1442. [UN-1 2.] **1.** Not authoritatively decided or settled. **b.** Not yet decided; still subject to alteration or uncertainty 1668. **2.** Not certainly known or identified 1588. **3.** Of indefinite meaning or application 1611. **4.** Not restrained within limits 1627. **5.** Not determined or fixed in respect of character, action, etc. 1676. **6.** Undecided, irresolute 1718.

1. The question..was..left u. in the case of Reg. *v.* Robson 1885. **b.** The combat was yet within the u. doom of Providence SCOTT. **2.** Though the date be u. 1697. **3.** Such u. expressions as wide, narrow, deep BERKELEY. **4.** Too absolute and vndetermined a power 1627.

Undete·rred *ppl. a.* [UN-1 2] 1607. **Undeve·loped** *ppl. a.* [UN-1 2] 1736. **Undeviating** *ppl. a.* [UN-1 4] 1732, **-ly** *adv.*

Unde·vil, *v. arch.* 1632. [UN-2 2 b, 4.] **1.** *trans.* To free from demoniacal possession. **2.** To deprive of the qualities of a devil 1726.

Undevi·sed *ppl. a.* [UN-1 2] 1766. **Undevou·red** *ppl. a.* [UN-1 2] 1661. **Undevou·t** *a.* [UN-1 1] late ME., **-ly** *adv.* **Unde·xt(e)rous** *a.* [UN-1 1] 1688, **-ly** *adv.* **Undiagno·sed** *ppl. a.* [UN-1 2] 1864. **Undicta·ted** *ppl. a.* [UN-1 2] 1797.

Undies (*v*·ndiz), *sb. pl. colloq.* 1918. [Intended as a euphemistic abbrev. of *underclothes, -garments*, prob. after *frillies* (1900).] Women's or children's undergarments.

Women's under-wear or 'undies' as they are coyly called 1918.

U·ndiffere·ntiated *ppl. a.* [UN-1 2] 1862. **Undi·g** *v.* [UN-2 3] 1641.

Undige·sted, *ppl. a.* 1528. [UN-1 2.] **1.** Not brought to a mature or proper condition by natural physical change. *arch.* **2.** Not digested in the stomach 1597. **3.** Not reduced to order or harmony; not arranged or classified; chaotic; confused 1598. **b.** Of discourse, ideas, etc. 1655.

1. When we behold the sunne through thicke clouds and u. vapors 1586. **2.** *fig.* His reading, too, though u., was of immense extent MACAULAY. **3. b.** A volume of u. observations 1742.

Undi·ght, *ppl. a. arch.* or *dial.* 1555. [UN-1 2.] Not decked, adorned, or put in order.

Undi·gnified, *ppl. a.* 1689. [UN-1 2.] †**1.** Of clergy: Not ranking as a dignitary –1833. **2.** Not dignified *by* or *with* something; undistinguished 1716. **3.** Lacking in dignity of manner, etc. 1782.

1. A great number of the u. clergy 1776. **2.** No prosperous event passed u. by poetry JOHNSON. **3.** Genuine emotion..is never u. 1836. Hence **Undi·gnifiedly** *adv.*

Undi·gnify *v.* [UN-2 4 c] 1702. **Undi·ligent** *a.* [UN-1 1] 1547, **-ly** *adv.* **Undilu·ted** *ppl. a.* [UN-1 2] 1756. **Undimi·nishable** *a.* [UN-1 1] 1653. **Undimi·nished** *ppl. a.* [UN-1 2] 1587. **Undi·mmed** *ppl. a.* [UN-1 2] 1723.

Undine (*v*·ndīn). Also **ondine.** 1657. [ad. G., ad. mod.L. *Undina* (Paracelsus), f. L. *unda* wave.] A female water-sprite; a nymph.

Spirits of nature, embodiments..of the four elements, sylphs, salamanders, gnomes, and ondines 1865.

Undi·ned *ppl. a.* [UN-1 2] 1500. **Undi·nted** *ppl. a.* [UN-1 2] SHAKS. **Undiploma·tic** *a.* [UN-1 1] 1831.

Undi·pped, *ppl. a.* 1648. [UN-1 2.] Not dipped. **b.** *spec.* Unbaptized 1693.

Undire·cted *ppl. a.* [UN-1 2] SPENSER. **Undisba·nded** *ppl. a.* [UN-1 2] 1641. **Undisce·rned** *ppl. a.* [UN-1 2] 1529. **Undisce·rnible** *a.* [UN-1 1] 1624, **-ness, -bly** *adv.* **Undisce·rning** *sb.* [UN-1 8] STEELE. **Undisce·rning** *ppl. a.* [UN-1 4] 1589, **-ly** *adv.*

Undischa·rged, *ppl. a.* 1585. [UN-1 2.] **1.** Not paid; not cleared off or settled. **2.** Not freed from obligations or engagements; not discharged in bankruptcy 1603. **3.** Not accomplished or carried out 1705. **4.** Not fired off 1798. **5.** Of cargo: Not unloaded 1864.

2. I know myself an u. debtor COLERIDGE.

Undi·sciplinable *a.* [UN-1 1] 1652. **Undi·scipline** [UN-1 6] 1827.

Undi·sciplined, *ppl. a.* late ME. [UN-1 2.] **1.** Not subjected to discipline; untrained. **2.** Not properly subjected or submissive to military discipline 1718.

Undisclo·sed *ppl. a.* [UN-1 2] 1571. **Undisco·loured** *ppl. a.* [UN-1 2] 1666. **Undisco·mfited** *ppl. a.* [UN-1 2] CHAUCER. **Undisconti·nued** *ppl. a.* [UN-1 2] 1629. **Undiscou·rageable** *a.* [UN-1 2] 1571. **Undiscou·raged** *ppl. a.* [UN-1 1] 1628. **Undisco·verable** *a.* [UN-1 1] 1642, **-bly** *adv.* **Undisco·vered** *ppl. a* [UN-1 2] 1542. †**Undiscree·t** *a.* [UN-1 1] –1704, †**-ly** *adv.* **Undiscri·minating** *ppl. a.* [UN-1 4] COWPER, **-ly** *adv.*, **-ness.** **Undiscu·ssed** *ppl. a.* [UN-1 2] ME. **Undisea·sed** *ppl. a.* [UN-1 2] 1450. **Undisfi·gured** *ppl. a.* [UN-1 2] 1720. **Undisgra·ced** *ppl. a.* [UN-1 2] 1748. **Undisgui·sable** *a.* [UN-1 1] 1673. **Undisgui·se** *sb.* [UN-1 6] 1804. **Undisgui·se** *v.* [UN-2 2] 1638. **Undisgui·sed** *ppl. a.* [UN-1 2] 1500, **-ly** *adv.*, **-ness.** **Undisho·noured** *ppl. a.* [UN-1 2] SHAKS. **Undismay·ed** *ppl. a.* [UN-1 2] 1615. **Undismi·ssed** *ppl. a.* [UN-1 2] COWPER. **Undispa·tched** *ppl. a.* [UN-1 2] 1589. **Undispe·lled** *ppl. a.* [UN-1 2] 1860.

Undispe·nsed, *ppl. a.* ME. [UN-1 2.] Not absolved or released by dispensation.

Undispo·sed, *ppl. a.* late ME. [UN-1 2 b.] †**1.** Unfitted –1449. †**2.** Disordered; out of condition –1645. †**3.** Ill-disposed, unfriendly –1621. **4.** Not disposed of; not put to any purpose 1483. **b.** With *of* (now usual) 1626. **5.** Without inclination, indisposed (*to* or *to do* something) 1590.

3. Some curse Fate, Others..rate Their vndisposed Starres 1621. **4.** The Fens and other Waste and u. Places 1653. The house took care..to prevent the recurrence of an u. surplus HALLAM. **5.** The greater part is carelesse and vndisposed to ioine with them HOOKER.

Undispro·ved *ppl. a.* [UN-1 2] 1579. **Undi·sputable** *a.* (now *rare*) [UN-1 1] 1598. **Undispu·ted** *ppl. a.* [UN-1 2] 1570, **-ly,** *adv.* **Undisse·mbled** *ppl. a.* [UN-1 2] 1651. **Undisse·mbling** *ppl. a.* [UN-1 4] 1613, **-ly** *adv.* **Undi·ssipated** *ppl. a.* [UN-1 2] 1661. **Undisso·lvable** *a.* [UN-1 1] 1611. **Undisso·lved** *ppl. a.* [UN-1 2] 1535. **Undiste·mpered** *ppl. a.* [UN-1 2] 1589. **Undisti·lled** *ppl. a.* [UN-1 2] 1600.

Undisti·nguishable, *a.* 1590. [UN-1 1.] **1.** Incapable of being made out or discerned; imperceptible. **2.** Not to be known apart, too much alike to be distinguished; of which the different elements cannot be distinguished 1679. Hence **Undisti·nguishably** *adv.*

Undisti·nguished, *ppl. a.* 1598. [UN-1 2.] **1.** Not separated or kept distinct. **b.** In which no distinction is or can be made 1608. **c.** Not distinguished *from* or *by* something 1612. **2.** Indistinctly articulated. Now *rare.* 1595. **b.** Not clearly seen; unrecognized 1814. **3.** Not marked by any distinction; not noted or elevated above others 1600.

1. U. clouds, and rocks WORDSW. **c.** Though undistinguish'd from the crowd By wealth or dignity COWPER. **2. b.** Finding herself u. in the dusk JANE AUSTEN.

Undisti·nguishing *ppl. a.* [UN-1 4] 1599, **-ly** *adv.* **Undisto·rted** *ppl. a.* [UN-1 2] 1647. **Undistra·cted** *ppl. a.* [UN-1 2] 1648, **-ly** *adv.*, **-ness.** **Undistre·ssed** *ppl. a.* [UN-1 2] 1582.

Undistri·buted, *ppl. a.* 1483. [UN-1 2.] Not distributed. **b.** *spec.* in *Logic.* Of a term: Not given its fullest extension, not made universal 1827.

b. It would have an u. middle WHATELEY.

Undistu·rbed *ppl. a.* [UN-1 2] 1610, **-ly** *adv.*, **-ness.** **Undive·rted** *ppl. a.* [UN-1 2] 1665. **Undive·rting** *ppl. a.* [UN-1 4] 1697. **Undivi·dable** *a.* (now *rare*) [UN-1 1] 1548. **Undivi·ded** *ppl. a.* [UN-1 2] late ME., **-ly** *adv.*, **-ness.** **Undivi·ne** *a.* [UN-1 2] 1685, **-ly** *adv.* **Undivi·ned** *ppl. a.* [UN-1 2] 1852. **Undivu·lged** *ppl. a.* [UN-1 2] SHAKS.

Undo (*v*ndū·), *v.* [OE. *an-, on-, undōn* = OFris. *un(d)dua*, OS. *antdōn*, OHG. *anttoan*: UN-2.] **1.** *trans.* To unfasten and open (a door, a receptacle, etc.) **2.** To unfasten by untying or by releasing from a fixed position OE. **b.** To unfasten the clothing of (a person) 1633. †**3.** To cut open; to open with a knife –1688. **4.** *intr.* To come open or undone. Now only *colloq.* ME. **5.** *trans.* To annul, cancel, rescind; to reduce to the condition of not having been done, decided, etc. Also *absol.* OE. **b.** To reverse the doing or making of (some material thing or effect) so as to restore the original form or condition. late ME. **6.** To destroy, put an end to; to take away, remove. Now *rare.* OE. **b.** To ruin, cause the downfall of. late ME. **c.** To ruin by seducing. *arch.* 1612. **7.** To explain, interpret, expound. Now *rare.* ME.

1. The wyndow she vndoth CHAUCER. Then made he men to vndo þe tombe 1450. **2.** Oure lady..vndyd his bondes 1450. **3.** George undid the Dragon just as you'd u. an oyster 1688. **5.** Warwicke as our Selfe, Shall do, and vndo as him pleaseth best SHAKS. **6.** Nor tell him that which will u. his Quiet 1703. **b.** Our Folly has undon us 1612. **c.** Losing Her I am undone, Yet would not gain Her to u. Her PRIOR. **7.** Such as can u. a Text..with as much ease as a bow-knot 1654. Hence **Undo·er.**

Undo·cked *ppl. a.* [UN-1 2] 1677. **Undo·ctor** *v.* [UN-2 4 b] 1833. **Undo·cumented** *ppl. a.* [UN-1 2] 1883. **Undogma·tic** *a.* [UN-1 1] PUSEY.

Undo·ing, *vbl. sb.* ME. [f. UNDO *v.*] †**1.** Interpretation –1440. **2.** The action of unfastening, opening, loosening, etc. late ME. **3.** The action of destroying or ruining; the fact of being so dealt with; also, an instance of this. late ME. **b.** With possessive. Chiefly in passive sense. late ME. **4.** A cause of ruin or destruction. late ME. **5.** The action of reversing, annulling, etc. 1540.

3. b. He was not the first that has..brought about his own u. THACKERAY. Phr. *To* (one's) *u.*; All his creditors came upon him to his utter undoinge 1621. **4.** The Chocolate-houses are his U. GAY. **5.** Our Trade of doing, and u., will be endlesse 1650.

Undo·ne, *ppl. a.*[1] ME. [UN-1 2.] Not done; unaccomplished, uneffected.

Nought done the Hero deem'd, while ought u. remain'd PRIOR.

Undo·ne, *ppl. a.*[2] ME. [pa. pple. of UNDO *v.*] **1.** Brought to decay or ruin; destroyed. **2.** Unfastened, untied, etc. 1565.

1. Keepe hop from sunne, and hop is vndunne 1573. Whichever way I turn, I am u. DICKENS.

Undou·ble, *v.* 1611. [UN-2 4.] **1.** *trans.* and *intr.* To unfold. **2.** *Chess.* (*trans.*) To move (pawns) so that one no longer stands directly in front of the other 1868.

Undou·bted, *ppl. a.* 1460. [UN-1 2.] **1.** Not held doubtful in respect of fact. **2.** Of persons: Not called in question in respect of status or character 1460. **3.** Not impaired by doubt; absolute, complete. Now *rare* or *Obs.* 1489. **4.** About the nature, truth, authenticity, etc., of which there is no doubt 1513.

Undou·btedly, *adv.* 1500. [UN-1 5.] **1.** Admittedly, certainly; beyond or without any doubt. †**2.** With verbs of statement: Positively, in no doubtful terms –1653.

Undou·btful *v.* [UN-1 1] 1450. **Undou·bting** *ppl. a.* [UN-1 4] late ME., **-ly** *adv.*, **-ness.** **Undow·ered** *ppl. a.* [UN-1 2] 1803. **Undrai·nable** *a.* [UN-1 1] 1611. **Undrai·ned** *ppl. a.* [UN-1 2] TUSSER.

Undrama·tic, *a.* 1754. [UN-1 1.] **1.** Lacking the essential qualities of drama, unsuited for the theatre. **2.** Not gifted with or exhibiting dramatic power 1769. **b.** Unappreciative of drama 1836. **3.** Not in the form of drama 1840. Hence **Undrama·tically** *adv.*

Undra·ped *ppl. a.* [UN-1 2] 1814. **Undra·peried** *ppl. a.* [UN-1 2] 1802.

Undraw·, *v.* 1677. [UN-2 1.] **1.** *trans.* To draw back (esp. a curtain); to unfasten by pulling. **2.** *intr.* Of bolts: To move back 1794.

Undraw·n *ppl. a.* [UN-1 2] 1527. **Undrea·ded** *ppl. a.* [UN-1 2] 1535. **Undrea·med, -drea·mt** *ppl. a.* [UN-1 2] SHAKS.

U·ndress, undre·ss, *sb.* 1683. [UN-1 6.] **1.** Partial or incomplete dress; dress of a kind not ordinarily worn in public; dishabille. Also (esp. of men), informal or ordinary as opposed to ceremonial or special dress. **b.** In the services, uniform authorized to be worn on ordinary occasions, as dist. from *full* or *service dress* 1748. **2.** *attrib.* Worn when in undress; constituting an undress 1829.

1. *fig.* This famine..'Tis death in an u. of skin and bone DRYDEN. b. A young officer, in a cavalry u. 1849. 2. *fig.* The simple, idiomatic, u., conversational tone of Lessing's blank verse 1806.

Undre·ss, *v.* 1596. [UN-2 2.] 1. *refl.* To divest (oneself) of clothes. b. *intr.* To take off one's clothes 1625. 2. *trans.* To divest or strip (a person) of clothes 1615. b. To strip *of* something 1641. †3. To undo (the hair) -1652.

2. *fig.* Till I slumber, and death shall undresse me 1633. b. The protestant religion..must undresse them of all their guilded vanities MILT. Hence **Undre·ssing** *vbl. sb.*

Undre·ssed, *ppl. a.* 1445. [UN-1 2.] 1. a. Of the hair, etc.: Not trimmed or put in order. b. Of textiles, leather, stone, wood, etc.: With the surface not artificially smoothed or prepared 1535. c. Not treated with surgical dressings 1597. d. Not pruned or clipped 1611. e. Not cooked or prepared for the table 1647. f. Of a shop-window: Not attractively set out 1883. 2. Not clothed; naked (or nearly so) 1613. b. In undress; not fully dressed; informally dressed 1605.

1. b. Strict Lawes are made..that the web vndressed be viewed by three skillfull men 1617. Enveloped in an u. seal-skin 1853. d. Thou shalt not.. gather the grapes of thy Vine vndressed *Lev.* xxv. 5. e. The flesh of an u. lobster 1806.

Undrie·d *ppl. a.* [UN-1 2] 1440. **Undri·nkable** *a.* [UN-1 1] 1611. **Undri·ven** *ppl. a.* [UN-1 2] 1615. **Undroo·ping** *ppl. a.* [UN-1 4] 1736. **Undrow·ned** *ppl. a.* [UN-1 2] 1573. **Undru·gged** *ppl. a.* [UN-1 2] 1868. **Undru·nk** *ppl. a.* [UN-1 2] 1637. **Undu·bbed** *ppl. a.* [UN-1 2] 1602. **Undu·bitable** *a.* (now *rare*) [UN-1 1] 1643, -bly *adv.*

Undue·, *a.* late ME. [UN-1 1.] 1. Not owing. 2. Not appropriate or suitable; improper; unseasonable. late ME. 3. Unjustifiable, illegal. late ME. 4. Going beyond what is appropriate, warranted, or natural; excessive 1684.

2. At an vndue houre of a leuen a clocke in the night 1541. The u. awarding of honours 1875. 3. Such miscreants..had by u. ways devoured the patrimony of the Church 1660. The Laws relating to Bribery, Treating, and u. Influence at Elections 1854. 4. Instances of u. Warmth and Zeal 1739.

Undu·g *ppl. a.* [UN-1 2] 1657. **Undu·ke** *v.* [UN-2 4 b] 1611.

Undulant (ʋ·ndiŭlănt), *a.* 1830. [ad. L. **undulant-*, *undulans*; cf. next.] Undulating. *U. fever* = MALTA *fever*.

Undulate (ʋ·ndiŭlĕt), *a.* 1658. [ad. L. *undulatus*, f. *unda* wave.] = UNDULATED *ppl. a.*; *spec.* in *Bot.* and *Zool.*

Undulate (ʋ·ndiŭleit), *v.* 1664. [ad. L. **undulat-*, ppl. stem of **undulare*, f. *unda* wave.] 1. *intr.* To move in, or like, waves. b. *transf.* Of sound, etc. 1760. 2. *trans.* To cause to move, esp. to rise and fall, like waves 1669. b. To impart a wavy appearance to 1730. 3. *intr.* To present a wavy surface, outline, or appearance 1833.

2. The first dancing of all Ghawâzi is..undulating the body 1873. 3. The vast plain undulates in hills and valleys 1833. Hence **U·ndulator** in *Wireless Telegr.*

Undulated (ʋ·ndiŭleitĕd), *ppl. a.* 1623. [Cf. prec.] 1. Having a wavy surface or outline. 2. Having wavy markings 1664. b. *spec.* In the names of birds or fishes 1785.

U·ndulating, *ppl. a.* 1700. [f. UNDULATE *v.*] That undulates. b. *fig.* Exhibiting variations comparable to the rising and falling of waves 1815.

b. The u. and tumultuous multitude BENTHAM. Hence **U·ndulatingly** *adv.*

Undulation (ʋndiŭlē·ʃən). 1646. [ad. L. **undulatio*; cf. UNDULATE *a.* and *v.*] 1. The action of moving in a wave-like manner; a gentle rising and falling in the manner of waves. b. A wave-like motion of the air, ether, etc., as in the propagation of light 1658. c. *transf.* Of sound 1668. 2. A wave-like curve or a series of these; a surface defined by such curves; an undulating rise and fall of level 1670. b. An instance of this; also, a single rise and fall of this nature 1823.

1. Porpoises progress by..undulations in a vertical plane 1854. Hence **Undula·tionist,** one who holds the undulatory theory of light.

Undulatory (ʋ·ndiŭlătəri), *a.* 1728. [ad. L. **undulatorius*; cf. UNDULATE *v.* and -ORY 2.] 1. Of the nature of undulation; exhibiting or consisting of wave-movement. b. *U. theory*, *hypothesis*, the theory that light consists in an undulatory movement of an elastic medium pervading space 1802. 2. Forming a series of wave-like curves; of ground, etc., having undulations 1796.

Undulous (ʋ·ndiŭləs), *a.* 1728. [ad. L. **undulosus*, f. *unda* wave.] Of an undulating nature.

Unduly (ʋndiū·li), *adv.* late ME. [UN-1 5.] 1. Without due cause or justification; unrightfully, undeservedly. 2. To excess; beyond the due degree 1779.

1. Malvern hills, for mountains counted Not u. MRS. BROWNING. 2. William had never been u. harsh FREEMAN.

Undu·rable *a.* [UN-1 1] COVERDALE. **Undu·sted** *ppl. a.* [UN-1 2] 1648. **Undu·teous** *a.* [UN-1 1] SHAKS. **Undu·tiful** *a.* [UN-1 1] 1582, -ly *adv.*, -ness.

U·ndy, *a.* 1592. [Anglicized f. UNDEE *a.*] *Her.* Wavy.

Undy·ing, *ppl. a.* ME. [UN-1 4.] That does not die; immortal.

Driven down To chains of Darkness, and th' u. Worm MILTON. The u. interest..felt by kindly women in a question of love or marriage 1885. Hence **Undy·ing·ly** *adv.*, -ness.

Unea·red, *ppl. a. arch.* OE. [UN-1 2.] Untilled.

Unea·rned, *ppl. a.* ME. [UN-1 2.] 1. Not earned by merit or desert; undeserved (as reward or punishment). 2. Not earned by work or service 1667. b. *U·nearned increment*, increase in the value of land or property not due to action or expenditure on the part of the owner 1873.

Unea·rth, *v.* 1450. [UN-2 3.] 1. *trans.* To exhume, dig out; to expose by removing earth. b. To force out of a hole or burrow 1622. 2. *fig.* To bring to light; to disclose, reveal, discover 1820. Hence **Unea·rthed** *ppl. a.*1

Unea·rthed, *ppl. a.*2 1513. [UN-1 2.] †1. Unburied. 2. *Electr.* Not furnished with an earth 1905.

Unea·rthly, *a.* 1611. [UN-1 1.] 1. Rising above what is characteristic of earth; sublime; heavenly. 2. Not belonging to this earth; supernatural, ghostly, weird 1802. b. colloq. *U. hour, time*, an absurdly early or inconvenient time 1865. Hence **Unea·rthliness.**

Unea·se [UN-1 6] ME. **Unea·seful** *a.* (now *rare*) [UN-1 1] 1515.

Unea·sily, *adv.* ME. [UN-1 5.] †1. With difficulty -1725. 2. Restlessly, with discomfort or embarrassment. late ME.

Unea·siness. late ME. [UN-1 6.] †1. The quality of being troublesome -1712. 2. Difficult nature or character -1691. †b. Reluctance -1737. 3. Discomfort, anxiety or trouble as affecting one's circumstances or welfare; an instance of this 1599. b. Bodily discomfort (falling short of actual or definite pain) 1665. c. Mental discomfort; anxiety, apprehension 1682.

Unea·sy, *a.* ME. [UN-1 1.] 1. Causing physical discomfort; preventing ease. †b. Disquieting to the mind -1798. c. Characterized by absence of ease or comfort; suggesting or manifesting discomfort of body or mind 1513. †2. Of persons: Disagreeable, unfriendly, dissatisfied -1737. b. Rigid, uncompromising 1819. 3. Not easy or simple; difficult, hard, troublesome. Now *rare*. late ME. 4. Disturbed in mind; anxious, apprehensive 1680. b. Restless, unsettled, fidgety 1855. c. Suffering physical discomfort 1725. 5. quasi-*adv.* Uneasily 1596.

1. Golden fetters are as uneasie as those of Iron 1660. 2. b. Ladies even of the most u. virtue BYRON. 3. 'The road will be u. to find,' answered Gurth SCOTT. 5. Vneasie lyes the Head, that weares a Crowne SHAKS.

Unea·table *a.* [UN-1 1] 1611. **Unea·ten** *ppl. a.* [UN-1 2] ME.

Uneath (ʋnī·þ), *adv. arch.* [OE. *unēaðe*, f. *un-* UN-1 5 + *ēaðe* EATH *adv.*] Not easily; (only) with difficulty; scarcely, hardly. So **Unea·th** *a.* difficult, hard, troublesome.

Uneclī·psed *ppl. a.* [UN-1 2] 1649.

U:necono·mic, *a.* 1909. [UN-1 1.] Not based on or out of relation to economics. b. *U. rent.* one too low to repay builder or owner.

Unecono·mical *adj.* [UN-1 1] BENTHAM, -ly *adv.* **Une·dge** *v.* [UN-2 2] 1614. **Une·dified** *ppl. a.* [UN-1 2] 1618. **Une·difying** *ppl. a.* [UN-1 4] 1641. **Une·dited** *ppl. a.* [UN-1 2] 1829. **Une·ducated** *ppl. a.* [UN-1 2] SHAKS., -ness. †**Une·ffable** *a.* [UN-1 1] -1689. **Unela·borate** *a.* [UN-1 1] 1663. **Unela·stic** *a.* [UN-1 1] 1728. **Unela·ted** *ppl. a.* [UN-1 2] 1710. **Une·lbowed** *ppl. a.* [UN-1 2] POPE. **Unele·cted** *ppl. a.* [UN-1 2] 1581. **Unele·ctrified** *ppl. a.* [UN-1 2] 1747. **Une·levated** *ppl. a.* [UN-1 2] 1627. **Une·loquent** *a.* [UN-1 1] 1565, -ly *adv.*

Unemba·rrassed, *ppl. a.* 1708. [UN-1 2.] 1. Not encumbered, hampered, or impeded. 2. Unconstrained; free from self-consciousness or awkwardness 1746.

Unemba·ttled, *ppl. a.* 1615. [UN-1 2; see EMBATTLED *ppl. a.*2]. Without battlements.

Unembe·llished *ppl. a.* [UN-1 2] 1630. **Unembi·ttered** *ppl. a.* [UN-1 2] 1711. **Unembo·died** *ppl. a.* [UN-1 2] 1662. **Unemo·tional** *a.* [UN-1 1] 1876, -ly *adv.* **Unempha·tic** *a.* [UN-1 1] 1800, -ally *adv.*

Unemploy·able, *a.* and *sb.* 1887. [UN-1 1.] (One) unfit to be employed as a paid worker.

Unemploy·ed, *ppl. a.* and *sb.* 1600. [UN-1 2.] 1. Not used; not occupied; not in use. 2. Of persons: Having no occupation; disengaged, at leisure; *spec.* temporarily out of work 1667. b. *absol.* or as *sb.* (chiefly pl. with *the*, occas. sing. with *an*) 1882. c. Pertaining to or connected with unemployed persons 1844.

2. Other Creatures all day long Rove idle unimploid MILT. The destinies of the u. workmen RUSKIN.

Unemploy·ment. 1888. [UN-1 6.] The state or fact of being unemployed; the prevalence or extent of this state.

Une·mptied *ppl. a.* [UN-1 2] 1624. **Unena·cted** *ppl. a.* [UN-1 2] 1802. **Unencha·nted** *ppl. a.* [UN-1 2] MILT. **Unenclo·sed** *ppl. a.* [UN-1 2] 1676. **Unencu·mbered** *ppl. a.* [UN-2 2] 1722. **Unenda·ngered** *ppl. a.* [UN-1 2] 1658.

Une·nded, *ppl. a.* Now *rare*. ME. [UN-1 2.] 1. Endless, infinite. 2. Unfinished. late ME.

1. For thi myche malice, and thi wickidnessis vnendid WYCLIF *Job.* xxii. 5.

Une·nding *ppl. a.* [UN-1 4] 1661, -ly *adv.*, -ness. **Unendow·ed** *ppl. a.* [UN-1 2] 1647. **Unendue·d** *ppl. a.* [UN-1 2] 1647. **Unendu·rable** *a.* [UN-1 1] 1630, -ly *adv.* **U:nenerge·tic** *a.* [UN-1 1] 1805. **Unenfo·rced** *ppl. a.* [UN-1 2] 1607. **Unenfra·nchised** *ppl. a.* [UN-1 2] 1832.

Unenga·ged, *ppl. a.* 1656. [UN-1 2.] 1. Not bound or committed. 2. *spec.* Not betrothed 1702. 3. Not hired 1654. 4. Not occupied or busied (*in* something) 1712. b. Not occupied or involved in fighting 1806. 5. Not allocated or assigned 1732.

4. If your Thoughts are u., I shall explain myself further POPE.

Un-E·nglish, *a.* 1633. [UN-1 1.] 1. Not English in character; lacking the qualities regarded as typically English. 2. Not English by occupation or possession 1738.

Une·nglished, *ppl. a. arch.* 1546. [UN-1 2.] Not translated into English.

Unenjoy·able *a.* [UN-1 1] 1797. **Unenjoy·ed** *ppl. a.* [UN-1 2] MILT. **Unenjoy·ing** *ppl. a.* [UN-1 4] 1697, -ly *adv.*

Unenli·ghtened, *ppl. a.* 1656. [UN-1 2.] 1. Not illuminated or lit up. Now *rare*. 1662. 2. Not mentally illuminated; uninstructed 1656. b. Uninformed *on* some matter 1829. 3. Marked by lack of enlightenment 1792.

Unenli·vened *ppl. a.* [UN-1 2] 1692. **Unenqui·ring** *ppl. a.* [UN-1 4] 1813, -ly *adv.* **Unenri·ched** *ppl. a.* [UN-1 2] 1723. **Unentai·led** *ppl. a.* [UN-1 2] 1713. **Unenta·ngled** *ppl. a.* [UN-1 2] 1586.

Une·ntered, *ppl. a.* 1482. [UN-1 2.] 1. Not recorded by an entry in a book. †2. Not initiated -1642. b. Of hounds: Not yet put into a pack 1896. 3. Of places: Not entered 1775.

Une·nterprising *ppl. a.* [UN-1 4] 1777. **Unentertai·ned** *ppl. a.* [UN-1 2] 1628. **Unentertai·ning** *ppl. a.* [UN-1 4] 1697, -ly *adv.*, -ness. **Unenthra·lled** *ppl. a.* [UN-1 2] MILT. **Unenthusia·stic** *a.* [UN-1 1] 1805. **Unenti·tled** *ppl.*

a. [UN-¹ 2] 1768. **Une·nviable** *a.* [UN-¹ 1] MILT., -bly *adv.*

Une·nvied, *ppl. a.* late ME. [UN-¹ 2.] †1. Unmixed with envy. late ME. only. 2. Not regarded with envy 1615. 3. Not enviously desired or grudged 1645.

Une·nvious *a.* [UN-¹ 1] 1656, -ly *adv.*

Unepi·scopal, *a.* 1659. [UN-¹ 1.] 1. Not controlled by bishops; not episcopalian in character or government. 2. Not pertaining to or befitting a bishop 1661.

2. The Bishop lost his temper, and used very u. language 1897. Hence **Unepi·scopally** *adv.*

Une·qual, *a., sb., adv.* 1535. [UN-¹ 1, 6.] A. *adj.* 1. Not equal in amount, size, quality, etc.: a. Of two or more things or persons in comparison with each other 1565. b. With abstract sbs. in the singular 1593. c. Of single persons or things 1677. 2. Not divisible into two equal numbers, odd 1697. 3. †a. Of things: Inadequate -1736. b. Not equal or adequate *to* some task, etc. 1694. 4. Variable or uneven in quality 1565. †5. Inequitable, unjust, unfair -1761. 6. In which the two parties are not on equal terms, or have not equal advantage 1552. b. *esp.* Of combats or contests 1654.

1. a. If your horses be unequall for height 1653. b. Halting on crutches of u. size COWPER. c. A match with one so u. in birth SCOTT. 2. Thrice bind about his thrice devoted Head,..U. numbers please the Gods DRYDEN. 3. b. Four..were..rejected as u. to the burden GIBBON. 4. A fine, but u. poem SCOTT. An u. distribution of heat 1836. 5. To punnish me for what you make me do Seemes much vnequall SHAKS. 6. So u. a bargain 1748. b. In such u. strife DRYDEN.

B. *sb. pl.* 1. Persons who are not on an equality with each other in rank or social standing 1565. 2. Things unequal to each other 1611.

1. Among unequals what societie Can sort, what harmonie or true delight? MILTON.

C. *adv.* or quasi-*adv.* Unequally 1602. So **Une·qual·ly** *adv.*, -ness.

Une·qualled *ppl. a.* [UN-¹ 2] 1622. **Une·quitable** *a.* [UN-¹ 1] 1647, -bly *adv.*

Unequi·vocal, *a.* 1784. [UN-¹ 1.] Of unmistakable meaning, free from ambiguity. Hence **Unequi·vocally** *adv.*, -ness.

Unera·dicable *a.* [UN-¹ 1] BYRON. **Une·rrancy** [UN-¹ 6] 1646.

Unerring (vnɔ̄·riŋ), *ppl. a.* 1621. [UN-¹ 4.] 1. Making no error; not going or leading astray 1660. 2. Not diverging from a standard or aim; exact 1665. 3. Of missiles, aim, etc.: Not going astray from the intended mark; sure 1621.

1. The U. Authority of the Catholic Church in matters of Faith 1732. 3. How deadly thine u. bow! SCOTT. Hence **Une·rring·ly** *adv.*, -ness.

Unesca·pable *a.* [UN-¹ 1] DONNE. **Unes·chew·able** *a.* [UN-¹ 1] CHAUCER. **Unesco·rted** *ppl. a.* [UN-¹ 2] 1774. **Unespie·d** *ppl. a.* [UN-¹ 2] CHAUCER. **Unessay·ed** *ppl. a.* [UN-¹ 2] 1642.

Une·ssence, *v.* 1642. [UN-² 2.] *trans.* To deprive of essence or essential properties.

Unesse·ntial, *a.* and *sb.* 1656. [UN-¹ 1.] 1. Having no essence or substance; immaterial 1667. 2. Not affecting or pertaining to the essence of a matter; unimportant 1656.

1. The void profound of u. Night MILT. 2. Those, who differed from him in the u. Parts of Christianity ADDISON.

B. *sb.* An unessential thing or feature 1828. b. That which is not essential 1840.

b. Who is to determine..the limit of the U.? 1841.

Unesta·blish *v.* [UN-² 1] MILT. **Unesta·blished** *ppl. a.* [UN-¹ 2] 1646. **Unesteem·ed** *ppl. a.* [UN-¹ 2] 1550. **Unestra·nged** *ppl. a.* [UN-¹ 2] 1851. **Une·thical** *a.* [UN-¹ 1] 1871. **Uneva·dable** *a.* [UN-¹ 1] 1839. **U·nevange·lical** *a.* [UN-¹ 1] 1648.

Une·ven, *a.* [OE. *unefen*, f. UN-¹ 1 + *efen* EVEN *a.*] 1. Not corresponding or matching; unequal. Now *rare.* b. Of numbers: Odd. Of things: Making up, or marked by, an odd number 1577. †2. Unequitable; unjust -1641. 3. Diverging from a straight or exactly parallel position. late ME. 4. Not smooth or level; irregular, broken, rugged ME. b. *transf.* and *fig.* (of immaterial things, sounds, etc.) 1596.

1. So forth they traueld an vneuen payre SPENSER. 3. The windows were u. 1862. 4. Which causeth cloth to cockle and be u. HAKLUYT. b. Such is the u. State of human Life DE FOE. Hence **Une·ven·ly** *adv.*, -ness.

Uneve·ntful *a.* [UN-¹ 1] 1800, -ly *adv.*, -ness. **Une·videnced** *ppl. a.* [UN-¹ 2] 1842. **Une·vident** *a.* [UN-¹ 1] late ME. **Unexa·ct** *a.* [UN-¹ 1] 1758. **Unexa·ggerated** *ppl. a.* [UN-¹ 2] 1770. **Unexa·lted** *ppl. a.* [UN-¹ 2] 1611. **Unexa·mined** *ppl. a.* [UN-¹ 2] 1495. **Unexa·mining** *ppl. a.* [UN-¹ 4] 1682.

Unexa·mpled, *ppl. a.* 1610. [UN-¹ 2.] Having no preceding or similar example; unprecedented, unparalleled.

Unexce·lled *ppl. a.* [UN-¹ 2] 1800. **Unexce·pted** *ppl. a.* [UN-¹ 2] 1614.

Unexce·ptionable, *a.* 1664. [UN-¹ 1.] 1. To whom or which no exception can be taken; perfectly satisfactory or adequate. 2. Admitting of no exception (*rare*) 1871. Hence **Unexceptionabi·lity.** **Unexce·ptionableness.** **Unexce·ptionably** *adv.*

Unexce·ptional, *a.* 1775. [UN-¹ 1.] 1. = prec. 1. 2. Admitting of or subject to no exception 1844.

2. The orders received..were imperative, and u. 1844.

Unexcha·nged *ppl. a.* [UN-¹ 2] 1618. **Unexci·sed** *ppl. a.* [UN-¹ 2, 3] 1871. **Unexci·table** *a.* [UN-¹ 1] 1839. **Unexci·ted** *ppl. a.* [UN-¹ 2] 1735. **Unexci·ting** *ppl. a.* [UN-¹ 4] 1833. †**Unexcu·sable** *a.* [UN-¹ 1] -1685. **Une·xecuted** *ppl. a.* [UN-¹ 2] 1585. **Unexe·mplary** *a.* [UN-¹ 1] 1649. **Unexe·mplified** *ppl. a.* [UN-¹ 2] 1634. **Unexe·mpt, unexe·mpted** *ppl. adjs.* [UN-¹ 2] MILT. **Une·xercised** *ppl. a.* [UN-¹ 2] late ME. **Unexe·rted** *ppl. a.* [UN-¹ 2] 1675. **Unexhau·sted** *ppl. a.* [UN-¹ 2] 1602. **Unexhau·stible** *a.* (now *rare*) [UN-¹ 1] 1656. **Unexi·stence** [UN-¹ 6] 1593. **Unexi·stent** *a.* [UN-¹ 1] 1682. **Unexi·sting** *ppl. a.* [UN-¹ 4] 1785. **Une·xorcised** *ppl. a.* [UN-¹ 2] 1750. **Unexpa·nded** *ppl. a.* [UN-¹ 2] 1664. **Unexpa·nsive** *a.* [UN-¹ 1] 1846. **Unexpe·ctable** *a.* [UN-¹ 1] 1598. **Unexpe·ctant** *a.* [UN-¹ 1] 1811. **Unexpe·cted** *ppl. a.* [UN-¹ 2] 1586, -ly *adv.*, -ness. **Unexpe·nded** *ppl. a.* [UN-¹ 2] 1571. **Unexpe·nsive** *a.* [UN-¹ 1] MILT., -ly *adv.*, -ness.

Unexpe·rienced, *ppl. a.* 1569. [UN-¹ 2.] 1. Not furnished with or taught by experience; not skilled or trained in this way. 2. Not known or felt by experience 1698.

Unexpe·rimented, *ppl. a.* 1594. [UN-¹ 2.] †1. Inexperienced -1635. 2. Not tried, known, or ascertained by experiment 1594.

†**Unexpe·rt** *a.* [UN-¹ 1] -1778. **Une·xpiated** *ppl. a.* [UN-¹ 2] 1681. **Unexpi·red** *ppl. a.* [UN-¹ 2] 1570. **Unexplai·nable** *a.* [UN-¹ 1] 1711. **Unexplai·ned** *ppl. a.* [UN-¹ 2] 1721. **Unexpla·natory** *a.* [UN-¹ 1] BENTHAM. **Une·xplicated** *ppl. a.* [UN-¹ 2] 1666. **Unexpli·cit** *a.* [UN-¹ 1] 1838, -ly *adv.* **Unexplo·red** *ppl. a.* [UN-¹ 2] 1697. **Unexpo·sed** *ppl. a.* [UN-¹ 2] 1691. **Unexpre·ssed** *ppl. a.* [UN-¹ 2] 1561. **Unexpre·ssible** *a.* [UN-¹ 1] 1621.

Unexpre·ssive, *a.* 1600. [UN-¹ 1.] †1. Inexpressible, beyond description -1637. 2. Not expressive; that fails to convey a meaning or feeling 1755.

1. The faire, the chaste, and vnexpressiue shee SHAKS. Hence **Unexpre·ssive·ly** *adv.*, -ness.

Unexpu·gnable *a.* (now *rare*) [UN-¹ 1] WYCLIF. **Unexpu·nged** *ppl. a.* [UN-¹ 2] 1826. **Une·xpurgated** *ppl. a.* [UN-¹ 2] 1882.

Unexte·nded, *ppl. a.* 1648. [UN-¹ 2.] 1. Not held out, opened, or spread. b. Of an athlete, horse, etc.: Without being obliged to exert himself to the full. 2. *spec.* Having no extension (EXTENSION 4) 1674.

2. Aristotle..did suppose Incorporeal Substance to be u. CUDWORTH. Hence (in sense 2) **Unexte·nded·ly** *adv.*, -ness.

Unexte·nuated *ppl. a.* [UN-¹ 2] JOHNSON. **Unexti·nct** *a.* [UN-¹ 1] 1622. **Unexti·nguishable** *a.* [UN-¹ 1] 1642, -ness, -bly *adv.* **Unexti·nguished** *ppl. a.* [UN-¹ 2] DRYDEN. **Une·xtirpated** *ppl. a.* [UN-¹ 2] 1663. **Unexto·rted** *ppl. a.* [UN-¹ 2] SWIFT.

Uneyed (vnəi·d), *ppl. a.* 1616. [UN-¹ 2.] Not looked at, unseen.

Unfa·ce, *v.* 1611. [UN-² 2.] *trans.* To strip of a facing or disguise; to expose the face of.

Unfa·dable *a.* [UN-¹ 1] 1626. **Unfa·ded** *ppl. a.* [UN-¹ 2] 1550. **Unfa·ding** *ppl. a.* [UN-¹ 4] 1652, -ly *adv.*, -ness.

Unfai·ling, *ppl. a.* late ME. [UN-¹ 4.] 1. Not failing or giving way. 2. Unceasing, continual. late ME. 3. Infallible, certain. late ME.

2. A country..watered by u. rivers 1876. 3. The undoubted truth of gods u. word 1553. Hence **Unfai·ling·ly** *adv.*, -ness.

Unfai·n, *a.* *arch.* and *dial.* [OE. *unfægen*, f. UN-¹ 1 + *fægen* FAIN *a.*]. Not glad; ill-pleased; reluctant.

Unfai·r, *a.* [OE. *unfæger*, f. UN-¹ 1 + *fæger* FAIR *a.*] †1. Not fair or beautiful; uncomely; ugly -1648. 2. Not fair or equitable; unjust 1713. b. *spec.* Not paying the usual rate of wages. Of wages, etc.: Below the normal rate. 1886. 3. Of the wind: Unfavourable. 1801. 4. *Ship-building.* Not fitting or corresponding exactly 1869. Hence **Unfai·rly** *adv.*, -ness.

Unfai·thful, *a.* late ME. [UN-¹ 1.] 1. Not holding the true faith; infidel. 2. Not keeping good faith; acting falsely or treacherously. late ME. b. *transf.* Of things: Disappointing expectation, deceptive, unreliable 1586. c. Misrepresenting the original; incorrect, inexact 1697. d. *spec.* Not faithful in wedlock 1828. 3. Of conduct: Characterized by want of good faith; not honest or upright 1565.

1. Vnfeithful men schulen be conuertid to thee WYCLIF *Ps.* l. 15. 2. The combined offence of two u. servants WELLESLEY. b. Sea-sand..is..u. in supporting great Weights 1726. c. He..is much blamed for his unfaithfull quotations 1697. Hence **Unfai·thful·ly** *adv.*, -ness.

Unfa·llen *ppl. a.* [UN-¹ 2] 1653. **Unfa·ltering** *ppl. a.* [UN-¹ 4] 1727, -ly *adv.* **Unfa·med** *ppl. a.* [UN-¹ 2] SHAKS. **Unfami·liar** [UN-¹ 1] 1594. **Unfamilia·rity** [UN-¹ 6] 1755. **Unfami·liarized** *ppl. a.* [UN-¹ 2] 1775. **Unfana·tical** *a.* [UN-¹ 1] 1826. **Unfa·ncied** *ppl. a.* [UN-¹ 2] 1655. **Unfanta·stic** *a.* [UN-¹ 1] 1794.

Unfa·shion, *v.* 1569. [UN-² 2.] *trans.* To undo the fashion or make of.

Unfa·shionable, *a.* and *sb.* 1563. [UN-¹ 1.] A. *adj.* †1. That cannot be fashioned or shaped -1607. †2. Badly shaped or formed -1663. 3. Of clothes, behaviour, opinions, etc.: Not in accordance with the prevailing fashion 1644. 4. Not belonging to fashionable society; not conforming to current fashions 1660.

1. The invisible and u. God 1563. 2. He was..of body somewhat grosse and vnfashionable 1611. 3. It is there u. not to be a man of business 1776.

B. *sb.* An u. person 1822. Hence **Unfa·shion·ableness.** **Unfa·shionably** *adv.*

Unfa·shioned, *ppl. a.* 1538. [UN-¹ 2.] 1. Not wrought into form or shape. †2. Not refined; lacking culture or elegance -1821.

2. A plump goodnatured u. girl 1821.

Unfa·sten, *v.* ME. [UN-² 1, 5.] 1. *trans.* a. To unfix; to make loose or slack. Also *absol.* b. To detach; to undo or release 1440. 2. *intr.* To become detached or loose; to open ME.

Unfa·stened *ppl. a.* [UN-¹ 2] 1587. **Unfasti·dious** *a.* [UN-¹ 1] 1815.

Unfa·thered, *a.*¹ 1597. [UN-¹ 3.] 1. Having no (known or acknowledged) father; illegitimate. 2. Of obscure origin; unauthenticated 1830.

Unfa·thered, *a.*² 1586. [UN-² 2, 6.] Deprived of a father.

Unfa·thomable, *a.* 1617. [UN-¹ 1.] 1. *fig.* Of feelings, qualities, conditions, etc.: Incapable of being fully ascertained, explored, exhausted, etc. 2. Incapable of being fathomed or measured; immeasureable, vast 1640. b. *fig.* Of the eyes 1817.

1. Thy Goodness is u. 1663. 2. O the u. Abysse of Eternity! 1672. Stretching into u. distance 1879. b. Her u. eyes THACKERAY. Hence **Unfa·thomable·ness.** **Unfa·thomably** *adv.*

Unfa·thomed *ppl. a.* [UN-¹ 2] 1623. **Unfati·guable** *a.* [UN-¹ 1] 1799. **Unfati·gued** *ppl. a.* [UN-¹ 2] 1705. **Unfati·guing** *ppl. a.* [UN-¹ 4] 1808. **Unfau·lty** *a.* [UN-¹ 1] 1548.

Unfa·vourable, *a.* 1548. [UN-¹ 1.] 1. Not favourable in various senses. 2. Ill-favoured; unprepossessing. Now *rare.* 1776.

1. An u. wind detained them GIBBON. Viewed with an u. eye 1835. The prognosis was u. 1890. 2. With

u., long, and saturnine countenances 1776. Hence **Unfa·vourableness. Unfa·vourably** *adv.*
Unfa·voured *ppl. a.* [UN-1 2] 1774. **Unfa·vouring** *ppl. a.* [UN-1 4] 1835. **Unfea·red** *ppl. a.* [UN-1 2] late ME. **Unfea·rful** *a.* [UN-1 1] 1544, -ly *adv.* **Unfea·ring** *ppl. a.* [UN-1 4] 1796, -ly *adv.* **Unfea·sible** *a.* [UN-1 1] 1527. **Unfea·ther** *v.* [UN-2 2] 1483.

Unfea·thered, *a.* 1570. [UN-1 3.] **1.** Of birds, etc.: Not provided or covered with feathers. **2.** Not of the feathered kind: applied spec. (after L. *implumis*) to man 1600. **3.** Of arrows: Not fitted with feathers 1611.
2. The *animal implume bipes*, the two-leg'd u. Philosopher 1754. **3.** U. arrows of reed LYTTON.
Unfea·tured *a.* [UN-1 3] DRYDEN. **Unfe·cundated** *ppl. a.* [UN-1 2] 1857. **Unfe·d** *ppl. a.* [UN-1 2] ME. **Unfee·d** *ppl. a.* [UN-1 2] SHAKS.

Unfee·ling, *ppl. a.* OE. [UN-1 4.] **1.** Devoid of sensation; insensible; *fig.* not sensitive to impressions, etc. **2.** Without kindly or tender feeling; callous, unsympathetic 1596.
1. So one..Woo'd an u. statue for his wife COWPER. **2.** Can it be? That men should liue with such vnfeeling soules? B. JONSON. Hence **Unfee·ling-ly** *adv.*, **-ness.**

Unfei·gned, *ppl. a.* late ME. [UN-1 2.] **1.** Not feigned or pretended; genuine, true, real. **2.** Of persons, the heart, etc.: Honest or sincere in feeling or action. late ME.
2. They parceyued well howe he spake them with all his herte vnfayned 1525. Your unfeined, trusty, and assured friend 1573. Hence **Unfei·gnedly** *adv.*
Unfei·gning *ppl. a.* [UN-1 4] late ME., -ly *adv.* **Unfe·lled** *ppl. a.* [UN-1 2] 1543. **Unfe·llowed** *a.* [UN-1 3] 1597. **Unfe·lt** *ppl. a.* [UN-1 2] 1586. **Unfe·minine** *a.* [UN-1 1] 1757, **-ness.**

Unfe·nced, *ppl. a.* 1548. [UN-1 2.] **1.** Undefended, unprotected. *arch.* **2.** Unenclosed; without fences 1608. **b.** Not provided with a guard or the like 1683.
Unferme·nted *ppl. a.* [UN-1 2] 1663. **Unfe·rtile** *a.* [UN-1 1] 1596. **Unfe·rtilized** *ppl. a.* [UN-1 2] 1893. **Unfe·tter** *v.* [UN-2 2 b] late ME.

Unfe·ttered, *ppl. a.* 1601. [UN-1 3.] Not in fetters. Chiefly in fig. use: Unrestrained, unrestricted. Const. *by*.
A new estate u. by conditions 1800. Accustomed.. to the u. exercise of their faculties PRESCOTT.

Unfi·gured, *ppl. a.* 1577. [UN-1 2, 3.] **1.** Not expressed in or employing figurative speech. **2.** Not marked with a numerical figure or figures 1596. **3.** *Zool.* etc. Not (yet) depicted by a figure 1822. **4.** *Logic.* Of a syllogism: Not belonging to one of the usual figures 1838.
1. The u. language of highly cultivated nations 1827.

Unfi·led, *ppl. a.*1 1590. [UN-1 2 + FILE *v.*1] **1.** Not smoothed with the file. **b.** *fig.* Rude, unpolished 1633. **2.** Of coin: Not reduced by filing 1774.
1. He was all armd in rugged steele vnfilde SPENSER. **2.** Unfil'd, unsweated, all of sterling weight 1774.

Unfi·led, *ppl. a.*2 1571. [UN-1 2 + FILE *v.*3] Not arranged in or as in a file; not placed on a file.
Unfi·lial *a.* [UN-1 1] SHAKS. **Unfi·llable** *a.* (now *rare*) [UN-1 1] ME. **Unfi·lled** *ppl. a.* [UN-1 2] late ME. **Unfi·ne** *a.* (now *rare*) [UN-1 1] late ME.

Unfi·ngered, (*ppl.*) *a.* 1603. [UN-1 2, 3.] **1.** Not provided with fingers. **2.** Not touched with the fingers 1811.

Unfi·red, *ppl. a.* 1590. [UN-1 2.] **1.** Not set on fire. **2.** Not subjected or exposed to fire 1791. **3.** Of firearms: Not discharged by firing 1892.
1. Not leave One house u. MASSINGER. *fig.* The human Brute, who view'd her Charms unfir'd 1729. **2.** These un-fired bricks lasted perfectly well 1888.

Unfi·rm, *a.* Now *rare.* 1592. [UN-1 1.] **1.** Lacking solidity or rigidity. †**2.** Weak, feeble, infirm -1660. †**3.** Unsteady, flighty. SHAKS. **4.** Unstable, unsteady; liable to slip or fall 1697.
1. What is the reason that most Veal is so u. and like a Jelly? 1683. **3.** Our fancies are more giddie and vnfirme..Then womens are SHAKS. So **Unfi·rmly** *adv.*

Unfi·t, *a.* 1545. [UN-1 1.] **1.** Not fit or suitable, not fitted or suited (*for* some purpose, action, or end, *to* do something, or *to be* done something to). **b.** Unsuitable, ill fitted for the purpose, etc. 1551. **2.** Not physically fit 1665. *sb.* an u. person. So **Unfi·t-ly** *adv.*, **-ness.**

Unfi·t, *v.* 1611. [UN-2 4.] *trans.* To render unfit; to disqualify.

Unfi·tted, *ppl. a.* 1592. [UN-1 2.] **1.** Not adapted or suited; unfit. **2.** Not fitted up or out; not properly furnished 1708. **3.** Not adjusted by fitting 1895.

Unfi·tting, *ppl. a.* 1590. [UN-1 4.] Not fitting or suitable; unbecoming, improper.
Qualities mis-seeming his place, and u. his calling FLORIO. A thing which..is altogether u. to be named 1656. This is an u., it is a dangerous, state of things BURKE. So **Unfi·tting-ly** *adv.*, **-ness.**

Unfi·x, *v.* 1597. [UN-2 1, 5.] **1.** *trans.* To unfasten, loosen. **b.** *spec.* in military use 1802. **2.** *fig.* To unsettle; to render uncertain or doubtful 1650. **3.** *intr.* To become unfixed 1844.
1. b. U. Bayonet, on which the soldier disengages the bayonet from his piece, and returns it to the scabbard 1802. **2.** The shock..had..unfixed all his opinions MACAULAY. **3.** But the ruthless talons refuse to u. HOOD.

Unfi·xed, *ppl. a.* 1598. [UN-1 2.] **1.** Not fixed in a definite place or position; loose, free. **b.** Of bayonets: Not attached to the rifles 1844. **2.** *fig.* Unsettled, uncertain, undetermined; fluctuating, variable 1654. **b.** Unstable; lacking permanency 1669.
1. In a rusty u. grate DICKENS. **2.** He is totally u. in his principles, and wants to puzzle other people JOHNSON.
Unfla·gging *ppl. a.* [UN-1 4] 1715, -ly *adv.* **Unfla·nked** *ppl. a.* [UN-1 2] 1553. **Unfla·ttered** *ppl. a.* [UN-1 2] 1634. **Unfla·ttering** *ppl. a.* [UN-1 4] 1581. **Unflaw·ed** *ppl. a.* [UN-1 2] 1665. **Unfle·cked** *ppl. a.* [UN-1 2] 1865.

Unfle·dged, *ppl. a.* 1602. [UN-1 2.] **1.** Not yet fledged; callow, unfeathered 1611. **b.** Of an arrow: Unfeathered 1752. **2.** Of persons: Immature, inexperienced 1602. **3.** Of things: Not fully developed; still in a crude or imperfect state 1615. **4.** Pertaining to or characteristic of youth and inexperience 1611.
1. The two-legged and u. species called mankind SCOTT. **3.** Newly hatched u. opinions 1790. **4.** In those vnfledg'd dayes, was my Wife a Girle SHAKS.

Unfle·sh, *v.* 1598. [UN-2 2.] *trans.* To strip of flesh. So **Unfle·shed** *ppl. a.*2

Unfle·shed, *ppl. a.*1 1542. [UN-1 2.] Not yet stimulated by tasting flesh; *fig.* untried, inexperienced, new.
Unfle·shly *a.* [UN-1 1] 1855. **Unfli·nching** *ppl. a.* [UN-1 4] 1728, -ly *adv.* **Unflu·ctuating** *ppl. a.* [UN-1 4] 1723. **Unfoi·led** *ppl. a.*1 [UN-1 2] 1579.

Unfoi·led, *ppl. a.*2 1640. [UN-1 2.] Not coated or backed with foil.

Unfo·ld, *v.*1 [OE. *unfealdan*, f. UN-2 + *fealdan* FOLD *v.*1] **1.** *trans.* To open or unwrap the folds of; to spread open; to expand; to straighten out. **b.** To open (the lips or eyes, a gate, etc.) ME. **2.** To disclose or reveal by statement or exposition; to explain OE. **3.** To disclose to view; to display. late ME. **4.** To unwrap; to release or extract from wrappings 1553. **5.** *intr.* To come open; to spread out or expand; to become patent or plain ME.
1. U. thy forehead gather'd into frowns 1633. U. your arms from about my patient SCOTT. *refl.* Would some new rosebud now u. itself? 1891. **b.** He would not once vnfold his lips SHELTON. Hell shall unfould ..her widest Gates MILT. **2.** I will vnto you all vnfold Our royall mind 1595. **3.** The lightning..That ..vnfolds both heauen and earth SHAKS. The hollow vales their smiling pride u. 1713. **5.** And now Olympus' shining gates u. POPE. The queen's scheme began gradually to u. 1759. So **Unfo·lded** *ppl. a.*1 **Unfo·lder.**

Unfo·ld, *v.*2 1530. [UN-2 2 b.] *trans.* To release (sheep) from a fold or folds. So **Unfo·lded** *ppl. a.*2
Unfo·llowed *ppl. a.* [UN-1 2] 1508. **Unfoo·l** *v.* [UN-2 4 b] SHAKS. **Unfoo·ted** *ppl. a.* [UN-1 2] 1808. **Unforbi·d** 1667, **unforbi·dden** 1535, *ppl. adjs.* [UN-1 2] -ly *adv.*, **-ness.**

Unfo·rced, *ppl. a.* 1598. [UN-1 2.] **1.** Not acting or done under compulsion, voluntary. **b.** Of plants: Not forced 1868. **2.** Not strained, arrived at or effected without abnormal effort, spontaneous, natural 1604.
2. A natural and unforc'd order of words 1665. Here we have a fair u. example of coincidence PALEY. Hence **Unfo·rcedly** *adv.*
Unfo·rdable *a.* [UN-1 1] 1611. **Unforeknow·n** *ppl. a.* [UN-1 2] MILT. **Unforesee·able** *a.* [UN-1 1] 1672, -bly *adv.*, **-ness. Unforesee·ing** *ppl. a.* [UN-1 4] 1602, -ly *adv.* **Unforesee·n** *ppl. a.* [UN-1 2] 1651. **Unfo·rested** *ppl. a.*1 [UN-1 2] 1885. **Unfo·rested** *ppl. a.*2 [UN-2 4 b, 6] 1502. **Unforewa·rned** *ppl. a.* [UN-1 2] 1651. **Unfo·rfeit** *a.* [UN-1 1] 1631. **Unfo·rfeited** *ppl. a.* [UN-1 2] SHAKS. **Unfo·rged** *ppl. a.* [UN-1 2] late ME. **Unforge·ttable** *a.* [UN-1 1] 1806. **Unforge·tting** *ppl. a.* [UN-1 4] 1777. **Unforgi·v(e)able** *a.* [UN-1 1] 1548, -bly *adv.* **Unforgi·ven** *ppl. a.* [UN-1 2] 1565. **Unforgi·veness** [UN-1 6] 1611. **Unforgi·ving** *ppl. a.* [UN-1 4] 1713, **-ness. Unforgo·t** (*arch.*) 1653, **Unforgo·tten** 1813, *ppl. adjs.* [UN-1 2]. **Unfo·rm** *v.* [UN-1 2] 1621. **Unfo·rmal** *a.* (now *rare*) [UN-1 1] 1449.

Unfo·rmed, *ppl. a.* ME. [UN-1 2.] **1.** Not formed or fashioned into a regular shape; formless. **b.** *transf.* Of immaterial things: Not brought to a definite or properly developed state; crude 1689. **c.** Of persons (or the mind): Not developed by education; unpolished 1711. **2.** Not formed or made; uncreated ME.
1. The u. matter of the World, was a God, by the name of Chaos HOBBES. **b.** Every science is in an u. state until its first principles are ascertained 1774. **3.** Vnfourmed is þe fader, vnfourmed is þe sone, vnformed is þe holi gost 1325. The New Ministry yet u. 1757.
Unfo·rmidable *a.* [UN-1 1] 1667. **Unfo·rmulated** *ppl. a.* [UN-1 2] 1866. **Unforsa·ken** *ppl. a.* [UN-1 2] 1648. **Unfo·rtified** *ppl. a.* [UN-1 2] 1525.

Unfo·rtunate, *a.* and *sb.* 1530. [UN-1 2.] **A.** *adj.* **1.** Not favoured by fortune; meeting with bad fortune; unlucky. **b.** euphemistically, *U. woman, female*, a prostitute 1796. **2.** Marked by or associated with misfortune or mishap; disastrous, inauspicious. Also, untoward, regrettable, unlucky 1548.
1. U. in most of his counsels 1652. She shall..fall a Sniveling and call herself the most u. of Women 1680. *absol.* Every gate is shut against the u. GIBBON. **2.** Sith that vnfortunate day 1548. My rash but more u. misdeed MILT. The word 'massage' seems rather an u. one to apply to the procedure 1890.
B. *sb.* **1.** An unfortunate person 1683. **2.** A prostitute 1844.
2. One more U...Gone to her death! HOOD.

Unfo·rtunately, *adv.* 1548. [UN-1 5.] **1.** In an unfortunate way, to a regrettable extent, not successfully, without good results, unaptly. Now *rare.* **2.** Used as a comment on the statement: = Sad to say; what is regrettable; a fact that has bad results. (The current use.) 1706. So **Unfo·rtunateness** 1561.
Unfo·rtune (*arch.*) [UN-1 6] 1470. **Unfo·stered** *ppl. a.* [UN-1 2] 1744. **Unfou·ght** 1523, **unfou·ghten** 1475 (*arch.*) *ppl. adjs.* [UN-1 2]. **Unfou·nd** *ppl. a.* [UN-1 2] 1584.

Unfou·nded, *ppl. a.* 1648. [UN-1 2.] Groundless, not based on facts; chiefly *fig.*, unwarranted. Hence **Unfou·ndedly** *adv.*
Unfra·me *v.* [UN-2 1] ME. **Unfra·med** *ppl. a.* [UN-1 2] 1548. **Unfra·nchised** *ppl. a.* [UN-1 2] 1648. **Unfra·nked** *ppl. a.* [UN-1 2] 1765. **Unfrate·rnal** *a.* [UN-1 1] 1865.

Unfree·, *a.* late ME. [UN-1 1.] **1.** Characterized by want of freedom; not possessed of personal liberty. **2.** Not holding the freedom of a corporation. *Obs.* or *arch.* 1442. **3.** Not free of duty, tax, or impost 1678. Hence **Unfree·man** (now *arch.*), one who is not a freeman of a corporation.
Unfree·d *ppl. a.* [UN-1 2] 1565. **Unfree·dom** [UN-1 6] late ME. **Unfree·ze** *v.* [UN-2 1, 5] 1584. **Un-Fre·nch** *a.* [UN-1 1] 1830. **Unfre·quency** (now *rare*) [UN-1 6] 1611. **Unfre·quent** *a.* [UN-1 1] 1611, -ly *adv.* **Unfreque·nted** *ppl. a.* [UN-1 2] SHAKS., **-ness. Unfre·tted** *ppl. a.* [UN-1 2] 1577.

Unfrie·nd. ME. [UN-1 6.] **1.** One who is not a friend (*to* or *of* a person, cause, etc.) In early use chiefly *Sc.*, app. revived in the 19th c. by Scott. **2.** One who is not a member of the Society of Friends 1828.
1. He is a very unquiet neighbour to his un-friends SCOTT. Mr. Courtney, certainly no u. of the Parnellites 1888. **2.** *attrib.* Adding the names of u. ladies to their committee 1846.

Unfrie·nded, *a.* 1513. [UN-¹ 2.] Not provided with friends; friendless.

Unfrie·ndly, *a.* late ME. [UN-¹ 1.] 1. Indicating or caused by dislike or hostility. 2. Not having the qualities or disposition of a friend; *esp.* unfavourably disposed, inimical, hostile 1483. 3. Not propitious or favourable (*to* or *for*) 1513.

1. This would be looked upon by other countries as an 'u. act' 1898. 3. A coarse, u., stiff soil 1805. Hence **Unfrie·ndliness.**

Unfrie·ndly *adv.* (now *rare*) [UN-¹ 5] OE. **Unfrie·ndship** (*arch.*) [UN-¹ 6] ME. **Unfri·ghted** *ppl. a.* [UN-¹ 2] 1611. **Unfri·ghtened** *ppl. a.* [UN-¹ 2] 1675.

Unfro·ck, *v.* 1644. [UN-² 2.] *trans.* To strip (an ecclesiastic) of his frock as a sign of degradation; hence, to deprive of the right of exercising the priestly function or office.

It is not the unfrocking of a Priest..that will make us a happy Nation MILTON. Who..had unfrocked himself to become a statesman L. HUNT. Hence **Unfro·cked** *ppl. a.*

Unfro·zen *ppl. a.* [UN-¹ 2] 1596. **Unfru·ctuous** *a.* (now *rare*) [UN-¹ 1] late ME. **Unfru·gal** *a.* [UN-¹ 1] 1629.

Unfrui·tful, *a.* late ME. [UN-¹ 1.] 1. Not producing offspring; barren. 2. Not productive of good results; unprofitable, fruitless. late ME. 3. Of trees: Not bearing fruit 1531. 4. Of ground, climate, etc.: Not yielding fruit or crops; unproductive 1545.

1. Unhappy and u. marriages BERKELEY. 2. A time of idle and u. laughter SCOTT. Hence **Unfrui·tful-ly** *adv.*, **-ness.**

Unfru·strable *a.* (*rare*) [UN-¹ 1] 1714, **-bly** *adv.* **Unfu·elled** (*ppl.*) *a.* [UN-¹ 2] 1687. **Unfulfi·lled** *ppl. a.* [UN-¹ 2] late ME. **Unfu·nded** *ppl. a.* [UN-¹ 2] 1776.

Unfu·rl, *v.* 1641. [UN-² 1.] 1. *trans.* To spread (a sail or flag) to the wind. b. *transf.* To open (a fan, umbrella, etc.) 1678. 2. *intr.* To open to the wind 1813.

1. b. The next Motion is that of unfurling the Fan ADDISON. 2. As to the breeze a flag unfurls 1854.

Unfu·rnish, *v.* 1580. [UN-² 2.] 1. *trans.* To remove the garrison or other means of defence of (a town, etc.). Now *rare*. 2. To strip of fittings or furniture; to dismantle 1598. †3. To deprive *of* something -1664.

1. English troops should, without unfurnishing Lisbon, co-operate for the relief of Oporto 1829. 3. That, which may Vnfurnish me of Reason SHAKS.

Unfu·rnished, *ppl. a.* 1541. [UN-¹ 2.] 1. Not furnished; unprovided (*with* or †*of* something), unequipped, unprepared. 2. Of houses or apartments: Not provided with furniture; *spec.* not furnished by the landlord or person letting; requiring to be furnished by the tenant 1581.

1. We shall be much vnfurnisht for this time SHAKS. The sayd place is..unfurnyshed with a convenient Schole howse 1611. To fill the void of an unfurnish'd brain COWPER. The treasury was u. 1860. 2. A Fair House to be Lett Furnished or U. 1680.

Unfu·rred (*ppl.*) *a.* [UN-¹ 2] 1450. **Unfu·rrowed** *ppl. a.* [UN-¹ 2] 1566. **Ungai·n** *a.* (now chiefly *dial.*) [UN-¹ 1] late ME. **Ungai·ned** *ppl. a.* [UN-¹ 2] SHAKS. **Ungai·nful** *a.* [UN-¹ 1] 1599.

Ungai·nly, *a.* 1611. [UN-¹ 1.] Awkward, clumsy, ungraceful.

The tall u. figure..of Ebenezer SCOTT. So **Ungai·nly** *adv.* in an u. manner.

Ungainsai·d *ppl. a.* [UN-¹ 2] 1587. **Ungainsay·able** *a.* [UN-¹ 1] 1618, **-bly** *adv.* **Unga·llant** *a.* [UN-¹ 1] 1710, **-ly** *adv.* **Unga·lled** *ppl. a.* [UN-¹ 2] SHAKS. **Unga·rbled** *ppl. a.* [UN-¹ 2] late ME. **Unga·rmented** *ppl. a.* [UN-¹ 2] 1798. **Unga·rnered** *ppl. a.* [UN-¹ 2] 1850. **Unga·rnish** *v.* [UN-² 2] 1530. **Unga·rnished** *ppl. a.* [UN-¹ 2] late ME. **Unga·rrisoned** *ppl. a.* [UN-¹ 2] 1660. **Unga·rter** *v.* [UN-² 2 b] 1594. **Unga·rtered** *ppl. a.* [UN-¹ 2] SHAKS. **Unga·thered** *ppl. a.* [UN-¹ 2] 1461. **Ungau·ged** *ppl. a.* [UN-¹ 2] 1745. **Ungau·ntleted** (*ppl.*) *a.* [UN-¹ 2] 1800.

Ungea·r, *v.* 1611. [UN-² 1, 2 b.] 1. *trans.* To unharness. Now *dial.* 2. To disconnect the gearing of 1828.

Ungea·red, *a.* [UN-¹ 3.] †1. Without fittings or accessories -1588. 2. Not provided with gears or gearing (cf. GEARING 3).

Unge·lded, unge·lt *ppl. a.* [UN-¹ 2] late ME.

Unge·nerated *ppl. a.* [UN-¹ 2] 1614. **Ungenero·sity** [UN-¹ 6] 1757.

Unge·nerous, *a.* 1641. [UN-¹ 1.] Not generous or large-minded; illiberal, ignoble, mean. Hence **Unge·nerous-ly** *adv.*, **-ness.**

Unge·nial *a.* [UN-¹ 1] 1726, **-ly** *adv.* **Ungentee·l** *a.* [UN-¹ 1] 1633, **-ly** *adv.*, **-ness.** **Ungenti·lity** [UN-¹ 6] 1822.

Unge·ntle, *a.* late ME. [UN-¹ 1.] †1. Not of gentle birth -1688. 2. Lacking the qualities associated with gentle birth or breeding; unchivalrous; discourteous, unmannerly. Now *arch.* late ME. b. Not appropriate to or befitting one of gentle birth or breeding 1565. 3. Not gentle in action; rough, harsh, unkind; rigorous, hard, severe 1509.

1. He is ashamed of hys vngentil lynage CHAUCER. 2. Sith the vngentle king Of Fraunce refuseth to giue aide..To this distressed Queene MARLOWE. b. Where so loose life, and so vngentle trade Was vsd of Knights and Ladies seeming gent SPENSER. 3. To crush our old limbes in vngentle Steele SHAKS. His temper, naturally u., had been exasperated by his domestic vexations MACAULAY.

Unge·ntleman *v.* (now *rare*) [UN-² 4 b] 1671. **Unge·ntlemanlike** *a.* and *adv.* [UN-¹ 1] 1592. **Unge·ntlemanly** *a.* and *adv.* [UN-¹ 1, 5] 1562. **Unge·ntleness** [UN-¹ 6] late ME. **Unge·ntly** *adv.* [UN-¹ 5] 1440. **Unge·nuine** *a.* (*rare*) [UN-¹ 1] 1665, **-ness.** **U:ngeome·trical** *a.* [UN-¹ 1] 1570. **Unge·t** *v.* [UN-² 1] 1775.

Unget-a·t-able, *a.* 1862. [UN-¹ 1.] Difficult to get at; inaccessible.

Ungho·stly, *a.* 1526. [UN-¹ 1.] 1. Not spiritual, secular. 2. Not of or like a ghost 1888.

1. Martin Luther the first preacher of this vnghostely ghospell 1565.

Ungi·fted (*ppl.*) *a.* [UN-¹ 2, 3] 1631. **Ungi·ld** *v.* [UN-¹ 2] 1611. **Ungi·lded** 1674, **ungi·lt** 1444 *ppl. adjs.* [UN-¹ 2] **Ungi·rd** *v.* [UN-¹ 2, 2 b] OE. **Ungi·rded** *ppl. a.* [UN-¹ 2] late ME. **Ungi·rdled** *ppl. a.* [UN-¹ 2] 1611.

Ungi·rt, *ppl. a.* ME. [UN-¹ 2.] 1. Not girded or wearing a girdle; with the girdle or belt removed or slackened. 2. *fig.* Not braced up for action; not drawn together; left loose or incompact 1579.

1. The idle and sluggish person..goeth loose and vngirt 1586. 2. What in most English wryters vseth to be loose, and as it were vngyrt, in this Authour is.. strongly trussed vp together SPENSER.

Ungi·rth *v.* [UN-² 2 b] 1580. **Ungi·rthed** (*ppl.*) *a.* [UN-¹ 2] 1628. **Ungi·ven** *ppl. a.* [UN-¹ 2] ME. **Ungi·ving** *ppl. a.* [UN-¹ 4] 1682. **Ungla·d** *a.* [UN-¹ 1] OE., **-ly** *adv.*, **-ness.** **Ungla·ddened** *ppl. a.* [UN-¹ 2] 1851.

Ungla·zed, *ppl. a.* 1599. [UN-¹ 2.] 1. Not glazed or having a smooth shining surface. 2. Not filled in with glass; without glass windows 1608.

Unglea·ned *ppl. a.* [UN-¹ 2] 1858. **Unglo·rified** *ppl. a.* [UN-¹ 2] late ME. **Unglo·rify** *v.* [UN-² 4 c] 1740. **Unglo·rious** *a.* (now *rare*) [UN-¹ 1] late ME. **Unglo·ssed** *ppl. a.* [UN-¹ 2] 1802. **Unglo·ssy** *a.* [UN-¹ 1] 1822. **Unglo·ve** *v.* [UN-² 2] late ME. **Unglo·ved** (*ppl.*) *a.* [UN-¹ 2] 1626.

Unglue·, *v.* 1548. [UN-² 1, 4.] 1. *trans.* To sever or detach (a glued article, joint, or part). b. *transf.* To part the lids of, open (the eyes) 1606. c. *fig.* To bring (a union, etc.) to an end, dissolve 1619. 2. *intr.* To lose cohesion, come apart 1693.

1. c. Enough to unglew all naturall and civill relations 1649.

Unglu·tted *ppl. a.* [UN-¹ 2] 1813. **Ungo·d** *v.* [UN-² 4 b] 1627. **Ungo·ddess** *v.* [UN-² 4 b] 1760. **Ungo·dlike** *a.* [UN-¹ 1] 1652.

Ungo·dly, *a.* 1526. [UN-¹ 1.] 1. Of persons: Not fearing or reverencing God; irreligious, impious, wicked. 2. Of actions, etc.: Not in accordance with the law or will of God; wicked 1526. 3. *colloq.* Outrageous, dreadful 1887.

1. They sayde it was vngodly to feyght..not beinge prouoked 1555. But no Success th' U. find WESLEY. 3. The wind['s] u. and unintermittent uproar STEVENSON. So **Ungo·dly** *adv.* (*arch.*) in an u. manner.

Ungo·rged *ppl. a.* [UN-¹ 2] 1623. **Ungo·spellike** *a.* [UN-¹ 1] 1574. **Ungo·t** *ppl. a.* [UN-¹ 2] late ME. **Ungo·tten** *ppl. a.* [UN-¹ 2] late ME.

Ungo·vernable, *a.* 1673. [UN-¹ 1.] That cannot be governed; uncontrollable.

The u. spirit of a Barbarian host GIBBON. The abbess..will have an u. penitent under her charge SCOTT. He fell into a most u. passion 1843. Hence **Ungo·vernableness. Ungo·vernably** *adv.*

Ungo·verned *ppl. a.* [UN-¹ 2] SHAKS. **Ungow·ned** *ppl. a.* [UN-¹ 2] 1611. **Ungra·ce** (now *rare*) [UN-¹ 6] late ME. **Ungra·ced** *ppl. a.* [UN-¹ 2] 1595. **Ungra·ceful** *a.* [UN-¹ 1] MILT., **-ly** *adv.*, **-ness.**

Ungra·cious, *a.* ME. [UN-¹ 1.] †1. Of persons: Devoid of spiritual grace; graceless, wicked -1820. †2. Unfortunate, unlucky, unfavourable -1634. †3. Rude, unmannerly -1606. †4. Not in favour; disliked -1761. b. Unpleasant and unappreciated 1807. 5. Ungraceful, unattractive 1647. 6. Not gracious; lacking in courtesy or responsiveness; offending the sensibilities of others 1745.

1. Emong yᵉ holy apostles vngratious Iudas 1579. 2. The .xv. day ys noght spedeful to be-gynne ony werke vp-on, for yt ys ongracyus 1445. 4. Prince Rupert, at that time, was generally very u. in England CLARENDON. b. The u. duties inseparable from his office 1844. 5. Show no parts which are u. to the Sight, as all fore-shortnings usually are DRYDEN. 6. The meek and affable duchess turned out an u. and haughty queen MACAULAY. Refusal on my part would be too u. DICKENS. Hence **Ungra·cious-ly** *adv.*, **-ness.**

Ungra·ded *ppl. a.* [UN-¹ 2] 1879.

Ungra·duated, *ppl. a.* 1783. [UN-¹ 2.] 1. That has not graduated at a university. 2. Without gradations; abrupt, not gradual 1841.

Ungra·fted *ppl. a.* [UN-¹ 2] 1657.

Ungramma·tical, *a.* 1654. [UN-¹ 1.] 1. Not grammatical; breaking or offending against the rules of grammar. 2. At variance with correct rule or method 1851.

2. Some really u. and false picture RUSKIN. Hence **Ungramma·tical-ly** *adv.*, **-ness.**

Ungra·nted *ppl. a.* [UN-¹ 2] 1570. **Ungra·spable** [UN-¹ 1] 1741.

Ungra·teful, *a.* 1553. [UN-¹ 1.] 1. Not feeling or displaying gratitude. b. Of soil etc.: Not responding to cultivation 1681. 2. Unpleasant, distasteful, unwelcome 1596.

1. b. The land is u. and barren BORROW. 2. Good wine which..is rendred..acid and u. to our palate 1663. Some sounds..are very harsh and u. 1690. The u. rumour reached his ears GIBBON. Then are these songs I sing of thee Not all u. to thine ear TENNYSON. Hence **Ungra·teful-ly** *adv.*, **-ness.**

Ungra·tified *ppl. a.* [UN-¹ 2] 1613. †**Ungra·titude** [UN-¹ 6] 1548. **Ungra·ve** *v.* [UN-² 3] 1664. **Ungra·vely** *adv.* (now *rare*) [UN-¹ 5] SHAKS. **Ungra·ven** *ppl. a.* [UN-¹ 2] late ME. **Ungrea·sed** *ppl. a.* [UN-¹ 2] 1440. **Un-Gree·k** *a.* [UN-¹ 1] 1846. **Ungree·ted** *ppl. a.* [UN-¹ 2] 1611. **Ungrou·nd** *ppl. a.* [UN-¹ 2] late ME.

Ungrou·nded, *ppl. a.* late ME. [UN-¹ 2.] 1. Not based or established *in* something. 2. Having no sound basis; unfounded, groundless. late ME. 3. Not properly instructed or informed (*in* a subject) 1449.

1. Euyle lawis vngroundid in holy writt & reson WYCLIF. 2. My former Letter, by which that conjecture will appear to be u. NEWTON. Hence **Ungrou·nded-ly** *adv.*, **-ness.**

Ungrow·n *ppl. a.* [UN-¹ 2] SHAKS. **Ungru·dged** *ppl. a.* [UN-¹ 2] 1631. **Ungru·dging** *ppl. a.* [UN-¹ 4] 1768, **-ly** *adv.*, **-ness.**

Ungual (v·ŋgwăl), *a.* and *sb.* 1834. [f. L. *unguis* nail + -AL.] A. *adj.* 1. *Anat.* Pertaining to, connected with, a nail or claw; esp. *u. phalanx*, the terminal bone of a digit. 2. *Path.* Affecting the nail 1872. B. *sb.* An ungual phalanx, claw, or bone.

Ungua·rd, *v.* 1745. [UN-² 2.] To deprive of a guard or defence; to lay open to attack. b. *Whist*, etc. To expose (a high card) to the risk of loss by discarding a lower and protecting card 1862.

Some well-chosen presents..so..unguarded the girl's heart FIELDING.

Ungua·rded, *ppl. a.* 1593. [UN-¹ 2.] 1. Not furnished with, or protected by a guard; left open to attack, spoliation, etc. b. *Chess*, *cards*, etc. Not protected by other pieces or cards 1808. 2. Not on one's guard; incautious 1640. b. Of times: Characterized by the absence of guard or caution 1680. c. Of actions, etc.: Incautious, imprudent; careless 1714. 3. Having no screen, shield, fence, case, etc. 1771.

1. The u. passes of the Apennine GIBBON. 2. Sir Robert was frequently very u. in his expressions 1763.

b. I'll..Wait on and watch her loose u. hours OTWAY. 3. Dust or gas..ignited by an u. lamp 1900. Hence **Ungua·rded-ly** *adv.*, **-ness.**

Unguent (*v*·ŋgwĕnt), *sb.* 1440. [ad. L. *unguentum*, f. *unguere* to anoint.] An ointment or salve. Hence **U·nguent** *v.* (*rare*) *trans.* to anoint.

‖**Unguentarium** (*v*ŋgwentē·riŏm). 1859. [L. *unguentarium* (sc. *vas*) neut. (see next).] *Archæol.* A vessel for holding ointment.

Unguentary (*v*·ŋgwĕntări) *sb.* and *a.* Now *rare.* late ME. [ad. L. *unguentarius*, f. *unguentum* UNGUENT *sb.*] **A.** *sb.* **1.** A maker of or dealer in (perfumed) ointment; a perfumer. **2.** = prec. 1911. **B.** *adj.* Adapted for use in, suitable for or connected with ointments 1657.

Ungue·rdoned *ppl. a.* [UN-1 2] late ME. **Ungue·ssable** *a.* [UN-1 1] 1832. **Ungue·ssed** *ppl. a.* [UN-1 2] late ME.

Unguiculate (*v*ŋgwi·kiŭlĕt), *a.* and *sb.* 1802. [ad. mod.L. *unguiculatus*, f. L. *unguiculus*, dim. of *unguis*.] **A.** *adj.* **1.** *Bot.* Of petals: Having an unguis. **2.** *Zool.* Ending in or of the form of a nail or claw 1826. **3.** *Zool.* Of quadrupeds: Having nails or claws; belonging to the order *Unguiculata* 1839. **B.** *sb.* An u. quadruped 1840. So **Ungui·culated** *a.* 1752.

Ungui·ded, *ppl. a.* 1585. [UN-1 2.] Not guided in a particular path or direction; left to take one's own course or way. **b.** *fig.* Of action, etc.: Undirected, uncontrolled 1597.

U·nguiform, *a.* 1726. [f. L. *unguis* nail + -FORM.] Having the form of a nail or claw.

Unguilloti·ned *ppl. a.* [UN-1 2] 1837. **Ungui·lty** *a.* [UN-1 1] OE.

‖**Unguis** (*v*·ŋgwis). *Pl.* **ungues** (-īz). 1728. [L., 'nail, claw'.] **1.** *Bot.* The narrow part of a petal, by which it is attached to the receptacle. **2.** *Zool.*, etc. A nail or claw 1790.

‖**Ungula** (*v*·ŋgiŭlă). 1710. [L., 'hoof', f. *unguis* nail.] *Geom.* An obliquely truncated cone or cylinder.

‖**Ungulata** (*v*ŋgiŭlē·tă), *sb. pl.* 1839. [L., neut. pl. *ungulatus*; see next.] The order or division of ungulate animals.

Ungulate (*v*·ŋgiŭlĕt), *a.* and *sb.* 1802. [ad. L. *ungulatus*, f. *ungula* hoof.] **A.** *adj.* **1.** Hoof-shaped. **2.** Of quadrupeds: Having hoofs 1839. **B.** *sb.* An u. animal 1842.

Unguled (*v*·ŋgiŭld), *a.* 1572. [f. L. *ungula* hoof.] *Her.* Of animals: With hoofs or claws of a different tincture from the body.

An ox gu., armed and u. or 1864.

Ungulite (*v*·ŋgiŭlait). 1850. [f. L. *ungula* hoof + -ITE 1.] *Palæont.* A Palæozoic brachiopod, the obolus.

Ungu·m *v.* [UN-2 2 b] 1598. **Ungu·mmed** *ppl. a.* [UN-1 2] 1799. **Ungy·ve** *v.* [UN-2 2 b] 1531. **Ungy·ved** *ppl. a.* [UN-1 2] 1607. **Unha·bitable** *a.* (now *rare*) [UN-1 1] late ME. **Unhabi·tuated** *ppl. a.* [UN-1 2] 1796. **Unha·cked** *ppl. a.* [UN-1 2] SHAKS. **Unha·ckneyed** *ppl. a.* [UN-1 2] 1759. **Unhai·led** *ppl. a.* [UN-1 2] 1715.

Unhai·r, *v.* late ME. [UN-2 2.] **1.** *trans.* To deprive (the head, etc.) of hair. **b.** *Tanning.* To remove the hair from (a skin) 1845. **2.** *intr.* To lose the hair; to become free of hair 1843.

Unha·llow *v.* [UN-2 2] COVERDALE.

Unha·llowed, *ppl. a.* [OE. *unhálgod*, f. UN-1 2 + pa. pple. of HALLOW *v.*] **1.** Not formally hallowed or consecrated; left secular or profane. **2.** Not having a hallowed or sacred character; unholy, impious, wicked 1588.

1. Men vnhallowed and vnconsecrated 1587. 2. In this unhallow'd air MILTON. In impious feasting, and unhallow'd joy POPE.

Unha·lter *v.* [UN-2 2 b] 1584. **Unha·lting** *ppl. a.* [UN-1 4] 1832. **Unha·mpered** *ppl. a.* [UN-1 2] 1699.

Unha·nd, *v.* 1602. [UN-2 2 b.] *trans.* To take the hand off; to release from one's grasp; to let go. Chiefly *arch.* in the phrase *unhand me*!

Unha·ndcuffed *ppl. a.* [UN-1 2] 1861. **Unha·ndily** *adv.* [UN- 5] 1706. **Unha·ndiness** [UN-1 6] 1706. **Unha·ndled** *ppl. a.* [UN-1 2] 1558.

Unha·ndsome, *a.* 1530. [UN-1 1.] **1.** Not handsome in appearance; plain, uncomely. †**2.** Unhandy, inconvenient -1690. †**3.** Inexpert, unskilful. SHAKS. **4.** Unfitting, unbecoming, unseemly; discourteous, mean 1645. **b.** Not generous or liberal 1800.

1. Socrates was the most nasty and unhandsom of all men living 1653. Being generally well-shaped, and not u. 1787. A large u. house 1895. 2. The night (perdy) is unhansome to woorke in UDALL. 4. The u. attributes you so often give me HOBBES. Let mee conjure you not to doe a thing soe unhandsom 1658. Hence **Unha·ndsome-ly** *adv.*, **-ness.**

Unha·ndy, *a.* 1664. [UN-1 1.] **1.** Not easy to handle or manage; inconvenient, awkward, clumsy. **2.** Not skilful in using the hands, lacking in dexterity 1669.

Unha·ng, *v.* late ME. [UN-2 1.] **1.** *trans.* To take down from a hanging position. **b.** *Naut.* To unship (a rudder) 1600. **2.** To undo the hanging of (a person) 1829.

Unha·nged, *ppl. a.* 1440. [UN-1 2.] Not (yet) executed by hanging.

There liues not three good men vnhang'd in England SHAKS. The greatest rascal u. THACKERAY.

Unha·ppily, *adv.* late ME. [UN-1 5.] **1.** By mischance; unfortunately, unluckily; regrettably. **b.** Used parenthetically or in loose construction 1586. **2.** In an unsatisfactory way; disastrously; unsuccessfully. late ME. **3.** Without happiness 1687. †**4.** Unpleasantly near the truth -1602. †**b.** Unfavourably. SHAKS.

1. Worc'ster (who had escap'd vnhappily His death in battel) on a Scaffold dies DANIEL. That War in which the King was so unhappyly engaged against Spain CLARENDON. b. U. the splendid qualities of John Churchill were mingled with alloy of the most sordid kind MACAULAY. 2. I promise you, the effects he writes of, succeede vnhappily SHAKS. The giddy girl who married u. 1779. Persons who manage so u. what they mean for civilities SCOTT. 3. Where little Rawdon passed the first months of his life, not u. THACKERAY. 4. *Ham.* IV. v. 13.

Unha·ppiness. 1470. [UN-1 6.] **1.** Misfortune, mishap, ill luck. *Obs.* or *arch.* **2.** The condition of being unhappy in mind 1722.

1. I haue not that vnhappinesse, to be A Rich Mans Sonne 1621.

Unha·ppy, *a.* ME. [UN-1 1.] **1.** Causing misfortune or trouble (to oneself or others); objectionable or miserable on this account. **2.** Ill-fated, unlucky; miserable in lot or circumstances. Also, in later use, wretched in mind, ill content. late ME. **b.** Unsuccessful; apt to make mistakes 1651. **c.** Of places: Subject to, suffering from, misfortunes or evils 1591. **3.** Associated with, bringing about or causing, misfortune or mishap; disastrous. late ME. **b.** Inauspicious 1533. **c.** Infelicitous 1719. **4.** Of conditions: Marked by misfortune or mishap; miserable, wretched. late ME.

1. These u. Highland clans are again breaking into general commotion SCOTT. 2. The seamen might conjecture some u. mortal to be shut up in the box SWIFT. b. He is as u. a person in Philology, as any that have pretended so much acquaintance with it 1662. c. The bands which..wasted these u. districts MACAULAY. 3. He had an u. propensity to drinking LOCKHART. b. Wretches borne vnder vnhappie starre SPENSER. 4. You oft declaim on man's u. fate 1712. Their u. social position 1838. So †**Unha·ppy** *v. trans.* to make u. or unfortunate -1653.

Unha·rbour, *v.* 1576. [UN-2 3.] *trans.* To dislodge (a deer) from covert.

Unha·rdened *ppl. a.* [UN-1 2] SHAKS. **Unha·rdy** *a.* [UN-1 1] late ME. **Unha·rmed** *ppl. a.* [UN-1 2] ME. **Unha·rmful** *a.* [UN-1 1] 1538, **-ly**, *adv.* **Unha·rming** *ppl. a.* [UN-1 4] 1795. **Unharmo·nious** *a.* [UN-1 1] 1634, **-ly** *adv.*

Unha·rness, *v.* late ME. [UN-2 2, 2 b.] **1.** *trans.* To divest of armour. **2.** To take off the harness from; to unyoke 1611.

2. *fig.* When two unfortunately met are by the Canon forc't to draw in that yoke..till death unharnesse 'em MILT. Hence **Unha·rnessed** *ppl. a.* 2

Unha·rnessed, *ppl. a.* 1 1513. [UN-1 2.] **1.** Not in armour. **2.** Not harnessed 1608. **b.** Not adapted for industrial use 1903.

2. b. U. rapids wasting fifty thousand head an hour KIPLING.

Unha·rvested *ppl. a.* [UN-1 1] 1867. **Unha·sp** *v.* [UN-2 2 b] late ME. **Unha·sting** *ppl. a.* [UN-1 4] 1839. **Unha·sty** *a.* [UN-1 1] SPENSER. **Unha·t** *v.* [UN-2 2, 5] 1611. **Unha·tched** *ppl. a.* 1 [UN-1 2] 1601.

†**Unha·tched,** *ppl. a.* 2 1601. [UN-1 2.] Unhacked; unstained -1619.

He is a knight dubb'd with vnhatch'd Rapier SHAKS.

Unha·tted *a.* [UN-1 3] 1832. **Unhau·nted** *ppl. a.* [UN-1 2] 1533. **Unha·zarded** *ppl. a.* [UN-1 2] 1588. **Unha·zardous** *a.* [UN-1 1] 1682.

Unhea·d, *v.* late ME. [UN-2 2.] **1.** *trans.* To behead. Now *rare.* **2.** To deprive or divest of a top, or end 1611.

Unhea·ded *a.* [UN-1 3] 1586. **Unhea·lable** *a.* [UN-1 1] late ME. **Unhea·led** *ppl. a.* [UN-1 2] ME. **Unhea·lth** [UN-1 6] OE. **Unhea·lthful** *a.* [UN-1 1] 1580, **-ness.**

Unhealthy (*v*nhe·lþi), *a.* 1595. [UN-1 1.] **1.** Not possessed of good health; weak, sickly 1611. **b.** *Path.* Not in a sound or healthy condition; diseased 1813. **2.** Prejudicial to health; insalubrious; unwholesome; in recent use, trivially (*War slang*), unsafe. 1595. **3.** *fig.* Deleterious to morals or character 1821.

1. b. When a wound becomes u., as surgeons term it 1877. 2. The most u. season of the year 1806. 3. I do feel the differences of mankind..to an u. excess LAMB. Hence **Unhea·lthily** *adv.*, **-ness.**

Unhea·rd, *ppl. a.* ME. [UN-1 2.] **1.** Not apprehended by the sense of hearing; not heard. **b.** Not having been allowed a hearing 1595. **2.** Not before heard of; unknown, new, strange. (Now always with *of.*) late ME.

1. He drew not nigh u. MILT. b. I will not condemn you u. 1655. 2. The vngracious and vnherde wickednesse of Iason COVERDALE 2 *Macc.* iv. 13. Inflicting vnheard-of tortures 1615.

Unhea·rt, *v.* 1593. [UN-2 2.] To deprive of heart; to dishearten.

Yet to bite his lip, And humme at good Cominius, much vnhearts mee SHAKS.

Unhea·rty *a.* (now *rare*) [UN-1 1] 1440. **Unhea·ted** *ppl. a.* [UN-1 2] 1691. **Unhea·ven** *v.* [UN-2 3] 1609. **Unhea·venly** *a.* [UN-1 1] 1752. **Unhe·dged** *ppl. a.* [UN-1 2] 1648. **Unhee·d** *v.* [UN-1 7] 1847. **Unhee·ded** *ppl. a.* [UN-1 2] 1611, **-ly** *adv.* **Unhee·dful** *a.* [UN-1 1] 1570, **-ly** *adv.*, **-ness.**

Unhee·ding, *ppl. a.* 1737. [UN-1 4.] **1.** Heedless, inattentive. **2.** Const. *of*, or with direct obj. 1795.

2. I ramble..u. of the storm 1795. Then, u. his proffered aid, Erma descends 1892. Hence **Unhee·dingly** *adv.*

Unhe·le, *v. Obs.* exc. *dial.* [OE. *unhelan*, f. UN-2 + HELE *v.*] To uncover; to strip of covering; *fig.* to discover, reveal.

Unhe·lm *v.* [UN-2 2, 5] late ME. **Unhe·lmed** (*ppl.*) *a.* [UN-1 2] 1795. **Unhe·lmeted** (*ppl.*) *a.* [UN-1 2] 1823. **Unhe·lpable** *a.* [UN-1 1] 1886. **Unhe·lped** *ppl. a.* [UN-1 2] late ME. **Unhe·lpful** *a.* [UN-1 1] SHAKS., **-ness.** **Unhe·lping** *ppl. a.* [UN-1 4] 1604. **Unhe·mmed** *ppl. a.* [UN-1 2] 1561. **Unhe·ralded** *ppl. a.* [UN-1 2] 1845. **Unhero·ic** *a.* [UN-1 1] 1732, **-ally** *adv.* **Unhe·sitating** *ppl. a.* [UN-1 4] 1753, **-ly** *adv.*, **-ness.** **Unhew·ed** *ppl. a.* [UN-1 2] late ME.

Unhew·n, *ppl. a.* late ME. [UN-1 2.] **1.** Not hacked or cut with weapons. **2.** Not hewn or cut into shape; not shaped by hewing. late ME. **b.** *fig.* Rugged, unpolished, rough 1659.

2. b. The difference between a rough, u. soldier, and a polish'd Gentleman 1703.

Unhi·d *ppl. a.* [UN-1 2] ME. **Unhi·dden** *ppl. a.* [UN-1 2] SHAKS. **Unhi·de** *v.* [UN-2 1] ME. **Unhi·ndered** *ppl. a.* [UN-1 2] 1615.

Unhi·nge, *v.* 1612. [UN-2 1.] **1.** *trans.* To take (a door, etc.) off the hinges; to remove the hinges from; to open in this way 1616. **2.** To unbalance, unsettle, upset, disorder (the mind, a person, his opinions, convictions, etc.) 1612. **3.** To deprive of stability or fixity; to throw into confusion or disorder 1664. **b.** *esp.* To unsettle (an established order of things) 1679. **4.** To detach or dislodge *from* something 1655.

1. Our hogges having found a way to unhindge their barne doores 1634. 2. The nerves of Mahomet were completely unhinged 1867. b. One Blow from unforeseen Providence unhing'd me at once DE FOE. 3. The supplies are coming in very irregularly and u. the trade 1886. 4. Minds that have been unhinged from their old faith and love GEO. ELIOT. Hence **Unhi·nged** *ppl. a.* **Unhi·ngement,** the act of unhinging; the fact of being unhinged.

Unhi·red *ppl. a.* [UN-1 2] 1617. **Unhisto·ric** *a.* [UN-1 1] 1862.

Unhisto·rical, *a.* 1611. [UN-1 1.] **1.** Not in accordance with history. **2.** Not recorded in true history; not having actually occurred 1848. Hence **Unhisto·rically** *adv.*

Unhi·tch, *v.* 1706. [UN-² 2 b.] **1.** *trans.* To detach (a horse, etc.) from a vehicle, etc. or from something to which its head is tied. **2.** To detach or unfasten (a thing) 1876.

Unhi·ve *v.* [UN-² 3] 1729. **Unhoa·rd** *v.* [UN-² 3] MILT. **Unho·lpen** *ppl. a.* (*arch.*) [UN-¹ 2] late ME.

Unho·ly, *a.* and *sb.* [OE. *unhálig*, f. UN-¹ + *hálig* HOLY *a.*] **1.** Not holy, impious, profane, wicked. **2.** *colloq.* Awful, dreadful 1865. **B.** *sb.* An u. person or thing (*rare*) 1831. Hence **Unho·lily** *adv.* **Unho·liness.**

Unho·mely *a.* [UN-¹ 1] 1871. **Unhomoge·neous** *a.* [UN-¹ 1] 1828.

Unho·nest, *a.* Now *arch.* or *dial.* ME. [UN-¹ 1.] **1.** Physically or morally objectionable, offensive, or unpleasant; indecent, filthy, vile. **b.** Unseemly, unbecoming, improper. late ME. **2.** Morally unfitting or unbecoming; unseemly, immodest, lewd; dishonourable, discreditable. late ME. **3.** Of persons: Not honourable, respectable, or of good repute; bad or immoral in character or conduct. late ME. **4.** Dishonest 1545.

1. Whatsoever thyng wer not of it self u., he affermed not to bee unhoneste in open presence UDALL. **2.** Taking delight in hearing u. things 1645. **3.** This untrew, u. and perjured persone HALL. **4.** How vnhonest is that labourer, who will not worke for his wages? 1603. So **Unho·nestly** *adv.* (*obs.* or *dial.*). **Unho·nesty** (*obs.* or *dial.*).

†**Unho·nourable** *a.* [UN-¹ 1] –1635. **Unho·noured** *ppl. a.* [UN-¹ 2] 1513. **Unhoo·d** *v.* [UN-² 2] 1575. **Unhoo·ded** *ppl. a.* [UN-¹ 2] 1575.

Unhoo·k, *v.* 1611. [UN-² 2 b.] **1.** *trans.* To detach from a hook; to unfasten or open in this way. **2.** To unfasten the hooks of (a dress). Also with personal obj. 1840. **3.** To disengage (one's arm) from another's 1865.

Unho·ped, *ppl. a.* late ME. [UN-¹ 2.] †**1.** Unforeseen –1697. **2.** Not hoped for. Now *rare.* late ME. †**b.** *advb.* By unexpected good fortune, beyond hopes –1830. **3.** Not hoped (†or looked) *for* 1598.

1. Amazed at this u. danger 1575. **2.** Such, as fill my heart with vnhop'd ioyes SHAKS. **b.** Though Jove hath given me to behold, Unhop'd, the land again COWPER. **3.** These u.-for circumstances 1857.

Unho·peful *a.* [UN-¹ 1] 1450, **-ly** *adv.*, **-ness.** **Unho·ping** *ppl. a.* [UN-¹ 4] 1628. **Unho·rned** *ppl. a.* [UN-¹ 2] 1570.

Unho·rse, *v.* late ME. [UN-² 1.] **1.** *trans.* To throw or drag (a rider) from his horse, esp. in battle. **b.** *fig.* To discomfit, overthrow. Now *rare.* 1577. **c.** *pass.* To be thrown from a horse 1583. **2.** To unharness the horses from (a carriage, gun, etc.) 1654.

1. b. Thou hast unhorsed me with that very word SCOTT.

Unho·spitable *a.* (now *rare*) [UN-¹ 1] SHAKS. **Unhou·se** *v.* [UN-² 3] late ME. **Unhou·sed** *ppl. a.* [UN-¹ 2] 1582.

Unhouseled (ʊnhau·z'ld), *ppl. a.* Now only after Shaks. [UN-¹ 2.] Not having received Holy Communion.

Vnhouzzled, disappointed, vnnaneld *Ham.* I. v. 77.

Unhu·man, *a.* 1549. [UN-¹ 1.] **1.** Inhuman, inhumane, unmerciful, cruel. Now *rare.* **2.** Transcending the human; superhuman 1782. **3.** Not pertaining to mankind 1885.

1. He was sent away pennyless..from the house of his u. father FIELDING. **2.** Exalted to u. happiness 1782. **3.** 'How is this?', he cried, in a sharp u., voice 1885.

Unhu·manize *v.* [UN-² 4 c] 1752. **Unhu·mble** *a.* [UN-¹ 1] 1611. **Unhu·mbled** *ppl. a.* [UN-¹ 2] 1604. **Unhu·morous** *a.* [UN-¹ 1] 1881.

Unhu·ng, *ppl. a.* 1648. [UN-¹ 2.] **1.** Not furnished with hangings. Now *rare.* **2.** Not (yet) hanged 1840. **b.** Not hung up (for exhibition) 1880.

2. One of the greatest scoundrels u. DICKENS.

Unhu·nted, *ppl. a.* 1572. [UN-¹ 2.] **1.** Of districts, etc.: Not hunted in. **2.** Not hunted or chased 1648.

Unhu·rried *ppl. a.* [UN-¹ 2] 1768, **-ly** *adv.* **Unhu·rrying** *ppl. a.* [UN-¹ 4] 1768. **Unhu·rt** *ppl. a.* [UN-¹ 2] ME. **Unhu·rtful** *a.* [UN-¹ 1] 1549, **-ly** *adv.*, **-ness.** **Unhu·rting** *ppl. a.* [UN-¹ 4] 1613.

Unhu·sbanded, *ppl. a.* 1538. [UN-¹ 2.] **1.** Not improved by husbandry; untilled, uncultivated. **2.** Having no husband 1797.

Unhu·sk, *v.* 1596. [UN-² 3.] **1.** *trans.* To divest of husk or shell 1598. **2.** *fig.* To strip of a covering or disguise; to expose 1596. Hence **Unhu·sked** *ppl. a.*²

Unhu·sked, *ppl. a.*¹ 1769. [UN-¹ 2.] Not stripped of the husk.

Unhygie·nic *a.* [UN-¹ 1] 1883, **-ally** *adv.* **Unhy·mned** *ppl. a.* [UN-¹ 2] 1851. **Unhypo·thecated** *ppl. a.* [UN-¹ 2] 1802. **Unhyste·rical** *a.* [UN-¹ 1] 1886.

Uni- (yū·ni), repr. L. *uni-*, comb. form of *unus* one, forming the first element in many words with the sense 'having, composed or consisting of, or characterized by one (thing specified by the second element)'. The older examples are directly adopted from French or Latin, as UNANIMOUS, UNIVERSAL. In the 15th and 16th centuries additional words were formed of L. elements and on L. analogy; in the 17th and 18th the prefix gained currency and appeared in some abnormal functions, as *unifold, unisoil*; and in the 19th it came into frequent use in forming scientific and technical terms, esp. in *Bot.* and *Zool.* The second element of these compounds is usually of L. origin, but the prefix has been combined with English forms or words, and has been used occas. in place of the Gr. equivalent MONO-. (In scientific works the figure 1 is often substituted for *uni-*, as in 1-*bracteate.*)

1. Forming adjs. with the general sense 'having, provided with, composed or consisting of, characterized by one (thing specified or connoted by the second element)'. Many of these compounds are self-explanatory. **U:niarti·culate** *Ent., Zool.*, having a single joint. **U:niauri·culate(d** *Zool.*, having a single auricle or auriculate process. **Unia·xial** *Optics* and *Cryst.*, having one optical axis; *Bot.* and *Zool.* = MONAXIAL *a.* **Unica·meral,** having, consisting of, or characterized by one legislative chamber. **Unico·lor, Unico·lorous, Unico·loured** *Nat. Hist.*, of a single uniform colour. **Unico·rneal** *Zool.*, of an ocellus: having a single cornea. **Unicu·spidate,** ending in one cusp or point. **U:nidime·nsional,** of one dimension. **U:nidire·ctional** *Electr.*, (of currents) moving in one direction. **Unifilar** (-fəi·lăɹ), of a magnetometer, etc., having or suspended by a single thread or fibre. **Uniflo·rous** *Bot.*, having or bearing only one flower. **Unifo·liate, -fo·liolate** *Bot.*, of leaves, etc.: consisting of one leaflet; of plants: having such leaves. **Unila·biate** *Bot., Ent.*, having one lip. **Unili·near** *Math.*, involving one line only. **Unili·ngual,** pertaining to one language only; knowing or employing only one language. **Unili·teral,** involving the use of, or consisting of, only one letter. **Unilo·bular** *Path.*, of cirrhosis: characterized by hypertrophy of single lobules; hypertrophic. **Unilo·cular,** having, consisting of, characterized by, only one loculus; one-celled. **Unino·dal,** having one node or nodal point. **Uninu·clear,** having, or characterized by, one nucleus. **Unio·cular,** of, pertaining to, or affecting one eye; *fig.* characterized by the use of one eye only. **Unio·vular, -o·vulate,** produced by or containing one ovule. **Unipa·rient** = UNIPAROUS 1. **Unipa·rtite** *Math.*, consisting of or involving a single part. **U·niped,** having only one foot (or leg). **Unipe·rsonal,** consisting of a single person or individual; having or existing as one person; hence **U:nipersona·lity.** **Unise·rial, -se·riate** *Bot., Zool.*, etc., arranged in or consisting of one series or row; characterized by such a form or arrangement. **U:nitenta·cular.** **U:niungui·culate,** having one unguis or claw.

2. Forming sbs. **U·nicell** *Bot.*, a unicellular plant. **U·nicode,** a telegraphic code in which one word or set of letters represents a sentence or phrase; a telegram or message in this. **U·nicycle** *U.S.*, a vehicle having only one wheel; esp. a monocycle used by acrobats or for gymnastic displays. **U·niped,** a creature having only one foot (or leg). **U·nireme** [L. *remus* oar], an ancient vessel or galley having one bank of oars. **Unitri·nity,** unity in trinity.

Uniat, Uniate (yū·niæt, -ĕt). 1833. [ad. Russ. *uniyatŭ*, f. *uniya* union, f. L. *unus* one.] A Russian, Polish, or other member of that part of the Greek Church which, while retaining its own liturgy, acknowledges the Pope's supremacy. **b.** *attrib.* or as *adj.* Of, adhering or pertaining to, or denominating the United Greek Churches 1855.

b. The much persecuted Uniate or Greek Catholic creed 1905.

Unica·psular, *a.* 1720. [ad. mod. L. *unicapsularis*; see UNI- and CAPSULAR *a.*] *Bot.* Of a pericarp: Having a single capsule. Of a plant: Having such a pericarp.

Unicellular (yūnise·liŭlăɹ), *a.* 1858. [ad. mod.L. *unicellularis*; see UNI- and CELLULAR *a.*] *Biol.* **1.** Composed or consisting of a single cell; applied esp. to organisms belonging to the primary divisions of the animal and vegetable kingdoms. Also as *sb.* **2.** Characterized by the formation or presence of a single cell or cells 1863. Hence **Unicellula·rity.**

Unicist (yū·nisist). 1807. [f. L. *unicus* one + -IST.] **1.** A believer in the unicity of the Godhead. **2.** *Med.* A believer in unicity 1890.

Unicity (yūni·siti). 1691. [f. L. *unicus*; see prec. and -ITY.] **1.** The fact of being or consisting of one; oneness. **b.** *Med.* The theory that syphilis is caused by one kind only of venereal virus 1861. **2.** The fact or quality of being unique 1859.

Unicorn (yū·nikǭɹn). ME. [a. AF., OF. *unicorne*, or ad. L. *unicornis* one-horned, f. *unus* one + *cornu* horn.] **1.** A legendary animal usu. regarded as having a horse's body and a single long straight horn projecting from its forehead. (The horn of this animal was reputed to possess medicinal or magical properties, esp. as an antidote to or preventive of poison.) **b.** Used in ME. and later versions of the OT. to render the Vulgate *unicornis* or *rhinoceros* (Greek *μονόκερως*), as tr. Heb. *rᵉ'em*, where the R. V. has *wild-ox*. ME. **2.** A representation of this animal, esp. in *Her.* as a charge or (usu.) as a supporter of the Royal Arms. late ME. **3.** *Sc.* One of the pursuivants of the Lyon King of Arms 1445. **4.** *Hist.* A Scottish gold coin (= 18 shillings Scots) current in the 15th and 16th centuries 1487. **5.** *Astr.* A southern constellation 1771. **6.** A carriage, etc., drawn by three horses, two abreast and one in front; now usu., a team of horses so arranged 1785. †**7.** The one-horned rhinoceros –1700. **8.** The narwhal or sea-unicorn 1694. **b.** A unicorn-shell 1711.

Comb., chiefly in names of animals or plants characterized by a projecting horn-like process or spine suggesting the unicorn's horn: **u.-bird,** the horned screamer, *Palamedea cornuta*; **-fish, narwhal** = sense 8; **-plant,** any of various N. Amer. plants, esp. *Martynia proboscidea*, the capsule of which terminates in two horn-like spines; **-shell,** a marine gasteropod having a horn-like lip projecting from the shell, now esp. one belonging to the genus *Monoceros*. **b.** Comb. with *unicorn's*: **unicorn's horn,** a horn of the rhinoceros, narwhal, or other animal reputed to be obtained from a u., freq. mounted or made into a cup, and employed as a preventive of or charm against poison; †the material of this powdered and used medicinally, esp. as an antidote against poison. Hence **Unico·rnic** *a.* (*rare*) resembling, having the form of, a u.

‖ **Unicum** (yū·nikŏm). *Pl.* **unica** (yū·nikă). 1885. [L., neut. sing. of *unicus* UNIQUE *a.*] A unique specimen.

Unicursal (yūnikʊ̄·ɹsăl), *a.* and *sb.* 1866. [f. UNI- + L. *cursus* course.] *Math.* **A.** *adj.* Having, traversing, or being on one course or path. **B.** *sb.* A unicursal curve.

Unidea'd (ʊn,əidī·ăd), *a.* 1752. [UN-¹ 2.] Not furnished with an idea.

Unideal (ʊn,əidī·ăl), *a.* 1751. [UN-¹ 1.] †**1.** Conveying or expressing no idea –1792. †**2.** Destitute of ideas –1801. **3.** Not following an ideal 1760. **4.** Not inspired by or exhibiting idealism 1846.

Unide·ntified *ppl. a.* [UN-¹ 2] 1860. **U:nidioma·tic** *a.* [UN-¹ 1] 1822. **Unido·latrous** *a.* [UN-¹ 1] 1841.

Unific (yuni·fik), *a.* 1788. [ad. L. **unificus*; see UNI- and -FIC.] That unifies; producing unity.

Unification (yū:nifikē¹·ʃən). 1851. [f. UNIFY *v.*] The action or process of unifying; reduction to unity or to a uniform system; the result of this.

Uniform (yū·nifǭɹm), *sb.* 1748. [subst. use of next.] **1.** A distinctive dress of uniform materials, colour, and cut, worn by all the members of a particular military, naval, or other force to which it is recognized as properly belonging and peculiar. **b.** A distinctive uniform dress worn by the members of any civilian body or association of persons 1837. **c.** A single suit of such dress 1783. **2.** *attrib.* **a.** Belonging to or forming part of a uniform, as *u. coat* 1807. **b.**

Wearing uniform, uniformed, as *u. policeman* 1895.

1. None shall fight who do not wear the u. of one of the armies engaged 1879. b. The proposed u., sir, of the Pickwick Club DICKENS. Hence **U·niformed** *a.* dressed in or wearing u.

Uniform (yū·nifǭɹm), *a.* 1540. [a. F. *uniforme*, or ad. L. *uniformis*; see UNI- and FORM.] 1. Having, maintaining, or occurring in the same form always; the same or alike under all conditions; unvarying. b. Of persons, etc. Hence, constant in respect of conduct or opinion; consistent. 1551. c. Of clothing, etc.: Of the same pattern, colour, and material amongst a number or body of persons 1746. 2. Having or presenting the same appearance or aspect; hence, having a plain, unbroken, or undiversified surface or exterior 1550. 3. Of motion, dimensions, etc.: Free from fluctuation or variation in respect of quantity or amount 1559. 4. Of the same form, character, or kind as another or others; conforming to one standard, rule, or pattern; alike, similar 1548.

1. That all our Subjects could be brought to agree in a uniforme Worship of God 1662. b. A man so u. as to have nothing of Inequality..in his Actions DRYDEN. c. The practice of clothing soldiers, by regiments, in one u. dress 1890. 2. The street..is one of the longest, straightest, and most u. in Europe 1756. His jerkin, hose, and cloak, were of a dark u. colour SCOTT. This piece of glass..being perfectly u. in its internal structure FARADAY. 3. Velocity..may be u., *i.e.* the same at every instant 1879. 4. How far churches are bound to be u. in their ceremonies HOOKER. When two figures are composed of similar parts, they are said to be u. 1762. The copies sold.. were found to be exactly u. 1867. Hence **U·niform-ly** *adv.* 1549, **-ness.**

U·niform, *v.* 1681. [f. prec.] 1. *trans.* To make uniform. 2. To put into uniform 1894.

1. The..travesties which words underwent before they were uniformed by Johnson and Walker 1870.

Unifo·rmal, *a.* Now *rare.* 1573. [f. L. *uniformis* + -AL.] Uniform.

U·niformist. 1885. [f. UNIFORM *a.* + -IST.] One who believes in or advocates uniformity, esp. in respect of religious doctrine or observance.

Uniformitarian (yū:nifǭɹmitē°·riăn), *sb.* and *a.* 1840. [f. next + -ARIAN.] A. *sb.* 1. *Geol.* One who attributes geological processes and phenomena to forces operating continuously and uniformly. (Opp. to CATASTROPHIST.) 2. = prec. (*rare*) 1890. B. *adj.* 1. *Geol.* Of, characteristic of, or held by uniformitarians 1840. b. In accordance with the theory of the uniformitarians 1869. c. Of persons: That is a uniformitarian 1864. 2. Of or pertaining to, advocating or practising, uniformity in something 1897. Hence **U:niformita·rianism.**

Uniformity (yūnifǭ·ɹmĭti). late ME. [a. F. *uniformité*, or ad. L. *uniformitas*, f. *uniformis* UNIFORM *a.*; see -ITY.] The quality or condition of being uniform, in various senses. b. Conformity to (or compliance with) one standard of opinion, practice, or procedure, esp. in religious observance 1549. c. *spec.* in *Geol.* Cf. UNIFORMITARIAN. 1837. d. With *a* and *pl.* A particular instance of this condition; a uniform feature, law, etc. 1665.

The u. of life must be sometimes diversified JOHNSON. Variety is more pleasing than u. HOGARTH. b. Three..Reverend Divines, who..can give a good Account of his Vertue, U., and Learning 1708. *Act of U.*, in *Eng. Hist.*, any of three Acts (1549, 1559, 1662) regulating public worship, which prescribed the use and acceptance of the Books of Common Prayer published in those years. c. It is very conceivable that catastrophes may be part and parcel of u. HUXLEY.

Unify (yū·nifəi), *v.* 1502. [ad. med.L. *unificare*, f. L. *uni-* UNI-; see -FY.] *trans.* To make, form into, or cause to become one; to unite, consolidate. Hence **U·nifying** *ppl. a.*

Unige·niture. 1659. [ad. eccl. L. *unigenitus* only-begotten + -URE.] 1. *Theol.* The fact of being the only-begotten Son. 2. The fact of being an only child; the practice of having only one child 1887.

Unila·teral, *a.* 1802. [ad. mod.L. *unilateralis*, or f. UNI- + LATERAL *a.*] 1. a. *Bot.* Of a raceme or panicle; Having the flowers on one side of the peduncle. Also, of a cyme: Having a branch or axis on one side only. b. *Bot., Zool.* Arranged or produced on one side of an axis or surface; directed towards one side 1870. 2. Of or pertaining to, occurring on or affecting, one side of an organ or part 1843. b. *Path.* Affecting or developed on one side of the body only 1876. c. *Phonetics.* Produced with the glottis open on one side only 1867. 3. Of one party or side only, not reciprocal 1802. b. *Law.* Binding or imposed on one party only; without reciprocal obligation 1802. 4. One-sided, partial, incomplete 1830.

4. This is a u. view of the social contract, and omits the element of reciprocity MORLEY. Hence **Unilatera·lity. Unila·terally** *adv.*

Unillu·minated, *ppl. a.* 1579. [UN-¹ 2.] 1. Not spiritually or mentally enlightened. 2. Not lighted up 1824.

Unillu·minating *ppl. a.* [UN-¹ 4] 1882. **Unillu·mined** *ppl. a.* [UN-¹ 2] 1826. **Uni·llustrated** *ppl. a.* [UN-¹ 2] 1828. **Uni·maged** *ppl. a.* [UN-¹ 2] 1648. **Unima·ginable** *a.* [UN-¹ 1] 1611, **-ness, -bly** *adv.* **Unima·ginative** *a.* [UN-¹ 1] WORDSW., **-ly** *adv.*, **-ness. Unima·gined** *ppl. a.* [UN-¹ 2] 1548. **Uni·mitated** *ppl. a.* [UN-¹ 2] 1610. **Unimme·rsed** *ppl. a.* [UN-¹ 2] 1835. **Unimmo·rtal** *a.* [UN-¹ 1] MILT. **Unimpai·rable** *a.* [UN-¹ 1] 1627. **Unimpai·red** *ppl. a.* [UN-¹ 2] 1583. **Unimpa·rted** *ppl. a.* [UN-¹ 2] 1655. **Unimpa·ssioned** *ppl. a.* [UN-¹ 2] 1744.

Unimpea·chable, *a.* 1784. [UN-¹ 1.] That cannot be called in question, doubted, or discredited of evidence, witnesses, good qualities, etc. Hence **Unimpeachabi·lity. Unimpea·chableness. Unimpea·chably** *adv.*

Unimpea·ched, *ppl. a.* late ME. [UN-¹ 2.] †1. Not impeded. -late ME. 2. Not assailed, accused, or called in question 1583.

Unimpe·ded *ppl. a.* [UN-¹ 2] 1760. **Unimplo·red** *ppl. a.* [UN-¹ 2] MILT. **Unimpo·rtance** [UN-¹ 6] JOHNSON. **Unimpo·rtant** *a.* [UN-¹ 1] 1727. **Unimpo·sing** *ppl. a.* [UN-¹ 4] 1736. **Unimpre·gnated** *ppl. a.* [UN-¹ 2] 1744.

Unimpre·ssed, *ppl. a.* 1743. [UN-¹ 2.] †1. Not under restraint. YOUNG. 2. Not affected by feelings of respect or awe 1861. 3. Not bearing an impression 1868.

Unimpre·ssible *a.* [UN-¹ 1] 1828. **Unimpre·ssionable** *a.* [UN-¹ 1] 1847. **Unimpre·ssive** *a.* [UN-¹ 1] 1796, **-ly** *adv.*, **-ness. Unimpri·soned** *ppl. a.* [UN-¹ 2] 1659.

Unimpro·vable, *a.* 1660. [UN-¹ 1.] 1. That cannot be cured of faults, etc.; hopelessly bad, not to be made better. 2. Perfect, having no fault or deficiency 1822.

1. A people the most unprincipled and unimproveable of all GROTE. 2. You show an absolute and u. acquaintance with..mankind SCOTT.

Unimpro·ved, *ppl. a.* 1665. [UN-¹ 2.] 1. Not made better; not raised in quality. 2. Not turned to use; not taken advantage of 1781.

2. They preferred leaving their victory u., to the hazard of a general battle 1850.

Unimpro·ving *ppl. a.* [UN-¹ 4] 1747. **Unimpu·gnable** *a.* [UN-¹ 1] 1832. **Unimpu·gned** *ppl. a.* [UN-¹ 2] 1838. **Unimpu·lsive** *a.* [UN-¹ 1] 1856, **-ness. Uninca·rnate** *a.* [UN-¹ 1] 1687. **Uncince·nsed** *ppl. a.* [UN-¹ 2] 1594. **Uninclu·ded** *ppl. a.* [UN-¹ 2] 1775. **Uninco·rporate** *a.* [UN-¹ 1] 1821. **Uninco·rporated** *ppl. a.* [UN-¹ 2] 1715. **Unincrea·sable** *a.* [UN-¹ 1] 1648. **Unincrea·sed** *ppl. a.* [UN-¹ 2] 1824. **Uninde·bted** *ppl. a.* [UN-¹ 2] DRYDEN, **-ness. Uninde·nted** *ppl. a.* [UN-¹ 2] 1750. **Uni·ndexed** *ppl. a.* [UN-¹ 2] 1832.

Unindi·fferent, *a.* 1565. [UN-¹ 1.] 1. Not impartial; prejudiced. Now *arch.* 2. Not unconcerned; interested 1813. So **Unindi·fference. Unindi·fferency** (now *arch.*). **Unindi·fferently** *adv.*

Unindu·strious *a.* [UN-¹ 1] 1599. **Uninfe·cted** *ppl. a.* [UN-¹ 2] 1628. **Uninfe·ctious** *a.* [UN-¹ 1] 1744. **Uninfe·sted** *ppl. a.* [UN-¹ 2] MILT.

Uninfla·med, *ppl. a.* 1626. [UN-¹ 2.] †1. Not set on fire -1794. 2. *fig.* Not fired with passion, enthusiasm, etc. 1714. 3. *Path.* Free from inflammation 1793.

1. Rise odours sweet from incense uninflam'd? YOUNG.

Uninfla·mmable *a.* [UN-¹ 1] 1666. **Uninfla·ted** *ppl. a.* [UN-¹ 2] 1861. **Uninfle·cted** *ppl. a.* [UN-¹ 2] 1713. **Uni·nfluenced** *ppl. a.* [UN-¹ 2] 1734. **Uninflue·ntial** *a.* [UN-¹ 1] 1661.

Uninfo·rmed, *ppl. a.* 1597. [UN-¹ 2.] 1. Not informed, instructed, or enlightened on some matter or in some respect. 2. Uneducated, uninstructed, ignorant 1647. b. Marked by lack of enlightenment, information, or knowledge 1796. 3. Not showing animation; lifeless, mechanical 1709.

3. Without this irradiating Power..her most perfect Features are Uninform'd and Dead STEELE.

Uninfo·rming *ppl. a.* [UN-¹ 4] 1709. **Uninfri·nged** *ppl. a.* [UN-¹ 2] 1610. **Uninge·nious** *a.* [UN-¹ 1] 1638. †**Uninge·nuous** *a.* [UN-¹ 1] -1670, †**-ly** *adv.* **Uninha·bitable** *a.* [UN-¹ 1] 1448, **-ness. Uninha·bited** *ppl. a.* [UN-¹ 2] 1571. **Unini·tiate** *ppl. a.* [UN-¹ 2] 1801. **Unini·tiated** *ppl. a.* [UN-¹ 2] 1678. **U:ninitia·tion** [UN-¹ 6] 1834. **Uni·njured** *ppl. a.* [UN-¹ 2] 1578. **Uninju·rious** *a.* [UN-¹ 1] 1809, **-ly** *adv.*

Unino·minal (yūni-), *a.* 1881. [a. F.; see UNI- and NOMINAL *a.*] 1. Based on the principle of one member being separately elected by each constituency. 2. Having or involving one name, *spec.* in *Nat. Hist.* 1885.

Uninqui·ring *ppl. a.* [UN-¹ 4] 1804. **Uninqui·sitive** *a.* [UN-¹ 1] 1609. **Uninscri·bed** *ppl. a.* [UN-¹ 2] 1704. **Uninspe·cted** *ppl. a.* [UN-¹ 2] 1858. **Uninspi·red** *ppl. a.* [UN-¹ 2] LOCKE. **Uninspi·ring** *ppl. a.* [UN-¹ 4] 1815.

Uninstru·cted, *ppl. a.* 1598. [UN-¹ 2.] 1. Not instructed or informed; unenlightened, ignorant. 2. Not furnished with instructions 1892. Hence **Uninstru·ctedness.**

Uninstru·ctive *a.* [UN-¹ 1] 1666, **-ly** *adv.* **Uni·nsulate** *v.* [UN-² 1] 1844. **Uni·nsulated** *ppl. a.* [UN-¹ 2] 1794. **Uninsu·rable** *a.* [UN-¹ 1] 1864. **Uninsu·red** *ppl. a.* [UN-¹ 2] 1799. **U:nintelle·ctual** *a.* [UN-¹ 1] 1676.

Uninte·lligent, *a.* 1609. [UN-¹ 1.] 1. Without knowledge or understanding *of* something. Now *rare.* 2. Devoid of intelligence 1664. 3. Deficient in intelligence; dull, stupid 1676. †4. Unintelligible -1756.

1. China,..too u. of us and too unintelligible to us CARLYLE. 2. Time,..the most spiritual of the u. creatures of God PUSEY. So (in sense 3) **Uninte·lligence. Uninte·lligently** *adv.*

U:nintelligibi·lity [UN-¹ 6] 1665. **Uninte·lligible** *a.* [UN-¹ 1] 1616, **-ness, -bly** *adv.* **Uninte·nded** *ppl. a.* [UN-¹ 2] MILT., **-ly** *adv.* **Uninte·ntional** *a.* [UN-¹ 1] 1782, **-ly** *adv.*

Uni·nterested, *ppl. a.* 1646. [UN-¹ 2.] †1. Impartial; disinterested -1767. 2. Taking no interest; indifferent 1771. Hence **Uni·nterestedly** *adv.*, **-ness.**

Uni·nteresting *ppl. a.* [UN-¹ 4] BURKE, **-ly** *adv.*, **-ness. U:nintermi·tted** *ppl. a.* [UN-¹ 2] 1611, **-ly** *adv.* **Unintermi·ttent** *a.* [UN-¹ 1] 1850, **-ly** *adv.* **Unintermi·tting** *ppl. a.* [UN-¹ 4] 1661, **-ly** *adv.*, **-ness. Unintermi·xed** *ppl. a.* (now *rare*) [UN-¹ 2] 1595. **Uninte·rpretable** *a.* [UN-¹ 1] 1625. **Uninte·rpreted** *ppl. a.* [UN-¹ 2] 1662. **Uninte·rred** *ppl. a.* [UN-¹ 2] 1648.

U:ninterru·pted, *ppl. a.* 1602. [UN-¹ 2.] 1. Not interrupted or broken in respect of continuity or sequence; unintermittent, continuous. b. Continuous in surface; having no intervals between the parts 1791. 2. Not disturbed or broken into; not interrupted *by* something 1657.

1. b. The cascade..falls..in one u. sheet 1791. Hence **U:ninterru·ptedly** *adv.*, **-ness.**

U:ninterru·ption [UN-¹ 6] 1647. **Uninti·midated** *ppl. a.* [UN-¹ 2] 1764. **Uninto·xicating** *ppl. a.* [UN-¹ 4] 1773. **U:nintrodu·ced** *ppl. a.* [UN-¹ 2] 1743. **Uninu·red** *ppl. a.* [UN-¹ 2] 1708. **Uninva·ded** *ppl. a.* [UN-¹ 2] 1647. **Uninve·nted** *ppl. a.* [UN-¹ 2] 1611. **Uninve·ntive** *a.* [UN-¹ 1] 1776, **-ness. Uninve·sted** *ppl. a.* [UN-¹ 2] 1802. **Uninve·stigable** *a.* [UN-¹ 1] 1677. **Uninve·stigated** *ppl. a.* [UN-¹ 2] 1816. **Uninvi·te** *v.* [UN-² 1 or UN-¹ 7] 1665. **Uninvi·ted** *ppl. a.* [UN-¹ 2] 1631. **Uninvi·ting** *ppl. a.* [UN-¹ 4] 1686. **Uninvo·ked** *ppl. a.* [UN-¹ 2] 1718. **Uninvo·lved** *ppl. a.* [UN-¹ 2] 1793.

‖**Unio** (yū·nio). *Pl.* **unios** (-ōuz), ‖**uniones** (-ōu·nīz). 1824. [L., 'a single large pearl'.] *Zool.* A genus of freshwater bivalves typical of the family *Unionidæ*; a mussel of this or a related genus, esp. one yielding pearls. Hence **U·nioid** *a.* resembling or shaped like (that of) a u.

Union¹ (yū·niən, yū·nyən). late ME. [a. F., ad. L. *unionem*, *unio*, f. *unus* one.] **1.** The action of uniting one thing to another or others, or two or more things together, so as to form one whole or complete body; the state or condition of being so joined or united; combination, conjunction. **b.** Of persons or countries with ref. to joint action or policy 1608. **c.** *spec.* in *Surg.* The growing together in the process of healing of parts separated by fracture, cutting, etc. 1631. **d.** With *a* and *pl.* An instance or occasion of this 1570. **e.** Sexual conjunction (*rare*) 1728. **2.** The uniting together of the different sections, parties, or individuals of a nation or other body so as to produce general agreement or concord; the condition resulting from this 1460. **b.** Harmony of colour or design between the parts of a picture 1704. **3. a.** *Scots Law.* The uniting into one tenantry of non-contiguous lands or tenements 1503. **b.** *Eccl.* The uniting of two or more churches or benefices into one 1529. **4.** The action of uniting, or fact of being united, into one political body; esp. formation or incorporation into a single state, kingdom, or political entity, usu. with one central legislature 1547. **b.** *Eng. Hist.* (with *the* and capital): The uniting of the English and Scottish crowns in 1603, or parliaments in 1707; or of the parliaments of Great Britain and Ireland, dating from 1 Jan. 1801. 1603. **5.** The joining of two persons in matrimony; an instance of this, a marriage 1595. **6.** That which is united or combined into one; a whole formed by conjunction of parts; a combination or compound 1660. **b.** An association or league of persons or states formed for some common purpose or action. Now esp. = TRADE-UNION. 1660. **c.** *spec.* A legislative confederacy of states or provinces; a confederation or federation; esp. the United States of America. (In American use occas. restricted to the northern or federal States.) 1775. **d.** A number of parishes combined under one Board of Guardians for poor-law administration; an area or sub-district so formed and administered 1834. **e.** A textile fabric composed of two or more different materials woven together, esp. of cotton with linen, wool, or jute 1844. **7.** That which unites or connects one thing to another; *techn.*, a coupling for pipes or tubes 1850. **8.** *Brewing.* One of a series of casks or vats used in the union system of cleansing beer 1876. **9.** *ellipt.* with *the* **a.** = *U.-flag*, UNION JACK 1769. (*b*) *spec.* The union flag inserted in the upper inner canton of the ensign; freq. in phr. *u. down* or *downwards*, i.e. with the flag inverted as a sign of distress 1804. **b.** = *U. House* 1843. **c.** = *U. Society*; also, the buildings of such a society 1835. **10.** *attrib.* and *Comb.*, passing into adj. **a.** With the sense 'of or belonging to, promoting or advocating, etc. (a particular) legislative union' 1707. **b.** *gen.* 1723. **c.** In sense 6 e, as *u. cloth, goods*, etc. 1862.

1. The U. of the human Nature with the Divine 1728. Persecution, said Mr. Fox, is a bond of u. 1789. By the u. and investigation of several data 1800. **d.** A colony having an u. of interest 1817. **2.** There shalbe perfite vnion amonges them without striffe CROMWELL. **b.** A figure.. though deviating from beauty, may still have a certain u. of the various parts SIR J. REYNOLDS. **5.** Her grandfather had been.. very much averse to our u. THACKERAY. **6. b.** The increase of wages is not confined to those trades which have unions 1878. **c.** The South will come back to the U. 1865. **9. a.** A barge with the U. hoisted at the stern 1865. **b.** I wonder..if I am doomed to die in the Union HARDY. **c.** There existed at Cambridge a certain debating club, called the 'Union' THACKERAY.

Special combs.: **U. flag**, the national flag of Great Britain, and (from 1801) of the United Kingdom, formed by combining the crosses of St. George, St. Andrew, and St. Patrick, retaining the blue ground of the banner of St. Andrew; **U. House**, the workhouse of a Poor Law u.; **-joint**, see sense 7; **u. nut**, (*a*) a nut used with a screw to unite one part to another; (*b*) the Australian timber tree *Bosistoa sapindiformis* or its wood; **-room** *Brewing*, the room containing the unions or cleansing vats; **-rustic**, a British moth, *Apamea connexa*; **U. Society**, at universities: a general club and debating society usu. open to all members or all undergraduates of the university; **u. suit** *U.S.*, men's or boys' combinations; **u. system** *Brewing*, a method of beer-cleansing. Hence **Unionic** (yūni̦·nik) *a.* of, pertaining to, characteristic of, a union or Union Society.

U·nion². *arch.* ME. [ad. L. *unionem*, *unio* UNIO.] A pearl of large size, good quality, and great value.

Unionid (yū·niənid). 1861. [a. mod.L. *Unionidæ*, f. L. *unio* UNIO; see -ID³.] *Zool.* A member of the *Unionidæ*, a family of bivalve molluscs typified by the genus *Unio*.

Unionism (yū·niəniz'm). 1845. [f. UNION¹ + -ISM.] The principle or policy of combining; combination in union as a system of social organization. **b.** = TRADE(S)-UNIONISM 1869. **c.** *U.S.* Advocacy of or belief in legislative union between States 1864. **d.** Loyalty to or advocacy of the principles, views, or programme of the Unionist party; the political tenets of a Unionist 1886.

Unionist (yū·niənist), *sb.* and *a.* 1799. [f. as prec. + -IST.] **A.** *sb.* **1.** A believer in unionism as a political principle or system of organization; esp. one who advocates or supports the formation of some particular legislative union (usu. with initial capital). **b.** *U.S.* A supporter of the Federal Union of the U.S.A.; esp. an opponent of Secession in the Civil War of 1861–5. 1830. **c.** *British Politics.* A member of the political party which advocated or supported maintenance of the parliamentary union between Great Britain and Ireland, formed by coalition between Conservatives and Liberal Unionists in 1886, and later known indifferently as 'Unionist' or 'Conservative' 1886. **2.** = TRADE-UNIONIST 1834. **3.** One who advocates or endeavours to promote the union of churches 1852.

2. The charges of conspiracy and violence brought against unionists 1879.

B. *attrib.* or as *adj.* **1.** Pertaining to or supporting a legislative union, esp. that between Great Britain and Ireland 1816. **b.** Of or belonging to the Unionist party 1886. **2.** Of or belonging to trade-unionism or trade-unionists 1879. Hence **Unioni·stic** *a.*

U·nionize, *v.* 1841. [f. UNION¹ + -IZE.] *trans.* To form into a union; to bring (work) under trade-union rules; to attract or form (workers) into trade-unions.

Union Jack. 1674. [JACK *sb.*³] Orig. and prop., a small British union flag flown as the jack of a ship; later extended to any size or adaptation of the union flag, whether used as a jack or not, and regarded as the national ensign. **b.** A figure or representation of this 1848.

Union pipes, *sb. pl.* 1851. [perh. ad. Ir. *píob uilleann*, f. *píob* pipe + *uilleann*, gen. sing. of *uille* elbow.] Irish bagpipes, in which the bag is inflated by bellows worked by the elbow.

Uniparous (yuni·părəs), *a.* 1646. [f. mod. L. *uniparus*; see UNI- and -PAROUS.] **1.** Bearing one at a birth; characterized by this kind of parturition. **2.** *Bot.* Of a cyme: Having only one axis or branch; developing a single axis at each branching 1839.

Unipla·nar, *a.* 1866. [f. UNI- + PLANAR *a.*] **1.** *Geom.* Having or characterized by coincident planes. *U. node* (or *point*), a form of node or conical point in which the tangent cone has become a pair of coincident planes. **2.** *Mech.* Of motion: Confined to one plane; of or pertaining to such motion 1882.

Unipo·lar, *a.* 1812. [f. UNI- + POLAR *a.*] **1.** *Electr.* Produced by, proceeding from, one magnetic pole; exhibiting one kind of polarity. **b.** Of apparatus: Having, or operating by means of, one magnetic pole 1876. **2.** *Biol.* Of nerve cells: Having one pole or fibrous prolongation; connected to the nerve-fibre by a single fibrous process 1859. Hence **Unipola·rity**.

Unique (yunī·k), *a.* and *sb.* 1602. [a. F., ad. L. *unicus*. In early use also directly ad. L. *unicus*.] **A.** *adj.* **1.** Of which there is only one; one and only; single, sole, solitary. **2.** Having no like or equal; superior to or different from all others; unparalleled, unrivalled 1618.

1. He hath lost..his unic Son 1645. A man..who made Latin scholarship his u. intellectual purpose 1873. **2.** This is a soueraigne and vnicke remedie 1618. Such a u. mortal..no man can describe 1871.

B. *sb.* **1.** A thing of which there is only one example, copy, or specimen; esp. such a coin or medal 1714. **2.** A thing, fact, person, etc., that is without equal or parallel in its kind 1758.

1. A coin, which I have reason to think is a Unic 1774. **2.** He is..quite an u. in this country COWPER. Of Lamb's writings..some were so memorably beautiful as to be uniques in their class DE QUINCEY. Hence **Uni·que-ly** *adv.*, **-ness**. **Uni·quity**, uniqueness.

Un·I·rish *a.* [UN-¹ 1] 1842. **Uni·roned** *ppl. a.* [UN-¹ 2] late ME. **Uni·rritating** *ppl. a.* [UN-¹ 4] 1797.

Unisexual (yūnise·ksiuăl) *a.* 1802. [ad. mod.L. *unisexualis*; see UNI- and SEXUAL *a.*] **1.** Of one sex; having the reproductive organs of one or other sex developed or present in individuals: **a.** *Bot.* Of flowers: With either stamens or pistils absent or suppressed. Of plants: Having such flowers. 1802. **b.** Of animals or their organs 1830. **2.** Pertaining or restricted to one sex 1885. Hence **U:nisexua·lity**, the condition of being u. **U:nise·xually** *adv.*

Unison (yū·nisən, -zən), *sb.* and *a.* 1574. [a. OF., or ad. late L. *unisonus*, f. L. *uni-* UNI- + *sonus* sound.] **A.** *sb.* **1.** *Mus.* and *Acoustics.* A note of the same pitch as another; also loosely, a note from which intervals are reckoned. Now *rare*. **b.** Identity of pitch; the relation of two notes of the same pitch reckoned as one of the musical 'intervals' 1575. **c.** In phr. *in u.*: with identity of note and pitch 1616. **d.** A passage in which different voices or instruments execute a melody that is the same for all parts (or, loosely, different only by an interval of an octave or octaves) 1724. **e.** *ellipt.* for *u. string* 1820. **2.** A union or combination of concordant sounds; a united and unanimous utterance 1806. **3.** *fig.* A thing perfectly agreeing or consonant with another. Now *rare* or *Obs.* 1650. **b.** Perfect agreement, concord, or harmony; harmonious combinations 1654. **c.** *In unison* (*with*), in agreement or harmony, consonant, harmonious 1780.

1. Unisons, 'tis plain, cannot possibly have any Variety 1728. **c.** The nymphs joined in u., and their swains an octave below them STERNE. **d.** In Unisons, or passages where all instruments play the same melody, though in different Octaves 1799. **3. b.** Friendship the Vnison of well tun'd Hearts 1674. **c.** It was all in u.; words, conduct,..told the same story JANE AUSTEN.

attrib.: **u. stop**, in an organ, a stop of the same pitch as the diapasons; **u. string**, in a pianoforte or other instrument, a string tuned to the same pitch as (or loosely an octave higher than) another; **u. tune**, one to be sung in u.; **-tuning**, the tuning of strings (of a pianoforte, etc.) in u.

B. *adj.* †**1.** Sounding together; *fig.* in complete agreement, unanimous –1762. **2.** Identical in pitch; singing or sounding in unison. Now *rare* or *Obs.* 1614. So **Uni·sonal** *a. Mus.* = next 1; **-ly** *adv.* **Uni·sonance** (*rare*), agreement or identity of sounds. **Uni·sonant** *a.* of the same pitch or sound.

Unisonous (yuni·sŏnəs), *a.* 1781. [f. late L. *unisonus* UNISON + -OUS.] **1.** *Mus.* Of the same pitch for the different voices or instruments; in unison or octaves, not in parts. **2.** Agreeing, concordant 1812.

Unit (yū·nit), *sb.* (and *a.*) 1570. [f. L. *unus* one; substituted for earlier *unity, unitie, unite*, perhaps in conformity with *digit*.] **1.** *Math.* A single magnitude or number regarded as an undivided whole and as the ultimate base of all number; *spec.* in *Arith.*, the least whole number; the numeral 'one', represented by the figure 1. **b.** Any determinate quantity, dimension, etc., adopted as a standard of measurement 1738. **c.** A substance adopted as a standard for estimating specific gravity 1829. **2.** One of the separate parts or members of which a complex whole or aggregate is composed or into which it may be analysed 1642. **b.** The lowest constituent part of a collective body or whole having a distinctive existence; such a division or group of individuals considered as a basis of formation or administration 1847. **3.** *attrib.*, passing into *adj.* Of, pertaining or equivalent to (that of) a unit; produced or caused by a u.; consisting of, containing, or forming a unit or units 1839. **4.** As *adj.* Having the distinct or individual existence of a unit 1870.

1. Note the worde, Vnit, to expresse the Greke Monas, and not Vnitie: as we haue all, commonly, till now, vsed JOHN DEE. If, as some affirm, the unite be no number, but only the source of all others 1726. **b.** The necessity..of the adoption of a money U. 1825. The ohm is a u. of resistance, in the same manner that an inch is a u. of length 1870. **c.** As water is taken as the u. for solids and liquids, so is

atmospheric air for gases 1829. **2.** The u. of that life ..was for ever withdrawn from the sum of human existence SCOTT. **b.** The village is a fraction, but the city is an u. 1847. A company is the u. of a regiment 1876. **3.** The u. current flowing through a conductor u. of length will exert the u. force on the u. pole at the u. distance 1867. The consumption of wheat per head of the population (u. consumption) was over 6 bushels per annum 1898. **4.** All things in the exterior world are u. and individual J. H. NEWMAN.

Unitable (yūnəi·tăb'l), *a.* [f. UNITE *v.* + -ABLE.] That can be united; capable of union.

Unital (yū·nităl), *a.* 1860. [f. UNIT or UNITY + -AL.] That unites; causing or producing unity or union; of the nature of a unit.

Unitarian (yūnitē^ə·riăn), *sb.* and *a.* 1687. [Partly f. mod.L. *unitarius* (f. L. *unitas* UNITY) + -AN; partly f. UNITY + *-arian.*] **A.** *sb.* **1.** *Theol.* One who affirms the unipersonality of the Godhead, esp. as opp. to an orthodox Trinitarian; *spec.* a member of a Christian religious body or sect holding this doctrine. (Usu. with initial capital.) **b.** Any monotheist, esp. a Mohammedan 1708. **2.** An advocate of a theory or system based on unity, e. g. of MONISM in philosophy, of centralization, federation, or national unity in politics, etc. 1836.

1. b. His preachers..called aloud on the unitarians, manfully to stand up against the Christian idolaters GIBBON.

B. *adj.* **1.** *Theol.* Of or pertaining to, connected with, the Unitarians or their doctrines; of the nature of, characteristic of, Unitarianism 1687. **b.** Accepting the doctrines, or belonging to a religious body or sect, of Unitarians 1691. **2.** Of or pertaining to, based or founded on, characterized by, unity, in various senses 1836.

1. The U. [conception], which conceives of Christ as an exalted human teacher merely 1889. **2.** These two theories, the one dualistic, the other u. 1875. The King of U. Italy 1865. Hence **Unitaˑrianism,** belief in or affirmation of the unity of God, esp. the tenets, principles, or views of the Unitarians.

Unitary (yū·nitări), *a.* 1842. [f. UNIT or UNITY + -ARY[1].] **1.** Of or pertaining to, characterized by, or based upon unity 1847. **2.** *Philos.* Of or pertaining to, involving, unity of being or existence 1842. **3.** Of the nature of a unit; individual, uncompounded 1861. **b.** Serving as a unit of measurement or calculation 1889. **4.** Of or pertaining to a unit or units. **a.** *Chem.* Applied to a theory or system in which the molecules of all bodies are regarded as units 1865. **b.** Of an alphabet, etc.: In which a single symbol represents each sound 1874. **c.** *Arith.* Applied to a modification of the 'rule of three', by which the value, extent, etc., of one unit being first determined, that of any number is found by multiplication 1877. **5.** Forming a unit *with* something 1868.

1. The national and u. tendencies of the people LOWELL. **2.** Man loves the Universal, the Unchangeable, the U. 1842. **3.** Each man is at once profoundly u. and almost infinitely composite 1901. Hence **U·nitarist,** an advocate of a u. system of government; *spec.* a supporter of the unity of Italy.

Unite (yū·nəit, yunəi·t), *sb.* 1604. [f. †*unite* pa. pple., united, ad. late L. *unitus, unire.*] *Numism.* An English gold coin first issued by James I in 1604 (named with ref. to the Union of the Crowns).

Unite (yunəi·t), *v.* late ME. [f. *unit-*, ppl. stem of late L. *unire* to join, f. L. *unus* one.] **1.** *trans.* To combine or join (a thing or things) *to* or *with* another or others, to bring or put (separate or divided things) together, so as to make a connected or contiguous whole; to form into, make or cause to be, one. **b.** To combine or amalgamate into one body 1591. **c.** To join (hands), esp. in the marriage ceremony 1602. **2.** To bring to agreement; to combine (persons, etc.) in action or interest, or for some purpose 1547. **b.** To join (persons) in marriage 1728. **3.** To have, possess, or exhibit (functions, qualities, etc.) in combination 1796. **4.** *intr.* To enter into association or union; to combine forces, act in concert *with* others (*in* some action or *to* do something) 1613. **b.** To become one in feeling or sentiment 1766. **5.** To form one material whole; to combine physically; to coalesce 1667. **b.** *spec.* in *Chem.* To combine by chemical affinity or attraction 1800. **c.** Of troops, etc.: To form one combined or conjoint body 1700. **d.** Of immaterial things or in non-physical connexion 1795.

1. Like a broken Limbe vnited SHAKS. Where the publique and private interest are most closely united HOBBES. **b.** Not believing that the enemy could be so soon united CLARENDON. **c.** Their hands were united by the Protestant preacher SCOTT. **2.** If Simpathy of Loue vnite our thoughts SHAKS. **3.** D'Aubigné's style, which unites the severe and the ludicrous 1798. **4.** Is it best for the States to u. or not to u.? WASHINGTON. **5. d.** The whole body of the coheirs.. must u. to constitute the heir 1795. Hence **Uni·ting** *vbl. sb.* and *ppl. a.*

United (yunəi·tėd), *ppl. a.* 1552. [f. prec.] **1.** Joined together; combined, made one. **2.** Conjoint, in combination; not of single origin or constituents; resulting from a union (freq. in titles of amalgamated churches and societies) 1586.

Special Collocations: *U. Brethren*, the Moravians; *U. Colonies*, †(*a*) the four colonies of the New England Confederation of 1643; (*b*) the thirteen colonies forming the original Republic of N. America; *U. Greek*, a Uniat; *U. Irishmen*, a political association orig. formed to promote union between Protestants and Catholics, which became a separatist secret society and was concerned in the rebellion of 1798; so *U. Irishman*; **U. Kingdom** (abbrev. *U.K.*), the kingdom of Great Britain or (from 1801 to 1922) of Great Britain and Ireland; **U. Provinces,** (*a*) the seven northern provinces of the Netherlands, allied from 1579, and later developed into the kingdom of Holland; (*b*) in full *U. Provinces of Agra and Oudh*, a district in north British India, consisting of the provinces of Agra and Oudh united under a governor. Hence **Uni·ted-ly** *adv.*, **-ness.**

United States. 1617. **1.** The proper name or title of a confederation, federation, or union of states. **a.** = United Provinces of the Netherlands (now *rare* or *Hist.*). **b.** The Republic of N. America. Abbrev. *U.S.* or *U.S.A.* 1781. **c.** In other applications 1864. **2.** The form of English spoken in the U.S. or regarded as distinctly American 1891.

Uni·ter. 1587. [f. UNITE *v.* + -ER[1].] A person or agency that brings about union.

Uniters of states and cities BACON. Money..the great u. of a most divided people SWIFT.

Unition (yuni·ʃən). Now *rare.* 1511. [ad. late L. *unitionem*, f. *unire* UNITE *v.*] The action of uniting; the fact or condition of being united; union, junction.

The vnition of two [livings] in one man 1587. The Union or rather U. of a particular Soul and particular Body 1733.

Unitive (yū·nitiv), *a.* 1526. [ad. late L. *unitivus*, f. *unit-*, *unire* UNITE *v.*; see -IVE.] **1.** Uniting; causing or involving union; *spec.* in *Anat.* of fibres. **2.** Bringing about spiritual union with God 1659. **b.** *spec.* in *unitive life, way*, etc., applied to the third and final stage of spiritual advancement 1649.

1. The u. power of the Intellect 1647. **2.** This u. power of the Eucharist 1879. **b.** The purgative, illuminative, and u. stages of devotion 1830. Hence **U·nitive-ly** *adv.*, **-ness.**

Unity (yū·nĭti). ME. [a. AF. *unite*, F. *unité*, or ad. L. *unitat-*, *unitas*, f. *unus* one.] **1.** The fact, quality, or condition of being one in number; oneness, singleness. **b.** *Math.* The condition of the unit or number one; the numeral one regarded abstractly as the basis of number 1570. **c.** A quantity, magnitude, or substance, adopted as the unit of comparison or measurement 1728. **2.** †**a.** = UNIT 1. –1837. **b.** One separate or single thing, quality, etc.; something complete in itself or regarded as such 1587. **3.** The quality or condition of being one in feeling, action, purpose, etc.; harmonious combination of parties or persons ME. **b.** *At unity*, in concord or harmony; at one. late ME. **c.** Agreement or concord between things. late ME. **4.** The fact of forming or being united into one whole; union (of persons or things, or one *with* another or others). late ME. **b.** A body formed by union, esp. *the Unity of the* (Moravian) *Brethren* 1780. **5.** The quality or fact of being one body or whole, esp. as made up of two or more parts; an undivided whole, as dist. from its parts. late ME. **6.** Singleness of design or effect in a work of art; consonance of parts with each other and the whole 1712. **b.** *The unities*, the three principles of the canon of dramatic composition laid down by Aristotle and observed in the classical French drama, according to which a play should consist of one main action, represented as occurring at one time (i.e. one day) and in one place 1668. **7.** Continuity, homogeneity; unvaried nature; singleness of aim, purpose, or action 1802. **8.** Law. *U. of possession*, the joint possession of two rights by separate titles 1607.

1. Our God is one, or rather very oneness, and meere unitie HOOKER. **b.** The quotient is u. when the Dividend and the Divisor are equal 1869. **2. b.** The life and strength of a multitude consisteth in vnities 1600. **3.** The vnity and married calme of States SHAKS. Laud..contemplated establishing u. by uniformity 1830. **b.** Ierusalem is buylded as a cite, that is at vnitie in it self COVERDALE *Ps.* cxxi. **c.** There is such vnitie in the proofes SHAKS. **4.** Our Lord claimed for himself a mysterious u. with the Father 1871. **5.** Every grain Is sentient both in u. and part SHELLEY. **6.** Aristotle..allows, that Homer has nothing to boast of as to the U. of his Fable ADDISON. **7.** The possession of this child would give u. to her life GEO. ELIOT.

Univalent (yuni·vălĕnt), *a.* 1869. [f. UNI- + L. *valent-*, *valere* to be worth.] *Chem.* Having a valency of one having the combining power of one atom of hydrogen. So **Uni·valence. Uni·valency.**

Univalve (yū·nivælv), *a.* and *sb.* 1661. [See UNI- and VALVE *sb.*[1]] *Nat. Hist.* **A.** *adj.* **a.** *Conch.* Of shells: Composed of a single valve or piece. Of molluscs: Having such a shell. **b.** *Ent.* Having one valve 1826. **B.** *sb.* *Conch.* A u. mollusc or shell 1668. Hence **U·nivalved, Univa·lvular** *adjs. Bot.* having or consisting of one valve.

Universal (yūnivɔ̄·ɹsăl), *a.* and *sb.* late ME. [a. OF. *universel, -al*, or ad. L. *universalis*, f. *universus* UNIVERSE; see -AL.] **A.** *adj.* **1.** Extending over, comprehending, affecting, or including the whole of something specified or implied. **b.** Proceeding from the whole body or number without exception; unanimous 1586. **c.** Qualifying agent-nouns, personal designations, or titles; freq. in *u. bishop*, a title assumed by or given to some popes. late ME. **d.** *Law.* Of or in respect of the whole estate or property 1669. **2.** Of or throughout the universe, the world, or all nature; existing or occurring everywhere or in all things. late ME. **b.** Of language, etc.: Adopted, (intended to be) used, understood, etc., everywhere or by all nations; freq. = Latin 1652. **3.** Of the Church: Including all Christians; catholic 1483. **4.** Constituting or forming, existing or regarded as, a complete whole; entire, whole. (In 16th c., freq. of the world, earth, etc.) 1470. **5.** Of persons, etc.: Having a wide range of knowledge or interest; widely accomplished; not specialized; versatile 1520. **c.** Embracing or covering all (or a great variety of) subjects, branches of knowledge, etc. 1638. **6.** *Logic.* Applicable to, relating to, involving, the whole of a class or genus, or all the individuals or species composing it; *spec.* of a proposition: Predicable of each of the things denoted by the subject 1551. **b.** Of a law or rule: Valid in all cases 1583. **7.** Of implements, machines or their parts, etc.: Adjustable to all requirements; adapted to various purposes, sizes, etc. Freq. *u. joint*, one allowing free movement in any direction of the parts joined. 1676. **8.** *absol.* The whole of, all of (something expressed or implied); *spec.* in *Logic* and *Philos.*, the whole class or genus, as dist. from the individuals comprising it. late ME.

1. Grammar u.; that grammar which..only respects those principles that are essential to them all 1751. The battle was general, the overthrow universal DISRAELI. **2.** Her inchanting son Whom U. nature did lament MILT. **3.** The Catholick Church, that is, God's whole or universall Assembly 1645. **4.** 'Twas for nothing in the u. world but for killing a rich Patient 1649. Thine this u. Frame MILT. **5.** Shakespeare had an u. mind DRYDEN. He sets up for an u. man, because he has a small tincture of every science SMOLLETT. **7.** An u. chuck for holding any kind of work which is to be turned 1825.

Collocations: **u. arithmetic,** algebra; **u. suffrage,** a suffrage extending to the whole of a community, esp. one in which all persons over a fixed age, except lunatics, aliens, and criminals, have the right to vote for representatives to a legislative assembly.

B. *sb.* **1.** *Logic* and *Philos.* What is predicated of all the individuals or species of a class or genus; an abstract or general concept regarded as having an absolute, mental, or nominal existence; a universal proposition; a general term or notion 1553. **2.** That which is universal; esp. one who or that which is universally potent, current, etc. Now *rare.* 1556.

1. An abstract u., which is properly nothing, a conception of our own making BENTLEY. The long controversies between the Realists and Nominalists concerning the nature of universals 1837.

Universalism (yūnivə̄·ɹsăliz'm). 1805. [f. prec. + -ISM.] 1. *Theol.* The doctrine of universal salvation or redemption. 2. The pursuit of universal knowledge or skill; extreme versatility 1827. 3. The fact or condition of being universal in scope or character; universality 1840. So **Unive·rsalist** *sb.* esp. *Theol.* one who believes or maintains the doctrine that redemption or election is extended to the whole of mankind; *spec.* in *U.S.* a member of a sect holding this doctrine; *adj.* universalistic. **U:niversali·stic** *a. Theol.* of or pertaining to Universalism; universal in scope or character.

Universality (yūnivəɹsæ·lĭti). late ME. [a. F. *universalité*, or ad. late L. *universalitas* f. *universalis* UNIVERSAL; see -ITY.] 1. The fact, quality, or condition of being universal, in various senses. 2. The collective whole *of* something regarded collectively, as the world, a people, a nation. Now *arch.* 1561. †b. The whole people or state -1675. †3. A general statement, a generality -1647.

1. The antiquitie, and vniuersalitie, of the Catholicke Religion 1559. The u. of this mathematical rule BERKELEY. 2. b. The Common happinesse of the vniuersalitie RALEIGH.

Universalize (yūnivə̄·ɹsăləiz), *v.* 1642. [f. UNIVERSAL *a.* + -IZE.] 1. *trans.* To make or render universal; to give a universal character to; to convert from particular or individual to general. 2. To bring into universal use, acceptance, or currency 1809.

Universally (yūnivə̄·ɹsăli), *adv.* late ME. [f. as prec. + -LY [2].] 1. In every instance; without any exception; in every part or place; by, among, to, etc., all the persons concerned. 2. *Logic* and *Metaph.* In relation to all the members of a class or genus 1551.

1. Rye is generally (nay u., I think) allowed to be a better bearer than wheat 1765. 2. The term 'necessary to life' is affirmed of food, but not u.; for it is not said of every kind of food WHATELY.

Universe (yū·nivə̄ɹs). 1589. [a. F. *univers*, ad. L. *universum* the whole world, orig. neut. sing. of *universus* universal, f. *unus* one and *versus*, *vertere* to turn.] 1. The whole of created or existing things regarded collectively; all things, including the earth, the heavens, and all that is in them, considered as constituting a systematic whole. b. With *a* and *pl.* 1667. 2. The world or earth, esp. as the abode of man or as the scene of human activities 1630. b. *transf.* The inhabitants of the earth; mankind in general 1742.

1. *transf.* The four Faculties are supposed to make the World or U. of Study 1728. Into the heights of Love's rare U. SHELLEY. b. A U. of death, which God by curse Created evil MILTON. To Newton and to Newton's Dog Diamond, what a different pair of Universes! CARLYLE. 2. [Wesley] took the u. for his parish 1791. b. Our good Edmund,..Who, born for the u.,..to party gave up what was meant for mankind GOLDSM.

Universitarian (yūnivəɹsitē·riăn), *a.* 1834. [f. UNIVERSITY + -ARIAN.] Of or pertaining to, characteristic of, obtaining in, a university.

‖**Universitas** (yūnivə̄·ɹsitæs). 1765. [L.; see next.] *Sc. Law.* The whole (of an estate or inheritance).

University (yūnivə̄·ɹsĭti). ME. [a. AF. *université*:—L. *universitat-*, *-itas* (1) the whole, universe, (2) a corporation or community, f. L. *universus* UNIVERSE. As the designation of a whole body, community, or guild of masters and scholars, the full phr. was *universitas magistrorum et scholarium*; *universitas* ultimately superseded *studium* for 'university'.] 1. The whole body of teachers and students pursuing, at a particular place, the higher branches of learning; such persons associated together as a society or corporate body, having the power of conferring degrees and other privileges, and forming an institution for the promotion of education in the higher branches of learning; the colleges, buildings, etc., belonging to such a body. †2. The whole number or aggregate *of* creatures, persons, things, etc. -1677. †b. The universe -1642. 3. Law. *University of rights and duties*, the complex aggregate of these attached to a succession, etc. 1832. †4. A class of persons regarded collectively; a corporate body -1678. 5. *attrib.* passing into *adj.* Of or belonging to, characteristic of, a u.; that is or has been a member of a u.; attached to or connected with a u.; etc. late ME.

1. They labour to put out the eyes of this land (the Vniuersityes I meane) 1579. The u. of the chancellor, masters, and scholars, is one corporation 1868. *transf.* I think you were broght vp in the vniuersitie of bridewell; you haue your rhetorick so ready at your toongs end 1595. 2. In al the hool vnyuersite of thingis and of beingis 1449. b. Man is a little world and beares the face And picture of the Vniuersitie 1598. 4. Although kings doe die, the people in the mean time (as niether any other Universitie) never dyeth 1643.

attrib., as *u. chair*, *chest* (CHEST *sb.*[1] 1), *course*, *extension* (EXTENSION 7), *lecturer*, *man*, *sermon*.

Univocal (yuni·vŏkăl), *a.* and *sb.* 1615. [f. late L. *univocus* having one meaning (f. L. *uni-* UNI- + *voc-*, *vox* voice) + -AL.] A. *adj.* 1. Having only one meaning or signification; not equivocal; unambiguous 1656. †2. Uniform, homogeneous -1727. †3. Of or belonging to, characteristic of, things of the same name or species; esp. in *u. generation*, normal generation between members of the same species -1822. †4. Uttered with or as with one voice; unanimous -1734. B. *sb.* A univocal term 1728. Hence **Uni·vocally** *adv.* 1593.

Univo·ltine, *sb.* and *a.* 1874. [ad. F. *univoltin*, *-tain*, f. *uni-* UNI- + It. *volta* turn.] A. *sb.* One of a breed of silkworms producing one brood a year. B. *adj.* Having only one brood each year 1883.

Unja·ded *ppl. a.* [UN-[1] 2] 1779. **Unjau·ndiced** *ppl. a.* [UN-[1] 2] 1792. **Unjea·lous** *a.* [UN-[1] 1] 1673. **Unjoi·n** *v.* (now *rare*) [UN-[2] 1] ME.

Unjoi·nt, *v.* late ME. [UN-[2] 1.] 1. *trans.* To take apart at the joints; to disjoint, dislocate. 2. *fig.* To disunite, sever 1561.

Unjoi·nted, *a.* 1588. [UN-[1] 3.] 1. *fig.* Incoherent, disjointed. *arch.* 2. Without joints 1681.

1. This bald, vnioynted Chat of his SHAKS.

Unjoy·ful *a.* [UN-[1] 1] ME., **-ly** *adv.* **Unjoy·ous** *a.* [UN-[1] 1] MILT. **Unju·dged** *ppl. a.* [UN-[1] 2] 1647. **Unjudi·cial** *a.* [UN-[1] 1] 1599, **-ly** *adv.* **Unjudi·cious** *a.* (now *rare* or *Obs.*) [UN-[1] 1] 1614. **Unju·mpable** *a.* [UN-[1] 1] 1886.

Unju·st, *a.* late ME. [UN-[1] 1.] 1. a. Not acting justly or fairly; not observing the principles of justice or fair dealing. b. Not in accordance with justice or fairness. late ME. 2. Not upright or free from wrong-doing; faithless, dishonest. Now *rare.* 1500.

1. a. To compare the universal with the limited is to be u. to both 1876. b. Vsurie and vniust gaine *Prov.* xxviii. 8. 2. The lorde commended the uniust stewarde TINDALE *Luke* xvi. 8. Hence **Unju·st-ly** *adv.*, **-ness.**

Unju·stifiable *a.* [UN-[1] 1] 1641, **-ness**, **-bly** *adv.*

Unju·stified, *ppl. a.* ME. [UN-[1] 2.] †1. Not brought to justice, not executed -1596. 2. Not justified, e.g. by faith 1651. 3. Lacking justification, done without due cause, improper, unwarranted. (The current use.) 1685.

Unked, unkid (ʊ·ŋkėd), *a.* Now *dial.* [ME. *unkid*(*d*, f. UN-[1] + pa. pple. of KITHE *v.*] 1. Unknown, strange. 2. Awkward or troublesome from unfamiliarity or novelty 1634. 3. Unfamiliarly lone or dreary; solitary, forlorn; lonely 1706. 4. Uncanny, eerie, weird 1800.

3. Weston is sadly u. without you COWPER. 4. They would not pass at night, Lest they should hear an u. strain Or see an u. sight CHRISTINA ROSSETTI.

Unkee·led *ppl. a.* [UN-[1] 2] 1807.

Unke·mbed, *ppl. a.* Now *rare.* late ME. [UN-[1] 2.] = next.

Unke·mpt, *ppl. a.* 1579. [UN-[1] 2.] 1. Of hair, etc.: Uncombed 1742. b. With uncombed hair, dishevelled 1748. c. Untidy; of neglected appearance; untrimmed; rough 1861. †2. Of language: Inelegant, unpolished; rude -1606.

1. c. Filthy habits and u. attire 1879. 2. To well I wote..howe my rymes bene rugged and vnkempt SPENSER.

Unke·nnel, *v.* 1576. [UN-[2] 3.] 1. *trans.* To dislodge (a fox) from its hole. Also *absol.* b. *intr.* To come out of a hole or lair 1760. 2. *fig.* (*trans.*) To dislodge, fetch out; to bring to light 1612. 3. To let (hounds) out of a kennel 1607.

Unke·pt *ppl. a.* [UN-[1] 2] ME. **Unkey·** *v.* [UN-[2] 2] 1751. **Unki·llable** *a.* [UN-[1] 1] 1878. **Unki·lled** *ppl. a.* [UN-[1] 2] 1535.

Unkind (ʊnkəi·nd), *a.* ME. [UN-[1] 1.] †1. Strange, foreign -late ME. 2. Of weather, etc.: Not mild or pleasant; ungenial. Now *dial.* or *arch.* ME. †b. Physically unnatural; contrary to the usual course of nature -1603. c. Naturally bad or hurtful; unsuitable; injurious. Now *dial.* late ME. †3. Lacking in natural gratitude, filial affection or respect, or natural goodness -1649. †4. Contrary to nature; *esp.* unnaturally bad or wicked -1656. 5. Lacking in kindness or kindly feeling; acting harshly or ungently. late ME. b. Of actions, etc.: Characterized by want of kindness. late ME.

2. The climate is u. and the ground penurious JOHNSON. b. They doe quench and allay thirst, and coole u. heat HOLLAND. c. The East-wind being cold..is verie vnkind for Bees 1609. 3. The Redeemer of unkinde mankinde 1649. 4. Such vnlawfull lust, such vnkinde desires GREENE. Making thyself unkinde and monstrous in murthering of thy mother 1635. 5. To the Noble minde, Rich gifts wax poore, when giuers proue vnkinde SHAKS. b. This was the most vnkindest cut of all SHAKS. Hence **Unki·nd-ly** *adv.*; phr. *to take u.*, to resent; **-ness**; *an u.*, an unkind act.

Unki·ndled *ppl. a.* [UN-[1] 2] 1513. **Unki·ndliness** [UN-[1] 6] 1470.

Unki·ndly, *a.* ME. [f. UN-[1] 1 + KINDLY *a.* Cf. OE. *ungecyndelic.*] †1. Unnaturally wicked or vile -1614. †b. Unrestrained by natural bonds of kindred, etc. -1647. †2. Unnatural in respect of physical qualities or actions -1639. b. Of weather, soil, etc.: Unnaturally bleak or cold; unfruitful; unfavourable. late ME. c. Of plants, animals, etc.: Ill-conditioned, not well developed. Now *dial.* or *arch.* late ME. †d. Prejudicial to health; not developing in a natural healthy manner -1827. 3. Devoid of kindness; unkind 1805.

Unki·ng, *v.* 1578. [UN-[2] 4 b.] 1. To deprive of the position of king; to depose from sovereignty. b. *refl.* To abdicate 1647. 2. To deprive (a country) of a king 1647.

1. These men do design To un-king the Queen 1711. 2. A wife's dishonour unking'd Rome for ever BYRON. Hence **Unki·nged** *ppl. a.* God saue King Henry, vn-King'd Richard sayes SHAKS.

Unki·ngly *a.* [UN-[1] 1] 1600; *adv.* [UN-[1] 5] late ME. **Unki·ss** *v.* [UN-[2] 1] 1562.

Unki·ssed, *ppl. a.* late ME. [UN-[1] 2.] Not kissed. †b. *Uncouth* (*unknown*, *unkent*), *u.*, the kiss of greeting is not given to strangers; *transf.* the unknown is neglected 1697.

Unkni·ght *v.* [UN-[2] 4 b] 1623. **Unkni·ghted** *ppl. a.* [UN-[1] 2] 1631. **Unkni·ghtly** *a.* [UN-[1] 1] late ME.; *adv.* [UN-[1] 5] 1586.

Unkni·t, *v.* [OE. *uncnyttan*, f. UN-[2] 2 b.] 1. *trans.* To undo (a knot or something tied). Now *arch.* b. *fig.* To loosen, dissolve (a bond, union). *poet.* and *arch.* ME. c. To relax (a knitted brow) 1596. d. To disjoint, disunite; to unclasp (*rare*) 1580. 2. *fig.* To disperse, dissolve, undo, destroy; to relax or weaken. Also *absol.* late ME. b. To sever, divorce. late ME. 3. *intr.* To become unknit, in various senses 1574.

1. c. Fie, fie, vnknit that threatning vnkinde brow SHAKS. 2. Logike is bound..to knit true arguments and u. false 1551. 3. The ligaments, hindring the parts from unknitting 1677.

Unkni·t *ppl. a.* [UN-[1] 2] 1607. **Unkno·t** *v.* [UN-[2] 1] 1598. **Unkno·tted** *ppl. a.* [UN-[1] 2] 1642. **Unknow·** *v.*[1] (now *rare*) [UN-[1] 7] late ME. **Unknow·** *v.*[2] [UN-[2] 1] 1586. **Unknow·able** *a.* [UN-[1] 1] late ME.

Unknow·ing, *ppl. a.* ME. [UN-[1] 4.] 1. Not knowing; ignorant, uninformed. 2. Without knowledge *of* something ME. b. Const. direct obj., or obj. clause. late ME. c. Const. with inf. 1666. 3. Unknown *to* (a person). Now *dial.* late ME. 4. As quasi-*adv.* Unknowingly. late ME.

1. Symple and unknouuing men 1386. Winds that pilfer from u. flowers Their balmy breaths 1845. 2. The residue wer vnknowying of this thyng UDALL. b. Mankind wanders, u. his way GOLDSM. U. where my course is bound SCOTT. c. U. whitherward to bend his way SOUTHEY. 3. He..sodenly departed (vnknowing to the Ladies) 1577. Hence **Unknow·ing-ly** *adv.*, **-ness.**

Unknow·n, *ppl. a.* and *sb.* ME. [UN-[1] 2.] A. *adj.* 1. Not known; unfamiliar, strange. 2. In absolute const.: Without its being known (*to*, one); without the knowledge *of* (some one). late ME.

1. Vnto the vnknowen God TINDALE *Acts* xvii. 23. To..walke through unknowen places without a guide 1586. Death is the knownest and vnknownest thing in the world 1622. The fishes of the u. deep COWPER. Some u.-of isle 1839. *U. warrior*: see WARRIOR 1. Phr. *U. quantity*, in algebra, a quantity of which the value is not determined; also freq. *fig*. Provb. phr. *U., unkissed* (see UNKISSED b); Unknowen vnkist, and beyng knowen I weene, Thou art neuer kist, where thou mayst be seene HEYWOOD. 2. Being done vnknowne, I should haue found it afterwards well done SHAKS. The Patient, u. to me, pursued his intention 1672.

B. *sb.* 1. An unknown person 1597. 2. That which is unknown 1656. 3. *Math.* An unknown quantity 1817.

1. The faire Unknowne 1652. 2. The dark u. of legal perplexities 1846.

Unla·belled *ppl. a.* [UN-1 2] 1844. **Unlabo·rious** *a.* [UN-1 1] MILT. **Unla·boured** *ppl. a.* [UN-1 2] 1473. **Unla·bouring** *ppl. a.* [UN-1 4] 1619.

Unla·ce, *v.* ME. [UN-2 1.] 1. *trans.* To undo the lace or laces of (armour, clothing, etc.); to unfasten or loosen thus. 2. To free or relieve (a person, the body, etc.) by undoing a lace or laces. Also *absol.* ME. †3. To carve (*spec.* a rabbit); to cut off in carving -1771.

1. He vnlaced his helme and gate hym wynde MALORY. Hence **Unla·ced** *ppl. a.*

Unla·de, *v.* late ME. [UN-2 2.] 1. *trans.* To take a load off (a horse, cart, etc.). b. To take the cargo out of (a ship) 1489. c. To unburden, relieve (*of* a load, care, sin, etc.) 1581. 2. To discharge (a cargo, etc.) from a ship. late ME. b. To lay down (a load, care, etc.); to unpack (goods); to bring forth (news, ideas) 1591. 3. *absol.* To discharge a cargo or cargoes, a burden, etc. 1547.

2. b. He..unlades his stock of ideas in perfect order LAMB. 3. What adventure is this you are so full of? come, u., u. 1717. Hence **Unla·ding** *vbl. sb.*

Unla·den *ppl. a.* [UN-1 2] 1802. **Unla·dylike** *a.* [UN-1 1] MISS MITFORD. **Unlai·d** *ppl. a.* [UN-1 2] 1468. **Unlame·nted** *ppl. a.* [UN-1 2] 1595. **Unla·nded** *a.* [UN-1 3] 1488.

Unla·nguaged, *a.* 1654. [UN-1 3.] 1. Not gifted with speech. 2. Not put into words 1846.

Unla·p, *v.* Now *rare.* late ME. [UN-2 2.] *trans.* To unwrap.

Unla·sh *v.* [UN-2 2 b] 1748. **Unla·tch** *v.* [UN-2 1] 1642. **Unla·tched** *ppl. a.* [UN-1 2] 1888. **Unlau·dable** *a.* [UN-1 1] 1550.

U·nlaw, *sb.* [OE. *unlagu.*] Illegal action; illegality. (Revived by recent writers.)

Unlaw·, *v.* 1491. [f. prec.] †1. *trans.* To fine. *Sc.* -1732. 2. To annul (a law). *rare.* 1644.

Unlaw·ful, *a.* ME. [UN-1 1.] 1. Prohibited by law; illegal. b. spec. *U. assembly*: the meeting of large numbers of people together with such circumstances of behaviour as to raise the fears of their fellow-subjects and to endanger the public peace 1485. c. Of offspring: Illegitimate 1606. 2. Offending against morals or religion 1475. 3. Of persons: Not obeying the law; acting illegally; with no right to the specified status. late ME. 4. Against rules; irregular 1729.

3. To execute worthy punishment on me as an u. wife ANNE BOLEYN. The u. opener of a letter DICKENS. 4. It is u. to divide the anapæst between two words 1836. Hence **Unlaw·ful·ly** *adv.*, **-ness.**

Unlay·, *v.* 1726. [UN-2 1.] *trans.* To untwist (a rope) into separate strands.

Unlead (vnle·d), *v.* 1591. [UN-2 2.] To strip (a roof or building) of lead. So **Unlea·ded** *ppl. a.* not weighted with lead; *Typog.* not spaced with leads.

Unlea·rn, *v.* 1450. [UN-2 1.] 1. *trans.* To discard from knowledge or memory; to give up knowledge of (something). b. *absol.* or const. with inf. 1530. 2. To unteach 1664.

1. The most necessary learning for mans life, is to u. that which is nought and vain 1686. 2. Legal learning..can never have unlearnt a man the difference between three and one and a half BENTHAM.

Unlearned (vnlə·ɹnėd), *ppl. a.* late ME. [UN-1 2.] 1. Having no learning; untaught; ignorant. 2. Not skilled or versed *in* something 1565. 3. Characterized by want of learning; pertaining to the unlearned class 1526. 4. (vnlə·ɹnd) Not acquired by learning 1534. 5. *absol.* Those who have no learning 1500.

3. The u. and vulgar passion of admiration BURKE. Hence **Unlea·rned·ly** *adv.*, **-ness.**

Unlea·rnt *ppl. a.* [UN-1 2] 1879. **Unlea·sed** *ppl. a.* [UN-1 2] 1716. **Unlea·sh** *v.* [UN-2 2 b] 1671. **Unlea·shed** *ppl. a.* [UN-1 2] 1821. **Unlea·vened** *ppl. a.* [UN-1 2] TINDALE. **Unle·d** *ppl. a.* [UN-1 2] 1569. **Unle·galized** *ppl. a.* [UN-1 2] 1830. **Unlei·sured** *a.* [UN-1 3] SIDNEY. **Unle·nt** *ppl. a.* [UN-1 2] 1887.

Unless (vnle·s), *prep. phr.*, *prep.*, *conj.* and *sb.* late ME. [f. LESS *a.* II. 2, preceded by *upon*, *on*, *in*, or *of*; unstressed *on* has been assimilated in form to UN-1.] †**A.** *prep. phr.* 1. On a less or lower condition, footing, etc., *than* (what is specified) -1500. 2. Except, if.. not. †a. With *than*, *that* -1596. b. With omission of conjunction before the subordinate clause, thus passing into *conj.* 1509. c. With ellipsis of verb, etc. in the clause 1548. **B.** *prep.* Except, but 1531. †**C.** *conj.* Lest. **D.** *sb.* An instance or utterance of the word; a reservation 1861.

2. a. Onlesse that our kyng haue more chyualry,..he shal be ouercome MALORY. b. For one is to much, onles it be well spent 1563. c. But I dare not shew them, u. to you 1789. B. All forbeare this place, vnlesse the Princess HEYWOOD. D. Let us have no unlesses, sir DICKENS.

Unle·ssoned *ppl. a.* [UN-1 2] 1550. **Unle·t** *ppl. a.* [UN-1 2] 1453.

Unle·ttered, *a.* ME. [UN-1 3.] 1. Not instructed in letters; not possessed of book-learning. b. Pertaining to or characterized by ignorance of letters 1588. 2. Not marked with or expressed in letters 1633.

1. Plain u. Men WESLEY. b. Learned men in an u. age HAZLITT. 2. This u. tomb 1782.

Unle·vel *a.* [UN-1 1] 1571. **Unle·vel** *v.* [UN-2 4 b] 1586. **Unle·velled** *ppl. a.* [UN-1 2] 1622. **Unle·vied** *ppl. a.* [UN-1 2] 1450. **Unli·able** *a.* [UN-1 1] 1624.

Unli·censed, *ppl. a.* 1608. [UN-1 2.] 1. Not authorized by a formal licence to carry on some occupation, etc. 1634. b. Not furnished with authority, sanction, or formal permission to do something 1608. 2. Of books, etc.: Published without licence 1643. b. Not authorized or sanctioned 1649. 3. Free from requiring a licence 1644.

1. b. The Papists restraint of the Laity u., from reading it translated in a known Tongue 1685. 3. For the Liberty of Vnlicenc'd Printing MILT.

Unli·cked, *ppl. a.* 1593. [UN-1 2.] 1. Not licked into shape (see LICK *v.* 4). Chiefly *fig.*, esp. with *cub* (or *whelp*). b. *fig.* Not reduced to form or order; unpolished, rude or crude 1661. 2. Not licked 1861.

1. b. Clumsy verse, unlickt DRYDEN.

Unli·d *v.* [UN-2 2] ME. **Unli·dded** *ppl. a.* [UN-1 2] 1819. **Unli·felike** *a.* [UN-1 1] 1818. **Unli·ghted** *ppl. a.* [UN-1 2] 1699. **Unli·ghtened** *ppl. a.* [UN-1 2] 1587. **Unli·ghtsome** *a.* (now *rare*) [UN-1 1] 1592.

Unlike (vnləi·k), *a.* and *sb.* [ME. *unliche*, *unlike* (corresp. to OE. *ungelīc*), f. UN-1 1.] **A.** *adj.* 1. Not like or resembling, different from (some other person or thing). b. Const. *to* ME. 2. Not like each other; dissimilar ME. 3. Dissimilar to the thing or person in question. late ME. 4. Not uniform or even; unequal. late ME. 5. Unlikely, improbable. Now *dial.* or *arch.* late ME.

1. He was unlich alle othre there GOWER. b. Vnlyk is my word to my dede 1400. 2. How much u. they look CRABBE. 3. Nor a muche vnlyke aunswere dyd Wylliam..gyue vnto me UDALL. 4. Whan an vnlike pare of oxen must drawe together COVERDALE *Ecclus.* xxvi. 7. 5. It is not vnlike but that the saide Duke hathe ben deceyued CROMWELL. He thought the Match very u. to be effected 1626.

B. *sb.* 1. *pl.* Dissimilar things or persons 1612. 2. A person unlike another or others ME.

1. In a comparison of unlikes 1612. 2. The just does not desire more than his like but more than his u. JOWETT.

Unli·ke, *adv.* ME. [UN-1 5.] †1. Unevenly, unequally. -late ME. 2. †a. Differently, diversely -1595. b. In a manner different from (that of a specified person) 1593. †3. Improbably -1596.

2. b. The Master had treated me u. a gentleman SCOTT.

Unli·k(e)able *a.* [UN-1 1] 1841. **Unli·ked** *ppl. a.* (now *rare*) [UN-1 2] 1561. **Unli·kelihood** [UN-1 6] 1483.

Unli·kely, *a.* late ME. [UN-1 1.] 1. Not likely to occur or come to pass. b. Not likely to be true or correct 1592. c. Not likely, in various senses 1535. 2. With complement: a. With *to* and inf. late ME. b. With *that* and clause. late ME. 3. Unseemly, unbecoming; of unattractive appearance. Now *dial.* 1456.

1. b. They tell, for news, such u. stories! DRYDEN. c. An U. way of gaining Proselytes 1694. A succession [of swifts] still haunts the same u. roofs G. WHITE. A poor lad was come, at that u. time, to fetch Mr. Rivers C. BRONTË. 3. The most u. person..that in any countrye might be found 1590. Hence **Unli·keliness.** late ME.

Unli·kely, *adv.* 1449. [UN-1 5.] Improbably. (Usu. with negative.)

The..epistle..ascryued vnlikeli to Constantyn 1449. [He] may fall not u...into an uncouth opinion MILT.

Unli·keness. ME. [UN-1 6.] †1. Strangeness. -late ME. 2. The quality of being unlike; dissimilarity. late ME. 3. With *a* and *pl.* An instance of this 1662. 2. A bad or poor likeness 1729.

Unli·king [UN-1 4, 8] late ME. **Unli·mber** *v.* [UN-2 3] 1802. **Unli·med** *ppl. a.* [UN-1 2] 1622.

Unli·mited, *ppl. a.* 1445. [UN-1 2.] 1. Of rule, power, etc.: Free from restriction or control. 2. Not limited or restricted in amount, extent, degree, or number 1586.

1. It must be an u. Monarchy SIDNEY. 2. Four Wives the Law tolerates, Concubines are u. 1665. My confidence in his talents..is u. 1846. Hence **Unli·mitedly** *adv.*, **-ness.**

Unli·neal *a.* [UN-1 1] 1593. **Unli·ned** *ppl. a.*[1] (see LINE *v.*[1]) [UN-1 2] 1521. **Unli·ned** *ppl. a.*[2] (see LINE *v.*[2]) [UN-1 2] 1865.

Unli·nk, *v.* 1600. [UN-2 2 b.] 1. *trans.* To undo the links of; to sever, unfasten (a chain, bond, connexion). b. To release or separate thus 1655. 2. *intr.* To lose connexion; to part; to become relaxed 1641.

Unli·nked *ppl. a.* [UN-1 2] 1813. **Unli·quid** *a.* [UN-1 1] 1547. **Unli·quidated** *ppl. a.* [UN-1 2] 1765. **Unli·quored** *ppl. a.* [UN-1 2] MILT. **Unli·stened** *ppl. a.* [UN-1 2] 1787. **Unli·stening** *ppl. a.* [UN-1 4] 1736. **Unli·t** *ppl. a.* [UN-1 2] 1852. **Unli·terary** *a.* [UN-1 1] LAMB.

Unli·ve, *v.* 1593. [UN-2 1, 2.] †1. *trans.* To deprive of life -1702. 2. To reverse, undo, or annul (past life or experience) 1614.

1. Where shall I live now Lucrece is unlived? SHAKS. 2. We must u. our former lives 1661.

Unli·v(e)able, *a.* 1869. [UN-1 1.] 1. Of life: Not to be lived, not worth living. 2. *U.* (*-in*), uninhabitable 1898.

Unli·vely *a.* [UN-1 1] 1563, **-liness.**

Unli·ver, *v.* Now *rare* or *Obs.* 1637. [UN-2 7.] *trans.* To discharge (a ship or cargo). Also *absol.*

Unli·very. 1805. [f. prec.] *Law.* Discharge of a ship or cargo.

Unli·ving *ppl. a.* [UN-1 4] 1561.

Unloa·d, *v.* 1523. [UN-2 1.] 1. *trans.* To take off (something carried or conveyed); to discharge (a cargo). Also *absol.* b. *absol.* Of vessels: To discharge cargo 1799. 2. *fig.* To give vent to (feelings); to communicate *to* another 1593. 3. *trans.* (and *refl.*) To free, relieve, or divest of a load, burden, or weight 1591. b. *Med.* To relieve by evacuation 1653. c. To relieve (the heart, etc.) by utterance 1720. d. To rid *of* something burdensome 1721. 4. To discharge the cargo from (a vessel) 1599. 5. To withdraw the charge from (a fire-arm, etc.) 1709. 6. *Stock Exch.* To get rid of, sell out (stock, etc.) Also *absol.* 1876. Hence **Unloa·ded** *ppl. a.*[2] **Unloa·ding** *vbl. sb.* 1522.

Unlo·aded *ppl. a.*[1] [UN-1 2] 1648. **Unlo·calized** *ppl. a.* [UN-1 2] LAMB. **Unloca·ted** *ppl. a.* [UN-1 2] 1776.

Unlo·ck, *v.* late ME. [UN-2 1.] 1. *trans.* To undo the lock of (a door, etc.) by turning the key. 2. To set free by undoing a lock; chiefly *fig.* late ME. b. To give or obtain access to; to bring to light 1593. 3. *fig.* To cause to open or unclose 1531. b. To explain, provide a key to (something obscure) 1636. 4. To open, or cause to open, by physical action 1586. b. To undo or unfasten by some mechanical operation, or by force 1606. c. To free from being fixed or immovable 1735. 5. *intr.* To become unlocked 1470.

1. This can u. the gates of Joy GRAY. 2. When the kind early Dew Unlocks th' embosom'd Odors 1708. Capital..is so very hard to u. 1884. b. These hoards of truth you can u. at will WORDSW. 3. I know you have a key to u. hearts GEO. ELIOT. b. With a Key Præfixed to vnlock the whole Story 1636. 4. [Claylands] hardning with the Sun and Wind, till they are unlocked by industry 1707. U. your jaws, sirrah SHERIDAN. b. Those stops, which..lock and u. the Clock in striking 1704. c. At first he could u. the knee easily 1902. Hence **Unlo·cked** *ppl. a.*[1]

Unlo·cked *ppl. a.*[2] [UN-[1] 2] 1603. **Unlocomo·tive** *a.* [UN-[1] 1] SCOTT. **Unlo·dge** *v.* (now *rare*) [UN-[2] 3, 7] 1560. **Unlo·gic** [UN-[1] 6] CARLYLE. **Unlo·gical** *a.* (now *rare*) [UN-[1] 1] 1661.

Unloo·ked, *ppl. a.* ME. [UN-[1] 2.] †1. Not looked to, neglected. ME. only. b. Not looked *at, on, to,* etc.; unexamined, unheeded, unregarded 1563. 2. Not looked *for*; unexpected, unanticipated 1535. †b. Unlooked for –1618.

2. b. But by some vnlook'd accident cut off SHAKS.

Unloo·sable *a.* [UN-[1] 1] late ME. **Unloo·se** *v.* [UN-[2] 7] late ME. **Unloo·sed** *ppl. a.* [UN-[1] 2] late ME. **Unloo·sen** *v.* [UN-[2] 7] 1450. **Unlo·pped** *ppl. a.* [UN-[1] 2] 1573. **Unlo·rd** *v.* [UN-[2] 4 b] 1572. **Unlo·rded** *ppl. a.* [UN-[1] 2] MILT. **Unlo·rdly** *a.* [UN-[1] 1] 1575. **Unlo·sable** *a.* [UN-[1] 1] 1647. **Unlo·st** *ppl. a.* [UN-[1] 2] 1513. **Unlo·v(e)able** *a.* [UN-[1] 1] 1570. **Unlo·ve** *v.* [UN-[2] 1] CHAUCER. **Unlo·ved** *ppl. a.* [UN-[1] 2] late ME.

Unlo·vely, *a.* late ME. [UN-[1] 1.] 1. Not evoking feelings of love or affection; unattractive, repellent. 2. Lacking beauty, ugly. late ME.

1. This very u. quarrel 1889. 2. A ful old man.. that onlovely was of face 1450. Hence **Unlo·veliness.**

Unlo·verlike *a.* [UN-[1] 1] JANE AUSTEN. **Unlo·ving** *ppl. a.* [UN-[1] 4] 1529, **-ly** *adv.*, **-ness.** **Unlu·ck** [UN-[1] 6] 1838.

Unlu·ckily, *adv.* 1530. [UN-[1] 5.] Unfortunately, unhappily (usu. parenthetic or in loose construction). b. With verbs of happening, succeeding, etc. With ill success or results, not well 1550.

Blind Fortune..made them u. to be killed SIDNEY. U. all our money had been laid out..in provisions GOLDSM. b. It has turned out u. SHELLEY.

Unlu·cky, *a.* 1530. [UN-[1] 1.] 1. Having an unfortunate character or issue; marked by misfortune or failure. 2. Boding or involving misfortune; ill-omened 1547. 3. Having ill-luck; meeting with misfortune or mishap 1552. 4. Bringing ill-luck; mischievous, malicious. Now *dial.* 1586. 5. Of an unfortunate or regrettable nature; not entitled to commendation 1628.

Brought hither in a most vnluckie houre SHAKS. The year..had certainly been u. MACAULAY. 2. The Scottes..thought John an unluckie name for a King 1568. 3. Some Ships..are so vnlucky, that they neuer make a good voyage 1627. 5. If some u. Barber notch my Hair 1746. Hence **Unlu·ckiness.**

Unlu·crative *a.* [UN-[1] 1] 1771. **Unlu·minous** *a.* [UN-[1] 1] 1773. **Unlu·strous** *a.* [UN-[1] 1] 1709. **Unlu·sty** *a.* (now only *dial.*) [UN-[1] 1] ME. **Unluxu·rious** *a.* [UN-[1] 1] 1700. **Unmaca·damized** *ppl. a.* [UN-[1] 2] 1840. **Unma·ddened** *ppl. a.* [UN-[1] 2] COLERIDGE.

Unma·de, *ppl. a.* ME. [UN-[1] 2.] 1. Not (yet) made, in senses of the vb. b. *spec.* Not trained 1856. c. With advs. Not made *out, up,* etc. 1600. 2. Existing without having been made; uncreated but existent ME.

1. Lawes..are farre better vnmade, then vnkept 1623. b. U. hunters and carriage-horses 1856. c. He wears his little Learning, unmade-up, puts it on, before it was half finished 1680. 2. U., Self-existent, independent Deities 1682.

Unmagna·nimous *a.* [UN-[1] 1] 1856. **Unmagne·tic** *a.* [UN-[1] 1] 1805. **Unma·gnetized** *ppl. a.* [UN-[1] 2] 1834. **Unmai·den** *v.* [UN-[2] 4 b] 1579. **Unmai·denly** *a.* [UN-[1] 1] 1634, **-liness.** **Unmai·lable** *a.* (*U.S.*) [UN-[1] 1] 1875. **Unmai·med** *ppl. a.* [UN-[1] 2] MALORY. **Unmaintai·nable** *a.* [UN-[1] 1] 1625.

Unma·ke, *v.* late ME. [UN-[2] 1.] 1. To reverse or undo the making of; to reduce again to an unmade condition. Also *absol.* 2. To deprive of a particular rank or station; to depose 1554. b. To deprive of a certain character or quality; to change the nature of 1616. 3. *fig.* To undo; to ruin; to bring to nothing 1605.

1. Prelaty..must be forc't to dissolve and u. her own pyramidal figure MILTON. When a statute..has been unmade by the authority that made it BENTHAM. 2. They made and unmade Popes at their pleasure 1670. b. You are so pure—That..Heaven would u. it sin! DRYDEN. 3. The machine unmakes the man EMERSON. Hence **Unma·ker.**

Unmali·cious *a.* [UN-[1] 1] 1649. **Unma·lleable** *a.* [UN-[1] 1] 1609, **Unmalleabi·lity.** **Unma·lted** *ppl. a.* [UN-[1] 2] 1651.

Unma·n, *sb. rare.* late ME. [UN-[1] 6.] †1. A being below the status of man –1641. 2. A monster 1879.

Unma·n, *v.* 1598. [UN-[2] 4 b.] 1. *trans.* To deprive of the attributes of a man; to remove from the category of men. 2. To reduce below the level of man; to degrade, brutalize 1637. 3. To deprive of manly courage or fortitude; to make weak or womanish 1600. b. *trans.* and *intr.* To bring or come back to childhood (*rare*) 1672. 4. To emasculate, castrate 1684. 5. To remove the men from (a vessel or fleet) 1687.

2. Habits of Vice u. Men's minds 1701. 3. The sight of her unmans me ADDISON. 5. He could not venture to u. his Fleet NELSON.

Unma·nacle *v.* [UN-[2] 2 b] 1582. **Unma·nacled** *ppl. a.* [UN-[1] 2] 1726.

Unma·nageable, *a.* 1632. [UN-[1] 1.] 1. Not amenable to control; unruly, headstrong. 2. Incapable of being properly or conveniently handled or manipulated 1658.

1. That tough, lofty, u. Monarch [Henry VIII] 1728. Each fresh gambade of his u. horse SCOTT. 2. An index of an u. length 1779. Hence **Unma·nageableness.** **Unma·nageably** *adv.*

Unma·naged, *ppl. a. arch.* 1603. [UN-[1] 2.] Not well trained or disciplined; not controlled. b. Of language: Unrestrained, immoderate 1771.

b. Accusations, so heavy in the matter and u. in the epithets BURKE.

Unma·nfully *adv.* [UN-[1] 5] late ME. **Unma·ngled** *ppl. a.* [UN-[1] 2] 1557. **Unma·nifest** *a.* [UN-[1] 1] 1535. **Unma·nifested** *ppl. a.* [UN-[1] 2] 1683. **Unma·nlike** *a.* and *adv.* [UN-[1] 1, 5] 1579.

Unma·nly, *a.* 1475. [UN-[1] 1.] 1. Dishonourable or degrading to a man. 2. Womanish; effeminate; cowardly; poor-spirited 1547. So **Unma·nliness.** **Unma·nly** *adv.* late ME.

Unma·nned, *ppl. a.* 1544. [UN-[1] 2.] 1. Not furnished with men. 2. Unsupported; unassisted 1620. b. Without inhabitants 1680. 3. Not trained or broken in; *spec.* of a hawk. Now *rare.* 1592.

3. Like a wild Kestrell or vnmand Hawke 1623.

Unma·nnered, *ppl. a.* 1594. [UN-[1] 2.] 1. Not possessed of good manners; unmannerly, rude. 2. Of conduct: Characterized by want of manners 1760. †3. Free from mannerisms. LAMB.

1. Vnmanner'd Dogge, Stand'st thou when I command SHAKS.

Unma·nnerly, *a.* late ME. [UN-[1] 1.] 1. Of persons: Ill-bred; lacking manners; behaving rudely or discourteously. 2. Of actions, etc.: Showing want of manners. late ME. So **Unma·nnerliness.** **Unma·nnerly** *adv.* in an u. fashion ME.

Unma·ntle, *v.* 1598. [UN-[2] 2, 5.] 1. *trans.* To take off a mantle or a covering from. b. *intr.* To take off one's mantle 1822. 2. *trans.* To dismantle (a room, etc.) *rare.* 1828.

2. The Tapestried Chamber to be unmantled SCOTT.

Unma·ntled *ppl. a.* [UN-[1] 2] 1800. **Unmanufa·ctured** *ppl. a.* [UN-[1] 2] 1796.

Unmanu·red, *ppl. a.* 1570. [UN-[1] 2.] †1. Not tilled –1721. †b. *fig.* Of the mind, etc.: Untrained, uncultivated –1700. 2. Without manure 1828.

1. All rough and u. places 1578. b. It argueth an u. wit 1594.

Unma·pped *ppl. a.* [UN-[1] 2] 1805.

Unma·rked, *ppl. a.* late ME. [UN-[1] 2.] 1. Having received no mark or impress. b. Not marked off or out, not distinguished or characterized (*by* something) 1815. 2. Unobserved, unnoticed 1533.

1. *Maverick*, used in Texas to designate an u. yearling 1872. b. Virgil's characters are mostly cold, u., and not attaching 1815. 2. The hours..have stol'n unmark'd away AKENSIDE.

Unma·rketable *a.* [UN-[1] 1] 1654. **Unma·rred** *ppl. a.* [UN-[1] 2] ME. **Unma·rriageable** *a* [UN-[1] 1] 1775.

Unma·rried, *ppl. a.* ME. [UN-[1] 2.] Not married. 2. Lived without marriage 1648.

Unma·rry, *v.* 1530. [UN-[2] 1, 5.] 1. *trans.* To dissolve the marriage of; to divorce. b. To put away (a wife) 1645. 2. *intr.* To free oneself from marriage 1635.

1. I did marry you;..I would there were a parson to u. us! 1637. b. Though he did not live with her, he could not u. her 1797. 2. We are unmarrying among the great; the Duke of Grafton's divorce was finished this morning 1769.

Unma·rtyred *ppl. a.* [UN-[1] 2] 1580. **Unma·sculine** *a.* [UN-[1] 1] MILT.

Unma·sk, *v.* 1586. [UN-[2] 2, 5.] 1. *trans.* To remove a mask or covering from (the face, a masked person, etc.). 2. *fig.* To strip of disguise; to disclose the real nature of; to bring into the light 1593. 3. *absol.* To take off one's mask 1603. b. *fig.* To reveal one's true character 1622. 4. *Mil.* To reveal the presence (of a gun or battery) by opening fire 1747. b. To make patent; to show plainly 1816.

1. If she vnmaske her beauty to the Moone SHAKS. 2. The true God hath vnmasked the errors of those times 1611. 4. The Chinese, unmasking a mountain gun, fired on the Bayard 1884. b. With a view of making the Afghan commandant..u. his force 1879. Hence **Unma·sked** *ppl. a.* **Unma·sking** *vbl. sb.*

Unma·stered *ppl. a.* [UN-[1] 2] 1561. **Unma·sticated** *ppl. a.* [UN-[1] 2] 1815. **Unma·tchable** *a.* [UN-[1] 1] 1544, **-bly** *adv.*

Unma·tched, *ppl. a.* 1581. [UN-[1] 2.] 1. Having no equal; matchless; unrivalled. 2. Not provided with something equal or alike 1645.

2. Old-fashioned u. chairs 1824.

Unma·ted *ppl. a.* [UN-[1] 2] 1614. **Unmate·rial** *a.* [UN-[1] 1] late ME. **Unmate·rnal** *a.* [UN-[1] 1] 1821. **Unmathema·tical** *a.* [UN-[1] 1] 1720, **-ly** *adv.*

Unmea·ning, *ppl. a.* 1704. [UN-[1] 4.] 1. Of features, etc.: Expressionless, vacant. b. Of persons: Having no serious aim or purpose 1746. 2. Having no meaning or significance; meaningless 1709. Hence **Unmea·ningly** *adv.*

Unmea·nt *ppl. a.* [UN-[1] 2] 1634. **Unmea·surable** *a.* [UN-[1] 1] late ME. **Unmea·surably** *adv.* (now *rare*) [UN-[1] 5] late ME.

Unmea·sured, *ppl. a.* late ME. [UN-[1] 2.] 1. Not limited or known by measurement; immense in size, extent, or amount. 2. Not composed of measured syllables 1715. 3. Immoderate, unrestrained 1820.

1. Gods vnmesured bountee 1450. Along th' unmeasur'd shore CHAPMAN. Of an u. fluid, we can only reason by conjecture 1794. 2. A kind of u. Poetry 1728. 3. The u. eulogies he bestows upon him 1839.

Unmecha·nical *a.* [UN-[1] 1] 1674, **-ly** *adv.* **Unme·chanize** *v.* [UN-[2] 4 c] 1687. **Unme·ddled** *ppl. a.* [UN-[1] 2] late ME. **Unme·ddling** *ppl. a.* [UN-[1] 4] 1765. **Unme·ditated** *ppl. a.* [UN-[1] 2] 1624. **Unme·ditative** *a.* [UN-[1] 1] 1842. **Unmee·k** *a.* (*arch.*) [UN-[1] 1] ME.

Unmee·t, *a.* [OE. *unmǣte*, f. UN-[1] 1 + MEET *a.*] †1. Immoderate or excessive in amount or size –1475. †2. Unequal; unevenly matched –1760. 3. Unbecoming, improper 1529. 4. Unfit or unsuited for some end or purpose 1513.

2. Litle Iulus..With wnmeit paiss his fader fast followand 1513. 3. While they contending were with words u. HOBBES. Christ thought..a ship no u. place to preach in 1703. 4. The lot fell oft vpon the vnmeetest 1598. The Pastor is the unmeetest person to meddle in it BAXTER. Mr. Blair was now infirm and u. for travel 1676. Hence **Unmee·t-ly** *adv.*, **-ness.**

Unme·llowed *ppl. a.* [UN-[1] 2] 1573. **Unmelo·dious** *a.* [UN-[1] 1] 1665, **-ly** *adv.* **Unme·lted** *ppl. a.* [UN-[1] 2] 1549. **Unme·lting** *ppl. a.* [UN-[1] 4] 1743. **Unme·morable** *a.* [UN-[1] 1] 1598. **Unme·naced** *ppl. a.* [UN-[1] 2] 1821. **Unme·ndable** *a.* [UN-[1] 1] 1584. **Unme·nded** *ppl. a.* [UN-[1] 2] 1880.

Unme·ntionable, *a.* and *sb.* 1830. [UN-[1] 1.] A. *adj.* Not fit to be mentioned; too scandalous, disgusting, etc., for mention 1837. B. *sb. pl.* Trousers 1830.

Hence **Unme·ntionably** *adv.*

With an unmentionably vulgar oath W. COLLINS.

Unme·ntioned *ppl. a.* [Un-[1] 2] 1545. **Unme·rcenary** *a.* [Un-[1] 1] 1643. **Unme·rchantable** *a.* [Un-[1] 1] 1602. **Unme·rciful** *a.* [Un-[1] 1] 1481, -ly *adv.*, -ness.

Unme·ritable, *a.* Now *rare.* 1594. [Un-[1] 1.] Of no merit.

This is a slight vnmeritable man Shaks.

Unme·rited *ppl. a.* [Un-[1] 2] 1648, -ly *adv.*, -ness. **Unme·riting** *ppl. a.* [Un-[1] 4] 1594. **Unmerito·rious** *a.* [Un-[1] 1] 1855, -ly *adv.* **Unme·rry** *a.* (now *rare*) [Un-[1] 1] OE. **Unme·sh** *v.* [Un-[2] 2 b] 1822. **Unme·t** *ppl. a.* [Un-[1] 2] 1603. **Unme·talled** *ppl. a.* [Un-[1] 2] 1843. **Unmeta·llic** *a.* [Un-[1] 1] 1757. **Unmetamo·rphosed** *ppl. a.* [Un-[1] 2] 1600. **Unmetaphy·sical** *a.* [Un-[1] 1] 1691. **Unmetho·dical** *a.* [Un-[1] 1] 1601, -ly *adv.* **Unme·thodized** *ppl. a.* [Un-[1] 2] 1677. **Unme·trical** *a.* [Un-[1] 1] 1791. **Unmew·** *v.* (*rare*) [Un-[2] 3] Keats. **Unmi·ghty** *a.* (*arch.*) [Un-[1] 1] OE.

Unmi·litary, *a.* 1777. [Un-[1] 1.] **1.** Not in accordance with military practice or standards. **2.** That is not a soldier, not belonging to the army. **b.** Of nations, etc.: Averse, or not prone, to soldiering. 1802.

1. Defence—the very word is u. 1806.

Unmi·lked *ppl. a.* [Un-[1] 2] 1648. **Unmi·lled** *ppl. a.* [Un-[1] 2] 1555. **Unmi·nded** *ppl. a.* [Un-[1] 2] 1513.

Unmi·ndful, *a.* late ME. [Un-[1] 1.] Not bearing something in mind; forgetful or oblivious *of* something; careless, heedless.

Dull vnmindfull Villaine, Why stay'st thou here? Shaks. Careless of Night, u. to return Dryden. Every person was willing to save himself, u. of others Goldsm.

Unmi·ngled *ppl. a.* [Un-[1] 2] 1548. **Unmi·nished** *ppl. a.* (*arch.*) [Un-[1] 2] 1533. **Unministe·rial** *a.* [Un-[1] 1] 1727. **Unmi·nted** *ppl. a.* [Un-[1] 2] 1611. **Unmira·culous** *a.* [Un-[1] 1] 1746. **Unmi·rthful** *a.* [Un-[1] 1] 1815, -ly *adv.* **Unmisgi·ving** *ppl. a.* [Un-[1] 4] 1693, -ly *adv.* **Unmi·ssed** *ppl. a.* [Un-[1] 2] late ME. **Unmista·kable** *a.* [Un-[1] 1] 1666, -ness, -bly *adv.* **Unmistru·sting** *ppl. a.* [Un-[1] 4] 1598. **Unmi·tigable** *a.* [Un-[1] 1] Shaks., -bly *adv.*

Unmi·tigated, *ppl. a.* 1599. [Un-[1] 2.] **1.** Not softened in respect of severity or intensity. **2.** Not modified or toned down; absolute 1840.

1. The u. glare of day Jane Austen. 2. An u. fib C. Bronte. An u. humbug 1860. Hence **Unmi·tigatedly** *adv.*

Unmi·tred *ppl. a.* [Un-[1] 2] 1688. **Unmi·x** *v.* [Un-[2] 1] 1558. **Unmi·xed** *ppl. a.* [Un-[1] 2] 1526, -ly *adv.*, -ness. **Unmo·cked** *ppl. a.* [Un-[1] 2] 1648. **Unmo·dern** *a.* [Un-[1] 1] 1757. **Unmo·dernized** *ppl. a.* [Un-[1] 2] Jane Austen. **Unmo·difiable** *a.* [Un-[1] 1] 1825. **Unmo·dified** *ppl. a.* [Un-[1] 2] Burke. **Unmo·dish** *a.* (*arch.*) [Un-[1] 1] 1665. **Unmo·dulated** *ppl. a.* [Un-[1] 2] Jane Austen. **Unmoi·st** *a.* [Un-[1] 1] 1611. **Unmoi·stened** *ppl. a.* [Un-[1] 2] 1625. **Unmole·sted** *ppl. a.* [Un-[1] 2] 1531, -ly *adv.* **Unmo·lten** *ppl. a.* [Un-[1] 2] 1525. **Unmo·narch** *v.* [Un-[2] 4 b] 1667. **Unmo·neyed** *ppl. a.* [Un-[1] 2] 1677.

Unmoo·r, *v.* 1497. [Un-[2] 2 b.] *Naut.* **1.** *trans.* To free from moorings; *spec.* to reduce the moorings of (a ship) till she rides by a single anchor. **2.** *intr.* To cast off moorings 1611.

1. They lye Unmored, and ride single, and intend to Sail 1681. 2. The next Morning we unmoor'd..and at Six weigh'd 1745.

Unmo·ral, *a.* 1841. [Un-[1] 1.] Non-moral; not influenced by, or connected with, moral considerations.

The Lower animism is not immoral, it is u. Tylor. So **Unmora·lity.**

Unmo·ralized *ppl. a.* [Un-[1] 2] 1668. **Unmo·rtared** *ppl. a.* [Un-[1] 2] 1656. **Unmo·rtgaged** *ppl. a.* [Un-[1] 2] 1638. **Unmo·rtified** *ppl. a.* [Un-[1] 2] 1450. **Unmo·thered** *ppl. a.* [Un-[1] 2] 1607. **Unmo·therly** *a.* [Un-[1] 1] 1593. **Unmo·tived** *ppl. a.* [Un-[1] 2] Coleridge.

Unmou·ld, *v.* 1611. [Un-[2] 1, 3, 5.] **1.** *trans.* To destroy the mould or form of. **b.** To take out of a mould 1900. **2.** *intr.* or *absol.* To lose form or shape 1834.

1. His baneful cup..unmoulding reasons mintage Character'd in the face Milt.

Unmou·lded *ppl. a.* [Un-[1] 2] 1620.

Unmou·nt, *v.* 1680. [Un-[2] 1, 6.] **1.** *trans.* To remove from a mount; to unfix and take down. **2.** To dismount. Also *intr.* (*rare.*) 1787.

2. The German Emperor has had to u. his high horse 1892.

Unmou·nted, *ppl. a.* 1592. [Un-[1] 2.] **1.** Not provided with or riding on a horse or horses. **2.** Of cannon: Not on carriages 1627. **3.** Of specimens, pictures, etc.: Not mounted; not provided with a mount or mounts 1888.

Unmou·rned *ppl. a.* [Un-[1] 2] 1650. **Unmo·vable** *a.* (now *rare*) [Un-[1] 1] late ME., -ness, -bly *adv.*

Unmo·ved, *ppl. a.* late ME. [Un-[1] 2.] **1.** Unaffected by emotion or excitement; collected, undisturbed; calm, steadfast. **2.** Not moved in position; remaining fixed or steady 1440.

1. He found the Duke u. by all the considerations and arguments..he had offered Clarendon. My soul is still the same, U. with fear Dryden. Hence **Unmo·vedly** *adv.*

Unmo·ving *ppl. a.* [Un-[1] 4] late ME., -ly *adv.* **Unmow·n** *ppl. a.* [Un-[1] 2] 1549. **Unmu·ffle** *v.* [Un-[2] 2] 1611. **Unmu·rdered** *ppl. a.* [Un-[1] 2] 1586. **Unmu·rmuring** *ppl. a.* [Un-[1] 4] 1784, -ly *adv.*

Unmu·sical, *a.* 1607. [Un-[1] 1.] **1.** Of sounds: Not musical; unmelodious, harsh. **2.** Of persons: Not appreciative of or not expert in music 1634. **3.** Not based on musical principles 1786.

1. A name vnmusicall to the Volcians eares Shaks. His voice was singularly u. 1880. 2. The u. admired her singing 1896. Hence **Unmu·sically** *adv.*

Unmu·tilated *ppl. a.* [Un-[1] 2] 1790. **Unmu·zzle** *v.* [Un-[2] 2 b] 1600. **Unmu·zzled** *ppl. a.* [Un-[1] 2] Shaks. **Unmyste·rious** *a.* [Un-[1] 1] 1746.

Unnai·l, *v.* 1470. [Un-[2] 1.] **1.** *trans.* To extract the nails or rivets from; to undo or unfasten thus. **2.** To detach by the removal of nails 1598.

1. They made all y[e] bridge to be vnnayled, redy to be broken downe Ld. Berners. Caus'd the Coffin to be unnail'd again 1704. 2. Whiles Joseph of Arimathea and Nicodemus un-nail our Lord Evelyn.

Unna·m(e)able, *a.* 1610. [Un-[1] 1.] That cannot be named.

God is celestiall, ineffable, and un-name-able 1610. Her lustrous eyes wide distended with unnamable horror 1874.

Unna·med, *ppl. a.* 1509. [Un-[1] 2.] **1.** Not mentioned or specified by name. **2.** Having no name 1611. **b.** *U. bone*, the Innominate bone 1845.

1. Throwing the burden..on some u. third person Meredith. 2. Flowers of u. colours bright Morris.

Unna·tional *a.* [Un-[1] 1] 1753. **Unna·tive** *a.* [Un-[1] 1] 1712.

Unna·tural, *a.* late ME. [Un-[1] 1.] **1.** Not in accordance with the physical nature of persons or animals. **2.** Not in accordance with the usual course of nature 1513. **b.** Monstrous, abnormal 1516. **c.** Devoid of natural qualities or characteristics; artificial 1746. **3.** Outraging natural feeling or moral standards, monstrously cruel or wicked 1529. **4.** At variance with what is natural, usual, or expected; unusual, strange 1586.

1. The tones of their voice sounded..hollow, hoarse, and u. 1846. 2. c. Timid, stiff, u., and ill at ease Lytton. 3. As vnnatural as children that seek the ruin of their parents 1685. In yon fatal apartment incest and u. murder were committed Scott. 4. It is u. for any one in a gust of passion to speak long together Dryden. Hence **Unna·tural-ly** *adv.*, -ness.

Unna·turalism [Un-[1] 6] 1754. **Unnatura·lity** (*rare*) [Un-[1] 6] 1548.

Unna·turalize, *v.* 1613. [Un-[2] 4 c.] **1.** *trans.* To change the nature of; to deprive of natural character; to make unnatural. **2.** To deprive of the status or privileges of a native-born subject 1698. **3.** To make unnatural or artificial 1741.

1. It may..u. the incidents Richardson.

Unna·turalized *ppl. a.* [Un-[1] 2] 1611. **Unna·ture** *sb.* (*rare*) [Un-[1] 6] 1843. **Unna·ture** *v.* [Un-[2] 4 b] 1586. **Unnau·tical** *a.* [Un-[1] 1] 1852. **Unna·vigable** *a.* [Un-[1] 1] 1579. **Unna·vigated** *ppl. a.* [Un-[1] 2] 1777. **Unnea·t** *a.* [Un-[1] 1] 1648.

Unne·cessary, *a.* and *sb.* 1548. [Un-[1] 1, 6.] **A.** *adj.* **1.** Not necessary or requisite; needless. **b.** With *it* (etc.) as subj., and usu. const. *to* with inf. 1597. †**2.** Not requiring much. Shaks.

1. From a nice, u. scruple Swift. Addicted to u. haste 1898. b. It is u. to pursue the argument any farther *Junius Lett.*

B. *sb. pl.* Unnecessary things 1559.

The unnecessaries of life 1881. Hence **Unne·cessarily** *adv.* **Unne·cessariness.**

Unnece·ssitated *ppl. a.* [Un-[1] 2] 1635. **Unnee·ded** *ppl. a.* [Un-[1] 2] 1844. **Unnee·dful** *a.* [Un-[1] 1] late ME., -ly *adv.* **Unnei·ghboured** *ppl. a.* [Un-[1] 2] 1657. **Unnei·ghbourly** *a.* and *adv.* [Un-[1] 1, 5] 1583.

Unne·rve, *v.* 1621. [Un-[2] 1.] **1.** *trans.* To destroy the strength of; to enfeeble, weaken. **2.** To deprive (the mind, etc., or a person) of courage or energy; to render incapable of acting with ordinary firmness or energy 1704.

1. Pale sudden feare vn-nerves his quaking thighs 1621. The Precepts..weaken and un-nerve his Verse Addison. 2. The fear..completely unnerved the Romans 1878. Hence **Unne·rved, Unne·rving** *ppl. adjs.*

Unne·st *v.* (chiefly *fig.*) [Un-[2] 3] late ME. †**Unne·stle** *v.* [Un-[2] 1] -1694. **Unne·tted** *ppl. a.* [Un-[1] 2] 1833. **Unneu·tralized** *ppl. a.* [Un-[1] 2] 1758. **Unni·mble** *a.* (now *rare*) [Un-[1] 1] 1566.

Unno·ble, *a.* late ME. [Un-[1] 1.] **1.** Not of noble birth or high rank. **2.** Without magnanimity or generosity; mean, base, ignoble *arch.* 1566.

1. The noble men bare a garment vnlyke to them that were vnnoble Caxton. It is an almost universal weakness of the u. in England to parade an acquaintance with the noble 1832.

Unno·table *a.* [Un-[1] 1] 1528. **Unno·tched** *ppl. a.* [Un-[1] 2] 1811.

Unno·ted, *ppl. a.* 1563. [Un-[1] 2.] **1.** Not noticed or observed; unmarked. **2.** Not specially noticed or observed; obscure, undistinguished 1592.

Unno·ticeable *a.* [Un-[1] 1] 1775, -ness, -bly *adv.* **Unno·ticed** *ppl. a.* [Un-[1] 2] 1720. **Unno·ticing** *ppl. a.* [Un-[1] 4] 1782. **Unno·tified** *ppl. a.* [Un-[1] 2] 1802. **Unnou·rishing** *ppl. a.* [Un-[1] 4] 1605. **Unnu·mberable** *a.* (now *rare*) [Un-[1] 1] ME.

Unnu·mbered, *ppl. a.* late ME. [Un-[1] 2.] **1.** Not numbered or reckoned up; countless. **2.** Not marked with or identified by a number or numbers 1533.

1. The Skies are painted with vnnumbred sparkes Shaks. 2. I have receaved yours (unnumbred) of the 8th of Dec. 1654.

Unnu·rsed *ppl. a.* [Un-[1] 2] 1875. **Unnu·rtured** *ppl. a.* [Un-[1] 2] 1548. **Unobe·dient** *a.* [Un-[1] 1] Wyclif. **Unobey·ed** *ppl. a.* [Un-[1] 2] 1595. **Unobje·cted** (*to*) *ppl. a.* [Un-[1] 2] Atterbury. **Unobje·ctionable** *a.* [Un-[1] 1] 1793, -ness, -bly *adv.* **Unobli·ged** *ppl. a.* [Un-[1] 2] 1648. **Unobli·terated** *ppl. a.* [Un-[1] 2] 1644.

Unobno·xious, *a.* 1609. [Un-[1] 1.] **1.** Not exposed or liable *to* something. **2.** Not objectionable or offensive 1678.

1. Unwearied, u. to be pain'd By wound Milt. The soul is..u. to error 1862.

Unobscu·red *ppl. a.* [Un-[1] 2] 1646. **Unobse·rvable** *a.* [Un-[1] 1] Hobbes. **Unobse·rvance** [Un-[1] 6] 1654. **Unobse·rvant** *a.* [Un-[1] 1] 1661, -ly *adv.* **Unobse·rved** *ppl. a.* [Un-[1] 2] 1612, -ly *adv.* **Unobse·rving** *ppl. a.* [Un-[1] 4] 1690. **Unobstru·cted** *ppl. a.* [Un-[1] 2] 1659, -ly *adv.* **Unobtai·nable** *a.* [Un-[1] 1] 1860. **Unobtai·ned** *ppl. a.* [Un-[1] 2] 1594. **Unobtru·sive** *a.* [Un-[1] 1] 1743, -ly *adv.*, -ness. **Uno·bvious** *a.* [Un-[1] 1] 1643.

Uno·ccupied, *ppl. a.* late ME. [Un-[1] 2.] **1.** Not occupied or engaged in some work or pursuit; at leisure. **2.** Not put to use; left idle. (In later use only of time) 1448. **3.** Without occupants or users; uninhabited, untilled, unfrequented. late ME. **b.** Not taken up or appropriated 1701.

1. She led a blameless, u., and apparently purposeless life 1898. 2. They..loste theyr puissaunce and brightnesse, lyke yron vnoccupied 1561. 3. The hye wayes were vnoccupied Bible (1560) *Judges* v. 6. Not an inch of ground lies waste and u. 1807. b. Leaving the ear u. for any measure which may follow 1832.

Unoffe·nded *ppl. a.* [Un-[1] 2] 1481, -ly *adv.* **Unoffe·nding** *ppl. a.* [Un-[1] 4] 1569. **Uno·ffered** *ppl. a.* [Un-[1] 2] 1526. **Uno·fficered** *ppl. a.* [Un-[1] 2] 1655. **Uno·fficerlike** *a.* [Un-[1] 1] 1803.

Unoffi·cial, *a.* 1798. [Un-[1] 1.] **1.** Not having an official character or stamp. **2.** Of persons: Not holding an official position; not acting in an official capacity 1829. Hence **Unoffi·cially** *adv.*

Unoffi·cious *a.* [UN-1 1] 1611. **Uno·ften** *adv.* [UN-1 5] 1741. **Unoi·led** *ppl. a.* [UN-1 2] 1728. **Uno·pened** *ppl. a.* [UN-1 2] 1600. (Cf. UNCUT *ppl. a.* 4 a.) **Unoppo·sed** *ppl. a.* [UN-1 2] 1659. **Unoppre·ssed** *ppl. a.* [UN-1 2] 1572. **Unoppre·ssive** *a.* [UN-1 1] 1648, **-ly**, *adv.*

Unordai·ned, *ppl. a.* ME. [UN-1 2.] †1. Not controlled. ME. only. 2. Not ecclesiastically ordained 1653. 3. Not appointed or decreed 1815.

Uno·rder *v.* [UN-2 1] 1440.

Uno·rdered, *ppl. a.* late ME. [UN-1 2.] †1. Not belonging to a religious order; not in ecclesiastical orders –1607. 2. Not put in order 1477. †3. Disorderly, uncontrolled –1611. 4. Not ordered or bespoken 1891.

1. Wedded or sengle, ordered or unordred,..clerk or seculeer CHAUCER. 2. Those various and u. ideas 1877. 3. The vnordred appetites of the body 1611.

Uno·rderly *a.* (now *rare*) [UN-1 1] 1483; *adv.* [UN-1 5] 1470. **Uno·rdinary** *a.* [UN-1 1] 1547.

Uno·rganized, *ppl. a.* 1690. [UN-1 2.] 1. Inorganic, not possessed of organs or life. 2. Not formed into an orderly whole 1836.

1. To me it seems that stones are vegetables u. BERKELEY. 2. The u. valour of the English nation 1836.

Unori·ginal, *a.* 1667. [UN-1 1.] †1. Without origin; uncreated. MILT. 2. Not original; derivative; borrowed or plagiarized 1774.

1. U. Night and Chaos wilde MILT. 2. The 'Song of Roland' is comparatively late and u. 1897. Hence **Unorigina·lity.**

Unori·ginate, *a.* and *sb.* 1719. [UN-1 2.] A. *adj.* Self-existent; without origin; not created.

One spirit,..self-existent, u., the first cause of the universe 1755.

B. *sb.* An u. being 1724. Hence **Unori·ginately** *adv.*, **-ness.**

Unori·ginated *ppl. a.* [UN-1 2] 1696. **Unorname·ntal** *a.* [UN-1 1] 1747. **Unorname·nted** *ppl. a.* [UN-1 2] 1697. **Uno·rthodox** *a.* [UN-1 1] 1657. **Uno·rthodoxy** [UN-1 6] 1704. **Uno·ssified** *ppl. a.* [UN-1 2] 1726. **Unostenta·tious** *a.* [UN-1 1] 1747, **-ly** *adv.* **Unoverco·me** *ppl. a.* [UN-1 2] late ME. **Unoverthrow·n** *ppl. a.* [UN-1 2] 1535.

Unow·ned, *ppl. a.* 1611. [UN-1 2.] 1. Not possessed as property; having no owner. 2. Unacknowledged; unadmitted 1715.

Uno·xidized *ppl. a.* [UN-1 2] 1827. **Unoxy·genated** *ppl. a.* [UN-1 2] 1790. **Unpaci·fic** *a.* [UN-1 1] 1774. **Unpa·cified** *ppl. a.* [UN-1 2] 1570.

Unpa·ck, *v.* 1472. [UN-2 1, 3.] 1. *trans.* To undo or open (a bale, luggage, etc.) and remove or release the contents. 2. To take (something) out of a pack or packing 1598. b. *refl.* or *pass.* To get one's furniture, luggage, etc., unpacked 1791. c. *absol.* To undo things from a packed state 1837. 3. To unload (a pack-horse, cart, etc.) 1570.

1. *fig.* That I..Must..vnpacke my heart with words SHAKS. 2. *transf.* A red-haired man..had unpacked himself from a cab DICKENS. 3. His first care was to u. his horses W. IRVING.

Unpa·cked *ppl. a.* [UN-1 2] 1495. **Unpa·dlocked** *ppl. a.* [UN-1 2] 1681. **Unpa·ged** *ppl. a.* [UN-1 2] 1874.

Unpai·d, *ppl. a.* late ME. [UN-1 2.] 1. To whom payment has not been made; not receiving payment. 2. Not met or cleared off by payment, undischarged; not handed over or given in payment. late ME. b. Not rendered or discharged 1611. 3. Not paid *for*. Also without prep. 1465.

1. Whilst thy unpay'd Musicians, Crickets, sing LOVELACE. Phr. *The* (*Great*) *U.*, the class of u. magistrates or judges. 2. She remembers she has u. bills 1887. *fig.* Coming to receive from us Knee-tribute yet u. MILT. b. What can atone..Thy fate unpity'd, and thy rites u.? POPE. 3. Rustling in vnpayd-for Silke SHAKS. Letters posted u. are charged double postage 1886.

Unpai·ned *ppl. a.* [UN-1 2] WYCLIF. **Unpai·nful** *a.* [UN-1 1] 1570, **-ly** *adv.* **Unpai·nt** *v.* [UN-2 2] 1611. **Unpai·ntable** *a.* [UN-1 1]. 1849. **Unpai·nted** *ppl. a.* [UN-1 2] 1555. **Unpai·red** *ppl. a.* [UN-1 2] 1648.

Unpa·latable, *a.* 1682. [UN-1 1.] 1. Not agreeable to the palate. 2. Unpleasant, distasteful, disagreeable 1711.

Unpa·lled *ppl. a.* [UN-1 2] 1770. **Unpa·lliated** *ppl. a.* [UN-1 2] 1798. **Unpa·lpable** *a.* (now *rare*) [UN-1 1] 1538. **Unpa·mpered** *ppl. a.* [UN-1 2] 1794. **Unpa·nelled** *ppl. a.* [UN-1 2] 1883. **Unpa·per** *v.* [UN-2 2] 1714. **Unpa·pered** *ppl. a.* [UN-1 2] 1851.

Unpa·radise, *v.* 1592. [UN-2 1, 4 b.] 1. *trans.* To expel from Paradise. 2. To deprive of the character of Paradise 1647.

Unpa·ragoned *ppl. a.* [UN-1 2] 1611. **Unpa·rallel** *a.* [UN-1 1] 1652. **Unpa·rallelable** *a.* [UN-1 1] 1640.

Unpa·ralleled, *ppl. a.* 1594. [UN-1 2.] That has no parallel or equal, unmatched. Hence **Unpa·ralleled·ly** *adv.*, **-ness.**

Unpa·ralyzed *ppl. a.* [UN-1 2] 1846. **Unpa·rcelled** *ppl. a.* [UN-1 2] 1840. **Unpa·rdonable** *a.* [UN-1 1] 1525, **-ness, -bly** *adv.* **Unpa·rdoned** *ppl. a.* [UN-1 2] 1565. **Unpa·rdoning** *ppl. a.* [UN-1 4] MILT. **Unpa·red** *ppl. a.* [UN-1 2] ME. **Unpa·rented** *ppl. a.* [UN-1 2, UN-2 6] 1650.

U·nparliame·ntary, *a.* 1626. [UN-1 1.] Not suitable or belonging to Parliament; unsanctioned by Parliament; transgressing parliamentary rules; applied esp. to discourteous language in debate.

I am come here to shew you your..u. proceedings in this Parliament JAS. I. All U. raising of Mony upon the Subjects HOBBES. A member had used u. language 1810. Hence **U·nparliame·ntarily** *adv.*

Unpa·rriable *a.* [UN-1 1] SCOTT. **Unpa·rted** *ppl. a.* [UN-1 2] 1561. **Unpa·rtial** *a.* (now *rare*) [UN-1 1] 1579. **Unparti·cipated** *ppl. a.* [UN-1 2] 1678. **Unparti·cipating** *ppl. a.* [UN-1 4] 1795. **Unparti·cularized** *ppl. a.* [UN-1 2] 1823. **Unpa·ssable** *a.* [UN-1 1] 1553. **Unpa·ssed** *ppl. a.* [UN-1 2] 1541. **Unpa·ssionate** *a.* [UN-1 1] 1593, **-ly** *adv.*, **-ness.** **Unpa·ssioned** *ppl. a.* [UN-1 2] 1618. **Unpa·storal** *a.* [UN-1 1] 1782. **Unpa·stured** *ppl. a.* [UN-1 2] 1548. **Unpa·tented** *ppl. a.* [UN-1 2] 1719. **Unpa·thed** *ppl. a.* [UN-1 2] SHAKS. **Unpathe·tic** *a.* [UN-1 1] 1782. **Unpatrio·tic** *a.* [UN-1 1] 1828, **-ally** *adv.* 1783. **Unpa·tronized** *ppl. a.* [UN-1 2] 1620.

Unpa·tterned, *ppl. a.* 1621. [UN-1 2.] 1. Unexampled, unequalled. *arch.* 2. Not decorated with a pattern 1884.

Unpau·sing *ppl. a.* [UN-1 4] 1837. **Unpa·ve** *v.* [UN-2 2] 1598. **Unpa·ved** *ppl. a.* [UN-1 2] 1533. **Unpavi·lioned** *a.* [UN-1 3] SHELLEY. **Unpa·wned** *ppl. a.* [UN-1 2] 1638. **Unpay·able** *a.* [UN-1 1] 1463. **Unpay·ing** *ppl. a.* [UN-1 4] 1682. **Unpea·ce** (*arch.*) [UN-1 6] ME. **Unpea·ceable** *a.* (now *rare*) [UN-1 1] 1520, **-ness,** 1475, **-bly** *adv.* **Unpea·ceful** *a.* [UN-1 1] 1611. **Unpeda·ntic** *a.* [UN-1 1] 1796. **Unpe·destal** *v.* [UN-2 3] 1821. **Unpe·digreed** *ppl. a.* [UN-1 2] 1827. **Unpee·led** *ppl. a.* [UN-1 2] 1599. **Unpee·red** *ppl. a.* (*arch.*) [UN-1 2] 1602. **Unpe·g** *v.* [UN-2 2 b] SHAKS. **Unpe·n** *v.* [UN-2 3] 1592. **Unpe·netrated** *ppl. a.* [UN-1 2] 1781. **Unpe·nitent** *a.* (now *rare*) [UN-1 1] 1546. **Unpe·nsioned** *ppl. a.* [UN-1 2] POPE. **Unpe·nt** *ppl. a.* [UN-1 2] SHELLEY. **Unpeo·ple** *v.* [UN-2 2] 1533. **Unpeo·pled** *ppl. a.* [UN-1 2] 1586. **Unpercei·vable** *a.* [UN-1 1] late ME., **-bly** *adv.* **Unpercei·ved** *ppl. a.* [UN-1 2] ME., **-ly** *adv.* **Unpercei·ving** *ppl. a.* [UN-1 4] 1723. **Unperce·ptive** *a.* [UN-1 1] 1668.

Unpe·rch, *v.* 1579. [UN-2 3.] *trans.* To dislodge from a perch.

Either rowse the Deer, or vnpearch the Phesant LYLY. If he but offers to tune his note contrary to the true Dialect of State he is straight unperched 1659.

†**Unpe·rfect** *a.* [UN-1 1] –1858. **Unpe·rfected** *ppl. a.* [UN-1 2] 1513. **Unpe·rforated** *ppl. a.* [UN-1 2] 1676. **Unperfo·rmed** *ppl. a.* [UN-1 2] 1442. **Unperfo·rming** *ppl. a.* [UN-1 4] 1670. **Unperfumed** *ppl. a.* [UN-1 2] 1706. **Unpe·rilous** *a.* [UN-1 1] 1621. **Unpe·rishable** *a.* (now *rare*) [UN-1 1] 1548. **Unpe·rished** *ppl. a.* [UN-1 2] late ME. **Unpe·rishing** *ppl. a.* [UN-1 4] 1561. **Unpe·rmanent** *a.* [UN-1 1] 1630. **Unpermi·tted** *ppl. a.* [UN-1 2] 1598. **Unperple·x** *v.* [UN-2 1] 1631.

Unperple·xed, *ppl. a.* 1558. [UN-1 2.] 1. Not puzzled or made uncertain. 2. Not involved or intricate 1653.

2. That good, plain, unperplext Catechism, that is printed with the old service book WALTON.

Unpe·rsecuted *ppl. a.* [UN-1 2] MILT. **Unpersua·dable** *a.* [UN-1 1] 1586, **-ness.** **Unpersua·ded** *ppl. a.* [UN-1 2] 1534. **Unpersua·sive** *a.* [UN-1 1] RICHARDSON, **-ly** *adv.* **Unpertu·rbed** *ppl. a.* [UN-1 2] late ME., **-ness.** **Unperve·rted** *ppl. a.* [UN-1 2] 1653. **Unpe·stered** *ppl. a.* [UN-1 2] 1588. **U·nphiloso·phical** *a.* [UN-1 1] MILT., **-ly** *adv.* **Unphone·tic** *a.* [UN-1 1] 1857. **Unphra·sed** *ppl. a.* [UN-1 2] 1663. **Unphy·sical** *a.* [UN-1 1] 1593. **Unphy·sicked** *ppl. a.* [UN-1 2] 1596.

Unpi·ck, *v.* late ME. [UN-2 7.] †1. *trans.* To pick (a lock); to open (a door, etc.) in this way –1661. 2. To take out (stitches); to undo the sewing of (a seam, garment, etc.) 1809.

Unpi·ckable *a.* [UN-1 1] 1612. **Unpi·cked** *ppl. a.* [UN-1 2] 1587. **Unpi·cketed** *ppl. a.* [UN-1 2] 1860. **U·npicture·sque** *a.* [UN-1 1] 1791, **-ly** *adv.*, **-ness.** **Unpie·rceable** *a.* [UN-1 1] 1600. **Unpie·rced** *ppl. a.* [UN-1 2] 1593.

Unpi·le, *v.* 1611. [UN-2 1, 3.] *trans.* To remove from a pile. b. Mil. *U. arms*, a command to detach rifles from stacks in which they are interlocked 1847.

Unpi·llowed *ppl. a.* [UN-1 2] MILT. **Unpi·loted** *ppl. a.* [UN-1 2] COLERIDGE.

Unpi·n, *v.* ME. [UN-2 1, 2.] 1. *trans.* To withdraw the pin or bolt of (a door). 2. To remove pins or pegs from; to unfasten or detach in this way 1611. 3. To undo the dress of (a person) by removing pins 1604. 4. To remove a pin or pins from (a garment, etc.); to detach by removing a pin or pins 1605.

1. Þe porter vnpynned þe ȝate LANGL. 2. When the upper part of the frame..is unpinned and removed 1825. 3. Mrs. Etoff, who had the honour to pin and u. the Lady Bellaston FIELDING. 4. She..began to u. her hood STEELE.

Unpi·nioned *ppl. a.* [UN-1 2] 1593. †**Unpi·teous** *a.* [UN-1 1] late ME., **-ly** *adv.* **Unpi·tiable** *a.* [UN-1 1] 1646. **Unpi·tied** *ppl. a.* [UN-1 2] SIDNEY. **Unpi·tiful** *a.* [UN-1 1] 1449, **-ly** *adv.* **Unpi·tying** *ppl. a.* [UN-1 4] DRAYTON, **-ly** *adv.* **Unpla·ce** *v.* (now *rare*) [UN-2 3] 1554.

Unpla·ced, *ppl. a.* 1512. [UN-1 2.] 1. Not assigned to, or set in, a definite place. b. *Racing.* Not among the placed competitors 1881. 2. Not appointed to a place or office 1558.

Unpla·gued *ppl. a.* [UN-1 2] 1550. **Unplai·t** *v.* [UN-2 1] CHAUCER. **Unplai·ted** *ppl. a.* [UN-1 2] 1659. **Unpla·ned** *ppl. a.* [UN-1 2] 1810. **Unpla·nted** *ppl. a.* [UN-1 2] late ME. **Unpla·stered** *ppl. a.* [UN-1 2] 1648. **Unplau·sible** *a.* [UN-1 1] 1575, **-bly** *adv.* **Unplay·able** *a.* [UN-1 1] 1833. **Unplay·ed** *ppl. a.* [UN-1 2] 1850. **Unplea·dable** *a.* [UN-1 1] 1716.

Unplea·sant, *a.* 1535. [UN-1 1.] 1. Not pleasant, disagreeable: a. To the senses 1538. b. To the mind or feelings 1535. 2. Unentertaining, unfacetious 1712. 3. Unamiable 1654.

1. Flies prefer u. smells 1879. b. Tho' your Majesty permitts me to wryte even on ane u. subject 1721. A commission which would require them to deliver many u. truths 1839. Hence **Unplea·santly** *adv.*

Unplea·santness. 1548. [UN-1 6.] The quality of being unpleasant. b. Ill-feeling or unpleasant relations between persons; an instance of this 1830. So **Unplea·santry** 1830.

Unplea·sed *ppl. a.* (now *rare*) [UN-1 2] 1450. **Unplea·sing** *ppl. a.* [UN-1 4] 1480, **-ly** *adv.*, **-ness.** **Unplea·surable** *a.* [UN-1 1] 1768, **-bly** *adv.* **Unplea·ted** *ppl. a.* [UN-1 2] 1612. **Unple·dged** *ppl. a.* [UN-1 2] 1605. **Unpli·able** *a.* [UN-1 1] late ME., **-ness.** **Unpli·ancy** [UN-1 6] 1737. **Unpli·ant** *a.* [UN-1 1] 1624. **Unplou·ghed** *ppl. a.* [UN-1 2] 1580. **Unplu·cked** *ppl. a.* [UN-1 2] 1568. **Unplu·mbed** *ppl. a.* [UN-1 2] 1623. **Unplu·me** *v.* [UN-2 2] 1587. **Unplu·med** *ppl. a.* [UN-1 2] 1601. **Unplu·ndered** *ppl. a.* [UN-1 2] 1655. **Unpo·cket** *v.* [UN-2 3] 1611. **Unpoe·tic** 1619, **-al** 1746, *adjs.* [UN-1 1], **-ly** *adv.*

Unpoi·nted, *ppl. a.* 1574. [UN-1 2.] †1. Of garments: Not tagged for tying. 2. Unpunctuated 1593. b. Without vowel points or diacritical marks 1640. 3. Without point; dull or irrelevant 1632. b. Without a point, not sharpened at the end 1887. 4. Not pointed *at* 1555.

Unpoi·sed *ppl. a.* [UN-1 2] 1600. **Unpoi·son**

v. [Un-2 4 b] 1598. **Unpoi·soned** *ppl. a.* [Un-1 2] 1821. **Unpo·larized** *ppl. a.* [Un-1 2] 1827. **Unpoli·ced** *ppl. a.* [Un-1 2] 1797. †**Unpo·licied** *ppl. a.* [Un-1 2] –1738. **Unpo·lishable** *a.* [Un-1 1] 1687. **Unpo·lished** *ppl. a.* [Un-1 2] late ME.

Unpoli·te, *a.* 1646. [Un-1 1.] †**1.** Without refinement, unpolished –1727. †**b.** Unfashionable, inelegant –1753. **2.** Lacking in politeness; impolite 1709. Hence **Unpoli·te·ly** *adv.*, **-ness.**

Unpo·litic *a.* (now *rare*) [Un-1 1] 1548. **Unpoli·tical** *a.* [Un-1 1] 1643. **Unpo·llarded** *ppl. a.* [Un-1 2] 1830. **Unpo·lled** *ppl. a.* [Un-1 2] 1647. **Unpollu·ted** *ppl. a.* [Un-1 2] Shaks. **Unpo·pe** *v.* [Un-2 4 b] 1563. **Unpo·pular** *a.* [Un-1 1] 1647. **Un:popula·rity** [Un-1 6] 1735. **Unpo·pulated** *ppl. a.* [Un-1 2] 1885. **Unpo·pulous** *a.* [Un-1 1] Scott. †**Unpo·rtable** *a.* [Un-1 1] –1782. **Unpo·rtioned** *ppl. a.* [Un-1 2] 1744.

Unposse·ssed, *ppl. a.* 1586. [Un-1 2.] **1.** Not possessed or owned; unoccupied 1594. †**2.** Unprejudiced –1685. **3.** Not having possession *of* something 1795.

1. A grace by thee unsought and unpossest Wordsw. 2. To any thinking and u. Man 1685.

Unpo·ssible *a.* (now *dial.*) [Un-1 1] late ME. **Unpo·sted** *ppl. a.* [Un-1 2] 1860. **Unpow·dered** *ppl. a.* [Un-1 2] 1440. **Unpow·erful** *a.* (*rare*) [Un-1 1] 1611. **Unpra·cticable** *a.* [Un-1 1] 1647, **-ness.** **Unpra·ctical** *a.* [Un-1 1] 1637, **-ly** *adv.*, **-ness.**

Unpra·ctised, *ppl. a.* 1540. [Un-1 2.] **1.** Not familiarized or skilled by practice; inexpert 1551. **2.** Not practised; unemployed 1540.

1. The most destructive arms in..u. hands 1748. 2. The old prouerbe..is not lefte vnpractised 1540.

Unprai·sed *ppl. a.* [Un-1 2] late ME. **Unpray·** *v.* [Un-2 1] 1611. **Unpray·ed** *ppl. a.* [Un-1 2] late ME. **Unprea·ch** *v.* [Un-2 1] 1692. **Unprea·ching** *ppl. a.* [Un-1 4] 1549. **Unpreca·rious** *a.* [Un-1 1] 1712.

Unpre·cedented, *ppl. a.* 1623. [Un-1 2.] For which no precedent can be cited; of an unexampled kind, degree, etc. Hence **Unpre·cedented·ly** *adv.*, **-ness.**

Unpreci·se *a.* [Un-1 1] 1782, **-ly** *adv.* **Unpredi·ctable** *a.* [Un-1 1] 1857. **Unpre·faced** *ppl. a.* [Un-1 2] 1801. **Unprefe·rred** *ppl. a.* [Un-1 2] 1483. **Unpre·gnant** *a.* [Un-1 1] Shaks.

Unpre·judiced, *ppl. a.* 1613. [Un-1 2.] †**1.** Not affected prejudicially. **2.** Free from prejudice 1637. Hence **Unpre·judiced·ly** *adv.*, **-ness.**

Unprela·tical *a.* [Un-1 1] 1647. **Unpreme·ditate** *ppl. a.* (*arch.*) [Un-1 2] 1551. **Unpremeditated** *ppl. a.* [Un-1 2] 1591, **-ly** *adv.*, **-ness.** **Unpreo·ccupied** *ppl. a.* [Un-1 2] 1827.

Unprepa·re, *v. rare.* 1598. [Un-2 1, or Un-1 7.] **1.** *trans.* To undo the preparation of. **2.** To make unprepared; to unfit 1645.

Unprepa·red, *ppl. a.* 1549. [Un-1 2.] **1.** Of persons: Not in a state of preparation; not ready (for defence, reply, etc.). **b.** Const. *for*, or *to* with inf. 1549. **c.** *spec.* Not prepared for death 1594. **2.** Left, introduced, taken, etc., without special preparation 1595.

2. Events..appear to us very often original, u., single, and un-relative 1751. So **Unprepa·red·ly** *adv.*, **-ness.**

U:npreposse·ssed *ppl. a.* [Un-1 2] 1648. **U:nprepossessing** *ppl. a.* [Un-1 4] 1816. **Unpre·scient** *a.* [Un-1 1] 1866. **Unprescri·bed** *ppl. a.* [Un-1 2] 1642. **Unprese·ntable** *a.* [Un-1 1] 1828, **-ness.** **U:npresentabi·lity** [Un-1 6] 1882. **Unprese·nted** *ppl. a.* [Un-1 2] 1523. **Unprese·rved** *ppl. a.* [Un-1 2] 1648. **Unpre·ssed** *ppl. a.* [Un-1 2] 1552. **Unpresu·ming** *ppl. a.* [Un-1 4] 1770, **-ness.** **Unpresu·mptuous** *a.* [Un-1 1] 1704, **-ly** *adv.* **Unprete·nding** *ppl. a.* [Un-1 4] 1697, **-ly** *adv.*, **-ness.** **Unprete·ntious** *a.* [Un-1 1] 1859, **-ly** *adv.*, **-ness.** **Unpre·tty** *a.* [Un-1 1] Mme D'Arblay. **Unprevai·ling** *ppl. a.* [Un-1 4] Shaks. **Unpreve·ntable** *a.* [Un-1 1] 1616, **-ness, -bly** *adv.* **Unpreve·nted** *ppl. a.* [Un-1 2] 1585. **Unpri·ced** *ppl. a.* [Un-1 2] 1857. **Unpri·cked** *ppl. a.* [Un-1 2] 1588. **Unprie·st** *v.* [Un-2 4 b] 1550. **Unprie·stly** *a.* [Un-1 1] 1537. **Unpri·mitive** *a.* [Un-1 1] 1708. **Unpri·ncely** *a.* [Un-1 1] 1536.

Unpri·ncipled, *ppl. a.* 1634. [Un-1 2.] †**1.** Not instructed or grounded *in* Milt. **2.** Not possessed of fixed, sound, or honourable principles of conduct 1644. **3.** Based upon, or exhibiting want of principle 1782.

1. I do not think my sister so..unprincipl'd in vertues book Milt. 2. A couple of u. rascals 1878. 3. Many who are esteemed good sort of persons, but whose goodness is u. 1782.

Unpri·ntable *a.* [Un-1 1] 1871. **Unpri·nted** *ppl. a.* [Un-1 2] More. **Unpri·son** *v.* [Un-2 3] late ME. **Unpri·vileged** *ppl. a.* [Un-1 2] 1590.

†**Unpri·zable,** *a.* 1601. [Un-1 1.] **1.** Not to be prized; of little worth. Shaks. **2.** Beyond all price; inestimable –1634.

1. A bawbling Vessell..For shallow draught and bulke vnprizable Shaks.

Unpri·zed *ppl. a.* [Un-1 2] 1445. **Unpro·bed** *ppl. a.* [Un-1 2] 1827. **Unproclai·med** *ppl. a.* [Un-1 2] 1648. **Unprocu·rable** *a.* [Un-1 1] 1607. **Unprodu·ced** *ppl. a.* [Un-1 2] 1674. **Unprodu·ctive** *a.* [Un-1 1] Burke, **-ly** *adv.*, **-ness.** **Unprofa·ned** *ppl. a.* [Un-1 2] 1650. **Unprofe·ssed** *ppl. a.* [Un-1 2] late ME.

Unprofe·ssional, *a.* and *sb.* 1806. [Un-1 1, 6.] **A.** *adj.* Not professional. **b.** Contravening the rules or etiquette of the profession concerned 1899. **B.** *sb.* One who belongs to no profession or is outside the one in question 1863. Hence **Unprofe·ssionally** *adv.*

Unpro·fit (now *rare*) [Un-1 6] late ME. **Unpro·fitable** *a.* [Un-1 1] ME., **-ness, -bly** *adv.* **Unpro·fited** *ppl. a.* [Un-1 2] Shaks. **Unpro·fiting** *ppl. a.* [Un-1 4] 1616. **Unprogre·ssive** *a.* [Un-1 1] 1851, **-ly** *adv.*, **-ness.** **Unprohi·bited** *ppl. a.* [Un-1 2] Milt. **Unproje·cted** *ppl. a.* [Un-1 2] Cromwell. **Unproli·fic** *a.* [Un-1 1] 1676. **Unpro·mise** *v.* (now *rare*) [Un-2 1] 1598.

Unpro·mising, *ppl. a.* 1632. [Un-1 4.] **1.** Not giving promise of excellence or success 1663. †**2.** Unprepossessing –1669. Hence **Unpro·misingly** *adv.*

Unpro·mpted *ppl. a.* [Un-1 2] 1659. **Unpro·mulgated** *ppl. a.* [Un-1 2] 1802. **Unpronou·nceable** *a.* [Un-1 1] Scott. **Unpronou·nced** *ppl. a.* [Un-1 2] 1611. **Unpro·per** *a.* (now *dial.*) [Un-1 1] late ME., †**-ly** *adv.* **Unpro·pertied** *ppl. a.* [Un-1 2] 1793. **Unprophe·tic** *a.* [Un-1 1] 1725. **Unpropi·tious** *a.* [Un-1 1] 1699. †**Unpropo·rtionable** *a.* [Un-1 1] –1766. **Unpropo·rtionate** *a.* (now *rare*) [Un-1 1] 1581, **-ly** *adv.* **Unpropo·rtioned** *ppl. a.* [Un-1 2] 1586. **Unpro·pped** *ppl. a.* [Un-1 2] 1616. **Unpro·secuted** *ppl. a.* [Un-1 2] 1655. **Unprospe·rity** [Un-1 6] 1628. **Unpro·sperous** *a.* [Un-1 1] 1578, **-ly** *adv.*, **-ness.** **Unpro·stituted** *ppl. a.* [Un-1 2] 1721. **Unprote·cted** *ppl. a.* [Un-1 2] 1593, **-ly** *adv.*, **-ness.** **Unpro·testant** *a.* [Un-1 1] 1841. **Unpro·testantize** *v.* [Un-2 4 c] 1833. **Unprou·d** *a.* [Un-1 1] 1570. **Unpro·vable** *a.* [Un-1 1] late ME.

Unpro·ved, *ppl. a.* 1440. [Un-1 2.] **1.** Not tested, untried. Now *rare.* **2.** Not demonstrated to be true or genuine 1532.

1. For to find a fresh vnproued knight Spenser.

Unprovi·ded, *ppl. a.* 1514. [Un-1 2.] **1.** Not furnished, supplied, or equipped (*with* something) 1523. **b.** Not provided for 1640. **2.** Not in a state of preparation or readiness; unprepared 1525. **3.** Against which provision has not been made; unforeseen 1514. **4.** Not provided *for* 1575. **5.** Not furnished, supplied, or made ready 1621.

1. Courts are seldom u. of persons under this character Swift. Since you will go, you must not go u. 1760. Assailants..u. with regular means of attack Kinglake. 2. If they dye vnprouided Shaks. 3. Sodayne tempeste, and unprovyded colde 1514. The u. expenditure of the year 1841. 4. The necessary Subsistence of the household was u. for Clarendon. Hence **Unprovi·ded·ly** *adv.*, **-ness.**

Unprovo·cative *a.* [Un-1 1] 1821. †**Unprovo·ke** *v.* [Un-2 1] Shaks. **Unprovo·ked** *ppl. a.* [Un-1 2] 1585, **-ly** *adv.*, **-ness.** **Unprovo·king** *ppl. a.* [Un-1 4] 1710. **Unprude·ntial** *a.* [Un-1 1] 1650. **Unpru·ned** *ppl. a.* [Un-1 2] 1588. **Unpu·blishable** *a.* [Un-1 1] 1815, **-bly** *adv.* **Unpu·blished** *ppl. a.* [Un-1 2] Shaks. **Unpu·lled** *ppl. a.* [Un-1 2] 1440. **Unpu·nctual** *a.* [Un-1 1] 1740, **-ly** *adv.* **Unpunctua·lity** [Un-1 6] 1828. **Unpu·nctuated** *ppl. a.* [Un-1 2] 1866. **Unpu·nishable** *a.* [Un-1 1] 1531. **Unpu·nished** *ppl. a.* [Un-1 2] ME. **Unpu·rchas(e)able** *a.* [Un-1 1] 1611. **Unpu·rchased** *ppl. a.* [Un-1 2] 1545. **Unpu·rged** *ppl. a.* [Un-1 2] 1530. **Unpu·rified** *ppl. a.* [Un-1 2] 1574. **Unpu·rposed** *ppl. a.* [Un-1 2] 1570.

Unpu·rse, *v.* late ME. [Un-2 3, 2, 1.] **1.** *trans.* To take (money) out of a purse; to disburse. **2.** To steal the purse of 1827. **3.** To relax from a pursed state. Also *intr.* 1871.

3. Now I permit your plump lips to u. Browning.

Unpursu·ed *ppl. a.* [Un-1 2] 1469. **Unpu·t** *ppl. a.* [Un-1 2] 1470. **Unpu·trefied** *ppl. a.* [Un-1 2] 1579. **Unquai·ling** *ppl. a.* [Un-1 4] 1836, **-ly** *adv.* **Unqua·kerish** *a.* [Un-1 1] Lamb. **Unqua·lifiable** *a.* [Un-1 1] 1734.

Unqua·lified, *ppl. a.* 1556. [Un-1 2.] **1.** Not qualified or fitted; not having the necessary qualifications. **2.** Not endowed with specific qualities 1678. **3.** Not modified, limited, or restricted 1796. Hence **Unqua·lified·ly** *adv.*, **-ness.**

Unqua·lify *v.* [Un-2 1] 1655. **Unqua·litied** *ppl. a.* (*rare*) [Un-1 2] Shaks. **Unqua·rried** *ppl. a.* [Un-1 2] 1788. **Unquee·n** *v.* [Un-2 2, 4 b] 1579. **Unquee·nly** *a.* [Un-1 1] 1865. **Unque·lled** *ppl. a.* [Un-1 2] late ME. **Unque·nchable** *a.* [Un-1 1] late ME., **-bly** *adv.* **Unque·nched** *ppl. a.* [Un-1 2] ME.

Unque·stionable, *a.* 1600. [Un-1 1.] **1.** Having an assured character or position; unexceptionable 1603. **2.** Incapable of being doubted or disputed; indubitable, certain 1631. **3.** Not submitting to question (*rare*) 1600.

2. Authentic facts, and u. evidence 1782. 3. An vnquestionable spirit Shaks. Hence **Unque·stionably** *adv.*

Unque·stioned *ppl. a.* [Un-1 2] 1601. **Unque·stioning** *ppl. a.* [Un-1 4] 1828, **-ly** *adv.* **Unqui·ckened** *ppl. a.* [Un-1 2] 1610.

Unqui·et, *sb.* 1551. [Un-1 6.] Absence or want of quiet; disquiet, disturbance.

Unqui·et, *a.* 1523. [Un-1 1.] **1.** Marked by unrest, disturbance, or disorder. **2.** Of persons, emotions, etc.: Restless, active, turbulent 1526. **3.** Perturbed, anxious, not at ease 1535. Hence **Unqui·et·ly** *adv.*, **-ness.**

Unqui·et, *v. arch.* late ME. [Un-2 1.] *trans.* To disturb the quiet of; to disquiet.

Unqui·vering *ppl. a.* [Un-1 4] 1811. **Unquo·table** *a.* [Un-1 1] 1843. **Unquo·ted** *ppl. a.* [Un-1 2] 1825. **Unrai·sed** *ppl. a.* [Un-1 2] 1523. **Unra·ked** *ppl. a.* [Un-1 2] Shaks. **Unra·nsacked** *ppl. a.* [Un-1 2] 1529. **Unra·nsomed** *ppl. a.* [Un-1 2] 1554. **Unra·table** *a.* [Un-1 1] 1629. **Unra·ted** *ppl. a.* [Un-1 2] 1648. **Unra·tified** *ppl. a.* [Un-1 2] 1611. **Unra·vaged** *ppl. a.* [Un-1 2] Burke.

Unra·vel, *v.* 1603. [Un-2 1.] **1.** *trans.* To undo from a ravelled, tangled or woven state; to disentangle; to untwist (rope). †**2.** *fig.* To reverse, undo, annul –1766. **3.** To free from intricacy or obscurity; to reveal or disclose 1660. **4.** *intr.* To come undone; to become unknit or disentangled 1650.

4. As the burning threads Of woven cloud u. in pale air Shelley. Hence **Unra·veller. Unra·velling** *vbl. sb.* **Unra·velment.**

Unra·vished *ppl. a.* [Un-1 2] 1622. **Unra·zored** *ppl. a.* [Un-1 2] Milt. **Unrea·chable** *a.* [Un-1 1] 1593, **-bly** *adv.* **Unrea·ched** *ppl. a.* [Un-1 2] 1611.

Unrea·d, *ppl. a.* 1456. [Un-1 2.] **1.** Not read; unperused. **2.** Not instructed by reading 1606. **b.** Const. *in* 1602.

2. The clown u., and half-read gentleman Dryden. b. Algernon was u. in the hearts of women Meredith.

Unrea·dable, *a.* 1802. [Un-1 1.] **1.** Too dull or distasteful to read. **2.** Illegible 1830. Hence **Unreadabi·lity, Unrea·dableness.**

Unrea·dy, *a.*[1] ME. [Un-1 1.] **1.** Not in a state of readiness or preparation. **2.** Not prepared or made ready. late ME. **3.** Undressed; in deshabille. *Obs.* or *dial.* 1591. **4.** Given to hesitation; irresolute; slow 1594.

1. For the most part our witts be best When wee be takyne most vnrediest 1560. I express'd my self u. to vote for it 1707. Hence **Unrea·dily** *adv.* **Unrea·diness.**

Unrea·dy, *a.*[2] 1580. [Later form of late ME. *unredy*, f. Un-1 1.] = Redeless *a.* (only as an epithet of Ethelred II, d. 1016).

Unreal (ɒnrī·ăl), *a.* 1605. [UN-1 1.] Not real. **b.** *Gram.* Applied to suppositions implying non-fulfilment.

Hence horrible shadow, Vnreall mock'ry hence SHAKS.

Unreali·stic *a.* [UN-1 1] 1865. **Unrea·lity** [UN-1 6] 1751. **Unre·alizable** *a.* [UN-1 1] 1840. **Unre·alize** *v.* [UN-2 1] 1804. **Unre·alized** *ppl. a.* [UN-1 2] 1803. **Unrea·ped** *ppl. a.* [UN-1 2] 1577.

Unrea·son. ME. [UN-1 6.] †**1.** Injustice, impropriety –1609. **2.** *Abbot of U.*: see ABBOT. *Hist.* 1496. **3.** Absence of reason; indisposition or inability to act or think rationally or reasonably 1827.

Unrea·sonable, *a.* ME. [UN-1 1.] **1.** Not having the faculty of reason; irrational. **2.** Not acting in accordance with reason or good sense; claiming or expecting more than is reasonable. late ME. **3.** Not based on reason or good sense ME. **4.** Going beyond what is reasonable or equitable; excessive. late ME. Hence **Unrea·sonableness. Unrea·sonably** *adv.*

Unrea·soned *ppl. a.* [UN-1 2] 1582. **Unrea·soning** *ppl. a.* [UN-1 4] 1751, **-ly** *adv.* **Unrebe·llious** *a.* [UN-1 1] 1570. **Unrebu·ked** *ppl. a.* [UN-1 2] 1445. **Unreca·lled** *ppl. a.* [UN-1 2] 1601. **Unrecei·pted** *ppl. a.* [UN-1 2] 1881. **Unrecei·vable** *a.* [UN-1 1] 1611. **Unrecei·ved** *ppl. a.* [UN-1 2] 1540. **Unrece·ptive** *a.* [UN-1 1] 1778. **Unre·ckoned** *ppl. a.* [UN-1 2] ME. **Unreclai·mable** *a.* [UN-1 1] 1577, **-bly** *adv.* **Unreclai·med** *ppl. a.* [UN-1 2] 1470. **Unrecogni·tion** [UN-1 6] 1869. **Unre·cognizable** *a.* [UN-1 1] 1817, **-bly** *adv.* **Unre·cognized** *ppl. a.* [UN-1 2] 1813. **Unre·cognizing** *ppl. a.* [UN-1 4] 1814, **-ly** *adv.* **Unrecolle·cted** *ppl. a.* [UN-1 2] 1733. **U:nrecomme·nded** *ppl. a.* [UN-1 2] 1550. **Unre·compensed** *ppl. a.* [UN-1 2] 1469. **Unre·concilable** *a.* [UN-1 1] 1577. **Unre·conciled** *ppl. a.* [UN-1 2] 1450. **Unreconstru·cted** *ppl. a.* [UN-1 2] 1869. **Unreco·rded** *ppl. a.* [UN-1 2] 1585.

Unreco·verable, *a.* late ME. [UN-1 1.] †**1.** That cannot be recovered; completely lost –1650. **2.** That cannot be recovered from; past remedy 1561.

Unreco·vered *ppl. a.* [UN-1 2] 1611. **Unrecrui·ted** *ppl. a.* [UN-1 2] 1649. **Unre·ctified** *ppl. a.* [UN-1 2] 1638. **Unredee·mable** *a.* [UN-1 1] 1584.

Unredee·med, *ppl. a.* 1548. [UN-1 2.] **1.** Not spiritually redeemed; unregenerate. **2.** Not recovered, ransomed, or released, by purchase or otherwise 1554. **b.** *spec.* Not recovered from pawn 1859. **3.** Having no redeeming qualities; unmitigated 1805. **4.** Of promises, etc.: Not performed or realized 1812.

Unredre·ssed *ppl. a.* [UN-1 2] 1563. **Unredu·ced** *ppl. a.* [UN-1 2] 1572. **Unredu·cible** *a.* [UN-1 1] MILT. **Unree·l** *v.* [UN-2 1] 1567. **Unree·lable** *a.* [UN-1 1] 1611. **Unree·ve** *v.* [UN-2 1] 1600.

Unrefi·ned, *ppl. a.* 1595. [UN-1 2.] **1.** Not refined in manners, feelings, or speech. **2.** Not freed from impurities; crude 1610.

Unrefle·cted *ppl. a.* [UN-1 2] 1670. **Unrefle·cting** *ppl. a.* [UN-1 4] 1665. **Unrefle·ctive** *a.* [UN-1 1] 1854, **-ly** *adv.* **Unrefo·rmable** *a.* [UN-1 1] 1583.

Unrefo·rmed, *ppl. a.* 1528. [UN-1 2.] **1.** Of faults, etc.: Not amended or made good. *arch.* **2.** Of persons, institutions, etc.: Not reformed or improved 1583. **3.** Of churches: Not affected by the Reformation 1788.

Unrefra·cted *ppl. a.* [UN-1 2] 1676. **Unrefre·shed** *ppl. a.* [UN-1 2] 1736. **Unrefu·ted** *ppl. a.* [UN-1 2] 1589. **Unre·gal** *a.* [UN-1 1] 1611. **Unrega·rded** *ppl. a.* [UN-1 2] 1561, **-ly** *adv.* **Unrega·rdful** *a.* [UN-1 1] 1598. **Unrega·rding** *ppl. a.* [UN-1 4] 1585.

Unrege·nerate, *a.* 1612. [UN-1 1.] Not regenerate; often used vaguely = wicked, bad. Also *sb.* So **Unrege·neracy** 1622. **Unrege·nerated** *ppl. a.* 1579. **U:nregenera·tion** 1625.

Unre·gistered *ppl. a.* [UN-1 2] 1604. **Unregre·tted** *ppl. a.* [UN-1 2] 1676. **Unre·gulated** *ppl. a.* [UN-1 2] 1721. **Unrehea·rsed** *ppl. a.* [UN-1 2] 1472. **Unrei·n** *v.* [UN-2 2 b] 1603. **Unrei·ned** *ppl. a.* [UN-1 2] 1609. **Unrejoi·cing** *ppl. a.* [UN-1 4] 1726.

Unrela·ted, *ppl. a.* 1661. [UN-1 2.] **1.** Not connected by blood; not akin. **2.** Not standing in relationship or connexion 1668. **3.** Not recounted or told 1764.

2. Detached and u. offences BURKE.

Unre·lative *a.* [UN-1 1] 1751. **Unrela·xed** *ppl. a.* [UN-1 2] 1508. **Unrela·xing** *ppl. a.* [UN-1 4] 1781. **Unrelea·sed** *ppl. a.* [UN-1 2] late ME. **Unrele·nting** *ppl. a.* [UN-1 4] SHAKS., **-ly** *adv.*, **-ness.**

Unreli·able, *a.* 1840. [UN-1 1.] That cannot be relied upon.

Alcibiades..was too unsteady, and (according to Mr. Coleridge's coinage) 'u.' DE QUINCEY. Hence **Unreliabi·lity, Unreli·ableness.**

Unrelie·vable *a.* [UN-1 1] 1586.

Unrelie·ved, *ppl. a.* 1533. [UN-1 2.] **1.** Not freed from an obligation; not provided with relief; not aided or assisted. **2.** Lacking the relief of diversity or contrast; monotonous, not varied (*by* something) 1764. Hence **Unrelie·vedly** *adv.*

Unreli·gious, *a.* late ME. [UN-1 1.] **1.** Irreligious. Now *rare.* **2.** Not connected with or related to religion 1855.

2. The popular poetry..became profane, u., at length in some parts irreligious MILMAN. Hence **Unreli·giously** *adv.*, **-ness.**

Unreli·nquished *ppl. a.* [UN-1 2] COWPER. **Unrelu·ctant** *a.* [UN-1 1] 1737, **-ly** *adv.* **Unrema·rkable** *a.* [UN-1 1] 1611. **Unrema·rked** *ppl. a.* [UN-1 2] 1793. **Unre·medied** *ppl. a.* [UN-1 2] 1563. **Unreme·mberable** *a.* [UN-1 1] 1803. **Unreme·mbered** *ppl. a.* [UN-1 2] late ME. **Unreme·mbering** *ppl. a.* [UN-1 4] 1540.

Unremi·tted, *ppl. a.* 1646. [UN-1 2.] **1.** Of debt, penalty, etc.: Not cancelled or forgiven. **2.** Of effort, etc.: Constant, sustained 1722. **b.** Of persons: Persistent in effort 1796. Hence **Unremi·ttedly** *adv.*

Unremi·tting, *ppl. a.* 1728. [UN-1 4.] Never relaxing or slackening; continuing with the same force; incessant. Hence **Unremi·ttingly** *adv.*, **-ness.**

Unremo·rseful *a.* [UN-1 1] 1611, **-ly** *adv.* **Unremo·vable** *a.* (now *rare*) [UN-1 1] 1500. **Unremo·ved** *ppl. a.* [UN-1 2] 1450. **Unremu·nerative** *a.* [UN-1 1] 1854, **-ly** *adv.*, **-ness.** **Unre·ndered** *ppl. a.* [UN-1 2] 1851. **Unrenew·ed** *ppl. a.* [UN-1 2] 1579. **Unrenow·ned** *ppl. a.* [UN-1 2] 1570. **Unre·nt** *ppl. a.* [UN-1 2] SPENSER. **Unrepai·d** *ppl. a.* [UN-1 2] 1655. **Unrepai·r** [UN-1 6] 1873. **Unrepai·red** *ppl. a.* [UN-1 2] 1523. **Unrepa·ssable** *a.* [UN-1 1] 1600. **Unrepea·lable** *a.* [UN-1 1] 1601. **Unrepea·led** *ppl. a.* [UN-1 2] 1479.

Unrepea·table, *a.* 1843. [UN-1 1.] **1.** Too coarse or indecent to be repeated. **2.** That cannot be done or made again 1880.

Unrepea·ted *ppl. a.* [UN-1 2] 1586. **Unrepe·lled** *ppl. a.* [UN-1 2] 1795. **Unrepe·ntance** [UN-1 6] late ME. **Unrepe·ntant** *a.* [UN-1 1] late ME., **-ly** *adv.* **Unrepe·nted** *ppl. a.* [UN-1 2] 1597. **Unrepe·nting** *ppl. a.* [UN-1 4] 1586, **-ly** *adv.*, **-ness.** **Unrepi·ning** *ppl. a.* [UN-1 4] 1637, **-ly** *adv.* **Unrepla·ceable** *a.* [UN-1 1] 1801. **Unreple·nished** *ppl. a.* [UN-1 2] 1562. **Unreply·ing** *ppl. a.* [UN-1 4] 1791. **Unrepo·rtable** *a.* [UN-1 1] 1611. **Unrepo·rted** *ppl. a.* [UN-1 2] 1622. **U:nrepresе·ntative** *a.* [UN-1 1] 1832. **U:nreprese·nted** *ppl. a.* [UN-1 2] 1681. **Unrepre·ssed** *ppl. a.* [UN-1 2] 1583. **Unreprie·vable** [UN-1 1] 1593, **-bly** *adv.* **Unreprie·ved** *ppl. a.* [UN-1 2] MILT. **Unrepri·nted** *ppl. a.* [UN-1 2] 1872. **Unreproa·ched** *ppl. a.* [UN-1 2] 1648. **Unreproa·chful** *a.* [UN-1 1] 1720, **-ly** *adv.* **Unreproa·ching** *ppl. a.* [UN-1 4] 1742. **U:nreprodu·cible** *a.* [UN-1 1] 1880. **Unrepro·vable** *a.* (now *rare*) [UN-1 1] late ME. **Unrepro·ved** *ppl. a.* [UN-1 2] late ME. **Unrepu·gnant** *a.* [UN-1 1] 1594. **Unreque·sted** *ppl. a.* [UN-1 2] 1576. **Unrequi·red** *ppl. a.* [UN-1 2] late ME. **Unrequi·table** *a.* [UN-1 1] 1584.

Unrequi·ted, *a.* *ppl. a.* 1542. [UN-1 2.] Not requited or reciprocated. Hence **Unrequi·tedly** *adv.*, **-ness.**

Unrese·mbling *ppl. a.* [UN-1 4] 1598. **Unrese·nted** *ppl. a.* [UN-1 2] 1705. **Unrese·ntful** *a.* [UN-1 1] 1773, **-ly** *adv.*, **-ness.** **Unrese·nting** *ppl. a.* [UN-1 4] 1716.

Unrese·rve. 1751. [UN-1 6.] Absence of reserve; frankness.

Unrese·rved, *ppl. a.* 1539. [UN-1 2.] **1.** Unrestricted, unlimited, absolute. **b.** Of seats, etc.: Not reserved for a particular person or persons. **2.** Frank, outspoken 1713. Hence **Unrese·rved·ly** *adv.*, **-ness.**

Unresi·sted *ppl. a.* [UN-1 2] 1526. **Unresi·stible** *a.* (now *rare*) [UN-1 1] 1608. **Unresi·sting** *ppl. a.* [UN-1 4] 1625, **-ly** *adv.*, **-ness.** **Unreso·lvable** *a.* [UN-1 1] 1611.

Unreso·lved, *ppl. a.* 1577. [UN-1 2.] **1.** Of questions, etc.: Undetermined, undecided, unsolved. **2.** Uncertain or undetermined how to act; irresolute 1594. **b.** Uncertain in opinion; undecided 1597. **3.** Not broken up or dissolved 1801.

Unrespe·ctable *a.* [UN-1 1] 1765. **Unrespe·cted** *ppl. a.* [UN-1 2] 1586.

Unrespe·ctive, *a.* Now *rare.* 1594. [UN-1 1.] †**1.** Inattentive, heedless –1633. **2.** Indifferent; undiscriminating 1606.

Unre·spirable *a.* [UN-1 1] 1807. **Unre·spited** *ppl. a.* [UN-1 2] 1593. **Unrespo·nsible** *a.* [UN-1 1] 1634. **Unrespo·nsive** *a.* [UN-1 1] 1668, **-ly** *adv.*, **-ness.**

Unre·st. ME. [UN-1 6.] Absence of rest; disturbance, turmoil, trouble.

Unre·stful, *a.* late ME. [UN-1 1.] **1.** Restless, stirring, unquiet. **2.** Marked by absence of rest or quiet. late ME.

2. The bedde of a persone beeyng in greate debte is an unrestefull thyng 1542. So **Unre·stfulness.**

Unre·sting *ppl. a.* [UN-1 4] 1582. **Unresto·red** *ppl. a.* [UN-1 2] 1445. **Unrestrai·nable** *a.* [UN-1 1] late ME.

Unrestrai·ned, *ppl. a.* 1586. [UN-1 2.] **1.** Not kept in check or under control; allowed free course or vent 1600. **b.** Not restricted or limited 1622. **2.** Not subject (or subjected) to restraint in respect of action or conduct 1586. **b.** *appositive.* Without restraint; unrestrainedly 1596. **3.** Not constrained; easy, natural 1856. Hence **Unrestrai·nedly** *adv.*

Unrestri·cted *ppl. a.* [UN-1 2] 1766, **-ly** *adv.*, **-ness.** **Unreta·rded** *ppl. a.* [UN-1 2] 1615. **Unrete·ntive** *a.* [UN-1 1] 1748. **Unretra·cted** *ppl. a.* [UN-1 2] 1646. **Unretu·rnable** *a.* [UN-1 1] 1513.

Unretu·rned, *ppl. a.* 1589. [UN-1 2.] **1.** Not having returned or come back. **2.** Not reciprocated, unrequited 1643.

Unretu·rning *ppl. a.* [UN-1 4] 1628, **-ly** *adv.* **Unrevea·led** *ppl. a.* [UN-1 2] 1529. **Unrevea·ling** *ppl. a.* [UN-1 4] 1628. **Unreve·nged** *ppl. a.* [UN-1 2] 1533. **Unre·verenced** *ppl. a.* [UN-1 2] 1470.

Unre·verend, *a.* 1562. [UN-1 1.] †**1.** Irreverent –1820. **2.** Unworthy of reverence 1828.

1. They rather hold such curiosities to be impertinent — u. LAMB.

Unre·verent *a.* (now *rare*) [UN-1 1] late ME. **Unreve·rsed** *ppl. a.* [UN-1 2] SHAKS. **Unreview·ed** *ppl. a.* [UN-1 2] 1819. **Unrevi·sed** *ppl. a.* [UN-1 2] 1845. **Unrevi·ved** *ppl. a.* [UN-1 2] 1631. **Unrevo·ked** *ppl. a.* [UN-1 2] 1479. **Unrewa·rded** *ppl. a.* [UN-1 2] late ME. **Unrewa·rding** *ppl. a.* [UN-1 4] 1653. **Unrheto·rical** *a.* [UN-1 1] 1822. **Unrhy·med** *ppl. a.* [UN-1 2] 1828. **Unrhy·thmical** *a.* [UN-1 1] 1777, **-ly** *adv.* **Unri·bbed** *ppl. a.* [UN-1 2] 1834. **Unri·dden** *ppl. a.* [UN-1 2] 1574.

Unri·ddle, *v.* 1586. [UN-2 1.] *trans.* To solve, explain (a mystery, etc.). Hence **Unri·ddler.**

Unrid(e)able *a.* [UN-1 1] 1881. **Unri·fled** *ppl. a.* [UN-1 2] 1603. **Unri·g** *v.* [UN-2 2] 1579. **Unri·gged** *ppl. a.* [UN-1 2] 1593. †**Unri·ght** *sb.* [UN-1 6] –1610. **Unri·ght** *a.* (*arch.*) [UN-1 1] OE., **-ly** *adv.* **Unri·ghted** *ppl. a.* [UN-1 2] 1883.

Unri·ghteous, *a.* [OE. *unrihtwīs*, f. UN-1 1 + RIGHTEOUS.] Not righteous; unjust, wicked. Hence **Unri·ghteous·ly** *adv.*, **-ness.**

Unri·ghtful *a.* (now *rare*) [UN-1 1] ME., **-ly** *adv.*, **-ness.** **Unri·nged** *ppl. a.* [UN-1 2] 1510. **Unri·nsed** *ppl. a.* [UN-1 2] 1661.

Unri·p, *v.* 1513 [UN-2 7.] **1.** *trans.* To strip (a house or roof) of tiles, etc. Now *dial.* **2.** To lay open, slit up, or detach, by ripping 1534.

Unri·pe, *a.* [OE. *unripe*, f. UN-1 1 + *ripe* RIPE *a.*] †1. Of death: Premature –1633. 2. Immature; not arrived at full development ME. b. Of fruit, etc.: Not matured by growth ME. Hence **Unri·pe·ly** *adv.*, **-ness.**

Unri·pened *ppl. a.* [UN-1 2] 1588. **Unri·ppled** *ppl. a.* [UN-1 2] 1816. **Unri·sen** *ppl. a.* [UN-1 2] 1806. **Unri·valled** *ppl. a.* [UN-1 2] SHAKS. **Unri·ven** *ppl. a.* [UN-1 2] late ME.

Unri·vet, *v.* 1591. [UN-2 1.] 1. *trans.* To unfasten or detach by the removal of rivets. 2. *fig.* To undo, loosen, detach, relax, etc. 1620.

2. Before I had..unriveted my gaze 1853.

Unroa·sted *ppl. a.* [UN-1 2] late ME. **Unro·bbed** *ppl. a.* [UN-1 2] late ME. **Unro·be** *v.* [UN-2 2] 1598. **Unro·bed** *ppl. a.* [UN-1 2] 1861.

Unro·ll, *v.* late ME. [UN-2 1, 2, 5.] 1. *trans.* To open out from a rolled-up state; to uncoil. b. To extend, spread out 1813. c. *fig.* To develop or expand fully 1854. 2. *intr.* To become unrolled 1588. †3. *trans.* To remove from a roll or list. SHAKS.

1. Time has unrowl'd her Glories to the last, And now clos'd up the Volume DRYDEN. The operation of unrolling the ancient papyri 1828. 2. Euen as an Adder when she doth vnrowle SHAKS.

Unro·lled *ppl. a.* [UN-1 2] 1573. **Un-Ro·man** *a.* [UN-1 1] 1682. **Unro·manized** *ppl. a.* [UN-1 2] 1771. **Unroma·ntic** *a.* [UN-1 1] 1731, **-ally** *adv.* **Unroo·f** *v.* [UN-2 2] 1598. **Unroo·fed** *ppl. a.* [UN-1 2] 1550. **Unroo·st** *v.* (now *rare*) [UN-2 3, 5] 1598.

Unroo·t, *v.* 1449. [UN-2 2 b, 5]. 1. *trans.* To tear up by the roots, overthrow from a fixed base, displace by force 1570. b. *fig.* To eradicate, get rid of 1449. 2. *intr.* To lose root-hold; to become detached (*rare*) 1616.

1. Whole plains unrooted from the main lands, by floods and tempests GOLDSM. b. Vices be so euill to be vnrooted where they once take place 1574.

Unroo·ted *out ppl. a.* [UN-1 2, ROOT *v.*1 II. 2] 1550. **Unro·pe** *v.* [UN-2 2 b] 1883. **Unro·ped** *ppl. a.* [UN-1 2] 1881. **Unro·tted** *ppl. a.* [UN-1 2] 1440. **Unro·tten** *a.* [UN-1 1] 1574. †**Unrou·gh** *a.* [UN-1 1] –1605. **Unrou·nd** *a.* [UN-1 1] 1588.

Unrou·nd, *v.* 1611. [UN-2 4 a.] 1. *trans.* To break or distort the roundness of 1611. 2. *Phonetics.* To delabialize (a vowel) 1874.

Unrou·nded *ppl. a.* [UN-1 2] 151.. **Unrou·sed** *ppl. a.* [UN-1 2] 1802. **Unroy·al** *a.* [UN-1 1] 1586, **-ly** *adv.* **Unru·bbed** *ppl. a.* [UN-1 2] late ME. **Unru·ffle** *v.* [UN-2 1, 5] 1697.

Unru·ffled, *ppl. a.* 1659. [UN-1 2.] 1. Not affected by any violent feeling; not agitated or disturbed; calm, unmoved. 2. Not physically ruffled or made rough 1713. 3. Not furnished with ruffles 1825. Hence **Unru·ffledness.**

Unru·ined *ppl. a.* [UN-1 2] 1610. **Unru·lable** *a.* [UN-1 1] 1680. **Unru·le** [UN-1 6] late ME. **Unru·led** *ppl. a.* [UN-1 2] late ME.

Unruly, *a.* late ME. [UN-1 1.] 1. Not amenable to rule or discipline; ungovernable; disorderly, turbulent. b. Characterized by disorder or disquiet. late ME. 2. Stormy, tempestuous, impetuous 1593.

1. Ouer kind fathers make vnruly daughters 1592. b. These vnrulye reuels 1582. 2. U. blasts wait on the tender spring SHAKS. Hence **Unru·liness.**

Unru·mple *v.* [UN-2 1] 1694. **Unru·mpled** *ppl. a.* [UN-1 2] 1641. **Unru·ng** *ppl. a.* [UN-1 2] late ME. **Unru·ptured** *ppl. a.* [UN-1 2] 1862. **Unru·sted** *ppl. a.* [UN-1 2] 1653. **Unru·th** (*arch.*) [UN-1 6] 1440. **U:nsacerdo·tal** *a.* [UN-1 1] 1847. **Unsa·cked** *ppl. a.* [UN-1 2] 1590. **Unsa·cred** *a.* [UN-1 1] 1608.

Unsa·ddle, *v.* late ME. [UN-2 2, 3.] 1. *trans.* To remove the saddle from (a horse, etc.) Also *absol.* 2. To dislodge from the saddle 1470.

Unsa·ddled *ppl. a.* [UN-1 2] 1623.

Unsa·fe, *a.* 1597. [UN-1 1.] 1. Not enjoying safety; exposed to danger or risk 1605. 2. Involving, or not free from, danger or risk 1597. b. Of places, etc.: Presenting or beset with dangers 1621. 3. Unreliable; not to be trusted to 1601. So **Unsa·fe·ly** *adv.*, **-ness. Unsa·fety.**

Unsai·d *ppl. a.* [UN-1 2] OE. **Unsai·led** *ppl. a.* [UN-1 2] 1572. **Unsai·lorlike** *a.* [UN-1 1] 1841. **Unsai·nt** *v.* [UN-2 4 b] 1572. **Unsai·nted** *ppl. a.* [UN-1 2] 1642. **Unsai·ntly** *a.* [UN-1 1] 1659. **Unsa·laried** *ppl. a.* [UN-1 2] DISRAELI. **Unsa·leable** *a.* [UN-1 1] 1565; hence **Unsaleabi·lity.** **Unsa·lted** *ppl. a.* [UN-1 2] 1440. **Unsa·lutary** *a.* [UN-1 1] 1770. **Unsalu·ted** *ppl. a.* [UN-1 2] 1542. **Unsa·lvable** *a.* [UN-1 1] 1624. **Unsa·mpled** *ppl. a.* [UN-1 2] 1890. **Unsa·nctified** *ppl. a.* [UN-1 2] 1570. **Unsa·nctify** *v.* [UN-2 4 c] 1594. **Unsa·nctioned** *ppl. a.* [UN-1 2] 1784. **Unsa·ndalled** *ppl. a.* [UN-1 2] 1772. **Unsa·nguine** *a.* [UN-1 1] 1728. **Unsa·nitary** *a.* [UN-1 1] 1871. **Unsa·ted** *ppl. a.* [UN-1 2] 1693. **Unsa·tiable** *a.* (now *rare*) [UN-1 1] late ME. **Unsa·tiated** *ppl. a.* [UN-1 2] 1701. **U:nsatisfa·ction** [UN-1 6] 1643.

U:nsatisfa·ctory, *a.* 1637. [UN-1 1.] That fails to meet requirements or fulfil hopes; giving ground for complaint, criticism, or suspicion. Hence **Unsatisfa·ctorily** *adv.*, **-ness.**

Unsa·tisfiable *a.* [UN-1 1] 1539.

Unsa·tisfied, *ppl. a.* late ME. [UN-1 2.] 1. Not satisfied in respect of something desired; not having obtained all that, or as much as, is wished for. 2. Not satisfied in respect of information or knowledge; doubtful, dubious 1575. 3. Not satisfied with some circumstance, result, etc.; displeased. Now *rare.* 1648. 4. Of requirements, debts, doubts, etc.: Not settled 1588.

3. Mr. Freeman is..u. with the review 1883. Hence **Unsa·tisfiedness.**

Unsa·tisfying *ppl. a.* [UN-1 4] 1656. **Unsa·turated** *ppl. a.* [UN-1 2] 1758. **Unsa·ved** *ppl. a.* [UN-1 2] 1648.

Unsa·voury, *a.* ME. [UN-1 1.] †1. Flavourless; insipid; tasteless –1634. 2. Disagreeable to the taste. late ME. b. Distasteful or offensive to the sense of smell, or to refined feelings 1539. 3. Unpleasant, disagreeable, distasteful. late ME. 4. Morally offensive; having an unpleasant or disagreeable character or association. late ME.

2. b. U. stench of oil POPE. 3. All that tended to safety was vnsauory 1591. 4. Grim anecdotes and u. details 1882. Hence **Unsa·vourily** *adv.* **Unsa·vouriness.**

Unsaw·n *ppl. a.* [UN-1 2] 1572. **Un-Sa·xon** *a.* [UN-1 1] 1848.

Unsay·, *v.* 1460. [UN-2 1, 5.] †1. *trans.* To deny. 2. To retract, revoke (something said or written). Also *intr.* 1483.

Unsca·bbard *v.* [UN-2 3] 1611. **Unsca·bbarded** *ppl. a.* [UN-1 1] 1562. **Unsca·lable** *a.* [UN-1 1] 1579. **Unsca·le** *v.* [UN-2 2, 2 b] 1510. **Unsca·led** *ppl. a.* [UN-1 2] 1812. **Unsca·lped** *ppl. a.* [UN-1 2] 1814. **Unsca·nned** *ppl. a.* [UN-1 2] 1577. **Unsca·red** *ppl. a.* [UN-1 2] 1742. **Unsca·rred** *ppl. a.* [UN-1 2] SHAKS.

Unsca·thed, *ppl. a.* orig. *Sc.* and *rare.* late ME. [UN-1 2.] Uninjured.

Unsce·nted *ppl. a.* [UN-1 2] COWPER. **Unsce·ptred** *ppl. a.* [UN-1 2] 1752. **Unscho·larlike** *a.* [UN-1 1] 1616. **Unscho·larly** *a.* [UN-1 1] 1784. **Unschola·stic** *a.* [UN-1 1] 1690. **Unschoo·l** *v.* [UN-2 1] 1820.

Unschoo·led, *ppl. a.* and *a.* 1589. [UN-1 2, 3.] 1. Uneducated, untaught 1594. b. *spec.* Not educated at school 1841. 2. Untrained, undisciplined 1589. b. Not affected or made artificial by education; natural, spontaneous 1815.

Unsci·ence. late ME. [UN-1 6.] 1. Lack of knowledge, ignorance. 2. False conceptions or methods in scientific inquiry 1878.

1. It nys nat oonly vnscience, but it is deceiuable oppinioun CHAUCER. 2. Un-science, not Science, Adverse to Faith PUSEY.

U:nscienti·fic, *a.* 1775. [UN-1 1.] Not versed in or concerned with science; now usu., not in accordance with or adopting scientific methods. So **Unscienti·fically** *adv.*

Unsci·ssored *ppl. a.* [UN-1 2] SHAKS. **Unsco·rched** *ppl. a.* [UN-1 2] SHAKS. **Unsco·red** *ppl. a.* [UN-1 2] 1596. **Unsco·rned** *ppl. a.* [UN-1 2] late ME. **Un-Sco·ttish** *a.* [UN-1 1] 1825. **Unscou·red** *ppl. a.* [UN-1 2] 1460. **Unscou·rged** *ppl. a.* [UN-1 2] late ME. **Unscra·ped** *ppl. a.* [UN-1 2] 1725. **Unscra·tched** *ppl. a.* [UN-1 2] SHAKS. **Unscree·n** *v.* (now *rare*) [UN-2 3] 1628. **Unscree·ned** (*ppl.*) *a.* [UN-1 2, 3] 1648.

Unscrew·, *v.* 1605. [UN-2 1, 5.] 1. *trans.* To slacken or detach by turning a screw; to remove or loosen (a screw) by turning. Also *fig.* 2. *intr.* To be unscrewed or admit of being unscrewed 1822.

2. Courtiers will..u. their features 1761.

Unscri·ptural, *a.* 1653. [UN-1 1.] Not authorized by or based on Holy Scripture. So **Unscriptura·lity. Unscri·ptural·ly** *adv.*, **-ness.**

Unscru·bbed *ppl. a.* [UN-1 2] 1900. **Unscru·pulous** *a.* [UN-1 1] 1803, **-ly** *adv.*, **-ness.** **Unscru·tinized** *ppl. a.* [UN-1 2] 1728. **Unscu·lptured** *ppl. a.* [UN-1 2] SHELLEY.

Unsea·l, *v.* late ME. [UN-2 1, 2.] 1. *trans.* To remove the seal from; to break the seal of (a letter, etc.) 2. To free from constraint; to allow free action to 1589. b. To free from the condition (or necessity) of remaining closed 1586. 3. To disclose, reveal 1640.

Unsea·led, *ppl. a.* late ME. [UN-1 2.] 1. Not stamped or marked with a seal. 2. Not closed with a seal; not having a seal imposed or attached. late ME. 3. *fig.* Not formally ratified 1601.

1. [They]..sell beere and wyne by vnlawful and vnsealled measures 1550. 2. A promissory note u. BERKELEY. 3. Prophecies..unseal'd by any divine Sign 1665.

Unsea·m, *v.* 1592. [UN-2 2.] 1. *trans.* To undo the seams of; to rip. 2. *fig.* To rip up, tear open 1605.

2. Till he vnseam'd him from the Naue to th' Chops SHAKS.

Unsea·manlike *a.* [UN-1 1] 1726. **Unsea·med** *ppl. a.* [UN-1 2] 1592.

Unsea·rchable, *a.* late ME. [UN-1 1.] That cannot be searched into; inscrutable. Hence **Unsea·rchableness. Unsea·rchably** *adv.*

Unsea·rched *ppl. a.* [UN-1 2] 1526. **Unsea·red** *ppl. a.* [UN-1 2] 1599. **Unsea·son** *v.* [UN-2 2] 1590.

Unsea·sonable, *a.* 1448. [UN-1 1.] 1. Not suited to or not in accordance with the time or occasion; untimely, inopportune. b. Of time: Not suitable; ill chosen, inconvenient; unusual 1595. 2. Of fish, etc.: Not in season 1450. 3. Of weather: Not appropriate to the season of the year; *esp.* stormy, tempestuous. Also of days, seasons, etc. 1513.

1. To chuse tyme is to save tyme, and an vnseasonable mocion is but beating the ayre BACON. The omission .. was u. and injudicious 1844. b. If he endeavoured at so u. an hour, to force an entrance LYTTON. Hence **Unsea·sonableness. Unsea·sonably** *adv.*

Unsea·soned, *ppl. a.* 1582. [UN-1 2.] 1. Not made palatable by seasoning. 2. Not matured by growth or time 1601. b. Not habituated by time or experience 1601.

Unsea·t, *v.* 1596. [UN-2 3.] 1. *trans.* To dislodge from a seat, *esp.* on horseback. 2. To dislodge from some place or position; to deprive of rank or office 1611. b. *spec.* To deprive of a seat in Parliament or other representative body 1834.

Unsea·worthiness [UN-1 6] 1824. **Unsea·worthy** *a.* [UN-1 1] 1820. **Unse·conded** *ppl. a.* [UN-1 2] SHAKS. **Unse·cret** *a.* (now *rare*) [UN-1 1] 1586. **Unsecta·rian** *a.* and *sb.* [UN-1 1, 6] 1847. **Unse·cular** *a.* [UN-1 1] 1846. **Unsecu·red** *ppl. a.* [UN-1 2] 1780. **Unsedu·ced** *ppl. a.* [UN-1 2] 1565. **Unsee·able** *a.* [UN-1 1] late ME.

Unsee·ing, *ppl. a.* ME. [UN-1 4.] †1. Invisible. ME. only. 2. Not seeing; lacking sight 1591. b. Without seeing (something) 1632.

2. I should haue scratch'd out your vnseeing eyes SHAKS. He looked at his friend's face with blank u. eyes 1873. b. I sat..u. all Around me SOUTHEY.

Unsee·mly, *a.* ME. [UN-1 1.] 1. Unbecoming, indecorous; indecent. 2. Uncomely, unhandsome. Now *rare.* ME. Hence **Unsee·mliness.**

Unsee·mly, *adv.* late ME. [UN-1 5.] In an unseemly or unbecoming manner.

English women..rode very unseemely astride, like as men doe 1610.

Unsee·n, *ppl. a.* and *sb.* ME. [UN-1 2, 6.] A. *adj.* 1. Not seen; not apprehended by sight; invisible. b. Const. *of* (= by) 1586. 2. Not seen previously or hitherto; *esp.* †unfamiliar, strange ME. b. Of passages for translation:

Not previously read 1879. B. *sb.* An unprepared passage for translation 1882.

Unse·gmented *ppl. a.* [Un-1 2] 1848. Unsei·zable *a.* [Un-1 1] 1862. Unsei·zed *ppl. a.* [Un-1 2] late ME.

Unse·ldom, *adv.* 1658. [Un-1 5.] *Not u.* (misused for) not rarely, not infrequently.

Unsele·ct *a.* [Un-1 1] 1826. Unse·lf *v.* [Un-2 4 b, 6] 1654. Unselfco·nscious *a.* [Un-1 1] 1866, -ly *adv.*, -ness. Unse·lfish *a.* [Un-1 1] 1698, -ly *adv.*, -ness. Unsensa·tional *a.* [Un-1 1] 1865, -ly *adv.* Unse·nse *v.* (now *rare*) [Un-2 4 b] 1611. Unse·nsed *ppl. a.* [Un-1 2] 1667. Unse·nsible *a.* (*Obs.* exc. *dial.*) [Un-1 1] late ME. Unse·nsitive *a.* [Un-1 1] 1610. Unse·nsualize *v.* [Un-2 4 c] 1792. Unse·nt *ppl. a.* [Un-1 2] 1501. Unse·ntenced *ppl. a.* [Un-1 2] 1526. Unse·ntient *ppl. a.* [Un-1 1] 1768. Unsentime·ntal *a.* [Un-1 1] 1810, -a·lity, -ly *adv.* Unse·parated *ppl. a.* [Un-1 2] 1545. Unse·pulchred *ppl. a.* [Un-1 2] 1611. Unse·rious *a.* [Un-1 1] 1655. Unse·rved *ppl. a.* [Un-1 2] ME. Unse·rviceable *a.* [Un-1 1] 1535, -ness, -bly *adv.* Unse·rvile *a.* [Un-1 1] 1701. Unse·t *v.* [Un-2 1, 5] 1602. Unse·t *ppl. a.* [Un-1 2] late ME. Unse·tting *ppl. a.* [Un-1 4] 1567.

Unse·ttle, *v.* 1598. [Un-2 1, 5.] 1. *trans.* To undo from a fixed position; to displace, unfix (*rare*). 2. To force out of a settled condition; to make insecure or unquiet; to disturb 1644. 3. *intr.* To become unsettled 1605. Hence Unse·ttling *ppl. a.*

Unse·ttled, *ppl. a.* 1591. [Un-1 2.] 1. Not peaceful or orderly; not (yet) quietly or firmly established. b. Of weather, etc.: Changeable, variable 1707. c. That has not yet settled down 1691. 2. Not settled in a particular place or position 1594. 3. Not settled, tranquil, calm, or staid in character; restless, turbulent 1594. 4. Undecided, undetermined 1593. 5. Unbalanced, disturbed 1611. b. Of persons: Mentally affected 1611. 6. Not assigned by will 1671. b. Undischarged, unpaid 1811. c. Not freed from doubt or uncertainty; undecided 1844. 7. Not occupied by settlers 1724. Hence Unse·ttledness.

Unse·ttlement. 1648. [f. Unsettle *v.* or Un-1 6.] 1. The act or process of unsettling. 2. Unsettled state or condition 1650.

Unse·vered *ppl. a.* [Un-1 2] 1453. Unsew· *v.* [Un-2 1] late ME. Unsew·ed *ppl. a.* [Un-1 2] ME. Unsew·n *ppl. a.* [Un-1 2] 1648.

Unse·x, *v.* 1605. [Un-2 4 b.] *trans.* To deprive or divest of sex, or of the typical qualities of one or other (*esp.* the female) sex. Hence Unse·xed *ppl. a.*

Unse·xual *a.* [Un-1 1] 1819, -ly *adv.* Unsha·ckle *v.* [Un-2 2 b] 1611. Unsha·ckled *ppl. a.* [Un-1 2] 1776. Unsha·ded *ppl. a.* [Un-1 2] 1668. Unsha·dow *v.* [Un-2 2 b] 1550. Unsha·dowed *ppl. a.* [Un-1 2] 1593. Unsha·keable *a.* [Un-1 1] 1611, -bly *adv.* Unsha·ken *ppl. a.* [Un-1 2] 1460. Unsha·med *ppl. a.* [Un-1 2] late ME. Unsha·pe *v.* [Un-2 1, 2] late ME. Unsha·ped *ppl. a.* [Un-1 2] 1572. Unsha·peliness [Un-1 6] 1741. Unsha·pely *a.* [Un-1 1] ME. Unsha·pen *ppl. a.* [Un-1 2] ME. Unsha·red *ppl. a.* [Un-1 2] 1616. Unsha·ttered *ppl. a.* [Un-1 2] 1634. Unsha·ved *ppl. a.* [Un-1 2] 1648. Unsha·ven *ppl. a.* [Un-1 2] late ME. Unshaw·l *v.* [Un-2 2, 5] 1817.

Unshea·the, *v.* late ME. [Un-2 2, 3.] †1. *trans.* To dislodge -1593. 2. To draw (a weapon) from the sheath or scabbard 1542. 3. To strip of a sheath or covering 1638.

1. Til I my soule out of my breste vnshethe Chaucer. 2. *To u. the sword*, to begin hostilities. Hence Unshea·thed *ppl. a.*

Unshe·d *ppl. a.* [Un-1 2] 1450. Unshe·ll *v.* [Un-2 3] 1599. Unshe·lled *ppl. a.* [Un-1 2] 1594. Unshe·ltered *ppl. a.* [Un-1 2] 1599. Unshe·ltering *ppl. a.* [Un-1 4] 1614. Unshe·nt *ppl. a.* (*arch.*) [Un-1 2] ME. Unshe·pherded *ppl. a.* [Un-1 2] 1850. Unshie·lded *ppl. a.* [Un-1 2] Dryden. Unshi·fted *ppl. a.* [Un-1 2] 1643. Unshi·fting *ppl. a.* [Un-1 4] Wordsw.

Unshi·p, *v.* 1450. [Un-2 3, 2, 5.] 1. *trans.* To take out of, remove, or discharge from a ship; to disembark. 2. *Naut.* To detach or remove (esp. a mast, rudder, or oar) from a fixed place or position 1598. b. *gen.* 1793. 3. *intr.* a. To admit of being detached or removed 1834. b. To become detached 1867. Hence Unshi·pment.

Unshi·pped *a.* [Un-1 3] 1720. Unsho·cked *ppl. a.* [Un-1 2] 1712.

Unsho·d, *ppl. a.* OE. [Un-1 2.] 1. Without shoes, barefooted. 2. Of horses: Having cast a shoe or shoes; not furnished with shoes 1523. 3. Not protected with an iron rim, toe-piece, etc. 1497.

Unshoe· *v.* [Un-2 2] 1481. Unsho·rn *ppl. a.* [Un-1 2] 1449. Unsho·rtened *ppl. a.* [Un-1 2] 1744. Unsho·t *ppl. a.* [Un-1 2] 1544. Unshou·lder *v.* [Un-2 2] 1598. Unshow·ered *ppl. a.* [Un-1 2] Milt. Unshow·n *ppl. a.* [Un-1 2] Shaks. Unshri·ne *v.* [Un-2 3] 1599. Unshri·nkable *a.* [Un-1 1] 1885. Unshri·nking *ppl. a.* [Un-1 4] Shaks., -ly *adv.* Unshri·ven *ppl. a.* [Un-1 2] ME. Unshrou·d *v.* [Un-2 1, 3] 1594. Unshrou·ded *ppl. a.* [Un-1 2] late ME. Unshru·nken *ppl. a.* [Un-1 2] 1862. Unshu·ffled *ppl. a.* [Un-1 2] 1775. Unshu·nnable *a.* [Un-1 1] Shaks. Unshu·t *v.* (now *rare*) [Un-2 1, 5] ME. Unshu·t *ppl. a.* [Un-1 2] late ME. Unshu·ttered *ppl. a.* [Un-1 2] 1845.

Unsi·fted, *ppl. a.* 1589. [Un-1 2.] 1. Not passed through a sieve; unstrained. 2. *fig.* Not classified, scrutinized, or tested 1620. †3. Untried, inexperienced. Shaks.

Unsi·ghing *ppl. a.* [Un-1 4] 1743.

Unsi·ght, *v.* 1615. [Un-2 2 b.] 1. *trans.* To blind (*rare*). 2. In *pa. pple.* Cut off from seeing an object 1825.

Unsi·ghted *ppl. a.* [Un-1 2.] 1584.

Unsi·ghtly, *a.* late ME. [Un-1 2.] Unpleasing to look at; ugly. b. Applied to immaterial things 1605. Hence Unsi·ghtliness.

Unsi·gnalled *ppl. a.* [Un-1 2] 1868. Unsi·gned *ppl. a.* [Un-1 2] 1598. Unsi·gnifying *ppl. a.* [Un-1 4] 1665. Unsi·lenceable *a.* [Un-1 1] 1678. Unsi·lenced *ppl. a.* [Un-1 2] 1615. Unsi·lvered *ppl. a.* [Un-1 2] 1772. Unsi·milar *a.* [Un-1 1] 1768. Unsi·mple *a.* [Un-1 1] 1541.

Unsi·n, *v.* 1628. [Un-2 2 b, 4 b.] 1. *trans.* To annul (a sin) by subsequent action. 2. To maintain or prove to be no sin 1682.

Unsince·re *a.* [Un-1 1] 1577. Unsi·new *v.* [Un-2 2, 4 b.] 1598. Unsi·newed *ppl. a.* [Un-1 2] 1541. Unsi·newy *a.* [Un-1 1] 1622. Unsi·nful *a.* [Un-1 1] 1598, -ly *adv.*, -ness. Unsi·nged *ppl. a.* [Un-1 2] 1599. Unsi·nkable *a.* [Un-1 1] 1655, -ness, -bi·lity. Unsi·nking *ppl. a.* [Un-1 4] 1705. Unsi·nning *ppl. a.* [Un-1 4] late ME. Unsi·ster *v.* [Un-2 4 b] 1875. Unsi·sterly *a.* [Un-1 1] 1747.

Unsi·zeable, *a.* 1653. [Un-1 1.] †1. Unequal in size -1716. †2. Too large, unwieldy -1759. 3. Of fish: Not grown to a proper size; immature 1746.

Unsi·zed, *ppl. a.*1 1700. [Un-1 2 + Size *v.*1] Not made to size, not sorted into sizes.

Unsi·zed, *ppl. a.*2 1794. [Un-1 2 + Size *v.*2] Not stiffened or coated with size.

Unski·lful, *a.* late ME. [Un-1 1.] †1. Ill-advised, unwise; ignorant *of* something -1667. 2. Lacking in skill; inexpert 1565. b. Displaying lack of skill; clumsy 1586. Hence Unski·lful-ly *adv.*, -ness.

Unski·ll (*arch.*) [Un-1 6; cf. ON. *úskil.*] ME.

Unski·lled, *ppl. a.* 1581. [Un-1 2.] 1. Not skilled or expert *in* something; ignorant *of*; not qualified *to* do something. b. Inexpert, inexperienced 1693. c. *spec.* Not skilled in some handicraft; without technical training 1851. 2. Not involving or requiring skill; displaying lack of skill 1833.

Unski·mmed *ppl. a.* [Un-1 2] 1634. Unski·n *v.* (now *rare*) [Un-2 2] 1598. Unski·nned *ppl. a.* [Un-1 2] 1882. Unsla·cked *ppl. a.* [Un-1 2] 1593. Unsla·ckened *ppl. a.* [Un-1 2] 1770. Unsla·ckening *ppl. a.* [Un-1 4] 1768. Unslai·n *ppl. a.* [Un-1 2] ME. Unsla·ked *ppl. a.* [Un-1 2] 1598. Unsla·te *v.* [Un-2 2] 1598. Unslau·ghtered *ppl. a.* [Un-1 2] 1719. Unsla·ve *v.* [Un-2 2 b] 1618. Unslee·ping *ppl. a.* [Un-1 4] Milt., -ly *adv.*

Unsle·pt, *ppl. a.* 1500. [Un-1 2.] 1. Not having slept. 2. Of a bed, etc.: Not slept *in.* 1864. 3. Of a carouse, etc.: Not slept *off* 1821.

1. Pale, as man longe u. 1500. I hurry on board, unsupped and u. Froude.

Unsli·ng *v.* [Un-2 1, 2 b] 1630. Unsli·p *v.* [Un-2 1, 2 b] 1611. Unsli·pping *ppl. a.* [Un-1 4] Shaks.

Unslui·ce, *v.* 1611. [Un-2 2 b, 5.] 1. To let out as from a sluice; to allow to flow. 2. To furnish with an outlet 1652.

Unslu·mbering *ppl. a.* [Un-1 4] 1718. Unsma·rt *a.* [Un-1 1] 1480. Unsme·lted *ppl. a.* [Un-1 2] 1824. Unsmi·led *ppl. a.* [Un-1 2] 1841. Unsmi·ling *ppl. a.* [Un-1 4] 1826, -ly *adv.*, -ness. Unsmi·rched *ppl. a.* [Un-1 2] Shaks. Unsmi·tten *ppl. a.* [Un-1 2] late ME. Unsmo·ked *ppl. a.* [Un-1 2] 1648. Unsmoo·th *a.* [Un-1 1] 1597. Unsmoo·th *v.* [Un-2 4 b] 1621. Unsmoo·thed *ppl. a.* [Un-1 2] 1614. Unsmo·therable *a.* [Un-1 1] Donne. Unsna·p *v.* [Un-2 1, 5] 1862.

Unsna·rl, *v.* 1555. [Un-2 1.] *trans.* To disentangle.

Unsnu·bbable *a.* [Un-1 1] 1847. Unsnu·ffed *ppl. a.* [Un-1 2] 1825.

Unso·ber, *a.* late ME. [Un-1 1.] †1. Uncontrolled, immoderate -1680. 2. Unregulated in conduct; not staid or grave 1542. 3. Affected by or addicted to drinking 1611.

1. The sea was vnsober 1400. Hence Unso·ber-ly *adv.*, -ness.

Unso·ciable, *a.* 1600. [Un-1 1.] 1. Not sociable or companionable; not readily or pleasantly associating with others. 2. Ill matched; incongruous, incompatible 1611. 3. Interfering with social intercourse 1638.

2. This..text..seemeth vnsociable to our begunne Subiect 1611. 3. Sunder'd by savage seas u. From kin and country 1861. So Unsociabi·lity. Unso·ciableness. Unso·ciably *adv.*

Unso·cial, *a.* 1731. [Un-1 1.] Not living or lived in communities, isolated or secluded or independent; ill adapted to or not fond of social life. Hence Unsocia·lity.

Unso·cket *v.* [Un-2 3] 1711. Unso·dden *ppl. a.* [Un-1 2] OE. Unso·ftened *ppl. a.* [Un-1 2] 1645. Unsoi·led *ppl. a.* [Un-1 2] Marlowe. Unso·ld *ppl. a.* [Un-1 2] late ME. Unso·lder *v.* [Un-2 1] 1538. Unso·ldered *ppl. a.* [Un-1 2] 1641. Unso·ldier *v.* [Un-2 2, 4 b] 1611. Unso·ldierlike *a.* [Un-1 1] 1590. Unso·ldierly *a.* [Un-1 2] 1598. Unso·lemn *a.* [Un-1 1] late ME. Unsoli·cited *ppl. a.* [Un-1 2] Shaks. Unsoli·citous *a.* [Un-1 1] 1668. Unso·lid *a.* [Un-1 1] 1593, -ly *adv.*, -ness. Unso·lvable *a.* [Un-1 1] 1821. Unso·lved *ppl. a.* [Un-1 2] 1665. Unso·n *v.* [Un-2 4 b] 1652. Unso·nlike *a.* [Un-1 1] 1657. Unsoo·thed *ppl. a.* [Un-1 2] 1648. Unsophi·stical *a.* [Un-1 1] Landor, -ly *adv.* Unsophi·sticate *ppl. a.* (now *rare*) [Un-1 2] 1607.

Unsophi·sticated, *ppl. a.* 1630. [Un-1 2.] 1. Unadulterated, unmixed. 2. Not tampered with, altered, or falsified; uncorrupted, genuine 1664. 3. Not sophisticated in habits, manners, or mind; natural, ingenuous 1665.

1. Vnsophisticated drinke, That neuer makes men stagger 1630. 2. The correspondence in its genuine u. state 1843. 3. What an u. little country creature you are! Thackeray.

Unsophistica·tion [Un-1 6] 1825. Unso·rted *ppl. a.* [Un-1 2] 1533.

Unsou·ght, *ppl. a.* ME. [Un-1 2.] 1. Not searched out or sought for. b. Not obtained by search or effort ME. 2. Unasked; without being requested 1500. 3. Unexamined, unexplored. late ME. 4. Not resorted to; untried 1582.

Unsou·l, *v.* 1634. [Un-2 2, 4 b.] 1. *trans.* To dispirit. Now *rare.* 2. To deprive of soul; to make soulless 1652.

1. Your sad appearance..Would half u. your army Chapman.

Unsou·led *ppl. a.* [Un-1 2] Spenser.

Unsou·nd, *a.* ME. [Un-1 1.] 1. Of persons, etc.: Not physically sound; unhealthy, diseased. b. *transf.* Of wounds, ailments, etc. late ME. c. Of substances, plants, etc.: Not in sound or good condition 1617. 2. Morally corrupt; wicked, evil. late ME. 3. Not mentally sound or normal; not sane 1547. 4. Not soundly based in fact or reasoning 1595. b. Holding such opinions, etc. 1597. 5. Lacking in solidity or firmness 1590. **6.** Of sleep: Broken or disturbed 1584.

2. Lewd my hauiour was, vnsound my carriage 1601. 4. b. St. John, I have even heard, was u. about Old Testament dates 1891. Hence **Unsou·nd·ly** *adv.*, -ness.

Unsou·ndable *a.* [Un-^{1} 1] 1627. **Unsou·nded** *ppl. a.*^{1} [Un-^{1} 2 + Sound *v.*^{1}] 1530. **Unsou·nded** *ppl. a.*^{2} [Un-^{1} 2 + Sound *v.*^{2}] Shaks. **Unsou·red** *ppl. a.* [Un-^{1} 2] Bacon. **Unsow·n** *ppl. a.* [Un-^{1} 2] late ME. **Unspa·red** *ppl. a.* [Un-^{1} 2] ME.

Unspa·ring, *ppl. a.* 1586. [Un-^{1} 4.] **1.** Showing no forbearance or mercy; sparing no effort; zealous. **2.** Not niggardly; liberal, lavish 1667. Hence **Unspa·ringly** *adv.*

Unspaw·ned *ppl. a.* [Un-^{1} 2] 1814. **Unspea·k** *v.* [Un-^{2} 1] Shaks.

Unspea·kable, *a.* late ME. [Un-^{1} 1.] **1.** Incapable of being expressed in words; inexpressible, ineffable. **b.** *spec.* Indescribably or inexpressibly bad or objectionable 1831. **2.** *U.S.* Unwilling or unable to speak 1888.

1. It is chaunged by an vnspeakeable woorking, although it seme bread to vs 1534. I had the u. mortification to see my favours sometimes not inserted 1754. b. The u. Turk should be immediately struck out of the question Carlyle. Hence **Unspea·kableness. Unspea·kably** *adv.*

Unspea·king *ppl. a.* [Un-^{1} 4] late ME. **Unspe·cialized** *ppl. a.* [Un-^{1} 2] 1874. **Unspeci·fic** *a.* [Un-^{1} 1] 1807. **Unspe·cified** *ppl. a.* [Un-^{1} 2] 1624. **Unspe·ctacled** *ppl. a.* [Un-^{1} 2] 1791. **Unspe·culative** *a.* [Un-^{1} 1] 1659.

Unspe·d, *ppl. a. arch.* ME. [Un-^{1} 2.] Not having succeeded or attained one's or its object; without success.

So was he come ayein u. Gower.

Unspe·ll, *v.* 1611. [Un-^{2} 1.] **1.** *trans.* To undo (a spell). **2.** To free from a spell 1635. **3.** *Typog.* In distributing type, to detach letter from letter in (a word) 1846.

Unspe·llable *a.* [Un-^{1} 1] 1852.

Unspe·nt, *ppl. a.* 1466. [Un-^{1} 2.] **1.** Not expended or used. Of money, food, cartridges, etc. **2.** Not at an end or worn out, with force or strength remaining, unexhausted 1611.

Unsphe·re, *v.* 1611. [Un-^{2} 3.] *trans.* To remove (a heavenly body, *fig.* a spirit) from its place in the sky.

Though you would seek t' vnsphere the Stars with Oaths Shaks. Unsphear The spirit of Plato Milton. Hence **Unsphe·red** *ppl. a.* 1598.

Unspi·ced *ppl. a.* [Un-^{1} 2] 1655. **Unspie·d** *ppl. a.* [Un-^{1} 2] late ME. **Unspi·ke** *v.* [Un-^{2} 1, 2 b] 1680. **Unspi·lled, -spi·lt** *ppl. a.* [Un-^{1} 2] 1573. **Unspi·n** *v.* [Un-^{2} 1] 1585. **Unspi·ritual** *a.* [Un-^{1} 1] Milt., -ly *adv.*, -ness. **Unspi·ritualize** *v.* [Un-^{2} 4 c] 1716. **Unspli·t** *ppl. a.* [Un-^{1} 2] 1656.

Unspoi·led, *ppl. a.* 1500. [Un-^{1} 2.] **1.** Not despoiled or plundered. **2.** Not spoiled or deteriorated 1732. So **Unspoi·lt** *ppl. a.* 1796, in sense 2.

Unspo·ken, *ppl. a.* late ME. [Un-^{1} 2.] **1.** Not spoken *of.* **2.** Not uttered; not expressed in speech 1449. **3.** Not spoken *to* 1616.

Unsponta·neous *a.* [Un-^{1} 1] 1791. **Unspo·rting** *ppl. a.* [Un-^{1} 4] 1859. **Unspo·rtsmanlike** *a.* [Un-^{1} 1] 1754.

Unspo·tted, *ppl. a.* late ME. [Un-^{1} 2.] **1.** Free from any spot or stain. **b.** *Nat. Hist.* Not marked with spots 1804. **2.** Not morally stained; unblemished, pure. late ME.

Unsprea·d *ppl. a.* [Un-^{1} 2] 1589. **Unspu·n** *ppl. a.* [Un-^{1} 2] 1545. **Unspu·rred** (*ppl.*) *a.* [Un-^{1} 2, 3] 1635. **Unsqua·ndered** *ppl. a.* [Un-^{1} 2] 1799. **Unsqua·red** *ppl. a.* [Un-^{1} 2] 1549. **Unsquee·zed** *ppl. a.* [Un-^{1} 2] 1683.

Unsta·ble, *a.* ME. [Un-^{1} 1.] **1.** Apt to move or be moved about; not stationary. **b.** Not steady in position; readily swaying or shaking; liable to swing or fall. late ME. **c.** Of movement: Unsteady; irregular 1549. **d.** *Mech.* Of equilibrium 1839. **2.** Not stable in purpose; vacillating, unreliable, changeable ME. **3.** Not fixed in character or condition; apt to change or alter; variable ME. **b.** *Chem.* Of compounds: Readily broken up 1849.

1. b. Thilke u. whel, Which evere torneth Gower. d. The body will be in a state of u. equilibrium 1839. 3. All oligarchies and democracies are u. 1863. So **Unstabi·lity** 1470. Hence **Unsta·bleness. Unsta·bly** *adv.*

Unstai·d *a.* (*arch.*) [Un-^{1} 1] 1550, -ly *adv.*, -ness. **Unstai·nable** *a.* [Un-^{1} 1] 1584. **Unstai·ned** *ppl. a.* [Un-^{1} 2] 1555. **Unsta·mped** *ppl. a.* [Un-^{1} 2] 1594. **Unsta·nchable** *a.* [Un-^{1} 1] late ME.

Unsta·nched, *ppl. a.* late ME. [Un-^{1} 2.] **1.** Not satisfied; unsated. *arch.* **b.** Of wounds: Still bleeding 1826. **2.** Not made staunch or water-tight. *arch.* 1607.

Unsta·rched *ppl. a.* [Un-^{1} 2] 1827. **Unsta·rred** *ppl. a.* [Un-^{1} 2] 1849. **Unsta·rtled** *ppl. a.* [Un-^{1} 2] 1659. **Unsta·te** *v.* [Un-^{2} 4 b] 1586. **Unsta·ted** *ppl. a.* [Un-^{1} 2] 1864. **Unsta·tesmanlike** *a.* [Un-^{1} 1] 1796. **Unsta·tutable** *a.* [Un-^{1} 1] 1634, -bly *adv.* **Unstay·ed** *ppl. a.*^{1} [Un-^{1} 2 + Stay *v.*^{1}] 1600. **Unstay·ed** *ppl. a.*^{2} [Un-^{1} 2 + Stay *v.*^{2}] 1594. **Unstay·ed** *ppl. a.*^{3} [Un-^{1} 2 + Stay *sb.*^{2}] 1820. **Unstay·ing** *ppl. a.* [Un-^{1} 4] 1616. **Unstea·dfast** *a.* [Un-^{1} 1] ME., -ly *adv.*, -ness.

Unstea·dy, *a.* 1598. [Un-^{1} 1.] **1.** Not steady in position; not firm or secure. **2.** Not steady or constant in conduct or purpose; fluctuating, fickle, wavering 1598. **3.** Marked or characterized by absence of steadiness or regularity; not regular, even, or uniform 1690. Hence **Unstea·dily** *adv.* **Unstea·diness.**

Unstea·dy *v.* [Un-^{2} 4 a] 1532. **Unstee·ped** *ppl. a.* [Un-^{1} 2] 1626. **Unste·p** *v.* [Un-^{2} 3, 5] 1853. **Unsti·ffen** *v.* [Un-^{2} 4] 1611. **Unsti·ffened** *a.* [Un-^{1} 2] 1648. **Unsti·fled** *ppl. a.* [Un-^{1} 2] 1742. **Unsti·lled** *ppl. a.* [Un-^{1} 2] 1648. **Unsti·mulated** *ppl. a.* [Un-^{1} 2] 1800. **Unsti·mulating** *ppl. a.* [Un-^{1} 4] 1844. **Unsti·nted** *ppl. a.* [Un-^{1} 2] 1480, -ly *adv.* **Unsti·nting** *ppl. a.* [Un-^{1} 4] 1845, -ly *adv.* **Unsti·rred** *ppl. a.* [Un-^{1} 2] ME. **Unsti·rring** *ppl. a.* [Un-^{1} 4] 1684. **Unsti·tch** *v.* [Un-^{2} 1] 1538. **Unsti·tched** *ppl. a.* [Un-^{1} 2] 1599.

Unsto·ck *v.* 1547. [Un-^{2} 2, 3.] **1.** *trans.* **a.** To remove (a ship) from the stocks. **b.** To dismount (a gun) 1598. **c.** To remove the stock from (a gun, etc.) 1706. **2.** To deplete of cattle, inhabitants, plants, etc. 1647.

2. The conflict of the Roses did not u...England 1865. So **Unsto·cked** *ppl. a.* [Un-^{1} 2] late ME.

Unsto·ckinged *ppl. a.* [Un-^{1} 2] 1812. **Unstoo·ping** *ppl. a.* [Un-^{1} 4] Shaks.

Unsto·p, *v.* late ME. [Un-^{2} 1.] **1.** *trans.* To free from being stopped up or closed. **2.** To pull out (an organ-stop) 1855. **3.** *Naut.* To let (the cable or engine) run again after stopping. Also *absol.* 1840.

1. The eares of the deafe shalbe vnstopped *Isaiah* xxxv. 5.

Unsto·ppable *a.* [Un-^{1} 1] 1836.

Unsto·pped, *ppl. a.* late ME. [Un-^{1} 2.] **1.** Not closed, stuffed up, corked, or bunged. **b.** Of a tooth or dental cavity: Not filled with stopping 1825. **c.** Of a hunting country: With the earths not stopped 1887. **2.** Not checked, unhindered 1621. **3.** *Phonetics.* Of a consonant: Open (cf. Stopped) 1874. **4.** Of blank verse: Not end-stopped (see End *sb.*) 1874.

Unsto·pper *v.* [Un-^{2} 1, 2] 1839. **Unsto·re** *v.* [Un-^{2} 2, 3] 1618. **Unsto·red** *ppl. a.* [Un-^{1} 2] 1603.

Unstow·, *v.* 1726. [Un-^{2} 1.] *Naut.* To take out of stowage; to clear (a hold, etc.) of the articles stowed in it.

Unstrai·ned, *ppl. a.* late ME. [Un-^{1} 2.] **1.** Not drawn tight; not subjected to a strain. **2.** Not forced or produced by effort 1580. **3.** Not passed through a strainer 1828.

Unstra·p *v.* [Un-^{2} 2 b] 1828. **Unstra·tified** *ppl. a.* [Un-^{1} 2] 1802. **Unstrea·ked** *ppl. a.* [Un-^{1} 2] 1861. **Unstre·ngthened** *ppl. a.* [Un-^{1} 2] 1597. **Unstre·ssed** *ppl. a.* [Un-^{1} 2] 1883. **Unstre·tch** *v.* [Un-^{2} 1, 5] 1611. **Unstri·cken** *ppl. a.* [Un-^{1} 2] 1548.

Unstri·ng, *v.* 1611. [Un-^{2} 2, 2 b.] **1.** *trans.* To relax or remove the string(s) of (a bow, lyre, etc.). **b.** To undo the strings of (a purse). Also *absol.* Now *rare.* 1681. **2.** To detach from a string 1697. **3.** To render lax or weak; to disorder (the nerves, etc.) 1700.

Unstri·nged *ppl. a.* [Un-^{1} 2] Shaks. **Unstri·p** *v.* (now *dial.* and *rare*) [Un-^{2} 7] 1596. **Unstri·ped** *ppl. a.* [Un-^{1} 2] 1841. **Unstri·pped** *ppl. a.* [Un-^{1} 2] 1676. **Unstru·ck** *ppl. a.* [Un-^{1} 2] 1615.

Unstru·ng, *ppl. a.* 1598. [f. Unstring *v.*, or Un-^{1} 2.] **1.** Having the string(s) removed or relaxed. **2.** Weakened, relaxed; unnerved 1692.

Unstu·died, *ppl. a.* late ME. [Un-^{1} 2.] **1.** Not meditated on; neglected as a subject of study or thought. **2.** Not having studied; unversed (*in* something) 1642. **3.** Not elaborated by study or care; not laboured or artificial 1657.

1. Þus..is goddis lawe vnstudied Wyclif. 2. I.. was not u. in those authors which are most commended Milt. 3. Express'd in ready and u. Words Dryden.

Unstu·dious *a.* [Un-^{1} 1] 1663. **Unstu·ffed** *ppl. a.* [Un-^{1} 2] 1480. **Unstu·ng** *ppl. a.* [Un-^{1} 2] 1615. **Unsty·lish** *a.* [Un-^{1} 1] 1863. **Unsubdu·able** *a.* [Un-^{1} 1] 1611. **Unsubdue·d** *ppl. a.* [Un-^{1} 2] 1590, -ness. **Unsu·bject** *a.* [Un-^{1} 1] late ME. **Unsubje·cted** *ppl. a.* [Un-^{1} 2] late ME. **Unsubli·med** *ppl. a.* [Un-^{1} 2] 1694. **Unsubme·rged** *ppl. a.* [Un-^{1} 2] 1883. **Unsubmi·ssive** *a.* [Un-^{1} 1] 1653, -ness. **Unsubmi·tting** *ppl. a.* [Un-^{1} 4] 1730. **Unsubo·rned** *ppl. a.* [Un-^{1} 2] 1656. **Unsubscri·bed** *ppl. a.* [Un-^{1} 2] 1571. **Unsubscri·bing** *ppl. a.* [Un-^{1} 4] 1790. **Unsu·bsidized** *ppl. a.* [Un-^{1} 2] 1756.

Unsubsta·ntial, *a.* 1455. [Un-^{1} 1.] **1.** Having no real basis or foundation in fact. **2.** Having no bodily or material substance 1592. **b.** Lacking in substance or solidity 1617.

1. These deep but u. meditations Gibbon. 2. Hill and plain, apparently u. as a mountain mist 1871. b. A nutriment that is watry and u. 1773. Hence **U:nsubstantia·lity. Unsubsta·ntially** *adv.*

U:nsubsta·ntiate *v.* [Un-^{2} 4] 1799. **U:nsubsta·ntiated** *ppl. a.* [Un-^{1} 2] 1837. **Unsubve·rted** *ppl. a.* [Un-^{1} 2] Wordsw. **Unsucce·ss** [Un-^{1} 6] Sidney. **Unsucce·ssful** *a.* [Un-^{1} 1] 1617, -ly *adv.*, -ness. **Unsucce·ssive** *a.* (now *rare*) [Un-^{1} 1] 1617. **Unsu·ccoured** *ppl. a.* [Un-^{1} 1] late ME. **Unsu·cked** *ppl. a.* [Un-^{1} 2] 1652. **Unsue·d** *ppl. a.* [Un-^{1} 2] 1594. **Unsu·fferable** *a.* (now *rare*) [Un-^{1} 2] ME., -bly *adv.* **Unsuffi·ced** *ppl. a.* [Un-^{1} 1] 1586. **†Unsuffi·cient** *a.* [Un-^{1} 1] –1656. **Unsu·gared** *ppl. a.* [Un-^{1} 2] 1592. **Unsugge·stive** *a.* [Un-^{1} 1] Lamb.

Unsui·t, *v.* 1635. [Un-^{1} 7.] **1.** *trans.* To be at variance with (*rare*). **2.** To render unsuitable 1869.

Unsui·table, *a.* 1586. [Un-^{1} 1.] Not suitable, unfitting. Const. *to, for.* Hence **Unsuitabi·lity. Unsui·tably** *adv.* **Unsui·tableness.**

Unsui·ted, *ppl. a.* 1598. [Un-^{1} 2.] **1.** Lacking the qualities required. Const. *to, for.* **2.** Not accommodated or supplied with what is desired 1796.

2. So that no constitution-fancier may go u. from his shop Burke.

Unsui·ting *ppl. a.* [Un-^{1} 4] 1596. **Unsu·llied** *ppl. a.* [Un-^{1} 2] Shaks., -ness. **Unsu·mmed** *ppl. a.* [Un-^{1} 2] late ME. **Unsu·mmerlike** *a.* [Un-^{1} 1] 1869. **Unsu·mmoned** *ppl. a.* [Un-^{1} 2] 1474.

Unsu·ng, *ppl. a.* late ME. [Un-^{1} 2.] **1.** Not sung. **2.** Not celebrated in or by song 1667.

Unsu·nk *ppl. a.* [Un-^{1} 2] ME.

Unsu·nned, *ppl. a.* 1607. [Un-^{1} 2.] **1.** Not penetrated or reached by sunlight; not exposed or accessible to the sun. **b.** *fig.* Not made patent or public 1809. **2.** Not touched or affected by the light or heat of the sun 1611. **b.** Not coloured or tanned by the sun 1821. **3.** Not lighted up by the sun 1840.

1. The unsun'd heaps Of Misers treasure Milt. b. The u. historical treasures in the possession of the London Corporation 1862. 2. As Chaste, as vn-Sunn'd Snow Shaks.

Unsupe·rfluous *a.* [Un-^{1} 1] 1571. **Unsupervised** *ppl. a.* [Un-^{1} 2] 1899. **Unsu·pped** *ppl. a.* [Un-^{1} 2] late ME. **Unsupplie·d** *ppl. a.* [Un-^{1} 2] 1599. **Unsuppo·rtable** *a.* [Un-^{1} 1] 1586.

Unsuppo·rted, *ppl. a.* late ME. [Un-^{1} 2.] **1.** Not supported by aid or assent; not backed up or corroborated. **b.** Const. *by.* 1694. **2.** Not physically supported or sustained 1635.

Unsuppo·sable *a.* [Un-^{1} 1] 1650. **Unsuppre·ssed** *ppl. a.* [Un-^{1} 2] 1621.

Unsure (vnʃūᵊ·ɪ), *a.* late ME. [Un-^{1} 1.] **1.** Not safe against attack or mishap; liable to danger or risk; exposed to peril; insecure. Now *rare.* **b.** Not affording or conducive to safety; unsafe, liable to yield or give way. late ME. **2.** Marked by uncertainty or unsteadfastness; dependent on chance or accident; precarious, uncertain. late ME. **3.** Of persons, etc.: Unreliable, untrustworthy. Now *rare.* 1445. **4.** Open to doubt; not fixed, sure, or certain; doubtful 1445. **5.** Lacking certainty, assurance, or confidence; in doubt; not sure *of* something; not knowing *whether, when,* etc. late ME. **6.** Irresolute, faltering, vacillating 1633. Hence **Unsu·re·ly** *adv.* (*rare*), **-ness.**

Unsurmou·ntable *a.* [Un-^{1} 1] 1611. **Unsurpa·ssable** *a.* [Un-^{1} 1] 1611, **-bly** *adv.* **Unsurpa·ssed** *ppl. a.* [Un-^{1} 2] 1818. **Unsurpri·sed** *ppl. a.* [Un-^{1} 2] 1591. **Unsurre·ndered** *ppl. a.* [Un-^{1} 2] 1800. **Unsurrou·nded** *ppl. a.* [Un-^{1} 2] 1813. **Unsurvey·able** *a.* [Un-^{1} 1] 1833. **Unsurvey·ed** *ppl. a.* [Un-^{1} 2] 1546. **U·nsusceptibi·lity** [Un-^{1} 6] 1805. **Unsusce·ptible** *a.* [Un-^{1} 1] 1692.

Unsuspe·cted, *ppl. a.* 1530. [Un-^{1} 2.] **1.** Not incurring suspicion; escaping suspicion or detection. **2.** Not suspected to exist, or to bear a certain character 1620.

1. The courage of our common seamen is hitherto generally u. 1747. I had..stolen unnotic'd on them, And u...heard the whole Coleridge. 2. A close, secret and u. Christian Fuller. Hence **Unsuspe·ctedly** *adv.*

Unsuspe·cting *ppl. a.* [Un-^{1} 4] 1595, **-ly** *adv.*, **-ness.** **Unsuspe·nded** *ppl. a.* [Un-^{1} 2] 1701. **Unsuspi·cion** [Un-^{1} 6] 1792. **Unsuspi·cious** *a.* [Un-^{1} 1] 1589, **-ly** *adv.*, **-ness.** **Unsustai·nable** *a.* [Un-^{1} 1] 1677. **Unsustai·ned** *ppl. a.* [Un-^{1} 2] 1630. **Unsustai·ning** *ppl. a.* [Un-^{1} 2] 1818. **Unswa·ddle** *v.* [Un-^{2} 2] 1580. **Unswa·llowed** *ppl. a.* [Un-^{1} 2] late ME. **Unswa·the** *v.* [Un-^{2} 2] late ME. **Unsway·ed** *ppl. a.* [Un-^{1} 2] Shaks. **Unswea·r** *v.* [Un-^{2} 1, 5] Shaks. **Unsweet** *a.* [Un-^{1} 1] OE., **-ly** *adv.* **Unswee·tened** *ppl. a.* [Un-^{1} 2] 1817. **Unswe·ll** *v.* (now *rare*) [Un-^{2} 1] late ME. **Unswe·pt** *ppl. a.* [Un-^{1} 2] 1597. **Unswe·rving** *ppl. a.* [Un-^{1} 4] 1694, **-ly** *adv.* **Unswo·llen** *ppl. a.* [Un-^{1} 2] 1648.

Unswo·rn, *ppl. a.* 1529. [Un-^{1} 2.] **1.** Not put on oath; not bound by or having taken an oath. **2.** Not confirmed by, or sworn as, an oath 1623.

Unsy·llabled *ppl. a.* [Un-^{1} 2] 1594. **Unsymme·trical** *a.* [Un-^{1} 1] 1755, **-ly** *adv.* **Unsympathe·tic** *a.* [Un-^{1} 1] 1823, **-ally** *adv.* **Unsy·mpathizing** *ppl. a.* [Un-^{1} 4] 1735, **-ly** *adv.* **U·nsystema·tic** 1770, **-al** 1780, *adjs.* [Un-^{1} 1], **-ly** *adv.* **Unsy·stematized** *ppl. a.* [Un-^{1} 2] 1849. **Unta·ck** *v.* [Un-^{2} 1] 1641.

Unta·ckle, *v.* 1552. [Un-^{2} 2, 2 b.] **1.** To strip (a vessel) of tackle. **2.** To unharness (a horse) 1573. **3.** To free from tackling or fastenings 1905.

Unta·ctful *a.* [Un-^{1} 1] 1860. **Untai·led** *ppl. a.* [Un-^{1} 2] 1611. **Untai·nted** *ppl. a.* [Un-^{1} 2] 1590. **Unta·ken** *ppl. a.* [Un-^{1} 2] ME. **Unta·king** *ppl. a.* [Un-^{1} 4] 1587. **Unta·lented** *ppl. a.* [Un-^{1} 2] 1753. **Unta·lked** *ppl. a.* [Un-^{1} 2] Shaks. **Unta·me** *a.* [Un-^{1} 1] late ME., **-ness.** **Unta·m(e)able** *a.* [Un-^{1} 1] 1567, **-ness, -bly** *adv.* **Unta·med** *ppl. a.* [Un-^{1} 2] ME., **-ly** *adv.*, **-ness.** **Unta·mpered** *ppl. a.* [Un-^{1} 2] 1682. **Unta·ngle** *v.* [Un-^{2} 1, 5] 1550. **Unta·nned** *ppl. a.* [Un-^{1} 2] 1535. **Unta·pped** *ppl. a.* [Un-^{1} 2] 1779. **Unta·rnished** *ppl. a.* [Un-^{1} 2] 1732. **Unta·rred** *ppl. a.* [Un-^{1} 2] 1579. **Unta·sted** *ppl. a.* [Un-^{1} 2] 1538.

Untau·ght, *ppl. a.* ME. [Un-^{1} 2.] **1.** Having had no teaching; uninstructed, untrained, ignorant. **b.** Const. with inf., *in,* or obj. complement 1581. **c.** Of animals, etc. 1697. **2.** Not imparted or acquired by teaching; hence, natural, spontaneous 1445.

1. Better it is to be wnborne than wntawght 1530. b. U. The knowledge of the world Cowper. 2. I have ..a pretty u. Step in Dancing Steele.

Unta·x *v.* [Un-^{2} 2 b] 1831. **Unta·xable** *a.* [Un-^{1} 1] 1610. **Unta·xed** *ppl. a.* [Un-^{1} 2] 1460. **Untea·ch** *v.* [Un-^{2} 1] 1531. **Untea·chable** *a.* [Un-^{1} 1] 1475. **Untea·m** *v.* (now *rare*) [Un-^{2} 2 b] 1548. **Untea·rable** *a.* [Un-^{1} 1] 1648. **Unte·chnical** *a.* [Un-^{1} 1] 1845, **-ly** *adv.* **Unte·llable** *a.* [Un-^{1} 1] late ME.; **-bly** *adv.* not recorded in 17th and 18th cc.; freq. from 1880.

Unte·mpered, *ppl. a.* late ME. [Un-^{1} 2.] **1.** Unregulated, uncontrolled; not held in check. **b.** Not modified or qualified (*by* something) 1768. **2.** Of lime or mortar: Not properly mixed and prepared 1440. **3.** Of steel, etc.: Not tempered or hardened 1820.

Unte·mpted *ppl. a.* [Un-^{1} 2] 1607. **Unte·mpting** *ppl. a.* [Un-^{1} 4] 1824. **Untenabi·lity** [Un-^{1} 6] 1644. **Unte·nable** *a.* [Un-^{1} 1] 1647, **-ness.** **Unte·nant** *v.* [Un-^{2} 2, 3] 1614. **Unte·nantable** *a.* [Un-^{1} 1] 1661. **Unte·nanted** *ppl. a.* [Un-^{1} 2] 1673. **Unte·nded** *ppl. a.* [Un-^{1} 2] 1598. **Unte·nder** *a.* [Un-^{1} 1] Shaks., **-ly** *adv.*, **-ness.** **Unte·ndered** *ppl. a.* [Un-^{1} 2] 1607. **Unte·nted** *ppl. a.* (*arch.*) [Un-^{1} 2 + Tent *v.*^{2}] Shaks. **Unte·rrified** *ppl. a.* [Un-^{1} 2] 1609. **Unte·rrifying** *ppl. a.* [Un-^{1} 4] 1691. **Unte·sted** *ppl. a.* [Un-^{1} 2] 1570. **Unte·ther** *v.* [Un-^{2} 2 b] 1888. **Untha·nked** *ppl. a.* [Un-^{1} 2] 1562.

Untha·nkful, *a.* late ME. [Un-^{1} 1.] **1.** Not earning thanks or gratitude; thankless, unappreciated; unwelcome. **2.** Giving no thanks, ungrateful (*to* a person, *for* a thing) 1499. **3.** Characterized by ingratitude 1614.

1. One of the most u. offices in the world Goldsm. Hence **Untha·nkful·ly** *adv.*, **-ness.**

Untha·tched *ppl. a.* [Un-^{1} 2] 1570. **Unthaw** *v.* (now *dial.*) [Un-^{2} 5, 7] 1598. **Unthaw·ed** *ppl. a.* [Un-^{1} 2] 1611. **Unthea·trical** *a.* [Un-^{1} 1] 1745. **U·ntheolo·gical** *a.* [Un-^{1} 1] Milt. **Unthi·ckened** *ppl. a.* [Un-^{1} 2] 1870. **Unthi·nk** *v.* [Un-^{2} 1] 1600.

Unthi·nkable, *a.* late ME. [Un-^{1} 1.] **1.** Beyond the scope of thought; too great, numerous, etc. to be conceived. **2.** Incapable of being framed or grasped by thought 1445. Hence **Unthi·nkably** *adv.*

Unthi·nking, *ppl. a.* 1676. [Un-^{1} 4.] **1.** Not exercising the faculty of thought; thoughtless; unreflecting; undiscriminating. **2.** Characterized by absence of thought 1688. **3.** Not possessing the faculty of thought 1688. Hence **Unthi·nking·ly** *adv.*, **-ness.**

Unthi·nned *ppl. a.* [Un-^{1} 2] 1648. **Unthou·ght** *ppl. a.* [Un-^{1} 2] 1538. **Unthou·ghtful** *ppl. a.* [Un-^{1} 1] 1456, **-ly** *adv.*, **-ness.** **Unthra·ll** *v.* [Un-^{2} 2 b] 1586. **Unthra·shed, -thre·shed** *ppl. a.* [Un-^{1} 2] 1561. **Unthrea·d** *v.* [Un-^{2} 1] Shaks. **Unthrea·tened** *ppl. a.* [Un-^{1} 2] 1647.

Unthrift (stress var.). late ME. [Un-^{1} 6.] †**1.** A fault or folly. **2.** Want of thrift or economy; wastefulness; †loose living. late ME. **3.** An unthrifty, shiftless, or dissolute person; a spendthrift, prodigal. Now *rare.* ME. **4.** *attrib.* or as *adj.* Prodigal, spendthrift 1562.

2. Ful of ydelnes and al maner vnthrifte 1400. 3. If he played the u. with this golden occasion 1639. 4. The u. Sunne shot vitall gold A thousand peeces Vaughan.

Unthri·fty, *a.* late ME. [Un-^{1} 1.] **1.** Not profitable or serviceable; leading to no good; tending to waste or harm. **2.** Not vigorous or thriving; weakly, unpromising. Now *rare.* 1440. **b.** Characterized by absence of well-being; unprosperous. late ME. †**3.** Unchaste, wanton, profligate –1571. **4.** Not thrifty; improvident; wasteful, extravagant, prodigal 1532. **b.** Prodigal or lavish *of* something 1620.

2. The Cow was very u., for which they gave her Cow Physick 1709. 3. Suche u. Carnall and abhomynable lyvyng 1535. 4. The wormes shall have his carkass, and u. heires his estate 1662. Hence **Unthri·ftily** *adv.* **Unthri·ftiness.**

Unthri·ving *ppl. a.* [Un-^{1} 4] ME., **-ly** *adv.*, **-ness.** **Unthro·ne** *v.* [Un-^{2} 2] 1611. **Unthrow·n** *ppl. a.* [Un-^{1} 2] 1547. **Unthu·mbed** *ppl. a.* [Un-^{1} 2] 1797. **Unthwa·rted** *ppl. a.* [Un-^{1} 2] Wordsw.

Unti·dy, *a.* ME. [Un-^{1} 1.] †**1.** Unseasonable; unsuitable, unseemly –1661. **2.** Not neat or orderly; not kept in good order ME. Hence **Unti·dily** *adv.* **Unti·diness.**

Unti·dy *v.* [Un-^{2} 1] 1891.

Untie (vntəi·), *v.* [OE. *untīgan,* f. Un-^{2} 1, 5 + Tie *v.*] **1.** *trans.* To release, set free, detach, by undoing a cord or similar fastening. **b.** To free from a confining or encircling cord, bond, etc. 1450. **c.** *fig.* ME. **2.** To undo (a cord, knot, etc.) 1590. **b.** *fig.* To solve (a difficulty); esp. with *knot* in fig. sense 1586. **c.** *fig.* To dissolve (a bond, esp. of union) 1634. **3.** *intr.* To become untied 1590. Hence **Untie·d** *ppl. a.*^{1}

Untie·d, *ppl. a.*^{2} [Un-^{1} 2.] Not tied.

For tunges vntayde be rennyng astray Skelton. Unty'd to a man Ramsay. An u. beerhouse 1888.

Until (vnti·l), *prep.* and *conj.* [ME. (orig. north.) *untill,* f. ON. *und* up to + Till *prep.* and *conj.*] **A.** *prep.* **1.** To, unto (a person or place). Now *Sc.* and *north.* **b.** Up to (a point or limit); so as to reach. Now *Sc.* and *north.* ME. **2.** Onward till (a time specified or indicated); up to the time of (an action, occurrence, etc.) ME. **b.** With (usu. after) a negative 1543. **c.** Followed by an adv. or (advb. phr.) of time ME. **3.** Before (a specified time) 1887.

1. Then came vntyll hym the tempter Tindale *Matt.* iv. 3. He..hastned them vntill Spenser. 2. To hang them up u. the end of February 1721. b. Things growing are not ripe vntill their season Shaks. c. U. four years ago 1873.

B. *conj.* Up to the time that; till the point when.

Now get you in, vntill I call for you 1602. A silly wench who has heard stories of apparitions u. she believes them H. Walpole. U. that the day began to daw 1802. After this, u. feathered, they should be fed on rich food 1855. *To think (it) long u.*: see Long *a.* II. 4, Think *v.*^{2} III. 2.

Unti·le *v.* [Un-^{2} 2] late ME. **Unti·led** *ppl. a.* [Un-^{1} 2] late ME. **Unti·llable** *a.* [Un-^{1} 1] 1714. **Unti·lled** *ppl. a.* [Un-^{1} 2] ME. **Unti·mbered** *ppl. a.* [Un-^{1} 2] 1606.

Unti·mely, *a.* 1535. [Un-^{1} 1.] **1.** Coming before the proper or natural time; premature, immature. **2.** Unseasonable (in respect of time of year) 1576. **3.** Ill-timed, inopportune, unseasonable 1581.

1. Euen as a figge tree casteth her vntimely figges Bible (Bishops') *Rev.* vi. 13. Abortion or u. birth 1634. 2. By u. rains or untimelier heat Longf. 3. All this u. activity Freeman.

Unti·mely, *adv.* ME. [Un-^{1} 5.] **1.** Unseasonably, inopportunely. **2.** Prematurely 1586.

Untimeous (vntəi·məs), *a.* Chiefly *Sc.* 1500. [Alteration of earlier *untimes,* advb. gen. of †*untīme* wrong time, by assimilation to adjs. in -(e)ous.] = Untimely *a.* Hence **Unti·meously** *adv.*

Unti·nctured *ppl. a.* [Un-^{1} 2] 1760. **Unti·nged** *ppl. a.* [Un-^{1} 2] 1664. **Unti·nned** *ppl. a.* [Un-^{1} 2] 1825. **Unti·rable** *a.* [Un-^{1} 1] 1607. **Unti·red** *ppl. a.* [Un-^{1} 2] Shaks. **Unti·ring** *ppl. a.* [Un-^{1} 4] 1822, **-ly** *adv.* **Unti·thed** *ppl. a.* [Un-^{1} 2] 1621. **Unti·tled** *ppl. a.* [Un-^{1} 2] Shaks.

Unto (v·ntu, *formerly also* vntū·), *prep.* and *conj.* Now chiefly *arch.* and *literary.* ME. [Modelled on Until *prep.* by substitution of To *prep.* for the northern equivalent *til* Till *prep.*] **A.** *prep.* **I.** Indicating spatial or local relationship. **1.** = To *prep.* I. 1, 2, 3, 5. **2.** Expressing relative location (esp. with *nigh* or *near*) 1526.

1. Wilt thou flout me thus vnto my face? Shaks. I will vnto Venice Shaks. The Root smelled vnto is good for the same purpose 1670. She..lean'd her head u. the kindly tree 1768. I bow'd fu' low u. this maid Burns. My throat is cut u. the bone Wordsw.

II. Indicating a temporal relationship. **1.** = To *prep.* II. 1. ME. †**2.** After a negative: = Until *prep.* 2 b. –1559.

1. The wulf..hyd hym self nyghe them vnto the nyght Caxton.

III. Expressing the relation of aim, design, destination, result, consequent status or condition. = To *prep.* III. ME.

Many bold knyghtes wente vnto mete Malory. For hokes and hengles u. the skolehouse dore 1487. Hee hath turnd a heauen vnto a hell! Shaks. To destroy and bring us u. nought Drayton. They..provoke Him u. ire Drayton. Such personal estate as he.. shall become..intitled u. 1738.

IV. Followed by an expression denoting or indicating a limit in extent, number, amount, or degree. = To *prep.* IV. 1 b. *arch.* ME. **b.** Down to (an ultimate grade, point, or number). *arch.* ME.

What may the Kings whole Battaile reach vnto? *Vernon.* To thirty thousand. Shaks. b. The whole world perished u. eight persons before the floud Sir T. Browne.

V. Expressing addition or accumulation, attachment, appurtenance, or possession. = To *prep.* V. ME.

A ful noble Knyghte nyghe kynne vnto sire Launcelot MALORY. There maye nothinge be taken from them, nothinge maye be put vnto them COVERDALE *Ecclus.* xviii. 6. Until the Earth seems join'd u. the Sky DRYDEN. So may'st thou be..a Father u. thy contemporaries SIR T. BROWNE.

VI. Expressing comparison or correspondence, relation to a standard, etc. = To *prep.* VI. ME.

Like vnto the turtill 1460. Likewise reckon yee also your selues to be dead indeed vnto sinne *Rom.* vi. 11. All thy passions, match'd with mine, Are as moonlight u. sunlight TENNYSON. U. all seeming, life went merrily WM. MORRIS.

VII. Expressing relations in which the idea of course or direction tends to blend with the dative use. = To *prep.* VII. ME.

He fell vnto his prayers 1440. Then gather strength, and march vnto him straight SHAKS. Now vnto thy bones good night SHAKS. These words of the Prophet vnto Heli 1610. To say Amen, u. Isaiahs Description of our Lord 1710.

VIII. Supplying the place of, assuming or taking over the functions of, the dative. = To *prep.* VIII. ME.

I am now in great haste, as may appeare vnto you SHAKS. This could not but be a great grief u. him BUNYAN. An excellent Lore, That u. your Wives you may teach 1714. The Lord be good u. me! 1796. One ..Known u. few WORDSW.

†**B.** *Conj.* = UNTIL *conj.* -1573.

Untoi·led, *ppl. a.* 1578. [UN-1 2.] †1. Not tilled -1683. 2. Not subjected to or overcome by toil 1598. 3. Not toiled *for* 1651.

Unto·ld, *ppl. a.* [OE. *untéald*: UN-1 2.] †1. Not counted up or counted out -1607. 2. Uncounted or unreckoned because of amount or numbers; indefinitely many or numerous, numberless, countless. late ME. b. Unmeasured, unlimited 1781. 3. Not related or recounted. late ME. †4. Not informed. SPENSER.

2. All the u. riches of his treasury 1853. *U. gold* (colloq.): any amount of money. b. It had..cost.. u. suffering 1875.

Unto·mb *v.* [UN-2 3] 1594. **Unto·mbed** *ppl. a.* [UN-1 2] 1560.

Unto·ngue, *v.* Now *rare.* 1598. [UN-2 2.] *trans.* To make speechless; to deprive of (the use of) the tongue. So **Unto·ngued** *ppl. a.*

Untoo·thsome *a.* [UN-1 1] 1548. **Untorme·nted** *ppl. a.* [UN-1 2] late ME. **Unto·rn** *ppl. a.* [UN-1 2] 1547.

Untou·chable, *a.* 1567. [UN-1 1.] †1. Intangible. b. Beyond the reach of touch 1622. c. *fig.* Unapproachable, unrivalled 1867. 2. Exempt from touch; that one may not touch; sacred 1607. b. *spec.* That cannot legally be interfered with or made use of 1734. 3. Too bad or unpleasant to touch 1873. *sb.* A Hindoo whose touch pollutes 1921.

Untou·ched, *ppl. a.* late ME. [UN-1 2.] 1. Not handled; not having suffered contact. b. Of places: Not reached or visited 1628. 2. Not affected physically; unhurt, intact. late ME. †b. Sexually intact; unviolated -1683. c. Not used or drawn upon; *esp.* untasted 1538. 3. Not worked upon or at; left or remaining in the previous state 1726. 4. Not subjected to discussion, amendment, or criticism; unedited; ignored in argument, etc.; unmentioned. late ME. 5. Not affected, modified, or influenced, esp. injuriously 1586. b. Not emotionally affected; unmoved, calm, undisturbed 1616. 6. Unequalled; unexampled, unparalleled 1736. **Untou·ching** *ppl. a.* [UN-1 4] 1602.

Untoward (ʋntō^u·wǎɹd, ʋntŭwǭ·ɹd), *a.* 1526. [UN-1 1.] †1. Averse *to*, not ready or disposed *for* something; disinclined -1665. 2. Intractable, unruly, perverse 1526. b. Of things: Hard to manage; stubborn, stiff 1566. †c. Ungainly; awkward -1791. 3. Unlucky; unfavourable; turning out badly 1570. 4. Unseemly, improper; foolish 1628.

2. The very u. Spanish Mules 1656. b. What a rascally vntoward thing this poetrie is B. JONSON. c. Knees that..grow u. and unshaped 1658. 3. When the times are u. 1868. She could hardly have made a more u. choice J. AUSTEN. 4. When I with these u. thoughts had striven WORDSW. Hence **Unto·ward·ly** *adv.*, **-ness.**

Unto·wardly, *a.* Now *rare.* 1483. [UN-1 1.] †1. Unbecoming, improper. b. Froward, perverse 1561. 2. Awkward, ungainly 1611. 3. Adverse, unfavourable 1756. Hence **Unto·wardliness.**

Untra·ceable *a.* [UN-1 1] 1661, **-ness, -bly** *adv.* **Untra·ced** *ppl. a.* [UN-1 2] 1641. **Untra·cked** (*ppl.*) *a.* [UN-1 2, 3] 1603. **Untra·ctable** *a.* (now *rare*) [UN-1 1] 1538, **-ness.** **Untrai·ned** *ppl. a.* [UN-1 2] 1548, **-ness.** **Untra·mmelled** *ppl. a.* [UN-1 2] 1795. **Untra·mpled** *ppl. a.* [UN-1 2] 1648. **Untra·nquil** *a.* [UN-1 1] KEATS. **Untra·nsferable** *a.* [UN-1 1] 1649. **Untransfo·rmable** *a.* [UN-1 1] 1570. **Untransfo·rmed** *ppl. a.* [UN-1 2] 1890. **Untransla·table** *a.* [UN-1 1] 1655, **-ness, -bly** *adv.* **Untransla·ted** *ppl. a.* [UN-1 2] 1530. **Untranspa·rent** *a.* [UN-1 1] 1591. **Untranspo·sed** *ppl. a.* [UN-1 2] JOHNSON. **Untra·pped** *a.* [UN-1 3] 1860.

Untra·velled, *ppl. a.* 1585. [UN-1 2.] 1. That has not travelled. 2. Not travelled over or through, unvisited 1646.

Untrea·d *v.* [UN-2 1] SHAKS. **Untrea·sure** *v.* [UN-2 2, 3] SHAKS. **Untrea·table** *a.* [UN-1 2] late ME. **Untrea·ted** *ppl. a.* [UN-1 2] 1456. **Untre·mbling** *ppl. a.* [UN-1 4] 1570, **-ly** *adv.* **Untre·nched** *ppl. a.* [UN-1 2] 1807.

Untre·ssed, *ppl. a.* late ME. [UN-1 2.] Not arranged in tresses; loose, dishevelled.

Untrie·d, *ppl. a.* 1526. [UN-1 2.] 1. Not tried, proved, or tested. 2. Not tried by a judge 1618.

2. Condemn'd u. COWPER. U. offenders DICKENS.

Untri·lled *ppl. a.* [UN-1 2] 1869. **Untri·m** *v.* [UN-2 1] SHAKS. **Untri·mmed** *ppl. a.* [UN-1 2] 1532. **Untro·d** 1593, **untro·dden** ME., *ppl. adjs.* [UN-1 2]. **Untrou·bled** *ppl. a.* [UN-1 2] 1484.

Untrue·, *a.* and *adv.* [OE. *untréowe, untrew(e,* etc., f. UN-1 1, 5.] **A.** *adj.* 1. Of persons: Unfaithful, faithless. 2. Contrary to fact; false. late ME. 3. Dishonest; unfair, unjust; wrong. Now *rare.* late ME. 4. Not straight; inexact; not agreeing with a standard ME.

3. Be cause it was of u. makyng, and untru stuff, no man sette therby 1444. 4. Untrewe Beames and Scales 1503. Whose hand is feeble, or his aim u. COWPER.

†**B.** *adv.* Untruly -1622.

Some fooles would say I flatter'd, spake untrue 1622. Hence **Untru·ly** *adv.*

Untru·ss, *v.* late ME. [UN-2 2 b.] 1. *trans.* To free from a pack or burden (*rare*). 2. To undo (a pack, etc.); to remove or free from some fastening. late ME. 3. *Hist.* To untie (a 'point' or tag of a garment) 1577. b. *absol.* To undo one's dress or breeches 1592. c. To undo or unfasten the garments of 1625. †4. To take apart, dissect, disclose -1651.

Untru·ssed *ppl. a.* [UN-1 2] ME. **Untru·st** (now *rare*) [UN-1 6] ME. **Untru·sted** *ppl. a.* [UN-1 2] 1552. **Untru·stworthiness** [UN-1 6] 1808. **Untru·stworthy** *a.* [UN-1 1] 1846. **Untru·sty** *a.* [UN-1 1] late ME.

Untru·th. [OE. *untréowþ, untríewþ,* f. UN-1 6.] 1. Unfaithfulness; disloyalty. *arch.* 2. Falsehood, falsity. late ME. b. A false or incorrect statement; a lie 1449.

Untru·thful *a.* [UN-1 1] 1847, **-ly** *adv.*, **-ness.** **Untu·ck** *v.* [UN-2 1] 1611. **Untu·mbled** *ppl. a.* [UN-1 2] 1675. **Untumu·ltuous** *a.* [UN-1 1] 1741. **Untu·nable** *a.* [UN-1 1] 1545, **-ness, -bly** *adv.* **Untu·ne** *v.* [UN-2 2] 1598. **Untu·ned** *ppl. a.* [UN-1 2] SHAKS. **Untu·neful** *a.* [UN-1 1] 1709, **-ly** *adv.*, **-ness.** **Untu·rned** *ppl. a.* [UN-1 2] 1550. **Untu·rning** *ppl. a.* [UN-1 4] 1591.

Untu·tored, *ppl. a.* 1593. [UN-1 2.] 1. Untaught; simple, unsophisticated; †boorish. 2. Not resulting from instruction; native, instinctive 1593. 3. Not subject to a tutor or tutors 1641.

1. The u. parts of the earth 1760. The u. many BENTHAM. 2. The u. wisdom of Romulus GIBBON. 3. A free and untutor'd Monarch MILT.

Untwi·ne, *v.* late ME. [UN-1 1.] 1. *trans.* To undo by untwisting or disentangling. b. *fig.* To dissolve, undo, destroy. late ME. 2. To detach, release, etc., by untwisting 1568. 3. *intr.* To become untwisted 1592.

Untwi·st *v.* [UN-2 1, 5] 1538. **Untwi·sted** *ppl. a.* [UN-1 2] 1575. **Unty·pical** *a.* [UN-1 1] 1848. **U:nundersta·ndable** *a.* [UN-1 1] 1631. **U:nundersta·nding** *ppl. a.* [UN-1 4] 1611. **U:nunderstoo·d** *ppl. a.* [UN-1 2] 1639. **Unu·niform** *a.* [UN-1 1] 1659, **-ly** *adv.* **Ununi·ted** *ppl. a.* [UN-1 2] 1587. **Unupbrai·ded** *ppl. a.* [UN-1 2] 1682. **Unupbrai·ding** *ppl. a.* [UN-1 4] 1780. **Unu·rged** *ppl. a.* [UN-1 2] SHAKS. **Unu·sable** *a.* [UN-1 1] 1825.

Unused (ʋnyū·zd), *ppl. a.* ME. [UN-1 2.] 1. Unaccustomed (esp. *to* something, or with inf.). 2. Not made use of. late ME. 3. Not in use; unusual. *arch.* 1513.

1. Albeit vn-vsed to the melting moode SHAKS. 3. Inuentyng..vnused termes 1568.

Unu·seful *a.* [UN-1 1] 1598, **-ly** *adv.*, **-ness.**

Unu·sual, *a.* 1582. [UN-1 1.] Not often occurring or observed, different from what is usual; out of the common, remarkable, exceptional. Hence **U:nusua·lity. Unu·sually** *adv.*, **-ness.**

Unu·tterable, *a.* and *sb.* 1586. [UN-1 1.] 1. Transcending utterance; inexpressible. b. In the phr. *u. things* 1711. 2. That may not be uttered or spoken 1656. b. Unpronounceable 1852.

1. He is, Sir, the most u. coward FLETCHER. Those u. Beatitudes 1746. U. scorn 1880. 2. Witness th' u. Name COWLEY.

B. *sb.* 1. An u. thing 1788. 2. *pl.* Trousers 1843. Hence **Unu·tterably** *adv.*

Unu·ttered *ppl. a.* [UN-1 2] 1463. **Unva·ccinated** *ppl. a.* [UN-1 2] 1871. **Unva·luable** *a.* (now *rare*) [UN-1 1] 1569. **Unva·lued** *ppl. a.* [UN-1 2] 1586. **Unva·nquishable** *a.* [UN-1 1] late ME. **Unva·nquished** *ppl. a.* [UN-1 2] late ME. **Unva·riable** *a.* (now *rare*) [UN-1 1] late ME. **Unva·ried** *ppl. a.* [UN-1 2] 1570.

Unva·rnished, *ppl. a.* 1604. [UN-1 2.] 1. *fig.* Of statements, etc.: Plain, straightforward; not adorned or specious. b. Of persons, etc.: Direct; unsophisticated 1827. 2. Not varnished 1758.

1. A round vn-varnish'd Tale SHAKS.

Unva·rying *ppl. a.* [UN-1 4] 1690, **-ly** *adv.*, **-ness.**

Unvei·l, *v.* 1599. [UN-2 2, 2 b.] 1. *trans.* To free (the eyes, etc.) from a veil. 2. To make (objects) visible by removing a veil or covering. Also *absol.* 1657. b. *spec.* To remove the covering from (a statue, etc.) so as to display it for the first time to the public 1865. 3. *fig.* To disclose, reveal 1606. b. To display to the sight; to make visible 1656. 4. *intr.* To emerge from a veil; to become visible 1655. Hence **Unvei·ling** *vbl. sb.*

Unvei·led *ppl. a.* [UN-1 2] 1606. **Unve·ndible** *a.* [UN-1 1] 1642. **Unve·nerable** *a.* [UN-1 1] SHAKS.

Unve·ntilated, *ppl. a.* 1712. [UN-1 2.] 1. Not provided with means of ventilation. 2. Not ventilated or discussed 1872.

Unve·ntured *ppl. a.* [UN-1 2] 1605. **Unvera·cious** *a.* [UN-1 1] 1845, **-ly** *adv.* **Unve·rified** *ppl. a.* [UN-1 2] 1816. **Unve·rsed** *ppl. a.* [UN-1 2] 1675. **Unve·st** *v.* [UN-2 2] 1609. **Unve·xed** *ppl. a.* [UN-1 2] 1456. **Unvi·ctualled** *ppl. a.* [UN-1 2] 1484. **Unview·ed** *ppl. a.* [UN-1 2] 1570. **Unvi·olated** *ppl. a.* [UN-1 2] 1555. **Unvi·rtuous** *a.* [UN-1 1] late ME., **-ly** *adv.*, **-ness.** **Unvi·sited** *ppl. a.* [UN-1 2] 1549. **Unvi·tal** *a.* [UN-1 1] 1661. **Unvi·tiated** *ppl. a.* [UN-1 2] 1632. **Unvi·trifiable** *a.* [UN-1 1] 1758. **Unvi·trified** *ppl. a.* [UN-1 2] 1779. **Unvo·cal** *a.* [UN-1 1] 1773.

Unvoi·ce, *v.* 1637. [UN-2 2.] *trans.* To deprive of voice; *spec.* in *Phonetics*, to utter with 'breath' instead of 'voice'.

Unvoi·ced, *ppl. a.* 1859. [UN-1 2.] 1. Of opinions, etc.: Not expressed. 2. Of organpipes: Not having had the tone regulated 1881. 3. *Phonetics.* Uttered without vibration of the vocal chords 1879.

Unvo·luntary *a.* (now *rare*) [UN-1 1] 1570. **Unvo·te** *v.* [UN-2 1, 5] 1647. **Unvou·ched** *ppl. a.* [UN-1 2] 1775. **Unvow·ed** *ppl. a.* [UN-1 2] 1570. **Unvoy·ageable** *a.* [UN-1 1] MILT. **Unvu·lgar** *a.* [UN-1 1] 1598. **Unwa·kened** *ppl. a.* [UN-1 2] 1621. **Unwa·lled** *ppl. a.* [UN-1 2] 1440. **Unwa·ndered** *ppl. a.* [UN-1 2] 1654. **Unwa·ndering** *ppl. a.* [UN-1 4] 1568. **Unwa·nted** *ppl. a.* [UN-1 2] 1697. **Unwa·rded** *ppl. a.* [UN-1 2] late ME. †**Unwa·re** *a.*, *sb.*, and *adv.* [UN-[1] 1, 5, 6] –1875. **Unwa·reness** (*arch.*) [UN-[1] 6] late ME.

Unwa·res, *adv. arch.* [Late OE. *unwæres*, f. *unwær* UNWARE, with advb. *-es*, -S *suffix*.] Unexpectedly, suddenly; unwittingly.

Unwa·rily *adv.* [UN-[1] 5] 1568. **Unwa·riness** [UN-[1] 6] 1544. **Unwa·rlike** *a.* [UN-[1] 1] 1590. **Unwa·rmed** *ppl. a.* [UN-[1] 2] 1625. **Unwa·rming** *ppl. a.* [UN-[1] 4] 1736. **Unwa·rned** *ppl. a.* [UN-[1] 2] OE. **Unwa·rp** *v.* [UN-[2] 1] 1659. **Unwa·rped** *ppl. a.* [UN-[1] 2] 1744. **Unwa·rrantable** *a.* [UN-[1] 1] 1612, **-ness, -bly** *adv.*

Unwa·rranted, *ppl. a.* 1577. [UN-[1] 2.] Not warranted or guaranteed, in various senses. Ignorant and u. Physitians 1633. The Assembly cannot Represent any man in things u. by their Letters HOBBES. I should be utterly u. in supposing that.. they were insane LYTTON.

Unwa·ry *a.* [UN-[1] 1] 1579.

Unwa·shed, *ppl. a.* late ME. [UN-[1] 2.] **1.** Not washed. **2.** *spec.* Of persons: Not having washed; not usually washed or in a clean state 1595. **b.** *absol.*, freq. in *The* (*Great*) *U.*, the lower orders 1833. **3.** Not washed *off* or *out* 1628.

2. Another leane, vnwash'd Artificer SHAKS. b. Whenever I speak of..the working classes, it is in the 'great-u.' sense 1868. So **Unwa·shen** *ppl. a.* (*arch.*) OE.

Unwa·sted *ppl. a.* [UN-[1] 2] ME. **Unwa·sting** *ppl. a.* [UN-[1] 4] late ME. **Unwa·tched** *ppl. a.* [UN-[1] 2] late ME. **Unwa·tchful** *a.* [UN-[1] 1] 1611, **-ly** *adv.*, **-ness.** **Unwa·ter** *v.* [UN-[2] 2] 1642.

Unwa·tered, *ppl. a.* 1440. [UN-[1] 2.] **1.** Not treated or supplied with water. **b.** Of silk fabrics, etc.: Plain, not watered 1535. **2.** Not diluted with water 1562. **b.** Of capital: Not increased merely in nominal amount by share-issuing 1893. **3.** Waterless, dry 1600.

Unwa·tery *a.* [UN-[1] 1] OE. **Unwa·vering** *ppl. a.* [UN-[1] 4] 1570, **-ly** *adv.* **Unwa·xed** *ppl. a.* [UN-[1] 2] late ME. **Unwea·kened** *ppl. a.* [UN-[1] 2] 1648. **Unwea·lthy** *a.* [UN-[1] 1] late ME. **Unwea·ned** *ppl. a.* [UN-[1] 2] 1581. **Unwea·poned** *ppl. a.* [UN-[1] 2] ME. **Unwea·riable** *a.* [UN-[1] 1] 1561, **-ness, -bly** *adv.* **Unwea·ried** *ppl. a.* [UN-[1] 2] ME., **-ly** *adv.*, **-ness.** **Unwea·ry** *a.* [UN-[1] 1] OE. **Unwea·rying** *ppl. a.* [UN-[1] 4] 1600, **-ly** *adv.* **Unwea·thered** *ppl. a.* [UN-[1] 2] 1843. **Unwea·ve** *v.* [UN-[2] 1, 5] 1542. **Unwe·bbed** *ppl. a.* [UN-[1] 2] 1768. **Unwe·d** 1513, **Unwe·dded** ME. *ppl. adjs.* [UN-[1] 2].

Unwe·dgeable, *a.* 1603. [UN-[1] 1.] Incapable of being split by wedges; uncleavable. The vn-wedgable and gnarled Oke SHAKS.

Unwee·ded *ppl. a.* [UN-[1] 2] 1602. **Unwee·ting** *ppl. a.* (*arch.*) [f. UN-[1] 4 + WEET *v.*[1]] ME., **-ly** *adv.* **Unwei·ghed** *ppl. a.* [UN-[1] 2] 1481. **Unwei·ghted** *ppl. a.* [UN-[1] 2] 1883. **Unwe·lcome** *a.* [UN-[1] 2] ME., **-ly** *adv.*, **-ness.** **Unwe·lcomed** *ppl. a.* [UN-[1] 2] 1548.

Unwe·ll, *a.* 1450. [UN-[1] 1.] Not in good health; slightly or temporarily ill; indisposed. (In early use chiefly *dial.* or *U.S.*) Hence **Unwe·llness** (*rare*).

Unwe·mmed, *ppl. a. arch.* or *dial.* [OE., f. UN-[1] 2.] Spotless, pure, immaculate; unblemished.

Unwe·pt, *ppl. a.* 1594. [UN-[1] 2.] Not wept or mourned for; unlamented. Unwept, unhonour'd, and unsung SCOTT.

Unwe·t *a.* [UN-[1] 1] late ME. **Unwe·tted** *ppl. a.* [UN-[1] 2] 1664. **Unwhi·pped, -whi·pt** *ppl. a.* [UN-[1] 2] SHAKS. **Unwhi·skered** *ppl. a.* [UN-[1] 2] 1812. **Unwhi·spered** *ppl. a.* [UN-[1] 2] 1821. **Unwhi·tewashed** *ppl. a.* [UN-[1] 2] 1846.

Unwho·lesome, *a.* ME. [UN-[1] 1.] **1.** Not beneficial, salutary, or conducive to morals, etc.; detrimental or prejudicial to health of mind. **b.** Hurtful, noxious. late ME. **2.** Unfavourable or injurious to bodily health ME. **3.** Of persons: Morally or physically unsound; tainted or corrupted. late ME.

1. b. Perhaps farther stay were u. for my safety SCOTT. 3. The people muddied, Thicke and vnwholsome in their thoughts and whispers SHAKS. Hence **Unwho·lesome·ly** *adv.*, **-ness.**

Unwieldy (vnwī·ldi), *a.* late ME. [UN-[1] 1.] †**1.** Of persons, etc.: Lacking strength; weak, feeble –1685. **2.** Moving ungracefully or with difficulty; not active; awkward, clumsy 1530. **b.** Of clumsy make or size; ponderously big 1582. **c.** Of action, etc.: Ungraceful, awkward 1635. **3.** Difficult to wield or manage owing to size, weight or shape 1547. **b.** *transf.* and *fig.* 1538. **4.** Restive, indocile; rejecting control. Now *rare.* 1513.

1. So vnweeldy was this sory palled goost CHAUCER. 2. b. Elephants and whales please us with their u. greatness HOGARTH. Two cases of u. corpulence 1793. 3. b. The u. haughtiness of a great ruling nation BURKE. 4. The Flemings grew vnweildie to his commandements 1611. Hence **Unwie·ldily** *adv.* **Unwie·ldiness.**

Unwi·lful *a.* [UN-[1] 1] late ME. **Unwi·ll** *v.* [UN-[2] 1] 1650. **Unwi·lled** *ppl. a.* [UN-[1] 2] 1540.

Unwi·lling, *ppl. a.* [OE. *unwillende*, f. UN-[1] 4 + WILLING *ppl. a.*] †**1.** Not intending the act in question –ME. **2.** Not willing or ready; reluctant, disinclined, loath OE. **b.** *transf.* of things 1592. †**3.** Involuntary, not intended –1687. **4.** Done, expressed, etc., reluctantly or unwillingly 1613.

2. I own I were u. he should learn what nowise concerns him SCOTT. b. Why shou'd you pluck the green distasteful Fruit From the u. Bough DRYDEN. 4. That sagacity..which had..extorted the u. admiration of his enemies MACAULAY. Hence **Unwi·lling·ly** *adv.* **-ness.**

Unwi·nd, *v.* ME. [UN-[2] 1.] **1.** *trans.* To wind off (a wrapping, bandage, etc.); to undo the windings of (thread, tape, or the like). **b.** To cause to uncoil; to free from a coiled state 1634. **2.** To roll, twist, or turn back the wrapping, bandaging or covering of (a body, etc.); to untwine thread from (a reel); to free (a person) *from* bonds 1596. **3.** *intr.* To become unwound or uncoiled 1656. **4.** *trans.* To trace or retrace to an issue, outlet, or end 1716.

1. *fig.* As you vnwinde her loue from him SHAKS. 2. †*fig.* You could u. yourself from all these dangers DRYDEN. 3. As the spring unwinds and acts with less power 1834. 4. Till Ariadne's clue unwinds the way GAY. Hence **Unwi·nding** *vbl. sb.*

Unwi·nged *ppl. a.* [UN-[1] 2] 1601. **Unwi·nking** *ppl. a.* [UN-[1] 4] 1782, **-ly** *adv.* **Unwi·nning** *ppl. a.* (*rare*) [UN-[1] 4] 1655. **Unwi·nnowed** *ppl. a.* [UN-[1] 2] 1552. **Unwi·ped** *ppl. a.* [UN-[1] 2] 1605. **Unwi·sdom** [UN-[1] 6] OE.

Unwi·se, *a.* [OE. *unwīs*, f. UN-[1] 1.] **1.** Lacking or deficient in (practical) wisdom, discretion, or prudence; foolish. Often *absol.* **2.** Not marked or prompted by (practical) wisdom; injudicious. late ME. Hence **Unwi·se·ly** *adv.*, **-ness.**

Unwi·sh, *v.* 1594. [UN-[2] 1.] **1.** *trans.* To revoke (a wish). **2.** To wish non-existent, desire the annihilation or absence of 1599. **b.** To wish or desire (a circumstance or thing) not to be 1628.

2. Now thou hast vnwisht fiue thousand men SHAKS. b. How many shall u. themselves Christians 1615.

Unwi·shed *ppl. a.* [UN-[1] 2] 1583. **Unwi·shful** *a.* [UN-[1] 1] 1876. **Unwi·st** *ppl. a.* (*Obs.* or *arch.*) [UN-[1] 2] late ME. †**Unwi·t** *v.* [UN-[2] 2] SHAKS. **Unwi·tch** *v.* (*arch.*) [UN-[2] 1] 1580. **Unwithdraw·ing** *ppl. a.* [UN-[1] 4] MILT. **Unwithdraw·n** *ppl. a.* [UN-[1] 2] 1829. **Unwi·thered** *ppl. a.* [UN-[1] 2] 1599. **Unwi·thering** *ppl. a.* [UN-[2] 4] 1743. **Unwithstoo·d** *ppl. a.* [UN-[1] 2] 1595. **Unwi·tnessed** *ppl. a.* [UN-[1] 2] late ME.

Unwi·tting, *ppl. a.* [OE. *unwitende*, f. UN-[1] 4. Rare after *c* 1600, until revived *c* 1800. Cf. UNWEETING.] **1.** Unconscious; not aware; without knowing; unheeding. Occas. quasi-*adv.* **b.** Const. *of*, or with direct obj. or obj. clause. late ME. †**2.** In absolute constructions –1622. †**3.** Without the knowledge *of* (or with poss. adj.), unbeknown *to* –1633. **4.** Done unwittingly; unintentional 1818.

1. Of which he had been the u. cause 1833. b. U. the frightful truth that lay in the words 1869. 2. Unwittand his ost, he passis fra his company 1456. 3. My wif delyvered all, myn unwetyng 1454. The two Earles .. vnwitting to the rest, presently withdrew themselues 1630. Hence **Unwi·tting·ly** *adv.*, **-ness.**

Unwi·tty, *a.* [OE. *unwittig*, f. UN-[1] 1.] **1.** Lacking in wit, intelligence, or knowledge; foolish; of weak understanding. Now *rare.* **2.** Lacking verbal wit; not witty 1637.

1. These u. wandering wits of mine TENNYSON. 2. It was an old, but not u. application 1637. Hence **Unwi·ttily** *adv.*

Unwi·ve *v.* [UN-[2] 1] 1611. **Unwi·ved** *ppl. a.* [UN-[1] 2] 1570. **Unwo·man** *v.* [UN-[2] 4 b] 1611. **Unwo·manly** *a.* [UN-[1] 1] 1529, *adv.* [UN-[1] 5] late ME. **Unwo·n** *ppl. a.* [UN-[1] 2] 1593. **Unwo·nt** *a.* (now *rare* or *Obs.*) [UN-[1] 1] late ME.

Unwo·nted, *ppl. a.* 1553. [UN-[1] 2.] **1.** Not wonted, usual, or habitual; infrequent. **2.** Not accustomed (*to* something or *to* do something) 1586.

1. New rules and u. tasks C. BRONTË. 2. Her feete, u. to feele the naked ground SIDNEY. These chambers..That with their splendour load my u. eyes 1822. Hence **Unwo·nted·ly** *adv.*, **-ness.**

Unwoo·ded *ppl. a.* [UN-[1] 2] 1628. **Unwoo·ed** *ppl. a.* [UN-[1] 2] 1570. **Unwo·rdable** *a.* [UN-[1] 1] 1660. **Unwo·rded** *ppl. a.* [UN-[1] 2] 1860.

Unwo·rkable, *a.* 1839. [UN-[1] 1.] **1.** Of systems, machines, etc.: That cannot be made to work or function. **b.** Too much, many, large, etc., to be rightly controlled or managed 1862. **2.** Of materials: Too hard, soft, brittle, etc., for shaping or using 1854. Hence **Unworkabi·lity. Unwo·rkableness.**

Unwo·rked, *ppl. a.* 1730. [UN-[1] 2.] **1.** Of flint, etc.: Not artificially shaped. **2.** Not worked in or operated upon 1817. **3.** Of persons, beasts, tools, etc.: Not set to work or used.

Unwo·rking *ppl. a.* [UN-[1] 4] 1696. **Unwo·rkmanlike** *a.* [UN-[1] 1] 1647. **Unwo·rld** *v.* [UN-[2] 4 b] 1647.

Unwo·rldly, *a.* 1707. [UN-[1] 1.] **1.** Of a type transcending or exceeding what is usually found or experienced in the world. **2.** Free from worldliness; spiritually minded 1825. **3.** Not belonging to this world; celestial 1765. Hence **Unwo·rldliness.**

Unwo·rn, *ppl. a.* 1586. [UN-[1] 2.] **1.** Not impaired, decayed, or wasted by use, weather, etc. **2.** Not deteriorated or weakened; unimpaired, fresh 1757. **3.** Never yet worn 1798.

Unwo·rried *ppl. a.* [UN-[1] 2] KEATS. **Unwo·rshipful** *a.* [UN-[1] 1] late ME. **Unwo·rshipped** *ppl. a.* [UN-[1] 2] late ME. **Unwo·rshipping** *ppl. a.* [UN-[1] 4] 1828. **Unwo·rth** *sb.* [UN-[1] 6] ME.

Unwo·rth, *a.* 1587. [UN-[1] 1.] Not worthy of. Chiefly in phr. *not u.* (one's) *while.*

Unworthy (vnwɒ̄·ɹði), *a.* ME. [UN-[1] 1.] **1.** Of little or no value; worthless. **b.** Discreditable; hurtful or injurious to reputation 1693. **2.** Of persons: Not worthy; undeserving; despicable ME. **b.** Used as a conventional or devotional expression of humility 1532. **3.** Not worthy *to* (with infin.) or *of* something ME. **4.** Of treatment, fortune, etc.: Not deserved or justified; unmerited. late ME. **5.** Unbecoming or inadequate to the character or dignity *of* a person, etc.; undeserving *of* notice, etc.; inferior to or below what is merited or deserved 1533. **6.** With ellipse of *of*. Not worthy of, not deserving (something). late ME. **b.** Not befitting or suiting, derogatory to (a person, one's repute, etc.) 1646. **7.** As *adv.* Unworthily. Now *rare.* 1661. **8.** As *sb.* An unworthy person 1616.

1. A litill toune and vnworthy 1375. b. Narrow schemings and u. cares SHELLEY. 2. An u. blackguard of that name 1835. 4. With tender ruth for her vnworthy griefe SPENSER. 5. I will take care to suppress things u. of him POPE. 6. How much he is vnworthy so good a lady SHAKS. b. Boyish folly, u. his experience and maturity 1885. 7. I hope I shall not behave u. of the good Instructions RICHARDSON. Hence **Unwo·rthily** *adv.* **Unwo·rthiness.**

Unwou·nd *ppl. a.* [UN-[1] 2] 1648. **Unwou·ndable** *a.* [UN-[1] 1] 1611. **Unwou·nded** *ppl. a.* [UN-[1] 2] OE. **Unwo·ven** *ppl. a.* [UN-[1] 2] late ME. **Unwra·p** *v.* [UN-[2] 1, 2, 5] late ME. **Unwrea·ked** *ppl. a.* [UN-[1] 2] 1590. **Unwrea·the** *v.* [UN-[2] 1] 1591. **Unwre·cked** *ppl. a.* [UN-[1] 2] 1748. **Unwre·nched** *ppl. a.* [UN-[1] 2] 1784. **Unwre·sted** *ppl. a.* [UN-[1] 2] 1653. **Unwri·nkle** *v.* [UN-[2] 1] 1611. **Unwri·nkled** *ppl. a.* [UN-[1] 2] 1576. **Unwri·te** *v.* [UN-[2] 1] 1586. **Unwri·teable** *a.* [UN-[1] 1] 1780.

Unwri·tten, *ppl. a.* late ME. [UN-[1] 2.] **1.** Not put in writing; unrecorded. **b.** Of laws, etc.: Not formulated in written codes or documents; oral 1456. **c.** Not written *of* 1651. **2.** Not written upon or *on* 1542.

1. b. The u., or common law; and..the written, or statute law BLACKSTONE. *U. law* (colloq.), the assumption that murder committed in the defence of personal honour (e.g. to avenge seduction) is justifiable.

Unwro·nged *ppl. a.* [UN-[1] 2] 1598.

Unwrou·ght, *ppl. a.* late ME. [UN-[1] 2.] **1.** Not brought to completion, left unfinished. 1375. **2.** Of materials, etc.: In the crude state, not fashioned or worked on. late ME. **3.** Of mines: Not worked 1669.

Unwru·ng *ppl. a.* [UN-[1] 2] SHAKS.

Let the gauled Iade winch, our withers are vnwrong *Ham.* III. ii. 253 (Q 2).

Unyie·lding, *ppl. a.* 1592. [UN-[1] 4.] **1.** Of substances: Not yielding to force or pressure 1658. **2.** Of persons, temper, etc.: Steadfast obstinate 1592. Hence **Unyie·lding·ly** *adv.*, **-ness.**

Unyo·ke, *v.* [OE. *ungeocian*; UN-[2] 2 b.] **1.** *trans.* To release (a beast) from the yoke. **b.** To disconnect (the plough) from a draught-animal. SCOTT. **2.** To free from oppression or subjection. late ME. **3.** To disjoin, unlink 1595. **4.** *absol.* To remove the yoke from an animal 1573. **b.** *fig.* To cease from labour, etc. 1594.

Unyo·ked *ppl. a.* [UN-[1] 2] 1573. **Unzo·ned** *ppl. a.* [UN-[1] 2] 1718.

-uous (-iuəs), a compound suffix repr. L. *-uosus*, OF. or AF. *-uous*, *-uos* (F. *-ueux*) occurring in adoptions from Latin or French, as *impetuous*, *tempestuous*, and by analogy, with the sense 'of the nature of, consisting of', in a few English formations on Latin stems, as *ambiguous*, *strenuous*.

Up (vp), *sb.* 1536. [f. UP *adv.*[1] and [2] or *a.*] **1.** A person or thing that is up (*rare*). **2.** Usu. *pl.* and assoc. with *downs* (see UP AND DOWN D): **a.** A rise in the ground 1637. **b.** A rise in life; a spell of prosperity 1844. **c.** A rise in price or value 1897. **3.** An 'up' train 1884.

Up (vp), *a.* ME. [f. UP *adv.*[1] and [2].] **1.** Of regions or their inhabitants: High, upland (*rare*). **2.** Of trains, coaches, etc.: Going or running up (see UP *adv.*[1] 6) 1784. **b.** Belonging to, connected with, such trains, etc. 1840. **3.** Of sparkling wines, beer, soda-water, etc.: Effervescing; effervescent. Usu. predic. 1815. **b.** *fig.* Animated, vivacious 1815. **4.** Ascending; upward 1869.

2. b. The booking-office..is on the up platform 1885. **4.** Horizontal, or with slight up gradient 1901.

Up, *v.* 1560. [f. UP *adv.*[1]] **1.** *trans.* To drive up (swans) for marking. **2.** To lift up (a weapon), esp. to or upon the shoulder 1885. **3.** *Naut.* To put (the helm) or haul (a trawl, etc.) up 1890. **4.** *intr.* To stand up; to get up; to rise from bed. **b.** colloq. *To up and* (do something), to do it abruptly or boldly 1831. **5.** *To up and down*, to rise and fall by turns 1737. **6.** *To up with*, to raise (the arm, a weapon, etc.) 1760.

2. Good..upped gun, and let drive at..a young cow 1885. **4. b.** All of a sudden the doctor ups and turns on them MARK TWAIN. **6.** He ups with the spade in a minute 1887.

Up (vp), *adv.*[1] [OE. *upp, up*, = OHG. *ûf* (G. *auf*), ON. *upp.*] **I. 1.** To or towards a point or place higher than another and lying directly (or almost directly) above it. **b.** Towards or above the level of the shoulders or head OE. **c.** So as to raise into a more erect (or level) as well as elevated position OE. **d.** So as to raise a thing from the place in which it is lying, placed, or fixed OE. **e.** So as to invert the relative position of things or surfaces; so as to have a particular surface facing upwards ME. **2.** Towards a point above the ground; into the air OE. **b.** To some height above the ground or other surface; *spec.* to a seat on horseback OE. **c.** So as to be suspended aloft or on high OE. **3.** Of stars, etc.: From below the horizon to the line of vision OE. **b.** From below to the surface of water, the ground, etc. OE. **c.** Out from the ground; from the stomach into, or out at, the mouth; out of the sea on to the shore, etc. OE. **4.** So as to extend or rise to a higher point or level, esp. above the surface of the ground OE. **b.** So as to form a heap or pile, or become more prominent ME. **5.** So as to raise or rise to an upright or nearly upright position OE. **b.** Upon one's feet from a recumbent or reclining posture; *spec.* out of bed OE. **c.** So as to rise from a sitting, stooping, or kneeling posture and assume an erect attitude OE. **6.** So as to mount or rise by gradual ascent, in contact with a surface, to a higher level; sometimes *spec.* = upstairs OE. **b.** To a point on a river, channel, etc., further from the sea OE. **c.** To or in any place regarded as important, e.g. London, a university, a capital city, etc. 1475. **d.** *Naut.* To windward 1591. **7.** So as to direct the sight to a higher point or level OE. **b.** So as to cause sound to ascend, increase, or swell OE.

1. After he has pulled up his stockings 1766. **b.** Eliza's hands went up in horror 1887. **e.** In trumps, if king or queen is turned up 1863. **2.** Doubting least S. Richard would haue blowne them vp and himselfe RALEIGH. The gentle larke..mounts vp on hie SHAKS. **3.** Never sleep the Sun up 1655. **b.** To se the water ryse up..out of a spring 1530. The taking up oysters from great depths 1748. **4.** Lighthouses ..put up to prevent shipwrecks 1873. **5.** Drew himself up in offended dignity 1850. I..did not get up till the lamps were being lighted 1865. **6.** The moving Moon went up the sky COLERIDGE. **c.** Resolved to go up to London 1820.

II. *transf.* and *fig.* **1.** From a lower to a higher status in respect of rank, affluence, credit, repute, etc. OE. **2. a.** To a higher spiritual or moral level or object OE. **b.** To a state of greater cheerfulness, resolution, etc. ME. **c.** Into a state of activity, commotion, or excitement ME. **d.** To or at a higher pitch, speed, rate, amount, number, price, etc. 1538. **3.** To or towards maturity or proficiency OE. **4.** Into existence, prominence, etc.; so as to appear or prevail OE. **b.** So as to be heard ME. **5.** To the notice of a person or body of persons (*spec.* of one in authority) ME. **b.** Before a judge, magistrate, etc. 1440. **c.** So as to divulge, reveal, etc. 1593. **d.** As a charge or accusation 1604. **6.** Into the hands or possession of another ME. **b.** So as to relinquish or forsake ME. **7.** Into a receptacle or place of storage ME. **8.** Into one's possession, charge, custody, etc. late ME. **9.** Into the position or state of being open ME. **10.** Into an open or loose condition of surface. late ME. **b.** So as to separate or divide, esp. into many fragments or parts. late ME. **11.** To or towards a state of completion or finality ME. **12.** By way of summation or enumeration. late ME. **b.** To a final or total sum or amount ME. **13.** Into a close or compact form; so as to be confined or secured. late ME. **b.** Into a closed or enclosed state 1489. **c.** So as to cover or envelop. late ME. **14.** Into a state of union, conjunction, or combination 1450. **b.** So as to supply deficiencies, defects, etc. 1568. **15.** To or towards a person or place; so as to approach or arrive. late ME. **b.** To or towards a particular point or state 1513. **c.** To or into later life 1535. **d.** So as to find, overtake, or keep on the track of 1622. **16.** To a stop or halt 1623.

1. Getting up in the world 1832. A preacher-up of Nature 1871. **2. b.** I..could not pluck up courage 1894. **c.** Work the crowds up 1901. **d.** Carry had better hurry up 1900. **3.** Brought up to no profession 1894. **4.** Smyth..had not turned up 1902. **b.** The bell..strikes up 1853. **5.** The writ went up to the Lords 1844. **c.** If his two companions..would not own up 1884. **7.** The heat of the sun is stored up in coal 1879. **10.** Taking up all the streets in South London 1895. **b.** Engaged in tearing up old newspapers 1837. **11.** Cloves..boil'd Up with the coffee BYRON. I polished up the handle of the big front door W. S. GILBERT. The spendthrift had..sold up the remainder 1894. **12.** All my years when added up are many JOWETT. **13.** Visitors huddled up in corners LAMB. **c.** If the wound is covered closely up 1837. **14.** That he could draw up..a hole in his breeches STERNE. **15.** The Spring comes slowly up this way COLERIDGE. **b.** To even up my account with his people 1901. **c.** From his youth up 1890. **16.** A man ..pulled up his coach 1623.

III. *ellipt.* **1.** *imper.* or with auxiliary vb. ME. **2.** Followed by a sb. in obj. relationship to an unexpressed verbal notion: Orig. in imper., later in other uses, thus passing into UP *v.* 2, 3. late ME.

1. Up, Guards, and at them', cried the Duke of Wellington SCOTT. **2.** We'll up anchor 1832. *Up Jenkins* = TIP-IT.

With preps., etc. **Up against —.** *To knock* or *run up against*, to fall in with. **Up till —.** = *up to*. **Up to —. a.** As high or as far as. **b.** Up towards. **c.** So as to arrive at. (*b*) Until. **d.** Confronting (a person) as a task. **e.** So as to reach or attain (a specified point or stage). (*b*) As many or much as (a specified number or amount). **Up with —. a.** So as to overtake. **b.** *To put up with*: see PUT *v.*[1] **c.** *ellipt.* (*a*) Denoting the raising of a weapon, the hand, etc., esp. so as to strike. (*b*) Denoting erecting, pulling up, etc. (*c*) To drink off, consume. (*d*) To 'come out' with (something). (*e*) Denoting support or advocacy of a person or thing. **Up and —,** *ellipt.*, denoting the act of rising or starting up, accompanied by subsequent action.

Up (vp), *adv.*[2] [OE. *uppe*, f. *upp* UP *adv.*[1]] **I. 1.** At some distance above the ground or earth; aloft. **b.** Of the heavenly bodies: Risen above the horizon OE. **2.** On high or (more) elevated ground; more inland OE. **3.** In an elevated position OE. **b.** Of an adjustable device or part: Raised 1599. **c.** *colloq.* On horseback, riding 1812. **4.** High, in respect of the river-bank or shore. late ME. **b.** On or above the surface of the ground or water 1835. **5. a.** In a standing posture; standing (and delivering a speech) ME. **b.** In an upright position 1669. **c.** Erected, built 1613. **6. a.** Out of bed; risen. late ME. **b.** Not (yet) gone to bed 1535. **c.** Of game: Roused, started 1611. **7.** Further away from the mouth of a river, etc. 1600. **b.** Towards a place or position; advanced in place 1613. **c.** At or in a place of importance (*spec.* London) 1845. **d.** *colloq.* At or in school or college 1847. **8.** Facing upward 1683. **9.** With the surface broken or removed 1886.

1. b. Tho' the Moon was up DE FOE. **2.** The City.. is 20 mile up in the Country 1697. **3. b.** His coat-collar was up MEREDITH. **c.** To pace the paddock when Archer 's up 1886. **4.** The tide was up DE FOE. **6. b.** They were up all last night DICKENS. **7. b.** If the ball is a half-volley or well up 1903. **9.** Streets that are up 1886.

II. *fig.* **1.** In a state of disorder, revolt, or insurrection. late ME. **b.** *Up in arms*, risen, levied, or marshalled as an armed host. Also *fig.* 1590. **c.** Actively stirring or moving about 1460. **d.** In a state of agitation, exaltation, confidence, etc. 1470. **2.** In a state of prevalency, performance, or progress (now chiefly with KEEP *v.*) ME. **b.** Much or widely spoken of. Now *rare.* 1618. **c.** *colloq.* Occurring (as an unusual or undesirable event); going on 1849. **d.** Amiss *with* a person, etc. 1887. **3.** Completed; expired; over; (at) the number or limit agreed on as the game; of an assembly: risen, adjourned, over. late ME. **b.** Come to a fruitless or undesired end 1787. **c.** *All up*, completely finished (*with*). Also, *all U.P.* (yū pī). 1825. **4.** Higher in respect of position, rank, fortune, etc. 1509. **b.** Increased in strength, power, etc.; ready for action 1547. **c.** Advanced or high in number, value, or price 1546. **d.** (So many points, etc.) in advance of a competitor 1894. **e.** At a high or lofty pitch 1902. **5.** Before a magistrate, etc., in court. **b.** Offered or exposed for sale 1921.

1. The eastern counties were up MACAULAY. **c.** Let us, then, be up and doing LONGF. **d.** When his temper is up 1891. **3.** As his leave was nearly up 1889. **4. b.** A Government steamer.., with steam up 1848.

With preps. **Up against —,** faced or confronted by (difficulties, etc.). *colloq.* (orig. *U.S.*). **Up in —,** expert or versed, etc., in a subject, etc. *colloq.* **Up to —. a.** Able to perform or undertake; fit or qualified for. (*b*) Prepared for; a match for. (*c*) Expert or versed in. (*d*) Ready for. **b.** Equal in quality or quantity to; on a level with. (*b*) *Not up to much*, of no great ability, importance, or worth. **c.** Engaged in or bent on (an activity, esp. of a reprehensible nature); doing or planning. **d.** *colloq.* Obligatory or incumbent upon. **Up with —.** On a level with (a person, place, etc.).

Up (vp), *prep.* 1509. [Elliptical use of UP *adv.*[1], by omission of a preposition.] **1.** Upwards on or along (an ascent). **2.** Towards the source or head of (a river, lake, etc.) 1513. **b.** *Up* (*the*) *wind*, towards the quarter it blows from 1611. **3.** Into or towards the interior of (a country); towards the upper end of (a room) 1596. **4.** Along towards the other end of (a street, town, passage, line, etc.) 1669. **5.** Of situation: In or at the higher, interior, or more remote part of (a stream, country, state, area) 1667. **6.** At the top of; at some distance above the bottom of 1645.

1. Phr. *Up hill and down dale*, over hill and valley (in pursuit or flight); *transf.* and *fig.*, headlong; thoroughly (as 'to curse up hill and down dale'). **2.** There was a nice up Channel breeze 1898. **3.** They passing in Went vp the hall SPENSER. William's army began to march up the country MACAULAY. **5.** All those five tenements up the yard 1799. *Up stage*: on a part of the stage distant from the footlights or the spectators; *fig.* (orig. *U.S.*) keeping oneself at a distance, distant (in behaviour). *Up-State* (U.S.), freq. with ref. to the State of New York. **6.** A small chamber up four pair of stairs 1714.

Up-, *prefix*, repr. OE. *up-*, *upp-*, identical with UP *adv.*[1]

I. In comb. with sbs. **1.** In OE. *up-* occurs freely with sbs., in the sense of 'occupying a higher position', 'upper', as in *upflôr*. In ME. this type practically disappears, and in later use is represented chiefly by UPLAND *sb.* and UPSIDE. b. In the sense of 'in a supported state', in OE. *upheald*, etc., ME. *uptie* (naut.), and the modern *upkeep*.

2. In the sense of 'upwards' OE. had compounds with nouns, mainly derived from intr. vbs., as *upyme*, *-spring*, etc. Many of these disappeared in ME., but new formations were added, and since 1800 the type has become common. Examples are *upbreak*, *-burst*, *-curve*, *-glance*, *-growth*, *-leap*, *-look*, *-shoot*, *-sweep*, *turn*. b. More rarely *up-* is employed in the sense of 'upwards' with other nouns than those of action, as OE. *upweg*, and the recent *up-grade*, *-road*, etc.

II. *Up-* is rarely employed in comb. with adjs.: **U·phand** *a.* operated, or performed by raising the hand or hands. †**U·pspring** *a.* upstart, newly arisen or come in.

III. 1. With vbs., participles, agent-nouns, etc. In OE., *up* was placed immediately before a vbl. form only in a limited number of instances, as *upgân*, *-hebban*, etc.; it is difficult to determine in how many of these the adv. had become a real prefix. In ME. the use of the prefix is thoroughly established and new formations have been constantly added during the following centuries. A considerable proportion, however, occur only in poetry, and are simple substitutions for the vb. followed by the adv., although they are regarded as real compounds and written as one word. Examples are: **uparise, -bear, -blaze, -blow, -boil, -break, -buoy, -call, -drag, -draw, -fill, -grow, -jet, -keep, -look, -move, -roll, -rouse, -shoot, -snatch, -stir, -tear, -thrust, -wind, -wrap.**

2. The use of *up* with pa. pples. gave rise to compounds of which several had already so far established themselves in OE. that derivatives in *-nes* and *-lice* were formed from them. The type is still usual, but at all periods these forms have been mainly employed in verse. When they are used *attrib.*, the stress is normally on the prefix. Examples are: **up-blown, -choked, -flung, -looped, -ploughed, -poised, -propped, -ripped, -rolled, -swept, -wrapped.**

3. The use of *up* before pres. pples. is somewhat rare in OE.; ME. furnishes a few instances, but this type of formation becomes common only after 1500. Examples are: **uparising, -blazing, -brimming, -gliding, -keeping, -rousing, -staring, -steaming, -swarming, -wreathing.** b. In the earlier periods these forms in *-ing* were not used *attrib.*; examples of this use begin to appear in the 16th c., but are not common before the 19th. As adjs., such compounds normally have the main stress on the prefix, but in verse the stress is freq. on the stem. Examples are: **upbearing, -creeping, -cropping, -flashing, -gushing, -lying, -pouring, -sticking, -stretching, -striving, -struggling.**

4. In OE. the comb. of *up-* with a vbl. sb. is limited to one instance, *uphebbing*; in ME. the type is also rare, but it becomes common in the 16th c. and again in the 19th. Examples are: †**uparising, -bubbling, †-crying, -gushing, -piling, -putting, -sealing, -surging, -swelling, -working.**

5. The use of *up-* with agent-nouns first appears in the 14th c., in *upstyer*, *uptaker*, etc. Similar forms appear in the 16th c. (but chiefly Sc.), as *up-creeper*, *-lifter*, *-looker*, and a few in the 17th as *upbringer*, *riser*. Later formations are mainly from the 19th c., as *upbuilder*, *-climber*, *-stander*.

U·p-a-daisy, *int.* Now *dial.* or *colloq.* 1711. [f. UP *adv.*[1]] An exclam. addressed to a child that has fallen, or when raising it in the arms.

Up-a·nchor, *v.* 1897. [UP *adv.*[1], UP *v.* 3.] *intr.* To weigh anchor.

Up and coming, *a. U.S.* 1889. [UP *adv.*[2]] Active, alert, wide-awake.

Up and down. *adv.*, *prep.*, *a.*, and *sb.* ME. [f. UP *adv.*[1] and *adv.*[2] + DOWN *adv.*] A. *adv.* 1. Alternately on or to a higher and a lower level or plane. 2. To and fro; backward and forward ME. 3. At various points; here and there ME. b. Here and there in a book or author; passim 1668. 4. *Naut.* In or into a vertical position; vertically 1669. 5. In every respect; entirely. Now *dial.* 1542. 6. *U.S. colloq.* Bluntly; in plain words 1869.

3. He..liu'd obscurely vp and downe in boothes, and taphouses B. JONSON. 4. When the cable is in that condition, the boatswain calls, 'Up and down, sir' 1867. 5. This is the Pharisee up and down, 'I am not as other men are' MILT.

B. *prep.* 1. To and fro, backward and forward, in, along or upon. late ME. b. Here and there in or upon 1597. 2. Alternately on or to higher and lower parts of (hills, etc.) 1665.

1. b. As is evident up and down the Scripture 1675.

C. *adj.* (now usu. hyphened). 1. Acting, directed, etc., alternately or indifferently upward and downward 1616. 2. Vertical; not horizontal or sloping 1710. b. *U.S.* Downright; straightforward 1836. 3. Having an uneven or irregular surface; consisting of ups and downs 1775. 4. Moving from place to place; migratory, oscillating 1824.

2. Clothes hanging in folds upon her up-and-down figure 1897.

D. *sb.* 1. *pl.* **Ups and downs.** a. Irregularities of surface 1682. b. Undulatory motions, tracings, etc. 1860. c. Vicissitudes 1659. 2. *sing.* (usu. hyphened). a. Alternate rise and fall, esp. *fig.* in respect of fortune, position, etc. 1775. b. An undulating surface or marking 1856.

Upanishad (upæ·nişæd). 1805. [a. Skr. *upa-nishād*, f. *upa* near to + *ni-shad* to sit or lie down.] In Sanskrit literature, one or other of various speculative metaphysical treatises forming a division of the Vedic literature.

‖**Upas** (yū·păs). 1783. [a. Malay *ūpas* poison, in the comb. *pōhun ūpas* poison-tree.] 1. In full *upas-tree*, a fabulous Javanese tree so poisonous as to destroy all life for many miles round. b. *fig.* A baleful power or influence 1801. 2. The Javanese tree *Antiaris toxicaria*, yielding a poisonous juice 1814. 3. The poison obtained from the upas-tree 1783.

U·pbeat. 1869. [UP- I. 2.] 1. *Mus.* An unaccented beat in a bar, during which the hand is raised in beating time. 2. *Pros.* a. An anacrusis. b. An arsis or stressed syllable. 1883.

Upbraid (ʌpbrē·d), *v.* [OE. *upbregdan*, f. *up-* UP- + *bregdan* BRAID *v.*[1]] †1. *trans.* To adduce or allege (a matter) as a ground for censure or reproach –1718. b. To censure, find fault with, carp at ME. 2. To reprove, reproach (a person, etc.) ME. b. Const. *with* or †*of* (the cause of censure) ME.

1. It shall bee vpbraided vs that wee haue turned our heartes backe 1583. b. How much doth thy kindnesse upbraide my wickednesse? SIDNEY. 2. b. Lest he of eny vntrouthe her vpbreyde CHAUCER. Hence **Upbrai·der. Upbrai·ding** *vbl. sb.* the action of the vb.; a reproach or reproof. **Upbrai·ding** *ppl. a.*

U·pbringing, *vbl. sb.* 1520. [f. †*upbring* to rear + -ING[1].] The action of bringing up; the fact of being brought up, or the manner of this; early rearing and training.

U·pcast, *sb.* 1611. [UP- I. 2.] 1. A chance or accident. Now *rare*. 2. *Mining* and *Geol.* An upward dislocation or shifting of a seam or stratum; a fault caused by this 1793. 3. *Upcast shaft* (or *pit*), the pit-shaft by which the ventilating air is returned to the surface 1816. 4. Material thrown up in digging 1883.

1. *Cymb.* II. i. 2.

Upca·st, *v.* late ME. [UP- III. 1.] *trans.* To cast or fling up. Hence **Upca·sting** *vbl. sb.*

U·pcast, *ppl. a.* late ME. [UP- III. 2.] 1. Of the eye or look: Turned or directed upwards. 2. Mining. *Upcast dyke* = UPCAST *sb.* 2. 1810. 3. Thrown upwards 1823.

U·p-country, up-cou·ntry, *sb.*, *a.*, and *adv.* 1835. [UP *a.* and *prep.*] A. *sb.* The inland or more remote part of a country 1837. B. *adj.* Of or situated in the inland part of a country 1835. C. *adv.* In or to the inland part of a country 1864.

Up-e·nd, *v.* orig. *dial.* 1823. [UP *adv.*[1]] 1. *trans.* To set (something) on its end; to turn end upwards. 2. *intr.* To rise up on end 1897.

U·p-grade, *sb.* and *adv.* orig. *U.S.* 1888. [UP- I. 2 b.] A. *sb.* An upward slope or incline. b. *On the up-grade*: ascending, rising; *fig.* improving, making progress 1892. B. *adv.* Uphill 1899. Hence **Upgra·de** *v. trans.* to raise to a higher grade of wages, etc.

Upheaval (ʌphī·văl). 1838. [f. next + -AL 2.] 1. *Geol.* The action of raising, or fact of being raised, above the original level, esp. by volcanic action. b. An instance of this; an upward displacement of some part of the earth's crust 1849. c. *gen.* 1890. 2. A great and sudden convulsion or alteration of society 1850. Hence **Uphea·valist,** one who attributes geological changes to upheaval.

Uphea·ve, *v.* ME. [UP- III. 1.] 1. *trans.* To heave or lift up; to raise. b. *esp.* To toss or throw up with violence; *spec.* in *Geol.* 1708. 2. *intr.* To rise up 1649.

1. The fader Eneas..His handis bayth vphevis towartis hevin 1513. 2. The surface of the bay..upheaved with a slow, majestic movement 1850. Hence **Uphea·ved** *ppl. a.* **Uphea·vement. Uphea·ver. Uphea·ving** *vbl. sb.* and *ppl. a.*

U·phill, u·p-hill, *sb.* and *a.* 1548. [f. UP *prep.*] A. *sb.* An ascent; a high or steep rise. B. *adj.* 1. Situated on high ground 1613. 2. Ascending; sloping upwards, esp. steeply 1622. b. Of a task, struggle, etc.: Difficult; involving prolonged effort; arduous 1622.

Uphi·ll, *adv.* 1607. [UP *prep.*] Towards higher ground; upwards on a (steep) slope. Hence **Uphi·llward** *adv.* and *a.*

Upho·ld, *v.* ME. [UP- III. 1.] 1. *trans.* To support or sustain physically; to keep from falling or sinking. 2. To support the cause or contribute to the preservation or prosperity of ME. b. To maintain at the same level or standard 1523. c. To sustain spiritually 1820. 3. To maintain in good condition or in a proper state of repair 1511. 4. To maintain or confirm the validity or truth of; to sustain against objection or criticism 1485. 5. To raise or lift up; to direct upwards. late ME.

1. Whose feeble thighes, vnhable to vphold His pined corse, him scarse..could beare SPENSER. 4. The decision of the registrar was upheld 1893.

Upho·lder. ME. [f. prec. + -ER[1].] 1. (also †*uphol(d)ster*). †a. A dealer in or maker of small wares, furniture, etc. –1812. b. An upholsterer. Now *rare*. 1688. c. An undertaker. Now *Hist.* 1709. 2. One who upholds a person, cause, doctrine, etc.; a supporter *of*. late ME. b. A support or prop. late ME.

1. c. Th' U., rueful Harbinger of Death, Waits with Impatience for the dying Breath GAY.

Upho·lster, *v.* orig. *U.S.* 1861. [Back-formation from UPHOLSTERER or UPHOLSTERY.] 1. *trans.* To cover with or as with upholstery 1864. 2. *intr.* To do upholstery work 1861.

Upho·lstered, *ppl. a.* 1837. [f. as prec.] Furnished or fitted with upholstery.

Upholsterer (ʌphōu·lstərəɹ). 1613. [f. †*upholster* sb., f. UPHOLD *v.* + -STER.] A maker, finisher, or repairer of articles of furniture and other house-furnishings in which woven or similar fabrics, or materials used for stuffing these, are employed. b. *transf.* Applied to certain bees and birds 1830.

Upho·lstery. 1649. [f. as prec.; see -ERY 2.] Upholsterer's work, materials, or products; the collective use of these in a room or house.

U·pkeep. 1884. [UP- I. 1 b.] Maintenance in good condition or repair; the cost of this.

Upland (ʌ·plænd), *sb.* and *a.* 1566. [f. UP *a.* 1 + LAND *sb.*] A. *sb.* 1. The part of a country lying away from the sea. *arch.* 1579. 2. High ground; a piece of high, hilly, or mountainous country. Usu. in *pl.* 1566. 3. (A stretch of) raised land not liable to flooding. Chiefly *local* and *U.S.* 1572. 4. *ellipt.* in *pl.* Upland cotton 1858.

1. He determined to draw these pirats from the sea into the vpland NORTH. 2. These to the u., to the valley those COWPER. At the foot of this hill, one stage or step from the uplands, lies the village 1787.

B. *attrib.* or as *adj.* 1. Lying away from the sea; inland, remote 1575. b. Living inland 1716. 2. Lying higher than the surrounding country 1610. b. Living, growing, or found on high ground 1622. c. Of water: Flowing from higher ground 1653.

1. The vpland townes are fairer and richer, then those that stand nearer the sea 1601. 2. *U. cotton*, a class of short-stapled cotton. Hence **U·plander,** an inhabitant or native of the uplands.

U·plift, *sb.* 1845. [UP- I. 2.] 1. The fact of being raised or elevated. b. *spec.* A rise in level, esp. of part of the earth's surface 1853. 2. *fig.* An elevating effect, result, or influence in the sphere of morality, emotion, physical condition, etc.; often *gen.* without article. Also *attrib.* orig. *U.S.* 1873.

Upli·ft, *v.* ME. [UP- III. 1.] 1. *trans.* To lift up to a higher level or more erect position; to raise. b. To raise to higher rank, repute, wealth, etc. Now *rare*. ME. c. To elevate morally 1883. 2. *Sc.* To levy (rents, etc.); to draw (wages) 1508. 3. To raise (the voice); to utter (hymns, cries, praise, etc.) 1816. Hence **Upli·ft** (*poet.*), **Upli·fted** *pa. pples.* and *ppl. adjs.* **Upli·fter. Upli·fting** *vbl. sb.*

U·plong. 1819. [f. UP *adv.*[2] + *long* ALONG.] A strengthening bar along the sail of a windmill.

Upmost (ʌ·pmǒst), *a.* 1560. [f. UP *adv.*[2] + -MOST.] = UPPERMOST *a.*

Upon (ɒpǫ·n), *prep.* [Early ME., f. UP *adv.* + ON *prep.*; prob. mainly modelled on ON. *upp á*. Though *upp on, uppe on*, occur in OE., the first word is there the independent adverb denoting elevation, whereas the ME. compound is, as in modern use, indistinguishable in meaning from the simple *on*.] = ON *prep.*, in all senses. (The use of one form or the other is usu. a matter of individual choice (on grounds of rhythm, emphasis, etc.) or of simple accident, although in certain contexts and phrases there may be a general tendency to prefer the one to the other.) **I.** Of position: = ON *prep.* I–V. **1.** Above and in contact with or supported by. **b.** Denoting that on which the hand is placed in taking the oath, or the basis of an oath ME. **c.** With *sit, serve*, etc.: On the panel of (a jury, inquest) 1516. **d.** In phrases now used *fig.* See esp. CARPET *sb.* 1, HAND *sb.* V. d, LEVEL *sb.* 1, 2. **2.** In contact with (any surface) ME. **b.** Of immaterial actions or *fig.* late ME. **c.** Conformably to (an axis, pivot, base) 1570. **3.** Close to, beside, near ME. **4.** Expressing position with ref. to a place or thing: = ON I. 4. ME. **b.** With vbs., as *border, touch, verge* ME. **c.** At close quarters with, about to attack 1568. **d.** Indicating the side or part espoused or supported by the agent. late ME. **5.** In the course of (a day, night, time) ME. **b.** With vbl. sbs., etc.: On the point of. late ME. **c.** On the occasion of, because of 1440. **d.** Immediately after; following upon. late ME. **6.** About, engaged in, intent on ME. **b.** Of state, condition, action: = ON IV. 3. ME. **c.** Indicating a sphere of activity or existence 1487. **7.** On the basis of, on the model of, by reason of, in reliance on, according to, on the strength of, by means of ME.

1. When they sawe him walkinge apon the see TINDALE *Mark* vi. 48. Gallantry strutting u. his Tiptoes STEELE. The castle u. yonder hill 1732. Mrs. Honour is u. the stairs FIELDING. U. her palfrey she is set SOUTHEY. 2. A greate clothe of redd silke..with lions of golde u. it 1552. Vpon the next Tree shall thou hang SHAKS. Those clothes would not look so well u. Oswald MARRYAT. b. Every one's eyes were u. me RICHARDSON. c. The Circle..is described u. the Centre A 1679. 3. Countries lying u. the Ocean 1662. 4. My Lord Ambassador beinge plac'd..u. his left hand 1644. c. The roundheads are u. us 1721. d. Famine..shall wage war u. our side! SHELLEY. 5. U. a Sabbath-day it fell KEATS. Phr. *Once u. a time*: see ONCE *adv.* b. The truce..was just u. expiring GOLDSM. c. If one kill another u. a suddaine quarrell BACON. They..were cast into Hell u. their Disobedience ADDISON. d. [They] conquered..townes and castels one vpon the other LD. BERNERS. 6. When Mankind..were u. Building a City together LOCKE. b. A Granadeer..absent u. Furlow 1706. c. The Reception these Gentleman met with u. Change STEELE. 7. Al min hope is uppon þe 1250. Let vs borowe money of the kinge vpon vsury COVERDALE. Aspshawe is a very poore man, and liveth apon his neibours 1564. Vpon my Blessing I command thee goe SHAKS. My life vpon her faith SHAKS. He has solved..Phænomena of Nature u. sound Principles 1697. He order'd every man u. the pain of death to bring in all the money he had 1699. A young Horse may look pretty sleek u. Hay only 1737. Mr. Belford gives the substance of it u. his memory RICHARDSON. The new constitution..is formed very much u. that of France 1863. A commission of over 60 per cent. u. the sums received 1892.

II. Of motion or direction towards something = ON *prep.* VI–VIII. **1.** Upward so as to place or be on a surface, etc. ME. **b.** To or towards a position on (a surface, etc.) ME. **c.** After vbs., etc., of seizing, striking, etc.: = ON VI. 1. ME. **d.** In pursuance of (a voyage, course, etc.) late ME. **2.** Into contact or collision with, against ME. **3.** In the direction of (esp. after vbs. of looking, etc.) ME. **4.** Into or on (some action, occupation, course, etc.) ME. **5.** Indicating the person or thing that action or feeling is directed towards or against, or that is influenced by it: with vbs., as *attend, bestow*, adjs., as *keen*, sbs., as *attempt, entrance*. ME. **6.** With regard or in reference to, as to, about. late ME.

1. He lep up on a stede HAVELOK. b. [They] fell vpon the kne, & worshipped him COVERDALE. Her head sunk down u. her breast MARSTON. A light broke in u. my brain BYRON. c. Sir Tristram gaf him suche a buffet vpon the helme MALORY. The paynes of hell gat holde vpon me COVERDALE *Ps.* cxiv. 3. Sent u. a long Voyage ADDISON. 2. *ellipt.* Aduance your standards, & vpon them Lords SHAKS. d. He cast his eye vpon Emelya CHAUCER. Our Fleet..bore down u. them 1716. 4. It put the Church u. the alert 1813. 5. The peple roos vp-on hym CHAUCER. Reuenge my death vpon his traiterous head 1595. Able to play vpon an oaten pipe 1621. They were sufficiently railed u. in the streets LAUD. He..had made their places be conferred u. men void of counsel 1656. Encroachments u. his Dominions 1678. The French have..refin'd too much u. Horace's Rule ADDISON. He shows me a bill u. me, drawn by my wife DE FOE. The constitution..is sacredly obligatory u. all 1796. O'Connell is bent u...disruption 1843. Softly turning the key u. him DICKENS.

†**Upo·n**, *adv.* ME. [ellipt. use of prec.] **1.** Upon it; upon its surface; upon one's person –1611. **2.** Thereupon, thereafter –1606.

1. His gloues, his gyrdell, the kynge had vpon 1513. A clothe..wroughte with goulde vpon 1567. 2. Indeed my Lord, it followed hard vpon SHAKS.

U·pper, *sb.* 1845. [f. next.] **1.** The upper part of a boot or shoe; that part above the sole and welt. Usu. *pl.* **b.** *U.S.* An ankle gaiter, spat 1891. **c.** *On* one's *uppers*, in want. *colloq.* (orig. *U.S.*) 1891. **2.** An upper jaw, dental plate, or tooth 1878.

Upper (ɒ·pəɹ), *a.* ME. [f. UP *a.* + -ER [3].] Comparative of UP *a.* **I. 1.** Consisting of or occupying higher (and usu. more inland) ground ME. **2.** Situated higher than or above another or others. Freq. in proper names of villages, etc. 1467. **b.** Of rooms, etc.: Occupying or forming (part of) the higher or highest portion of a building 1522. **3.** With partitive terms, esp. *end, part, side* 1484. **4.** That forms the higher of a pair of corresponding things or sets 1460. **5. a.** Of garments, etc.: Outer, exterior 1526. **b.** Furthest removed from the door or entrance; innermost. Usu. with *end*. 1590. **6.** That is on or above the earth's surface, not subterranean or infernal 1667. **7.** Of strata: Lying nearer the surface or formed later 1696. **8.** Occurring in a higher or the highest position; directed upwards 1607.

1. The Lower and U. Cossacks 1790. 2. Clouds..driven along by the u. currents of air 1873. b. *fig.* 'Ill-furnished in the u. story'; a head without brains 1870. 4. *U. case* (Printing): see CASE *sb.*[2] 6. *U. bench*, during the exile of Chas. II, the KING'S BENCH (*Hist.*). 6. Longing the common Light again to share, And draw the vital breath of u. Air DRYDEN. 8. During the u. stroke [of the piston] 1815. *U. cut* (Pugilism) a blow delivered upwards 'when an opponent leads off or rushes in with his head down'.

II. *transf.* **1.** Of higher (or the highest) rank, station, authority, wealth, or dignity 1477. **2.** Of studies or students: More advanced 1629. **3.** Of notes, voices, etc.: Of higher pitch 1843.

1. By the Extortion of U. Servants STEELE. Finishing schools for the u. classes EMERSON. 3. The u. or female voice part of the scale 1843.

Special collocations. **Upper crust**: **a.** The top crust of a loaf. †**b.** The surface of the earth. **c.** *slang.* The human head. **d.** *colloq.* The aristocracy. **Upper deck**, the highest continuous deck of a ship. **Upper hand. a.** The mastery or control (*of, over*); predominance, rule, dominion. Usu. after vbs., as *get, have, gain*. †**b.** The place of honour; precedence. **Upper house.** The House of Lords; the higher of the two chambers of any deliberative assembly. **Upper leather. a.** (Leather forming) the upper of a boot or shoe. **b.** Leather prepared or suitable for this. **Upper lip. a.** The superior lip of a person, animal, or insect. *To keep a stiff upper lip*, to show no sign of weakening, yielding, or suffering. **b.** The higher of two edges of an organ-pipe mouth. **c.** *Bot.* The superior division of a bilabiate corolla or calyx. **Upper ten**, the upper classes; the aristocracy. *colloq.* Orig. (U.S.) *u. ten thousand.* **Upper works. a.** The part of a ship above the water-line when it is ready or laden for a voyage. **b.** *slang.* The head, brains, wits.

U·pperest, *a.* Now *rare* or *Obs.* ME. [f. prec. + -EST.] Uppermost.

On what might be called the u. Thames W. MORRIS.

Uppermost (ɒ·pəɹmōst), *adv.* and *a.* 1481. [f. as prec. + -MOST.] **A.** *adv.* **1.** In or to the highest or upmost position or place. **b.** In the first place in respect of precedence, rank, importance, etc. 1526. **2.** Foremost in or into the mind, thoughts, conversation, etc. 1693.

1. Shee was turned topse-turvie, her Kele vppermost 1622. 2. Perpetual Chat on whatever comes u. 1693.

B. *adj.* **1.** Occupying the highest position or place; loftiest; furthest up (on a river, etc.) 1500. **b.** Outermost, most external 1548. **2.** Highest in rank, importance, precedence, etc. 1680. **b.** Having the chief power, control, or authority; predominant 1691.

1. Ye love the vppermost seates in the sinagoges TINDALE *Luke* xi. 43. The vppermost village neere the mountaines 1623. b. The Adder..casteth off yearely his u. skin 1567.

U·pping, *vbl. sb.* 1560. [f. UP *v.*] **1.** = SWAN-UPPING. **2.** The action of getting up; only *attrib.* in *u.-block, -stock, -stone*, a mounting-stone 1796.

Uppish (ɒ·piʃ), *a.* 1678. [f. UP *adv.*[2] + -ISH.] †**1.** Flush of money –1700. **2.** †**a.** Elated –1802. †**b.** Excited with drink –1728. **c.** Irritable, testy. Now *dial.* or *Obs.* 1778. **2.** Characterized by presumption or affectation of superiority 1734. **3.** Slightly elevated or directed upwards 1862. Hence **U·ppishness.**

Uprai·se, *v.* ME. [UP- III. 1.] †**1.** *trans.* To raise from the dead –1533. †**2.** To laud, extol –1595. **3.** To raise to a higher level; to lift up (esp. the head, hands, etc.) ME. **b.** To raise from a prostrate, low, or dejected state; to assist, encourage, or cheer ME. **4.** To erect, build. Now *rare.* ME. Hence **U·praised** *ppl. a.* **Uprai·sing** *vbl. sb.* and *ppl. a.*

Uprea·r, *v.* ME. [UP- III. 1.] **1.** *trans.* To raise up, elevate, erect, etc. **b.** To raise in dignity; to exalt. late ME. **2.** To bring up; to tend. late ME. **3.** To excite, stir up. *arch.* 1486. **4.** *intr.* To rise up 1828.

1. So in the field..Uprears some antient Oak his rev'rend head 1718. b. Now I shal ben enhauncid, now I shal ben vp rered WYCLIF *Isaiah* xxxiii. 10. 4. Steeds Were seen uprearing 1828. Hence **U·preared** *ppl. a.* **Uprea·ring** *vbl. sb.*

Upright (ɒ·prəit, †ɒprəi·t), *a.* and *sb.* [OE. *up(p)riht* (f. *up* UP *adv.*[1] + RIGHT *a.*) = OFris. *upriucht*, MLG. *uprěcht*, OHG. *ûfrěht*, ON. *uprěttr*.] **A.** *adj.* **1.** *predic.* Erect on the feet or end; in or into a vertical position; perpendicular to the ground or other surface. †**2.** *predic.* Lying or so as to lie at full length on the back; supine. Usu. with *lie* vb. –1627. **3.** Having the chief axis or distinctive part perpendicular to a surface; pointed or directed upwards; not inclined or leaning over. late ME. **b.** Marked by perpendicular position or attitude; erect OE. **4.** Of persons: Erect in carriage. late ME. **5. a.** Of a hill, etc.: Very steep 1596. **b.** Of a rectangular superficies: Having the height greater than the breadth 1888. †**6.** Of a shoe: That may fit either foot –1642. **7.** *fig.* Of persons, principles, conduct: Of unfailing integrity or rectitude; morally just, honest, or honourable 1530.

1. My stiffned haire stands vpright 1607. Supported by pillows, she sat almost u. MISS BURNEY. *fig.* While the honour of the Britons stood vpright 1570. 2. Sleeping u. upon the back be not healthfull 1620. 3. It cost me a Month to shape it..to something like the Bottom of a Boat, that it might swim u. DE FOE. *U. pianoforte*: see PIANOFORTE. *U. Grand Piano*..applied..to the better kinds of the cottage piano 1896.

B. *sb.* †**1.** A vertical front, face, or plane –1726. †**b.** = ELEVATION II. 3. –1842. **2.** An upright or vertical position; the perpendicular 1683. **3.** Something set or standing upright; a perpendicular stone, post, part, etc. 1742. **b.** *spec.* One of the vertical members of a framing, etc. 1700. **c.** An upright pianoforte 1860. **d.** A kind of fly-hook 1878. **4.** *slang.* A drink of beer and gin mixed 1796.

1. b. There are not many uprights, but several ground plans of some of the palaces H. WALPOLE. 2. The mullion was much out of u. 1905. 3. A beam laid cross-wise upon two uprights 1845.

U·pright, *adv.* 1509. [f. prec.] †**1.** = UPRIGHTLY 1. –1624. **2.** Vertically upwards 1590.

2. Wownded on his hed by his own wanton throwing of a brik-bat u., and not well avoyding the fall of it 1591.

U·pright, *v.* ME. [f. as prec.] *trans.* To raise to an upright or vertical position; to erect.

Upri·ghteousness. 1549. [f. UPRIGHT *a.*, after RIGHTEOUSNESS.] †**1.** = Uprightness –1623. **2.** Show of virtue, sanctimony (*rare*) 1904.

U·prightly, *adv.* 1549. [f. as prec. + -LY [2].] **1.** In a just or upright manner; with strict observance of justice, honesty, or rectitude. †**b.** Candidly –1630. **2.** In an upright position. Now *rare.* 1601.

2. I have..seen him..walk..as u. as you can walk 1826.

U·prightness. 1541. [f. as prec. + -NESS.] **1.** The state or condition of being upright; moral integrity or rectitude. b. Const. *of* (heart, conduct, etc.) 1560. 2. The state or character of being vertical, erect, or upright; erectness 1645.

2. Mrs. Croft..had a squareness, u., and vigour of form JANE AUSTEN.

Upri·sal. 1871. [f. UPRISE *v.* + -AL 2.] Uprising.

Uprise (vprəi·z, v·prəiz), *sb.* ME. [UP-I. 2.] †1. Resurrection. ME. only. 2. Rising (of the sun, etc.); dawn (of day) 1588. b. The act of rising to a higher level; ascent 1690. c. The beginning of an ascent; an ascending shaft in a mine 1875. 3. Ascent to power or dignity; rise to wealth or importance 1810. b. The act of coming into existence or notice 1817.

Uprise (vprəi·z), *v.* ME. [UP-III. 1.] 1. *intr.* To rise to one's feet; to stand up. b. To rise from bed ME. 2. Of the sun: To rise ME. 3. To rise from the dead ME. b. To come from the underworld 1550. 4. To rise or ascend to a higher level; to rise into view ME. b. To become erect 1796. 5. To ascend as a sound 1503. 6. To come into existence 1471. Hence **Upri·sen**, **Upri·sing**, *ppl. adjs.*

Upri·sing, *vbl. sb.* ME. [UP-III. 4.] 1. The action of rising from death; resurrection. Now *rare.* 2. The action of rising from bed; or from a sitting, kneeling, or recumbent posture ME. 3. The action of rising after a fall ME. 4. The rising of the sun ME. 5. Advancement in place or power; increase of prosperity. Now *rare.* late ME. 6. An insurrection; a popular rising 1587. 7. The process or fact of coming into existence or notice 1587.

2. Thou knowest my downe syttinge & my vprisynge COVERDALE *Ps.* cxxxviii. 2. 6. The great communistic u. under Wat Tyler 1861. 7. The u. of a new aristocracy of wealth and intellect 1851.

U·p-ri·ver, *a.* 1877. [UP *prep.* 2.] Belonging to, situated, etc. farther up, or near the source of, a river. b. Leading or directed towards the source of a river 1890.

Uproar (v·prōᵊɹ), *sb.* 1526. [ad. Du. *oproer*, f. *op-* UP- + *roer* confusion; in sense 2 assoc. with ROAR *sb.*[1]] 1. An insurrection or popular rising; a serious tumult or outbreak of disorder among the people or a body of persons. Now *rare.* 2. Loud outcry; noise of shouting or tumult 1544. b. With article and in pl. 1572. 3. *In* (*an*) *u.*, in a state of tumult, commotion, or excitement 1548.

1. Athalia rente hir clothes, & sayde vproure, vproure COVERDALE 2 *Kings* xi. 14.

Uproa·r, *v. rare.* 1605. [f. prec.] 1. *trans.* To throw into confusion. 2. *intr.* To make an uproar 1831.

1. I should..Vprore the uniuersall peace SHAKS.

Uproarious (vprōᵊ·riəs), *a.* 1819. [f. UPROAR *sb.* + -IOUS.] 1. Making, or given to making, an uproar. 2. Characterized by uproar 1849. Hence **Uproa·riously** *adv.*, **-ness.**

Uproo·t, *v.*[1] 1620. [UP- III. 1 + ROOT *v.*[1]] *trans.* To tear up by the roots; to remove from a fixed position 1695. b. *fig.* To destroy as by tearing up; to exterminate, eradicate 1620. So **Uproo·ted** *ppl. a.* 1593.

Uproo·t, *v.*[2] 1726. [UP- III. 1 + ROOT *v.*[2]] *trans.* To grub up.

U·prush, *sb.* 1873. [UP- I. 2.] An upward rush or flow.

Upru·sh, *v.* 1818. [UP- III. 1.] *intr.* To rush up.

U·psaddle, *v. S. Afr.* 1863. [ad. Du. *opzadelen*, f. *op-* UP- + *zadelen* SADDLE *v.*] *intr.* To saddle a horse.

Upset (v·pset), *sb.* late ME. [UP- I. 2.] †1. A revolt. late ME. only. †2. *north.* and *Sc.* (The fee paid upon) setting up in business as a master or becoming a freeman in a trade -1687. 3. The overturning of a vehicle or boat; the fact of being overturned 1804. b. An overturning or overthrow *of* ideas, plans, etc. 1822. c. A physical or (more commonly) mental disturbance or derangement 1866. d. A quarrel; a misunderstanding 1887.

3. b. What a strange u. of old principles and old measures! SOUTHEY.

Upset (vpse·t), *v.* 1440. [UP- III. 1.] 1. *trans.* †a. To set up, establish -1608. b. *techn.* To force back the end of (a metal bar, etc.) by hammering or beating, esp. when heated 1677. 2. *intr.* To be overturned or capsized (said of a vehicle, boat, etc., or of persons in it) 1799. 3. *trans.* To overturn; to capsize; to knock over 1803. b. To involve (persons) in the accidental overturning of a vehicle or boat. Chiefly *pass.* 1807. c. *fig.* To overthrow, undo, put out of joint 1818. 4. To throw into mental disorder or discomposure; to trouble, distress: freq. *pass.* 1805. b. To disorder physically 1845.

3. Phr. *To u.* a person's or the *applecart*, fig. to overthrow his projects. 4. I never was so shocked or so completely upset 1805. b. A young person..easily upset by any imprudence in diet 1845. Hence **Upse·tter.** **Upse·tting** *vbl. sb.* and *ppl. a.*

U·pset, *pa. pple.* and *ppl. a.* ME. [UP- III. 2.] 1. Set up, erected, raised up, etc. Now *rare.* 2. Of price: Stated as the lowest sum for which property exposed to auction will be sold; named as the sum from which bidding may start. Orig. *Sc.* and *U.S.* 1814. 3. Overturned, capsized 1842.

U·pshot. 1531. [UP- I. 2.] †1. A final shot in a match at archery; chiefly *fig.* a closing or parting shot -1618. †2. A mark aimed at -1754. †3. An end, conclusion, or termination; the climax or completion *of* something -1662. b. The extreme limit (*rare*) 1699. 4. The result, issue, or conclusion (*of* some course of action, etc.) 1604.

1. As it were for an vp-shot to all the fooles thunderbolts they had let flie 1614. 2. The U. of all Religion is to please God 1754. 3. Through fear of death the u. of evils 1617. b. That threescore years and ten make the u. of man's pleasurable existence DE QUINCEY. 4. The u. of all was, our Lord vanquished the devil 1680. Phr. *In the upshot*, in the end, at last.

Upsidaisy, var. UP-A-DAISY.

U·pside. 1611. [UP- I. 1.] 1. The upper side or part (*of* a thing). 2. The side of a railway or station on or into which the 'up' trains run 1880.

U·pside dow·n, *adv.* (*a.*) ME. [orig. *up so down*, the *so* perh. meaning 'as if'.] A. *adv.* 1. So that the upper part or surface becomes the under or lower. Freq. in phr. *to turn u.* 2. *fig.* In or into a state of overthrow, reversal, or disorder ME. B. *adj.* (Written with hyphen or as one word.) Inverted 1866.

A. 1. The cradel and the child thai found Up so doun upon the ground ME. Transuersed or turned vp set downe 1520. 2. As for the waye of yᵉ vngodly, he turneth it vpsyde downe COVERDALE *Ps.* cxlv[i]. 9.

U·pside dow·nward(s), *advs.* 1611. [f. prec. + -WARD, -WARDS.] = prec. A.

U·psides, *adv.* 1746. [f. UPSIDE + -S.] 1. *U. with*, even, equal, or quits with (a person). *dial.* (orig. *Sc.*) or *colloq.* 2. *colloq.* On a level *with*, alongside *of* 1883.

Upsilon (yupsəi·lǫn). 1642. [a. Gr. ῦ ψιλόν 'slender u.'] The Greek letter Υ, υ, representing the vowel *u.* Also *attrib.* = having the form of this letter. (Cf. HYPSILOID.)

Upspri·ng, *v.* OE. [UP-III. 1.] 1. *intr.* Of plants, etc.: To spring up, to grow. b. *fig.* To come into being. late ME. 2. To ascend; to spring or leap upwards; to start to one's feet. late ME.

1. b. The hour When Paradise upsprung BYRON. 2. Upsprang she then, and kiss'd them R. BRIDGES. Hence **Upspri·nging** *ppl. a.*

U·pstair, *adv.* and *a.* 1627. [UP *prep.* 1, 6.] = next A. 1, B.

Upstairs, *adv.*, *sb.*, and *a.* 1596. [UP *prep.* 1, 6.] A. *adv.* (vpstēᵊ·ɹz, exc. when contrasted with *dow·nstairs*). 1. So as to ascend a flight of stairs; to the floor at the top of a staircase. 2. At the top of, on a floor or in a room reached by, a flight of stairs; in an upper story 1781. b. quasi-*sb.* 1842. c. as *sb.* An upper story or floor. Also *transf.*, a person or persons living on an upper floor. 1884.

1. *Phr. To kick u.*; see KICK *v*, 5. 2. b. The ogre's voice from u. LOVER.

B. *adj.* (v·pstēᵊɹz). Situated on an upper story or at the top of a flight of steps 1782. b. Belonging to, connected with, the upper rooms or parts of a house 1839.

U·pstanding, *ppl. a.* OE. [UP- III. 3.] 1. Standing up; erect. 2. Of animals (esp. horses) or persons: Having an erect carriage; well set up 1835. b. *fig.* Of independent, open, or honest bearing; straightforward, downright 1863. 3. *U. wage*, a regular or fixed wage (as opp. to one dependent on circumstances) 1888.

1. A coronal of high u. plumes SOUTHEY.

Upstart, (v·pstaɹt), *sb.* and *a.* 1555. [UP- I. 2, II.] A. *sb.* 1. One who has newly or suddenly risen in position, rank, or importance; a parvenu. 2. The meadow-saffron, *Colchicum Autumnale* 1852.

1. Mary gyp goodman vpstart, who made your father a gentleman? 1592.

B. *adj.* 1. Of things: Lately come into existence or notice; new-fangled 1565. b. Characteristic of upstarts 1593. 2. Of persons, families, etc.; Lately or suddenly risen to prominence or dignity 1566.

1. This up-start fansie is far from God's ordinance 1593. b. He dreaded their u. ambition GIBBON.

Up-stream, *adv.* and *a.* 1681. [UP *prep.* 2, 5.] A. *adv.* (even stress, and freq. as two words). In a direction contrary to the flow of a stream; towards the source of a stream. B. *adj.* (v·pˌstrīm). 1. Situated higher up a stream 1838. 2. Directed or taking place up-stream 1826.

U·p-stroke. 1828. [UP- I. 2.] 1. A stroke delivered upwards. 2. The upward stroke of a pen, etc. 1848.

†U·psy. 1590. [ad. Du. *op zijn* on his (her, its), used e. g. in *op zijn Vriesch* 'in the Frisian fashion'.] *U. Friese*, *u. Dutch*, deeply, heavily, to excess 1592. *U. Friese*, a mode of drinking or carousing 1590. *U. Dutch*, suggestive of having drunk too deeply, heavy 1610.

Drinke Duch like gallants, lets drinke vpsey freeze 1601. Sit downe Lads, And drink me upsey-Dutch FLETCHER.

U·ptake. 1816. [UP- I. 2.] 1. The action of, or capacity for, understanding; comprehension. Usu. *quick* (etc.) *in the u.*; orig. (and still chiefly) *Sc.* 2. = TAKE-UP 4. 1839. 3. A ventilating shaft by which foul air ascends 1889.

Upthrow (v·pþrōᵘ). 1807. [UP- I. 2.] 1. *Geol.* and *Mining.* An upward dislocation of a stratum or seam. 2. *Geol.* An upheaval of part of the earth's crust or surface 1833. 3. The action of throwing up 1898.

1. *attrib.* A true fault with an u. and downthrow side 1882.

U·pthrust. 1846. [UP- I. 2.] The action of thrusting or the fact of being thrust upwards, esp. by volcanic action.

Up to date, *adv. phr.* and *a.* 1868. [UP *adv.*[1]] A. *adv. phr.* (u·p to da·te). 1. Until the present time, the time in question, or the time of writing. 2. Not behind the times; with the latest information, appliances, etc. 1889.

2. The improvements..render this camera quite 'up to date' 1892.

B. *adj.* (predic. *u·p-to-da·te*; attrib. *u·p-to-date*). 1. Extending to the present time; presenting or inclusive of the latest facts, details, etc.; employing or involving the latest methods or devices 1888. 2. Of persons: Having or employing the latest information, facts, or methods; keeping abreast of the times; having tastes, manners, etc., regarded as prevailing at or characteristic of the present time 1891. Hence **Up-to-da·teness.**

1. General up-to-date smartness 1894.

Up town, up-tow·n, *adv.*, **u·p-town**, *a.* 1838. [UP *prep.*] A. *adv.* In, to, or into the higher or upper part of a town, or (*U.S.*) the residential portion of a town or city 1855. B. *adj.* Situated or dwelling up-town 1838.

A. I had heard of Miss Havisham up town DICKENS.

Uptu·rn, *v.* ME. [UP- III. 1.] †1. *trans.* To overthrow, subvert. -late ME. 2. To turn, throw, or tear up; to cast or turn over 1567. 3. To turn (the eyes, face, etc.) upwards 1667. 4. *intr.* To turn or move up or upwards 1805.

2. Boreas and Cæcias..rend the Woods and Seas u. MILTON. Hence **Uptu·rning** *vbl. sb.*

U·pturned, *ppl. a.* 1592. [UP- III. 2.] 1. Turned or directed upwards. 2. Turned upside-down; overturned; turned up by digging, etc. 1816. 3. Turned upwards at the point or end; curved 1843.

Upward (v·pwǫ̈ɹd) *adv.*, *prep.*, *a.*, and *sb.* [OE. *upweard*, f. *up* UP *adv.*[1] + *-weard* -WARD.] A. *adv.* I. 1. To or towards a higher position or plane: a. In ref. to movement or extension through space. b. In ref. to aspect, attitude, or direction OE. c. *fig.* In respect of thought, life, merit, rank, etc. ME. **d.** Higher in respect of price or value 1874. **2.** Up along the course of a stream, etc.; further into the interior of a country; to or towards a centre, metropolis, source, etc. ME. **b.** Towards the body or head 1600. **3.** In, occupying, or so as to occupy a higher or the highest position or place ME. **b.** In respect of the upper part or parts. late ME. **4.** With (vertical) extension *from* a point or part (esp. of the body) to another expressed or implied. late ME.

1. a. Herons,..mounting u... soar above the Sight DRYDEN. *fig.* U. steals the life of man, As the sunshine from the wall LONGF. **b.** If yee looke u., yee see there infinite bodies SIDNEY. **c.** *Macb.* IV. ii. 24. **2.** Trace the Muses u. to their spring POPE. **3.** Lying with the face u. JOHNSON. **b.** U. Man And downward Fish MILT. **4.** A Spaniard from the hip vpward SHAKS.

II. 1. Backward in order of time; continuously into the past OE. **2. a.** To or into later life 1530. **b.** *And (or) u.* = UPWARDS *adv.* 2. 1555. **3.** *U. of*, more than; also, rather less than 1613.

1. Consider now from this day, and vpward *Haggai* ii. 18. **2. a.** I am, and ever have been from my Youth u., one of the greatest Liars STEELE. **b.** To the number of two thousand people and vpward 1608. **3.** I haue beene your Wife, in this Obedience, Vpward of twenty yeares SHAKS.

†**B.** *prep.* Up; along the line of ascent of –1818. **C.** *adj.* †**1.** Facing upwards; supine –1646. **2.** Directed, taking place, or inclined upwards; ascending 1607. **b.** Having a course which indicates advance, progress, or increase 1596. **3.** Situated above; higher; lofty 1622. **4.** Directed, moving, taking place, etc. upstream 1731. †**D.** *sb.* The top part. SHAKS.

2. b. The u. movement which raised the lower labouring classes 1914. **3.** With strong wings Scaling the u. sky SHELLEY. **4.** The..chief Boatman of any u. boat 1731. Hence **U·pward-ly** *adv.*, **-ness.**

Upwards (ʊ·pwǫ̈ɹdz), *adv.* and *prep.* [OE. *up(p)weardes*, f. *upweard* UPWARD + *-es* of advb. gen.; see -WARDS.] **A.** *adv.* **1.** = UPWARD *adv.* I. **b.** *U. of*, to or at a higher level than; above 1853. **2.** To a higher aggregate, figure, or the like. Usu. *and u.*, *or u.* 1523. **c.** To later life 1805. **3.** Backwards in time; into the past 1654. **4.** *U. of*, rather more than; rather less than 1721. †**B.** *prep.* = UPWARD *prep.* –1601.

1. Prisoners..of the degree of a Baron, or uppwardes 1557. A Fire that naturally mounts u. ADDISON. Looking u. we saw a series of coloured rings TYNDALL. We followed this stream u. 1869. **2.** Hotel accommodation..for two and a half or three guineas a week, u. 1910. **4.** U. of three thousand years ago 1893.

Up-wind (ʊ·pwi·nd), *adv.* 1838. [UP *prep.* 4.] Contrary to the course of or against the wind.

Ur (ɔ̄ɹ). Also **-er.** 1846. [Echoic.] An inarticulate sound, uttered instead of a word that the speaker is unable to remember or bring out.

‖**Ur-** (ūᵊr), *prefix*, repr. G. *ur-* 'primitive, original, earliest', and occurring in a few terms.

The *Ur-Hamlet* may have contained a number of these borrowings 1901. **Ursprache** (ū·rʃpraχə) *Philol.*, hypothetically primitive language reconstructed from a group of historically cognate languages.

‖**Urachus** (yūᵊ·răkɒs). 1578. [mod.L., ad. Gr. οὐραχός urinary canal of a fœtus.] *Anat.* A fibrous cord binding the apex of the bladder to the anterior abdominal wall and the peritoneal folds. Hence **U·rachal** *a.*

‖**Uræmia** (yurī·miă). 1857. [mod.L., f. Gr. οὖρον urine + αἷμα blood.] *Path.* A morbid condition resulting from presence in the blood of urinary constituents normally eliminated by the kidneys. So **Uræ·mic** *a.* of, marked by, or affected by uræmia 1855.

‖**Uræus** (yurī·ɒs). *Pl.* **uræi** (-əi). 1832. [mod. Latinization of Gr. οὐραῖος (perh. influenced by Gr. οὐραῖος, f. οὐρά tail) repr. the Egyptian word for 'cobra'.] *Egypt. Antiq.* A representation of the sacred asp, or of its head and neck, employed as an emblem of supreme power, occas. *spec.* as worn on the head-dress of ancient Egyptian divinities and sovereigns.

Ural[1] (yūᵊ·răl, yurā·l). 1785. The name of a mountain-chain (more freq. *Urals, U. mountains*) forming the north-eastern boundary of Europe with Asia, used attrib. in specific appellations of animals, etc., as *U. duck, lizard.* **b.** *U.-Altaic*, pertaining or belonging to the region including the Ural and Altaic mountains, its people, or their speech. Also *absol.*, the family of agglutinative languages spoken in eastern Europe and northern Asia; Turanian; Finno-Tartar 1855.

Ural[2] (yūᵊ·răl). 1891. [irreg. f. URETHANE.] *Med.* A preparation of chloral hydrate and urethane, used as a hypnotic.

‖**Urali** (urā·li). 1862. [var. of OORALI.] The urari-plant, *Strychnos toxifera*, or the poison obtained from this.

Uralian (yurē̆·liăn), *a.* 1801. [f. URAL[1] + -IAN.] Of or pertaining to, dwelling in or near, the Ural mountains; also, Ural-Altaic. So **Uralic** (yuræ·lik), *a.*

Uralite (yūᵊ·răləit). 1835. [ad. G. *uralit*, f. URAL[1] + -ITE[1].] *Min.* Pyroxene altered to amphibole. Hence **Urali·tic** *a.*

Uralium (yurē̆·liɒm). 1889. [See URAL[2] and -IUM.] *Med.* = URAL[2].

Uralo- (yurē̆·lo), comb. form of URAL[1], as in *Uralo-Altaic, -Caspian, -Finnic.*

Uramil (yuræ·mil). 1839. [G., f. UREA + AMMONIA + *-il*, -YL.] *Chem.* Murexan. Hence **Urami·lic** *a.* 1839.

Uran- (yūᵊ·răn), comb. form of URANITE, URANIUM, as in *uran-mica, -ochre.*

Uranate (yūᵊ·rănēt). 1842. [f. URANIC *a.*[2] + -ATE[1].] *Chem.* A salt produced by the action of uranic oxide upon a base.

Urania (yurē̆·niă). 1614. [L. (the muse of astronomy), ad. Gr. Οὐρανία fem. of οὐράνιος heavenly, f. οὐρανός heaven.] **1.** As the title of a book or poem dealing with celestial or astronomical themes, etc. **2.** *Astr.* One of the planetoids or asteroids 1865.

Uranian (yurē̆·niăn), *a.*[1] 1600. [f. prec. + -AN.] **1.** Pertaining to or befitting heaven; heavenly, celestial. **b.** As a distinctive epithet of Venus (or Aphrodite): Heavenly, spiritual 1768. **2.** Pertaining, belonging, or dedicated to (the muse) Urania 1656. **b.** Astronomical 1761.

1. He sees the earthly image of U. Love SHELLEY.

Uranian (yurē̆·niăn), *a.*[2] and *sb.* 1844. [f. URANUS + -IAN.] **A.** *adj.* Of or pertaining to the planet Uranus. **B.** *sb.* An inhabitant of Uranus 1870.

Uranic (yuræ·nik), *a.*[1] 1837. [f. URANIUM + -IC.] Formed from or related to the higher oxide of uranium.

Ura·nic, *a.*[2] 1901. [f. Gr. οὐρανός palate + -IC.] *Anthropol.* Pertaining or relating to the palate. Freq. in *u. index.*

Uraninite (yuræ·ninəit). 1879. [f. URANIUM + -IN[1]; see -ITE[1] 2 b.] *Min.* Pitchblende.

Uranism (yūᵊ·răniz'm). 1899. [ad. G. *uranismus*, f. Gr. οὐράνιος heavenly, taken to mean 'spiritual'; see -ISM.] Homosexuality.

Uranite (yūᵊ·rănəit). 1794. [a. G. *uranit*, or F. *uranite*, f. next + -ITE[1] 4, 2 b.] †**1.** *Chem.* = next 1. –1821. **2.** *Min.* An ore or mineral composed largely of uranium, and occurring in two varieties, autunite and torbernite 1802. Hence **Urani·tic** *a.* of, pertaining to, or containing u. or uranium.

Uranium (yurē̆·niɒm). 1797. [mod.L., f. URANUS + -IUM.] **1.** A rare, heavy, grayish metallic element, found esp. in pitchblende and uranite. **2.** *ellipt.* A solution of a salt or nitrate of uranium 1878.

Urano-[1] (yūᵊ·răno, yūᵊrănǫ·), comb. form of Gr. οὐρανός sky, heaven(s), roof of the mouth.

Urano·graphy, the science of describing or delineating, a delineation or description of, the sidereal heavens; hence **Urano·grapher.** **Uranogra·phic, -al** *adjs.* **Urano·logy,** (a treatise or discourse on) astronomy; hence **Uranolo·gical** *a.* **Urano·metry,** (a treatise on) the measurement of the magnitudes and relative distances of heavenly bodies, esp. the fixed stars; hence **Uranome·trical** *a.* **U·ranopla·sty** *Surg.*, plastic surgery of the hard palate; hence **U·ranopla·stic** *a.* **Urano·scopus,** *Ichth.* = STAR-GAZER 2.

Urano·so-, comb. form of next occurring in a few chemical terms, as *uranoso-ammonic, -potassic, -uranic.*

Uranous (yūᵊ·rănəs), *a.* 1842. [f. URANIUM + -OUS c.] *Chem.* **1.** Formed from or related to the lower oxide of uranium. **2.** Of, pertaining to or typical of uranium 1878.

Uranus (yūᵊ·rănɒs, pop. yurē̆·nɒs). [L., a. Gr. Οὐρανός husband of Gæa (Earth) and father of Cronos (Saturn).] *Astr.* The most remote but two of the planets, situated between Saturn and Neptune, and discovered in 1781 by Sir Wm. Herschel.

Uranyl (yūᵊ·rănil). 1850. [f. URANIUM + -YL.] *Chem.* A radical (UO_2) held to exist in many compounds of uranium. Hence **Urany·lic** *a.*

‖**Urari** (urā·ri). 1838. [See CURARE, and cf. URALI.] = CURARE.

Urate (yūᵊ·rēt). 1800. [a. F.; see URIC *a.* and -ATE[1].] *Chem.* A salt produced by the action of uric acid on a base. Hence **Ura·tic** *a.* of or pertaining to, containing or consisting of, a u. or urates.

Urban (ɔ̄·ɹbăn), *a.* and *sb.* 1619. [ad. L. *urbanus*, f. *urbs* city. Rare before 19th c.] **A.** *adj.* **1.** Pertaining to or characteristic of, situated or occurring in, a city or town. **b.** Constituting, forming, or including a city, town, or burgh 1841. **2.** Exercising authority, control, etc., in or over a city or town 1651. **b.** Residing, dwelling, or having property in a city or town 1837.

1. The strength of u. Toryism GLADSTONE. **2.** All Magistrats are either U. or Forren, viz. of Town or Countrey 1651. **b.** The vehemence of u. democracy 1849.

B. *sb.* A town-dweller (*rare*) 1891.

Urbane (ɒɹbē̆·n), *a.* 1533. [ad. F. *urbain*, or L. *urbanus.*] **1.** Of or pertaining to, characteristic of or peculiar to, a town or city. Now *Obs.* or *arch.* **2.** Having the manners, refinement, or polish regarded as characteristic of a town; courteous, at ease in society; also, blandly polite, suave 1623. **b.** Characterized by urbanity, courtesy, or politeness 1679.

1. Raising..savage life To rustic, and the rustic to u. WORDSW. Béranger, an u. or city poet LOWELL. **2.** I feel never quite sure of your u. and smiling coteries STEVENSON. **b.** His manners were gentle, affable, and u. W. IRVING. Hence **Urba·nely** *adv.*

U·rbanist. 1523. [f. the papal name *Urban* + -IST.] **1.** An adherent of Pope Urban VI against Clement VII (*rare*). **2.** A nun of a branch of the Poor Clares, following the rule as mitigated in 1264 by Pope Urban IV. 1687.

Urbanity (ɒɹbæ·nĭti). 1535. [a. F. *urbanité*, or ad. L. *urbanitas*, f. *urbanus* URBAN.] **1.** The character or quality of being urbane; refined or bland politeness or civility. **b.** *pl.* Civilities, courtesies 1646. †**2.** Cheerful, witty, or pleasant talk; polished wit or humour –1693. **3.** The state, condition, or character of a town or city; life in a city 1549.

1. His U., that is, his Good Manners DRYDEN. **b.** The passages of societie and daily urbanities of our times SIR T. BROWNE. **2.** Moral Doctrine,..and U., or well-manner'd Wit,..constitute the Roman Satire DRYDEN.

Urbanize (ɔ̄·ɹbănəiz), *v.* 1642. [In sense 1, f. URBAN *a.* + -IZE; in sense 2, ad. F. *urbaniser.*] **1.** To make urbane, or more refined or polished. Now *rare.* **2.** To make of an urban character; to convert into a city 1884.

1. In order to..u. their savage Disposition 1785. Hence **Urbaniza·tion.**

Urceolate (ɔ̄·ɹsiŏlēt), *a.* 1760. [ad. mod.L. *urceolatus*, f. L. URCEOLUS.] **1.** Pitcher-shaped; esp. in *Bot., Anat.*, etc. **2.** Furnished with or contained in an urceolus 1891. So **U·rceolated** *a. Zool.* = sense 1. 1752.

‖**Urceolus** (ɒɹsī·ŏlɒs). 1832. [L., dim. of *urceus* pitcher.] A pitcher-shaped sheath or tube, esp. as a protective part in plants or animals.

Urchin (ɔ̄·ɹtʃin). ME. [var. of HURCHEON; cf. †*irchin.*] **1.** = HEDGEHOG 1. †**b.** A goblin or elf –1614. **2.** A sea-urchin; = ECHINUS 1. 1601. **3.** One who is deformed in body; a hunchback. Now *dial.* 1528. **4.** A pert, mischievous, or roguish youngster; a brat 1530. **b.** *poet.* Applied to Cupid 1709. **5.** A little fellow; a boy or youngster 1556. **6.** *techn.* One of a pair of rapidly rotating small card cylinders of a carding-machine 1835.

1. b. An old wiues tale of diuells and vrchins 1594. **2.** The Vrchins of the sea called Echini 1601. **3.** An vrchine: by which name also we call a man that holdeth his Necke in his bosome 1607. **4. b.** The subtile line Wherewith the u. angled for my Heart SOUTHEY. **5.** The gutter urchins 1839.

Urdee (ɒ·ɹdi), *a.* Also **urdé, urdy.** 1562. [Origin obsc.; perh. due to a misreading of F. *vidée* in the phr. *croix aiguisée et vidée.*] *Her.* **1.** Of a cross: Having the extremities pointed. **2.** Of a bend, etc.: Having the margin broken into parallel pointed projections. Also of a line broken thus. 1688.

Urdu (ū·ɹdū), *sb.* and *a.* 1796. [a. Hindustani (Pers.) *urdū* camp, ad. Turkī *ordu* HORDE; ellipt. for *zabān-i-urdū* 'language of the camp'.] **A.** *sb.* = HINDUSTANI *sb.* 2. **B.** *adj.* Of or pertaining to, printed, written, or composed in the Hindustani language 1845.

†**Ure**[1]. late ME. [a. AF. *eure, = OF. *uevre* (F. *œuvre*):—L. *opera* work.] **1.** *In ure*, in or into use, practice, or operation -1711. **2.** *Out of ure*, disused, obsolete -1600. **3.** Custom, habit -1600.

†**Ure**[2]. *Orkney* and *Shetland.* 1534. [ad. ON. *øyrir* (= Sw. *öre*), ad. L. *aureus* a gold solidus. Cf. ORA[1].] *Urisland* [ON. *øyrisland*], *u. of land*, land yielding rent of one-eighth of a mark; also *ellipt.*

-ure (iūɹ), *suffix*, repr. F. *-ure*, L. *-ura*, in words of F. or L. origin. The meaning, in L. action or process, hence the result of this office, rank, dignity, after further development in Fr. and Eng. is now extended to action or process, the results or product of this (e.g. *enclosure*, *figure*, *scripture*), state, rank, office or function (e.g. *judicature*, *prefecture*), a collective body (e.g. *legislature*), and that by which the action is effected (*ligature*). Many words are early adoptions from Fr. (as *figure*, *censure*, *tonsure*), a few direct adaptations from L. (*aperture*), some formed by addition of *-ure* to Eng. stems of L. origin (e.g. *composure*, *unigeniture*). The suffix was further used with stems of Romance origin and with native or other stems, as in *wafture*.

‖**Urea** (yūᵊ·rīă). 1806. [Latinized f. F. *urée*, f. Gr. οὖρον urine.] *Chem.* A soluble crystalline compound, forming an organic constituent of the urine in mammalia, birds, and some reptiles, and also found in blood, milk, etc.; carbamide, $CO(NH_2)_2$. Hence **U·real** *a.*

Uredine (yurī·dəin), *sb.* and *a.* 1889. [f. the pl. UREDINES.] *Bot.* **A.** *sb.* A fungus of the family *Uredineæ* of minute ascomycetal fungi (including mildew, rust, smut, etc.), parasitic on plants. **B.** *adj.* Pertaining or belonging to the Uredines 1889.

‖**Uredines** (yurī·dinīz). 1753. [L., pl. of UREDO.] *Bot.* Species of fungi parasitic upon and injurious to plants, etc.

Uredinous (yurī·dinəs), *a.* 1865. [f. L. *uredin-* (see next) + -OUS.] **1.** *Bot.* Of the nature of a uredine; belonging to the *Uredines.* **2.** *Path.* Affected with or of the nature of nettlerash 1891.

‖**Uredo** (yuᵊrī·do). 1706. [L. (pl. *uredines*) blight, blast, itch, f. L. *urere* to burn.] *Bot.* **1.** A form of blight, = BRAND *sb.* 6 (*rare*). **2.** The intermediate stage of the *Uredineæ* or rust fungi, parasitic on grain and other plants; formerly regarded as a separate genus. Usu. with capital. 1836. **b.** A species or plant of this 1836. **3.** *attrib.*: **u.-fruit**, a group of uredospores; **u. stage**, the summer stage of certain rust fungi.

Ure·dospore. 1875. [f. prec. + SPORE.] *Bot.* One of the peculiar summer spores developed during the uredo stage in rust fungi.

Ureide (yūᵊ·rīəid). 1857. [f. UREA + -IDE.] *Chem.* A derivative of urea containing acid radicles.

Ureo- (yūᵊ·rīo), comb. form of UREA, as in *ureo-carbonate*, *ureometer.*

Ure-ox (yūᵊ·rǫks). 1607. [ad. MHG. *ûrochse* UROCHS.] = AUROCHS.

-uret (iūret), *Chem.*, a suffix, ad. mod.L. *-uretum*, *-oretum*, now replaced by -IDE, forming names of simple compounds of an element with another element or a radical.

Ureter (yurī·təɹ). 1578. [a. medical L., a. Gr. οὐρητήρ, f. οὐρεῖν to make water.] *Anat.* Either of the fibro-muscular tubes or vessels conveying urine from the kidneys to the bladder; a urinary duct. Usu. in pl. Hence **Ure·teral**, **Ureteric** (yūᵊrite·rik) *adjs.* pertaining to, affecting, or connected with a u. or the ureters.

Ureteritis (yurītěrəi·tis). 1823. [f. prec. + -ITIS.] *Path.* Inflammation of a ureter.

Uretero- (yurī·tĕro), comb. form of URETER, occurring in various surgical and medical terms, as in **uretero·tomy, -ge·nital, -ve·sical** *adjs.*, etc.

Urethane (yure·þēⁱn). 1838. [a. F. *uréthane*; see UREA and ETHANE.] *Chem.* Ethyl carbamate, valued as an anæsthetic.

Urethra (yurī·þrā). 1634. [a. late L., a. Gr. οὐρήθρα, f. οὐρεῖν to make water.] *Anat.* The membranous tube through which the urine is discharged from the bladder. Hence **Ure·thral** *a.* of or pertaining to, connected with, or affecting the u.; adapted for, used in, operating on the u.

Urethritis (yūᵊrīþrəi·tis). 1823. [f. prec. + -ITIS.] *Path.* Inflammation of the urethra.

Urethro- (yurī·þro), comb. form of URETHRA, as in **urethrocele, -meter, -rrhaphy, -scope, -tomy; -plastic, -sexual** *adjs.*

Urethylane (yure·þilēⁱn). 1844. [f. UREA; see ETHYL and -ANE 2.] *Chem.* Methyl-urethane; methyl carbamate.

Urge (ɒ̄ɹdʒ), *sb.* 1618. [f. next.] **1.** The action of urging or fact of being urged or prompted (*rare*). **2.** An impelling motive, force, pressure, etc.; an inner striving or yearning towards development or action 1884.

1. That we may pray without all u. 1618. 2. There is an inward u. that forces it upwards 1914.

Urge (ɒ̄ɹdʒ), *v.* 1560. [ad. L. *urgere* to press, drive.] **1.** *trans.* To bring forward, present or press upon the attention (a fact, reason, etc.) in an urgent manner; to plead as an excuse or argument; to allege or state, esp. in justification, extenuation, or defence. **2.** To advocate (a course of action, etc.); to claim or demand pressingly 1592. **3.** To entreat or plead with pertinaciously; to importune, ply with arguments or strong persuasion. Also, with impersonal subject: To incite or impel strongly. 1565. **4.** To serve or act as a constraining influence on (a person's feelings, etc.). **5.** To press forward, prosecute vigorously (a proceeding, enterprise, etc.) 1565. **6.** To drive or force in some direction. Also with preps. or advs., as *against*, *through.* 1594. **b.** To accelerate the pace of; to speed up. Usu. with advs. or preps. 1721. **c.** To pursue (one's flight, way, the chase); to hasten (one's pace, etc.) 1697. **7.** To stimulate to expression or action; to provoke; to increase or intensify 1594. **8.** To ply vigorously 1697. **9.** *intr.* To adduce or bring forward arguments, allegations, etc.; to press by inquiry 1592. **b.** To press solicitously, make a strong claim *for* something 1607. **10.** To press, push, or hasten on 1605. **11.** To act as an impelling or prompting motive, stimulus, or force; to exercise pressure or constraint 1645.

1. I am at a loss what more to u. BERKELEY. 'Don't break out, Lammle,' urged Fledgeby DICKENS. 2. He hath ever urged peace with the malignants SCOTT. 3. The barbarian..moves when he is urged by appetite J. H. NEWMAN. 5. While Turnus urges thus his Enterprise DRYDEN. 6. From Stage to Stage the licens'd Earl may run,..the Senator at Cricket u. the Ball POPE. Evening must usher night, night u. the morrow SHELLEY. b. Vesper! u. thy lazy car! SHELLEY. 7. Then u. the fire gradually 1800. 9. He again urged for her hand, and for a private marriage RICHARDSON. 11. The combat urges, and my soul 's on fire POPE. Hence **U·rger. U·rging** *vbl. sb.* and *ppl. a.*, **-ly** *adv.*

Urgence (ɒ̄·ɹdʒěns). 1592. [a. F., or f. URGENT *a.*; see -ENCE.] **1.** = next 1, 2. **2.** Expedition, haste 1612. **3.** = next 4. 1874.

1. At the united u. of France and England..[he] resigned 1893. 2. Late despatches sent With u. GEO. ELIOT.

Urgency (ɒ̄·ɹdʒěnsi). 1540. [f. next, or ad. late L. *urgentia.*] **1.** The state, condition, or fact of being urgent; pressing importance. **b.** *spec.* The status of parliamentary business that has been voted urgent 1883. **2.** Pressure by importunity or entreaty; urgent solicitation 1611. **3.** Stress *of* wind, weather, etc. 1660. **4.** Impelling or prompting force or quality 1816. **5.** An urgent need or situation 1647. **6.** A driving or constraining impulse or motive 1664. **7.** *pl.* Earnest representations or entreaties 1823.

2. By your great and frequent u., you prevailed on me SWIFT. 4. From no apparent impulse but the u. of conscience SCOTT. 5. Collections through the Kingdom being too slow for such an u. 1647. 6. Quick urgencies of Devotion 1664.

Urgent (ɒ̄·ɹdʒěnt), *a.* 1496. [a. F., ad. L. *urgent-*, *urgens*, *urgere* to URGE.] **1.** Pressing; demanding prompt action; marked or characterized by urgency. **b.** Of messages, commands, etc., by which a matter is strongly pressed upon a person's attention 1611. **2.** Of persons: Importunate, insistent 1548. **b.** Eagerly desirous *to* do something 1753. **3.** Pressing forward, hurrying on. Now *poet.* 1546. †**4.** Oppressive; severe; heavy -1699. †**5.** Of time: Pressing; passing quickly -1791.

1. U. appetites of the flesche 1559. 2. Most vrgent suiters for my loue MARLOWE. His family have been very u. for him to make an expedition to Margate W. IRVING. 3. A shapen prow Borne by the mastery of its u. wings R. BRIDGES. 4. The heat is very vrgent HAKLUYT. 5. *Wint. T.* I. ii. 465. Hence **U·rgently** *adv.*

-uria (yūᵊ·riă), a second element, latinized from Gr. -ουρία, employed in pathological terms denoting morbid conditions of the urine, as *albuminuria*, *glycosuria*, *hæmaturia*, *pyuria.*

Uric (yūᵊ·rik), *a.* 1797. [ad. F. *urique*, f. *urine* URINE; see -IC.] *Chem.* **1.** *U. oxide*: earlier name of XANTHINE. **2.** *U. acid*, a crystallizable acid, $C_5H_4N_4O_3$, found in the urine of man and certain of the lower animals 1800.

Comb.: **u.-acidæmia** = URICÆMIA; **u. acidity**, the condition of containing an excess of u. acid.

Uricæmia (yūᵊrisī·miă). 1867. [mod.L., f. *uricus* URIC *a.* + Greek αἷμα blood + -IA[1].] *Path.* = LITHÆMIA. Hence **Uricæ·mic** *a.*

Uriconian (yūᵊrikōᵘ·niăn), *a.* 1886. [f. *Uriconium*, name of a Roman town at Wroxeter + -AN.] *Geol.* Consisting of or pertaining to a series of volcanic rocks such as constitute the Wrekin in Shropshire.

-urient (yūᵊ·riěnt), *suffix*, ad. L. *-urient-*, pres. pple. stem of desiderative vbs., occurring in a few direct adoptions from L., as *parturient*, and hence occas. added to L. stems to form adjs. with the meaning 'desiring, characterized by a desire (to do something)', as *nupturient.*

‖**Urim** (yūᵊ·rim). 1537. [a. Heb. *ūrīm* pl., referred to *ōr* light, pl. *ōrīm*, and by some taken as = lights, φωτισμοί 'illuminations'.] Certain objects, the nature of which is not known, worn in or upon the breastplate of the Jewish high-priest, by means of which the will of Jehovah was held to be declared. (Chiefly in *Urim and Thummim*, rendered in the LXX δήλωσις καὶ ἀλήθεια, in the Vulgate *doctrina et veritas*, whence Wyclif *doctryne and trewthe*, and in Coverdale *light and perfectnesse*, following Luther's *licht und recht*; in later English versions the words are left untranslated.)

The Counsel would be as the Oracle U. and Thummim, those oraculous gems On Aaron's breast MILT.

Urinal (yūᵊ·rinăl), *sb.* ME. [a. OF., a. L. *urinal*, f. *urina* URINE.] †**1.** A glass vessel for the medical examination or inspection of urine -1858. †**2.** *Alchemy.* A phial for solutions, etc. -1738. **3.** A chamber-pot 1475. **b.** *Med.* A bottle for passing urine in bed. **4.** A vessel with conductor worn on the person for incontinence of urine 1855. **5.** A place of accommodation for passing urine 1851.

U·rinal, *a.* Now *rare* or *Obs.* 1541. [a. F., ad. late L. *urinalis*, f. *urina* URINE.] = URINARY *a.*

Urinary (yūᵊ·rinări), *a.* 1578. [ad. med. L. *urinarius, f. L. *urina* URINE.] **1.** Affording passage to urine; effecting or assisting in the secretion and discharge of urine. **2.** Of the nature of urine; excreted as urine 1646. **3. a.** Adapted for using on the urinary passage 1688. **b.** Adapted for receiving urine 1822. **4. a.** Lodged or formed in the urinary organs or bladder; excreted in the urine 1793. **b.** Of, pertaining to, affecting, or occurring in the urinary system or organs 1822.

Urinate (yūᵊ·rineⁱt), *v.* 1599. [f. med.L. *urinat-*, *urinare* to pass water, f. L. *urina* URINE.] **1.** *intr.* To discharge urine; to make water. **2.** *trans.* To wet with urine 1768. **b.** To pass as or after the manner of urine 1915.

So **Urina·tion**, the action of passing water, micturition 1599.

†**U·rinator.** 1648. [a. L., f. *urinari* to dive.] A diver -1691.

Urine (yūᵊ·rin), *sb.* ME. [a. OF., ad. L. *urina*, related to Greek οὖρον.] The fluid secreted from the blood by the kidneys in man and the higher animals, stored in the bladder, and voided at intervals through the urethra. (Freq. in *Path.* with qualifying terms, denoting morbid condition.) **b.** With *an* and *pl.* 1483.

A physycyen, truely, can lyttel descerne Ony maner sekenes wythout syght of uryne 1509. Hence **U·rine** *v.* (now *rare* or *Obs.*) = URINATE.

Urini·ferous, *a.* 1744. [ad. mod.L. *uriniferus*; see -(I)FEROUS.] *Anat.* Conveying urine. Usu. with *tube*, also with *duct*, *tubule*.

Urino- (yūᵊ·rino, -ǫ·), comb. form of L. *urina* URINE.

U·rinoge·nital *a.*, = UROGENITAL *a.*, affecting or occurring in the urogenital organs. **Urino·logy** = UROLOGY; hence **Urino·logist**. **U·rinomancy**, diagnosis of diseases by examination of the urine. **Urino·meter**, an instrument for determining the specific gravity of urine. **U·rinosco·pic** *a.*, of or pertaining to the inspection of urine as a means of diagnosing diseases; hence **Urino·scopist**, **-scopy**.

Urinous (yūᵊ·rinəs), *a.* 1644. [ad. mod.L. *urinosus*, f. L. *urina* URINE.] **1.** Having or partaking of the essential properties of urine. **b.** Characteristic or suggestive of that of urine 1670. **2.** Of the nature of urine 1669. **3.** Marked by the presence or prevalence of urine 1788.

Urn (ɒ̄ɹn), *sb.* late ME. [ad. L. *urna*, f. *urere* to burn.] **1.** An earthenware or metal vessel of a rounded or ovaloid form and with a circular base, used by the ancient Greeks and Romans and others to preserve the ashes of the dead. **2.** A receptacle for holding voting-tablets, lots, or balls, in casting lots, voting, etc. Chiefly *Rom. Antiq.* 1513. **b.** A ballot-box 1888. **3.** A hollow vessel, usu. of earthenware, of an oviform or rounded shape, and having a circular base, used for various purposes 1639. **b.** A sculptured ornament representing or shaped like an urn 1653. **4.** An oviform pitcher or vessel for water, wine, etc. 1613. **b.** The source of a stream, etc.; a spring or fountain 1728. **c.** A tear-bottle (freq. with *lachrymal*) 1753. **d.** *Astr.* The constellation of Aquarius 1633. **5.** Short for *tea-urn* 1781. **6. a.** *Bot.* The spore-case or capsule of urn-mosses 1840. **b.** *Biol.* An urn-shaped process or part 1877.

1. Alasse, how small an Vrne containes a King! DEKKER. **3.** *fig.* The haughty day Fills his blue u. with fire EMERSON. **b.** Her statue..set uppon an Urne or Pedestall 1653. **4. b.** Ten thousand rivers poured.. From urns that never fail COWPER.

Comb.: **u.-moss** (see sense 6 a). Hence **Urn** *v. trans.* to deposit (ashes, bones) in a cinerary u.; to enclose in or as in an u. †**U·rnal** *a.* of the nature of a cinerary u.; effected in a sepulchral u.

Urning (ɒ̄·ɹniŋ). 1890. [Ger. (Ulrichs). Cf. URANISM.] A homosexual person.

Uro-[1] (yūᵊ·ro), comb. form of Greek οὖρον urine, in terms of physiological chemistry, etc., denoting esp. (*a*) pigments present in or derived from urine, as *urocy·anin*; (*b*) morbid conditions of the urine or urinary organs, as *urocysti·tis*; (*c*) instruments for examining urine, as *urogravi·meter*; also in adjs., as *urose·xual*.

Urobe·nzoate, = HIPPURATE. **Urobenzo·ic** *a.*, in *u. acid*, hippuric acid. **Urobilin** (-bei·lin), a brownish resinous pigment found in the urine; hence **U·robilinu·ria**, a morbid condition characterized by excess of urobilin. **U·rochrome**, a yellow amorphous pigment found in the urine. **Uroe·rythrin**, a reddish pigment found in the urine of persons suffering from fevers, esp. rheumatic fever. **Uroglaucin** (glǭ·sin), a blue pigment found in the urine in certain diseases, as scarlet fever. **Urohæ·matin**, a variety of hæmatin forming the colouring matter of the urine. **Uroto·xic**, *a.* of or pertaining to the toxicity or toxic materials of the urine. **U·rotoxy, -toxi·city**, the toxic quality of the urine; a unit of urine in respect of its toxicity. **Uroxa·nic** *a.*, of an acid, obtained by oxidation of uric acid in alkaline solution. **Uroxanthin** (-zæ·nþin), = INDICAN.

Uro-[2] (yūᵊ·ro), comb. form of Greek οὐρά tail, occurring in terms of comparative anatomy, etc., designating or relating to a posterior, caudal, or tail-like part, region, segment, or process.

U·rochord, the notochord of ascidians and tunicates, regarded as corresponding to the primordial spinal column in vertebrates; one of the *Urochorda*, a branch of *Chordata* comprising ascidians and tunicates. **U·rodele** [Gr. δῆλος evident] *sb.* a member of the order *Urodela* of amphibians, in which the larval tail persists in adult life; *adj.* belonging to this order; so **Urode·lan**. **Urohy·al** *a.* forming or relating to a median posterior process or part of the hyoid arch in fishes or birds; *sb.* the bone forming this. **U·rostyle**, *Biol.* the posterior unsegmented portion of the vertebral column in certain fishes and amphibians.

‖**Urochs** (ūᵊ·ɹ-, yūᵊ·rǫks). 1839. [G., var. of *auerochs*.] = AUROCHS.

Uroge·nital, *a.* 1848. [f. URO-[1] + GENITAL *a.*] Pertaining or belonging to the urinary and genital organs or products.

Urology (yuᵊrǫ·lŏdʒi). 1753. [f. URO-[1] + -LOGY.] †**a.** A treatise or discourse on urines. **b.** The scientific study of urine. Hence **Uro·lo·gical** *a.* **Uro·logist**.

Uroo (yūᵊ·ru). *Austral.* 1866. [Native name.] A species of kangaroo.

Uropoietic (yūᵊropoi,e·tik), *a.* 1783. [ad. mod.L. *uropoieticus*: see URO-[1] and POIETIC *a.*] Of, pertaining to, concerned with the secretion of urine; secreting or excreting urine.

‖**Uropygium** (-pi·dʒiǒm). 1813. [med.L. *uropygium*, ad. Gr. οὐροπύγιον.] *Ornith.* The rump in birds. So **Uropy·gial** *a.* situated on or belonging to the u.; *sb.* a rump-feather.

Uroscopy (yurǫ·skŏpi). 1646. [ad. med.L. *uroscopia*; see URO-[1] and -SCOPY.] The scientific examination of urine, esp. as a means of diagnosing diseases. Hence **Urosco·pic** *a.* **Uro·scopist**.

Urrhodin (yūᵊ·rŏdin). 1846. [ad. G. *urorhodin*, f. *uro-* URO-[1] + Gr. ῥόδον rose.] *Chem.* A red pigment found in the urine in certain morbid conditions. Hence **Urrhodi·nic** *a.*

‖**Ursa** (ɒ̄·ɹsă). OE. [L., bear (esp. she-bear), the Great Bear.] *Astr.* **1.** = sense 2. **2.** *Ursa Major*: The northern constellation also called the Great Bear, the Plough, and Charles's Wain. late ME. **b.** *joc.* A bearish person 1773. **3.** *Ursa Minor*: the northern constellation called the Little Bear 1597.

U·rsal, *a.* 1837. [f. L. *ursus* bear + -AL.] Bear-like; *fig.*, bearish.

Ursine (ɒ̄·ɹsəin), *a.* 1550. [ad. L. *ursinus*, f. *ursus* bear.] **1.** Of or pertaining to, characteristic of, or due to a bear or bears. **2.** Of the nature of, resembling, or having the essential characteristics of a bear; consisting of bears 1833. **b.** In specific names of beasts 1778. **3.** Suggesting that or those of a bear; bear-like 1837.

1. Full corpolent he was with breist ursyne,..and sperit leonine 1550. The u. fate of prophet-mockers 1841. **3.** Noted for u. manners SOUTHEY.

Urson (ɒ̄·ɹsən). 1774. [a. F. *ourson*, dim. of *ours* bear.] *Zool.* The Canada porcupine, *Erethizon dorsatus*.

Ursone (ɒ̄·ɹsoun). 1866. [*f.* L. (*uva*) *ursi* (see UVA) + -ONE.] *Chem.* A crystalline principle obtained esp. from the leaves of the bearberry.

Ursuline (ɒ̄·ɹsiuləin, -in, -īn), *sb.* and *a.* 1693. [f. name of St. *Ursula* + -INE[1].] **A.** *sb. pl.* An order of nuns established in 1572 with the rule of St. Augustine, for the teaching of girls, nursing of the sick, and the sanctification of the lives of its members. **B.** *adj.* Pertaining or belonging to the Ursulines 1739.

‖**Urtica** (ɒ̄·ɹtikă, vɹtəi·kă). 1706. [L., f. *urere* to burn.] A genus of apetalous plants, typical of the family *Urticaceæ*, including the true nettles; also, a plant of this, a stinging-nettle. So **Urtica·ceous** *a.* belonging to, consisting of, the *Urticaceæ*; resembling a nettle.

Urtical (ɒ̄·ɹtikăl, vɹtəi·kăl), *a.* and *sb.* 1846. [f. L. *urtica* nettle + -AL.] *Bot.* **A.** *adj.* Pertaining or belonging to the stinging-nettles. **B.** *sb.* An exogenous plant of the genus *Urtica* 1846.

‖**Urticaria** (ɒ̄tikēᵊ·riă). 1771. [mod.L., f. L. URTICA.] *Path.* = NETTLE-RASH. Hence **Urtica·rial**, **Urtica·rious** *adjs.* of or pertaining to, appearing in, characteristic of, or resembling u.

Urticate (ɒ̄·ɹtikeit), *v.* 1843. [a. med.L. *urticat-*, *urticare*, f. L. URTICA.] **1.** *intr.* To have the property of stinging like a nettle; to affect with a tingling pain or stinging sensation. **2.** *trans.* To flog with stinging-nettles 1861. **b.** To affect with a stinging pain; to produce urtication in or on 1862. **3.** To nettle, irritate 1873.

Urtication (vɹtikēⁱ·ʃən). 1655. [ad. med.L. *urtication-*, f. *urticare* to URTICATE.] **1.** The action or function of stinging like or as a nettle. **b.** A sensation suggestive of sting 1859. **2.** The flogging or pricking of a benumbed part or paralytic limb with nettles as a means of restoring sensation, etc. 1837.

‖**Urubu** (ūrubū·). 1672. [a. Brazilian (Tupi) *urubú*.] The black vulture, *Cathartes fœtens* or *atrata*, of the southern U.S. and South America.

‖**Urucu** (ūrukū·). 1613. [a. Brazilian (Tupi) *urucú* anatta.] = ROUCOU 1, †2.

‖**Urucuri** (ūrukū·ri). 1863. [a. Brazilian (Tupi) *urucurí* palm.] The Brazilian palm-tree, *Attalea excelsa*.

‖**Urus** (yūᵊ·rɒ̆s). *Pl.* **uri** (yūᵊ·rəi), **uruses**. 1601. [a. L., = Gr. οὖρος, OTeut. **ūrus*; see AUROCHS.] *Zool.* **1.** = AUROCHS. **2.** Applied to species of fossil or prehistoric oxen 1823.

Us (ɒs), *pers.* and *refl. pron.* [Com. Teut.; OE. *ús* (see I *pron.*) with loss of *n* retained in Du. *ons*, G. *uns*:—wk. grade of Indo-Eur. **nes*.] The objective case of the pron. WE, repr. the OE. acc. and dat. **I.** With ref. to two or more persons. **1. a.** As direct obj. of a verb. **b.** As indirect obj., = To us OE. **c.** As obj. of a prep. (or other governing word or phrase) OE. **d.** With participles in absolute construction 1549. **e.** In ethic dative. *arch.* 1685. **2.** *refl.* Ourselves. Now only *arch.* or *dial.*, after some verbs of motion or posture. OE. **3.** With defining term. late ME. **4.** As nom., in place of WE. Now *dial.* or *vulg.* 1607. **b.** With sb. or adj. numeral in apposition 1489. **c.** In continuative or exclamatory clauses after *and* 1848. **d.** *predic.* after the vb. *to be*. *dial.* and *colloq.* 1883. **5.** *Naut.* = Our ship 1622.

1. a. To the soper sette he vs anon, And serued vs with vitaille CHAUCER. **b.** We myȝte be lordes aloft and lyue as vs luste LANGL. It mighte cost vs oure neckes COVERDALE 1 *Chron.* xiii. 19. Give us clothes, father! SHELLEY. **c.** Spanish men of warre..came vp with vs and fired at vs 1659. **d.** Vntill he ascended vp (all vs beholdyng hym) to heauen 1549. **e.** They wounded us only one Man 1711. **2.** For we may not hide us from þin iȝe 1430. Let's make vs Med'cines of our great Reuenge SHAKS. Let vs hye vs to Wakefield 1599. We sat us dahn on a wall top 1892. **3.** Bacon-fed Knaues, they hate vs youth SHAKS. Concerning the loyalty of us Catholics 1641. **4.** Come my Lords, shall vs march? 1607. **b.** A thing us men ought..to bless God for 1814. **c.** And him so rich.. And us so poor! DICKENS. **d.** It 's us must break the treaty when the times come STEVENSON. **5.** We had taken the Vice-admirall, the first time shee bourded with vs 1622.

II. With ref. to a single person. **1.** Used by a sovereign or other potentate or magnate ME. **b.** In editorial or authorial use 1835. **2.** *dial.* and *colloq.* Me; to me 1828.

1. Tell Our Army from Vs Q. ELIZ. His Holiness was pleased to raise us..to the rank of Cardinal Priest of the Holy Roman Church CDL. WISEMAN. **b.** The one public man who is supposed never to read Us 1895.

Usable (yū·zăb'l), *a.* Also **useable**. late ME. [a. OF., f. *user* USE *v.*; see -ABLE.] That may or can be used.

The candelstik, lanterns, and the vsable thingis of it WYCLIF *Exod.* xxxix. 36. Hence **Usabi·lity**. **U·s(e)ableness**.

Usage (yū·zédʒ). ME. [a. AF., OF., = med.L. *usaticum*, f. L. *usus* USE *sb.*] **1.** Habitual use, established practice, customary mode of action, on the part of a number of persons. **2.** With *a* and *pl.* An established or recognized mode of procedure, action, or conduct; a custom; *spec.* one which has force in law ME. **b.** *The Usages*, the eucharistic ceremonies of mixing water with the wine, prayer for the dead, prayer for the descent of the Holy Spirit on the elements, and the prayer of oblation 1718. **c.** *local.* A right-of-way 1829. **3.** The rules and customs *of* a particular body, class, craft, or pursuit ME. †**4.** Manner of (ordinarily) bearing or comporting oneself; usual conduct or behaviour; a practice or habit -1655. **5.** The action of using something; the fact of being used; employment, use. late ME.

6. Action, behaviour, or conduct towards a person, etc.; manner of using or being used; treatment 1563. 7. Established or customary use of words, language, expressions, etc. 1697.

1. Laws..corrected, altered, and amended by acts of parliament and common u. BLACKSTONE. 2. Dyvers Privileges, Liberties and free Usages 1473. All I have here related was a receiv'd u. 1734. c. Crooked U. is a narrow lane..[in] Chelsea 1884. 3. Of woodecraft wel koude he al the vsage CHAUCER. Married.. according to the u. of the church of England 1827. 5. Þe vsage and exercitacioun of pacience CHAUCER. Thou haste the vsage of reason CAXTON. 6. Another ..surrendred of her own accord, in hopes of better u. 1687. To inquire into the u. of children legally bound out 1799. Without fear of their being injured by the roughest u. 1892. Hence **U·sager**, a member of that section of nonjurors which observed 'the Usages'.

Usance (yū·zăns). late ME. [a. OF., = med.L. *usancia*, f. *usant-*, *usare* to USE.] 1. = prec. 1, 1 b. Now *arch.* or *poet.* 2. = prec. 5. *arch.* 1460. 3. †a. The practice or fact of lending or borrowing of money at interest (*rare*) –1611. b. Interest on money lent. (In 19th c. as a literary revival.) 1584. 4. The period allowed by commercial usage or law for the payment of a bill of exchange, esp. as drawn in a foreign or distant land 1617. b. In the phr. *at u., at..usance(s)* 1487.

1. Edicts, which have lost their validity by contrary u. 1656. I have in this way heard something of the prospects and usances of teachers 1860. Things to which we have grown so accustomed.., that u. has begotten familiarity 1862. 3. a. You have rated me About my monies and my vsances SHAKS. b. The old Catholic doctrine that no u. whatever could be unsinfully received for the use of money 1862. 4. Touching the exchange from London to Venice farther distant, by the word vsance three moneths are signified, and by double vsance six moneths 1617. b. No bills are now drawn in London at u. 1878.

Use (yūs), *sb.* ME. [a. AF., OF. *us* :—L. *usus*, f. ppl. stem *us-* of *uti* to use.] I. Act of using or fact of being used. 1. The act of using a thing for any (esp. a profitable) purpose; the fact, state, or condition of being so used; utilization or employment for or with some aim or purpose; application or conversion to some (esp. good or useful) end. b. In *Law*, coupled with *occupation* (or *occupancy*) 1738. c. Freq. *to make* or *take* (*free, full*, etc.) *use of* 1591. 2. In special senses: a. The act of using or fact of being used as food, etc.; consumption 1586. b. Employment or maintenance for sexual purposes 1565. 3. *Law*. The act or fact of using, holding, or possessing land or other property so as to derive revenue, profit, or other benefit from it 1535. b. A trust or confidence reposed in a person for the holding of property, etc., of which another receives or is entitled to the profits or benefits 1535. 4. The fact of using money borrowed or lent at a premium 1603. b. Such premium; interest, usury. Now *dial.* or *arch.* 1598. 5. Employment or usage resulting in or such as to cause impairment, wear, etc. 1440.

1. To lend me the vse of one of your maskes 1558. The..confusion that is so hard to be avoided in the U. of Words LOCKE. c. Perhaps she had only made u. of him as a convenient aid to her intentions HARDY. Phrases. *In u.*; A low word not in u. JOHNSON. *To u.*; Every moment may be put to some u. CHESTERF. *Out of u.*; The name..had in some way gone out of u. 1892. *Of u.*; Words..of very frequent u. in the New Testament 1648. 2. a. A moderate u. of generous liquors 1772. b. His step-mother desired the u. of his body 1647. 3. The property or possession of the soil being vested in one man, and the u., or profit thereof, in another BLACKSTONE. b. The Statute of Uses (A.D. 1535) was passed in order to prevent the severance of legal from beneficial ownership 1882. 4. When money is lent on a contract to receive..an increase by way of compensation for the u. BLACKSTONE. b. Human life Is but a loan to be repaid with u. COWPER. Phr. *At, to*, †*u.* (now *dial.*); You are my own son; — you have put my money out to u. already 1785. †*U. upon u.*, compound interest. 5. Everything told of long u. and quiet slow decay DICKENS.

II. Habit of using. 1. The habitual, usual, or common practice; continual, repeated, or accustomed employment or exercise; habit, custom ME. 2. A custom, habit, or practice ME. 3. Without article: Accustomed practice or procedure; usage, wont, habit. Often *use and wont*. 4. Opportunity, occasion, habit or practice of using. Chiefly *to have the u. of*. ME. b. The power of using some faculty, etc.; ability to use or employ 1483. 5. Long practice in something; practised condition, skill. late ME. 6. *Eccl.* The distinctive ritual and ceremonial of a particular church, diocese, community, etc. late ME. b. Religious rite or ceremony observed in particular services of the church; a customary form of religious observance or service. late ME. 7. The usage or fashion obtaining or prevailing in a country or community. late ME.

1. His vse was to ride with a thousande horses 1568. It is the vse of Cowards to doe that which thou dost 1612. According to the U. of those Days 1720. 2. Englande hath an euyll vse in syttynge longe at dyner 1542. She knows not yet the uses of the world SHELLEY. 3. Long U. obtaineth the authority of a Law HOBBES. 4. The Pict..hath generally no vse of apparell HOLINSHED. b. Till a Person is come to the U. of Reason 1753. 'Little darling' has lost the u. of an arm 1860. 5. When men can by muche vse, leape, wrastle, or cast the barre, better then any other 1551. I frequented all the fencing-schools to keep my hand in vse GOLDSM. 6. Some folowyng Salsbury vse, some Herford vse, some the vse of Bangor 1548. b. Some very remarkable 'uses'.., such as mixing water with the wine 1877. 7. The vse of that cuntre differethe from the rite of Englonde in clothenge 1432.

III. Manner of using. Manner or a manner or method of employing, applying, turning to account, etc.; an instance of this ME.

Perverts best things To worst abuse, or to thir meanest u. MILT. As its u. is very easie, so its convenience is very great 1703. Some of these uses of the word are confusing JOWETT.

IV. Purpose served. 1. A purpose, object, or end, esp. of a useful or advantageous nature ME. †b. A practical application of doctrine in a sermon or homily –1816. 2. The fact or quality of serving the needs or ends *of* a person or persons ME. 3. *Law*. The advantage *of* a specified person or persons in respect of profit or benefit from lands, etc. late ME. 4. Office; function; service 1509. 5. The character, property, or quality which makes a thing useful or suitable for some purpose; utility; advantage, benefit 1598. b. In the phr. *of* or *to* (*no, little*, etc.) *use*. late ME. c. With ellipsis of prep. 1820. 6. Need or occasion for using; necessity, demand 1604. b. *To have no use for*: to find superfluous, regard as a nuisance; to dislike. *colloq.*, orig. *U.S.* 1887.

1. The prestes..take the golde.., and put it to their owne vses COVERDALE *Baruch* vi. 10. I had the tallow..for greasing my boat, and other uses SWIFT. b. I proceed now to the Uses which may be drawn from the Truths delivered 1679. 2. Coffee..for the u. of the Grand Seignior MILT. 3. A rente charge paiable to the vs and profit of his chanterie 1393. 4. The u. of the sand in these processes is to prevent the amber.. from passing over into the receiver 1811. 5. Their u. is not answerable to the great Stress which seems to be laid on them LOCKE. What is the u. of making up my mind? 1880. b. Birds..that are of Assistance and U. to Man ADDISON. I had good reason to hope that I was being of u. 1859. c. Alas! it is no u. to say, 'I'm poor!' SHELLEY. 6. Giue it me..I haue vse for it SHAKS.

Use (yūz), *v.* ME. [a. OF. *user* = med.L. *usare*, f. L. *us-*, ppl. stem of *uti* to use.] I. †1. *trans.* To observe (a rite, custom, etc.); to keep as a custom; *pass.*, of a practice: to be customary –1889. †2. To comply with, put in practice (a law, etc.) –1609. 3. To prosecute or pursue (a course of action). Now *rare*. ME. †4. To follow (a trade, etc.); to perform the functions of (an office) –1773. †b. To follow or pursue (a manner or course of life) –1821. c. To spend (a period of time) in a certain way. (Now only with implication of sense II. 1.) 1477. †d. To frequent (a person's company) –1599. †5. To engage in or practise (a game, etc.) –1801. 6. To put into practice or operation; to carry into action or effect. late ME.

1. It shall be lawful, as it hath been used heretofore, to make Probates of wills..in the Colony 1650. 2. Al Barons sall receaue, and vse the lawes, as they are vsed in the Kings court 1609. 3. The chiefest Market place, where all the buying and selling was used 1648. 4. Then let them vse the office of a Deacon 1 *Tim.* iii. 10. b. The wicked life that I did vse 1578. c. *Timon* III. i. 39. 5. A corpulent Man, who lived freely and used no Exercise 1764. 6. 'Twas a good world when such simplicitie was vsed 1589.

II. 1. To make use of (some immaterial thing) as a means or instrument; to employ for a purpose ME. b. To employ (a standard, type, etc.) ME. 2. To employ (an article, etc.), esp. for a profitable end; to turn to account ME. b. To wear as an article of apparel. late ME. 3. To work, manipulate (a member, tool, etc.) ME. 4. To employ (a person, animal, etc.) in some function or capacity, esp. for an advantageous end. late ME. b. To have sexual intercourse with. Now *dial.* late ME. 5. To take or partake of as food, drink, etc. Now *rare*. late ME. 6. To expend, consume, or exhaust by use 1440. 7. *To use up*: a. To come to the end of (a stock, etc.) 1785. b. To exhaust the vigour of, tire out (a person) *colloq.* 1850. 8. To speak or write (a language) ME. b. To avail oneself of, express oneself by or in (a style, a word, etc.) ME. 9. To frequent, haunt (a place). Now *rare*. late ME. b. *To use the sea(s)*, to be a sailor. *arch.* 1634. 10. To treat or deal with (a person or thing), behave to (a person) in a specified way 1483. †b. *refl.* To conduct or comport oneself –1860.

1. Freedom is either a blessing or a curse as men u. it BERKELEY. The arguments used..to detain her brother 1798. 2. b. Buskins of shels all siluered vsed she MARLOWE. 3. Good Launcelot Iobbo, vse your legs,..run awaie SHAKS. I am against the prophets ..that vse their tongues *Jer.* xxiii. 31. He..used a *perspicillum* or simple lens 1880. 4. Were not his purpose To u. him further yet in some great service MILT. 5. And vse these thynges, Cowe mylke, Almon mylke, yolkes of rere egges 1542. 6. A Cook that used six Pounds of Butter to fry twelve Eggs MRS. GLASSE. 7. The genuine Roman race must have been almost used up in the desperate warfare 1875. b. We have used up no fewer than six Irish Secretaries 1887. 8. [He] should be able to u. Latin, not merely to understand it 1888. b. A man y^t vseth moch swearing BIBLE (Great) *Ecclus.* xxiii. 11. 9. Like a wilde Asse, that vseth the wildernesse COVERDALE *Jer.* ii. 23. He useth the Queen's-head Ale-house 1708. b. These many years..have I used the seas 1681. 10. My Colonel useth me with very greate courtesy 1639. b. He used himself more like a Fellow to your Highness, than like a Subject 1648.

III. 1. To make (a person, etc.) familiar or accustomed by habit or practice; to habituate, accustom; to inure. Const. †*in*, †*with*, *to*. Now chiefly in pa. pple. ME. 2. *intr.* To do a thing customarily; to be wont to do. (Now only literary and chiefly in clauses introduced by *as*.) late ME. 3. To be accustomed or wont *to* do something. Now only in pa. t. *used to* (yūst tu, yū·stŭ). ME. 4. To frequent a place; to go often *to* a person or place. Now *dial.* and *U.S.* 1470.

1. This man had accesse unto the queene..to u. hir with..courtlie pastimes HOLINSHED. You shall do well also to u. your Horse to Swimming 1643. As soon as it perceives any thing it is not us't to 1682. I'm not used to be used in this manner! MME D'ARBLAY. He wanted to u. her by degrees to live without meat SCOTT. 2. We should, as learned Poets u., Invoke the Assistance of some Muse 1663. 3. Your silke-worme useth to fast every third day WEBSTER. Jewels do not u. to lie upon the surface of the earth 1662. 4. Sertaine lewde fellowes..doe frequente and and u. about Layton heath 1599. Ye valleys low where the milde whispers u., Of shades and wanton winds MILT. Hence **U·ser**[1], one who uses or employs a thing.

Used (yūzd), *ppl. a.* late ME. [f. prec. + -ED[1].] †1. Usual, wonted –1655. b. That is or has been made use of 1594. 2. **Used up.** a. Thoroughly exhausted by physical exertion; tired out, 'done up'; exhausted by use, rendered unserviceable. *slang* or *colloq.* 1840. b. *U.S.* Fully discussed 1839. c. Worn out, debilitated, rendered useless, as with hard work, dissipation, age, etc. 1848.

Useful (yū·sfŭl), *a.* 1483. [f. USE *sb.* + -FUL.] Having the qualities to bring about good or advantage; helpful in effecting a purpose; suitable for use; serviceable. Hence **U·seful-ly** *adv.*, **-ness.**

Useless (yū·slės), *a.* 1593. [f. as prec. + -LESS.] That is of no use; unserviceable, ineffectual, unavailing. b. Of persons: Incompetent, inefficient; performing no service 1670. Hence **U·seless-ly** *adv.*, **-ness.**

U·se-mo:ney. Now *dial.* 1616. [f. USE *sb.* I. 4 b.] = INTEREST *sb.* II. 2.

User[2] (yū·zəɪ). 1835. [a. F. *user* to use, or inferred from NON-USER.] *Law.* Continued use, exercise, or enjoyment of a right; presumptive right arising from use.

‖**Ushabti** (*u*ʃa·bti). 1912. [Egyptian.] Statuettes of servants deposited in the tomb of a mummy.

Usher (ʋ·ʃəɹ), *sb.* late ME. [a. AF. *usser*, OF. *ussier, uissier*, var. of *huisier* HUISHER.] **1.** An official or servant who has charge of the door and admits people to a hall, chamber, etc.; in later use, esp. an officer in a law-court or an attendant who conducts people to seats in a church or place of assembly. **2.** An officer at court, in a great household, etc., who walks before a person of high rank; also, a chamberlain 1518. †**b.** A male attendant on a lady –1809. **3.** One who precedes or arrives before another, esp. a higher dignitary or personage; a precursor 1548. **b.** *transf.* That which precedes or gives intimation of the approach or advent of a person or thing 1586. **c.** *Ent.* A species of moth 1819. **4.** A schoolmaster's assistant; an under-master. Now only as a traditional title, or as a depreciatory synonym for (*assistant-*)*master*. 1512.

1. *fig.* Arminianisme is but a Bridge, an Vsher vnto grosse Popery PRYNNE. **2.** The Duke of Northfolke ..claymethe to be highe vssher the daye of the coronacion 1553. *U. of the Black Rod*: see BLACK ROD; The U. of the Black-Rod commanded their Attendance in the House of Lords 1718. *U. of the Green Rod*, an officer of the Order of the Thistle. *transf.* The wife of Antony Should haue an Army for an Vsher SHAKS. **3.** By his ussher and messenger John UDALL. **b.** Fasts haue beene set as Vshers of festiuall dayes HOOKER. **4.** Country Vshers..are vnder the Headmaister, equall with the chiefe Schollers, and aboue the lesser boyes 1632. Hence **U·sheress, -ette,** a female usher. **U·sherless** *a.* lacking an u., herald, or harbinger. **U·shership,** the functions or office of an u.

Usher (ʋ·ʃəɹ), *v.* 1594. [f. prec.] **1.** *trans.* To act as usher to; to conduct, attend, or introduce with ceremony *from, to*, or esp. *into* (a place), etc.; to announce or bring *in*, show *in* or *out*. **2.** To precede or escort (a dignitary) ceremonially as an usher 1612. **b.** To precede; to lead up to 1607. **3.** To introduce or preface (an utterance, etc.) 1635. **4.** To introduce or bring *into* the world 1679.

1. *fig.* The blushing dawn out of the chearful east Is ushering forth the day DRAYTON. **2. b.** Pitchy tempests threat, Usher'd with horrid gusts of wind CHAPMAN. **3.** Oh name for ever sad!..still ushered with a tear POPE.

To usher in: (see also 1). **a.** To bring in (a banquet, etc.) in state. **b.** To inaugurate (a period). **c.** To precede, come before. **d.** To mark the introduction, beginning, or occurrence of. **e.** To preface. Hence **U·sherer, U·shering** *vbl. sb.* and *ppl. a.*

‖**Usine** (yuzī·n, Fr. üzin). 1858. [Fr.] A factory, *esp.* a West Indian sugar factory.

‖**Usnea** (ʋ·snĭă). 1597. [med.L., ad. Arab. and Pers. *ushnah* moss.] A genus of gymnocarpous lichens, typical of the family *Usneidæ*.

Usnic (ʋ·snik), *a.* 1847. [f. prec. + -IC 1 b.] *Chem. U. acid*, an acid found in lichens.

Usnin (ʋ·snin). 1861. [f. as prec. + -IN[1].] *Chem.* Usnic acid.

Usquebaugh (ʋ·skwĭbǭ). 1581. [a. Irish and Sc. Gaelic *uisge beatha* 'water of life', f. *uisge* water, and *beatha* life.] = WHISKY *sb.*[1]

‖**Ustilago** (ʋstilē·go). *Pl.* **-agines** (-ē·dʒinīz). 1578. [Late L., a kind of thistle.] *Bot.* Smut on grain; *spec.* a genus of parasitic fungi, typical of the family *Ustilagineæ* (brand fungi). So **Ustilagi·neous** *a.* of or pertaining to the *Ustilagineæ*. **Ustila·ginous** *a.*, resembling, or belonging or allied to *U.*

†**U·stion.** 1567. [a. OF., ad. L. *ustionem*, f. *ustus, urere*, to burn.] **1.** The action of burning or fact of being burnt –1802. **2.** Cauterization –1737.

Ustulation (ʋstiŭlē·ʃən). 1658. [ad. med. L. *ustulatio*, f. L. *ustulare* to burn.] The action of burning or fact of being burnt; *spec.* in later use, roasting.

Usual (yū·ʒ'uăl, yū·ziuăl), *a.* late ME. [a. OF., or ad. L. (post-class.) *usualis*, f. *usus* USE *sb.*] **1.** That is in ordinary use or observance; commonly observed or practised; current, prevalent. **2.** Ordinarily used; in common use; ordinary, customary 1444. **b.** Of persons: Commonly employed or serving in a particular capacity 1590. **3.** That ordinarily happens, occurs, or is to be found; common, wonted 1577. **b.** Customary on the part of a person or persons *to* do something 1605. **c.** Common or habitual *to* a person or thing 1655. **d.** *As* (or *than*) *u.*, as (or than) is or was customary or habitual. Also, in facetious use, *as per u.* 1716. **4.** *absol. The* (*his*, etc.) *usual*, what is usual, customary, or frequent (esp. with a person or persons) 1876.

1. Fortie markis wsuall money of Scotland 1575. He never goes thither but at the u. hours 1687. **2.** The u. expressions of friendship 1836. Beer in the u. stately German flagons with pewter covers 1883. **b.** Where is our vsuall manager of mirth? SHAKS. **3. b.** It was u. for him to show the Delicacy of his Taste by [etc.] ADDISON. **d.** Our Conversation opened, as u., upon the Weather ADDISON. The huddled buildings looked lower than u. DICKENS. **4.** To-day the drivers outdid their u. 1892. Hence **U·sualness.**

Usually (yū·ʒ'uăli, yū·ziuăli), *adv.* 1477. [f. prec. + -LY[2].] **1.** In a usual or wonted manner; according to customary, established, or frequent usage; as a rule. †**2.** In a regular manner –1605.

1. Phr. †*As u.*: The company behaved as u. on these Occasions FIELDING. *Than u.* (now only when followed by an adj.); The mind of man has been more than u. active in thinking about man JOWETT.

Usuca·pient. 1875. [ad. L. *usu-capient-*, *usu-capere*; see next.] *Roman Law.* An owner or claimant by usucapion.

Usucapion (yūziukē·piǫn). 1606. [a. L. *usu-capion, usu-capio*, f. *usu-capere* to acquire ownership by prescription.] *Roman* and *Civil Law.* The acquisition of ownership by long use or enjoyment.

Usucapt (yū·ziukæpt), *v.* 1880. [ad. L. *usu-capt-, usu-capere*; see prec.] *Roman Law. trans.* To acquire ownership of or title to (a property, etc.) by usucapion. So **Usuca·ption** = USUCAPION 1656.

Usufruct (yū·ziufrʋkt). 1630. [ad. late L. *usufructus*, for L. *usus-fructus* (abl. *usu-fructu*).] **1.** *Law.* The right of temporary possession, use, or enjoyment of the advantages of property belonging to another, so far as may be had without causing damage or prejudice to it. **2.** Use, enjoyment, or profitable possession (*of* something) 1811.

2. In the rich man's houses and pictures..I have a temporary u. at least LAMB.

Usufructuary (yūziufrʋ·ktiuări), *sb.* 1618. [ad. late L. *usufructuarius*, f. *usufructus* USUFRUCT.] **1.** *Law.* One who enjoys the usufruct of a property, etc. **2.** *gen.* One who has the use or enjoyment *of* something 1621.

1. The Parsons of Parishes are not in Law accounted Proprietors, but only Usufructuaries 1726. **2.** The present usufructuaries of the blessings of civilization 1886.

Usufru·ctuary, *a.* 1710. [ad. late L. *usufructuarius*; see prec.] Pertaining or relating to, or of the nature of usufruct.

†**U·sufruit.** 1478. [a. OF., ad. late L. *usufructus* USUFRUCT.] = USUFRUCT –1728.

†**Usure.** ME. [a. OF., ad. L. *usura*.] = USURY.

Usurer (yū·ʒŭrəɹ, yū·ziŭrəɹ). ME. [a. AF., ad. med. L. *usurarius*, f. *usura* USURY.] One who practises usury; a money-lender, esp. one who charges an excessive rate of interest.

No Christian is an vsurer 1551. The u., who derived from the interest of money a silent and ignominious profit GIBBON. I know myself to be an u. as long as I take interest on any money RUSKIN.

Usurious (yuʒūᵊ·riəs, yuziūᵊ·riəs), *a.* 1610. [f. USURY + -OUS.] **1.** Characterized by, of the nature of, or involving usury or excessive interest. **b.** Of interest, etc.: Charged by way of usury; exorbitant, excessive 1611. **2.** Practising usury; exacting excessive interest on loaned money 1631. **b.** Characteristic of a usurer 1727. Hence **Usu·riously** *adv.*

Usurp (yuzʋ̄·ɹp), *v.* ME. [a. OF. *usurper*, ad. L. *usurpare* to seize for use.] **1.** *trans.* To appropriate wrongfully to oneself (a right, prerogative, etc.); *esp.* to assume or arrogate to oneself (political power, rule, authority, etc.) by force; to claim unjustly. **2.** To take possession or assume rule of (territory, etc.) wrongfully or illegally. late ME. **b.** *transf.* To take the place of or encroach upon physically 1635. **c.** Of feelings: To gain control of or fill (the heart, etc.) 1749. **d.** *To usurp the place of*, to oust, be substituted for 1573. †**3.** To appropriate by ruse or violence; to steal –1643. **4.** To make use of, employ (something not properly belonging to one or one's estate). late ME. **b.** To pretend to, assume as one's own (a name or style) 1549. **c.** To take into use, borrow (a word, etc.) from another language, source, etc. Now *rare.* 1531. **6.** To oust, supplant (*rare*) ME. **7.** *intr.* To play the usurper. Now *rare.* late ME. **8.** *To usurp on* or *upon*: **a.** To practise usurpation upon (a person) 1470. **b.** To encroach upon or infringe (a right, sphere, etc.) 1493. **c.** To intrude upon and seize (territory, etc.) without right or just cause 1630.

2. Whereat a sudden pale..Usurps her cheek SHAKS. Blasphemous and ignorant mechanics usurping the pulpets every where EVELYN. **b.** The white-mouth'd Water now usurpes the Shore QUARLES. **c.** Distemper'd passion..Usurped my troubled bosom SMOLLETT. **3.** *Ham.* I. i. 46. **4.** Some inferior dauber has usurped the pencil of Apelles SCOTT. **b.** Love to heaven is fled, Since sweating Lust on earth usurp'd his name SHAKS. **c.** Stadium..is vsurped, for a place where men exercise ther horse 1559. **6.** The erle..wyllynge to usurpe her of her duchy 1512. **8. a.** When any of the three estates have usurped upon the others 1760. The Saxon and the Norman kings gradually usurped upon the freedom of the Church MANNING. Hence **Usu·rping** *vbl. sb.* and *ppl. a.*

Usurpation (yūzʋɹpē·ʃən). late ME. [a. OF. *usurpacion*, ad. L. *usurpatio*, f. *usurpare* to USURP.] **1.** Unwarranted assumption of or pretension to something. **2.** Unlawful seizure or occupation of other's property; encroachment on or intrusion into the office, right, etc., of another. late ME. **b.** *esp.* The unlawful or forcible seizure or occupation of a throne, sovereign power, etc. 1470. **c.** With *a* and *pl.* An act of usurping or encroachment 1638. **3.** *Eccl. Law.* The action on the part of a stranger of dispossessing a lawful patron of the right of presenting to a benefice 1596. †**4.** Usurpatory rule or power (*rare*) –1761. **b.** *The u.*, the period of the Commonwealth 1682. **5.** The action of taking a thing into use; usage, employment. Now *rare.* 1583.

1. As he usurped divine honours, so he made a figure suitable to his u. DE FOE. **2.** Whatsoeuer the Popes of Rome gained upon us..was meer tyranny and u. 1654. **b.** Nameinge hymself, by usurpacion, King Richard the IIId 1485. **c.** Usurpations of unconstitutional powers by the House of Commons 1863. **5.** Which worde [*sc.* priests] is taken vp by common vsurpation, to signifie sacrificers 1583.

Usurpative (yuzʋ̄·ɹpătiv), *a.* 1797. [ad. late L. *usurpativus*, f. L. *usurpare*.] Of the nature of, marked by, or characterized by usurpation.

Usurpatory (yuzʋ̄·ɹpătəri), *a.* 1847. [ad. late L. *usurpatorius*, f. *usurpator*, f. L. *usurpare*.] Marked or characterized by usurpation; usurping.

Usurpature (yū·zʋ̄ɹpē·tiŭɹ). *poet.* 1845. [f. L. *usurpat-*, *usurpare* to usurp + -URE.] Usurpation.

Usurper (yuzʋ̄·ɹpəɹ). late ME. [a. OF. *usurpeur*, or f. USURP *v.* + -ER[1].] One who usurps a crown or throne, or supreme power or authority. **b.** One who illegally or unjustly seizes or intrudes into any office, property, rights, etc. late ME.

Usury (yū·ʒŭri, yū·ziŭri). ME. [a. AF. **usurie*, ad. med.L. *usuria*, f. L. *usus, uti* to use.] **1.** The fact or practice of lending money at interest; esp. in later use, the practice of charging excessive or illegal rates of interest for money on loan. **2.** Premium or interest on money (or goods) lent. Also *fig.* Now *arch.* 1440.

1. To whom þat vsery ys lefe, Gostely he ys a þefe 1303. The crime of u., before the Reformation, consisted in the taking of *any* interest for the use of money; and now in taking an higher rate of interest than is authorised by law 1754. I know of but two definitions that can possibly be given of u.: one is, the taking of a greater interest than the law allows of...The other is the taking of a greater interest than it is usual for men to give and take BENTHAM. The statutes against u...are repealed, so that you may take for your money whatever amount of interest you can get LD. ST. LEONARDS. **2.** Þer was ane vsurar þat wolde neuer restore his vsurie agayn 1440. I repay you with u. yor kinde Wishes PEPYS.

Usward (ʋ·swəɹd), *adv.* Now *arch.* late ME. [f. US; see -WARD.] orig. (and chiefly) *to u.*, towards us. Also *from u.*

Ut (ut, ʋt). ME. [L. *ut* 'that', the notes of the hexachord being the initial syllables of half-lines of the sapphic stanza of the office hymn for the Nativity of St. John Baptist, *Ut* queant laxis *re*sonare fibris *Mi*ra gestorum *fa*muli tuorum, *Sol*ve polluti *la*bii reatum, *S*ancte

Johannes (SJ = si). Cf. GAMUT.] *Mus.* The first note in Guido's hexachords, and in the modern octave, now commonly Do *sb.*[2]; the note C in the natural scale of C major.

Utas (yū·tæs). *Hist.* late ME. [Reduced form of *utaves*, obs. pl. of OCTAVE.] = OCTAVE 1 a, b.

The Octave or U. of each Feast 1833.

Utensil (yute·nsil). late ME. [a. OF. *utensile*, a. med.L. *utensile*, f. L. *utensilis* useful.] †1. *collect. sing.* Domestic vessels, appliances, and furniture. Chiefly *Sc.* –1535. 2. Any article useful or necessary in a household; a domestic implement, vessel, or article of furniture; now *esp.*, an instrument or vessel in common use in a kitchen, dairy, etc. 1484. b. Any vessel (†or other article) serving a useful end or purpose 1502. c. *esp.* A tool or implement used by artisans, farmers, etc. 1604. 3. One who is made use of (*rare*) 1678. 4. A sacred vessel, etc., belonging to, and esp. used in the services of a place of worship 1650. 5. (*Chamber*) *utensil*, a chamber-pot 1699.

1. Y be-qweythe to lucye my wyfe..alle þe vtensyl of myn hows 1411. 2. He ha's braue Vtensils..Which when he ha's a house, hee'l decke withall SHAKS. No expences are calculated for the dairy, such as wood, utensils, &c. 1767. b. Waggons fraught with Utensils of war MILT. *transf.* A large Library, and other literary utensils 1657. 3. A Sot, a Beetle, a Droan of a Husband, a mere U. OTWAY.

Uterine (yū·tĕrəin, -rin), *a.* late ME. [a. OF. *uterin(e*, or ad. late L. *uterinus*, f. L. UTERUS.] 1. Born of one womb; having the same mother, but not the same father. b. Related through the mother (*rare*) 1632. 2. *Surg.* Adapted for using or operating on or in the womb 1615. 3. Of, pertaining or belonging to, situated in, or connected with the womb 1646. b. Affecting, occurring, or taking place in the uterus 1661. 4. Of vellum: Made from the skin of a fœtal or abortive calf or lamb 1870.

1. Brothers or sisters of the deceased by the mother only, who are called *u.* ERSKINE. b. The property.. devolves to his brothers or u. uncles 1816.

Utero- (yū·tĕro), comb. form of UTERUS in medical and surgical terms, esp. with the sense 'of or for the womb and another part'.

Utero-abdo·minal, *a.* relating to or suitable for the womb and the abdomen. **Utero-gesta·tion**, the development of the embryo in the womb from conception till birth. **Utero-inte·stinal**, *a.* of the womb and intestines. **Utero-ova·rian**, *a.* of or pertaining to the uterus and ovary. **U·terotome**, an instrument for incising the womb. **Utero·tomy**, surgical incision of the uterus. **Uterovaginal** (stress var.) *a.* pertaining to or connected with the uterus and the vagina.

‖**Uterus** (yū·tĕrʊs). *Pl.* **uteri** (əi). 1615. [L.] 1. In the primates: The organ in which the young are conceived, developed, and protected till birth; the female organ of gestation; the womb. b. In other animals: The matrix; the ovary 1753. 2. *Bot.* a. = PERICARP 1676. b. In fungi: The envelope of the sporophore 1829.

Utile (yū·təil), *a.* Now *rare.* 1484. [a. OF., ad. L. *utilis*, f. *uti* to use.] Useful, profitable, advantageous.

Utilitarian (yutilitē·riăn), *sb.* and *a.* 1781. [f. UTILITY, after TRINITARIAN, UNITARIAN, etc.] A. *sb.* An adherent of utilitarianism; one who considers utility the standard of whatever is good for man; *loosely*, a person devoted to mere utility or material interests.

I thought they had more sense than to secede from Christianity to become Utilitarians 1821.

B. *adj.* 1. Of philosophy, principles, etc.: Based upon utility; *spec.* that regards the greatest good or happiness of the greatest number as the chief consideration or rule of morality 1802. b. Of, pertaining, or relating to utility or mere material interests 1830. c. More useful than beautiful, made, etc., primarily for utility 1847. 2. Of persons: Believing in or supporting utilitarianism; also, preferring mere utility to beauty or amenity 1802. 3. Of times: Marked or characterized by prevalence of utilitarian doctrine, principles, or views 1828.

1. The u. doctrine is, that happiness is..the only thing desirable, as an end MILL. b. Turning from the picturesque or romantic, to the u. view of this tree 1859. c. All exceedingly u., well kept, stiff, and disagreeable 1847. 3. In these hard, unbelieving u. days CARLYLE.

Utilitarianism (yutilitē·riăniz'm). 1827. [f. prec. + -ISM.] Utilitarian doctrine, principles, theories, or practices; *spec.* in *Philos.*, the doctrine that the greatest happiness of the greatest number should be the guiding principle of conduct.

A life..of sordid godless U. 1827. U., therefore, could only attain its end by the general cultivation of nobleness of character MILL.

Utility (yuti·lĭti). late ME. [a. OF. *utilite*, ad. L. *utilitat-*, *utilitas*, f. *utilis* UTILE.] 1. The fact, quality, or character of being useful; fitness for a purpose; usefulness, serviceableness. b. In the phr. *Of* (*great, no,* etc.) *utility* 1440. c. *Philos.* The ability or capacity of a person, action, or thing to satisfy the needs or gratify the desires of the majority, or of the human race as a whole 1751. †2. Personal convenience or profit –1752. 3. A useful thing or feature; a use. Chiefly in pl. 1483. b. *Pol. Econ.* An object that can satisfy a human need 1848. 4. Short for *u. actor*, etc. (see 5) 1885. 5. *attrib.* passing into *adj.* a. U. actor, an actor of the smallest speaking-parts in a play; u. man, a u. actor, also (U.S.) an all-round substitute at base-ball. b. Of a dog, fowl, etc.: That is bred or kept for some useful object as dist. from purposes of display, show, etc. 1877.

1. The u. of Prayer for the Dead HOBBES. The circular court is a picturesque thought, but without meaning or u. H. WALPOLE. c. The creed which accepts as the foundation of morals, U., or the Greatest Happiness Principle MILL. 2. This is ayenst your prosperite and utilite CAXTON. 3. Of several of his creatures, whereof men..make some uses, they shall hereafter discover other utilities BOYLE. Heinzman wanted the improvements..sold as a public u. to the highest bidder S. E. WHITE. Also *pl.* = *public utilities* (PUBLIC *a.* I. 1). b. A good or u. is anything which can satisfy a human want 1904. 4. She was playing u., that is to say, going on for anything 1889.

Utilize (yū·tiləiz), *v.* 1807. [ad. F. *utiliser*, f. *utile* UTILE; see -IZE.] *trans.* To make useful, turn to account. So **U·tilizable** *a.* **Utiliza·tion.** **U·tilizer.**

Utmost (ʊ·tmoᵘst, -məst), *a.* and *sb.* [OE. *ūt(e)mest*, double superl. from *ūte* or *ūt* OUT + *-m-est*; see -MOST.] I. 1. Situated, dwelling, etc., farthest from the centre; most external or remote; outermost, uttermost. b. Reaching furthest; of greatest length, extent, etc. 1709. 2. Of the greatest or highest degree; of the largest amount, etc.; extreme ME. 3. Latest in order or time; last, final. Now *rare.* 1460.

1. The u. extremities of the north of Britain 1729. b. All..that I could reach with my u. sight and keenest listening was still KINGLAKE. 3. In these sad words she spent her vtmost breath SPENSER.

II. *absol.* and as *sb.* 1. That which is most outward, distant, or remote; the farthest part *of* something. *arch.* OE. 2. That which is greatest or of the highest degree; the utmost point, extreme limit or degree (*of* something) 1472. b. With possessive adjs.: The highest, greatest, or best of one's ability, powers, etc. Often with *do.* 1611. 3. The end, finish, or issue *of* something. Now *rare.* 1603. 4. *To the u.*, to the extreme (*of* one's power, etc.) 1450. 5. *At the u.* (†*at u.*), at the most; taking the highest possible estimate 1618.

1. A City..on the u. of the ridge of a hill 1615. 2. Thinking the vtmost of their force to trie SPENSER. b. To rally up all one's little U. into one Discourse 1660. 3. *Meas. for M.* II. i. 36. 4. The wrath off God is come on them, even to the vtmost TINDALE 1 *Thess.* ii. 16. 5. The Modern Age of Men at the u. is not 80. 1722.

Utopia (yutōᵘ·piă). 1551. [mod.L., f. Greek οὐ not + τόπος place; see -IA[1].] 1. An imaginary island, depicted by Sir Thomas More as enjoying a perfect social, legal, and political system. b. *transf.* Any imaginary or indefinitely-remote region, country, or locality 1610. 2. A place, state, or condition ideally perfect in respect of politics, laws, customs, and conditions 1613. b. An impossibly ideal scheme, esp. for social improvement 1734.

1. b. Ignorant where this River rises,..whether in Asia, in Africa, or in U. 1684. 2. b. Averse to all enthusiasm, mysticism, utopias, and superstition LECKY.

Utopian (yutōᵘ·piăn), *a.* and *sb.* 1551. [ad. mod.L. *Utopianus*; see prec. and -AN.] A. *adj.* 1. Of or belonging to the imaginary island of Utopia or its people. †b. Nowhere existing –1689. 2. Impracticably ideal; of impossible and visionary perfection, esp. in respect of politics, social organization, etc. 1613. 3. Indulging in impracticably ideal projects for social welfare, etc.; believing in or aiming at the perfecting of polity or social conditions 1597.

1. b. In certain intermundane spaces and U. regions without the world 1678. 2. When he was laying out so magnificent, charitable, and philosophic an U. villa H. WALPOLE. An U. sketch of a perfect government 1798. 3. You are..a Theoretical Common-wealths-man, an U. Dreamer COWLEY.

B. *sb.* 1. A native or inhabitant of Utopia; a dweller in some Utopia 1551. 2. One who conceives or proposes schemes for the perfecting of social and political conditions; an advocate of visionary reform 1873.

2. Utopians who are equally ignorant of capital, labour, or hard work 1887. Hence **Uto·pianism.** **Uto·pianize** *v. trans.* to render U. **U·topism** = UTOPIANISM. **U·topist** = sense B. 2.

Utraquist (yū·trăkwist), *sb.* and *a.* 1836. [ad. mod.L. *Utraquista*, f. L. *utraque* each, both, in the phr. *sub utraque specie* under each kind; see -IST.] A. *sb. Hist.* = CALIXTIN 1. B. *adj. Hist.* Belonging to the Utraquists; insisting on Communion in both kinds 1894. So **U·traquism**, the doctrine of the Utraquists.

Utrecht (yū·trekt, ṻ·trext). 1848. The name of a Dutch town and province, used attrib. in *U. velvet*, a strong thick kind of plush used in upholstery.

Utricle[1] (yū·trik'l). 1731. [ad. F. *utricule*, or L. UTRICULUS[1].] 1. *Bot.* A small sac or bladder-shaped body; a bottle-shaped part. 2. *Anat.* and *Biol.* A small cell, sac, or bladder-like process 1822. b. The larger of two sacs in the membranous labyrinth of the ear 1837. 3. *gen.* A small bladder-like body; a globule 1858. So **Utri·cular** *a.*[1] of the nature of or resembling a u.; composed of utricles or small bladders.

U·tricle.[2] 1861. [ad. F. *utricule*, or L. UTRICULUS[2].] *Anat.* A small cul-de-sac in the prostatic portion of the urethra in man; the prostatic vesicle.

Utricular (yutri·kiŭlăɪ), *a.*[2] 1827. [f. L. UTRICULUS[2] + -AR[1].] Of or pertaining to the uterus or abdomen; uterine.

‖**Utricularia** (yutrikiŭlē·riă). *Pl.* **-iæ** (i,ī). 1753. [mod.L., f. UTRICULUS[1].] *Bot.* A genus of scrophulariaceous plants, bearing small bladders at the margins of the leaves; bladderwort, hooded (water) milfoil; a species or plant of this.

‖**Utriculus**[1] (yutri·kiŭlʊs). 1753. [L., dim. of *uter* leathern bottle or bag.] 1. *Bot.* = UTRICLE[1] 1. 2. *Anat.* = UTRICLE[1] 2 b. 1847.

‖**Utri·culus.**[2] 1848. [L., dim. of *uterus* UTERUS.] *Anat.* = UTRICLE[2].

Utriform (yū·trifǭɹm), *a. rare.* 1860. [ad. mod.L. *utriformis*, f. *utris*, *uter* bag, bottle; see -FORM.] Shaped like a leathern bottle.

‖**Utrum** (yū·trŏm). *Obs.* or *Hist.* ME. [L., which, whether, neut. sing. of *uter*.] A writ authorizing the holding of an assize to decide the status of a property. Usu. *assize of utrum.*

Utter (ʊ·təɹ), *sb.* 1853. [See quot.] *Mech. pl.* Irregular marks made on a surface by the vibration or too great pressure of a tool.

Fine lines or striæ, also called 'utters',..from the sound emitted by the work when in vibration against the tool 1879.

Utter (ʊ·təɹ), *a.* [OE. *ūtera*, *ūttera*, compar. adj. f. *ūt* OUT *adv.* Cf. OUTER *a.*] 1. That is farther out than another; forming the exterior part or outlying portion; exterior, outward, external; also, indefinitely remote. Now only *poet.* exc. in *u. bar, barrister* (taken after 1600 to mean a junior counsel pleading outside the bar in lawcourts, as distinguished from a K.C. within it: see BAR *sb.*[1] III. 3, BARRISTER). b. With partitive words, as *end, part, side.* Now *rare.* ME. †2. = OUTER *a.* 2. –1450. †3. = OUTWARD *a.* 4. –1593.

1. The kyngis cote, vndir his vttir garnement 1435. Cast that vnprophetable servaunt into vtter derckness TINDALE *Matt.* xxv. 30. 3. Lyke the Geometritians, they square about poynts and lynes, and the vtter shew of things NASHE.

II. 1. Going to the utmost point; extreme, absolute, complete, total. Freq. of destruction, ruin, etc. late ME. b. Of answers, decisions, etc.: Unqualified, decisive, definite 1456. c. Of darkness, etc.: Complete, absolute 1596.

2. Of persons: That is such to an absolute degree; out-and-out, complete, 'perfect'. late ME. b. In affected use: Indescribably beautiful, intense, or æsthetic 1881.

1. The vtter losse of all the Realme SHAKS. Two Things which were his u. Aversion PRIOR. b. This is my vtter minde and will, That [etc.] 1560. The u. refusal of the..regiments..to march farther CLARENDON. c. They blew out their lights.., and left the knight in u. darkness SCOTT. 2. The Kinges u. enemye 1555. Ye be u. strangers to me BUNYAN. b. Are they not quite too all-but?..They are indeed jolly u. W. S. GILBERT. Hence **U·tterness** (*rare*).

Utter (*v*·tər), *v.* late ME. [Partly from OUT *adv.* or *v.*, partly ad. MDu. *uteren* (Du. *uiteren*) to drive away, announce, speak, show, make known.] I. †1. *trans.* To put (goods, wares, etc.) forth or upon the market; to vend, sell –1863. 2. To give currency to (money, coin, etc.); esp. to pass or circulate (forged coin, notes, etc.), as legal tender. Also *absol.* 1483. 3. To put or thrust forth, shoot or urge out; to discharge, emit, eject. Now *dial.* 1536.

1. Booksellers were..prohibited from uttering Tindal's translation of the Bible 1863. 2. To u. or cause to be uttered false mony knowing it to be false 1602. *absol.* The punishment of forging, uttering, and the like 1863.

II. 1. To give vent to (joy, etc.) in sound; to burst out with (a cry, etc.); to give out in an audible voice. late ME. b. With advs., esp. *forth* 1594. 2. To give utterance to (words, speech, etc.). late ME. b. To give expression to, put in words, describe (thoughts, a subject, theme, etc.); to speak of or about 1449. c. With clause as obj. 1449. †3. To disclose or reveal (something unknown, secret, or hidden); to declare, divulge –1677. 4. *refl.* To express oneself in words 1600. 5. *intr.* To exercise the faculty of speech; to speak. late ME. b. Of words, etc.: To be spoken; to undergo utterance. *rare.* 1857.

1. A shout..sweet As from blest voices, uttering joy MILT. 2. While he was uttering the words of Consecration HOBBES. b. His heart will worke iniquitie, ..to vtter errour against the Lord *Isaiah* xxxii. 6. This dire change, Hateful to u. MILT. c. Then didst thou vtter, I am yours for euer SHAKS. 3. With what gravity..his Tongue and Pen uttered Heavenly Mysteries WALTON. 4. *transf.* An excellent Musician ..cannot u. himself upon a defective instrument 1648. 5. My trembling was so great..that I could not u. 1774. b. Wishes that cannot be understood, and words that will not u. 1857.

Utterable (*v*·tərăb'l), *a.* 1581. [f. prec. + -ABLE.] †1. That may be disposed of by sale –1611. 2. That can be said; expressible in words 1648. Hence **Utterabi·lity.**

Utterance[1] (*v*·tərăns). late ME. [f. as prec. + -ANCE.] †1. The disposal of goods, etc. by sale or barter –1632. 2. The action of uttering with the voice; vocal expression; speaking, speech. *To give utterance to,* to express in words. 1456. b. *transf.* Musical or visible expression 1602. 3. The faculty or power of speech; manner of speaking 1474. 4. That which is uttered; a spoken (or written) statement or expression; an articulated sound 1454.

2. Oftetymes they selle as welle theyr scilence as theyr vtterance CAXTON. 3. Because God has not bestow'd on them the gift of u. DRYDEN. The King's difficult u. rendered his addresses..painful to himself and the Parliament 1828. 4. To hear a whole series and river of the most memorable utterances CARLYLE.

U·tterance[2]. Now *literary* or *arch.* late ME. [ad. OF. *oultrance, outrance* OUTRANCE.] *To the u.*, to the last extremity; to the bitter end. Freq. with *fight*, etc.

Come Fate into the Lyst, And champion me to th' vtterance SHAKS. I will fight him to the u. upon this quarrel SOUTHEY.

Utterer (*v*·tərər). 1509. [f. UTTER *v.* + -ER[1].] †1. A seller, vendor –1653. b. One who utters counterfeit coin, etc. 1731. 2. One who utters, speaks, or expresses in language 1509. †b. A revealer –1590.

b. The coiners manufacture, and the utterers buy and distribute 1887. 2. Falsehood..brings dishonour on its u. 1785. b. The vterer of which conspiracie was one White HOLINSHED.

U·tterest, *a.* Now *rare.* ME. [f. UTTER *a.* + -EST.] †1. Most remote, furthest –1491. 2. = UTMOST *a.* I. 2. late ME. †3. Last, final –1470. 4. *absol.* or as *sb.* †a. = UTMOST II. 2, 2 b. –1577. b. *To the u.* = To the utmost. late ME.

2. The u. fool..in all the universe 1873.

Utterless (*v*·tərlĕs), *a.* 1643. [f. UTTER *v.* + -LESS.] Incapable of being uttered; unutterable. b. Inexpressible 1832.

Utterly (*v*·tərli), *adv.* ME. [f. UTTER *a.* + -LY[2].] †1. Sincerely, outspokenly –1559. 2. In a complete or utter manner; altogether, entirely; fully, out-and-out. late ME. b. Freq. with verbs of perishing, refusal, etc. late ME. c. Qualifying adjs. (esp. with words implying negation, defect or opposition). late ME.

Uttermost (*v*·tərmoust, -məst), *a.* ME. [f. as prec. + -MOST.] 1. Farthest out or off; remotest. b. Greatest in extent; longest (*rare*) 1586. 2. Extreme ME. †3. Last in time; final –1600. b. Last of a series, store, etc.; usu. in *u. farthing* 1553. 4. *absol.* = UTMOST II. ME.

1. From the u. parts of the Earth HOBBES. b. The vttermost time presupposed in it, should be..but one day SIDNEY. 2. As they will answere..for the same att their u. perilles 1544. A voice of u. joy WORDSW. 3. To the vttermest dayes of my lyf MALORY. b. Thou shalt by no meanes come out thence, till thou hast payd the vttermost farthing *Matt.* v. 26. 4. Ile ..seeke to effect it to my vttermost SHAKS. To withstand the stranger to the u. FREEMAN.

‖**Utu** (*ū*·tū). *New Zealand.* 1840. [a. Maori, = requital.] Satisfaction, price paid for injuries received.

Uva (yū·vă). 1670. *Pl.* **uvæ** (yū·vī). [L.] 1. *Bot.* A grape or raisin; a grape-like fruit. 2. *U. ursi,* the bearberry, *Arctostaphylos Uva-ursi,* a trailing plant furnishing an astringent tonic 1753. b. *Med.* (An infusion of) bearberry leaves 1805.

Uvarovite (*u*væ·rŏvəit). 1837. [Named after Count S. S. *Uvarov*; see -ITE[1] 2 b.] *Min.* An emerald-green variety of garnet.

‖**Uvea** (yū·vĭă). 1525. [med.L., f. L. *uva* UVA.] *Anat.* †1. The posterior coloured surface or choroid coat of the eye –1797. 2. A layer of pigmented cells forming the posterior covering of the iris; the choroid, iris, and ciliary body, forming the vascular tunic of the eye 1745. Hence **U·veal** *a.* **Uveitis** (yūvĭəi·tis), inflammation of the u.

Uvula (yū·viŭlă). late ME. [a. med.L., dim. of L. *uva* UVA.] *Anat.* The conical fleshy prolongation hanging from the middle of the pendent margin of the soft palate in man and some other primates. b. A small eminence forming the apex of the trigone, and projecting into the urethral orifice 1835. c. A lobe or triangular elevation between the two tonsils of the cerebellum 1848. Hence **U·vulatome, U·vulotome,** an instrument for cutting or removing the u. **Uvula·tomy, -o·tomy.**

Uvular (yū·viŭlăr), *a.* (*sb.*). 1843. [ad. mod.L. *uvularis,* f. UVULA.] 1. Pertaining or belonging to the uvula. 2. *Phonetics.* Produced by vibration of the uvula 1873. b. as *sb.* A uvular consonant 1884.

2. The u. trill in French Paris 1873. Hence **U·vularly** *adv.* with a thick utterance, as when the uvula is unduly long.

‖**Uvularia** (yūviulē·riă). 1829. [Early mod.L., f. med.L. UVULA.] *Bot.* One or other species of *Uvularia,* a liliaceous genus typical of the family *Uvularex* of melanthaceous plants.

Uvulitis (yūviulai·tis). 1848. [f. UVULA + -ITIS.] *Path.* Inflammation of the uvula.

Uxorial (*v*ksō·riăl), *a.* 1800. [f. L. *uxorius* UXORIOUS *a.* + -AL.] 1. Of or pertaining to a wife or wives. 2. = UXORIOUS *a.* 2. 1853.

1. The rather generous u. laws of Islam 1896.

Uxoricide[1] (*v*ksō·risəid). 1860. [ad. mod. L. **uxoricida,* f. L. *uxor* wife; see -CIDE 1.] One who murders his wife.

Uxo·ricide[2]. 1854. [ad. med.L. *uxoricidium*; see -CIDE 2.] The murder of one's wife.

Uxorious (*v*ksō·riəs), *a.* 1598. [f. L. *uxorius,* f. *uxor* wife.] 1. Dotingly or submissively fond of a wife; devotedly attached to a wife. 2. Of actions, etc.: Marked or characterized by excessive affection for one's wife 1623.

1. Effeminate and U. Magistrates, govern'd and overswaid at home under a Feminine usurpation MILT. Hence **Uxo·rious-ly** *adv.*, **-ness.**

V

V (vī), the 22nd letter of the modern English and the 20th of the ancient Roman alphabet, was in the latter an adoption of the early Greek vowel-symbol V, now also represented by U and Y, but in Latin was employed also with the value of the Greek digamma, viz. (w), to which it corresponds phonologically. Under the Empire, the semi-vocalic sound gradually changed to a bilabial consonant, and finally became the labio-dental voiced open consonant (spirant) now denoted by this letter in English and various other languages.

The use of *v* in English first became established with the influx of French words into literature, and it is subsequently used freely in native words as well as in those of Latin or other origin. It had a double function, like U (q.v.), until in the 17th century *u* and *v* were finally distinguished as vowel and consonant symbols; even in the 19th century words beginning with either letter continued to form one series in some dictionaries, and this arrangement survives still in some catalogues.

Elision of *v* when not initial has taken place extensively in dialects. In standard English this is represented by such words as *hawk, head, lark, lord,* and is specially indicated in a few archaic or poetic forms, as *e'en* even, *e'er* ever, *ne'er* never, *o'er* over.

I. 1. The letter or its name. 2. Used with ref. to the shape of the letter; an object having this shape; a V-shaped, acute-angled formation; also *attrib.*, freq. in the sense 'shaped like the letter V'; *v.-neck,* a neck (as of a dress) cut in front in the shape of a letter V. 3. Used to denote serial order, as V Battery, MS. V, or as a symbol of some thing or person.

II. The Roman numeral symbol for: Five (for fifth). b. *V, V-spot, V-note,* a five-dollar note. *U.S.*

III. *Abbreviations.* a. Of various Latin words or phrases: v. = *verso* the back of the leaf, *versus* against, *vide* see; v.g. = *verbi gratia.* b. Of English words and phrases: V. = various proper names, as Victoria, Vincent, etc.; the chemical symbol of Vanadium; v. = verb, verse, vision (in *Med.*), volt, etc.; very (as v.g. very good, v.h.c. very highly commended, etc.); V.A. = Vicar-Apostolic; V.C. = Victoria Cross; v.d. = various dates; V.M. = Virgin Mary; V.P. = Vice-President; v.r. = variant or various reading; V.S. = veterinary surgeon. c. In music an abbrev. of various Italian words, as *verte* turn, *violino* violin, *voce* voice, *volta* time.

Vac (væk). 1709. Abbreviation (chiefly in University colloq. use) of VACATION *sb.*

Vacancy (vē·kănsi). 1580. [f. next (see -ANCY), or ad. late and med.L. *vacantia,* f. *vacant-, vacans* VACANT.] I. 1. = VACATION 2. Also in pl. Now *arch.* †2. Temporary freedom from business or some usual occupation –1775. †b. Unoccupied time; leisure –1656. †c. An interval of leisure –1748. 3. The state or condition of being unoccupied; absence of occupation; idleness; inactivity. Now *rare.* 1615. †b. Freedom from mental preoccupation –1856.

3. Nor does the v. of a Bath life suit complaints 1782. b. The fishers..whistle o'er their lazy task In happy v. 1856.

II. †1. An unoccupied period or interval; a time of absence *of* some activity –1663. 2. The fact or condition of an office or post being, becoming, or falling vacant; an occasion or occurrence of this 1607. 3. A vacant or unoccupied office, post, or dignity 1693.

1. *Twel. N.* v. i. 90. 2. The V. of a Bishoprick 1726. The v. among the Chancery taxing masters 1896. 3. How could there be an election without a v.? MACAULAY.

III. 1. Empty or void space 1602. 2. A vacant, unfilled, or unoccupied space; an open space between objects or things, or in a row or series; a breach, gap, or opening 1652. b. *transf.* A blank, gap, or deficiency 1759. 3. The state or condition of being vacant, empty, or unoccupied; emptiness 1788. b. Lack of intelligence; inanity; vacuity 1841.

1. You bend your eye on vacancie, And with the incorporall ayre do hold discourse SHAKS. 3. He contemplated with horror the v. and solitude of the city GIBBON.

Vacant (vē·kănt), *a.* ME. [a. OF., or ad. L. *vacant-, vacans,* pres. pple. of *vacare* to be empty.] 1. Of a benefice, office, position, etc.: Not filled, held, or occupied. 2. Devoid of all material contents or accessories; empty, void. late ME. **b.** Devoid of an occupant; not taken up by any one 1599. **c.** Of land, houses, etc.: Uninhabited, unoccupied, untenanted. Also of a room: Not in use, disengaged. 1518. Also *transf.* in *v. possession.* **d.** Marked by the absence of life, activity, or sound 1791. **3.** With *of*: Devoid or destitute of, entirely lacking or free from something. late ME. **4.** Of time: Free from or unoccupied with affairs, business, or customary work; leisure 1531. †**b.** Of persons: At leisure; also, having nothing or little to do -1782. **c.** Characterized by or arising or proceeding from absence of occupation, leisure, or idleness; undisturbed by business or work. Now *rare.* 1615. **5.** Of the mind or brain: Devoid of or unoccupied with thought or reflection. Chiefly *poet.* 1579. **6.** Characterized by, proceeding from, or exhibiting absence of intelligence or thought; inane 1712.

2. Instant to his aid The Goddess hasted, to his v. hand His whip restored COWPER. **b.** To see the v. chair, And think 'How good! how kind! and he is gone' TENNYSON. **d.** The stillness of the v. night COWPER. **3.** A company of select friends, v. of business, and full of chearfulness 1663. **4.** The Memory relieves the Mind in her v. Moments ADDISON. **c.** An idle and v. life 1866. **5.** The loud laugh that spoke the v. mind GOLDSM. **6.** Yet folly ever has a v. stare COWPER. Hence **Va·cantly** *adv.*

Vacate (văkēⁱ·t, *U.S.* vēⁱ·keⁱt), *v.* 1643. [f. L. *vacat-*, *vacare* to be empty.] **1.** *trans.* To make void in law; to annul or cancel. **b.** *transf.* To deprive of force, efficacy, or value; to render inoperative. Now *Obs.* or *rare.* 1655. **2.** To make or render (a post or position) vacant; to deprive of an occupant or holder 1697. **b.** To leave (an office, position, etc.) vacant by death, resignation, or retirement; to give up, relinquish, or resign the holding or possession of. Also *absol.* 1812. **3.** To leave or withdraw from (a place, seat, etc.); to quit or give up 1791.

1. Such omission..will not v. the contract 1817. **2.** As a Garter was vacated by the death of Lord Strafford 1697. **3.** I have determined..to remove him to the berth Riley has vacated 1856.

Vacation (văkēⁱ·ʃən, *U.S.* veⁱkēⁱ·ʃən). late ME. [a. OF., or ad.L. *vacation-*, *vacatio*, f. *vacare* (see prec.).] **I. 1.** Freedom, release, or rest *from* some occupation, business, or activity. **b.** Without const. Freedom or respite from work, etc.; time of rest or leisure. late ME. **2.** A period during which there is a formal suspension of activity; one or other part of the year during which the normal functions of law-courts, universities, or schools are suspended; holidays 1456. **3.** †**a.** A state or period characterized by the intermission or absence *of* something -1711. **b.** A state or period of inactivity 1644. **4.** A time of freedom or respite 1614.

1. What vacacion had they from the warres? 1531. **2.** In the Easter V. we went for a short walking tour in Norfolk 1904. *attrib.* At a V. Exercise in the Colledge MILT. **b.** A holiday (chiefly *U.S.*) 1878. **3. a.** Sleep's a V. of our Pow'rs 1711. **4.** Let..a V. from Labour be given him 1748.

†**II.** The fact of an office or post becoming or being vacant; the time during which the vacancy lasts -1709.

III. The action of vacating, of leaving (or being left) vacant or unoccupied 1876.

Hence **Vaca·tion** *v. intr.* (U.S.), to take a v. or holiday; to pass one's v. 1896.

Vaccary (væ·kări). Now *Hist.* 1471. [ad. med.L. *vaccaria*, f. L. *vacca* cow.] A place where cows are kept or pastured; a dairy-farm.

Vaccinal (væ·ksinăl, væksəi·năl), *a.* 1888. [f. VACCINE *sb.* + -AL, or a. F.] Of, pertaining to, or connected with vaccine or vaccination.

Vaccinate (væ·ksineⁱt), *v.* 1803. [f. VACCINE *a.*] **1.** *trans.* To inoculate with the virus of cow-pox as a protection against small-pox. **b.** *transf.* To inoculate with a virus 1904. **2.** *intr.* To perform or practise vaccination 1837.

Vaccination (væksinēⁱ·ʃən). 1800. [f. VACCINE *a.*; see -ATION.] The action or practice of inoculating with vaccine matter as a preventative of small-pox. **b.** Inoculation with a virus 1891.

attrib. as *v. act, law, scar.* Hence **Vaccina·tionist.**

Vaccinator (væ·ksinēⁱtəɪ). 1808. [f. VACCINATE *v.*; see -OR.] **1.** One who performs, practises, or advocates vaccination. **2.** An instrument used in performing vaccination 1875.

Vaccine (væ·ksīn, -in), *sb.* 1846. [f. as next, or a. F.] Vaccine matter used in vaccination. **b.** A preparation of some virus used for the purpose of inoculation 1894.

Vaccine (væ·ksīn, -in), *a.* 1799. [ad. L. *vaccinus* (f. *vacca* cow), esp. in *variolæ vaccinæ* cow-pox (Dr. Jenner, 1798).] **1.** *V. disease, pock* = COW-POX. **b.** Appearing in or characteristic of the disease of cow-pox 1800. **2.** *V. lymph, matter, virus*, the characteristic virus of cow-pox (obtained directly or from human subjects) which is employed in vaccination 1799. **3.** *V. inoculation* = VACCINATION 1799. **b.** Connected with vaccination 1812. **4.** Derived from, pertaining or relating to, cows 1804.

4. We have milk..butter..cheese. All this is v. matter. 1804.

‖**Vaccinia** (væksi·niă). 1803. [mod.L., f. L. *vaccinus* VACCINE *a.*] *Path.* Cow-pox.

Vaccinist (væ·ksinist). 1847. (Cf. *anti-vaccinist* 1822.) [f. VACCINE *sb.* or *a.* + -IST.] A vaccinator; a supporter or advocate of vaccination.

‖**Vaccinium** (væksi·niə̆m). 1706. [L., perh. 'bilberry'.] *Bot.* **a.** A large genus of plants, chiefly belonging to the northern hemisphere, many species of which bear edible berries. **b.** One or other species of this genus; *spec.* a bilberry.

Vacillant (væ·silănt), *a.* 1521. [ad. L. *vacillant-*, *vacillans*, *vacillare*; see next.] **1.** Uncertain, hesitating, wavering. **2.** *Ent.* Unsteady; swaying readily 1860. Hence **Va·cillancy** (now *rare*), vacillation.

Vacillate (væ·sileⁱt), *v.* 1597. [f. L. *vacillat-*, *vacillare* to sway, stagger.] **1.** *intr.* To swing or sway unsteadily; to be in unstable equilibrium; to stagger. **b.** To hover doubtfully 1841. **2.** To alternate or waver between different opinions or courses of action 1623.

1. When a spheroid..turns upon an axis which is not permanent..it is always liable to shift and v. from one axis to another 1802. **2.** He may..tremble, but he must not v. RUSKIN.

Va·cillating, *ppl. a.* 1814. [f. prec.] **1.** Of persons: Given to vacillation. **2.** Of conduct, etc.: Marked by vacillation 1828. **3.** Of things: **a.** Varying, changeful. **b.** Unsteady, swaying. 1822.

2. The v. expression of a mind unable to concentrate itself strongly 1863. Hence **Va·cillatingly** *adv.*

Vacillation (væsilēⁱ·ʃən). late ME. [ad. L. *vacillatio, -onem*, f. *vacillare* VACILLATE *v.*] **1.** The action or quality of alternating or wavering in respect of opinion or conduct; hesitation, uncertainty; an instance of this. **2.** The action or an act of swaying or swinging unsteadily to and fro 1632.

1. Christopher Smart, with whose unhappy v. of mind he..sympathised BOSWELL. The agents..were shocked at the vacillations of their own Cabinets 1828.

Vacillatory (væ·silătŏri), *a.* 1734. [f. VACILLATE *v.*] **1.** Marked by vacillation. **2.** Of persons: Tending to vacillate 1854.

†**Va·cuate,** *v.* 1572. [f. L. *vacuat-*, *vacuare* to empty, clear, free, f. *vacuus.*] *trans.* = EVACUATE *v.* 1, 4, 5. -1765.

†**Vacua·tion.** 1590. [ad. med.L. *vacuatio*, f. L. *vacuare* VACUATE *v.*] = EVACUATION 1 a, b. -1721.

Vacuity (văkiū·iti). 1541. [ad. L. *vacuitas* empty space, f. *vacuus*; see VACUUM.] **I. 1.** Absolute emptiness of space; complete absence of matter 1546. **2.** Emptiness consisting in the absence of solid or liquid matter 1579. **b.** Complete emptiness in respect of things or persons 1660. **c.** The fact of being unfilled or unoccupied 1664. **3.** *fig.* The quality or fact of being empty, in various fig. senses; esp. emptiness as a condition or state having a kind of real existence 1603. **4.** Complete absence of ideas; vacancy of mind or thought 1594. **5.** Complete absence or lack *of* something, or †freedom or exemption *from* something 1601. **6.** Lack of occupation; idleness 1817.

1. There is no voidnesse or v. in nature HOLLAND. **2. b.** Sunbeams..lost themselves in the v. of the vaults SCOTT. **3.** The emptiness, v., and no worth of man FLORIO. Thou all-sufficient art, and I Am nothing but v. 1711. **4.** The mental v. of the savage 1885.

II. 1. A hollow or enclosed space empty of matter; *esp.* a small internal cavity or interstice of this kind in a solid body 1541. **b.** A cosmic space empty of matter 1643. **2.** An empty space left or contrived in something 1624. **b.** An open space, gap, or interval left between or among things (*rare*) 1658. **c.** An empty space due to the disappearance or absence of some special thing 1822. **3.** *fig.* An emptiness, an empty space, a blank 1631. **4.** An empty or inane thing 1648.

1. b. That seat soon failing, [he] meets A vast vacuitie MILT. **2. b.** The Scots and Picts..rushed with redoubled violence into this v. BURKE. **3.** A filling of all former vacuities, a supplying of all emptinesses in our souls DONNE.

Vacuole (væ·kiu,ōul). 1853. [ad. F., f. L. *vacuus* empty.] **1.** A small cavity or vesicle in organic tissue or protoplasm, freq. containing some fluid. **2.** An empty or open space (in a comet) 1881. So **Va·cuolar** *a.* of, pertaining to or of the nature of a v. or vacuoles 1852. **Va·cuolated** *ppl. a.* rendered vacuolar; modified or altered by vacuolation. **Vacuola·tion,** the formation of vacuoles, change to a vacuolar state.

Vacuous (væ·kiu,əs), *a.* 1655. [f. L. *vacuus* empty + -OUS.] **1.** Empty of matter; not occupied or filled with anything solid or tangible. **b.** Empty of air or gas; in which a vacuum has been produced 1669. **2.** Empty of ideas; unintelligent; expressionless 1848. **3.** Devoid of content or substance 1870. **4.** Unoccupied, idle, indolent 1872.

1. The water..is not able to fill it, hence a v. space must be formed in the cell TYNDALL. **2.** A v., solemn ..Snob THACKERAY. **4.** Many rich people..lead such mean and v. lives 1897. **Va·cuous-ly** *adv.*, **-ness.**

Vacuum (væ·kiu,ə̆m). *Pl.* **vacua, vacuums.** 1550. [L. *vacuum*, neut. of *vacuus* empty.] **1.** Emptiness of space; space unoccupied by matter. Now *rare* or *Obs.* **2.** A space entirely empty of matter 1607. **b.** A space empty of air, esp. one from which the air has been artificially withdrawn 1652. **3.** An empty space; a portion of space (left) unoccupied or unfilled with the usual or natural contents 1589.

2. There are objections against a *plenum*, and objections against a *vacuum*; yet one of them must..be true JOHNSON. **b.** Count Rumford proved the passage of heat through a Torricellian v., that is, the space left at the top of a barometer by the mercury falling 1829. **3.** *fig.* They filled up the v. of the unrecorded past GROTE.

attrib. and *Comb.*: **v.-brake,** a form of steam-operated brake used on railways; **-cleaner,** an apparatus for removing dust, etc., by suction; **-flask,** a flask with two walls separated by a vacuum, the existence of which keeps the contents of the inner receptacle at their original temperature for a considerable period; **-gauge,** a contrivance for testing the pressure consequent on the production of a v.; **-pan,** a large closed metallic retort, so connected with an exhausting apparatus that a partial v. is formed within; used in sugar manufacture for boiling down syrup; **-pump,** a pump for producing a v.; **-tube,** a tube from which the gas has been exhausted, or in which the gas pressure is less than normal, as the bulb of an electric incandescent light or a wireless valve; **-valve,** a safety-valve opening inwards (cf. SAFETY-VALVE 1).

†**Vade,** var. of FADE *v.* -1678.

Seize the short Ioyes then, ere they v. MARVELL.

Vade-mecum (vēⁱ·dɪ mī·kə̆m). Also **vade mecum.** 1629. [L., 'go with me'.] **1.** A book or manual suitable for carrying about with one for ready reference. **2.** A thing commonly carried about by a person as being of some service to him 1632.

Vagabond (væ·găbǫnd), *a.* and *sb.* late ME. [a. OF., or ad. L. *vagabundus*, f. *vagari* to wander.] **A.** *adj.* **1.** Of persons, etc.: Roaming or wandering from place to place without settled habitation or home; nomadic. **2.** Leading an unsettled, irregular, or disreputable life; good-for-nothing, rascally, worthless 1630. **3.** Of or pertaining to, characteristic or distinctive of a homeless wanderer 1585. **4.** *fig.* Roving, straying; not subject to control or restraint 1635.

1. A v. and useless tribe there eat Their miserable meal COWPER. *fig.* To Heav'n thir prayers Flew up, nor missd the way, by envious windes Blow'n v. or frustrate MILT. **2.** A most v. crew! 1777. **3.** Voyages by Sea and Land, and a v. life 1653. **4.** My heart is a vain heart, a v. and unstable heart QUARLES.

B. *sb.* **1.** One who has no fixed abode or

home, and who wanders about from place to place; *spec.* an itinerant beggar, idle loafer, or tramp; a vagrant 1485. **2.** A disreputable or worthless person; an idle good-for-nothing fellow; a rascal or rogue 1686.

1. A Bill..for the more effectual punishing Rogues and Vagabonds 1736. 2. The dishonest, scheming vagabonds! 1890. Hence **Va·gabond** *v. intr.* to wander (*about*) as or like a v. **Va·gabondism** = next. **Va·gabondry** = next 1.

Vagabondage (væ·găbǫ̆ndėdʒ). 1813. [f. prec. + -AGE, or a. F.] **1.** The state, condition, or character of a vagabond; idle or unconventional wandering or travelling; vagabondism. **2.** Vagabonds collectively 1855.

Vagabondize (væ·găbǫ̆ndəiz), *v.* 1611. [f. as prec. + -IZE.] *intr.* To live, wander, or go about as, or in the manner of, a vagabond; to play the vagabond. Also with *it.*

Vagal (vē̆i·găl), *a.* 1854. [f. VAGUS + -AL.] *Anat.* and *Path.* **a.** *V. nerve*, the vagus or pneumogastric nerve. **b.** Of, pertaining to, or affecting this.

Vagarious (văgē̆ə·riəs), *a.* 1827. [f. VAGARY *sb.*] **1.** Marked or characterized by, full of, or subject to vagaries; erratic. **2.** Wandering, roving 1882.

Vagary (văgē̆ə·ri, vē̆i·gəri). 1577. [prob. ad. L. *vagari* to wander.] †**1.** A wandering or devious journey or tour; an excursion, ramble, stroll –1826. †**2.** A wandering in speech or writing; a digression or divagation –1762. **3.** A departure or straying from the ordered, regular, or usual course of conduct, decorum, or propriety; a frolic or prank, esp. one of a freakish nature. Now *rare* or *Obs.* 1588. **4.** A capricious, fantastic, or eccentric action or piece of conduct 1629. **b.** A caprice or trick *of* fortune, fancy, the brain, a malady, etc. 1717. **5.** A fantastic, eccentric, or extravagant idea or notion 1753.

3. Strait they chang'd thir minds, Flew off, and into strange vagaries fell, As they would dance MILT. 4. The Vagaries of a Child STEELE. b. To follow the vagaries of fashion 1871. 5. The vagaries of Apocalyptic interpretation 1882.

Vagina (vădʒəi·nă). *Pl.* **-æ**(*i*), **-as.** 1682. [L., sheath, scabbard.] **1.** *Anat.* and *Med.* The membranous canal leading from the vulva to the uterus in women and female mammals. **b.** A genital passage in other animals 1826. **2.** A sheath-like covering, organ, or part; a theca 1713. **b.** *Bot.* = SHEATH *sb.* 2 b. 1720.

Vaginal (vădʒəi·năl, væ·dʒinăl), *a.* and *sb.* 1726. [f. prec. + -AL.] **A.** *adj.* **1.** *Anat.* and *Med.* Of the nature of or having the form or function of a sheath; serving as a sheath. **2.** Of, pertaining to, or affecting the vagina 1825. **b.** Of instruments: Used in dealing with or operating on the vagina 1825. **B.** *sb.* A vaginal artery or muscle 1872.

Va·ginant, *a.* 1760. [ad. mod.L. *vaginant-, vaginans*, f. *vagina* sheath.] *Bot.* Constituting an investing sheath.

Va·ginate, *a. rare.* 1849. [ad. mod.L. *vaginatus*, f. as prec.] Enclosed in a sheath or vagina; invaginate. So †**Vaginated** *ppl. a.*

Vaginitis (vædʒinəi·tis). 1846. [f. L. *vagina* + -ITIS.] *Path.* Inflammation of the vagina.

Vagino- (vădʒəi·no), used as a comb. form of L. *vagina*, as in **vagi·noscope**, an instrument for examining the vagina.

‖**Vaginula** (vădʒəi·niŭlă). *Pl.* **-æ** (*i*). 1843. [L., dim. of VAGINA.] *Zool.* and *Bot.* A little sheath or vagina; *esp.* in *Bot.* the capsule or theca enclosing the base of the seta in certain mosses. So **Vagi·nule.**

Vagrancy (vē̆i·grănsi). 1642. [f. VAGRANT *a.*; see -ANCY.] **1.** The action or fact of wandering or digressing in mind, opinion, thought, etc.; an instance of this. **2.** The state, condition, or action of roaming abroad or wandering about from place to place 1677. **b.** *spec.* Idle wandering with no settled habitation, occupation, or obvious means of support; conduct or practices characteristic of vagrants 1706.

2. b. He ought to be taken up for v. as having no visible means of support 1876.

Vagrant (vē̆i·grănt), *sb.* and *a.* 1444. [Late ME. *vagraunt, vagaraunt*, perh. an alteration of earlier AF. *wakerant* vagrant, through association with L. *vagari.*] **A.** *sb.* **1.** One of a class of persons who, having no settled home or regular work, wander from place to place, and maintain themselves by begging or in some disreputable or dishonest way; an itinerant beggar, idle loafer, or tramp. **2.** One who leads a wandering life; a rover 1590.

1. Vagrants who on falsehood live, Skill'd in smooth tales, and artful to deceive POPE. 2. The Israelites, poor vagrants who had not a foot of ground of their own 1770.

B. *adj.* **1.** Wandering about without proper means of livelihood; of or belonging to the class of vagrants or itinerant beggars 1461. **2.** *fig.* Wandering, roving; unsettled, wayward 1522. **3.** Leading a wandering or nomadic life; ranging or roaming from place to place; straying, straggling 1546. **4.** Of or belonging to a vagrant or wanderer; characterized by, peculiar to, or devoted to vagrancy or wandering 1583. **5.** Of things: Not fixed or stationary; moving hither and thither; *spec.* in *Path.* of certain blood-cells 1586.

1. His house was known to all the v. train GOLDSM. 2. The offspring of a v. and ignoble love MACAULAY. 3. The v. soldiers were recalled to their standard GIBBON. The soft murmur of the v. Bee WORDSW. 4. That Beauteous Emma v. Courses took; Her Father's House and civil Life forsook PRIOR. 5. Those v. worlds, the comets 1794. Hence **Va·grantly** *adv.*

Vagrom (vē̆i·grəm), *a.* 1599. [Illiterate alteration of VAGRANT *a.* In mod. use only after SHAKS.] Vagrant, vagabond, wandering.

You shall comprehend all v. men SHAKS.

Vague (vē̆ig), *a.* (*adv., sb.*). 1548. [ad. F., or its source L. *vagus* wandering.] **1.** Of statements, ideas, etc.: Couched in general or indefinite terms; not precisely expressed; lacking in definiteness or precision; indefinite. **2.** Lacking physical definiteness of form or outline; indistinctly seen or perceived; obscure, shadowy 1822. **3.** Of persons, the mind, etc.: Unable to think with clearness or precision; indefinite or inexact in thought or statement 1806. **4.** Of the Egyptian month or year: Beginning at varying seasons; moveable, shifting 1656. **5.** As *adv.* Vaguely; indistinctly 1864. **6.** *absol.* as *sb.*, esp. *the v.*, the vague aspect or consideration of things 1851. **b.** The vague or undefined expanse *of* something 1870.

1. Their answers, v., And all at random COWPER. An indiscriminate use of v. terms 1813. A v. analogy 1881. Man's sense of v. wonder in the presence of powers whose force he cannot measure 1885. 2. Countries where every feature of the scenery is v. 1879. 6. *In the v.*, in a v. or indefinite state or condition; in general. Hence **Va·gue-ly** *adv.*, **-ness.**

Vague (vē̆ig), *v.* Chiefly *Sc.* Now *rare* or *Obs.* late ME. [ad. L. *vagari* to wander.] *intr.* To wander; to range, roam; to ramble idly or as a vagrant.

These robbers that v. about our country HOLLAND.

Vagus (vē̆i·gǫ̆s). *Pl.* **vagi** (vē̆i·dʒəi). 1840. [a. L. *vagus* wandering, straying.] *Anat.* and *Path.* The pneumogastric nerve.

Vail (vē̆il), *sb.*[1] Now *arch.* or *dial.* late ME. [f. VAIL *v.*[1] Cf. AVAIL *sb.*] †**1.** Advantage, profit –1550. **2.** Usu. *pl.* Now *arch.* or *Obs.* A casual or occasional profit or emolument in addition to salary or other regular payment, esp. one accruing or attached to an office or position; a fee or offering of this nature. 1450. **b.** A dole or gratuity given to one in an inferior position 1622. **3.** A gratuity given to a servant or attendant; a tip; *spec.* one of those given by a visitor on his departure to the servants of the house in which he has been a guest. *arch.* 1605. **4.** *pl.* = PERQUISITE 3 b. Now *rare.* 1592.

3. Why should he, like a Servant, seek Vails over and above his Wages? MILT.

†**Vail,** *sb.*[2] 1606. [f. VAIL *v.*[2]] The going down or setting *of* the sun. SHAKS.

†**Vail,** *v.*[1] ME. [ad. OF. *vail-, vaill-*, subjunctive and ppl. stem of *valoir* to be of value :—L. *valere*. Cf. AVAIL *v.*] **1.** *intr.* To be of use or service; to avail or profit –1601. **2.** *trans.* To be of use, advantage, or benefit to; to aid, assist, or help –1813.

Vail (vē̆il), *v.*[2] *arch.* or *Obs.* ME. [a. OF. *valer* (rare), or aphetic f. AVALE *v.*] **I.** *trans.* **1.** To lower (a weapon, banner, etc.); to cause or allow to descend or sink. **b.** *spec.* To lower in sign of submission or respect 1599. **c.** To lower or cast down (the eyes); to bend, bow down (the head, etc.); to hang (the tail) 1586. **2.** To doff or take off (a bonnet, hat, crown, etc.), esp. out of respect or as a sign of submission; also *fig.* with *bonnet*, to manifest submission; to yield, give way; to show respect *to* 1460. †**3.** *Naut.* To lower, to let or haul down (a sail) –1635. †**4.** *fig.* To abase, humble, or lower (one's courage, the heart, etc.); to submit, subject, or yield (one thing) *to* (another) –1827.

1. c. Voice of the wise of old! Go..teach proud Science where to v. her brow KEBLE. 2. The bonnets, which hitherto each Chief had worn..were now at once vailed in honour of the royal warrant SCOTT. 4. Now vaile your pride you captiue Christians 1592.

II. *intr.* †**1.** To fall (*down*); to descend –1624. **2.** Of a bonnet or banner: To be doffed or lowered in token of respect or submission 1550.

1. His jollity is down, valed to the ground 1624.

III. *absol.* †**1.** *Naut.* To lower the sail –1650. **2.** To doff or take off the cap or hat (*to* a person, etc.) 1599. **3.** *fig.* To submit, yield, give place *to* (or *unto*); to acknowledge the superiority or supremacy of 1610. †**b.** To do homage *to.* SHAKS.

3. The Ministry v. to every measure to humour the people 1779.

†**Vai·lable,** *a.* ME. [f. VAIL *v.*[1] + -ABLE.] **1.** Of avail, advantage, or benefit; beneficial; profitable, efficacious –1577. **2.** Legally valid or effective –1652.

Vain (vē̆in), *a.* and *sb.* ME. [a. OF. :— L. *vanus* empty, idle.] **A.** *adj.* **1.** Devoid of real value, worth, or significance; idle, unprofitable, useless; of no effect, force, or power; fruitless, unavailing. †**2.** Empty, vacant, void. Also const. *of.* –1544. **3.** Of persons: Devoid of sense or wisdom; foolish, thoughtless; of an idle or futile disposition. Now *rare* or *Obs.* late ME. **4.** Given to indulging in personal vanity; having an excessively high opinion of one's own appearance, attainments, qualities, possessions, etc.; delighting in or desirous of attracting the admiration of others; conceited. Const. *of.* 1692.

1. For the loue of a vayn thynge men ought not to leue that whiche is certeyn CAXTON. In v. regrets for the past, in vainer resolves for the future 1853. 3. He is veyne that puttiþ his hope in men or in creatures 1450. 4. A good, honest, plain girl, and not v. of her face FIELDING.

In vain, to no effect or purpose; ineffectually, uselessly, vainly. *To take..in v.* (with *name* as object): To use or utter (the name of God) lightly, needlessly, or profanely; *transf.* to mention or speak of casually or lightly. [After L. *in vanum*, F. *en vain.*]

†**B.** as *sb.* Vanity; a vain thing –1742. Hence **Vai·n-ly** *adv.*, **-ness.**

Vainglorious (vē̆inglō̆ə·riəs), *a.* 1480. [f. VAINGLORY *sb.*] **1.** Filled with, given to, or indulging in, vainglory; inordinately boastful or proud of one's own abilities, actions, or qualities; excessively and ostentatiously vain. **2.** Characterized by, indicative of, or proceeding from vainglory 1533.

1. Where is the fame Which the v. mighty of the earth Seek to eternize? SHELLEY. 2. Wandring..in a vayne glorious oppinion of their owne wit GASCOIGNE. Hence **Vainglo·rious-ly** *adv.*, **-ness.**

Vainglory (vē̆inglō̆·ri), *sb.* ME. [ad. med.L. *vana gloria.*] **1.** Glory that is vain, empty, or worthless; inordinate or unwarranted pride in one's accomplishments or qualities; disposition or tendency to exalt oneself unduly; idle boasting or vaunting. **2.** A vainglorious thing, action, etc. (*rare*) 1450.

1. For he that doth a thing secretly..how seketh he vaynglory? 1535. 2. What needs these Feasts, pompes, and Vaine-glories? SHAKS. Hence **Vainglo·ry** *v. intr.* to indulge in v.

Vair (vē̆əɪ), *sb.* ME. [a. OF. *vair, veir* :—L. *varium*, acc. sing. masc. of *varius* particoloured.] **1.** A fur obtained from a variety of squirrel with grey back and white belly, much used in the 13th and 14th centuries as a trimming or lining for garments. Now *arch.* **2.** A weasel or stoat. Now *dial.* late ME. **3.** *Her.* One of the heraldic furs, represented by bell- or cup-shaped spaces of two (or more) tinctures, usu. azure and argent, disposed alternately (in imitation of small skins arranged in a similar manner) 1562.

Vairy (vē°·ri), *a.* 1486. [a. OF. *vairy*, f. *vair* VAIR.] *Her.* Of a coat, charge, etc.: Varied or variegated with two or more colours; having divisions and tinctures like those of vair.

Vaisya (vai·syă). 1794. [Skr. *vaiśya* peasant, labourer.] The third of the four great Hindu castes, comprising the merchants and agriculturists; a member of this caste.

Vaivode (vēɪ·vǭd). Now *Hist.* 1560. [Ult. ad. early Magyar *vajvoda* (now *vajda*), repr. the common Slavonic *voj(e)voda* VOIVODE.] A local ruler or official in various parts of south-eastern Europe (in older use esp. in Transylvania).

‖**Vakeel, vakil** (vǎkī·l). *India.* 1622. [Urdū *vakīl, wakīl.*] 1. An agent or representative; *esp.* a minister, envoy, or ambassador. 2. A native attorney or barrister; a pleader in the Hindu law-courts 1858.

Valance (væ·lăns), *sb.* 1450. [perh. a. AF. *valance*, f. *valer* = OF. *avaler* to descend.] 1. A piece of drapery attached lengthways to a canopy, altar-cloth, or the like, so as to hang in a vertical position 1463. 2. *spec.* a. A border of drapery hanging round the canopy of a bed; in later use, a short curtain around the frame of a bedstead, etc. serving to screen the space underneath 1450. b. A short window-curtain (*rare*) 1726. 3. A pendant border or edging of velvet, leather, or other material 1700. b. A flap attached to a head-dress, esp. as a protection against the sun 1791.

1. A tent, striped with white and gold..and the v., of the same colours H. WALPOLE. 2. a. An iron bed-stead (no vallance, of course), and hair mattress FLOR. NIGHTINGALE. 3. b. Like the cap with a v. named from the East Indian hero 'Havelock' 1875. So **Va·lance** *v.* (*rare*) *trans.* to drape or fringe with, or as with, a v.

Valanced (væ·lănst), *ppl. a.* 1548. [f. prec.] Provided or furnished *with* a valance or draped edging of a specified material. b. *transf.* Also *ellipt.*, fringed with hair 1602.

An old set-stich'd chair, v. and fringed around with worsted bobs STERNE. b. *Haml.* II. ii. 403.

Vale (vēɪl), *sb.*[1] ME. [a. OF. *val*:—L. *vallem, vallis* valley.] A tract of land lying between two ranges of hills, or stretches of high ground, and usu. traversed by a river or stream; a dale or valley. In later use chiefly *poet.* Freq. const. *of* (the distinctive name of the v.). b. The world regarded as a place *of* trouble, sorrow, etc., or as the scene of life. late ME.

And thou Moon [stand] in the v. of Aialon, Till Israel overcome MILT. A slumber seems to steal O'er v. and mountain WORDSW. b. What could you find in the vail of tears? RALEIGH. Phr. *The v. of years*, the declining years of a person's life, old age; I am declin'd Into the v. of yeares SHAKS.

Vale (vēɪ·li), *int.* and *sb.*[2] 1550. [L., 2nd pers. sing. imper. of *valere* to be well.] A. *int.* Farewell; goodbye; adieu. B. *sb.* A farewell greeting, letter, etc.; a goodbye, farewell, or leave-taking 1580.

I am going to say my *vales* to you for some weeks SCOTT.

Valediction (vælǐdi·kʃən). 1614. [ad. L. type *valedictio, f. *vale-dicere*, f. L. *vale* VALE *int.* and *dicere* to say, speak.] 1. The action of bidding or saying farewell (*to* a person, etc.); an instance of this; a farewell or leave-taking. 2. An utterance, discourse, etc. made in (or by way of) leave-taking or bidding farewell 1619.

2. Their last v., thrice uttered by the attendants, was..very solemn SIR T BROWNE.

Valedictory (vælǐdi·ktŏri), *a.* and *sb.* 1651. [f. L. *valedictum*, pa. pple. of *vale-dicere* + -ORY[2].] A. *adj.* 1. Uttered or bestowed in bidding or on taking farewell; of the nature of a valediction. 2. Manifested, performed, or done by way of valediction 1806.

1. The Bishop who delivered the v. address SOUTHEY. Lord Ripon's v. tour..in the Punjab 1884.

B. *sb.* 1. *U.S.* A valedictory oration 1847. 2. A statement or speech made by way of valediction on leaving a position, person, etc. 1892.

2. In his V. on retiring from the Editorship 1892. Hence **Valedicto·rian** (*U.S.*), in colleges, academies, etc., the student appointed on grounds of merit to deliver the v. oration on Commencement Day.

Valence (vēɪ·lěns). 1884. [ad. L. *valentia*; see VALENCY.] *Chem.* = VALENCY 2.

Valencia (văle·nʃiă). Also **Valentia.** 1796. [See def.] 1. *attrib.* Of, pertaining to, cultivated in, or obtained from Valentia, a province and town of eastern Spain. 2. A mixed fabric for waistcoats, etc., having a wool weft with a warp of silk, silk and cotton, or linen, and usu. striped 1850. 3. *ellipt.* in *pl.* Valencia almonds or raisins 1867. b. A variety of orange. So **Vale·ncian** *a.* 1753.

Valenciennes (valaṅsyęn, vælənsī·nz). 1717. [See def.] 1. The name of a town in northern France, celebrated for the manufacture of lace, used *attrib.* in *V. lace.* 2. *ellipt.* A variety of lace orig. manufactured at Valenciennes; a ruffle or the like made of this 1764.

Valency (vēɪ·lĕnsi). 1869. [ad. L. *valentia* vigour, capacity, f. *valere* to be well or strong.] 1. *Physics.* Energy, active force. 2. *Chem.* The power or capacity of certain elements to combine with or displace a greater or less number of hydrogen (or other) atoms; atomicity 1876. b. A unit of this capacity. Usu. in pl. 1891.

Valentine (væ·lĕntəin). late ME. [a. OF. (also mod.F.) *Valentin*, or ad. L. *Valentinus*, the name of two early Italian saints, both commemorated on the 14th of February.] 1. (*St.*) *Valentine's day*, the 14th of February. (Freq. mentioned with ref. to the choosing of sweethearts or the mating of birds.) 2. A person of the opposite sex chosen, drawn by lot, or otherwise determined, on St. Valentine's day, as a sweetheart, lover, or special friend for the ensuing year 1450. 3. A folded paper inscribed with the name of a person to be drawn as a valentine 1553. b. A written or printed letter or missive, a card with verses or other words, esp. of an amorous or sentimental nature, sent on St. Valentine's day to a person of the opposite sex; in later use also, a printed sheet consisting of a more or less grotesque picture with humorous or satirical rhymes (more exactly called a *mock v.*) 1824.

1. *ellipt.* Saint V. is past, Begin these wood birds but to couple now? SHAKS.

Valentinian (vælĕnti·niăn), *sb.* and *a.* 1449. [See def.] A. *sb.* A follower of the Egyptian theologian Valentinus (*c*150 A.D.), founder of a Gnostic sect. B. *adj.* Adhering or belonging to the Gnostic sect instituted by the heresiarch Valentinus; taught or disseminated by Valentinus or his followers 1579. Hence **Valenti·nianism.**

Valerate (væ·lĕrĕɪt). 1852. [f. VALERIC *a.* + -ATE[1] c.] *Chem.* = VALERIANATE.

Valerian (văliə·riăn). late ME. [ad. OF. *valeriane* or med.L. *valeriana*, app. fem. sing. of L. adj. *Valerianus*, f. the personal name *Valerius.*] 1. Any of the various species of herbaceous plants belonging to the genus *Valeriana*, many of which have been used medicinally as stimulants or antispasmodics. 2. With distinctive terms, denoting varieties of true v., or plants of other genera 1548. 3. The drug derived from the rootstocks of the wild valerian or other species 1794.

2. *Red, spur-v.* = *Centranthus ruber. Greek v.*, Jacob's ladder, *Polemonium cæruleum.*

Valerianate (văliə·riănĕɪt). 1845. [f. prec. + -ATE 1 c.] *Chem.* A salt produced by the action of valeric acid on a base.

Valerianic (văliəriæ·nik), *a.* 1838. [f. mod.L. *Valeriana* VALERIAN + -IC.] *Chem.* Derived or obtained from valerian. So **Valeric** (văliə·rik) *a.* esp. in *valeric acid*, a fatty acid of the formula $C_5H_{10}O_2$. **Valerin** (væ·lĕrin), a glyceride produced by heating valeric acid with glycerin.

Valero- (væ·lĕro-), before a vowel **valer-**, comb. form of VALERIAN or VALERIC *a.*; e.g. *valerolactic*, in *valerolactic acid*, ethyl-lactic acid; *valero-nitrile*, cyanide of tetryl.

Valerone (væ·lĕrǭn). 1839. [f. VALERIAN + -ONE.] *Chem.* A transparent, colourless, mobile liquid, a ketone of valeric acid.

Va·leryl. 1852. [f. as prec. + -YL.] *Chem.* The hypothetical radical, C_5H_2O, of valeric acid.

Valet (væ·lĕt, væ·leɪ), *sb.* 1567. [a. F., OF. *valet, vaslet*, prob. related to VASSAL.] A manservant performing duties chiefly relating to the person of his master; a gentleman's personal attendant. Hence **Va·let** *v. trans.* to wait upon, to attend or serve, as a v. **Va·letry,** valets collectively; the office of a v.

‖**Valetaille** (valtaˡy). 1858. [F., f. prec.] A number or retinue of valets.

‖**Valet-de-chambre** (vale d ʃāṅbr). 1646. [F., lit. 'chamber-valet'.] = VALET *sb.*

No man is a hero to his valet de chambre 1764.

‖**Valet-de-place** (vale də plas). 1750. [F., lit. 'place-servant'.] A man who acts as a guide to strangers or tourists; a cicerone.

†‖**Valetudinaire,** *a.* and *sb. rare.* 1682. [F. *valétudinaire.*] = next -1715.

Valetudinarian (væ:lǐtiūdinē°·riăn), *sb.* and *a.* 1703. [See next and -IAN.] A. *sb.* A person in weak health, esp. one who is constantly concerned with his own ailments; an invalid.

Every one knows how hard..it is to cure a v. 1787.

B. *adj.* = next A. 1713.

The v., feeble Part of Mankind 1713. Hence **Valetudina·rianism,** the condition of a v.; *esp.* tendency to be much concerned about one's own health.

Valetudinary (vælǐtiū·dinări), *a.* and *sb.* 1581. [ad. L. *valetudinarius*, f. *valetudin-*, *valetudo* state of health.] A. *adj.* 1. Not in robust or vigorous health; more or less weakly, infirm, or delicate; invalid. (In later use freq. implying anxious attention to the state of one's own health.) 2. Of conditions, etc.: Characterized by weak or feeble health 1620.

1. I carry an infirm and V. body DONNE. Though v., he lived to be nearly ninety SCOTT.

B. *sb.* prec. A. 1785.

‖**Valgus** (væ·lgŏs). 1800. [L., bandy-legged.] *Path.* A variety of club-foot in which the foot is turned outwards (or †inwards).

Valhalla (vælhæ·lă). 1768. [a. mod.L., ad. ON. *Valhall-, Valhǫll*, f. *valr* (= OE. *wæl*) those slain in battle + *hǫll* hall.] In Scandinavian mythology, the hall assigned to those who have died in battle, in which they feast with Odin. b. *transf.* and *fig.* A place or sphere assigned to persons, etc., worthy of special honour 1845.

V., the hall of Odin, or paradise of the Brave GRAY. b. That St. Paul's might fitly become a V. for English worthies 1868.

‖**Vali** (vălī·). 1753. [Turk. (Arab.) *valī.*] A civil governor of a Turkish province or vilayet.

Valiance (væ·liăns). 1456. [a. AF., or ad. OF. *vaillance*, f. *valiant, vaillant*; see next.] 1. Bravery, valour. 2. A valiant act or deed; a feat of valour or bravery. Now *arch.* 1470.

1. In spite of our v., The victory lay with Malbrook THACKERAY. So **Va·liancy.**

Valiant (væ·liănt), *a.* (and *sb.*). ME. [ad. OF. *vailant, vaillant*, pres. pple. of *valoir* to be of worth:—L. *valere.*] A. *adj.* †1. Of persons: Stalwart *of* body, bone, hands -1548. 2. Having or possessing courage; *esp.* acting with boldness or bravery on the field of battle; brave, stout-hearted ME. b. *absol.* with *the* 1560. 3. Characterized by, performed with, or exhibiting valour or courage; of a valorous character or nature ME. 4. As *sb.* One who is valiant; a brave or courageous person 1609.

1. Sir Moreau of Fyennes..was a right valyant man of his handes 1523. 2. In all these castles..William placed trusty and v. captains FREEMAN. b. O harmless Death! whom still the v. brave DAVENANT. 3. The v. deeds of the great reign of Elizabeth 1907. Hence **Va·liant-ly** *adv.*, **-ness.**

Valid (væ·lid), *a.* 1571. [ad. F. *valide*, or L. *validus* strong, f. *valere* to be strong.] 1. Good or adequate in law; legally binding or efficacious. b. *Eccl.* Technically perfect or efficacious 1674. 2. Of arguments, assertions, etc.: Well founded and applicable; sound and to the point; against which no objection can fairly be brought 1648. b. *gen.* Effective, effectual; sound 1651. 3. Of things: Strong, powerful. Now *arch.* 1656. 4. Of persons: Sound or robust in body; possessed of health and strength. Also said of health. 1652.

1. The nature of Justice, consisteth in keeping of v. Covenants HOBBES. Those, who held rent-free lands by titles that might be declared v. 1844. 2. For when One's Proofs are aptly chosen; Four are as v. as four Dozen PRIOR. b. The only v. method of investigating the relation between thought and speech 1860. 4. The Boers have evidently put every v. male into the field 1899. Hence **Va·lid-ly** *adv.*, **-ness.**

Validate (væ·lidĕɪt), *v.* 1648. [f. med.L. *validat-*, *validare*; see VALID *a.* and -ATE[3].] 1. *trans.* To render or declare legally valid; to confirm the validity of (an act, contract, deed, etc.); to legalize. **b.** *spec.* [Now after F. *valider.*] To declare (an election) valid; to declare (a person) duly and properly elected 1658. **2.** To make valid or of good authority; to confirm, corroborate, substantiate, support 1775.

1. b. The Chamber has validated the election for Passy of M. Cailla 1883. **2.** You must v. my report, for I learnt it of you 1803. Hence **Valida·tion,** the action of validating.

Validity (văli·dĭti). 1550. [ad. late L. *validitas*, f. *validus* VALID *a.*] **1.** The quality of being valid in law; legal authority, force, or strength. **2.** The quality of being well-founded and applicable to the case or circumstances; soundness and strength (of argument, proof, authority, etc.) 1581. †**3.** The quality or state of being (physically) strong or sound –1750. **4.** Value or worth; efficacy 1593.

1. Much as they hated him, they could not question the v. of his commission MACAULAY. **2.** A mere coniecture, and of no valydytye 1599. I do not..understand the v. of this objection 1804. **4.** The v. of regular troops 1788.

Valise (vălī·s, vălī·z). 1633. [a. F., ad. It. *valigia*, corresp. to med.L. *valisia*, of doubtful origin.] A travelling case or portmanteau, now usu. made of leather and of a size suitable for carrying by hand, formerly also for strapping to the saddle of a horse. Now chiefly *U.S.* **b.** *Mil.* A cylindrical cloth or leather case for carrying the kit or outfit of a soldier, esp. of a cavalryman or artilleryman 1833.

Valkyrie (væ·lkiri, vælki·ri, -kī·ri, -kəi·ri). 1768. [a. ON. *valkyrja*, f. *valr* the slain in battle + *-kyrja* chooser, f. **kur-*, stem of *kjósa* to CHOOSE.] In Scandinavian mythology, any of the twelve war-maidens who hovered over battlefields and conducted the fallen warriors (of their choice) to Valhalla. Hence **Valky·rian** *a.* of or concerning the valkyries.

Vallar (væ·lăı), *a.* 1542. [ad. L. *vallaris*, f. *vallum* or *vallus* rampart.] *Rom. Antiq.* Of a crown or garland: Bestowed as a distinction on the first soldier to mount the enemy's rampart. So **Va·llary** *a.*

‖**Vallecula** (væle·kiŭlă). *Pl.* -æ(*i*). 1856. [Late L., var. of L. *vallicula*, dim. of *valles*, *vallis* VALLEY *sb.*] **1.** *Anat.* A furrow, fissure, or fossa; *spec.* = next 4. 1859. **2.** *Bot.* A groove or channel; a sulcus or stria 1856. Hence **Valle·cular** *a.*

Valley (væ·li). ME. [a. OF. *valee*, *vallee* (mod.F. *vallée*), f. L. *vallis*, *valles* VALE *sb.*[1]] **1.** A long depression or hollow lying between hills or stretches of high ground and usu. having a river or stream flowing along its bottom. (Usu. dist. from a *vale* as having less width and a steeper slope on either side.) Freq. in *fig.* uses. **b.** The extensive stretch of flattish country drained or watered by one or other of the larger river-systems of the world 1790. **2.** *transf.* A depression or hollow suggestive of a valley; *esp.* a trough between sea-waves 1611. **3.** *techn.* The depressed angle formed by the meeting (at the bottom) of two sloping sides of a composite roof, or by the slope of a roof and a wall; a gutter 1690. **4.** *Anat.* A depression between the hemispheres of the cerebellum 1842.

1. Euery v. shalbe fylled, and euery mountayne & hyll shalbe brought lowe COVERDALE *Luke* iii. 5. The pleasant Vally of Hinnom MILT. *Valleys of elevation*, those which seem to have originated in a fracture of the strata, and a movement of the fractured part upwards 1839. fig. *V. of the shadow* (*of death*): see SHADOW *sb.* I. 1. *V. of tears*: the world regarded as a place of trouble, sorrow, misery, or weeping.

‖**Vallum** (væ·lŏm). 1610. [L., f. *vallus* stake, palisade.] **1.** A wall or rampart of earth, sods, or stone, erected as a permanent means of defence; *esp.* one of those constructed by the Romans in northern England and central Scotland. **2.** In Roman castrametation, a palisaded bank or mound, formed of the earth cast up from the ditch or fosse around a camp or station 1806.

Valonia (vălōᵘ·niă). 1722. [ad. It. *vallonia*, *vallonéa*, ad. mod. Gr. βαλάνια, βελάνια, pl. of. βαλάνι, βελάνι acorn.] **1.** The large acorn-cups and acorns of *Quercus ægilops* (and the related *Q. vallonea*), a species of oak of the north-eastern Mediterranean region, valued for the abundant tannin they contain. **2.** *V. Oak*, the Levantine species *Q. ægilops*. Also *ellipt.*

Valor (væ·lŏɹ). 1467. [var. of VALOUR, after med.L.] †**1.** = VALUE *sb.* I. 2. –1676. **2.** Power, import, significance 1676. **3.** Courage, bravery. Now chiefly *U.S.* 1586.

1. An horse..to such a v. 1577. **2.** If I may make an English word to express the v. of the Greek word 1808. **3.** The v. of the French 1586.

Valorization (væ:lŏrəizēⁱ·ʃən). 1907. [f. prec.: see -IZATION.] Fixing the price or value of a commodity, etc., esp. by a centrally organized scheme. So **Va·lorize** *v. trans.*

Valorous (væ·lərəs), *a.* 1477. [ad. OF. *valeureux*, f. *valeur* VALOUR, or med.L. *valorosus* valiant, valuable, f. *valor.*] **1.** Of persons: Endowed with valour; valiant, courageous; brave, bold. **2.** Of actions, etc.: Characterized by valour, courage, or bravery 1490. Hence **Va·lorously** *adv.*

Valour (væ·ləɹ). Also (now *U.S.*) **valor.** ME. [a. OF. *valour*:—late L. *valor*, f. *valere* to be strong.] **1.** †**a.** Worth or importance due to personal qualities or to rank –1586. **b.** The quality of mind which enables a person to face danger with boldness or firmness; courage or bravery, esp. as shown in warfare or conflict; valiancy, prowess 1581. **c.** Used as a personal name or as a quasi-title; also, a person of courage 1606. †**2.** = VALUE *sb.* II. 2. –1642.

1. a. A damisel of gret v. 1330. **b.** Our fortunate and oft prooued v. in warres abroad JAS. I. **2.** A launce he tok of gret v. 1330.

Valsalvan (vælsæ·lvăn), *a.* 1878. [f. the name of the Italian anatomist A. M. *Valsalva* (1666–1723).] *Med.* Associated with Valsalva's researches on the organs of hearing; introduced or used by Valsalva.

Valse (vǫls), *sb.* 1796. [a. F., ad. G. *walzer* WALTZ.] A round dance in triple time, a waltz; the music for this. So **Valse** *v. intr.* to waltz.

Valuable (væ·liu,ăb'l), *a.* and *sb.* 1589. [f. VALUE *v.* + -ABLE.] **A.** *adj.* **1.** Of material or monetary value; having value for use or for exchange. **2.** Having value or worth, of great use or service, *to* a person or *for* a purpose 1647. **b.** Possessed of qualities which confer value or bring into high estimation 1638. †**c.** Of persons: Estimable –1730. †**3.** That can be valued (*rare*) –1690.

1. Jewels, or other v. effects 1776. Phr. *V. consideration*: see CONSIDERATION 6; Natural affection was formerly called *good consideration*, as contrasted with *v. consideration*, or that which is deemed to have value in a pecuniary sense N.E.D. **2.** Quinine is v. for curing fevers 1878. **b.** Yᵉ ancient Classicks, and other v. authors H. WALPOLE. **c.** Mr. Pepys, who was a very v. person..is dead 1703.

B. *sb.* An article of worth or value. Usu. in pl., valuable goods or possessions 1775.

I..sent all my valuables to the hammer LYTTON.

Valuation (væliu,ēⁱ·ʃən). 1529. [a. OF. *valuacion*, *-ation*, f. *valuer* VALUE *v.*] **1.** The action of valuing; the process of assessing the value of a thing. **b.** Estimated value 1631. †**2.** Value or worth; *spec.* Current value (of money) –1776. **3.** Appreciation or estimation of anything in respect of excellence or merit 1548.

1. A new v. of all private property had been made THIRLWALL. **b.** Mr. Hardwicke..had also taken the furniture at a v. 1888. **3.** The outside public appear disposed to take Mr. Chaplin at his own v. 1884.

Valuator (væ·liu,ēⁱtəɹ). 1731. [f. VALUE *v.* + -ATOR.] One who estimates the value of things; *esp.* one appointed or licensed to do so; an appraiser.

Value (væ·liu), *sb.* ME. [a. OF., fem. pa. pple. of *valoir* to be worth:—L. *valere.*] **I. 1.** That amount of some commodity, medium of exchange, etc., which is considered to be an equivalent for something else; a fair or adequate equivalent or return. **2.** The material or monetary worth of a thing; the amount at which it may be estimated in terms of some medium of exchange or other standard of a like nature ME. **3.** The equivalent (in material worth) *of* a specified sum or amount. late ME. **b.** The extent or amount *of* a specified standard or measure of length, quantity, etc. Now *dial.* 1600. **4.** *Ethics.* That which is worthy of esteem for its own sake; that which has intrinsic worth.

1. We hardly could be said to have had v. for our money 1806. **2.** The v. of the stock I hold has doubled 1885. Phr. *Of v.*, valuable. *Of..v.*, possessed of (a specified) material or monetary worth; Gold and Siluer is of no v. amongst them 1634. *Under v.*, below the proper v. **3.** Bronze coinage..to the v. of £57,563. 1887.

II. †**1.** Worth or worthiness (of persons) in respect of rank or personal qualities –1639. †**b.** Valour –1614. **2.** The relative status of a thing, or the estimate in which it is held, according to its real or supposed worth, usefulness, or importance. late ME. †**b.** Estimate *of* or liking *for* a person or thing –1794. **3. a.** *Math.* The number or quantity represented by a figure or symbol 1542. **b.** *Mus.* The relative length or duration of a tone signified by a note 1662. **c.** Of cards, chessmen, or the like: Relative rank or importance according to the conventions of the game; the amount at which each (or each set) is reckoned in counting the score 1670. **d.** *Painting.* Due or proper effect or importance; relative tone of colour in each distinct section of a picture; a patch characterized by a particular tone 1778.

1. b. Alceste by his v. brought My father..to such distress 1591. **2.** [Let men] rate themselves at the highest V. they can; yet their true V. is no more than it is esteemed by others HOBBES. **b.** I must esteem one for whom..Mr. Allworthy hath so much v. FIELDING. Phr. *To set a..v. on* or *upon*, to estimate at a specified rate; Wolsey set much v. upon the study of Greek 1868. **3. d.** A certain quantity of cold colours is necessary to give value and lustre to the warm colours SIR J. REYNOLDS.

Value (væ·liu), *v.* 1482. [f. the sb.] **I. 1.** *trans.* To estimate or appraise as being worth a specified sum or amount. **2.** To estimate the value of (goods, property, etc.); to appraise in respect of value 1509. **3.** To estimate or regard as having a certain value or worth 1589.

1. I valued it at Ten Pounds 1686. **3.** The Queene is valued thirtie thousand strong SHAKS. He..does not v. his life at a boot-lace 1892.

II. 1. To consider of worth or importance; to rate high; to esteem; to set store by 1549. †**2.** With neg.: To take account of; to heed or be concerned about; to care –1765. **3.** *refl.* **a.** To pride or plume (oneself) *on* or *upon* a thing 1667. **b.** To think highly of (oneself) *for* something 1687.

1. He valued money, as a man values it who has been poor 1880. **2.** People infected..valued not who they injur'd DE FOE. **3. b.** Every one is in danger of valuing himself for what he does J. H. NEWMAN.

†**III.** To equal in value; *esp.* to have the value of (so much money); to be worth (nothing, more, etc.) –1799.

Valued (væ·liŭd), *ppl. a.* 1605. [f. prec.] †**1.** In which value is indicated. SHAKS. **2.** Estimated, appraised 1607. **3.** Highly esteemed 1665.

1. The v. file Distinguishes the swift, the slow, the subtle SHAKS. **3.** The Epicureans..were the only valued Sects of Philosophers 1665.

Valueless (væ·liulės), *a.* 1595. [f. VALUE *sb.*] Having no value. Hence **Va·luelessness.**

Valuer (væ·liu,əɹ). 1611. [f. VALUE *v.*] **a.** One who estimates values; a valuator. **b.** One who values something; an appreciator.

†**Valure.** late ME. [app. an alteration of OF. *valur* or *valeur* VALOUR, after forms in -URE.] = VALOUR, VALUE *sbs.* –1641.

‖**Valuta** (văl*ū*·tă). 1924. [It. 'value'.] A standard money.

Valvate (væ·lvėt), *a.* 1829. [ad. L. *valvatus* having folding-doors, f. *valva* VALVE *sb.*] **1.** Of sepals or petals: Applied to each other by the margins only 1830. **b.** Of a calyx: Composed of sepals so united 1858. **2.** Of æstivation or vernation: Characterized by this arrangement of parts 1829.

Valve (vælv), *sb.* late ME. [ad. L. *valva* leaf of a door (usu. pl. *valvæ* a folding door).] **I. 1.** One or other of the halves or leaves of a double or folding door. **b.** A door controlling the flow of water in a sluice 1790. **2.** *Conch.* One of the halves of a hinged shell; a single shell of similar form; a single part of a compound shell 1661. **3.** *Bot.* **a.** One of the halves or sections of a dehiscent pod, pericarp, or capsule 1760. **b.** A lid-like portion of some anthers 1812.

1. Throwing open the valves, we entered the chapel BECKFORD.

II. 1. *Anat.* A membranous fold in an organ

or passage of the body (esp. in the heart, arteries, and veins), which automatically closes after the manner of a trap-door to prevent the reflux of blood or other fluid 1615. †2. A supposed check (similar to above) to the reflux of sap in plants –1807. 3. *Mech.* A device of the nature of a flap, lid, plug, etc., applied to a pipe or aperture to control the passage of air, steam, water, or the like, usu. acting automatically by yielding to pressure in one direction only 1659. b. *Electr.* An arrangement of filaments, etc., in a vacuum bulb, designed to regulate or modify a current; a vacuum tube. Also, *thermionic, wireless v.* 1905.

Comb.: **v.-shell**, a gasteropod of the genus *Valvata*; **v. set**, a wireless receiving apparatus with thermionic valves. Hence **Va·lval** *a.* (*Bot.*) in *valval view*, that aspect of a diatom in which one of the valves is turned to the observer; a side-view. **Va·lvar** *a.* (*rare*) of the nature of or pertaining to a v. **Valve** *v.* (*rare*) *trans.* to furnish with a v. or valves; to govern, check, or hold *back* by a v. or similar device; *intr.* to make use of a v. or valves, *spec.* in ballooning, to open a v. in order to descend. **Valved** (vælvd) *a.* provided with a v. or valves. **Va·lveless** *a.*

‖**Valvula** (væ·lviŭlă). *Pl.* **-æ** (ī). 1615. [med. or mod.L., dim. of *valva* VALVE *sb.*] *Anat.* A valve or valvule.

Valvular (væ·lviŭlăı), *a.* 1797. [f. prec.] 1. Having the form or function of a valve; composed or consisting of valves. Chiefly *Anat.* and *Bot.* 2. Furnished with a valve or valves 1808. 3. Of or pertaining to a valve or valves 1866.

1. The calyx is v. LINDLEY. 3. V. disease of the heart 1881.

Valvule (væ·lviŭl). 1755. [a. F.] A small valve. b. *Bot.* = PALÆA.

‖**Valvulitis** (vælviuləi·tis). 1891. [f. VALVULA + -ITIS.] *Path.* Inflammation of the valves of the heart.

Valylene (væ·lilīn). 1868. [f. VALERIAN *sb.* + -YL + -ENE.] *Chem.* A hydrocarbon, C_5H_6, found among the products of the action of alcoholic potash on valerylene.

Vambrace (væ·mbrēˈs). Now *Hist.* [ME. *vaumbras, vambras*, var. of *vaunt-*, VANTBRACE.] Defensive armour for the (fore-)arm. Hence **Va·mbraced** *a.* (*Her.*) of an arm: defended or covered by a v.

Vamose (vămōu·s), **vamoose** (vămū·s), *v.* orig. *U.S. colloq.* 1848. [ad. Sp. *vamos* let us go.] 1. *intr.* To depart, make off, decamp, disappear. 2. *trans.* To decamp or disappear from; to quit hurriedly 1852.

2. On the old Californian principle of 'making a "pile" and vamosing the ranche' 1852.

Vamp (væmp), *sb.*[1] ME. [ad. AF. **vampé*, **vanpé*, = OF. *avanpié* (later F. *avant-pied*), f. *avan(t)* before + *pié* foot.] 1. That part of hose or stockings which covers the foot and ankle; also, a short stocking, a sock. Now *dial.* 2. The part of a boot or shoe covering the front of the foot; *U.S.*, that part between the sole and the top in front of the ankle-seams 1654.

Vamp (væmp), *sb.*[2] 1884. [f. VAMP *v.*[1]] Anything vamped, patched up, or refurbished; a patchwork; a book of this nature.

Vamp (væmp), *sb.*[3] 1918. *colloq.* [abbrev. of VAMPIRE *sb.*] A woman who sets out to charm or captivate men (freq. from disreputable or dishonest motives) by an unscrupulous use of sexual attractiveness. Hence **Vamp** *v.*[2] *trans.* **Va·mpish** *a.* **Va·mpishness.**

Vamp (væmp), *v.*[1] 1599. [f. VAMP *sb.*[1]] I. 1. *trans.* To provide or furnish with a (new) vamp; to mend or repair with or as with patches; to furbish up, renovate, or restore. Also with *up.* 2. *transf.* To make or produce by or as by patching; to serve up (something old) as new by addition or alteration. Also with *up.* 1644. 3. *Mus.* To improvise or extemporize (an accompaniment, tune, etc.) Also *intr.* 1789.

1. *fig.* The expedient of vamping up an old Sermon 1825. 2. The veriest drudge that vamps books together for his daily bread 1880.

II. *intr.* To make one's way on foot; to tramp or trudge. Now *dial.* 1654. Hence **Va·mper**, one who vamps.

Vampire (væ·mpəiəɹ). 1734. [a. F., ad. Magyar *vampir*, a word of Slavonic origin; perh. ult. f. north. Turkish *uber* witch.] 1. A preternatural being of a malignant nature (in the orig. and usual form of the belief, a reanimated corpse), supposed to seek nourishment, or do harm, by sucking the blood of sleeping persons; a man or woman endowed with similar habits. 2. *transf.* A person of a malignant and loathsome character, esp. one who preys ruthlessly on others; a vile and cruel exactor or extortioner 1741. 3. *Zool.* One or other of various bats, chiefly S. Amer., known or popularly believed to be blood-suckers 1774. 4. A double-leaved trap-door, closing by means of springs, used in theatres to effect a sudden disappearance from the stage 1881.

1. Walter Mapes..gives some curious stories of English vampires in the twelfth century 1846.

attrib. and *Comb.*: **v.-bat**, = sense 3; **v. trap**, = sense 4. Hence **Vampirism** (væ·mpəiriz'm), the collective facts or ideas connected with the supposed existence and habits of vampires.

Vamplate (væ·mplēˈt). Now *Hist.* ME. [f. AF. *va(u)n-*, *va(u)nt-* VANT- + *plate* PLATE *sb.*] A plate fixed on a spear or lance to serve as a guard for the hand, esp. in tilting.

Van (væn), *sb.*[1] 1450. [Southern var. of FAN *sb.*, perh. partly a. OF., or ad. L. *vannus.*] 1. A winnowing basket or shovel. b. A shovel used for lifting charcoal or testing ore 1664. c. A process of testing ore on a shovel; the amount of metal obtained by this test 1778. 2. = FAN *sb.*[1] 4. Chiefly *poet.* 1667. 3. A sail of a windmill 1837.

2. Strait a fiery Globe Of Angels on full sail of wing flew nigh, Who on their plumy Vans receiv'd him soft MILT. 3. With his arms flying..like the vans of a windmill 1860.

Van (væn), *sb.*[2] 1610. [Shortening of VANGUARD.] 1. The foremost division or detachment of a military or naval force when advancing or set in order for doing so 1633. 2. The foremost portion of, or the foremost position in, a company or train of persons moving or prepared to move forwards or onwards 1610.

1. Standards, and Gonfalons twixt V. and Reare Streame in the Aire MILT. 2. *fig.* Moses led the v. of these testimonies 1772. Our position in the v. of industrial nations 1879.

Van (væn), *sb.*[4] 1829. [Shortened f. CARAVAN.] 1. A covered vehicle chiefly employed for the conveyance of goods, usu. resembling a large wooden box with arched roof and opening from behind, but varying in size and form. 2. A closed carriage or truck used on railways for conveying passengers' luggage and the guard of the train, or in goods trains for smaller articles 1868. Hence **Van** *v.*[2] *trans.* to send in a v.

Van, *sb.* Abbrev. of VANTAGE *sb.* 5.

Van (væn), *v.*[1] ME. [Southern var. of FAN *v.*[1]] †1. *trans.* To winnow with a fan –1706. 2. To separate and test (ore) by washing on a van or shovel 1839.

Vanadate (væ·nădēˈt). 1835. [f. VANADIUM + -ATE [1].] *Chem.* A salt produced by the combination of vanadic acid with a base. So **Vanadiate** (vănē·diēt).

Vanadic (vănæ·dik, vănēˈ·dik), *a.* 1835. [f. VANADIUM + -IC.] *Chem.* Of, pertaining to, or derived from vanadium; *spec.* containing vanadium in its higher valency, as opp. to VANADIOUS *a.* Chiefly in *v. acid.*

Vanadinite (vănæ·dinəit). 1855. [f. VANADIUM + -IN [1] + -ITE [1].] *Min.* A mineral consisting of vanadate of lead and chloride of lead, occurring in brilliant crystals of various colours.

Vanadious (vănēˈ·diəs), *a.* 1868. [f. VANADIUM + -OUS.] *Chem.* Containing vanadium in its lower valency, as opp. to VANADIC *a.*; esp. in *v. acid.* So **Va·nadite**, a salt of v. acid.

Vanadium (vănēˈ·diŏm). 1835. [mod.L., irreg. f. ON. *Vanadís*, one of the names of the Scandinavian goddess Freyja; see -IUM.] *Chem.* A rare chemical element (symbol V), occurring in certain iron, lead, and uranium ores, some of the compounds of which are used in the production of aniline blacks and other dyeing materials.

Vanbrace, -bras, vars. VAM-, VANTBRACE.

Van-courier (væ·nkūəːriəɹ). 1581. [Variant of *vant-*, VAUNT-COURIER.] A vaunt-courier or forerunner.

Vanda (væ·ndă). 1801. [mod.L., a. Skr. and Hindī *vandā.*] *Bot.* A genus of epiphytal orchids of tropical Asia, having large showy flowers; a plant of this genus.

Vandal (væ·ndăl), *sb.* and *a.* 1555. [ad. L. *Vandalus.*] A. *sb.* 1. A member of a Germanic tribe, which in the 4th and 5th centuries invaded Western Europe, and established settlements, esp. in Gaul and Spain, finally in 428–9 migrating to Northern Africa. Chiefly in pl. 2. *transf.* One who acts like a Vandal or barbarian; a wilful or ignorant destroyer of anything beautiful, venerable, or worthy of preservation 1663.

1. Till Goths, and Vandals, a rude Northern race, Did all the matchless Monuments deface DRYDEN. 2. The Vandals of our isle..Have burnt to dust a nobler pile Than ever Roman saw! COWPER.

B. *adj.* 1. Of or pertaining to the Vandals (or a Vandal) 1613. 2. Acting like a Vandal; recklessly or ruthlessly destructive; barbarous, rude, uncultured 1700. 3. Characterized by vandalism or lack of culture 1752. So **Vanda·lic** *a.* characteristic of the Vandals; barbarously or ignorantly destructive; of, pertaining to, or consisting of the Vandals. **Vandali·stic** *a.* characterized by or given to vandalism. **Va·ndalize** *v. trans.* to render V. in respect of culture; to treat in a vandalistic manner.

Vandalism (væ·ndăliz'm). 1787. [a. F. *vandalisme.*] The conduct or spirit characteristic of the Vandals in respect of culture; ruthless destruction or spoiling of anything beautiful or venerable; in weakened sense, barbarous, ignorant, or inartistic treatment.

Vandyke (vændəi·k, væ·ndəik), *sb.* 1751. [f. name of Sir Anthony *Vandyke* (anglicized spelling of *Van Dyck*), Flemish painter (1599–1641).] 1. A painting or portrait by Vandyke. 2. A broad lace or linen collar or neckerchief with a deeply cut edge, imitating a type of collar freq. depicted in portraits by Vandyke and fashionable in the 18th c. 1755. 3. usu. *pl.* One of a number of deep-cut points on the border or fringe of an article of apparel. 1827. 4. *transf.* A notched, deeply indented, or zigzag border, edging, or formation 1846. 5. *attrib.* or as *adj.* designating things associated in some way with Vandyke or his paintings, as *V. beard*, a small pointed beard, *V. brown, collar* 1757.

1. The whole-length Vandykes went for a song! H. WALPOLE. 5. *V. Brown*,..a species of peat or bog-earth, of a fine deep semi-transparent brown colour 1850.

Vandyke (vændəi·k, væ·ndəik), *v.* 1800. [f. as prec.] 1. *trans.* To furnish or provide (a dress material) with vandykes or deep-cut points, after the manner represented in Vandyke's paintings; to cut or shape with deep angular indentations. Chiefly in pa. pple. b. Said of the thing forming the indentations 1854. †2. *intr.* To go or proceed in an irregular zigzag manner; to take a zigzag course –1845.

1. b. Tongues of sea-sand..vandyking its borders 1854.

Vane (vēˈn). late ME. [Southern var. of FANE *sb.*[1]] 1. A plate of metal, usu. of an ornamental form, fixed at an elevation upon a vertical spindle, so as to turn readily with the wind and show the direction from which it is blowing; a weather-cock. b. *fig.* An unstable or constantly changing person or thing 1588. c. *Naut.* A piece of bunting fixed to a wooden frame, which turns on a spindle at the mast-head to show the direction of the wind 1706. 2. a. A sail of a windmill 1581. b. A blade, wing, or similar projection attached to an axis, wheel, etc., so as to be acted upon by a current of air or liquid or to produce a current by rotation 1815. c. A revolving fan or wheel 1810. 3. A sight of a levelling-staff, forestaff, quadrant, or other surveying instrument 1594. 4. The web of a feather 1713.

1. b. What plume of feathers is hee that indited this Letter? What veine? What Wether-cocke? SHAKS.

‖**Vanessa** (văne·să). 1863. [mod.L.] *Ent.* A genus of butterflies (including the *red admiral* and *peacock*); a butterfly of this genus.

Va·n-foss(e. 1728. [ad. F. *avant-fossé*, after *vanguard*, etc., and FOSSE.] *Mil.* A ditch usu. full of water at the outer foot of the glacis.

Vang (væŋ). 1769. [var. FANG *sb.*] *Naut.* One or other of the two ropes used for steadying the gaff of a fore-and-aft sail.

Vanguard (væ·ngāɹd). 1487. [ad. OF. *avangarde*, var. of *avant-garde.*] 1. *Mil.* The foremost division of an army; the forefront or van. 2. *ellipt.* The name of a variety of peach 1786.

Vanilla (văni·lă). 1662. [orig. in various forms ad. early Sp. *vaynilla*, now *vainilla*, dim. of *vaina* (:—L. VAGINA) sheath. The mod. spelling is assim. to bot.L. *Vanilla.*] 1. A pod produced by one or other species of the genus *Vanilla* (see sense 2), esp. *V. planifolia.* Chiefly in pl. 2. The climbing orchid *V. planifolia*, or other species related to this; the tropical (Amer.) genus to which these belong 1698. b. With pl. One or other species of this genus 1827. 3. The aromatic substance composed of or obtained from the slender pod-like capsule of *V. planifolia* or related species, much used as a flavouring or perfume 1728. b. A kind or variety of this 1753.

attrib. and *Comb.*, as *v. bean, essence, ice*; **v. grass**, Seneca grass, *Hierochloa borealis*; **v. plant** (*a*) = sense 2; (*b*) an Amer. species of *Liatris.*

Vanille (văni·l). 1845. [a. F., ad. mod.L. *Vanilla*; see prec.] 1. = prec. 3. 2. *V. ice*, ice cream flavoured with vanilla essence 1846.

Vanillic (văni·lik), *a.* 1868. [f. VANILLA + -IC 1 b.] *Chem.* In *v. acid*, vanillin, or an oxidized form of this.

Vanillin (văni·lin). 1868. [f. as prec. + -IN.] *Chem.* The neutral odoriferous principle of vanilla, $C_8H_8O_3$.

Vanish (væ·niʃ), *v.* ME. [Aphetic ad. OF. *evaniss-* EVANISH *v.*] 1. *intr.* To disappear from sight or become invisible, esp. in a rapid and mysterious manner. 2. To disappear by decaying, coming to an end, or ceasing to exist ME. b. *Math.* Of numbers or quantities: To become zero 1715. 3. *trans.* To cause to disappear; to remove from sight 1440.

1. Therwith merlyn vanysshed awey sodenly MALORY. 2. The heauens shal v. awaye like smoke COVERDALE *Isa.* li. 6. The cold began to v. and the north-east wind change 1695. If the cock be heard to crow The charm will v. into air HOGG. 3. Then he vanishes a birdcage and its occupant 1886. Hence **Va·nish** *sb.* †disappearance; *spec.* a gradual cessation of sound; a glide. **Va·nisher. Va·nishment.**

Vanishing (væ·niʃiŋ), *vbl. sb.* late ME. [-ING [1].] The action or fact of disappearing.

V. point, in perspective, the point in which receding parallel lines, if continued, appear to meet. Similarly *v. line, plane.*

Vanishing (væ·niʃiŋ), *ppl. a.* late ME. [-ING [2].] 1. Disappearing from sight or from existence. 2. *Math.* Becoming zero 1823.

1. *V. cream*, invisible face cream. 2. Much discussion has arisen as to whether v. fractions have values or not 1838. Hence **Va·nishing-ly** *adv.*

Vanity (væ·niti). [ME. *vanite*, a. OF. *vanite* (F. *vanité*), ad. L. *vanitat-, vanitas*, f. *vanus* VAIN *a.*] 1. That which is vain, futile, or worthless; that which is of no value or profit. b. Vain and unprofitable conduct or employment of time ME. 2. The quality of being vain or worthless; the futility or worthlessness *of* something ME. †b. The quality of being foolish or of holding erroneous opinions –1660. 3. The quality of being personally vain; high opinion of oneself; self-conceit and desire for admiration; an instance of this ME. b. A thing of which one is vain 1837. 4. A vain, idle, or worthless thing; a thing or action of no value ME. †b. An idle tale or matter –1660.

1. All is but vanite (sayeth the preacher) all is but playne Vanite COVERDALE *Eccl.* xii. 8. b. In V. ye waste your Days 1751. 2. He hath pleasure in the vanyte of wickednes COVERDALE *Ecclus.* xvii. 31. 3. The intention of this discourse was not fond ambition or the v. to get a Name MILT. His v. was so mingled with good nature that it became graceful LYTTON. 4. I had forsaken the vanytees of the world MALORY.

attrib. and *Comb.*: **v.-bag, -box, -case**, a small hand-bag, etc., fitted with a mirror and powder-puff; **V. Fair** (after Bunyan *Pilgrim's Progress*), a place where all is frivolity and empty show; the world or a section of it as a scene of idle amusement and unsubstantial display.

Vanner (væ·nəɹ). 1552. [f. VAN *sb.*[1] and *v.*[1]] 1. One who winnows with a fan (*rare*). 2. *Mining.* One who tests the quality of ore by washing it on a shovel 1671. b. An apparatus for separating minerals from the gangue 1882.

Va·nning, *vbl. sb.* 1552. [f. VAN *v.*[1]] †1. The action of winnowing with a fan –1626. 2. The action or process of separating ore on a shovel 1671.

Vanquish (væ·ŋkwiʃ), *v.* [ME. *vencu(s)che, -quissh*, etc., ad. OF. *vencus* pa. pple. and *venquis* pa. t. of *veintre* (:—L. *vincere*), mod.F. *vaincre* to conquer; see -ISH [2].] 1. *trans.* To overcome or defeat (an opponent or enemy) in conflict or battle; to reduce to subjection or submission by superior force. b. *fig.* To overcome by spiritual power. late ME. 2. To overcome (a person) by other than physical means. Also const. *of* (= in respect of). late ME. 3. With impers. object: To overcome, subdue, suppress or put an end to (a feeling, state of things, etc.). late ME. †4. To win or gain (a battle or other contest) –1548. 5. *absol.* To be victorious; to have the victory. late ME.

1. David vanquished the Ammonites NEWTON. b. The Son of God Now entring his great duel,..to v. by wisdom hellish wiles MILT. 2. I my self, Who vanquisht with a peal of words..Gave up my fort of silence to a Woman MILT. 3. Till it thus v. shame and fear SHELLEY. Hence **Va·nquishable** *a.* capable of being vanquished. **Va·nquisher**, a conqueror, subduer. **Va·nquishment**, the act of vanquishing.

Vansire (væ·nsīəɹ). 1774. [a. F., formed by Buffon from the Malagasy name.] *Zool.* The marsh-ichneumon (*Herpestes galera*) of S. Africa.

Vant-, *prefix*, repr. AF. *vant-*, aphetic f. *avant-* AVANT-; see VANT-BRACE, etc. In a number of compounds the *t* was elided, as in VANBRACE, -COURIER. Before labials the *n* by assimilation became *m*, as in VAMBRACE, VAMPLATE; and a further reduction appears in *vamure* VAUMURE and VAWARD.

Vantage (vɑ·ntédʒ), *sb.* ME. [a. AF., var. of OF. *avantage* ADVANTAGE *sb.*] 1. Advantage, benefit, profit, gain. Now *arch.* †2. An additional amount or sum –1706. 3. Advantage or superiority in a contest; position or opportunity likely to give superiority; vantage-ground 1523. †4. With *a* and *pl.* An advantage; a position or state of superiority. Freq. with *at* or *for*. –1642. 5. *Lawn Tennis.* = ADVANTAGE *sb.* 2. 1884.

1. Then at my commynge shulde I have receaved my money with vauntage TINDALE *Matt.* xxv. 27. 2. *For* or *to the v.*, in addition. 3. To each knight their care assigned Like v. of the sun and wind SCOTT. Phr. *Coign* (see COIGN 1), *place, point*, (etc.) *of v.* *To catch, have, hold, take* (one) *at v.*

Vantage (vɑ·ntédʒ), *v.* Now *arch.* 1460. [f. prec.] *trans.* To profit or benefit (one). Hence †**Va·ntageable** *a.* profitable –1610.

Va·ntage-ground. 1612. [VANTAGE *sb.*] A position which places one at an advantage for defence or attack.

Va·ntbrace. Now *arch.* or *Hist.* late ME. [a. AF. *vantbras*, aphetic f. *avantbras*, f. *avant* before + *bras* arm.] = VAMBRACE.

†**Va·ntguard.** 1450. [Aphetic f. AVANT-GUARD.] = VANGUARD 1, 1 b. –1754.

Va·nward, *a.* 1820. [f. VAN *sb.*[2]] Situated in the van or front. So **Va·nward** *adv.* towards or in the front; forward.

Vapid (væ·pid), *a.* 1656. [ad. L. *vapidus* savourless, insipid.] 1. Devoid of briskness; flat, insipid. b. *Med.* Of blood: Devoid of strength or vigour; weak, inert 1684. 2. *fig.* Devoid of animation, zest, or interest; dull, flat, lifeless, insipid 1758. †3. Of a damp or steamy character; dank; vaporous –1690.

1. He..made his own cold tea, and drank it weak and v. MME D'ARBLAY. It gives to the beer a v. disagreeable flavour 1826. 2. Conversation would become dull and v. JOHNSON. One continued round of v. amusements 1825. A smile is..in general v. DISRAELI. Hence **Vapi·dity**, the quality or fact of being v.; a v. remark, idea, feature, etc. **Va·pid·ly** *adv.*, **-ness.**

Vaporable (vēⁱ·pŏrăb'l), *a.* late ME. [ad. med.L. *vaporabilis*; see VAPOUR *sb.* and -ABLE.] Capable of being converted into vapour. Hence **Va:porabi·lity**, capability of being vaporized.

Vaporific (vēⁱpŏri·fik), *a.* 1781. [ad. mod. L. *vaporificus*, f. L. *vapori-*, VAPOUR *sb.*; see -FIC.] 1. Associated, connected with, producing, or causing vaporization. 2. Vaporous 1797.

1. A great quantity of v.,..or, as it is called, latent heat 1799.

Vapori·meter (vēⁱpŏr-). 1878. [f. L. *vapori-, vapor* VAPOUR *sb.* + -METER.] An instrument for measuring the amount of vapour.

Vaporize (vēⁱ·pŏrəiz), *v.* 1634. [f. L. *vapor-* VAPOUR *sb.* + -IZE.] †1. *trans.* To smoke (tobacco). SIR T. HERBERT. 2. To convert into vapour 1803. 3. *intr.* To become vaporous 1828. 4. *trans.* To spray with fine particles of liquid 1900.

1. Forty load of Tobacco vaporized 1634. 3. *fig.* Money seems somehow to have vaporised away, and none knows anything about it 1892. Hence **Va·porizable** *a.* vaporable. **Vaporiza·tion**, the action or process of converting or of being converted into vapour. **Va·porizer**, a device or apparatus by which conversion into vapour is accomplished.

†**Vaporo·se**, *a.* *rare.* late ME. [ad. L. *vaporosus*, f. *vapor* VAPOUR *sb.*] Vaporous, easily vaporizing –1731. So **Vaporo·sity** (*rare*), vaporous quality or qualities.

Vaporous (vēⁱ·pŏrəs), *a.* 1527. [f. L. *vaporus* or ad. L. *vaporosus*, f. *vapor* VAPOUR *sb.*] †1. Of a bath: Consisting or composed of vapour –1706. 2. Emitting or exhaling vapour; †*spec.* of food in the stomach 1544. 3. Filled with vapour, thick or dim with mist; foggy, misty 1593. b. Covered or obscured with vapour 1687. 4. Having the form, nature, or consistency of vapour 1604. b. *fig.* Of ideas, feelings, etc.: Fanciful, idle, unsubstantial, vain 1605. c. Of fabrics or garments: Gauzy, filmy 1863. 5. Of persons or minds: Inclined to be fanciful, vague, or frothy, in ideas or discourse 1605. 6. Of state or condition: Characteristic of vapour 1661.

2. Such things as bee most v. do most dispose us to sleepe 1584. 3. The waveless plain of Lombardy, Bounded by the v. air SHELLEY. b. The lower cloud field—itself an empire of v. hills TYNDALL. 4. b. Such v. conjecture passed away as quickly as it came GEO. ELIOT. 6. We have matter in the v. or gaseous form TYNDALL. Hence **Va·porous-ly** *adv.*, **-ness.**

Vapour (vēⁱ·pəɹ), *sb.* Also (now *U.S.*) **vapor.** late ME. [a. AF. (OF., F. *vapeur*), or ad. L. *vapor* steam.] 1. Without article: Matter in the form of a steamy or imperceptible exhalation; *esp.* the form into which liquids are naturally converted by the action of a sufficient degree of heat. 2. An exhalation of the nature of steam, or an emanation consisting of imperceptible particles, usu. due to the effect of heat upon moisture. late ME. b. An exhalation rising by natural causes from the ground or from some damp place; freq., a mist or fog. late ME. c. *fig.* Used esp. to denote something unsubstantial or worthless. late ME. 3. *pl.* In older medical use: Exhalations supposed to be developed within the organs of the body (esp. the stomach) and to have an injurious effect upon the health. late ME. b. A morbid condition supposed to be caused by the presence of such exhalations; depression of spirits, hypochondria, hysteria, or other nervous disorder. Now *arch.* 1662. c. So *The vapours* 1711. †4. A fancy or fantastic idea; a foolish brag or boast –1738.

1. V. is a moist kinde of fume extracted chiefly out of the water 1610. 2. The vapoure of the fyre brenneth his flesh COVERDALE *Ecclus.* xxxviii. 28. Vapours of ammonia will be evolved if nitrogen be present 1857. b. The vapours which are raised by the Sun under the Torrid Zone 1698. c. Forsothe what is ȝoure lijf? A v., to a litel semynge. WYCLIF *Jas.* iv. 15. 3. Vapours from an empty Stomach DE FOE. b. Sometimes, thro' pride, the sexes change their airs; My lord has vapours, and my lady swears YOUNG. 4. These are mere vapours, indeed—Nothing but vapours STEELE.

attrib. and *Comb.*: **v.-burner**, a device for burning previously vaporized liquid hydrocarbons; **-density**, the density of a substance in a state of v. Hence **Va·poured** *ppl. a.* affected with the vapours, suffering from nervous depression.

Vapour (vēⁱ·pəɹ), *v.* Also (now *U.S.*) **vapor.** late ME. [f. prec.] 1. *intr.* To rise, ascend, be emitted or diffused in the form of vapour. Also with *out, up.* b. To pass *away* in the form of vapour 1555. c. To pass *into* a state of vapour or moisture (*rare*) 1567. 2. *trans.* a. To cause to rise *up* or ascend in the form of vapour. late ME. b. To cause to pass *away* in the form of vapour 1460. c. With *out* or *forth*: To evaporate 1530. d. To convert into vapour. Chiefly with *to.* 1591. 3. *intr.* To use language as light or unsubstantial as vapour; to talk fantastically, grandiloquently, or boastingly; to brag or bluster 1628. b. *trans.* To declare or assert in a boasting or grandiloquent manner 1658. 4. *intr.* To act in a fantastic or ostentatious manner; to show off; to swagger 1652. 5. *trans.* †To give (one) the vapours; to depress or bore -1804.

1. b. *fig.* Their whole life hath vapoured away in hopes 1638. 2. b. Then upon a gentle heat v. away all the Spirit of Wine BACON. 3. Poets indeed use to vapor much after this manner MILT. Strutting and vapouring about his own pretensions HAZLITT. 4. The robbers vapouring about in the court below BORROW. Hence **Va·pouring** *ppl. a.*, **-ly** *adv.*

Va·pour-bath. Also **vapour bath.** 1719. 1. A bath consisting of vapour. Also, an apartment in which such a bath is used. 2. *Chem.* A vessel or receptacle in which hot vapour is generated in order to heat or melt a substance 1728.

1. *transf.* One day in August, when all Chowringhee is a vast v. TREVELYAN.

Vapourer (vē̆ⁱ·pərəɪ). 1653. [f. VAPOUR *v.*] 1. One who vapours; a bragging, grandiloquent, or fantastical talker. 2. *V. moth*, a British moth of the genus *Orgyia*, esp. *O. antiqua*, the male of which flies with a rapid quivering motion 1782.

Vapourish (vē̆ⁱ·pəriʃ), *a.* Also (*U.S.*) **vaporish.** 1647. [f. VAPOUR *sb.* + -ISH.] 1. Of the nature of vapour; dim through the presence of vapour; vapoury. 2. Apt to be troubled with the vapours; inclined to depression or low spirits 1716. b. Of the nature of, connected with, or arising from nervous depression 1733.

2. For, as most other old Maids, she is exceedingly v. and fanciful 1716. Hence **Va·pourishness.**

Vapoury (vē̆ⁱ·pəri), *a.* Also (*U.S.*) **vapory.** 1598. [f. VAPOUR *sb.* + -Y [1].] 1. Of the nature or consistency of vapour; composed of or caused by vapour. b. *fig.* Unsubstantial, indefinite, vague 1818. 2. Rendered dim or obscure by the presence of vapour 1818.

1. The Jungfrau..had wrapped her v. veil around her TYNDALL.

‖**Va·ppa.** Now *rare* or *Obs.* 1629. [L.] Flat or sour wine.

Vapulate (væ·piŭleⁱt), *v. rare.* 1603. [ad. L. *vapulat-*, *vapulare* to be beaten.] 1. *trans.* To beat or strike. b. *absol.* To administer a flogging 1818. 2. *intr.* To suffer flogging 1783.

Vapulation (væpiulēⁱ·ʃən). *rare.* 1656. [ad. L. **vapulatio*; see prec.] A beating or flogging.

‖**Vaquero** (vākē·ro). 1837. [Sp., f. *vaca* cow.] In Spanish America: A cowboy or cowherd; a herdsman or cattle-driver.

‖**Vara** (vā·rā). 1674. [Sp. and Pg., 'rod, yard-stick':—L., 'forked pole, trestle', f. *varus* bent.] A linear measure used in Spain, Portugal, and S. America, usu. about 33 inches long; a Spanish yard.

Varan (væ·răn). 1843. [ad. mod.L. *Varanus*, f. Arab. *waran*, var. of *waral* monitor lizard.] *Zool.* A lizard belonging to the genus *Varanus* or family *Varanidæ*; a monitor or varanian.

Varangian (vărǣ·ndʒiăn), *sb.* and *a.* 1788. [f. med. or mod.L. *Varangus*, ad. med.Gr. Βάραγγος (pl. Βάραγγοι), ad. (through Slavonic languages) ON. *Væringi* (pl. *Væringjar*), app. f. *vár-* plighted faith.] A. *sb.* One of the Scandinavian rovers who in the 9th and 10th centuries overran parts of Russia and reached Constantinople; a Northman (latterly also an Anglo-Saxon) forming one of the bodyguard of the later Byzantine Emperors. B. *adj.* Of or pertaining to the Varangians, e.g. *V. Guard*; composed of Varangians 1788.

Varanian (vărēⁱ·niăn), *sb.* and *a.* 1840. [f. mod.L. *Varanus* VARAN + -IAN.] A. *sb.* A lizard belonging to the family *Varanidæ* of scaled saurians; a monitor or varan 1841. B. *adj.* Belonging to or characteristic of the varans or monitors 1840.

†**Va·rdingale.** 1552. [ad. obs. F. *verdugale*, ad. Sp. *verdugado*, f. *verdugo* rod, stick.] = FARTHINGALE -1753.

†**Vare.** 1545. [ad. Sp. *vara* or its source L. VARA.] 1. = VARA -1604. 2. A rod, staff, or wand, esp. as a symbol of judicial office or authority -1681.

2. His Hand a V. of Justice did uphold DRYDEN.

‖**Varec** (væ·rek). Also **varech.** 1676. [F., ad. prehist. Scand. **wrek*; see WRECK *sb.*] 1. Seaweed. 2. An impure carbonate of soda obtained from sea-weed 1844.

†‖**Varella** (văre·lă). 1588. [Pg. and It., of doubtful origin.] A pagoda -1662.

‖**Vari** (vā·ri). 1774. [f. *vari(kandama)* or *vari(anda)*, the Malagasy name.] The ruffed lemur, *Lemur varius.*

Variability (vē̆ᵊriăbi·lĭti). 1771. [f. next + -ITY, or a. F. *variabilité.*] 1. The fact or quality of being variable in some respect; tendency towards or capacity for variation or change. 2. *spec.* a. The fact of, or capacity for, varying in amount, magnitude, or value 1816. b. *Biol.* Capability in plants or animals of variation or deviation from a type 1832.

Variable (vē̆ᵊ·riăb'l), *a.* and *sb.* late ME. [a. OF., ad.L. *variabilis*, f. *variare* to VARY.] A. *adj.* 1. Liable or apt to vary or change; (readily) susceptible of variation; mutable, changeable, fluctuating, uncertain. 2. Of persons: Apt to change from one opinion or course of action to another; inconstant, fickle, unreliable. late ME. 3. a. Of the weather, seasons, etc.: Liable to vary in temperature or character; changeable 1480. b. Of wind or currents: Shifting 1665. c. Of a star: That varies periodically in respect of brightness or magnitude 1788. d. *Biol.* Liable to deviate from a type; admitting of such deviation 1859. †4. Differing, diverse, various -1613. 5. Susceptible or admitting of increase or diminution in respect of size, number, amount, or degree 1607. b. Of quantity, number, etc.: Liable to vary 1710. 6. That may be varied, changed, or modified; alterable 1597. 7. *Nat. Hist.* Of various colours, or varying in colour according to the season, etc. 1776.

1. A doubtfull and v. fight 1610. Subjects of v. fancy RUSKIN. 2. My word nor I shall not be v., But alwaies..firme and stable WYATT. 3. a. The weather ..was very v., but upon the whole mild 1808. b. We had the wind v. DE FOE. d. Beings low in the scale of nature are more v. than those which are higher DARWIN. 5. The pressure of the atmosphere is v. 1815.

B. *sb.* 1. *Math.* and *Phys.* A quantity or force which, throughout a mathematical calculation or investigation, is assumed to vary or be capable of varying in value 1816. 2. a. A variable or shifting wind; *spec.* in *pl.*, parts of the sea where a steady wind is not expected 1846. b. A variable star 1868. 3. Something which is liable to vary or change; a changeable factor, feature, or element 1846.

2. a. The Variables, which are found South of the border of the South-east Trades 1857. Hence **Va·riableness. Va·riably** *adv.*

Variance (vē̆ᵊ·riăns). ME. [a. OF., ad. L. *variantia*, f. *variare* to VARY.] I. 1. The fact or state of undergoing change or alteration; tendency to vary or become different; variation. †b. Inconstancy in persons; variableness, changeableness -1520. 2. The fact or quality of varying or differing; difference, divergency, discrepancy. late ME. 3. a. *Law.* A difference or discrepancy between two statements or documents. late ME. b. *gen.* A difference or discrepancy; a divergent feature 1497.

1. Uncarefull of Fortunes varyaunce 1559. 2. It is evident that v. of opinion proves error somewhere 1839. 3. b. Variances in the spelling of proper names 1860.

II. 1. The state or fact of disagreeing or falling out; discord, dissension, contention, debate. late ME. 2. A disagreement, quarrel, or falling out; a dispute. late ME.

1. She makes V. betwixt Rulers and Subjects, betwixt Parents and Children BUNYAN.

Phr. **At v.** a. Of persons: In a state of discord, dissension, or enmity. b. Of things: In a state of disagreement or difference; conflicting, differing. Usu. const. *with.*

Variant (vē̆ᵊ·riănt), *a.* and *sb.* late ME. [a. OF., a. L. *variant-*, *varians*, *variare* to VARY.] A. *adj.* 1. Of persons: Changeful in disposition or purpose; inconstant, fickle. Now *rare.* 2. Of things: Exhibiting variation or change; tending to vary or alter; not remaining uniform. late ME. 3. Exhibiting difference or variety; diversified; diverse. late ME. 4. Differing or discrepant *from* something. late ME. b. *Biol.* Varying from type 1881.

1. Calm and resolute, if occasionally v. of mood 1890. 3. They who would trauerse earths v. face 1632.

B. *sb.* 1. A form or modification differing in some respect from other forms of the same thing 1848. b. A various reading 1861. 2. A variation of the original work, story, song, etc. 1872. 3. *Nat. Hist.* A variant form or type 1895.

†**Va·riate,** *v.* 1566. [a. L. *variat-*, *variare* to VARY.] *trans.* and *intr.* To alter, vary, change -1770.

Variation (vē̆ᵊriēⁱ·ʃən). late ME. [a. OF., a. L. *variation-*, *variatio*, f. *variare* to VARY.] †I. Difference, divergence, or discrepancy between two or more things or persons -1637. II. 1. The fact of varying in condition, character, degree, or other quality; the fact of undergoing modification or alteration, esp. within certain limits 1502. b. The action of making some change or alteration 1704. 2. *V. of the compass* or *needle*, = DECLINATION 8 b. Also *ellipt.* 1556. 3. The fact, on the part of the mercury, of standing higher or lower in the tube of a barometer or thermometer; the extent or range of this 1719. 4. *Astr.* = LIBRATION 2. 1704. 5. *Math.* †a. = PERMUTATION 3. -1728. b. Change in a function or functions of an equation due to an indefinitely small increase or decrease in the value of the constants 1743. 6. *Biol.* Deviation or divergence in the structure, character, or function of an organism from those typical of or usual in the species or group 1859.

1. According to the varying gravity of the atmosphere; which v. has..a very considerable influence on the weather-glass BOYLE. b. Powers..to control the v. of investments 1885.

III. 1. An instance of varying or changing; an alteration or change in something, esp. within certain limits; a difference due to the introduction or intrusion of some change 1611. b. *Biol.* A slight departure or divergence from a type 1835. c. A variety, variant 1863. 2. A deviation or departure *from* something 1647. 3. Math. *Calculus of variations*, a form of calculus applicable to expressions or functions in which the law relating the quantities is liable to variation 1810. 4. *Mus.* A modification with regard to the tune, time, and harmony of a theme, by which on repetition it appears in a new but still recognizable form; *esp.* in *pl.*, embellishments in an air for giving variety on repetition after playing it in its simple form 1801.

1. Variations of the Compass DE FOE. c. The Matadore Game..is a v. of All Fives 1868. 4. She ran a set of variations on 'Kenmure's on and awa'' SCOTT. Hence **Varia·tional** *a.* characterized by, dealing with, or concerning v.

‖**Varicella** (værise·lă). 1771. [mod.L., irreg. dim. of *variola* VARIOLA.] *Path.* Chickenpox. Hence **Varice·llous** *a.* of, relating to, affected with, or of the nature of v.

Varicocele (væ·rikosīl). 1736. [mod.L., f. L. *varic-* VARIX + Gr. κήλη tumour; see -O-.] *Path.* Varicose condition or dilatation of the spermatic veins.

Vari-coloured, varicoloured (vē̆ᵊ·rikɒ:ləɪd), *a.* 1665. [f. L. *varius* VARIOUS *a.* + COLOURED *ppl. a.*] Of various or different colours; variegated in colour. b. *fig.* Different, diverse, diversified 1855.

Varicose (væ·rikōus), *a.* 1730. [ad. L. *varicosus*, f. *varic-* VARIX; see -OSE.] 1. *Path.* or *Med.* Affected with, characterized by, or of the nature of a varix or varices. b. Of veins: Unnaturally swollen or dilated 1797. 2. *Ent.* and *Bot.* Unusually enlarged or swollen; resembling a varix 1826. 3. Of appliances: Designed or used for the treatment of varicose veins 1858.

1. b. *fig.* Milton has..not a sinew sharp or rigid, not a vein v. or inflated LANDOR. So †**Va·ricous** *a.* -1786.

Varicosity (værikɒ·sĭti). 1842. [f. prec. + -ITY.] 1. A varicose swelling or distension. 2. The state or condition of being varicose or abnormally swollen; an instance or case of this 1876. 3. The state of having varicose veins 1879.

1. Irregular dilatations or varicosities of the absorbent vessels 1842.

Varied (vē°·rid), *ppl. a.* 1588. [f. VARY *v.*] 1. Differing from one another; of different or various sorts or kinds. 2. Marked by variation or variety; presenting different forms or qualities on this account 1732. 3. Vari-coloured; *esp.* in the names of birds or beasts 1715.

1. So v., extensive and pervading are human distresses 1851. 2. Observe.. What vary'd Being peoples ev'ry star POPE. The v. actor flies from part to part CHURCHILL. Hence **Va·ried·ly** *adv.*, **-ness** (*rare*).

Variegate (vē°·rigeˈt), *v.* 1653. [f. L. *variegat-*, *variegare* to make varied, f. *varius* VARIOUS *a.*] 1. *trans.* To diversify; to invest with variety; to enliven with differences or changes. b. *esp.* To mark or cover with patches of different colours or objects 1728. 2. To vary by change or alteration (*rare*) 1674.

1. b. The Shells are filled with a white Spar, which variegates and adds to the Beauty of the Stone 1728.

Variegated (vē°·rigēˈtėd), *ppl. a.* 1661. [f. prec. or L. *variegatus* + -ED [1].] 1. Marked with patches or spots of different colours; varied in colour; many-coloured, vari-coloured; *spec.* in *Bot.* (see next 1). 2. Marked or characterized by variety; of a varied character, form, or nature; diverse 1662. 3. Varied or diversified *with* something 1678.

1. A v. flowing robe of silk GIBBON. 3. Corolla blue v. with white inside 1870.

Variegation (vērigēˈ·ʃən). 1646. [f. VARIEGATE *v.*; see -ATION.] 1. The quality or condition of being variegated or varied in colour; diversity of colour or the production of this; *spec.* in *Bot.*, the presence of two or more colours in the leaves, petals, or other parts of plants; also, defective or special development leading to such colouring. b. With *a* and *pl.* Also, a variegated marking. 1664. 2. The action or process of diversifying; an instance or occasion of this 1668.

Varietal (vărəi·ĕtăl), *a.* 1866. [f. next + -AL 1.] *Zool.* and *Bot.* Of, pertaining to, or connected with, indicating, etc., a distinct variety of animal or plant. Opp. to *specific* or *generic*. Hence **Vari·etally** *adv.*

Variety (vărəi·ĕti). 1533. [a. F. *variété*, or ad. L. *varietat-*, *varietas* difference, diversity, etc., f. *varius* VARIOUS *a.*; see -TY.] †1. a. Variation or change of fortune –1617. b. Tendency to change; fickleness –1579. 2. Difference or discrepancy between things or in the same thing at different times 1552. 3. The fact, quality, or condition of being varied; absence of monotony, sameness, or uniformity 1548. b. *pl.* A series or succession of different forms, conditions, etc.; variations 1604. 4. Used as a collective to denote a number *of* things, qualities, etc., different or distinct in character 1553. 5. A different form *of* some thing, quality, or condition; a kind or sort 1617. b. *Zool.* and *Biol.* A plant or animal differing from those of the species to which it belongs in some minor but permanent or transmissible particular; a group of such individuals constituting a sub-species or other subdivision of a species; also, a plant or animal which varies in some trivial respect from its immediate parent or type 1629. c. So in the classification of inorganic substances or of diseases 1753. 6. *attrib.* a. *V. shop* or *store* (*U.S.*), one in which small goods of various kinds are sold; a general store 1824. b. Used to designate music-hall or theatrical entertainments of a mixed character (songs, dances, impersonations, etc.). Also applied to things or persons connected with such entertainments. c. *ellipt.*, v. performances or entertainments. 1886. d. attrib., *v. theatre.*

2. Many, according to the varietie of their opinions, attribute this to diverse causes 1604. 3. Age cannot wither her, nor custome stale Her infinite v. SHAKS. V. is the mother of enjoyment DISRAELI. b. He had passed through all varieties of fortune, and had seen both sides of human nature MACAULAY. 4. Like Proteus, he transforms himself into a v. of shapes 1875. A v. of hooks were used for different kinds of fish 1887. 5. Even the varieties of good character are almost infinite 1860.

Variform (vē°·rifǭɹm), *a.* 1662. [f. L. *vari-*, stem of *varius* VARIOUS *a.* + -FORM.] Of various forms; varied or different in form; diversiform.

†**Va·rify**, *v.* 1606. [f. L. *vari-*, stem of *varius* VARIOUS *a.*; see -FY.] *trans.* To make varied; to vary; to variegate –1741.

‖**Variola** (vărəi·ŏlă). 1771. [med.L., pustule, pox, f. L. *varius* speckled, variegated.] *Path.* The small-pox. So **Vari·olar** *a.* of, pertaining to, or resembling (that of) v. **Vario·lic** *a.* (*rare*) of v.

Variolate (vē°·riŏleˈt), *v.* 1792. [f. prec.; see -ATE.] *Med. trans.* To infect with variola; to inoculate with the virus of variola or small-pox. Hence **Va:riola·tion,** inoculation with the virus of small-pox.

Variolite (vē°·riŏləit). 1796. [f. med.L. *variola* VARIOLA + -ITE [1] 2.] *Geol.* A kind of rock embedded with spherulites which give it the appearance of being pock-marked; esp. the diabase (diorite) of Brongniart. Hence **Va:rioli·tic** *a.* of the nature of or containing v.; spherulitic.

Varioloid (vē°·riŏloid), *a.* and *sb.* 1821. [See VARIOLA and -OID.] *Path.* A. *adj.* Resembling variola or small-pox; like that of variola. B. *sb.* A modified form of variola, esp. a mild variety occurring after vaccination or in those who have previously had small-pox 1828.

Variolous (vărəi·ŏləs), *a.* 1668. [f. med. L. *variola* VARIOLA; see -OUS.] 1. Of the nature of or resembling (that of) variola or small-pox; of, pertaining to, appearing in, or characteristic of variola 1676. 2. Of persons: Affected with or suffering from small-pox 1668.

1. *V. matter* (*fluid* or *virus*), the virus of small-pox, esp. as used for inoculation.

Variometer (vē°rip·mėtəɹ). 1889. [f. *vario-*, taken as comb. form of L. *varius* VARIOUS + -METER.] An instrument used to show or determine variations in barometric pressure, magnetic force, etc.; in wireless telephony and telegraphy, a tuning coil the inductance of which is varied by altering the relative position of its two parts.

‖**Variorum** (vē°riō°·rŏm). 1728. [L., gen. pl. masc. of *varius* VARIOUS *a.*, in the phr. *editio cum notis variorum* (see def.).] An edition, esp. of the complete works of a classical author, containing the notes of various commentators or editors. Also *v. edition.*

V. Shakespeare; The book-sellers have chosen to call the 1803 and 1813 editions of Johnson and Steevens the *First* and *Second V. Shakespeares*, and the 1821 edition of Malone, although of different origin, the *Third V.* E. K. CHAMBERS.

Various (vē°·riəs), *a.* 1552. [f. L. *varius* changing, diverse: see -IOUS.] †I. 1. Of things: Undergoing, exhibiting, or subject to variation or change; variable, changeful –1775. 2. Of persons: Unstable; fickle –1820.

1. As the condition of the Court is ever v. and unconstant 1647. 2. The v. character of that emperor, capable, by turns, of the meanest and the most generous sentiments GIBBON.

II. †1. Of persons: Versatile in knowledge or acquirements; exhibiting variety in work or writings –1681. 2. a. Varied in colour; vari-coloured. Chiefly *poet.* 1618. b. Exhibiting variety in appearance 1656. 3. Characterized by variation or variety of attributes or properties; varied in nature or character 1633. †b. Calculated to cause difference. MILT. 4. Marked by variety of incident or action 1634. 5. a. Exhibiting variety of subject or topic 1677. b. Exhibiting variety in the different persons or things forming a collective whole 1769.

1. A delectable Author, very v. SIR T. BROWNE. 2. a. Birds of v. plumage LONGF. b. A prospect wide And v. MILT. 3. After conviction their behaviour was very v. 1780. 5. a. One whose conversation was so v., easy, and delightful THACKERAY. b. A v. host they came SCOTT.

III. 1. With pl. sb. Different from one another; of different kinds or sorts 1634. b. With a sing. sb., and freq. preceded by *each* or *every* 1721. 2. In weakened sense, as an enumerative term: Different, divers, several, many, more than one 1696.

1. The woodland scene, Diversified with trees of ev'ry growth, Alike, yet v. COWPER. b. In every v. Change of Life the same 1746. Phr. *V. reading(s)*; It may rest upon a v. reading in the Hebrew 1910. Hence **Va·rious·ly** *adv.*, **-ness**.

‖**Varix** (vē°·riks). *Pl.* **varices** (vē°·risīz). late ME. [L.] 1. *Path.* An abnormal dilatation or enlargement of a vein or artery, usu. accompanied by a tortuous development; a varicose vein. b. The diseased condition characterized by this, as a specific malady 1813. 2. *Conch.* A longitudinal elevation or swelling on the surface of a shell 1822.

Varlet (vā·ɹlėt). 1456. [a. OF., var. of *vaslet*, *vallet* VALET.] 1. A man or lad acting as an attendant or servant; a menial, a groom. Now *arch.* b. *spec.* An attendant on a knight or other person of military importance. Now *Hist.* 1470. 2. A person of a low, mean, or knavish disposition; a knave, rogue, rascal. (In later use, freq. without serious implication of bad qualities.) 1550. †3. The knave in cards. [So F. *valet.*] –1625.

2. A little contemptible v., without the least title to birth, person, wit SWIFT.

Varletry (vā·ɹlĕtri). 1606. [f. prec. + -RY.] Varlets collectively; a crowd of menials.

Shall they hoyst me vp, And shew me to the showting Varlotarie Of censuring Rome? SHAKS.

Varment, varmint (vā·ɹmĕnt), *sb. dial.* and *U.S.* 1539. [Variant of *varmin* VERMIN, with excrescent *-t.*] 1. a. *collect.* Vermin. b. An animal of a noxious or objectionable kind 1689. c. In hunting parlance, the fox. 2. An objectionable or troublesome person or persons; a mischievous boy or child 1773.

1. b. The granger came out with his rifle and shot the varmint [*viz.* a panther] 1889.

Varnish (vā·ɹniʃ), *sb.*[1] ME. [ad. OF. *vernis*: a Com. Rom. word of unkn. origin.] 1. Resinous matter dissolved in some liquid and used for spreading over a surface in order to give this a hard, shining, transparent coat, by which it is made more durable or ornamental. b. With *a* and *pl.* A special preparation of this nature 1667. c. A solution of this kind spread on a surface; the coating or surface so formed 1643. 2. *fig.* A specious gloss or outward show; a pretence 1565. 3. A means of embellishment or adornment; a beautifying or improving quality or feature 1591. 4. An external appearance or display of some quality without underlying reality. (Cf. VENEER *sb.*) 1662.

2. For the better v., the Duke would not be his own Judge 1647. 3. A cloudy and rainy day takes the v. off the scenery HAWTHORNE. 4. The youth comes up with a v. of accomplishment beyond his real powers 1868.

attrib. and *Comb.*: **v. sumach**, the Japanese tree *Rhus vernicifera* from which lacquer is obtained; **-tree**, one or other of various trees yielding a resinous substance used as a v.

Va·rnish, *sb.*[2] 1601. [f. the vb.] An act of varnishing; an application of varnish.

Varnish (vā·ɹniʃ), *v.* late ME. [ad. OF. *verniss(i)er*, *vernic(i)er* (F. *vernisser*), or *verniss-*, *vernir*, f. *vernis* VARNISH *sb.*[1]] 1. *trans.* To paint *over* or coat with varnish; to overlay with a thin coating composed of varnish. b. *transf.* To invest with a bright or glossy appearance; to smear or stain with some substance similar to varnish. late ME. 2. To embellish or adorn; to improve, trick out, furbish *up*. late ME. 3. To cover or overlay with a specious or deceptive appearance; to gloss over, disguise 1571.

1. These pictures, I am persuaded, were afterwards constantly varnished 1821. b. The Leaves fresh varnisht lively green SYLVESTER. 2. To dress up and v. the Story of Pausanias BENTLEY. 3. Cato's voice was ne'er employed To clear the guilty, and to vernish crimes ADDISON. To v. over these distinctions 1871. Hence **Va·rnisher**, one who varnishes; *spec.* one who makes a business or trade of varnishing.

Varnishing (vā·ɹniʃiŋ), *vbl. sb.* 1505. [f. prec.] The action of applying varnish or of coating anything with varnish.

attrib. In the year 1809..the 'v. days' were appointed, whereby the members of the Academy were granted the privilege of retouching and varnishing their pictures after they were hung, and prior to the opening of the exhibition 1862.

Varronian (værō·niăn), *a.* 1693. [ad. L. *Varronianus*, f. *Varron-*, *Varro*; see def.] Of or pertaining to the Roman author M. Terentius Varro (116–27 B.C.); admitted as genuine by Varro.

Varsal (vā·ɹsăl), *a.* Now *dial.* 1696. [Illiterate abbrev. of UNIVERSAL *a.*] 1. Universal, whole. Only in the phr. *in the v. world.* 2. Single, individual (*rare*) 1765.

Varsity (vā·ɹsĭti). Also **'varsity.** 1846. Colloquial abbrev. of UNIVERSITY.

Vartabed (vā·ɹtăbed). Also **-bied, -bet.** 1718. [Armenian.] An ecclesiastic in the Armenian church whose function it is to teach and preach.

‖**Varus**[1] (vē°·rɒ̆s). 1800. [L., 'knock-kneed'.] *Path.* A physical deformity in which the foot is turned inwards.

‖**Varus**[2] (vē°·rɒ̆s). 1822. [L., 'pimple'.] *Path.* **a.** Stone-pock. **b.** A papule (of small-pox).

Varvel (vā·ɹvĕl). 1537. [a. OF. *vervelle, varvele*, app. a reduced form of *vertvelle, vertevelle*, repr. a pop. L. deriv. of L. *vertibulum* joint.] A metal ring attached to the end of a hawk's jess and serving to connect this with the leash.

Va·ry, *sb. rare.* 1660. [f. next.] A variation; †a hesitation or vacillation.

Vary (vē°·ri), *v.* ME. [ad. OF. (also F.) *varier*, or L. *variare*, f. *varius* VARIOUS *a.*] **I.** *intr.* **1.** Of things: To undergo change or alteration; to pass from one condition, state, etc., to another. late ME. **2.** To differ, to exhibit or present divergence, *from* something else. late ME. **3.** Of persons: To differ, diverge, or depart, in respect of practice or observance (*from* some standard). late ME. †**4.** To differ in respect of statement; to give a different or divergent account –1607. **b.** Const. *from* (another or each other). In later use, to depart *from* an author by some change of statement. 1513. †**5.** To differ in opinion, to disagree (*about, for, in,* or *of* something); to dissent *from* another –1657. †**b.** To fall at variance –1577. **6.** To change or alter in respect of conduct, direction, etc. 1481. **7.** To be inconsistent in one's statements; to introduce a difference or discrepancy 1557.

1. When the organisation has once begun to v., it generally continues to v. for many generations DARWIN. **2.** This edition varies very little from its predecessor 1891. **3.** I v. from his wordes, as all Translators must doe 1621. **4. b.** I have in..other places varied somewhat from him 1653. **7.** For drawing wittnesses to varie from their former depositions 1637.

II. *trans.* **1.** To cause to change or alter; to introduce changes or alterations into (something); in later use freq., to adapt to certain circumstances or requirements by appropriate modifications ME. **b.** To dispose, obtain, occupy in a manner characterized by variety or variation 1697. †**2.** To express in different words –1682.

1. The court, after such notice,..may v. such order in such manner..as it may think fit 1891. **b.** To v. a whole week with joy, anxiety, and conjecture JOHNSON. **2.** Let your ceasless change Varie to our great Maker still new praise MILT. Hence **Va·rier** †(*a*) = PREVARICATOR 4; (*b*) one who varies or dissents *from* something. **Va·rying** *vbl. sb.*

Varying (vē°·riˌiŋ), *ppl. a.* ME. [f. prec. + -ING[2].] That varies.

V. hare, a species of hare, inhabiting northern or elevated regions, the fur of which turns white in winter; the Alpine, blue, or mountain hare. Hence **Va·ryingly** *adv.*

‖**Vas** (væs). *Pl.* **vasa** (vē¹·să). 1651. [L., vessel.] **a.** *Anat.* A hollow organ serving for the conveyance of a liquid in the body: often *ellipt.* for *vas deferens*, etc. **b.** *Bot.* (See quot.) 1843.

b. *Vasa*, the tubes which occur in the interior of plants, and serve for the conveyance of sap or air 1866. Hence **Va·sal** *a.*

Vascular (væ·skiŭlăɹ), *a.* 1672. [ad. mod.L. *vascularis*, f. L. *vasculum*, dim. of *vas* VAS.] **1.** *Bot.* Of fibres, tissue, etc.: Having the form of tubular vessels; consisting of continuous tubes of simple membrane. **b.** Of structure: Characterized by the prevalence of tubular vessels 1728. **c.** Of plants: Having a vascular structure 1830. **2.** *Anat.* or *Phys.* Having the character or properties of a conveying vessel or vessels 1728. **b.** Affecting the vascular system or tissue 1869.

1. The v. fibres of the bark 1791. *V. system*, the aggregate of tubular vessels in a plant. **2.** All the Flesh in an animal Body is found to be V. 1728. *V. system*; The v. system comprises the heart, arteries, veins, and capillaries; the lymphatic glands and vessels, together with certain ductless glands; and the blood with its tributary fluids 1876. Hence **Vascula·rity**, v. form or condition. **Va:sculariza·tion**, conversion to a v. condition. **Va·scularize** *v. trans.* to render v. **Va·scularly** *adv.*

Vasculose (væ·skiŭlǫus). 1883. [f. VASCULAR + -OSE[2].] The principal constituent of the vascular tissue in plants.

‖**Vasculum** (væ·skiŭlɒ̆m). 1832. [L., dim. of *vas* vessel.] **1.** *Bot.* = ASCIDIUM 2. **2.** A special case used by botanists for carrying newly-collected specimens 1844.

Vase (vāz, *occas.* vǭz; earlier and still *U.S.* vē¹s, vē¹z). 1563. [a. F., ad. L. *vas* vessel; see VAS.] **1.** *Arch.* †**a.** = BELL *sb.*[1] 4. –1753. **b.** An ornament having the form of a vase (sense 2) 1706. **2.** A vessel, usu. of an ornamental character, commonly of circular section, tall in proportion to its diameter, and made either of earthenware, metal, glass, etc., but varying greatly in form and use 1629. **b.** A calyx or other growth resembling a vase 1728.

2. No chargers then were wrought in burnish'd gold, Nor silver vases took the forming mold POPE.

Vaseline (væ·sĕlīn, -in, væ·z-), *sb.* 1874. [irreg. f. G. *wasser* water + Gr. ἔλαιον oil + -INE[5] (irreg. used).] Proprietary name (introduced by R. A. Chesebrough, 1872) of a soft greasy substance used as an ointment or lubricant, obtained by evaporating petroleum and passing the residuum through animal charcoal. Hence **Va·seline** *v. trans.* to lubricate, rub, or anoint with v.

Vasiform (vē¹·zifǭɹm, vē¹·s-), *a.* 1835. [f. F. *vasi-* VAS + -FORM.] **1.** Having the form of a duct or similar conveying vessel; tubular. **2.** Shaped like a vase 1846.

1. *V. tissue*, ducts, that is tubes having the appearance of spiral vessels and bothrenchyma 1866.

Vaso- (vē¹·so), comb. form, on Gr. types, of L. *vas* VAS, employed in terms of *Phys.* and *Path.* relating to the vascular system or parts of this, as **vaso-cellular** *a.*, **-constrictor, -dentine, -dilator, -ganglion, -inhibitory** *a.*, **-motive** *a.*

Va·so-mo·tor, *a.* and *sb.* 1865. [f. prec.] *Phys.* **A.** *adj.* **1.** Acting upon the walls of the blood-vessels, so as to produce constriction or dilatation of these and thus regulate or affect the flow of the blood. Chiefly with *nerve* and *centre*. **2.** Affecting the vaso-motor nerves or centres 1879. **B.** *sb.* A vaso-motor nerve 1887.

Vassal (væ·săl), *sb.* and *a.* ME. [a. OF., :—med.L. *vassallus* man-servant, retainer, of Celtic origin; the simpler form *vassus* (cf. VAVASOUR) corresp. to OBreton *uuas* (Bret. *goaz*), W. *gwas*, Ir. *foss* servant, serf.] **A.** *sb.* **1.** In the feudal system, one holding lands from a superior on conditions of homage and allegiance; a feudatory; a tenant-in-fee. Now *Hist.* **2.** *transf.* One who holds, in relation to another, a position similar or comparable to that of a feudal vassal 1563. **b.** *esp.* A humble servant or subordinate; one devoted to the service of another 1500. **c.** One who is completely subject to some influence. Const. *of* or *to*. 1614. **3.** A base or abject person; a slave 1589. **4.** *attrib.* or *adj.* **a.** Subject, subordinate. Chiefly *fig.* 1593. **b.** Of, pertaining to, or characteristic of a v. 1588.

2. b. Damoyselle,..as to my part, your vassall & seruaunt shal I euer be 1500. *transf.* Thy thoughts, low vassals to thy state SHAKS. **c.** The feeble vassals of wine and anger and lust TENNYSON. **3.** *Lear* I. i. 163. **4. a.** Thy proud hearts slaue and vassall wretch to be SHAKS. Hence **Va·ssalize** *v. trans.* = next. **Va·ssalry** = VASSALAGE 3, 4. **Va·ssalship.**

Vassal (væ·săl), *v.* Now *rare.* 1606. [f. prec.] **1.** *trans.* To make subject or subordinate *to* some thing or person 1613. **2.** To reduce to the position of a vassal; to subdue or subjugate 1606.

Vassalage (væ·sălėdʒ). ME. [a. OF. *vassal(l)age*, f. *vassal* VASSAL *sb.*] **1.** Action befitting a good vassal or a man of courage and spirit; prowess. *Obs.* exc. *arch.* **2.** The state or condition of a vassal; subordination, homage, or allegiance characteristic of or resembling that of a vassal 1594. **3.** Subjection, subordination, servitude; service 1595. **4.** A body or assemblage of vassals 1807.

2. Like v. at vnawares encountring The eye of Maiestie SHAKS. Phr. *To hold* (lands) *in v.* **3.** Princes .., Born to the pompous v. of state 1767.

Vast (vɑst), *sb.* 1604. [f. the adj.] **1.** A vast or immense space. Chiefly *poet.* **2.** *dial.* A very great number or amount 1793.

1. Thou god of this great v., rebuke these surges SHAKS. The v. of Heav'n MILT. **2.** I took a v. of trouble (as the country folks say) about it HUXLEY.

Vast (vɑst), *a.* and *adv.* 1575. [ad. L. *vastus* void, immense.] **A.** *adj.* **1.** Of very great or large dimensions or size; huge, enormous. **2.** Of great or immense extent or area; extensive, far-stretching 1590. **3.** Of the mind, etc.: Unusually large or comprehensive in grasp or aims 1610. **4.** Very great in respect of amount, quantity, or number 1637. **5.** As a mere intensive 1695.

1. A v. ruff, a vaster fardingale H. WALPOLE. **2.** One sees more diuels then vaste hell can hold SHAKS. His v. breadth of shoulder 1865. Science is grown too v. for any one head KINGSLEY. **4.** V. herds of cattle 1838. His reading was v. 1856. I saw a v. number 1884. **5.** Their wise heads go..nodding with v. solemnity 1861.

B. *adv.* Vastly. Now *dial.* 1687. Hence **Va·st·ly** *adv.* immensely; in weakened sense as a mere intensive, exceedingly, very (freq. in fashionable use in the 18th cent.); **-ness.**

Vastation (væstē¹·ʃən). 1545. [ad. L. *vastation-*, *vastatio*, f. *vastare*, f. *vastus* waste.] †**1.** The action of laying waste, devastating, or destroying –1663. †**2.** The fact or condition of being devastated or laid waste –1653. **3.** The action of purifying by the destruction of evil qualities or elements 1847.

Vastitude (vɑ·stitiŭd). 1623. [ad. L. *vastitudo*, f. *vastus*.] **1.** The quality of being vast; immensity. **2.** A vast extent or space 1841.

Vastity (vɑ·stĭti). Now *rare.* 1545. [ad. L. *vastitas*; see VAST *a.* and -ITY.] †**1.** The fact or quality of being desolate, waste, void, or empty –1651. **2.** The quality of being vast or immense 1603.

2. Th' unbounded Sea and Vastitie of shore HEYWOOD.

Vasty (vɑ·sti), *a.* 1596. [f. VAST *a.* + -Y[1].] Vast, immense. (In mod. use after Shaks.)

I can call Spirits from the vastie Deepe SHAKS. Hence **Va·stily** *adv.*

Vat (væt), *sb.* ME. [Southern var. of FAT *sb.*[1]] **1.** A cask, tun, or other vessel used for holding or storing water, beer, or other liquid; usu. one of some size in which a liquor, esp. beer or cider, undergoes fermentation or is prepared. **b.** A vessel, cauldron, or cistern containing the liquid used in dyeing or some other process 1548. **2.** *spec.* **a.** = CHEESE-*vat* 1669. **b.** = TAN-*vat* 1777. **c.** *Mining.* A wooden tub used in washing ore, etc. 1802. **d.** *Salt-making.* A salt-pit 1860. **3.** = FAT *sb.*[1] 3. 1766. †**b.** Formerly used as a measure of capacity for coal –1821. **4.** *Dyeing.* The liquid solution in which the material to be dyed is immersed; the dyeing liquor 1755. Hence **Vat** *v. trans.* to place or store in a v.; to immerse in a dyeing solution or v.

‖**Vates** (vē¹·tīz). 1625. [L.] **1.** A poet or bard, esp. one who is divinely inspired; a prophet-poet. **2.** *pl.* One of the classes of the old Gaulish druids 1728. Hence **Va·tic**, †**-ical** *adjs.* of, pertaining to, or characteristic of a prophet or seer; prophetic, inspired 1594.

Vatican (væ·tikăn). 1555. [a. F., or ad. L. *Vaticanus* (sc. *collis, mons*).] **1.** (With initial capital, and now always with *the*.) The palace of the Pope built upon the Vatican Hill in Rome. Also, in recent use, the papal authorities or the system which they represent; the papacy. **b.** Used with ref. to the artistic or literary treasures of the Vatican 1600. **2.** *attrib.* or as *adj.* Of or pertaining to the Vatican or its library 1638.

1. b. I..would not part with his Book for half a V. 1694. **2.** *V. Council*, the council of 1869–70 which proclaimed the infallibility of the Pope.

Vaticanism (væ·tikăniz'm). 1875. [f. prec.] The policy or principles of the Vatican, esp. in respect of papal infallibility and particularly with ref. to the Vatican Council of 1869–70.

Vaticanist (væ·tikănist), *sb.* and *a.* 1846. [f. as prec. + -IST.] **A.** *sb.* An adherent or supporter of the Vatican or of Vaticanism. **B.** *adj.* Of or pertaining to Vaticanism or its adherents 1892.

Vaticide[1] (væ·tisəid). 1728. [f. L. *vati-*, stem of *vates* + -CIDE 1.] One who kills a prophet.

Vaticinal (văti·sinăl), *a.* 1586. [f. L. *vaticinus* prophetic (see next) + -AL.] Of the nature of or characterized by vaticination; prophetic, vatic.

Vaticinate (văti·sineit), *v.* 1623. [f. L. *vaticinat-*, *vaticinari* to prophesy, etc., f. *vates* VATES.] 1. *intr.* To speak as a prophet or seer; to utter vaticinations; to foretell events. 2. *trans.* To foretell, predict, prognosticate, or prophesy (a future event) 1652.

Vaticination (vătisinēi·ʃən). 1603. [ad. L. *vaticination-*, *vaticinatio*; see prec.] 1. A prediction of an oracular or inspired nature; a prophecy, a prophetic utterance or forecast. 2. The action or fact of vaticinating; also, the power or gift of this 1623.

2. The ambiguous v. of the heathen oracles 1874.

Vaticinator (væti·sineitəɹ). Now *rare* or *Obs.* 1652. [ad. L., f. *vaticinari* to VATICINATE.] One who writes or utters vaticinations; a prognosticator or prophet.

Vatted (væ·tėd), *ppl. a.* 1843. [f. VAT *v.*] Placed or stored in a vat; said esp. of wine. Also *fig.*, mellow.

‖**Vaudeville** (vōu·dəvil, Fr. vodvīl). 1739. [F., earlier *vau* (pl. *vaux*) *de ville*, *vau de vire*, and in full *chanson du Vau de Vire* a song of the valley of Vire (in Calvados, Normandy).] 1. A light popular song, commonly of a satirical or topical nature; *spec.* a song of this nature sung on the stage. Now *rare* or *Obs.* 2. A play or stage performance of a light and amusing character interspersed with songs. Also, without article, this species of play or comedy. 1833. 3. orig. *U.S.* = VARIETY 6 c, d. 1891.

2. Country people always go to see tragedies. None of your flimsy vaudevilles for them! 1862. So **Vaudevi·llian** *a.* and *sb.* **Vau·devillist.**

‖**Vaudois** (vodwa), *sb.* and *a.* 1560. [F., repr. med.L. *Valdensis*; see WALDENSES.] A. *sb. pl.* Waldensians. B. *adj.* Waldensian.

‖**Vaudoux** (vodu). 1864. [F.] = VOODOO *sb.*

Vault (vǭlt), *sb.*[1] [Late ME. *voute*, a. OF. *voute*, *vaulte*, *vaute* (mod.F. *voûte*) :—pop. L. **volta*, ppl. sb. f. L. *volvere* to turn.] 1. A structure of stones or bricks so combined as to support each other over a space and serve as a roof or covering to this; an arched roof or ceiling. b. *transf.* An arching roof or covering resembling a structure of this kind 1470. c. The apparent concave surface formed by the sky. Chiefly *poet.* 1586. d. *Anat.* One or other of certain concave structures or surfaces normally facing downwards 1594. e. The inner portion of a steel furnace 1825. 2. An enclosed space covered with an arched roof; *esp.* a lower or underground apartment or portion of a building constructed in this form. late ME. b. A place of this kind used as a cellar or storeroom for provisions or liquors 1500. 3. †a. An arched space under the floor of a church, used for ecclesiastical purposes; a crypt -1511. b. A burial chamber (orig. with arched roof), usu. altogether or partly under ground 1548. †4. A covered conduit for carrying away water or filth; a drain or sewer -1700. 5. A natural cavern, cave, or overarched space; †a deep hole or pit 1535.

1. The long-drawn isle and fretted v. GRAY. b. They frequently passed under vaults, formed by fragments of the rock 1773. c. When evening turns the blue v. grey COWPER. d. The cranial v. 1849. 2. A paper currency is employed, when there is no bullion in the vaults EMERSON. 3. b. In as few years their successors will go to the family v. of 'all the Capulets' BURKE. 5. The v. at the end of the glacier TYNDALL.

Vault (vǭlt), *sb.*[2] 1576. [f. VAULT *v.*[2]] An act of vaulting; a leap or spring.

Vault (vǭlt), *v.*[1] late ME. [ad. OF. *vouter* (mod.F. *voûter*), f. *voute* VAULT.] 1. *trans.* To construct with or cover in with a vault or arched roof. Also with *over*. b. Of things: To form a vault over (something); to cover like a vault; to overarch 1667. 2. To bend, arch, or raise (something) after the manner of a vault 1552. 3. *intr.* To curve in the form of a vault 1805.

1. The various attempts made to v. the naves 1894. b. Have I not seen whole armies vaulted o'er With flying jav'lins? 1719. 2. Hateful is the dark-blue sky, Vaulted o'er the dark-blue sea TENNYSON. 3. Her mighty orbit vaults like the fresh rainbow into the deep EMERSON.

Vault (vǭlt), *v.*[2] 1568. [app. ad. OF. *volter* to gambol, leap, assim. in form to prec.] 1. *intr.* To spring or leap; *spec.* to leap with the assistance of the hand resting on the thing to be surmounted, or with the aid of a pole. 2. *trans.* To get over, surmount in this way 1884.

1. Vaulting from the ground, His saddle every horseman found SCOTT. *fig.* He was ordained priest a day or two only before he vaulted into the Archbishopric of Canterbury 1882. 2. The foot-passengers have to v. the gate 1884. Hence **Vau·lter**, one who vaults or leaps.

Vaultage (vǭ·ltėdʒ). 1599. [f. VAULT *sb.*[1]] A vaulted place or area; a series of vaults.

Vaulted (vǭ·ltėd), *ppl. a.* 1553. [f. VAULT *sb.*[1] or *v.*[1]] 1. Having the form of a vault; arched or rounded. 2. Constructed or furnished with an arched roof; covered in or roofed by a vault 1601.

Vaulting (vǭ·ltiŋ), *vbl. sb.*[1] and *sb.* 1512. [f. VAULT *sb.*[1] and *v.*[1]] 1. The construction of a vault or vaults; the operation of covering or roofing with a vault. 2. The work or structure forming a vault 1513. b. With *a* and *pl.* A species, example, or piece of such work 1750.

Vaulting (vǭ·ltiŋ), *vbl. sb.*[2] 1531. [f. VAULT *v.*[2]] The action of leaping with a vault, esp. as a gymnastic exercise.

V. horse: †a. a horse mounted by vaulting, esp. one used for the exercise of leaping into the saddle without the help of a stirrup; b. in gymnastics, a wooden figure of a horse employed for exercise in vaulting.

Vaulty (vǭ·lti), *a.* 1545. [f. VAULT *sb.*[1]] Resembling a vault; having the arching form of a vault.

Sound..which resounds in v. and hollow places 1651.

†**Vaumure.** 1475. [Reduced f. AF. **vauntmur*; see VAUNTMURE.] An advanced wall or earthwork thrown out in front of the main fortifications; the outer wall or series of walls of a fortification or fortress -1656.

Vaunt (vǭnt, *U.S.* vānt), *sb.*[1] Now *rhet.* or *arch.* late ME. [Aphetic f. AVAUNT *sb.*[1]] 1. Boasting, bragging; arrogant assertion or bearing. 2. A boasting assertion, speech, or statement; a boast or brag 1597. 3. A cause or subject of boasting (*rare*) 1791.

1. With all the v. and insolent port of a conqueror 1838. Phr. *To make* (*one's* or *a*) *v.*, to boast or brag (now *rare*). 2. The spirits beneath, whom I seduc'd With other promises and other vaunts Then to submit, boasting I could subdue Th' Omnipotent MILT. Hence **Vau·ntful** (*arch.*) *a.* boastful; *adv.* (*rare*) boastfully.

†**Vaunt,** *sb.*[2] 1589. [Independent use of VANT-, VAUNT- *prefix*.] A front part or portion, *esp.* the van of an army -1624.

Vaunt (vǭnt, *U.S.* vānt), *v.* Now *rhet.* or *arch.* late ME. [a. OF. *vanter* :—pop. L. **vanitare*; cf. AVAUNT *v.*[1]] 1. *intr.* To boast or brag; to use bragging or vainglorious language. Now *rare* or *Obs.* 2. *trans.* To boast of (something); to commend or praise in a vainglorious manner 1592.

1. He talk'd little, never vaunted, observ'd much, was very secret TEMPLE. Attila vaunted that the grass never grew again after his horse's hoof 1853. 2. This country, which does not always err in vaunting its own productions H. WALPOLE. So **Vau·nter** (now *arch.*) a boaster, braggart. **Vau·ntery** (now *Obs.* or *arch.*) vaunting, boasting; †a vaunt. **Vau·ntingly** *adv.*

Vaunt-, *prefix*, an AF. variant of VANT-.

Vaunt-courier (vǭnt-, vāntˌkūᵊ·riəɹ). Also †**vantcourier.** 1560. [ad. F. *avant-coureur* AVANT-*courier*, with assimilation to forms in VAUNT-, and to COURIER.] †1. A soldier or horseman sent out in advance of the main body. Usu. in pl. -1677. 2. *transf.* One who goes or is sent out in advance in order to prepare the way or to announce the approach of another; a forerunner. Freq. of things. 1561.

†**Vauntmure.** 1562. [Aphetic f. AVANTMURE; see VANT-, VAUNT-.] = VAUMURE -1605.

Vauquelinite (vōu·klinəit). 1823. [f. the name of the French chemist L. N. *Vauquelin* (1768–1829) + -ITE[1].] *Min.* Chromate of lead and copper, found in amorphous masses or crystalline crusts of a green or brownish colour.

‖**Vaurien** (voryæ̃n). Also **vaut-rien, vautrien.** 1825. [F., f. *vaut*, 3rd sing. pres. ind. of *valoir* to be worth + *rien* nothing.] A worthless good-for-nothing fellow; a scamp.

Vavasour (væ·văsūᵊɹ). Now *arch.* and *Hist.* ME. [a. OF. *vavas(s)our*, or med.L. *vavassor*, app. f. *vassi vassorum* vassals of vassals.] A feudal tenant ranking immediately below a baron.

Was nowher such a worthi vauaser CHAUCER. So **Va·vasory**, an estate held by a v.

Va·ward. *Obs.* exc. *arch.* late ME. [Reduced form of †*vaumward*, †*vamward* vanguard. See VANT- *prefix*.] *Mil.* = VANGUARD 1. b. *fig.* The forefront; the early part 1597.

b. We that are in the v. of our youth SHAKS.

've, reduced form of HAVE *v.* appended to pronouns in rapid or unstudied speech; e.g. *they've* = they have.

Veal (vīl), *sb.* late ME. [a. AF. *vel*, OF. *veel*, *veal* (mod.F. *veau*) :—L. *vitellus*, dim. of *vitulus* calf.] 1. The flesh of a calf as an article of food. 2. A calf, esp. as killed for food or intended for this purpose. Now *rare.* late ME. Hence **Veal** *v. trans.* (*U.S.*) to rear (calves) for use as v. **Vea·ly** *a.* resembling v.; *fig.* imperfectly developed; immature.

‖**Vectis** (ve·ktis). 1648. [L., 'lever, crowbar'.] †1. A lever -1674. 2. *Surg.* a. An obstetrical instrument used as a lever to free the head of the child 1790. b. An instrument employed in operations on the eye 1882.

Vectita·tion. *rare.* 1656. [f. L. *vectitare*, freq. of *vectare* to carry.] The action of carrying or conveying; the fact of being carried or conveyed.

Vector (ve·ktəɹ). 1704. [a. L., f. *vehere* to carry.] †1. *Astr.* An imaginary straight line joining a planet moving round a centre, or the focus of an ellipse, to that centre or focus. Also *v. radius* = *radius v.* (RADIUS 3 d) -1796. 2. *Math.* A quantity having direction as well as magnitude, denoted by a line drawn from its original to its final position 1865. 3. A carrier of disease 1926. Hence **Vecto·rial** *a.* of, pertaining to, or connected with a v. or radius vector.

‖**Veda** (vē·dă). 1734. [a. Skr. *vēda* knowledge, sacred book, from the root *vid-* to know; see WIT *v.*] One or other of the four ancient sacred books of the Hindus (called the *Rig-*, *Yajur-*, *Sāma-*, and *Atharva-vēda*); the body of sacred literature contained in these books. Hence **Veda·ic** *a.* = VEDIC *a.*; **Ve·daism** = VEDISM.

‖**Vedanta** (vėdā·ntă, -æ·ntă). 1823. [Skr. *vēdānta*, f. *vēda* VEDA + *anta* end.] One of the leading systems of Hindu philosophy.

The V. system shows us..how pantheism must logically result in scepticism 1849. Hence **Veda·ntic** *a.* **Veda·ntism. Veda·ntist.**

Vedda (ve·dă). Also **Wedda.** 1681. [Sinhalese *veddā* archer, hunter.] A member of a primitive race inhabiting the forest districts of Ceylon.

‖**Vedette** (vĭde·t). 1690. [F., ad. It. *vedetta*, prob. f. *vedere* to see.] *Mil.* A mounted sentry placed in advance of the outposts of an army to observe the movements of the enemy.

V. boat, a small vessel used for scouting purposes in naval warfare.

Vedic (vē·dik), *a.* and *sb.* 1859. [f. VEDA + -IC.] A. *adj.* Of, pertaining to, contained, mentioned in, or contemporary with the Vedas. B. *sb.* The language of the Vedas, an early form of Sanskrit.

Vedism (vē·diz'm). 1882. [f. VEDA + -ISM.] The system of religious beliefs and practices contained in the Vedas.

‖**Vedro** (vedrō·). 1753. [Russ., 'pail'.] A Russian liquid measure equal to 2·7 imperial gallons.

Veer (vīᵊɹ), *sb.* 1611. [f. VEER *v.*[2]] An act or instance of veering; a change of direction.

Veer (vīᵊɹ), *v.*[1] 1460. [a. MDu. *vieren* to let out, slacken, = OHG. *fieren* to give direction to.] †1. *trans.* To allow (a sheet or other sail-line) to run out to some extent; to let *out* by releasing -1694. b. To let *out* (any line or rope); to allow to run *out* gradually to a desired length 1574. 2. To allow (a boat, buoy, etc.) to drift further off by letting out a line attached to it 1539. **3.** To let out or pay out (a cable) 1604.

1. b. They rowed it towards the rock, veering out a rope, which they had fastened to the large boat 1793. 2. They veered out a buoy with a line, which we got hold of MARRYAT. 3. After veering cable we went to quarters 1870. *To v. and haul*, is to haul and slack alternately on a rope, as in warping, until the vessel or boat gets headway R. H. DANA.

Veer (vīᵊɹ), *v.*² 1582. [ad. F. *virer* to turn, veer; of obsc. origin.] **1.** *intr.* Of the wind: To change gradually; to pass by degrees from one point to another, *spec.* in the direction of the sun's course. orig. *Naut.* **2.** *Naut.* Of a ship: To change course; *spec.* to turn round with the head away from the wind in order to sail on another tack 1620. **3.** To turn round or about; to change from one direction or course to another 1633. **4.** *fig.* To change or alter; to pass from one state, position, tendency, etc. to another; to be variable or changeable 1669. **5.** *absol.* To alter the course of a ship, *spec.* by causing it to swing round with the stern to windward so as to sail on another tack. Also of a ship: To admit of veering. 1625. **6.** *trans.* To turn from one course or direction to another 1647.

1. The next night the wind veered to the eastward 1899. 2. A-head of all the Master Pilot steers, And, as he leads, the following navy veers DRYDEN. 3. Grief a fixed star, and joy a vane that veers SWINBURNE. The amazed horse veered quickly to one side 1879. 4. Seldom has the fortune of war veered round so rapidly 1878. He is a man to v. about like a weathercock 1884. 5. My lads, lie to, then v. and sail against the wind 1884.

Veery (vīᵊ·ri). *U.S.* 1845. [perh. imitative.] A N. Amer. thrush (*Turdus fuscescens*), also called *tawny* and *Wilson's thrush*.

‖**Vega**¹ (vēⁱ·gă). 1645. [Sp. and Catal.; origin obsc.] In Spain and Spanish America, an extensive, fertile, and grass-covered plain or tract of land.

Vega² (vī·gă). 1638. [a. Sp. or med.L., ad. Arab. *wāqiᵉ* falling, in (*al nasr*) *al wāqiᵉ* 'the falling (vulture)', the constellation Lyra.] The brightest star in the constellation Lyra; *α Lyræ*.

Vegetability (ve:dʒĭtăbi·lĭti). late ME. [ad. med.L. **vegetabilitas*, f. L. *vegetabilis* VEGETABLE *a.*; see -ITY.] †**1.** A vegetable organism. late ME. only. **2.** Vegetable character, quality, or nature 1646.

Vegetable (ve·dʒĭtăb'l), *sb.* 1582. [f. the adj.] **1.** A living organism belonging to the vegetable kingdom or the lower of the two series of organic beings; a growth devoid of animal life; = PLANT *sb.* I. 2. †**b.** *pl.* in collective sense: Vegetation –1821. **2.** A plant cultivated for food; *esp.* an edible herb or root used for human consumption and commonly eaten, either cooked or raw, with meat or other articles of food 1767.

2. At a stinted repast of milk and vegetables 1796. *attrib.*, as *v. dish, garden, soup.*

Vegetable (ve·dʒĭtăb'l), *a.* late ME. [a. OF., (mod.F. *végétable*), or ad. L. *vegetabilis* animating, vivifying, f. *vegetare* VEGETATE *v.*] †**1.** Having the vegetating property of plants; living and growing as a plant or organism endowed with the lowest form of life –1678. **2.** Of or pertaining to, composed or consisting of, or derived or obtained from plants or their parts; of the nature of or resembling a vegetable. Freq. as contrasted with animal or mineral products. 1582. **3.** *V. creation, kingdom, world*, etc., that division of organic nature to which plants belong 1668. **4.** Of, composed or consisting of, or made from esculent vegetables 1746. **5.** Resembling that of a vegetable; *esp.* uneventful, monotonous, dull 1854.

1. Comparysownyd..To a sowle þat were v., þe whiche, with-oute sensibilite, Mynystreth lyf in herbe, flour, and tre LYDG. 2. The superiority of coal to v. tar 1800. The subject of v. development 1842. 5. The pauper peasantry, weary of a merely v. life, were glad of any pretext for excitement 1854.

Special collocations: **V. acid**, an organic acid derived from a plant. **V. alkali**, carbonate of potash. **V. butter**, the name given to the concrete oil of certain vegetables, because of its resemblance to the butter obtained from the milk of animals, and because it is employed for similar purposes. *V. casein* = LEGUMIN. *V. ivory* (see IVORY 2); also *attrib.* **V. leather**, the plant *Euphorbia punicea*; also, imitation leather made from cotton waste. **V. marrow**: see MARROW¹ 3. **V. mould**, mould having a large proportion of decayed v. matter in it. **V. parchment**: see PARCHMENT 1. **V. silk**, a cotton-like material obtained from the seed-pods of *Chorisia speciosa*. **V. tallow**, a fatty substance obtained from *Stillingia sebifera*, and other plants. **V. wax**, a wax or wax-like substance obtained from plants or v. growths.

Vegetal (ve·dʒĭtăl), *a.* and *sb.* late ME. [ad. med.L. **vegetalis*, f. L. *vegetare*; see VEGETATE *v.*] **A.** *adj.* **1.** Characterized by, exhibiting, or producing the phenomena of physical life and growth. Now usu. in contrast with *animal*. **b.** In expressed or implied contrast with *sensible* (or *sensitive*) and *rational*. *Obs.* exc. *Hist.* 1621. **2.** Of or pertaining to, derived or obtained from, plants or vegetables 1596. **3.** = prec. 3. 1664.

1. Phenomena of animal and v. life SPENCER. b. All creatures, v., sensible, and rational BURTON. 2. Manna, Cassia, and v. Salt 1758.

B. *sb.* = VEGETABLE *sb.* 1. 1599.

Vegetant (ve·dʒĭtănt), *a.* and *sb.* 1576. [a. F. *végétant*, or ad. L. *vegetant-*, *vegetans*, *vegetare*; see VEGETATE *v.*] **A.** *adj.* †**1.** Animating, vivifying, invigorating (*rare*) –1615. **2.** Vegetating; vegetable, vegetal. Now *rare*. 1610. †**B.** *sb.* = VEGETABLE *sb.* 1. –1610.

Vegetarian (vedʒĭtēᵊ·riăn), *sb.* and *a.* 1842. [irreg. f. VEGETABLE + -ARIAN.] **A.** *sb.* **1.** One who lives wholly or principally upon vegetable foods; *esp.* one who abstains from animal food obtained by the direct destruction of life. **2.** A member of a fanatical Chinese sect 1895. **B.** *adj.* **1.** Of or pertaining to vegetarians or vegetarianism; practising or advocating vegetarianism 1849. **2.** Of animals: Living on vegetables 1856. **3.** Consisting of vegetables or plants 1868.

Vegetarianism (vedʒĭtēᵊ·riăniz'm). 1853. [f. prec. + -ISM.] The principles or practice of vegetarians; abstention from eating meat, fish, or other animal products.

Is it contrary to the rules of V. to eat eggs? TYNDALL.

Vegetate (ve·dʒĭtēⁱt), *v.* 1605. [f. L. *vegetat-*, *vegetare* to animate, enliven, f. *vegetus* VEGETE *a.*] **1.** *intr.* Of plants, seeds, etc.: To exercise or exhibit vegetative faculties or functions; to grow or develop, or begin to do so. **b.** *transf.* To increase as if by or present the appearance of vegetable growth 1744. **2.** *fig.* Of persons, etc.: To live a merely physical life; to lead a dull, monotonous existence, devoid of intellectual activity or social intercourse; to live in dull retirement or seclusion 1740. †**3.** *trans.* To cause to grow; to animate, quicken –1678.

1. A young oak, just vegetating from the acorn 1791. b. Naturalists have observed that ore in swamps and pondy ground vegetates and increases 1796. 2. In short, we rather vegetated than lived 1777. The vast empire of China..has vegetated through a succession of drowsy ages W. IRVING.

Vegetation (vedʒĭtēⁱ·ʃən). 1564. [ad. (late and) med.L. *vegetatio*, f. *vegetare* VEGETATE *v.*] **I. 1.** The action of vegetating or growing; the faculty, process, or phenomena of growth and development as possessed by certain organic substances; vegetal activity or property. †**2.** *transf.* The production of a plant-like formation –1842. **3.** *fig.* Existence similar or comparable to that of a vegetable; dull, empty, or stagnant life spent in retirement or seclusion 1797.

2. The Influence of the Air and Light upon the V. of Salts 1823. 3. Hedouville..went to spend a life of mere v. in Spain 1854.

II. 1. †**a.** A vegetable form or growth; a plant –1707. **b.** A plant-like growth or formation due to chemical action 1790. **c.** *Path.* A morbid fungoid growth or excrescence occurring on some part of the body 1835. **2.** Plants collectively; plants or vegetal growths as a product of the soil 1727.

2. When an American forest is cut down, a very different v. springs up DARWIN.

Vegetative (ve·dʒĭtēⁱtiv), *a.* and *sb.* late ME. [ad. med.L. *vegetativus*, f. *vegetat-*, *vegetare* VEGETATE *v.*; see -IVE.] **A.** *adj.* **1.** Having the function of vegetation; endowed with the power or faculty of growth. **b.** *spec.* in *Phys.* and *Bot.* Concerned with growth and development, as opp. to *reproductive* 1857. **2.** Of or pertaining to, concerned or connected with, or characterized by vegetation or growth. late ME. **3.** Causing or promoting vegetation; productive, fertile 1594. **4.** = VEGETABLE *a.* 3. 1677. **5.** *Path.* Characterized by the exercise or activity of the physical functions only 1893.

3. Fullers-earth is..very full of that v. Salt that helps the growth of Plants 1707. 5. Idiots of v. grade 1899.

†**B.** *sb.* An organic body capable of growth and development but devoid of sensation and thought; a vegetable or plant –1764. Hence **Ve·getative-ly** *adv.*, **-ness**.

Vegete (vĭdʒī·t), *a.* Now *rare*. 1639. [ad. L. *vegetus*, f. *vegere* to be active or lively.] **1.** Healthy and active; flourishing in respect of health and vigour. **2.** Of plants or their parts: Healthy, vigorous; growing strongly or promoting active growth 1651.

1. Even her body was made aëry and v. JER. TAYLOR. 2. The lower leaf dies..as the upper leaf becomes v. 1800.

Vegetive (ve·dʒĭtiv), *a.* and *sb.* 1526. [Reduced f. VEGETATIVE *a.*, after L. *vegetare* or *vegetus*.] **A.** *adj.* **1.** = VEGETATIVE *a.* 2. **2.** Endowed with the faculty of vegetation or growth 1615. †**B.** *sb.* = VEGETABLE *sb.* 2. –1819.

Vegeto- (ve·dʒĭto), irregular comb. form of the L. stem *veget-*, used in the sense of 'vegetable and..' or 'having a vegetable origin', as *v.-animal, -mineral*.

†**Vegetous**, *a.* 1609. [f. L. *vegetus* VEGETE; see -OUS.] = VEGETE *a.* –1696.

Vehemence (vī·ĭmĕns, vī·hĭmĕns). 1529. [a. late OF., or ad. L. *vehementia*; see next. In this and the related words the pronunc. (vī·h-) is now chiefly *U.S.*] **1.** Intensity or strength *of* smell or colour (*rare*) 1535. **2.** Impetuosity, great force or violence, of physical action or agents 1542. **3.** Great or excessive ardour, eagerness, or fervour of personal feeling or action; passionate force or violence 1529.

3. With an almost savage v. of gesticulation 1839.

Vehemency (vī·ĭmĕnsi, vī·h-). Now *rare*. 1538. [ad. L. *vehementia*, f. *vehement-* VEHEMENT *a.*; see -ENCY.] **1.** = prec. 3. **2.** Intensity or severity 1543. **3.** = prec. 2. 1555.

1. You'll learn henceforth to chide with far less v. 1830. 2. The vehemencie of the fire forceth..vp an abboundance of vapours 1604.

Vehement (vī·ĭmĕnt, vī·h-), *a.* 1485. [a. OF. (F. *véhément*), or ad. L. *vehement-*, *vehemens* violent, impetuous, usu. taken as f. *vehe-* (= *ve-* in *vecors*) lacking + *mens* mind.] **I. 1.** Intense, severe; rising to a high degree or pitch. **2.** Of natural forces: Operating with great strength or violence; *esp.* of wind, blowing very strongly or violently 1531. **3.** Of actions: Characterized by great physical exertion; performed with unusual force or violence 1531. †**4.** Of remedies, etc.: Having a powerful effect upon the system –1656.

1. V. dolour and payne 1563. Salt of Tartar requires a v. fire to flux it BOYLE. 2. The Rain was so v. 1701. 3. *transf.* These v. exertions of intellect cannot be frequent JOHNSON.

II. 1. a. Of suspicion or likelihood: Very strong. Now *arch.* 1516. †**b.** Of proof, etc.: Strong, cogent; capable of producing conviction –1731. **2.** Of thoughts, feelings, etc.: Extremely strong or deep; eager, passionate; violent, intense 1526. **3.** Of language: Very forcibly or passionately uttered or expressed; resulting from strong feeling or excitement 1533. **4.** Of persons, their character, etc.: Acting or tending to act in a manner displaying passion or excitement 1560. **5.** Of debate, strife, etc.: Characterized by great heat or bitterness 1620.

2. The Queen's v. partisanship 1907. 3. The most v. protestations of gratitude and fidelity 1848. 4. For the woman..Ever prefers the audacious, the wilful, the v. hero 1848. 5. Powerful and v. opposition 1844. Hence **Ve·hement-ly** *adv.*, **-ness**.

Vehicle (vī·ĭk'l; chiefly *U.S.* vī·hik'l), *sb.* 1612. [ad. F. *véhicule*, or L. *vehiculum*, f. *vehere* to carry.] **I. 1.** A substance, *esp.* a liquid, serving as a means for the readier application or use of another substance mixed with or dissolved in it: **a.** *Med.* A medium in which strong or unpalatable drugs or medicines are administered. **b.** *Painting.* A fluid (as water, oil, etc.) with which pigments are mixed for use 1787. **2.** That which serves as a means of transmission, or as a material embodiment or manifestation of something 1650. **3.** A means or medium by which ideas or impressions are communicated or made known; a medium of expression or utterance 1652. 4. The form, the material or other shape, in which something spiritual is embodied or manifested 1652.

2. If the water be in reality the v. of this disease 1779. The..use of paper as the v. of writing instead of parchment 1837. 3. Music is not made the v. of poetry, but poetry of music HAZLITT. 4. When our souls are divested of their grosser vehicles 1670.

II. 1. A material means, channel, or instrument by which a substance or some property of matter (as sound or heat) is conveyed or transmitted from one point to another 1615. 2. A means of conveyance provided with wheels or runners and used for the carriage of persons or goods; a carriage, cart, wagon, sledge, etc. 1656. 3. A receptacle in which anything is placed in order to be moved 1678.

1. Air is the usual v. of Sound 1803. 2. The rumbling and jolting v. stopped at the door of a tavern 1829. Hence **Ve·hicle** *v. trans.* to place or convey in a v.

Vehicular (vǐhi·kiŭlăɹ), *a.* 1616. [ad. late L. *vehicularis*, f. *vehiculum* VEHICLE *sb.*] **a.** Of, pertaining to, associated or connected with a (wheeled) vehicle. **b.** Made, performed, or carried on by means of a vehicle or vehicles 1742. **c.** Of the nature of or serving as a vehicle 1807.

b. V. traffic was almost entirely suspended 1879.

Vehiculate (vǐhi·kiŭlēᵗt), *v. rare.* 1660. [f. L. *vehiculum*; see -ATE [3].] **a.** *trans.* To carry or convey in or as in a vehicle. **b.** *intr.* To travel, ride, or drive, in a vehicle. So **Vehicula·tion**, conveyance by means of a vehicle or vehicles; vehicular activity or traffic. **Vehi·culatory** *a.* of the nature of, pertaining or relating to, vehicles.

‖**Vehiculum** (vǐhi·kiŭlɒ̆m). Now *rare* or *Obs. Pl.* vehicula. 1624. [L.] = VEHICLE *sb.* I. 1, 2, 4, II. 2.

‖**Vehme** (vē·mə, ‖fē·mə). *Hist.* Also **Fehm.** 1829. [a. early mod.G. *Vehme*, now *Fehme*, *Feme*, MHG. *veme*, *veime* judgement, punishment.] = next. Hence **Veh·mic** *a.* pertaining to or connected with the Vehmgericht.

‖**Vehmgericht** (vē·m-, ‖fē·mgərixʸt). *Hist.* 1829. [a. early mod.G. *Vehm-*, now *Fehm-*, *Femgericht* (pl. *-gerichte*), f. prec. + *gericht* court, tribunal.] A form of secret tribunal which exercised great power in Westphalia from the end of the 12th to the middle of the 16th century.

Veil (vēᵗl), *sb.* ME. [a. AF. and ONF. *veile* and *veil* = OF. *voile* and *voil*:—L. *vela* (neut. pl. taken as fem. sing.) and *velum* curtain, veil.] 1. A piece of woollen material forming the outer part of the distinctive head-dress of a nun, and worn so as to drape the head and shoulders. 2. An article of attire worn, esp. by women, over the head or face, either as a part of the ordinary head-dress, or in order to conceal or protect the face; freq. a piece of net or thin gauzy material tied to the hat and covering the face in order to protect it from the sun or wind ME. 3. A piece of cloth or other material serving as a curtain or hanging: **a.** *Jewish Antiq.* The piece of precious cloth separating the sanctuary from the body of the Temple or the Tabernacle ME. **b.** *Eccl.* The curtain hung between the altar and the choir, esp. during Lent. Now *Hist.* late ME. 4. A piece of silk or other material used as a covering, *spec.* (*Eccl.*) to drape a crucifix, image, picture, etc., esp. during Lent, or to cover the chalice, etc. late ME. 5. *fig.* Something which conceals, covers, or hides; a disguising or obscuring medium or influence; a cloak or mask. late ME. 6. In various specific uses: A veil-like membrane; a membranous appendage or part serving as a cover or screen; a velum 1760.

1. Phr. *To take the v.*, to become a nun; to enter a convent or nunnery. *The v.*, the life of a nun. 2. Over her face a v., so transparent as not to conceal 1774. A bridal v. of old Brussels lace (*mod.*). 3. a. Phr. *Behind*, *beyond*, or *within the v.*: used fig. or allus., chiefly after Heb. vi. 19; now commonly with ref. to the next world. 5. The v. of anonymity 1882. Phr. *To draw*, *throw*, or *cast a v. over*: to hide or conceal, to refrain from discussing, to hush up or keep from public knowledge. Hence **Vei·lless** *a.* having no v.; unshaded, unclouded.

Veil (vēᵗl), *v.* late ME. [f. prec.] 1. *trans.* To cover (a person, etc.) with or as with a veil; to conceal or hide (the face, etc.) by means of a veil or other material; to enveil. **b.** *refl.* To hide, cover, or wreathe (oneself) *in* something 1799. 2. To bestow the veil of a nun upon (a woman); to admit into the religious life as a nun. late ME. 3. To cover, enshroud, or screen as or in the manner of a veil; to serve as a veil to (something) 1513. 4. *fig.* To conceal (some immaterial thing, condition, quality, etc.) from apprehension, knowledge, or perception; to hide the real nature or meaning of (something): freq. with implication of bad motives. 1538. 5. To render less distinct or apparent; to reduce, soften, tone down 1843.

1. She bow'd as if to v. a noble tear TENNYSON. Psyche, all in lily-whiteness veil'd BRIDGES. 3. Ornament is but..The beautious scarfe Vailing an Indian beautie SHAKS. Yonder blazing Cloud that veils the Hill MILT. 4. Pythagoras learned to v. his precepts 1770.

Veiled (vēᵗld), *ppl. a.* 1593. [f. VEIL *v.* or *sb.*] 1. Covered with or wearing a veil; shrouded in a veil. **b.** *Bot.* Having a velum; velate 1793. 2. Concealed, covered, hidden, as if by a veil; obscure, unrevealed 1612. **b.** *fig.* Covert, disguised; not openly declared, expressed, or stated 1875. 3. Of sound, the voice, etc.: Indistinct, muffled, obscure 1834.

1. What v. form sits on that ebon throne? SHELLEY. 2. The more vailed and pregnant parts of Scripture 1612. b. The scarcely v. sneer which marked his tone of voice 1891.

Veiling (vēᵗ·liŋ), *vbl. sb.* late ME. [f. as prec. + -ING [1].] 1. The action of VEIL *v.* 1586. 2. Something serving as a veil, curtain, or screen. late ME. **b.** Material of which veils are made. Also *pl.* 1882.

2. *Nun's v.*: see NUN *sb.*

Vein (vēᵗn), *sb.* ME. [a. OF. *veine*:—L. *vena.*] I. 1. One or other of the tubular vessels in which the blood is conveyed through the animal body; in later use *spec.* one of those by which the blood is carried back to the heart from the extremities (opp. to *artery*). 2. *Bot.* A slender bundle of fibro-vascular tissue forming an extension of the petiole in the parenchyma of a leaf 1513. **b.** *Ent.* A nervure of an insect's wing 1817. 3. A marking or an appearance suggestive of a vein; *esp.* an irregular stripe or streak of a different colour in marble or other stone 1642. **b.** A streak or seam of a different material or texture from the main substance 1663.

1. *fig.* In equity and reason the benefitt of trade should be equally disposed into all the vaines of the Commonwealth 1651. 3. The blue veins of the glacier are beautifully shown TYNDALL. b. The spectrum formed by a fine prism of flint glass, free of veins 1831.

II. 1. A small natural channel or perforation within the earth through which water trickles or flows; a flow of water through such a channel ME. 2. *Min.* A deposit of metallic or earthy material having an extended or ramifying course under ground; a seam or lode; *spec.* a continuous crack or fissure filled with matter (esp. metallic ore) different from the containing rock. late ME. 3. †**a.** A strip of ground or soil, *esp.* one having a particular character or quality -1693. **b.** A channel or lane of water 1606. **c.** A current of wind; the track in which this moves 1792. III. *fig.* 1. A strain or intermixture *of* some quality traceable in personal character or conduct, in a discourse or writing, etc. 1565. **b.** A line or course *of* thought, etc.; a source *of* information 1704. 2. A natural tendency towards or a special aptitude or capacity for the production of literary or artistic work; a particular strain of talent or genius 1577. 3. A special or characteristic style of language or expression in writing or speech 1548. †4. A habit or practice -1725. †**b.** An inclination or desire towards something specified -1673. 5. Personal character or disposition; also, a particular element or trait in this 1565. **b.** A humour or mood 1577.

1. A v. of Superstition ran through all his Actions 1701. b. Delay opens new veins of thought JOHNSON. 2. If I had Virgilles vayne to indite, or Homers quill 1577. 3. An inscription, somewhat in the v. of Ancient Pistol SCOTT. 5. When the peacock v. rises, I strut a Gentleman Commoner LAMB. b. Phr. *In the v.*, in a fit or suitable mood for something; Nobody can be more amusing when she is in the v. 1905. Hence **Vei·nless** *a.* having no veins: chiefly *Bot.* of leaves.

Vei·nlet, a small or minor v.; *spec.* in *Bot.* a branch or subdivision of a v.

Vein (vēᵗn), *v.* 1686. [f. prec.] 1. *trans.* To ornament with coloured, incised, or impressed lines or streaks suggestive of veins. Also with *in.* 2. Of things: To extend over or through (something) after the manner of veins. Chiefly *poet.* 1807.

2. All the gold That veins the world TENNYSON.

Veined (vēᵗnd), *ppl. a.* 1529. [f. as prec.] 1. Furnished or marked with veins (in various senses). 2. Intersected or marked *with* something (esp. a colour) suggestive of veins 1612.

1. The v. structure of the ice TYNDALL. The million leaves, v. and edge-cut, on bush and tree 1883.

Veining (vēᵗ·niŋ), *vbl. sb.* 1686. [f. VEIN *sb.* or *v.*] 1. The action or process of ornamenting with vein-like markings. 2. The arrangement of veins or vein-like markings on or in something; a veined appearance or structure; venation 1826.

Veinous (vēᵗ·nəs), *a.* 1634. [f. as prec. + -OUS.] 1. *Physiol.* **a.** Full of or traversed by veins. **b.** Occupying the veins 1801. 2. Having large or prominent veins (also *transf.*); formed by out-standing veins 1848.

2. She clasped her v. and knotted hands together DICKENS.

Vei·n(-)stone. 1709. [f. VEIN *sb.*] 1. Stone or earthy matter composing a vein and containing metallic ore; gangue, matrix. **b.** With pl.: A portion or variety of this 1728. 2. = PHLEBOLITE, -LITH 1835.

Veiny (vēᵗ·ni), *a.* 1594. [f. VEIN *sb.*] Full of veins; traversed by veins; marked by veins of colour.

Six blocks of very superior veiny marble 1800.

‖**Velamen** (vǐlē·mĕn). *Pl.* **-amina.** 1882. [L., f. *velare* to cover.] *Bot.* The outer envelope or covering of the aerial roots of some arums and orchids.

Velar (vī·lăɹ), *a.* and *sb.* 1726. [ad. L. *velaris*, f. *velum* sail, curtain.] **A.** *adj.* 1. *Arch. V. cupola*: a cupola or dome, terminated by four or more walls. 2. *Phonetics.* Of sounds: Produced by contact with the soft palate 1876. 3. *Zool.* Of or pertaining to a velum 1878. **B.** *sb.* A velar guttural 1886.

‖**Velarium** (vǐlēᵊ·riɒ̆m). *Pl.* **-ia.** 1834. [L., 'awning', f. *velum* sail.] 1. *Rom. Antiq.* A large awning used to cover a theatre or amphitheatre as a protection against sun or rain. 2. *Zool.* A thin marginal rim on the bell of certain hydrozoans 1888.

Velate (vī·lĕt), *a.* 1857. [f. L. *velum* VELUM, or ad. L. *velatus*, *velare* to cover.] **a.** *Bot.* Furnished with a veil; veiled. **b.** *Zool.* Having a velum. So **Ve·lated** *a.* 1835.

Veld, veldt (velt, felt). Also **velt.** 1801. [a. early Du. *veldt*, now *veld*; see FIELD *sb.*] In South Africa, the unenclosed country, or open pasture-land.

Comb.: **v.-cornet**, = *field-cornet*; **v. pig**, the Ethiopian wart-hog (*Phacocœrus ethiopicus*); **v. rat**, the striped rat of S. Africa.

Veld-, veldt-shoe (ve·lt,ʃū, felt-). *S. Afr.* Also velschoen (*pl.*); veldtschoon. 1822. [a. or ad. Cape Du. *veldschoen*, earlier *velschoen*, f. Du. *vel* skin, FELL *sb.*[1] + *schoen* SHOE *sb.*] A light shoe made of untanned hide.

‖**Velella** (vėle·lă). 1834. [mod.L., f. L. *velum* sail.] *Zool.* A genus of siphonophorous oceanic hydrozoans; a member of this genus.

Veliferous (vǐli·fĕrəs), *a.* 1656. [f. L. *velifer*, f. VELUM; see -FEROUS.] †1. Carrying sails -1697. 2. *Zool.* Bearing a velum; membranous 1871.

Veliger (vī·lidʒəɹ). 1877. [mod.L., f. L. *veli-* VELUM + *-ger* bearing.] *Zool.* A molluscan larva furnished with a velum or ciliated swimming-membrane.

Veligerous (vǐli·dʒĕrəs), *a.* 1877. [f. as prec.: see -GEROUS.] *Zool.* Of certain larval forms: Bearing or furnished with a velum.

Velitation (velitēᵗ·ʃən). Now *rare.* 1607. [ad. L. *velitatio*, f. *velitari*, f. *velit-*, *veles*; see next.] 1. A slight engagement; a skirmish 1616. 2. *fig.* A wordy skirmish or encounter 1607.

2. All the velitations were peaceably furled up in this result 1702.

Velites (vī·litīz), *sb. pl.* 1600. [L., pl. of *velit-, veles.*] Light-armed soldiers employed as skirmishers in the Roman armies. So †**Ve·litary** *a.* of or pertaining to light-armed troops.

Velleity (velī·iti). 1618. [ad. F. *velléité*, or med.L. *velleitat-, velleitas*, f. *velle* to will, wish; see -ITY.] **1.** The fact or quality of merely willing, wishing, or desiring, without any effort or advance towards action or realization. **2.** With *a* and *pl.* A mere wish, desire, or inclination 1624.

Vellicate (ve·likeᵉit), *v.* Now *rare* or *Obs.* 1604. [f. L. *vellicat-, vellicare*, freq. of *vellere* to pull, pluck.] **1.** *trans.* Of things: To act upon or affect so as to irritate; *esp.* to pluck, nip, pinch, or tear by means of small or sharp points. **b.** Of persons: To tickle or titillate 1755. †**2.** *fig.* To carp at -1686. **3.** *intr.* To twitch; to contract or move convulsively (*rare*) 1670.

1. A hairy, bristly substance, which..will, by pricking and vellicating the coats of stomach and bowels, many times occasion sickness 1783.

Vellication (velikēⁱ·ʃən). Now *rare* or *Obs.* 1623. [ad. L. *vellicatio*, f. *vellicare* to VELLICATE.] **1.** The action or process of pulling or twitching; irritation or stimulation by means of small or sharp points; titillation or tickling. **2.** An instance or occasion of this; also, a twitching or convulsive movement, esp. of a muscle or other part of the body 1665.

‖**Vellon** (velyō·n). 1676. [Sp.; cogn. w. BILLON.] Copper, as used in Spanish coinage: esp. in *real (of) v.*

Vellum (ve·lŏm). [late ME. a. *velym, -um*, OF. *velin* (mod.F. *vélin*), f. *vel* VEAL *sb.* For the change of final *n* to *m* cf. *pilgrim, venom.*] **1.** A fine kind of parchment prepared from the skins of calves (lambs or kids) and used especially for writing, painting, or binding; also, any superior quality of parchment or an imitation of this 1440. **2.** A piece or sheet of this material; a manuscript or testimonial written on vellum. late ME.

attrib. and *Comb.*: **v. cloth**, tracing-cloth; **v. paper**, a paper made to imitate v. Hence **Ve·llumy** *a.* relating to or resembling v.

Velocimeter (velǫsi·mītəɹ). 1842. [f. L. *veloci-, velox* swift + -METER.] An instrument or apparatus (variously constructed) for measuring the velocity of engines, vessels, projectiles, etc.

Velocipede (vīlǫ·sipīd). 1819. [ad. F. *vélocipède*, f. L. *veloci-, velox* swift + *ped-, pes* foot.] **1.** = HOBBY *sb.*[1] 4. *Obs.* exc. *Hist.* **2.** A travelling-machine having wheels turned by the pressure of the foot upon pedals; *esp.* an early form of the bicycle or tricycle; a 'bone-shaker'. Now *rare.* 1849. Hence **Velo·cipedist** [ad. F. *vélocipédiste*], one who rides a v.

Velocity (vīlǫ·siti). 1550. [ad. F. *vélocité* or ad. L. *velocitat-, velocitas*, f. *veloci-, velox* swift, rapid; see -ITY.] **1.** Rapidity or celerity of motion; swiftness, speed. Also, relative rapidity or rate of motion. **2.** Rapidity (absolute or relative) of operation or action; quickness 1674.

1. His Blood flows with its due V. 1704. A v. of upwards of three knots per hour 1880. **2.** Colonel Braithwaite was instructed to anticipate resistance by v. of completion JAS. MILL.

‖**Velours** (vəlūᵊ·ɹ). Also **velour.** 1706. [F., 'velvet'.] **1.** A hatter's velvet pad for smoothing and polishing a hat. **2. a.** A kind of velvet or plush for furniture, carpets, etc. manufactured in Prussia 1858. **b.** A woollen dress-stuff with a velvet pile; also, a material for making hats, usu. with a short soft pile like velvet 1884.

‖**Velum** (vī·lŏm). *Pl.* **vela** (vī·lă). 1771. [L., 'sail, curtain'.] **1.** *Anat.* **a.** The soft palate; the membranous septum extending backwards from the hard palate. **b.** One or other of two membranes extending from the vermiform process of the brain 1840. **c.** A triangular fold of the pia mater lying between the third ventricle and the fornix of the brain 1845. **d.** A small triangular space in the inferior region of the bladder 1835. **2.** *Zool.* A membrane or membranous integument, esp. one occurring in molluscs, medusæ, or lower forms of animal life 1826. **3.** *Bot.* A membranous structure or covering in certain fungi 1832.

Velure (vīliūᵊ·ɹ). 1587. [ad. OF. *velour*; see VELOURS.] †**1.** Velvet -1748. **2.** = VELOURS 1. 1880. **3.** A fabric of linen, silk, or jute resembling velvet.

Velu·tinous, *a.* 1826. [f. mod.L. *velutinus*, f. med.L. *velutum* velvet.] *Ent.* and *Bot.* Having a surface resembling velvet; velvety.

Ve·lveret. Now *rare.* 1769. [irreg. f. next.] A variety of fustian with a velvet surface.

Velvet (ve·lvėt). ME. [ad. med.L. *velvetum (-ettum)*, ult. f. L. *villus* shaggy hair.] **I. 1.** A textile fabric of silk having a short, dense, and smooth piled surface; a kind or variety of this. **b.** A piece of this material (*rare*). late ME. **2.** *transf.* The soft downy skin which covers a deer's horn while in the growing stage. late ME. **3.** A surface, substance, etc. comparable to velvet in respect of softness or general appearance 1597. **4.** Profit, gain, winnings 1901.

1. Phr. *On v.*, in a position of ease or advantage; in an advantageous or prosperous condition. *colloq.*

II. *attrib.* **a.** In the sense 'made of v.', as *v. bag, gown*, or 'covered with v.', as *v. cushion* ME. **b.** In the sense 'smooth or soft like v., velvety', as *v. down, hand, leaf.* Also with names of colours, esp. *v. black.* 1588.

Comb.: **v.-brush**, a velvet-covered brush used to remove dust, etc. from garments made of v.; **-cloth**, a plain cloth with a gloss, used in eccl. embroidery, and as a material for womens' jackets; **-cork**, the best kind of cork bark, which is of a reddish colour; **-pile** (a carpet or cloth) having a pile like that of v.

b. In names of plants or animals, as **v.-bean**, an annual climbing plant (*Mucuna utilis*) bearing velvety pods; **v. crab**, a species of swimming crab (*Portunus puber*); **-dock**, common mullein; **-duck**, a species of scoter (*Œdemia fusca*); **-grass**, *Holcus lanatus*; †**v. runner**, the water-rail; **v. scoter** = *velvet-duck*; **v. wheat**, a variety of white wheat with downy ears. Hence **Ve·lveted** *a.*, covered with or dressed in v. **Ve·lveting**, velvet as a commercial fabric, esp. *pl.* v. goods.

Velveteen (velvėtī·n, *attrib.* ve·lvėtīn). 1776. [f. VELVET *sb.*] **1.** A fabric having the appearance and surface of velvet, but made from cotton in place of silk. **b.** *attrib.* Made of this material 1824. **2.** *pl.* **a.** Trousers or knickerbockers made of v. 1863. **b.** *transf.* A gamekeeper (as usu. wearing velveteen clothes) 1857.

†**Velvet head.** 1576. [f. VELVET 2.] The head of a deer while the horns are still covered with velvet -1674.

Velvet-leaf. 1707. [f. VELVET II. *b.*] **1.** The tropical shrub *Cissampelos Pareira*, the root and bark of which are employed medicinally. **2.** The tree-mallow, *Lavatera arborea*, or a leaf of this 1728.

Velvety (ve·lvėti), *a.* 1752. [f. VELVET.] **1.** Having the smooth and soft appearance or feel of velvet. **b.** Applied to colours 1819. **2.** Characteristic of velvet; similar to that of velvet 1846. **3.** *fig.* Unusually or attractively smooth, soft, or gentle 1861.

1. b. The v. brown of a stag's throat 1883. **3.** The other's v. manner made him chafe and fret 1861.

‖**Vena** (vī·nă). *Pl.* **venæ** (vī·nī). late ME. [L.] A vein. (Used only in conjunction with Latin adjs. or genitives.)

The abdominal branches of the v. portæ 1822. The aortic and v. cava pressures 1899.

Venal (vī·năl), *a.*[1] 1652. [ad. L. *venalis*, f. *venum* that which is sold or for sale.] **1.** Of things: **a.** Exposed or offered for sale, that may be bought, as an ordinary article of merchandise. Also, associated or connected with ordinary sale or purchase. Now *arch.* 1662. **b.** Of offices, privileges, etc.: Capable of being acquired by purchase, instead of being conferred on grounds of merit or regarded as above bargaining for 1675. **c.** Of support, favour, etc.: That may be obtained for a price 1652. **2.** Of persons: Capable of being bought over; of an unprincipled and hireling character 1670. **3.** Subject to mercenary or corrupt influences 1718.

1. a. The figs..might be v. at the nearest stall 1888. **b.** The V. Indulgences and pardons of the Church of Rome 1839. **c.** You may command a v. vote *Junius Lett.* **2.** Rome was as v. under the popes as Jugurtha found her under the Republic FROUDE. **3.** Corruption on her v. throne THOMSON.

Venal (vī·năl), *a.*[2] Now *rare* or *Obs.* 1615. [f. L. *vena* VEIN *sb.* + -AL.] **1.** Of blood: Contained in the veins. **2.** Of, connected with, forming, or of the nature of a vein or veins 1661.

Venality (vīnæ·liti). 1611. [ad. F. *vénalité*, or late L. *venalitas* f. L. *venalis* VENAL *a.*[1]] **1.** The quality or fact of being for sale (*rare*). **2.** The quality of being venal; readiness to give support or favour in return for profit or reward; prostitution of talents or principles for mercenary considerations 1683.

Venatic (vīnæ·tik), *a.* 1656. [ad. L. *venaticus*, f. *venari* to hunt.] Of, pertaining to, employed in, or devoted to hunting.

I adore, with a sort of v. worship, both a fox and a hound 1889. So **Vena·tical** *a.*, **-ally** *adv.*

Vena·tion [1]. Now *rare* or *Obs.* late ME. [ad. L. *venatio*, f. *venari* to hunt.] The action or occupation of hunting wild animals.

Venation [2] (vinēⁱ·ʃən). 1830. [f. L. *vena* VEIN *sb.*] *Bot.* and *Ent.* The arrangement or structure of the veins in the leaves of plants or the wings of insects.

Venatorial (venătōᵊ·riăl), *a.* 1830. [f. L. *venatorius* + -AL.] **1.** Connected with hunting. **2.** Given to hunting; addicted to the chase 1881. So **Ve·natory** *a.*

Vend, *sb.* 1618. [f. next.] **1.** Sale; opportunity of selling. **2.** *spec.* Sale of coals from a colliery; the total amount sold during a certain period 1708.

Vend (vend), *v.* 1622. [ad. F. *vendre* or L. *vendere* to sell.] **1.** *intr.* To be disposed of by sale; to find a market or purchaser. **2.** *trans.* To sell; to dispose of by sale; to trade in as a seller 1651. **3.** *fig.* To give utterance to, to put forward, advance (an opinion, etc.) 1657.

1. No Books v. so nimbly, as those that are sold (by Stealth as it were) and want Imprimaturs 1689. **2.** The right to v. books and newspapers 1879. **3.** He is not free to v. in his pulpit the extravagances of an eccentric individualism 1907. Hence **Ve·ndable** *a.* (now *rare*) = VENDIBLE *a.* late ME.

Vendace (ve·ndės). 1769. [app. ad. OF. *vendese, vendoise* (mod.F. *vandoise*) dace.] **a.** A species of small freshwater fish (*Coregonus vandesius*) belonging to the same genus as the pollan, found in the lake of Lochmaben in Scotland. **b.** A closely-allied species (*C. gracilior*) found in Derwentwater.

Vendean (vendī·ăn), *sb.* and *a.* 1796. [ad. F. *vendéen*, f. F. *Vendée*, a maritime department in western France.] **A.** *sb.* An inhabitant of La Vendée, esp. one who took part in the insurrection of 1793 against the Republic. **B.** *adj.* Of or pertaining to La Vendée, esp. in connexion with that insurrection 1796.

Vendee (vendī·). 1547. [f. VEND *v.* + -EE.] The person to whom a thing is sold; the purchaser.

Vender (ve·ndəɹ). 1596. [f. VEND *v.* + -ER [1].] One who sells; a seller; occas., a street-seller.

‖**Vendetta** (vende·tă). 1855. [It. :—L. *vindicta* vengeance.] **1.** A family blood-feud, usu. of a hereditary character, as customary among the Corsicans. **2.** A similar blood-feud in other communities 1861.

Vendible (ve·ndĭb'l), *a.* and *sb.* late ME. [ad. L. *vendibilis*, f. *vendere* to sell.] **A.** *adj.* **1.** Capable of being vended or sold; that may be disposed of by sale; saleable, marketable. **b.** = VENAL *a.*[1] 1 b, c. 1579. †**c.** Of persons: = VENAL *a.*[1] 2. -1668. †**2.** Offered for sale; that may be bought -1756. †**3.** *fig.* Current, accepted, acceptable -1678.

1. They cannot therefore bee v. because they are not valuable 1633. **2.** Houses, like our Tauernes. Where is v. Wine. 1634.

B. *sb.* A thing admitting of being sold or offered for sale 1681. Hence **Ve·ndibleness. Ve·ndibly** *adv.*

†**Ve·nditate**, *v.* 1600. [f. L. *venditat-, venditare*, frequent. of *vendere* to sell.] *refl.* and *trans.* To set out as if for sale; to exhibit ostentatiously -1678. So †**Vendita·tion**, the action of putting forward or displaying in a favourable or ostentatious manner -1854.

Vendition (vendi·ʃən). 1542. [ad. L. *venditio*, f. *vendere* to sell.] The action of selling; disposal or transfer by sale.

Vendor (ve·ndǫ̆ɪ). 1594. [a. late AF., earlier *vendour* (F. *vendeur*), f. *vendere* VEND *v.*] orig. *Law.* One who disposes of a thing by sale; a seller.

Vendue (vendiū·). *U.S.* and *W. Indies.* 1686. [a. Du. *vendu*, ad. early mod.F. (now dial.) *vendue* sale, f. *vendre* to sell.] A public sale; an auction: freq. in phr. *at v., by v.*

Veneer (vǝ-, vǐnīǝ·ɪ), *sb.* 1702. [ad. G. *furni(er), fourni(e)r*; see next.] **1.** One of the thin slices or slips of fine or fancy wood, or other suitable material, used in veneering. **2.** Material prepared for use in veneering, or applied to a surface by this or some similar process 1750. **3.** *fig.* A merely outward show or appearance *of* some good quality 1868. **4.** One or other of many species of moths of the genus *Crambus* or family *Crambidæ*; a grass-moth 1819.

3. Heartfelt courtesy..was replaced by a superficial v. of forced politeness 1882.

Veneer (vǝ-, vǐnīǝ·ɪ), *v.* 1728. [Later form of FINEER *v.*[1], ad. G. *furni(e)ren*, ad. F. *fournir* FURNISH *v.*] **1.** *trans.* To apply or fix as veneering. **2.** To cover or face with veneer 1742. **b.** *fig.* To invest with a merely external or specious appearance of some commendable or attractive quality. Usu. const. *with.* 1847.

2. b. And one the Master, as a rogue in grain Veneer'd with sanctimonious theory TENNYSON.

Venee·ring, *vbl. sb.* 1706. [Later f. *faneering, fineering*, ad. G. *furni(e)rung, fourni(e)rung*; see prec.] **1.** The process of applying thin flat plates or slips of fine wood (or other suitable material) to cabinet-work or similar articles; also, the result obtained by this process. Often *fig.* **2.** Wood or other material in the form of veneer; a facing of this 1789.

†**Vene·fic,** *a.* 1646. [ad. L. *veneficus*, f. *venenum* poison; see -FIC.] Practising, or dealing in, poisoning; acting by poison; having poisonous effects -1702. So †**Vene·fical** *a.* venefic; practising or associated with malignant sorcery or witchcraft 1584-1716.

†**Ve·nefice.** late ME. [ad. L. *veneficium*, f. *veneficus.*] The practice of employing poison or magical potions; the exercise of sorcery by such means -1652. Hence †**Venefi·cial, Venefi·cious** (now *rare*) *adjs.* = VENEFICAL *a.*

Venenose (ve·nĕnōᵘs), *a.* Now *rare.* 1673. [ad. late L. *venenosus*, f. *venenum* poison; see -OSE.] Poisonous, venomous. So **Vene·nous** *a.* (now *rare*). late ME. †**Veneno·sity,** poisonous quality or property 1539.

Venerable (ve·nĕrăb'l), *a.* and *sb.* late ME. [ad. L. *venerabilis*, f. *venerari* to venerate.] **1.** Of persons: Worthy of being venerated, revered, or highly respected and esteemed, on account of character or position. **a.** As an epithet of ecclesiastics (or ecclesiastical bodies), now *spec.* of archdeacons or, in the R. C. Church, of those who have attained the first degree of canonization. (Abbreviated *Ven.*) late ME. **b.** *gen.* (*rare*) 1641. **2.** Commanding veneration or respect in virtue of years and high personal qualities 1480. **b.** Applied to personal features or attributes of these 1726. **3.** Of things: **a.** Worthy of religious reverence 1504. **b.** Worthy of veneration or deep respect on account of noble qualities or associations 1601. **c.** Impressive, august 1615. **4.** Worthy of veneration or respect on account of age or antiquity 1610. **b.** Ancient, antique, old 1792. †**5.** Reverent, reverential -1710.

1. The Archbishop of Arles, v. for his years and his virtues 1849. **a.** Peter the V., of Cluny 1834. **2.** A white beard which made him look v. 1862. **3. b.** Holy Writers, and such whose names are v. unto all posterity SIR T. BROWNE. **4.** His looks adorn'd the v. place GOLDSM. **b.** Those muskets cased with v. rust 1792. Hence **Venerabi·lity. Ve·nerableness. Ve·nerably** *adv.*

Venerate (ve·nĕreɪt), *v.* 1623. [ad. L. *venerat-, venerari* (also *venerare*) to reverence, worship.] **1.** *trans.* To regard with feelings of respect and reverence; to look upon as something exalted, hallowed, or sacred; to reverence or revere. **2.** To pay honour to (something) by an act of reverence 1844.

1. Who v. themselves, the world despise YOUNG. The ruined chapels are still venerated 1851. **2.** Thrice he venerated the sacred remains 1844. So **Ve·nerator,** one who venerates; a reverencer of something.

Veneration (venĕrēɪ·ʃǝn). late ME. [ad. L. *veneration-, veneratio*, f. *venerari* to venerate.] **1.** A feeling of deep respect and reverence directed towards some person or thing. **2.** The action or fact of showing respect and reverence; the action or practice of venerating 1526. **3.** The fact or condition of being venerated 1625.

1. She expressed a great v. for the liturgy of the Church of England 1759. Phr. *To have* or *hold in v.* **2.** The v. paid to Mary in the early Church 1852. **3.** Princes are like to Heauenly Bodies..which haue much V., but no Rest BACON.

Venereal (vǐnīǝ·rĭăl), *a.* and *sb.* late ME. [f. L. *venereus*, f. *Vener-, Venus* VENUS.] **1.** Of or pertaining to, associated or connected with sexual desire or intercourse. **2.** Resulting from or communicated by sexual intercourse with an infected person; symptomatic of or associated with a disease so caused 1658. **b.** Of persons: Infected with or suffering from venereal disease 1683. **c.** *ellipt.* as *sb.* Venereal disease 1843. †**3.** Of persons: Under the influence of Venus; addicted to venery or lust -1728.

1. Such is hunger and thirst, and the venereall affect, vsually called lust 1610. **2.** A lusty robust Souldier dangerously infected with the V. Disease 1667.

†**Vene·rean,** *a.* (and *sb.*). 1550. [f. as prec. + -AN.] **1.** Connected or associated with; relating or pertaining to Venus or her service -1685. **2.** Of or pertaining to sexual desire or intercourse -1700. **3.** Addicted to venereal pleasures. Also as *sb.*, a person of this character. -1631.

†**Vene·reous,** *a.* 1509. [f. L. *venereus* + -OUS.] **1.** Addicted to or desirous of sexual enjoyment; libidinous, lustful -1713. **2.** = VENEREAL *a.* 1. -1795. **3.** Exciting or stimulating sexual desire -1694.

Ve·nerer. *arch.* 1845. [f. VENERY[1].] A huntsman.

†**Ve·nerous,** *a.* 1562. [f. L. *Vener-, Venus* see -OUS.] **1.** = VENEREAL *a.* 1. -1651. **2.** = VENEREOUS *a.* 3. -1651.

Venery[1] (ve·nĕri). Now *arch.* ME. [a. OF. *venerie*, f. *vener*:—L. *venari* to hunt; see -ERY.] **1.** The practice or sport of hunting beasts of game; the chase. †**2.** Wild animals hunted as game -1630.

1. Phr. *Beasts, game, hounds of v.*

Venery[2] (ve·nĕri). 1497. [f. L. *Vener-*, VENUS + -Y[3].] **1.** The practice or pursuit of sexual pleasure; indulgence of sexual desire *arch.* †**2.** *fig.* A source of great enjoyment -1625.

Venesection (venǐse·kʃǝn). 1661. [ad. med. or mod.L. *venæ sectio* cutting of a vein.] *Med.* **1.** The operation of cutting or opening a vein; phlebotomy; the practice of this as a medical remedy. **2.** An instance of this 1834. Hence **Ve·nesect** *v. intr.* to practise v.

Venetian (vǐnī·ʃăn, vǝ-), *sb.* and *a.* late ME. [a. OF. *Venicien* (F. *Vénitien*) or ad. med. L. *Venetianus*, f. *Venetia* VENICE.] **A.** *sb.* **1.** A native or inhabitant of Venice. †**2.** *pl.* Hose or breeches of a particular fashion originally introduced from Venice -1612. †**3.** A sequin of Venice, as current in India, etc. -1835. **4.** A closely-woven cloth having a fine twilled surface, used as a suiting or dress material 1710. **5.** *ellipt.* A Venetian blind 1816. **B.** *adj.* **1.** Of or pertaining to Venice 1554. **2.** In special collocations, denoting things characteristic of Venice, esp. articles produced there, or others made in imitation of these 1548.

1. *V. School*, (*a*) a school of painting, distinguished by its mastery of colouring, which originated in the 15th c. and reached its climax in the 16th; (*b*) a school of Italian architecture originating in the early part of the 16th c. **2. V. blind,** a window blind composed of narrow horizontal slats so fixed on strong tapes as to admit of ready adjustment for the exclusion or admission of light and air. **V. carpet,** a common make of carpet, usu. striped, in which the warp alone is shown. **V. chalk,** a white compact talc or steatite, used for marking on cloth. **V. door,** a door having side lights on each side for lighting an entrance hall. **V. glass,** Venice glass. †**V. hose,** = sense A. 2. **V. mast,** a tall pole ornamented with spiral bands of colour, used in the decoration of streets or open spaces on special occasions. **V. pearl,** a solid artificial pearl. **V. point,** a variety of point-lace. **V. sumach,** the southern European shrub *Rhus Cotinus.* **V. window,** a window in three separate apertures, the two side ones being narrow, and separated from the centre by timber only.

Venge (vendʒ), *v.* Now *arch.* ME. [ad. OF. *vengier, venger*:—L. *vindicare* VINDICATE *v.*] = AVENGE *v.* So **Ve·nger,** an avenger (now *poet.* or *rhet.*) †**Ve·ngeress.**

Vengeable, *a. Obs.* or *dial.* late ME. [a. AF., f. *venger* VENGE *v.*] **1.** Inclined or ready to take vengeance or inflict retaliative injury. **2.** Characterized by or arising from vengeance or revenge; cruel, dreadful. late ME. **3.** As an intensive: Very great, severe, intense, etc. 1532. Hence **Ve·ngeably** *adv.* late ME.

Vengeance (ve·ndʒăns), *sb.* (and *adv.*). ME. [a. AF. *venia(u)nce, veng(e)a(u)nce*, = (O)F. *vengeance*, f. *venger* VENGE *v.*] **1.** The act of avenging oneself or another; retributive infliction of injury or punishment. **2.** With *a* and *pl.* An act or instance of retributive or vindictive punishment ME. **b.** In imprecations, usu. with *on. Obs.* or *arch.* 1500. †**3.** Used to strengthen interrogations -1828. †**b.** As *adv.* Extremely, intensely -1711.

1. Thou God to whom vengeaunce belongeth, shewe thy self COVERDALE *Ps.* xciii. 1. Where was thine arm, O V.! CAMPBELL. Phr. *To take v.* **2.** Taking ..a cruel v. on these deluded wretches BURKE. **b.** A veng'ance on't, there 'tis SHAKS.

Phr. *With a v.*: †**a.** With a curse or malediction. **b.** As an intensive: With great force or violence; in an extreme degree; to an unusual extent.

Vengeful (ve·ndʒfŭl), *a.* 1586. [f. VENGE *v.*, after *revengeful.*] **1.** Harbouring revenge; seeking vengeance; vindictive 1599. **b.** Inflicting vengeance; serving as an instrument of vengeance. Said of a weapon, the hand or arm, etc. 1586. **2.** Of actions or feelings: Characterized or prompted by revengeful motives; arising from a desire for vengeance 1635.

1. Ulysses is..subtle, v., cunning 1873. **b.** So could he bid the v. fire fall from heaven 1869. **2.** Pond'ring v. Wars PRIOR. Hence **Ve·ngeful·ly** *adv.*, **-ness.**

Venial (vī·niăl), *a.* and *sb.* ME. [a. OF., (mod.F. *véniel*), or ad. L. *venialis*, f. *venia* forgiveness, pardon.] **A.** *adj.* **1.** Worthy or admitting of pardon, forgiveness, or remission; not grave or heinous; pardonable, light: **a.** Of sin; *spec.* in *Theol.* as opp. to *deadly* or *mortal.* **b.** Of crimes, offences. etc. 1604. **2.** Of an error or fault: That may be excused or overlooked; light, unimportant, trivial 1581. †**3.** Permissible; blameless (*rare*) -1725.

1. **a.** In þis wise skippith v. in to dedly synne CHAUCER. **b.** If they do nothing, 'tis a Veniall slip SHAKS. **2.** If a boy has committed some..quite v. fault 1876. **3.** Where God..With Man..us'd To sit indulgent,.. permitting him the while V. discourse unblam'd MILT.

†**B.** *sb.* A venial sin or offence; a light fault or error -1671. Hence **Venia·lity,** the property or quality of being v.; a matter of favour or grace. **Ve·nially** *adv.*

Venice (ve·nis). 1506. [a. F. *Venise*:—L. *Venetia*; see def.] The name of a city (the capital of the province of the same name) in the north-east of Italy, used attrib. to designate various articles made there or having some connexion with the locality.

V. crown, (*Her.*) the crown, or cap of state, worn by the Doge of V. **V. glass** (*a*) a very fine and delicate kind of glass, orig. manufactured at Murano, near V.; (*b*) an article made of this, esp. a drinking vessel or vial; (*c*) a Venetian mirror. **V. talc,** steatite or soap-stone. **V. treacle** (now *arch.*), in old pharmacy, an electuary composed of many ingredients and supposed to possess universal alexipharmic and preservative properties.

‖**Venire** (vǐnəɪǝ·ri). 1665. [ellipt. for next.] *Law.* = next 1.

V. de novo = next 1 b. *V. man* (*U.S.*) one summoned to serve on a jury under a writ of *V. facias*, a juryman.

‖**Venire facias** (vǐnəɪǝ·ri fēɪ·ʃiæs). 1444. [L., lit. 'make or cause to come'.] *Law.* **1.** A former judicial writ directed to a sheriff requiring him to summon a jury to try a cause or causes at issue between parties. *Obs.* or *Hist.* **b.** *Venire facias de novo*, an order for a new trial of a cause, upon the same record, owing to some defect or irregularity in the first trial 1797. †**2.** A writ issued against a person indicted of a misdemeanour, summoning him to appear before the court -1769.

Venison (ve·nz'n, ve·niz'n). ME. [a. AF. and OF. (mod.F. *venaison*):—L. *venationem* hunting, f. *venari* to hunt. The pronunc. (ve·nz'n) is usual in England, (ve·niz'n) in U.S.] **1.** The flesh of an animal killed in the chase or by hunting and used as food; formerly applied to the flesh of the deer, boar, hare, or other game animal, now almost entirely restricted to the flesh of various species of deer. **2.** Any beast of chase or other wild animal, esp. of the deer kind, killed by hunting. Now *arch.* ME. **b.** *collect.* Now *arch.* ME.

‖**Venite** (vīnəi·tĭ). ME. [L.; 2nd pers. pl. imp. of *venire* to come.] The ninety-fifth psalm (beginning *Venite, exultemus Domino* 'O come, let us sing unto the Lord') used as a canticle at Matins or Morning Prayer; the invitatory psalm; also, a musical setting of this.

Venom (ve·nəm), *sb.* and *a.* ME. [orig. *venym*, a. AF. and OF. *venim*, var. of *venin* :—L. *venenum* poison, potion, dye, etc. For the change of final *n* to *m* cf. *pilgrim, vellum.*] **A.** *sb.* **1.** The poisonous fluid normally secreted by certain snakes and other animals and used by them in attacking living creatures. **2.** Poison, esp. as administered to or drunk by a person; any poisonous or noxious substance, preparation, or property; a morbid secretion or virus. Now *rare.* ME. **3.** *fig.* Something comparable to or having the effects of poison; any baneful, malign, or noxious influence or quality; bitter or virulent feeling, language, etc. ME. **4.** With *a* and *pl.* A poison; a particular kind of poison or virus. late ME.

1. What the..hurtfull Worm with canker'd v. bites MILT. **2.** Anoynted let me be with deadly Venome SHAKS. **3.** The veneme of this Book wrought upon the hearts of men CLARENDON. So **Ve·nom** *v.* (*Obs.* or *arch.*) *trans.* = ENVENOM *v.*

Venomous (ve·nəməs), *a.* ME. [a. AF. *venimus* = OF. (and mod.F.) *venimeux*, f. *venim* VENOM *sb.*, after L. *venenosus.*] †**1.** *fig.* Morally or spiritually hurtful; pernicious -1610. **2.** Containing, consisting or full of, infected with venom; destructive of, harmful or injurious to life on this account ME. †**b.** Of a wound, etc.: Envenomed -1774. †**c.** Harmful or injurious *to* something -1691. **3.** Of animals, *esp.* snakes, or their parts: Secreting venom; having the power or property of communicating venom by means of bites or stings; inflicting or capable of inflicting poisonous wounds in this way ME. **4.** *fig.* Having the virulence of venom; rancorous, spiteful, malignant; embittered, envenomed ME. †**5.** Treated with venom or poison -1631. **6.** Of, pertaining to, or of the nature of venom. late ME.

1. That venemous Pelagian Heresie 1610. **2.** Of the venemous apples wherwith the Canibales inuenime theyr arrowes 1555. **c.** *Cor.* IV. i. 23. **3.** The poisonous Snakes are divided into two groups—the Viperiform Snakes and the V. Colubrines 1880. **4.** The Venemous Mallice of my swelling heart SHAKS. The doctor seemed to me a v. little creature 1911. **6.** The glands that serve to fabricate this v. fluid GOLDSM. Hence **Ve·nomous-ly** *adv.*, **-ness.**

Venose (vī·nōᵘs), *a.* 1661. [ad. L. *venosus*, f. *vena* VEIN *sb.*] Venous; *spec.* in *Bot.* and *Ent.* Hence **Veno·sity** *Path.*, the state of being venous; *spec.* of the blood.

Venous (vī·nəs), *a.* 1626. [ad. L. *venosus*, or f. L. *vena* + -OUS.] **1.** Filled with, full of, or having veins; veined; veiny. **2.** *Anat.* and *Phys.* Of, pertaining to, or of the nature of a blood-vein or veins; having the form or function of a vein 1681. **b.** Of blood: Contained in the veins; characterized by a dusky or blackish red colour due to loss of oxygen. (Opp. to *arterial.*) 1728. **c.** Consisting or composed of veins 1826. **3.** Of, pertaining to, or characteristic of vein-blood 1845.

1. If the veins diverge from the midrib towards the margin, ramifying as they proceed, such a leaf has been called a v. or reticulated leaf 1832. **2. c.** *V. system*, the aggregate of veins by which the blood is conveyed from the various parts of the body to the heart. Hence **Ve·nous-ly** *adv.*, **-ness.**

Vent (vent), *sb.*¹ late ME. [Variant of FENT *sb.*] An opening or slit in a garment; now *spec.* the slit in the back of a coat.

Vent (vent), *sb.*² 1508. [Partly a. F. :—L. *ventus* wind; partly ad. F. *évent* (OF. *esvent*), vbl. sb. from *éventer.*] **I. 1.** The action of emitting or discharging; emission or discharge *of* something; utterance *of* words (*rare*). **2.** The action, usu. on the part of something confined or pent up in a comparatively small space, of escaping or passing out; means, power, or opportunity to do this; issue, outlet 1558. **b.** The windage of a firearm or gun 1644. **3.** *fig.* Means of outlet afforded to or obtained by a feeling, faculty, activity, etc.; expression or utterance, or the relief afforded by these 1603. **4.** With *a*: An opportunity or occasion of escaping or issuing from a receptacle; a discharge or evacuation 1644. **5.** Something which serves as an outlet for an emotion, energy, etc. 1667.

1. Phr. †*To make v. of*, to speak or talk of; Thou didst make tollerable v. of thy trauell SHAKS. **2.** Phr. *To find, get, have, make, want v.*; The smoke found ample v. through the holes TYNDALL. *To give v.*, (*a*) to cause or allow to issue or flow out; (*b*) *fig.* to give outlet, expression, or utterance (to an emotion, faculty, etc.); to relieve in this way. †*To take v.*, (*a*) of news, etc., to become known, to be divulged or let out; (*b*) of a mine or powder, to explode imperfectly; to lose explosive power. **3.** Passion found v. in words 1880. **4.** *fig.* For, though in whispers speaking, the full heart Will find a v. WORDSW. **5.** Laughter is a v. of any sudden joy 1713.

II. 1. †**a.** An opening by which blood issues from the body -1606. **b.** The anus, anal or excretory opening of (†persons or) animals, esp. of certain non-mammalians, as birds, fishes, and reptiles 1587. **2.** An aperture or opening occurring or made in something and serving as an outlet for air, liquid, or other matter; a passage or hole by which matter is carried off or discharged from the interior of something; a vent-hole 1570. **b.** *spec.* The funnel or pipe of a volcano 1604. **3.** An opening, aperture, or hole; occas., one by which air, etc. enters or is admitted 1593. **b.** The hole or channel in the breech of a cannon or firearm through which fire is communicated to the charge; the touch-hole; the adjustable part of a gun containing this, a vent-piece 1667. **4.** Any outlet or place of issue; a passage, exit, or way out. Chiefly *fig.* 1602.

1. a. *Ant. & Cl.* V. ii. 353. **2. b.** A 'solfatara' or v. emitting only gaseous discharges 1882. **3.** Through little vents and crannies of the place The wind wars with his torch to make him stay SHAKS. **4.** Winds for ages pent In earth's dark womb have found at last a v. COWPER.

III. Of an otter: The action of coming to the surface of the water in order to breathe; an instance or occasion of this 1653.

attrib. and *Comb.*, as *v.-cock, -pipe*; **v. feather**, one of the feathers covering or surrounding a bird's v.; **v.-piece** *Gunnery*, (*a*) a plug of steel or wrought iron containing the v.; (*b*) the block which closes the rear of the bore in a breech-loader.

Vent, *sb.*³ *Obs.* exc. *arch.* 1545. [a. F. *vente* :—pop. L. **vendita*, from L. *venditus*, *vendere* to sell. In sense 3 directly ad. Sp. *venta.*] **1.** The fact of commodities being disposed of by sale or of finding purchasers. **2.** The fact, on the part of persons, of disposing of goods by sale; opportunity for selling; market or outlet for commodities 1548. †**3.** An inn or tavern; a baiting or posting house -1625.

1. Like fish that could not find v. in London H. WALPOLE. **2.** If husbandmen..have a ready v. for their commodities HUME.

Vent (vent), *v.*¹ late ME. [f. VENT *sb.*², or ad. F. *éventer.*] **I.** *trans.* †**1.** To provide (a liquor cask, etc.) with a vent or outlet for gas or vapour -1703. **b.** *fig.* To relieve or unburden (one's heart or soul) in respect of feelings or emotions. Also *refl.* 1626. †**2.** To discharge, eject, cast or pour out (liquid, smoke, etc.); to carry off or away; to drain in this way. Also with advs. -1793. †**b.** Of persons, animals, or their organs: To cast out, expel, or discharge, esp. by natural evacuation -1846. **3.** *fig.* To give vent to (an emotion, feeling, a sigh, groan); to give free course or expression to; to make manifest or known 1596. **b.** To let loose, pour out, wreak (one's anger, spleen, etc.) *on* or *upon* a person or thing 1697. **4.** *fig.* To give out or forth, publish or spread abroad, by or as by utterance; to utter (a word, expression, etc.). Now *rare* or *arch.* 1602. **5.** *refl.* Of a thing: To discharge itself; to find issue or exit; *esp.* of an emotion, faculty, quality, etc.: to express or show itself *in* something 1650. **6.** To supply (a gun) with a vent or vent-piece 1828.

1. b. To v. an Heart overflowing with Sense of Success STEELE. **3.** I..v. a heaving sigh MARSTON. I must v. my griefes, or heart will burst MARSTON. **b.** To v. their spleen on the first idle coxcomb they can find 1816. **5.** The Presidency v. the most bitter complaints 1817. **6.** The coffee houses were the chief organs through which the public opinion of the metropolis vented itself MACAULAY.

II. *intr.* **1.** Of an exhalation, liquid, smoke, etc.: To find or make an outlet or way of escape from a confined space; to come, flow, pass, or pour *out* or *away* by a vent or opening. Now *rare.* 1540. †**2.** Of a bottle, confined space, etc.: To have or obtain an outlet by which the contained matter can escape -1655.

1. New wine..by venting bursteth the bottle 1604.

III. †**1.** *intr.* Of an animal: To snuff up the air, esp. in order to pick up the scent of something -1660. †**2.** = SCENT *v.* **1.** -1735. **3.** Of an otter, or beaver: To rise to the surface in order to breathe 1590.

2. The Fox,..if he vents any thing which causes fear, returns to ground again 1660. Hence **Ve·nter**², one who gives vent to a statement, doctrine, etc., esp. of an erroneous, malicious, or objectionable nature.

Vent, *v.*² Now *dial.* 1478. [f. F. *vente* VENT *sb.*³] **1.** *trans.* To sell or vend (commodities or goods); to dispose of by sale. †**2.** *intr.* Of goods: To have or find sale; to sell, go off (well or ill) -1670.

‖**Venta** (ve·ntă). 1610. [Sp. :—L. *vendita*; see VENT *sb.*³] A Spanish hostelry or wayside inn.

Ventage (ve·ntėdʒ). 1602. [f. VENT *sb.*² + -AGE.] **1.** One of the series of apertures or holes in the length of a wind instrument for controlling the notes; a finger-hole. (In mod. use, perh. after Shakespeare.) **2.** An air-hole or vent-hole 1623.

Ventail (ve·ntēˡl). Now *Hist.* ME. [a. OF. *ventaille* (mod.F. *ventail*), f. *vent* wind.] †**1.** A piece of armour protecting the neck, upon which the helmet fitted; a neck-piece -1450. **2.** The lower movable part of the front of a helmet, as distinct from the vizor; latterly, the whole movable part including the vizor. late ME.

2. Through whose bright ventayle..His manly face ..lookt foorth SPENSER.

Venter¹ (ve·ntəɹ). 1544. [a. AF. *ventre*, *venter*, or L. *venter* paunch, womb.] **I. 1.** One or other of two or more wives who are sources of offspring to the same person; orig. (and in later use chiefly) *Law.* **2.** The womb as the source of one's birth or origin; hence *transf.*, a mother in relation to her children 1579.

1. To his Sons by another V...he gave Money-portions 1665. **2.** My Sister, by one V. 1630.

II. †**1.** In man, quadrupeds, etc.: One or other of the three chief cavities containing viscera, consisting of the abdomen, thorax, and head. Usu. in pl. or qualified -1771. **2.** †**a.** One of the four stomachs in ruminants -1706. **b.** *Anat.* The abdomen, the belly 1706. **c.** That part in lower forms of animal life corresponding in function or position to the belly of mammals 1790. **3.** *Anat.* †**a.** The belly or body of a muscle, into which are inserted arteries and nerves -1728. **b.** The belly or hollowed surface of a bone 1851.

Ve·nt-hole. Also **venthole, vent hole.** 1577. [f. VENT *sb.*² + HOLE *sb.*] **1.** A hole or opening for the admission or passage of air, light, etc. **2.** A hole or opening in a furnace, etc., for the escape of smoke and gases or the admission of fresh air 1612. **b.** Any hole by which an enclosed space communicates with the outside air 1750. **3.** *spec.* An air-hole in a cask; a vent 1669.

Ventiduct (ve·ntidʊkt). 1615. [f. L. *venti-*, *ventus* wind + *ductus* a conducting.] A pipe or passage serving to bring cool or fresh air into an apartment or place, esp. in Italy and other warm climates. **b.** A conduit for the passage of wind, air, or steam 1685.

Ventil (ve·ntil). 1876. [a. G., ad. med.L. *ventile* sluice, shutter, f. *ventus* wind.] *Mus.* One or other of the valves or shutters which control the wind-supply of the various groups of stops in an organ.

Ventilate (ve·ntilēˡt), *v.* 1527. [f. L. *ventilat-*, *ventilare* to brandish, fan, f. *ventus* wind.] **I. 1.** To fan or winnow (corn, etc.) 1609. †**2.** To increase (a fire or flame) by blowing or fanning -1742. †**3.** To put or set (air) in motion; to move or agitate; to renew or freshen in this way -1775. **4. a.** To expose (blood) to the chemical action of the air; to aerate, oxygenate 1668. **b.** To expose (substances, etc.) to fresh air so as to keep in or restore to good condition 1755. **5.** Of air: To blow upon, to pass over or circulate through, so as to purify or freshen 1695. **6.** To supply (a room, building, mine, etc.) with fresh air in place of that which is vitiated, exhausted, or stagnant; to produce a free current of air in (some enclosed space) so as to maintain a fresh supply 1758.

4. a. Lungs v. the blood 1891. b. The wheat should be kept cool, well ventilated, and frequently moved 1855. 5. Sweeping breezes v. each street 1810. 6. How to v. and purify his cottages 1888.

II. 1. *trans.* To examine or investigate (a question, topic, etc.) freely or thoroughly by discussion or debate; to bring to public notice or consideration in this way 1527. **2.** To publish *abroad*; to make public (*rare*) 1530. **3.** To utter; to make known to others 1637. †**4.** To carry on or take part in (a controversy) –1678.

1. Politicians do not 'discuss' subjects in the year of grace 1857: they 'v.' them 1857. 3. The habit..of using novels to v. opinions 1855. Hence **Ve·ntilative** *a.* of, pertaining to, or promoting v.

Ventilation (ventilēⁱ·ʃən). 1456. [a. L. *ventilation-*, *ventilatio*, f. *ventilare* VENTILATE *v.*] **I.** †**1.** A stir or motion of the air; a current of air; a breeze –1752. **2.** Movement or free course of the air 1605. **3.** Oxygenation of the blood, *spec.* in the act of respiration 1615. **4.** The admission of a proper supply of fresh air, esp. to a room, building, mine, or other place where the air readily becomes stagnant and vitiated; the means or method by which this is accomplished 1664.

2. Upon such consideration of winds and v. the Ægyptian granaries were made open SIR T. BROWNE. 3. The lungs,..in which the air undergoes the important process of v. 1822. 4. Before v., the foul air..became infectious 1753.

II. 1. The action of fanning or blowing; †the winnowing of corn in this way 1519. **2.** *fig.* Free or open discussion or debate upon a doctrine, question, or subject of public interest; the action or fact of bringing to public notice in this way 1614.

2. Careful v. of questions 1850.

Ventilator (ve·ntilēⁱtəɹ). 1743. [f. VENTILATE *v.* + -OR, or a. L.] **1.** A mechanical contrivance or apparatus by which the vitiated or heated air is drawn or removed from a building, ship, mine, etc., and a fresh supply introduced; also freq., a simple opening or open shaft, so placed or contrived as to facilitate renewal of the air. **b.** The former Ladies' Gallery in the House of Commons 1832. **2.** One charged with ventilating a building, etc. 1750.

†**Ventose**, *sb.* 1500. [a. OF., ad. L. *ventosa* (sc. *cucurbita*), fem. of *ventosus*, f. *ventus* wind.] *Surg.* A species of cupping-glass –1704.

Ventose (ve·ntōᵘs), *a. rare.* 1721. [ad. L. *ventosus* (mod.F. *venteux*) windy, conceited, f. *ventus* wind.] Windy, flatulent.

Ventosity (ventǫ·sĭti). Now *rare* or *Obs.* late ME. [a. (O)F. *ventosité*, ad. L. *ventositas* windiness, conceit, f. *ventosus* VENTOSE *a.*] **1.** *Path.* The state of having the stomach or other part of the alimentary canal charged with wind; flatulency. **b.** *pl.* Gases generated in the stomach or bowels; attacks of flatulence. late ME. †**2.** A blast or puff of wind, esp. one coming from the stomach –1725. †**3.** The state of being windy; windiness –1661. **4.** *fig.* Pompous conceit, vanity, or bombast 1550. †**b.** An instance of this; an idle conceit –1681.

4. Vaine glory..is windy and full of v., consisting of popular applause 1631.

Ve·nt-peg. 1707. [f. VENT *sb.*²] A small peg for inserting in the vent-hole of a cask; a spile.

Ventrad (ve·ntræd), *adv.* 1847. [f. L. *ventr-*, *venter* abdomen + -AD.] *Anat.* and *Zool.* Toward the ventral surface of the body.

Ventral (ve·ntrăl), *a.* and *sb.* 1739. [a. F., or ad. L. *ventralis*, f. *venter* abdomen.] **A.** *adj.* **1.** Occurring or taking place in the region of the abdomen; abdominal. **2.** *Anat.* and *Zool.* Of, pertaining to, or situated in or on the abdomen; abdominal 1752. **3.** *Bot.* Of or belonging to the anterior or lower surface 1832. **4.** *V. segment*, in Acoustics: the part of a vibrating string, air column, etc. between two nodes 1830.

1. V. rupture is a protrusion of some of the bowels through the interstices of the abdominal muscles 1797. To..shake luxuriously with a silent v. laughter GEO. ELIOT. 2. The v. fins, serve to raise and depress the fish 1802. The v. (or front) aspect of the body HUXLEY.

B. *sb.* **1.** A ventral fin; one of the fins corresponding to the hind legs of quadrupeds 1834. **2.** *Ent.* One or other of the segments of the abdomen, esp. in *Coleoptera* 1891. Hence **Ve·ntrally** *adv.* in a v. direction; with respect to the venter or abdomen.

Ventri- (ve·ntri), comb. form of L. *ventri-*, *venter* VENTER¹, as in **Ventrico·rnu** *Anat.*, the ventral extension of gray matter in the substance of the spinal cord; hence **Ventrico·rnual** *a.*; **Ventrime·son** *Anat.*, the median line on the ventral surface of the body; hence **Ventrime·sal** *adj.*

Ventricle (ve·ntrik'l). late ME. [ad. L. *ventriculus* or F. *ventricule.*] *Anat.* and *Zool.* **1.** One or other of the two cavities in the heart by means of which the blood is circulated through the body; also, the cavity of the heart in certain animals which fulfils this function. **2.** One or other of a series of cavities in the brain (normally numbering four in the adult human being) formed by enlargements of the neural canal. late ME. †**3.** The stomach in man or quadrupeds –1806. **b.** The digestive sac or organs in birds, fishes, insects, and certain reptiles 1575. **4.** Any small hollow or cavity in an animal body, serving as a place of organic function; in later use, the recess or space between the true and false vocal cords on each side of the larynx 1641.

2. *Pineal v.*: see PINEAL *a.* b. 3. Whether I will or not,..my Heart beats,.. my V. digests what is in it 1676. So **Ve·ntricule.**

Ventricose (ve·ntrikōᵘs), *a.* 1756. [ad. mod.L. *ventricosus*, f. L. *ventr-*, *venter* belly; see -IC and -OSE.] **1.** Swelling out in the middle or on one side, after the manner of an animal's belly; bellied, protuberant, strongly convex. **2.** Of persons: Big-bellied 1843.

1. The flowers are white and v. 1841. So **Ve·ntricoseness, Ventrico·sity. Ve·ntricous** *a.* (1702).

Ventricular (ventri·kiŭlăɹ), *a.* 1822. [f. L. *ventriculus* + -AR.] **1.** Of or pertaining to the stomach; abdominal, gastral, ventral. **2.** Of, pertaining to, forming part of, or affecting a ventricle 1838. **3.** Of the nature of a ventricle 1841.

Ventriculite (ventri·kiŭləit). 1822. [ad. mod.L. *Ventriculites*, f. L. *ventriculus* ventricle; see -ITE¹ 2.] A fossil sponge belonging to the genus *Ventriculites* or the family *Ventriculitidæ*.

‖**Ventriculus** (ventri·kiŭlŏs). 1710. [L., dim. of *venter* VENTER¹.] **1.** *Anat.* and *Zool.* = VENTRICLE 2. **b.** The gizzard in birds and insects 1891. **2.** = VENTRICLE 1. 1771. **3.** The body-cavity of a sponge 1877.

Ventriloquial (ventrilōᵘ·kwiăl), *a.* 1836. [f. VENTRILOQUY + -AL.] **1.** Of sounds: Such as are produced by ventriloquism. **2.** Of, belonging to, or consisting of ventriloquism 1838.

Ventriloquism (ventri·lŏkwiz'm). 1797. [f. VENTRILOQUY + -ISM.] **1.** The art or practice of speaking or producing sounds in such a manner that the voice appears to proceed from some person or object other than the speaker, and usu. at some distance from him. **b.** An instance of this; a ventriloquial sound 1839. **2.** The fact or practice of speaking or appearing to speak from the abdomen 1818.

Ventriloquist (ventri·lŏkwist). 1656. [f. as prec. + -IST.] One who practises or is expert in ventriloquism. Also applied to birds and beasts. Hence **Ventriloqui·stic** *a.* using or practising ventriloquism; ventriloquial.

Ventriloquize (ventri·lŏkwəiz), *v.* 1832. [f. as prec. + -IZE.] **1.** *intr.* To use or practise ventriloquism; to cast the voice. **2.** *trans.* To utter as a ventriloquist 1865.

Ventriloquous (ventri·lŏkwəs), *a.* 1713. [f. L. *ventriloquus* (used 1644–1762 in Engl.) ventriloquist, f. *ventri-*, VENTER¹ + *loqui* to speak, after Gr. ἐγγαστρίμυθος + -OUS.] **1.** Using or practising ventriloquism. **2.** Produced by or as by ventriloquy; ventriloquial 1768.

Ventriloquy (ventri·lŏkwi). 1584. [ad. med. or early mod.L. *ventriloquium*, f. L. *ventriloquus*; see prec.] = VENTRILOQUISM.

Ventripotent (ventri·pŏtĕnt), *a.* Now *rare.* 1611. [a. F. (Rabelais), f. L. *ventri-*, VENTER¹ + *potens* POTENT.] **a.** Big-bellied. **b.** Gluttonous 1823.

Ventro- (ve·ntro), comb. form, on Gr. models, of VENTER¹, as in **v.-i·nguinal** *a.*, of or pertaining to the abdominal cavity and the inguinal canal; **-la·teral** *a.*, of or belonging to the ventral and lateral sides of the body.

Venture (ve·ntiŭɹ, -tʃəɹ), *sb.* 1450. [Aphetic f. *aventure* ADVENTURE *sb.*] †**1.** Fortune, luck; chance. **b.** *At a v.*, at random, by chance, without due consideration or thought 1509. †**2.** Danger, jeopardy, hazard, or peril; the chance or risk of incurring harm or loss –1823. **3.** A course or proceeding the outcome of which is uncertain, but which is attended by the risk of danger or loss 1566. **4.** A commercial enterprise in which there is considerable risk of loss as well as chance of gain 1584. **b.** That which is ventured in a commercial enterprise or speculation 1597. **5.** The (or an) act of venturing upon something; also, the means or result of so venturing 1842.

1. b. A certaine man drew a bow at a v. 1 *Kings* xxii. 34. 3. I'll be your scholar, I cannot lose much by the v. sure FLETCHER. 4. Hath all his ventures faild, what not one hit? SHAKS. b. He lost his v., sheep and gold 1764. 5. On her great v., Man, Earth gazes MEREDITH.

Venture (ve·ntiŭɹ, -tʃəɹ), *v.* late ME. [Aphetic f. *aventure* ADVENTURE *v.*] **I. 1.** *trans.* To risk the loss of (something); to hazard, risk, or stake. **2.** *refl.* To risk (oneself); to dare to go. Now *arch.* 1572. **3.** To take the risk of sending or causing to go where loss or detriment is possible. Now *rare.* 1599.

1. To v. a greater Good for a less LOCKE. Provb. *Nought* (or *nothing*) *v.*, *nought* (or *nothing*) *have*. 3. The streame..he found so exceeding swift, that it was like to be dangerous to v. our horses ouer 1617.

II. 1. To run or take the risk of (something dangerous or harmful); to brave the dangers of (ice, water, etc.). Now *rare.* 1548. **b.** To risk trusting or confiding in (a person) 1777. **2.** To dare or have the courage to attempt or undertake (some action); to risk the issue or result of; to venture upon 1595. **b.** To dare to give, put forth, or express (an opinion, statement, etc.); to make or utter tentatively or with some degree of presumption 1638.

1. That they had rather venter hanging than starving 1675. 2. I am afraide, and yet Ile v. it SHAKS. b. I..ventured a sly joke at the good effects of matrimony LYTTON.

III. 1. *intr.* To risk oneself; to brave the risks or chances of a journey, voyage, etc.; to dare to go or proceed 1534. **2.** To run or take risks; to incur the chance of danger, peril, loss, disapproval, etc. 1560. **3.** With inf.: To dare, presume, go so far as, be so bold as (*to* do something) 1559.

1. Your marchantes .. venteryng to Iseland for Fysshe 1534. 2. You have deeply ventured; But all must do so who would greatly win BYRON. 3. I humbly v. to say, all these things may be done 1687.

Phr. **To v. on** or **upon**: †**a.** To dare to advance upon, approach, or attack (a person or animal). **b.** To accept or take the risk of (an action, etc.), to dare to do, make, or take (something), realizing that a risk is being run. *To v. at*, to make a venture or attempt at; to guess at. Hence **Ve·nturer**, one who ventures, an adventurer; one who undertakes or shares in a commercial or trading venture, esp. by sending goods or ships beyond seas, a merchant-venturer.

Ve·nturesome, *a.* 1661. [f. VENTURE *sb.* or *v.* + -SOME.] **1.** Of persons: = next 1. 1677. **2.** Hazardous, risky 1661.

1. He was most v. in his schemes for action 1863. Hence **Ve·nturesome·ly** *adv.*, **-ness.**

Venturous (ve·ntiŭrəs, ve·ntʃərəs), *a.* 1565. [Aphetic f. ADVENTUROUS *a.*, after VENTURE *sb.* and *v.*] **1.** Of persons, etc.: Disposed to venture upon or undertake something of a dangerous or risky nature; bold, daring, or enterprising in action or opinion; adventurous. **2.** Of the nature of a venture; hazardous, risky 1570. **3.** Arising from or indicative of a readiness to encounter hazard or risk; bold, daring 1584. **b.** Of opinions, etc.: Daringly bold or original; going further than the evidence or facts appear to warrant 1608.

1. Those who at the Spear are bold And vent'rous MILT. He..drives his v. plough-share to the steep GOLDSM. 2. Bloody Wreaths in vent'rous Battels won PRIOR. 3. There was something of romance in Jeanie's v. resolution SCOTT. Hence **Ve·nturous-ly** *adv.*, **-ness.**

Venue (ve·niu). ME. [a. OF., 'coming', f. *venir.*] †I. 1. An assault or attack. ME. only. 2. A thrust or hit in fencing; a stroke or wound with a weapon -1662. 3. A bout or turn of fencing -1659.

II. *Law.* The county, district, or locality where an action is laid; the place where a jury is summoned to come for the trial of a case 1531. b. The scene of a real or supposed action or event; also *fig.*, a position taken up by a disputant 1843. c. An appointed place of meeting, esp. for a match or competition 1857.

Thus we say, Twelve of the Assize ought to be of the same Venew where the Demand is made 1728. The Attorney-General may lay the venue where he pleases 1838. Phr. *To change the v.*, (*a*) *change of v.* b. Here Mr. Froude changes the v. and joins issue on the old battle ground SPENCER.

Venule (ve·niul). 1850. [ad. L. *venula*, dim. of *vena* VEIN *sb.*] A small or minor vein.

Venus (vī·nǝs). *Pl.* **Venuses, †Veneres.** OE. [L.] I. 1. *Myth.* The ancient Roman goddess of beauty and love (esp. sensual love), or the corresponding Greek goddess Aphrodite. b. A representation, esp. a statue or image, of Venus 1568. c. A local or other distinct conception of the goddess; also *transf.* a goddess in other mythologies corresponding to Venus 1770. d. A beautiful or attractive woman 1579. †2. The desire for sexual intercourse; indulgence of sexual desire; lust, venery -1746. †3. A quality or characteristic that excites love; a charm, grace, or attractive feature -1711.

1. c. Under the special protection of Hathor, the Egyptian V. 1877. d. The dreams..of the sable Venuses which they were to find on the banks of the Congo 1816. 3. All the Graces, Veneres, pleasures, elegances attend him BURTON.

II. 1. *Astr.* The second planet in order of distance from the sun, revolving in an orbit between those of Mercury and the earth; the morning or evening star ME. †2. *Alch.* Copper. So in *crystals, saffron, salt, vinegar, vitriol of V.* -1807. †3. *Her.* A name for the tincture green or vert when the names of planets are used in blazoning -1704. 4. The highest cast or throw in playing with huckle-bones 1611. 5. *Zool.* A genus of bivalve molluscs typically representing the family *Veneridæ*; a member of this genus or family; a venerid 1770.

Comb. (of the possessive, with or without *'s*): **Venus's hair-stone, pencil,** names applied to rock crystals enclosing slender hair-like or needle-like crystals of hornblende, asbestos, oxide of iron, oxide of manganese, etc.

b. *Bot.* **Venus's basin, bath,** the wild teasel, *Dipsacus sylvestris*; **Venus's comb,** the shepherd's needle, *Scandix Pecten-Veneris*; **Venus's flytrap,** the N. Amer. marsh-plant *Dionæa muscipula*; **Venus' hair,** the maiden-hair, *Adiantum Capillus-Veneris*; **Venus('s) looking-glass,** one or other of certain plants belonging to the genus *Specularia*, esp. *S.* (or *Campanula*) *Speculum*; **Venus's navel-wort,** (*a*) the pennywort, *Cotyledon Umbilicus*; (*b*) one or other species of annual plants belonging to the genus *Omphalodes*, esp. *O. linifolia*; **Venus's slipper,** the lady's slipper, *Cypripedium Calceolus*.

c. *Zool.* **Venus's comb,** the shell of *Murex tribulus*, which has many long thin spines; **Venus's fan,** a sea-fan, esp. *Rhipodogorgia* (*Gorgonia*) *flabellum*; **Venus's flower-basket, purse,** a glass-sponge of the genus *Euplectella*, esp. *E. aspergillum*; **Venus-shell,** a bivalve mollusc belonging to the family *Veneridæ* or related species; a venus, murex, or cowry **Venus's slipper,** any shell of the genus *Carinaria*.

Ve·ny. *Obs.* exc. *dial.* 1578. [Phonetic var. of VENUE.] 1. = VENUE 2. Also *fig.*, *esp.* a sharp retort, a pungent remark. 2. = VENUE 3. 1594.

†Ver. late ME. [a. L., or OF.] The season of spring; springtime -1630.

Veracious (vĕrē¹·ʃǝs), *a.* 1677. [f. L. *verac-*, *verax* truthful + -IOUS.] 1. Habitually speaking or disposed to speak the truth; observant of the truth; truthful. 2. Characterized by veracity; conforming to truth; true, accurate 1777. 3. That estimates or judges truly or correctly 1851.

1. The testimony of the two v. and competent witnesses DICKENS. 2. The v. narrative of Balaam and his ass 1868. 3. The young ardent soul that enters on this world..with v. insight,..will find this world a very mad one CARLYLE. Hence **Vera·cious-ly** *adv.*, **-ness.**

Veracity (vĕræ·sĭti). 1623. [ad. F. *véracité*, or med. L. *veracitat-*, *veracitas*, f. L. *veraci-*, *verax*, f. *verus* real, true.] 1. The quality or character in persons of speaking or stating the truth; habitual observance of the truth; truthfulness, veraciousness. 2. Agreement of statement or report with the actual fact or facts; accordance with truth; correctness, accuracy 1736. 3. Correspondence with external facts; exactness in the indication of these 1666. 4. That which is true; a truthful statement; a truth 1852.

1. Phr. *Of v.*, trustworthy, veracious, truthful; Authors..of the greatest authority and v. 1671. 2. Narratives where historical v. has no place JOHNSON. 3. He was under the painful necessity of omitting the v. of his optics DICKENS.

Veranda, verandah (vĕræ·ndă). 1711. [orig. introduced from India, where the word occurs in several native languages; ad. Pg. and older Sp. *varanda* (mod. *baranda*) railing, balcony.] An open portico or roofed gallery extending along the front (and occas. other sides) of a dwelling or other building, erected chiefly as a protection or shelter from the sun or rain.

After dinner we will sit in the verandah 1879. Hence **Vera·nda(h)ed** *a.* furnished with a v. or verandahs.

Veratr-, comb. form or stem of VERATRUM, occurring in chemical terms, as **veratrate,** a salt of veratric acid; **veratric** *a.*, derived from or contained in species of *Veratrum*; **veratrol,** a colourless aromatic oil obtained by distilling veratric acid with excess of baryta.

Veratria (vĕrē¹·triă). 1821. [f. VERATR-UM + -IA¹.] *Chem.* = next.

Veratrine (ve·rătrīn). 1822. [a. F. *vératrine*, f. next + -INE⁵.] *Chem.* A poisonous vegetable alkaloid or mixture of alkaloids, obtained esp. from various species of *Veratrum*, and used medicinally as an ointment for the relief of neuralgia, rheumatism, etc.; veratria.

‖**Veratrum** (vĕrē¹·trǝm). 1577. [L., hellebore.] *Bot.* A perennial genus typical of the family *Veratreæ* of liliaceous plants; a plant belonging to this genus, esp. the white hellebore (*V. album*); also, the rhizome of this.

Comb.: **v.-resin,** a brownish resin extracted from the seeds of sabadilla (*V. Sabadilla*).

Verb (vǝ̄ɹb). late ME. [a. OF. (mod. F.) *verbe*, or ad. its source, L. *verbum* word, verb.] *Gram.* That part of speech which is used to express action or being.

Active, auxiliary, deponent, desiderative, frequentative, inchoative, intransitive, transitive, etc. *verb*: see the adjs. *Principal v.*, the chief verb in a sentence; †*fig.* the chief or most important thing; The violin was scarce knowne tho' now the principall v. 1728.

Verbal (vǝ̄·ɹbăl), *a.* and *sb.* 1484. [a. OF., or ad. L. *verbalis* consisting of words, pertaining to words, f. *verbum* word, VERB.] A. *adj.* 1. Of persons: a. Dealing in or with words, esp. with mere words. †b. Using many words; talkative, verbose -1647. c. Interested in or attending to the mere words of a literary composition 1709. 2. Consisting or composed of words; also, pertaining to or manifested in, words 1530. b. Of the nature of or denoting a word 1605. 3. Concerned with, affecting, or involving words only, without touching things or realities 1605. b. Finding expression in words only, without being manifested in action 1622. c. Consisting merely in words or speech 1618. 4. Expressed or conveyed by speech instead of writing; stated or delivered by word of mouth; oral 1591. 5. = VERBATIM *a.* 1. 1612. b. In respect of each single word 1790. 6. Of, pertaining to, or derived from a verb 1530.

1. b. *Cymb.* II. iii. 111. c. The labours of v. critics 1782. 2. A series of v. quibbles and jingles 1791. Phrases. *V. inspiration*: see INSPIRATION II. 1 a. *V. note*, in diplomacy, an unsigned note or memorandum sent as a mere reminder of some matter not of immediate importance. 3. The opposition between these two modes of speaking is rather v. than real JOWETT. 4. He did it by v. order from Sir W. Coventry PEPYS. 5. You will perceive that it is almost a v. Copy 1786. b. The sacred writers never aim at v. accuracy in their quotations FARRAR. 6. *Verbals* or *V. Nouns*, those Nouns that are derived from Verbs 1706.

B. *sb.* A noun or other part of speech derived from a verb 1530.

Verbalism (vǝ̄·ɹbăliz'm). 1787. [f. prec. + -ISM.] 1. A verbal expression; a word or vocable. 2. Predominance of what is merely verbal over reality or real significance 1871.

Verbalist (vǝ̄·ɹbălist). 1609. [f. as prec. + -IST.] 1. One who deals in or directs his attention to words only, apart from reality or meaning. 2. One who is skilled in the use or knowledge of words 1794.

Verbality (vǝɹbæ·lĭti). 1645. [f. as prec. + -ITY.] The quality of being (merely) verbal; that which consists of mere words or verbiage. b. *pl.* Verbal expressions or phrases 1840.

Verbalize (vǝ̄·ɹbălǝiz), *v.* 1609. [a. F. *verbaliser*, or f. VERBAL *a.* + -IZE.] 1. *intr.* To use many words; to be verbose. 2. *trans.* To make into a verb 1659. 3. To express in words 1875. Hence **Ve:rbaliza·tion,** the action of verbalizing or the fact of being verbalized.

Verbally (vǝ̄·ɹbăli), *adv.* 1588. [f. VERBAL *a.* + -LY².] 1. Word for word; in respect of each word. 2. In or with (mere) words, without accompanying action or reality 1610. b. So far as words (only) are concerned 1855. 3. In actual words; by means of words or speech 1646. b. In speech, as contrasted with writing 1637.

2. This passion of Christ, the reprobate preach verballie only 1610.

Verbarian (vǝɹbēᵊ·riăn), *a.* and *sb.* 1830. [f. L. *verbum* word, after forms in -ARIAN.] A. *adj.* Having to do with words. B. *sb.* An inventor or coiner of words 1873.

In *The Doctor*, Southey gives himself free scope as a v. 1873.

‖**Verbascum** (vǝɹbæ·skǝm). 1562. [L. (Pliny).] = MULLEIN 1; one or other species of this.

Verbatim (vǝɹbē¹·tim), *adv.*, *a.*, and *sb.* 1481. [a. med. L., f. L. *verbum* word.] A. *adv.* 1. Word for word; in the exact words. †2. In so many words; exactly, precisely -1638.

1. A translation v. from the french 1815. Phr. *V. et literatim*; It was, *v. et literatim*, a copy of the log-book of the brig 1828.

B. *adj.* 1. Corresponding with or following an original word for word 1737. 2. *transf.* Able to take down a speech word for word (in shorthand) 1882.

1. A machine for *v.* reporting 1880. 2. The fastest 'v.' hands seemed to be embarrassed 1897.

C. *sb.* A verbatim report 1898.

Verbena (vǝɹbī·nă). 1562. [In sense 1, a. L. (usu. in pl. *verbenæ*), in sense 2, med. and mod. L. (= L. *verbenaca*).] 1. *Rom. Antiq.* In *pl.*, the leaves or twigs of certain plants or shrubs (as olive, myrtle, laurel, etc.) having a sacred character and employed in religious ceremonies 1600. 2. The plant VERVAIN; also, one or other plant of the genus *Verbena* or the order *Verbenaceæ* 1562. 3. A perfume obtained from the leaves of vervain 1858.

2. The *Aloysia citriodora* is the Lemon-scented V. of the gardens 1866. Hence **Verbena·ceous** *a.* *Bot.* of or pertaining to the *Verbenaceæ*, an extensive family of monopetalous (chiefly tropical) plants.

Verberate (vǝ̄·ɹbĕrē¹t), *v.* 1587. [f. L. *verberat-*, *verberare* to beat, flog, f. *verber* whip, lash.] 1. *trans.* a. To strike so as to produce a sound (*rare*). b. To beat or strike so as to cause pain, esp. by way of punishment 1625. 2. *intr.* To vibrate or quiver 1755.

1. The sounde..Reboundes againe, and verberates the skies 1587.

Verberation (vǝ̄ɹbĕrē¹·ʃǝn). 1610. [ad. L. *verberationem*; see prec.] 1. The action of beating or striking, or the fact of being struck, so as to produce sound; percussion. 2. The action of beating or striking so as to cause pain or hurt; also, a blow or stroke 1730.

Verbiage (vǝ̄·ɹbiēdʒ). 1721. [a. F., irreg. f. L. *verbum* word; see -AGE.] 1. Abundance of words without necessity or without much meaning; excessive wordiness. 2. Diction, wording, verbal expression 1804.

1. The Homeric phrase is thus often muffled and deadened by Pope's v. 1880. 2. All that is nothing; the previous v. [of the treaty] is thought sufficient to bind us WELLINGTON.

Verbify (vǝ̄·ɹbifǝi), *v.* 1813. [f. VERB + -(I)FY.] *trans.* To convert (a noun, etc.) into a verb. Also *absol.*

Verbigerate (vǝɹbi·dʒĕrē¹t), *v.* 1892. [f. ppl. stem of L. *verbigerare* to chat, f. *verbi-*, *verbum* word + *gerere* to carry on.] *Path. intr.* To go on repeating the same word or phrase in a meaningless fashion, as a symptom of mental disease. So **Verbigera·tion** 1891.

Verbose (vəɹbōu·s), *a.* 1672. [ad. L. *verbosus*, f. *verbum* word.] **1.** Expressed in an unnecessary number of words; prolix, wordy. **2.** Using an excessive number of words; long-winded 1692.

1. Any v. circumlocutory appeal 1826. Countless papers, expressed in..v. and tedious tenor 1870. 2. The conveyances of a v. attorney ADAM SMITH. Hence **Verbo·se·ly** *adv.*, **-ness.**

Verbosity (vəɹbǫ·sĭti). 1542. [a. F. *verbosité*, or ad. post-cl. L. *verbositas*, f. *verbosus* VERBOSE *a.*] The state or quality of being verbose; superfluity of words; wordiness, prolixity. **b.** With pl. An instance of this 1665.

He draweth out the thred of his verbositie, finer then the staple of his argument SHAKS.

‖**Verbum sap.** 1818. Also **verb. sap.** (sæp). [Shortening of L. *verbum sapienti sat est* 'a word is sufficient to a wise man'.] A phrase used in place of making a full statement or explanation, implying that an intelligent person may easily infer what is left unsaid, or understand the reasons for reticence.

‖**Verbum sat.** Also **sat verbum.** 1649. [See prec.] A phrase used to conclude a statement, implying that further comment is unnecessary or unadvisable.

Verdancy (vō·ɹdănsi). 1631. [See next and -ANCY.] **1.** The quality, condition, or character of being verdant; greenness. **2.** *fig.* Innocence, inexperience; rawness, simplicity 1849.

Verdant (vō·ɹdănt), *a.* 1581. [f. *verd-* (as in *verdure*) + -ANT, perh. partly after L. *viridant-*, *viridans*, *viridare*, f. *viridis* green.] **1.** Of a green hue or colour; green. **2.** Green with vegetation; characterized by abundance of verdure 1590. **3.** *fig.* Of persons: Green, inexperienced, gullible 1824.

1. When eve embrowns the v. grove 1764. 2. As I tread The walk, still v., under oaks and elms COWPER. 3. With the..object of warning 'v.' purchasers 1854. Hence **Ve·rdantly** *adv.*

‖**Verd-antique, verd antique** (vōɹd æntī·k). 1745. [Older F. (now *vert antique*) 'antique green'. Cf. next.] **1.** An ornamental variety of marble, consisting chiefly of serpentine mixed with calcite and dolomite. **b.** *Oriental v.*, green porphyry 1852. **2.** A green incrustation on brass or copper; verdigris 1835.

‖**Verde antico.** 1753. [It.] = prec. 1.

Verderer (vō·ɹdərəɹ). Also **-or.** 1541. [a. AF. *verderer*, f. (ult.) OF. *verd* (var. of *vert*):—L. *viridis* green.] 'A judicial officer of the King's forest..sworn to maintain and keep the assises of the forest, and also to view, receive, and enroll the attachments and presentments of all manner of trespasses of the forest, of vert and venison' (Manwood).

†**Verdet.** 1558. [a. OF., dim. of *verd* green.] *Chem.* An acetate of copper; verdigris -1896.

Verdict (vō·ɹdikt). ME. [a. AF. *verdit* (= OF. *voirdit*), f. *ver, veir* true + *dit*, pa. pple. of *dire* to say.] **1.** *Law.* The decision of a jury in a civil or criminal cause upon an issue which has been submitted to their judgement. **2.** *transf.* and *fig.* A judgement given by some body or authority acting as or likened to a jury. late ME. **3.** *transf.* A finding, conclusion, or judgement upon some matter or subject. late ME.

1. The Agreement of Twelve Men is a V. in Law 1726. 2. They are here presently to abide the verdite of battaile 1611. 3. No controversy is supposed to be closed till the *Times* has given its v. 1882.

Verdigris (vō·ɹdigris, -grīs). ME. [a. AF. and OF. *vert de Grece*, *vert-de-gris* (also mod. F.), lit. 'green of Greece'.] A green or greenish blue substance obtained artificially by the action of dilute acetic acid on thin plates of copper (or as a green deposit naturally forming on copper or brass), and much used as a pigment, in dyeing, the arts, and medicine; basic acetate of copper.

attrib.: **v. green,** a green of a bright, bluish hue; æruginous green. Hence **Ve·rdigrised** *ppl. a.* coated or tainted with v.

Verditer (vō·ɹditəɹ). 1505. [a. OF. *verd de terre* (later F. *vert de terre*), lit. 'green of earth.'] **1.** A pigment of a green, bluish green, or (more freq.) light blue colour, usu. prepared by adding chalk or whiting to a solution of nitrate of copper, and much used in making crayons and as a water-colour. **2.** The blue or green colour characteristic of verditer 1819.

†**Verdour.** 1447. [a. OF., f. *verd* green; see -OR 1.] = VERDURE, in various senses -1646.

Verdoy, *a.* 1562. [ad. F. *verdoyé*, pa. pple. of *verdoyer*, f. *verd* VERD *sb.*] *Her.* Of a bordure: Charged with leaves, flowers, fruits, etc.

Verdure (vō·ɹdiŭɹ, -dʒəɹ). late ME. [a. OF., f. *verd* green + -URE.] **I. 1.** The fresh green colour of vegetation; greenness, viridity. **2.** Green vegetation; plants or trees, or parts of these, in a green and flourishing state. late ME. **b.** *esp.* Green grass or herbage 1447. †**c.** *pl.* Green plants or herbs -1722.

1. The perennial v. of cypress and pine 1910. 2. b. [Thoughts] and the pleasant v. of the fields Made me forget the way COWLEY.

II. †**1.** Freshness or agreeable briskness of taste in fruits or liquors; also simply, taste, savour -1630. †**2.** Smell; odour -1716. **3.** *fig.* Fresh or flourishing condition 1586.

3. Those years make the prime and v. of our lives 1829. Hence **Ve·rdured** *ppl. a.* clad with v. or vegetation, covered with grass. **Ve·rdureless** *a.* destitute of v.; bare, bleak.

Verdurous (vō·ɹdiŭrəs, -dʒərəs), *a.* 1604. [f. VERDURE + -OUS.] **1.** Of vegetation: Rich or abounding in verdure; flourishing thick and green. **b.** Of places, etc.: Displaying a rich (green) vegetation 1717. **2.** Consisting or composed of verdure 1667. **3.** Of, pertaining to, or characteristic of verdure 1820.

1. Where the lowing Herd Chews verd'rous Pasture 1708. b. That v. hill with many a resting-place COLERIDGE. 3. Through v. glooms and winding mossy ways KEATS. Hence **Ve·rdurousness.**

Verecund (ve·rĭkʊnd), *a.* 1550. [ad. L. *verecundus*, f. *vereri* to reverence, fear.] Modest, bashful; shy, coy.

Veretilliform (verĭti·lifǫɹm), *a.* 1838. [f. mod.L. *Veretillum* + -(I)FORM.] *Zool.* Having the form of a member of *Veretillum*, the typical genus of *Veretillidæ*, a family of pennatuloid polyps.

Verey (*lights*), variant of VERY.

Vergaloo (vōɹgălū·). *U.S.* Also **virgalieu.** 1828. [var. of VIRGOULEUSE, prob. taken as a pl.] The white doyenné or Warwickshire bergamot.

Verge (vōɹdʒ), *sb.* late ME. [a. OF. (also mod.F.) *verge*:—L. *virga* rod, etc.] **I. 1.** †**a.** The penis. late ME. only. **b.** *Zool.* [after mod.F. use.] The male organ of a mollusc, crustacean, or other invertebrate 1774. **2. a.** A rod or wand carried as an emblem of authority or symbol of office; a staff of office; a warder, †sceptre, mace 1494. †**b.** A rod or wand put in a person's hand when taking the oath of fealty to the lord on being admitted as a tenant, and delivered back on the giving up of the tenancy. Also in phr. *tenant by the v.* -1651. **3.** *Watchmaking.* The spindle or arbor of the balance in the old vertical escapement 1696. **b.** *ellipt.* A verge watch 1871. **4.** *U.S.* That part of a linotype machine which carries the pawls by which the matrices are released 1909.

†**II.** *V. of land* [tr. OF. *verge de terre*, med.L. *virga terræ*] = VIRGATE (*rare*) -1672.

III. 1. *Within the v.* [AF. *dedeinz la verge*], within an area subject to the jurisdiction of the Lord High Steward, defined as extending to a distance of twelve miles round the King's court. In the 18th c. commonly denoting the precincts of Whitehall as a place of sanctuary. *Obs.* exc. *Hist.* 1509. **b.** Hence *The v.* (*of the court*), etc., employed to designate this area or jurisdiction 1529. **2.** The bounds, limits, or precincts *of* a particular place 1641. †**3.** In phrases. **a.** The range, sphere, or scope *of* something -1734. **b.** The pale or limit *of* a class or community -1768. **c.** The power, control, or jurisdiction of a person or persons -1704.

2. She should be beheaded within the v. of the Tower HUME. 3. a. They do not fall within the V. of my Undertaking in the present 1734.

IV. 1. The edge, rim, border, or margin *of* some object of limited size or extent. Now *rare.* †**b.** With *a* and *pl.*, etc.: A brim or rim; a circle of metal, etc. -1710. **c.** *Arch.* The edge of the tiling projecting beyond the gable of a roof 1833. **2.** The extreme edge, margin, or bound *of* a surface of an extensive nature, but regarded as having definite limits 1593. **b.** *fig.* The end *of* life 1750. **c.** The utmost limit to which a thing or matter extends; the distinctive line of separation between one subject and another 1796. **3. a.** The extreme edge of a cliff or abrupt descent 1605. **b.** The margin *of* a river or the sea 1606. **c.** *poet.* The horizon 1822. **4.** With *a* and *pl.* A limit or bound; a limiting or bounding belt or strip. Somewhat *rare.* 1660. **b.** *spec.* A narrow grass edging separating a flower border, etc. from a walk 1728. **5.** The brink or border *of* something towards which there is progress or tendency (from without); the point at which something begins. Usu. in phrases *on* or *to the v. of.* 1602. **6.** The space within a boundary; room, scope 1690.

2. The furthest V. That euer was suruey'd by English eye SHAKS. c. Having lived up to the very v. of his yearly income MME D'ARBLAY. 3. *fig.* You see him often tottering on the v. of laughter GRAY. c. The v. where brighter morns were wont to break BYRON. 5. He seems to have been driven to the very v. of despair 1842. Phr. *On the v. of* (with vbl. sbs.), on the very point of (doing something); Twice she was on the v. of telling all 1887. 6. Give ample room, and v. enough The characters of hell to trace GRAY.

Verge (vōɹdʒ), *v.*[1] 1605. [f. prec.] †**1.** *trans.* To provide *with* a specified kind of verge or border; to edge. Chiefly in pass. -1708. **2.** *intr.* **a.** To be contiguous or adjacent to; to lie on the verge of. Const. *on* or *upon, along.* 1787. **b.** To border *on* or *upon* some state, condition, etc. 1825.

2. b. Your generosity must have verged on extravagance C. BRONTE.

Verge (vōɹdʒ), *v.*[2] 1610. [ad. L. *vergere* to bend, turn.] **1.** *intr.* Of the sun: To descend towards the horizon; to sink, or begin to do so. **2.** To move in a certain direction (esp. downwards); also, to extend or stretch 1661. **b.** To diverge or deflect 1692. **3.** To incline or tend, to approach or draw near, *towards* or *to* some state or condition 1664. **b.** To pass or undergo gradual transition *into* something else 1756. **4.** To have a particular direction; to lie or extend towards a specified point 1726.

3. A man of light wit, verging towards fourscore CARLYLE. b. Fast verging into a state of monomania 1854. 4. Whose rays..V. to one point and blend for ever there SHELLEY.

Ve·rge-board. 1833. [f. VERGE *sb.* IV. 1 c.] *Arch.* = BARGE-BOARD.

Vergency (vōɹ·dʒĕnsi). 1649. [f. VERGE *v.*[2] + -ENCY.] †**1.** The act or fact of verging or inclining towards some condition, etc.; tendency, leaning; an instance of this -1702. **2.** The fact or condition of being inclined toward some object or in some direction 1668. **b.** *Optics.* The reciprocal of the focal distance, being the measure of the degree of divergence or convergence of a pencil of rays 1832.

†**Ve·rger**[1]. ME. [a. OF.:—L. *virdiarium*, f. *viridis* green.] A garden or orchard; a pleasure-garden -1501.

Verger[2] (vō·ɹdʒəɹ). 1472. [prob. a. AF. **verger*, f. *verge* VERGE *sb.*] An official who carries a rod or similar symbol of office before the dignitaries of a cathedral, church, or university. **b.** One whose duty it is to take care of the interior of a church, and to act as attendant 1707. See also VIRGER.

Vergobret (vō·ɹgǒbret). 1563. [ad. L. *vergobretus*, of Gaulish origin.] The chief magistrate among the ancient Ædui of Gaul.

Veridical (vĭri·dikăl), *a.* 1653. [f. L. *veridicus*, f. *verum* truth + *dic-*, stem of *dicere* to speak.] **1.** Speaking, telling, or relating the truth; veracious. **2.** *spec.* in *Psychol.* Of hallucinations, phantasms, etc.: Coincident with, corresponding to, or representing real events or persons 1884.

Verifiable (ve·rifəi,ăb'l), *a.* 1593. [f. VERIFY *v.* + -ABLE.] That can be verified or proved to be true, authentic, accurate, or real; capable of verification. Hence **Ve:rifiabi·lity. Ve·rifiableness. Ve·rifiably** *adv.*

Verification (ve:rifikēi·ʃən). 1523. [a. OF. *verificacion*, f. *verifier*, or ad. med.L. **verifica-*

tion-, verificatio, f. *verificare* VERIFY *v.*; see -ATION.] **1.** The action of demonstrating or proving to be true or legitimate by means of evidence or testimony; formal assertion of truth. Now *rare.* **2.** Demonstration of truth or correctness by facts or circumstances 1541. **3.** The action of establishing or testing the truth or correctness of a fact, theory, statement, etc., by means of special investigation or comparison of data 1603. **b.** The action of verifying or testing the correctness of an instrument, or the quality of goods 1832. **4.** [After F.] Ratification 1845.

4. By the old constitution of France, these letters patent required the v. of the Parliament M. ARNOLD.

Verificatory (ve·rifikēi:təri), *a.* 1834. [f. med.L. *verificat-, verificare* VERIFY *v.* + -ORY [2].] That verifies; of the nature of or serving as a verification.

Verify (ve·rifəi), *v.* ME. [ad. OF. *verifier*, ad. med.L. *verificare*, f. L. *verus* true.] **1.** *trans. Law.* To prove by good evidence or valid testimony; to testify or affirm formally or upon oath. **b.** *gen.* To testify to, to assert as true or certain. Now *rare.* 1525. **†c.** To support by testimony. SHAKS. **2.** To show to be true by demonstration or evidence; to substantiate. Now *rare* of persons. late ME. **3.** *pass.* To be proved true or correct by the result or event, or by some confirming fact or circumstance; to be fulfilled or accomplished in this way. late ME. **b.** Used actively of the circumstances, person, etc., serving as proof or confirmation. late ME. **4.** To ascertain or test the accuracy or correctness of (something), esp. by examination or by comparison with known data or some standard; to check or correct in this way 1527. **5.** To establish by investigation 1801.

1. The said charge to be verified by the oath of the said Frazer BURKE. 2. 'Prosperitee is blynd':.. and verifie I can wel it is so HOCCLEVE. The strongest evidence by which the fact of a death was ever verified MACAULAY. 3. If he doth, I fear it will be verified in him, that a 'fool and his money is soon parted' 1645. 4. Hours..spent in casting up and verifying accounts 1802. Hence **Ve·rifier**, one who or that which verifies.

Verily (ve·rili), *adv.* Now *arch.* or *rhet.* ME. [f. VERY *a.* + -LY [2].] In truth; as a matter of truth or fact; in deed, fact, or reality; really, truly. **b.** Placed in front of a sentence or statement as an emphatic asseveration of its truth or accuracy; freq. connoting the truth of a preceding statement ME. **c.** Used to emphasize a negative or affirmative particle 1489.

He..v. believes him an honest man *Junius' Lett.* b. V., Mr. Spectator, we are much offended at the Act for Importing French Wines 1711. c. Yes, v.,.. you must 1865.

Verisimilar (verisi·milăɹ), *a.* 1681. [f. L. *verisimilis, veri similis*, after SIMILAR *a.*] Having the appearance of truth or reality; appearing true or real; probable.

Are these dramas of his not v. only but true? CARLYLE.

Verisimilitude (ve:risimi·litiūd). 1603. [ad. L. *verisimilitudo, veri similitudo*, f. *veri similis, veri*, gen. of *verum* truth + *similis* like.] **1.** The fact or quality of being verisimilar; the appearance of being true or real; probability. **2.** A statement, etc., which has the mere appearance or show of being true or in accordance with fact 1783.

1. Truth has no greater Enemy than v. and likelihood 1654. 2. I felt..that there was more truth in the verisimilitudes of fiction than in the assumptions of history L. HUNT. So **†Verisimi·lity** -1706.

Verist (vīə·rist). 1884. [f. L. *verum* or It. *vero* true + -IST.] One who believes in or practises the rigid representation of the truth or reality in literature or art. So **Ve·rism**, the style practised or advocated by the verists. **Veri·stic** *a.*

Veritable (ve·rităb'l), *a.* 1474. [ad. OF. and AF., f. *verite* VERITY; see -ABLE.] **†1.** Of a statement, etc.: That is in accordance with the truth; true -1649. **†b.** Of persons: Veracious -1594. **2.** Genuine, real, true; correctly or properly so called 1483. **3.** In extended use, denoting possession of all the distinctive qualities of the person or thing specified 1862.

1. *Oth.* III. iv. 76. 2. A v. personage was Whittington 1852. A moral relish for v. proofs of honesty 1872. 3. They had a succession of governors who were v. brigands 1869. Hence **Ve·ritably** *adv.*

Verity (ve·rĭti). late ME. [a. AF. and OF. *verite, veritet*:—L. *veritat-, veritas*, f. *verus* true, VERY *a.*; see -ITY.] **1.** Without article. Truth; conformity to fact or reality. **2.** With article or pronoun. The truth; the true or real facts or circumstances. late ME. **b.** Said of God or Christ. Usu. with defining adj. preceding. 1535. **†c.** The exact wording and meaning of the original Hebrew or Greek text of the Bible -1771. **d.** The actuality or reality *of* something 1633. **3.** With *a* and *pl.* A true statement, doctrine, or opinion; an established fact, a reality; a truth 1533. **†4.** Truthfulness, veracity, sincerity -1848.

1. Betweene veritie & falsitie there is no meane 1579. 2. Telle me what ye be, and of youre felowes telle me the verite 1450. The v. of his Miracles HOBBES. b. God being the Prime V. 1645. 3. The quarrel and the reconciliation are unquestionable verities FREEMAN. Phr. *Of a v.*, truly, assuredly. 4. Thou hast sworen to Dauid in thy verite 1565.

Verjuice (vɔ̄·ɹdʒūs), *sb.* ME. [a. OF. *verjus*, f. *vert* green, unripe + *jus* JUICE.] The acid juice of green or unripe grapes, crab-apples, or other sour fruit, expressed and formed into a liquor; formerly much used in cooking, etc.

fig. Miss Budd, although she said nothing, looked vinegar and v. 1833. Hence **Ve·rjuice** *v. trans.* to make sour.

Vermeil, vermil (vɔ̄·ɹmil), *a.* and *sb.* late ME. [a. AF. and OF. *vermeil* adj. and sb.:— L. *vermiculum* (acc.); see VERMICLE, and cf. VERMILION.] **A.** *adj.* Of a bright scarlet or red colour; vermilion. Chiefly *poet.* **b.** With names of colours; esp. *v. red* 1590.

Take not colde water in stede of vermayll wine 1509. b. In her cheekes the vermeill red did shew SPENSER.

B. *sb.* **1.** Vermilion hue or colour 1590. **†b.** *transf.* Blood (*rare*) -1812. **2.** An orange-red garnet 1796. **3.** Silver gilt; gilt bronze 1858. Hence **Vermeil, vermil** *v. trans.* to colour or suffuse, to stain *over*, with or as with vermilion.

‖**Vermes** (vɔ̄·ɹmīz). 1693. [L., pl. of *vermis* worm.] **1.** *Path.* A disease caused by the presence of parasitic worms. **2.** *Zool.* One or other of the primary divisions, sub-kingdoms, or groups of the animal kingdom proposed or adopted at various times, comprising worms and allied forms 1771.

Vermetid (vɔ̄·ɹmĕtid). 1860. [ad. mod.L. *Vermetidæ*, f. L. VERMES.] *Zool.* An individual of the family *Vermetidæ* of holostomatous gasteropods.

Vermi- (vɔ̄·ɹmi), comb. form of L. *vermis*, as in VERMICIDE, VERMIFORM, VERMIFUGE, *adjs.*; also in other terms, as **Vermi·ferous**, *a.* producing worms; **-i·gerous** *a.* infested with worms.

Vermian (vɔ̄·ɹmiăn), *a.* 1878. [f. VERMES + -IAN.] **1.** Of or pertaining to *Vermes*; characteristic of worms; worm-like. **2.** *Anat.* Pertaining or belonging to the vermis of the cerebellum.

Vermicelli (vɔ̄ɹmise·li, vɔ̄ɹmitʃe·li). 1669. [a. It., pl. of *vermicello*, dim. of *verme*:—acc. sing. of L. *vermis* worm.] **1.** A wheaten paste, of Italian origin, now usu. made of flour, cheese, yolks of eggs, sugar and saffron, prepared in the form of long, slender, hard threads, and used as an article of diet. **2.** *ellipt.* Vermicelli soup 1771.

Vermicide (vɔ̄·ɹmisəid). 1849. [f. VERMI- + -CIDE 1.] *Med.* A medicine for killing intestinal worms; an anthelmintic.

Vermicle (vɔ̄·ɹmik'l). late ME. [ad. L. *vermiculus.*] **†1.** = VERMILION *sb.* 3. WYCLIF. **2.** *Biol.* A vermicule 1657.

Vermicular (vəɹmi·kiŭlăɹ), *a.* 1672. [ad. med.L. *vermicularis*, f. L. *vermiculus* VERMICULE.] **1.** = PERISTALTIC *a.* **2.** Having the sinuous shape or form characteristic of a worm; consisting of or characterized by tortuous outlines or markings; sinuous, wavy 1712. **3.** Of, pertaining to, or characteristic of a worm or worms; resembling or like a worm 1713. **b.** Accomplished or made by worms; performed by means of worms 1715. **4.** Of the nature of a worm; consisting of worms 1784. **5.** *Path.* Of diseases: Due to or caused by intestinal worms 1794.

1. The v. motion of the intestine 1881. 2. A generation more refin'd..made three legs four, Gave them a twisted form v. COWPER. 4. *V. ascaris*, the thread-worm, *Oxyurus* (*Ascaris*) *vermicularis*. Hence **Vermi·cularly** *adv.*

Vermiculate (vəɹmi·kiŭlĕt), *a.* 1605. [ad. L. *vermiculatus, vermiculari*, f. *vermiculus*, dim. of *vermis* worm.] Vermiculated, vermicular, sinuous.

Subtile, idle, vnholesome, and (as I may tearme them) v. questions BACON.

Vermiculated (vəɹmi·kiŭleɪtĕd), *ppl. a.* 1623. [See prec. and -ED [1].] **1.** Worm-eaten; covered or ornamented with vermicular markings. **b.** *Arch.* Of stone-work or other surfaces so carved or moulded as to present the appearance of worm-tracks 1788. **2.** Of mosaic work (after L. (*opus*) *vermiculatum*): Wrought, ornamented, or inlaid in a pattern resembling the sinuous movements or tracks of worms 1656. **3.** Ornamented *with* sinuous or wavy lines or markings of a specified colour 1872.

Vermiculation (vəɹmikiŭlēi·ʃən). 1611. [ad. L. *vermiculation-, vermiculatio*, f. *vermiculari.*] **1.** The fact or condition of being infested with or eaten by worms; conversion into small worms. **†2.** *Path.* Peristalsis -1710. **3.** With *pl.* A tortuous boring or marking made by or assembling the track of a worm 1670. **b.** Without article. Vermicular marking or ornamentation 1866.

3. The face of the boards is shown to be eaten into innumerable vermiculations T. HARDY.

Vermicule (vɔ̄·ɹmikiŭl). 1713. [ad. L. *vermiculus*, dim. of *vermis* worm.] *Biol.* A small worm or worm-like creature; a maggot or grub.

Vermiculite (vəɹmi·kiŭləit). 1824. [f. L. *vermiculari* + -ITE [1].] *Min.* Any of a number of hydrous silicates, chiefly resulting from alterations of mica, and occurring in small foliated scales.

Vermiculous (vəɹmi·kiŭləs), *a.* 1690. [ad. late L. *vermiculosus*, f. *vermiculus* VERMICULE; see -OUS.] **†1.** Full of worms (*rare*). **2.** Of or pertaining to worms 1813. **3.** Having a wormy appearance 1818. So **Vermiculo·se** *a.* (*rare*) infested with worms, worm-like.

Vermiform (vɔ̄·ɹmifǭɹm), *a.* 1730. [ad. med.L. *vermiformis*, f. L. *vermis* worm; see -FORM.] **1.** Having the form of a worm; long, thin, and more or less cylindrical. **2.** Of, pertaining to, or characteristic of a worm; like or resembling that of a worm; vermicular 1822.

1. *V. appendix* (or *appendage*), a small worm-like process or diverticulum extending from the cæcum in man and a few other mammals. *V. process*, the median lobe of the cerebellum, the upper and lower laminæ of which are distinguished as the *superior* and *inferior v. processes.*

Vermifuge (vɔ̄·ɹmifiūdʒ), *a.* and *sb.* 1697. [a. F., or ad. mod.L. **vermifugus*, f. L. *vermis* worm; see -FUGE.] **A.** *adj.* Causing or promoting the expulsion of worms or other animal parasites from the intestines; anthelmintic. **B.** *sb.* An anthelmintic 1718. So **Vermi·fugal** *a.*

Vermilion (vəɹmi·lyən), *sb.* and *a.* ME. [a. AF. and OF. *vermeillon* (mod.F. *vermillon*), f. *vermeil* VERMEIL *a.*] **A.** *sb.* **1.** Cinnabar or red crystalline mercuric sulphide, esp. in later use that obtained artificially, much valued on account of its brilliant scarlet colour, and used as a pigment or in the manufacture of red sealing-wax; also, any red earth resembling this and similarly used as a pigment. **2.** The colour of this pigment; a bright red or scarlet. late ME. **†3.** Scarlet wool or fabric -1641.

2. Streight the Vermillion vanish'd from her Face 1708.

B. *adj.* Having the colour of vermilion; of a bright red or scarlet colour 1589. Hence **Vermi·lion** *v. trans.* to colour or paint with, or as with v.; to give the colour of v. to (the face, etc.).

Vermin (vɔ̄·ɹmin), *sb.* ME. [a. AF. and OF. *vermin(e)*:—pop.L. **verminum*, f. L. *vermis* worm.] **1.** *collect.* Animals of a noxious or objectionable kind: **a.** Orig. applied to reptiles, stealthy or slinking animals, and various wild beasts; now, exc. in *U.S.* and *Austral.*, almost entirely restricted to those animals or birds which prey upon preserved game. **b.** Applied to creeping or wingless insects (and other minute animals) of a loathsome or offensive appearance or character, esp. those which infest or are parasitic on living beings and plants ME. †2. With *a*, *that*, *this*, etc. a. A kind or class of obnoxious animals -1774. b. A single animal or insect of this kind -1809. 3. *fig.* Applied to persons of a noxious, vile, objectionable, or offensive character or type 1562.

1. A hole..filled with Snakes, Lizards, and other poisonous Virmin 1684. That the stock of partridges, grouse, and hares on any large estate depends chiefly on the destruction of v. DARWIN. b. Vermyn, as flees, lyse, wormes, etc. 1552. 2. a. This Crocodile is..a dangerous vermine used to both elements HOLLAND. 3. Knaves, cheats, hypocrites; the v. of this earth 1690.

Verminate (vɔ̄·ɹmineɪt), *v. rare.* 1693. [f. L. *verminat-*, *verminare* to have worms, f. *vermis* worm.] *intr.* To breed parasitic vermin.

Vermination (vɔ̄ɹminē¹·ʃən). 1628. [ad. L. *vermination-*, *verminatio*, f. *verminare*; see prec.] †1. The fact or condition of being gnawed by worms; vermiculation. DONNE. †2. The breeding, growth, or production of vermin, esp. parasitic vermin -1713. 3. The fact of being infested with parasitic vermin; esp. *Med.*, the morbid condition due to this 1818.

Verminous (vɔ̄·ɹminəs), *a.* 1616. [f. VERMIN *sb.* + -OUS, or ad. L. *verminosus*, f. *vermis* worm.] 1. Of the nature of or consisting of vermin; like vermin in character; noxious, objectionable, offensive. 2. Infested with vermin, esp. parasitic vermin; foul or offensive on this account 1632. 3. Of diseases or morbid conditions, etc.: Due to or characterized by the presence of parasitic vermin or intestinal worms 1666. b. Of persons: Subject to vermin or intestinal worms 1860.

2. A v., over-crowded vagrant ward 1865. 3. Instances of v. abscess 1897. Hence **Ve·rminous·ly** *adv.*, **-ness.**

Vermi·parous, *a. rare.* 1646. [f. VERMI- + -PAROUS.] 1. Producing young, or produced as young, in the form of small worms or maggots. 2. Producing verminous parasites 1860.

‖**Vermis** (vɔ̄·ɹmis). 1890. [L., worm.] *Anat.* The vermiform process of the cerebellum.

Vermivorous (vəɹmi·vŏrəs), *a.* 1704. [f. mod.L. *vermivorus* worm-eating + -OUS.] Feeding on worms, grubs, or insect vermin; said esp. of certain birds.

Vermouth (vēə·ɹmūt, vɔ̄·ɹmūþ). Also **vermuth.** 1806. [a. F. *vermout*, ad. G. *wermuth* wormwood.] A liqueur consisting of white wine flavoured with wormwood or other aromatic herbs and taken to stimulate the appetite. b. A glass of vermouth 1899.

Vernacular (vəɹnæ·kiŭlăɹ), *a.* and *sb.* 1601. [f. L. *vernaculus* domestic, indigenous, f. *verna* a home-born slave, a native.] A. *adj.* 1. That uses the native or indigenous language of a country or district. 2. Of a language or dialect: That is naturally spoken by the people of a particular country or district; native, indigenous 1645. 3. Of literary works, etc.: Written, spoken in, or translated into the native language of a particular country or people 1661. 4. Of words, etc.: Of or pertaining to the native language 1716. 5. Connected or concerned with the native language 1845. 6. Of arts, etc.: Native or peculiar to a particular country or locality 1857.

1. The Learned v. Editor of Hippocrates's Works in French 1716. 2. The congregation here being chiefly peasants, and artisans, a sermon was delivered in the v. dialect 1832. He began to translate the Bible into clear v. German FROUDE. 3. A history of our v. literature D'ISRAELI. 4. A word entirely English and v. POPE. 6. The v. cottage-building of the day 1857.

B. *sb.* 1. The native speech or language of a particular country or district 1706. 2. With *a* and *pl.* A native or indigenous language 1715. 3. *transf.* The phraseology or idiom *of* a particular profession, trade, etc. 1876.

1. No one of them was qualified..to preach in the v. 1889. 3. To use the v. of engineers 1876. Hence **Verna·cularism**, a v. word, idiom, or mode of expression. **Vernacula·rity**, the fact of belonging or adhering to the v. or native language. **Verna·cularly** *adv.*

Vernacularize (vəɹnæ·kiŭlărəiz), *v.* 1821. [f. prec. + -IZE.] *trans.* To render or translate into the native speech of a people; to make vernacular. Hence **Verna·culariza·tion.**

†**Verna·culous**, *a.* 1605. [f. L. *vernaculus*; see -OUS.] 1. Low-bred, scurrilous. B. JONS. 2. Indigenous, native -1657. 3. = VERNACULAR *a.* 1, 2. -1682.

†**Ve·rnage.** late ME. [a. OF., ad. It. *vernaccia.*] A kind of white Italian wine -1500.

Vernal (vɔ̄·ɹnăl), *a.* (and *sb.*). 1534. [ad. L. *vernalis* (rare), f. *vernus* pertaining to spring, f. *ver* VER *sb.*] 1. Coming, appearing, happening, etc., in spring. 2. Pertaining or belonging to the spring-time; spring-like 1611. b. *fig.* Suggestive of spring; having the mildness or freshness of spring; early, youthful 1790. 3. Of flowers, plants, etc.: Appearing or blooming in spring-time 1695. b. *V. grass*, one of the grasses commonly cultivated for hay 1762. 4. *ellipt.* or as *sb.* = *V. grass* 1771.

1. V. Birds, such as the Cuckow 1709. Sweet is the breath of v. shower GRAY. *V. equinox* (or †*equinoctial*): see EQUINOX 1, 2. 2. The freshest v. airs 1847. *V. season*, the season of spring. b. Late in beauty's v. bloom SOUTHEY. 3. As thick as bees o'er v. blossoms fly POPE. b. The sweet scented v. grass (anthoxanthum odoratum) 1799. Hence **Ve·rnally** *adv.* (*rare*).

Vernant, *a.* Now *rare* or *Obs.* 1440. [a. OF., ad. L. *vernant-*, *vernans*, pres. pple. of *vernare* to flourish, be verdant.] Flourishing or growing in or as in spring.

Vernation (vəɹnē¹·ʃən). 1793. [ad. mod.L. *vernatio* (Linn.), f. L. *vernare*; see prec.] *Bot.* The arrangement or formation of the leaves of plants or fronds of ferns in the bud; the manner in which the rudimentary or unexpanded leaves are disposed; prefoliation.

Verneuk (vərnū·k), *v. S. Afr.* To humbug.

Vernicle (vɔ̄·ɹnik'l). late ME. [a. AF., OF., = OF. *veron(n)icle*, var. of *veronique*, ad. med.L. *veronica*; see VERONICA [2].] 1. The picture of the face of Christ said to have been impressed upon the handkerchief of St. Veronica; any similar picture of Christ's face; an ornament or token bearing this as worn by pilgrims. 2. The cloth or kerchief, alleged to have belonged to St. Veronica, with which, according to legend, she wiped the face of Christ on the way to Calvary, and upon which his features were miraculously impressed. late ME.

1. A vernycle hadde he sowed vp on his cappe CHAUCER.

Vernier (vɔ̄·ɹniəɹ). 1766. [Named after the inventor, Paul *Vernier* (1580–1637).] A device consisting of a short movable scale, by which more minute measurements may be readily obtained from the divisions of the graduated scale of astronomical, surveying, or other mathematical instruments to which it is attached.

attrib., as *v. circle*, *scale*; also in the names of instruments or tools having a v. scale or attachment, as *v. caliper*, *compass*.

Veronal (ve·rŏnăl). 1903. [a. G.] *Chem.* Diethyl-malonyl-urea, a white crystalline substance used as a hypnotic.

Veronese (verŏnī·z, ve·rŏnīz), *a.* and *sb.* 1757. [a. It., f. *Verona*; see -ESE.] A. *adj.* Of, belonging to, made in, or obtained from Verona in the north of Italy. B. *sb.* The natives or inhabitants of Verona. Also as *sing.* 1757.

‖**Veronica** [1] (vĕ-, vĕrǫ·nikă). 1527. [med.L., app. from the name of St. Veronica.] 1. *Bot.* A large genus of scrophulariaceous plants (herbs or shrubs) having leafy stems and blue (rarely white or pink) flowers borne in racemes or spikes. 2. With *a* and *pl.* A plant or species of the genus Veronica 1855.

Vero·nica [2]. 1700. = VERNICLE, q.v.

‖**Verruca** (verū·kă). *Pl.* **verrucæ** (verū·sī). 1565. [L., wart, excrescence on precious stones.] a. A wart. B. *Bot.*, *Conch.*, *Ent.* A wart-like formation, growth, or prominence. So **Ve·rrucated** *a. Conch.* having or covered with verrucæ or warty growths.

Verruci- (si), combining form of L. *verruca* VERRUCA, as in **Verruci·ferous** *a.*, of a zoophyte, bearing verrucæ. **Verru·ciform** *a.*, wart-shaped.

Verrucose (ve·rukōus), *a.* 1686. [ad. L. *verrucosus.*] 1. Covered, furnished with, or full of verrucæ or wart-like excrescences or growths. Now *Nat. Hist.* and *Path.* 2. *Bot.* Studded with warty swellings or protuberances; tuber cular 1802.

Verrucous (verū·kəs), *a.* 1656. [ad. L *verrucosus*, f. *verruca.*] 1. = prec. (*rare*). 2 *Path.* Of the nature of a wart or warts; cha racterized by the formation of warts 1728.

Verruculose (verū·kiŭlōus), *a.* 1846. [ad mod.L. *verruculosus*, f. L. *verrucula*, dim. c *verruca* VERRUCA.] Covered with small ve rucæ or warts.

‖**Verruga** (verū·gă). 1897. [Sp., wart:- L. *verruca* VERRUCA.] *Path.* A febrile diseas endemic in Peru and characterized by wart eruptions or tumours on the skin; Peruvia wart.

†**Ve·rry**, *a.* (and *sb.*). 1550. [var. of *varr* VAIRY *a.*] *Her.* = VAIRY *a.* 1. -1780.

†**Versabi·lity.** 1673. [f. L. *versabilis*, f *versare*; see -ITY.] a. = VERSATILITY. b Aptness or readiness to be changed or turne (round). -1762.

Versal (vɔ̄·ɹsăl), *a.* *Obs.* or *dial.* 159 [Illiterate or colloq. abbrev. of UNIVERSAL *a* Cf. VARSAL *a.*] 1. Universal; whole. Usu. cou pled with *world*. 2. Single; individual 1709.

Versant (vɔ̄·ɹsănt), *sb.* 1851. [a. F., *verser*; see VERSE *v.*[2]] 1. The slope, side, c descent of a mountain or mountain-chain; th area or region covered by this. 2. Tendenc to slope or descend; declination 1859.

Versant (vɔ̄·ɹsănt), *a.* 1645. [f. L. *ve sant-*, *versans*, pres. pple. of *versare*, *versar* VERSE *v.*[2]] 1. Concerned *about*, occupied c engaged *in* or *with*, something. 2. Of person a. = VERSED *ppl. a.*[1] Now *rare*. 1766. b. Co versant or intimately acquainted *with* a subje or person 1787.

2. b. A man not v. with courts of justice SYD. SMIT

Versatile (vɔ̄·ɹsătəil, vɔ̄·ɹsătil), *a.* 160 [a. F., or ad. L. *versatilis*, f. *versare* VERSE *v.* I. 1. Marked by changeability or inconstancy subject to change or fluctuation; variabl changeable. b. Of persons: Fickle, inconsta (*rare*) 1682. 2. Characterized by readiness c facility in turning from one subject, pursu etc., to another; marked by many-sidedness c variety of talent 1656. 3. Of persons: Turnin easily or readily from one subject or occupatio to another; showing facility in varied subjects many-sided 1762.

1. The v. tenderness which marks the irregular an capricious feelings of the populace BURKE. 2. Cha cer's genius was vast, v. and original 1828. 3. H was an able man of business, v., politic 1874.

II. Capable of being turned round on, or a on, a pivot or hinge; that may be turned diffe ent ways 1658. b. *Bot.* Of an anther: Swingin or turning about freely on the filament to whic it is attached 1760.

The Head..is sometimes v. 1826. Hence **Ve·rsa tile·ly** *adv.*, **-ness.**

Versatility (vɔ̄ɹsăti·lĭti). 1755. [a. F *versatilité*, or from prec. + -ITY.] The conditio or quality of being versatile, in various sense

Verse (vɔ̄ɹs), *sb.* [OE. *fers*, ad. L. *versus* line or row, spec. a line of writing (so name from turning to begin another line), f. *verte* to turn; in ME. reinforced by AF., OF. *ve* from the same source.] 1. A succession words arranged according to rules of prosod and forming a complete metrical line; one c the lines of a poem or piece of versification. 2 *Liturg.* = VERSICLE 1. Now *rare*. OE. 3. O of the sections of a psalm or canticle corre sponding to the compound unit (usu. a couple of Hebrew poetry. (Now merged in next.) M b. One of the sections into which a chapter c the Bible is divided 1560. 4. A stanza ME 5. Without article: Metrical composition, form or structure; language or literary work writte or spoken in metre; poetry, esp. with ref. t metrical form. Opp. to *prose*. ME. 6. Th metrical or poetical compositions of a particula author, etc.; a certain amount of metrical wor or poetry considered as a whole 1586.

1. Some mens behauiour is like a v. wherein euer sillable is measured BACON. 3. b. The first editio of the New Testament divided into our present verse was printed by Robert Stephens at Geneva in 1551. 4 I remember the two last lines of a v. in some of the ol songs of 'Logan Water' BURNS. 5. In antient tim before letters were in common use, the Lawes we

many times put into v. HOBBES. Phr. *In v.*, in metrical form. *Adonic, Alexandrine, blank, elegiac, heroic(al, hexameter, Leonine, Saturnian v.*: see these words. 6. Thus your V. Flow'd with her Beautie once SHAKS. Hence **Ve·rselet**, a small poem. **Ve·rsema:ker**, one who makes or writes verses; a versifier. **Ve·rseman**, a man who writes v.; a poet, esp. (in recent use) a minor poet or versifier. **Ve·rsemonger**, a versifier, esp. one who writes poor or indifferent v.

Verse (vɔ̄ɪs), *v.*[1] OE. [f. prec.] 1. *intr.* To compose or make verses; to versify. Also with *it.* 2. *trans.* To tell in verse; to turn into verse 1446.

2. Versing loue To amorous Phillida SHAKS. Hence **Versed** (vɔ̄ɪst) *ppl. a.*[2] composed in verse, turned into verse. **Ve·rser**, a writer of verse, a verseman.

Verse (vɔ̄ɪs), *v.*[2] 1556. [ad. F. *verser* or L. *versare*, freq. of *vertere* to turn.] †1. To turn over (a book) in study or investigation -1656. 2. To instruct, to make (a person) conversant or experienced *in* something. Now *refl.* 1673.

Versed (vɔ̄ɪst), *a.* 1596. [f. mod.L. *versus* (sc. *sinus*), pa. pple. of *vertere* to turn.] *V. sine.* 1. *Trig.* orig. The segment of the diameter intercepted between the foot of the sine and the extremity of the arc; in mod. use, the ratio of this line to the radius, or (equivalently, as a function of an angle) the quantity obtained by subtracting the cosine from unity. b. *Bridge-building.* The rise of an arch 1838.

Versed (vɔ̄ɪst), *ppl. a.*[1] 1610. [f. L. *versatus, versari* to be experienced; see -ED[1].] Of persons: Experienced, practised, or skilled *in* a subject, matter, art, etc.; conversant with or having an intimate knowledge of something.

Versed, *ppl. a.*[2]: see VERSE *v.*[1]

Verset (vɔ̄·ɪsėt). ME. [a. OF., dim. of *vers* VERSE *sb.*] 1. = VERSICLE 1. Now *Hist.* 2. A little or short verse, esp. one of the Bible or a similar book; a short piece of verse 1625.

Versicle (vɔ̄·ɪsik'l). late ME. [ad. L. *versiculus*, dim. of *versus* VERSE *sb.*] 1. *Liturg.* One of a series of short sentences, said or sung antiphonally in divine service; *spec.* one said by the officiant and followed by the RESPONSE of the congregation or people; often *collect. pl.*, a set of these with their accompanying responses. 2. A little verse. †a. A short clause or sentence -1721. b. †A verse of the Psalms or the Bible; now *spec.* one of the subdivisions of a Hebrew verse 1624. c. A short or single metrical line; a little verse 1573.

2. b. That v. of Psal. 119, ' Righteous art thou, O Lord, and right are thy Judgements' 1641. So **Versi·cular** *a.* of, pertaining to, characterized by, or consisting of versicles or verses, esp. Biblical verses.

Versicoloured (vɔ̄·ɪsikɒləɪd), *a.* 1721. [f. L. *versicolor*, f. *vers-, vertere*, after COLOURED *ppl. a.*] Changing or varying in colour; iridescent; also, variegated.

A rocket..drops its v. shower 1873.

Versification (vɔ̄ɪsifikēⁱ·ʃən). 1603. [ad. L. *versification-, versificatio*, f. *versificare* to versify.] 1. The action of composing verse; the art or practice of versifying. 2. The form or style in which the words in a poetical composition are arranged; the structure of poetry or verse; measure, metre 1693. 3. A metrical version *of* something 1821.

Versificator (vɔ̄·ɪsifikēⁱ:təɪ). 1611. [a. L., f. *versificare.*] One who writes verse; a poet, versifier.

Statius, the best V. next to Virgil DRYDEN.

Versifier (vɔ̄·ɪsifəi,əɪ). ME. [a. AF. *versifiour*, OF. *versifiere*, f. *versifier*; see next and -ER[1].] 1. One who versifies or composes verses; a verse-maker; a poet. 2. A mere or poor writer of verse(s); a rhymester, poetaster 1531.

1. He was a good classic and an excellent v. 1828. . She thought Byron an ephemeral v. 1880.

Versify (vɔ̄·ɪsifəi), *v.* late ME. [a. OF. *versifier*, ad. L. *versificare*, f. *versus* VERSE *sb.* + *facere* to make.] 1. *intr.* To make or compose verses; to write poetry. 2. *trans.* To narrate or recount in verse; to treat as the subject of verse. late ME. 3. To turn or convert (a literary piece) into verse; to translate or rewrite in verse-form 1735.

1. Never straining hard to v. BYRON. 2. I v. the truth, not poetize DANIEL. 3. Bolingbroke really wrote the 'Essay on Man', which Pope versified D'ISRAELI. Hence **Ve·rsifying** *vbl. sb.*

Version (vɔ̄·ɪʃən), *sb.* 1582. [a. F., or ad. L. *version-, versio*, f. *vertere* to turn.] 1. A rendering of some text or work, or of a single word, passage, etc., from one language into another; a translation; also (*rarely*), the action or process of translating. 2. The particular form of a statement, account, report, etc., given by one person or party; an account resting upon limited authority or embodying a particular point of view 1788. b. A particular form or variant of something 1835. †3. A turning about; a change of direction -1706. b. *Obstet.* The operation of manually turning the child so as to facilitate delivery 1853. †4. Conversion, transformation -1666.

1. The English v. of the Bible 1874. 2. The v. generally received of what he actually did say FROUDE. b. This painting is a larger v. of one at Windsor Castle 1908. 4. The V. of Aire into Water BACON. Hence **Ve·rsion** *v. trans.* to translate. **Ve·rsionist**, a translator.

‖**Vers libre** (vẹr lībr). 1909. [F., 'free verse'.] Versification in which the ordinary rules of prosody are or may be disregarded; verse consisting of an irregular alternation of long and short lines, freq. unrhymed. Hence **Vers-li·brist**, a writer of such verse.

‖**Verso** (vɔ̄·ɪso). 1839. [L. (sc. *folio* leaf), abl. sing. neut. of *versus*, pa. pple. of *vertere* to turn.] 1. The back of a leaf in a manuscript or printed book; the side presented to the eye when the leaf has been turned over in a forward direction. Abbreviated *v.*, *v°*. 2. The reverse of a coin, medal, or the like 1891.

1. The left-hand page of a book is the verso of that leaf, and faces the RECTO of the next N.E.D.

Versor (vɔ̄·ɪsǫ̈ɪ). 1640. [a. L. **versor*, f. *vers-, vertere* to turn.] †1. The needle of a compass. 2. *Math.* In quaternions, an operator which changes the direction of a vector without altering its length 1865.

Verst (vɔ̄ɪst). 1555. [ad. Russ. *verstá*, partly through G. *werst* and F. *verste.*] A Russian measure of length equal to 3500 English feet or about two-thirds of an English mile.

‖**Versus** (vɔ̄·ɪsɒ̆s), *prep.* 1447. [L.] Against; employed in *Law* to denote an action by one party against another. Freq. abbrev. *v.* (also *vs.*).

The jugement by twene..John Husset *versus* John Notte 1447. *transf.* Free will *versus* necessity H. SPENCER.

Versute (vəɪsiū·t, vɔ̄·ɪsiut), *a.* Now *rare.* 1616. [ad. L. *versutus*, f. *vers-, vertere* to turn.] Cunning, crafty, wily.

Vert (vɔ̄ɪt), *sb.*[1] (and *a.*). late ME. [a. AF. and OF. :—L. *viridem, viridis* green.] 1. Green vegetation growing in a wood or forest and capable of serving as cover for deer. 2. *ellipt.* The right to cut green trees or shrubs in a forest. Now *arch.* 1639. †3. A green colour or pigment -1582. 4. *spec.* in *Her.* The tincture green. Also as *adj.* 1507.

1. The oversight of verte and venyson, in all the Parkes 1455.

Vert (vɔ̄ɪt), *sb.*[2] Also **'vert.** 1864. [Short for CONVERT *sb.*, PERVERT *sb.*] A convert or pervert from one religion to another, esp. to the Roman Catholic faith.

Vert, *v.*[1] 1590. [ad. L. *vertere* to turn.] *trans.* To turn in a particular direction; to turn or twist out of the normal position. Now *spec.* in *Path.* or *Anat.*

Vert, *v.*[2] Also **'vert.** 1888. [f. VERT *sb.*[2]] *intr.* To become a convert or pervert from one religion to another, esp. to Roman Catholicism

Vertebra (vɔ̄·ɪtĭbrā). *Pl.* **-æ** (*ī*). 1615. [a. L., joint, joint of the spine, f. *vertere* to turn.] 1. *Anat.* and *Zool.* One or other of the joints composing the spinal column in man or other vertebrate animals; any segment of the backbone. 2. *pl.* (with *the*). The vertebral column; the spine or backbone 1627. 3. *Zool.* One or other of the axial ossicles of the arms of starfishes 1704.

Vertebral (vɔ̄·ɪtĭbrăl), *a.* and *sb.* 1681. [ad. med. or mod.L. *vertebralis*, or f. prec. + -AL.] A. *adj.* 1. Of, pertaining to, or situated on or near the vertebræ; spinal. 2. Composed of vertebræ; spinal. Freq. in *v. column.* 1822. 3. Of the nature of a vertebra 1847. 4. = VERTEBRATE *a.* 1. 1816. B. *sb.* A vertebral artery or vein 1718. Hence **Ve·rtebrally** *adv.*

Vertebrarterial (vɔ̄:ɪtĭbraɪtiᵊ·riăl), *a.* 1884. [f. VERTEBRA + ARTERIAL *a.*] *Anat.* and *Zool.* Of or belonging to a vertebra and an artery; vertebro-arterial.

‖**Vertebrata** (vɔ̄ɪtĭbrēⁱ·tă). 1826. [mod.L., a. L. (sc. *animalia*), neut. pl. of *vertebratus* VERTEBRATE *a.*] 1. With *the.* A division of the animal kingdom including all animals which have a backbone or its equivalent. 2. A group or class of these; a number of vertebrate animals 1851.

Vertebrate (vɔ̄·ɪtĭbrĕt), *a.* and *sb.* 1826. [ad. L. *vertebratus* jointed, articulated, f. *vertebra* VERTEBRA.] A. *adj.* 1. *Zool.* Of or belonging to the Vertebrata; characterized by having a backbone or spinal column. 2. Of, pertaining to, characteristic of, or found in a vertebrated animal or animals 1848. 3. *fig.* Of writings, etc.: Connectedly put together; characterized by strength or consistency 1882. B. *sb.* A member of the Vertebrata 1826. Similarly **Ve·rtebrated** *ppl. a.* 1828. (*a*) = sense A. 1; (*b*) consisting of vertebræ; (*c*) *transf.* constructed in a manner suggestive of vertebræ.

Vertebration (vɔ̄ɪtĭbrēⁱ·ʃən). 1884. [f. VERTEBRA.] Vertebral formation; division into segments like those of the spinal column; *fig.* 'backbone', strength or firmness.

†**Ve·rtebre.** 1578. [a. F. *vertèbre*, ad. L. *vertebra.*] = VERTEBRA 1 -1843.

Vertebro- (vɔ̄·ɪtĭbro), used as comb. form (see -O-), of VERTEBRA, as in *v.-arterial, -costal, -iliac.*

Vertex (vɔ̄·ɪteks). *Pl.* **vertices** (vɔ̄·ɪtisīz); also vertexes. 1570. [a. L., whirl, whirlpool, VORTEX, highest point, summit, f. *vertere* to turn.] 1. *Geom.* The point opposite to the base of a (plane or solid) figure; the point in a curve or surface at which the axis meets it; an angular point, as of a triangle or polygon. b. *Optics.* The point at which the axis cuts the surface of a lens 1704. 2. The point in the heavens vertically overhead, or directly above a given place; the zenith 1646. 3. *Anat.* and *Zool.* The crown or top of the head; *esp.* in man, the part lying between the occiput and the sinciput 1638. 4. The top, summit, or highest point of something, esp. a hill or structure; the crown of an arch. Also, †a high piece of land, an eminence. 1641.

†**Ve·rtible**, *a.* 1447. [a. OF., or ad. med.L. *vertibilis*, f. L. *vert-, vertere* to turn; see -IBLE.] Capable of turning or being turned; inconstant, mutable -1667. So †**Vertibi·lity** -1675.

Vertical (vɔ̄·ɪtikăl), *a.* and *sb.* 1559. [a. F., or ad. late L. *verticalis*, f. *vertic-*, stem of *vertex* VERTEX.] A. *adj.* 1. Of, pertaining to, placed or situated at, or passing through the vertex or zenith; occupying a position in the heavens directly overhead or above a given place or point; †*fig.* pertaining to or denoting the period or position of greatest eminence or perfection. 2. *V. angle*: a. Either of the two angles lying on opposite sides of two intersecting lines or planes; an opposite angle. †b. The angle opposite the base of a triangle or polygon. 1571. c. *Astr.* An angle measured on a vertical circle. 3. Placed or extending at right angles to the plane of the horizon; perpendicular, upright 1704. b. Of mechanical appliances or structures. Also in techn. use applied to machines which operate vertically. 1825. 4. Having a position at right angles to the plane of the axis, body, or supporting surface; pointing or situated directly upwards or downwards 1776. 5. *Zool.*, *Anat.*, etc. Of, pertaining to, situated on, or affecting the vertex of the head 1826.

1. At each equinox the sun appears v. over the equator 1880. †*V. point*, = VERTEX 2. *V. circle*, an azimuth-circle (see AZIMUTH 1). 3. The adaptation of the Virginian Creeper to climbing up v. walls 1882. b. *V. Boring-machine*, a drill..having a v. spindle 1875. *V. engine*, an upright engine, as distinct from a 'horizontal one' 1888.

Special collocations: **v. anthers**, anthers attached to the top of the filaments and pointing in the same direction as the filaments; **v. escapement**, *Watchmaking*, an old type of escapement in which the balance staff was at right angles to the axis of the escape wheel; **v. fire** (*Naval* and *Mil.*), fire at such a high angle that it will fall nearly vertically on the target; **v. index**, the ratio of the height of the cranium to its length; **v. limb**, a graduated arc attached to a theodolite or other instrument for measuring v. angles; **v. line**, a line at right angles to the plane of the horizon, or to any other line or plane taken as a base.

B. *sb.* [The adj. used ellipt.] †**1.** The vertex or zenith –1655. **2.** A vertical circle, line, or plane 1669. **3.** A vertical dial 1669.

2. *Prime v.*: see PRIME *a.* Phr. *The v.*, the perpendicular. Hence **Ve·rtical-ly** *adv.*, **-ness.**

Verticality (vɔ̄ɹtikæ·lĭti). 1570. [f. prec. + -ITY.] **1.** The condition of the sun or other celestial body when it is vertical or at the vertex or zenith. **2.** Vertical position; perpendicularity 1799.

1. For unto them the Sunne is verticall twice a year, making two distinct Summers in the different points of v. SIR T. BROWNE.

Verticil (vɔ̄·ɹtisil). 1793. [ad. L. VERTICILLUS.] *Bot.* A number or set of organs or parts arranged, disposed, or produced in a circle round an axis; a whorl.

Verticillaster (vɔ̄ɹtisilæ·stəɹ). 1832. [mod. L., f. L. VERTICILLUS + -ASTER.] *Bot.* A form of inflorescence occurring in certain labiate plants; a false whorl.

Verticillate (vɔ̄ɹtisi·lĕt, vəɹti·silĕt), *a.* Also †**verticellate.** 1668. [ad. mod.L. *verticillatus*, f. L. *verticillus* VERTICILLUS; see -ATE [2] 2.] *Bot.* and *Zool.* Arranged in whorls; disposed in or forming verticils or whorls; having leaves, flowers, hair, etc. so disposed or arranged. So **Verti·cillated** *a.* (now *rare.*) **Verticilla·tion**, the formation of verticils; a verticil.

‖**Verticillus** (vɔ̄ɹtisi·lŭs). *Pl.* **-li** (-ləi). 1760. [L., whorl (sc. of a spindle), dim. of *vertex* VERTEX.] *Bot.* A verticil or whorl.

Verticity (vəɹti·sĭti). Now *rare.* 1625. [ad. mod.L. *verticitas*, f. L. *vertic-*, *vertex* VERTEX.] **1.** The faculty of turning, or tendency to turn, towards a vertex or pole, esp. as exhibited in the loadstone or magnetic needle. Now *rare* or *Obs.* †**2.** The power of turning or revolving; rotation, revolution –1819.

1. The little magnet or needle turned itself briskly, ..shewing great v. 1837.

Vertiginate (vəɹti·dʒineᵉt), *v. rare.* 1767. [f. L. *vertigin-*, VERTIGO.] *intr.* To turn round, spin, or rush dizzily.

Vertiginous (vəɹti·dʒinəs), *a.* 1608. [ad. L. *vertiginosus* one suffering from giddiness, f. *vertigin-*, *vertigo* VERTIGO.] **1.** Of persons, the head, etc.: Affected with vertigo or giddiness; giddy, dizzy 1621. **b.** *fig.* Inconstant; marked by instability or rapid change 1609. **2.** Of the nature of or characterized by vertigo 1608. **3.** Liable to cause vertigo; inducing giddiness 1649. **4.** Of motion: Having the character of rotation or revolution; rotatory 1663.

1. They grew v. and fell from the battlements of heaven JER. TAYLOR. **2.** V. attacks became troublesome at times 1901. **3.** Crowded rooms and the v. influence of the dance 1899. **4.** We see, with whirl v., the Sun From west to east around his axis run 1766. Hence **Verti·ginous-ly** *adv.*, **-ness.**

‖**Vertigo** (vɔ̄·ɹtigo, vəɹtəi·go, vəɹtī·go). 1528. [L., a whirling about, giddiness, f. *vertere* to turn.] **1.** *Path.* A disordered condition in which the person affected has a sensation of whirling, either of external objects or of himself, and tends to lose equilibrium and consciousness; swimming in the head; giddiness, dizziness. **2.** *fig.* A disordered state of mind, or of things, comparable to giddiness 1634.

‖**Verumontanum** (viəːru,mɒntēⁱ·nŏm). 1728. [f. L. *veru* spit + *montanum*, neut. of *montanus* hilly.] *Anat.* A small prominence at the point where the seminal ducts enter the prostatic part of the urethra.

Vervain (vɔ̄·ɹvēⁱn). late ME. [a. AF. and OF. *verveine*, ad. L. *verbena* VERBENA.] **1.** The common European herbaceous plant *Verbena officinalis*, formerly much valued for its reputed medicinal properties. Also rarely, some other species of the genus *Verbena*, or the genus itself. **b.** With distinguishing terms, denoting varieties of this or other species of *Verbena*. Also applied to other plants resembling or allied to the vervains. 1578. **c.** With *a* and *pl.* A single species or plant of the genus *Verbena* 1597. **2.** Incorrectly used to render L. *verbena*; see VERBENA **1.** 1548.

attrib.: **v. humming bird**, the small Jamaican species, *Mellisuga minima*; **v. mallow**, a species of mallow, *Malva alcea*.

Verve (vɔ̄ɹv). 1697. [a. F.; origin obsc.] **1.** Special bent, vein, or talent in writing. Now *rare* or *Obs.* **2.** Intellectual vigour or energy, esp. as manifested in literary productions; great vivacity of ideas and expression 1803. **3.** *gen.* Energy, vigour, spirit 1863.

2. That thorough enjoyment of the labour, which is necessary to give life and v. to any creation, whether of the poet or the orator 1879.

Vervet (vɔ̄·ɹvĕt). 1884. [a. F.; origin obsc.] *Zool.* A species of monkey (*Cercopithecus pygerythrus* or *C. lalandii*) native to various parts of Africa.

Very (ve·ri). Also **verey.** The name of the inventor, Samuel W. *Very*, used attrib. in *V. lights*, lights used in night-signalling or for illuminating the enemy's position; so *V. flare*; *V. pistol*, the pistol from which these lights or flares are fired 1915.

Very (ve·ri), *a.* and *adv.* ME. [a. AF. *verrey*, *verai*, OF. *verai*, *vrai* (mod.F. *vrai*), f. the stem of L. *verus* true.] **A.** *adj.* **I.** †**1.** Really or truly entitled to the name or designation; = TRUE *a.* 5. **2.** With limitation (usu. expressed by *the* or a possessive) to particular instances: The true or real; that is truly or properly entitled to the name. Now *arch.* late ME. **3.** In emphatic use, denoting that the person or thing may be so named in the fullest sense of the term, or possesses all the essential qualities of the thing specified. late ME. **4.** †**a.** Truthful, true; sure, reliable –1505. **b.** Of truth: Exact, simple, real, actual. late ME. †**5.** Exact or precise, as opp. to *approximate* –1657. †**6.** Of a friend, servant, etc.: True, faithful, sincere, staunch –1676. †**7.** Of persons: Rightful, lawful, legitimate –1606.

1. Very God of very God *Bk. Com. Pr.*, *Nicene Creed* 1549. God is a v. spirit 1615. The Law of Nature [is] v. justice HOBBES. **2.** What would you say to me now, and I were your verie, verie Rosalind? SHAKS. The reall, and v. object HOBBES. **3.** They shall become a v. desolacion and curse COVERDALE *2 Kings* xxii. 19. A Region, which is the v. Reverse of Paradise ADDISON. A thing..so v. a nothing in itself 1747. A verier knave ne'er stepped the earth 1856. The veriest schoolboy 1859. **4. a.** Phr. *In* (or †*of*) *v. deed*; see DEED. **b.** To speak the v. truth 1668. **6.** A Gentleman a verie friend of mine 1608.

II. 1. Used as an intensive, either to denote the inclusion of something regarded as extreme or exceptional, or to emphasize the exceptional prominence of some ordinary thing or feature. late ME. **b.** Emphasizing sbs. which denote extremity of degree or extent. late ME. **2.** Neither more nor less than (that expressed by the sb. qualified); sheer. late ME. **b.** = MERE *a.* 5. 1546. **3.** Used (after *the, this, that*, etc.) to denote or emphasize complete or exact identity 1582. **b.** Of words: Exactly corresponding to those of an original or previous statement 1598.

1. The v. heauens declare his rightuousnes COVERDALE *Ps.* xcvi. 6. The room was crammed to the v. door 1832. His v. defects were a main cause of his popularity 1880. **b.** A bankrupt from the v. outset 1851. **c.** Coupled with *own*; I had to have it for my v. own. 1884. **2.** The sailors mutinied from v. hunger MACAULAY. **b.** The Governor-General treated the v. request as a high offence 1817. **3.** She died just this v. Day Seven Years SWIFT. Phr. *The v. thing*, the thing exactly suitable or requisite. **b.** Those were my v. words! 1865.

B. *adv.* †**1.** Truly, really, genuinely; in or with truth or reality; truthfully –1593. **2.** In a high degree or measure; to a great extent; exceedingly, extremely 1448. **b.** Qualifying pa. pples. used predic. or attrib.: = Very much 1641. **c.** With a neg., freq. denoting: Only moderately or slightly 1710. **d.** Repeated in order to convey greater emphasis 1649. **3.** In purely intensive use 1500.

2. My father..ys a verye old man 1588. V. near as long as the Iliad it self ADDISON. **b.** A v. over-rated man 1804. **c.** Then it went off, leaving me sickish, but not v. SWIFT. **d.** It was indeed v., v., v. dreadful DE FOE. **3.** The City was now reduc'd to the v. last Extremity 1684. The v. same day the year before 1662.

‖**Vesania** (vĭsēⁱ·niă). 1693. [L., f. *vesanus* mad, f. *ve-* not + *sanus* sane.] *Path.* Mental derangement.

‖**Vesica** (vĭsəi·kă). 1683. [L., bladder, blister.] **1.** *Anat.* A bladder 1693. †**2.** A copper vessel used in distilling –1728 **3.** In full, *V. piscis* (also *piscium*): a pointed oval figure, the sides of which are properly parts of two equal circles passing through each other at their centres, freq. employed as an architectural feature and by early artists as an aureole enclosing figures of Christ, the Virgin, etc. 1809.

3. Vesica piscium cannot, therefore, signify a fish's bladder, but a bladder which when filled with wind, would be in the form of a fish 1813. Hence **Ve·sical** *a.* of, pertaining to, or formed in the urinary bladder; having the form of a v.

Vesicant (ve·sikănt), *sb.* and *a.* 1661. [ad. mod.L. *vesicant-*, *vesicans*, pres. pple. of *vesicare*; see next and -ANT.] *Med.* **A.** *sb.* A vesicatory. **b.** A blister gas 1938. **B.** *adj.* Causing blisters; vesicatory 1826.

Vesicate (ve·sikeᵉt), *v.* 1657. [f. ppl. stem of mod.L. *vesicare*; see VESICA and -ATE [3].] Chiefly *Med.* **1.** *trans.* To cause to rise in a blister or blisters; to raise blisters on (the skin, etc.). **b.** In *pa. pple.* Covered with or converted into blisters 1676. **2.** *absol.* To produce blisters 1809. **3.** *intr.* To become blistered 1899.

Vesication (vesikēⁱ·ʃən). 1543. [ad. mod. L. *vesicatio*, f. *vesicare*; see prec.] *Med.* **1.** The result of blistering or of rising in blisters; a blister or a group of these. **2.** The formation or development of blisters; the action or fact of blistering 1753.

Vesicatory (ve·sikeᵉtəri, vesi·kătəri), *sb.* and *a.* 1604. [ad. med. or early mod.L. *vesicatorius*, f. L. VESICA.] *Med.* **A.** *sb.* An ointment, plaster, or other application for raising blisters on the skin. **B.** *adj.* Of the nature of a vesicatory; capable of or characterized by raising blisters 1612.

Vesicle (ve·sik'l). 1578. [ad. F. *vésicule* or L. *vesicula* VESICULA.] **1. a.** *Anat.*, *Bot.*, *Zool.* A small bladder-like vessel; a cavity or cell with a membranous integument; a small sac or cyst. (Freq. with defining terms, as *blood-seminal, umbilical vesicles.*) **b.** *Physics.* A minute bubble or spherule of liquid or vapour, esp. one of those composing a cloud or fog 1731. **c.** *Geol.* A small spherical or oval cavity produced by the presence of bubbles of gas or vapour in volcanic rocks 1811. **2.** *Path.* A small, usually round, elevation of the cuticle containing fluid matter 1799.

Vesico- (ve·siko), used as comb. form (see -O-) of VESICA, occurring in terms referring to the bladder in connexion with some other part of the body denoted by the second element, as *v.-cervical, -prostatic, -rectal.*

‖**Vesicula** (vĭsi·kiŭlă). *Pl.* **-æ** (*i*). 1715. [L., dim. of VESICA.] = VESICLE **1** (usu. in pl.), 2.

Vesicular (vĭsi·kiŭlăɹ), *a.* 1715. [ad. early mod.L. *vesicularis*, f. L. *vesicula.*] **1.** Having the form or structure of a vesicle; bladder-like 1720. **2.** Characterized by the presence of vesicles; composed of parts having the form of vesicles 1715. **3.** *Path.* **a.** Characterized by the formation or presence of vesicles on the skin 1818. **b.** Affecting or connected with the vesicles or air-cells of the lungs 1829.

1. It was formerly advanced that these minute drops of rain or fog were v.—that is, hollow spheres! 186[illegible] **2.** V. Lava 1811. **3. a.** V. Fever 1818. **b.** It is commonly called the 'v. murmur', having been so named when the idea that it arose in the air cells of the lung was accepted without question 1883.

Vesiculated (vĭsi·kiŭlēⁱtĕd), *a.* 1703. [f. mod.L. *vesiculatus* (f. L. VESICULA) + -ED.] **1** Having or full of small cavities or air-cells. **2.** Of the nature of a vesicle or vesicula 1898. **3.** *Path.* Covered with vesicles 1858.

Vesiculation (vĭsikiŭlēⁱ·ʃən). 1876. [f. VESICULA + -ATION.] *Path.* The formation of vesicles, esp. on the skin; a vesicular condition or pustule.

‖**Vesiculitis** (vĭsikiŭləi·tis). 1861. [f. VESICULA + -ITIS.] *Path.* Inflammation of a vesicle, esp. of the seminal vesicles.

Vesiculose (vĭsi·kiŭlōᵘs), *a.* 1817. [ad. L. *vesiculosus*; see VESICULA and -OSE.] Full of vesicles; vesicular. So †**Vesi·culous** *a.* –1712.

Vesper (ve·spəɹ). late ME. [Partly a. L. evening star, cogn. w. Gr. ἕσπερος HESPERUS

Partly ad. early F. *vespres* (mod.F. *vêpres*) vespers, ad. L. *vesperas*, acc. pl. of *vespera*.] I. In the sing. form. 1. *poet.* (or *rhet.*). With capital. The evening star; Hesper, Hesperus. †2. Evening, eventide; an evening -1849. 3. Vespers, evensong 1636. 4. *ellipt.* The vesper-bell 1808.

4. But, hark! the v. calls to pray'r MOORE.

II. In collect. pl. Vespers. †1. a. In University use: The public disputations and accompanying ceremonies immediately preceding the inception or commencement of a Bachelor of Arts; esp. in later use at Oxford, the day on which these were held, the eve *of* the Act -1715. †b. The eve *of* a festival or *of* the Passion -1697. 2. *Eccl.* The sixth of the canonical hours of the breviary, said or sung (orig.) towards evening; evensong; also, the time of this office 1611. b. *poet.* Evening prayers or devotions 1814. 3. *transf.* The evening song of a bird. Chiefly *poet.* 1678.

2. *Sicilian vespers*: see SICILIAN *a.*

Vesperal (ve·spĕrăl), *a.* and *sb.* 1623. [ad. late L. *vesperalis*, f. L. *vespera*; see prec.] A. *adj.* Pertaining to the evening or to vespers (*rare*). B. *sb. Eccl.* An office-book containing the psalms, canticles, antiphons, etc., used at vespers; an antiphonary containing the vesper-chants 1869.

‖**Vespertilio** (vespəɹti·lio). 1665. [L., f. *vesper* VESPER.] A bat (*rare*); in mod. *Zool.*, one of the many genera of *Cheiroptera*.

Vesperti·lionid, *a.* 1875. [ad. mod.L. *Vespertilionidæ*.] *Zool.* Of or belonging to the *Vespertilionidæ*, a large family of insectivorous bats including the common British species.

Vespertine (ve·spəɹtəin, -in), *a.* 1502. [ad. L. *vespertinus*, f. *vesper* VESPER; see -INE [1].] 1. Of or pertaining to the evening; coming, occurring, or taking place in the evening. b. Of animals, birds, etc.: Appearing or especially active in the evening 1607. 2. *Astr.* and *Astrol.* Of a star, planet, etc.: Setting at or just after sunset 1601. 3. *Geol.* Used to designate the lowest carboniferous formation of the Pennsylvanian coal-measures 1858. So Vesperti·nal *a.*

Vespiary (ve·spiări). 1817. [irreg. f. L. *vespa* wasp, after *apiary*.] A wasps' nest.

Vespine (ve·spəin), *a.* 1843. [f. L. *vespa* wasp + -INE [1].] Of or pertaining to a wasp or wasps; consisting of wasps.

Vessel (ve·sĕl), *sb.* ME. [a. (1) AF. and OF. *vessel* (mod.F. *vaisseau*), masc.:—L. *vascellum*, dim. of *vas* VAS; (2) AF. and OF. *vessele* fem., repr. the L. pl. *vascella* and used in a collective sense.] †1. In collect. sing.: = PLATE *sb.* II. 3. -1664. 2. A receptacle for a liquid or other substance, often one of circular section and made of some durable material; *esp.* a utensil of this nature in domestic use, employed in connexion with the preparation or serving of food or drink, and usu. of a size suitable for carrying by hand ME. 3. *fig.* (chiefly in or after Biblical use). a. Said of a person regarded as having the containing capacity or function of a vessel. Now *arch.* ME. †b. Said of the body, esp. as the receptacle of the soul -1704. 4. A craft or ship of any kind, now usu. one larger than a rowing-boat and often restricted to sea-going craft or those plying upon the larger rivers or lakes ME. 5. *Anat.* and *Zool.* One of the membranous canals, ducts, or tubes in which the fluids of the body are contained and by means of which they are circulated; freq., a blood-vessel. late ME. b. *Bot.* One of the cellular or tubular structures composing the vascular system of plants and having the function of containing or carrying sap or other secretion; a duct 1671. 6. *Bot.* = PERICARP (*rare*) 1691.

1. All his Vessell was of golde and siluer, pottis, basons, ewers, dysshes, flagons, barels, cuppes, and all other thyngis LD. BERNERS. 2. To my great Misfortune, I had no V. to boil or stew any Thing DE FOE. *fig.* When creeping Murmure..Fills the wide Vessell of the Vniuerse SHAKS. *Prov.* But the saying is true, The empty v. makes the greatest sound SHAKS. 3. a. We know there are vessels of wrath 1597. Phr. *The weaker v.*: see WEAK *a.* 3. b. WYCLIF 1 *Thess.* iv. 4. 4. *fig.* In 1832 the v. of Reform was still labouring heavily 1876. Hence †Ve·ssel *v. trans.* to put or enclose (a liquid, etc.) in a v. Ve·sselful, as much or as many as a v. will hold.

Vest (vest), *sb.* 1613. [ad. F. *veste*, a. It. *veste* (also *vesta*) robe, gown:—L. *vestem*, *vestis*, cogn. w. Gr. ἐσθής, Skr. *vastra*.] 1. A loose outer garment worn by men in Eastern countries or in ancient times; a robe or gown. b. A similar garment worn by women. Chiefly *poet.* 1700. c. A garment, in various fig. uses 1655. 2. An ecclesiastical vestment (*rare*) 1663. 3. a. A sleeveless garment of some length worn by men beneath the coat. (Introduced by Charles II.) Now *Hist.* b. A waistcoat. (Now in tradesman's use and *U.S.*) 1666. c. A knitted or woven under-garment for the upper part of the body, worn next to the skin 1851. d. A piece of lace, net, silk, or other soft material worn so as to be completely or partly visible at the front of the bodice of a low-necked garment 1887.

1. The Persians make their long vests of such cloths DE FOE. b. Attended by her Maiden Train, Who bore the Vests that Holy Rites require DRYDEN. c. Ev'ning in her sober v. COWPER.

Vest (vest), *v.* late ME. [ad. OF. *vestir* (mod.F. *vêtir*):—L. *vestire* to clothe, f. *vestis* clothing; see prec.] I. 1. *trans.* = INVEST *v.* I. 5, 6. Chiefly in pass., and usu. const. *in*. b. To invest (a person) *with* some quality, esp. power, authority, etc. Chiefly in pass. 1674. 2. *intr.* To become vested *in* a person; to descend or devolve *upon* a person as possessor 1592.

1. No Legiance is due to him, before the Crown is vested upon him 1651. There is a particular jurisdiction vested in the officers 1756. Miltiades thus vested in the supreme command GOLDSM. b. They may be reasonably supposed to be vested with the same powers 1727. 2. The property vests in the official receiver *qua* trustee 1885.

II. 1. *trans.* In pa. pple.: Dressed, clothed, robed (*in* some garment) 1513. 2. Of a garment: To clothe or cover (a person) 1582. 3. To dress (a person) in a robe or garment, esp. as a formal act or ceremony 1648. b. *Eccl.* To drape or cover (an altar) 1867. 4. *refl.* To apparel or robe oneself, esp. in ecclesiastical vestments. Also *absol.* 1668.

1. My late espoused Saint..Came vested all in white, pure as her mind MILT. 4. Just before the Bishop vested himself to say Mass 1771.

III. *trans.* = INVEST *v.* II. 1719.

Vesting this Hundred Pounds in English Goods DE FOE.

‖**Vesta** (ve·stă). late ME. [L., corresp. to Gr. Ἑστία, identical with ἑστία hearth, house, household.] 1. *Myth.* A Roman female divinity, the daughter of Saturn and goddess of the hearth and household. 2. *Astr.* One of the minor planets, revolving in an orbit between Mars and Jupiter 1807. 3. orig. *v. match*: A kind of short match, orig. of wax 1839.

Vestal (ve·stăl), *a.* and *sb.* late ME. [ad. L. *vestalis*, f. VESTA.] A. *adj.* 1. *V. virgin*, one of the priestesses (orig. four, subseq. six in number) who had charge of the sacred fire in the temple of Vesta at Rome. 2. Of fire, etc.: Of or pertaining to Vesta 1599. 3. Resembling a priestess of Vesta in respect of chastity; chaste, pure, virgin 1595. 4. Pertaining to or characteristic of a vestal virgin or virgins; marked by chastity or purity 1592.

2. She sprinkl'd thrice, with Wine, the V. Fire DRYDEN. 3. *transf.* V. primroses KEATS. 4. A Song fit for a v. Ear 1729.

B. *sb.* 1. A vestal virgin 1579. 2. A virgin; a chaste woman; a nun 1590.

2. She was the most hospitable and jovial of old vestals, and had been a beauty in her day THACKERAY.

Vested (ve·stĕd), *ppl. a.* 1671. [f. VEST *v.* + -ED.] 1. Clothed, robed, dressed, *spec.* in ecclesiastical vestments. 2. Established, secured, or settled in the hands of, or definitely assigned to a certain possessor; *esp.* with *right* or *interest* 1766.

1. The V. Priest before the Altar stands WORDSW. 2. V. remainders..are where the estate is invariably fixed, to remain to a determinate person, after the particular estate is spent BLACKSTONE.

Vestiarian (vesti,ē·riăn), *a.* 1850. [f. VESTIARY + -IAN.] Of, relating to, or concerned with ecclesiastical vestments.

Vestiary (ve·sti,ări), *sb.* ME. [a. OF. *vestiarie* (mod.F. *vestiaire*), or ad. L. *vestiarium* clothes-chest, wardrobe, neut. sing. of *vestiarius* adj.] The vestry of a church. Now *rare* or *Obs.* b. A room or building, esp. in a monastery or other large establishment, in which clothes were kept. *Hist.* 1450.

Vestiary (ve·sti,ări), *a.* 1622. [ad. L. *vestiarius*; see prec. and -ARY [1].] Of, pertaining to, or relating to clothes or dress.

Vestibular (vesti·biŭlăɹ), *a.* 1836. [f. next + -AR [1].] Of, pertaining to, of the nature of, resembling, or serving as a vestibule.

The v. termination of the auditory nerve 1899.

Vestibule (ve·stibiūl). 1623. [ad. L. *vestibulum* entrance-hall, fore-court, entrance.] 1. The enclosed or partially enclosed space in front of the main entrance of an ancient Roman or Greek house or building; an entrance-court or fore-court. b. A chamber or hall immediately between the entrance-door and the interior of a building or house (usu. one of some size), to which it gives admittance; an ante-chamber, entrance-hall, or lobby 1730. c. An enclosed and covered-in portion at either end of a railway carriage, serving as a means of passage from one carriage to another. Also *attrib.* in *v. train*. orig. *U.S.* 1889. 2. *Anat.* and *Zool.* One or other of various cavities or hollows regarded as forming an approach or entrance to another, usu. a larger or more important part 1728.

2. *V. of the ear*, the osseous cavity which forms the central portion of the labyrinth of the ear and is situated between the tympanum and the internal auditory canal immediately behind the cochlea.

‖**Vestibulum** (vesti·biŭlŏm). 1662. [L.; see prec.] a. = prec. 1, 2. b. *Zool.* The cavity or chamber in certain infusorians into which the œsophagus and anus open 1859.

Vestige (ve·stidʒ). 1602. [a. F., ad. L. *vestigium* footprint, trace.] I. 1. A mark, trace, or visible sign *of* something which no longer exists or is present; a piece of material evidence of this nature; something which remains after the destruction or disappearance of the main portion. b. A surviving memorial or trace *of* some condition, quality, practice, etc., serving as an indication of its former existence. Usu. in pl. 1700. c. A very small or slight trace, indication, or amount (*of* something) 1756. 2. *Biol.* A surviving trace *of* some part formerly existing in the species; a vestigial organ or structure 1859.

1. Descending the Mons Cælius we come against the vestiges of the Palazzo Maggiore EVELYN. b. The vestiges of a patriarchal state still surviving 1875. c. Not a v. of green pasturage was to be descried 1834. 2. Rudimentary organs,..as..the v. of an ear in earless breeds DARWIN.

II. A mark or trace left on the ground by the foot; a footprint; a track (*rare*) 1656.

Vestigial (vesti·dʒiăl), *a.* 1884. [f. L. *vestigium* (see prec.) + -AL [1].] Of the nature of a vestige; remaining or surviving in a degenerate, atrophied, or imperfect condition or form.

‖**Vestigium** (vesti·dʒiŏm). *Pl.* **-ia.** Now *rare* or *Obs.* 1637. [L.] A vestige or trace; a mark or indication left by something destroyed, lost, or no longer present.

†**Ve·stiment.** ME. [a. OF., or ad. L. *vestimentum* clothes, f. *vestire* to clothe.] A vestment, esp. one worn by an ecclesiastic -1850. Hence Vestime·ntal (*rare*), Vestime·ntary *adjs.* of or pertaining to clothes or dress; vestiary.

Ve·sting. 1828. [f. VEST *sb.* 3 b.] Cloth or other material for making vests or waistcoats. Usu. in pl.

Vestiture (ve·stitiŭɹ, -tʃəɹ). late ME. [ad. med.L. *vestitura*, f. L. *vestire* to VEST.] 1. = INVESTITURE 2, 3. (*rare*). 2. *concr.* Clothes, clothing, vesture 1842.

Vestment (ve·stmĕnt). ME. [a. AF. and OF. *vestement* (mod.F. *vêtement*), ad. L. *vestimentum* VESTIMENT.] 1. A garment or article of clothing, esp. one of the nature of a robe or gown. Also *collect.*, clothing, dress, vesture. 2. A garment worn by a priest or ecclesiastic on the occasion of some service or ceremony; a priestly robe ME. b. An article of attire worn by the clergy, or by certain of their assistants, during divine service or on some special occasion; *spec.* a chasuble ME. c. *transf.* and *fig.* Something which covers as a garment; a covering 1483.

2. The Surplice, a v. of the Pagan Priests, introduced into churches 1796. 3. Green,..which colour nature hath chosen for the v. of the earth HOGARTH.

Vestry (ve·stri). late ME. [prob. a. AF. **vest(e)rie*, f. VEST *v.* + -(E)RY, substituted for *vestiarie* VESTIARY.] **1.** A room or part of a church in which the vestments, vessels, records, etc. are kept, and in which the clergy and choir robe for divine service; a room used for similar purposes in connexion with any church, chapel, or other place of worship. **b.** A place or room where clothes (†or valuables) are kept 1574. **2.** In English parishes: An assembly or meeting of the parishioners or a certain number of these, held usu. in the vestry of the parish church, for the dispatch of parochial business 1589. **b.** The body of parishioners meeting in this way and constituting a parochial board or council of management 1672.

1. b. Then said the Interpreter.., Go into the V. and fetch out Garments for these People BUNYAN. 2. I did speechify once at a v. 1762. b. The Lower House..had degenerated into something noisier than a v. 1882.

Comb.: **v.-book,** (*a*) a book in which the proceedings of the parish v. are recorded; (*b*) a book kept in a v. in which the births, marriages, and deaths of the parishioners are registered; **-clerk,** the clerk of a parochial v.; **-room,** the v. of a church; the room in which the parochial v. assembles. Hence **Ve·stryman,** a member of a parochial v.

Vestuary (ve·stiuări). Now *arch.* 1490. [ad. OF. *vestuaire*. Cf. VESTIARY *sb.*] A vestiary or vestry; a wardrobe.

Vesture (ve·stiŭı, -tʃəı), *sb.* late ME. [a. AF. and OF. (mod.F. *vêture*), f. *vestir* VEST *v.*] **1.** That with which a person is clothed or dressed; clothes, clothing. **2.** *Law.* All that grows upon or covers the land, with the exception of trees; one or other of the products of land, such as grass or corn 1455.

1. Pharaoh..arayed him in vestures of fine linnen *Gen.* xli. 42. *collect.* They haue cast lottes vpon my v. COVERDALE *Ps.* xxi. 18. *fig.* To clothe ourselves with the comely v. of innocency 1575. 2. In English Law it has been held that one person may have a freehold in the soil and another in the v. 1869. Hence **Ve·stured** *ppl. a.* clothed or dressed in v.; wearing v.

Vesuvian (vĭsiū·viăn), *a.* and *sb.* 1673. [f. *Vesuvius*, the active volcano on the Bay of Naples in Italy.] **A.** *adj.* Of or pertaining to Vesuvius; *esp.* like or resembling Vesuvius, or that of Vesuvius, in volcanic violence or power. **B.** *sb.* **1.** *Min.* A silicate of aluminium, lime, and iron or other base, occurring massive but more freq. in square crystals of various colours, and found orig. in the ancient Vesuvian lavas; idocrase 1796. **2.** A kind of match or fusee, used esp. for lighting cigars or pipes in the open air 1853. Hence **Vesu·vianite** = B 1.

Vesuvin (vĭsiū·vin). 1885. [a. G., f. *Vesuvius*, from its explosive property; see -IN [1].] *Chem.* Phenyl-brown, used esp. as a staining matter for histological preparations.

Vet, *sb.* 1862. [colloq. contr. of VETERINARIAN or VETERINARY.] A veterinary surgeon. Hence **Vet** *v. trans.* to submit (an animal) to veterinary examination or treatment 1891; *transf.* to examine or treat (a person) medically; *fig.* (*colloq.*) to examine, scrutinize, test 1904.

Vet. U.S. abbrev. of VETERAN.

Vetch (vetʃ). late ME. [a. ONF. *ve(c)che*, = OF. *vecce*, (mod.F. *vesce*):—L. *vicia*.] **1.** The bean-like fruit of various species of the leguminous plant *Vicia*. **2.** *pl.* Plants belonging to the genus *Vicia*, esp. to the species *V. sativa*, the common tare. late ME. **3.** In generic use as a plant-name (or, in early use, as that of a grain); also occas., with *a* and *pl.*, one or other species of the genus *Vicia*. late ME. **4.** Applied, with distinguishing terms, to plants of various genera more or less resembling vetches 1562. Hence **Ve·tchy** *a.* composed of or abounding in vetches.

Vetchling (ve·tʃliŋ). 1578. [f. prec. + -LING [1].] *Bot.* A plant or species of the genus *Lathyrus*; the genus itself.

Veteran (ve·tĕrăn), *sb.* and *a.* 1509. [a. early mod.F., or ad. L. *veteranus*, f. *veter-*, *vetus* old.] **A.** *sb.* **1.** One who has had long experience in military service; an old soldier. **2.** One who has seen long service in any office or position, an experienced or aged person 1597.

3. An ex-service man (*U.S.*) 1906.

B. *adj.* **1.** Of soldiers: Long practised or exercised in war 1611. **2.** Of persons in general: Grown old in service; experienced by long usage or practice 1728. **3.** Of things: Old; long-continued (*rare*) 1653.

1. The loss of a v. army GIBBON. 2. The self-possession of a v. courtier MACAULAY. Hence **Ve·teranize** *v.* (*U.S.*) *trans.* to render a v.; *intr.* to re-enlist as a soldier.

Veterinarian (ve:tĕrinē·riăn), *sb.* and *a.* 1646. [f. L. *veterinarius* + -AN.] **A.** *sb.* One who is skilled in or professionally occupied with the medical and surgical treatment of cattle and domestic animals; a veterinary surgeon. **B.** *adj.* = next A. 1656.

Veterinary (ve·tĕrinări), *a.* and *sb.* 1790. [ad. L. *veterinarius*, f. *veterinus* of or pertaining to (draught) cattle (f. *vehere* to draw).] **A.** *adj.* Of, pertaining to, connected or concerned with the medical or surgical treatment of cattle or domestic animals.

V. surgeon = prec. A.

B. *sb.* = prec. A. 1861.

Vetiver (ve·tivəı). Also **-vert.** 1858. [ad. F. *vétyver*, ad. Tamil *vețțivēru* (f. *vēr* root).] = CUSCUS [2].

Veto (vī·to), *sb.* 1629. [a. L., I forbid, the word by which the Roman tribunes of the people opposed measures of the Senate or actions of the magistrates.] **1.** A prohibition having for its object or result the prevention of a proposed or intended act; the power of thus preventing or checking action by prohibition. **2.** *spec.* The act on the part of a competent person or body of preventing or checking legislative or other political action by the exercise of a prohibitory power; the right or power to interpose prohibition against the passing or putting in force of an enactment or measure 1792.

1. Phr. *To put* (also *place, set*) *a v. on* or *upon* (something); The Rector had beforehand put a v. on any Dissenting chairman GEO. ELIOT. 2. The President's v kills off some vicious measures 1888. Hence **Ve·toist,** one who exercises the right, or supports the use, of the v.

Veto (vī·to), *v.* 1706. [f. prec.] **1.** *trans.* To put a veto on, refuse consent to; to stop or block by this means. **2.** To refuse to admit or accept (a person) 1885.

1. Washington vetoed..two bills only 1888.

‖**Vettura** (vetū·ra). 1792. [It.:—L. *vectura* conveyance, carriage, f. *vect-*, *vehere* to convey.] A four-wheeled carriage used in Italy.

‖**Vetturino** (veturī·no). *Pl.* **-ini.** 1617. [It., f. *vettura*; see prec.] **1.** In Italy: One who lets out carriages or horses on hire; also, a driver of a vettura. **2.** = prec. 1789.

Vex (veks), *v.* late ME. [a. OF. (also mod.F.) *vexer*, ad. L. *vexare* to shake, agitate, disturb.] **I. 1.** *trans.* To trouble, afflict, or harass (a person, etc.) by aggression, encroachment, or other interference with peace and quiet. **2.** Of diseases, etc.: To afflict or distress physically. Now *poet.* 1489. **3.** To afflict with mental agitation or trouble; to make anxious or depressed; to distress deeply or seriously. late ME. **4.** To affect with a feeling of dissatisfaction, annoyance, or irritation; to cause (a person) to fret, grieve, or feel unhappy 1450. **b.** To irritate or tease (an animal) 1700. †**5.** *intr.* To be distressed in mind; to feel unhappy or dissatisfied; to fret or grieve. Also const. *at.* -1804.

1. When intestine divisions v. a state 1845. 2. Sore vexed with the gout 1548. 3. V. not his ghost, O let him passe SHAKS. Why will you v. yourself about your father? 1873. 4. Your letter very much vexed me 1714.

II. 1. *trans.* To disturb by causing physical movement, commotion, or alteration; to agitate, toss about, work, etc. 1627. **b.** *fig.* To press, strain, or urge 1678. **2.** To subject (a matter) to prolonged or severe examination or discussion 1614.

1. Some English wool, vex'd in a Belgian Loom, And into Cloth of spungy softness made DRYDEN. 2. And not vexing a question let us own that he was.. a gentleman 1869. Hence **Ve·xer,** one who or that which vexes or annoys.

Vexation (veksē¹·ʃən). late ME. [a. OF., or ad. L. *vexation-*, *vexatio*, f. *vexare* VEX *v.*] **1.** The action of troubling or harassing by aggression or interference (occas. *spec.* by unjustifiable claims or legal action); the fact of being troubled or harassed in this way. †**2.** The action of troubling, disturbing, or irritating by physical means; the fact or state of being so troubled or distressed -1704. **3.** The state or fact of being mentally troubled or distressed, in later use esp. by something causing annoyance, irritation, dissatisfaction, or disappointment 1465. **4.** A source or cause of mental trouble or distress; a grief or affliction. Chiefly with *a.* 1594.

1. I still had hopes, my long vexations past, Here to return GOLDSM. 2. The fierce v. of a dreame SHAKS. 3. The King..heard of this new trouble with much v. SCOTT. Phr. *V. of mind, spirit.* 4. Your Children were v. to your youth, But mine shall be a comfort to your Age SHAKS.

Vexatious (veksē¹·ʃəs), *a.* 1534. [f. prec.; see -IOUS.] **1.** Causing or tending to cause vexation. **b.** *spec.* Of legal actions: Instituted without sufficient grounds for the purpose of causing trouble or annoyance to the defendant 1677. †**2.** Full of trouble or uneasiness -1671.

1. The Townsmen..are..turbulent and v. to the Regiment 1715. b. Their courts were unceasingly occupied with v. suits FROUDE. 2. Riches and honours which bring not a pleasant, but rather a careful and v. life 1671. Hence **Vexa·tious·ly** *adv.*, **-ness.**

Vexed (vekst), *ppl. a.* 1440. [f. VEX *v.*] **1.** Troubled, harassed. **2.** Distressed, grieved; annoyed, irritated 1602. **3.** Subjected to physical force or strain; tossed about, agitated 1610. **4.** *V. question*, a much debated or contested question 1657. Hence **Ve·xed·ly** *adv.*

Vexillary (ve·ksilări). 1591. [ad. L. *vexillarius* standard-bearer, f. *vexillum* standard.] **a.** One of the oldest class of veterans in the Roman army, who served under a special standard. **b.** A Roman standard-bearer.

Vexillation (veksilē¹·ʃən). 1656. [ad. L. *vexillatio*, f. *vexillum*.] A company of veteran soldiers (see prec. a) or of soldiers grouped under one standard.

‖**Vexillum** (veksi·lŏm). 1726. [L. (in sense 1), f. the stem of *vehere* to carry.] **1. a.** A flag or banner carried by Roman troops; a body of men grouped under one banner. **b.** *Eccl.* A piece of linen or silk attached to the upper part of a crozier 1877. **2.** *Bot.* The large external petal of a papilionaceous flower 1727. **3.** *Ornith.* The vane or web of a feather 1867.

‖**Via** (vəi·ă), *sb.* 1615. [L., a road, way.] **1.** *V. Lactea*, the Milky Way. **2.** A way or road; a highway 1787. **3.** *V. media*, a middle way; an intermediate course 1845.

‖**Via** (vəi·ă), *int. Obs.* exc. *arch.* 1596. [It. (special use of *via* way; see prec.).] **1.** As an exclam. = Onward, come on, come along. **2.** As an exhortation or command to depart = Away, be off, begone 1596. **b.** Used to check argument or reply, or to dismiss a subject 1598.

1. Then *v.* for the spatious bounds of Fraunce 1596. 2. b. *Merry W.* II. ii. 159.

‖**Via** (vəi·ă). *prep.* Also **viâ.** 1779. [L., abl. sing. of VIA *sb.*] By way of; by the route which passes through or over (a specified place).

To proceed through Spain and *viâ* Paris, home 1882.

Viability (vəi,ăbi·lĭti). 1843. [ad. F. *viabilité*, or f. VIABLE *a.*; see -ITY.] The quality or state of being viable; capacity for living; ability to live under certain conditions.

Viable (vəi·ăb'l), *a.* 1828. [a. F., f. *vie* life; see -ABLE.] Capable of living; able to maintain a separate existence.

Such..deformity of the female pelvis..as will absolutely preclude the birth of a v. child 1881.

Viaduct (vəi·ădəkt). 1816. [f. L. *via* way, after AQUEDUCT.] An elevated structure, consisting of a series of arches or spans, by means of which a railway or road is carried over a valley, road, river, etc.

Viage, obs. f. VOYAGE.

Vial (vəi·ăl), *sb.* late ME. [var. *fiol*, *fiall*, etc., PHIAL *sb.*] A vessel of a small or moderate size used for holding liquids; *spec.*, in later use a small glass bottle, a phial.

Put a spoonful of this Water in a V. WESLEY. *fig.* (after Rev. xvi. 1) The vials of God's wrath poured out KINGSLEY. Hence **Vi·al** *v. trans.*, to put into a v.

Viand (vəi·ănd). late ME. [a. AF., OF. *viande*:—pop. L. **vivanda*, for *vivenda*, neut. pl. gerundive of L. *vivere* to live.] **1.** *pl.* Articles of food; provisions, victuals. **2.** *sing.* **a.**

collect. Food, sustenance 1450. **b.** With *a* and *pl.* An article or kind of food 1527.

1. Flesche and dyverse vyaundes MAUNDEV. 2. All things necessary both for viande and apparell 1643.

†**Vi·ander**[1]. ME. [a. AF. *viaundour, viandere*, f. *viande* VIAND.] 1. One who provides viands or good cheer for his household or guests; a (liberal) host or entertainer –1577. 2. One who provides himself with good cheer; one who is fond of good living –1780. 3. A supplier or seller of provisions –1622.

†**Vi·ander**[2]. 1548. [ad. OF. *viandier*, f. as prec.] Viands, victuals, food –1625. So †**Vi·andry.**

Viatical (vəi,æ·tikăl), *a.* and *sb. rare.* 1855. [f. L. *viaticus* or *-um*; see next.] **A.** *adj.* Of or pertaining to a way or road; relating to a journey. **B.** *sb. pl.* Articles for use on a journey.

‖**Viaticum** (vəi,æ·tikŏm, vi-). *Pl.* **viatica.** 1562. [L., travelling-money, provision for a journey, neut. sing. of *viaticus* (rare), f. *via* way.] 1. *Eccl.* The Eucharist when administered to or received by one who is dying or in danger of death. 2. A supply of money or other necessaries for a journey; a sum given or taken to cover travelling expenses 1582. **b.** Provisions taken for use on a journey 1663.

Viator (vəi,ē¹·tǭɹ). 1504. [a. L., f. *via* way.] A traveller, wayfarer.

‖**Vibex** (vəi·beks). *Pl.* **vibices** (vəi-, vibəi·sīz). 1771. [L., weal.] *Path.* A long and narrow mark or patch in the skin caused by the subcutaneous extravasation of blood, occurring esp. in some fevers. Usu. in pl.

‖**Vibraculum** (vəibræ·kiŭlŏm). *Pl.* **-cula.** 1854. [mod.L., f. L. *vibrare* to shake.] *Zool.* One of the long whip-like movable processes or organs possessed by certain polyzoans; now regarded as a modified zooid. Hence **Vibra·cular** *a.* of, pertaining to, or furnished with vibracula.

Vibrant (vəi·brănt), *a.* 1616. [ad. L. *vibrant-, vibrans, vibrare* to VIBRATE.] 1. Moving or quivering rapidly; vibrating. 2. Of sound, the voice: Characterized by or exhibiting vibration; resonant 1848. Hence **Vi·brancy,** the condition or quality of being v.

Vibrate (vəibrē¹·t, vəi·brē¹t), *v.* 1647. [f. L. *vibrat-, vibrare* to move rapidly to and fro, to brandish, shake.] **I.** 1. *intr.* Of a pendulum, etc.: To swing to and fro; to oscillate 1667. 2. **a.** Of sounds: To strike *on* or sound *in* the ear, etc., with an effect like that of a vibrating chord; to resound; to continue to be heard. Chiefly *poet.* 1735. **b.** To circulate *about*, move or pass *through*, pierce or penetrate *to*, by or as by vibration 1756. 3. To move or swing backwards and forwards, or upwards and downwards, with some degree of rapidity; to quiver, shake, tremble 1756. **b.** *spec.* in *Physics* (see VIBRATION 2) 1774. 4. *fig.* To move or oscillate *between* two extreme conditions, opinions, etc.; to fluctuate or vary *from* one extreme *to* another. Also without const. To vacillate in opinion. 1782.

1. Long pendulums v. more slowly than short ones 1827. 2. **a.** Music, when soft voices die, Vibrates in the memory SHELLEY. **b.** Those powers that..Catch every nerve, and v. through the frame GOLDSM. 3. Palm trees vibrating in the breeze 1816. **b.** When a hammer strikes a bell, the latter vibrates TYNDALL. 4. The life of a man of fashion vibrated between frivolity and excess 1874.

II. 1. *trans.* To throw with vibratory motion; to launch or hurl (a thunderbolt, sentence, etc.). Now *Obs.* or *arch.* 1641. **b.** To emit, give forth (light, sound, etc.) by or as by vibration or vibratory motion 1643. 2. Of a pendulum, etc.: To measure (seconds) by vibration; also, to swing (so many times) 1667. 3. To give a vibratory motion to (something); to set in vibration 1700.

1. **b.** Star to star vibrates light TENNYSON. 2. A pendulum which vibrates seconds in very small arcs 1803. 3. Virginian rattlesnakes..swiftly vibrating and shaking their tailes EVELYN.

Vibratile (vəi·brătəil, -il), *a.* 1826. [ad. mod.L. **vibratilis*; see prec. and -ILE.] 1. Of the nature of vibration; vibratory. 2. Of cilia, etc.: Endowed with the power of vibration; having a rapid and constant oscillatory movement 1835.

1. The v., lashing action of the spermatozoon 1881.

Vibration (vəibrē¹·ʃən). 1655. [ad. L. *vibration-, vibratio*, f. *vibrare* to VIBRATE.] 1. The action on the part of a pendulum, etc. of moving or swinging to and fro; oscillation 1668. **b.** A single instance of this 1667. 2. *Physics.* The rapid alternating or reciprocating motion to and fro or up and down, produced in the particles of an elastic body by the disturbance of equilibrium; the motion in the particles of a sonorous body by which sound is produced 1656. **b.** A single movement of this kind 1666. **c.** *spec.* A supposed movement of this kind in the nerves, regarded as the means by which external impressions are conveyed to the mind. *Obs.* exc. *Hist.* 1728. 3. In wider sense: Movement to and fro or up and down, esp. when quick and more or less continuous; a quivering, swaying, or tremulous motion of any kind; an instance of this 1655. 4. The action or fact of vacillating in respect of conduct or opinion; an instance of this 1785.

2. The v. of the Air and its Undulation PRIOR. **b.** The deep vibrations of his witching song THOMSON. 3. The vibration and smells of the modern steamer 1901. 4. In Virginia there had been a great v. of opinion 1882. Hence **Vibra·tional** *a.* of or pertaining to v.; vibratory.

Vibratiuncle (vəibrē¹·ʃiŏŋk'l). 1718. [ad. mod.L. *vibratiuncula*, dim. of L. *vibratio* VIBRATION.] A minute or slight vibration.

Vibrative (vəi·brătiv), *a.* Now *rare.* 1667. [f. L. *vibrat-, vibrare*; see VIBRATE *v.* and -IVE.] Vibrating, vibratory.

‖**Vibrato** (vībrā·to), *adv.* and *sb.* 1861. [It., = L. *vibratus.*] *Mus.* **A.** *adv.* With much vibration of tone. **B.** *sb.* A tremulous quality of tone 1876.

Vibrator (vəibrē¹·tǭɹ, vəi·brē¹təɹ). 1862. [f. VIBRATE *v.* + -OR.] That which vibrates or causes vibration. **a.** One of the vibrating reeds of an organ, harmonium, etc. **b.** One or other of various appliances, instruments, or parts which have or cause a vibratory motion or action 1888.

Vibratory (vəi·brătəri), *a.* 1728. [f. VIBRATE *v.* + -ORY[2].] 1. Of the nature of vibration; characterized by or consisting of vibration. 2. Causing or producing vibration 1756. 3. Of or pertaining to vibration 1831. 4. Capable of vibrating; readily admitting of vibration 1839. **b.** Of the voice: Vibrant 1890.

1. The v. Motion of the Nerves 1728. 2. Human throats Have v. powers 1812. 3. The v. theory of light 1889. 4. The v. rays of the spectrum 1862. **b.** A voice v. with excitement 1891.

‖**Vibrio** (vəi·brio, vi·brio). *Pl.* **vibriones** (-ōᵘ·nīz), **vibrios.** 1835. [mod.L., f. L. *vibrare.*] †1. A genus of minute nematode worms; an anguillule –1839. 2. A group or genus of bacterioid or schizomycetous organisms characterized by vibratory motion; a member of this genus; *spec.* in *Bacteriol.*, a form of bacterium having vibratile cilia and closely resembling spirilla 1870.

†**Vi·brion.** 1853. [ad. mod.L. *vibrion-*, VIBRIO.] 1. A vibratile filament or appendage. 2. *Bacteriol.* A vibrio 1882.

‖**Vibrissæ** (vəibri·sī), *sb. pl.* 1693. [L., f. *vibrare.*] 1. *Anat.* The hairs which grow in the nostrils. 2. *Zool.* Stiff or bristly hairs, esp. those growing about the mouth or other parts of the face in certain animals 1839. **b.** *Ornith.* The coarse hairs or bristles growing about the rictus of certain birds, esp. of insectivorous species 1874.

Vibro- (vəi·bro), irreg. comb. form of L. *vibrare* to vibrate, as in **vibro-massage; vi·broscope,** an instrument used for counting the vibrations of a tuning-fork.

‖**Viburnum** (vəibɔ̄·ɹnŏm). 1731. [L., the wayfaring-tree.] An extensive genus of shrubs, natives of Europe, Asia, and N. America, to which the guelder-rose and laurustinus belong; a species or plant of this genus.

Vicar (vi·kăɹ). ME. [a. AF. *vica(i)re* (OF., F. *vicaire*), ad. L. *vicarius* substitute, f. **vicis* change, occasion, place (of another).] One who takes the place of or acts instead of another; a substitute, representative, or proxy. Chiefly *Eccl.* 1. Applied to persons, etc., as earthly representatives of God or Christ. **b.** *spec.* (*V. of Christ*, etc.) Applied to the Pope; also to St. Peter in a similar sense ME. 2. In early use, a person acting as priest in a parish in place of the parson or rector, or as the representative of a religious community to whom the tithes had been appropriated; hence, in later and mod. use, the incumbent of a parish of which the tithes are impropriated or appropriated, in contrast to a RECTOR ME. 3. One of the minor clergy or laymen (also called *lay vicar*) in a cathedral whose duty it is to sing parts of the services. Cf. VICAR-CHORAL. late ME. 4. One who takes the place of, or acts as the representative of, another (esp. the Pope or other high dignitary) in the performance of ecclesiastical functions; *spec.* in the R. C. Ch., a bishop's deputy. late ME. 5. In general use: One acting or appointed to act in place of another, esp. in administrative functions; a vicegerent. late ME.

1. **b.** Proclaiming that to the Pope, as God's v., all mankind are subject, and all rulers responsible BRYCE. 2. *V. of Bray*, one who readily changes his principles to suit the times or circumstances (chiefly in allusion to the song of that name). 4. *V. apostolic*; Where the succession of the Catholic hierarchy has been interrupted, as in England,..the bishops who superintend the Catholic church and represent the papal authority, are known by the name of vicars apostolic 1836. *V. forane*, in the R. C. Ch., a dignitary or parish priest appointed by a bishop to exercise a limited jurisdiction in a particular town or district of his diocese 1888.

Vicarage (vi·kărĕdʒ). late ME. [f. VICAR + -AGE.] 1. The benefice or living of a vicar. 2. The house or residence of a vicar; also, its occupants 1530. †3. The position, office, or duties of a vicar or representative (*rare*) –1734.

Vicar(-)choral. 1530. = VICAR 3.

Vicaress (vi·kărĕs). 1613. [f. VICAR + -ESS[1].] 1. The sister ranking immediately below the abbess or mother superior in a nunnery or convent. 2. The wife of the vicar of a parish 1770.

Vicar(-)general. late ME. [VICAR 4, after med.L. *vicarius generalis.*] †1. The title assumed by or bestowed upon the Pope as head of the Church under Christ –1651. 2. An ecclesiastical officer, usu. a cleric, appointed by a bishop as his representative in matters of jurisdiction or administration; also, in post-Reformation use in the Church of England, *spec.* a permanent lay official serving as a deputy or assistant to a bishop, or to the Archbishop of Canterbury or York, in certain ecclesiastical causes 1450. 3. *Hist.* The title given to Thomas Cromwell in 1535 as representative of the King in ecclesiastical affairs 1679.

Vicarial (vəi-, vikē^ə·riăl), *a.* 1617. [f. L. *vicarius* VICAR.] 1. Delegated, deputed; vicarious. 2. Of or belonging to a vicar or vicars 1744.

1. V. and deputed power 1803. 2. A v. tithe 1765.

Vicarian (vəi-, vikē^ə·riăn), *sb.* and *a.* 1598. [ad. late L. *vicarianus*, f. L. *vicarius* VICAR.] **A.** *sb.* †1. A substitute or deputy. MARSTON. 2. One who accepts the view of religious vicariousness 1851. **B.** *adj.* Of, pertaining to, or governed by a deputy ruler 1643.

Vicariate (vəi-, vikē^ə·riĕt). 1610. [ad. med.L. *vicariatus*, f. L. *vicarius* VICAR.] 1. The office or authority of a vicar in a religious or ecclesiastical sense. 2. A political office held by a person as deputy for another; deputed exercise of authority by a person or governing body 1619. 3. **a.** A district under the rule of a deputy governor 1755. **b.** *R. C. Ch.* A district under the charge of a vicar apostolic; the see of a vicar apostolic 1818.

2. The vicariat of that part of Germany which is governed by the Saxon laws, devolved to the elector of Saxony ROBERTSON.

Vicarious (vəi-, vikē^ə·riəs), *a.* 1637. [f. L. *vicarius*, f. **vicis* change, stead; see -ARIOUS.] 1. That takes or supplies the place of another thing or person; substituted instead of the proper thing or person. 2. Of punishment, etc.: Endured or suffered by one person in place of another; accomplished or attained by the substitution of some other person, etc., for the actual offender. Freq. in *Theol.* with ref. to the suffering and death of Christ. 1692. 3. Of power, authority, etc.: Exercised by one person or body of persons as the representative or deputy of another 1706. 4. Performed or achieved by means of another, or by one person, etc., on behalf of another 1806. **b.** Of qualities, etc.: Possessed by one person but reckoned to the credit of another 1812. **c.** Of methods, principles, etc.: Based upon the substitution of one person for another 1857. **5.** *Physiol.* Denoting the performance by or through one organ of functions normally discharged by another; substitutive 1780.

1. The University and Colleges are thus neither identical, nor v. of each other 1831. 2. V. Punishments may be..absolutely necessary 1736. 3. Exercising a kind of v. jurisdiction JOHNSON. Hence **Vica·rious·ly** *adv.*, **-ness.**

Vi·carship. 1534. [f. VICAR + -SHIP.] The office or position of a vicar.

†Vi·cary[1]. ME. [ad. L. *vicarius* VICAR.] = VICAR -1648.

†Vi·cary[2]. late ME. [a. AF. and OF. *vicarie*, or ad. med.L. *vicaria*, f. L. *vicarius* VICAR.] The office or position of a vicar; a benefice held by a vicar -1712.

Vice (vəis), *sb.*[1] ME. [a. AF., OF., :— L. *vitium* fault, defect.] **1.** Depravity or corruption of morals; evil, immoral, or wicked habits or conduct; indulgence in degrading pleasures or practices. **2.** A habit or practice of an immoral, degrading, or wicked nature ME. **b.** In horses: A bad habit or trick 1726. **3.** A character in a morality play representing one or other vice; hence, a stage jester or buffoon. Now *Hist.* (with cap.) 1551. **4.** Moral fault or defect (without implication of serious wrong-doing); a flaw in character or conduct ME. **5.** A fault, blemish, or imperfection. late ME. **6.** Viciousness, harmfulness 1837.

1. Fy upon slouth, the nourysher of vyce 1509. 2. The Gods are iust, and of our pleasant vices Make instruments to plague vs SHAKS. b. Of all the vices incidental to the horse, shying is one of the worst 1847. 3. A favourite piece of horse-play in the old miracles and morals, when the V. belabours the Devil 1886. 4. Contempt, prior to examination, is an intellectual v. PALEY. 5. I perceive I doe anticipate the vices of age SIR T. BROWNE.

Vice (vəis), *sb.*[2] Also (now *U.S.*) **vise.** ME. [a. OF. *vis*:—L. *vitis* vine, with ref. to the spiral growth of the tendrils.] **1.** A winding or spiral staircase. *Obs.* exc. *arch.* **†2.** A mechanical contrivance or device by which some piece of apparatus, etc., is worked -1650. **†3.** A screw -1611. **†4.** A tap of a vessel; a screw-stopper -1653. **5.** A tool composed of two jaws, opening and closing by means of a screw, which firmly grip and hold a piece of work in position while it is being operated upon; used esp. by workers in metal and carpenters 1500. **6.** A tool used for drawing lead into grooved rods for lattice windows 1706.

5. To secure him with a grasp like that of his own iron v., was, for the powerful Smith, the work of a single moment SCOTT.

Vice (vəis), *sb.*[3] 1597. [absol. use of VICE-*prefix.*] One who acts in the place of another; a substitute or deputy.

Vice (vəis), *v.* 1602. [f. VICE *sb.*[2]] *trans.* To force, strain, or press hard as by the use of a vice; to fix, jam, or squeeze tightly.

‖**Vice** (vəi·sī), *prep.* 1770. [L., abl. of **vicis* change, place, stead.] In place of; in succession to.

Vice- (vəis), *prefix*, repr. L. *vice* in place of; see prec. The older examples in English, having been taken immediately from French, also present the prefix in the reduced forms *vis-* (*vys-*, *viz-*) and *vi-* (*vy-*), subsequently replaced by *vice-*, except in VISCOUNT.

a. With personal designations, especially titles of office, indicating that the person so called acts temporarily or regularly in place of, in the absence of, or as assistant to another who properly holds the office or bears the title or name, as *v.-abbot, -agent, -architect, -captain*, etc. A group of these words appears in English in the 16th and early 17th cc. which includes *vice-god, -governor, -king, -rector*; **vice-chamberlain,** *spec.* an officer of the Royal Household under the Lord Chamberlain; **-legate,** one who acts as the representative or deputy of a (Papal) legate; **-queen,** (*a*) a woman ruling as the representative of a queen; (*b*) the wife of a viceroy; **-treasurer,** *spec.* formerly in the government of Ireland; **-warden,** *esp.* a deputy warden of the Stannaries or the Borders. **b.** With nouns or adjs. derived from personal designations, as *v.-apostolical, -deity, -duchy*, etc., or associated in some way with the holding of office, as *v.-chair, -government, -throne.*

Vice-a·dmiral. 1520. [a. AF. *visadmirail* (OF. *visamiral*); see VICE- and ADMIRAL.] **1.** A naval officer ranking next to an admiral. **b.** A civil officer appointed by the lords-commissioners of the Admiralty for the execution of jurisdiction 1618. **†2.** A vessel commanded by a vice-admiral -1693.

Vice-a·dmiralty. 1602. [f. prec. + -TY.] The office or jurisdiction of a vice-admiral (in sense 1 b); an area under the jurisdiction of a vice-admiral.

V. courts, branches of the High Court of Admiralty, instituted for carrying on the like duties in several of our colonies, prize-courts, &c. 1867.

Vice-cha·ncellor. late ME. [See VICE- and CHANCELLOR *sb.*] **1.** The deputy or substitute of an ecclesiastical chancellor; *spec.* the cardinal at the head of the Papal Chancery. **2.** The acting representative of the Chancellor of a university, usu. the head of a college, appointed to the office for a limited time, or the principal of the university 1530. **3.** A deputy or subordinate of one or other state official bearing the title of Chancellor 1587. **b.** *spec.* One of the higher judges in the former Court of Chancery 1813. Hence **Vice-cha·ncellorship,** the office or dignity of a v.; the period during which this is held.

Vice-co·nsul. 1559. [VICE-.] **†1.** A Roman proconsul -1601. **2.** The assistant or deputy of a consul 1601.

Vice-cou·nty. 1859. [f. VICE- + COUNTY[1] 2.] A division of a large county treated as a county-area with regard to the distribution of species of plants, etc.

Vicegerency (vəis,dʒī³·rĕnsi, -dʒe·rĕnsi). 1596. [See next and -ENCY.] The office, dignity, or rule of a vicegerent; the fact of ruling or administering as representative of another. **b.** A district or province ruled by a vicegerent 1865. So **Vicege·rence** (now *rare*) 1527.

Vicegerent (vəis,dʒī³·rĕnt, -dʒe·rĕnt), *sb.* and *a.* 1536. [ad. med.L. *vicegerent-, vicegerens*, f. L. *vicem* (acc.) place, office, and *gerens, gerere* to carry, hold.] **A.** *sb.* **1.** A person appointed by a king or other ruler to act in his place or exercise certain of his administrative functions. **b.** *gen.* One who takes the place of another in the discharge of some office or duties 1549. **c.** A ruler or commander *of* a country, etc., in virtue of deputed power 1577. **2.** Applied to rulers and magistrates as representatives of the Deity. Also to priests, and *spec.* to the Pope, as representatives of God or Christ. 1547. **b.** Similarly applied to man in general, and to persons as representing some other supernatural or spiritual power 1588.

1. He was trusted by the sultan as the faithful vicegerent of his power GIBBON. c. Aspasius the v. of Rome 1610. 2. Princes, being by God put in authority, are His vice-gerents, and should therefore require obedience 1547. The Pope, Christ's Vicar and V. 1593.

B. *adj.* (or *attrib.*). **1.** Taking the place or performing the functions of another 1577. **2.** Characterized by deputed or vicarious power 1667.

2. Under his great Vice-gerent Reign abide,..For ever happie MILT.

Vice-pre·sident. 1574. [VICE-.] One who acts as the representative or deputy of a president; an official ranking immediately below a president. **Vice-pre·sidentship, -pre·sidency.**

Vice-re·gal, *a.* 1839. [f. VICE- + REGAL.] Of, pertaining to, or associated with a viceroy.

Vice-re·gent. 1556. [VICE-.] One who acts in place of a regent. Hence **-re·gency.**

‖**Vicereine** (vəi·srēn). 1823. [a. F., f. *vice-* VICE- + *reine* queen.] The wife of a viceroy; also (less usu.), a woman ruling as the representative of a queen.

Viceroy (vəi·sroi). 1524. [a. late MF. *vice-roy, visroy* (F. *vice-roi*), f. *vice-* VICE- + *roi* king.] **1.** One who acts as the governor of a country, province, etc., in the name and by the authority of the supreme ruler; a vice-king. **2.** *transf.* One having authority or rank comparable to that of a viceroy 1590. **3.** *Ent.* An Amer. species of butterfly, *Basilarchia archippus*, distinguished by handsome red and black colouring 1881. Hence **Vi·ceroyal** *a.* of or pertaining to a v. **Vi·ceroyship,** viceroyalty.

Viceroyalty (stress variable). 1703. [ad. F. *vice-royauté*; see VICE- and ROYALTY.] **1.** The office, rank, or authority of a viceroy. **b.** In quasi-concr. use: A viceroy or viceregal household 1842. **2.** A province or dependency commonly administered by a viceroy 1715. **3.** The period during which a particular viceroy holds office 1849.

Vice versa (vəi·sī vɔ̄·ɪsă), *adv. phr.* 1601. [L., f. *vice*, abl. sing. of *vicis* turn, etc., and *versa*, abl. sing. fem. of *versus, vertere* to turn.] With a reversal or transposition of the main items in the statement just made; contrariwise, conversely.

Nor can we ask his favour upon occasion, and so *vice versa* he can make no use of us 1710.

‖**Vichy** (vi·ʃi). 1858. [See def.] The name of a town in the department of Allier in Central France, used *attrib.* and *ellipt.* to designate a mineral water obtained from springs there.

Vicinage (vi·sinėdʒ). ME. [ad. OF. *visenage* (*visnage*), *vicenage*, or *voisinage* (see VOISINAGE), with assimilation of the stem to the original L. *vicinus*; see VICINITY.] **1.** A number of places lying near to each other taken collectively; an area extending to a limited distance round a particular spot; a neighbourhood. **b.** *transf.* The people living in a certain district or neighbourhood 1647. **2.** The fact of being or living close to one another or others; nearness, proximity 1598.

1. The Metropolis and its V. BURKE. The French ladies in my v. H. WALPOLE. 2. Common because of v., or neighbourhood, is where the inhabitants of two townships, which lie contiguous to each other, have usually intercommoned with each other BLACKSTONE.

Vicinal (vi·sinăl, visəi·năl), *a.* 1677. [ad. L. *vicinalis*, f. *vicinus* neighbour.] **1.** *V. way* or *road*, a local common way as dist. from a highway; a by-road or cross-road. **2.** Neighbouring, adjacent, near 1739. **b.** *Math.* and *Min.* Nearly coincident with a given surface or plane 1895. **c.** *Organ. Chem.* Of substituted groups or atoms: Lying in consecutive order; adjacent to each other 1898.

Vicinity (visi·nĭti). 1560. [ad. L. *vicinitas*, f. *vicinus*; see prec. and -ITY.] **1.** The state, character, or quality of being near in space; propinquity. **†2.** Nearness in degree or quality; close relationship or connexion; resemblance, likeness -1676. **3.** = VICINAGE 1. 1781.

1. The Abundance and v. of country seats SWIFT. This v. to the great capital 1858. 3. We were glad.. to escape the v. of that ugly crevasse TYNDALL.

Phr. *In the v.* (*of*), in the neighbourhood (of), near or close (to).

Vicious (vi·ʃəs), *a.* ME. [a. AF. (F. *vicieux*), or ad. L. *vitiosus*, f. *vitium* VICE *sb.*[1]] **I. 1.** Of habits, practices, etc.: Of the nature of vice; contrary to moral principles; depraved, immoral, bad. **2.** Of persons: Addicted to vice or immorality; of depraved habits; profligate, wicked. late ME. **3.** Falling short of or varying from what is morally or practically commendable; reprehensible, blameworthy, mischievous. late ME. **4.** Of animals (*esp.* horses): Inclined to be savage or dangerous, or to show bad temper; not submitting to be thoroughly tamed or broken in 1711. **b.** Full of malice or spite; malignantly bitter or severe 1825.

1. Richard Iohnson caused the English, by his v. liuing, to bee worse accounted of then the Russes 1613. 2. V. as the stage was, it only reflected the general vice of the time 1874. 3. It had beene v. To haue mistrusted her SHAKS. 4. A v. animal, having injured any person, was forfeited 1818. b. Three nasty v. letters 1908.

II. 1. *Law.* Marred or rendered void by some inherent fault or defect; not satisfying legal requirements or conditions; unlawful, illegal. late ME. **2.** Impaired or spoiled by some fault, flaw, blemish, or defect; faulty, defective, imperfect, bad; corrupt, impure, debased 1589. **†3.** Foul, impure, noxious, morbid -1831. **†4.** Of a part or function of the body: Morbid, diseased; irregular -1733.

2. If from true premisses follows what is false, it is a sign that the form of the syllogism is vitious 1697. The foundations of the bridge were originally v. 1846.

Phr. *V. circle.* **a.** *Logic.* See CIRCLE *sb.* Also *gen.* **b.** *Path.* A morbid process consisting in the reciprocal continuation and aggravation of one disorder by another. The practice proceeds, in a v. circle of habit 1839. The authority of the law is demanded, and he cites the disputed passage. A more..v. circle was never devised 1876. Hence **Vi·cious·ly** *adv.*, **-ness.**

Vicissitude (vəi-, visi·sitiūd). 1570. [a. OF. and F., or ad. L. *vicissitudo*, f. *vicis* turn, change.] **1.** The fact of change or mutation taking place in a particular thing or within a certain sphere; the uncertain changing or mutability *of* something. **2.** Without article: Change, mutation, mutability; successive substitution of one thing or condition for another taking place from natural causes 1596. **3.** A change or alteration in condition or fortune; an instance of mutability in human affairs 1616. **4.** Alternation, mutual or reciprocal succession, of things or conditions 1624. **5.** An instance of alternation or succession 1648.

1. The notice, that our Senses take of the constant V. of Things LOCKE. 2. This is a world of conflict, and of v. amid the conflict 1833. 3. The vicissitudes of War 1665. 4. The succession of light and darkness,..the v. of the seasons 1835. 5. The vicissitudes of tides are scarcely felt in those seas GIBBON. Hence †**Vicissitu·dinary** *a.* marked by alternation -1650. **Vicissitu·dinous** *a.* marked by vicissitudes.

†**Vico·ntiel**, *sb.* and *a.* 1548. [a. AF., f. *viconte* VISCOUNT.] **A.** *sb. pl.* Certain sums regularly payable to the Crown by a sheriff and charged against him in the Exchequer accounts -1738. **B.** *adj.* **1.** Of or pertaining to a sheriff -1798. **2.** Of a writ: That is to be executed by the sheriff -1768.

Victim (vi·ktim). 1497. [ad. L. *victima.*] **1.** A living creature killed and offered as a sacrifice to some deity or supernatural power. **2.** A person who is put to death or subjected to torture by another; one who suffers severely in body or property through cruel or oppressive treatment 1660. **b.** One who is reduced or destined to suffer under some oppressive or destructive agency 1718. **c.** One who perishes or suffers in health, etc. from some enterprise or pursuit voluntarily undertaken 1726. **d.** In weaker sense: One who suffers some injury, hardship, or loss, is badly treated or taken advantage of, or the like 1781.

1. Select four Brawny Bulls for Sacrifice,..From the slain Victims pour the streaming Blood DRYDEN. 2. If he had not died the v. of a tyrant 1839. b. The houses..continued to collapse and make fresh victims 1890. d. He went off.., and left his respected v. to settle the bill DICKENS.

Phr. *To fall a v. to* (some thing or person).

Victimize (vi·ktiməiz), *v.* 1830. [f. prec.] **1.** *trans.* To make a victim of; to cause to suffer discomfort, inconvenience, etc.; to cheat, swindle, or defraud. **2.** To put to death as, or in the manner of, a sacrificial victim; to slaughter 1853. **b.** To spoil or destroy (plants) completely 1849. Hence **Victimiza·tion. Vi·ctimizer.**

Victor (vi·ktəɪ), *sb.* ME. [a. AF. or L., f. *vict-*, *vincere* to overcome.] One who overcomes or vanquishes an adversary; the leader of an army which wins a battle or war. Sometimes *collect. sing.* with *the*, the winning army or nation. **b.** *transf.* and *fig.* One who overcomes in any contest or struggle. late ME.

1. The Huns..soon withdrew from the presence of an insulting v. GIBBON. b. There, V. of his health, of fortune, friends, And fame, this lord of useless thousands ends POPE. Hence †**Vi·ctor** *v. trans.* to overcome, vanquish -1683.

‖**Victoria**[1] (viktōᵊ·riă). 1638. [L.; see VICTORY *sb.*] A word employed as a shout of triumph.

Victoria[2] (viktōᵊ·riă). 1846. [Name of Queen *Victoria* of England (1837–1901) used attrib. or ellipt.] **1.** A light, low, four-wheeled carriage having a collapsible hood, with seats (usu.) for two persons and an elevated seat in front for the driver 1870. **2.** *Bot.* A gigantic species of water-lily, *Victoria regia*, indigenous to South America 1846. **3.** *Astr.* One of the minor planets, discovered in 1850 by Hind. **4.** A variety of domestic pigeon 1879. **5.** A variety of plum characterized by its luscious flavour and rich red colour 1860. **6.** attrib. *V. Cross* (abbrev. V.C.), the highest British military and naval decoration, bestowed for conspicuous bravery in battle. 1856. *V. Day*, the anniversary of the birthday of Queen Victoria, May 24 (now usu. called *Empire Day*).

Victo·rian, *a.*[1] 1728. [f. the name of *Victorius*, an ecclesiastic of the 5th c.] *V. cycle, period* (see quot. and DIONYSIAN *a.*).

V. period, an Interval of 532 Julian Years, which elaps'd, the new and full Moons return on the same Day of the Julian Year 1728.

Victorian (viktōᵊ·riăn), *a.*[2] and *sb.* 1875. [f. VICTORIA[2].] **A.** *adj.* Of, belonging to, designating, or typical of the reign of Queen Victoria (1837–1901). **B.** *sb.* A person who lived in or has the characteristics typical of the reign of Queen Victoria 1876. Hence **Victo·rianism.**

Victo·rian, *a.*[3] 1857. [See def.] Of, belonging, or native to the colony of Victoria in Australia (named in 1851 after Queen Victoria).

Victorine (vi·ktŏrīn). 1849. [perh. f. VICTORIA[2] + -INE[4].] A kind of fur tippet formerly worn by ladies, fastening in front of the neck and having two loose ends hanging down.

Victorious (viktōᵊ·riəs), *a.* late ME. [a. AF., or ad. L. *victoriosus*, f. *victoria* VICTORY *sb.*] **1.** Having gained victory or obtained supremacy as victor; successful in any contest or struggle. **2.** Of, belonging to, or characterized by victory; producing victory; emblematic of victory 1490.

1. Giacomo da Pesaro,..v. over the Turks in war, and over himself in peace 1757. *transf.* Now the distemper, spite of draught or pill, V. seem'd COWPER. 2. Those just Spirits that wear v. Palms MILT. Hence **Victo·rious·ly** *adv.*, **-ness.**

Victory (vi·ktŏri). ME. [a. AF. and OF. *victorie* (var. of OF. and F. *victoire*), ad. L. *victoria*, f. *victor* VICTOR *sb.*] **1.** The position or state of having overcome an enemy or adversary in combat, battle, or war; supremacy or superiority achieved as the result of armed conflict. **b.** Used interjectionally as an expression of triumph or encouragement 1591. **2.** An instance or occasion of overcoming an adversary in battle, etc. ME. **3.** Supremacy, superiority, triumph, or ultimate success in any contest, struggle, or enterprise ME. **4.** The Roman goddess representing or typifying victory; a figure or statue of this 1569.

1. V. is the fruit of moral as well as military virtue GIBBON. *personified* Fortune, and V. sit on thy Helme SHAKS. Phr. *To have* (*get*, *win*) *the v.* b. Saint George, and V.; fight Souldiers, fight SHAKS. 2. Phr. *Cadmean, Pyrrhic v.*: see these words. *Moral v.*: see MORAL *a.* 7 b. 3. Such is euer-more the finall victorie of all truth HOOKER. 4. Crowned with a winged figure of Victory GIBBON.

Victress (vi·ktrės). 1601. [f. VICTOR + -ESS, after L. *victrix.*] A female victor or vanquisher.

‖**Victrix** (vi·ktriks). 1651. [L., fem. of VICTOR.] = prec. So †**Vi·ctrice** -1633.

Victual (vi·t'l), *sb.* ME. [a. AF. and OF. *vitaile*, *-aille* :—late L. *victualia*, neut. pl. of post-cl. L. *victualis*, f. *victus* food, sustenance. The spelling has been assimilated to the L. original, while the pronunciation still represents the older forms *vittel*, *vittle.*] **1.** *collect.* Whatever is normally required or may naturally be used for consumption in order to support life; food or provisions of any kind. †**b.** Produce of the ground capable of being used as food -1799. **2.** *pl.* Articles of food; supplies or various kinds of provisions; in later use *esp.* articles of ordinary diet prepared for use ME.

1. Twise a day giue him fresh vittle and drinke 1573. A fair-hair'd youth, that in his hand Bare v. for the mowers TENNYSON. 2. The Wages of a..Labourer ..is 4s. per week without Victuals 1687. Hence **Vi·ctualage** (*rare*) victuals.

Victual (vi·t'l), *v.* ME. [ad. AF. and OF. *vitailler*, f. *vitaille* VICTUAL *sb.*] **1.** *trans.* To supply or furnish (a ship, castle, garrison, body of troops, etc.) with victuals, esp. with a store to last for some time. **2.** *intr.* **a.** To partake of victuals; to eat. Also of animals, to feed or pasture. 1577. **b.** To lay in or obtain a supply of victuals 1615.

1. This squadron..was victualed for twelve months 1777. 2. b. Which was a voyage of such a length, that no ship could v. for DE FOE. Hence **Vi·ctualled** *ppl. a.*

Victualler (vi·t'ləɪ). late ME. [a. AF. and OF. *vitaill(i)er*, f. *vitaille* VICTUAL *sb.*] **1.** A purveyor of victuals or provisions; *spec.* the keeper of an eating-house, inn, or tavern; a licensed victualler. **2.** *spec.* **a.** One who supplies or undertakes to supply an army or armed force with necessary provisions; †*pl.* those engaged in bringing up victuals to an armed force late ME. **b.** One who furnishes a ship or navy with provisions. late ME. **3.** A ship employed to carry provisions for a fleet or squadron (or for troops over-seas); a victualling ship 1572.

1. *Licensed v.*, one who has a licence to sell food or drink, but esp. the latter, to be consumed on the premises; a publican.

Victualling (vi·t'liŋ), *vbl. sb.* 1462. [f. VICTUAL *v.*] **1.** The action of providing or storing a ship, town, army, etc. (now esp. the Navy) with victuals. **b.** The business of supplying food and drink for payment; supply of food for this purpose 1534. **2.** A supply of food for personal use 1532.

attrib.: **v.-house**, an eating-house, inn, or tavern; **-office**, an office concerned with the v. of ships, esp. of ships of the Royal Navy; *Boxing slang*, the stomach.

‖**Vicuña** (vikū·nʸă), **vicuna** (vikiū·nă). 1622. [a. Sp. *vicuña*, the Quichuan name of the animal.] **1.** A S. Amer. animal (*Auchenia vicunna*), closely related to the llama and alpaca, inhabiting the higher portions of the northern Andes and yielding a fine silky wool used for textile fabrics. **2.** *ellipt.* Vicuña cloth; also, a garment made of this 1851.

Comb.: **v.-cloth,** cloth made of **v. wool,** (*a*) wool or fur of the v.; (*b*) a mixture of fine wool and cotton.

‖**Vidame** (vī·dam). 1523. [a. F. *vidame*, :—med.L. *vicedominum*, *-us*, f. *vice-* VICE- + *dominus* lord.] Formerly in France, one who held lands from a bishop as his representative and defender in temporal matters.

‖**Vide** (vəi·dī), *v. imp.* 1565. [L., imp. sing. of *videre* to see.] 'See, refer to, consult': a direction to the reader to refer elsewhere for fuller or further information.

‖**Videlicet** (vəi-, vide·liset, vəidī·liset, vi-), *adv.* and *sb.* 1464. [L., f. *vide-*, stem of *videre* + *licet* it is permissible.] **A.** *adv.* That is to say; namely; to wit; used to introduce an amplification or more precise explanation of a previous statement or word. Abbrev. *viz.*

One of Rob's original profession, *v.* a drover SCOTT.

B. *sb.* The word itself as used to introduce an explanation or amplification, esp. in legal documents 1658.

Vidian (vi·diăn), *a.* 1831. [f. Vidus *Vidius*, latinized form of Guido Guidi, an Italian anatomist (died 1569).] *Anat.* The special designation of certain anatomical features of the head, as *V. artery, canal, nerve.*

‖**Vidimus** (vəi·dimŏs). late ME. [L., = 'we have seen'.] **1.** A copy of a document bearing an attestation that it is authentic or accurate. **b.** An examination or inspection, as of accounts 1850. †**2.** *Arch.* A design for a painted or stained-glass window -1762.

‖**Vidonia** (vidōᵘ·niă). 1723. [Origin obsc.] A dry white wine made in the Canary Islands.

Viduage (vi·diu,ėdʒ). 1832. [f. L. *vidua* widow; see -AGE.] The condition of widowhood, viduity; widows collectively.

Vidual (vi·diu,ăl), *a.* 1550. [ad. late L. *vidualis*, f. *vidua* widow.] Of or belonging to, befitting, a widow or widowhood; widowed.

Viduity (vidiū·iti). late ME. [a. OF. *viduite* or ad. L. *viduitas*, f. *vidua* widow; see -ITY.] The state of being or remaining a widow; the time during which a woman is a widow; widowhood.

†**Vie**, *sb.* 1533. [Aphetic ad. F. *envi* increase of stake (in OF., challenge, provocation), f. *envier* to increase the stake :—L. *invitare* to INVITE.] **1.** In card-playing: A challenge, venture, or bid; a sum staked on one's cards -1680. **2.** A challenge to contest or rivalry; a display of rivalry or emulation; a contest or competition -1674. **3.** A challenge as to the accuracy of something; an objection or difficulty (*rare*) -1640.

2. They..beganne a v., who should be first in shewing their alteration 1611.

Vie (vəi), *v.* 1565. [f. prec., or aphetic ad. F. *envier*; see prec.] †**1.** *intr.* In card-playing: To make a 'vie'; to hazard a sum on the strength of one's hand -1640. †**2.** *trans.* To hazard (a certain sum, etc.) on a hand of cards -1659. †**3.** To back (cards) for a certain sum; to declare oneself able to win (a game, etc.) -1655. **4.** To display, advance, practise, etc., in competition or rivalry *with* another person or thing; to contend or strive *with* in respect of (something). *Obs.* or *arch.* 1570. **5.** To match (one thing) *with* another by way of return, rivalry, or comparison. Now *arch.* 1583. **†6.** To increase in number by addition or repetition –1633. **7.** *intr.* To enter into or carry on rivalry; to be rivals or competitors; to compete for superiority in some respect 1615.

1. They v. and reuie till some ten shillings bee on the stake 1591. 4. One eye vied drops with the other 1660. 5. I will take your advice, and v. my state with others 1685. 6. *Tam. Shr.* II. i. 311. 7. Fruits that v. In glowing colours with the Tyrian dye POPE. They all vied in paying me every attention 1806.

‖**Vielle** (vie·l). 1768. [F.; origin obsc.] A musical instrument with four strings played by means of a small wheel; a hurdy-gurdy.

Vienna (vi₁e·nă), name of the capital of Austria used in various collocations, as **V. caustic,** = *V. paste*; **V. paste,** a paste made up of equal parts of caustic potash and quicklime. **b.** The distinctive name of a grade of wheat-flour, and of certain forms of plain or fancy bread.

Viennese (viĕ₁nī·z), *sb.* and *a.* 1839. [f. prec. + -ESE.] **A.** *sb.* **a.** A native or inhabitant of Vienna; also *collect.* **b.** The variety of German spoken in Vienna. **B.** *adj.* Of or belonging to Vienna; originating in Vienna 1839.

View (viū), *sb.* late ME. [a. AF. *vewe, viewe,* = OF. *veue* (F. *vue*), from *veoir* (F. *voir*) to see.] **I. 1. a.** A formal inspection or survey of lands, tenements, or ground for some special purpose. Now *rare* or *Obs.* **†b.** A formal examination or inspection of something, made by a properly appointed or qualified person; the charge or office of inspecting something –1827. **†c.** A review (of troops, etc.) –1721. **2.** *gen.* An examination, inspection, or survey 1568. **3.** The exercise of the faculty of sight; the faculty or power of vision; the possibility or opportunity of seeing something 1573. **b.** Range of sight or vision 1591. **4.** An act of looking or beholding; a sight, look, or glance 1581. **5.** The sight or vision *of* something 1588. **b.** = VIEW-HALLOO 1825. **†6.** Visual appearance or aspect –1812. **7. †a.** *Hunting.* The footprints of a buck or fallow-deer –1679. **b.** A sight or prospect of some landscape or extended scene; an extent or area covered by the eye from one point 1606. **c.** A drawing, painting, print, etc. representing a landscape or other prospect 1700.

1. b. *V. of frank-pledge*: see FRANK-PLEDGE. 2. Surveying Nature with too nice a v. DRYDEN. 3. Tom was already lost to v. 1852. b. Somewhere, out of human v., Whate'er thy hands are set to do Is wrought TENNYSON. 4. The first v. would displease many 1581. 5. Pisa's Mount, that intercepts the v. Of Lucca GRAY. b. From a find to a check, from a check to a v., From a v. to a death in the morning *c*1825. 6. A happy rural seat of various v. MILT. 7. b. From the flat roof of the church we had a delightful v. of the village 1808. c. A photographist preparing to take a v. of the castle 1854.

II. 1. Mental contemplation or vision; observation, notice 1440. **b.** A single act of contemplation or attention to a subject 1570. **2.** A particular manner or way of considering or regarding a matter or question; a conception, opinion, or theory formed by reflection or study 1573. **b.** An aspect or light in which something is regarded or considered 1713. **c.** *pl.* Opinions, ideas, or theories of an individual or speculative character held or advanced with regard to some subject 1769. **3.** A survey; a general or summary account 1604. **4.** An aim or intention; a design or plan; an object or purpose 1634. **5.** A prospect, anticipation, expectation, or outlook 1719.

1. But I hate to have my secrets laid open to everybodie's v. 1642. *Point of v.*: see POINT *sb.*[1] 2. Let us take the most impartial V. we can 1679. c. Nor did his political views and maxims seem less strange 1769. 3. It may not be amiss to give the reader the whole argument here in one v. 1729. 4. I have told you my views for Jemima 1831. 5. I entertain no v. of any emolument whatever from the present publication 1827.

Phrases. †*At, to the v.* (in hawking or hunting): By sight. **In** (..) **v.**: **a.** *In (the) v. of,* in the sight of, so as to be seen by; also, within sight of, near enough to see. **b.** *In v.,* in sight; also (*b*) in contemplation or notice, under attention; (*c*) as an end or object aimed at. **c.** *In v. of,* (*a*) in prospect or anticipation of, with a view to; (*b*) in consideration or regard of, on account of. **On** (..) **v.**: **a.** *On* or *upon (the) v of,* on ocular inspection or perception of, *spec.* by way of inquest. **b.** *On v.,* on exhibition, open to general or public inspection. **With** (..) **v.**: **a.** *With the* (or *a*) *v. of,* with the object or design of (doing something). **b.** *With a v. to,* (*a*) with the aim or object of attaining, effecting, or accomplishing something; (*b*) with regard to; (*c*) in view of. **c.** *With this* (or *that*) *v.,* with this intention or aim, for this purpose. *To take a v. of,* to take a look at, to make an examination or survey of. *To take the long v.,* to provide for the future.

Comb.: **v.-finder,** an attachment to a camera by which it is more readily adjusted to photograph a particular view.

View (viū), *v.* 1523. [f. prec.] **1.** *trans.* To inspect or examine in a formal or official manner; to survey carefully or professionally; †to review (troops). **†b.** *spec.* To inspect or examine (records, accounts, etc.) by way of check or control –1647. **†c.** To survey or explore (a country, coast, etc.) –1796. **2.** To look at (something) more or less attentively; to scrutinize; to observe closely 1548. **b.** To see or behold; to catch sight of 1586. **c.** *Hunting.* With *away*: To see (a fox) break cover; to give notice of (the fox as doing so) by hallooing 1853. **3.** To survey mentally; to consider 1591. **b.** To regard or consider in a certain light 1765.

1. The Surgeon,..having viewed the wound,..ordered his Patient instantly to bed FIELDING. 2. Looke where she comes: Æneas, viewe her well 1593. b. The fox was viewed several times by the horsemen 1810. 3. Bede viewed the world only from the retirement of his cell 1845. b. A third manner of viewing mixed governments 1832.

Viewer (viū·əɹ). late ME. [f. VIEW *v.* + -ER [1].] **1.** One who views. **2.** A person appointed to examine or inspect something, either on a special occasion or permanently; in later use *esp.* an inspector or examiner of goods supplied by contract; †*spec.* in *Law,* one appointed by a court to inspect a place, property, etc., and report upon it. late ME.

View-halloo (viū₁hălū·). 1761. [f. VIEW *v.* + HALLOO.] The shout given by a huntsman on seeing a fox break cover.

Viewless (viū·lės), *a.* 1603. [f. VIEW *sb.* or *v.*] **1.** That cannot be perceived by the eye; incapable of being seen; invisible. orig. and chiefly *poet.* **2.** Devoid of a view or prospect 1840. **3.** Having no views or opinions 1885.

1. To be imprison'd in the viewlesse windes SHAKS. Hence **View·lessly** *adv.* invisibly.

View·-point, view·point. 1856. [f. VIEW *sb.*] A point of view.

Viewy (viū·i), *a.* 1848. [f. VIEW *sb.*] Given to adopting speculative views on particular subjects; inclined to be unpractical or visionary. **2.** *slang.* Attractive in appearance; showy 1851.

1. I doubt whether the public care much about v. books 1883. 2. Odds and ends of the ham, such as isn't quite v. enough for the public 1851. Hence **Vie·winess.**

Vigesimal (vəi-, vidʒe·simăl), *a.* 1656. [f. L. *vigesimus,* var. of *vicesimus,* f. *viceni* distrib. of *vicinti* twenty.] Of or pertaining to twenty; based on the number twenty.

Vige·simo-qua·rto. 1864. = TWENTY-FOURMO.

‖**Vigia** (vi·dʒiă). 1867. [Sp. or Pg., look-out:—L. *vigilia* (see next).] A warning on a sea chart to denote some hidden danger.

Vigil (vi·dʒil). ME. [a. AF. and OF. *vigile*:—L. *vigilia* watch, wakefulness, f. *vigil* awake, alert.] **1.** *Eccl.* The eve of a festival or holy day, esp. as an occasion of religious observance. **b.** A devotional watching, *esp.* the watch kept on the eve of a festival or holy day; formerly, a nocturnal service or devotion. Chiefly in pl. late ME. **c.** *pl.* Prayers said or sung at a nocturnal service, *spec.* for the dead. *arch.* 1483. **†2.** One or other of the four watches into which the Romans divided the night –1656. **3.** An occasion or period of keeping awake for some special reason or purpose 1711. **b.** Without article: Watching, watch 1816. **4.** A state or period of wakefulness or inability to sleep. Somewhat *rare. poet.* 1747.

1. He that shall see this day, and liue old age, Will yeerely on the V. feast his neighbours, And say, to morrow is Saint Crispian SHAKS. b. The solemnity of the Easter v. 1896. Phr. *To keep* (*a*) *v.* or *vigils.* 3. His delicate frame worn out by the labours and vigils of many months MACAULAY. b. Hermas and the twelve virgins keep v. by the tower 1892.

Vigilance (vi·dʒilăns). 1570. [a. F., or ad. L. *vigilantia*; see next and -ANCE.] **1.** The quality or character of being vigilant; alertness or closeness of observation. **†b.** A guard or watch. MILT. **2.** The state of being awake; *spec.* in *Path.,* abnormal wakefulness, inability to sleep, insomnia 1748.

1. What constant v. it requires to preserve the public health in a large city 1875. b. In at this Gate none pass The v. here plac't MILT.

attrib.: **v. committee** *U.S.,* a self-appointed committee for the maintenance of justice and order in an imperfectly organized community; hence *v. man, work.*

†Vi·gilancy. 1537. [ad. L. *vigilantia,* f. *vigilant-, vigilans*; see next and -ANCY.] = prec. –1767.

Vigilant (vi·dʒilănt), *a.* 1480. [a. F., or ad. L. *vigilant-, vigilans,* pres. pple. of *vigilare* to keep awake, f. *vigil* awake.] **1.** Wakeful and watchful; keeping steadily on the alert. **2.** Of attention, etc.: Characterized by vigilance 1531.

1. Be sober, be v. 1 *Pet.* v. 8. Disperse then to your posts: be firm and v. BYRON. 2. They kept a v. eye ..upon every height where a scout might be posted 1836. Hence **Vi·gilant-ly** *adv.,* **†-ness.**

Vigilante (vidʒilā·nte). 1865. [a. Sp., = VIGILANT *a.*] *U.S.* A member of a vigilance committee.

‖**Vigneron** (vin[y]əroṅ). 1456. [F., f. *vigne* VINE *sb.*] One who cultivates grape-vines; a wine-grower.

Vignette (vinye·t, vine·t), *sb.* 1751. [a. F.; see VINET.] **1.** An ornamental or decorative design, usu. of relatively small size, on a blank space in a book or among printed matter, esp. at the beginning or end of a chapter or other division; *spec.* any embellishment, illustration, or picture unenclosed in a border, or having the edges shading off into the surrounding paper; the head-piece or tail-piece of a book or article. **b.** An ornamental design, drawing, or picture in a manuscript or written document 1830. **2.** A photographic portrait, showing only the head or the head and shoulders, with the edges of the print shading off into the background 1862.

Vignette (vinye·t, vine·t), *v.* 1853. [f. prec.] *trans.* To make a vignette of; *spec.* in *Photogr.,* to produce (a picture or portrait) in the style of a vignette by softening away or shading off the edges, leaving only the central portion.

‖**Vigogne** (vigon[y]). 1660. [F., ad. Sp. VICUÑA.] **1.** = VICUÑA **1.** **2.** Vicuña-cloth 1876. **3.** *V. yarn,* a mixture of vicuña wool or other fine wool, and cotton 1885.

Vigonia (vigōu·niă). 1763. [app. a latinization of prec.] = prec. **1, 2.**

Vigorous (vi·gŏrəs), *a.* ME. [See next and -OUS.] **1.** Of persons or animals: Strong and active in body; robust in health or constitution. So of the body or its parts, health, etc. **b.** Of plants, etc.: Growing strongly and freely 1706. **c.** Marked by, requiring or involving physical strength or activity 1697. **2.** Full of or characterized by vigour or active force; powerful, strong 1548. **b.** Of language, etc.: Energetic, forcible, powerful 1821. **3.** Of actions, measures, etc.: Characterized by, attended, carried out, or enforced with vigour or energy 1599. **b.** Of persons, etc.: Acting, or prepared to act, with vigour 1638.

1. Men are Conservatives when they are least v., or when they are most luxurious EMERSON. The..v. pulse, and undimmed eye 1870. b. Some Trees are weak, others strong and v. 1706. c. The keenness of youth's v. day 1836. 2. *Elaterium* is a v. Purge 1728. The air was dark and heavy, for want of that v. heat which clears..it 1770. Where the opportunities of v. intellectual exercise were frequent MACAULAY. b. A copious fount of v. English 1864. 3. A v. defence 1777. b. An able, v., and well-informed statesman BURKE. Hence **Vi·gorous-ly** *adv.,* **-ness.**

Vigour (vi·gəɹ). Also (*U.S.*) **vigor.** late ME. [a. AF., OF. *vigor,* ad. L. *vigor* liveliness, force, f. *vigere* to thrive.] **1.** Active physical strength as an attribute or quality of living things; active force or power; activity or energy of body or constitution. **2.** Mental or moral strength, force, or energy; activity, animation, or liveliness of the mind or the faculties 1587. **3.** Active force or strength as an attribute of things, natural agencies, conditions, or qualities; intensity of effect or operation 1445. †4. Legal or binding force; validity. *In v.*, in force or operation. –1678. 5. Strong or energetic action, esp. in administration or government; the power, exercise, or use of this, esp. as possessed by or as an attribute of a ruler or governor. (Freq. implying some degree of severity or rigour.) 1618. 6. The condition or state of greatest strength or activity, esp. in the life of a man; *spec.* in *Med.*, the height or acme of a disease 1563.

1. The sinnowy v. of the trauailer SHAKS. In order to.. maintain a sufficient degree of v. in the vines 1842. 2. The mind retains its utmost v. to forty-nine 1823. 3. My bones beares witnesse, That since haue felt the vigor of his rage SHAKS. The whole picture is wanting in v. and contrast 1873. 4. The Five Mile Act and the Conventicle Act were in full v. MACAULAY. 5. The Star Chamber.. was invested with a v. beyond the laws 1830. 6. He was then in the V. of his years 1697.

Viking (vəi·kiŋ, vī·kiŋ). Also **vikingr**, wi(c)king. 1807. [ad. ON., Icel. *víkingr*, = OE. *wīcing*: perh. formed from OE. *wīc* camp, the formation of temporary encampments being a feature of viking raids; but commonly regarded as f. ON. *vík* creek, inlet + *-ingr* -ING^{3}.] *Hist.* One of those Scandinavian adventurers who practised piracy at sea, and committed depredations on land, in northern and western Europe from the 8th to the 11th c.; occas. *gen.*, a warlike pirate or sea-rover.

A fleet of vikings from Norway ravaged the western coasts 1848.

‖**Vilayet** (vilā·yet). 1869. [Turkish, ad. Arab. *welāyeh*, *-yet* district, dominion.] A province of the Turkish empire ruled by a vali or governor-general.

Vild (vəild), *a.* *Obs.* exc. *arch.* or *dial.* 1560. [Variant of VILE *a.*, with excrescent *d.*] = VILE *a.* Hence **Vi·ldly** *adv.*

Vile (vəil), *a.* and *adv.* ME. [a. AF. and OF. (also mod.F.) *vil* masc., *vile* fem.:—L. *vilem*, *vilis* cheap, common, mean, base.] **A.** *adj.* 1. Of actions, conduct, character, etc.: Despicable on moral grounds; characterized by baseness or depravity. **b.** Of epithets, etc.: Implying (moral) baseness or depravity 1560. 2. Of persons: Of a base or despicable character; morally depraved or degraded ME. 3. Physically repulsive, esp. through filth or corruption; horrid, disgusting ME. **b.** Of clothes, etc.: Mean, wretched 1526. 4. Of conditions, situations, treatment, etc.: Base or degrading in character or effect; ignominious ME. 5. Of little worth or account; mean or paltry in respect of value; held in no esteem. Also *absol.* ME. †**b.** Cheap, low (in price) –1601. 6. Of poor or bad quality; wretchedly bad or inferior ME. **b.** Used as an intensive emphasizing some bad quality or condition; also *colloq. trivially* (cf. *foul*). late ME.

1. Let their v. thoughts the thinckers ruine be SIDNEY. **b.** The vilest epithet in the English language 1868. 2. A victim to the snare, That v. attorneys for the weak prepare CRABBE. 3. My v. body I bequeath to the dust 1637. **b.** A poore man in vyle raiment TINDALE *Jas.* ii. 2. 4. He had been a slave, in the vilest of all positions 1879. Phr. *Durance v.*: see DURANCE 5. 5. The vilest and commonest stones 1677. A clamorous v. plebeian POPE. 6. A V. compound.. called Olla podrida 1841.

B. *adv.* = VILELY *adv.* Now only in combs. ME. Hence **Vi·le·ly** *adv.*, **-ness.**

†**Viliaco.** 1593. [ad. It. *vigliacco* :—pop.L. **viliaccum*, *-us*, f. L. *vilis* vile.] A vile or contemptible person –1651.

Vilification (vi:lifikēi·ʃən). 1653. [ad. L. **vilificatio*; see next and -FICATION.] The action of vilifying by means of abusive language; reviling; an instance of this.

Vilify (vi·lifəi), *v.* 1450. [ad. late L. *vilificare*, f. *vilis* VILE *a.*; see -(I)FY.] 1. *trans.* To lower or lessen in worth or value; to reduce to a lower standing or level. Also *refl.* Now *rare* or *Obs.* †**b.** To make morally vile; to degrade; also, to defile or dirty –1781. †**c.** To bring disgrace or dishonour upon –1749. 2. †To depreciate or disparage in discourse; to defame or traduce; to speak evil of 1586. †3. To regard as worthless or of little value; to contemn or despise –1671.

1. **b.** Thir Makers Image..then Forsook them, when themselves they villifi'd To serve ungovern'd appetite MILT. 2. Mother-in-Lawes, Poets much Vilifie 1659. Hence **Vi·lifier**, a defamer or abuser.

Vilipend (vi·lipend), *v.* 1470. [a. OF. *vilipender*, or ad. L. *vilipendere*, f. *vilis* vile, worthless + *pendere* to consider, esteem.] 1. *trans.* To rate or regard as being of little value or consequence; to contemn or despise; to treat slightingly. 2. To abuse or vilify 1529.

2. Even Dryden, who speaks with proper respect of Corneille, vilipends Racine 1806. Hence †**Vilipe·ndency**, the expression of disparagement or contempt (*rare*).

Vility (vəi·lĭti). *Obs.* exc. *arch.* late ME. [a. OF. *vilité*, ad. L. *vilitas*, f. *vilis* VILE *a.*; see -ITY.] 1. Vileness of character or conduct; moral baseness. †2. Meanness or lowliness of condition –1696. †**b.** Cheapness –1674.

Vill (vil). 1596. [a. AF., OF. *vile*, *ville* farm, country-house, village (mod.F. *ville* town) :—L. *villa* VILLA *sb.*] 1. *Law* and *Hist.* A territorial unit or division under the feudal system, consisting of a number of houses or buildings with their adjacent lands, more or less contiguous and having a common organization; corresponding to the Anglo-Saxon tithing and to the modern township or civil parish. 2. *poet.* A village 1700.

1. Any Parish, Township, Vill, or Extraparochial Place 1721. 2. Parochial Priests were fix'd in ev'ry Vill 1700.

Villa (vi·lă). 1611. [Partly a. L., country-house, farm, perh. a dim. from the stem of *vicus* village; partly a. It., from the same source.] *orig.* A country mansion or residence, together with a farm, farm-buildings, or other houses attached, built or occupied by a person of some position and wealth; a country seat or estate; later, a residence in the country or in the neighbourhood of a town, usu. standing in its own grounds. **b.** Hence, any residence of a superior type, in the suburbs of a town or in a residential district, such as is occupied by a person of the middle-class; also, any small better-class dwelling house, usu. one which is detached or semi-detached 1755. Hence **Vi·lladom**, the world of villas; suburban villas or their residents collectively.

Village (vi·lėdʒ), *sb.* late ME. [a. OF. :—L. *villaticum*, neut. sing. of *villaticus* of or pertaining to a villa, f. *villa* VILLA; see -AGE.] 1. A collection of dwelling-houses and other buildings, larger than a hamlet and smaller than a town, or having a simpler organization and administration than the latter. Sometimes applied joc. to a large town or city. **b.** *U.S.* A minor municipality with limited corporate powers 1888. 2. The inhabitants or residents of a village; the villagers 1529. 3. *transf.* A small group or cluster of the burrows of prairie-dogs 1808.

1. A wall'd Towne is more worthier then a v. SHAKS. Birmingham is called 'the hardware village' 1874. Hence **Vi·llage** *v. intr.* to settle down to a villeggiatura. **Vi·llager**, one who lives in a v.; now usu., a working-class inhabitant of a v. **Vi·llagery**, villages collectively.

Villain (vi·lən), *sb.* ME. [a. AF. and OF. *vilein*, *villain* :—pop. L. **villanum*, **villanus*, f. L. *villa* VILLA. Cf. VILLEIN.] 1. *orig.* A low-born, base-minded rustic; a man of ignoble ideas or instincts; in later use, an unprincipled or depraved scoundrel; a man naturally disposed to base or criminal actions, or deeply involved in the commission of disgraceful crimes. **b.** Used playfully. Also applied to a woman 1590. **c.** (Usu. with *the.*) That character in a play, novel, etc., whose evil motives or actions form an important element in the plot 1822. 2. A person or animal of a troublesome character in some respect. Const. *to* with inf. 1895.

1. Now knocke when I bid you: sirrah villaine SHAKS. There were two desperate Villains among them DE FOE. **b.** Ile fetch her; it is the prettiest villaine SHAKS. I shall telegraph to the young v. 1908. **c.** Arnulf, as usual, appears as the v. of the piece 1867. Hence **Vi·llainess**, a female v.

Villain (vi·lən), *a.* Now *rare.* ME. [a. AF. and OF. *vilein*, *vilain*; see prec.] †1. Boorish, clownish. -late ME. 2. Base in character or disposition; given to committing vile or criminal acts ME. 3. Partaking of the nature of villainy ME. 4. Low or mean in respect of birth or position 1483.

2. Where gloomily retired The v. spider lives, cunning and fierce THOMSON. 3. Narrowness or spite, Or v. fancy fleeting by TENNYSON.

Villain: see VILLEIN.

Villainize (vi·lănəiz), *v.* 1623. [f. VILLAIN *sb.*] 1. *trans.* To render villainous; to debase or degrade. 2. To treat or revile as a villain 1857.

Villainous (vi·lənəs), *a.* late ME. [f. VILLAIN *sb.* + -OUS.] 1. Of persons: Having the character or disposition of a villain; infamously depraved or wicked; vilely criminal 1550. 2. Of actions: Of the nature of villainy; marked by depravity or vileness of conduct. late ME. **b.** Of looks, etc.: Indicative of villainy 1828. 3. Of words, etc.: Pertaining to or characteristic of a villain 1470. †4. Shameful, atrocious, horrible –1616. 5. Extremely bad or objectionable; atrocious, detestable 1596. 6. Low or base in respect of social position; servile –1766.

1. There is nothing but Roguery to be found in Villanous man SHAKS. 2. A Vilanous and shamefull act 1573. **b.** A most sinister and v. squint DICKENS. 3. A. v., low oath STEVENSON. 4. Phr. †*V. judgement*, a sentence of extreme severity passed on one found guilty of conspiracy or other grave offence. 5. Thou art ugly and old, And a v. Scold ADDISON. The weather was v. 1884. Hence **Vi·llainous·ly** *adv.*, **-ness.**

Villainy (vi·lăni). ME. [a. AF. and OF. *vile(i)nie*, *vilanie*, *vilenie*; see VILLAIN *sb.* and -Y^{3}. Until the 19th c. *villany* was the more prevalent spelling.] 1. Action or conduct befitting, characteristic or typical of a villain; evil or wrongdoing of a foul, infamous, or shameful nature; extreme wickedness on the part of a person in dealing with others. **b.** With *a* and *pl.*: An instance or case of this. late ME. †2. Ill-usage, indignity, insult –1590. †3. Disgrace, dishonour; ignominy; discredit –1594. †4. Lack of courtesy or politeness; incivility, rudeness; boorishness –1694. †5. The condition or state of a villein; bondage, servitude; hence, moral degradation –1543.

1. Age's firm, cold, subtle v. SHELLEY. **b.** Robberies and all manner of Villanies 1691. 2. To see villanie offered him, and to holde his peace 1590.

Phrases. †*To say* or *speak* (*a*, *no*, etc.) *v.*, to speak (no) evil, to use (refrain from) low, obscene, or opprobrious language. †*To speak v. of*, to defame (a person). So †*words of v.*

Villakin (vi·lăkin). 1730. [f. VILLA + -KIN.] A little villa; a villa-residence. Chiefly *familiar* or *joc.*

I am every day building villakins and have given over that of castles GAY.

Villan (vi·lăn). *Hist.* 1552. [ad. med.L. *villanus* villager, f. L. *villa* VILLA.] A villein; an occupier of land in the feudal vill.

‖**Villanella** (vilăne·lă). *Pl.* **-elle.** 1597. [It., fem. of *villanello* rural, rustic, f. *villano*; see VILLAIN *sb.* and *a.*] An unaccompanied part-song, of light rustic character.

‖**Villanelle** (vilăne·l). 1586. [a. F., ad. It. *villanella*; see prec.] †1. = prec. –1685. 2. A poem of fixed form, usu. of a pastoral or lyric nature, consisting normally of five three-lined stanzas and a final quatrain, with only two rhymes throughout 1877.

2. A dainty thing 's the V. Sly, musical, a jewel in rhyme HENLEY.

Villarsite (vilā·ɹzəit). 1846. [a. F., f. name of D. *Villars* (1745–1814), a French botanist.] *Min.* A hydrous silicate of magnesium occurring massive or in rounded grains at Traversella, Piedmont.

Villatic (vilæ·tik), *a.* 1671. [ad. L. *villaticus*, f. *villa* VILLA.] Of or pertaining to a villa or villas or to the inhabitants; *esp.* rural, rustic.

The perched roosts, And nests in order rang'd Of tame v. Fowl MILT.

‖**Villeggiatura** (viledʒātū·ră). 1742. [It., f. *villeggiare* to live at a villa or in the country, f. *villa* VILLA.] Residence at a country villa or in the country; a holiday spent in this way.

Lord Byron is in *v.*, near Leghorn SHELLEY.

Villein (vi·lĕn). Now *Hist.* Also **villain.** ME. [a. AF. *villein*, *villain* VILLAIN *sb.*] One of the class of serfs in the feudal system; *spec.* a peasant occupier or cultivator entirely subject to a lord (*v. in gross* GROSS *sb.*^{3} 2 e.) or attached to a manor (*v. regardant* REGARDANT *a.* 1.); a tenant in villeinage; also applied to a person regarded as holding a similar position in other communities; a bondsman. †Hence formerly in general use, a peasant, country labourer, or low-born rustic.

The villain was not a slave, but a freeman minus the very important rights of his lord 1876.

attrib.: **v. service,** service which a villein was bound to render to his lord as a condition of holding his land: **-socage,** socage or tenure by v. service.

Villeinage (vi·lĕnėdʒ). ME. [a. AF. (OF.) *vil(l)enage*, perh. ad. med.L. *villenagium*; see prec. and -AGE.] 1. The tenure by which a feudal villein held or occupied his land; tenure of lands by bond-service rendered to the lord or superior. Also called *tenure in v.* 2. The state or condition of a feudal villein; complete subjection, bondage, serfdom, servitude 1531.

1. Copy-holders is but a new Name, for anciently they were called Tenants in villenage 1672. 2. Reduced to the terms of the Peasants of France, of v. and slavery MILT. *fig.* As if sin were condemn'd in a perpetual v...never to be manumitted MILT.

Villiform (vi·lifǭɹm), *a.* 1849. [ad. mod.L. *villiformis*; see VILLUS and -FORM.] *Zool.* Of the teeth of certain fishes: Having the form of villi; so numerous, slender, and closely set as to resemble the pile of velvet.

Villose (vi·lōus), *a.* 1727. [ad. L. *villosus* hairy, rough, f. *villus* VILLUS.] *Bot.* and *Ent.* = VILLOUS *a.*

Villosity (vilǫ·sĭti). 1777. [See prec. and -ITY.] 1. *Bot.*, *Zool.*, etc. The condition or fact of being villose or villous. 2. a. A villous formation or surface. b. A villus. 1828.

Villous (vi·ləs), *a.* late ME. [ad. L. *villosus* VILLOSE *a.*] 1. *Anat.* Covered with numerous thick-set slender projections resembling short hairs. 2. Of the nature of villi 1664. 3. *Bot.* Of parts of plants: Thickly covered with long soft hairs 1766. Hence **Vi·llously** *adv.*

‖**Villus** (vi·lɒ̆s). *Pl.* **villi** (vi·ləi). 1704. [L., tuft of hair, shaggy hair.] 1. *Bot.* A long, slender, soft hair. 2. *Anat.* A slender hair-like process or minute projection forming one of a number closely set upon a surface 1728.

Vim (vim). orig. *U.S.* 1850. [perh. interjectional, but commonly taken as a. L. *vim*, acc. sing. of *vis* strength, energy.] Force or vigour, energy, 'go'.

Vimineous (vimi·niəs), *a.* Now *rare.* 1657. [f. L. *vimineus*, f. *vimin-* osier + -OUS.] 1. Made of pliable twigs or wickerwork. 2. *Bot.* Producing long, flexible shoots or twigs 1664.

‖**Vina** (vī·nă). 1796. [Skr. and Hindī *vīṇā*.] An Indian musical instrument consisting of a fretted fingerboard, to which seven strings fitted with pegs are attached, with a gourd at each end; an Indian lyre.

Vinaceous (vəinē¹·ʃəs), *a.* 1688. [f. L. *vinaceus*, f. *vinum* wine; see -ACEOUS.] Of the reddish colour of wine; wine-coloured. Also *ellipt.* or as *sb.*

‖**Vinaigrette** (vinēgre·t). 1698. [F., f. *vinaigre* VINEGAR *sb.*] 1. A small two-wheeled carriage drawn or pushed by hand, formerly in use in France. Now *Hist.* 2. A small ornamental bottle or box usu. containing a sponge charged with some aromatic or pungent salts; a smelling-bottle 1811.

Vinal (vəi·năl), *a.* Now *rare.* 1658. [ad. L. *vinalis* (rare), f. *vinum* wine.] Produced by or originating in wine.

Vincentian (vinse·nʃăn), *sb.* and *a.*[1] 1854. [f. *Vincent* (see def.) + -IAN.] A. *sb.* A member of the Congregation of the Priests of the Mission founded by St. Vincent de Paul (1576–1660). B. *adj.* Of or pertaining to this.

Vincentian (vinse·nʃăn), *a.*[2] 1875. [f. *Vincent* (see def.) + -IAN.] Originating or associated with St. Vincent of Lerins (died *c* 450 A.D.).

The meaning of 'Semper' in the Vincentian Canon [viz. *quod ubique, quod semper, quod ab omnibus creditum est*] LIDDON.

Vincible (vi·nsĭb'l), *a.* 1548. [ad. L. *vincibilis*, f. *vincere* to overcome; see -IBLE.] 1. Of persons: That may be overcome or vanquished; susceptible of defeat or overthrow. 2. Of material or immaterial things, obstacles, arguments, etc.: That may be overcome; conquerable, surmountable 1568.

1. He not easily v. in spirit..drew his sword 1630. 2. Nought is so hard but v. by paines FULLER. *V. ignorance*, an ignorance the means of overcoming which are possessed by the ignorant person himself. Hence **Vincibi·lity, Vi·ncibleness. Vi·ncibly** *adv.*

‖**Vinculum** (vi·ŋkiŭlɒ̆m). *Pl.* **vincula.** 1678. [L., f. *vinc-*, *vincire* to bind + *-ulum* -ULE.] 1. A bond of union; a tie. Usu. *fig.* 2. *Math.* A straight line drawn over two or more terms, denoting that these are to be considered as subject to the same operations of multiplication, division, etc., by another term 1710. 3. *Anat.* A ligament or frenum 1859.

Vindemiate (vindī·miē¹t), *v.* 1664. [f. L. *vindemiat-*, *vindemiare*, f. *vindemia* vintage.] *intr.* To gather ripe fruit, esp. grapes (*rare*). So **Vindemia·tion,** the gathering of grapes or other fruit 1609.

‖**Vindemiatrix** (vindīmiē¹·triks). 1704. [med. or mod.L. fem. of *vindemiator* vintager, star in Virgo, f. L. *vindemiare.*] A bright fixed star in the constellation Virgo.

Vindicable (vi·ndikăb'l), *a.* 1647. [ad. late L. *vindicabilis*, f. L. *vindicare* to vindicate.] Capable of being vindicated, justified, or maintained.

Vindicate (vi·ndikē¹t), *v.* 1623. [f. L. *vindicat-*, *vindicare* (also *vendicare*) to claim, set free, punish, f. *vim*, acc. sing. of *vis* force + *dic-*, *dicere* to say.] †1. *trans.* To avenge or revenge (a person, cause, wrong, etc.) –1713. †b. To punish –1770. †2. To make or set free; to deliver or rescue. Usu. const. *from.* –1761. 3. To clear from censure, criticism, suspicion, or doubt, by means of demonstration; to justify or uphold by evidence or argument 1635. b. To provide justification for (something); to justify by facts or results 1702. 4. To assert, maintain, or make good by one's action, esp. in one's own interest; to defend against encroachment or interference 1650. 5. To claim as properly belonging *to* oneself or another; to assert or establish possession of (something) *for* oneself or another 1680. b. Without const.: To claim for oneself or as one's rightful property; *spec.* in *Law* 1725.

1. But Cupid, full of mischief, longs To v. his mother's wrongs SWIFT. b. Because our grievances are..not..those which we bore from the Tudors, or vindicated on the Stuarts BURKE. 3. The design of this treatise is not to v. the character of God 1736. I must v. Sterne from a charge of plagiarism 1798. b. What have I ever shewn to v. this presumption of yours? FARQUHAR. 4. Arise and v. Thy Glory, free thy people from thir yoke MILT. 5. Though Christ's Appeal to the 110th vindicates that Psalm to David 1737. b. Is thine alone the seed that strews the plain? The birds of heav'n shall v. their grain. POPE.

Vindication (vindikē¹·ʃən). 1484. [a. OF. (now F. dial.), vengeance, or ad. L. *vindicatio*, f. *vindicare*; see prec.] †1. The action of avenging or revenging –1690. 2. The action of vindicating against censure, calumny, etc.; justification by proof or explanation 1647. b. A justifying fact or circumstance 1846. 3. The action of asserting or maintaining 1871.

2. Leave the v. of your character to your children 1825. Phr. *In v. of.* 3. The bulk of the members supported Eliot in his last v. of English liberty 1874.

Vindicative (vi·ndikē¹tiv, vindi·kătiv), *a.* 1521. [ad. OF. *vindicatif* (also mod.F.), or med.L. *vindicativus*; see VINDICATE *v.* and -IVE.] †1. = VINDICTIVE *a.* 1. –1734. 2. = VINDICTIVE *a.* 2. Now *rare.* 1610. 3. Serving to vindicate by defence or assertion 1660.

1. They discerned not between a zealous and a v. spirit DONNE. 2. They will find it ill striving against the Stream and Current of V. Justice 1679. Hence **Vindi·cativeness,** vindictiveness.

Vindicator (vi·ndikē¹təɹ). 1566. [a. late L. (eccl.), f. *vindicare* VINDICATE *v.*] One who vindicates. Hence **Vi·ndicatress.**

Vindicatory (vi·ndikē¹təri), *a.* 1647. [f. VINDICATE *v.* + -ORY [2].] 1. Serving to vindicate; justificatory, defensive. 2. Avenging; punitive; retributive 1655.

2. The afflictions of Job were no v. punishments to take vengeance of his sins 1655. Hence **Vi·ndicatorily** *adv.* in a v. manner.

Vindictive (vindi·ktiv), *a.* 1616. [f. L. *vindicta* vengeance, revenge + -IVE.] 1. Of persons: Given to revenge; having a revengeful disposition. b. Of actions, qualities, etc.: Characterized by a desire for, or the exercise of, revenge 1627. 2. Involving retribution or punishment; punitive, retributive; avenging. Now *rare.* 1623. b. Of deities: Inflicting punishment for wrongdoing 1703.

1. He is as v. as a demon 1875. b. When..you engage To meet high Heaven's v. Rage 1743. 2. The.. debts we owe to thy v. justice 1711. *V. damages*, damages awarded not only as compensation to the plaintiff but also as a punishment to the defendant. b. V. Jove prepares his Thunder 1703. Hence **Vindi·ctive·ly** *adv.*, **-ness.**

Vine (vəin), *sb.* ME. [a. OF. *vigne, vine* (mod.F. *vigne*):—L. *vinea* vineyard, vine, f. *vinum* wine.] I. 1. The trailing or climbing plant, *Vitis vinifera*, bearing the grapes from which ordinary wine is made (= GRAPE-VINE); also gen., any plant of the genus *Vitis.* b. A single plant or tree of this species or genus ME. c. A representation of a vine in metal, embroidery, etc. late ME.; also, an ornamental figure cut by a skater. 2. *fig.* a. Applied to Christ, in renderings or echoes of John xv. 1 and 5. ME. b. In allusion to Ps. cxxviii. 3. 1787. 3. Applied, with distinguishing epithets, to some species of *Vitis* distinct from the ordinary grape-vine, and to many plants of other genera which in some feature resemble this. late ME. 4. The stem of any trailing or climbing plant. Also *collect.* without article. 1563. b. *U.S.* A trailing or climbing plant 1842.

1. Then sayde the trees vnto the vyne: Come thou and be oure kinge COVERDALE *Judg.* ix. 12. b. Raisins from the Grapes of Psythian Vines DRYDEN. 2. a. That true V. whereof wee both spiritually and corporally are branches HOOKER. b. A wife, who bids fair to be a fruitful v. 1787. 3. *Wild v.*, the fox-grape, *Vitis Labrusca* (now *rare* or *Obs.*); also, one or other of several climbing or trailing plants, esp. bryony and traveller's joy.

II. †1. A vineyard –1560. 2. A grape. *Obs.* or *poet.* late ME. 3. *Rom. Antiq.* = VINEA (*rare*) 1563.

attrib. and *Comb.*, as *v.-branch, -grounds, -leaf, -prop, -stock.* **v. bower,** a species of clematis (*Clematis Viticella*); **-disease,** one or other disease attacking vines, esp. v.-mildew and the v.-pest (*Phylloxera*); **-fretter** (now *rare* or *Obs.*), **-grub,** a grub or insect (esp. a species of aphis) feeding upon vines; **-leek,** round-headed garlic (*Allium ampeloprasum*); **-louse,** the phylloxera; **-mildew,** a disease of vines caused by the fungus *Oidium Tuckeri*; the fungus or mould itself; **-moth,** a species of pyralis infesting vines; **-pest,** the phylloxera; **-rod,** a rod of v.-wood, *spec.* as the staff of a Roman centurion; **-sawfly,** a species of sawfly, the larvæ of which feed on the v.; **-scrub,** in Australia, scrub abounding in various species of *Vitis*; **-snail** [F. *escargot des vignes*], the Roman snail; **-weevil,** a small weevil destructive to vines. Hence **Vine** *v. trans.* to graft (*in* or *into* a vine); *intr.* to develop tendrils like a vine.

‖**Vinea** (vi·niă). 1601. [L.; see VINE *sb.*] A kind of protective shed or penthouse anciently used in siege operations.

Vineal (vi·niăl), *a.* *rare.* 1659. [ad. L. *vinealis*, f. *vinea* VINE *sb.*] Of or pertaining to vines or wine; living on vines; consisting of wine.

Vi·ne-dre:sser. 1560. [VINE *sb.*] One occupied in the pruning, training, and cultivation of vines.

Vinegar (vi·nėgăɹ), *sb.* ME. [a. OF. *vyn egre, vinaigre* (so mod.F.), f. *vin*:—L. *vinum* wine + *egre, aigre* EAGER *a.*] 1. A liquid (consisting of acetic acid in a dilute form) produced by the acetous fermentation of wine and some other alcoholic liquors or special compounds, and employed in the preparation of food (or as a relish to this), and in the arts, etc. b. With *a* and *pl.* A particular kind or special preparation of vinegar 1839. 2. *fig.* Speech, temper, etc. of a sour or acid character 1601.

1. *allus.* Our desire is..not to pour Vineger but Oyl into the Wounds 1656. 2. Heere 's the Challenge..: I warrant there 's v. and pepper in 't SHAKS.

attrib. and *Comb.*, as *v. bottle, -cruet*; (= sour) *v.-faced* adj. **V. Bible,** an edition printed by Baskett in 1717, so called from an error in the running title at St. Luke, chap. xxii, where it reads 'the parable of the v.', instead of 'the parable of the vineyard'; **v.-eel,** a minute nematoid worm (*Anguillula aceti*) breeding in v.; **v. mother,** = *vinegar-plant* (b); **-plant,** (*a*) the Virginian sumach, *Rhus typhina*; (*b*) a mould which grows on the surface of liquids undergoing acetous fermentation; **-tree,** = *v.-plant* (*a*); **-yard,** a yard or open space in which v. casks are arranged. Hence **Vi·negar** *v. trans.* to treat with v. in some way; to add or apply v. to; to restore by means of v. **Vi·negary** *a.* resembling v.; sour like v.

Vinery (vəi·nəri). late ME. [ad. med.L. *vinarium*, or f. VINE *sb.* + -ERY.] †1. A vineyard –1513. **2.** A glass house or hot-house constructed for the cultivation of the grape-vine 1789. **3.** Vines collectively 1883.

†**Vinet.** late ME. [ad. OF. *vignete, vignette*, dim. of *vigne* VINE *sb.* Readopted in 18th c. as VIGNETTE.] **1.** A running or trailing ornament or design in imitation of the branches, leaves, or tendrils of the vine, employed in architecture or decorative work –1601. **2.** = VIGNETTE *sb.* 1, 1 b. –1637. **3.** An ornamental title-page or the like containing various symbolical designs or figures –1625.

Vineyard (vi·nyăɹd). ME. [f. VINE *sb.* + YARD *sb.*, after the earlier *wineyard*, OE. *winʒeard*.] A piece of ground in which grape-vines are cultivated; a plantation of vines. **b.** *fig.* A sphere of action or labour, esp. of an elevated or spiritual character. (See Matt. xx. 1 and xxi. 28, 40.) late ME.

b. The v. of methodism lies before you SMOLLETT. Hence **Vi·neyardist**, one who engages in vine-growing.

‖**Vingt-et-un** (væ̃nte ö̃n), **vingt-un** (væ̃nt-ö̃n). 1781. [F., 'twenty-one'.] A round game of cards in which the object is to make the number twenty-one or as near this as possible without exceeding it, by counting the pips on the cards, court-cards counting as ten, the ace one or eleven as the holder chooses.

Vinic (vəi·nik), *a.* 1835. [f. L. *vinum* wine.] *Chem.* Obtained or derived from wine or alcohol.

Viniculture (vəi·ni-). 1871. [f. L. *vini-, vinum* wine + CULTURE *sb.*] The cultivation of grapes for the production of wine. Hence **Vinicu·ltural** *a.*

Vinification (vəi:nifikēⁱ·ʃən). 1880. [f. as prec.; see -FICATION.] The conversion of grape juice or the like into an alcoholic liquid by fermentation.

Vino- (vəi·no), used as comb. f. L. *vinum* wine, as in *vino-acetous, -sulphureous*, adjs.

Vinolent (vəi·nŏlĕnt), *a.* late ME. [ad. L. *vinolentus*, f. *vinum* wine.] Addicted to drinking wine; tending to drunkenness. So **Vi·nolence, Vi·nolency**, drunkenness. *rare.*

Vinose (vəi·nōᵘs), *a.* 1727. [ad. L. *vinosus* full or fond of wine.] = VINOUS *a.*

Vinosity (vəinǫ·sĭti). 1624. [ad. L. *vinositas* the flavour of wine, f. *vinosus*; see prec. and -ITY.] The quality or state of being vinous.

Vinous (vəi·nəs), *a.* 1664. [ad. L. *vinosus*, f. *vinum* wine.] **1.** Of the nature of wine; having the qualities of wine; tasting or smelling like wine; made of or prepared with wine. **2.** Pertaining to or characteristic of wine 1708. **3.** Caused by or resulting from indulgence in wine 1776. **b.** Affected by the use of wine 1847. **4.** Addicted to wine 1816. **5.** With names of colours: Like that of (red) wine; having a wine-coloured tinge 1834.

1. So will the Liquor be V. in Smell 1694. **2.** A v. and delicious Taste 1719. **3.** I was seized with a v. inspiration 1874. **b.** Winking..with a pair of v. eyes THACKERAY. **5.** Cup..rough, vinous-brown 1887. Hence **Vi·nous-ly** *adv.*, **-ness.**

Vint, *sb.* 1898. Also **wint.** [Russ.] A Russian card-game resembling auction bridge.

Vint (vint), *v.* 1857. [Back-formation from VINTNER or VINTAGE.] *trans.* To make (wine or strong liquor).

The best wine that ever was vinted TROLLOPE.

Vintage (vi·ntĕdʒ), *sb.* 1450. [a. AF., altered f. *vindage, vendage*, ME. *vendage*, OF. *vendange*, by association with VINTNER.] **1.** The produce or yield of the vine, either as grapes or wine; the crop or yield of a vineyard or district in a single season. Now *rare* or *Obs.* **b.** *poet.* Wine, esp. of good or rare quality 1604. **c.** Used with ref. to the age or year of a particular wine, usu. connoting one of good or outstanding quality; now *spec.* a wine made from the grape-crop of a certain district in a good year and kept separate on account of its quality 1746. **2.** The gathering of the ripe grapes in order to make them into wine, including the preliminary processes of wine-making, as pressing and placing the juice in the fermenting vats, etc.; the grape-harvest 1540. **b.** The season or time when this is done. Also with *a* and *pl.* 1616.

1. The gen'rous V. of the Chian Vine DRYDEN. **b.** O! for a draught of v., that hath been Cool'd a long age in the deep-delved earth KEATS. **c.** Taste my wine; 'Tis of an ancient v. BYRON. *attrib.* The market for v. wines 1895. **2.** The grape-gatherer in time of Vintage HOLLAND.

Vintage, *v.* 1618. [f. prec.] *trans.* †**a.** To strip (vines or a vineyard) of grapes at the vintage –1694. **b.** To gather (grapes) in order to make wine; to make (wine) from gathered grapes 1888. Hence **Vi·ntaging** *vbl. sb.* the action or process of gathering the grapes at the v.

Vintager (vi·ntădʒəɹ). 1588. [f. prec. + -ER, after med. or mod.L. VINDEMIATRIX.] **1.** One who gathers grapes in the vintage 1589. **2.** A bright star in the constellation Virgo 1588.

‖**Vintem** (vinte·m). 1584. [Pg., f. *vinte* twenty.] A small silver (or copper) coin of the value of 20 reis.

†**Vi·nter.** ME. [a. AF., f. L. *vinum* wine.] A vintner –1486.

Vintner (vi·ntnəɹ). late ME. [Alteration of prec.] One who deals in or sells wine; a wine-merchant; †an innkeeper selling wine.

Vintry (vi·ntri). Now *arch.* or *Hist.* ME. [f. VINTER; see -RY.] A place where wine is sold or stored; a wine-shop; a wine-vault, or a number of these. **b.** With *the* (and usu. with initial cap.): A large wine-store formerly existing in the City of London; also, the immediate neighbourhood of this as a part of the city 1456.

Viny (vəi·ni), *a.* 1570. [f. VINE *sb.* + -Y[1].] **1.** Of, pertaining to or of the nature of vines; composed or consisting of vines. **2.** Abounding in, full of, or covered with vines; bearing vines 1612.

Vinyl (vəi·nil). 1863. [f. L. *vinum* + -YL.] *Chem.* The compound univalent radical CH_2CH, isomeric with ethenyl, and characteristic of many derivatives of ethylene (which is the hydride of vinyl).

Viol[1] (vəi·əl). 1483. [orig. ad. AF., OF. *viele, vielle* VIELLE, subseq. assim. to OF., F. *viole* (= It., Sp., Pg. *viola*, Prov. *viula*).] **1.** A musical instrument having five, six, or seven strings and played by means of a bow. Now *Hist.* or *arch.* **2.** With distinguishing terms, denoting esp. the form or tone of the instrument. See also BASS-VIOL, VIOL DA GAMBA, etc. 1611. **b.** *Viol d'amore* or *viol(e d'amour*, a viol with five or six metal strings 1700.

1. For I wil not heare the melodie of thy violes BIBLE (Genev.) *Amos* v. 23.

†**Vi·ol**[2]. Also **voyol, voyal.** 1627. [Origin obsc.] *Naut.* A large rope formerly used in weighing an anchor. Also *attrib.*, esp. in *v.-block.* –1869.

Viola[1] (vəi·ŏlă). late ME. [a. L., violet.] †**1.** The violet (*rare*) –1480. **2.** A large genus of herbaceous plants of the order *Violaceæ*, including violets and pansies; a plant or species of this genus 1731. **b.** A hybrid garden-plant of this genus, distinguished from the pansy by a more delicate and uniform colouring of the flowers 1871. **3.** *attrib.* In chemical terms denoting substances derived from the violet or pansy 1868.

‖**Viola**[2] (vəi,ōᵘ·lă, vi,ōᵘ·lă). 1797. [It. and Sp., = F. *viole* VIOL.[1]] **1.** A four-stringed musical instrument slightly larger than a violin; the alto or tenor violin. **b.** One who plays the viola 1894. **2.** *V. da* (also *di*) *gamba*, = VIOL DA GAMBA 1724. **3.** *V. d'amore* (or †*d'amour*) = viol d'amore (see VIOL[1] 2 b) 1724.

Violable (vəi·ŏlăb'l), *a.* 1552. [ad. L. (poet.) *violabilis*, f. *violare* to violate.] Capable of being violated. Hence **Vi·olableness.**

Violaceous (vəiŏlēⁱ·ʃəs), *a.* 1657. [f. L. *violaceus* violet-coloured, f. *viola* VIOLA[1]; see -ACEOUS.] **1.** Of a violet colour; purplish blue. **2.** *Bot.* Belonging to or resembling the family *Violaceæ* 1889.

Violan (vəi·ŏlăn). 1850. [f. L. *viola* VIOLA[1].] *Min.* A silicate of aluminium, calcium, magnesium, and sodium.

Violate (vəi·ŏlēⁱt), *v.* late ME. [f. L. *violat-, violare* to treat with violence.] **1.** *trans.* To break, infringe, or transgress unjustifiably; to fail to keep or observe duly. **2.** To ravish or outrage (a woman) 1440. **3.** To do violence to; to treat irreverently; to desecrate, dishonour, profane, or defile 1490. **b.** To destroy (a person's chastity) by force 1592. **c.** To interfere with by appropriation 1823. †**4.** To vitiate, corrupt, or spoil, esp. in respect of physical qualities –1656. †**b.** To damage or injure by violence –1675. **5.** To break in upon; to interrupt or disturb; to interfere with rudely or roughly 1667. **6.** To treat without proper respect or regard; to do violence or injury to (feelings, etc.) in this way 1692.

1. If any man be affraid to violat the oth of obedience, which they haue made to suche monstres KNOX. Her priests haue violated my law *Ezek.* xxii. 26. He that would not v. truth, must avoid all injustice 1722. **5.** Legislation passes its limits when it violates the purse JOHNSON. So **Vi·olate** *pa. pple.* and *ppl. a.* (now *poet*). **Vi·olater** (now *rare*) = VIOLATOR. **Vi·olative** *a.* (chiefly *U.S.*) involving or causing violation (*of* something).

Violation (vəiŏlēⁱ·ʃən). late ME. [a. OF. *violacion* (F. *violation*), or ad. L. *violation-, violatio*, f. *violare* to violate.] The action of violating. **1.** Infringement, flagrant disregard, or non-observance *of* some principle or standard of conduct or procedure, as an oath, promise, law, etc.; an instance of this. †**2.** The action of treating or handling violently and injuriously –1699. **3. a.** Defilement *of* chastity, etc.; in later use esp. by means of violence 1497. **b.** Ravishment, outrage, rape 1599. **4.** Desecration or profanation of something sacred 1546.

1. V. of the principles of the constitution GIBBON. A flagrant v. of treaty 1863. **4.** The v. of a sacred place by murder 1856.

Violator (vəi·ŏlēⁱtŏɹ, -əɹ). late ME. [a. L., f. *violare* to violate.] One who violates; a ravisher or outrager of women; a desecrator or profaner; an infringer, breaker, or transgressor (of a law, compact, etc.).

‖**Viol da gamba** (vi·ŏl da ga·mbă). 1597. [ad. It. *viola da gamba* 'leg-viol'.] **1.** A viol held between the legs of the player while being played; in later use restricted to the bass viol corresponding to the modern violoncello. **2.** An organ-stop having a tone resembling that of the viol da gamba 1852.

Violence (vəi·ŏlĕns), *sb.* ME. [a. AF. and OF., ad. L. *violentia* vehemence, f. *violentus* VIOLENT *a.*] **1.** The exercise of physical force so as to inflict injury on or damage to persons or property; action or conduct characterized by this. **b.** In weakened sense: Improper treatment or use of a word; wresting or perversion of meaning or application; unauthorized alteration of wording 1596. **c.** Undue constraint applied to some natural process, habit, etc. 1715. **2.** With *a* and *pl.* An instance or case of violent, injurious, or severe treatment. late ME. **3.** Force or strength of physical action or natural agents; forcible, powerful, or violent action or motion (in early use freq. connoting destructive force or capacity). late ME. **4.** Great force, severity, or vehemence; intensity *of* some condition or influence. late ME. **5.** Vehemence of personal feeling or action; great, excessive, or extreme ardour or fervour; also, violent or passionate conduct or language; passion, fury. late ME.

1. Promises proceeding from fear of death, or v., are no Covenants HOBBES. The v. of war admits of no distinction JOHNSON. Phr. *To do v. to, unto* (or with indirect object), to inflict harm or injury upon; to outrage or violate. **b.** The v. of the proposed interpretation is..conspicuous 1875. **2.** The violences inseparable from the best-ordered ancient society 1864. **3.** He knocked a fourth time, and with v. 1841. **4.** All the v. of her disorder was passed 1794. **5.** The v. of party spirit 1818. Hence †**Vi·olence** *v. trans.* to do v. to, to violate; to compel or constrain.

†**Vi·olency.** 1545. [ad. L. *violentia*; see prec.] Violence –1660.

Violent (vəi·ŏlĕnt), *a.* ME. [a. OF. *violent*, or ad. L. *violentus*, f. *vis* strength.] **I. 1.** Of things: Having some quality or qualities in such a degree as to produce a very marked or powerful effect (esp. in the way of injury or discomfort); intense, vehement, very strong or severe. **b.** Of colour: Intensely or extremely bright or strong; vivid. Also *fig.* of outline. 1768. **2.** Of natural forces: Possessed of or operating with great force or strength; moving, flowing, blowing, etc. strongly and impetuously. late ME. **b.** Of noise: Extremely loud 1602. **3.** Of persons: Acting with or using physical force or violence, esp. in order to injure, control, or intimidate others; committing harm or destruction in this way; †acting illegally, taking illegal possession. late ME. **b.** Of the hand. Chiefly in phr. *to lay v. hands on* or *upon*. late ME. **4.** Of actions: **a.** Characterized by the doing of harm or injury; accompanied by the exercise of violence. late ME. **b.** Characterized by the exertion of great physical force or strength; done or performed with intense or unusual force, and with some degree of rapidity; not gentle or moderate. late ME. **5.** †**a.** Due or subject to constraint or force; forced –1667. **b.** Of death: Caused by or due to physical violence; not natural 1588. **6.** Of persons, their temper, etc.: Displaying passion, excessive ardour, or lack of moderation in action or conduct 1647. **7.** Of language or writings: Resulting from, indicating, or expressive of strong feeling 1749.

1. So v. and fervent was þe hete LYDG. Parker was a man of v. passions 1808. b. Her hair, which was a very v. red 1873. 2. For v. fires soone burne out themselues SHAKS. 3. A man so v. and unprincipled as Goodenough MACAULAY. 4. a. [To use] v. thefts, And rob in the behalfe of charitie SHAKS. b. Feverish with v. exercise 1798. 5. b. I pray thee doe on them some v. death SHAKS. 6. Some of the violenter sort of the other partie 1654. 7. He wrote v. letters, protesting his innocence 1826.

II. In intensive use: Very or extremely great, strong, or severe 1516.

V. presumption is many times equal to full proof BLACKSTONE. I cannot make use of so v. a metaphor 1807. The intemperate life has v. delights, and still more v. desires 1875. Hence **Vi·olent-ly** *adv.*, †**-ness.**

†**Vi·olent,** *v.* 1598. [ad. OF. (also mod.F.) *violenter*, or ad. med.L. *violentare* to compel by force; see prec.] **1.** *trans.* To constrain or force by violence; to compel or coerce (a person) –1730. **2.** To perpetrate or attempt with violence –1661.

Violer (vəi·ŏləɹ). Chiefly *Sc.*, now *arch.* 1551. [ad. OF. *violeur*; see VIOL [1] and -ER [1].] A player of the viol.

Violet (vəi·ŏlėt), *sb.* ME. [(ult.) dim. of OF. *viole* VIOLA [1].] **1.** A plant or flower of the genus *Viola*, esp. *V. odorata*, the sweet-smelling violet, growing wild, and cultivated in gardens; the flowers are usu. purplish blue, mauve, or white. **b.** *collect.* and *pl.* The plant, or more usu. the flowers, pulled or plucked for use in medicine or in making confections. late ME. **2.** With specific epithets: **a.** Denoting species of *Viola*, or varieties of the common violet 1578. **b.** Applied to plants of other genera, as *bulbous, dog's-tooth, false v.* 1578. **3.** Cloth, dress, or vestments of a violet colour. late ME. **4.** A purplish blue colour resembling that of the violet; a pigment or dye of this colour. late ME.

1. Underfoot the V., Crocus, and Hyacinth with rich inlay Broiderd the ground MILT. *fig. Rich. II*, v. ii. 46. 2. a. *Viola canina syluestris.* Dogs Violets, or wilde Violets. 1597. 3. Where be my gounes of scarlet,..Grenes also, and þe fayre v.? HOCCLEVE.

Comb.: **v.-blind** *a.* colour-blind as regards the violet rays of the spectrum; **-powder,** a violet-scented variety of toilet-powder; **-wood,** (*a*) kingwood; (*b*) the wood of the Australian *Acacia pendula*; (*c*) the wood of *Andira violacea*, a tree of Guiana.

Violet (vəi·ŏlėt), *a.* late ME. [a. OF.; see prec.] **1.** Having the colour of violets; of a blue or bluish-purple colour. **2. a.** In names of varieties of fruits or plants, as *v. clover, maize, plum* 1706. **b.** In names of birds, insects, etc., as *v. bee, cormorant, crab, heron, swallow*; **v.-ear,** one or other species of the genus *Petasophora* of humming-birds; **v.-fly,** an artificial fly used in angling; **v.-tip,** an American butterfly (*Polygonia interrogationis*) 1676.

V. ray, the shortest ray of the visible spectrum, producing v. colour; also = *ultra-violet ray* 1903.

Violet (vəi·ŏlėt), *v.* 1623. [f. VIOLET *sb.* or *a.*] **1.** *trans.* To tinge with a violet hue. **2.** *intr.* To gather violets 1813.

Vi·olet-co:loured, *a.* 1552. [VIOLET *sb.* or *a.*] Of bluish-purple colour.

Violin (vəi,ŏli·n). 1579. [ad. It. *violino*, f. *viola* VIOLA [2].] **1.** A musical instrument having four strings tuned in fifths and played with a bow; a fiddle. **2.** One who plays on the violin; a violinist 1667.

1. Phr. *To play first v.*, freq. fig., to take the leading part.

Violine [1] (vəi·ŏləin). 1831. [a. F., f. *viole* VIOL [1] + -INE [5].] *Chem.* A bitter emetic principle found in the common violet.

Violine [2] (vəi·ŏləin). 1859. [f. L. *viola* VIOLA [1] + -INE [5].] *Chem.* A violet-blue colouring matter or colour.

Violinist (vəi,ŏli·nist). 1670. [ad. It. *violinista*, f. *violino* VIOLIN *sb.*] A player of or performer on the violin.

Violist (vəi·ŏlist). 1670. [f. VIOL *sb.* [1] + -IST.] A player on the viol.

Violon (vəi·ŏlǫn). 1552. [a. F., violin, or (in sense 2) It. *violone* bass-viol.] †**1.** A violin. Also, a violinist. –1606. **2.** A variety of organ-stop 1852.

‖**Violoncello** (vəiŏlǫntʃe·lo, vī,ŏ-). 1724. [It., dim. of *violone*; see VIOLON.] **1.** A large four-stringed instrument of the violin class; a bass violin. Abbreviated 'CELLO. **2.** An organ-stop having a tone similar to that of a violoncello 1876. Hence **Violonce·llist.**

‖**Violone** (vī,ŏlō·ne). 1724. [It., f. *viola* VIOLA [2].] The double-bass viol.

Violuric (vəi,ŏliū·rik), *a.* 1866. [f. VIOL(ET) + URIC *a.*] *Chem.* In *v. acid*, an acid produced by the action of nitric on hydurilic acid. Hence **Violu·rate,** a salt of v. acid.

Viper (vəi·pəɹ). 1526. [a. OE. *vipere, vipre* (mod.F. *vipère*), or ad. L. *vipera* viper, snake, contr. f. *vivi-pera*, f. *vivus* alive, and *parere* to bring forth.] **1.** The small ovo-viviparous snake *Pelias berus* (formerly *Coluber berus* or *Vipera communis*), abundant in Europe and the only venomous snake found in Great Britain; the adder; in general use, any venomous, dangerous, or repulsive snake or serpent. **b.** *Zool.* Applied with distinguishing terms to other species of the genus *Vipera*, the sub-order *Viperina*, or snakes resembling the common viper 1736. **c.** *Zool.* One or other of the snakes belonging to the genus *Vipera*, of which the common viper is the type, or to the family *Viperidæ* 1802. **2.** *fig.* A venomous, malignant, or spiteful person; a villain or scoundrel 1591. **3.** †**a.** In allusion to the supposition that the female viper was killed by her young eating their way out at birth –1608. **b.** In allusion to the fable of the viper reared or revived in a person's bosom 1596.

3. a. *Per.* I. i. 64. b. He is the brother of that wicked v. which I have so long nourished in my bosom FIELDING.

Comb.: **v.-fish,** a deep-sea fish of the family *Chauliodontidæ*, esp. *Chauliodus sloani*; **-grass,** = *viper's grass.* **b.** Special collocations with *viper's*, forming names of plants, as **viper's bugloss,** the plant *Echium vulgare* or a variety of this; **viper's grass,** a plant of the genus *Scorzonera*, esp. *S. hispanica.* Hence **Vi·perish** *a.* viper-like; *fig.* venomous, viperish.

Viperine (vəi·pĕrəin, -in), *a.* and *sb.* 1550. [ad. L. *viperinus*, f. *vipera* VIPER; see -INE [1].] **A.** *adj.* **1.** Resembling a viper or that of a viper; having the nature or character of a viper; venomous, viperous; viper-like. **2.** Of or pertaining to a viper; obtained from or natural to vipers 1608. **3.** *Zool.* Of snakes: Resembling or related to the common viper; now *spec.* belonging to the sub-order *Viperina* (*Solenoglypha*) 1802. **B.** *sb. Zool.* A snake belonging to the *Viperina* 1887.

Viperous (vəi·pĕrəs), *a.* 1535. [f. VIPER + -OUS.] **1.** Of or pertaining to a viper or vipers. **2.** Composed or consisting of vipers 1538. **3.** Of actions, qualities, etc.: Worthy of or befitting a viper; malignant, treacherous, venomous. Now *rare* or *arch.* 1542. **4.** Of the nature of a viper; having the attributes or evil qualities of a viper. Now *rare.* 1591.

1. Censure spreads the v. hiss around 1765. 2. Phr. *V. brood* or *generation.* 3. The v. malice of this Monkish broode 1631. 4. *fig.* The stings of v. remorse WORDSW. Hence **Vi·perously** *adv.* **Vi·perousness** (*rare*).

Viraginian (virădʒi·niăn), *a.* and *sb.* 1642. [f. L. *viragin-, virago* + -IAN.] **A.** *adj.* = next. **B.** *sb.* The language of a virago 1899.

Viraginous (viræ·dʒinəs), *a.* 1666. [f. as prec. + -OUS.] Of the nature of or having the characteristics of a virago.

Virago (virē·go, virā·go). OE. [a. L., a man-like or heroic woman, f. *vir* man.] †**1.** Woman. (Only as the name given by Adam to Eve, after the Vulgate rendering of Gen. ii. 23.) –1576. **2.** A man-like, vigorous, and heroic woman; a female warrior; an amazon. Now *rare.* late ME. †**b.** Applied to a man (*rare*) –1601. **3.** A bold, impudent (or †wicked) woman; a termagant, a scold. late ME.

1. And Adam seide..This schal be clepid v., for she is takun of man WYCLIF *Gen.* ii. 23. 2. To arms! to arms! the fierce v. cries, And swift as lightening to the combate flies POPE. b. *Twel. N.* III. iv. 300. 3. God sets this black brand upon this v. Jezabel 1680.

Virelay (vi·rĕlē). Now *Hist.* or *arch.* late ME. [a. OF. *virelai*, an alteration (prob. after *lai* LAY *sb.* [2]) of *vireli*, prob. a meaningless refrain.] A song or short lyric piece, of a type originating in France, usu. consisting of short lines arranged in stanzas with only two rhymes, the end rhyme of one stanza being the chief one of the next.

He made..manye an ympne for your halydayis That hightyn baladis, roundelys, & vyrelayes CHAUCER.

Virent (vəi·rĕnt), *a.* 1595. [ad. L. *virent-, virens, virere* to be green.] †**1.** Verdant; fresh, not faded –1646. **2.** Green in colour 1830.

Vireo (vi·ri,o). 1834. [a. L. *vireo*, perhaps the greenfinch.] *Ornith.* Any small Amer. bird belonging to the genus *Vireo* or the family *Vireonidæ*; a greenlet, a fly-catcher.

Virescent (vire·sĕnt), *a.* 1826. [ad. L. *virescent-, virescens, virescere* to become green.] Greenish; turning or becoming green. Hence **Vire·scence,** (*a*) *Bot.* regular or abnormal development of a green colour in leaves or flowers; (*b*) greenness.

Virgate (vō·ɹgĕt), *sb. Hist.* 1655. [ad. med.L. *virgata* (sc. *terræ*), f. L. *virga* rod, used as tr. OE. *ȝierdland* YARDLAND.] **1.** An early English land-measure, varying greatly in extent, but in many cases averaging thirty acres. **2.** As a linear measure: A rod or pole 1772.

Virgate (vō·ɹgĕt), *a.* 1821. [ad. L. *virgatus*, f. *virga* rod.] *Bot.* and *Zool.* Rod-like; long, slender, and straight. So **Vi·rgated** *a.* (*rare*) 1752.

†**Virge.** 1540. [var. of VERGE *sb.*, after L. *virga.*] **1.** = VERGE *sb.* III. 1. –1671. **2.** A rod or wand; *esp.* a rod of office –1727.

Vi·rger. 1671. [var. of VERGER [2], after prec.] An official rod-bearer; a verger.

This spelling is still retained in various cathedrals, e.g. St. Paul's and Winchester.

Virgilian (vəɹdʒi·liăn), *a.* and *sb.* 1513. [ad. L. *Virgilianus*, f. *Virgilius*; see -AN.] **A.** *adj.* **1.** Of, pertaining to, or characteristic of the poet Virgil; agreeing with or suggestive of the style of Virgil. **2.** Of agriculture: Practised according to the methods described in the *Georgics* of Virgil. Also of persons following these methods. 1724.

B. *sb.* One who is specially devoted to or skilled in the study of Virgil's works 1577.

Virgin (vō·ɹdʒin), *sb.* and *a.* ME. [a. AF. and OF. *virgine, virgene*, etc., ad. L. *virginem*, acc. of *virgo* maiden.] **I. 1.** *Eccl.* An unmarried or chaste maiden or woman, distinguished for piety or steadfastness in religion, and regarded as having a special place among the members of the Christian church on account of these merits. **2.** A woman (esp. a young woman) who is or remains in a state of inviolate chastity; an absolutely pure maiden or maid. Also *transf.* of things. ME. **b.** *Ent.* A female insect producing fertile eggs by parthenogenesis 1883. **3.** A young woman or maiden of an age and character affording presumption of chastity ME. **4.** *The* (*Blessed*) *V. Mary* (abbrev. B.V.M.), or *the* (*blessed, holy*) *V.*, the mother of Jesus Christ. Also (now *rare*) an image or picture representing her, a madonna ME. **b.** *attrib.* or in possessive, in pop. names of plants 1703. **5.** A youth or man who has remained in a state of chastity ME. **6.** *Astr.* = VIRGO 1480. **7.** *Ent.* Applied to species of moths and butterflies 1832.

1. St. Ursula and her eleven thousand virgins 1862. 2. [Thou] toldst her doubting how these things could be To her a V., that on her should come The Holy Ghost MILT. *transf.* In Africa, the highest mountain is still a v. 1897. 3. She seemed a v. of the Spartan blood DRYDEN. 4. God, that of the vyrgyn was borne

in bedeleym CAXTON. 5. He was reputed a Pure V. 1700.

II. *attrib.* passing into *adj.* 1. Of persons (usu. of the female sex): Being a virgin or virgins; remaining in a state of chastity 1560. b. *The V. Mother*, the Virgin Mary 1711. c. *V. widow*, a widow who has been deprived of her husband before the consummation of the marriage 1644. d. Of a fortress, city, etc.: That has never been taken or subdued 1780. e. *V. generation, procreation*, or *(re)production*, parthenogenesis 1849. 2. Composed or consisting of virgins 1586. 3. Of or pertaining to a virgin; appropriate to or characteristic of virgins 1586. 4. Comparable to a virgin in respect of purity or freedom from stain; unsullied; not yet touched, handled, or employed for any purpose. late ME. 5. Employed for the first time; coming at the beginning or outset 1627.

1. Pardon, goddesse of the night, Those that slew thy v. knight SHAKS. *The V. Queen*, Queen Elizabeth of England. d. Kerak, whose proud boast is that it yet remains a v. city 1873. 2. In this tryumphant song, A v. army did their voices try 1586. 3. Yet ne'er again .. the v. snood did Alice wear SCOTT. Humble v. simplicity 1848. 4. The v. Lillie, and the Primrose trew SPENSER. Salmon..hatched in perfectly v. waters 1867. 5. His v. sword Ægysthus' veins imbru'd POPE. The v. energy of the session 1891.

Collocations: **v. earth, soil**, soil which has not been brought into cultivation, freq. *fig.*; **v. forest**, a forest of natural growth untouched by man.

Comb.: **v.-bower**, = VIRGIN'S BOWER; **-stock**, the Virginian stock; **-tree**, Oriental sassafras. Hence **Vi·rginhood**, virginity.

Virginal (vɜ̄·ɹdʒinăl), *sb.* 1530. [app. f. as next, but the reason for the name is obsc.] A keyed musical instrument (common in England in the 16th and 17th centuries), resembling a spinet, but set in a box or case without legs. a. in plural form, applied to a single instrument. Also *a pair of virginals*. b. as sing., with *pl.* denoting more than one instrument 1566.

Virginal (vɜ̄·ɹdʒinăl), *a.* late ME. [a. OF., or ad. L. *virginalis*, f. *virgin-, virgo*; see VIRGIN *sb.* and -AL.] 1. Of or pertaining to a virgin or to virginity. 2. Of qualities, actions, etc.: Proper to or characteristic of a virgin. late ME. 3. Of persons: Continuing in a state of virginity 1483. 4. *transf.* Fresh, pure, unsullied, untouched 1659.

1. In the vyrgynall wombe of blessed marye 1513. Phr. *V. generation*, parthenogenesis. 2. A..v. and spotless innocence 1850. 3. The vyrgynal companye of thynnocentes CAXTON. 4. Mountain flowers More v. and sweet than ours M. ARNOLD. Hence **Vi·rginally** *adv.*

Virginia (vəɹdʒi·niă). 1609. [f. L. *virgin-, virgo* VIRGIN *sb.* (in honour of Queen Elizabeth) + -IA [1].] 1. The name of that part of North America in which the first English settlement was made in 1607, subsequently one of the original thirteen States of the North American Union, used attrib. in *V. company, tobacco, trade*, etc. 2. *ellipt.* A variety of tobacco grown and manufactured in Virginia 1618. 3. *Astr.* One of the minor planets 1868.

1. **V. creeper**, *Ampelopsis hederacea* and *quinquefolia*, common climbing plants of the family *Vitaceæ*; **V. fence**, a rail fence made in a zig-zag manner; **V. nightingale**, the cardinal grosbeak; **V. reel**, a country-dance; **V. stock** = *Virginian stock* (STOCK *sb.*[1] V. 4 b).

Virginian (vəɹdʒi·niăn), *sb.* and *a.* 1588. [f. prec. + -AN.] A. *sb.* One of the aboriginal natives or inhabitants of Virginia. b. A white settler in Virginia; a native or inhabitant of the modern State of Virginia 1797. B. *adj.* Belonging or relating to the State of Virginia; connected with or interested in Virginia 1609.

V. creeper, = VIRGINIA *creeper*.

Virginity (vəɹdʒi·nĭti). ME. [a. AF. and OF. *virginite* (mod.F. *virginité*), ad. L. *virginitat-, virginitas*, f. *virgin-, virgo* VIRGIN; see -ITY.] 1. The condition of being or remaining in a state of chastity; abstinence from or avoidance of all sexual relations; bodily chastity; the mode of life characterized by this, esp. as adopted from religious motives. 2. The state or condition of a virgin or chaste woman; chastity; maidenhood. Also, a condition affording presumption of chastity; spinsterhood. ME. 3. *fig.* The state of being virgin, fresh, or new 1610.

2. Some pleaded their unspotted V.; others their numerous issue ADDISON.

Virgin's bower. 1597. [VIRGIN *sb.*] The British climbing shrub *Clematis Vitalba*, traveller's joy. b. Applied to other species of *Clematis*, esp. to the Amer. species *C. virginiana*, or employed as a book-name for the whole genus 1668.

†Virgin's milk. 1600. [tr. med.L. *lac virginis.*] A chemical preparation having a milky appearance; a cosmetic preparation or wash for cleansing or purifying the face or skin -1835.

Virgin wax. Also **virgin-wax; †virgin's wax.** ME. [tr. med.L. *cera virginea.* So F. *cire vierge.*] *orig.* Fresh, new, or unused bees-wax; in later and more general use, a purified or fine quality of wax, esp. as used in the making of candles; white wax.

‖**Virgo** (vɜ̄·ɹgo). OE. [L.; see VIRGIN *sb.*] a. The zodiacal constellation lying between Leo and Libra; the Virgin. b. The sixth sign of the zodiac, which the sun enters about Aug. 20–23.

‖**Virgouleuse** (virgulöz). 1698. [F., f. *Virgoulée*, the pop. pronunc. of *Villegoureix*, name of a village in Limousin. Cf. VERGALOO.] In full *V. pear*: A juicy variety of winter pear.

Virgule (vɜ̄·ɹgiŭl). 1837. [a. F., or ad. L. *virgula*, dim. of *virga* twig, rod.] A thin sloping or upright line (/, |) occurring in mediæval MSS. as a mark for the cæsura or as a punctuation-mark (freq. with the same value as the modern comma).

Virial (vi·riăl). 1870. [a. G., f. L. *vir-, vis* force, strength.] *Physics.* In Clausius' kinetic theorem of gases, half the product of the stress due to the attraction or repulsion between a pair of particles multiplied by the distance between them; also, half the sum of such products for all pairs in a system.

Virid (vi·rid), *a. poet.* and *rhet.* 1600. [ad. L. *viridis.*] Green, verdant.

‖**Viridarium** (viridē·riŏm). 1700. [L., pleasure-garden, f. *viridis* VIRID *a.*] *Rom. Antiq.* A pleasure-garden or green court of an ancient Roman villa or palace.

Viride·scent, *a. rare.* 1847. [ad. ppl. stem of late L. *viridescere* to become green, f. *viridis*; see -ESCENT.] Somewhat green or virid. So **Viride·scence** (*rare*), the quality of being v. 1841.

Viridian (viri·diăn), *sb.* and *a.* 1882. [f. L. *viridis* VIRID *a.*] A. *sb.* Veronese green. B. *adj.* Of or pertaining to this colour.

Viridine (vi·ridin). 1837. [f. as prec. + -INE.] 1. *Bot.* = CHLOROPHYLL, CHROMULE. 2. *Dyeing.* A green aniline dye 1875. 3. *Chem.* = JERVINE 1877.

Viridite (vi·ridəit). 1879. [f. as prec. + -ITE [1] 2 b.] *Min.* A mineral compound occurring in certain rocks in the form of minute greenish particles.

Viridity (viri·dĭti). Now *rare.* late ME. [ad. L. *viriditat-, viriditas*, f. *viridis* VIRID *a.*] 1. The quality or state of being virid or green; greenness, verdancy. 2. *fig.* = VERDANCY 2. 1825.

Virile (vi·rəil, vəi·rəil), *a.* 1490. [a. OF. *viril*, or ad. L. *virilis*, f. *vir* man; see -ILE.] 1. Of, belonging to, or characteristic of a man; manly, masculine; marked by strength or force. b. Of dress: Denoting the attainment of man's estate; distinctively belonging to men in contrast to youths (or women) 1603. 2. Of persons: Full of masculine energy or strength; not weak or effeminate; also *spec.* (cf. next 2) 1512.

1. The V. Age..*viz.* from thirty to forty-five Years 1728. *V. member* [L. *membrum virile*], the male organ of generation. b. The assumption of the v. jacket and pantaloons THACKERAY.

Virility (viri·lĭti). 1586. [ad. F. *virilité* or L. *virilitas*, f. *virilis* VIRILE *a.*; see -ITY.] 1. The period of life during which a person of the male sex is in full vigour; fully developed manhood or masculine force. b. Masculine vigour; masculinity of sex 1890. 2. Capacity for sexual intercourse 1721. 3. Manly strength and vigour of action or thought; energy or force of a virile character 1597.

1. b. Literary men of more sensitiveness than v. 1898.

Virose (vəiə·rōus), *a.* Now *rare.* 1680. [ad. L. *virosus*, f. *virus* VIRUS.] Poisonous; suggestive of poisonous qualities; rank and unwholesome. So **Vi·rous** *a.* (*rare*).

‖**Virtu, vertu** (vɜ̄ɹtū·, vēɹtū). Also **vertù, virtù.** 1722. [a. It. *virtù*:—L. *virtutem, virtus* VIRTUE; the form *vertu* follows French spelling without justification.] 1. A love of or taste for works of art or curios; a knowledge of or interest in the fine arts; the fine arts as a subject of study or interest. 2. *collect.* Objects of art; curios 1746.

1. Phr. *Man* (or *gentleman*) *of v.*, a virtuoso. *Article, object, piece*, etc., *of v.*, an article such as virtuosos are interested in; a curio, antique, etc. 3. My books, my *v.*, and my other follies and amusements H. WALPOLE.

Virtual (vɜ̄·ɹtiuăl), *a.* late ME. [ad. med. L. *virtualis*, f. L. *virtus* virtue, after L. *virtuosus.*] 1. Possessed of certain physical virtues or capacities; effective in respect of inherent natural qualities or powers; capable of exerting influence by means of such qualities. Now *rare.* b. Of herbs: Possessing specific virtues (*rare*) 1660. †2. Capable of producing a certain effect or result; effective, potent, powerful -1683. 3. That is so in essence or effect although not formally or actually; admitting of being called by the name so far as the effect or result is concerned 1654. b. *Optics.* Applied to the apparent focus or image resulting from the effect of reflection or refraction upon rays of light 1704. c. *Dynamics.* Of velocity or momentum (see quot.); (usu. =) possible and infinitesimal 1818.

1. See if the Virtuall Heat of the Wine, or Strong Waters will not mature it BACON. 3. One part of it could not be yielded..without a v. surrender of all the rest BURKE. The simplest conscious action involves actual or v. thought 1883. b. The image of an object under water is *v.* 1859. c. If the point of application of a force be displaced through a small space, the resolved part of the displacement in the direction of the force has been called its V. Velocity. ..The product of the force, into the v. velocity of its point of application, has been called the V. Moment of the force THOMSON & TAIT. So *v. displacement, eccentric, work.*

Virtuality (vɜ̄ɹtiuæ·lĭti). 1483. [f. VIRTUAL *a.* + -ITY.] †1. The possession of force or power. CAXTON. 2. Essential nature or being, apart from external form or embodiment 1646. 3. A virtual (as opp. to an actual) thing, capacity, etc.; a potentiality 1836.

2. In one graine of corne..there lyeth dormant the v. of many other, and from thence sometimes proceed an hundred eares SIR T. BROWNE.

Virtually (vɜ̄·ɹtiuăli), *adv.* late ME. [f. VIRTUAL *a.* + -LY [2].] 1. As far as essential qualities or facts are concerned. b. In effect; practically; to all intents; as good as 1600. 2. Virtuously, morally (*rare*) 1539.

Virtue (vɜ̄·ɹtiu). ME. [a. AF., OF. (mod. F.) *vertu*, ad. L. *virtut-, virtus* manliness, valour, f. *vir* man.] I. As a quality of persons. 1. The power or operative influence inherent in a supernatural or divine being. Now *arch.* or *Obs.* b. An embodiment of such power; esp. *pl.*, one of the orders of the celestial hierarchy ME. †c. An act of superhuman or divine power; a 'mighty work'; a miracle -1526. 2. Conformity of life and conduct with the principles of morality; voluntary observance of the recognized moral laws or standards of right conduct ME. b. *spec.* Chastity, sexual purity, esp. in women. *Of easy v.*: see EASY *a.* II. 1599. 3. With *a* and *pl.* A particular moral excellence; a special manifestation of the influence of moral principles in life or conduct ME. 4. Superiority or excellence; unusual ability, merit, or distinction. late ME. b. An accomplishment. Now *rare* or *Obs.* 1550. †5. Physical strength, force, or energy -1500. 6. The possession or display of manly qualities; manly excellence, manliness, valour ME.

1. In his owne vertue he rose agayne *N.T.* (Geneva) Epist. *iiii. b. Dominations first; next them, Virtues; and powers the third CARY. 2. Lessons of honour, courage,..humanity, and in one word, v. in its true signification CHATHAM. 3. Neither faith, hope, nor charity enters into the virtues of a savage 1865. *Cardinal virtues*: see CARDINAL *a.* 1. *Theological virtues*: see THEOLOGICAL *a.* 1. 4. That un-

sparing impartiality which is his most distinguishing v. MACAULAY.

Phr. *To make (a) v. of necessity* [after F. *faire de nécessité vertu*, L. *facere de necessitate virtutem* (Jerome)], to do as if performing a meritorious action what one in reality cannot help doing; to submit to circumstances with a good grace. *To make a v. of*, to make a merit of, to gain credit by.

II. As a quality of things. **1.** In the prep. phrases *in* or *by* (also †*through* or *with*) *v. of*, by the power or efficacy of; hence, in later use, by the authority of, in reliance upon, in consequence of, because of ME. **2.** †**a.** Of precious stones: Occult efficacy or power; in later use, great worth or value –1509. **b.** Of plants, waters, etc.: Efficacy arising from physical qualities; strengthening, sustaining, or healing properties ME. **c.** Efficacy of a moral nature; influence working for good upon human life or conduct ME. **d.** Worth or efficacy of any kind. late ME. **3.** With *a* and *pl.* A particular power, efficacy, or good quality inherent in or pertaining to something. late ME.

1. The planets..rise and set by v. of the Earth's rotation 1868. He remained a senator in v. of his quæstorship FROUDE. 2. b. All Simples that haue Vertue Vnder the Moone SHAKS. d. There is v. in a bushel of coals properly consumed, to raise seventy millions of pounds weight a foot high 1830. 3. I declare also the vertues of euery herbe 1551. If the Loadstone be of such a vertue, let it show it by attracting the Iron to it 1628. Hence **Vi·rtued** *a.* (*rare*) endued with v. or efficacy.

Vi·rtueless, *a.* late ME. [-LESS.] **1.** Destitute of efficacy or excellence; ineffective, worthless. **2.** Destitute of moral goodness; immoral, vicious. late ME.

1. Wo worth þe faire gemme vertules CHAUCER.

‖**Virtuosa** (vəɹtiu̯ō^u·sä). Now *rare*. 1668. [It., fem. of VIRTUOSO.] A female virtuoso.

Virtuosity (vǝɹtiu̯ǫ·sĭti). 1673. [f. next + -ITY.] **1.** The pursuits, interests, or temperament characteristic of a virtuoso; interest or taste in the fine arts, esp. of a dilettante or trifling nature. **b.** *spec.* Excessive attention to technique or to the production of special effects in vocal or instrumental music (also *transf.* in art or literature) 1865. **2.** Virtuosi collectively 1831.

1. Charles-Augustus had imbibed..a taste for merit, a v. in human excellence, to employ his preceptor's phrase 1823.

‖**Virtuoso** (vǝɹtiu̯ō^u·so). *Pl.* **virtuosi, virtuosos.** 1651. [It., learned, skilful:—L. *virtuosus* VIRTUOUS *a.*] †**1.** One who has a general interest in arts and sciences, or who pursues special investigations in one or more of these; a learned person; a scientist, savant, or scholar –1778. **2.** One who has a special interest in, or taste for, the fine arts; a student or collector of antiquities, natural curiosities or rarities, etc.; a connoisseur; freq., one who carries on such pursuits in a dilettante or trifling manner 1662. **3.** One who has special knowledge or skill in music; *spec.*, in mod. use, one who devotes special attention to technique in playing or singing 1743.

1. Another excellent V. of the same Assembly, Mr. John Evelyn, hath very considerably advanced the History of Fruit and Forest-Trees 1676. 3. All these *virtuosi*..were either *contraltos* of the softest note, or *sopranos* of the highest squeakery 1834. Hence **Virtuo·soship.**

Virtuous (vǝ·ɹtiu̯ǝs), *a.* ME. [a. AF. and OF. *vertuous*, OF. *vertuos, vertueux*, ad. late L. *virtuosus*, f. L. *virtus* VIRTUE *sb.*; see -OUS.] **I.** Of persons, personal qualities or actions, etc. †**1.** Distinguished by manly qualities; valiant, valorous –1611. †**b.** Of an act: Evincing a manly spirit; brave, heroic, courageous (*rare*) –1653. **2.** Possessing or showing virtue in life and conduct; acting with moral rectitude or in conformity with moral laws; good, just, righteous ME. **b.** Of women. Freq. = CHASTE *a.* late ME. †**c.** Used as a title of courtesy in addressing or referring to persons, esp. ladies of rank or eminence –1700. **d.** *absol.* (as *pl.*), chiefly with *the*. late ME. **3.** Of acts, life, manners, etc.: Characterized by or of the nature of virtue; morally good or justifiable. late ME.

1. But young Deiphobus, Old Priam's son, amongst them all was chiefly v. CHAPMAN. 2. A man may be counted a vertuous man, though hee haue made many slips in his life 1611. b. A vertuous woman is a crowne to her husband *Prov.* xii. 4. c. I saw the tragedy of 'Horace' (written by the v. Mrs. Phillips) EVELYN. d. The esteem of the noble and v. 1846. 3. Can any act be truly v., if done in pride? 1836.

II. Of things, their operations, etc. **1.** Producing or capable of producing (great) effect; powerful, potent, strong ME. **2.** Endowed with or possessed of inherent or natural virtue or power (often of a magical, occult, or supernatural kind); potent in effect, influence, or operation on this account; *spec.* having potent medicinal qualities; efficacious in healing. late ME.

1. With one vertuous touch Th' Arch-chimick Sun, so farr from us remote..Produces..so many precious things MILT. 2. Canace.., That own'd the vertuous Ring and Glass MILT. These our mountaines are full of vertuous herbes 1632. Hence **Vi·rtuous-ly** *adv.*, **-ness.**

Virulence (vi·ri̯ŭlĕns). 1663. [ad. L. *virulentia*; see next and -ENCE.] **1.** Extreme acrimony of temper or speech; violent malignity or rancour. **2.** The property or quality of being physically virulent or full of virus; malignity or violence (of disease) 1748.

1. Our v. is thrown On others' fame, thro' fondness for our own YOUNG. 2. The v. of distemper 1815. So **Vi·rulency** 1617.

Virulent (vi·ri̯ŭlĕnt), *a.* late ME. [ad. L. *virulentus* poisonous, f. *virus* VIRUS.] **1.** *Med.* †**a.** Of wounds or ulcers: Characterized by the presence of corrupt or poisonous matter –1728. **b.** Of diseases, etc.: Extremely malignant or violent 1563. **2.** Of serpents, material substances, plants, etc.: Possessing venomous or strongly poisonous qualities; extremely noxious 1577. **3.** *fig.* Violently bitter, spiteful, or malignant; full of acrimony or enmity 1607.

1. b. Scurvy in its most v. form 1866. 2. Herbs or mineralls, with V., and Deleterious Qualities 1671. 3. The v. Pen of that Rascal the Examiner STEELE. His enemies here are as v. as ever 1792. She was hated by Whig beauties with v. wrath 1867. Hence **Vi·rulent-ly** *adv.*, **-ness** (*rare*).

‖**Virus** (vəi^ə·rǝ̆s). 1599. [L., slimy liquid, poison, offensive odour or taste.] **1.** Venom, such as is emitted by a poisonous animal. **2.** *Path.* A morbid principle or poisonous substance produced in the body as the result of some disease, esp. one capable of being introduced into other persons or animals by inoculation or otherwise and of developing the same disease in them 1728. **3.** *fig.* A moral or intellectual poison or poisonous influence 1778.

1. Cleopatra..pouring the V. of an Asp into a Wound ..in her Arm 1702. 2. The pustules..contain a perfect Small-pox v. 1800. 3. Venice is a stink-pot, charged with the very v. of hell! 1778.

‖**Vis** (vis). *Pl.* **vires** (vəi^ə·rīz). 1601. [L.] Strength, force, energy, vigour.

V. a fronte, a force operating from in front (as in attraction or suction); **v. a tergo,** a force operating from behind, a propulsive force; **v. inertiæ,** the resistance naturally offered by matter to any force tending to alter its state in respect of rest or motion; also *transf.* tendency on the part of persons, etc., to remain inactive or unprogressive; **v. major,** such a degree of superior force that no effective resistance can be made to it; **v. vitæ,** vital force; **v. viva,** the operative force of a moving or acting body, reckoned as equal to the mass of the body multiplied by the square of its velocity.

‖**Visa** (vī·ză), *sb.* 1831. [F., a. L. *visa* (sc. *carta*), fem. pa. pple. of *videre* to see.] = VISÉ *sb.* Hence **Vi·sa** *v. trans.* to visé.

Visage (vi·zėdʒ), *sb.* ME. [a. AF. and OF. (also mod.F.), f. L. *visus* face; see -AGE.] **1.** The face, the front part of the head, of a person (rarely of an animal). **2.** The face with reference to the form or proportions of the features ME. **3.** The face or features as expressive of feeling or temperament; the countenance ME. **4.** *transf.* The face or visible side of the sun or moon. late ME. **5.** An appearance or aspect. late ME. †**6.** An assumed appearance; an outward show; a pretence or semblance –1684.

1. There are no wrinkles in his v. 1797. 2. I neuer sawe..soo fayre a creture in ye v. 1533. 3. A plodding invalid..with..dreary v. 1860. 4. And thou fair Moon ..Stoop thy pale v. through an amber cloud, And disinherit Chaos MILT. Hence †**Vi·sage** *v. trans.* to confront; to regard, observe –1531. **Vi·saged** *a.* having a v. of a specified kind.

‖**Vis-à-vis** (vīz-, vizävī), *sb.*, *prep.*, and *adv.* 1753. [F., face to face; f. *vis*:—L. *visum*, *visus* sight, face.] **A.** *sb.* **1.** A light carriage for two persons sitting face-to-face. *Obs.* exc. *Hist.* **2.** One or other of two persons or things facing or situated opposite to each other 1757. **3.** A meeting face to face; an encounter 1867.

2. Partners were scrambling for v. and places 1877.

B. *prep.* Over against, in comparison with, in relation to; also *lit.*, face to face with 1755.

He is responsible v. the Government for their efficiency 1907.

C. *adv.* Opposite, so as to face (another or each other) 1807. Hence **Vis-à-vis** *v. trans.*

Viscacha (viska·tʃă). Also **vizcacha.** 1604. [a. Sp. (also *biscacha* BISCACHA), ad. Quichuan (*h*)*uiscacha.*] One or other of two large burrowing rodents of S. America, related to the chinchilla. **a.** The *Lagidium cuvierii*, inhabiting the upper Andes from Chili to Ecuador; the Alpine viscacha. **b.** The *Lagostomus trichodactylus* of the southern Argentine pampas 1836.

‖**Viscera** (vi·sĕră), *sb. pl.* 1651. [L., internal organs, pl. of *viscus* VISCUS.] **1.** *Anat.* The soft contents of the principal cavities of the body; *esp.* the internal organs of the trunk; the entrails or bowels together with the heart, liver, lungs, etc. **2.** *transf.* The interior; the inner parts 1709.

Visceral (vi·sĕrăl), *a.* 1575. [ad. med.L. *visceralis*, f. *viscera*; see prec.] †**1.** Affecting the viscera or bowels regarded as the seat of emotion; pertaining to or touching deeply inward feelings –1640. **2.** *Phys.* Of disorders or diseases: Affecting the viscera or internal organs 1794. **3.** *Anat.* Of, pertaining to, consisting of, or situated in or among the viscera 1826. **4.** Pertaining to the viscera of animals used as a means of divination 1833. **5.** *Anat.* **a.** *V. layer*, a portion of the arachnoid membrane 1840. **b.** *V. arch*, one of a set of parallel ridges in the region of the mouth in the embryonic skull. *V. cleft*, one of the intervals between the visceral arches. 1870.

3. *V. cavity*, that part of an animal body in which the viscera are contained.

Vi·scerate, *v. rare.* 1727. [f. VISCERA + -ATE[3], after *eviscerate.*] *trans.* To eviscerate, disembowel.

Viscero- (vi·sĕro), used as comb. form (see -O-) of L. *viscera* VISCERA, as in *v.-branchial*, *-pericardial.*

Viscid (vi·sid), *a.* 1635. [ad. late L. *viscidus*, f. L. *viscum* birdlime.] **1.** Of fluid or soft substances: Having a glutinous or gluey character; sticky, adhesive, ropy. **2.** Of surfaces: Covered with a glutinous or sticky secretion. Chiefly *Bot.* of leaves. 1760.

Viscidity (visi·dĭti). 1611. [f. prec. + -ITY.] **1.** The quality of being viscid; glutinousness, stickiness, ropiness. **2.** Viscid matter or substance 1720.

Viscin (vi·sin). 1838. [a. F., f. L. *viscum* birdlime; see -IN.] *Chem.* A substance which forms the main constituent of birdlime, chiefly obtained from the berries and other parts of the misletoe.

Viscose (vi·skō^us). 1896. [ad. L. *viscosus* VISCOUS.] Cellulose reduced to a viscous solution, largely used in the manufacture of artificial silk. Also *attrib.*, as *v. silk.*

Viscosimeter (viskǫsi·mĭtǝɹ). 1868. [f. L. *viscosus* VISCOUS *a.*; see -METER.] An instrument for measuring the viscosity of liquids.

Viscosity (viskǫ·sĭti). late ME. [a. OF. *viscosite* (F. *viscosité*) or ad. med.L. *viscositas*, f. L. *viscosus* viscous; see -ITY.] **1.** The quality or fact of being viscous; viscidity. **2.** A viscous substance; a collection of viscous matter 1545.

1. *Magnetic v.*, tendency on the part of a magnetic medium to retard the magnetizing force.

Viscount (vəi·kaunt). late ME. [a. AF. *ves-, viscounte*, OF. *visconte, viconte* (F. *vicomte*), f. *vis-* VICE- + *counte* COUNT *sb.*[2], after med.L. *vicecomes.*] **1.** *Hist.* One acting as the deputy or representative of a count or earl in the administration of a district; in Eng. use *spec.* a sheriff or high sheriff. **2.** A member of the fourth order of the British peerage, ranking between an earl and a baron. Abbreviated *Visc., Visct.* 1450. Hence **Vi·scountcy,** the title, dignity, or rank of a viscount. **Vi·scountship,** the dignity of a v.; a viscountcy.

Viscountess (vəi·kauntès). 1475. [See prec. and -ESS.] The wife of a viscount; a peeress of the fourth order of nobility.

Viscounty (vəi·kaunti). 1611. [f. VISCOUNT + -Y [3].] 1. *Hist.* The office or jurisdiction of or the territory under the authority of a viscount 1611. 2. = VISCOUNTCY 1859.

Viscous (vi·skəs), *a.* late ME. [a. AF. *viscous*, or ad. L. *viscosus*, f. *viscum* (also *viscus*) misletoe, birdlime.] 1. Of substances: Having a glutinous or gluey character. b. *Physics.* Imperfectly fluid; adhesively soft 1830. 2. *fig.* Adhesive, sticky 1605. 3. *Bot.* Of leaves: = VISCID *a.* 2. 1712. Hence **Vi·scous-ly** *adv.*, -ness (now *rare*). So †**Vi·scuous** *a.*

‖**Viscus** (vi·skɒ̆s). 1728. [L., usu. in pl. *viscera* VISCERA.] *Anat.* One or other of the soft internal organs of the body.

Vise, var. (now usu. *U.S.*) of VICE *sb.*[2]

‖**Visé** (vī·zeⁱ), *sb.* 1858. [F., pa. pple. of *viser* to examine, view.] An entry or note on a passport, certificate, or other official document signifying that it has been examined and found correct; a formal official signature or entry of this nature. Hence ‖**Visé** *v. trans.* to put a v. on (a passport or other document); to endorse or sign as correct and in due order.

Vishnu (vi·ʃnu). 1638. [Skr. *Vishṇu*, prob. from the root *vish*, and meaning 'all-pervader' or 'worker'.] One of the principal Hindu deities, holding the second place in the great triad, but by his worshippers identified with the supreme deity and regarded as the preserver of the world. Hence **Vi·shnuism**, the worship of V. **Vi·shnuite**, a worshipper of V.

Visibility (vizĭbi·lĭti). 1581. [ad. late L. *visibilitat-*, *visibilitas*, f. L. *visibilis*; see next and -ITY.] 1. The condition, state, or fact of being visible; capacity of being seen (in general, or under special conditions). b. *spec.* The possibility of (a vessel, etc.) being seen under the conditions of distance, light, atmosphere, etc., existing at a particular time; hence conversely, the possibility of seeing, or the range of vision, under such conditions 1914. 2. With *a* and *pl.* A visible thing or object 1628. †3. Sight, vision (*rare*) -1733.

1. b. The v. early on 1st June (three to four miles) was less than on 31st May SIR J. JELLICOE.

Visible (vi·zĭb'l), *a.* and *sb.* ME. [a. OF., or ad. L. *visibilis*, f. *vis-*, ppl. stem of *videre* to see.] A. *adj.* 1. Capable of being seen; perceptible by the sense of sight. 2. That may be mentally perceived or observed; clearly or readily evident; manifest, obvious 1613. 3. That can be seen under certain conditions, at a certain time, or by a particular person; in sight; open or exposed to sight or view 1667. b. *Comm.* Of stocks or supply: Actually in hand or to be seen 1882. 4. Of persons: Capable of being seen or visited; accessible to others; now *esp.*, 'at home' to visitors 1722. 5. *V. direction*, in *Optics*, the apparent direction in which an object is seen 1829.

1. He was neuer visyble to the mortall eye COVERDALE. It pleased God to unite Christians in communities or visible churches BUTLER. The conversion of v. energy into heat 1878. *V. speech*, a system of phonetic notation devised by A. M. Bell, consisting of characters or symbols intended to represent the actual position of the vocal organs in the production of speech-sounds. 2. Pneumonia..may..arise without any v. cause 1908. 3. On this Mount he appeerd, under this Tree Stood v. MILT. *V. horizon*: see HORIZON *sb.* 1. b. Statistics relating to the v. supply of grain 1882.

B. *sb.* 1. A visible thing or entity. Chiefly in pl. 1614. 2. *The v.*, that which is visible, esp. the visible world 1742. Hence **Vi·sibleness**. **Vi·sibly** *adv.*

Visigoth (vi·zigɒþ). 1647. [ad. late L. *Visigothus*, usu. in pl. *Visigothi*; perh. meaning 'West Goths', as opp. to *Ostrogothi* (OSTROGOTH).] 1. A member of that branch of the Gothic race which entered Roman territory towards the end of the fourth century and subsequently established a kingdom in Spain, overthrown by the Moors in 711–12; a West-Goth. Chiefly in *pl.* 2. *transf.* An uncivilized or barbarous person 1749. Hence **Visigo·thic** *a.*

Visile (vi·zəil), *a.* and *sb.* 1909. [f. L. *vis-*, ppl. stem. of *videre* to see + -ILE.] (One who is) characterized by strong visual perception.

Vision (vi·ʒən), *sb.* ME. [a. AF. *visiun*, *visioun*, OF. *vision*, or ad. L. *vision-*, *visio* seeing, thing seen, f. *vis-*, ppl. stem of *videre* to see.] 1. Something which is apparently seen otherwise than by ordinary sight; *esp.* an appearance of a prophetic or mystical character, or having the nature of a revelation, supernaturally presented to the mind in sleep or in an abnormal state. b. A mental concept of a distinct or vivid kind; a highly imaginative scheme or anticipation 1592. c. A person seen in a dream or trance 1611. d. *transf.* A person, scene, etc. of unusual beauty 1823. 2. The action or fact of seeing or contemplating something not actually present to the eye; mystical or supernatural insight or foresight. late ME. 3. The action of seeing with the bodily eye, the exercise of the ordinary faculty of sight, or the faculty itself 1491. b. An instance of seeing; a look 1855. 4. A thing actually seen; an object of sight. SHAKS.

1. Visions of glory, spare my aching sight GRAY. The art renown'd, V. and omen to expound SCOTT. b. The visions of romantic youth CAMPBELL. c. The v. bright, As with a smile more brightn'd, thus repli'd MILT. 2. Ministers..neither have v. to foretell, nor power to confer, blessing 1657. 3. Even the v. of natural objects presents to us insurmountable difficulties 1832.

Vision (vi·ʒən), *v.* 1594. [f. prec.] 1. *trans.* To show as in a vision; to display to the eye or mind. 2. To see as in a vision; to bring before the eye of the mind 1795.

2. We in the morning eyed the pleasant fields Vision'd before SOUTHEY.

Visional (vi·ʒənăl), *a.* 1588. [f. VISION *sb.* + -AL.] 1. Connected with, relating to, based upon, a vision or visions. 2. Of the nature of a vision; seen or occurring in a vision; visionary, unreal 1647. Hence **Vi·sionally** *adv.* as or in a vision.

Visionary (vi·ʒənări), *a.* and *sb.* 1648. [f. VISION *sb.* + -ARY.] A. *adj.* 1. Able or accustomed to see visions; capable of receiving impressions by means of visions 1651. b. Given to fanciful and unpractical views; speculative, dreamy 1727. 2. Of the nature of a vision; presented or apprehended in a vision 1648. b. Seen only in a vision; unreal, spectral 1697. c. Connected with or pertaining to visions 1727. 3. Existing in imagination only; not actual or real 1725. b. Of schemes, plans, etc.: Incapable of being carried out or realized; fantastic, unpractical 1727. c. Characterized by fantasy or imagination without corresponding reality 1777.

1. What spells entrance my v. mind 1792. b. Knox was no v. enthusiast 1902. 2. The v. emblem seen By him of Babylon COWPER. b. The v. fabric melted into air GIBBON. c. The v. hour, When musing midnight reigns THOMSON. 3. Vanish'd are all the v. joys POPE. b. Vain, idle, v. thoughts SWIFT. c. To withdraw from active life into a v. world 1840.

B. *sb.* 1. One who has visions; one to whom unknown or future things are revealed in visions 1706. 2. One who indulges in fantastic ideas or schemes; an unpractical enthusiast 1702.

1. Of such honourable repute was the name Seer, or v., in those times 1778. Hence **Vi·sionarily** *adv.* **Vi·sionariness.**

Visioned (vi·ʒənd), *ppl. a.* 1510. [f. VISION *sb.* or *v.*] 1. Seen in a vision. 2. Associated with or arising from a vision or visions 1817. 3. Having the power of seeing visions 1813. 4. Full of visions 1815.

3. The v. poet in his dreams SHELLEY.

Visionist (vi·ʒənist). 1665. [f. VISION *sb.*] One who has or professes to have visions; a professed visionary.

Visionless (vi·ʒənlès), *a.* 1820. [f. VISION *sb.* + -LESS.] 1. Destitute of vision; sightless, blind. 2. Devoid of higher insight or inspiration 1856.

Visit (vi·zit), *sb.* 1621. [ad. F. *visite*, or f. next.] 1. An act of visiting a person; a friendly or formal call upon a person or a shorter or longer stay with him, as a feature of social intercourse. b. An excursion *to* a place for the purpose of sight-seeing; a short or temporary stay at a place. Also *transf.* of animals or birds. 1800. c. An occasion of going *to* a doctor, dentist, etc., for examination or treatment 1884. 2. a. A call made by a minister of religion as part of his pastoral duties 1724. b. A professional call made by a doctor on a patient 1719. 3. An instance (or the action) of going to a place, house, etc., for the purpose of inspection or examination 1787.

1. Phr. *To make, pay a v., to return a v.* b. A v. to Lyme 1839. 3. The right of v. and search. A belligerent has the right..to visit and search every merchant ship at sea in time of war. 1897.

Visit (vi·zit), *v.* ME. [a. OF. (F.) *visiter* or ad. L. *visitare* to go to see, frequentative of *visare*, f. *vis-*, ppl. stem. of *videre* to see.] I. 1. *trans.* Of the Deity: To come to (a person) in order to comfort or benefit him. †2. To come to (a person) in order to observe or examine his conduct or disposition; to make trial of; to subject to test or scrutiny -1667. 3. To inflict hurt, harm, or punishment upon; to deal severely or hardly with (persons or things); †to cut off, cause to die. late ME. b. To afflict or distress *with* sickness, poverty, or the like. late ME. 4. Of sickness, etc.: To come upon, assail, afflict ME. 5. To punish or requite (wrongdoing) ME. b. To avenge, or inflict punishment for (wrongdoing) *on* or *upon* a person. late ME. 6. *absol.* To take vengeance or inflict punishment. late ME.

1. For He..Shall v. earth in Mercy COWPER. 3. Therfore will I vyset you in all youre wickednesses COVERDALE *Amos* iii. 2. b. It pleased God to visite me with a quartan 1624. 5. Mild offences were visited with the loss of eyes or ears 1879. b. The Lorde.. vysiteth the myszdede of the fathers vpon the children COVERDALE *Numb.* xiv. 18.

II. 1. To go to see (a person in sickness or distress) in order to comfort or assist him, out of charity or devotion or in the fulfilment of pastoral duty ME. 2. To go to see (a person) in a friendly or sociable manner; also, to stay with for a short time as a guest ME. b. Of a medical man: To attend (a patient) professionally 1585. c. *transf.* To go to (a person, etc.) with hostile intentions 1533. d. *absol.* To make a call or calls; to pay calls; to maintain friendly or social intercourse by this means; also, to spend a short time with one as a guest; to pay visits of this kind; *spec.* to make pastoral visits 1626. 3. To go to look at (†or explore); to inspect or examine; to look into or see to (something); in later use *esp.* to examine (vessels, goods, baggage, etc.) officially ME. b. *spec.* To go to (an institution) for the purpose of seeing that everything is in due order; to exercise a periodical surveillance or supervision over, or make a special investigation into (management or conduct) ME. 4. To go to (a temple, shrine, etc.) for the purpose of worship or as a religious duty ME. b. To go to (a place) for the purpose of sight-seeing or on some special errand. late ME. c. Of birds, etc.: To resort to or frequent (land or sea, a country, etc.) for a limited period or at certain seasons 1774.

1. Ye must v. the Sick and these who are in Distress 1687. Sent for..to v. a sick parishioner 1808. 2. He comes here visiting his relation DICKENS. c. *Cor.* IV. v. 148. d. A spinster..who spends her life visiting from place to place 1894. 3. Go se and vysyte our wethers in the cote 1514. b. A faculty empowering Wolsey to v. those English monasteries 1868. 4. He had visited the Holy Land SCOTT. *transf.* Dear, as the light that visits these sad eyes GRAY. Hence **Vi·sitable** *a.* liable to visitation; capable of being visited; such as admits of receiving visitors.

Visitant (vi·zitănt), *sb.* and *a.* 1599. [a. F., or ad. L. *visitant-*, *visitans*, *visitare* to VISIT.] A. *sb.* 1. One who pays a visit; a visitor. b. Applied to supernatural beings or agencies, etc., esp. as revealing themselves to mortals 1667. 2. One who visits some place or object of interest 1677. b. A stranger who spends a short time in a place; a temporary resident 1751. 3. A thing which comes to one in a casual or temporary manner 1742. 4. A migratory bird, etc., as temporarily frequenting a particular locality 1770.

1. b. Adam..to Eve, While the great V. approachd, thus spake MILT. 4. The Hooded Crow..being..in some localities a winter visitant only, in others a resident 1894.

B. *adj.* Paying a visit or visits; having the position or character of a visitor 1653.

Visitation (vizitēⁱ·ʃən). ME. [a. AF. *visitacioun* (F. *-ation*), or ad. L. *visitatio*, f. *visitare* to visit. Now rare in I. 2, 3, 4.] I. 1.

The action, on the part of one in authority, or of a duly qualified or authorized person, of going to a particular place in order to make an inspection and satisfy himself that everything is in order; an instance of such inspection or supervision. **b.** *esp.* A visit by an ecclesiastical person (or body) to examine into the state of a diocese, parish, religious institution, etc.; *spec.* in English use, such a visit paid by a bishop or archdeacon; a meeting of persons concerned in such a visit ME. **c.** A periodic visit made to a district by heralds to examine and enrol arms and pedigrees. Now *Hist.* 1572. **d.** Examination of goods by a customs officer or similar official; the action on the part of a belligerent vessel of ascertaining, by entry or close examination, the character of a merchant ship belonging to a neutral state 1755. **2.** The action of going to a place, either for some special purpose or merely in order to see it; an instance of this. late ME. **3.** The action or practice of visiting sick or distressed persons as a work of charity or pastoral duty. late ME. **4.** The action of making a friendly or formal call or calls; social intercourse of this nature; visiting 1586. **b.** An instance of this; a visit 1581.

1. d. The law of nations gives to every belligerent cruiser the right of v. and search of all merchant ships 1867. 3. The Church of England..retains private confession in the rubric for v. of the sick 1862. *The V.* (*of our Lady, of the Blessed Virgin Mary*), the visit paid by the Virgin Mary to Elizabeth, recorded in Luke i. 39 ff. and commemorated by the Church on July 2; hence *ellipt.*, the day on which this is commemorated, the feast so observed; also, a picture representing the event. *The* (*order of the*) *V.*, the Order founded in 1610 by Mme de Chantal (St. Frances) under the direction of St. Francis of Sales.

II. 1. The action, on the part of God or some supernatural power, of coming to, or exercising power over, a person or people for some end ME. **2.** A heavy affliction, blow, or trial, regarded as an instance of divine dispensation; retributive punishment operating by this means 1450. **3.** The fact of some violent or destructive agency or force coming or falling upon a people country, etc. 1535. **4.** The fact of some immaterial power or influence acting or operating on the mind 1791.

1. Mercies are visitations; when God comes in kindness and love to do us good, he visiteth us 1643. A verdict of 'died by the v. of God' was recorded 1820. 2. War is here regarded..as a punitive v., as a form of retribution for our sins 1885. 3. The period..was marked by the visitations of pestilence, as well as those of war 1838. 4. Or was he moved by some v. of compunction? 1873.

Visitatorial (vizitătō°·riăl), *a.* 1688. [f. L. *visitat-*, *visitare*; see -ORIAL.] **1.** Pertaining to, connected with, involving or implying, official visitation. **2.** Having the power of visitation; exercising authority of this kind 1880.

1. Deriving the v. power from the property of the donor 1834. 2. Leave of absence granted by v. boards 1881.

Visite (vizī·t). 1852. [F., visit.] A light cape or short sleeveless cloak worn by women in the 19th c.

Visiter (vi·zitəɹ). Now *rare.* late ME. [f. VISIT *v.* + -ER.] = VISITOR.

Visiting (vi·ziting), *vbl. sb.* ME. [f. VISIT *v.*] The action of coming or going to a person or place for some special purpose.

attrib.: **v.-book**, a book containing the names of persons to be visited; **-card**, a small card bearing a person's name (and address), to be presented or left on paying a visit; **-list**, a list of persons to be visited.

Visiting (vi·ziting), *ppl. a.* 1606. [f. VISIT *v.*] **1.** That visits; that pays visits or is engaged in visiting. **2.** That visits officially for the purpose of inspection or examination 1713.

1. *V. ant*, the driver ant.

Visitor (vi·zitəɹ). late ME. [a. AF. *visitour*, OF. *visiteor*, *visiteur* (F. *visiteur*), f. *visiter* to visit.] **1.** One who visits officially for the purpose of inspection or supervision, in order to prevent or remove abuses or irregularities. **2.** One who visits from charitable motives or with a view of doing good. late ME. **3.** One who pays a visit to another person or to a household; one who is staying for a time with friends 1607. **4.** One who visits a place, country, etc., esp. as a sightseer or tourist 1728. **b.** An animal or bird which occasionally or at regular seasons frequents a certain locality or area 1859.

1. In certain Colleges..fundamental statutes can only be changed by visitors 1832. 2. Vertuous visitour to folkys in prisoun LYDG. 3. You see this confluence, this great flood of visitors SHAKS. 4. Visitors to the Montauvert 1860. b. The Glead or Kite..is a very rare v. 1870.

Visitress (vi·zitrĕs). 1827. [f. VISITOR; see -ESS.] **1.** A female visitor. **2.** *spec.* A woman who undertakes regular visiting of the poorer households of a district in order to help or advise 1861.

†Vi·sive, *a.* 1543. [ad. med.L. *visivus*, f. L. *visus* seeing, sight; see -IVE.] Of or pertaining to sight or the power of seeing; visual. **1.** *V. faculty, power, virtue*, etc.: the faculty of sight; the power of vision –1838. **2.** Forming the object of vision; capable of being seen –1647. **b.** *Optics.* Falling upon or appearing to the eye –1690.

Visne (vī·ni). 1449. [a. AF., OF. *visné*, f. *vesin*, *visin*, *veisin* (F. *voisin*):—L. *vicinus* neighbour.] *Law* or *Hist.* **1.** A neighbourhood or vicinage, esp. as the area from which a jury is summoned. **2.** A jury summoned from the neighbourhood in which the cause of action lies 1633.

Visnomy (vi·znŏmi). Now *arch.* or *dial.* 1509. [var. of ME. *fisnomye* PHYSIOGNOMY.] = PHYSIOGNOMY 3.

Vison (vəi·sən). 1781. [a. F.; origin unkn.] The American mink.

Visor, vizor (vəi·zəɹ), *sb.* ME. [a. AF. *viser*, f. F. *vis* face.] **1.** The front part of a helmet, covering the face but provided with holes or openings to admit of seeing and breathing, and capable of being raised and lowered; sometimes spec. the upper portion of this. **b.** *U.S.* The peak of a cap 1864. **2.** A mask to conceal the face; a vizard ME. **3.** *fig.* An outward appearance or show under which something different is hid; a mask or disguise 1532. **†4.** A face or countenance; an outward aspect or appearance –1693.

2. They were disguised in cloaks and visors 1797. 3. He concealed his dislike (their enmity being covered yet under a fair visour) 1653.

Comb.: **v.-mask**, (*a*) a form of disguising mask, a domino (*Hist.*); †(*b*) a prostitute. Hence **Vi·sor, vi·zor** *v.* (*rare*) *refl.* to disguise (oneself) with a v.; *trans.* to cover *up* with a v.

Visored, vizored (vəi·zəɹd), *ppl. a.* late ME. [f. prec. + -ED.] **1.** Of persons: Having the face covered or hid with a visor or mask. **2.** Of helmets: Furnished with a visor 1834.

1. Visor'd falshood, and base forgery MILT.

‖Viss (vis). 1626. [ad. Tamil *vīsai.*] A weight used in Southern India and Burmah equal to about $3\frac{1}{2}$ lbs.

Vista (vi·stă). Also **†visto.** 1657. [It. *vista*, f. L. *vis-*, *videre* to see.] **1.** A view or prospect, esp. one seen through an avenue of trees or other long and narrow opening. **2.** A long narrow opening in a wood, etc., through which a view may be obtained, or which in itself affords a pleasant prospect; an avenue or glade 1671. **b.** An open corridor or long passage in or through a large building; an interior portion of a building affording a continuous view 1708. **3.** *fig.* A mental view or vision of a far-reaching nature 1673. **4.** *In v.*, in continuous view 1758.

1. A Visto by Canalleto 1742. A piny dell gave some v. of the broad sea we were leaving 1873. 2. He employed hands to cut a v. through a coppice RICHARDSON. b. The central aisle..forming in itself the grandest architectural v. in Europe 1806. 4. A long v. of years stretching out before them 1888.

Vistaed (vi·stăd), *a.* 1835. [f. prec.] **1.** Placed or arranged so as to make a vista or avenue. **2.** Provided with vistas 1862. **3.** *fig.* Seen as it were in prospect by the imagination 1849.

3. The vista'd joys of Heaven's eternal year 1851.

Visual (vi·ʒiuăl, vi·ziu,ăl), *a.* and *sb.* late ME. [a. OF., or ad. late L. *visualis*, f. L. *visus* sight, VISION.] **A.** *adj.* **1.** Of beams: Coming, proceeding, or directed from the eye or sight. *Obs.* or *arch.* **2.** Of power or faculty: Pertaining or relating to, concerned or connected with, sight or vision 1603. **3.** Of organs: Endowed with the power of sight; having the function of producing vision 1626. **4. a.** Of knowledge: Attained or obtained by sight or vision 1651. **b.** Carried out or performed by means of vision 1849. **c.** Of impressions, etc.: Received through the sense of sight; based upon something seen 1833. **5.** Of or pertaining to vision in relation to the object of sight; optical; as in *v. angle, axis, focus, point* 1710. **6.** Perceptible, visible 1756. **7.** Of the nature of a mental vision 1845.

1. For inward light alas Puts forth no v. beam MILT. *V. line*, the direct line from the eye to the object or point of vision; the line of sight. *V. ray*, a ray proceeding from the eye to the object seen, or in later use from the object to the eye. 2. The Spirits of the Mind Are busy..Upon the rights of v. sense Usurping WORDSW. 3. The virtue of the V. nerve SWIFT. 4. b. The v. test however is independent 1882. c. A' parts of the retina are not equally sensitive to v. impressions 1879.

B. *sb.* **1.** A visual ray 1726. **2.** One whose memory, imagination, etc., is wholly or largely visual 1886. **Visua·lity**, mental visibility; a mental picture or vision. CARLYLE. **Vi·sually** *adv.*

Visualize (vi·ʒiuăləiz, vi·ziu-), *v.* 1817. [f. prec. + -IZE.] **1.** *trans.* To form a mental vision, image, or picture of. **2.** *absol.* To construct a visual image in the mind 1871.

Vi·sualiza·tion, the action, fact, or power of visualizing; a picture formed by visualizing. **Vi·sualizer**

Vita glass (vəi·tă glɑs). 1925. [f. L. *vita* life.] Trade name of a variety of glass which permits the passage of a large part of the ultra-violet rays of sunlight.

Vital (vəi·tăl), *a.* and *sb.* late ME. [a. OF., or ad. L. *vitalis*, f. *vita* life.] **A.** *adj.* **I. 1.** Consisting in, constituted by, that immaterial force or principle which is present in living beings or organisms and by which they are animated and their functions maintained. Now chiefly *Phys.* or *Biol.* **2.** Maintaining, supporting, or sustaining life 1450. **3.** Of parts, organs, etc.: Essential or necessary to life 1482. **b.** *trans.* 1647. **4.** Of, pertaining or relating to, accompanying, or characteristic of life 1565. **b.** *V. statistics*: Concerned with or relating to the facts of life, e. g. birth, marriage, death, etc. 183[illegible]. **5.** Invigorating, vitalizing; life-giving. Chiefly *poet.* 1590. **6.** Affecting life; fatal to or destructive of life 1612. **7.** *fig.* That is essential to the existence of something; absolutely indispensable, necessary, or requisite. Also, in wider sense, of supreme importance. 1619. **b.** Paramount, supreme, very great 1810.

1. This internal energy, which is peculiar to living protoplasm, is frequently spoken of as v. force BENTLEY. Phr. *V. spark* (†or *flame*); The v. spark was extinct 1826. 2. The Spirit of God..v. vertue infus'd, and v. warmth throughout the fluid Mass MILT. Dream not that the amorous Deep Will yet restore him to the v. air SHELLEY. Phr. *V. fluid*, in *Bot.* = LATEX 2. †*V. air*, in *Old Chem.* = OXYGEN 1. 3. The V. Parts are the Heart, Brain, Lungs and Liver 169[illegible]. b. Such v. parts as the machinery, magazines, and steering gear 1889. 4. When I haue pluck'd thy Rose, I cannot giue it vitall growth againe SHAKS. A gradual decay of the v. powers from old age 1826. *V. affinity*, see AFFINITY 9. *V. capacity*, in *Phys.*, the breathing or respiratory capacity of the lungs. 5. Vitall and comfortable heate..from the bodie of the sunne 160[illegible]. 6. Those that hold the v. shears MILT. 7. Our own interests 1809. A cause which was so v. to both nations 1860. This question—quite v. to all social happiness RUSKIN. b. This inquiry..is..of v. moment 1850.

II. 1. Endowed with or possessed of life; animate, living. Now *poet.* or *rhet.* 1513. **b.** Of places: Full of life or activity 1742. **†2.** As an epithet of *life* –1645. **†3.** = VIABLE *a.*[1] –164[illegible].

1. That bright shape of v. stone which drew the heart out of Pygmalion SHELLEY.

B. *sb.* A vital part or organ (*rare*) 1710. Hence **Vi·tally** *adv.*

Vitalism (vəi·tăliz'm). 1822. [a. F. *vitalisme*, or f. prec. + -ISM.] *Biol.* The doctrine that the origin and phenomena of life are due to or produced by a vital principle, as dist. from a purely chemical or physical force.

Vitalist (vəi·tălist). 1860. [Cf. prec.] A advocate of or believer in vitalism. Also as *adj.* = next.

Vitalistic (vəităli·stik), *a.* 1865. [f. prec. + -IC.] **1.** Of, pertaining to, involving, or denoting vitalism, or a hypothetical vital principle. **2.** Pertaining to or denoting the germ-theory, esp. in its relation to fermentation 1891.

Vitality (vəitæ·līti). 1592. [ad. L. *vitalitat-*, *vitalitas*, f. *vitalis*; see -ITY.] **1.** Vi force, power, or principle as possessed or manifested by living things; the principle of life; animation. **b.** Of plants or vegetative organisms. Also *spec.* of seeds: Germinating power. 1829. **2.** *fig.* Power of enduring or continuing 1844. **3.** *fig.* Active force or power; mental or physical vigour 1858. **4.** With *a* and *pl.* Something possessed of vital force 1851.

2. The v. of Pope's writings 1874. **3.** Such was the intense v. of the Béarnese prince 1860.

Vitalize (vəi·tăləiz), *v.* Also **-ise.** 1678. [f. VITAL *a.* + -IZE.] **1.** *trans.* To give life or animation to (the body, etc.); to endow with vital force or principle. **2.** *fig.* To make living or active; to infuse vitality or vigour into (something); to animate 1805. **b.** To put life into (a literary or artistic conception) 1884.

2. b. He is not an artist. He cannot v. his material. 1907. Hence **Vitaliza·tion,** the action or process of vitalizing, or the state of being vitalized; an instance of this.

Vitals (vəi·tălz), *sb. pl.* 1610. [ad. L. *vitalia*, neut. pl. of *vitalis*, or f. VITAL *a.*] **1.** Those parts or organs of the body, esp. the human body, essential to life, or upon which life depends; usu. applied vaguely, but occas. *spec.* the brain, heart, lungs, and liver. **2.** *transf.* Essential parts or features 1657. **b.** The vital parts of a ship 1884.

1. The weapon has missed your v. 1760. *fig.* Such immense sums, drawn from the v. of all France BURKE. **2.** The very vitals of religion 1702.

Vitamin (vi·tămin, vəi·tă-, -īn). 1912. Also **-ine.** [Coined by Casimir Funk; f. L. *vita* life + AMINE (the early view being that these substances were amines).] Any of the accessory food-factors (distinguished as *v. A, B*, etc.) occurring naturally in minute quantities in many foodstuffs and regarded as essential to normal growth. Hence **Vitami·nic, Vita·minous** *adjs.* **Vi·taminize** *v. trans.*

Vitascope (vəi·tăskōup). *U.S.* 1896. [f. L. *vita* + -SCOPE.] A variety of cinematograph.

‖**Vitellarium** (vitelēə·riŏm). *Pl.* **-aria.** 1865. [mod.L., f. L. *vitellus*.] *Anat.* An accessory gland in the female productive organs of some worms, by which the vitellus for the eggs is secreted; a yolk-gland. Hence **Vitella·rian** *a.*

Vitellary (vi·telări, vite·lări, vəi-), *sb.* and *a.* 1650. [f. L. *vitellus* + -ARY.] †**A.** *sb.* The place or part where the yolk of an egg is formed –1687. **B.** *adj.* Vitelline 1846.

Vitelli-, comb. f. L. *vitellus* VITELLUS, as in vitelli·genous *a.* producing the vitellus.

Vitellin (vite·lin, vəi-). 1857. [f. VITELLUS + -IN[1].] *Chem.* **1.** The albuminoidal substance in the yolk of an egg, a mixture of albumin and casein. **2.** A related substance found in the seeds of plants 1882.

Vitelline (vite·ləin, -in, vəi-), *a.* and *sb.* late ME. [ad. med.L. *vitellinus*, f. L. *vitellus* VITELLUS.] **A.** *adj.* **1.** Coloured like the yolk of an egg; deep-yellow with a tinge of red. **2.** *Biol.* Of or belonging to the vitellus or yolk of an egg 1835. **b.** *V. membrane, sac*, the transparent membrane which surrounds the yolk of an egg; the yolk-sac; the investing membrane of the embryo 1845. **B.** *sb.* The yolk, the vitellary substance 1891.

Vite·llo-, comb. f. VITELLUS, as in **vitello·genous** *a.*, producing the vitellus or yolk.

‖**Vitellus** (vite·lŏs, vəi-). 1728. [L.] **1.** *Embryol.* The yolk of an egg; the germinative contents of an ovum-cell. **2.** *Bot.* A fleshy sac situated between the albumen and the embryo in a seed 1807.

Viti-, comb. form of L. *vitis* vine, as in viti·ferous *a.* [L. *vitifer*].

Vitiate (vi·ʃiĕt), *ppl. a.* Now *rare.* late ME. [ad. L. *vitiatus, vitiare*.] Vitiated.

Vitiate (vi·ʃieit), *v.* 1534. [f. L. *vitiat-*, *vitiare*, f. *vitium* VICE *sb.*[1]] **1.** *trans.* To render incomplete, imperfect, or faulty; to impair or spoil. **b.** To corrupt (*a*) literary works or (*b*) language by carelessness, arbitrary changes, or the introduction of foreign elements 1659. **2.** To render corrupt in morals; to lower the moral standard of (persons) 1534. **b.** Similarly with impersonal objects 1584. **c.** To pervert (the eye, taste, etc.), so as to lead to false judgements or preferences 1806. †**3.** To deflower or violate (a woman) –1791. **4.** To corrupt in respect of substance; to make bad, impure, or defective 1572. **5.** To render of no effect; to invalidate either completely or in part; *spec.* to destroy or impair the legal force of (a deed, etc.) 1621. **b.** To render (an argument, etc.) unsatisfactory 1748. †**6.** To adulterate– 1728.

1. A continual Anxiety for Life vitiates all the Relishes of it ADDISON. **b.** Many barbarous terms and phrases, by which other dictionaries may v. the style, are rejected from this JOHNSON. **2.** The suppression of those habits with which I was vitiated JOHNSON. **b.** One sin of youth vitiates a protracted life 1847. **4.** A malady that has permanently vitiated the sight 1863. The impurity of the air vitiated by respiration 1869. **5.** If an undefined portion of a bequest is to be applied to a purpose void by the statute, it vitiates the whole 1827. Hence **Vi·tiated** *ppl. a.*

Vitiation (viʃiē·ʃən). 1635. [f. prec.] The action of vitiating, the fact or state of being vitiated.

Viticulture (vi·tikɒltiŭr, vəi·ti-, -tʃəɹ). 1872. [f. VITI- + CULTURE.] The cultivation of the vine; vine-growing. Hence **Viticu·ltural** *a.* of or pertaining to v. 1865. **Viticu·lturer, Viticu·lturist,** a vine-grower.

‖**Vitiligo** (vitiləi·go). 1657. [L.] *Path.* A skin disease characterized by the presence of smooth white shining tubercles on the face, neck, and other parts of the body; a species of leprosy. Hence **Vitili·ginous** *a.* of, connected with, or of the nature of v.

Vitiosity (viʃiǫ·sĭti). 1538. [ad. L. *vitiositas*, f. *vitiosus*; see -ITY.] †**1.** A defect or fault; an imperfection –1665. **2.** The state or character of being morally vicious 1603. †**b.** An instance of this; a vice –1657. †**3.** The quality of being physically impaired or defective –1651. **4.** *Sc. Law.* The quality of being legally faulty or improper 1765.

2. My untamed affections and confirmed v. makes mee dayly doe worse SIR T. BROWNE.

‖**Vitrage** (vi·trāʒ). 1886. [F., f. *vitre* glass.] *V. net* (also *cloth*), a lace-net or thin fabric suitable for window-curtains.

Vitreous (vi·trĭəs), *a.* 1646. [f. L. *vitreus*, f. *vitrum* glass; see -OUS.] **1.** Of, belonging to, or consisting or composed of glass; of the nature of or resembling glass; glassy. **b.** *Geol.* and *Min.* Resembling glass in brittleness, hardness, lustre, and mode of cleavage 1774. **c.** *Chem.* Resembling glass in composition 1800. **2.** *V. humour* (or *body*), the transparent gelatinous substance occupying the posterior and larger part of the eyeball 1663. **b.** *ellipt.* as *sb.* = a. 1869. **3.** *V. electricity*, positive electricity obtained from glass by friction 1759. **4.** Resembling that of glass; characteristic of glass 1811. **b.** Having the colour or appearance of glass 1874.

1. The final stiffening of a v. mass into solid stone 1882. **b.** V. lava 1811. Hence **Vi·treousness.**

Vitreously (vi·trĭəsli), *adv.* 1794. [f. prec. + -LY[2].] In a vitreous manner: **a.** With positive electricity. **b.** Like glass 1904.

Vitrescence (vitre·sĕns). 1796. [f. next; see -ENCE.] The state of becoming vitreous or glassy; vitrified or vitreous condition. So **Vitre·scency** (*rare*) 1756.

Vitrescent (vitre·sĕnt), *a.* 1756. [f. L. *vitrum* glass + -ESCENT.] Tending to become glass; susceptible of being turned into glass; glassy.

Vitrescible (vitre·sib'l), *a.* 1754. [f. L. **vitrescere*, or a. F.] That can be vitrified; vitrifiable. Hence **Vitrescibi·lity.**

Vitrifaction (vitrifæ·kʃən). 1728. [See VITRIFY *v.* and -FACTION.] = VITRIFICATION.

Vitrifiable (vi·trifəiăb'l), *a.* 1646. [f. VITRIFY *v.* + -ABLE.] Capable of being vitrified; admitting of conversion by heat into a glassy substance.

Vitrification (vi:trifikē¹·ʃən). 1612. [ad. med. or mod.L. **vitrificatio*, f. **vitrificare* to vitrify.] **1.** The action or process of vitrifying; conversion into a glassy substance by fusion due to heat; the fact of being so converted. **b.** With *a* and *pl.*: An instance of such conversion 1626. **3.** The result or product of vitrifying; a vitrified substance or body 1651.

3. He had but to cover this material with a v. of transparent glaze 1860.

Vitrified (vi·trifəid), *ppl. a.* 1646. [f. VITRIFY *v.*] Converted into glass or a glassy substance by exposure to heat; rendered glassy; glazed. †**b.** *fig.* Icy, frozen. CRABBE.

V. fort, a hill-fort of a type occurring in Scotland and some parts of the Continent, the stones of which have been converted into a vitreous substance by the action of fire.

Vitriform (vi·trifǭɹm), *a.* 1796. [f. L. *vitrum* glass.] Having the form or appearance of glass.

Vitrify (vi·trifəi), *v.* 1594. [ad. F. *vitrifier* or med.L. **vitrificare*, f. L. *vitrum* glass; see -FY.] **1.** *trans.* To convert into glass or a glass-like substance; to render vitreous by fusion due to heat. **2.** *intr.* To become vitreous; to turn into glass or a glass-like substance 1626.

‖**Vitrine** (vi·trīn). 1886. [a. F., f. *vitre* glass.] A glass show-case for specimens or for objects of art.

Vitriol (vi·triǫl). late ME. [a. OF., or ad. med.L. *vitriolum*, f. L. *vitrum* glass.] **1.** One or other of various native or artificial sulphates of metals used in the arts or medicinally, esp. sulphate of iron. **b.** *Oil of v.*, concentrated sulphuric acid 1580. Also, short for this. **2.** *fig.* (In allusion to the corrosive properties of v.) Virulence or acrimony of feeling or utterance 1769.

1. *Blue, green, red, white v.*, sulphate of copper, iron, cobalt, and zinc respectively. *Oil of v.*, concentrated sulphuric acid. *Spirit(s of v.*, a distilled essence of v.

†**Vi·triolate,** *a.* 1646. [ad. med. or mod.L. **vitriolatus*, f. *vitriolum* vitriol.] **1.** Of, belonging to, or resembling that of vitriol –1672. **2.** Treated with vitriol –1782. **3.** Affected by or impregnated with vitriol –1751.

Vi·triolated, *ppl. a.* 1626. [f. prec.] **1.** Impregnated with vitriol. **b.** Of minerals, etc., affected by native sulphates 1794. **2.** Treated with vitriol, as *v. tartar*, sulphate of potassium 1694.

Vitriolic (vitriǫ·lik), *a.* and *sb.* 1670. [ad. F. *vitriolique*, or f. VITRIOL + -IC.] **A.** *adj.* **1.** Of or belonging to vitriol; having the nature or qualities of vitriol; impregnated with vitriol. **2.** *fig.* Of language, persons, etc.: Extremely caustic or scathing; bitterly malignant 1841.

1. *V. acid*, oil of vitriol. **2.** A.. Parliamentary critic of the acrid and v. style 1879.

Vitriolize (vi·triŏləiz), *v.* 1694. [f. VITRIOL + -IZE.] **1. a.** *trans.* To convert into vitriol; to vitriolate. Also *absol.* **b.** *intr.* To become vitriolated or vitriolic 1757. **2.** *trans.* To injure with vitriol; to throw vitriol at (a person) with intent to injure 1886. Hence **Vitrioliza·tion,** the process of converting, or of being converted, into a vitriol. **Vi·triolizer,** one who throws vitriol with intent to injure.

Vitrite (vi·trəit). 1866. [f. L. *vitrum* glass + -ITE[1].] *Min.* 'The matrix of Bohemian pyrope, related to pitchstone'.

Vi·tro-, comb. form on Gr. models of L. *vitrum* glass, as in **v.-de·ntine,** the hard external layer of dentine in a tooth.

Vi·trous, *a. rare.* 1657. [f. L. *vitrum* glass.] Vitreous.

Vitruvian (vitrū·viăn), *a.* 1762. [f. the name of M. *Vitruvius* Pollio, a Roman architect and writer (*c* 10 B.C.).] Of, relating to, or in the style of Vitruvius. **b.** *V. scroll*, a convoluted scroll-pattern employed as an architectural ornament 1837.

†**Vi·try.** late ME. [ad. F. *Vitré*, name of a town in Brittany.] In full *V. canvas*, a kind of light durable canvas –1867.

‖**Vitta** (vi·tă). *Pl.* **-æ** (*i*). 1819. [L.] **1.** *Zool.* A band or stripe of colour. **2.** *Bot.* One of the oil-tubes occurring in the pericarp of the fruit of most umbelliferous plants. Usu. in pl. 1830.

Vittate (vi·tet), *a.* 1826. [ad. L. *vittatus* bound with a fillet or chaplet, f. *vitta* fillet + -ATE[2].] **1.** *Zool., Bot.*, etc. Marked or striped with vittæ. **2.** *Bot.* Having a vitta or vittæ 1870. So **Vi·ttated** *a.* (*rare*) = sense 1. 1790.

Vituline (vi·tiŭləin), *a. rare.* 1656. [ad. L. *vitulinus*, f. *vitulus* calf.] Of or belonging to a calf or calves; resembling that of a calf.

Vitu·perable, *a.* Now *rare* or *Obs.* 1450. [a. OF., ad. L. *vituperabilis*, f. *vituperare*.] That deserves vituperation; censurable; reprehensible; disgraceful.

Vituperate (vəitiū·pĕrėⁱt, vi-), *v.* 1542. [f. L. *vituperat-*, *vituperare*, f. *vitu-* for *viti-*, stem of *vitium* VICE *sb.*[1] + *parare* to prepare.] *trans.* To blame, speak ill of, find fault with, in strong or violent language; to assail with abuse; to rate or revile. Also *absol.* or *intr.*

Vituperation (vəitiūpĕrēⁱ·ʃən, vi-). 1481. [a. OF., or ad. L. *vituperation-*, *vituperatio* blaming, censuring, etc., f. *vituperare*; see prec. and -ATION.] The action, fact, or process of vituperating; blame, censure, reproof, or (esp. in later use) the expression of this, in abusive or violent language; abuse, railing, rating. Also, vituperative or abusive language.

Few nations can surpass the Spaniards in the language of v. 1845.

Vituperative (vəitiū·pĕrėtiv, vi-), *a.* 1727. [ad. L. **vituperativus*, or f. VITUPERATE *v.* + -IVE.] 1. Of words, language, etc.: Containing, conveying, or expressing strong depreciation; violently abusive or fault-finding; contumelious. Also, of or pertaining to vituperation. 2. Characterized by vituperation or abuse 1754. 3. Of persons: Given to vituperation 1819.

1. In utter despair at this v. epithet SCOTT. 3. A Whig is a v. animal 1819. Hence **Vitu·peratively** *adv.*

Vituperator (vəitiū·pĕrėⁱtəɹ, vi-). 1837. [a. L., f. *vituperare*.] One who vituperates; an abuser.

Vitu·peratory, *a.* Now *rare* or *Obs.* 1586. [See VITUPERATE *v.* and -ORY[2].] Expressive of blame or censure; vituperative, violently abusive.

‖**Viva** (vī·vă), *sb.*[1] 1700. [It., 3rd pers. sing. pres. subj. of *vivere* (:—L. *vivere*) to live.] A cry of *viva!* ('long live') as a salute or greeting; a shout of applause; a cheer or hurrah.

Viva (vəi·vă), *sb.*[2] *Univ. colloq.* 1891. [abbrev. of VIVA VOCE.] = VIVA VOCE *sb.* Hence **Vi·va** *v. trans.* to subject to a viva voce examination; *intr.* to examine viva voce.

‖**Vivace** (vivā·tʃe), *adv.* (and *sb.*). 1683. [It., 'brisk, lively':—L. *vivac-*, *vivax*; see next.] *Mus.* A direction indicating brisk or lively performance.

Vivacious (vəivēⁱ·ʃəs, vi-), *a.* 1645. [f. L. *vivaci-*, *vivax* tenacious of life, long-lived, lively, vigorous, f. *vivere* to live; see -ACIOUS.] 1. Full of, characterized by, or exhibiting vivacity or liveliness; animated, brisk, lively, sprightly. 2. Continuing to live; remaining alive for a long time; long-lived. Now *rare* or *Obs.* 1655. b. Of plants; †*spec.* perennial 1676. 3. Possessing or exhibiting tenacity of life; difficult to kill or destroy (*rare*) 1660.

1. V. nonsense 1788. V. pupils should from time to time be accustomed to an exact enumeration of particulars 1798. 2. Hitherto the English Bishops had been v. almost to wonder FULLER. Hence **Viva·cious-ly** *adv.*, **-ness**.

Vivacity (vəivæ·sĭti, vi-). late ME. [a. OF. *vivacite*, or ad. L. *vivacitat-*, *vivacitas* natural vigour, vital force, liveliness, f. *vivaci-*, *vivax*; see -ITY.] 1. Intellectual or mental animation, acuteness, or vigour; quickness or liveliness of conception or perception. †2. Vital force or power; vitality –1747. b. *transf.* and *fig.* Active force, power, vigour 1649. 3. Longevity. Now *rare*. 1616. †b. Tenacity of life –1664. 4. Vigorous or energetic action; activity, energy, vigour; spirit. Now *rare*. 1652. 5. The quality, condition, or fact of being vivacious; animation or liveliness of demeanour or disposition; briskness, sprightliness 1647. b. A vivacious or lively act, expression, scene, etc. Usu. in *pl.* 1692. 6. Brightness, brilliancy (of light or colour) 1734.

1. He hath this viuacite or quycknes of wytte 1526. His conceptions were..full of fire and v. 1704. 2. b. The v. of an excellent example JER. TAYLOR. 3. The v. of some of these Pensioners is little lesse than a Miracle, they survived so long FULLER. 5. As V. is the Gift of Women, Gravity is that of Men ADDISON.

‖**Vivandier** (vivandye). 1591. [F., a supplier of victuals or provisions, f. pop. L. **vivanda* for *vivenda*; see VIAND[1].] In the French or other continental armies: A person who supplies victuals to troops in the field; a sutler. So **Vivandière** *fem.*

Vivarium (vəivēə·riŏm, vi-). *Pl.* **vivaria**, also **-iums**. 1600. [L., neut. sing. of *vivarius*, f. *vivus* alive, living.] 1. A place where living animals, esp. fish, are maintained or preserved for food; a fish-pond or fish-pool. 2. A place specially adapted or prepared for the keeping of living animals under their normal conditions, either as objects of interest or for the purpose of scientific study; freq. in later use, an aquarium 1684. b. A glass bowl, case, etc., in which fish or other aquatic animals are kept, esp. for study 1855.

Vivary (vəi·vări). 1601. [ad. L. *vivarium* VIVARIUM; see -ARY[1].] 1. = prec. 2. Now *rare* or *Obs.* 2. = prec. 1. 1628.

1. That cage and vivarie Of fowles, and beasts DONNE. 2. In stagnant vivaries they lie Forgetful of their ancient haunts 1858.

Vivat (vəi·væt), *int.* and *sb.* 1663. [a. L., 3rd pers. sing. pres. subj. of *vivere* to live.] A. *int.* A word of acclamation wishing a person (long) life and prosperity, or expressing applause or approval. B. *sb.* An utterance of this word by way of acclamation or applause 1821.

‖**Viva voce** (vəi·vă vōᵘ·si), *adv. phr.*, *a.* and *sb.* 1581. [med.L., lit. 'by or with the living voice', f. L. *viva*, abl. sing. fem. of *vivus* living, and *voce*, abl. sing. of *vox* voice.] A. *adv.* By word of mouth; in speech; orally.

The Apostles taught *viua voce*, by liuely voyce 1581.

B. *adj.* Conveyed or expressed in speech instead of writing; spoken; oral 1718. b. Of an examination, etc.: Conducted by speech 1815. C. *sb.* A viva voce examination; freq. abbrev. VIVA *sb.*[2] 1842. Hence **Viva-voce** *v. trans.* to examine orally.

Vi·vda. *Orkn.* and *Shetl. dial.* Also **vifda**. 1688. [perh. ad. ON. *vǫðva* muscular flesh.] Meat smoked, or dried in the air, without being salted.

Vive, *a.* Now only *Sc.* or *arch.* 1477. [a. OF. *vive* fem. of *vif*:—L. *vivum*, *vivus* living, or ad. L. *vivum*.] 1. Lively, forcible, or brisk (*rare*). 2. Of images, pictures, etc.: Life-like 1585. 3. Of colours: Bright, vivid 1591. Hence **Vi·vely** *adv.* (now *Sc.* or *Obs.*).

Vivency (vəi·vĕnsi). *rare*. 1646. [f. L. *vivere* to live + -ENCY.] Manifestation of the principle of life; vitality.

‖**Viverra** (vive·ră, vəi-). 1706. [L., ferret.] *Zool.* †a. The ferret. b. The civet-cat (*V. civetta*), or other species of the type-genus of the civet family (*Viverridæ*).

Viverrine (vive·rəin, vəi-), *a.* and *sb.* 1800. [ad. mod.L. *viverrinus*, f. VIVERRA; see -INE[1].] A. *adj.* Resembling or related to the civet, or the civet family; *spec.* belonging to the subfamily *Viverrinæ*. B. *sb.* An individual of the sub-family *Viverrinæ* 1880.

Vivers (vəi·vəɹz), *sb. pl.* orig. and chiefly *Sc.* 1536. [ad. OF. *vivres*, pl. of *vivre* food, sustenance, sb. use of *vivre* to live.] Food, provisions, victuals, eatables.

Vives (vəivz), *sb. pl.* 1523. [Aphetic f. AVIVES.] Hard swellings of the submaxillary glands of a horse.

Vivi- (vi·vi), comb. form of L. *vivus* alive, living, as in **vivise·pulture**, burying alive.

Vivianite (vi·viănəit). 1823. [f. name of J. G. *Vivian* the discoverer.] *Min.* A phosphate of iron usu. occurring in crystals of blue and green colour.

Vivid (vi·vid), *a.* 1638. [ad. L. *vividus*, f. *vivere* to live.] 1. Full of life; vigorous, active, or energetic on this account; lively or brisk. 2. Of actions or operations: Proceeding or taking place with great vigour or activity 1702. b. Of utterances: Strongly or warmly expressed 1806. c. Of intellectual faculties: Capable of ready and clear creation of ideas or concepts 1814. d. Of description, etc.: Presenting subjects or ideas in a clear and striking manner 1837. 3. Of colour, light, etc.: Brilliant, fresh, lively, bright 1665. b. Of things in respect of colour or brightness 1686. 4. Clearly or distinctly perceived or perceptible 1690. b. Intensely or strongly felt 1704. 5. Quasi-*adv.* Vividly, brightly 1819.

1. They have a sprightly v. countenance 1769. This v. and volatile instrument [*sc.* the violin] 1818. Her face expressed v. interest 1860. 2. The combustion that ensues is exceedingly v. and beautiful 1815. c. Edward's power of imagination..was v. SCOTT. d. A most v. history of the time FREEMAN. 3. A deep v. blue 1815. b. Like a v. circular rainbow quite round the sun TYNDALL. 4. A..v. impression of the growth of Russian influence 1869. Hence **Vi·vid-ly** *adv.*, **-ness**.

Vividity (vivi·dĭti). 1616. [f. prec. + -ITY.] †1. Living force, vitality. 2. The quality or state of being vivid; vividness 1772.

Vivific (vivi·fik), *a.* 1551. [ad. L. *vivificus*, f. *vivus* living; see -FIC.] Life-giving, enlivening, vivifying. So †**Vivi·fical** *a.*

Vivificate (vivi·fikeⁱt), *v.* late ME. [ad. L. *vivificat-*, *vivificare*, f. *vivus* alive; see -ATE[3].] *trans.* = VIVIFY *v.* 1.

Vivification (vi:vifikēⁱ·ʃən). 1548. [ad. L. *vivificatio*, f. *vivificare*; see prec. and -ATION.] 1. The process or fact of being vivified in a spiritual sense. 2. The action or fact of enduing with life; the fact of being vivified physically 1626. †3. Restoration of a metal to its original state –1728. 4. The action or fact of investing with an air of vitality or reality 1858.

4. An industrious scholar..but we do not know that he has the gift of v. 1890.

Vivify (vi·vifəi), *v.* 1545. [ad. F. *vivifier*, ad. L. *vivificare*; see VIVIFICATE *v.*] 1. *trans.* To give life to; to endue with life; to animate; to quicken. 2. To make brighter, more brilliant, or more striking 1791. 3. *absol.* To impart life or animation 1626. 4. *intr.* To acquire life; to become alive 1737.

1. An indraught—slight no doubt, but..sufficient to contaminate or vivify the infusion TYNDALL. *fig.* That Promethean fire, which..vivifies the marble SIR J. REYNOLDS. 3. It [a fire] talks to us;..it is vivified at our touch; it vivifies in return L. HUNT. Hence **Vi·vifier**, one who or that which gives life.

Viviparity (vivipæ·rĭti). 1864. [f. L. *viviparus* (see next) + -ITY.] *Zool.* and *Bot.* The condition or character of being viviparous.

Viviparous (vivi·părəs, vəi-), *a.* 1646. [f. L. *viviparus*, f. *vivus* alive + *parere* to bring forth; see -OUS.] 1. Involving the production of young in a living state. 2. Of animals: Bringing forth young in a live state. (Usu. in contrast with *oviparous*.) 1651. 3. *Bot.* Reproducing from seeds or bulbs which germinate while still attached to the parent plant 1777. b. Characterized by this mode of reproduction 1802. Hence **Vivi·parous-ly** *adv.*, **-ness**.

Vivisect (vi·visekt), *v.* 1864. [Back-formation from next.] 1. *trans.* To dissect (an animal) while living; to perform vivisection upon. 2. *intr.* To practise vivisection 1883.

Vivisection (vivise·kʃən). 1707. [f. L. *vivi-*, comb. form of *vivus* living + *sectio* cutting.] The action of cutting or dissecting some part of a living organism; *spec.* the action or practice of performing dissection or other painful experiment upon living animals as a method of physiological or pathological study. b. An operation of this nature 1859.

Vivisectional (vivise·kʃənăl), *a.* 1866. [f. prec.] 1. Of, belonging to, or of the nature of vivisection. 2. Performing vivisection 1882.

Vivisectionist (vivise·kʃənist). 1879. [f. as prec. + -IST.] One who practises or defends vivisection.

Vivisector (vi·visektəɹ). 1863. [f. as VIVISECT *v.* + -OR.] One who vivisects or practises vivisection.

†‖**Vivres** (vī·vəɹz). 1650. [F.; see VIVERS.] Victuals, provisions –1852.

Vixen (vi·ks'n), *sb.* and *a.* [Late ME. *fixen* repr. OE. **fyxen* (recorded only as adj.), fem. of *fox* FOX.] 1. The female of the fox; a she fox. 2. An ill-tempered quarrelsome woman; a shrew, a termagant 1575. †b. Applied to a child or a man (*rare*) –1738. 3. *attrib.* a. Appositive with *fox*, = sense 1. late ME. b. = VIXENISH *a.* 1660.

2. She's a pestilent v. when she's angry, and as proud as Lucifer 1644. 3. b. What a Vixon trick is this? CONGREVE. The old v. queen 1842.

Vixenish (vi·ks'niʃ), *a.* 1828. [f. prec. + -ISH[1].] 1. Resembling a vixen in temper; cross, ill-tempered, snappish. 2. Characteristic of o.

appropriate to a vixen 1838. Hence **Vixenishly** *adv.*, **-ness.**

Vixenly (vi·ks'nli), *a.* and *adv.* 1677. [f. as prec. + -LY.] **A.** *adj.* Like a vixen in disposition. **B.** *adv.* Crossly, ill-naturedly.

‖**Viz.**, *adv.* and *sb.* 1540. [abbrev. of VIDELICET; the abbrev. repr. the ordinary med.L. symbol of contraction for *-et.*] **A.** *adv.* = VIDELICET *adv.* **B.** *sb.* = VIDELICET *sb.* Also, a special clause in a deed introduced by *viz.* 1750.

†**Vizament,** alteration of ADVISEMENT or *visement* (1414–1568). SHAKS.

Vizard (vi·zăɹd), *sb.* Now *arch.* 1558. [Altered form of *vysar, viser, vizar* VISOR, by confusion of ending; see -ARD.] **1.** = VISOR *sb.* 2, 3. †**2.** In depreciatory use: A face suggestive of a mask –1625. †**3.** A person wearing a visor or mask; *spec.* a woman of loose character wearing a mask in public, a prostitute –1719.

1. Men are glad to pull of their Vizards, and resume themselves again SIR T. BROWNE. Hypocrisy and Superstition wear the V. of Piety WATTS.

Vi·zard, *v.* Now *rare.* 1609. [f. prec.] †**1.** *trans.* To conceal or disguise (something) under a false outward show or appearance; to represent falsely or speciously –1660. **2.** To cover or disguise (the face, etc.) with or as with a vizard; to mask 1609. Hence **Vi·zarded** *ppl. a.* disguised with or wearing a vizard; *fig.* assumed, pretended 1593.

Vizard-mask. *arch.* 1667. [f. as prec.] **1.** A mask worn to conceal the face; a domino. **2.** A woman who wears such a mask; a prostitute 1670.

Vizier (vizī·əɹ, vi·zyəɹ, vi·ziəɹ). 1562. [ad. Turk. *vezīr*, a. Arabic *wazīr, wezīr*, orig. porter, hence one who bears the burden of government, a minister or lieutenant of a king, f. *wazara* to carry, carry on.] **1.** In the Turkish empire, Persia, or other Mohammedan country: A high state official or minister, freq. one invested with vice-regal authority; a governor or viceroy of a province; now esp. the chief minister of a sovereign. **2.** *Grand v.*, the chief minister or administrator of a Mohammedan ruler, esp. of the Sultan of Turkey 1597.

1. All Pashas, before whom are carried the three horse-tails, have the title of Visier 1819.

Vizierate (vizīə·rĕt). 1687. [ad. (through F. *vizir(i)at*) Arab. *wizārat, -et*, f. *wezīr* VIZIER.] **1.** The dignity, position, or authority of a vizier or grand vizier; also, the period of office of a vizier. **2.** A province or district governed by a Turkish vizier 1876.

Vizierial (vizīə·riăl), *a.* 1849. [f. VIZIER + -IAL.] **1.** Of a letter or rescript: Issued by or under the authority of a vizier or grand vizier. **2.** Of or pertaining to a vizier 1876.

Viziership (vizīə·ɹʃip). 1655. [f. VIZIER + -SHIP.] The office or function of a vizier; rule or government as a grand vizier.

Vlach (vlæk). 1841. [a. Bulg. and Serb. *Vlach'*, = OSlav. *Vlachŭ* Roumanian, Italian, Czech *Vlach* Italian, etc.; Slavonic adoptions of Germanic * *Walh-* foreigner, applied esp. to Celts and Latins. Cf. WALACH and WELSH *a.*] A member of the Latin-speaking race occupying parts of south-eastern Europe; a Walachian or Roumanian. Hence **Vlachian** (vlē·kiăn) *a.*

‖**Vlei** (vləi). 1849. [Du. dial., reduced f. Du. *vallei* valley.] **1.** In South Africa: A shallow pool of water; a piece of low-lying ground covered with water during the rainy season. **2.** *local U.S.* A swamp 1880.

Vocable (vōᵘ·kăb'l), *sb.* 1530. [a. F., or directly ad. L. *vocabulum*, f. *vocare.*] **1.** A word or term. (app. reintroduced in the 18th c.) †**2.** A name or designation (*rare*) –1623.

Vo·cable, *a.* [f. L. *vocare* + -ABLE.] Capable of utterance. MEREDITH. Hence **Vo·cably** *adv.*

Vocabular (vŏkæ·biŭlăɹ), *a.* 1608. [f. L. *vocabulum* VOCABLE *sb.* + -AR[1].] Of, pertaining to, or concerning words.

Vocabulary (vŏkæ·biŭlări). 1532. [ad. med.L. *vocabularius, -um*, f. L. *vocabulum* VOCABLE *sb.*; see -ARY[1].] **1.** A collection or list of words with brief explanations of their meanings; now *esp.* one given in an elementary grammar or reading-book of a foreign language. **2.** The range of language of a particular person, class, profession, or the like 1753. **3.** The sum or aggregate of words composing a language 1782.

1. This is the proper signification of the word,.. Greeke vocabularies thus expound it SIR T. BROWNE. 2. An Innocent, in Shakesperian v., signifies an Idiot 1851. The rank v. of malice and hate 1872.

Vocal (vōᵘ·kăl), *a.* and *sb.* late ME. [ad. L. *vocalis*, f. *voc-, vox* voice + -AL.] **A.** *adj.* **I. 1.** Uttered or communicated by the voice; spoken, oral. **b.** Of sound: Produced by the voice; *spec.* of the nature of words or speech 1623. **2.** Of music: Performed by or composed for the voice. (Opp. to *instrumental.*) 1586. **b.** Connected with singing 1799. **3. a.** Having the character of a vowel; vocalic 1589. †**b.** Actually sounded. JOHNSON. **c.** *Phonetics.* Uttered with voice (as dist. from *breath*); voiced, sonant 1668.

1. They were not vocall but mentall Prayers 1641. The human pair..joynd thir v. Worship to the Quire Of Creatures wanting voice MILT. **b.** V. sound is the Matter of speech 1864.

II. 1. Endowed with a voice, possessed of utterance; exercising the power of speech or of uttering sounds 1601. **2.** *fig.* Conveying impressions or ideas as if by speech; expressive, eloquent 1608. **3.** Operative or concerned in the production of voice. Freq. in *v. chords, organs*, etc. 1644. **4.** Of or belonging to the voice (†or sound) 1644. **b.** Of the nature of voice or sound 1826. **5.** Full of voice or sound; sounding, resounding 1667. **6.** Readily or freely expressing oneself in speech; giving vent to one's views or opinions 1871.

1. These insects are generally v. in the midst of summer GOLDSM. *transf.* The v. statue of the supposed Memnon is of Amunoph III. 1837. 4. His vocall impediment 1654. 5. Hill, or Valley, Fountain, or fresh shade Made v. by my song MILT. 6. The most v. class in the whole community 1887.

B. *sb.* †**1.** A vowel –1586. **2.** A member of a Roman Catholic body who has a right to vote in certain elections 1660.

Vocalic (vokæ·lik), *a.* 1814. [f. VOCAL *a.* + -IC.] **1.** Rich in vowels; composed mainly or entirely of vowels. **b.** Characterized by a vowel or vowels 1874. **2.** Consisting of a vowel or vowels; of the nature of a vowel 1852. **3.** Of, pertaining to, affecting, or concerning a vowel or vowels 1861.

1. The Gaelic language being uncommonly v. SCOTT. **b.** The varying v. forms of the Imperfect 1874. **2.** The series of v. and consonantal sounds 1852.

Vocalion (vokē·liən). 1882. [f. VOCAL *a.* + -ION.] A musical instrument of the nature of a harmonium with broad reeds, producing sounds somewhat resembling the human voice.

Vocalism (vōᵘ·kăliz'm). 1864. [f. VOCAL *a.* + -ISM.] **1.** The exercise of the voice or vocal organs in speech. **b.** The art of exercising the voice in singing 1884. **2.** A vocal sound or articulation 1873. **b.** A system of vowels; the use of vowels; vocalic conditions 1873.

Vocalist (vōᵘ·kălist). 1613. [f. as prec. + -IST.] †**1.** A speaker. **2.** A vocal musician; a singer 1834.

Vocality (vokæ·lĭti). 1597. [f. VOCAL *a.* + -ITY.] **1.** The quality of having voice or utterance; the possession or exercise of vocal powers. **2.** The quality or fact of being uttered or utterable; vocal quality or nature 1623. **b.** *pl.* Vocal properties or sounds, *spec.* as displayed in singing 1667. **3.** *Phonetics.* The quality of being (*a*) voiced or (*b*) vocalic 1669.

Vocalization (vōᵘ:kăləizē·ʃən). 1842. [f. next + -ATION.] **1.** The action of vocalizing or the fact of being vocalized; utterance with the voice. **b.** Mode of pronunciation, esp. of vowel sounds 1855. **2.** *Mus.* The action or art of producing musical sounds with the voice; exercise of the voice in singing 1852. **b.** *spec.* The action of singing upon a vowel to one or more notes 1889. **3.** The insertion of vowel-signs in forms of writing consisting mainly or entirely of consonants 1845. **4.** *Phonetics.* Conversion into a voiced sound 1874.

3. The question of v...is one of the highest importance in Biblical criticism 1848.

Vocalize (vōᵘ·kăləiz), *v.* 1669. [f. VOCAL + -IZE. Cf. F. *vocaliser* (1835).] **1.** *trans.* To form into voice; to utter or articulate. **b.** To sing 1798. **2.** *Phonetics.* **a.** To convert into a vowel 1844. **b.** To utter with voice (as dist. from *breath*); to render sonant 1836. **3.** To endow with voice; to render vocal or articulate 1858. **4.** To furnish with vowels or vowel-signs 1845. **5.** *intr.* To perform vocal music; to sing 1830. **b.** *spec.* To sing upon a vowel to one or more notes 1873.

1. A faithful copy of the native pronunciation which readers in all countries will v. alike 1867. Hence **Vo·calizer.**

Vocally (vōᵘ·kăli), *adv.* 1483. [f. VOCAL *a.* + -LY[2].] **1.** In a vocal manner; in spoken words. **2.** By means of singing; in vocal music 1716. **3.** In respect of vowels 1873.

1. I 'never told my love' v. EMILY BRONTE.

Vocation (vŏkē·ʃən). late ME. [a. OF. or ad. L. *vocation-, vocatio*, f. *vocare* to call, summon.] **1.** The action of God in calling a person to exercise some special (esp. spiritual) function, or to fill a certain position; divine influence or guidance towards a definite (esp. religious) career; the fact of being so called or directed towards a special work in life; natural tendency to or fitness for such work. **b.** The action of God (or Christ) in calling persons or mankind to a state of salvation or union with Himself; the fact or condition of being so called 1502. **2.** The particular function or station to which a person is called by God 1487. **b.** One's ordinary occupation, business, or profession 1553. †**c.** *collect.* Those who follow a particular business or profession –1651. **3.** The action on the part of an ecclesiastical body of calling a person to the ministry or to a particular office or charge in the Church 1578.

1. None are to enter the Ecclesiastick or Monastick State, without a particular Vocation 1728. 2. Heaven is his v., and therefore he counts earthly employments avocations FULLER. **c.** Euerie function and seuerall v. strieueth with other 1587. 3. A v. to pastoral duty in the manufacturing districts 1860. Hence **Voca·tional** *a.* **-ly** *adv.*

Vocative (vǫ·kătiv), *a.* and *sb.* 1440. [a. OF. *vocatif, -ive*, or ad. L. *vocativus* (sc. *casus*; also as sb.), *f. vocat-, vocare* to call.] **A.** *adj.* **1.** *V. case*: That case of nouns, adjectives, or pronouns, which in inflected languages is used to express address or invocation. **2.** Characteristic of or pertaining to calling or addressing 1644. **B.** *sb.* **1.** The vocative case 1522. †**2.** An invocation or appeal. RICHARDSON.

Vociferance (vosi·fĕrăns). 1838. [f. next; see -ANCE.] **a.** Clamour or noise of shouting. **b.** Vociferant quality.

Vociferant (vosi·fĕrănt), *a.* 1609. [ad L. *vociferant-, vociferans*, pres. pple. of *vociferari*; see next.] Clamouring, bawling, vociferating.

Vociferate (vosi·fĕrēⁱt), *v.* 1623. [f. L. *vociferat-, vociferari*, f. *voci-, vox* voice + *ferre* to carry.] **1.** *intr.* To cry out loudly; to bawl, shout. **2.** *trans.* To utter in a loud voice; to shout out clamorously; to declaim or assert with loud vehemence 1748.

1. So they vociferating to the Greeks, Stirr'd them to battle COWPER. 2. He entered, vociferating oaths dreadful to hear EMILY BRONTE. Hence **Voci·ferator,** one who or that which vociferates.

Vociferation (vosifĕrē·ʃən). late ME. [a. OF. *vociferacion*, or ad. its source L. *vociferation-, -atio*, n. of action f. *vociferari*: see prec.] The action or an act of vociferating, shouting, or speaking loud.

Vociferous (vosi·fĕrəs), *a.* 1611. [f. L. *vociferari* (see prec.) + -OUS.] **1.** Uttering loud cries or shouts; clamorous, bawling, noisy. **2.** Of the nature of vociferation; uttered with or accompanied by clamour; characterized by loud declamation 1631.

1. The whole audience..became v. 1875. 2. V. ill-nature CIBBER. Hence **Voci·ferous-ly** *adv.*, **-ness.**

Vocular (vǫ·kiŭlăɹ), *a. rare.* 1813. [f. L. *vocula* VOCULE + -AR.] **1.** Vowel, vocalic. **2.** Vocal. DICKENS.

Vocule (vǫ·kiŭl). 1833. [ad. L. *vocula*, dim. of *vox* voice.] The faint final sound produced in pronouncing certain consonants.

‖**Vodka** (vǫ·dkă). Also **vodki, -ky, votky.** 1802. [Russ., pronounced (vo·tka), f. *vodá* water.] An ardent spirit peculiar to Russia, chiefly distilled from rye.

Voe (vōᵘ). *Orkn.* and *Shetl. dial.* 1688. [ad. Norw. *vaag.*] A bay, creek, or inlet.

‖**Vogt** (vǭ*γ*t, fǭ*γ*t). 1694. [a. G., ad. med. L. *vocatus*, pa. pple. of *vocare* to call.] A steward, bailiff, or similar official.

Vogue (vǭg). 1571. [a. F., rowing, course, success, f. *voguer*, ad. It. *vogare* to row.] †**1.** *The v.*, the principal or foremost place in popular repute or estimation; the greatest currency or prevalence –1788. **2.** Without article: Popularity; general acceptance or currency; success in popular esteem 1604. **3.** With *a*, *the*, etc.: A prominent place in popular favour or fashion; a course or period of success or distinction in this connexion 1645. †**4.** General course or tendency; general character or condition –1729. †**5.** The current opinion or belief; the general report or rumour –1730. **6.** The prevailing fashion or tendency 1648.

1. A theory of electricity, which then had the general v. FRANKLIN. 2. Mr. —..seems to have a good deal of v. as a sculptor HAWTHORNE. Phr. *In* (or *out of*) *v.*, *in full v.*, etc. 3. Authority..may give a temporary v. to a bad poet 1752. 4. They go with the v. and stream of times 1660. 6. An age when burlesque is the v. 1860.

Voice (vois), *sb.* ME. [a. AF. *voiz*, *voice*, OF. *voiz*, *vois*, (mod.F.) *voix*:—L. *vocem*, *vox* voice, sound.] **I. 1.** Sound, or the whole body of sounds, made or produced by the vocal organs of man or animals in their natural action; esp. sound formed in or emitted from the human larynx in speaking, singing, or other utterance; vocal sound as the vehicle of human utterance or expression. Also occas., the faculty or power of producing this; or concretely, the organs by which it is produced. **b.** Utterance or expression (of feeling, etc.) 1855. **c.** *Phonology.* Sound uttered with vibration or resonance of the vocal chords, as dist. from BREATH 10. 1842. **2.** The right of speaking or voting in a legislative assembly, etc.; part or share in the control, government, or deciding of something. late ME **3.** The expressed opinion, judgement, will, or wish *of* the people, a number of persons, a corporate body, etc.; occas. as indicated by the exercise of the suffrage. late ME. †**4.** That which is generally or commonly said; common talk; rumour or report –1652. †**b.** A report or rumour –1652. **5.** *Gram.* The form of a verb by which the relation of the subject to the action implied is indicated; one or other of the modes of inflecting or varying a verb according to the distinctions of *active*, *passive*, or *middle*. late ME.

1. A..iustice, which speaketh in action though not in voyce 1608. They that haue the voyce of Lyons, and the act of Hares: are they not Monsters? SHAKS. Phr. *In* (..) *v.*, (of persons) having the v., or vocal organs in fit condition for speaking or singing; so *out of v.* **b.** Phr. *To give v. to*, *to find v. in*. 2. If we had more v. in the management of affairs 1873. 3. The whole v. of the commons was to yelde, yeld, rather then starue HALL. The common voyce do cry it shall be so SHAKS.

II. 1. In limited sense: The sounds naturally made by a single person or animal in speech or other form of vocal utterance; these sounds regarded as characteristic of the person and as distinguishing him from another or others; also freq., the individual organic means or capacity of producing such sounds ME. **b.** Used in ref. to the expression of opinion or protest, or the issuing of a command 1667. **2. a.** The sound *of* prayer, etc. ME. **b.** *transf.* A sound or sounds produced or emitted by something inanimate, as a stream, thunder, the wind, etc., or musical instruments ME. †**3.** An articulate sound; a vocable, term, or word –1697. **4.** An expression of opinion, choice, or preference uttered or given by a person; a single vote. late ME. †**b.** Support or approval in a suit or petition. SHAKS. **c.** A right or power to take part in the control or management of something. Chiefly in the phr. *to have a v. in*. 1835. **5.** *Mus.* The vocal capacity of one person in respect of its employment for musical purposes, esp. in combination with others; a person considered as the possessor of a voice so employed; a singer. Chiefly in pl. 1607. **b.** A vocal part in music 1666. **6.** The agency or means by which something specified is expressed, represented, or revealed 1600.

1. Return Alpheus, the dread v. is past, That shrunk thy streams MILT. A talent for music and a good v. H. WALPOLE. Within such distance as a v. may reach COWPER. Phr. *The v. of God*, freq. = 'the expressed will or desire of God, etc.; the divine command, ordinance, or word'. *To lose the v.*, to be (temporarily) deprived of the power of using the voice for singing or speaking. **b.** A convention..ratified the constitution without a dissenting v. 1796. Phr. *With one v.*, unanimously. †*In my v.*, in my name. SHAKS. 2. **a.** Thou heardest the v. of my supplications when I cryed vnto thee *Ps.* xxxi. 22. **b.** Fro the voises of manye watris WYCLIF *Ps.* xcii[i]. 3. Two Voices are there; one is of the sea, One of the mountains; each a mighty V. WORDSW. *fig.* The v. of tradition 1839. 4. **b.** *Merry W.* I. iv. 167. **c.** A v. in the management of the workhouse 1888. 5. [He] hath sent for voices and painters and other persons from Italy PEPYS. 6. Poetry is the v. of imagination 1854. Lord Cranborne, the present v. of the Foreign Office in the House of Commons 1903.

Comb., as *v.-production*, *-trainer*, *-training*; **v.-box**, the larynx; **-figure**, a figure or graphic representation of a vocal sound; **-part**, *Mus.* a part or melody written for the v., a vocal part; **-pipe**, **-tube**, a tube or pipe for conveying the v., a speaking-tube, esp. as used on ships.

Voice (vois), *v.* 1453. [f. prec.] **I.** *trans.* †**1.** *pass.*: To be commonly said or stated; to be spoken of generally or publicly; to be reported, rumoured, or bruited *abroad* –1822. †**2.** To speak of, state, report, proclaim, etc. –1672. †**3.** To speak much or highly of; to cry *up* (a person or thing). Usu. *pass.* –1673. †**4.** To elect (a person) by voice or vote; to nominate or appoint to an office –1670. **5.** To speak or utter (a word, etc.) 1638. **6.** To give voice, utterance, or expression to (an emotion, opinion, etc.); to proclaim openly or publicly 1607. **b.** To act as the mouthpiece or spokesman of, to express the opinions of (a body of persons) 1893. **7.** *poet.* or *rhet.* To endow with voice, or the faculty of speech or song 1711. **b.** *Organ-building.* To give the correct quality of tone to (an organ or organ-pipe) 1708. **8.** *Phonology.* To utter (a sound) with vibration of the vocal chords 1877.

1. Your father was voiced generally as..one of the bravest men of Scotland SCOTT. 5. Words..voyced like the Irish 1638. 6. Rather assume thie right in silence..then voyce it with claimes and Challenges BACON. **b.** To v. the Opposition 1893. 7. The God of Harmony voic'd all their Throats KEN.

†**II.** *intr.* **1.** To use the voice; to cry out, exclaim. Also *to v. it.* –1682. **2.** To vote –1642. Hence **Voi·cer**, esp. in sense I. 7 b.

Voiced (voist), *ppl. a.* 1600. [f. VOICE *sb.* and *v.*] **1.** Endowed with or possessing a voice. **b.** Having a voice of a specified kind, quality, or tone 1637. †**2.** Much spoken of; famed –1661. **3.** *Phonetics.* Uttered with voice (or vibration of the vocal chords) as opp. to *breath*; sonant. Said esp. of certain consonants, in opposition to VOICELESS *a.* 5. 1867.

Voiceful (voi·sfŭl), *a.* Chiefly *rhet.* or *poet.* 1611. [f. VOICE *sb.* + -FUL.] **1.** Endowed with or as with a voice; having voice or power of utterance; vocal. **b.** Vocal *with* or expressive *of* something 1856. **2.** Of or pertaining to the voice; uttered by the voice or voices 1821.

1. That blind Bard, who..Beheld the Iliad and the Odyssee Rise to the swelling of the v. sea COLERIDGE. **b.** The mountains were thus v. with perpetual rebuke RUSKIN. Hence **Voi·cefulness.**

Voi·celess, *a.* 1535. [-LESS.] **1.** Having no voice; uttering no words or speech; dumb, mute. †**b.** Having no voice in the management of affairs –1634. **c.** Silent, mute 1863. **2.** Characterized by the absence of sound; silent, still 1815. **3.** Unspoken, unuttered 1816. **4.** Characterized by or causing loss of speech or vocal utterance; speechless 1818. **5.** *Phonetics.* Produced or uttered without voice or vocalic tone; surd. Said esp. of certain consonants in opposition to VOICED *ppl. a.* 3. 1867.

1. Mute As creatures v. thro' the fault of birth TENNYSON. **c.** The v., helpless masses of the population 1884. 2. A silent and v. desert 1868. 3. The spirit's v. prayer LONGF. 4. The Niobe of nations! there she stands, Childless and crownless, in her v. woe BYRON. Hence **Voi·celess-ly** *adv.*, **-ness.**

Void (void), *a.* and *sb.* ME. [a. AF., OF. *voide* (mod.F. *vide*), fem. of *voit*, *vuit*, *vuis*:—pop. L. **vocita*, *-um*, *-us*, replacing L. *vacuus*.] **A.** *adj.* **I. 1.** Of a see, benefice, etc.: Unoccupied, vacant. Also of secular offices. **2.** Of a seat, saddle, etc.: Having no occupant; empty ME. **b.** Of a house or room: Unoccupied; untenanted. Now chiefly *dial.* 1479. **3.** Of places: Not occupied or frequented by living creatures; deserted, empty ME. **b.** Not occupied by buildings or other useful structures; vacant 1442. **4.** Not occupied by visible contents; empty, unfilled. late ME. †**b.** Of paper: Blank –1748. **5.** †**a.** Of persons, etc.: Worthless –1728. **b.** Ineffective, useless, leading to no result. late ME. **6.** Having no legal force; legally null, invalid, or ineffectual. late ME. **b.** *gen.* Null, invalid 1526. **7.** Of time: Unemployed, idle, leisure. Now *rare.* 1450. †**b.** Vacant in respect of office –1614.

1. Winchester lay v. six, and Sherburn seven years FULLER. 2. I..sate down on the first v. Seat 1713. 3. As for Ierusalem, it laye voyde, and was as it had bene a wyldernesse COVERDALE 1 *Macc.* iii. 45. 4. The Spaces between..left v. to admit the Light 1697. 6. **a.** They that do persecute, be voyde, and without all truth FOXE. **b.** The end ought to be, from both philosophies to separate..whatsoever is empty and v., and to preserve..whatsoever is solid and fruitful BACON. 6. The Force us'd on me made that Contract v. DRYDEN. *Null and v.*: see NULL *a.* 1. **b.** This makes v. that common conceit and tradition of the Fish called *Faber marinus* SIR T. BROWNE.

II. Const. *of* (occas. †*from*). **1.** Devoid of, free from, or not tainted with (some bad quality, fault, or defect); not affected or impaired by (something unpleasant or hurtful). late ME. **2.** Destitute of (some virtue or good quality); lacking or wanting (something desirable or natural). late ME.

1. The lambish peple, voyd of alle vyce CHAUCER. V. of Care and Strife, To lead a soft, secure, inglorious Life DRYDEN. 2. Bad Fruit of Knowledge,..Which leaves us naked thus, of Honour v. MILT. It would not at first view be altogether v. of probability BERKELEY.

B. *sb.* **1.** A state or condition devoid *of* something; a lack or want (*rare*) 1786. **2.** Emptiness, vacancy, vacuity, vacuum 1618. **3. a.** *Arch.* A space left in a wall for a window or door; the opening of an arch; any unfilled space in a building or structure 1616. **b.** An empty or vacant space, an unoccupied place or opening; a vacancy caused by the removal of something 1697. **c.** *spec.* An absolutely empty space; a vacuum 1727. **d.** One of the small unoccupied spaces in a heap or mass which is not perfecty solid 1837. **4.** *spec.* With *the*: The empty expanse of space 1667. **b.** Const. *of* (heaven, etc.) 1667. **5.** *fig.* **a.** An unsatisfied feeling or desire 1779. **b.** A blank in a record 1866. **6.** A period during which a house or farm is unoccupied or unlet 1885.

1. Men in whom pride..supplies the v. of sense WESLEY. 3. **b.** Phr. *To fill the v.* 4. He sung.. How Seas, and Earth, and Air, and active Flame, Fell through the mighty V. DRYDEN. **b.** To tempt with impious wings the v. of air 1743. *fig.* The dark v. of infidelity 1829. 5. **a.** They have left an aching v., The world can never fill COWPER. Hence **Voi·dness**, the state or condition of being v.; a v. or vacant space.

Void (void), *v.* ME. [Partly ad. AF. and OF. *voider*, *vuider* (mod.F. *vider*):—pop. L. **vocitare* to make empty, f. **vocit-* VOID *a.*; partly an aphetic form of AVOID *v.*] **I. 1.** *trans.* To clear (a room, house, place) *of* (or †*from*) occupants; to empty or clear (a place, receptacle, etc.) *of* something. Now *arch.* **b.** To rid *of* (or †*from*) some quality or condition ME. †**2.** Without const. To clear (a table) of dishes, etc.; to clear or empty (some thing or place) of its contents or occupants –1658. †**b.** To render (a benefice) vacant –1703. **3.** To deprive (something) of legal validity; to annul or cancel ME. **b.** To deprive of efficacy, force, or value; to set aside or nullify. Now *rare.* ME. †**c.** To confute or refute –1699.

1. Whan that the house voyded was of alle CHAUCER. **b.** Having voided thy mind of what is earthly and carnal 1668. 3. Unless you intend to..v. Bargains lawfully made LOCKE. **b.** We defeat our own hope and v. our own prayer 1874.

II. †**1.** To send or put (a person) away; to dismiss or expel –1644. †**2.** To go away, depart, or withdraw from (a place); to move out of (the way) –1732. **3.** To remove (something) so as to leave a vacant space; to take, put, or clear away; occas., to remove by emptying or taking out. Now *rare.* late ME. †**b.** With immaterial obj. –1656. **4.** Of persons, animals, or their organs: To discharge (some matter) from the body through a natural vent or orifice, esp. through the excretory organs; also, †to spit or pour forth (venom). late ME. **b.** *absol.*

To evacuate; to vomit. late ME. †5. To carry off or drain *away* (water, etc.); to discharge or let out -1707.

2. To voyde the realme of Fraunce 1523. The whole shoal of virtuosoes..voided the room 1732. 4. My brother..fell, and voided much blood at the nose 1617. *fig.* That 's base wit, That voyds but filth and stench VAUGHAN.

†III. 1. To leave alone, avoid; to abstain or refrain from; to have nothing to do with -1681. 2. To escape from or evade (something injurious or troublesome) -1677. 3. To prevent; to keep or ward *off* -1722.

1. For if I had fear'd death, Of all the Men i th' world I would haue voided thee SHAKS.

IV. 1. *intr.* To go away, withdraw; to retire or retreat; to give place; to vanish. Now *Obs.* or *arch.* ME. †2. Of a benefice, etc.: To become, fall, or remain vacant -1531. †3. Of matter, etc.: To come, flow, or pass out, esp. in or by evacuation or excretion; to issue -1774. Hence **Voi·ding** *vbl. sb.* the action of the vb.; also *concr.* that which is voided or evacuated.

Voidable (voi·dăb'l), *a.* 1485. [f. prec. + -ABLE.] 1. Capable of being annulled or made legally void; *spec.* (as dist. from *void*) that may be either voided or confirmed. 2. Capable of being voided or evacuated (*rare*) 1663.

1. These civil disabilities make the contract void *ab initio*, and not merely v. BLACKSTONE. Hence **Voidabi·lity. Voi·dableness.**

Voidance (voi·dăns). late ME. [a. AF. *voidaunce*, OF. *vuidance*, f. *voider* VOID *v.*; or aphetic f. AVOIDANCE.] The action of voiding or making void. 1. The action or process of emptying out the contents of something. Now *rare.* †2. The action or fact of removing, clearing away, or getting rid of something; removal -1677. 3. *Eccl.* The fact of a benefice, etc., becoming or being void. late ME. 4. Annulment 1488. †5. A verbal evasion; an evasive answer or argument. BACON.

Voi·ded, *ppl. a.* late ME. [f. VOID *v.*] †1. Made void or empty; emptied or cleared of contents -1563. 2. Having a part or portion cut out so as to leave a void or vacant space. †a. of shoes or a garment -1623. b. *Her.* of a charge or ordinary 1572. 3. Evacuated (*rare*) 1784.

2. b. *V.* is a term applied to any ordinary, ..when it is pierced through, so that the field appears, and nothing remains of the charge but its edge 1780.

Voidee (voi·dī). Now only *Hist.* late ME. [a. AF. **voidé(e*, pa. pple. of *voider* VOID *v.*, with ref. app. to the withdrawing from a hall or chamber of those who were not to sleep there.] A collation consisting of wine with spices, comfits, or the like, partaken of before retiring to rest or before the departure of guests; a repast of this nature following upon a feast or fuller meal; a parting dish.

Voider (voi·dəɹ). late ME. [f. VOID *v.* + -ER[1].] †1. That which keeps off or away; a screen or defence -1550. 2. A receptacle intc which something is voided or emptied: a. A tray, basket, etc. in which dirty dishes, fragments of broken food, etc. are placed in clearing the table or during a meal. *Obs.* exc. *dial.* 1466. †b. A tray, basket, or large plate for holding, carrying, or handing round sweetmeats. Also *transf.* a quantity or amount carried in this. -1706. c. A clothes-basket; a wicker basket of any kind. *dial.* 1707. 3. *Her.* As the name of an ordinary (see quot.) 1562. 4. One who or that which voids, clears away, or empties (*rare*) 1589.

2. a. I sent my old silver voyder..to be exchandged for a new 1620. 3. *V.*, is an ordinary much resembling the flanch, but is not quite so circular towards the centre of the field 1780.

‖**Voile** (voil, vwal). 1889. [F., VEIL *sb.*] A thin semi-transparent cotton or woollen material much used for blouses and dresses.

‖**Voir dire** (vwār dīɹ). 1676. [OF. *voir* true, the truth + *dire* to say.] *Law.* (See quot.)

If however the court has, upon inspection, any doubt of the age of the party,..it may..examine the infant himself upon an oath of *voir dire, veritatem dicere*, that is, to make true answer to such questions as the court shall demand of him BLACKSTONE.

‖**Voiture** (vwatūr). 1698. [F.:—L. *vectura*, f. *vect-*, *vehere* to convey.] A carriage or conveyance; a vehicle.

‖**Voiturier** (vwatūrye). 1763. [F., f. prec.; see -IER.] The driver of a carriage or coach.

‖**Voiturin** (vwatūræṅ). 1768. [F., f. *voiture*, after It. *vetturino*.] 1. = prec. 2. A carriage for hire, a voiture 1768.

Voivode (voi·vōud). 1570. [ad. Bulg., Serb *vojvoda*, Czech *vojevoda*, etc., mod. L. *voivoda*, mod. Gr. βοεβόδα(ς) = VAIVODE.

Vol (vǫl). 1722. [F., f. *voler* :—L. *volare* to fly.] *Her.* Two wings displayed and joined at the base.

Vol., abbrev. of VOLUME.

Volage (volā·ʒ), *a.* late ME. [a. OF. and F. *volage*, f. *voler* :—L. *volare* to fly. (Re-introduced in the 19th c. from mod. French.)] Giddy, foolish, fickle, inconstant.

Not yit twelve yeer of age, With herte wylde, and thought v. CHAUCER.

Volant (vōu·lănt), *a.* and *sb.* 1548. [a. F., pres. pple. of *voler*, also as sb.] A. *adj.* †1. a. Riding at full gallop (*rare*). b. *Mil.* So constituted as to be capable of rapid movement or action -1647. 2. *Her.* Of birds, etc.: Represented as flying; having the wings expanded as if in flight 1572. 3. Flying; capable of flight 1665. 4. Of things: Passing rapidly through the air or space, as if by flight; floating lightly in the air 1603. b. Moving rapidly or lightly; active, nimble. Also *fig.* of discourse. 1650. 5. Characterized by or of the nature of flight 1818.

1. b. Sir Henrie Powers squadron v. (or flying Regiment) 1617. 3. A kind of v. beetle MRS. PIOZZI. 4. The v. shadows that cross our British hills MRS. PIOZZI. b. Bards with v. touch Traverse loquacious strings 1708.

B. *sb.* †1. *To act* or *keep* (*upon*) *the v.*, to hover between two parties, sides, or opinions -1734. 2. A flounce or frill 1882.

‖**Volante** (vola·nte). 1791. [Sp.] A two-wheeled covered carriage drawn by a horse ridden by a postilion (freq. with another horse attached at the side), used in Spanish countries.

Volapük, -puk (vǫ·lăpük, -puk). 1885. [f. *vol* world (alteration of Eng. *world*) + *a*, connecting vowel + *pük* speech (alteration of Eng. *speak*).] An artificial language, invented in 1879 by a German priest, Johann M. Schleyer, as a means of international communication.

Volar (vōu·lăɹ), *a.* 1814. [f. L. *vola* + -AR.] *Anat.* Of or belonging to the palm of the hand or the sole of the foot; palmar.

Volary (vōu·lări). Now *rare.* 1630. [app. ad. F. *volière*, after types in -ARY, -ERY.] 1. A large bird-cage; an aviary. 2. *collect.* The birds kept in an aviary 1693.

Volatic (vŏlæ·tik), *sb.* and *a.* Now *rare* or *Obs.* 1643. [ad. L. *volaticus*, f. *volat-*, *volare* to fly.] A. *sb.* A winged creature. B. *adj.* That flies or flits about; *spec.* in *Path.* of a variety of itch 1684.

Volatile (vǫ·lătəil, -il), *sb.* and *a.* ME. [a. OF. and F. *volatil*, *-ile*, or ad. L. *volatilis*, f. *volat-*, *volare*.] A. *sb.* †1. *collect.* Birds, *esp.* wild-fowl -1660. 2. A winged creature; a bird, butterfly, or the like; a fowl. Usu. in pl. ME. 3. A volatile matter or substance 1686. B. *adj.* 1. Flying, capable of flying, volant 1626. b. Moving or flitting from one place to another, esp. with some degree of rapidity 1654. 2. Of substances: Liable to or susceptible of evaporation and diffusion at ordinary temperatures 1605. 3. Changeable, fickle; marked or characterized by levity or flightiness 1647. 4. Evanescent, transient; readily vanishing; difficult to seize, retain, or fix permanently 1665.

1. Conveyed by some v. insect 1865. 2. Sulphur is fixt and not v. 1671. *V. salt* or *salts*, sal volatile. *V. alkali*, ammonia. *V. oil*: see ESSENTIAL 5. 3. The fickle, inconstant, v. temper of the people 1861. 4. The incidents which give excellence to biography are of a v. and evanescent kind BOSWELL. Hence **Vo·latileness, Volati·lity,** the quality, state, or condition of being v.

Volatilize (vǫ·lătiləiz, volæ·tiləiz), *v.* 1657. [f. VOLATILE *a.* + -IZE.] 1. *trans.* To render volatile; to cause to evaporate or disperse in vapour. b. *fig.* To render light, airy, unsubstantial, etc. 1664. 2. *intr.* To become volatile; to evaporate 1728.

1. Hence we see how necessary heat is, to v. the rancid oil 1755. Hence **Vo·latili·zable** *a.* capable of being volatilized. **Vo·latiliza·tion,** the action or process of making volatile; volatilized state.

†**Vo·latize**, *v.* 1650. [f. as prec.] = prec. -1826.

‖**Vol-au-vent** (volovaṅ). 1828. [F., lit. 'flight in the wind'.] A kind of raised pie, formed of a light puff paste filled with meat, fish, or the like.

Volborthite (vǫ·lbǫɹþəit). 1844. [Named after its discoverer, A. von *Volborth*, a Russian scientist.] *Min.* Hydrous vanadate of copper, barium, and calcium, found in small yellowish-green crystals.

Volcan (vǫ·lkăn). Now *rare.* 1577. [a. F. and Sp., ad. L. *Volcanus*, *Vulcanus* VULCAN.] = VOLCANO 1.

Volca·nian, *a.* *rare.* 1820. [f. VOLCANO + -IAN.] = next.

Volcanic (vǫlkæ·nik), *a.* 1774. [a. F. *volcanique*, f. *volcan* VOLCAN.] 1. Discharged from or produced or ejected by a volcano or volcanoes. 2. Due to or caused by a volcano or volcanoes 1776. b. Of or pertaining to a volcano or volcanoes 1797. 3. Characterized by the presence of volcanoes; composed of volcanoes; consisting of materials produced by igneous action 1789. b. Of the nature of a volcano 1833. 4. *fig.* Resembling or characteristic of a volcano, or the attributes of this; violently explosive, latently capable of sudden and violent activity 1854.

1. V. cinders 1774. *V. tufa, tuff*: see TUFA. *V. glass*, obsidian. 2. V. shocks 1817. 3. Hot springs are common to the v. districts of different parts of the world 1832. 4. His v. soul was tossed with an inward ocean of fire 1870. Hence **Volca·nically** *adv.* like or in respect of a volcano or volcanoes.

Volcanicity (vǫlkăni·sĭti). 1836. [ad. F. *volcanicité* or f. prec. + -ITY.] Volcanic action, activity, or phenomena.

Volcanism (vǫ·lkăniz'm). 1869. [a. F. *volcanisme*.] The state, condition, or character of being volcanic; volcanic action or phenomena.

Volcanist (vǫ·lkănist). 1796. [f. VOLCANO + -IST, or a. F. *volcaniste*.] 1. One who asserts the igneous origin of certain geological formations; a Plutonist or Vulcanist. 2. One who studies or is versed in volcanoes 1828.

Vo·lcanized, *ppl. a.* *rare.* 1792. [ad. F. *volcanisé*, f. *volcan* VOLCAN; see -IZE.] Affected or altered by volcanic action or heat. Hence **Vo·lcanize** *v. trans.*

Volcano (vǫlkē̆ⁱ·no). *Pl.* **volcanoes** (†-os, -o's). 1613. [a. It. *vol-*, *vulcano*:—L. *Vol-*, *Vulcanum*, *Volcanus* VULCAN.] 1. *Physiog.* A more or less conical hill or mountain, composed wholly or chiefly of discharged matter, communicating with the interior of the globe by a funnel or crater, from which in periods of activity steam, gas, ashes, rocks, and freq. streams of molten materials are ejected. 2. *fig.* A violent feeling or passion, esp. one in a suppressed state 1697. b. A state of things liable to burst out violently at some time 1853.

2. Nursing this v. of wrath in his breast 1872. b. The social v. which some think exists below modern society 1890.

Vole (vōul), *sb.*[1] 1679. [a. F., app. f. *voler*, ad. L. *volare* to fly.] The winning of all the tricks in certain card-games, as écarté, quadrille, or ombre. Phr. *to win the v.* b. *To go the v.*, to run every risk in the hope of great gain; to try all shifts. Hence **Vole** *v. intr.* to win the v. POPE.

Vole (vōul), *sb.*[2] 1805. [orig. *vole-mouse*, ad. Norw. **vollmus*, f. *voll* field + *mus* mouse.] One or other of various rat- or mouse-like quadrupeds; esp. the short-tailed field-mouse, *Microtus* (formerly *Arvicola*) *agrestis*; the water-rat, *M. amphibius*; and the red or bank vole, *Evotomys glareolus*.

Volent (vōu·lĕnt), *a.* *rare.* 1654. [a. L. *volent-*, *volens*, *velle* to will, wish, desire.] Exercising or capable of exercising will or choice in respect of one's conduct or course of action.

‖**Volet** (vole). 1847. [F., shutter, etc., f. *voler*, a. L. *volare* to fly.] One of the wings or side compartments of a triptych.

Volitant (vǫ·litănt), *a.* 1847. [ad. L. *volitant-, volitare.*] Flitting, flying, or constantly moving about.

Volitate (vǫ·liteᶦt), *v.* 1866. [f. L. *volitat-, volitare*, frequentative of *volare* to fly.] To fly with a fluttering motion.

Volitation (vǫlitēᶦ·ʃən). 1646. [ad. med.L. *volitation-, volitatio*, f. L. *volitare.*] Flying, flight.

Volition (vǒli·ʃən). 1615. [a. F., ad. med. L. *volition-, volitio*, f. L. *volo* I wish, will.] 1. With *a* and *pl.* An act of willing or resolving; a decision or choice made after due consideration or deliberation. 2. The action of consciously willing or resolving; exercise of the will 1660. b. The power or faculty of willing 1738. c. Will-power 1844.

1. A determination to suspend a v. is, in fact, another v. 1777. 2. b. The individuality of a mind..or its v., that is, its power of originating motion PALEY. c. Montacute..acted upon a stronger v. than his own DISRAELI. Hence **Voli·tional** *a.* of or belonging to v.; endowed with or exercising the faculty of v.; leading or impelling to action; arising from the exercise of v.

Volitive (vǫ·litiv), *a.* and *sb.* 1660. [ad. med. or mod.L. **volitivus*, or f. prec. + -IVE.] A. *adj.* 1. Of or pertaining to the will; volitional. 2. Arising from the will 1675. 3. *Gram.* Expressive of a wish or desire; desiderative 1864.

1. The V. or chusing faculty JER. TAYLOR.

B. *sb.* A desiderative verb, mood, etc. 1813.

Volitorial (vǫlitōᵊ·riăl), *a.* 1872. [f. mod.L. *Volitores* birds capable of flight + -IAL.] Of or pertaining to flight; having the power of flight.

‖**Volksraad** (vǫ·lksrāt). 1852. [f. Du. *volk* FOLK + *raad* senate, council.] The chief legislative assembly in either of the former South African republics of the Transvaal or the Orange Free State.

Volley (vǫ·li), *sb.* 1573. [ad. F. *volée*:— Rom. *volata*, f. L. *volatus, volare* to fly.] 1. A simultaneous discharge of a number of firearms or artillery; a salvo. 2. A shower or simultaneous flight of many missile weapons, as arrows, stones, etc. 1598. b. *poet.* A storm or shower of hail, rain, etc. 1737. 3. An uttering or outpouring *of* numerous words, oaths, shouts, etc., in smart or rapid succession. Also without const. 1590. 4. *Tennis.* The flight of a ball in play before it has touched the ground 1596. b. *Tennis, Lawn-tennis, Cricket*, etc. A return stroke or hit at a ball before it has touched the ground; the action of so returning the ball 1862.

1. A v. of small shot SCOTT. After firing a v., the troops charged 1844. *fig.* Large black eyes that flash on you a v. Of rays BYRON. 2. *P. L.* VI. 213. 3. Volleys of laughter 1786. 4. c. *attrib.* v.-ball (*U.S.*) a game played by volleying a large inflated ball with the hands over a high net.

Volley (vǫ·li), *v.* 1591. [f. prec.] I. *trans.* a. To utter (words, etc.) rapidly or impetuously. Usu. with advs. as *forth, off, out.* b. To discharge (arrows, shot, etc.) in a volley 1839. c. *Tennis*, etc. To return (a ball) in play before it touches the ground; to reply to (a service) in this way 1875. 2. *absol.* a. To fire a volley or volleys 1606. b. *Tennis*, etc. To hit or return the ball before it bounces; to make a volley-stroke 1819. 3. *intr.* a. To emit or produce sounds simultaneously or continuously, in a manner suggestive of firearms or artillery 1810. b. To rush, roll, or stream with simultaneous motion 1853. c. To issue or be discharged in or after the manner of a volley 1887. Hence **Vo·lleyer** *Tennis*, etc. one who volleys.

Volleyed (vǫ·lid), *ppl. a.* 1616. [f. prec. + -ED.] 1. Shouted or uttered in the manner of a volley. 2. Of thunder or lightning: Discharged with the continuous effect of a volley 1667. 3. Of missiles, etc.: Discharged or cast in or as in a volley 1759.

2. When in Battel to thy aide The blasting volied Thunder made all speed MILT. 3. Our vollied darts 1759.

Volplane (vǫ·pleᶦn), *sb.* 1910. [orig. two words, *vol plane*, prop. *vol plané*, f. F. *vol* flight + *plané*, pa. pple. of *planer* PLANE *v.*[2]] A dive, descent, or downward flight at a steep angle on the part of an aeroplane under control, and with the engine stopped or shut off. Hence **Vo·lplane** *v. intr.* to make a v.

Volscian (vǫ·lʃiăn), *sb.* and *a.* 1513. [f. L. *Volsci* + -AN.] A. *sb.* 1. *Hist.* One of an ancient warlike people formerly inhabiting the east of Latium, subdued by the Romans in the 4th century B.C. 2. The Italic language spoken by the Volscians 1897. B. *adj.* Of, pertaining to, or belonging to the Volscians; that is a Volscian 1601.

Volt (vōᵘlt, vǫlt), *sb.* 1873. [f. the name of *Volta*; see VOLTAIC *a.*] The practical unit of electromotive force; the difference of potential capable of sending a current of one ampère through a conductor whose resistance is one ohm. Also *attrib.* (with numeral preceding).

Volt (vǫlt, vōᵘlt), *v.* 1692. [ad. F. *volter*, f. *volte* VOLTE.] *Fencing.* To make a volte.

‖**Volta** (vǫ·ltă). 1642. [It., turn, etc., fem. pa. pple. of *volgere, volvere* to turn, used as a sb.] = LAVOLTA.

Volta- (vǫ·ltă), comb. form of VOLTAIC used in a few technical terms, as *v.-electric, -electrometer.*

Voltage (vōᵘ·ltėdʒ, vǫ·ltėdʒ). 1890. [f. VOLT *sb.* + -AGE.] Electromotive force reckoned or expressed in volts.

Voltaic (vǫltēᶦ·ik), *a.* 1812. [f. name of Alessandro *Volta*, Italian physician and scientist (1745–1827).] 1. Of apparatus: Used in producing electricity by chemical action after the method discovered by Volta; esp. *v. battery, v. pile.* 2. Of electricity: Generated by chemical action 1816. b. Of a current: Consisting of voltaic electricity 1834. 3. Of, pertaining to, connected with, or caused by electricity due to chemical action 1820. b. *V. brass*, brass deposited by the action of electricity 1860.

2. The application of v. electricity to the welding and fusion of metals 1890. Hence **Volta·ically** *adv.* by means of or in respect of v. electricity; after the manner of a v. battery.

Voltairean, Voltairian (vǫltēᵊ·riăn), *sb.* and *a.* 1871. [f. the later name, *de Voltaire*, of the French author François Marie Arouet (1694–1778).] A. *sb.* A follower or adherent of Voltaire; one whose views on social and religious questions are characterized by a critical and mocking scepticism. B. *adj.* Of, belonging to, or resembling Voltaire; holding opinions like those of Voltaire, or expressing them in his style 1876. So **Voltai·rianism** 1848, **Voltai·rism** 1776, the body of opinions or views expressed by Voltaire; the mocking and sceptical attitude characteristic of these.

Voltaism (vǫ·ltă,iz'm). 1811. [f. *Volta* (see VOLTAIC *a.*) + -ISM.] The production of an electric current by the chemical action of a liquid on metals; galvanism as produced by Volta's methods.

Voltameter (vǫltæ·mĭtəɹ). 1836. [See VOLTA- and -METER.] An instrument used for the quantitative measurement of electricity by means of the results of electrolysis.

Volte, volt (vǫlt, vōᵘlt). 1586. [a. F., ad. It. *volta*; see VOLTA.] †1. = LAVOLTA –1610. 2. *Fencing.* A sudden dexterous movement to avoid a thrust 1688. 3. In the manège, a circular movement executed by a horse 1727.

‖**Volte-face** (volt(ə)fas). 1819. [F., ad. It. *volta faccia*, f. *volta* turn + *faccia* face.] The act of turning so as to face in the opposite direction; *fig.* a complete change of attitude or opinion.

‖**Voltigeur** (voltizōr). 1805. [F., f. *voltiger* to hover, flutter, vault, etc.] Formerly in the French Army, a member of a special skirmishing company attached to each regiment of infantry.

Voltmeter (vōᵘ·ltmītəɹ, vǫ·lt-). 1882. [f. VOLT *sb.* + METER.] An instrument for measuring the pressure of electricity in volts.

‖**Vo·lto.** 1700. [It.] = VAULT *sb.*[1] 1.

Voltzite (vǫ·ltsəit). 1835. [f. name of P. L. *Voltz*, French inspector of mines.] *Min.* A native oxysulphide of zinc.

Volubility (vǫliŭbi·lĭti). 1579. [ad. F. *volubilité*, or ad. L. *volubilitas*, f. *volubilis*; see next and -ITY.] †1. Versatility (*rare*) –1605. 2. The capacity of rolling, revolving, or turning round; aptness to rotate about an axis or centre 1594. †3. Changeableness, mutability –1699. 4. Ready flow *of* speech, etc. 1589. b. Smooth, easy, or copious flow of verse 1589. 5. The character or state of being voluble in speech; fluency, garrulousness 1596. 6. Extreme readiness *of* the tongue, voice, etc. in speech or discourse 1612.

Voluble (vǫ·liŭb'l), *a.* 1575. [a. F., or ad. L. *volubilis*, f. *volu-, volvere* to turn; see -BLE.] I. 1. Liable to change; inconstant, variable, mutable. Now *rare.* 2. Capable of ready rotation on a centre or axis; apt to revolve in this manner. Now *rare.* 1589. 3. Moving rapidly and easily, esp. with a gliding or undulating movement 1589. 4. *Bot.* Twining, twisting 1753.

1. Nothing abides at a stay; all things are unstable, and v. 1647. 4. Plants with v. stems 1789.

II. 1. Characterized by fluency or glibness of utterance; fluent 1588. 2. Of discourse, words, etc.: Characterized by great fluency or readiness of utterance 1588.

1. A most acute Iuuenall, v. and free of grace SHAKS. Her tongue, so v. and kind, It always runs before her mind PRIOR. 2. A discours, v. anough, and full of sentence MILT. Hence **Vo·lubleness. Vo·lubly** *adv.*

Volume (vǫ·liŭm), *sb.* late ME. [a. OF. *volum(e*, ad. L. *volumen* coil, wreath, roll, f. *volvere* to roll.] I. 1. *Hist.* A roll of parchment, papyrus, etc. containing written matter; a literary work or part of one, recorded or preserved in this form, which was customary in ancient times. 2. A collection of written or printed sheets bound together so as to form a book; a tome. late ME. 3. *fig.* Something comparable to a book; *esp.* something which may be studied after the manner of a book 1592. 4. A separately bound portion or division of a work; one of a number of books forming a related set or series 1523.

1. In history a great v. is unrolled for our instruction BURKE. 2. Lo, here a little v., but great book! CRASHAW. *The sacred v.*, the Bible. *The Christian v.*, the New Testament. 3. This night you shall.. Read ore the v. of young Paris face, And find delight, writ there with Beauties pen SHAKS. Phr. *To speak* (also *tell, express*) *volumes*, to be highly expressive or significant. 4. Thus endeth the first v. of sir Johan Froissart LD. BERNERS.

II. †1. Size, bulk, or dimensions (of a book) –1683. 2. A particular bulk, mass, or quantity as an attribute of a thing 1621. b. *concr.* A quantity or mass (esp. a large one) regarded as matter occupying space 1647. c. *Chem.* A determinate quantity or amount, in terms of bulk, of any substance 1812. 3. The bulk, size, or dimensions *of* a thing. Also *concr.*, the mass or solid body *of* something. 1792. b. *gen.* The amount or quantity *of* something 1882. c. *spec.* The cubic contents of any enclosed space or solid, e.g. as determined by the length × breadth × height 1841. 4. Without article: Bulk, mass, dimensions 1794. 5. *Mus.* Quantity, strength or power, combined mass, of sound 1801.

2. Certain gases, which, in assuming a larger v., have caused the explosion 1862. b. The v. of mercury in the stem of a thermometer 1871. c. Instead of a given v. or measure, a given weight of air is examined HUXLEY. 3. The v. of the Sun is 1,200,000 times greater than that of the Earth 1868. b. The v. of business 1892. 4. The brook is..of..moderate v. 1868. 5. *V.*, a term applied to the power and quality of the tone of a voice or instrument 1876.

III. *poet.* A coil, fold, wreath, convolution, esp. of a serpent 1648. b. A winding of a stream 1716.

So glides some trodden Serpent on the Grass, And long behind his wounded V. trails DRYDEN. The ivy and the wild-vine interknit The volumes of their many-twining stems SHELLEY. Hence †**Vo·lumist**, one who writes a v. MILT.

Volume (vǫ·liŭm), *v.* 1815. [f. prec.] 1. a. *trans.* To send up, pour out, in volumes. b. *intr.* To rise or roll in a volume or cloud 1824. 2. *trans.* To collect or bind in a volume 1853.

1. a. More and more the nightingales volumed their notes MEREDITH.

Volumed (vǫ·liŭmd), *a.* 1596. [f. VOLUME *sb.* and *v.*] 1. Made into a volume or volumes of a specified size, number, etc. b. Filling a volume or volumes 1746. 2. Formed into a rolling, rounded, or dense mass 1803.

1. Margents of great volum'd bookes 1609. 2. Gasping with the v. smoke BYRON.

Volumetric (vǫliumeˑtrik), *a.* 1862. [f. VOLUME *sb.* + METRIC *a.*²] Of, pertaining to, or noting measurement by volume. So **Volumeˑtrical** *a.* 1853; -ly *adv.*

Voluminosity (vǒliūminǫˑsiti). 1782. [See next and -OSITY.] 1. The state of being voluminous in respect of literary production. 2. The fact of turning or winding; an instance of this 1841.

Voluminous (vǒliūˑminəs), *a.* 1611. [ad. late L. *voluminosus*, f. *volumin-*, *volumen* VOLUME *sb.*] 1. Full of turnings or windings; containing or consisting of many coils or convolutions. 2. Writing so much as to fill volumes; writing or discoursing at great length 1611. 3. Forming a large volume; extending to or consisting of many volumes; extensive or copious in treatment 1612. 4. Of matter of discourse: Extremely full or copious; forming a large mass or collection 1647. b. *gen.* Extensive, vast 1652. 5. Of great volume or size; massive, bulky, large, swelling 1635.

1. Many a scaly fould V. and vast, a Serpent arm'd With mortal sting MILT. 2. The very learned and v. Grotius 1782. 3. Fames v. booke DEKKER. 4. V. roundabout descriptions HAZLITT. 5. That young lady with the v. light brown hair 1872. Hence **Voluˑminous-ly** *adv.*, **-ness.**

Voluntariate (vǫlǒnteˑriět). 1881. [ad. F. *volontariat*, f. *volontaire* VOLUNTARY *a.*] Voluntary service, *spec.* of a military character.

Voluntarily (vǫˑlǒntărili), *adv.* late ME. [f. VOLUNTARY *a.* + -LY².] In a voluntary manner; of one's own free will or accord; naturally, spontaneously.

Voˑluntariness. 1612. [f. as prec. + -NESS.] The state or condition of being voluntary; absolute freedom or liberty in respect of choice, determination, or action; spontaneity; also, an instance of this.

Voluntarism (vǫˑlǒntăriz'm). 1838. [irreg. f. VOLUNTARY *a.* + -ISM.] 1. = VOLUNTARYISM 1. 2. *Philos.* One or other theory or doctrine which regards will as the fundamental principle or dominant factor in the individual or the universe 1896.

Voluntarist (vǫˑlǒntărist). 1841. [f. as prec. + -IST.] An advocate or adherent of the voluntary principle or method in the Church or in philosophy. Also, in more recent use, an advocate of voluntary military service, as opp. to conscription.

Voluntary (vǫˑlǒntări), *a.*, *adv.*, and *sb.* late ME. [ad. OF. *voluntaire*, *volontaire*, or ad. L. *voluntarius*, f. *voluntas*.] A. *adj.* I. 1. a. Of feelings, etc.: Arising or developing in the mind without external constraint; purely spontaneous. b. Of actions: Performed or done of one's own free will, impulse, or choice; not constrained, prompted, or suggested by another 1449. c. Of oaths, etc.: Proceeding from the free, unprompted, or unconstrained will of a person; *spec.* in *Law* 1595. d. *Law.* Of documents, proceedings, etc. 1625. 2. *Physiol.* Of bodily actions: Subject to the will. late ME. 3. Of conditions, etc.: Freely chosen or undertaken. late ME. b. Brought about by one's own choice or deliberate action; self-inflicted, self-induced 1548. c. Entered into of free choice 1612. 4. Done of deliberate intent or purpose; designed, intentional 1495. b. *Law.* Of escapes: Deliberately permitted or connived at 1660. 5. Of gifts, etc.: Freely or spontaneously bestowed, rendered, or made; contributed voluntarily 1580.

1. Albeit we sweare A v. zeale, and an vn-urg'd Faith SHAKS. b. Thy v. wandring, and vnconstrayned exyle 1632. d. V. conveyances of estates in land, that is, conveyances without any consideration, such as money or marriage 1875. 2. Imagination is the first internal beginning of all V. Motion HOBBES. 3. They discover what nothing but v. blindness before had concealed JOHNSON. b. Voluntarie death ought not to be attempted of any wise man 1576. c. *V. association*,..a society which is unincorporated, but is not a partnership, in that the members are not agents for one another 1889. 4. Waste is either v., which is a crime of commission, as by pulling down a house; or it is permissive BLACKSTONE. 5. Nor is it every contribution, called v., which is according to the free will of the giver BURKE.

II. †1. Of the will: Free, unforced, unconstrained -1563. 2. Of persons: That is such of one's own accord or free choice; acting voluntarily, willingly, or spontaneously in a specified capacity; also, endowed with the faculty of willing 1594. †b. Serving as a volunteer soldier; that is a volunteer; also, composed of volunteers -1647. c. *poet.* Of a sword: Offered freely or willingly in aid of some cause 1761. †3. Willing, ready (*to* do something) -1768. 4. Of institutions: Maintained or supported solely or largely by freewill offerings or contributions, and free from State interference or control 1745. b. Of, pertaining to, concerned, or connected with voluntaryism 1834. c. Of persons: Advocating or supporting the voluntary principle as opp. to State establishment and control 1835. 5. Of muscles, etc.: Acting in response to the volition; directing or controlling voluntary movements 1788.

2. V. exiles GIBBON. c. At Aix his v. sword he drew GRAY. 4. Private or V. Schools 1837. b. The v. system..is almost universal in Australia 1891.

†III. Growing wild or naturally; of spontaneous growth -1718.

The wilde or v. Strawberries 1620.

†B. *adv.* = VOLUNTARILY *adv.* -1769.

C. *sb.* I. †1. Free will or choice -1633. 2. †a. Music added at the will of the performer to a piece played or sung -1597. b. A musical piece or movement performed spontaneously or of one's free choice, esp. by way of prelude to a more elaborate piece, song, etc. 1598. c. *esp.* A piece or solo played upon the organ before, during, or after any office of the Church; also, the music for this 1712. 3. An extempore, optional, or voluntary piece of writing or composition 1690. 4. The parting of a rider from his horse without adequate cause. Phr. *to cut a v.* = VOLUNTEER *v.* 2 b. 1863. 5. A voluntary examination 1894.

2. b. *fig.* He..ran off in a wild v. of fanciful mirth SCOTT.

II. †1. = VOLUNTEER *sb.* 1. -1670. 2. = VOLUNTEER *sb.* 2. 1609. 3. One who holds or advocates that the Church (or educational institutions) should be maintained by voluntary contributions instead of by the State 1834.

Voluntaryism (vǫˑlǒntări,izm). 1835. [f. prec.] 1. The principle or tenet that the Church and educational institutions should be supported by voluntary contributions instead of by the State. 2. A system which rests upon voluntary action or principles 1883.

Voluntaryist (vǫˑlǒntări,ist). 1842. [f. as prec. + -IST.] = VOLUNTARY C. II. 3. Also, in recent use, an advocate of voluntary military service.

Voluntative (vǫˑlǒntětiv), *a.* and *sb.* 1870. [ad. med.L. *voluntativus*, f. L. *voluntat-*, *voluntas* VOLUNTY.] A. *adj.* a. *Hebrew Gram.* Of a verbal form: Expressive of a desire; desiderative. b. Having the ability to act or accomplish at will; voluntary. B. *sb. Hebrew Gram.* A verbal form expressive of a desire to do the action denoted by the verb; a desiderative 1870.

Volunteer (vǫlǒntīˑɹ), *sb.* and *a.* Also †**-ier.** 1600. [ad. F. *volontaire*, †*voluntaire*, ad. L. *voluntarius* VOLUNTARY *a.*, with ending assim. to the suffixes -IER and -EER.] A. *sb.* 1. *Mil.* One who voluntarily offers or enrols himself for military service, in contrast to those who are under obligation to do so, or who form part of a regular army or military force. b. *spec.* A member of an organized military company or force, formed by voluntary enrolment and distinct from the regular army. In later use, a civilian forming part of the 'auxiliary forces' of a country as a member of such a body. 1642. †c. One voluntarily serving in the Navy -1720. 2. One who of his own free will takes part in any enterprise 1638. 3. *Law.* One to whom a voluntary conveyance is made; one who benefits by a deed made without valuable consideration 1744. B. *attrib.* or as *adj.* 1. a. Of troops, etc.: Consisting or composed of persons undertaking military service as volunteers 1662. b. Of persons: Serving as a volunteer in the army (†or the navy) 1649. c. Of or pertaining to a volunteer or volunteers 1724. 2. Voluntarily undertaking or performing any action or service 1661. b. Of vegetation: Growing spontaneously 1794. 3. Of services, actions, etc.: Rendered or performed voluntarily 1724.

1. a. Officers of..V. Corps 1811. c. Trailing a v. pike in the Artillery ground SHERIDAN. 2. b. V. or self-sown oats 1882. 3. I am not very fond of any v. modes of raising money for public service BURKE.

Volunteeˑr, *v.* 1755. [Back-formation from next.] 1. *intr.* To undertake military service voluntarily, esp. on a special occasion. Freq. const. *for.* 2. To offer of one's own accord *to* do something 1840. b. To be thrown from a horse without adequate cause 1890. 3. *trans.* To offer (one's services) for some special purpose or enterprise 1800. 4. To offer to undertake or perform (something) 1818. 5. To communicate (information, etc.) on one's own initiative 1839. 6. To offer to give or supply 1873.

1. John Sheffield..volunteered to serve at sea against the Dutch MACAULAY. 2. My guide volunteered to cut the steps for me TYNDALL. 5. He volunteered no information about himself GEO. ELIOT.

Volunteeˑring, *vbl. sb.* 1691. [f. VOLUNTEER *sb.*] The action of serving or offering one's services as a volunteer.

†**Volunty.** [ME. *volunte*, a. OF. *volonte*, ad. L. *voluntat-*, *voluntas* will, f. *vol-*, *velle* to will.] Will, desire, pleasure; that which one wishes or desires -1652.

Voluptuary (vǒlɒˑptiu,ări), *sb.* and *a.* 1605. [ad. L. *voluptuarius*, post-cl. form of *voluptarius*, f. *voluptas* pleasure.] A. *sb.* One who is addicted to sensuous pleasures; one given up to indulgence in luxury or the gratification of the senses; a sybarite 1610.

A good-humoured, but hard-hearted, v. SCOTT.

B. *adj.* Of, pertaining to, or characterized by sensuous or luxurious pleasures 1605.

Voluptuoˑsity. Now *rare* or *Obs.* late ME. [a. OF. *voluptuosite*, or ad. med.L. *voluptuositas*, f. L. *voluptuosus*; see next.] The quality or state of being voluptuous; voluptuousness.

Voluptuous (vǒlɒˑptiu,əs), *a.* late ME. [ad. OF. *voluptueux*, *-euse*, or L. *voluptuosus*, f. *voluptas* pleasure.] 1. Of, pertaining to, derived from, resting in or characterized by gratification of the senses, esp. in a refined or luxurious manner; marked by indulgence in sensual pleasures; luxuriously sensuous. 2. Addicted to sensual pleasure or the gratification of the senses; inclined to ease and luxury; fond of elegant or sumptuous living 1440. 3. Imparting a sense of delicious pleasure; suggestive of sensuous pleasures, esp. of a refined or luxurious kind 1816. b. Suggestive of sensuous pleasures by fullness and beauty of form 1839.

1. V. liuing, one of the thornes that choke the worde 1582. V. Feasts 1638. The luxuriant charms of v. Italy 1832. 2. The poore are not so v.: they content themselves with drie ryce, herbs, roots SIR T. HERBERT. 3. And when Music arose with its v. swell, Soft eyes look'd love to eyes which spake again BYRON. b. The v. image of a Corinthian courtezan JOWETT. Hence **Voluˑptuous-ly** *adv.*, **-ness.**

†‖**Voluta** (vǒliūˑtă). 1563. [L., prop. fem. of *volutus*, *volvere* to turn.] *Arch.* = VOLUTE *sb.* 1. -1753.

Volutation (vǫliutēˑʃən). Now *rare* or *Obs.* 1610. [ad. L. *volutation-*, *volutatio*, f. *volutare* to roll or wallow, f. *volut-*, *volvere* to roll.] The action of rolling or causing to roll; revolution combined with progression. b. Wallowing 1655.

Volute (vǒliūˑt), *sb.* 1696. [ad. L. *voluta* VOLUTA, or a. F.] 1. *Arch.* A spiral scroll forming the chief ornament of the Ionic capital and employed also in those of the Corinthian and Composite orders. 2. A spiral conformation; a convolution, twist, or turn; a thing or part having a spiral form 1756. 3. The spiral shell of a gasteropod of the genus *Voluta*; also, the animal itself 1753.

Volute (vǒliūˑt), *a.* 1845. [ad. L. *volutus*; or attrib. use of prec.] Having the form of a volute; forming a spiral curve or curves.

Voluˑted, *a.* 1801. [f. as prec. + -ED².] 1. Spirally twisted or grooved. 2. *Arch.* Furnished with a volute or spiral scroll 1810.

Volution (vǒliūˑʃən). 1610. [f. L. *volut-*, *volvere*, after *revolution*, etc.] 1. A rolling or revolving movement. 2. A spiral turn or twist;

a coil or convolution 1752. 3. A whorl of a spiral shell 1884.

‖**Volva** (vǫ·lvă). 1753. [L., f. *volvere* to roll, wrap.] *Bot.* The membranous covering which completely encloses many fungi in the early stage of growth.

Volvelle (vǫ·lvel). *Obs.* exc. *Hist.* late ME. [ad. med.L. *volvella* or *volvellum*, app. f. *volvere* to turn.] An old device consisting of one or more movable circles surrounded by other graduated or figured circles, serving to ascertain the rising and setting of the sun and moon, the state of the tides, etc.

‖**Volvox** (vǫ·lvǫks). 1798. [mod.L., f. L. *volvere.*] *Bot.* A genus of freshwater organisms having a spherical form and provided with cilia which enable them to roll over in the water; an individual of this genus.

‖**Volvulus** (vǫ·lviūlǒs). 1679. [med. or mod. L., f. L. *volvere* to turn, twist.] *Path.* A form of intestinal obstruction caused by a twisting or knotting of the bowel. †Also in pl. *volvuli.* b. With *a*: An instance of this 1758.

Vomer (vōu·məɪ). 1704. [a. L., 'ploughshare'.] 1. *Anat.* A small thin bone forming the posterior part of the partition between the nostrils in man and most vertebrate animals. 2. *Ichth.* A bone forming the front part of the roof of the mouth, and often bearing teeth 1828. 3. *Ornith.* The pygostyle 1872. Hence **Vo·merine** *a.* of or belonging to the v.; composing the v.; of teeth, situated on the v.

‖**Vomica** (vǫ·mikă). *Pl.* **vomicæ** (-isī), vomicas. 1572. [L., 'boil, ulcer', f. *vomere* to eject, vomit.] 1. †a. A vent or opening. b. A place at which water issues 1838. 2. *Path.* An ulcerous cavity or abscess in the substance of the lungs or (more rarely) some other internal organ 1693.

Vomit (vǫ·mit), *sb.* late ME. [a. AF. *vomit(e*, OF. *vomite*, or ad. L. *vomitus*, f. *vomere*; see next.] 1. The act of ejecting the contents of the stomach through the mouth. 2. Matter ejected from the stomach by vomiting. late ME. 3. An emetic. late ME.

1. Nvx vomica..causeth a strong vomite 1579. 2. *Black v.*, a blackish matter, resembling coffee grounds and due to hæmorrhage, vomited in severer cases of yellow fever; also, the disease of yellow fever itself. *fig.* (with allusion to *Prov.* xxvi. 11); Now that ye have started back from the purity of Scripture..to the old v. of your traditions MILT. 3. I have taken a v. to-day, and hope I shall be better SWIFT.

Vomit (vǫ·mit), *v.* late ME. [a. L. *vomit-*, *vomere*, or ad. *vomitare*, frequent. of *vomere* to vomit.] 1. *intr.* To bring up and eject the contents of the stomach by the mouth. 2. *trans.* To bring up and discharge (swallowed food or drink) through the mouth; to cast out (a matter or substance) in this way 1541. 3. *fig.* To eject, reject, cast *out* or *up*, esp. with abhorrence or loathing 1562. b. To give vent to or utter (abusive or objectionable language) 1592. 4. *transf.* To discharge, to give, send, or throw out copiously or with force; to send *out* or pour *forth* in a manner suggestive of vomiting 1552. 5. (All now *rare* or *Obs.*) *absol.* Of emetics: To cause vomiting 1651. b. *trans.* To cause (a person) to vomit 1662. c. Said of a person administering the emetic; or *pass.* of the patient 1684. 6. *intr.* To issue with force or violence; to rush *out*, to spout *up* 1632.

2. The fish..vomited out Jonas upon the dry land BIBLE (Douay) *Jonah* ii. 11. 3. b. All these abominable names Thou vomits forth so fluently COTTON. 4. He and his curst crew..like the sons of Vulcan, v. smoke MILT. An incredible quantity of nonsense is vomited from the press 1834. Hence **Vo·miting** *vbl. sb.* the act of ejecting the contents of the stomach through the mouth; an instance of this; †*concr.* matter which is vomited.

Vomition (vǫmi·ʃən). 1656. [a. obs. F., or ad. L. *vomition-*, *vomitio*, f. *vomere.*] The action of vomiting.

†**Vo·mitive**, *a.* and *sb.* 1580. [a. F. *vomitif*, *-ive*, ad. med.L. **vomitivus*; see VOMIT *v.* and -IVE.] A. *adj.* 1. Of medicines: Causing vomiting; vomitory; emetic -1754. 2. Of or pertaining to vomiting -1691. B. *sb.* = VOMITORY *sb.* 1. -1756.

‖**Vomito** (vǫ·mitǫ). 1833. [Sp. (and Pg.) *vómito*, ad. L. *vomitus.*] The yellow fever in its virulent form, when it is usu. accompanied by black vomit.

Vomitorium (vǫmitōᵊ·riǒm). *Pl.* **-ia.** 1754. [neut. sing. of L. *vomitorius* (cf. next); recorded only in pl.] A passage or opening in an ancient amphitheatre or theatre, leading to or from the seats. Usu. *pl.*

Vomitory (vǫ·mitŏri), *sb.* 1601. [ad. L. *vomitorium*; see prec. and next.] †1. An emetic -1753. 2. An opening, door, or passage in a theatre, playhouse, or the like, affording ingress or egress to the spectators; orig. (and usu.) = prec. 1730. 3. A funnel, vent, or other opening through which matter is emitted or discharged 1822.

2. Sixty-four *vomitories*..poured forth the immense multitude GIBBON.

Vomitory (vǫ·mitŏri), *a.* 1620. [ad. L. *vomitorius*, f. *vomere* to vomit; see -ORY [2].] 1. Of or pertaining to vomiting. 2. Efficacious in promoting vomiting; causing vomiting; emetic 1634.

Vomiturition (-iuri·ʃen). 1842. [a. F., or ad. med. or mod.L. *vomiturition-*, *vomituritio-*, **vomiturire* to desire to vomit.] Ineffectual attempts to vomit.

Voodoo (vū·dū), *sb.* 1880. [Dahomey *vodu.* Cf. VAUDOUX, HOODOO.] 1. A body of superstitious beliefs and practices, including sorcery, serpent-worship, and sacrificial rites, current among negroes and persons of negro blood in the West Indies and southern United States, and ultimately of African origin. 2. One who practises voodoo; a negro sorcerer or witch 1880. 3. *attrib.* as *v. dance, doctor, priest* 1885. Hence **Voo·doo** *v. trans.* to bewitch by means of v. arts. **Voo·dooism**, the system of beliefs and practices constituting v.; the belief in or practice of v. as a superstition or form of sorcery.

‖**Voorlooper** (vōrlō·pəɪ). *S. Afr.* 1852. [Du., f. *voor-* before + *loopen* to run.] A native boy who walks with the foremost pair of a team of oxen in order to guide them.

‖**Voortrekker** (vōrtre·kəɪ). *S. Afr.* 1878. [Du., f. *voor-* before + *trekken* TREK *v.*] One of the original Dutch emigrants into the Transvaal; a Boer pioneer.

Voracious (vŏrēⁱ·ʃəs), *a.* 1635. [f. L. *voraci-*, *vorax*, f. *vorare* to devour + -OUS.] 1. Of animals (rarely of persons, or of the throat): Eating with greediness; devouring food in large quantities; gluttonous, ravenous. Also const. *of.* 1693. b. *fig.* Of persons: Excessively greedy or eager in some desire or pursuit. Also const. *of.* 1746. c. *transf.* Of things 1767. 2. Characterized by voracity or greediness 1635. b. *fig.* Of desires, interests, etc.: Insatiable 1712.

1. The v. and highly organized tribe of sharks 1855. b. A v. reader 1883. 2. He had such a v. appetite that he would take with indifference either medicine or food 1800. b. His appetite for argument was..v. 1854. Hence **Vora·cious-ly** *adv.*, **-ness.**

Voracity (vŏræ·sĭti). 1526. [a. F. *voracité*, or ad. L. *voracitas*, f. *voraci-*, *vorax*; see prec. and -ITY.] The quality or character of being voracious; greediness in eating.

†**Vora·ginous**, *a.* 1624. [ad. L. *voraginosus*, f. *voragin-*, *vorago.*] 1. Of or belonging to an abyss or whirlpool; resembling a chasm or gulf -1747. 2. Devouring, voracious -1691.

‖**Vorago** (vŏrēⁱ·go). Now *rare.* 1654. [L., f. *vorare* to devour.] An abyss, gulf, or chasm.

Vorant (vōᵊ·rănt), *a.* 1618. [ad. L. *vorant-*, *vorans*, *vorare* to devour.] †1. Devouring (*rare*) -1639. 2. *Her.* Of animals: Devouring or swallowing something 1766.

-vorous, *suffix*, forming adjs., after L. *-vorus* devouring, eating, in *carnivorus, omnivorus.* Examples are *carnivorous, herbivorous, omnivorous.*

Vortex (vǫ·ɹteks). *Pl.* **vortices** (-isīz). 1652. [a. L. (var. of *vertex*), f. *vort-*, *vertere* to turn.] 1. a. In older theories of the universe (esp. that of Descartes), a supposed rotatory movement of cosmic matter round a centre or axis, regarded as accounting for the origin or phenomena of the terrestrial and other systems; a body of such matter rapidly carried round in a continuous whirl 1653. b. In mod. scientific use: A rapid movement of particles of matter round an axis; a whirl of atoms, fluid, or vapour 1847. 2. An eddying or whirling mass of fire or flame 1652. 3. A whirl or swirling mass of water; a strong eddy or whirlpool 1704. 4. A violent eddy or whirl of the air; a whirlwind or cyclone, or the central portion of this 1700. 5. *fig.* A state or condition of human affairs or interests comparable to a whirl or eddy by reason of rush or excitement, rapid change, or absorbing effect 1761. b. A constant round *of* excitement or pleasure 1792. c. A situation into which persons or things are steadily drawn, or from which they cannot escape 1779.

5. To be drawn into the v. of New York politics W. IRVING. b. She..lived in a v. of gaiety 1877. c. Whirled round again in the v. of dissipation and gaming 1779.

attrib. **v. turbine** or **wheel**, a turbine in which the water enters tangentially at the circumference and is discharged at the centre.

Vortical (vǭ·ɹtikăl), *a.* 1653. [f. L. *vortic-*, *vortex* VORTEX + -AL.] 1. Of motion: Like that of a vortex; rotating, eddying, whirling. 2. Moving in a vortex; whirling round 1728. Hence **Vo·rtically** *adv.*

‖**Vorticella** (vǭɹtise·lă). 1787. [mod.L., dim. of L. *vortic-*, *vortex* VORTEX.] *Zool.* The typical genus of *Vorticellidæ*, a family of sedentary infusorians; an individual belonging to this genus; a bell-animalcule. So **Vortice·llid**, an individual belonging to the *Vorticellidæ*.

Vorticist (vǭ·ɹtisist). 1866. [f. L. *vortici-*, VORTEX + -IST.] 1. An advocate of the theory of vortices (VORTEX 1). 2. *Painting*, etc. One of a school of artists who emphasize the expression of movement and activity and are characterized by a dynamic quality; also *attrib.* 1915. So **Vo·rticism.**

Vorticose (vǭ·ɹtikōᵘs), *a.* 1783. [ad. L. *vorticosus*, f. *vortic-*, *vortex*; see -OSE.] 1. Of motion: = VORTICAL *a.* 1. 2. Resembling a vortex 1870.

Vorticular (vǭɹti·kiŭlăɪ), *a.* 1838. [Cf. prec. and -ULAR.] Of motion: Vortical, vorticose.

Vortiginous (vǫɹti·dʒinəs), *a.* 1671. [f. L. *vortigin-*, *vortigo*, var. of *vertigo*; see VERTIGINOUS *a.*] 1. Of motion: Vortical, vorticular. 2. Moving in a vortex or vortices; rushing in whirls or eddies 1791.

Votal (vōᵘ·tăl), *a.* 1610. [f. L. *votum* vow, wish + -AL.] †1. Existing in will or wish, though not carried out in fact -1624. 2. Of the nature of a vow or solemn engagement 1632. †3. Bound by vows; devoted to a religious life; appropriate to one under vows -1656. 4. Of offerings: Votive 1846.

2. Strong objections to take any further v. obligations 1855.

Votaress (vōᵘ·tărés). 1589. [f. VOTARY + -ESS. See also VOTRESS.] A female votary; *esp.* a woman devoted to a religious life or to a special saint.

Votarist (vōᵘ·tărist). 1603. [Cf. next and -IST.] One bound by a vow; a devotee, votary.

Votary (vōᵘ·tări), *sb.* 1546. [f. L. *vot-*, *vovere* to vow + -ARY [1].] I. 1. One who is bound by vows to a religious life; a monk or nun. b. One who has made or is bound by a special vow 1588. 2. One who is devoted to a particular religion, or to some form of worship or religious observance 1704. b. A devout worshipper 1823. 3. A devoted or zealous worshipper of God, Christ, a saint, etc. 1690.

1. b. The votarie that will not cut his haire, Vntill the expiration of his vow 1596. 3. Hear, Goddess, hear thy V. PRIOR.

II. 1. One who is devoted or passionately addicted to some particular pursuit, occupation, study, aim, etc. 1591. 2. A devoted adherent or admirer of some person, institution, etc. 1647.

1. We know..You are already loues firme v. SHAKS.

†**Votary**, *a.* 1564. [Cf. prec.] 1. Consecrated by a vow; subject to vows -1656. 2. Of the nature of a vow -1612.

Votation (votēⁱ·ʃən). 1816. [f. VOTE *v.* + -ATION.] The action of voting in an election or at a meeting.

Vote (vōᵘt), *sb.* 1460. [ad. L. *votum* vow, prop. pa. pple. neut. of *vovere.*] †I. 1. A vow -1715. 2. A prayer -1664. 3. An ardent wish or desire -1667. II. 1. An indication, by some approved method, of one's opinion or choice on a matter under discussion; an intimation that one approves or disapproves, accepts or rejects, a proposal, motion, candidate for office, or the like 1460. **b.** A means of signifying choice, approval, etc.; a voting tablet or ticket 1817. **2.** The collective opinion or assent of an assembly or body of persons 1582. **b.** In phr. *To put to the v.*, to submit to the decision of a meeting. Similarly (of a question), *to go to the v.* 1599. **c.** The collective support of a special number or class of persons in a deliberative decision, election, etc. 1851. **3.** The right or privilege of exercising the suffrage; esp. in phr. *to have a v.* 1585. †**b.** A person regarded merely as an embodiment of the right to vote; also, a person possessing the right to vote; a voter -1806. **c.** The aggregate of voters, esp. of a certain class 1888. **4.** A resolution or decision passed by, or carried in, an assembly as the result of voting; an expression of opinion formally adopted by a meeting of any kind 1641. †**5.** A declaration or statement of opinion -1680.

1. *Casting v.*: see CASTING *ppl. a.* 2. **b.** *To give (record) a v.* The citizens of each tribe cast their votes of condemnation or acquittal into one urn 1838. 2. Phr. *To take a v.*, to ascertain the opinion of a meeting by formal reference. 3. The common people ceased to have votes 1782. **b.** To enter the votes' houses up and down WOLCOT. 4. A v. of thanks DICKENS. Marlborough was..condemned as guilty by a v. of the House of Commons 1874. A v. of censure 1881.

Comb.: **V. Office**, the office from which Parliamentary bills and papers are issued to members of the House of Commons.

Vote (vōᵘt), *v.* 1533. [f. L. *vot-*, *vovere* to vow, desire, or ad. med.L. *votare* to devote by a vow, from the same stem.] **1.** *refl.* and *trans.* To assign by a vow; to devote religiously. Now *rare.* **2.** *intr.* To give a vote; to express a choice or preference by ballot or other approved means 1552. **3.** *trans.* Of assemblies, etc.: To choose, elect, enact, or establish by vote; to ratify or determine by formal expression of will 1568. **4.** *To v. down*, to defeat, put down, or suppress by a vote 1642. **5.** To grant, allow, or confer by vote 1710. **6.** To declare by common assent; hence *gen.* to characterize by an expression of opinion; to pronounce 1663. **b.** *colloq.* To propose, suggest 1814.

2. The right to v. makes a safety-valve of every voter 1887. 3. They v. a message to their absent chief DRYDEN. 6. He..spoke no more during the whole debate, which I am sure he was ready to v. a bore MME D'ARBLAY. 7. *U.S.* To influence or control in voting; also, to present for voting, to record the votes of (electors) 1859.

Voter (vōᵘ·təɹ). 1578. [f. prec.] One who has a right to vote; *esp.* an elector. **b.** One who gives a vote (*rare*) 1701.

Voting (vōᵘ·tiŋ), *vbl. sb.* 1575. [f. VOTE *v.* + -ING [1].] The action of giving a vote.

attrib.: v.-paper, a paper on which a vote is recorded; a ballot-paper.

†**Vo·tist.** *rare.* 1613. [f. VOTE *sb.* or *v.* + -IST.] One who makes a vow; a votary -1711.

Votive (vōᵘ·tiv), *a.* 1611. [ad. L. *votivus*, f. *votum* VOTE *sb.*] **1.** Dedicated, consecrated, offered, erected, etc. in consequence of or in fulfilment of a vow. **b.** Observed, practised undertaken, etc. in consequence of a vow 1628. **2.** Consisting in or expressive of a vow, desire, or wish 1597. **3.** *V. mass*, a special or extraordinary mass said at the personal desire of the priest 1738.

1. The jewels given as v. offerings 1789. V. pictures 1841. **b.** Votiue Abstinence 1628. 2. Fanes..that echoed to the v. strains WORDSW. 3. Masses..called v. masses, because said according to the votum, i. e. the intention or desire of the celebrant 1881. Hence **Vo·tively** *adv.*

Votress (vōᵘ·trės). 1590. [var. of VOTARESS.] A female votary.

The imperiall Votresse passed on, In maiden meditation, fancy-free SHAKS.

Vouch, *sb.* 1603. [f. next.] †**1.** = VOUCHER *sb.*[1] 1. -1621. **2.** An assertion, allegation, or declaration; a formal statement or attestation of truth or fact. Now chiefly *colloq.* 1603.

2. *Oth.* II. i. 147.

Vouch (vautʃ), *v.* ME. [a. AF. and OF. *vocher, voucher* to call, summon, invoke, claim, etc., obscurely ad. L. *vocare* to call.] **1.** *trans.* Law. *To v. to warrant* or *to* (also †*for*) *warranty*, to cite, call, or summon (a person) into court to give warranty of title. Also *ellipt.* (with omission of *to warrant*). **b.** With *over.* Of a vouchee: To cite (another person) into court in his stead. Also *absol.* 1511. **2.** To take or call (a person) to witness. late ME. **b.** To cite or appeal to (authority, example, doctrine, authors, works, etc.) in support of one's views or statements or as justification for a course of action 1531. **3.** To allege, assert, affirm, or declare. Also const. *upon* or *against* (a person). Now *rare* or *Obs.* late ME. **4.** To assert or affirm to be true or according to fact; to attest or certify. Also const. *against* (a person). 1591. **5.** To support or uphold by satisfactory evidence; to back with proofs of a practical or substantial character 1579. **b.** To attest or substantiate by written evidence 1745. **6.** To become sponsor for (a person or thing). *rare.* 1590. **b.** To affirm or guarantee (the truth of a statement) 1607. **7.** *intr.* with *for.* **a.** To speak or bear witness on behalf of (a person); to be surety or sponsor for 1687. **b.** Of things: To supply evidence or assurance of (some fact) 1755. **c.** To give personal assurance of the truth or accuracy of (a statement or fact) 1777. †**8.** To guarantee the title to or legal possession of (something). *rare.* -1661. †**9.** = VOUCHSAFE *v.*, in various senses -1848.

1. If the Heir at Common Law be vouched for Warranty 1741. **b.** He vouches the tenant in tail, who vouches over the common vouchee BLACKSTONE. 2. **b.** A solicitor cannot v. his privilege in such a case as this 1885. 3. What can you v. against him, Signor Lucio? SHAKS. 4. The saying of Pliny..that there is no lie so impudent which is not vouched by authority 1750. Peter vouches that he had seen our Saviour 1806. 5. He afterwards honourably vouched his words by his deeds 1828. **b.** All expenses so claimed must be strictly vouched 1886. 6. **b.** *Cor.* V. vi. 5. 7. **c.** I dare swear the Lady will v. for the truth of every word of it SHERIDAN. 8. *Ham.* V. i. 117.

Vouchee (vautʃī·). 1485. [f. prec. + -EE.] **1.** *Law.* The person vouched or summoned into court to give warranty of title. **2.** A person cited or appealed to as an authority for some fact or statement, or in evidence of some assertion 1654.

1. *Common v.*; The cryer of the court (who, from being frequently thus vouched, is called the common v.) BLACKSTONE.

Voucher (vau·tʃəɹ), *sb.*[1] 1531. [a. AF. *voucher* VOUCH *v.*; see -ER [4].] **1.** *Law.* The summoning of a person into court to warrant the title to a property. **2.** *transf.* A piece of evidence; a fact, circumstance, or thing serving to confirm or prove something; a guarantee 1611. **b.** A written document or note, or other material evidence, serving to attest the correctness of accounts or monetary transactions, to prove the delivery of goods or valuables, etc. 1696. **c.** A written warrant or attestation 1796.

1. *V. over*: cf. VOUCH *v.* 1 b. *Double v.*; You shall finde in bookes a recouery..with a double V., and that is when the Vouchee voucheth over COKE. 2. It has no V. but the Epistles of Phalaris, the very Book that 's under debate BENTLEY.

Voucher (vau·tʃəɹ), *sb.*[2] 1612. [f. VOUCH *v.* + -ER [1].] **1.** One who vouches for the truth or correctness of a fact or statement; an author or literary work serving this purpose. **b.** One who vouches for the good faith or respectability of another, or who undertakes to guarantee some procedure 1667. **c.** *transf.* Of things 1718. †**2.** *Law.* **a.** = VOUCHEE 1. **b.** = VOUCHOR. -1672.

1. They would make him a V. of all their Falshood PENN. **b.** All the great Writers of that Age..stand up together as Vouchers for one another's Reputation ADDISON.

Vouchor. *rare.* 1628. [AF., f. *voucher* VOUCH *v.*] One who calls another into court to warrant a title.

Vouchsafe (vautʃsēⁱ·f), *v.* ME. [f. VOUCH *v.* + SAFE *a.* used predic. In early use often treated as two words; e.g. *I vouche hur safe.*] **I.** †**1.** *trans.* To confer or bestow (some thing, favour, or benefit) *on* a person -1671. **2.** To give, grant, or bestow in a gracious or condescending manner. late ME. **b.** To deign or condescend to give (a word, answer, etc.) in reply or by way of friendly notice 1597. †**3. a.** To condescend to engage in (some pursuit) -1667. **b.** To deign to accept -1607. **c.** To be prepared to bear or sustain. SHAKS. †**4.** To acknowledge (a person) in some favourable relationship or manner -1634.

2. Nature indeed vouchsafes, for our delight, The sweet vicissitudes of day and night COWPER. **b.** V. a word, yong sister, but one word SHAKS. 3. **a.** Nor other strife with them do I voutsafe MILT. **b.** *Timon* I. i. 152.

II. †**1.** To grant, permit, or allow, as an act of grace or condescension -1639. **2.** To show a gracious readiness or willingness, to condescend or deign, *to* do something ME. Now only *literary.* †**3.** *ellipt.* To grant; to agree graciously; to condescend -1736.

1. *Jul. C.* III. i. 130. 2. She did not even v. to answer him 1880. 3. If you pleased, or would v., or condescend, or think proper, I would rather that you would..charge only five per cent. SHERIDAN.

Vouchsafement (vautʃsēⁱ·fmĕnt). 1628. [f. prec. + -MENT.] **1.** An act of condescension, grace, or favour; a boon, benefit, or blessing. **2.** The action of conferring or granting some boon, favour, advantage, etc. 1666.

‖**Voussoir** (vū·swǫɹ, -aɪ). ME. [a. OF. *vausoir, vaussoir*, etc., F. *voussoir*:—pop. L. **volsorium*, f. **volsum*, L. *volvere* to turn. Reintroduced in the 18th c.] One of the stones which form part of an arch or vault, usu. having the sides slightly inclined towards each other.

Vow (vau), *sb.* ME. [a. AF. *vu(u, vou, vo* (F. *vœu*):—L. *votum* VOTE *sb.*] **1.** A solemn promise made to God, or to any deity or saint, to perform some act or make some gift or sacrifice in return for some special favour; more generally, a solemn engagement, undertaking, or resolve to achieve something or to act in a certain way. **2.** *Eccl.* A solemn engagement to devote oneself to a religious life of a definite nature, such as that of a monastic or conventual order. Freq. in pl.; *to take the vows*, to enter a religious order. late ME. **3.** A solemn promise of fidelity or faithful attachment 1590. **4.** An earnest wish or desire; a prayer; a supplication 1563. **5.** A solemn affirmation or asseveration 1593. †**6.** A votive offering (*rare*) -1700.

1. Holy vows of chastity TENNYSON. The v. of Poverty was turned into a stern reality J. R. GREEN. (The three monastic vows are of poverty, chastity, and obedience.) Phr. *To make, hold, keep, pay a v., to break a v.*; Thou shalt make thy prayer vnto him,.. and thou shalt rendre thy vowes BIBLE (Geneva) *Job* xxii. 27. 3. They stood beside the altar, and their vows were exchanged 1829. 4. They haue nothing more in their vowes, then her Maiesties ruine 1600. 5. *Wint. T.* I. ii. 47.

Vow (vau), *v.*[1] ME. [ad. OF. *vouer, vower* (F. *vouer*), f. *vou* VOW *sb.*] **1.** *trans.* To promise or undertake solemnly, *spec.* by a vow to a deity or saint. **2.** To dedicate, consecrate, or devote *to* some person or service 1526. **3.** To make a solemn resolve or threat to inflict (injury), exact (vengeance), harbour (hatred), etc. 1592. **4.** *intr.* To make a vow or solemn undertaking; to bind oneself by a vow ME.

1. Vowing to do what there is no Use in doing, is trifling with our Creator 1768. Vowing large sacrifice COWPER. To pray the prayer, and v. the vow SCOTT. 2. He to heaven was vowed WORDSW. 3. The Empress..could not forbear vowing revenge SWIFT. 4. It is better that thou shuldest not vowe, then that thou shuldest vowe and not paye it BIBLE (Geneva) *Eccl.* v. 4.

Vow, *v.*[2] ME. [Aphetic f. AVOW *v.*[1]] †**1.** *trans.* To acknowledge, admit -1560. **2.** To affirm or assert solemnly; to asseverate ME. **b.** *I vow*, used to strengthen an assertion 1590. In later use chiefly *U.S.* **c.** To make solemn assertion of (a feeling or quality) 1742.

2. She vowed that it was a delightful ball THACKERAY. **b.** I v., child, you are vastly handsome GOLDSM. **c.** To her again they v. their truth GRAY.

Vowel (vau·ĕl), *sb.* ME. [a. OF. *vouel*:— L. *vocalem* or *vocale*, *vocalis* VOCAL *a.*] A sound produced by the vibrations of the vocal cords; a letter or character representing such a sound (as *a, e, i*, etc.).

At meetings young men should be Mutes, and old men Vowels 1657. A v. may be defined as voice (voiced breath) modified by some definite configuration of the super-glottal passages, but without audible friction (which would make it into a consonant) SWEET.

attrib. and *Comb.*: **v.-point**, a sign used to indicate a vowel in certain (esp. the Semitic) alphabets; also as *v. trans.* to supply with points to indicate vowels.

Vowel (vau·ĕl), *v.* 1597. [f. prec.] †**1. a.** *intr.* To utter the vowels in singing. **b.** *trans.*

To sing with vowel-articulation. -1646. †2. *trans.* To convert into a vowel; to vocalize 1611. 3. To supply with vowels or vowel-points 1681. †4. *slang.* To pay (a creditor) with an I O U. -1796.

Vowelism (vau·ĕliz'm). 1842. [f. VOWEL *sb.* + -ISM.] A system of vowel-sounds; articulation in respect of vowels.

Vowelize (vau·ĕləiz), *v.* 1816. [f. as prec. + -IZE.] 1. *trans.* To modify or produce by means of vowel-sounds. 2. To render vocalic 1867. 3. To supply with vowel-points or signs representing vowels 1883.

Vowelled (vau·ĕld), *ppl. a.* 1662. [f. VOWEL *sb.* or *v.* + -ED.] Of language or words: Supplied or provided with vowels, esp. to an unusual extent. b. Having vowels of a specified kind or quality 1783.

Vower (vau·əɹ). 1546. [f. VOW *v.* + -ER[1].] One who makes a vow, or has taken vows.

Vowess (vau·ės). Now *Hist.* or *arch.* 1506. [Cf. prec. and -ESS.] 1. A woman, *esp.* a widow, who has taken a vow of chastity for the remainder of her life. 2. A nun 1533.

†**Vow·son.** ME. [Aphetic f. *avowson* ADVOWSON.] Advowson, patronage -1570.

‖**Vox** (vǫks). 1550. [L., 'voice'.] 1. *Vox populi*, the voice of the people; expressed general opinion; common talk or rumour. 2. *V. angelica, v. humana*, varieties of organ-stops imitative of vocal sounds 1726.

Voyage (voi·ėdʒ), *sb.* [ME. *ve(i)age, vayage, voiage*, a. AF., OF. (F. *voyage*):—L. *viaticum* provision for a journey, VIATICUM.] 1. An act of travelling (†or transit), a journey (†or passage), by which one goes from one place to another. Now *rare.* †b. A pilgrimage -1518. †2. A journey or expedition undertaken with a military purpose; a warlike enterprise or undertaking -1686. †3. An enterprise of a private character (in early use implying the making of a journey) -1611. 4. A journey by sea or water from one place to another (usu. to some distant place or country); a course or spell of sailing or navigation, *spec.* one in which a return is made to the starting-point; a cruise ME. b. A flight through the air (or through space); *esp.* a trip in a balloon or airship 1667. 5. Used *fig.* (in senses 1 or 4) to denote the course of human life (or some part of it) or the fate of persons after death. late ME. 6. A written account of a voyage 1587.

1. The utmost extent of her voyages [from home] had been about two and a half miles COBBETT. 2. †*V. royal*, an expedition undertaken by a king in person. 4. b. So stears the prudent Crane Her annual Voiage, born on Windes MILT. 5. *Jul. C.* IV. iii. 220.

Voyage (voi·ėdʒ), *v.* 1477. [ad. F. *voyager*, or f. prec.] 1. *intr.* To journey by land; to travel. Now *rare.* 2. To go by sea; to sail or cruise; to make a voyage or voyages 1604. b. *transf.* of things: To move through the water or air 1834. 3. *trans.* To cross or travel over; to traverse; to sail over or on 1667.

2. *fig.* His..silent face, The marble index of a mind for ever Voyaging through strange seas of Thought, alone WORDSW. b. Grand clouds still voyaged in the sky STEVENSON. 3. Like far-off music, voyaging the breeze COLERIDGE.

Voyageable (voi·ėdʒăb'l), *a.* 1819. [f. prec. + -ABLE.] That can be sailed over; navigable.

Voyager (voi·ėdʒəɹ). 1477. [ad. OF. *veaigier, voi-, voyag(i)er*, or f. VOYAGE *v.* + -ER[1].] 1. One who journeys; a traveller by land. 2. One who goes upon or takes part in a voyage or voyages by sea; a navigator 1622.

‖**Voyageur** (vwayaʒȫr). 1809. [F.; see prec.] In Canada, a man employed by the fur companies in carrying goods to and from the trading posts on the lakes and rivers a Canadian boatman.

Vraic (vrēk). 1610. [F. dial.; cf. VAREC, WRACK *sb.*[2] 3.] A seaweed found in the Channel Islands, used for fuel and manure.

‖**Vraisemblance** (vręsaṅblāṅs). 1831. [F., f. *vrai* + *semblance.*] 1. Verisimilitude. 2. A representation, picture 1853.

Vril. 1871. [Coined by Bulwer-Lytton.] A mysterious force discovered by the imaginary people described in Bulwer-Lytton's *The Coming Race* (1871).

‖**Vrouw, vrow** (vrau). 1620. [Du. and Flem.] A (Dutch) woman, matron, goodwife.

Vug (vɒg). 1818. [ad. Cornish *vooga.*] *Cornish mining.* A cavity in a rock; a cave, a hollow. Hence **Vu·ggy** *a.* full of cavities.

Vulcan (vɒ·lkăn). 1513. [ad. L. *Vulcanus.*] I. 1. *Rom. Myth.* The god of fire and of metal-working, corresponding to the Greek Hephæstus; the lame son of Jupiter and Juno, and the husband of Venus. b. *fig.* A lame slow-moving person 1682. 2. *transf.* A blacksmith; an iron-worker 1638. 3. A planet supposed to have its orbit between the Sun and Mercury 1870.

2. His Sire, the blear-ey'd V. of a Shop DRYDEN.

II. †1. A volcano -1707. 2. Fire; a fire. Chiefly *poet.* 1674.

Vulcanian (vɒlkēⁱ·niăn), *a.* 1602. [f. L. *Vulcanius*, f. *Vulcanus* VULCAN.] 1. Of, pertaining to, characteristic of, or associated with Vulcan. b. Fashioned or forged by Vulcan 1603. 2. Sprung from or related to Vulcan 1630. 3. Volcanic 1656. 4. = PLUTONIAN *a.* 2. 1840.

Vulcanic (vɒlkæ·nik), *a.* 1774. [In sense 1, ad. F. *vulcanique.* In sense 2, f. L. *Vulcanus* VULCAN.] 1. = VOLCANIC *a.* 2 b. 2. (With initial capital.) Of, belonging to, or having the character of Vulcan 1807. b. Of or pertaining to fire; fiery 1866.

Vulcanicity (vɒlkăni·sĭti). 1873. [f. prec. + -ITY.] 1. = VOLCANICITY. 2. The study of volcanic action 1879.

Vulcanism (vɒ·lkăniz'm). 1877. [ad. F. *vulcanisme*, var. of *volcanisme.*] Volcanic action or condition.

Vulcanist (vɒ·lkănist). 1593. [In early use f. VULCAN + -IST. In sense 2, ad. F. *vulcaniste*, var. of *volcaniste.*] †1. One who works by fire; *spec.* an alchemist, a blacksmith -1603. 2. = VOLCANIST 1. 1802.

Vulcanite (vɒ·lkănəit). 1836. [f. VULCAN + -ITE[1].] †1. Pyroxene -1840. 2. A preparation of india-rubber and sulphur hardened by exposure to intense heat; ebonite 1860. b. *attrib.* Made of vulcanite 1866.

Vulcanization (vɒlkănəizēⁱ·ʃən). 1846. [f. next.] The method or process of treating crude india-rubber with sulphur and subjecting it to intense heat, by means of which it is rendered more durable and made adaptable for various purposes.

Vulcanize (vɒ·lkănəiz), *v.* 1827. [f. VULCAN.] 1. *trans.* To commit to the flames (*rare*). 2. To subject (india-rubber, etc.) to the process of vulcanization 1846. 3. *intr.* To undergo vulcanization 1890. Hence **Vu·lcanizer**, one who or that which vulcanizes; *esp.* the apparatus used in vulcanizing india-rubber.

Vulcano·logy. 1858. [f. *vulcan-* as in VULCANIC, etc. + -OLOGY.] The science or scientific study of volcanoes. So **Vulcanolo·gical** *a.* **Vulcano·logist.**

Vulgar (vɒ·lgăɹ), *sb.* late ME. [absol. use of next.] †1. The common language of a country; the vernacular -1665. 2. †a. *pl.* Persons belonging to the ordinary or common class of the community -1678. b. A person not reckoned as belonging to good society 1763. 3. *The v.*, the common people 1590. †4. *pl.* Sentences or passages in English to be translated into Latin as a school-exercise -1612. †5. = VULGATE *sb.* 1 b. -1711.

1. Translations into the v. 1611. 2. a. For these vile vulgars are extreamly proud CHAPMAN. b. A Mr. Brereton (a sad v.) 1767.

Vulgar (vɒ·lgăɹ), *a.* late ME. [ad. L. *vulgaris*, f. *vulgus* the common people.] I. 1. Employed in common or ordinary reckoning of time, distance, etc.; esp., in later use, *v. era*, the ordinary Christian era. b. *V. fraction*: see FRACTION *sb.* 5. 1674. †c. *V. arithmetic*, ordinary arithmetic as opp. to *decimal* -1728. 2. In common or general use; common, customary, ordinary. late ME. †b. Used to designate the Vulgate version of the Bible -1823. 3. Of language or speech: Ordinary, vernacular. Now *arch.* 1513. b. Qualifying the name of the language 1483. 4. Of words or names: Employed in ordinary speech; common, familiar 1676. 5. Common or customary in respect of the use or understanding of language, words, or ideas 1553. 6. Commonly current or prevalent, generally or widely disseminated, as a matter of knowledge, assertion, or opinion 1549. 7. Of or pertaining to the common people 1597.

2. The v. Method of Grammar-Schools LOCKE. b. The v. Latine interpretation, of the olde Testament 1583. 3. To be instructed in their Duties in the known or v. Tongue STEELE. b. This in v. English may be called a corner 1766. 5. By a Month, in the v. way of speaking, is meant 30 Days 1696. 6. The v. cry against the Dutch MACAULAY. This mode of interpreting Scripture is fatal to the v. notion of its verbal inspiration M. ARNOLD. One of the vulgarest fallacies of statecraft 1879. 7. An habitation giddy and vnsure Hath he that buildeth on the v. heart SHAKS.

II. 1. Of persons: Belonging to the ordinary or common class in the community; plebeian 1530. 2. Of the common or usual kind; of an ordinary commonplace character 1555. 3. Of an ordinary unartificial type; not refined or advanced beyond the common 1580. †4. Common in respect of use or association -1602. 5. Having a common and offensively mean character; coarsely commonplace; lacking in refinement or good taste. 1643. Now the only sense in ordinary colloq. use.

1. Superior to the v. Herd PRIOR. 2. Copper mettall, adorned with v. precious stones 1617. Yet shall he mount,..Beyond the limits of a v. fate GRAY. 4. Be thou familiar; but by no meanes v. SHAKS. 5. The mean malice of the same V. Scribler MARVELL. A coarse, v. spirit KINGLAKE. His features were v., his lips thick and coarse 1846. The v. sort of trade which is carried on by lending money JOWETT. Mean little houses and v. streets 1905. Hence **Vu·lgar-ly** *adv.*, **-ness** (now *rare* or *Obs.*).

Vulgarian (vɒlgēᵊ·riăn), *a.* and *sb.* 1650. [f. prec. + -IAN.] A. *adj.* = VULGAR *a.* B. *sb.* A vulgar person; freq. a well-to-do or rich person of vulgar manners 1804.

Vulgarism (vɒ·lgăriz'm). 1644. [f. VULGAR *a.* + -ISM.] †1. A common or ordinary expression. 2. A vulgar phrase or expression; a colloquialism of a low or unrefined character 1746. 3. Vulgarity; a vulgar action, practice, habit, etc. 1749.

2. She leads him and his mother (to use a v.) a devil of a life MRS. SHELLEY.

Vulgarity (vɒlgæ·rĭti). 1579. [ad. L. (post-classical) *vulgaritas* the mass or multitude, or f. VULGAR *a.* + -ITY.] †1. The commonalty; the common people -1659. †b. The ordinary sort or run (*of* a class, etc.) -1681. †2. The quality of being usual, ordinary, or commonplace; an instance of this -1716. 3. The quality of being vulgar, unrefined, or coarse; an instance of this 1774.

3. The ignorant zealotry and sordid v. of the leaders of the day! COLERIDGE.

Vulgarization (vɒlgărəizēⁱ·ʃən). 1656. [See next and -ATION. Cf. F. *vulgarisation*, etc.] 1. The action of making usual or common; the process of rendering familiar or popular. 2. The action or process of rendering coarse or unrefined 1819.

Vulgarize (vɒ·lgărəiz), *v.* 1605. [f. VULGAR *a.* + -IZE.] 1. *intr.* To act in a vulgar manner; to become vulgar. 2. *trans.* To make common or popular; to reduce to the level of something usual or ordinary 1709. 3. To make vulgar or commonplace; to debase, degrade 1756.

3. They vulgarise and degrade whatever is interesting or sacred to the mind HAZLITT.

Vulgate (vɒ·lgĕt), *a.* and *sb.* 1609. [ad. L. *vulgata* (sc. *editio* or *lectio*), and *vulgatus* (sc. *textus*), pa. pple. of *vulgare*, f. *vulgus* the common people.] A. *adj.* 1. In common use as a version of the Bible (or portion of this); occurring in one of these versions. 2. Forming (part of) the common or usual version of a literary work 1861. B. *sb.* with *the.* 1. a. The old Italic version of the Bible, preceding that of St. Jerome 1728. b. The Latin version of the Bible made by St. Jerome (completed in 405) 1728. c. The usual or received text or version of the Bible or of some portion of this 1815. d. with *a* and *pl.* An edition of the Vulgate 1865. 2. The ordinary reading in a text; the ordinary text of a work or author 1861. 3. Common or colloquial speech 1855.

||**Vulgo** (vʊ·lgo), *adv.* 1623. [L. adv., abl. of *vulgus*.] Commonly, popularly.

||**Vulgus**[1] (vʊ·lgŏs). 1687. [L.] The common people; the ordinary ruck.

||**Vulgus**[2] (vʊ·lgŏs). 1857. [prob. alteration of *vulgars*; see VULGAR *sb.* 4.] In some public schools, a short set of Latin verses on a given subject.

Vulnerable (vʊ·lnĕrăb'l), *a.* 1605. [ad. late L. *vulnerabilis*, f. *vulnerare*, f. *vulner-*, *vulnus* wound.] †1. Having power to wound; wounding (*rare*) –1609. 2. That may be wounded; susceptible of receiving wounds or physical injury 1605. b. *fig.* Open to attack or injury of a non-physical nature 1678. 3. Of places, etc.: Open to attack or assault by armed forces; liable to be taken or entered in this way 1790. b. *Contract Bridge.* Of a side: That has won one game, and is therefore liable to heavier 'penalties' if its 'contract' is not fulfilled 1927.

1. To throw the V. and Ineuitable darte 1609. 2. Let fall thy blade on v. Crests, I beare a charmed Life SHAKS. b. Yet even calumny is sagacious enough to discover and to attack the most v. part GIBBON. 3. Every v. point was guarded 1800. She felt herself v. in Ireland, and on the Scottish border MOTLEY. Hence **Vulnerabi·lity, Vu·lnerableness**, the quality or state of being v. **Vu·lnerably** *adv.*

Vulnerary (vʊ·lnĕrări), *a.* and *sb.* 1599. [ad. L. *vulnerarius*, f. *vulner-*, *vulnus* wound; see -ARY.] A. *adj.* 1. Useful in healing wounds; curative in respect of external injuries. 2. Causing a wound or wounds; wounding 1615.

1. Let him drinck a vulnerarye potione 1599. The Flowers are v.; the Seed pectoral 1712.

B. *sb.* Any preparation, plant, or drug used in the cure of wounds 1601.

†**Vu·lnerate**, *v.* 1599. [f. L. *vulnerat-*, *vulnerare* to wound.] *trans.* To wound. Also *Her.* –1750. So †**Vulnera·tion**, the action of wounding; the fact of being wounded –1688.

Vulpanser (vʊ·lpænsəɹ). 1706. [mod.L., f. *vulpes* fox + *anser* goose, after Gr. χηναλώπηξ.] *Ornith.* The sheldrake (*Anas tadorna*).

Vulpic (vʊ·lpik), *a.* 1886. [f. L. *vulpina* + -IC.] *Chem.* In *v. acid*, an acid occurring in the lichen *Cetraria vulpina*, and extracted from this or obtained artificially.

Vulpicidal (vʊlpisəi·dăl), *a.* Also **vulpe-**. 1826. [f. next + -AL.] Committing or taking part in, connected with, or of the nature of vulpicide.

Vulpicide[1] (vʊ·lpisəid). Also **vulpe-**. 1826. [f. L. *vulpi-*, *vulpes*, fox + -CIDE 1.] One who kills a fox otherwise than by hunting it with hounds.

Vu·lpicide[2]. Also **vulpe-**. 1873. [f. as prec. + -CIDE 2.] The act of killing a fox otherwise than by hunting it with hounds.

Vulpine (vʊ·lpəin), *a.* 1628. [ad. L. *vulpinus*, f. *vulpes*; see -INE[1].] 1. Characteristic of a fox; similar to that of a fox. 2. Resembling a fox; *spec.* in *V. Opossum* or *Phalanger* 1789. b. *fig.* Cunning, sly 1830. 3. Consisting of foxes 1849. 4. Of or pertaining to a fox or foxes 1854. Hence **Vu·lpinism**, foxy character.

Vulpinite (vʊ·lpinəit). 1823. [f. *Vulpino*, (*Volpino*), near Bergamo in Lombardy + -ITE[1] 2 b.] *Min.* A granular variety of anhydrite.

Vulture (vʊ·ltiŭɹ, -tʃəɹ). late ME. [a. AF. *vultur* and *voutre*, OF. *voltour*, *voultour*, *voutour* (F. *vautour*), or L. *vultur*, or ad. L. *vulturius*.] 1. One of a number of large birds of prey of the order *Raptores* which feed almost entirely upon carrion and have the head and neck altogether or almost featherless. (The American vultures belong to different genera from those of the Old World.) b. With distinguishing terms 1575. c. *King of the vultures*, the king-v. (*Sarcorhamphus papa*) 1743. 2. *fig.* Something which preys upon a person, the mind, etc., after the manner of a vulture; *esp.* a consuming or torturing passion 1582. b. A person of a vile and rapacious disposition 1603. 3. Either of two northern constellations, dist. as the *falling v.* = LYRA 2, and *flying v.* = EAGLE *sb.* 4. 1638.

1. As when a Vultur on Imaus bred..flies toward the Springs Of Ganges or Hydaspes MILT. *attrib.* Victorious Wrong, with v. scream, Salutes the rising sun SHELLEY. 2. The vulturs of the mind, Disdainful Anger, pallid Fear, And Shame GRAY. b. They sent for the vultures of physic—I was bled copiously 1828.

Vulturine (vʊ·ltiŭrəin), *a.* 1647. [ad. L. *vulturinus*, f. *vultur*; see -INE.] 1. Of or belonging to the vulture tribe; resembling a vulture. 2. Of or pertaining to a vulture or vultures; characteristic of or like that of a vulture 1656.

2. The v. nose which smells a carrion in every rosebed KINGSLEY.

Vulturish (vʊ·ltiŭriʃ), *a.* 1826. [f. VULTURE *sb.* + -ISH.] Somewhat vulture-like.

Vulturous (vʊ·ltiŭrəs), *a.* 1623. [f. as prec. + -OUS.] Resembling a vulture or that of a vulture; ravenous.

||**Vulva** (vʊ·lvă). 1548. [L., 'wrapper, uterus'.] 1. *Anat.* The external organ of generation in the female; *esp.* the opening or orifice of that organ. 2. *Conch.* An impression behind the umbones of Venus-shells 1840. Hence **Vu·lval, Vu·lvar** *adjs.* of or belonging to the v.

||**Vulvitis** (vʊlvəi·tis). 1859. [f. VULVA + -ITIS.] *Path.* Inflammation of the vulva.

Vulvo- (vʊ·lvo), comb. form on Gr. models of L. *vulva* VULVA, in *v.-uterine*, *-vaginal*, etc.

Vum (vʊm), *v. U.S. colloq.* 1785. [Alteration of VOW *v.*[2]] *intr.* To vow, swear.

W

W (dʊ·b'l,yū), the 23rd letter of the modern English alphabet, is an addition to the ancient Roman alphabet, having originated from a ligatured doubling of the Roman letter represented by the U and V of modern alphabets. The English sound represented by *w*, a gutturally-modified bilabial voiced spirant, acoustically almost identical with the devocalised (*u*) or (u) which was the sound orig. expressed by the Roman U or V as a consonant-symbol, was at first usu. written *uu*; but in the 8th c. this sign began to be superseded by the Runic character ƿ (*wyn*, Kentish *wen*). In the 11th c. the ligatured form was introduced into England by Norman scribes, and ƿ finally went out of use about A.D. 1300.

In OE. the sound (w) occurred initially not only before vowels but also before (l) and (r); the combination *wl* became obs. in the 15th c., and *wr*, though still written, is now pronounced (r) in standard English. OE. had also the initial combination (hw): see WH.

The chief etymological sources of Eng. (w) are (1) OE. (w), repr. Indo-Eur. *w*, *gh*^{w}, *kw*, *k*^{w}; (2) ON. (w) of the same origin; (3) OF. (w), later becoming (gw) and finally (g), except in north-eastern F. dialects. The sound also occurs in words of L. origin containing the combinations *qu* (kw) and *su* (sw), as *question*, *persuade*, and in a few F. words, as *reservoir* (-vwāɹ).

As a consonant symbol, the letter always denotes (w), but in a few words it has ceased to be pronounced (as in *answer*, *sword*, *two*, and in the combination *wr*). In the unstressed second element of a compound, (w) tends to be elided in colloquial speech; this pronunciation is in some words a mere vulgarism (marked by spellings like *allus* for *always*) but in *Norwich* and some other place-names in *-wich* and in the nautical terms *forward* (*forrard*), *gunwale* it is the only one regarded as correct.

In ME a new (w) arose from the development of intervocalic or final (γ), as in *bowe* :— *boȝe* :—OE. *boga* BOW *sb.*[1]; but this sound has not survived as a consonant, since every (w) after a stressed vowel became a *u*-glide, the terminal element of a diphthong. In modern spelling *aw*, *ew*, *ow* are phonetically equivalent to *au*, *eu*, *ou*, though *ow* now never stands for (*ū*) except in the surname Cowper; the choice between *u* and *w* is mainly arbitrary, but at the end of a word *w*, not *u*, is used almost invariably.

In south-eastern dialects (w) is regularly substituted for (v), and many writers of the first half of the 19th c. attribute to the Cockney dialect the habit of misusing (w) for (v), and also the (probably merely occasional) reverse substitution of (v) for (w) on all occasions.

A mispronunciation of (w) for (v), in some persons due to a physical defect, has sometimes been a fashionable affectation.

1. The letter, its sound or name 1465. 2. The letter considered with regard to its shape 1798. 3. Abbrevs. W. = various personal names, as William, Winifred; †W. (*Calendar*) = Whitsunday; W. = West (W.C., the West Central postal district of London); W (*Chem.*) = tungsten (mod.L. *wolframium*); W. (Electr.) = watt; W.C. = water-closet; W.I. = West Indies; W.S. (*Scotland*) = Writer to the Signet.

Wa, obs. f. WAY, WOE.

Wa', Sc. f. WALL *sb.*[1]

Waac (wæk). 1917. A member of the *Women's Army Auxiliary Corps.*

Wabble: see WOBBLE.

Wacke (wæ·kə). 1796. [a. G., a miners' word, adopted by Werner as a geological term.] *Geol.* A sandstone-like rock, resulting from the decomposition of basaltic rocks *in situ*.

Wad (wǫd), *sb.*[1] 1540. [Origin obsc. With sense 3 cf. Sw. *vadd*, G., Du. *watte*, F. *ouate*.] 1. A bundle of hay or straw; esp. a small bundle of hay, peas, beans, etc., made at the time of cutting or reaping. Now *dial.* 1573. 2. A small bundle of a soft, flexible material; esp. for use as a plug, pad, or rubber 1580. b. Something rolled up tightly, as a roll of banknotes. Chiefly *U.S.* 1778. †3. = WADDING 2. –1761. 4. A plug of tow, cloth, etc., a disk of felt, etc., to retain the powder and shot in position in charging a gun or cartridge 1667.

1. Where he encradled was In simple cratch, wrapt in a w. of hay SPENSER.

Comb.: **w. hook**, (*a*) a spiral tool for withdrawing wads or charges from guns; (*b*) *Mining*, a tool 'for removing fragments from the bottom of deep boreholes'.

Wad (wǫd), *sb.*[2] 1614. [Origin obsc.] 1. *local.* Plumbago or black lead. 2. An impure earthy ore of manganese 1783.

Wad (wǫd), *v.* 1579. [f. WAD *sb.*[1]] I. 1. To lay up (the cut haulm of beans, peas, etc.) in bundles 1677. 2. To press (loose or fibrous material) into a small compass or a compact mass; *U.S.* to roll up tightly 1675. II. 1. To put a wad in (a gun, a cartridge) 1579. 2. To line, fill out, pad, as with wadding; to quilt 1759. 3. To plug (the ears) with wads 1876.

2. You say your prayers in carved stalls wadded with velvet cushions THACKERAY. Hence **Wa·dded** *ppl. a.* lined with wadding.

Wadable, wadeable (wē¹·dăb'l), *a.* 1611. [f. WADE *v.* + -ABLE.] That can be waded.

Wadding (wǫ·diŋ), *vbl. sb.* 1627. [-ING[1].] The action of WAD *v.* Also, *concr.*: 1. Any soft, pliable material from which gun-wads are made; also, a wad. 2. Any loose fibrous material for use as a padding, stuffing, quilting, etc. Now chiefly, cotton wool formed into a fleecy layer. 1734.

2. The seat, with plenteous w. stuff'd COWPER.

Waddle (wǫ·d'l), *sb.* 1691. [f. next.] The action of waddling; a waddling gait.

That must be my sweet Duckling—I know her by her pretty W. in her Gate 1691.

Waddle (wǫ·d'l), *v.* 1592. [frequent. f. WADE *v.*; see -LE. Some earlier instances perh. mean 'to move heavily or clumsily'.] To walk with short steps, swaying alternately from one leg to the other, as is done by a stout short-legged person; also said of animals, esp. of ducks or geese. b. *transf.* said of inanimate things 1728. †c. *Stock Exch. slang.* To become a 'lame duck' (DUCK *sb.*[1] 6) –1834.

Next a fat Author wadled into view 1681. b. Like bias to the bowl, Which, as more pond'rous, made its aim more true, Obliquely wadling to the mark in view POPE.

Waddy (wǫ·di). *Austral.* 1814. [perh. native word, but possibly alteration of Eng. *wood*.] An aboriginal war club.

Wade (wē¹d), *v.* [Com. Teut. (orig. str.) vb.; OE. *wadan* :—OTeut. **wad-*, *wōd-* :— pre-Teut. **wadh-*; cf. L. *vadere*. The str. inflexion became obs. in the 16th c.] †1. *intr.* To go, proceed (physically or in thought, etc.) –1709. 2. To walk through water or any liquid or soft substance which impedes motion ME. 3. *transf.* Of the sun or moon: To move (apparently) *through* clouds or mist. Chiefly *Sc.* and *north.* late ME. 4. *trans.* To walk through (water, etc.) ME. 5. To cause (a horse) to walk through water 1838.

1. Farewell,..Steepy wayes by which I waded 1648. I have sufficiently waded in this various Doctrine 1653. 2. A rill of water, through which we were compelled to w. as high as the knee BORROW. Phr. *To w. in*, to make a vigorous attack on one's opponent. *To w. into*, to assail energetically.

Wader (wēⁱ·dəɹ). 1673. [f. prec. + -ER [1].] 1. One who wades; *esp.* as the distinctive appellation of those long-legged birds (as the heron, plover, snipe, etc.) which wade in shallow water. 2. *pl.* Waterproof boots reaching above the knee, used by anglers, etc., for wading 1841.

Wadge, variant of WODGE.

‖**Wadi, wady** (wā·di). 1839. [Arab. *wādī*.] In some Arabic-speaking countries, a ravine or valley which in the rainy season becomes a watercourse; the stream running through such a ravine.

Wadmal (wǫ·dmăl). late ME. [a. ON. *vaðmál*, believed to be from *váð* (= OE. *wǣd* WEED) + *mál* measure.] A kind of woollen cloth. a. In England, a coarse woollen material. *Obs.* exc. in *wadmiltilt*. b. *Hist.* A woollen fabric woven in Orkney and Shetland 1572. c. A woollen fabric worn by country people in Scandinavia and Iceland 1682.

Comb.: **wadmiltilt**, a kind of tarpaulin covering for artillery stores.

Wadset (wǫ·dset), *sb.* *Sc. obsol.* 1449. [f. next.] 1. *Sc. Law.* The conveyance of land in satisfaction of or as security for a debt, the debtor having the right to recover the lands on payment of the debt. (Cf. MORTGAGE *sb.*) 2. A thing pledged 1796.

Wa·dset, *v.* Chiefly *Sc. obsol.* ME. [Sc. form of ME. *wedset*, f. WED *sb.* + SET *v.*] To put in pledge; to pawn, mortgage. Hence **Wa·dsetter**, *Sc.* a mortgagor (*rare*); a mortgagee.

Wae, obs. or dial form of WOE.

Wafer (wēⁱ·fəɹ), *sb.* [Late ME. *wafre*, a. AF., ad. MLG. *wâfel* WAFFLE.] 1. A very light thin crisp cake, baked between wafer-irons; formerly often eaten with wine, now chiefly with ices. 2. The thin disk of unleavened bread used at the Eucharist in the Western Church 1559. 3. A small disk of flour mixed with gum, or of gelatine or the like, used for sealing letters, attaching papers, or receiving the impression of a seal 1635. 4. *Med.* A cachet made of paste, for the administration of a powder 1887.

1. A womans oathes are wafers, breake with making 1625. 2. The adoration of the Sacrament, in the Countrey where they knocke and kneele to a W., is a popishe pollicie 1570.

Combs.: †**w.-cake** = sense 1, 2; also *fig.* as a type of fragility; **-iron**, an apparatus for baking wafers. Hence **Wa·fer** *v. trans.* to fasten or seal with a w. **Wa·ferer**, a maker or seller of wafers. **Wa·ferish, Wa·fery** *adjs.* like a w., extremely thin or fragile.

Wafery (wēⁱ·fəri), *sb.* 1455. [a. AF. *wafrie*, f. *wafre* WAFER *sb.*] A room or building in which wafers or thin cakes are made; the department of the royal household occupied with the making of wafers.

Waff (wɑf), *v.* Chiefly *north.* 1513. [var. of WAVE *v.*] 1. *trans.* To cause (something) to move to and fro. b. *intr.* To wave to and fro; to flutter in the wind 1834. 2. To produce a current of air by waving something to and fro 1688.

Waffle (wǫ·f'l). *U.S.* 1808. [a. Du. *wafel* WAFER.] A kind of batter-cake, baked in a waffle-iron, and eaten hot with butter or molasses.

Comb.: **w.-iron**, an iron utensil for baking waffles over a fire.

Waft (wɑft, wǫft), *sb.* 1542. [app. noun of action f. WAFT *v.*[1] or [2].] 1. A taste or flavour, esp. an ill taste; a scent or odour passing through the air or carried on the breeze. 2. A current or rush of air; a breath of wind 1607. b. A sound carried by the breeze 1697. c. A puff (of smoke or vapour) 1896. †3. An act of transporting or a passage over water -1786. 4. An act of waving; a waving movement 1652. 5. *Naut.* A flag, etc. hoisted as a signal; the act of displaying such a signal 1613.

1. The Strongest Sort of Smells are best in a weft, a farre off BACON. 2. *fig.* Tost too and fro with wafts of appetite 1607. 5. We..saw her make a W. with her Antient, as a Signal for the Boat to come on Board DE FOE.

Waft (wɑft, wǫft), *v.*[1] 1513. [Back-formation f. WAFTER.] †1. *trans.* To convoy -1670. 2. To convey safely by water; to carry *over* or *across* a river, sea, etc. Now *poet.* 1593. †b. *intr.* To sail *about*, *off*, etc. -1814. 3. *trans.* Of the wind: To propel (a vessel), convey (a navigator or passenger) safely 1653. 4. To carry or send (something, esp. a sound, scent, etc.) through the air or through space 1704. b. To carry in flight: said chiefly of angels 1718. c. *fig.* To transport, as by magic or in imagination 1781. 5. *intr.* To pass through the air or through space; to float upon the wind 1664. b. Of the breeze: To blow softly 1804. 6. *trans.* To drive or carry *away* by producing a current of air 1839.

2. Away with her, and w. her hence to France SHAKS. b. Satan..Wafts on the calmer wave by dubious light And like a weather beaten Vessel holds Gladly the Port MILT. 3. In vain you tell your parting Lover You wish fair winds may w. Him over PRIOR. 5. And now the Shouts w. near the Cittadel DRYDEN. Hence **Wa·ftage**, the action of wafting; conveyance across water (occas. the Styx) by ship or boat; passage through the air; the action or power of propulsion of the wind or breeze.

†**Waft**, *v.*[2] 1578. [app. alteration of WAFF *v.*] 1. *trans.* To wave (the hand or something held in the hand), esp. as a signal; to signal to (a person, etc.) thus -1719. b. To move (something) *aside* with a wave of the hand. COWPER. 2. To turn (the eyes) aside. SHAKS.

†**Wa·fter.** 1482. [app. a. Du. or LG. *wachter*, f. *wachten* to guard.] 1. An armed vessel employed as a convoy -1670. 2. The commander of a convoying vessel -1622.

Wafture (wɑ·ftiŭɹ, wǫft-). 1601. [f. WAFT *v.*[2] and *v.*[1] + -URE.] 1. The action or an act of waving (the hand or something held in the hand). b. The waving (of a wing or wings) 1790. 2. The action of wafting; propulsion by air or current 1755.

1. You answer'd not, but with an angry wafter of your hand, Gaue signe to me to leaue you SHAKS.

Wag (wæg), *sb.*[1] 1553. [prob. f. next.] †1. A mischievous boy (often as a term of endearment); in wider application, a youth, young man, 'fellow' -1672. 2. 'Any one ludicrously mischievous; a merry droll' (J.); a habitual joker 1584. 3. *To play (the) wag*: to play truant (*slang*) 1851.

1. But I prythee sweet Wag, shall there be Gallowes standing in England when thou art King? SHAKS. 2. Phr. *To play the wag*; Hauing wit enough..to plaie the wagge 1604.

Wag (wæg), *v.* [ME. *wagge*, f. root of OE. *wagian* to oscillate, shake.] I. *intr.* 1. To be in motion; to stir, move. Now *colloq.* (chiefly w. neg.) to stir, move one's limbs. 2. To oscillate, shake, or sway alternately in opposite directions. late ME. 3. Of a limb, etc.: To be moved briskly from side to side 1484. b. Of the tongue, †lips: To move briskly in animated talk: often with implication of foolish or indiscreet speech 1590. †4. To move, budge *from* a place -1730. 5. To go, depart, be off. Now *colloq.* 1594. b. To travel or make one's way 1684. 6. *slang.* To play truant 1848.

1. Driven to fly with her heavie burden with which she is scarce able to w. 1636. 3. It is a common proverbe, it is mery in hall when beardes wagges all 1550. 5. *Merry W.* I. iii. 7. b. They made a pretty good shift to wagg along BUNYAN. Provb. phr. *How the world wags*, how affairs are going. *To let the world w.* (*as it will*), to regard the course of events with unconcern.

II. *trans.* 1. To brandish (a weapon). Also, to wave (something) defiantly or as a signal, etc. *Obs.* exc. *joc.* ME. 2. To move (a limb or part of the body) to and fro, up and down, from side to side, etc.: usu. implying rapid and repeated movement. late ME. b. (Chiefly in neg. context.) To stir (a limb, finger, etc.). Now *colloq.* 1596. c. To shake (the head) ME. d. To move (the tongue, †lips) in animated speech: esp. with implication of indiscretion or malignity 1569. e. Of an animal: To move (its tail) from side to side. late ME.

1. While there's one Scottish hand that can w. a claymore, sir SCOTT. 2. b. I most positively declined to ask him or anyone to w. a finger to get me there 1898. d. Every one who owed him grudge would eagerly begin to w. his tongue 1871. Hence **Wag** *sb.*[2] an act of wagging; power or disposition to wag.

Wage (wēⁱdʒ), *sb.* ME. [a. AF., = OF. *g(u)age*:—pop. L. **wadium*, of Teut. origin.] †1. = GAGE *sb.*[1] 1 -1590. 2. A payment to a person for service rendered; now esp. the amount paid periodically for the labour or service of a workman or servant. Freq. *pl.* (after F. *gages*). ME. b. *fig.* Reward, recompense. late ME.

2. The produce of labour constitutes the natural recompence or wages of labour ADAM SMITH. b. The wagis of synne is deth WYCLIF *Rom.* vi. 22.

attrib. and *Comb.*, as *w.-earner*, *-slave*; **wage(s)-fund**, *Pol. Econ.* that part of the capital of a community which is available for paying wages; **wage(s)-sheet**, the list of wages paid by an employer of labour; **w.-worker** (*U.S.*), a wage-earner. Hence **Wa·geless** *a.* that does not earn or receive wages.

Wage (wēⁱdʒ), *v.* [ME., a. ONF. *wagier*, :—pop. L. **wadiare*, f. **wadium* WAGE *sb.*] I. To gage, pledge. 1. *trans.* To give as a pledge or security -1585. 2. *spec.* in *Law.* Now only *Hist.* a. *To w. battle*: To pledge oneself to judicial combat 1568. b. *To w. one's* (or *the*) *law*, to defend an action by 'wager of law'; erron. to go to law 1455. †3. To put to hazard, venture; *esp.* to stake, wager, bet -1825.

3. I would w. a shilling that the pedestrian outstripped the equestrian travellers FIELDING. Their lives have been freely waged and wasted SCOTT.

II. †1. To engage or employ for wages; to hire, spec. for military service -1662. 2. To pay wages to. Now *rare* or *Obs.* late ME.

1. *fig.* I seem'd his Follower, not Partner; and He wadg'd me with his Countenance, as if I had bin Mercenary SHAKS.

III. To carry on (war, a contest) 1456. Hence **Waged** *ppl. a.* hired for or paid by wages; †of soldiers, mercenary.

‖**Wagenboom** (vā·γ'nbōm). *S. Afr.* Also vaboom. 1822. [Du., f. *wagen* WAGGON + *boom* tree.] A tree (*Protea grandiflora*), the wood of which is used for making waggon-wheels.

Wager (wēⁱ·dʒəɹ), *sb.* ME. [a. AF. *wageure*, f. *wager* WAGE *v.* In branch II perh. f. WAGE *v.* + -ER [4].] I. 1. Something (esp. a sum of money) laid down and hazarded on the issue of an uncertain event; a stake. Now *rare* exc. in phr. *to lay, win, lose, a w.* 2. An agreement or contract under which each of the parties promises to give money or its equivalent to the other according to the issue of an uncertain event 1548. b. A contest for a prize 1615. 3. The subject of a bet or bets 1586.

1. Most men..Will back their own opinions with a w. BYRON. 2. Wee'le make a solemne w. on your cunnings SHAKS.

II. *Law* (now *Hist.*). a. *W. of law*: an offer to make oath of innocence or non-indebtedness, to be supported by the oaths of eleven compurgators 1521. b. *W. of battle*: a challenge by a defendant to decide his guilt or innocence by single combat 1625.

Comb.: **w.-boat**, a light racing sculling-boat used in contests between single scullers; **-insurance, -policy**, an insurance policy in which the insurer has no insurable interest in the thing insured.

Wager (wēⁱ·dʒəɹ), *v.* 1602. [f. prec.] 1. *trans.* To stake or hazard (something of value) on the issue of an uncertain event or on some question to be decided 1611. b. To venture on the issue of a contest 1819. 2. *intr.* To offer or lay a wager, to make a bet 1602.

1. *Cymb.* V. v. 182. 2. I'll w. that your stopping here to-night would please him better than it would please me DICKENS.

Waggery (wæ·gəri). 1594. [f. WAG *sb.*[1] + -ERY.] 1. The action or disposition of a wag; drollery; in early use chiefly, practical joking. 2. A waggish action or speech; in early use, a practical joke 1604.

1. So good a fellow, so full of fun and w.! 1824.

Waggish (wæ·giʃ), *a.* 1589. [f. as prec. + -ISH [1].] 1. Of a person: Having the qualities of a wag. †Also, wanton, loose. 1590. 2. Pertaining to or characteristic of a wag. Of an act, etc.: Done in a spirit of waggery. 1589. Hence **Wa·ggish-ly** *adv.*, **-ness**.

Waggle (wæ·g'l), *v.* 1586. [Frequentative of WAG *v.*] 1. *trans.* a. To move (anything held or fixed at one end) to and fro with short quick motions; *esp.* to shake (any movable part of the body) 1594. **b.** *absol. Golf.* To swing the club-head to and fro over the ball in the line of the intended stroke 1897. **2.** *intr.* **a.** With advs. or advb. expressions: To shake or wobble while in motion; to waddle 1611. **b.** Of things held or fixed at one end: To move backwards and forwards with short quick motions 1706.

1. She hinted, she sighed, she waggled her head at me THACKERAY. Hence **Wa·ggle** *sb.* the action or an act of waggling; *spec.* in *Golf.* **Wa·ggly** *a.* waggling, unsteady.

Waggon, wagon (wæ·gən), *sb.* 1523. [Early mod.E. *wagan, waghen*, a. Du. *wagen, waghen* = OE. *wæʒn* WAIN.] **1.** A strong four-wheeled vehicle designed for the transport of heavy goods. **b.** *transf.* The constellation CHARLES'S WAIN 1867. †**2.** A carriage of any kind for the conveyance of persons, their luggage, etc. Also *poet.* a triumphal car, car of state. –1638. **3.** An open four-wheeled vehicle built for carrying hay, corn, etc., consisting of a long body furnished with 'shelboards' 1573. **4.** A covered vehicle for the regular conveyance of commodities and passengers by road. (Now only *colonial* and *U.S.*) 1615. **5. a.** *Mining.* A truck used to convey minerals along the roadways of a mine or from the mine to the place of shipment 1649. **b.** An open truck or closed van for the transport of goods on a railway. †Formerly applied to the open carriages for conveying passengers at the lowest fares. 1756. **6.** *U.S.* A light four-wheeled vehicle used for various business purposes and for pleasure 1837. **7.** A covered four-wheeled vehicle used as a living-house by gipsies, travelling showmen, etc. 1851. **8.** Short for *dinner-w., tea-w.* 1906.

2. *Tit. A.* v. ii. 51. 4. The two London waggons came in with sixteen and fourteen horses 1776.

Comb.: **w.-bed** *U.S.*, the body of a w.; the bottom of the body; **-ceiling**, a boarded roof of the Tudor period, of either semicircular or polygonal section; **-drift** *S. Afr.*, a passage for waggons across a river; **-head** *Arch.*, a cylindrical ceiling, roof, or vault; **-load**, as much as a w. can carry; **-road**, a road for the passage of waggons; spec. in *Coal-mining*, a prepared road or railway for the haulage of waggons; **-train** *Mil.*, a train, collection, or service of transport waggons; also, a train of waggons used by colonial settlers; **-tree** = WAGENBOOM; **-vault** = *w.-head*; **-way** = *w.-road.* Hence **Wa·ggonful. Wa·ggonry,** (*rare*) conveyance or transport by w.

Waggon, wagon (wæ·gən), *v.* 1606. [f. prec.] **1.** *intr.* To travel in a waggon, transport goods by waggon. Chiefly *U.S.* **2.** *trans.* To put into a waggon for conveyance 1649. **3.** *U.S.* To transport (goods) in a waggon or waggons 1755.

Waggonage, wagonage (wæ·gənėdʒ). Now *U.S.* 1609. [f. WAGGON *sb.* or *v.* + -AGE.] Conveyance or transport by waggon; money paid for this.

Waggoner, wagoner[1] (wæ·gənəɹ). 1544. [f. WAGGON *sb.* + -ER[1]; perh. orig. a. Du. *waghenaer.*] **1.** One who has charge of a waggon as driver. **b.** Used as the designation of a particular class of farm servant, whose special duties include the driving of a waggon 1790. †**2.** The driver of a chariot, a charioteer; freq. applied to Phoebus or to Phaethon –1638. **3. a.** The northern constellation AURIGA 1607. †**b.** Applied to the constellation Boötes, viewed as the driver of 'Charles's Wain' –1697.

2. Her W., a smal gray-coated Gnat SHAKS. 3. **b.** By this the Northerne wagoner had set His seuenfold teme behind the stedfast starre SPENSER.

Waggoner, wagoner[2] (wæ·gənəɹ). *Obs.* exc. *Hist.* 1687. [Anglicized form of the Du. surname *Waghenaer.*] *orig.* The atlas of charts, *Spieghel der Zeevaerdt*, published by Lucas Janssen Waghenaer in 1584. Hence *gen.* a book of charts for nautical use.

Waggonette, wagonette (wægəne·t). 1858. [f. WAGGON *sb.* + -ETTE.] A four-wheeled carriage, made open or with a removable cover and furnished with a seat or bench at each side facing inwards and with one or two seats arranged crosswise in front.

Wagnerian (vāgnī·riăn), *a.* and *sb.* 1873. [-IAN.] **A.** *adj.* Of or pertaining to the German operatic composer Richard Wagner (1813–83), his music and theories of musical and dramatic composition. **B.** *sb.* An admirer or adherent of Wagner 1882. So **Wagnere·sque** *a.* resembling the style of Wagner. **Wa·gnerism,** the influence or cult of Wagner. **Wa·gnerist, Wa·gnerite** = B.

‖**Wagon-lit** (vagonlī). 1884. [F.; *wagon* railway coach + *lit* bed.] A sleeping coach on a Continental train.

Wagtail (wæ·gtēˡl), 1510. [f. WAG *v.* + TAIL *sb.*[1]] **1.** A small bird belonging to the genus *Motacilla* or family *Motacillidæ*, so called from the continual characteristic wagging motion of the tail. In Great Britain chiefly applied to *M. lugubris*, the *pied w.*, called also *water w.* **b.** With qualifying words, indicating native country, colour, habits, etc., as *grey, Siberian, white, winter w.* 1668. **2.** Applied to other birds, e.g. *U.S.* a water-thrush, *Seiurus nævius* or *S. motacilla* 1868. †**3.** *transf.* A familiar or contemptuous epithet applied to a man or young woman; *esp.* a contemptuous term for a profligate or inconstant woman; hence, a harlot –1783.

1. I..had my spirit as full of life as a wagtayle 1604. 3. *Lear* II. ii. 73.

Wahabi, Wahabee (wăhā·bī). 1807. [a. Arab. *Wahhābī*, f. *Wahhāb.*] A follower of Abd-el-Wahhab, a Mohammedan reformer (1691–1787) whose sect flourishes in central Arabia.

Wahoo (wăhū·). 1860. [N. Amer. Indian.] The N. Amer. shrub *Euonymus atropurpureus.*

Waif (wēˡf), *sb.*[1] (and *a.*) late ME. [a. AF., = OF. *gaif*; prob. of Scandinavian origin; cf. ON. *veif.*] **A.** *sb.* **1.** *Law.* A piece of property which is found ownerless and which, if unclaimed within a fixed period after due notice given, falls to the lord of the manor; freq. in *w. and stray.* **2.** *transf.* and *fig.*, *esp.* a person who is without home or friends; one who lives uncared-for; an outcast; an unowned or neglected child 1624.

1. Prowling about the shore after the waifs of the storm KINGSLEY. 2. They are the waifs and strays, and cast-aways of society 1862.

B. *attrib.* and as *adj.* (indicating lost property, a strayed animal, etc.) 1609.

A Home for W. Boys 1898.

Waif (wēˡf), *sb.*[2] 1530. [perh. a. ON. *veif*, something waving or flapping.] A small flag used as a signal. Now *Naut.*

Waif (wēˡf), *sb.*[3] 1854. [Cf. Sc. *waff*, f. WAFT *v.*] Something borne or driven by the wind; a puff (of smoke), a streak (of cloud).

Wail (wēˡl), *sb.* late ME. [Belongs to next.] **1.** The action of wailing; esp. sound of lamentation for the dead. **2.** A cry of pain or grief, esp. if loud and prolonged 1863. **3.** *transf.* A sound resembling a cry of pain 1825.

2. *fig.* A long w. of anguish was rising from the persecuted all over France 1867. 3. The w. Of plover, or the pipe of quail 1858.

Wail (wēˡl), *v.* ME. [prob. a. ON. **veila*, f. *vei* WOE *int.*] **1.** *intr.* To express pain or sorrow by prolonged piteous cries. **b.** To cry piteously *for* (something desired) 1573. **2.** *transf.* Of birds, the wind, etc.: To give forth mournful sounds 1595. **3.** To utter persistent and bitter lamentations or complaints; to say lamentingly ME. **4.** To grieve bitterly. late ME. **5.** *trans.* To bewail, lament, deplore (sin, misfortune, suffering); to mourn bitterly for (the dead). Now *poet.* or *rhet.* late ME.

1. My Mother weeping: my Father wayling: my Sister crying SHAKS. **b.** I heard 'em w. for Bread GRAY. 3. 'I wish I was dead,' wailed the poor creature 1894. 5. Yet I must not..but wayle his fall, Who I my selfe struck downe SHAKS. They neither esteemed him while he was liuing, nor wailed him at all, after that he was dead 1631. Hence **Wai·ler,** one who wails; *spec.* a professional mourner. **Wai·ling** *pl. a.*, **-ly** *adv.*

Wailful (wēˡ·lfŭl), *a.* Chiefly *poet.* 1544. [f. WAIL *sb.* + -FUL.] **1.** Having the character of a wail, expressive of pain or sorrow; resembling a wail, plaintive. **2.** Full of lamentation, sorrowful 1579. **b.** *transf.* Of animals, etc.: Producing plaintive sounds 1818. †**3.** That is to be bewailed, lamentable –1620.

1. The w. sweetness of the violin 1899. 2. **b.** A w. gnat KEATS. 3. Woe and wailefull miserie SPENSER. Hence **Wai·lfully** *adv.*

Wailing (wēˡ·liŋ), *vbl. sb.* ME. [f. WAIL *v.* + -ING[1].] The action of the verb. *attrib.*: **w. place, wall,** *spec.* in *Jews' W. Place*, part of the Solomonic wall in Jerusalem where the Jews assemble to lament the destruction of the Temple.

Wain (wēˡn), *sb.* [OE. *wæʒen, wæn* = Du., G. *wagen*:—OTeut. **wagnoz*:—pre-Teut. **woghnos*, f. Indo-Eur. root **wegh-, wogh-*; cf. WEIGH *v.*, WAY *sb.*] **1.** A large open vehicle, usu. four-wheeled, drawn by horses or oxen, and used for carrying heavy loads, esp. of agricultural produce. Now chiefly *dial.* or *poet.* **b.** *poet.* A car or chariot. Chiefly *fig.* or in mythological use. ME. **2.** In full CHARLES'S WAIN: The group of seven bright stars in the Great Bear. *Lesser W.*, the similar group of stars in the Little Bear. OE.

1. From the sun-burnt hay-field, homeward creeps The loaded w. COWPER. **b.** Fresche Appollo with his golden Wayn LYDG. Hence †**Wain** *v. trans.* to transport in a w. **Wai·ner,** the driver of a w. (*rare*). **Wai·nman,** a wainer; †the constellation Boötes. **Wai·nwright,** a waggon-builder.

Wainscot (wēˡ·nskŏt, we·n-), *sb.* ME. [ad. MLG. *wagenschot*, app. f. *wagen* WAGGON; the meaning of the second element is uncertain.] **1.** A superior quality of foreign oak imported from Russia, Germany, and Holland, chiefly used for fine panel-work; logs, planks, or boarding of this oak. Now *techn.* **2.** Panel-work of oak or other wood, lining or used to line the walls of a room 1548. **3.** *attrib.* passing into *adj.* Made of wainscot; (of a room) lined with wainscot panelling; †resembling wainscot in hardness or colour 1575.

1. *fig.* This kind of men haue faces of wainscote 1630. Hence **Wai·nscot** *v. trans.* to line (a wall etc.) with wooden panel-work, or *transf.* with panels of other materials. **Wai·nscot(t)ing** *vbl. sb.* the action or process of lining a room with w.; *concr.* panelling of w.

Waist (wēˡst). [Late ME. *wast*, believed to represent OE. **wæst*, **weahst*, f. Teut. root **wahs-*; see WAX *v.*[1]] **1.** The portion of the trunk of the human body that is between the ribs and the hip-bones; the middle section of the body, normally slender in comparison with the parts above and below it. **b.** Applied to the corresponding part in an insect 1713. **2.** †**a.** A girdle –1611. **b.** The part of a garment that covers the waist; the narrowed part of a garment corresponding to the narrowing of the body at the waist (but sometimes, in accordance with fashion, worn higher or lower than the position of this) 1650. **c.** The part of a garment between the shoulders and the narrowed part 1607. **d.** A bodice, blouse. Chiefly *U.S.* 1816. **3.** *Naut.* The middle part of the upper deck of a ship, between the quarter-deck and the forecastle 1495. **4.** Applied to the narrowed part of an object which is smaller in breadth or girth near the middle than at the extremities; esp. of a bell, a violin or similar instrument, a boot or shoe 1612. †**5.** Affectedly used for: Middle (of day or night) –1651.

1. Young Virgins..who..strive..by straight-lacing themselves, to attaine unto a wand-like smalnesse of waste 1650. 2. **a.** *John* II. i. 217. 5. *Ham.* I. ii. 198.

attrib. and *Comb.*: **w.-band,** a band fitting about the w., *esp.* one forming the upper part of a garment (skirt, pair of trousers, etc.) and serving to stiffen or maintain it; **-boat,** one carried in the w. of a ship; **-cloth,** †(*a*) *pl.* coloured cloths hung about the upper works of a ship as an adornment or to screen men stationed there; (*b*) a loin-cloth worn by natives of hot climates. Hence **Wai·sted** *a.* having a w. (usu. of specified size or form, as *long-w., short-w.*). **Wai·ster,** a man stationed in the w. of a ship. **Wai·sting** *vbl. sb.* (*U.S.*) material for waists (sense 2 d). **Wai·stless** *a.*

Waistcoat (wēˡ·s(t)kōᵘt; *colloq.* or *vulgar* we·skit, -kət). 1519. [f. prec. + COAT *sb.*] A garment covering the upper part of the body down to the waist: **1.** A garment (in early use often elaborate and costly) forming part of ordinary male attire, worn under a coat or jacket, and intended to be partly exposed to view when in wear. †**b.** A plainer and less costly garment, usu. of knitted wool, worn chiefly for additional warmth –1711. †**2.** A short (woollen) garment worn next the skin –1806. **3.** †**a.** A short garment, often elaborate and costly, worn by women about the upper part of the body (usu. underneath an outer gown, but so as to be seen) –1711. **b.** A woman's garment or dress-front designed in imitation of a man's waistcoat 1711. †**c.**

A short (sleeveless) under-garment; a camisole –1785.

1. Phr. *Under one's w.*, in one's breast; We Irish have good warm hearts under our waistcoats 1859. *transf.* A woodpecker with black wings, a white w., and a crimson crest 1898. Hence **Wai·stcoated** *a.* **Waistcoatee·r**, a low-class prostitute (*Obs.* exc. *Hist.*). **Wai·stcoating**, a textile fabric made esp. for men's waistcoats.

Wait (wēⁱt), *sb.* ME. [Partly a. ONF. *wait, wet, f. *waitier* (see WAIT *v.*) and *waite*. The word adopted from F. has coalesced with an Eng. formation on WAIT *v.*] **I.** The action of WAIT *v.* **1.** In phrases with the general sense: To lurk in ambush. **2. a.** (*Day's*) *w.*: the duty of keeping guard by day performed by the warders of the Tower 1694. **b.** The period of attendance at court of a lord- or lady-in-waiting 1884. **3.** The state or condition of waiting 1873. **4.** A period of waiting; spec. *Theatr.*, the time of waiting between the acts of a play, etc. 1855.

1. †*To sit in w.*; *to lie* (†*lay*) *in w.* *To lay w.*, †*lay one's w.*; They layed w. for him..and murdered him 1597. 4. The waits between the acts being very much longer than the acts themselves DICKENS.

II. A person who watches or waits. †**1.** A watchman; a scout, spy –1802. **2.** *pl.* †**a.** A small body of wind instrumentalists maintained by a city or town at the public charge –1764. **b.** A band of musicians and singers who perambulate the streets by night at Christmas and the New Year playing and singing carols, etc., for gratuities 1773.

1. At the last..he came to a Castel and there he herd the waytes vpon the wallys MALORY.

Wait (wēⁱt), *v.* [Early ME. *waite(n*, a. AF., ONF. *waitier* = OF. *guaitier* to watch, a. OHG. *wahtên*, f. *wahta* watch, f. OTeut. *wak-; see WAKE *v.*] †**1.** *trans.* To watch, observe constantly; esp. to watch with hostile intent; to spy upon, lie in wait for –1597. †**2.** *intr.* To keep watch, be watchful; to act as a watchman –1605. **3.** *trans.* To look forward to (esp. with desire or apprehension); to continue in expectation of. Now somewhat *rare* and superseded by AWAIT *v.* late ME. **b.** *intr.* Chiefly *to w. for* = 3. 1577. **c.** To remain for a time without something expected or promised 1550. **4.** *trans.* To continue stationary or quiescent, in expectation of (a person or thing, an event). Now *rare*; superseded by *w. for* and AWAIT *v.* late ME. **b.** *transf.* Of things: To remain in readiness for, to await 1745. **5.** *intr.* or *absol.* Often *to w. for.* **a.** To remain in a place, defer one's departure until something happens. late ME. **b.** To defer action until some event has taken place; to delay *to do* something 1633. **c.** Of a thing: = 4 b; also, to remain for a while neglected 1838. **d.** quasi-*trans.* To postpone (a meal) in expectation of the arrival of some one (*colloq.*) 1838. **6.** To be in readiness to receive orders; hence, to be in attendance as a servant. Chiefly const. *on*: 1526. **b.** To serve as an attendant at table 1568. †**c.** quasi-*trans.* *To w. attendance*: to remain in attendance –1607. †**7.** To attend or escort –1816.

2. Where be these Warders, that they w. not here? SHAKS. 3. c. He would agree to w. for his money 1897. 4. Phr. *To w. one's* (or *the*) *time, hour, opportunity*, etc., to defer action until a fitting season or opportunity presents itself. b. Better mansions w. the just, prepar'd above the sky 1745. 5. a. The old adage, 'time and tide w. for no man' DICKENS. Phr. *To w. about*, to linger expectantly, 'hang about' where something is likely to happen (*colloq.*); also (chiefly *U.S.*) *to w. around.* *To w. on*, (*a*) *Sc.* to linger about a place; also, to linger in expectation of death; (*b*) *Hawking*, of a falcon, to soar in circles above the falconer, waiting for the game to be flushed. *To w. up*, to defer going to bed in expectation of some one or something. *To w. and see*, to wait the course of events (recently often used with allusion to Mr. H. H. Asquith's answers to many questions in parliament during the war of 1914–18). d. It's a trying thing waiting supper for lovers DICKENS. 6. b. Phr. *To w. at table*; She had not prudence enough to hold her tongue before the servants, while they waited at table JANE AUSTEN.

With preps. **Wait for** —. (See 3 b, 5.) **W. of** —. †**a.** = *w. on* e, f. **b.** = *w. for.* Now *dial.* **W. on** or **upon** —. †**a.** To observe, watch; to lie in wait for. †**b.** To await, expect with desire or anxiety. †**c.** In Bible phrase, to place one's hope in (God). **d.** To attend as or in the manner of a servant to the personal requirements of. *To w. on hand and foot*: see HAND *sb.* **e.** To accompany on one's way (as a mark of respect or to render service or assistance): to escort (now *rare*). **f.** To call upon with the intention of showing respect, asking a favour, or the like. **g.** Of things: To accompany; to be associated with. *literary.*

Wai·t-a-bit. Also **wait-a-while.** 1785. [tr. Cape Du. *wacht-een-beetje.*] Usu. *attrib.* with *thorn*, etc. Any of various S. African plants and shrubs, with joc. ref. to their hooked and clinging thorns; e.g. various species of *mimosa.* Also applied to plants of a similar character in other parts of the world.

Waiter (wēⁱ·təɹ). late ME. [orig. a. AF. *waitour, f. *waitier* WAIT *v.* In later use f. WAIT *v.* + -ER [1].] **I.** †**1.** One who watches or is on the look-out –1687. **2.** †**a.** *Sc.* A watchman at the city gates –1818. **b.** A warder of the Tower of London 1551. **c.** An officer in the employ of the Customs. *Obs.* exc. *Hist.* 1473. **II.** One who waits expectant of some event, opportunity, etc. 1592.

W. upon Providence, †*time*, one who awaits the turn of events when required by duty or honour to come to a personal decision.

III. †**1.** One who visits or pays court to a superior –1611. †**2.** One whose office or privilege it is to attend upon a superior –1714. **3.** A man (rarely a woman) of lower rank employed as a household servant; *esp.* a servant whose particular duty it is to wait at table. *Obs.* exc. *U.S.* 1483. **4.** A man who waits upon the guests (*esp.* at table), at inns, eating-houses, etc. Also, a man hired for a similar purpose on special occasions in a private household. 1663.

2. Gentlemen Wayters of the Court 1630. Ministers about holy things, and waiters at God's altar 1711. 4. The sum is six pounds, and be pleased to remember the Waiters 1663.

IV. 1. A salver, small tray 1738. †**2.** = DUMB-WAITER 2. –1861.

Waiting (wēⁱ·tiŋ), *vbl. sb.* ME. [-ING [1].] The action of WAIT *v.* in various senses, *esp.* **a.** Remaining stationary or quiescent in expectation of something. **b.** Attendance *upon* a superior; official attendance at court; one's period or term of such attendance 1560.

a. *In w.*, (predic.), remaining in one place or condition so as to be ready for some expected event; The coach was in w. 1760. b. See LADY-, LORD- *in-w.*

Comb.: **w. game**, applied to the tactics of a player who abstains from attempting to secure advantages in the earlier part of the game, with a view to more effective action at a later stage; also *fig.*; **w. list**, a list of persons waiting for appointments, etc.; **-room**, a room set apart for those who are obliged to wait (now *esp.* in a railway-station; also at a doctor's or dentist's).

Waiting (wēⁱ·tiŋ), *ppl. a.* 1538. [-ING [2].] **1.** That waits upon or attends to another. Often hyphened to the qualified sb., as in *w.-gentlewoman, -lady.* **2.** That waits for some person or thing; expectant 1654.

1. **W.-maid**, a superior female servant in personal attendance on a lady. **W.-woman** (now *arch.*), a female servant or personal attendant.

Waitress (wēⁱ·très). 1834. [f. WAITER + -ESS [1].] A woman who waits upon the guests at a hotel, restaurant, etc. Also, one hired for similar duties (on special occasions) in a private household.

Waive (wēⁱv), *v.* Also freq. †**wave.** [ME. *weyve*, a. AF. *weyver* to allow to become a 'waif', f. *weyf* WAIF *sb.*[1]] **1.** *trans. Law.* To outlaw (a woman). *Hist.* **2.** *Law.* To abandon (stolen goods). *Hist.* 1531. †**3.** To abandon, relinquish, desert, forsake –1817. **4. a.** *Law.* To relinquish (a right, claim, or contention) either by express declaration or by some intentional act which by law is equivalent to this 1469. **b.** To give up (a privilege, right, claim, etc.); to forbear to claim or demand 1625. **c.** To forbear persistence in (an action, etc.); to refrain from pressing (an objection, etc.) 1681. **d.** To dispense with (formality, ceremony, etiquette) 1781. **5.** To evade (doing something); to shun, avoid 1440. †**6.** To avoid acceptance of, reject (an offer, something offered); to decline (an honour) –1753. †**7.** To neglect, ignore, overlook –1713. **8.** To refrain from applying or enforcing (a rule, law); to make an exception to 1665. **9.** To abstain from entering upon (an action, discussion, etc.). Often with some notion of reserving for a future opportunity: To allow to stand over, put aside for the present. 1650. †**b.** To refrain from dealing with in statement or narrative –1742. ¶**10.** [Confused with WAVE *v.*] To put *aside, away, off* with or as with a wave of the hand 1832.

3. For this Reason, he hoped, the Hon. Gentleman would..wave the Motion he had made 1736. He once entertained a desire of taking a tour to Scythia; but waved it 1787. 4. b. Congreve waved his title to dramatic reputation and desired to be considered only as a gentleman JOHNSON. 5. The most effectual mode of solving all difficulties and waiving all discussions SCOTT. There appears to be no concealment on the part of the officers in thus waiving the exercise of their duty HAWTHORNE. 9. b. To wave therefore a circumstance, which..is not greatly material FIELDING.

Waiver (wēⁱ·vəɹ). 1628. [a. AF. *weyver*, subst. use of *weyver* WAIVE *v.*; see -ER [4].] *Law.* The action or an act of waiving.

W. clause, a clause in the prospectus of a joint-stock company, by which the subscribers are made to contract themselves out of the provision of the Companies Act requiring the prospectus to contain certain particulars respecting the contracts made with the promoters.

Wakari (wăkā·ri). 1909. [Native name.] A S. Amer. monkey of the genus *Cacajao.*

Wake (wēⁱk), *sb.*[1] ME. [app. in part repr. OE. *wacu (in *nihtwaco* night-watch), in part a new formation in ME. f. WAKE *v.* With sense 4 cf. ON. *Jónsvaka* St. John's Eve, Midsummer festivities.] **1.** The state of wakefulness, *esp.* during normal hours of sleep; †the act of awaking. *Obs.* exc. in *sleep and w.* †**2.** Abstinence from sleep practised as a religious observance: often coupled with *fasting.* Also, an instance of this. –1641. **3.** The watching (*esp.* by night) of relatives and friends beside the body of a dead person; the drinking, feasting, and other observances incidental to this. Now chiefly *Anglo-Irish* or with ref. to Irish custom. late ME. **4. a.** The vigil or eve of a festival and the observances belonging to this: also, a festival. *Obs.* exc. *dial.* 1550. **b.** The local annual festival of an English parish, observed (orig. on the feast of the patron saint of the church, but now usu. on some particular Sunday and the two or three days, or the week, following) as an occasion for making holiday, village sports, etc. Now only *dial.* (chiefly northern and west midland) and usu. *pl.* with sing. meaning and construction. ME.

1. Making such difference betwixt W. and Sleepe, As is the difference betwixt Day and Night SHAKS. 4. a. Their Wakes and Vigils, in all riot and excesse of eating and drinking 1629. b. Every town had its fair, every village its w. THACKERAY. *transf.* The Wood-Nymphs..Their merry wakes and pastimes keep MILTON.

Wake (wēⁱk), *sb.*[2] 1547. [Directly or mediately a. ON. *vaku, *vǫk* hole or opening in ice.] **1.** The track left on the water's surface by a ship. **2.** *transf.* Anything compared to the wake of a vessel, as the disturbance caused by a body swimming in water, the air-currents behind a body in flight, etc. 1711. **3.** A course that a ship has taken, or is to take 1595.

1. The foaming w. far widening as we go CLOUGH. Phr. *To fetch* (*get, get into, have*) *the w. of* (a pursued vessel), to get so close to her as to be able to see and steer by her wake. **In the w. of**: (*a*) *Naut.*, immediately behind, and (properly) in the actual track made by a vessel; also *transf.*, in the direct line aft from (any object, etc. on a ship), in the line of sight of (an observed object), in the line of recoil of (a gun); (*b*) *transf.* and *fig.*, following close behind, in the train or track of; following as a result or consequence. 2. Morn in the white w. of the morning star Came furrowing all the orient into gold TENNYSON. Outside it's merry in the wind's w. ROSSETTI. They had left a wide, discoloured w. upon the snow STEVENSON. 3. They were..quite out of the w. of the Bermudas DE FOE.

Wake (wēⁱk), *v.* Pa. t. **woke** (wōᵘk), waked (wēⁱkt). OE. [Two words; (1) OE. (*wæcnan*), *wóc, wócon*, *wacen, str. vb.; (2) OE. *wacian*, wk. vb.; both f. Teut. *wak- (: *wōk-*, as in OE. *wōcor* increase, usury) :—pre-Teut. *wag-, weg- (cf. L. *vegere, vigere, vigil*, Skr. *vājas* vigour).] **I.** To remain awake. **1.** *intr.* To be or remain awake. Also, to be still up and about (at night). Now *rare* exc. in pres. pple. and ppl. adj. †**b.** To sit up late for pleasure or revelry –1602. **c.** with advb. obj. *the night, a night* (poet.). Also quasi-*trans.* with complement. 1480. **2.** To keep watch while others sleep, be on guard at night. Now only *dial.*, to sit up at night *with* a (sick) person. ME. **3.** To stay awake or pass the night in prayer; to keep vigil in church, in the presence of a corpse, etc. *Obs.* exc. *dial.* OE. **4.** *trans.* To watch or guard (one who sleeps, etc.); to keep watch upon or over. *Obs.* exc. *dial.* ME. **b.** To hold a wake over. Now *dial.* ME.

1. They cannot .. be waking at this late hour DICKENS. Phr. *To keep* (†*hold*) *waking*, to prevent from sleeping; to keep watchful or on the alert; This confusion of my Thoughts kept me waking all Night DE FOE. **b.** I could w. a winter night For the sake o' somebody BURNS. **2.** You promised to w. with me the night before my wedding C. BRONTE.

II. To come out of the state of sleep or unconsciousness; to be roused from sleep. Often with *up.* ME. **b.** *transf.* and *fig.*, esp. of inanimate things. Of persons: To become animated, alert, or lively; to throw off lethargy. Of conditions, etc.: To be stirred up or aroused. 1450. **c.** *To w.* (*up*) *to*, to become conscious or aware of 1836.

I..have almost ever since woke at that hour and fancied it morning NEWMAN. **b.** W. vp, w. vp, & be stronge: O thou arme of the Lorde COVERDALE *Isa.* li. 9. Truths that w., To perish never WORDSW. The sleeping zephyrs woke 1814. **c.** The Church..had woke up to the sense of her true position 1863.

III. 1. *trans.* To rouse from sleep or unconsciousness. Also with *up.* late ME. **2.** To rouse to action, activity, or liveliness. Also with *up.* late ME. **3.** To raise, stir up (war, strife, woe, etc.); to arouse, excite (an activity, emotion); to evoke (a sound, echo, etc.) ME.

1. Phr. *To w. snakes* (U.S. slang), to cause trouble or disturbance. **2.** Hands, that..might have..wak'd to extasy the living lyre GRAY. **3.** To w. and wage a danger profitlesse SHAKS. Every melody that wakes the echoes 1889. Hence **Wa·king** *vbl. sb.*

‖**Wakeel** (wǎkī·l). *India.* 1803. [See VAKEEL.] = VAKEEL 1, 2.

Wakeful (wē¹·kful), *a.* 1549. [f. WAKE *v.* + -FUL.] **1.** Keeping awake, esp. while others sleep. **2.** Habitually keeping awake; *fig.* keeping on the alert, vigilant, watchful 1550. **3.** Unable to sleep, restless 1675. **4.** Marked by want of sleep 1628. **5.** Said of dreams, or what is normally characteristic of sleep: Waking 1638. †**6.** Rousing (one) from sleep. MILT.

1. The w. Bird Sings darkling, and in shadiest Covert hid Tunes her nocturnal Note MILT. **2.** W. jealousy GRAY. **4.** They..pass the w. Night in Feasts and Play DRYDEN. **5.** In sort of w. swoon, perplex'd she lay KEATS. A. w. doze TENNYSON. Hence **Wa·keful·ly** *adv.*, **-ness.**

Wakeman (wē¹·kmæ̆n). *Obs.* exc. *arch.* ME. [f. WAKE *sb.*[1] + MAN *sb.* Survives as a surname.] A watchman.

In the borough of Ripon. **a.** In the 15–16th c. one of a class of municipal officers whose duties included attendance on the shrine of St. Wilfrid. **b.** The title, until 1604, of the chief magistrate of the borough 1478.

Waken (wē¹·k'n), *v.* [OE. *wæcnan*, f. root **wak-* (see WAKE *v.*) + *-n-* suffix of inchoative verbs of state.] **I.** *intr.* **1.** To cease to sleep; to become awake. Const. *from*, *out of*, etc. Also with *up.* ME. **b.** *transf.* and *fig.*, of inanimate things, etc. OE. **c.** Of a person: To become lively or animated 1825. †**2.** To remain awake, keep watch or vigil. BUNYAN.

1. An he sleeps in this damp hole, he'll maybe wauken nae mair SCOTT. **b.** It was then a great calm,..and afterwards the wind wakened 1634.

II. *trans.* **1.** To rouse (a person or animal) from sleep or unconsciousness. Also with *up.* ME. **2.** To rouse to activity, to stir up, excite. Also with *up.* late ME. **3.** To raise, stir up (war, wind, etc.); to kindle (fire, flame); to arouse, excite (an activity, emotion); to evoke (sound). ME. **4.** *Scots Law.* To revive (a process) which, after calling a summons, has been allowed to 'sleep' for a year and a day 1560.

1. *fig.* Your sleepie thoughts, Which here we w. to our Countries good SHAKS. **3.** Speake to that Lion Lord, w. his anger 1616. Hence **Wa·kened** (wē¹·kənd), **Wa·kening** *ppl. adjs.* **Wa·kener,** a person or thing that wakens or arouses. **Wa·kening** *vbl. sb.*

Wakerife (wē¹·krəif), *a.* *Sc.* and *north.* 1480. [f. WAKE *v.* + RIFE *a.*] Wakeful, vigilant.

Wa·ke-ro:bin. 1530. [app. f. WAKE *v.* + ROBIN.] **1.** The plant *Arum maculatum*, also commonly called cuckoo-pint, lords-and-ladies, etc. **2.** In U.S. applied (*a*) to certain araceous plants, esp. *Peltandra undulata*, arrow-arum; (*b*) to liliaceous plants of the genus *Trillium* 1711. **3.** In the West Indies and tropical America, applied to certain araceous plants of either of the genera *Anthurium* (tail-flower) and *Philodendron* 1864.

Waking (wē¹·kiŋ), *ppl. a.* ME. [-ING [2].] **1.** That is awake or keeps watch. **2.** Pertaining to or characteristic of one who is awake 1567.

2. A w. vision WALPOLE.

‖**Wakon** (wē¹·kən). 1778. [Dakota *wakaŋ* 'a spirit, something consecrated'.] = MANITOU.

Walach, Wallach (wǫ·lăk). 1786. = VLACH.

Walachian, Wallachian (wǫlē¹·kiăn), *sb.* and *a.* 1603. [f. *Walachia*, one of the two principalities which united to form the kingdom of Rumania + -AN.] **A.** *sb.* **1.** = prec. Also, a native of Walachia. **b.** A Walachian sheep 1837. **2.** The language spoken by the Walachians 1864. **B.** *adj.* Of or pertaining to Walachia or the Walachians 1791.

Walcheren (va·lχərən). 1810. [The name of a Dutch island at the mouth of the Schelde.] Used in comb., as *W. ague, fever.*

Waldenses (wǫlde·nsīz), *sb. pl.* 1537. [a. med.L., app. f. *Waldensis*, a variant form of the cognomen of Peter Waldo.] *Eccl. Hist.* The adherents of a religious sect which originated in the south of France about 1170 through the preaching of Peter Waldo. Hence **Walde·nsian** *a.* and *sb.* of or pertaining to (a member of) the sect of the W.

Wale (wē¹l), *sb.*[1] [OE. *walu.*] **1.** = WEAL *sb.*[2] **2.** *Textile-manuf.* A ridge or raised line in a textile fabric; also *collect.* with epithet, as indicating the texture of a particular fabric 1583. **3.** *Naut.* **a.** The gunwale of a boat ME. **b.** *pl.* The horizontal planks or timbers, broader and thicker than the rest, which extend along a ship's sides, at different heights, from stem to stern; also *sing.*, each of such timbers ME. **4.** Each of the horizontal timbers connecting and bracing the piles of a dam 1754. **5.** *Basket-making.* Each of the horizontal bands round the body of a basket composed of rods intertwined as a finishing-off course 1907.

Comb.: **w.-piece** = 4; **w.-streak** = 3 a. Hence **Wa·ling** = sense 4; also *collect.*

Wale (wē¹l) *sb.*[2] *Sc.* and *north.* ME. [a. ON. *val*, f. Teut. *wal-*, **wel-*; see WILL *v.*] **1.** The action or an act of choosing; choice. **2.** That which is chosen or selected as the best; the choicest individual, kind, etc. 1513.

Wale (wē¹l), *v.*[1] *Sc.* and *north.* ME. [f. prec.] **1.** *trans.* To choose, select, pick out, sort. Also with *out, through.* **b.** *Coal-mining.* To clean (coal) by picking out the refuse by hand 1860. **2.** *intr.* To make choice. late ME.

1. He wales a portion with judicious care BURNS.

Wale (wē¹l), *v.*[2] late ME. [f. WALE *sb.*[1]] **1.** *trans.* To mark (the flesh) with wales or weals. **2.** To fasten or protect with a wale 1909. **3. a.** *Mil.* To weave or wattle (a gabion, hurdle) 1842. **b.** *Basket-making.* To intertwine (rods) in making a wale; to supply (a basket) with a wale 1907.

Waler (wē¹·ləɪ). *India.* 1849. [f. *Wales* (for New South Wales) + -ER [1].] A horse imported from Australia, esp. from New South Wales.

Walhalla, var. VALHALLA.

‖**Wali** (wā·lī). 1811. [Arab. *wālī*, f. *wala* to be foremost.] = VALI.

Walk (wǭk), *sb.* late ME. [f. next.] **I.** Action or manner of walking. **1.** An act or spell of walking or going on foot from place to place; *esp.* a short journey on foot taken for exercise or pleasure. **2.** A procession, ceremonial perambulation. Now *dial.* 1563. **3.** An act of walking as dist. from other more rapid modes of locomotion on foot; the slowest gait of a horse, etc.; a walking pace 1601. **b.** A walking race 1887. **4.** A manner of walking; *esp.* the distinctive manner of walking of an individual 1656. **5.** *fig.* **a.** In religious language (see WALK *v.*[1] 4 a): Manner of behaviour, conduct of life 1586. †**b.** A course of conduct –1786.

1. Phr. *To take a* (*one's*) *w.* **3.** The horses were never suffered to go off a w. 1788. Exchanging her faltering w. for a good, swift, steady run DICKENS. **4.** By her graceful W., the Queen of Love is known DRYDEN.

II. Place or path for walking. †**1.** The usual place of walking, the haunt or resort (of a person or animal). late ME. **2.** A place prepared or set apart for walking. **a.** In a church or other public building: An ambulatory; a place where people can walk, as a cloister, aisle, etc.; *esp.* in the Royal Exchange, each of the portions of the ambulatory formerly allotted to different classes of merchants; designated by special names, as *East India, Virginia,* etc. *w.* 1530. **b.** An avenue bordered by trees 1596. **c.** A broad path in a garden or pleasure-ground. Also *U.S.*, a foot-walk, side-walk. 1533. **d.** A public promenade in or near a town 1840. **e.** The circular pavement on which a mill-horse walks in driving the mill 1734. **f.** A rope-walk 1794. **3.** A tract of forest land comprised in the circuit regularly perambulated by a superintending officer; a division of a forest placed in the charge of a forester, ranger, or keeper 1541. **b.** *West Indian.* A plantation 1793. **4. a.** A fowl-run 1538. **b.** The place in which a game-cock is kept 1615. **5.** Land, or a tract of land, used for the pasture of animals, esp. sheep. *Obs.* exc. in SHEEP-WALK. 1549. **6.** A farm, cottage, etc. to which a young hound is sent in order to get accustomed to a variety of surroundings 1735. **7.** The 'beat', round, or circuit of an itinerating official, tradesman, etc. 1703. **8.** A distance or length of way to be walked; *esp.* such a distance as defined by a specified length of time spent in walking 1562. **9.** A course or circuit which may be chosen for walking 1617.

1. *transf.* Far as the solar w. or milky way POPE. **4. b.** *Cock of the w.* (fig.), a person whose supremacy in his own circle is undisputed. **6.** Phr. *At w.* *To put, send, to w.*; When about ten or twelve weeks old puppies are sent out to w. 1881. **8.** 'A cheerful musical home in a select private family, residing within ten minutes' w. of'—everywhere DICKENS. **9.** One of the sweetest walks in Matlock 1757.

III. Department of action. **1.** A department of action; a particular branch or variety of some specified activity 1759. **2.** *W. of life* (more rarely *w. in life*): **a.** A social grade, station of life, rank 1752. **b.** A trade, profession, or occupation 1848. **3.** = 2 a and b (*rare*) 1836.

3. Children in the lower ranks were beginning to choose chimney-sweeping as their particular walk DICKENS.

Comb.: **w.-clerk,** a banker's clerk whose duty it is to collect payment of cheques in a particular district. Hence **Wa·lksman,** an officer charged with the care of a certain length of the banks of a river or canal.

Walk (wǭk), *v.*[1] Pa. t. and pa. pple. walked (wǭkt). [OE. *wealcan* redupl. str. vb. to roll, toss, and *wealcian* wk. vb. to muffle up, curl. To these correspond OHG. *walchan* str. vb., (M)LG., (M)Du. *walken* wk. vb., to full, to cudgel, ON. *valka* to drag about, torment, etc.] **I.** *intr.* †**1.** To go from place to place; to journey, wander. Also of things, to circulate, pass from hand to hand; to move, be in motion. –1815. †**2.** To go about in public, live, move (in a place or region) –1559. **b.** With complementary adj. or phrase: = Go *v.* I. 6. Now *rare* or *Obs.* 1604. **3.** To travel or move about on foot ME. **b.** with cognate obj.; also with advb. accus. of distance. 1460. **c.** In express or implied contrast with *ride.* Also colloq. *to w. it.* 1668. **d.** More explicitly, *to w. on foot.* late ME. **e.** With advs. *in, up,* and const. *into,* the use of this vb. instead of the indefinite *come* or *go* sometimes implies an additional notion of absence of pausing or hesitation ME. **f.** To move about or go from place to place on foot for the sake of exercise, pleasure, or pastime; to take a walk or walks ME. **g.** *To w.* (*out*) *with, to w. together*: in rustic use, said of a young man and young woman 'keeping company' with a view to marriage 1876. **h.** quasi-*trans.* with complementary adj., adv., or phrase 1669. **i.** *Naut.* (*trans.*) To turn (the capstan) by walking round it; to haul by walking round the capstan or by walking away with a rope 1836. **4.** *fig. intr.* **a.** Chiefly in religious use, after Bible examples: To conduct oneself, behave (ill or well, etc.). *To w. with God* (Gen. v. 22), interpreted to mean 'to lead a godly life', or to have intimate communion with God. 1526. **b.** To direct one's conduct *by, after* a rule, etc. 1581. **5. a.** Of human beings or other bipeds: To progress by alternate movements of the legs, so that one of the feet is always on the ground 1762. **b.** Of a horse or other quadruped: To advance by a gait in which there are always two feet on the ground, and during a part of the step three or (in slow walking) four feet: opp. to *amble, trot, gallop*, etc. 1681. c. *trans.* To go through (a dance) at a walk 1810. 6. *intr.* To go away. Now only *colloq.*, to go away perforce; also *slang*, to die. 1460. †b. *transf.* Of animals and things: To be stolen, carried off; to be got rid of -1611. c. With *off*: To depart suddenly or abruptly. *To w. off with*, to carry away as a prize or plunder. 1604. 7. Of a ghost, fiend, etc.: To be seen walking, to appear. Of a dead person: To 'come back' as a ghost. ME. 8. To walk about or perform other actions as a somnambulist. *rare* exc. in phr. *to w. in one's sleep.* 1605. 9. To go on foot in procession; also, to go in a regular circuit or to and fro over a prescribed track in the course of official duty. Also with cognate accus., as in *to w. one's round(s*, etc., said esp. of a sentinel. 1594. b. *Oxford University.* (*a*) Of a proctor or pro-proctor: To perambulate the streets at night, in the exercise of his function. (*b*) Of the proctors: To march to and fro in the Convocation House, as part of the ceremony of conferring degrees. 1530. 10. **W. into —.** (*slang* or *colloq.*) a. To make a vigorous attack upon 1794. b. To assail with invective or reproof 1859. c. To eat or drink heartily of 1837. d. To make large inroads on (one's stock of anything) 1859.

1. Ther was brybes walking, money makynge, makynge of handes LATIMER. Ever as she went, her toung did walke In foule reproch SPENSER. A wonderfull erroneous obseruation that walketh about BACON. 3. *To w. with* (a stick), to use it as a partial support in walking. *To w. on crutches*, to support oneself by crutches in walking. *To w. upon air*, to be in an exultant state of mind. c. We alighted and walked up all the hills DICKENS. e. 'Will you w. into my parlour?' said the Spider to the Fly 1834. g. A certain young woman I'm walking out with 1902. i. The men..walked the anchor up to the bows MARRYAT. j. *To w. out*, to go on strike. 5. a. *To w. through* (a dance) = sense 5 c. b. *To w. over* (*the course*), of a horse, to go over the course at a walking pace, so as to be accounted the winner of a race in which there is no opposition; *transf.* and *fig.* to win a race or other contest with little or no effort. *To w. round* (U.S. colloq.), to beat easily. 7. I am thy Father's Spirit Doom'd for a certaine terme to walke the night SHAKS. Everybody knows that it's an awful thing for a dead man to *w.* 1882. 10. b. He walks into us..as if it were our faults 1861. c. He..with most voracious swallow Walks into my mutton chops 1871.

II. *trans.* 1. To go over or traverse on foot ME. b. To walk on or along (a road) 1530. 2. To walk about upon (the ground, etc.). So *Naut.*, of an officer, *to w. the deck, the quarter-deck.* 1634. 3. To walk along (a line); to perambulate (a boundary) 1602. †4. To attend, frequent (the exchange, a market) -1750. b. *To w. the hospitals* (*a hospital*), to receive regular clinical instruction and assist in surgical work 1781. 5. *Shooting.* To start (game-birds) by beating up the ground with pointers or setters. Usu. *to w. up.* 1873.

1. b. *To w. the street(s*: see STREET *sb.* 2. 2. The dear might of him, that walk'd the waves MILT. *To w. the plank*: see PLANK *sb.* 3. *To w. the chalk* (slang), to walk along a chalked line (as a proof of being sober). *To w. one's chalks* (slang): see CHALK *sb.*

III. Causative uses. 1. To lead, drive, or ride (a horse) at a walk; to exercise (a horse, dog) by causing it to walk 1470. 2. To cause or induce (a person) to walk; to conduct on a walk 1630. b. To force to walk (by holding the arms or pushing before one). Also, to help to walk. 1809. 3. a. To take charge of (a puppy) 'at walk' 1845. b. To keep (a game-cock) in a 'walk' 1854. 4. *Cribbage.* To cheat by moving one's own pegs forward, or those of one's opponents back 1803.

Comb.: **w.-around** (*a*) *Colonial*, a kind of rotary mill turned by oxen; (*b*) *U.S.*, among negroes, a dance in which the performers go round in a large circle; music for such a dance; **-mill**, a mechanical contrivance, the driving power of which is furnished by the walking of a horse; **-on** *Theatr.*, a walking-on part (see WALKING *vbl. sb.* 1 a); **-out**, a strike of workmen.

Walk (wǭk), *v.*[2] Now only *dial.* and *Hist.* late ME. [orig. identical w. prec.] *trans.* = FULL *v.*[2] 1.

Comb.: **w.-mill** a fulling mill (now *rare*). Hence **Walked** (wǭkt) *ppl. a.* (*a*) of cloth, etc., fulled; (*b*) felted, matted (now *dial.* and *Hist.*).

Walker (wǭ·kəɹ), *sb.*[1] late ME. [f. WALK *v.*[1] + -ER[1].] 1. One who walks; *esp.* with the construction of the vb. in various senses, e.g. One who walks *in* (a place), *about.* 2. A person (or animal) that journeys or goes about on foot 1578. b. One who takes part in walking-matches 1778. 3. One who acts in a particular manner or pursues a certain line of conduct. Now *rare* or *Obs.* 1680. 4. *Sport.* One who 'walks up' partridges 1913. 5. A bird, insect, etc. characterized by walking, as dist. from other modes of progression. Also, a stick-insect. 1658.

2. She was an excellent w. 1880. 3. Cast out of the ..Communion of the Faithful as disorderly Walkers 1716.

Walker (wǭkəɹ), *sb.*[2] *Obs.* or *dial.* [OE. *wealcere*, agent-n. f. OTeut. **walkan* WALK *v.*[2]] One who fulls cloth, a fuller.

attrib. **walker('s earth, clay** (now *dial.*) = FULLER'S *earth.*

Walker (wǭ·kəɹ), *int.* More fully **Hookey Walker.** 1811. [Always written with initial capital; prob. a use of the surname *Walker.*] An exclamation expressive of incredulity.

Walkerite[1] (wǭ·kərəit). 1830. [f. the proper name *Walker* + -ITE[1] 1.] A member of an extreme Calvinistic sect founded in Ireland by John Walker (1768–1833).

Walkerite[2] (wǭ·kərəit). [Named by Heddle 1880, after Prof. John *Walker* (1731–1803) who discovered it; see -ITE[1] 2 b.] *Min.* = PECTOLITE.

Walking (wǭ·kiŋ), *vbl. sb.* late ME. [f. WALK *v.*[1] + -ING[1].] 1. The action or an act of the verb. a. The action of moving on the feet at any pace short of breaking into a run or trot. Also, the manner or style in which a person walks. b. *fig.* Manner of conducting or behaving oneself. late ME. c. The action of a somnambulist 1605. d. The action of appearing as a ghost 1727. 2. A walk or journey on foot, the distance covered in a certain time 1542. 3. The condition of a path or road for walking on 1631.

1. a. *attrib.* The 'w.-out' habits of the servant girls 1905. *W.-on part* Theatr., one in which the actor is required only to 'walk on' to the stage, without speaking. 3. Empty heads and tongues a-talking Make the rough road easy w. HOUSMAN.

attrib. and *Comb.*, as *w.-match, -race, -shoe, -tour*; **w.-day**, a day on which school-children walk in procession; **-rapier, -sword**, (now *Hist.*) a rapier or sword such as was worn by gentlemen in civil life.

Walking (wǭ·kiŋ), *ppl. a.* late ME. [-ING[2].] 1. Moving about from place to place, travelling; †vagrant. Now only with implication of sense 2. b. Going about from place to place 1663. 2. That travels or goes about on foot at a walk 1697. 3. Theatr. *W. gentleman*, an actor who plays a 'walking-on' part. Similarly *w. lady.* 1815. 4. That goes about in the semblance of a human being. Often in fig. or similative expressions; e.g. *w. corpse, dictionary, encyclopædia, library* 1605. 5. Of a spectre: That 'walks' or appears 1607. 6. Of a bird: That walks, as dist. from one that hops. *W. tyrant*, a South Amer. flycatcher, *Machetornis rixosa.* 1837. 7. *W. fern*, a club-moss 1829.

Comb.: **w.-leaf**, (*a*) an Amer. evergreen fern *Camptosorus rhizophyllus*; (*b*) a phasmid insect belonging to the genus *Phyllium* or some related genus; also *w.-leaf insect.*

Wa·lking-stick. 1580. [WALKING *vbl. sb.*] 1. A stick or short staff carried in the hand when walking. 2. = *Stick-insect* (STICK *sb.*[1]). Also *w.-s. insect.* 1760.

2. The walking-sticks..resembling the twig upon which they rest 1885.

Comb.: **w. palm**, an Australian palm, *Bacularia monostachya*, used for making walking-sticks.

Wa·lk-o·ver. 1838. [f. phr. *walk over*; see WALK *v.*[1] I. 5 b.] A race in which through absence of competitors the winner has merely to 'walk over'; in extended use, a contest in which through the inferiority of his competitors the winner has virtually no opposition. b. *transf.* Anything that is easy to accomplish 1902.

Walksman. See WALK *sb.*

Walkyrie (wǫlki·ri). [repr. OE. *wælcyrie, -cyrge*, f. *wæl* WALE *sb.*[2] + **cur-*, ablaut-root of *céosan* CHOOSE *v.*] = VALKYRIE.

Wall (wǭl), *sb.*[1] [OE. *wall* (WS. *weall*), a Saxon and Anglo-Frisian adoption of L. *vallum* rampart.] I. 1. A rampart of earth, stone, or other material constructed for defensive purposes. b. An embankment to hold back the water of a river or the sea ME. 2. A defensive structure enclosing a city, castle, etc. Chiefly *pl.*, fortifications. OE. b. *Her.* A representation of an embattled wall used as a bearing 1688. 3. *fig.* a. Applied to a person or thing that serves as a defence. late ME. b. Applied to the sea, the navy, or shipping (as Britain's external defence). late ME. 4. An enclosing structure composed of bricks, stones, or similar materials laid in courses; each of the sides and vertical divisions of a building; an enclosing structure round a garden, yard, or other property; also, each of the portions between the angles of such a structure OE. b. The inner side of a footpath or pavement; the side next the wall 1606. c. (*a*) In phr. *at the w.*, designating a species of football peculiar to Eton played against a wall. (*b*) Applied to each of the players who form the 'bully' or scrimmage against the wall. 1864. 5. *fig.* Something which is a barrier or impediment to intellectual, moral, spiritual or social union or intercourse ME. 6. A wall considered with regard to its surface. a. The interior wall of an apartment OE. b. A garden- or house-wall upon which fruit-trees and flowering trees are trained 1699.

1. The Great W. of China 1850. 2. *Within the walls*: within the ancient boundaries (of a city) as dist. from the suburbs; hence *fig.* within the limits (of the Church, †Christendom, etc.) 3. a. It is Aiax the strong, Who is best hope, defence and w., that to the Greeks belong 1581. b. *Wooden walls*: see WOODEN *a.* 4. Four gray walls, and four gray towers, Overlook a space of flowers TENNYSON. *Hollow w.*, a w. built with an interior cavity or composed of hollow bricks. Prov. *Walls have ears*: see EAR *sb.*[1] 4. b. A rev'rend sire..Shov'd from the w. perhaps, or rudely press'd By his own son POPE. 5. A w. of tradition, which may not be broken through RUSKIN. 6. a. In the mean time, the Preacher speaks to the bare walls 1639. b. Grapes, long ling'ring on my only w. POPE. *fig.* Women grow on the sunny side of the w. TROLLOPE.

II. *transf.* 1. Something that resembles a wall in appearance; a perpendicular surface forming an enclosure or barrier 1697. 2. Something that confines or encloses; chiefly *pl.*, the containing sides of a vessel, the vertical sides of a tent, and the like 1594. 3. *Mining.* The coating or crust of a lode or vein; also, the side of a mine next to this 1728. 4. *Engraving.* A border of wax surrounding the plate, to contain the aquafortis 1797. 5. *Anat.* and *Zool.* The membranous investment or lining tissue (of any organ or cavity of the body, or of a tumour or the like). Also *Bot.* the cellulose membrane (of a cell). 1677. b. The outer horny covering of the foot of a horse 1830.

1. The black w. of forest 1859. A w. of water 1859. 2. Within this w. of flesh There is a soule counts thee her Creditor SHAKS.

Phrases: *To go to the w.* (†*walls*): (*a*) to give way, succumb in a conflict or struggle; (*b*) of a business, etc., to give precedence (to something else); (*c*) to fail in business. Prov. *The weakest goes* (*must go*) *to the w.* *To send to the w.*, to thrust aside into a position of neglect. *To drive* (*push*) *to the w.*, to drive to the last extremity. *With one's back to the w.*, hard-pressed, struggling against odds. *To give a person the w.*, to allow a person the right or privilege of walking next the w. as the cleaner and safer side of a pavement, etc.; so *to have, take, the w.* (*of* a person). †*To lie* (*lay*) *by the w.* (or *walls*), to lie on one side, remain idle or useless; of a ship, to lie up (in dock or harbour). (*To be able*) *to see*, etc. *through* or *into a* (*brick, mud, stone*) *w.*, to have great keenness of perception or understanding. *To turn one's face to the w.*, said of a person on his deathbed conscious of the approach of the end (app. after 2 Kings xx. 2, Isa. xxxviii. 2).

attrib. and *Comb.*: **w. box**, a postal collecting box affixed to a w. as dist. from a pillar-box; **-fruit**, fruit grown against a w.; **-game**, the Eton game of football played 'at the w.'; **-plate**, a timber placed horizontally on or in a w., to form a support for joists or rafters; **-stone**, a stone for building; also, masonry; stone suitable for building. b. In the names of animals frequenting or living in walls: **-bird** (*dial.*), the Spotted Flycatcher; **-brown**, a common British butterfly *Satyrus megæra.*

Wall (wǭl), *sb.*[2] 1834. *Naut.* Short for WALL-KNOT. Hence **Wall** *v.*[4] *trans.* to make a wall-knot on (a rope).

Wall (wǭl), *sb.*[3] 1884. = LABLAB.

Wall, *v.*[1] *Obs.* exc. *dial.* [OE. *weallan* :—Teut. **wallan*; cf. WELL *sb.* and *v.*] †To boil -1450. b. *absol.* To boil brine in salt-making 1600. Hence **Wa·ller**[2], in the Cheshire salt-works, a brine-boiler.

Wall (wǭl), *v.*² [OE. **weallian* (only in pa. pple. *geweallod*), f. *weall* WALL *sb.*¹] **1.** *trans.* To furnish with a wall or walls. Also with *about, round, up,* etc. **b.** To line (a well, cistern) with a wall 1707. **2.** *transf.* and *fig.* To enclose, defend, bound, or divide, as with a wall, or as a wall does. late ME. **b.** To form the sides of (a room) like walls; to line the walls of (an apartment) 1832. **3.** To shut up (a person or thing) within walls; to build *up* or entomb in a wall 1530. **4.** To close (a gate or other aperture) with or as with a wall. Chiefly with *up.* 1503. **5.** To build (stone) into a wall 1621. **6.** *absol.* or *intr.* To construct a wall or walls 1588.

1. *To w. in,* to enclose with a wall. *T. w. off, out,* to shut off or out with a wall. 2. A Lady wal'd about with Diamonds SHAKS. A canyon..was here walled across by a dump of rolling stones STEVENSON. b. The rest of the room was walled from the floor to the roof with books 1832. 4. Some of the windows had been walled up DICKENS.

Wall (wǭl), *v.*³ Now only *U.S.* [MSc. *wawle* :—**waȝle*, related to first element in WALL-EYED *a.*] *trans.* To roll (the eyes). Also *absol.* and *intr.* of the eyes.

Wallaba (wǫ·lăbă). 1825. [perh. a. native name.] A large South Amer. timber-tree, *Eperua falcata.*

Wallaby (wǫ·lăbi). 1828. [Native Australian *wolabă.*] A kangaroo belonging to any of the small species of the genus *Macropus* or of the genera *Onychogale* (Nail-tailed W.), *Petrogale* (Rock W.), *Lagorchestes* (Hare W.) and *Lagostrophus* (Banded W.). **b.** *pl.* Australians 1908.

On the w. track, hence *on the w.,* on tramp.

Wallah (wǫ·lă). *India.* 1776. [a. Hindī *-wālā*, suffix, expressing relation, forming adjs. and sbs.; Europeans have commonly apprehended it as a sb. = 'man', 'fellow'.] **a.** In certain Hindī or Hindustānī words adopted in Anglo-Indian use, as *howdah-w.,* an elephant accustomed to carry a howdah, *jungle-w.,* man of the jungle, *lootie-w.,* a member of a band of looties or robbers, *punkah-w.,* etc. **b.** Used as sb. with Eng. word prefixed attrib., as in *box-w.* (BOX *sb.*²), *competition-w.* (COMPETITION) 1785. **c.** Short for *competition-w.* 1863.

Wallaroo (wǫlărū·). 1827. [Native Australian *wolarū.*] A large species of kangaroo, *Macropus robustus*; in Queensland and New South Wales chiefly the black variety.

Walled (wǭld), *ppl. a.* OE. [f. WALL *v.*² + -ED ¹.] **1.** Furnished with or as with a wall; enclosed with a wall. **2.** With advs. *W.-up,* closed or blocked up with masonry. *W.-in, -up,* entombed in a wall. 1826. **3.** *Anat.* and *Zool.* Furnished with a 'wall' or investing structure: chiefly in parasynthetic formations 1875.

1. Twelue Cities, and seuen w. Townes of strength SHAKS. A..large walled-in garden 1826.

Waller ¹ (wǭ·ləɹ). 1440. [f. WALL *v.*² + -ER ¹.] A builder of walls.

Waller ². See WALL *v.*¹

Wallerian (wǫlī·riăn), *a.* 1877. [f. the name of A. V. *Waller* (1816–70) + -IAN.] *Physiol.* Of or pertaining to Waller, or to the kind of degeneration of tissue discovered by him.

Wallet (wǫ·lėt). late ME. [Origin obsc.] **1.** A bag for holding provisions, clothing, etc., esp. on a journey; a pilgrim's scrip, a pedlar's pack, or the like. **b.** *spec.* A bag having the opening in the middle and a receptacle at each end 1528. **c.** A beggar's bag 1546. **2.** A flat bag, usu. of leather closed by a flap fastened with a button or clasp, or secured by a band; *esp.* a pocket-book for holding paper money without folding, or documents. Orig. *U.S.* 1845.

1. With her scanty wardrobe packed up in a w., she set out on her journey on foot GOLDSM. *transf. Temp.* III. iii. 46. c. *fig.* Time hath (my lorde) a w. at his backe Wherein he puts almes for obliuion SHAKS.

Wall eye, wall-eye (wǭ·lˌəi·, wǭ·lˌəi). 1523. [Back-formation from next.] An eye the iris of which is whitish, streaked, particoloured, or different in hue from the other eye, or which has a divergent squint.

Wall-eyed (wǭlˌəid; stress var.), *a.* [Late ME. *wawil-eȝed*, a. ON. *vagl-eygr.* The first element is of obsc. origin.] **1.** Having one or both eyes of an excessively light colour, so that the iris is hardly distinguishable from the white. Also, in ME. and in mod. dialects, having parti-coloured eyes, eyes of different colour, or a divergent squint. **†2.** app. = Having glaring eyes –1613. **3.** *U.S.* Of fishes: Having large prominent eyes 1868.

1. Vulgar opinion has decided that a w. horse is never subject to blindness 1831. *transf.* A little, pale, w., woe-begone, inn DICKENS. 2. Wall-ey'd wrath, or staring rage SHAKS.

Wallflower (wǭ·lˌflau:əɹ). 1578. [f. WALL *sb.*¹] **1.** A plant of the cruciferous genus *Cheiranthus,* esp. *C. Cheiri,* growing wild on old walls, on rocks, etc., and cultivated in gardens for its fragrant flowers. Also called GILLYFLOWER. **b.** Applied to plants of other genera 1804. **2.** *colloq.* A lady who keeps her seat at the side of a room during dancing, usu. because she cannot find a partner 1820.

1. b. *Native w.,* the Tasmanian plant *Pultenæa subumbrosa*; also, in Australia, one of the poison-bushes, *Gastrolobium grandiflorum. Western w.,* any of certain Amer. species of *Erysimum.*

Wa·lling, *vbl. sb.* late ME. [f. WALL *v.*² + -ING ¹.] **1.** The action of the verb; the making of walls, furnishing with a wall. Also with advs. 1450. **2.** *concr.* Wall-work; also, walls collectively; also, the materials of which a wall is made. late ME.

Wall-knot (wǭ·lnǫt), **wale-knot** (wē̆·lnǫt). 1627. [First element obsc.] A secure knot made on the end of a rope by unlaying and intertwining the strands.

Walloon (wǫlū·n), *sb.* and *a.* 1530. [a. F. *Wallon* :—med.L. *Wallonem*, f. Teut. **walhoz*, foreigner; see WELSH *a.*] **A.** *sb.* **1.** A man or woman of the race, of Gaulish origin and speaking a French dialect, which forms the chief portion of the population of the south-eastern provinces of Belgium 1567. **2.** The language or dialect of the Walloons 1642. **B.** *adj.* Pertaining to the Walloons 1530.

Wallop (wǫ·ləp), *sb.* ME. [a. ONF. *walop* = F. *galop*, related to *galoper* to gallop; see next.] **†1.** A horse's gallop –1489. **2.** *dial.* (esp. *Sc.*) and *colloq.* A violent, heavy, clumsy, noisy movement of the body 1820. **b.** Used *quasi-advb.* with vbs. of motion to represent the noise of such movements 1540. **3.** *colloq.* and *joc.* A heavy resounding blow; a whack. Also (in boxing slang) the capacity to deliver such a blow 1823.

2. b. Souple Tam Gaed w. ower the stile 1885. 3. His opponent..has a prodigious 'w.', but no great amount of skill 1914.

Wallop (wǫ·ləp), *v.* late ME. [a. ONF. **waloper* = F. *galoper* to gallop, of unkn. origin.] **†1.** *intr.* To gallop –1721. **2.** To boil violently and with a noisy bubbling 1579. **3.** To make violent heavy movements (accompanied by noise); to flounder, plunge. *colloq.* and *dial.* 1715. **4.** To dangle, flap, wobble. *colloq.* and *dial.* 1822. **5.** *trans.* To beat soundly, belabour, thrash. *colloq.* 1825.

3. The gallop of a cow or a cart-horse is a good specimen of wallopping 1825.

Wallow (wǫ·lo͡u), *sb.* 1591. [f. next.] **1.** The act of wallowing or rolling in mud or filth. Also *concr.,* the filth in which swine wallow. **b.** A mud-hole or dust-hole formed by the wallowing of a buffalo, elephant, or rhinoceros 1841. **2.** †**a.** A rolling walk or gait. DRYDEN. **b.** The roll or swell of the sea. *poet.* 1868.

Wallow (wǫ·lo͡u), *v.* [OE. *wealwian* :—OTeut. **walwōjan* :—pre-Teut. **wolw-, welw-* whence Gr. ἐλυσθείς rolled, wrapped, L. *volvere* to roll.] **I.** *intr.* **1.** Of a person or animal: To roll about, toss or tumble from side to side, while lying down or stretched out. Now *rare* exc. as in 2. **b.** To move about heavily or clumsily; to go along with a rolling or floundering gait 1570. **2.** To roll about, or lie prostrate and relaxed in or upon some liquid, viscous, or yielding substance (e.g. mire, water, sand). Often implying sensual enjoyment or indifference to defilement. OE. **3.** Of a ship: To roll from side to side ME. **4.** Of the sea, waves: To roll, surge. Of wind: To blow gustily. Of a liquid, smoke, etc.: To spout, gush; to surge *up.* late ME.

1. b. Toads..shrugged and wallowed up from their torpid beds 1845. 2. Part huge of bulk Wallowing unweildie, enormous in thir Gate Tempest the Ocean MILT. *fig.* The godly..shall not w. in their sinnes *Ecclus.* xxiii. 12. I wallowed in sloth and voluptuous ease DE FOE. A man that wallows in gold and silver WESLEY. I mean to w. in strawberries and cream 1887.

†II. *trans.* **1.** To cause (a rounded object) to roll on the ground; to trundle –1662. **2.** To cause (a person or animal) to roll or toss about; to cause to lie prostrate or immersed (*in* something) –1673.

2. Gird thee with sackcloth, and wallowe thy selfe in ashes *Jer.* vi. 26. Hence **Wa·llower,** a person or animal that wallows; *Mech.* a trundle, lantern-wheel.

Wa·ll-pa:per. 1858. Paper, freq. printed in ornamental designs, used for covering the interior walls of buildings.

Wallsend (wǭ·lzend, wǭ:lze·nd). 1827. The name of a town in Northumberland, used *attrib.* (and *ellipt.* as *sb.*), orig. as the designation of coal from a local seam, subseq. as the trade name for coal of a certain quality.

Wallwort (wǭ·lwɒɹt). [OE. *wealhwyrt*, f. *wealh* foreigner + *wyrt* WORT ¹.] The caprifoliaceous plant *Sambucus Ebulus,* also called Dwarf Elder, Danewort, Danes' Blood, etc. It has a nauseous taste and an offensive odour, and was formerly valued as a styptic.

Walnut (wǭ·lnɒt). [OE. *walhhnutu.* The first element is OTeut. **walhoz* (OE *wealh* WELSH *a.*).] **1.** The nut of the common walnut-tree, *Juglans regia,* consisting of a two-lobed seed (the edible kernel) enclosed in a spheroidal shell covered with a green fleshy husk. **2.** The nut-bearing tree *Juglans regia.* Also applied to other species of *Juglans* and related genera. 1600. In U.S. = SHAGBARK 2. **b.** With defining adj. **Common W.,** *Juglans regia,* called in the U.S. **English W. Black W.,** the American species, *Juglans nigra.* **Grey** or **White W.**: see BUTTERNUT 1. 1754. **3.** The wood of the walnut-tree 1585.

1. In after-dinner talk, Across the walnuts and the wine TENNYSON. *Oil of walnuts,* the essential oil expressed from the kernels of walnuts. 3. Dust-proof cases of solid w. shaped in the best style of the art 1868.

attrib. and *Comb.*: **w.-brown,** the brown colour produced by the application of w.-juice to the skin; **-juice,** the juice expressed from the green husk of the w., used as a brown stain for the skin; **-tree,** the tree that bears walnuts (*Prov.* A woman, asse, and walnut-tree, the more you beat the better be 1639).

Wa·lnut-shell. 1523. **1.** The hard shell enclosing the seed of the walnut; either of the boat-shaped halves of this. **2.** *transf.* Applied to a boat, as a hyperbolical expression for extreme lightness and fragility 1614.

Walrus (wǭ·lrɒs). 1655. [prob. a. Du. *walrus, -ros*, perh. metathesized f. the word represented by OE. *horschwæl*, Norw. *russhval*, etc.] The sea-horse, or morse (*Trichechus rosmarus*), a carnivorous pinniped marine mammal allied to the *Phocidae* (seals) and *Otariidae* (sea-lions), and chiefly distinguished by two tusks (exserted upper canine teeth). It inhabits the Arctic seas.

attrib. and *Comb.,* as *w.-beef, -hide, -ivory.*

†Walt, *a.* 1539. [OE. **wealt*, found only in *unwealt* steady; cogn. w. WALLOW. Cf. *walt, walter* vbs. (dial.), to roll, overturn, etc.] *Naut.* Of a ship: Unsteady –1769. So **Walty** (wǫ·lti) *a.* 1702.

Waltonian (wǫltōu·niăn), *a.* and *sb.* 1830. [f. name of Izaac *Walton,* author of *The Compleat Angler* (1653); see -IAN.] **A.** *adj.* Of or pertaining to Izaac Walton. **B.** *sb.* A disciple of Walton, an angler 1832.

Waltz (wǭls, †wǭlts), *sb.* 1781. [ad. G. *walzer*, f. *walzen* to roll, revolve, waltz.] **1.** A dance performed to music in triple time by couples who swing round and round in the same direction with smooth and even steps, moving on as they gyrate. **2.** A piece of music to accompany this dance 1816.

1. *W.*,..the name of a riotous and indecent German dance 1825. 2. The band..played a w. 1837.

Waltz (wǭls, †wǭlts), *v.* 1794. [f. prec., or directly ad. G. *walzen*: see prec.] *intr.* To dance a waltz. Also, to be addicted to or practised in the waltz. **b.** quasi-*trans.*: To move (a person, oneself) as in a waltz 1853.

transf. With a fair wind she waltzed beautifully round the coast 1900. **b.** He seized me and waltzed me around the little dining-room 1883. Hence **Wa·ltzing,** *vbl. sb.* and *ppl. a.*; *waltzing-mouse* = WALTZER (*b*). **Wa·ltzer,** (*a*) one who dances waltzes; (*b*) one of a breed of domesticated mice which have the habit of spinning round rapidly.

Waly (wǫ·li, wǟ·li), *int.* *Sc.* and *north.* 1724. [Origin obsc.] An exclamation of sorrow.
O w., w. up the bank, And w., w. down the brae 1724.

Wamara (wămā·rā). 1840. [Native name.] The brown ebony of British Guiana.

Wambais. *Obs.* exc. *Hist.* 1761. [a. dial. OF.] = GAMBESON.

Wamble (wǫ·mb'l, wæ·mb'l), *sb.* Now *colloq.* or *dial.* 1603. [f. next.] **1.** A rolling or uneasiness in the stomach; a feeling of nausea. **2.** An unsteady movement (of a person or thing); a roll of the body; a rolling or staggering gait 1825.

Wamble (wǫ·mb'l, wæ·mb'l), *v.* Now *dial.* late ME. [In branch I perh. corresp. to Da. *vamle* to feel nausea, f. Teut. root **wem-*, *wam-* (cf. L. *vomere*, Gr. ἐμεῖν); with branch II cf. Norw. *vamla*, *vamra* to stagger, etc.] **I.** *intr.* †**a.** To be qualmish, feel nausea –1500. **b.** Of the stomach or its contents: To be felt to roll about (in nausea) 1518.
fig. The pains o' love'll work and wommle in the inside of ye like a knot o' adders! 1898.
II. 1. To turn and twist the body about, roll or wriggle about, roll over and over. late ME. **2.** To roll about in walking; to go with an unsteady gait 1611. **b.** Of things: To move unsteadily, stagger, reel 1589.
2. b. His feet wambling one over the other like those of a mummer's bear 1896. Hence **Wa·mbling** *vbl. sb.* and *ppl. a.*, **-ly** *adv.* **Wa·mbly** *a.* affected with nausea; shaky, tottering, unsteady.

Wame (wēⁱm). *Sc.* and *north.* late ME. [Northern form of WOMB.] **1.** The belly, abdomen. **b.** The womb, uterus. late ME. †**2.** In the 17th c. the word seems to have been adopted (in the forms *wem*(*b*, *weamb*) in southern use as a joc. substitute for 'belly' –1764.
1. *transf.* In a wreath o' snaw, or in the w. o' a wave, what signifies how the auld gaberlunzie dies? SCOTT. **2.** If not their Purse, their Wems they fill 1691. Hence **Wa·meful** = BELLY-FUL.

Wampee (wǫmpī·). 1830. [a. Chinese *hwang-pī* 'yellow skin'.] The fruit of an Asiatic tree *Clausena Wampi*, also, the tree itself.

Wampum (wǫ·mpŏm). 1636. [See next.] **1.** Cylindrical beads made from the ends of shells rubbed down, polished, and threaded on strings; used among N. Amer. Indians as currency, for ornament, and (as a substitute for writing) for mnemonic and symbolic purposes, according to the arrangement of the beads. **2.** Short for *w.-snake.*
1. *transf.* He arrayed himself in the w. and war-paint proper for such engagements as manufactured by Mr. Poole, of Saville Row 1890.
Comb.: **w.-snake,** a colubrid snake, *Farancia abacura*, of the southern U.S.

Wampumpeag (wǫ·mpŏmpīg). Now *rare.* 1631. [Adopted from the northerly dials. of the Algonkin language.] = prec.

Wamus (wæ·mŏs). *U.S.* 1805. [a. Du. *wammes*, contracted f. *wambuis*, a. OF. *wambois* WAMBAIS, GAMBESON.] In southern and western U.S., a warm knitted jacket resembling a cardigan.

Wan (wǫn), *a.* [OE. *wann* dark, gloomy, black.] †**1.** Lacking light, or lustre; dark-hued, gloomy, dark –1591. **b.** *esp.* in conventional application in poetry to the sea (waves, etc.) or other waters. (In recent use, prob. always with some ref. to sense 3.) OE. †**2.** Of an unwholesome colour; livid, leaden-hued: applied *esp.* to wounds, corpses, etc. –1655. **3.** Pallid, faded, sickly; unusually or unhealthily pale ME. **b.** Applied to the (light of) heavenly bodies, etc.: Faint, sickly, partially obscured 1601. **4.** *absol.* (quasi-*sb.*) Wan hue, wanness. *poet.* 1821.
1. With vysage w. As swarte as tan SKELTON. **3.** As pale and w. as ashes was his looke SPENSER. *A w. smile*, a faint or forced smile (as of one sick or unhappy). **b.** The blasted Starrs lookt w. MILT. **4.** Melissa, tinged with w. from lack of sleep TENNYSON. Hence **Wan** *v.* to grow or make pale (*rare*). **Wa·n-ly** *adv.*, **-ness.**

Wan- (wǫn), a prefix expressing privation or negation (approximately equivalent to UN-[1] or MIS-), repr. OE. *wan-*. A similar prefix appears in most Germanic langs. Most of the surviving words formed with this prefix are *Sc.* and *north.*; as **Wanchancy,** *a.* unlucky, dangerous; eerie, uncanny. **Wan-thriven,** *a.* ill-developed, stunted in growth, etc.

Wand (wǫnd). ME. [a. ON. **vandur*, *vǫndr*:—OTeut. **wanduz* (not found in WGer.), prob. f. root **wend-*, *wand-* to turn, WEND.] **1.** A straight slender stick. Now *Sc.* and *dial.* **b.** As a type of slenderness or straightness 1508. †**c.** A light walking-stick, cane –1762. **d.** A stick used as a pointer 1589. **2.** A young shoot, a slender stem of a shrub or tree, a sapling. *Obs.* exc. *poet.* and *dial.* ME. **3.** A young shoot of willow cut to be used in basket-making, wattled buildings, or the like. Now *Sc.* and *dial.* ME. **4.** A stick or switch for urging on a horse. *Obs.* exc. *dial.* late ME. **5.** A rod or staff borne as a sign of office; esp. a tall slender rod of white wood, sometimes of ebony or silver, carried erect by an officer of the royal household or of a court of justice, by a verger or beadle, etc. late ME. **b.** Applied to the *caduceus* of Hermes or Mercury. late ME. †**6.** A measuring rod –1829. **7.** A magic rod; the staff used in enchantments by a fairy or a magician. late ME. **8.** A fishing-rod. Now chiefly *Sc.* 1565.
1. Looke you, she is as white as a lilly, and as small as a w. SHAKS. **2.** The stem bends like a hazel w. 1919. **4.** Fodder, a w., and burdens, are for the asse *Ecclus.* xxxiii. 24. **7.** If a good fairy had built the house for me with a wave of her w. DICKENS.
Comb.: **w.-bearer,** one who carries a w. in a procession, etc., as a sign of office; *spec.* as a title of certain honorary lay officials of St. Paul's Cathedral, London. Hence **Wa·ndsman,** an official who carries a w.; a verger of a cathedral.

Wander (wǫ·ndəɹ), *v.* [OE. *wandrian*:—OTeut. **wandrōjan* f. **wand-*: see WEND *v.*] **I.** *intr.* **1.** Of persons, etc.: To move hither and thither without fixed course or certain aim; to go idly or restlessly about. Also with adv., as *about, up and down.* **b.** quasi-*trans.* with cognate obj. *poet.* ME. **c.** To go or take one's way casually or without predetermined route; to go *to* a place by a devious and leisurely course. Also with *forth, out.* 1596. **2.** Of an inanimate thing: To travel, move, or be carried about in an uncertain course; to stray OE. **b.** Of rumours, etc.: To be in circulation 1547. **c.** Of the eyes: To turn this way and that; to rove. Hence, of the vision: To pass (idly or restlessly) from one point to another. 1574. **d.** Of the mind, thoughts, desires, etc.: To move (hither and thither) uncontrolled. late ME. **e.** Of rivers, roads, etc.: To pursue a devious or winding course; to meander 1742. **3.** To deviate from a given path, or determined course; to stray from one's home or company, or from protection or control 1500. **b.** *fig.* or in fig. context: Of persons (also of thoughts, desires, etc. personified): To turn aside from a purpose, from a determined course of conduct, or train of thought; to pass out of the control of reason or conscience; to fall into error (moral or intellectual), etc. OE. **4.** To be unsettled, or incoherent, in mind, purpose, etc. Hence, later, to be temporarily disordered in mind; to be delirious; to ramble, rave. late ME.
1. With Caine go w. through the shade of night SHAKS. Multitudes wandering about they knew not whither, in quest they knew not of what JOHNSON. *fig.* Not in Fancy's maze he wander'd long, But stoop'd to Truth POPE. **2.** In some, the gout wanders through the whole body 1764. **b.** There was no evidence..: but strange whispers wandered about the camp MACAULAY. **c.** Their eyes wandered over the glorious scene 1794. **d.** Thoughts that w. through Eternity MILT. **3.** If the Moone should w. from her beaten way HOOKER. **b.** Madam, you w. from the goode We ayme at SHAKS. **4.** They said he was wandering in his head yesterday DICKENS.
II. *trans.* **1.** To roam over, in, through (a place). Now only *poet.* 1573. **2.** To cause to wander, lead astray; also *fig.* to confuse in mind, bewilder. Chiefly *colloq.* or *joc.* 1897.
1. She wandred many a wood, and measurd many a vale SPENSER. Hence **Wa·nder** *sb.* an act of wandering. **Wa·ndered** *ppl. a.* that has wandered; astray; bewildered. late ME.

Wanderer (wǫ·ndərəɹ). 1440. [f. prec. + -ER[1].] **1.** A person or thing that is wandering, or that has long wandered. **b.** as tr. L. *planeta* or Gr. πλανήτης: A wandering star, planet 1614. **c.** *Hist.* One of the Covenanters who left their homes to follow their dispossessed ministers in 1669. 1724. **2.** *Zool.* As tr. various mod. L. terms of classification; a bird of the group *Vagatores* in Macgillivray's system; one of the wandering spiders (*Vacabundæ*) 1837.

Wandering (wǫ·ndəriŋ), *vbl. sb.* ME. [f. WANDER *v.* + -ING[1].] **1.** Travelling from place to place or from country to country without settled route or destination; roaming. late ME. **b.** Of inanimate things: Devious movement from place to place 1827. **c.** Of the eyes: Irregular turning this way and that 1818. **d.** Of the mind, thoughts, etc.: Aimless passing from object to object ME. **2.** Deviation from the right or intended path or direction, straying, aberration 1711. **3.** Disordered action of the mind due to illness; delirium; in *pl.*, delirious fancies, esp. as expressed in speech 1837.

Wandering (wǫ·ndəriŋ), *ppl. a.* OE. [-ING[2].] **1.** That moves from place to place or from country to country without readily apparent purpose; roving; vagrant. **b.** Of primitive peoples, etc.: Nomadic, migratory. Frequently tr. scientific L. *errans, vagus*, etc. late ME. **2.** Of things: Travelling (or carried) along in an uncertain or frequently changing direction 1590. **b.** Of the mind, thoughts, etc.: Not directed by reason or fixed purpose; random; wanton 1450. **c.** Of the eyes: Roving, restless 1578. **d.** Of the moon or stars (*esp.* tr. L. *planeta*, or Gr. πλανήτης): Not fixed, having a separate individual motion 1526. **e.** Of plants: Trailing; sending out long tendrils or runners 1590. **f.** *W. fire* or *light*, will-o'-the-wisp 1666. **g.** *Phys.* and *Path.* Of diseases, pains, etc.: Moving from one part of the body to another (without clearly ascertained cause). Also (in recent use), *W. cells*: amœboid cells. 1585. **h.** Of roads, rivers, etc.: Winding, meandering. Also *transf.* (*Phys.*) as the distinctive epithet of a particular pair of nerves (after mod.L. *nervi vagi*). 1667. **3.** Deviating from the proper or determined course; †*fig.* disloyal 1600. **4.** Characterized by wandering 1582.
1. To sie that thair be no w. persones efter the hour of ten 1607. **The W. Jew,** a legendary personage who (according to a popular belief first mentioned in the 13th c.), for having insulted Our Lord on his way to the Cross, was condemned to wander over the earth without rest until the Day of Judgement. **2.** O cuckoo, shall I call thee Bird, Or but a. w. Voice? WORDSW. **e.** *W. Jew, Sailor(s, Jenny, Willie*, popular names of certain plants. **f.** *fig.* How often..This chance of noble deeds will come and go Unchallenged, while ye follow w. fires Lost in the quagmire! TENNYSON. Hence **Wa·ndering-ly** *adv.*, **-ness.**

‖**Wanderlust** (va·ndəlust, wǫ·ndəɹlŏst). 1902. [G.] Eager desire or fondness for wandering or travelling.

Wanderoo (wǫndərū·). 1681. [a. Sinhalese *wanderu* monkey.] A name properly belonging to the langur monkeys (genus *Semnopithecus*), inhabiting Ceylon, but until recently almost always misapplied, after Buffon, to the Lion-tailed Macaque of Malabar.

Wa·nder-year. 1895. [f. WANDER *v.*, after G. *wanderjahr* a year spent in travel for the purpose of perfecting one's skill and knowledge after the completion of apprenticeship.] A year of wandering or travel (usu. with more or less direct ref. to German usage).

Wandoo (wǫndū·). 1884. [Native Australian.] The White Gum-tree (*Eucalyptus redunca*) of Western Australia.

Wane (wēⁱn), *sb.*[1] ME. [f. WANE *v.* Cf. OE. *wana*, ME. *wane* want, lack.] †**1.** Decrease in size. -late ME. **2.** The waning or gradual decrease of the visible illuminated area on the moon. Now *rare* exc. in phrases *on, upon* the *w.*, *in* (*the, her, its*) *w.* 1548. **b.** The period characterized by the waning of the moon, *esp.* regarded as a favourable, or unfavourable, time for various (usu. agricultural) operations 1563. **3.** Gradual decrease or decline in splendour, power, importance, or the like, esp. as following on the culmination of a process of gradual increase; the declining period (of a person's life, an institution, etc.). late ME.
2. b. In Suffolk it is considered unlucky to kill a pig

In the w. of the moon 1866. 3. The day was in its w., and still..she slept on DICKENS. It is quite possible that his power may be on the w. 1885.

Wane (wēⁱn), *sb.*² 1662. [a. LG. *wan-*, G. *wahn-* in *wanhout*, *wahnholz*, *-kante* (*wa(h)n-* = OE. *wana*).] The bevelled edge left on a plank (by reason of one face being narrower than the other), or the imperfect angles of a rough-hewn log (the section of which is thus octagonal). Hence **Waney** (wēⁱ·ni) *a.* [cf. G. *wahnig*].

Wane (wēⁱn), *v.* [OE. *wanian* :—OTeut. *wanōjan, f. *wano- (OE. *wana*) lacking.] 1. *intr.* To decrease in size or extent; to dwindle. Now *rare.* †b. To grow less in quantity or volume. Of the sea, water: To subside, ebb. -1815. 2. Of the moon: To undergo the periodical decrease in the extent of its visible illuminated portion, characteristic of the second half of the lunation OE. 3. Of light, luminous objects, colour, etc.: To decrease in brilliance or splendour; to become faint or dim OE. 4. Of a person, etc.: To decline in power, importance, prosperity, or renown OE. 5. Of qualities, activities, feelings, etc.: To become gradually less in degree, to decline in intensity ME. 6. Of a period of time: To draw to its close (usu. with some notion of sense 3 or 5) 1590.

2. But oh, methinkes, how slow This old Moon wanes SHAKS. 3. The light waned without, it grew dusk DICKENS. 4. Plato..had seen the Athenian empire..wax and w. JOWETT.

Wangle (wæ·ŋg'l), *v. slang* and *colloq.* 1888. [Origin obsc.] *trans.* To accomplish (something) in an irregular way by scheming or contrivance; to bring about or obtain by indirect or insidious means; to manipulate, 'fake' (an account, report, prices, etc.); also, to influence or induce (a person) to do something. Also *intr.* Hence **Wa·ngle** *sb.*

Wangun (wæ·ŋgŏn). *U.S.* 1848. [Shortened f. Montagnais Indian *atawangan*, f. *atawan* to buy or sell.] A receptacle for small supplies or a reserve stock; *esp.*, a boat or chest containing outfit supplies for a lumber camp; also, stores.

Wa·nhope. *Obs.* exc. *arch.* ME. [f. WAN- + HOPE *sb.*¹] Hopelessness, despair.

Waning (wēⁱ·niŋ), *vbl. sb.* OE. [f. WANE *v.* + -ING ¹.] 1. Decrease or diminution in magnitude, importance, etc. 2. Of the moon: Periodical decrease in apparent size; the half of the lunar month in which this takes place OE. †3. Decline (of life); concluding part (of a period) -1594.

Wa·ning, *ppl. a.* OE. [f. WANE *v.* + -ING ².] That wanes or is on the wane. 1. Of the moon. 2. Decreasing or declining in power, importance, etc. 1596. 3. Of light, or a luminary: Declining in lustre 1700. b. Of the day: Drawing to a close 1767. 4. Becoming scanty, running short. Now *rare.* 1632.

2. *Tam. Shr.* Induct. ii. 65.

Wanion, wannion (wǫ·nyən). *Obs.* exc. *arch.* 1549. [An altered form of obs. *waniand* waning (moon), used in phr. *in the (wild) waniand* in an unlucky hour, (hence) with a vengeance.] a. *In a w.*, later *with a (wild) w.*: with a plague, with a vengeance. b. *A (wild) w. on, a w. to*: May a curse or plague light on (a person, etc.)! 1570.

a. Come away, or Ile fetch'th with a w. SHAKS. b. I'll teach you to take place of Tradesmens Wives with a wannion to you DRYDEN.

Want (wǫnt), *sb.* ME. [a. ON. *vant*, neut. of *vanr* adj. (= OE. *wana*, ME. *wane*) lacking, missing, also quasi-sb. In later Eng. usage often directly f. WANT *v.*] 1. Deficiency, shortage, lack (*of* something desirable or necessary). 2. The state of lacking the necessaries of life; penury. Also, the condition of lacking food; starvation. ME. †b. Straits, circumstances of want, hardship, etc. -1731. †3. The fact that a person (*rarely* a thing) is not present; absence -1831. 4. A condition marked by the lack of some necessary thing; need; also, an instance of this; hence quasi-*concr.*, something needed or desired. Freq. *pl.* 1578.

1. Three votes of w. of confidence 1859. *For* (occas. *by, from, in, through*) *w. of*, because of the absence or deficiency of; Many, for W. of Wit, shall sell their Freehold for Tobacco-pipes and red Petticoats 1608. 2. *To come to w.*, to be reduced to penury. Prov. *Wilful waste makes woeful w.* 4. I would..Supplie your present wants SHAKS. Still by the pillow of the unconscious sufferer, still anticipating his every w. DICKENS. Phr. *A (long-)felt w.*: something of which the want has (long) been felt. *In w. of*, in need of; not having, or having in insufficient measure. *In no w. of*, having abundantly. Provb. phr. *Then W. must be your master*, used in refusing a demand expressed by 'I want —'. Hence **Wa·ntless** *a.*

Want (wǫnt), *v.* ME. [a. ON. *vanta* to be lacking, to lack: cf. prec. and WANE *v.*] 1. *intr.* To be lacking or missing; not to be forthcoming; to be deficient in quantity or degree. Now *rare arch.* †b. To be lacking to complete a certain total or achieve a result. Const. *of* or with neg. clause. -1768. 2. *trans.* To lack; to be destitute of or deficient in. Now *rare*, exc. with obj. a desirable quality or attribute. ME. b. To come short by (so much) of completing a certain total or attaining a certain result. Now chiefly *impers.* in telling the time of day. late ME. †c. To be deprived of, to lose -1724. d. *Wanting* (pres. pple.): deprived of, without; lacking, less, minus. *Obs.* exc. *Sc.* 1536. e. To go or do without. *Obs.* exc. *dial.* 1562. 3. *intr.* †a. To be in want of something implied by the context, or of the necessaries of life -1684. b. *To w. for* (chiefly in neg. context): to suffer from the want of; to be ill-provided with; in later use also, to be lacking in (some quality). *To w. for nothing*, to have no lack of any of the necessaries or comforts of life. 1607. 4. *trans.* To suffer the want of; to need, require; to stand in need of (something salutary, but often not desired) 1470. b. With *vbl. sb.* or *inf.* (esp. *pass.*) as obj. (now chiefly *colloq.*). *It wants doing* (dial. *to be done*), it needs doing, should be done. 1563. 5. To desire, wish for 1706. b. To desire, with *accusative* and *inf.* Also *U.S.*, with clause as object. 1845. c. To wish to see or speak to (a person); to desire the presence or assistance of (for a specified purpose). Freq. *pass.* 1760. d. *Wanted* (pa. pple.): colloq. or joc. ellipsis for *wanted by the police.* 1812.

1. In France there neuer wanted discontented Persons, who would joyn with his Forces 1648. 2. Some hae meat, and canna eat, And some wad eat that w. it BURNS. b. 'Wants a few minutes of five o'clock, sir' DICKENS. It only wants five minutes to dinner TROLLOPE. d. What a wearie way From Rauenspurgh to Cottshold will be found.., wanting your companie SHAKS. e. A worthless old play-fellow of mine, whose company I would rather w. than have SCOTT. 4. Man wants but little here below, Nor wants that little long GOLDSM. b. 'Your hair wants cutting', said the Hatter L. CARROLL. 5. *What does he w. with* (dial. and U.S. *of*) (a certain person or thing)? = What is his object in dealing with (the person)?, why should he care to possess (the thing)? Hence **Wa·nted** *ppl. a.*, *esp.* of a person, sought for by the police (also *absol.* as *sb.*). **Wa·nter**, one who is deficient in something; one who is in need or desirous of something; (*dial.*) one who seeks a husband or wife.

Wanting (wǫ·ntiŋ), *pres. pple.* and *ppl. a.* ME. [f. prec. + -ING ².] A. *pres. pple.* (only predic.). 1. That is absent or lacking; not forthcoming, not supplied or provided. †2. Needful, requisite -1802. 3. That lacks, or is without something. Usu. const. †*of*, *in*. 1592. 4. Mentally defective, weak-minded (*dial.*) 1877.

1. Were our Teares w. to this Funerall SHAKS. *To be w. to*: to fail to help or satisfy; to prove unequal to. *To be w. to oneself*, to fail to do justice to oneself (*arch.*). 3. Thou art weighed in the balances, and art found w. *Dan.* v. 27. England is not w. in a Learned Nobility DRYDEN.

B. *ppl. a.* (in attrib. use). 1. Absent, lacking, missing 1573. †2. Deficient, lacking; esp. lacking in money or necessaries of life; needy 1616.

Wanton (wǫ·ntən), *a.* and *sb.* [ME. *wantowen*, f. WAN- + *-towen* :—OE. *togen* pa. pple. of *tēon* to discipline, train.] A. *adj.* †1. Undisciplined, ungoverned; unmanageable, rebellious -1697. b. Said of boys, with mixture of sense 4; often (after Shakespeare) with ref. to childish cruelty 1605. 2. Lascivious, unchaste, lewd. late ME. 3. (Chiefly *poet.*) of young animals: Frisky, frolicsome. Of moving objects, viewed as if endowed with life: Sportive, impelled by caprice or fancy, unrestrained. 1565. †4. 'Spoiled', petulant (of children); hence self-indulgent, luxurious -1835. †b. Said of money or wealth, as tempting to extravagance or luxury -1770. †5. Insolent in triumph or prosperity; merciless -1764. b. Of cruelty, injury, etc.: Unprovoked and reckless of justice or compassion; arbitrary, gratuitous 1651. 6. Profuse in growth, luxuriant, rank (*poet.*) 1590. †7. Of speech, etc.: Unrestrained, extravagant, impetuous -1759.

1. b. *Lear* IV. i. 38. 5. b. W. and superfluous insults JOHNSON. Protecting beasts against the w. cruelty of men MACAULAY. 6. *Mids. N.* II. i. 99. Where w. Ivy twines POPE. 7. How does your Tongue grow w. in her Praise! ADDISON.

B. *sb.* †1. A person, esp. a child, spoiled by over-indulgence and excessive leniency -1656. †2. A sportive or roguish person, child, animal, etc. -1812. 3. A lascivious or lewd person 1540.

Phr. *To play the w.*: to dally, trifle; †to behave lewdly or lasciviously. Hence **Wa·ntonize** *v. intr. arch.* to play the w.

Wanton (wǫ·ntən), *v.* 1582. [f. prec.] 1. *intr.* To sport amorously 1588. b. To play sportively, heedlessly, or idly, to gambol 1582. c. To go idly or heedlessly *up and down, over, through*, etc. 1682. 2. To run into excesses or extravagances of conduct, language, thought, etc. 1631. b. *transf.* Of a garden, plant: To flourish profusely or extravagantly 1800. 3. To deal carelessly or wastefully (*with* property, etc.). Also *trans.* with *away*, to dissipate (life, time, resources). 1646.

1. b. Dancing Leaves, that wanton'd in the Wind DRYDEN. 2. Wantoning on venison and champagne KINGSLEY. *fig.* A Wilderness of sweets; for Nature here Wantoned as in her prime MILT.

Wantonly (wǫ·ntənli), *adv.* late ME. [-LY ².] a. Lewdly, lasciviously. b. Sportively, lightheartedly. c. Recklessly, unadvisedly; without regard for consequences; wilfully.

Wantonness (wǫ·ntən,nės). ME. [f. WANTON *a.* + -NESS.] 1. The quality of being wanton. 2. An instance of wantonness; a caprice, whim 1630. †3. As the name of an allegorical personage in a morality play; also *transf.* 1506.

Wa·nt-wit. 1448. [f. WANT *v.* + WIT *sb.*] One who lacks wit or sense.

Wanze (wǫnz), *v. Obs.* or *dial.* [OE. *wansian*, f. *wane* wanting.] *trans.* and *intr.* To diminish; to decrease; to waste.

Wap (wǫp), *sb. Obs.* exc. *dial.* late ME. [Belongs to next.] 1. A blow, knock, thump. 2. *Sc.* A sudden storm 1818. 3. A shake, flap; a sweeping or tossing movement 1663.

Wap (wǫp), *v.* Now *dial.* late ME. [Origin obsc.; cf. SWAP *v.* and WHOP *v.*] 1. *trans.* To throw quickly or with violence. 2. *intr.* To strike, knock *upon*; to strike *through.* late ME.

‖**Wapacut** (wǫ·păkɒt). 1785. [Amer. Indian.] A large white spotted owl, believed to be the snowy owl, *Nyctea scandiaca.*

Wapentake (wǫ·p-, wæ·p'ntēⁱk). late OE. [a. ON. *vápnatak*, f. *vápna* genit. pl. of *vápn* WEAPON + *tak* act of taking.] A subdivision of certain English shires, corresponding to the 'hundred' of other counties. b. The judicial court of such a subdivision. late ME.

The shires which have divisions so termed are Yorkshire, Derbyshire, Notts, Lincolnshire, Northamptonshire, and Leicestershire, all of which have a large Danish element in the population.

Wapiti (wǫ·piti). 1817. [a. Cree *wapitik* (Shawnee *wahpetee*) lit. 'white deer'.] The North Amer. stag or elk, *Cervus canadensis.* Also attrib., *w. deer, stag.*

Wappato(o (wǫ·pătŏ, -ū). *U.S.* 1807. [a. Cree *wapatowa* white mushroom.] The tubers of the plant *Sagittaria variabilis*, used for food by Indians.

Wappens(c)haw (wæ·p'nʃǭ). Also **weapon-.** *Sc.* 1503. [f. *wapen* WEAPON + *schaw* SHOW *sb.*; prob. orig. a shortening of next.] 1. *Hist.* = next. 2. A volunteer rifle-meeting 1868. b. *S. Africa.* Used to render Du. *wappenschouwing*, applied by the Boers to a rifle-shooting competition 1899.

Wappens(c)hawing (wæ·p'nʃǭiŋ). Also weapon-. *Sc. Hist.* 1624. [f. *wapen* WEAPON + *schawing* SHOWING *vbl. sb.*; = Du. *wapenschouwing.*] A periodical muster or review of the men under arms within a particular lordship or district.

War (wǭɹ), *sb.* [Late OE. *werre*, a. ONF. *werre* (F. *guerre*), a. OHG. *werra* confusion, discord, strife, f. Teut. root *werz-, *wers-, whence also WORSE *a.*] 1. Hostile contention by means of armed forces, carried on between nations, states, or rulers, or between parties in the same nation or state; the employment of armed forces against a foreign power or against an opposing party in the state. Formerly freq. *pl.* in sing. sense. b. *transf.* and *fig.* Applied *poet.* or *rhet.* to any kind of active hostility or contention between living beings, or of conflict between opposing forces or principles ME. 2. A contest between armed forces carried on in a campaign or series of campaigns. (Often with identifying word or phrase, as in *the Trojan war, the Wars of the Roses, the Thirty Years' War.*) ME. †3. Actual fighting; a battle, engagement (chiefly *poet.*) –1827. 4. The kind of operations by which the contention of armed forces is carried on; fighting as a department of activity, as a profession, or as an art. ME. 5. *concr.* Used *poet.* for: †a. Instruments of war, munitions –1713. †b. Soldiers in fighting array –1822.

1. *W. to the knife*: see KNIFE *sb.* 1 b. *Open w.*, avowed active hostility. Phr. *To have been in the wars* (colloq.), to show marks of injury or of rough usage. *At* (*open*) *w.*, †*wars*, engaged in w. *To go to w.*, to enter on hostilities. *To go to the war(s* (arch.), to go abroad as a soldier. *To make w.* b. Such railing eloquence and w. of words POPE. 2. *Holy w.*, a war waged in a religious cause: applied e.g. to the Crusades. *Sacred W.* [= Gr. ἱερὸς πόλεμος], in *Gr. Hist.*, the designation of two wars waged by the Amphictyonic Council against Phocis in punishment of alleged sacrilege.

attrib. and *Comb.*: **w.-baby**, one born during a war while the father is on active service; **-correspondent**, a journalist engaged by a newspaper to send home first-hand descriptions of a campaign; **war-craft**, cunning and skill in warfare; w.-vessels collectively; **-cry**, a cry uttered by a body of fighters to encourage each other in a charge, etc. (also *fig.*); **-dance**, a dance performed by savage tribes before a warlike excursion or to celebrate a victory; **-dog**, a dog trained for use in w.; also *fig.*, a fierce warrior; **-game** = KRIEGSPIEL; **-horse**, a powerful horse ridden in w. by a knight or trooper; also, a veteran soldier or politician; **-kettle**, among North Amer. Indians, a kettle which was set on the fire as part of the ceremony of inaugurating a w.; **-lord**, a military commander; often used to render *Kriegsherr* as a title of the German Emperors; **-man**, a fighting-man, warrior (now *rare*); **-monger**, †(*a*) a mercenary soldier; (*b*) one who seeks to bring about w.; **-note**, a musical summons to w.; **-paint**, among North Amer. Indians, paint applied to the face and body before going into battle; *colloq.*, one's best clothes and finery; **w. savings certificate**: see SAVINGS; **-song**, a song inciting to w., or celebrating martial deeds; **-worn** *a.* wasted, etc. by w.

War, waur (wār, wǭɹ), *a.* and *adv.* *Sc.* and *north.* ME. [a. ON. *verre* adj., *verr* adv.; see WORSE *a.* and *adv.*] = WORSE *a.* and *adv.* Hence **War** *v.*[2] *trans.* to worst; to surpass.

War (wǭɹ), *v.*[1] ME. [f. WAR *sb.* Cf. OF. *guerrer*; also *werreier* WARRAY *v.*] 1. *intr.* To make or carry on war; to fight. Now only *literary.* b. To serve as a soldier 1535. 2. *fig.* Of persons: To contend, fight with immaterial weapons. Of things, forces, etc.: To be in strong opposition. ME.

2. Carnal desires which warre against the soule BIBLE (Rheims) 1 *Pet.* ii. 11. So **Wa·rrer**, †one who engages in warfare –1482; one who wars or contends (*against* something) 1836. **Wa·rring** *vbl. sb.*

Waratah (wǫ·rătā). 1793. [Native Australian name.] 1. Any Australian shrub of the genus *Telopea*, esp. *T. speciosissima* and *T. oreades*, which bear crimson or scarlet flowers in terminal clusters; also, the flower. 2. In full *w. camellia*: a variety of the camellia 1824.

Warble (wǭ·ɹb'l), *sb.*[1] late ME. [a. OF. *werble*; see WARBLE *v.*[1]] *orig.* A tune or melody performed on an instrument or sung; subseq. (influenced by WARBLE *v.*[1]), the action or an act of warbling; gentle and melodious singing, esp. of birds. b. Manner of warbling 1547. c. *collect.* The united sound of bird-songs 1776.

Warble (wǭ·ɹb'l), *sb.*[2] 1585. [Origin obsc. Cf. WARNEL.] 1. Usually *pl.* A small hard tumour, caused by the pressure of the saddle on a horse's back 1607. 2. A small tumour or swelling on the back of cattle, deer, etc., produced by the larva of a gad-fly 1585. 3. In full *w.-fly*: The gadfly or its larva which produces 'warbles' 1808. Hence **Wa·rbled** *a.* of hides: injured by warbles.

Warble (wǭ·ɹb'l), *v.*[1] 1530. [a. north-eastern OF. *werbler, werbloier*, f. *werble* WARBLE *sb.*[1], a. OHG. *werbel*, f. OTeut. root **hwerƀ-* to revolve; see WHIRL, WHORL.] 1. *intr.* To modulate the voice in singing; to sing with trills and quavers. In later use (influenced by sense 3), to sing softly and sweetly, in a birdlike manner. b. *poet.* Of a small stream: To make melody as it flows 1579. 2. *trans.* To sing with quavering trills and runs, to carol 1576. b. To express or celebrate in song or verse 1591. 3. *intr.* Of birds To sing clearly and sweetly 1606.

2. The Sky-lark warbles high His trembling thrilling ecstacy GRAY. b. You..w. out your groans with uncommon elegance JOHNSON. Hence **Wa·rbling** *vbl. sb.* soft and melodious singing. **Wa·rbling** *ppl. a.* that warbles; occas. in specific names of birds, as the Warbling Flycatcher, *Vireo gilvus.*

Warble (wǭ·ɹb'l), *v.*[2] 1486. [Origin obsc.] *Falconry.* (*trans.*) To cross (the wings) together over the back after 'rousing' and 'mantling'.

Warbler (wǭ·ɹbləɹ). 1611. [f. WARBLE *v.*[1] + -ER[1].] 1. One who warbles or sings; a singer, songster. 2. a. In the Old World: Any of the numerous small plain-coloured singing-birds of the family *Sylviinae*, including the blackcap, whitethroat, and others having names in which *w.* is the second element, as *garden-w.*, REED-WARBLER, etc. 1733. b. In America: One of the small, usu. bright-coloured, birds, with little power of song, of the family *Mniotiltidae* 1783. c. In Australia and New Zealand: A bird of the genera *Gerygone, Malurus*, and others 1790. 3. *Sc.* A group of grace-notes on the bagpipe 1875. 4. *The W.*: the title of a song-book 1760.

Ward (wǭɹd), *sb.* [OE. *weard*:—OTeut. **warđō*, f. **warđ-*, extended form of **war-* to watch, guard.] I. Action of watching or guarding. 1. The action or function of a watchman, sentinel, or the like; look-out, watch, guard; also, surveillance. 2. Guardianship, keeping, control (now *rare*); *spec.* guardianship of a child, a minor, or other person legally incapable of conducting his affairs. Also, the condition of being subject to a guardian. ME. b. *Feudal Law.* The control and use of the lands of a deceased tenant by knight-service, and the guardianship of the infant heir, which belonged to the superior until the heir attained his majority ME. c. *Court of Wards*: a court established by Hen. VIII (and abolished in 1660) for the trial of causes relating to wardships. Also, in British India, a court which deals with cases pertaining to the property of minors. 1560. 3. Care or charge of a prisoner; the condition of being a prisoner. Now *rare.* ME.

1. Phr. *To hold, keep w. Watch and w.*: see WATCH *sb.* II. 2. 2. b. *All's Well* I. i. 5. c. Called also *Court of Wards and Liveries. Master of the Wards* (*and Liveries*), the presiding judge of the Court of Wards. 3. *Free w.*: see FREE *a.*

II. A person 'in ward'. 1. A minor under the control of a guardian; *transf.* one who is under the protection or control of another. late ME. †2. An orphan under age –1592.

1. *W. in chancery, w. of court*, a minor for whom a guardian has been appointed by the Court of Chancery, or who has become directly subject to the authority of that Court.

III. Defence. 1. *Fencing.* A defensive posture or movement; a mode of parrying 1586. †b. Defence, protection, shelter –1697. 2. *Scots Law.* Tenure by military service. Also, a payment in commutation of military service; more explicitly *taxed w.* Now *Hist.* 1508.

IV. A body of guards. 1. A company of watchmen or guards. Now *rare.* OE. †2. A garrison –1660. †3. One of the three main divisions of an army –1656.

3. The fore-w. foremost, the battell in the middest, the rere-w. hindermost, ech w. hauing his troope of horssemen HOLINSHED.

V. Place for guarding. 1. In a fortress: The circuit of the walls of a castle; the ground between two encircling walls. *Obs.* exc. *arch.* late ME. 2. †a. A prison. b. Each of the divisions or separate departments of a prison. ME. 3. An apartment or division in a hospital or lunatic asylum, containing a certain number of beds, or allocated to a particular class of patients 1749. 4. An administrative division of a borough or city; orig. a district under the jurisdiction of an alderman; now usu., a district which elects its own Town Councillors. late ME. 5. One of the administrative districts into which Cumberland, Northumberland, and some Scottish counties are divided. late ME.

3. He was lodged in the Fever W. 1758. 4. *Meas. for M.* II. i. 281.

VI. An appliance for guarding. a. Each of the ridges projecting from the inside plate of a lock, serving to prevent the passage of any key the bit of which is not provided with incisions of corresponding form and size 1440. b. Each of the incisions in the bit of a key, corresponding to the 'wards' of the lock. late ME.

Comb.: **wardcorn** (*Feudal Law*), a periodical payment of corn in commutation of military service; **w.-maid**, a maidservant who performs the menial offices of a hospital w.; **-penny** (*Feudal Law*), a rent paid to the superior in commutation of military service; **-woman** (*arch.*), a woman in charge of her mistress's wardrobe. Also, with *genitive*, **wardsman**, an inmate appointed to supervise his w. in a prison or workhouse. Hence **Wa·rdable** *a.* liable to pay castle-guard.

Ward (wǭɹd), *v.* [OE. *weardian*:—OTeut. **warđōjan, -ǣjan*, f. **warđō*; see prec.] 1. *trans.* To guard, stand guard over; to defend, protect. *arch.* or *obsol.* Also †*intr.* (*absol.*), to keep guard. 2. With *in, off, up*: To enclose, hem in, shut off (esp. for safety or protection). *rare.* 1586. 3. To parry, fend off, turn aside (a blow, attack, weapon, etc.). Now usu. with *off.* 1571. b. *absol.* or *intr.* To parry blows; to stand on the defensive in a combat. *Obs.* or *arch.* late ME. 4. *trans.* To avert, keep off (harm, danger, etc.) 1586. †5. To take up a position of defence, take precautions *against* –1755. 6. *trans.* To place (a patient) in a particular hospital ward; to lodge (a vagrant) in a 'casual ward' 1879. 7. Of a dog: To line or cover (a bitch) 1781.

1. S. Michels Mount..That wardes the Westerne coste SPENSER. *To watch and w.* see WATCH *v.* I. 6, II. 2. 2. The machinery not warded off or guarded in any way DICKENS. 3. b. A Nation..redier to strike than w. LYLY. 5. Regard must be had..to w. against the bleak Northwind 1726.

-ward *suffix*, OE. *-weard*, primarily forming adjs. with the sense 'having a specified direction':—OTeut. **-warđo-*, f. **warđ-*, var. of **werþ-*:—pre-Teut. **wert-* (L. *vertere*) to turn.

1. The suffix, usu. denoting direction of movement, was orig. appended only to local advs., and in OE, was still confined to this use. 2. The adjs. in *-weard*, like the corresponding words in other Teut. langs., admitted of being used advb. in the accus. (OE. *-weard*) or in the gen. (OE. *-weardes* -WARDS) of the neut. sing. On the analogy of the older advs. with this suffix, there were formed in ME. several compounds in which *-weard* was added to advs., esp. to compound advs. of phrasal origin, as in *abackward, adownward, awayward* (which were soon displaced by the aphetic forms *backward, downward, wayward.* 3. In OE. the adv. *tóweard* was also used as a prep., with the sense 'in the direction leading to', and in early ME. †*fromward* acquired a similar use. Later there are isolated examples of this development of function in some other advs. in *-ward* (e.g. *inward, onward*). 4. In OE. the suffix was sometimes attached to a phrase consisting of a sb. or pronoun governed by a prep. The description of this type of expression (represented by the obs. or arch. forms 'to heavenward(s', 'to the city ward(s', 'to us-ward'), as a 'tmesis' of the preps. *toward(s*, †*fromward(s*, is not historically correct. 5. On the analogy of the abvb. compounds originating from the omission of *to* (e.g. *heavenward* adv. from *to heaven ward*), the suffix has in the mod. Eng. period been added freely to sbs. to form advs. expressing direction, aspect, or tendency. From the 16th c. onwards there has been a growing disposition to use the advs. in *-ward* as adjs.; in the 19th c. or the last years of the 18th c. several new adjs. of this formation appear for the first time: e.g. *earthward, Godward, skyward*; these, however, have been confined to literary use.

Warden[1] (wǭ·ɹd'n). ME. [a. OF. *wardein*, north-eastern var. of *guarden(e* GUARDIAN.] 1. One who has the care of something specified; a keeper. *Obs.* exc. *poet.* b. A gatekeeper, porter, sentinel. Now *rare.* ME. †2. = GUARDIAN 2. –1700. 3. A regent or viceroy appointed to rule a country in the king's absence or minority. *Obs.* exc. *Hist.* ME. b. The governor of a town, province, or district; the commander of a fortress. *Obs.* exc. *Hist.* in the title *W. of the Marches.* ME. 4. In certain guilds, esp. in the Livery Companies of the City of London: A member of the governing body under the authority of the Master or the Prime W. late ME. b. *Freemasonry.* Either of two officers (called *Senior* and *Junior W.*) in a symbolic lodge, whose duty it is to assist the Worshipful Master 1723. 5. The superintendent of a harbour, market, or the like 1538. 6. = CHURCHWARDEN 1 late ME. b. *transf.* Applied to an official with similar functions in a Jewish synagogue 1879. 7. In the titles of officers holding positions of trust under the Crown. a. (*Lord*) *W. of the Cinque Ports*: see CINQUE PORTS. 1435. b. *W. of the Mint*: until 1823 the title of the chief officer of the Mint 1463. c. (*Lord*) *W. of the Stanneries*: an officer appointed by the Duke of Cornwall to preside over the mining parliaments of Cornwall 1485. d. *W. of the Standards*: an officer of the Board of Trade having the custody of the standards of weight and measure 1878. 8. The title given to the head or presiding officer of certain colleges and schools, hospitals, etc. 1575. 9. An officer to whose custody prisoners are committed; the governor of a prison, esp. in the old title *W. of the Fleet* (*Prison*) ME. 10. A member of a committee appointed to take charge of the repair and make regulations for the use of a bridge, a highway, etc. 1486. 11. *U.S.* (and earlier in colonial use). The officer who presides at ward-meetings or elections 1763. 12. *Canada.* The head of a county council 1873. 13. *Australia.* The government official, with magisterial powers, in charge of a goldfield 1861.

1. b. Female wardens made a fit outpost for this palace of many women STEVENSON. 5. *Fire-w.* (U.S.): see FIRE *sb.* 5. *Fish-w.* (U.S.). an official in charge of fisheries. *Game w.*, an officer having the superintendence of the game of a particular locality. 6. Rival candidates for the office of the people's w. 1914. 8. I'll..talke as superciliously, and walke As stately, as the W. of a colledge 1632.

attrib.: **w.-court** (*Hist.*), a court held by the W. of the Marches. Hence **Wa·rdency,** the position of a w.; the sphere or district in which a w. exercises his functions. **Wa·rdenry,** the office or position of w.; the jurisdiction of, or district under the care of, a W. of the Marches. **Wa·rdenship,** the office or position of a w.

Warden[2] (wǭ·ɹd'n). late ME. [Origin obsc.] An old variety of baking pear.

attrib. and *Comb.*, as *w.-pear, -pie, -tree.*

Warder (wǭ·ɹdəɹ), *sb.*[1] late ME. [a. AF. *wardere, wardour*, f. *warder* (OF. *garder*) to GUARD.] 1. A soldier or other person set to guard an entrance; also, a watchman on a tower. 2. An official in charge of prisoners in a jail 1855.

1. Late wardours in the Tower of London 1679. *fig.* Memorie, the W. of the Braine SHAKS. Hence **Wa·rder** *v. trans.* to provide with a w. or sentinel. **Wa·rdership,** the office or position of w.; the carrying out of the duties of a w.

Warder (wǭ·ɹdəɹ), *sb.*[2] 1440. [Origin obsc.] In early use: A staff or wand. Later, the baton or truncheon carried as a symbol of office, etc., esp. as used to give the signal for the commencement or cessation of hostilities in a battle or tournament.

Wa·rderer. *Obs.* exc. *Hist.* late ME. [Identical with prec.] A warder or truncheon.

Wardian (wǭ·ɹdiăn), *a.* 1842. [f. the name of the inventor, N.B. *Ward* + -IAN.] In *W. case*, a close-fitting case with glass sides and top for growing small ferns and other moisture-loving plants.

Warding (wǭ·ɹdiŋ), *vbl. sb.* late ME. [f. WARD *v.* + -ING[1].] 1. The action of guarding (a place); the action or duty of keeping guard. 2. *Sc.* Imprisonment 1497. 3. The fashioning of the wards of keys, in *w. file* 1846.

1. *Watching and w.*; see WATCHING *vbl. sb.* 1 b. 2. He was put under w. for a time SCOTT. 3. A thin flat file called a 'w. file' 1881.

Wardmote (wǭ·ɹdmout). late ME. [f. WARD *sb.* + *mote* MOOT *sb.*] A meeting of the citizens of a ward; esp. in the City of London, a meeting of the liverymen of a ward under the presidency of the alderman.

attrib.: **w. inquest, quest,** (*a*) a judicial inquiry made by a w.; (*b*) the body of men composing a w.

Wardour-street (wǭ·ɹdəɹ,strīt). The name of a street in London, mainly occupied by dealers in antique and imitation-antique furniture. Used *attrib.* in *W. English*, applied to the pseudo-archaic diction affected by some writers, esp. of historical novels 1888.

Wardress (wǭ·ɹdrės). 1878. [f. WARDER *sb.*[1] + -ESS[1].] A female warder in a prison.

Wardrobe (wǭ·ɹd,rōub). late ME. [a. AF. north-eastern OF. *warderobe*, var. of *garderobe* GARDEROBE.] †1. A room in which wearing apparel was kept; esp. a room adjoining the sleeping apartment; hence, a dressing-room –1859. b. A room in which theatrical costumes and properties are kept 1711. c. A movable closed cupboard, fitted with hooks or pegs, often also with shelves or movable trays and drawers, in which wearing apparel is kept; esp. as a piece of bedroom furniture 1794. 2. The office or department of a royal or noble household charged with the care of the wearing apparel. late ME. 3. A person's stock of wearing apparel. late ME.

1. *transf.* France appears to be the w. of the world 1754. c. Their intellectual w...has few whole pieces in it LAMB. 2. The Lady of the Strachy, married the yeoman of the wardrob SHAKS. 3. *transf.* Flowers, that their gay wardrop wear MILT.

attrib. and *Comb.*: **w. bedstead,** a bedstead adapted to fold up into a w.; **w. book,** a book in which the accounts of a w. were kept; **w. dealer,** a dealer in second-hand clothes; **w. master, mistress,** one who has charge of the professional w. of an actor or actress or of a theatrical company; **-room** = 1 b; **-trunk,** a trunk designed to stand on end and serve as a wardrobe. Hence **Wa·rdrober** (now *Hist.*), an officer of a royal household who had charge of the robes, wearing apparel, etc. late ME.

Wa·rd-room. 1801. [WARD *sb.*] 1. The mess-cabin of naval commissioned officers above the rank of sub-lieutenant; hence, the commissioned officers as a body. 2. = GUARD-ROOM 1853.

-wards, *suffix*, OE. *-weardes*, corresp. to OS., MLG. *-wardes*, OHG., MHG. *-wartes*, the ending of the neut. genit. sing. (used advb.) of adjs. in OTeut. **-wardo-*; see -WARD.

1. The history of *-wards* as an advb. suffix is identical with that of *-ward*; beside every adv. in *-ward* there has existed (at least potentially) a parallel formation in *-wards*, and vice versa. The two forms are so nearly synonymous that the choice between them is mostly determined by some notion of euphony in the particular context. Where, however, the meaning to be expressed includes the notion of manner as well as direction of movement, *-wards* is required, as in 'to walk backwards'. In other instances the distinction seems to be that *-wards* is used when the adv. is meant to express a definite direction in contrast with other directions: thus we say 'it is moving *forwards* if it is moving at all', but 'to come forward', not 'forwards'. 2. In OE. the suffix *-weardes*, like *-weard*, was added to phrases containing the preps. *tō* and *wið* (see -WARD 4). In *to..ward(s, from..ward(s*, the two forms of the suffix were formerly equally common, but *-wards* now survives only in dialects.

To Troyewardes CHAUCER. To me-wards HERRICK. The nobles come peoplewards THACKERAY. He was growing downwards, brutewards 1893.

Wardship (wǭ·ɹdʃip). 1454. [f. WARD *sb.* + -SHIP.] 1. The office or position of a guardian; *spec.* in *Feudal law*, the guardianship and custody of the person and lands of a minor with all profits accruing during his minority. 2. The state or condition of being a ward; *spec.* in *Feudal law*, the condition of being under guardianship as a minor 1549.

1. This is the master-piece of a modern politician,.. how the puny Law may be brought under the w. and controul of lust and will MILT.

Ware (wēᵊɹ), *sb.*[1] *Sc.* and *dial.* [OE. *wār*, repr. OTeut. **wairom*, f. **wai-, *wī-* to bind; see WIRE *sb.*] Seaweed; *esp.* large drift seaweed used as manure. In *Scots Law*, the right of gathering seaweed on the shore. Also SEA-WARE.

Ware (wēᵊɹ), *sb.*[2] [OE. *waru* = OFris. *were*, MLG., MDu. *ware*, ON. *vara.*] 1. *collect. sing.* or *pl.* Articles of merchandise or manufacture; the things which a merchant, tradesman, or pedlar has to sell; goods, commodities. b. An article of merchandise, a saleable commodity (*rare*) 1881. 2. With defining word, as *dye-, grocery-, peltry-ware.* Also HARDWARE, HOLLOW-WARE, IRONWARE, SMALL-WARE(S, etc.) late ME. 3. *spec.* a. Vessels, etc., made of baked clay. Chiefly with defining word, as BROWN-, CHINA-, DELF-, GLASS-*ware*: see these words, and EARTHENWARE, STONEWARE 1761. †b. Textile fabrics –1748. c. The spat of oysters in its third year 1877. 4. *transf.* and *fig.* ME. b. Applied *joc.* to women 1558. c. *The hale w.* (Sc.): the whole number, quantity, or amount 1563.

1. *pl.* A capricious man of fashion might sometimes prefer foreign wares, merely because they were foreign, to cheaper and better goods..made at home ADAM SMITH. 3. b. Euerything he wore was substantial honest, home-spun w. ADDISON. 4. There is nothing immodest..in the advertisement of a man's literary wares 1865.

Ware (wēᵊɹ), *a. arch.* [OE. *wær*:—OTeut. **waro-*, f. **war-* to observe, take care.] *predic.* 1. = AWARE *a.* 2. 2. Prepared, on one's guard, vigilant, cautious. OE. 3. Careful or cautious in avoiding. Const. *of.* late ME. 4. Prudent, sagacious, cunning, skilled. Frequently coupled with *wise.* OE.

1. Thou speak'st wiser then thou art w. of SHAKS. 2. They shall find him w. an' wakin', as they found him long ago! 1897. 3. 'Be ye waure o' judgin' the Almichty' 1868.

Ware (wēᵊɹ), *v.*[1] [OE. *warian*:—OTeut. **warōjan*, f. **war-* to guard, watch. In ME. the native word coalesced with *ware* from AF. *warer* (OF. *garer*), adopted from Teut.] †1. *intr.* To give heed, take care, be on one's guard; esp. *imper.*, as a warning cry, a call to animals, and in hunting –1825. b. with clause. *Obs.* or *arch.* OE. 2. *trans.* To beware of, guard against; to avoid, shun. Chiefly in imper. = look out for! *arch.* OE. b. In hunting and in cries to animals, as *w. hawk* (fig. = look out for police, detectives, etc.), *w. horse*, etc. Now chiefly in *w. wheat* (= don't ride over it), *w. holes, w. wire.* Occas. pron. (wǭɹ). 1529.

1. W. there, roome for Sir Adam Prickeshaft DEKKER. b. W. what you do B. JONS.

Ware (wēᵊɹ), *v.*[2] Now *Sc.* and *dial.* late ME. [a. ON. *verja* to invest (money), lay out.] *trans.* To spend, lay out (money, goods). Const. *in, on, upon.*

fig. There would be little love wared on the matter SCOTT.

Warehouse (wēᵊ·ɹhaus), *sb.* ME. [f. WARE *sb.*[2] + HOUSE *sb.* Cf. Du. *warenhuis*, G. *warenhaus.*] A building or part of a building used for the storage of merchandise; the building in which a wholesale dealer keeps his stock of goods for sale; a building in which furniture or other property may be stored; a government building (more fully BONDED *w.*) where goods are kept in bond. †b. Used as a more dignified synonym for 'shop' –1857. c. In a printing office, the department responsible for printed work and 'white' paper 1888.

transf. The kidney-pie man has just walked away with his w. on his arm DICKENS.

attrib.: **w.-room,** storage in a w.

Warehouse (wēᵊ·ɹhaus), *v.* 1799. [f. prec.] *trans.* To deposit or secure (goods, furniture, bonded wares) in a warehouse. Hence **Wa·rehousing** *vbl. sb.*, the depositing goods, etc., in a warehouse; also, money paid for the accommodation of a warehouse.

Warehouseman (wēᵊ·ɹhausmæ̆n, wēᵊ·ɹəsmæ̆n). 1635. [f. WAREHOUSE *sb.* + MAN *sb.*] 1. A man employed in or having the charge of a warehouse. 2. A wholesale merchant (esp. a trader in textile materials) who has a warehouse for the storing of merchandise 1677. b. *Italian w.*: see ITALIAN *a.*

Wa·reless, *a. arch.* 1562. [f. †*ware* care, heed, + -LESS.] 1. Unwary, incautious. 2. Unguarded, unconscious (*of* danger) 1562.

Wa·rely, *adv. Obs.* or *arch.* [OE. *wærlice*, f. *wær* WARE *a.*; see -LY.[2]] Watchfully, cautiously; prudently.

Warfare (wǭ·ɹfēᵊɹ), *sb.* 1456. [f. WAR *sb.* + FARE *sb.*[1]] *orig.* A going to war, in phrases, as †*to go a w.*; now, the action of carrying on war; the act or state of conflict.

The Philistines gathered their armies together for w. 1 *Sam.* xxviii. 1. Hence †**Wa·rfare** *v. intr.* to wage war, take part in war.

†**Wa·riangle.** OE. The shrike.

Warily (wēᵊ·rili), *adv.* 1552. [f. WARY *a.* + -LY[2].] In a wary manner, cautiously, †watchfully.

Wariness (wēᵊ·rinės). 1552. [f. as prec. + -NESS.] The quality of being wary; cautiousness, circumspection.

†**Wa·rison.** ME. [a. OF., north-eastern f. *g(u)arison* GARRISON *sb.*] 1. A gift bestowed by a superior; a reward –1572. ¶2. Misused by Scott for: A note of assault.

1. Mynstrells, playe vp for your waryson And well

quyt it schall bee 1460. 2. Straight they sound their w. And storm and spoil thy garrison SCOTT.

Wark, obs. and dial. f. WORK.

Warlike (wǭ·rləik), *a.* late ME. [f. WAR *sb.* + -LIKE.] 1. Naturally disposed to warfare or fighting; skilled in war, martial; valiant; bellicose 1470. †2. Equipped for fighting or war -1711. 3. Of or pertaining to war 1560. 4. Of or belonging to a warrior (*poet.*) 1551.

1. The w. sound Of Trumpets loud and Clarions MILT. 2. A Pyrate of very Warlicke appointment SHAKS. 3. Thirtie Carts loaden with Munition, carriages, and other w. utensils 1652.

Warlock (wǭ·rlǫk). [OE. *wǽrloga* traitor, enemy, devil. The mod. forms with final -(*c*)*k* are Sc. in origin.] †1. The Devil; Satan -1568. 2. One in league with the Devil and so possessing occult and evil powers; a sorcerer, wizard; the male equivalent of *witch*. *Sc.* and *n. dial.* late ME. b. *Sc.* A magician, conjurer 1721. 3. *attrib.* or as *adj.* That is a warlock. late ME. b. Pertaining to a warlock or warlocks 1786.

2. The gipsy..sneaks out at night with the bats and the owls,—So do Witches and Warlocks, Ghosts, Goblins, and Ghouls BARHAM. Hence **Wa·rlockry** (*Obs.* or *arch.*), the practice of magic; wizardry.

Warm (wǭrm), *a.* (and *sb.*[1]) [Com. Teut.; OE. *wearm*:—OTeut. **warmo-*, probably to be identified with Indo-Eur. *g^{w}hormo-, *g^{w}hermo-, repr. by Gr. θερμός hot, L. *formus* warm, etc.] A. *adj.* 1. Having a fairly high temperature; affording or giving out a considerable degree of heat (less than that indicated by *hot*). 2. Of the body, the blood, etc.: Having the degree of heat natural to the living organism OE. b. Of persons: Glowing with exertion or exercise, with eating and drinking, etc. Of exercise: Strenuous enough to raise one's temperature. 1606. c. Applied to tears, kisses (combining the literal idea of bodily warmth with that of affection), etc. late ME. 3. Of clothing, etc.: Made of material which retains heat in the body ME. 4. Of a drug or edible: Producing a sensation of heat in the body 1737. 5. Of a scent or trail: Fresh, strong 1713. 6. Of the person chosen to seek or guess, in children's games: Near the object sought; on the verge of finding or guessing 1860. †7. Comfortably settled (*in* a seat, office); securely established *in* (possession of) -1809. 8. Comfortably off, well to do. Now chiefly *colloq.* 1571. 9. Of fighting, etc.: Vigorously conducted. Of a combatant: Dangerous to tackle. Of a locality: Dangerous to live in. 1627. 10. Of persons, controversy, the passions, etc.: Ardent, zealous, keen; prone to excitement, impulsive. Now somewhat *rare.* late ME. 11. Hot-tempered, angry 1547. 12. Full of love, gratitude, etc.; very cordial or tender 1480. 13. Characterized by, of the nature of, or prone to sexual desire; amorous 1592. 14. Of fancy, ideas, etc.: Ardent, lively, glowing 1668. b. Of imaginative composition: Indelicate in its appeal to sexual emotion 1814. 15. Of colour: Suggestive of warmth 1764.

1. Promise me to take a little something w. before you go to bed DICKENS. *fig. To keep a seat* or *place w.*, to occupy it temporarily for another. 2. A fur'd gowne to keepe him warme SHAKS. c. In Winter with warme teares Ile melt the snow SHAKS. 3. W. clothing for the poor 1917. 7. The conquering King was scarce w. in his Throne 1647. 8. A w. man; a fellow who will cut up well MACAULAY. 9. Phr. *W. work*, hot fighting. *To make it* (or *things*) *w. for* (a person), to attack or 'go for' him. *A w. reception*, a vigorous onslaught or resistance; a demonstration of hostile feeling. 12. My warmest vows of constancy GOLDSM. A very w. friendship DICKENS. They were now w. friends 1891.

B. *absol.* and *sb.*[1] 1. That which is warm; warmth (*rare*) ME. 2. *British* (*Service*) *w.*, a warm short overcoat worn especially by officers of the army 1901.

Comb.: **w. bath**, a bath of w. water (often as medical treatment); **-blooded** *a.*, having w. blood; *spec.* of mammals and birds, which have a uniform high temperature; **-hearted** *a.*, having a w. heart; of a generous and affectionate nature; **-house**, a kind of hot-house; **w. water**, water heated to a degree considerably below boiling-point; the seas of warmer regions as opposed to the Arctic Ocean; **w. with** *colloq.*, (spirits) mixed with hot water and sugar. Hence **Wa·rmish** *a.* somewhat w. **Wa·rm-ly** *adv.*, **-ness** (now *rare*).

Warm (wǭrm), *adv.* [OE. *wearme*, f. the adj.] Warmly; so as to be warm.

Warm (wǭrm), *v.* [Two formations: (i) OE. (**wierman*), *węrman*:—OTeut. **warmjan*; (ii) OE. *wearmian*:—OTeut. **warmæjan*; both f. OTeut. **warmo-* WARM *a.*] I. 1. *trans.* To make (the body, etc.) warm by approach to a fire, by exercise, clothing, etc.; to impart warmth to. 2. *fig.* To inspire with affection or kindly feelings; to render eager or zealous; †to exhort to valour; †to provoke (temper). Of drink: To excite, stimulate. 1526. 3. To make (a material object or substance) warm; to heat moderately OE. b. To impart warmth of colour to 1853. 4. To heat (a building, a room) to a moderate temperature 1858. †5. To inaugurate (a new house) by a feast or entertainment -1800. †6. *Mil.* To throw (an enemy) into commotion by a cannonade -1720. 7. *dial.* To beat, flog 1824.

1. Warming themselves in the sun 1798. The blood that warms an English yeoman 1896. *absol.* There shall not be a coale to w. at *Isa.* xlvii. 14. 2. It will w. my heart to witness the happiness of those friends who are dearest to me DICKENS. Anne, who is so difficult to w. up to bare satisfaction point 1857. 3. *To w. up* (U.S. *to w. over*), to make warm again (cooked food that has become cold). Also *fig.*; All the old anti-Turk abuse was warmed up again 1876. 7. Take out your strap and w. him 1853.

II. *intr.* 1. To be raised in temperature OE. b. Of colour: To become 'warmer' or more ruddy 1831. 2. To become affectionate, kindly, or genial (*to*, *towards* a person). late ME. 3. To become eager, animated, or enthusiastic. Also with *up*. 1749.

2. Your Grace's heart wad w. to the tartan SCOTT. 3. *To w.* (*up*) *to*, to acquire zest for, 'put one's back into'. Hence **Warm** *sb.*[2] an act of warming or state of becoming warm (somewhat *colloq.*). **Wa·rmer**, a person who warms (*poet.*); a contrivance for warming (usu. with defining word prefixed, as *foot-*, *plate-w.*). **Wa·rming**, *vbl. sb.* the action of making warm, the state of becoming warm; (*dial.*) a thrashing, trouncing; also *attrib.* **Wa·rming** *ppl. a.* **Wa·rmish** *a.* somewhat warm.

Wa·rming-pan. 1573. 1. A long-handled covered pan of metal (usu. of brass) to contain live coals, etc., formerly in common use for warming beds. 2. *Hist.* With allusion to the story that James II's son, afterwards called the Old Pretender, was a supposititious child introduced into the Queen's bed in a warming-pan 1689. 3. *slang.* A person who temporarily holds a place or employment until the intended occupant is ready to take it 1846.

2. Our immortal deliverer from papists and pretenders, and wooden shoes and warming pans SCOTT. 3. A *locum tenens* (ecclesiasticè, a w.) was wanted for a Yorkshire living 1846.

Warmth (wǭrmþ). ME. [OE. **wiermþu*, **wærmþu* = MLG., MHG. *wermede*, *warmte*:—OTeut. **warmiþō*, f. **warmo-*: see WARM *a.* and -TH.] 1. A moderately hot or pleasantly heated state of the atmosphere; a temperate heat radiating from the sun, a fire, etc. 2. The natural heat of a living body; vital heat 1592. 3. A moderate degree of heat inherent or produced in a substance or liquid 1748. 4. An excited or fervent state of the feelings; strength or glow of feeling; ardour, enthusiasm; heartiness 1596. b. A heated state of the temper approaching anger; the expression or exhibition of this 1710. 5. A glowing hue; *spec.* in *Painting*, a glowing effect produced by the use of warm colours 1717.

2. No w., no breath shall testifie thou livest SHAKS. 4. The matter was taken up with unexpected w. 1893. 5. Titian's w. divine POPE. His skin had a truly Spanish w. and intensity of colouring 1834. Hence **Wa·rmthless** *a.* (*rare*) devoid of warmth.

Warn (wǭrn), *v.*[1] [OE. *war*(*e*)*nian*, *wearnian*:—OTeut. **waranōjan* (-*æjan*), f. **war-* to be cautious; see WARE *a.*] 1. *trans.* To give timely notice to (a person) of impending danger or misfortune. 2. To put (a person) on his guard, to caution *against* some person or thing as dangerous ME. 3. To give (a person) cautionary notice or advice with regard to actions or conduct OE. 4. To inform, notify. Now only in restricted use, to notify of something requiring attention. ME. b. To give previous notice to ME. c. *absol.* or *intr.* Of a clock: To make the clicking or whirring noise which indicates that it is about to strike. *dial.* 1846. 5. To notify of something commanded; to order under penalties. late ME. b. To notify (a person) to go *from*, *out of* (a place), *away* 1592. 6. To summon (a person *to* a duty, place, etc.). In later use chiefly, To summon officially; to command the attendance of. Now only *Mil.* ME.

1. They say it often comes to w. people of their death MRS. RADCLIFFE. 3. *absol.* A perfect Woman, nobly planned, To w., to comfort, and command WORDSW. I w. you not to do so; I w. you to read what I have written 1852. 4. The broker did not w. us of the arrival of the vessel 1886. b. But I w. you I will call again very soon 1866. 5. He had warn'd them from the Seas DRYDEN. His royal summons warn'd the land, That all..Should instant take the spear SCOTT. *To w. off*, to notify (a person) to keep at a distance, or to keep *off* (private ground). *To w. off* (*the course*) (Racing), to prohibit (a defaulter against the laws of the Jockey Club) from riding or running horses at meetings under its jurisdiction. 6. *Rich. III.* I. iii. 39. Officers and soldiers are warned for guard 1802. Hence **Wa·rner**, one who warns or gives warning to others; *transf.* esp. a mechanical device for giving warning.

†**Warn**, *v.*[2] [Two formations: (i) OE. *wiernan*:—OTeut. **warnjan*; (ii) OE. *wearnian*:—OTeut. **warnōjan*; both f. OTeut. **warnō* (OE. *wearn*), f. the root **wer-*, *war-* to obstruct, defend.] *trans.* To refuse, deny, forbid; to prevent, hinder, restrain -1611.

Warnel (wǭ·rnĕl). Now *dial.* [OE. *wernægel.*] = WARBLE *sb.*[2] 2, 3.

Warning (wǭ·rniŋ), *vbl. sb.* [OE. *war*(*e*)*nung*, *wearning*, f. *war*(*e*)*nian*, *wearnian* WARN *v.*[1]; see -ING[1].] †1. Taking heed, precaution -1590. 2. Previous intimation or threat of impending evil or danger; a portent of coming evil OE. 3. Advice to beware of a person or thing; cautionary advice against imprudent or vicious action, etc. OE. b. A deterrent example 1613. 4. Previous notice of an event whether good or bad ME. b. In some clocks, the rattling or whirring noise which precedes the striking 1775. 5. Notice of the termination of a business relation given by one of the parties to the other; esp. by a landlord to a tenant, a master to a servant, etc., or vice versa. late ME. †6. Intimation, notification of a fact or a present occurrence -1821.

2. Phr. *To give w.* (*to*); Looke to thy selfe; I gyue thee fayre w. 1600. †*Scarborough w.*: see SCARBOROUGH. 3. A wyse man wil receaue warnynge, but a foole wil sooner be smytten in the face COVERDALE *Prov.* x. 8. *To take w.*, to alter one's course of action when warned of its danger. b. Such a man is a spectacle and a w. to us all 1857. 4. *Tam. Shr.* IV. iv. 60. An Angel gave the Blessed Virgin three days w. of her Death 1701. 5. Mary Dishley gave her mistress w.: no fault to find with her place, but wanted a change 1872.

Comb.: **w.-bell**, (*a*) a bell for giving alarm of fire or invasion; (*b*) a bell announcing the imminent departure of a vessel; **-gun**, a gun sounded as an alarm or announcement; **-lever**, *Horology*, the lever that sets in motion the w.-wheel; **-piece**, (*a*) = *w.-gun*; (*b*) *Horology*, the piece that 'warns' that the clock is about to strike; **w.-pipe**, an overflow pipe serving to show when a cistern is too full; **w.-wheel**, *Horology*, the wheel that produces the 'warning'.

Warning (wǭ·rniŋ), *ppl. a.* 1552. [f. as prec. + -ING[2].] That warns, in senses of the verb; *spec.* in *Biol.* of coloration or other distinctive marks found in caterpillars, etc. Hence **Wa·rningly** *adv.*

Wa·r O·ffice. 1721. a. The department of the British Government, presided over by the Secretary of State for War, which is charged with the administration of the Army; the building in which the business of this department is carried on. b. *U.S.* The War Department.

Warp (wǭrp), *sb.* [OE. *wearp*:—OTeut. **warpo-*, f. **werp-*, *warp-* to throw; see next.] 1. *Weaving.* The threads which are extended lengthwise in the loom, usu. twisted harder than the weft or woof, with which these threads are crossed to form the web or piece. 2. *Naut.* A rope or light hawser attached at one end to some fixed object, used in hauling or in moving a ship from one place to another in a harbour, road, or river ME. b. *Trawl-fishing.* A rope attached to a net 1835. c. *Whaling.* A rope fastened to a harpoon 1897. 3. A tale of four (occas. three or a couple) esp. used of fish and oysters. late ME. 4. Alluvial sediment deposited by water; silt 1698. b. A bed or layer of this 1678. 5. A twist or bending, esp. in wood not properly dried; also, the state of being warped or twisted 1679. 6. *fig.* A perversion or perverse inclination of the mind; a mental twist 1764.

1. *fig.* Sorrow is..the..woof which is woven into the w. of life 1849. 4. The tide is let in at high water to deposit the w. 1805. 5. A w. in the glass made him look as if he had taken poison 1871.

attrib. and *Comb.*: (sense 1) *w.-twist, -yarn*; (sense 2) *w.-anchor, -rope*; **w.-beam**, the roller on which the w. is wound; **-lace**, a kind of lace having threads so placed as to resemble the w. of a fabric; **-wire**, one of the lengthwise wires in a wire-loom.

Warp (wǭɹp), *v.* [Com. Teut. str. vb.; OE. *weorpan* (*wearp, wurpon, worpen*) :—OTeut. **werpan-, warp-, wurp-*; cf. prec. The str. conjugation did not survive later than the 15th c.] †**I.** *trans.* To cast, throw, fling –1513. **II. 1.** To bend, curve, or twist (an object) out of shape; *spec.* to curve (timber) by the application of steam; also, to distort, contort (the body or a limb, the features). late ME. **2.** *intr.* To become bent, twisted, or uneven, by shrinkage or contraction: *esp.* said of timber 1440. **3.** *trans.* To cause to shrink, shrivel, corrugate (*rare*) 1600. **b.** *intr.* To shrink or shrivel, become contracted or wrinkled (*rare*) 1579. **4.** *trans.* To pervert, distort (the mind, judgement, principles, etc.); to turn (*aside*) from rectitude or the straight path. Also const. *from, out of, to, into.* 1599. **5.** To distort, wrest, misinterpret (a fact, account, etc.) 1717. **6.** To turn aside (a moving body) from its path or orbit. Also, to deflect (one's journey). *rare.* 1725. †**7.** *intr.* To turn from the straight path; to deviate, swerve, go astray –1817.

2. Old wood seldom warps in the wetting SCOTT. 3. *A.Y.L.* II. vii. 187. b. The Fames of Shakespear and of Ben Must w., before my nobler fire To their regardless Tombs retire TUTCHIN. 4. I have no private considerations to w. me in this controversy ADDISON. By the present mode of education we are forcibly warped from the bias of nature GOLDSM. 5. Warping the Scriptures into Erastianism SCOTT. 7. *Meas. for M.* I. i. 15.

III. 1. *trans.* To arrange (threads, yarn) so as to form a warp; to wind on a warp-beam 1598. **2.** *Rope-making.* To stretch (yarn) into lengths to be tarred 1815. †**3.** To twist, entwine, insert (something *into* something else) –1822. **4.** *Angling.* To fasten (the materials of an artificial fly) to the hook 1676.

3. Those strings of pearl, which you fret me by warping into my tresses SCOTT.

IV. 1. *Naut.* To move (a ship) along by hauling on a 'warp'. Also *absol.* and *intr.* of a ship: To move by warping. 1513. **2.** *intr.* To progress slowly or with effort by using the hands as well as the feet. Also *refl.* 1796. **3.** To float or whirl through the air. Chiefly *poet.* 1565.

1. Phr. *To w. one's way.* 2. The first mate..warping himself from one belaying-pin to another 1859.

V. 1. *trans.* To choke *up* (a channel) with alluvial deposit. Also *intr.*, to become choked *up.* 1745. **2.** To cover (land) by natural or artificial flooding, with a deposit of alluvial soil 1799. Hence **Warped** *ppl. a.* bent, contorted, or twisted out of shape; enriched with alluvial warp. **Wa·rper,** one who winds yarn in preparation for weaving; one who lays the warp for the weaver.

Wa·r-path. 1768. Among North Amer. Indians: The path or route taken by a warlike expedition.

To be or *go on the w.*, to go to war, be out for scalps; also *transf.* and *fig.*

Wa·rping, *vbl. sb.* 1440. [f. WARP *v.* + -ING [1].] **1.** The action of preparing a warp for weaving. **2.** The action of moving a ship from one place to another by means of warps 1513. **3.** The process of flooding low-lying land near a tidal river so that the muddy alluvium may be deposited when the water is withdrawn 1799. **4.** The action of twisting or bending, or the fact of becoming twisted or bent; an instance of this 1440. **5.** *Carpentry.* A strengthening brace 1833. **6.** *Angling.* The wound thread which attaches the artificial fly to the hook 1676.

4. *fig.* The w. of opinion which the bias of patriotism causes SPENCER.

‖ **Warracoori** (wǫrăkūᵊ·ri). 1858. [Native name.] The wood of the white cedar of Demerara.

Warrandice (wǫ·răndis). Chiefly *Sc.* 1466. [a. AF. *warandise*, var. of *warantise*, f. *warantir* WARRANT *v.*] **a.** A guarantee, an undertaking to secure another against risk. Chiefly in *Scots Law*; now only as a literary archaism 1488. **b.** *spec.* in *Scots Law.* The obligation to indemnify the grantee or purchaser of land if an evictive or paramount claim should be established against the lands through defect of title 1466.

a. I'se be caution for them—I'se give you my personal w. SCOTT.

Warrant (wǫ·rănt), *sb.*[1] ME. [a. OF. *warant, warand*, dial. var. of *g(u)arant*, f. Teut. source repr. by MLG. *warend, -ent* warranty, subst. use of pres. pple. of *waren* to warrant.] **I.** †**1.** A protector, defender –1829. †**2.** A guarantor, surety (*Sc.*); assurance, pledge, guaranty –1828. **3.** One who is answerable for a fact or statement; an authoritative witness ME. †**4.** One whose command justifies an action –1821. **5.** Command or permission of a superior which frees the doer of an act from blame or legal responsibility; authorization, sanction ME. **b.** A token or evidence of authorization. late ME. **6.** Justifying reason or ground for an action, belief, or feeling 1576.

1. I will be thy warrand for a year and a day SCOTT. 2. *Rich. II*, IV. 235. *To take w. on oneself*, to pledge oneself. 4. Use axe and lever, Master Foster—I will be your w. SCOTT. 5. b. Fayth is willing to obey, as soone as it seeth a Warrand 1635. 6. Good intentions are no w. for irregular actions 1703. Phr. †*Of w.*, warranted. †*Out of w.*, unlawful, unwarranted.

II. 1. A writing issued by the sovereign, an officer of state, or an administrative body, authorizing those to whom it is addressed to perform some act 1513. **2.** A writ or order issued by some executive authority, empowering a ministerial officer to make an arrest, a seizure, or a search, to execute a judicial sentence, etc. 1450. **3.** A writing which authorizes one person to pay or deliver, and another to receive, a sum of money. late ME. †**4.** A voucher, certificate –1598. **5.** A form of receipt given to a person who has deposited goods in a warehouse, by assignment of which the title to the goods is transferred 1825. **6.** *Mil.* and *Naval.* An official certificate of appointment issued to an officer of lower rank than a commissioned officer 1786. **b.** Short for WARRANT OFFICER 1706. **7.** *W. of attorney* = letter, power of attorney (see ATTORNEY *sb.*[2]) 1512.

2. There's a w. out against me, and I must fly 1859. *General w.*, a w. for the apprehension of the persons suspected of an offence, no individual being named or particularly described.

Comb.: **w. holder**, a tradesman who has written authority to supply goods to the household of the king or a member of the royal family.

Warrant (wǫ·rănt), *sb.*[2] *Mining.* 1847. [Origin obsc.] Under-clay.

Warrant (wǫ·rănt), *v.* [Early ME. *warant(i, warand*, a. OF. *warantir, warandir*, dial. var. of *g(u)arantir, -dir*; Com. Rom. f. the sb.; see WARRANT *sb.*[1]] †**1.** *trans.* To keep safe from danger, to protect –1600. **2.** *Law.* To guarantee the security of (land, possessions *to* a person); to give warranty of (title); to give warranty of title to (a person). late ME. **3.** To guarantee (goods, etc.) to be of the quality, quantity, etc. specified. late ME. **b.** To promise under guarantees 1849. **4.** To guarantee as true, make oneself answerable for (a statement) ME. †**b.** To promise or predict as certain. Also, of a thing: To be a sure presage of. –1821. **5.** To give (a person) assurance of a fact. Chiefly in *I (I'll) w. you*, used colloq. = 'I'll be bound'. 1520. **6.** To attest the truth or authenticity of; to authenticate. †Also with clause as obj. or with obj. and complement. 1591. †**7.** To furnish (a person) with a guarantee or assurance –1597. **8.** To guarantee the security or immunity of (a person or thing). Now *rare.* 1530. **9.** To give (a person) warrant or authority, authorize (*to* do something); to authorize, sanction (a course of action, a payment, etc.) 1579. **10.** Of things: To furnish good and sufficient grounds for (a course of action); to justify (a person *in* or *to* a course of action) 1654.

1. Hym I beseche to kepe and waraunt thee..from evyl CAXTON. 3. The manuscript sermons of a clergyman lately deceased, all warranted originals, and never printed FIELDING. One French roll rasped, one egg new laid (or warranted to be) DICKENS. 4. I will w. her a good Huswife BUNYAN. *I w., I will w.*, often used *colloq.* as a mere expression of strong belief = 'I'll be bound'; I w. she kissed thee DE FOE. Some chapel where she comforts herself with brimstone doctrine, I w. DICKENS. b. My fainting words doe w. death SHAKS. 5. ¶ *I w. me* (orig. quasi-*arch.*) = 'I w.' (see 4). 6. A thousand oathes..W. me welcome to my Protheus SHAKS. 9. The Lord warrants us to suspect the inconstant 1642. 10. We are not warranted in referring our sensations to a cause MILL. Hence **Wa·rranted** *ppl. a.* allowed by law or authority; sanctioned; furnished with a legal or official warrant. **Wa·rrantee·**, (*Law*) the person to whom a warranty is given.

Warrantable (wǫ·răntăb'l), *a.* 1581. [f. prec. + -ABLE.] **1.** That may be authorized, sanctioned, or permitted; justifiable 1597. †**2.** That may be guaranteed as good, true, genuine, or the like; praiseworthy, acceptable –1821. **3.** That can be legally guaranteed 1876. **4.** *Venery.* Applied to a stag which is of an age to be hunted (5 or 6 years) 1677.

2. Grave and w. personages LAMB. Hence **Wa·rrantableness** 1586. **Wa·rrantably** *adv.*

Warranter (wǫ·răntəɹ). 1583. [f. WARRANT *v.* + -ER [1].] One who warrants or guarantees. **b.** *Law.* = WARRANTOR 1706.

Warrantise (wǫ·răntəiz). *arch.* ME. [a. OF. *warentise*, f. *warantir* WARRANT *v.*] **1.** *Law.* = WARRANTY 1 a; often in *clause of w.* **2.** *gen.* The action of warranting; the state or fact of being guaranteed. Also *predic.*, of a thing or person that serves as a guarantee or security. ME. **3.** Authorization, permission, sanction 1580.

2. Breake vp the Gates, Ile be your warrantize SHAKS. 3. *Ham.* V. i. 250.

Wa·rrant o·fficer. 1693. **1.** An officer of the army or navy who holds office by warrant, as dist. from a commissioned officer. (In the army, the warrant officers are now intermediate in rank between the commissioned and the non-commissioned officers.) **2.** An officer whose duty it is to serve warrants 1895.

Warrantor (wǫ·răntǫ̆ɹ, wǫrăntǭ·ɹ). 1685. [f. WARRANT *v.* + -OR.] *Law.* One who gives warranty.

Warranty (wǫ·rănti). ME. [a. AF. *warantie* (OF. *guarantie* GUARANTEE), f. *warant* WARRANT *sb.*] **1.** *Law.* An act of warranting: in certain specific applications. **a.** A covenant (either expressed by a *clause of w.* or implied) annexed to a conveyance of real estate, by which the vendor warrants the security of the title conveyed. **b.** An undertaking, express or implied, given by one of the parties to a contract to the other, that he will be answerable for the truth of some statement incidental to the contract; esp. an assurance given by the seller of goods that he will be answerable for their possession of some quality attributed to them 1543. **c.** In a contract for insurance, an engagement by the assured that certain statements are true or that certain conditions shall be fulfilled 1817. **2.** *transf.* A guarantee, an assurance. Now *dial.* 1555. **3.** Formal or official sanction; authorization = WARRANT *sb.*[1] I. 5. Now *rare.* 1591. **4.** Justifying reason, ground (*for* an action or belief) 1836. **5.** Substantiating evidence or witness 1561.

1. a. *Covenant of w.* (U.S.) corresp. to English 'covenant for quiet enjoyment'. 3. From your loue I haue a warrantie To vnburthen all my plots and purposes SHAKS. 4. The smallest civility was sufficient w. for the opening of an acquaintanceship 1877.

†**Warray,** *v.* [ME. *werreye*, a. OF. *werreier*, dial. var. of *guerreier* (mod.F. *guerroyer*), f. **werra* WAR *sb.*] **1.** *trans.* To make war upon, ravage by war –1768. **2.** *intr.* To make war –1600.

1. With this she oft hath Villainy warray'd 1768.

War(r)ee (wǫ·rī). 1684. [Origin obsc.] The white-lipped peccary, *Dicotyles labiatus*, native to Central and South America.

Warren (wǫ·rĕn, -ən). late ME. [a. AF. *warenne* (OF. *garenne*); of Teut. origin, f. **war-* to protect, guard.] **1.** A piece of land enclosed and preserved for breeding game. *Obs.* exc. *Hist.* **2.** *spec.* A piece of land appropriated to the breeding of rabbits (formerly also of hares). More fully *rabbit-w., cony-w., hare-w.* Now usu. a piece of uncultivated ground in which rabbits breed wild in burrows. late ME. **3.**

The inhabitants of a warren; *transf.* any collection of small animals 1607. 4. A building, etc., likened to a rabbit-warren; †a brothel; a building or number of buildings densely populated by poor tenants 1649. †5. An old name for the site of Woolwich Arsenal. Hence *gen.* –1805.

1. As melancholy as a Lodge in a W. SHAKS. †(*Free*) *w.*, a right of keeping or hunting *beasts* and *fowls of w.* 4. A large passenger steamer..is..an amazing w. of passages 1919.

Warrener (wǫ·rĕnəɹ, -ənər). ME. [a. AF. *warrennier*, f. *warenne* WARREN.] 1. a. An officer employed to watch over the game in a park or preserve. *Obs.* exc. *Hist.* b. A servant who has the charge of a rabbit-warren. 2. One who owns or rents a warren 1846.

Warrigal (wǫ·rigăl), *sb.* (and *a.*) *Austral.* Also **warragal.** 1852. [Alteration of native name *warringin.*] A. *sb.* 1. = DINGO. 2. A wild Australian aboriginal 1890. 3. A wild or untamed Australian horse 1881. B. *adj.* Wild 1890.

Warring (wǭ·riŋ), *ppl. a.* 1608. [f. WAR *v.*¹ + -ING ².] 1. That makes or carries on war; that contends in warfare 1702. 2. *fig.* Engaged in strife, contending; *esp.* with plural subject, mutually contending, discordant 1608.

1. W. nations BYRON. 2. All the w. Winds that sweep the Skies DRYDEN. W. Passions 1703. What means this senseless din of w. tongues? 1883.

Warrior (wǫ·riəɹ). [Early ME., a. AF. *werreieor, werrieur*, etc. (OF. *guerreieor*, etc., mod.F. *guerroyeur*), agent-n. f. *werreier* WARRAY *v.*] 1. One whose occupation is warfare; a fighting man; in eulogistic sense, a valiant or an experienced man of war. Now chiefly *poet.* and *rhet.*, exc. as applied to the fighting men and heroes of past ages and of uncivilized peoples. b. occas. applied to a woman. late ME. c. *transf.* Applied to an animal 1697. 2. (*Bloody*) *w.*: (*local*) the wallflower, *Cheiranthus Cheiri* 1825. 3. A South Amer. humming-bird of the genus *Oxypogon* 1861. 4. *Black w.*, an Amer. bird of prey, *Buteo harlani* 1884.

1. Then should al captaines..be tendre ouer there poore warriours and base souldiours 1551. *The Unknown W.*, a member of one of the fighting forces (army, navy, or air force) who was buried in Westminster Abbey on 11 Nov. 1920, as the representative of all members of the British Empire who lost their lives in the war of 1914–18. *Warrior's belt*, three bright stars in the constellation Orion. b. *Oth.* II. i. 184.

attrib.: (*a*) quasi-adj., belonging to or characteristic of a w., martial, as *w.-blood, hymn, laurel, lay, spirit, trumpet*; (*b*) appositive, that is a w., as *w.-angel, chief, dame, god, guest, king, love, maid, queen, son, steed*; consisting of warriors, as *w.-host, -train*; (*c*) similative, as *w.-like* adj. and adv., *-wise* adv. Hence **Wa·rrioress**, a female w. 1594.

Warsaw (wǭ·ɹsǫ). *U.S.* 1884. [An attempt to pronounce the Sp. name *guasa.*] a. The American fish guasa, *Garrupa nigrito.* b. The jew-fish, *Promicrops itaiara.*

Warship, war-ship (wǭ·ɹʃip). 1533. [f. WAR *sb.* + SHIP *sb.*] A ship armed and manned for war.

Warsle (wa·ɹs'l), *v. Sc.* and *north.* ME. [Metathetic form of WRESTLE *v.* Cf. WORSLE.] *intr.* and *trans.* = WRESTLE *v.*

1. Ye'll soon hae poets o' the Scottish nation, Will ..w. Time, and lay him on his back BURNS. Hence **Wa·rsle** *sb.*, a struggle; a wrestling bout 1792. **Wa·rsler**, a wrestler.

Wart (wǭɹt). [Com. Teut. (not in Gothic): OE. *wearte*:—OTeut. **wartōn-*.] 1. A small, round, dry, tough excrescence on the skin; especially common on the hands of young persons. Also applied to other small excrescences on animals, etc. b. = CONDYLOMA 1552. c. A normal callosity on the legs of a horse, ass, etc. 1523. 2. *Bot.* A rounded protuberance or excrescence on the surface of a plant 1793. 3. *transf.* and *fig.* (from sense 1). A relatively small or disfiguring protuberance 1602. 4. *Mil. colloq.* A very young subaltern 1894.

1. Vp on the cope right of his nose he hade A werte CHAUCER. An unhealthy-looking boy, with warts all over his hands DICKENS. 3. *Ham.* v. i. 306. You will not deny you are..A nuisance, a w., a blot, a stain upon the face of nature! 1792.

attrib. and *Comb.*: **w.-biter** [= G. *warzenbeisser*], a grasshopper (*Gryllus verrucivorus*) supposed to destroy warts by biting them; **-cress**, the genus *Senebiera*; **-hog**, a swine of the African genus *Phacochœrus*, having w.-like excrescences on the face; **-snake**, a colubriform snake of the family *Acrochordidæ*, having w.-like scales; **-weed** = WARTWORT. Hence **Wa·rted** *a.* covered with warts (*rare*); *Bot.*, *Zool.*, etc. verrucose.

Warth. *Obs.* exc. *dial.* [OE. *waroð*:—OTeut. **waruþoz.*] A shore, strand; in mod. use 'a flat meadow, esp. one close to a stream; a stretch of coast' (*Eng. Dial. Dict.*).

Wa·r-time. late ME. The time when war is being waged.

These war times were hard, and everything was dear C. BRONTË. *attrib.* A W. Journal 1915.

Wartwort (wǭ·ɹt,wɒɹt). late ME. [f. WART + WORT ¹.] A name for *Euphorbia Helioscopia, E. Peplus* and *E. Peplis* (Sea Wartwort), the juice of these plants being used to cure warts. Also applied to other plants, as *Chelidonium majus* and *Senebiera Coronopus.*

Warty (wǭ·ɹti), *a.* 1483. [f. WART + -Y ¹.] 1. Afflicted with warts on the skin. 2. Chiefly *Zool.*, *Bot.*, etc. Having wart-like excrescences or protuberances 1693. 3. Of the nature of or resembling a wart 1762. 4. *fig.* Rocky, rough 1648.

1. Freckled, wartie, and wodden-faced wenches CAMDEN. 2. Tall, w., black-boled trees 1894.

War-whoop (wǭ·ɹ,hūp). 1761. The cry or yell of Amer. Indians and other savage peoples on rushing into battle.

transf. The accustomed maternal warwhoop BYRON.

Warwickite (wǫ·rikəit). 1838. [f. *Warwick*, New York, where it was found; see -ITE ¹.] *Min.* A borotitanate of magnesium and iron in dark-brown acicular crystals.

Wa·r-wolf. 1610. 1. *Hist.* A kind of siege engine. †2. A fierce warrior. SCOTT.

Wary (wēᵊ·ri), *a.* 1552. [f. WARE *a.* + -Y ¹.] 1. Given to caution, habitually on one's guard against danger, deception, or mistake; circumspect. 2. On one's guard, cautious, careful 1575. 3. Of action, behaviour, etc.: Proceeding from or characterized by caution 1557. †4. Careful in expenditure, thrifty –1812.

1. A w. man he is in Grammar; very nice as to Solœcism or Barbarism DRYDEN. W. old alligators KINGSLEY. 2. The day is broke, be w., looke about SHAKS. Thus men cannot be too w. what they inscribe on Tombs FULLER. To be very cautious and w. in the choice of our words 1680. A tradesman ought to be very w. of taking too much credit 1745. 3. I shall keep a w. eye upon all that passes 1794. 4. I have, by leading a very w. Life, laid up a little Money STEELE.

†**Wary**, *v.* [OE. *wierȝan, wærȝan*:—OTeut. **warȝjan*, f. **warȝoz*, OE. *wearȝ* felon.] *trans.* and *intr.* To curse –1746.

Was (wǫz), *sb.* ME. [pa. t. sing. of BE *v.*] What was; something past.

If the 'w.' is hard to face, how much harder the 'might have been' 1876.

Was (wǫz, wəz), 1st and 3rd pers. sing. pa. t. of BE *v.*

Wash (wǫʃ), *sb.* 1440. [f. WASH *v.*] I. Act of washing. 1. An act or process of washing or cleansing with water 1663. b. An act of washing oneself, esp. of washing one's hands and face 1825. 2. An act, spell, or task of washing clothes, etc.; the process of washing undergone by clothes or the like; *concr.* the quantity of clothes or other textile articles washed (or set apart to be washed) on one occasion 1704. 3. A washing with some liquid for the purpose of producing a particular effect; a liquid preparation used or intended to be used in this manner 1626. 4. A thin coat of water-colour or distemper spread over a wall or similar surface; a preparation used for this purpose (cf. WHITEWASH) 1698. b. *Water-colour Painting.* A broad thin layer of colour laid on by a continuous movement of the brush 1597. 5. A solution applied to metals for producing an appearance of gold or silver 1697.

1. b. What we really did want was a w. and a brush up 1912. 2. The family w...flutters gracefully in the breeze 1889. (*To be lost, damaged,* etc.) *in the w.*, in course of being washed. *At the w.*, of clothes, etc., sent away or set aside to be washed. 3. Essences, powders, pastes, washes for the hair, washes for the skin, recal the days of one's grandmothers 1859. *Black, yellow w.*, various liquid preparations of mercury for application to ulcers or to the skin in eruptive diseases. *White w.*, dilute liquor of subacetate of lead. 4. *transf.* One broad w. of shadow STEVENSON.

II. Washing movement of water. 1. The washing of the waves upon the shore; surging movement of the sea or other water 1579. b. A surge raised by the passage of a vessel 1883. c. The sound of the surge of water 1845. d. Wear or attrition due to the action of waves 1791. 2. A sandbank or tract of land alternately covered and exposed by the sea 1440. b. A low-lying tract of ground, often flooded, and interspersed with shallow pools and marshes 1483. c. *Western U.S.* The dry bed or portion of the bed of a winter torrent 1894. 3. A tract of shallow water, a lagoon. Also, a shallow pool or runnel formed by the overflow of a river; a stream running across a road. 1530.

1. The long w. of Australasian seas TENNYSON. 2. †*The Washes*, applied *spec.* to the fordable portion of the estuary between Lincolnshire and Norfolk; hence as a name for the estuary itself, now called *The W.*

III. 1. Waste water discharged after use in washing; liquid refuse. Now *rare.* 1440. 2. *Sc.* and *north.* Stale urine 1480. 3. Kitchen swill or brewery refuse as food for swine; HOG-WASH, PIG-WASH. 1585.

3. *Rich. III*, v. ii. 9.

IV. Matter washed away or deposited by running water; alluvial deposit 1707. b. *Mining.* A formation of gravel, etc. over an abraded coal seam 1888. V. Soil from which gold (or diamonds) can be extracted by washing 1875. VI. Watery infusion or mixture. 1. Orig., the partially fermented wort remaining after ale or beer has been brewed from it. In later use, malt or other fermentable substance or mixture of substances steeped in water to undergo fermentation preparatory to distillation. 1700. 2. Washy or vapid liquor. Also *fig.*, vapid discourse or writing. 1548.

2. Coffee; not the vile and vapid w. which is usually made in England 1819.

VII. Senses of doubtful origin. 1. A measure for oysters and whelks 1481. 2. The underground den of a beaver or a bear 1809. 3. *slang.* a. *Printers.* An act of 'washing' 1841. b. *Stock Exch.* A fictitious sale of securities by a broker who has a commission from an intending buyer and also from an intending seller, and who simply transfers from the one account to the other, the difference going to his own profit 1891.

Comb.: **w.-basket**, a basket for clothes sent to the w.; **-day**, the day for the washing of clothes in a household; **-drawing**, the method of water-colour drawing in which washes of colour are extensively used; a picture produced by this method; **-land**, a tract of land periodically overflowed by a river; **-linen**, linen sent to the w.; **-plain**, a tract of land formed by alluvial deposits.

†**Wash**, *a.* 1548. [perh. f. WASH *v.*] Washy, weak, tender –1639.

Wash (wǫʃ), *v.* Pa. t. and pa. pple. **washed** (wǫʃt). [Com. Teut. str. vb.; OE. *wæscan* (*wósc, wósc, wóxon, -wæscen*):—OTeut. **waskan*:—**watskan*, f. root **wat-* as in WATER *sb.* The strong forms seldom occur exc. dial. after the 16th c.] I. To cleanse by means of water. Also with compl. adj., *to w. white, clean.* 1. *trans.* To cleanse, remove the dirt from (something) by affusion of or immersion in water. 2. To cleanse (soiled clothes, etc.) by rubbing in water, with soap or some equivalent. Also *to w. clean, white.* OE. b. *absol.* To wash clothes (as an occupation or as part of one's household duties) 1591. c. *trans.* To wash clothes for (a customer or lodger). *dial.* 1795. d. *absol.* To have one's clothes washed. *joc.* DICKENS. e. *trans.* Of water, etc.: To have the property of cleansing (clothes) easily and well (*rare*) 1697. f. *intr.* Of a fabric, a dye: To bear cleansing with soap and water without damage to colour or texture 1765. g. *fig.* (*colloq.*) To bear trial or investigation, stand the test. Chiefly in phr. (*it*) *won't w.* 1849. h. *pass.* or *intr.* with *out.* To lose colour in the wash. Hence *fig.* to lose all vigour or freshness. 1848. 3. To cleanse (the body or part of it) with water ME. b. said of the water as agent. late ME. c. Of a cat, etc.: To cleanse (itself, its face) by licking and rubbing with its paw 1661. d. *refl.* and *intr.* To cleanse one's body or (often) merely one's face and hands, with water ME. e. To cleanse, rinse (the mouth, etc.) with a douche or medicinal application 1538. f. Said with ref. to baptism ME. g. *fig.* To cleanse *from* the stain of sin ME. 4. To flush or drench (a substance) with water or other liquid, in order to remove impurities or to dissolve out some component 1650. **b.** Of running water, rain, etc.: To pass over (a surface) so as to carry off adherent matter 1523.

1. Take cockles at a full moon and w. 'em 1764. Prov. †*To w. a wall of loam, a brick or tile*, to labour in vain. *To w. out*, to cleanse the interior of (a vessel). *To w. up*, to w. (table utensils) after a meal; also *absol.* *To w. down*, to wash from top to bottom or from end to end 1877. **2.** *To w. one's dirty linen at home, in public* (said *fig.* with ref. to domestic quarrels or grievances). *To w. out*, to rinse so as to remove soap, etc. from the web of the stuff. **b.** What wilt thou do to the Germans, who w. scarce twice in a year? 1671. Goes out charing and washing by the day DICKENS. **c.** That'd be nigh enough for me to w. 'im an' mend 'im 1895. **f.** Only eighteenpence a yard, ma'am, and warranted to w. 1883. **h.** I'm quite washed out and unfit for anything 1886. **3.** Keep your Temper, w. your Face, and go to Bed STEELE. Prov. *To w. an Ethiop, a blackamoor (white)*; *to w. an ass's head* (or *ears*), to labour in vain. Phr. *To w. one's hands of*, to disown responsibility for, refuse to have any further connexion with (orig. an allusion to Pilate's washing his hands; see *Matt.* xxvii. 24). *To w. one's hands*, to rub the hands together, in imitation of the act of washing them. **d.** No Earl is to w. with a Duke without the Dukes Permission 1694. **f.** The Anabaptist washt and washt, and shrunk in the washing 1653. **g.** Washed in the blood of the Lamb 1874.

II. To subject to the action of water or other liquid. **1.** To bathe, lave (the body, limbs, etc.) with water or other liquid ME. **b.** To moisten (the throat) with wine. late ME. †**c.** *intr.* for *refl.* To use cosmetic washes -1693. †**2.** To plunge, bathe (a person) in a river or lake -1660. †**b.** *refl.* To bathe -1775. **c.** *intr.* for *refl.* To bathe. *Obs.* exc. of animals. late ME. **3.** To wet or moisten thoroughly; to saturate with water (esp. rain) or other liquid; to sprinkle or pour water upon ME. **b.** To form *in* holes by running or dropping water; to form (a hole or depression) by such erosion 1766. †**4.** To sweat (coin) by the application of acids -1643. **5.** To cover or smear (a surface) with a liquid; to cover (a wall, etc.) with pigment mixed with water or watery liquid, to whitewash, colour-wash; *Water-colour Painting*, to cover with a broad layer of colour by a continuous movement of the brush; to depict by this means; to lay (colour) in washes 1604. **b.** *transf.* in *pass.* in Natural History, said of surfaces that appear to have a superficial layer of colour spread over them 1844. **c.** To cover *with* a film of metal deposited from a solution 1792. **6.** *Mining.* To agitate in water, or to pass a stream of water through (metalliferous earth) in order to separate the metallic particles. Also *absol.* 1543.

1. †*To w. the eyes* (joc.): to clear or sharpen the sight of the eyes with strong drink; His eyes washed with only a single cup of canary SCOTT. **b.** †*To w. one's brain, head*, etc., as jocular expressions for wine-drinking; *Ant. & Cl.* II. vii. 105. **2. b.** He went but forth to w. him in the Hellespont, and being taken with the crampe, was droun'd SHAKS. **3.** Reyn shal thee wasshe, and sonne shal thee drye CHAUCER. Morning Roses newly washt with dew SHAKS. He, a marble to her teares, is washed with them, but relents not SHAKS. **5. c.** Any of the current Coin which shall have been gilt, silvered, washed, coloured, or cased over 1861.

III. Of a sea or river: To flow over or past (the sand, shore, coast); to beat upon (walls, cliffs, etc.); to touch, adjoin (a town, country, etc.). Also of a river: To pass through, 'water' (a country). ME. **b.** *intr.* Of waves: To sweep *over* a surface; to break or surge *against* (the shore, etc.); to break *in.* Also used by onomatopœia to suggest the sound of moving water. 1774.

The land By Danube wash'd 1814. *transf.* Great spaces washed with sun KIPLING. **b.** I heard the ripple washing in the reeds TENNYSON.

IV. 1. *trans.* To remove (dirt, a stain, colouring, etc.) by the application of water or other liquid. Chiefly with adv., as *away, out, off.* ME. **b.** *transf.* and *fig.* To blot out, obliterate, cancel. late ME. **c.** *intr.* with *out.* Of colouring matter: To disappear from a fabric when washed 1755. **2.** trans. *To w. down*: to swallow liquor along with or after (solid food), in order to assist deglutition or digestion 1600. **3.** Of waves, running water, etc.: To remove, dislodge, carry away. late ME. **b.** To separate (metallic particles) by treating the containing earth with water 1555. †**c.** Of a hard surface: To beat *off* waves, etc. DRYDEN. **d.** *intr.* To be carried away or detached by moving water 1590. **4.** To be tossed about, to be carried or driven along, by waves, etc. 1623. **5.** *Rowing.* trans. To steer so as to impede (a competitor) by the 'wash' of one's own boat 1865.

1. *fig.* Nor Tears, that w. out Sin, can w. out Shame PRIOR. **b.** This Wilford..thirsts to w. out the insult he has received in blood 1850. **2.** In this one draught I w. my sorrow downe 1600. **3.** What wilt thou w. him from his graue with teares? SHAKS.

V. *Mech.* With *off*: to cut to a slope or bevel 1833. **VI.** *slang.* **a.** *Printing.* To punish or 'rag' (a fellow-workman for telling falsehoods) by hammering on his desk 1841. **b.** *Stock-broking.* To subject (stock) to a 'wash' 1895.

attrib. and *Comb.*: **w.-ball**, a ball of soap used for washing the hands and face, and for shaving (now *rare*); **-basin**, a w.-hand basin (now chiefly *U.S.*); **-bottle**, *Chem.* (*a*) a bottle containing liquid through which gases may be passed for purification; (*b*) a bottle with a mouthpiece and issue tube, for directing a stream of liquid on to a substance or utensil to be washed; **-bowl**, †(*a*) a w.-tub; (*b*) a w.-hand basin; **-day** = WASHING-*day*; **-dirt** *Mining*, auriferous soil or gravel to be submitted to washing; **-gourd**, the loofah; **-kitchen**, a kitchen used for washing clothes; **-leather**, a soft kind of leather, usu. of split sheep-skin, dressed to imitate chamois leather; also *attrib.*, made of w. leather; *Path.* of eruptions resembling w.-leather in appearance; **-man**, (*a*) = WASHERMAN; (*b*) a workman employed in applying the w. of tin in the manufacture of tinplate; **-mill**, (*a*) in *Brick-making*, etc., a machine for washing clay or materials for cement; (*b*) in *Leather Manuf.*, a machine for washing skins after unhairing by the application of lime; **-pool**, a pool for washing sheep; **-room**, *U.S.* a lavatory; **-stand**, a w.-hand stand; **-strake** *Naut.* = WASHBOARD 1; **-trough** *Mining*, a trough in which ore is washed; **-tub**, a tub in which clothes are washed; **-water**, water for washing or that has been used for washing; **-woman**, (now *U.S.*) = WASHERWOMAN. Hence **Wa·shable** *a.* that can be washed without damage to texture or colour. **Washabi·lity.** **Wa·shery**, a place at which the washing of coal, ore, wool, etc. is carried on.

Wa·shaway. *Colonial.* 1893. [f. vbl. phr. *to wash away.*] The removal by flood of a portion of a hillside; the destruction of a portion of railway or road track by flood; a hole or breach produced by the washing away of soil.

Wa·sh-bear. *U.S.* 1891. [f. WASH *v.* In G. *waschbär*, a transl. of *Ursus lotor* (Linn.); cf. WASHER¹ 4 b.] The racoon.

Wa·shboard. 1742. [f. WASH *sb.*; cf. G. *waschbrett.*] **1.** *Naut.* A board on the side of a boat, or the sill of a lower-deck port, to prevent the sea breaking over. **2.** *dial.* A skirting-board 1828. **3.** *U.S.* A hardwood board, with a fluted surface or covered with corrugated zinc, on which clothes are rubbed in washing 1882.

Wa·shbrew. *dial.* 1620. [f. WASH *sb.* or *v.*] Oatmeal boiled to a stiff jelly.

Washed (wǫʃt), *ppl. a.* 1575. [f. WASH *v.* + -ED¹.] **1.** Cleansed by rubbing in water or other liquid; treated with water or other liquid so as to remove impurities or soluble matter, etc. †**b.** Of coin: Sweated -1711. **c.** Covered with a coating of precious metal 1772. **d.** Having the tints produced by colour laid on in 'washes' 1770. **2. W. out**, of a fabric, dye, etc.: That has faded, or lost freshness, in the wash 1837. **b.** *fig.* Lacking in colour, animation, vigour, etc. 1850.

Washen (wǫ·ʃ'n), *ppl. a.* *arch.* and *dial.* 1483. [str. pa. pple. of WASH *v.*] Washed.

Washer (wǫ·ʃəɹ), *sb.*¹ ME. [f. WASH *v.* + -ER¹.] **1.** One who washes 1450. **2.** One who sweats coin -1771. **3.** One whose occupation or profession is the cleansing of materials, vessels, etc.; †a launderer or laundress 1515. **b.** One who washes sheep before shearing 1520. **c.** One who washes (ore, etc.) as a mining operation 1531. **4. a.** A popular name of the wagtail, *Motacilla lugubris* (cf. F. *lavandière*) ME. **b.** The racoon 1891. **5.** An apparatus for washing; a washing-machine used in various industries, e.g. for washing rags in paper-making, or for washing domestic linen, photographic plates or prints, etc. 1808. **6.** A cock or outlet valve of a water-supplying pipe; the outlet valve of a basin, cistern, etc., to which a waste-pipe is attached 1596.

Comb.: **w.-wife** (*Sc.*) = WASHERWOMAN.

Washer (wǫ·ʃəɹ), *sb.*² ME. [Origin obsc.] A perforated annular disk or flattened ring of metal, leather, etc., placed between two surfaces subject to rotative friction, to relieve friction and prevent lateral motion and unsteadiness. **b.** An annular disk of leather, rubber, or other material placed between the flanges of abutting water-pipes, beneath the plunger of a screw-down water-tap, etc., to prevent leakage 1850. **c.** A bearing-plate of iron placed under the nut of a bolt or tie-rod 1821. Hence **Wa·sher** *v.* *trans.* to furnish with a w.

Wa·sherman. 1715. [f. WASHER *sb.*¹ + MAN *sb.*] A man whose occupation is the washing of clothes. (Chiefly designating the Chinese laundryman of the U.S. and the Asiatic native washer of clothes.)

Wa·sherwoman. 1632. [f. WASHER *sb.*¹ + WOMAN. Cf. G. *wäscherfrau.*] **1.** A woman whose occupation is the washing of dirty linen; one who takes in washing. **2.** = WASHER *sb.*¹ 4 a. 1817.

1. *Washerwoman's fingers, hand*, a condition of the hands, characteristic of cholera, resembling the wrinkling of the skin produced in the hands of washerwomen by the action of soap and soda. *Washerwoman's itch, scall*, a form of eczema incident to the hands of washerwomen.

Wa·sh-hand, *a.* 1759. [f. WASH *v.* Cf. F. †*lavemain(s* sb. wash-hand stand.] Intended for use in washing the hands. Only in certain combs. (sometimes hyphened or written continuously as single words): *w. basin*, a basin for washing the hands; *w. stand*, a piece of furniture for holding the w. basin, ewer, soap-dish, etc.; *w. table*, a table serving the purpose of a w. stand.

Wash-house (wǫ·ʃhaus). 1577. [f. WASH *v.* + HOUSE *sb.* Cf. Du. *waschhuis*, G. *waschhaus.*] **a.** An outbuilding or apartment used for washing clothes. **b.** A building in which goods are washed in the process of bleaching, or calico printing 1701. **c.** *U.S.* A laundry 1873. **d.** A building, provided with suitable accommodation, at which the public may wash clothes 1846.

Washiness (wǫ·ʃinės). 1631. [f. WASHY *a.* + -NESS.] The quality or state of being washy.

The w. of the following line is only surpassed by that of the two which succeed it 1814.

Washing (wǫ·ʃiŋ), *vbl. sb.* ME. [-ING¹.] **I.** The action of WASH *v.* **1.** The action or an act of cleansing by water, or of laving or bathing with water or other liquid. Also *fig.* with ref. to spiritual or moral purification. *W. up*: the washing of table utensils after a meal. **b.** A ceremonial ablution ME. **c.** *spec.* = 'washing of clothes', esp. as one of the regular requirements of a person or household 1480. **d.** In chemical and mining operations 1600. **e.** With advs. *away, off, out, up* 1612. **2.** *Painting.* The action of laying on a thin coat of colour. Also *w. in.* 1650. **3.** Sweating of coin by means of acids. late ME. **4.** Surging, overflowing (of waves); the action of moving water in carrying off loose matter 1471. **5.** *Printers' slang.* See WASH *v.* VI. 1825.

1. Abstention from w. was a common form of asceticism 1911. **b.** Their pilgrimages to Idols, their shauings and their washings 1606. **c.** Meat, drink, w., and lodging 1765. †*At (the) w.* = 'at the wash.'

II. *Concr.* **1.** *pl.* (formerly also *sing.*) The liquid that has been used to wash something; matter removed when something is washed ME. **b.** Matter carried away by rain or running water; metal obtained by washing ore or soil 1604. **c.** Places containing soil from which gold or diamonds are obtained by washing 1865. **2.** Clothes newly washed or set apart to be washed 1854.

Comb.: **w.-bill**, a statement of laundry charges; **-book**, a book in which a person's laundry-charges are entered; **-crystals**, crystallized soda used for washing clothes, etc.; **-day**, the day on which the dirty clothes of a household are washed; **-machine**, a machine for washing clothes, etc.

Wa·shing, *ppl. a.* 1560. [-ING².] **1.** That washes; *spec.* of a garment, a textile fabric: That will admit of being washed without injury to colour or texture. †**2.** Of a blow: = SWASHING *ppl. a.* 2. -1625. **3.** *W. bear, racoon* = WASH-BEAR 1891.

Wa·sh-out. 1876. [f. vbl. phr. *to w. out.*] **1.** An act of washing out a cistern, etc.; a pipe or other appliance for doing this 1877. **2.** *Mining.* A place where a portion of coal or ironstone seam has been carried away by a stream, a deposit of sandstone being left in its place 1876. **3.** The removal by flood of a portion of a hillside; a hole or breach in a railway or road track caused by flood or erosion. Orig. (and chiefly) *U.S.* 1883. **4.** *slang.* A disappointing failure, a 'sell' 1902.

Wa·sh-pot. 1535. [f. WASH *v.*] †**1.** A servant employed to wash pots; *spec.* the designation of a servant employed at the Inns of Court –1816. **2.** A vessel for washing one's hands. *Obs.* exc. *fig.* in allusion to Ps. lx. 8. 1535. **3.** A vessel containing melted tin, into which iron plates are plunged to be converted into tin-plate 1839. **4.** A vessel used in separating silver from lead 1879.

2. Moab is my washpotte, ouer Edom wil I stretch out my shue COVERDALE *Ps.* lx. 8.

Wa·sh-up. 1884. [f. vbl. phr. *to wash up.*] **1.** = *washing up.* **2.** *Mining.* The washing of a collected quantity of ore; the quantity of gold that has been obtained by washing 1890.

Wash-up, joc. or vulgar f. WORSHIP *sb.*

Washy (wǫ·ʃi), *a.* 1566. [f. WASH *sb.* or *v.* + -Y[1].] †**1.** Having too much moisture, water-logged. Of wind or weather: Bringing moisture or rain. –1726. **2.** Of food, drink, etc.: Too much diluted, weak, sloppy, thin. Hence *fig.* of literary style, productions, etc. 1615. **3.** Of colour, painting, etc.: Lacking body, weak, pale 1639. **4.** Of the stomach: Having an accumulation of liquid and undigested food; relaxed 1622. **5.** Of a horse or cow: Poor in quality or condition; esp. liable to sweat or scour after slight exertion 1639. **6.** Of a person: Lacking strength or stamina; weak, feeble, insipid; = WISHY-WASHY. Now *rare* or *Obs.* 1631.

1. The washie Oose MILT. 2. Other persons' w. opinions GEO. ELIOT. 3. Sir Joshua's w. Virtues WALPOLE. Blue eyes like hers..look so mild and gentle and w. 1886. 6. What w. Rogues are here, are these the Sons of Beef, and English Beer? 1719.

Wasn't (wǫ·z'nt), colloq. contraction of *was not.*

Wasp (wǫsp). [OE. *wæfs, wæps, wæsp* :—OTeut. **wabisoz, -isō, *waps-* :—pre-Teut. **wobhes-, *wops-* (cf. L. *vespa*, from another grade of the stem). The root is believed to be **webh-* to weave, the name having ref. to the nests which the insect constructs.] **1.** In pop. lang. any insect of the genus *Vespa*; chiefly applied to *V. vulgaris*, the Common W., and other species not readily distinguishable from this; sometimes taken to include the hornet, *V. crabro.* The obvious characteristics of the genus are the alternate rings of black and yellow on the abdomen, the narrow stalk or petiole by which the abdomen is attached to the thorax, and the formidable sting (peculiar to the females and the workers). In scientific lang. applied gen. to two divisions of hymenopterous insects, the Diploptera or true wasps, and the Fossores or digger wasps. **2.** *fig.* **a.** Applied to persons characterized by irascibility and persistent petty malignity 1508. **b.** Something that irritates or offends one 1588. **3.** An artificial fly for salmon fishing (made to imitate the appearance of a w.) 1867. **4.** *Conchol.* A variety of cowry 1815.

1. Angry as a waspe HEYWOOD. Then the wasps arrived. They killed three in the jam alone. 1905. 2. *Tam. Shr.* II. i. 210. I raised a nest of holy wasps and hornets about my ears 1721. **b.** *Hen. VIII*, III. ii. 55.

attrib. and *Comb.*, as *w.-sting*, etc.: **w.-bee,** a bee of the genus *Nomada*, a cuckoo-bee; **-beetle,** a beetle of the genus *Clytus*, esp. *C. arietis*; **-fly,** a syrphid fly somewhat resembling a hornet; also = sense 3; **-paper,** the paper-like material, produced by mastication, of which wasps' nests are made; **-waist,** a very slender waist, *esp.* one produced by tight-lacing; so **w.-waisted** *a.* **b.** with genit.: **wasp's nest,** the nest of a w., often used *fig.* like *hornet's nest.* Hence **Wa·spy** *a.* wasp-like; abounding in wasps.

Waspish (wǫ·spiʃ), *a.* 1566. [f. prec. + -ISH.] Pertaining to or resembling a wasp or some characteristic of it; *esp.* quick to resent any trifling affront; irascible, petulantly spiteful.

If I be w., best beware my sting SHAKS. W., dogmatical, over-bearing fellows 1861. Hence **Wa·spish-ly** *adv.*, **-ness.**

Wassail (wæ·s'l, wǫ·s'l, -eˈl), *sb.* Now only *arch.* and *Hist.* [ME. *wæs hail*, a. ON. *ves heill*, corresp. to OE. *wes hál* lit. 'be in good health' or 'be fortunate'.] **1.** A salutation used when presenting a cup of wine to a guest, or drinking the health of a person, the reply being DRINK-HAIL. **2.** The liquor in which healths were drunk; esp. the spiced ale used in Twelfth-night and Christmas-eve celebrations ME. **3.** †A custom formerly observed on Twelfth-night and New-Year's eve of drinking healths from the w.-bowl –1661; a carousal, riotous festivity, revelling 1602. †**4.** A carol or song sung by wassailers –1650.

2. The Wassell well spiced, about shall go round 1661. *Wine and w.* (now *arch.*, echoing Shaks.), *vaguely*, strong drink in abundance; *Macb.* I. vii. 64. 3. The King doth wake to night, and takes his rouse, Keepes wassels SHAKS. Merry Eastcheap, that ancient region of wit and w. 1820.

attrib. and *Comb.*, as *w.-candle, -singer*, etc.; **w.-bowl, -cup,** a large bowl or cup in which w. was made, and from which healths were drunk; also the liquor contained in the bowl. Hence **Wa·ssailry,** carousing, revelry (*rare*) 1814.

Wassail (wæ·s'l, wǫ·s'l, -eˈl), *v.* ME. [f. prec.] **1.** *intr.* To 'keep wassail'; to sit carousing and health-drinking. **2.** *trans.* (*local.*) To drink to (fruit-trees, cattle) in wassail, in order to ensure their thriving 1648.

2. The old Christmas custom of wassailing the apple-trees 1895. Hence **Wa·ssailer,** one who takes part in riotous festivities; a reveller; one who takes part in Twelfth-night or Christmas-tide 'wassailing'. **Wa·ssailing** *vbl. sb.* the action of the vb.; carousing; the action of going from house to house at Christmas-time, singing a song expressive of good wishes for Christmas and the coming year, usu. with the addition of carols or other songs.

Wast (wǫst, wəst). *arch.* and *poet.* 2nd pers. sing. pa. t. of BE *v.*

Wastage (wēˈ·stėdʒ). 1756. [f. WASTE *v.* + -AGE.] **1. a.** Loss or diminution by use, decay, leakage or the like 1756. **b.** The action of spending uselessly or using wastefully; loss incurred by wastefulness 1885. **2.** The product of wear or decay, waste 1898. **3.** *Sc.* A ruined or deserted place; also, a waste piece of ground 1823.

Waste (wēˈst), *sb.* ME. [a. AF. *wast(e*, = OF. *g(u)ast(e*, partly repr. L. *vastum*, neut. of *vastus* WASTE *a.*, partly a verbal noun f. *waster* WASTE *v.*] **I.** Waste or desert land. **1.** Uninhabited (or sparsely inhabited) and uncultivated country; a wild and desolate region, a wilderness; also *transf.*, applied e.g. to the ocean or to land covered with snow. **2.** A piece of land not cultivated or used for any purpose, and producing little or no herbage or wood. In legal use *spec.* a piece of such land not in any man's occupation, but lying common. late ME. †**3.** A devastated region –1697. **4.** *Coal-mining.* A disused working 1695.

1. Satan..in the emptier w., resembling Air, Weighs his spread wings MILT. Tartary's extended W. PRIOR. *fig.* A dreary w. of cold potatoes, looking as eatable as Stonehenge DICKENS. 3. They shall build the olde wastes, they shall raise vp the former desolations *Isa.* lxi. 4.

II. Action or process of wasting. **1.** Useless expenditure or consumption, squandering (*of* money, time, etc.); †the consumption or using up of material, resources, etc. ME. **b.** An instance or example of wasting 1612. **c.** A profusion, lavish abundance *of* something 1725. **2.** Destruction or devastation caused by war, floods, fire, etc. Now *rare* or *Obs.* 1560. †**b.** *pl.* Ravages –1738. †**c.** *concr.* Something wasted or destroyed –1640. **3.** *Law.* 'Any unauthorized act of a tenant for a freehold estate not of inheritance, or for any lesser interest, which tends to the destruction of the tenement, or otherwise to the injury of the inheritance' (F. Pollock) ME. **4.** Gradual loss or diminution from use, wear and tear, decay or natural process; *spec.* with ref. to animal tissues and structures; (now *dial.*) a wasting of the body by disease. Now somewhat *rare.* late ME.

1. The clocke vpbraides me with the w. of time SHAKS. These insulting Words, this w. of Breath DRYDEN. *Prov.* Haste maketh w. 1641. Phr. †*To make w.*, to be wasteful. †*In w.*, in vain, to no purpose. *To run to w.*, to flow away so as to be wasted. *fig.* of wealth, powers, etc., to be wasted. *To go to w.*, to be wasted; *To cut to w.*, lit. to cut (cloth) in a wasteful manner. *fig.* (*slang.*) to apportion (time) wastefully. **b.** Prefaces..are great wastes of time BACON. **c.** And there the garden yields a w. of flow'rs POPE. 2. **b.** Pleas'd with the Work of thy own Hands, Thou dost the Wastes of Time repair WESLEY. **c.** Then of thy beauty do I question make That thou among the wastes of time must goe SHAKS. 4. Sudden W. made upon Fat Persons by violent Fevers 1695. Her mother went off in a w. 1878.

III. Waste matter, refuse. **1.** Refuse matter; the useless by-products of any industrial process; material or manufactured articles so damaged as to be useless or unsaleable. late ME. **b.** = COTTON-*waste* 1886. **c.** *Printing*, etc. The surplus sheets of a work 1785. **2.** A pipe, conduit, or other contrivance for carrying off waste matter or surplus water, steam, etc. 1707.

Combs.: **w.-basket** (now chiefly *U.S.*) = WASTE-PAPER *basket*; **-land,** land in its natural, uncultivated state; **-man** *Mining*, a man whose duty is to inspect the w., and to secure the proper ventilation of the mine; **-pipe** = III. 2; **-way** *U.S.*, a channel for the passage of waste water; †**-yard,** app. a yard for the reception of odds and ends of little value. Hence **Wa·steless** *a.* without diminution, unwasting. **Wa·sty** *a.* liable to waste from deterioration; *U.S.*, that resembles cotton-w.

Waste (wēˈst), *a.* ME. [a. AF. *wast*, = OF. *g(u)ast* :—Rom. **wasto*, repr. (with influence from the cogn. OHG. *wuosti*) L. *vastus* waste, desert.] **1.** Of land: **a.** Uncultivated and uninhabited or sparsely inhabited. Sometimes with stronger implication: Incapable of habitation or cultivation; barren, desert. **b.** In weaker sense: Not applied to any purpose; not utilized for cultivation or building. late ME. †**2.** Of former places of habitation or cultivation, buildings, etc.: Devastated, ruinous –1823. †**3.** Of speech, thought, or action: Profitless, serving no purpose –1598. †**b.** Superfluous, needless –1618. †**4.** Spare, unoccupied, unused –1772. **5.** Of materials, etc.: Eliminated or thrown aside as worthless after the completion of a process; refuse. Of manufactured articles: Rejected as defective; also, produced in excess of what can be used. 1450.

1. Eden rais'd in the wast Wilderness MILT. *fig.* This w. weary life 1825. *To lie w.*, to remain in an uncultivated or ruinous condition. *To lay w.*, to devastate, ravage (land, buildings); I will lay thy cities w., and thou shalt be desolate *Ezek.* xxxv. 4. 4. Shee took penne and inke and in those wast leaues wrote a most Godly and learned exhortation 1615. I was locked up and confined in a w. room 1772. 5. The duty of the kidneys is to filter w. matters from the blood as it circulates through them 1908. *W. water*, superfluous water, or water that has served its purpose, allowed to run away. *W. steam*, the superfluous steam discharged from a boiler, or the spent steam discharged from the cylinder of a steam-engine.

Comb.: **w.-book** *Book-keeping*, a rough account-book (now little used) in which entries are made of all transactions at the time of their occurrence, to be 'posted' afterwards in the more formal books.

Waste (wēˈst), *v.* ME. [a. AF. *waster* = OF. *g(u)aster* :—Com. Rom. **wastare*, repr. (with influence from the cognate Teut. **wōstjan*) L. *vastare*, f. *vastus* WASTE *a.*] **I.** *trans.* **1.** To lay waste, devastate, ruin (a land, town, its inhabitants, etc.). **2.** *Law.* To destroy, injure, damage (property); to cause to deteriorate in value 1450. **3.** To consume, use up, wear away, exhaust by gradual loss; to consume or destroy (a person, etc.) by decay or disease; to emaciate, enfeeble ME. †**b.** To destroy, put an end to (something immaterial, e.g. sin, sorrow) –1689. †**4.** To diminish or consume the livelihood of, impoverish (a person) –1727. †**b.** To spend, diminish one's store of (money, etc.); to spend, pass (time); to get over (a distance in travelling) –1764. **5.** To spend, consume, employ uselessly, unprofitably or without adequate return; to make prodigal or improvident use of; to squander ME. **b.** *pass.* (without distinct ref. to an agent). To fail to be appreciated; to make no impression; to have no opportunities for displaying useful qualities 1898. **c.** To fail to take advantage of (an opportunity) 1836. **d.** To cause or allow (a substance, etc.) to be used unprofitably or lost 1826.

1. *absol.* For now I see Peace to corrupt no less then Warr to w. MILT. 3. To..wast huge stones with little water drops SHAKS. Would he were wasted, Marrow, Bones, and all SHAKS. **b.** The pryde off Iordane is wasted awaye COVERDALE *Zech.* xi. 3. 4. **b.** I like this place, And willingly could w. my time in it SHAKS. The Goddess wasts her Days In joyous Songs DRYDEN. 5. The yonger sonne..wasted his

substance with riotous liuing *Luke* xv. 13. Full many a flower is born to blush unseen, And w. its sweetness on the desert air GRAY. To w. a great deal of time in novel-reading 1881. *To w. words, breath*, to speak to no purpose; similarly *to w. paper, space*. **b.** Two such amusing liars as we were utterly wasted on after-dinner oratory 1898.

II. *intr.* **1.** To lose strength, health, or vitality; to lose flesh, pine, decay. Also with *away*. ME. **b.** *Sport.* To reduce one's weight by training. Also *refl.* 1763. **2.** To be used up or worn away; to lose substance or volume by gradual loss or wear or decay; to be consumed or spent. late ME. †**3.** Of time: To pass away, be spent –1847.

1. Shall I wasting in Dispaire, Dye because a Womans faire? 1622. **2.** Euphues had rather shrinke in the wetting then wast in the wearing LYLY. Hence **Wa·stable** *a.* liable to be wasted, subject to waste; also in *Law*, said of things in respect of which a tenant may be chargeable with waste. **Wa·sting** *vbl. sb.* the action of the vb.; *ppl. a.* that wastes.

Wasteful (wēⁱ·stfŭl), *a.* late ME. [f. WASTE *sb.* + -FUL.] **1.** That causes devastation, desolation or ruin; that destroys or lays waste. †**2.** Useless, worthless, vain; unused –1577. **3.** Of a place: Desolate; unfrequented, uninhabited. *Obs.* exc. *arch.* and *poet.* 1572. **4.** Addicted to waste; given to useless or excessive expenditure. Of expenditure, etc.: Characterized by waste or extravagance. 1451. **5.** That wastes, consumes or expends unprofitably. Const. *of.* 1587. **6.** That causes bodily waste or decay. Now *rare.* 1600.

1. Wastefull vengeance SHAKS. **3.** The Throne Of Chaos, and his dark Pavilion spread Wide on the w. Deep MILT. W. Tartarus BRIDGES. **6.** Leane and w. Learnings SHAKS. This w. excess of grief 1824. Hence **Wa·steful·ly** *adv.*, **-ness.**

Wastel (wǫ·st'l). *Obs.* exc. *Hist.* ME. [a. AF., = OF. *g(u)astel* (F. *gâteau*).] **1.** Bread made of the finest flour; a cake or loaf of this bread. **2.** *Her.* = TORTEAU 1. 1486.

Wasteness (wēⁱ·stnės). late ME. [-NESS.] **1.** †**a.** Desolation, destruction, ruin. (Chiefly *biblical.*) –1863. **b.** The state of lying waste, being uncultivated or barren 1608. **2.** An uninhabited or unfrequented region or place. *Obs.* exc. *dial.* 1500.

1. a. Desolacion shal remayne in the cities, and the gates shalbe smytten with waistnesse COVERDALE *Isa.* xxiv. 12.

Wa·ste-pa·per. 1585. Paper cast aside as spoiled, superfluous, or useless for its original purpose.

The securities..proved to be little better than waste paper 1905.

attrib.: **w.-basket,** a basket into which waste paper is thrown.

Waster[1] (wēⁱ·stəɹ). ME. [orig. a. AF. *wastere, -our*, f. *waster* WASTE *v.* This coalesced with later formation on WASTE *v.* + -ER[1].] **I. 1.** One who lives in idleness and extravagance; a squanderer, spendthrift. Now chiefly with some notion of sense II, a 'ne'er-do-well'. **b.** One who, or something which wastefully dissipates or consumes (something specified). late ME. **2.** One who lays waste, despoils or plunders. late ME. **3.** The designation of a class of thieves mentioned in a statute of Edw. III. *Obs.* exc. *arch.* 1543. **4.** An animal, etc. that is wasting away or losing flesh, or that will not fatten. late ME. **5.** Something which causes or allows waste or loss of material 1788. **b.** *Path.* = COMEDO 1899.

1. Ye will think I am turned w., for I wear clean hose and shoon every day SCOTT. Here was a wretched invertebrate fellow, an absolute 'w.' 1904. **b.** Building and marrying of Children are great wasters 1633. **4.** *A bad w.*, said of a jockey who has difficulty in 'wasting'. **5.** Oft on the wick there hangs a w., Which makes the candle burn the faster 1788.

II. Something rejected as waste. **a.** An article of faulty or inferior manufacture 1800. **b.** An animal, etc., which is not good enough to be kept for breeding purposes 1722.

†**Wa·ster**[2]. 1455. [Origin obsc.] **1.** A wooden foil used in sword-exercise and fencing; a cudgel, staff, club –1661. **2.** Fencing with a 'waster'; single-stick –1636.

Waster[3] (wēⁱ·stəɹ). *Sc.* 1580. [Altered f. synonymous *wawsper.*] A fishing-spear.

Wastrel (wēⁱ·strĕl), *sb.* and *a.* 1589. [f. WASTE *v.* + -REL.] **A.** *sb.* **1.** In Cornwall, a tract of waste land; now only, a strip of road-side waste. **2.** *dial.* = WASTER[1] II. 1790. **3.** An idle, worthless, disreputable person 1847. **b.** A street arab 1877. **4.** A wasteful person, a spendthrift 1887. **B.** *adj.* **1.** Of manufactured articles: Waste, rejected as imperfect 1790. **2.** Of an animal: Feeble, lacking strength or vigour 1880. **3.** Spendthrift 1894.

Wat[1] (wǫt). *Obs.* exc. *dial.* 1500. [prob. a use of *Wat*, short for *Walter.*] A hare.

‖**Wat**[2] (wat). 1871. [Siamese.] A Siamese Buddhist temple.

Watap, wattap (wǫ·tæp). 1789. [Narragansett Indian *wattap* root of a tree.] Thread or fibre from the roots of the spruce fir, used by Indians for weaving, sewing, etc.

Watch (wǫtʃ), *sb.* [OE. *wæcce*, f. stem of *wæccan* WATCH *v.*] **I.** Wakefulness, vigil. †**1.** The state of being awake; going without sleep –1631. †**2.** Watching as a devotional exercise or religious observance; an act or instance of this. *Obs.* exc. in *w.-night.* –1526. †**b.** A wake or revel held on St. John the Baptist's (Midsummer) Eve (23 June) –1592. **c.** A 'wake' over a dead person (*rare*) ME. **3.** The action or a continued act of watching; a keeping awake and vigilant for the purpose of attending, guarding, or the like OE. **4.** [tr. L. *vigilia*, Gr. φυλακή, Heb. *ashmōreth.*] Each of the (three, four, or five) periods into which the night was anciently divided OE.

1. *Ham.* II. ii. 148. **4.** And about the fourth w. of the night, he commeth vnto them, walking vpon the Sea *Mark* vi. 48. *The watches of the night*, now often rhet. = 'the night-time'.

II. Action of watching or observing. **1.** The action or an act of watching or observing with continuous attention; a continued look-out, as of a sentinel or guard. late ME. **b.** The duty, post, or office of watchman or sentinel. *Obs.* exc. in Bible phr. *to stand upon one's w.* 1535. **c.** Surveillance *over* a person 1611. **2.** *W. and ward*, the performance of the duty of a watchman or sentinel, esp. as a feudal obligation. Now only a rhetorical and more emphatic synonym of *w.* in sense II. 1. late ME. †**3.** The action of keeping guard and maintaining order in the streets, esp. during the night, performed by a picked body of the community –1878. †**4.** A lying in wait, an ambush –1653. **5.** One who watches; a look-out man. late ME. **b.** *Cricket.* A fieldsman; also a fielding position. (*Winchester Coll.*) 1836. **6.** One who watches, or those who watch, for purposes of guarding and protecting life and property, and the like; *esp.* before the introduction of the new Police, a watchman or body of watchmen, who patrolled and guarded the streets of a town, proclaimed the hour, etc. 1539. **7.** A sentinel; also, the body of soldiers constituting the guard of a camp, town, etc. *Obs.* exc. *Hist.* late ME. **8.** In the early 18th c., the designation of certain companies of irregular troops in the Highlands 1739.

1. Vse carefull W., chuse trusty Centinels SHAKS. Phr. *to keep* (*a, the*) *w.*, *to set a w.* *On, upon* (*the*) *w.*, on the look out, exercising vigilance. **b.** As I did stand my w. vpon the Hill I look'd toward Byrnane SHAKS. **c.** Am I a sea, or a whale, that thou settest a w. ouer me? *Job* vii. 12. **6.** The Sherife and all the W. are at the doore: they are come to search the House SHAKS. **8.** *Black W.*, a name given (from the dark-coloured tartan worn by them) to some companies of irregular Highland troops raised *c* 1729–30, and afterwards embodied as the 42nd Regiment, which still retains the name.

III. Naut. uses. **1.** That period of time for which each of the divisions of a ship's company alternately remains on deck; usu. four hours, with the exception of the DOG-WATCHES 1585. **b.** A sailor's turn or period of duty 1725. **2.** That part, usu. one half, of the officers and crew, who together attend to the working of a vessel during a 'watch' 1626. **b.** *W. and w.*, the arrangement by which the two halves of a ship's crew take duty alternately every four hours 1780.

1. (One's) *w. below, off*, the time one is off duty. **2.** 'The grub's horrid', said both watches 1913.

IV. A timepiece. **1.** †**a.** A dial or clock-face; the circle of figures on a dial –1672. †**b.** The going-part of a clock –1816. **2.** A small timepiece with a spring-driven movement, and of a size to be carried in the pocket 1588. **b.** A chronometer as used on board ship 1778. **3.** A trial-piece of glass, pottery, copper, etc. put in a furnace and taken out again, to enable the workman to judge of the degree of heating, etc. [App. a mistranslation of F. *montre*, in this application used in the sense of 'show-piece'.] 1606.

1. a. *Rich. II*, v. v. 52. **2.** Dictionaries are like watches, the worst is better than none, and the best cannot be expected to go quite true JOHNSON.

attrib. and *Comb.*: **w.-bell,** (*a*) a bell on which the half-hourly periods in each w. are struck on board ship; (*b*) a bell rung at the setting and relief of a military w., or to sound an alarm; **-boat,** a boat on patrol-duty; **-box,** a small structure to shelter a person on w.; a small wooden shelter resembling a sentry-box, but furnished with a seat and half-door, used by a municipal watchman (now only *Colonial*); **-bracelet,** a bracelet carrying a wrist-watch; †**-candle,** = *watching-candle*; **-case,** a hinged case or cover of an old-fashioned w. enclosing the w. proper; now, the metal cover enclosing the works of a w.; **-chain,** a metal chain used as a w.-guard; **w. committee,** the committee of a borough council which deals with all matters pertaining to the policing and public lighting of the borough; **-cry,** the periodical cry of a watchman; *fig.* = WATCHWORD 3 b; **-dog,** a dog kept to guard a house, etc., and give warning of the approach of intruders; **-fire,** a fire maintained during the night as a signal or for the use of a party or person on w.; **-guard,** a chain, cord, ribbon, or the like used to secure a w. when it is worn on the person; **-house,** (*a*) a house in which a w. or guard is stationed; (*b*) a house used as a station for municipal night-watchmen (now only *U.S.* and *Colonial*); **-light** = NIGHT-LIGHT 2 b; **-night,** orig. a religious service extending over midnight held monthly by Wesleyan Methodists; in later use a service held on New Year's eve, lasting until midnight; also the night on which the service is held; **-oil,** a highly refined lubricating oil used for watches and clocks; **-spring,** the mainspring of a w.; also (without article) as a material; **-stand,** a small case or stand in or upon which a w. may be placed so that its face may be seen; **-wheel,** the balance-wheel of the 'w.-work' of a clock. Hence **Wa·tchless** *a.*, keeping no w.; unwatched, unguarded; not having or possessing a watch (IV. 2).

Watch (wǫtʃ), *v.* Pa. t. and pa. pple. **watched** (wǫtʃt). [OE. **wæccan* (only in pr. pple. *wæccende*), a doublet of *wacian* WAKE *v.*, repr. WGer. **wakōjan* (OHG. *wahhēn*).] **I.** *intr.* †**1.** To be or remain awake –1667. **b.** To remain awake *with* a sick person or at his bedside 1691. **2.** To remain awake for purposes of devotion; to keep vigil OE. **3.** To be on the alert, to be vigilant; to be on one's guard ME. **4.** To be on the look out; to keep a person or thing in sight, so as to be aware of any movement or change. late ME. **b.** To be on the watch for opportunities *to do* something. late ME. **c.** To be on the watch *for* (something expected) 1831. **5. W. over** —. To exercise protecting care over 1526. **6.** To fulfil the duty of a watchman, sentinel, or guard. late ME. **b.** Of a sailor: To be on duty during a watch 1799.

1. Sleepest thou? Couldest not thou w. one houre? W. ye and pray. *Mark* xiv. 38, 39. **4.** To w. as the cat for the mous 1547. They watch'd what the end would be TENNYSON. *To w. after*, to follow with one's looks (*rare*). *To w. out* (Cricket), = FIELD *v.* 5; (orig. *U.S. colloq.*) to look out, be on one's guard. **5.** There is a Providence..that watches over innocence and folly GIBBON. **6.** †*To w. and ward*, to keep 'watch and ward'. **b.** Each man watches four hours, and rests eight 1820.

II. *trans.* †**1.** To keep under surveillance; to set an armed watch upon –1579. **b.** To guard (a dead body, goods) 1450. †**2.** To guard against attack; to provide with a body of guards or armed watchmen; to serve as a guard to. Also *to w. and ward.* –1819. **3.** To keep (a person or thing) in view in order to observe any actions, movements, or changes that may occur 1515. **4.** To keep in mental view; to keep oneself informed about 1675. **b.** To be on the alert to avail oneself of (opportunities, etc.); to be vigilant to choose (one's time for action) 1578. **c.** Of a barrister: To attend the trial of (a case) in order to note and act upon any point that may arise to affect the interests of a client who is not a party in the litigation 1890. **5.** To exercise protecting vigilance over; to tend (a flock); to sit up beside (a sick person); to keep watch beside (a dead body) 1526. †**6.** To do (a person a good or bad turn) –1705. **7.** To provide (a town) with watchmen; *pass.* to be policed *by* a specified body of men 1806. **8.** *Falconry.* To prevent (a hawk) from sleeping, in order to tame it 1575.

3. Didn't I w. him into Codger's commercial boarding-house, and w. him out, and w. him home to his hotel DICKENS. 4. Youth should w. joys, and shoot 'em as they flie DRYDEN. The natural jealousy of the Spaniards watched every naval enterprise of Englishmen 1868. 5. While Shepherds watch'd their Flocks by Night 1700. 8. *Tam. Shr.* IV. i. 198. Hence †**Wa·tchment** (*rare*), a task of watching.

Watcher (wǫ·tʃəɹ). 1525. [f. WATCH *v.* + -ER¹.] One who watches or keeps watch; *spec.* (*a*) one who watches by a sick bed, or by the dead; (*b*) a watchman, guard, sentry; (*c*) as the title of a class of angels, or of angels generally [tr. Aramaic *'îr* one who is wakeful].

Beholde, a w. (euen an holy angel) came downe from heauen COVERDALE *Dan.* IV. 13. An eye like mine A lidless w. of the public weal TENNYSON.

Watchet (wǫ·tʃėt), *sb.* and *a. Obs.* or *arch.* late ME. [app. a. AF. *wachet, waschet*, of obsc. origin.] A. *sb.* 1. A light blue colour; cloth or garments of this colour. 2. In full *w. fly*: A fly used by anglers; an artificial fly made to imitate this 1799. B. *adj.* Light blue, sky-blue; sometimes prefixed to *blue* as a qualifying term 1496.

Watchful (wǫ·tʃfŭl), *a.* 1548. [f. WATCH *sb.* + -FUL.] 1. Wakeful, sleepless; accustomed to keeping awake. Of time: Passed in wakefulness. *arch.* 2. Engaged in or accustomed to watching or close observation; vigilant 1601. 3. Characterized by vigilance; in which one must be vigilant 1582.

1. W. nights and laborious days 1878. 2. A w. mamma and governess in chaperonage 1882. 3. The souldier may not moue from watchfull sted SPENSER. Keeping w. guard HAWTHORNE. Hence **Wa·tchful-ly** *adv.* 1538, **-ness**.

Wa·tch-glass. 1637. [WATCH *sb.*] †1. A sand-glass or hour-glass used to measure the time of keeping watch, esp. on board ship –1769. 2. A thin piece of glass, usu. concavo-convex in form, fitted into the case of a watch over the dial-plate 1773. b. as a receptacle for small objects or portions of material to be subjected to scientific observation 1757.

Watching (wǫ·tʃiŋ), *vbl. sb.* late ME. [-ING¹.] 1. The action of WATCH *v.*; an act or instance of this. b. Sc. *W. and warding*: see WATCH *v.* I. 6, II. 2. 1579. 2. The state or condition of being awake, wakefulness; an instance of this 1550.

Comb.: **w. brief**, a brief instructing counsel to 'watch' a case; **w. candle**, a candle used at the 'watching' of a shrine or a corpse.

Wa·tchma:ker. 1630. One whose trade it is to make watches. So **Wa·tchm:aking** *vbl. sb.*

Watchman (wǫ·tʃmæ̆n). late ME. [f. WATCH *sb.* + MAN *sb.*] 1. A member of a military guard, a sentinel or sentry; a look-out. (Now *rare* exc. with allusion to Bible uses.) †2. One who keeps vigil; one who watches over or guards a person or thing –1628. †b. Applied to angels –1613. 3. One of a body of men formerly appointed to keep watch and ward in all towns from sunset to sunrise; later, a constable of the watch who, before the Police Act of 1839, patrolled the streets by night to safeguard life and property. late ME. 4. A man employed to guard private property, a building, etc., esp. during the night 1600. 5. The dor-beetle, *Geotrupes stercorarius* 1864.

1. Excepte the Lorde kepe the cite, the w. waketh but in vayne COVERDALE *Ps.* cxxvi. 1. 2. 1 *Hen. VI*, III. i. 66. 3. A face..that had just as much play of expression as a watchman's rattle DICKENS.

Wa·tch-tow:er. 1544. [WATCH *sb.*] 1. A tower or station from which observation is kept of the approach of danger; a look-out station. †2. A pharos or lighthouse –1804.

1. *fig.* Morning sought Her eastern w. SHELLEY.

Watchword (wǫ·tʃwɔ̄ɹd). late ME. [WATCH *sb.*] 1. *Mil.* A word or short phrase used as a password. *Obs.* in techn. use. †b. The call of a sentinel on his rounds –1797. †2. A preconcerted signal to begin an attack –1834. 3. A password used among members of the same sect, society, etc. *Obs.* or *arch.* 1534. b. A word or phrase used as embodying the guiding principle or rule of action of a party or individual 1738. †4. A cautionary word or speech –1761.

2. *transf.* Which giues the watch word to his hand ful soon, To draw the clowd that hides the siluer Moon SHAKS. 3. Classical quotations are the watch-words of scholars, by which they distinguish each other from the ignorant and the illiterate SYD. SMITH. b. When the rude rabble's watch-word was—destroy COWPER.

Watchwork (wǫ·tʃwɔ̄ɹk). 1667. [WATCH *sb.*] That part of the movement of a timepiece which is concerned with the measuring of the hours, as distinguished from the 'clockwork' or striking part; also the 'works' or parts composing the movement of a watch.

Water (wǭ·təɹ), *sb.* [Com. Teut.: OE. *wæter* :—OTeut. **watar-* :—Indo-Eur. **wod-* (as in Russ. *vodá*, cf. VODKA): **wĕd-* (OTeut. **wǣt-* WET *a.*): *ud-* (as in Skr. *udán*, Gr. ὕδωρ, genit. ὕδατος :—**udn̥tos*, L. *unda* wave).] I. 1. The liquid of which seas, lakes, and rivers are composed, and which falls as rain and issues from springs. When pure, it is transparent, colourless (except as seen in large quantity, when it has a blue tint), tasteless, and inodorous. b. With various qualifying words, as *ice-w.*, RAIN-W., etc. c. Considered as antagonistic to fire. late ME. d. As supplied for domestic needs, esp. as distributed through pipes to the houses of a district 1535. 2. As a drink, as satisfying thirst, or as necessary aliment for animals and plants OE. 3. As used for dilution of liquors OE. b. *fig.* (*Stock Exch.*) Fictitious capital created by the 'watering' of the stock of a trading company 1883. 4. As used for washing, steeping, boiling, etc. OE. b. Each of the quantities of water used successively in a gradual process of washing ME. 5. Water of a mineral spring or a collection of mineral springs used medicinally for bathing or for drinking, or both. Freq. *pl.* with *the*. 1542. 6. Water regarded as collected in seas, lakes, etc., or as flowing in rivers or streams. (The pl. is often used instead of the sing., esp. with ref. to flowing water or water moving in waves.) OE. b. *Hunting*, etc. Streams or ditches which a horse is required to leap 1860. 7. Quantity or depth of water, as sufficient or insufficient for navigation 1546. b. With prefixed adj., a particular state of the tide; see HIGH W., LOW W. late ME. 8. Water received into a boat or ship through a leak, or by the breaking of the waves over the sides. late ME. 9. As an enveloping or covering medium; in various phrases. late ME. 10. A body of water on the surface of the earth. (In sense 'a stream, river', now chiefly *Sc.* and *north.*) OE. 11. *pl.* Floods: esp. in phr. *the waters are out*. 1523.

1. W., w., every where, Nor any drop to drink COLERIDGE. All else..runs off them like w. off a duck's back 1871. Phr. *To write on* or *in w.*, to fail to leave abiding record of (something). (To spend money) *like w.*, profusely, recklessly. d. *To cut off, turn on the w.* 2. *Bread and w.*, the type of extreme hard fare, as of a prisoner or penitent. *W. bewitched* (colloq.), excessively diluted liquor; now chiefly, very weak tea. 3. *Brandy-and-w., whisky-and-w.*, etc.; hence joc. in nonce-combs.; The weak Addison-and-w. of the 'Mirror' 1882. 5. It is..very long, Mr. Pickwick, since you drank the waters DICKENS. A wine-glass of Orezza w. after breakfast every morning 1879. 6. Thy waye was in the see, and thy pathes in the great waters COVERDALE *Ps.* lxxvii. 19. *fig.* Therfore she loves to fish in troubled Waters 1628. Phrases. *Deep waters* (after *Ps.* lxix. 2, 14), grave distresses and anxieties; also difficult or dangerous affairs. *To make a hole in the w.* (slang), to commit suicide by drowning. *By w.*, by ship or boat on the sea or a lake or river or canal. *On* or *upon the w.*, on the sea, in naval employments or enterprises. *Across, over, on this side the w., to cross the w.*, across, etc. the sea; (in London *the w.* in such phrases is often = the Thames). *The king over the w.*: see OVER *prep.* IV. 4. *To take* (*the*) *w.*, (*a*) to enter the sea, or lake, or river, and begin to swim; (*b*) to embark, take ship; (*c*) *U.S.* 'to abandon one's position'; (*d*) of a ship, to be launched. 7. *To draw* (so much) *w.*: see DRAW *v.* I. 11. 8. *To make w.*, *take* (*in*) *w.*, to leak, or to admit or 'ship' w. over the side, etc. 9. *Under w.*, below the surface of w.; (of land) flooded, submerged; hence *fig.* unsuccessful in life; also (*Sc.*) in debt. *Above w.*, above the surface of the w.; also *fig.*, esp. in *to keep one's head above w.*, to avoid ruin by a continued struggle. 10. By the waters of Babilon we sat downe and wepte COVERDALE *Ps.* cxxxvii. 1. The winters..are seldom severe enough to freeze any considerable w. BURKE. Within a little [we] found ourselves crossing the w. of Leith 1793. On one side lay the Ocean, and on one Lay a great w., and the moon was full TENNYSON.

II. The substance of which the liquid 'water' is one form among several; the chemical compound of two volumes of hydrogen and one of oxygen (formula H_2O); in ancient speculation regarded as one of the four (or later, five) elements of which all bodies are composed. OE.

III. A liquid resembling (and usu. containing) water. 1. An aqueous decoction, infusion, or tincture, used medicinally or as a cosmetic or perfume ME. b. With defining word, applied to liquid preparations of various kinds (see LAVENDER-W., LIME-W., SODA-W., etc.). late ME. 2. Used to denote various watery liquids found in the human or animal body, either normally or in disease 1533. b. The fluid contained in the amniotic cavity (*liquor amnii*); now usu. *pl.* 1688. c. Tears. late ME. d. Saliva; now only, flow of saliva provoked by appetite 1598. 3. *esp.* Urine. late ME. 4. Applied to vegetable juices 1585.

2. *W. on the brain, in the head*, hydrocephalus. c. A dexterous rap on the nose..which brought the w. into his eyes DICKENS. 3. *To make w.*, to urinate. *To pass w.*, to void urine (usu. with ref. to obstruction or the absence of it).

IV. The transparency and lustre characteristic of a diamond or a pearl 1607.

The three highest grades of quality in diamonds were formerly known as the *first, second*, and *third w.*; the phrase *of the first w.* survives in pop. use as a designation of the finest quality N.E.D. *fig. Of the first* (occas. *purest, finest*) *w.*, orig., of the highest excellence or purity: now only with the sense 'out-and-out', 'thorough-paced'.

attrib. and *Comb.*, as *w-biscuit, -brook, -broth, -bucket, -cask, -cock, -diet, -drainage, -gauge, -pole, -pool, -pump, -sprite, -supply, -tap, -trough, -turbine*, etc.; *w.-cooled* adj.; also (designating substances which harden under water) *w.-cement, -lime, -mortar*.

Comb.: a. **w. authority**, a municipal body administering a system of w.-supply; **-balance**, a machine for raising loads to a height by the weight of w.; **-ballast**, cisterns filled with w., placed in the hold of a vessel to serve as ballast; **-bearing** *a.* producing w., not arid; *Geol.* through which w. percolates; **W. Board**, an administrative body having control of the supply of w. to a town or district; **-boot**, a boot intended for those who have to stand or walk in w.; **-bound** *a.* of macadam roads: solidified by watering and rolling; **-breather**, any animal capable of breathing in w. (by means of gills); **-cell**, each of the cells in the walls of the stomach of the camel, in which w. is stored; **-company**, a commercial association for the purpose of supplying w. to a town or district; **-diviner**, one who finds subterranean springs or supplies of w. by means of a divining-rod; **-doctor**, (*a*) = W.-CASTER; (*b*) a hydropathist; **-finder** = *w.-diviner*; **-gilding**, the process of gilding metal surfaces by applying liquid amalgam, the mercury being afterwards removed by evaporation; so **-gilt** *a.*; **-head**, the head or source of a stream; **-jacket**, a casing containing w., placed about something to prevent its becoming unduly heated or chilled; hence **-jacketed** *ppl. a.*; **-jump**, a place where a horse is required to leap a stream or ditch; **-knot**, a knot used in joining together lengths of fishing-line; **-lead** (lĭd), (*a*) a mill-lead; (*b*) an open channel through an ice-field; †**-leader**, one who carts w. for sale; **-leaf** *Arch.*, an ornament used on capitals, supposed to represent the leaf of some w.-plant; **-mouth**, (*Sc.*), the mouth of a river; **-organ**, the hydraulicon or hydraulic organ; **-parting** = WATERSHED 1; **-pistol**, a weapon constructed to discharge a sudden jet of w. or other liquid; **-plane**, an aeroplane that can rise from or alight on water; a hydroplane; **-plate**, a plate with a receptacle underneath for hot w. to keep the food warm; **-power**, the power of moving or falling w. employed to drive machinery; **-quake**, a seismic disturbance in the sea; **-rate**, a rate or tax levied by a municipality or a w.-company for the supply of w.; **-spaniel**, a variety of spaniel, much used for retrieving w.-fowl; **-splash**, a shallow stream or ford crossing a road; **-stone**, a nodule of chalcedony having an internal cavity containing w.; **-tower**, (*a*) a tower serving as a reservoir to deliver w. at a required head; (*b*) a long iron tube, carried vertically on a wheeled frame, for discharging w. to extinguish fires in the upper stories of buildings; **-waggon**, *U.S.* = W.-CART; also *slang* in phr. *on the w.-waggon* = teetotal; **-worn** *a.* (chiefly *Geol.*), worn or corroded by the action of w.

b. Prefixed to names of animals to denote species inhabiting the w.: **w.-bear**, a sloth-animalcule; **-beetle**, a beetle of the group *Hydradephaga*; **-boatman**, a w.-bug of either of the families *Notonectidæ* or *Corixidæ*; **-buffalo**, the common domestic Indian buffalo, *Bos bubalus* or *Bubalus buffelus*; **-bug**, (*a*) any heteropterous insect of aquatic habit; (*b*) *U.S.* the cockroach, *Blatta orientalis*; **-flea**, any of the small crustaceans that hop like fleas; **-fly**, a fly that frequents w. and the w.-side; **-lawyer** *joc.*, a shark; **-mole** *Austral.*, the ornithorhyncus or duck-bill; **-mouse**, the w.-vole; **-rail**, a bird, *Rallus aquaticus*, having a general resemblance to the landrail; **-scorpion**, an aquatic bug of the family *Nepidæ*; **-serpent, -snake**, any snake that inhabits or frequents the w.; **-vole**, the common w.-rat, *Arvicola amphibius*; **-worm**, any aquatic annelid.

c. Denoting vegetable growths that live in w., as

w.-plant, *-reed*, etc.; also **w.-blob** *dial.*, a name for the marsh-marigold and similar plants; **-elder**, the guelder-rose; **-flag**, the yellow flag, *Iris Pseudacorus*; **-oak**, a hard coarse-grained oak, *Quercus aquatica*, of the southern U.S.; also applied to certain Australian trees of the genera *Casuarina* and *Callistemon*; **-parsley**, name for *Sium latifolium* or other aquatic umbellifers; **-parsnip**, name for aquatic umbelliferous plants of the genus *Sium*, esp. *S. latifolium*; **-plantain**, the plant *Alisma Plantago*, with leaves somewhat like those of the plantain, growing in ditches, etc.; **-violet**, the feather-foil, *Hottonia palustris*.

d. *Med.* Designating specific ailments, eruptions, etc., as *w.-blister*; also **w.-blebs**, pemphigus; **-pox**, chicken-pox.

Water (wǭ·təɹ), *v.* [OE. *wæterian*, f. *wæter* WATER *sb.*] **I.** *trans.* **1.** To give a drink of water to (an animal, esp. a horse on a journey); also, to take (cattle) to the water to drink. **2.** To furnish with a supply of water OE. **3.** To supply water as aliment to (a plant, crop, etc.), esp. by pouring or sprinkling with a watering-can, hose, or the like; to pour or sprinkle water on (soil) OE. **b.** To supply (land, crops) with water by flooding or by means of irrigation-channels; to irrigate 1555. **4.** Of a river, etc.; To supply water to (land, etc.). Now chiefly passive. OE. **5.** *To w.* (something) *with one's tears*; to make wet or moist with copious and continued weeping. *Obs.* or *arch.* Also †said of the tears. ME. †**6.** To soak in or with water, to steep in a liquor -1675. **b.** To sprinkle or drench (a road, pavement, etc.) with water, in order to lay the dust 1662. **c.** To sprinkle or drench (a material) with water in order to moisten it or with a solution to impregnate it 1474. **d.** *To w. one's clay*, to take liquid refreshment 1769. **7.** To add water to as a diluent or solvent, thereby increasing the bulk and reducing the strength. late ME. **a. To w. down.** To reduce the strength of (liquor) by dilution; *fig.* to weaken the force or strength of (language) by addition or alteration; to reduce in efficacy or potency 1850. **b.** *Comm.* To increase in nominal amount (the stock or capital of a trading company) by the creation of fictitious stock 1870. **8.** To produce a moiré or wavy lustrous finish on (silk or other textile fabrics) by sprinkling them with water and passing them through a calender 1450.

1. *Cymb.* II. iii. 23. 2. Lord Hood has gone to w. the Fleet NELSON. In a campaign like this..It should be easy to w. troops at fixed intervals 1898. 3. *fig.* The Apostles..planted this Faith..and watred it with their blood 1672. 4. That pleasant district..which is watered by the river Don SCOTT. 7. Tea twice watered with a good deal of sugar in it 1902.

II. *intr.* **1.** Of the eyes: To fill and run with moisture; to flow with tears ME. **2.** Of the mouth, also (now *Sc.*) of the teeth: To secrete abundant saliva in the anticipation of appetizing food or delicacies 1530. **3.** Of a ship, ship's company, etc.: To take on board a fresh store of water 1557. **4.** To drink water; to obtain water to drink 1607.

1. *Mids. N.* III. i. 200. The smoke..got into the Captain's eyes, and made them blink and w. DICKENS. 2. He sees no green cheese but his mouth waters after it 1639. 4. Cattle were watering in a lake 1839. Hence **Wa·tered** *ppl. a. spec.* of silk, etc., having a wavy lustrous damask-like pattern or finish; of steel, damascened. **Wa·terer**, one who waters (plants, etc.); one who is sent ashore to obtain fresh water for a ship's company; one who supplies animals with drinking-water.

Wa·ter-bag. 1638. A bag of skin or leather used for holding or carrying water, esp. one used in Eastern countries for transporting and distributing water.

Wa·ter-bai:lage. 1669. A duty or tax levied on all goods brought into or carried out of the Port of London.

Wa·ter-bai:liff. late ME. †**1.** An officer in various port towns, charged with the enforcement of shipping regulations, the collection of customs, and the like -1871. **2.** An official responsible for the enforcement of by-laws relating to fishing-waters 1667. **b.** A river-policeman employed to prevent poaching, etc. 1860.

Wa·ter-bath. 1824. **1.** *Chem.* A vessel containing water heated to a given temperature in or over which preparations are placed in suitable vessels to be digested, evaporated, or dried. **2.** A bath of water, as dist. from a vapour-bath 1891.

Wa·ter-bea:rer. late ME. One who carries water; *spec.* one whose employment is to carry water from a spring, etc. for domestic use.

Wa·ter-bed. 1791. **1.** A stratum through which water percolates. **2.** A water-tight mattress partly filled with water, designed to serve as a bed for an invalid, esp. for the prevention of bed-sores 1853. **3.** *Anat.* The cavity between the arachnoidea and pia mater containing cerebrospinal fluid, upon which the brain rests 1899.

‖**Waterbok** (wǭ·təɹbǫk). 1850. [Du., f. *water* WATER + *bok.*] = WATER-BUCK.

Wa·ter-borne, *a.* 1558. [BORNE *ppl. a.*] **1.** Of a boat: Supported by the water so as to be clear of the bottom upon which it has rested; afloat 1608. **2.** Of goods: **a.** Carried or transported by water. Hence of traffic, commerce. 1702. **b.** Put aboard a vessel for shipment 1558. **3.** Of disease: Propagated by the use of contaminated drinking-w. 1892.

Wa·ter bo:ttle. 1591. **1.** A vessel of leather or skin used in certain countries to convey water for domestic use. **2.** A bottle to hold drinking-water. **a.** One placed on the table for use at meals or in a bedroom 1825. **b.** A kind of flask used by soldiers and travellers 1889.

Wa·ter-break. 1806. Broken water; a piece of broken water.

Wa·ter-buck. 1850. [Anglicized f. WATERBOK.] A species of antelope, *Cobus ellipsiprymnus*, found in watered districts in central South Africa; an animal of this species. Sometimes applied to other species.

Wa·ter-butt. 1833. A large open-headed cask set up on end to receive the rain-water from a roof. **b.** Contempt. epithet for a teetotaller 1898.

Wa·ter-can. late ME. **1.** A portable vessel (in mod. use, of tin-plate or other metal) for holding or conveying water. **2.** The yellow water-lily, *Nuphar lutea*, so called from the shape of the seed-vessels. Also, the white water-lily, *Nymphæa alba*. 1622.

Wa·ter-ca:rriage. 1536. **1.** Conveyance or transportation by water. **b.** Carrying away (of sewage) by water 1873. **2.** Means or facilities for transporting by water 1727.

Wa·ter-ca:rrier. 1764. **1.** One who transports goods, etc. by water, not by land. **2.** A man (or animal) that carries water; *esp.* in oriental countries, the native who supplies an establishment or a number of troops with water 1787. **3.** A tank or other vessel for carrying water 1854.

Wa·ter-cart. 1707. A cart, usu. a barrel or tank on wheels, carrying water; chiefly, an apparatus of this kind intended for watering the streets, the receptacle being fitted with an arrangement by which the water escapes through a number of small holes or is forced through a nozzle, as the vehicle goes along.

†**Water-caster.** 1603. One who practises inspection of patients' urine as a means of diagnosis; latterly, used as = quack -1828.

Wa·ter-clock. 1601. [CLOCK *sb.*[1]] An instrument actuated by water for the measurement of time.

Wa·ter-clo:set. 1755. A small room fitted up to serve as a privy, and furnished with water-supply to flush the pan and discharge its contents into a waste-pipe below. Abbreviated W.C., w.c.

Wa·ter-co:lour. 1596. **1.** A pigment for which water and not oil is used as a solvent. Usu. in *pl.* **2.** A picture painted with water-colours 1854. **3.** The art or method of painting with water-colours 1843. **4.** *attrib.*, as *w. drawing, painting*, etc. 1698. Hence **Wa·ter-co:lourist**, one who paints in water-colours.

Wa·tercourse. 1510. **1.** A stream of water, a river or brook; also, an artificial channel for the conveyance of water. **2.** The bed or channel of a river or stream 1566.

1. They shall spring vp..as willowes by the water courses *Isa.* xliv. 4.

Wa·ter-cress. ME. [= MLG., MDu. *waterkerse.*] **1.** The hardy perennial, *Nasturtium officinale* (family *Cruciferæ*), found in abundance near springs and in small running streams, and now widely cultivated for use as a salad. *sing.* and *pl.* **2.** Applied (chiefly as book-names) to some other cruciferous plants, esp. *Cardamine amara*, *C. pratensis*; also to *Helioscadium nodiflorum*. late ME.

1. Watercresses doth cure tothe ache 1528. He loved..his brook with its water-cresses LONGF. I grew in my stream, some Watercress 1881.

Wa·ter-cure. 1842. [CURE *sb.*[1] 4; after G. *wasserkur.*] A method or course of medical treatment by means of water.

Wa·ter-dog. ME. **1.** A dog bred for or trained to the water; esp. one trained to retrieve water-fowl. Formerly as a specific name, the barbet or poodle imported from the Continent. **2.** A man thoroughly at home on or in the water; a sailor; a good swimmer 1674. **3.** A name for various animals. †**a.** The otter -1856. **b.** *U.S.* One of the various species of salamanders, *esp.* the hellbender or the mud-puppy 1859.

Wa·ter-dri:nker. 1440. **1.** A drinker of water, one who drinks water in preference to wine or other liquors; now usu. *spec.* a total abstainer. **2.** One who drinks the 'waters' at a spa 1707. So **Wa·ter-dri:nking** *vbl. sb.*; *ppl. a.* that drinks water and abstains from stronger liquors.

Wa·ter-drop. 1593. **1.** A drop or globule of water. Usu. *pl.* **2.** A tear, tear-drop 1605.

1. When water drops haue worne the Stones of Troy SHAKS. 2. Let not womens weapons, water drops, Staine my mans cheekes SHAKS.

Wa·ter-e:ngine. 1677. †**1.** A fire-engine -1802. **2.** An engine to raise water; a water-pumping engine 1685. **3.** An engine driven by water-power 1858.

Waterfall (wǭ·təɹfǭl). late ME. [f. WATER *sb.* + FALL *sb.*; OE. had *wætergefeall.*] **1.** A more or less perpendicular descent of water from a height over a ledge of rock or precipice; a cascade, cataract. **2.** Such an inclination of the ground as will facilitate the fall or drainage of water 1522. †**3.** A swift stream tumbling in a rocky bed, a rapid -1748. **4.** *Coal-mining.* A special 'head' of water to be turned down a pit-shaft when needed 1797. **5.** (orig. *U.S.*) A chignon; also, a wave of hair falling down the neck below the chignon or net 1866.

3. To..steep In wholsom Water-falls the woolly Sheep DRYDEN. 5. The young lady that affects waterfalls, the Grecian bend, or the kangaroo hop 1875.

Wa·ter-flood. [OE. *wæterflōd.*] **1.** A moving flood or overflowing of water; a tempestuous sea. **2.** A body or mass of water in flood. late ME.

1. The Lorde stilleth the water floude COVERDALE *Ps.* xxix. 10.

Waterfowl (wǭ·təɹfaul). ME. [Cf. G. *wasservogel.*] Any bird that frequents the water, or inhabits the margin of lakes, rivers, seas, etc.; in mod. use chiefly applied to the larger kinds of swimming birds, esp. those which are regarded as game. Often *collect. sing.* for *pl.*

Wa·ter-front. orig. *U.S.* 1856. Land or buildings abutting on a river, a lake, the sea, etc.; the frontage of a town on the water-side.

Wa·ter-fu:rrow, *sb.* OE. A deep furrow made for conducting water from the ground and keeping it dry. Hence **Wa·ter-fu:rrow** *v. trans.* to make water-furrows in (land).

Wa·ter-gall. Now *dial.* 1594. [GALL *sb.*[2] Cf. G. *wassergalle.*] A secondary or imperfectly-formed rainbow; also applied to various other phenomena in the clouds that are believed to portend rain.

Wa·ter-gas. 1851. **1.** A gas made by forcing steam over incandescent carbon; used as fuel, and when carburetted as an illuminator. **2.** Water in the form of vapour 1881.

Wa·ter-gate. late ME. [GATE *sb.*[1]] †**1.** A sluice or floodgate -1755. **2.** A gate (of a town, a castle, etc.) giving access to the water-side. late ME. **3.** A place through which water-traffic passes 1893.

Wa·ter-glass. 1612. **1.** A water-clock or clepsydra 1661. †**2.** A glass finger-bowl -1784. **3.** A glass vessel to contain water; esp. such a vessel intended for keeping plants in water 1612. **4.** An instrument for making observations beneath the surface of water, consisting of a bucket with a glass bottom 1848. **5.** An aqueous solution of silicate of soda or potash (or of both), which solidifies when exposed to the air. It is used as a vehicle for fresco-painting, for pickling eggs, etc. 1859.

Wa·ter-gruel. late ME. **1.** Thin gruel made with water instead of milk. †**2.** *fig.* as the type of what is insipid. Chiefly *attrib.* (quasi-*adj.*), namby-pamby. -1811.

2. A pretty, sweet, smiling, flexible, insipid, w. girl 1784.

Wa·ter-ha·mmer. 1805. **1.** An instrument used to illustrate the fact that in a vacuum liquids and solids fall at the same rate. (It consists of a hermetically sealed tube exhausted of air and partly filled with water. When the tube is quickly reversed the water falls on the end with a noise like that of a hammer.) **2.** *Hydraulics.* The concussion or sound of concussion of water in a pipe when its flow is suddenly stopped, or when live steam is admitted 1891. **b.** Path. *W. pulse*, a jerky pulse with a full expansion, followed by a sudden collapse 1899.

Wa·ter-hen. 1529. Any of the various ralline birds, esp. the MOOR-HEN, *Gallinula chloropus*. **b.** *W. hackle*, an artificial fly made of the hackle feathers of the w. 1837.

Wa·ter-hole. 1679. A hole or depression in which water collects, a pond or pool; a reservoir. *Obs.* exc. *dial.* and *Colonial*. **b.** A cavity in the bed of a river, esp., in Colonial use, one that retains water when the river itself is dry 1792.

Wa·ter-horse. late ME. †**1.** The hippopotamus -1642. **2.** A fabled water-spirit appearing in the form of a horse 1800.

Wa·ter-ice. 1818. **1.** A confection of water and sugar, flavoured and frozen. **2.** Ice formed by the freezing of water, not by the compacting of snow 1882.

Watering (wǭ·təriŋ), *vbl. sb.* OE. [f. WATER *v.* + -ING [1].] **I.** The action of the verb WATER; an instance of this. **1.** The action or an act of pouring or sprinkling water on plants, crops, or the soil. **2.** The action or an act of soaking or steeping in water or of impregnating with a liquor. late ME. **3.** The application of water to a road, etc., in order to lay the dust 1673. **4.** The action of giving drinking-water to cattle, etc.; also, the action (of an animal) of going to the water to drink 1440. **5.** The action of procuring fresh water for a ship 1613. **6.** The action or process of giving a 'watered' appearance to the surface of a material 1665. **7.** Dilution with water 1888. **8.** Dilution of the capital of a trading company 1884. **9.** Running (of the eyes); filling with tears. late ME. **10.** Salivation of the teeth, mouth, or 'chops' induced by the thought or anticipation of appetizing food 1601. †**11.** Taking the waters -1765.

4. *transf.* 1 *Hen. IV*, II. iv. 17. 7. Six drops to the half-pint seems a sinful w. of grog 1896.

II. *concr.* **1.** A ditch for draining a marsh; the tract drained by such a ditch 1790. **2.** The wavy variegated appearance given to silk, metal, etc. 1670.

Comb.: **w-can** = WATERING-POT 1; **-cart** = WATER-CART; †**-house**, an inn or public house where coachmen may obtain water for their horses and refreshment for themselves.

Wa·tering-pla·ce. 1440. **1.** A place in a river or lake where animals come or are brought to drink; also, a pool or trough prepared for the use of cattle and horses. **2.** A place where a ship's company goes to fill the ship's casks with fresh water 1613. **b.** *gen.* A place where a supply of water can be obtained 1621. **3.** [See prec. II.] A resort of fashionable or holiday visitants, either for drinking or bathing in the waters of a mineral spring, or for sea-bathing 1757.

Wa·tering-po·t. 1580. **1.** A portable vessel for watering plants; now usu. of tinned iron, and furnished with a long tubular spout, often ending with a rose for scattering the water. **2.** *Zool.* A mollusc of the genus *Aspergillum*, so named from the shape of its shell 1815.

Wa·terish, *a.* 1542. [f. WATER *sb.* + -ISH [1].] **1.** Resembling water in appearance or sensible properties 1583. **2.** Containing excess of water. Of liquids: Dilute, thin, poor. Of solids: Loose in texture, not firm or compact. 1542. **3.** Of weather, air, mist: Charged with water, watery 1650. **4.** Of light or of luminous bodies: Dimmed by watery vapour 1607.

2. *fig.* Out of a w. and queasy conscience MILT. 4. The w. moonlight 1845.

Wa·ter-lane. 1872. **1.** *dial.* A green lane with a stream running along it. **2.** A narrow passage of open water, e.g. between masses of reeds or between lines of shipping 1883.

Waterless (wǭ·təɹlės), *a.* [OE. *waterlēas* = Du. *waterloos*, OHG. *wazzerlôs*.] Destitute of water; containing no water; unsupplied with water.

Wa·ter-level. 1563. **1.** A levelling instrument in which water is used instead of alcohol. **2.** *Mining.* A road driven on the strike of a seam to carry off water 1698. **3.** The plane below which the rock or soil is saturated with water; the situation of this plane 1839. **4.** The horizontal surface of still water. Also, the position of the surface of water. 1860.

Wa·ter-lily. 1549. The common name for many aquatic plants with large flowers, belonging to the family *Nymphæaceæ*. In England chiefly applied to the white water-lily *Nymphæa alba*, and the yellow water-lily *Nuphar lutea*. **b.** Applied to aquatic plants of other orders 1653.

Wa·ter-line. 1625. **1.** *Naut.* The line of floatation of a ship; the line supposed to be described on the hull by the surface of the water when a ship is afloat. Often = LOAD-WATER-LINE. **2.** *Shipbuilding.* Any one of certain structural lines of a ship, parallel with the surface of the water which represent the contour of the hull at various heights above the keel 1750. **3.** = WATER-LEVEL 3. 1849. **4.** The outline of a coast 1791. **5.** A linear watermark in paper 1847.

Waterlog (wǭ·təɹlǫg), *v.* 1779. [app. f. WATER *sb.* + LOG *v.*[1] (in the sense of 'to reduce to a log-like condition').] **1.** *trans.* To render (a ship, etc.) unmanageable by flooding with water. **2.** To saturate with water so as to render inert 1868.

Waterlogged (wǭ·təɹlǫgd), *ppl. a.* 1769. [f. prec. + -ED [1].] **1.** Of a ship, boat: Flooded with water so as to become impaired in buoyancy, heavy, and unmanageable. **2.** Of floating bodies: Saturated with water so as to be deprived of buoyancy 1832. **3.** Suffering from, deteriorated or rendered unserviceable by, excessive saturation with water 1829.

1. *transf.* That water-logged country called Holland 1840. 3. W. mines 1895. Rotten water-logged earth 1897.

Waterloo (wǭtəɹlū·). 1816. The battle fought outside the village of Waterloo, near Brussels, on June 18, 1815, in which Napoleon was finally defeated. Hence, something which is a 'settler'; a decisive and final contest; chiefly in phr. *to meet one's W.*

Waterman (wǭ·təɹmæ̆n). late ME. [Cf. G. *wassermann*, WFris. *wetterman*.] †**1.** A seaman, mariner -1682. **2.** A man working on a boat or among boats, *esp.* a boatman who plies for hire on a river, etc. 1458. **b.** *colloq.* One having a (good) knowledge of boating, etc. 1912. **3.** A man employed in the supply or distribution of water; *e.g.* a water-carrier, a turncock or fireman; *esp.* an attendant at cab-stands whose duty was to water the horses 1705. Hence **Wa·termanship**, the art of a w.; skill in rowing or managing boats, etc.

Wa·ter-mark, wa·termark, *sb.* 1678. [MARK *sb.*[1]] **1.** The line (whether actually marked or not) forming the limit to which the tide, or the water of a river, well, etc., has risen or usu. rises. Cf. HIGH-WATER *mark*, LOW-WATER *mark*. **2.** A mark left by a flood 1822. **3.** The line showing the draught of a ship 1764. **4.** A distinguishing mark or device impressed in the substance of a sheet of paper during manufacture, usu. barely noticeable except when the sheet is held up against the light 1708. **b.** The metal design from which the impression is made 1854. Hence **Wa·ter-mark** *v. trans.* to mark or stamp with a w.; to embody as a w.

Wa·ter-meadow. 1733. A meadow periodically overflowed by a stream.

Wa·ter-measure. 1465. A kind of measurement formerly used for coal, salt, etc., sold on board vessels in port or in the river.

Wa·ter-melon. 1615. [So called from the abundance of watery juice.] A kind of gourd, *Citrullus vulgaris*.

Wa·ter-mill. late ME. **1.** A corn-mill whose machinery is driven by water. **2.** A water-wheel or a machine driven by a water-wheel 1580.

Wa·ter-mint. 1542. Any aquatic plant of the labiate genus *Mentha*; chiefly the Bergamot Mint (*Mentha aquatica*) or the Brook-mint (*M. hirsuta*).

Wa·ter-nymph. late ME. **1.** A nymph inhabiting or presiding over water; a naiad. **2.** A water-lily of the genus *Nymphæa* 1866.

Water of Ayr. 1805. The name of the river at the mouth of which the town of Ayr stands. Used *attrib.* in *Water of Ayr stone*, a kind of stone found on its banks, used for whetstones and for polishing.

Water of life. late ME. **1.** *fig.* A drink which gives life or immortality to the drinker. **2.** A name for brandy or whisky; tr. med.L. *aqua vitæ*, F. *eau-de-vie*. rare. 1576.

Wa·ter-pipe. late ME. **1.** A pipe through which water is conducted. **2.** A hookah, narghile, or kalian 1824.

1. One depe calleth another because of yᵉ noyse of thy water pipes *Ps.* xlii. 8 (Great Bible): see note s.v. WATER-SPOUT.

Wa·ter-pot. late ME. **1.** A vessel, usu. of earthenware, for holding water. **b.** *Astr.* The portion of the zodiacal constellation Aquarius which is figured as a vase or urn 1546. **2.** = WATERING-POT 1. 1530. **3.** = WATERING-POT 2. 1815.

Waterproof (wǭ·təɹprūf), *a.* and *sb.* 1736. [See PROOF *a.* 1 b.] **A.** *adj.* Impervious to water; capable of resisting the deleterious action of water.

Neat w. travelling suits 1871. *fig.* Tears were not the things to find their way to Mr. Bumble's soul; his heart was w. DICKENS.

B. *sb.* A fabric or garment rendered impervious to water by treatment with india-rubber or the like 1799. Hence **Wa·terproof** *v. trans.* to make w. **Wa·terproofed** (-prūft) *ppl. a.* **Wa·terproofing** *vbl. sb.* the action or process of making materials, etc. w.; material with which a substance is made w.

Wa·ter-rat. 1552. **1.** An aquatic rodent of the family *Muridæ*; in British use, the water-vole, *Arvicola amphibius*. In the U.S. applied to the MUSK-RAT, and in Australia to the genus *Hydromys*. **2.** *fig.* A water-thief, pirate. Also contempt., a sailor, boatman, or the like. 1596.

Watershed (wǭ·təɹʃed). 1803. [SHED *sb.*[1]] **1.** The line separating the waters flowing into different rivers or river basins; a narrow elevated tract of ground between two drainage areas. **2.** *loosely.* **a.** The slope down which the water flows from a watershed 1839. **b.** The whole gathering ground of a river system 1874. **3.** A structure for throwing off water 1881.

Wa·tershoot. 1625. **1.** †**a.** Outflow of drainage water from land; water carried off by drainage -1721. **b.** A gutter or channel for the overflow of water 1819. **2.** An artificial cascade contrived for the amusement or exercise of 'shooting the rapids' in a boat or by swimming 1900.

Wa·terside. late ME. **1.** The side or brink of water; the bank or margin of the sea, or of a river, stream, or lake. **2.** The side towards the water 1868.

Water-souchy (-sū·tʃi, -sū·ʃi). 1731. [a. Du. *waterzootje*, f. *water* WATER *sb.* + *zootje*, *zoodje* boiling (of fish).] Fish (prop. perch) boiled and served in its own liquor.

Wa·ter-spout, wa·terspout. late ME. **1.** A spout, pipe, or nozzle, through which water is discharged; also †a squirt, syringe. **2.** *Meteorol.* A gyrating column of mist, spray, and water, produced by the action of a whirlwind on a portion of the sea and the clouds immediately above it 1738. **b.** A sudden and violent fall of rain; a cloudburst 1779.

In Ps. xlii. 7 (version of 1611), the word is now commonly apprehended as an example of sense 2; it was, however, probably intended as a metaphorical use of sense 1.

Wa·ter-spring. 1440. = SPRING *sb.*[1] I. 2. Now chiefly in echoes of the Bible.

Wa·ter-stream. Now *rare.* OE. [Cf. G. *wasserstrom.*] A stream or current of water; a river or brook; †a flood.

Wa·ter-table. late ME. [See TABLE *sb.* IV. 2, 3.] **1.** *Arch.* **a.** The sloping top of a plinth. **b.** A projecting ledge or moulding sloping on the top, set along the side of a wall so as to throw off rain. **2.** A channel or gutter on each side of or across a road 1707. **3.** A window-ledge or sill in a ship or railway carriage 1883. **4.** = WATER-LEVEL 3. 1879. Hence **Wa·ter-tabling** *Arch.*, water-tables collectively; a line of water-tables.

Watertight (wǭ·təɹtəit), *a.* late ME. [See TIGHT *a.* 2.] **1.** So closely constructed or fitted that water cannot leak through. **b.** *fig.* 1647. **2.** As *sb. pl.* Watertight boots 1880.

1. *W. compartment*, each of the many compartments, with w. partitions, into which the interior of a large ship is now usu. divided for safety; hence often *fig.*

Wa·ter-wa·gtail. 1611. **1.** The common pied wagtail, *Motacilla lugubris.* Also applied with distinctive epithet to other species. **2.** *U.S.* A bird of the Amer. genus *Seiurus* 1865.

Wa·ter-wave. 1560. **1.** A wave of water. **2.** A wave in the hair produced by **W.-waving,** a method of waving the hair with w. 1882.

Wa·ter-way. 1440. **1.** A channel for the escape or passage of water. **2.** *Naut.* A long piece of timber, hollowed in the middle, serving as a channel for carrying off water from the deck of a ship 1635. **3.** A route for travel or transport by water; a river, canal, or a portion of a sea or lake, viewed as a medium of transit 1858. **4.** The breadth of a navigable watercourse; esp. the breadth allowed for the watercourse of a canal or the like passing under a bridge or tunnel 1739. **5.** An opening for the passage of vessels, esp. entering and leaving a harbour, the fairway 1883. **6.** The full-open passage area in a cock or valve 1744.

Wa·ter-weed. 1842. Any aquatic plant with inconspicuous flowers; spec. the Amer. weed *Elodea canadensis*, common in Eng. waters.

Wa·ter-wheel. late ME. **1.** A wheel designed to drive machinery with water as the motive power. **2.** A wheel for raising water by means of buckets or boxes fitted on its circumference 1639. †**3.** A paddle-wheel –1822.

Wa·ter-witch. 1680. **1.** A witch inhabiting the water. **2.** *U.S.* A name for several water-birds noted for their quickness in diving 1789. **3.** *U.S.* = WATER-*diviner* 1859.

Waterwork (wǭ·təɹwɒɹk). 1443. [f. WATER *sb.* + WORK *sb.*] †**1.** A structure built in the water or serving as a receptacle for water or a defence against the force of water –1791. **2.** †**a.** A system of machinery for raising, conveying, or distributing water –1775. **b.** *collect. pl.* (Sometimes construed as sing.) The machinery, buildings, and engineering constructions, used for the purpose of supplying a town, etc., with water distributed through pipes 1621. †**3.** Any contrivance for producing a pleasing spectacle by means of water in motion; an ornamental fountain or cascade –1779. **b.** *transf.* Chiefly in joc. ref. to shedding of tears or making water 1647. **4.** An operation or department of labour concerned with hydraulic engineering, irrigation, or the like. Now *rare.* 1564.

Watery (wǭ·təri), *a.* OE. [f. WATER *sb.* + -Y[1].] **1.** Of land or soil: Full of water; moist, plashy. **b.** Of clouds: Full of moisture which is ready to fall as rain. Also of wind, etc. late ME. **c.** *transf.* Covered with or permeated by water; set or built in the water 1593. **2.** Resembling water in consistence; thin, fluid OE. **3.** Having the appearance of water; resembling water in colour. Of colour: Looking as if diluted with water. late ME. **4.** Of the nature of water 1477. **b.** applied to the rainbow. *poet.* 1600. **c.** Of a chemical solution, etc.: Made with water, aqueous 1826. **5.** Consisting of water. Chiefly *poet.* or *rhet.* 1535. **6.** Of, belonging to, or connected with the water; aquatic. Now *rare.* late ME. **7.** Of food: Containing too much moisture; tasting too much like water 1440. **8.** Of the eyes: Suffused with tears, tearful; exuding moisture, as a result of weakness or disease in the lachrymal glands 1447. **9.** Of the skin, etc.: Exuding or suffused with a humour or moisture resembling water. late ME. **10.** *fig.* Of thought, feeling, expression, etc.: Vapid, washy, poor, thin ME.

1. c. The Lark now leaves his watry Nest DAVENANT. 3. A w. sunbeam SCOTT. 5. *W. grave*, †*tomb*, (*a*) the place in which a person lies drowned; (*b*) death by drowning; A youth..was rescued from the w. grave 1802; similarly *w. death.* 6. W. Neptune SHAKS. The sev'ral sorts of watry Fowls, That swim the Seas, or haunt the standing Pools DRYDEN. Swithin ..the w. saint 1818. 7. W. soup for beggars 1871. 10. A w. but harmless story of London society 1904.

Watt (wǫt). 1882. [f. name of James *Watt* (1736–1819), the inventor of the modern steam-engine.] *Physics.* A unit of activity or power (used chiefly with ref. to electricity), corresponding to the rate of work represented by a current of one ampère under a pressure of one volt.

Comb.: **w.-hour,** the work done by one w. in one hour; **wattmeter,** an instrument for measuring electric energy. Hence **Wa·ttless** *a.*

Watteau (wǫ·tou, ‖vato). 1833. The name of Antoine *Watteau* (1684–1721), a French painter, used *attrib.* in *W. school, W.-like* adj.; also in designations of articles of female costume similar to those represented in Watteau's pictures, as *W. bodice, hat.* Hence **Wa·tteauish** *a.* resembling the style of Watteau.

Wattle (wǫ·t'l), *sb.*[1] [OE. *watul*, of obsc. origin.] **I. 1.** *pl.* and *collect. sing.* Rods or stakes, interlaced with twigs or branches of trees, used to make fences, walls, and roofs. Also, rods and branches of trees collected for this purpose. **2.** *dial.* A hurdle 1640. **3.** *dial.* A wand, rod 1570.

1. *W. and daub*, interwoven twigs plastered with clay or mud, as a building material for huts, etc.

II. *Australian.* [orig. *w.-tree*, from the use of the long pliant branches for making wattled fences, etc.] The common name in Australia for indigenous trees of the genus *Acacia.* Also with defining word indicating the particular species, as *Black, Silver W.* 1810.

Wattle (wǫ·t'l), *sb.*[2] 1513. [Origin obsc.] **1.** A fleshy lobe (usu. bright-coloured) pendent from the head or neck of certain birds, as the domestic fowl, the turkey, etc. **2.** A flap of skin pendent from the throat or neck of some swine. Also, a similar excrescence on the jaws of sheep or goats, and *joc.* of human beings 1570. **3.** A fleshy appendage hanging from the mouths of some fishes; a barb 1655. Hence **Wa·ttled** *a.* of a bird, having wattles or a w.; in *Heraldry*, having the wattles of a specified tincture distinct from that of the body.

Wattle (wǫ·t'l), *v.* late ME. [f. WATTLE *sb.*[1]] **1.** *trans.* To construct (a building, fence, etc.) of wattle. **2.** To interlace (boughs, twigs, etc.) so as to form wattle-work 1486. **3.** To bind together (posts, laths, etc.) with interlaced osiers, twigs, or flexible branches 1602. Hence **Wa·ttled** *ppl. a.* constructed of wattle; interlaced. **Wa·ttling** *vbl. sb.* (*a*) an assemblage of rods or laths interlaced with twigs, osiers, or the like, serving as the material of a wattled wall, fence, etc.; (*b*) boughs and twigs for use in wattle-work.

Wave (wēⁱv), *sb.* 1526. [f. WAVE *v.*] **I. 1.** A movement in the sea or other collection of water, by which a portion of the water rises above the normal level and then subsides, at the same time travelling over the surface; a moving ridge or swell of water between two depressions; one of the long ridges or rollers which, in the shallower parts of the sea, follow each other at regular intervals, and successively break on the shore. **b.** *poet.* Used in collect. sing. for 'water', 'sea' 1588. **2.** *transf.* **a.** An undulatory movement, or one of an intermittent series of movements, of something passing over or on a surface or through the air 1810. **b.** A forward movement of a large body of persons (chiefly invaders or immigrants overrunning a country, or soldiers advancing to an attack), who either recede and return after an interval, or are followed after a time by another body of persons repeating the same movement 1852. **c.** A long convex strip of land between two long broad hollows; also occas. a rounded ridge of sand or snow 1788. **3.** *fig.* and in fig. context 1548. **4.** An undulating conformation; each of the undulations of such a conformation 1547. **5. a.** *Physics.* Each of those rhythmic alternations of disturbance and recovery of configuration in successively contiguous portions of a body or medium, by which a state of motion travels in some direction without corresponding progressive movement of the particles successively affected 1832. **b.** *Meteorol.* A change of atmospheric pressure or temperature, consisting of gradual rise and fall or fall and rise, taking place successively at successive points in some particular line of direction on the earth's surface. (In pop. lang., a 'heat-wave', etc. denotes a spell of abnormal heat, etc., which is assumed to be travelling over the country in a particular direction) 1843. **c.** *Seismology.* A seismic disturbance of the crust or surface of the earth, travelling continuously for a certain distance 1862. **d.** *Physics* (see quots.) 1851. **6.** A book-name of certain geometrid moths 1819.

2. a. The..waves of wheat, That ripple round the lonely grange TENNYSON. b. Europe was peopled by several successive migrations, or..waves of population, all flowing from one point in the east 1852. They send forward w. after w. of men, regardless of the punishment 1915. 3. Man, on the dubious waves of error toss'd COWPER. A w. of militarism sweeps through the nation 1915. 4. Freedom's northern wind will take all the w. out of your hair 1886. 5. a. Examples are the waves in the surface of water, the waves of the air which convey sound, and the waves of the ether which are concerned in the transmission of light, heat, and electricity. N.E.D. *Hertzian waves*, a class of ether-waves (discovered by the German physicist Heinrich Hertz in 1888) similar to light waves but of much greater w.-length. d. *W. of contraction*, the onward contraction of a muscle from the point where the stimulus is applied. *W. of stimulation*, the (hypothetical) impulse of molecular vibration travelling along a nerve from the point at which it is stimulated.

II. An act of waving. **1.** A motion to and fro of the hand or of something held in the hand, used as a signal or as an expressive sign 1688. **2.** A swaying to and fro 1648. **3.** An act of waving the hair.

attrib. and *Comb.*: **w.-front** *Physics*, the continuous lines or surface including all the waves or radiatory emissions which are in the same phase; **-length,** (*a*) the distance from crest to crest or from hollow to hollow of a wave of water or other liquid; (*b*) the distance between two successive points of maximum compression or maximum rarefaction in sound-waves; (*c*) the distance between points in the same phase on two successive heat, light, electro-magnetic, or other waves; *esp.* the length of electro-magnetic wave employed by a broadcasting station; also *fig.*; **-line,** (*a*) *Shipbuilding*, an outline recommended by some naval architects for the hull of a vessel as facilitating movement through the waves; (*b*) *Physics*, the path of a w. of light, sound, etc.; also, the graphic representation of the path. Hence **Wa·veless** *a.* having no waves, not agitated or disturbed by waves. **Wa·velet,** a little w., a ripple.

Wave (wēⁱv), *v.* [OE. *wafian*, corresp. to MHG. *waben* to wave:—Teut. root **wab-*.] **I.** To move to and fro or up and down. **1.** *intr.* Of a thing having a free end: To move to and fro, shake or sway in the air by the action of the wind or breeze. late ME. **b.** *trans.* Of the wind, etc.: To cause (a thing) to sway or move to and fro 1602. †**2.** *intr.* To move to and fro restlessly or uncertainly; to waver; also, to hover –1728. †**3.** To be restless in mind; to vacillate, waver –1796. **4.** Of water: To move in waves, undulate; also *transf.* of a crowd 1530. **b.** Of a field of corn, etc.: To undulate like the waves of the sea 1667. †**5.** To make a movement to and fro (with the hands). OE. only. †**6.** To make motions (with the uplifted hands or something held in the hands) by way of signal –1644. †**b.** *trans.* To signal to (a person) –1627. †**7.** *trans.* and *intr.* To move to and fro or up and down regularly or rhythmically –1808. **8.** *trans.* To move through the air with a sweeping gesture (the uplifted or extended arm or hand, or something held in the hand), often as a sign of greeting or farewell, or as an expression of exultation; usu. implying repeated movements. Said also (chiefly *poet.*) of impersonal things personified 1607. **b.** To brandish (a weapon) 1601. **c.** *intr.* (for *pass.*) To be moved to and fro 1605. **9.** To signify (something) by a wave of the hand or arm 1810. **b.**

To motion (a person, etc.) *aside, away, off,* etc.; also with preps. *from, to,* etc. 1840. **c.** *intr.* To make a sign by a wave of the hand 1803.

1. A stately Ship..Sails fill'd, and streamers waving MILT. 3. *Cor.* II. ii. 19. 4. b. Fair waved the golden corn In Canaan's pleasant land 1851. 7. At last,.. thrice his head thus wauing vp and downe, He rais'd a sigh SHAKS. Colours that change whene'er they w. their wings POPE. 8. Maidens w. Their 'kerchiefs, and old women weep for joy COWPER. Cypresses that seldom w. their boughs SHELLEY.

II. [from WAVE *sb.*] **1.** *trans.* To ornament with an undulating design; to make wavy in outline 1547. **2.** *intr.* To undulate in form or outline 1789.

1. Hair that has been waved by hot irons till it is broken and irregular 1909.

Comb., in the names of the several offerings which, according to the Levitical law, were 'waved' by the priest when presented in sacrifice, as **wavebread, -breast, -loaf, -offering, -sheaf.** Hence **Waved** (wēⁱvd) *ppl. a.* having the form of waves, presenting a wavy outline or appearance, having wavy markings or a wavy texture; held aloft and moved to and fro. **Wa·ver** *sb.*[2] one who waves or causes to wave; an implement for making the hair wavy; *Printing*, an inking roller which has a waving motion, because placed diagonally in the machine.

Wa·ve-like, *a.* and *adv.* 1685. [f. WAVE *sb.* + -LIKE.] **A.** *adj.* Resembling a wave, or what pertains to a wave. **B.** *adv.* After the manner of a wave or waves 1872.

Wavellite (wēⁱ·vělait). 1805. [f. name of Dr. *Wavel*, its discoverer; see -ITE [1] 2 b.] *Min.* Hydrous phosphate of aluminium, found in globular aggregates with a radiated structure.

Waver (wēⁱ·vəɹ), *sb.*[1] 1555. [Origin obsc.; perh. f. WAIVE *v.*, in the sense 'to leave untouched'.] A young tree left standing when the surrounding wood is felled.

Waver (wēⁱ·vəɹ), *v.* [ME. *waver, wever* = MHG. *waberên*, ON. *vafra*; a frequentative f. Teut. root **wab-*.] **1.** *intr.* To sway to and fro, as if in danger of falling; to reel, stagger, totter. Now *rare.* late ME. **2.** To swing or wave in the air; to float or flutter 1440. **3.** To exhibit doubt or indecision; to change or vary; to fluctuate or vacillate (*between*); to become unsteady, flinch, give way ME. **4.** Of things (or a person as an unconscious agent): To change, vary, fluctuate 1490. **5.** Of the voice, the eye, etc. (or a person in respect of these): To become unsteady; to shake, tremble, falter 1621. **6.** Of light, shade, objects seen indistinctly: To flicker, quiver 1664.

3. Vertue that wavers is not vertue MILT. The line wavered and broke 1915. Hence **Wa·ver** *sb.*[3] the act or condition of wavering. **Wa·verer,** one who wavers. **Wa·vering** *vbl. sb.* and *ppl.*; hence **wa·veringly** *adv.* **Wa·very** *a.* characterized by wavering or fluttering; tremulous, unsteady 1820.

Wavey (wēⁱ·vi). 1795. [See WAWA.] A northern (Amer.) goose of the genus *Chen*, esp. the common w., *C. hyperboreus.*

Wavy (wēⁱ·vi), *a.* 1562. [f. WAVE *sb.* or *v.* + -Y [1].] **1.** Full of waves, abounding in waves, billowy 1593. **2.** *transf.* Said of the air, clouds, etc. 1586. **3.** *fig.* Fluctuating, wavering, changing 1795. **4.** Moving to and fro or up and down with a wave-like motion 1700. **b.** Of movements: Taking place in undulating curves, sinuous 1836. **5.** Rising and falling gently in a succession of waves and hollows; forming an undulating line or a series of wave-like curves 1701. **b.** *Bot.* and *Zool.* Undulate, sinuate; having undulate or sinuate markings 1832. **c.** *Her.* = UNDEE 1562. **d.** Of a dog (short for *w.-coated*): Having the coat in waves, not curly 1884.

2. *W. breathing, respiration* (Path.), respiration in which the inspiratory, and sometimes the expiratory, sounds are broken into two or more separate parts. 4. Let her glad Vallies smile with w. Corn PRIOR. 5. Her dark hair flowed behind, w. but uncurled 1858. A fine w. chalk down 1891. c. *Barry w.*, of the field, divided into waving bands of generally horizontal direction. Hence **Wa·vi-ly** *adv.*, **-ness.**

†**Waw.**[1] [ME. *waȝe*, related to OE. *wagian* to wave, shake, totter.] A wave -1600.

‖**Waw,**[2] **wau.** 1832. The 6th letter in the Hebrew and the corresponding letter in the Arabic and other Semitic alphabets.

‖**Wawa** (wēⁱ·wǎ). 1768. [Cree *wehwew* goose. Cf. WAVEY.] An Amer.-Indian name for the wild goose.

Wax (wæks), *sb.*[1] [Com. Teut.; OE. *weax* :—OTeut. **wahsom*, of disputed origin.] **1.** A substance (also distinctively called BEESWAX) produced by bees and used by them as the material of the honeycomb; when slightly warmed it is readily moulded into any shape. **2.** Beeswax as melted down, bleached, or otherwise prepared for some special purpose in the arts, in medicine, or in manufactures OE. **b.** As used for the coating of writing tablets 1533. **c.** A particular variety of wax. Usu. with adj., as *white, yellow w.* 1545. **d.** An object made of wax; a wax candle; a figure or model in wax 1844. **3.** In fig. and similative uses, referring to the easy fusibility of wax, its softness, adhesiveness, etc. OE. **4.** = SEALING-WAX OE. **b.** With designation of colour 1485. **5.** Any of a class of substances, found in nature in greater or less purity, including beeswax and other compounds resembling it in general properties and (more or less) in chemical composition. **a.** A vegetable product obtained from various trees and plants 1799. **b.** A substance resembling beeswax secreted or produced by various species of scale-insects 1802. **c.** A mineral product somewhat resembling beeswax 1838. **d.** *gen.* 1866. **6.** = EARWAX 1706. **7.** A thick resinous composition used by shoemakers for rubbing their thread. More fully *cobblers', shoemakers' wax.* 1622. **8.** *U.S.* A thick syrup produced by boiling down the sap of the sugar-maple tree 1845. **9.** *attrib.* (quasi-*adj.*) = composed of or modelled in w. 1585.

2. Effigies..Curiously done in W. to the Life 1702. The Art of Painting in Wax 1787. 3. I'll work her as I go, I know shee 's w. 1612. His heart was..W. to receive, and marble to retain BYRON. Phr. *Close, tight, neat as w.; to stick like w.; to fit like w. Man, lad of w.*, used as a term of emphatic commendation (now *arch.* and *dial.*). 5. c. *Fossil, mineral w.* = OZOCERITE. *Paraffin w.*: see PARAFFIN *sb.*

Comb.: **w.-berry,** (*a*) the fruit of plants of the genus *Myrica*, esp. *M. cerifera*; also, the plant itself; (*b*) = *Symphoricarpus racemosus*; **-bill,** any one of numerous small birds of the *Ploceidæ* or Weaver-bird family, whose bills have a waxy appearance; **-billed** *a.*, having a bill resembling sealing-w.; **-cloth,** cloth coated with w. as a protection from wet; **w. doll,** (*a*) a doll with head and bust (often also the limbs) of w.; (*b*) *pl.* = FUMITORY; **-end,** thread coated with cobblers' w., used by shoemakers; hence **-ended** *a.*, bound with w.-ends; **-flower,** (*a*) an imitation flower made of w.; (*b*) the genus *Hoya*; (*c*) *Clusia insignis* of British Guiana; (*d*) *Stephanotis floribunda*; **-leather,** leather 'waxed' or finished on the 'flesh' side; **-light,** a candle, taper, or night-light made of w.; **-maker,** a worker-bee that makes w.; **-myrtle** = *w.-berry* (*a*); **-plant,** any one of various plants either yielding a vegetable w. or having a waxy appearance; esp. *Myrica cerifera*, any species of *Hoya*, and *Monotropa uniflora*; **w. tablet,** a board coated with w., to be written on with a stylus; **w. taper,** a taper made of w.; **-tree,** any of various trees yielding vegetable w.; esp. *Myrica cerifera*, of N. America, the privet, *Ligustrum lucidum*, of China, the genus *Vismia* of S. America, the varnish-tree of S. America, *Elæagia utilis*, the Japanese shrub *Rhus succedanea.*

Wax (wæks), *sb.*[2] *colloq.* or *slang.* 1854. [Origin obsc.] Angry feeling; a fit of anger; chiefly *to be in a w.*

I used to rush out in a frightful state of w., and show a leg 1854.

Wax (wæks), *v.*[1] Now chiefly *literary* or *arch.* Pa. t. and pa. pple. **waxed** (wækst); pa. pple. also **waxen.** [Com. Teut. str. vb.; OE. *weaxan* (*weox, weaxen*) :—OTeut. **wahs-* :—pre-Teut. **woks-*, abl. var. of Indo-Eur. **aweks-*, **auks-*, **uks-*, extended f. **aweg-*, **aug-*, **ug-* (L. *augere* to increase, Skr. *ōjas* strength, Lith. *augu* I grow, OTeut. **auk-* in OE. *ēacian* EKE *v.*).] **I.** To grow, increase. (Opp. to *wane.*) **1.** *intr.* To increase gradually in size and strength; to grow, develop. *arch.* and *dial.* **2.** To advance *in* power, importance, prosperity, etc. OE. **3.** Of inanimate things: To increase in size, quantity, volume, intensity, etc. OE. **4.** Of the moon: To undergo the periodical increase in the extent of its visible illuminated portion, characteristic of the first half of the lunation OE. **5.** Of a quality, state of things, activity, etc.: To become gradually greater or more striking; to increase in potency or intensity OE.

1. There wex..euery holsum spice CHAUCER. Thy bairn waxes fast, she 's taller ivery time I see her 1889. 2. *Cor.* II. ii. 103. A democratic party..was waxing in size and strength 1873. 3. The river, which I observed to be somewhat waxen SCOTT. Glaciers..w. and wane in some mysterious manner 1884. 4. States thrive or wither, as moons w. and wane COWPER.

II. With complement: To change by growth or increase; to turn, become, grow ME.

When her sonne to mans estate did wex SPENSER. What? Art thou like the Adder waxen deafe? SHAKS. It was now waxing towards morning 1831. Mr. Chuckster waxed wroth at this answer DICKENS. As time waxed on 1870.

Wax (wæks), *v.*[2] late ME. [f. WAX *sb.*[1]] **1.** *trans.* To cover with a layer of wax; to dress with wax; to polish or stiffen with a dressing of wax. †**2.** To stop up (an aperture) with or as with wax -1709. **3.** *Leather-manuf.* To dress (a skin) with a mixture of lamp-black, oil, etc. 1885.

1. As a Shoemaker waxeth his thread 1615. The elegant ignoramus whose sole accomplishments consist in parting his hair, waxing his moustaches, and smoking a meerschaum 1863. Hence **Waxed** (wækst) *ppl. a.* coated with a layer of wax; polished or stiffened with wax; dressed or saturated with wax, e.g. for water-proofing; of a skin, dressed on the flesh side with a mixture of lamp-black and oil.

Wax candle. OE. A candle made of wax.

Wa·x-cha:ndler. late ME. One whose trade is to make or sell wax candles.

Waxen (wæ·ks'n), *a.* [OE. *wexen*, superseded by a new formation f. WAX *sb.*[1] + -EN [4].] **1.** Made of wax. **2.** *transf.* and *fig.* As if made of wax (with ref. to its softness, impressibility or fusibility, or to the smooth and lustrous surface of things modelled in wax) 1591. **3.** Covered or coated with wax, loaded with wax 1590.

1. *W. image*, spec. an effigy in wax representing a person whom it was desired to injure by witchcraft; The W.-Image being found and broken,..the King did..recover 1685. 2. For men haue marble, women w. mindes SHAKS. His rosy neck, and w. arms 1743. W. paleness 1853.

Comb.: **w.-chatterer,** the Bohemian waxwing, *Ampelis garrulus.*

†**Wa·xen,** *v.* 1540. = WAX *v.*[1] -1647. (See N.E.D.)

Wa·x-shot. *Obs.* exc. *Hist.* 1550. [f. WAX *sb.*[1] + SHOT *sb.*[1]] A customary payment made for the maintenance of lights in churches.

Waxwing (wæ·ks,wiŋ). 1817. A passerine bird of the genus *Ampelis* (*Bombycilla*), esp. *A. garrulus*, the Bohemian w.

Waxwork (wæ·ks,wɔɹk). 1697. **1.** Work executed in wax; *esp.* modelling in wax; an object modelled in wax; usu. applied to life-size effigies of persons, with head, hands, and bust of wax, coloured and clothed to look like life. **2.** An exhibition of wax figures representing celebrated or notorious characters; also, the place of exhibition. Now *pl.* 1796. **3.** *U.S.* The climbing bitter-sweet, *Celastrus scandens*; so called from the waxy scarlet aril of the fruit 1856.

1. I've seen wax-work quite like life DICKENS.

attrib. and *Comb.*, as *w.-figure, -show*, etc. So **Wa·x-wo:rker,** a worker in wax; *spec.* a bee that makes wax. **Wa·x-wo:rking** *a.* making wax.

Waxy (wæ·ksi), *a.*[1] 1596. [f. WAX *sb.*[1] + -Y [1].] **1.** Having the nature or distinctive properties of wax; *fig.* of a person, etc., soft, plastic, impressionable like wax. **2.** Resembling wax in colour or consistence; (of a quality) like that of wax 1835. **b.** *Med.* Affected with amyloid degeneration 1845. Hence **Wa·xi-ly** *adv.*, **-ness.**

Waxy (wæ·ksi), *a.*[2] *colloq.* or *slang.* 1853. [f. WAX *sb.*[2] + -Y [1].] Angry, 'in a wax'.

Way (wēⁱ), *sb.* [Com. Teut.; OE. *weg* :— OTeut. **wegoz*, f. **weg-* to move, journey, carry (see WEIGH *v.*) :— Indo-Eur. **wegh-* (*wogh-*) as in L. *vehere* to carry, Gr. ὄχος vehicle.] **I.** Road, path. **1.** A track prepared or available for travelling along; a road, street, lane, or path. **b.** A road considered with ref. to the condition of its surface, etc. OE. **c.** A place of passage, e.g. an opening made through a crowd, a door or gate, etc. ME. **d.** *Railways.* See PERMANENT *w.*, SIX-FOOT *w.*, etc. **2.** *pl.* Parallel wooden planks or balks for heavy loads, ships, etc. to slide upon 1639. **b.** *Mech.* Parallel sills forming a track for the slides of the uprights of a planing machine, the carriage of a lathe, or the like 1869.

1. Broad on the left before him lay, For many a mile, the Roman w. SCOTT. *Beside, over, across the w., the other side of the w.*, etc.; He called out to a gentleman on the opposite side of the w. DICKENS. For the most part, no English creature ever does see farther than over the w. RUSKIN. *transf.* The Via lactea, or 'milky w.', which the peasantry of the North frequently designate 'the w.' 1844. *fig.* But in the beaten w. of friendship, What make you at Elsonower? SHAKS. b. The weather was cold, the ways dirty and dangerous 1663. d. *Line of w.*, a track formed by a pair of rails.

II. Course of travel or movement. 1. A line or course of travel or progression by which a place may be reached, or along which a person or thing may pass OE. 2. Course or line of actual movement. late ME. 3. *gen.* Opportunity for passage or advance; absence of obstruction; hence *fig.* freedom of action, scope, opportunity. late ME. b. In legal documents sometimes = RIGHT OF W. 1766. 4. Travel or motion along a particular route or in a particular direction OE. b. *Naut.* Progress (of a ship or boat) through the water; rate of progress, velocity 1663. 5. Distance travelled or to be travelled along a particular route OE. 6. Direction of motion, relative position, or aspect. Chiefly in advb. phr., as *this w.* (= hitherwards), *my w.* (= towards me, into my neighbourhood), *that w.*, *which w.*, *all ways*, etc. ME.

1. Mr. Bourne..asked if I were going his w. 1856. *fig.* That go the Primrose w. to th' euerlasting Bonfire SHAKS. *Prov.* There be mo waies to the wood than one HEYWOOD. The Longest w. about is the nearest W. Home 1661. Phrases. *To hold, keep* (a certain) *w.*, to follow it without deviation. *To know one's w. about*, to know how to get from place to place in a neighbourhood; *fig.* to know how to act in any emergency, to possess wide experience of the ways of the world, esp. with derogatory implication. †*There lies your w.*, please to go away. *To go the wrong w.*, of food or drink, to go into the windpipe instead of the gullet when being swallowed. *W. of the Cross* (= eccl. L. *Via Crucis*), a series of (fourteen) images or pictures representing the 'Stations of the Cross' (STATION *sb.* IV. 3), ranged round the interior of a church, or on the road to or in the vicinity of a church or shrine, esp. as used as an object of devotion; hence, a series of devotions used in connexion with the Stations. 2. The weie of an egle in heuene,.. the weie of a ship in the myd se WYCLIF *Prov.* xxx. 19. The series of parallel paths hewn out by the rocker on a mezzotint is technically termed a *w.* 1891. 3. Phr. *To give w., make w.*; also *Way!* (= 'make w.') 4. *To take* (a place, etc.) *in one's w.*, to visit in the course of one's journey; We may take Chatsworth in our w. 1777. *To go, wend one's w.*, (now *arch.*) almost = to go away; Then she railed on me, and I went my w. BUNYAN. *Go, come your* (*thy*) *w.* (see also IV), now *dial.*; Go your w. for a simpleton, and say no more about the matter 1772. *To go the w. of all the earth* (Josh. xxiii. 14, 1 Kings ii. 2), to die; so (by confusion with other Bible passages) *the w. of all flesh* (sometimes used to mean the experience common to all men in their passage through life), *of all living*; I heard that Don Rodrigo had gone the w. of all flesh 1809. *To force, push, squeeze*, etc., *one's w.*, to effect a forward movement by the action denoted by the verb; to accompany one's advance by the specified action; The plowman homeward plods his weary w. GRAY. *To hold, keep one's w.*, to travel without interruption; *fig.* to 'keep going'. b. *transf.* A..short dark man came into the room with so much w. upon him, that he was within a foot of Clennam before he could stop DICKENS. 5. Long w. he traveiled before he heard of ought SPENSER. The village..is not a great w. off 1882. (*By*) *a long w.*, fig., qualifying a comparative, = 'far' (better, etc.). †*A great w.*, to a great extent; I..Thinke him a great w. foole SHAKS. *All the way from —— to ——* (U.S.), expressing the lower and upper limits of value, number, etc. 6. *fig. Lear* III. iv. 21. *The other w. about, round*, conversely, vice versa. *One w. or* (*the*) *other, either w.*

III. Course of life or action, means, manner. 1. A path or course of life; the activities and fortunes of a person; a prescribed course of life or conduct OE. b. *pl.* Habits of life, esp. with regard to moral conduct OE. c. *The w.* or *ways of God*, the course of God's providence OE. 2. A course of action ME. †b. (One's) best or most advisable course. SHAKS. 3. A course of action; a device, expedient method, or means by which some end may be attained. Sometimes coupled with MEAN *sb.*; see WAYS AND MEANS. ME. 4. Manner in which something is done or takes place; method of performing an action or operation OE. b. advb. phrases without prep. (now *rare*) ME. 5. In advb. phrases like (*in*) *all ways*, (*in*) *any w.*, etc., the sense of 'manner' passes into that of: An aspect, feature, or respect; a point or particular of comparison 1598. 6. A condition regarded as hopeful or the contrary (usu. with qualifying adj.) 1467. 7. Kind, sort, description. Now only in phr. *in the w. of*, of the nature of, belonging to the class of; so *in the — w.* 1647. 8. Kind of occupation, work, or business 1690. 9. *In a great, small w.*, (living) on a large or small scale of income and expenditure 1750. 10. The customary or usual manner of acting or behaving 1613. b. *pl.* Customary modes of behaviour; usages 1742. 11. A habitual or characteristic manner of action, expression, or the like 1709.

1. They kept the noiseless tenor of their w. GRAY. *The W.*, in the Acts of the Apostles, the Christian religion. 2. He told me that I went the wrong w. to work SMOLLETT. *To have* (*get*, etc.) *one's* (*own*) *w.*, to be allowed to follow or to enforce on others the course of action on which one is resolved; hence *to love, be fond of one's own w.* 3. Mr. Huxley..can see but one w. of arriving at truth; which he calls experience 1892. Prov. *Where there's a will there's a w.* 4. After dinner we rode in like way two miles MORYSON. There are several Ways of making Sauce for a Pig 1747. *The humid, moist*, or *wet w., the dry w.*, (F. *voie humide, voie sèche*), Chem. and Assaying, processes distinguished by the presence or absence of liquid. *In his* (*her*, etc.) *w.*, appended to expressions of praise, implying that the praise is to be understood in a limited sense appropriate to the object; so *in a w. W. of thinking*, a set of opinions or principal characteristic of a party or sect. *W. of living, life*, habits with regard to food, habitation, etc. *To have everything one's own w., to have it all one's own w.*, to have one's wishes carried out; to meet with no resistance or opposition. *No two ways about it*, there can be no doubt of the fact. *It is always the w. with* (*him*), (he) always acts so. b. Without..his being any manner of ways connected in it 1705. I..hope she will..allow them to be happy their own way JOHNSON. 5. A teetotaler, however admirable in other ways, is not the fit person to edit Burns 1893. 6. *In the family w.*: see FAMILY (Phr.). *To be in a w.*, to be in a state of mental distress or anxiety. 7. I should want for nothing in the bread and water w.! 1809. 8. It was a new house, but did a tremendous business in the fig and sponge w. THACKERAY. 9. Contractors and builders in a large w. of business 1864. 10. Even so Sir, 'tis the w. of the World CONGREVE. 11. *It is* (*only*) *his w.*, often said of some perverse or annoying habit of behaviour which the friends of the person guilty of it are accustomed to regard with toleration; And all that's madly wild, or oddly gay, We call it only pretty Fanny's w. PARNELL. (Parnell's phr. is often used allus.) *To have a w. with one*, to have a persuasive manner.

IV. Ways (orig. genitive) used as sing. OE.

To go, come one's ways (now *dial.*); Go thy ways for a true Pattern of the Vanity, Impertinence,..and Ostentation of thy Country FARQUHAR. *A good, great, little, long ways* (now only *dial.* and *U.S.*).

Phrases. **Have w.** †a. To be allowed liberty of action SHAKS. b. Of feelings, etc.: To find vent. **Make w.** a. To open a passage (*for*, †*to*), remove obstacles to progress. b. To move from one's place so as to allow a person to pass. c. To leave a place vacant *for* a successor or substitute. d. To make progress on a journey or voyage. **Make one's (its) w.** a. To travel or proceed in an intended direction or to a certain place. *To make the best of one's w.*, to go as quickly as one can. b. To make progress in one's career; to advance in wealth, station, etc., by one's own efforts. c. Of a thing: to travel, make progress; of an opinion, etc., to gain acceptance. **Pay one's (its) w.** To succeed in paying one's expenses as they arise, without incurring debts. Of a business undertaking: To be self-supporting. **See one's w.** To have a view of the portion of the road or route immediately before one, so as to be able to avoid wandering or stumbling; hence *fig.*, now often (chiefly with neg.) to feel justified in deciding *to do* something. **Take one's w.** To set out on a journey; to journey, travel.

By the w. a. Along or near the road by which one travels. b. In the course of one's walk or journey; *fig.* incidentally, in passing, as a side-topic. c. Used parenthetically to apologize for introducing a new topic, a casual remark, or the like. d. As a by-work, as a subordinate piece of work. †e. Indirectly. SHAKS. **By w. of —.** †a. By means of, through the medium of. b. As an instance or a mode of; in the capacity or with the function of. c. Followed by gerund, used *predic.* with the sense: In the habit of (doing something); also, usu., making a profession of, having a reputation for (being or doing so-and-so). *colloq.* d. = VIA *prep.* **In the** (etc.) **w.** (see also III senses 7–9). a. (Usu. *in one's w.*) On or along the road by which one travels; so as to be met, encountered, or observed. b. *fig.* in phr. *to come, fall, lie*, etc., *in* (one's) *w.*, to be met with in one's experience, to come within (one's) range of possible observation, attainment, etc. So *to lay, put, throw in* (a person's) *w.* c. In such a position or of such a nature as to obstruct, impede, or be an annoyance. d. Within reach or call, at hand; in a place where things are going on or where one can be found readily. Now *rare*. e. *Once in a w.*, on a single (rare or exceptional) occasion; as a solitary or rare instance. Also *for once in a w.* **In the way of —.** (See also III. 7.) †a. = *By w. of* b. b. By means of. Now *rare*. c. In the course or routine of. †d. When one is concerned with. SHAKS. e. *To be in the w. of*, to be likely to do or obtain (something), to have a good chance of (doing or attaining something). So *to put* (a person) *in the w. of*. Also with *to* and inf. †f. *In* (*the*) *w. of marriage, in w. to marriage*, with a view to matrimony. **On the** or **one's w.** On, or in the course of, a journey. *To be well on one's w.*, to have made some progress; also *fig.* **Out of the w.** (See also OUT-OF-THE-W.) a. Away from the road by which one is travelling; off the track or proper route. b. With *of* or possessive. Away from the path in which a person or thing is moving; in a position where one does not meet or impede another; out of reach of, not in danger from. *Out of harm's w.*: see HARM *sb.* 1. c. *To go out of one's w. to* (do something), to do something which the circumstances do not call for or invite. d. *To put* (a person) *out of his w.*: to disturb, inconvenience, trouble; often *refl.* to submit to inconvenience or bother for the sake of others. e. Away from the resort or society of other persons; in a position remote or inconvenient to get at. f. Away from an obstructive position. g. *To put out of the w.*, to make away with, kill. *Out of the w.*, no longer alive. h. *predic.* as adj.: Beside the mark, out of place; odd, bizarre. **Under w.** *Naut.* [ad. Du. *onderweg*.] Having begun to move through the water. Often spelt *under weigh*: see WEIGH *sb.*[2] Also *transf.* and *fig.*, beginning to advance or make progress.

Comb.: **w.-board**, *Mining* and *Geol.*, any thin layer or bed of rock, clay, etc. separating thicker strata; **-leave**, permission to make and use a way for conveying coal from the pit-head across a person's land; the rent paid for such permission; the way or road constructed for the purpose; permission to carry telephone wires over buildings, drains or water-pipes across private land, etc.; also, the rent or charge for such permission; **-man**, a workman employed on the permanent w. of a railway, a plate-layer; **-mark**, any object which serves as a guide to the traveller; **w. passenger**, *U.S.*, a passenger picked up or set down at a stage or station intermediate between the main stopping-places; **-station**, *U.S.*, an intermediate station on a railway route, a wayside station; **-wise** *a. dial.* and *U.S.*, of a horse, familiar with the roads he is required to travel; also *fig.* of persons; **-wort**, a name for the pimpernel. Hence **Way·less** *a.* having no way or road; trackless, pathless; **-ness**.

Way (wēⁱ), *adv.* Now *Sc.*, *north.*, and *U.S.* ME. [Aphetic f. AWAY.] 1. = AWAY *adv.* 2. *esp.* At or to a (great) distance, far 1849. Hence **W.-off** *a.* distant. **W.-back** *U.S. slang*, in phr. *from w.-back*, from a remote or rural district; hence attrib. and quasi-adj.

Way (wēⁱ), *int.* 1836. [Cf. WO *int.*] A call to a horse to stop.

-way (weⁱ), as terminal element of advs., is identical with WAY *sb.* Cf. -WAYS.

1. Phrases consisting of the sb. qualified by an adj. are often used advb., and some of the combinations thus used have come to be apprehended as single words, and to be so pronounced and written; e.g. *anyway, someway; broadway, crossway, straightway.* 2. The few advs. f. sb. + *-way* are genuine compounds; *edgeway, endway, sideway*, etc., are not older than the 16th c. These words may also be used as adjs.

Way·-bill. 1791. 1. A list of passengers booked for seats in a stage-coach or other public vehicle for places on the road. Also, a detailed statement of goods entrusted to a public carrier for delivery. 2. A list of places to be visited on a journey. 3. *U.S.* A label attached to an article in transport to indicate its destination, etc. 1887. 4. A kind of pass by producing which a man 'on the road' can obtain relief at certain stages of his journey. So *w. system*. 1893. Hence **Way·-bill** *v. U.S. trans.* to enter (goods) on a w.

Waybread, waybred (wēⁱ·bred). [Com. WGer.: OE. *wegbrǣde, wegbrǣde*; f. WAY *sb.* + OTeut. *braidjōn- broad object, f. *braid- BROAD *a.*] = PLANTAIN[1] 1. Also *water w.* = water plantain: see PLANTAIN[1] 2.

Wayfare (wēⁱ·feəɹ), *sb. arch.* late ME. [f. WAY *sb.* + FARE *sb.*[1], after WAYFARING *a.*] Wayfaring, travelling.

Wayfare (wēⁱ·feəɹ), *v.* Now *rare* and *arch.* 1547. [Back-formation from WAYFARING *sb.*] *intr.* To journey or travel, esp. on foot.

Wayfarer (wēⁱ·fēᵊ:rəɹ). 1440. [f. WAY *sb.* + *farer* (f. FARE *v.*[1]).] A traveller by road, esp. one who journeys on foot. b. *Wayfarer's-tree*, the hobble-bush. *U.S.* 1858.

Wayfaring (wēⁱ·fēᵊ:riŋ), *vbl. sb. arch.* 1536. [f. WAY *sb.* + *faring* vbl. sb. f. FARE *v.*[1], after next.] Journeying, travelling; an instance of this.

fig. This earthly waifaring 1561. That I may dare, in w., To stammer where old Chaucer used to sing KEATS.

Wayfaring (wēⁱ·fēᵊ:riŋ), *ppl. a. arch.* [OE. *wegfarende*, f. *weg* WAY *sb.* + pres. pple. of *faran* FARE *v.*[1]] Travelling or journeying by road. Usu. *w. man*, a traveller by road. *Isa.* xxxv. 8.

Way·fa:ring-tree:. 1597. [Short for *wayfaring man's tree*; cf. *traveller's joy*.] **1.** The tall shrub *Viburnum Lantana*, growing wild in hedges and underwood. **2.** *U.S.* The hobble-bush 1814.

Waygoose. Now *dial.* or *Obs.* 1683. [Etym. obsc.: see N.E.D.] = WAYZGOOSE.

Waylay (wēⁱlēⁱ·), *v.* Pa. t. and pa. pple. **waylaid** (wēⁱlēⁱ·d). 1513. [f. WAY *sb.* + LAY *v.*[1], after MLG., MDu. *wegelāgen*, f. *wegelage* :—OS., OHG. **wega lâga* besetting of ways.] **1.** *trans.* To lie in wait for with evil or hostile intent; to seize or attack in the way. **b.** To intercept and seize (a thing in transit) 1599. **2.** *transf.* To wait for and accost (a person) in the way; to stop (a person) in order to converse with him 1612. †**3.** To impede or intercept; to block the path or progress of –1688. †**4.** To beset or blockade (a road, position, etc.) with an armed force or the like –1828.

1. *fig.* The..Miseries, which way-lay our Passage through the World JOHNSON. **2.** I have held it the first principle of manners not to w. people RUSKIN.

†**Wayment,** *v.* late ME. [a. OF. *waimenter, guaimenter*, f. *wai, guai* alas, prob. after *lamenter* to lament.] *intr.* To lament, wail; to sorrow bitterly –1861.

-ways, terminal element of advs., was orig. a use of the genitive of WAY *sb.*

1. Many phrases consisting of the genitive of *way* qualified by an adj. were formerly used advb., and later apprehended as one word; see ALWAYS, OTHERWAYS, etc. On the analogy of these were subsequently formed *anyways, crossways, longways, straightways*, etc. **2.** In advs. f. sb. + *-ways*, as *endways, lengthways, sideways*, the general sense is 'in a specified direction'. **3.** Most advs. in *-ways* have synonyms in -WAY, and often also in -WISE, which is often preferred to *-ways* or *-way* because it is supposed to be the more 'correct' form. **4.** The combs. of *-ways*, except SIDEWAYS, are hardly ever used as adjs.

Ways and means. late ME. Formerly also †**means and ways.** **1.** The methods and resources which are at a person's disposal for effecting some object. **2.** *spec.* In *Legislation*: Methods of procuring funds or supplies for the current expenditure of the state 1644. **b.** Pecuniary resources in general 1738.

2. *Committee of Ways and Means*, (*a*) a committee of the whole House of Commons, which sits to consider the budget (see BUDGET 4); (*b*) *U.S.* a standing committee of the House of Representatives, to which are referred bills dealing with revenue, tariff, etc.

Way·side. late ME. The side of a road or path; the land bordering either side of the way. **b.** *attrib.* passing into *adj.* Of or pertaining to the w.; situated on, growing by, etc., the w. 1817.

Wayward (wēⁱ·wǫ̈ɹd), *a.* Not now in colloq. use. late ME. [Aphetic f. AWAYWARD.] **1.** Disposed to go counter to the wishes or advice of others or to what is reasonable; wrong-headed, intractable, self-willed, perverse. **2.** Capriciously wilful; conforming to no fixed rule or principle of conduct; erratic 1533.

1. A! thou generacioun vnbyleeful and weiward WYCLIF *Matt.* xvii. 16. Pericles Is now againe thwarting thy w. seas SHAKS. Mutt'ring his w. fancies GRAY. Hence **Way·ward·ly** *adv.*, **-ness.**

Waywarden (wēⁱ·wǭ:ɹd'n). 1776. [f. WAY *sb.* + WARDEN[1].] A person (later, one of a board) elected to supervise the highways of a parish or district.

Way-wiser (wēⁱ·wəi:zəɹ). Now *Hist.* 1651. [Formed after G. *wegweiser*, f. *weg* WAY *sb.* + *weiser*, agent-n. f. *weisen* to show.] An instrument for measuring and indicating a distance travelled by road.

Waywode (wēⁱ·wōud). Now *Hist.* 1661. [var. of VAIVODE, repr. an early Magyar form of a common Slavonic title.] = VOIVODE. Hence **Way·wodeship,** the province or district ruled by a w.

Way·-worn, *a.* 1777. Worn or wearied by travel.

Wayzgoose (wēⁱ·zgūs). 1731. [Alteration of WAYGOOSE.] orig. An entertainment given by a master-printer to his workmen in August, marking the beginning of the season of working by candle-light. Later, an annual festivity held in summer by the employees of a printing establishment, consisting of a dinner and (usu.) an excursion into the country.

‖**Wazir** (wăzīᵊ·ɹ). 1715. [Arab. *wazīr*.] = VIZIER I.

We (wī, wi), *pron.* [Com. Teut.; OE. *wĕ̄* :—ablaut-var. (**wĕz* or **wēz*) of OTeut. **wīz* (:—pre-Teut. **weis*, extension of Indo-Eur. **wei*, as in Skr. *vāyam*), or pre-Teut. **wĕ*.] **1.** The pronoun of the first person plural nominative, denoting the speaker and one or more other persons whom he associates with himself as the subject of the sentence. **b.** Used confidentially or playfully to mean the person addressed, with whose interests the speaker thus identifies himself. **c.** Used indefinitely in general statements in which the speaker or writer includes those whom he addresses, his contemporaries, or the like OE. **2.** Used by a single person to denote himself: **a.** by a sovereign or ruler OE. **b.** by a speaker or writer (e.g. in editorial or unsigned articles in newspapers or other periodicals), in order to secure an impersonal style and tone OE. **c.** Hence joc. as quasi-*sb.*: The editor of a periodical; the periodical itself 1853. **3.** Used for the accusative *us* (now *local*) 1500.

1. Vppon the texte whee sware, both I and my wiffe 1460. Put we our quarrell to the will of heauen SHAKS. When shall we three meet againe? SHAKS. We, Your Majesty's most dutiful and loyal subjects, the Commons of the United Kingdom..in Parliament assembled 1918. **b.** Well, Jane, and how are we this morning? 1884. **c.** There is nothing which we receive with so much Reluctance as Advice ADDISON. What do we, as a nation, care about books? RUSKIN. **2. b.** There is a mysterious authority in the plural *we*, which no single name..can acquire 1807. **3.** You must ride On horseback after we COWPER.

Weak (wīk), *a.* ME. [a. ON. *veikr*, corresp. to OE. *wāc* (ME. *wōk*) :—OTeut. **waikwo-*, f. **waikw-* : **wīkw-* to give way. The vocalism of the present form is difficult.] **1.** Wanting in moral strength for endurance or resistance; lacking fortitude or courage, strength of purpose or will. late ME. **b.** Used to render Gr. ἀσθενής, ἀσθενῶν, applied by St. Paul (esp. in Rom. xiv and 1 Cor. viii) to believers whose scruples, though unsound, should be treated with tenderness, lest they should be led into acts condemned by their conscience. Hence allus. in *weaker brethren*. 1526. **c.** Of features, expression, tears, etc.: Indicating weakness; of persons, etc., deficient in power to control emotion; unduly swayed by grief, compassion, or affection 1768. **2.** Wanting in strength and skill as a combatant; deficient in numbers, resources, etc.; relatively deficient in fighting power as shown by the result of the contest ME. **b.** Wanting in or exhibiting want of skill in a game, sport, contest, etc. 1827. **3.** Deficient in bodily or muscular strength; esp. of a child or woman, inferior in respect of physical strength ME. **4.** Deficient in bodily vigour through age, sickness, privation, etc.; wanting in strength of the vital functions of the body ME. **5.** Constitutionally feeble; not vigorous or robust in health 1523. **6.** Of bodily organs or their functions: Deficient in functional strength 1480. **7.** Of the mind or mental faculties: Deficient in power. late ME. **b.** Lacking force of intellect or strength of mind; easily deceived; feeble (*in* one's intellect, the head, etc.). late ME. **8.** Of a person, his qualities, productions, etc.: Inefficient, ill-qualified. late ME. **9.** Wanting in power or authority over others. late ME. **b.** Of power, strength, authority, etc. late ME. **10. a.** *Card-playing.* Of a hand, suit, etc.: Not of a commanding nature or value. Of a player: Ill-provided with commanding cards (*in* a specified suit). 1680. **b.** Of money or stock: Insufficient to meet a demand or to carry on operations. Similarly of a holder of stock. 1875. **11.** Not strong or energetic in action; lacking in force or power ME. **12.** Wanting in effectiveness; not convincing 1538. †**13.** Of a thing: Of little account or worth –1822. **14.** Having less than the full or proper amount of a specific ingredient. Of an infusion: Over diluted. 1597. **15.** Wanting in material strength, unsound, insecure. late ME. **16.** Wanting in solidity or firmness; of a texture: easily broken, fragile 1581. **17.** Not strongly marked; faint 1585. **18.** *Comm.* Of market prices, commodities, etc.: Having a downward tendency; not firm 1856. **19.** *Phonetics* and *Prosody*. Of a sound or syllable: Pronounced with less force than the adjacent sound or sounds; unstressed. Of stress: Having relatively little force. Of the cæsura: Falling after a short syllable. 1637. **20.** *Philol.* (Opp. to STRONG *a.* 22). **a.** Of Germanic nouns and adjs.: Belonging to any of the declensions in which the stem in Primitive Germanic ended in *-n* 1841. **b.** Of Germanic verbs: Forming the preterite by means of a suffix 1841. **c.** In Greek grammar, applied to the sigmatic or 'first' aorist 1875. **d.** In Sanskrit grammar, the designation of the reduced stems of nouns, and of the cases in which the reduced stem occurs 1863. **e.** In Hebrew and Syriac grammar, applied to certain consonants and to verbs which have any of these in the root 1874. **f.** Applied to the ablaut-grade which results from absence of stress 1888.

1. The spirite ys willynge but the flesshe is weeke TINDALE *Matt.* xxvi. 41. Disraeli, in a w. moment, offered him office again 1878. **c.** You must have a w. spot in your heart for him 1886. **2. b.** The Surrey bowling was w. 1862. Seek for the w. spot in the batsman's defence 1891. **3.** *The weaker vessel*, in 1 Pet. iii. 7 said of the wife as compared with the husband; hence occas. *joc.* = wife. **5.** Stake and bind up the weakest Plants 1696. Laws to prevent the education of w. children 1772. **6.** My weake stomacke SHAKS. A woman of w. nerves 1825. **7. b.** By these means w. men are often deceived by others 1736. **8.** My w. oratorie SHAKS. The weakest Part of a very w. Book 1713. W. to perform, though mighty to pretend COWPER. **11.** My loue is strengthned, though more weake in seeming SHAKS. A w. Pulse 1707. If these terms are w., or ambiguous 1771. W., sad voices CRABBE. **12.** My w. endeavours to amuse you 1741. Justin..is..a w. authority for any disputed historical fact 1863. **14.** A little brandy and water, not too w. 1891. **15.** The strength of the chain is in the weakest link 1885. *W. side* (of a fortified place), a side unsound in its defences; also *fig.*; The Love of Mutton was his W. side 1692. *W. point*, the point or feature where a thing is defective or unsound; a (moral or intellectual) failing or weakness. **19.** *W. ending*, the occurrence of an unstressed or proclitic monosyllable in the normally stressed place at the end of an iambic line.

Comb.: **w.-headed** *a.*, lacking strength of mind or purpose; **-hearted** *a.*, faint-hearted, tender-hearted; **-sighted** *a.*, having w. sight. Hence **Wea·kish** *a.* somewhat w.

Weaken (wī·k'n), *v.* 1530. [f. prec. + -EN[5].] **I.** *trans.* To make weak or weaker. **1.** To lessen the physical strength or vigour of; to lessen the functional vigour of 1568. **2.** To enfeeble or decrease the vigour of (the mind, etc.) Now *rare*. 1536. **3.** To lessen (authority, credit, etc.) 1530. **4.** To reduce the strength of (a body of men) in numbers or fighting power; to render (a position) less secure 1560. **5.** To render weaker in resources, authority, power, or the like 1568. **6.** To render less efficacious 1606. **7.** To render (a material thing) less strong 1827. **8.** To reduce the intensity of (a colour, sound, fire) 1683. **b.** *Phonetics.* To reduce in force or intensity of utterance 1863. **9.** *Card-games.* To lessen the strength of (one's hand, etc.) 1742. **10.** To render (market prices, a market) less firm 1875.

6. *Tr. & Cr.* I. iii. 195. Another fragment of the true cross..weakened in virtue, doubtless, by sojourning with infidels SCOTT. **7.** This weakened the central tower, which fell with a crash 1914.

II. *intr.* To grow or become weak or weaker 1541. **b.** (orig. *U.S.*) To take a less firm attitude; to give way 1876.

Weakfish (wī·kfiʃ). *U.S.* 1838. [ad. Du. †*weekvisch*, f. *week* soft + *visch* fish.] A marine sciænoid food-fish of the genus *Cynoscion*, esp. *C. regalis*, the sea-trout of the Atlantic.

Weak-kneed (stress var.), *a.* 1870. Having weak knees; chiefly *fig.* wanting in resolution or determination.

Weakling (wī·kliŋ). 1557. [f. WEAK *a.* + -LING[1].] **1.** A person or animal that lacks physical strength or is weak in health or constitution 1576. **2.** One who is weak in character or intellect 1577. **3.** *appos.* or as *adj.* Weak, feeble 1557.

Weakly (wī·kli), *a.* 1577. [f. WEAK *a.* + -LY [1].] **1.** Weak in constitution, not strong or robust, delicate. **2.** Characterized by moral weakness 1890. Hence **Wea·kliness,** w. quality.

Weakly (wī·kli), *adv.* late ME. [-LY [2].] **1.** With little force or strength. **2.** With slight defensive strength 1582. **3.** Sparsely, meagrely, slightly. Now *rare.* 1605. **4.** With weakness of mind or character 1610. **5.** Inefficiently 1663. **6.** With little force of argument 1662.

Weak-minded, *a.* 1782. **1.** Having a weak mind; lacking strength of purpose. Of actions, etc.: Indicating weakness of mind. **2.** Mentally deficient; half-witted 1883.

1. It is my misfortune to be w. I can't say 'no' to people. 1863. Hence **Wea·kmi·ndedness.**

Weakness (wī·knės). ME. [f. WEAK *a.* + -NESS.] **1.** The quality or condition of being weak. **2. a.** A weak point, a circumstance of disadvantage 1597. **b.** An infirmity of character, a failing 1645. †**c.** A weakened bodily condition; an attack of faintness -1756. **3.** An unreasonable or self-indulgent liking or inclination *for* (a person or thing) 1712. **b.** quasi-*concr.* Something for which one has an unreasonable liking 1822.

2. a. The brakes of the Britannia cars have always been their w. 1914. c. *Ham.* II. ii. 148. 3. b. Fashion and whiskers have been my weaknesses, and I don't care who knows it DICKENS.

Weal (wīl), *sb.*[1] [OE. *wela*:—OTeut. **welon-*, f. root **wel-*; see WELL *adv.*] †**1.** Wealth, riches, possessions -1838. **2.** Welfare, well-being; happiness, prosperity (often contrasted with *woe*) OE. **3.** *contextually.* The welfare of a country or community; the general good. Now *arch.* 1444.

2. For the w. of Michael's soul SCOTT. In w. and woe I have ever had the true sympathy of all my people Q. VICTORIA. Hence †**Weal-public** [after F. *le bien public*, L. *bonum publicum*], the general good of the community; public welfare or interest; also, a state, community, commonwealth.

Weal (wīl), *sb.*[2] 1821. [var. of WALE *sb.*[1]] The mark or ridge raised on the flesh by the blow of a rod, lash, etc.

Weal (wīl), *v.* 1722. [var. of WALE *v.*[2]] = WALE *v.*[2] 1.

Weald (wīld). Also †**wild.** [OE. (WS.) *weald* forest, ME. *wēld(e*, *weeld*; the mod. spelling, due to Lambarde, is a re-adoption of the OE. form.] **1.** The tract of country, formerly wooded, including the portions of Sussex, Kent, and Surrey which lie between the North and South Downs. **2.** A wooded district or an open country; a wold (now only *poet.*) 1544.

1. A native of the Wild of Kent, which is none of the most polite parts of the world 1801.

attrib. and *Comb.*: **W. clay,** the upper stratum of the Wealden formation immediately above the 'Hastings sand'; **W. saurian** = HYLÆOSAURUS.

Wealden (wī·ldən), *a.* and *sb.* 1828. [f. WEALD + -EN.[4]] **A.** *adj.* **1.** Of or pertaining to the geological formation known as the Wealden (see B). **2.** Of or pertaining to the Weald 1870.

1. *W. lizard* = HYLÆOSAURUS.

B. *sb. Geol.* A formation or series of estuarine and freshwater deposits of Lower Cretaceous age, extensively developed in the Weald 1828.

Wealth (welþ). [ME. *welþe*, f. WELL *adv.* or WEAL *sb.*[1] + -TH, on the analogy of *health.*] **1.** The condition of being happy and prosperous; well-being. *Obs.* exc. *arch.* †**b.** Chiefly *pl.* An instance or kind of prosperity; a felicity, blessing -1652. **2.** Prosperity consisting in abundance of possessions; riches, affluence ME. **b.** Abundance of possessions or of valuable products, as characteristic of a people, country, or region; the collective riches of a people or country 1666. **c.** said of a specific commodity as the chief source of a country's riches 1645. **3.** *Economics.* A collective term for those things the abundant possession of which constitutes riches, or 'wealth' in the popular sense 1821. **4.** Plenty, abundance, profusion (*of* what is specified) 1596.

1. *Merch. V.* v. 249. 2. *fig.* No time more..prolific of intellectual w. HAZLITT. b. An Inquiry into the Nature and Causes of the W. of Nations A. SMITH. Not for all the w. of India would he have given up his lamb to that young wolf TROLLOPE. 3. W..., all useful or agreeable things which possess exchangeable value MILL. 4. Dark Italian eyes, and a w. of deep black hair 1894. Hence **Wea·lthful** *a.* (now *rare*) abounding in w. ME. **Wea·lthless** *a.* without w.; having no money.

Wealthy (we·lþi), *a.* late ME. [f. prec. + -Y [1].] **1.** Having wealth or abundant means at command; opulent; prosperous, flourishing. **2.** Rich *in* some possession or advantage; plentifully furnished with something 1601. †**3.** Of great worth or value -1746.

1. The southern provinces, the most fertile and wealthiest of the kingdom SOUTHEY. *Prov.* Earely to bed and earely to rise, makes a man healthy, w., and wise 1639. Hence †**Wea·lthi·ly** *adv.* †**-ness.**

Wean (wīn, wēn), *sb. Sc.* and *n. dial.* 1692 (wie-one). [Contraction of *wee ane*; see WEE *a.* and ONE.] A young child.

Wean (wīn), *v.* [OE. *węnian* to accustom, wean:—OTeut. **wanjan*, f. **wano-* accustomed (cf. WON *v.*).] **1.** *trans.* To accustom (a child or young animal) to the loss of its mother's milk; to cause to cease to be suckled. **2.** *fig.* To detach or alienate *from* some accustomed object of pursuit or enjoyment to reconcile by degrees to the privation of something 1526.

2. A long continuance of ill health has weaned me from the world 1741. A love of secular learning from which Edmund found it hard to w. himself 1874.

Weanling (wī·nliŋ), *sb.* and *a.* 1532. [f. prec. + -LING [1].] **A.** *sb.* A young child or animal newly weaned. **B.** *adj.* Recently weaned 1637.

Weapon (we·pən, we·p'n), *sb.* [Com. Teut.; OE. *wǣpen*:—OTeut. **wǣpnom*:—pre-Teut. **wēbnom.*] An instrument of any kind used in warfare or combat to attack and overcome an enemy. **b.** *transf.* Any part of the body (esp. of a bird or beast) which is or may be used as a means of attack or defence, as a claw, horn, or the like 1635.

fig. Let not womens weapons, water drops, Staine my mans cheekes SHAKS. So voluble a w. is the tongue POPE. †*At all, any weapons*, with weapons of any kind. (To challenge, fight, etc., an adversary) *at, with, his own w.* or *weapons*, i.e. with such as he is expert in; chiefly *fig.* Hence **Wea·ponless** *a.* without a w.; unarmed; of an animal, without natural means of attack or defence OE.

Weapon (we·pən, we·p'n), *v.* Now *rare* exc. in pa. pple. [OE. *wǣpnian*, f. *wǣpen* WEAPON *sb.*] *trans.* To furnish with weapons or a weapon; to arm. Hence **Wea·poned** *ppl. a.*

Wear (wēᵊɹ), *sb.* 1464. [f. next.] **I. 1.** The action of wearing or carrying on the person (an article of clothing, an ornament, or the like); the condition or fact of being worn or carried upon the person. **2.** What one wears or should wear; the thing or things worn or proper to be worn in a particular period or on a particular occasion 1570. **3. a.** Capacity for being worn or for further advantageous use 1699. **b.** Advantage of continued wearing 1836.

1. A charming coat for restaurant w. 1912. *The worse for w.*, deteriorated through wearing. *To be in w.*: (*a*) of a garment, etc., to be actually on the person of the wearer; also, to be (still) habitually worn by a person, not to have been discarded; (*b*) of a kind or style of garment, etc., to be worn by people generally; to be in vogue or fashion. 2. Motley's the onely weare SHAKS. 3. a. The shoe that has still w. in it 1881.

II. The process or condition of being worn or gradually reduced in bulk or impaired in quality by friction, exposure, etc.; loss or diminution of substance or deterioration of quality due to these causes 1666.

W. and tear, wearing or damage due to ordinary usage; deterioration in the condition of a thing through constant use or service; (a common formula in leases and similar documents); also *transf.* and *fig.*; Unequal to the w. and tear of daily life DICKENS.

III. The anterior surface of the lower part of the mouth of a carpenter's plane 1850.

Wear (wēᵊɹ), *v.*[1] Pa. t. **wore** (wōᵊɹ); pa. pple. **worn** (wǭɹn). [Com. Teut. wk. vb.; OE. *węrian*:—OTeut. **wazjan*, f. **was-* (cf. L. *vestis*: see VEST *sb.*) The change from the wk. to the str. conjugation, due to analogy with *bear, tear*, etc., began in the 14th c.] **I. 1.** *trans.* To carry or bear on one's body or on some part of it, for covering, warmth, ornament, etc.; to be dressed in. **b.** To dress oneself habitually or at a particular season in (a material, garment) of a particular sort or fashion. Also *pass.*, of the material or garment. ME. **2.** To bear or carry (arms, also a stick or cane) OE. **3.** To allow (one's hair, beard) to grow in a specified fashion, or as opposed to shaving or to the use of a wig ME. **4.** Of a ship (or its commander): To fly (a flag, colours) 1558. **5.** *transf.* To bear or possess as a member or part of the body 1513. **6.** To exhibit or present (a particular look, expression, etc.) 1611. **7.** *fig.* To carry about with one in one's heart, mind, or memory; to have as a quality or attribute; to bear (a name, title) 1586. **b.** To possess and enjoy as one's own 1573.

1. Miss McFlimsey..was in utter despair, Because she had nothing whatever to w.! 1857. b. When the Court went into mourning, she always wore black THACKERAY. 3. The Officers, Petty Officers, and Seamen of the Fleet are not to w. moustaches or beards 1862. 5. *A.Y.L.* II. i. 14. 7. *Ham.* III. ii. 77. I shame To weare a Heart so white SHAKS. b. *To win and w.* (a lady as one's wife).

Phrases. *To w. a crown, diadem, palm, the purple*, etc., to hold the dignity or office of which the ornament is a symbol. †*To w. the horn(s*, to be a cuckold. *To w. one's heart on one's sleeve*: see HEART *sb.* *To w. the breeches*: see BREECH *sb.* *To w. the willow*: see WILLOW *sb.*

II. To waste, damage, or destroy by use. **1.** To waste and impair (a material) gradually by use or attrition. Also with adv., as *away, out*, and with pred. extension, as *to w. smooth.* late ME. **2.** To sap the strength or energy of (a person, his faculties, etc.) by toil, age, grief, etc. (Chiefly with adv., as *away, out*, or advb. phr.) 1508. **3.** *fig.* with object a quality, condition, etc.: To cause to weaken, diminish, or disappear gradually. late ME. **4.** To form or produce by attrition 1597.

1. All the linnen is quite worne out 1647. She would w. a gown to rags, because he had once liked it THACKERAY. 2. You that haue worne your eyes almost out in the seruice SHAKS. She tells you that her patience is quite wore out 1729. 3. *To w. down*, to blunt the force of and overcome by steady resistance or counter-attack.

III. *intr.* To suffer waste or decay by use or by lapse of time (usu. with adv. or advb. phr.) ME.

All thyng weareth save the grace of God 1530. My Suit begins to w. out 1687. In a little Time..the Fear of their Coming wore off DE FOE. A Man had better w. out than rust out 1720.

IV. To last or hold out in use or with the lapse of time; to resist (well or ill) the attrition or waste of use and age; also, to stand the test of experience, criticism, etc. 1568.

I..chose my wife, as she did her wedding-gown, not for a fine glossy surface, but such qualities as would w. well GOLDSM. How are you, Minns? 'Pon my soul you w. capitally! DICKENS.

V. In ref. to time, change, etc. **1.** In *pa. pple.* of time, a period of time: Past, spent, passed away. Now chiefly *poet.* late ME. **2.** *trans.* To spend, pass (one's time, a period of time). Chiefly *poet.* Also with adv., as *away, out.* 1535. **3.** *intr.* Of time, a period of time: To pass on or advance gradually to its conclusion; to pass away 1597. **4. a.** To pass gradually *into* (a condition, etc.) 1555. **b.** *trans.* To bring (a person) gradually *into* (a habit or disposition) 1690.

1. Winter is worne that was the flowers bale 1547. 2. We wore away a good part of the night in..drinking 1809. 3. The daye began to weare awaye TINDALE *Luke* ix. 12. Away I say, time weares SHAKS.

VI. With ref. to movement in space. **1.** *intr.* Chiefly *Sc.* To go, proceed, advance (usu. of a slow or gradual movement); with adv. or advb. phr. indicating direction 1470. **2.** *Sc.* To conduct (sheep or cattle) to the fold or other enclosure 1724. Hence **Wea·rable** *a.* capable of being worn; fit or suitable to be worn; also as *sb.* (chiefly *pl.*) a wearable commodity, an article of clothing. **Wea·ring** *ppl. a.* exhausting, tiring; that gradually destroys or impairs by continued use or attrition; that is undergoing wear by continued use or attrition.

Wear (wēᵊɹ), *v.*[2] Pa. t. and pa. pple. **wore.** 1614. [Origin obsc.] *Naut.* **1.** *intr.* Of a ship: To come round on the other tack by turning the head away from the wind (opp. to *tack*). **2.** *trans.* To put (a ship) about, bringing her stern to windward 1719.

Weariful (wīᵊ·riful), *a.* 1454. [f. WEARY *v.* + -FUL.] **1.** That causes weariness; that tires one's endurance or patience. **2.** Full of weariness; utterly fatigued 1862.

Weariless (wī°·rilės), *a.* late ME. [f. as prec. + -LESS.] That does not weary or become weary.

Weariness (wī°·rinės). OE. [f. WEARY *a.* + -NESS.] **1.** Weary condition, extreme tiredness or fatigue. **2.** Tedium or distaste induced by monotonous or uncongenial conditions or occupations; tiredness *of* a course of action, a state of things, etc. 1526. **3.** Something that wearies 1560.

1. A man would die..only vpon a wearinesse to do the same thing, so oft ouer and ouer BACON. 3. There is none end in making manie bokes: and muche readinge is a wearines of the flesh BIBLE (Genev.) *Eccl.* xii. 12.

Wearing (wē°·riŋ), *vbl. sb.* ME. [f. WEAR *v.*[1] + -ING[1].] †**1.** The fact or habit of being clothed in a particular way; kind or style of clothing; also *concr.* what a person wears or might wear -1690. **2.** The action of carrying on the body (an article of dress, an ornament, or the like). Also *attrib.* in *w. apparel, w. gear*, articles of clothing collectively. late ME. **3.** The condition or process of being continuously in wear or use 1546. **4.** The action of wearing, or the process of being worn, by continuous use or exposure 1473. **5.** Passing, elapsing (of a period of time). *rare.* 1876.

1. Giue me my nightly w., and adieu SHAKS. 2. The opposition..wished..to make the crown of England not worth the w. MACAULAY. 3. *In (the) w., (the) worse for w.*

Wearisome (wī°·risŏm), *a.* 1450. [f. WEARY *v.* and *a.* + -SOME.] **1.** Causing weariness through monotony, or the continuance of uncongenial conditions; tedious. **2.** Causing weariness from bodily or mental exhaustion or protracted pain. Now somewhat *rare.* 1594.

1. This w. murder-mongering 1891. 2. The w. gallery stairs 1883. Hence **Wea·risome·ly** *adv.* **-ness.**

Weary (wī°·ri), *a.* [OE. *wērig* :—W. Ger. **wōrigo-*.] **I. 1.** Having the feeling of loss of strength, languor, and need for rest, produced by continued exertion (physical or mental), endurance of severe pain, or wakefulness; tired, fatigued. Now usu., Intensely tired, worn out with fatigue. **2.** Discontented at the continuance or continued recurrence *of* something, and desiring its cessation; having one's patience, tolerance, zeal, or energy exhausted ME. **b.** Tired *of* (a person). 1472. **3.** Depressed and dispirited through trouble, anxiety, disappointment, etc. OE.

1. Come vnto me all ye that are wearie and laden N.T. (Genev.) *Matt.* xi. 28. W. with his Toyl DRYDEN. *W. Willie*: see TIRED *ppl. a. absol.* There the wearie be at rest *Job* iii. 17. 2. Brethren be not w. in well doynge TINDALE 2 *Thess.* iii. 13. I grew w. of the sea SWIFT. b. I am w. of her TENNYSON. 3. So wearie with Disasters, tugg'd with Fortune SHAKS.

II. Causing weariness. **1.** Fatiguing, toilsome, exhausting. (Sometimes indistinguishable from sense 2.) ME. **2.** Irksome, wearisome, tedious; burdensome to the spirit 1465. †**b.** Of a speaker, etc.: Tedious, wearisome -1603. **3.** *Sc.* and *north.* Sad, sorrowful, hard to endure 1785. **b.** *Sc.* Tiresome, 'wretched'; in phr. *weary fa'*, etc., a curse on 1785.

1. It was w. work with any tool but the hatchet 1832. 2. b. *Meas. for M.* I. v. 25. 3. A w. lot is thine SCOTT. Hence **Wea·rily** *adv.*

Weary (wī°·ri), *v.* [OE. *wer(i)gian* intr., and *gewergian* trans., f. *werig* WEARY *a.*] **I.** *intr.* To grow weary.

I had not ridden four miles when one of the horses wearyed 1686. She..wearied of passing all her time by herself 1782. Diligence which never wearies 1829. I was beginning to w. for a letter from you 1856.

II. *trans.* To make weary OE.

I will wearie you then no longer with idle talking SHAKS. A mighty curtal axe, which would have wearied the arm of any other than Cœur de Lion SCOTT. He..wearied Heaven and every saint with prayers..for the prolongation of his life SCOTT. **Wea·rying** *ppl. a.* that cause fatigue, weariness, tedium, or ennui.

Weasand (wī·zănd). Now chiefly *dial.* [OE. *wāsend*, corresp. to OFris. *wāsande*, OS. *wāsend*, OHG. *weisant*; etym. obsc. The mod. *weasand* may represent an OE. **wǣsend*.] **1.** The œsophagus or gullet. **2.** The trachea or windpipe. late ME. **3.** The throat generally 1450.

3. There thou maist braine him..Or cut his wezand with thy knife SHAKS.

Weasel (wī·z'l). [OE. *wes(u)le* :—OTeut. **wisulōn-*, of obsc. origin.] **1.** A carnivorous animal (*Putorius nivalis*), the smallest European species of the genus (of the family *Mustelidæ*) which includes the polecat, stoat, etc. **b.** Confused with the STOAT, sometimes called *ermine w.*, *white w.* 1607. **2.** Applied to various animals of the family *Mustelidæ*, or having some resemblance to the weasel 1771. **3.** *U.S.* Nickname for a native of S. Carolina 1875.

2. *Four-toed w.* = SURICATE. *Malacca w.* = RASSE, *Mexican w.* = KINKAJOU. 4. *attrib.* **w.-word** (*U.S.*), a word which destroys the force of a statement, as a weasel ruins an egg by sucking out its contents. Hence **Wea·sel** *v.*, to deprive of its meaning by using weasel-words. **Weaselly** (wī·z'li) *a.* weasel-like.

Weather (we·ðəɹ), *sb.* [Com. Teut.; OE. *weder* :—OTeut. **weðrom*; prob. f. Indo-Eur. root **wē-* to blow + suffix *-dhro-* or *-tro-*.] **1.** The condition of the atmosphere (at a given place and time) with respect to heat or cold, presence or absence of rain, etc. **b.** *pl.* Kinds of weather. Now *rare* exc. in phr. (*in*) *all weathers.* OE. **c.** With unfavourable implication: Adverse, unpleasant, hurtful, or destructive condition of the atmosphere; rain, frost, etc. as destructive agents ME. **d.** Violent wind accompanied by heavy rain or agitation of the waves (now *dial.* and *Naut.*) OE. †**e.** What falls from the clouds; rain, snow, etc. late ME. **2.** *Naut.* The direction in which the wind is blowing. late ME. **3.** The angle (more fully *angle of w.*) which the sails of a windmill make with the perpendicular to the axis 1759.

1. In Autumne when the whether is milde and pleasant 1578. The conversation began about the w. 1779. *Wind and w.*: see WIND *sb.* †*To make fair w.*, to be conciliatory, make a show of friendliness, goodness, etc. *In the w.*, in an exposed situation, unprotected from rain, cold, wind, etc. *Under the w.* (orig. *U.S.*), indisposed, not quite well. *W. permitting*, often appended to an announcement (e.g. of the sailing of a vessel) to indicate that it is conditional on the weather being favourable. *Clerk of the w.*, an imaginary functionary humorously supposed to control the w. c. *To make good, bad*, etc. *w. of it*, (of a ship) to behave well or ill in a storm. *fig.* The ..muddle-headed, making heavy w. of the simplest tasks 1915. 2. *To drive with the w.*, to drift with the wind and waves. *To have the w. of*, to be to windward of (another ship).

attrib. and *Comb.*, as *w.-chart, forecast, report*, etc.; **w.-bitt**, *Naut.* an extra turn of the cable about the bitts in bad w.; also *v. trans.* to give this extra turn to (the cable); †**-bitten**, nipped, gnawed, or worn by the weather; **-bound** *a.*, detained by bad w.; prevented by stress of w. from sailing, travelling, etc.; **-brained** = W.-HEADED: **-breeder**, a day of exceptionally sunny and calm w., pop. supposed to presage a coming storm; **-cloth**, *Naut.* a covering of canvas or tarpaulin used as a protection against the w., or against wind and spray; **-driven**, driven by stormy w.; **-fend** *v. trans.*, to defend from the w., to shelter (SHAKS.); **-gall** = WATERGALL; **-gleam**, **-glim** *Sc.* and *north.*, clear sky near a dark horizon; **-house**, a toy hygroscope in the form of a small house with figures of a man and woman standing in two porches; by the varying torsion of a string the man comes out of his porch in wet w., and the woman out of hers in dry; **-moulding**, *Arch.* a drip-stone; **-proof** *a.*, impervious to the w.; **-prophet**, one who foretells the w.; one who is w.-wise; **-side**, the side (e.g. of a building, a tree) that is most exposed to injury from w.; **-stain**, a stain or discoloration caused by the w.; **-tiled** *a.*, covered with overlapping tiles; so **-tiling.**

b. *Naut.* in the sense 'situated on the side which is turned towards the wind; windward', as *w.-beam, -port, -quarter, -tack*, etc.; **w.-bow**, the bow that is turned towards the wind; hence as *v. trans.* to turn the w.-bow to; **-gage, -gauge**, (see GAUGE *sb.* I. 5); **-helm**, a tendency in a ship under sail to come too near the wind; **-side**, the windward side.

Weather (we·ðəɹ), *v.* late ME. [f. prec.] **1.** *trans.* To subject to the beneficial action of the wind and sun; to air. **2.** *trans.* and *intr.* To change by exposure to the weather; to wear away, disintegrate, discolour, under atmospheric influences 1757. **3.** *Naut.* **a.** *trans.* To sail to the windward of (a point or headland, another ship, etc.) 1595. **b.** *fig.* To get safely round; to get the better of 1626. **c.** intr. *To w. on* or *upon*, to gain upon in a windward direction; also *fig.*, to get the advantage of 1595. **4.** *trans.* **a.** *Naut.* To withstand and come safely through (a storm) 1655. **b.** *gen.* To pass through and survive (severe weather) 1680. †**c.** To take shelter from (a storm) -1798. **5.** To set (the sails of a windmill) at the proper angle to obtain the maximum effect of the wind-force 1745. **6.** *Arch.* To slope or bevel (a surface) so as to throw off the rain; to furnish (a wall, buttress) with a weathering 1833.

1. It shall be well done to w. your garmentes in Marche for feare of mothes 1530. 2. The face of the limestone is hollowed out and weathered LYELL. 3. b. That soule which is but neare destruction, may w. that mischiefe DONNE. 4. a. *fig.* He Weathered out the Raign of Queen Mary FULLER. The Government..could not have weathered the session 1834. b. I began..to fear I should never be able to w. out the winter in so lonely a dwelling COWPER.

Wea·ther-bea:ten, *pa. pple.* and *ppl. a.* 1530. **1.** Beaten or buffeted by wind and rain; that has been exposed to severe weather 1560. **2. a.** Of things: Worn, defaced, or damaged by exposure to the weather 1547. **b.** Of persons, etc.: Bronzed, coarsened, hardened by exposure to all kinds of weather 1530.

2. a. Pancras Church..old and wetherbeaten 1593. b. Two weatherbeaten old seamen MACAULAY.

Wea·therboard. 1539. **1.** One of a series of boards nailed horizontally, with overlapping edges, as an outside covering for walls. **b.** A board laid over builders' work or material as a protection 1851. **2.** A board placed sloping over a window or other opening to throw off or keep out rain 1568. **3.** *Naut.* The windward side of a ship 1625. Hence **Wea·therboard** *v. trans.* to nail weatherboards upon (a wall or roof). **Wea·therboa:rding** *vbl. sb.* the covering a building with weatherboards; *concr.* weatherboards collectively.

Wea·thercock, *sb.* ME. **1.** A vane in the form of a cock, which turns with its head to the wind. Also *gen.*, a vane of any form. Often as a symbol of mutability or fickleness; also *fig.* of persons or things. **2.** *attrib.* and *appos.*, passing into *adj.* = changeable, inconstant 1680.

1. As a wedercok, that turneth his face With every wind CHAUCER. 2. The wavering and w. resolutions of men 1680. Hence **Wea·thercock** *v. trans.* to provide with a w.; to serve as a w. for.

Weathered (we·ðəɹd), *ppl. a.* 1879. [f. WEATHER *v.* + -ED[1].] **1.** Worn, stained, or seasoned by the weather or by atmospheric influences. Chiefly *Geol.* **2.** Of a crop of grain or hay: Deteriorated by too long exposure to the elements 1875. **3.** *Arch.* Made sloping, so as to prevent the lodgement of water; furnished with a weathering 1840.

Wea·ther-eye. 1839. [app. a joc. use of WEATHER *sb.* used *attrib.*] In fig. phrases, as *to keep one's w. open*, to be watchful and alert, keep one's wits about one.

Wea·ther-glass. 1626. †**1.** A kind of thermometer used to ascertain the temperature of the air, and also to prognosticate changes in the weather -1720. **2.** A barometer 1695.

2. *Poor Man's, Shepherd's W.*, the scarlet pimpernel, *Anagallis arvensis* (from its closing its flowers before rain).

†**Weather-headed**, *ppl. a.* 1652. [prob. f. WETHER.] Light-headed, foolish -1822.

Weathering (we·ðəriŋ), *vbl. sb.* ME. [In sense 1, repr. OE. *wederung*, f. *wed(e)rian*; in late uses f. WEATHER *v.* + -ING[1].] †**1.** Weather conditions; (good or bad) weather -1565. **2.** The action of the atmospheric agencies or elements on substances exposed to them; the discoloration, disintegration, etc., resulting from this action 1665. **3.** *Naut.* The action of passing (an object) on the windward side 1878. **4.** *Arch.* A projecting course on the face of a wall, serving to throw off rain-water; a sloped 'set-off' of a wall or buttress; the inclination or slope given to a surface in order to prevent the lodgement of water 1739.

Weatherly (we·ðəɹli), *a.* 1729. *Naut.* Of a sailing-vessel: Able to sail close to the wind without drifting to leeward. Hence **Wea·therliness.**

Weatherology (weðərǫ·lŏdʒi). 1823. [f. WEATHER *sb.* + -OLOGY.] The science and study of the weather and its phenomena.

Weather-wise (we·ðəɹwəiz), *a.* late ME. [f. WEATHER *sb.* + WISE *a.*] Skilled in prognostics of the weather. So **Wea·ther-wi:sdom** 1822.

Weave (wīv), *sb.* 1581. [f. next.] †1. Something that has been woven, a woven fabric -1646. 2. A particular method or pattern of weaving 1888.

Weave (wīv), *v.*[1] Pa. t. **wove** (wōuv); pa. pple. wo·ven. [Com. Teut. str. vb.; OE. *wefan* (*wæf, wǣfon, wefen*) :—OTeut. **weƀ-* (: **waƀ-* : **wǣƀ-*) :—Indo-Eur. **webh-* (: **wēbh-* : **ubh-*), repr. in Gr. ὑφή, ὕφος web, ὑφαίνειν to weave.] 1. *trans.* To form or fabricate (a stuff or material) by interlacing yarns or other filaments of a particular substance in a continuous web; to manufacture in a loom by crossing the threads or yarns called the warp and the weft. Also with obj. the web itself, a garment made up of such a stuff or material. b. *fig.* To contrive, fabricate, or construct (a mental product) with elaborate care. late ME. c. To form (e.g. a basket, a wreath) by interlacing rods or twigs, flowers, etc. late ME. 2. *absol.* or *intr.* To practise weaving; to work with a loom OE. 3. *trans.* Of a spider, insect: To spin (a web, a cocoon) ME. 4. To form a texture with (threads, filaments, strips of some material); to interlace or intertwine so as to form a fabric 1538. b. To entwine or wreathe together 1578. 5. To cause to move in a devious course; to direct (one's steps) in a devious or intricate course, as in dancing 1650. b. To go through the intricate movements of (a dance) 1792.

1. O what a tangled web we w., When first we practise to deceive! SCOTT. b. I had already woven a little romance..in my imagination 1819. The evil arts of brewing charms and weaving spells 1876. 3. 2 *Hen. VI*, III. i. 340. 4. *fig.* Untruth is so maliciously weaved with truth 1545. Put the melody in the bass, ..and w. in a new melody with it in the upper part 1875.

Weave, *v.*[2] 1593. [Continuation of ME. *weve*(*n.* app. repr. OE. **wǣfan*, or perh. a dial. var. of *weyve, waive*, a. ON. *veifa* to wave, swing.] 1. *intr.* To move repeatedly from side to side; to sway the body alternately to one side and the other; to pursue a devious course 1596. 2. *trans.* To make a signal to (a ship or its occupants) by waving a flag or something used as a substitute 1593. 3. *Pugilism.* To creep close into (one's opponent) before delivering one's blow 1818.

Weaver[1] (wī·vəɹ). late ME. [f. WEAVE *v.*[1] + -ER[1].] 1. One who weaves textile fabrics; a workman or workwoman whose occupation is weaving. 2. (Also *w.-bird.*) One of numerous Asiatic or African tropical birds of the family *Ploceidæ*, so called from the elaborately interwoven nests that many of them build 1828. 3. = WHIRLIGIG *sb.* 4. 1864.

1. *fig.* Sedentary weavers of long tales Give me the fidgets COWPER.

Comb., with possessive, as **weaver's knot**, a sheet-bend or single bend, used for joining threads in weaving.

Wea·ver[2]. 1847. [f. WEAVE *v.*[2] + -ER[1].] A horse that 'weaves' or rolls the neck and body from side to side.

Weazen (wī·z'n), *a.* 1765. Altered f. WIZEN *a.* Hence **Wea·zeny** *a.* somewhat w.

Weazen (wī·z'n), *v.* 1821. [Altered f. WIZEN *v.*] *intr.* To shrink, shrivel. Hence **Wea·zened** *ppl. a.*

Web (web), *sb.* [OE. *web*(*b* :—OTeut. **waƀjom*, f. **waƀ-*, ablaut-var. of **weƀ-* to WEAVE *v.*[1]] I. 1. A woven fabric; *spec.* a whole piece of cloth in process of being woven or after it comes from the loom. Also *collect.*, woven stuff. b. *transf.* and *fig.* Something likened to a woven fabric; also, the texture of such a fabric 1599. c. Used for WARP 1538. 2. An article made of woven stuff. Also *collect.* woven stuff of a particular material or pattern. (Now chiefly literary or *arch.*) OE. 3. A band of material woven strongly without pile. Also *collect.* = WEBBING. ME. b. *attrib.* (and *Comb.*) Made of webbing 1844. 4. A cobweb. Also applied to the filmy textures spun by some caterpillars. ME. b. = COBWEB 1 b. 1877. c. *fig.*, esp. (*a*) a subtly-woven snare or entanglement; (*b*) something flimsy and unsubstantial 1574. 5. *Paper-making.* a. An endless wire-cloth working on rollers and carrying the pulp. b. A large sheet or roll of paper made in this way. 1825.

1. b. The webbe of our life is of a mingled yarne, good and ill together SHAKS. The w. of diplomatic negotiation and court-intrigue 1860. 4. c. Entangled in a w. of crime and guilt 1859.

II. 1. A tissue or membrane in an animal body or in a plant; also applied to similar pathological formations ME. b. The omentum or caul of cattle 1808. †2. A thin white film or opacity growing over the eye -1827. 3. The membrane or fold of skin which connects the digits of an animal; esp. that which connects the toes of an aquatic bird or beast, forming a palmate foot 1576. b. *Path.* An extension of the normal fold which occurs as a congenital malformation in the human hand or foot 1866. 4. The series of barbs on each side of the shaft of a bird's feather; the vane or vexillum 1713.

2. †*Pin and w.*: a disease of the eye, perh. characterized by a pin-like spot and a film.

III. †1. A sheet of lead, such as is used for roofing and for coffins -1852. 2. The piece of bent iron which forms a horseshoe 1587. 3. a. The thin sharp part of the coulter of a plough 1784. b. The detachable long narrow blade of a frame-saw or fret-saw 1831. 4. The bit of a key; also, each of the 'steps' or incisions in this 1773. 5. The vertical plate which connects the upper and lower laterally-extending plates in a beam or girder 1851. b. The upright portion between the tread and the bottom flange of a rail 1838. c. The arm of a crank, connecting the shaft and the wrist 1875. d. The thinner part of an anvil, between the head and the base 1874. 6. The basket-work of a gabion 1852.

Comb.: **w.-fingered** *a.*, having the fingers united for a considerable part of their length by a fold of skin; also, applied to a fish, *Prionotus carolinus* or *palmipes*; **-machine, (-perfecting) press,** a printing machine which is automatically supplied with paper from a roll or w.; **-printing,** printing on a w.-press; **-saw,** a frame-saw; **-toed** *a.*, w.-footed; **-worm** *U.S.*, any of various lepidopterous larvæ which are more or less gregarious and spin large webs in which they feed or rest. Hence **Webbed** (webd) *ppl. a.* furnished with a w. or connecting membrane; *esp.* of the feet of certain birds; covered with or as with cobweb. **We·bby** *a.* consisting of w.; resembling w. or a w.; of the digits, palmated.

Web (web), *v.* [In sense 1, OE. *webbian*, f. WEB *sb.* In other senses, f. WEB *sb.*] †1. *trans.* To weave (a fabric) in the loom -1892. 2. To cover with a (spider's) web, or something resembling this 1853. b. To stretch threads of spider's web across (a micrometer, etc.) 1883. 3. To entangle or envelop in or as in a (spider's) web 1864. 4. To connect (fingers, toes, etc.) with a web or membrane 1774.

We·b-beam. OE. The roller in a loom on which the web is wound as it is woven.

Webbing (we·biŋ), *vbl. sb.* 1440. [f. WEB *v.* + -ING[1].] †1. The action or process of weaving -1657. 2. *concr.* A woven material 1754. b. Woven material in the form of a strong wide band, used by upholsterers, etc. 1794. 3. = PALMATION *concr.* Also *Path.*, a webbed state of the fingers or toes. 1872.

Weberian (wībiə·riăn), *a.* 1849. [f. name of E. H. *Weber* (1795–1833), a German anatomist + -IAN.] *W. corpuscle, organ,* a tubular vesicle in the prostatic portion of the urethra. *W. ossicles,* a chain of small bones between the ear and the air-bladder in certain fishes; *W. apparatus,* the set of structures which connect the air-bladder with the ear.

We·b-foot. 1765. 1. A foot with webbed toes. Also, the condition of being web-footed. 2. †a. A nickname for a dweller in the Fens. b. A native of the State of Oregon (so called on account of the moist climate) 1873. So **We·b-foo·ted** *a.* having web-feet 1681.

Webster (we·bstəɹ). *Obs.* exc. *Hist.* [OE. *webbestre*, fem. of *webba* weaver; see -STER.] A weaver: a. as the designation of a woman; b. extended, or applied *spec.*, to a male weaver.

Websterite (we·bstərəit). 1823. [f. name of T. *Webster*, who discovered it; see -ITE[1] 2 b.] *Min.* = ALUMINITE.

Wed (wed), *sb. Obs.* exc. *dial.* [Com. Teut.; OE. *wed*(*d* :—OTeut. **waðjom*, cogn. w. L. *vad-*(*vas*) surety; cf. WAGE *sb.*] 1. A pledge, something deposited as security for a payment or the fulfilment of an obligation; occas., a hostage. 2. A stake in a game or wager ME.

Wed (wed), *v.* Pa. t. and pa. pple. **wedded** (*dial.* wed). [Com. Teut. :—OE. *weddian* :—OTeut. **waðjōjan*, f. **waðjom* WED *sb.*] 1. *trans.* To wager, stake. *Obs.* exc. *Sc.* and *north.* late ME. 2. *orig.* To make (a woman) one's wife by the giving of a pledge or earnest; hence, to take in marriage; to become the husband or wife of (a person) by participating in a prescribed ceremony or formal act OE. 3. To bind (the contracting parties) in wedlock; to conduct the marriage ceremony for OE. 4. *pass.* To be joined in wedlock; to be married *to,* †*with,* †*unto* (a husband or wife) ME. 5. *intr.* To enter into the matrimonial state; to take a wife or husband ME. 6. *trans.* To unite as in marriage. late ME.

2. With thys ring I thee w. *Bk. Com. Prayer.* 3. The sayd incumbent shuld..burye, wedde, and christen wythin the sayd chappell 1546. 6. The quene was wedded to her awne opinion 1548. A book in which matter and manner are wedded as in few other books of the same kind 1887.

Wedded (we·dėd), *ppl. a.* OE. [f. prec. + -ED[1].] 1. Joined in wedlock; living in the married state. 2. Of or pertaining to marriage or to married persons 1592. 3. Obstinately attached (to a habit, opinion, etc.) 1579.

1. My lawful, w. wife 1798. 2. *Rom. & Jul.* I. v. 137 (Fo.).

Wedding (we·diŋ), *vbl. sb.* OE. [f. WED *v.* + -ING[1].] 1. The action of marrying; marriage, espousal. 2. The performance of the marriage-rite; the ceremony of a marriage, with its attendant festivities ME.

2. *Penny w.*: see PENNY. *Silver w.*, the 25th anniversary of a w. (see SILVER *sb.*). *Golden w.*, the 50th anniversary. *Diamond w.*, the 60th anniversary.

attrib., as *w.-bell, -dress, -feast, -guest, journey*; **w.-breakfast,** the entertainment given to the wedding-guests after the marriage-ceremony and before the departure for the honeymoon; **-cake,** a large rich cake, covered with icing and decorated with sugar ornaments, cut and distributed to the guests at the w.-feast or sent in small portions to absent friends; **-garment,** usu. *fig.* (with ref. to *Matt.* xxii. 11–12); **-march,** a march (Mendelssohn's, if not otherwise specified) composed for performance at a w.; **-ring,** a ring placed by the bridegroom on the third finger of the bride's left hand as part of the marriage ceremony.

Wedge (wedʒ), *sb.* [Com. Teut.; OE. *wecg* :—OTeut. **wagjoz*, perh. cogn. w. Gr. ὀφνίς ploughshare, Lith. *vągis* pin, plug.] 1. A piece of wood, metal, or other hard material, thick at one end and tapering to a thin edge at the other; chiefly used as a tool operated by percussion applied to the thick end, for splitting wood, etc., dilating a fissure or cavity, tightening or securing some part of a structure, and other similar purposes. Hence, in *Mechanics*, the type of simple machine of which this is an example, and which includes also knives, chisels, etc.; now regarded as a variety of the inclined plane. b. *Grafting.* (*a*) A peg to keep the cleft open. (*b*) The tongue or tapered end of a scion or stock. 1523. c. *Arch.* A voussoir 1726. †2. An ingot of gold, silver, etc. -1719. b. *Cant.* Silver, whether money or plate 1725. 3. *transf.* a. A formation of troops tapering to the front or van, in order to cleave a way through an opposing force. Now more widely of a body of people. 1614. b. The V-shaped formation adopted by a number of geese or other wildfowl when flying 1869. c. *gen.* Something in the form of a wedge; a wedge-shaped part or piece of anything 1821. d. *Meteorol.* A narrow w.-shaped area of high pressure between two adjacent cyclonic systems; also, the representation of this on a weather-chart 1887. e. The wedge-shaped stroke in cuneiform characters 1821. 4. *Geom.* a. A triangular prism. b. A simple solid formed by cutting a triangular prism by any two planes. 1710. 5. *Her.* A charge consisting of an isosceles triangle with a very acute angle at its vertex 1716.

1. *The thin end of the w.*, fig. a small beginning which it is hoped or feared may lead to something greater. 3. c. A pot of the real draught stout, and.. wedges of cheese DICKENS.

Comb.: **w.-bill,** a bird with a w.-shaped bill; **-shaped** *a.*, shaped like a w., cuneiform, *Bot.* and *Zool.* = CUNEATE *a.*; **-shell,** a marine bivalve, belonging to *Donax* or allied genera; **-tailed** *a.*, having a w.-shaped tail; used *spec.* in the names of birds, as the w.-tailed gull, *Rhodostethia rosea*. Hence **We·dgewise** *adv.* after the manner or in the form of a w.

Wedge (wedʒ), *v.*[1] 1440. [f. prec.] 1. *trans.* To tighten, fasten tight by driving in a wedge or wedges. Also with *in, on, up.* 2. To cleave or split by driving in a wedge 1530.

b. To split *off*, force *apart*, *asunder*, or *open*, by driving in a wedge 1853. **3.** *transf.* To drive, push, or squeeze (an object) into something where it is held fast; to fix firmly by driving in, or by pressing tight 1513. **4.** To pack or crowd (a number of persons or animals) in close formation, or in a limited space 1720.

2. My heart, As wedged with a sigh, would riue in twaine SHAKS. **3.** *fig. Cor.* II. iii. 30. Hence **We·dging** *vbl. sb.* the action of driving in a wedge or wedges; *Geol.* the jutting *out* or flaking *off* (of rock, etc.), as if by the operation of a wedge.

Wedge (wedʒ), *v.*² 1686. [Origin obsc.] *trans.* To cut (wet clay) into masses and work them by kneading and throwing down, in order to expel air-bubbles.

Wedgwood (we·dʒwud). 1787. [Proper name.] **1.** Used *attrib.* to designate the pottery made by Josiah Wedgwood (1730–95) and his successors at Etruria, Staffs. **b.** Used to designate the blue colour which is characteristic of Wedgwood ware 1900. **c.** as *sb.* = Wedgwood pottery or ware 1863. **2.** Designating the scale of temperature used in the pyrometer invented by Josiah Wedgwood for testing the heat of kilns 1807.

Wedgy (we·dʒi), *a. rare.* 1799. [f. WEDGE *sb.* + -Y¹.] Resembling a wedge; shaped like a wedge.

Wedlock (we·dlǫk). OE. [OE. *wedlác*, f. *wed* pledge + *-lác* -LOCK.] †**1.** The marriage vow or obligation -1611. **2.** The condition of being married; marriage as a state of life or as an institution; matrimonial relationship. Now only in literary or legal use. ME. **b.** *Born in, out of w.*, said distinctively of legitimate or illegitimate offspring ME. **c.** A matrimonial union; a married life. late ME. †**3.** A wife -1690.

1. *Oth.* v. ii. 142. **3.** The most true constant lover of his w. FLETCHER.

Wednesday (we·nzdeⁱ, -di, we·d'nzdeⁱ). [OE. *Wódnes dæg* 'day of (the god) Woden', tr. late L. *Mercurii dies* 'day of Mercury'. N.E.D.] The fourth day of the week. Also *attrib.* **b.** In names of certain days of the ecclesiastical calendar, as ASH WEDNESDAY. Also *Good W.*, *Holy W.*, *Spy W.* (Anglo-Ir.), the W. before Easter.

Wee (wī), *sb.* and *a.* orig. *Sc.* [Northern ME. *wei*, repr. Angl. *wǽg(e* = WS. *wǽg(e*; see WEIGH *sb.*¹] **A.** *sb.* In early use almost always *a little w.*, later also *a w.* (chiefly as advb. acc.) **1. a.** To a small extent, in a small degree 1513. **b.** Qualifying and adj. or adv.: Somewhat, rather 1816. **2.** A short time ME.

1. a. I have been drinking a wi, and I believe the Devil was in me 1793. **2.** Bide a w. — bide a w.; you southrons are aye in sic a hurry SCOTT.

B. *adj.* Extremely small, tiny 1450. **b.** *A w. bit*: = 'a wee'. Often quasi-*adj.* and quasi-*adv.* 1661. **c.** *The w. folk*, the fairies 1819. **d.** *The W. Free Kirk*, a nickname given to the minority of the Free Church of Scotland which stood apart when the main body amalgamated with the United Presbyterian Church to form the United Free Church in 1900. Hence *W. Frees*, members of the 'W. Free' church. 1904.

Weed (wīd), *sb.*¹ [OE. *wéod* = OS. *wiod*; ult. etym. unkn.] **1.** A herbaceous plant not valued for use or beauty, growing wild and rank, and regarded as cumbering the ground or hindering the growth of superior vegetation. **b.** A plant that grows wild in fresh or salt water. Cf. PONDWEED, SEAWEED, WATERWEED. 1538. **c.** Used, with defining word, to form the names of wild plants, as BINDWEED, DUCKWEED, KNAPWEED, etc. **2.** *gen.* Any herb or small plant. Chiefly *poet.* OE. **b.** Applied to a shrub or tree, *esp.* to a large tree, on account of its abundance in a district 1697. **3.** *spec.* Tobacco 1606. **b.** A cigar or cheroot. *colloq.* 1847. **4.** *fig.* An unprofitable, troublesome, or noxious growth. late ME. **5.** *slang.* **a.** A poor, leggy, loosely-built horse 1845. **b.** A lank delicate person without muscle or stamina 1869.

1. They bid thee crop a w., thou pluckst a flower SHAKS. In the garden there was not a w. to be seen DICKENS. Prov. *Ill weeds grow apace.* **2. b.** The elm..is still known as the 'Warwickshire w.' 1890. **4.** *Oth.* IV. ii. 67.

Comb.: **w.-killer**, a preparation of arsenic used for killing weeds. Hence **Wee·dery**, weeds collectively; also, a place where weeds abound. **Wee·dling**, a small w.; a slight, weakly person.

Weed (wīd), *sb.*² *arch.* exc. in sense 6 b. OE. [ME. *wede*, repr. (1) OE. *wǽd* :—OTeut. *wǣdiz; (2) OE. *wǽde*, prob. shortened f. *gewǽde* :—OTeut. *gawǣdjom.] **1.** An article of apparel; a garment. **2.** *collect. sing.* Clothing, raiment, dress OE. **3.** *transf.* and *fig.* ME. **4.** Used contextually for: Defensive covering, armour, mail ME. **5.** A garment, or garb, distinctive of a person's sex, profession, or state of life ME. **6.** With defining word: A black garment worn in token of bereavement. Also, a scarf or band of crape worn by a mourner. 1536. **b.** *spec.* The deep mourning worn by a widow. Now always *pl.* 1595.

2. Deposed..for apparelling himselfe in such weede as was not decent for the dignity and order of priesthood 1576. **3.** There the snake throwes her enammel'd skinne, W. wide enough to rap a Fairy in SHAKS. **5.** They who to be sure of Paradise Dying put on the weeds of Dominic MILT. This poor gown,..this beggar-woman's w. TENNYSON. **6. b.** An afflicted Widow in her Mourning-Weeds ADDISON.

Weed (wīd), *v.* [OE. *wéodian*, f. *wéod* WEED *sb.*¹] **1.** *intr.* (or *absol.*) To clear the ground of weeds; to pull up weeds. **2.** *trans.* To free (land, a crop, plant) from weeds ME. **3.** To remove (weeds) from land, esp. from cultivated land or from a crop. Also with *out*, *up*. late ME. **b.** *fig.* To eradicate (errors, faults, etc.); to remove (things or persons) as noxious or useless 1526. **4.** To clear *away* (plants, not necessarily noxious or useless); to take *out* (plants or trees) to prevent overcrowding; to thin (a crop). 1543. **b.** *transf.* To remove (inferior or superfluous individuals) from a company, herd, etc.; also with *out* 1863.

2. *fig.* Prouided that you w. your better judgements Of all opinion that growes ranke in them SHAKS. **3. b.** Those who are so active to w. out the prejudices of education BERKELEY. **4.** The Flowers of the Forest are weeded away 1760. **b.** All her old society (excepting such as she had judiciously weeded out) 1889. Hence **Wee·der**, an implement used to eradicate weeds, a person employed to remove weeds from a crop, land, etc.; an extirpator (of weeds).

Wee·d-hook. OE. [f. WEED *sb.*¹ + HOOK *sb.*] A hook for cutting away weeds. Also **Wee·ding-hook** ME.

Weedy (wī·di), *a.*¹ late ME. [f. WEED *sb.*¹ + -Y¹.] **1.** Full of, abounding, or overgrown with weeds. **2.** Of the nature of or resembling a weed; made or consisting of weeds 1602. **3.** *colloq.* **a.** Of animals, esp. horses and hounds: Lean, leggy, loose-bodied, and lacking in strength and mettle 1800. **b.** Of persons: Unhealthily thin and tall; lanky and wanting physical vigour 1852.

2. When downe the w. Trophies, and her selfe, Fell in the weeping Brooke SHAKS.

Weedy (wī·di), *a.*² 1848. [f. WEED *sb.*² + -Y¹.] Wearing widow's 'weeds'; clad in mourning.

I think there was some compromise in the cap; but otherwise she was as w. as in the early days of her mourning DICKENS.

Week (wīk), *sb.* [Com. Teut.; OE. *wice* :—OTeut. *wikōn-.] **1.** The cycle of seven days, recognized in the calendar of the Jews and thence adopted in the calendars of Christian, Mohammedan, and various other peoples; a single period of this cycle, beginning with the day traditionally fixed as the first of the week. **b.** With prefixed word, denoting some particular week of the year OE. **2.** A space of seven days, irrespective of the time from which it is reckoned OE. **b.** Seven days as a term for periodical payments (of wages, rent, or the like), or as a unit of reckoning for time of work or service. late ME. **c.** Used vaguely for an indefinite time. late ME. **d.** Feast of weeks *Heb. Antiq.* [tr. Heb. *ḥag šābūʿōth*] = PENTECOST **1.** late ME. **3.** The six working days, as opp. to Sunday; the period from Monday to Saturday inclusive OE.

1. b. In Cristemesse wike 1450. Being the Tuesday in Easter w. 1622. **2.** She was within six weeks of seventeen 1856. There came a w. of rain 1865. **b.** In two days..the week's rent would be due 1882. A week's notice 1886. **c.** *A w. or two*, a moderate space of time. *Weeks*, a time which is felt as long; He *did* feel the same, Elinor—for weeks and weeks he felt it J. AUSTEN. **3.** *Ham.* I. i. 76.

Phrases. *A w.*, every w., weekly; A good woman.. that fasted .iij. tymes a woke 1450. *This day, tomorrow, Monday*, etc. *w.*, seven days before or after the day specified. *Yesterday, Monday*, etc., *was a w.* (dial.), seven days before the day mentioned. †*To be in by the w.*, to be ensnared, caught; *fig.* to be deeply in love. *Too late a week*, joc. understatement for 'far too late'; *A.Y.L.* II. iii. 74. *A w. of Sundays*, seven Sundays or weeks as repr. a long time. *To knock* (a person) *into the middle of next w.*, to give (him) a decisive blow, to punish severely.

Comb.: **w.-long** *a.*, continuing for a w.; **-night**, a night in the w. other than Sunday night; also *attrib.*; **-old** *a.*, that has lived or lasted a w.

Week (wīk), *int.* 1588. Imitation of the squeak of a pig or mouse.

Weekday (wī·kdeⁱ). [OE. *wicdæg*, f. *wicu* WEEK.] †**1.** A day of the week -1456. **2.** A day of the week other than Sunday 1546.

2. A hard-working man on week-days, and a preacher on Sundays 1860. *attrib.* Week-day services GEO. ELIOT.

Week-end (stress var.). 1878. **a.** (with *a* and *pl.*). The holiday period at the end of a week's work, usu. extending from Saturday noon or Friday night to Monday morning 1879. **b.** The period from Saturday to Monday during which business is suspended and shops are closed 1878.

a. They had evidently taken the house for weekends 1892. *attrib.* W. tickets 1887. Hence **Weekend** *v. intr.* to spend a w. holiday.

Weekly (wī·kli), *a.* and *sb.* 1489. [f. WEEK *sb.* + -LY¹.] **A.** *adj.* That occurs, is done, made, given, etc. once a week. **b.** With a personal designation: Performing some action, or employed in some capacity, once a week; that has a contract by the week 1712.

The w. charge in this establishment..is three dollars DICKENS. *W. tenancy*, one determinable at the end of any week. **b.** *W. tenant*, one paying rent by the week, and subject to removal at a week's notice.

B. *sb.* A newspaper or review published once in each week 1846.

A new literary W. of high pretensions 1863.

Weekly (wī·kli), *adv.* 1465. [f. WEEK *sb.* + -LY².] In each or every week; week by week. Usu., once in seven days.

Wee·k-work. *Hist.* [OE. *wicweorc*, f. *wic(u* WEEK + *weorc* WORK *sb.*] In Old English Law, work done for the lord by the tenant so many days a week.

Weel¹ (wīl). *Sc.* and *north.* [OE. *wǽl* = MDu. *wael*, MLG. *wêl*.] A deep pool; a deep place in a river or the sea; a whirlpool or eddy.

Weel² (wīl). ME. [OE. *wile-* (in *wilewíse*), reduced form of *wilige* WILLY *sb.*¹] **1.** A wicker trap for catching fish, esp. eels. **b.** *Her.* A conventional representation of such a fish-trap, borne as a charge 1688. **2.** A basket, *esp.* one in which fish are kept. late ME.

Weem (wīm). 1792. [a. early Gael. *uaim* a cavern.] Applied in Scotland to a cave or underground dwelling-place used by early inhabitants of the country.

Ween (wīn), *v.* *Obs.* exc. *arch.* [Com. Teut. wk. vb.; OE. *wénan* :—OTeut. *wǣnjan.] **1.** *trans.* To think, surmise, suppose, conceive, believe, consider. **b.** used parenthetically (esp. in *I w.*) ME. **2.** In regard to what is future or contingent; To expect, anticipate, count on; to think possible or likely OE. †**3.** *intr.* with *of*, *for*: To dream of, look for, expect -1613.

1. *absol.* I know you better than ye wene MALORY. **b.** Nor turnd I weene Adam from his fair Spouse MILT. A stalwart knight, I w., was he BARHAM. **2.** Weening in his pride to make the land nauigable 2 *Macc.* v. 21. **3.** *Hen. VIII*, v. i. 136.

Weeny (wī·ni), *a.* *dial.* and *colloq.* 1790. [f. WEE, with ending imitated from TINY.] Very small, tiny.

Such a little tiny w. pill can never cure such a great big headache 1833.

Weep (wīp), *sb.* ME. [f. next.] †**1.** Weeping, lamentation -1545. **b.** A fit or bout of weeping 1836. **2.** An exudation, percolation, or sweating of moisture 1838.

Weep (wīp), *v.* Pa. t. and pa. pple. **wept.** [Com. Teut.; OE. *wépan* (pa. t. *wéop*), f. OTeut. *wōpo- (OE. *wóp*) weeping, lamentation.] **I.** *intr.* **1.** To manifest the combination of bodily symptoms (instinctive cries or moans, sobs, and shedding of tears) which is the natural expression of painful (and sometimes of intensely pleasurable) emotion; also, and in mod. use chiefly, to shed tears (more or less silently). **b.**

said of animals. late ME. c. Const. *for*, *over*, †*on* (a person or thing regretted or commiserated), *for* (the emotion that prompts weeping). Also with *to* and inf., or a *that*-clause. OE. 2. Of the eyes: To shed tears 1567. b. *fig.* of the heart ME. 3. *transf.* Of things: To shed water or moisture in drops; to exude drops of moisture. late ME. b. To issue in drops; to trickle or fall as tears 1596. c. Of a boiler, etc.: To allow small drops of water to percolate or trickle through 1869. d. Of a sore, etc.: To exude a serous fluid 1882. 4. Of a tree: To droop its branches 1764.

1. I am a foole To weepe at what I am glad of SHAKS. I could have wept like a child 1860. It is a sight to make the angels w. 1889. Phr. *To w. one's fill.* b. Þeise serpentes [crocodiles] slen men & þei eten hem wepynge MAUNDEV. c. Weepe thou for me in France; I, for thee heere SHAKS. Faire Daffadills, we w. to see You haste away so soone HERRICK. She embrac'd him, and for joy Tenderly wept MILT. 3. The sky ceased to w. 1854. 4. The Willow weeping o'er the fatal wave 1764.

II. *trans.* 1. To shed tears over; to lament with tears OE. 2. To let fall from the eyes, to shed (tears) ME. b. *fig.* Of the heart, or a wound: *To w.* (*tears of*) *blood* 1592. c. To declare, express, utter with lamentation. *rare* (chiefly *poet.*) 1599. 3. quasi-*trans.* with adv. or compl. a. in phrases expressing excessive or prolonged weeping; esp. *to w. out one's eyes* or *heart* ME. b. To bring into a specified state or condition by weeping 1591. c. with advs. 1590. 4. To shed (water or moisture) in drops; to exude 1634.

1. Now they 'gin to weepe The mischiefe they haue done B. JONSON. 2. When we vowe to weepe seas SHAKS. *To w. crocodile tears*, to feign grief (see CROCODILE 2). †*To w. millstones*, said of a hard-hearted person. 3. b. She wept her true eyes blind for such a one TENNYSON. Phil wept herself to sleep 1891. c. *To w.* (a thing) *back*, to recover it by weeping. *To w. out*, to remove, put out, extinguish, by weeping; also, to expend (one's life) in weeping. *To w. down*, to w. until the setting of (the sun). *To w. away*: (*a*) to spend, consume in tears and lamentation; (*b*) to remove or wash *away* with tears of commiseration. 4. Groves whose rich Trees wept odorous Gumms and Balme MILT.

Weeper (wī·pəɹ). late ME. [f. prec. + -ER [1].] 1. One who weeps or sheds tears, *esp.* one who is constantly weeping. b. *spec.* A hired mourner at a death-bed or funeral. late ME. c. One of a number of little images in niches on a funeral monument, representing mourners 1656. d. *Church Hist.* One of the lowest class of penitents (προσκλαίοντες, *flentes*) in the early Eastern Church 1841. 2. The Capuchin monkey (*Cebus capucinus*) of S. America 1781. 3. A conventional badge of mourning. Usu. *pl.* a. A strip of white linen or muslin formerly worn on the cuff of a man's sleeve (cf. F. *pleureuse*) 1724. b. A broad white cuff worn by widows 1755. c. A long black hat-band formerly worn by men 1832. d. The long black crape veil of a widow 1860. 4. Usu. *pl.* Long flowing side-whiskers as worn by 'Lord Dundreary' in the play *Our American Cousin* 1894. 5. A hole or pipe in a wall for the escape of dripping water 1890.

Weeping (wī·piŋ), *vbl. sb.* ME. [f. as prec. + -ING [1].] The action of the vb. in various senses; an instance of this.

Comb.: **w.-hole**, an opening through which moisture percolates; **-ripe** *a.*, ready to weep.

Weeping (wī·piŋ), *ppl. a.* OE. [f. as prec. + -ING [2].] 1. That weeps. 2. Tearful, lachrymose; accompanied with or expressed by weeping OE. 3. Falling or issuing in drops like tears. Now *rare*. 1686. 4. Exuding moisture; (of soil), oozing, swampy 1550. b. *Path.* Of the eyes: Running, watering. Also of diseased tissues or structures from which moisture exudes. 1580. 5. Of climate, skies, etc.: Dripping, rainy 1597. 6. Applied to trees (less usu. to other plants) the branches of which arch over and hang down drooping. Chiefly in distinctive names of particular species or varieties. 1606.

4. b. *W. eczema*, a variety of eczema characterized by abundant exudation. 6. *W. oak*, the Californian white oak, *Quercus lobata*; also, a cultivated variety of the English oak, *Quercus Robur*. Hence **Wee·pingly** *adv.*

Weeping Cross. 1575. A place-name occurring in several English counties, presumably indicating the site of a stone cross formerly known by this designation.

Provb. phr. *To come home by Weeping Cross*, to suffer grievous disappointment or failure.

Weeping willow. 1731. [See WEEPING *ppl. a.* 6. Cf. F. *saule pleureur*.] A species of willow, *Salix babylonica*, having long and slender pendulous branches, cultivated in Europe as an ornamental tree and regarded as symbolical of mourning.

Weepy (wī·pi), *a.* 1825. [f. WEEP *v.* + -Y [1].] 1. Inclined to weep or shed tears, tearful 1863. 2. *dial.* Exuding moisture, damp, oozy 1825.

Weeshy (wī·ʃi), *a.* *Anglo-Irish.* 1830. [Origin obsc. Cf. WEE *a.*] Very small, tiny.

Weet (wīt), *v.* [1] *arch.* 1547. [repr. ME. *wēte(n*, var. f. *wite(n* WIT *v.* Frequent as a literary archaism in 16th and 17th c.] a. *trans.* To know (a fact, the answer to a question). b. *intr.* To know of something.

Weet (wīt), *int.* and *v.* [2] 1852. [Echoic.] A. *int.* An imitation of the cry of certain small birds. B. *v. intr.* Of a bird: To chirp or twitter.

Weetless (wī·tlės), *a.* *arch.* 1579. [app. coined by Spenser; f. WEET *v.* [1] + -LESS.] Unknowing, unconscious. Also, †meaningless.

Weet-weet, *int.* and *sb.* [1] 1808. [Echoic.] A. *int.* (wī·tˌwī·t). An imitation of the cry of certain birds, esp. the sandpiper and chaffinch. Also *sb.* as the name for this cry. B. *sb.* (wī·t-wīt). The sandpiper 1852.

‖**Weet-weet** (wī·tˌwīt), *sb.* [2] 1878. [Native Australian.] An Australian toy, consisting of a head and a stem, and so constructed as to be capable of being thrown to a great distance.

Weever (wī·vəɹ). 1622. [prob. orig. *wīver*, a. OF. *wivre*, transf. use of *wivre* serpent, dragon, repr. L. *vipera* VIPER.] A fish of the genus *Trachinus* or family *Trachinidæ* (esp. *T. draco* the Greater, and *T. vipera* the Lesser W.), having sharp dorsal and opercular spines with which they can inflict painful wounds.

Weevil (wī·vĭl). [OE. *wifel* :—OTeut. **weðiloz*, f. **weð-* to move about briskly (see WAVE *v.*).] In OE., a beetle of any kind; in later use, any beetle classed under the group *Rhyncophora*, the larvæ of which, and sometimes the beetles themselves, are destructive by boring into grain, nuts, the bark of trees, etc.; *esp.* a beetle belonging to any species of the family *Curculionidæ*, the true weevils. Hence **Wee·vily** *a.* infested with weevils.

Weft [1] (weft). [OE. *wefta*, *weft*, repr. OTeut. types **wefton-*, **weftoz*, f. **weð-* to WEAVE.] 1. *Weaving.* The threads that cross from side to side of a web, at right angles to the warp threads with which they are interlaced. b. The strips of cane, palm-leaf, etc. used as the filling, in weaving baskets, mats, etc. 1845. 2. Yarn to be used for the weft-threads 1795. 3. That which is spun or woven. late ME. 4. *transf.* A layer of closely interwoven hyphæ produced in certain fungi 1875. 5. A streak of cloud; a thin layer of smoke or mist 1822. Hence **We·ftage**, the arrangement of the threads of a woven fabric. **We·fted** *a.* composed of interwoven hyphæ.

†**Weft.** [2] 1579. Variant or perversion of WAIF *sb.* [1] –1838.

Wegotism (wī·gǒtiz'm). 1797. [joc. f. WE *pron.* and EGOTISM.] An obtrusive and too frequent use of the first person plural by a speaker or writer.

Wehee (wĭhī·), *int.*, *sb.*, *v.* *Obs.* exc. *dial.* late ME. [Echoic.] A. *int.* A conventional representation of the sound uttered by horses. B. *sb.* An utterance of this sound; a whinny or neigh. late ME. †C. *v. intr.* To neigh or whinny, as a horse does –1847.

Weierstrassian (vəiəɹstrā·siăn), *a.* 1878. [f. name of Karl W. *Weierstrass* (1815–97), a German mathematician + -IAN.] *Math.* Pertaining to or invented by Weierstrass, esp. *W. function.*

‖**Weigel(i)a** (wəidʒī·lă, -ī·liă). 1846. [mod. L., f. name of C. E. *Weigel* (1748–1831), a German physician.] *Bot.* A genus of caprifoliaceous shrubs from China and Japan cultivated for its flowers; a plant of this genus.

Weigh (wēˡ), *sb.* [1] *Obs.* exc. *dial.* [OE. *wǽg*, *wǽge* :—OTeut. **wǣʒō-*, *-ōn-*, f. **wǣʒ-*; see WEIGH *v.*] A balance, pair of scales. †a. *sing.* –1450. b. *pl.* (sometimes construed as *sing.*). Now *dial.* OE.

Weigh (wēˡ), *sb.* [2] 1785. In *under w.*, common var. of *under way*, from erron. association with the phr. 'to weigh anchor'. See WAY *sb.*

Weigh (wēˡ), *v.* [Com. Teut. str. vb.; OE. *wegan* (*wæg*, *wǽgon*, *wegen*) :—Teut. **weʒ-*, *waʒ-*, *wǣʒ-* :—Indo-Eur. **wegh-*, *wēgh-*, *wogh-* (Gr. ϝόχος, ὄχος vehicle, L. *vehere* to convey, Skr. *vah* to carry). Related are WAG *v.*, WAGGON, WAIN *sb.*] I. To bear, carry; to heave up, lift. †1. *trans.* To bear from one place to another; to carry, transport. –late ME. 2. *Naut.* To heave up (a ship's anchor) from the ground, before sailing. Now usu. *to w. anchor.* ME. b. *absol.* = to w. anchor. Hence, to sail (*from*, *out of* a port, etc.). 1513. 3. To raise (a sunk ship, gun, etc.) from the bottom of the water. Also with *up.* 1500. II. To balance in the scales; to ascertain the weight of. 1. *trans.* To ascertain the exact heaviness of (an object or substance) by balancing it in a pair of scales, or on a steelyard, against a counterpoise of known amount. Also *absol.* OE. b. In Horse-racing. *To weigh out, in*: to take the weight of (a jockey) respectively before and after a race 1890. 2. To measure a definite quantity of (a substance) on the scales. Usu. with *out*: To portion out (a quantity measured by weight) from a larger mass; to apportion (such a quantity) *to* (a person or persons). late ME. 3. *intr.* in *Horse-racing.* Of a jockey: To take his place in the scales, in order that his declared weight may be verified by the clerk. *To w. out*, *in*, to do this before and after a race. 1805. b. Hence *To w. in with*: to introduce or produce (something that is additional or extra). *colloq.* 1885. 4. *trans.* To hold (an object) in the hand (or hands) in order to observe or estimate its weight; to balance an object in the hand as if estimating its weight 1540. 5. *fig.* To estimate, assess the value of (a person, quality, etc.) as if by placing in the scales ME. b. To balance *with* or *against* (another object regarded as a counterpoise) in order to a comparative estimate 1513. 6. To consider (a fact, circumstance, statement, etc.) in order to assess its value or importance; to balance in the mind with a view to choice or preference. late ME. b. To ponder and examine the force of (words or expressions) ME. c. with object-cl. Now *rare.* 1526. d. *To w. up*, to appraise, form an estimate of (a person). *colloq.* 1894. †7. To esteem, value, think highly of; to ascribe value or importance to. Often with negative: (Not) to care for or regard. Also with adj. compl. –1681.

3. *To w. in*, also of boxers before a fight, or in gen. use. 5. Not waiyng our merites, but pardonyng our offences *Bk. Com. Prayer.* b. Weighing anxiously prudence against sentiment LAMB. 6. I weighed the consequences on both sides as fairly as I could FIELDING. The jurymen..little accustomed to w. evidence MACAULAY. b. *To w. one's words*, to speak deliberately and in calculated terms. c. Let any one w. well what it is to translate such a collection of documents 1841. 7. All that she so deare did way, Thenceforth she left SPENSER. You waigh me not, O that 's you care not for me SHAKS.

III. To have heaviness or weight. 1. *intr.* To have a greater or less degree of heaviness, as measured by the scales. a. To be equal to or balance (a specified weight) in the scales OE. b. with adv. or pred. adj. ME. 2. *fig.* ME. †b. *To w. with*, to counterpoise in power, value, etc.; to be of equal value or importance with –1656. c. *To w. against*, to counterbalance, countervail. late ME. d. quasi-*trans.* To equal (something else) in weight or value 1583. 3. *intr.* To be of (much or little) value or account; to have influence *with* (a person) when he is forming an estimate or judgement. late ME.

2. For synne is not lyȝt, but it is hevy, and weythe more than lede 1440. b. *Timon* I. i. 146. d. The heads of all thy Brother-Cardinals..Weigh'd not a haire of his SHAKS. 3. In truth, their testimonie did little w. with me EVELYN.

IV. To affect, or be affected, by weight. 1. trans. *To w. down*: to draw, force, or bend down by pressure of weight; *fig.* to depress, oppress, lie heavy on ME. 2. Of an object set in the scales (with *down, up*): To turn the scale when weighed against (something else); to outweigh, cause to rise in the scale. Also *to w. down* (the balance or scale). late ME. **3.** *intr.* with *on* or *upon.* Of a thought, feeling, etc.: To lie heavy upon, depress (a person, his spirits, etc.) 1775.

1. Weighed down by this habitual Sorrow of Heart ADDISON. The people were weighed down by an insufferable taxation 1857. 2. *Rich. II*, III. iv. 89. One Whig shall w. down ten Tories SWIFT. 3. While care weighs on your brow KEATS. Something seemed to w. upon her spirits LYTTON.

Comb.: **w.-beam**, a balance or steelyard; **-box**, (*a*) one of a set of boxes, used in 'drawing' wool, in which the wool is more accurately weighed; (*b*) a w.-house; **-house**, a public building to which commodities are brought to be weighed; **-lock** *U.S.*, a canal-lock at which barges are weighed and their tonnage settled; **-man**, in a colliery, one who weighs the tubs of coal as they leave the cage at the pit-mouth; **-master**, the official in charge of a w.-house or public scales; **-out**, the verification of a jockey's declared weight before a race. Hence **Wei·ghable** *a.* that can be weighed; heavy enough to be weighed in scales. †**Wei·ghage**, a duty or toll paid for the weighing of goods. **Wei·gher**, a person employed to weigh commodities; an official appointed to w. or supervise weighing, to test weights, etc.

Wei·gh-bridge. 1796. A platform scale, flush with the road, for weighing vehicles, cattle, etc.

Weighing (wē¹·iŋ), *vbl. sb.* late ME. [f. WEIGH *v.* + -ING [1].] The action of WEIGH *v.*

Comb.: **w.-engine, -machine**, an apparatus (e.g. a combination of levers, a spring-balance) for weighing heavy bodies.

Weighment (wē¹·mĕnt). *India.* 1878. [f. WEIGH *v.* + -MENT, after *measurement.*] The action of weighing (commodities).

Wei·gh-scale. orig. *north.* ME. [ad. Du. *waagschaal* or MLG. *wageschale.* In recent use perh. a new formation.] The pan of a balance; *pl.* a pair of scales.

Weight (wē¹t), *sb.* [OE. *wiht*:—OTeut. **wehtiz*, f. root **weg-*; see WEIGH *v.* The normal mod. representative would be **wight*; the mod. vowel is mainly due to the vb.] **I.** Measurement of quantity by means of weighing; quantity as determined in this way. **1.** *By w.*: as determined by weighing. **2.** Assoc. with *measure* and *number*, esp. in fig. expressions referring to due proportion ME. **3.** Ponderability, as a general property of material substances; relative heaviness. late ME. **b.** Impetus (of a heavy falling body; also of a blow). late ME. **4.** The amount which an article of given price or value ought to weigh. late ME. **5.** Ponderable matter; that which weighs 1663.

3. As clocks to w. their nimble motion owe, The wheels above urg'd by the load below POPE. *fig.* I would rather be knock'd down By w. of argument than w. of fist WOLCOT. 4. It was near two ounces more than w. in a pound DE FOE. To see if the money he was going to pay was w. 1850. *Short w.*: see SHORT *a.* III. 1. Phr. *In w.*, added to adjs. such as *heavy, light*, etc. 5. Overcharged with W. laid upon them 1755.

II. An amount determined or determinable by weighing. **1.** A portion or quantity weighing a definite amount. Often preceded by an expression indicating the amount. Abbrev. *wt.* OE. **2.** *Its, his*, etc. *w. in* or *of gold, silver*, etc.: a quantity of gold, silver, etc. of the same weight. Chiefly in hyperbolical statements of value. ME. **3.** The amount that something weighs; the quantity of a portion of matter as measured by the amount of its downward force due to gravitation. late ME. **4.** A heavy mass; usu., something heavy that is lifted or carried; a burden. late ME. **5.** *spec.* **a.** In horse-racing or riding: The amount (expressed in stones and pounds) which the jockey or rider is expected or required to weigh or which the mount can without difficulty carry 1692. **b.** Without article 1734. **c.** *Boxing.* A match between boxers of a particular weight 1914.

3. The w. of an hayre will turne the Scales betweene their Haber-de-pois SHAKS. *fig.* We have seen such a system fall by its own w. 1794. People round us were not pulling their w. 1921. Phr. *Atomic w.* (Chem.), the relative w. of the atom of any element. *Live w.*: see LIVE *a.* 7. 4. The greater weighte that is cast on, the soner it breakes 1562. The simplest form of work is the raising of a w. TYNDALL. 5. b. He carries w.! he rides a race! COWPER.

III. *fig.* **1.** A burden (of responsibility, obligation, years, etc.). late ME. **2. a.** The force of an onslaught or encounter in the field; pressure exerted by numbers 1500. **b.** *To feel the w. of*, to suffer from (by receiving a heavy blow or undergoing severe pressure) 1553. **3.** Importance, moment, claim to consideration 1521. **4.** Persuasive or convincing power (of utterances, arguments, evidence); impressiveness (of matter or speech) 1534. **5.** Weightiest or heaviest part; greatest stress or severity; preponderance, superior amount on one side or the other of a question 1568. **6.** Influence or authority (of a person) due to character, position, wealth, or the like 1710.

1. The w. of seventy Winters prest him down DRYDEN. For my Part, I had a W. taken off from my Heart DE FOE. 2. b. He that ones wincheth shall fele the waite of my fiste 1553. 3. Obedience..due to them in matters of small waight 1583. The objection is of w. BURKE. 5. A new trial on the ground..that the verdict was against the w. of evidence 1883.

Phrases. *To lay w. upon*, to attach importance or value to. *To have w.*, to make an impression on, weigh *with* (those who judge a matter); to be recognized as valid or important; so *to carry w.* *To give* (full, due) *w. to*, to allow its proper force; to treat as valid or important.

IV. A standard of quantity determined by or employed in weighing. **1.** †**a.** A standard of weight. late ME. **b.** With qualifying word, as in *troy, avoirdupois w.*: Any of the systems used for stating the weight of a quantity of matter 1500. **2.** A unit or denomination of ponderable quantity ME. **b.** In pl. and coupled with *measures.* late ME. **3.** A piece of metal or other substance, weighing a known amount and identical with one of the units or with a multiple or aliquot part of a unit in some recognized scale ME. **b.** *Athletics.* A heavy lump of stone, or ball of metal, which is thrown from one hand placed close to the shoulder: chiefly in *putting the w.* 1865. **4.** A block or lump of metal or other heavy substance, or a heavy object, used to pull or press down something, to give an impulse to machinery (e.g. in a clock), to act as a counterpoise, or the like. late ME.

2. b. Certaine brief Tables of English waights, and Measures 1596.

attrib. and *Comb.*: **w.-clock**, a clock operated by weights; **-plate**, a plate on which articles are set to be weighed in a weighing-machine. Hence **Wei·ghtless** *a.* without w., having comparatively little w.

Weight (wē¹t), *v.* 1647. [f. prec.] †**1.** *trans.* To oppress the mind; also *pass.*, to be oppressed in mind or spirit –1728. **2.** To load with a weight; to supply with an additional weight; to make weighty 1747. **b.** *techn.* To add weight to (an inferior commodity) by the admixture or use of an adulterant 1862. **c.** *Statistics.* To multiply the components of (an average) by compensating factors 1901. **3.** To assign to (a horse) the weight he must carry in a handicap race 1846. Hence **Wei·ghting** *vbl. sb.* the action of the vb.; *concr.* something used as a weight to press down, steady, or balance.

Weighty (wē¹·ti), *a.* 1489. [f. WEIGHT *sb.* + -Y [1].] **I. 1.** Of a considerable or appreciable weight; that weighs a good deal, heavy 1500. **b.** Of persons or animals: Of more than the usual size, large or bulky of body 1581. **c.** Of great weight in proportion to its bulk, of high specific gravity 1585. **2.** Bearing down heavily as if weighted or of great weight; falling with force or violence 1583.

1. c. It look'd like a fungus, but was w. like metall EVELYN. 2. [I]..Prest the sinking sands With w. steps POPE.

II. 1. a. Of great gravity or significance; highly important, serious, grave, momentous 1489. **b.** Of a substantial or solid nature; ranking high in respect of importance or value 1558. **2. a.** Of an argument, etc.: Producing a powerful effect; adapted to influence or convince 1560. **b.** Of persons: Having great authority or influence; important in respect of position, views, or utterance 1662. **3.** Hard to bear or endure without failing or giving way; oppressive; burdensome 1540. †**b.** Rigorous, severe. SHAKS. †**4.** Expressing seriousness or gravity, earnest, solemn –1677.

1. a. 1 *Hen. VI*, II. i. 62. b. Were they weightie Treatises? NASHE. 2. b. There is not any necessity that men should aim at being important and w. in every sentence they speak 1729. 4. *Hen. VIII*, Prol. I. 2. Hence **Wei·ghti·ly** *adv.*, **-ness.**

Weir (wī³r), *sb.* [OE. *wer*, f. stem of *werian* to dam up.] **1.** A barrier or dam to restrain water, *esp.* one placed across a river or canal in order to raise or divert the water for driving a mill wheel; now gen., a dam constructed on the reaches of a canal or navigable river to retain the water and regulate its flow. **2.** A fence or enclosure of stakes made in a river, harbour, etc., for taking or preserving fish OE. **b.** A weel for catching fish 1611. **3.** A pond or pool. *Obs.* exc. *dial.* ME. **4.** *local.* A fence or embankment to prevent the encroachment of a river or sea-sand, or to turn the course of a stream 1599.

attrib. and *Comb.*: **w.-hatch**, the flood-gate or sluice of a w.; **w. house**, a trap for salmon at a salmon w. Hence **Weir** *v. trans.* (usu. in pa. pple.) to provide with a w. **Wei·ring** *vbl. sb.* the constructing of a w. or weirs; *concr.* materials used for making a w.

Weird (wī³ɹd), *sb.* Now *Sc.* or *arch.* [OE. *wyrd*, from the wk. grade of the stem **werþ-*, *warþ-*, *wurþ-* to become.] **1.** The principle, power, or agency by which events are predetermined; fate, destiny. **2.** *pl.* The Fates OE. **b.** One pretending or supposed to have the power to foresee and to control future events 1625. **3.** That which is destined or fated to happen to a particular person, etc.; one's appointed lot or fortune, destiny OE. **b.** *spec.* An evil fate inflicted by supernatural power, esp. by way of retribution 1874. **4. a.** A happening, event, occurrence OE. **b.** That which is destined or fated to happen; predetermined events collectively 1470. **c.** A supernatural or marvellous occurrence or tale 1814.

2. b. With this green nettle And cross of metal I witches and wierds defy 1899. 3. My w. maun be fulfilled SCOTT. *To dree one's w.*: see DREE *v.* 1. 4. a. Prov. *After word comes w.*, the mention of a thing is followed by its occurrence or appearance. Hence **Wei·rdly** *a. Sc.* (*a*) favoured by fate, prosperous; (*b*) pertaining to or suggestive of witchcraft or the supernatural.

Weird (wī³ɹd), *a.* late ME. [orig. attrib. use of prec. in *weird sisters* (see sense 1).] **1.** Having the power to control the fate or destiny of men; claiming such power. Orig. in *the W. Sisters* = †(*a*) the Fates; (*b*) the witches in Shakespeare's *Macbeth*. **2.** Partaking of or suggestive of the supernatural; of a mysterious or unearthly character; uncanny 1817. **3.** Of strange or unusual appearance, odd-looking 1815. **4.** Out of the ordinary course, strange, unusual; hence, odd, fantastic 1820.

2. Awakened by a w. and unearthly moaning 1876. 3. Mutable As shapes in the w. clouds SHELLEY. 4. A w. belief..that no one could count the stones of Stonehenge twice, and make the same number of them DICKENS. Hence **Wei·rdish** *a.* somewhat w. **Wei·rd·ly** *adv.*, **-ness.**

Weird (wī³ɹd), *v.* *Sc.* and †*north.* ME. [f. WEIRD *sb.*] **1.** *trans.* To preordain by the decree of fate; esp. in *pass.* to be destined or divinely appointed *to.* **2.** To assign to (a person) as his fate, destiny, or lot 1550.

Weism (wī·iz'm). 1800. [f. WE *pron.* + -ISM, after EGOISM.] The too frequent use of 'we' (see WE *pron.* 2 b) by a speaker or writer.

Weismannian (vəi·smæniăn), *a.* and *sb.* 1903. [f. as next + -IAN.] **A.** *adj.* Of or pertaining to Weismann or his biological theory. **B.** *sb.* One who accepts the theory of Weismannism.

Weismannism (vəi·smăniz'm). 1894. [f. name *Weismann* + -ISM.] The theory of evolution and heredity propounded by the German biologist, August Weismann, esp. in regard to the continuity of the germ-plasm and the non-transmission of acquired characteristics.

Weissite (vəi·səit). 1836. [f. name of C. S. *Weiss*, German crystallographer + -ITE [1] 2 b.] *Min.* An altered form of iolite.

Weka (we·ka, wē¹·kă, wī·kă). 1845. [Maori, so named from its cry.] Either of the flightless rails, *Ocydromus australis* and *O. brachypterus* of New Zealand.

Welcome (we·lkŏm), *sb.*[1], *int.*, and *a.* [orig. OE. *wilcuma* (f. *wil-* desire, pleasure + *cuma* comer), with later alteration of first element to *wel-* WELL *adv.* under influence of OF. *bien venu* (or ON. *velkominn*).] †**A.** *sb.* One whose coming is pleasing or desirable; an acceptable person or thing. OE. only. **B.** *predic.*, passing into *adj.* **1.** Of a person: Acceptable as a visitor, companion, etc.; also in phr. *to make* (a person) *w.* OE. **b.** *attrib.* 1579. **2.** Of a thing: Acceptable, agreeable, pleasing ME. **b.** *attrib.* 1577. **3.** Freely permitted or allowed, cordially invited (*to* do or have something) ME.

1. The oftner they come to him, the welcomer they are 1667. **b.** They..with full Mirth receive the w. Guest PRIOR. **2.** Praise is not so w. to the Idler as quiet JOHNSON. **b.** He hath brought vs smooth and w. newes SHAKS. **3.** You're very w. to pass another night here DICKENS. *And w.*, added to a statement to imply: and he is (you are, etc.) freely permitted or cordially invited to do so, to have it, or the like; And if this be done, let them judge and w. 1755.

C. Used in the vocative as a form of address to a visitor or guest; hence as *int.*, serving as an expression of good will or pleasure at the coming of a person OE.

To bid, wish (a person) *w.* (*home*), to tell him that he is gladly received (*home*, as a guest, etc.). Hence **We·lcome·ly** *adv.*, **-ness.**

Welcome (we·lkŏm), *sb.*² 1525. [f. prec. or next.] **1.** An assurance to a visitor or stranger that he is welcome; a pleasant or hearty greeting or reception given to a person on arrival. **b.** *transf.* (esp. with *adjs.*) A greeting or reception of an unpleasant or unsatisfactory nature 1548. **2.** *W. home*: entertainment provided to celebrate the return home of a person; also, expressions of greeting made at a person's homecoming 1530. **3.** Hearty or hospitable reception of a stranger or guest 1590. **4.** A welcoming salute 1615.

1. And to thee, and thy Company, I bid A hearty w. SHAKS. *To outstay* or *overstay one's w.*, to remain in a place longer than one is desired. **b.** We met but with a cold w. 1725. **3.** Small cheere and great w., makes a merrie feast SHAKS.

Welcome (we·lkŏm), *v.* [orig. OE. *wilcumian*, f. *wilcuma* WELCOME *sb.*¹, with later alteration of the first element, as in the noun.] **1.** *trans.* To greet (a person) with 'welcome!'; to receive gladly and hospitably; to make welcome. Also const. *to, into* (a place), and with advs. of place, as *back*; esp. *to w. home.* **2.** To greet or receive *with* (or *by*) something (esp. of an unpleasant nature) 1590. **3.** To greet heartily or with pleasure (the return of a person, the occurrence of an event, etc.) 1697.

1. I know no cause Why I should w. such a guest as greefe SHAKS. Your wiues shall w. home the Conquerors SHAKS. **2.** If you return..you will be welcomed by a brace of bullets 1791. Hence **We·lcomer,** one who, or something which, welcomes or greets (a person or thing). **We·lcoming** *ppl. a.* that welcomes or gives a welcome.

Weld (weld), *sb.*¹ late ME. [OE. **wealde* = MLG. *walde*, MDu. *woude.*] The plant *Reseda Luteola*, which yields a yellow dye. Also, the dye obtained from this plant.

Weld (weld), *sb.*² 1831. [f. next.] **1.** A joining or joint made by welding. **2.** The act, process, or result of welding; the state or fact of being welded 1862. Hence **We·ldless** *a.* made without a w.

Weld (weld), *v.* 1599. [Altered f. WELL *v.*, q.v. sense 2.] **1.** *intr.* To undergo junction by welding; to admit of being welded. **2.** *trans.* To soften by heat and join together (pieces of metal, esp. iron or iron and steel) in a solid mass, by hammering or by pressure; to forge (an article) by this method 1677.

2. A steel blade welded to a wrought-iron socket 1880. Hence **We·ldable** *a.* capable of being welded; so **Weldabi·lity.** **We·lder,** one who welds; *spec.* a smith employed exclusively in welding.

Welding (we·ldiŋ), *vbl. sb.* 1603. [f. prec. + -ING¹.] The action of the vb. WELD; the process of joining with a weld. **b.** Capacity for uniting under the operation of heat and pressure 1825.

Comb.: **w. heat,** the degree of heat to which iron is brought for w.; **w. point,** degree of heat requisite for w.; **w. powder,** a flux used in w.

Welfare (we·lfēəɹ), *sb.* ME. [f. the verbal phr. *wel fare* (WELL *adv.* II. 3, FARE *v.*¹ 8).] The state or condition of doing or being well; good fortune, happiness, or well-being (of a person, community, or thing); prosperity.

One continued Series of Actions, for the W. of the People 1718. Her first wish in life is for your happiness and w. 1838.

Comb. in sense 'concerned with or devoted to the w.' (of workers, etc.), as *w. policy, work, -worker.*

†**We·lfare,** *vbl. phr.* 1534. [f. as prec.] The optative phr. *well fare* (you, it, etc.) = 'May it go well with', 'good luck to' -1672.

‖**Weli, -y** (we·li). 1819. [Arab.] **1.** A Mohammedan saint. **2.** A tomb or shrine of this 1838.

Welk (welk), *v.* *Obs.* exc. *dial.* [ME. *welken*, prob. of Continental origin.] **1.** *intr.* Of a flower, plant, etc.: To lose freshness or greenness; to wilt, wither, fade. **2.** *trans.* To cause to fade or wither 1579. Hence **Welked** *ppl. a.*

Welkin (we·lkin). [OE. *wolcen, wolcn* = OFris. *wolcn-*, OS. *wolcan*, OHG. *wolkan.*] †**1.** A cloud -ME. **2.** The apparent arch or vault of heaven overhead; the sky, the firmament. (In later use chiefly *poet.* and *dial.*) ME. **3.** The upper atmosphere; the region of the air in which the clouds float, birds fly, etc. late ME.

2. *By the w.*; This villanous poetrie will vndoe you, by the w. B. JONSON. *To make the w. ring, to rend the w.*, etc., said of loud sounds; Making the w. ring with the music of their deep-toned notes SURTEES.

Well (wel), *sb.* [Anglian form of OE. *wielle* and **wiell* (*wyll, will*), f. stem of *weallan* to boil or bubble up.] **1.** A spring of water rising to the surface of the earth and forming a small pool or flowing in a spring. Now *arch.* or *dial.* **b.** A spring of water supposed to be of miraculous origin or to have supernatural healing powers; also, a medicinal or mineral spring OE. **c.** *pl.* A place where medicinal springs exist; a watering-place or spa (cf. the place-name *Wells*) 1673. **2.** *transf.* and *fig.* **a.** In allusive contexts directly suggestive of the nature or uses of a spring OE. **b.** That from which something springs or arises; a source or origin OE. **c.** Applied to persons regarded as a source or abundant manifestation of some quality or virtue ME. **d.** A whirlpool 1654. **3.** A pit dug in the ground to obtain a supply of spring-water; *spec.* a vertical excavation, usu. circular in form and lined with masonry, sunk to such a depth as to penetrate a water-bearing stratum OE. **4.** *Naut.* **a.** A vertical shaft protecting the pump below the lower (or upper) deck in a ship's hold 1611. **b.** A cistern or tank in a fishing-boat, in which the catch of fish is preserved alive 1614. **5.** A shaft or pit bored or dug in the ground. In various specific uses. **a.** An excavation for the storage of ice 1681. **b.** A shaft sunk to obtain oil, brine, gas, etc. 1799. **c.** A shaft to carry water through a retentive to a porous stratum or to a drain 1856. **d.** A hollow cylinder or shaft of masonry sunk and filled in solid to form a foundation 1885. **6. a.** The central open space, from roof to basement, of a winding, spiral, or elliptical staircase; the open space in which a lift operates 1700. **b.** The space on the floor of a law-court where the solicitors sit 1853. **c.** A deep narrow space formed by the surrounding walls of a building or buildings, serving for the access of light and air 1859. **7.** In *Ship-* and *Boat-building*, applied to various vertical apertures 1874. **8. a.** A box-like receptacle in the body of a vehicle, for articles of luggage 1783. **b.** A deep receptacle at the bottom of a piece of furniture, esp. of one fitted with trays, drawers, etc. 1841. **9.** A hole or cavity containing or to contain a liquid. **a.** The water-tank at the base of a shot-tower, into which the drops of melted lead fall 1851. **b.** A cavity at the bottom of a furnace, into which the molten metal falls 1864. **c.** A sunk receptacle for a liquid, as ink (*ink-w.*), etc. 1873.

1. **b.** Where meete we?..At Saint Gregories w. SHAKS. **2. a.** O sleep,..Holding unto our lips thy goblet filled Out of Oblivion's w. LONGF. **b.** Understandyng is a w. of life vnto him that hath it BIBLE (Great) *Prov.* xvi. 22. **c.** Dan Chaucer, w. of English vndefyled SPENSER. **3.** No: 'tis not so deepe as a w., nor so wide as a Church doore, but 'tis inough SHAKS. *fig.* With ioy shall yee draw water out of the wels of saluation *Isaiah* xii. 3. Provb. phr. If Truth, as Democritus fansied, lies at the bottom of a deep W. 1691. 'He 's as deep as a w.' 1860. *A w. of a* (place), like a w., as being damp and cold, or deep and dark; The veriest old w. of a shivering best-parlour that ever was seen DICKENS. **4. a.** *To sound the w.*, to ascertain, by means of a sounding-rod, the depth of water in the hold.

Comb.: **w.-beam,** the wooden beam or roller over which the rope of a w.-bucket runs; **-boat,** a fishing boat provided with a w.; **-bucket,** a bucket used to draw water from a w. by means of a rope and pulley or windlass; **-curb,** the stone border round the mouth of a w.; **-deck,** an open space on the main deck of a ship, lying at a lower level between the forecastle and poop; **-dish,** a meat-dish with a depression at one end as a receptacle for gravy; **-drain** *Agric.*, a drain for wet land with a boring through which the water rises to be carried off by the drain; **-grate,** a grate in which the fire burns on the hearth, receiving its air supply from below; **-house,** a small building or room enclosing a w. and its apparatus; **-staircase, -stairs, -stairway,** a winding or geometrical staircase with a w. or open centre; **-trap,** a depression in a drain, in which water lies and prevents the escape of foul air; **-water,** water issuing, or drawn, from a w. or spring.

Well (wel), *a.* (*predic.*). ME. [Arising from WELL *adv.* in impers. use of sense II. 3.] **1.** In a state of good fortune, welfare, or happiness -1825. **2.** In favour, in good standing or estimation, on good terms *with* (a person) ME. **b.** *spec.* On terms of intimate friendship or familiarity *with* (a woman) 1704. **3.** = WELL OFF 1 c. Now *rare* exc. in *w. to do, w. off.* late ME. **b.** = WELL OFF 1 a. Now *rare.* 1440. **4.** In a sound or undamaged state; *spec.* in marine insurance, of a vessel 1450. **5.** Sound in health; free or recovered from sickness or infirmity 1555. **b.** *attrib.*, esp. with *man.* Now only *U.S.* 1628. **c.** *absol.* (as pl.) Those who are sound in health 1676. **d.** Of a person's health or spirits: Sound, good. Of sickness: Cured. 1712. **6.** In phr. (*It is*) *w.* (*that*) or *to*: **a.** Advisable, desirable, to be recommended 1475. **b.** Fortunate, lucky; forming a matter for satisfaction or thankfulness 1665. **c.** *As w... if* or *that*, in preceding senses 1753. **7.** Of a state of things, an undertaking, etc.: Satisfactory; of such a nature or in such a condition as to meet with approval. Also, formerly, of material things. late ME. **8.** Good; of a character or quality to which no exception can be taken. *arch.* or *Obs.* 1661. **9.** †**a.** Of good or satisfactory appearance -1748. **b.** *W. to see, to be seen*: good to look upon, comely (*rare*) 1804. **10.** In concessive use, followed by an objection or contrary view expressed or implied 1560.

1. O w. were wee in the daies of Queene Elizabeth 1595. **2.** Good reasons for standing w. with his neighbours 1883. **3.** *To leave* (a person) *w.*, *to be w. left*, to leave or be left w. off by devise or inheritance. **b.** Apparently they found themselves very w. as they were M. ARNOLD. **5.** Where young Adonis oft reposes, Waxing w. of his deep wound MILT. *Not w.* = UNWELL *a.* *W. day*, a day on which one is free from sickness, esp. from an attack of an intermittent disorder. **d.** He had..determined, if his cold was w. enough, to ride over to Snailswell SURTEES. **6. a.** 'Twer w., It were done quickly SHAKS. **c.** I think it would be as w. if John was to go off..this afternoon 1801. **7.** Though it is vastly w. to be here for a few weeks, we would not live here for millions J. AUSTEN. *Prov.* All is w. that endes well HEYWOOD. *To let* (or *leave*) *w. alone*, to refrain from trying to make better that which is already w. *All's w.*, a sentry's reply when he has received the password in answer to his challenge. **8.** No weakness,..or blame, nothing but w. and fair MILT. **10.** *It is all very w.*, it is right and proper in itself or under certain circumstances; Written contracts are all very w., but if the contractor stops payment—where are you? RUSKIN. *He* (*it*, etc.) *is all very w.*, *is w. enough*, there is no fault to be found with him, it, etc. *W. and good* (without vb.); 'If you like to bow and scrape to rich people, w. and good', I said 1888.

Well (wel), *v.* Now only *literary* or *dial.* [OE. *wiellan* (Anglian *wællan, wellan*), causative of *weallan* to boil.] †**1.** *trans.* To boil -1450. †**2.** To liquefy (metal) by heat; to cast, found -1570. **b.** To weld. *Obs.* exc. *dial.* late ME. **3.** *intr.* To boil. Also with *up.* late ME. **4.** Of liquids, esp. of a well or spring of water: To rise (*up*) to the surface (of the earth) and flow in a copious stream. late ME. **5.** Of tears: To rise (*up*) to the eyes in a copious flood. late ME. **6.** Of blood or corrupt matter: To flow from the body, a wound, or sore. late ME. **7.** *fig.* To spring or originate; to issue or flow *forth* or *out* ME. **8.** *trans.* Of a spring, etc.: To pour forth (water, etc.). late ME.

4. *transf.* What sweet sounds from her fast-closed lips are welling KINGSLEY. Smoke welled slowly through the leaves 1895. *To w. over*: (*lit.* and *fig.*) to overflow; His heart welled over with joy 1883. **8.** *fig.* Mary welle of mercy, wellyng euer pite 1425.

Well (wel), *adv.* [Com. Teut.; OE. *wel*(*l*. The stem is regarded as identical with that of WILL *sb.*¹, *v.*¹ and ².] **I. 1.** In accordance with a good or high standard of conduct or morality; in a way which is morally good. **b.** Satisfactorily in respect of conduct or action OE. **2.** In such a manner as to constitute good treatment or confer a benefit; kindly, considerately; in a kind and friendly manner; with favour or welcome OE. **b.** With equanimity or good nature; without resentment. Chiefly with *take*. 1753. **3.** With courage and spirit; gallantly, bravely. ME.

1. **b.** Ye swear that ye w. and trulie shall serve our Sovraigne Lord the King 1534. **2.** We grete you wele 1483. Each man desireth to bee w. thought of 1576. His forward voyce now is to speake w. of his friend SHAKS. He was w. receiv'd at Court 1706. At least I meant w. 1729. We wished the man w. DICKENS. *To deserve w. of*, to be entitled to gratitude or good treatment from.

II. 1. Faithfully; heedfully, carefully, attentively OE. **2.** In a way appropriate to the facts or circumstances; fittingly, properly OE. **3.** Prosperously, successfully, fortunately, happily; without harm or accident OE. **4. a.** In a state of plenty or comfort OE. **b.** Satisfactorily or excellently in respect of health or recovery from illness: usu. with *do*. 1440. **5.** With good reason; as a natural result or consequence OE. **6.** Without difficulty or hindrance; readily, easily OE. **b.** Denoting the possibility or likelihood of an occurrence or fact. late ME. **c.** In negative or comparative clauses 1523.

1. Take him and looke w. to him, and doe him no harme *Jer.* xxxix. 12. After thinking the matter w. over, we have determined not to compete 1873. **2.** This is wel sayd, saide Morgan le fay MALORY. I think it will do very w. RICHARDSON. *To do w.*, to act prudently or sensibly; You will do w. to keep a watchful eye over..Villiams SMOLLETT. **3.** What a father doth to marie his daughter wel, is to give her a great portion 1604. In Iudah things went w. 2 *Chron.* xii. 12. Blessing ourselves that we had come off so w. SMOLLETT. All went w. as far as the foot of the ice-fall 1899. Formerly freq. in impers. construction †*Well is me* (etc.): I (etc.) am fortunate or happy. Wel is me that I haue mette with you MALORY. **4. a.** He would be able to live w. and good all his days 1874. **b.** A fine child, and the Queen doing w. 1841. **5.** Back to the Thicket slunk The guiltie Serpent, and w. might MILT. A regulation of which the legality might w. be questioned MACAULAY. **6.** Nor were the refugees such as a country can w. spare MACAULAY. **b.** This was as strong a case as could w. come before the Court 1818. **c.** He can praise a sharp remark before it is w. out of another's mouth JOWETT.

III. 1. Effectively; successfully as regards result or progress OE. **2.** In a manner, or to an extent, approaching thoroughness or completeness OE. **3.** Used as an intensive to strengthen the idea implied in the verb, or to denote that the action, etc., indicated by it attains a high point or degree. Similarly with pa. pples. OE. **4.** Clearly, definitely, without any doubt or uncertainty ME. **b.** Intimately, familiarly; closely, in detail ME. **5.** In a skilful or expert manner OE. **b.** In a sufficient or satisfactory manner ME. **c.** With good appearance or effect; elegantly ME.

1. The printer gets on w. with my History SOUTHEY. **2.** The market here is not very w. supplied 1799. **3.** Wel loued he garleek, oynons, and eek lekes CHAUCER. W. instructed in sciences 1538. Many moo..had w. deserued to be whipped UDALL. Your plainnesse and your shortnesse please me w. SHAKS. I am neither w. litter'd, nor w. provender'd..nor indeed w. any thing'd 1639. The twain had got on very w. together 1877. **4.** The parties know perfectly w...what are the points in dispute 1895. **b.** He being w. known to us all STEELE. **5. b.** She appears moping, but eats very w. 1855. **c.** Carrying my six feet w. 1898.

IV. As an intensive with adjs., numerals, advs., etc. OE.

They were wel at peace, when I did leaue 'em SHAKS. A seemely..tree, and w. worth the hauing 1612. Nor w. alive nor wholly dead they were DRYDEN. You are w. able to settle this affair STEELE. The Captain stood w. to the westward, to run inside the Bermudas 1840. She held her head w. up 1883.

V. 1. As w. as: a. In as good, efficient, satisfactory (etc.) a way or manner as. late ME. **b.** To the same extent, in the same degree, as much, as. late ME. **c.** With weakened force, passing into the sense of 'both..and', 'not only..but also'. late ME. **d.** Used to denote the inclusion of one thing or class with another 1449. **2. As w: a.** Also, in addition; in the same way ME. **b.** With *may*, *might*, etc., implying the equivalence or equal result of one action in comparison with another 1440. **3.** With qualifying adv. prefixed, as *too w.*, *pretty w.* OE. **b.** *W. enough*: sufficiently well, adequately. late ME.

2. **b.** He thought he might as w. strive to promote his own ends 1870. **3. b.** The vulgar translation is known welinough 1585.

VI. Employed without construction to introduce a remark or statement, sometimes implying that the speaker accepts a situation, etc., already expressed or indicated, or desires to qualify this in some way, but frequently used merely as a preliminary or resumptive word OE. **b.** *sb.* An instance of this use of the word 1866.

W., my boy, what have you brought us from the fair? GOLDSM. W., and what of that? 1826. *W., w.*, denoting surprise, resignation, or acquiescence; W., w., you may banter as long as you please STEELE. *Very w.*, denoting agreement, approval, or acquiescence. *W. then*, introducing a conclusion or further statement, or implying that one can naturally be drawn or made.

Comb.: *Well* is extensively employed in comb. with various parts of the vb., esp. the past and present pples., and in parasynthetic adjs. ending in *-ed*. In modern practice the latter are regularly hyphened. The more important are entered as Main words; the following illustrate the wider extent of the use with some indications of date; *well-aimed* CHAPMAN, *-aired* SCOTT, *-apaid* (= satisfied) ME. and mod. dial., *-apparelled* SHAKS., *-applied* SIDNEY, *-appointed* COVERDALE, *-approved* SPENSER, *-armed* ME., *-arrayed* CHAUCER, *-attested* GLANVILL, *-behaved* SHAKS., *-bodied* 1481, *-built* CHAPMAN, *-clad* CAXTON, *-concerted* POPE, *-conducted* 1749, *-considered* 1769, *-covered* 1697, *-cultivated* CONGREVE, *-cut* COWLEY, *-defined* NEWTON, *-deserved* *-directed* SIDNEY, *-disciplined* 1595, *-dressed* 1576, *-earned* THOMSON, *-educated* SHAKS., *-endowed* LOCKE, *-established* 1709, *-featured* 1500, *-fed* CHAUCER, *-filled* CHAPMAN, *-flavoured* 1771, *-formed* 1520, *-framed* SIDNEY, *-furnished* 1474, *-governed* late ME., *-horsed* late ME., *-inclined* SIDNEY, *-informed* 1440, *-instructed* 1553, *-intended* SIDNEY, *-intentioned* 1598, *-kept* late ME., *-learned* 1426, *-lettered* ME., *-limbed* LYDG., *-looked* PEPYS, *-looking* STEELE, *-managed* 1665, *-manned* 1450, *-marked* 1797, *-matched* DRYDEN, *-minded* SIR T. MORE, *-mounted* SHAKS., *-mouthed* late ME., *-natured* 1561, *-ordered* SHAKS., *-placed* CHAPMAN, *-pleased* LYDG., *-polished* CHAPMAN, *-practised* SPENSER, *-prepared* SPENSER, *-proportioned* CHAUCER, *-proved* PECOCK, *-regulated seasoned* 1583, *-shaped* ME., *-shapen* late ME., *-skilled* SHAFTESB., *-remembered* 1482, *-rooted* CHAPMAN, UDALL, *-sounding* ME., *-spread* 1577, *-stocked* MILTON, *-stored* 1591, *-tasted* COWLEY, *-taught* CHAUCER, *-timbered* SPENSER, *-toned* 1460, *-trained* CHAPMAN, *-trimmed* 1667, *-tuned* COVERDALE, *-watered* 1450, *-weighed* SIDNEY, *-won* SHAKS., *-woven* SPENSER, *-written* 1598.

Such compounds carry even stress (or strong secondary stress on *well-*) when used predicatively, but *well-* bears the main stress in attributive positions.

Well(-)acquai·nted, *ppl. a.* 1565. †**1.** Familiarly known (to others) –1590. **2.** Having a good acquaintance *with* a person or thing; familiar *with*. Also without const. 1728.

1. *Com. Err.* IV. iii. 2. **2.** Time was when Love and I were well acquainted W. S. GILBERT.

Welladay (we·lădēⁱ), *int.* (*sb.*) Now *arch.* and *dial.* 1570. [Altered f. WELLAWAY, by substitution of DAY, as in *lackaday*.] **A.** *int.* An exclam. expressing sorrow or lamentation; = alas! **b.** redupl. *wella, welladay* 1805. **B.** *sb.* The utterance of this; lamentation, a lament 1582.

Well(-)advi·sed, *ppl. a.* (In mod. use chiefly *predic.*) late ME. **1.** Of persons: Prudent, wary, circumspect. **b.** In one's right mind, sane. SHAKS. **2.** Of actions, etc.: Based on wise counsel or careful consideration 1470.

Well(-)affe·cted, *ppl. a.* 1563. **1.** Favourably disposed, inclined to be favourable or friendly; *spec.*, well-disposed towards existing authority, loyal. **2.** Adroitly assumed or simulated 1907.

Well-anea·r, *int.* *Obs.* exc. *dial.* 1600. [app. altered f. WELLAWAY by substitution of ANEAR.] Alas, alack-a-day!

Wellaway (we·lăwēⁱ), *int.* and *sb.* *arch.* [OE. *weg lá weg, wei lá wei*, alteration of *wá lá wá* by substitution of OScand. *wei for OE. *wá*.] **A.** *int.* An exclam. of sorrow or lamentation. **B.** *sb.* The utterance of this; hence, lamentation, a lament ME.

Well-ba·lanced, *ppl. a.* 1629. **1.** Exactly poised or equilibrated. **2.** Having an orderly or harmonious disposition of parts 1859. **3.** Having or betokening a good balance of the mental faculties; sane and sensible; not flighty or eccentric 1861.

Well-being (we·lˌbī·iŋ, we·lˌbī·iŋ), *vbl. sb.* 1613. [After F. *bien-être*, mod.L. *bene esse*.] The state of being or doing well in life; happy, healthy, or prosperous condition; welfare. **b.** Satisfactory condition (of a thing) 1702.

Most healthy persons feel..a sense of w. after a meal 1883. **b.** His loudly-expressed anxiety..respecting the..w. of the two bags, the leather hat-box, and the brown-paper parcel DICKENS.

Well-belo·ved, *ppl. a.* and *sb.* late ME. **A.** *ppl. a.* **1.** Dearly loved, greatly beloved. **2.** In letters, etc., of a sovereign or lord, prefixed to the names or designations of the persons addressed or referred to. Usu. '(right) trusty and w.' late ME. **B.** *sb.* A dearly loved one. late ME.

A bundle of myrrhe is my welbeloued vnto me *Cant.* i. 13.

Well(-)born, *ppl. a.* OE. **1.** Of good birth or lineage, of gentle blood. **b.** *absol.* 1787. **2.** [after F. *bien-né*.] Having the personal qualities naturally associated with good birth; noble in nature or character 1450.

Well-breathed (-brīðd, -breþt), *a.* 1470. Sound or strong of wind; exercised so as to be in good wind; not out of breath.

Well-bred, *ppl. a.* 1597. **1.** Of good family and upbringing. Usu., displaying good breeding; having refined manners; courteous in speech and behaviour. **b.** of speech, behaviour, etc. 1699. **2.** Of animals: Of good breed or stock 1815.

Well(-)cho·sen, *ppl. a.* 1586. Carefully or happily selected; esp. of words or language.

A w. Library 1697. The Conversation of a well chosen Friend ADDISON. A w. epithet 1828.

Well-condi·tioned, *a.* 1482. **1.** Of good disposition, morals, or behaviour; right-minded. **2.** Having a good physical condition; being in a sound, healthy, or satisfactory state; *spec.* in *Surg.*, of a wound, etc. 1613. **3.** Established on good terms or conditions 1645.

Well(-)conne·cted, *ppl. a.* 1734. **1.** Linked together in good order or sequence; exhibiting proper sequence or coherence of thought. **2.** Of good family and connexions. Also *absol.* 1840.

Well(-)conte·nt, *a.* *arch.* 1440. Highly pleased, gratified, or satisfied. So **Well-conte·nted** *ppl. a.* 1555.

We·ll-cress. Now *dial.* [OE. *wyllecærse*; see WELL *sb.* and CRESS.] Water-cress, *Nasturtium officinale.*

†**Well-dese·rver.** 1617. One who deserves well (*of* another) –1709.

Well-dispo·sed, *ppl. a.* late ME. †**1.** In good physical condition; healthy –1716. **2.** Suitably or skilfully placed, arranged, or adjusted 1470. **3.** Of good disposition; *esp.* disposed to be friendly or favourable 1455.

Well-doing (we·lˌdū·iŋ), *vbl. sb.* late ME. **1.** The action or practice of doing good; virtuous life and behaviour. **2.** Thriving condition; health, prosperity, success. late ME.

1. Brethren be not weary in well doynge TINDALE. **2.** *Thess.* iii. 13. So **We·ll-do·er.** **We·ll-do·ing** *ppl. a.* that does good or well; diligent in performance of work or duty; well-behaved ME.

Well(-)done (we·lˌdɒ·n), *ppl. a.* 1449. **1.** Skilfully or rightly performed or executed. **b.** as exclam., expressing approval of what some one has done 1460. **c.** quasi-*sb.* The utterance of this, as an expression of commendation 1628. **2.** Of meat: Thoroughly cooked 1846.

1. *Twel. N.* I. v. 253. **b.** Well done, my dear boy! —O bravo! SMOLLETT.

Welled (weld), *ppl. a.* 1848. [f. WELL *sb.* + -ED[2].] **1.** Having a well or hollow in the surface. **2.** Having a tank or cistern in which fish are carried or preserved alive 1864.

Welleresque (welərе·sk), **Wellerian** (welīə·riăn), *adjs.* 1868. Typical or reminiscent of Sam Weller or his father, two celebrated characters in Dickens's *Pickwick Papers.* So **We·llerism**, a speech or expression employed by or typical of either of these characters.

Well-fa·voured, *a.* late ME. Handsome or attractive in appearance, good-looking. Hence †**Well-fa·vouredly** *adv.* in a w. manner; *iron.*, in ref. to punishment, etc.: severely, soundly. **Wellfa·vouredness.** *Obs.* or *rare.*

Well(-)found, *ppl. a.* 1601. †**1.** Of tried goodness, merit, or value –1887. **2.** Fully furnished or equipped 1793.

1. *All's Well* II. i. 105.

Well(-)fou·nded, *ppl. a.* late ME. Built on a good and solid base; esp. of a belief, statement, etc.: Having a foundation in fact; based on good or sure grounds or reasons.

Well-groomed (grūmd), *ppl. a.* 1886. **a.** *lit.* of a horse 1890. **b.** of persons: Neat and trim, with hair, skin, etc. carefully tended 1886.

Well-grou·nded, *ppl. a.* late ME. Of immaterial things: Based on good grounds; having a good basis or foundation.

No man..can be w. in any branch of learning, who has not been at one of our famous Universities RICHARDSON. To determine whether our fears are w. 1888.

Well-grown, *ppl. a.* 1597. Showing satisfactory or adequate growth.

We·ll-head. ME. [WELL *sb.*] **1.** The place at which a spring breaks out of the ground; the head-spring or source of a stream or river. **b.** *Sc.* A spring in a marsh or morass 1816. **2.** *fig.* The chief source or fountain-head of anything 1542. **3.** The top of a draw-well; also, a more or less elaborate structure erected over this 1613.

We·ll-hole. 1680. [WELL *sb.*] **1. a.** An opening through a floor or series of floors, for a staircase, chimney-stack, or for the admission of light, etc. **b.** The space round which the stairs of a winding staircase turn 1823. **c.** A vertical passage-way (for machinery, a lift, etc.); a shaft 1841. **2.** The compartment at the lower end of a ship's pump 1774.

Well-hung, *ppl. a.* 1611. **1. a.** Furnished with large pendent organs (*rare*). **b.** Decorated with rich hangings or tapestry (*rare*) 1667. **2.** Of the tongue: Working readily and freely; glib, fluent 1678. **3.** Suspended or attached so as to hang well 1762. **4.** Of meat or game: Hung up for a sufficient time 1877.

Wellington (we·liŋtən). 1817. [Named after Arthur, first Duke of *Wellington* (1769–1852).] **1.** *attrib.* **a.** *W. boot* = sense 2. 1818. **b.** Used to designate other articles of clothing, as *W. coat, hat, trousers* 1818. **2.** In military use, a high boot covering the knee in front and cut away behind. Also, a somewhat shorter boot worn under the trousers. More recently, a waterproof rubber boot reaching to the knee and worn by women, girls, and children as a protection against rain, etc. 1817. **3.** A variety of cooking apple, large, roundish, and with yellowish white flesh 1821.

Wellingtonia (weliŋtōu·niă). 1853. [f. prec. + -IA [1].] The pop. name in England of *Sequoia* (*Wellingtonia*) *gigantea*, a large coniferous tree, native to California.

Wellingtonian (weliŋtōu·niăn), *a.* 1854. [f. as prec. + -IAN.] Belonging to or characteristic of the Duke of Wellington.

Well-knit, *ppl. a.* 1445. **1.** Firmly conjoined or compacted; closely linked or connected. **2.** Of a person, his frame: Strongly and compactly built, not loose-jointed 1588.

Well(-)known, *ppl. a.* 1470. **1.** Known to many, widely or generally known. **2.** Intimately or thoroughly known 1590.

Well-li·king, *ppl. a. arch.* ME. In good condition and of lusty appearance; thriving, healthy and plump.

They..shalbe fat and wel lyking *Bible* (Great) Ps. xcii. 13.

Well-lined, *ppl. a.* 1562. Furnished with a good lining. **b.** *spec.* Of a purse: Full of money 1820.

Well-made, *ppl. a.* ME. **1.** Of a person or animal: Well-proportioned, of good build. **2.** Of things: Skilfully fabricated, constructed, or contrived 1530.

Well-ma·nnered, *a.* late ME. **1.** Of good morals –1597. **2.** Having good manners, courteous 1547.

Well-mea·ning, *ppl. a.* late ME. Having or actuated by good intentions; animated by a kindly purpose or friendly disposition.

'Tis the fault of many a w. Man, to be officious in a wrong place DRYDEN.

Well-meant, *ppl. a.* 1476. Rightly, honestly, or kindly intended; said or done with good intention.

Well-near, *adv. Obs.* exc. *dial.* [Early ME. *wel-ner*, f. WELL *adv.* + NEAR *adv.*[2]] = WELL-NIGH.

Wellness (we·lnės). 1654. [f. WELL *a.* + -NESS.] The state of being w. or in good health.

Well(-)nigh (we·l,nəi), *adv.* [OE. *wel néah*, f. WELL *adv.* + NIGH *adv.*] Very nearly, almost wholly or entirely.

Well off, *adv.* and *a.* 1733. **1.** *predic.*, normally without hyphen: **a.** Favourably circumstanced, fortunately situated. **b.** Well provided, having no lack 1800. *esp.* **c.** In easy circumstances, well-to-do 1849. **2.** *attrib.* or *adj.* (with hyphen). In sense 1 c. Also *absol.* 1884.

1. a. She was a silly little thing, and did not know when she was well off 1865. **b.** We are well-off for wild-flowers here MEREDITH. **c.** He was rich (or at least certainly well off) 1889.

Well-oiled, *ppl. a.* 1740. Sufficiently lubricated; also *fig.* smoothly expressed; *slang*, in liquor.

I was courteous, every phrase well-oil'd TENNYSON.

Well-prese·rved, *ppl. a.* 1854. (Often used to describe elderly persons who carry their years well.)

Well(-)read, *ppl. a.* 1596. **1.** Well-informed by reading, learned *in* (a subject); also *gen.*, versed or skilled (*in*). **2.** Of a book: Read in a proper, attentive, or profitable way 1865.

Well(-)seen, *ppl. a.* ME. †**1.** Well provided or furnished –1450. **2.** Skilled, versed, proficient *in* (some subject or affair). *arch.* 1528. †**3.** Plainly visible, evident –1725.

Well(-)set, *ppl. a.* ME. **1.** Skilfully, fittingly, or happily placed, arranged, or adjusted. late ME. **2.** Of a person, etc.: Strongly built, firmly knit ME. **b.** Now usu. *well set-up* 1867. **3.** *Cricket.* Said of a batsman who is playing the bowling with ease, and seems unlikely to get out 1880.

Well-spent, *ppl. a.* 1534. **1.** Of time, life: Passed profitably and virtuously. **2.** Expended judiciously or to advantage 1749.

Well(-)spo·ken, *ppl. a.* 1440. **1.** Of a person: Gifted with good or ready speech; courteous and refined in speech. **2.** Of words: Spoken well or with propriety 1592. **3.** With *of*: Favourably mentioned –1538.

We·ll-spring. [OE. *welspryng*, f. WELL *sb.* + SPRING *sb.*[1]] The source or headspring of a stream; a fountain-head; *fig.* a source of perennial emanation or supply.

Well-te·mpered, *ppl. a.* 1422. †**1.** Having a good bodily constitution –1716. **b.** †Having a well-balanced mental temperament; good-tempered. †**2.** Of climate: Temperate –1628. **3.** Of metal, clay, etc.: Properly tempered 1597.

Well-thought, *ppl. a.* 1579. In comb. with a prep. or adv., as *of, on, upon, out.*

Well-timed, *ppl. a.* 1635. **1.** Occurring, done, or made at a good or fitting time; timely, opportune. **2.** Actuated in regular time or at the right moment 1697.

Well-to-do·, *adj. phr.* 1825. [See WELL *a.* 3.] **1.** Possessed of a competency; in easy circumstances; thriving, prosperous. Also *well to do in the world.* **b.** *transf.* Indicative of easy circumstances, prosperous-looking 1863. **2.** Of an animal or plant: Thriving 1875.

1. It is only idle and w. people who kill themselves 1850. For Corsicans they were w. 1874. *absol.* He has strayed into the paradise of the w. 1851.

Well to live, *adj. phr.* Now *rare. Sc.* and *U.S.* 1579. [See WELL *a.* 3.] Prosperous, well-to-do. **b.** Partly intoxicated 1619.

Well to pass, *adj. phr.* Now *Sc.* 1610. [See WELL *a.* 3.] Well off, well to do.

Well-tried, *ppl. a.* 1449. Often tried or tested with good result; thoroughly tried.

Well-turned, *ppl. a.* 1616. [TURN *v.* II.] **1.** Skilfully turned or rounded 1725. **2.** Of the body, etc.: Symmetrically shaped or rounded 1616. **3.** Of speech: Neatly finished, felicitously expressed 1623.

Well-wa·rranted, *ppl. a.* 1603. Authorized, guaranteed, or approved by good warrant.

Well-wi·lled, *a.* late ME. Now *Sc.* and *north.* Kindly or favourably disposed (*to*).

We·ll-wi·ller. Now *rare.* 1448. One who bears good will or wishes well (to another, a cause, etc.); one who is disposed to be kind or friendly; †one who is addicted or devoted *to* a study. So **We·ll-wi·lling** *a.* (now *rare* or *dial.*) wishing well to another; disposed to be kind or friendly; loyal, well-affected OE.

We·ll-wi·sher. 1590. One who wishes well to another, a cause, etc. So **Well-wish** (now *rare*), an act of wishing well to another; a good wish. **Well-wi·shing** *vbl. sb.* and *ppl. a.*

Well-worn, *ppl. a.* 1621. **1.** Much worn or used; *fig.* trite, hackneyed. **2.** Becomingly carried or displayed 1814.

Well-wrought, *ppl. a.* ME. Well made or fashioned, skilfully constructed or put together. **b.** of immaterial things, esp. literary or musical composition 1460.

Welsh (welʃ), *a.* and *sb.* [OE. (Angl. and Kentish) *Welisc, Wælisc*, f. *Wealh, Walh* Celt, Briton: see -ISH. The var. *Walsh* survives as a surname.] **A.** *adj.* **1. a.** *orig.* Belonging to the native British population of England in contrast to the Anglo-Saxons. *Hist.* **b.** In later use, belonging to Wales by birth and descent; forming (part of) the native population of Wales. **2.** Of things: Pertaining to Wales or its inhabitants, †or to the British race in Anglo-Saxon times OE. **3.** As the designation of the language of the Welsh people; written or spoken in the Welsh language; of or belonging to the language or literature of Wales 1547.

2. The Pump-room..crowded like a W. fair SMOLLETT. Yesterday I returned from my Welch journey JOHNSON. Prob. phr. As long as a W. pedigree 1661.

B. *sb.* (Elliptical uses of the adj.) **1. a.** *pl.* The Britons as dist. from the Anglo-Saxons. *Obs.* exc. *Hist.* OE. **b.** The inhabitants or natives of Wales ME. **2.** The Welsh language OE. **b.** *transf.* A strange language; speech that one does not understand 1648. **3.** Short for: Welsh coal 1898.

Collocations: **a.** in the names of various products of, and commodities obtained from, Wales, as **W. coal,** coal obtained from the South Wales coal-fields; anthracite; **W. dresser,** a kind of dresser orig. made on the borders of Staffordshire and Shropshire; **W. flannel,** a heavy variety of flannel with a bluish tinge, made from Welsh fleeces; **W. mutton,** mutton obtained from a small breed of sheep pastured on the W. mountains, highly esteemed for the delicacy of its flavour. **b.** in the names of plants, beasts, insects, etc. indigenous to or found chiefly in Wales, as *W. cattle, pony*; **W. poppy,** a perennial poppy of the genus *Meconopsis.* **c.** In other collocations: **W. ambassador,** the cuckoo; **W. mile,** a distance of a mile and more; a long and tedious mile (chiefly provb.); **W. niece,** a first cousin; **W. onion** = CHIBOL 1; **W. wig,** a worsted cap.

Welsh (welʃ), *v.* 1857. [Origin obsc.] *Racing. trans.* To swindle (a person) out of money laid as a bet; also *absol.* or *intr.*

Welsher (we·lʃəɹ). 1860. [Cf. prec.] A book-maker at a race-meeting, who takes money for a bet, and absconds or refuses to pay if he loses.

Welsh harp. 1637. Applied spec. to the triple-strung harp; also called *Welsh triple harp.*

†**Welsh hook.** 1593. A bill-hook; a weapon of this form –1694.

Welshman (we·lʃmăn). OE. [f. WELSH *a.* + MAN *sb.*] **1.** †**a.** A native Briton. **b.** A native of Wales. **2.** *U.S.* Applied locally to the black bass (*Micropterus*) and other fishes 1714. So **We·lshwoman,** a woman of Welsh nationality 1442.

Welsh rabbit. 1725. A dish consisting of cheese and a little butter melted and mixed together, with seasoning, the whole being stirred until it is creamy, and then poured over buttered toast.

Welsh rarebit. 1785. [Etymologizing alteration of prec.] = prec.

Welshry (we·lʃri). 1603. [f. WELSH *a.* + -RY.] **1.** That part of a town or county (inhabited by English and Welsh) which is appropriated to the Celtic population, as dist. from the ENGLISHRY. **2.** Welsh origin or nationality 1894.

Welt (welt), *sb.* late ME. [Origin obsc.] **1.** *Shoemaking.* A strip of leather placed between and sewn to the edge of the sole and the turned-in edge of the upper in soling a boot or shoe. **2.** A narrow strip of material put on the edge of a garment, etc., as a border, binding, or hem; a frill, fringe, or trimming 1506. **3.** †A narrow ridge, a raised stripe; spec. in *Nat. Hist.* (now *rare*) 1578. b. A ridge in the flesh, esp. the mark of a healed wound; a seam 1800. 4. In various techn. applications, as a flange on a horseshoe, a strip or fillet laid over a seam or joint or placed in an angle to secure or strengthen it, the ribbed border of a piece of knitting 1770. 5. A stroke with a lash or pliant stick; also, a heavy blow with the fist 1863. Hence **We·lted** *ppl. a.* furnished with a w. **We·lter** *sb.*[2] a worker who makes or inserts the w. (in a manufactured article). **We·lting** *vbl. sb.* (often *concr.* an edging, a border).

Welt (welt), *v.* 1483. [f. prec.] I. *trans.* To furnish (shoes) with welts; to repair or renew the welts of. 2. To border, hem, or ornament (a garment) with welts or strips of material. Now *rare* or *Obs.* 1489. 3. *techn.* a. To bind with strips or a strip of leather 1795. b. *Plumbing.* To join (the ends of a pipe, etc.) by turning the edges one over the other and pressing them together 1888. 4. To beat, thrash (chiefly *dial.*) 1823.

Welter (we·ltəɹ), *sb.*[1] 1596. [f. WELTER *v.*] 1. A state of confusion, upheaval, or turmoil. 2. The rolling, tossing, or tumbling (of the sea or waves) 1849. 3. A surging or confused mass: a. of material things, persons, etc. 1857; b. of immaterial things 1851.

Welter (we·ltəɹ), *sb.*[3] 1804. [Origin obsc.] 1. A heavy-weight horseman or pugilist. b. *Horse-racing.* Used *attrib.* with the meaning 'for heavy-weight riders', as *w. handicap.* Also *ellipt.* (= w. race, etc.) 1843. 2. Something exceptionally big or heavy of its kind. *colloq.* and *dial.* 1865.

Welter (we·ltəɹ), *v.* ME. [a. MDu. *welteren* or MLG. *weltern.*] *intr.* 1. To roll or twist the body; to turn or tumble about; to writhe, to wriggle. Now *rare* or *Obs.* b. To roll about (*in* the mire, etc.). Now *rare* or *Obs.* 1530. c. To roll or lie prostrate (*in* one's blood); hence (hyperbolically) to be soaked with blood or gore; also *fig.* of a nation, etc. Now only *poet.* 1590. 2. *fig.* a. = WALLOW *v.* 2. *fig.* (now *rare*) 1535. b. To be sunk or deeply involved *in* 1629. c. *transf.* of inanimate things 1847. 3. Of a ship, a dead body: To roll to and fro, be tossed about (on the waves); to roll or tumble about (in water). late ME. 4. To roll down in a stream; to flow. late ME. 5. Of waves, water: To roll; to toss and tumble; to surge. Now only *poet.* late ME. b. *transf.* of a mass of persons or things: To be in a state of turmoil or confusion 1837. 6. To go with a heavy rolling gait; to flounder 1595.

1. c. Down dropt the Hero, welt'ring in his Gore 1744. 2. a. Numbers of them lay senslesse and weltring in wine 1611. Those that w. in sin TENNYSON. 3. He must not flote upon his watry bear Unwept, and w. to the parching wind MILT.

Welter weight. 1825. [WELTER *sb.*[3]] 1. †a. Heavy weight (of a horseman). b. A heavy-weight rider 1850. c. *Horse-racing.* An extra weight sometimes imposed in addition to weight for age 1880. 2. A boxer or wrestler whose weight is from 10 st. 7 to 9 st. 9. 1896.

Wem (wem). Now *arch.* or *dial.* [ME., substituted for OE. *wam(m, wom(m,* under the influence of †*wem* vb. (OE. *wemman*).] 1. Moral defilement; stain (of sin). Obs. exc. *arch.* 2. Material blemish, defect, injury, or stain. Now *dial.* ME. 3. Bodily blemish, disfigurement, or defect; also, the mark of a bodily injury, a scar. *arch.* ME.

Wen[1] (wen). [OE. *wen(n*; ultimate etym. obsc.] 1. †a. A lump or protuberance on the body, a wart. b. *Path.* A sebaceous cystic tumour under the skin, occurring chiefly on the head. c. Applied to the swelling on the throat characteristic of goitre 1530. d. An excrescence or tumour on the body of a horse 1559. †e. An excrescence on a tree –1791. f. *transf.* and *fig.* (occas. applied *spec.* to London) 1597. †2. A spot, blemish, stain –1593.

1. f. 2 *Hen. IV*, II. ii. 115. But what is to be the fate of the great w. of all? The monster, called.. 'the metropolis of the empire'? COBBETT. Hence **We·nny** *a.* of the nature of or similar to a w.; afflicted with wens.

Wen[2] (wen). [OE.; Kentish var. of *wyn* WIN *sb.*[2]] The name of the OE. runic letter ƿ (= w) and of the manuscript form of this (ƿ) in Old and early Middle English.

Wench (wenʃ), *sb.* [ME. *wenche,* shortened f. early ME. *wenchel*:—OE. *wencel* a child.] 1. a. A girl, maid, young woman; a female child. Now *dial.* b. A girl of the rustic or working class 1575. c. As a familiar or endearing form of address. Now only *dial.* or *arch.* 1581. 2. A wanton woman; a mistress. *Obs.* exc. *arch.* late ME. 3. A female servant, maid-servant. late ME. b. *U.S.* A coloured female servant. *colloq.* 1765.

1. a. Prythee how many Boyes and Wenches must I haue SHAKS. b. She was but a milkmaide, and a plaine cuntrie w. 1575. 2. I am a gentil womman and no wenche CHAUCER.

Wench (wenʃ), *v.* *Obs.* exc. *arch.* 1599. [f. prec.] *intr.* To associate with common women. Hence **We·ncher. We·nching** *ppl. a.* that habitually associates with common women.

Wend (wend), *sb.* 1786. [ad. G. *Wende, Winde* (pl. *Wenden, Winden* = OHG. *Winida,* OE. *Winedas, Weonodas*), of obsc. origin.] A member of the Slavonic race now inhabiting Lusatia in the east of Saxony, but formerly extending over Northern Germany; a Sorb.

Wend (wend), *v.* Pa. t. and pa. pple. **wended, †went.** [Com. Teut.; OE. *wendan,* f. **wand-*, pret. stem of *windan* WIND *v.*[1], of which *wendan* is the causative. The pa. t. and pa. pple. *wente, went* appear from *c* 1200; *went* finally replaced the older pa. t. of GO and from *c* 1500 is most naturally regarded as the pa. t. of that vb., *wend* itself being provided with the new form *wended.*] I. *trans.* and *refl.* 1. †a. To alter the position or direction of; to turn (something) round or over –1450. b. *Naut.* To turn (a ship's bow or head) to the opposite tack 1556. †2. *refl.* To turn, direct, or betake (oneself) –1635. II. *intr.* †1. *Naut.* Of a ship: To turn her head about –1704. †2. To turn from one condition or form to another; to change *to* or *into* –1579. 3. To go off, away, or out; to depart. Now *arch.* OE. 4. To go forward, proceed; to journey, travel; to take one's way. Now *arch.* ME. 5. *transf.* and *fig.* of things: To move, flow, run (in a specified course or direction) ME. 6. With advb. acc., esp. *way*: To go or journey in a certain way or direction. Now only *to w. one's way,* a phr. revived *c* 1800. ME.

2. Must not the world w. in his commun course From good to badd, and from badde to worse? SPENSER. 4. Whither away w. you so late? 1635.

Wendic (we·ndik), *a.* and *sb.* 1861. [f. WEND *sb.* + -IC.] A. *adj.* Of or pertaining to the Wends. B. *sb.* The language of the Wends, Sorabian.

Wendish (we·ndiʃ), *a.* and *sb.* 1614. [f. as prec. + -ISH, or ad. G. *Wendisch.*] A. *adj.* Of or pertaining to the Wends. B. *sb.* The language of the Wends, esp. the Sorabian tongue spoken in Saxony 1617.

Wenlock (we·nlǫk). 1834. Name of a town in Shropshire, used attrib. in **W. formation, group,** a formation of upper Silurian age, typically developed near W. Also **W. limestone, shale, slate.**

Wensleydale (we·nslidēˈl). Name of a district of the North Riding of Yorkshire, used *attrib.*, and hence *ellipt.* as sb., to designate a. A breed of long-woolled sheep orig. raised there; b. A local variety of blue-mould cheese.

Went (went). *Obs.* exc. *dial.* ME. [Related to WEND *v.*] A course, path, way, or passage.

Went, orig. pa. t. (and pa. pple.) of WEND *v.*; now used as the pa. t. of GO *v.*

Wentletrap (we·nt'ltræp). 1758. [a. Du. *wenteltrap* winding stair, spiral shell.] A marine shell of the genus *Scalaria* or family *Scalariidæ*, esp. *S. pretiosa.*

Were (wīəɹ). *Hist.* 1607. [OE. *were,* abbreviation of *wer(e)gild.*] = WERGELD.

Were- (wīəɹ). The first element of WEREWOLF used in comb., chiefly with names of animals, to indicate a human being imagined to be transformed into a beast; as *w.-bear,* etc.

Werewolf, werwolf (wīə·ɹ-, wɔ̄·ɹwulf). Also *Sc.* **warwolf.** [OE. *werewulf* = MDu. *weerwolf,* MHG. *werwolf.* The first element has usu. been identified with OE. *wer* man, but this is somewhat doubtful.] A person who (according to mediæval mythology) was transformed or was capable of transforming himself at times into a wolf.

Wergeld (wɔ̄·ɹgeld), **-gild.** *Hist.* ME. [ad. OE. (Anglian and Kentish) *wergeld* (WSaxon) *wergield, -gild,* f. *wer* man + *geld* YIELD *sb.*] In ancient Teut. and OE. law, the price set upon a man according to his rank, paid by way of compensation or fine in cases of homicide and certain other crimes to free the offender from further obligation or punishment.

Wernerian (wəɹnīə·riăn), *a.* and *sb.* 1811. A. *adj.* Of or relating to A. G. *Werner* (1750–1817), a German mineralogist and geologist, who advocated the theory of the aqueous origin of rocks; agreeing with Werner's system or theory. B. *sb.* A supporter of Werner's theory; a Neptunian 1815.

Wernerite (wɔ̄·ɹnərəit). 1811. [f. name of A. G. *Werner* (see prec.) + -ITE.] *Min.* Silicate of aluminium and calcium, the most important member of the scapolite group.

Werowance (we·rowɑns). 1588. [Amer.-Indian.] A chief of the Indians of Virginia and Maryland in old colonial days.

Wertherian (vəɹtīə·riăn), *a.* 1831. [f. G. *Werther,* hero of Goethe's romance 'Die Leiden des jungen Werther' (1774).] Morbidly sentimental and melancholy. So **Wertherism** (vɔ̄·ɹtəriz'm), morbid sentimentality.

Werwolf: see WEREWOLF.

Wesleyan (we·sliăn, we·zliăn, wezlī·ăn), *a.* and *sb.* 1771. [f. name of John *Wesley* (1703–1791), originator of Methodism + -AN.] A. *adj.* Of or pertaining to Wesley or his teachings; belonging to the Wesleyans as a religious organization.

W. Methodist, a member of the society of Methodists as constituted by John Wesley; also *attrib.* passing into *adj.*, of or pertaining to the W. Methodists as an organization. *W. Methodism,* the religious principles, practice, and organization of the W. Methodists.

B. *sb.* A follower of John Wesley; a W. Methodist 1791. Hence **We·sleyanized** *pa. pple.* affected by Wesleyanism.

Wesleyanism (see prec.). 1774. [f. prec. + -ISM.] The system of Arminian theology introduced and taught by John Wesley; the doctrines and church polity of the Wesleyans; Wesleyan Methodism. So **We·sleyism.**

West (west), *adv., sb.* and *a.* [Com. Teut.; OE. *west* adv.: OTeut. **wes-t-*, app. an extension of the **wes-* in Gr. ἕσπερος, ἑσπέρα, L. *vesper, vespera.*] A. *adv.* Towards or in the direction of that part of the horizon where the sun sets. 1. a. With ref. to movement, extension, or direction. b. (*a*) *To go w.*, of the sun; also *fig.* to die, perish, disappear. late ME. (*b*) To America, or to the Western States 1839. 2. With ref. to a place or location OE. 3. With modifying addition, as *w. by south,* etc. 1577.

1. b. (*a*) All the Lewis guns gone w. 1919. 2. The Kenet ryseth..v or vj miles w. of Marleborow 1577. A nice little flat somewhere, not too far w. 1905.

B. 1. quasi-*sb.* = C. ME. 2. *By w.* †a. In the w.; on the w. side –1596. b. *Naut.* Indicating certain points of the compass (see BY *prep.* 1 d). late ME.

1. East is East, and W. is W., and never the twain shall meet KIPLING.

C. *sb.* (usu. with *the*). 1. That one of the four cardinal points which lies opposite the east and at right angles to the north and south; that part of the horizon or of the sky which is near the place of the sun's setting ME. b. That quarter which with regard to the speaker or some particular place lies in a westerly direction 1537. 2. *spec.* a. The western part of the world. Now usu., Europe and America as dist. from Asia ME. b. The western portion of the Roman world after its division into two empires in A.D. 395. 1577. 3. The western part of a country, region, or area; *spec.* a. of England, Great Britain, Scotland, or Ireland. late ME. b. The western states of N. America. (Sometimes dist. as *the Far, Middle W.*) 1829. c. The western part *of* a specified country, etc. 1613. d. The W. End of London 1823. 4. *Ch. Hist.* The Catholic Church in the Western Roman

Empire and countries adjacent to it; the Roman or Latin church 1586. **5.** The w. wind 1604.

1. Pikes..never bite more freely, than when the Wind is in the W. 1712. **b.** A Sunny hill..Back'd on the North and W. by a thick wood MILT. **2. a.** Once did She hold the gorgeous east in fee; And was the safeguard of the w. WORDSW. **5.** As roses, when the warm W. blows, Break to full flower SWINBURNE.

D. *adj.* **1.** Lying towards the w.; situated at or in the w.; western, westerly. late ME. **b.** Of western Europe, as opp. to the east; *esp.* belonging to the Roman or Latin church. Now *rare* or *Obs.* 1553. **c.** Of or pertaining to the w. 1572. **2.** With proper names: a. Denoting the western part of a country, district, etc., or the more westerly of two places having the same name 1470. **b.** Denoting the western division of a race, nation, or people 1561. **c.** With sbs. and adjs. derived from the names of countries, districts, or peoples 1614. **3.** *Eccl.* Situated in or at that part of a church (normally the actual w.) which is farthest from the altar or high altar. late ME. **4.** Facing to the w. 1593.

2. a. The mountainous district of the W. Riding of Yorkshire 1811. **c.** The W. African River Shrew 1877.

Comb.: **w.-bound** *a.* (orig. *U.S.*), travelling to the w. or in a westerly direction; connected with travel in this direction; **-central** *a.* (abbrev. W.C.), belonging to the western half of the central postal division of London; **-land** (chiefly *Sc.*), the western part of a country, *esp.* the W. of Scotland; also *attrib.*; **w. wind,** the (or a) wind blowing from the w.

West (west), *v. poet.* or *rhet.* late ME. [f. prec.] *intr.* To move towards the west. Chiefly of the sun: To draw near to the west, to sink in the west.

West country. late ME. [WEST *a.*] The western part of any country; the district or region towards the west; *spec.* of England or of Scotland. Sometimes *spec.* the south-western counties (Somerset, Devon, etc.) of England.

attrib. Zome honest plain West-Country-mon 1678. A west-country whig frae Kilmarnock SCOTT.

We·st e·nd. [OE. *westende.* In later use f. WEST *a.*] **1.** The western quarter, district, end, or extremity. **2.** *spec. The West End,* that part of London lying westward of Charing Cross and Regent St. and including the fashionable shopping district, Mayfair, and the Parks; also, those living within this area 1807. **3.** *transf.* The fashionable or aristocratic quarter of a town or other place 1823.

Wester (we·stəɹ), *v.* late ME. [f. WEST *adv.* + -ER [5].] **1.** *intr.* Of the sun, moon, or a star: To travel westward in its course; to draw near the west. **2.** Of the wind: To shift to the west 1580.

Westering (we·stəriŋ), *ppl. a.* 1637. [f. prec.] **1.** That declines from the meridian towards the west (chiefly of the sun when it is nearing the western horizon). **2.** That moves in a westward direction. Of the wind: That shifts to the west. 1747.

1. Earthward he slopes again his w. wheels COWPER. Hills..illumined by the w. sun SOUTHEY.

Westerly (we·stəɹli), *a.* and *sb.* 1577. [f. WEST *adv.*] **A.** *adj.* **1.** Coming from the west. **2.** Situated in or towards the west 1577. **3.** Situated near the western horizon 1801. **4.** Extending towards the west; facing the west. Of motion, etc.: Directed towards the west or the western horizon. 1637.

1. A fine gentle westerlie sea winde blowing 1690. **3.** Till over the w. heaven The shadows of evening had spread SOUTHEY.

B. *sb. pl.* The prevailing w. winds found in certain latitudes 1876.

Westerly (we·stəɹli), *adv.* 1625. [f. as prec.] **1.** In a westward direction; towards the west. **2.** (Blowing) from the west 1708.

We·stermost, *a.* 1555. Now *rare* or *Obs.* [f. *wester* adj. (OE. *westra* lying towards the west) + -MOST.] = WESTERNMOST.

Western (we·stəɹn), *a.* and *sb.* [OE. *westerne,* f. *west* WEST *adv.* + *-erne* (:—OTeut. *-rônjo-*).] **A.** *adj.* **1.** Coming from the west. **2.** Dwelling in the west; *spec.* living or originating in the 'West country' or south-western counties OE. **b.** Of or belonging to the south-western counties 1545. **3.** Having a position relatively west; lying towards or in the west. late ME. **b.** Of or belonging to the west; found or produced in the west 1590. **c.** in the specific names of animals or plants 1784. **4.** Of or pertaining to the Western or European countries as dist. from the Eastern or Oriental 1600. **b.** Of, belonging to, connected with, or characteristic of the Western Church 1699. **5.** With *States*: Constituting the more westerly of the United States of America 1829. **b.** Of or belonging to the W. States 1834. **6.** Directed towards the west; facing westward 1589. **7.** *fig.* Of a person's life or days: Declining 1615. **8.** Hinder, posterior 1829.

1. A westerne milde, and pretty whispering gale 1613. An amazing strong w. current NELSON. **3.** The Sun begins to guild the westerne skie SHAKS. *W. hemisphere,* the hemisphere containing America. **4.** *W. Church,* the Latin as dist. from the Greek or Eastern Church. *W. Empire,* the more westerly of the two parts into which the Roman Empire was divided in 395 A.D.; so *W. emperor,* etc.

B. *sb.* **1.** A member of a Western race; a native or inhabitant of the west, as dist. from an Oriental or Asiatic 1708. **2.** A member of the W. or Latin Church 1860. **3.** *U.S.* An inhabitant or native of the W. States 1846. Hence **We·sternism,** an idiom or expression peculiar to the W. States of America; W. characteristics, practices, etc. 1884.

Westerner (we·stəɹnəɹ). 1837. [f. prec. + -ER.] **1.** An inhabitant or native of the Western States of America. **2.** One belonging to a western race, as dist. from an Oriental 1910.

Westernize (we·stəɹnəiz), *v.* 1842. [-IZE.] *trans.* To make western in character; esp. to make (an Oriental race or country) Western in ideas, institutions, etc.

We·sternmost, *a.* 1703. [f. as prec. + -MOST.] Farthest towards the west; most westerly.

Westfalite (we·stfăləit). 1896. [ad. G. *Westfalit,* f. *Westfalisch* WESTPHALIAN, in the name of the original manufacturing company.] An explosive compound, of which the principal ingredient is ammonium nitrate.

West I·ndia. 1555. †**1.** = WEST INDIES –1648. **2.** *attrib.* Of, pertaining to, or connected with the West Indies 1656.

2. *West India Islands,* the islands lying between N. and S. America.

West-I·ndiaman. 1689. [f. prec. **2.**] A vessel engaged in the West India trade.

West I·ndian, *sb.* and *a.* 1584. [f. WEST INDIA.] **A.** *sb.* †**a.** *pl.* The original inhabitants of the West Indies –1658. **b.** An inhabitant or native of the West Indies, of European origin or descent 1661. **B.** *adj.* Of, pertaining to, situated in, or connected with the West Indies 1611. **b.** in specific names, as *West Indian pike* 1781.

West I·ndies. 1555. [Cf. EAST INDIES.] †**a.** The parts of America first discovered by Columbus and other early navigators. **b.** The West India Islands.

Westing (we·stiŋ), *vbl. sb.* 1628. [f. WEST *adv.* or *v.*] **1.** *Naut.* The net distance made by a vessel towards the west. **2.** Direction towards the west 1825. **3.** Of winds: The fact of blowing from or shifting to the west 1860.

Westland (we·stlǣnd). Chiefly *Sc.* 1470. Also **-lin.** [WEST *a.*] The western part of a country. Also *attrib.*

Westminster (we·s[t]minstəɹ). 1549. The name of the City of Westminster in London, the Abbey of St. Peter on the north bank of the Thames, the Palace which was superseded by the Houses of Parliament (hence *allus.* for parliamentary life or politics), the Hall used as a court of justice and for the assembly of divines held in 1643 (hence of the Confession drawn up by them), or to St. Peter's College. **b.** An alumnus of St. Peter's College, W.

West-north-west, *adv.* late ME. In or from the direction situated between west and north-west. Also as *sb.* and *adj.*

Westphalia (westfē[i]·liă). 1650. [med.L., f. OHG. *Westfalo* an inhabitant of the district of *Westfalen.*] The name of a province of western Germany lying between Hanover and Rhenish Prussia, used *attrib.* with *bacon, gammon,* or *ham.* Hence **Westpha·lian** *a.* of, belonging to, or connected with W.; *sb.* a native or inhabitant of W. 1604.

Westralian (westrē[i]·liăn), *a.* and *sb.* 1896. [f. *Westralia,* telegraphic abbrev. of *Western Australia.*] **A.** *adj.* Of or pertaining to West Australia. **B.** *sb.* A native or inhabitant of West Australia; *pl.* West Australian mining shares 1896.

West Saxon, *sb.* and *a.* *Hist.* late ME. [f. WEST + SAXON, after OE. *Westseaxan* pl.] **A.** *sb.* **1.** *pl.* The division of the Saxons in England occupying the area south of the Thames and westward from Surrey and Sussex; also *sing.* an individual belonging to this group or area. **2.** The dialect of Old English spoken by the West Saxons 1844. **B.** *adj.* Of, pertaining to, or characteristic of the West Saxons or their speech 1570.

West-south-west, *adv.* late ME. In or from the direction situated midway between west and south-west. Also as *sb.* and *adj.*

Westward (we·stwəɹd), *adv., sb.,* and *a.* [OE. *westweard,* f. WEST *adv.* + -WARD.] **A.** *adv.* **1.** Towards the west; in a westerly direction. **2.** quasi-*sb.* = B. 1697.

1. W. there are people..whose king hath but one eie HOLLAND. W. to the Sea the Sun declin'd DRYDEN.

B. *sb.* That direction or part which lies to the west of a place, etc. 1652. **C.** *adj.* Having a westerly situation or direction; lying, facing, moving, etc., towards the west 1872. Hence **We·stwardly** *a.* blowing from the w.; moving w.; situated to the w.; *adv.* in or to the w.; in a westerly direction.

We·stwards, *adv.* and *sb.* 1540. [See -WARDS.] **A.** *adv.* = prec. A. **1.** **B.** *sb.* = prec. B. Now *rare.* 1574.

Wet (wet), *sb.* [Partly OE. (1) *wǣt,* (2) *wǣta* (whence ME. *wete*); partly f. WET *a.*] **1.** Moisture; liquid or moist substance. **2.** Rainy or damp weather ME. **b.** Atmospheric moisture precipitated as rain, mist, or dew ME. **c.** Rain, water, or damp regarded as deleterious or detrimental. Also, standing water which collects in pools, or makes the ground muddy. late ME. **d.** (With *pl.*) A burst, storm, or downpour of rain 1440. **3.** Liquor, drink. In mod. use only *slang.* OE. **b.** A drink or draught of some alcoholic beverage; a glass of liquor 1719. **4.** One who is in favour of the sale and consumption of alcoholic liquor; an anti-prohibitionist 1906. **5.** An incompetent or futile person. *slang.*

1. The floor of the staircase was covered with w. and slime 1897. **2.** This distempered messenger of w., The manie colour'd Iris SHAKS. Make haste in out of the w. DICKENS. **c.** All our rations..being..saturated with w. 1858. **3.** *Heavy w.,* malt liquor.

Wet (wet), *a.* [OE. *wǣt* = OFris. *wēt,* ON. *vátr*; finally superseded, exc. dial., by late ME. *wet(t,* prop. the pa. pple. of the vb.] **1.** Consisting of moisture, liquid. Chiefly as a pleonastic rhetorical epithet of water or tears. **2.** Rainy OE. **3.** Of land or soil: Holding water, saturated with water OE. **b.** Of a crop: Grown in a moist or watery soil 1885. **4.** Made damp or moist by exposure to the elements or by falling in water; sprinkled, covered, or permeated with rain, dew, etc. OE. **b.** with prefixed intensive pple., as *wringing, dripping w.* 1500. **5. a.** Suffused with tears; moist with weeping or with being wept upon ME. **b.** Moist or damp with perspiration. late ME. **6.** Made moist or damp by dipping in, or sprinkling or smearing with, water or other liquid. late ME. **7.** Of timber: Full of sap, unseasoned. late ME. **8.** Of paint, varnish, ink: Not yet dry, sticky, liable to smudge 1519. **9.** *Fort.* Of a ditch: Containing water 1590. **10.** Of fish: **a.** Cured with salt or brine 1580. **b.** Fresh, not dried 1851. **11.** Of confections: Preserved in syrup; of a syrupy nature. Of surgical or natural history specimens: Bottled in spirits. 1612. †**12.** Of measure: Used for liquid articles –1638. **13.** *Med.* **a.** Designating certain diseases which are characterized by moist secretions 1565. **b.** Designating various modes of hydropathic treatment, as in *w. compress, pack* 1843. **14.** *colloq.* **a.** Primed with liquor; more or less intoxicated 1704. **b.** Addicted to drink (*dial.* or *slang*) 1700. **c.** *transf.* 1592. **15.** *colloq.* Of a Quaker: Not very strict in the observances of his sect 1700. **16. a.** Consisting of alcoholic liquor; concerned with the sale and consumption of alcoholic liquor 1779. **b.** *U.S.* Permitting the sale of alcoholic liquor; opposed to the prohibition of the liquor traffic 1888. **17.** Designating various technical processes or operations 1800. **18.** *Naut.* Of a vessel: Liable to ship water over the bows or gunwale 1832.

2. Upon Thursday which was a wete day 1461. The wettest spot in England being near Seathwaite in Cumberland 1877. *transf.* Scotland was evidently bent on giving us a w. welcome 1872. 4. I hate to get w. 1861. Mad as a w. hen because I refuse to take his word for it 1918. *W. through, to the skin,* having one's clothes completely saturated. 6. *W. from the press,* freq. of new-printed matter (newspapers or books). †*With a w. finger,* easily, with little effort. *To come with a w. sail,* to make swift progress, like a ship with sails wetted in order to keep close to the wind. 14. c. Some of us had a w. night of it, last night 1905. 16. b. Like a cow-hand with three month's pay hitting a w. town 1919.

Collocations and *Comb.*: **w. bob,** a boy at Eton who devotes himself to boating; **-bulb,** applied to that one of the two thermometers of a psychrometer the bulb of which is covered with muslin, which is wetted at the time of observation; **w. dock**: see DOCK *sb.*[3] 4; **w. fly** *Angling,* a fly allowed to sink under the surface of the water; **w. meter,** a gas-meter in which the gas passes through a body of water; **w. plate** *Photogr.,* a sensitized collodion plate exposed in the camera while the collodion is moist; **-shod** *a.* (now *dial.*) having the feet wet. Hence **We·t·ly** *adv.*, **-ness** (OE.). **We·ttish** *a.* somewhat w.

Wet (wet), *v.* Pa. t. **wet, wetted.** [OE. *wǣtan,* f. *wǣt* WET *a.*] **I.** *trans.* **1.** To make (an object) humid or moist by the application of water or other liquid; to moisten, sprinkle, drench, bathe *with* (water, etc.); to dip, soak *in.* **2.** To suffuse with tears, bedew with weeping. Also said of the tears. OE. **3.** To make moist or damp by exposure to rain, by a fall into water, or the like ME. **4.** To get (oneself, one's body or clothes, also another person or object) moist or damp by contact with, or immersion in, water or other liquid ME. **b.** To void urine in (one's bed, clothes) 1767. **5. a.** *To w.* (one's) *whistle, weasand,* etc., to take a drink. late ME. **b.** *To w. the other eye,* to drink one glass after another 1745. **c.** *absol.* To drink alcoholic liquor; to 'liquor *up*' 1840. **d.** *trans.* To accompany (solid or dry food) with liquor 1878. **6.** To celebrate by drinking; to have a drink over 1687. **7. a.** To steep or soak (grain) in water in order to convert it into malt 1695. **b.** To infuse (tea) by pouring boiling water on the leaves. *dial.* 1905.

2. Who wets my graue, can be no friend of mine B. JONSON. 3. *To wet through, to the skin,* to drench the clothes of (a person); I had been w. to the skin in the afternoon 1775. *To w. one's line,* to start fishing, to fish. *To w. down,* to damp (sails, paper, embers) with water. *To w. out* (Dyeing), to soak in water. 6. He was as Drunk as a Chaplain of the Army upon wetting his Commission 1687.

II. *intr.* **1.** To become wet. Also *to w. through.* ME. **2.** To rain, drizzle. *dial.* 1740. **3.** *Naut.* Of a vessel: To ship water 1875. Hence **We·tter** one who wets; *spec.* one who damps paper to be used in printing.

Wet blanket. 1662. **1.** A blanket that has been drenched in water; esp. one used for quenching a conflagration. **2.** *fig.* **a.** Something that acts as a damper to activity, enthusiasm, or cheerfulness 1810. **b.** A person who has a depressing or dispiriting effect on those around him 1857. Hence **Wet-bla·nket** *v. trans.* to throw a damper on, discourage, depress.

2. b. She would spoil the whole evening: she is such a w.

Wether (we·ðəɹ). [Com. Teut.; OE. *weðer* = OS. *withar,* OHG. *widar,* ON. *veðr,* Goth. *wiþrus.*] **1.** A male sheep, a ram; *esp.* a castrated ram. **b.** *transf.* of a man; *spec.* a eunuch 1548. **2.** *Grey wethers,* boulders of hard sandstone found lying on the surface of the Downs in Wiltshire and Devonshire 1661. **3.** *Comm.* The fleece obtained from the second or any subsequent shearing of a sheep 1879.

1. b. I am a tainted Weather of the flock Meetest for death SHAKS.

Comb.: **w.-gammon,** a leg of mutton; **w.-head,** a sheep's head; *fig.* a stupid person; **w. hog,** a male sheep before its first shearing; **w. sheep** = sense 1.

Wet nurse, we·t-nurse, *sb.* 1620. A woman who is hired to suckle and nurse another woman's child. Cf. DRY-NURSE. Hence **We·t-nurse** *v. trans.* to serve as wet-nurse to; *fig.* to treat tenderly or take under special care, as if helpless.

We've, contracted f. *we have.*

Wey (wēⁱ). OE. [orig. identical w. WEIGH *sb.*[1]] A standard of dry-goods weight used for cheese, wool, salt, coal, corn, etc., varying greatly with different commodities.

Weymouth (wēⁱ·məþ). 1766. [Title of the first Lord *Weymouth,* by whom the tree was extensively planted after its introduction to England in 1705.] *W. pine,* the Amer. white pine, *Pinus Strobus.*

Wh, a consonantal digraph, normally represents initial *hw* in words of OE. origin; in words of other origin its occurrence may be due to analogy; it sometimes varies with *h* or simple *w*; e.g. *whoop* and *hoop, whelked* and *welked.* Historically OE. initial *hw* represents OTeut. *hw,* under which Indo-European q^w and *kw* were levelled. The normal OE. spelling *hw* was generally preserved in ME. till late in the 13th c.; the modern spelling *wh* is first found in regular use in the *Ormulum.*

In OE. the pronunciation symbolized by *hw* was probably in the earliest periods a voiced bilabial consonant preceded by a breath. This was developed in two different directions: (1) it was reduced to a simple voiced consonant (w); (2) by the influence of the accompanying breath, the voiced (w) became unvoiced. The first of these pronunciations (w) is now universal in English dialect speech except in the four northernmost counties and north Yorkshire, and is that prevailing among educated speakers. The second pronunciation, denoted in this dictionary by the conventional symbol (hw), is general in Scotland, Ireland, and America, and is used by a large proportion of educated speakers in England, either from social or educational tradition, or from a preference for what is considered a careful or correct pronunciation.

The symbol (hw) is used systematically in this Dictionary in the pronunc. of words beginning with *wh.*

Whack (hwæk), *sb. colloq.* 1737. [Either echoic, or alteration of THWACK (cf. WHANG *sb.*[1]).] **1.** A vigorous stroke with a stick or the like; a heavy resounding blow; also, the sound of this. **2.** A portion, share, allowance; *esp.* a full share, a large portion or amount 1785. **3.** As *int.* or *adv.*: With a w. (in sense 1) 1812.

1. *To have* or *take a w. at* (orig. *U.S.*), to make an attempt or attack upon. 2. Phr. *To get, have, take one's w. Out of w.,* not in proper condition; disordered.

Whack (hwæk), *v. colloq.* 1719. [See prec.] **1.** *trans.* To beat or strike vigorously, as with a stick, to thrash 1721. **b.** *fig.* To beat in a contest 1877. **2.** *transf.* and *fig.* Substituted for 'put', 'bring', 'get', etc., with implication of vigorous or violent action 1719. **3.** To share, divide (*up*) 1812. Hence **Wha·cking** *vbl. sb.*

Whacker (hwæ·kəɹ). *colloq.* 1823. [f. prec. + -ER [1].] **1. a.** A heavy blow. *dial.* **b.** A driver of animals, a drover. *U.S.* 1880. **2.** Anything abnormally large of its kind; *esp.* a 'thumping' lie; a 'whopper' 1825. So **Wha·cking** *ppl. a.* that is a w.; 'thumping', 'whopping'; often quasi-*adv.* in *whacking big, great.*

Whale (hwēⁱl), *sb.* [OE. *hwæl,* corresp. to OHG. *wal,* ON. *hvalr.* The mod. form (as dist. from †*whall* from the OE. nom.) is from the oblique cases.] **1.** Any of the larger fish-like marine mammals of the order *Cetacea,* which have fore-limbs like fins and a tail with horizontal flukes, and are hunted for their oil and whalebone; in wider (scientific) use, any cetacean of the groups *Mystacoceti* or whalebone-whales, and *Odontoceti* or toothed whales. **b.** With specific names 1755. **2.** Applied to the 'great fish' which swallowed Jonah (*Jonah* i. 17) OE. **3.** *transf.* An object resembling a w.; *Astron.* (with cap.) the constellation *Cetus* 1551.

1. *allus.* Amid a shoal of minnows they..pose as authoritative whales 1914. fig. phr. *A w. on,* having a great capacity or appetite for, very good at or keen on. *A w. of* (colloq., orig. U.S.), 'no end of'. *Very like a w.,* used in ironical assent to an absurd statement (after Shaks. *Ham.* III. ii. 399). **b. Right w.,** a whalebone-w., esp. of the genus *Balæna.*

attrib. and *Comb.*: **w.-bird,** any of various birds which inhabit the places where whales are found, or which feed on their oil or offal; (*a*) a petrel of the genus *Prion* or *Procellaria*; (*b*) the turnstone; (*c*) the red or grey phalarope; (*d*) the ivory gull; **-boat,** (*a*) a long carvel-built boat, sharp at both ends, and steered with a rudder or an oar, used in w.-fishing; (*b*) a boat of this kind carried by a large ship as a life-boat; **†-fin,** whalebone, formerly supposed to be the fin of the w.; **-fisher** = WHALER 1; **-fishery**; **-fishing,** the occupation of taking whales, whaling; **-man** = WHALER 1, 2; **-oil,** oil from w.-blubber; **-shark** (*a*) a very large shark, *Rhinodon typicus*; (*b*) the BASKING-*shark.* Hence **Whale** *v.*[1] *intr.* to engage in w.-fishing.

Whale *v.*[2] Now *U.S. colloq.* 1790. [Origin obsc.] **1.** *trans.* To beat, flog, thrash. **2.** *transf. intr.* To do something implied by the context continuously or vehemently 1897. Hence **Wha·ling** *vbl. sb.*[2] (*dial.* and *U.S.*) beating, thrashing.

Whaleback (hwēⁱ·lbæk). 1886. [f. WHALE *sb.* + BACK *sb.*] **1.** = TURTLE-BACK 1. **2.** A kind of steam vessel having a spoon bow and the main decks covered in and rounded over, suggesting the back of a whale 1891. **3.** *Geol.* A large mound of the shape of the back of a whale 1893. **4.** *attrib.* or as *adj.* Furnished with a w.; of the shape of the back of a whale 1891. Hence **Wha·le-backed** (-bækt) *a.* shaped like a whale's back 1879.

Whalebone (hwēⁱ·lbōun). ME. **†1.** Ivory from the walrus or some similar animal confused with the whale; chiefly in phr. *white as whale's bone* -1848. **2.** The elastic horny substance which grows in a series of thin parallel plates in the upper jaw of certain whales in place of teeth; baleen 1604. **3.** A strip of w., esp. used as stiffening in women's stays, dresses, etc. 1601. **b.** A riding-whip of w. 1842. **4.** *attrib.* as *adj.* Stiffened with strips of w.; made of or containing w.; *fig.* 'stiff', affected 1601.

1. *L.L.L.* v. ii. 332. 2. A female who is thus invested in W. is sufficiently secured against the Approaches of an ill-bred Fellow ADDISON. 4. A few words in defence of sacks, long waists, and w. stays MARIA EDGEWORTH.

attrib. and *Comb.*: **w.-tree,** an Australian urticaceous tree, *Pseudomorus brunoniana*; **-whale,** a whale of the family *Balænidæ,* having plates of w. developed from the palate instead of teeth. Hence **Wha·leboned** *pa. pple.* and *ppl. a.* stiffened with w.

Whaler (hwēⁱ·ləɹ). 1684. [f. WHALE *sb.* or *v.*[1] + -ER [1].] **1.** A person engaged in whaling; a whale-catcher. **2. a.** A vessel used in whaling. **b.** = WHALE-BOAT b. 1806. **3.** Anything unusually large of its kind; a 'whacker', 'whopper'. *U.S. slang.* 1860.

Whalery (hwēⁱ·ləri). 1683. [f. WHALE *sb.* + -ERY.] The industry of whale-fishing, or the establishment for carrying it on.

Whaling (hwēⁱ·liŋ), *vbl. sb.*[1] 1716. [f. WHALE *sb.* or *v.*[1] + -ING [1].] The action, practice, or business of catching whales. Also *attrib.* or as *ppl. a.*, as *w. ship, voyage.*

Whang (hwæŋ), *sb.*[1] *Sc.* and *dial.* 1536. [var. of *thwang* THONG.] **1.** = THONG *sb.* **2.** A large or thick slice, esp. of cheese, bread, etc. 1684. So **Whang** *v.*[1] *trans.* to beat as with a thong, to lash; *gen.* to beat, strike, or knock violently.

Whang, *sb.*[2] Chiefly *dial.* 1824. [Echoic.] A resounding blow or stroke, or the sound of such a blow; a bang. So **Whang** *v.*[2] *intr.* to make a loud resounding noise, as of a heavy blow or explosion; also used advb.

Whangee (hwæŋgī·). 1813. [Chinese *huang* bamboo sprouts too old for eating.] A cane made of the stem of one or other species of *Phyllostachys,* Chinese and Japanese plants allied to and resembling bamboos. Also *w.-cane.*

‖ **Whare** (hwā·re, hwǫ·ri, wǫ·ri). Also **ware, wharry.** 1833. [Maori *whare, ware* house.] A Maori hut or native dwelling.

Wharf (hwǭɹf), *sb.* Pl. **wharfs** (hwǭɹfs), **wharves** (hwǭɹvz). [Late OE. *hwearf,* corresp. to MLG. *warf, werf.*] **1.** A substantial structure of timber, stone, etc. built along the water's edge, so that ships may lie alongside for loading and unloading. **2. †a.** An embankment, mole, or dam -1601. **b.** †The bank of a river; also, a gravel or sandbank 1602. **c.** A place raised or otherwise marked out on which anything is deposited for subsequent removal to another place 1725.

2. b. *Ant. & Cl.* II. ii. 218.

attrib. and *Comb.*: **w.-boat,** (*a*) *U.S.* a boat supporting a platform and moored at a bank, used as a w.; (*b*) a boat employed about a w.; **-rat,** (*a*) the common brown rat, *Mus decumanus,* which infests wharfs; (*b*) a man or boy who loafs about wharfs, often with the intention of stealing (*slang*). Hence **Wha·rfless** *a.* having no w.

Wharf (hwǭɹf), *v.* 1569. [f. prec.] †1. *trans.* To strengthen with a wall of timber or stone -1793. 2. To discharge at a wharf 1629. 3. To accommodate (vessels) at a wharf 1902. 4. *intr.* To come to wharf 1891.

Wharfage (hwǭ·ɹfėdʒ). 1469. [f. as prec. + -AGE.] 1. The provision of or accommodation at a wharf; the stowage of goods on a wharf; the loading and unloading at a wharf. 2. The charge or dues exacted for the use of a wharf 1535. 3. Wharf accommodation 1807.

Wharfe (hwǭɹf). 1888. Short for **Wharfedale** (*machine*), a cylindrical printing machine made at Wharfedale in Yorkshire.

Wharfing (hwǭ·ɹfiŋ). 1691. [f. WHARF *sb.* + -ING [1].] A structure in the form of a wharf; materials of which a wharf is constructed.

Wharfinger (hwǭ·ɹfindʒəɹ). 1552. [app. for earlier *wharfager (f. WHARFAGE + -ER [1]); cf. *messager* MESSENGER.] An owner or manager of a wharf.

Wharl (hwāɹl), *v.* late ME. [Imitative.] = BURR *v.* 1. **Wharl** *sb.* **Wha·rl-er, -ing** *vbl. sb.*

Wharrow (hwæ·rou). Now *dial.* 1519. By-form of WHARVE. Also attrib. *w.-spindle.*

Whartonian (hwǫɹtōu·niăn), *a.* 1840. *Anat.* Discovered or described by Thomas *Wharton*, English anatomist (1610-73).

Wharve (hwǭɹv). [OE. *hweorfa*: cf. OE. *hweorfan* to turn.] The whorl of a spindle.

What (hwǫt), *pron.*, *a.*, *adv.*, *conj.*, *int.* (*sb.*) [OE. *hwæt*:—OTeut. **hwat*:—Indo-Eur. **qʷod* (cf. L. *quod*), neut. sing. of **qʷos* WHO.] **A.** Interrogative and allied uses. **I.** *pron.* *In direct questions. 1. As the ordinary interrogative pronoun of neuter gender; orig. sing., in later use also pl.: used of a thing or things. 2. Of a person (or persons) in predic. use: formerly gen., in ref. to name or identity; in later use only in ref. to nature, character, function, or the like OE. 3. In rhetorical questions, implying an emphatic contrary assertion OE. **b.** *predic.*, quasi-*adj.* Of what account, consequence, value, or force? OE. 4. **a.** With ellipsis, esp. of the remainder of the question; hence (*colloq.*) short for 'What did you say?' or 'What is it?' ME. **b.** Substituted for a word or phr. of which explanation is asked 1676. **c.** As an interrogative expletive, usu. at the end of a sentence, esp. in recent trivial or affected colloq. use 1785. **In dependent clauses. 5. In indirect questions, and clauses of similar meaning: corresp. to the direct use in 1. OE. 6. Of a person, in predic. use OE. ***Various special uses. 7. With intensive additions, as *w. the deuce* (*devil, dickens*), *w. in the name of . .*, *w. in the world, on earth*, etc. late ME. 8. Of quantity, amount, or price: How much, how many. So of the time of day, in *what's o'clock, what's the time.* OE. 9. *W. for* (introducing a clause); Sc. and n. dial; now in polite colloq. use, only *W. . . . for*, or *W. for?*: For w. purpose, With w. object? Why, Wherefore? ME. **b.** When subordinated *w. . . . for* comes to mean 'the reason why' 1714. **c.** As sb. phr. (slang) in *to give* (one) *w. for*, to inflict severe pain or chastisement 1873. 10. As indefinite final alternative in a disjunctive question. Chiefly *colloq.* 1766.

1. W. is your broders name? MALORY. W. do you meane by Catholike Religion? 1582. Odd people? and in w. are we so very odd? MISS BURNEY. 2. W. are these which are arayed in longe whyte garmentes? TINDALE *Rev.* vii. 13. W. were they?..They were ..atheists COWPER. 3. W. cannot Praise effect in Mighty Minds? DRYDEN. Give a young woman admiration, and w. more can she wish for? 1780. b. What 's death? You'll love me yet! BROWNING. W. would your assertion be against mine? 1885. 4. b. 'Your chummage ticket will be on twenty-seven, in the third.'..'My w., did you say?' DICKENS. c. Goodbye, Miss Thornton, awfully jolly evening — w.? 1906. 5. Demaunding of them w. the matter was 1568. More money than he knew w. to do with 1883. 6. And knowing w. I am, I know w. she shallbe SHAKS. Who or w. he was,..no one ever cared to inquire 1854. 9. W. for should I burn a' my..bukies? 1760. W. are you staring..like that for? 1879. 10. Have you supposed me dead or w.? 1842.

Phrases. *W. if* (†*W. and, W. an(d if)*)..? W. is or would be the case if..? What does it matter if..? etc.; often = 'Suppose..', 'Supposing..'. *W. of..?* w. is to be said of..? What comes of or follows from..? etc. *W. then?* What happens or would happen in that case? W. of that?; so *W. next? W. though..?* W. happens or would happen in view of the fact that..? (implying some opposition between the circumstance mentioned and the possible one implied); also *absol.*, W. if it is (or were) so? W. does it matter? †*W. lack you? W. do you lack?* a salesman's cry; hence as an appellation for an itinerant vendor or pedlar. *W. say you* (*W. do you say*) *to..? W. think you* (*W. do you think*) *of..?* Are you inclined for..? How would you like..? *To know what's what.*, to have a good judgement or apprehension, to know what is fitting or profitable. *To know w. it is*, to apprehend w. it implies or may involve; hence, to have had experience of it; Though I am always serious, I do not know w. it is to be melancholy ADDISON. *I('ll) tell you w.* (†*I know w.*, †*wot you w.*), used to emphasize or call special attention to what is said (= let me tell you), or (*mod. colloq.*) in making a proposal.

Phrases used as sbs. *I know* (or *wot*) *not w.*, *Lord* or *God knows w.* (cf. L. *nescio quid*, F. *je ne sais quoi*), something unknown or only vaguely apprehended or suggested; so..*and I don't know w. all* (colloq.) = '..and all sorts of things besides'. *You know w.*, something that need not be specified.

II. *adj.* 1. As the ordinary interrogative adj., used of a thing or things, a person or persons, in direct questions ME. **b.** In rhetorical questions, implying a contrary assertion. late ME. 2. In indirect questions, and dependent clauses of similar meaning ME. 3. In ref. to quality or character: = W. kind of (= L. *qualis*) ME. 4. In ref. to quantity or amount: How much, how many. late ME. 5. In predic. use, corresp. to a predic. adj. in a direct statement: usu. referring to quality, = of what kind, character, or disposition ME. 6. In parasynthetic compounds, as *w.-fashioned* adj. (= of w. fashion). So *w. countryman* (= a man of w. country). 1559.

1. W. impossible matter wil he make easy next? SHAKS. W. good would it do? 1880. b. W. hope of refuge, or retreat, or aid? SHELLEY. 2. *I know not w.*, *Heaven knows w.*, used as adj. phr. = some unknown or undefined.., some..or other; There was present..I knowe not w. poetical preacher 1635. 3. Þou..askist w. life this man hath had 1445. 4. Pray thee w. money hast thou brought? 1820. 5. I see you w. you are, you are too proud SHAKS.

III. *adv.* †1. For w. cause or reason? For w. end or purpose? -1677. 2. In w. way? In w. respect? How? *Obs.* or *arch.* ME. **b.** To w. extent or degree? How much? late ME. 3. As a mere sign of interrogation, introducing a question. *Obs.* exc. *dial.* OE.

1. W. sit we then projecting Peace and Warr? MILT. 2. But alas, w. can I helpe you? COVERDALE *Baruch* iv. 17. b. W. shal it profit vs if we sleen oure brother? WYCLIF *Gen.* xxxvii. 26. 3. *Rom. & Jul.* I. v. 57.

B. Exclamatory and allied uses. **I.** *int.* 1. As an exclam. of surprise or astonishment (sometimes mixed with indignation) ME. **b.** With intensive additions, esp. in *What ho!* late ME. 2. Used to hail, summon, or call the attention of a person. *arch.* and *dial.* late ME.

1. W.! no go-to-meeting clothes? 1886. b. W. the deuyll! can ye agre no better? SKELTON. 3. W. ho, thou iollye shepheards swayne, Come vp the hyll to me SPENSER. *Rom. & Jul.* I. iii. 3, 4.

II. *adj.* Used to express the surprising or striking nature of the thing(s or person(s denoted by the sb.; in *sing.* now always followed by indef. art., exc. with sb. in collective or abstract sense ME. **b.** In dependent clauses, after vbs. of thinking or perceiving ME.

W. a piece of worke is a man! SHAKS. W. shocking times we live in! 1798. b. You cannot imagine w. a parcel of cheating brutes the work people here are 1708.

C. Relative and allied uses. **I.** *pron.* 1. That which, the thing which ME. **b.** In ref. to a prec. sb., esp. after *but, except, than, like*, etc., with quasi-adj. force: The one which; chiefly as *pl.* those which 1597. 2. **a.** So much (or many) as, as much as 1646. **b.** Such as; the kind of thing (or person) that 1658. **c.** Expressing parallel relation or correspondence 1673. 3. **a.** In a parenthetic phr. (chiefly with *call*) qualifying a following word or phr.; equivalent to an adj. phr., or to a following phr. with *as* 1697. **b.** Introducing a prefatory (usu. parenthetic) qualifying clause, equivalent to a following clause with *which* 1697. 4. = WHATEVER 2 a. ME. 5. *But w.* (after a negative expressed or implied): except w. (or who); which (or who)..not 1596. **b.** *loosely* as conj. phr.: But that, that..not *colloq.* 1662. 6. Redundantly after *than* introducing a clause. *dial.* or *vulgar.* 1818. 7. As simple relative (*sing.* or *pl.*): Which (or who); that. Now *dial.* or *vulgar.* ME.

1. He..abetted them in w. they did MILT. b. *The Usurper*, which is no good play, though better than w. I saw yesterday PEPYS. All fevers, except w. are called nervous 1824. 2. a. Their service was six biscuits a-piece, and w. they pleased of burnt claret PEPYS. c. Intellect is to the mind w. sight is to the body BERKELEY. 3. a. I..am still w. men call young 1856. b. She wore, what was then..unusual, a coat, vest, and hat resembling those of a man SCOTT. 4. Twelfe Night, Or w. you will SHAKS. It may have been murdered, for w. I can tell SCOTT. *W. else*, orig. ellipt. = whatever else there may be; hence, anything else, anything and everything; 3 *Hen VI*, III. i. 51. 5. Padua affords nothing but w. is kinde SHAKS. b. Not but w. many changes had been wrought 1894. 7. To tell that w. ye see needs not SPENSER. Long Forster, w. walked to Colne and back before breakfast 1842.

II. *adj.* 1. That (or those)..which (or who); such..as; so much (or many)..as ME. 2. Any..which (or who), any..that. Now only in certain collocations. late ME. **b.** Followed by *ever, so, soever, somever* (now only, exc. with *soever*, immediately following: see WHATEVER, etc.) ME. **c.** Usu. with *soever*, in indef. (non-relative) sense: = WHATEVER 4. 1597. 3. *W. time*, as conj. phr.: At the time at which; when; whenever ME.

1. I will peece out the comfort with what addition I can SHAKS. 2. Spirits..Assume w. sexes and w. shapes they please POPE. c. I loue thee not a Iarre o' th' Clock, behind W. Lady she her Lord SHAKS. Things of w. Nature or Value soever 1736.

D. Indefinite (non-relative) uses. †**I.** *pron.* Something; anything; only OE. exc. in phrases in which *w.* is qualified by a quantitative or identifying word -1596.

They..gaue him for to feed Such homely w., as serues the simple clowne SPENSER.

II. *adv.* or *conj.* Introducing (*a*) each, or (*b*) only the first, of two or more alternative or coordinate words or phrases. Now *rare.* ME. **b.** Introducing advb. phrases formed with preps., implying 'in consequence of, on account of; in view of, considering' ME.

(*a*) Seven Children at the least (w. Male w. Female) were brought forth 1693. (*b*) They rode so long w. night and day 1523. b. W. with hunting, fishing,.. and bad weather, the progress..was..slow 1867.

E. Substantival nonce-uses. 1. The question 'W.?', 'W. is it?', or the like, or the answer to such question; the essence or substance of the thing in question 1656. 2. A something 1654. 3. An instance of the exclam. 'What!' 1779.

1. My lady will know all the w. and the why 1844. 2. We are not seeking a W.; we are seeking a Whom 1903.

What-d'ye-call-'em, -her, -him, -it (hwǫ·tdyə-, wǫ·tʃəkǫləm, etc.) *colloq.* 1639. An appellation for a thing or person whose name the speaker forgets, does not know or wish to mention, or thinks not worth mentioning. Also in contracted forms, as †**whatd'ecalt**, †**whatsha-callum**, etc.; so **what-ye** (or **-you**) **-call** (**-it**, etc.).

There is no What 's-his-name but Thingummy, and What-you-may-call-it is his prophet! DICKENS.

Whatever (hwǫtˌe·vəɹ), *pron.* and *a.* Also *poet.* **whate'er** (hwǫtˌē·ɹ). ME. [WHAT C. II. 2 b.] 1. *interrog.* (prop. as two words.) Emphatic extension of *what*, implying perplexity or surprise. Now *colloq.* 2. As compound relative. **a.** *pron.* Anything at all which, anything that; sometimes (esp. *poet.*), all that, everything that. late ME. **b.** *adj.* Any..at all which (or who), any..that; occas. (*poet.*), all or every..that. late ME. 3. Introducing a qualifying dependent clause, often with vb. in subjunctive: **a.** *pron.* = 'No matter what'; frequently = 'Notwithstanding anything that' ME. **b.** *adj.* 1561. 4. As indefinite adj. or pron., with loss of the relative force: Any (thing) ..at all. late ME.

1. W. can you want to emigrate for? 1880. 2. a. Being mou'd he strikes, whatere is in his way SHAKS. 3. a. Take no repulse, what euer she doth say SHAKS. W. the defects of American universities may be, they disseminate no prejudices DICKENS. b. Money, in w. hands, will confer power JOHNSON. 4. If thence he scape into what ever world, Or unknown Region MILT. I know nothing w. of Mr. Jellyby DICKENS.

What-like, *interrog. a. arch.* and *dial.* 1821. [orig. Sc.] Of what appearance or aspect. (Usu. predic.)

Whatman (hwǫ·tmăn). 1880. [From the name of the maker.] In full *W. paper*: A kind of paper used for drawings, engravings, etc.

Whatness (hwǫ·tnės). 1611. [f. WHAT *pron.* + -NESS; tr. L. *quidditas*.] = QUIDDITY 1.

What(-)not (hwǫ·tnǫt). 1540. [prop. ellipt. interrog. phr.] 1. Usu. as two words (hwǫ·t nǫ·t): Anything whatever; everything; 'all sorts of things'; now only as final item of an enumeration: = various things besides. b. A thing or person that may be variously named or described (*rare*) 1602. 2. An article of furniture consisting of an open stand with shelves one above another, for keeping or displaying various objects 1808.

1. *Tam. Shr.* v. ii. 110. Fencing, dam-making, cattle-droving, what not 1890.

What's-his-name (hwǫ·tshizneim). *colloq.* 1697. Substituted for the name of a man or boy (loosely, of a thing) which the speaker forgets, does not know, or is unwilling to mention. So **What's-her-name, What's-its-name, What's-your-name**; also in ambiguous form, **Whatsename.**

Whatso (hwǫ·tsou), *pron.* and *a. arch.*, chiefly *poet.* [ME. *what so, what se*, reduced f. OE. *swá hwæt swá*.] = WHATEVER 2 a, b, 3 a, b, 4.

Whatsoever (hwǫtsoue·vəɹ), *poet.* **whatsoe'er** (hwǫtsouē·əɹ), *pron.* and *a.* ME. [f. prec. + EVER *adv.*] = WHATEVER 2 a, b, 3 a, b, 4 (as adj.). †b. *pron.* Whoever -1628.

W. ye axe in my name, that will I do TINDALE *John* xiv. 13. W. thyngs are true, w. thyngs are honest,..those same have ye in youre minde TINDALE *Phil.* iv. 8. I woll not be dyspleased what so euer thou sayest 1533. In w. shape he lurk, of whom Thou telst MILT. In every circumstance of government and legislation w. 1792. b. *Twel. N.* I. iii. 124.

Whatsomever (hwǫtsŏme·vəɹ), *pron.* and *a. Obs.* exc. *dial.* ME. [f. WHAT *pron.* + SOMEVER.] = WHATEVER 2 a, b, 3 a, b, 4 (as adj.). †b. = prec. b. -1601.

b. What somere he is He's brauely taken heere SHAKS.

Whaup (hwǭp, hwāp). 1538. *Sc.* and *north.* [perh. for **whalp*, and allied to OE. *huilpe*:—**hwalpjon-*, f. **hwalp-*, **hwelp-*, a stem imitative of the bird's cry.] The larger curlew, *Numenius arquata*.

Wheal (hwīl), *sb.* 1808. [Misspelt form of WEAL *sb.*[2]] a. = WEAL *sb.*[2] 1811. b. *Med.* A flat, usu. circular, hard elevation of the skin, esp. that characteristic of urticaria 1808. c. *gen.* A ridge 1855. So **Wheal** *v. trans.* to mark with wales or weals 1698.

Wheat (hwīt). [OE. *hwǣte* :—OTeut. **hwaitjoz*, deriv. of **hwīt-* WHITE.] 1. The grain of a cereal (see sense 2), furnishing a meal or flour which constitutes the chief breadstuff in temperate countries. 2. The cereal plant (closely related to barley and rye) which yields this grain, esp. common wheat, *Triticum vulgare* (*sativum*). OE. 3. *pl.* Wheat-plants; crops of wheat; kinds of wheat 1795.

2. When wheate is greene, when hauthorne buds appeare SHAKS.

attrib. and *Comb.*, as *w.-bread, -crop, -flour, -harvest*; **w.-corn**, a grain of w.; **-duck**, the Amer. widgeon, *Mareca americana*, found in flocks in w.-fields; **-grass**, any of various species of the genus *Triticum*, esp. couch-grass, *T. repens*; **-land**, land on which w. is grown, or suitable for growing w. on.

Wheatear[1] (hwī·tˌiəɹ). late ME. [EAR *sb.*[2]] An ear of wheat.

Wheatear[2] (hwī·tˌiəɹ). 1591. [app. orig. *wheatears* for **whiteeres*, f. *whit-* WHITE *a.* + *eeres, ers* ARSE, in allusion to the bird's white rump.] A small passerine bird, *Saxicola œnanthe*, widely distributed over the Old World, having a bluish-grey back, white belly, rump, and upper tail-coverts, and blackish wings.

Wheaten (hwī·t'n), *a.* Now *rare.* [OE. *hwǣten*; see -EN[4].] 1. Composed of the grain or flour of wheat. 2. Of or belonging to wheat as a plant; made of the stalks or straw of wheat OE.

Wheatmeal (hwī·tmīl). [OE. *hwǣtemelu*; see MEAL *sb.*[1]] Meal or flour of wheat.

Wheatstone (hwī·tstən). 1872. [Called after Sir Charles *Wheatstone*.] Short for *Wheatstone('s bridge*: an apparatus for measuring electrical resistances.

Wheedle (hwī·d'l), *v.* 1661. [Origin obsc.] 1. *trans.* To entice or persuade by coaxing or cajolery; to bring into a specified condition by such action. 2. To do (a person) *out of* a thing, or to get (a thing) *out of* a person, by such action 1670. 3. *absol.* or *intr.* To use soft flattering words; (of an animal) to fawn 1664.

1. Smooth words he had to w. simple souls WORDSW. How to w. a man into ordering something he doesn't want DICKENS. Hence **Whee·dle** *sb.* (now *rare*) an act or instance of wheedling, wheedling speech; †a wheedler.

Wheel (hwīl), *sb.* [OE. *hweogol, hwéol* :—OTeut. **hwe(g)ula-*: —Indo-Eur. **qʷeqʷlo-*, repr. by Gr. κύκλος CYCLE; redupl. f. **qʷelo-*, **qʷolo-*, repr. by Gr. πόλος axis, L. *colus* distaff.] I. A circular frame of wood, metal, or other hard substance (sometimes in the form of a solid disk, but usu. of a ring (*rim* or *felloe*) with spokes radiating from the central part or *nave*) attached or capable of being attached at its centre to an axle around which it revolves. a. In a vehicle, etc., each of two or more such appliances which support it and, by rolling upon the ground or other surface, enable it to move along with the least possible friction. b. *gen.*, in machinery or mechanical apparatus of any kind OE. c. With prefixed defining words indicating kind, use, etc., as COG-W., DRIVING-W., FLY-W., etc.

a. *At* or *in the w.*, of horses, next to the carriage, in the place of the wheelers. *On the w.*, *on wheels*, riding in wheeled vehicles. b. Some wheels were taken off..so the Clock was spoild 1616. *W. and axle*, one of the mechanical powers (see POWER III. 2. 12). c. *Fifth w.*; see FIFTH *a.* *Idle w.*: see IDLE *a.* 5.

II. A wheel or wheel-like structure, or an instrument or appliance having a wheel as its essential part, used for some specific purpose. 1. A large wheel, or a contrivance resembling one, used as an instrument of torture or punishment OE. 2. Various mechanical contrivances. a. The revolving part of a turning-lathe, or of a potter's lathe. late ME. b. = MILL-W. late ME. c. = SPINNING-W. 1467. d. = TREAD-W.; also, a treadmill 1623. e. = PERAMBULATOR 2. 1696. f. = GRINDING-*w.* 1707. g. *Naut.*, etc. = STEERING-*w.* 1743. h. = PADDLE-W. 1842. 3. In full *w. of fortune* = LOTTERY-*w.* 1698. 4. a. A rotatory firework in the form of a w. 1629. b. *W. of colour* = CHROMATROPE 1877. c. *W. of life* = ZOETROPE 1872. 5. orig. and esp. *U.S.* A bicycle or tricycle; also, the practice of riding on one, cycling 1884.

1. *To break on the w.*: see BREAK *v.* II. 1.

III. Something resembling a w. 1. An object having the form or figure of a w.; a circle, or something circular OE. 2. The celestial sphere or firmament, or one of the spheres of the planets, etc. in the ancient astronomy, regarded as revolving like a w. *Obs.* or only *fig.* ME. 3. *techn.* One of the wards of a lock, which are rotated by the key 1784. IV. *fig.*, *allus.*, etc. 1. a. The w. which Fortune is fabled to turn, an emblem of mutability OE. b. With allusion to the wheels of the chariot of the Sun. *poet.* 1557. 2. In direct fig. use from I. 1, esp. in ref. to the course or sequence of events, procedure, the passage of time ME. 3. With allusion to sense I. 1 b, denoting a constituent part of something figured as a machine 1625. 4. *fig.* A reiterated or recurring course of actions, events, or time; an endless round or cycle ME. 5. A movement like that of a w. a. A movement in a circular or curved course; a revolution 1604. b. A movement about an axis or centre; *spec.* (*Mil.*) such a movement of a rank or body of troops about a pivot (PIVOT *sb.* 2) 1660. 6. *Prosody.* A set of short lines forming the concluding part of a stanza, usu. five in number (also *bob and w.*) 1838.

1. Turn, Fortune, turn thy w. and lower the proud TENNYSON. 2. To oyl the Wheels of Mens utmost Endeavours 1675. *On wheels*, with rapid and continuous movement or action; *to go* or *run on wheels*, to go smoothly or swiftly, make good progress; (joc., of a clock) to go too fast or irregularly. 3. *Wheels within wheels* (after *Ezek.* i. 16), a complexity of forces or influences; a complication of motives, designs, plots, etc. 5. Satan..Throws his steep flight in many an Aerie wheele MILT.

Comb.: **w.-animal, -animalcule** = ROTIFER; **-back**, a back resembling a w., characteristic of chairs made by Hepplewhite about 1775; **-base**, the distance between the points of contact of the front and back wheels of a vehicle with the ground or a rail; **-carriage**, a carriage moving on wheels, a wheeled vehicle; also as part of a machine; **-chair**, a chair with wheels, *esp.* a Bath chair; **-guard**, (*a*) a circular guard on a sword or dagger; (*b*) a guard to protect a w. (or adjacent parts) from dirt or injury; **-horse**, a horse harnessed between the shafts of a vehicle, next to the wheels, as dist. from a *leader*; **-house**, (*a*) a structure enclosing a large w.; *spec.* a pilot-house; (*b*) a building in which cart-wheels are stored; **-lock**, a form of gun-lock in which the powder was fired by the friction of a small w. against a piece of iron pyrites; **-man**, (*a*) a man who attends to a w.; *U.S.* a helmsman; (*b*) a man who rides a bicycle or tricycle (*colloq.*); **-pit**, a space enclosed by masonry for a large w. to turn in; **-tracery**, tracery radiating from a centre, as in a **w.-window**, a circular window with mullions radiating from the centre like the spokes of a w.; **-work**, a set of connected wheels forming part of a machine or mechanical contrivance. Hence **Whee·lage** (*Hist.*) a toll paid for the passage of a wheeled vehicle; cost of carriage in a wheeled vehicle. **Wheeled** (hwīld, *poet.* hwī·lėd) *a.* furnished with a w. or wheels; effected on wheels or by wheeled vehicles. **Whee·ly** *a. rare*, of or pertaining to a w.

Wheel, *v.* ME. [f. prec.] I. To move like a wheel. 1. *intr.* To turn or revolve about an axis or centre, like a wheel on its axle; to rotate, to whirl. b. To reel, as from giddiness; to be affected with giddiness 1593. 2. *trans.* To turn (something) on or as on a wheel; to cause to revolve about an axis, or to move in a circle or cycle. late ME. 3. *intr. Mil.* Of a rank or body of troops: To turn, with a movement like that of the spokes of a wheel, about a pivot (PIVOT *sb.* 2), so as to change front 1579. b. *trans.* To cause to turn in this way 1634. 4. *intr.* To turn so as to face in a different direction; to turn round or aside, esp. quickly or suddenly 1639. b. *trans.* To cause to turn round or aside 1805. 5. *intr.* To move like a point in the circumference of a wheel; to move in a circle, spiral, or similar curve. *poet.* 1600. b. *trans.* To cause (something) to move in this way; to perform (a movement), trace (a course) in this way. *poet.* 1725. 6. *intr.* To roll along like a wheel (*rare*) 1667.

4. *fig.* Who had wheeled from his Loyalty during the War 1663. 5. The gulls that w. and dip around me DICKENS. b. Save where the beetle wheels his droning flight GRAY.

II. To move on or by means of wheels. 1. *trans.* To convey in a wheeled vehicle or on a chair, etc. moving on wheels 1601. 2. *intr.* To travel in or drive a wheeled vehicle; to go along on wheels, as a vehicle 1721. 3. *trans.* To push or draw (something) on wheels 1784.

3. The other man..had a bad puncture and was wheeling his machine 1896.

III. 1. *trans.* To make like a wheel; to give a circular or curved form to (*rare*) 1656. 2. To furnish with a wheel or wheels 1661.

Wheelbarrow (hwī·lbæːrou). ME. A barrow or shallow open box mounted between two shafts that receive the axle of a wheel at the front ends, the rear ends being shaped into handles and having legs on which it rests; also, a similar contrivance with more than one wheel.

Wheeler (hwī·ləɹ). 1497. [f. WHEEL *sb.* and *v.* + -ER[1].] 1. A wheelwright. 2. A wheel-horse or other draught-animal in the same position 1813. 3. Something, as a vehicle, boat, etc., furnished with a wheel or wheels; chiefly in comb., as FOUR-W. 1886. 4. One who wheels a vehicle, or conveys something in a wheeled vehicle 1683. 5. *Mil.* The man at the outermost end of the rank in wheeling 1798.

Wheelerite (hwī·lərəit). 1874. [f. name of Lieut. G. M. *Wheeler*, of the U.S. Army.] *Min.* A yellowish fossil resin occurring in lignite in the cretaceous strata of New Mexico.

Wheelwright (hwī·lrəit). ME. A man who makes wheels and wheeled vehicles.

Wheen (hwīn), *a.* and *sb.* *Sc.* and *n. dial.* late ME. [repr. OE. *hwǣne*.] (A) few.

Wheep (hwīp). 1891. [Echoic.] A long-drawn sound of a steel weapon drawn from its sheath.

Wheeze (hwīz), *sb.* 1834. [f. next.] 1. An act of wheezing; a whistling sound caused by difficult breathing; *transf.* a sound resembling this. 2. orig. *Theatr. slang.* A joke or comic gag introduced into a performance by a clown or comedian; hence (*slang* or *colloq.*) a catch phrase constantly repeated; a trick or dodge frequently used 1864.

Wheeze (hwīz), *v.* 1460. [prob. a. ON. *hvæsa* to hiss. (Not conn. w. OE. *hwōsan*, to cough, dial. *hoose*.)] 1. *intr.* To breathe hard with a whistling sound from dryness or obstruction in the throat, as in asthma. b. *transf.* To make a similar sound 1854. 2. *trans.* To utter with a sound of wheezing 1849. Hence **Whee·zer** one who wheezes; *esp.* a broken-winded horse.

Wheezy (hwī·zi), *a.* 1818. [f. WHEEZE *sb.* + -Y [1].] Characterized by wheezing; resembling a wheeze. Also *transf.*

A lean, w. old clock 1859.

Whelk [1] (hwelk). [OE. *wioloc*, *weoloc*, of obsc. origin.] A marine gasteropod mollusc of the genus *Buccinum*, having a turbinate shell, esp. *B. undatum*, much used for food.

Whelk [2] (hwelk). [Late OE. *hwylca*, prob. for **hwelca*, f. *hwelian* to suppurate.] 1. A pustule, pimple. 2. Used by confusion for WEAL *sb.*[2] 1761.

1. His face is all bubukles and whelkes SHAKS.

Whelked, welked (hwelkt, welkt), *ppl. a.* 1560. [f. WHELK [1] + -ED [2].] 1. Formed like a whelk; twisted, convoluted, or ridged like the shell of a whelk. 2. Marked with ridges on the flesh; waled, wealed 1727.

Whelm (hwelm), *sb.* 1576. [f. next.] 1. A wooden drain-pipe; orig. a tree-trunk halved vertically, hollowed, and turned with the concavity downwards to form an arched water-course. Now *dial.* 2. The overwhelming surge of waters *poet.* 1842.

Whelm (hwelm), *v.* ME. [perh. repr. OE. **hwelman*.] 1. *trans.* To turn (a hollow vessel) upside down, or *over* or *upon* something so as to cover it. Now *dial.* b. To throw (something) over violently or in a heap upon something else, esp. so as to cover or to crush or smother it 1624. †2. *intr.* (*poet.*) To come or pass over something so as to cover it -1700. 3. *trans.* a. To cover completely with water or other fluid so as to ruin or destroy; to submerge, drown 1555. b. To bury under a load of earth, snow, or the like 1555. 4. *transf.* To engulf or bear down like a flood, storm, avalanche, etc.; hence, to involve in destruction or ruin 1553.

2. The Waves whelm'd over him DRYDEN. 3. a. *Merry W.* II. ii. 143. 4. Sorrow whelm'd his soul COWPER.

Whelp (hwelp), *sb.* [OE. *hwelp* = OS. *hwelp*, OHG. *(h)welf*, ON. *hvelpr*.] 1. The young of the dog. (Now mostly superseded by *puppy*.) 2. The young of various wild animals, *esp.* and now only (chiefly as a literary archaism) of such as the lion, tiger, bear, and wolf, to the young of which the name *cub* is usu. applied OE. 3. a. Applied to the offspring or young of a noxious creature or being ME. b. An ill-conditioned or low fellow; later, a saucy or impertinent young fellow, a 'puppy' ME. 4. *Naut.* One of the longitudinal projections on the barrel of a capstan or the drum of a windlass ME.

2. *fig.* 1 *Hen. IV*, III. iii. 167. 3. a. The Son,.. A frekelld whelpe, hagborne SHAKS.

Whelp (hwelp), *v.* ME. [f. prec.] 1. *trans.* To bring forth (a whelp or whelps). b. *transf.* and *fig.* To bring forth: often *contempt.* 1581. 2. *intr.* To bring forth whelps. late ME.

1. b. Having whelped a prologue with great pains COWPER.

When (hwen), *adv.* (*conj.*, *sb.*) [OE. *hwanne*, *hwonne*, *hwenne*, deriv. of the interrog. stem *hwa-* WHO, WHAT, as *then* is of *þa-* THE, THAT; cf. L. *quom*, *cum* when, OIr. *can*, W. *pan*.] I. *interrog.* 1. In a direct question: At what time? on what occasion? Sometimes passing into the sense: In what case or circumstances? †b. *ellipt.* as exclam. of impatience -1623. 2. In a dependent question or clause: At what time; on what occasion; in what case or circumstances. Also *ellipt.* OE. 3. After a prep.: = What time? (Cf. F. *depuis quand*, G. *seit wann*.) ME.

2. To know w. to speake, and w. to be silent 1676. I haven't seen such food I don't know w. 1888. *Say w.*, colloq. formula used by a person pouring out a drink for another, to ask him to say when he shall stop. 3. Since w. have you missed her? 1861.

II. Relative and conjunctive uses. 1. As compound relative, or as correlative to *then* (implied and sometimes expressed): At the (or a) time at which: on the (or an) occasion on which OE. 2. Introducing a clause as the object of a verb, or (later) governed by a prep.: = The or a time at which OE. 3. As simple relative: At which time, on which occasion; and then. Sometimes implying suddenness: = and just then, and at that moment. OE. b. quasi-*pron.* after a prep.: = which time ME. 4. With *time*, *day*, etc. as antecedent: = at or on which ME. 5. With the notion of time weakened or modified: In the, or any, case or circumstances in which ME. b. As simple relative: In which case; whereupon 1803. 6. a. It being the case that, considering that, since ME. b. While on the other hand, whereas ME.

1. W. I begin, I wil also make an end BIBLE (Geneva) 1 *Sam.* iii. 12. I could not say Amen, W. they did say God blesse vs SHAKS. W. God will, all winds bring raine 1639. 2. Expecting w. our turn shall come to die MORRIS. 3. b. Till w., thou Charmer of my Soul, Farewel 1712. 4. In A somer sesun whon softe was þe sonne LANGL. 5. Most confident, w. palpably most wrong COWPER. 6. a. What 's the good of my pretending to stand out, w. I can't help myself? DICKENS. b. You rub the sore, W. you should bring the plaister SHAKS.

III. as *sb.* The time at which something happens (or did or will happen); also *vaguely*, Time, duration 1616.

The *hows* and *whens* of life STERNE.

Whenas, when as (hwen,æ·z, hwe·n æ̆z), *adv.*, *conj. arch.* late ME. [f. prec. + AS *adv.*] 1. = WHEN II. 1, 5. 2. a. = WHEN II. 6 a. 1551. b. = WHEN II. 6 b. 1578.

1. Subjects must vail, w. their Sov'raigne's by 1638. 2. b So Iudas kist his master, And cried all haile, whenas he meant all harme SHAKS.

Whence (hwens), *adv.*, *conj.* (*sb.*) [ME. *whannes*, *whennes*, f. *whanne* (:—OE. *hwanone*): see -S *suffix*.] I. *interrog.* in direct and indirect questions. (Now repl. in colloq. use by *where.. from*.) 1. From what place? 2. *gen.* and *transf.* From what source, origin, or cause? ME. II. Relative or conjunctive uses. 1. From which place; from or out of which. late ME. †b. as *compound relative*: From where. SHAKS. 2. *gen.* and *transf.* From which source or origin; from which cause; from which fact or circumstance 1568.

1. Let me alone that I may take comfort a litle, Before I goe w. I shall not returne *Job.* x. 21. b. *All's Well* III. ii. 124.

III. as *sb.* That from which something comes or arises; place of origin; source 1832. Hence **Whencesoe·ver, -soe'er, Whence·ver** *advs.* and *conjs.* from whatever place or source; wherever.. from.

Whenever (hwene·vəɹ), *adv.*, *conj.* Also *poet.* **whene'er** (hwenēᵊ·ɹ). late ME. [f. WHEN + EVER *adv.*] 1. At any time when; every time that, as often as; at whatever time, no matter when. Also, in any or every case in which. 2. As soon as. Now *Sc.* and *Irish.* 1655. 3. As interrog. adv., emphatic extension of *when*. (prop. two words.) Now *colloq.* 1713.

Whenso (hwe·nsou), *adv.*, *conj. arch.* [ME., repr. OE. **swā hwanne swā*.] = WHENEVER 1.

Whensoever (hwensoue·vəɹ), *adv.*, *conj.* Also *poet.* **whensoe'er** (-ēᵊ·ɹ). ME. [f. prec. + EVER *adv.*] = WHENEVER 1. b. *ellipt.* At any time 1604.

b. *Ham.* v. ii. 210. So **Whensome·ver** (now *dial.* or *vulgar*).

Where (hwēᵊɹ), *adv.* and *conj.* [OE. *hwǣr*, *hwār*, deriv. of interrog. stem **hwa-*.] I. *interrog.* 1. In or at what place (region, country, etc.)? b. colloq. *W. ... from?* = whence? *w. ... to?* = whither? 1760. 2. In what position or situation? At what point or stage? In what passage or part? In what particular? In what? also (contextually, with *get*, etc.) From what source? ME. 3. To what place? Now, in ordinary use, replacing WHITHER. OE. 4. In rhetorical questions having the effect of emphatic negations OE.

1. My dearest Edith,.. w. on earth have you been? DICKENS. You come from no one knows w.; you live no one knows how 1882. *Lo, see, look, behold w.* (he comes) = Here or there (he comes)! *arch.* b. I must go.., but w. to? 1760. 2. That is all very well; but w. do I come in? 1908. 3. Unconscionable dogs! W. do they expect to go when they die? 1809. 4. W. would be the good of.. quarrelling over it? DICKENS.

II. Relative and conjunctive uses. 1. as compound relative, or as correlative to *there*: In or at the (or a) place in or at which; at the part at which ME. b. To the (or a) place in or at which. late ME. 2. Introducing a clause as obj. of a vb. or prep., or as predicate: = a or the place in (or to) which ME. 3. as simple relative: In or at which; in or at which place; and there ME. 4. (In or to the place) to which; whither ME. 5. In, or to, any (or every) place in, or to, which; wherever ME. 6. as compound rel.: a. In the passage or part (of a writing) in which; at or to the point or stage at which, late ME. b. In a or the case in which; in the circumstances, position, or condition in which; in that respect in which. late ME. c. †A case in which; †a person to whom; the point or particular in which ME. 7. as simple rel.: In or at which; and there; †whereupon. late ME.

1. Wher God buildes a church, the deuill builds a chappell 1583. b. Me seemes I see them going W. mulberies are growing 1586. 2. Within about twenty paces of w. we were sitting GOLDSM. 3. Russet Lawns, and Fallows Gray, W. the nibling flocks do stray MILT. Th' unhappy climes, w. Spring was never known DRYDEN. 4. He is in heauen, w. thou shalt neuer come SHAKS. 5. W. he arriues, he moues All hearts against vs SHAKS. G. w. you like DICKENS. 6. a. I marked the booke w. there is a passage full of treason 1661. b. We cannot be easy w. we are not safe 1766. Thee know'st we canna love just w. other folks 'ud have us GEO. ELIOT. c. *Cymb.* II. iv. 111. 7. The Yorkshire Tragedy, a play.. w. a Rake.. throws his wife down stairs SCOTT. The precise spot w. confidence merges into conceit 1887.

III. 1. With preceding qualifying words, forming advb. phrases: In or at (one, another, etc.) place. (Chiefly in compounds: see ANYWHERE, ELSEWHERE, etc.) 1508. 2. as *sb.* Place, locality; now *esp.* the place at which the thing spoken of is or happens 1443.

Comb. with advs. and preps.: **wherea·fter**, after which (now *formal* or *arch.*); **whereane·nt** (chiefly *Sc.*), anent or concerning which; **whereaway**, whither, in what direction; **wherefro·m** (now *formal* or *arch.*), from which, whence; **whereinsoe·ver** (now *formal* or *arch.*), in whatever matter, respect, etc.; **wherei·nto** (*arch.*), into which; **whereou·t** (*arch.*), out of which, out from which; **whereu·nder** (*arch.*), under which; **whereunti·l** (*dial.*), **whereunto** (now *formal* or *arch.*), unto what? unto which. Hence **Whe·reness**, the condition, quality, or fact of being w. it is; position, location, *ubi*.

Whereabout (hwēᵊ·răbau·t: stress var.), *interrog.* and *rel. adv.*, *sb.* ME. [f. WHERE *adv.* + ABOUT *prep.*] 1. *interrog.* About where? In or near what place, part, situation, or position? Now *rare.* †2. *interrog.* and *rel.* About, concerning, or in regard to what or which -1653. 3. as *sb.* With possessive or *of*: The place in or near which a person or thing is; (approximate) position or situation. Now repl. by next. 2. 1605.

Whe·reabou·ts (stress var.), *adv.*, *sb.* 1450. [f. prec. + advb. *-s*.] 1. *interrog.* = prec. 1. 2. as *sb.* (hwēᵊ·răbauts). = prec. 3. 1795.

2. The prisoner.. succeeded in concealing his w. 1903.

Whereas (hweᵊræ·z), *rel. adv.*, *conj.* (*sb.*). [See AS VI. 5.] †I. As rel. adv. or advb. phr. = WHERE II. 1, 3-7. -1868. II. As illative or adversative conj. 1. In view or consideration of the fact that; forasmuch as, inasmuch as. (Chiefly, now only, introducing a preamble or recital in a formal document.) late ME. 2. Introducing a statement of fact in contrast or opposition to that expressed by the principal clause 1535.

2. His father, whom he had always imagined to be a gentleman; w. he was only a sergeant in a Line regiment 1882.

III. as *sb.* A statement introduced by 'w.'; the preamble of a formal document 1795.

Whereat (hweᵊræ·t), *adv.* Now *formal* or *arch.* ME. 1. *interrog.*: At what? *rare.* 2. *rel.* At which. late ME.

1. W. are you offended? JOHNSON. 2. W. his speech he thus renews MILT. The spot w. the Squire kept.. watch 1891.

Whereby (hweᵊɹbəi·), *adv.* ME. I. *interrog.* a. By, beside, or near what? In what direction? b. By what means? how? II. *rel.* 1. By means of or by the agency of which; according to which, in the matter of which, etc. ME. 2. In consequence of, as a result of, or owing to which; wherefore. *Obs.* exc. *dial.* late ME. †b. Upon which, whereupon. *dial.*

-1748. **3.** Beside or near which; along, through, or over which. Now *rare*. ME.

2. 1 *Hen. IV*, v. i. 67. **b.** 2 *Hen. IV*, II. i. 104.

Wherefore (hwēə·ɹfǫɹ), **wherefor** (hweəɹfǭ·ɹ), *adv.* (*sb.*) ME. [FOR *prep.*] **I.** *interrog.* **1.** For what? *esp.* For what purpose or end? **2.** For what cause? On what account? Why? ME.

1. W. was I borne? SHAKS. **2.** You..ran away.. without leaving me word why or w. 1809.

II. *rel.* **1.** (Now *wherefo·r*). For which ME. **2.** On account of or because of which; in consequence of which. *arch.* ME. **3.** (Now always *whe·refore*.) Introducing a clause expressing a consequence or inference from what has just been stated. ME.

1. Peace to this meeting, w. we are met SHAKS. **2.** The causes wherfore this playe was founden 1474. **3.** And ryght forth said geffray, 'I chalenge the, wherfor deffende the' 1500.

III. as *sb.* A question beginning with *wherefore*, or (more usu.) the answer to such question; cause, reason 1590.

They *will* have the why and the w., and will take nothing for granted DICKENS.

Wherein (hweəri·n), *adv.* Now *formal* or *arch.* ME. [IN *prep.*] **I.** *interrog.* In what (thing, matter, respect, etc.)?

To what can I be useful, w. serve My Nation? MILT.

II. *rel.* **1.** In which (place, material, etc.); where. late ME. **b.** In, at, during, or in the course of which (time) 1535. **2.** In which (matter, action, condition, etc.); in respect of which. late ME.

1. b. The yeares wherin we haue suffred aduersite COVERDALE *Ps.* lxxxix. 15. **2.** He taketh from him his harnes wherein he trusted TINDALE *Luke* xi. 22.

Whereof (hweəɹǫ·v, -ǫ·f), *adv.* Now *formal* or *arch.* ME. [OF *prep.*] **I.** *interrog.* Of what.

To know..how this World..first began, When, and w. created MILT.

II. *rel.* **1.** From or out of which ME. **b.** Of which material substance ME. **2.** For, by reason of, on account of; wherefore ME. †**3.** By means of which, with which, whereby, wherewith -1607. **4.** About or concerning which; in regard to or in respect of which ME. **5.** Of which or whom, in *obj.*, *poss.*, and *partitive* senses. late ME.

2. The Lorde hath done greate thynges for vs.. wherof we reioyse BIBLE (Great) *Ps.* cxxvi. 3. **3.** *Timon* IV. iii. 194. **4.** Thys newe doctrine wher off thou speakest TINDALE *Acts* xvii. 19. **5.** In wittenesse qwherof I haue set to myn seele 1469. The greene sowre Ringlets..W. the Ewe not bites SHAKS.

Whereon (hweəɹǫ·n), *adv.* Now *formal* or *arch.* ME. [ON *prep.*] **I.** *interrog.* On what?

W. do you looke? SHAKS.

II. *rel.* On which. **1.** Of local position ME. **2.** Of time, esp. with antecedent *day* 1588. **3.** Of immediately subsequent or consequent action. (Now usu. WHEREUPON.) 1597. **4.** Of motion or direction to or towards ME. **5.** In ref. to the object of an action, feeling, etc. ME.

2. On that day at noone, w. he sayes, I shall yeeld vp my Crowne SHAKS. **4.** His triple-colour'd Bow, w. to look And call to mind his Cov'nant MILT. **5.** *Wint. T.* I. i. 2.

Whereso (hwēə·ɹsoᵘ), *adv.*, *conj. arch.* [ME., repr. OE. *swā hwǣr swā*.] = WHEREVER 2-5.

Wheresoever (hwēəɹsoᵘe·vəɹ), *adv.*, *conj.* Now *formal* or *arch.* Also *poet.* wheresoe'er (-ēə·ɹ). ME. [f. prec. + EVER.] = WHEREVER 2-5. So **Wheresome·ver** (*Obs.* exc. *dial.*).

Wherethrough (hweəɹþrū·), *adv.* Now *formal* or *arch.* ME. [THROUGH *prep.*] Through which. **1.** In ref. to movement or direction in space, etc., or to duration in time. **2.** By means of which, whereby, wherewith. Now *rare* or *Obs.* ME. **3.** By reason of which, on account of which; in consequence of which, whereby, whence (as result or inference); *rarely* = by whom ME.

Whereto (hweəɹtū·), *adv.* Now *formal* or *arch.* ME. [TO *prep.*] **I.** *interrog.* **1.** To what? In what direction, Whither? †**2.** To what end? For what reason? -1790.

2. W. serues mercy, But to confront the visage of Offence? SHAKS.

II. *rel.* To which ME.

I hold an old accustom'd Feast, W. I haue inuited many a Guest SHAKS.

Whereupon (hwēəɹǫpǫ·n), *adv.* Now *arch.* or *formal* exc. in sense II. 3. ME. [UPON *prep.*] **I.** *interrog.* = WHEREON I; †At what? Upon what ground? Wherefore? **II.** *rel.* **1.** = WHEREON II. **1.** late ME. **2.** Upon which as a basis of action, argument, etc. 1521. †**b.** (with clause as antecedent.) On which account, for which reason, wherefore -1674. **3.** Upon (the occurrence or occasion of) which; immediately after and in consequence of which 1461. **4.** About, as to, or concerning which. Now *rare.* 1533. **5.** = WHEREON II. 4, 5. 1560.

2. b. *Wint. T.* IV. iv. 763. **3.** Last month I receiv'd my fortune..; w. I have taken a house in one of the principal streets DE FOE. **4.** *Hen. VIII*, II. iv. 201. **5.** The desire of their eyes, and that w. they set their minds *Ezek.* xxiv. 25.

Wherever (hweəre·vəɹ). Also *poet.* wher-e'er (-ēə·ɹ), *adv.*, *conj.* ME. [EVER *adv.*] **1.** *interrog.* An emphatic extension of *where*? implying perplexity or surprise. Now *colloq.* **2.** *rel.* At (or to) any place at which ME. **b.** *ellipt.* At any place whatever, at some place or other. Now *rare* or *Obs.* 1667. **3.** To (or at) any place to which; whithersoever. late ME. **4.** Introducing a qualifying dependent clause, often with vb. in subjunctive: In (or to) whatever place; no matter where. late ME. **5.** *gen.* or *fig.* In any case, condition, or circumstances in which 1600.

2. To Oxford, or where ere these Traitors are SHAKS. **4.** W. they come from,..they have perform'd very well 1703. **5.** W. there is genius there is pride GOLDSM.

Wherewith (hweəɹwi·ð, -wi·þ), *adv.* (*sb.*) Now *formal* or *arch.* ME. [WITH *prep.*] **I.** *interrog.* With what? **II.** *rel.* With which. **1.** By means of which; whereby ME. **b.** With ellipsis of antecedent, or as compound relative: That, or something, with which; the means by which ME. **2.** With which as cause or occasion; on account of or by reason of which; by the agency or effect of which. late ME. **3.** Along with or together with which; against which; in addition to or besides which. late ME. **b.** With which occurrence, act, etc.; whereat, whereupon 1533.

Wherewithal (hwēəɹwiðǭ·l), *adv.* (*sb.*) 1535. **I.** *interrog.* = prec. I. *arch.*

Wherewithall shall wee be clothed? *Matt.* vi. 31.

II. *rel.* = prec. II. 1. *arch.* 1578. **b.** = prec. II. 1 b. 1583. **c.** Preceded by the definite (rarely the indefinite) article: (*a*) followed by inf. with *to* = means by which, resources with which (*to do* something) 1809; (*b*) with ellipsis of inf. (chiefly *colloq.*), thus becoming a *sb.* = means, *esp.* pecuniary means 1809.

b. My husband and I cannot live by Love..; we must have w. DRYDEN. He had not w. to buy a coat FIELDING. **c.** The design comprised a harbour..but the w. failed 1861.

Wherret (hwe·rėt), *v.* Now *rare.* 1599. [perh. echoic.] *trans.* To give a blow or slap to. So **Whe·rret** *sb.* a sharp blow; esp. a box on the ear or slap on the face 1577.

Wherry (hwe·ri), *sb.* 1443. [etym. obsc.] **1.** A light rowing-boat used chiefly on rivers to carry passengers and goods. **2.** *local.* A large boat of the barge kind 1589. **3.** *local.* A large four-wheeled dray or cart without sides 1881. Hence **Whe·rry** *v. trans.* to carry in or as in a w. **Whe·rryman,** a man employed on a wherry (sense 1 and 2).

Whet (hwet), *sb.* 1628. [f. next.] **1.** An act of sharpening; *transf.* the interval between two sharpenings of a scythe, etc.; *fig.* an occasion, turn. Now *dial.* **2.** *fig.* Something that incites or stimulates desire; an incitement or inducement to action 1698. **b.** Something that whets the appetite; *esp.* an appetizer in the form of a small draught of liquor; a dram, a drink (cf. WET *sb.* 4 b) 1688.

2. b. I have seen turnips..not as a dessert, but by way of *hors d'œuvres*, or whets SMOLLETT.

Whet (hwet), *v.* [OE. *hwęttan* :—OTeut. **hwatjan*, f. **hwat-* (whence OE. *hwæt* active, brave).] **1.** *trans.* To sharpen, put a sharp edge or point upon. **b.** *absol.*; also *fig.* to get ready for an attack (like a boar whetting his tusks). late ME. †**2.** *fig.* To incite, instigate, egg or urge *on to* or *to do* something -1761. **3.** To sharpen, render (more) acute, keen, or eager (a person's wits, appetite, interest, etc.). late ME. **4.** *To w. one's whistle,* to clear the throat or voice by taking a drink 1674.

1. Like an ill Mower, that mowes on still, and neuer whets his Syth BACON. The eagle whets his beak BYRON. Hence **Whe·tter,** *spec.* (from sense 4) a habitual drinker of whets; a dram-drinker.

Whether (hwe·ðəɹ), *pron.*, *adj.*, *conj.* (*sb.*) [OE. *hwæþer, hweþer* :—OTeut. **hwaþar-*, **hweþar-*, f. **hwa-*, *hwe-* WHO + compar. suffix as in OTHER. EITHER is a compound of *whether*.] **I.** *pron.* and *adj. Obs.*, *arch.*, or *dial.* **1.** Which of the two. (In direct and indirect questions.) **2.** In generalized or indef. sense: Whichever of the two: (*a*) as *compound rel.*; (*b*) introducing a qualifying clause: No matter which of the two ME.

1. What children.., and how many, Of w. sex 1598. W. doest thou professe thy selfe, a knaue, or a foole? SHAKS. I am troubled With the toothach, or with love, I know not w. MASSINGER.

II. *conj.* **1.** As an interrogative particle introducing a disjunctive direct question, expressing doubt between alternatives: usu. with correl. *or.* *Obs.* or *rare arch.* OE. **2.** Introducing a disjunctive dependent question or its equivalent expressing doubt, choice, etc. between alternatives: usu. with correlative *or.* Sometimes repeated after (or without) *or* before the second or later alternative. OE. **3.** By suppression of the second alternative, *whether* comes to introduce a simple dependent question, and = IF II. OE. **4.** Introducing a disjunctive clause (usu. with correl. *or*) having a qualifying or conditional force: *w... or* = in either of the cases mentioned ME. **b.** with ellipsis in both alternatives: often virtually equivalent to *either* ME. **5.** *W. or no* (*not*). **a.** as *conj. phr.* introducing a dependent interrog. clause 1650. **b.** introducing a qualifying clause 1665. **c.** *ellipt.* as *adv. phr.* In any case, at all events 1784. **6.** as *sb.* (*nonce-use*) 1827.

1. *Merch V.* III. ii. 117. **2.** W. this be, Or be not, I'le not sweare SHAKS. **3.** A loud chearful Voice enquiring w. the Philosopher was at Home ADDISON. **4.** Ye shal abyde w. ye will or nyll MALORY. **b.** This, I say, w. right or wrong 1732.

Whetstone (hwe·tstoᵘn). [OE. *hwetstān*, f. WHET *v.* + STONE *sb.*] **1.** A shaped stone used for giving a smooth edge to cutting tools when they have been ground. **b.** Any hard fine-grained rock of which whetstones are made; hone-stone 1578. **2.** *allus.* and *fig.*: freq. in allusion to the former custom of hanging a w. round the neck of a liar. late ME. *Obs.* or *dial.*

2. Wits w., want 1618. He serves for nothing but a mere W. of your Ill-humour 1763. *To lie for the w.*, to be a great liar.

Whew (hwiū̆, hiū̆), *sb.* 1513. [Echoic.] **1.** A sound as of whistling or of something rushing through the air; *spec.* the cry of the plover. **2.** An utterance of the interjection *whew!* 1751. **3.** (Also *w.-duck*) = WHEWER 1804. So **Whew** *v.*[1] *intr.* to whistle; to utter the interjection *whew!* 1475. **Whe·wer** (*dial.*) the female widgeon, *Mareca penelope.*

Whew (hwiū̆, hiū̆), *int.* late ME. An exclam. of the nature of a whistle uttered by a person as a sign of astonishment, disgust, dismay, etc.

Whewellite (hiū̆·ėləit). 1852. [f. name of Professor William *Whewell* (1794-1866) + -ITE [1].] *Min.* Calcium oxalate, occurring in colourless or white monoclinic crystals.

Whey (hwēⁱ). [OE. *hwæg, hweg* :—OTeut. **hwajo-* (a word of the LG. area).] The serum or watery part of milk which remains after the separation of the curd by coagulation, esp. in the manufacture of cheese.

W. of butter, butter milk; *alum w.*, w. formed in the coagulation of milk by powdered alum; *celery, mustard, sack, wine w.*, names of beverages or medicinal drinks.

Comb.: **w.-butter,** butter made from w. or from **w.-cream,** the cream remaining in the w. after the curd has been removed; **-face,** a person having a pale face; so **w.-faced** *a.* Hence **Wheyey** (hwēⁱ·i) *a.* of the nature of w.; consisting of, containing, or resembling w. **Whey·ish** *a.* having the nature or quality of w.; like or resembling w.

Which (hwitʃ), *a.* and *pron.* [OE. *hwelc, hwilc, hwylc* :—OTeut. *hwalīk-, hwilīk-*, f. **hwa-*, *hwi-* WHO + **līko-* (cf. LIKE *a.*).] **I.** *interrog.* **1.** †**a.** *adj.* = WHAT A. II. 1, 2. **b.** *pron.* = WHAT A. I. 1, 6. *Obs.* exc. as joc. substitute for *what*. OE. **2.** *adj.* and *pron.* Expressing a request for selection from a definite number: What one (or ones) of a (stated or implied) set of persons, things, or alternatives OE. **3.** *adj.* and *pron.* Repeated (in prec. sense): **a.** in each of two (or more) separate clauses, usu. connected by a conj. OE. **b.** in the same clause, in abbreviated expressions, esp. *w. is w.*; also with another interrog., as *who is to have w.* ME.

1. *L. L. L.* IV. i. 105. **b.** 'I want a so-and-so' he says..'A w.?' says the Captain DICKENS. **2.** I know on w. syde my bread is buttred 1562. Of these two I doe not know w. to prefer 1601. W. way shall I flie? MILT. But w. is it to be? Fight or make friends? STEVENSON. **3. b.** To see w. went best with w. 1881. Phr. (joc.) *To tell tother from w.*, to distinguish between (two things or people).

II. *rel.* **1.** *adj.* The ordinary relative adj. ME. **2.** *pron.* Introducing an additional statement about the antecedent, the sense of the principal clause being complete without the relative clause ME. **3.** Introducing a clause defining or restricting the antecedent and thus completing the sense (= THAT *rel. pron.* I. 1) ME. **4.** Used of persons. Now only *dial.* exc. of people in a body ME. **b.** Still regularly used of a person in ref. to character, function, or the like 1645. **5.** Rarely used after an antecedent to which the ordinary correlative is *as* ME. †**6.** as compound *rel. pron.* That which, one which, something that ME. **7.** *adj.* or *pron.* Any (person or thing) that, whatever; usu., now always, with limitation of reference, as in I. 2. OE. **8. The w.** *arch.* as *adj.* (= II. 1), or *pron.* (= II. 2, 3). ME. †**b.** Of persons: = II. 4. -1606. **9.** (as *pron.* or *adj.*) With pleonastic personal pronoun or equivalent in the latter part of the relative clause, referring to the antecedent, *which* thus serving merely to link the clauses together. late ME. ¶**b.** Hence, in vulgar use, without any antecedent as a mere connective or introductory particle 1723. ¶ **10.** In sylleptic construction, e.g. as obj. of two different verbs or of a prep. and a verb, etc.; giving the effect of ellipsis of a personal pronoun 1687. **11.** Preceded by *and* 1579. ¶**b.** in erroneous or illogical use, either *and* or *which* being superfluous 1606.

1. It rain'd all Night and all Day,..during w. time the Ship broke in pieces DE FOE. **2.** A letter..qwych I send yow a copy of 1451. I spy'd a small Piece of a Rope, w. I wondered I did not see at first DE FOE. We have no Methodists settled amongst us, w. is very fortunate 1787. A similar experiment, w. was soon discontinued 1875. W. when he saw, thither full fast ran he 1883. **3.** This is the path w. leads to death J. H. NEWMAN. A bar upon w. the sea breaks 1839. **4.** Euery one heares that, w. can distinguish sound SHAKS. I am all the Subiects that you haue, W. first was min owne King SHAKS. **b.** He was not quite the craven..w. she thought him J. H. NEWMAN. **5.** There is not any argument so absurd, w. is not daily received BENTHAM. **6.** I am a wise fellow, and w. is more, an officer, and w. is more, a housholder SHAKS. **7.** W. waye I flie is Hell; my self am Hell MILT. Place it w. way they would, it could not be prevented from shewing 1844. **9.** The history of myself, w., I could not die in peace unless I left it as a legacy to the world STERNE. **b.** If anything 'appens to you — w. God be between you and 'arm — I'll look after the kids 1905. **10.** A quality..w., if we could obtain, would add nothing to our honour 1741. **11. b.** This is their Due, and w. ought to be rendered to them by all people G. WHITE.

Whichever (hwitʃ,e·vəɹ), *a.* and *pron.* late ME. **1.** As compound relative: Any or either (of a definite set of persons or things, expressed or implied); that one (or those) who or which. **2.** Introducing a qualifying dependent clause: Whether one or another (of a definite set); no matter which 1690. So **Whichsoe·ver** *pron. arch.* 1450.

Whicker (hwi·kəɹ), *v. dial.* and *U.S.* 1656. [Imitative.] **1.** *intr.* To utter a half-suppressed laugh; to snigger, titter. **2.** Of a horse: To whinny 1808. So **Whi·cker** *sb.* a snigger; a whinny.

Whid (hwid). 1567. [Possibly dial. development of OE. *cwide* speech.] **1.** A word. *Cant.* **2.** A lie, fib. *Sc.* 1791.

Whidah, whydah (hwi·dă). 1781. [Name of a town in Dahomey, West Africa.] **1.** In full *w.-bird*, alteration of WIDOW-BIRD 1783. **2. W. goat,** a West African goat, *Capra reversa.* **W. thrush,** *Pholidauges leucogaster.* 1781.

Whiff (hwif), *sb.*[1] 1591. [perh. partly alteration of ME. *weffe*, partly a new onomatopœic formation.] **I. 1.** A slight puff or gust of wind, a breath. **b.** *transf.* and *fig.* A 'breath', 'blast', 'burst' 1644. **2.** An inhalation of tobacco smoke; smoke so inhaled 1599. **3.** A wave or waft of (usu. unsavoury) odour 1668. **4.** A puff of smoke or vapour, esp. of tobacco-smoke 1714. **b.** *transf.* A small cheroot 1881. **5.** A puffing or whistling sound, as of a puff or gust of wind through a small opening; a short or gentle whistle 1712. **b.** A discharge of shot or explosive 1837.

1. **b.** The whiffe of every new pamphlet MILT. **3.** *fig.* Apologising for some whiffs of orthodoxy which Voltaire scented MORLEY.

II. A flag hoisted as a signal 1693. **III.** A light kind of outrigged boat for one sculler, used on the Thames 1859.

Whiff, *sb.*[2] 1713. [perh. same word as prec.] A name for various flat-fishes or flounders, as the sail-fluke, *Rhombus megastoma*, the smear-dab, *Pleuronectes microcephalus.*

Whiff, *v.*[1] 1591. [f. WHIFF *sb.*[1]] **1.** *intr.* To blow with a whiff or slight blast; to move with or make the sound of this. **b.** *trans.* To utter with a whiff or puff of air 1765. **2.** To drive or carry (*off*, *away*, etc.) by or as by a whiff 1601. **b.** *intr.* To move with or as with a puff of air 1686. **3.** *trans.* To puff out tobacco-smoke from a pipe, etc.; hence, to smoke. Also *absol.* or *intr.* 1602. **4.** *trans.* To inhale, sniff; also *intr.* to smell, sniff 1635.

Whiff, *v.*[2] 1836. [perh. same as prec.] *Angling. intr.* To angle for mackerel, etc. from a swiftly moving boat with a hand-line towing the bait near the surface. Hence **Whi·ffing** *vbl. sb.*

Whiffle (hwi·f'l), *v.* 1568. [f. WHIFF *v.*[1] + -LE.] **1.** *intr.* To blow in puffs or slight gusts; hence, to veer or shift *about* (of the wind or a ship). **2.** *trans.* To blow or drive with or as with a puff of air. Often *fig.* 1641. **3.** *intr.* To move lightly as if blown by a puff of air; to flicker or flutter as if stirred by the wind. Often *fig.* 1662. **4.** To make a light whistling sound; *trans.* to utter with such a sound 1832. So **Whi·ffle** *sb.* an act of whiffling; a slight blast of air; a veering *round.* Hence **Whi·ffling** *ppl. a.* that whiffles; inconstant, shifting, evasive; trifling, paltry, insignificant.

Whiffler[1] (hwi·fləɹ). *Obs.* exc. *Hist.* 1539. [f. †*wifle* :—OE. *wifel* javelin, axe + -ER[1].] One of a body of attendants armed with a javelin, battle-axe, sword, or staff, and wearing a chain, employed to keep the way clear for a procession or at some public spectacle. **b.** *transf.* A swaggerer, braggadocio 1581.

Whiffler[2] (hwi·fləɹ). 1617. [f. WHIFFLE *v.* + -ER[1].] †**1.** A smoker of tobacco -1836. **2.** A trifler; an insignificant or contemptible fellow; also, a shifty or evasive person 1659.

Whig (hwig), *sb.*[1] Now *Sc.* and *dial.* 1528. [Origin obsc.] Variously applied to (*a*) sour milk or cream, (*b*) whey, (*c*) buttermilk, (*d*) a beverage consisting of whey fermented and flavoured with herbs.

Whig (hwig), *sb.*[2] and *a.* 1657. [Origin obsc.; prob. shortening of WHIGGAMORE.] **1.** An adherent of the Presbyterian cause in Scotland in the seventeenth century. *Hist.* **2.** Applied to the Exclusioners who opposed the succession of James, Duke of York, to the Crown, on the ground of his being a Roman Catholic. *Hist.* 1679. **3.** Hence, from 1689, an adherent of one of the two great parliamentary parties in England. (Opp. to TORY; now mostly superseded by *Liberal.*) 1702. **4.** *Amer. Hist.* **a.** An American colonist who supported the American War of Independence 1768. **b.** A member of a party formed in 1834 from a fusion of the National Republicans and other elements opposed to the Democrats; it was succeeded in 1856 by the Republican party 1834.

1. I am as sorry to see a man day, even a whigue, as any of themselfs CLAVERHOUSE. **3.** All that opposed the Court came in contempt to be called Whiggs BURNET. I have always said, the first W. was the Devil JOHNSON.

B. *adj.* That is a W.; of, pertaining to, or characteristic of a W. or Whigs; holding the opinions or principles of a W. 1681. Hence **Whig** *v. trans.* to behave like a W. towards; *intr.* to play the W. **Whi·ggish** *a.* having something of the character of a W., inclined to Whiggism (usu. *hostile* or *contempt.*); *transf.* liberal, 'broad'; **Whi·ggish-ly** *adv.*, **-ness.**

Whiggamore (hwi·gămōəɹ). *Hist.* 1649. [Origin obsc. N.E.D.] One of a body of insurgents of the West of Scotland who in 1648 marched on Edinburgh; later (*contempt.*) = WHIG *sb.*[2] 1.

Whiggery (hwi·gəri). 1682. [f. WHIG *sb.*[2] + -ERY.] Whig principles or practice; Whiggism. (Mostly *hostile* or *contempt.*)

Whiggism (hwi·giz'm). 1666. [f. WHIG *sb.*[2] + -ISM.] The principles, tenets, or methods of the Whigs; moderate or antiquated Liberalism.

While (hwəil), *sb.* [Com. Teut.: OE. *hwīl* time = OS., OHG. *hwīl*, ON. *hvīla* bed, Goth. *hweila* :—OTeut. **hwīlō*, f. Indo-Eur. **qʷi-* (cf. L. *quies*, *tranquillus*).] **I. 1.** A portion of time considered with respect to its duration. Now almost always in certain connexions (see below). **b.** with adj. expressing quantity, as *good, great, little, short*, etc.: forming esp. advb. phr. = for a (long, etc.) time OE. **2.** *spec.* The time spent (connoting the trouble taken or labour performed) in doing something. Now only in phr. *worth the w.* (now rare or arch.), *worth* one's *w.*, *worth w.*: often = worth doing, profitable, advantageous. ME.

1. *A w.* (*a*) as sb. phr., a time, esp. a short or moderate time; contextually = a considerable time, some time, as in *quite a w.* (colloq.); (*b*) as adv. phr. = for a (short or moderate) time. *Once in a w.*: see ONCE. *That* or *this w.* (now only with *all* preceding); I haue this w. with leaden thoughts beene prest SHAKS. *The w.*: (*a*) as advb. phr., during the time, meanwhile; (*b*) followed by conj. †*the* or *that*, and later with ellipsis = WHILE *conj.* 1 (*arch.*). *All the w.*, during the whole time (that). **2.** It is worth w. being a soldier in Ireland 1842. *To make it worth* (a person's) *w.*, to give (him) sufficient recompense.

II. Time at which something happens or is done; occasion. *Obs.* exc. *arch.* or *dial.* OE. **b.** In exclams. of grief. Chiefly *poet. Obs.* or *arch.* late ME. **c.** With pl. *At whiles*, at times, sometimes, at intervals. *Between whiles*: see BETWEEN-WHILES. 1540.

There are whiles..when ye are altogether too.. Whiggish to be company for a gentleman like me STEVENSON. †*One w.*, at one time, on one occasion, in one case (usu. opp. to *another w.*). **b.** God helpe the w., a bad world I say SHAKS.

While (hwəil), *adv.*, *conj.*, (*prep.*). [As adv., OE. *hwīle*, instr. of *hwīl* WHILE *sb.*; as conj., abbrev. of OE. phr. *þā hwīle þe.*] †**A.** *adv.* At a time or times; *esp.* at one time... at another time; now... then -1632. **B.** *conj.* (or in *conj. phr.*) and *prep.* **1.** *W.* (*that*): during the time that ME. **b.** (*a*) During the whole, or until the end, of the time that ME.; (*b*) within, or before the end of, the time that ME. **c.** During which time; and meanwhile. late ME. **2.** *transf.* **a.** As long as, so long as (implying 'provided that', 'if only'). late ME. **b.** At the same time that; *adversatively*, when on the contrary or the other hand; *concessively*, it being granted that; occas. nearly = although 1588. **c.** At the same time that, in addition to the fact that; often = and at the same time, and besides 1860. **3.** Up to the time that; till, until. Now *dial.* (chiefly *north.*) ME. **b.** as *prep.* Up to (a time), up to the time of; until. Now *dial.* (chiefly *north.*) 1450.

1. **b.** (*a*) She told her 'w. there was life there was hope' FIELDING. (*b*) Lett ws be mery wyll we be here! 1450. **c.** Moses sate reading, w. I taught the little ones GOLDSM. **2. b.** W. they deny a Deity, they assert other things on far less reason 1662. **c.** The walls..are decorated with white enamelled panelling, w. the frieze and ceiling are in modelled plaster 1904. **3.** They drank of the byshopis wyne Quhill they culde drynk ne mair 1813. **b.** W. then, God be with you SHAKS.

While (hwəil), *v.* 1635. [f. WHILE *sb.*] *trans.* To cause (time) to pass without wearisomeness; to pass or get through (a vacant time), esp. by some idle or trivial occupation. Usu. with *away.* Also, to beguile (sorrow, pain). **b.** *intr.* Of time: To pass tediously. Now *dial.* 1712.

Whilere (hwəil,ēə·ɹ), *adv. arch.* OE. [orig. two words, WHILE *adv.* and ERE.] = EREWHILE.

That cursed wight, from whom I scapt whyleare SPENSER.

Whiles (hwəilz), *sb.* (*advb. gen.*) *conj.* (*prep.*), *adv. Obs.* or *arch.* ME. [orig. in advb. and conj. phr., as *sume-hwiles* SOMEWHILE(S, *oðerhwiles* OTHERWHILE(S, formed with advb. -s on *sumhwile, oðerhwile.*] **I.** †**1.** In advb. phrases: e.g. *that w.*, at or during that time; *long w.*, for a long while -1654. **2.** *The w.*, advb. and conj. phr. = *the while* (WHILE *sb.* 2.) ME.

2. We wyll walke vp and downe..the whyles 1540.

II. 1. *conj.* = WHILE *conj.* 1. ME. †b. *transf.* = WHILE *conj.* 2. -1665. †2. *conj.* and *prep.* Till, until -1601. 3. *adv.* = WHILE *adv.* 1. (In mod. use apprehended as sb. pl.) Chiefly *Sc.* 1480.

1. Fyghte ye, my myrry men, whyllys ye may 1465. 2. *Twel. N.* IV. iii. 29. 3. She took w. fits of distraction 1722. W. whispering, w. lying still STEVENSON.

Whillywha (hwi·lihwā, -ǫ), *sb. Sc.* 1680. [Origin obsc.] 1. A wheedling or insinuating person; a flattering deceiver. 2. Wheedling speech, cajolery 1816. So **Whi·llywha, Whi·lly** *vbs. trans.* to take in or persuade by flattery; to wheedle, cajole.

Whilom (hwəi·ləm), *adv.* (*adj.*) *Obs.* or *arch.* [OE. *hwīlum*, dat. pl. of WHILE *sb.*] †1. At times -1600. 2. At some past time; once upon a time. ME. b. as *adj.* That existed, or was such, at a former time; former. 1452.

2. b. Mexico..that w. dependency of the Spanish Crown 1868.

Whilst (hwəilst), *adv.* and *conj.* late ME. [f. WHILES + -*t* as in *amongst, amidst.*] 1. a. In advb. phr. *the w.* (obs. or rare arch.), also as simple adv. (obs. exc. dial.): During that time, meanwhile. b. *The w.*, conj. phr.: During the time that, while. *Obs.* or *rare arch.* late ME. 2. *conj.* = WHILE *conj.* 1, b, c. late ME. 3. *transf.* = WHILE *conj.* 2 a, b, c 1548. 4. *conj.* Till, until. *Obs.* exc. *dial.* 1520.

Whim (hwim), *sb.* 1678. [See WHIM-WHAM.] I. †1. A fanciful or fantastic creation; a whimsical object -1821. †b. A whimsical fellow. ADDISON. 2. A capricious notion or fancy; a fantastic or freakish idea 1697. b. *gen.* Capricious humour or disposition of mind 1721.

2. The scheme was no w. of the moment 1832.

II. A machine, used esp. for raising ore or water from a mine, consisting of a vertical shaft with one or more radiating arms to which a horse or horses, etc. may be yoked and by which it may be turned 1738. Hence **Whim** *v. trans.* to desire capriciously, to have an odd fancy for; *intr.* of the head: to be giddy (now *dial.*). **Whi·mmy** *a.* of the nature of a w.; full of whims.

Whimberry (hwi·mbĕri). *local.* OE. [Assimilated f. *whinberry*, alteration of *winberry* (OE. *wīnberige*), by assoc. w. WHIN[1].] The bilberry or whortleberry.

Whimbrel (hwi·mbrĕl). 1530. [perh. f. WHIMPER *v.*, from the bird's cry.] Applied to various small species of curlew, esp. *Numenius phæopus.*

Whimper (hwi·mpəɹ), *sb.* 1700. [f. next.] A feeble, broken cry, as of a child about to burst into tears; a fretful cry. b. A similar cry of dogs, etc. 1810.

Whimper (hwi·mpəɹ), *v.* 1513. [Echoic.] 1. *intr.* To utter a feeble, whining, broken cry, as a child about to burst into tears; to make a low complaining sound. b. *trans.* To utter or express in a whimper 1784. 2. *intr.* Of an animal, esp. a dog: To utter a feeble querulous cry 1576. 3. Of running water or the wind: To make a continuous plaintive murmur 1795.

1. The poore boye whympereth a lytell, but he dare nat wepe for his lyfe 1530. *fig.* The great Grecian youth, Who whimper'd for more worlds to conquer 1815. Hence **Whi·mperer.**

Whimsical (hwi·mzikăl), *a.* (*sb.*) 1653. [f. WHIMS(Y + -ICAL.] 1. Full of, subject to, or characterized by a whim or whims; actuated by or depending upon whim or caprice. 2. Characterized by deviation from the ordinary as if determined by mere caprice; fantastic, fanciful; freakish 1675. †b. Subject to uncertainty -1748.

1. One Sir Roger de Coverley, a w. Country Knight ADDISON. 2. The Germans are w. animals in their appearance 1826. b. Must the bread of Life be ground only by the winde of every Doctrine? and whimsicall Wind-Mills? 1654.

B. *sb.* (in *pl.*) A cant name for a section of the Tories in the reign of Queen Anne 1714. Hence **Whimsica·lity**, the quality or state of being w.; oddity, fantasticalness. **Whi·msically** *adv.*, **-ness.**

Whimsy, whimsey (hwi·mzi), *sb.* 1605. [perh. related to next as *flimsy* to *flim-flam.*] I. †1. Dizziness, vertigo -1656. 2. = WHIM *sb.* I. 2. 1605. b. = WHIM *sb.* I. 2 b. *arch.* 1680. 3. = WHIM *sb.* I. 1. 1712.

2. Those vain Attempts of Flying, and Whimsies of passing to the Moon 1713.

II. = WHIM *sb.* II. *local.* 1789. Hence **Whimsy-whamsy** = next 2.

Whim-wham (hwi·mˌhwæm). 1529. [A reduplication with vowel-variation, like *flim-flam, trim-tram*, similarly applied to trivial or frivolous things.] 1. A fanciful or fantastic object; *fig.* a trifle; in early use chiefly, a trifling ornament of dress, a trinket. 2. A fantastic notion, odd fancy 1580.

1. I have spent 700 pounds..for her to learn music and whim-whams 1808. 2. Such blind vnreasonable whimwhams 1588.

Whin[1] (hwin). late ME. [app. orig. northern, and prob. of Scand. origin.] 1. The common furze or gorse, *Ulex europæus.* (Often *collect. pl.* and *sing.*) 2. Applied to other prickly or thorny shrubs, as rest-harrow and buckthorn; also to heather 1530. 3. With distinctive additions, in local names of various prickly shrubs. late ME.

3. **Cammock, Lady-, Land-w.** = *petty w.* (*a*). **Heather-, Moor-, Moss-, Needle-w.** = *petty w.* (*b*). **Petty w.**, (*a*) the rest-harrow, *Ononis arvensis*; (*b*) the needle-furze, *Genista anglica.* Hence **Whi·nbush**, a furze-bush.

Whin[2] (hwin). *Sc.* and *n. dial.* ME. [Origin obsc.] = WHINSTONE.

Comb.: **w.-rock**, whinstone; **w.-sill**, a sill or layer of whinstone; also, whinstone.

Whinchat (hwi·nˌtʃæt). 1678. [f. WHIN[1] + CHAT *sb.*[2]] A small European bird, *Pratincola rubetra*, closely allied to the stonechat.

Whine (hwəin), *sb.* 1633. [f. next.] An act of whining; a low somewhat shrill protracted cry, usu. expressive of pain or distress; a suppressed nasal tone, as of feeble, mean, or undignified complaint; a complaint uttered in this tone.

A peevish w. in his voice like a beaten schoolboy HAZLITT.

Whine (hwəin), *v.* [OE. *hwīnan* (only of the whizzing of an arrow) = ON. *hvína.*] 1. *intr.* Of persons, also of animals, esp. dogs: To utter a low somewhat shrill protracted sound or cry, usu. expressive of pain or distress; to cry in a subdued plaintive tone ME. 2. To utter complaints in a low querulous tone; to complain in a feeble, mean, or undignified way 1530. 3. *trans.* a. To cause to pass *away* by whining; to waste in whining 1607. b. To utter in a whining tone 1698.

1. Yet canne thys peuyshe gyrl neuer ceace whining and pulyng for fear SIR T. MORE. Thrice the brinded Cat hath mew'd..Thrice, and once the Hedge-Pigge whin'd SHAKS. The bullets..whined through the air 1901. 3. a. *Cor.* v. vi. 98. Hence **Whi·ner**, a person or animal that whines. **Whi·ning** *ppl. a.*, **-ly** *adv.*

Whing (hwiŋ), *int.* and *sb.* 1912. [Imitative.] A word expressing a high-pitched ringing sound.

Whing (hwiŋ), *v.* 1882. [Onomatopœic.] *trans.* and *intr.* To move with great force or impetus.

Whinge (hwindʒ), *v. Sc.* and *n. dial.* 1513. [Northern form of OE. *hwinsian*:—OTeut. **hwinisōjan*, f. root of *hwīnan* to WHINE.] *intr.* To whine. Hence **Whinge** *sb.* a whine 1500.

Whinger (hwi·ŋgəɹ, hwi·ndʒəɹ). Chiefly *Sc. Obs.* exc. *Hist.* 1540. = WHINYARD.

Whinner (hwi·nəɹ), *v. local.* 1700. [Frequentative of WHINE *v.*] *intr.* To whine (feebly). Also as *sb.*

Whinny (hwi·ni), *sb.* 1823. [f. WHINNY *v.*] An act of whinnying; the sound of this.

Whinny (hwi·ni), *a.* 1482. [f. WHIN *sb.*[1] + -Y[1].] Covered or abounding with whins or furze-bushes.

Whinny (hwi·ni), *v.* 1530. [Imitative; cf. earlier *whine, whrinny*, and L. *hinnire.*] 1. *intr.* Of a horse: To neigh, esp. in a low or gentle way; also occas. of other animals or of inanimate objects. 2. *trans.* To utter with a whinnying sound; to express by whinnying 1815.

Whinstone (hwi·nstoun). 1513. [f. WHIN[2] + STONE *sb.*] A name for various very hard dark-coloured rocks or stones, as greenstone, basalt, chert, or quartzose sandstone. b. A boulder or slab of this rock 1585.

b. Despair..such as would have melted the heart of a whinstane SCOTT.

Whiny (hwəi·ni), *a.* 1854. [f. WHINE *sb.* or *v.* + -Y[1].] Characterized by whining; disposed to whine; fretful.

Whinyard (hwi·nyăɹd). Now *Hist.* 1478. [Origin obsc; cf. WHINGER.] A short-sword, a hanger.

Whip (hwip), *sb.* ME. [Partly f. next; partly a. (M)LG. *wippe, wip* quick movement, leap, etc.] I. 1. An instrument for flogging or beating, consisting either of a rigid rod or stick with a lash of cord, leather, etc. attached, or of a flexible switch with or without a lash, used for driving horses, chastising human beings, spinning a top, and other purposes. b. *transf.* The occupation or art of driving horses; coachmanship 1792. 2. An object resembling a whip; a slender flexible branch of a plant, a switch; a collection or growth of such branches 1585. 3. A blow or stroke with or as with a whip; a lash, stripe. Now only *Sc.* late ME. 4. One who wields a driving-whip; a driver of horses. (Usu. with descriptive adj. or phr. expressing skill or style.) 1775. 5. *Hunting.* = WHIPPER-IN 1. 1848. 6. (orig. *whipper-in.*) A member of a particular party in Parliament whose duty it is to secure the attendance of members of that party on the occasion of an important division 1853. 7. a. The action of 'whipping *up*' the members of a party for a Parliamentary division, or any body of persons for some united action 1828. b. A call or appeal to a number of persons for contributions to a sum or fund; now esp. *w.-round* (for some object of charity) 1861. c. The written appeal issued by a Parliament 'whip' to summon the members of his party 1879. 8. A preparation of whipped cream, eggs, or the like 1756. 9. A movement as of a whip or switch; *spec.* a slight bending movement produced by sudden strain, as in a piece of mechanism 1889.

1. *fig.* And I forsooth in loue, I that haue beene loues whip! SHAKS. Phr. *W. and spur* (advb. usu. with *ride*), at one's utmost speed, at a furious pace. *W. behind!*, a cry to the driver of a horse vehicle calling his attention to the presence of some one riding on the back of the vehicle without his knowledge. 3. *Ham.* III. i. 70. 4. You're a wery good w., and can do what you like with your horses DICKENS.

II. †a. A sudden, brisk, or hasty movement; a start -1631. b. *Fencing.* A thrust in which the blade slides along the adversary's blade 1771. III. Something moved briskly. †1. *Naut.* = WHIPSTAFF 2. -1625. 2. Each of the arms carrying the sails in a windmill 1759. 3. A simple kind of tackle or pulley, consisting of a single block with a rope rove through it (*single w.*); used on board ship, etc., for hoisting, esp. light objects 1769.

2. *Double w., w. on w., w. and runner*, a standing block and a running block, the 'fall' of the former being attached to the latter. *W. and derry* = WHIPSY-DERRY.

IV. 1. *Needlework.* An overcast stitch (see WHIP *v.* III. 2); the portion of the stuff between such stitches 1592. 2. *Weaving.* (See quot.) 1825.

2. In the weaving of ribands and other ornamental works, many extraneous substances, totally unconnected with the warp or weft, are thrown in...These ..are..denominated whips. 1825.

Whip, *v.* ME. [Early history uncertain; cf. (M)LG., Du. *wippen* to swing, leap, dance, Du. *wipstaart* wagtail, LG. *wipwap* seesaw, etc.] I. To move briskly. 1. *intr.* †a. To flap violently with the wings. ME. only. b. *gen.* To make a sudden brisk movement; to move hastily or nimbly (almost always with advb. extension) 1440. 2. *trans.* To move (something) suddenly or briskly; to take, pull, strike, etc. with a sudden vigorous movement or action; *fig.* to 'come *out* with', utter suddenly. Almost always with advb. extension. late ME. b. *slang.* To drink quickly, 'toss off' (usu. with *off* or *up*) 1600. c. To make *up* quickly or hastily 1611. †3. *slang.* To run *through* with a sword thrust -1842. 4. *Fencing. intr.* To make a thrust in which the blade slides along the opponent's blade. Also *trans.* with the blade as obj. 1771. 5. *Naut.*, etc. *trans.* To hoist or lower with a whip 1769.

1. b. I whipt behind the Arras SHAKS. 2. He.. leapes behind me, whippes my purse away 1600.

II. To use a whip, strike with a whip. 1. To strike or beat with or as with a whip. a. To punish or chastise with a whip or rod; to scourge. Also *loosely*, to beat (esp. a child) with the hand or otherwise; to spank. late ME. b. To drive *away, out*, etc. with a whip 1567. c. To drive or urge on (a horse, etc.) with strokes of a whip. Also (occas.) *absol.* 1587. d. Hunting. *W. in*: to drive (hounds) with the whip back into the pack so as to prevent them from straying; *absol.* to act as whipper-in. *W. off*: to drive (the hounds) with the whip away from the chase; *absol.* to give over the chase. 1739. e. To spin (a top) by striking it with a whip 1588. 2. To beat up into a froth (eggs, cream, etc.) with a fork, spoon, or other instrument; to prepare (a fancy dish) in this way 1673. 3. *Angling*. To cast the line upon the water with a movement like the stroke of a whip; to draw a fly or other bait along the surface by such a movement; *intr.*, or *trans.* with the bait or (usu.) the water as obj. 1653. 4. *trans.* To strike like a whip, lash; to move or drive in this way 1699. b. *intr.* To lash; also, to bend or spring like a whip or switch 1872. 5. *trans.* To bring, get, render, make or produce by whipping 1635. 6. *fig.* To vex, afflict, torment; to punish, chastise; to administer severe reproof or satire to 1530. †b. esp. *imper.* as a mild execration: = 'confound', 'hang' –1872. 7. To overcome, vanquish; to surpass, outdo. Now *U.S. colloq.* 1571. 8. To urge, incite, rouse; to revive 1573. 9. (orig. *fig.* from II. 1 d.) To summon to attend, as the members of a party for a division in Parliament. Const. *in, up*; also simply or *absol.* 1769. †10. *pa. pple.* Streaked, striped. (After F. *fouetté*.) –1721.

1. She deserves to be whipped, and sent to bed THACKERAY. b. For whipping dogges from ye churche 1567. e. Thou disputes like an Infant: goe w. thy Gigge SHAKS. 6. b. W. me such honest knaues SHAKS. 7. The British can w. the whole airth, and we can w. the British 1836.

Phrases. *To w. the cat* (chiefly *dial.* or *techn. colloq.*), †(*a*) to get drunk; (*b*) to work as an itinerant tailor, carpenter, etc. at private houses by the day; (*c*) to play a practical joke; (*d*) to practise extreme parsimony; (*e*) to shirk work on Monday; (*f*) to win all the tricks at whist. *To w. the devil* (or *the old gentleman*) *round the post* (U.S. *around the stump*): to accomplish by underhand or roundabout means what cannot be done openly or directly.

III. To bind round or over. 1. *trans.* To overlay (a rope, string, or other object) with cord, thread, or the like wound closely and regularly round and round. Also, to bind (cord, etc.) in this way round something. 1440. b. To fasten or 'seize' by binding in this way 1760. 2. *Needlework*. a. To sew over and over; to overcast. b. To draw into gathers, as a frill, by a combination of overcast and running stitch. 1592.

†Whip, *int.* and *adv.* 1460. [The vb.-stem used as int. and adv.] Suddenly, forthwith, in a trice; quick! presto! –1806.

Whip- in combination.

1. Combs. of the sb.: as *w.-leather, -maker, -mark, -smacking*; *w.-shaped, -wielding* adjs.; **w.-beam**, the white-beam; **-bird**, an Australian bird (*Psodophes crepitans*) with a note resembling the crack of a whip; **-crane**, a crane with a 'whip' for hoisting; **-crop**, local name for several trees whose stems are used for w.-stocks, as the white-beam (*Pyrus Aria*); **-fish**, a chætodont fish, *Heniochus macrolepidotus*, having a dorsal spine elongated into a filament like a w.-lash; **-handle** = *w.-stock*; **-line** (*a*) = WHIPCORD 1; (*b*) the rope of a 'whip' (WHIP *sb.* III. 3); **-man**, a driver of horses; *dial.* a carter; **-master**, a master who uses the whip; a flogger; **-net**, techn. name of a simple kind of network; **-ray**, a fish of the family *Trygonidæ*, having a long slender flexible tail resembling the lash of a whip; a sting-ray; **-scorpion**, an arachnid of the genus *Thelyphonus* or some allied genus having a long slender abdomen like a w.-lash; **-snake**, name for various serpents of long slender form like a w.-lash, as *Masticophis flagelliformis* of N. America, *Hoplocephalus flagellum* of Australia; **-socket**, a socket fixed to the dash-board of a vehicle to hold the butt-end of a whip; **-stalk** (*dial.*), **-stick**, **-stock**, the stick or staff to which the lash of a whip is attached; the handle of a whip; **-tail**, name used (simply or attrib.) for any one of various animals having a long slender tail like a w.-lash; **-worm**, a parasitic nematoid worm of the genus *Trichocephalus*, consisting of a stout posterior and slender anterior part, like a w.-stock with a lash.

2. The vb.-stem in comb. a. with second element in objective relation: **w.-belly (-vengeance)**, *slang*, weak thin beer or other liquor; **-cat**, a workman who 'whips the cat' (see WHIP *v.* II). b. in attrib. relation to second element: **†w.-gig** = *w.-top*; **-rod**, a fishing-rod whipped or wound round with twine; **-sillabub**, whipped sillabub; **-top** = WHIPPING-*top*.

Whipcord (hwi·pkǭɹd). ME. [prob. f. WHIP *v.* III, with later association of WHIP *sb.* I.] 1. A thin tough kind of hempen cord, of which whip-lashes or the ends of them are made. b. A piece of this material, as a whip-lash or its extremity 1500. c. *attrib.* Tough as w. 1879. 2. *transf.* a. A kind of catgut 1880. b. A close-woven ribbed worsted material used for dresses, riding-breeches, etc. 1897. 3. Applied (simply or attrib.) to a. species of willow with very flexible shoots, as *Salix purpurea* or *S. vitellina*; b. species of seaweed with long slender fronds, as *Chorda Filum* or *Chordaria flagelliformis* 1812.

1. He looks as hard as iron, and tough as w. 1861.

Whi·p-gra:fting. 1657. [f. WHIP *v.* I. 2.] *Hort.* (See quot.)

The old-fashioned system of 'w.'..The stock is headed down and cut on one side only to receive the scion, which is cut with a long splice-cut and partially cleft or notched 1878.

Whip-hand (hwi·phæ·nd). 1680. [f. WHIP *sb.* I. 1.] 1. The hand in which the whip is held in driving or riding; the driver's or rider's right hand 1809. 2. fig. phr. *To have the w. of*: to have the advantage or upper hand of, control. Hence in similar phr. 1680.

†Whi·p-jack. 1556. [app. f. WHIP *v.* II. + JACK *sb.*[1]] A vagabond or beggar who pretends to be a distressed sailor –1753.

Whi·p-lash. 1573. [f. WHIP *sb.* I. 1 + LASH *sb.*[1] 2.] 1. The lash of a whip. 2. *transf.* An object resembling the lash of a whip, as the *vibraculum* of certain polyzoans; *spec.* a species of seaweed with long narrow fronds 1850.

1. *fig.* The sharp w. of furious voices in the room below 1915.

Whippable (hwi·păb'l), *a.* 1853. [f. WHIP *v.* II. 1 + -ABLE.] Liable to be whipped.

Whipper (hwi·pəɹ). 1552. [f. WHIP *v.* + -ER[1].] One who or that which whips. 1. One who beats or chastises with (or as with) a whip; *spec.* an official who inflicts whipping as a legal punishment. †b. = FLAGELLANT A. 1. –1782. 2. A workman who hoists coal with a 'whip' 1835. 3. One who runs the coloured thread along the edge of a blanket 1881.

Whipper-i·n. 1739. [f. phr. *to whip in*; see WHIP *v.* II. 1 d.] 1. A huntsman's assistant who keeps the hounds from straying by driving them back into the pack with a whip. b. In the game of hare and hounds, a runner whose business it is to keep the hounds in order 1855. c. *Racing slang.* The horse last in a race or at any given moment of a race 1892. 2. = WHIP *sb.* I. 6. *Obs.* exc. *Hist.* 1771.

Whi·pper-sna:pper. 1674. [app. jingling extension of **whip-snapper* a cracker of whips, on the model of the earlier *snipper-snapper*.] A diminutive or insignificant person, *esp.* a sprightly or impertinent young fellow.

Whippet (hwi·pėt). 1550. [perh. f. WHIP *sb.* or *v.* + -ET.] 1. A lively young woman; a light wench; now *dial.* a nimble, diminutive, or puny person. 2. A small breed of dog; now *spec.* a cross between a greyhound and a terrier or spaniel, used for coursing and racing, esp. in the north of England 1610. b. *transf. Mil.* A light kind of 'tank' used in the last year of the war of 1914–18.

Whipping (hwi·piŋ), *vbl. sb.* 1540. [f. WHIP *v.* + -ING[1].] The action of WHIP *v.* in various senses.

attrib. and *Comb.*: **†w.-cheer** (*joc.*), flogging, flagellation; **-post**, a post set up, usu. in a public place, to which offenders are or were tied to be whipped; so **-cart, -house**; **-top**, a top spun by whipping.

Whi·pping, *ppl. a.* 1530. [f. WHIP *v.* + -ING[2].] That whips. 1. Moving briskly or nimbly; acting vigorously or violently; characterized by such movement or action. 2. Beating with or as with a whip; flogging; lashing 1598.

2. *W. Tom*, a man who whips others or flagellates himself.

Whi·pping-boy. 1647. A boy educated together with a young prince or royal personage, and flogged in his stead when he committed a fault that was considered to deserve flogging; hence *allus.*

Whippletree (hwi·p'ltrī). 1733. [The first element is app. f. WHIP.] = SWINGLETREE 2.

Whi·p-poor-wi·ll. 1747. [Echoic, from the bird's note.] Popular name in U.S. and Canada for a species of Goatsucker, *Antrostomus* (*Caprimulgus*) *vociferus*.

Whippy (hwi·pi), *a.* 1867. [f. WHIP *sb.* + -Y[1].] Resembling a whip; *esp.* bending like a whip, flexible, springy.

Whip-saw (hwi·pˌsǭ), *sb.* 1538. [f. WHIP *sb.* or *v.* + SAW *sb.*[1]] a. A long narrow two-handed saw. b. A frame-saw with a narrow blade, used esp. for curved work 1875. c. *fig.* (cf. the verb). Hence **Whi·p-saw** *v. intr.* to work a w.; *trans.* to cut with a w.; *fig.* (*U.S. slang*) to have or get the advantage of in two ways; *spec.* at cards. **Whi·p-saw:yer, -saw:ing** *vbl. sb.*

Whipstaff (hwi·pˌstɑf). 1599. [STAFF *sb.*[1]] 1. The handle of a whip. †2. A handle attached to the tiller, formerly used in small ships –1769.

Whipster (hwi·pstəɹ). 1589. [app. f. WHIP *v.* + -STER.] 1. A vague term of reproach, contempt, or the like. a. A lively, smart, reckless, violent, or mischievous person. *Obs.* or *dial.* b. A wanton or licentious person, a debauchee. *Obs.* or *dial.* 1593. c. A slight, insignificant, or contemptible person. (Often with the epithet *puny*, after Shaks.) 1604. 2. One who wields a whip: a. a driver of horses; b. one addicted to whipping or flogging –1825.

1. c. I am not valiant neither: But euery Punie w. gets my Sword SHAKS.

Whip-stitch (hwi·pˌstitʃ), *sb.* (*adv.*) 1640. [f. WHIP *sb.* + STITCH *sb.*] 1. = WHIP *sb.* IV. 1. †2. As *adv.* or *int.* expressing sudden movement or action *slang* or *colloq.* –1706.

1. Phr. (*At*) *every w.*, at short or frequent intervals (*dial.* and *U.S.*). Hence **Whi·p-stitch** *v. trans.* to sew with a w.

Whi·psy-de:rry. 1865. [app. connected w. WHIP *sb.* III. 2 and DERRICK *sb.*] A contrivance for hoisting (esp. ore in shallow mines), consisting of a derrick with a 'whip' attached, and worked by a horse or horses.

Whip-tom-kelly. 1756. [Imitative, from the bird's note.] Popular name for the Red-eyed Greenlet or 'Flycatcher' (*Vireo olivaceus* or *Vireosylvia olivacia*) of eastern N. America, and the Black-whiskered Greenlet (*Vireo barbatulus* or *Vireosylvia calidris*) of the W. Indies.

Whirl (hwɜ̄ɹl), *sb.* late ME. [Partly a. MLG., MDu. *wervel* or ON. *hvirfill*, partly f. the vb.] I. 1. The fly-wheel or pulley of a spindle. b. *Rope-making.* A cylindrical piece of wood furnished with a hook on which the ends of the fibre are hung in spinning 1794. 2. *Bot.* and *Zool.* = WHORL 2. 1713. 3. *Conch.* = WHORL 3. 1681. 4. = WHORL 4. 1862. 5. *Angling.* A spinning bait 1888.

II. 1. The action or an act of whirling; (swift) rotatory or circling movement; a (rapid) turn, as of a wheel, around an axis or centre 1480. 2. Something, as a body of water or air, in (rapid) circling motion, or the part at which this takes place; an eddy, a vortex 1547. 3. Swift or violent movement, as of something hurled or flung, or of a wheeled vehicle, etc.; rapid course; rush; *transf.* and *fig.* Confused and hurried activity of any kind 1552. b. A confused, distracted, or dizzy state of mind or feeling 1707.

3. The w. of dissipation 1780. b. His head was in a complete w. 1854. Hence **Whi·rl-about**, the action of whirling about; something that whirls about; *attrib.* characterized by whirling about. **Whi·rly** *a.* (*rare*) characterized by whirling or rotatory movement.

Whirl (hwɜ̄ɹl), *v.* ME. [prob. a. ON. *hvirfla* to turn about, whirl:—OTeut. **hwerƀil-*, f. **hwerƀ-* to rotate.] 1. *intr.* To move in a circle or similar curve; to circle, circulate; more vaguely, to move *about* in various directions, esp. with rapidity or force; to be in commotion. 2. To turn, esp. swiftly, around an axis, like a wheel; to spin. late ME. b. To turn round or aside quickly 1861. 3. *trans.* To cause to rotate or revolve, esp. swiftly or forcibly; to move (something) around an axis, or in a circle or the like. late ME. 4. *intr.* To move along swiftly or as if on wheels; *gen.* to go swiftly or impetuously, rush or sweep along. late ME.

5. *trans.* To drive (a wheeled vehicle) or convey in a wheeled vehicle swiftly; *gen.* to drive or carry along impetuously, as a strong wind or stream (now only with implication of circular movement). late ME. **6.** To throw or cast with violence, hurl (esp. with rotatory movement, as from a sling). Also *absol.* 1440. **7.** *intr.* To be affected with giddiness; to reel: usu. (now only) of the head or brain 1561. †**b.** *trans.* To affect with giddiness, to put in a whirl or tumult –1829.

1. This world is not certeine ne stable, But whirlyng a bowte and mutable 1475. 2. Fortunes wheele, Howe constantly it whyrleth styll about 1563. 4. *Tit. A.* v. ii. 49. 5. The winds begin to rise..; The last red leaf is whirl'd away TENNYSON. 7. b. I am giddy: expectation whirles me round SHAKS. Hence **Whi·rler**, one who or that which whirls; a revolving piece of mechanism, as a potter's whirling-table, etc.

Whirl-, the sb. or vb. stem in Comb.

†**Whi·rlbat, who·rlbat.** 1565. [Alteration of HURLBAT by substitution of WHIRL for the first syllable.] = CESTUS[2] –1700.

Whi·rl-blast. 1798. [app. a Cumberland dial. wd., for which Wordsworth is the earliest literary authority.] A whirlwind, hurricane.

Whi·rlicote. *Obs.* exc. *Hist.* late ME. [Form doubtful; app. orig. *whirlecole*, f. WHIRL *v.*; recorded by Stow in the form *whirlicote*, whence its later use.] A coach, carriage.

Whirligig (hwɔ̄·ɹligig), *sb.* 1440. [f. WHIRL- or WHIRLY- + GIG *sb.*[1]] **1.** Name of various toys that are whirled, twirled, or spun round; *spec.* †(*a*) a top or teetotum; (*b*) a small spindle turned by means of a string; (*c*) a toy with four arms like windmill-sails, which whirl round when it is moved through the air. **2.** Applied to various mechanical contrivances having a whirling or rotatory movement; *spec.* a roundabout or merry-go-round 1477. **3.** *gen.* and *fig.* in various applications: (*a*) Something that is continually whirling, or in constant activity of any kind; (*b*) circling course, revolution (of time or events); (*c*) an antic; (*d*) a circling movement, a whirl 1589. **b.** A fickle, inconstant, giddy, or flighty person 1602. **4.** A water-beetle of the family *Gyrinidæ*, esp. the common species *Gyrinus natator*, found in large numbers circling rapidly over the surface of the water in ponds and ditches 1713. **5.** *advb.* Like a w.; with rapid circling movement 1598.

3. And thus the whirlegigge of time brings in his reuenges SHAKS. *attrib.* That intoxicating, inflammatory, and w. dance, the waltz 1807. Hence **Whi·rligig** *v. intr.* to turn like a w.; to whirl or spin round.

Whirling (hwɔ̄·ɹliŋ), *ppl. a.* late ME. [f. WHIRL *v.* + -ING[2].] That whirls, in various senses of the verb.

fig. These are but wild and wherling words, my Lord SHAKS.

Collocations: **w. blue, dun,** artificial flies used in angling; **w. plant**, the 'telegraph-plant', *Desmodium gyrans*; **-table,** (*a*) a machine consisting essentially of a table contrived to revolve rapidly, used for experiments or demonstrations in dynamics, etc.; (*b*) a horizontally rotating disk in a potter's lathe, carrying a mould which shapes the inside of a plate or other circular piece of ware. Hence **Whi·rlingly** *adv.*

†**Whi·rlpit.** 1570. [PIT *sb.*[1]] = next –1724.

Whirlpool (hwɔ̄·ɹlpūl). 1529. [f. WHIRL- + POOL *sb.*[1]] A place in, or part of, a river, the sea, or any expanse of water where there is constant (and usu. rapid) circular movement; a (large and violent) eddy or vortex 1530. **b.** *fig.* esp. a destructive or absorbing agency by which something is figured as engulfed or swallowed up; a scene of confused and turbulent activity 1529.

b. In yᵉ deepest whoorlpools of aduersities, faith may hold vs vp 1571. The Whirl-pool of Poetry suck'd me in, and I fell a Rhiming 1704.

Whirlwig (hwɔ̄·ɹlwig). 1816. = WHIRLIGIG 4.

Whirlwind (hwɔ̄·ɹlwind). ME. [f. WHIRL- + WIND *sb.*, prob. after ON. *hvirfilvindr*.] **1.** A whirling or rotating wind; a body of air moving rapidly in a circular or upward spiral course around a vertical or slightly inclined axis which has also a progressive motion over the surface of land or water. **2.** *transf.* and *fig.* Something rushing impetuously like a whirlwind; a violent or destructive agency; a confused and tumultuous process or condition. late ME.

2. Mr. Pickwick concluded amidst a w. of applause DICKENS. Phr. *To sow the wind and reap the w.* (Hos. viii. 7), to indulge in reckless wickedness or folly, and suffer the disastrous consequences.

Whirly-, obs. or dial. var. of WHIRL-, as †**whirly-pool, -wind** = WHIRLPOOL, -WIND.

Whirr, whir (hwɔ̄ɹ), *sb.* late ME. [See next.] †**1.** Violent or rapid movement, rush, hurry; the force or impetus of such movement –1553. †**b.** *fig.* Commotion of mind or feeling; a mental or nervous shock –1728. **2.** A continuous vibratory sound, such as that made by the rapid fluttering of a bird's or insect's wings, by a wheel turning swiftly, or by a body rushing through the air 1677.

2. A w. of unseen wings SOUTHEY.

Whirr, whir, *v.* (*adv.*, *int.*) late ME. [prob. of Scand. origin; cf. Da. *hvirre*, Norw. *kvirra*.] **1.** *trans.* †**a.** To throw or cast with violence and noise –1605. **b.** To carry or hurry along, to move or stir, with a rushing or vibratory sound (now *causal* from 2) 1608. **2.** *intr.* To move swiftly in some way with a continuous vibratory sound, as various birds, rapidly revolving wheels, etc. late ME. **3.** To make or emit a vibratory sound 1804. **b.** *dial.* To snarl or growl; to purr 1706. **4.** The vb.-stem as *int.* or *adv.*, expressing a sudden or rapid movement with vibratory sound 1600.

1. b. *Per.* IV. i. 21. 3. Grasshoppers whirring in the grass STEVENSON.

Whish (hwiʃ), *sb.*, *int.*[2] 1808. [Imitative.] A soft sibilant sound, as of something moving rapidly through the air or over the surface of water. Also as *int.*

Whish (hwiʃ), *v.* 1518. [Imitative.] **1.** *intr.* To utter the syllable 'whish' or a sound resembling it; *trans.* to drive or chase by crying 'whish!' **2.** To make a soft sibilant sound of this kind; as a body rushing through air or water, the wind among the trees, etc. 1540.

Whish, *int.*[1] Now *dial.* 1635. = Hush!

Whisht (hwiʃt), *sb.* 1553. [f. WHISHT *int.*] **1.** An utterance of 'whisht!' to enjoin silence. **2.** Silence; in phr. *to hold one's w.*, to keep silence. *Sc.* 1785.

Whisht (hwiʃt), *a.* Now *dial.* 1570. [Variant of WHIST *a.*] Silent, still, hushed. Hence **Whi·shtly** *adv.* 1548.

Whisht (hwiʃt), *int.* Now *dial.* late ME. [A natural utterance.] An exclamation enjoining silence: Hush! Hence **Whisht** *v.* (*dial.*) *intr.* to be silent; *trans.* to silence, hush.

Whisk (hwisk), *sb.*[1] late ME. [orig. *wisk*, *wysk*; partly f. WHISK *v.*, partly ad. ON. *visk*.] **I.** A brief rapid sweeping movement; a light stroke of a brush or other sweeping implement.

fig. The whiske of one of his Epigrams 1644. *With a w.*, *in a w.*, in an instant, in a flash.

II. 1. A neckerchief worn by women in the latter half of the 17th c. *Obs.* exc. *Hist.* 1654. **2.** A small instrument, usu. made of wire, for beating up eggs, cream, or the like 1666. **3.** A bundle or tuft of hairs, feathers, etc. fixed on a handle, used for brushing or dusting 1729. **b.** A slender hair-like or bristle-like part or appendage, as those on the tails of certain insects 1618. **c.** The panicle or other part of certain plants used for making into brushes or brooms; *esp.* the panicle of the common millet or 'broom-corn' (*Sorghum vulgare*); hence, the plant itself 1757. **d.** A small bunch or tuft 1845. **4.** A mechanical appliance having a whisking movement: **a.** A kind of winnowing-machine. **b.** A machine for winding yarn. **c.** A cooper's plane for levelling the chimes of casks. 1813.

1. My wife..brought her a white w. and put it on PEPYS.

attrib. and *Comb.*: **w. broom** = sense II. 3; **w. seed**, millet seed.

Whisk, *sb.*[2] *Obs.* or *dial.* 1621. [perh. f. next.] The earlier name of the card-game now called whist.

Whisk, *v.* (*adv.*, *int.*). 1480. [orig. Sc.; prob. of Scand. origin; cf. Sw. *viska* to whisk (off), Da. *viske*.] **1.** *intr.* To move with a light rapid sweeping motion; to make a single sudden movement of this kind; to move about or travel swiftly or briskly. **b.** as *adv.* or *int.* With a whisk, or sudden light movement 1750. **2.** *trans.* To move (something) *about*, *away*, etc. with a light sweeping motion 1513. **b.** in ref. to rapid travel 1694. **3.** To brush or sweep lightly and rapidly from a surface, esp. with a light instrument, as a feather or small brush 1621. **4.** To beat or whip with a rod of twigs or the like. *Obs.* in *gen.* sense: now, to beat up (eggs, cream, or the like) with a light rapid movement by means of a whisk. 1530.

2. The squirrel..there whisks his brush, and perks his ears COWPER. 3. The beadle..whisked the crumbs off his knees DICKENS. 4. Whites of Eggs beat up and whisk'd 'till it stand all in froth 1710.

Whisker (hwi·skəɹ). late ME. [f. WHISK *v.* + -ER[1].] **1.** Something that whisks or is used for whisking; applied to various objects, as a fan, a bunch of feathers used as a brush. *Obs.* or *dial.* **2.** *slang* or *colloq.* Something great or excessive; esp. a great lie. Now *rare* or *Obs.* 1668. **3.** The hair that grows on an adult man's face; formerly commonly applied to the *moustache*, and sometimes to (or including) the *beard*; now restricted to that on the cheeks or sides of the face. **a.** *pl.*: usu. collective 1600. **b.** *sing.*: formerly, a moustache; now, the hair on one side of the face; also *collect.* 1706. **4.** Each of a set of projecting hairs or bristles growing on the upper lip or about the mouth of certain animals; also applied to a similar set of feathers in certain birds 1678. **5.** *Naut.* Each of two spars extending laterally on each side of the bowsprit, for spreading the guys of the jib-boom 1844. **b.** A lever for exploding a torpedo 1880.

3. a. A tall fellow, with..very thick bushy whiskers meeting under his chin DICKENS. Hence **Whi·skered** *a.* having whiskers; *spec.* as a descriptive appellation of particular species of animals, as *whiskered auk*, *tern*. **Whi·skerless** *a.* **Whis·kery** *a.* having large whiskers.

Whiskey: see WHISKY.

Whiskied (hwi·skid), *a. rare.* 1850. [f. WHISKY *sb.*[1] + -ED[2].] Saturated or tainted with whisky.

Whiskified (hwi·skifəid), *a.* 1802. [f. WHISKY *sb.*[1]; see -FY.] Affected by excessive drinking of whisky.

Whisky, whiskey (hwi·ski), *sb.*[1] 1715. [Short for † *whiskybae*, var. USQUEBAUGH. In mod. trade usage, Scotch *whisky* and Irish *whiskey* are thus distinguished in spelling.] A spirituous liquor distilled orig. in Ireland and Scotland, and in the British Islands still chiefly, from malted barley, in U.S. chiefly from maize or rye. With *a* and *pl.*, a drink of whisky.

W.-and-milk, *-soda*, *-water*, mixed or diluted drinks. He..went home..for his whiskey-and-water DICKENS. *attrib.* and *Comb.*, as *w.-punch*, *-still*, *-toddy*; **w. insurrection, rebellion** *U.S. Hist.*, an outbreak in Pennsylvania in 1794 against an excise duty on spirits; **w. ring** *U.S. Hist.*, a combination of distillers and revenue officers formed in 1872 to defraud the government of part of the tax on spirits; **-straight** *U.S. slang*, whisky without water.

Whisky, whiskey, *sb.*[2] 1769. [app. f. WHISK *v.* + -Y[1], from its swift movement.] A kind of light two-wheeled one-horse carriage, used in England and America in the late 18th and early 19th c.

Whi·sky, *a. rare.* 1782. [f. WHISK *v.* + -Y[1].] Light and lively, flighty.

Whisky jack (hwi·skiˌdʒæk). 1772. [Altered f. next by substitution of *jack* for *john*.] Popular name for the Common Grey Jay of Canada, *Perisoreus canadensis.*

Whisky john (hwi·skiˌdʒǫn). 1772. [Corruption of Amer. Indian name (Cree *wiskatjan*).] = prec.

Whisper (hwi·spəɹ), *sb.* 1596. [f. next.] **1.** An act or the action of whispering the low non-resonant quality of voice which characterizes this 1608. **b.** *Phonetics.* Speech or vocal sound without vibration of the vocal cords and with contraction of the glottis 1856. **c.** A whispered word, phrase, or speech 1599. **2.** A secret or slight utterance, mention, or report; a suggestion, insinuation, hint; with negative, the slightest mention, the 'least word' 1596. **3.** *fig.* A soft rustling sound resembling or suggesting that of a whispering voice 1637. **4.** *attrib.* Uttered in a whisper 1626.

1. Secrets which he always communicates in a w. JOHNSON. *Stage w.*: see STAGE *sb.* c. *Hen. V*, IV.

Chor. 7. **2.** At least the w. goes so SHAKS. No one raises even a w. of reproach against Peel 1827.

Whisper (hwi·spəɹ), *v.* [OE. **hwisprian* (only Northumb., glossing L. *murmurare*), of imitative origin. Cf. G. *wispern*, ON. *hviskra.*] **1.** *intr.* To speak softly 'under one's breath', i. e. without the resonant tone produced by vibration of the vocal cords; to talk or converse in this way, esp. in the ear of another, for the sake of secrecy. **2.** *trans.* To say, tell, communicate, utter, or express by whispering 1588. **3.** To address in a whisper; to tell, inform, bid, or ask in a whisper 1540. **4. a.** *intr.* To speak or converse quietly or secretly about something (usu. implying hostility, malice, etc.); also (with negative) to speak ever so slightly, to say 'the least thing' about something 1515. **b.** *trans.* To say, report, or utter quietly, secretly, or confidentially; also (with negative), to say the least word of 1562. **c.** with *adv.* or *advb. phr.* To bring *into* or *out of* something, or to take *away*, by secret (esp. malicious or slanderous) speech 1631. **5.** *intr. fig.* To make a soft rustling sound resembling or suggesting a whisper 1653. **6.** *trans. fig.* To suggest secretly to the mind; also, to express or communicate by a soft rustling sound 1640. **b.** with the person, etc. as obj. 1605.

2. What did you w. in your Ladies eare? SHAKS. **3.** Miss Jane.. whispered her sister to observe how jealous Mr. Cheggs was DICKENS. **4. a.** All myne enemyes w. together agaynst me BIBLE (Great) *Ps.* xli. 7. **b.** This newes was first wispered here the 19th November. 1628. Some vague rumour..which had been whispered abroad DICKENS. **5.** No tree is heard to w., bird to sing GRAY. **6. b.** What devil whispered thee to marry such a woman? 1761. Hence **Whi·spered** *ppl. a.* **Whi·spering** *ppl. a.* that whispers; uttered in a whisper; reporting something secretly or confidentially; **-ly** *adv.*

Whisperer (hwi·spərəɹ). 1547. [f. prec. + -ER [1].] One who whispers. **1.** One who speaks in a whisper 1567. **b.** An appellation for certain horse-breakers, said to have obtained obedience by whispering to the horses 1810. **2.** One who communicates something quietly or secretly; *esp.* a secret slanderer or tale-bearer 1547.

Whispering (hwi·spəriŋ), *vbl. sb.* OE. [f. as prec. + -ING [1].] The action of WHISPER *vb.* in various senses.

Foule whisp'rings are abroad SHAKS. The Gazings and Whisperings of the Ladies and Gentlemen RICHARDSON. The w. of the leaves,..and the plashing of the fountains SCOTT. The whisperings of her womanly nature..caused her to shrink from any unmaidenly action MRS. GASKELL.

attrib. **w.-gallery,** a gallery or dome, usu. of circular or elliptical plan, in which a whisper or other faint sound at one point can be heard by reflexion at a distant point where the direct sound is inaudible.

Whist (hwist), *sb.*[1] *Irish.* 1897. [f. WHIST *v.* or *int.*] Silence: in phr. *to hold one's w.*, to keep silence.

Whist (hwist), *sb.*[2] 1663. [Altered f. WHISK *sb.*[2]] A game of cards played (ordinarily) by four persons each having a *hand* of 13 cards; one of the suits is *trumps* (see TRUMP *sb.*[2] 1); the players play in rotation, each four successive cards played constituting a *trick*, in which each player after the leader must follow suit if he holds a card of the suit led, otherwise may discard or trump; points are scored according to the number of tricks won and sometimes also by *honours* or highest trumps held by each pair of partners.

Dummy w.: see DUMMY *sb.* 2. *Duplicate w.*, a form in which the hands played are preserved and played again by the opposing partners. *Long w.*, a form in which the score is ten points with honours counting. *Short w.*, the form now usual in England, in which the score is five points with honours counting.

attrib. and *Comb.*, as *w.-club, -party, -player*; **w.-drive,** a party of progressive w. (see PROGRESSIVE *a.* 2 b) usu. played for prizes.

Whist (hwist), *a. arch.* and *dial.* late ME. [f. WHIST *int.*] Silent, quiet, hushed; free from noise or disturbance. (Usu. predic.) **b.** Keeping silence in relation to something; saying nothing about the matter 1577.

Curtsied when you haue, and kist the wilde waues w. SHAKS. **b.** The Heybrooks were w. folks about their concerns 1880. Hence **Whi·stly** *adv.*

Whist, *v.* Pa. t. and pple. **whi·sted, whist.** 1541. [f. next.] **1.** *intr.* To become or be silent, keep silence. *arch.* and *dial.* 1547. †**2.** *trans.* To put to silence; to hush -1602.

Whist (hwist), *int.* Now *dial.* late ME. [A natural utterance.] An exclam. to command silence: Hush!

Whistle (hwi·s'l), *sb.* [OE. *hwistle*, related to *hwistlian* (see next).] **1.** A tubular wind instrument of wood, metal, or other hard substance, having a more or less shrill tone; a shrill pipe. **2.** *colloq.* A joc. name for the mouth or throat as used in speaking or singing. late ME. **3.** An act of whistling; the sound of this, esp. as a call or signal to a person or animal, or as an expression of surprise or astonishment. Also, the act of sounding or the sound made by a whistle or pipe. 1447. **b.** *fig.* or in fig. phrases: Call, summons 1529. **c.** The clear shrill voice or note of a bird or of certain other animals 1784. **d.** Any similar sound, as of wind blowing through trees, etc. 1648.

1. Boatswain with your w. command the Saylors to the upper deck 1610. The w. sounded, and the train began..to glide out of the station 1898. *Penny w., tin w.*, a musical toy, usu. of tin and pierced with six holes. *As clean, clear, dry as a w.*; A first rate shot; ..head taken off as clean as a w. 1849. †*Box* or (Sc.) *kist of whistles*: a contemptuous phr. for a church organ. *To pay (too dear) for one's w.*, to pay more for something than it is worth. **2.** *To wet* (erron. *whet*) *one's w.*, to take a drink (esp. of alcoholic liquor). **3. b.** Ready to run at every mans w. 1639. Phr. (*Not*) *worth a w.*; I haue beene worth the w. SHAKS.

Whistle (hwi·s'l), *v.* [OE. *hwis(t)lian, wistlian*, f. an echoic root + -LE 3.] **I. 1.** *intr.* To utter a clear, more or less shrill sound or note by forcing the breath through the narrow opening formed by contracting the lips: esp. as a call or signal, also as an expression of derision, etc., later more usu. of surprise or astonishment; also, to utter a melody or tune consisting of a succession of such notes, esp. by way of idle diversion. **2.** To utter a clear shrill sound, note, or song, as various birds and certain other animals; to pipe OE. **3.** To produce a shrill sound of this kind in any way, esp. by rapid movement, as the wind, a missile, etc. 1480. **b.** To rustle shrilly, as silk or other stiff fabric. *Obs.* or *dial.* 1633. **4.** To blow or sound a whistle; to sound as a whistle 1530. **5.** *trans.* To produce or utter by whistling, as a tune or melody; to express by whistling 1530. **6.** To shoot or drive with a whistling sound 1697. **b.** To make (one's way) with whistling 1853.

1. He whistled thrice for his little foot-page SCOTT. Richard, whistling to the dog, led the way 1905. *To w. for a wind*, in ref. to the common superstitious practice among sailors; The more we whistled for the wind The more it did not blow HOOD. **3.** The wind whistled through the cracked walls DICKENS. **b.** Brave Glorie puffing by In silks that whistled G. HERBERT. **5.** Those tunes..that he heard the Car-men w. SHAKS.

II. 1. a. To call, summon, bring, or get by or as by whistling 1486. **b.** (With *away, off*, etc.) To send or dismiss by whistling (esp. as a term of falconry); also *fig.* to cast off or abandon lightly: so *to w. down the wind* (the hawk being usu. cast off against the wind in pursuit of prey, but with the wind when turned loose) 1555. **2.** *To go w.*: to go and do what one will, to occupy oneself idly or to no purpose (esp. in phrases expressing contemptuous dismissal, or the like). *To w. for*: to seek, await, or expect in vain, to go without. *colloq.* 1513. †**3.** *intr.* and *trans.* To speak, tell, or utter secretly; to give secret information, turn informer -1815.

1. b. *Oth.* III. iii. 262. Having accepted my love you cannot w. me down the wind as though I were of no account TROLLOPE. **2.** This being done, let the Law goe w. SHAKS. She..rode off, telling him he might w. for his money 1882. **3.** *Wint. T.* IV. iv. 248.

Whistler (hwi·s'ləɹ). [OE. *hwistlere*, f. *hwistlian* WHISTLE *v.*] A person, animal, or thing that whistles. **1. a.** One who sounds or plays upon a whistle or pipe. Now *rare.* **b.** One who whistles with the lips 1440. **c.** A keeper of a 'whistling-shop' 1821. **2. a.** A bird that whistles: applied locally to various species; also *spec.* used of some nocturnal bird having a whistling note believed to be of ill omen 1590. **b.** (tr. Canadian F. *siffleur.*) A large species of marmot, *Arctomys pruinosus*, found in mountainous parts of N. America 1820. **c.** A broken-winded horse that breathes hard with a shrill sound 1824. **3.** Something that makes a whistling sound 1812.

2. a. The W. shrill, that who so heares, doth dy SPENSER.

Whistling (hwi·s'liŋ), *vbl. sb.* [OE. *hwistlung*, f. *hwistlian* WHISTLE *v.*] The action of the vb. WHISTLE, in various senses.

attrib.: **w. post,** a post beside a railway-line, on passing which the engine-whistle is sounded; **-shop** *slang*, a room in a prison in which spirits were secretly sold without a licence (a signal being given by whistling to escape detection).

Whi·stling, *ppl. a.* late ME. [f. WHISTLE *v.* + -ING [2].] That whistles, in various senses.

To dance our ringlets to the w. Winde SHAKS. *Prov.* A w. woman and a crowing hen Is neither fit for God nor men.

W. buoy, a buoy fitted with a whistle which is automatically sounded by the movement of the waves; **w. dick,** any of various species of thrush, esp. of the Australian genus *Collur icincla*; **w. duck,** various species of duck, as the golden-eye and the widgeon; **w. marmot** = WHISTLER 2 b; **w. thrush,** local name for the song-thrush.

Whit (hwit), *sb.*[1] Now *arch.* or *literary.* 1480. [Early modE. *whyt, wyt*, app. an alteration of *wight* in *no wight, little wight* (see WIGHT *sb.*).] A very small or the least portion or amount; a particle, jot; freq. in phrases used advb., esp. with negative expressed or implied.

Every w., the whole. *Never a w., not a w.*, none at all. *A w.*, to a very small extent, very little; *any w., one w.*, to the least amount, in the least degree; *every w.*, completely, thoroughly, quite (in late use almost always with *as* in comparisons of equality); I have written..a whole cartload of things, every w. as good as this 1672. *Never, not* (etc.) *a w., no w.*, not in the least, not at all; You don't seem one w. the happier at this SHERIDAN.

Whit, *int.* (*adv.*), *sb.*[2], *v.* 1833. [Imitative.] A word expressing a shrill abrupt sound, as of a bird's chirp, etc.

White (hwəit), *sb.* OE. [absol. uses of WHITE *a.*] **1.** The translucent viscous fluid surrounding the yolk of an egg, which becomes white when coagulated (usu. in full, *the w. of an egg*, pl. *whites of eggs*, or, as a substance, *w.* or *the w. of egg*). **2.** The white part (sclerotic coat) of the eyeball, surrounding the coloured iris (usu. in full, *the w. of the eye*). late ME. **3.** The white or light-coloured part of some substance or structure, as flesh, wood, etc. late ME. **4.** *Archery.* **a.** The white target usu. placed on the butt. *arch.* or *Hist.* 1456. **b.** In modern practice, a circular band of white on the target, or each of two such bands (*inner* and *outer w.*); hence, a shot that hits this 1687. **5. a.** *Printing.* The blank space in certain letters or types; a space left blank between words or lines 1594. **b.** *Drawing*, etc. *pl.* White or blank parts 1892. **6.** White cloth or textile fabric: applied *spec.* to various particular kinds; often in *pl.* ME. **7.** White clothing or array; usu. in phr. *in w.* ME. **b.** *pl.* White garments or vestments; *spec.* (*a*) surplices worn by clergymen, choristers, etc. (now chiefly *Hist.*); (*b*) white trousers or breeches 1622. **8.** = BLANK *sb.* 1. *Hist.* 1716. **9.** White wine. late ME. **10.** An animal of a species, breed, or variety distinguished by a white colour (chiefly as a fancier's abbrev.) 1530. **11.** A white man; a person of a race distinguished by light complexion 1671. **12.** Either of the white balls in billiards 1856. **13. a.** Applied variously to any white body or substance 1540. **b.** As a specific name (chiefly in *pl.*) for various manufactured articles and products of a white colour; as pins, sugar, flour, etc. 1690. **14.** *pl.* Pop. name for leucorrhœa 1572. **15.** White colour or hue; white coloration or appearance. Sometimes semi-*concr.* OE. **b.** Whiteness or fairness of complexion ME. **16.** A white pigment; often with defining word denoting a particular kind, as *Chinese, flake, Spanish w.*, etc. 1546. **17.** A member of any one of certain political parties (from the colour of the badge worn) 1680. **18.** Short for *white squadron* 1704. **19.** The player who holds the white pieces at chess or any similar game 1750.

2. Phr. *To turn up the whites of one's eyes* (usu., in affected devotion, but also in death, in astonishment, horror, etc.). **4. a.** *fig.* 'Twas I wonne the wager, though you hit the w. SHAKS. **5. b.** If a plate is over-exposed..the whites will be muddy, and the blacks lacking in richness 1892. **11.** *Poor whites* = 'poor white folks' (see next 4). **13. a.** †*To spit w.*, to eject frothy-white sputum from a dry mouth. 15. Provb. phr. *To call w. black, to turn w. into black.* b. Varying her Cheeks by Turns, with w. and red DRYDEN.

Phrases. *In black and w.*: see BLACK *a.* *In the w.*, said of cloth in an undyed state; hence of manufactured articles generally in an unfinished state.

White (hwəit), *a.* [Com. Teut: OE. *hwít*:–OTeut. **hwītoz*, f. (ult.) Indo-Eur. base **kwid-* to be bright.] 1. Of the colour of snow or milk; having that colour produced by reflection, transmission, or emission of all kinds of light in the proportion in which they exist in the complete visible spectrum, without sensible absorption, being thus fully luminous and devoid of any distinctive hue. b. Of the colour of the hair or beard in old age; also *transf.* white-haired, hoary ME. 2. a. Of a light or pale colour: applied to things of various indefinite hues approaching white, esp. dull or pale shades of yellow OE. b. Of metal, or objects made of metal, of a light grey colour and lustrous appearance OE. c. Colourless, uncoloured, as glass or other transparent substance OE. d. Blank, not written or printed upon 1466. 3. Of or in ref. to the skin or complexion: Light in colour, fair. Now *rare* or *Obs.* OE. 4. Applied to those races of men (chiefly European or of European extraction) characterized by light complexion 1604. b. *slang* or *colloq.* (orig. *U.S.*) Honourable; square-dealing 1877. 5. Pale, pallid, esp. from fear or other emotion. Also in allusive phrases expressing cowardice, and *transf.* (as in *w. rage*). 1508. 6. a. Clothed or arrayed in white; *spec.* belonging to an eccl. order distinguished by wearing a white habit ME. b. Regarded as specially associated with royalist and legitimist causes (as in the white flag of the Bourbons); hence applied in recent times to certain constitutional or anti-revolutionary parties and the policy for which they stand (cf. RED *a.* I. 9 b) 1749. 7. *fig.* Morally or spiritually pure or stainless; spotless, innocent OE. b. Free from malignity or evil intent; innocent, harmless, esp. as opp. to something characterized as *black*: chiefly in phr. *w. lie* (LIE *sb.*[1] 1), *w. magic* (MAGIC *sb.* 1) 1651. 8. Chiefly of times and seasons: Propitious; auspicious, happy. Now *rare.* 1629. †9. Highly prized, precious; dear, beloved –1821 (see WHITE BOY 1). †10. Specious, plausible –1825.

1. *As w. as* (or *whiter than*) *snow, milk, a lily*, etc.; I am as w. as driven snow compared to some blackguards 1885. 3. Fair be their wives, right lovesom, w. and small DUNBAR. 4. The W. Australia policy—the determination to keep Australia w. 1921. *Poor w. folks* or *trash*, a contemptuous name given in America by negroes to white people of no substance. b. As w. a man as I ever knew 1877. 5. I shame to weare a Heart so w. SHAKS. She is as w. as a sheet 1866. *To bleed* (a person, etc.) *w.*, to drain completely of resources. 6. b. Boswell, in the year 1745,..wore a w. cockade, and prayed for King James. JOHNSON.

Special collocations and Combs.: **w. ash**, a species or variety of ash with light-coloured wood; hence (*colloq.*) an oar; **w. bonnet** [BONNET *sb.* 7.], a fictitious bidder at an auction; **w.-book** [tr. med.L. *liber albus*], a book of official records or reports bound in white; **w. brass**, an alloy of copper and zinc, containing a large proportion of the latter; **w. bread**, bread of a light colour, made from fine wheaten flour, as dist. from *brown bread*; **w. corpuscle**, a colourless blood-corpuscle, a leucocyte; **-ear**, a gasteropod resembling, or having some part resembling, a w. ear; e.g. one of the family *Vanicoridæ*, having a w.-ribbed shell with a wide opening; **w. elephant** (see ELEPHANT 1); **w. ensign**, an ensign (ENSIGN 5) with a white ground; **-face**, a name for Hereford cattle; **w. feather** (see FEATHER *sb.* 1); **-fellow**, applied by Australian natives to a w. man; **w. flag**, (*a*) a flag of a w. colour displayed in token of peaceful intention, desire for parley, or surrender; (*b*) the national flag of France before the Revolution; **w. flux**, leucorrhœa; **-heart** (in full *w.-heart cherry*), a light-coloured variety of cultivated cherry; **W. House**, pop. name for the official residence of the President of the U.S. at Washington; **w. iron**, (*a*) tinned iron, tin-plate; (*b*) cast iron of a silvery colour containing a large proportion of carbon; **w. lead**, a compound of lead carbonate and hydrated oxide of lead, much used as a w. pigment; *w. lead ore*, native carbonate of lead, cerusite; **w. letter** *Printing*, occasional name for the (now) ordinary or 'roman' style of type, as dist. from BLACK-LETTER; **w. lie** (see 7 b); **w. matter**, the fibrous matter of the brain and spinal cord, as dist. from the *grey matter*; **w. metal**, applied to various alloys of a light grey colour; **w. monk**, a Cistercian monk, so called from the colour of his habit of undyed wool; **w. mouse**, (*a*) an albino variety or fancy breed of the common house mouse; (*b*) the collared lemming, *Cuniculus torquatus*; **w. night** (tr. F. *nuit blanche*), a sleepless night; **w. note** *Mus.*, a note with an open head, as a semibreve or minim; **w. paper**, (*a*) paper of a w. colour; (*b*) *techn.* blank paper, not written or printed upon; (*c*) an official document printed on w. paper; **w. plague**, tuberculosis; **w. point**, a moth (*Leucania albipuncta*) having a w. dot on each forewing; **-pot**, a dish made (chiefly in Devonshire) of milk or cream boiled with eggs, flour, spices, etc.; so **w. pudding**; **w. rose**, the emblem, and hence a designation, of the House of York in the Wars of the Roses; also adopted by the Jacobites in the 18th c.; **W. Russian**, (*a*) a Russian of the stock inhabiting the western part of Russia; (*b*) the dialect of these; **w. sale**, a sale of linen (LINEN *sb.* 3) and the like; **w. sauce**, a sauce made with flour, milk, and butter, seasoned or sweetened and used as a dressing for food; **w. scourge**, tuberculosis; **w. sheet**, in phr. referring to the performance of penance in a sheet; **-skin**, a w. man (cf. *redskin*); **w. slave**, a w. person who is or is treated like a slave; freq. attrib. in *w.-slave traffic*, so **w. slaver**, **w. slavery** (*spec.* in ref. to prostitution); **w. squadron**, one of the three squadrons into which the Royal Navy was formerly divided; **w. squall** (see SQUALL *sb.*[3] 1 c); **-stocking**, one who wears w. stockings; occas. applied to a horse with w. legs; **w. stone**, in provb. phr. *to mark with a w. stone*, to reckon as specially fortunate or happy (in allusion to the use of a w. stone among the ancients as a memorial of a fortunate event); **-tip**, an artificial fly; **w. vine**, (*a*) the common bryony, *Bryonia dioica*; (*b*) traveller's-joy, *Clematis Vitalba*; **-weed**, name in N. America for the ox-eye daisy (*Chrysanthemum Leucanthemum*); **w. wheat**, wheat with w. or light-coloured grain; **w.-wing**, local name for (*a*) the chaffinch; (*b*) *U.S.* the w.-winged scoter, *Œdemia fusca deglandi*; (*c*) *w.-wing dove*, a dove of the genus *Melopelia*; **w. wings**, (*a*) sails; (*b*) (*U.S.*) a person, esp. a street sweeper, wearing a white uniform; **w. witch**, a witch (or wizard) who uses witchcraft for beneficent purposes: cf. WHITE *a.* 7 b; **-wood**, any of various trees with w. or light-coloured wood, as the N. Amer. tulip-tree, the W. Indian wild cinnamon, etc.; also, the wood.

Parasynthetic Combs., as *w.-armed, -handed, -hatted, -lipped, -whiskered*, etc.; **w.-blooded**, having light-coloured or colourless blood, without red corpuscles, as most invertebrates; **-eyed**, having w. eyes; having the iris of the eye white, or having w. plumage round the eyes; **-haired**, having w. hair, esp. from age; also, covered with w. hairs or down, as a plant; **-winged**, having w. wings; often in specific names of birds having the wings wholly or partly w. Hence **Whi·te-ly** *adv.* so as to be or appear w.; with a w. colour or aspect.

White (hwəit), *v.* [OE. *hwītian*, f. *hwīt* WHITE *a.*] †1. *intr.* To become white –1471. †2. *trans.* To make white –1721. b. *spec.* To cover or coat with white; to whitewash. Now *rare.* ME. †c. To bleach; to blanch –1714. d. *Printing.* To space *out* (matter) with 'white'.

White ant: see ANT.

Whitebait (hwəi·tbeᶦt). 1758. [f. WHITE *a.* + BAIT *sb.*; so called from its former use as bait.] A small silvery-white fish (the fry of various fishes, chiefly the herring and sprat), caught in large numbers in the estuary of the Thames and elsewhere, and esteemed as a delicacy. b. Applied to other small fishes in different parts of the world resembling this and used as food 1882.

Whitebeam (hwəi·tbīm). 1705. [Origin obsc.] A small tree, *Pyrus Aria*, having large leaves with white silky hairs on the under side.

Whitebeard (hwəi·tbīəɹd). 1450. 1. An old man with a white beard. 2. *Australia.* The plant *Styphelia ericoides*, from the white hairs on the corolla 1898.

White boy, whi·teboy. 1599. †1. A favourite, pet, or darling boy: a term of endearment for a boy or (usu.) man –1821. 2. (usu. with capital.) Adopted by or applied to the members of various illegal, rebellious, or riotous associations 1644; *spec.* in *Irish Hist.* a member of a secret agrarian association formed in 1761. Hence **Whi·teboyism**, the principles or practices of the Irish Whiteboys.

Whitecap, white-cap (hwəi·tkæp). 1668. [CAP *sb.*[1]] 1. Any of several birds having a white or light-coloured patch on the head. 2. *pl.* Local name for species of mushroom 1818. 3. A white-capped or crested wave; a breaker 1773. 4. A person wearing a white cap; *spec.* one of a self-constituted body in the U.S. who commit outrages upon persons under the pretence of regulating public morals 1891.

Whitechapel (hwəi·t,tʃæ·p'l). 1700. [Name of a district of London, inhabited chiefly by persons of low character.] 1. a. In various slang uses, mostly *attrib.* (see quots.) b. *attrib.* or *absol.* Applied to certain irregular or unskilful methods of play in whist and billiards *colloq.* 1755. 2. In full *W. cart*, a kind of light two-wheeled spring-cart 1842. 3. as *adj.* Low, vulgar 1901.

1. a. *W. beau*, who dresses with a needle and thread, and undresses with a knife 1785. A 'W. shave' (..which is, in fact, whitening, judiciously applied to the jaws with the palm of the hand) DICKENS. b. Avoid the hateful 'W.', *i.e.* the lead from a single card 1899.

Whi·tecoat. 1555. 1. A soldier wearing a white or light-coloured coat. *Hist.* b. An Austrian soldier 1861. 2. A young seal, having a coat of white fur; also, the fur itself 1792.

White-collar. *U.S.* 1929. Applied *attrib.* to persons engaged in non-manual work, or to the occupations of these; 'black-coated'.

Whited (hwəi·tėd), *ppl. a.* Now *rare* or *arch.* ME. [f. WHITE *v.* + -ED[1].] 1. Covered or coated with white; *spec.* plastered over with white, whitewashed; now chiefly in biblical phr. *w. sepulchre* (Matt. xxiii. 27) used *allus.* 2. Whitened by deprivation of colour; also, peeled so as to expose the white interior 1529.

Whitefieldian, Whitfieldian (hwəit-, hwi·tfīldiăn), *sb.* and *a.* [f. proper name *Whitefield* or *Whitfield* + -IAN.] A. *sb.* A follower of George Whitefield; a Calvinistic Methodist. B. *adj.* Of or belonging to George Whitefield or the Whitefieldians. So **Whi·t(e)fieldism. Whi·t(e)fieldite**, a W.

Whitefish (hwəi·tfiʃ). 1461. 1. A general name for fishes of a white or light colour, as cod, haddock, whiting, etc. 2. The Great Sturgeon (= BELUGA 1); the White Whale (= BELUGA 2) 1662. 3. Any fish of the genus *Coregonus* (family *Salmonidæ*), found in the lakes of N. America, and valued as food 1748. Hence **Whi·tefisher**, one who catches white fish (sense 1). **Whi·tefishery, -fishing.**

Whitefoot (hwəi·tfut). 1753. [Cf. OE. *hwītfōt* adj.] 1. *Farriery.* A white marking on a horse's foot; also, a horse with such a mark. 2. Collector's name for a species of moth 1832. 3. *Hist.* A member of a secret society in Ireland who committed murders and outrages about 1832.

White friar. late ME. [WHITE *a.* 6 a.] 1. A Carmelite friar (whose habit is distinguished by a white cloak and scapular). Also, loosely, a Premonstratensian. Hence in *pl.*, the quarters of these friars, in London or elsewhere 1561.

Whi·teha·ll. A thoroughfare in London which is bordered by government offices; hence *fig.* British imperial government or policy.

Whitehead (hwəi·thed), *a.* and *sb.*[1] 1577. A. *adj.* = WHITE-HEADED (*rare*). B. *sb.* 1. Any of various species of birds having the head (wholly or partly) white 1686. 2. A West Indian feverfew, *Parthenium Hysterophorus* 1864.

Whitehead, *sb.*[2] 1884. A kind of torpedo, invented by Robert Whitehead.

White-headed (hwəi·the:dėd), *a.* 1525. 1. Of an animal: Having the head (wholly or partly) white; having white hair, plumage, etc. on the head. 2. Of a person: White-haired; also, flaxen-haired 1815. b. with *boy*: Favourite, darling. *Irish colloq.* 1820. 3. Of a wave: White-capped, white-crested; also of a sea covered with such waves 1897.

White heat. 1710. That degree of heat or temperature at which metals and some other bodies radiate white light; the state of being white-hot. b. *fig.* A state of intense emotion 1839.

White horse. 1647. 1. The figure of a white horse; freq. used for an inn-sign, and hence as the name of an inn. 2. The W. Indian shrub *Portlandia grandiflora* (family *Rubiaceæ*), with large white flowers 1866. 3. A tough sinewy substance lying between the upper jaw and junk of a sperm whale 1874.

White-hot (stress var.), *a.* 1820. Heated to such a degree as to radiate white light; at white heat.

White lime, white-lime, *sb.* Now *rare* or *Obs.* 1528. [LIME *sb.*[1]] Lime mixed with water as a coating for walls, etc.; whitewash. So **Whi·telime** *v.* (*Obs.* or *dial.*) *trans.* to coat or cover with white lime, to whitewash ME.

White line, white-line, *sb.* 1598. **1.** *Anat.* **a.** (tr. L. *linea alba.*) A longitudinal band of tendinous tissue extending from the sternum to the pubis. **b.** A whitish band in the pelvic fascia extending from the symphysis pubis to the spine of the ischium. **2.** *Printing.* A line left blank between two lines of type 1683. **3. a.** = BOBBIN *sb.* 2. 1824. **b.** An untarred 'line' or rope 1867. **c.** A line of white paint on the surface of a road used as a mark for the regulation of traffic 1927. So **White-line** *v. trans.* to mark with white lines.

White-livered (-livəɹd), *a.* 1549. Having (according to an old notion) a light-coloured liver, supposed to be due to a deficiency of bile or 'choler', and hence of vigour, spirit, or courage; feeble-spirited, cowardly, dastardly.

A double-faced, w., sneaking spy DICKENS.

Whitely (hwəi·tli), *a.* Now only *Sc.* late ME. [f. WHITE *a.* + -LY [1].] Whitish; pale; light-complexioned.

A whitly wanton, with a veluet brow, With two pitch bals..for eyes SHAKS.

White man. 1691. **†1.** A man clothed in white -1693. **2.** A man belonging to a race having naturally light-coloured skin or complexion: chiefly applied to those of European extraction 1695. **b.** orig. *U.S. slang.* A man of honourable character such as one associates with a European (as dist. from a negro) 1883.

White meat, whi·temeat. *Obs.* exc. *dial.* late ME. **a.** *collect. sing.* or *pl.* Foods prepared from milk; dairy produce (occas. including eggs.) **b.** *pl.* Certain white or light-coloured flesh foods, as chicken, etc. 1752.

Whiten (hwəi·t'n), *v.* ME. [f. WHITE *a.* + -EN [5].] **1.** *trans.* To make or render white; to impart a white colour or appearance to. **b.** To cover, coat, or overspread with something white; *spec.* to whitewash; to coat (metal) with tin; to tin. late ME. **c.** To make white by depriving of the natural colour; to blanch; to bleach 1693. **d.** *fig.* To free or clear from evil, guilt, or the like; also, to give a specious appearance to 1440. **2.** *intr.* To become or turn white; to assume a white colour or aspect; *vaguely,* to appear white 1633. **b.** To turn pale, esp. from fear or other emotion 1783.

1. b. Sails unnumber'd w. all the stream 1719. **2.** Willows w., aspens quiver,..By the island in the river TENNYSON. Hence **Whi·tener,** one who whitens, *spec.* a person employed in bleaching or other whitening process; a thing that whitens, *spec.* an agent used for bleaching, etc.

Whiteness (hwəi·tnės). [OE. *hwītnes.*] The quality or condition of being white; white colour or appearance. **b.** Of the human skin or face: †(*a*) Fairness of complexion; (*b*) Paleness, pallor. late ME. **c.** quasi-*concr.* A white substance or part of something 1560. **d.** Purity, stainless character or quality 1555.

Whitening (hwəi·t'niŋ), *vbl. sb.* 1601. [f. WHITEN *v.* + -ING [1].] **1.** The action or process of making white; bleaching, whitewashing, tinning, etc. Also, the fact or process of becoming white. **2.** *concr.* = WHITING *vbl. sb.* II. 1710.

Whitesmith [1] (hwəi·tˌsmiþ). ME. **a.** A worker in 'white iron', a tinsmith. **b.** One who polishes or finishes metal goods, as dist. from one who forges them; also, more widely, a worker in metals.

Whi·tesmith [2]. 1860. [f. WHITE *a.* + surname of Sir William Sidney *Smith* (1764–1840).] A variety of gooseberry with white fruit.

White staff. *Pl.* **-staves.** 1581. [STAFF *sb.*[1] 6.] **1.** A white rod or wand carried as a symbol of office by certain officials, as the steward of the king's household; hence, the office held by these. **2.** An official who carries a white staff 1601.

attrib.: **white staff officer** = sense 2. So **White stick.**

White-tail (hwəi·tˌtēˡl). 1611. [TAIL *sb.*[1]] **1.** = WHEATEAR [2]. *Obs.* or *dial.* **2.** The white-tailed deer (*Cariacus virginianus*), a common N. Amer. species, having the under side of the tail white 1888.

Whitethorn (hwəi·tþǭɹn). ME. [After L. *alba spina.*] The common hawthorn, *Cratægus Oxyacantha*: so called from the lighter colour of its bark as compared with that of the BLACKTHORN.

Whitethroat (hwəi·tþrōᵘt), *sb.* (*a.*) 1676. **1.** Any of several species of warbler (*Sylvia*), esp. the common w., *S. cinerea*, and the lesser w., *S. curruca.* **2.** The white-throated sparrow of N. America, *Zonotrichia albicollis* 1889. **B.** *adj.* White-throated. *W. warbler* = sense 1 above. 1876.

Whitewash (hwəi·tˌwǫʃ), *sb.* 1689. [prob. f. the vb.] **†1.** A cosmetic wash used for imparting a light colour to the skin -1764. **2.** A liquid composition of lime and water, or of whiting, size, and water, for whitening walls, ceilings, etc. 1697. **3.** *fig.* Something that conceals faults or gives a fair appearance 1865. **4.** An act of 'whitewashing', as of a bankrupt; also (*U.S. colloq.*) a victory at baseball or other game in which the opponents fail to score 1851.

3. The w. of diplomacy 1885. **4.** The Report is a fairly comprehensive w. of everybody concerned 1920.

Whi·tewash, *v.* 1591. [f. WHITE *sb.* 16 + WASH *v.* II. 5.] **1.** *trans.* To plaster over (a wall, etc.) with a white composition; to cover or coat with whitewash. Also *absol.* **b.** *intr.* To become coated with a white efflorescence: see next b. 1889. **2.** *fig.* To give a fair appearance to; to cover up, conceal, or gloss over the faults or blemishes of 1762. **b.** *spec.* To clear (a bankrupt or insolvent) by judicial process from liability for his debts. Also with the debts, etc. as obj., and *intr.* for *pass.* to go through the bankruptcy court. 1762. **3.** In *Baseball* and other games: To beat (the opponents) so that they fail to score. *U.S. colloq.* 1884.

1. To w. a church is..a profanity 1834. **2. b.** If I'm dunned, I w. THACKERAY. Hence **Whi·tewa·sher,** one who or that which whitewashes; *slang* or *colloq.* a final glass of white wine taken after dinner.

Whitewashing (hwəi·tˌwǫːʃiŋ), *vbl. sb.* 1663. [f. prec. + -ING [1].] The action or process of coating with whitewash; also *fig.* **b.** The production of a white efflorescence (saltpetre rot) on a brick wall 1889.

I think the book an altogether foolish..book..having but one object, the w. of James KINGSLEY. *attrib.* We allege that no assets have been recovered, and that this is a w. case 1890.

White water. 1586. **1.** Shallow or shoal water; water with breakers or foam, as in shallows or rapids. **2.** Water mixed with oatmeal or bran, as a medicinal drink for horses 1737.

Whitey: see WHITY *a.*

White wine. ME. [WHITE *a.* 2 a.] Any light-coloured transparent wine: a general designation for wines of various colours from pale yellow to amber, in contradistinction to *red wine.*

attrib.: **white wine vinegar,** vinegar made from white wine; **white wine whey,** a medicinal drink consisting of white wine and whey.

Whither (hwi·ðəɹ), *adv.* (*sb.*) Now only *arch.* or *literary.* [OE. *hwider*, earlier (Northumb.) *huidir*, f. Teut. **hwi-* (cf. WHO).] **I.** *interrog.* **1.** To what place? **2.** *gen.* or *fig.* To what result, condition, action, cause? OE.

1. W. will you go? and what can you do? DE FOE. Wandering they knew not w. DICKENS. **2.** Thou tedious varlet, w. tends This putrid stuff? 1746.

II. *rel.* **1. a.** as compound relative: To the place to (or in) which OE. **b.** as simple relative: To which place; after a noun of place = to which; also with ellipsis = a place to which. late ME. **2.** To (or in) any place to which; whithersoever ME.

1. a. And whother the head went thither must the bodye folow 1535. **b.** He which..is a fugitive, may have..w. to escape BIBLE (Douay) *Deut.* xix. 3. Dined at Melville Castle, w. I went through a snowstorm SCOTT. **2.** I haue hyred this shyppe..to sayle whyder as me lyst 1523.

B. as *sb.* (*nonce-use.*) Place or state to which a person or thing moves or tends 1875.

Whi·therso, *adv. arch.* [ME. *hwiderse*, repr. OE. *swā hwider swā.*] = next.

Whithersoever (hwiːðəɹsoᵘeˑvəɹ), *adv.* ME. [f. prec. + EVER *adv.*] To whatever place. **a.** To (or in) any place to which. **b.** Whether to one place or another; no matter to what place 1583.

Whitherto (hwiðəɹtū·, hwi·ðəɹtu), *adv.* Now *rare* or *Obs.* 1549. [f. WHITHER *adv.* + To *prep.*] To what place, result, etc.? to what? whither?

Whitherward (hwi·ðəɹwǫɹd), *adv.* (*sb.*) *arch.* ME. [f. WHITHER *adv.* + -WARD.] **1.** *interrog.* Towards or to what place? Whither? Also *fig.* or *gen.* Towards what? **2.** *rel.* **a.** as compound relative: Towards the place that; usu., towards any place that, whithersoever ME. **b.** as simple relative: Towards which. late ME.

Whiting (hwəi·tiŋ), *sb.* late ME. [ad. (M)Du. *wijting*, app. f. WHITE *a.* + -ING [3].] A gadoid fish of the genus *Merlangus*, a small fish with pearly-white flesh, highly esteemed as food. **b.** Locally applied to fishes of other genera: (*a*) some freshwater fish found in Wales; (*b*) *U.S.*, a fish of the genus *Menticirrus*; also applied to the silver hake, and the menhaden; (*c*) in Australia, a fish of the genus *Sillago* 1587.

Comb., in names of fishes resembling the w., as **w. perch** (*Perca alburnus*); *w.* POLLACK, *w.* POUT; **w. salmon** (*Salmo phinoc*).

Whiting (hwəi·tiŋ), *vbl. sb.* 1440. [f. WHITE *v.* + -ING [1].] **†I.** The action or process of making white; whitening; **a.** by covering or coating with white; **b.** by depriving of colour -1683. **II.** *concr.* A preparation of finely powdered chalk, used for whitewashing, etc. 1440.

Whitish (hwəi·tiʃ), *a.* late ME. [f. WHITE *a.* + -ISH [1].] **1.** Somewhat white; of a colour inclining to or approaching white. **2.** Qualifying other adjs. (or sbs.) of colour, indicating a pale or light tint of the colour specified 1653. Hence **Whi·tishness.**

Whitleather (hwi·tleːðəɹ). late ME. [f. WHITE *a.* + LEATHER *sb.*] **1.** Leather of a white or light colour and soft pliant consistence, prepared by dressing with alum and salt, so as to retain the natural colour. **b.** In comparisons, or as a type of toughness, elasticity, softness, etc. 1605. **2.** = PAXWAX 1713.

Whi·tley Cou·ncil. 1923. [f. the name of J. H. *Whitley*, chairman of the committee of 1916 which recommended the setting up of such councils.] A council of representatives of employers and workers for discussing and settling industrial relations and conditions. Hence **Whi·tleyism,** the use of such methods.

Whitling (hwi·tliŋ). *Sc.* and *north.* 1597. [f. WHITE *a.* + -LING.] A fish of the salmon family; app. the young of the bull-trout.

Whitlow (hwi·tloᵘ). late ME. [app. orig. *whitflaw, -flow* = WHITE *a.* + FLAW *sb.*[1], but perh. of alien origin (cf. early mod. Du. *vijt, fijt*, LG. *fīt* whitlow).] = PARONYCHIA **1.**

attrib.: **w.-grass,** book-name for *Saxifraga tridactylites*, rue-leaved w.-grass, and *Draba* (*Erophila*) *verna*, formerly reputed to cure whitlows; **-wort,** a plant of the genus *Paronychia*, formerly reputed to cure whitlows.

Whitneyite (hwi·tniˌəit). 1861. [f. the name of J. D. *Whitney*, an Amer. geologist; see -ITE [1].] *Min.* A native arsenide of copper, of a reddish-white colour, found in America.

Whitsun (hwi·tsɒ̆n). [ME. *w(h)itsone(n*, the first two elements of WHIT SUNDAY, analysed as *Whitsun Day.*] **1.** Used attrib. to denote something belonging to, connected with, or occurring on Whit Sunday or at Whitsuntide. **2.** *sb.* Short for WHITSUNTIDE (*rare*) 1849.

1. W. ale *Hist.*, a parish festival formerly held at Whitsuntide, marked by feasting, sports, and merry-making; **W. week,** the week beginning with Whit Sunday, Whit-week.

Whit Sunday, Whitsunday (hwi·t sɒ·ndi, hwi·tsɒ̆ndeˡ). [Late OE. *Hwīta Sunnandæᵹ* lit. 'white Sunday'. The epithet 'white' is generally taken to refer to the ancient custom of the wearing of white baptismal robes by the newly-baptized at the feast of Pentecost.] **1.** The seventh Sunday after Easter, observed as a festival of the Christian Church in commemoration of the descent of the Holy Spirit upon the Apostles on the Day of Pentecost. **2.** (In form *Whitsunday*, or *Whitsun Day.*) One of the Scottish quarter-days or term-days, ordinarily May 15th, but in certain cases May 26th (= May 15th, Old Style) or May 28th. 1450. So **Whit Monday, Whit Tuesday,** the Monday and Tuesday following Whit Sunday; also (in occas. recent use) *W. Saturday*, the day before Whit Sunday. **W.-week,** the week beginning with Whit Sunday.

Whitsuntide (hwi·tsɒ̆ntəid). ME. [f. WHITSUN + TIDE *sb.*] The season of Whit

Sunday; Whit Sunday and the days immediately following.

Tis Whitson-tyde, and we must frolick it MARSTON.

Whittawer (hwi·tǭəɹ). Now *Hist.* or *dial.* ME. [f. WHITE *a.* + TAWER.] One who taws skins into WHITLEATHER. In mod. dial., a saddler, harness-maker.

Whitten (hwi·t'n). *dial.* ME. [In full *w.-tree*, repr. OE. *hwītingtrēow*, f. *hwīting* (f. as WHITING *sb.*) + *trēow* tree.] The water elder or wild guelder-rose (*Viburnum Opulus*), and the wayfaring-tree (*V. Lantana*). Also (by confusion with *whicken* QUICKEN *sb.*[1]), the mountain-ash (*Pyrus aucuparia*), and some allied plants.

Whittle (hwi·t'l), *sb.*[1] Now *dial.* [OE. *hwītel*, f. *hwīt* WHITE *a.* + -LE.] †a. A cloak, mantle. †b. A blanket. c. A baby's woollen napkin or flannel petticoat. d. A shawl or wrap.

Whittle (hwi·t'l), *sb.*[2] Now *dial.* late ME. [Variant of ME. *þwitel* (f. OE. *þwītan* to cut + -EL[1], -LE[1]).] A knife, esp. one of a large size, as a carving-knife; also, a clasp-knife.

†Whi·ttle, *v.*[1] 1530. [Origin obsc.] *trans.* To ply with drink, to make drunk, intoxicate –1694.

Whittle (hwi·t'l), *v.*[2] 1552. [f. WHITTLE *sb.*[2]] 1. *trans.* To cut thin slices or shavings from the surface of (a stick, etc.); to dress or pare with a knife; to reduce or sharpen by doing this. Also *absol.* or *intr.* b. *transf.* To wear away or reduce by a process analogous to paring 1736. 2. *fig.* To reduce or make smaller by successive abstractions; to diminish the amount, force, or importance of; to take *away* by degrees, so as to reduce to nothing 1746. 3. To make or shape by whittling; to carve 1848.

1. Cambyses..whitling a sticke to passe away the time 1614.

Whitworth (hwi·twɔ̈ɹþ). 1858. In full, *W. gun* or *rifle*: A form of rifle invented by Sir Joseph Whitworth (1854), having a hexagonal bore with a rapid twist, and firing an elongated shot.

W. metal or *steel*, a specially strong make of steel cast under hydraulic pressure, used for ordnance.

Whity, whitey (hwəi·ti), *a.* (*adv.*) 1593. [f. WHITE *a.* + -Y[1].] = WHITISH. b. *esp.* (quasi-*adv.*) with other adjs. (or *adj.* with sbs.) of colour 1856.

b. The insipid w.-grey bread of towns DE QUINCEY.

Whi·ty-brow·n, *a.* (*sb.*) 1777. [prec. b.] 1. Of a brown colour inclining to white; whitish brown: most commonly of paper. As *sb.* (prop. two words) a whitish brown; *ellipt.* = w. paper. 2. *fig.* Neither one thing nor another, neutral, half-and-half 1892.

Whizgig (hwi·zgig). *Obs.* or *U.S.* 1848. [f. WHIZ(Z + GIG *sb.*[1]] An object that whizzes round, as a revolving humming toy.

Whizz, whiz (hwiz), *sb.* 1620. [f. next.] 1. An act, or the action, of whizzing; a sibilant sound between a hiss and a buzz; a swift movement producing such a sound. 2. *U.S. slang.* An agreement, 'bargain' 1869.

1. Their shot would go by their ears with a W. BUNYAN. 2. They said,..Let us sleep here..And each ..said, It is a whiz MARK TWAIN.

Whizz, whiz, *v.* 1547. [Echoic.] I. *intr.* To make a sound as of a body rushing through the air; of trees, to rustle; of a burning or hot object, to hiss, sizzle. Now *dial.* 2. To move swiftly with or as with such a sound 1591. b. *fig.* To have a sensation of such a sound 1797. 3. *trans.* To cause to whizz; to hurl, shoot, or convey with a whizz; *spec.* to dry by centrifugal force in a rapidly revolving apparatus 1836.

2. *Jul. C.* II. i. 44. b. Reading makes my head whiz DARWIN. Hence **Whi·zzer,** something that whizzes; *spec.* (*a*) a toy that whizzes when whirled round; (*b*) a machine for drying articles by the centrifugal force of rapid revolution. **Whi·zzing,** *vbl. sb.* and *ppl. a.* **Whi·zzy** *a* (*rare*) characterized by whizzing; *dial.* dizzy, giddy.

Whizz, whiz (hwiz), *int.* 1812. An exclam. imitating a whizzing sound; also *advb.* = with a whizz. b. *Comb.* **whi·zz-bang** *colloq.*, the shell of a small-calibre high-velocity German gun 1915.

Who (hū, unstressed hu), *pron.* (*sb.*) Infl. WHOM, WHOSE, q.v. [OE. *hwā* :—OTeut. **hwoz* :—Indo-Eur. **qʷos* : **qʷes* : *qʷis* (Skr. *ka*, Lith. *kàs*, L. *quis*, Gr. τίς); cf. WHAT, WHEN, WHETHER, WHICH, WHITHER, WHY.] I. *interrog.* 1. As the ordinary interrogative pronoun, in the nominative singular or plural, used of a person or persons. b. With intensive additions, as *w. the devil*, etc. 1470. c. In pregnant or emphatic sense, referring to a person's origin, character, position, or the like. late ME. d. Substituted for the name of a person in asking for an explanation 1749. 2. In rhetorical questions, suggesting or implying an emphatic contrary assertion OE. 3. In a dependent question or clause of similar meaning OE. ¶4. Used ungrammatically for the objective WHOM (common in colloq. use as obj. of a vb., or of a prep. following at the end of a clause) 1450.

1. c. Jesus I knowe, and Paul I knowe: but w. are ye? TINDALE *Acts* xix. 15. W. is the Lord that I should obey him? *Exod.* v. 2. d. 'My Lord Fellamar.' 'My Lord w.?' FIELDING. 2. W. stands if freedom fall? KIPLING. *W. would..?* = No one would ...*W. would not..?* = Any one would... *W. knows..?* = No one knows... *W. but..?* = no one but, no one else than... Then came brave Glorie puffing by, In silks that whistled, w. but he! 1633. 3. They throng w. should buy first SHAKS. Did he know w. I was? 1677.

Phrases. *W. is w.*, w. is one and w. is the other; w. each of a number of persons is, or what position each holds. †*W. and w. are* (or *who's*) *together*, w. is allied with or engaged to whom. *Who's W.*, the title of a reference manual of contemporary biography first issued in 1849. *I know not* (mod. *I don't know*) *w.*, *Lord knows w.*, etc., some person or persons unknown, or of unknown origin, status, etc.; so *and I don't know w. all* (colloq. rare) = 'and various other persons unspecified'. *W. not*, any one whatever, any one and every one (now rare or obs.). *Who's-afraid* adj. phr., defiant, swaggering; A vagabondish who's-afraid sort of bearing DICKENS.

II. *rel.* 1. As compound relative in the nominative in general or indefinite sense: Any one that. *arch.* or *literary.* ME. †b. = WHOEVER 2 –1556. 2. As who (freq. followed by *would* or *should*): as or like one who; hence, as if one. *arch.* late ME. b. With the vb. *say*: (*a*) †*as w. saith* or *say*, as they say, as the saying is –1611; (*b*) *as w. should say* (arch.). late ME. 3. As compound relative, of persons (less freq. a person): The persons (or person) that. *arch.* (Chiefly a latinism; esp. in 'There are w...' = L. *Sunt qui...*) 1596. 4. As simple relative (of a person or persons), introducing a clause defining or restricting the antecedent and thus completing the sense ME. 5. As simple relative introducing an additional statement about the antecedent; thus sometimes = 'and he (she, they)' 1466. 6. a. With antecedent denoting or connoting a number of persons collectively: usu. with pl. concord 1593. b. Used in ref. to an animal (or animals) or an inanimate thing (or things): usu. with personification or implication of personality 1585. ¶7. In irregular constructions: a. with pleonastic personal pronoun in the relative clause, *who* thus becoming a mere link between the clauses; b. preceded by redundant *and* 1523. ¶8. Used ungrammatically for the objective WHOM (still common colloq. in indefinite sense, = *whomsoever*) ME.

1. W. that holdeth ageynst it we wille slee hym MALORY. Be good, sweet maid, and let w. can be clever KINGSLEY. 2. b. They command Regard, as w. should say, We are your Defenders 1717. 3. *Macb.* I. iii. 109. 4. A man w. hath anie honestie in him SHAKS. 5. I should do Brutus wrong, and Cassius wrong, Who (you all know) are Honourable men SHAKS. Scots, wha hae wi' Wallace bled BURNS. 7. a. *Tit. A.* III. i. 37.

III. Substantival nonce-uses. a. A person, indefinitely or abstractly; a 'some one' 1654. b. with *the*: The question 'who?' 1771.

Who (wǭu), *int.* 1450. [Variant of Ho *int.*[2]] Stop! esp. as a call to a horse = next 2.

Whoa (wǭu), *int.* 1623. [Variant of prec.] †1. *W. ho ho*, used to call attention from a distance. SHAKS. 2. A word of command to a horse or other draught-animal to stop or stand still; hence used joc. to a person as a command to stop or desist 1849.

Whoever (hu,e·vəɹ), *pron.* Also (*poet.*) **whoe'er** (-ēᵊ·ɹ). ME. [orig. two words, WHO *pron.* and EVER *adv.*] I. 1. As compound relative, or with correlative in principal clause: Whatever person or persons; any one who, any who. 2. Introducing a qualifying clause with conditional or disjunctive force: If any one at all; whether one person or another; no matter who 1500. ¶3. Used ungrammatically for the objective: Any one whom; whomsoever 1592.

2. W. you may be, sir,.. I am deeply grateful to you DICKENS. 3. Who ere you find attach SHAKS.

II. *interrog.* An emphatic extension of *who*, implying perplexity or surprise (prop. written as two words). *colloq.* 1875.

Who ever would have thought it? 1875.

Whole (hōᵘl), *a.*, *sb.*, *adv.* [Com. Teut.: OE. *hāl* :—OTeut. **hailoz* :—Indo-Eur. **qoilos.* On the spelling *whole* (the *wh* appears first in the 15th c.) see WH; pronuncs. with (w) exist in many dials. For derivs. of the same root with mutated vowel see HAIL *sb.*[2], HEAL *sb.*, *v.*[1]] A. *adj.* I. In good condition, sound. 1. Of a man or animal, the body, limbs, skin: Uninjured, unwounded, unhurt; (contextually) recovered from injury or a wound; †(of a wound) healed. *arch.* 2. Of inanimate objects: Free from damage or defect; uninjured, unbroken, intact ME. 3. In good health; free from disease; healthy; (contextually) restored to health, recovered from disease. *arch.* OE.

1. Phr. *As w. as a fish* (*a trout*); They are both as w. as a fish SHAKS. *In* (or *with*) *a w. skin*, uninjured. 2. *Hen. V*, III. ii. 37. 3. Goo in peace, and be w. off thy plage TINDALE *Mark* v. 34. *fig.* My life is yet w. within me COVERDALE 2 *Sam.* i. 9.

II. Complete, total. 1. Having all its parts or elements; having its complete or entire extent or magnitude ME. b. Containing all its proper or essential constituents; of milk, unskimmed 1794. 2. The full or total amount of; all, all of. (Only attrib., and now always preceding the sb.) OE. †b. In phr. *w. and some*, 'the whole lot', all; in all, altogether –1566. c. With rhetorical emphasis, implying an unusually large quantity or number 1628. 3. Not divided into parts or particles; undivided, entire OE. b. *Math.* Of a number: Denoting a complete and undivided thing or a set of such things; integral, not fractional. late ME. 4. Constituting the total amount, without admixture of anything different; full, unmixed, pure: often opp. to *half.* late ME. b. *Bookbinding.* Forming the whole of the cover, as *w. calf* 1839.

2. The roare Of a w. heard of Lyons SHAKS. The.. captain,..upon whom they fix Their w. attention COWPER. The w...manner of looking at things alters 1845. b. Sitting..W. days and nights 1664. W. towns ..were left in ruins MACAULAY. 3. One pint of w. oatmeal 1756. Apples..baked w. in a dish 1842. 4. *W. blood*: see BLOOD *sb.* III. 2; so *w. brother, sister*, a brother or sister of the w. blood. *W. holiday*, a day the w. of which is observed as a holiday.

B. *sb.* 1. The full, complete, or total amount; the assemblage of all the parts, elements, or individuals (*of*). late ME. b. In a charade, *my w.* denotes the complete word of which the syllables, called *my first, my second*, etc., are the parts 1789. 2. Something made up of parts in combination or mutual connexion; a complex unity or system 1697.

1. The good of the w.,..is the same with the good of all its parts JOHNSON. Thicken with flour, and pour the w. on the deer when roasted 1853. 2. The complex w. which we call Civilization 1865.

Phrases. **As a w.**, as a complete thing; as a unity; in its entirety, all together. **In (the) w.**, (*a*) to the full amount, in full, entirely, completely; (*b*) in total amount, all together, in all (now *rare*). **On** or **upon the w.**, (*a*) on the basis of the affair as a w., all things considered; hence †(*b*) as the upshot, or summing up, of the whole matter, as a final result, ultimately; (*c*) in respect of the w., notwithstanding exceptions in detail; for the most part; The clergy were regarded as, on the w., a plebeian class MACAULAY.

C. *adv.* Wholly, entirely, fully, perfectly. *Obs.* exc. in nonce-use in explicit or implied opposition to *half.* ME.

The ills thou dost are w. thine own COWLEY. Laying a half-dirty cloth upon a w.-dirty deal table SCOTT.

Special collocations and Combs., etc.: **w.-bred** *a.* of pure breed; **w. cloth**, a piece of cloth of the full size as manufactured; also *fig.* esp. in phr. *cut* (etc.) *out of the w. cloth*; now esp. (*U.S. colloq.* or *slang*) of a statement wholly fabricated or false; **-colour, -coloured** *adjs.*, of the same colour throughout; **-feather**, a variety of pigeon having all the feathers of one colour; so **w.-feathered** *a.*; **-footed** *a.*, †having 'whole' feet, i. e. with the toes united, web-footed, solid-footed; treading with the w. foot on the ground, not lightly or on tip-toe; **-hearted** *a.*, having one's w. heart in something (orig. and chiefly *U.S.*); done with one's w. heart, thoroughly earnest or sincere; **w. hog**, in slang phr. *to go the w. hog* (see Hog *sb.*[1]); hence *w.-hogger*, *-hoggery*, etc.; **-hoofed** *a.*, having undivided hoofs; **-length** *a.*, (*a*) of a portrait, etc., representing the w. human figure, usu. standing; also *ellipt.* as *sb.*; (*b*) *gen.* exhibited at full length; **w. meal**, meal or flour made from the w. grain of wheat, etc. (occas. including the bran); **-minded** *a.* giving one's w. mind to something, completely interested; **w. note** *Mus.*, a semibreve, as the longest note in ordinary use (now *U.S.*); **w. plate** *Photogr.*, see Plate *sb.* I. 5 c; **-souled** *a.*, (orig. *U.S.*) = *w.-hearted*; **-time** *a.*, occupying the w. of some particular time, esp. of the working time; (of a person) employed during the w. time; **-timer** = Full-timer. Hence **Who·leness**, the quality or condition of being w.

Wholesale (hōu·lsēl), *sb.*, *a.*, *adv.* late ME. **I. 1.** orig. two words, in phr. *by whole sale*, now usu. ellipt. as adv., qualifying *buy*, *sell*, etc.: In large quantities, in gross (opp. to *by retail*). **2.** *fig.* In a large way, in large numbers or amount, in abundance, indiscriminately 1601.

2. They .. throw contempt upon it by w. 1741. Homer never allows distinguished Greeks to fall w. by the Trojan sword 1869.

II. *attrib.* or *adj.* **1. a.** Selling a commodity by w. 1645. **b.** Pertaining to sale in gross; used for a commodity sold by w. 1724. **2.** *fig.* Having an extensive application; unlimited or indiscriminate in range; doing something, or done, profusely or in great quantities 1642.

1. a. A w. Dealer in Silks and Ribbons Addison. 2. A w. admirer of our legal solemnities Dickens. A w. creation of peers for the purpose of obtaining a majority 1863. Hence **Who·lesaler**, one who sells goods w., a w. dealer.

Wholesome (hōu·lsəm), *a.* (*sb.*) ME. [OE. **hālsum*, corresp. to OHG. *heilsam*, ON. *heilsamr*; see Whole *a.* and -some *suffix*[1].] **1.** Conducive to well-being in general, esp. of mind or character; tending or calculated to do good; beneficial, salutary. **2.** Promoting or conducive to health; health-giving or health-preserving; salubrious. late ME. †**b.** Having the property of restoring health; curative, medicinal –1651. **3.** Sound in (physical or moral) condition or constitution; free from disease or taint; healthy. Now *rare*. 1533. **b.** *transf.* of a quality, condition, place, etc. 1604.

1. To enjoy better air, keep better hours, and employ herself in quieter and wholesomer pleasures Southey. 2. Abrecockes..are lesse then the other peches and are holsummer for the stomack 1562. 3. A plump rosy-cheeked w. apple-faced young woman Dickens. b. In wholsome Wisedome He might not but refuse you Shaks.

B. as *sb.* in *pl.* Wholesome things 1731. Hence **Who·lesome-ly** *adv.*, **-ness.**

Wholly (hōu·lli, hōu·li), *adv.* [ME. *hol(l)iche*, *iholliche*, repr. OE. *(*ʒe*)*hāllīce*; see Whole *a.* and -ly[2]. The normal development *holly* (hǫ·li), which survives in some dials., was generally superseded by a form influenced by *hǭl* Whole, whence the present pronunc. The current sp. *wholly* derives from ME. *holliche*, and has superseded the once frequent *wholely*, *wholy*.] **1.** As a whole, in its entirety, in full, throughout, all of it (now *rare*). **2.** Completely, entirely, to the full extent; altogether, thoroughly, quite ME. **b.** Entirely, so as to exclude everything else; hence practically = exclusively, solely, only. late ME.

1. *Non omnis moriar*, I shall not w. die 1681. 2. Sleepe hath ceiz'd me w. Shaks. We were w. at a loss what to do 1833. b. A creature w. given to brawls and wine Tennyson.

Whom (hūm), *pron.* [repr. formally OE. *hwām*, later variant of *hwǣm* (:—**hwaimi*), dat. of *hwā* Who, *hwæt* What. In its usage, *whom* combines the functions of OE. *hwǣm* and OE. *hwone*, *hwane*, *hwæne*, acc. masc. of *hwā*.] The objective case of Who: no longer current in unstudied colloquial speech. ¶**b.** Used for the nominative Who, esp. (in later use only) when taken as obj. of a vb. of which the whole clause is really the obj. 1467. ¶**c.** In irregular constructions. (*a*) With pleonastic personal pronoun; often also with anacoluthon, *whom* serving as apparent obj. to a vb. whose real obj. is a dependent clause of which the pron. is subj.; (*b*) preceded by redundant *and* 1556.

To w. lesse is forgiuen, the same doeth lesse loue Tindale *Luke* vii. 47. W. shall I sende, and who wilbe oure messaunger? Coverdale *Isa.* vi. 8. Chose you this daye w. ye wyll serue Coverdale *Josh.* xxiv. 15. W. he wolde, he set vp: & w. he list, he put downe Coverdale *Dan.* v. 19. This is the man, w. I spake to the of Bible (Great) 1 *Sam.* ix. 17. I..am come to see of w. such noise Hath walk'd about Milt. For w. in the world do you think that I was kept so long kicking my heels? 1780. 'W. the gods love die young' was said of yore Byron. b. Tel me in sadnes whome she is you loue Shaks. c. Let him be w. he will 1603.

Whomever (hūme·vəɹ), *pron.* Also (*poet.*) **whome'er** (-ēᵊɹ). *literary.* ME. [orig. two words, Whom and Ever *adv.*] The objective case of Whoever. (Less frequent than Whomsoever.)

Whomso (hū·msou), *pron. arch.*, chiefly *poet.* [Early ME. *swa hwam swa*; see Whom and So *adv.*] = next.

Whomsoever (hūmsoue·vəɹ), *pron.*; also (*poet.*) **whomsoe'er** (-ēᵊ·ɹ). *literary.* 1450. The objective case of Whosoever. ¶**b.** Used for Whosoever, chiefly by attraction to the case of the unexpressed antecedent 1560.

b. They shall not be impeded by w. it may be Ruskin.

Whoo (hwū), *int.* 1608. [Variant of Hoo *int.*] An exclam. of surprise, grief, or other emotion; *occas.* an imitation of an owl's hoot. So **Whoo** *sb.* an utterance of this, or a similar sound. **Whoo** *v. intr.* to utter this sound.

Whoof (hwūf, hwuf), *int.* (*sb.*, *v.*). 1766. Imitation of a gruff abrupt cry or noise; as *vb.* to utter such a cry.

Whoop (hūp), *sb.* 1600. [f. Whoop *int.*] **1.** An act of whooping; a cry of 'whoop!', or a shout or call resembling this; *spec.* as used in hunting, esp. at the death of the game, or by N. Amer. Indians, etc. as a signal or war-cry. **b.** The characteristic sonorous inspiration following a fit of coughing in whooping-cough 1873. **2.** A form of the game of hide-and-seek 1798.

Whoop (hūp), *v.* late ME. [Parallel w. next.] **1.** *intr.* To utter a cry of 'whoop!' or a loud vocal sound resembling this; to shout (as in summons, exultation, defiance, or mere excitement). **b.** *trans.* with obj. of cognate meaning, or indef. *it*: To utter with a whoop; to express by whooping 1576. **c.** with adv. or advb. phr.: To bring, summon, or urge by or with whooping. late ME. **d.** To shout at, hoot (a person). *rare.* 1690. **e.** *U.S.* To increase or raise 1896. **2.** *intr.* To hoot, as an owl. Also *trans.* 1658. **3.** To utter the 'whoop' in whooping-cough 1887.

1. With that the shepheard whoop'd for ioy Drayton. 2. Owls whooping after Sunset..foreshews a fair day to ensue 1658. Hence **Whoo·per**, a person or animal that whoops; *spec.* the wild or whistling swan, *Cygnus musicus* (*ferus*). **Whoo·ping** *ppl. a.* that whoops; esp. in **whooping crane**, the large white crane of America, *Grus americana*, **whooping swan**, the whooper.

Whoop (hūp), *int.* 1568. [A natural exclam.] An exclam., or representation of a shout or cry, expressing excitement, etc.

W. Iugge I loue thee Shaks. Whop Sir, thought I, and what ado's here? 1691.

Whoopee (hū·pi), *int.* orig. *U.S.* 1845. An exclam. accompanying or inviting to hilarious enjoyment; also *sb.*, esp. in *to make w.*, to have a good time, go on the razzle-dazzle.

Whooping-cough (hū·piŋ,kǭf). 1739. The now prevalent spelling of Hooping-cough.

Whoosh (hwūʃ, hwuʃ), *v.* 1856. [Imitative.] *intr.* To utter or emit a dull soft sibilant sound, like that of something rushing through the air. So **Whoosh** *sb.* a sound of this nature.

Who(o)-whoop (hūhū·p), *int.* and *sb.* 1611. The shout of huntsmen at the death of the game. Hence **Whoo-whoo·p** *v.* to utter this cry.

Whop (hwǫp), *v.* (*adv.*) late ME. [Variant of Wap *v.*] **1.** *trans.* To cast, pull out, etc. violently; to take or put suddenly. *dial.* **2.** To strike with heavy blows; to beat soundly, flog. *colloq.* or *vulgar.* 1575. **b.** *fig.* To overcome, vanquish, defeat utterly; hence, to surpass or excel greatly. *colloq.* or *vulgar* 1836. **3.** The vb.-stem used as *adv.*: With a 'whop'; with a sudden movement or impact 1812.

2. Ain't nobody to be whopped for takin' this here liberty, sir? Dickens. b. Nelson, as was a British General and wopped the French 1865. Hence **Whop** *sb.* an act of whopping; a heavy blow or impact (*colloq.* or *vulgar*). **Who·pping** *vbl. sb.* the action of the vb.; a severe beating or flogging.

Whopper (hwǫ·pəɹ). *colloq.* or *vulgar.* 1785. [f. prec. + -er[1].] Something uncommonly large of its kind; a very big thing, animal, or person. **b.** *spec.* A great lie, a monstrous falsehood 1791.

b. Better to get a licking than to tell a w. 1870.

Who·pping, *ppl. a.* *colloq.* or *vulgar.* 1625. [f. as prec. + -ing[2].] That whops; usu. *fig.* that is a 'whopper'; abnormally large or great; 'thumping'.

Whore (hōᵊɹ), *sb.* [Late OE. *hōre* (perh. a. ON. *hóra*) :—OTeut. **hōrōn-* :—Indo-Eur. **qār-* (cf. L. *carus* dear). *Whore* is now confined to coarse and abusive speech, exc. in occasional echoes of historical expressions, as *the w. of Babylon*. The pronunc. (hūᵊɹ), now dial., is the normal repr. of OE. *hōre*.] **1.** A woman who prostitutes herself for hire; a prostitute, harlot. **b.** More gen.: An unchaste or lewd woman; a fornicatress or adulteress; occas. applied opprobriously to a concubine or kept mistress; also, with distinguishing epithet, to a catamite. ME. **2.** *fig.*; *spec.* in bibl. use, applied to a corrupt or idolatrous community, and hence in controversial use, esp. in phr. *the w. of Babylon*, to the Church of Rome (in allusion to Rev. xvii. 1, 5, etc.). late ME.

1. *Whore's bird* (also dial. *wosbird*), prop., the child of a w.; but usu. as a mere vulgar term of abuse or reprobation. b. *To play the w.* (of a woman) to commit fornication or adultery.

Comb.: †**w.-house**, a brothel; †**-hunt** *v.*, *intr.* to go after whores, practise fornication; **-master** (*Obs.* or *arch.*), a whoremonger.

Whore, *v.* 1583. [f. prec.] **1.** *intr.* To have to do with a whore or whores; to commit whoredom; (of a woman) to play the whore. †**2.** *trans.* To make a whore of; to debauch (a woman) –1740. Hence **Who·ring** *vbl. sb.* the action of the vb.; also *fig.*, *spec.* in bibl. use: chiefly in phr. *to go a whoring*.

Whoredom (hōᵊ·ɹdəm). *arch.* ME. [prob. a. ON. *hórdómr*.] **1.** The practice of playing the whore or of intercourse with whores; illicit sexual indulgence in general. **b.** *pl.* Acts of sexual immorality ME. **2.** *fig.*, *esp.* in bibl. and religious use, applied to idolatry or other form of unfaithfulness to the true God. late ME.

Whoremonger (hōᵊ·ɹmɒ:ŋgəɹ). *arch.* 1526. [f. Whore *sb.* + Monger.] One who has dealings with whores; one who practises whoredom; a fornicator. So **Who·remo:nging**, the practice of a w.

Whoreson (hōᵊ·ɹsən). *Obs.* or *arch.* ME. [f. Whore *sb.* + Son *sb.*, after AF. *fiz a putain*.] prop. The son of a whore, but commonly used as a coarse term of reprobation, abuse, or contempt; occas. even of jocular familiarity. **b.** *attrib.*: commonly as a coarsely abusive epithet, applied to a person or thing; also sometimes expressing humorous familiarity or commendation.

Whorish (hōᵊ·riʃ), *a.* Now *rare* or *Obs.* 1535. [f. Whore *sb.* + -ish[1].] **1.** Having the character of a whore; addicted to whoredom; lewd, unchaste 1560. **b.** Belonging to or characteristic of a whore; lewd, unchaste 1552. **2.** *fig.*, esp. in religious and controversial use (often = idolatrous) 1535. Hence **Who·rish-ly** *adv.*, **-ness.**

Whorl (hwǭɹl, hwɔ̄ɹl). 1440. [Late ME. *wharwyl*, *whorwhil*, app. variants of Whirl influenced by Wharve *sb.*] **1.** A small fly-wheel fixed on the spindle of a spinning-wheel to maintain or regulate the speed; a small pulley by which the spindle is driven in a spinning-machine. **2.** *Bot.* A set of members, as leaves, flowers, or parts of the flower, springing from the stem or axis at the same level and encircling it. Also in *Zool.* a set of parts or structures similarly arranged. 1578. **3.** *Conch.* and *Anat.* Each of the turns, coils, or convolutions of a spiral shell, or of any spiral structure 1828. **4.** *gen.* A convolution, coil, curl (esp. of something whirling, or suggesting a whirling movement) 1592.

3. See what a lovely shell, Small and pure as a pearl, ..With delicate spire and w. Tennyson.

Comb.: **w.-flower**, a plant of the genus *Morina* (family *Dipsacaceæ*), having the flowers in dense whorls; **-grass**, a grass of the genus *Catabrosa*.

Hence **Whorled** (hwǭɹld) *a.* having or arranged in a w. or whorls; verticillate; convoluted, turbinate.

Whort (hwɒ̄ɹt). *dial.* 1578. [South-western dial. f. HURT *sb.*[3]] = WHORTLEBERRY.

Whortle (hwɒ̄·ɹt'l). 1597. [Short for WHORTLEBERRY.] = next.

Whortleberry (hwɒ̄·ɹtl'lbĕri). 1578. [South-western dial. f. HURTLEBERRY; now the usual book-name.] The blue-black fruit of the dwarf shrub *Vaccinium Myrtillus*, or the plant itself; the BILBERRY. Also extended to the genus *Vaccinium* as a whole (excepting the species called CRANBERRY, *V. Oxycoccos* and *V. macrocarpon*).

Bear's w., the Bearberry, *Arctostaphylos Uva-ursi*. **Bog w.**, *Vaccinium uliginosum*. **Red w.**, *V. Vitis-Idæa*. **Victorian w.**, *Wittsteinia vacciniacea* a shrub allied to *Vaccinium*, found in Victoria.

Whory (hōə·ri), *a. rare.* 1682. [f. WHORE *sb.* + -Y[1].] = WHORISH.

Whose (hūz), *pron.* [ME. *hwās*, later *hwǭs*, *whǭs*, altered form of *hwas*, *hwes*, OE. *hwæs* (:—**hwasa*), genitive of *hwā* and *hwæt*, through the influence of *hwā* WHO, *hwām* WHOM.] The genitive case of WHO (and in OE. of the neuter WHAT). Used, in all senses, either before a sb. as a possessive adj., or *absol.*: in the latter case chiefly *interrog.* as predicate. In ref. to things now usu. replaced by *of which*, exc. where this would produce an intolerably clumsy form.

I could a Tale vnfold, w. lightest word Would harrow vp thy soule SHAKS. Arrest me? at w. sute? 1607. The man w. these are *Gen.* xxxviii. 25. Any thing w. loss they can so easily supply 1754. Fishermen, who's humanity he had occasion to remember GOLDSM. I cheer a dead man's sweetheart, Never ask me w. HOUSMAN. So **Whosesoe·ver** (h·ūzsoue·vəɹ) *pron. arch.* whatever person's; of whomsoever.

Whoso (hū·sou), *pron. arch.* [ME. *hwa swa*, *hwa se*, reduced form of OE. *swā hwā swā*; see So *adv.*] = WHOEVER 1, 2.

W. eats thereof, forthwith attains Wisdom MILT.

Whosoever (hūsoue·vəɹ), *pron.* Also *poet.* **whosoe'er** (-ē·əɹ). ME. [f. prec. + EVER *adv.*] **1.** = WHOEVER 1. **2.** = WHOEVER 2; also formerly = 'if any one' ME. **3.** With loss of relative force: Any one at all. Now *rare* or *Obs.* 1583. **b.** qualifying a preceding sb. or *any*: now usu. replaced by WHATEVER 1586.

1. Let w. wyll, take of the water of lyfe fre TINDALE *Rev.* xxii. 17. **2.** Margaret my name, and daughter to a King, . . who so ere thou art SHAKS. **3. b.** Gentlemen, and curteous Readers whosoeuer 1586.

†**Whosome**, *pron.* ME. [f. WHO + -SOME[3]. *adv.*] = WHOEVER 1, 2. -late ME.

Whosomever (hūsŏm͵e·vəɹ), *pron. Obs.* or *dial.* late ME. [f. prec. + EVER *adv.*] = WHOEVER.

Who some euer you take him to be, he is Aiax SHAKS.

Whuff (hwɒf), *v.* 1896. [Imitative.] *intr.* To make a sound as of a forcible blast of breath or wind; *trans.* to utter with such a sound.

Why (hwəi), *adv.*, *sb.*, *int.* [OE. *hwī*, *hwȳ*, instr. case of *hwæt* WHAT:—OTeut. **hwī*:—Indo-Eur. **qᵘei*, locative of **qᵘo-* WHO.] **I. 1.** In a direct question: For what reason? From what cause or motive? For what purpose? Wherefore? **b.** Implying or suggesting a negative assertion (= 'there is no reason why . .'); hence often expressing a protest or objection OE. **c.** With ellipsis of the remainder of the sentence, or of all except the principal word or words (esp. when emphatic); also with simple inf. (= 'W. should one . . ?'). late ME. **2.** In an indirect question or dependent clause of similar meaning OE. **3.** With intensive additions: see DEVIL *sb.*, DICKENS, etc. 1475. **4.** With a negative particle immediately following OE.

1. W. don't you learn Italian? 1883. **b.** Whie should our faults at home be spred abroad? 1608. W., w. was I born to undergo such unmerited misfortunes? THACKERAY. **c.** W. so Cold, and w. so Coy? VANBRUGH. But w. prolong the tale? WORDSW. **2.** I dare give him no counsell, and I will tell you w. 1581. **3.** W. in the name of all patience should you work so hard as this? 1860. **4.** You can't marry me? W. not? When I offer you a fortune? 1882.

II. As relative: On account of which, because of which, for which. Usu., now almost always, after *reason*. Also *ellipt.* ME. **b.** Introducing a subject or predicative clause: = 'the reason w.' 1605.

Reasons w. Catholiques refuse to go to Church 1581. I'll have my Earl, as well as She, or know the Reason w. PRIOR. **b.** And this is w. I sojourn here KEATS.

III. as *sb.* (pl. *whys*). **a.** Reason, cause (now only with conscious allusion to the interrogative use) ME. **b.** A question beginning with (or consisting of) the word 'Why?'; a question as to the reason of something; hence, a problem, an enigma 1532. **c.** Conjoined with *wherefore* similarly used 1590.

a. As may perchance be done for sum gude quhy 1560. The when, and the how, and the w. of the surrender SOUTHEY. **c.** The savage is no authority on the w. and wherefore of his customs 1911.

IV. Used interjectionally before a sentence or clause. **a.** As an expression of surprise (sometimes only momentary or slight, sometimes involving protest), either in reply to a remark or question, or on perceiving something unexpected 1519. **b.** Emphasizing or calling more or less abrupt attention to the statement following, in opposition to a possible or vaguely apprehended doubt or objection 1545. †**c.** As an emphasized call or summons, expressing some degree of impatience. SHAKS. †**d.** *W., so!* an expression of content, acquiescence, or relief -1826.

a. *Bene.* Doo not you loue me? *Beat.* W. no, no more then reason SHAKS. W., I believe I've been asleep! 1893. **b.** Take an honest woman from her husband! w., it is intollerable 1596. If you will have Caesar for your master, w. have him GOLDSM. Not a doubt . . W., it stands to reason. 1882. **c.** *Rom. & Jul.* IV. v. 2, 3. **d.** *Macb.* III. iv. 107.

V. For w.: **a.** *interrog.* For what reason; **b.** *rel.* For which reason, wherefore; **c.** *conj.* For the reason that, because, for. *Obs.*, *arch.*, or *dial.* (Now commonly apprehended as the adv. *why* with a redundant *for* prefixed.) OE.

As for what he was like I cannot tell, . . for w. I never saw un SCOTT. Hence **Whye·ver** *adv.* for whatever reason. †**Why-for, why for** *advb.* and *conj. phr.*

Why-not (hwəi·nǫt). 1611. [The phr. *why not?* used as sb.] An argument of the form 'why not?', which attempts to leave the opponent without a reply.

Wibble-wobble (wi·b'lwǫ·b'l). *colloq.* 1847. Reduplication of WOBBLE. So **Wi·bbly-wo·bbly** *a.* characterized by 'wibbling and wobbling', unsteady.

Wich, wych (witʃ, *locally* wəitʃ). *local.* 1601. [app. a differentiated variant of WICK *sb.*[2] Cf. the place-names (of salt-making towns) *Droitwich* (formerly *Wich*), *Nantwich*, *Northwich*.] A salt-works, salt-pit, or brine-spring, in the salt-manufacturing district of Cheshire and neighbouring parts; *pl.* the salt-making towns of these parts.

Comb.: **w.-house**, a building in which brine is evaporated for making salt; **-man**, a man employed in salt-making; **-waller**, a salt-boiler.

Wick[1] (wik). [OE. *wēoce*, *wēoc* (in *candelwēoc*), corresp. to MDu. *wiecke*, MLG. *wêke*, *weike*, OHG. *wioh*.] The bundle of fibre, now usu. loosely twisted or woven cotton, in a lamp, candle, or taper (formerly also in a torch), immersed or enclosed except at one end in the oil or grease, which it absorbs and draws up on being kindled at the free end, so as to maintain the flame. **b.** Without article = WICKING. late ME. **c.** Used as a tent or dressing in surgery 1658.

Wick[2] (wik). Now only *local.* [OE. *wīc* = OS. *wīc*, OHG. *wīch*; app. ad. L. *vicus* row of houses, village (cogn. w. Gr. οἶκος, Goth. *weihs*).] †**1.** An abode, dwelling, dwelling-place -ME. **2.** A town, village, or hamlet. *Obs.* or *dial.* (Surviving as an element of place-names, in forms *-wich*, *-wick*.) OE. **3.** A farm; *spec.* a dairy farm: Now *local.* OE.

-wick, *suffix*, shortened form of †*wike* (OE. *wīce*) office, function of an official, as in BAILIFFWICK, BAILIWICK, SHERIFFWICK.

Wicked (wi·kėd), *a.*[1] (*sb.*, *adv.*) [ME. *wicked*, *wikked*, app. f. *wicke*, *wikke*, perh. adj. use of OE. *wicca* wizard + -ED.] **I. 1.** Bad in moral character, disposition, or conduct; practising or disposed to practise evil; morally depraved. **2.** Bad, in various senses. Freq. in ME.; later chiefly *dial.*, or *colloq.* as a conscious metaphor (now often joc.) from sense 1, = 'very or excessively bad', 'beastly'. **a.** In ref. to character or action: Cruel, severe, fierce. Of animals: Savage, vicious. ME. **b.** Actually or potentially harmful, destructive, or pernicious; baleful ME. **c.** Of bad quality; poor, vile, 'sorry' ME. **3.** In weakened sense, usu. more or less joc.: Malicious; mischievous, sly 1600.

1. The Divine Vengeance on a W. World 1696. Vice increases, and men grow daily more and more w. BERKELEY. 'Yes, hang it' (said Sir Pitt, only, he used, dear, a much wickeder word) THACKERAY. **2. b.** *Temp.* I. ii. 321. It was a w. country for fever 1895. **3.** That same w. Bastard of Venus, . . that blinde rascally boy SHAKS.

II. *absol.* or as *sb.* **a.** *absol.* in *pl.* sense: Wicked persons. (Usu., now always, with *the.*) ME. **b.** *absol.* or as *sb.* in *sing.* sense: A wicked person. *Obs.* or *rare arch.* 1484.

b. Let the w. forsake his waies BIBLE (Geneva) *Isa.* lv. 7.

III. as *adv.* Wickedly; fiercely, savagely, furiously; 'cruelly', 'terribly'. late ME.

Yesterday was . . a w. hot day 1663. A hungry louse bites w. sair HOGG. Hence **Wi·cked-ly** *adv.*; **-ness**, the quality of being w.; w. action or conduct; a piece of wickedness, a w. act or proceeding.

Wicked (wikt), *a.*[2] 1507. [f. WICK[1] + -ED[1].] Furnished with or having a wick or wicks; usu. in comb., as *two-w.*

Wicker (wi·kəɹ), *sb.* ME. [East Scandinavian; f. root of Sw. *vika* to bend.] **1.** A pliant twig or small rod, usu. of willow, esp. as used for making baskets and various other objects; an osier. Chiefly in *pl.* late ME. **2.** (without *pl.*) Wickers collectively, or as plaited together; wickerwork ME. **3.** A basket, cradle, chair, etc. of wicker 1646. **4. a.** *attrib.* Made or consisting of wicker, as a basket, chair, etc.; also, covered with or encased in wicker, as a bottle 1502. **b.** *W. wings*, attributed to various sinister creatures 1637.

4. b. The Goblin plys his w. wings CONGREVE. Hence **Wi·cker** *v. trans.* to furnish, fit, cover, or enclose with w. **Wi·ckered** (-əɹd) *a.* encased in w.; made of w. **Wi·ckerwork**, work consisting of wickers; a structure of flexible twigs or the like plaited together; basket-work.

Wicket (wi·kėt). ME. [a. AF. = ONF. *wiket* = OF. *guichet*; usu. referred to the Teut. root appearing in ON. *vīkja* to move, turn; but perh. from some other source.] **1.** A small door or gate made in or placed beside a large one, for ingress and egress when the large one is closed; also, any small gate for foot-passengers, as at the entrance of a field. **2.** *Cricket.* A set of three sticks called *stumps*, fixed upright in the ground, and surmounted by two small pieces of wood called *bails*, forming the structure at which the bowler aims the ball, and at which (in front and a little to one side of it) the batsman stands to defend it with the bat 1733. **b.** In various expressions referring to a batsman's tenure of the wicket, or that part of an innings during which some particular batsman is (or might be) 'in', i. e. at the wicket 1738. **c.** *transf.* The ground between and about the wickets, esp. in respect of its condition; the pitch 1862. **3.** *U.S. Croquet.* A hoop 1868. **4.** In various techn. senses, as (*a*) a small gate or valve for emptying the chamber of a canal-lock, etc.; (*b*) one of a set of gratings in the form of which the lead is made up in the manufacture of white lead 1875.

2. *Single w.*, a form of cricket in which there is only one w., and therefore only one batsman 'in' at a time. *Double w.*, the ordinary form, in which there are two wickets placed 22 yards apart, between which the two batsmen run. *To keep w.*, to act as w.-keeper. **b.** *To take* so many *wickets* (said of a bowler), to put so many batsmen 'out'. *Three wickets* (or *third w.*) *down*, three men having been put out. *The sixth w. fell for 75* = the sixth batsman was put out after 75 runs had been made in the innings. *To win by eight wickets*, i. e. by exceeding the opponents' full score of runs with eight wickets yet to 'fall' (= with two men 'not out' and seven not having been 'in' in the innings). **c.** The w. did not seem to play particularly well 1881. The English eleven commenced batting on a perfect w. 1884.

attrib. and *Comb.*: **w.-gate** = sense 1; **-keep** (*colloq.*), **-keeper** *Cricket*, a player stationed behind the w. to stop the ball if it passes by, and if possible to put the batsman 'out' by 'stumping' or 'catching'.

Wicking (wi·kiŋ). 1873. [f. WICK[1] + -ING[1].] Material for making wicks; cord or tape of cotton or other fibre, to be cut into lengths for wicks.

Wickyup (wi·ki͵ɒp). *U.S.* 1857. [Amer. Indian (Menominee *wikiop*, Saki *wekeab*); perh. a variant of *wikiwam* WIGWAM.] A rude hut consisting of a frame covered with brushwood or the like, used by nomadic tribes in the west and south-west. Hence extended to any small hut or shanty.

Wicopy (wi·kǫpi). 1778. [Amer. Indian (Cree *wikupiy*).] **a.** The leatherwood or moosewood of N. America, *Dirca palustris*; also the basswood, *Tilia americana*. **b.** An Amer. name for species of willow-herb (*Epilobium*): distinctively *Indian* or *herb w.*

Widdershins: see WITHERSHINS.

Widdy (wi·di). Chiefly *Sc.* 1450. [Sc. and n. dial. var. of WITHY.] **1.** A band or rope, prop. one made of intertwined osiers or the like 1470. **2.** A rope for hanging, a halter; freq. *allus.* 1450.

Wide (wəid), *sb.* ME. [absol. use of next.] **1.** †**a.** The open sea. ME. only. **b.** A wide, extensive, or open space *poet.* 1833. **2.** *Cricket.* [Short for *wide ball.*] A ball bowled wide of the wicket, counting one against the bowler's side 1850. **3.** *The w.* (short for 'the wide world') in slang. phr., as *done, whacked to the w.*, utterly done up; *broke to the w.*, completely broke.

Wide (wəid), *a.* [Com. Teut.; OE. *wīd*:— OTeut. **wīdoz* (G. *weit*); further relations obsc.] **I. 1.** Having great extent (esp. horizontally); vast, spacious, extensive. *Obs.* exc. as generalized use of II. 1. **b.** as a conventional epithet of words denoting an extensive area, esp. the earth and the sea (*poet.* and *rhet.*); as an epithet of *world*, sometimes implying contrast to the privacy or security of one's own home or country OE. **c.** Of a garment, etc.: Capacious; large and loose. *Obs.* exc. *dial.* in *w. coat*, a greatcoat. ME. **2.** *transf.* Extending over or affecting a large space or region; far-reaching. Chiefly *poet.* OE. **3.** *fig.* Having a large range; extensive, largely inclusive; (of a word or term) having a large extent of meaning 1534. **b.** Of views or opinions, or *transf.* of a person: = BROAD *a.* 10. 1824.

1. *A.Y.L.* II. vii. 137. **b.** I shall be turn'd a drift to the w. World DE FOE. **c.** And there the Snake throwes her enammel'd skinne, Weed w. enough to rap a Fairy in SHAKS. **3.** A definition of art w. enough to include all its varieties of aim RUSKIN. His w. knowledge of ethnography 1865.

II. 1. Having great extent from side to side; large across, or in transverse measurement (now dist. from *broad* in so far as it tends to be restricted to applications in which actual mensuration is possible, and in which there is no implication of superficial extent) OE. **b.** *transf.* of the lateral boundaries: Having a wide space between, far apart 1840. **2.** Having a specified or particular transverse measurement indicated by a numerical quantity or by a comparison; (so much) across OE. **3.** Opened widely, expanded; of the arms, stretched widely apart. (Now superseded in general use by *w. open.*) 1508. **b.** *Phonetics.* Of a vowel-sound: Pronounced with the tongue relaxed, or with a wider opening between it and some other part of the mouth than the corresponding *narrow* vowel 1867.

2. 'Tis not so deepe as a well, nor so w. as a Church doore SHAKS. A Bed-chamber..Thirty foot w. 1663.

III. 1. Extending far between limits; existing between two things which are far apart, *lit.* or *fig.* 1589. †**2.** Situated a great way off, distant, far–1854. **b.** *fig.* Far, far apart (in nature, views, etc.); not in accordance, disagreeing, different. Const. *from, of.* Now *rare.* 1542. **3.** Deviating from the aim, or from the direct or proper course; missing the mark or the way. **a.** *lit.*; *spec.* in *Cricket*, of a ball bowled too far aside from the wicket for the batsman to strike it 1588. **b.** *fig.* (*a*) without prep. (now *rare*): often = Astray in opinion or belief, mistaken 1561. (*b*) Const. *of, from* (now rare or obs.): esp. in phr. *w. of the mark* 1566. **4. a.** Going beyond bounds of restraint, propriety, or virtue; loose, immoral. Now *colloq.* or *slang.* 1574. **b.** Going beyond bounds of moderation; excessive, immoderate 1858. **c.** *slang.* Wide-awake, cute 1887.

1. The w. difference 'Twixt Amorous, and Villanous SHAKS. *To give a w. berth to*, to keep well away from, steer quite clear of. **3. b.** *Lear* IV. vii. 50. **4. a.** W. females in pink 1902. **c.** Well, she was tipsy; but she was very 'w.' 1891.

Comb.: *w.-brimmed* adj.; **w.-angle** *a.*, applied to a lens of short focus, the field of which extends through a w. angle, used for photographing at short range; **-eyed** *a.*, having w. eyes; usu., having the eyes wide open, gazing intently; **-watered**, having a w. expanse of water; watered over a w. extent; bordered or traversed by w. waters.

Wide (wəid), *adv.* [OE. *wīde*, advb. f. *wīd* WIDE *a.*] Widely. **1.** Over or through a large space or region; so as to affect many or various persons or places. Chiefly *poet.* (exc. as in b). **b.** in phr. *far and w.* (rarely *w. and far*); †*w. and side* OE. **2.** With a large space or spaces between; at a wide interval or intervals; far apart or asunder OE. **b.** Of a horse: With the legs apart: opp. to NEAR *adv.*[2] I. 10. 1680. **c.** Loosely asunder; so as not to remain close or in contact 1784. **3.** With a wide or broad opening; esp. with *open* vb. or adj. = fully; with *fling, fly*, etc. = *wide open* OE. **4.** At (to, from) a (great, or specified) distance; far, far away, far off. Now only *dial.* OE. **5.** At a distance to one side; aside from the aim, or from the direct or proper course 1534.

1. There..W. roams the Russian exile THOMSON. **b.** They scoured the country far and w. 1862. **2. c.** Shaking w. thy yellow hair SHELLEY. **3.** This is a strange repose, to be asleepe With eyes w. open SHAKS. The doors were flung w. 1895. **5.** Is my Lord well, that he doth speake so w.? SHAKS. You hurt not me, Your anger flies so w. FLETCHER. A..ball..pitched a little w. of the off stump 1833.

Wi·deawa·ke, *adj. phr.*, **wi·de-awake**, *a.* and *sb.* 1818. [f. prec. + AWAKE *pred. a.*] **A.** *adj.* (or *adj. phr.*) **1.** Awake with the eyes wide open; full awake (usu. *predic.*). **2.** *fig.* Thoroughly vigilant or on the alert; fully aware of what is going on or of what it is best to do; sharp-witted, knowing (*colloq.*, orig. *slang*) 1833. **3.** Applied joc. to a soft felt hat with broad brim and low crown: app. so called as having no 'nap'. Now usu. *absol.* as *sb.* 1841.

2. Our governor's wide awake, he is..He knows what's o'clock DICKENS.

B. *sb.* **1.** A 'wide-awake' hat 1837. **2.** A sailor's name for the Sooty Tern (*Sterna fuliginosa* and allied species) from its cry 1881. Hence **Wide-awa·keness**, the state or character of being wide awake.

Widely (wəi·dli), *adv.* 1663. [f. WIDE *a.* + -LY [2].] **1.** Over or through a wide area; in or to various places 1697. **2.** Over a wide range; in relation to many or various things, subjects, etc. 1695. **3.** With or at a wide interval; far apart; to a considerable width 1663. **4.** To a large extent, greatly, far 1688.

Wide-mouthed (-mauðd, -mauþt), *a.* 1593. **1.** Having a wide mouth 1611. **2.** Having the mouth wide open: (*a*) loud-spoken; (*b*) voracious.

Widen (wəi·d'n), *v.* 1607. [f. WIDE *a.* + -EN [5].] †**1.** *trans.* To open wide, set wide open –1627. **2.** To make wide or wider 1669. **3.** *intr.* To become wide or wider 1650.

1. *Cor.* I. iv. 44. **2.** I would cleanse, w., and deepen the river Stort 1785. The society is widening its scheme of operations 1885. **3.** A reall quarrell widening 1650. The streamlet widens into a pond 1920. Hence **Wi·dener**, one who or that which widens; *spec.* a drill constructed to bore a hole of greater diameter than its own.

Wideness (wəi·dnės). OE. Also **widness** (*Obs.* or *dial.*). [f. WIDE *a.* + -NESS.] Width: **a.** Large extension, vastness (in later use only as transf. use of 3) ME.; **b.** Transverse measurement, breadth OE. (in standard Eng. replaced by WIDTH); **c.** Large transverse measurement 1548. **d.** *concr.* A wide space or expanse. **e.** Largeness of range, wide reach 1551.

Wide-open, *a.* 1610. [WIDE *adv.* 3.] **1.** Open to a wide extent. **2.** *U.S.* Free from limitations or restrictions; also, characterized by overt law-breaking 1902.

Wide-spread, *a.* 1705. [f. WIDE *adv.* + *spread*, pa. pple. of SPREAD *v.*] **1.** Extended over or occupying a wide space; broad in spatial extent 1735. **2.** Distributed over a wide region; extensively or generally diffused 1705.

Wide-spreading, *a.* 1591. **1.** Extending over a wide space. **2.** Extending to many places or persons, far-reaching 1766.

†**Wide-where**, *adv.* *Obs.* exc. *rare arch.* ME. [f. WIDE *adv.* + WHERE *adv.*] In or to various places, widely, far and wide; in or to a distant place, far away –1906.

Widgeon, wigeon (wi·dʒən). 1513. [etym. obsc., possibly formed with L. suffix *-ion-* on onomatopœic base.] **1.** A wild duck of the genus *Mareca*, esp. *M. penelope* of Europe and Northern Asia. (Collective pl. in later use usu. *widgeon.*) **b.** Applied locally to various wild ducks of other genera, as *Anas fusca*, the Red-headed W. 1668. †**2.** Of a person, in allusion to the supposed stupidity of the bird: A fool, simpleton, ninny –1741.

attrib. and *Comb.*: **w.-grass**, **-weed**, (*local*) the grass-wrack, *Zostera marina*.

Widish (wəi·diʃ), *a.* 1780. [f. WIDE *a.* + -ISH [1].] Somewhat wide.

Widow (wi·dou), *sb.*[1] [OE. *widewe, widuwe, wuduwe*; orig. an Indo-Eur. adj. formation **widhewo-*, *-wā* (cf. Skr. *vidhavā* widow, L. *viduus* void, *vidua* widow) on the base * *widh-* to be empty, be separated.] **1.** A woman whose husband is dead (and who has not married again). **b.** Prefixed as a title to the name. Now chiefly *dial.* or *vulgar.* 1576. **c.** In extended sense: A wife separated from or deserted by her husband; esp. in colloq. or dial. phr. *a w. bewitched*; see also GRASS WIDOW 2. 1461. **d.** *Eccl.* One of a class or order of devout or consecrated widows in the Early Church 1572. **e.** *transf.* A female animal, esp. a hen bird, that has lost its mate ME. **2. a.** A bird of the subfamily *Viduinæ*. **b.** Collector's name for a geometrid moth, *Cidaria luctuata*; also *mourning w.* **c.** *Mournful* or *mourning w.*, pop. names of certain plants with dusky flowers. 1747. **3.** *colloq.* or *slang.* **a.** An extra hand dealt to the table in certain card-games. **b.** *The w.*: champagne. [From 'Veuve Cliquot', the name of a firm of wine merchants.] 1891.

1. Take example by your father, my boy, and be wery careful o' widders DICKENS. **c.** Has Mr. Balfour never heard of the Golf Widow? 1908.

Comb.: as *w. lady, woman* (arch. or dial.), etc.; **w.-duck**, a species of tree-duck, *Dendrocygna viduata*; **-finch** = W.-BIRD; **w. right**, that part of a deceased husband's estate to which a w. has a right. **b.** with genitive: **widow's cruse**, an inexhaustible source of supply (after 1 Kings xvii. 14); **widow's lock**, a lock or tuft of hair growing apart from the rest, supposed to presage early widowhood; **widow's mite**, a small money contribution (in allusion to Mark xii. 43); **widow's peak** (see PEAK *sb.*[2] I. 1 b, and cf. *widow's lock*); **widow's weeds**, the mourning apparel of a w.

Widow, *sb.*[2] *Obs.* exc. *dial.* [OE. *widewa*, masc. corresp. to *widewe* WIDOW *sb.*[1]] = WIDOWER.

Wi·dow, *v.* ME. [f. WIDOW *sb.*[1] or [2].] **1.** *trans.* To make a widow (*rarely*, a widower) of; to bereave of one's husband (or wife). Most commonly in *pa. pple.* **b.** *fig.* To deprive *of* a valuable or highly prized possession; to bereave. Usu. in *pa. pple.* 1595. †**2.** To survive as a widow, become the widow of. SHAKS. †**3.** To endow with a widow's right. SHAKS.

Wi·dow-bird. 1772. [Representing L. generic name *Vidua* (widow).] A bird of the genus *Vidua* or subfamily *Viduinæ* of the family *Ploceidæ* (Weaver-birds), found in various parts of Africa; so called from the prevailingly black plumage of the males. (Cf. WHIDAH.)

Widowed (wi·doud), *ppl. a.* 1600. [f. WIDOW *sb.*[1] or [2] or *v.* + -ED.] **1.** Made or become a widow (or widower). Also of an animal, esp. a bird: Bereaved of its mate. **2.** *fig.* Deprived of a partner, friend, companion, or mate; bereaved; hence, deserted, desolate, solitary 1633. **b.** Of an elm: Not 'mated' with a vine; conversely of the vine. (After L. *ulmus* and *vitis vidua.*) 1743.

1. *transf.* Sleepelesse she spent in her now widow'd bed..the night that followed 1627.

Widower (wi·douəɹ). late ME. [f. WIDOW *sb.*[1] + -ER [1].] **1.** A man whose wife is dead (and who has not married again); a husband bereaved of his wife. †**2.** One of an ecclesiastical class or order of men corresp. to the order of 'widows' –1610. Hence **Wi·dowerhood** [after WIDOWHOOD], the condition of a w., or the time during which a man is a w.

Widowhood (wi·douhud). [OE. *widewanhād*, f. gen. of WIDOW *sb.*[1] or [2] + *-hād* -HOOD.] **1.** The state or condition of a widow or widower, or (contextually) the time during which one is a widow or widower; also *transf.* of an animal, esp. a bird. †**2.** An estate settled on a widow, a widow's right. SHAKS.

1. In my wedowhode, afore I maried this gentilwoman 1528. Lucretia..in the deep weeds of w. 1846.

Wi·dow-wail. 1597. **a.** The shrub Mezereon (*Daphne Mezereum*) or other species of *Daphne*. **b.** A shrub of the genus *Cneorum* (family *Simarubaceæ*), esp. *C. tricoccum*, a dwarf shrub with evergreen leaves and pink sweet-scented flowers, found in Spain and the south of France.

Width (widþ, witþ). 1627. [A literary formation of the 17th century, taking the place of *wīdness* WIDENESS. 'A low word' (J.).] **1.** Extent across or from side to side; transverse dimension; *occas.* extent of opening, distance apart (of the two parts of something). **2.** Large extent across, or in general 1697. **3.** *concr.* = BREADTH 2. 1876. Hence **Wi·dthless** *a.* having no (great) w., narrow. **Wi·dthways, -wise** *adv.* in the direction of the w., transversely.

Wield (wīld), *v.* [Two OE. vbs.; (1) Com. Teut. str. vb., OE. (WS.) *wealdan*, (Anglian) *waldan*, pa. t. *wēold*, pa. pple. *gewealden*; (2) wk. vb., OE. (WS.) **gewieldan, wyldan*, Anglian *wældan*, containing a mutated form of the same stem **walđ-*.] †**1.** *trans.* To rule or reign over, govern, command. *Obs.* exc. as merged in 4. –1633. †**2.** To have at command or disposal, hold, own, possess; to have the advantage of, enjoy –1603. **3.** To direct the movement or action of, to control; to use, have the use of, as a bodily member or faculty; *gen.* to deal with, have to do with; to deal with successfully. *Obs.* or *dial.* exc. as in 4. OE. †**b.** To express, utter –1635. **4.** To use or handle with skill and effect; to manage, ply (a weapon, tool, or instrument, now always one held or carried in the hand) OE. **b.** To exercise (power, authority, influence) 1612. **c.** To use after the fashion of a tool or weapon for the performance of something 1601.

3. b. *Lear* I. i. 56. 4. Monstrouse cudgells..as bigge as the partie is well able to wild 1603. *To w. a* or *the sceptre* (and similar phrases), to exercise supreme authority, to reign or rule (also *fig.*). c. A trained soldier wielding a graphic and powerful pen 1882. Who could w. such scathing invective? 1918. Hence **Wie·lder**, one who wields.

Wieldy (wī·ldi), *a.* late ME. [f. prec. + -Y [1].] **1.** Capable of easily 'wielding' one's body or limbs, or a weapon, etc.; vigorous, active, nimble. *Obs.* exc. *dial.* **2.** Easily wielded, controlled, or handled; manageable, handy. [In later use a back-formation from *unwieldy*.] 1583.

1. So fressh so yong so weldy semed he CHAUCER.

Wife (wəif). *Pl.* **wives** (wəivz). [Com. WGer. and Norse str. n.: OE. *wīf* = OFris., OS. *wīf*, OHG., MHG. *wīp* (G. *weib* woman); origin obsc. (Gothic used *qinō* woman, QUEAN, *qēns* wife, QUEEN.)] **1.** A woman: formerly in general sense; in later use restricted to a woman of humble rank, esp. one engaged in the sale of some commodity. Now *dial.*, exc. with prefixed descriptive word, esp. in compounds such as FISHWIFE, etc. **b.** Qualified by *old*, esp. in the phr. *old wives' tale*: see OLD WIFE 1. OE. **2.** A woman joined to a man by marriage; a married woman OE. **b.** *transf.* The female of a pair of the lower animals; the mate of a male animal. late ME. **3.** The mistress of a household; the hostess or landlady of an inn. *Obs.* exc. as surviving in GOODWIFE 1, HOUSEWIFE 1. late ME. **4.** Collector's name for a moth, *Catocala nupta*, also called Willow Red Underwing 1832.

1. Where ginger-bread wives have a scanty sale KEATS. 2. He was still on the look-out for a w. with money DICKENS. Phrases. *To w.*, for a w., to be one's w. *To take a w.*, to marry (somewhat *arch.*). †*To have to w.*, to have as one's w., be the husband of. *All the world and his w.* (joc. colloq.), all men and women, everybody: usu. hyperbolically for a large and miscellaneous company of people of both sexes. *W. of the left hand*: see LEFT HAND. Hence **Wi·fedom** = WIFEHOOD 1, 2; also, wives collectively, married women as a class. **Wi·feless** *a.* having no wife; unmarried, celibate.

Wifehood (wəi·fhud). late ME. [f. prec. + -HOOD.] **1.** The position or condition of a wife; married state (of a woman). **2.** The character of or befitting a wife; wifeliness. late ME.

Wifelike (wəi·f,ləik), *a.* and *adv.* 1598. [f. as prec. + -LIKE.] **A.** *adj.* Resembling, or having the character of, a wife; characteristic of or befitting a wife 1613. **B.** *adv.* In the manner of a wife 1598.

Wifely (wəi·f,li), *a.* [OE. *wīflic*; see -LY [1].] †**1.** Of or pertaining to a woman or women; womanly (*rare* exc. OE.) –1533. **2.** Pertaining to, characteristic of, or befitting a wife OE. **3.** Having the character befitting a wife; such as a wife should be 1633.

2. A picture of w. patience 1863. 3. A w. wife, a motherly mother, and above all, a lady 1853. Hence **Wi·feliness**, w. character or quality.

Wifie (wəi·fi). 1825. [f. WIFE *sb.* + -IE, -Y [6].] Little wife: used as a term of endearment.

Wifish (wəi·fiʃ), *a.* 1535. [f. WIFE *sb.* + -ISH [1].] †**1.** Belonging to or characteristic of a woman; womanly; womanish –1560. **2.** Belonging to or characteristic of, having the character of, a wife 1616.

Wig (wig), *sb.*[1] Now *dial.* late ME. [a. MLG., MDu. *wigge* wedge, wedge-shaped cake.] A kind of bun or small cake made of fine flour.

Home to the only Lenten supper I have had of wiggs and ale PEPYS.

Wig, *sb.*[2] 1675. [Shortened f. PERIWIG.] **1.** An artificial covering of hair for the head, worn to conceal baldness or to cover the inadequacy of the natural hair, as part of professional, ceremonial, or formerly of fashionable, costume (as still by judges and barristers), or as a disguise (as by actors on the stage). **b.** Applied joc. to a (natural) head of hair, esp. of a child. **2.** *transf.* A person who wears a wig (professionally); a dignitary. *colloq.* 1828. (Cf. BIGWIG.) **3.** *techn.* The coarse hair on the shoulders of a full-grown male fur-seal; the seal itself when bearing this 1830. **4.** A severe rebuke or scolding; an act of WIGGING. *slang* or *colloq.* 1804.

1. The disappearance of the bishops' wigs, which he said had done more harm to the church than anything else! GLADSTONE. Phr. *Dash my wig(s* (colloq.), a mild imprecation. *My wig(s!* (colloq.), a trivial expression of surprise, etc. *Wigs on the green*, a colloquial expression (orig. Irish) for coming to blows or sharp altercation (wigs being liable to fall or be pulled off in a fray).

attrib. and *Comb.*: **w.-block**, a rounded block for placing a w. upon when being made or not in use; **-tail**, (*a*) a bird of the tropics, from its long tail-feathers; (*b*) the tail of a w.; **-sumach, -tree**, the Venetian sumach (*Rhus Cotinus*), from its hairy inflorescence. Hence **Wi·gdom**, judges or lawyers as a body. **Wigged** (wigd) *a.* furnished with or wearing a w. **Wi·ggery**, wigs collectively, the practice of wearing a w.; used by Carlyle for empty formality (in legal proceedings), 'red tape'. **Wi·ggy** *a.* wearing, or distinguished by, a w., bewigged. **Wi·gless** *a.* destitute of a w., not wearing a w. †**Wi·gsby** [-BY 2] *joc. slang* or *colloq.*, a person wearing a w.

Wig, *v.* 1826. [f. prec.] **I.** *trans.* To supply with a wig; to put a w. upon; *spec.* to provide with wigs in preparation for a theatrical performance. **2.** To rebuke or censure severely, scold, rate. *slang* or *colloq.* 1829.

Wigging (wi·giŋ), *vbl. sb. slang* or *colloq.* 1813. [f. WIG *sb.*[2] 4 + -ING [1].] A severe rebuke, reproof or reprimand; a scolding.

Wiggle (wi·g'l), *v.* Now *colloq.* or *dial.* ME. [Cognate with or a. (M)LG. *wiggelen*; frequent. f. dial. *wig*.] **1.** *intr.* To move to and fro or from side to side irregularly and lightly; to walk with such a movement, to stagger, reel; to go or move sinuously, to wriggle. **2.** *trans.* To move (something) in this way; also *refl.* 1685. Hence **Wi·ggle** *sb.* an act of 'wiggling'.

Wiggle-waggle (wi·g'l,wæ:g'l), *v. colloq.* 1825. Redupl. form combining WIGGLE *v.* and WAGGLE *v.*, emphasizing the alternation of movement. *trans.* or *intr.* So **Wiggle-waggle** *a.* that 'wiggle-waggles'; *fig.* vacillating 1778.

Wiggly (wi·gli), *a. colloq.* 1903. [f. WIGGLE *v.* or *sb.* + -Y [1].] Characterized by or suggestive of 'wiggling'; (in ref. to form) having small irregular undulations. Also in redupl. form **Wi·ggly-wa·ggly.**

Wight (wəit), *sb. arch.* [OE. *wiht* = OS., OHG., MHG. *wiht*, ON. *vættr, vitr*, Goth. *waiht* (*ni...waiht* nothing); ulterior connexions unc. Cf. AUGHT, NAUGHT, NOUGHT.] †**1.** A living being; a creature –1587. **b.** orig. and chiefly with (good or bad) epithet, applied to supernatural, preternatural, or unearthly beings. *Obs.* or *rare arch.* OE. **2.** A human being, man or woman, person. Now *arch.* or *dial.* (often implying contempt or commiseration). ME. †**3.** In advb. phrases, qualified by *no, any, a little*, or the like: (A certain) amount; for (any, a little, etc.) time or distance –1470.

1. b. These were the good wights (fairies) dwelling in the court of Elfland SCOTT. 2. Of fayre Elisa be your siluer song, that blessed w. SPENSER. The unlucky w...is doomed 1869.

Wight (wəit), *a.* (*adv.*) *arch.* and *dial.* ME. [a. ON. *vīgt*, neut. of *vīgr* of fighting age, skilled in arms, f. OTeut. **wīg-*, (*waig-, wig-*), as in OE. *wīg* battle, fight, *wiga* warrior.] **1.** Of persons, actions, etc.: Strong and courageous, esp. in warfare; having or showing prowess; valiant, doughty, bold. **2.** Strong, vigorous, robust, stalwart; exercising strength, energetic ME. **3.** Moving briskly or rapidly; active, agile; swift, fleet. late ME.

1. Where is Robin Hood, and yᵉ w. Scarlet? 1601. 3. Mount thee on the wightest steed SCOTT.

B. *adv.* Actively, nimbly, energetically; quickly, rapidly ME. Hence **Wi·ght·ly** *adv.* (*arch.* and *dial.*); **-ness** (*Obs.* or *arch.*).

Wig-wag (wi·g,wæg), *v. colloq.* or *techn.* 1846. [Reduplicated formation; cf. *wiggle-waggle, zig-zag*.] *trans.* and *intr.* To move lightly to and fro, to wag; *esp.* to wave a flag or other object to and fro in signalling; to signal in this way. Also as *adv.* = with a to-and-fro movement. So **Wi·g-wag** *sb.* 1582.

Wigwam (wi·gwæm, -wǫm). 1628. [a. Ojibwa *wigwaum, wigiwam*, var. of Algonkin *weekuwom, wikiwam* lit. 'their house'.] A lodge, cabin, tent, or hut of the N. Amer. Indian tribes of the region of the Great Lakes and eastward, formed of bark, matting, or hides stretched over a frame of poles converging at the top. **b.** Extended to similar structures among native tribes in other parts of the world 1743. **c.** Applied *joc.* to a house or dwelling in general 1818.

Wild (wəild), *a.* and *sb.* [Com. Teut.; OE. *wilde*:—OTeut. **wilþijoz*, of doubtful ulterior relationship; possibly connected with **walþus* forest, WOLD.] **A.** *adj.* **I. 1.** Of an animal: Living in a state of nature; not tame, not domesticated (freq. in names of particular species or varieties, for which see the sbs.). **2.** Of a plant (or flower): Growing in a state of nature; not cultivated (freq. in names of particular species or varieties, for which see the sbs.) OE. **3.** Produced or yielded by wild animals or plants; sometimes, having the characteristic (usu. inferior) quality of such productions ME. **b.** *Mining.* Applied to impure or inferior minerals or ores 1778. **4.** Of a place or region: Uncultivated or uninhabited; hence, waste, desert, desolate OE. **b.** *transf.* Belonging to or characteristic of a wild region; of or in a wilderness 1690. **5.** Of persons (or their attributes): Uncivilized; savage; uncultured, rude; also, not accepting the constituted government, rebellious ME.

1. Eight Wilde-Boares rosted whole SHAKS. 2. I know a banke where the wilde time blowes SHAKS. With woodbine and w. roses mantled o'er COWPER. *attrib. phr.* A young lady with a w.-rose complexion 1890. 3. Their flesh is hot and unsauorie, and hath a wilde tast 1600. 4. The scenery was w. without being grand 1849. 5. When w. in woods the noble Savage ran DRYDEN. The 'slim' ways of the w. Boer 1901.

II. 1. Not under or not submitting to control or restraint; taking or disposed to take one's own way; uncontrolled OE. **b.** Shy; *esp.* of game, afraid of or avoiding the pursuer 1594. **2.** *spec.* Not submitting to moral control; taking one's own way in defiance of moral obligation or authority OE. **b.** Giving way to sexual passion; also, licentious, dissolute, loose ME. **3.** Fierce, savage; furious, violent, cruel ME. **4.** Of the sea, the weather, etc.: Violently agitated, rough, stormy; hence *fig.* or *gen.* Full of disturbance or confusion, tumultuous, turbulent ME. **b.** Of vocal sounds: Loud and unrestrained 1549. **5.** Of feelings or their expression: Highly excited or agitated; passionately vehement or impetuous 1594. **6.** Of persons: **a.** Extremely irritated or vexed; angry, 'furious' 1653. **b.** Passionately or excitedly desirous *to do* something 1797. **c.** Elated, enthusiastic, 'raving' 1868. 7. Not having control of one's mental faculties; demented, out of one's wits; hence, extremely foolish or unreasonable ME. b. Of the eyes or look: Having an expression of distraction 1592. 8. Of actions, statements, etc.: Going beyond prudent or reasonable limits; rashly or inconsiderately venturesome; fantastically unreasonable 1515. 9. Artless, free, unconventional or romantic in style; having a somewhat barbaric character 1632. b. Of strange aspect; fantastic in appearance 1605. 10. Aimed wide of the mark or at random; random: usu. *advb.* at random, astray 1810.

1. Depriving Cupid's wing of some w. feathers SCOTT. The children w. in the streets, the mother a destitute widow DICKENS. Phr. *To run w.*: (*a*) of an animal or plant, to live in or revert to a state of nature, not under domestication or cultivation; (*b*) of a person; He had a bold spirit, and he ran a little w., and went for a soldier DICKENS. b. *Much Ado* III. i. 35. 2. I am afraid he has turned out very w. JANE AUSTEN. b. If a young man is w., and must run after women and bad company JOHNSON. 5. A fit of w. weeping 1885. 6. c. She had accepted me, and I was w. with joy 1891. 7. Her misery had actually drove her w. DICKENS. 8. This vnheedfull, desperate, wilde aduenture SHAKS. 9. If..sweetest Shakespear fancies childe, Warble his native Wood-notes wilde MILT. 10. The Chinese shells..' went wild' 1895.

Special collocations: **w. beast**, orig. in sense I. 1, now always with mixture of sense II. 3; also *attrib.*, as in *w. beast show*, etc.; **w. boar**: see BOAR *sb.* c; **w. horse**, a horse not domesticated or broken in; esp. in phr., referring to a mode of punishment or torture, *to draw with w. horses*, and hence joc. with negative; **w. Irish**, the less civilized Irish; formerly, those not subject to English rule.

B. *sb.* †1. A wild animal, or wild animals collectively; *spec.* a beast, or beasts, of the chase; game -1599. 2. A wild or waste place; a waste, wilderness. Now mostly *rhet.* or *poet.* 1637. b. *pl.* (Chiefly in *the wilds of* a specified region.) 1596.

2. *transf.* A lighthouse o'er the w. of dreary waves SHELLEY. b. *fig.* Striving to cut a new road through the wilds of jurisprudence 1832. Hence **Wi·ldish** *a.* somewhat w., inclining to wildness. **Wi·ldling** = WILDING A. 2, 3. **Wi·ld·ly** *adv.*, **-ness**.

Wi·ldbore. *local.* 1784. [Origin unkn.] A stout and closely woven unglazed tammy.

Wild cat. late ME. [Cf. MLG. *wildkatte*, MHG. *wilde katze*.] 1. The European wild species of cat, *Felis catus*; also applied to other wild animals of the cat tribe, esp. in U.S. to species of lynx. 2. *fig.* Applied to a savage, ill-tempered, or spiteful person, esp. a woman 1573. 3. *fig.* a. One who forms a rash project, or engages in a risky enterprise. b. An unsound business undertaking, as a 'wild-cat bank'. Chiefly *U.S. colloq.* 1812. 4. *attrib.* (usu. with hyphen). *fig.* Applied to banks in the western United States which fraudulently issued notes with little or no capital, or to their notes or transactions; hence extended to unsound, risky, or illicit business enterprises generally; and more widely to reckless or rash undertakings, statements, etc. 1838.

2. But will you woo this Wilde-cat? SHAKS. Hence **Wild-catter, -catting**, one who engages, the action of engaging, in a 'wild-cat' business or enterprise.

Wild deer. OE. [In sense 1, OE. *wil(d)-dēor*, *wildedēor*, alteration of *wildor, pl. *wildru*.] †1. A wild animal -ME. 2. Deer in a wild state 1748.

‖ **Wildebeest** (vi·ldəbēst). 1838. [S. African Du., f. *wild* WILD *a.* + *beest* BEAST *sb.*] The gnu.

Wilder (wi·ldəɹ), *v. arch.* (now chiefly *poet.*) 1613. [Origin obsc.; perh. f. WILD *a.* (in the sense 'astray' of ON. *villr*) or f. WILD *sb.* 2; freq. apprehended as aphetic f. BEWILDER, and occas. spelt '*wilder*.] 1. *trans.* To cause to lose one's way, as in a wild or unknown place; to lead or drive astray; also *refl.* b. *fig.*; *esp.* to render at a loss how to act or what to think; to perplex, bewilder 1642. 2. *intr.* To lose one's way, go astray, stray; to be bewildered 1658.

1. Young Actæon, wilder'd in the wood ADDISON. b. You shall be left wildred with strange Revelations 1654. Hence **Wi·ldered** (wi·ldəɹd) *ppl. a.* straying, 'lost'; perplexed, bewildered; of a place, etc., pathless, wild. **Wi·ldering** *ppl. a.* that 'wilders'.

Wilderness (wi·ldəɹnės). ME. [OE. *wild(d)ēornes = MLG., MDu. *wildernisse*; either f. OE. *wil(d)dēor* WILD DEER + -NESS, or f. OE. *wildēorern* wild + -NESS.] 1. a. (without article) Wild or uncultivated land. b. A wild or uncultivated region or tract of land, uninhabited, or inhabited only by wild animals ME. c. A piece of ground in a large garden or park, planted with trees, and laid out in an ornamental or fantastic style, often in the form of a maze or labyrinth 1644. 2. *transf.* or *gen.* A waste or desolate region of any kind, e.g. of open sea 1588. 3. *fig.* Something figured as a region of a wild or desolate character, in which one wanders or loses one's way; in religious use applied to the present world or life as contrasted with heaven or the future life ME. b. Rhetorically applied to a building, town, etc., which is regarded as 'desolate' or in which one is lonely or 'lost' 1842. 4. A mingled, confused, or vast assemblage or collection *of* persons or things (usu. coloured by other senses) 1588. †5. Wildness, uncultivated condition -1667. †b. *fig.* Wildness of character. SHAKS.

2. Inuiron'd with a wildernesse of Sea SHAKS. 3. As I walk'd through the w. of this world BUNYAN. 4. I would not haue given it for a wildernesse of Monkies SHAKS. 5. b. *Meas. for M.* III. i. 142.

Wild-fire, wildfire (wəi·ldfəiəɹ). OE. †1. Furious or destructive fire; a conflagration -1634. 2. *spec.* a. Will-o'-the-wisp, *ignis fatuus* 1663. b. Lightning; *esp.* sheet lightning without audible thunder, 'summer lightning' 1795. 3. A composition of highly inflammable substances, readily ignited and very difficult to extinguish, used in warfare, etc. ME. 4. A name for erysipelas and various inflammatory eruptive diseases, esp. those in which the eruption spreads from one part to another OE. 5. *fig.* or in fig. allusions, in ref. to a destructive agency, etc. ME.

5. The wilde-fire of my Passions burnèd me 1612. *Like w.*, with immense rapidity and effect; very swiftly and forcibly; The report..spread like w. through the town DISRAELI.

Wi·ld-fowl. (Also as one word, or as two.) OE. A wild bird, or (usu.) wild birds collectively; chiefly applied to those caught for food, game birds. b. *joc.* misapplied to a wild beast; hence *allus.* 1590.

b. There is not a more fearefull wilde foule then your Lyon liuing SHAKS.

Wild goose. OE. 1. Any wild bird of the goose kind; in Britain usu. the greylag (*Anser ferus* or *cinereus*), in N. America the Canada goose (*Bernicla canadensis*). 2. *fig.* a. Used of or in ref. to a flighty or foolish person. b. *Eng. Hist.* (*pl.*) A nickname for the Irish Jacobites who went over to the Continent on the abdication of James II and later. 1592. 3. *attrib.* [after next 2.] Wild, fantastic, very foolish or risky 1770.

3. Gone away upon some wild-goose errand, seeking his fortune DICKENS.

Wild goo·se chase. 1592. †1. A kind of horse-race in which the second or any succeeding horse had to follow accurately the course of the leader, like a flight of wild geese -1685. 2. *fig.* An erratic course taken by one person (or thing) and followed (or that may be followed) by another; in later use apprehended as 'a pursuit of something as unlikely to be caught as the wild goose' (J.); a foolish, fruitless, or hopeless quest 1592.

2. Don't let me think..you will set out upon every wild-goose chase, sticking to nothing H. WALPOLE.

Wilding (wəi·ldiŋ), *sb.* and *a.* 1525. [f. WILD *a.* + -ING[3].] A. *sb.* 1. A wild apple or apple-tree; a crab-apple or crab-tree. 2. *gen.* A wild plant, flower, or fruit 1577. 3. A wild animal (*rare*) 1897. 4. *fig.* (applied to a person or thing) 1621. B. *attrib.* or *adj.* 1. Applied to a crab-apple or crab-tree 1538. 2. Of a plant, etc.: Growing wild. Chiefly *poet.* 1697.

2. *fig.* That growth of w. art 1884.

Wild man. ME. [Cf. ON. *villumaðr*.] 1. A man who is wild. a. A man of savage, fierce, uncultured, or unruly nature or character. b. A man of an uncivilized race or tribe; a savage, or one reverted to a savage state ME. c. *pl.* The extremists of a political party, profession, etc. 1923. 2. The orang-outang: also *wild man of the woods* 1791.

Wildwood (wəi·ld,wud). Now chiefly *poet.* OE. [orig. two words, WILD *a.* and WOOD *sb.*] A forest of natural growth, or one allowed to grow naturally; an uncultivated or unfrequented wood.

attrib. When With wild wood-leaues & weeds, I ha' strew'd his graue SHAKS.

Wile (wəil), *sb.* ME. [Origin and early history obsc. Early ME. *wil* perh. represents Scand. *wihl-, whence ON. *vél* craft, artifice.] 1. A crafty, cunning, or deceitful trick; a sly, insidious, or underhand artifice; a stratagem, ruse. Chiefly *pl.* (in *sing.* now *arch.* or *poet.*). †b. Without implication of deceit: A subtle contrivance; a skilful device or scheme -1830. c. In lighter sense: An amorous or playful trick; a piece of sportive cunning or artfulness 1600. d. *spec.* A cunning turn or other trick of the hare to escape the hunters 1691. 2. Deceit or deceitfulness; craft, cunning, subtlety. Now *rare.* late ME.

1. The wiles by which its members are lured..to their goal 1888. c. Haste thee nymph, and bring with thee..Quips and Cranks, and wanton Wiles, Nods, and Becks, and Wreathed Smiles MILT.

Wile, *v.* late ME. [f. prec.] 1. *trans.* To bring, draw, or get by a wile; to lead, induce, or obtain by craft or cunning. 2. (as substitute for WHILE *v.*) To divert attention pleasantly from (something tedious); to charm *away*; *esp.* to cause (time) to pass *away* pleasantly or insensibly 1796.

1. She talk'd, she smil'd, my heart she wil'd BURNS. She could neither be driven nor wiled into the parish kirk STEVENSON. 2. I was reading a book..to w. the time away DICKENS.

Wilful (wi·lfŭl), *a.* (*adv.*, *sb.*) ME. [f. WILL *sb.*[1] + -FUL.] 1. Asserting or disposed to assert one's own will against persuasion, instruction, or command; governed by will without regard to reason; obstinately self-willed or perverse. †2. Willing; consenting; ready to comply with a request, desire, or requirement -1598. †3. Proceeding from the will; done or suffered of one's own free will or choice; voluntary -1687. 4. Done on purpose or wittingly; purposed, deliberate, intentional. (Chiefly, now always, in bad sense, of a blameworthy action; freq. implying 'perverse, obstinate'.) Also *transf.* of the agent. ME.

1. The seid Henry is sklanderus and a wylfull person and wyll not be ordered but after his owne wyll 1529. 2. *Merry W.* III. ii. 44. 3. Amazed to see Contempt of wealth, and w. poverty DRYDEN. 4. Wylfull murtherers, whom God commaundeth to be taken from the aulter 1548. *Prov.* Wilful waste makes woeful want.

†B. as *adv.* = WILFULLY 3, 4. -1611.

Since from thee going, he went wilfull slow SHAKS.

C. as *sb.* A wilful person; *rarely*, a wilful act 1819. Hence **Wi·lfulness**.

Wilfully (wi·lfŭli), *adv.* [Late OE. *wilfullīce*, f. *wilfull WILFUL *a.*] †1. Willingly, readily; patiently, submissively -1513. †2. Of one's own free will, of one's own accord, voluntarily -1705. †b. According to one's own will; at will, freely -1600. 3. Purposely, on purpose, intentionally, deliberately. Chiefly, now always, in bad sense; occas. implying 'maliciously'. late ME. 4. In a self-willed manner; perversely, obstinately, stubbornly 1586.

2. Martyrs are to die willingly but not w. FULLER. 3. For those that set houses on fire w., they are smoked to death 1617.

Wilga (wi·lgă). 1889. [Native name in New South Wales.] An Australian tree of the rutaceous genus *Geijera*, esp. *G. parviflora*.

Wilily (wəi·lili), *adv.* late ME. [f. WILY *a.* + -LY[2].] In a wily manner; craftily, cunningly, by stratagem.

Wiliness (wəi·linės). 1450. [f. as prec. + -NESS.] The quality or character of being wily; craftiness, cunning, guile.

Will (wil), *sb.*[1] [OE. *willa* :—OTeut. *wiljon- :—pre-Teut. *weljon-: cf. WILL *v.*[1]] I. 1. Desire, wish, longing; inclination, disposition (*to do* something). Now coloured by or merged in sense II. 1. b. An inclination *to do* something, as contrasted with power or opportunity 1594. †2. *spec.* Carnal desire or appetite -1603. 3. *transf.* That which one desires, (one's) 'desire'. Now *arch.* or *poet.* OE. b. A desire or wish as expressed in a request; hence (contextually) the expression of a wish, a request. *arch.* or *dial.* ME.

1. b. They desired the power, and want not the w., to do us an ill turn 1667. 2. *Meas. for M.* II. iv. 164. 3. Would'st haue me weepe? why now thou hast thy w. SHAKS. A lad that lives and has his w. Is worth a dozen dead HOUSMAN. b. *Ant. & Cl.* I. ii. 7. *What's your w.?* (now arch. or dial., esp. Sc.), What do you want? What do you wish me to do?

II. 1. The action of willing or choosing to do something; the movement or attitude of the mind which is directed with conscious intention to (and, normally, issues immediately in) some action, physical or mental OE. †**b.** Intention, purpose, determination -1712. **c.** *W. to* with sb. or inf. (after G. *wille zu*) 1823. **2.** The power or capacity of willing; power of choice in regard to action OE. **3.** Intention or determination that something shall be done by another or others, or shall happen or take place; (contextually) an expression or embodiment of such intention or determination OE. **b.** Intent, purport (of a document). late ME. **4.** Qualified by possessive: That which one wills should be done; one's 'pleasure' OE.

1. c. Wherever I found living matter I found w. unto power 1896. The triumph of the w. to live 1908. **2.** All is not lost; the unconquerable W.,.. And courage never to submit or yield MILT. A girl of high spirit and strong w. 1907. *A w. of one's own*, implying a strong or self-assertive w., and hence used as a euphemism for 'wilfulness'. **3.** Is it your w. Claudio shall die to morrow? SHAKS. Such was the w. of Heav'n MILT. My w. is law TENNYSON. **4.** Direct me, if it be your w., where great Auffidius lies SHAKS. If then he wreak on me his wicked w. GRAY.

III. A person's formal declaration (usu. in writing) of his intention as to the disposal of his property or other matters to be performed after his death; commonly *transf.* the document in which such intention is expressed. late ME.

She threw her w. into the fire JOHNSON. To make the gentleman's last w. and testament STERNE.

Phrases. *Good w., ill w.*, see GOODWILL, ILL WILL. *With the best w.* (*in the world*); With the best w. we found it impossible to eat anything 1857. *To take the w. for the deed*; The reasonable will accept the w. for the deed 1661. *Where there's a w. there's a way* (WAY *sb.*[1] 13). See also FREE WILL. **Against** (one's) **w.** In opposition to (one's own) inclination or liking, unwillingly; in opposition to (another's) choice, intention, or desire. **At** (one's) **w. a.** According to one's volition or choice; as (when, where) one will. **b.** In readiness to be dealt with as one will; at one's command or disposal. **c.** In ref. to an estate held during the owner's or lessor's pleasure, from which the tenant may be ousted at any time; chiefly in phr. *estate, tenant*, etc. *at w.* †**By** (one's) **w.** With one's consent, or of one's own free will, willingly; according to one's desire. **Of** (one's) **w.** Of one's own accord, spontaneously, voluntarily. (Now only with poss. and *own*, e.g. 'He did it of his own (free) w.') **With** (one's) **w.** †**a.** Intentionally; willingly; voluntarily. **b.** *With a w.*. with determination, resolutely, energetically. Hence **Willed** (wild) *a.* having a w. of a specified kind: chiefly in *comb.*, as SELF-WILLED; having the w. directed to some (specified) action. **Wi·ll-less** *a.* not having 'a w. of one's own'; not involving exercise of the w.; destitute of the faculty of volition.

Will, *sb.*[2] Abbrev. form of the Christian name *William*. **b.** *dial.* = WILL-O'-THE-WISP 1718.

Will, *sb.*[3] 1677. [f. WILL *v.*[1]] **a.** An utterance of the verb 'will'; a determination expressed by this. **b.** The verb 'will' as used in contradistinction to 'shall.'

Will *a. Sc.* and *dial.* [a. ON. *villr* WILD.] Astray; 'lost'; perplexed.

Will (wil), *v.*[1] *Pres. t.* 1st and 3rd pers. sing.; pl. **will**; 2nd sing. **wilt** (*arch.*). *Pa. t.* **would** (wud). Abbreviated (colloq.) forms: **'ll** = *will*, esp. after prons., e.g. *I'll* (†*Ile*), *they'll* (†*theile*); **'lt** = *wilt*; **'ld, 'd** = *would*, esp. after prons., e.g. †*I'ld, I'd, we'd*; **won't** (wōunt) = †*wonnot* for †*wol not*. [OE. **willan, wyllan*, pres. t. *wille, wilt, willaþ*, pa. t. *wolde*, Anglian *walde*:—OTeut. **wel(l)jan*, parallel w. **wal(l)jan*: f. Indo-Eur. **wel-, wol-, wl-*, represented by L. *velle, volo*, W. *gwell* better, Skr. *vārati* chooses: see also WALE *sb.*[2], WELL *adv.*, and cf. WILL *v.*[2]] **I.** *The present tense* **will.** †**1.** *trans.* Desire, wish for, have a mind to (something); sometimes implying 'intend, purpose' -1734. †**b.** with neg. = have no desire for, do not wish for; often implying 'refuse, decline' -1606. **2.** with obj. clause: Desire, wish; sometimes implying also 'intend, purpose' (that something be done or happen). *Obs.* or *arch.* OE. †**3.** Denoting expression (usu. authoritative) of a wish or intention: Determine, decree, give order (*that* something be done) -1682. **b.** *spec.* in a direction or instruction in one's will or testament; hence, to direct by will OE. †**c.** *fig.* of an abstract thing: Demands, requires -1597. **4.** Desire to, wish to, have a mind to (do something); often implying intention. *Obs.* or *arch.*, or merged in other senses. OE. **5.** In relation to another's desire, etc., or to an obligation of some kind: Am (is, are) disposed or willing to consent to OE. **b.** In 2nd person, interrog., or in a dependent clause after *beg* or the like, expressing a request (usu. courteous; with emphasis, impatient) ME. **6.** Expressing voluntary action, or conscious intention directed to the doing of what is expressed by the principal verb (without emphasis as in 9, and without temporal ref. as in 10) OE. **7.** Expressing natural disposition to do something, and hence habitual action: Has the habit of -ing; is addicted or accustomed to -ing; habitually does; sometimes connoting 'may be expected to' OE. **8.** Expressing potentiality, etc.: Can, may, is capable of -ing; is (large) enough or sufficient to. late ME. **9.** *emphatically.* Is fully determined to; insists on or persists in —ing. Also *fig.* = must inevitably, is sure to. 1611. **b.** In phr. of ironical or critical force referring to another's assertion or opinion. Now *arch.* exc. in *w. have it.* 1591. **10.** *As auxiliary of the future tense* with implication of intention or volition. **a.** In 1st pers.: *occas.* = intend to, mean to OE. **b.** In 2nd and 3rd pers., in questions or indirect statements OE. **11.** With neg.: commonly = refuse or decline to; *emphatically* insist on or persist in not —ing OE. **12.** In 1st pers., expressing immediate intention: = 'I am now going to', 'I proceed at once to'. With neg., used with *say* or the like: *I w. not* = 'I do not venture so far as to'. ME. **b.** In 1st pers. pl., expressing a proposal = 'let us' ME. **13.** In 2nd and 3rd pers., as auxiliary expressing mere futurity, forming (with pres. inf.) the future, and (with pf. inf.) the future pf. tense OE. **b.** As auxiliary of future substituted for the imper. in mild injunctions or requests 1824. **14.** As auxiliary of future expressing a contingent event, or a result to be expected, in a supposed case or under particular conditions OE. **b.** Expressing a voluntary act or choice in a supposed case, or a conditional promise or undertaking: esp. in asseverations (e.g. *I w. die sooner than..., I'll be hanged if...*). late ME. **c.** Expressing a determinate or necessary consequence (without the notion of futurity). late ME. **d.** With the notion of futurity obscured or lost: = w. prove or turn out to; may be supposed to, presumably does. Hence (chiefly *Sc.* and *n. dial.*) in estimates of amount, etc., the future becoming equivalent to a present with qualification: e.g. *it w. be..* = I think it is..., it is about... 1450. **15.** Used where *shall* is now the normal auxiliary; since 17th c. chiefly in Scottish, Irish, provincial, or extra-British use OE. **16.** *absol.* or with ellipsis of obj. clause as in 2: = sense I. 4–6. OE. **17.** With ellipsis of a verb of motion. *arch.* OE. **18.** With ellipsis of active inf. to be supplied from the context; also with generalized ellipsis, and with *so* or *that* (now usu. at the beginning of the sentence) substituted for the omitted inf. phr. OE. **b.** In a qualifying phr. with relative, equivalent to a phr. with indef. relative in *-ever*: e.g. *shout as loud as you w.* = 'however loud you (choose to) shout'. late ME. **19.** In a disjunctive qualifying clause or phr. (usu. parenthetical), as *whether he w. or no, w. he nill he*, etc. late ME.

1. (*title*) Twelfe Night, Or what you w. SHAKS. **b.** Ile no Swaggerers;..shut the doore, there comes no Swaggerers heere SHAKS. **3. b.** I wyll that Rose Plandon shall haue x marc 1504. **c.** 2 *Hen. IV*, IV. i. 157. **4.** Sen now al men wilbe theologis 1562. **5. b.** O, O, O,..O, w. you have done! HARDY. **7.** Crabs move sideling, Lobsters w. swim swiftly backward SIR T. BROWNE. **8.** My periwig is arrived,..my head w. only go into the first half of it COWPER. **9.** Fate's such a shrewish thing, She w. be mistris CHAPMAN. An impulse which w. vent itself in some form or other 1845. **b.** The Rosie-cross Philosophers, Whom you w. have to be but Sorcerers 1664. **10. a.** I haue both glorified it, and w. glorify it agayne BIBLE (Great) *John* xii. 28. **b.** Her..sonne..Swears he will shoote no more SHAKS. **11.** I cannot, I wo'not sit down at Table with her RICHARDSON. **12.** My host (whom I w. call Mr. Newman) 1856. **b.** We w. forget Mistress Dods for the present, if you please SCOTT. **13.** They w. probably return this day fortnight COWPER. **b.** In your intercourse with their chiefs,..you w. take care to give no offence to their natural presumption SCOTT. **14.** *Lear* III. vi. 85. You'll be surprised when you find how easy it is 1882. **b.** I'll take you five children from London, who shall cuff five Highland children JOHNSON. **c.** Then ioyn the Points *A* and *f* with a Right-line, and it w. form the Angle requir'd 1709. **d.** What lights w. those out to the northward be? M. ARNOLD. This word we have only once heard, and that w. be twenty years ago 1876. **15.** Perchance I w. be there as soone as you SHAKS. I expect we w. have some good singing SCOTT. **16.** *If you w.*, sometimes = 'if you choose or prefer to call it so'; Very savage! monstrous! if you w. RUSKIN. *If God w., God willing*, if it be the will of God, 'D.V.' **17.** Ile to my booke SHAKS. **18.** Wilt thou haue thys woman to thy wedded wyfe..? I w. *Bk. Com. Prayer.* I hope it may do you some good, as it won't me RUSKIN. Prov. He that w. not when he may, When he would he shall haue nay 1562. **b.** *Come what w.* = 'whatever may come'; Well, come what w., Ile tarry at home SHAKS. *Be that as it w.* = 'however that may be'.

II. *The pa. t.* **would** *with temporal function.* **1.** Desired, wished for, wished; often implying 'intended'. With †simple obj., with obj. cl. or acc. and inf. *Obs.* or *rare arch.* OE. **2.** Wished to; often implying 'intended to'. *Obs.* or *arch.* exc. in dependence on a vb. in pa. time. OE. **3.** Was (were) willing to, consented to; chose to. Now only in dependence on a vb. in pa. time. OE. **b.** In a dependent clause after an expression of request, command, or the like, where the principal vb. is in pa. time. Now *rare.* ME. **4.** Was (were) accustomed to; used to OE. **5.** Was capable of —ing; could (usu. in relative cl.). late ME. **6.** Was determined to; insisted on or persisted in —ing 1706. **7.** In indirect reports, usu. in 3rd pers., of past utterances, etc.; in the 1st pers. (now) implying intention OE. **8.** With neg., commonly denoting refusal ME. **9.** Forming (with pres. inf.) the auxiliary of the 'anterior future' or 'future in the past', and (with pf. inf.) of the 'anterior future perfect', in the 2nd and 3rd pers. OE. **b.** without notion of futurity: Probably or presumably did 1857. **10.** Used where *should* is now the normal auxiliary (cf. I. 15) 1760. **11.** Elliptical and quasi-elliptical uses as in I. 16–19. Now *rare* or *Obs.* exc. with ellipsis of active inf. to be supplied from the context, or in disjunctive qualifying clauses OE.

1. Heauen would that shee these gifts should haue SHAKS. When we would no Pardon, they laboured to punish us 1643. **2.** Certaine, which would be counted pillars of the State A.V. *Transl. Pref.* **3.** I said you would be all right in a few days if you would only hold on 1884. **4.** There..His listless length at noontide would he stretch GRAY. **8.** Editors and publishers.. would have none of it 1918. **9.** This he protested to be true, as he would answer before God 1582. **10.** My aunt did not expect that I would be plucked in any examination 1870. **11.** Look where you would, some exquisite form glided..through the throng DICKENS. I wanted Mr. Meyers to come with us but he wouldn't 1882.

III. *The pa. t.* **would** *with modal function.* **1.** with simple obj.: Could or might desire; should like. *Obs.* or *rare arch.* **2.** with obj. cl., with vb. in past subj. (*arch.* exc. in *would rather* or *sooner*), or with acc. and inf. Hence (*arch.*) with ellipsis of 1st pers. pron. as an expression of longing; also, by confusion with 3, in the form (*I*) *would to God* ME. **3.** *Would God* = 'O that God would', as an expression of earnest desire or longing. *Obs.* or *rare arch.* late ME. **4.** The past subj. used with potential or conditional force as a softening of the pres. indic. in sense I. 4: Could or should wish to; should like, wish, or desire to. *arch.* or *dial.* exc. in *would have* = should like or wish (a person or thing) to be or to do something OE. **b.** Am (is, are) disposed or inclined to; often (in 1st pers. sing.) = 'wish to... if I may'. late ME. **5.** In the apodosis of a conditional sentence (expressed or implied), forming the auxiliary of the periphrastic past subj. with implication of intention or volition: = 'should choose or be willing to' ME. **b.** *I would* (sc. 'if I were you') often = 'I advise or recommend you to'. So *I wouldn't* = 'I advise you not to'. 1591. **c.** *Would you..?* = 'Will you, please..? 1607. **6.** In the apodosis of a conditional sentence (expressed or implied), in the 2nd or 3rd pers., forming the auxiliary of the simple 'conditional mood', expressing merely a possibility or contingency in the supposed case OE. **b.** With the hypothetical notion obscured, the 'conditional mood' becoming a qualification of the pres. indic. expressing some degree of hesitation or uncertainty 1449. **c.** Used in the 1st pers. instead of the normal auxiliary *should* 1448. **7.** In a question or indirect statement in the 2nd or 3rd pers., where *should* would be used in the corresponding direct statement in the 1st. late ME. **8.** In a conditional (or equivalent) clause with implication of intention or volition: = 'chose to', 'were willing to' OE. **b.** With inversion of subj., expressing desire or longing 1593. **9.** In a noun-clause expressing the object of desire, advice, or request 1555. **10.** Elliptical and quasi-elliptical uses, as in I. 16–19. ME.

1. But, in a word, what would you with me? BYRON. 2. I am wearie of this Moone; would he would change SHAKS. I am not mad, I would to heauen I were SHAKS. Would to God that we had peace! 1777. 4. I would not..be thought to share Mr. St. John's extreme scepticism 1869. **b.** I would..humbly propose to the ladies, to be good-humoured 1779. *Would say* = 'intend to say, mean'. *Would have* = 'is inclined to believe or assert (something *to be* so-and-so)'. 5. I wouldn't do such a thing here, sir..upon my word and honour, I wouldn't DICKENS. 6. **b.** *It would seem* = 'it almost or somewhat seems'. *One would think* = 'one is inclined to think'; You'd think she'd get off of her luxurious pillows for once 1882. **c.** He makes everything turn out exactly as we would wish it COLERIDGE. 7. Would you believe it, Sir, my daughter Elizabeth..said it was fanatical to find fault with card-playing on Sunday 1779. Would you like to see it? 1886. 8. **b.** O wad some Pow'r the giftie gie us To see oursels as others see us! BURNS. 9. I wish the lady would favour us with something more than a side-front SHERIDAN. 10. Who so mounted hyher than he shold he falleth lower than he wold CAXTON. Letting I dare not, wait vpon I would SHAKS.

IV. Followed by *to* with inf., esp. after an intervening word or words; now the regular constr. only with pres. pple. *willing* ME.

†**V.** Pa. pple. **would:** chiefly in sense I. 6 = wished, chosen –1633.

Many tymes he myghte haue had her and he had wold MALORY. If hee had would, he might easily ..occupied the Monarchy 1633.

VI. Conjoined with NILL *v.* **1.** *absol.* or *intr.* **a.** In disjunctive qualifying phr., as *whether he w. or nill*, willingly or unwillingly; voluntarily or compulsorily. *Obs.* or *rare arch.* OE. **b.** esp. with inversion of subj. (usu. a pron.), as *w. I* (*or*) *nill I* (*he*, etc.); occas. vaguely = 'one way or another', 'in any case'. Now chiefly in WILLY-NILLY. OE. **2.** (Always inflected *willeth* (*wills*), *willed*; thus prop. belonging to WILL *v.*[2]) **a.** *trans.* To desire, have a mind to, choose (as opp. to *nill* = 'refuse'); to determine by the will (as opp. to *nill* = 'negative', 'prevent') 1585. **b.** *absol.* or *intr.* 1577.

Will (wil), *v.*[2] Pres. t. 3rd pers. sing. **wills, willeth** (*arch.*); pa. t. and pple. **willed** (wild). [OE. *willian*, f. WILL *sb.*[1]] **1.** *trans.* = prec. I. 1, 2, 4. *Obs.* or *rare arch.* **b.** with NILL: see prec. VI. **2. a.** To direct by one's will or testament (*that* something be done, or something *to be* done) OE. **b.** To dispose of by will; to bequeath or devise 1460. **3.** To determine by the will; to aim at effecting by exercise of the will; to set the mind with conscious intention to the performance or occurrence of something OE. **b.** *intr.* To exercise the will; to perform the mental act of volition 1582. **c.** *trans.* To control (another person), or induce (another) *to do* something, by the mere exercise of one's will, as in hypnotism 1882. **4.** To express or communicate one's will or wish with regard to something. **a.** To enjoin; to decree, ordain. *Obs.* or *arch.* ME. †**b.** To pray, request, entreat –1690. †**c.** *fig.* of a thing: To require, demand –1667.

2. **b.** Was it not enough that I should have been willed away, like a horse? DICKENS. 3. If I *w.* to move my Arm, it is presently moved 1710. All shall be as God wills CARLYLE. 4. **a.** It is common with Princes..to w. contradictories BACON. Willing and requiring all Officers and men to obey you NELSON. **c.** *Cor.* II. iii. 125. Hence **Willed** (wild) *ppl. a.* disposed of by will or testament; determined by the will; controlled by another's will.

Willemite (wi·lĕməit). 1850. [ad. Du. *Willemit*, f. *Willem* William I of the Netherlands.] *Min.* Native silicate of zinc, found in masses or crystals of various colours from light greenish-yellow to flesh-red.

Willet (wi·lĕt). 1862. [From its cry, *pill-will-willet*.] A N. Amer. bird of the snipe family, *Symphemia semipalmata*.

William (wi·lyăm). 1597. A common masculine personal name, used in the names of certain species of pinks and other flowers: now only in SWEET-WILLIAM. ¶*W. pear*: see WILLIAMS.

Williamite (wi·lyăməit). 1689. [f. the name *William* + -ITE[1].] A supporter of William of Orange (King William III): opp. to JACOBITE *sb.*[4]

Williams (wi·lyămz). 1814. In full, *Williams'*, *Williams's* (erron. *William*) *Bon Chrétien*: A very juicy variety of the Bon Chrétien pear (see BON *a.*), so called from the name of its first distributor in England.

Williamsite (wi·lyămzəit). 1833. [f. the surname *Williams* + -ITE[1].] **1.** A follower of Roger Williams, an Amer. colonist of the 17th c. **2.** *Min.* An impure variety of serpentine, named after L. W. Williams, an Amer. mineralogist 1848.

Willing (wi·liŋ), *ppl. a.* ME. [OE. **willende*, in *selfwillende*, *unwillende*, *willendlice* WILLINGLY, etc.; f. WILL *v.*[1] + -ING[2].] †**1.** Wishing, wishful, desirous –1825. **2.** Having a ready will; disposed to consent or comply; ready to do (what is specified or implied) without reluctance; *spec.* disposed to do what is required, ready to be of use or service ME. **b.** *transf.* Given, rendered, offered, performed, assumed, borne, or undergone willingly 1568. **c.** *fig.* of things: Compliant, yielding; (of the wind) favourable 1500. **d.** *advb.* Willingly, consentingly, without reluctance. Now *rare* or *Obs.* 1578. †**3.** That is so, or is done or borne, of one's own will; voluntary, intentional –1613. **4.** Exercising or capable of exercising the will, volitional; conveying impulses of the will 1875.

2. He snatch'd the w. Goddess to his Arms DRYDEN. The king was willinger to comply with anything than this DE FOE. Barkis is willin' DICKENS. *W. horse* (in provb. phrases), applied to one who is w. to work or to take trouble. **d.** *W.* (*or*) *nilling* (arch.), with or against one's will, willy-nilly. 3. The willing'st sinne I euer yet committed SHAKS.

Comb., as *w.-hearted*, *-minded* adjs. Hence **Wi·lling·ly** *adv.*, **-ness.**

Williwaw (wi·liwǭ). 1842. [Origin unkn.] A sailor's name for a sudden violent squall, orig. in the Straits of Magellan.

Willock (wi·lək). *local.* 1631. [f. WILL *sb.*[2] + -OCK.] The GUILLEMOT; also, the puffin and the razor-bill.

Will-o'-the-wisp (wi:ləðəwi·sp). 1608. [orig. **Will with the wisp**; see WILL *sb.*[2] and WISP *sb.*] **1.** = IGNIS FATUUS; *fig.* a thing (rarely a person) that deludes or misleads by means of fugitive appearances. **2.** An alga, *Nostoc commune*, so called from the inexplicable suddenness of its appearance 1866.

1. Wenches..Use to call me Willy Wispe 1628. To play Will in the Wisp with Men of Honour VANBRUGH. Those Wills-o-the-wisp, the Reviewers 1806. *attrib.* A fluttering, shadowy, will-o-the-wisp style 1860.

Willow (wi·lo[u]), *sb.* [OE. *welig*, f. Teut. **walg-*, *welg-*. The phonological history is obsc.; the precursor of the present form, *wilwe*, appears in the 14th c.] **I. 1.** Any plant of the genus *Salix*, which consists of trees and shrubs of various sizes, growing for the most part by the side of watercourses, characterized by very pliant branches and long narrow drooping leaves. **b.** The wood or osiers of any tree of this genus 1489. **c.** Taken as a symbol of grief for unrequited love or the loss of a mate; esp. in phr. *to wear* (*the*) *w.*, *the w. garland*, or *the green w.*: to grieve for the loss of a loved one 1584. **2.** With qualification, denoting a particular species or variety of the genus *Salix*, and extended to plants of other genera having some resemblance to the w. 1548.

1. By the rushy-fringed bank, Where grows the W. and the Osier dank MILT. (*allus.*, with ref. to pliability) Burleigh..was of the w., and not of the oak MACAULAY. *Bat w.*, a species of willow from which cricket-bats are made. **c.** In such a night Stood Dido with a W. in her hand Vpon the wilde sea bankes SHAKS. 2. ALMOND, GOAT, GROUND, WEEPING *w.*, etc.: see these wds. *Bay*, *flowering*, *French*, *Persian w.*, the WILLOW-HERB, *Epilobium angustifolium*.

II. 1. = WILLY[1] 3. 1835. **2.** A cricket-bat (made of willow-wood). Similarly, the bat at baseball. 1866.

attrib. and *Comb.*: **w. bay**, *Salix pentandra*; **-earth**, compost made of rotten w.-branches; **-grouse**, the common ptarmigan of N. America, *Lagopus albus*; **-lark**, the sedge-warbler; **-leaf**, a leaf of the w.-tree, or a figure resembling this; *pl.* the luminous filaments of the sun's surface; **w. myrtle**, a myrtaceous w.-leaved tree (*Agonis flexuosa*) of Western Australia; **w. pattern**, a design in blue, upon domestic crockery originated by Thomas Turner in the late 18th c., having w.-trees as a prominent feature; so **w. ware**; **-tree** = sense 1; **-warbler, -wren**, a small bird, *Sylvia trochilus*. **b.** In several names of insects or their larvæ which infest willows, as **w.-beauty** (*Boarmia rhomboidaria*), **-butterfly, -caterpillar, -fly, -worm.** Hence **Wi·llow** *v. trans.* to put (cotton, etc.) through a w. (sense II. 1). **Wi·llowed** (-o[u]d) *a.* bordered or grown with willows. **Wi·llower,** one who tends a w. (sense II. 1). **Wi·llowish** *a.* resembling that of a w., esp. in ref. to the colour of w.-leaves; like a w., *fig.* of a pliant character (*rare*).

Wi·llow-herb. 1578. [So named from the resemblance of the leaves to the willow's.] **1.** Yellow Loosestrife, *Lysimachia vulgaris*. **2.** Any plant of the genus *Epilobium*, esp. *E. angustifolium* and *hirsutum* 1578. **3.** *Spiked* or *Purple-spiked W.*: Purple Loosestrife, *Lythrum Salicaria* 1578. **4.** In full *Hooded W.*: *Scutellaria galericulata* or *S. minor* 1597.

Willowy (wi·lo[u]i), *a.* 1766. [f. WILLOW *sb.* + -Y[1].] **1.** Bordered, shaded, or clad with willows. **2.** Resembling a willow in its flexible or drooping gracefulness 1791. **3.** Suggesting the sound of willows agitated by the wind 1895.

2. A fragile form, With a w. droop MRS. HEMANS.

Wi·ll-wo:rship. 1549. [f. WILL *sb.*[1] + WORSHIP *sb.*, rendering Gr. ἐθελοθρησκεία (Col. ii. 23).] Worship according to one's own will or fancy, or imposed by human will without divine authority.

Willy, willey (wi·li), *sb.*[1] [OE. *wilige*.] **1.** A basket. *dial.* **2.** *local.* A fish-trap 1602. **3.** A revolving machine of a conical or cylindrical shape armed internally with spikes for opening and cleaning wool, cotton, and flax 1835. Hence **Wi·ll(e)y** *v. trans.* to treat with the w. **Wi·ll(e)yer,** one who tends a w.

Willy *sb.*[2], **Willie** (wi·li). 1849. [Pet form of the name *William*.] Applied locally to various animals; e.g. the guillemot.

attrib.: w.-**goat**, a he-goat (= BILLY-GOAT); **-wagtail,** (*a*) the water-wagtail; (*b*) in Australia, the black-and-white fantail, *Rhipidura tricolor*.

Willy-nilly (wi·li ni·li), *adv.* and *a.* 1608. [= *will I, nill I* (*he, ye*); see WILL *v.*[1] VI.] **A.** *adv.* Whether it be with or against the will of the person or persons concerned; whether one likes it or not; *nolens volens*.

Carrying her off and marrying her willy nilly at Gretna Green 1884.

B. *adj.* **1.** That is such, or that takes place, whether one will or no 1877. ¶**2.** *erron.* Undecided, shilly-shally 1883.

Willy-willy (wi·liwi:li). *Austral.* 1894. [Native name.] A cyclonic storm or tornado.

Wilsome (wi·lsə̆m), *a. Obs.* exc. *dial.* ME. [a. ON. *villusamr*, f. *villr* WILL *a.*] **1.** Desert, dreary. **2.** Erring, perplexed. **3.** Wilful, obstinate.

Wilt (wilt), *sb.* 1855. [f. next.] The action or an act of wilting; *spec.* (also *w. disease*) any fungous disease of plants which is characterized by wilting.

Wilt (wilt), *v.* 1691. [orig. dial. (in early 19th c. largely U.S.); perh. alteration of *wilk*, WELK *v.*] **1.** *intr.* Of plants or their parts: To become limp or flaccid, through heat or drought. **b.** *transf.* and *gen.* To become limp; to lose energy or vigour; to become dispirited or nerveless 1787. **2.** *trans.* To cause to become limp; to deprive of stiffness, energy, vigour, or spirit 1809.

1. **b.** The major..pale as death; and wiltin' away, like a cabbage leaf, in the hot sun 1825.

Wilt, 2nd pers. sing. pres. ind. of WILL *v.*[1]

Wilton (wi·ltən). 1773. Name of a town in the south of Wiltshire, noted for the manufacture of carpets; applied to †(*a*) a kind of cloth, (*b*) a carpet of which the manufacture resembles that of a Brussels carpet but differing in having the rib cut so as to produce a velvet pile.

Wiltshire (wi·ltʃəɪ). 1794. Name of an English county, applied to (*a*) a breed of sheep, (*b*) a kind of 'smoked' bacon, (*c*) a kind of cheese (also Wilts).

Wily (wəi·li), *a.* ME. [f. WILE *sb.* + -Y[1].]

Full of or characterized by wiles; crafty, cunning, sly, artful.

The serpent that was moost w. of alle othere beestes CHAUCER. The w. suttleties and refluxes of mans thoughts MILT. Here w. Jesuits simple Quakers meet CRABBE.

Comb.: **w. beguile,** also freq. in jingling form **w. beguily**: orig. in phr. *to play w. beguile oneself*, to act wilily in such a way as to be oneself beguiled; hence as sb. phr. (*a*) a person who acts thus, or (simply) who acts wilily or craftily; (*b*) an act of this kind, or (simply) a w. act or action.

Wimble (wi·mb'l), *sb.* Now *dial.* or *techn.* ME. [a. AF. **wimble*, ad. MLG. *wiemel, wemel.*] **1.** A gimlet. **2.** An auger; also, a brace. late ME. **3.** An instrument for boring in soft ground or for extracting rubbish from a bore-hole in mining 1692. Hence **Wi·mble** *v.* (*Obs.* exc. *dial.*) *trans.* to pierce with or as with a w., to make (a hole) with a w.; *intr.* to bore *into*; chiefly *fig.*, to penetrate or insinuate oneself *into*.

Wimble (wi·mb'l), *a. dial.* 1579. [app. a northern word taken up by Spenser.] Active, nimble.

Wimple (wi·mp'l), *sb.* [Late OE. *wimpel* = (M)LG., (M)Du. *wimpel*, OHG. *wimpal*, ON. *vimpill*; ult. origin obsc.] **I.** A garment of linen or silk formerly worn by women, so folded as to envelop the head, chin, and sides of the face, and neck: now retained in the dress of nuns. **II. 1.** A fold or wrinkle; a turn, winding, or twist; a ripple or rippling in a stream 1513. **2.** A crafty turn or twist; a wile. *Sc.* 1638. Hence **Wi·mpler,** a maker of wimples (*Obs.* exc. *Hist.*).

Wi·mple, *v.* ME. [f. prec.] **I. 1.** *trans.* To envelop in a wimple; loosely, to veil. **2.** *fig.* To veil, cover. late ME. **3.** *pass.* and *intr.* To fall in folds 1590.

1. Al wayes she was wympeld that no man myȝt see her vysage MALORY. 3. A vele, that wimpled was full low SPENSER.

II. 1. *intr.* Of a stream: To meander, twist and turn; also, to ripple. Chiefly *Sc.* 1721. **2.** To move shiftily or unsteadily 1819.

Wimpled (wi·mpl'd), *ppl. a.* 1579. [f. WIMPLE *v.* or *sb.* + -ED.] **1.** Enveloped in or wearing a wimple; hence, veiled, *occas.* blindfolded. **2.** Arranged or falling in folds like a wimple; hence, wrinkled; rippled 1599. **3.** *fig.* Involved, intricate. *Sc.* 1722.

1. This w., whyning, purblinde waiward Boy SHAKS.

Win (win), *sb.*[1] [OE. *win(n* labour, strife, conflict. The modern senses are from WIN *v.*] **I.** †**1.** Strife, contention; tumult, disturbance, agitation -ME. †**2.** Gain, acquisition, profit; also, advantage, benefit -1535. **II.** *colloq.* **1.** A victory in a game or contest 1862. **2.** A gain; *pl.* gains, winnings 1891.

1. I was real pleased with the w., for lots of my pals had backed Actea 1894.

†**Win,** *sb.*[2] [OE. *wyn(n*, f. Teut. **wun-*: see WISH *v.*] Joy, pleasure, bliss, or a source of this -1700. (See also WEN[2].)

Win, *sb.*[3] *slang.* 1567. [Origin obsc.] A penny.

Win (win), *v.* Pa. t. and pple. **won** (wʊn). [Com. Teut. str. vb.: OE. *winnan* (*wann, wunnen*); ult. origin obsc.] †**1.** *intr.* To work, labour; to strive, contend, fight -ME. †**2.** *trans.* To conquer, subdue, defeat, vanquish -1610. **3.** To be victorious in (a contest of any kind). Also *to w. the day, the field.* ME. **4.** *absol.* or *intr.* To overcome one's adversary, opponent, or competitor; to be victorious, gain the victory (now chiefly in sports or games of skill) ME. **5.** *trans.* To subdue and take possession of; to seize, capture, take (a place). *arch.* ME. **b.** To seize, capture, take as spoil; to capture, take captive (a person). *Obs.* exc. in euphemistic slang, to steal. ME. **c.** *Cards.* (*a*) To be of higner value than, to 'beat' (another card, hand, suit); (*b*) to gain possession of, take (a trick) 1680. **6.** To get, obtain, acquire; *esp.* to get as something profitable or desired; to gain, procure. **a.** with material obj. *Obs.* or *arch.* ME. **b.** with immaterial obj., or *gen.* OE. **7.** *spec.* **a.** To obtain (a woman) as a wife or 'lady' by action or effort of some kind: usu. with implication of gaining her affection and consent ME. **b.** To gain by effort or competition, as a prize or reward, or in gaming or betting, as a wager, etc. Also *absol.* ME. **c.** To get by labour, to earn (now *dial.*); †to get as profit, to gain ME. **d.** To get, gather (crops or other produce); to gather in, harvest. Now *dial.* late ME. **e.** To get or extract (coal, or other mineral) from the mine, pit, or quarry; also, to sink a shaft or make an excavation so as to reach (a seam of coal or vein of ore) and prepare it for working 1447. †**f.** To gain (ground) *upon*; to gain (time) -1717. **8.** To overcome the unwillingness or indifference of; to attract, allure; to prevail upon; to gain the affection or allegiance of. Also with adv. or prep., as *away, over, to, from,* etc., and with *to* and inf. (*arch.*). ME. **9.** *intr.* with *upon, on.* †**a.** To gain an advantage over, get the better of; to gain or encroach upon -1791. **b.** To gain influence over; to prevail with; to gain the favour or engage the affections of (esp. gradually or increasingly). Also with *affection, esteem,* or the like as obj. 1601. **10.** *trans.* To reach, attain, arrive at; *occas.* to get at, get hold of (an object); to overtake (a person); to be in time for, 'catch'. *arch.* 1471. **11.** *intr.* To make or find one's way; also, to arrive at or come to some place, etc. Formerly chiefly *Sc.* and *n. dial.* ME. **b.** In ref. to a desired end, a condition, experience, proceeding, etc.: with various preps. and advs. ME. **c.** with adj. as compl.: = GET *v.* V. 3. 1886. **12.** *intr.* with *to* and inf.: To succeed in doing (what is denoted by the vb.); to contrive *to do* something. Now *Sc.* and *dial.* ME. **13.** *trans.* To succeed in bringing, putting, etc. *Obs.* or *arch.* ME.

3. Won the toss—first innings—seven o'clock a.m. DICKENS. 4. *2 Hen. IV*, I. i. 132. Now freq. with *out* (cf. 11 b). orig. *U.S.* 5. He that will Fraunce wynne must with Scotlande firste begyn 1548. 6. b. *To w. confidence, esteem, fame, love, praise, respect*; I am glad to have won your confidence DICKENS. *To w. the* (or *a*) *victory*, to be victorious. *To w. one's way*, to make or find one's way, succeed in getting somewhere. 7. a. Faint heart never won faire lady 1639. *To w. and wear*: see WEAR *v.*[1] I. 7 b. b. Frank took dummy; and I won sixpence DICKENS. 8. The worst temper of minds are wonne 1653. She could not w. him.. to any conversation J. AUSTEN. 10. And if they once may w. the bridge, What hope to save the town? MACAULAY. 11. The Germans never won through to the Channel ports 1923. *To w. up*, to get up, get up on one's feet; to get on horseback, mount. b. *To w. by..*, to escape, avoid. *To w. out* or *through*, to come out successfully, succeed in attaining one's end. c. To w. free from every form and observance 1886.

Wince (wins), *sb.*[1] 1612. [f. WINCE *v.*[1]] **1.** A kick. Now *dial.* **2.** An involuntary, shrinking movement 1865.

Wince (wins), *sb.*[2] 1688. [Variant of WINCH *sb.*] **1.** = WINCH *sb.* 1, 2. **2.** *Dyeing.* A reel or roller placed over the division between two vats so that a fabric spread upon it may be let down into one or the other 1839. Hence **Wince** *v.*[2] *trans.* to immerse in or pass through a vat by means of a w. **Wi·ncer,** one who tends a w.

Wince (wins), *v.*[1] ME. [a. AF. **wencir* or **wencier* = OF. *guencir, -ier*, dial. vars. of *guenchir, -ier* WINCH *v.*[1]] **1.** *intr.* To kick restlessly from impatience or pain. Now *dial.* **2.** To start or make an involuntary shrinking movement in consequence of or in order to avoid pain, or when alarmed or suddenly affected 1748.

1. Wynsynge she was as is a ioly colt CHAUCER. Let the galld iade w. SHAKS.

Wincey (wi·nsi). 1808. [orig. Sc.; app. alteration of *woolsey* in LINSEY-WOOLSEY, through the medium of the assimilated form **linsey-winsey*.] A very durable cloth having a linen warp and a woollen weft.

Winch (winʃ), *sb.* [Late OE. *wince*:—OTeut. **winkjo-*, **wenkjo-*, f. Indo-Eur. root **weng-* (cf. WINK *v.*).] **1.** A reel, roller, or pulley. **b.** *spec.* An angler's reel 1662. **c.** *Naut.* A small machine used for making ropes and spun-yarn 1640. **2.** The cranked handle by means of which the axis of a revolving machine is turned 1660. **3.** A hoisting or hauling apparatus consisting essentially of a horizontal drum round which a rope passes, and a crank by which it is turned 1577. **b.** In the navigation of the river Thames, a revolving apparatus at the river-side, round which a rope was wound to haul craft through difficult places; a toll levied for the use of this 1623. **4.** *Dyeing.* = WINCE *sb.*[2] 2. 1791.

Winch (winʃ), *v.*[1] *Obs.* exc. *dial.* ME. [a. AF. **wenchier, -ir* = OF. *guenchier, -ir* to turn aside, avoid, a. Teut. **wenkjan*: cf. prec.] **1.** *intr.* To start back or away, recoil, flinch; to wince. †**b.** *fig.* To recoil in fear or disgust (*at*) -1709. †**2.** = WINCE *v.*[1] 1. -1718.

Winch, *v.*[2] 1529. [f. WINCH *sb.*] **1.** *trans.* To hoist or draw *up*, etc. with or as with a winch. **2.** *Dyeing.* = WINCE *v.*[2] 1831.

Winchester (wi·nˌtʃėstəɹ). 1550. [Proper name.] **I.** The name of a city in Hampshire, the capital of Wessex and later of the Anglo-Saxon kingdom: used *attrib.* in specific designations.

W. measure, dry and liquid measures the standards of which were orig. deposited at Winchester. So *W. bushel, gallon, quart*, for which *W.* is used for short (in druggists' use = W. quart). *W. goose*: see GOOSE *sb.* 3.

II. The name of Oliver F. *Winchester* (1810–1880), an American manufacturer, used as the designation of a breech-loading rifle having a tubular magazine under the barrel and a horizontal bolt operated by a lever on the underside of the stock 1871.

Wind (wind, *poet. also* wəind), *sb.*[1] [OE. *wind*:—OTeut. **windoz*:—pre-Teut. **wentos*, cogn. w. L. *ventus*; orig. a pres. ppl. formation (**wēnto-*) f. root **wē-* of OE. *wawan*, Goth. *waian* to blow, Gr. ἄ(ϝ)ησι, Skr. *vâti* blows. The normal development is (wəind), as in *hind, rind*; (wind) became current in polite speech in the 18th c.; the short vowel is prob. due to the influence of *windy*, where it is normal.] **I. 1.** Air in motion; a state of movement in the air; a current of air, of any degree of force perceptible to the senses, occurring naturally in the atmosphere, usu. parallel to the surface of the ground. **2.** With specific ref. to the direction from which it blows; usu. qualified by the name of a point of the compass, or in *pl.* by a numeral, esp. *four* (hence sometimes *transf.* = points of the compass, directions) OE. **3.** In ref. to navigation, as the means of propulsion of a sailing-vessel OE. **b.** *Naut.* in various expressions referring to the direction or position of the wind in relation to the ship; hence also *allus.* late ME. **4.** As conveying scent, esp. the scent of a person or animal in hunting, etc. ME. **5.** In alliterative conjunction with *weather*: now always *w. and weather* ME. **6.** As a thing devoid of sense or perception, or that is unaffected by what one does to it: in phrases usu. expressing futile action or effort ME. **7.** As a type of violence or fury, swiftness, freedom, or unrestrainable character, mutability or fickleness, lightness or emptiness. late ME.

1. Hither the winds blow, here the spring-tide roar MARLOWE. There was just such a w. and just such a fall of snow, a good many years back DICKENS. Not a breath of w. crossed the heavens 1849. *fig.* Lady Petherwin crashed out of the room in a w. of indignation HARDY. 2. O, wild West W., thou breath of Autumn's being SHELLEY. The cousins disperse to the four winds of heaven DICKENS. 3. I set up my sail, the w. being fair SWIFT. b. *To gain, get, take the w. of*, to get to windward of (another ship) so as to intercept the w.; so *to give, have the w. of*. *To take the w. out of the sails of* (fig.), to deprive of the means of progress, put a check upon the action of, put at a disadvantage. 4. *To take, have, get, gain the w. of*, to scent or detect by or as by the w. *To keep the w.*, to keep the game on the windward side so as to scent it, or so that it does not scent one; Hee knowes the Game, how true hee keepes the winde? SHAKS. *Within w. of*, near enough to be detected by. 6. This I tell her, but talk to the winds SWIFT. 7. About the wood, goe swifter then the winde SHAKS. Thou shalt be as free As mountaine windes SHAKS.

II. *transf.* **1.** Air in general, as a substance or 'element'. *Obs.* exc. in *w. and water.* ME. **2.** 'Air' or gas in the stomach or intestines; flatus OE. **3.** Air inhaled and exhaled by the lungs. *Obs.* exc. as coloured by c. OE. **b.** Breath as used in speaking; hence *transf.* speech, talk. *Obs.* or *arch.* (exc. as implied in LONG-WINDED 2). ME. **c.** Easy or regular breathing; power or capacity of breathing; condition with regard to respiration. Now only in sporting phrases. ME. (*b*) in ref. to diseased or disordered breathing in horses 1523. **d.** *transf.* (*Pugilistic slang*). That part of the body in front of the stomach a blow upon which takes away the breath by checking the action of the diaphragm 1823. **4.** Air as used for 'blowing' or sounding a musical instrument (*w.-instrument*) such as a horn, trumpet, flute, etc., or an organ-pipe. late ME. **b.** *transf.* The wind-instruments of an orchestra (or their players) collectively, as dist. from the 'strings' and 'percussion' 1876. **5.** A blast of air artificially produced, *e.g.* by bellows; the rush of air caused by a rapidly moving body 1556.

1. *Between* (or *betwixt*) *w. and water* (Naut.), referring to that part of a ship's side which is sometimes above water and sometimes submerged, in which part a shot is peculiarly dangerous. *W. and water line*, the part of a ship's side between w. and water. *To break w.*, to discharge flatus from the stomach or bowels. *To get the w. up* (slang), to get into a state of alarm or 'funk'. 3. She..fetches her winde so short, as if she were fraid with a sprite SHAKS. **b.** *Com. Err.* I. ii. 53. **c.** *Second w.*, a condition of regular breathing regained after breathlessness during long-continued exertion. *W. and limb, limb and w.*: see LIMB *sb.*[1] 2. (*b*) A very handsome English coach-horse (a little touched in the w.) 1777. 4. Heaving a long sigh, like w. in a trombone G. B. SHAW. 5. He was knocked down by the w. of the shell 1804.

III. *fig.* and *allus.* **1.** Applied to something empty, vain, trifling, or unsubstantial, as empty talk, vain imagination or conceit ME. **2.** In provb. and other expressions, figuring or denoting a force or agency that drives or carries along or that strikes upon some person or thing OE. **b.** In expressions referring to a tendency, turn, or condition of affairs. late ME. **3. a.** *To get* or *take w.*: to be revealed or divulged, become known. Now *rare.* 1667. **b.** *To get w. of*, to receive information or a hint of. Hence, in recent use, *w.* = a hint or slight intimation (*of*). 1809.

1. I hope the Lord has let some of the w. out of you, that I thought was in you when first I knew you 1779. Hard words..are but w. SCOTT. Is Society become wholly a bag of w., then, ballasted by guineas? CARLYLE. 2. *What w. blows you here? It's an ill w. that blows nobody good. To sow the w. and reap the whirlwind*: see WHIRLWIND 2. *To raise the w.*: see RAISE *v.* I. 7. **b.** *To know which way the w. blows. The w. has changed.* †*Is the w. in that corner? To sail with every* (*shift of*) *w.*, to turn every change of circumstances to one's advantage.

With preps. **Before the w.:** said of a ship sailing directly with the w.; also *fig.* **By the w.** (*Naut.*): as near as possible to the direction from which the w. is blowing. **Down (the) w.:** in the direction in which the w. is blowing; along the course of the w. Also *down-w.* (attrib.), situated in this direction, 'lee'. **In the w.: a.** In (or into) the direction from which the w. is blowing; to windward. **b.** *fig.* So as to be 'scented' or perceived (or so as to 'scent' or perceive something). **c.** *predic.* Happening or ready to happen; astir, afoot; (of a person or thing) as the subject of what is going on, 'in the business'. **d.** *To hang in the w.*: to remain in suspense or indecision. **e.** *Naut. slang* (predic.). Intoxicated; the worse for liquor: usu. with qualification, esp. *three sheets in the w.* **Into the w.:** into or towards the direction from which the w. is blowing; so as to face the w. **Near the w.:** nearly in the direction from which the w. is blowing; hence *fig.* nearly up to the possible or permissible limit. **Off the w.** (*Naut.*): away from the w. **On a** (less commonly **the**) **w.** (*Naut.*): towards or close to the direction from which the w. is blowing. **To the w.: a.** *Naut.* Towards the direction from which the w. is blowing. *Close to the w.*, very nearly in this direction. **b.** *To fling, give*, etc. *to the winds* (fig.): to cast away, reject utterly. **Under the w.:** on the side away from the w.; *spec.* in a position of shelter from the w.; under the lee of something. Chiefly *Naut.* and *dial.* **Up (the) w.:** in the direction contrary to that in which the w. is blowing; against the w. **With the w.:** in the direction in which the w. is blowing.

Comb.: **w.-ball**, an inflated ball; a game played with such a ball by striking it with the fist; **-band**, a band of w.-instruments, as a military band; **-belt**, a belt of trees planted for protection from the w.; **-blown** *a.*, blown up or inflated; blown along or about; blown upon by (the) w.; **-break**, something, esp. a row of trees, used to break the force of the w. (chiefly *U.S.*); **-chest**, an air-tight chest or box in an organ or similar instrument, which is filled with w. from the bellows, and from which the w. is admitted to the pipes or reeds; **-driven** *a.*, driven, carried, or impelled by the w.; †**-gun** = AIR-*gun*; **-hole**, (*a*) an opening in brickwork for the passage of air; (*b*) the hole in the lower board of a pair of bellows; (*c*) a ventilating shaft in a mine; (*d*) each of the openings in the sound-board of an organ, through which w. is admitted to the pipes; **-jammer** *U.S. slang*, a sailing vessel; **-porch**, a chamber constructed on the inner side of a doorway to keep the w. out; **-pump**, a pump driven by a w.-wheel; **-rode** *a. Naut.*, swung by the w., as a ship riding at anchor; **-screen**, a screen for protection from the w., now esp. in front of the driver's seat on a motor-car; **-suck** *v.*, *intr.* of a horse, to have the vice of noisily drawing in and swallowing air; **-sucker**, a horse addicted to w.-sucking; **-tight** *a.*, solidly constructed to keep out w.; also of a vessel = AIR-*tight*; **-wheel**, a wheel turned by the w. to drive some mechanism, as in a windmill or w.-pump.

Wind (wəind), *sb.*[2] late ME. [Partly a. MDu., MLG. *winde* windlass; partly f. WIND *v.*[1]] **1.** An apparatus for winding, a winch or windlass. *Obs.* exc. *dial.* **2.** An act or instance of winding; curved or twisted form; *techn.* bend or twist, esp. in phr. *out of w.*, not twisted 1825.

Wind (wəind), *v.*[1] Pa. t. and pple. **wound** (waund). [OE. *windan* :—OTeut. **wendan*, related to **wand-* in WANDER *v.*, WEND *v.*] †**1.** *intr.* To go on one's way, take oneself; to proceed, go –1608. **2.** *trans.* To wield (a weapon, an implement). *Obs.* or *dial.* OE. **3.** *intr.* To turn this way and that; to writhe. *Obs.* exc. *dial.* OE. †**4.** *trans.* To put into a curved or twisted form or state; to bend –1624. **b.** *intr.* To take or have a bent form; now only *dial.* or *techn.* of a board, door, etc., to be twisted. late ME. **5. a.** *refl.* = 6 a, b. *arch.* ME. **b.** *trans.* To turn; to cause to move in a curve. *arch.* ME. **6. a.** *intr.* To move in a curve; to turn, esp. in a specified direction. *Obs.* exc. as in b, c. late ME. **b.** To move along in a sinuous course; to go or travel *along, up, down*, etc. a path or road which turns this way and that 1682. **c.** *transf.* Of a line, road, or the like: To have a curved (esp. a sinuous) course; to lie or extend in a curve or succession of curves 1555. **d.** with advb. acc., or *trans.* with obj. (*one's* or *its*) *way*, etc. 1667. **e.** *trans.* To traverse in a curved or sinuous course. *arch.* 1648. **7.** *Naut.* **a.** *intr.* Of a ship: To turn in some direction, e.g. to swing round when at anchor; to lie with her head towards a particular point of the compass. **b.** *trans.* To turn (a vessel) about, or in some particular direction. 1613. **8.** To turn or deflect in a particular direction; *esp.* to turn or lead (a person) according to one's will; also *to turn and w.* Now *rare* or *Obs.* late ME. †**b.** To draw, bring, or involve (a person) *in*, attract *into*, by alluring or enticing methods –1655. **9.** *intr.* To pursue a devious, circuitous, or intricate course in argument, statement, or conduct; to use circumlocution or subtle terms of argument. *arch.* late ME. **10.** *intr.* and *refl.* †**a.** With *out*: To extricate or disentangle oneself from a state of confinement or embarrassment –1667. **b.** With *in, into*: To insinuate oneself 1548. **11.** *trans.* To turn or pass (something) around something else so as to encircle or enclose it and be in contact with it; to turn, twist, or wrap (something) *about, round*, or *upon* something else ME. **12.** To put (thread, tape, or the like) in coils or convolutions around something, as a reel, or upon itself, so as to form it into a compact mass (hank, skein, ball, etc.). Also with *from* or *off*, to undo the coils of (thread, etc.) by rotating the object on which they are wound; to unwind. ME. **13.** To encircle *with* or enclose in something passed round and in contact; now only of binding a thing *round* with tape, wire, or the like ME. **b.** *spec.* To wrap (a corpse) in a shroud or *winding-sheet*; to shroud. *Obs.* exc. *dial.* ME. **c.** Chiefly in pa. pple. and *fig.*: To involve, entangle ME. **14.** *intr.* To turn so as to encircle and lie in contact with something else; to twist or coil *about, around*, or *upon* something. So *to w. off*, to unwind. 1575. †**15.** *trans.* To plait, wreathe, weave –1601. **16.** To haul or hoist by turning a winch, windlass, or the like, around which a rope or chain is passed. **a.** *gen.* late ME. **b.** *Naut.* To move or warp (the ship), by hauling, as on a capstan or windlass. Also *absol.* or *intr.* 1515. **c.** *Mining.* To hoist (coal, etc.) to the surface 1883. **17.** To set (a watch, clock, or other mechanism) in order for going by turning an axis with a key or other device so as to coil the spring tighter or draw up the weights 1601. **b.** *fig.* To exalt or 'screw up' *to* a certain pitch 1635.

1. But winde away, bee gone I say SHAKS. 6. **b.** The lowing herd winds slowly o'er the lea GRAY. **d.** He..windes..his oblique way Amongst innumerable Starrs MILT. 8. He can w. the proud Earl to his will SCOTT. 9. *Merch. V.* I. i. 154. 10. **b.** Of your having..wound yourself..almost into his confidence DICKENS. 11. *To w.* (a person, etc.) *round one's* (*little*) *finger*, to make him do anything. 13. Her twin-brother couldn't w. up a top for his life DICKENS. **b.** She had winded a many of them in her time 1860.

W. up.: a. *trans.* To draw up or hoist with a winch or the like. †**b.** *fig.* To involve, implicate. **c.** †(*a*) To coil, roll, or fold up; to furl; (*b*) to coil (thread, etc.) into a compact mass: chiefly in phr. †*to w. up a bottom, one's bottoms*, usu. *fig.* to sum up, conclude. **d.** †(*a*) To sum up; (*b*) to bring to a close or conclusion; to form the conclusion of, be the final event in; (*c*) to bring (an affair) to a final settlement; *spec.* to arrange and adjust the affairs of (a company or business concern) on its dissolution; (*d*) *absol.* or *intr.* to bring the proceeding to a close; to conclude *with* something. **e.** = 17 a. **f.** *fig.* To set in readiness for action; to raise (feeling) to a high degree; now usu., to put into a state of tension or intensity of feeling, etc.; to excite.

Wind (wind, wəind), *v.*[2] Pa. t. and pple. **winded.** late ME. [f. WIND *sb.*[1]] **I.** *trans.* To get the wind of; to perceive (an animal, a person, or thing) by the scent conveyed by the wind. **b.** *intr.* Of an animal: To sniff in order to scent or on scenting something. late ME. **c.** *fig.* (*trans.*) To perceive by some subtle indication; to smell or nose *out* 1583.

They had winded two lions 1850. **c.** No nose to.. winde out all your tricks 1611.

II. 1. *trans.* To expose to the wind or air; to air. late ME. **b.** *intr.* To become tainted by exposure to air; *trans.* to taint by such exposure (*dial.*) 1842. **2.** *trans.* (usu. wəind). To sound by forcing the breath through, to blow (a wind-instrument, esp. a horn). Often with pa. t. and pple. *wound.* 1586. **b.** To blow (a blast, call, or note) on a horn, etc. 1599. **c.** To supply (an organ-pipe) with wind at a particular pressure 1879. **3.** To deprive of 'wind' or breath, put out of breath 1811.

2. Where the Beetle winds His small but sullen Horn COLLINS. **b.** *Much Ado* I. i. 243. 3. Parkes was very faint, and apparently quite winded 1811.

Windage (wi·ndėdʒ). 1710. [f. WIND *sb.*[1] + -AGE.] **1.** An allowance of space (for expansion of gas in firing) between the inner wall of a fire-arm and the shot or shell with which it is charged. **2.** Allowance made (esp. in shooting) for deflexion from the direct course by the wind; such deflexion itself 1867. **3.** = WIND *sb.*[1] II. 5; also, the friction of the air upon a moving part of a machine 1889.

Wind-bag, windbag (wi·ndbæg). 1470. [f. WIND *sb.*[1] + BAG *sb.*] **1.** A bag containing 'wind' or air, as the bag of a bagpipe, the lungs, the chest or body considered as a receptacle of breath (now only *joc.*). **2.** *fig.* (*contempt.*) An empty pretender, or something pretentious but unsubstantial; *esp.* a voluble and senseless talker 1827.

Wi·nd-bound, *a.* [f. WIND *sb.*[1] + BOUND *ppl. a.*[2]] Detained by contrary winds.

Winded (wi·ndėd), *a.* 1440. [f. WIND *sb.*[1] + -ED[2].] Having wind, i.e. (usu.) breath, of a specified kind or in a specified condition; chiefly in parasynthetic combs., as LONG-W., SHORT-W.

Wi·nded, *ppl. a.* 1595. [f. WIND *v.*[2] + -ED[1].] **1.** (wi·ndėd) Exposed to or spoilt by wind or air. **2.** (wəi·ndėd) Blown, as a wind-instrument 1622. **3.** (wi·ndėd) Put out of breath, blown 1597.

Wind-egg (wi·nd,eg). late ME. [f. WIND *sb.*[1] + EGG *sb.*] An imperfect or unproductive egg, esp. one with a soft shell.

Winder[1] (wəi·ndəɹ). 1552. [f. WIND *v.*[1] + -ER[1].] A person or thing that winds, in various senses. **1.** One who turns or manages a winch or windlass, esp. at a mine 1747. **2.** An operative employed in winding wool, etc. 1552. **3.** One who winds a clock or other mechanism 1823. **4.** An apparatus (of various kinds) for winding something, or upon which something is wound or coiled 1585. **5.** A key for winding a jack, clock, or other mechanism 1606. **6.** A winding step in a staircase: usu. in *pl.*, opp. to *flyers* 1667.

Wi·nder[2]. 1611. [f. WIND *v.*[2] + -ER[1].] **1.** (wəi·ndəɹ). One who blows a wind-instrument. **2.** (wi·ndəɹ). Something that takes one's breath away; a blow that 'knocks the wind' out of one; a run or other exertion that puts one out of breath *colloq.* 1825.

Windfall (wi·ndfǭl). 1464. [perh. of foreign origin; cf. MHG. *wintval.*] **1.** Something blown down by the wind, or the fall of something so blown down: **a.** a tree or branch, or a number of trees or branches; *spec.* (chiefly *U.S.*) a heap or tract of fallen trees blown down by a tornado; **b.** fruit from a tree or bush (*rarely* flowers). 1592. **2.** *fig.* A casual or unexpected acquisition or advantage 1542.

2. This man..by these windfalles and unexpected cheats became very wealthy HOLLAND. So **Wi·nd-fallen** *a.* blown down by the wind.

Wi·nd-flow:er. 1551. [Turner's rendering of L. *anemone*, Gr. ἀνεμώνη.] The wood-anemone (*Anemone nemorosa*), or any plant or flower of the genus *Anemone.* **b.** A species of gentian 1866.

Windgall[1] (wi·ndgǭl). 1523. A soft tumour on either side of a horse's leg just above the fetlock, caused by distension of the synovial bursa. Hence **Wi·ndgalled** *a.* affected with a w. or windgalls.

Wi·nd-gall[2]. 1840. [Cf. G. *windgalle, -gelle.*] = WEATHER-*gall.*

Wi·nd-gauge. 1774. [f. WIND *sb.*[1] + GAUGE.] **1.** = ANEMOMETER 1. **2.** A graduated attachment to the sights of a gun, to enable allowance to be made for the effect of the wind on the projectile 1862. **3.** = ANEMOMETER 2. 1876.

Windhover (wi·ndhǫ:vəɹ, -hʌ:vəɹ). 1674. [f. WIND *sb.*[1] + HOVER *v.*] A name for the kestrel, from its habit of hovering in the air with its head to the wind.

Windily (wi·ndili). *adv.* 1866. [f. WINDY *a.* + -LY [2].] In a windy manner; as if driven or agitated by the wind.

Windiness (wi·ndinės). 1450. [f. WINDY *a.* + -NESS.] **1.** Windy condition of the atmosphere; prevalence of windy weather 1687. **2.** Flatulence. Now *rare.* 1450. **b.** Quality of causing or tendency to cause 'wind'. Now *rare.* 1576. **3.** *fig.* 'Airiness', emptiness, want of substance; inflated or verbose style 1614.

Winding (wəi·ndiŋ), *vbl. sb.* OE. [f. WIND *v.*[1] + -ING [1].] **I.** The action of WIND *v.*[1], or the resulting condition. **1.** Motion in a curve; sinuous progress or movement. late ME. **2.** *fig.* Turning this way and that in thought or conduct; usu. *pl.* devious or intricate motions; tortuous or crooked ways or dealings 1621. **3.** *Carpentry*, etc. Condition of being twisted; chiefly in phr. *out of w.* = *out of wind* (WIND *sb.*[2] 2); *in w.*, twisted 1711. **4.** The action of twining a flexible object round another or itself, *esp.* the coiling or twining of thread, silk, etc. late ME. **5.** Hoisting or hauling by means of a winch, windlass, or the like 1440. **6.** Usu. with *up*, of a clock or other mechanism 1630. **7.** *W. up*, conclusion, finish; now usu., the bringing to an end the activities of a business concern 1560. **II.** That which winds or is wound. **1.** An object that winds or is wound round; a coil or coiled object OE. **2.** A curved, sinuous, or meandering line, path, or the like; esp. *pl.* meanderings, twists and turns. late ME. **3.** A flexible rod or withy. *Obs.* or *dial.* late ME.

1. To nurse the Saplings tall, and curl the grove With Ringlets quaint, and wanton windings wove MILT. 2. I..follow'd long The windings of the stream COWPER.

Winding (wəi·ndiŋ), *ppl. a.* 1530. [f. WIND *v.*[1] + -ING [2].] That winds, in various senses. **a.** That follows a sinuous course or is full of bends and turns; esp. of a staircase: Spiral. **b.** Of a narrative: Circuitous, rambling 1887. Hence **Wi·nding·ly** *adv.*, **-ness.**

Winding-sheet (wəi·ndiŋʃīt). late ME. [f. WINDING *vbl. sb.* + SHEET *sb.*[1]] **1.** A sheet in which a corpse is wrapped for burial. **2.** A mass of solidified drippings of grease clinging to the side of a candle, resembling a sheet folded in creases, and regarded as an omen of death or calamity 1708.

1. A thousand Coarses, some standing bolt vpright in their knotted winding sheetes DEKKER. 2. She..sees..gifts in her finger-nails, letters and winding-sheets in the candle 1824.

Wi·nd-i:nstrument. 1582. (Often as two words.) A musical instrument played by means of 'wind', supplied either by the breath of the player or by bellows: most commonly applied to portable instruments of this kind, such as those used in an orchestra. (Strictly, applied to instruments whose sounds are produced by vibration of air in a pipe or tube, or in a number of pipes; but usu. also including those sounding by vibration of reeds.)

Windlass (wi·ndlăs), *sb.*[1] late ME. [prob. alteration, by association w. *windle* (now dial.) to wind, of †*windas* (AF. *windas* = OF. *guindas*, a. ON. *vinddáss*, f. *vinda* WIND *v.*[1] + *áss* pole).] A mechanical contrivance working on the principle of the wheel and axle, on a horizontal axis; consisting of a roller or beam, resting on supports, round which a rope or chain is wound, and used for various purposes, as on board ship for weighing the anchor, for raising a bucket from a well, etc.

attrib.; **w.-bar**, any of a set of bars inserted in holes in a ship's w., by which it is turned; **w.-bitt, -chock**, each of the supports of a ship's w. Hence **Wi·ndlass** *v.*[2] *trans.* to hoist or haul with a w.

†Windlass, *sb.*[2] 1530. [Alteration of †*wanlace* (AF., of obscure origin) by association with WIND *v.*[1]] **1.** A circuit made to intercept the game in hunting; *gen.* a circuit, circuitous movement –1602. **2.** *fig.* A circuitous course of action; a crafty device –1734.

2. *Ham.* II. i. 65. Hence **†Windlass** *v.*[1] *trans.* to decoy or ensnare; *intr.* to make a circuit, to act circuitously or craftily –1660.

Windle (wi·nd'l). [OE. *windel*, f. *windan* WIND *v.*[1]] **1.** A basket. Now *dial.* **2.** A measure of corn and other commodities; of wheat, usu. about 3 bushels. *local.* ME.

Windless (wi·nd,lės), *a.* late ME. [f. WIND *sb.*[1] + -LESS.] **1.** Breathless, out of breath. Now *rare.* **2.** Free from wind; not exposed to or stirred by the wind, in or upon which no wind blows 1591. Hence **Wi·ndless-ly** *adv.*, **-ness.**

Windlestraw (wi·nd'l,strǭ). *Sc.* and *dial.* [OE. *windelstrēaw*, perh. f. *windel* WINDLE + *strēaw* STRAW *sb.*] **1.** A dry thin withered stalk of grass, such as is left standing after the flower or seed is shed. **2.** Any of various long-stalked species of grass, as *Cynosurus cristatus* (dog's-tail grass), *Lolium perenne* (rye-grass), and *Agrostis Spicaventi* OE.

1. *fig.* He grippit me..and drew his windlestrae of a sword 1895.

Windmill (wi·ndmil, wi·nmil). ME. [f. WIND *sb.*[1] + MILL *sb.*[1]] **1.** A mill the machinery of which is driven by the wind acting upon sails, used (chiefly in flat districts) for grinding corn, pumping water, etc. **2.** A figure of a windmill; a sign or character resembling this, as a cross or asterisk. Now *rare* or *Obs.* late ME. **3. a.** A model of a windmill. **b.** A toy consisting of a cross-shaped piece of card or other light substance fixed at the end of a stick so as to revolve like the sails of a windmill when moved through the air. 1557. **4.** *fig.* and *allus.* **†a.** A fanciful notion, a crotchet –1749. **b.** In allusions to the story of Don Quixote tilting at windmills under the delusion that they were giants 1644. **c.** *To fling* (*throw*) *one's cap over the w.* [= F. *jeter son bonnet par-dessus les moulins*]: to act recklessly and defiantly, fly in the face of convention 1885.

4. a. Thy head is full of Windemils 1622.

Comb.: **w.** aero(plane = AUTOGIRO; **w.-cap**, the upper story of a w. when made movable so as to turn the sails to the wind; **w. plant** = TELEGRAPH-*plant*; **-pump**, a wind-pump.

Window (wi·ndo[u]), *sb.* [ME. *windoȝe*, a. ON. *vindauga*, f. *vindr* WIND *sb.*[1] + *auga* EYE *sb.*[1]] **1.** An opening in a wall or side of a building, ship, or carriage, to admit light or air, or both, and to afford a view of what is outside or inside; now usu. fitted with sheets of glass, horn, mica, etc., a frame containing a pane or panes of glass, or glazed sashes. **2.** *transf.* A window space or opening; *esp.* in phr. *in the w.*, now chiefly with ref. to the exhibition of notices, advertisements, etc., or the display of goods (as in a shop-w.) ME. **3.** Applied to openings, resembling or likened to a window in shape or function, e.g. *pl.* a pattern of squares made with sugar on bread and butter; soap-bubbles blown between the finger and thumb. late ME. **b.** *Windows of heaven*: openings in the sky through which rain was thought to pour. late ME. **c.** *Anat.* = FENESTRA 1. 1615. **4.** *fig.* Applied to the senses or organs of sense, esp. the eyes, regarded as inlets or outlets to or from the mind or soul ME. **b.** *fig.* and in allusive or provb. expressions. late ME.

1. At the chekker hous windo 1583. Storied Windows richly dight MILT. 2. *To dress a w.*: cf. *w.-dresser*, *-dressing*. 3. A large..lamp, having side windows 1892. 4. The eyes..are the windowes of the minde 1544. **b.** *To throw the house out at (the) w.* [= F. *jeter la maison par la fenêtre*], to make a great commotion, turn everything topsy-turvy. *To come in by the w.* [= F. *entrer par la fenêtre*], to come in stealthily.

Comb.: **w.-box**, a box placed outside a w., in which ornamental plants are cultivated; **-cleaner**, a person whose business it is to clean windows; **-dresser**, one whose business it is to arrange and display goods to the best advantage in a shop-w.; **-dressing**, (*a*) the dressing of a w. with goods attractively displayed; (*b*) *fig.* a display made in such a way as to give a falsely favourable impression of the facts; *esp.* the arrangement of a balance-sheet so as to suggest that the business concerned is more prosperous than it is; **-envelope**, an envelope with an opening or transparent 'panel' in the front through which the address is visible; **w. gardening**, the cultivation of plants in w. spaces or on w.-sills; **-mirror**, a mirror fixed outside a w. and adjustable so as to reflect the image of objects in the street; **-pane**; **-seat**, a seat fixed under a w. or windows, often upholstered; **-sill** = SILL [1] 2; **-tax**, a duty levied upon windows, imposed in 1695 and abolished in 1851. Hence **†Wi·ndow** *v.* (*rare*) *trans.* to furnish with windows or w.-like openings; to place in a w. **Wi·ndowless** *a.* not having or furnished with windows.

Windowed (wi·ndo[u]d), *ppl. a.* 1483. [f. prec. + -ED [2].] **1.** Furnished with or having windows. Also with prefixed word in comb. **2.** Having decorative openings 1483. **3.** Full of holes. (In later use echoing Shaks.) 1605.

3. Your lop'd, and window'd raggednesse SHAKS.

Windpipe (wi·ndpəip, wəi·ndpəip). 1530. [f. WIND *sb.*[1] + PIPE *sb.*[1]] **1.** = TRACHEA 1 a. **2.** An artificial pipe or tube for conducting a blast of air (*rare*) 1688.

Wind rose (wi·nd,rōuz). 1597. [f. as prec. + ROSE *sb.*; in sense 2, after G. *windrose.*] **1. a.** The 'bastard wild poppy', *Argemone mexicana*, or the common wild poppy, *Papaver Rhœas*; **b.** the violet horned poppy, *Rœmeria hybrida.* **2.** *Meteorol.* A diagram indicating the relative frequency, force, etc. of the winds from the various points of the compass at some given place 1846.

Windrow (wi·nd,ro[u]), *sb.* 1523. A row in which mown grass or hay is laid before being made up into heaps or cocks, in which sods, peats, etc. are set up to be dried by the wind, or in which dead branches, etc. are gathered to be burnt. Hence **Wi·ndrow** *v. trans.* to set or lay in windrows.

Windsail (wi·ndsē[i]l). 1725. [f. WIND *sb.*[1] + SAIL *sb.*[1]] **1.** *Naut.* A long wide tube or funnel of sail-cloth used for ventilating a ship 1741. **2.** A sail of a windmill 1725.

Wind-shake (wi·ndʃē[i]k). 1545. [f. WIND *sb.*[1] + SHAKE *sb.* II. 1.] A flaw or crack in timber, supposed to be due to a strain caused by the force of the wind.

Wind-shaken (wi·ndʃē[i]:k'n), *ppl. a.* 1550. [f. WIND *sb.*[1] + *shaken*, pa. pple. of SHAKE *v.*] **1.** Shaken or agitated by the wind. **2.** Of timber: Affected with wind-shake 1565. So **†Wi·nd-shaked** *ppl. a.* (*rare*) = sense 1.

Windsor (wi·nzəɹ). Name of a town in Berkshire, on the right bank of the Thames, at which is W. Castle, a royal residence. **1.** *attrib.* in names of various things now or formerly obtained, made, etc. at or near W., or of persons connected with W. Castle 1473. **2.** Short for *W. bean*, *brick*, *soap* 1786.

1. **W. bean**, the common broad bean; **brick**, a kind of red fire-resisting brick formerly made at Hedgerley, near W.; **W. chair**, a kind of wooden chair with the back formed of upright rod-like pieces surmounted by a cross-piece, and often with arms; **W. herald**, an officer whose duties are now performed by the Garter King of Arms; **W. knight**, one of a body of military pensioners residing within the precincts of W. Castle; **W. soap**, a kind of toilet soap, usu. brown; **W. tie** (*U.S.*), a kind of broad silk necktie, tied in a double bow; **W. uniform**, a uniform introduced by King George III, worn on certain occasions at W. Castle by members of the royal household.

Wind-up (wəi·nd,ʌp), *sb.* and *a.* 1573. [f. the phr. *to wind up.*] **A.** *sb.* The action of 'winding-up', or something that 'winds up' or concludes a course of action, etc.; close, conclusion;

final settlement; closing act or proceeding. **B.** *adj.* **1.** Constructed to be wound up 1784. **2.** Forming the conclusion of something; concluding, closing 1843.

Windward (wi·nd,wǫ̈ɹd), quasi-*sb.* in *phr.*, *a.*, and *adv.* 1549. [f. WIND *sb.*[1] + -WARD.] **A.** Phr. *To (the) w.*, to the w. side or direction. *To get to w. of* (fig.), to gain an advantage over. *To keep to w. of*, to keep out of the reach of.

B. *adj.* **1.** Having a direction towards, *i.e.* opposite to that of, the wind; moving against the wind 1627. **b.** = WEATHERLY *a.* 1895. **2.** Situated towards the direction from which the wind blows; facing the wind. *W. tide*, a tide running contrary to the direction of the wind. 1687. **C.** *adv.* Towards the wind, to w. 1690. Hence **Wi·ndwardly** *a.* = B 1 b, 2. So **Wi·ndwards** = A.

Windy (wi·ndi), *a.* [OE. *windig*; see WIND *sb.*[1] and -Y[1].] **I. 1.** Consisting of wind; of or pertaining to (the) wind; indicating or suggesting wind. **b.** Produced, or actuated, by 'wind' or compressed air: said of a wind-instrument, or its music 1841. **2. a.** Of places, etc.: Full of, exposed to, or blown upon or through by the wind OE. **b.** Of times, conditions, etc.: Characterized by wind, in which wind is frequent or prevalent; accompanied by (much) wind OE. **c.** Situated towards the wind, windward 1599. **3.** Resembling the wind in storminess, quality of sound, swiftness, etc. OE. **4. a.** = FLATULENT 3. OE. **b.** = FLATULENT 2. late ME.

1. March, departed with his w. rage 1602. **2. a.** The w. tall elm-tree TENNYSON. **c.** Phr. *On the w. side of* (fig.): out of the reach of, away from, clear of (in modern use echoing SHAKS.); Still you keepe o' th windie side of the Law: good. SHAKS.

II. *fig.* **1.** Having 'nothing in it', intangible, empty, vain, trifling, worthless 1593. **2. a.** Of speech or discourse: Verbose; violent, vehement; empty and high-sounding; extravagant. late ME. **b.** Of a speaker or writer: Full of talk or verbiage, long-winded; violent or extravagant in utterance, bragging, boastful 1513. **3.** †**a.** That 'puffs one up'; inducing pride or vain-glory -1784. **b.** 'Puffed up'; inflated with, or showing, pride or vain conceit. Now *Sc. colloq.* 1603. **4.** Apt to 'get the wind up'; 'funky'. *slang.* 1916.

1. The Prince of Wales had some w. projects of encouraging literature..and the arts THACKERAY. **2. a.** The w. speeches made at..political meetings 1886.

Wine (wəin), *sb.* [Com. Teut. loanword: OE. *wīn*:—OTeut. **wīnom*, a. L. *vinum* (whence also the Balto-Slavic and Celtic words), prob. borrowed with Greek οἶνος, etc. from a common Mediterranean source.] **1.** The fermented juice of the grape used as a beverage. **b.** As one of the elements in the Eucharist OE. **c.** Regarded as the usual accompaniment of dessert 1824. **2.** In wider use, usu. with qualifying word: A fermented liquor made from the juice of other fruits, or from grain, flowers, the sap of various trees, etc.: sometimes called *madew.* late ME. **3.** *Pharmacy.* A solution of a medicinal substance (denoted by a qualifying word) in wine; a medicated wine 1652. **4.** A wine-party, esp. of undergraduates 1860. **5.** *Spirit(s) of w.*, alcohol, rectified spirit; *oil of w.*, œnanthic ester; also, a heavy oily liquid (*heavy oil of w.*) consisting of etherin, etherol, and ethyl sulphate 1646. **6.** *pl.* Short for: Wine-glasses 1848.

1. Wyne to make glad yᵉ herte of man COVERDALE *Ps.* ciii[i]. 15. The Sons Of Belial, flown with insolence and w. MILT. The..W. and Spirit Merchant 1828. *fig. Macb.* II. iii. 100. Phrases. *In w.*: in a state of intoxication with w.; in one's cups. *To take w.*, to drink w. *with* another person in a ceremonial manner, esp. as a token of friendship or regard. Provb. phrases. *New w. in old bottles* (see Matt. ix. 17). *To look on the w. when it is red* (see Prov. xxiii. 31). *Good w. needs no (ivy) bush* (see BUSH *sb.*[1] 5). *When w. is in, wit* (or *truth*) *is out. W. and women*; Those two maine plagues and common dotages of humane kind, W. & Women BURTON. **c.** In after-dinner talk Across the walnuts and the w. TENNYSON. **2.** *The w. of the country*: prop., the wine made in a particular locality for local consumption; usu. *transf.* the alcoholic beverage most drunk in a particular country. **3.** W. of Ipecacuanha 1811.

attrib. and *Comb.*: **w.-bibber** (now *literary*). [Coverdale's rendering in Prov. xxiii. 20, Matt. xi. 19 of Luther's (*wein*)*säufer*], a tippler, a drunkard; **-biscuit**, a small light biscuit served with w.; **-card** [G. *weinkarte*], a list of the wines that may be obtained at a restaurant; **-cellar**, a cellar used for storing w.; **-cooler**, a vessel in which bottles of w. can be immersed in ice or iced liquid; **-dark** *a.*, of the colour of deep-red w.; used esp. to render Gr. οἰνοψ as an epithet of the sea; **-fly**, any fly the larva of which lives in w.; **-glass**, a small drinking-glass for w.; **-grape**, *U.S.* a grape from which w. is made; **-grower**, one who cultivates vines for the production of w.; **-lees**, the sediment deposited in a vessel containing w.; **-measure**, the standard of liquid measure used for w.; **-party**, a party, the chief object of which is to drink w.; **-sap**, a large red Amer. winter apple; **-sour**, a small acid variety of plum; **-taster**, (*a*) one who judges the quality of w. by tasting; (*b*) an instrument for drawing a small sample of w. from a cask; **-vat**, a w.-press; **-vault(s**, (*a*) a vault in which w. is stored; (*b*) a pretentious name for a public-house; **vinegar**, vinegar made from w., as opp. to *malt vinegar*. Hence **Wine** *v. intr.* to take w., esp. at an undergraduates' w.-party (*colloq.*) 1829; *trans.* to entertain to w.: usu. in jingling phr. *dine and w.* (colloq.) 1862. **Wi·neless** *a.* lacking or destitute of w.

Wineberry (wəi·nbeːri). [OE. *wīnberige*; f. WINE *sb.* + BERRY *sb.*[1]] †**1.** A grape -1562. **2.** Applied formerly or now locally to various berries, e.g. †the bilberry; *dial.* the currant, the gooseberry. late ME.

Wi·ne-house. 1607. [Cf. OE. *wīnhūs*.] A public-house where wine is drunk. Now chiefly *Hist.* or with particular local reference. **2.** A house that deals in wine; a firm of wine-merchants 1834.

Wi·ne-press. 1526. [f. WINE *sb.* + PRESS *sb.*[1] III. 2.] A press in which the juice is extracted from the grapes in the manufacture of wine. Also *fig.*, esp. with ref. to Isa. lxiii. 3, Rev. xiv. 19, 20, xix. 15.

He must Tread the w. alone, calling no God-fearing man his friend FROUDE.

Winery (wəi·nəri). orig. *U.S.* 1882. [f. WINE *sb.*[1] + -ERY.] An establishment for making wine.

Wing (wiŋ), *sb.* [ME., first in pl. forms *wenge, wengen, wenges*, a. ON. *vængir*, pl. of *vængr*.] **I. 1.** Each of the organs of flight of any flying animal, as a bird, bat, or insect. **b.** The wing of a bird, used as food. Also, the shoulder of a hare or rabbit. 1470. **c.** The wing of a bird (usu. of a hen, goose, or turkey) used as a brush 1573. **d.** A figure or imitation of a wing (e.g. on an angler's artificial fly) 1552. **2. a.** Attributed to supernatural beings, as angels, demons, etc., and to fabulous creatures, as dragons, etc. ME. **b.** Attributed to inanimate or abstract things represented as flying, or as carrying one swiftly along (esp. in phr. *on the wings of*). late ME. **3.** *transf.* and *fig.* **a.** Power or means of flight, or of action figured as flight; action or manner of flying ME. **b.** In biblical and derived expressions referring to a mother bird's use of her wings for the protection of her young; thus virtually = protecting care ME. **4.** *transf.* †**a.** In phr. *of* (such-and-such) *w.*, = kind or description of bird (usu. *fig.*) -1630. **b.** Qualified by a restrictive word, or in techn. phr., = bird or birds 1601. **c.** A flock (of plover) 1805.

1. b. Something light for supper—the w. of a roasted fowl DICKENS. **2. b.** Thou..goest vpon the wynges of the wynde COVERDALE *Ps.* ciii[i]. 3. **3. a.** The self same place where hee First lighted from his Wing MILT. **b.** Under the shelter of her aunt's w. 1883. Give w. to your desires, and let 'em fly DRYDEN.

II. 1. An appliance or appendage resembling or analogous to a wing in form or function ME. **2.** A lateral part or appendage: in various connexions, as an outlying portion of a space or region, the mudguard of a motor vehicle, each of two side pieces at the top of an arm-chair against which the head may be rested. late ME. **3.** Either of the two divisions (*right w.*, *left w.*) on each side of the main body of an army or fleet in battle array; also, each of the two divisions of a regiment, a division of the Royal Air Force (so *w. commander*, etc.) late ME. **b.** *Football*, etc. The position of the forwards on either side of the centre; a player or players occupying this position (so *w. forward*, etc.) 1889. **c.** A section of a party, holding views deviating in one direction or the other from those generally held 1879. **4.** One of a pair of lateral projecting pieces of a garment on or near the shoulder, as of a doublet; also, a side-flap of a cap, etc. late ME. **5. a.** A subordinate part of a building on one side of the main or central part 1523. **b.** *Theatr.* Each of the side-scenes on the stage; also (usu. *pl.*) the space at each side of the stage where these stand 1790. **6.** *Anat.* = ALA 1. 1650. **7.** *Bot.* **a.** Each of the two lateral petals of a papilionaceous flower 1776. **b.** A thin membranous appendage of a seed or fruit, serving for its dispersal by the wind; a thin lateral projection extending along a stem 1776.

1. Your Argosies..with their wouen wings SHAKS. Wind milles..hauing ten wings a piece 1609. Being unable to swim he had made use of a pair of swimming wings 1908. Aeroplanes..depend for their support in the air upon the spread of surfaces which are ..called wings..or planes 1910. *Wings*, in the Royal Air Force, a certificate of ability to pilot an aeroplane, the badge representing a pair of wings.

Phrases. **On** or **upon the w.: a.** *lit.* Flying, in flight. **b.** *fig.* (*a*) Moving or travelling swiftly or briskly; astir, active. (*b*) Going off or away; ready to start or depart. **c.** *On the wings of*: see I. 2 b. **On wings:** going with light steps as one in a joyously exalted mood. **Under (..) w.:** *Under the w. of, under —'s w.*, under the protection, care, or patronage of. †**Make w.:** to make one's way by flying, to fly. **Take w.: a.** Of a bird, etc.: To take flight, begin flying. **b.** *fig.* To 'take flight', take one's departure, make off. **W.-and-w.:** (of a ship) sailing before the wind with the foresail hauled over one side and the mainsail over the other.

Comb.: **w.-case**, each of the structures (modified fore-wings) which cover the functional wings in certain insects, as the *elytra* of beetles and the *tegmina* of *Orthoptera*; **-covert**, any one of the small feathers overlying the flight-feathers of a bird's w.; **-fish**, (*a*) = PTERICHTHYS; (*b*) a flying-fish, esp. of the genus *Prionotus*; **w. rib**, the end rib of a loin of beef; **-shell**, any of several kinds of molluscs having the shell or some part of it resembling a w., as the genus *Pinna*; also, a w.-snail; **-snail** = PTEROPOD; **-spread**, (*a*) the extent of a bird's wings when spread; (*b*) the surface or area of an aeroplane's wings; **-tip**, (*a*) the tip of the w. of a bird, bat, or insect; (*b*) the outer end of the 'wing' of an aeroplane. Hence **Wi·nger** *Football*, a player on the (right or left) w.; in the Rugby game, a forward whose place is on the 'wing' in the back row of the scrum.

Wing, *v.* 1486. [f. prec.] **I.** †**1.** *trans.* To carve (a quail or partridge) -1804. **2.** *intr.* (†occas. *refl.*) To use one's wings, take flight, fly. *poet.* or *rhet.* 1611. **b.** In pa. pple. = flying, on the wing. *Obs.* or *arch.* 1591. **3.** *trans.* **a.** To fly through, upon, or across; to traverse by flying 1605. **b.** With cognate obj. 1697. **4.** To put wings upon, to furnish or fit with wings for flying; to feather (an arrow) 1616. **b.** *fig.* To 'give wings to'; to give speed or swift motion to; to speed, hasten 1599. **5.** To convey by or as by means of wings; to carry through the air as if flying; to waft 1628. **6.** To send flying, let fly (as a missile); to send off swiftly, to dart 1718. **7.** To shoot (a bird) in the wing, so as to disable it from flying without killing it; *transf.* to wound (a person, etc.) with a shot in the arm or shoulder, or some other not vital part 1802.

2. b. *Cymb.* IV. ii. 348. **3. a.** The Crowes and Choughes, that w. the midway ayre SHAKS. **4. b.** The Thunder, Wing'd with red Lightning and impetuous rage MILT. **7.** *transf.* One aeroplane was winged by Russian soldiery 1914.

II. †**a.** *Mil.* To furnish (a force) *with* additional troops on the wings; also of such troops, to form the wings of -1699. **b.** To furnish with side parts or projections, as a building, etc. 1700.

Winged (wi·ŋėd, *less freq.* wiŋd), *a.* late ME. [f. WING *sb.* + -ED [2].] **1.** Having wings, as a bird, bat, insect, supernatural or mythical being, etc.; represented or figured with wings. **b.** *poet.* Applied to a ship with sails set 1586. †**c.** Full of wings; crowded with flying birds. MILT. **2.** Furnished with or having a wing or wings, i. e. lateral part(s), appendage(s), or projection(s) 1597. **3.** *Bot.*, etc. **a.** Having lateral processes or appendages, as a stem, seed, fruit, etc. 1776. **b.** in names of plants dist. by having w. stems or other parts 1650. **4.** *fig.* Capable of or performing some movement or action figured as flight; flying or passing swiftly, swift, rapid 1513. **b.** *esp.* of words or speech (rendering or imitating the Homeric phr. ἔπεα πτερόεντα) 1616.

1. c. Th'earth cumber'd, and the wing'd air dark't with plumes MILT. **3. b. W. elm**, a small N. Amer. species of elm (*Ulmus alata*) with corky w. branches. **W. pea**, a plant of the S. European genus *Tetragonolobus* (now included in *Lotus*), having four-w.

pods. 4. Oswald leaves her with w. heels to make his arrangements 1877.

Wi·ngless, *a.* 1591. Having no wings; also, having rudimentary wings, as an apteryx.

Winglet (wi·ŋlėt). 1611. [f. WING *sb.* + -LET.] 1. A little wing. 2. a. *Entom.* A small appendage at the base of each wing or wing-sheath, as in certain flies and beetles, or on each side of the rostrum in certain weevils. b. *Ornith.* A process on the terminal joint of a bird's wing, having small feathers 1816. 3. A small wing-like appendage on some article of dress 1611.

Wingy (wi·ŋi), *a.* 1596. [f. WING *sb.* + -Y [1].] †1. Of, pertaining to, or resembling a wing or wings -1694. 2. Having wings, winged (*poet.*); having large or conspicuous wings 1566. 3. *fig.* Capable of 'flight', soaring, aspiring; eluding grasp or comprehension 1643.

Winish (wəi·niʃ), *a.* Now *rare.* 1540. [f. WINE *sb.* + -ISH [1].] Having the quality or nature of wine; resembling wine.

Wink (wiŋk), *sb.* ME. [f. WINK *v.*] 1. A closing of the eyes for sleep; a (short) spell of sleep, a nap. *rare* exc. in phr. (*not*) *a w.* (*of sleep*). 2. A glance or significant movement of the eye (often accompanied by a nod) expressing command, assent, invitation, or the like. *Obs.* exc. in prov. *A nod's as good as a w. to a blind horse,* and phr. *to tip, give,* or *get the w.* 1500. 3. *transf.* a. A moment of time, as being that occupied by a glance of the eyes 1585. b. (*Not*) *a w.*: (not) the slightest amount 1596. 4. A nictitation of the eyelid; a blink 1611. 5. An act of winking (see WINK *v.* 6) 1837.

1. *Temp.* II. i. 285. I will go to-bed; but not one W., I fear, shall I get this Night RICHARDSON. *Forty winks* (colloq.) a brief sleep, a short nap. 2. He gave me the w. that the lady was a friend of his 1872. 3. a. *In a w.*, in a trice. b. Ambition cannot pierce a winke beyond SHAKS. 5. A knowing w. or a sarcastic smile 1891.

Wink (wiŋk), *v.* [OE. *wincian,* f. Teut. **wink-* :—Indo-Eur. **weng-* to move, turn (cf. WINCH *v.*[1]).] †1. *intr.* To close one's eyes -1816. b. Said of the eyes: To close. *Obs.* or *rare arch.* ME. 2. To open and shut one's eyes momentarily and involuntarily; to blink, nictitate ME. b. Said of the eyes or eyelids: To blink. Now *rare.* 1661. c. Of a light, etc.: To emit quick intermittent flashes; to twinkle. (Now assoc. with sense 6.) 1591. †3. To have the eyes closed in sleep; to sleep. late ME. 4. To 'shut one's eyes' to something faulty, wrong, or improper; to be complaisant. (Now *rare* exc. with *at.*) 1480. †5. To give a significant glance, as of command, direction, or invitation -1835. †b. *trans.* To bring into a specified state by a glance or nod -1728. 6. *intr.* To close one eye momentarily, in a flippant or frivolous manner, esp. to convey intimate information or to express good-humoured interest 1837. 7. *trans.* To close (an eye, the eyes) for a moment 1838. b. *To w. away*: to remove (tears) by blinking one's eyes 1876. c. To give (a signal), express (a message), etc. by means of flashlights 1918.

1. *Cymb.* v. iv. 194. 2. c. A beaker..With beaded bubbles winking at the brim KEATS. 3. *Temp.* II. i. 216. 4. W. at: a. To 'shut one's eyes to' (an offence, fault, impropriety or irregularity), to connive at. b. To disregard, overlook, pass unnoticed (now *rare* or *Obs.*). c. To be complaisant with (an offending or contumacious person); to connive at the doings of. 5. Davis winked to his friends that it was all right 1819. Winking at me not to take any notice 1821. Hence **Wi·nker,** one who winks (*rare*); *pl.* applied to the eyes or eyelashes (now *dial.* or *slang*); *pl.* = BLINKER 2 b. **Wi·nking** *ppl. a.* that winks; -ly *adv.*

Winking (wi·ŋkiŋ), *vbl. sb.* ME. [f. prec. + -ING [1].] The action of WINK *v.*

Like w., in a flash, in a twinkling; very rapidly or suddenly. So, *as easy as w.*

Winkle (wi·ŋk'l). 1585. Shortened from PERIWINKLE [2].

A typical family..lives..on a nutriment of winkles and gin 1899. Hence **Wi·nkler,** one who gathers winkles. **Wi·nkling** *gerund* and *vbl. sb.*

Winnable (wi·năb'l), *a.* 1544. [f. WIN *v.* + -ABLE.] Capable of being won, in various senses.

Winner (wi·nəɹ). ME. [f. WIN *v.* + -ER [1].] One who or that which wins, in various senses; *spec.* a horse, dog, etc. that wins a race; a winning shot; in recent slang, a thing that scores a success.

I'd ridden seven great winners before I was eighteen 1859.

Winning (wi·niŋ), *vbl. sb.* ME. [f. WIN *v.* + -ING [1].] The action of WIN *v.*; *concr.* something won. 1. Conquest, capture, taking (of a place). 2. The action of gaining, getting, or obtaining; acquisition ME. 3. *concr.* That which is won; a thing or amount obtained or gained; gain, profit. Now *rare* or *Obs.* exc. as in 4. ME. 4. *pl.* Things or sums gained, gains, profits; earnings (*obs.* or *dial.*); in mod. use chiefly applied to money won by gaming or betting. late ME. 5. *spec.* Getting, gathering, taking (of produce, coal, stone, etc.) 1473. 6. Gaining of a person's affection or allegiance; also with *over.* late ME.

attrib.: **w.-gallery** *Tennis,* the last gallery on the hazard-side of a tennis-court; **-post,** a post set up at the goal of a race-course, the racer who first passes it being the winner.

Wi·nning, *ppl. a.* 1592. [f. WIN *v.* + -ING [2].] That wins. 1. Gaining or resulting in victory or superiority in a contest or competition; victorious. 2. Persuasive (now *rare* or *obs.*); alluring, attractive, 'taking' 1596.

1. *W. hazard*: see HAZARD *sb.* 6 b. *W. stroke,* a stroke that gains a point in a game, or one by which the game is won. 2. The W. Air, the Bewitching Glance, the Amorous Smirk 1700. Hence **Wi·nning-ly** *adv.*, **-ness.**

Winnow (wi·nǫᵘ), *v.* [OE. *windwian,* f. *wind* WIND *sb.*[1] The form *window* survives dial.] 1. *trans.* To expose (grain or other substances) to the wind or to a current of air so that the lighter particles (as chaff or other refuse matter) are separated or blown away; to clear of refuse material by this method. Also *absol.* or *intr.* b. *fig.* To subject to a process likened to the winnowing of grain, in order to separate the various parts or elements, esp. the good from the bad; hence, to clear of worthless or inferior elements. late ME. 2. a. To separate or drive off (lighter or refuse particles) by the process described in 1; also *fig.* OE. b. To separate (the valuable part *from* the worthless); now esp. with *out,* to extract, select, or obtain (something desirable) by such separation 1611. c. To waft, diffuse. *poet.* 1764. 3. *transf.* a. To beat (the air) with or as with wings; to flap (the wings), to wave (the fins); also *intr.* 1579. b. Of the air, etc.: *trans.* To fan with a breeze. *intr.* To blow fitfully or in gusts. 1796.

2. a. Do but w. their chaffe from their wheat, ye shall see their great heape shrink MILT. 3. a. He.. with quick Fann Winnows the buxom Air MILT. b. Falling snows that w. by CLARE. Hence **Wi·nnow** *sb.* a contrivance for winnowing grain; an act of winnowing or a motion resembling it. **Wi·nnower,** one who winnows; an apparatus for winnowing, a winnowing-machine. **Wi·nnowing** *vbl. sb.* also in combs., esp. in names of appliances for winnowing, as *winnowing-fan, -machine, -sheet.*

Winsome (wi·nsŏm), *a.* [OE. *wynsum,* f. *wyn(n* WIN *sb.*[2] + *-sum* -SOME [1].] †1. Pleasant, delightful, agreeable -ME. 2. [In the mod. lit. lang. from north. dial.] Pleasing or attractive in appearance, handsome, comely; of attractive nature or disposition, of winning character or manners 1677. Hence **Wi·nsome·ly** *adv.*, **-ness.**

Winter (wi·ntəɹ), *sb.*[1] [OE. *winter* :— OTeut. **wentrus,* prob. f. nasalized form of the Indo-Eur. base **wed-, wod-, ud-* to be wet, found in WET *a.*, WATER, OTTER.] 1. The fourth and coldest season of the year, coming between autumn and spring; reckoned astronomically from the winter solstice to the vernal equinox, i. e. in the northern hemisphere from the 22nd of December to the 20th of March; pop. comprising the months of December, January, and February; also often in contradistinction to *summer,* the colder half of the year. b. With ref. to the chilling or injurious effect of winter, esp. on plants; *transf.* a period resembling winter, wintry or cold weather OE. c. *fig.* and *allus.*, esp. in ref. to old age, or to a time or state of affliction or distress 1590. 2. Put for 'year': nearly always *pl.* with a numeral; often in expressions referring to a person's age; now *poet.* or *rhet.*, chiefly in ref. to advanced age or to a protracted period of hardship or misfortune OE. 3. *attrib.* passing into *adj.* a. = Of, pertaining to, or characteristic of winter; adapted or appropriate to, used or occupied in, winter; existing, appearing, flourishing, or performed in winter OE. b. The possessive *winter's* is similarly used, chiefly with *day, night, morning, evening* OE. c. Applied to autumn-sown crops that stand through the winter; also to fruits that ripen late, or keep well until or during winter; *spec.* in names of late-ripening apples, pears, etc. late ME. d. *fig.*; †occas. = Old, aged 1593.

1. God bless us in the spring, after this green w. LAUD. Store of fire-wood for the w. DICKENS. c. Now is the W. of our Discontent, Made glorious Summer by this Son of Yorke SHAKS. 2. I knew a man Of eightie winters 1612. 3. a. W.-flies, all Anglers know,..are as useful as an Almanack out of date WALTON. Black Velvet Scarfs..are a handsome W.-wear GAY. The w.-sleep..of hibernating animals 1836. d. The tasteless, dry embrace Of a stale virgin with a w. face POPE.

Comb.: **w. bud** *Zool.*, a statoblast (formed at the approach of, or quiescent during, w.); **-fallow** *sb.* a lying fallow, or land that lies fallow, during the w.; *v. trans.* to lay (land) fallow during the w.; **-feed** *v. trans.* to feed or maintain (animals, etc.) during w.; **w. garden,** (*a*) a garden of plants that flourish in w., as evergreens; (*b*) a greenhouse or conservatory in which plants are kept flourishing in w.; **-long** *a.* as tediously long as w.; *adv.* through a whole w.; **w. ova,** eggs produced by certain invertebrates at the approach of w.; **-pride,** the condition of being w.-proud; **-proud** *a.* (of wheat or other crops) too luxuriant in w.; **w. quarters,** (*a*) the place occupied by troops, or by members of an expedition, during the w. (between two campaigns or periods of activity or travel); (*b*) the place in which certain animals find shelter during the w.; **-rot,** a disease incident to sheep in the w.; **w. solstice,** the time at which the sun reaches the w. tropic, i. e. in the northern hemisphere the tropic of Capricorn, in the southern the tropic of Cancer; the middle of the w. half of the year; **-tide** (*arch.*) = *w.-time*; **-time,** the season of w. b. In names of animals and plants that are active or flourish in w. or in the w. half of the year, or of late-ripening fruits: **w. berry,** any of several N. Amer. species of holly with berries, usu. scarlet, which persist through the w., esp. *Ilex verticillata* and *I. lævigata*; **-bloom,** (*a*) a late-flowering species of *Azalea*; (*b*) the Amer. witch-hazel, *Hamamelis virginica,* which blossoms late in autumn and ripens its fruit the following day; **-bunting,** the snow bunting; **w. corn,** corn sown in w., or in autumn and remaining in the ground through the w.; **-cress,** any of the cruciferous herbs of the genus *Barbarea,* the leaves of which were formerly used as a w. salad; **w. grape,** an Amer. species of grape-vine, *Vitis cordifolia*; **w. queening,** a late-ripening variety of apple, which keeps well through the w.; **w. rocket,** the common w.-cress, *Barbarea vulgaris*; **w. snipe,** the purple sandpiper or rock-snipe, *Tringa striata* or *maritima*; **w. strawberry** = ARBUTUS. Hence **Wi·nterish** *a.* (somewhat) winterly or wintry. **Wi·nterless** *a.* having no w.; free from or not experiencing w. **Wi·nterling,** a yearling 1825.

Wi·nter, *sb.*[2] 1683. [Origin obsc.] In a hand-printing press, a block of wood about nine inches broad by nine deep, supporting the carriage and having a tenon at each end to fit into corresponding mortices in the cheeks.

Wi·nter, *v.* late ME. [f. WINTER *sb.*[1] after L. *hiemare, hibernare.*] 1. *intr.* To pass or spend the winter; to stay or reside (at a specific place) during the winter; (of animals) to find or be provided with food and shelter in the winter. 2. *trans.* To keep or maintain during winter; *esp.* to provide (animals) with food and shelter in winter 1440. 3. To affect like winter, subject to wintry conditions; to chill, freeze. Chiefly *fig.* 1622. Hence **Wi·nterer,** one who spends the winter in a specified place; *spec.* a servant of the Hudson's Bay Company who was employed in the far interior of N. America 1801.

Winterbourne (wi·ntəɹbōᵊɹn). [OE. *winterburna,* f. WINTER *sb.*[1] + *burna* BURN *sb.*[1]] An intermittent stream, such as those found in chalk and limestone districts, which flows only in winter or at long intervals.

Winter cherry. 1548. 1. Any of several plants of the nightshade family (*Solanaceæ*) with cherry-like fruit which is ripe in winter; also, the fruit itself. a. = ALKEKENGI; also applied to other species of *Physalis,* as the Cape Goooseberry, *P. edulis.* b. Applied to species of *Solanum* with cherry-like fruit, as *S. Pseudo-capsicum,* also called Jerusalem Cherry 1629. 2. Applied to species of *Cardiospermum* (family *Sapindaceæ*), having fruit enclosed in an inflated calyx like that of *Physalis*; esp. *C. Halicacabum*, also called Balloon Vine 1597.

Winter day. [OE. *winterdæg*.] A day in winter. (More commonly **winter's day**.)

Wintered (wi·ntəɹd), *a.* [OE. *gewintred*, f. *ge-* Y- + *winter* WINTER *sb.*[1] + *-ed* -ED.] †1. Having lived through or experienced many winters or years; aged; veteran –1599. 2. Exposed to the influence of winter; subjected to wintry conditions; chilled or blasted by winter ME. †3. Adapted for or used in winter. SHAKS.

1. W. souldiers vs'd to conquering KYD. 3. *A.Y.L.* III. ii. 111.

Wintergreen (wi·ntəɹ,grīn). 1548. [After Du. *wintergroen*, G. *wintergrün*.] 1. Name for various plants of low growth or creeping habit whose leaves remain green in winter. a. Any plant of the genus *Pyrola*, esp. *P. minor*, a woodland plant with roundish drooping white flowers. Also applied to plants of the allied genus *Chimaphila*, as *C. maculata* (Spotted W.). b. The N. Amer. plant *Gaultheria procumbens* (Aromatic, Creeping, or Spring W.), bearing drooping white flowers and edible scarlet berries 1778. c. **Chickweed W.**, either species of *Trientalis* (*T. europæa* or *americana*), woodland plants of high latitudes or altitudes 1760. d. **Flowering W.**, the Fringed Milkwort of N. America, *Polygala paucifolia* 1856. 2. Usu. *pl.* (with hyphen, or as two words). An evergreen. *rare* or *Obs.* 1681. 3. (With hyphen, or as two words.) Green vegetables for winter use 1846.

1. b. *Oil of w.*, *w. oil*, a heavy volatile oil obtained from the leaves of *Gaultheria procumbens*, used as an aromatic stimulant, and for flavouring confectionery, etc.

Wi·nter-house. [OE. *winterhūs*.] A house for winter occupation.

Winterly (wi·ntəɹli), *a.* [OE. *winterlic*, f. WINTER *sb.*[1] + -LY[1]; in mod. use a new formation.] 1. Of, belonging to, or occurring in winter. 2. Having the character of or characteristic of winter; wintry 1611.

2. *fig.* *Cymb.* III. iv. 13.

Winter's bark. 1622. [= mod.L. *cortex Winteranus*, named from its discoverer, Captain William *Winter*, who accompanied Francis Drake to the Magellan Straits in 1578.] a. The pungent aromatic bark of *Drimys winteri*, used as a stimulant tonic and antiscorbutic; also called **Winter's cinnamon.** b. Extended to other medicinal barks, as that of the W. Indian whitewood or wild cinnamon, *Canella alba*. c. Any of the trees themselves.

Wintry (wi·ntri), *a.* [OE. *wintrig*, f. WINTER *sb.*[1] + -Y[1]; in mod. use a new formation.] 1. Of or pertaining to winter; occurring, existing, or found in winter; adapted or suitable for winter. Now *rare* or merged in 2. 2. Having the quality of winter; of such a kind as occurs in winter; characteristic of winter 1590. 3. Exposed or subject to the effect or influence of winter; chilled or blasted by winter 1697. 4. *fig.* esp. (*a*) Aged, infirm or withered from age; (*b*) devoid of fervour or affection, 'cold'; (*c*) destitute of warmth or brightness, dreary 1633.

1. The w. Misleto DRYDEN. 3. The w. top of giant Lebanon HEBER. 4. (b) A somewhat w. welcome 1895. Hence **Wi·ntri-ly** *adv.*, **-ness.**

Winy, winey (wəi·ni), *a.* late ME. [f. WINE *sb.* + -Y[1].] 1. Of, belonging to, or characteristic of wine; having the nature or properties of wine; *occas.* producing wine; vinous. 2. a. Accompanied by the drinking of wine (*rare*) 1586. b. Affected by or due to (excessive) consumption of wine 1594.

1. Ful of a redde wynie sappe or iuyce 1578. 2. b. If their w. wits must needs be working NASHE.

Winze (winz). 1757. [perh. derived from WIND *sb.*[2]] *Mining.* A shaft or an inclined passage sunk from one level to another, but not rising to the surface.

Wipe (wəip), *sb.* 1550. [f. next.] 1. An act of wiping 1642. 2. A slashing blow; a sweeping cut; a swipe 1550. †b. *transf.* A mark as of a blow or lash; a scar. SHAKS. 3. *fig.* A cutting remark; a sarcastic reproof or rebuff; a jeer 1596. 4. *slang.* A handkerchief 1789. 5. = WIPER 4. 1884.

1. A brush to give the gemman a w. down 1822. 2. The cove used to fetch me a w. over the knuckles with his stick 1851. 4. Three boys brought in for prigging of wipes 1800.

Wipe (wəip), *v.* [OE. *wīpian*, ult. f. base *wib-, as in L. *vibrare* to brandish, shake.] 1. *trans.* To rub (something) gently with a soft cloth or the like, or *on* something, so as to clear its surface of dust, dirt, moisture, etc.; to clean or dry in this way. 2. To remove or clear away (moisture, dust, etc.) from something by the action described in 1. OE. 3. To apply or spread a soft or liquid substance over the surface of a body by rubbing it on with a cloth, pad, or the like (with the substance or the body as obj.); *spec.* in *Plumbing*, to apply solder by this method so as to unite and finish off a joint 1799. †4. *fig.* To deprive, rob, defraud, do out of some possession or advantage –1746. 5. To clear away, remove: usu. with adv. (*away*, *off*, *out*). a. To remove the guilt, blame, or dishonour of; to clear a person, or oneself, of (a charge or imputation). late ME. b. To destroy the trace of, obliterate; to destroy the effect or value of, bring to naught 1564. c. To do away with, put an end to, annihilate. Now always with *out*. 1538. d. *spec.* To put all to death, destroy completely (a body of persons); usu. with *out*. 1577. e. With *off*, †*out*: To cancel (an account or score); to discharge, pay off (a debt) 1667. 6. To strike, beat, or attack with blows, or with mockery, rebuke, or the like. Now *dial.* or *slang.* 1523. 7. *intr.* for *pass.* To be rubbed *away*, removed, obliterated, etc. ME.

1. Wiping his lips, after having finished his draught SCOTT. Stopping on the mat to w. his shoes all round DICKENS. *fig.* I..wyll wype out Ierusalem, euen as one wypeth a platter COVERDALE 2 *Kings* xxi. 13. 5. b. *Wint. T.* IV. ii. 11. The anxiety wiped away from his face as if by magic 1898. d. A tragedy which wiped out an entire crew 1898.

Phrases. *To w. a person's eye* (slang or colloq.): (*a*) to get the better of, 'score off'; (*b*) to 'give a black eye to'. *To w. one's boots on*, to inflict the utmost indignity upon. *To w. the floor with*, to 'bring to the ground' utterly, inflict a crushing defeat on.

Wiper (wəi·pəɹ). 1552. [f. prec. + -ER[1].] 1. A person who wipes; *spec.* in various industries, a workman employed in wiping something clean or dry. 2. A cloth or other appliance used for wiping; *slang*, a handkerchief (cf. WIPE *sb.* 4) 1587. b. See *screen-w.* s.v. SCREEN *sb.* 3. One who or that which strikes or assails. *slang.* 1611. 4. In machinery, a projecting piece fixed on a rotating or oscillating part, as an axle or wheel, and periodically communicating movement by a rubbing action to some other part; a cam, eccentric, or tappet 1796.

Wiping (wəi·piŋ), *vbl. sb.* late ME. [f. as prec. + -ING[1].] The action of WIPE *v.*

Comb.: **w.-rod, -stick,** a rod fitted with a piece of cloth or tow for cleaning out the bore of a gun.

Wire (wəi³ɹ), *sb.* [OE. *wīr*; referred to the base *wi- of L. *viere* to plait, weave.] I. Metal wrought into the form of a slender rod or thread, formerly by hammering, now by the operation of wire-drawing. b. used as fencing; esp. *barbed* (earlier *barb*) *w.*: A fencing wire composed of two or more strands twisted together, with barbs or short spikes fastened a few inches apart in the strands; also, the fencing or defence so constructed 1876.

Gold wir ME. Shakt his long lockes, colourd like copper-w. SPENSER. b. I was in hopes that a country like the Bicester..would be free of such an enemy as w. 1876.

II. *1. A piece, length, or line of wire used for various purposes OE. b. *spec.* One of the fine platinum cross-wires fixed horizontally and vertically at the focus of a telescope 1774. c. connecting a bell with the bell-pull or -push 1837. 2. A line of wire used as a conductor of electric current 1747. b. *spec.* The line of wire connecting the transmitting and receiving instruments of a telegraph or telephone; *transf.* the telegraphic system (e.g. *by w.*). Also (*colloq.*) a telegraphic message, a telegram. 1854. **Senses used mainly in pl. or collect. sing. 3. Metallic strings (of a musical instrument). late ME. 4. Metallic bars (of a cage) 1656. 5. *Croquet.* The iron hoops or arches through which the balls are driven. Now *rare.* 1868. 6. The metallic lines by which puppets are worked 1607.

2. *Live w.*, a w. charged with electricity; *fig.* (*colloq.*) an energetic or vigorously active person. 3. Apollo sings To th' touch of golden wires MILT. 6. Phr. *To pull* (*the*) *wires* (cf. WIRE-PULLER); A demagogue..may..pull the wires of a President whom he has put into the chair 1888. *To be on wires* (fig.), to be in a state of nervous excitement or jumpiness.

III. Network or framework of wire. a. Wire-work; now usu., wire netting 1547. †b. A frame of wire (*a*) to support the hair, (*b*) to support the ruff. –1690. c. *Paper-making.* Woven brass wire-cloth 1700. d. A snare for hares or rabbits 1749.

a. In the middle of this garden was a cupola made of wyre, supported by slender pillars of brick EVELYN.

IV. 1. Something resembling wire or a wire; e.g. a long thin plant-stem, as a strawberry runner; a cylindrical piece of native silver 1601. 2. *pl.* Applied to hairs, or rays, as resembling shining wires (*poet.* and *rhet.*). Now *rare.* 1589. 3. *slang.* A pickpocket (from the practice of extracting handkerchiefs from pockets with a piece of wire) 1851. 4. Short for: a. Wire rope or cable 1882. b. Wire-haired fox terrier 1892.

Comb.: **w. bar,** a bar of copper cast into a suitable form for drawing into w.; **w. bridge,** (*a*) a suspension bridge supported by wires; (*b*) a kind of electric bridge furnished with a w. and a graduated scale; **-cutter,** nippers or pliers for cutting w.; also, a man employed to cut w., e.g. in war operations; **w. edge,** the turned-over strips of metal produced on the edge of a cutting tool by faulty grinding or honing; **w. entanglement** *Mil.*, an abatis of (barbed) w. stretched over the ground in order to impede the advance of an enemy; **-glass,** sheet glass in which w. netting is embedded; **-hair,** a wire-haired terrier; **-haired,** *a.* having a rough coat of a hard and wiry texture, esp. designating a kind of fox-terrier as dist. from the smooth-haired variety; **-mark** *Paper-making*; (*a*) *pl.*, the faint lines made by the impression of the wires of the mould in the substance of laid paper; (*b*) = WATER-MARK 4; **w. saw,** a kind of saw of which the cutting-part is made of w.; **w. silver,** native silver found in w.-shaped pieces; **-walker,** an acrobat who performs feats on a w. rope.

Wire (wəi³ɹ), *v.* ME. [f. prec.] †1. *trans.* To adorn with (gold) wire. ME. only. 2. To fasten, join, or fit with a wire or wires; *spec.* to secure (the cork of a bottle, the bottle itself) with wire. late ME. b. To furnish with a wire support; to stiffen with wire 1834. c. To fence with wire: chiefly *to w. in*, to enclose with a wire fence 1691. d. To strengthen or protect with (barbed) wire 1881. e. To furnish with electric wires 1892. 3. To catch or trap in a wire snare 1749. 4. *Croquet.* To place (one's own or an opponent's ball) so that a hoop intervenes between it and its object; also with the player as obj. Chiefly *pass.* 1866. 5. To send (a message) 'over the wires', to telegraph; also *absol.* or *intr.*; *transf.* to send a telegraph message to. *colloq.* 1859. 6. intr. *To w. in*, to get to work with a will, to apply oneself energetically to something; *to w. into* (a meal, etc.), to set about it with avidity. *colloq.* or *slang.* 1865.

4. Red..has wired the player for all the balls 1874. 5. I am going to w. my broker fellow to buy a couple of thousand Bs and Cs 1876.

Wired (wəi³ɹd), *ppl. a.* late ME. [f. WIRE *sb.* or *v.* + -ED.] 1. Supported, strengthened, or stiffened with wire. 2. Furnished with or consisting of a wire fence or netting for confinement or protection 1748. 3. Fastened or secured with wire 1798.

1. A lovely bouquet..—not a nasty w. affair, but just a lot of loose flowers 1885. 3. *W. on*, designating a kind of tyre which is secured to the wheel-rim by means of wire.

Wire-draw (wəi³·ɹ,drǭ), *v.* Now *rare.* 1598. [Back-formation from next.] 1. *trans.* To draw out (metal) into wire 1666. 2. *transf.* To draw out (a material thing) to an elongated form; to stretch, elongate 1598. b. To cause (steam or water) to pass through a small aperture, thereby diminishing its pressure 1744. 3. *fig.* a. To protract excessively, spin out 1598. b. To draw out to an extreme tenuity; to reduce to a subtle fineness 1660. c. To strain, force, or wrest by subtle argument or the like 1610. †d. To draw, get, induce, extract, etc. by some subtle device –1748.

3. c. Do not wrest, and wiredraw, and colour my words WESLEY.

Wire-drawer (wəi³·ɹ,drǭ:əɹ). ME. [f. WIRE *sb.* + DRAWER.] One who draws metal into wire; one who practises or is skilled in wire-drawing. So **Wi·re-dra:wing** *vbl. sb.*

Wire-drawn (wəi³·ɹ,drǭn), *ppl. a.* 1603. [pa. pple. of WIRE-DRAW *v.*] 1. Drawn out to a great length or with subtle ingenuity; fine-spun. 2. Of steam, water: see WIRE-DRAW *v.* 2 b, 1744. 3. *nonce-uses.* Attenuated; 'weak'; 'thin' 1856.

1. The..w. distinctions..of the Schoolmen BERKELEY.

Wi·re-grass. 1793. [f. WIRE *sb.* + GRASS *sb.*] A name for various grasses or grass-like plants having wiry stems. 1. *U.S.* The British flat-stemmed meadow-grass, *Poa compressa*, or the annual grass *Elusine indica*, naturalized in N. America. 2. One of several other plants, as the West Indian *Paspale filiforme*, the Australian *Tetrarrhena juncea*, the N. Amer. *Sporobolus junceus* and species of *Aristida* 1824.

Wireless (wəiᵊ·ɹ,lės), *a.* (*sb*). 1894. [f. WIRE *sb.* + -LESS.] Without a wire or wires; spec. *Electr.* dispensing with the use of a conducting wire. b. as *sb.* Short for *w. telegraphy, telephony, message, apparatus, receiver* 1904.

W. telegraphy, a system of telegraphy in which no conducting wire is used between the transmitting and receiving stations, the signals or messages being transmitted through space by means of electric waves; so *w. telegraph, telephone, telephony.* Hence **Wi·reless** *v. intr.* to send a message by w.; *trans.* to send (a message) or inform (a person) by w. 1899.

Wire-puller (wəiᵊ·ɹ,pu:ləɹ). orig. *U.S.* 1848. [See WIRE *sb.* II. 6 and PULL *v.* II. 3.] One who 'pulls the wires'; one who works secretly to further the interests of a person or party; *esp.* a politician or political agent who privately influences and directs others. Hence **Wi·re-pull** *v. trans.* to actuate or promote by wire-pulling. **Wi·re-pu:lling** *vbl. sb.* and *ppl. a.*

Wirework (wəiᵊ·ɹwɒ̄ɹk). 1587. 1. The making of wire; work done in or with wire; fabrics or objects made of wire. 2. *pl.* An establishment where wire is made or where wire goods are manufactured 1598.

Wire-worker (wəiᵊ·ɹwɒ̄:ɹkəɹ). 1670. 1. An artisan who works in wire. 2. One who pulls the wires of a puppet-show 1843. 3. *U.S.* = WIRE-PULLER 1835.

Wireworm (wəiᵊ·ɹwɒ̄ɹm). 1790. 1. The slender hard-skinned larva of any of the click-beetles (family *Elateridæ*), which is destructive to the roots of plants; also applied to similar larvæ, *esp.* the leather-jacket grub of the crane-fly. 2. A myriapod, esp. one belonging to the genus *Iulus*; a millepede 1875.

Wi·re-wove, *ppl. a.* 1799. [f. WIRE *sb.* + *wove*, pa. pple. of WEAVE *v.*] 1. Denoting a very fine kind of paper used chiefly for letter-paper. 2. Made of woven wire 1888.

Wirra (wi·rə), *int. Irish.* 1839. [Preceded by *oh*, = Ir. *a muire.*] An exclam. of sorrow or lament.

Wiry (wəiᵊ·ri), *a.* 1588. [f. WIRE *sb.* + -Y[1].] 1. Made or consisting of wire; in the form of wire. 2. Resembling wire in form and consistence: said esp. of hair (hence of a dog's coat), grass, stems of plants 1595. b. *Med.* Of the pulse: Small and tense 1801. 3. Of sound: Produced by or as by the plucking or vibration of a wire; (of a voice) thin and metallic 1819. 4. Of a person or animal: Lean, tough, and sinewy. Hence *fig.* of personal attributes. 1808.

1. Her yeolow locks, like wyrie golde, About her shoulders careleslie downe trailing SPENSER. 4. Mrs. Blimber..was a lady of great suavity, and a w. figure DICKENS.

†**Wis,** *v.*[1] [OE. *wissian*, f. *wis* certain (cf. IWIS *adv.*).] *trans.* To make (a thing) known; to direct, guide, instruct (a person) -1550.

Wis (wis), *v.*[2] *pseudo-arch.* 1606. orig. in *I wis* for IWIS *adv.*, erron. taken as = 'I know'; hence occas. as a synonym of 'know' in other parts of the verb, being apprehended as the present of *wist*, pa. t. of WIT *v.*[1]

Where my morning haunts are he wisses not MILT.

Wisdom (wi·zdəm). [Com. Teut. (not in Gothic): OE. *wīsdōm*; see WISE *a.* and -DOM.] The quality or character of being wise, or something in which this is exhibited. 1. Capacity of judging rightly in matters relating to life and conduct; soundness of judgement in the choice of means and ends; sometimes, less strictly, sound sense, esp. in practical affairs: opp. to *folly*. b. as one of the manifestations of the divine nature in Jesus Christ; hence used as a title of the Second Person of the Trinity (*the W. of the Father*); also occas. applied to God or the Trinity OE. c. Contextually, usu. predic. with following inf.: = a wise thing to do; also with *a* and *pl.*, a wise action or proceeding. *arch.* late ME. d. *pl.* as attribute of a number of persons: hence, with possessive, as a title of dignity or respect, esp. for the members of a deliberative assembly; also, less commonly, in *sing.* of a single person. Now *joc.* late ME. 2. Knowledge (esp. of a high or abstruse kind); learning, erudition, in early use often = philosophy, science. Now only *Hist.* OE. 3. Wise discourse or teaching; with *a* and *pl.*, a wise saying or precept. Now *rare* or *arch.* ME. b. In the titles of two books of the Apocrypha, viz. *The W. of Solomon* (often abbrev. *W.* or *The Book of W.*), and *The W. of Jesus the son of Sirach* (commonly called *Ecclesiasticus*). late ME. †4. Sanity, 'reason'. SHAKS.

1. The feare of the Lorde is the begynnynge of wysdome COVERDALE *Prov.* ix. 10. c. Till then, 'tis wisdome to conceale our meaning SHAKS. d. Even folly ..freely on your Wisdom cracks her jokes WOLCOT. 2. Moses was learned in all manner off w. of the Egipcians TINDALE *Acts* vii. 22. 4. *Meas. for M.* IV. iv. 5.

Wisdom tooth. 1848. [Usu. pl.; orig. *teeth of wisdom*, rendering L. *dentes sapientiæ* = Arab. *adrāsu 'lḥikmi*, after Gr. σωφρονιστῆρες; so called as not appearing till the attainment of years of discretion.] The hindmost molar tooth on each side of both upper and lower jaws in man, usu. 'cut' about the age of twenty. Often in phr. *to cut one's wisdom teeth*, to attain to wisdom or discretion.

Wise (wəiz), *sb.*[1] *arch.* [OE. *wīse* :— OTeut. **wīsōn-*, **wīsō*, f. **wit-* WIT *v.*[1]; for the sense cf. Gr. εἶδος shape, kind, state of things, course of action.] †I. Manner, mode, fashion, style; *spec.* habitual manner of action, habit, custom -1572. II. OE. *wīse* was used in various kinds of advb. expressions meaning 'in such-and-such a manner, way, or respect', in which it was qualified by an adj. or a sb. with or without a governing prep. Several of these, with similarly-formed later ones, have survived as simple words, e.g. *crosswise, likewise, nowise, otherwise.* The free use of *wise* in such expressions, apart from the established simple words, is now only arch. (Cf. -WAYS.) 1. a. With demonstr., interrog., or indef. adj. in an oblique case, e.g. OE. *ōðre wīsan* OTHERWISE. b. With general adjs., forming an equiv. of -LY[2], e.g. †*humble wise.* 2. a. With prep. (orig. *on*, later *in*), and demonstr., interrog., or indef. adj., as *on nāne wīsan* NOWISE. b. With general adjs., e.g. *in like wise* (see LIKEWISE), *in gentle wise.* 3. With prep. and sb. in comb. with *wise*, e.g. OE. *on scipwīsan* like a ship, ME. *on crosse wyse* (see CROSSWISE), *in maiden wise.* b. without prep., e.g. *festoon-wise.*

The nyghtes longe Encressen double wise the peynes stronge CHAUCER. I will..that ye be wel bisene in the richest wyse MALORY. Are we better then they? No in no wyse TINDALE *Rom.* iii. 9. Humble w. To thee my sighes in verse I sacrifise 1592. Let them tie upon a stick, posie w., a little piece of sponge 1631. Whilst things stand this w. with me 1649. The Houses, that can no w. afford above one Garden EVELYN. Geraldine, in maiden w.,..turned her from Sir Leoline COLERIDGE. Timothy or Titus-wise 1876.

Wise (wəiz), *a.* (*sb.*[2], *adv.*) [OE. *wīs* :— OTeut. **wīsoz* :—pre-Teut. **wīttos*, f. Indo-Eur. **weid-* (see WIT *v.*[1]) + ppl. suffix *-to-*. The pronunc. with (z) comes from the obl. forms.] 1. Having or exercising sound judgement or discernment; having the ability to perceive and adopt the best means for accomplishing an end; characterized by good sense and prudence: opp. to *foolish.* b. Of action, speech, personal attributes, etc.: Proceeding from, indicating, or suggesting sound judgement or good sense; sage OE. 2. †Skilled, expert; *spec.* skilled in magic or hidden arts. Now only *dial.* OE. 3. Having knowledge; well-informed; learned. *Obs.* exc. as in b. OE. b. Informed or aware *of* something specified or implied. Now only in such phrases as *none the wiser, as w. as before* = knowing no more than before (i.e., usu., nothing) about the matter. ME. (*b*) U.S. colloq. *To be* (or *get*) *w. to*, to be (or become) aware of; *to put* (a person) *w.* (*to*), to inform (of), enlighten (concerning) 1901. 4. In one's right mind, sane. Now *Sc.* and *dial.* ME. 5. *absol.* or as *sb. pl.* Wise men or persons: now always with *the* OE. b. The compar. *wiser* as sb. (with pl. *wisers*): One who is wiser; usu. with possessive, (one's) superior in wisdom. Now *rare.* ME. 6. Used as *adv.* = WISELY. In later use only in compar. *rare.* late ME.

1. Fyve of them were folysshe, and fyve were wyse TINDALE *Matt.* xxv. 2. W. to frustrate all our plots and wiles MILT. The w. Ant her wintry Store provides DRYDEN. *Prov. phr.* It is a w. Father that knowes his owne childe SHAKS. The proverb of being w. behind the time 1717. b. Full of w. sawes, and moderne instances SHAKS. By a w. dispensation of Providence MACAULAY. 3. Where ignorance is bliss, 'Tis folly to be w. GRAY. 4. *Oth.* IV. i. 245. 5. *A word to the w.* (*is enough*): = VERBUM SAP. b. Of þi wysers lern bettyr gouernaunce 1447. 6. Thou speakst wiser then thou art ware of SHAKS. Hence **Wi·se-ly** *adv.* [OE. *wīslīce*] with wisdom, sagacity, or good sense; †carefully; †skilfully; **-ness** (*rare*).

Wise (wəiz), *v.*[1] *Obs.* exc. *Sc.* and *n. dial.* [OE. *wīsian*, f. OTeut. **wīsoz* WISE *a.* Cf. WIS *v.*[1]] 1. *trans.* To show the way to (a person); to guide, direct. 2. To direct the course or movement of; to move in some direction or into some position; to convey, conduct ME. 3. To show, point out (the way). late ME.

Wise (wəiz), *v.*[2] 1919. [f. WISE *a.* 3 b (*b*).] *To w. up* (U.S. slang) *trans.* and *intr.*: to 'get wise'; to 'put wise'.

Wiseacre (wəi·zē̆ɪ:kəɹ). 1595. [ad. Du. *wijsseggher* (wai·sze:gər) soothsayer, app. ad. OHG. *wīzago* (= OE. *wītega*), assim. to *wijs* WISE *a.* and *seggher* SAYER.] 1. One who thinks himself or wishes to be thought wise; a foolish person with an air of wisdom. 2. A wise or learned person. (Usu. *contempt.*) 1753.

Wisecrack. *U.S. slang.* 1924. A smart sententious saying; a clever witticism. So **Wi·se-crack** *v. intr.*, **-cracker, -cracking** *vbl. sb.*

Wisehead (wəi·zhed). 1756. [f. WISE *a.* + HEAD *sb.*] One who has a wise head; always *iron.* one who fancies himself wise, a wiseacre.

Wise man. OE. 1. *gen.* A man who is wise; a discreet or prudent man. (Often opp. to *fool.*) b. Applied *iron.* to a fool or simpleton, as in *the wise men of Gotham* (see GOTHAM 1) 1526. 2. *spec.* a. A man deeply versed in some subject of study, or in studies generally; a learned man, sage. Now *rare* or *arch.* OE. †b. A man who utters wise sayings or maxims; *esp.* as a title for any of the writers of the Jewish 'Wisdom Literature' -1750. 3. A man versed or skilled in hidden arts, as magic, witchcraft, and the like; *spec.* applied to the three Oriental astrologers or Magi who came to worship the infant Jesus. In general sense now *dial.* or *vulgar.* late ME.

1. *Worldly wiseman*: see WORLDLY. 2. *The seven wise men* = the seven sages: see SAGE *sb.*[2] B. b. There is no new thing vnder the Sunne, saith the wiseman 1611. So **Wise woman,** a woman skilled in magic or hidden arts; a witch, sorceress; *esp.* a harmless or beneficent one, who deals in charms against disease, etc. (now *dial.* or *arch.*).

Wisent (wī·zĕnt). 1866. [a. Gr.; see BISON.] *Antiq.* The aurochs.

Wish (wiʃ), *sb.* ME. [f. next.] 1. An instance of wishing; a feeling in the mind directed towards something which one believes would give satisfaction if attained, possessed, or realized. 2. A desire expressed in words, or the expression of such; sometimes nearly = 'request' 1513. b. *spec.* An expression of desire for another's welfare: often as a farewell greeting. Usu., now always, in *pl.* 1593. c. An imprecation; a malediction. *Obs.* or *dial.* 1592. 3. *transf.* An object of desire; what one wishes or wishes for ME.

1. Thy w. was Father (Harry) to that thought SHAKS. *Prov.* If Wishes were Horses, Beggars would ride 1721. Phr. *To one's w.*, as one wishes; *esp.* to the full extent of one's desire (now *rare* or *Obs.*). 2. b. Take from my mouth, the w. of happy yeares SHAKS. 3. *Two Gent.* IV. ii. 93.

Comb.: **w.-bone** = MERRYTHOUGHT.

Wish (wiʃ), *v.* [OE. *wyscan* :—OTeut. **wunskjan*, f. **wunska, -skō-*; cf. Skr. *vāñchā* :— **wānskā-*, f. base **wen-* to hold dear, love, desire; see also WIN *sb.*[2], WEEN *v.*, WONE.] 1. *trans.* To have or feel a wish for; to desire: with various const.; with simple obj. now *dial.* 2. *intr.* To have or feel a wish; in early use often, to long, yearn ME. b. *trans.* with cognate obj.

late ME. **3.** *trans.* To express a wish for; to say that one wishes..; *spec.* to imprecate, invoke (an evil or curse) OE. **4.** *spec.* To desire (something, usu. good) for or on behalf of a person, etc.: esp. in formulæ of greeting or expressions of goodwill; hence, to express such a wish for, esp. as a formal greeting OE. **b.** To desire, or express a desire for, the welfare or misfortune of (a person); only in *evil wished*, ILL-WISH *v.*, *well-wished* 1577. **5.** In expressions of desire for something to be done by another, thus conveying a request; hence, to request, entreat; formerly sometimes, to bid, command 1533. **6.** To recommend (a person) *to* another, or *to* a place, etc. *Obs.* or *dial.* 1596.

1. I am as well nowe, I thanke God, as I could wysshe 1530. 'Tis a consummation Deuoutly to be wish'd SHAKS. I neuer wish'd to see you sorry, now I trust I shall SHAKS. Kings for such a Tomb would w. to die MILT. He is certainly bewitched: I w. the old hag upon the green has done him no mischief 1756. Heigh ho! I w. I was drunk—but I have nothing but this damned barley-water BYRON. I wished both magazine and review at the bottom of the sea LAMB. Would you w. a little more hot water, ma'am? DICKENS. **2.** Having nothing to do and nothing to w. for, she naturally imagined she must be very ill DICKENS. **3.** *Rich. III*, I. iii. 218. **4.** We w. you good lucke in the name of the Lorde COVERDALE *Ps.* cxxix. 8. I w. Jane Fairfax very well; but she tires me to death JANE AUSTEN. **5.** There is another thing I w. you to notice specially RUSKIN. Hence **Wi·shable** *a.* (*rare*). **Wished** (wiʃt, *poet.* wi·ʃéd) *ppl. a.*; **-ly** *adv.* (*rare* or *Obs.*). **Wi·sher. Wi·shing** *ppl. a.*

Wishful (wi·ʃfŭl), *a.* 1523. [f. WISH *sb.* + -FUL.] †**1.** Such as is or is to be wished; desirable; desired -1645. **2. a.** Of the eye or look, feeling, etc.: Full of desire; longing, wistful. *Obs.* or *dial.* 1593. **b.** Of a person: Possessed by a wish for something specified or implied; wishing, desirous. Now *rare* in literary prose. 1733.

2. a. To greet mine owne Land with my wishfull sight SHAKS. Hence **Wi·shful-ly** *adv.*, **-ness.**

Wishing (wi·ʃiŋ), *vbl. sb.* ME. [f. WISH *v.* + -ING[1].] The action of WISH *v.*; an instance of this.

attrib. and *Comb.* in many designations of objects supposed to be capable of magically conferring the fulfilment of one's wishes, as *w.-cap*, *-gate*, *-well.*

Wishmay (wi·ʃmeⁱ). 1863. [transl. ON. *óskmær*, f. *ósk* wish + *mær* MAY *sb.*[1]] A Valkyrie.

Wisht (wiʃt), *a.* Chiefly *s.w. dial.* 1800. [Origin obsc.] **1.** Dreary, dismal; melancholy 1829. **2.** Uncanny, eerie, weird 1800. **3.** Sickly, wan 1868.

Wishtonwish (wi·ʃtənwiʃ). 1806. [Imitative, from the cry of the animal.] Native name for the prairie-dog of N. America.

Wish-wash (wi·ʃ,wǫʃ). 1786. [redupl. formation from WASH *sb.*] **1.** A contemptuous name for weak, insipid, or unsubstantial drink (or liquid food). **2.** *fig.* Wishy-washy talk or writing 1842. Hence †**Wi·sh-wa:shy** *a.* = next.

Wishy-washy (wi·ʃi,wǫ:ʃi), *a.* (*int.*) 1693. [redupl. formation on WASHY *a.*] **1.** Of drink (or liquid food): Weak and insipid; sloppy 1791. **2.** *fig.* **a.** Feeble or poor in constitution, condition, or aspect; weakly, sickly. Now *rare* or *Obs.* 1703. **b.** Feeble or poor in quality or character; unsubstantial, 'milk-and-watery'. †Also rarely as *int.* = pish! tush! 1693.

1. Their w., watery wine 1898. **2. b.** Isabel painted w. looking flowers on Bristol-board from Nature 1865. Hence **Wi·shy-wa:shiness.**

Wisp (wisp), *sb.* ME. [Origin obsc.] **1.** A handful, bunch, or small bundle (of hay, straw, grass, etc.). **b.** Used to wipe something dry or clean; now chiefly to rub down a horse. late ME. **c.** in various special uses, e. g. as an ale-house sign; hung outside a house as a sign of the plague; as a plug, strainer, or wad 1508. **2.** A twisted band, esp. of hay or straw; a ring or wreath of twisted material, used as a pad. late ME. †**b.** A twist or figure of straw for a scold to rail at -1698. **3.** A bunch or twisted bundle of hay or straw, used for burning as a torch, etc. late ME. **b.** A WILL-o'-THE-w. In recent use *poet.* 1618. **4.** *transf.* and *allus.* **a.** A twist of paper 1597. **b.** A heap or bundle (of clothes) 1736. **c.** A thin, narrow, filmy, or slight piece, fragment, or portion (*of* something) 1836. **d.** A small broom; a whisk 1875.

2. b. 3 *Hen. VI*, II. ii. 144. **4. c.** A rusty black neckerchief with a red border, tied in a narrow w. round his neck DICKENS. A thin w. of smoke on the horizon 1919.

Wisp (wisp), *v.* 1598. [f. prec.] **1.** *trans.* To rub (an animal, esp. a horse) *down* or *over* with a wisp. **2.** To twist into or as a wisp; *dial.* to rumple 1753. **3.** *intr.* To pass *away*, as a wisp of vapour 1883.

Wispish (wi·spiʃ), *a.* 1896. [f. WISP *sb.* + -ISH[1].] Of the nature of or resembling a wisp.

Wispy (wi·spi), *a.* 1717. [f. WISP *sb.* + -Y[1].] Consisting of or resembling a wisp or wisps.

Wist (wist), *v. pseudo-arch.* 1508. [Partly from *I wist*, corrupt form of IWIS (cf. WIS *v.*); partly erron. use of pa. t. *wist* of WIT *v.*[1]] To know.

Wist, pa. t. of WIT *v.*[1]

Wistaria (wistē·riă). Also **wisteria** (-ī^ə·riă). 1842. [mod.L., f. name of Caspar *Wistar* (or *Wister*) 1761–1818, Amer. anatomist; named by T. Nuttall in 1818.] Any plant of the leguminous genus *Wistaria*, native to N. America, Japan, and China, the species of which are hardy, climbing, deciduous shrubs bearing racemes of blue-lilac papilionaceous flowers.

Wistful (wi·stfŭl), *a.* 1613. [app. f. WISTLY *adv.* In early use chiefly poet.] †**1.** Closely attentive, intent -1711. **2.** Expectantly or yearningly eager, watchful, or intent; mournfully expectant or longing. (Chiefly in ref. to the look.) 1714. Hence **Wi·stfulness.**

Wistfully (wi·stfŭli), *adv.* 1663. [f. prec. + -LY[2].] †**1.** Attentively, intently -1833. **2.** With expectant or yearning eagerness; with mournful expectancy or longing 1663.

Wistiti (wi·stiti). 1774. [ad. F. *ouistiti* (imitative); named by Buffon from the cry of the animal.] A S. Amer. monkey of the family *Hapalidæ*; a marmoset, esp. the Common Marmoset, *Hapale jacchus.*

†**Wi·stly,** *adv.* 1500. [Origin obsc.; perh. var. of WHISTLY *adv.*] With close attention; intently (occas. with implication of WISTFULLY 2).

Wit (wit), *sb.* [OE. *wit*, *gewit(t*; f. **wit-* (see WIT *v.*[1]).] **I.** Denoting a faculty (or the person possessing it). †**1.** The seat of consciousness or thought, the mind -1660. **2.** The faculty of thinking and reasoning in general; mental capacity, intellect, reason. *arch.* (now esp. in phr. *the w. of man* = human understanding). OE. **b.** Often denoting indifferently the faculty or the person possessing it, and hence sometimes used definitely for the person in respect of this faculty. Usu. in pl., of a number of persons. *arch.* 1536. **c.** Phr. *At one's wit's end*: utterly perplexed; at a loss what to think or what to do. So *to bring* (*drive*) *to one's wit's end.* late ME. †**d.** *W., whither wilt thou?*: phr. addressed to a person who is letting his tongue run away with him -1637. †**3.** = SENSE *sb.* I, 7. Also *common w.* = COMMON SENSE 1. -1592. **b.** *Five wits*: usu., the five (bodily) senses; often vaguely, the perceptions or mental faculties generally. *Obs.* or *rare arch.* ME. **c.** *pl.* Mental faculties, intellectual powers. late ME. **4.** The understanding or mental faculties in respect of their condition; chiefly = 'right mind', 'senses', sanity. **a.** *sing.* (*Obs.* or *dial.*) OE. **b.** *pl.* = SENSE *sb.* I. 9: esp. in phr. *in* or *out of one's wits* ME.

1. If a mans w. be wandring, let him study the Mathematiks BACON. **2. b.** A schole for the training up of young wits HOLLAND. **d.** *A.Y.L.* IV. i. 167. **3. b.** Alone and warming his five wits, The white owl in the belfry sits TENNYSON. **c.** *To have one's wits about one*, to have one's mental powers in full exercise, to be mentally alert. *To live by one's wits*, to get one's living by clever or (now esp.) crafty devices, without any settled occupation. **4. a.** *In* (*one's right*) *w.*, sane, of sound mind. *Out of* (*one's*) *w.*, insane, out of one's mind. **b.** The governor..was frightened out of his wits MACAULAY.

II. Denoting a quality (or the possessor of it). **1.** Good or great mental capacity; genius, talent, cleverness; mental quickness or sharpness, acumen. *arch.* ME. †**b.** Practical talent or cleverness; skill, ingenuity -1726. **2.** Wisdom, good judgement, discretion. *Obs.* exc. in phr. like *to have the w. to.* ME. **3.** Quickness of intellect or liveliness of fancy, with capacity of apt expression; talent for saying brilliant or sparkling things, esp. in an amusing way. *arch.* 1579. **4.** That quality of speech or writing which consists in the apt association of thought and expression, calculated to surprise and delight by its unexpectedness; later always with ref. to the utterance of brilliant or sparkling things in an amusing way 1542. **5.** (*transf.* from II. 1.) A person of great mental ability; a learned, clever, or intellectual person; a man of talent or intellect. *arch.* or *Hist.* 1470. **6.** (*transf.* from II. 3.) A person of lively fancy, who has the faculty of saying smart or brilliant things, now always so as to amuse; a witty person 1692.

1. *Meas. for M.* II. i. 282. **b.** It..spake the praises of the workmans w. SPENSER. **2.** Since Breuitie is the Soule of Wit,..I will be breefe SHAKS. **3.** Men of all sorts take a pride to gird at mee:..I am not onely witty in my selfe, but the cause that w. is in other men SHAKS. **4.** W.; which is a just mixture of Reason and Extravagance 1693. True W. is Nature to advantage dress'd, What oft was thought, but ne'er so well express'd POPE. A species of minor w., which is much used,..I mean Raillery CHESTERF. **5.** There goes an Author! One of the Wits! 1638. **6.** Uncle Bill..is evidently the w. of the party DICKENS. Hence **Wit** *v.*[2] (in nonce-uses) (*a*) *intr.* with *it*, to play the w.; (*b*) *trans.* as a meaningless repetition of the word just used, by way of a vague threat; (*c*) to call (a person) a w., attribute w. to.

Wit, *v.*[1] *arch.* exc. in *to wit.* Pres. t. **wot;** pa. t. and pple. **wist.** [Com. Teut. pret.-pres. vb.; OE. *witan*, pa. t. *wisse*, *wiste*, pa. pple. *gewiten*; f. OTeut. **wait-*, *wĭt-*:—Indo-Eur. **woid-*, *weid-*, *wid-* to see (cf. Skr. VEDA, Gr. οἶδα, ἴδμεν know, L. *videre* to see). Various attempts were made to normalize the app. anomalous conjugation of the orig. pret.-pres. vb. For new formations or differentiated forms see WEET *v.*[1], WIST *v.*, WOT *v.* Forms with prefixed negative are NIST, NOT *v.*[2]] **1.** *trans.* To have cognizance or knowledge of; to be aware of; to know (as a fact or an existing thing). **2.** *intr.* with *of*: To be aware of (as existing, or as happening or having happened); to know of ME. †**3.** Passing into the sense: To become aware of, gain knowledge of, get or come to know; to find out; to be informed of, learn. *trans.* and *absol.* or *intr.* with *of.* -1795. **4.** *trans.* with *to* and *inf.*: To know how, be able ME. †**5.** In imper. = 'be assured', and later in monitory formulæ and polite phrases = 'you must know', 'allow me to inform you' -1608. **6.** To recognize; to distinguish, discern, detect. *Obs.* or *rare arch.* ME.

1. For aught I woot, he was of Dertemouthe CHAUCER. Hee never wist the matter to bee haynous 1571. As witting I no other comfort haue SHAKS. Whether they speak Gaelic or no I wotna SCOTT. **3.** O Lassie, are ye sleepin yet, Or are ye waukin, I wad w.? BURNS. **4.** Fear wist not to evade, as Love wist to pursue F. THOMPSON. **5.** Please you w.: The Epitaph is for Marina writ SHAKS.

Phrases. †**Do to w.** To cause (a person) to know, make known to. **Let w.** To let (a person) know (a thing); to inform (one), or to make (something) known; to disclose, reveal. *Obs.* exc. *dial.* **To w.:** †**a.** *It is to w.*: it is to be observed, noted, or ascertained. †**b.** *That is to w.* = AF. *cestasavoir*, L. *scilicet*, *videlicet*; occas. = *id est.* **c.** *To w.*: (*a*) 'To be sure', truly, indeed (*Obs.* or *rare arch.*) (*b*) That is, namely, *scilicet.* **God wot**: God knows.

Witan (wi·tăn). *Hist.* 1807. [OE., pl. of *wita* wise man, councillor.] The members of the national council in Anglo-Saxon times; the council itself.

Witch (witʃ), *sb.*[1] Now *dial.* [OE. *wicca* masc.] A man who practises witchcraft or magic; a magician, sorcerer, wizard.

Witch (witʃ), *sb.*[2] [OE. *wicce* fem., corresp. to *wicca* WITCH *sb.*[1], app. derivative of *wiccian* WITCH *v.*] **1.** A female magician, sorceress; in later use, *esp.* a woman supposed to have dealings with the devil or evil spirits and to be able by their co-operation to perform supernatural acts. **2.** *fig.* **a.** *gen.* 1659. **b.** (*a*) A young woman or girl of bewitching aspect or manners 1740. (*b*) *Old w.*: a contemptuous appellation for a malevolent or repulsive-looking old woman. late ME. **3.** Applied to various animals and objects. **a.** The stormy petrel 1784. **b.** A kind of snail 1815. **c.** In a loom: = DOBBY 3. 1883. **d.** *W. of Agnesi* (Math.): a plane curve named after M. G. Agnesi (1718–99) of the university of Bologna 1875.

1. *The w. is in it*, it is bewitched. *As nervous as a w.*: a New England phr., applied to a very restless person. 2. b. (*a*) For my part I find every woman a w. LYTTON. (*b*) A lusti galaunt that weddithe an olde wiche LYDG.

Comb.: **w.-bell(s**, *Sc.* the harebell, *Campanula rotundifolia*; **-finder**, one formerly employed to search for and obtain evidence against witches; **-fire** = CORPOSANT; **-grass**, *U.S.* (*a*) *Panicum capillare*, a weed-grass found throughout the U.S.; (*b*) couch-grass, *Triticum* (*Agropyrum*) *repens*; **-hat**, a hat with a conical crown and flat brim, represented as worn by witches; **-lock** = W. KNOT I; **-mark**, a mark on the body, supposed by w.-finders to denote that its possessor was a w.; **-monger**, one who has dealings with witches, or who believes in witchcraft; **-weed**, *S. Afr.* a parasitic plant, *Striga lutea*.

Combs. with *witch's*, *witches'*: **witch's bells**, the foxglove; **witches' besom, broom**, a bushy tuft developed on the branches of trees by a fungus; **witches' bridle**, an iron collar and gag formerly used as an instrument of torture in Scottish w.-trials; **witches' butter**, pop. name for certain gelatinous algæ and fungi, esp. *Tremella Nostoc*; **witches' Sabbath** = SABBATH 3.

Witch, wych (witʃ), *sb.*[3] [OE. *wice* and *wic*; app. f. Teut. *wik- to bend.] Applied gen. or vaguely to various trees having pliant branches: *esp.* †a. the WYCH ELM; b. (now *dial.*) the mountain ash, *Pyrus aucuparia*. Also *attrib.*; **w. alder**, a w. hazel with alder-like leaves, *Fothergilla alnifolia*, native to Virginia and N. Carolina.

Witch (witʃ), *sb.*[4] *local.* 1879. [prob. a use of WITCH *sb.*[2], the name being given on account of the uncanny appearance of the fish; cf. L. *saga*, F. *sorcière*.] The flat-fish *Pleuronectes cynoglossus*, resembling the lemon sole.

Witch (witʃ), *v.* [OE. *wiccian*, of obsc. origin. In later senses, prob. aphetic from *bewitch*.] †1. *intr.* To practise witchcraft; to use sorcery or enchantment –1623. 2. *trans.* = BEWITCH *v.* 1. ME. b. (with prep. or adv.) To bring, draw, put, or change by witchcraft 1597. 3. *fig.* = BEWITCH *v.* 2. 1590.

2. Thou art a W...and diddest procure Mother Bale to w. the Cattell of J. S. 1647. 3. 1 *Hen. IV*, IV. i. 110. Hence **Wi·tching** *vbl. sb.* the use or practice of witchcraft OE.

Witchcraft (wi·tʃ,krɑft). [OE. *wiccecræft*, f. *wicca*, *wicce* WITCH *sb.*[1] and [2] + *cræft* CRAFT *sb.*] 1. The practices of a witch or witches; the exercise of supernatural power supposed to be possessed by persons in league with the devil or evil spirits. b. *pl.* Acts or instances of this; magic arts OE. 2. *fig.* Power or influence like that of a magician; bewitching or fascinating attraction or charm 1599.

1. The Sickness is more than natural, and W. is to be feared 1671. 2. You haue Witch-craft in your Lippes, Kate. SHAKS.

Wi·tch-do·ctor. 1718. One who professes to cure disease and to counteract witchcraft by magic arts. b. A magician among African tribes, esp. Kaffirs, whose business it is to detect witches, and to counteract the effects of magic 1836.

Witchen (wi·tʃĕn). Now *dial.* 1594. [f. WITCH *sb.*[3] + -EN[4].] 1. In full *w. elm*: = WYCH ELM. 2. The mountain ash, *Pyrus aucuparia* 1664.

Witchery (wi·tʃəri). 1546. [f. WITCH *sb.*[2] or *v.* + -ERY.] 1. The use or practice of witchcraft. b. *pl.* Deeds of witchcraft 1591. 2. *fig.* Charming or fascinating power or influence 1582.

2. He never felt The w. of the soft blue sky! WORDSW.

Witchetty (wi·tʃĕti). *Austral.* 1891. [Native name.] The larva of some species of longicorn beetles, used as food by Australian natives.

Wi·tch ha·zel, wy·ch ha·zel. 1541. [WITCH *sb.*[3]] 1. = WYCH ELM. Also, the hornbeam. 2. A N. Amer. shrub, *Hamamelis virginica*; also, an extract of the leaves and bark of this shrub, used as an astringent remedy 1760.

Witching (wi·tʃiŋ), *ppl. a.* late ME. [f. WITCH *v.* + -ING [2].] 1. That casts a spell; enchanting, bewitching. 2. *transf.* Of or belonging to witchcraft; concerned with the practice of witchcraft or sorcery 1584. b. *spec.* Of time: Belonging or appropriate to the deeds of witches and witchcraft, and hence to supposed supernatural occurrences. (In later use echoing Shaks.) 1602. 3. *fig.* 'Bewitching', fascinating 1600. b. *advb.* Bewitchingly 1821.

2. b. 'Tis now the verie w. time of night, When Churchyards yawne, and Hell it selfe breaths out Contagion to this world SHAKS.

Wi·tch knot. 1598. 1. A tangled knot of hair supposed to be made by witches. 2. = *witches' besom* (see WITCH *sb.*[2]) 1806.

Wite, wyte (wəit), *sb. Obs.* exc. *Hist.* and *n. dial.* [OE. *wīte*; see next.] †1. a. Punishment, penalty; pain inflicted in punishment or torture, *esp.* the torments of hell –ME. b. In Anglo-Saxon law, a fine imposed for certain offences or privileges; often as second element in compounds, as BLOODWITE. Now *Hist.* OE. 2. Blame, reproach; blameworthiness, fault. Now *Sc.* and *n. dial.* ME.

Wite, wyte (wəit), *v. Obs.* exc. *Sc.* and *n. dial.* [OE. *wītan* f. Teut. *wit-; see WIT *v.*[1]] 1. *trans.* To impute the guilt or lay the blame of (something) to or upon a person (his action, conduct, or character) or a thing, condition, or event. 2. To impute the guilt or fault to, blame (a person) OE. 3. To lay the fault or blame upon (a thing) ME.

Witenagemot (wi·tĕnăgĕmōᵘt, *popularly* witĕnæ·gĕmǫt). *Hist.* [OE. *witena gemōt* assembly of wise men.] The assembly of the WITAN, the national council of Anglo-Saxon times; *transf.* of modern parliaments or other deliberative assemblies.

Wi·tereden. *Hist.* [OE. *wīterǣden*, f. *wīte* WITE *sb.* + *rǣden* -RED.] A fine (erron. explained by antiquaries as a royal imposition or aid).

With (wiþ), *sb.* 1708. [perh. corruption of WIDTH.] A partition between flues in a chimney stack.

With (wið; *chiefly north.* wiþ), *prep.* [OE. *wið*, app. a shortening (peculiar to the Anglo-Fris. and Scand. areas) of Com. Teut. *wider-; see WITHER *a.* and *adv.*, and N.E.D.] I. Denoting opposition and derived notions. †1. In a position opposite to; over against –ME. b. In exchange, return, or payment for. *Obs.* exc. *dial.* OE. 2. Of conflict, rivalry, and the like: In opposition to, adversely to. (Still the normal prep. with such words as *battle*, *compete*, *vie*, and phrases like *go to law*, *at odds*, but now assoc. with or merged in other senses.) OE. 3. †a. Towards, in the direction of. OE. only. b. Near or close to, against, alongside. Now only *Naut.* with words denoting proximity. OE.

2. Let us go and have t'other Brush w. them DE FOE. 3. b. A man..saw..some dark troubled object close in w. the land DICKENS.

II. Denoting personal relation, agreement, association, union, addition. 1. After words denoting speech or other verbal communication between persons (with the person as obj.) OE. b. Followed by refl. pron., in ref. to soliloquy, consideration, etc. *arch.* 1530. 2. a. After words expressing transaction or dealing between persons (with the person as obj.) OE. b. After words expressing conduct or feeling towards (a person, etc.). Now sometimes repl. by other preps., e.g. envious *of*. OE. 3. In the matter of, in regard to, concerning; in regard to the condition or fortune of OE. b. After an adv. or phr. with ellipsis of or equivalent to a vb., usu. imper.: e.g. *away w. it* = 'take it away'. late ME. c. In phr. *w. reference, regard*, or *respect to*: concerning, anent, respecting. 4. In the opinion, view, or estimation of; 'in the sight of' OE. 5. In the practice or experience of, in the life or conduct of; sometimes *spec.* in the language or statement of, according to. (With pl. obj. = AMONG A. 5.) ME. b. After words expressing influence or the like 1573. 6. Following words expressing comparison, likeness, equality, or identity. (Sometimes varying with or now replaced by *to*.) OE. 7. Following words expressing agreement, conformity, sympathy, and the like OE. b. By extension, after words expressing disagreement 1646. 8. On the side or party of; in favour of; on behalf of ME. b. In ref. to wind, tide, etc.: Favourable to, in a favourable direction for 1647. 9. In the same way as; as — does or did, is or was, etc.; like ME. b. Followed by *the* and a superlative used *absol.*: As well or thoroughly as; (as) one of, 'among': forming advb. phrases denoting 'to the full or fullest extent', '(nearly) as — as any or as possible' ME. 10. Expressing simultaneous occurrence and association. a. At the same time as; on the occurrence of (and because of); at, on, upon ME. b. Followed by a sb. or pron., forming a phr. = a clause with *when* in which the vb. is identical with that in the principal clause; e.g. *to rise w. the lark*, i.e. when the lark rises (= early in the morning). late ME. c. In the course or duration of, in process of, 'in' (time, etc.) 1440. d. After words denoting change or variation: At the same rate as; in proportion to, according to 1697. 11. Expressing agreement or accordance, esp. in opinion or statement 1456. 12. In the same direction as; along the course of: opp. to AGAINST III. 1. 1489. 13. Following words expressing accompaniment or addition, as *associate*, *connect*, *join*, *marry*, *share*, *unite* vbs.; *connexion*, *company*, *contact* sbs.; *together* adv. OE. b. Following words expressing acquaintance or familiarity ME. c. By extension, following words expressing separation, as *break*, *part* ME. 14. Expressing association or participation in some act, proceeding, or experience; *spec.* = acting on the same side as (another lawyer) in an action at law ME. 15. a. (with such vbs. as *bring*, *take*, *come*, *go*) Followed by a sb. or (most commonly) pron. denoting the person (vessel, etc.) that leads, conveys, or carries a person or thing, thus having it in charge ME. b. In the possession, keeping, care, or charge of (a person); in the hands of ME. c. In the nature or character of; as a quality or attribute of. Now chiefly after *way*. late ME. 16. In the company, society, or presence of ME. b. *spec.* At the house of, or in the same house or meeting-place as; in the household, retinue, or service of; on a visit to, being the guest of ME. c. *fig.* in ref. to an abstract thing: *to be w.*, to accompany, 'attend'. Also in ref. to God. ME. †d. *To be w.*, used in menace, etc. = to be avenged on, chastise, be even with –1825. 17. Having in one's hold, keeping, or charge; having within its compass, limits, area, etc.; leading, bringing, carrying, wearing, etc. ME. b. In phr. *w. child*, *w. young*, etc., said of a pregnant woman or animal ME. c. In phr. *w. costs*, *w. damages*: in early use = 'in possession of', 'having as awarded'; later, in ref. to the verdict = 'accompanied by an order to the losing party to pay' 1466. 18. Accompanied by; having as an addition; having in one's company. Often = 'and in addition', 'and besides', or simply 'and'. ME. b. Comprising in the whole number or total; including ME. c. Having the advantage of (favourable wind, weather, etc.) 1536. 19. Expressing association, conjunction, or connexion in thought, action, or condition. late ME. 20. Expressing collocation in space 1480. b. Expressing mixture or combination of material substances. late ME. (*b*) *ellipt.* in slang use, in ref. to liquor = mixed with sugar, having sugar added; usu. in phr. *hot* (*warm*) or *cold w.* 1835. 21. Having, possessing; having in or upon it, containing, bearing ME. 22. Indicating a quality or attribute of the action spoken of: forming phrases equivalent to advs., e.g. *w. one accord* = unanimously. Similarly after an adj., in phr. expressing a particular kind or degree of the quality denoted by the adj. ME. 23. Indicating a feeling, purpose, or other mental state accompanying the action spoken of ME. b. In expressions of devotion, affection, or gratitude accompanying what is said or written, esp. by way of greeting 1454. 24. Indicating an attribute, quality, or condition of the person or thing spoken of: Having, possessing, characterized by 1450. b. Still having; without loss of or detriment to; consistently with 1440. (*b*) Though having; notwithstanding, in spite of. (Usu. followed by *all* qualifying the sb.) ME. 25. Indicating an accompanying or attendant circumstance, or a result following from the action expressed by the verb ME. 26. Indicating something granted, received, or assumed: often with conditional implication, as in *w. your permission* = 'if you will allow me'. late ME. 27. Followed by a sb. denoting some alteration or modification, or something imposed in the way of a demand or requirement: e.g. *exception*, *proviso*, *qualification* 1450. 28. a. Followed by a sb. denoting misfortune or evil, in imprecations and intensive phrases: now usu. *w. a vengeance* (in intensive sense) ME. **b.** Introducing a refrain (often meaningless) in a poem or ballad. late ME. **29.** In various preceding senses, followed by object and complement ME.

1. White handed Mistris, one sweet word w. thee SHAKS. **2. a.** All who had business to transact w. him 1838. **b.** Be opposite w. a kinsman, surly w. seruants SHAKS. 3. We tooke more Cod then we knew what to doe w. 1624. 4. Juan stood well both w. Ins and Outs BYRON. 5. It is an accustom'd action w. her, to seeme thus washing her hands SHAKS. 6. A sniveling Gentleman of not half the sense w. the late poor spirited Dick Cromwell 1710. 7. Spain..on friendly terms with France 1796. **b.** Impossibilities and things inconsistent w. truth SIR T. BROWNE. 8. He that is nat w. me, is aȝeinus me WYCLIF *Matt.* xii. 30. Shakespeare was of us, Milton was for us, Burns, Shelley, were w. us BROWNING. 9. Whether we should love everbody w. Tolstoy, or spare nobody w. Nietzsche 1905. **b.** At your age..I could have wept w. the best TENNYSON. 10. *W. that*, when (and, often, because) that occurred, thereupon; saying or having just said that. *W. this*, hereupon. **c.** Mans labours and skill wil faile w. yeeres 1611. **d.** The probability of an error diminishes w. its magnitude 1838. 11. *To be w.*, to be of the same opinion as, to agree with; Ah, it's a fine dance—I'm w. you there STEVENSON. 12. W. the Grain of the wood 1678. 13. **b.** He is..a man of sorrows, and acquainted w. griefe *Isa.* liii. 3. **c.** *To break w.* = to break off connexion w.; It cannot be The Volsces dare breake w. vs. SHAKS. 14. I will..for the future be merry w. the Vulgar STEELE. 15. **a.** Ten poundes..To carie in your pursse about w. ye 1596. **b.** The 'burden of proof' lies w. the accusers 1828. **c.** He had such an honest way w. him 1711. 16. I have no one to go w. 1914. *Face to face w.*, looking in the face of, confronting. *W. God*, in heaven. **c.** Luck, my lads, be w. you still HOUSMAN. **d.** *Mids. N.* III. ii. 403. 17. A tall..Man, ..w. Ruffles and a light bag Wig 1722. **c.** A verdict ..for the plaintiff, w. one pound eleven shillings and sixpence damages 1775. 18. Imprisonment w. or without hard labour 1911. **b.** 'What's the terms?' ..'Five guineas a week, ma'am, w. attendance.' DICKENS. 19. *One (day, etc.) w. another*; see ONE IV. 3; One week w. another she earned about half-a-crown 1784. 20. The aristocracy dare not ask the professors to dinner for fear lest..they should wear green ties w. their dress clothes 1914. 21. A Man with a sour rivell'd Face ADDISON. 22. I look'd vpon her with a souldiers eie SHAKS. 23. A land of exile, visited with reluctance and quitted w. delight MACAULAY. **b.** Here: take George his hat and stick w. my compliments 1898. 24. She had a tongue with a tang SHAKS. In a cool sweat, w. a low pulse 1776. **b.** He vnnethis gatt away w. his life 1440. *(b)* England, w. all thy faults, I love thee still COWPER. 25. The frosty silence..w. which it is received 1806. 26. Another gentleman..collars that glass of punch, without a 'w. your leave', or 'by your leave' DICKENS.

III. Denoting instrumentality, causation, or agency. **1.** Indicating the means or instrument of any kind of action: By means of, by the use of ME. **b.** Formerly used in many cases where *by* is now the usual or only construction, e.g. with obj. a person, or an action ME. **c.** Used where other preps. are now usual, as *at* (a charge or cost), *on* or *upon* (food, etc.) ME. **†d.** In ref. to procreation: = BY *prep.* 5. –1714. **e.** After *begin* or *end* and words of like sense. late ME. **2.** After words of furnishing, filling, covering, and the like ME. **3.** In consequence of, as a result of, by the action of; because of ME. **4.** After a passive verb or participle, indicating the principal agent. *Obs.* exc. *dial.* ME.

1. They build w. vnburnt clay 1634. The people w. a shout Rifted the Air MILT. **b.** W. all this the King was convinced 1715. **c.** You shall fast a Weeke w. Branne and water SHAKS. **d.** I had but two children w. my wife 1709. **e.** We may close her national history w. the seventeenth century RUSKIN. 'Middle' begins with 'm' 1887. *To begin w.*, to take what is mentioned or indicated as one's starting-point; To begyne w., we shall interdyte the lond 1550. 2. Her wombe then rich w. my yong squire SHAKS. 3. Went they not quickly, I should die w. laughing SHAKS. Now glow'd the Firmament W. living Saphirs MILT. None shall tax me with base Perjury DRYDEN. Men and horses..nearly spent w. toil 1839. *It is pouring w. rain* = rain is pouring. *Dripping w. dew*, having dew dripping from it. 4. He was torne to pieces w. a Beare SHAKS. This island is inhabited..w. monkies and myself 1727.

With-, repr. OE. *wiþ-* used as a prefix to vbs. (and derived sbs.) with the meanings (1) away, back, as in OE. *wiþgān*; so WITHDRAW, WITHHOLD; (2) away from one, as in several OE. vbs. meaning 'reject, refuse', *wiþcēosan*, *wiþsacan*; (3) against, in opposition, as in OE. *wiþhabban* to resist, *wiþstandan* WITHSTAND *v.*

Withal (wiðǭ·l), *adv.* and *prep. arch.* ME. [prop. two words, orig. *with al(le*; ultimately superseding earlier *mid alle* (MID *prep.*[1]).] **A.** *adv.* **1.** Along with the rest; in addition; moreover; as well. **b.** Contextually: 'At the same time'; notwithstanding, nevertheless 1596. **2.** = THEREWITH 1 c, 2. ME.

1. **b.** He confessed that his master was rather severe, but w. a very good man 1859. 2. *To begin w.* = to begin with (see WITH *prep.* III. 1 e); I wyll (to begyn w.) shew you what repentance is 1553.

B. *prep.* Substituted for WITH *prep.* in post-position, esp. at the end of a relative clause or its equivalent or of a direct or indirect question, governing a relative or an interrogative ME.

Ile tel you who Time ambles withall, who Time trots w.,..and who he stands stil withall SHAKS.

Withamite (wi·ðəməit). 1825. [f. the name of its discoverer, H. *Witham*; see -ITE [1].] *Min.* A red or reddish-yellow variety of epidote, found at Glencoe in Scotland.

Withdraw (wiðdrǭ·, wiþdrǭ·), *v.* Pa. t. **withdrew** (-drū·), pa. pple. **withdrawn** (-drǭ·n). ME. [f. WITH- (1) + DRAW *v.*] **I.** *trans.* **1.** To take back or away (something that has been given, allowed, possessed, experienced, or enjoyed). **2.** To draw back, take away, remove (a thing) *from* its place or position ME. **b.** To take (one's eyes, etc.) off something 1477. **c.** To remove (money) *from* capital, or *from* a bank or other place of deposit 1776. **d.** To draw (a veil, curtain, etc.) back or aside; to draw back (a bolt). Now *rare.* 1797. **3.** To remove *from* the scope of an inquiry, *from* a particular category, or the like 1725. **b.** To take back, retract (one's words, an expression). Often *absol.* in imper., in parliamentary procedure, to demand the withdrawal by a member of an expression or statement. 1793. **c.** To refrain from proceeding with or prosecuting (a course of action, etc.); to cease to support or present (a candidate, etc.) 1781. **4.** To draw away, deflect, divert (a person, his mind, etc.) *from* an object, pursuit, etc. Now *rare.* ME. **5.** To remove (a person) *from* a position; to cause to retire or recede; *spec.* to cause (a force, troops) to retire *from* a position, an engagement 1450. **b.** *Law.* To remove (a juror) from the panel in order to put an end to the proceedings 1676.

1. They..said they'd w. their subscriptions from the hounds SURTEES. 2. In prosperous days They swarm, but in adverse w. their head MILTON. 3. **b.** Burke got up twice, but..nothing was heard but *W., w.* 1793. **c.** Amendment, by leave, withdrawn 1880. 4. With how contrarious thoughts am I withdrawne GREENE. 5. Walter Scape was withdrawn from Eton THACKERAY.

II. *refl.* Now *rare* or *arch.* **1.** To remove oneself *from* a place or position. ME. **2.** To remove oneself *from* a condition, sphere, society, etc. ME.

1. W. your selues, and leaue vs here alone SHAKS.

III. *intr.* **1.** To go away, depart, or retire *from* a place or position, *from* some one's presence, to another room or a private place, etc. ME. **b.** Of combatants, troops, etc.: To retire *from* the field of battle or any contest, or *from* an advanced position ME. **2.** To draw away *from* a person; to remove oneself or retire *from* a society or community, etc.; to retire from participation in or pursuit of something. late ME.

1. Sophia now took the first Opportunity of withdrawing with the Ladies FIELDING. 2. Withdrawing into his own soul 1911. So **Withdrau·ght** (*obs.* exc. *arch.*) withdrawal; †a place of withdrawal; a sewer, a privy (now *local*). **Withdraw·** *sb.* withdrawal, removal. **Withdraw·able** *a* capable of being withdrawn. **Withdraw·er**, *spec.* in *Sc. Church Hist.* one who did not conform to the established church in the 17th century. **Withdraw·ment** (now *rare*) = WITHDRAWAL. **Withdraw·n** *ppl. a.* in various senses; occas. secluded; also, of mental state, detached.

Withdrawal (wiðdrǭ·ăl, wiþ-). 1824. [f. prec. + -AL. (Superseding the earlier WITHDRAWMENT.)] **1.** The act of taking back or away what has been held, occupied, or enjoyed 1839. **b.** The removal of money or securities from a bank or other place of deposit 1861. **2.** The act of withdrawing a person or thing *from* a place or position, *esp.* the removal of troops by way of retreat 1838. **3.** The retractation of a statement, proposal, etc. 1835. **4.** The act of retiring or retreating *from* a place or position 1824.

Withdrawing (wiðdrǭ·iŋ, wiþ-), *vbl. sb.* ME. [f. WITHDRAW *v.* + -ING [1].] The action of WITHDRAW *v.* in various senses.

attrib.: **†w.-chamber, -room** (*arch.* or *Hist.*), a room to withdraw to; = DRAWING-ROOM 1.

Withe, with (wiþ, wið, waið), *sb.* [OE. *wiþþe*:—OTeut. *wiþjōn-, *wiþi- (cf. Gr. ἰτέα willow, L. *vitis* vine); cf. WITHY.] **1.** A band, tie, or shackle consisting of a tough flexible twig or branch, as of willow or osier, or of several twisted together; such a twig or branch used for binding or tying, and occas. for plaiting. **b.** *gen.* A pliant twig or bough 1817. **c.** With allusion to the story of Samson in *Judges* xvi. 7. 1835. **†2.** A halter, prop. one made with withes –1694. **3.** A willow. Now *dial.* ME. **b.** The creeping plant *Heliotropium fruticosum*, of Jamaica, the stems of which are used for making baskets 1657. **4.** Applied to various iron implements resembling a withe in some respect 1688.

1. If they binde me with seuen greene withs, that were neuer dried, then shall I be weake *Judges* xvi. 7. Hence **Withe** *v.* (now *dial.* and *U.S.*) *trans.* to twist like a w.; to bind with a w. or withes; *U.S.* to take (deer) with a noose made of withes.

Wither (wi·ðəɹ), *sb.* 1652. [f. WITHER *v.*] **†1.** A disease of cows –1722. **2.** *Tea-manuf.* The process of withering 1897.

Wi·ther, *a.* and *adv.* *Obs.* or *dial.* [OE. *wiþer* adv. or adj., related to *wiþer* prep. = OS. *withar*, OHG. *widar*, ON. *viðr*, Goth. *wiþra*; f. Indo-Eur. *wi- denoting separation or division + comp. suffix *-tero-*.] **A.** *adj.* **1.** Hostile, adverse; fierce. **†2.** Contrary, opposite; wrong (side) –1450. **†B.** *adv.* Hostilely; perversely, fiercely –ME.

Wither (wi·ðəɹ), *v.* late ME. [app. var. of WEATHER *v.*, ult. differentiated for certain senses.] **1.** *intr.* Of a plant: To become dry and shrivel up. **2.** Of other animate things: To become dried up or shrivelled; to lose vigour from lack of animal moisture; to pine or fade *away.* late ME. **3.** *fig.* Of persons, or of inanimate and immaterial things: To lose vigour or freshness, to pine *away*, languish, fade, fall into decay 1508. **4.** *Tea-manuf.* (*trans.*) To dry (tea-leaf) before roasting. Also *absol.* Also *intr.* of the leaf. 1753. **5.** To cause (a plant, flower, etc.) to dry up and shrivel 1555. **6.** To cause (the body or the physical powers) to become wasted or decayed; to cause to shrink, become wrinkled, or lose freshness 1599. **7.** *fig.* To destroy the vitality or vigour of; to cause to decline, decay, or waste; now somewhat *rare* exc. in hyperbolical use, to blight or paralyse with a look of scorn or the like 1590.

1. Like a neglected rose, It withers on the stalk MILT. 2. Now I wax old,..As muk apon mold I widder away 1460. 3. An honest gentellman witheringe in pouerty 1647. 6. Age cannot w. her SHAKS. 7. Like to a Step-dame, or a Dowager, Long withering out a yong mans reuennew SHAKS. Dr. Slammer.. withering the company with a look DICKENS.

Withered (wi·ðəɹd), *ppl. a.* 1470. [f. prec. + -ED [1].] **1.** Of a plant, fruit, etc.: Shrivelled or shrunken through lack of moisture, and so deprived of its natural colour, freshness, or bloom; hence of fields, etc., and *gen.*: Dried up, arid. **2.** Of men or the lower animals: Physically shrunken, shrivelled, wasted, or decayed 1500. **b.** Of the body, or parts of it: Shrivelled or shrunken, esp. by the wasting of disease or age. Formerly, and now *colloq.* or *dial.*, often applied to a paralysed limb 1513. **3.** *fig.* Deprived of or having lost vigour, freshness, or 'bloom'; shrunken and decayed 1561.

2. **b.** There was a man which had a widdred honde TINDALE *Mark.* iii. 1. 3. The curse of the wither'd heart SCOTT. Hence **Wi·thered-ly** *adv.*, **-ness.**

Witherite (wi·ðərəit). 1794. [f. name of W. *Withering*, who first described and analysed it.] *Min.* Native barium carbonate.

Withernam (wi·ðəɹnām). *Law.* Now *Hist.* ME. [Law-French, app. a. ON. *viðrnām*, f. *viðr* WITHER *adv.* + *nām* NAAM.] *Law.* In an action of replevin, the reprisal of other goods in lieu of those taken by a first distress and eloigned; also, the writ (*capias in w.*) commanding the sheriff to take the reprisal. **b.** A process of distress (or arrest) for debt, formerly current in the Cinque Ports (and other towns) ME.

Withers (wi·ðəɹz), *sb. pl.*, occas. *sing.* **wither.** 1580. [app. a reduced form of *widersome* or *-sone*, f. *wider* WITHER *adv.* + an obsc. element; cf. G. *widerrist*, f. *wider* WITHER *adv.* + *rist* WRIST.] In a horse, the highest part of the back, lying between the shoulder-blades. Also, the corresponding part in some other animals, as the ox. (Often in fig. use, esp. after Shaks. with allusion to the 'wringing' of a horse's withers.)

Let the gall'd iade winch: our w. are vnrung SHAKS.

Withershins, widdershins (wi·ðəɹ-, wi·dəɹʃinz), *adv. dial.* (chiefly *Sc.*) 1513. [a. MLG. *weddersin(ne)s*, a. MHG. *widersinnes*, f. *wider* WITHER *adv.* + gen. of *sin* way, direction. In sense 2, assoc. with SUN *sb.*] †1. In a direction opposite to the usual; the wrong way –1721. 2. In a direction contrary to the apparent course of the sun (considered as unlucky or causing disaster) 1545.

Withhold (wiðhōu·ld, wiþ-), *v.* Pa. t. and pa. pple. **withheld.** ME. [See WITH- (1) and HOLD *v.* The pa. pple. **withholden** was still freq. in the 19th c.] 1. *trans.* To keep *from* doing something; to hold back, restrain. b. *refl.* To restrain oneself ME. †c. *intr.* To refrain *from*; occas. const. inf., or *trans.* with gerund –1817. 2. To keep back; to keep in one's possession (what belongs to, is due to, or is desired by another); to refrain from granting or giving ME. †3. To detain; to keep in bondage, in custody, or under control –1714.

1. What cause with-holds you then to mourne for him? SHAKS. Had not some awe of the company.. withheld his rage FIELDING. 2. From such an inference, I must..w. my assent 1794. [Parliament's] acknowledged power to give or to w. supplies 1861. Hence **Withhe·ld, -ho·lden** (*arch.*) *ppl. adjs.* kept or held back. **Withho·lder.**

Within (wiði·n), *adv., prep.* (*adj.*). [Late OE. *wiþinnan*, f. *wiþ* WITH *prep.* + *innan* INNE, the second element being assim. to IN *adv.* in ME.] **A.** *adv.* 1. In the inner part or interior, or on the inner side (of a receptacle or other material thing). b. In the interior of the body or some part of it ME. c. In this writing or document; herein. *Obs.* exc. *techn.* late ME. 2. a. In the limits of, or in the inner part of, a space or region, esp. a city or country ME. b. In (or into) the house or dwelling, indoors; also, in the inner part of the house, in an inner chamber; *Theatr.* (esp. in stage-directions) behind the scenes ME. 3. *fig.* In the inward being; in the mind, soul, or heart; inwardly OE. 4. Preceded by *from*, in various senses 1489.

1. b. Why should a man whose bloud is warme w., Sit like his Grandsire, cut in Alablaster? SHAKS. 2. b. Apartments furnished for a single gentleman. Inquire w. DICKENS. 3. Be suche wiþ-ynne, as ȝe outward seme 1421.

B. *prep.* 1. In the inner part or interior of, inside of. (*a*) as a mere synonym of IN *prep.* I. 1 (*arch.*) ME. (*b*) with emphasis on the restriction or confinement by limits or boundaries: In the limits of, not outside or beyond ME. b. In (an enclosure or enclosing boundary); so as to be included, contained, surrounded, or confined by. late ME. (*b*) Appended to names of places lying within a certain boundary or area, as *Bishopsgate W.* (i. e. w. the walls of London) 1598. c. On the inner (esp. landward) side of; further in than. Now *rare* or *Obs.* 1743. d. *transf.* In the membership of (a class, society, etc.); (in predicate) included in, forming a part of 1697. 2. To the interior of; into. *Obs.* or *arch.* ME. †3. In or into the midst of, among, with; *spec.* in the house of –1609. 4. *transf. W. oneself* (*itself*, etc.): (*a*) so as to be self-contained or independent (now *dial.*) 1518; †(*b*) in self-command or self-control –1606; (*c*) without external supply or aid (now *dial.*) 1738; (*d*) not beyond one's normal capacity of exertion; without strain 1737. 5. *fig.* In the (inner) being, soul, or mind of OE. 6. In the limits of (a period of time); most usu., before the end of, after not more than; also, since the beginning of; *gen.* in the course of, during ME. †b. (without ref. to limits) At some time during –1651. 7. Not beyond or above (a specified or implied amount or degree); so as not to exceed or surpass; *esp.* in expressions of a small difference or margin of error from a larger amount: = with a difference of not more than (so much) above or, usu., below. late ME. b. Not beyond or outside (a specified distance); nearer or not farther away than 1440. 8. In expressions referring to the physical range of some action or perception: Not beyond, not farther than the extent of: as *w. reach*, near enough to reach, or to be reached 1533. b. Inside the guard, defence, or point of; *Fencing*, on the inside of (one's sword, arm, etc.). Now *rare* or *Obs.* 1565. 9. *fig.* In the extent of (something abstract figured as a region, or as having extension); *esp.* in the scope or sphere of action of (authority, knowledge, a law, etc.) 1493.

1. (*a*) Her head leaning on one side w. her hand STERNE. b. *W. board* (Naut.), in the inside of a ship. (*b*) The united parishes of Saint Simon Without, and Saint Walker W. DICKENS. 2. I would Haue suncke the Sea w. the Earth SHAKS. 5. *W. oneself*, spec. (after *say, think*, etc.) = in thought, mentally, without outward expression. 6. The Hours w. which Marriages may be lawfully solemnized 1918. b. *Hen. V*, I. ii. 60. 7. She has a tall Daughter w. a Fortnight of Fifteen STEELE. Determined to live w. my income 1783. 8. *W. call*, near enough to hear a call. *W. sight* or *hearing*, near enough to see or hear, to be seen or heard. b. Some get w. him, take his sword away SHAKS. 9. A written warranty w. the meaning of the above section 1891.

C. *adj.* That is within; †(of a letter or document) enclosed (*rare*) 1748.

†**Withi·n-doo:r,** *adv. phr.* (*a.*) 1579. = next –1821.

Speak within door, 'do not clamour so as to be heard beyond the house' (J.).

Withi·n(-)doors, *adv. phr.* (*adj., sb.*) *arch.* 1581. In (or into) the house. b. (with hyphen) †*attrib.* or as *adj.* = INDOOR 1; also as *sb.* that which is, or those who are, indoors 1612.

Withi·nside, *adv., prep.* Now *arch.* or *dial.* 1595. [f. WITHIN + SIDE *sb.*[1], after *inside*.] **A.** *adv.* 1. On the inner side. 2. In (or to) the inner part or interior (*of*) 1598. **B.** *prep.* = INSIDE *prep.* 1686. So **Withi·nsides** *adv.* (*arch.* or *dial.*) 1891.

Without (wiðau·t), *adv., prep., conj.* [Late OE. *wiþūtan*, f. *wiþ* WITH *prep.* + *ūtan* from the outside.] **A.** *adv.* Outside: opp. to WITHIN *adv.* Now only *literary* and somewhat *arch.* 1. On the outside or outer surface (of a material thing); externally. 2. Outside (or out of) the place mentioned or implied; *esp.* outside the house or room; out of doors OE. b. *transf.* Outside of a class, body, or community; in an alien or foreign community. (Now only in echoes of 1 *Cor.* v. 12.) ME. 3. *fig.* and *gen.* Outside of the inward being, soul, or mind; with regard to external actions or circumstances; sometimes, in outward appearance as opp. to inward reality OE. 4. Preceded by *from*; in above senses. late ME.

2. b. *Those* (*that are*) *w.* = 'outsiders'. 3. Then you will be at ease w. and at peace within 1832.

B. *prep.* I. Outside of, beyond: opp. to WITHIN *prep.* Now only *literary* or *arch.* 1. Outside of, on or at the outside of, in the space external to (a space, receptacle, enclosing boundary, etc.) OE. b. (with verb of motion). So as to be outside of, out of. *Obs.* or *arch.* OE. c. On the outer side of; further out than; beyond 1623. 2. *transf.* and *fig.* Outside of, not in the limits of, external(ly) to OE. †3. Beyond the extent of, outside the range of (some action or perception); beyond the scope or sphere of action of –1809. 4. Used *absol.* by ellipsis of obj., in opposition to *within* (or *in*) prep. ME.

1. The church of S[t]. Agnes w. the City BERKELEY. 3. Conjectures of things w. our knowledge 1676. 4. Placez within the shire of Couentre & withoute 1480.

II. Expressing absence, privation, or negation: opp. to WITH *prep.* II. 1. With absence of; not with the presence or addition of; not having with it or with one, not accompanied by (a thing or person) ME. 2. In a state of not possessing (a part, an advantage, a possession of any kind); in want of, destitute of, lacking ME. b. Not with (something that might be given or obtained); not getting or receiving, or having got or received ME. c. In the construction of certain verbs: see DO *v.* V. 6, GO *v.* VI. 1458. 3. With no use, employment, or action of (an instrument, means, etc.); with no action or agency of (a person); *esp.* with no co-operation of, or support from ME. 4. (with obj. an abstract thing, as a quality, action, etc.): a. (depending on or referring to a verb). With absence or lack of, or freedom from: often forming phrases equivalent to neg. advs., e.g. *w. end* = endlessly, *w. success* = unsuccessfully, etc. ME. b. (depending on or referring to a sb.) Characterized by absence of, lacking or free from: often forming phrases equivalent to neg. adjs., e.g. *w. end* = endless, etc. ME. c. With no possibility of; so, or such, as not to admit of ME. 5. Followed by a gerund or vbl. sb. in *-ing*: = 'so as not to' or 'and not' with the corresp. vb., or 'not' with the pres. pple. ME. b. By ellipsis of the gerund: Not counting, leaving out of account. *colloq.* 1871. 5. With conditional implication (mostly with neg., expressed or implied): If one have (or had) not, if there be (or were) not, in the absence or, in default of ME. 6. With ellipsis of the obj. Now *colloq.* (exc. in contrast with *with*). late ME. b. *slang.* in ref. to liquor: Not mixed with sugar 1835. 7. Qualified by a negative: *not w.* = not lacking, with or having some (implying or suggesting a somewhat slight or not very great amount) 1596.

1. There is no fyre w. some smoke 1546. If you can live w. me 1877. 2. I do believe you are better w. the money GEO. ELIOT. b. They are all Guilty of Felony, w. Benefit of the Clergy 1723. 3. Imprisoned for burying a Catholic w. a minister 1592. Withouten wind, withouten tide, She steddies with upright keel COLERIDGE. *W. book*: without authority; also lit. without the aid of a book, from memory, by rote; hence (with hyphen) attrib. or as adj., recited w. book or from memory; Weele haue..no withoutbooke Prologue faintly spoke After the Prompter SHAKS. 4. I hope I may say it w. vanity 1779. He..let her go w. a word 1881. c. These wounds..are w. cure JOHNSON. 5. I can hardly stir abroad w. catching cold 1734. b. My father has enough to do to keep the rest, w. me GEO. ELIOT. 6. Nober man ne womman schulde be punsched wiþ oute gilt 1387. 7. You must have given him some encouragement..A man wouldn't offer to lend a lady his opera-glasses w. 1898.

C. *conj.* (or in *conj. phr.*) 1. The prep. governing a clause introduced by *that*, so that *w. that* becomes a conjunctional phr. a. Without its being the case that. Now *rare* or *Obs.* 1450. †b. *W. that* (or *this*) *that*: legal phr. introducing an exception, *spec.* in pleading [tr. law-Fr. *sans ceo que*], a form, obs. since 1852, whereby a defendant asserted special matter of exception or justification against the plaintiff's claim while reserving his denial of the whole cause of action –1824. 2. Hence, by omission of *that*, simply as a conjunction: If... not, except, unless. In later use *colloq.* or *arch.*, and now chiefly *illiterate*. late ME.

2. I'm but a working woman, and cannot live w. I gets my due 1814.

†**Withou·t doo:r,** *adv. phr.* (*adj.*) ME. = next –1739. b. *attrib.* or as *adj.* = OUT-DOOR *a.*; also *transf.* or *fig.* –1611.

Withou·t doo:rs, *adv. phr.* (*adj.*) *Obs.* or *rare arch.* 1617. 1. Out of doors, outside the house, in the open air. 2. *transf.* and *fig.* Outside the community (family, nation, etc.) 1697. 3. *attrib.* or as *adj.* = prec. b. 1654.

Withou·tside, *adv.* and *prep.* Now *rare* or *Obs.* 1578. [f. WITHOUT + SIDE *sb.*[1], after *outside*.] **A.** *adv.* 1. On the outer side or surface. 2. In (or to) the place or space without 1700. 3. W. of, *prep. phr.* = *outside of* 1638. **B.** *prep.* = A. 3. 1686.

Withstand (wiðstæ·nd, wiþ-), *v.* Pa. t. and pa. pple. **withstood.** [OE. *wiþstandan*; see WITH-.] 1. *trans.* To stand or maintain one's or its position against; to offer resistance to: often with implication that the resistance is successful or effectual. b. To resist the attraction, influence or cogency of; occas. to abstain from (doing something) 1725. 2. To stand in the way of; to oppose or hinder the performance, operation, or progress of. *Obs.* or merged in 1. late ME. 3. *intr.* To offer resistance or opposition OE.

1. To w. your enemyes in tyme of nede 1434. And sturdy strokes he did w. 1558. Rage must be withstood SHAKS. 2. I hope you will not w. your own preferment FIELDING.

Withwind (wi·þwəind). Now *dial.* [OE. *wiþowinde, wiþe-*, f. *wiþo-, wiþe-* (related to WITHE) + *winde* WIND *sb.*[2]] Bindweed, *Convolvulus arvensis* or *C. sepium*; also *C. Solda-*

nella (Sea W.). Applied also to other climbing plants, e. g. dodder, smilax.

Withy (wi·ði). [OE. *wiþig*; see WITHE.] **1.** A willow of any species: sometime *spec.* the osier willow, *Salix viminalis.* **b.** With qualification, applied to various species of willow. late ME. **2.** A flexible branch of a willow, esp. as used for tying or binding, as a halter, etc.; any similar flexible branch or twig; a leash, hoop, or the like made of a w. late ME.

Withywind (wi·ðiwəind). Now *dial.* 1578. [Alteration of WITHWIND, after prec.] = WITHWIND.

Witless (wi·tlės), *a.* Now only *literary* and somewhat *arch.* [OE. *witléas*; see WIT *sb.* and -LESS.] **1.** Lacking wisdom or sense; not guided by reason; foolish, heedless ME. **2.** Mentally deficient or deranged; crazy, out of one's wits OE. **3.** Deficient in understanding; having undeveloped or imperfect intellectual power; stupid, dull-witted 1562. **b.** Not understanding (something specified or implied); inapprehensive 1614. **4.** Not knowing; unaware, unconscious *of* 1584. **5.** Devoid of wit (*rare*) 1753.

1. I was witlesse, wanton, fond, and yong 1559. 4. Guiltlesse and witlesse of the crime 1597. 5. Solemn dinners, ..and w. tea-parties 1859. Hence **Wi·tless-ly** *adv.*, **-ness.**

Witling (wi·tliŋ). 1693. [f. WIT *sb.* + -LING¹ 2.] A petty wit; one who fancies himself a wit; one who utters light or feeble witticisms.

‖**Witloof** (wi·tlōf). 1885. [Du. lit. 'white leaf'.] = CHICORY.

Witness (wi·tnės), *sb.* [OE. *witnes*, f. *wit* WIT *sb.* + *-nes* -NESS.] †**1.** Knowledge, understanding, wisdom -1482. **2.** Attestation of a fact, event, or statement; testimony, evidence OE. **b.** Applied to the inward testimony of the conscience; after 2 *Cor.* i. 12. ME. **3.** Testimony by signature, oath, etc. Chiefly in phr. *in w. of*, *whereof*, etc. ME. **4.** One who gives evidence in relation to matters of fact under inquiry; *spec.* one who gives or is legally qualified to give evidence upon oath or affirmation in a court of justice or judicial inquiry OE. **5.** One who is called on, selected, or appointed to be present at a transaction, so as to be able to testify to its having taken place; *spec.* one who is present at the execution of a document and subscribes it in attestation thereof (*attesting* or *subscribing w.*) ME. †**b.** A sponsor or godparent at baptism (orig. in Puritan use) -1837. **6.** One who is or was present and is able to testify from personal observation; one present as a spectator or auditor ME. **b.** In asseverative formulæ, in which a deity or a person is invoked as one who is cognizant of a fact; as *God is my w. that...* Chiefly in phr. *to call* or *take to w.*: to call upon or appeal to as one's surety; to swear by. ME. **7.** *fig.* Something that furnishes evidence or proof of the thing or fact mentioned; an evidential mark or sign, a token ME. **b.** Introducing a name, designation, phrase, or clause denoting a person or thing that furnishes evidence of the fact or exemplifies the statement. (After L. *teste..*, F. *témoin..*) ME. **c.** *spec.* In textual criticism, a manuscript or an early version which is regarded as evidence of authority for the text. (Usu. in *pl.*) 1853. **8.** One who testifies for Christ or the Christian faith, esp. by death; a martyr. *Obs.* exc. as literal rendering of Gr. μάρτυς MARTYR. late ME.

2. b. May we with..the witnesse of a good conscience, pursue him with any further reuenge? SHAKS. 3. In witnesse whereof I have hereunto set my hand and seal 1658. 4. False witnesses are much cheaper than in Christendom 1718. *transf.* Well, let my Deeds be witnesse of my worth SHAKS. *Hostile w.*, one who gives evidence adverse to the party by whom he is called. *Ultroneous w.*, see ULTRONEOUS b. 6. No man might haue accesse to him, nor speake wᵗ him without a witnesse 1560. I..stood the helpless w. of thy fate POPE. b. The tall boy..called those about him to w. that he had only shouted in a whisper DICKENS. 7. b. Nature oftentimes recompenceth deform'd bodies with excellent wits. Witnesse Æsop. FULLER. And novels (w. ev'ry month's review) Belie their name, and offer nothing new COWPER.

Phrases. *In w.*, as a testimony or piece of evidence (*rare* or *Obs.* exc. as in 3). *To bear w.*, (said prop. of a person, a book, etc.) to give oral or written testimony or evidence; hence *fig.* to furnish or constitute evidence or proof. *To bear* (one) *w.*, to corroborate one's statement or be a witness of one's action. †*To take w. of*, to call or take to w. (see 6 b). *With a w.*, with clear evidence, without a doubt, 'and no mistake' (*obs.* or *rare arch.*).

attrib. and *Comb.*: **w. action**, an action in which witnesses are summoned, as dist. from one in which only matters of law are argued; **-box**, an enclosed space in which a w. is placed while giving evidence; **-stand** *U.S.*, the place where a w. is stationed while giving evidence.

Witness (wi·tnės), *v.* ME. [f. prec.] **1.** *trans.* To bear witness to (a fact or statement); to furnish oral or written evidence of. **b.** *transf.* Of a document: To furnish formally attested evidence of 1474. **c.** *fig.* To furnish evidence or proof of; to be a sign or mark of, betoken. late ME. †**d.** To give evidence of by one's behaviour; to make evident -1728. **e.** To show forth evidence of or as to (an object of allegiance) by faithful speech or conduct; to be a witness for. Now *rare* or *Obs.* 1526. **2.** *intr.* To bear oral or written witness; to testify. Now usu. with *to* or *against.* ME. **3.** *trans.* **a.** To give formal or sworn evidence of (a fact, etc.); to depose in evidence. Now *rare.* ME. **b.** To attest formally by signature; to sign (a document) as a witness of its execution. Also *absol.* ME. **c.** To be formally present as a witness of (a transaction). late ME. **4.** (*transf.* from 3 c.) To be a witness, spectator, or auditor of (something of interest, importance, or special concern); to experience by personal (esp. ocular) observation; to see with one's own eyes. (In loose writing often used merely as a synonym of 'see'.) 1582. **b.** *fig.* Of a place, time, etc.: To be associated with (a fact or event); to be the scene or setting of; to 'see' 1785.

1. c. Thy face, and thy behauiour, Which..Witnesse good bringing vp SHAKS. And there it stands unto this day To w. if I lie MACAULAY. 4. Never did I w. a more melancholy scene of devastation SOUTHEY. Large crowds witnessed their departure, but no demonstration occurred 1912. b. These fertile plains.. once witnessed the defeat and death of a Gothic monarch 1813. Hence **Wi·tnessable** *a.* (*rare*) that may be witnessed. **Wi·tnesser** (now *rare*), one who witnesses, a witness.

Witney (wi·tni). 1716. A heavy loose woollen material with a nap, manufactured and made up into blankets at Witney, a town in Oxfordshire; also, formerly, a kind of cloth or coating made there. Also *attrib.*, esp. in *W. blanket.*

Witted (wi·tėd), *a.* late ME. [f. WIT *sb.* -ED².] Having wit or wits (of a specified quality or amount): in parasynthetic comb. with an adj., as *dull-*, HALF-WITTED, *quick-*, *sharp-*, *slow-w.*

A quick-w. though not whole-w. lad 1904.

Wittichenite (wi·tikĕnəit). 1868. [ad. G. *wittichenit*, f. *Wittichen* in Baden, where found; see -ITE¹.] *Min.* Native sulphide of bismuth and copper.

Witticism (wi·tisiz'm). 1677. [Coined by Dryden; f. WITTY *a.*, after *criticism.*] A piece of wit; a witty saying or remark. In earlier use often *contempt.*, or applied esp. to a joke made at another's expense, a jeer.

Maternal witticisms upon his uncouth appearance MARIA EDGEWORTH. Hence **Wi·tticize** *v. intr.*, to utter witticisms.

Wittily (wi·tili), *adv.* ME. [f. WITTY *a.* + -LY².] †**1.** Intelligently, cleverly; wisely, discreetly, sensibly -1825. **2.** In a manner characterized by wit; in a cleverly amusing way; with smart jocosity 1553.

1. W. wicked SIR T. BROWNE. Dr. Pritchard.. preached..very allegorically..yet very gravely and wittily EVELYN. 2. In conversation w. pleasant, and pleasantly gamesome SIDNEY.

Wittiness (wi·tinės). 1533. [f. WITTY *a.* + -NESS.] The quality or character of being witty.

Witting (wi·tiŋ), *vbl. sb.* *Obs.* exc. *dial.* late ME. [Partly (in forms †*witand*, †*wetand*) a. ON. *vitand* in phr. *at minni*, *várri* (etc.) *vitand* to my, our (etc.) knowledge; partly f. WIT *v.*¹ + -ING¹.] **1.** The fact of knowing or being aware of something; knowledge, cognizance. Most freq. in phr. *at*, *by* (*etc.*) *one's w.* (cf. OF. *a son escient*): to one's knowledge, as one knows. **2.** Knowledge obtained or (esp.) communicated; information, tidings; notice, warning. Chiefly in *to get* or *have w.* late ME.

Wi·tting, *ppl. a.* late ME. [f. WIT *v.*¹ + -ING².] **a.** *advb.* = WITTINGLY. **b.** Chiefly *predic.*: Aware, cognizant 1500. **c.** Conscious as an agent; that is consciously what the sb. denotes 1678. **d.** *transf.* of the action: Done consciously (and so with responsibility), deliberate 1553.

a. No man wyttyng and wyllyng wyl hurt hymselfe 1538. d. The notion of w. and wilful vice 1879.

Wittingite (wi·tiŋəit). 1868. [ad. G. *wittingit*, f. *Wittingi* in Finland; see -ITE¹.] *Min.* A variety of neotocite.

Wittingly (wi·tiŋli), *adv.* ME. [f. prec. + -LY².] With knowledge or awareness of what one is doing; knowingly, consciously; often implying 'designedly, deliberately'.

Wittol (wi·təl). *Obs.* or *arch.* [Late ME. *wetewold*, app. formed after *cokewold* CUCKOLD, with substitution of *wete* WIT *v.*¹ for the first part of the word.] **1.** A man who is aware of and complaisant about the infidelity of his wife; a contented cuckold. **b.** *transf.* (app. with pun on *wit-all.*) One who has little sense; a half-witted person 1588. **2.** *attrib.* That is a wittol; pertaining to or characteristic of a wittol; *transf.* half-witted 1604.

1. *Merry W.* II. ii. 313. Hence **Wi·ttolly** *a.* having the character, or characteristic, of a w.

Witty (wi·ti), *a.* [OE. *wit(t)ig*, f. WIT *sb.* + -Y¹.] †**1.** Having wisdom, wise -1611. **2.** Having (good) intellectual ability; intelligent, clever; skilful, capable. *Obs.* exc. *dial.* OE. †**b.** Crafty, cunning, wily, artful -1706. †**3.** *transf.* Showing or demanding intellectual ability; (later, esp. of discourse) clever, ingenious, or subtle in conception or expression -1700. †**b.** Skilfully devised for an evil purpose; (of torment, etc.) ingeniously contrived -1686. †**4.** *transf.* Showing, or springing from, good judgement or discernment; wise, discreet -1710. **5.** Possessing wit; capable of or given to saying (or writing) brilliant or sparkling things, esp. in an amusing way 1590. †**b.** Sharply critical, censorious, sarcastic -1748. **6.** Of speech or writing: Characterized by or full of wit; cleverly amusing, smartly facetious or jocular; †sarcastic 1588.

2. Iudges ought to be more Learned, then Wittie BACON. b. *Much Ado* IV. ii. 27. 3. I wisedome dwell with prudence, and find out knowledge of w. inuentions *Prov.* viii. 12. The Fallacies that are often concealed in florid, witty or involved Discourses LOCKE. 5. I know a wench of excellent discourse, Prettie and wittie SHAKS. b. My Mother..says, I am too w.; Anglicè, too pert RICHARDSON. 6. He told the wittiest stories in the world without omitting anything in them but the point LYTTON.

Witwall (wi·twǫl). Now *dial.* 1544. [a. G. †*wittewal(e* = MLG. *weddewale*, early Flem. *widewael.*] †**1.** The Golden Oriole, *Oriolus galbula* -1678. **2.** The Green Woodpecker, *Gecinus viridis*, or the Greater Spotted Woodpecker, *Dendrocopus major* 1668.

Wive (wəiv), *v.* [OE. *wīfian*, f. *wīf* WIFE.] **1.** *intr.* To take a wife, get married, marry. **2.** To be a wife, act as a wife (*rare*) 1583. **3.** *trans.* To take to wife, make one's wife, wed (a woman); *pa. pple.* made or become a wife, married (*to* a man) 1592. **4.** To furnish with a wife, obtain a wife for: chiefly in *pa. pple.* married (of a man). *Obs.* or *arch.* 1513. **5.** To become the wife of, marry (a man). *Obs.* or *arch.* 1621.

1. Ther as myn herte is set ther wol I wyue CHAUCER. 3. It is no vulgar nature I have wived MEREDITH. 4. 2 *Hen. IV*, I. ii. 61. Hence **Wi·ving** *vbl. sb.* taking a wife, marrying, marriage.

Wiwi¹ (wī·wī). 1842. [Maori, = 'rushes'.] A New Zealand rush used to make an outer covering for the roof and walls of a house.

Wi-wi² (wī·wī). *Austral. slang.* 1845. [ad. F. *oui, oui* yes, yes, taken as typical of the French language.] A Frenchman; as *pl.*, the French.

Wizard (wi·zəɹd), *sb.* and *a.* [Late ME. *wysar(d*, f. *wys*, *wis* WISE *a.* + -ARD.] **A.** *sb.* †**1.** A philosopher, sage. Often *contempt.* -1841. **2.** A man who is skilled in occult arts; in later use, a man who practises witchcraft 1550. **b.** *transf.* and *fig.*: *esp.* a man who 'does wonders' in his profession: in recent use often trivially applied to an expert 1620. **c.** A witch-doctor or medicine-man 1845.

1. Therefore the antique wisards well inuented, That Venus of the fomy sea was bred SPENSER. 2. The Star-led Wisards haste with odours sweet MILT. I call myself a w. as well; but that 's only the polite term for conjurer 1851. **b.** *The W. of the North*, Sir Walter Scott.

B. *adj.* **1.** Having the powers or properties of a wizard; hence *gen.* having magical or witching power or influence 1579. **2.** Of, pertaining to, or associated with wizards or wizardry; hence *gen.* magic, enchanted, bewitched 1638.

2. Nor on the shaggy top of Mona high, Nor yet where Deva spreads her wisard stream MILT. Hence **Wi·zard** *v.* (*rare*) to practise wizardry upon, to bewitch. **Wi·zardly** *a.* (now *rare*) of, pertaining to, characteristic of, or resembling a w. or wizardry.

Wizardry (wi·zəɹdri). 1583. [f. WIZARD *sb.* + -RY.] **1.** The art or practice of a wizard or wizards; wizardly or magic skill; witchcraft. **2.** *fig.* 'Magical' or 'bewitching' art, power, or influence 1884.

Wizen (wi·z'n), *a.* 1786. [Clipped f. WIZENED.] = WIZENED 2.

Wizen (wi·z'n), *v.* [OE. *wisnian, weosnian*, f. Teut. **wis-*; cf. L. *viescere* to wither, W. *gwyw* (:—**wiswo-*) withered.] **1.** *intr.* Of plants: To dry up, shrivel, wither. Also *transf.* of persons, their features, etc. **2.** *trans.* To cause to wither or shrivel. *Sc.* 1513.

Wizened (wi·z'nd), *a.* 1513. orig. *Sc.* and *north.* [f. prec. + -ED[1].] **1.** Of plants, foliage, etc.: Dried up, withered, shrivelled. **2.** Of persons or animals, their features, etc.: Shrunken and dried up, thin and shrivelled 1513.

1. The w. pomegranate HAWTHORNE. 2. A w. old hen instead of the plump pullet you look for MEREDITH. *transf.* A w. old city hidden among the hills 1905.

Wo (wōᵘ), *int.* 1588. [var. of WHO *int.*] **1.** In *wo ho, wo ho ho, wo ha ho*: a falconer's call to a hawk; also *allus.* **2.** A call to a horse to stop. Also used in conjunction with other interjections, as *wo-back, wo-ho.* 1787.

2. I pulled very hard, and cried out, Wo! but he wouldn't: and on I went galloping for the dear life THACKERAY. Hence **Wo** *v. intr.* to call 'wo' to a horse.

Woa (wōᵘ), *int.* 1840. [var. of WHOA *int.*] = prec. 2. Hence **Woa** *v.* to stop (*trans.* and *intr.*) with the call of 'woa'.

Woad (wōᵘd), *sb.* [OE. *wād* :—OTeut. **waido-* (whence OF. *gaide*. It. *guado*), by-form of **waizdo-* (whence med.L. *waizda*, OF. *guesde*, F. *guède*); ulterior connexions doubtful.] **1.** A blue dye-stuff prepared from the leaves of *Isatis tinctoria* powdered and fermented: now generally superseded by indigo. **2.** The plant *Isatis tinctoria*, formerly extensively cultivated for the blue colouring matter furnished by it; sometimes called *Dyer's* or *Garden W.* Also applied to other species of *Isatis.* OE. **b.** **Wild W.**, the plant *Reseda Luteola* 1578.

1. Al the Britons doe dye themselves wyth woade, which setteth a blewish color uppon them 1563.

Comb.: †**w.-ashes**, (*a*) the ashes of burnt winelees, used by dyers; (*b*) the ashes of burnt wood used to make a lye. Hence **Woad** *v. trans.* to dye, colour, or stain with w., sometimes (in dyeing) as a ground for another colour; to treat with w., in dyeing. **Woa·der** (*rare*), a dyer with w.; a cultivator of w.

Wobble, wabble (wǫ·b'l), *sb.* 1699. [f. next.] The action or an act of wobbling; an unsteady rocky motion or movement. **b.** *pl.* (*Austral.*) A disease in cattle caused by eating the leaves of the palm-tree 1895.

Wobble, wabble (wǫb'l), *v.* 1657. [corresp. to LG. *wab(b)eln*, f. Teut. **wab-*.] **1.** *intr.* Of a person or animal: To move from side to side unsteadily or with uncertain direction. **b.** Of a piece of mechanism, a top, a missile, etc. 1677. **c.** To shake or quiver like a jelly or fleshy body 1748. **d.** To move unsteadily from side to side or backwards and forwards (without progression) 1858. **2.** *fig.* To hesitate or waver between different opinions or courses of action; to be inclined to favour first one side and then the other 1884. **3.** *trans.* To cause to move unsteadily from side to side 1831.

1. Such a figure *I* never saw on a horse!..bumping when she trots, and wobbling when she canters 1856. **c.** Her chin wobbled pathetically 1875.

Comb.: **w.-saw**, a circular saw mounted askew on its spindle so as to cut a groove wider than its own thickness. Hence **Wo·bbler**, one who or that which wobbles. **Wo·bbly** *a.* inclined to w.

Wodenism (wōᵘ·dəniz'm). *rare.* 1891. [f. *Woden* (see ODINISM) + -ISM.] Odinism.

Wodge (wǫdʒ). *dial.* and *colloq.* 1860. Also wadge. [Cf. WAD *sb.*[1] and WEDGE *sb.*] A lumpy bundle or mass. Hence **Wo·dgy** *a.*

Woe (wōᵘ), *int., adv., sb., a.* [Com. Indo-Eur. interjection, used as a natural exclam. of lament; OE. *wā*, also *wǣ* :—OTeut. **wai*; cf. L. *væ*, Lett. *wai*, OIr. *fē*, and WAIL *v.*, WELL-AWAY.] **A.** *int.* and *adv.* **I.** As an exclam. of grief or lamentation: = Alas! *arch.* **II.** Construed with dat. or its equivalent. **1.** In prophetic or denunciatory utterances, as *w. be to us* = may affliction or distress light upon us; *w. is him* = cursed is he. *Obs.* or *arch.* OE. **2.** In merely declaratory statements of the type of ME. *him is* (*full*) *wo* = he is (much) distressed or grieved. *Obs.* exc. in *w. is me*: I am distressed, afflicted, unfortunate, grieved (now *arch.* and *dial.*). OE. **3.** *W. worth*: may evil befall or light upon; a curse upon: freq. in phr. *w. worth the day*, (*the while, the time*). *arch.* ME. **b.** Similarly, *W. betide you* (etc.): In mod. use colloq. = You (etc.) will get into trouble (if..). late ME. **4.** Without vb. OE. †**5.** *To do* or *work* (a person) *w.*: to inflict distress or trouble upon; to do harm to OE.

1. W. is him whose bed is made in hell 1636. 3. Then they all wept again, and cryed out: Oh, Wo worth the day BUNYAN. *W. worth me!* used occas. = *W. is me.* 4. Then w. mine eyes vnlesse they beautie see GREENE. Now wae to thee, thou cruel lord, A bluidy man I trow thou be BURNS.

B. *sb.* **1.** A condition of misery, affliction, or distress; misfortune, trouble. *poet.* or *rhet.* ME. **b.** in conjunction with *weal* ME. **c.** In particularized use: chiefly *pl.*, Misfortunes, troubles, griefs. late ME. **2.** Sorrow, grief, anguish (as a state of mind or feeling). *Obs.* or merged in 1. ME. **3.** An utterance of the word 'woe' in denunciation; an anathema, curse. late ME.

1. The Fruit Of that Forbidden Tree, whose mortal tast Brought Death into the World, and all our w. MILT. **c.** One w. makes another w. seeme lesse DRAYTON. 3. The wo denounced against our original mother SCOTT.

C. *adj.* (orig. and chiefly predic.) **1.** Grieved, wretched, miserable, sorrowful. *Obs.* exc. *Sc.* and *n. dial.* ME. **b.** attrib. *Obs.* or *dial.* 1670. †**2.** Of an event, situation, etc.: Woeful, miserable, 'sorry' -1795.

1. An' mony a time my heart's been wae BURNS. Poor Queen!..I was wae to look at her, wae to think of her MRS. CARLYLE. She was not there, and my heart is w. R. BRIDGES. **b.** I am a w. woman this heavy day 1778. 2. Oh! woe it is to think So many men shall never see the sun Go down! SOUTHEY.

Woe-begone (wōᵘ·bɪ̆gǫn), *a.* (*sb.*) ME. [From constructions in which an object is governed by a compound tense of BEGO *v.* (q.v., sense 4), as *me is woe begone* = woe has beset me.] **1.** 'Beset with woe'; oppressed with misfortune, distress, sorrow, or grief. *Obs.* or *arch.* **2.** Of persons in respect of their looks, manner, etc.: Exhibiting or betraying a state of distress, misery, anguish, or grief 1802. **b.** as *sb.* A w. creature 1879.

1. Euen such a man, so faint, so spiritlesse, So dull, so dead in looke, so woe-be-gone SHAKS. 2. A poor mendicant..old and woebegone LOCKHART. *transf.* It was the most woebegone excavation..you ever saw 1862.

Woeful (wōᵘ·fŭl), *a.* ME. [f. WOE *sb.* + -FUL. (Revived or newly formed *c* 1750.)] **1.** Full of woe; afflicted with sorrow, distress, or misfortune; sorrowful, mournful. **2.** Of times, places, etc.: Fraught with woe, affliction, or misery; miserable ME. **3.** In weakened or trivial senses: Such as to excite commiseration or dissatisfaction; 'grievous'; 'pitiful', 'deplorable', 'wretched' 1619. **4.** In comb. with another adj., as *w.-wan*; also advb. = woefully 1750.

1. A w. wight was he 1802. 2. The wofulest anniversary in the whole year HAWTHORNE. 3. What woful stuff this madrigal would be POPE. So **Woe·fulness.** **Woe·some** (*Sc.* waesome) *a.* woeful.

Woefully (wōᵘ·fŭli), *adv.* 1390. [f. prec. + -LY[2].] **1.** Miserably; mournfully, sadly. *arch.* **2.** Grievously, deplorably, 'sadly' 1648.

2. Thou hast once wofully, irreparably deceived me GOLDSM.

Woggle (wǫ·g'l), *v.* 1648. Variant of WAGGLE *v.*

Wogul, vogul (w-, vōᵘ·gul). 1780. [Russian *vogulŭ*, G. *Wogul*, etc.] One of a tribe of the Ugrian stock inhabiting Tobolsk and Perm.

Woke, pa. t. and pa. pple. of WAKE *v.*

Wo·ken, *ppl. a. rare.* 1649. [pa. pple. of WAKE *v.*] Awakened.

Wold (wōᵘld). [Com. Teut.; OE. (Anglian) *wald* (WS. *weald*, artificially preserved as WEALD):—OTeut. **walþuz*; ulterior relations doubtful. After the early 16th c., the word became restricted to local (toponymic) usage, from which the gen. literary use in sense 3 was derived.] †**1.** Forest, forest land; wooded upland -1450. †**2.** A hill, down -1513. **3.** A piece of open country; a plain; in later use chiefly, an elevated tract of open country or moorland; also *collect. pl.* or *sing.* rolling uplands ME. **4.** Used in specific designations of certain hilly tracts in England, viz. the hill country of the East and North Ridings (*Yorkshire Wolds*), the Cotswold district, the hilly districts of Leicestershire and Lincolnshire 1472.

3. Swithold footed thrice the old SHAKS. On they went, through wild and over w. SCOTT. The long pure line of the rising w. 1905.

Wolf (wulf), *sb.* *Pl.* **wolves** (wulvz). [Com. Teut.; OE. *wulf* :—OTeut. **wulfoz*, :—Indo-Eur. **wlqʷos* (Skr. *vṛkas*, Gr. λύκος, L. *lupus*).] **1.** A somewhat large canine animal (*Canis lupus*) found in Europe, Asia, and N. America, hunting in packs, and noted for its fierceness and rapacity. Also applied, with or without defining word, to various other species of *Canis* resembling or allied to this. **b.** In comparisons, with allusion to the fierceness or rapacity of the beast OE. **2.** A figure or representation of a wolf 1562. **b.** *Astron.* The constellation *Lupus* 1551. **3.** Applied to other animals in some way resembling wolves. **a.** (*a*) In S. Africa, a hyena; (*b*) a Tasmanian marsupial, *Thylacinus cynocephalus* 1812. **b.** A name for various voracious fishes (after Gr. λύκος, L. *lupus*) 1555. **c.** A name for various destructive insect larvæ, esp. that of the w.-moth, which infests granaries 1682. **4.** A person or being having the character of a wolf; one of a cruel, ferocious, or rapacious disposition OE. †**b.** Applied to a person, etc. that should be hunted down like a wolf -1638. **5.** As a type of a destructive or 'devouring' agency, esp. hunger or famine; often in such phrases as *to keep the w. from the door* (now always = to ward off hunger or starvation) 1470. **b.** Applied to a ravenous appetite or craving for food 1576. **6.** A name for certain malignant or erosive diseases in men and animals; *esp.* = LUPUS 1. *Obs.* or *dial.* 1559. **7.** A name for apparatus of various kinds. †**a.** An ancient military engine with sharp teeth, employed for grasping battering-rams used by besiegers -1632. **b.** A kind of fishing-net 1725. **c.** *Textile Manuf.* A willow or willy 1875. **8.** *Mus.* [after G. *wolf*] **a.** 'The harsh howling sound of certain chords on keyed instruments, particularly the organ, when tuned by any form of unequal temperament' (Grove); a chord or interval characterized by such a sound 1788. **b.** In instruments of the viol class, a harsh sound due to faulty vibration in certain notes 1876.

1. The wolves howled from the prairies LONGF. **b.** Hog in sloth, Foxe in stealth, Wolfe in greedinesse SHAKS. The Assyrian came down like the w. on the fold BYRON. 3. **b.** The Pike..is called the Wolfe of the water 1634. 4. **b.** 3 *Hen. VI*, II. iv. 13. 5. That Hee or Shee should have wherewith to support both,..at least to keep the Woolf from the door, otherwise 'twere a meer madnes to marry 1645.

Phrases. *To cry w.*, to raise a false alarm (in allusion to the fable of the shepherd boy who deluded people with false cries of 'Wolf!'). *To keep the w. from the door*: see 5. *A w. in a lamb's skin, in sheep's clothing*, etc., a person who conceals malicious intentions under an appearance of gentleness or friendliness (in allusion to *Matt.* vii. 15). *To see* or *have seen a w.* [= Gr. λύκον ἰδεῖν, etc.], to be tongue-tied (from the old belief that a man on seeing a w. lost his voice). *To wake a sleeping w.*, to invite trouble or disturbance.

attrib. and *Comb.* as *w. cub, -hunter, pack*; **w.-berry**, a N. Amer. shrub, *Symphoricarpus occidentalis*, allied to the snowberry; **-fish**, a large and voracious sea-fish, *Anarrhichas lupus*, having numerous sharp teeth and edible flesh; also applied to other fishes of the same genus; **-moth**, a moth, *Tinea granella*, infesting granaries; **-skin**, the skin or pelt of a w.; a garment, etc. made of this; **-spider**, a spider of the family *Lycosidæ*, which hunts after and springs upon its prey. **b.** Combs. with genitive: **wolf's claw**, club-moss.

Wolf (wulf), *v.* 1862. [f. prec.] **1.** *trans.* To eat like a wolf; to devour ravenously. **2.** To delude with false alarms 1910.

1. [She] used to w. her food with her fingers 1862.

Wo·lf-dog. 1652. [Cf. G. *wolfshund.*] **1.** Any of several large varieties of dog formerly kept for hunting wolves, *esp.* the Irish greyhound or wolf-hound. **2.** A cross of a domestic dog and a wolf 1736. **3.** *Alsatian w.*, the official name adopted by the Kennel Club for the German sheep-dog or shepherd-dog (*deutscher schäferhund*) 1924.

Wolffian (vǫ·lfiăn, wu·lfiăn), *a.* 1844. [f. name of K. F. *Wolff* (1733–94), German embryologist + -IAN.] *Anat.* and *Zool.* In *W. body*, the mesonephron or primitive kidney; either of the two renal organs of the embryo of vertebrates; so *W. duct.*

Wolf-hound. 1823. = WOLF-DOG 1.

Russian w. (or borzoi), a slender type with silky, usu. white, hair. *Irish w.*, a heavy type, resembling the deerhound, with a hard wiry coat.

Wolfian (vǫ·lfiăn, wu·lfiăn), *a.*[1] and *sb.*[1] 1791. [f. name of Christian *Wolf* or *Wolff* (1679–1754), German philosopher + -IAN.] **A.** *adj.* Pertaining to the philosophical system of Wolf, which was an eclectic adaptation of Leibnitzianism and scholasticism. **B.** *sb.* An adherent of this system.

Wo·lfian (see prec.) *a.*[2] and *sb.*[2] 1875. [f. name of F. A. *Wolf* (1759–1824), German philologist + -IAN.] **A.** *adj.* Of or pertaining to F. A. Wolf or his theory regarding the Homeric poems. **B.** *sb.* One who accepts this theory.

Wolfish (wu·lfiʃ), *a.* 1570. [f. WOLF *sb.* + -ISH [1].] **1.** Of or pertaining to a wolf or wolves. †**b.** Abounding in wolves. COLLINS. **2.** Characteristic of, befitting, or resembling that of a wolf 1674. **3.** Resembling a wolf, wolf-like 1775. **b.** Ravenously hungry. *U.S. colloq.* 1848.

2. The eyes of the three men, with a fierce and w. glare LYTTON. Hence **Wo·lfish-ly** *adv.*, **-ness.**

Wo·lfling. ME. [-LING [1].] A young or little wolf.

Wolfram (wu·lfrăm, vǫ·lfrăm). 1757. [a. G., of obsc. formation; perh. f. *wolf* wolf + *rahm* cream, or MHG. *râm* dirty mark, soot.] **1.** *Min.* A native tungstate of iron and manganese. **2.** The metal tungsten, obtained from this 1845.

attrib.: **w. lamp, -steel** = TUNGSTEN *lamp, steel*; **-ochre** = TUNGSTITE.

Wolf's-bane (wu·lfsbēin), †**wolfbane.** 1548. [f. genit. of WOLF *sb.* + BANE *sb.*, rendering L. *lycoctonum*, a. Gr. λυκοκτόνον, f. λύκος WOLF + κτον- (: κτεν-) to slay.] A plant of the genus *Aconitum*, esp. *A. lycoctonum*, with dull yellow flowers, occurring in mountainous regions in Europe. Also applied to *Arnica montana* (*winter w.*), and to the winter aconite, *Eranthis hyemalis.*

Wo·lf's-head, wolf-head. OE. **1.** The head of a wolf; a figure of this, e.g. as a heraldic bearing. **2.** *Old English Law.* A cry for the pursuit of an outlaw as one to be hunted down like a wolf; *transf.* an outlaw ME.

Wo·lfskin. late ME. The skin or pelt of a wolf, or a garment made of this.

Wo·lf's-milk. 1575. **1.** The sun-spurge, *Euphorbia Helioscopia*, having an acrid milky juice. **2.** The milk of a wolf 1847.

Wollastonite (wu·lǝstǝnǝit). 1823. [f. name of W. H. *Wollaston* (1766–1828), chemist and physicist + -ITE [1].] *Min.* Native metasilicate of calcium; tabular spar.

Wolve (wulv), *v.* 1702. [f. inflexional stem of WOLF *sb.*] **1.** *intr.* (also with *it*). To behave like a wolf, play the wolf. **2.** Of an organ: To give forth a hollow wailing sound like the howl of a wolf, from deficient wind-supply 1864. So **Wo·lver** (*rare*), one who behaves like a wolf, a ravenous or savage creature; one who searches or hunts for wolves 1593.

Wolverene, -ine (wu·lvǝrīn). 1574. [Obscurely f. inflexional stem of WOLF *sb.*] **1.** The glutton (*Gulo luscus*), now esp. the N. Amer. variety. **2.** The fur of the wolverene 1596. **3.** A nickname for an inhabitant of Michigan. So *W. State*, Michigan. 1835.

†**Wo·lvish,** *a.* late ME. [f. *wolv-*, inflexional stem of WOLF *sb.*] = WOLFISH –1817.

The w. howl BLAKE. If superstition and despotism have been suffered to let in their woolvish sheep COLERIDGE.

Woman (wu·măn), *sb.* *Pl.* **women** (wi·mĕn). [OE. *wīfmon(n, -man(n*, pl. *wīfmen(n*, f. *wīf* woman, WIFE + *mon(n* MAN *sb.* A formation peculiar to English, and not extant in the earliest period of OE. In the mod. period five pronuncs. of the sing. have been current: wu·măn, wū·măn, wʌ·măn, u·măn, ʌ·măn. The last four are now only in vulgar or dial. use; (u·măn) was in educated use in the early 19th c. The standard sing. form represents a divergence (due to the rounding influence of w) from the normal phonetic development, which is preserved in the (wi-) of the pl.] **1.** An adult female human being. **b.** *generically* without article: The female human being; the female sex. Hence gen. *woman's* = womanly, female, feminine. OE. **c.** *pl.* in pregnant use with ref. to (irregular) intercourse with women ME. **d.** As a mode of address. Now (exc. *dial.*) used chiefly derogatorily or joc. ME. **e.** With allusion to qualities attributed to the female sex, as mutability, proneness to tears, or physical weakness; also to their position of inferiority or subjection. late ME. **f.** (Now always with *the.*) The essential qualities of a woman; womanly characteristics; *occas.* the feminine side or aspect 1611. **g.** In contrast, explicit or implicit, with 'lady' 1788. †**h.** In the 16th and 17th cc. freq. with play on a pseudo-etymol. association with *woe* –1653. **2.** A female servant, *esp.* a lady's maid or personal attendant. Often *pl.* OE. **3.** †**a.** A lady-love, mistress. **b.** A kept mistress, paramour. ME. **4.** A wife. Now only *dial.* and *U.S.* 1450. **5.** The reverse of a coin, in ref. to the figure of Britannia upon it 1785.

1. I saw women acte, a thing that I neuer saw before 1611. A perfect W., nobly planned, To warn, to comfort, and command WORDSW. A girl she was not, but a w. of at least nine and twenty 1889. Provbs. A woman, asse, and walnut-tree, the more you beat, the better be 1639. Three Women make a Market 1659. *Little w.*, a female child; also, an affectionate or playful form of address to a girl or young w., esp. one in whom womanly qualities are conspicuous. *New w.* (Hist.), a w. of 'advanced' views, advocating the independence of her sex and defying convention. **b.** W. is the glory of all created existence:—But you, madam, are *more* than w.! RICHARDSON. **c.** Aboue all thynges let hym keepe hym self from Women 1577. **e.** Frailty, thy name is w. SHAKS. Don't make such a fuss; you're as bad as a w. 1850. **f.** Teach her to subdue The w. in her nature 1834. **g.** Defendant pleaded ..that the person described as a w. was in fact a lady 1847. **h.** A woman! As who saith, woe to the man! 1546. **2.** In Town I visit none but the Women of Women of Quality FIELDING. From Mrs. Crouch, ma'am, her Grace's w. 1898. **4.** *Merry W.* II. ii. 305.

attrib. and *Comb.*, simple attrib. or appos. = 'feminine', 'womanly', 'female', as *w. friend, guard, helper, slave, wit*; **w.-boat** = *women's-boat*; **-grown** *a.*, that has become a w.; **w. movement**, the movement for the emancipation of women, or the recognition and extension of women's rights; **-suffrage**, the right of women to vote in public affairs. **b.** Comb. with *woman's, women, women's*: **woman's, women's-boat**, a boat to be used by women only = OOMIAK; **women's courses** = CATAMENIA; **women-house**, *Sc.* a building set apart for women only; **woman's man**, a lady's man, a gallant. Hence **Wo·mandom**, the realm of women, womankind. **Wo·manfully** *adv.* (after *manfully*) with womanly courage or perseverance; like a w. of spirit. †**Wo·manhead** = WOMANHOOD. **Wo·manism**, advocacy of or enthusiasm for the rights, achievements, etc. of women. **Woma·nity** (after *humanity*) *rare*, the normal disposition or character of womankind. **Wo·manless** *a.* without a w. or women; having or containing no women. **Wo·manness** (*rare*), womanliness.

Woman (wu·măn), *v.* 1595. [f. prec.] †**1.** Nonce-uses. **a.** *intr.* To become woman-like; with *it*, to behave as a woman. **b.** *trans.* To make like a woman in weakness or subservience. **c.** *pa. pple.* Accompanied by a woman. –1613. **2.** *trans.* To furnish or provide with women; to equip with a staff of women. (After MAN *v.*) 1706. **3.** To address (contemptuously) as 'woman': see prec. 1 d. 1740.

3. She call'd her another time Fat-face and woman'd her most violently RICHARDSON.

Wo·man-child. *Pl.* **wo·men-chi·ldren.** *arch.* 1558. A female child.

Wo·man-ha·ter. 1607. One who hates women, a misogynist.

Womanhood (wu·mănhud). late ME. **1.** The state or condition of being a woman. **b.** The state of being a grown woman; the period of life succeeding to girlhood 1608. **2.** The disposition, character, or qualities natural to a woman or womankind; womanliness. late ME. **3.** Women collectively, womankind 1523.

1. She.., contrarie to Gods lawe, and the honest estate of w., was clothed in mans apparell 1568.

Womanish (wu·măniʃ), *a.* late ME. [-ISH [1] 2.] **1.** Of or belonging to a woman or women; used or done by women. Now *rare.* **2.** Characteristic of or proper to a woman or women; womanly, feminine. late ME. **b.** In derogatory use. late ME. **3.** Resembling a woman, woman-like: in later use chiefly derogatory. late ME.

1. Spinning, weaving, and the like w. chares 1624. **2. b.** Her questions.. wer like to be but friuolous & womannish 1532. Hence **Wo·manish-ly** *adv.*, **-ness.**

Womanize (wu·mănǝiz), *v.* 1593. [f. WOMAN *sb.* + -IZE.] **1.** *trans.* To make a woman of (a man); *gen.* to render effeminate. †**2.** *intr.* To become womanlike; to behave like a woman –1736. **3.** To consort illicitly with women (*colloq.*) 1893. Hence **Wo·manizer**, one who goes after or consorts illicitly with women.

Womankind (wu·mănkǝind). late ME. [f. WOMAN *sb.* + KIND *sb.*] **1.** The female part of the human race; women in general. **2.** The women of a family, household, company, country, etc.; (one's) women-folk 1573. †**3.** A female human being; a woman –1823.

1. I do admire Of w. but one COWPER. **2.** The persecution which his w. had inflicted upon him THACKERAY.

Womanlike (wu·mănlǝik), *a.* and *adv.* 1440. [f. WOMAN *sb.* + -LIKE.] **A.** *adj.* Like, resembling, or characteristic of a woman or women; in derogatory use, womanish, effeminate. **B.** *adv.* In a manner characteristic of women, after the fashion of women; like a woman 1440.

Looking, w., straight on to the purpose she had in view 1857.

Wo·manliness. 1538. [f. next + -NESS.] The quality of being womanly; womanly character.

Womanly (wu·mănli), *a.* ME. [f. WOMAN *sb.* + -LY [1].] **1.** Possessing the attributes proper to a woman; having the qualities (as of gentleness, devotion, etc.) characteristic of women; also said of these qualities or of actions which exhibit them. late ME. **b.** In derogatory use, with ref. to the bad qualities attributed to women ME. **2.** Having the character of, befitting or characteristic of, a woman as contrasted with a girl 1709. **3.** Belonging or proper to the female sex 1863.

1. **b.** Has she baffled me by some piece of w. juglery? 1862. **2.** A very little girl.. wearing a w. sort of bonnet much too large for her DICKENS.

Wo·manly, *adv.* *Obs.* or *arch.* ME. [f. as prec.; see -LY [2].] In a womanly manner; like a woman.

Wo·man-se·rvant. 1529. A female servant.

Woman's rights. Also **women's rights.** 1840. The rights claimed by women of equal privileges and opportunities with men. Hence Woman's (women's) righter, a believer in or supporter of woman's rights.

Womb (wūm), *sb.* [Com. Teut.; OE. *wamb, womb*; ulterior relations obsc.] †**1.** = BELLY. **a.** The abdomen –1684. **b.** The stomach (as the receptacle of food) –1756. **2.** The uterus OE. **3.** *transf.* A hollow space or cavity, or something conceived as such (*e.g.* the depth of night) OE. **4.** *fig.* A place or medium of conception and development; a place or point of origin and growth 1593.

1. **a.** 2 *Hen. IV*, IV. iii. 25. **3.** Yee sootie coursers of the night, Hurrie your chariot into hels black wombe MARSTON. **4.** Some vnborne sorrow, ripe in fortunes wombe SHAKS. Hence **Womb** *v. trans.* to enclose as in a w. **Wombed** (wūmd) *a.* having a w. or belly (of a specified kind). **Womby** (wū·mi) *a.* (*rare*) having a w.-like cavity; hollow.

Wombat (wǫ·mbæt). 1798. [Native Australian name.] Any of the burrowing marsupials of the genus *Phascolomys*, native to S. Australia and Tasmania, characterized by a thick heavy body, short legs, and a general resemblance to a small bear.

Womenfolk (wi·mĕnfōᵘk). 1833. [f. pl. of WOMAN *sb.* + FOLK.] **a.** Women collectively, womankind. Now *dial.* **b.** The women of a household, a party, or the like: *dial.* the female servants.

Womenkind (wi·mĕnkəind). late ME. [f. as prec. + KIND *sb.*] **1.** = WOMANKIND **1.** **2.** = WOMANKIND 2. 1648.

1. This behaviour disgusted Mr. Bousfield with w. 1889. 2. The old gentleman evidently took a secret pride in his w. 1852.

Won, wone (wɒn, wōᵘn), *v. Obs.* exc. *Sc.* and *n. dial.*, and *arch.* [OE. *wunian*:—OTeut. **wunōjan*, *-ǣjan*, related to WEAN *v.*, WIN *sb.*[2]] **I. 1.** *intr.* To stay habitually, dwell, live (in a place or with some one). †**2.** To continue to be, remain; to have existence, live –1633. †**3.** *trans.* To dwell in, inhabit –1600. †**II.** *intr.* To be accustomed or used *to do* something –1642.

To be wont: see WONT *pa. pple.*

Won (wɒn), *ppl. a.* 1500. Pa. pple. of WIN *v.*

A w. battle SCOTT.

Wonder (wɒ·ndəɪ), *sb.* [OE. *wundor* = OS. *wundar*, OHG. *wuntar*, ON. *undr*; origin unkn.] **I.** Something that causes astonishment. **1.** A marvellous object; a marvel, prodigy. **b.** Marvellous character or quality; marvels collectively ME. **c.** (*transf.* from II. 1.) The object of astonishment (usu. implying profound admiration) for a particular country, age, or the like 1591. **d.** A marvellous specimen or example (*of* something) 1721. **e.** *U.S.* = CRULLER 1848. **2.** A deed performed or an event brought about by miraculous or supernatural power; a miracle. *arch.* OE. †**b.** An extraordinary natural occurrence, esp. when regarded as supernatural or taken as an omen or portent. Chiefly *pl.* –1681. **3.** A marvellous act or achievement ME. **4.** *gen.* An astonishing occurrence, event, or fact; a wonderful thing ME.

1. *The seven wonders of the world* (= L. *septem mira, miracula*, or *spectacula*), the seven monuments regarded as the most remarkable structures of ancient times. *Nine days' w.*: see NINE *a.* b. Great things and full of w. in our eares MILT. c. She 's the w. of the Court, And talke oth' Towne 1639. *World's w.*, the Marvel of Peru. 2. *To do* or *work wonders*, to perform miracles. 3. *To work, do*, or *perform wonders*, to do marvellous acts or bring about marvellous results; hence *gen.* to do surprising things; Inspired by your Ladyship's approbation, my steward has really done wonders DISRAELI. 4. Bee you in the Parke about midnight,..and you shall see wonders SHAKS.

Phrases. *To a w.*, marvellously, wonderfully, marvellously well. (*Obs.* or *arch.*) *It is* (*was, were*, etc.) *no w.*, it is (etc.) not surprising; usu. with dependent *that-* or *if-* clause. Also, without vb., *No w. that, if*, or *though*; similarly *Small w. that* (etc.), *what w. if..?* Also interjectionally in (*and*) *no w.!*, *and what w.!* *The w. is..*, what is surprising is.. *For a w.*, as an instance of a surprising fact; strange to say. *In the name of w.*, used with an interrogative word to give emphasis to a question.

II. 1. The emotion excited by the perception of something novel and unexpected, or inexplicable; astonishment mingled with perplexity or bewildered curiosity. Also, the state of mind in which this emotion exists. ME. †**b.** Profound admiration –1607. **2.** [f. WONDER *v.* 2.] A state of wondering (*whether*, etc.). *rare.* 1853.

1. Satan..Looks down with w. at the sudden view Of all this world at once MILT. b. *Macb.* I. iii. 92.

III. *attrib.* and *Comb.*, as *w.-book, -child, -story, -world*; *w.-loving, -struck* adjs.; *w.-monger* 1552.

†**Wo·nder,** *a.* ME. [repr. OE. *wundor* WONDER *sb.* in compounds, as *wundorcræft* marvellous skill or power.] Wonderful, wondrous, marvellous –1590.

Wonder (wɒ·ndəɪ), *v.* [OE. *wundrian*, f. WONDER *sb.*] **1.** *intr.* To feel or be affected with wonder; to be struck with surprise or astonishment, to marvel. Also *occas.* to express wonder in speech. **2.** Usu. with clause: To ask oneself in wonderment; to feel some doubt or curiosity (*how, whether, why*, etc.); to be desirous to know or learn ME. †**3.** *trans.* To regard with wonder; to marvel at –1821. **b.** *impers.* pass. *It is to be wondered* = it is to be wondered at. Now *rare* or *Obs.* 1654.

1. That to hymself..he seme a stoute felow and one to be wondered at 1549. I w. of this being heere together SHAKS. I w. that you will still be talking, signior Benedicke, no body markes you SHAKS. I w. at you RICHARDSON. He wondered to hear a Man of his Sense talk after that Manner ADDISON. *I shouldn't w.* (colloq.), I should not be surprised (*if*, etc.). 2. *I w.!*, colloq. exclam. expressing doubt, incredulity, or reserve of judgement. Hence **Wo·ndering** *vbl. sb.* and *ppl. a.*, **-ly** *adv.*

Wo·nder, *adv. Obs.* or *arch.* (in later use *Sc.*) ME. [Partly OE. *wundor* WONDER *sb.* in compounds; partly OE. *wundrum*, advb. dat. pl. of *wundor*.] Wondrously, marvellously; exceedingly, very.

Wonderful (wɒ·ndəɪfŭl), *a.*, (*sb.*), and *adv.* [Late OE. *wunderfull*, f. WONDER *sb.* + -FUL.] **A.** *adj.* Full of wonder; such as to excite wonder or astonishment; marvellous; sometimes used trivially, = surprisingly large, fine, excellent, etc. **b.** *The w.*: that which is wonderful. †Also *sb. pl.* wonderful things. 1727.

Whereof ensued unto me..a wonderfull payne in my stomacke 1596. There be three things which are too wonderfull for me; yea foure, which I know not *Prov.* xxx. 18. He trimmed his whiskers, and put on a w. waistcoat 1880.

B. *adv.* Wonderfully. Now *dial.* late ME. Hence **Wo·nderful·ly** *adv.*, **-ness.**

Wonderland (wɒ·ndəɪlænd). 1790. [f. WONDER *sb.* + LAND *sb.* Cf. G. *wunderland.*] **a.** An imaginary realm of wonder and faery. **b.** A country, realm, or domain which is full of wonders or marvels.

a. Alice's Adventures in Wonderland LEWIS CARROLL. b. The w. of molecular physics 1903.

Wonderment (wɒ·ndəɪmĕnt). Chiefly *literary.* 1535. [f. WONDER *v.* + -MENT.] **1.** The or a state of wonder. **b.** An expression of wonder: chiefly in *to make a w.*, to express wonder 1553. **2.** An object of or matter for wonder; a wonderful thing 1542. **b.** A wonderful example or instance (*of* something) 1606. **3.** Wonderful quality 1596.

1. Whom all..gazd vpon with gaping w. SPENSER. 2. It 's a w. to me..how you got us off 1841.

†**Wo·nders,** *a.* and *adv.* ME. [genit. of WONDER *sb.*; a Scand. idiom: cf. MSw. *unders.*] = WONDROUS *a.* and *adv.* –1602.

Wo·nder-work. [OE. *wundorweorc*, f. WONDER *sb.* + WORK *sb.* In mod. use a new formation.] **1.** A marvellous or miraculous act; a miracle. **2.** A wonderful work or structure ME. **3.** Marvellous work or workmanship 1513.

2. Wonder-works of God and Nature's hand BYRON.

Wo·nder-wo·rker. 1599. [f. WONDER *sb.* + WORKER; tr. med.L. *thaumaturgus*, Gr. θαυματουργός.] One who performs wonders; *esp.* a worker of miracles; a thaumaturge.

That he may be accounted a stupendious W., a Creatour of his Creatour H. MORE. So **Wo·nder-wo·rking** *ppl. a.*

Wondrous (wɒ·ndrəs), *a.* and *adv. literary.* 1500. [Alteration of WONDERS *a.* by substitution of suffix -OUS, after *marvellous.*] Wonderful.

A faire young man, Of w. beautie SPENSER. Some of Serpent kinde W. in length and corpulence MILT.

B. *adv.* In a wondrous manner; to a wonderful degree 1557.

They tell me she is grown w. pretty RICHARDSON. Hence **Wo·ndrous·ly** *adv.*, **-ness.**

†**Wone,** *sb.*[1] [ME. *wune, wōne*, aphetic f. OE. *ȝewuna*, f. Teut. **ga-* Y- + **wun-* WON *v.*] **1.** Habit, custom –1562. **2.** A dwelling-place, abode; *spec.* this world –1748.

†**Wone,** *sb.*[2] ME. [prob. a. ON. *ván*; see N.E.D.] A dwelling place; a country –1570.

†**Wone,** *sb.*[3] ME. [a. ON. *ván.*] **I.** Hope, expectation; opinion, belief –1583. **II.** Resources, abundance, wealth –1570.

Wone, *v.*: see WON *v.*

‖**Wonga-wonga** (wǭ·ŋgăwǫ·ŋgă). *Austral.* 1827. [Native name.] An Australian pigeon, *Leucosarcia picata.*

Wonky (wǫ·ŋki), *a. slang.* 1925. [Fanciful.] Shaky; ailing.

Wo·nning, wo·ning, *vbl. sb. Obs.*, *dial.*, or *arch.* [OE *wunung*, f. *wunian* WON *v.*] **1.** The action or state of dwelling or abiding. **2.** A place of habitation, dwelling-place OE. **3.** A dwelling-house or dwelling-room, dwelling, habitation OE.

Wont (wōᵘnt; *now chiefly U.S.* wɒnt), *sb. arch.* 1530. [Early history and origin doubtful.] Habitual or customary usage, custom, habit.

As merry as that fellow Joyce could make us with his mad talking, after the old w. PEPYS. *Use and w.*: see USE *sb.* II. 3.

Wont (wōᵘnt; *now chiefly U.S.* wɒnt), *v. arch.* 1440. [f. WONT *pa. pple.* or back-formation from WONTED.] **1.** *trans.* To make (a person, etc.) accustomed or used *to.* **b.** *refl.* (rarely *intr.* for *refl.*) 1603. **2.** *intr.* To be wont or accustomed; to be in the habit of (doing that which is expressed by the inf.) 1547.

2. Talbot is taken, whom we w. to feare SHAKS. To bouze old Wine, mad Pindar wonted 1700.

Wont (wōᵘnt; *now chiefly U.S.* wɒnt), *pa. pple.* and *ppl. a.* [OE. *gewunod*, pa. pple. of *ȝewunian* WON *v.*] **A.** *pa. pple.* †**1.** Accustomed, used *to*, familiar *with* –1520. **2.** Conjugated with the verb 'to be' and const. inf.: Accustomed, used; in the habit of (doing something). Also without inf. OE. **b.** Conjugated with the verb 'to have': in *had w.*, had been accustomed. Now *rare.* 1594.

2. He was wonte to boste, brage, and to brace SKELTON. The longer your letters were the more they were woont to please mee 1647. All is going on as it was w. DICKENS.

†**B.** *ppl. a.* = WONTED B. –1596.

Won't (wōᵘnt), colloq. contraction of *wol(l) not* = *will not.* Also as *sb.* = refusal.

Wonted (wōᵘ·ntĕd; *now chiefly U.S.* wɒ·ntĕd), *pa. pple.* and *ppl. a.* late ME. [Either f. WONT *sb.* + -ED, or an extension of WONT *pa. pple.*] **A.** *pa. pple.* †**1.** = WONT *pa. pple.* 2. –1612. **2.** = WONT *pa. pple.* 1. Now *U.S.* 1610. **b.** *absol.* Made familiar with one's environment. Now *U.S.* 1610.

2. She was w. to the Place, she said, and would not Remove 1692.

B. *ppl. a.* Accustomed, customary, usual. Now *arch.* or *U.S.* late ME.

E'en in our Ashes live their w. Fires GRAY. Hence **Wo·nted·ly** *adv.* (now *rare* or *Obs.*), **-ness** (*rare*).

Woo (wū), *v.* Now *literary.* [Late OE. *wōȝian* intr. (*āwōȝian* trans.), of obsc. origin.] **I.** *intr.* (or *absol.*) **1.** To solicit or sue a woman in love; to court, make love. **2.** To make solicitation or entreaty; to sue *for* 1615.

1. To wo is a pleasure in a young man, a fault in an old 1670.

II. *trans.* **1.** To sue to or solicit (a woman) in love, esp. with a view to marriage; to court ME. **2.** To move or invite by alluring means; to entreat or solicit alluringly. late ME. **3.** To sue for or solicit the possession or achievement of; hence *fig.* to 'court', 'invite', 'tempt' 1440.

1. Wooe hir, win hir, and weare hir LYLY. See that you come Not to wooe honour, but to wed it SHAKS. 2. I..will w. my pillow For thoughts more tranquil BYRON.

Wood (wud), *sb.* [OE. *widu, wiodu*, later *wudu*:—OTeut. **widuz* (also in OHG. and ON.), rel. to OIr. *fid* tree, wood.] **I.** †**1.** A tree –ME. **2.** A collection of trees growing more or less thickly together (esp. naturally, as dist. from a *plantation*), of considerable extent, usu. larger than a *grove* or *copse* (but including these), and smaller than a *forest*; a piece of ground covered with trees OE. **b.** *Woods and Forests*, more fully *Woods, Forests, and Land Revenues*, a department of the Civil Service 1803. **3.** Without article: Wooded country, woodland; trees collectively (growing together). Now *rare* exc. as in BRUSHWOOD 2, UNDERWOOD. OE. **4.** *transf.* and *fig.* A collection or crowd of spears or the like (suggesting the trees of a wood); *gen.* a collection, crowd, 'forest'. (After L. *silva.*) Now *rare* or *Obs.* 1584.

4. In such a w. of words MILT.

Phrases, etc. †*In a w.*, in a difficulty, trouble, or perplexity; at a loss. *Out of the w.* (U.S. *woods*), clear or free from difficulties. *Man of the woods* = ORANG-OUTANG. *Not to see the w. for the trees*, to lose the view of the whole in the multitude of details.

II. 1. The substance of which the roots, trunks, and branches of trees or shrubs consist;

trunks or other parts of trees collectively (whether growing or cut down ready for use) OE. **b.** as prepared for and used in arts and crafts ME. **c.** as used for fuel; firewood OE. **d.** *Hort.* The substance forming the head of a tree or shrub; branch-wood; in a fruit-tree, primarily leaf-bearing, as dist. from fruit-bearing, branches 1523. **e.** In bibl. use, as the material of an idol or image 1535. **f.** *spec.* (*Hort.* and *Bot.*) The hard compact fibrous substance lying between the bark outside and the pith within 1600. **g.** A particular kind of wood; freq. *pl.* kinds of wood 1580. **h.** In echoes of the L. proverb *Ne e quovis ligno Mercurius fiat*; hence the 'material' of which a person is 'made' 1594. (Cf. Gr. ὕλη HYLE.) **2.** Something made of wood: *spec.* **a.** The wooden part, as the shaft of a spear 1683. **b.** The cask or barrel as a receptacle for liquor, as opp. to the bottle 1826. **c.** *slang.* The pulpit 1854. **d.** The wooden wind-instruments in an orchestra collectively (also called *the w.-wind*) 1879. **e.** Each of the bowls in the game of bowls 1884.

1. **c.** Heape on muche w.: kindle the fyre BIBLE (Geneva) *Ezek.* xxiv. 10. **e.** The Heathen, in his blindness, Bows down to wood and stone! HEBER. **h.** I know better than most men of what w. a minister is made DISRAELI. **2. b.** Ordinary clarets from the w. 1882. Phrases. *W. of Jerusalem*, a variety of pear. *W. of life* = GUAIACUM.

III. a. *attrib.* or as *adj.* Made or consisting of wood, wooden 1538. **b.** *attrib.* in sense I. 2 or 3. OE. **c.** attrib. uses and comb. of pl. (sense I. 2) *U.S.* 1849. (Cf. WOODSMAN.)

a. Fower woodd bottels, one lether botle 1578. The ..Sap of thir W.-fewel burning on the fire MILT. **b.** Begin these w. birds but to couple now? SHAKS. **c.** Bands of woods-creatures 1902.

Comb.: **w.-alcohol** = WOOD-SPIRIT 2; **-ash, -ashes,** the ash or ashes of burnt wood; **-bill,** an implement used for cutting w., etc.; **-block,** a block of w., *esp.* one on which a design is cut for printing from; **-borer,** *esp.* any one of certain insects and other invertebrates which make perforations in w.; **-carving,** the ornamental carving of wooden utensils, furniture, etc.; **-coal,** (*a*) charcoal obtained from w.; (*b*) = LIGNITE; **-engraver,** (*a*) one who engraves on w.; (*b*) any of various species of N. Amer. w.-boring beetles, esp. *Xyleborus cælatus*; **-engraving,** the process or art of engraving on w. or of making woodcuts; *concr.* a woodcut; **-gum** = XYLAN; **-house,** a house, shed, or room in which w. is stored; **-knife,** a dagger or short sword used by huntsmen for cutting up the game, or gen. as a weapon (*Obs.* or *Hist.*); **-monger,** a dealer in wood; a timber-merchant, or (*esp.*) a seller of w. for fuel (now *rare* exc. *Hist.*); **-note,** a natural untrained musical note or song like that of a wild bird in a w. (in later use echoing Milton); **-oil,** any of several oils or oily substances, obtained from various trees; (*a*) the East Indian *Dipterocarpus alatus* and other species; (*b*) the East Indian Satin-wood, *Chloroxylon Swietenia*; (*c*) (called also *tung-oil*) the seeds of the Chinese Oil-tree or Varnish-tree, *Aleurites cordata* (the *tung-tree*), used chiefly for varnishing woodwork; **-pulp,** a pulp made by mechanical or chemical disintegration of w.-fibre, and used for making paper; **-ranger** *U.S.*, one who ranges woods; a scout or sharpshooter in Amer. armies; **-reeve,** the steward or overseer of a w. or forest; **†-shaw,** a thicket; **-spell** *U.S.*, a spell or turn of work at piling or storing w. for fuel; **-sugar** = XYLOSE; **-vinegar,** vinegar or crude acetic acid obtained by distillation of w.; **-wind,** the wooden wind-instruments in an orchestra collectively; **-wool,** fine shavings of w., usu. pine-w., used as a surgical dressing and for various other purposes; **-yard,** a yard or enclosure in which w. is chopped, sawn, or stored, esp. for use as fuel. **b.** In names of animals, chiefly birds and insects, that live in woods or trees, or that live, bore, or burrow in w., as **w.-ant,** (*a*) a large ant, *Formica rufa*, living in woods; (*b*) a termite or white ant, which burrows in w.; **-dove** = W.-PIGEON; **-duck,** a species of duck inhabiting woods, *esp.* the N. Amer. summer duck *Æx sponsa*, and the Australian *Bernicla jubata*; **-frog,** a species of frog found in woods, as the N. Amer. *Rana sylvatica*; **-grouse,** (*a*) the capercailye *Tetrao urogallus*; (*b*) the spotted Canada grouse, *Canace* (*Dendragapus*) *canadensis*, or allied species; **-lark,** a species of lark (*Alauda arborea*) which perches on trees; dist. from the skylark by having a shorter tail, more variegated plumage, and a different song; **-warbler,** (*a*) the w.-wren, *Phylloscopus sibilatrix*; (*b*) a general name for the Amer. warblers, esp. those of the genus *Dendrœca*. **c.** In names of plants or their products (usu. designating particular species) growing in woods, as **w. anemone,** the common wild anemone, *A. nemorosa*, abundant in woods; **-lily,** (*a*) the lily-of-the-valley, *Convallaria majalis*; (*b*) the common winter-green, *Pyrola minor*; (*c*) any plant of the N. Amer. genus *Trillium*; **-rush,** any plant of the genus *Luzula* (prop. the sylvan species, as *L. sylvatica*), comprising grass-like herbs allied to the rushes, with clusters of chaffy brown flowers; **-sage,** a common name for the W. Germander (*Teucrium Scorodonia*), a labiate herb with dull greenish-yellow flowers, and leaves having a heavy aromatic smell like sage. Hence **Woo·dish** *a.* somewhat woody; †sylvan. **Woo·dlet** (*rare*), a little w.

Wood, *a.* (*adv.*) *Obs.* exc. *dial.* or *rare arch.* [OE. *wōd*, f. Teut. *wōð- :—Indo-Eur. *wāt-, repr. by L. *vates* seer, poet, OIr. *fáith* poet.] **1.** Out of one's mind, insane, lunatic. **b.** Of a dog or other beast: Rabid OE. **2.** Going beyond all reasonable bounds; extremely rash or reckless, wild; vehemently excited OE. **a.** Extremely fierce or violent, ferocious; irascible, passionate ME. **b.** Violently angry or irritated; enraged, furious ME.

1. The folk in Lunnon are a' clean wud about this bit job SCOTT. **2. b.** Heere am I, and w. within this wood, Because I cannot meet my Hermia SHAKS.

†B. *adv.* Madly, frantically, furiously (chiefly in *wood wroth*) -1601. Hence (*Obs.* or *dial.*) **Woo·d-ly** *adv.*, **-ness.**

Wood (wud), *v.* 1538. [f. WOOD *sb.*] **I.** †**1.** *trans.* To surround with a wood or trees; *refl.* and *intr.* to hide or take refuge in a wood -1645. **2.** *trans.* To cover (land) with trees; to convert into woodland (cf. WOODED *ppl. a.*) 1807. **II. a.** *trans.* To supply with wood for fuel; to load (a vessel) with wood 1628. **b.** *intr.* To take in a supply of wood for fuel 1630.

Woodbine[1] (wu·dbəin), **woodbind** (-bəind). [OE. *wudubind(e*, f. *wudu* WOOD *sb.* + root of BIND *v.*] **1.** A name for various plants of a climbing habit; in early use (later only *dial.*), convolvulus and ivy; now chiefly (*U.S.*), the Virginia Creeper, *Ampelopsis quinquefolia*, and the West Indian *Ipomœa tuberosa* (Spanish W.). **2.** *esp.* The common honeysuckle, *Lonicera Periclymenum*; also extended to other species, as the N. Amer. *L. grata* ME.

2. I know a banke where the wilde time blowes,.. Quite ouer-canoped with luscious w. SHAKS. Hence **Woo·dbined** (-bəind) *a.* overgrown or adorned with w.

Woo·dbine[2]. 1915. A cigarette of the *Wild Woodbine* brand.

Woodbury (wu·dbəri). 1869. The name of Walter Bentley *Woodbury* (1834–1885), used attrib. in designation of processes connected with photography invented by him; esp. **Woo·dburytype,** a process in which a design on a film of gelatine, obtained from a photographic negative, is transferred by heavy pressure to a metal plate from which it may be printed; a print thus produced.

Woodchat (wu·d,tʃæt). 1705. [First found in a posthumous work of Ray's, where it appears to be for *woodcat, a literal rendering of G. *waldkatze* or *-kater*.] A species of shrike, *Lanius rutilus* (*rufus*, or *auriculatus*), a rare summer visitor to England; also called *w.-shrike.*

Woodchuck (wu·d,tʃɒk). 1689. [Alteration, by association with WOOD *sb.*, of Amer. Indian name (cf. Cree *wuchak*, *otchock*).] A common N. Amer. species of marmot, *Arctomys monax*, of a large stout form, which burrows in the ground and hibernates in winter.

Woodcock (wu·dkɒk). [Late OE. *wudu-*, *wudecoc(c*, f. WOOD *sb.* + COCK *sb.*[1]] **1.** A common European migratory bird, *Scolopax rusticula*, allied to the snipe, having a long bill, large eyes, and variegated plumage, and much esteemed as food. Also, the allied *Philohela minor* of N. America. **2.** *allus.* (from the ease with which the w. is taken in a snare or net), in ref. to capture by some trickery, or as a type of gullibility or folly; hence applied to a person: A fool, simpleton, dupe. *Obs.* or *arch.* late ME. **3.** *transf.* **a.** = *w. shell* 1815. **b.** A variety of apple 1700. **c.** *Scotch w.*, a savoury dish of eggs, anchovy, etc. 1879.

2. *Twel. N.* II. v. 92.

attrib. and *Comb.*: **w. clay** = *w. soil*; **-shell,** one of several species of *Murex* having a long spout resembling a woodcock's bill; **-snipe,** the great snipe, *Scolopax major*. **w. soil,** a loose soil consisting of a mixture of clay and gravel.

Woodcraft (wu·dkraft). Also *U.S.* **woodscraft.** late ME. (revived or re-formed by Scott). [f. WOOD *sb.* + CRAFT *sb.*] **1.** Skill in or skilled practice of matters pertaining to woods or forests, esp. (in early use) to the chase; now (chiefly *U.S.* and *Colonial*) esp. such knowledge of forest conditions as enables one to maintain oneself or make one's way. **2.** Skill in woodwork, or in constructing something of wood 1833.

Woodcut (wu·dkɒt). 1662. [f. WOOD *sb.* + CUT *sb.*[2] IV. 4.] A design cut in relief on a block of wood, for printing from; a print or impression obtained from this.

Wood-cutter (wu·dkɒtəɹ). 1774. **1.** One who cuts wood; one who cuts down trees, or cuts off their branches, for the wood. **2.** A maker of woodcuts, a wood-engraver 1821. So **Woo·d-cu:tting** *sb.* 1722.

Wooded (wu·dėd), *ppl. a.* 1605. [f. WOOD *sb.* or *v.* + -ED.] Furnished with wood or woods; abounding in woods or forests.

Wooden (wu·d'n), *a.* 1538. [f. WOOD *sb.* + -EN[4].] **1.** Made or consisting of wood. **b.** *transf.*: Made or produced by means of wood; dull or dead, as the sound of wood when struck; relating to or occupied with wood; hard and stiff like wood 1606. **2.** *fig.* Having some quality likened to the hard dry consistence of wood, or to its inferior value as compared with precious metal or the like. **a.** Expressionless, spiritless; dull and inert; stiff and lifeless 1566. **b.** Mentally dull; insensitive; unintelligent, blockish 1586. **†c.** Of inferior character, poor, worthless -1719.

1. **b.** *Tr. & Cr.* I. iii. 155. **2. a.** He wyll neuer blush, he hath a wodden face 1566. **b.** When people have w. heads..it can't be helped GEO. ELIOT.

Collocations: **†w. cut** = WOODCUT; **†w. dagger,** the dagger of lath worn by Vice in the old moralities; **w. horse,** (*a*) a ship (*Obs.* or *arch.*); (*b*) an instrument of punishment, chiefly military, formerly in use; (*c*) the w. figure of a horse (ἵππος δουράτεος, *Odyssey* VIII. 492, 512) in which the Greek invaders were concealed at the siege of Troy; (*d*) a w. structure in a gymnasium, for vaulting exercise; **w. leg,** an artificial leg made of wood; **w. pear,** an Australian tree, *Xylomelum pyriforme*, bearing hard pear-shaped seed-vessels; **w. shoe,** a shoe made of wood, as the French sabot; in the 18th c. pop. taken as typical of the miserable condition of the French peasantry; **w. spoon,** a spoon made of wood; *spec.* one presented by custom at Cambridge to the lowest of those taking honours in the Mathematical Tripos; hence, this position in the examination, or the person who takes it; **w. tongue,** an infectious disease in horses and cattle, in which the tongue is enlarged and hardened; **w. walls** (after ξύλινον τεῖχος, Herodotus vii. 141), ships or shipping, as a defensive force; **w. wedding** *U.S.*, the fifth anniversary of one's wedding, on which it is appropriate to give presents made of wood

Comb. as *w.-faced*, *-featured* adjs.; **w.-head,** a blockhead; **w.-headed** *a*, blockish, stupid. Hence **Woo·den-ly** *adv.*, **-ness.**

Woo·d-hen. ME. **1.** A female woodcock. Now *rare.* **2.** Any flightless rail of the genus *Ocydromus*, of New Zealand and other Pacific islands; = WEKA. 1773.

Woodhouse; see WOODWOSE.

Woodiness (wu·dinės). 1601. [f. WOODY *a.* + -NESS.] The quality or condition of being woody. **1.** Woody texture, consistence, or appearance. **2.** The condition of being full of woods or forests; prevalence or abundance of woodland 1796.

Woo·d-kern(e. *Hist.* 1548. [tr. Ir. *ceithearnach* (KERN *sb.*[1]), *coille* (wood).] An Irish outlaw or robber haunting woods or wild country; such outlaws collectively.

Woodland (wu·dlǽnd). [OE. *wuduland.*] Land covered with wood, i. e. with trees; a wooded region or piece of ground. **b.** *attrib.* Of or pertaining to w.; used, situated, dwelling, or growing in w.; consisting of or containing w.; sylvan ME.

What is now the W. in Warwickshire, was heretofore part of a larger..Forest, called Arden SELDEN. **b.** I am a w. fellow sir, that alwaies loued a great fire SHAKS. Hence **Woo·dlander,** an inhabitant of the w. 1774.

Wood-louse (wu·dlaus). *Pl.* **wood-lice** (-ləis). 1611. **1.** A small isopod crustacean of the genus *Oniscus* or family *Oniscidæ*; esp. the common species *O. asellus*, found in old wood, under stones, etc., and having the property of rolling itself up into a ball. **2.** Locally or occas. applied to various other small invertebrates found in woodwork or in woods, or resembling the crustacean described in 1, as a white ant or termite, various insects of the family *Psocidæ*, etc. 1666.

Woodman[1] (wu·dmǣn). *Pl.* **-men.** ME. [f. Wood *sb.* Cf. WOODSMAN.] **1.** One who hunts game in a wood or forest; a huntsman. *Obs.* or *arch.* **2.** One who looks after the trees in a wood or forest; one who fells or lops trees for timber or fuel; also, one who provides or purveys wood. late ME. †**3.** = WOODWOSE –1780. **4.** A workman who makes something of wood, esp. the woodwork of a carriage 1879.

1. *Merry W.* v. v. 30. *fig.* Has the old Cupid, your Father, chosen well for you? is he a good W.? DRYDEN. **2.** Spare, w., spare the beechen tree CAMPBELL.

†**Woo·dman**[2]. ME. [WOOD *a.*] A madman, lunatic, maniac –1512.

Woo·d-nymph. 1577. **1.** A nymph of the woods; a dryad or hamadryad. **2. a.** Any of certain species of humming-bird, esp. of the genus *Thalurania*. **b.** Collectors' name for moths of the genus *Eudryas* 1861.

1 By dimpled Brook, and Fountain brim, The Wood-Nymphs deckt with Daisies trim, Their merry wakes and pastimes keep MILT.

‖**Woodoo** (wudū·). 1794. [Turkish *wazū*.] The minor ablution of the Mohammedans.

Woodpecker (wu·dpe:kəɪ). 1530. [f. WOOD *sb.* + PECK *v.*[1] + -ER[1]. Cf. Gr. δρυ(ο)κολάπτης, δρυοκόπος.] A bird of the family *Picidæ*, esp. of the sub-family *Picinæ*, usu. having variegated plumage of bright contrasted colours; characterized by their habit of pecking the trunks and branches of trees in search of insects. **b.** With defining words, denoting various species 1668.

b. The three British species are the Green W. (*Gecinus viridis*), the Pied or Greater Spotted W. (*Dendrocopus major*), and the Barred or Lesser Spotted W. (*D. minor*).

Woo·d-pi:geon. 1668. Any of the species of pigeon that live in woods, as the stock-dove, *Columba œnas*, and (now esp.) the ring-dove, *C. palumbus*.

Woodruff (wu·drɒf). [OE. *wudurofe*, f. *wudu* WOOD *sb.* + **rofe*, **rife*, of unkn. meaning.] A low-growing rubiaceous herb (*Asperula odorata*) found in woods in Britain and Europe generally, with clusters of small white flowers, and strongly sweet-scented leaves in whorls. **B.** Extended to other species of *Asperula* 1597.

A-way is huere [= their] wynter wo, when woderove springeth 1310.

Wood-sear, -seer, -sere (wu·dsiəɪ). *Obs.* or *dial.* 1573. [perh. f. WOOD *sb.* + SERE *a.*] **1.** A frothy exudation on plants, produced by an insect; cuckoo-spit; also, the insect itself 1585. **2.** The season in which a tree or shrub will decay or die if its wood be cut 1573. **3.** *attrib.* or *adj.* Applied to loose, spongy ground. *local.* 1670.

Woodshock (wu·dʃǫk). 1829. [app. popular alteration of a native form of WOODCHUCK.] A N. Amer. species of marten or its fur = PEKAN.

Woodside (wu·dsəid). ME. The side or edge of a wood.

By or *under the* or *a w.* = beside a wood; I would have been glad to have lived under my w., to have kept a flock of sheep, rather than undertaken such a government as this CROMWELL.

Woodsman (wu·dzmǣn). *Pl.* **-men.** Chiefly *U.S.* 1688. [f. *woods*, pl. of WOOD *sb.* Cf. BACKWOODSMAN.] A man who inhabits, frequents, or ranges the woods, as a huntsman, wood-cutter, etc.; one acquainted with or accustomed to the woods.

Woo·dso:rrel. 1525. [Englishing of *sorrel de boys*, superseding WOODSOUR; so called from the sour taste of the leaves, resembling that of sorrel.] The common name of *Oxalis Acetosella*, a low-growing woodland plant having delicate trifoliate leaves and small white flowers streaked with purple, appearing in spring. **b.** Applied with defining words to other species of *Oxalis*; also in the W. Indies to species of *Begonia* 1770.

†**Woo·d-sour.** late ME. [f. WOOD *sb.* + SOUR *sb.*] = prec. –1597.

Woo·d-spi:rit. 1842. [f. WOOD *sb.* + SPIRIT *sb.*] **1.** *Myth.* A spirit or imaginary being, fabled to dwell in or haunt woods 1845. **2.** Crude methyl alcohol obtained from wood by destructive distillation 1842.

Woodspite (wu·dspəit). Now *dial.* 1555. [f. WOOD *sb.* + SPEIGHT.] A woodpecker; *esp.* the Green Woodpecker, *Gecinus viridis*.

Woodsy (wu·dzi), *a.* *U.S.* 1861. [f. f. *woods*, pl. of WOOD *sb.* + -Y[1]; formed thus for distinction from *woody*.] Of, pertaining to, characteristic or suggestive of the woods; sylvan.

Woodwall (wu·dwǫl). Now *dial.* [ME. *wodewale*, ad. or cogn. w. MLG. *wedewale*, f. *wede* WOOD *sb.* + **wale*, of obsc. origin.] †**1.** A singing bird, the Golden Oriole, *Oriolus galbula*, which has a loud flute-like whistle –1667. **2.** A woodpecker; *esp.* the Green Woodpecker, *Gecinus viridis* 1489.

1. Nyghtyngales, Alpes, fynches, and wodewales, That in her swete song deliten CHAUCER.

Woodward (wu·dwǫ̆ɪd). *Hist.* [Late OE. *wuduweard*, f. WOOD *sb.* + WARD *sb.*[1] Survives as a surname.] The keeper of a wood; an officer of a wood or forest, having charge of the growing timber. **b.** As the title of an officer of the 'Ancient Order of Foresters' 1886.

Woodwax (wu·dwæks). *Obs.* or *dial.* [OE. *wuduweaxe*, f. *wudu* WOOD *sb.* + **weaxe*, app. f. Teut. **wahs-* WAX *v.*[1]] = next.

Woodwaxen (wu·dwæ:ksən). late ME. [app. oblique case of OE. *wuduweaxe* (*wuduweaxan*) taken as nom.] The plant dyer's broom or greenweed, *Genista tinctoria*.

Woodwork, wood-work (wu·dwɒ̄ɪk). 1650. **1.** †**a.** An article made of wood, or such articles collectively –1792. **b.** (without *pl.*) Work in wood; *esp.* those parts or details of a manufactured object or artificial structure which are made of wood; the wooden part *of* something 1684. **2.** Work done in wood, as carpentry 1913.

1. a. I give vnto my sonne..all my plate,..hangings, wood worke, houshold stuffe, and furniture 1650. Hence **Woo·dwo:rker,** (*a*) a worker in wood, one who makes things of wood; (*b*) a machine for working in wood.

Woo·dwose, woo·dhouse. *Obs.* (exc. *Hist.*). [Late OE. *wudewása*, f. *wudu* WOOD *sb.* + **wása*, of obsc. origin.] A wild man of the woods; a savage; a satyr, faun; a person dressed to represent such a being in a pageant. **b.** A figure of such a being, as a decoration, a heraldic bearing or supporter, etc. ME.

Woody (wu·di), *a.* late ME. [-Y[1].] **I. 1.** Covered or overgrown with wood; having a growth of trees or shrubs; wooded. †**2.** Belonging to, inhabiting, or growing in woods or woodland; sylvan –1655. **b.** Of, pertaining to, or situated in a wood 1721.

2. A grassie hillock..With woodie primroses befreckeled 1610.

II. 1. Of the nature of or consisting of wood; of or belonging to the wood as a constituent part of the plant; ligneous 1597. **b.** Of a plant: Of which wood is a constituent part; forming wood; having the stem and branches of wood; *spec.* in distinctive names of particular species, as *w. nightshade* 1578. **c.** Resembling wood; having the texture or consistence of wood 1791. **2.** Pertaining to or characteristic of wood; resembling that of wood 1830. **b.** Having a dull sound like that of wood when struck 1875.

1. b. *W. plant*, a tree or shrub, as dist. from a *herb*. Hence **Woo·diness.**

Wooer (wū·əɪ). [OE. *wōgere*, f. *wōgian* WOO *v.*] One who woos (a woman); a suitor.

Woof (wūf), *sb.*[1] [OE. *ōwef* (later *āwef*), f. *ō-* + *wefan* to WEAVE. ME. **owf*, *oof* became *woof* partly by association with WARP *sb.* or with WEFT.] **1.** = WEFT[1] **1.** **2.** Thread used to make the woof 1540. **3.** A woven fabric, esp. as being of a particular texture; also, the texture of a fabric 1674.

1. *fig.* Where euery English thread is ouercast with a thicke woollen woofe of strange wordes 1627. **3.** Flames dart their glare o'er midnight's sable w. SCOTT. Hence **Woof** *v.*[1] (*rare*) to arrange (threads) so as to form a w.; to weave. **Woo·fed** (wūft, *poet.* wūfĕd) *ppl. a.* woven; *fig.* intricate. **Woo·fy** *a.* (*rare*) resembling a w. or woven fabric; of dense texture.

Woof (wuf), *int.*, *sb.*[2] and *v.*[2] 1804. Imitation of a gruff abrupt bark of a dog. (Cf. WHOOF.)

Wooing (wū·iŋ), *vbl. sb.* OE. [f. WOO *v.* + -ING[1].] The action of WOO *v.*; amorous solicitation, courtship.

Hys vnaduised wowyng, hasty louyng and to spedy mariage 1548. What? Michael Cassio, That came a woing with you? SHAKS. *Prov.* Happy is the woing, that is not long in doing 1670.

Wooing (wū·iŋ), *ppl. a.* late ME. [f. as prec. + -ING[2].] That woos. **a.** That solicits in love; courting, as a lover. **b.** *fig.* Alluring, enticing 1549. Hence **Woo·ingly** *adv.*

Wool (wul), *sb.* [Com. Teut. and Indo-Eur.; OE. *wull*:—OTeut. **wullō*:—pre-Teut. **wl̥nā*: cf. Gr. λῆνος wool, οὖλος (:—*ϝολνος) woolly, L. *lana* (:—**wlānā*) wool, *vellus* (:—**welnos*) fleece.] **1.** The fine soft curly hair forming the fleecy coat of the domesticated sheep (and similar animals), characterized by its property of felting (due to the imbricated surface of the filaments) and used chiefly in a prepared state for making cloth; freq., the material in a prepared state as a commodity. **b.** The fleece or complete woolly covering of a sheep, etc. late ME. **c.** The short soft under-hair or down forming part of the coat of certain hairy or furry animals 1605. **2.** Applied to substances resembling sheep's wool. **a.** A downy substance or fibre found on certain trees and plants; also, the thick furry hair of some insects or larvæ. late ME. **b.** Any fine fibrous substance naturally or artificially produced 1599. **c.** The short crisp curly hair of a negro. Also *gen.* (joc.), the hair of the head. 1697. **3.** Woollen clothing or material ME. **b.** The nap of a woollen fabric 1563. **c.** Twisted woollen yarn used for knitting and mending garments 1840. **4.** A quantity or supply, or a particular kind or class, of wool. Chiefly in *pl.* late ME.

1. *Spanish* or *oriental w.*, w. treated with a dye, used as a cosmetic; I am ashamed to tell you that we are indebted to Spanish W. for many of our masculine ruddy complexions 1755. Phr. *Against the w.*, contrary to the direction in which w. naturally lies, the wrong way. *To draw, pull, the w. over* (a person's) *eyes*, to hoodwink, deceive (orig. *U.S.*). *To dye in the w.*, to dye the w. before spinning; *fig.* in *pass.* to be thoroughly imbued; *dyed in the w.* (chiefly *U.S.*), thoroughgoing, out-and-out. *Great* (or *much*) *cry and little w.* (etc.), much talk or clamour with insignificant results. **b.** *Out of the w.*, shorn. **c.** Eye of Newt, and Toe of Frogge, Wooll of Bat, and Tongue of Dogge SHAKS. **2. c.** 'Keep your w. on', don't get angry BARRÈRE & LELAND *Dict. Slang*.

Comb.: *w. blanket, mattress, tax*; *w.-cleaner, -dresser, -grower, -monger, -picker, -washer*; *w.-lined* adj.; **w.-bearer,** an animal that bears w., *esp.* a sheep; **-card,** an instrument used in carding w.; **-comb,** the toothed instrument used in carding wool by hand; later also, a machine to perform the same operation; **-comber,** one who combs or cards wool; **-fat** (*a*) = SUINT; (*b*) = LANOLIN; **-fell** = *w.-skin* (*Hist.*); **-needle,** a blunt needle used for w.-work; **-packer,** one who makes up packages of w. for transport or sale; also, a machine for packing w.; **-shed,** *Austral.*, the large building at a sheep-station in which shearing and w.-packing are done; **-skin,** a sheepskin with the fleece on it; **-sorter,** a sorter of w.; *wool-sorter's disease*, anthrax; **-winder,** one who 'winds' or packs up fleeces for transport or sale.

Wool (wul), *v.* 1660. [f. prec.] †**1.** *trans.* To coat or line with wool. **2.** *U.S. slang.* To pull the 'wool' or hair of (a person) in sport or (esp.) in anger 1854.

Woold (wūld), *sb.* 1628. [Related to next.] **a.** *Naut.* = WOOLDING. **b.** *attrib.* in *w. cord, rope*, binding cord or rope.

Woold (wūld), *v.* 1616. [Back-formation from next, or ad. MLG. *wolen, wōlen*, MDu. *woelen*.] *trans.* (*Naut.*) To wind rope or chain round (a mast or the like) to strengthen it where it is broken, or where it is fished or scarfed. Also said of the rope. **b.** *gen.* To wrap or bind round 1775. Hence **Woo·lder,** †*Naut.* a woold rope; *Rope-making*, a stick used as a lever in woolding; also, a workman operating this.

Woolding (wū·ldiŋ), *vbl. sb.* [Late ME. *wol(l)ing*, prob. ad. MLG. **woling*, MDu. **woeling*, f. MLG. *wolen*, etc. WOOLD *v.*] **1.** The action of binding an object tightly with cord; esp. *Naut.* of winding rope or chain round a mast or yard, to support it where it is fished or broken 1440. **2.** *concr.* A wrapping, swathing; esp. *Naut.* (often *pl.*) the rope or chain used in woolding a mast, spar, etc. late ME.

Woo·l-ga:thering, *vbl. sb.* and *gerund.* 1553. **1.** The action of gathering fragments of wool torn from sheep by bushes, etc. 1581. **2.** In fig. phr. *to go* (*run, be*) *w.*, to indulge in wandering fancies or purposeless thinking; to be in a dreamy or absent-minded state 1553. **b.** Hence, Indulgence in idle imagining or aimless speculation 1607.

2. Hackyng & hemmyng as though our wittes and our senses were a woll gatheryng 1553. So **Woo·l-ga·ther-ing** *a.* indulging in wandering thoughts or idle fancies.

Woollen (wu·lĕn, wu·lən), *a.* and *sb.* Also (now *U.S.*) woolen. [Late OE. *wullen*, f. *wull* WOOL *sb.* + -EN[4].] **A.** *adj.* **1.** Made of or manufactured from wool. †**2.** Wearing woollen clothing, (*a*) as a mark of penance, (*b*) as a mark of poor or lowly status -1607.

2. *Cor.* III. ii. 9.

B. *sb.* Cloth or other fabric made of wool or chiefly of wool. Now *rare.* ME. **b.** *pl.* Woollen cloths or clothes 1800.

†*To lie in the w.*, to sleep with a blanket next to one; I could not endure a husband with a beard on his face, I had rather lie in the w. SHAKS. *To be buried in w.*, to have a w. shroud, as required by the Act of 18 and 19 Chas. II for the encouragement of the w. manufacture.

Woo·llen-dra:per. Now *Hist.* 1554. [f. prec. sb. + DRAPER *sb.*] A dealer in woollen goods.

Woolliness (wu·linĕs). 1597. [f. WOOLLY *a.* + -NESS.] The quality or condition of being woolly, in various senses; also *concr.* a woolly substance.

Woolly (wu·li), *a.* (*sb.*) 1578. [f. WOOL *sb.* + -Y[1].] **1.** Consisting of wool. Also *transf.* relating to wool; containing wool (or sheep) 1591. **2.** Of the nature, texture, or appearance of wool; resembling wool 1586. **b.** Having a soft and clinging texture; said esp. of edible things which are consequently unpleasant to the palate 1687. **3.** Having a natural covering of wool, wool-bearing 1596. **b.** Having hair resembling wool: applied esp. to negroes 1767. **c.** In specific names of animals, often rendering L. *lanatus, laniger* 1781. **d.** *Wild and w.*, orig. applied to the Far West of the U.S., on account of its rude and uncivilized character; hence *gen.* barbarous, lacking culture 1891. **4.** Of parts of plants: Covered with a pubescence resembling wool; downy, lanate, tomentose 1578. **b.** In specific names of plants, often rendering L. *lanatus* or *tomentosus* 1597. **5.** *gen.* Having a wool-like texture, surface, or covering 1796. **6.** *transf.* and *fig.* Lacking in definiteness or incisiveness; confused and hazy; lacking in clearness or definition 1815.

1. Silent was the flock in w. fold KEATS. **3. b.** It was a large, w. poodle, snowy white 1886. **c. W. bear** *colloq.* (esp. *children's*), a large hairy caterpillar, esp. the larva of the tiger-moth. **4. b. W. butt,** Australian name for species of *Eucalyptus*, esp. *E. longifolia.* **6.** Pusey's w. mind 1865. A drawing to look into, but rather w. at a few paces off 1884.

B. *sb.* A woollen garment or covering; now esp. *pl.*, garments or wraps knitted of (fleecy) wool 1865.

Woo·lly-head. 1859. A person with woolly hair, *esp.* a negro; hence, a nickname for an abolitionist in America.

Woolly-headed, *a.* 1650. Having a woolly head: **a.** in specific names of plants; **b.** Woolly-haired 1708; **c.** *fig.* Dull-witted 1883.

Woo·lman. Now chiefly *Hist.* late ME. A dealer in wool; a wool-merchant.

Woo·l-pack. ME. [PACK *sb.*[1]] **1.** A large bag into which a quantity of wool or of fleeces is packed for carriage or sale. †**b.** = next 2. -1710. **2.** *transf.* Something resembling a wool-pack. †**a.** A large mass of white water -1733. **b.** orig. *w. cloud*: A fleecy cumulus cloud. Chiefly *pl.* (or *collect. sing.*). 1648.

Woolsack (wu·lsæk). ME. [SACK *sb.*[1]] **1.** A large package or bale of wool. **b.** Applied joc. to a corpulent person. SHAKS. **2.** A seat made of a bag of wool for the use of judges when summoned to attend the House of Lords (in recent practice only at the opening of Parliament); also, the usual seat of the Lord Chancellor in the House of Lords, made of a large square bag of wool without back or arms and covered with cloth. Often *allus.* with ref. to the position of the Lord Chancellor as the highest judicial officer; hence, *the w.*, the Lord-Chancellorship. 1577.

She drags her husband on to the w., or pushes him into parliament 1862.

‖**Woolsaw** (wu·lsǭ). 1757. [Mosquito *wulasha.*] Among people of African descent in Central America, an evil spirit or demon.

Woolsey (wu·lzi), *a. rare.* 1839. [f. WOOL *sb.* + *-sey* derived from LINSEY-WOOLSEY.] Woolly; woollen.

Woo·l-sta:ple. 1593. [STAPLE *sb.*[2]] A market appointed for the sale of wool. So **Woo·l-sta:pler,** a merchant who buys wool from the producer, grades it, and sells it to the manufacturer.

†**Woo·lward,** *a.* [ME. *wolleward*, prob. alteration of **wollewerd*, from OE. **wullwerd*, f. *wull* WOOL *sb.* + *-werd*, *-wered* wearing, clothed (in), f. stem of *werian* WEAR *v.*[1]] Wearing wool next the skin, esp. as a penance: chiefly in *to go w.* -1822.

The naked truth of it is, I haue no shirt, I go w. for penance SHAKS. To walk wool-ward in winter SCOTT.

Woolwich (wu·lidȝ). 1794. The name of a town in Kent, used attrib., esp. to designate productions of its old dockyard and the Royal Arsenal, as *W. gun, hulk*; *W. infant*, a joc. name for certain heavy guns.

Woo·l-work. 1475. †**1.** Working in wool; manufacture of woollen goods -1630. **2.** Needlework executed in wool usu. on a canvas foundation. Also, knitted wool fabric. 1871. So **Woo·l-wo:rker,** one who works in wool. late ME.

Woomera (wū·mərǎ). *Austral.* 1817. [Native name.] A throwing-stick used by Australian aboriginals. Also = next.

Woomerang (wū·məræŋ). *Austral.* 1849. [Native name. Cf. BOOMERANG.] A missile club used by Australian aboriginals.

Woon (wūn). 1800. [Burmese *wun.*] A Burmese administrative officer.

Woorali, wourali (wurā·li). 1769. [See CURARE.] A S. Amer. climbing plant, *Strychnos toxifera*, from the root of which one of the ingredients of the poison CURARE is obtained; also, the poison itself.

Wootz (wūts). 1795. [app. orig. misprint for *wook*, repr. Canarese *ukku* (pron. with initial *w*) steel.] A crucible steel made in southern India by fusing magnetic iron ore with carbonaceous matter.

Woozy (wū·zi), *a. U.S. slang.* 1897. [Origin unkn.] Fuddled with drink; hence, muzzy.

Wop (wǫp). *U.S. slang.* 1916. [Obscure.] A Mid- or South-European (esp. Italian) immigrant in the United States of America.

Worcester (wu·stəɹ). 1551. The name of the county town of Worcestershire, used *attrib.* to designate articles originating there, e.g. †a fine cloth, (now chiefly) a kind of China ware; also *ellipt.*

W. sauce = Worcestershire sauce (see next).

Worcestershire (wu·stəɹʃəɹ, -ʃiəɹ). 1686. The name of an English county: *attrib.* in *W. sauce*, a sauce made in Worcester; also *ellipt.*

Word (wɒ̄ɹd), *sb.* [OE. :—OTeut. **wurdom* :—pre-Teut. **wr̥dho-* (cf. Lett. *wàrds*, OPruss. *wirds*), app. ult. cogn. with Gr. ἐρέω I shall say, ῥήτωρ speaker, L. *verbum* word.] **I.** Speech, utterance, verbal expression. **1.** *collect. pl.* Things said, or something said; speech, discourse, utterance; *esp.* with possessive, what the person mentioned says or said; (one's) form of expression or language. **b.** *spec.* The text of a song or other vocal composition, as dist. from the music; also, the text of an actor's part 1450. **2.** *sing.* Something said; a speech or utterance *arch.* OE. **b.** with negative expressed or implied, or with *every*: Any or the least utterance, statement, or fragment of speech OE. **c.** *A w.*: a (short or slight) utterance or statement; a brief speech or conversation; similarly *a w. or two* 1485. **d.** *spec.* Something said on behalf of another; esp. in such phrases as *to speak a (good) w. for* 1540. **e.** *spec.* A watchword or password 1533. †**3.** *abstr.* or *collect. sing.* Speech, speaking: often as dist. from writing, esp. in phr. *by w.*; also, the faculty of speech -1728. **4.** *sing.* and *pl.* Speech, verbal expression, in contrast with action or thought OE. **5.** *pl.* orig. in various phr. denoting verbal contention or altercation, e.g. †*to be* or *fall at words*, etc., now chiefly *to have words (with)*; hence *words* = contentious or violent talk between persons; altercation 1462. **6.** *sing.* (without article). Report, tidings, news, information OE. **b.** Common report or statement, rumour. Now *rare* or *Obs.* OE. **7.** A command, order, bidding; a request OE. **8.** A promise, undertaking. Almost always with possessive. late ME. **9.** With possessive: Assertion, affirmation, declaration, assurance; esp. as involving the veracity or good faith of the person who makes it 1601. **10. a.** An utterance or declaration in the form of a phrase or sentence. *arch.* OE. **b.** A pithy or sententious utterance; a saying; a maxim, proverb. Now *rare* exc. in BYWORD 1, NAYWORD 2, *household w.* late ME. †**c.** A significant phrase or short sentence inscribed upon something -1630. **11.** Religious and theological uses; often more fully *word of God* (or *the Lord*), *God's word*, freq. with cap. **a.** A divine communication, command, or proclamation, as one made to or through a prophet or inspired person; *esp.* the message of the gospel OE. **b.** The Bible, or some part or passage of it, as embodying a divine communication 1553. **c.** *The W.* (*of God, of the Father*), *the Eternal W.*, etc., as a title of Jesus Christ: = LOGOS. OE.

1. Words can't describe the figures the women dress here 1813. I have no words..to express the very great thanks which I..owe you 1878. *In these, other,* etc. *words*, in (such-and-such) language. *To give words to, to put into words*, to express by means of language. *Beyond words*, incapable of being expressed in language, unutterable. **b.** Songs without words (tr. G. *Lieder ohne Worte*). **2.** At this worde which he coupled with an othe, came I in FOXE. He bless'd the bread, but vanish'd at the w. COWPER. **b.** They never heard a w. of English DE FOE. **c.** To speake a worde in season to him that is wearie *Isa.* l. 4. **e.** *To give the w.*: (*a*) to utter the password in answer to a sentinel's challenge; (*b*) to inform officers or men of the password to be used. **4.** Thy actions to thy words accord MILT. **5.** High words passed between them. They parted in passion. RICHARDSON. My old man said he was a bloodsucker, and that led to words 1913. **6.** Bid you Alexas Bring me w., how tall she is SHAKS. Send me W...whether he has so great an Estate STEELE. **b.** W. gae'd she was nae canny 1718. **7.** In my time a father's w. was law TENNYSON. *To say the w.*, to give the order, say 'go' or the like; Say the w., Ile have him by the eares HEYWOOD. **8.** Having solemnly pledged his w...not to attempt anything against the government MACAULAY. *To be as good as one's w.*, to keep one's promise. *A man of his w.*, one who keeps his promises. **9.** I give you my w. that my brother did not leave a shilling to his son THACKERAY. **10. a.** The hopelesse w., of Neuer to returne, Breath I against thee SHAKS. **c.** And round about the wreath this w. was writ, *Burnt I do burne* SPENSER. **11. b.** *Merry W.* III. i. 44.

II. An element of speech: A combination of vocal sounds, or one such sound, used in a language to express an idea (e.g. to denote a thing, attribute, or relation), and constituting an ultimate minimal element of speech having a meaning as such; a vocable OE. **b.** †(*a*) A name, title, appellation. (*b*) A term, expression. OE. **c.** A written (engraved, printed, etc.) character or set of characters representing this OE. **d.** In contrast with the thing or idea signified 1450. **e.** *The w.* (predicatively): the right word for the thing, the proper expression; hence contextually denoting or indicating the thing spoken of, esp. the business in hand (*colloq.*) 1596.

Sometimes with ref. to the writing of a word as an indivisible unit, e.g. *as one or a single w.*, *as two words* N.E.D.

d. A business of words only, and ideas not concerned in it 1782. **e.** Come Sir, are you ready for death?.. Hanging is the w., Sir. SHAKS. Contempt? Why, damsel, when I think of man, Contempt is not the w. 1885.

Phrases. **At a** or **one w.: a.** Upon the utterance of a single w.; without more ado; at once, forthwith. **b.** In short, briefly, in a word. *Obs.* exc. *arch.* or *dial.* *To take* a person *at his w.*, to accept what he says and act accordingly. **In a w.** In a simple or short, (esp. comprehensive) statement or phrase; briefly, in short. **In so many words** (tr. L. *totidem verbis*), lit. in precisely that number of words; in those very words. **On** or **upon one's w.: a.** On the security of, or as bound by, one's promise or affirmation; hence as an asseveration, *on, upon my w.* = Assuredly, truly, indeed. **b.** (with ellipsis of prep.) *My w.!* as an ejaculation of surprise (*colloq.* or *vulgar*). **A w. and a blow.** A brief utterance of anger or defiance, followed immediately by the delivery of a blow, as the beginning of a fight; hence in ref. to hasty or sudden action of any kind. **W. of command.** A w. or short phrase uttered by an officer to a body of soldiers as an order for some particular movement or evolution. **W. of honour.** An affirmation or promise by which one pledges one's honour or good faith. **By w. of mouth.** By speaking, as dist. from writing or other method of expression; orally. Hence *w.-of-mouth* attrib., oral. **W. for w.** In the exact or (in ref. to translation) precisely corresponding words; verbatim. Also *attrib.* **Fair words.** Pleasant or attractive speech (usu. implying deceitfulness or insincerity). **Of few words.** Not given to much or lengthy speaking; taciturn. **Good w.** A friendly, favourable, or laudatory utterance; something said on behalf of or in commendation of a person or thing. *To give* (a person) *a good w.*, to speak well of. *To say* or *speak a good w. for*, (*spec.*) to recommend to the favour of another. *Half a w.*, a very short utterance, a slight fragment of speech or conversation. **Last w.: a.** The final utterance in a conversation or (esp.) dispute. **b.** *pl.* The latest utterance of a person before death. *The Seven Last Words*, the seven utterances of Jesus Christ on the Cross. **c.** The final or conclusive statement, after which there is no more to be said; hence *transf.* the final achievement, the latest thing. **Of many words.** Given to much or lengthy speaking, loquacious, verbose.

Make words. with neg.: (Not) to say anything (more) about a matter. **Take (up) the w.** To begin speaking, esp. immediately after or instead of some one else. **b.** *To take* (a person's) *w.*, to accept his statement or assertion as true or trustworthy: usu. with *for*, esp. in the phr. *take my w. for it* = I can assure you, you may be sure, believe me.

Comb.: *w.-order*, *-stock*; *w.-building*, *-formation*; **w.-blind** *a. Path.*, affected with **w.-blindness**, inability to understand written or printed words when seen, owing to disease of the visual w.-centre; **-centre**, *Anat.* each of certain centres in the brain which govern the perception and use of words (spoken or written); **-deaf** *a. Path.*, affected with **w.-deafness**, inability to understand words when heard, owing to diseases of the auditory w.-centre; **-hoard**, literal rendering of OE. *wordhord* treasure of speech; **-lore**, (*a*) the study of words and their history; (*b*) the doctrine of the forms and formation of words, morphology (= G. *wortlehre*); **-man**, a man who deals with or has command of words; a master of language; **-monger**, *contempt.* one who deals in words, esp. in strange or pedantic words, or in empty words without sense; **paint**, *v. trans.* to 'paint' in words, describe vividly; so **-painter**, **-painting**; **-perfect**, *a.* knowing perfectly every w. of one's lesson, part, etc.; **-picture**, a vivid description in words, presenting the object to the mind like a picture; **w. square**, a set of words of the same number of letters to be arranged in a square so as to read the same horizontally or vertically; a puzzle in which such a set of words has to be guessed.

Word (wɒɹd), *v.* ME. [f. prec.] **1.** *intr.* To utter words; to speak, talk. *Obs.* or *arch.* **b.** *To w. it*: to talk, esp. excessively or violently; to have (high) words *with*. *Obs.* or *dial.* 1612. **2.** *trans.* To utter in words, say, speak (occas. as dist. from singing). *Obs.* or *arch.* late ME. †**3. a.** To ply or urge with words. SHAKS. **b.** To bring by the use of words (into or out of a specified condition, etc.) –1716. **4.** To express in or put into words; to compose, draw up. *Obs.* exc. as in b. –1831. **b.** esp. with ref. to the kind of language or form of words used 1619. **c.** *nonce-use.* To represent as in words. SHAKS.

3. a. *Ant. & Cl.* v. ii. 191. 4. Songs of Mourning… Worded by Tho. Campion. 1613. b. 'Tis in reality one and the same question, only differently worded 1701.

Word-book (wɒ·ɹdbuk). 1598. [f. WORD *sb.* + BOOK *sb.*; in sense 1, cf. G. *wörterbuch*, Icel. *orðabók*, etc.] **1.** A book containing a list of words (as of the vocabulary of a language, a book, an art, or science) arranged in alphabetical or other systematic order. (Often implying less elaboration or fullness than *dictionary* or *lexicon*.) **2.** The 'book of the words' or libretto of a musical composition 1878.

Worded (wɒ·ɹdėd), *ppl. a.* 1606. [f. WORD *sb.* or *v.* + -ED.] **1.** Formed into words; expressed in or put into words (*rare*). **b.** Qualified by an adv.: Expressed in a particular kind of language or form of words; phrased in such-and-such a manner 1848.

Wordily (wɒ·ɹdili), *adv.* 1522. [f. WORDY *a.* + -LY [2].] In a wordy manner or style, with excess or abundance of words; verbosely. So **Wo·rdiness**, verbosity.

Wording (wɒ·ɹdiŋ), *vbl. sb.* 1564. [f. WORD *v.* or *sb.* + -ING [1].] **1.** Speaking, talking, utterance. *Obs.* or *arch.* 1604. †**2.** Angry or abusive speech; 'having words' –1614. **3.** The action of putting or condition of being put into words; composition or expression in language, esp. in ref. to the words used; mode of speech, form of words 1649. **4.** A set of written words, an inscription (*rare*) 1908.

3. Things for which no w. can be found KEATS. I entreat the attention of the jury to the w. of this document DICKENS.

Wordless (wɒ·ɹdlės), *a.* ME. [f. WORD *sb.* + -LESS.] **1.** Inexpressible in words; unspeakable, unutterable. *Obs.* or merged in 2. **2.** Not expressed in words; unspoken, unuttered 1500. **3.** Not uttering a word; silent, speechless 1500. **b.** Lacking the faculty or power of speech 1648. **c.** Lacking words for expression 1881. **4.** Not accompanied by words; (of a play) acted without words 1598.

2. So sat she joylesse down in wordless grief complaining 1633. Hence **Wo·rdless-ly** *adv.*, **-ness.**

Wordsworthian (wɒɹdzwɒ·ɹðiăn, -wɒ·ɹþiăn), *sb.* and *a.* 1815. [f. the name of the English poet William *Wordsworth* (1770–1850) + -IAN.] **A.** *sb.* An admirer or imitator of Wordsworth, or a student of his works. **B.** *adj.* Of, belonging to, or characteristic of Wordsworth; (of a poem) composed by or in the style of Wordsworth.

Wordy (wɒ·ɹdi), *a.* [Late OE. *wordig*, f. WORD *sb.* + *-ig* -Y [1].] **1.** Full of or abounding in words. **a.** Of speech or writing: Consisting of or containing many words; verbose. **b.** Of persons: Using an excess of words; *occas.* garrulous, talkative. late ME. †**2.** Skilled in the use of words (*rare*) –1680. **3.** Consisting or expressed in words; of words; verbal. Now chiefly in phr *w. war(fare).* 1627.

1. To deal in w. Compliment Is much against the Plainness of my Nature 1713. 3. All that w. tempest for a girl COWPER.

Work (wɒɹk), *sb.* [OE. *weorc*:—OTeut. **werkom*, cogn. w. Gr. ἔργον.] **I. 1.** Something that is or was done; what a person does or did; an act, deed, proceeding, business; *pl.* actions, doings (often *collect.*) *arch.* or *literary* in gen. sense. **b.** *Theol.* (*pl.*) Moral actions considered in relation to justification: usu. as contrasted with *faith* or *grace.* late ME. **2.** Something to be done, or something to do; occupation, business, task, function OE. **b.** *Cricket, Rowing*, etc. What a batsman, an oarsman, etc. has to do, esp. with ref. to the points at which his force is to be applied 1851. **3. a.** Action (of a person or thing) of a particular kind: in various connexions 1440. **b.** *Cricket.* Deflexion of the ball after touching the ground, resulting from the spin or twist imparted to it by the bowler 1846. **4.** Action involving effort or exertion directed to a definite end, esp. as a means of gaining one's livelihood; (one's) regular occupation or employment OE. **b.** *gen.* in ref. to any action requiring effort or difficult to do 1518. **c.** *spec.* The labour done in making something, as dist. from the material used (in ref. to the cost) 1737. **d.** Exercise or practice in a sport or game; also, exertion or movement proper to a particular sport, game, or exercise 1856. **5.** A particular piece or act of labour; a task, job. Also *gen.* something difficult to do. *Obs.* or *arch.* OE. **6. a.** Trouble, affliction; in later use, disturbance, fuss. **b.** Pain, ache. *dial.* OE. **7.** *Math.* The process of or an operation in calculation; a process of calculation written out in full. Now *rare* or *Obs.* 1557. **8.** *Physics* and *Mech.* The operation of a force in producing movement or other physical change, esp. as a definitely measurable quantity 1855.

1. Their workes are workes of iniquitie BIBLE (Genev.) *Isa.* lix. 6. It is a damned, and a bloody worke SHAKS. I have another W. of Charity upon my hands,..to reform an extravagant Husband 1703. *The w. of..*, a proceeding occupying (a stated length of time); All this was..but the w. of a few minutes 1834. So *a w. of time*, a proceeding which takes a long time. 2. Fie vpon this quiet life, I want worke SHAKS. Euerie bodies worke is no bodies worke 1611. 3. a. *To do its w.* (of a thing, in ref. to result), to produce its effect: The brandy-and-water had done its w. DICKENS. 4. Doinge certen Iobbes of woorke 1557. I do all the w. of the house DICKENS. b. It was hard w. rowing, for the wind was against him 1902. 7. Take a few Examples without their W. at large 1709.

II. 1. With possessive: The product of the operation or labour *of* a person or other agent; creation, handiwork. Also vaguely, the result of one's labour, something accomplished. OE. **b.** The result of the action or operation of some person or thing; (one's) 'doing'; the device or invention *of* some one. late ME. **2.** A thing made; a manufactured article or object; a structure or apparatus of some kind, esp. one forming part of a larger thing. Now chiefly in gen. sense with qualification, esp. in compounds like BRICKWORK, FIREWORK, etc. OE. †**3.** An architectural or engineering structure; a building, edifice –1667. **b.** *pl.* Architectural or engineering operations 1700. **4.** *spec.* (*Mil.*) A fortified building; a defensive structure, fortification; any one of the several parts of such a structure OE. **5.** A literary or musical composition (viewed in relation to its author or composer); often *pl.* and *collect. sing.*, (a person's) writings or compositions as a whole ME. **6.** A product of any of the fine arts (in relation to the artist), as a painting, a statue, etc.: in the phr. *a w. of art* including literary or musical works, and connoting high artistic quality. 1531. †**7.** Make, workmanship; *esp.* ornamental workmanship –1795. **8.** The operation of making a textile fabric or (more often) something consisting of such fabric, as weaving or (usu.) sewing, knitting, or the like; *esp.* any of the lighter occupations of this kind, as a distinctively feminine occupation; also *concr.*, the fabric or the thing made of it, esp. while being made or operated upon. late ME. **9.** An excavation in the earth, made for the purpose of obtaining metals or minerals; a mine. *Obs.* exc. = WORKING *vbl. sb.* II. 1475. **10.** *pl.* An establishment where some industrial labour, esp. manufacture, is carried on, including the whole of the buildings and machinery used. Now commonly construed as sing. (in earlier use also sing. in form) 1581. **11.** A set of parts forming a machine or piece of mechanism: orig. *sing.*, esp. as the second element of compounds; as an independent word now only *pl.*, the internal mechanism of a clock or watch 1628.

1. We all are the worke of thy hondes COVERDALE *Isa.* lxiv. 8. b. Other Hereticks..condemned Marriage as the W. of the Devil 1753. 3. b. *Clerk of the Works*, an officer who superintends the erection of buildings, etc. 5. A Man who publishes his Works in a Volume ADDISON. 6. They breake downe all y[e] carued worcke therof BIBLE (Great) *Ps.* lxxiv. 6. 10. We went to see..silk works 1748. 11. He took to pieces the eight-day clock..under pretence of cleaning the works DICKENS.

Phrases. **At w.: a.** Occupied with labour; engaged in a task; working, esp. at one's regular occupation. **b.** *gen.* Occupied in some action or process; actively engaged; operating. **In w.** In regular occupation. **Of w.** — *of all w.*, employed in all kinds of w., esp. in a household: chiefly in *maid-of-all-w.*; hence allus. **Out of w.** Having no w. to do, unemployed, workless. Also *attrib.*, or as *sb.* **To go to w.** To proceed to some action (expressed or implied); to commence operations. So *to fall to w.* **To set to w.: a.** *trans.* To set (a person, the faculties, etc.) to a task, or to do something; *refl.* to set about doing something. **b.** *intr.* for *refl.* **To cut out w.** *for* (a person). To prepare work to be done by him, to give him something to do; now only in *to have (all) one's w. cut out* (colloq.), to have as much as one can manage to do. **To make w.: a.** (also *to make a w.*) To work havoc or confusion; hence, to make a to-do or fuss. **b.** *To make w. for*, to give (a person, etc.) something to do. **c.** with qualifying adj., as *to make good, short*, etc. *w.* (*of* or *with*) a person or thing, to do the business, or deal with the person or thing, well, shortly, etc.; often with special implication, as *to make short w. of*, to destroy or put an end to quickly. **Good w.** A morally commendable or virtuous act (also colloq. = as *int.* in commendation of some action or performance); *esp.* an act of piety; usu. *pl.* such acts done in obedience to divine law, or as the fruits of faith or godliness. *Prov.* Meny hondys makyth lyght werke 1530. All w. and no play, makes Jack a dull boy 1670.

attrib. and *Comb.*, as *w.-girl*, *-place*, *-room*, etc.; **w.-bag**, **-basket**, a bag, or basket, to contain implements and materials for needlework; **-bench**, a bench, with accessories, at which mechanics work; **-box**, a box to contain instruments and materials for needlework; **-hand**, (*a*) a person employed by another to do w.; (*b*) with defining adj., as *a good w.-hand*, one who is a 'good hand' at w., a capable worker; **-mate**, a fellow-labourer; **-shy** *a.*, shy of or disinclined for w., lazy; **-table**, a table for supporting working materials and tools; *esp.* a small table with compartments and drawers, and sometimes with a well for needlework; **-train**, a train of waggons or trucks for conveying materials for construction or repair of a railway, etc.

Work (wɒɹk), *v.* Pa. t. and pple. **worked** (wɒɹkt), *arch.* and *techn.* **wrought** (rǭt). [(1) OE. *wyrcan* (*worhte, geworht*):—OTeut. **wurkjan*, **wurht-*; (2) OE. (Mercian) *wircan*:—OTeut. **werkjan*, **warht-* (**wurht-*); (3) late

OE. *wercan, weorc(e)an*, partly after the sb. The Indo-Eur. base *worg-, werg-, wrg- appears in Gr. ἔρδω, ῥέζω I do, perf. ἔοργα, ὄργανον ORGAN, ὄργιον ORGY. The normal descendant of OE. *wyrcan* would be *worch; the substitution of *k* was due mainly to the sb. The new pa. t. and pa. pple. *worked* has supplanted the original *wrought* in most senses.] **I.** *trans.* **1.** To do, perform, practise (a deed, course of action, task, process, etc.). Now *arch.*; chiefly with cogn. obj., or in such phr. as *to w. a miracle, to w. wonders.* **b.** To do (something evil or harmful). *arch.* OE. **2.** To perform, carry out, execute (a person's will, advice, etc.). *Obs.* or *arch.* OE. **3.** To produce by (or as by) labour or exertion; to make; to fashion. *Obs.* or *arch.* in gen. sense; often, now usu., implying artistic or ornamental workmanship. OE. **b.** Said of God: To create. Also in *pass. Obs.* or *rare arch.* OE. **c.** To construct, build (a house, wall, etc.). *Obs.* or *rare arch.* OE. **d.** const. *of*, rarely *out of* (the material or constituents); also *in* (some material), usu. implying artistic or ornamental workmanship. (Now almost always in pa. pple. *wrought.*) OE. †**4.** To compose (a book or writing), to write –1746. **5.** To make (a 'web' or textile fabric), to weave; to make (something consisting of such fabric) by means of needlework, to sew or knit; to embroider ME. **6.** To make (an image or figure); to delineate, paint, draw, or carve; also, to represent by an image, portray. *Obs.* or *arch.* exc. in special connexions. ME. †**7.** To cause to be.., make, render; to bring into a specified state; also, to make or create in the form of –1639. **8.** To make, form, or fashion *into* something; to make up 1538. **9.** To put in, insert, incorporate, esp. in the way of construction or composition 1663. **b.** To graft (*on* a stock) 1658. **10.** To effect, bring about, bring to pass; to cause, produce ME. †**11.** To act in order to or so as to effect (something); to plan, contrive; to manage (a business or proceeding) –1667. **12.** To bestow labour or effort upon; to operate upon: *esp.* **a.** To till, cultivate (land) OE. **b.** To get (stone or slate from a quarry, ore or coal from a mine, etc.) by labour; also with the quarry, etc. as obj. ME. **c.** To manipulate (a substance) so as to bring it into the required condition; *esp.* to knead, press, etc. (a plastic substance), or to mix or incorporate (such substances) together by this means. late ME. **d.** To shape (stone, metal, or other hard substance) by cutting or other process; also, to beat out or shape (metal) by hammering 1665. **e.** *colloq.* or *slang.* To go through or about (a place) for the purposes of one's business or occupation; to carry on some operation in; *spec.* of a hound, of an itinerant vendor, beggar, etc., of a clergyman, and of a canvasser 1834. **f.** *slang.* To deal with in some way; to get, or to get rid of, esp. by artifice 1839. **g.** To operate upon so as to get into some state or convert into something else; *refl.* with *compl. adj.* to go through some process so as to become 1594. **13.** *Math.*, etc. = *w. out* 1593. **14. a.** To act upon the mind or will of; to influence, induce, persuade (esp. by subtle or insidious means); to bring into a particular mental state, etc. 1595. **b.** To act upon the feelings of; to stir, move, incite 1605. **c.** Of medicine: To take effect upon 1712. **d.** To practise on, hoax, cheat. *U.S.* 1892. **15.** To move (something) into or out of some position, or with alternating movement (to and fro, etc.): usu. with some implication of force exerted against resistance or impediment 1617. **16.** To direct or manage the movement of; to guide or drive in a particular course; *spec.*, *Naut.* to direct the movement of (a ship) by management of the sails and rudder 1667. **17.** *refl.* To make one's (or its) way 1576. **18.** with *way*, etc. as obj. 1713. **19.** To set or compel (a person, animal, etc.) to work; to employ or use in work 1445. **b.** To bring or get into some condition by labour or exertion 1628. **20.** To set in action, cause to act; to exercise (a faculty, etc.); to actuate, operate, manage. late ME. **b.** In fig. or allusive phrases expressing cunning management or manœuvring, as *to w. the oracle, the ropes* 1859.

1. She worcketh knittinge of stockings 1600. **b.** Depart from me, ye that worke iniquity *Matt.* vii. 23. **5.** Now she vnweaues the web that she hath wrought SHAKS. I'm going to w. Mr. Laurence a pair of slippers 1868. **7.** *Hen. VIII*, II. ii. 47. **9.** Those occasional Dissertations, which he has wrought into the Body of his History STEELE. **10.** He wirkis sorrow to himsell DUNBAR. The ravages that confinement and sorrow had worked upon him 1831. **11.** To w. in close design, by fraud or guile What force effected not MILT. **12.** *To w. one's passage* (etc.), to pay for one's passage on board ship by working during the voyage. **e.** A professional beggar, who 'works' seventy or eighty streets in a few hours 1897. **14. b.** My dull Braine was wrought with things forgotten SHAKS. Endeavouring to w. herself into a state of resentment DICKENS. **16.** Having no Sails to w. the Ship with DE FOE. **17.** The women worked themselves into the centre of the crowd DICKENS. **19.** Whether it was right to w. little boys and girls in the mills, longer than from six o'clock in the morning to six o'clock in the evening 1841. **b.** She worked herself to death DICKENS. Richard said that he would w. his fingers to the bone for Ada. DICKENS. **20.** They are..dead dolls, wooden, worked with wires KINGSLEY.

II. *intr.* **1.** To do something, or to do things generally; to conduct oneself, behave, 'do'. *Obs.* or *arch.* OE. **2.** To act for a purpose or so as to gain an end; to plot, contrive. *arch.* OE. **3.** Of a thing: To do something; to perform a function, or produce an effect; *esp.* to act in the desired way, do what is required; to be practicable or effectual, to succeed ME. **b.** Of a machine or apparatus: To perform its proper function; to act, operate 1610. **c.** Of a part of mechanism: To have its proper action or movement in relation to another part with which it is in contact 1770. **4.** To do something involving effort (of body or mind); to exert oneself for a definite purpose, esp. in order to produce something or effect some useful result, to gain one's livelihood OE. **b.** const. *at*, *on* or *upon* (a material object, a subject of study or literary treatment, an occupation, etc.) ME. **5.** To exert oneself in order to accomplish something or gain some end (expressed by context) ME. **6.** To do one's ordinary business; to pursue a regular occupation. Also more widely, to do something for a definite end, to engage in some systematic occupation. (Often coinciding with II. 4.) ME. **b.** const. *in* the material upon which labour is expended in some business or manufacture 1471. **c.** *spec.* of sporting dogs 1832. **7.** To perform the work proper or incidental to one's business or avocation. *Obs* exc. as in b. ME. **b.** Said esp. of the performance of artistic work or the practice of an artist 1539. **8.** *Math.*, etc. To proceed (in a particular way) in calculation; to go through the process of solving a problem. late ME. **9.** Of a substance: To behave in a particular way while being worked 1489. **10.** To operate *upon* (physically, mentally, or morally), produce an effect upon; to take effect *on*, affect, influence. late ME. **b.** To ache (Now north. dial. chiefly in the form *wark* from OE. *wærcan.*) late ME. **11.** Of liquor: To ferment 1570. **12.** To go or move along, or in a particular course; to make one's (or its) way; now usu., to make way slowly, laboriously, with some exertion or difficulty, or in an indirect course. late ME. **b.** To make one's (or its) way slowly or with effort through something. late ME. **c.** *Naut.* Of a sailing vessel: To sail in a particular course, to make sail; *esp.* to beat to windward, to tack 1633. **d.** To proceed in a particular direction in some operation 1877. **13.** To move restlessly, violently, or convulsively; to be in a state of agitation or commotion; to toss, seethe; *Naut.* of a ship, to strain or 'labour' so that the fastenings become slack; so of an engine or carriage 1581. **14.** With complement: To move irregularly or unsteadily so as to become out of gear 1770.

1. *All's Well* IV. ii. 29. **2.** Without the King's assent or knowledge, You wrought to be a Legate SHAKS. **3.** All thynges worke for the best [A.V. worke together for good] vnto them that love god TINDALE *Rom.* viii. 28. Lady Lufton was beginning to fear that her plan would not w. TROLLOPE. **c.** The four bevelled nuts w. into the bevelled wheels..and so turn them 1825. **4.** For men must w., and women must weep KINGSLEY. **b.** Vulcan working at the Anvil PRIOR. How hard some folks do w. at what they call pleasure 1840. **5.** 1 *Hen. VI*, III. iii. 27. **6.** Rude Mechanicals, That worke for bread vpon Athenian stals SHAKS. **7. b.** *Timon* I. i. 200. **10.** He toke poison..but..it would not worke vpon hym UDALL. She..worked on his feelings by pretending to be ill MACAULAY. **12. d.** The paper hanger generally works from left to right 1877. **13.** With his face all working with sorrow STEVENSON. **14.** The anchor on the lee bow had worked loose 1840.

With advs. **W. in.**: **a.** *trans.* To insert, introduce, incorporate. **b.** *intr.* To make one's (or its) way in. **W. off.**: **a.** *trans.* To print off (as from a plate); esp. to print in final form, so as to be ready for publication or distribution. **b.** To perpetrate, 'play off'. **c.** To take off or away by a gradual process; to get rid of, disburden oneself of, free oneself from, by some continuous action or effort. **d.** To finish working at; to dispose of and get done with. **e.** To put to death; to hang (*slang.*). **W. out.**: **a.** *trans.* To bring, fetch, or get out by some process or course of action; to get rid of. **b.** *intr.* To make its way out, esp. from being embedded or enclosed in something. **c.** *trans.* To work (a mine, etc.) until it yields no more. **d.** To discharge (a debt or obligation) by labour instead of a money payment. **e.** To bring about, effect, produce, or procure (a result) by labour or effort; to carry out, accomplish (a plan or purpose). **f.** To go through a process of calculation or consideration so as to arrive at the solution of (a problem or question), to solve; also, to reckon out, calculate. **g.** *intr.* for *pass.*: (*a*) of a course of events, narrative, etc.: To proceed so as to issue in a particular result; (*b*) with *at*, of a quantity: To amount to (so much) when reckoned up, to 'come to'. **h.** To bring to a fuller or finished state; to develop, elaborate. **W. up.**: †**a.** *trans.* To build up, construct (a wall, etc.). **b.** *intr.* To make one's (or its) way up, esp. against impediment or indirectly; to ascend, advance. **c.** *trans.* To stir up, mix, or compound, as a plastic substance. **d.** To make up (material) *into* something by labour; also, to bring into some condition, esp. so as to be ready for use. **e.** *gen.*, or in ref. to something immaterial: To make up, develop, expand, enlarge (*to* or *into* something). **f.** To bring by labour or effort *to* or *into* a higher state or condition. **g.** To make up, form, construct, produce (something material or immaterial): with special ref. to the process, or to the labour, etc. expended upon it. **h.** *Naut.* To set to or keep at needless and disagreeable hard work as a punishment. **i.** To 'get up' (a subject) by mental labour; to master by research. **j.** To bring by effort, or by some influence, into a particular state of mind or feeling, esp. one of strong emotion; to induce or persuade by effort *to do* something; to put into a state of excitement, excite, agitate. Also *refl.* **k.** *intr.* To be gradually stirred up or excited. Hence **Worked** (wɒ̄ɹkt) *ppl. a.* in senses of the vb.; *esp.* executed or ornamented with needlework, engraving, or the like.

Workable (wɒ̄·ɹkăb'l), *a.* 1545. [f. prec. + -ABLE.] **1.** Of substances or materials: That can be worked, fashioned, or manipulated for use; said also of the state in which they are capable of being worked. **2.** That can be worked, managed, or conducted, as a contrivance, establishment, institution, etc. 1756. **b.** of a plan, system, scheme, or the like 1865.

2. The only w. boat of the Lord Hood was manned 1881. Hence **Workabi·lity. Wo·rkableness.**

Workaday, work-a-day (wɒ̄·ɹkădēi), *sb.* and *a.* [orig. north. ME. *werkeday*, a. ON. *virkr dagr* working day, weekday.] **A.** *sb.* A day on which work is ordinarily done (dist. from *holiday*); a working-day. *Obs.* or *dial.* **B.** *attrib.* passing into *adj.* Belonging to or characteristic of a work-day or its occupations; characterized by a regular succession or round of tasks and employments; of ordinary humdrum everyday life: freq. in phr. *this w. world* 1554.

Prythee tel her but a worky day Fortune SHAKS. We cannot long indulge in day-dreams in this w. world 1859.

Work-day (wɒ̄·ɹkdēi), *sb.* and *a.* late ME. [OE. *weorcdæg* does not seem to have survived; ME. *werkday* is prob. a new formation.] **A.** *sb.* A day on which work is ordinarily performed; a week-day. **B.** *attrib.* passing into *adj.* Belonging to or characteristic of a work-day; performed, worn, etc. on a work-day 1500.

My woorkday gowne..thre woorkday aprens, one woorkday band 1622.

Worker (wɒ̄·ɹkəɹ). late ME. [f. WORK *v.* + -ER [1].] **1.** One who makes, produces, or contrives. †**a.** Applied to God as maker or creator –1602. **b.** An author, producer, contriver, or doer. *arch.* late ME. **c.** *transf.* of things ME. **2.** One who works or does work of any kind; esp. one who works *in* a certain medium, *at* a specified trade, etc. or in a certain position or status (often denoted by prefixed sb., etc., as *cloth-w.*, *iron-w.*; *brain-w.*, *hand-w.*). late ME. **b.** In emphatic use, esp. as opp. to *idler*, or the like 1628. **c.** One who is employed for a wage, esp. in manual or industrial work; now often in the language of social economics, a 'producer of wealth', as opp. to *capitalist* 1848. **d.** Of animals: (*a*) A horse, dog, etc. that works (well) 1844. (*b*) The neuter or undeveloped female of certain social hymenopterous or other insects, as ants and bees, which supplies food and performs other services for the community 1747. **e.** *U.S. Politics.* One of a class of political agents or partisans subordinate to a 'boss' 1888. **3.** Applied to apparatus or pieces of machinery, as (*a*) one of the small card-covered cylinders in a carding-machine; (*b*) *pl.* in pillow lace-making, the bobbins that are worked across a pattern, etc. 1594. **4.** With advs., as *w.-up* 1656.

2. b. The distinction between workers and idlers, as between knaves and honest men RUSKIN.

attrib., as *w.-ant, -bee*: **w. bobbin** = 3 (*b*); **w. card** = 3 (*a*).

Workfolk (wʊ̄·ɹkfōᵘk). 1475. = WORKPEOPLE, *esp.* farm labourers.

Workful (wʊ̄·ɹkfŭl), *a.* ME. [f. WORK *sb.* + -FUL.] †**1.** Active, operative -1674. **2.** Full of (hard) work; hard-working 1854. Hence **Wo·rkfulness**, †activity; laborious activity.

Workhouse (wʊ̄·ɹkhaus). [OE. *weorchūs*; f. WORK *sb.* + HOUSE *sb.*¹] **1.** A house, shop, or room in which work is regularly performed; a workshop or factory. *Obs.* or *Hist.* **2.** *spec.* orig. A house established for the provision of work for the unemployed poor of a parish; later, an institution, administered by Guardians of the Poor, in which paupers are lodged and the able-bodied set to work. (Formerly †*house of work*, †*working-house*, †*house of industry*; see also POORHOUSE, UNION 9 b.) 1652. **3.** A prison or house of correction for petty offenders. *U.S.* 1888.

2. Most well-regulated Bridewells are Paradises compared to the Oxford Work-house 1797.

Working (wʊ̄·ɹkiŋ), *vbl. sb.* ME. [f. WORK *v.* + -ING¹.] The action of WORK *v.*; the result of this. **I. 1.** Performance of work or labour; †also, that which is done, work. †**2.** Performance, execution, achievement (of some particular work or action) -1693. †**3.** Making, construction; handiwork, workmanship -1726. **4.** The action of operating or performing work upon something; manipulation, management; exploitation (of a mine, etc.) 1450. **b.** The carrying on or putting into operation (of a scheme, system, legislation, etc.) 1832. **5.** Action, operation. **a.** Of a person; esp. *collect. sing.* and *pl.* actions, doings, deeds. late ME. **b.** Of a drug, medicine, etc. late ME. **c.** Of the mind, conscience, etc. Often *pl.* 1588. **d.** The conduct or operations collectively of a factory, vessel, or the like 1873. **6.** Influential operation; influence; also, the result or effect of operation or influence. late ME. **7.** Mathematical calculation; now chiefly, the statement of the operations involved in solving a mathematical problem. late ME. **8.** Fermentation of liquor 1565. **9.** Restless movement of water (esp. the sea); straining of a ship, vehicle, etc. so as to loosen the fittings 1582. **b.** Involuntary movement of the face or mouth, esp. due to emotion 1800. **10.** The proper action or movement of a piece of mechanism or the like 1645. **11.** Gradual movement or progress (as against resistance) 1683.

5. b. After my physicks w. 1648. **c.** I am sicke with w. of my thoughts SHAKS. **6.** The w. of clerical prejudice in..a liberal mind 1861. **7.** A knowledge of mathematics may be gained without the perpetual w. of examples 1873. **10.** The workings of his lungs pumped great jets of blood out KINGSLEY.

II. *concr.* A place in which mineral is or has been worked; a mining excavation 1766. **III.** With advs., as *w.-off, -together, -up* 1623.

attrib. and *Comb.*: *w. hour(s; w. capital, expenses*; **w. drawing**, usu. pl., the drawings made of the plan, etc. of a building from which the workmen carry out the construction of the work; †**-house**, = WORKHOUSE; **w. load**, the maximum load that a member in a machine or other structure is designed to bear; **w. order**, a condition in which a machine, system, etc. works (well, badly, etc.); **w. room**, (*a*) space in which one may work, room for the performance of work; (*b*) a work-room.

Working (wʊ̄·ɹkiŋ), *ppl. a.* late ME. [-ING².] That works. **1.** Of a person, etc.: Active, operative; energetic. *Obs.* or *arch.* †**b.** Of a thing: Operative, effective -1709. **2.** That works or labours; *esp.* that works for an employer in a manual or industrial occupation 1639. **b.** In contrast with: (*a*) 'master', 'managing', etc., in designations of trade or occupation; (*b*) 'sleeping', in ref. to partners in a firm 1708. **c.** Mil. *W. party*: a party of men detailed for a special piece of work outside their ordinary duties 1744. **d.** Of horses and cattle: Employed in work, esp. in agricultural work 1613. **e.** Of a bee or ant: That is a 'worker' 1766. **3.** Of the sea, etc.: Agitated, tossing. *poet.* 1581. **4.** Of the features: Moving involuntarily or convulsively, esp as the result of emotion 1753. **5.** Of an organism, piece of machinery, etc.: That performs its function (esp. in a specified manner); that 'goes' (as opp. to being stationary) 1608. **b.** *Naut.* applied to certain sails 1882. **6. a.** Of a majority: Sufficient to secure the passing of measures 1858. **b.** Of a theory, etc.: That provides a basis upon which to work 1849.

1. b. Things..Sad, high, and w., full of State and Woe SHAKS. **4.** The w. lip was loosened; and the tears came streaming forth DICKENS. **5.** But are you flesh and bloud? Haue you a w. pulse, and are no Fairie? SHAKS. **6. a.** A w. majority of about a hundred in the House of Commons 1858. **b.** No one asks more of Evolution at present than permission to use it as a w. theory 1894.

Wo·rking(-)cla·ss. Chiefly pl. **wo·rking cla·sses.** 1813. [f. prec.] The grade or grades of society comprising those who are employed to work for wages in manual or industrial occupations. **b.** *attrib.*, as *w. family, vote*, etc. 1869.

What are termed *the* working-classes, as if the only workers were those who wrought with their hands 1844.

Wo·rking(-)day·. 1478. [f. WORKING *vbl. sb.* + DAY *sb.*] **1.** A work-day. **b.** *attrib.* or as *adj.* 1533. **2.** The portion of a day devoted to work or allotted to labour as a day's work 1875.

1. They quite forgot the days, and knew not a Sunday from a w. any longer DE FOE. **2.** Leaving the length of the working day unchanged 1875.

Wo·rking-ma·n. 1816. A man of the working classes; a man employed to work for a wage, esp. in a manual or industrial occupation. So **Wo·rking-wo·man.**

The word 'working-man' was held to include a clerk or small shopkeeper, or anyone whose total income did not exceed £150 a year 1896.

Workless ((wʊ̄·ɹklės), *a.* 1484. [f. WORK *sb.* + -LESS.] **1.** Doing no work; inactive, idle. *Obs.* or *arch.* **2.** Unprovided with work; out of work, unemployed. Often *absol.* with *the.* 1848. Hence **Wo·rklessness.**

Workman (wʊ·ɹkmǣn). *Pl.* **workmen.** [OE. *weorcmann.*] **1.** A man engaged to do work or (usu.) manual labour, esp. one employed upon some particular piece of work; often (contextually) a skilled worker. **b.** Connoting a class or grade, or in correlation with 'employer', 'capitalist', or the like 1704. **2.** A skilled or expert craftsman. *Obs.* exc. in *Glassmaking*, the first man of a 'chair'. 1478. **b.** *transf.*; e.g. applied to a rider, esp. in hunting, who manages his horse well or is conversant with the technique of the field; also to a horse that takes its fences well, etc. 1832. **3.** One who works or practises his craft or art (in some specified manner) 1484.

2. b. The Squire having hit off his fox like a w. 1832. **3.** Never had ill workeman good tooles 1633. Hence **Wo·rkmanly** *a.* and *adv.* = WORKMANLIKE 1467.

Workmanlike (wʊ̄·ɹkmǣnləik), *adv.* and *a.* 1447. [See -LIKE.] **A.** *adv.* In a manner or style characteristic of a good workman.

To be all plastered over with lyme and hayer workeman lyke 1618.

B. *adj.* **1.** Of or pertaining to a workman; characteristic of or suitable to a workman (*rare*) 1663. **2.** Characteristic of or resembling (that of) a good workman 1739.

2. To compleat the intended Bridge..in a..w. Manner 1739. Two very workmanlike little horses 1878.

Workmanship (wʊ̄·ɹkmǣnʃip). late ME. [f. WORKMAN + -SHIP.] †**1.** The performance or execution of work or a work; work, labour -1818. †**2.** Action, agency, operation -1641. **3.** That which is wrought or made by a workman or craftsman; (a person's) work. Also *transf.* something produced: *arch.* exc. as in *piece of w.* 1523. **4.** Skill or cunning as a workman; craftsmanship as exhibited in a piece of work 1529.

3. A little Hut,..the W...of some Indian 1751. There's no denying she's a rare bit o' w. GEO. ELIOT. **4.** Idiots admire in things the Beauty of their Materials, but Artists that of the Workmanship BOYLE.

Wo·rk-ma·ster. Now *rare.* 1533. A master workman; an overseer or employer of workmen. **b.** *fig.*: esp. applied to God as creator and ruler; rarely of a thing 1535. So **Wo·rk-mi·stress**, only *fig.*, chiefly of Nature.

Workpeople (wʊ̄·ɹkpī:p'l). 1708. [WORK *sb.*] People employed in manual or industrial labour for a wage; workmen and (or) workwomen.

Workshop (wʊ̄·ɹkʃǫp). 1562. [f. WORK *sb.* + SHOP *sb.* 3.] A room, apartment, or building in which manual or industrial work is carried on.

transf. England..the w. for the world DISRAELI.

Workwoman (wʊ̄·ɹkwu:măn). 1530. [f. after *workman.*] A woman who works; a female worker; †a woman who does needlework.

Worky (wʊ̄·ɹki). *U.S.* 1833. [f. WORK *sb.* + -Y⁶.] A worker or operative; one of the working class.

World (wʊ̄ɹld). [Com. Teut.; OE. *weorold, worold, world*; a formation peculiar to Germanic, f. **wer-* man + **alđ-* age.] **I.** Human existence; a period of this. **1. a.** Chiefly *This w., the w.*: the earthly state of human existence; this present life. **b.** *The other, another, the next, a better w., the w. to come* or *to be*: the future state, the life after death. Sometimes viewed as the 'realm' of departed spirits. OE. **c.** *gen.* A state of (present or future) existence ME. **2.** The pursuits and interests of this present life; *esp.*, in religious use, the least worthy of these; temporal or mundane affairs OE. **3.** The affairs and conditions of life; chiefly in phr., esp. with the verb *go*, as *how the w. goes*, how events shape themselves, etc.; also *to let the w. wag* OE. †**b.** State of human affairs, state of things; hence, season of time as marked by the state of affairs -1614. **4.** Secular (or lay) life and interests, as dist. from religious (or clerical); also, secular (or lay) people OE. **b.** In the Society of Friends applied to those outside their own body 1648. †**c.** *To go to the w., to be* (a man, woman) *of the w.*, to be married -1601. **d.** In biblical and religious use: Those who are concerned only with the interests and pleasures of this life or with temporal or mundane things; the worldly and irreligious. late ME. †**5.** An age or (long) period of time in earthly or human existence or history; *pl.* ages -1674. **b.** A period or age of human history characterized by certain conditions or indicated by the character of those living in it. *Obs.* exc. as coloured by III. 3. 1530. **6.** *W. without* (ME. *abuten* or *buten*) *end*, earlier also †*in world(s of world(s*, etc. (tr. eccl. L. *in secula seculorum, in seculum seculi*): for ever and ever, for all time, through eternity. Later used hyperbolically: Endlessly, eternally. Hence as *adj. phr.* = perpetual, everlasting, eternal; and as *subst. phr.* = eternal existence, endlessness, eternity. ME.

1. She was too good for this w. and for me, and she died six weeks before our marriage-day DICKENS. *To the world's end*, as long as human things shall last, to the end of time; similarly *as long as the* or *this w. lasts, in this w.* *To bring into the w.*, to give birth to. *To come into* (or *to*) *the w.*, to be born; *fig.* (of a book) to be published. *To go* or *depart out of this w.*, to die. **c.** Both the worlds I giue to negligence, Let come what comes SHAKS. **2.** The w. is too much with us WORDSW. **3.** Some must watch, while some must sleepe; So runnes the w. away SHAKS. How's the w. used you since this morning? DICKENS. *How goes the w. with* (a person), how are his affairs. *As the* (or *this*) *w. goes*, as things are, considering the state of affairs. **b.** This is no w. To play with Mammets SHAKS. **4.** How happy is the blameless Vestal's lot! The w. forgetting, by the w. forgot POPE. Having resigned the situation I held in the w. 1888. **d.** The W. with fruitless Pain Seek Happiness below WESLEY. **5.** *Tr. & Cr.* III. ii. 180. **6.** A time me thinkes too short, To make a w.-without-end bargaine in SHAKS.

II. The earth or a region of it; the universe or a part of it. **1.** The earth and all created things upon it; the terraqueous globe and its inhabitants OE. **b.** In generalized sense, usu. qualified by *a.* 1676. **c.** *pl.* Used hyperbolically for: 'a great quantity'; often advb. 'a great deal', infinitely'. (*a*) pl. *Not..for worlds*, not on any account; (*b*) sing. *Not for (all) the w.*, *not for anything in the w.* 1586. **2.** Any part of the universe considered as an entity, as *lower* or *nether w.*, Hades or hell, less freq. the earth; UNDERWORLD ME. **b.** A planet or other heavenly body, esp. one viewed as inhabited 1713. **3.** The material universe as an ordered system; the system of created things; the cosmos ME. **4.** The sphere within which one's interests are bound up or one's activities find scope; (one's) sphere of action or thought 1586. **5.** A section or part of the earth at large, as a place of inhabitation or settlement 1555. **6.** A division of created things; *esp.* each of the three primary divisions of natural objects (the animal, vegetable, and mineral kingdoms) 1695. **7.** A group or system of things or beings associated by common characteristics (denoted by a qualifying word or phr.), or considered as constituting a unity 1673.

1. The W. was all before them, where to choose Thir place of rest, and Providence thir guide MILT. *Citizen of the w.*: see CITIZEN 2. *Universal w.*: see UNIVERSAL *a.* 4; cf. VARSAL. *Wide w.*: see WIDE *a.* I. 1 b. Phr. (chiefly *fig.*) with *go round*: Their fame it shall last while the w. goes round BURNS. It's Love that makes the w. go round! W. S. GILBERT. *The world's end*, the farthest limit of the earth (chiefly hyperbolical). **b.** Each thinks a W. too little for his sway DRYDEN. **c.** Nor doth this wood lacke worlds of company SHAKS. I'm sure I wouldn't stand in his way for worlds 1874. **4.** [His] w. was a narrow one, consisting as it did of himself and his bank-book 1898. **5.** *New W.*, a continent or country discovered or colonized at a comparatively late period, esp. the continents of America, as dist. from the *Old W.*, or the continents of the Eastern Hemisphere, esp. Europe and Asia, as being known before the discovery of America. **7.** Then, all the w. of waters sleeps again COWPER. The Outdoor W.: or, Young Collector's Handbook 1893.

III. The inhabitants of the earth, or a section of them. **1.** The human race; the whole of mankind; human society OE. **2.** The body of living persons in general; society at large, 'people'; often with ref. to its judgement or opinion 1603. **3.** Usu. with qualification: A particular division, section, or generation of the earth's inhabitants or human society, with ref. to the time or place of their existence or to their interests or pursuits. late ME. **4.** Human society considered in relation to its activities, difficulties, and the like; hence, the ways, practices, or customs of the people among whom one lives; the occupations and interests of society at large 1449. **b.** with ref. to social status or worldly fortune 1687. **5.** High or fashionable society. More explicitly *the w. of fashion, the great w.*, etc. 1673.

1. *Against the w.*, in opposition to or in the face of all mankind; hence, against all opposition. †*World's shame, shame of the w.*, universal or public disgrace. **2.** There are all sorts of stories of the Lord High Admiral, and the w. says he is mad 1828. **3.** A gentleman well known in the theatrical w. SHERIDAN. The whole w. of ruffiandom 1882. Theodosius left the Roman w. in peace 1890. **4.** Olde folkes you know, haue discretion,..and know the w. SHAKS. He was a perfect child in the world's ways 1882. *To begin the w.*, to begin to take an active part in the affairs of life; to start one's career. **b.** Indications of the good gentleman's having gone down in the w. of late DICKENS. **5.** To know the w.! a modern phrase For visits, ombre, balls, and plays SWIFT.

Phrases. **A world**: **a.** A vast quantity, an 'infinity': sometimes more emphatically *a whole w. of*. **b.** Used advb.: Infinitely, vastly (*arch.*). †**c.** *It is a w.*, it is a great thing, it is a marvel. **The w.**: **a.** *In the w.*, on earth, in existence; (*a*) as an intensive phr. after a superlative or *all, no, nothing*, etc.; (*b*) intensifying an interrogative, as *how, why, what in the w...?* †**b.** *Of the w.* = *in the w.* **c.** *Of (all) the w.*, out of the whole w., above all others. **d.** *To think the w. of*, to have the highest possible opinion of or regard for. **e.** See MAN OF THE W. So *woman of the w.*, a woman who is experienced in the ways of life or the conventions of society. **f.** Living the secular as opposed to the religious life. **All the w.**: **a.** The whole of the inhabited globe; the entire earth (or universe). **b.** (= F. *tout le monde*.) Everybody in existence; in narrower sense, everybody in the community, the public. *Against all the w.*, in opposition to or competition with everybody. *All the w. and his wife*: see WIFE 2. **c.** Everybody in fashionable society; everybody of account. **d.** Everything in existence: often in intensive emotional use = All that is of value or account *to* a person, something supremely precious. **e.** *For all the w.*, in regard to or taking into consideration everything in the w.; hence, in every respect, exactly (like, etc.). **The whole w.** = *all the w.* a, b.

attrib. and *Comb.* in simple attrib., objective, and advb. uses (sometimes echoing German compounds), as *w. sadness, -sorrow; w.-famous, -renowned, -weary*, adjs.; often passing into adj., with the meaning 'of or pertaining to the whole w., world-wide, universal', as *w.-commerce, -empire, -war*; also **w.-history** [G. *weltgeschichte*], history embracing the events of the whole w.; **-old** *a.* [G. *weltalt*] as old as the world; **-policy, -politics** [G. *weltpolitik*], a policy or politics based upon considerations affecting the w. as a whole; **-ruler**, a ruler of the (known) w.; **w.('s series** *Baseball*, a series of games to decide the professional championship of the U.S.; **-soul** [G. *weltgeist, -seele*], the animating principle which informs the physical world; **-state**, (*a*) a state comprising the whole w.; (*b*) a state possessing w.-power. Hence **Wo·rldish** *a.* (*rare*) of or belonging to this w., worldly. **Wo·rldless** *a.* (*rare*) not having a w. to live in; not containing a w. or worlds; free from the w., unworldly.

Worldliness (wɒ̄·ɹldlinės). late ME. [f. WORLDLY *a.* + -NESS.] The condition of being worldly; devotion to worldly affairs to the neglect of religious duties or spiritual needs; love of the world and its pleasures.

Worldling (wɒ̄·ɹldliŋ). 1549. [f. WORLD + -LING.] **1.** One who is devoted to the interests and pleasures of the world; a worldly or worldly-minded person. †**2. a.** A 'citizen of the world', cosmopolite. **b.** An inhabitant of the world. –1816.

1. The various pretexts under which Worldlings delude themselves and neglect the welfare of their Souls 1844.

Worldly (wɒ̄·ɹldli), *a.* [OE. *woruldlic.*] **1.** Of or belonging to this world (as dist. from the other world); earthly, mundane. †**2.** Of, belonging to, or connected with this world and its inhabitants; earthly, human, mortal –1674. †**3.** Of or belonging to the world (as dist. from the church or the cloister); secular –1658. **4.** Devoted to the world and its pursuits ME.

1. With al my w. Goodes I thee endowe *Bk. Com. Prayer, Matrimony.* Too much a child in w. matters DICKENS. **4.** W. prelatis ful of coueitise symonye & heresie WYCLIF.

Comb.: **w.-minded** *a.*, having a w. mind, having the thoughts set upon the things of this world.

Worldly (wɒ̄·ɹldli), *adv.* ME. [f. after prec. + -LY².] In a worldly manner; with a worldly intent or disposition.

Worldly-wise (stress variable), *a.* late ME. Wise in a worldly manner or in worldly affairs; *transf.* of actions or conduct.

Worldly wiseman, a w. man; now only with allusion to the character so named in Bunyan's *Pilgrim's Progress*.

Wo·rld-power. 1866. [After G. *weltmacht.*] **1.** The power of 'this world' (as dist. from the spiritual world); secular power. **2.** Any of the powers (nations, empires) that dominate the world 1901.

2. The foundation of England's greatness as a w. 1904.

Worldward (wɒ̄·ɹldwǫ̆ɹd), *adv.* (*a.*) 1583. [f. WORLD + -WARD.] **1.** (orig. *To the w.*) In regard to the world; in worldly respects. **2.** Towards or in the direction of the world 1642. **B.** *adj.* Directed towards or facing the world 1857.

World-wide (stress variable), *a.* 1632. [f. WORLD + WIDE *a.*] 'As wide as the world'; extending over or covering the whole world.

Worm (wɒ̄ɹm), *sb.* [OE. *wyrm* :—**wurmiz*; related to L. *vermis* worm, Gr. *ῥόμος*, *ῥόμοξ* wood-worm. The spelling *wo-* is an early substitution for *wu-* which is a reversion through the influence of the following *r* to the unmutated vowel.] **I. 1.** A serpent, snake, dragon. Now only *arch.* †**2.** Any animal that creeps or crawls; a reptile, an insect –1820. **3.** A member of the genus *Lumbricus*; a slender, creeping, naked, limbless animal, usu. brown or reddish, with a soft body divided into a series of segments; an earthworm. More widely, any annelid. OE. **4.** Any endoparasitic helminth breeding in the living body of men and other animals. Usu. *pl.* Also, the disease or disorder constituted by the presence of these parasites. OE. **5.** The larva of an insect; a maggot, grub, or caterpillar, esp. one that feeds on and destroys flesh, fruit, leaves, textile fabrics, and the like. Also collect. *the w.*, as a destructive pest. OE. **b.** The larva or grub of many kinds of beetles, destructive to trees, timber, furniture, etc. OE. **c.** *contextually.* A silkworm OE. **6.** A maggot, or, in popular belief, an earthworm, supposed to eat dead bodies in the grave OE. **b.** *fig.* as one of the pains of Hell (Mark ix. 48, Isa. lxvi. 24) OE. **7.** †**a.** A tick or mite breeding in the hand, foot, or other part of the body –1605. **b.** *pop.* = COMEDO 1730. **8.** An earthworm, or a larva: **a.** as the food of birds ME. **b.** as bait for fish ME. **9.** A name for various long slender crustaceans and molluscs (e.g. *Teredo navalis*, the ship-w.) which destroy timber by boring. Also collect. *the w.*, as a destructive pest. 1621.

1. Hast thou the pretty worme of Nylus there, That killes and paines not? SHAKS. **3.** Prov. *Tread on a w. and it will turn*, i.e. even the humblest will resent extreme ill-treatment; also, *even a w. will turn*, etc. See also DEW-W., EARTHWORM, SAND-*w.*, etc. **4.** See ROUND-W., TAPEWORM, etc. **5.** She..let concealment like a worme i'th budde Feede on her damaske cheeke SHAKS. See also BOOK-W., CADDIS-*w.*, PALMER-W., etc. **6.** Men haue died from time to time, and wormes haue eaten them SHAKS. *Worm's* or *worms' meat*, said of a man's dead body, or of man as mortal; also, *food* or *meat for worms*. **7. a.** *Rom. & Jul.* I. iv. 65.

II. 1. *fig.* A human being likened to a worm or reptile as an object of contempt, scorn, or pity; an abject miserable creature OE. †**b.** With qualification expressing tenderness, playfulness, or commiseration –1626. **2.** *fig.* A grief or passion that preys stealthily on a man's heart or torments his conscience (like a worm in a dead body or a maggot in food); esp. the gnawing pain of remorse OE. †**b.** A whim or 'maggot' in the brain; a streak of insanity –1705. **3.** *The w.*: formerly a pop. name for various ailments supposed to be caused by the working of a 'worm'. †**a.** Colic. *Sc.* –1654. **b.** Toothache. *Sc. Obs.* or *rare.* 1583.

1. Sith that wickide worme, Wiclyf..began to sowe the seed of cisme in the erthe 1402. **b.** *Temp.* III. i. 31. **2.** The Worme of Conscience still begnaw thy Soule SHAKS.

III. 1. A small vermiform ligament or tendon in a dog's tongue, often cut out when the animal is young, as a supposed safeguard against rabies 1530. **b.** A tendon in a dog's tail, often cut or pulled out when the tail is being docked 1877. **2.** An artificial or natural object resembling an earthworm 1702. **b.** *pl.* The coiled pods of *Astragalus hamosus* 1849. **3.** As the name of various implements of spiral form (supposed to resemble the sinuous shape and movement of an earthworm). **a.** A screw fixed on the end of a rod, used for withdrawing the charge or wad from a muzzle-loading gun 1591. **b.** The thread or spiral ridge of a male screw 1677. **c.** The spiral of a female or hollow screw 1725. **d.** An endless or tangent screw the thread of which gears with the teeth of a toothed wheel (or similar device) 1729. **e.** A long spiral or coiled tube connected with the head of a still, in which the vapour is condensed 1641. **f.** A spiral heating flue in a furnace or coiled steam pipe in a boiler 1758. **g.** A spring or strip of metal of spiral shape 1724.

attrib. and *Comb.*: **w.-bark**, the anthelmintic bark of the W. Indian cabbage-tree, *Andira inermis*; **-cast**, the convoluted mass of mould thrown up by an earthworm on the surface of the soil after passing through the worm's body; **-eater**, a bird or other creature that feeds on worms; *spec.* the W.-eating Warbler, *Helminthotherus vermivorus* of the eastern U.S.; **-grass**, the Pinkroot, *Spigelia marilandica*, of the Southern U.S., used as a vermifuge; **-hole**, a hole made by a burrowing worm or insect in wood, fruit, books, etc.; **-shell**, the twisted shell or tube of a marine annelid or mollusc, as *Serpula* and *Vermetus*; **-snake**, any of various small harmless snakes, as *Typhlops nigrescens* and *Carphophis amœna*; **-spring**, a spiral spring. Hence **Wo·rmless** *a.* (*rare*) free from or destitute of worms. **Wo·rm-like** *a.* resembling a w., vermiform; *adv.* after the manner of a w. **Wo·rmling**, a small w. chiefly *fig.*, a poor despicable creature.

Worm (wɒ̄ɹm), *v.* 1564. [f. prec.] **I. 1.** *intr.* To hunt for or catch worms 1576. **2.** *trans.* To cause to be eaten by worms; to devour, as a burrowing worm does. Chiefly *pass.*, to be eaten by worms. 1604. **II. 1.** To extract the 'worm' or lytta from the tongue of (a dog) as a safeguard against madness 1575. **b.** *transf.* and *fig.* (as a remedy for madness, a ribald

tongue, or greediness) 1564. **2.** To rid (plants, esp. tobacco) of 'worms' or grubs 1624.
1. b. He is such a froward testy old fellow, he should be Wormed like a mad dog SHADWELL.

III. †1. To pry into the secrets of (a person); to play the spy upon –1807. **2.** *To w.* (a person) *out of*: to deprive or dispossess of (property, etc.) by underhand dealing. Now *rare* or *Obs.* 1617. **3.** *To w. out*: to thrust out, get rid of, by subtle and persistent pressure or undermining 1594. **4.** *To w. out*: to extract (information, a secret, etc.) by insidious questioning 1715. **5.** *intr.* To move or progress sinuously like a worm; also *transf.* of things. Usu. with adv. 1610. **b.** *refl.* in same sense 1865. **c.** With advb. acc. as *to w. one's way* 1822. **6.** *fig.* To make one's way insidiously like a worm *into* (a person's confidence, secret affairs, etc.); to burrow *in* so as to hurt or destroy 1627. **b.** *refl.* To insinuate oneself *into* (a person's favour or confidence, a desirable position, etc.) 1711. **7.** *trans.* with predicate-extension: To move (an object) *off, down,* etc. by a gradual tortuous propulsion or dragging 1861.
4. Old Wood knew all her history... He had wormed it out of her, day by day THACKERAY. 6. Vse subtle and crafty men, they will search, and skrew, and worme into busines of difficulty 1639. b. W. yourself into her secrets DICKENS.

IV. 1. To make a screw-thread on 1598. **2.** *Naut.* To wind spun-yarn or small rope spirally round (a rope or cable) so as to fill up the grooves between the strands and render the surface smooth 1644. **3.** To remove the charge or wad from (a gun) by means of a worm 1802. Hence **Wormed** (wɒ̄ɹmd) *ppl. a.* eaten into or bored by worms, infested with worms; formed with a screw-thread; furnished with a (specified) number of screw-threads. **Wo·rmer.**

Wo·rm-ea:ten, *pa. pple.* and *ppl. a.* late ME. Eaten into by a worm or worms. **b.** *transf.* Applied to organic tissue which is indented with small holes 1592. **c.** *fig.* (of persons and things). Decayed, decrepit; antiquated, outworn 1575.
Smircht w. tapestrie SHAKS. c. That worme-eaten name of Liberall..It's a name of the old fashion DEKKER.

Wo·rm-ea:ting, *ppl. a.* 1817. That eats worms for food.
W. Warbler, the bird *Helminthotherus vermivorus* of the eastern U.S.

Wormian (wɒ̄·ɹmiăn), *a.* 1831. [ad. mod. L. (*ossa*) *Wormiana*, f. the name of the Danish physician Olaus *Worm* (1588–1654).] *Anat.* The designation of small bones of irregular shape, freq. found in the sutures of the skull.

Wormseed (wɒ̄·ɹmsīd). late ME. [WORM *sb.* I. 4.] **1.** Any of various plants considered to have anthelmintic properties, e.g. swine's fennel or sulphurwort, *Peucedanum officinale*; *Erysimum cheiranthoides* (Treacle or English W.); *Chenopodium anthelminticum* and *Ambrina anthelmintica* (American W.); *Halogeton tamariscifolium* (Spanish W.). **2.** The dried flower-heads of one or other of these plants, used as an anthelmintic 1502. **3.** The eggs of the silkworm moth 1733.

Wormwood (wɒ̄·ɹmwud). late ME. [Altered f. OE. *wermod* (cf. VERMOUTH), of obsc. origin, as if f. WORM *sb.* + WOOD *sb.*] **1.** The plant *Artemisia Absinthium*, proverbial for its bitter taste. **b.** With qualifying word, designating species of *Artemisia* and some similar plants 1548. **c.** *Salt of w.*, an impure carbonate of potash, obtained from the ashes of w. 1617. **2.** *fig.* An emblem or type of what is bitter and grievous to the soul 1535. **3.** Used as a name or specific epithet for certain moths 1832. **4.** Short for *w. ale* 1843. **5.** *fig.* attrib., passing into adj. = bitter, tart, unpleasant to experience 1593.
1. b. **Pontic, Roman w.,** *Artemisia pontica* or *A. Absinthium*; **Sea w.,** *A. maritima*; **Tree w.,** *A. arborescens* of the Mediterranean; **Wild w.,** *Parthenium Hysterophorus*. 2. *To be w.* (or *gall and w.*), to be acutely mortifying or vexing (*to* a person). 5. Thy secret pleasure turnes to open shame,..Thy sugred tongue to bitter w. tast SHAKS.
attrib. and *Comb.*: **w.-ale, -beer,** ale or beer in which w. is infused; **w. water, wine,** a cordial prepared (like absinthe or vermouth) from w.

Wormy (wɒ̄·ɹmi), *a.* late ME. [f. WORM *sb.* + -Y[1].] **1.** Attacked, gnawed, or bored by worms or grubs; worm-eaten. **b.** *fig.* = WORM-EATEN c. (*rare*) 1611. **2.** Of the body, etc.: Infested or affected with worms, itch-mites, etc. 1599. **3.** Of soil, the grave, etc.: Infested with worms, full of worms 1590. **4.** Resembling a worm; worm-like 1545. **b.** *fig.* Grovelling; earthy; crooked, tortuous 1640. **5.** Of or pertaining to worms. *poet.* 1801.
3. Damned spirits all,..Alreadie to their wormie beds are gone SHAKS. 4. Long w. feelers instead of fins 1888.

Worn (wɒ̄ɹn, wōᵊɹn), *ppl. a.* 1508. [pa. pple. of WEAR *v.*[1]] **1.** Impaired by wear, use, or exposure; showing the results of use or attrition. **b.** *fig.* Of words or ideas: Hackneyed, trite 1569. **2.** Wasted, enfeebled, or exhausted by toil, exposure, age, anxiety, or ill-health; showing signs of such enfeeblement 1508. †**3.** Of time, a period: Past, spent. SHAKS. **4.** With adv. **a.** *W.-down* = 1, 2. 1814. **b.** *W.-in*, ingrained by attrition or exposure to weather 1883.
2. The President..looked somewhat w. and anxious, and well he might DICKENS. 3. *Wint. T.* v. i. 142.

Worn-out, *ppl. a.* 1593. **1.** Injured, damaged, defaced by wear, attrition, or exposure, esp. to such a degree as to be no longer of use or service 1612. **2.** Utterly exhausted and wasted in strength or vitality 1700. **3.** Of ideas, etc.: Hackneyed by use, trite, stale, out of fashion. Of institutions: Effete. 1713. †**4.** Of time: Past, departed. SHAKS.
1. The w. carpets and old-fashioned chairs TROLLOPE. 2. Every w. Preacher shall receive, if he wants it, at least ten pounds a-year WESLEY. 3. The House of Lords..was an effete and w. institution 1882. 4. This patterne of the worne-out age SHAKS.

Worricow (wʌ·rikau). *Sc.* 1711. [f. WORRY *v.* + COW *sb.*[2]] A scarecrow; a hobgoblin. Also *transf.* of persons.

Worried (wʌ·rid), *ppl. a.* 1559. In senses of WORRY *v.*
'I don't mean that', said Mrs. Boffin, with a w. look DICKENS.

Worrier (wʌ·riəɹ). 1536. [f. WORRY *v.* + -ER [1].] **1.** An animal that kills or injures others by biting and rough treatment. **2.** One who harasses or persecutes another 1712. **3.** One who causes distress of mind to another; also, one who gives way to anxiety or mental disquietude 1891.

Worriment (wʌ·rimĕnt). Chiefly *U.S.* 1855. [f. WORRY *v.* + -MENT.] The act of worrying or causing anxiety; the state of being worried or troubled in mind. Also, something that harasses or causes worry.

Worrisome (wʌ·risɒ̆m), *a.* 1869. *dial.* [f. WORRY *sb.* or *v.* + -SOME [1].] Apt to cause worry or distress; given to worrying.

Worrit (wʌ·rit), *sb. dial.* and *vulgar.* 1836. [f. next.] A state of worry or mental distress; a fretting care or anxiety. Also, a person that worries others or himself.

Worrit (wʌ·rit), *v. dial.* and *vulgar.* 1818. [app. vulgar alteration of WORRY *v.*; but cf. dial. *wherrit* (1762), *werrit* (1825), of app. different origin.] **1.** *trans.* To worry, distress, vex, pester. **2.** *intr.* To give way to worry; to experience or display mental disquietude, impatience, etc. 1854.
1. Don't w. your poor mother DICKENS. It will worret you to death, Lucy; *that* I can see GEO. ELIOT.

Worry (wʌ·ri), *sb.* 1804. [f. next.] **I.** A troubled state of mind arising from the frets and cares of life; harassing anxiety or solicitude. **b.** An instance or case of this; a cause of or matter for anxiety; *pl.* cares, solicitudes 1813. **2.** The act of biting and shaking an animal so as to injure or kill it. (Properly of hounds when they seize their quarry.) 1847.
1. It is not work that kills, but 'w.' 1879. b. Delicious spot to come and repose in from the cares and worries of life LEVER.

Worry (wʌ·ri), *v.* Pa. t. and pple. **worried.** [OE. *wyrgan*:—OTeut. **wurgjan* related to **werg-* (cf. MHG. *irwergen* to throttle).] †**1.** *trans.* To strangle (a person or animal) –1606. †**2.** To choke (a person or animal) with a mouthful of food –1779. **3.** To seize by the throat with the teeth and tear or lacerate; to kill or injure by biting and shaking. Said e.g. of dogs or wolves attacking sheep, or of hounds when they seize their quarry. late ME. **b.** *transf.* To bite at or upon (an object); to kiss or hug vehemently 1567. **c.** *intr.* To pull or tear *at* (an object) with the teeth 1882. **d.** *trans.* To devour. Chiefly *north.* ME. **4.** *trans.* To harass by rough or severe treatment, by repeated aggression or attack; to assail with hostile or menacing speech 1553. **b.** *transf.* With adv. or advb. phr.: To get or bring into a specified condition by harassing treatment, persistent aggression, or dogged effort 1727. **c.** To irritate (an animal) by a repetition of feigned attacks, etc. 1807. **d.** *U.S.* To afflict with physical fatigue or distress 1828. **5.** To vex, distress, or persecute by inconsiderate or importunate behaviour; to plague or pester with reiterated demands, requests, or the like 1671. **6.** To cause distress of mind to; to afflict with mental trouble or agitation; to make anxious and ill at ease. Freq. *refl.* or *pass.* 1822. **b.** in pa. pple., denoting a state of mind 1863. **c.** *intr.* (for *refl.*) To give way to anxiety or mental disquietude 1860. **7.** with advb. extension. **a.** To advance or progress by a harassing or dogged effort; to force or work one's way *through* 1699. **b.** To get *through* (a business, piece of work) by persistent effort or struggle 1873.
3. She bit me..She worried me like a tigress C. BRONTË. 4. Thus she worries him out of his senses 1678. b. Worrying out a knotty point in the 'Original Hebrew' 1894. 5. You w. me to death with your chattering DICKENS. They won't really do anything but w. you with questions 1927. 6. c. When she can find nothing to do, then she worries 1861. *I should w.* (U.S. colloq.), it does not trouble me at all. 7. b. *To w. along* (orig. U.S.), to contrive to live, 'keep going', in the teeth of trials or difficulties. Hence **Wo·rrying** *vbl. sb.* and *ppl. a.*

Worse (wɒ̄ɹs), *a.* and *sb.* [OE. *wyrsa, wiersa*:—OTeut. **wersizon-*, f. root **wers-* (cf. WAR *sb.*) + compar. suffix *-izon-* (see -ER [3]).] **A.** *adj.* Used as the comparative of BAD, EVIL, ILL, or as the opposite of BETTER. **1.** More reprehensible morally; more wicked, depraved, or vicious; more cruel, unkind, or ill-conditioned. **2.** More harmful, painful, grievous, unpleasant, unlucky, etc. OE. **b.** More unattractive; more unsuitable or unfitting; more faulty, incorrect, etc. 1640. **c.** With agent-noun: More unskilful or inefficient. Also, more addicted to some (specified) bad habit. 1719. **3.** Less good, not so good, inferior; of lower quality or value OE. **4.** *predic.* **a.** Of persons: Less fortunate, less well off; in less favourable circumstances or position *for* (some person or thing that causes deterioration or loss) OE. **b.** Less well in health, physical condition, or spirits OE. **c.** Of things: In less good condition; showing signs of damage, deterioration, or loss of quality ME. **5.** *Comb.*, as *w.-natured, -tempered* adjs. 1648.
1. Three Iudasses, each one thrice w. then Iudas SHAKS. I only hope and trust he wasn't a w. liver than we think of GEO. ELIOT. 2. Come, you drop that stick or it'll be w. for you DICKENS. No very good news; but then it might be w. GEO. ELIOT. b. She has bad Features, and a w. Complexion SWIFT. 3. *To be w. than one's word*, to fail to carry out or act up to what one has promised. *W. half*, corresp. to *better half* (HALF *sb.* II. 2). 4. a. To make fayre promyse, what are ye the w.? SKELTON. Nobody seem'd one penny the w.! BARHAM. b. He was at first very ill, then got better; he is now w. 1776. *The w. for*, overcome or intoxicated by (liquor, drink). c. Blue satin shoes and sandals (a *leetle* the w. for wear) DICKENS. *It would be none the w. for*, it would be improved by (colloq.). *W. and w.*, w. in an increasing degree, progressively w.

B. *absol.* or as *sb.* Chiefly ellipt. or absol. uses. **1.** A person that is less good, virtuous, kindly, etc. ME. **2.** Something worse; a greater degree of badness OE. **b.** *To do w.*: to behave more wickedly, badly, foolishly, etc. ME. **c.** What is less good or precious or valuable 1586. **d.** Used as an alternative or addition to an unfavourable epithet or characterization = something worse still: usu. *or w.*, *and w.* late ME.
1. I feare there will a w. come in his place SHAKS. 2. You had better take yourself off peaceably, before w. comes of it 1864. d. I might say more of this, but it might be thought curiosity or worse WALTON.
Phrases. *For better, for w.*, also *for better or (for) w.*: used where an issue is doubtful or beyond human control; I N. take the N. to my wedded wif to haue and to holde fro this day forward for bettere for wers for richere for pouerer 1500. *For the w.*: chiefly used to indicate the result of a change in condition or quality, fortune, or circumstances. *From bad to w.*;

Thus will this latter, as the former World, Still tend from bad to w. MILT. *The w.*, the losing or less desirable part (in a contest, or the like); disadvantage. *To have the w.*, to be worsted or defeated in a contest; also *gen.* to have the disadvantage in a comparison with another. †*To put to the w.*, to defeat, worst, discomfit.

Worse (wɒ̄ɹs), *v.* *Obs.* exc. in nonce-use. [OE. *wyrsian*, f. *wyrsa* WORSE *a.*] **1.** *intr.* To become or grow worse, deteriorate. **2.** *trans.* To make worse, impair, injure, blemish ME.

Worse (wɒ̄ɹs), *adv.* [OE. *wyrs, wiers*; see WORSE *a.*] **1.** More badly or wickedly; more censurably or foolishly in regard to conduct. **b.** More severely, hardly, harshly, etc. ME. **c.** More carelessly, faultily, imperfectly, etc. ME. **2.** More unfortunately, unluckily, or unhappily OE. **3. a.** As an intensive, with verbs of hurting, fearing, hating, etc.: More greatly, severely, or intensely; in a greater degree 1596. **b.** With a verb of liking, loving, pleasing, etc.: In a lesser or lower degree, less well. Similarly *w. at ease*, less well at ease. OE. **4.** *W. than*, used before an adj. (sb., vb.) as a form of pejorative comparison ME. **5.** Used parenthetically or continuatively to introduce an additional clause or sentence containing a further and stronger instance of action which incurs reprobation 1784.

1. I judg'd a man of sense could scarce do w. Than caper in the morris-dance of verse COWPER. **b.** You are sure you won't think the w. of me, if I tell it? 1881. **c.** I may put all the good I have ever got by you in my eyes, and see never the w. FIELDING. **2.** With ruin upon ruin, rout on rout, Confusion w. confounded MILT. *W. off*, in w. circumstances, less happily or fortunately situated. *To go w. with*, to be the worse for (a person). Prov. *To go further, and fare w.* **4.** Brutish Villaine; w. then brutish SHAKS. He ..chose to w. than waste his opportunities and his talents 1897. **5.** They stir us up against our kind; And worse, against ourselves WORDSW.

Worsement (wɒ̄·ɹsmĕnt). 1884. [f. WORSE *v.* + -MENT, after *betterment*.] Deterioration and depreciation of real property caused by the action of persons outside without the owner's consent.

Worsen (wɒ̄·ɹs'n), *v.* ME. [f. WORSE *a.* + -EN [5]. Common in dialect, and reintroduced to literature *c* 1800–1830 by writers like Southey and De Quincey.] **1.** *trans.* To make worse; to impair, vitiate, cause to deteriorate. **b.** *spec.* To inflict loss upon (a person, locality) in respect of real property (see prec.) 1894. **c.** To represent (a thing) as worse than it is; to depreciate 1885. **d.** *refl.* To make oneself worse or (*dial.*) worse off 1828. **2.** *intr.* To become worse, deteriorate 1795.

1. Life..is not worsened by being long 1647. **2.** I am still much engaged with my sick friend; and sorry am I to add that he worsens daily WORDSW.

Worsen (wɒ̄·ɹs'n). 1634. dial. or illiterate alteration of WORSE.

It stinket..w. than ony brimstone 1634.

Worseness (wɒ̄·ɹsnĕs). late ME. [-NESS.] The quality or condition of being worse.

Worser (wɒ̄·ɹsəɹ), *a.* and *adv.* 1495. [f. WORSE *a.* + -ER [3]. Cf. *lesser*.] **A.** *adj.* = WORSE *a.* **b.** *absol.* and *ellipt.* 1586.

Chang'd to a w. shape thou canst not be SHAKS. You might ha' made a w. guess than that, old feller DICKENS.

B. *adv.* = WORSE *adv.* 1560.

Oth. IV. i. 105. Your poor dear wife as you uses w. nor a dog DICKENS. Also **Wo·rserer**, a further extension (joc. or vulgar) of WORSER; e.g. *wusserer and wusserer* 1752.

Worship (wɒ̄·ɹʃip), *sb.* [OE. *weorðscipe*, f. *weorð* WORTH *a.* + *-scipe* -SHIP. The formation is peculiar to English.] **I. 1.** The condition (in a person) of deserving or being held in esteem or repute; honour, renown; good name, credit. *Obs.* exc. *arch.* **2.** The condition of holding a prominent place or rank; dignity, importance, high standing or degree. *arch.* OE. †**b.** With *a* and *pl.* A distinction or dignity; a position of honour or high place -1606. **3.** *Man, gentleman*, etc., *of w.*: a person of repute and standing. *arch.* ME. **4.** With *your* or *his*: A title of honour used in addressing or speaking to a person of note. In later use *spec.* as the title of a magistrate. 1548.

1. †*To win (one's) w.*, to gain honour or renown. **2.** She was as fine as Fi'pence; but truly, I thought there was more Cost than W. SWIFT. **b.** *Lear* I. iv. 288. **4.** What does your w. know about farming? LAMB. This here 's Pickwick, your wash-up DICKENS.

II. †**1.** Respect or honour shown to a person or thing -1610. **2.** Reverence or veneration paid to a being or power regarded as supernatural or divine; the action or practice of displaying this by appropriate acts, rites, or ceremonies ME. **b.** *transf.* Veneration similar to that paid to a deity 1838. **3.** With *a* and *pl.* A form or type of veneration or adoration 1604.

1. †*To do* (a person) *w.*, to show honour or pay respect or homage to. **2.** *Place of w.*: see PLACE *sb.* Hence **Wo·rshipless** *a.* not practising w.; unworshipped.

Worship (wɒ̄·ɹʃip), *v.* [Early ME. *wurþ-, worþscipien*, f. prec.] **1.** *trans.* To honour or revere as a supernatural being or power or as a holy thing; to adore with appropriate acts, rites, or ceremonies. **b.** *transf.* To regard with extreme respect or devotion; to 'adore' 1720. **c.** *absol.* To engage in worship; to perform or take part in the act of worship 1703. †**2.** *trans.* To honour; to regard or treat with honour or respect; to salute, bow down to -1737. †**3.** To invest with or raise to honour or repute; to confer honour or dignity upon -1601.

1. I come from Ierusalem, where I have worshypd the holy grave CAXTON. **b.** I worshipped the very ground she walked on! 1856. Hence **Wo·rshipable** *a.* †entitled to honour or respect, worshipful; capable of being worshipped. **Wo·rshipper**, one who worships; one engaged in, or taking part in, divine worship; *transf.* one who regards a person or thing with feelings akin to worship.

Worshipful (wɒ̄·ɹʃipfŭl), *a.* (*sb.*) ME. [f. WORSHIP *sb.*] **1.** Of things: Notable or outstanding in respect of some (good) quality or property; imposing; reputable, honourable. *arch.* **2.** Of persons: Distinguished in respect of character or rank; entitled to honour or respect on this account. *arch.* ME. **3. a.** As an honorific title for persons or bodies of distinguished rank or importance: now restricted to justices of the peace, aldermen, recorders, the London city companies, and freemasons' lodges and their masters. *Right w.* is applied to mayors, and the sheriffs, aldermen, and recorder of London. late ME. **b.** Used in forms of address, as *w. sir*, (*right*) *w. master*, etc. late ME. **c.** *absol.* (chiefly pl.) or as *sb.* In later use *spec.* a magistrate. 1450. **4.** Imbued with the spirit of worship or veneration 1809. **5.** Deserving or capable of being worshipped; worshipable 1872.

3. **a.** The Master and Wardens of the W. Company of Mercers 1768. **b.** Ryght wyrshypfull and my ryght tendre modre, I recommaunde me to yow 1473. Hence **Wo·rshipful-ly** *adv.* (now *rare*), **-ness.**

Wo·rsle, *v.* 1513. *Sc.* and *north.* var. of WARSLE *v.*

Worst (wɒ̄ɹst), *a.* and *sb.* [OE. *wierresta, wyrresta, wyrsta, wersta* :—OTeut. **wersistoz*, f. *wers-* (see WORSE *a.*) + *-istoz* superl. suffix (see -EST).] **A.** *adj.* Used as the superlative of the adjs. *bad, evil*, or *ill*. **1.** Most bad or evil in regard to moral character or behaviour; also qualifying an agent-noun or the like. **2.** Most grievous, painful, unlucky, or unpleasant OE. **b.** Hardest, most difficult to deal with. late ME. **c.** U.S. colloq. phr. *the w. kind*; also used advb. = most severely, most thoroughly; so *the w. way* 1839. **3.** Most wanting in the good qualities required or expected; least good, valuable, desirable, or successful; least considerable or important ME. †**4.** *predic.* Most unfortunate or badly off 1603.

1. His worst fault is that he is giuen to prayer SHAKS. My w. enemies..never accused me of being meek DICKENS. **2.** They ought to be every one of them put to the w. of Deaths DE FOE. **b.** The best things are w. to come by 1639. **3.** One of that class..who, with the best intentions, have made the w. citizens LYTTON. **4.** *Lear* IV. i. 2.

B. *sb.* (absol. uses of the adj.) **1.** *The w.*: one who is or those who are most objectionable, or least estimable in moral character, behaviour, etc. 1606. **2.** What is most objectionable or deplorable in regard to morals, taste, etc. late ME. **3.** What is most grievous, unlucky, painful; a state of things that is most undesirable or most to be dreaded. late ME. **b.** A course of action ill-advised in the highest degree 1568. **c.** The worst part, degree, or phase *of* 1615. **4.** What is least good in quality or least valuable; the most inferior kind. late ME. **5.** The harshest view or judgement; as *to speak* or *think the w.* (*of* a person or thing) 1586. **6.** Defeat in a contest 1460.

2. Do you know the w. of your father? DICKENS. **3.** I am prepared for the w. LYTTON. *The w. is*, the most unfortunate thing or circumstance is (*that..*). Also, *the w. of* (something), *the w. of it is*, etc. *If the w. comes to the w.*, if things fall out as badly as possible or conceivable. **6.** †*To put to the w.*, to defeat, overcome. *To have the w.*, to be defeated.

Phrases. *At (the) w.*: (*a*) in the most evil or undesirable state that can be; at the greatest disadvantage; (*b*) even on the most unfavourable view, estimate, or surmise. (*To do*) *the w.* or *one's w.*, the utmost evil or harm possible. *To make the w. of*, to regard or represent in the most unfavourable light.

Worst (wɒ̄ɹst), *v.* 1602. [f. WORST *a.*] †**1.** *trans.* To make worse, impair, damage, inflict loss upon -1783. †**b.** *intr.* To grow worse, deteriorate (*rare*) -1815. **2.** *trans.* To defeat, overcome, get the better of (an adversary) in a fight or battle 1636. **b.** To defeat in argument, in a suit, attempt, etc.; to outdo, prove better than 1651.

1. **b.** Anne haggard, Mary coarse, every face in the neighbourhood worsting JANE AUSTEN. **2. b.** Johnson could not brook appearing to be worsted in argument BOSWELL. Hence **Worsted** (wɒ̄·ɹstĕd) *ppl. a.*

Worst (wɒ̄ɹst), *adv.* [OE. *wyrrest, wyrst*; cf. WORST *a.*] In a manner or to a degree that is most (or extremely) bad or evil. **b.** With a vb. of liking, loving, pleasing, etc.: Least well, least OE.

Worsted (wu·stĕd), *sb.* ME. [From the name of a parish in Norfolk, orig. (OE.) *Wurðestede*, now written *Worstead*.] **1.** A woollen fabric or stuff made from well-twisted yarn spun of long-staple wool combed to lay the fibres parallel. **b.** with *pl.* A particular variety of this fabric ME. **2.** A closely twisted yarn made of long-staple wool in which the fibres are arranged to lie parallel to each other. Later, a fine and soft woollen yarn used for knitting and embroidery. 1465. **3.** *attrib.* or *adj.* Made of worsted or worsted yarn; often in specific names of fabrics or materials, as *w. braid, damask*, etc. late ME.

†**Wo·rsum.** Survived in 19th c. in north. dial. [OE. *worsm, wursm.*] Pus.

Wort [1] (wɒ̄ɹt). [OE. *wyrt* root, plant = G. *wurz*; the stem is related to those of ON. *rót* ROOT *sb.* and of L. *radix*, Gr. ῥίζα.] **1.** A plant, herb, or vegetable used for food or medicine; often = pot-herb. *arch.* exc. as second element of various plant-names, as *colewort, liverwort.* †**2.** Any plant of the cabbage kind (genus *Brassica*); colewort -1755.

Wort [2] (wɒ̄ɹt). [OE. *wyrt* = G. *würze*; related to prec.] **1.** The infusion of malt or other grain which after fermentation becomes beer (or may be used for the distillation of spirits). **2.** An infusion or decoction of malt formerly used in the treatment of ulcers, of scurvy, and other diseases 1694.

Worth (wɒ̄ɹþ), *sb.*[1] [OE. *weorþ, wurþ, worþ*; cf. WORTH *a.*] **1.** Pecuniary value; †price; †money. **b.** The equivalent *of* a specified sum or amount (cf. HALFPENNYWORTH, PENNYWORTH, SHILLINGSWORTH). OE. **2.** The relative value of a thing in respect of its qualities or of the estimation in which it is held ME. **b.** High or outstanding value, excellence. *Obs.* or *arch.* 1617. **3.** The character or standing of a person in respect of moral and intellectual qualities; *esp.* high personal merit or attainments 1591. **4.** The position or standing of a person in respect of property; hence *concr.* possessions, property, means. *Obs.* or *arch.* 1592.

1. Some poverty-stricken legatee,..selling his chance ..for a twelfth part of its w. DICKENS. **2.** The w. of man's homage to God 1877. **3.** He was a iust Prince, full of w. and magnanimitie 1615. How hard for real w. to gain its price! YOUNG. **4.** They are but beggers that can count their w. SHAKS.

Phrases. *Of great, little, no*, etc. *w.*; Euerie day Men of great w. resorted to this forrest SHAKS. *Of w.*, of high merit or excellence. †*To take at, of*, or *to w.*, *to take, bear, have in (good) w.*, *to take well in w.*: to take at its true value, take in good part, be content with.

Worth (wɒ̄ɹþ), *sb.*[2] *Hist.* 1575. [OE. *worþ, wurþ* as the second element of place-names.] An enclosed place; a homestead.

Worth (wɒɹþ), *a.* [OE. *weorþ, worþ, wurþ,* also *wierþe, wyrþe* (whence ME. *wurthe*), *weorþe*; the relationships of the stem are obsc.] Almost always (now only) *predic.*, or following the sb. as part of a qualifying phrase. **I. 1.** Of the value of a specified amount or sum; equivalent to (something) in material value. **b.** Of (such-and-such) value *to* a person 1484. **c.** In contemptuous comparisons ME. **2.** Of material value; capable of being estimated in terms of money or some other material standard. *arch.* ME. **b.** Of value in other than material respects. *arch.* ME. **3.** Of a specified or certain value in other than material respects ME. **4.** Of standing in respect of possessions, property, or income; possessed of, owning: usu. with specification of the sum 1460.

1. There is a fayre Diamond, what is it w.? 1605. It is esteem'd w. its weight in Gold ADDISON. c. She knewe it to be but a feigned & peinted mattre & not woorth two strawes 1548. Manufacturers, and meagre mechanicks? fellows not w. powder and shot 1776. 2. b. Little w. is woman's beauty, So oft an image dumb we see 1871. 3. I thought an howers rest w. a Kings ransome 1617. *As much as.. is w.*; It is as much as my Life is w., if she should think we were intimate STEELE. *For all one* or *it is w.* (orig. U.S.): to the utmost of one's or its powers or possibilities; to the fullest extent. Prov. *A bird in the hand is w. two in the bush.* 4. I shall be w. Fifty thousand Pound STEELE.

II. 1. Deserving or worthy of the bestowal or expenditure of (something) OE. **2.** Sufficiently valuable or important to be an equivalent or good return for (something). late ME. **b.** With vbl. sbs., or a noun having the force of a vbl. sb., as obj. 1540.

1. The captain..is not w. his salt MARRYAT. 2. To reign is w. ambition though in Hell MILT. b. An Ass like this was w. the stealing! WORDSW. 'They are not w. your notice', said the dismal man DICKENS. Is Life w. living? 1877. *W. it* (colloq.), having a value or importance commensurate with what is expended upon it, WORTH-WHILE.

Worth (wɒɹþ), *v. Obs.* exc. *arch.* [Com. Teut.; OE. *weorðan, wurðan* (*wearþ, wurdon, geworden*), cogn. w. L. *vertere* to turn; cf. -WARD.] **1.** *intr.* To come to be, come to pass, happen; in subjunctive, expressing a wish for something to happen to one. **2.** To become, come to be OE. **b.** To become *of* (= happen to, betide). late ME.

1. Phr. *Woe w.*, †*well w.*, followed by a noun or pronoun orig. in the dative = May evil or good betide; Woo worthe the oure that euer I was made in! 1440. Woe w. the chase, woe w. the day! SCOTT.

Worthful (wɒ·ɹþfŭl), *a.* [OE. *weorþ-, wurþful*, f. *weorþ* WORTH *sb.*[1] In later use app. re-formed in 16–17th and again in 19th cent.] **1.** Of persons: Honourable; meriting respect or reverence; full of worth or merit. **2.** Having worth or value; valuable, precious ME.

Worthily (wɒ·ɹðili), *adv.* ME. [f. WORTHY *a.* + -LY[2].] †**1.** With due dignity, pomp, or splendour –1522. **2.** In a manner befitting one of high standing or character; in accordance with one's own dignity or personal worth. late ME. **3.** According to desert or merit; deservedly, justly, rightly ME. **b.** Fittingly (in respect of subject or matter) 1553. **4.** With due devotion or reverence; in a fitting spirit; also, with real desert by reason of faith or good life ME.

2. An incident of a life w. spent 1858. 4. The vertue and efficacie of this Sacrament duely and worthely received 1565. So **Wo·rthiness**, the character or quality of being worthy ME.

Worthless (wɒ·ɹþlės), *a.* 1588. [f. WORTH *sb.*[1] + -LESS.] **1.** Of things, etc.: Destitute of (material) worth; having no intrinsic value. **2.** Of persons: Lacking worth or merit; contemptible, despicable 1591. †**3.** Unworthy *of* –1639.

2. Am I then doom'd to fall..for a w. woman? ADDISON. A w. adventurer, whose only recommendation was that he was a Papist MACAULAY. 3. A peeuish School-boy, worthles of such Honor SHAKS. Hence **Wo·rthless-ly** *adv.*, **-ness.**

Worth-while, *a.* 1884. Chiefly *predic.* [See WHILE *sb.* 3 b.] That is worth while; of sufficient value or importance.

Worthy (wɒ·ɹði), *a., adv., sb.* [ME. *wurði, worði*, etc., f. WORTH *sb.*[1] + -Y[1].] **A.** *adj.* **I. 1.** Of things: Having worth; possessed of value or importance; valuable; excellent. *arch.* **2.** Of persons: Distinguished by good qualities; entitled to honour or respect on this account. Now often with patronizing implication (e.g. *She's a very w. woman*). ME. **b.** *absol.* in sing. or pl. sense. late ME. **c.** Of mind or character: Having a high moral standard 1753. †**3.** Of things: Honourable; held in honour or esteem –1721. **4.** Of sufficient worth or value; appropriate, fitting, suitable ME. †**b.** Deserved; merited by default or wrong-doing, condign –1622. **5.** Of persons: Possessed of sufficient worth, desert, or merit 1552. **b.** Of actions, etc.: Adequate or suitable in respect of moral excellence or noble aims 1563.

1. Cows and Oxen are w. Beasts, and in great request with the Husbandman 1669. 2. A small collection of your late dear and w. Pastor's sermons 1758. c. Such as are styled, in the cant term of the day, men of w. characters WESLEY. 4. b. He has much w. blame laid vpon him SHAKS. 5. A w. successor to Mr. Russell Lowell 1885.

II. 1. Of sufficient merit, excellence, or desert *to* be or have something, or †*for* (some purpose) ME. **2.** Deserving *of* something by reason of merit or excellence; also with ellipsis of *of* ME. **3.** Deserving or meriting by fault or wrong-doing ME. **4.** Corresponding to the worth of; appropriate or suitable (to), fit (for). Const. noun as obj. (now *arch.* and *rare*), or *of*. ME.

1. He is as w. for an Empresse loue, As meet to be an Emperors Councellor SHAKS. The only knowledge w. to be called knowledge JOWETT. 2. Be w. me, as I am w. you DRYDEN. 'Twere matter W. the hearing WORDSW. 3. Thou arte w. to be hanged 1508. 4. The stern joy which warriors feel In foemen w. of their steel SCOTT.

B. *adv.* or quasi-*adv.* Worthily; in a manner worthy *of* (something). *Obs.* or *poet.* late ME.

C. *sb.* **1.** A distinguished or eminent person; esp. a man of courage or of noble character. late ME. **b.** *spec.* A hero of antiquity 1552. **c.** Applied colloq. or joc. to any person, esp. one having a marked personality 1751. †**2.** A thing of worth or value. SHAKS.

1. b. *The Nine Worthies*: nine famous personages of ancient and mediæval history and legend; the number is composed of three Jews (Joshua, David, and Judas Maccabæus), three Gentiles (Hector, Alexander, and Julius Cæsar), and three Christians (Arthur, Charlemagne, and Godfrey of Bouillon). Hence †**Worthy** *v. trans.* to render, or hold, w. (*of* something); to raise to honour or distinction –1624.

-worthy, the adj. as a second element in a number of compounds, of which only a few are in regular use, as *blame-, note-, praise-, sea-worthy* (so *airworthy*). The earliest examples replace compounds of OE. *-wyrþe*.

Wortle (wɒ·ɹt'l). late ME. [Origin obsc.] An implement used in drawing wire or lead-pipe.

Wot (wǫt), *v. arch.* ME. [New formation due to the carrying over of the pret.-pres. stem *wot* of WIT *v.*[1] into other parts of the verb.] To know.

He she wots of remained here..expecting to see her SCOTT. There are more dangers around than you w. of 1841.

Wou·bit, oo·bit. *dial.* [ME. *wolbode, -bede*, app. f. *wol* WOOL *sb.* with obscure second element.] A hairy caterpillar; a woolly bear.

Wough[1] (wōᵘ, wǫ). *Obs.* exc. *dial.* [OE. *wāg, wāh.*] **1.** A wall of a house; a partition. **2.** *Mining.* The side of a vein 1653.

Wough[2] (wuf). 1824. [Imitative. Cf. WHOOF, WOOF.] The bark of a dog, etc.

Would (wud). late ME. [pa. t. subj. of WILL *v.*[1] used subst.] The feeling or expression of a conditional or undecided desire or intention. **b.** With *the*, denoting desire or intention in contrast to duty or necessity 1753.

Would-be (wu·dbī), *a.* and *sb.* ME. [The verbal nexus *would be* used attrib. and absol.] **A.** *adj.* Of persons: That would be; wishing to be; posing as. **b.** Of things: Intended to be what is denoted by the sb. 1839. **c.** With following adj., forming a hyphened phr. 1826.

B. *sb.* One who fain would be (something specified or implied) 1605.

Would-have-been, *a.* 1744. [Verbal nexus used attrib.] That would have liked to be, that aimed at being (something specified).

Woulfe (wulf). 1800. [The surname of Peter *Woulfe* (? 1727–1803), a London chemist.] *Woulfe's apparatus*, a series of glass receivers (called *Woulfe's bottles*), formerly used in distillation.

Wound (wūnd), *sb.* [Com. Teut.; OE. *wund.* The normal mod. pronunc. would be (waund); cf. WOUNDY, ZOUNDS.] **1.** A hurt caused by the laceration or separation of the tissues of the body by a hard or sharp instrument, a bullet, etc.; an external injury. **b.** esp. in *the (Five) Wounds* of Christ ME. **c.** Used as an oath or strong exclam., as *By Christ's wounds, Wounds of God*, etc. (see SWOUNDS, ZOUNDS, WOUNDS) ME. **2.** *transf.* An incision, abrasion, or other injury due to external violence, in any part of a tree or plant 1574. **b.** In other transf. uses 1667. **3.** *Surgery.* An incision or opening made by a surgical operator 1668. **4.** Something which causes a wound 1715.

1. *fig.* She..Pours balm into the bleeding lover's wounds POPE. The wounds of honour never close 1744. 2. b. Her rash hand..Forth reaching to the Fruit, she pluck'd, she eat: Earth felt the w. MILT.

Combs.: **w.-cork**, a protective layer formed on a damaged trunk or branch of a plant or tree; **-fungus**, a fungus which grows on the injured part of a plant; **-stripe**, a stripe of gold braid worn by a wounded soldier on the left sleeve, vertically, above the cuff; **-weed** = WOUNDWORT. Hence **Wou·ndless** *a.* unwounded; †invulnerable; harmless.

Wound (wūnd), *v.* [OE. *wundian*, f. *wund* WOUND *sb.*] **1.** *trans.* To inflict a wound on (a person, the body, etc.) by means of a weapon; to injure intentionally in such a way as to cut or tear the flesh: freq. in pass. Also said of the weapon, etc. **2.** *fig.* To injure, inflict pain or hurt upon, in a manner comparable to the infliction of a wound; in later use *esp.* to pain or grieve deeply ME. **b.** Used to express the effect of harsh or disagreeable sounds upon the ear 1669. **3.** *absol.* or *intr.* To inflict a wound or wounds; to do harm, hurt, or injury (physically or otherwise); to impair in any way OE. **4.** *transf.* To pierce or cut as if to wound; to damage in this way ME. **b.** *fig.* Of wine: To overpower (*rare*) 1613.

1. An honest Man that has been wounded in the Queen's Service ADDISON. 2. *A. Y. L.* v. ii. 25. Moore's vanity was easily wounded at any time 1884. 4. When she would with sharpe needle w. The Cambricke SHAKS. Hence **Wou·nded** *ppl. a.* **Wou·nded-ly** *adv.* in a wounded manner, as though wounded. **Wou·nding** *vbl. sb.* and *ppl. a.* **Wou·nder.**

Wound (waund), pa. t. and pa. pple. of WIND *v.*[1]

Woundily (wau·ndili), *adv. Obs.* exc. *arch.* 1706. [f. WOUNDY *a.* + -LY[2].] Excessively, extremely, dreadfully.

I own I's w. afraid of dead men 1796.

Wounds (waundz), *int. Obs.* exc. *arch.* 1610. [ellipt. for *God's wounds*; see WOUND *sb.* 1 c. Cf. OONS, ZOUNDS.] Used as an oath or asseveration.

Wound-up (waund,ʋp), *a.* 1837. [f. *wound*, pa. pple. of WIND *v.*[1] + UP *adv.*] That has undergone winding-up.

Woundwort (wū·ndwɒɹt). 1548. [f. WOUND *sb.* + WORT *sb.*[1], after Du. *wondkruid*, G. *wundkraut.*] A popular name for various plants, from their use in healing wounds, *esp.* (*a*) one of the species of *Stachys*; (*b*) the golden-rod, *Solidago Virgaurea*; (*c*) the kidney-vetch, *Anthyllis vulneraria*; (*d*) the comfrey, *Symphytum officinale*.

Woundy (wau·ndi), *adv.* and *a.* 1621. [f. WOUNDS *int.* + -Y[1]. Cf. *bloody.*] **A.** *adv.* Very, extremely, excessively.

He was w. angry when I gav 'n that wipe CONGREVE.

B. *adj.* Very great; extreme 1681.

He flew into a w. passion 1794.

Wove (wōᵘv), *ppl. a.* and *sb.* 1710. [var. of WOVEN.] **1.** = next. **b.** *W. mould*, the particular kind of mould used in making w. paper (see 2) 1839. **2.** Of paper: Made on a mould of closely woven wire 1809. **b.** *absol.* or as *sb.* Paper so made 1859.

Woven (wōᵘ·v'n), *ppl. a.* 1470. [pa. pple. of WEAVE *v.*[1]] **1.** That has undergone the process of weaving; formed or fabricated by weaving. **2.** Formed by interlacing or intertwining after the manner of weaving 1590. **3.** Interlaced, intertwined; wreathed 1815.

2. Soone after comes the cruell Sarazin, In wouen maile all armed warily SPENSER. 3. The kiss, The w. arms TENNYSON.

Wow (wau), *sb.* 1811. [Imitative.] A bark or similar sound; a cat's howl. So **Wow** *v. intr.* to howl; to waul.

Wow (wau), *int.* and *sb. Sc.* and *U.S.* 1513. An exclamation of surprise, admiration, aversion, or commiseration. **b.** phr. *It's a wow* (U.S.), used to express admiration or approval 1927.

Wowser (wau·zəɹ). *Austral.* 1909. [Origin obsc.] A Puritanical enthusiast or fanatic.

‖**Wow-wow** (wau·wau). 1827. [a. Malay *wauwau*, Javanese *wawa*, imitative of the animal's cry.] The silver gibbon of Java, *Hylobates leuciscus*; also *H. agilis*.

Wr- (r), a consonantal combination occurring initially in a number of words (freq. implying twisting or distortion), the earlier of which usu. have cognates with the same initial sounds in the older Germanic langs. The combination was regularly preserved in Gothic, OS., OFris., and OE., but in OHG. and ON. was reduced to *r*.

In English, signs of the dropping of the *w* in pronunciation begin to appear about the middle of the 15th cent., and become common in the 16th cent. In standard English the *w* was finally dropped in the 17th cent.; it has remained (though now *obsol.*) in Scottish, and in some south-western dialects is represented by *v*, which is also regular in north-eastern Scottish.

Wrack (ræk), *sb.*[1] [OE. *wræc*, f. gradation-var. of *wrecan* WREAK *v.*] **I. 1.** Retributive punishment; vengeance, revenge; later also, active enmity, persecution. *Obs.* exc. *arch.* or *poet.* **2.** Damage, disaster, or injury to a person, state, etc., by reason of force, outrage, or violence. late ME. **3.** A disastrous change in a state or condition of affairs; wreck, ruin. late ME. †**b.** The ruin, downfall, or overthrow of a person or persons –1699.

1. *fig.* Hath he not lost much wealth by w. of sea? SHAKS. 2. Phr. *To bring, go, put, run to w.* (*and ruin*). Cf. RACK *sb.*[4] 3. *All's Well* III. v. 24.

II. †**1.** An instance of causing or suffering wreck, ruin, destruction, etc. –1632. †**b.** A means or cause of subversion, overthrow, or downfall –1682. **2.** A thing or person in an impaired, wrecked, or shattered condition 1586. **b.** That which remains after the operation of any destructive action or agency; a vestige or trace left by some subversive cause 1602.

1. b. And thus I feare at last, Humes Knauerie will be the Duchesse Wracke SHAKS. 2. b. I am a poore, poore orphant—a weake, weake childe. The w. of splitted fortune. MARSTON.

Wrack (ræk), *sb.*[2] late ME. [a. MDu. *wrak* or MLG. *wra(c)k*, a parallel formation to OE. *wræc* WRACK *sb.*[1]] **1.** A wrecked ship or other vessel. Now *dial.* **b.** Remnants of or goods from a wrecked vessel, esp. as driven or cast ashore; wreckage. *arch.* late ME. **2.** = SHIPWRECK *sb.* 2. *rare* or *Obs.* 1579. **3.** Marine vegetation, seaweed or the like, cast ashore by the waves or growing on the tidal sea-shore 1513. **b.** Weeds, rubbish, etc., floating on or washed down or ashore by a river, pond, or the like 1598. **c.** Field-weeds, roots of couch-grass or the like, esp. as loosened from the soil to be collected for burning 1715.

1. b. As rich.. As is the Owse and bottome of the Sea With sunken Wrack SHAKS. Hence **Wra·ckful** *a.* (now *rare arch.*) causing shipwreck, causing destruction or devastation, subject to or attended by harm, injury, etc.

Wrack (ræk), *sb.*[3] 1472. [a. (M)LG. or Du. *wrak.*] **1.** That which is of an inferior, poor, or worthless quality; waste material; rubbish. Now *rare.* **2.** An inferior grade of flax 1879.

†*World's w.* (Sc.): earthly 'dross'; worldly possessions.

Wrack (ræk), *v.* Now *arch.* or *dial.* 1470. [f. WRACK *sb.*[2]] †**1.** *intr.* To suffer or undergo shipwreck –1632. **2.** *trans.* To wreck; to ruin or cast ashore by shipwreck: chiefly *pass.* 1562. **3.** To cause the ruin, downfall, or subversion of (a person, etc.); to ruin, overthrow 1564. **b.** To render useless by breaking, etc.; to injure or spoil severely; to destroy 1587. **4.** *intr.* To undergo ruin or subversion 1586.

3. b. Eightie odde yeeres of sorrow haue I seene, And each howres ioy wrackt with a weeke of teene SHAKS. Hence **Wracked** (rækt) *ppl. a.*

Wraith (rēþ). orig. *Sc.* 1513. [Origin obsc.] **1.** An apparition or spectre of a dead person; a phantom or ghost. **b.** An immaterial or spectral appearance of a living being, freq. regarded as portending that person's death 1513. **2.** A water-spirit 1742. **3.** An appearance or configuration suggestive of a wraith or spectre 1882.

1. b. The shape of the warning w. haunts the mountaineer 1838.

Wrangle (ræ·ŋg'l), *sb.* 1547. [f. next.] **1.** An angry dispute or noisy quarrel; an altercation or bitter disputation. **2.** Without article: The action of wrangling; angry altercation or argument 1797.

1. The disgraceful wrangles of the religious newspapers 1859.

Wrangle (ræ·ŋg'l), *v.* late ME. [Cf. LG. *wrangeln*, MHG. *rangelen*, frequent. f. *rangen* to struggle, make uproar.] **1.** *intr.* To dispute angrily and noisily; to bicker. **2.** To argue or debate; to engage in controversy; †to dispute or discuss publicly, as at a university, for or against a thesis, etc. 1570. †**3.** *trans.* To argue *out* (a case, dispute, etc.) –1728. **4.** To influence (a person) by wrangling or contention; to argue *out of* a possession, etc. 1633. **5.** *Western U.S.* To take charge of (horses) 1903.

1. Wrangling about trifles 1746. 4. To w. the Church of England out of a good possession 1658.

Wrangler (ræ·ŋgləɹ). 1515. [f. prec. + -ER[1].] **1.** One who wrangles or quarrels; an angry or noisy disputer or arguer. **b.** One who engages in argument, debate, or controversy 1561. **c.** One who has been placed in the first class in the mathematical tripos at Cambridge University 1750. **2.** *Western U.S.* One who is in charge of a string of horses or ponies on a stock-farm 1888. Hence **Wra·nglership**, the position or rank of a w. at Camb. Univ.

Wrap (ræp), *sb.* 1460. [f. next.] **I. a.** A wrapper or covering. **b.** A blanket, rug, or the like for laying over or drawing about the person when travelling, resting, etc. 1861. **2.** A loose garment or article of feminine dress used to wrap about the person; a shawl, scarf, or the like 1827. **b.** An additional outer garment worn as a protection against cold, wind, and weather, etc. Usu. *pl.* = outdoor garments. 1817.

1. b. We have heard.. Livingstone.. say that at night no w. could equal the beard 1861. 2. b. I was taking off my wraps, and making ready to go up stairs 1855.

Wrap (ræp), *v.* ME. [Origin obsc.] **I. 1.** *trans.* To cover, enwrap, or swathe (a person or part of the body) with a cloth or the like; now *esp.* to envelop or enshroud in a garment: freq. with *up*; esp. *pass.* = attired in warm or protective clothing. **b.** *absol.* for *refl.* 1848. **2.** To cover or envelop (an object) by winding or folding something round or about it, esp. so as to protect from injury, loss, etc. late ME. **3.** To envelop or enclose *in* a surrounding medium, as flames, water, etc. late ME. **b.** To clasp, embrace 1588. **4.** To envelop or implicate (a person, etc.) *in* some (esp. prejudicial) condition of things, as sin, trouble, sorrow, etc. late ME. **b.** To involve or enfold (a person, etc.) *in* some soothing or tranquillizing state or influence. Freq. *pass.* late ME. **5.** To involve or enfold (a subject or matter) so as to obscure or disguise the true or full nature of it. late ME. **6.** Of qualities, etc.: To invest or environ (a person, etc.); encompass *in* some condition. late ME. **b.** To form a wrap or covering for (a person or thing); to clothe; to veil 1602. **c.** Of flames, etc.: To spread or extend around, about, or over (something); to surround, encompass 1656.

1. Are you well wrapped up?.. It's a desperate sharp night DICKENS. 2. We can't be kept in bandboxes and wrapped in cotton wool all our lives 1890. 4. It is a Man wrapped in woe 1659. **b.** The house is wrapped in slumbers DICKENS. 5. The religion of the Egyptians.. was all mystery, wrapt in obscurity 1770. Without troubling to w. up his resolve in smooth-sounding words 1897. See also WRAPPED. 6. b. Cauld's the clay, That wraps my Highland Mary! BURNS.

II. 1. To wind or fold up or together, as a pliant or flexible object; to roll or gather up in successive layers ME. **2.** To fold, wind, or roll (a covering, garment, or the like) about a person, etc.; to arrange or dispose (a wrapping, etc.) so as to cover or envelop. late ME. **b.** To twist or coil (a pliable or flexible substance, etc.) *round, about,* or *on* something 1523. **3.** *intr.* for *refl.* To twine, encircle, or wreathe *round* or *about* something 1608. **b.** Of a garment, etc.: To extend *over* something so as to cover it, or form a lap 1798.

2. Wrapping my plaid around me, I wandered up towards Charmoz 1860. **b.** Again she wrapped her arms about me RICHARDSON. Hence **Wra·ppage**, that which wraps, enfolds, or covers; a wrap or outer covering; a wrapper; something wrapped up, a package 1827.

Wrap-, the vb. stem in comb. with a sb. or adv., in the sense 'that which wraps or is wrapped about', as w. tobacco (also *ellipt.*) = WRAPPER *sb.* 4.

Wrapped (ræpt), *pa. pple.* and *ppl. a.* Formerly often **wrapt**. late ME. [f. WRAP *v.* + -ED[1].] **I.** In senses of the vb.: Covered, enwrapped; (with *up*) involved, complicated; etc. **II.** In predic. use. **1.** Deeply interested or absorbed *in*. Often with *up*. 1548. **b.** *W.* (*up*) *in*, entirely associated or bound up with, involved in 1648. **2.** Absorbed or engrossed *in* thought. (Cf. RAPT *pa. pple.* 4.) 1601.

1. b. His young Wife (in whom all his Happiness was wrapt up) ADDISON. 2. Wrapt in a pleasing fit of melancholy MILT. As if wrapt in prayer or meditation GEO. ELIOT.

Wrapper (ræ·pəɹ), *sb.* 1460. [f. WRAP *v.* + -ER[1].] **1.** That in which anything is wrapped; a piece of fabric or other material forming a wrapping; esp. in later use, a protective covering for a parcel or the like. **b.** A detachable outer paper cover of a book, etc., intended to protect the print, boards, or binding 1806. **c.** A covering to protect and compact a newspaper or the like when sent by post, etc. 1846. **d.** A dust sheet 1848. **2.** A head-dress wrapped about the head (*rare*) 1548. **b.** A shawl, mantle, etc., for wearing about the person. Now *rare* 1782. **3.** A garment, esp. for indoor wear, designed for loosely enveloping the whole (or nearly the whole) figure; a loose robe or gown. Now chiefly *U.S.* 1734. **b.** An article of dress, esp. for men, intended to wrap about or fit loosely over the person; also, an overall. Now *dial.* 1799. **4.** Tobacco-leaf of a superior grade used for the outer covering of cigars or of plug tobacco; a covering made of this. Chiefly *U.S.* 1688. **b.** *U.S.* A cigar 1849. **5.** *Bot.* In fungi, = VOLVA 1796. **6.** One who wraps or packs up anything; *spec.* one whose occupation is wrapping parcels 1591.

3. His wife.. had just risen—or so it seemed, for she wore a rose-colored w. 1883. 6. Women & Girls as Lacquerers.. Press Women, & Wrappers-up 1866. Hence **Wra·pper** *v. trans.* to enclose or envelop in a w., cover *up* in or as in a w. **Wra·ppering**, coarse fabric used or designed for wrapping or covering; a wrap or wrapper.

Wrapping (ræ·piŋ), *vbl. sb.* late ME. [f. WRAP *v.* + -ING[1].] **1.** The action of covering with or enveloping in a wrap or wrapper 1440. **2.** Something used or designed for enveloping or wrapping up; a wrap or covering. late ME. **b.** An article of dress enveloping the figure; a loose or warm outer garment 1635.

2. Tearing the paper wrappings off the big box of sweeties 1894. **b.** A gentleman in the coach who.. looked very large in a quantity of wrappings DICKENS.

Comb.: †**w.-gown**, a nightgown; **-paper**, a special make of strong paper for packing or wrapping up parcels.

Wrap-rascal (ræ·pˌrɑːskăl). 1716. Now *arch.* or *dial.* [f. WRAP *v.* + RASCAL *sb.* 3.] A loose overcoat or greatcoat; a surtout.

Wrasse (ræs). 1672. [ad. Cornish *wrach*, mutated f. *gwrach* = Welsh *gwrach.*] **1.** Any species belonging to the acanthopterygian family *Labridæ*, esp. of the genus *Labrus* of bony, thick-lipped marine fishes; e.g. the ballan, *Labrus maculatus*, or *L. mixtus*, found on the British coasts. **b.** With distinguishing epithet, as *cook, rainbow, striped w.*, etc. 1769. **2.** Without article: Wrasses collectively 1750.

Wrath (rǭþ, *U.S.* and *Sc.* rāþ), *sb.* [OE. *wrǣððu, -o*, f. *wrāþ* WROTH *a.* + *-þu* :—Teut. **-iþō*; see -TH[1].] **1.** Vehement or violent anger; intense exasperation or resentment; deep indignation. **b.** The righteous indignation (of God or a deity) OE. **c.** *transf.* Violence or extreme force of a natural agency, regarded as hostile to mankind or growth 1579. **2.** An instance of deep or violent anger; a fit or spell of ire or fierce indignation ME. †**3.** Impetuous ardour, rage, or fury -1601. 4. Anger displayed in action; the manifestation of anger or fury, esp. by way of retributory punishment; vengeance OE. †5. An act done in anger or indignation -1754.

1. Upon every triffle they shall be provoked to W. 1691. When he had respectfully suffered her w. to vent itself, he made apologies MME D'ARBLAY. b. As when the w. of Jove Speaks thunder MILT. c. Thou barrein ground, whome winters w. hath wasted SPENSER. 2. *Temp.* III. iii. 79. 3. They are in the verie w. of loue, and they will together SHAKS. 4. Remembre that the w. shall not be longe in tarienge COVERDALE *Ecclus.* vii. 16. The wrauth Of stern Achilles on his Foe MILT. Phr. (orig. biblical). *The w. of God, the day of w.*

Wrath (rǭþ), *a.* Somewhat *rare.* 1535. [var. of WROTH *a.*, infl. by association with prec.] = WROTH *a.*

Wrathful (rǭ·þfŭl), *a.* ME. [f. WRATH *sb.* + -FUL.] 1. Harbouring wrath; full of anger; enraged, incensed. Also *transf.* of things. 2. Marked or characterized by, expressive of, or of the nature of wrath or anger. late ME.

1. The wrathfull Skies SHAKS. The Bees, a w. Race DRYDEN. Hence **Wra·thful-ly** *adv.*, -ness.

Wrathy (rǭ·þi, *U.S.* rā·þi), *a.* orig. and chiefly *U.S.* 1828. [f. WRATH *sb.* + -Y[1].] Feeling or inclined to wrath; wrathful, incensed. Also *transf.* of things. b. Marked or characterized by wrath; expressing or evincing deep anger or indignation 1873.

†Wray, *v.* [Com. Teut.: OE. *wrēgan* = OHG. (G. *rügen*), f. **wrōg-* (as in ON. *rōg* slander, strife).] 1. *trans.* To accuse, denounce -1450. 2. = BEWRAY *v.* 2, 3, 4. -1587.

Wreak (rīk), *sb.* Now *arch.* or *Obs.* ME. [Northern form of ME. *wreche* (OE. *wræc*) vengeance; in later use prob. substituted for this under the influence of the vb.] 1. Hurt or harm done from vindictive motives; vengeance, revenge. †2. An instance of taking revenge or exacting retribution -1626. †3. Harm, injury, damage -1600.

2. Where mortall wreakes their blis may not remoue SPENSER. Hence **Wrea·kless** *a. rare*, unpunished, unavenged.

Wreak (rīk), *v.* [Com. Teut.; OE. *wrecan* (*wræc, wræcon, wrecen*), f. Teut. stem **wrek-*:— pre-Teut. **wreg-*, cogn. w. L. *urgere* to URGE.] I. 1. *trans.* To give vent or expression to, exercise or gratify (wrath, anger, etc.); to vent. b. *refl.* Of a passion, feeling, etc.: To give expression to (itself); to find utterance or free course 1590. c. To bestow or spend *on* a person, etc.; to expend (*rare*) 1586. †2. To punish or chastise; to visit with retributive punishment -1683.

1. The more to wreake his wrath, the King spoyled many Religious houses of their goodes HOLINSHED. I wreaked my Resentment upon the innocent Cause of my Disgraces SMOLLETT.

II. 1. To avenge (a person) OE. †b. To revenge (a person) *of* a wrong, injury, etc. -1591. 2. *refl.* and (now arch. or obs.) *pass.* To take vengeance. 3. *trans.* To take vengeance or inflict retributive punishment for; to avenge or revenge (a wrong, harm, or injury) OE. †4. To visit (a fault, misdeed) with punishment -1610. 5. To inflict (vengeance, etc.) *on* or *upon* a person; to execute or carry out by way of punishment or revenge 1489. b. To cause or effect (harm, damage, etc.) 1817. c. To inflict or deliver (a blow, etc.) 1817.

1. To wreake the Loue I bore my Cozin, Vpon his body that hath slaughter'd him SHAKS. 2. He micht hae spared my lady's life, And wreakit himsell on me! *Ballad, Capt. Car.* 5. Resolv'd.. To w. his Vengeance, and to cure her Love DRYDEN. Hence **Wrea·ker** (now *arch.* and *rare*), an avenger.

Wreakful (rī·kfŭl), *a.* 1531. [f. WREAK *sb.* + -FUL.] 1. Given or addicted to revenge; vengeful. b. *transf.* Of natural agencies 1561. 2. Marked or characterized by desire for revenge; of the nature of vengeance or retribution 1532.

Wreath (rīþ). *Pl.* **wreaths** (rīðz). [OE. *wriþa*, f. wk. grade of *wrīþan* WRITHE *v.*] I. 1. Something wound, wreathed, or coiled into a circular shape or form; a twisted or wreathed band, fillet, or the like. b. A ring, band, or circlet of (usu. precious) metal, etc., esp. for wearing as an ornament OE. c. *Her.* A representation of a ring or circlet used as a bearing; *spec.* the circular fillet or twisted band by which the crest is joined to the helmet 1478. 2. Something resembling or comparable to a twisted or circular band; *esp.* a coil of a spiral column of smoke, steam, or the like 1667. b. A bank or drift of snow. Orig. and chiefly *Sc.* 1725. 3. Each of the turns, convolutions, or coils of a ringed or spiral structure; a whirl, whorl 1641. b. *Conch.* A member of the genus *Turbo*; a turbinated shell; a turbinate 1777. 4. A twist, coil, or winding (of some material thing or natural growth); a sinuosity 1589. 5. A curve in the handrail or string of a geometrical stair 1814.

2. Clouds began To darken all the Hill, and smoak to rowl In duskie wreathes MILT.

II. A chaplet or garland of flowers, leaves, or the like, esp. worn or awarded as a mark of distinction, honour, etc., or laid upon a grave, etc. 1450. b. A trailing cluster of flowers, tendrils, etc. 1610. c. As the title of a book comprising a collection of short literary pieces 1753. d. A representation of a wreath in decorative work, metal, stone, etc. 1847.

A Crown, Golden in shew, is but a w. of thorns MILT.

Comb.: **w. shell** = I. 3b; **-wort**, the early purple orchis, *Orchis mascula.* Hence **Wrea·thless** *a.* having no w. **Wrea·thlet**, a small w.

Wreathe (rīð), *v.* 1530. [Partly back-formation from *wrethen* WREATHEN *ppl. a.*, partly f. WREATH *sb.*] I. 1. *trans.* To twist or coil (something); to form into a coil or coils 1535. b. To wind or turn (some pliant object) about or over something; to form or adjust as a wreath or encircling coil 1530. 2. To surround or invest with or as with something twisted or turned; to encircle or surround with a wreath or garland; to adorn with or as with a wreath; to form a wreath about (something) 1558. 3. To unite (two or more things) by twining or twisting together; to entwine, intertwine 1553. b. To combine (several things into one structure) by interweaving; to form or make by intertwining 1547. 4. To arrange or dispose flowers, etc., in the form of a wreath; to fashion (flowers, etc.) into a garland or chaplet 1595.

1. An adder Wreathed up in fatal folds SHAKS. b. An ill-adjusted turban.. wreathed around their sunburnt brows WORDSW. 2. With Laurels wreath your posts, And strow with Flow'rs the Pavement DRYDEN. Each flower that wreath'd the dewy locks of Spring COLERIDGE. 3. Enter Andrugio and Antonio wreathed together MARSTON. 4. The Garland wreath'd for Eve MILT.

II. †a. To strain or turn forcibly round or to one side; to wring, wrench, or wrest -1737. b. To twist, turn, or contort (the body, limbs, etc.); to writhe 1642. c. To alter (the features, etc.) *in, into,* or *to* a smile, etc. 1813.

b. Even in death their lips are wreathed with fear SHELLEY.

III. *intr.* 1. To undergo writhing, twisting, or deviation; to bend, turn, or coil 1584. 2. To assume the form of or circle in the manner of a wreath 1776.

2. The flames of fire shall round him w. 1776. Hence **Wreathed** (rīðd) *ppl. a.* **Wrea·thing** *vbl. sb.* the action of twisting or contorting, or of entwining or intertwining; an instance of this *concr.* something wreathed or twisted.

Wreathen (rī·ð'n), *ppl. a.* [Late ME. *wrēðen*, var. of *wriðen*, pa. pple. of *wrīðen* WRITHE *v.*] 1. Wreathed; contorted, twisted. 2. Entwined, intertwined 1611.

Wreathy (rī·þi), *a.* 1644. [f. WREATH *sb.* + -Y[1].] 1. Of the form of a wreath; marked or characterized by convolution, twisting, or twining. 2. Decked with a wreath 1697. 3. Of the nature of, forming, or constituting a wreath or garland 1718.

Wreck (rek), *sb.* ME. [a. AF. *wrec, wrech*, a. ON. **wrec* (Norw., Icel. *rek*), f. the stem of *wrekan* to drive.] I. 1. *Law.* That which is cast ashore by the sea in tidal waters; *esp.* goods or cargo from a wrecked, stranded, or foundered vessel. 2. A vessel broken, destroyed, or totally disabled by being driven on rocks, cast ashore, or stranded; a wrecked or helpless ship 1500. 3. a. *Law.* A piece or article of wreckage. Freq. *pl.* 1570. b. Without article: = WRECKAGE 2. 1744. 4. That which remains *of* something that has suffered ruin, demolishment, waste, etc. 1713. 5. That which is in a state of ruin; anything that is broken down or has undergone wrecking, shattering, or dilapidation 1814. b. A person of undermined, shattered, or ruined constitution 1795. ¶6. = WRACK *sb.*[1] II. 2b. 1787.

1. A warrant against 11 Britton men for riotously taking a whale and other wrecke 1666. 2. The ship.. struck upon a reef of rocks.., and shortly became a total w. 1805. 3. b. Several chests, broken masts, and other pieces of w. floating in the sea 1744. 4. As Mamma surveyed the w. of luncheon 1854. The Republican party was formed.. out of the wrecks of the Whig party 1888. 5. b. I was a nervous w. 1899. I feel a perfect w. 1901. 6. These ruins soon left not a w. behind SHELLEY.

II. 1. The disabling or destruction of a vessel by any disaster or accident of navigation; = SHIPWRECK *sb.* 2. 1463. 2. The action of subverting or overthrowing an established order of things, etc., or of wrecking or breaking apart; the fact of being brought to disaster or wrecked; destruction, downfall, demolition 1577.

1. A range of rocks, the terrible scene of many a disastrous w. 1809. 2. Books, which.. may.. perish only in the general W. of Nature ADDISON. The w. of their ancient liberties PRESCOTT. Phr. *To go to w.* (*and ruin*); cf. RACK *sb.*[4]

Wreck (rek), *v.*[1] late ME. [f. prec.] †1. *trans.* To cast on shore -1821. 2. To cause the wreck of (a vessel). Chiefly *pass.* 1570. b. To make or cause (a person) to suffer or undergo shipwreck; also, to cause the loss of (goods or cargo) by shipwreck. Chiefly *pass.* 1617. 3. To cause or bring about the ruin or destruction of (a structure, etc.) as by violence or misuse; to shatter, ruin, destroy 1510. b. To cause or bring about the subversion or overthrow of (some condition or order of things) 1749. c. To frustrate or thwart; to prevent the passing of (a measure, etc.) 1855. 4. To bring (a person) to ruin or disaster 1590. b. To shatter (a person's health, constitution, or nerves) by sickness, hardship, or the like: usu. *pass.* 1850. 5. *intr.* To suffer or undergo shipwreck 1671. 6. To seize or collect wreck or wreckage; to search *for* wreck 1843.

2. The shallop of my peace is wrecked on Beauty's shore 1845. 3. b. Their want of tact and judgment has wrecked the party 1826. 4. b. I wonder your nervous system isn't completely wrecked KIPLING. 5. Honour, glory, and popular praise; Rocks whereon greatest men have oftest wreck'd MILT.

†Wreck, *v.*[2] 1570. [Late var. of WREAK *v.*] = WREAK *v.* -1793.

Wreckage (re·kėdʒ). 1837. [f. WRECK *v.*[1] + -AGE.] 1. The action or process of wrecking; the fact of being wrecked. 2. Fragments or remains of a shattered or wrecked vessel; wreck 1846. 3. Material of or from a wrecked or shattered structure; a ruined fabric, building, etc. 1874. b. *fig.* Persons whose lives have been wrecked or who have failed to maintain a position in society 1883.

3. The venerable w. of a feudal keep 1894.

Wrecker[1] (re·kəɹ). 1820. [f. WRECK *v.*[1] + -ER[1].] One who causes shipwreck, esp. for purposes of plunder by showing luring lights or false signals; a person who makes a business of watching for and plundering wrecked vessels; *transf.* one who destroys machinery or the like. b. One who wrecks or ruins a structure, institution, etc.; one who successfully obstructs the passing of a measure, etc. 1882.

Wrecker[2] (re·kəɹ). orig. and chiefly *U.S.* 1804. [f. WRECK *sb.* + -ER[1].] 1. A person engaged in salvaging wrecked or endangered vessels or cargo; a salvager, salvor. 2. A ship or vessel employed in salvaging sunk, wrecked, or stranded vessels 1864. **Wre·cking** *vbl. sb.*

Wren[1] (ren). [OE. *wrenna*, obscurely related to OHG. *wrendo, wrendilo*, Icel. *rindill.*] 1. Any species of small dentirostral passerine birds belonging to the genus *Troglodites*, esp. the common w. (jenny- or kitty-w.), *T. parvulus*, native to Europe. 2. Applied, esp. with distinguishing term, to various other small birds of the family *Trogloditidæ* or *Sylviidæ*, resembling the common w. in appearance or habits; esp. the gold-crest, *Regulus cristatus* 1674. b. Applied to various Australasian species of w.-like birds 1848.

1. Thus the fable tells us, that the w. mounted as high as the eagle, by getting upon his back ADDISON.

Comb.: **w.-boys**, in Ireland, a party of boys or young men, carrying a decorated holly-bush with a w. or wrens hanging from it, who go about on St.

Stephen's day singing verses; **w. song,** the song sung by the w.-boys.

Wren[2] (ren). 1918. A member of the *W*omen's *R*oyal *N*aval *S*ervice.

Wrench (renʃ), *sb.* 1530. [f. next.] **1.** An act of wrenching or the fact of being wrenched; a twisting or putting aside, awry, or out of shape. **b.** A sudden or sharp twist or jerk causing pain or injury to a limb, person, etc. 1530. **c.** An instance of this in horses 1578. **d.** *fig.* A parting or separation causing painful or violent emotion; pain or anguish resulting from separation 1849. **e.** *Mech.* A system made up of a force and a couple in a plane perpendicular to it 1876. †**2.** A sharp turn, bend, or deflexion -1654. **b.** *Coursing.* A turning or bringing round of the hare at less than a right angle 1615. **3.** A strained or wrested meaning; a forced or false interpretation 1603. **4.** A mechanical screw 1552. **b.** A tool or implement consisting essentially of a metal bar with jaws adapted for catching or gripping a bolt-head, nut, etc., to turn it; a screw-key, screw-wrench, or spanner 1794. **c.** *Surg.* Applied to various instruments having adjustable jaws, *spec.* one for gripping a deformed foot to be rectified by torsion 1895.

Wrench (renʃ), *v.* [OE. *wrencan* = OHG. *renchan*; origin obsc.] **I.** †**1.** *intr.* To perform or undergo a quick or forcible turning or twisting motion; to turn or writhe -1716. **2.** *Coursing.* Of a hare, etc.: To veer or come round at less than a right angle 1576.

II. *trans.* **1.** To twist or turn forcibly or with effort; to jerk or pull with a violent twist ME. **b.** To tighten with or as with a wrench 1577. **2.** To injure or pain (a person, the limbs, etc.) by undue straining or stretching; to rick, sprain, strain 1530. **b.** To affect with severe pain, suffering, or anguish; to distress or pain greatly 1798. **3.** To pull or draw with a wrench or twist; to twist or wrest out; to force, turn, etc., by a twisting movement 1582. **b.** To seize or take forcibly 1605. **4.** To twist, alter, or change from the right or true form, application, or import 1549. **5.** *Coursing.* To divert, turn, or bring round (a hare, etc.) at less than a right angle 1622. **6.** *absol.* To pull or tug (*at* something) with a turn or twist 1697.

1. b. *fig.* For thy Reuenge W. vp thy power to th' highest SHAKS. 2. You wrenched your foot against a stone, and were forced to stay SWIFT. 3. W. his Sword from him SHAKS. He went up to the door, wrenched off the fastenings 1825. Hence **Wre·ncher,** a machine or instrument for wrenching or wringing (*rare*); one who or that which wrenches or twists.

Wrest (rest), *sb.*[1] ME. [f. the vb.] **1.** The action of twisting or writhing; a twist, wrench; a tug or violent pull. **2.** An implement for tuning certain wire-stringed instruments, as the harp or spinet; a tuning-key. Now *arch.* late ME.

Comb.: **w.-pin,** the peg round which the ends of the strings or wires of certain musical instruments are coiled, a tuning-pin; **-plank,** the board in a piano in which the w.-pins are fixed.

Wrest, *sb.*[2] Now *dial.* 1653. [Variant spelling of dial. *reest* (OE. *rēost*), by association w. prec.] *Agric.* A piece of iron (†or wood) fastened beneath the mould-board in certain ploughs. **b.** A mould-board.

Wrest (rest), *v.* [OE. *wrǣstan* :—OTeut. **wraistjan.*] **1.** *trans.* To subject (something) to a twisting movement; to turn or twist. **2.** To pull, pluck, drag away, or detach (a person or thing) with a wrench or twist; to twist, tear, or wrench out, etc. ME. †**3.** To turn or dispose (some one, his heart) to a person or thing; to incline or influence (a person, etc.) *to* do something -1618. **4.** To usurp, arrogate, or take by force (power, lands, etc.) from another or others; to assume forcibly (a dignity or office). late ME. **b.** To obtain or gain (money, information, etc.) by extortion, persistency, or strong persuasion; to wring 1565. **5.** To strain or overstrain the meaning or bearing of (a writing, passage, word, etc.); to twist, pervert 1533. **b.** To put a wrong construction on the words or purport of (a writer); to interpret perversely 1555. **6.** To turn or deflect (a matter, etc.); to divert *to* some different (esp. undue or improper) purpose, end, etc. 1524. **b.** To deflect (the law, etc.) from its proper course or interpretation; to misapply, pervert 1530. †**7.** *intr.* To struggle or contend *against* something -1594. †**8.** To force a way (*out*), make way with effort, find egress -1590.

2. You w. the Bolt from Heav'ns avenging Hand PRIOR. 4. I had wrested from fortune her favours and smiles 1890. b. Did not she..reveal The secret wrested from me? MILT. 5. You try to w. Scripture and history to your own use KINGSLEY. 6. b. The law was generally supposed to be wrested, in order to prolong their imprisonment HUME.

Wrestle (re·s'l), *sb.* 1593. [f. next.] **1.** The action of wrestling or struggling; the fact of having wrestled. **2.** A struggle between two persons, each trying to throw the other by grasping his body or limbs; also, a wrestling-match 1670. **b.** *fig.* A struggle or contest 1850.

2. b. The body politic..straining every nerve in a w. for life or death MACAULAY.

Wrestle (re·s'l), *v.* [OE. **wrǣstlian,* frequent. of *wrǣstan* WREST *v.*] **I.** *intr.* **1.** To strive with strength and skill to throw a person to the ground by grappling with him; to endeavour to overpower another, esp. in a contest governed by fixed rules, by grasping his body or limbs and tripping or overbalancing him. **b.** To struggle (*with* something) after the manner of wrestling 1589. **2.** To contend or struggle in hostility or opposition (*with* or *against* another or others) ME. **b.** *fig.* To strive or labour (*with* or *against* difficulties, personal feelings, etc.) ME. **c.** To strive earnestly (*with* God) in prayer 1612. **3. a.** To labour, toil, or exert oneself; to strive (*for* something); to tussle. late ME. **b.** To engage strenuously in argument, debate, or controversy 1450. **c.** To busy, occupy, or concern oneself closely or earnestly *with* a subject, etc. 1454. **4.** To twist or writhe about; to wriggle, move sinuously. late ME. **b.** To move or proceed with effort or toil; to struggle *out* (*of*) or *through* some place or condition 1591.

1. A handsome sum of money has been subscribed to be wrestled for 1811. He challenges all comers to w. with him 1856. Learnin' her son to box..and wrastle 1896. b. I must w. here with death 1844. 2. b. I had to w. with my self-respect DICKENS. 3. b. Hosius doth w. maruelously about the word 1565. c. After wrestling with French history or German poetry 1905.

II. *trans.* **1.** To engage in (a wrestling-bout or match). late ME. **2. a.** To contend with (a person) in wrestling; to overcome by wrestling 1818. **b.** *Western U.S.* To throw (a calf, etc.) for branding 1888.

1. Wilt thou w. a fall with me? SCOTT. 2. a. A stout girl of twenty, strong enough to w. any man 1881.

Phr. *W. down,* to put down by wrestling or striving. *W. out,* to go through, perform, or execute with effort. Hence **Wre·stler** [OE. *wrǣstlere*].

Wrestling (re·sliŋ), *vbl. sb.* OE. [f. prec. + -ING[1].] **1.** The action or exercise of two persons grappling or gripping in a contest of strength and adroitness, each endeavouring to throw the other by tripping or overbalancing him; the fact of contending or throwing in this manner. **b.** With *the.* The sport of grappling and throwing; a contest in wrestling; a w.-match ME. **c.** With *a* and *pl.* A w.-bout or match ME. **2.** The action of striving or contending; maintenance of resistance, opposition, or strife OE. **b.** The action of striving earnestly in prayer; an instance of this 1722.

attrib. and *Comb.*, as *w. bout, -match*; **w. school,** *Gr. Antiq.* = PALÆSTRA.

Wretch (retʃ), *sb.* and *a.* [OE. *wrecca, wrǣcca* = OHG. *reccho* exile, adventurer (G. *recke* warrior, hero) :—OTeut. **wrakjon-,* f. **wrak-, wrek-*; see WREAK *v.*] **A.** *sb.* †**1.** One driven out of or away from his native country; an exile -1450. **2.** One who is sunk in deep distress, sorrow, misfortune, or poverty; a miserable, unhappy, or unfortunate person OE. **b.** Applied to animals ME. **c.** A person or little creature. (Used as a term of playful depreciation, or to denote slight commiseration or pity.) 1450. **3.** A vile, sorry, or despicable person; one of opprobrious or reprehensible character; a mean or contemptible creature OE. **b.** Used without serious imputation of bad qualities; *a w. of a,* a miserable 1688.

2. Poore wretches, which (were it not for your charity) would perish in your streetes 1623. Poor w., I pity thee SHELLEY. c. Excellent w.: Perdition catch my Soule But I do loue thee SHAKS. 3. W.!..look back upon a mis-spent Life DE FOE. The wickedness of the w. who would import a cargo of spirituous liquors into the..Society Islands 1805. b. A w of a pedant who knows all about tetrameters 1847.

†**B.** *adj.* = next 1, 2. -1596.

Wretched (re·tʃėd), *a.* ME. [f. prec. + -ED[1].] **1.** Living in a state of misery, poverty, or degradation; very miserable or unhappy. **b.** *absol.* late ME. **2.** Of conditions, etc.: Marked or distinguished by misery or unhappiness; attended by distress, discomfort, or sorrow ME. **b.** Of weather, etc.: Causing discomfort; very unpleasant or uncomfortable 1711. **3.** Distinguished by base, vile, or unworthy character or quality; contemptible ME. **b.** Of a poor, mean, or paltry character; mean, sorry, trifling. late ME. **4.** Contemptible in character or quality; despicable; hateful. late ME. **5.** Poor in ability, capacity, character, etc. 1482.

1. We are no Spinsters; nor..So w. as you take us 1622. b. who might be your mother That you insult, exult,..Ouer the w.? SHAKS. 2. Myserabul penury and wrechyd pouerty 1538. 3. The thing was clearly some w. court intrigue 1868. b. Their lean and flashy songs Grate on their scrannel Pipes of w. straw MILT.

Wretchedly (re·tʃėdli), *adv.* ME. [f. prec. + -LY[2].] In a wretched manner. **1.** In a miserable or unhappy fashion; miserably. **b.** In a way suggestive of indisposition or bad health 1728. **2.** So as to cause or involve in misery, distress, or discomfort ME. **3.** To a distressing, vexing, or unsatisfactory degree; deplorably, very badly 1546. **4.** In an inexpert, unsatisfactory, or crude manner; inefficiently, very poorly 1677.

1. b. Methinks I look so w. to-day! YOUNG. 3. Miss Berry..looking w. ill 1810. 4. A statue of Coilus in wood, w. carved EVELYN. So **Wre·tchedness.**

†**Wretchless** (re·tʃlės), *a.* 1598. [erron. form of *retchless,* obs. var. of RECKLESS *a.*] = RECKLESS *a.* 1, 2, 3 -1853. So **Wre·tchlessness** (now *arch.*).

Wretchock (re·tʃɔk). Now *dial.* 1529. [f. WRETCH *sb.* + -OCK.] The smallest or weakest of a brood, etc.; a diminutive person, little wretch.

Wried (rəid), *ppl. a. arch.* 1576. [f. WRY *v.* + -ED[1].] That has undergone contortion or twisting; writhed, contorted.

Wriggle (ri·g'l), *sb.* 1709. [f. next.] **1.** A quick writhing movement or flexion of the body, etc. **b.** A sinuous or tortuous formation, marking, etc.; a wriggling or meandering course 1825. **2.** *local.* The sand-eel or sand-launce 1816.

Wriggle (ri·g'l), *v.* 1495. [a. (M)LG. *wriggeln,* frequent. of †*wriggen* to twist or turn.] **1.** *intr.* To twist or turn about with short writhing movements; to move sinuously; to writhe, squirm, wiggle. **2.** To move, proceed, or go with a writhing or worming movement 1602. **b.** To flow or run sinuously; to meander 1640. **3.** To advance, 'creep' or get *in,* to insinuate oneself *into* favour, place, etc., by wheedling or ingratiation; to get *out of,* escape *from* (a condition or position by evasion, mean artifice, or contrivance) 1598. **4.** *trans.* To cause to writhe, twist, or bend tortuously; to move or turn writhingly or with quick jerks 1573. **b.** To bring into a specified state, form, etc., by writhing or twisting 1677. **5.** To introduce, insert, or bring *in* (something) by wriggling; to insinuate (*into* something) 1599. **b.** To insinuate or introduce (a person) gradually (*into* favour, office, etc.), esp. by subtle or shifty means 1670. **c.** To make (one's way) by sinuous motion 1863. **6.** To form in a tortuous or sinuous manner 1760.

1. His nose at the same time wriggling with most portentous agitation 1831. 2. Truth..forbids us to riggle into her sacred presence through by-paths WARBURTON. 3. He wriggled out of his bargain 1858. 4. The wretched Patient cannot lie down,..wrigling his body all manner of ways 1684. 5. b. While he was wriggling himself into my favour SWIFT. Hence **Wri·ggler,** one who or that which wriggles; one who makes his way by subtle, ingratiating, or underhand means. **Wri·ggly** *a.* given to wriggling.

Wright (rəit). [OE. *wyrhta, wryhta* :—OTeut. **wurh-*; see WORK *v.*] **1.** An artificer or handicraftsman; *esp.* a constructive workman. Now *arch.* or *dial.* **2.** One who works in wood; a carpenter, a joiner. See also CARTWRIGHT, SHIPWRIGHT, WAINWRIGHT, WHEELWRIGHT. ME.

Wring (riŋ), *sb.*[1] Now *dial.* [OE. *wringe*, f. *wringan* WRING *v.*] **1.** A cider-press or wine-press. **2.** A cheese-press 1670.

attrib.: **w.-house**, the house or shed where a cider- or cheese-w. is kept.

Wring (riŋ), *sb.*[2] 1460. [f. next.] **1.** The act of wringing, twisting, or writhing; an instance of this. **b.** The action of squeezing, pressing, or clasping; a squeeze or clasp of the hand 1599. **2.** A sharp or griping pain, esp. in the intestines 1500.

1. She gave the shirt..a vicious w. 1889.

Wring (riŋ), *v.* Pa. t. and pa. pple. **wrung** (rɒŋ). [OE. *wringan* (*wrang, wrungon, wrungen*). Another grade of the base is repr. by WRONG *a.*] **I.** *trans.* **1.** To press, squeeze, or twist (a moist substance, juicy fruit, etc.), esp. so as to drain or make dry. **b.** To strain (juice, moisture, etc.) from a moist or wet substance by squeezing or torsion OE. **c.** *transf.* To force (tears) *out of* the eye, *from* a person, etc. late ME. **2.** To twist, writhe, or wrest (a person or thing); to force (a limb, etc.) *round* or *about* so as to cause a sprain or pain OE. **b.** To contract or contort (the features, etc.); to screw, distort, turn awry ME. **3.** To twist (a wet garment, cloth, etc.) in the hands, so as to force out water; also in recent use, to pass through a wringer ME. **b.** To clasp and twist (the hands or fingers) together, esp. in token or by reason of distress or pain ME. **4.** Of a shoe or boot: To press painfully upon (the foot, toe, etc.); to hurt (a person) in this way. Also *absol.* late ME. **5.** To cause anguish or distress to (a person, his heart, etc.); to vex, distress, rack. late ME. **b.** To affect (a person, etc.) with bodily pain, hurt, or damage (sometimes *spec.* by torsion or pressure). Now *dial.* or *arch.* (after Shaks.) 1520. †**c.** To distress or afflict (a person) by exaction, severity, etc.; to oppress, keep down -1742. **6.** To wrench or wrest out of position or relation; to cause to change place by turning or twisting ME. **b.** To bring out (words, etc.) with effort ME. **7.** To acquire or gain (money, property, a right, etc.) by exaction or extortion ME. **b.** To exact, extort, or draw (an admission, consent, etc.) *from* or *out of* a person, etc. 1444. **8.** To press, clasp, or shake (a person's hand); to press (a person) *by* the hand; to shake hands with 1534. **9. a.** To subject (something) to a writhing, wresting, or turning movement; to press, drive, or impel in this way ME. †**b.** To strain the purport or meaning of (a writing, words, etc.) -1645. **c.** To wreathe, twist, or coil (something flexible); to wind or dispose in coils 1585.

1. b. A laundress wringing water out of a piece of linen EVELYN. **2.** I shall w. that Budd's neck if he comes in my way 1881. **b.** When pain and anguish w. the brow SCOTT. **3. b.** Persons in violent grief w. their hands MAR. EDGEWORTH. **4.** Provb. phr. *To know where the shoe wrings* (*one*): cf. PINCH *v.* 1 b. **5. b.** *fig.* The poore Iade is wrung in the withers SHAKS. **6.** I'll wring his calf's head off his body STEVENSON. **7.** The fields which the usurer has wrung from the orphan 1868. **b.** I wrung a promise from him he would try YOUNG. **9. a.** It is a hint That wrings mine eyes too't SHAKS.

With advs. **W. down.** To force, squeeze, or press down. †**W. in.** To insert, insinuate, or bring in with or as with a twisting movement. **W. off.** To wrest or force off by twisting or turning round. **W. out. a.** To force out (moisture) by or as by twisting; to squeeze out. **b.** To strain (a wet fabric, etc.) with a twisting motion, so as to press out most of the moisture. Also const. *of* (the liquid). **c.** To express or bring out with effort. **d.** To obtain or draw (something) from another by pressure, application, or art; to extract, elicit. **W. up.**: **a.** To squeeze, press, or compact by torsion; to twist or screw up. **b.** *Mining.* In pass., of a lode: To become diminished or dwindled.

II. *intr.* **1.** To be engaged in, to perform the action of, writhing or twisting; *esp.* of the hands. late ME. **2.** To twist the body in struggling or striving *with* or *against* something; to contend, labour, or endeavour earnestly 1470. **b.** To twist, turn, or struggle in pain or anguish; to writhe 1485. †**c.** To suffer or undergo grief, pain, punishment, etc. (*for* something) -1882.

Wringer (ri·ŋəɹ). ME. [f. prec. + -ER [1].] **1.** An exactor, extortioner; an oppressor. **2.** One who wrings clothes or the like after washing; one whose occupation consists in wringing 1598. **3.** A wringing-machine 1799. **4.** A device for wringing hot fomentations before application 1884.

Wringing (ri·ŋiŋ), *vbl. sb.* ME. [f. as prec. + -ING [1].] The action of the verb WRING in various senses; the fact of being wrung.

attrib.: **w. machine**, a machine for wringing clothes, etc., after washing. So **Wri·nging** *ppl. a.*

Wrinkle (ri·ŋk'l), *sb.* late ME. [Origin obsc.; perh. a back-formation from WRINKLED *a.*] **I.** †**1.** A sinuous or tortuous movement, formation, etc. -1513. **2.** A crease, fold, or ridge caused by the folding, puckering, or contraction of a fabric, cloth, or other pliant substance. late ME. **b.** A slight narrow ridge or depression on a surface; a longitudinal mark; a corrugation 1523. **3.** A small fold or crease of the skin, esp. due to age, care, displeasure, etc. late ME. **b.** A ripple or ruffle on the surface of water; a wavelet. Chiefly *poet.* 1633. **4.** *fig.* A moral stain or blemish. late ME. **5.** *Anat., Zool., Bot.* = RUGA 1545.

2. With their hosen hanging about their heels, ful of wrinckles 1594. **b.** *transf.* Every point and w. in the headland 1849. **3.** The calm..forehead that had as yet no w. of age or care 1877. **4.** A glorious congregacion with oute spot or wrynckle TINDALE *Eph.* v. 27.

II. †**1.** A crooked or tortuous action; a trick or wile -1579. **2.** *colloq.* A clever or adroit expedient or trick; a happy device; a 'dodge' 1817. **b.** A piece or item of useful information, knowledge, or advice; a helpful or valuable hint; a 'tip' 1818.

2. He could put her up to a w. or two 1817. Hence **Wri·nkly** *a.* full of or marked with wrinkles; creased, puckered.

Wrinkle (ri·ŋk'l), *v.* 1528. [app. back-formation from next.] **1.** *intr.* To suffer or undergo contraction or puckering into wrinkles or small folds; to become corrugated. **b.** Of persons, the face, etc.: To become creased or puckered; to assume or undergo marking with wrinkles, creases, or lines; also, to crease *into* smiles, etc. 1530. **2.** *trans.* To form or cause corrugations, wrinkles, or folds in or on (a surface, etc.); to corrugate 1611. **b.** To contract or draw (the skin, countenance, etc.) into creases or wrinkles 1566. **c.** To screw up (the eyes) 1840. **3.** To manifest (something) in or by facial wrinkles 1586.

1. b. The finest Skin wrinkles in a few Years ADDISON. **2. b.** *fig.* A Grecian Queen, whose youth & freshnesse Wrinkles Apolloes SHAKS.

Wrinkled (ri·ŋk'ld), *a.* late ME. [f. WRINKLE *sb.* + -ED [2], or in early use repr. the rare OE. pple. *gewrinclod* winding, serrated.] †**1.** Formed or disposed in convolutions, sinuosities, or windings -1587. **2.** Having, distinguished by, or formed into wrinkles, corrugations, or creases 1523. **3.** Of persons, the face, etc.: Marked with small folds, wrinkles, or furrows; creased, lined, furrowed 1529. **b.** Marked or characterized by wrinkles 1576. **4.** *Bot., Anat., Zool.* Marked by rugæ or wrinkles; rugose; freq. in specific names 1563.

2. Every Ribbon was w., and every Part of her Garments in Curl ADDISON. **3.** I am..crabbed, wrinkled, olde 1616. The w. face of antiquity CLARENDON. So **Wri·nkling** *vbl. sb.* the action or fact of becoming w.; *concr.* a series or collection of wrinkles, a w. surface, formation, etc.

Wrist (rist). [OE. *wrist*, prob. f. *wrið-, weak grade of the stem of *wrīðan* WRITHE *v.*] **1.** *Anat.* That part of the human frame between the fore-arm and the metacarpus; the joint by which the hand is united to the fore-arm; the carpus or radio-carpal joint of primates. (Cf. HAND-WRIST.) **b.** *transf.* That part of a garment, sleeve, or glove which covers the wrist 1828. **2.** The ankle; the instep. Usu. *w. of the foot.* (Cf. Ger. and ON. *rist.*) Now *dial.* 1530. **3.** A part or joint analogous or answering to the wrist in man: **a.** The carpus or carpal joint in birds 1843. **b.** The knee or knee-joint in the forelegs of animals 1843. **c.** In some spinous fishes, an elongation of the carpal bones, to the extremity of which the pectoral fin is attached 1840. **4.** *Mech.* A pin or stud projecting from the side of a wheel, crank, etc., to which a connecting-rod is attached 1864.

Comb.: **w.-bone**, any of the small bones of the w.; a carpal bone; **-drop**, *Path.* an affection marked by inability to extend the hand and fingers, resulting from paralysis of the fore-arm extensor muscles; **w. jerk**, *Path.* spasmodic contraction of the muscles of the hand, produced by sudden backward pressure; **-joint**, the radio-carpal articulation or joint; **-pin**, *Mech.* = sense 4; **-watch**, a small watch worn in a wristlet or strap around the w. Hence **Wri·sted** *a.* having a (specified kind of) w.; carried on the w.

Wristband (ri·sᵗbænd, ri·zbănd). 1571. **1.** The band or part of a sleeve (esp. of a shirt-sleeve) which covers or fastens about the wrist; a cuff or sleeve-band. **2.** A bracelet or wristlet 1585. **b.** A band for shackling the wrist 1884. **3.** A bandage for fastening round the wrist 1663.

Wristlet (ri·sᵗlėt). 1851. [f. WRIST + -LET.] **1. a.** A bracelet. **b.** A handcuff 1881. **c.** A small strap for wearing on the wrist. Also *attrib.*, in *w. watch* = wrist-watch. 1891. **2.** An ornamental band or covering for the wrist 1851.

Writ (rit). [OE. *writ*, f. weak grade of *wrītan* WRITE *v.*] **1.** Something written, penned, or recorded in writing. Now *rare.* †**b.** A written work, a book -1687. **c.** *spec.* Sacred writings collectively, the Bible or Holy Scriptures: freq. in *Holy* or *Sacred W.* OE. †**d.** A written communication, letter -1592. **2. a.** Without article. That which is written; written record ME. **b.** Written command, order, or authority. late ME. **3.** A formal writing or paper of any kind; a legal document or instrument OE. **b.** *Law.* A written command, precept, or formal order issued by a court, directing or enjoining the person or persons to whom it is addressed to do or refrain from doing some act specified therein. late ME. **c.** *spec.* A document issued by the crown conveying a summons to a spiritual or temporal lord to attend Parliament, or directing a sheriff to hold an election of a member or members of Parliament. late ME. †**4.** WRITING *vbl. sb.* I. 5. -1684.

1. c. *transf.* At Tarsus, where each man Thinks all is w. he speken can *Per.* II. Prol. 12. **3. b.** Writts are out for me, to apprehend me 1602.

Writable (rəi·tăb'l), *a.* 1782. [f. WRITE *v.* + -ABLE.] **1.** That may be written; capable of being reduced to or set down in writing. **2.** Suitable for writing with 1844.

Writative (rəi·tătiv), *a. rare.* 1736. [f. as prec. + -ATIVE, after *talkative.*] **1.** Disposed to write; given or addicted to writing. **2.** Marked by inclination or addiction to writing 1746.

Write (rəit), *sb.*[1] Chiefly *Sc.* ME. [var. of WRIT *sb.* after WRITE *v.*, or directly f. the vb.] †**1.** = WRIT *sb.* 1. -1762. †**2.** *Holy W.* = WRIT *sb.* 1 c. -1567. †**b.** = WRIT *sb.* 2. -1825. †**3.** = WRIT *sb.* 3 b. -1550. **4.** *Sc.* Handwriting; manner or style of calligraphy 1614.

4. *Hand of w.*, handwriting, style of writing.

Write, *sb.*[2] [f. the vb.] *W.-off*, a cancellation in or by writing. *W.-up*, a written account or description commending or praising a person or thing (orig. and chiefly *U.S.*).

Write (rəit), *v.* Pa. t. **wrote** (rōut). Pa. pple. **written** (ri·t'n); from 16th to 18th c., later dial. or illiterate **wrote**. [OE. *wrītan* (*wrāt, writon, (ge)writen*) = OHG. *rīzan* to tear (G. *reissen*), ON. *rīta* to score, write.] **I.** *trans.* **1.** †**a.** To score, outline, or draw the figure of (something) -1590. **b.** To form (letters, symbols, words, etc.) by carving, engraving, or incision; to record in this way OE. **c.** *transf.* To impress or stamp marks indicating (some condition or quality) *on, in,* or *over* a person, etc. 1603. **2.** To form or delineate (a letter, symbol, ideogram, etc.) on paper or the like with a pen, pencil, brush, etc. OE. **b.** To enter or record (a name); to mention (a person) in this way ME. **3. a.** To set down in writing; to express or present (words, etc.) in written form. Also said of the pen, etc. OE. **b.** To form by painting or the like; to paint (a sign, etc.). late ME. **c.** Of a manuscript, etc.: To bear or exhibit in writing 1607. **d.** To print by means of a typewriter; to typewrite 1883. **4.** To state or relate in writing; to draw up or frame a written statement of (circumstances, events, etc.) OE. **b.** To convey (tidings, information, etc.) by letter; to send (a message) in writing. late ME. **c.** To decree, ordain, or enjoin in writing 1560. **5. a.** To give a written account or enumeration of; to describe or depict in writing OE. **b.** To treat of (a subject, theme, etc. in writing OE. **c.** To give expression to (one's feelings, thoughts, etc.) by means of writing ME. **6.** To compose and set down on paper (a literary composition, narrative, verse, etc.); to put into or produce in literary form, to bring out (a book or literary work) as an author OE. **b.** To compose and set down (music, a melody, etc.) in notes 1672. **7.** To pen (a document, etc.); to put into proper written form; to draft or draw up OE. **b.** To pen (a letter, note, etc.); to communicate with a person by (letter, etc.) OE. **c.** To fill in (a cheque) 1837. **8.** To describe or designate (a person) in writing as something; to set down in a particular class. late ME. **b.** *refl.* To name (oneself) in writing; to sign 1821. **c.** To bring or reduce (a person, etc.) to a specified state by writing. Freq. *refl.* 1735. **9.** To spell (a word, name, etc.) in a specified or particular manner in writing ME. **10.** To cover, fill, or mark (a paper, etc.) with writing ME. **11. a.** To employ or be able to employ (a particular language) in writing ME. **b.** To employ (a name, word, etc.) in designating oneself 1591. **12.** To execute (a particular style of handwriting). late ME.

1. **b.** fig. *To w. in the dust, in sand, water, the wind*, etc., with ref. to absence of abiding record; Here lies one whose name was writ in water KEATS. **c.** Duty is written all over him 1899. **2. b.** To hae your name Wrote in the bonny book of fame 1772. **3.** *Writ* (*written*) *large*, penned or exhibited in large characters (chiefly *fig.*). **4. b.** She writes me..what conflicts she had endur'd EVELYN. You will..w. me word how it looks 1850. **e.** = UNDERWRITE *v.* 2 b. 1882. **5. a.** If I could w. the beauty of your eyes SHAKS. **b.** The Difficulties of writing History 1711. **c.** I did w. my mind plainly to you 1524. **6.** Some-body had written a Book against the 'Squire ADDISON. **7.** A lawyer..to w. her last will SMOLLETT. **8.** The Author Writes himself a Church-of-England-Man 1687. *fig.* Nature had writ him villain on his face DICKENS. *To w. oneself man*, etc., to arrive at man's (or woman's) estate; to attain manhood, or a specified age. **c.** That no man was ever written out of reputation, but by himself WARBURTON. **9.** Many words written alike are differently pronounced JOHNSON. **11. b.** † *To w. man* = to w. oneself man (see 8). **12.** *2 Hen. VI*, IV. ii. 100.

With advs. **W. down.**: **a.** To put or set down in writing. **b.** To overcome or suppress, to disparage or depreciate, by writing; to w. in disparagement of. **c.** *refl.* To diminish or destroy one's literary reputation by inferior writing. **d.** To reduce (an account, assets, etc.) to a lower amount in writing. **W. in.** To insert (a fact, statement, etc.) in writing. **W. off. a.** To note the deduction of (money) in an account or financial statement; now *spec.* to record the cancelling of (a sum, as a bad debt, etc.). **b.** To compose (a letter, etc.) with facility or expedition. **W. out. a.** To make a (fair or perfect) transcription or written copy of (something, a rough draft, etc.); also, to transcribe in full or detail, as from brief notes or shorthand. **b.** *refl.* To exhaust one's resources or stock of ideas by excessive writing. **W. over.**: **a.** To rewrite. **b.** To cover the whole or remaining surface of (a book, etc.) with writing. **W. up**: **a.** To put in writing a full account, statement, or record of (something); to give an elaborate description of, describe fully; to pen or write in full or detail. **b.** To form, trace, or place (something) in writing in an elevated position. **c.** To commend (something) to notice or favour by appreciative writing; to laud by way of advertisement. **d.** To bring (a journal, report, etc.) up to date, or down to the latest event, fact, or transaction; to complete some record in writing.

b. *W.-down, -off, -up* are also used as sbs.

II. *intr.* **1.** To inscribe letters *in, on*, or *upon* a hard or plastic surface by scoring, tracing, engraving, etc. OE. **2.** To engage in or perform the action of writing (esp. with pen and ink); to produce (a specified kind of) writing. Also said of the pen, etc. OE. **b.** To depict or paint on glass, etc. 1854. **c.** To typewrite 1875. **3.** To perform the action of composing and putting on paper; to practise literary composition; to engage in authorship or literary work ME. **b.** To compose music, a melody, etc. 1672. **4.** To compose a letter, note, etc.; to communicate information, etc. by writing; to conduct epistolary correspondence ME. **b.** With preps., e.g. *to*, or indirect personal obj. OE. **5.** To follow or practise writing as a profession or occupation. late ME. **6.** To spell words in writing; to represent words, etc. orthographically 1620.

2. My having at last found a Pen that writes GRAY. *transf.* The Moving Finger writes; and, having writ, Moves on FITZGERALD. **3.** A gentleman who had wrote for the stage SMOLLETT. I should be sorry to w. down to their comprehension 1809. **4.** He wrote to request my aid 1842. Tell Mary she hasn't written for an age 1890. **b.** Wrote me, and write you (merchant's language) PEGGE. Ferrers wrote to a friend of his 1888.

Writer (rəi·təɪ). [OE. *wrītere*, f. *wrītan* WRITE *v.* + -ER [1].] **1.** A person who can write; one who practises or performs writing; occas., one who writes in a specified manner. **b.** A sign-writer 1837. **2.** One whose business or occupation consists in writing; a functionary, officer, etc., who performs clerical or secretarial duties OE. **b.** Sc. *W. to the Signet* (abbrev. *W.S.*), orig., a clerk in the Secretary of State's office, who prepared writs to pass the royal signet; now, one of an ancient society of law-agents who conduct cases before the Court of Session, and have the exclusive privilege of preparing crown writs, charters, etc. 1488. **c.** *Sc.* An attorney or law-agent; an ordinary legal practitioner in country towns 1540. **d.** A clerk in the service of the former East India Company. Now *Hist.* 1676. **3.** One who writes, compiles, or produces a literary composition; a literary man or author OE. **b.** One who is writing 1578. **c.** A composer of music 1688. **4.** A make of paint-brush 1884. **5.** A pen, etc. that writes in a specified manner 1907.

1. *Writer's cramp* (*palsy, paralysis*), a form of cramp or spasm affecting certain muscles of the hand and fingers essential to writing, and resulting from excessive use of these. **3.** I saw the other day in an American w. a humorous account 1859. **b.** *The* (*present*) *w.*, the w. hereof; The present Writer's belief on this subject 1895. Hence **Wri·tership**, the office or position of a w. in the service of the East India Company (now *Hist.*); the office or employment of a clerk.

Writhe (rəið), *sb.* 1513. [f. next.] †**1.** Something twisted, wreathed, or formed into a circular shape -1569. **b.** A curled or twisted formation; a wreath or twist 1857. **2.** An act of writhing; a contortion 1611.

Writhe (rəið), *v.* [OE. *wrīðan* (*wrāþ, wriðon, gewriðen*); cf. WREATHE *v.*] **I.** *trans.* **1.** To twist or coil (something); to fashion into coils or folds; to bend or distort by twisting. †**2.** To unite, combine, or make compact by twisting, entwining, or interweaving; to intertwine -1671. †**3.** To turn or wrench round or to a side; to wring -1713. **4.** To subject (the body, limbs, etc.) to a contorting or twisting movement; to twist, contort. late ME. **b.** To distort (the face, etc.) 1480. **c.** To utter or speak *out* with a writhe 1889. **d.** To make or pursue (its way) by writhing 1867. **5.** To twist or wrench (something) out of place, position, or relation. late ME.

4. Then Satan first knew pain, And writh'd him to and fro convolv'd MILT. **5.** She writhed herself free 1859.

II. *intr.* **1.** To move or stir in a turning or sinuous manner; to twist about ME. **b.** To contort the body, limbs, etc., as from agony, emotion, or stimulation; to twist *under* or *with* pain, distress, etc. late ME. **2.** To change place or position, to turn, move, or go, with a writhing or twisting motion ME.

1. Human wrecks, writhing in anguish 1890. **b.** *fig.* His heart writhing with hatred 1846. Hence **Wri·thing** *vbl. sb.*

Writhen (ri·ð'n), *ppl. a.* ME. [pa. pple. of prec.] **1.** Subjected to writhing, twisting, or turning; contorted. **2.** Combined, made by, or subjected to twining or plaiting OE. **3.** Disposed or arranged in coils, folds, or windings; formed or fashioned by or as by coiling 1542.

1. 'Till, with a w. Mouth,.. He tastes the bitter Morsel 1708. The w. elder spreads its creamy bloom 1850.

Writhled (ri·ð'ld), *a. Obs.* exc. *arch.* 1565. [app. f. stem of WRITHE *v.* (see -LE 3); but perh. an alteration of RIVELLED *a.*] Wrinkled, shrivelled, withered.

Writing (rəi·tiŋ), *vbl. sb.* ME. [f. WRITE *v.* + -ING [1].] **I. 1.** The action of one who writes, in various senses. **2.** The art or practice of penmanship or handwriting 1440. **b.** Style, form, or method of fashioning letters or other conventional signs (esp. in handwriting or penmanship); the 'hand' or HANDWRITING of a particular person 1440. **3.** The action of composing and committing to manuscript; literary composition or production. late ME. **b.** Style or manner of composition or literary expression 1509. **c.** The composition of music 1782. †**4.** Spelling, orthography -1728. **5.** The state or condition of having been written or penned; written form. late ME.

1. *At this* (*present*) *w.*, at the time of writing this. **2.** The three R's—Reading, Writing, and Rithmetic 1828. **b.** It wes his awne propir hand and writting 1476. **3. b.** Fine w. is, next to fine doing, the top thing in the world KEATS. **5.** The author's agreement ..is in w. 1887.

II. 1. That which is in a written (now also typewritten) state or form; written information, composition, or production ME. **2.** A written composition; freq. *pl.*, the work or works of an author or group of authors; literary productions ME. **b.** *The* (*sacred* or *holy*) *writings*, the Scriptures ME. **3. a.** A written document, note, etc.; a letter or missive 1456. **b.** A written paper or instrument, having force in law; a deed, bond, agreement, or the like 1448. **4.** Wording or lettering scored, engraved, or impressed on a surface; an inscription. late ME. **5.** Words, letters, etc. embodied in written (or typewritten) form; written lettering ME.

3. b. The Lawyers finished the Writings..and they were married STEELE. **4.** The width between the lines of w. 1899.

Comb.: **w.-board**, a board on which to rest the paper while writing; **-book**, (*a*) a blank book in which to write, a book containing or consisting of w.-paper; (*b*) a copy-book; **-case**, a portable case for holding writing requisites, and providing a surface to write on; **-centre**, a physical centre in the brain which controls the action of writing; **-desk**, (*a*) a desk used or designed for writing on; such a desk fitted with conveniences for holding writing materials, papers, etc.; (*b*) a portable w.-case which on being opened forms a desk or surface for writing on; **-ink**, ink or writing-fluid prepared or suitable for writing with the pen; **-master**, (*a*) a teacher of w., penmanship, or calligraphy: (*b*) the yellow-hammer, *Emberiza citrinella*; **-paper**, a special kind of paper, usu. with a smooth surface and sized, for w. upon; now *esp.*, notepaper; **-pen**, a pen suitable or adapted for w.; **-school**, †(*a*) a school in which w. is taught; (*b*) at Oxford University, a room used or set apart for written examinations.

Wri·ting-ta:ble. 1526. [f. prec. + TABLE *sb.*] †**1.** A small thin tablet, sheet, or plate of wood, ivory, or other material for writing (esp. notes or memoranda) upon -1829. †**2.** = ESCRITOIRE -1722. **3.** A table used, suitable, or adapted for writing on, having usu. drawers and other accessories or conveniences 1833.

Written (ri·t'n), *ppl. a.* ME. [pa. pple. of WRITE *v.*] **1.** That is composed, recorded, preserved, or mentioned in writing; committed to writing; also, that is in writing (as opp. to *oral* or *printed*); manuscript. **b.** Of laws: Reduced to or established by writing; formulated in documents, codes, or printed works ME. **2. a.** That is inscribed or carved upon 1440. **b.** Bearing, inscribed or covered with, writing 1580. †**3.** *W. hand*, cursive form of writing; a form of running hand -1849. **4.** Of letters, etc.: Traced or formed with the pen, pencil, etc. 1582. **5.** That has been written *to, about, down, out*, or *up* 1748.

1. He will consent to accept a w. apology DICKENS. **2. b.** A flat bundle of w. Papers 1692. **3.** We appoint him our Secretary for he can read w. hand 1764.

Wrizzled (ri·z'ld), *a.* Now *dial.* 1590. [perh. var. of WRITHLED *a.*] Marked with creases, wrinkles, or corrugations; wrinkled, shrivelled.

Wrong (rǫŋ), *sb.* OE. [Substantival use of next.] **I. 1.** That which is morally unjust, unfair, amiss, or improper; the negation of equity, goodness, or rectitude. (Freq. contrasted w. *right.*) **2.** Unjust action or conduct; evil or damage inflicted or received; injustice, unfairness ME. **b.** *Law.* Violation, transgression, or infringement of law; invasion of right to the damage or prejudice of another or others. orig. *Sc.* ME. †**3.** Claim, possession, or seizure that is unjustifiable or unwarranted on legal or moral grounds -1590. **b.** In the phr. *by, in*, †*of*(...) *w.* ME. **4.** With poss. pron. or genitive: †**a.** Injustice, harm, or evil inflicted upon another or others -1642. **b.** Injury, hurt, harm, or prejudice received or sustained by a person or persons. late ME. **5.** Physical hurt or harm caused to or sustained by some thing or person. late ME. **6.** *The w.*, that which is wrong; absence of right or fairness; unjust or wrongful action ME. **7.** The fact or position of acting unjustly or indefensibly; the state of being wrong in respect of attitude, procedure, or belief ME.

1. They put no difference betuix wrang and right 1578. 2. Expos'd To daily fraud, contempt, abuse and w. MILT. *To do* (a person or thing) *w.*, to act unjustly or unfairly *to*. 4. *a.* Loue knowes it is a greater griefe To beare loues w., then hates knowne iniury SHAKS. b. Wail, for the world's w.! SHELLEY. 6. If the w. has been wholly on one side PALEY. 7. Phr. *To be* or *put in the w.*; He had now put himself in the w. MACAULAY.

II. A wrongful, unjust, or unfair action; an injury received or inflicted; a mischief OE. b. *Law.* An invasion of right to the damage, harm, or prejudice of another or others; a violation of law or statute. late ME.

As thou lou'st me, do him not that w. SHAKS. Beare not hatred to thy neighbour for euery w. *Ecclus.* x. 6. Trees bent their Heads to hear him sing his Wrongs DRYDEN. The Earl deeply resented the w. done to himself SCOTT.

Wrong (rɒŋ), *a.* and *adv.* [Late OE. *wrang*, *wrong*, a. ON. **wrangr*, *rangr*; related to WRING *v.*] A. *adj.* †I. Having a crooked or curved course, form, or direction; twisted or bent in shape or contour –1613. II. 1. Of actions, etc.: Deviating from equity, justice, or goodness; not morally right or equitable. ME. 2. Of persons: Doing or prone to do that which is evil, noxious, or unjust; opprobrious, vicious ME. †b. Actively opposed; antagonistic (*rare*). 3. Not in conformity with some standard, rule, or principle; contrary to or at variance with what one approves or regards as right ME. b. Not in consonance with facts or truth; incorrect, false, mistaken. late ME. c. Of belief, etc.: Partaking of or based on error; erroneous. late ME. 4. Not right or satisfactory in state or order; in unsatisfactory or bad condition; amiss. late ME. 5. Not adapted, according, or answering to intention, requirement, or purpose; not proper, fitting, or appropriate. late ME. b. *Typog.* Not of the proper size, character, or face. Freq. in *w. fount* (abbrev. *w. f.*). 1771. 6. Of a way, course, etc.: Leading in or having a trend or aspect to a direction other than one intends, desires, or expects. late ME. 7. W. side. a. That side of a thing, a fabric, etc., which lies or is normally turned inward, downward, or away from one; the side opposite to the usual or principal, the reverse surface 1511. b. The side, party, or principle of which one disapproves 1649. c. The disadvantageous, undesirable, or unsafe side *of* some place, object, etc. 1719. 8. Of persons, etc.: a. Judging, believing, or acting contrary to the facts of the case; mistaken, in error 1693. b. Not normal or sound *in the head*, etc. (*dial.* or *colloq.*) 1765.

1. There is nothing..morally w. in a strike 1878. It was very w. of him to make such a request 1879. 2. It don't make black white, 'cause I'm a w. 'un 1896. 3. b. Her watch..being seldom more than twenty minutes w., either way 1871. 4. You see,..it might put us w. with our son-in-law DICKENS. *What's w. with* (mod. colloq.), what objection is there to, why not have (etc.)? 5. You are barking up the w. tree, Johnson 1833. Does he want..money?..He's come to the w. shop for that. DICKENS. *The w. end*, the end, extremity, or limit less adapted, suitable, or proper for a required or particular purpose; This was..beginning at the w. end 1809. See also STICK *sb.*[1] Phr. 6. *To go the w. way*, of food, etc.: see WAY *sb.* II. 1. *The* (or *a*) *w. way*, the way or method least conducive to a desired end or purpose; advb., in a contrary or opposite direction or position to the proper or usual one. 7. Advb. phr. (*The*) *w. side out, before*; My sicke Foole Rodorigo, Whom Loue hath turn'd almost the w. side out SHAKS. *To laugh on the w. side of one's face, mouth*: see LAUGH *v.* 1. *On the w. side of the blanket*: see BLANKET *sb.* 2. *On the w. side of*, older than (a specified age). *To get out of bed* (*on*) *the w. side*, with allusion to the supposed disturbing effect on one's temper. c. The poor meagre home in a dingy street; the w. side of Oxford Street 1893.

B. *adv.* 1. In a direction differing from the right or true one; by an erroneous course or way; astray ME. 2. Not in accordance with good morals or a just standard of actions; in a manner contrary to equity or uprightness ME. 3. Out of accordance or consistence with facts or the truth of the case; mistakenly, erroneously; incorrectly ME. 4. Not in the right or proper way; improperly, unduly, amiss ME. b. Out of proper order or due place 1573.

1. Lock-a-daisy, my masters, you're come a deadly deal w.! GOLDSM. 3. You took my meaning w. 1681. In spite of her care..she guessed w. THACKERAY. To go w.: a. To take a wrong way, road, or course; to go astray: freq. *fig.* b. To deviate or depart from moral rectitude or integrity, to take to evil courses; also, to fall from virtue. c. To happen amiss or unfortunately; to issue or result unsuccessfully or unprosperously. d. To get out of gear or working order; (of a clock, etc.) to fail to keep correct time. e. To fail in some undertaking or enterprise, or in the general conduct of life. Hence **Wro·ngness.**

Wrong (rɒŋ), *v.* ME. [f. prec.] 1. *trans.* To do wrong or injury to (a person); to treat with injustice, prejudice, or harshness. b. To violate or do violence to; to treat unfairly or without due respect 1449. 2. To deprive or dispossess (a person) wrongfully *of* something; to cheat, defraud 1484. 3. To do injustice to (a person) by statement, imputation, opinion, etc.; to discredit or dishonour by word or thought 1594. †4. To impair or injure the quality or substance of (something); to mar, spoil –1784. 5. *Naut.* To outsail (another vessel); to outdo or surpass in sailing 1685.

2. Ask anybody..whether I have ever wronged them of a farthing DICKENS. 3. He says that the Duke of York is suspected..; but that he do know that he is wronged therein PEPYS. Hence **Wro·nger.**

Wrong-doer (rɒ·ŋdū·əɪ). late ME. [f. WRONG *sb.* + DOER.] 1. One who commits wrongful, unjust, or blameworthy acts; one who transgresses or offends against the moral law. 2. *Law.* One who is guilty of a wrong, tort, or trespass; a law-breaker 1501. So **Wro·ng-do·ing** *vbl. sb.*

Wrongful (rɒ·ŋfŭl), *a.* ME. [f. WRONG *sb.* + -FUL.] 1. Full of wrong, injustice, or injury; marked or characterized by wrong, unfairness, or violation of equity. b. Of actions: Performed, executed, or done unjustly, unfairly, or harmfully ME. †2. That commits wrong; that does wrong or injustice *to* (or *against*) another –1614. 3. a. That is contrary to law, statute, or established rule; unlawful, illegal. late ME. b. Holding office, possession, etc., unlawfully or illegally; having no legal right or claim 1567.

1. He regarded slavery simply as an unnatural and w. accident 1879. 2. Mighty wrongfull foes, Who do evill for good SIDNEY. Hence **Wro·ngfully** *adv.*, **-ness.**

Wrong-headed (stress variable), *a.* 1732. [f. WRONG *a.*] 1. Having a perverse judgement or intellect; persistent or obstinate in erroneous opinion. 2. Marked or characterized by perversity of judgement 1735. So **Wro·nghead** *sb.* a w. person; *adj.* wrong-headed 1729. **Wrong-hea·ded·ly**, **-ness.**

Wrongly (rɒ·ŋli), *adv.* ME. [-LY [2].] 1. Unfittingly, improperly. b. Inaccurately, incorrectly 1633. c. By mistake or misapprehension 1755. 2. Unfairly, wrongfully ME.

Wrongous (rɒ·ŋəs), *a.* Now *Sc.* (and *n. dial.*) [Early ME. *wrangwīs*, f. *wrang* WRONG *a.* + *-wīs*, after *rihtwīs*, RIGHTEOUS *a.*] †1. Of persons: Acting wrongfully, inequitably, or unjustly –1625. 2. = WRONGFUL *a.* 1, 1 b. ME. 3. Not right or justifiable in nature or application; unfitting, unsuitable ME. 4. *Scots Law.* Contrary to law; unlawful, illegal 1671. Hence **Wro·ngously** *adv.*

Wroot, original form of ROOT *v.*[2]

Wroth (rōᵘþ, rɒþ), *a.* [OE. *wrāþ*, f. var. stem of *wrīðan* to WRITHE.] 1. Stirred to wrath; very angry or indignant; wrathful, incensed. †2. Of animals: Of a fierce or violent nature; enraged –1526. b. *transf.* Of the wind, sea, etc.: Moved to a state of turmoil or commotion; violent, stormy. *poet.* late ME.

1. When the kyng hearde that, he was w. TINDALE *Matt.* xxii. 7. Then got Sir Lancelot suddenly to horse, W. at himself TENNYSON. Why should not Heaven be w.? TENNYSON. 2. b. The most holy heart of the deep sea, Late w. now full of quiet SWINBURNE. Hence **Wro·thful** *a.* (*Obs.* or *arch.*) = WRATHFUL *a.* 1. **Wro·thy** *a.* wrathful, angry 1422.

Wrought (rɒt), *ppl. a.* [ME. *wroȝt*, *worht*, pa. pple. of *wirchen*, *wurchen* WORK *v.*] Worked into shape or condition. †1. Created, shaped, moulded. –late ME. b. That is made or constructed by means of labour or art; fashioned, formed. late ME. c. Shaped, fashioned, or finished from the rough or crude material; cut 1560. 2. a. Of textile materials, esp. silk: Manufactured; spun 1463. b. Decorated or ornamented, as with needlework: embellished, embroidered 1455. c. Of articles: Made, manufactured, or prepared for use or commerce 1580. 3. a. Of metals: Beaten out or shaped with the hammer or other tools 1535. b. *W. iron*, slag-bearing malleable iron 1703. c. Of metal-work: Made by hammering or hand-work (in contrast to *cast*) 1807.

1. b. Handsomely chased and w. silver garlands 1890. 2. b. The old Tapestry Hangings and W. Bed pulled down 1711. 3. b. Great old w.-iron gates 1885. With advs. *W.-off*, worked off; printed. *W.-up*, stirred up, excited or stimulated.

Wrung (rɒŋ), *ppl. a.* late ME. [pa. pple. of WRING *v.*] 1. Subjected to wringing, twisting, or squeezing; pressed, squeezed. 2. That has suffered or undergone distress, grief, or pain; racked, distressed 1730. b. Marked by distress, worry, or pain 1862.

2. The refuge of many a w. and broken heart 1841.

Wry (rəi), *a.* and *adv.* 1523. [f. WRY *v.*[2]] A. *adj.* 1. Of the features, neck, etc.: Abnormally deflected, bent, or turned to one side; distorted. b. Temporarily twisted, contorted, or writhed by reason or in manifestation of disrelish, disgust, or the like 1598. c. Of a smile, etc.: Made with a twisting of the features expressing dislike or distaste 1883. 2. That has undergone twisting, contortion, or deflexion; twisted, crooked, bent 1552. b. Deflected from a straight course; inclined or turned to one side 1587. 3. Of words, thoughts, etc.: Contrary to that which is right, fitting, or just; cross, ill-natured 1599. b. Wrested; perverted; distorted 1663. 4. Marked or characterized by perversion, unfairness, or injustice 1561.

1. With faire black eyes and haire, and a w. nose B. JONSON. b. Physic to be quickly swallowed with w. face 1876. He..shook his head with a w. smile 1883. 2. b. A w. step COWPER. *W. look*, one expressive of displeasure or dislike.

B. *adv.* In an oblique manner, course, or direction; awry 1575.

Comb.: **w.-faced** *a.*, having the face out of line with the neck and chest; also, that has or makes a w. face; **-mouth** *U.S.*, (*a*) one or other fish belonging to the genus *Cryptacanthodes* of blennioid fishes; (*b*) the electric ray or torpedo; *attrib.* = *w.-mouthed* (*a*); **-mouthed** *a.* (*a*) having a w. mouth; (*b*) marked or characterized by contortion of the mouth. Hence **Wry·ly**, *adv.*, **-ness.**

Wry (rəi), *v.*[1] *Obs.* exc. *dial.* [OE. *wrēon.*] To cover, veil, conceal.

Wry (rəi), *v.*[2] [OE. *wrigian.*] I. *intr.* †1. To have a particular or specified tendency, disposition, or inclination –1581. †2. Of persons: To move or go, to swerve or turn *aside*, *away*, etc.; *fig.* to deviate or swerve from the right or proper course; to go wrong –1634. 3. To contort the limbs, features, etc., as from pain or agony; to writhe ME.

2. How many Must murther Wiues much better then themselues For wrying but a little? SHAKS.

II. *trans.* †1. To deflect or divert (a person or thing) from some course or in some direction –1650. 2. To twist or turn (the body, neck, etc.) round or about; to contort, wring, wrench 1460. b. To twist out of shape, form, or relationship; to pull, contort, make wry 1586. 3. To twist or distort (the face or mouth), esp. so as to manifest disgust or distaste 1510.

3. I made my eyes to roll, and wrayed my face in a frightful manner 1779. She wried her mouth to a smile 1898.

Wryneck (rəi·nek). 1585. [f. WRY *a.* + NECK *sb.*] 1. One or other species of the genus *Iynx* of small migratory scansorial picoid birds; esp. the common species, *I. torquilla*, distinguished by its habit of writhing the neck and head. 2. a. One who has a wry neck 1607. b. *attrib.* = next 2. 1586. 3. *Path.* = TORTICOLLIS 1753.

Wry-necked (stress var.), *a.* 1596. [f. WRY *a.*] 1. Having a wry or crooked neck. 2. Affected with distortion of the neck; having wryneck 1608.

1. The vile squealing of the wry-neckt Fife SHAKS.

Wuff (wɒf). 1824. [Cf. *waff*, *woof*, *wough.*] A dog's low suppressed bark. Also as vb.

Wulfenite (wu·lfĕnəit). 1849. [a. G. *wulfenit*, f. F. X. von *Wulfen* (1728–1805), Austrian scientist + -ITE [1].] *Min.* Native molybdate of lead, found in brilliant-coloured crystals; called also *yellow lead ore.*

Wurley (wɒ̄·ɹli). *Austral.* 1847. [Native word.] An aboriginal's hut.

Wurtzite (wūᵊ·ɹtsəit). 1868. [f. C. A. *Wurtz* (1817–84), a French chemist + -ITE [1].] *Min.* Native zinc sulphide.

Wyandotte (wəi·ǎndǫt). 1884. [f. name of a tribe of N. Amer. Indians.] One of a handsome breed of medium-sized domestic fowls.

Wych elm, witch elm (wi·tʃ,elm). 1626. [f. WITCH *sb.*[3] + ELM.] A species of elm, *Ulmus montana*, having broader leaves and more spreading branches than the common elm; the witch hazel; also, the wood of this.

Wyclif(f)ian (wikli·fiǎn), *sb.* and *a.* 1570. [ad. med.L. *Wyclivianus*, or directly f. *Wycliffe*, *-clif*, etc.] †**A.** *sb.* = WYCLIFFITE A –1717. **B.** *adj.* Of, pertaining to, or characterizing the teaching of Wyclif or his followers 1720.

Wyclif(f)ism (wi·klifiz'm). 1675. [f. as next + -ISM.] The religious doctrines or tenets advocated or propagated by Wyclif or held by his followers. So **Wy·clif(f)ist** *sb.* and *a.* = next.

Wyclif(f)ite (wi·klifəit), *sb.* and *a.* Also Wic-. 1580. [ad. med.L. *Wiclefita*, etc., f. name of John *Wyclif* or *Wycliffe* (*c* 1320–1384), English theologian and religious reformer + -ITE [1].] **A.** *sb.* One who held or propagated the religious tenets or doctrines of Wyclif; a follower of Wyclif. **B.** *adj.* **1.** Of, pertaining to, written or made by Wyclif or his followers 1843. **2.** That is a follower of Wyclif; holding, advocating, or propagating the religious views of Wyclif and his school 1875.

Wykehamical (wikæ·mikǎl), *a.* 1758. [See next and -AL **1.**] **1.** Of or pertaining to Winchester College, or the pupils or staff of this. **2.** That is or has been a pupil of, or connected with, Winchester College 1844.

Wykehamist (wi·kǎmist), *sb.* and *a.* [ad. mod.L. *Wykehamista*, f. name of William of *Wykeham* (1324–1404), Bishop of Winchester and founder of Winchester College.] **A.** *sb.* One who is or has been a pupil at Winchester College. **B.** *adj.* = prec. **1.** 1865.

Wynd (wəind). Chiefly *Sc.* and *n. dial.* late ME. [app. f. the stem of WIND *v.*[1] (cf. OE. *gewind* spiral, etc.).] A narrow street or passage turning off from a main thoroughfare; a narrow cross-street.

Wyvern (wəi·vəɹn). 1610. [f. ME. †*wyver*, a. OF. *wyvre*, var. *vivre* serpent.] **1.** *Her.* A representation of a chimerical animal imagined as a winged dragon with two feet like those of an eagle, and a serpent-like barbed tail. **b.** An image or figure of this monster 1863. **2.** Such a monster conceived as having a real existence 1700.

2. Lakes which..Blaze like a w. flying round the sun BROWNING.

X

X (eks), pl. X's, *Xs* (e·ksėz), the 24th letter of the modern and 21st of the ancient Roman alphabet, corresp. to Gr. X, representing (ks) in the Chalcidian alphabet.

Most English words with initial *x* (pronounced as *z*) are of Gr. origin; but in a few (as *xebec*, *Xerez*) *x* represents the early Spanish *x*, now *j*. In OE. *x* was used medially and finally as a variant spelling of *cs* (as in *áxian* = *ácsian*, *ásciàn* to ASK, *fixas* pl. of *fisc* FISH.) Some East Anglian texts of the 14th c. have *x* for initial *sh*, *sch*, as in *xal* shall. In early forms of some oriental words *x-* stands for *sh-* (or *s-*), as *xerif* SHEREEF. Temporary uses of *x* are seen e.g. in obsolete spellings of ACCESS (*axes*, *axis*), EXCELLENT (*exelent*), EXCITE (*exite*); cf. the forms *pox* (= pocks), which has survived, and *sox* (= socks), which has been adopted in trade use.

Phonetically, the normal value of *x* is (ks), as in *axis*, *excuse*; but the prefix *ex-* followed by a vowel or *h*, is usu. pronounced (ėgz) if the stress is not on the prefix, but (eks) if *ex-* is stressed; so *exact* (ėgzæ·kt), *exhort* (ėgzǭ·ɹt), but *exile* (e·ksəil). The same general principle governs the pronunciation of *anxious* (æ·ŋkʃəs), *anxiety* (aŋgzəi·ėti), *luxury* (lɒ·kʃəri), *luxurious* (lɒgzūᵊ·riəs). In all words having initial *x*, (gz) is reduced to (z), e.g. *Xerxes* (zɔ̄·ɹksīz), *xylophone* (zəi·lǒfōᵘn).

I. The letter or its sound. **b.** The letter considered with regard to its shape; chiefly *attrib.* and *Comb.* Hence identified with a cross. *X's and O's*, the game of noughts and crosses (see NOUGHT 3 b). **c.** Denoting serial order.

II. Symbolic uses. **1.** The Roman numeral symbol for ten; so xx = 20, xxx = 30. OE. **b.** U.S. colloq. *X*, *XX*, a ten-, twenty-dollar note 1837. **2.** In *Algebra* and *Higher Math.* used as the symbol for an unknown or variable quantity (or for the first of such quantities, the others being denoted by *y*, *z*, etc.); *spec.* the sign for an abscissa 1660. Hence *allus.* for something unknown or undetermined. 1859. See also X RAYS. **b.** Used *attrib.* as an indeterminate numeral adjective = 'an unknown number of'. Chiefly *joc.* 1848. **c.** Put for a person's name when unknown or left undetermined 1797. **d.** In wireless telegraphy: A discharge of atmospheric electricity causing irregular signals, atmospherics 1906. **3.** In designations of brands of malt liquor, XX or double X denotes a medium quality; XXX or treble X the strongest quality. Also in the marking of qualities of tin-plate. 1827. **4.** XYZ: used to denote some thing or person unknown or undetermined 1808.

III. *Abbreviations.* **1.** In writing the name *Christ*, esp. in abbreviations, X represents the first letter of Gr. XPICTOC, and XP or xp the first two letters (kəi rōᵘ). Hence in early times Xp̄, in modern times Xt, X[t], and X, are used as abbreviations of the syllable *Christ*, alone or in derivatives, thus *Xtian(ity)* = CHRISTIAN(ITY); *Xmas* = CHRISTMAS. **2.** For *ex* or a word with initial *ex-*: **a.** *slang.* *X's* (e·ksėz), expenses 1894. **b.** Stock Exchange. *xd* = ex dividend (see Ex 2 b) 1885. Hence **X** *v. trans.*, to supply with x's in place of types that are wanting 1849.

Xanth- (zænþ), = XANTHO- in derivatives and compounds before a suffix or second element beginning with a vowel.

Xa·nthate, *Chem.* a salt of xanthic acid. **Xa·nthein** (-iˌin), *Chem.* the water-soluble part of the yellow colouring-matter of flowers. ‖ **Xanthelasma** (-æ·zmǎ) [Gr. ἔλασμα metal plate], *Path.* = XANTHOMA. **Xa·nthic** *a.*, (*a*) *Chem.* in *xanthic oxide*, earlier name for XANTHINE; *xanthic acid*, a complex acid, $C_3H_6OS_2$, many of whose salts are yellow; (*b*) *Bot.* applied to a series of flower-colours of which the type is yellow. **Xa·nthin,** (*a*) *Chem.* a yellow colouring-matter obtained from madder; (*b*) the insoluble part of the yellow colouring-matter of flowers. **Xa·nthine** (-əin), a substance ($C_5H_4N_4O_2$) allied to uric acid found in animal organs and secretions, and forming a lemon-yellow compound with nitric acid. **Xa·nthite,** *Min.* a variety of vesuvianite occurring in yellowish crystals. ‖**Xantho·ma** [Gr. -ωμα, cf. *sarcoma*], *Path.* a skin-affection characterized by the growth of yellowish patches or tubercles; hence **Xantho·matous** (-ōᵘ-) *a.* **Xantho·psia, Xa·nthopsy** [Gr. ὄψις sight], *Path.* yellow vision. **Xantho·psin** [as prec.], *Chem.* yellow pigment of the retina. ‖**Xantho·sis** [-OSIS], *Path.* yellow discoloration as in cancerous tumours. **Xa·nthous** *a.*, *Ethnol.* characterized by yellowish hair and light complexion; also said of the hair, etc.

Xanthian (zæ·nþiǎn), *a.* (*sb.*). 1685. [f. *Xanthus* + -IAN.] Of, pertaining to (or an inhabitant of) Xanthus, an ancient town in Asia Minor; *spec.* of the marbles found near it.

Xantho- (zæ·nþo), repr. Gr. ξανθο-, comb. form of ξανθός yellow, in many terms chiefly of chemistry, botany, pathology, and mineralogy.

Xanthoca·rpous *a.* [Gr. καρπός fruit], *Bot.* having yellow fruit. ‖ **Xanthochroi** (-ǫ·kroˌəi, -ōᵘ·kroi) *sb. pl.* [mod.L., app. meant as f. Gr. ξανθός yellow + ὠχρός pale], *Anthrop.* in Huxley's classification of the varieties of mankind, a subdivision of the *Leiotrichi* or smooth-haired class, having light-coloured hair and pale complexion; **Xanthochro·ic, Xanthochroid** (-ōᵘ·kroid), **Xanthochrooid** (-ǫ·kroˌoid), **Xanthochroous** (-ǫ·kroˌəs), **Xanthochrous** (-ōᵘ·krəs), *adjs.* **Xanthochroism** (-ǫ·kroˌiz'm), *Ornith.* abnormal replacement of another colour by yellow in the plumage of certain birds. **Xanthocy·anopsy, -cya·nopy** [Gr. κύανος blue + ὄψις, ὦπή sight], *Path.* colour-blindness, in which yellow and blue are the only colours discerned. **Xanthode·rm(i)a,** [Gr. δέρμα skin], *Path.* yellowness of skin. **Xa·nthodont, Xanthodo·ntous** *adjs.* [Gr. ὀδούς, ὀδοντ- tooth], *Zool.* (of rodents) yellow-toothed. **Xa·nthogen,** *Chem.* the hypothetical radical of xanthic acid. ‖**Xanthome·lanoi** *sb. pl.* [mod.L; cf. MELANOI], *Anthropol.* in Huxley's classification, a subdivision of the *Leiotrichi* or smooth-haired class of mankind, having black hair and yellowy-brown, or olive complexion; hence **Xanthome·lanous** *a.* **Xantho·pa·thia, Xantho·pathy** [-PATHY], *Path.* yellow discoloration of the skin. **Xa·nthophyll** [Gr. φύλλον leaf], *Chem.* the yellow pigment of autumn leaves. **Xanthophy·llite,** *Min.* a micaceous mineral, a species of seybertite, occurring in yellowish crusts or implanted globules in talcose schist. ‖**Xanthorrhœa** (zænþorī·ǎ) [Gr. ῥοία flow], *Bot.* a genus of Australian liliaceous plants, some of which yield a yellow resin. **Xanthospe·rmous** *a.* [Gr. σπέρμα seed], *Bot.* with yellow seeds. ‖**Xantho·xylon, -um** [Gr. ξύλον wood], *Bot.* a large genus of trees and shrubs of the family *Rutaceae*, yielding various products, esp. pungent and aromatic drugs and condiments; hence **Xantho·xyl,** a plant of the genus; **Xanthoxyla·ceous** *a.*

Xantippe (zænti·pi). 1596. [prop. *Xanthippe*, Gr. Ξανθίππη.] The wife of Socrates; *allus.*, a shrewish wife.

As curst and shrow'd As Socrates Zentippe SHAKS.

Xebec (zī·bek, zíbe·k). 1756. [Altered f. CHEBEC after Sp. *xabeque*.] A small three-masted (orig. two-masted) Mediterranean ship, lateen-rigged but with some square sails, used formerly as a war-ship and now as a merchant ship.

Xeme (zīm). 1836. [ad. arbitrary mod.L. *Xema*.] *Ornith.* A bird of the genus *Xema*; a fork-tailed gull.

‖**Xenia** (zī·niǎ). 1899. [mod.L., ad. Gr. ξενία state of a guest, f. ξένος guest.] *Bot.* A supposed direct action or influence of foreign pollen upon the seed or fruit which is pollinated.

‖**Xenium** (zī·niɒm); usu. in pl. **xe·nia.** 1706. [L., ad. Gr. ξένιον, f. ξένιος.] *Gr.* and *Rom. Antiq.* A present (esp. of table delicacies) given to a guest or stranger; *transf.* in mediæval usage, an offering made (occas. compulsorily) by subjects to their prince on the occasion of his passing through their estates.

Xeno- (ze·no, zėnǫ·), before a vowel **xen-**, repr. Gr. ξενο-, ξεν-, comb. form of ξένος strange, foreign, stranger, guest, used in various scientific and other terms.

Xenaca·nthine (-ǎkæ·nþəin) *a.* (*sb.*) [Gr. ἄκανθα spine], *Zool.* (a fish) of an extinct selachian order with long slender spines. **Xena·rthral** *a.* [Gr. ἄρθρον joint], *Zool.* having peculiar accessory articulations in the vertebræ, as the Amer. edentates. **Xenobiosis** (-bəiōᵘ·sis) [Gr. βίωσις manner of life], *Zool.* a symbiosis of two colonies of ants of different species, living together but not interbreeding. ‖**Xenodochium** (-dǫki·ɒm) [Gr. δέχεσθαι to receive], a hostel, guest-house, esp. in a monastery. **Xeno·gamy** [Gr. γάμος marriage], *Bot.* cross-fertilization. **Xenoge·nesis,** *Biol.* production of offspring permanently unlike the parent; so **Xenogene·tic, Xenoge·nic** *adjs.* **Xe·nolite** [-LITE], *Min.* a silicate of aluminium. **Xenomo·rphic** *a.* [Gr. μορφή form], *Geol.* applied to mineral constituents of a rock having an abnormal form in consequence of the pressure of other constituents. **Xeno·phoran** *a.* [Gr. -φορος -carrying], *Zool.* belonging or allied to the genus *Xenophora* of gasteropod molluscs distinguished by the habit of cementing foreign bodies to their shells. **Xe·nurine** [Gr. οὐρά tail], *Zool. a.* belonging to the genus *Xenurus* of armadillos, having the tail nearly naked; *sb.* an armadillo of this genus, a kabassou.

Xenon (ze·nǫn). 1898. [ad. Gr. ξένον, neut. of ξένος strange.] *Chem.* A heavy inert gaseous element present in minute quantity in the atmosphere. Symbol Xe or X.

Xenophontean, -ian (zenǒfǫ·ntiǎn), *a.* 1593. [f. Gr. Ξενοφῶν, -ῶντος Xenophon, an ancient Greek historian and biographer (*c* 444–354 B.C.) + -EAN, -IAN.] Pertaining to, characteristic of, or resembling (that of) Xenophon. So **Xenopho·ntic** *a.* 1822.

Xenotime (ze·notəim). 1844. [Named 1832, as if f. Gr. ξένος strange + τιμή honour; but app. in error for **kenotime* f. Gr. κενός empty, vain.] *Min.* A native phosphate of yttrium.

Beudant named the species *xenotime*.., but in the next line gives the derivation 'κενος, vain, et τιμή, honneur', as if the word were *kenotime*, and adds.. that this name is intended to recall the fact that the mineral was erroneously supposed by Berzelius..to contain a new metal DANA.

‖**Xeranthemum** (ziᵊræ·nþ*ĭ*mɒm). 1741. [mod.L., f. Gr. ξηρός dry + ἄνθεμον blossom.] *Bot.* A genus of composites having flower-heads with purplish or whitish dry chaffy bracts; a plant of this genus; one kind of the plants commonly called *everlasting* or *immortelle*.

‖**Xerasia** (ziᵊrē¹·ziǎ). 1706. [a. Gr. ξηρασία dryness.] *Path.* Excessive dryness of the hair.

Xeres (ze·rės, ziᵊ·rėz). 1661. Name of an Andalusian town famous for its wine; in full, *X. sack*, *wine*, = SHERRIS, SHERRY.

Xeriff (ze·rif, zīə·rif), var. of SHEREEF.

Xero- (zīə·ro), before a vowel **xer-**, repr. Gr. ξηρο-, ξηρ-, comb. form of ξηρός dry, in scientific and technical terms.

Xerode·rm(i)a [Gr. δέρμα skin], *Path.* a disease characterized by excessive dryness of the skin; hence **Xeroderma·tic, -de·rmatous, -de·rmic** *adjs.* **Xero·ma**, *Path.*, abnormal dryness of some parts; *spec.* = XEROPHTHALMIA; hence **Xero·matous** *a.* **Xero·phagy** [ad. Gr. ξηροφαγία, see -PHAGY], the eating of dry food, esp. as a form of fasting practised in the early church. **Xero·philous** *a.* [Gr. -φιλος -loving], *Bot.* adapted to dry conditions: so **Xe·rophil(e**, a xerophilous plant; **Xero·phily**, the condition or character of being xerophilous. **Xerophtha·lmia**, *Path.* inflammation of the conjunctiva of the eye with abnormal dryness and corrugation. **Xe·rophyte** [Gr. φυτόν plant], *Bot.* = *xerophil*; so **Xerophy·tic** *a.*, **Xero·phytism.** **Xero·sis** [-OSIS], *Path.* = XEROMA; *spec.* = *xeroderma*; so **Xero·tic** *a.*

Xiphias (zi·fiæs). 1667. [L., a. Gr. ξιφίας, f. ξίφος sword.] **1.** A swordfish, esp. *X. gladius*; the genus of fishes to which this belongs, characterized by having the upper jaw prolonged into a sword-like weapon. **2.** *Astron.* A southern constellation, also called Dorado or the Swordfish 1728. Hence **Xi·phioid** *a.* resembling or allied to the genus *X.*; *sb.* a xiphioid fish.

Xiphi-, xipho- (zi·fi, zi·fo), comb. form. of Gr. ξίφος sword in terms of *Anat.* and *Zool.*

‖**Xiphipla·stron** (pl. -a), each of the hindmost pair of lateral plates in the plastron of a turtle; hence **Xiphipla·stral** *a.*; *sb.* a xiphiplastron. **Xiphiste·rnal**, *a.* belonging to or constituting the xiphisternum; *sb.* a xiphisternal part or appendage. **Xiphiste·rnum** [STERNUM], the cartilaginous or bony process ending the sternum (in man, the xiphoid cartilage); also, = *xiphiplastron.* ‖**Xipho·pagus** [Gr. πάγος something firmly fixed], a twin monster united by a band extending downwards from the xiphoid cartilage, as in the case of the Siamese twins; hence **Xipho·pagous** *a.* **Xiphosu·ran** [irreg. f. Gr. οὐρά tail], *Zool.* *a.* belonging to the arachnid order *Xiphosura*, including the king-crab with a long sharp telson; *sb.* an arachnid of this order; so **Xi·phosure,** a xiphosuran.

Xiphoid (zi·foid), *a.* (*sb.*) 1746. [ad. mod. L. *xiphoides*, a. Gr. ξιφοειδής, f. ξίφος sword + εἶδος; see -OID.] *Anat.* Sword-shaped; applied to the bony or cartilaginous process at the lower or posterior end of the sternum in man and other animals, and to a projecting bone at the back of the head in the cormorants and related birds.

Xmas, earlier also **X't-, Xst-.** 1551. Common abbrev. in writing of CHRISTMAS; see X III. **1.** Sometimes vulgarly pronounced (e·ksmæs).

Xoanon (zōu·ănǫn). *Pl.* **-a.** 1706. [Gr. ξόανον, related to ξύειν to scrape.] *Gr. Antiq.* A primitive rudely-carved image (orig. wooden), esp. of a deity.

Xonotlite (zonǫ·tlait). Also **xonaltite.** 1868. [f. *Xonotla*, a village in Puebla, Mexico, where found; see -ITE [1].] *Min.* A hard massive hydrated silicate of calcium.

X rays (eks rēi·z), *sb. pl.* Also **X-rays.** 1896. [tr. G. *x-strahlen*, the name given by the discoverer, Prof. Röntgen, expressing the fact that their essential nature is unknown; see X II. 2.] A form of radiation capable of penetrating many substances impervious to light, and of affecting a sensitized plate and producing shadow-photographs of objects enclosed within opaque bodies; they produce phosphorescence, fluorescence, and electrical effects, and have a curative effect in certain skin-diseases; much used in recent surgical and medical practice. Also called *Röntgen rays.* **b.** *attrib.* and *Comb.* (in sing. form *X-ray*), as *X-ray examination, photograph* 1897. Hence **X-ray** (e·ksrē^i·) *v. trans.* to examine or treat with X rays. So **X-radia·tion.**

Xylan (zəi·læn). 1894. [f. Gr. ξύλον wood + -AN.] *Chem.* A gelatinous compound contained in wood, also called *tree-gum, wood-gum.*

Xylem (zəi·lem). 1875. [f. Gr. ξύλον wood; cf. PHLOEM.] *Bot.* Collective name for the cells, vessels, and fibres forming the harder portion of the fibrovascular tissue; the wood.

Xylite (zəi·ləit). 1843. [ad. G. *xylit*, f. Gr. ξύλον wood.] **1.** *Chem.* A volatile liquid obtained from wood-spirit. **2.** *Min.* An impure silicate of iron, occurring in brown fibrous masses resembling asbestos or 'mountain-wood' 1850.

Xylo- (zəi·lo), before a vowel **xyl-**, repr. Gr. ξυλο-, ξυλ-, comb. form of ξύλον wood, in scientific and technical terms.

Xy·lene [-ENE], *Chem.* a mixture of three isomeric hydrocarbons, obtained as a volatile colourless liquid from wood-spirit or coal-naphtha; any one of these three; dimethylbenzene; also called *xylol*; hence **Xy·lic** *a.* in *xylic acid*, dimethylbenzoic acid. **Xy·lidine** [-ID [4], -INE [5]], *Chem.* (*a*) an amine-derivative of xylene, homologous with aniline, used in the preparation of artificial dyes; (*b*) = *xyloidin.* ‖**Xyloba·lsamum** [ad. Gr. ξυλοβάλσαμον; see BALSAM], the fragrant wood of the tree *Balsamodendron gileadense*, which yields OPOBALSAMUM or Balm of Gilead. **Xylo·copid** *a.* [Gr. -κοπος -cutting] *a.*, *Entom.* belonging or related to the genus *Xylocopa*, comprising the carpenter-bees. **Xylo·graphy** [ad. F. *xylographie*, see -GRAPHY], wood-engraving, esp. of the early period or of a primitive kind; printing from wood-blocks as distinct from type; so **Xy·lograph**, *sb.* a wood-engraving; *v. trans.* to produce by xylography; **Xylo·grapher, -graphist; Xylogra·phic, -al** *adjs.*; **Xylogra·phically** *adv.* **Xyloi·din, -ine** [-OID, -IN[1]], *Chem.* an explosive substance obtained by treating starch or vegetable fibre with nitric acid. **Xy·lol** = *xylene.* **Xylo·phagous** [Gr. -φαγος eating] *a.*, *Zool.* wood-eating, destructive to wood (of larvæ, etc.); so **Xylo·phagan** *a.* (*sb.*), (a member) of the *Xylophaga* or *Xylophagi*, various groups of insects with wood-devouring larvæ. **Xylo·philan** *a.* (*sb.*), (a beetle) of the group *Xylophili* of beetles, which live in decayed wood; so **Xylo·philous** *a.* living or growing in or on wood, as an insect or a fungus. **Xylo·stein** (-tīn) [Gr. ὀστέον bone, -IN [1]], *Chem.* a poisonous bitter substance found in the berries of the fly-honeysuckle, *Lonicera Xylosteum.* **Xy·lotil(e)** (-təil, -til), [Gr. τίλος down]. *Min.* an asbestos-like mineral called also *mountain-wood.* **Xylo·tomous** [Gr. -τομος cutting], *a.* cutting or boring wood (of insects). **Xy·lotypogra·phic** *a.*, printed from wooden blocks or types.

Xylonite (zəi·lŏnəit). 1869. [irreg. f. Gr. ξύλον wood + -ITE [1].] A proprietary name for CELLULOID.

Xylophone (zəi·lŏfōun). 1866. [f. XYLO- + Gr. φωνή voice, sound.] A musical instrument consisting of a graduated series of flat wooden bars, played by striking with a small hammer or rubbing with rosined gloves.

Xylose (zəi·lous). 1894. [-OSE [2].] *Chem.* A colourless carbohydrate, $C_5H_{10}O_5$, obtained by the action of sulphuric acid on xylan; wood-sugar.

Xylyl (zəi·lil). 1862. [f. XYL- + -YL.] *Chem.* The hypothetical radical of xylene.

Xyrid (zəiə·rid). 1846. [ad. mod.L. *Xyrid-*, *Xyris*, ad. Gr. ξυρίς a species of iris with sharp-edged leaves, f. ξυρόν razor.] *Bot.* A plant of the monocotyledonous family *Xyridaceæ*, typified by the genus *Xyris*, sedge-like herbs having flowers with three coloured petals; chiefly N. Amer. and tropical. So **Xyridaceous** (ziridē^i·ʃəs) *a.* belonging to the *Xyridaceæ.*

‖**Xyster** (zi·stəɹ). 1684. [mod.L., a. Gr. ξυστήρ, f. ξύειν to scrape.] *Surg.* An instrument for scraping bones.

‖**Xystus** (zi·stŏs). *Pl.* **xysti** (-əi). Also anglicized **xyst.** 1664. [L., ad. Gr. ξυστός smooth (course), f. ξύειν to scrape.] In ancient Greece, a long covered portico or court for athletic exercises; in ancient Rome, an open colonnade, or walk planted with trees, used for recreation and conversation.

Y

Y (wəi), pl. Y's, *Ys* (wəiz), the 25th letter of the modern and the 23rd of the ancient Roman alphabet, repr. ult. Greek Υ, ϒ (u psilon), a differentiated form of the primitive V which has given also U and V. The Latin alphabet adopted first the V form for the sounds (*u*) and (w), and later the Y form for the ϒ of borrowed Greek words. The French and German names for y (*i grec, ipsilon*) preserve the fact of its Greek origin. The English name *wy* (wəi) is of obscure origin.

In early OE. the letter expressed the *i/j*-mutation of *u*; its forms varied from those resembling Gr. ϒ to ẏ, the latter prevailing in ME. and becoming identical with debased forms of þ, whence the *y^e*, *y^t*, etc., for *the, that*, etc., which continued to be extensively employed in manuscript in the 17th and 18th centuries; *y^e* is still often used pseudo-archaically or jocularly, and vulgarly pronounced as *ye.* In later (West-Saxon) OE. *y* was written alternatively for *i*, e.g. as repr. older *ie*; and as its function of expressing rounded *i* (*ü, ǖ*) was taken over by *u* in imitation of French usage, it became ultimately a possible substitute for vocalic *i* in any position. This use had become established by the middle of the 13th century, and thenceforward *y* served as a convenient means of breaking up an ambiguous series of minims produced by a succession of *i, u, n, m*, as *nym, myn*, for *nim, min*, etc. This free use of *y* continued long after the introduction of printing, but usage has now restored *i*, except (1) in final *i*-sounds of all but alien words (as in *fly, family, daily, destroy*); (2) for Greek upsilon (as in *hymn*); (3) in verb-inflexions before *i* (as in *lying*); (4) in plurals of nouns in *-ay, -ey, -oy* (as in *rays, alleys, boys, moneys*, but also *monies*). Particular usages, not falling under these categories, are the use of *y* to distinguish *dye* from *die*, and the fluctuation between *tire* and *tyre, flyer* and *flier, siphon* and *syphon, silva* and *sylva*, etc.

As a consonant, *y* represents the voiced palatal spirant (y), which was one of the values of the obsolete letter ȝ (see YOGH); *y* began to occur as a variant of ȝ in this use about 1250.

Pronunciation. The vocalic sounds now normally expressed by *y* are :—(1) i, as in h*y*mn (him), sill*y* (si·li); (2) əi, as in m*y* (məi), den*y* (dǐnəi·); (3) əiə, as in l*y*re (ləiəɹ); (4) ɜ̄, as in m*y*rtle (mɜ̄·ɹt'l); (5) ə as in sat*y*r (sæ·təɹ). With other vowels it forms combinations having special values :—*ay* (final) = ē^i, as in l*ay* (lē^i), ess*ay* (e·se^i), = əi in *aye* (əi), = ī in qu*ay* (kī), = e in s*ay*s (sez); *ey* = ē^i, as in ob*ey* (obē^i·), = i, as in all*ey* (æ·li), = əi in *eye* (əi) and its derivatives, = ēə in *eyre* (ēəɹ); *oy* = oi, as in b*oy* (boi); *uy* (*rare*) = əi in b*uy* (bəi), g*uy* (gəi).

1. The letter. OE. **b.** Used for the Greek Υ (*upsilon*), esp. as a Pythagorean symbol. late ME. **2.** The letter considered with regard to its shape; a figure or marking of this shape. Also comb. *Y-shaped* adj. 1513. **3.** A Y-shaped contrivance or piece of apparatus, *esp.* a forked support for a telescope, theodolite, etc. Also *attrib.*, as *Y bearing*; **Y branch,** a piece of piping with a branch at an acute angle to the main; **Y cross,** (*a*) a y-shaped ornament on ecclesiastical vestments, (*b*) a piece of piping diverging into three; **Y level,** the common spirit-level, used with a telescope, etc. resting on Y's; **Y track,** a piece of railway line at right angles to the main line, and connected with it by two switches in opposite directions, for reversing an engine or car. Also in names of natural structures, as *Y cartilage.* 1793. **b.** As a name for various moths of the genus *Plusia*, having markings resembling the letter Y 1775. **4.** *Math.* Used to denote the second of a set of unknown or variable quantities (cf. X II. 1 b); *spec.* in Analytical Geometry the symbol for an ordinate 1728. **5.** Used in abstract reasoning (usu. in connexion with X) for the name of a person or thing. Also *Y.Z.*, as initials of an anonymous person (cf. X). 1765. **6.** Denoting serial order. **7.** *Abbreviations.* y. = year(s); Y = Yttrium; Y.M.C.A., Y.W.C.A. = Young Men's (Women's) Christian Association; also colloq. abbrev. YM (wəi,e·m), YW (wəi,dɒ·b'lyu).

Y- *prefix* represents OE. *ge-* :—OTeut. **ga-* (G., Du. *ge-*), perh. identical w. L. *co-, com-* (cf. OE. *gemæne*, L. *communis*). The original (physical) meaning 'with', 'together', yielded the notions of (1) association, and hence of suitability or appropriateness, and (2) collectivity, the final stage being (3) a perfective, completive, or intensive notion evolved in some measure from each of the others. Its use as a prefix of pa. pples. is an instance of the latter meaning. The prefix survives in such archaic pa. pples. as YCLEPT and YCLAD, and in a disguised form in the first syllables of ALIKE, AWARE, AFFORD, ENOUGH, AMONG, q. v.; HANDIWORK (OE. *handgeweorc*), EITHER (OE. *æghwæðer*) also contain it. Its use as a mark of the pa. pple. continued regularly in southern ME. into the 15th c., and, in the form *a-*, is not yet extinct in south-western dialects. The OE. *ge-* was succeeded first by *ie-, i-*, and later by *y-*, which, being adopted by Spenser and his imitators in their archaistic forms, has remained the accepted spelling in such use.

-y *suffix*[1] descends from the OE. adj. suffix *-ig* :—OTeut. *-*īga-*, and *-*aga-*. With sbs. ending in *y*, *-ey* it takes the form *-ey*, e. g. *clayey*; sbs. ending in mute *e* preceded by a vowel retain the *-e* (as in *gluey*); in other cases there may be variation, as *homey, homy, nosey, nosy*.

1. The general sense of the suffix is 'having the qualities of' or 'full of' that which is denoted by the sb. to which it is added, as *icy*=(1) of the nature of or having the coldness, hardness, etc. of ice; (2) full of or covered with ice. Such adjs. were numerous in OE., and large additions were made at particular periods, esp. in the 14th c. (as *angry, hearty, milky, naughty*) and 16th c. (as *frothy, dirty, healthy, saucy*). Later formations tend to be colloquial, undignified, or trivial, as *bumpy, hammy, messy, oniony*. A sense 'addicted to', as in *booky, doggy, horsy*, is of modern growth. 2. Some monosyllabic adjs. were extended by means of this suffix as early as the 15th c., apparently with the design of giving them a more adjectival appearance; so *chilly, dusky, paly, vasty*. Similarly *slippery*, f. *slipper*. The majority of such words arose in the 16th and 17th cc. The suffix has not infrequently come to express the same notion as *-ish*, particularly with colour-epithets, and esp. when these are used quasi-advb., as *greeny-blue*. 3. From the 13th c. the suffix has been added to verb-stems to express the meaning 'inclined or apt to' do something, or 'giving occasion to' a certain action; e. g. *blowy, drowsy, sticky*. 4. From the early years of the 19th c. the suffix has been used in nonce-words, connoting characteristics which call for condemnation as *beery, catty, fuggy*.

-y *suffix*[2], represents the OE. infin. ending *-ian* (:— *-*ōjan*, whence also OS. *-ōian, -ôn*, OHG., Goth. *-ōn*), and *-*æjan* (whence OHG. *-ēn*) of the second class of weak verbs, surviving in Somerset, Devon, and Dorset, as the infin. ending of any verb used intransitively.

-y *suffix*[3] represents, through F. *-ie*, the Com. Romanic *-ia* = L. *-ĭa* (Gr. *-ία, -εια*). Many English words in *-y*, such as *glory, history, victory*, were adopted from AF., which preferred learned adoptions in *-ie* of L. nouns in *-ia* to the popular or semi-popular OF. forms in *-e*. This suffix has never been in English a prolific formative, but the correspondence of adjs. in *-ic* and *-ous* to sbs. in *-y* has made possible in modern times the formation after Gr. types of such words as *brachycephaly, synchrony* from *brachycephalic, synchronous*. The suffix also constitutes the final element of a great number of compound suffixes, e. g. -ACY, -CY, -ERY, -GRAPHY, -LATRY, -LOGY, -PATHY, -PHILY, -RY, -TOMY.

-y *suffix*[4] represents (first through AF. forms in *-ie*) L. *-ium* as appended to vbl. roots to denote an act; so *remedy* (L. *remedium*, f. *mederi* to heal); *colloquy, perjury, subsidy* are similarly from L. originals. The suffix has not been independently used in English, except, perhaps helped by the false analogy of -RY, in *expiry* and *inquiry*, and in *entreaty*, f. *entreat* vb. on the analogy of *treat, treaty*.

-y *suffix*[5] represents AF., OF. *-e, -ee*, mod.F. *-é, -ée* :—L. *-atu-, -ata-* (see -ATE[1], -ATE[2]). a. In sbs. = -ATE[1]; as in (i) COUNTY, F. *comté*, L. *comitatus*, DUCHY, etc. (ii) ARMY, F. *armée*, L. *armata*. b. In adjs. = -ATE[2]; as in *easy*, OF. *aisié*; chiefly in heraldic terms, as *barry, lozengy*; also with var. in *-é*, as *tenné, tenny*; *wavy* (after *undy*) is a rare instance of an analogical use of *-y* with a native word.

-y *suffix*[6], **-ie**, forming pet names and familiar diminutives. The spelling varies, sometimes in the same word, but with a tendency to *-y* in proper names (as in BILLY, TOMMY, *Fanny*, but with many exceptions) and transferred applications of these (as JEMMY, DICKY, JENNY, PEGGY, but CHARLEY, CHARLIE), and to *-ie* (after Sc. usage) in general hypocoristic forms (*laddie, dearie*). The earliest appearance of the suffix is in Scottish pet forms of proper names, *c* 1400, many of which have survived as Sc. surnames, e. g. *Christie, Pirrie, Ritchie, Jamieson. Bookie* for *bookmaker* (1885) shows an extension of the type; cf. *nighty* for *nightdress, undies* for *underclothes, frillies*, f. *frill, movie, talkie*.

Yabber (yæ·bəɹ), *sb. Austral.* 1874. [Native Austral. *yabba*.] Speech, language, applied to the speech of the Australian aborigines. So **Ya·bber** *v. trans.* and *intr.* to talk.

‖**Yaboo** (yabū·). 1753. [Hindustani = Persian *yābū*.] One of a breed of large ponies or small stout horses in Afghanistan, Persia, and adjacent countries.

‖**Yacca** (yæ·kă). 1843. [Native name.] A W. Indian evergreen tree (*Podocarpus coriacea* or *P. purdieana*), or its wood, used in cabinet-work, etc.

Yacht (yǫt), *sb.* 1557. [ad. early mod.Du. *jaghte* = *jaghtschip* fast piratical ship, f. *jag(h)t* hunting, f. *jagen* to hunt.] A light fast-sailing ship, in early use esp. for the conveyance of royal or other important persons; later, a vessel, usu. light and comparatively small, for cruising, now esp. one built and rigged for racing. 1886.

I sailed this morning with his Majesty in one of his Yatchts EVELYN.

attrib. and *Comb.*, as *y.-club, -race, -squadron*; **Ya·chtsman** 1862, **-woman**. Hence **Yacht** *v. intr.* to cruise or race in a yacht; **Ya·chting** *vbl. sb.* and *ppl. a.* 1836.

Yaffingale (yæ·fiŋgəl). *south.* and *s.w. dial.* 1609. [Echoic, with termination modelled on *nightingale*.] = next.

Yaffle (yæ·f'l). *dial.* 1792. [Echoic of its laughing cry.] The green woodpecker.

Yager (yēⁱ·gəɹ). 1804. [Anglicized spelling of G. *jäger* JÄGER.] = JÄGER 1, 2. b. *U.S.* A rifle 1840.

Yah (yā), *int.* 1812. [Echoic.] An exclamation of disgust, aversion, or malicious defiance.

Yah!.. Never thinking of anybody but yourself DICKENS.

Yah, in pseudo-phonetic representations (*y.! y.!*) of the House of Commons ejaculation *Hear! hear!* 1886.

Yahoo (yahū·). 1726. A name invented by Swift in *Gulliver's Travels* for an imaginary race of brutes having the form of men; hence *transf.* and *allus.*, a human being of degraded or bestial type.

attrib.: Some Corruptions of my Y. Nature have revived in me SWIFT. Hence **Yahoo·ism**.

Yahveh, -vism, etc., **-weh**, etc.: see JEHOVAH, JAHVISM.

Yair, yare (yēᵊɹ). *Sc.* and *n. dial.* [OE. *gear* (in comb. *mylengear* mill-yair).] An enclosure extending into a tideway, for catching fish; a fishgarth.

Yak (yæk, yāk). 1799. [Tibetan *gyag*.] A silky-haired bovine animal (*Poephagus grunniens*), found wild and domesticated in Tibet and other high regions of central Asia.

Yale[1] (yēⁱl). late ME. [ad. L. *eale* (Pliny).] A fabulous beast with horns and tusks; used *Her*.

Yale[2] (yēⁱl). 1882. A form of cylinder lock invented by Linus *Yale*.

Yam (yæm). 1588. [a. Pg. *inhame* or Sp. *igname*; ult. origin obsc.] 1. The starchy tuberous root of various species of *Dioscorea*, taking the place in tropical and subtropical countries of the potato; also, any plant of the genus *Dioscorea*, comprising twining herbs or shrubs with spikes of small inconspicuous flowers. 2. Applied to †(*a*) the mangrove; (*b*) varieties of the common potato, cultivated in Scotland; (*c*) a variety of the sweet potato (*Batatas edulis*) largely eaten by negroes in America 1753.

1. **Chinese** or **Japanese Y.**, *D. Batatas*. **Coco Y.**=Cocco. **Common Y.**, *D. sativa*. **Granada** or **Guinea Y.**, *D. bulbifera*. **Indian Y.**, *D. trifida*. **Long Y.**, of Australia, *D. transversa*. **Native Y.**, applied to Australian species of *Ipomœa* with edible tubers. **Red, White, Negro Country, Winged Y.**, *D. alata*. **Round Y.**, (*a*) a species with a round tuber; (*b*) the Burdekin Vine of Australia, *Vitis (Cissus) opaca*. **Wild Y.**, *D. villosa* of N. America, also called *colic-root*; also applied to other plants.

attrib. and *Comb.*: **yam-bean**, either of two tropical leguminous plants with edible pods and tubers, *Pachyrrhizus (Dolichos) tuberosus* and *angulatus*; **y. potato**, = 2 (*b*); **y.-stick**, a long sharp stick used by Australian natives for digging and as a weapon; **y.-stock**, a nickname for an inhabitant of St. Helena; **y.-vine**, (*a*) a species of y., *Dioscorea bulbifera*; (*b*) the 'vine' or climbing stem of the y.-plant.

Yammer (yæ·məɹ), *v. Obs.* exc. *Sc.* and *dial.* 1481. [Alteration (after MDu., MLG. *jammeren*) of ME. *ȝomer* :—OE. *ȝeómrian*, f. *ȝeómor* sorrowful.] 1. *intr.* To lament, mourn; to utter cries of lamentation or distress, to wail. b. To murmur, complain, grumble; also *trans.* 1786. 2. To make a loud, unpleasant noise or outcry 1513. Hence **Ya·mmer** *sb.* the action or an act of 'yammering'; a wail; a loud outcry; lamentation, complaint.

‖**Yamstchick** (yæ·mstʃik). 1753. [Russ.] The driver of a post-horse.

‖**Yamun, yamen** (yā·mǝn). 1827. [Chinese *ya* official residence, office + *mun* gate.] A mandarin's office or official residence; hence, any department of the Chinese public service, as the *tsung li y.*, or Chinese 'foreign office'.

Yank (yæŋk), *sb.*[1] (*a.*) 1778. Colloq. abbrev. of YANKEE.

As clever at a trick as a Y. 1886.

Yank (yæŋk), *v. dial.* and *U.S.* 1822. [Origin unkn.] 1. *trans.* To pull with a jerk; to jerk or twitch vigorously 1848. 2. *intr.* To pull or jerk vigorously; *fig.* to be vigorously active 1822. Hence **Yank** *sb.*[2], a sharp stroke (*Sc.*); a jerk, tug (*U.S.*) 1818.

Yankee (yæ·ŋki), *sb.* and *a.* 1758. [Origin unknown. None of the several attempts that have been made to establish the etymology are convincing. As a surname or nickname with Dutch associations *Yank(e)y, Yankee* is recorded as early as 1683.] A. *sb.* 1. a. *U.S.* A nickname for a New-Englander, or an inhabitant or native of the northern States generally; during the War of Secession applied by the Confederates to the soldiers of the Federal army. b. In English use: A native or inhabitant of the U.S., an American 1784. 2. The New England dialect; *loosely*, American English 1772. 3. pl. *Stock Exch. slang.* American stocks or securities 1887.

1. Our hero being a New-Englander by birth, has a right to the epithet of Yankey; a name of derision 1765. b. I..am determined not to suffer the Yankies to come where the ship is NELSON.

B. *adj.* That is a Yankee; pertaining to or characteristic of Yankees (often connoting cleverness, cunning, or cold calculation); of or pertaining to the United States, American 1781.

Comb., etc.: **Y. Doodle**, a popular air of the U.S., considered to be characteristically national; also, a Y.; **Ya·nkeeland**, New England, the United States of America; **Y. notions**, small wares or useful articles made in New England or the northern States; **Y. State**, a nickname for Ohio. Hence **Ya·nkeedom** = YANKEELAND; Yankees collectively. **Ya·nkeefied** *ppl. a.*; **Ya·nkeeish** *a.* Americanized or as of Americans. **Ya·nkeeism**, Y. character or style, a Y. idiom. **Ya·nkeeize** *v. trans.* to give a Y. character to.

Yanolite (yæ·nǝləit). 1850. [a. F. *yanolithe*, perh. f. Gr. *ἴανθος* violet; see -LITE.] *Min.* = AXINITE.

‖**Yaourt** (yā·uɹt). 1819. [Turkish *yōghurt*.] = YOGURT.

Yap (yæp), *v.* 1668. [Echoic.] 1. *intr.* To bark sharply, as a small dog. 2. *transf.* To speak snappishly 1864. So **Yap** *sb.* a short sharp bark or cry. **Ya·pping** *vbl. sb.* and *ppl. a.*

Yapo(c)k (yæ·pǫk). 1827. [f. *Oyapok*, name of a river between French Guiana and Brazil.] The S. Amer. water opossum, *Chironectes variegatus*.

Yapon, yaupon (yǭ·pǫn). 1712. [North Carolina.] An evergreen shrub or small tree (*Ilex Cassine* or *vomitoria*) of Southern U.S.; a decoction of the leaves (*y. tea*) is used as an emetic and purgative.

Yapp (yæp). 1882. [Name of a London bookseller for whom first made about 1860.] A style of bookbinding in limp leather with overlapping edges or flaps. Hence **Yapped** (yæpt) *a.*

Yarak (yæ·ræk). 1855. [perh. Pers. *yārakī* strength.] Falconry. *In y.*, (of a hawk) in condition for hunting.

Yarborough (yā·ɹbǝrǝ). 1900. [Said to be so called because an Earl of Yarborough used to bet 1,000 to 1 against its occurrence.] *Cards.* In whist and bridge, a hand which contains no card above a nine.

Yard (yāɹd), *sb.*[1] [OE. *geard* fence, dwelling, house (the second element of OE. *ortgeard* ORCHARD); cf. GARTH[1], GARDEN. Ulterior relations (as with Gr. *χόρτος*, L. *hortus, cohors*) uncertain.] 1. A comparatively small uncultivated area attached to a building or enclosed by it; esp. such an area surrounded by walls or buildings within the precincts of a castle, house, inn, etc. (Cf. *back-y.*, *inn-y.*, *stable-y.*) **b.** *spec.* (*a*) *Sc. pl.* a school playground 1808; (*b*) = COURT *sb.*[1] I. 3 (esp. in proper names) 1851. **c.** = CHURCHYARD 1791. **d.** An enclosure attached to a prison, in which the prisoners take exercise 1777. **e.** *The Yard*, short for *Scotland Yard*, the chief London police office 1888. **2.** An enclosure forming a pen for cattle or poultry, a storing place for hay, or the like, belonging to a farm-house, or surrounded by farm-buildings ME. **3.** A garden. Now *dial.* and *U.S.*, a kitchen- or cottage-garden ME. **4.** **a.** An enclosure devoted to some work or business; cf. *brickyard*, DOCKYARD, etc. late ME. **b.** The space used for storing rolling-stock, making up trains, etc., adjacent to a railway station or terminus; also, an enclosure in which cabs, trams, etc. are kept when not in use 1827. **5.** *U.S.* and *Canada.* = MOOSE-YARD 1829.

attrib. and *Comb.*: **y.-dog**, a watch-dog kept in the y.; **-money**, fees payable by cab-hirers to stablemen, etc., on returning them to the y.

Yard (yāɹd), *sb.*[2] [OE. **gierd*, *gyrd*, *gird* twig, stick :—OTeut. **gazdjō* GAD *sb.*[1]. L. *hasta* spear, is prob. related.] †**1.** A branch, twig, shoot –1450. †**2.** A staff, stick –1538. †**3.** A stick or rod used as an instrument for administering strokes –1450. †**b.** *fig.* A means or instrument of punishment; hence, chastisement –1530. †**4.** A wand, rod, or staff of office –1470. **5.** *Naut.* A spar slung at its centre from, and forward of, a mast and serving to support and extend a square sail OE. †**6.** A measuring-rod; *spec.* a yard-measure –1751. **7.** A unit of linear measure of 16½ ft. (but varying locally); a rod, pole, or perch. Now *local.* OE. **8.** The standard unit of English long measure, equal to three feet or thirty-six inches. Also the corresponding measure of area (*square y.* = 9 sq. ft.) or of solidity (*cubic y.* = 27 cub. ft.). In *Building*, used as a measure of lime, mortar, stone, etc. late ME. **b.** Vaguely, hyperbolically, or fig. late ME. **9.** **a.** In full *y. of land* = YARDLAND OE. **b.** A quarter of an acre, a rood 1450. †**10.** The virile member, penis –1884.

6. *fig.* We imagine God to be lyke ourselues, & we measure him by our owne y. 1583. 8. Phrases. *Y. of ale, wine*, a long slender glass and its contents. *Y. of clay*, a long clay pipe. *Y. of satin* (slang), a glass of gin. *Y. of tin*, a coachman's horn. **b.** He could talk by the y. of what little he did know 1869.

Yard, *v.*[1] *Colonial* and *U.S.* 1828. [f. YARD *sb.*[1]] **1.** *trans.* To enclose (cattle, etc.) or store (wood) in a yard. **2.** *intr.* Of moose, etc.: To resort to winter quarters (see MOOSE-YARD) 1852.

Yard, *v.*[2] [f. YARD *sb.*[2] after Manx *slattys.*] *trans.* In the Isle of Man, to summon for hiring.

Yardage[1] (yā·ɹdėdʒ). 1889. [f. YARD *sb.*[1] + -AGE.] The use of or charge for a yard for storing, etc.

Ya·rdage[2]. 1877. [f. YARD *sb.*[2] + -AGE.] **1.** The cutting of coal at a fixed rate per yard. **2.** The aggregate number of yards; amount reckoned in yards 1900.

Ya·rd-arm. 1553. [f. YARD *sb.*[2] 5 + ARM *sb.*[1] II. 3.] *Naut.* Either end of a yard; *esp.* that part which is outside the sheave-hole often used for the yard as a whole. **b.** in ref. to hanging or ducking a person from the extremity of a yard as a punishment 1553.

Y. and (or *to*) *y.*, said of two ships so near that their yard-arms touch or cross.

Yardland (yā·ɹdlænd). 1450. [= *yard of land*, OE. *gyrd landes*; see YARD *sb.*[2] 9 a.] An area of land, usu. of 30 acres, but varying locally: commonly taken as = a fourth of a hide.

Yardman[1] (yā·ɹdmæn). 1825. [YARD *sb.*[1]] A man in charge of or employed in a yard.

Ya·rdman[2]. 1886. [YARD *sb.*[2]] *Naut.* *Royal, upper*, etc. *y.*, a sailor occupied on the royal yards, the upper yards, etc.

Ya·rd-mea·sure. 1831. [YARD *sb.*[2]] A rod, bar, or tape for measuring by the yard (but not necessarily restricted to that length).

Yardsman (yā·ɹdzmæn). 1872. [f. genit. of YARD *sb.*[1]] = YARDMAN[1]. So **Ya·rdswoman** 1817.

Yardstick (yā·ɹdstik). orig. *U.S.* 1828. [YARD *sb.*[2]] A three-foot measuring-rod. Often *fig.* = a standard of comparison.

Ya·rd-wand. late ME. [YARD *sb.*[2]] A 3-ft. measuring-rod.

Yare (yēəɹ), *a.* and *adv.* *arch.* and *dial.* [OE. *gearu, -o* adj. (*geara, -o, -e* adv.), prob. a compound of OTeut. **ga-* Y- prefix and **arw-*, represented by OE. *earu* ready.] **A.** *adj.* **1.** Ready, prepared OE. **2.** Brisk, quick ME. **b.** Of a ship: Responsive to the helm. late ME.

1. The gunner held his linstock y. SCOTT. 2. A halter'd necke, which do's the Hangman thanke, For being y. about him SHAKS.

B. *adv.* †Quickly, promptly –1513. **b.** As exclam.: = QUICK! esp. in nautical use. *arch.* 1606.

b. Cheerely my harts: y., y.: Take in the toppe-sale SHAKS.

Ya·rely, *adv.* *arch.* [OE. *gearolīce*; see YARE *a.* and -LY[2].] Promptly, briskly.

Come y. my mates DRYDEN.

Yark. See YERK.

Yarl. See JARL.

Yarmouth (yā·ɹməþ). 1614. Name of a fishing town on the Norfolk coast; used *attrib.* in *Y. bloater*, a slightly salted and smoked herring; also *transf.* a native of Y.

Yarn (yāɹn), *sb.* [OE. *gearn*, related (outside Teut.) to Lith. *žarna* intestine, L. *hira* empty gut, *haruspex* diviner by entrails, Gr. χορδή gut.] **1.** *orig.* Spun fibre, as of wool, flax, silk, cotton; now usu., fibre spun and prepared for use in weaving, knitting, etc. **b.** In Rope-making, one of the threads composing a strand, or these threads collectively 1627. **2.** *To spin a y.* (*fig.*, orig. *Naut. slang*), to tell a tale. Hence, *yarn* = a (long) tale, esp. a marvellous or incredible one 1812.

1. *fig.* The webbe of our life, is of a mingled yarne, good and ill together SHAKS. 2. Come, spin us a good y., father MARRYAT.

attrib. and *Comb.*: **y.-beam** *Weaving*, the roller on which y. is wound; **-spinner**, one who spins y. or who 'spins a y.'; **-wind, -windle**, an appliance for winding a skein of y. into a ball (*obs.* exc. *dial.*). Hence **Yarn** *v. colloq. intr.* to 'spin a y.', tell a story.

Yarrow (yæ·rou). [OE. *gearwe*, of uncertain etym.] The composite herb *Achillea Millefolium* or MILFOIL, common on waste land, with finely divided bipinnate leaves and close flat flower-clusters of a somewhat dull white, often varying to pink or crimson. **b. Soldier's Y.**, *Stratiotes aloides*. **Water Y.**, any of various water-plants with finely-divided leaves, as *Ranunculus aquatilis* and *Hottonia palustris*.

‖**Yashmak** (yæ·ʃmæk). 1844. [Arab. *yashmaq.*] The double veil concealing the lower part of the face, worn by Mohammedan women in public.

Yataghan (yæ·tăgæn). 1819. [Turk. *yātāghan.*] A sword of Mohammedan countries, having a handle without a guard and often a double-curved blade.

Yate (yēᵗ). 1830. [Native name.] Either of two species of gum-tree (*Eucalyptus cornuta* and *E. occidentalis*), of S.W. Australia, with tough wood; also, the wood itself.

Yaud (yǭd, yād). *Sc.* and *north.* 1500. [a. ON. *jalda.*] A mare, an old mare; a worn-out horse (assoc. w. JADE).

‖**Yava** (yā·vă). 1804. Variant of KAVA. Cf. AVA.

Yaw (yǭ), *sb.*[1] 1546. [Related to YAW *v.*] *Naut.* An act of yawing; a movement of deviation from the direct course, as from bad steering.

The boat took a sudden y. or sheer, which canted me overboard SMEATON.

Yaw, *sb.*[2] 1679. [Back-formation from YAWS apprehended as pl.] Each of the spots of eruption in yaws. **b.** As attrib. form of YAWS: **y.-house**, a hospital for persons affected with yaws; **y.-weed**, the shrub *Morinda Royoc*, used in the West Indies as a remedy for yaws.

Yaw, *v.* 1584. [Origin obsc.] **1.** *Naut.* *intr.* Of a vessel: To deviate temporarily from the straight course, as through faulty or unsteady steering. **2.** *trans.* To cause to yaw 1746.

1. *transf.* I shot ahead, and yawed a little—caught a peep at her through her veil MARRYAT.

Yaw-haw (yǭ·hǭ·), *sb.* and *v.* 1836. [Imitative.] = GUFFAW.

Yawl (yǭl), *sb.*[1] 1670. [app. ad. MLG. *jolle* or Du. *jol*, of unkn. origin.] **1.** A ship's boat resembling a pinnace, but smaller, usu. with four or six oars. **2.** A small sailing-boat of the cutter class, with a jigger 1684. **3.** A small fishing-boat 1670.

Yawl, *v.* Now *dial.* late ME. [Parallel to YOWL.] *intr.* and *trans.* To cry out loudly from pain, grief, or distress; to howl, scream, bawl: also said of the howling of dogs, the 'wauling' of cats, etc. Hence **Yawl** *sb.*[2], a howl, scream, yell.

Yawn (yǭn), *sb.* 1602. [f. next.] **1.** Something that yawns; a gaping aperture; *esp.* a chasm, abyss. **2.** The or an act of yawning. **a.** Gaping 1697. **b.** Involuntary opening of the mouth, as from drowsiness 1706.

1. Spaces of fire, and all the y. of hell KEATS. 2. b. Our salutation is a Y. and a Stretch STEELE.

Yawn, *v.* [OE. *ginian, geonian*; related to GANE *v.* The phonology of the present form is obscure.] †**1.** *intr.* To open the mouth wide voluntarily, esp. in order to swallow or devour something; to gape. Said also of the mouth. –1603. **2.** To lie, stand, or be wide open, as a chasm, gap, etc.; to have or form a wide opening, gap, or chasm OE. **3.** To show fatigue, drowsiness, or boredom by making (usu. involuntarily) a prolonged inspiration with the mouth wide open and the lower jaw dropped. late ME. **b.** *trans.* To say or utter with a yawn. Also with cognate obj. 1718. **c.** To open the mouth wide from surprise or the like, to gape. *Obs.* exc. *dial.* 1604. **d.** To bring into some position or condition by or to the accompaniment of yawning 1742. **4.** *intr.* To open wide as a mouth; to form a chasm; to gape 1599. **5.** *trans.* To make, produce, or afford by opening wide. *rare.* 1605.

1. Crocodiles lyinge in the sande, and yanyng to take the heate of the soonne 1555. 2. The gashes That bloodily did yawne vpon his face SHAKS. 3. The audience yawned through the play THACKERAY. c. *Oth.* v. ii. 101. d. Who y. away their existence in the assemblies of London 1817. 4. Graues yawne and yeelde your dead SHAKS. Hence **Yaw·ner**, one who yawns; something that yawns, a wide ditch.

Yawning (yǭ·niŋ), *ppl. a.* OE. [f. prec. + -ING[2].] That yawns. **b.** *transf.* Characterized by or producing yawning; drowsy, soporific 1575.

b. The shard-borne Beetle, with his drowsie hums, Hath rung Nights y. Peale SHAKS. Hence **Yaw·n-ingly** *adv.*

Yawny (yǭ·ni), *a.* 1805. [f. YAWN *sb.* + -Y[1].] Inclined to or provocative of yawning.

Yawp, yaup (yǭp), *v.* Chiefly *dial.* late ME. [Echoic.] To utter a strident call; to yelp, as a dog; to cry harshly or querulously, as a bird. Hence **Yawp, yaup** *sb.* a harsh, hoarse, or querulous cry, esp. of a bird; *fig.* speech or utterance likened to this.

Yaws (yǭz). 1679. [Origin uncertain.] A contagious disease of negroes, characterized by raspberry-like tubercles on the skin; also called *frambœsia*. Hence **Yaw·y** *a.*

Yaw-yaw (yǭ·yǭ·), *v.* 1854. [Echoic.] *intr.* To talk affectedly.

They liked fine gentlemen..and they yaw-yawed in their speech like them DICKENS.

†**Yble·nt**, *pa. pple.*[1] ME. [f. BLEND *v.*[1]; see Y- 4.] Blinded; dazed –1590.

The eye of reason was with rage y. SPENSER.

†**Yble·nt**, *pa. pple.*[2] late ME. [f. BLEND *v.*[2]; see Y- 4.] Mingled –1748.

†**Ybo·rn**, *pa. pple.* [OE. *geboren*; pa. pple. of (*ge*)*beran* BEAR *v.*[1]] **1.** Born –1755. **2.** Borne –1642.

†**Ybre·nt**, *pa. pple.* ME. [See BURN *v.*[1] and Y- 4.] Burnt –1767.

With feverish Thirste y. 1767.

Yclad (iklæ·d), *pa. pple.* *arch.* ME. [See CLAD and Y- 4.] Clothed.

Spring y. in grassy dye BYRON.

Yclept (ikle·pt), **ycleped** (iklī·pt, *poet.* iklī·pėd), *pa. pple.* *arch.* [OE. *geclypod*, pa. pple. of (*ge*)*clypian* CLEPE; see Y- 4.] Called (so-and-so), named, styled. (A frequent poetic or serio-comic archaism.)

But com thou Goddes fair and free, In Heav'n yclept Euphrosyne MILT. The sweet wood yclept sassafras LAMB.

Ye (yī, yĭ), *pers. pron. 2nd pers. nom.* (*obj.*), *pl.* (*sing.*). Now *arch.*, *poet.*, or *dial.*; in ordinary use replaced by YOU. [OE. *ge*, modified (on the analogy of *we*) f. OTeut. **jūs*, **juz.* (Gothic *jus*; cf. Lith. *yūs*, Skr. *yū-yám*). Orig. restricted to the nom. pl., *ye* came in the 13th c. to be used instead of the sing. to a superior, and later to any single person; and, when *you* displaced it as the ordinary nom., it came to be used, vice versa, as obj. sing. and pl.] **1.** As the nom. or voc. pl. of THOU, used in addressing a number of persons OE. **b.** In apposition with a following sb. in the vocative. late ME. **2.** Used instead of *thou* in addressing a single person (orig. as a sign of respect or deference) ME. **3.** Used instead of *you* as obj. sing. or pl. 1449.

1. Ye [*1st Pr. Bk.* 1549 You] that do truly and earnestly repent you of your sins *Bk. Com. Pr.* 1662. But ye at home, ye bore the brunt BRIDGES. b. Ye holy Angels bright 1681. 2. Good lord, ye created & made our fader Adam CAXTON. 'Damsel', he said, 'ye be not all to blame' TENNYSON. 3. As I haue made ye one Lords, one remaine SHAKS.

Ye, ye, graphic var. *þe, þe* THE; see Y.

Yea (yē¹), *adv.* (*sb.*). Now *dial.* and *arch.* [OE. (WS.) *gēa*, (Anglian) *gē*:—OTeut. **ja, je.*] **A.** *adv.* A word used to express affirmation or assent: now ordinarily replaced by YES. **1.** = YES 1, 2, 3, 4. **†2.** Even, truly, verily –1581. **3.** Introducing a question or remark in reply to a statement, etc., expressing either vague assent or (more commonly) opposition or objection: = 'Indeed?'; 'Well', 'well then' ME.

1. Thei..seiden to hym, 3oure maister payeth nat tribute? And he seith, 3he WYCLIF *Matt.* xvii. 23. He asked whether our countrey had warres? I answered him y. 1611. Some of them use improper, yea, indecent, expressions in prayer WESLEY. *To say y.*, to answer in the affirmative; hence, to give assent; They praed them to say..playnly ye or nay 1440. 2. They fell a chydynge..Ye, dyd they so? SKELTON. Y., is it come to this? SHAKS.

B. *sb.* **1.** An utterance of the word 'yea'; an affirmative reply or statement; an expression of assent ME. **b.** Affirmation, assurance, certainty, absolute truth. late ME. **2.** An affirmative vote; a person who votes in the affirmative. Usu. *pl.* Still in use in U.S. Congress. 1657. **3.** *Yea and nay* (or *no*): positive and negative statement (or command); affirmation and denial; *occas.*, shilly-shally. late ME. **b.** *By yea and nay*, a substitute for an oath 1588.

1. Let youre ye be ye, and youre naye naye TINDALE *James* v. 12. Their No should be as welcome unto him as their Yea 1611. b. Love God. This is the Everlasting Yea. CARLYLE. 2. If one fifth of a quorum demand a call of yeas and nays, this is taken BRYCE. 3. These two went on, With yea and nay, and pro and con PRIOR. *attrib.* One of your water-gruel, yea-and-nay good boys 1781. b. He swore by yea and nay He would have no denial 1661.

Comb.: **y.-forsooth** *a.*, addicted to saying 'yea forsooth' in the way of superficial assent; **-word**, a word of assent. Hence **Yea** *v. intr.* to say y.; to reply affirmatively.

Yean (yīn), *v.* *arch.* and *dial.* late ME. [perh. OE. **geēanian*, related to *geēan* pregnant; see Y- and EAN *v.*] **1.** *trans.* Of a ewe: To bring forth (a lamb); also said of goats. **2.** *intr.* To bring forth young, as a sheep 1548.

Yeanling (yī·nliŋ). *arch.* 1637. [f. prec. + -LING¹.] A young lamb or kid. **b.** appositive or as *adj.* That is a y.; young or new-born; esp. of a lamb.

Year (yīəɹ). [OE. (WS.) *gēar*, (Anglian) *gēr*:—OTeut. **jǣrom*, cogn. with Gr. ὧρος year, ὥρα season, OSl. *jarŭ* spring. The OE. pl. *gēar* is represented still in dial. usage.] **1.** The time occupied by the sun in its apparent passage through the signs of the zodiac; the period of the earth's revolution round the sun, forming a natural unit of time (nearly = 365¼ days); hence, a space of time approximately equal to this in any conventional practical reckoning OE. **b.** Following and qualifying a date: = a year before or after... 1533. **c.** In ref. to the duration of some (usu. painful) experience, as a term of imprisonment, etc. ME. **d.** *pl.* with numeral, expressing a person's age ME. **2. a.** With qualifying words, denoting periods differing in length according to the manner in which they are computed in some scientific or conventional reckoning, as *anomalistic, astronomical, canicular, civil, embolismic, equinoctial, Gregorian, Julian, lunar, lunisolar, natural, sidereal, solar, Sothic, tropical, vague year.* **b.** *transf.* Applied to a very long period or cycle. late ME. **c.** The period of a planet's revolution round the sun (*planetary y.*) 1728. **3.** A space of time, of the length stated in sense 1, with fixed limits. **a.** *esp.* Such a space of time as reckoned in a calendar and denoted by a number in a particular era; also called the *civil y.*; in the ordinary or Roman calendar beginning on 1st Jan., divided into twelve months, and having 365 (or 366) days OE. **b.** Such a space of time, with limits not necessarily coinciding with those of the civil year, forming a division of a period (or the whole period) of office, study, etc., or taken between definite dates for some special purpose, e.g. taxation, etc. OE. **c.** Such a space of time as arranged for religious observance in the Christian Church, beginning with Advent. late ME. **4.** The round of the seasons. late ME. **5.** *pl.* Age (of a person) OE. **b.** Maturity; old age (esp. in phr. *in years* = old, aged). Now *arch.* or *poet.* 1579. **6.** *pl.* Times; a spell of time, one's time or period of life ME. **b.** Chiefly *pl.* A very long time, 'ages' 1692.

1. He will last you some eight yeare SHAKS. b. On the day y. on which he had received our Lord's servants into his house 1873. c. If he was not careful she could get him fifteen years 1901. d. A nurse of ninety years TENNYSON. 2. b. *Cynic y.*: see CYNIC *a.* 3. *Great y.* (Gr. μέγας ἐνιαυτός), the period (variously reckoned) after which all the heavenly bodies were supposed to return to their original positions; also called *Platonic y.* c. According to the Neptunian calendar, it is only thirty-six years since the creation of Adam 1870. 3. Dr. Pauli.. gives the day and the month, without remembering to add the y. 1861. *Y. of Christ, of our Lord, of grace*, a particular year of the Christian era (denoted by a number following). b. The relative positions which the boys of each y. had occupied in the school 1848. c. The first Sunday in Advent was not always the beginning of the liturgical y. 1875. 4. Shatter your leaves before the mellowing y. MILT. The varying y. with blade and sheaf Clothes and reclothes the happy plains TENNYSON. 5. Vane, young in yeares, but in sage counsell old MILT. 6. The state of painting in this country of late years H. WALPOLE. b. We live years of emotion in a few weeks THACKERAY.

Phrases. **A y.**, every y., *per annum.* **Y. after y., y. by y., from y. to y.**, through a succession of years; every y. successively. **Y. in (and) y. out**, as each y. begins and until it ends; continually throughout the y. (and through successive years). **Y. and day** (*Law*), a period constituting a term for some purposes, in order to ensure the completion of a full y.

Year-book (yīə·ɹbuk). 1588. **1.** *pl.* The books of reports of cases in the English law-courts published annually during several periods from the reign of Edw. II to that of Hen. VIII. **2.** A book published annually and containing the latest information for the year; an annual on its subject 1710.

Yearling (yīə·ɹliŋ), *sb.* and *a.* 1465. [f. YEAR + -LING¹.] **A.** *sb.* **1.** An animal a year old, or in its second year (esp. a sheep, calf, or foal). **b.** *transf.* The fleece of a y. sheep 1888. **2.** A plant a year old; *spec.* applied to hops of the previous year's growth 1849. **B.** *adj.* A year old; in its second year; of the previous year's growth 1528.

Yea·r-long, *a.* 1813. [f. YEAR + LONG *a.*¹; cf. OE. *gēarlanges* adv. for a year.] Lasting for a year; lasting for years in succession; *occas.*, age-long.

Through y. hours of hope and woe 1871. The year-long alliance between philosophy and theology 1886.

Yearly (yīə·ɹli), *a.* [OE. *gēarlic*; see YEAR and -LY¹.] **†1.** Of the year; belonging or relating to a year (*rare*) –1811. **2.** Of or in each year; happening, etc., once a year; annual OE.

1. The varietie..of the yearely seasons PURCHAS.

Yea·rly, *adv.* [OE. *gēarlīce*; see YEAR and -LY².] Every year, once a year, annually.

He gave y. great sums in charity 1715.

Yearn (yɔ̄ɹn), *v.*¹ [OE. (Northumb.) *giorna*, (Mercian) *geornan*, (WS.) *giernan*, related to *georn* eager:—Teut. **ger-*; cf. Gr. χαίρειν to rejoice, L. *hortari* to cheer.] **†1.** *trans.* To long for –1568. **2.** *intr.* To have a longing: **a.** Const. inf. with *to* OE. **b.** Const. *after, for, †to, towards.* Also *absol.* OE. **†3.** Of hounds: To give tongue –1680. **4.** To express yearning or strong desire; also *trans.* to utter in an emotional voice 1816. **5.** To be deeply moved, esp. with pity or tenderness 1500. **†6.** *trans.* To move to compassion –1641.

2. a. The child yearned to be out of doors DICKENS. b. His heart yearned after the damsel W. IRVING. 4. The music, yearning like a God in pain KEATS. The faces of thy ministers Yearned pale with bitter ecstasy ROSSETTI. The kind of voice..in which..actresses y. out passages from 'The Cenci' 1894. 5. Her bowelles yerned vpon her sonne BIBLE (Great) 1 *Kings* iii. 26. Her Heart yearns towards you ADDISON. 6. She laments Sir for it, that it would yern your heart to see it SHAKS. Hence **Yearn** *sb.* a yearning. **Yea·rner. Yea·rnful** *a.* mournful. **Yea·rning** *vbl. sb.*¹ the action of the vb., an instance of this; *ppl. a.* that yearns; **-ly** *adv.*

Yearn (yɔ̄ɹn), *v.*² Chiefly *Sc.* and *n. dial.* late ME. [prob. dial. var. of EARN *v.*²] **a.** *intr.* To coagulate, curdle. **b.** *trans.* To curdle (milk); to make (cheese) of curdled milk. Hence **Yea·rning** *vbl. sb.*² rennet.

Yea·r-old, *a.* and *sb.* 1539. **A.** *adj.* A year old. 1767. **B.** *sb.* A yearling 1539.

Year's mind, yea·r-mind. [OE. *gēargemynd*; see YEAR and MIND *sb.*] The commemoration of a deceased person by requiem services on the first or on each anniversary of his death or funeral.

The 'Year's Mind' of her late Majesty Queen Victoria 1902.

Yeast (yīst); *formerly and now dial.* **yest**, *sb.* [OE. *gist*; related to Gr. ζέω I boil.] **1.** A yellowish substance produced by the propagation of a fungus (*Saccharomyces cerevisiæ*) as a froth (*top* or *surface y.*) or sediment (*bottom, under*, or *sediment y.*) during the alcoholic fermentation of malt worts and other saccharine fluids, and used in making beer, leavening bread, and medicinally. **b.** *fig.* = LEAVEN *sb.* 2 a. 1760. **2.** *transf.* Foam or froth 1611.

1. b. The best of men have but a portion of good in them—a kind of spiritual y. KEATS.

attrib. and *Comb.*: **y.-cake**, y. drained and pressed for keeping; also, a cake resembling a dough-cake; **-plant**, any plant of the genus *Saccharomyces*, esp. *S. cerevisiæ.* Hence **Yeast** *v. intr.* to ferment, to form froth (*rare*).

Yeasty (yī·sti), *a.* 1598. [f. prec. + -Y¹.] **1.** Of, full of, or like yeast 1599. **2.** *fig.* In a ferment; acting like leaven; turbid and restless; light and superficial 1598. **3.** *transf.* Frothy, foamy 1605. Hence **Yea·stily** *adv.* **Yea·stiness.**

Yegg (yeg). *U.S.* 1903. [Said to be a surname.] A burglar or safe-breaker. So **Ye·ggman.**

Yeld (yeld), *a.* (*sb.*). *Sc.* and *n. dial.* [Late OE. **gielde, gelde*; cf. GELD *a.* and *v.*¹] **A.** *adj.* **1.** Of an animal: Barren; that has missed having her young, or is not old enough to bear. **2.** Of cattle: Not yielding milk 1670. **3.** *transf.* Unproductive 1721. **B.** *sb.* A barren cow or ewe; a hind that is not pregnant 1856.

‖**Yelek** (ye·lek). 1836. [Turk.] A long vest worn by Turkish women.

Yelk: see YOLK.

Yell (yel), *sb.* late ME. [f. next.] An act of yelling; a sharp loud outcry. **b.** *U.S.* The distinctive cheer used by the students of any particular college. 1889.

Once or twice the Indian y. was given 1841.

Yell, *v.* [OE. (Anglian) *gellan*, (WS.) *giellan*, related to *galan* GALE *v.*¹] **1.** *intr.* To utter a loud strident cry, esp. from some strong or sudden emotion, as rage, horror, or agony ME. **b.** Of some birds and beasts: To emit a strident cry, either as their natural utterance or when hurt or from rage OE. **2.** *trans.* To utter with a yell ME.

1. She yelled out on seeing him SCOTT. b. The Dogges did y. SHAKS. 2. Yelling their uncouth dirge BYRON.

Yelloch (ye·ləχ), *sb.* and *v.* *Sc.* 1513. [app. f. prec.] = YELL *sb.* and *v.*

Yellow (ye·loᵘ), *a.* and *sb.* [OE. *geolu, -o*:—OTeut. **gelwo-*:—Indo-Eur. **ghelwo-* (cf. L. *helvus* and GOLD *sb.*).] **A.** *adj.* **1.** Of the colour of gold, butter, yolk of egg, etc.; constituting the most luminous primary colour, occurring in the spectrum between green and orange. **b.** Of the complexion in age or disease; also as the colour of faded leaves, ripe corn, or old paper;

hence *allus.* OE. c. Having a naturally yellow skin or complexion, as the people of the Mongolian races; hence = MONGOLIAN A. 2. 1834. d. Applied to naval captains retired as rear admirals in H.M. Fleet without being attached to a particular squadron (red, white, or blue) 1788. e. *transf.* Dressed in yellow 1848. †2. *fig.* Jealous –1858. 3. Applied to newspapers (or writers of newspaper articles) of a recklessly or unscrupulously sensational character (orig. *U.S.*: from a picture in the *New York World*, 1895, with the central figure in a yellow dress) 1898.

1. This Pardoner hadde heer as yelow as wex CHAUCER. b. *Macb.* v. iii. 23. c. *The y. peril*, a supposed danger of a destructive invasion of Europe by Asiatic peoples. 2. Your y. humour interprets this to be too much familiarity 1665. Phr. † *To wear y. hose* or *stockings*, to be jealous. b. Craven, cowardly 1896.

B. *sb.* 1. The colour described in A. 1, or a pigment, fabric, or stuff of this colour ME. b. With qualifying words, denoting shades of the colour, as *brass-, primrose-, sulphur-y.*, or various pigments and dyes, as *aniline, Naples y.*, etc., for which see the first element 1532. 2. A yellow object, substance, part, etc., as the yolk of an egg, sulphur, a kind of turnip, etc. 1738. b. A particular yellow species or variety of bird, butterfly, or moth 1816. 3. A member of a yellow race, a Mongolian. Only *pl.* 1808. 4. As the colour of a party badge; hence *transf.* a member of a party whose colour is yellow 1755. 5. A 'yellow' newspaper (see A. 3) 1898. 6. In specialized uses of the pl. in sing. sense: a. (*The*) *yellows*, jaundice, esp. in beasts 1561. †b. (*The*) *yellows*, jealousy –1638. c. (*The*) *yellows*, a disease of wheat or of peach-trees (*peach-yellows*) 1771. d. *Yellows*, a name for certain plants yielding a yellow dye, as *Genista tinctoria* and *Reseda luteola*; *dial.*, the yellow-flowered wild mustard and the wild cabbage 1601.

1. Elms, whose fallen leaves have made the road one y. 1824. c. Cowardice; meanness (cf. A. 2 b) 1896.

Collocations and *Combs.*: **y. admiral** (see A. 1 d); **-ammer**, see YELLOW-HAMMER; **y. atrophy**, atrophy and y. discoloration of the liver with jaundice; **-back**, a cheap y.-backed (esp. French) novel; **y. bark**, any kind of Peruvian bark of a y. colour; **-beak** = BEJAN; **-belly**, a frog; *transf.* a native of the fens; a kind of tortoise, or its shell; western *U.S.* a Mexican or half-caste; any of various fishes having the underparts y.; **y. berries**, the fruit of *Rhamnus infectorius* and other species, yielding a y. die; **-bill**, any of various birds with a y. bill, as the Amer. scoter; **-bird**, any of several birds having y. plumage; now esp. the N. Amer. goldfinch, *Chrysomitris* (*Spinus, Carduelis*) *tristis*, and the N. Amer. summer warbler (*summer y.-bird*), *Dendrœca æstiva*; **-boy** (*slang*; now *rare* or *Obs.*), a gold coin, a guinea or sovereign; **y. cartilage**, *Anat.* cartilage containing y. *fibres*; **-cup**, a buttercup; **y. deal**, the wood of the Scotch fir, *Pinus sylvestris*; **y. earth**, a yellowish clay, coloured by iron, used as a pigment; **y. fever**, a highly fatal infectious febrile disease of hot climates, characterized by vomiting, constipation, jaundice, etc.; **y. fibre**, *Anat.* one of the elastic fibres of a y. colour occurring in certain tissues; **-fin**, any of various fishes with y. fins; **-fish**, any of various fishes with y. coloration; now esp. a species of rock-trout, *Pleurogrammus* (*Hexagrammus*) *monopterygius*, of the coast of Alaska; **y. flag**, one displayed on a ship as a signal of infectious disease or quarantine; **Y. George** (see GEORGE II. 2); **y. gum**, jaundice in infants, characterized by yellowness of the gums; **y. jack** *slang* = *y. fever*; **-jacket**, *U.S. colloq.* a wasp or hornet; **y. metal**, an alloy of two parts of copper and one of zinc, used for sheathing vessels; **y. ore**, copper pyrites; **-pate**, the yellow-hammer; **y. peril** (see A. 1 c); **y. plague**, jaundice; **ye·llowplush**, plush of a y. colour, as worn by footmen; hence *transf. joc.*, a footman; **y. press** (see A. 3); **-rattle** (see RATTLE *sb.* I. 3 a); **-root**, (the root of) two N. Amer. ranunculaceous plants, *Hydrastis canadensis* (*Canadian y.-root* or *golden seal*) and *Xanthorrhiza apiifolia* (*shrub y.-root*), yielding y. dyes, and used as tonics; **Y. Sally**, a species of stone-fly used as a bait by anglers; **yellowseed**, *Lepidium campestre*, mithridate mustard (pepperwort); **y. sickness**, jaundice; **y. soap**, a common soap made of tallow, rosin, and soda; **y. spot**, *Anat.* a yellowish circular depression in the middle of the retina, being the region of most distinct vision; **yellowtail**, (*a*) any of various fishes, chiefly of N. America and Australasia as species of *Seriola, Caranx*, and *Latris*; (*b*) collector's name for a species of moth, also called *gold-tail*; **y. ware**, y. earthenware or stoneware; **-weed**, (*a*) *dial.* dyer's-weed, *Reseda luteola*; (*b*) common ragwort, *Senecio Jacobæa*; (*c*) *U.S.* various species of golden-rod (*Solidago*); **-wood**, any of various trees and shrubs having y. wood, or the wood of any of these; **-wort**, y. centaury. Hence **Ye·llow-ly** (*rare*) *adv.*, **-ness. Ye·llowy** *a.* = YELLOWISH.

Ye·llow, *v.* OE. [f. YELLOW *a.*] 1. *intr.* To become yellow. 2. *trans.* To make yellow 1598. b. *Naut. colloq.* To make a 'yellow admiral' of (see YELLOW A. 1 d) 1747.

Yellow dog. *U.S.* 1840. 1. A mongrel dog or cur, of a yellow or yellowish colour. 2. *fig.* A person or thing of no account or of a low type 1903. b. *attrib.*; applied *spec.* to organizations, etc. opposed to trade-unionism 1902.

Ye·llow-ha:mmer, -a:mmer. 1556. Also **Ye·llow ham** 1544, now *dial.* [The earliest recorded form, *yelambre*, is prob. f. YELLOW *a.* + OE. *amore* (*omer, emer, emær*) an unidentified bird; the origin and identity of the forms *ham, hamer, -ere* are uncertain.] A species of bunting, *Emberiza citrinella*, with yellow head, throat, and under parts. b. *U.S.* The golden-winged woodpecker, *Colaptes auratus* 1857.

Ye·llowish, *a.* late ME. [-ISH¹.] Somewhat yellow. Hence **Ye·llowishness.**

Yelm (yelm), *sb. dial.* [OE. *gielm* handful, sheaf.] A bundle of straw laid straight for thatching. **Yelm** *v.* (*dial.*) *trans.* and *intr.*

Yelp (yelp), *sb.* [OE. *gielp* vainglory; cf. next.] †1. Boasting. –late ME. 2. A dog's shrill bark of excitement or distress 1500.

2. *transf.* How is it that we hear the loudest yelps for liberty among the drivers of negroes? JOHNSON.

Yelp (yelp), *v.* [OE. *gielpan*:—**galpjan.*] †1. To boast –late ME. †2. To cry aloud; to sing shrilly –1549. 3. *intr.* To utter a yelp or yelps 1553. 4. *fig.* To complain, whine 1706. 5. *trans.* To express yelpingly 1654. Hence **Ye·lping** *vbl. sb.* and *ppl. a.*

Yelper (ye·lpəɹ). ME. [f. prec. + -ER¹.] †1. A boaster. ME. only. 2. An animal or person that yelps; e. g. a whelp, the avocet (*local*), a young partridge 1673. b. *slang.* A town-crier 1725. 3. *contempt.* A speaker or writer whose utterance is compared to a dog's yelp 1673.

3. In the house of commons he was the terror of that species of orators called the Yelpers SCOTT.

Yelt (yelt). *dial.* [Late OE. *gilte*:—**galtjōn-*. Cf. GILT *sb.*²] A young sow.

‖**Yen** (yen). 1875. [Japanese, ad. Chin. *yüan* round, dollar.] A gold or silver coin, the monetary unit of Japan since 1871, formerly of about the value of the U.S. dollar, now of about two shillings. Also *collect.* as *pl.*

Yengees (ye·ŋgīz), *pl.* 1819. Stated to be a N. Amer. Indian corruption of *English*, applied to the people of New England.

Yeoman (yōᵘ·măn). *Pl.* **yeomen** (yōᵘ·mĕn). [ME. *ȝoman, ȝeman*, etc., prob. reduced forms of *ȝongman* = *youngman* servant, attendant, f. YOUNG *a.* + MAN *sb.*] 1. A servant or attendant in a royal or noble household, usu. ranking between a sergeant and a groom or between a squire and a page. b. An attendant or assistant to an official, etc. late ME. c. *Yeoman('s) service*, good, efficient, or useful service 1602. 2. With *of* (or *for*), in official titles, as *y. of the cellar, revels, robes, wardrobe, y. for the household* ME.; also in burlesque titles, as *y. of the cord*, hangman 1640. b. *Y. of the Guard*, a member of the sovereign's body-guard, instituted at the accession of Henry VII 1485. *Y. extraordinary* (*of the Guard*), any of the warders of the Tower 1552. c. In the British and U.S. navies, an inferior officer in charge of stores, as *y. of the signals, engineer's y.* 1669. 3. Appositive in the titles of various attendants and officials, as *y. bedel, farrier, pricker, usher.* late ME. 4. A man owning and cultivating a small estate; a freeholder under the rank of gentleman; *loosely*, a countryman of respectable standing, a farmer. late ME. 5. A yeoman (as in 4) serving as a (foot) soldier. Now *arch.* or *Hist.* late ME. b. *spec.* A member of the (Imperial) Yeomanry (see YEOMANRY 2) 1798.

1. Knyȝt, squiere, ȝomon & page 1420. The kyng callyd vpon hys knyghtes squyers and yemen MALORY. b. The senior Sheriff's y. read Her Majesty's writ 1861. c. I once did hold it..A basenesse to write faire; ..but Sir now, It did me Yeomans seruice SHAKS. 2. William Pratte, Yoman for the King's mouth 1455. Extraordinary Y.: see BEEFEATER 2. 3. The Yeomen Ushers of Devotion MILT. 4. Yeoman: which worde now signifieth among vs, a man well at ease and hauing honestlie to liue, and yet not a gentleman 1577. My father was a Yoman, and had no landes of his owne, onlye he had a farme LATIMER. Those only who rent..are, properly speaking, farmers. Those who till their own land are yeomen. COBBETT.

Yeomanly (yōᵘ·mănli), *a.* 1576. [f. prec. + -LY¹.] 1. Having the rank or the character of a yeoman. 2. Of, characteristic of, or befitting a yeoman; sturdy; homely 1626.

Yeo·manly, *adv.* ME. [f. as prec. + -LY².] In a yeomanly manner.

Wel koude he dresse his takel yemanly CHAUCER.

Yeomanry (yōᵘ·mănri). late ME. [f. YEOMAN + -RY.] 1. The body of small landed proprietors; yeomen collectively. b. *Hist.* The freemen of a livery company 1497. 2. A British volunteer cavalry force first embodied in 1794 and consisting chiefly of men of the yeomanry class or status 1794.

Imperial Y., a corps recruited for service in the South African War (1899–1902) from the y., the volunteers, and civilians; the title was subsequently extended to the original y. and was retained till 1908.

Yeowoman (yōᵘ·wu:măn). *Pl.* **yeowomen** (-wi:mĕn). 1852. [After YEOMAN.] A woman having the rank or position of a yeoman.

Yep, *dial.* (esp. *U.S.*) pron. of YES. Cf. NOPE².

-yer, *suffix*, var. of -IER, esp. after *w*, as *bowyer, lawyer, sawyer.*

‖**Yerba-maté** (yɔ̄·ɹbă mæ·te). Also simply yerba (yerva). 1818. [Sp. *yerba* herb + *mate* MATÉ.] = MATÉ 2.

‖**Yercum** (yɔ̄·ɹkŏm). 1826. [Tamil.] Either of two East Indian shrubs, *Calotropis gigantea* and *C. procera*, or the fibre of their bark, used medicinally.

Yerk, yark (yɔ̄ɹk, yāɹk), *v.* Now *Sc.* and *dial.* [Late ME. *yerk*; origin obsc.] 1. In shoe-making: *intr.* To draw stitches tight, to twitch; *trans.* to sew (leather, etc.) thus. 2. *trans.* To strike smartly, esp. with a rod or whip 1520. b. To crack (a whip) 1566. 3. *fig.* To lash, beat (as with sharp words or treatment) 1593. b. *intr.* To carp *at* 1621. 4. *trans.* To push or pull suddenly; to jerk 1568. 5. To fling out (the heels, etc.), *intr.* to lash or strike *out* with the heels, to kick 1565.

1. His hands and feet are yerked as tight as cords can be drawn SCOTT. 2. Like as the carter..yerketh his horsse with the whyp COVERDALE. 3. Aye, Satan! does that y. ye? KEATS. 5. Their wounded steeds.. Yerke out their armed heeles at their dead masters SHAKS. Hence **Yerk, yark,** *sb.* a smart blow; a horse's kick; a jerk 1509.

Yerva: see YERBA.

Yes (yes), *adv.* (*sb.*). [OE. *gēse, gise, gȳse*, pointing to early WS. **gīese*:—**gēasī*, prob. f. *gēa* YEA + *sī*, 3 sing. pres. subj. of *bēon* to be.] A word used to express an affirmative reply to a question, statement, command, etc. A. *adv.* 1. In answer to a question not involving a negative; = 'It is so'. (Formerly usu. more emphatic than *yea* or *aye*; in later use taking the place of these.) 2. a. In answer to a question involving a negative. (Formerly regularly used thus, and as in b, in distinction from *yea*; the distinction became obsolete soon after 1600 (but is retained in the 1611 transl. of the Bible), and since then *yes* has been the ordinary affirmative particle in reply to any question positive or negative.) OE. b. In contradiction of or opposition to a negative statement expressed or implied, or a negative command or request. (Now usu. accompanied by a short asseverative phr. echoing the preceding statement.) ME. 3. Expressing assent to a command, request, proposal, or summons ME. b. Expressing assent to a statement or implication. late ME. c. In iron. assent, or conceding something as true but irrelevant or immaterial; often *Yes, but* or impatiently *Yes, yes* 1596. d. (Usu. interrog.) Inviting a speaker to repeat, confirm, or amplify what he has said, or expressing provisional acceptance of a statement 1842. 4. Used to emphasize or strengthen the speaker's own preceding statement 1598. ¶*O yes*: see OYEZ.

1. Þanne þe kyng com, and þe pope axede of hym ȝif he hadde i-holde his oth..Þe kyng..seide 'Ȝis al at þe fulle' TREVISA. *To say y.*, to assent, comply; *spec.* to accept a proposal of marriage. *Yes and No*, a round game, in which questions are asked which must be answered only by one of these words. 2. Myn hertes greef, mote I not wepe? O yis. 1400. b. Knowest hym ought? *Lamaunt.* Yhe, dame, parde.

Raisoun. Nay, nay. *Lamaunt.* Yhis, I. 1400. 3. c. *Jew*..May I speake with Anthonio? *Bass.* If it please you to dine with vs. *Jew.* Yes, to smell porke. SHAKS. 'It was the *best* butter..' 'Yes, but some crumbs must have got in as well.' 'L. CARROLL'. d. My landlady's daughter..Says 'Yes?' when you tell her anything. O. W. HOLMES. 4. 'The race of Dermid, whose children murdered—yes, she added, with a wild shriek, 'murdered your mother's fathers' SCOTT.

B. *sb.* (Pl. *yes's, yeses.*) An utterance of the word 'yes'; an affirmative reply, or expression of assent 1712. **Yes** *v. intr.* to say 'yes' 1820.

attrib. **Yes-man** (*U.S. slang*), a person who agrees with everything that is said to him.

Yester (ye·stəɹ), *a. poet.* 1577. [The first element of *yesterday*, etc. treated as a separate word.] Of yesterday.

Yester-, in comb. or as prefix = immediately preceding the present, last; in *y.-afternoon, -age, -noon, -week*; YESTEREVE, etc.

Yesterday (ye·stəɹdeⁱ, -di), *adv.* and *sb.* [OE. *geostran, gystran dæg*; the first element, which was used in the other Teut. languages without *day*, has the form of a comp. *ghistr-, *ghjestr-, of Indo-eur. *ghjes; cf. Skr. *hyás*, Gr. χθές, L. *heri* yesterday.] A. *adv.* 1. On the day immediately preceding the present day. Also, in reported speech, on the day before. 2. *transf.* Not long ago, recently. late ME.

1. He..was to dine, as y., with the Frasers JANE AUSTEN. 2. Towns that y. were hamlets 1856. Provb. phr. *Not born y.*, too old to be gulled.

B. *sb.* 1. The day next before this, also *pl.* past days OE. 2. *transf.* Time not long past. late ME. 3. *attrib.* with times of the day: *y. afternoon, evening, morning, night, noon* sbs. or advs. 1654.

1. Did you receive my yesterday's note? BYRON. 2. Lo, all our pomp of y. Is one with Nineveh and Tyre! KIPLING. So **Yestere·ve** *adv.* and *sb.* (*poet.*) 1603 = y. evening. **Yester·e·ven, -e'en** (-ī·n) *arch.* and *dial.* late ME. **Yester·e·vening** *adv.* and *sb. arch.* 1715 (in) the evening of y. **Yestermo·rn** *adv.* and *sb.* (*poet.*) 1702. **Yester-mo·rning** *adv.* and *sb.* (*arch.* and *dial.*) (in) the morning of y. 1654.

Yesternight (yestəɹnəi·t), *adv.* and *sb.* Chiefly *dial.* and *arch.* [OE., f. *gystran* (see YESTERDAY) + *niht* NIGHT *sb.*] A. *adv.* On the night of yesterday, last night. B. *sb.* The night last past 1513.

Yester-year (yestəɹyīə·ɹ). 1870. [Coined by D. G. Rossetti to render F. *antan* (Villon).] Last year.

Yestreen (yestrī·n), *adv.* and *sb.* Chiefly *Sc.* and *poet.* late ME. [MSc. *ȝystrewin* = *ȝystir-* YESTER- + *ewin* EVEN *sb.* in the 16th c. contr. to *ȝistrene*; taken up by English writers in the 18th c.] A. *adv.* On the evening of yesterday. B. *sb.* Yesterday evening 1816.

Yet, *v. dial.* [OE. *ġēotan*.] To pour, shed; to cast (metal, a metal object).

Yet (yet), *adv.* and *conj.* [OE. *ġīet(a* of obsc. origin.] A. *adv.* 1. In addition, or in continuation; besides; moreover. With numerals, etc. = 'more', as *y. a, y. one* = 'another', 'one more'. Now *arch.* exc. with *again* or *once more.* b. Used to strengthen a comparative: Even, still OE. c. Emphasizing *nor*: *nor y.* = and also not ME. 2. Temporal uses: a. Now (or then) as before; still OE. b. Followed by an inf. referring to the future, and thus implying incompleteness 1659. c. Up to this (or that) time; thus far; with a superlative, *only*, etc., = at any time up to now (or then) OE. d. By this (or that) time, so soon as this (or that). Usu. in questions to which the negative answer would be *not y.* ME. e. *Ere yet*, before the coming of the time when. *arch.* 1643. f. *Not* or *never yet*, not by this (or that) time, not up to now (or then): implying the possibility of subsequent change OE. g. With neg. following. *Obs.* or *arch.* exc. when preceded by *even* or *as.* OE. h. At some future time; hereafter; before all is over; after all, even now OE. i. Even now (though not till now); sometimes implying 'while there is still time' OE. j. Henceforth (or thenceforth). Usu., now only, with words denoting time; often replaceable by 'to come'. OE. k. *As y.*, hitherto, up to this time. late ME.

1. Yet once more, O ye Laurels..I com to pluck your Berries MILT. b. I purpose to dive y. more deeply into the depth of my Text 1626. c. I..founde noo faute in this man..No nor yett Herode TINDALE *Luke* xxiii. 15. 2. a. While her Beauty was y. in all its Height and Bloom ADDISON. Till you have finish'd these that are y. unprinted POPE. c. This is the queerest thing y.! SCOTT. d. Haue you enquir'd y. who pick'd my Pocket? SHAKS. e. Ere y. from Orleans to the war we went SOUTHEY. f. The tyme of fygges was not y. BIBLE (Great) *Mark.* xi. 13. g. Even y. not quite finished MOORE. h. He sees that he may y. be happy GOLDSM. i. Cum ȝytt, and thou schalt fynde Myne endlys mercy and grace SKELTON. j. There are yet xl. dayes, and then shal Niniue be ouerthrowen COVERDALE *Jonah* iii. 4. k. I failled neuere of my trouthe as yit CHAUCER. As yet the Duke professed himself a member of the Anglican Church MACAULAY.

B. *conj. adv.* or *conj.* For all that, nevertheless, but. Sometimes preceded by *and* or *but*; sometimes strengthened by *nevertheless*, etc.; often correlative to *though*, etc. ME.

Oftymes we doo many thynges that we wene it be for the best & y. peraduenture hit torneth to the werst MALORY. Though his belief be true, y. the very truth he holds, becomes his heresie MILT. The splendid y. useless imagery SCOTT.

Yew (yū). [OE. *īw, ēow*:—OTeut. **īhwoz*, **īgwoz.*] 1. A tree of the genus *Taxus*, esp. the common y. of Europe and Asia, *T. baccata*, having heavy coniferous elastic wood, dark foliage, and red berries; often planted in churchyards, and associated with mourning. b. The wood of this tree, esp. as the material of bows. late ME. c. Branches or sprigs of the tree, esp. as signs of mourning 1450. 2. A bow of yew-wood 1598.

1. Beneath a Bow'r for sorrow made,..Of the black Yew's unlucky green COWLEY. b. Ewe of all other thynges, is that, wherof perfite shootyng woulde haue a bowe made ASCHAM. c. My shrowd of white, stuck all with Ew SHAKS. 2. To send the arrow from the twanging Y. PRIOR. *attrib.* **y.-tree.** late ME. Hence **Yew·en** *a.* (*arch.*) of y.-wood or y.-trees 1563.

Yex (yeks), **yesk** (yesk), *v.* Now *Sc.* and *dial.* [OE. *geocsian, giscian*, of imitative origin.] †1. *intr.* To sob -1629. 2. To hiccup. late ME. 3. *trans.* To belch forth. late ME. So **Yex, yesk** *sb.* †a sob; a hiccup or the hiccups.

Yezidi, -dee (ye·zidi). 1818. [Of disputed origin.] One of a religious sect found in Kurdistan, Armenia, and the Caucasus, which, while believing in a Supreme God, regards the Devil with reverential fear.

†**Yfere**, *adv.* ME. [prob. a predic. use of pl. of *yfere* sb., OE. *ġefēra* companion, f. *faran* to go; see Y-.] In company, together.

O goodly golden chaine, wherewith yfere The vertues linked are in louely wize SPENSER.

Yggdrasil (i·gdrăsil). [ON. *yg(g)drasill* (app. f. *Yggr*, name of Odin + *drasill* horse).] *Myth.* In later Scand. mythology, the great tree whose branches and roots extend through the universe and support it.

Yiddish (yi·diʃ), *sb.* (*a.*) 1886. [Anglicization of G. *jüdisch* (*deutsch*) Jewish (-German).] The language used by Jews in Europe and America, consisting mainly of German (orig. from the Middle Rhine area) with admixture of Balto-Slavic or Hebrew words, and written in Hebrew characters. So **Yid** *U.S. slang.*, a Jew. **Yi·ddisher**, a y.-speaking Jew.

Yield (yīld), *sb.* [In senses 1, 2, OE. *gield* payment, f. stem of OTeut. **gelđan*; in 3, f. YIELD *v.*] †1. Payment, a sum paid or exacted -1582. †b. Payment for loss or injury, compensation -1500. 2. Recompense; retribution. ME. only. 3. The action of yielding crops or other products; *esp.* produce; amount of produce 1440. b. The amount obtained from an investment, undertaking, tax, etc. 1877.

3. The yong plants ought daily to be plucked vp from the old, for feare of hindring the yeeld of the old 1563.

Yield (yīld), *v.* [A Com. Teut. str. vb.; OE. (WS.) *ġieldan*, (Anglian) *ġeldan* (*ġeald, guldon, golden*):—OTeut. **gelđan*; ult. etym. obsc.] †1. To give in payment, render as due (money, a debt, tribute, etc.) -1652. 2. To give (service, obedience, thanks, etc.) as due or of right, or as demanded or required. Now somewhat *arch.* OE. †3. To repay; to restore -1552. †4. To give in return for something received, to render, return (a benefit, injury, etc.) -1586. 5. To return (an answer, greeting, or the like). Now only, to vouchsafe (an assent) *to.* ME. †6. With personal obj. (orig. dat.; occas. with *to*): To reward, requite, repay. Now *arch.* OE. 7. To give forth from its own substance by a natural process or in return for cultivation or labour; to produce, bear, put forth (fruit, seed, minerals, vegetation, etc.) Now chiefly *arch.* or *poet.* ME. b. To furnish (a produce of so much) ME. c. *absol.* To bear produce ME. 8. †a. To deliver, present, offer -1807. b. To give as a favour: to grant, accord ME. c. To give forth, emit, discharge. *Obs.* exc. as a weakened use of other senses. 1450. 9. To supply for use, furnish, afford 1548. b. To give rise to, occasion (a state or feeling). Now *rare.* 1576. c. To produce as profit, bring in 1573. 10. To give up, hand over, surrender, relinquish (a place, possession, advantage, opinion, point). *arch.* or *poet.* ME. b. *To y. up the ghost, life,* etc., to die ME. 11. *refl.* To give oneself *up*, surrender, submit, as to a conqueror. Now *rare.* ME. 12. *intr.* To give oneself up, surrender, submit (as overcome in fight) ME. b. To give way, be subjected, submit 1576. c. To be inferior *to.* Now *rare.* 1604. 13. To comply, give consent *to* persuasion, entreaty, etc.; to comply, submit 1500. †b. To consent (*to do* something, *that* something should be done, etc.) -1814. 14. *trans.* To admit, confess: †a. with compl. adj. or adj. phr. -1744. †b. with clause or acc. and inf. -1703. c. With simple obj. Now *rare.* 1571. 15. *intr.* To give way under some natural or mechanical force, so as to collapse, bend, stretch, crack, etc. 1552. b. To submit *to* some physical action or agent (e. g. pressure, friction, heat) so as to be affected by it 1794.

3. Yeld eftesones a thinge receiued, or taken 1552. 4. It with kinde nevere stod A man to yelden evil for good GOWER. 6. Tend me to night two houres, I aske no more, And the Gods yeeld you for't SHAKS. 7. For want of seede, land yeeldeth weede 1573. 8. b. To y. him loue she doth deny SPENSER. The King yielded the citizens the right of justice 1874. 9. The narrow valley..yielded fresh pasturage W. IRVING. b. Curved forms and winding movements y. of themselves a certain satisfaction 1855. 10. The besieged did yeeld the place to the Queene 1617. Constantius, yielding to fear what he denied to justice NEWMAN. b. He..yeelded vp the ghost, and was gathered vnto his people *Gen.* xlix. 33. 11. I yelde my self prisoner to you 1560. 12. England shall couch downe in feare, and yeeld SHAKS. b. The night has yielded to the morn SCOTT. c. Their mutton yields to ours SWIFT. 13. I haue yeelded vnto those my freindes which pressed me in the matter HAKLUYT. b. How hast thou yeelded to transgress The strict forbiddance? MILT. 14. a. Ȝeldynge him self gylty, and cryenge him mercy 1400.

Comb.: **y.-capacity**, capacity for producing; **-point**, the degree of force at which a particular substance, etc. begins to yield (see 15). Hence **Yie·lder**, one who or that which yields or produces, now esp. with qualifying word referring to the amount or quality of the produce.

Yie·lding, *ppl. a.* ME. [f. prec. + -ING [2].] †1. Indebted. ME. only. †2. Productive, fertile -1777. 3. Submissive, compliant, unresisting 1578. 4. Not rigid, giving way to pressure or other physical force 1577. Hence **Yie·ldingly** *adv.*, **-ness.**

Yike (yəik), *sb.* 1891. [Echoic.] An imitation of the cry of the woodpecker. So **Yike** *v.* 1889.

Yill, Sc. var. of ALE.

Yite (yəit). *dial.* 1812. [Obscure.] The yellow-hammer.

-yl (il, əil), a terminal element of chemical terms, ad. F. *-yle*, f. Gr. ὕλη wood, substance, used for 'chemical principle, radical'. It is used in forming the names of radicals compounded of two or three elements in various atomic proportions, which behave in combination like simple elements and are the constant bases of series of compounds; the majority are compounds of carbon and hydrogen, either alone, as *amyl, ethyl*, or with oxygen, as *acetyl.*

Ylang-ylang (ī·læŋ ī·læŋ). 1876. [Tagalog *álang-ílang.*] A Malaysian tree (*Canangium odoratum*) with fragrant greenish-yellow flowers; hence, the perfume distilled from these.

Yo (yōᵘ), *int.* late ME. An exclamation of incitement, warning, etc. In nautical use = YOHO.

Yod (yǫd, yōᵘd). 1735. 1. The name of the tenth letter in the Hebrew alphabet. 2. *Philol.* The consonantal *i* = (y), the front voiced open consonant, denoted in prehistoric forms by *j.*

†**Yode, yede,** *v.* ME. [Early ME. *ȝeode, ȝede*, var. of *eode, ede* (OE. *ēode*).] Past tense of Go *v.* -1808.

So forth they yode, and forward softly paced SPENSER. In other pace than forth he yode, Returned Lord Marmion SCOTT.

Yodel (yōᵘ·dĕl), *v.* Also **jodel.** 1830. [ad. G. *jodeln.*] *intr.* To sing or warble with interchange of falsetto and the natural voice, in the manner of Swiss and Tyrolese mountaineers. **b.** *trans.* To utter (a song, refrain) thus. Hence **Yo·del, jo·del** *sb.* a melody or musical phrase sung thus. **Yo·del(l)er.**

‖**Yoga** (yōᵘ·gă). 1820. [Hind., Skr. *yoga* lit. union, YOKE.] In Hindu philosophy, union with the Supreme Spirit; a system of ascetic practice, abstract meditation, and mental concentration, pursued as a method of obtaining this.

Yogh (yǫg, yoɣ). Also **ȝok**, etc. ME. [Origin doubtful; see N.E.D.] The name of the ME. letter ȝ; see G, Y.

‖**Yogi** (yōᵘ·gi). 1619. [Hind. *yogī*, f. YOGA.] An Indian devotee practising YOGA. So **Yo·gism, Yo·geeism,** the system of yoga.

‖**Yogurt** (yōᵘ·guət). 1625. [Turkish *yōghurt.*] A sour fermented liquor made from milk in Turkey and other countries of the Levant.

Yo-heave-ho (yōᵘ·hī·vhōᵘ·), *int.* (*sb.*). Also **yeo-.** 1803. [See YO *int.* and HEAVE HO.] A sailor's accompaniment to hauling and heaving motions.

Yohi·mbenine, Yohi·mbine. 1898. [See def. and -INE [5].] *Chem.* Either of two colourless alkaloids obtained from the bark and leaves of a W. African tree, the *yohimbé.*

Yoho, yo-ho (yŏhōᵘ·), *int.* 1769. [See YO *int.*, HO *int.*[3]] An exclamation (orig. *Naut.*) used to call attention; also occas. used like YO-HEAVE-HO. Hence **Yoho·** *v. intr.* to shout 'yoho!'

Yoi, *int.* 1826. A huntsman's cry to encourage the hounds.

Yoicks (yoiks), *int.* 1774. [app. related to HYKE *int.* (*hike hallow, hyke a Bewmont*, Turbervile).] A fox-hunting cry urging on the hounds; also *gen.* as an exclam. of excitement or exultation. Hence **Yoicks, yoick** *v. int.* to cry 'y.!'; *trans.* to urge on with this cry.

‖**Yojan** (yōᵘ·dʒăn), **yojana** (yōᵘ·dʒănă). *India.* 1784. [Hindi *yójan*, Skr. *yójana* yoking, distance travelled at one time without unyoking, f. *yóga*; see next.] A measure of distance, varying locally from about four to ten miles.

Yoke (yōᵘk), *sb.* [Com. Teut.; OE. *ȝeoc*, corresp. to L. *jugum*, Gr. ζυγόν, Skr. *yugám* :—Indo-Eur. **jugóm*; cf. Skr. *yuj*, Gr. ζευγνύναι, L. *jungere* to yoke, join, Skr. *yóga* YOGA.] **1.** A contrivance by which two oxen or other beasts are coupled together for drawing a plough or vehicle; usu. a curved bar of wood fitted with 'bows' or hoops at each end which are passed round the beasts' necks, and having an attachment in the middle for the trace or chain OE. **b.** A similar appliance anciently placed on the neck of a captive or conquered enemy; a symbol of this, consisting of three spears arranged as an arch beneath which vanquished enemies were forced to pass by the ancient Romans and others OE. **2.** A wooden frame fixed on an animal's neck to prevent it from breaking through or leaping over a hedge, fence, etc. 1573. **3.** A frame fitted to the neck and shoulders of a person for carrying a pair of pails, baskets, etc. 1618. **b.** A part of a garment, made to fit the shoulders (or the hips), and supporting the depending parts 1882. **4.** Applied to various objects resembling the yoke of a plough. late ME. **b.** *Naut.* A board or bar fixed transversely to the head of the rudder, and having two ropes (*y.-lines*) attached for steering 1625. **5.** *transf.* A pair of animals, esp. oxen, that are or may be coupled by a yoke (in this sense the pl. after a numeral is freq. *yoke*) OE. **6.** A quarter of a SULING, about 50 or 60 acres; hence, later applied vaguely to small manors OE. **7.** *fig.* or in fig. phrases denoting servitude, subjection, restraint, etc. OE. **b.** Cooperation, union; the marriage bond. late ME.

1. In time the sauage Bull doth beare the yoake SHAKS. **b.** His army was routed, and passed under the y. 1875. **2.** I have..seen a number of hens all wearing yokes 1886. **3.** The speaker, who had been carrying a pair of pails on a y. HARDY. **5.** A deep well whence they draw water, with a wheel turned round by a y. of Bulls 1660. A M. yock oxen COVERDALE *Job* xlii. 12. [A.V. a thousand yoke of oxen.] **7.** He brouȝte alle þe kynges þat were nyh hym under his ȝok TREVISA. **b.** We haue byn ioyned togyther with the y. of holy matrimonie 1555.

Comb.: **y.-band,** a band for fastening the y. to the pole; **-elm,** the hornbeam, the wood of which is used for yokes; **-fellow,** a person 'yoked' or associated with another; a fellow-worker, *spec.* a husband or wife, spouse; **-mate** (now *rare*), a y.-fellow.

Yoke, *v.* [OE. *geocian*, f. *geoc* YOKE *sb.*] **1.** *trans.* To put a yoke on (draught beasts); to couple with a yoke OE. **2.** To attach (a draught-animal) *to* a plough or vehicle; to 'put in', 'put to'. late ME. **b.** With the plough or vehicle as object 1568. **c.** *fig.* To set (a person, force, etc.) to work; to harness 1606. **3.** To fasten a yoke round the neck of (a hog, etc.) 1530. **4.** To suspend (a heavy bell) on a yoke 1701. **5.** To bring into or hold in subjection or servitude; to subjugate, oppress. Now *rare* or *Obs.* ME. **6.** *fig.* To join, link, couple, connect ME. **b.** With ref. to marriage; only in *pa. pple.* 1604. **7.** *intr.* (for *refl.*) To consort, to be associated or matched. Now *rare.* 1500.

1. It was cautioned in the Law not to yoake an Oxe, and an Asse together 1641. **2.** Lions have been yoked to the chariots of conquerors GOLDSM. **b.** Without his license the pleugh cannot be yoked 1638. **c.** It is by wisdom and knowledge that the Forces of Nature ..are yoked to service 1867. **3.** You muste y. your hogge, for he ronneth thorowe every hedge PALSGR. **5.** But foul effeminacy held me yok't Her Bond-slave MILT. **6.** Oh then,..my Name Be yoak'd with his, that did betray the Best SHAKS. **b.** He that is yoaked with a wife must not put her away 1632. **7.** 'Twere pittie, to sunder them, That yoake so well together SHAKS. Hence **Yo·keless** *a.* (*rare*) used as tr. L. *absque jugo* 'without yoke', Jerome's explanation of *b'lī-yaʿal* BELIAL. **Yo·king** *vbl. sb.*; *spec.* a spell of work at the plough or with a cart, etc., done at a stretch.

Yokel (yōᵘ·k'l). 1812. [Origin obsc.] A countryman, rustic; a country bumpkin.

Yokohama (yōᵘkohā·mă). 1882. The name of a city in Japan, used as a specific epithet of a breed of fowls, etc.; also as *sb.* (*ellipt.*).

Yo·ldring, ye·ldring. *Sc.* and *north. dial.* 1790. [var. of earlier †*yowlring.*] A yellow-hammer.

Yolk [1], **yelk** (yōᵘk, *formerly* yelk). [OE. *geolca, -leca, -loca*, f. *geolu* yellow. The spelling *yelk*, still found in scientific and technical works, is otherwise now rare.] **1.** The yellow internal part of an egg, surrounded by the 'white' or albumen, and serving as nourishment for the young before it is hatched. **b.** *Biol.* Extended to the part in any animal ovum that nourishes the embryo (*nutritive* or *food-y.*) and to the protoplasmic substance from which the embryo is developed (*formative* or *germ-y.*) 1835. †**2.** *fig.* Centre; innermost part, 'core' -1730. **3.** (Also *y. of egg*) A gasteropod of the genus *Nerita*, from the appearance of its shell 1796. **4.** A rounded opaque or semi-opaque part in window-glass 1808.

An Addle-egg with double Yoalk 1666. Beat up the yolks of three eggs MRS. HAYWOOD. The leather is ..soaked in liquor made of the yelks of eggs 1884.

attrib. and *Comb.*: **y.-bag, -sac,** the sac or vesicle enclosing the y., esp. when attached to the umbilicus, as an organ of nutrition; it is connected with the embryo by the **y.-duct** or **y.-stalk**; **y.-cleavage,** the division of the (formative) y. as the initial process in the development of the embryo. Hence **Yolked** (yōᵘkt) *ppl. a.* (chiefly in comb., as *double-y.*). **Yo·lk-less** *a.*

Yolk [2] (yōᵘk). 1607. [OE. **eowoca* (see YOLKY *a.*[2]), corresp. to Flemish *ieke.*] The greasy substance secreted by the sebaceous glands in the skin of a sheep, which serves to moisten and soften the wool; also called *suint, wool-oil*, and *lanolin.*

Yolky (yōᵘ·ki), *a.*[1] 1528. [f. YOLK [1] + -Y [1].] Like, of, or abounding in (egg) yolk.

Yolky (yōᵘ·ki), *a.*[2] [OE. *eow(o)cig*, f. **eowoca* YOLK [2].] Containing 'yolk'; greasy with yolk, as unwashed wool.

Yon (yǫn), *dem. a., pron.* and *dem. adv.* [OE. had *ȝeon* adj.; and *ȝeond, ȝeondan* prep. and adv., as well as *biȝeonan, beȝeondan* BEYOND *adv.* and *prep.* From these the various parallel uses of *yon, yond*, and *yonder* (ME. *ȝonder*) have arisen by interchange of functions.] **A.** *adj.* That, those; applied chiefly to what is visible but not close: = 'that' (those)... over there'. *arch.* and *dial.* **B.** *pron.* The adj. used *absol.*: = 'That *or* those' (over there). Now only *Sc.* and *dial.* ME. **C.** *dem. adv.* = YONDER *adv. Obs.* exc. *dial.* 1475. **b.** *Hither and y.*, hither and thither, this way and that. *dial.* 1787.

A. Because of his being of this or this, or that, or y., or of that other Religion 1652. **B.** Was y. the messenger? SCOTT. **C.** But..with thee bring, Him that y. soars on golden wing MILT. **b.** She swayed hither and y. 1836.

Yond (yǫnd), *a., pron., prep.*, and *adv. Obs.* exc. *dial.* [OE. *geond, geondan* prep.] **A.** *adj.* †**1.** Qualifying *half, side*, or the like. The farther, 'the other' -1623. **2.** = prec. A. ME. **B.** *pron.* That or those person(s) or thing(s) ME. **C.** *prep.* †**1.** Over, throughout, across -ME. **2.** On (or to) the farther side of, beyond. Now *poet.* or *Sc.* late ME. **D.** *adv.* = YONDER *adv.* Now *dial.* OE.

A. 1. To y. side o' th' riuer lies a wall WEBSTER. **2.** Y. same Starre that's Westward from the Pole SHAKS. **B.** Who is yonde that for the dothe call? SKELTON. **C. 1.** He..sette tweyne and tweyne to gon ȝond al þe world to prechen vchon 1320. **2.** Thou God of grace,..y. whome we can not roaue Or raunge aright 1579. **D.** Say what thou see'st y. SHAKS.

Yonder (yǫ·ndəɹ), *adv., a.*, and *pron.* Now only *literary* and somewhat *arch.* or *dial.* [ME. *ȝonder, ȝender.* Cf. OS. *gendra*, Goth. *jaindrē.*] **A.** *adv.* At or in that place; there: usu. implying that the object spoken of is at some distance but within sight; over there, away there. **b.** To that place, thither ME. **c.** *Here* (*hither*) *and y.*, here and there, to and fro. late ME.

But, as I live, y. comes Moses. GOLDSM. **b.** As for me and the childe, we wyl go y. COVERDALE.

B. *adj.* **1.** With *the.* Farther, more distant, 'other'. late ME. **2.** That is yonder. late ME.

1. O she was fair as a beech in May With the sun on the y. side MEREDITH. **2.** Y. bank hath choice of Sun or shade MILT.

C. *pron. sing.* or *pl.* = YON *pron.* Now *dial.* late ME.

An inquiry whether 'y. was a lad or a lass' 1880.

Yondmost (yǫ·ndməst), *a. Sc.* 1608. [f. YOND *a.* + -MOST.] Farthest, extreme, uttermost.

‖**Yoni** (yōᵘ·ni). 1799. [Skr.] A figure or symbol of the female organ of generation as an object of veneration among Hindus and others.

Yonside (yǫ·nsəid), *sb., adv.* and *prep.* Now *dial.* and *literary.* 1535. [f. YON *a.* + SIDE *sb.*] **A.** *sb.* The farther side. **B.** *adv.* On the farther side (*of*) 1681. **C.** *prep.* Beyond 1856.

Yoop (yūp), *sb.* and *int.* 1848. A word expressing the sound made by convulsive sobbing.

Yore (yōᵊɹ), *adv. arch.* [OE. *geāra, geāre, geāro*, of obsc. origin.] †**1.** A long time ago, of old -1613. †**2.** Formerly, before -1574. †**3.** For a long time (past, or *rarely* to come) -1522. **4.** Of yore: **a.** *advb.* Of old, anciently, formerly. late ME. **b.** as *adj.*: Ancient, former 1598.

4. a. A form, not now gymnastic as of y. COWPER. **b.** This is altogether different from the village politics of y. COLERIDGE.

York (yǭɹk), *sb.* [OE. *Eoforwic*, ME. *Everwik, Yerk, York*, ad. L. *Eboracum* + *wīc* dwelling.] **1.** The name of the capital of Yorkshire, used attrib. in names of things originating from or peculiar to York or Yorkshire, as *Y. ham, tan* 1794. **b.** Short for *Yorkshire cabbage* 1823. **2.** *attrib.* Pertaining to the royal house of York; *spec.* = YORKIST 1 b. late ME. **3.** One of the heralds of the College of Arms 1630.

1. Y. paving, paving with Yorkshire stone. **Y. pitch** (of a plane) an angle of the iron of 50°; hence **Y.-pitched** *a.* **2. Y. pence,** copper coins of the reign of Henry VI.

York (yǭɹk), *v.* 1888. [Back-formation f. YORKER [2].] *Cricket. trans.* To bowl (a batsman) out or strike (the wicket) with a yorker.

Yorker [1] (yǭ·ɹkəɹ). 1599. [f. YORK *sb.* + -ER [1].] **1.** An inhabitant of York or Yorkshire. **2.** An inhabitant or soldier of New York 1776.

Yorker [2] (yǭ·ɹkəɹ). 1870. [perh. same word as prec.] *Cricket.* A ball that pitches directly beneath the bat.

Yorkish (yǭ·ɹkiʃ), *a. rare.* 1548. [f. YORK *sb.* + -ISH [1].] = next 1 b.

Yorkist (yǭ·ɹkist), *sb.* (*a.*). 1601. [f. YORK *sb.* (see below) + -IST.] 1. An adherent of the royal house of York, which descended from Lionel, Duke of Clarence, and Edmund, Duke of York, third and fifth sons of Edward III; or one of the party (whose emblem was the white rose) which supported this family in the Wars of the Roses. b. as *adj.* 1823. 2. A supporter of the claim of James, Duke of York, to succeed his brother, Charles II. 1681.

Yorkshire (yǭ·ɹkʃəɹ, -ʃiəɹ). 1683. [f. YORK *sb.* + SHIRE.] The largest of the counties of England. 1. *attrib.* Of, made or grown or used in, or characteristic of Yorkshire. 2. *allus.*, esp. with ref. to the bargaining skill, cunning, or sharp practices attributed to Yorkshire people. Phr. *To come* or *put Y. on* (a person), to dupe or overreach (him). 1620. 3. *ellipt.* as the designation of thick coarse cloth made in Yorkshire, a breed of canary, (pl.) soldiers of a Yorkshire regiment; also, short for *Y. dialect*, etc. 1726.

1. *Y. ale, cabbage, grit* (GRIT *sb.*[1] 2), *kidney* (potato), *stone, tyke* (TYKE 3); **Y. pudding**, a batter-pudding cooked under a joint of meat or in meat juice. **Y. terrier**, one of a small shaggy breed. Hence **Yorkshireman** (yǭ·ɹkʃəɹmæn), a man of Y.

You (yū, yŭ), *pers. pron.*, *2nd pers. obj.* (*nom.*), *pl.* (*sing.*). [OE. *éow*, acc. and dat. pl. :—OTeut. **iwwiz*. See THOU. Orig. restricted to acc. and dat. pl. uses, *you* gradually replaced *ye* as nom. pl. in 14th–15th centuries, and also by extension of the deferential plural (see YE) came into general use for *thou* and *thee*; it is now, in ordinary use, the 2nd pers. pron. for any number and case.] 1. As *pl.* The persons or things addressed: a. As direct or indirect obj of a vb., or as obj. of a prep. b. As *refl. pron.* Yourselves. *arch.* OE. c. As *nom.* = YE ME. d. As *vocative*, chiefly in apposition with a sb. following 1569. e. In apposition with a sb., a numeral, *all*, or *both* ME. 2. As sing., used in addressing a person (or thing); orig. as a mark of respect, later *gen.* a. As direct or ind. obj. of a vb., or obj. of a prep.: Thee ME. b. As *refl. pron.* Thyself, yourself. *arch.* late ME. c. As *nom.* replacing THOU. late ME. d. As *vocative*, chiefly in apposition with a sb. following; in reproach or contempt often repeated after the sb. 1500. 3. Any hearer or reader, any one concerned 1577. b. Used with no definite meaning as indirect obj. ('ethic dative') 1590. 4. Qualified by a preceding adj. 1600. 5. As *sb.*: a. The word as used in addressing a person or persons 1645. b. The person (or such a person as the one) addressed 1700.

1. a. I graunte you leue, seyth what yow semyth 1400. Ryght trusty & wele-beloued, we grete yewe wele 1482. I will..make y. both friends 1607. You have killed me between y. 1896. b. Home y. idle Creatures, get y. home SHAKS. c. What ye rede, se you practise it in lyfe and dede 1526. Do y. assure us that y. are all sound men? DE FOE. d. Farwell y. Ladies of the Court 1569. e. If y. men durst not vndertake it..women would 1596. *You-all* (U.S.) = YOU (as sing. or plur.) 1919. 2. a. Myn lord,..þis ringe, þat I yu present now, Me gafe a pilgram to gyf ȝow 1375. Unto you that bene a member of chirche 1455. Hold, woman, hold!..the dog will not do y. harm SCOTT. b. Pray set it downe, and rest y...Pray now rest your selfe. SHAKS. c. 'Syr Gye', he seyde,..'To morowe schall yow weddyd bee,' late ME. Old year, y. shall not go TENNYSON. d. Fie, fie, y. counterfeit, y. puppet, y. SHAKS. 3. Nay more, y. shall haue Atheists striue to get Disciples BACON. Y. can talk a mob into anything RUSKIN. b. I will roare y. as gently as any Sucking Doue SHAKS. 5. a. Several Sober Reasons against Hat-Honour, Titular Respects, Y. to a Single Person PENN. b. If your flesh and blood be new, You'll be no more the former y. SWIFT.

Phrasal combs.: **y.-be-damned** *a.*, addicted to saying 'y. be damned!'; contemptuously overbearing; **y.-know-what**, used instead of the name of something which it is needless or undesirable to specify. Hence **You** *v. trans.* to address (a person) as 'you' (instead of 'thou').

Young (yvŋ), *a.* (*sb.*). See also YOUNGER, YOUNGEST. [OE. *geong, gung, iung*:—OTeut. **jungoz*, contraction of **juwungoz* :—Indo-Eur. **juwṇkós* (whence L. *juvencus* young bull), f. **juwen-* (*jūn-, jun-*); cf. Skr. *yúvan-, yūn-*, L. *juvenis* (compar. *junior*) young, L. *juventus, -ta*, OIr. *óitiu* youth.] A. *adj.* 1. That has lived a relatively short time; not mature or fully developed; youthful: opp. to OLD *a.* I. 1. b. Used to distinguish the younger of two persons of the same name or title in a family (esp. a son from his father) ME. 2. *transf.* Belonging or pertaining to a young person or persons, or to youth OE. 3. Having the characteristics of young persons, or of youth; *esp.* having the vigour or freshness of youth 1513. 4. That has newly or not long since entered upon some course of action, or having the character of such a one; newly or recently initiated; 'raw' OE. 5. Of a thing: That is in an early stage or phase; lately begun, formed, introduced, etc.; not far advanced; recent, new. late ME. b. Applied to the moon in the early part of the lunar month, soon after 'new moon'. late ME. 6. *fig.* Small, diminutive, miniature, not full-sized. Now *colloq.* and *joc.* 1550.

1. Philip..died y. before his Father 1617. That they might..set a meet example to the *y. folk* SCOTT. The heart wood is..of a darker colour than the soft or y. wood 1842. The expression 'y. person' means a person under eighteen years of age who is no longer a child *Act* 8 & 9 *Geo. V*, c. 39, § 48. *Y. one*, a young person; *pl.* offspring, progeny; *y. 'un* (colloq.) = YOUNGSTER. See also YOUNG LADY, YOUNG MAN, YOUNG WOMAN. b. The chief leaders, Nathaniel Fynes and y. Sir H. Vane CLARENDON. 2. Hauyng a yonge and a lusty courage,..he set on hys enemyes 1548. A remnant of my y. days 1852. 3. To se the a quene wyll make vs yonge agayne 1513. Mr. Gresham was y. for his age TROLLOPE. 4. I was but y. at the work DE FOE. We are still so y. in the study of Nature 1796. 5. A little yonge yellowe bearde 1569. *Rom.* Is the day so y.? *Ben.* But new strooke nine SHAKS. A severe tax on a y. concern not earning profits 1913. 6. Such a weapon is really a y. cannon 1885.

B. *absol.* or as *sb.* 1. *absol.* in pl. sense (with def. art., or in *y. and old, old and y.*): Young people OE. 2. Young animals collectively in relation to the parent; offspring 1484. b. Phr. *With* (also *in*) *y.*, of a female animal: Pregnant 1535.

1. Thus there was killing of yong and old 2 *Macc.* v. 13. That Vigour which the Y. possess STEELE. 2. The brinded lioness led forth her y. SHELLEY.

Collocations and *Comb.*: a. (with the names of countries, etc., in the designations of political parties chiefly composed of y. men, as **Y. England**, name assumed by a group of Tory politicians in the early part of the reign of Queen Victoria (hence **Y.-Englander, Y.-Englandism**); **Y. Europe**, the republican agitators of various countries (*Y. France, Y. Italy*, etc.) working together after the July revolution (1830) in France; **Y. Ireland**, Irish agitators of 1840–50. **Y. Pretender** (see PRETENDER 1 c); **Y. Turk**, a member of a party of Turkish agitators which brought about the revolution of 1908. (Such phrases may also be used in gen. sense, as *Y. England* = the typical young Englishman, or the rising generation of Englishmen.) b. **y.-eyed** *a.* having the bright or lively eyes of a y. person; **y.-old**, *a.*, vigorous or young in disposition in spite of age; **y. thing**, said playfully or indulgently of a child or woman. Hence **You·ngish** *a.* somewhat y. **You·ng-like** *a.* resembling one that is y.

Younger (yv·ŋgəɹ), *a.* (*sb.*). OE. [f. YOUNG *a.* + -ER[3]. (The normal mutated OE. *gyngra, gingra* did not survive.)] The comparative of YOUNG *a.* 1. Of less age: opp. to ELDER *a.*, OLDER. Also *absol.* or as *sb.* b. Used after a person's name for distinction from an older person of the same name. Chiefly *Sc.* late ME. c. Belonging to the earlier part of life, earlier 1578. 2. Less advanced in practice or experience, later, more recent 1593. b. *Y. hand*, at cards, the second player in a two-handed game 1744.

1. It is fit that the yonger obey the elder 1612. Not many a moon his y. TENNYSON. The y. brother may not marry the elder brother's widows 1897. c. To shake all cares and busines of our state, Confirming them on yonger yeares SHAKS. 2. The y. the science, the smaller will be the amount of known facts 1874.

Youngest (yv·ŋgėst), *a.* OE. [f. YOUNG *a.* + -EST. (The normal mutated OE. form *gyngest, gingest* did not survive.)] The superlative degree of YOUNG *a.*: opp. to ELDEST, OLDEST, in uses corresp. to those of prec. b. *Y. hand*, at cards, the last player, or the last except the dealer 1680.

Young lady. late ME. 1. A young woman, usu. unmarried, of superior social position: formerly often used to connote the primness, etc. attributed to these. (Now, exc. in old-fashioned polite use or as playfully applied to a girl, only applied, with the intention of avoiding the implications of *young woman*, to female shop assistants or clerks of good appearance and manners.) 2. A fiancée. *vulgar* or *joc.* 1896.

1. Young Lady Wanted, with good experience, as Book-keeper 1920.

Youngling (yv·ŋliŋ). *arch.* [OE. *geongling*; see YOUNG and -LING.] 1. A young person. †b. A beginner, novice, tiro –1682. 2. A young animal ME. 3. A young plant, sapling; a young shoot or blossom of a plant 1559. 4. *attrib.* That is a 'youngling'; youthful; pertaining to or characteristic of a 'youngling', juvenile. late ME.

1. Like as a yongling that to schoole is set QUARLES. b. Younglynges in the feith UDALL. 2. The linnet.. was bringing out her younglings 1772. 3. Masses of precipitous ruin, overgrown with the younglings of the forest SHELLEY. 4. The y. Cottagers retire to rest BURNS.

Youngly (yv·ŋli), *adv.* Now *rare.* 1530. [f. YOUNG *a.* + -LY[2].] 1. In youth 1559. 2. In a youthful way 1530.

Young man. late OE. 1. One in early manhood. Also applied playfully to a boy. b. A youth employed by a tradesman, etc. 1751. 2. A lover; a fiancé. *vulgar* or *joc.* 1851.

Youngness (yv·ŋnės). 1510. [f. YOUNG *a.* + -NESS.] The state or quality of being young; youthfulness 1528. †b. The time when one is young, one's youth –1579.

Youngster (yv·ŋstəɹ). Chiefly *colloq.* 1589. [f. YOUNG *a.* + -STER, suggested by YOUNKER.] 1. A young person, *esp.* a young man: now usu. connoting inexperience or immaturity. 2. Familiarly applied to a boy or junior seaman on board ship; also to a junior officer in the army or navy 1608. 3. A child, *esp.* a boy. *colloq.* 1732. 4. A young animal 1849.

Young woman. late OE. 1. One in early womanhood. Also applied playfully to a girl. 2. A female sweetheart; a fiancée. *vulgar* or *joc.* 1858.

Younker (yv·ŋkəɹ). 1505. [ad. MDu. *jonckher* = *jonc* YOUNG + *hēre* lord; cf. JUNKER.] †1. A young nobleman or gentleman (orig. Dutch or German) –1645. 2. A young man, in early use *esp.* a gay or fashionable young man 1513. †b. = YOUNGSTER 2 –1818. 3. A child. Now *rare.* 1601.

Your (yūəɹ, *usu. unemphatic* yŭɹ, yŏɹ), *poss. pron.* and *a.* [OE. (1) *éower*, genit. of *gé* YE; (2) *éower, éowru, éower*, poss. adj.; corresp. to G. *euer.*] †1. As genit. of the 2nd pers. pron.: Of you (*pl.*, in partitive sense). late ME. 2. As poss. pron. and adj. of the 2nd pers.: Of or belonging to you, that you have. a. as poss. pl., referring to a number of persons addressed OE. b. as poss. sing., referring to one person addressed ME. c. In titles of honour substituted for *you* in addressing a person (or persons) of high rank, as *y. Excellency, y. Honour, y. Majesty.* late ME. d. Qualifying a sb. denoting the speaker or writer himself, esp. in the subscription of a letter. late ME. †3. *absol.* or as *pron.* = YOURS. –1625. 4. Used more or less vaguely of something which the person(s) addressed may be expected to possess, or to have to do with in some way ME. b. Without definite meaning, or vaguely implying 'that you know of': often expressing contempt 1568. 5. As poss. of the indef. pron. (YOU 3) One's, any one's 1598.

2. b. 'Madame, mercy,' quod I 'me liketh wel ȝowre wordes' LANGL. d. Yor loving Father Charles R. CHAS. I. 3. For ye are myne and i am y. 1400. 4. The most ancient of all histories, you will read in y. Bible 1773. b. There is not a more fearefull wilde foule then y. Lyon liuing SHAKS. I hate y. accomplished women FITZGERALD. 5. Here there is no living without them [curtains], one whole side of y. house being glass 1708.

Yourn (yūəɹn), *poss. pron. dial.* late ME. [f. prec. + -*n* as in HERN, HISN.] = next.

Yours (yūəɹz), *poss. pron.* ME. Also (now illiterate) your's. [f. YOUR + -*s* as in HERS, OURS.] The absol. form of YOUR, used when no sb. follows: That or those, belonging to you. 1. *predic.* late ME. b. In the subscription of a letter, often qualified by an adv. or advb. phr. late ME. c. = Your affair or task 1841. 2. Standing for *your* and a sb. to be supplied from the context ME. b. Those who belong to you; your relations or friends: chiefly in *you and yours* ME. c. = Your letter, the letter from you. (Now chiefly commercial.)

1536. **3.** Used instead of *your* before another possessive, etc., qualifying the same sb. Now *rare* or *Obs.* 1534. **4.** *Of yours*, that is yours, belonging to you ME.

1. b. *Y. truly*, etc., *joc.* for 'I' or 'me', 'myself'; The verdict will be 'Guilty..' against y. truly 1860. c. Be it your's to help him 1841. 4. She hath that Ring of y. SHAKS.

Yourself (yuəɹse·lf), *pron.* [ME. *ȝour selfe, ȝour selven*; see SELF.] The emphatic and reflexive pronoun corresp. to *you* (now only in sing. sense). **b.** In pregnant sense: Your being or personality; also, you as you are in your natural or normal condition 1590. **c.** Used as simple subject, with the vb. either in the pl. or in the 3rd pers. sing. late ME.

Ye proude galants that thus your selfe disguise 1509. Here is a Table of Latitudes..and the way to calculate it your self 1669. Not one of them equals y. or Southey 1807. b. What euill starre On you hath frownd,..That of your selfe ye thus berobbed are SPENSER. You will soon come to y. again FIELDING. c. Madam, your selfe is not exempt from this SHAKS. Conversation is but carving; Carve for all, y. is starving SWIFT.

Yourselves (yuəɹse·lvz), *pron. pl.* 1526. [f. prec. with pl. inflexion.] The emphatic and reflexive pronoun corresp. to *you* in pl. sense: replacing the earlier *yourself*.

‖ **Yourt** (yūəɹt). 1784. [ad. Russ. *yurta*.] A semi-subterranean native hut of northern and central Asia, usu. formed of timber covered with earth or turf.

Youth (yūþ). [OE. *geoguþ*:—Com. WGer. **jugunþi-*, f. **juwunþi-*:—pre-Teut. **juwənti-* (cf. L. *juventa*); see YOUNG and -TH [1].] **1.** The fact or state of being young; youngness. **b.** *fig.* Newness, recentness 1596. **2.** The early part of life, esp. the period between childhood and adult age OE. **b.** *transf.* and *fig.* Early stage of existence 1602. **3.** A quality or condition characteristic of the young; e.g. freshness, vigour, wantonness, rashness, youthful appearance OE. **4.** Personified, or vaguely denoting any young person or persons. late ME. **5.** Young people, the young. Now always construed as *pl.* OE. **6.** A young person; *esp.* a young man between boyhood and mature age ME.

1. b. If that the y. of my new interest here Have power to bid you welcome SHAKS. 2. The ymaginacion of mans hert is euell, euen from the very y. of him COVERDALE *Gen.* viii. 21. 3. Though..that youthe of wytte haue made hym to defye the kynge LD. BERNERS. 4. We haue an olde prouerbe y. wil haue his course LYLY. 5. Now all the Y. of England are on fire SHAKS. 6. Profitable to bee read of all godly and vertuous Youthes of both sexe 1580.

Youthful (yū·þfŭl), *a.* 1561. [f. YOUTH + -FUL.] **1.** That is still young 1590. **2.** *transf.* Juvenile; of, characteristic of, or suitable for youth or the young 1561. **3.** *fig.* In the early stage, new; having the freshness or vigour of youth 1588.

1. The y. Socrates JOWETT. 2. In a very y. costume DICKENS. 3. The larger stature..of men in those youthfull times and age of the world PURCHAS. Hence **You·thful-ly** *adv.*, **-ness**.

Youthhead (yū·þhed). Chiefly *Sc.* ME. [f. YOUTH + -HEAD.] = YOUTH 1, 2, 5.

Youthhood (yū·þhud). Now *rare* or *arch.* [OE. *geoguþhād*; see YOUTH and -HOOD.] = YOUTH 1, 2, 3, 5.

Youthly (yū·þli), *a.* Now *rare.* [OE. *geoguþlic*; see YOUTH and -LY [1].] = YOUTHFUL 1, 2.

Youthy (yū·þi), *a.* Now *rare.* 1712. [f. YOUTH + -Y [1].] Having or affecting youth.

A withered beauty who persists in looking y. SCOTT. Hence **You·thily** *adv.*, **You·thiness**.

Youward(s, in phr. *to y.*: see -WARDS.

Yow (yau), *int.* 1820. [Imitative.] Representing the cry of a cat or dog; also as *sb.* and *vb.* (redupl. *yow-yow*).

Yowl (yaul), *v.* [ME. *ȝoȝele, ȝoule*.] **1.** *intr.* To utter loud wailing cries; to howl. **2.** *trans.* To utter with a yowl 1842. Hence **Yowl** *sb.* an act of yowling; a prolonged loud cry, now esp. of a dog or cat.

Yo-yo (yōu·yo). 1932. A toy resembling the old BANDALORE. Also as vb.

Ypight (ipəi·t), *pa. pple. arch.* ME. [See PITCH *v.*[1] and Y-.] Set, pitched.

Far underneath a craggy cliff y. SPENSER.

Ypocras: see HIPPOCRAS.

Ypsiliform (ipsi·lifǭɹm), *a.* 1886. [f. *ypsilon* = UPSILON + -(*i*)FORM.] Shaped like the Greek letter upsilon; Y-shaped.

Yt, y[t], graphic var. *that*; see Y.

Ytter (i·təɹ). 1805. *Min.* The first element of *Ytterby* (see next) used attrib. = combined with *yttria, yttrious.*

Ytterbite (i·təɹbəit). 1839. [Named from *Ytterby* in Sweden, where found; see -ITE [1].] *Min.* = GADOLINITE. So **Ytterbia** (itə̄·ɹbiă) *Chem.*, oxide of ytterbium. **Ytte·rbic** *a.* containing ytterbium. **Ytte·rbium**, a rare metallic element occurring in gadolinite, etc.

Ytterite (i·tərəit). 1849. [f. *Ytter(by)* (see prec.) + -ITE [1].] *Min.* = GADOLINITE.

Yttria (i·triă). 1800. [mod.L., f. *Ytterby*; see prec.] *Chem.* Sesquioxide of yttrium (Y_2O_3), obtained as a white earth from gadolinite and other rare minerals.

Yttrium (i·triŏm). 1822. [mod.L., f. prec.; see -IUM.] *Chem.* A rare metal of the cerium group, the base of yttria. Symbol Y. Hence **Yttrialite** (i·triăləit) *Min.*, a silicate of thorium and the yttrium metals. **Y·ttric** *a.* related to or containing y. **Yttri·ferous** *a.* containing y. **Y·ttrious** *a.* pertaining to or containing yttria. **Yttrite** (i·trəit) *Min.*, = GADOLINITE.

Yttro- *Min.*, comb. form of YTTRIUM.

Yuan (yū·ăn). The monetary unit of China since 1933, superseding the TAEL.

Yucca (yɒ·kă), **yuca** (yū·kă). 1555. [Of Carib origin.] **1.** (usu. *yuca.*) The common name in S. and Central America for the CASSAVA. **2.** Any plant of the N.-Amer. liliaceous genus *Yucca*, characterized by a woody stem, a crown of sword-like leaves, and a spike of white bell-shaped flowers 1664.

attrib. and *Comb.*: **y.-borer**, (*a*) a N.-Amer. moth, *Megathymus yuccæ*, whose larva bores into y.-roots; (*b*) a Californian weevil, *Yuccaborus frontalis*; **y.-moth**, a tineid moth of the genus *Pronuba*, esp. *P. yuccasella*; **-tree**, any arborescent species of Y.

Yuffrouw (yu·frau). 1494. [ad. early mod. Du. *jongvrouw*, later *juffrouw, juffer*, f. *jong* YOUNG + *vrouw* woman. Cf. EUPHROE, UFER.] **1.** A young lady, girl 1589. **2.** *Naut.* = EUPHROE.

‖ **Yuft** (yɒft). 1799. [a. Russ. *yuftĭ*.] Russia leather.

‖ **Yug** (yug), **yuga** (yu·gă). 1784. [Hindī *yug*, Skr. *yugá-* YOKE, an age of the world.] In Hindu cosmology, any of the four ages in the duration of the world, the four ages comprising 4,320,000 years and constituting a *Mahāyuga*.

Yugoslav: see JUGOSLAV.

Yuke (yuk), *v. Sc.* and *n. dial.* [Alteration of ME. *ȝeke, ȝike.*] To itch. **Yu·ky** *a.*, itching.

‖ **Yulan** (yū·lăn). 1822. [Chinese, f. *yu* a gem + *lan* plant.] A Chinese species of magnolia, *Magnolia conspicua.*

Yule (yūl). [OE. *geōl, geōla* Christmas day or Christmastide:—Teut. **jeul-*, **jehul-*:—pre-Teut. **jeqwəl-*; cf. ON. *jól* pl. a heathen feast lasting twelve days; ult. origin obscure. See N.E.D.] †**1.** December or January -ME. **2.** Christmas and its festivities (still the name in *Sc.* and *north. dial.*; now a literary archaism in England) OE. †**3.** An exclam. of joy or revelry at Christmas -1853.

2. The kynge is now deed sithe Martin-masse, and fro hens to yoole is but litill space 1450. At Ewle we wonten, gambole, daunce, to carrole, and to sing 1589. Ye ken a green Y. makes a fat kirk-yard SCOTT. The merry merry bells of Y. TENNYSON.

attrib. and *Comb.*: **y.-day** (chiefly *Sc.*), Christmas day; **-even** (*Sc.*), Christmas Eve; **-log**, a large log burnt on the hearth at Christmas; **-song** (*dial.*), a Christmas carol.

Ywrought (irǭ·t), *pa. pple. arch.* [OE. *geworht*: see WORK *v.*] Wrought, worked.

A plesaunt herber, wel y-wrought *a*1500.

Z

Z (zed), the twenty-sixth and last letter of the English alphabet, the twenty-third of the later Roman, and seventh of the earlier Roman, Greek, and Phœnician alphabets, derives its form from Phœnician and ancient Hebrew I Z Z.

Z was used in OE. in alien words, and in certain loan-words, with the value (ts), which is preserved in and indicated by the spelling of mod. *assets* (AF. *asetz*, OF. *asez* enough) and *Fitz-* (AF. *fiz* = *fius, fils*, L. *filius*); but by the end of the 13th c. it is found with its modern value (voiced *s*) in some words, and by the end of the 14th was in general use with that value. Similarity between the tailed *z* and *ȝ* led to confusion in MSS. from 1300, and in the typography of early Scottish printers, who represented the two sounds (y) and (z) by the same characters; this confusion has led to the general mispronunciation by Englishmen of *capercailzie* (-kē·lyi) and proper names such as *Dalziel* (diye·l), *Mackenzie, Menzies* (mi·ŋis).

The letter has been called in England by other names besides *zed*, of which *izzard, ezod, uzzard, zad*, survive in dialects, and *zee* is the general U.S. form. Initially and medially *z* occurs largely in words of Greek or Oriental origin, and in this dictionary the spelling of the suffix derived ultimately from Gr. -ίζειν has been normalized throughout as -IZE. In other classes of words the use of *z* has been determined by various circumstances, e.g. the immediate source of the word, as in *bronze*, or the desirability of an unambiguous or distinctive spelling, as in *ooze, prize*; but the difficulty of writing the character rapidly and intelligibly has told against an extensive use of it instead of *s* to represent the sound (z).

Z is normally employed to denote (z), the blade-open-voice consonant, the voiced analogue of (s). In the combination *-zure* in *azure* it denotes (ʒ).

1. The letter, or its sound OE. 2. As a shape or figure; a Z-shaped object or figure. Also *attrib.*, as *Z-bar* (see ZED 2), *-iron, -crank.* 1680. 3. As the last letter of the alphabet; hence *allus.* for 'end', esp. in phr. *from A to Z*, from beginning to end 1819. 4. Used (usu. repeated) to represent a buzzing sound 1852. 5. *Math.* Used as a symbol for the third unknown or variable quantity (cf. X, Y) 1660. 6. Used abstractly for the name of a person or thing 1755. 7. Denoting serial order 1842.

‖ **Zabra** (þa·bra, zā·bră). 1523. [Sp.] A small vessel used off the coasts of Spain and Portugal.

Zaffre, zaffer (zæ·fəɹ). 1662. [ad. It. *zaffera*, of uncertain origin.] An impure oxide of cobalt, used in preparing smalt and as blue colouring-matter (cobalt blue) for pottery, glass, etc.

†**Zagai·e, -ay·e.** 1590. [a. F. *zagaie*, reduced f. *azagaye.*] = ASSAGAI -1869.

Zalambdodont (zălæ·mdŏdǫnt), *a.* 1885. [f. Gr. ζα- intensive prefix + λάμβδα lambda + ὀδούς, ὀδοντ- tooth.] *Zool.* Belonging to the *Zalambdodonta*, insectivorous mammals having short molar teeth with a single Λ- or V-shaped ridge.

‖ **Zamang** (zæ·mæŋ). 1819. [Native name.] A giant mimosa (*Pithecolobium Saman*) of tropical S. America, having a vast spreading head of branches.

‖ **Zamarra** (þama·rra). 1842. [Sp.] A sheepskin jacket worn by Spaniards.

Zambo (zæ·mbo). 1819. [Sp.; see SAMBO.] **1.** = SAMBO 1. **2.** A species of American monkey 1851.

‖ **Zambra** (þa·mbra, zæ·mbră). 1670. [Sp.] A Spanish or Moorish dance.

‖ **Zamia** (zē¹·miă). 1819. [mod.L., due to a misreading of *azaniæ* (in Pliny) pine-nuts which open on the tree.] *Bot.* A genus of cycadaceous palm-like plants, of tropical and subtropical N. America, the W. Indies, and S. Africa, having fern-like leaves and oblong cones; a plant of this genus.

‖ **Zamorin** (zæ·mŏrin). *India.* 1582. [a. Pg. *samorim, ça-*, ad. Malayālam *sāmūri.*] 'The title for many centuries of the Hindu Sovereign of Calicut and the country round' (Yule).

Zander (zæ·ndəɹ). 1854. [G.] A common European species of pike-perch, *Stizostedion lucioperca* (*Lucioperca sandra*).

Zany (zē¹·ni), *sb.* 1588. [a. F. *zani*, or its source It. *zani, zanni* (Venetian form of

Gianni, Giovanni John), name of the servants who act as clowns in the 'Commedia dell'arte'.] **1.** A clown's or mountebank's comic assistant; a merry-andrew, jack-pudding; occas. vaguely, a professional jester or buffoon in general. *Hist.* or *arch.* 1588. **2.** An attendant; an underling, parasite. Now *rare.* 1601. **b.** One who plays the fool for the amusement, or so as to be the laughing-stock, of others. Now *rare* or *Obs.* 1606. **c.** A fool, simpleton, 'idiot'. *dial.* 1784.

1. Hee 's like a *Zani* to a Tumbler, That tries trickes after him to make men laugh B. JONS. 2. Pitt and his z. Beckford quarrelled H. WALPOLE. c. The printers are awful zanies, they print erasures and corrections too TENNYSON. Hence **Za·ny** *v.* (*Obs.* or *rare arch.*) *trans.* to play the z. to, to imitate poorly or awkwardly; hence *gen.* to mimic. **Za·nyism.**

‖**Zaptieh** (zæ·ptie). 1869. [Turkish *ḍabtiyeh*, f. Arab. *ḍabt* administration.] A Turkish policeman.

Zarathustrian (zærăþu·striăn), *a.* and *sb.* 1871. [f. *Zarathustra*, Old Iranian f. *Zoroaster.*] = ZOROASTRIAN.

Zaratite (zæ·rătəit). 1858. [a. Sp. *zaratita*, named from Señor *Zarate*; see -ITE[1].] *Min.* A green hydrous carbonate of nickel.

‖**Zariba** (zărī·bă), *sb.* 1849. [Arab. *zarībah* pen or enclosure for cattle.] In the Soudan, an enclosure, usu. of thorn-bushes, for defence against enemies or wild beasts; a fenced camp.

We employed ourselves..in cutting thorn branches, and constructing a zareeba 1867. Hence **Zari·ba** *v. trans.* to enclose with a z.; *intr.* to make a z.

‖**Zayat** (zā·yăt). 1823. [Burmese.] A public hall for meetings or shelter.

‖**Zea** (zī·ă). 1577. [Late and mod.L., a. Gr. ζειά.] †**1.** Spelt -1611. **2.** *Bot.* Adopted by Linnæus as the name of a genus of graminaceous plants, comprising one species, *Z. Mays* (occas. anglicized as *z. maize*), maize 1787.

Zeal (zīl). [Late ME. *zele*, ad. L. *zelus*, a. Gr. ζῆλος.] **1.** In biblical language, tr. L. *zelus*, denoting ardent feeling (taking the form of love, wrath, 'jealousy', or righteous indignation). †**2.** Eager desire; longing -1697. **3.** Ardour in the pursuit of an end or in favour of a person or cause; active enthusiasm. Const. *for.* 1520.

1. He brought an honger vpon them and in his zele he made them few in nombre COVERDALE *Ecclus.* xlviii. 2. 2. This doth inferre the zeale I had to see him SHAKS. 3. He joined with his drinking propensities a great z. for the Episcopal Church 1860. Hence **Zea·lful, Zea·lless** *adjs.*

Zealander (zī·lændəɹ). 1573. [f. *Zealand* = Du. *Zeeland* + -ER[1].] A native or inhabitant of Zealand in the Netherlands.

See also NEW ZEALANDER.

Zealot (ze·lət). 1537. [ad. eccl.L. *zelotes*, a. Gr. ζηλωτής, f. ζηλοῦν to be zealous, f. ζῆλος ZEAL.] **1.** A member of a Jewish sect which aimed at a Jewish theocracy over the earth and resisted the Romans till the fall of Jerusalem in A.D. 70. **2.** A zealous person (*for* a cause, etc.); esp. one who is carried away by excess of zeal; a fanatical enthusiast 1638.

2. The true Z. whom God approveth, namely, He whose Spirit is in Fervency and not in Shew 1638. The queen [Elizabeth] was as a mark for the pistol or dagger of every z. HALLAM. Hence **Zea·lotry**, action or feeling characteristic of a zealot; an instance of this 1656.

Zealous (ze·ləs), *a.* 1535. [ad. med.L. *zelosus*; see ZEAL and -OUS.] **1.** Full of or incited by zeal; fervent; actively enthusiastic. Const. *for.* (In the 17th cent. occas. connoting puritanical zeal.) **2.** Eagerly desirous 1605. Hence **Zea·lous-ly** *adv.*, **-ness** (now *rare*).

Zebra (zī·bră, ze·bră). 1600. [Congolese.] **1.** A S. African equine quadruped (*Equus* or *Hippotigris z.*), of a whitish ground-colour striped all over with black bars; noted for its wildness and swiftness. Also applied to other species of *Hippotigris*, or occas. to the whole subgenus, comprising all the striped species of African wild horses. **2.** *transf.* Applied to things having zebra-like stripes, as a kind of agate, a striped shawl, scarf, or the like 1811.

attrib. and *Comb.*: **z. fish**, an Australian fish, *Neotephræops z.*; **z. opossum**, = THYLACINE; **-poison**, the S. African tree, *Euphorbia arborea*, with poisonous milky juice; **-wolf** = THYLACINE; **-wood**, any of several kinds of ornamentally-striped wood used in cabinet-making.

Zebu (zī·biu). 1774. [ad. F. *zébu.*] The small humped ox, *Bos indicus*, domesticated in India, China, Japan, and parts of Africa.

Zecchin (ze·kin). 1575. [ad. It. *zecchino*, f. *zecca* the mint at Venice.] = SEQUIN 1.

‖**Zechstein** (ze·kstəin). 1823. [G., lit. minestone.] *Geol.* A limestone stratum of the Permian system in Germany; also extended to the series of rocks containing this, forming the upper division of the Permian.

Zed. late ME. [a. F. *zède*, ad. L. *zeta*, a. Gr. ζῆτα.] **1.** Name of the letter Z. **2.** *Zed* (*-bar*), a metal bar of Z-shaped cross-section 1891.

1. *allus.* Thou whoreson Zed, thou vnnecessary Letter *Lear* II. ii. 69.

Zedoary (ze·doări). 1475. [ad. med.L. *zedoarium*, ad. Arab. *zedwār.*] The aromatic tuberous root of one or more E. Indian species of *Curcuma*, used as a drug, having properties resembling those of ginger; the plant itself. *Yellow z.*, = CASSUMUNAR.

Zee (zī). 1677. A name, esp. now in U.S., of the letter Z.

Zeilanite (zəi·lănəit). 1851. [ad. G. *zeilanit*, f. *Zeilan* CEYLON.] *Min.* = CEYLONITE.

Zein (zī·in). 1822. [f. ZEA + -IN[1].] *Chem.* A protein found in maize, analogous to gluten.

‖**Zeitgeist** (tsai·tgaist). 1884. [G., f. *zeit* time + *geist* spirit.] The thought or feeling peculiar to a generation or period.

Zel. 1817. [Turk. *zil.*] A kind of cymbal.

Zelator (ze·lătǫɹ). 1460. [a. OF. *zelateur* or eccl. L. *zelator*, f. *zelare* to be zealous.] **1.** A zealous defender or supporter (*rare*). **2.** = ZEALOT 1, 2. (*rare*) 1644. **3.** A sister in a religious community with the duty of admonishing the mother superior or other members of the community when necessary 1851. So (in sense 3) **Ze·latrice** (-tris), **Ze·latrix.**

Zelotic, zealotic (zīlǫ·tik), *a.* 1657. [f. ZEALOT + -IC.] Of or like a zealot. So **Ze(a)·lotism**, zealotry.

Zeme, zemi (zī·mi). 1613. [Carib *cemi.*] An idol or tutelary spirit worshipped by the aborigines of the W. Indian islands. Hence **Ze·meism. Zemei·stic** *a.*

Zemindar (zĕmī·ndaɹ). *India.* 1683. [Hind., a. Pers. *zamīndār*, f. *zamīn*, *zamī* earth + *dār* holder.] Formerly, a collector of the revenue from land held by a number of cultivators; now, a native who holds land for which he pays revenue direct to the British government. Hence **Zemi·ndarship.**

Zemindary (zĕmī·ndări). *India.* 1757. [Hind., a. Pers. *zamīndārī*, f. *zamīndār.*] **1.** The system of holding lands and farming revenue by means of zemindars; the office or jurisdiction of a zemindar. **2.** The territory administered by a zemindar 1764.

‖**Zemni** (ze·mni). 1785. [Short for Russ. dial. *shchenók zemnói* 'puppy of earth'.] The blind mole-rat, *Spalax typhlus.*

Zemstvo (ze·mstvo). 1865. [Russ., f. *zemlya* land.] An elective provincial council in Russia for purposes of local government.

Zenana (zĕnā·nă). 1761. [Hind. *zenāna*, *zanāna*, a. Pers. *zanāna*, f. *zan* (= Gr. γυνή) woman.] **1.** In India and Persia, the women's apartments; an E. Indian harem. **2.** (Also *z.-cloth.*) A light thin dress-fabric 1900. **3.** *attrib.*, esp. of Christian missionary work among native Indian women 1810.

Zend (zend). 1700. [See next.] **1.** = next 1715. **2.** The language of the Avesta: also called *Avestic* and *Old Bactrian*, forming with Old Persian the Iranian group of Indo-European languages 1700. Hence **Ze·ndic, Ze·ndish** *adjs.* **Ze·ndist**, one versed in Z.

Zend-Avesta (zendăve·stă). 1630. [Alteration of *Avestá-va-Zend* the Avesta with the interpretation. The word *Zend* was mistaken for the name of the language and acquired that sense.] The sacred writings of the Parsees, usu. attributed to Zoroaster.

Zendic (ze·ndik). 1842. [a. Arab. *zindīq* atheist, Pers. *zandīq* fire-worshipper.] In the East, a disbeliever in revealed religion or a practiser of heretical magic. Hence **Ze·ndicism**, the belief of a z. 1697.

Zenick (zī·nik). Also **-ik.** 1843. [a. F. *zénik.*] The African suricate.

Zenith (ze·niþ, zī·niþ). late ME. [a. OF. *cenit*(*h* or med.L. *cenit*, ad. Arab. *samt* (*ar-rās*) way or path over the head.] **1.** The point of the sky directly overhead; the upper pole of the horizon. †**b.** *transf.* Course towards the zenith. MILT. **c.** *Magnetic z.*, the point of the sky directly above the magnetic pole of the earth 1885. **2.** *loosely.* The upper region of the sky; the highest or culminating point of a heavenly body 1631. **3.** *fig.* Highest point or state, climax, acme 1610.

1. The stars..near the z. shine with a steady light TYNDALL. 2. The conscious Moon, now in her Z. SWIFT. 3. The hand of God, whereby all Estates arise to their Z. and verticall points SIR T. BROWNE.

attrib. and *Comb.*: **z. distance**, the angular distance of a heavenly body from the z. (the complement of its *altitude*); **z. sweep**, a series of observations of the sky passing through the z. Hence **Ze·nithal** *a.*

Zenonian (zīnōu·niăn), *a.* and *sb.* 1843. [f. L. *Zeno*, *Zenon*, Gr. Ζήνων + -IAN.] **A.** *adj.* (*a*) Of or pertaining to Zeno of Elea, a philosopher of the 5th century B.C., and author of a disproof of the possibility of motion. (*b*) Of or pertaining to Zeno of Citium (*c* 300 B.C.), the founder of the Stoic philosophy. **B.** *sb.* A follower of (esp. the Stoic) Zeno; a Stoic. So **Zenonic** (zīnǫ·nik) *a.* **Zenonism** (zī·nŏniz'm), Stoicism.

Zeolite (zī·ŏləit). 1777. [ad. Sw., G., etc. *zeolit*, f. Gr. ζεῖν to seethe; see -LITE.] *Min.* Generic name for a group of hydrous silicates in which the bases are alumina and the alkalies and alkaline earths; generally characterized by swelling up and fusing to a glass or enamel under the blowpipe; commonly found in the cavities of igneous rocks. Hence **Zeolitic** (-i·tik) *a.*

Zep, colloq. abbrev. of ZEPPELIN.

Zephyr (ze·fəɹ). Also **zephyrus**, †**zefferus.** [OE. *zefferus*, a. L. *zephyrus* a. Gr. ζέφυρος.] **1.** The west wind, esp. as personified, or the god of the west wind. **2.** A mild soft gentle breeze or wind 1611. **3. a.** A shawl, coat, shirt, etc., of light gauzy material 1774. **b.** A fine light cotton dress-material, having the colours woven into the fabric 1849. **4.** A butterfly of the genus *Zephyrus.* **5.** A (French) Algerian light-infantryman 1854.

1. Zephirus..with his swete breeth CHAUCER. Zephir with Aurora playing MILT. 2. The zephyrs breathed softly from the south 1883. Hence **Zephyre·an, Zephy·rian, Ze·phyrous, Ze·phyry** *adjs.*

Zephyranth (ze·firænþ). 1845. [ad. mod.L. *Zephyranthes*, f. Gr. ζέφυρος + ἄνθος flower: with allusion to the waving flower-stalks.] A plant of the genus *Zephyranthes.*

Zeppelin (ze·pəlin). 1900. [f. name of the German Count F. von *Zeppelin.*] A dirigible airship of the type constructed by Count Zeppelin in 1900. Often colloq. abbrev. *Zep*(*p.* Hence **Ze·ppelin** *v. trans.* to bomb from a Z.

Zerda (zə̄·ɹdă). 1781. [So called by the 'Moors'.] = FENNEC.

Zereba, -iba, var. ff. ZARIBA.

Zero (zīə·ro). *Pl.* **zeroes** (-ouz). 1604. [ad. F. *zéro* or its source It. *zero*, ad. Arab. *çifr* CIPHER.] **1.** The symbol 0, 'nought'. Now *rare.* **b.** The compartment numbered 0 on a roulette table 1859. **2.** The point marked 0 on a graduated scale, from which the reckoning begins; esp. in a thermometer or other measuring instrument 1795. **3.** The temperature or degree of heat reckoned as zero in any thermometric scale, e.g. the freezing-point of water in Centigrade 1800. **4.** Nought or nothing reckoned as a number denoted by the figure 0, and constituting the starting-point of the series of natural numbers; the total absence of quantity considered as a quantity (in *Alg.*, etc. as intermediate between positive and negative quantities); hence = 'none at all' 1823. **b.** In the theory of functions, a value of a variable for which a function vanishes 1893. **5.** *fig.* A person or thing of no account; a 'cipher', nonentity 1813. **6.** *fig.* The lowest point; vanishing-point; nullity 1820. **b.** The starting-point of a process or reckoning 1849.

3. *Absolute z.*, the lowest temperature possible in the nature of things, at which the molecular motion

which constitutes heat, would cease; the z. of absolute temperature reckoned as −273° C. 4. Dante's direct acquaintance with Plato may be reckoned at z. LOWELL. 5. The other gentlemen are zeros MARIA EDGEWORTH. 6. My courage sinks to z. HOOD. b. He..makes 1788 his z. of human history 1866.

attrib., as *z. line, point* (sense 2), *z. value* (sense 4), *z. weather* (sense 3); **z. creep,** spontaneous displacement of the z.-point on a graduated scale; **z. hour** *Mil.*, the hour at which an attack or operation is timed to begin; *fig.* the moment at which any ordeal is to begin; the hour at which the lowest value of anything is reached or recorded; **z. magnet,** a magnet for adjusting the z., e.g. of a galvanometer; **z. mark, post,** a mark or post from which road distances are measured.

The coming of the z. hour of 3.30 in the morning 1917.

Zerumbet (zīrʋ·mbet). 1555. [Pg., ad. Hind., Pers. *zerunbād*.] An E. Indian plant (or its aromatic root) of the genus *Curcuma*, yielding a tonic drug.

Zest (zest), *sb.* 1674. [a. F. *zeste* orange or lemon peel; origin obsc.] 1. Orange or lemon peel used as a flavouring or for preserving. Now *rare* or *Obs.* 2. *fig.* Something that gives savour, relish, or piquancy; piquant quality 1709. 3. Keen relish or enjoyment displayed in speech or action; gusto, appetite or strong inclination (*for*) 1791. 4. *transf.* An appetizer or appetizing food; also, a relish, a piquant flavour 1835.

1. To prepare lemon-juice you must first carefully remove the z. and then the white part 1800. 2. The sense that, perhaps, it was imprudent to take a cab or drink a bottle of wine added a z. to those enjoyments THACKERAY. 3. She went to a lying-in or a laying-out with equal z. DICKENS. 4. Private zests and flavours on a side-table DICKENS. Hence **Zest** *v. trans.* to flavour with 'z.'; to add a relish to; to give a piquant quality to. **Ze·stful** *a.*, **-ly** *adv.*, **-ness.**

Zeta (zī·tă). 1840. [Gr. ζῆτα the letter Z, ζ.] The sixth letter of the Greek alphabet, used *attrib.* in **z.-function** *Math.*, one of a set of functions (denoted by Z or ζ prefixed to the variable) connected with elliptic integrals.

Zetetic (zĭte·tik), *a.* and *sb. rare.* 1645. [ad. Gr. ζητητικός, f. ζητεῖν to seek.] **A.** *adj.* Investigating; proceeding by inquiry.

This was called the Zetetick Philosophy, from its continual enquiry after Truth 1660.

B. *sb.* 1. (*sing.* or *pl.*) Investigation, scientific inquiry 1679. 2. An inquirer; *spec.* an adherent of the ancient Greek sceptic school of philosophy 1660.

2. The ancient Pyrrhonists were called Zetetics or seekers 1838. Hence **Zete·tically** *adv.*

‖**Zeuglodon** (ziū·glodǫn). 1839. [mod.L., f. Gr. ζεύγλη strap or loop of a yoke + ὀδούς, ὀδόντ- tooth.] *Palæont.* A genus of extinct Eocene cetaceans. Hence **Zeu·glodont** *sb.* and *a.* (a cetacean) of this genus. **Zeuglodo·ntoid** *a.* and *sb.* having the characters of this genus; (a cetacean) of the family *Zeuglodontidæ*.

‖**Zeugma** (ziū·gmă). 1586. [a. Gr. ζεῦγμα a yoking, f. ζευγνύναι to yoke.] *Gram.* and *Rhet.* A figure by which a single word is made to refer to two or more words in the sentence; esp. when applying in sense to only one of them, or applying to them in different senses. (Example: *She came in a flood of tears and a Bath chair.*) Hence **Zeugma·tic** *a.* **Zeugma·tically** *adv.*

Zeunerite (zoi·nərəit). 1873. [f. name of Gustav *Zeuner* of Freiberg, Saxony.] *Min.* A hydrous arseniate of uranium and copper, occurring in bright-green crystals.

‖**Zeus** (ziūs). 1706. [Gr. Ζεύς, related to L. *Jovis*; see JOVE.] 1. *Myth.* The supreme deity of the ancient Greeks 1839. 2. *Ichth.* A genus of spiny-finned fishes, including the John Dory, *Z. faber*, anciently sacred to Zeus 1706.

Zeuxite (ziū·ksəit). 1836. [f. Gr. ζεῦξις yoking, joining, tr. 'unity' in *Huel Unity*, name of the mine where found.] *Min.* A variety of tourmaline.

‖**Zho** (ʒōᵘ). 1841. [Tibetan *mdso*.] A hybrid animal, bred from the yak bull and a common cow, used for domestic purposes in northern India. Also called ‖**Zo·bo, zo·bu** [with masc. affix *-bo*]. So **Zho·mo,** a female zho.

Zibeline (zi·bĕlin, -əin). 1585. [ad. F. *zibeline*, deriv. of Slav. *sobol* SABLE *sb.*[1]] 1. The sable. 2. The fur of the sable 1869. 3. (In full *z. cloth.*) A soft woollen dress-material with a slightly furry surface 1892.

Zibet (zi·bĕt). 1594. [ad. med.L. *zibethum*; see CIVET *sb.*[1]] Variant of CIVET, esp. the Asiatic species.

Ziczac (zi·kzæk). Also **siksak, sagsag, sicsac, zi(c)kza(c)k.** 1844. [ult. a. Arab. *zaqzāq, saqsaq*.] An Egyptian plover, *Pluvianus ægyptius*, which warns the crocodile of approaching danger; perhaps identical with TROCHILUS[1].

Zigan, var. TZIGANE.

Zigzag (zi·gzæg), *sb., a., adv.* 1712. [ad. F.; ult. origin unkn.] **A.** *sb.* 1. A series of short lines inclined at angles in alternate directions; a line or course having sharp turns of this kind; *concr.* something characterized by such lines or turns. b. Chiefly in *pl.*: Each of the such lines or turns 1728. c. *fig.* 1781. 2. A road or path turning sharply at angles in alternate directions esp. so as to reduce the gradient on a steep slope 1728. b. *Fortif.* An attacking trench dug in zigzag to prevent enfilading 1733. c. *Arch.* A chevron-moulding 1814. d. A shell, or a moth, with zigzag marking 1815.

1. The hieroglyphic use of the z., for water, by the Egyptians RUSKIN. b. A winding road, which forms thirteen zig-zags 1775. c. The little zigzags of embarrassment JANE AUSTEN.

B. *adj.* 1. Having the form of a z.; turning sharply at angles in alternate directions; characterized by such turns 1750. b. *Bot.* Applied to the stem of a plant, or to a plant having such a stem 1796. 2. Chiefly *Nat. Hist.* Having z. markings 1785.

1. The chevron-work (or zig-zag moulding) GRAY. Flashes of forked, or zig-zag lightning 1767. Up from the lake a z. path will creep WORDSW. *fig.* All the brood of zig-zag politicians 1863.

C. *adv.* In a zigzag manner or direction 1730.

It may go straight forward, or zig-zag 1846. Hence **Zi·gzag** *v. intr.* to go or move in a z. course, to have a z. direction; *trans.* to give a z. form or motion to 1777. **Zi·gzagged** *ppl. a.* 1774; **Zi·gzagging** *vbl. sb.* and *ppl. a.*; **Zi·gzaggery,** z. course or proceeding 1760; **Zi·gzaggy** *a.* 1845.

‖**Zikkurat, ziggurat** (zi·kŭrăt, zi·g-). 1877. [Assyrian *ziqquratu* height, pinnacle.] A staged tower in which each storey is smaller than that below it; an Assyrian or Babylonian temple-tower.

‖**Zillah** (zi·lă). 1800. [Hind. *ḍilah* division.] An administrative district in British India. Hence **Zi·lladar,** the collector of a zillah.

‖**Zimb** (zimb). 1790. [Amharic.] An Abyssinian dipterous insect allied to the tsetse.

Zinc (ziŋk), *sb.* 1651. [ad. G. *zink*, of obsc. origin.] A hard brittle bluish-white metal (commercially called SPELTER), malleable and ductile between 200° and 250° F., obtained from various ores (BLENDE, CALAMINE, SMITHSONITE, ZINCITE), and used for roofing, for 'galvanizing' iron, etc., and as a component in alloys, esp. with copper in BRASS. Chemical symbol Zn; atomic weight 65. b. (with *pl.*). A plate of zinc used as the electropositive metal in a voltaic battery 1876.

attrib. and *Comb.*, as *z. filings, wire; z. lotion, ointment; z. carbonate, oxide; z. etching; z. lined, roofed* adjs. **z.-blende,** native zinc sulphide, blende; **-bloom,** hydrous carbonate of zinc; **-dust,** z. in the form of a fine powder, used as a deoxidizing agent and as a paint; **-grey,** (*a*) z.-dust obtained by grinding in oil, used as a preservative paint for ironwork; (*b*) a colour resembling that of z.; **-powder,** = *z.-dust*; **-spinel,** = GAHNITE; **-white,** oxide of z. used as a white paint. Hence **Zinc** *v. trans.* to coat or treat with z. or some compound of z. **Zi·ncate** *Chem.*, a compound of zincic oxide with the oxide of a more electropositive metal. **Zincic** (zi·ŋkik) *a.* of, pertaining to, or containing z. **Zinciferous** (ziŋki·fĕrəs) *a.* producing z. **Zi·ncify** *v. trans.* to coat or impregnate with z. **Zincite** (zi·ŋkəit) *Min.*, red oxide of z., red z. ore. **Zi·ncous** *a. Chem.* and *Electr.* pertaining to or of the nature of zinc; having the affinity of z.; relatively electropositive.

‖**Zincalo** (zi·ŋkălo), *fem.* **-ala.** *Pl.* **-ali, -ale.** 1842. The name by which the Gitanos or gipsies of Spain call themselves.

Zinco (zi·ŋko). 1887. Abbreviation of ZINCOGRAPH. Also, a zincographic plate or block.

Zinco-, comb. form of mod.L. *zincum* ZINC, in names of chemical compounds of zinc and another element or radical, as *z.-sulphate*. Also **Zincolysis** (ziŋkǫ·lisis), decomposition by an electric current, electrolysis. **Zincolyte** (zi·ŋkoləit), a substance so decomposed, an electrolyte. **Zincopo·lar** *a.*, having the polarity of a zincode. **Zi·ncotype** = ZINCOGRAPH.

Zincode (zi·ŋkoᵘd). [f. ZINC *sb.*, after ANODE.] *Electr.* = ZINC *sb.* b.

Zincography (ziŋkǫ·grăfi). 1834. [f. ZINCO- + -GRAPHY.] The art or process of engraving or etching designs on zinc, or of printing from such designs. Hence **Zi·ncograph** *sb.* a design or print produced by z.; *v. trans.* to engrave or print by z. **Zinco·grapher,** an engraver on zinc. **Zincogra·phic** *a.*

Zincoid (zi·ŋkoid). 1842. [f. ZINC *sb.* + -OID.] = ZINCODE.

Zinfandel (zi·nfændel). 1896. A red or white dry Californian wine.

‖**Zingano** (zi·ŋgăno), *fem.* **-ana.** *Pl.* **-ani, -e.** 1581. [It.] = next.

‖**Zingaro** (zi·ŋgăro), *fem.* **-ara.** *Pl.* **-ari, -e.** 1617. [It.] A gipsy; also *attrib.* or as *adj.*

‖**Zingel** (tsi·ŋgəl). 1803. [G.] Any fish of the percoid genus *Aspro*; esp. *A. zingel* of the Danube.

Zingiberaceous (zi:ndʒibĕrēⁱ·ʃəs), *a.* 1846. [f. mod.L. *Zingiberaceæ*; see GINGER *sb.* and -ACEOUS.] *Bot.* Belonging to the family *Zingiberaceæ* of monocotyledonous plants, typified by the genus *Zingiber* (GINGER).

‖**Zinke** (zi·ŋkĕ, tsi·ŋkĕ). 1776. [G.] A cornet-like musical instrument, formerly common in Europe; a loud reed-stop in an organ.

Zinked, pa. t. and pa. pple. of ZINC *v.*

Zinkenite (zi·ŋkĕnəit). 1835. [ad. G. *zinkenit*, named from J. K. L. *Zincken*.] *Min.* A steel-grey sulphide of antimony and lead.

Zinkiferous, -ify, -ing, -ite. See ZINC.

Zinky (zi·ŋki), *a.* 1757. [f. ZINC *sb.* + -Y[1].] Pertaining to or containing zinc.

‖**Zinnia** (zi·niă). 1767. [mod.L., f. name of J. G. *Zinn*, German botanist.] *Bot.* A plant of the Amer. composite genus *Zinnia*, extensively cultivated for the beauty of its flowers.

Zinnwaldite (zi·nwǫldəit). 1861. [ad. G. *zinnwaldit*, f. *Zinnwald* in Bohemia.] *Min.* A kind of mica containing lithium and iron.

Zion (zəi·ən). OE. [eccl. L. *Sion*, a. Heb. *tsīyōn*.] One of the hills of Jerusalem, on which the city of David was built, and which became the centre of Jewish life and worship; hence, the house of God, Israel, the Jewish religion, the Christian Church, Heaven, a place of worship. Hence **Zi·onism,** a movement aiming at the re-establishment of a Jewish nation in Palestine 1896; so **Zi·onist** *sb.* and *a.* **Zi·onward(s** *adv.* usu. *fig.* = heavenwards.

Zip (zip). *colloq.* 1875. [Imitative.] 1. A light sharp sound as of a bullet in flight or of the tearing of canvas or the like; movement accompanied by such a sound. 2. *fig.* Energy, impetus, 'go' 1900. 3. *attrib.* in the trade name of a 'lightning fastener', a device by which an opening is closed by the interlocking of metal strips placed on adjacent edges 1925. (Also **Zi·pper.**) Hence **Zip** *v. intr.*, to make a zip-like sound.

Ziphioid (zi·fi,oid), *a.* and *sb.* 1870. [f. mod.L. *Ziphius*, erron. for *Xiphius*, ad. Gr. ξίφιος, var. of ξιφίας XIPHIAS swordfish; see -OID.] *Zool.* **A.** *adj.* Resembling or allied to the genus *Ziphius* of whales. **B.** *sb.* A z. whale. So **Zi·phiiform** *a.*

Zippeite (zi·pĭ,əit). 1854. [ad. G. *zippeit*, named after F. X. M. *Zippe*, German mineralogist; see -ITE[1] 2 b.] *Min.* A sulphate of uranium, occurring in small yellow needles.

Zircon (zɔ̄·ɪkǫn). 1794. [ad. F. *zircone*; see JARGON *sb.*[2]] *Min.* A native silicate of zirconium, occurring in tetragonal crystals of various colours, some of which are used as gems. Hence **Zi·rconate,** a salt of zirconic acid. **Zirconia** (-kōᵘ·niă), a white earth, zirconium dioxide, ZrO_2, used in incandescent burners. **Zirconian** (-kōᵘ·niăn), **Zirconic** (-kǫ·nik) *adjs.* of, pertaining to, or like z.; containing zirconia or zirconium; **Zircon(i)o-, zirco-,** comb. ff. in names of zirconium compounds, as **Zi·rcon(i)oflu·oride. Zi·rconite,** a greyish or brownish variety of z. **Zirconium** (-kōᵘ·niəm), a metallic element obtained from z. as a black powder or in greyish crystals; symbol Zr.

Zither (zi·þəɹ). 1850. [See CITHERN.] An Austrian musical instrument having from thirty to forty strings let into the lower rim of a shallow resonance-box, and played by striking with the fingers and thumb. So **Zi·thern.**

‖**Zizania** (zi-, zəizē·niă). 1829. [mod.L. fem. sing. = late L. neut. pl., a. Gr. ζιζάνια pl. darnel.] *Bot.* (Any aquatic grass of) the genus *Zizania*, esp. *Z. aquatica* (Canada, Indian, water, or wild rice). Also †**Zizany**, tares ME.

Zizel (zi·zĕl). 1785. [ad. G. *ziesel.*] The ground-squirrel, *Spermophilus citillus.*

‖**Zizyphus** (zi·zifɒ̆s). 1440. [Late L., ad. Gr. ζίζυφον.] *Bot.* A plant of the genus *Zizyphus*, comprising spiny shrubs or trees of the buckthorn family, various species of which bear an edible fruit called JUJUBE. Also †**Zi·zypha,** the fruit itself, = JUJUBE 1. 1546.

Zoantharian (zōuænþē·riăn), *a.* and *sb.* 1887. [f. mod.L. *Zoantharia*, neut. pl., f. Gr. ζῷον animal + ἄνθος flower.] *Zool.* (A member) of the *Zoantharia*, one of the main divisions of *Actinozoa*, comprising the sea-anemones and other (often flower-like) animals, usu. with simple tentacles and parts arranged in sixes. So **Zoa·nthid,** a member of the zoantharian family *Zoanthidæ*. **Zoa·nthodeme** (-dīm) [Gr. δέμα bundle], a compound organism formed of coherent z. zooids or polyps. **Zoa·nthoid** *a.* of or like the zoanthids.

Zoanthropy (zouæ·nþrŏpi). 1856. [ad. mod.L. *zoanthropia*, f. Gr. ζῷον animal + ἄνθρωπος man.] *Path.* A form of mania in which a man imagines himself to be a beast. Hence **Zoanthropic** (-ǫ·pik) *a.*

‖**Zoarium** (zoē̆ə·riɒ̆m). 1880. [mod.L., as if f. Gr. ζῷον + -ARIUM.] *Zool.* The supporting structure of a colony of polyps; also, the colony or compound organism as a whole.

Zobo: see ZHO.

Zodiac (zōu·diæk). late ME. [a. OF. *zodiaque*, ad. L. *zodiacus*, a. late Gr. ζῳδιακός (sc. κύκλος circle) of signs, f. ζῴδιον sculptured figure (of an animal), dim. of ζῷον animal.] **1.** *Astr.* A belt of the celestial sphere extending 8 or 9 degrees on each side of the ecliptic, within which the apparent motions of the sun, moon, and principal planets take place; it is divided into twelve equal parts called *signs*. **b.** *Signs of the z.*: the twelve equal parts of the zodiac, through one of which the sun passes in each month; they are named after the twelve constellations (Aries, Taurus, Gemini, Cancer, Leo, Virgo, Libra, Scorpio, Sagittarius, Capricornus, Aquarius, Pisces) with which at a former epoch they severally coincided approximately 1532. **c.** *Z. of the moon, a planet*, etc.: that belt of the heavens to which its apparent motion is confined 1704. **2.** A representation of the zodiac. late ME. **3.** *transf.* (*a*) Recurrent series, round, course. (*b*) Compass, range. (*c*) Set of twelve. 1560.

1. Thus Phœbus through the Zodiack takes his way POPE.

Zodiacal (zodəi·ăkăl), *a.* 1576. [f. L. *zodiacus*; see prec. and -AL.] Of, pertaining to or situated in the zodiac. **b.** *Z. light*: a tract of nebulous light sometimes visible before sunrise or after sunset extending along the zodiac on each side of the sun in the form of an elongated ellipse 1734.

‖**Zoea** (zo,ī·ă). *Pl.* **zoeæ** (zo,ī·ī). 1828. [mod.L., f. Gr. ζωή life.] *Zool.* A larval stage of development in crustaceans, esp. decapods, usu. characterized by one or more spines on the carapace, and rudimentary thoracic and abdominal limbs. Hence **Zoeal** (zo,ī·ăl) *a.*

Zoetrope (zōu·ītroup). 1869. [irreg. f. Gr. ζωή life + -τροπος turning.] The 'wheel of life', a mechanical toy consisting of a revolving cylinder in which the effect of motion is produced by pictures on the inner surface of successive positions of a moving object, viewed through slits in the circumference.

Zoic (zōu·ik), *a.* 1863. [ad. Gr. ζωικός, taken as f. ζωή life, after AZOIC.] Showing traces of life; *Geol.* containing organic remains.

Zoilus (zōu·ilɒ̆s). 1567. [L., a. Gr. Ζωΐλος, the grammarian and critic of Homer.] A censorious, malignant, or envious critic. Hence **Zo·ilism,** carping criticism like that of Zoilus. **Zo·ilist.**

Zoisite (zoi·səit). 1805. [ad. G. *zoisit*, named from Baron von *Zois.*] *Min.* A native silicate of alumina and lime, occurring in orthorhombic prismatic crystals.

Zoism (zōu·iz'm). 1843. [f. Gr. ζωή life + -ISM.] The doctrine that life depends on a peculiar vital principle, and is not a mere resultant of combined forces; esp. in connexion with animal magnetism. So **Zo·ist. Zoi·stic** *a.*

Zolaism (zōu·lă,iz'm). 1882. [f. name of Émile *Zola* (1840–1902), French novelist + -ISM.] Excessively realistic treatment of the coarser sides of life, as in Zola's novels. So **Zolaesque** (-e·sk) *a.* characteristic of or resembling the style of Zola.

‖**Zollverein** (tsǫ·lfərəin). 1843. [G., f. *zoll* TOLL *sb.*[1] + *verein* union.] A union of states for free trade among themselves and uniform customs rates against others; orig. between certain states of the German empire, later including all the states; hence *gen.* of other countries.

‖**Zolotnik** (zolotni·k). 1783. [Russ., f. *zoloto* gold.] A Russian unit of weight, $\frac{1}{96}$ of the funt or Russian pound.

‖**Zona** (zōu·nă). 1706. [L., = ZONE.] **1.** *Archæol.* A girdle 1800. **2.** In Latin medical or anatomical terms, as **z. ignea** [= fiery girdle], also simply z., the disease shingles; **z. pellucida,** the transparent cell-wall of the ovum in Mammalia.

Zonal (zōu·năl), *a.* 1867. [ad. mod.L. *zonalis*, f. L. *zona* ZONE *sb.*] **1.** Characterized by or arranged in zones; of the nature of or forming a zone 1873. **b.** Of varieties of pelargonium: Having the leaves marked with zones of colour 1868. **2.** *Math.* and *Cryst.* Relating to a zone or zones of a sphere or of a crystalline form 1867. **3.** Pertaining or relating to, involving, or constituting a 'zone' or 'zones' 1882. Hence **Zona·lity,** z. character or distribution. **Zo·nally** *adv.*

Zone (zōun), *sb.* 1500. [ad. L. *zona*, a. Gr. ζώνη girdle.] **1.** *Geog.*, etc. Each of the five 'belts' or encircling regions, differing in climate, into which the tropics of Cancer and Capricorn and the arctic and antarctic circles divide the surface of the earth; viz. the *torrid* (†*burning*) *z.* between the tropics, the (north and south) *temperate zones* extending from the tropics to the polar circles, and the *frigid* (†*frozen*) *zones* (arctic and antarctic) within the polar circles. **b.** Any region extending round the earth and comprised between definite limits, e.g. between two parallels of latitude. Also applied to a similar region in the heavens or on the surface of a planet, etc. 1559. **2.** A region or tract of the world, esp. in relation to its climate 1599. **b.** A limited area distinguished from those adjacent by some quality or condition, freq. indicated by a defining word or phrase 1822. **3.** A girdle or belt, as a part of dress. Chiefly *poet.* Hence, any encircling band. 1608. **b.** *Astron.* The girdle of Orion 1599. **4.** A circumscribing or enclosing ring, band, or line 1591. **b.** A band or stripe of colour, etc. extending around something or over any surface or area; freq. one of a number of concentric or alternate markings of this kind 1752. **5.** *Astr.* A region of the sky comprised between definite limits 1795. **6.** *Anat., Zool., Bot.* A growth or structure surrounding some part in the form of a ring or cylinder; also, a region or area of some special character extending around or over some part 1811. **7.** *Geol.* and *Physical Geog.* A region comprised between definite limits, as of depth or height, and distinguished by special characters 1829. **8.** *Math.* The part of the surface of a solid of revolution contained between two planes perpendicular to the axis 1795. **b.** *Cryst.* A series of faces extending round a crystal and having their lines of intersection parallel 1868.

1. The Sun, with Rays directly darting down, Fires all beneath, and fries the middle Z. DRYDEN. **b.** We have, extending entirely around the earth, two zones of perpetual winds 1860. **2.** We may..in some milde Z. Dwell not unvisited of Heav'ns fair Light Secure MILT. **b.** All extensions should be performed before entering within the fire z. 1873. **3.** Shall these course hands untie The sacred Z. of thy Virginitie? QUARLES. **4.** Tentacles disposed in a z. around the mouth 1856. **b.** All such white marbles as are marked with green-coloured zones 1816.

attrib. and *Comb.*, as *z.-like* adj.; **z.-plate,** a glass plate with concentric rings alternately opaque and clear, for focusing light; **z. system,** division of a country into regions for railway travel, etc., travellers paying according to the number of zones traversed; so **z.-tariff**; **z. time,** the local time for any longitude as opposed to Greenwich time.

Hence **Zo·nary** *a.* having the form of a z. or girdle. **Zonate** (zōu·nēˈt), **Zo·nated** *adjs.* marked with rings or bands of colour. **Zona·tion,** distribution in zones; also, formation of zones or concentric layers.

Zone, *v.* 1792. [f. prec.] **1.** *trans.* To furnish with or encircle like a zone or girdle 1795. **2.** *Nat. Hist.* To mark with zones, rings, or bands of colour. Only in *pa. pple.* 1792. **3.** To distribute or arrange in zones 1904.

Zoned (zōund), *a.* 1718. [f. ZONE *sb.* or *v.* + -ED.] **1.** Wearing a zone or girdle. Hence, virgin, chaste. **2.** Characterized by or arranged naturally in zones, rings, or bands; marked with zones of colour 1792. **3.** Arranged according to zones or definite regions 1795.

Zonite (zōu·nəit). 1860. [ad. mod.L. *zonites*; see ZONE *sb.* and -ITE [1].] **1.** A snail of the genus *Zonites*. **2.** Any of the body-rings of a segmented animal, as an annelid 1880.

Zono- (zǫ·no), repr. Gr. ζωνο-, comb. form of ζώνη ZONE *sb.*, occurring in a few scientific and technical words; **Zonociliate** (-si·liĕt) *a.* *Zool.*, having a circlet of cilia. **Zo:noplace·ntal** *a.* *Zool.*, having a zonary placenta.

Zonule (zǫ·niul). 1831. [ad. mod.L. *zonula*, dim. of L. *zona* ZONE *sb.*; see -ULE.] *Anat.* A little zone: *spec.* the ring-shaped suspensory ligament of the crystalline lens (*z. of Zinn*). Hence **Zo·nular** *a.* pertaining to or forming a z. or little zone; *spec.* belonging to or affecting the z. of Zinn.

Zonure (zōu·niuəɹ). 1883. [ad. mod.L. *Zonurus*, f. Gr. ζώνη ZONE + οὐρά tail.] *Zool.* A lizard of the genus *Zonurus*, having rings of spiny scales on the tail.

Zoo (zū). *colloq.* 1847. [First three letters of ZOOLOGICAL taken as one syllable.] The Zoological Gardens in London; also, any similar collection of animals elsewhere.

Zoo- (zōu·o, zo,ǫ·), before a vowel properly **zo-**, repr. Gr. ζῳο-, comb. form of ζῷον animal, occurring in numerous scientific and technical terms; occas. denoting the power of spontaneous movement.

‖**Zo·ocarp** [Gr. καρπός fruit], a zoospore. **Zooche·mistry,** the chemistry of animal bodies; so **Zooche·mical** *a.* **Zo·oculture** = *zootechny*; so **Zoocu·ltural** *a.* **Zo:odyna·mics,** the dynamics of animal bodies. ‖**Zoœcium** (zo,ī·ʃ[1]ɒ̆m) [Gr. οἶκος house], the thickened and hardened part of the cuticle of each polyp in a colony of Polyzoa, forming a cell or sheath in which it is lodged. **Zo·ogamete,** a motile gamete. **Zooge·nic** *a.*, produced from animals; *Geol.* applied to formations of animal origin. **Zo:ogeo·graphy,** the geographical distribution of animals; hence **Zo:ogeo·grapher, Zo:ogeogra·phical** *a.*, **-ally** *adv.* **Zo:ogeo·logy,** that branch of geology which deals with fossil animal remains; **-lo·gical** *a.*, **-o·logist.** ‖**Zooglœa** (-glī·ă) [Gr. γλοιά glue], a gelatinous mass of bacteria; hence **Zooglœ·ic** *a.* ‖**Zo:ogoni·dium,** pl. **-ia,** a motile gonidium. **Zoo·graphy** (now *rare*), descriptive zoology 1593; hence **Zoo·grapher, -gra·phic, -al** *adjs.*, **-ally** *adv.* **Zoogyroscope** (-dʒəiə·rŏ-), a revolving glass cylinder enabling successive photographs of an animal to be thrown on a screen as continuous motion. **Zoo·latry** [-LATRY], the worship of animals. **Zo·olite,** a fossil animal or animal substance. **Zooma·gnetism,** animal magnetism. **Zo·omancy** [Gr. μαντεία], divination by observing the actions of animals. **Zo:omecha·nics,** = *zoodynamics*; hence **Zo:omecha·nical** *a.* **Zo:onoso·logy** [Gr. νόσος disease], the study of the diseases of animals. **Zoo·phagous** *a.* [Gr. -φαγος -eating], feeding on animals; carnivorous. **Zo·ophile,** a zoophilous plant; a zoophilist. **Zoo·philist** [Gr. -φιλος -loving], a lover of animals; an opponent of cruelty to animals, *spec.* an antivivisectionist. **Zoo·philous** *a.*, loving animals; also (*Bot.*) applied to plants whose seeds are disseminated by animal agency. **Zoophy·sics,** the study of physics in relation to animal bodies; so **Zoophy·sical** *a.* **Zo:ophysio·logy,** animal physiology. **Zoopla·nkton,** floating animal organisms collectively. **Zoopra·xiscope** [Gr. πρᾶξις action], a form of zoogyroscope. **Zoo·scopy,** a species of hallucination in which imaginary animal forms are seen, as in delirium tremens; so **Zoosco·pic** *a.* **Zoo·sophy,** the knowledge or study of animals. **Zo·osperm,** (*a*) a spermatozoon, (*b*) a zoospore; hence **Zo·osperm·atic** *a.* **Zo·ospore,** a motile spore, swarm-spore, occurring in some Algæ, Fungi, and Protozoa. **Zo:ospora·ngium,** a receptacle containing zoospores. **Zoo·sporous** *a.*, producing, of the nature of, or affected by zoospores. **Zo·otaxy** [Gr. τάξις arrangement], zoological classification, a systematic zoology. **Zo·otechny** [Gr. τέχνη art], the art of rearing and using animals for any purpose; so **Zoote·chnic** *a.*, **Zoote·chnics** *sb.* **Zoo·theism,** the attribution of deity to animals; so **Zoothei·stic** *a.* **Zo·otype,** an animal, or figure of one, used as the type of a deity, as in Egyptian hieroglyphics. **Zootypic** (-ti·pik) *a.*, pertaining to the animal type or types.

Zooid (zōu·oid). 1851. [f. Gr. ζῷον animal + -OID.] *Biol.* Something that resembles an animal (but is not one in the strict or full sense): now chiefly restricted to an animal arising from another by asexual reproduction, i. e. gemmation or fission; *spec.* each of the distinct beings which make up a compound or 'colonial' animal organism, and often have different forms and functions, thus more or less corresponding to the various organs in the higher animals.

The sexual z. is developed from the asexual, either directly by metamorphosis, or indirectly by gemmation or fission, thus giving rise to an Alternation of Generations 1888. Hence **Zo₁oi·dal** *a.* **Zo₁oidio·gamous** *a.* characterized by or of the nature of fertilization by the union of a motile cell with another cell.

Zookers (zu·kəɪz), *int. Obs.* or *arch.* and *dial.* 1620. [Short for *gadzwookers*; cf. next.] = next.

Zooks (zuks), *int. Obs.* or *arch.* and *dial.* 1634. [Short for *gadzooks* (GAD *sb.*⁵ 3).] An exclam. or minced oath, expressing vexation, surprise, or other emotion.

Zoological (zōu₁ŏlǫ·dʒikăl, *popularly* zū-lǫ·dʒ-), *a.* 1815. [f. ZOOLOGY + -ICAL.] Pertaining or relating to zoology; belonging or devoted to the scientific study of animals. **b.** *transf.* (freq. *joc.*) Animal 1855.

Z. Garden(s), the grounds of the London Z. Society in which its collection of wild animals is housed; hence *gen.* a garden or park in which wild animals are kept for public exhibition. **b.** One of the apartments has a zoological papering on the walls DICKENS. So **Zo₁olo·gic** *a.* (*rare*) 1816. **Zo₁ologi·cally** *adv.*

Zoologist (zo₁ǫ·lŏdʒist). 1663. [f. mod.L. *zoologia* + -IST.] One versed in zoology.

Zoologize (zo₁ǫ·lŏdʒəiz), *v.* 1861. [f. next or prec.; see -IZE.] *intr.* To study zoology practically; to examine animals zoologically; *trans.* to explore or study zoologically.

Zoology (zo₁ǫ·lŏdʒi). 1669. [ad. mod.L. *zoologia*, mod.Gr. ζωολογία, f. ζῷον animal + -λογία -LOGY. See N.E.D.] The science which treats of animals, one of the two branches (*z.* and *botany*) of Natural History or Biology, and itself divided into ornithology, ichthyology, entomology, etc.; also, a treatise on, or system of, this science. So **Zoo·loger** (*rare*) = *zoologist* 1663.

Zoom (zūm), *v.* 1886. [Echoic.] **1.** *intr.* To make a continuous low-pitched buzzing sound. **2.** *Aircraft slang.* To rise very steeply after flying horizontally at a low level 1917.

Zoomorph (zōu·omǭɪf). 1895. [f. Gr. ζῷον animal + μορφή shape.] A zoomorphic design or figure.

Zoomorphic (zōuomǭ·ɪfik), *a.* 1872. [f. as prec. + -IC.] **1.** Representing or imitating animal forms, as in decorative art. **2.** Attributing the form or nature of an animal to something, esp. to a deity or superhuman being 1880. **b.** Having, or represented as having, the form of an animal 1886.

Zoomorphism (zōu·omǭɪfiz'm). 1840. [f. prec. + -ISM.] **1.** Attribution of animal form or nature to a deity or superhuman being. **2.** Imitation or representation of animal forms in decorative art or symbolism 1879.

‖**Zoon** (zōu·ǫn). *Pl.* **zoa** (zōu·ă). 1864. [mod.L., a. Gr. ζῷον animal.] *Biol.* An organism scientifically regarded as a complete animal, whether constituting a single being as in the higher animals, or a number of zooids as in the various 'persons' that make up a 'colonial' animal.

Zoophyte (zōu·ŏfəit). 1621. [ad. mod.L. *zoophyton*, a. Gr. ζωόφυτον (Aristotle), f. ζῷον animal + φυτόν plant.] Any of the various animals of low organization formerly classed as intermediate between animals and plants, resembling the latter in being usu. fixed and in having a branched or radiating structure: as crinoids, sea-anemones, corals, sponges. So **Zo·ophytal, Zoophytic** (-fi·tik), *adjs.* **Zo:ophyto·graphy,** description of zoophytes. **Zo:ophyto·logy,** the department of zoology which treats of zoophytes; so **Zo:ophytolo·gical** *a.*

Zootomy (zo₁ǫ·tŏmi). 1663. [ad. mod.L. *zootomia*: see ZOO- and -TOMY.] The anatomy of animals; the dissection of animal bodies; in mod. use *esp.* comparative anatomy. So **Zooto·mic, -ical** *adjs.*, **-ically** *adv.* **Zoo·tomist,** a dissector of animal bodies, a comparative anatomist.

‖**Zophorus** (zōu·fŏrɒs), **zoophorus** (zo₁ǫ·fŏrɒs). 1563. [L., ad. Gr. ζῳ(ο)φόρος, f. ζῷον animal + -φορος -bearing.] *Anc. Arch.* A frieze bearing figures of men and animals carved in relief.

‖**Zopilote** (zōu·pilout). 1787. [Sp., a. Mex. *azopilotl.*] A vulture of the family *Cathartidæ*, esp. the Amer. carrion vulture or turkey-buzzard, *Cathartes aura.*

Zoril (zǫ·ril). Also **zo·rille, zori·llo.** 1774. [ad. F. *zorille*, ad. Sp. *zorrilla, -illo*, dim. of *zorra* ZORRO.] An animal of the African genus *Zorilla*, allied to the skunks; also applied to some Central and S. Amer. skunks.

Zoroastrian (zǫroæ·striăn), *a.* and *sb.* 1743. [f. L. *Zoroastres*, a. Gr. Ζωροάστρης, ad. Zend *Zarathustra*; see -IAN.] **A.** *adj.* Of or pertaining to Zoroaster or his dualistic religious system. **B.** *sb.* A follower of Zoroaster; a Parsee 1811. Hence **Zoroa·strianism.**

‖**Zorro** (þǫ·rro, zǫ·ro). 1838. [Sp., = fox.] The S. Amer. fox-wolf. Also **Zorri·no,** a kind of skunk, or its fur.

‖**Zoster** (zǫ·stəɪ). 1706. [L., a. Gr. ζωστήρ girdle.] **1.** The disease shingles, *Herpes zoster.* **2.** *Gr. Antiq.* A belt or girdle, esp. as worn by men 1824.

‖**Zostera** (zǫstīə·ră). 1819. [mod.L.; see prec. and -A¹.] *Bot.* A marine plant of the genus *Zostera*, esp. grasswrack, *Z. marina.*

‖**Zosterops** (zǫ·stĕrǫps). 1867. [mod.L., f. Gr. ζωστήρ girdle + ὤψ eye.] *Ornith.* Any small bird of the tropical and sub-tropical genus so named, characterized by a ring of white feathers round the eye; a silver-eye or white-eye.

Zouave (zuā·v). 1848. [F., f. native name *Zouaoua.*] **1.** One of a body of French light infantry, orig. recruited from the Algerian Kabyle tribe of Zouaoua, but afterwards composed of selected French soldiers, formerly retaining the Oriental uniform. **b.** (Also *Pontifical* or *Papal Z.*) One of a French corps organized at Rome in 1860 for the defence of the Pope, and disbanded after 11 years. 1864. **c.** Applied to certain Northern volunteers in the American civil war (1861–5) 1865. **2.** In full *z. jacket, bodice*: A woman's short embroidered jacket or bodice, resembling the jacket of the Z. uniform 1859.

Zounds (zaundz), *int. Obs.* or *arch.* 1600. A euphemistic abbrev. of *by God's wounds* used in oaths and asseverations. See 's.

Zubr (zūbr). 1847. [Russ.] The European bison or aurochs.

‖**Zucchetto** (tsuke·to). 1853. [Incorrect but usual form for It. *zucchetta*, dim. of *zucca* gourd, the head.] The skull-cap of an ecclesiastic.

Zulu (zū·lu), *sb.* and *a.* 1824. [Native name.] **1.** Also *Z.-Kaffir.* (A member) of a warlike S. African race of blacks of a type resembling the Kaffir, and inhabiting Natal. **2.** Applied to the language spoken by the Zulus 1850. **3.** An artificial fly used in angling 1898.

Zumbooruk (zɒ·mburɒk). 1825. [ad. Hindustani *zambūrak*, f. Pers. *zambūr* hornet.] A small swivel-gun, esp. one mounted on the back of a camel.

Zunyite (zū·nyəit). 1885. [f. *Zuñi*, name of a mine in Colorado + -ITE¹.] *Min.* A fluo-silicate of aluminium.

Zurlite (zɒ·ɪləit). 1826. [f. name of Signor *Zurlo* of Naples + -ITE¹.] *Min.* A white or green variety of melilite.

‖**Zwanziger** (tsva·ntsigəɪ). 1828. [G., f. *zwanzig* twenty.] An Austrian silver coin, equivalent to twenty kreutzers.

Zwieselite (tsvī·zĕləit). 1861. [ad. G. *zwiselit*, f. *Zwiesel* in Bavaria.] *Min.* A clove-brown variety of triplite.

Zwinglian (zwi·ŋgliăn, tsvi·-), *sb.* and *a.* 1532. [f. *Zwingli* (see below) + -AN.] **A.** *sb.* A follower of Ulrich Zwingli (1484–1531), the Swiss religious reformer. **B.** *adj.* Of or pertaining to Ulrich Zwingli or his doctrine, esp. concerning the Eucharist 1565. Hence **Zwi·nglianism.**

Zygadite (zi·gădəit). 1861. [ad. G. *zygadit*, f. Gr. ζυγάδην in pairs, f. ζυγόν yoke.] *Min.* A variety of albite occurring in reddish or yellowish-white tabular twin crystals.

‖**Zygæna** (zəidʒī·nă). 1683. [mod.L., ad. Gr. ζύγαινα.] **a.** *Ichth.* Any fish of the genus formerly so named (now *Sphyrna*), comprising the hammer-headed sharks. **b.** *Entom.* A genus of moths (also called *Anthrocera*), comprising the burnet-moths 1837.

Zygal (zəi·găl), *a.* 1886. [f. ZYGON + -AL.] *Anat.* Pertaining to or having a zygon.

‖**Zygantrum** (zəigæ·ntrɒm, zig-). *Pl.* **-antra.** 1854. [mod.L., f. Gr. ζυγόν yoke + ἄντρον cave.] *Anat.* A double cavity on the posterior side of the neural arch of each ordinary vertebra in serpents and some lizards, into which the *zygosphene* of the next vertebra fits.

‖**Zygapophysis** (zəigăpǫ·fisis, zig-). *Pl.* **-physes** (fisīz). 1854. [mod.L., f. Gr. ζυγόν yoke + ἀπόφυσις APOPHYSIS.] *Anat.* and *Zool.* A lateral process on the neural arch of a vertebra articulating with the corresponding process of the next vertebra. Hence **Zygapophysial** (-ăpofi·ziăl) *a.*

Zygite (zəi·dʒəit). 1888. [ad. Gr. ζυγίτης, f. ζυγόν yoke, thwart.] *Gr. Antiq.* A rower in the upper tier of a bireme or the middle tier of a trireme; cf. THALAMITE, THRANITE.

Zygnemaceous (zignīmēi·ʃəs), *a.* 1887. [f. mod.L. *Zygnemaceæ*, f. *Zygnema*, irreg. f. Gr. ζυγόν yoke + νῆμα thread; see -ACEOUS.] *Bot.* Belonging to the family *Zygnemaceæ* of filamentous freshwater algæ, which propagate by conjugation. So **Zygnemid** (zignī·mid), a member of this order.

Zygo- (zəi·go, zi·go), before a vowel properly **zyg-,** repr. Gr. ζυγο-, comb. form of ζυγόν yoke; occurring in various scientific terms (in *Biol.* freq. with ref. to *zygosis* as a method of reproduction).

Zygobranchiate (-æ·ŋki₁ĕt) *a.* and *sb.* (a gasteropod mollusc) having paired (right and left) gills. **Zygoda·ctyl** *a.*, having the toes arranged in pairs; yoke-toed; *sb.* a yoke-toed bird; so **Zygodacty·lic, Zygoda·ctylous** *adjs.* **Zy·godont** [Gr. ὀδούς, ὀδοντ- tooth] *a.*, of a molar tooth, having an even number of cusps arranged in pairs; of an animal, having such molar teeth. **Zygomo·rphic, Zygomo·rphous** *adjs.* [Gr. μορφή form] *Bot.*, of a flower, symmetrical about a single plane, divisible into similar lateral halves in only one way. **Zygophylla·ceous** [Gr. φύλλον leaf] *a. Bot.*, belonging to the family *Zygophyllaceæ*, typified by the genus *Zygophyllum* (bean-capers). **Zy·gophyte** (-fəit) [Gr. φυτόν plant], a plant which reproduces by conjugation. **Zygopleu·ra** [Gr. πλευρά side] *sb. pl. Morphology*, organic forms having bilateral symmetry, with either two or four antimeres; hence **Zygopleu·ral** *a.* **Zygo·pterid** [Gr. πτερόν wing] *sb.* and *a.*, (a member) of the *Zygoptera*, a division of dragon-flies, having all the wings nearly or quite equal in size. **Zy·gosperm,** = *zygospore.* **Zy·gosphere,** either of the two conjugating cells or gametes forming a zygospore. **Zy·gospore,** a germ-cell arising from the fusion of two similar cells (gametes), as in certain Algæ and Fungi. **Zygozo·ospore,** a motile zygospore.

‖**Zygoma** (zəigōu·mă, zig-). *Pl.* **-o·mata, -o·mas.** 1684. [a. Gr. ζύγωμα, f. ζυγόν yoke.] *Anat.* The bony arch on each side of the skull in vertebrates, consisting of the malar or jugal bone (cheekbone) and its connexions, and joining the facial to the cranial bones; also, some part of this arch, as the malar bone itself, o either of the two processes by which the cheekbone and the temporal bone articulate. So **Zygomatic** (-æ·tik) *a.* pertaining to, forming part of, or articulating with the zygoma; *sb.* a zygomatic muscle or bone. **Zygoma·tico-, zygo·mato-,** comb. forms of ZYGOMATIC, ZYGOMA.

‖**Zygon** (zəi·gǫn). *Pl.* **zyga** (zəi·gă). 1886. [ad. Gr. ζυγόν yoke.] *Anat.* The bar or stem connecting the two branches of an H-shaped fissure (*zygal fissure*) of the brain.

‖**Zygosis** (zəigōu·sis, zig-). 1880. [mod.L., ad. Gr. ζύγωσις, f. ζυγοῦν to yoke, f. ζυγόν yoke.] *Biol.* = CONJUGATION 5.

Zygosphene (zəi·gosfīn, zi·g-). 1854. [f. Gr. ζυγόν yoke + σφήν wedge.] *Anat.* and *Zool.* A double wedge-shaped projection on the anterior side of the neural arch of each ordinary vertebra in serpents and some lizards, which fits into the *zygantrum* of the next vertebra.

Zygote (zəi·gout). 1891. [ad. Gr. ζυγωτός yoked, f. ζυγοῦν to yoke.] *Biol.* A germ-cell resulting from the union of two reproductive cells or gametes; also *attrib.* or as *adj.* Hence **Zygotic** (-ǫ·tik) *a.* pertaining to or of the nature of a zygote; produced or characterized by zygosis. **Zygo·toblast** [-BLAST], one of a number of germ-cells or sporozoites produced by budding from a zygotomere. **Zygo·tomere** [Gr. μέρος part], one of a number of cells formed by segmentation of a zygote in the malaria parasite or other *Sporozoa.*

Zymase (zəi·mēⁱs). 1875. [ad. F. *zymase*, f. Gr. ζύμη leaven + *-ase* (in *diastase*).] *Biochem.* Any of a group of enzymes which convert glucose into carbon dioxide and water or into alcohol and carbon dioxide according as oxygen is present or absent.

Zyme (zəim). 1882. [ad. Gr. ζύμη leaven.] The substance causing a zymotic disease.

Zymo- (zəi·mo), before a vowel **zym-**, comb. form repr. Gr. ζύμη leaven, used in the general sense 'ferment'.

Zymogen (zəi·modʒen) *Biol. Chem.*, a substance formed in an organism and producing a ferment; so **Zymogene·tic, Zymoge·nic** *adjs.* **Zymo·logy,** the science of ferments and their action; so **Zymolo·gical** *a.*, **Zymo·logist.** **Zymo·lysis** [Gr. λύσις loosening], decomposition by means of a (esp. an unorganized) ferment; so **Zymoly·tic** *a.* **Zymo·meter,** an instrument measuring the degree of fermentation of a fermenting liquor. **Zy·mophyte** [Gr. φυτόν plant], a vegetable organism which causes fermentation. **Zy·motechny,** the art of fermentation; so **Zymote·chnic, -ical,** *adjs.*; **Zymote·chnics. Zy:motechno·logy,** the scientific study of the principles of zymotechny.

‖**Zymosis** (zəimōu·sis). *Pl.* **-oses** (-sīz). 1842. [f. Gr. ζύμωσις, f. ζυμοῦσθαι to ferment, f. ζύμη leaven; see -OSIS.] Fermentation; *spec.* the morbid process, regarded as analogous to or involving fermentation, which constitutes a zymotic disease.

Zymotic (zəimǫ·tik), *a.* (*sb.*). 1842. [ad. Gr. ζυμωτικός causing fermentation; see prec.] **A.** *adj.* A general epithet for infectious diseases, orig. because regarded as being caused by a process analogous to fermentation; pertaining to this theory of disease; causing such disease. **b.** Fermentative 1874. **c.** *transf.* Containing putrefactive germs 1881. **B.** *sb.* A zymotic disease 1842. Hence **Zymo·tically** *adv.*

Zymurgy (zəi·mɒɹdʒi). 1868. [f. Gr. ζύμη leaven + -ουργία working.] The practice or art of fermentation, as in wine-making, brewing, distilling, etc.

ADDENDA AND CORRIGENDA

*** An asterisk placed before a word in the course of an article indicates that it will be found in its alphabetical place below.**

A. III.

A = adult, designating cinema films suitable for adult audiences; A = atomic, as in *A-bomb*; = Australian, as £A 1,246; A or a = ampère; a.a., in photography = take one of each; A.A. = Automobile Association 1905, Anti-aircraft 1917; A.A.F. = Army Air Force (*U.S.*); A.B.A. = Amateur Boxing Association; A.B.C., applied to a process of sewage treatment in which *a*lum, *b*lood, *c*lay, and *c*harcoal are employed as precipitants (*Chambers's Techn. Dict.*); A.B.C.A. = Army Bureau of Current Affairs; A.B.C.D. = *A*merican, *B*ritish, *C*hinese, *D*utch powers in the Pacific 1941; A.C., a.c. = alternating current; A.C. = Aircraftman; A.C.C. = Army Cadet College; A.D.C. = AIDE-DE-CAMP; A.D.G.B. = Air Defence of Great Britain 1925–44; A.E.A. = Atomic Energy Authority 1954; A.E.R.E. = Atomic Energy Research Establishment; A.E.U. = Amalgamated Engineers' Union; A.F., a.f. = audio-frequency; A.F.C.(M.) = Air Force Cross (Medal) 1919; A.F.N. = American Forces Network; A.F.S. = Auxiliary Fire Service; A.I. = artificial insemination; A.L.(s.) = autograph letter (signed); A.M.G., see *AMGOT; A.R.P. = Air Raid Precautions 1936; A.S.C. = Army Service Corps; A.S.L.E.F. = Associated Society of Locomotive Engineers and Firemen; A.S.R. = Air-Sea Rescue 1941; A.T.C. = Air Training Corps 1941; A.T.S. = Auxiliary Territorial Service (women) 1938; Å.U., AU. = Ångstrom unit; A.V.R.E. = Armoured Vehicle Royal Engineers.

‖**Aasvogel** (ā·sfōu:gəl). 1887. [Afrikaans, f. Du. *aas* carrion + *vogel* bird, FOWL.] A South African vulture, *Gyps kolbii.*

A.B.C. (ēⁱbīsī·). 1894. Initials of *A*erated *B*read *C*ompany; a tea-shop conducted by this company.

Abdomen. Add pronunc. (æ·bdŏmĕn), now the more usual.

Aberdeen (æbəɹdī·n), name of a city and county in Scotland; *A. terrier*, a rough variety of Scotch terrier 1880. The adj. is Aberdonian (æbəɹdōu·niăn) 1670 [f. med.L. *Aberdonia*].

Ablative, *a.* Hence **Ablatival** (æblătəi·văl) 1854.

Aboard, *adv.* **3.** *U.S.* On or on to a railway train, etc.; esp. in *All aboard!*, a conductor's direction to intending passengers to enter a train, car, etc. 1837. Similarly as *prep.*

‖**Aboulia** (ăbau·liă), **abulia** (ăbiū·liă). 1848. [mod.L., f. Gr. ἀ- privative + βούλεσθαι to will; cf. Gr. ἀβουλία thoughtlessness.] *Path.* Loss of will-power, as a mental disorder.

Above, *prep.* **3.** Phr. *A. oneself*: orig. applied to horses that are over-fed and under-exercised, or have not undergone the full training for a race; hence, (of persons) not self-controlled, out of hand (*colloq.*) 1893.

Abrasive (ăbrēⁱ·ziv), *sb.* 1853. [subst. use of the adj.] A substance used for the removal of matter by abrasion.

Abreaction (æbriæ·kʃən). 1916. [f. AB- + REACTION, after G. *abreagierung* (Jung).] *Psychotherapy.* The liberation by revival and expression of the emotion associated with forgotten or repressed ideas of the event that first caused it. Hence **Abrea·ct** *v.* to eliminate by a.

Abridge, *v.* **2. b.** Illogically used for: To produce by a process of shortening *from.*

A Vocabulary Persian, Arabic, and English a–d from the quarto edition of Richardson's dictionary as edited by Charles Wilkins 1810. Any Dictionaries compiled or abridged from the principal Dictionary *Indenture between Philological Society and O.U.P.* 1875.

‖**Absolvitor** (æbsǫ·lvitǫɹ). 1547. [3rd pers. sing. imper. pass. of L. *absolvere* to ABSOLVE; 'let him be absolved or discharged from the action'.] *Sc. Law.* A decision of the court in favour of the defender.

Abstract, *a.* In the fine arts, characterized by lack of or freedom from representational qualities. So **Abstra·ction,** a state of freedom from these; hence **Abstra·ctionism,** the pursuit or cult of this.

The contention..that abstract or non-representational pictures can be appreciated whichever way they are hung...that two of his abstract pictures have been deliberately hung sideways in an exhibition at the Tate Gallery *Daily Tel.* 25 Mar. 1952. Ours is the age of atomic energy,..of psycho-analysis and abstractionism in the arts *Lit. Guide* Apr. 1952.

Acade·micism. Academic quality or style.

It was dry academicism at its worst, but was admired at the time 1948 BOASE in *Jrnl. Warburg & Courtauld Inst.* X. 99.

Acadian. Add: 1705 (*Dict. Amer. Eng.*) ¶F. *Acadie* included Nova Scotia and New Brunswick.

‖**Acapnia** (ēⁱkæ·pniă). 1907. [mod.L., f. A- 14 + Gr. καπνός smoke; see -IA [1]. Cf. F. *acapnie* (1903).] *Path.* Diminution or deficiency of carbon dioxide in the blood.

Accent, *sb.* **8.** Also, a mark or feature as distinctive of an individual, national, local, etc. style or method.

Since the difference between good and bad design.. may be a question of millimetres in the thickness of a part of a letter..even these slight national accents are of great importance to the bibliophile 1947.

Accinge (æksi·nᵈʒ). 1657. [ad. L. *accingere.*] *refl.* To 'gird oneself' *to* action.

Acheulian (ăʃiū·liăn), *a.* [After F. *acheuléen.*] *Archæol.* Of the palæolithic epoch represented by remains at *St. Acheul*, France.

Achilles (ăki·līz). L. form of Gr. Ἀχιλλεύς, a hero of Greek story, son of Peleus and Thetis; phr. *A. heel* or *heel of A.*, the one vulnerable spot; with allusion to the dipping of A. by Thetis in the river Styx, which left the heel vulnerable by which he was held, so that he died from a wound in it. Cf. ACHILLEAN.

Ireland, that vulnerable heel of the British A.! COLERIDGE, 1810. Hanover, the Achilles'-heel to invulnerable England CARLYLE, 1864. He only discloses his own Achilles' heel 1930. **A. tendon**: see TENDON.

Acholic (ēⁱkǫ·lik), *a.* [f. Gr. ἄχολος (see A- 14, CHOLIC) + -IC.] *Path.* = ACHOLOUS.

Acid. *A. drop*: short for *acidulated drop* 1836 (Dickens).

Ack (æk), used in telephone communications and in oral transliterations of code messages for *a.*, as in *ack emma*, for *a.m.* (see A III. 2); cf. *EMMA, *PIP; so **Ack-ack** (ækæ·k), for *a.-a.*, i.e. anti-aircraft.

Acoustic, *a.* **1. b.** *A. mine*, a submarine mine that can be exploded by sound-waves transmitted under water.

Across, *adv.* In phr. (orig. U.S.), for *a. the footlights*, as *to get* or *come a.*, to reach the audience or the public, gain acceptance (*with* something). So *to get* or *put* (something) *a.*: see GET *v.* VII, *PUT *v.* 1913.

Acrost (ăkrǫ·st), *adv.* and *prep.* Widespread dial. and U.S. f. ACROSS 1759.

Act, *sb.* †An interval or interlude in a play.

Acte..an Act, or Pause in a Comedie, or Tragedie COTGR. 1611. They sleep all the Act SHAKS. *Mids.N.D.* III. ii ad fin. (Folio 1, 1623). In the act-time De Flores hides a naked rapier behind the door MIDDLETON *Changeling* (1653) III. i. 11. We call Act that Fifth part of a Drammatick Poem which is begun and ended with Musick HEDELIN *Whole Art of Stage* (1684) 66.

ACTH, Acth (ēⁱsītīēⁱ·tʃ). 1943. Initial-formed name of the drug *A*drenocortico*t*ropi*c h*ormone.

Actino-.

a:ctinothe·rapy [see *-THERAPY], healing by means of radiation.

Action. II. 3. *attrib.*

a. stations, positions in a ship, etc., to be taken up when going into action or proceeding to a manœuvre.

Actioned (æ·kʃənd), *a.* [f. ACTION + -ED[2].] Having an action of a specified kind.

He was a particular a. horse 1835.

Activate, *v.* Delete †*Obs.* and add: **b.** *Physics.* To make active, *spec.* radioactive 1902.

Schönbein..found that sulphurous acid had a remarkable 'activating' (*activierende*) effect on various oxidising substances 1902. *Activated sludge*, aerated sewage containing aerobic bacteria. So **Activa·tion, A·ctivator.**

Active, *a. A. list*, a list of naval, military, or air force officers who are performing active service, or are available for doing so, and are receiving full pay 1852. *A. service*, war service in an armed force 1838.

Ad (æd), colloq. abbrev. of ADVERTISEMENT 1852 (*U.S.*). Also *ADVERT.

Adapt, *v.* Illogically used for: To construct or produce by adaptation (*from*).

A lost husband. A drama..written and a-d from the French (*title*) C. READE 1852. The Concise Oxford Dictionary of Current English adapted..from the Oxford Dictionary 1911.

Address, *v.* **II. 1.** *Golf.* To put oneself in position to strike (the ball).

Aden (ē·dən). 1954. [f. initials of *Armament Development Establishment Enfield.*] A 30-millimetre cannon for aircraft.

Ad lib. (æd li·b): see AD LIBITUM. Hence Ad-lib *v.* (orig. *U.S.*) to announce without script, improvise (words, etc.) in the course of a broadcast performance.

‖**Ad nauseam** (æd nǭ·siæm). 1814. [L., 'to sickness'.] So as to excite disgust. Also *et ad nauseam* (1647), *ad nauseam usque* (*a* 1683), *usque ad nauseam* (1819).

Adsorption. Hence (by back-formation) **Adso·rb** *v.* to collect by adsorption 1882. **Adso·rbate**, the material adsorbed. **Adso·rbent** *a.*, *sb.*, (that is) an adsorbing agent.

Advance, *sb. attrib.* applied to measures taken in advance of publication or issue; so also *a. agent*, *a. copy* (of a book) 1885.

Advert (æ·dvəɹt), *sb. c* 1935. Commercial abbrev. of ADVERTISEMENT.

Aerobe. So the adjs. **Aero·bian, Aero·bious** 1879, **Aero·bic** (-ǫ·bik), **Aerobio·tic** 1885.

Ae:rodynamicist (-dəinæ·misist). One skilled in aerodynamics; see -IST.

Aerodyne (ē·rŏdəin). 1940. [Back-formation from AERODYNAMIC.] Generic term for heavier-than-air aircraft.

Aerofoil (ē·rŏfoil). 1910. [f. AERO- + FOIL *sb.*[1]] A wing, aileron, tailplane, or other lifting surface of an aeroplane.

Aerostat. 3. Generic term for lighter-than-air aircraft 1940.

Affiliate, *sb.* An affiliated organization, company, etc.

Two a.-s of the internationally owned Iraq Petroleum Company 1953.

Afghan (æ·fgæn), *a.* and *sb.* 1798. Pertaining to, a native of, Afghanistan, a country lying to the NW. of India.

A. hound: a swift hunting dog of the Near East, having thick silky hair.

After, *prep.* **2.** Used provincially for 'past' in stating the time of day, as in *half* (*a quarter*) *a. three* 1847.

A·fter-care. 1894. [AFTER-, CARE *sb.*[1]] Attention given to a subject after a specific period (e.g. of medical treatment, imprisonment, etc.).

The A. Association 1894.

Age, *sb.* **1.** phr. *Be your a.* (orig. *U.S.*): behave as becomes your years.

Age, *v. techn.* To fix the colours and mordants in (cloth, etc.) by exposing the printed goods to the action of a warm moist atmosphere; orig. in gerund or vbl. sb. 1849. Hence **Ager** (ē·dʒəɹ), an ageing apparatus or chamber; *attrib.*, as *a.-man*, *-minder*.

Agene (ē·dʒīn). 1951. [f. AGE *v.* + -ENE.] Nitrogen trichloride used in bread-making for improving, stabilizing, and artificially ageing the flour. Hence **A·genator**, an apparatus used for the operation [see *-ATOR]. **A·genize** *v. trans.* to treat with agene, as *agenized flour*.

‖**Agent provocateur** (aʒaṅ provokatör). 1896. [F., 'provocative agent'.] An agent employed to induce or incite a person to commit an incriminating act.

Agin (ăgi·n), *prep.* 1857. Widespread dial. var. of AGAIN *prep.*, against; often used joc. in phr. *a. the government*, taken to represent the typical Irishman's or countryman's attitude in politics.

I wur niver agin the raäte TENNYSON *Northern Farmer*, 1864.

Agreeable, as *sb.* with *the*, in *to do the a.*, to make oneself pleasant and affable 1851.

Agricu·lturally, *adv.* 1821. [f. AGRICULTURAL + -LY[2].] With regard or reference to agriculture.

Agro- (æ·grǭ), irreg. comb. form of L. *ager* countryside (cf. ACRE), as in **a.-town**, a town established in the midst of a rural area 1952.

Ahead, *adv.* **4.** esp. with *to go*: Forward or onward with what is in hand 1838.

Aid, *sb.* **1. b.** phr. *In a. of*: used derisively, with allusion to the freq. use of the phr. in appealing for the public support of a cause.

That 's your disillusioned expression..what 's it in a. of? 1935.

3. *spec.* A physical device to aid persons whose organs are disabled, e.g. *hearing a.* 1951.

‖**Aide-mémoire** (ē·dmemwāɪ, ‖ędmemwār). 1856. [F., f. *aider* to AID + *mémoire* MEMORY.] A manual of formulæ, etc. to serve as an aid to the memory; in diplomatic use, a memorandum.

Aileron (ē·lĕrǫn). 1909. [a. F. *aileron*, dim. of *aile* (:—L. *ala*) wing.] A hinged plane or flap on the wing of an aeroplane, for maintaining lateral control.

Air, *sb.* **I. 1. b.** *On the a.*: broadcast or broadcasting by wireless telegraphy 1927.

3. fig. phr. (slang). *Up in the air*: excited, as in anger (orig. *U.S.* 1906).

a.-borne, carried through the air; (of aircraft) that is in the air; (of troops) belonging to a unit trained for transportation and attack by air 1940; **a.-conditioned** *a.*, (of a building, room) provided with conditions of temperature and humidity suited to the proper accommodation of its occupants or conservation of its contents 1936; also **a.-conditioning** 1910; **a.-field**, an area of land devoted to the accommodation and maintenance of aircraft; **a.-lift**, transport or supply by aircraft; **a. liner** (see *LINER[2]); **a.-mail**, correspondence conveyed by aeroplane 1914; **a.-minded** *a.*, interested in or enthusiastic for the use and development of aircraft; **a.-power**, power of defensive and offensive action dependent upon a supply of aircraft 1936; **a.-raid**, also *attrib.*, as *a.-r. precautions* (1935), *shelter*, *warden*, *warning* (cf. A.R.P. s.v. *A); **a.-screw**, a power-driven screw for producing pull or thrust by rotation in the air, a propeller 1914; **a.-sea rescue**, applied to a branch of the R.A.F. whose task is to rescue airmen and passengers from the sea, and to such operations 1941; **a.-speed**, the speed of a flying-machine in relation to the air, as dist. from ground-speed 1910; **a.-stop**, a point on the route of aircraft at which stops are regularly made; **a. strip**, a strip of country used or usable for air-fields 1944; **A. Training Corps**, an organization for the training of cadets for the R.A.F.; **a. umbrella**, a force of aircraft used to 'cover' (i.e. give air protection to) a military operation; **a. warden** = *air-raid warden* 1937.

Aircraft. Also, a single flying machine 1907. The official form of the compound with *man* is **Aircraftman** (so **-woman**).

Airdrome. *U.S.* = AERODROME.

Airgraph (ē·ɹgraf). 1941. [f. AIR *sb.* + -GRAPH.] A form of air-mail registered by Kodak Ltd., in which the correspondent's letter is photographed on a reduced scale.

Airplane. The official and popular word for *aeroplane* in U.S.A.

[**Air,** *sb.* p. 39, col. 1, **b. -port**[2]: substitute:]

Airport (ē·ɹpōəɹt). 1926. [PORT *sb.*[1], in transf. use of sense 2.] An aerodrome on a route served by aircraft with customs facilities.

Alarm, *sb.* II. 2, 8. *Alarms* (or *alarums*) *and excursions*, a stage direction occurring in varying forms in Shaks. *Hen. VI* and *Rich. III* (e.g. *3 Hen. VI* v. ii. *init.*); used playfully by recent writers for: Skirmishing, confused fighting, sudden divagations, and the like 1895.

Albanian (ælbē·niăn), *a.* and *sb.* 1813. [f. med.L. *Albania*, med.Gr. Αλβανία + -AN. Cf. *ARNAOUT.] Of or pertaining to, a native of, Albania, a country of the western part of the Balkan peninsula. **B.** The language of modern Albania.

Albion (æ·lbiən). *poet.* or *rhet.* ME. [L. *Albiōn* (Gr. 'Αλουίων Ptolemy, 'Αλβίων), a. Celtic **Albiō(n-)*, referred to **albho-* (L. *albus* white), with ref. to the white cliffs of Dover.] Great Britain.

Perfidious A., rendering F. *le perfide Albion*, a rhetorical expression for 'England', with ref. to her alleged treacherous policy towards foreigners.

Aldis (ǫ·ldis). Name of Arthur Cyril Webb *Aldis*, registered trademark designating inventions of his, as *A. lens* (for hand cameras), *A. lamp* (for signalling), *A. unit sight* (for aeroplanes).

Aleck: see *SMART.

Alert. C. 3. a. A state of preparedness for resistance to a possible gas attack 1915. **b.** A signal given by means of a siren or hooter to indicate that enemy aircraft are in the neighbourhood; the period lasting from this to the all-clear 1940.

Alexin (ăle·ksin). 1896. [ad. G. *alexin*, f. Gr. ἀλέξειν to ward off + -IN[1].] *Physiol.* Any of a class of substances found in blood serum capable of destroying bacteria.

Algo- (æ·lgo, ælgǫ·), comb. form of Gr. ἄλγος pain.

algo·meter, an instrument for measuring degrees of sensitiveness to pain 1890.

Algol (æ·lgǫl). [Arab. *rās al-ghūl* head of the Medusa (spec. use of *ghūl* GHOUL).] *Astron.* The star β Persei.

Alibi, *sb.* **b.** *U.S.* A plea of innocence, an excuse 1912. Hence **Alibi** *v.* 1917.

Alicyclic (ælisi·klik), *a.* 1891. [f. *ali-* of next + CYCLIC.] *Org. Chem.* Combining the qualities of aliphatic and cyclic compounds.

Aliphatic (ælifæ·tik), *a.* 1895. [f. Gr. ἀλειφατ-, ἄλειφαρ unguent, fat + -IC.] *Org. Chem.* Pertaining to fats or fatty acids; (hence) epithet of organic compounds (of which these are typical) having a chain structure.

All. A. 7. In scoring at games, denoting that both sides have made the stated score; *love all* = neither side has scored 1837.

all-clear, a signal giving information that there is no danger; *spec.* the signal that hostile aircraft have left the neighbourhood ('raiders passed') 1939; **all-in,** (*a*) exhausted 1902, (*b*) inclusive of all 1890; *Wrestling*, without restrictions; **all-out**, using or involving all one's (or its) strength or resources; fully extended; at top speed 1895; **all-way** *a.*, from and to which there is movement in all possible directions.

C.

colloq. phr. **all there**: having all his wits about him; often in *not all there*, not 'compos mentis', 'wanting' 1864.

E.

all-star (of a dramatic company, performance, etc.) in which all performers are theatrical (etc.) stars; *transf.* of a performance, meeting, etc. in which the participants are of the first rank 1889.

The old O.U.D.S. will present a special All-Star Matinee at the New Theatre 1949.

Alleluiatic, *a.*

A. Sequence, the hymn 'Cantemus cuncti melodum' (B. Notker, 840–912), translated by J. M. Neale as 'The strain upraise of joy and praise, Alleluya!'.

Allergy (æ·lɘɹdʒi). 1913. [ad. G. *allergie* (1906), f. Gr. ἄλλος other, different + ἔργον work (used for 'reaction'): see -Y[3].] *Path.* orig. The altered state of a body produced by a sensitizing dose of foreign material; now, more widely, sensitiveness to the action of particular foods, pollens, insect-bites, or the like. Hence **A·llergen** [after *pollen*], a substance producing a.; **Allergic** (ælɜ̄·ɹdʒik) *a.*, pertaining to or characterized by a.; *fig.* sensitive (esp. antipathetic) *to*; **Allergist** (ælɜ̄·ɹdʒist), one who specializes in allergic phenomena.

Perennial hay fever or allergic coryza 1939.

Allure, *sb.*[1] In the 20th c. a direct adoption of F. *allure*: Personal charm or power of attraction 1901.

Altar, *sb.* **2.** phr. *To raise to the altars of the Church*: to give (a person) the status of one who is commemorated in the service of the altar, as by sanctification or beatification.

Alter, *v.* **1. b.** Used illogically in *altered from*: produced by alteration of, e.g. '*be wi' you*, altered from *buy you*'.

Alternator (ǭ·ltəɹnētǫɹ). 1893. [f. ALTERNATE + -OR 2 c.] *Electr.* A dynamo giving an alternating current.

Altero- (æ·ltĕro), comb. form (see -O-) of L. *alter* other, as in *altero-centric*, *-referent*.

Amalgamate, *v.* **4.** *esp.* To combine (bodies of people, societies, or organizations) into a whole; freq. in *ppl. a.*

Amalgamated Railway Servants 1894. Amalgamated Engineers' Union 1938.

Ambi- (æmbi), repr. L. *ambi-*, comb. form of *ambo* both.

Ambivalent (æmbi·vălənt), *a.* 1921. [f. *AMBI-, after *equivalent*.] Having either or both of two contrary or parallel values, qualities, or meanings. Hence **Ambi·valently** *adv.*, **Ambi·valence.**

Amerind (æ·mĕrind), **Amerindian** (æmĕri·ndiăn), *sbs.* and *adjs.* 1897–8. contr. of *American Indian.*

Amgot (æ·mgǫt). A word made up from the initials of *Allied Military Government of Occupied Territory*, title of a body first set up in Sicily in 1943 during World War II. Later called *A.M.G.*

Amharic (æmhæ·rik), *a., sb.* 1813. [f. *Amhara*, province of Ethiopia + -IC.] The name of the official and court language of Ethiopia.

Amitosis (æmitōu·sis). 1888. [mod.L., f. Gr. privative α- A- 14 + MITOSIS.] Direct division of a nucleus or cell without mitosis.

Ammo (æ·mo). *Service slang.* [See *-O.] Ammunition 1938.

Ammonal (æ·mǒnæl). 1903. [f. AMMON(IUM + AL(UMINIUM.] A high explosive consisting of 3 parts ammonium nitrate and 1 part aluminium.

Amorce (ămǭ·ɹs). 1802. [ad. F. *amorce* bait, lure, priming, f. OF. *amordre* to bite, attract, f. *à* A- *prefix* 7 + *mordre* to bite (cf. MORSEL).] A charge of powder for priming a fire-arm; now, a cap for a toy pistol.

Ampoule, ampule (æ·mpūl). [F., ad. L. AMPULLA.] A small glass vessel containing a hypodermic injection.

Anabolism (ănæ·bǒliz'm). 1886. [f. Gr. ἀναβολή 'throwing up', ascent + -ISM.] *Biol.* Constructive METABOLISM. Cf. KATABOLISM. So Anabolic (ænăbǫ·lik) *a.* 1885.

‖**Anaclasis** (ănæ·klăsis). [mod.L., Gr. ἀνάκλασις, f. ἀνακλᾶν to bend back, f. ἀνά ANA- + κλᾶν to break, bend.] *Prosody.* Overlapping of the elements of a metron. So **Anacla·stic** *a.* 3, pertaining to or involving this.

The hypodochmins, or 'anaclastic' dochmins *Oxf. Classical Dict.* (1949) 566/2. The view..that the anacreontic is derived from the ionic dimeter by the interchange of the final long of the first metron with the opening short of the second ('anaclasis') *Ibid.* 567/1.

Anaerobe (ænēə·rōub). 1884. [ad. mod.L. *Anaerobia*; see AN- 10, A- 14, and AEROBE.] *Biol.* Any of a group of microbes or bacteria which live without free oxygen. Hence **Anaerobic** (ænēərǫ·bik), *a.*

Analysis. phr. *In the last a.* [after F. *en dernière analyse*]: at the conclusion of the investigation or examination involved, all things duly considered and weighed.

‖**Anaphylaxis** (æ:năfilæ·ksis). 1907. [mod. L., f. ANA-, after *prophylaxis.*] *Path.* Extreme sensitiveness to the introduction of foreign matter into the body. Hence **Anaphyla·ctic** *a.*

Serum sickness is a simple example of an anaphylactic reaction in man 1939.

‖**Anaptyxis** (ænăpti·ksis). 1895. [mod.L., a. Gr. ἀνάπτυξις unfolding.] *Phonetics.* The development of a vowel between two consonants. So **Anapty·ctic** *a.* 1885.

A:nastigma·tic, *a.* 1897. [AN- 9.] Not astigmatic: applied to a compound lens for correcting astigmatic aberration. So **Anasti·gmat** [G.], an a. lens or system of lenses.

And, *conj.*[1] B. 7. *and/or*: formula denoting that the items joined by it are to be taken either together or as alternatives.

The movement of the tongue and/or lips 1930.
¶The medieval Latin *vel* will often stand for *and*.. Often it is like the $\frac{and}{or}$ of our mercantile documents POLLOCK & MAITLAND *Hist. Eng. Law* I. 152 n.

Anderson (æ·ndəɹsən). *A. shelter*: an arched corrugated-steel air-raid shelter adopted during the Home-Secretaryship of Sir John *Anderson* (1939–40).

Angle, *sb.*[2] 2. b. Used for: The point or direction from which one views or approaches an object, circumstance, event, subject of inquiry, etc.; hence (loosely), aspect or phase of a matter.

I find it strange, writing from the a. of today to conceive it possible.. H. WALPOLE 1922. Hero hasn't much of a notion of the technique yet, has she?..She hasn't got the right a. yet ROSE MACAULAY 1934. Of all the a-s of approach to Shakespearian Comedy, the master a. is..the a. of femininity G. S. GORDON. BAYER & GREEN (*title*) Kitchen strategy: the family a. on nutrition.

Angled (æ·ŋg'ld), *ppl. a.*

a. deck, a flight deck on an aircraft carrier on which the landing path is inclined to the ship's fore-and-aft axis 1952.

Anglo-Israelite (æŋglōui·zrĕələit). 1886. [f. ANGLO- + ISRAEL + -ITE.] One who accepts the theory that the English race consists of descendants of the tribes of the kingdom of Israel. Also as adj. So **Anglo-I·sraelism.** Cf. *BRITISH ISRAELITE.

Anglo-Israelite Theory, ..the contention that the British people in the United Kingdom, its Colonies, and the United States, are the racial descendants of the 'ten tribes' forming the kingdom of Israel, large numbers of whom were deported by Sargon, King of Assyria, on the fall of Samaria in 722 B.C. The theory (which is fully set forth in a book called *Philo-Israel*) rests on premisses which are deemed by scholars..to be..unsound *Encycl. Brit.* 1910.

Anglophil(e) (æ·ŋglǒfil), *a.* and *sb.* 1867. See ANGLO- and -PHIL.] (One who is) favourably disposed towards the English.

Anhedral (ænhe·drăl, -hī·drăl), *a.* 1939. [f. AN- 9 + Gr. ἕδρα seat, face of a solid + -AL[1].] Of the angle at which the main planes of an aircraft are inclined downwards to the lateral axis; also called *negative dihedral* and earlier *kathedral.*

Animatograph (ænimæ·tǒgrɑf). 1896. [irreg. f. ANIMATE + -O- + -GRAPH.] An obs. name of the CINEMATOGRAPH. Cf. BIOGRAPH, *BIOSCOPE.

‖**Anopheles** (ănǫ·fĕlīz). 1899. [mod.L., ad. Gr. ἀνωφελής unprofitable, useless.] *Ent.* A mosquito of the genus so named, which conveys the parasite of malaria.

‖**Anosmia** (ænǫ·zmiă). [mod.L., f. AN- 10 + Gr. ὀσμή smell + -IA[1].] *Path.* Lack of the sense of smell.

Another. 1 b. *You're a.*: colloq. phr. primarily used in retorting a charge upon the person who makes it (cf. TU QUOQUE); hence humorously as a vaguely contemptuous (often meaningless) retort 1553. 3. *A. place*: euphem. phr. used by members of parliament in referring to the other House, i.e. the House of Lords or the House of Commons 1883.

‖**Anoxæmia** (ænǫksī·miă). [mod.L., f. AN- 10 + OX(YGEN + Gr. αἷμα blood + -IA[1].] *Path.* Defective aeration of the blood.

‖**Anschluss** ('a·nʃlus). 1922. [G., 'addition, annexation, union', f. *anschliessen* to join, annex.] Annexation, spec. of Austria to Germany.

The decline of interest in the *A.* idea, due to the calamitous condition of Germany 1923.

Answer, *v.* II. *To a. back*: to make a rude or impertinent retort; cf. *back-answer* (1884), s.v. BACK *adv.*

Ante (æ·ntī). 1835. [a. L. *ante* before.] In poker, a stake put up by a player (usu. the eldest hand) before drawing new cards; *transf.* a price. Hence **Ante** *v.* to put up (an ante); *transf.* to bet, stake; also, to pay *off, up.*

Anthroposophy. 2. A movement inaugurated by Rudolf Steiner to develop the faculty of cognition and the realization of spiritual reality 1922.

Anti-, *pref.*[1] *Anti-British* 1845; *Anti-Comintern* 1937; *a.-gambling* (*league*); **anti-clockwise** = COUNTER-CLOCKWISE; **a.-personnel,** applied to aerial bombs, etc. designed to kill or injure human beings; **a.-tank,** used in defence against tanks 1918.

Antibiotic (æ:ntibəiǫ·tik), *a.* and *sb.* 1892. (A substance) that destroys or impairs living organisms, e.g. bacteria. Hence **Antibiosis** (æ:ntibəiōu·sis), the conditions pertaining to antibiotics.

Antifogmatic(al) (æ:ntifǫgmæ·tikăl), *a.* 1789. [f. ANTI-[1] 7 b + FOG *sb.*, prob. after *ant(i)asthmatic.*] *U.S.* An alcoholic drink intended to be useful in counteracting the effects of damp or wet. Also *adj.*

Antigen (æ·ntidʒen). 1909. [f. *anti-* of ANTIBODY + -GEN 'producing'.] *Biochem.* A substance which causes the formation of antibodies.

Anting (æ·ntiŋ), *vbl. sb.* 1938. [f. ANT + -ING[1], after G. *einemsen* (E. Stresemann, 1935).] The action of birds in rubbing on their plumage ants, or other insects that secrete acrid juices, sour fruits, etc.

McAtee in *The Auk* LV (1938) 98 'Anting' by Birds. F. W. Lane, *Animal Wonderland* (1948), 111 ff. The Mystery of Bird Anting.

Anting-anting (æ·ntiŋ,æ·ntiŋ). 1890. [Tagalog.] A supposed supernatural influence possessed by a person, by which he is protected from harm; also, a charm having such properties.

Anti-Semitism (æntise·mitiz'm, -sī·məitiz'm). 1893. [f. ANTI- + SEMITE + -ISM.] Theory, action, or practice directed against the Jews. Hence **Anti-Se·mite** *a.* and *sb.*, **-Semi·tic** *a.*

Anti-social. 3. Contrary to the interest or welfare of one's fellow-men 1934.

Anybody. 1. colloq. phr. *Anybody's guess*: an unpredictable matter.

Anzac (æ·nzæk). 1916. A word made up from the initial letters of *Australian and New Zealand Army Corps*, used colloq. for a member of that corps; later gen. pertaining to Australia and New Zealand together. *A. Day*: 25 April 1915, when A. troops landed in the Gallipoli Peninsula; an anniversary of the day.

Anzus (æ·nzǒs). 1952. [f. *Anz-* of *ANZAC + U.S.] The combination of Australia, New Zealand, and the United States for the security of the Pacific; *attrib.* in *A. pact.*

‖**Apartheid** (apā·ɹtheit). 1949. [S. Afr. Du., f. Du. *apart* (ad. F. *à part* APART) + *heid* -HOOD.] Segregation of the coloured natives from the whites in S. Africa.

This Congress [of the Dutch Reformed Church] adopted a resolution calling for full territorial 'apartheid' *Ann. Register for 1950*, 112.

‖**Apologia** (æpǒlōu·dʒiă). 1883. [L., a. Gr. ἀπολογία speech in defence.] A defence of the opinions or conduct of a writer or speaker, the advocate of a project, etc.

The currency of the word is largely derived from J. H. Newman's *Apologia pro vita sua*, 1864.

Apostolic. 2. *esp.* Characteristic of or resembling the Apostles in zeal or devotion.

Its active members brought to their task an a. enthusiasm 1937.

Appeasement. Often used derogatorily with allusion to the Prime Minister Mr. Neville Chamberlain's attempts from 1937 onwards to preserve peace with the Axis powers. Similarly **Appease** *v.* and **Appeaser.**

Apperceive (æpəɹsī·v), *v.* Delete † and add: 2. *Psychol.* To be or become conscious of perceiving; to comprehend (something perceived) by a mental act which unites and assimilates the perception to a mass of ideas already possessed 1876 (Sully). So **Apperce·ption.**

Apple. 5. b. A thermionic valve used in an audio-frequency amplifier.

a. sauce *U.S.* (*a*) insincere flattery, (*b*) nonsense.

Apport, *sb.* Transfer †*Obs.* to senses 1 and 2 and add: 3. *pl.* Material things introduced, professedly by occult means, at a spiritualistic séance 1902 (Oliver Lodge).

Approach, *sb.* 3. b. *Golf.* A stroke intended to land the ball on the putting green; chiefly *a. shot, stroke* 1879. So **Approach** *v.* 1887.

Approved, *ppl. a.*

a. school, a place of training for boys or girls who have been found guilty of offences or exposed to moral danger.

‖**A priori.** Also *attrib.* or *predic.* (as *adj.*). Hence **Apriorism** (ēprəiǭ·riz'm).

The most important opposition to modern philosophy as that between empiricism or 'apriorism' 1930. A.. fatalism creed that to them is divine law or *a priori* 1952.

Apron, *sb.* 4. g. A defence against hostile aircraft consisting of a series of wires suspended from a cable to which captive balloons are attached 1917. **h.** An area near the hangars on an aerodrome for the accommodation of aeroplanes manœuvring on the ground 1940.

Arabesque. B. 3. *Ballet.* A pose in which the performer stands on one foot with one arm extended in front and the other leg and arm extended behind.

Araroba (powder) = *GOA *powder* 1876.

Arbitrary, *sb.* **b.** *Typogr.* A character used to supplement the letters and accents of an ordinary fount of type; orig. *a. character* 1890.

Armagnac (ārmæ·nyæk). 1910. A superior brandy made in the former province of *Armagnac* (department of Gers, France).

Armour, *sb.* **6. b.** The protective metal covering of military vehicles and aircraft. **c.** Armoured vehicles collectively, e.g. armoured cars, tanks 1942.

Armoured (ā·ɹməɹd), *ppl. a.* Also of military vehicles and aircraft provided with a protective covering of metal plates.

Armour-plated: also *fig.* Insensitive to attack or influence 1894.

Army. *Royal A. Service Corps*: that part of the army establishment which is concerned with commissariat and transport 1871.

Arnaout (ā·ɹnaut). 1802. [Turkish, ad. med.Gr. Ἀρβανῆτες, var. of Ἀλβανῆτες *ALBANIAN.] An Albanian, esp. one serving in the Turkish army.

Around, *prep.* Of time, amount, etc.: Something near, about. *U.S.* 1888.

arr. (in time-tables) = arrives.

Arrestor (ăre·stəɹ). 1935. [f. ARREST *v.* + -OR 2.] An attachment for bringing an object to a stop.

He lowered his a. hook—used for landing on carriers 1944.

Arrive, *v.* **7. b.** [after mod.F. *arriver.*] To be successful, establish oneself or itself. Also *ppl. a.* **Arrived,** after F. *arrivé* 1896. So ‖ **Arriviste** (arivist), one who is bent on succeeding or making a good position for himself 1912.

Art, *v.*[2] **5.** *To a. up*: to make arty, decorate in an arty fashion (*colloq.*).

(Substitute for **Artifact**:)

Artefact (ā·ɹtĭfækt). Also **arti-**. 1821 (Coleridge). [f. L. *arte,* abl. of *ars* ART + *factum* FACT). A thing made by human art; an artificial product; *Archæol.* a product of aboriginal art as dist. from natural remains.

Arterio-.

a.-sclerosis, a condition of thickening and hardening (loosely, any degeneration) of the arteries 1890.

Articulated, *ppl. a.* [See -ED [1].] Of a vehicle: Consisting of elements joined in a flexible arrangement, as *a. lorry.*

Arty (ā·ɹti), *a.* 1901. [f. ART *sb.* + -Y [1].] Of artistic pretensions; also applied to persons who wish to be regarded as artistic in taste, dress, etc. (*joc. colloq.*).

The house filled with badly made 'a.', not artistic furniture 1910.

Aryanize, *v.* **b.** Under the Nazi régime, to confer 'Aryan' status upon (a 'non-Aryan', e.g. a Jew); also *transf.* Hence **A·ryaniza·tion.**

Aryanizing street names in Austria 1938.

As, *adv.* **VIII. 1.** *As for, as to*: in respect of, with regard to.

‖ **Asbestosis** (æzbestōᵘ·sis). 1938. [mod.L., f. ASBESTOS + -OSIS.] *Path.* A disease of the lungs caused by inhaling particles of asbestos.

Ascorbic (ăskǭ·ɹbik), *a.* 1940. [f. A- 14 + SCORB(UT)IC.] Chem. *A. acid*: Vitamin C, the anti-scorbutic vitamin.

Asdic (æ·zdik). 1940. [f. initials of *Anti-submarine detection investigation committee.*] A device for the detection of submarines.

-ase (ēⁱz), suffix taken from the ending of DIASTASE and used in naming ferments.

‖ **Ashkenazim** (æʃkĭnā·zīm). 1842. [with Heb. pl. suffix *-īm* f. *Ashkenaz,* name of a son of Gomer and grandson of Noah (Gen. x. 3), taken as the progenitor of one of the nations of the world (cf. 'the kingdoms of Ararat, Minni, and Ashchenaz', Jer. li. 27).] That section of the Jews in Europe having Yiddish as the mother tongue, esp. German Jews; cf. SEPHARDIM.

Asian. Delete *arch.* and add: In recent official use superseding *Asiatic* because of the alleged depreciatory implication of the latter term; e.g. Asian Relations Conference (1947); Africans and Asians.

Asianic (ēⁱ:ʃiæ·nĭk), *a.* 1883. [f. prec. + -IC.] **1.** Of or pertaining to Asia Minor. **2.** Pertaining to or characterized by the florid and inflated style of Asiatic Greeks in the three centuries before Christ 1920.

Ask, *v.* **IV. 6.** *To a. for it*: to act so as to bring trouble upon oneself, invite punishment or retaliation (*slang* or *colloq.*) 1909.

Asking, *vbl. sb.* *attrib.* **a. price,** the price that is asked for a thing (*U.S.*). Cf. sense 3.

Mod. The a. price is $45,000, but I'm pretty sure you could get it for $43,000.

Aslib (æ·zlib). f. initials of A*ssociation of special libraries and information bureaux* 1924.

Assemble, *v.*[1] **1. b.** To put together (the separately manufactured parts of a composite machine or mechanical structure); also with the machine as obj. 1852. So **Assembly** 1897; often attrib., as *a. line, room, shop, worker.*

Assignment. 5. b. A task assigned to one; a commission, an appointment (orig. *U.S.*) 1897.

Association. 9. Used attrib. in *a. book, copy,* a volume showing some mark of personal connexion with its author or a former owner (of note) 1912.

Assonant, *sb.* One of a series of assonant words.

Bergère and *pimprenelle* are a-s 1904.

Assonantal (æsᵒunæ·ntăl), *a.* 1897. [f. ASSONANT + -AL [1].] Of the nature of an assonance.

Astral, *a.* 3. *Theosophy.* Pertaining to or consisting of a supersensible substance considered to be next above the sensible world in refinement and held to pervade all space 1877. *A. body,* the ethereal counterpart of a human or animal body 1881.

Astro-.

a.-fix [FIX *sb.*], the position of an aircraft on its course as determined by the stars.

Astrodome (æ·strŏdōᵘm). 1940. [f. ASTRO- + DOME.] A transparent dome on the top of the fuselage of an aeroplane through which the sky is observed or fire is directed. Similarly **A·stro-hatch** [HATCH *sb.*[1]].

Astronomical, *a.* **b.** Of figures: Of dimensions similar to those used in astronomy, e.g. the numbers expressing stellar distances (*colloq.*).

Astrophysics (æstrofi·ziks). 1890. [f. ASTRO- + PHYSICS.] That branch of astronomy which deals with the physical and chemical composition of the heavenly bodies.

At (æt), *sb.* *colloq.* A woman of the A.T.S. (æts, treated as a pl.). See *A.

At, *prep.* **I. 14.** With verbs of speaking, implying indirect attack aimed *at* as opp. to direct address *to* a person.

The Parson is always preaching at the 'Squire 1711. Mrs. Parsons talked *to* Miss Littleton and *at* her better half DICKENS.

Atcha, Atchoo, Ati(s)choo (æ·tʃə, *-ū,* ăti·ʃū). 1873. Representations of the characteristic noises accompanying a sneeze.

Athematic (æþ-, ēⁱþĭmæ·tik), *a.* [f. A- 14 + THEMATIC.] *Philol.* Formed by immediate addition of a suffix to a stem without a thematic vowel.

Athetize (æ·þĭtəiz), *v.* 1886. [Formed to render Gr. ἀθετεῖν: see -IZE.] *trans.* To set aside (a reading) as spurious.

Atlantic, *a.* *A. Charter,* a document laying down eight points of policy and conduct concerning international relations, drawn up by the British Prime Minister, Mr. Winston Churchill, and President Franklin D. Roosevelt, on behalf of the British Empire and the U.S.A., at their meeting in the Western Atlantic on the battleship *Prince of Wales* in August 1941. *A. Pact,* an agreement made in 1948 to ensure the adequate defence of the countries with seaboards on the A. Ocean.

A. wall, the line of fortifications constructed by the Germans to defend the Atlantic coast of Europe in World War II.

Atom, *sb.* Loosely used *attrib.* for *atomic* (see next), as in *a. age, a. bomb, a. scientist* 1945.

The effect of the a. bomb on Japan *Ann. Register for 1946.*

Atomic, *a.* **1.** *A. number*: (of a chemical element) the number of unit positive charges carried by the nucleus of its atom, being the physical property which determines the position of the element in the periodic table 1912. *A. weight*: (since the adoption of oxygen as a standard) the ratio between the weight of one atom of the element and $\frac{1}{16}$ of the weight of an atom of oxygen.

1, 2. Now *spec.* applied to energy produced by the disintegration of atoms of uranium or similar metals; also to a bomb of which the explosive force is derived from such energy; hence, of research and researchers in a. energy, of warfare involving the use of a. bombs, and (in journalistic and colloq. use) of the age or era (etc.) marked by the invention and use of the a. bomb; e.g. *a. energy, a. bomb, a. research, a. scientist, a. age* (1945), *a. war.*

1952 J. B. CONANT (*title*) Anglo-American relations in the Atomic Age.

-ator (ēⁱtəɹ), suffix formed by combination of the *-ā*-stem of L. vbs. in *-āre* + *-tor,* e.g. *creator* CREATOR; a few, like *senātor,* were formed otherwise. The earliest exx. in Eng. came through F. forms in *-ateur* (†*-our,* etc.). Since the 17th cent. used in names of instruments, and from the 19th widely extended; e.g. *escalator, incubator, perambulator, ventilator.*

Attested (ăte·stėd), *ppl. a.* [pa. pple. of ATTEST *v.*] Of cattle: That are approved by authority to be free from disease.

‖ **Aubrietia** (ǭbri‚ī·ʃă). Also very freq. in erron. form **Aubretia.** 1829. [mod.L., f. the name of Claude *Aubriet*; see -IA [1].] A (plant of a) genus of spring-flowering dwarf perennial plants of the family *Cruciferæ.*

‖ **Au courant** (*o* kuraṅ). 1849. [F. 'in the (regular) course (of events)'.] Acquainted with what is going on: const. *with, of.*

Audile (ǭ·dəil), *a.* and *sb.* 1886. [irreg. f. L. *audire* to hear + -ILE.] **A.** *adj.* Pertaining to or involving hearing. **B.** *sb.* A person to whom auditory images are more prominent than motile or visual images.

Audio- (ǭ·diōᵘ). [f. L. *audire* to hear + -O-.]

a.-frequency, a frequency which gives rise to aural perception.

Aurignacian (ǭrinyēⁱ·ʃăn, -ign-), *a.* 1920. [f. the place-name *Aurignac,* France; see -IAN.] *Archæol.* Of or pertaining to the Aurignac cave in the Pyrenees or to the Aurignac era or period represented by the remains there.

Aussie (ǫ·zi). 1918. [f. first syll. of *Australian* + -IE.] An Australian; orig. of Australian troops that took part in World War I.

Austerity. Applied *attrib.* to clothes, etc. in which non-essentials were reduced to the minimum, as a war-time measure of economy.

Before the year ended several features of 'austerity' life common to Great Britain, especially in the matter of catering, had been introduced [into S. Africa] 1942.

Auto-.

au·toclave, (*b*) a vessel, usu. of steel, for carrying out chemical reactions at high temperatures under pressure; an apparatus for sterilizing by steam at high pressure; hence **au·toclaving.**

Automatic, *a.* **2. b.** Of a firearm: Furnished with mechanism for successively and continuously loading, firing, and ejecting a cartridge as long as ammunition is supplied; also *sb.* = *a. pistol* 1902.

Automatism. 2. Also, an instance of this, an automatic act.

If we attempt to explain how such expressions as 'nearly a tumble', 'scarcely a promise', 'easily a foul' can be more than automatisms 1951.

Autotype, *v.* [f. the sb. 2.] *trans.* To produce by the process of autotype.

Beowulf, the unique MS. autotyped and transliterated by J. Zupitza 1882.

Autotomy (ǭtǫ·tŏmi). [f. AUTO- + -TOMY.] *Zool.* The casting-off by an animal of a damaged or useless member, as a tail by a lizard, a leg by a spider, a claw by a crab.

Avestic (ăve·stik), *a.* and *sb.* 1922. [f.

Avesta (see ZEND-AVESTA) + -IC.] (Pertaining to) the language of the Avesta, also called *Zend* and *Old Bactrian*.

Avid, *a.* **b.** *transf.* in weaker sense: Eager. So **Avidity,** eagerness.

Had Mr. Tupman..offered 'a back', Mr. Pickwick would have accepted his offer with the utmost avidity DICKENS.

Avitaminosis (ēⁱvi:tăminōᵘ·sis). 1941. [mod.L., f. A- 14 + VITAMIN + -OSIS.] *Path.* The condition of lacking vitamins; a disease caused by such deficiency.

Axiology (æksiǫ·lŏdʒi). 1929. [f. Gr. ἀξία worth, value + -LOGY.] *Philos.* The theory or doctrine of values. Hence **A:xiolo·gical** *a.*, **Axio·logist.**

Axis. The name given in 1936 to the political association (becoming in 1939 an offensive-defensive alliance) formed between Italy and Germany (more particularly *Rome–Berlin* or *Berlin–Rome A.*); later extended to that between Germany, Italy, and Japan (*Berlin–Rome–Tokio A.*). Often used attrib., as in *A. forces, A. powers,* and ellipt. for such phrases, with consequent pl. concord.

The illusory hope of seeing the break-up of the Rome–Berlin axis and the anti-Communist triangle *Ann. Register for 1939.* A. activity in South America 1940. Official lists..of A. and British aircraft losses. *Ibid. 1942.* The A. were strongly placed 1943.

Axon (æ·ksǫn). 1884. [mod.L., ad. Gr. ἄξων axis.] *Anat.* **a.** The axis of a vertebrate body. **b.** The central process of a nerve-cell or neuron, constituting the essential portion of nerve-fibre.

Azilian (ăzi·liăn), *a.* 1899. [f. *Azil* in Mas d'Azil (Ariège, France); see -IAN.] *Archæol.* Of or pertaining to the transition period between the palæolithic and eolithic ages, characterized by remains discovered at Mas d'Azil.

B. III.

= bloody, in b.f. (fool), b.h. (hell); B.A.O.R. = British Army of the Rhine: B.C.P.A. = British Commonwealth Pacific Airlines; B.(D.)S.T. = British (Double) Summer Time; B.E.A. = British Electrical Authority; B.E.A.C., B.O.A.C. 1939, B.S.A.A.C. = British European (Overseas, South American) Airways Corporation; B.F.N. = British Forces Network; B.I.F. = British Industries Fair; B.L.A. = British Liberation Army; B.O. = body odour; B.P. = British Public, British Pharmacopœia; B.R. = British Railways; B.R.M. = British Racing Motors; b.t.m. (bĭtī·m), euphem. for *bottom* (i.e. posterior); B.U.P. = British United Press; B.V.(M.) = Blessed Virgin (Mary).

Babbit(t)[1] (bæ·bit), name of Isaac *Babbitt*, of Boston, Mass., inventor of *B. metal*, a soft alloy of tin, antimony, and copper, used in bearings 1874.

Babbitt[2] (bæ·bit). 1923. *U.S. colloq.* A type of vulgar self-satisfied business man conforming to the standards of his set: generalized from Sinclair Lewis's novel *Babbitt.* Hence **Ba·bbittry.**

Baby, *sb.* **1. b.** *transf.* The youngest member of a family or group of persons (*colloq.*) 1897. **c.** A girl, sweetheart (orig. *U.S. slang*) 1911. **d.** phr. *To carry* or *hold the b.*, to be saddled with an unwelcome responsibility.

b.-sitter, a person engaged to 'sit in' for the purpose of minding a baby.

Bach (bætʃ), *v.* orig. *U.S.* 1878. [Shortened f. next.] *intr.* To live as a bachelor.

Bachelor. 4. b. *transf.* One of the young male fur-seals which are kept away from the breeding-grounds by the adult bulls 1881.

attrib. **b. girl, woman** (orig. *U.S.*), an unmarried woman who lives independently 1899.

Back bench. 1902. [BACK *a.* 1, BENCH *sb.* 3.] Any of the benches in the House of Commons or similar assembly occupied by members not entitled to places in the front benches on either side; also *attrib.* Hence **Ba·ck-be·ncher,** a member who occupies a seat on the back benches.

Mr. Baldwin filled the modest rôle of a back-bencher in the House for many years 1923.

Ba·ck-chat. *slang.* 1901. [BACK *adv.* 5.] Saucy or impertinent replies to a superior; altercation. Also, rapid interchange of talk between comedians. Cf. *BACK-TALK.

Ba·ck-cloth. 1886. [BACK *a.* 1, BACK-.] *Theatr.* The painted cloth hung across the back of the stage as the principal part of the scenery. So **Ba·ck-drop** *U.S.*

Background. 1. b. The contemporary conditions of a literary (etc.) period, movement (etc.), e.g. *the social and political b. of this poetical activity.*

Back number. 1812. See NUMBER *sb.* I. 5.

Backra, var. of BUCKRA.

Back room. [BACK *a.* 1.] A room at the back of a house or other building: *spec.* in *back-room boys (girls)*, a group of men (women) engaged in secret research (*colloq.*).

[The boys in the back rooms, who do not sit in the limelight BEAVERBROOK April 1941.] The German 'b. r. boys' produced a number of gadgets in 1943.

Back seat. 1859. [BACK *a.*, BACK-.] A seat towards the back of a hall, etc.; hence *colloq.* a position of inferiority or comparative obscurity (orig. U.S. in phr. *to take a b. s.*).

b. s. driver, *fig.* one who controls affairs from a subordinate position.

Ba·ck-talk. 1858. = *BACK-CHAT.

Backwoodsman. b. A member of the House of Lords who rarely attends meetings of that body except when whipped up to vote 1909.

Bacon. Phr. *To bring home the b.*: to achieve success in an undertaking (*slang*) 1924.

Bacteriological, *a.* Used loosely for: Involving the use of bacteria for the propagation of disease, as *b. warfare.*

Bacteriolysis (bæktīᵊriǫ·lisis). 1900. [mod. L., f. *bacterio-*, used as comb. form of BACTERIUM + Gr. λύσις dissolution.] The destruction of bacteria by an anti-bacterial serum. Hence **Bacterioly·tic** *a.* 1901.

Badian (bēⁱ·diən). = *BARBADIAN. Also colloq. Bajun (bēⁱ·dʒən).

Baedeker (bēⁱ·dekəɹ). Any of the series of guide-books issued by Karl *Baedeker* (1801–59) at Coblenz, or his successors. *B. raids,* raids by the Luftwaffe undertaken in April and May of 1942 as a reprisal for the bombing of Lübeck, and concentrated on cities of England marked with two stars in 'Baedeker'.

Baff (bæf), *v.*[2] 1910. [f. BAFF *sb.*] *Golf.* 'To strike the ground with the club when playing, and so loft the ball unduly'.

Bags I (bægz əi). 1866. [dial. 1st pers. pres. ind. of BAG *v.*[1] 6.] A formula used (orig. by children) to assert a claim to some article on the ground that one is the first to speak for it.

Bailey bridge. 1944. A form of pontoon bridge for spanning rivers and chasms, invented by D. C. *Bailey.*

Balance, *sb.* **16. b.** *On b.* (earlier *upon the b.*); balancing one thing with another, taking all things into consideration 1861.

19. Also in gen. use: *The b.*, what is left, the rest, the remainder (recorded from late 18th cent. in Amer. use).

Bale, *v.* *To b. out*: (of an airman) to make a descent by parachute from his machine 1940. Usu. so spelt, as if the action were that of letting a bundle fall through a trapdoor; but also as *bail*, as if a use of BAIL *v.*[3], to lade out.

Balibuntal (bælibʊ·ntăl). Also abbrev. **bali.** 1918. [Short for *Baliuag buntal*, a weave of *BUNTAL originating from Baliuag in Bulacan, Philippine Islands.] A fine straw of a very close weave, used for hats.

Ball, *sb.*[1] *attrib.*

b. pen or **b. point pen,** one of which the writing point is a minute ball which is inked from an inner reservoir; **b. turret,** a spherical turret that protects the exterior of an aircraft 1942.

Ball, *sb.*[2] For sense 2 substitute: A social assembly for dancing, often of people belonging to the same or a connected establishment, society, profession, etc., with an organized programme and often accompanied by special entertainment 1632. Also *attrib.*, as *b.-room* (1752).

Balletically (bæle·tikăli), *adv.* 1951. [f. BALLET + -ICALLY.] In relation to the ballet.

‖**Ballon d'essai** (balon dese). 1883. [F., 'trial balloon'.] An experimental project put forward to test individual or popular feeling.

Balloon,

b. barrage, a defence against hostile aircraft consisting of a connected system of balloons carrying wire cables reaching to the ground 1897.

Baltic (bǫ·ltik), *a.* and *sb.* 1588. Name of a sea (Russ. *Baltigskoe More*), called by the neighbouring Germanic countries 'East Sea' (G. *Ostsee*, etc.), extending between 54° and 66° N. lat., and 9° and 30° E. long.

1588 A. ASHLEY (*title*) The second part of the Mariners Mirrorr..with all the sounds of Denmark, and the Baltick Sea. 1720 *Phil. Trans.* Abr. VI. 498 Observations on the variations of the needle in the B.

Balto-Slavic (bǫltoslæ·vik), *a.* and *sb.* 1902. [f. *Balto-*, used as comb. form of BALTIC + SLAVIC.] Designation of the group of Indo-European languages comprising the Baltic branch (Lithuanian, Lettish, and Old Prussian) and the Slavonic branch (Russian, Polish, Czech, etc.). Also **Ba:lto-Slavo·nic.**

Band, *sb.*[2] **12.** In radiotelephony, a group of frequencies that may be tuned in together.

Band, *sb.*[3] **4. b.** Phr. *When the b. begins to play*: when matters become serious or exciting 1891. *To beat the b.*: lit. so as to drown the noise made by the b.; hence, to surpass or beat some stated or implied project 1897.

b.-wag(g)on *U.S.*, the waggon carrying the band at the head of a procession 1855; *to be on the b.-w.*, fig., to be in the forefront of an enterprise.

‖**Bandar** (bʊ·ndăɹ). 1886. [Hind.] The rhesus monkey, *Macacus rhesus*; *attrib.* in *b.-log* [Hind. *log* people], Kipling's nation of monkeys; *fig.* a body of irresponsible chatterers.

Bangalore. [Name of a city in India.]

B. torpedo: a tube containing explosive for blowing wire.

Banner, *sb.* **6.** *attrib. U.S.* Entitled to a banner as a distinction (orig. in *b. county, state*); hence as *adj.* pre-eminent, supreme (latterly familiar in *b. headline* in newspapers) 1840.

Bar (bāɹ), *sb.*[4] 1914. [ad. Gr. βάρος weight.] *Meteorol.* A unit of barometric pressure equivalent to a pressure of 29·53 inches or 750·1 mm. of mercury at 32° F. in latitude 45°. So **Ce·ntibar, De·cibar, Mi·llibar,** a hundredth, tenth, thousandth of a bar.

Barbadian (bāɹbēⁱ·diăn), *a.* and *sb.* Pertaining to (a native of) Barbados; see -IAN.

Barbituric (bāɹbitiūᵊ·rik), *a.* 1866. [ad. F. *barbiturique*, f. G. *barbitur(säure)*.] Chem. *B. acid*: an acid ($C_4H_4O_3N_2$) from which various hypnotic and sedative drugs are derived. Hence **Barbitu·rate** [-ATE[1] 1 c]. Also **Ba·rbitone:** = VERONAL; in U.S. Pharmacopœia **Ba·rbital.**

Sulphonal..and Methylsulphonal..were formerly used..as hypnotics but they have now been superseded almost entirely by the barbituric acid derivatives 1940.

Barbola (bāɹbōᵘ·lă). 1927. [Trade name.] *B. (work)*, decorative work chiefly of flowers and fruit modelled in a plastic paste and coloured.

Bargain, *sb.* **3.** *esp.* An article of which the price is professedly reduced for the purpose of a special sale in a shop or stores; also *attrib.* and *Comb.* designating persons and things associated with the practice of offering goods for sale in this way, e.g. *b.-counter* 1886, *-day, -hunter* 1868, *-hunting, -price, -sale*; **b. basement,** the basement floor of a stores devoted to the display of bargains.

Bark, *v.*[1]

To b. up the wrong tree (fig. phr., from the action of a dog in mistaking the tree in which its quarry is): to misdirect one's efforts by pursuing the wrong object (orig. *U.S.*) 1832.

Barlow (bā·ɹlōᵘ). *U.S.* 1779. [Maker's name.] *B. knife*, a large single-bladed pocket knife.

Barn[2] (bāɹn). 1941. [Said to have originated in the phrase 'as big as a *barn*'.] In nuclear physics, 10^{-24} sq. cm., a unit of area representing the order of magnitude of the geometrical projected area of a nucleus.

Baron. 8. *U.S.* A great merchant in a particular commodity, an industrial or commercial 'magnate' 1887.

The 'money barons' were using the whole of their influence to restrict the raising of money for national development 1931.

Baroque. In literary criticism, applied to a heavily or grotesquely ornamented style.

Barrage. Also said of the firing of anti-aircraft guns 1916. See also *BALLOON, *BOX.

Baseball. 'The history of the word in the U.S. before 1850 is obscure' (*Dict. Amer.*

English). *Base ball* as used by Jane Austen (*Northanger Abbey* i) appears to be applied to rounders.

Basement. **3.** See also *BARGAIN.

Basic, *a.*

B. English, a variety of the English language, comprising a select vocabulary of 850 words, invented by C. K. Ogden, of Cambridge, and intended for use as a medium of international communication (see quot. below); **b. petrol** (also ellipt. *the basic*); **b. slag,** slag from the basic or Bessemer process of steel manufacture, used as a fertilizer when finely ground 1888.

It is the continuous approximation of East and West, as a result of the analytic character of Chinese and English..which makes this particular [panoptic] form of English *basic* for the whole world. Many special captions or trade-marks for the system have been suggested, but Basic = British American Scientific International Commercial (English)—is for the time being as good as any. 1929 *Psyche* IX. 4. Translation into B. English *Ibid.* 97.

Bastard, *sb.* **1. b.** Used vulgarly as a term of abuse for a man, and, with weakened force, as the equiv. of 'fellow', 'chap', also trivially for 'thing'.

'We've knocked the b. off' (reported remark of Sir Edmund Hillary after his ascent of Mount Everest in 1953).

Bat, *sb.*[1] Phr. *To have bats in the belfry*: to be crazy or eccentric **1911.** Hence **Bats** as adj. in predic. use = BATTY *a.* 2.

1935 MARSH & JELLETT *Nursing-home murder* xi, I had a great-aunt who left all her money to a muffin-man with coloured blood..She was undoubtedly bats.

Bat (bæt), *sb.*[4] 1892. [Hindī.] *The b.*: the colloquial language of a foreign country; chiefly in phr. *to sling the b.*, to speak the lingo.

An' 'ow they would admire for to hear us sling the *b.* KIPLING.

Batch. **5.** Also, in jute manufacture, a selection of kinds of jute for a particular yarn; in glass-making, the mixture of raw materials from which glass is produced in the furnace. Hence **Ba·tching** [-ING [1]], the addition of oil to textile fibres to facilitate spinning (*Chambers's Techn. Dict.*).

The first process in the manufacture of jute is batching. Batch setting is the first part of this operation; it consists of selecting the different kinds of jute for any predetermined kind of yarn. The number of bales for a batch seldom exceeds twelve. 1911 *Ency. Brit.* XV. 607.

Batho- (bæþo), **Bathy-** (bæþi), comb. forms respectively of Gr. βάθος depth and βαθύς deep, in various techn. terms, e.g. **ba·tho-, ba·thylith** [see -LITH], a mass of intrusive igneous rock having no visible floor; **batho·-, bathy·meter** [see -METER], an instrument used for deep-water soundings; **bathophilous** (bæþǫ·filəs), adapted to life in deep water.

Bathyscaph (bæ·þiskæf). 1953. [ad. F. *bathyscaphe*, f. Gr. βαθυς BATHY- + σκάφος ship.] A vessel constructed for deep-sea diving and exploration. Also **Ba·thysPHERE.**

The new bathysphere in which Prof. Auguste Piccard, the Swiss scientist, will try to descend more than two miles into the Mediterranean 15 Jan. 1953.

Batsman (bæ·tsmæ̆n). [f. pl. of BAT *sb.*[2] + MAN *sb.*] A man on the deck of an aircraft carrier having a pair of bats with which he signals to the pilot of an incoming aircraft; also, one who guides aircraft on the ground in this way.

Battery. **13.** A series of hutches, cages, or nesting-boxes in which laying hens are confined for intensive laying or poultry reared and fattened.

Battle, *sb.*

b. dress, a soldier's uniform consisting of a belted blouse and trousers, often with ankle-leggings 1939.

Battleship. 1794 (*Dict. Americanisms*).

Bay, *sb.*[3] **3. b.** *Mil.* A passing-place in a trench.

b.-line, a side line of a railway terminating in a station on the main line.

Bazooka (bāzū·kă). *U.S.* 1935. [Cf. U.S. *bazoo* trumpet.] **1.** A crude pipe-shaped musical instrument. **2.** An anti-tank rocket-launcher 1943.

Beach, *sb.*

b. head [illogically formed after *bridge head*], a fortified position of troops landed on a beach.

Beach-la-mar (bīt∫lamā·ɹ). 1910. [Alteration, by association with Pg. *bicho do mar*, of BÊCHE-DE-MER *English* (quasi 'English spoken by bêche-de-mer fishermen').] The commercial jargon English used in the Western Pacific.

Beat, *v.*[1] **I. 10. b.** To get the better of by fraud 1886 *U.S.* **c.** To get ahead of (as in *to b. one to it*) 1898 *U.S.*

b. it, orig. *U.S.*, to be off, decamp 1908; **b. up,** (*d*) *U.S.* to beat severely, as with a truncheon, cudgel, etc. 1906.

Beatemest (bī·təmĕst). *U.S.* 1831. [app. f. *beat 'em* + -EST, later interpreted as f. *beating* ppl. a.] Most excellent or splendid.

‖**Beau geste** (bo ʒest). 1922. [F., 'fine gesture'.] A display of magnanimity.

Beautician (biūti·∫ăn). *U.S.* 1926. [irreg. f. BEAUTY; cf. *MORTICIAN.] One who runs a beauty parlour, a beauty specialist.

Bebop (bī·bǫp). 1946. A kind of syncopated music. Also abbrev. **Bop.**

Becquerel (be·krĕl). 1896. The name of a French physicist, A. H. *Becquerel* (1852–1908) used attrib. to denote rays discovered by him in uranium.

Before. **A. 3.** phr. *To have been there b.*: to have already experienced the thing implied.

If it's a question of the male sex, I may say that I've been there before 1912.

Begin, *v.* **1. c.** (Not) to take the first step or make the least approach (orig. *U.S.*) 1833.

Behavioural (bĭhē·vyərəl), *a.* [See -AL [1].] Pertaining or relating to behaviour.

Bel (bel). *Electr.* 10 decibels 1936.

Belay, *v.* **3. b.** *Climbing.* To secure a rope in a position. Hence **Belay** *sb.*, the position so secured or the point providing it.

Belisha (bəlī·∫ă). Surname of Leslie Hore-*Belisha*, Minister of Transport 1931–7.

B. beacon, a post about seven feet high surmounted by an amber-coloured globe and erected on the pavement at officially recognized pedestrian crossings of the highway, first used in 1934.

Bell, *sb.*[1] **1.** colloq. phr. *To ring the b.*: to carry off the prize; to be the best of a lot: in allusion to the ringing of the bell attached to a strength-testing machine 1928. *To ring a b.*: to call up the memory of or suggest an earlier occurrence of the thing referred to.

Belly, *sb.*

b. landing, the landing of aircraft on the under surface of the fuselage without the use of the undercarriage 1939.

Bellyache (be·liēⁱk), *v.* 1889. [f. *belly-ache* (see BELLY *sb. Comb.*)] *intr.* (*U.S. colloq.*) To whimper, whine, grizzle.

You can overcome anything if you don't b. 1951.

Belt, *sb.*[1] **1. c.** *To tighten, pull in* (etc.) one's *b.*: see TIGHTEN *v.* 1. **2. d.** A zone or district characterized by specific natural features (orig. *U.S.*) 1871. **3. b.** In a machine gun, a length of woven fabric or of metal plates pinned together, fitted with cartridges and revolving on the feed-block 1885.

Bench, *sb.* *attrib.*

b. hook, 'a flat piece of wood having a wooden block at the back edge of the top and a similar block fixed on the underside along the front edge, used to steady the work and prevent injury to the bench top' (*Chambers's Techn. Dict.*).

Beneficial, *a.* **4.** Carrying a salary or stipend.

A Beneficial Post required by refined girl..holding School Certificate 1944.

‖**Bene esse** (bī·nī e·sī). 1621. [L., *bene* well, *esse* to be.] Well-being, fully satisfactory state.

So long as your clergy believe that Episcopacy is essential not only to the b. e., but to the esse of the Church 1899.

Benefit, *sb.* **4. e.** A performance, as of a play, a game, a concert, or the like, the proceeds from which go to a particular player or company.

Benelux (be·nĭlʋks). 1948 (1 Jan.). A customs union of *Be*lgium, *The Ne*therlands, and *Lux*embourg.

Benzedrine (be·nzĕdrīn). [f. BENZYL + *-edrine*, as in *EPHEDRINE.] A drug used by inhalation to relieve respiratory trouble and internally as a nerve stimulant.

‖**Berceuse** (bɛrsö̆z). 1876. [F., f. *bercer* to rock + fem. agent-suffix *-euse*.] *Mus.* A cradle song.

‖**Beret** (be·rēⁱ). Now forming part of many British service and other uniforms.

Berry, *sb.*[1] **1.** Also, a grain of wheat.

Bespoke (bĭ͵spōᵘ·k), *ppl. a.* 1865. [See BESPEAK *v.*] Made to order, as distinguished from READY-MADE. Also said of the maker.

Best, *a.* and *adv.* **A. I. 2. b.** *B. girl* (GIRL *sb.* 2 c): favourite sweetheart or female companion (orig. *U.S.*) 1904. **B. 3. b.** *B.-seller* (orig. *U.S.*): see SELLER 2. 1905.

Betatron (bī·tătrǫn). [f. BETA + *-tron* of *cyclotron*.] A machine designed for the acceleration of β particles.

Bevin (be·vin). Name of Ernest *Bevin*, Minister of Labour and National Service 1940–5.

B. boy, a boy selected by lot to serve in a coal-mine.

Bhoy, B'hoy, intended to represent the Ir. pronunc. of BOY. **a.** A rough or rowdy 1846 (*bo-hoy*). **b.** A 'lad', a 'knut' 1911.

Bi-[2]. **I. bi·partisa·n,** pertaining to, characterized by, or involving two parties 1920 (orig. *U.S.*); earlier **bi-party** 1898.

Bib-cock. 1797. [? BIB *sb.*[1]; COCK *sb.*[1] IV. 1.] A cock or tap with a turned-down nozzle, as dist. from STOPCOCK.

Bid, *sb.* phr. *To make a b. for*: to make an attempt to obtain, try to get 1885. Hence the simple sb. is freq. used, esp. in journalese, for: Attempt to secure or win something.

Germany's b. for sea-power 1915. Crash ends Polish air record bid (*Mod. newspaper*).

Big, *a.* **3. d.** colloq. phr. *Too b. for one's boots* (*breeches, trousers*): above oneself.

b. bug [see BUG *sb.* 1 b] orig. *U.S.*, a person of importance, great man 1830; **b. four, b. five** orig. *U.S.*, a combination of four (five) persons or things, companies, etc. of the highest standing 1886; **b. gun** orig. *U.S.*, a person of importance 1865; **b. noise** (see NOISE *sb. phr.*); **b. shot** *U.S. slang*, a prominent member of an organization, e.g. a notorious gangster 1929; **B. Smoke,** (*a*) *Austral.*, aboriginal name for a town 1848; (*b*) London; **b. stick** [STICK *sb.*[1] 4] orig. *U.S.*, a display of force 1904.

Bijugy (bəi·dʒugi). 1950. [See -Y [3].] The condition of being bijugate.

Comparison is made with the bijugy of apices of *Salvia horminoides.*

Bikini (bikī·ni). Name of one of the Marshall Islands, in the Pacific Ocean, which was used, in 1950, as the locale of an atomic bomb explosion; applied to a scanty two-piece swimming outfit for women in vogue at the time.

Bilateral, *a.* **b.** *spec.* Pertaining to or concerning two countries (only), esp. of the trade and financial agreements made between them; so **Bila·teralism,** with such spec. reference. Cf. *MULTILATERAL.

Bill, *sb.*[3] **8. b.** phr. *To fill the b.*: to fulfil the required conditions; to meet requirements (orig. *U.S.*) 1860.

Bim. *colloq.* A native of Barbados. Hence **Bi·mshire,** Barbados.

Bio-. **Bioche·mistry,** the study of chemical processes which take place in living organisms 1902; hence **Bioche·mical** *a.*, **Bioche·mist** 1913; **Bi·olumine·scence,** the luminescence emitted by living animals and plants; **Bio·metry,** (2) the science which deals with the application of statistical methods to biological facts 1901; hence **Biome·tric, Bi·ometri·cian**; **Biono·mics,** the branch of biology which deals with the life of organisms in their natural surroundings 1888; **Biophy·sics,** the science which applies the laws of physics to biological phenomena 1892; **Bi·o·scope,** (2) an earlier form of cinematograph (cf. BIOGRAPH) 1897.

Bipod (bəi·pǫd). 1939. [f. BI-[2] + *-pod*, as in *tripod*.] A two-legged support, e.g. for an automatic rifle.

Birdlore (bɔ̄·ɹdlōᵊɹ). [f. BIRD *sb.* + LORE *sb.*[1]] The facts and beliefs concerning birds and their life and habits.

[Ornithology should be birdlore 1830 *Gentleman's Mag.* June 503/2.]

Birthday. **2.** *B. honours*, the titles or honour conferred by the Sovereign on an anniversary of his or her birthday 1888.

Biscuit. **I. b.** A small square army mattress, three of which form a full-size mattress.

Bite, *v.* **I.** phr. *To b. off more than one can*

chew: to undertake more than one can accomplish (orig. *U.S.*) 1877. **b.** intr. *To b. on*: to 'set one's teeth into', get hold of 1904.

‖**Bizonia** (bəizōᵘ·niă). [BI-², ZONE *sb.*, -IA¹.] The combination of the British and the U.S. zones of occupation in Germany after World War II. Also **Bi·zone**; hence **Bizo·nal** *a.*, **Bizo·nial** *a.*

Black, *a.*

B. and Tans, pop. name for an armed force specially recruited to combat the Sinn-Feiners in 1921, so named from the mixture (black and khaki) of constabulary and military uniforms worn by them. **b.-coated** (also **b.-coat**), of a clerical or professional as dist. from an industrial worker 1893. **b. market,** traffic dealing surreptitiously in commodities that are rationed or of which the supply is otherwise restricted, and thereby involving exorbitant prices (*b. m. prices*) 1941; hence *b. marketeer* (also abbrev. *blacketee·r*).

Black, *v.* **2. b.** *To b. out*: to obscure or obliterate with black material, fog, or the like 1850; *spec.* to prevent the emission of light from buildings and to minimize street lighting as a precaution against observation by hostile aircraft (*trans.* and *intr.*) 1938.

Bla·ck-out. [f. phr. *to black out* (see prec.)] **1.** Temporary complete loss of consciousness 1935; esp. in flying, temporary blindness resulting from physical derangement when a sudden turn or change of speed is made. **2.** The action of blacking out, the state of being blacked out; also *attrib.* as *b. material* 1938. **b.** *fig.* A condition of obfuscation or obscuration.

2. On the same night [9 August] a complete 'b.' was carried out over nearly half the country 1939. **b.** Kept in the dark by the political b. as to what was really happening in France 1944.

Blah (blā). orig. *U.S. slang.* 1921. [Imitative of rapid talk.] Nonsense, humbug.

Blanket, *sb.* *attrib.* passing into *adj.* Covering all cases, inclusive (orig. *U.S.*) 1886.

‖**Blanquette** (blā·ŋket). 1933. [F., f. *blanc* white: see -ETTE.] *Cookery.* A stew of white meat (esp. veal) with white sauce.

Blast, *sb.* **7. b.** A wave of highly compressed air resulting from the explosion of a bomb and causing heavy damage 1940.

Blatant, *a.* **4.** *colloq.* used loosely (perh. assoc. with *patent*): Palpably prominent or obvious. So **Bla·tantly** *adv.*

The transactions were more than open; they were b. W. S. CHURCHILL 1950.

Blessed, *ppl. a.* **1.** *The Blessed Sacrament*: see SACRAMENT *sb.* 2.

Blessing, *vbl. sb.* **4.** *A b. in disguise*: said of a misfortune that works to the eventual good of the sufferer.

Ev'n Crosses from his sov'reign Hand Are Blessings in Disguise J. HERVEY 1746.

Blimp (blimp). 1916. [Said to have been coined by Horace Short, an aviator.] **1.** A non-rigid airship consisting of a gas-bag with the fuselage of an aeroplane slung underneath. **2.** (*Colonel*) *Blimp*: a character invented by David Low (1891–), cartoonist and caricaturist; an obese, pompous-looking elderly figure, pop. interpreted (often gen. *a blimp*) as typifying a diehard or reactionary.

Blind, *sb.* **6.** In Poker, a stake put up by a player before seeing his cards 1857. **7.** [f. *BLIND *a.* 1. d] A drunken bout or orgy, binge.

Blind, *a.* **1. d.** Blind-drunk 1625. **e.** Applied to flying and aerial bombing executed by means of instruments without direct observation or visual identification 1935. **f.** In Poker, *to go b.*: to put up a blind (see BLIND *sb.* 6); hence, *to go* (a specified stake) *b.*; fig. *to go it b.*, to act without previous investigation of the circumstances, plunge without regard to the risks involved 1846.

Blind, *a.* *Comb.*

b.-stamped, (of book-covers) stamped without colour or gold leaf (cf. *blind-blocking, -tooling*).

Blind alley. 1724. [BLIND *a.* 10.] An alley closed at one end; a cul-de-sac; also *fig.* esp. in *b. employment, occupation,* one that 'leads nowhere' or offers no prospects 1909.

Blip (blip). 1945. In radiolocation, an image of an object as projected on to a screen.

Blister, *sb.*

b. gas, a poison gas which causes blisters on or intense irritation of the skin 1938.

‖**Blitz** (blits). 1940. [Short for next.] An attack or offensive launched suddenly with great violence with the object of reducing the defences immediately; *spec.* an air-raid or a series of them conducted in this way. Hence **Blitz** *v. trans.* to attack in this way; to hit, blast, etc. by an air-raid; **Blitzed** (blitst) *ppl. a.*

A piece of blitzed timber 1944.

‖**Blitzkrieg** (bli·tskrīg, ‖-krīk). 1939. [G., 'lightning-war'.] See prec.

The British b. on the grand scale 1944.

‖**Bloc** (blǫk). 1905. [F.; see BLOCK *sb.*] In Continental politics, a combination of parties of divergent views which supports the government in power; also, a combination of groups or nations formed to foster a particular interest.

The Rome *b.* states (Italy, Austria, and Hungary) 1937.

Block, *sb.* *attrib.* and *Comb.*

b.-buster [see *BUSTER], an aerial bomb of a type designed to wreck a block of buildings; **b. capitals,** capital letters in 'printed' as opposed to script form.

Blocked (blǫkt), *ppl. a.* [f. BLOCK *v.* + -ED¹.] *Finance.* Applied to a currency, or to assets of any kind, the use of which is restricted (e.g. in respect of current expenditure).

Blood, *sb.* **I. 1. b.** (*You cannot get*) *b. out of a stone*, i.e. sympathy from the hardhearted or money from the avaricious 1865. **3. c.** *B. and thunder*, bloodshed and violence, used *attrib.* in *b.-and-thunder book, tale,* etc., one describing or relating the exploits of men of violence or desperadoes 1870; also (orig. *U.S.*) abbrev. to *blood* (esp. in pl.), e.g. *b. books*, (*penny*) *b-s* 1897. **d.** *B. and iron* [tr. G. *blut und eisen*], military force as opp. to diplomacy, esp. in *the man of b. and iron*, Prince Bismarck, Prussian statesman 1872.

attrib.

b. sports, outdoor sports that involve the shedding of blood, as hunting; **b. stock** [see III. 5], thoroughbred horses collectively.

Blot, *v.* **1.** colloq. phr. *To b. one's copybook*: to make a blunder that stains one's record.

Blotto (blǫ·to), *a. slang.* 1919. [?] Fuddled with drink.

Blow, *v.*¹ **10. c.** *fig.* To lay out or get through (money) extravagantly (*slang*) 1874. Cf. *BLUE *v.*²

Blow-.

b. lamp, b. torch, a lamp designed to direct a condensed heat on a selected spot.

Blower¹. **3. b.** An apparatus for producing an artificial current of air by pressure, a blast in a furnace, etc. 1858. **c.** *slang.* A speaking-tube, telephone.

Blue, *a.* **3. b.** Of affairs, etc.: Dismal, unpromising, depressing 1833. **c.** Of musical tone: Characteristic of 'the *BLUES'.

b. It's a b. look out, Master 1833. The situation looked b. 1878. **c.** The melody is characterized by the frequent use of the 'blue' tone 1950.

b. bag, a barrister's (orig. a solicitor's) brief-bag of blue stuff 1837; **b. pencil,** a blue 'lead pencil' as used in marking corrections, obliterations, and the like 1893; hence **b.-pencil** *v.*, to mark, scron through, or obliterate with a blue pencil: to make cuts in, censor; **b.-pencilled** *ppl. a.* (substituted for a profane or obscene epithet); **b. print,** a photo-print composed of white lines on a blue ground or vice versa, used for making copies of plans and designs 1887; *fig.* a plan, scheme.

Blue (blū), *v.*² 1859. [?] To spend lavishly or improvidently; = *BLOW *v.*¹

Blues (blūz). orig. *U.S.* 1921. [See BLUE *sb.* ad fin.] A melody of a mournful and haunting character, originating among the negroes of the Southern U.S.; hence, dance tunes of this kind, and the dances themselves.

Board, *v.* **7 b, 8 b.** *To b. out*: to supply, be supplied with, food and lodging away from one's place of residence.

Boart, var. of BORT.

The abrasives are produced from the lowest quality of diamond material, known as 'crushing boart' 1953.

Bob, *sb.*¹ 10.

b. and wheel: see WHEEL *sb.* III. 6.

‖**Bock** (bǫk). 1867. [F., G. *bock*, in full *bockbier*, shortening of *Einbockbier*, now *Einbecker bier*, f. *Einbeck*, a town in Hanover, Germany.] A strong dark-coloured variety of German beer; also with *a* and *pl.* a glass of this.

Bofors (bōᵘ·fǫɪz). 1938. [Name of a manufacturing town in Örebro Län, Sweden.] *B. gun*: a type of light anti-aircraft gun.

Bohunk (bōᵘ·hɒŋk). 1914. [perh. f. the initial syllables of *Bohemia* and *Hungarian*.] *U.S. slang.* A labourer of Central or Southern Europe; *transf.* a low rough fellow.

Boiled, *ppl. a.* *B. shirt* (U.S.): a white or dress shirt with starched front 1869.

Boloney (bəlōᵘ·ni). 1900. *U.S. slang.* [?] Humbug, nonsense.

Bolt, *sb.*¹

b. position [tr. G. *riegelstellung*], a disposition of military forces designed to bar the way to an advance at a vital point.

Bo·lt-hole. 1851. [BOLT *v.*²] A hole or burrow into which an animal or a human being bolts for safety; *fig.* an avenue of escape.

Bomb, *sb.*

b.-aimer 1936; **Bomb Alley** *colloq.*, a path followed by flying bombs 1944; **b.-bay,** a compartment in an aircraft to hold bombs 1939; **b.-disposal,** the removal and detonation of delayed-action bombs by experts 1940; **b.-load,** the weight of bombs carried by an aircraft 1936; **b.-proof** *a.* (see PROOF *a.* 1 b); **b.-sight,** a device in an aircraft for the aiming of bombs 1938.

The b.-disposal squads..displayed remarkable coolness 1941.

Bomb, *v.* *To b. out*: to cause to leave one's dwelling or place of business by aerial bombing 1940. *To b. up*: to load (an aircraft) with bombs 1939.

Bombard, *v.* **2. b.** *Nuclear physics.* To impart energy to (a body) by means of moving particles from an external source. So **Bomba·rdment.**

Bombardier. **2. c.** orig. *U.S.* A bomb-aimer in aircraft.

Bombay duck (bǫ·mbeɪ dɒk). [Alteration of native name *bombil* by assimilation to the place-name *Bombay* + DUCK *sb.*, fancifully used.] A small fish of S. Asiatic coasts eaten dried with curry.

‖**Bombe** (boṅb). [F., 'bomb'.] *Cookery.* A cone-shaped dish or confection.

Bomber (bǫ·məɪ). [f. BOMB *sb.* or *v.* + -ER¹.] **1.** One who throws a bomb, one of a bombing party 1915. **2.** An aircraft used for bombing 1919. **3.** *attrib.*, as in *B. Command.*

Bone, *sb.*² **4.** Used for: Insensitive or insensible matter (e.g. instead of brain); hence *bone-head, -headed,* blockhead(ed) 1903.

B. from the eyes up 1935.

Bonzer (bǫ·nzəɪ), *a.* *Austral. slang.* 1915. [perh. from BONANZA.] Excellent.

Booby, *sb.*

b. trap, (also) *Mil. colloq.* a harmless-looking object concealing an explosive charge, designed to go off if the object is disturbed 1918. Hence **b.-trap** *v.*

Mined and booby-trapped 1944. To booby-trap the bodies of the fallen 1944.

Boogie-woogie (bū·giwūgi). 1935. A style of playing blues on the piano marked by a persistent bass rhythm.

Book, *sb.*

b. token, a voucher for a sum of money to pay for the purchase of a book or books from a named bookseller 1932; **b. value,** the value of a commodity as shown by a firm's books, as dist. from its market value.

Boot, *sb.*³

b.-licker, [cf. *b.-lick* vb.] a toady, sycophant.

Borrovian (bǫrōᵘ·viăn), *a.* [See -IAN.] Pertaining to or characteristic of George *Borrow* (1803–81).

‖**Borsch, bortsch** (bǭɪʃ, bǫɪtʃ). 1887. [Russ. *borshch* (borʃtʃ).] A Russian ragout of various ingredients, coloured with beetroot juice.

Borstal (bǭ·ɪstəl). Name of a village on the river Medway, Kent, where the first experiments were made under the Prevention of Crime Act (1908) in segregating and reforming young delinquents; also *attrib.*, as *B. Association* (which is responsible for the after-care of ex-Borstal subjects), *B. system.*

Boss (bǫs), *v.*³ *dial.* and *slang.* 1887. [Cf. next.] *trans.* To miss or bungle (a shot); *gen.* to make a mess of. Hence **Boss** *sb.*⁶ (*b. shot*), a bungled shot 1898.

Boss-eyed, *a.* *dial.* and *slang.* 1860. [Cf. BOSS *v.*³] Squint-eyed, cross-eyed. Also *fig.* oblique, crooked.

Boswell (bǫ·zwĕl). Name of James *Boswell*, reporter of Samuel Johnson's doings and sayings. Used allus. for: A constant companion or attendant who witnesses and records what a person does. Cf. BOSWELLIAN.

'I think that I had better go, Holmes.' 'Not a bit, Doctor. Stay where you are. I am lost without my Boswell.' CONAN DOYLE.

Bottle, *sb.*[2]

b. neck, (also) a restricted or crowded condition which causes obstruction or delay of production; **b. party,** a party to which each guest contributes a bottle of wine or spirits 1934.

Bottom. B. *attrib.* passing into *adj.*, = that is at the b., that is the lowest or among the lowest, e.g. *the b. line, row*; *one's b. dollar*, one's last remaining resources (1857). Hence BOTTOMMOST.

Botuline (bǫ·tiŭlǝin). 1901. [f. L. *botulus* sausage: see -INE[5].] *Med.* A poisonous ptomaïne found in decaying meats, etc. So **-inic** (i·nik) *a.* 1899.

Bounty. 5. c. *King's* or *Queen's b.*: a sum of money given from the royal purse to a mother who has given birth to triplets 1910.

Box, *sb.*[1] Phr. *To be in the same b.*: to be in the same predicament 1884.

b. barrage, anti-aircraft barrage in which shells are fired so as to form a box-like figure; **b.-kite,** (*a*) a toy kite made in the form of a box; (*b*) a kite used in meteorological experiments and consisting of two light rectangular boxes secured together horizontally; (*c*) = **b.-kite aeroplane,** an early form of biplane in which the arrangement of the planes resembles a box-kite 1908.

Boxer[3] (bǫ·ksǝɹ). **2.** A smooth-coated brown breed of dog of the bulldog type.

Boy, *sb.* **2.** *U.S.* A university student. **3.** In various oversea countries, a male servant, e.g. *cow-b., garden-b., yard-b.* **6.** One of a 'fraternity' or gang of professional thieves or swindlers (usu. pl. *the boys*) 1898.

Boykin (boi·kin). 1547. [f. BOY + -KIN.] A young boy: mainly a term of affection.

Bra (brā). Slang abbrev. of BRASSIÈRE.

Bracket, *sb.* **5. b.** The (specified) distance between a pair of shots fired, one beyond the target and one short of it, in order to find the range for artillery 1899. So **Bracket** *v.* 3. To drop shot beyond (the target) and short of it.

The German gun had got its b. 1916.

Brain, *sb. attrib.*

b. fag, exhaustion of the brain by prolonged mental strain 1857; **b. fagged** *a.*, suffering from brain fag; **b. storm** (see STORM *sb.* I. 4); **b.-washing** *colloq.*, clearing or purging the mind of established ideas by persistent suggestion and indoctrination; **b. wave,** (*a*) a hypothetical telepathic vibration which conveys a thought from one mind to another without recourse to the usual methods of communication 1871; (*b*) *colloq.* a sudden inspiration or bright thought 1890; **Brain Trust** [transf. use of TRUST *sb.* 7], *U.S.* a group of experts appointed to advise and to direct policy 1933; **Brains Trust,** a group of persons chosen to give their opinions on problems presented to them.

Brash, *a.*[2] Latterly in general colloq. use, in imitation of U.S. currency. Other U.S. senses are: **b.** Rough, harsh 1880; **c.** Active, quick 1884. Hence **Bra·shly** *adv.* (1865), **Bra·shness.**

Brass, *sb.*[1] **1.** *transf.* 'Brass hats' collectively (*U.S. slang*) 1899.

attrib. **b. hat** (*slang*), an officer of high rank in one of the services, the reference being to the gold braid worn on the hat; **b. tacks** (see TACK *sb.*[1] I. 2).

Brass, *v.* phr. *To be brassed off* = 'to be browned off' (see *BROWN *v.*). *Services slang.*

Break, *sb.*[1] **1.** A break-away, break-down, break-out (*U.S.*) 1827. **5.** *A bad b.*, a serious blunder or failure (*U.S.*) 1883. **b.** A short play time between lessons in the middle of morning or afternoon school 1921. **9.** A (fair, equal) chance (*U.S.*) 1911.

Break, *v.* **II. 1.** *To b. one's arm*, etc.: to suffer fracture of the bones of the limb 1586.

Break-away (brē¹·kăwē¹). 1885. [f. phr. *to break away*: see BREAK *v.*] Severance 1897; the act of breaking away or getting free; spec.: **a.** *Athletics* (*Running*). A premature start. **b.** *Boxing.* The separating of the combatants after a spell of in-fighting. **c.** *Football.* A sudden rush of players with the ball towards their opponents' goal, after a period of pressure.

Breakdown. 3. The act of decomposing, disintegrating, or analysing a substance; a result of this; also *attrib.*, as *b. product* 1929.

Brea·k-out. The act of breaking out, escaping, or rushing from a place, etc.

Brea·k-through. 1924. [f. phr. *to break through*, after G. *durchbruch*.] The making of a breach in the enemy's lines.

Breast, *sb.*

b.-fed *a.* (of infants), nourished at the mother's b.; so *b.-feeding*; opp. to *bottle-fed, -feeding*.

Breeder. b. An apparatus which produces more radioactive material than is put into it 1954.

Bren gun. 1937. [f. *Brno*, town in Czechoslovakia, where it was orig. made + first syll. of *Enfield*, town in Middlesex, England, seat of a small-arms factory.] A type of light machine-gun.

‖**Brevi manu** (bre·vi mæ·niu). 1650. [L., 'with immediate action', lit. 'with short hand'.] *Sc. Law.* In a summary manner, summarily.

Bridge, *sb.*

b.-head, latterly extended to cover any military position established in the face of the enemy, e.g. by a landing force.

Allied forces were pressing forward on Bougainville Island, from the widening bridgeheads, in a bid to capture the whole island 1943.

‖**Brie** (brī). 1876. A kind of soft cheese made at *Brie* in N. France.

Brief, *v.*[2] **3. b.** To give instructions to (an aircraft crew) for an air-raid 1940. So **Brief** *sb.*

Britisher was preceded by *Britishite* (1788).

British Israel, title of an organization that maintains that the British Commonwealth and the United States of America are the principal Israel nations in the world. Hence **B. Israelite.** Cf. *ANGLO-ISRAEL.

Brolly (brǫ·li). *colloq.* 1874. Clipped and altered form of UMBRELLA. **b.** *slang.* A parachute.

‖**Bronco.**

b.-buster, a breaker-in of broncos 1888.

Brown, *v.* **3.** *To be browned off*: to be surfeited, disgusted, or 'fed up' (*R.A.F. slang*) 1920.

Brow·nshirt. 1933. A Nazi; so called from the brown shirt worn as part of the uniform.

Buchan (bʊ·kăn). The name of a Scottish meteorologist, Alexander *B.* (1829–1907), used to designate specified periods of cold weather forecast by him as of annual occurrence 1923.

Buchmanism (bu·k-, bʊ·kmăniz'm). 1933. [f. name of Frank *Buchman*, the founder + -ISM.] The religious tenets and practice propagated by Buchman in the Group Movement, the adherents of which work by means of groups of persons who are encouraged to make 'total recall' of their past, to 'share' this with others, and so to become 'changed'. So **Bu·chmanite.**

Buck (bʊk), *sb.*[7] 1872. [?] In Poker, any article placed in the pool with the chips. *To pass the b. to* (fig.): to make a scapegoat of, shift responsibility to.

Buckshee (bʊ·kʃī). orig. *Army slang.* 1916. [Alteration of BAKSHEESH.] An allowance above the usual amount, e.g. extra rations; hence *adj.* and *adv.*, gratuitous(ly), free, gratis.

Bud (bʊd), *sb.*[2] *U.S.* 1851. [Childish or negro pronunc. of BROTHER.] Brother used as a form of address. Also **Bu·ddy** [-Y[6]].

Buffer[2].

b.-state, in international politics, a state lying between two others, owing allegiance to neither, and serving as a means of preventing hostile collision between them 1883.

Build, *v.* **4.** *To b. up*: to bring together the elements necessary to constitute or establish (a thing); to collect and organize men and materials for (also *absol.*).

The desire to 'build-up' the figure of the Leader (*El Caudillo*) in the approved Fascist style 1938. Once we build up on the Seine we will break through 1944. Hence **Bui·ld-up** *sb.* 1934.

Bui·lt-up, *a.* [See prec.] **1.** Constructed of separately prepared parts which are afterwards joined together 1829. **2.** Covered or closed in with buildings, as *b. area*.

Bulge, *sb.* **b.** Phr. *To get the b. on*: to have the advantage over (*slang*, orig. *U.S.*) 1860. **2.** A bulging part of a military front.

He..managed to overrun the British position between the two gaps, which he then turned into a 'bulge' 1942.

Bull-doze, *v.*

b.-dozer, (also) a large mechanical navvy for levelling surfaces, felling trees, or other obstacles 1930.

Bulling (bu·liŋ), *ppl. a.* in sense 1 b of BULL *v.*[1], e.g. *b. heifer*.

Bum, *v.*[4] *U.S. colloq.* 1863. [? back-formation from BUMMER.] *intr.* To wander *around* idly. So **Bum** *sb.*[3] 1887 = BUMMER.

Bumble-puppy. c. A game in which a ball slung to a post is struck with a racket by each player in opposite directions, the object being to wind the string entirely round the post 1900.

Bumf (bʊmf). *slang.* 1889. [Short for *bumfodder* 'anitergium' (BUM *sb.*[1]).] Toilet paper; hence, paper (esp. with contemptuous implication), documents collectively.

Bumper[1]. **2.** esp. in attrib. use = exceptionally full or abundant 1865. **5. b.** A log, bar, etc. used as a balance 1868; one used as a fender or shock-absorber 1883. **6.** One who or a thing which bumps; an operative employed in bumping; *Cricket*, a bumping ball 1881.

Bunker. 5. A military dug-out 1940; (gen.) a hide-out.

‖**Buntal** (bʊ·ntăl). 1910. [Philippine.] A straw prepared from the talipot.

Bunyip (bʊ·nyip). 1848. Aboriginal name for a fabulous monster inhabiting rushy swamps and lagoons in Australia. **b.** *transf.* An impostor 1852.

Bus, *sb.* **1. b.** Phr. *To miss the b.*: (fig.) to lose an opportunity, fail in an undertaking or attempt (*slang*) 1915. **2.** *colloq.* **a.** An aeroplane 1913. **b.** A motor car 1921.

attrib., as *b. company, conductor* (CONDUCTOR 3); **b.-bar, -conductor** *Electr.*, a system of conductors in a generating station on which all the power of all the generators is collected for distribution or, in a receiving station, on which the power from the generating station is received for distribution; **busman,** the driver of a bus; *a busman's holiday*, leisure time spent in occupations of the same nature as those in which one engages for a living.

‖**Bushido** (bū·ʃidōu). 1899. [Jap., 'way of a soldier or knight'.] In feudal Japan, the ethical code of the Samurai.

Busker (bʊ·skǝɹ). 1859. [f. BUSK *v.*[2] + -ER[1].] *slang.* An itinerant musician or actor.

Buster. 3. As the second element of an objective compound, e.g. **bronco-b.** *U.S.* (see *BRONCO), **dam-b.,** wrecker of a dam; in familiar designations of guns, bombs, etc., e.g. **block-b.,** an aerial bomb capable of destroying a whole block of buildings; **tank-b.,** a gun or an aircraft powerful enough to 'knock out' a tank 1940.

Busy, *a.* **6.** phr. *To get b.*: to go into action, start up 1904.

Buy, *sb.* orig. *U.S.* 1882. [f. BUY *v.*] A purchase, bargain.

I believe it's a good b.! 1911.

Buzz, *sb.*[1] **1. b.** *Phonetics.* A voiced hiss 1877.

Buzz, *v.*[1] **6. b.** *Phonetics.* To pronounce as or with a b. 1877. **7.** To telephone or signal (a call, etc.) by the 'buzzer'. *To b. off*: to ring off the telephone. Also *intr.* of a message: To come *in* by the buzzer 1914. **b.** To go *off* or *away* quickly (*slang*) 1925. **8.** To throw swiftly or forcibly (*colloq.*) 1893. **9.** Of a pilot of aircraft: To fly fast and close to.

b.-bomb *colloq.*, a flying bomb 1944; **b.-saw** *U.S.*, a circular saw 1860.

Buzzer. 4. An electric mechanism for producing an intermittent current and a buzzing sound or series of sounds, used chiefly as a call or signal 1884.

By. B. *adv.* **By and large. a.** *Naut.* To the wind and off it 1669. **b.** *To take.. by and large*: to regard in a general aspect, without entering into details; (also, without *take*) everything considered, on the whole (orig. *U.S.*) 1833.

They soon find out one another's rate of sailing, by and large 1833. Taking it by and large, as the sailors say, we had a good run 1869. By and large the bookstore in the South is a sorry institution 1926.

Bye. 1. e. *Golf.* 'The holes remaining after one side has become more holes up than remain to play' (*Encycl. Brit.* 1910).

Bye-spot (bəi·spɒt). *dial.* [f. By(e) *a.* + Spot *sb.*] A solitary or secluded spot.

Through heights and hollows, and bye-spots of tales Rich with indigenous produce 1805–6 Wordsworth *Prelude* v. 236.

‖**Byssinosis** (bisinōu·sis). 1949. [mod.L., f. Gr. βύσσινον cotton + -osis.] *Path.* Chronic bronchitis resulting from inhalation of cotton dust.

C. II. **C 3,** used by extension to denote a very low standard of physical health and capacity, as in *C3 population.*

III. 3.

C = *Cmd, Conservative; C.B. = confined to barracks (as a punishment in the army); C.B.E. = Commander of the Order of the British Empire; C.B.S. = Confraternity of the Blessed Sacrament, Columbia Broadcasting System; C.C.F. = Co-operative Commonwealth Federation (of Canada); c.d. = cum dividend; C.D. = Canada Decoration; C.D.(S.) = Civil Defence (Service); C.E.A.(C.) = Central Electrical Authority (Corporation); C.E.E.C. = Council for European Economic Co-operation; C.E.M.A. = Council for the Encouragement of Music and the Arts; C.G.S. = centimetre-gramme-second; C.G.T. = Confédération Général du Travail; C.H. = Companion of Honour; C.I.D. = Committee for Imperial Defence, Criminal Investigation Department; C.I.E. = Companion of the Order of the Indian Empire; C.I.F., c.i.f. = Cost, Insurance, plus Freight; C.I.G.S. = Chief of the Imperial General Staff; C.-in-C. = Commander-in-Chief; C.M.G. = Companion of the Order of St. Michael and St. George; C.O. = Commanding Officer, Colonial Office, conscientious objector; C.S.M. = Company Sergeant Major; C.U. (A.C., etc.) = Cambridge University (Athletic Club, etc.); C.W. = continuous wave; C.W.S. = Co-operative Wholesale Society.

Cab, *sb.*³ **1.** Applied also to motor-driven vehicles (see Taxi-cab).

The c.-without-a-horse 1899.

Cabinet, *sb.* **III.**

c. pudding, a pudding made of bread or cake, dried fruit, eggs, and milk, usu. served with a sauce 1822.

Cabotage. b. The reservation to a nation of traffic within its territory 1944.

Cabriole (kæ·briōul). Transfer † to 1, 2, 3 and add: 4. A form of curved leg, frequent in Queen Anne and Chippendale furniture, so called from its resemblance to the front leg of a leaping or capering quadruped 1781.

Cabriolet. b. A motor car with fixed side and a folding top.

‖**Cacique. 2.** In Sp. politics, a man who owes his ascendancy to his power or influence; *transf.* a system in which the power is in the hands of such men. So Caci·qu(e)ism 1903.

Cacomistle (kæ·kəmis'l). 1869. (*cacomixl*, Dict. Americanisms.) [Amer.-Sp.] A raccoon-like animal, *Bassaris astuta.*

‖**Cadet**² (käde·t). 1906. [ad. Russ. *Kadet*, pl. *Kadeti*, repr. the pronunc. of *K. Dti*, abbrev. of *Konstitutsionalnyie Demokrati* Constitutional Democrats.] A member of the Constitutional Democratic (Liberal) party.

‖**Café.** Spelt **cafe** and pronounced (kēⁱf). *U.S.* (käfē·), (kæf).

‖**Cafeteria** (kæfētiə·riă). orig. *U.S.* 1839. [Sp. *cafetería* coffee-shop.] A restaurant in which the customer fetches his own food.

‖**Cagoulard** (kagulār). [F., f. *cagoule* sleeveless hooded garment + *-ard.*] A member of a secret organization whose aim was to substitute a dictatorship in France with a view to restoring the monarchy.

The papers of the Right..alleged that the police had got up the whole affair of the 'C—s' in order to conceal the existence of the Communist plot 1937.

Cake, *sb.* **1.** phr. *A piece of c.*: something pleasant and easy (*colloq.*, orig. *R.A.F. slang*) 1940.

I was in Crete, and that was a piece of c. compared with the bridgehead at Arnhem 1944.

Cake-walk (kēⁱ·k,wǭk), *sb.* 1889. [f. Cake *sb.* + Walk *sb.*] **1. a.** A walking competition among negroes, in which the couple who put on most style 'take the cake'. **b.** A dance modelled on this. **2.** A promenade moved by machinery on which people walk to the accompaniment of music 1902.

Calamity. U.S. colloq. phr., as *c. howler*, *c. Jane*, *c. prophet*, a prophet of disaster 1890.

‖**Calque** (kælk). [F., 'exact copy', f. *calquer* to trace (a design, etc.), ad. It. *calcare*, ad. L. *calcare* to tread.] An exact reproduction or imitation.

‖**Calypso** (käli·pso). [Of unkn. origin.] A song, characteristic of the West Indies, composed spontaneously on some topic of present interest, to the accompaniment of a band. Hence **Calypsonian** (kælipsōu·niăn).

Camber, *sb.* **1. b.** The arch of a road 1905. **c.** The curvature of the wings of aircraft 1909

‖**Camembert** (kæ·maṅbēəɹ). 1878. [Name of a village near Argentan, France.] A rich soft cheese made in the vicinity of C.

Camp, *sb.* **4. b.** Quarters for the accommodation of detained or interned persons, e.g. *concentration c.* (1901).

Campshed (kæ·mpʃed). 1531. Var. (the second element = Shide *sb.*) of Camp-shot.

The starting-boats..moored in mid-stream at Putney opposite the end of the c. on the Fulham side 1888.

Canalize, *v.* **2.** *fig.* To lead in a desired direction, so as to control or regulate 1922.

Canarese (kænărī·z), *a.* and *sb.* Also **Kan-.** 1875. [See -ese.] Pertaining to (a native, the Dravidian language) of Canara in W. India.

‖**Canariensis** (kănēəriе·nsis). 1901. [app. pop. alteration of spec. name *canariense* in *Tropæolum canariense*, a former systematic name.] Canary-creeper, *Tropæolum aduncum.*

‖**Canasta** (känæ·stă). 1948. [Sp., 'basket'.] A card game, of Uruguayan origin, in which two packs are used with four jokers, and combining features of rummy, pinochle, and bridge (*canasta* is the name of a meld having a high bonus value).

Candid, subst. use of the adj. with sense: An ingenuous, unsophisticated, or unposed photograph 1931.

(*Mod.*) He is known for his particular art in children's candids 1943.

Cannibalize (kæ·nibăləiz), *v.* 1941. [f. Cannibal + -ize.] *trans.* To take parts from (a machine, etc.) to make up deficiencies in another.

Cannon, *sb.*¹ **2. b.** *U.S. slang.* A pistol, revolver 1901. **c.** An aircraft gun of heavy calibre 1939.

Canon¹. **4.** *transf.* of other sacred books. Also, the list of the writings of an author accepted as authentic.

Skeat (*title*) The Chaucer C. 1900. The c. and text of Plato appear to have been fixed by Dercyllides and Thrasyllus *Encycl. Brit.* (14th ed.) s.v. *Plato.*

Canroy (kæ·nroi). Also **candroy.** 1836. [?] A machine, used in calico-printing, through which cotton-cloth is passed before printing.

Canuck (känʊ·k). *U.S.* Also **Kanuck, Canack.** 1855. [app. f. the first syll. of *Canada.*] **1.** A Canadian; *spec.* a French Canadian. **2.** A Canadian horse or pony 1860.

Cape, *sb.*³ *attrib.*

C. cart, a two-wheeled horse-drawn cart peculiar to S. Africa.

Capital, *sb.*

c. goods, economic goods (e.g. railways, ships, machinery, buildings) destined for use in production, opp. to *consumers' goods* 1928; **c. levy,** confiscation by the State of a proportion of all private property 1919.

Capitalize, *v.* **1. b.** *transf.* To make capital out of; to make profit or obtain advantage for oneself; also *absol.* orig. *U.S.* 1926.

Mod. [To] capitalize on another's mistake.

Carbon, *sb.* **1. b.** Short for Carbon paper 1895; also attrib., as *c. copy.*

Card, *sb.*² **1.** Phr. *To have a c. up one's sleeve*: to have a plan in reserve. *To play with* or *lay one's cards on the table*: to reveal all one's resources. **4. b.** A programme giving names, score, and other details of a race, game, etc. **5. b.** A c. held by a delegate of a trade union meeting or congress and representing a certain number of his constituents 1902 (**c. vote**).

Cardan (kā·ɹdăn). 1902. Name of *Cardan* (Geronimo *Cardano*, Italian mathematician, 1501–76).

c. joint, a universal joint; **c. shaft,** a shaft having a universal joint at one or both ends for transmitting motion from one shaft to another not in a direct line with it.

Cardboard. *attrib.* (*fig.*) Unsubstantial, unreal 1893.

The c. family that has become larger than life 1952.

Cardiotonic (kāːɹdiotǫ·nik), *a.* [f. Cardio- + Tonic.] *Med.* Serving to invigorate the heart.

Digitalis and other c. drugs 1953.

Care, *v.* **2.** *I couldn't c. less*: pop. catch-phrase implying indifference = I'm not interested 1945.

Careerist (kărīə·rist). 1910. [f. Career *sb.* + -ist.] One who is mainly intent on personal advancement to the exclusion of other considerations.

Caretaker.

C. Government: an administration retained in office temporarily until another general election should be held or other decisive step is taken; e.g. W. S. Churchill's Conservative government which lasted from 25 May to 26 July, 1945, succeeding to his War administration of 10 May 1940 to 23 May 1945 and preceding C. R. Attlee's Labour government of 5 August 1945 to October 1951.

Carley float (kā·ɹli flōut). 1940. An emergency raft used like a lifeboat.

Carrel (kæ·rəl). Variant of Carol *sb.* 5 revived in the 19th c. and used as the designation of an apartment in a library for the accommodation of a particular reader.

Carrier. 1. As the second element of comps. denoting a vessel or vehicle for carrying machines or men, e.g. *aircraft-c.* (1913), *Bren-(gun-) c.*, *troop-c.* **5. b.** A high-frequency current used for multiple transmission. Also *attrib.*, as *c. wave.*

Carry, *v.* With advs.

C. on. f. (transf. from **d**) To continue doing what one is occupied with 1916.

In verbal phrases used subst. **c.-forward,** the balance carried to the next account after declaration of dividend 1898; **c.-over,** on the stock exchange, postponement of payment of an account until the next settling-day, the amount so kept over 1894; also *transf.* of the leaving-over of business of any kind.

Cartel, *sb.* **4.** After G. *kartell* (ad. F. *cartel* or It. *cartello*): In Germany and Austria, an association of business houses for the regulation of output, prices, etc.; the houses so combined; a trust, syndicate; later *gen.* 1902. **5.** *Hist.* The combination of German Conservatives and National Liberals in 1887 for the support of each others' candidates; also used for similar combinations in other countries 1918.

Cartoon, *sb.* **2.** Earlier date: 1843 (*Punch* 24 June, 15 July). (No longer restricted to full-page drawings.)

‖**Cascara. 2.** pop. pronounced (kæskā·ră). In full *cascara sagrada*: A preparation of the bark of Californian buckthorn, *Rhamnus purshiana*, used as a laxative 1879.

Case, *sb.*¹ *In case*: **e.** esp. in *just in c.*, orig. with aposiopesis, *in case —*, i.e. of something happening. *colloq.*

A picture of a London policeman directing the traffic at a busy point in Paris, with a French traffic constable standing by, just in case 1951.

Casease (kēⁱ·siēⁱz). 1899. [f. Casein + *-ase.] *Chem.* A ferment capable of decomposing casein.

Casemate. 1. b. *Naut.* An armoured enclosure for guns in a warship 1934.

Cash, *v.*² **C. in.** *U.S.* To settle accounts in the game of poker; *gen.* to clear or close accounts; to die 1888; *to c. in on*, to acquire a stake in.

Cashable (kæ·ʃăb'l), *a.* 1891. [f. Cash *v.*² + -able.] That may be cashed.

It is part of the nature of a concept to be c. by instances 1953 H. H. Price *Thinking & Exper.* 229. There can be no symbols unless *some* symbols are empirically c. *Ibid.* 36. Hence **Cashabi·lity.**

Cast, *v.* **C. off. e.** *Printing.* To estimate how much printed matter will correspond to (a piece of 'copy') 1683. Hence **C.-off** *sb.*, the estimation of this 1898.

Catabolism 1889: see Katabolism.

Catalo (kæ·tălo). 1889. Also **cattalo.** [f. Cat(tle + Buff)alo.] *U.S.* A cross between the male buffalo or bison and the domesticated cow.

Catalyse (kæ·tăləiz), *v.* 1890. [f. Catalysis, after *analyse, analysis.*] *trans.* To break down, decompose. Hence **Ca·talysator, -lyser.** So **Ca·talyst** [after *analyst*], a catalytic agent 1902.

Cat-lap. Also *fig.* Poor or feeble stuff.
With a lot of c. added about the break being no fault of hers 1901.

‖**Caudillo** (kaudī·lʸo). 1938. [Sp., 'leader', 'chief':—late L. (Rom.) *capitellum*, dim. of *caput* head.] Title (*El C.*) assumed by General Francisco Franco as head of the Spanish State, in imitation of *Duce* and *Führer*.

Caudine Forks (kǭ·dəin fǭɹks). The name of passes in the mountains of Samnium where Romans on surrendering to the Samnites (321 B.C.) passed under a yoke of spears; used allus. for the imposition of a trial.
Their passing through the C. f. of the selective examination at the age of 11. 1952.

‖**Causalgia** (kǭ·zældʒiă). 1939. [mod.L., f. Gr. καῦσις burning (f. καίειν to burn) + -αλγία, ἄλγος pain; see -IA[1].] *Path.* An affection of the skin characterized by burning pain.

Cavault, early var. of CAVORT 1829.

Cave, *sb.*
c. man, a prehistoric dweller in caves; (hence) a man of primitive passions, instincts, or behaviour 1897.

Cease-fire. 1859. [CEASE *v.*, FIRE *sb.* 14.] *Mil.* The signal to cease firing; formerly *cease firing* and simply *cease* (1847).

Ceiling, *sb.* **4. b.** Also *fig.* Maximum height or uppermost limit of prices, expenditure, wages, etc.
Prices hit a new c. 1944.

Celanese (selănī·z). 1923. [Arbitrarily f. CELLULOSE.] Proprietary term for artificial silk made by British Celanese Ltd.

Cell. I. 4. b. *pl.* Imprisonment in solitary confinement as a punishment for offences against military law 1891. III. 3. A nucleus or centre of persons engaged in furthering a cause or propagating principles, esp. of a revolutionary kind 1930.

Cellophane (se·lŏfēⁱn). 1921. [f. CELL(ULOSE + -O- + *-phane*, as in DIAPHANE.] Proprietary term for a transparent material made from wood pulp and used as a wrapping.

Celtic, often pronounced (ke·ltik).
C. Fringe [FRINGE *sb.* 2], joc. collective designation of the Scots, Irish, Welsh, Manx, and Cornish in their geographical relation to England.

Cema (sī·mă). See C.E.M.A. s.v. *C. 1944.

Centibar (se·ntibāɹ): see *BAR *sb.*[4]

Central, *a.* 4. *C. heating,* a system of heating a building by hot water or steam conveyed through pipes from a c. source 1921.

Cereal, *sb.* **b.** An article of diet consisting of a cereal 1899. orig. *U.S.*

‖**Cestui que trust.** Pronounced (se·tiki-trɒ·st).

Cha: see also *CUPPA.

Chad (tʃæd). [?] The figure of a human head appearing above a wall, etc. with the legend 'Wot, no ——?'
[He] returned [the papers] to the Inspector of Taxes, ornamented with a chad, exclaiming: 'Wot, no number?' 1946.

Chagas (tʃæ·găs), in *Chagas('s) disease,* a form of sleeping-sickness of South and Central America, named after its discoverer.

Chain, *sb.* = *c. store*; a combine of associated newspapers.
c. reaction *Chem.*, reaction forming intermediate products which react with the original reactant and are repeatedly renewed; esp. in nucleonics; also *fig.*; **c.-smoker** [tr. G. *kettenraucher*], one who smokes cigarettes or cigars in unbroken succession, esp. one who lights a fresh one from the one in hand 1890; **c. store,** *U.S.*, one of a series of commercial establishments owned and controlled by one and the same firm, etc. and dealing in the same goods 1910.

Chair, *sb.* *The* (*electric*) *c.*: the chair in which a condemned criminal is placed for electrocution 1890.

Champion, *sb.* *attrib.* passing into *adj.* Excellent, first-class (*dial.* and *slang*) 1889.
'It was c.', he added 1914.

Chance, *v.* 4. *To c. one's arm*: to perform an action in the face of probable failure, take one's chance of success (*colloq.*) 1889.

Change, *v.* 6. *intr.* (also *pass.*) To reform one's way of life in accordance with the methods of the Group Movement 1933.

Charge, *v.* 8. Chiefly *U.S.* To bring as a charge *against* a person *that*.. 1891.

‖**Charisma** (kări·zmă). *c* 1640. [eccl.L., a. Gr. χάρισμα.] *Theol.* A spiritual gift.

Charlady (tʃā·ɹlēⁱdi). [CHAR-.] 1895. joc. substitute for CHARWOMAN.

Chaser[1]. 4. = CHASSE[2]; also, a small quantity of water, etc. taken after spirits, etc., to wash them down 1897.

‖**Chaud-froid** (ʃofrwa). 1892. [F., 'hot-cold'.] *Cookery.* A dish composed of meat, etc. cooked to be served cold in jelly or sauce.

Check-list (tʃe·klist). 1853. *U.S.* [CHECK-, LIST *sb.* 5.] A list of titles, etc. forming a means of reference or verification, spec. a list of qualified voters.

Check-roll. Used in India and some other Asiatic countries for: A record of the work done on an estate by labourers under a contract of service, and of the wages so earned.
A complete register of all labourers employed on his estate, whether borne on the c., or working on any form of contract 1889.

Check-up (tʃe·kɒp). orig. *U.S.* 1924. [f. *to check up*: see CHECK *v.*[1] IV.] A detailed scrutiny or verification of the items of an account, statement, etc.

Chemical, *a.* and *sb.*
c. warfare, that in which chemicals (other than explosives) are used, as gases, smoke, incendiary compounds; **fine c-s,** those handled in small lots and in a purified state; **heavy c-s,** those handled in large lots and in a more or less crude state.

Che:milumine·scence. 1910. [f. CHEMI-(CO-).] Emission of light accompanying a chemical reaction, as in the oxidation of phosphorus.

‖**Chemin de fer** (ʃəmæ̃n d fĕɹ). 1902. [F., 'road of iron', railway.] A form of baccarat. Whence slang or colloq. **Chemmy** (ʃe·mi) 1923.

Chemo- (ke·mo), used as comb. form = CHEMIC(AL), as in **Che:mokine·sis,** increased activity of an organism induced by a chemical substance 1900; **Chemothe·rapy,** treatment of internal diseases by chemical reagents 1922.

Chew, *v.* Phr. *To c. the rag* or *fat*: to discuss things complainingly, reiterate an old grievance, dispute, etc. (*Army slang*) 1885.

Chicken. *attrib.*
c. feed, food for poultry 1865; *fig.* poor or inferior stuff, 'small change' 1931; **c. meat** *slang*, applied to matter of 'pale' or 'bloodless' quality.
A milk and water chicken meat publication 1824.

Chikhor, chikor (tʃi·kǭɹ). 1815. [Hind.] Sportman's name for various Indian game-birds, esp. the red-legged partridge (*Caccabis chukar*).

Chilled (tʃild), *ppl. a.* 1598. [CHILL *v.* II.] 1. Made cold; injuriously or unpleasantly affected with cold. 2. Of cast iron: Rapidly cooled and so hardened 1831. 3. Of meat: Kept at a moderately low temperature 1894.

Chimp (tʃimp), colloq. abbrev. of CHIMPANZEE 1928.

Chip, *sb.*[1] 1. b. A piece sliced from a potato and fried, usu. *pl.* as in *fish and chips.*

Chi-rho (kəi rōᵘ). (1611, Florio), 1868. The first two letters of Gr. XPICTOC CHRIST, often joined in a monogram ☧ and used to symbolize the name.

Chirurgery. Survives in the title of the Professor of Anatomy and Chirurgery in the University of Dublin.

Cholelithiasis (kǫ:lĭlipəi·ăsis). 1897. [f. Gr. χολή bile, CHOLE- + LITHIASIS.] *Path.* The presence of stones in the gall bladder and bile ducts.

Choosy (tʃū·zi), *a.* 1862. [f. CHOOSE *v.* + -Y[1].] orig. *U.S.* Disposed to be particular in one's choice.

‖**Chota hazri** (tʃōᵘ·tă hā·zri). *Anglo-Indian.* 1863. [Hindī *chhota hāẓ(i)ri* little breakfast.] A light early breakfast. So **Chota Peg** (*sb.*[1] 4).

‖**Chou** (ʃū). 1889. [F., 'cabbage'.] 1. A knot of ribbon, chiffon, etc. 2. A kind of puff pastry with a flaky surface 1892.

Christ. *C. child* (after G. *Christkindchen, -lein*), Christ as a child, the infant Jesus 1842.

Christadelphian (kristăde·lfiăn). 1864. [f. Gr. Χριστοῦ ἀδελφοί brethren of Christ (with ref. to Heb. ii. 11) + -IAN.] A member of a religious body which professes a millenarian theology, claims sole possession of the true exegesis of Scripture (as against general Christian practice), and has no ministry or organization.

Christiania (kristiā·niă). 1924. [Former name of the capital of Norway, now Oslo.] A swing in ski-ing, used to stop short. Abbrev. **Chri·stie.**

Chromatography (krōᵘmătǫ·grăfi). Also *Chem.* The separation of a mixture of compounds by their adsorption in separate coloured layers. So **Chro·matogram,** a series of such layers. **Chro·matogra·phic** *a.*

Chukar, -or, vars. of *CHIK(H)OR.

Church, *sb.*
C. Army, an English religious body, having a quasi-military organization, founded by the Rev. Wilson Carlisle in 1886 to work for the betterment of outcasts and criminals; **C. Assembly,** short title of the National Assembly of the Church of England, a body established by Statute in 1919 (the C. of England Assembly (Powers) Act); **C. Congress,** an annual meeting of members of the C. of England to discuss spiritual, moral, and social matters under the presidency of the bishop of the diocese in which it is held 1861; **c. parade,** (*a*) divine service performed as part of the routine of military duty 1869; (*b*) a turn-out of fashionable church-goers after the late Sunday morning service 1891; **c.-people,** people belonging to the C. of England 1842.

Chute[2] (ʃūt), colloq. abbrev. of PARACHUTE 1940.

Cine (si·nĭ), colloq. and commercial abbrev. of Gr. κίνημα movement, CINEMA, as in *cine-film* (1897), *cine-goer*, *-variety* (1928), *-worker.*

Cinerama (si·nĭrāmă). 1952. [f. CINE- + *-rama* of PANORAMA, etc.] A form of three-dimensional film. So **Ci·nemascope.**

Circs (sōɹks), colloq. abbrev. of pl. of CIRCUMSTANCE, esp. in *under the c.* 1883.

Ci·rcumcircle. [CIRCUM-.] *Math.* A circle which passes through the three apices of a triangle.

Circus. 2. b. *transf.* A raiding party; a squadron of aeroplanes used for raiding 1917.

Citation. 5. orig. *U.S.* Mention in an official dispatch or recommendation to an honour 1918.

Citified (si·tifəid), *ppl. a.* [f. CITY + -IFY + -ED[1].] Conformed to the fashion or style of a city or the City.
Taken by his son, a young man who looked like a slighter and citified version of his father 1945.

City. *attrib.*
c. state, a city that is an independent sovereign state.
The City-State of the Greeks and Romans (*title*) WARDE FOWLER 1893.

Civil, *a.*
C. Defence Service, the organization in which were co-ordinated the former A.R.P. services 1940; **c. disobedience,** in India, refusal to obey the laws as part of a political campaign.
[London's Civil Defence organization *Illustrated* 16 Sept. 1939.]

Civvy (si·vi). Also **civy.** *slang.* Short for CIVILIAN, as in *c. clothes* (also *pl.* **Civvies** 1889), *c. life*, *C. Street* (= civilian life).

Class, *sb.* 2. In adj. use, put for 'high class', e.g. *not c. enough* 1874, *no c.* 1897. b. *attrib.* and *Comb.*, as in *c. conflict*, *war* 1920; *c.-conscious(ness)* 1887.

Clean, *a.* 4. b. *The c. thing*: honesty, straightforwardness (*U.S.*) 1835. c. Free from impropriety or indecency 1908. d. *To come c.*: to make a c. breast of it, confess (*slang*) 1926.

Clearing, *vbl. sb.*
c. hospital, a field hospital for the temporary treatment of the sick and wounded 1916.

Clerihew (kle·rihiū). [Name of Edmund *Clerihew* Bentley (1875–).] A short comic or nonsensical verse, professedly biographical, usu. of two couplets differing in length.

Clerk, *sb.* 5. c. *U.S.* (klōɹk) A shop assistant 1771.

Click, *v.*[1] 1. b. *fig.* To meet *with* fortunately or at the right moment; to come to an agreement or understanding 1915.

Climate, *sb.* 3. b. *fig.* The mental or moral attitude of a body of people in respect of some aspect of life, policy, etc.
We have reached a 'climate' of opinion where figures rule BAGEHOT 1866. *Mod.* Writers have the power and the duty to alter their c. of opinion. A religious c. of the puritanical kind.

Clippie (kli·pi). *colloq.* 1940. [f. CLIP *v.*[2] (with allusion to the clipping of tickets) + *-ie*, -Y[6].] A bus or tram conductress.

Clock, *v.* **1. b.** Also to put *in* (so many hours) *at* a piece of work. Also **Clocking-in**, etc. (*attrib.* in *clocking-in apparatus*).

Clone (klōun). 1903. [ad. Gr. κλών twig, slip.] *Bot.* **a.** A group of cultivated plants the individuals of which are transplanted parts of one original seedling or stock. **b.** A group of individuals produced asexually from a sexually produced ancestor.

Close, *a.*

c. call *U.S.*, an incident that came near to disaster, a near shave 1887.

Close-down (klōu·zdəun). 1889. orig. *U.S.* [f. phr. *close down*; see CLOSE *v.* II. 2.] The action of closing down, bringing to a close or conclusion, as work in a factory.

Cloth, *sb.* **II. b.** A piece of such woven (etc.) stuff of a particular kind used for a specific purpose (denoted by a qualifying word), as CERECLOTH 1540, *dish-cloth* 1828, FLOOR-CLOTH 1746, GREENCLOTH 1536, HAIRCLOTH 1500, OILCLOTH 1697, SACKCLOTH ME.

Clothette (klǫþe·t). [f. CLOTH + -ETTE.] An inferior kind of binding cloth.

Cloud-cuckoo-town or **-land.** 1903. tr. Gr. Νεφελοκοκκυγία (f. νεφέλη cloud + κόκκυξ, -υγ- cuckoo), name of the town in Aristophanes' *Birds* (l. 819) built by the birds to separate the gods from mankind. Used allusively for: A fanciful or ideal realm or domain.

Clouded (klau·dėd), *ppl. a.* [f. CLOUD *sb.* or *v.* + -ED[1].] Marked with stripes, spots, or veins of colour, as in *C. leopard, tiger*, a handsome cat of the E. Indies and Asia, *Felis nebulosa.*

Cmd (formerly *C* and *Cd*) = *COMMAND *paper.*

Co-. *Co-belligerent* 1813; *Co-prosperity* (*sphere*).

The Japanese 'Co-Prosperity Sphere' embraced Japan, Manchukuo, a large and rich part of China, Indo-China, Thailand, Malay, the Philippines, Burma, and the Dutch East Indies *Ann. Register for 1942*, 280.

Coach, *sb.*

c.-built, (of a motor body) built of wood throughout by craftsmen, or on a wood framework with metal panels 1904.

Coal-mine (kōu·lməin). 1613. [f. COAL *sb.* + MINE *sb.*] A mine in which coal is dug. (Earlier COAL-PIT.) So **Co·al-mi:ner** 1639.

Coca-cola (kōu:kăkōu·lă). 1887. Trade name of a soda-fountain beverage; f. *coca* and *cola*, names of vegetable products from which stimulants are extracted; abbrev. **Coke** (kōuk) 1909.

Cocktail. 3. The origin of this application to a drink (1806 in Thornton's *American Glossary*) is unknown.

Cocoon, *v.* [f. COCOON *sb.*] *trans.* To wrap up, lay up or aside for the future.

With cocooned Sabre jets on her deck 1951.

‖**Cocotte** (kokǫ·t). 1867. [F.] A light or loose woman.

C.O.D. (sī·ōudī·). orig. *U.S.* Initials of cash (costs, or collect) on delivery 1863.

Cœlacanth, *sb.* (Specimens of this fish recently found have been systematically named *Latimeria chalumnæ* and *Morlania anjouanæ.*) Also **Cœlaca·nthid** [-ID[2]] *attrib.* or *adj.*

A further Cœlacanthid Fish *Nature* 3 Jan. 1953, p. 17/1.

Co-existence. b. With special reference to peaceful existence side by side of states professing different ideologies 1954.

Coke, *sb.*[2], short for *COCA-COLA.

Cold, *a.*

c. war, hostilities short of armed conflict, consisting in threats, violent propaganda, political warfare, or the like.

Colfarm (kǫ·lfāɪm), anglicization of *KOLKHOZ.

Collaborate *v.*, **Collaboration.** In World War II *spec.* applied to traitorous co-operation with the enemy 1940. Hence **Collabora·tionist**; so **Colla·borator.**

Collect, *v.* **1. b.** To retrieve from a place 1875.

Collins (kǫ·linz). 1904. A letter of thanks for hospitality and entertainment sent by a departed visitor to his host: named after William *Collins* in Jane Austen's *Pride & Prejudice* xxiii.

Collizh (kəli·ʒ), colloq. abbrev. of COLLISION.

Naturally she had a little collizh now and again 1934 R. MACAULAY *Going Abroad* xi.

Colonialism (kŏlōu·niăliz'm). 1886. [f. COLONIAL + -ISM.] A colonial system; a policy involving the relation of countries as colonial dependencies on another.

Colonic (kouləˈnik), *a.* [f. COLON[2] + -IC.] Pertaining to or concerning the colon.

Colonic irrigation *Times* 27 Nov. 1951.

Colour, *sb.*

c. scheme, (*a*) an arrangement of colours according to a thought-out design 1921; (*b*) a pattern of protective coloration in nature; **c. wash,** coloured distemper; hence as vb. 1887.

Colourful (kʊ·ləɪfŭl). 1889. [f. COLOUR *sb.* + -FUL 1.] Full of colour, of bright and varied colour, highly-coloured.

Colouristic (kʊləri·stik), *a.* [f. COLOUR *sb.* + -ISTIC.] Marked by fulness of colour.

In a flat linear conception instead of a highly c. one 1948 BOASE in *Jrnl. Warburg & Courtauld Inst.* X. 103.

Columnist (kǫ·ləmist, kǫ·liŭmist). orig. *U.S.* 1920. [f. COLUMN 2 + -IST.] A writer who contributes a column regularly to a journal.

Combination.

c. bolt, lock, one that can be opened only after a set combination of movements has been performed 1851.

Combined, *ppl. a.* *C. operations*, operations of war in which all three arms are combined.

Comb-out (kōu·maut). 1919. [f. phr. *comb out*: see COMB *v.* 4.] An act of combing out or clearing out.

Come, *v.*

II. 2. slang phr. *To have it coming to* (one): to be 'in for it'. **VII. C. again?**: an off-hand slang equiv. of 'What is that?', 'Beg pardon'. **VIII. C. back** *U.S.*, to retort, retaliate 1896. (Cf. COME-BACK 1.) **C. off** *U.S. slang*, to stop, desist; also *c. off it* 1889. **C. through** *U.S.*, to succeed, attain an end; *spec.* to attain conversion 1886.

Come-hither (kʊmhi·ðəɪ). [COME *v.*, HITHER.] As an imper., a summons to come towards one (*dial.*) 1819; as *sb.*, attraction, lure 1952. Hence **Come-hither(y)** *a.* attractive.

Comic, *a.* **4.** *C. strip*, in journals, a series of humorous pictures arranged consecutively (orig. *U.S.*) 1920. *sb.* **1.** Delete † and add: Now, a comedian in a dramatic sketch or variety entertainment (also in F. form **Comique**) 1927.

Cominform (kǫ·minfǫɪm). [Russ., f. *kommunist* COMMUNIST, *inphormatziya* information.] A bureau set up (5 Oct. 1947) for the communist countries of eastern Europe for interchange of experience and coordination of activities. Also *attrib.*, as *C. country.*

Comintern: dissolved 22 May 1943.

Command, *sb.* **7. b.** *The Higher C.*: the general staffs collectively of the British army; more particularly, the commander-in-chief 1916; *the High C.*: orig. tr. foreign designations, as G. *hochbefehl*, F. *haut commandement* 1917. **8. b.** A unit of the R.A.F. detailed for a particular service, as *Bomber C., Coastal C., Fighter C.* 1936.

c. paper (see *CMD), a paper laid before Parliament by c. of the Crown; **c. performance,** a theatrical, musical, etc. performance given by royal c. 1922; **c. post,** (*a*) a post from which artillery fire is directed; (*b*) *U.S.* army headquarters.

Commandant. Revived in World War I as the title of an officer holding a special command, as of a place, depot, etc.

Commando. b. *pl.* Bodies of picked men trained orig. (in 1940) as shock troops for the repelling of an invasion of England, later for the carrying out of raids on the Continent, etc.; *sing.* a member of such a unit. Also *attrib.*, as *c. raid.*

Commend, *v.* **2. b.** *refl.* To be acceptable *to* 1886.

Commie (kǫ·mi). f. first syll. of COMMUNIST + -IE.

‖**Commissar** (kǫmisā·ɪ). 1918. [Russ. *kom(m)issár*, ad. F. *commissaire.*] The head of a state department in the U.S.S.R. (since 1946 replaced by *minister*). So **Commissa·riat**[2], such a department.

Commissioner. 1. c. *High C.*: the chief representative in London of a British Dominion or of India; e.g. *H. C. for Canada* 1881 (superseding *Resident Minister*).

Commodore. 4. *Air C.*, R.A.F. officer equivalent in rank to a brigadier in the army 1918.

Commonwealth. 2. b. transf. *British C. of Nations*, designation of the British Empire coined by Gen. J. C. Smuts in 1919; more recently *British C.* (*and Empire*) has been used.

Community. II. 4. *spec.*, *Bot.* and *Zool.* A group of plants or animals growing together in natural conditions or found inhabiting a restricted area.

Compact (kǫ·mpækt), *sb.*[2] Delete † and add: Compact powder or make-up, case containing this 1930. (Cf. F. *poudre compacte, fard compact.*)

Compassionate, *a.* **1. b.** Granted out of compassion, e.g. in a manner exceeding the official terms or rates, as *c. allowance, c. leave.*

Comrade. b. Used by socialists and communists of and to each other 1884.

Con (kǫn). *U.S.* 1896. Short for CONFIDENCE in attrib. use, as *c. game, man, talk.* Hence **Con** *v.*, to swindle, dupe.

Concentration.

c. camp 1901; (also), quarters for the detention of political prisoners, internees, and suspects.

Conceptualist. *Philos.* (See quot.)

Two theories of the nature of universals will be considered, the conceptualist belief that they are mental entities, and the *in re* form of realism which maintains that they inhere in objects and are so apprehended by the mind 1951 HOLLOWAY *Lang. & Intell.* ii. 16.

‖**Condemnator** (kǫ·ndemnēitǭɪ). 1557. [L. *condemnator* let him (her) be condemned, 3rd pers. sing. imper. pass. of *condemnare* to CONDEMN.] *Sc. Law.* A decree of the court in favour of the pursuer.

Condition, *v.* **9.** To bring to a desired or required condition 1849. Cf. *AIR-*conditioned.*

When my hunters were being conditioned 1908.

Conditioned, *ppl. a.* **2.** Dependent upon specific conditions, as *c. reflex* 1915.

Conduct, *sb.*[1] **II. 4.**

c. sheet, the record of a soldier's offences and punishments 1927.

Conductimetric (kǫndʊktime·trik), *a.* [f. CONDUCTANCE + METRIC.] *Chem.* Applied to volumetric analysis in which the end-point of a titration is determined by measurements of the conductance of the solution.

Condy's fluid (kǫ·ndiz flū·id). 1859. [Name of H. B. *Condy*, English physician.] A disinfecting fluid usu. consisting of an aqueous solution of permanganate of calcium and of sodium. Also (*colloq.*) **Condy.**

Cone, *v.* *trans.* To catch or trap in a cone of searchlights.

We got coned over the target 1944.

Conk (kǫŋk), *v. colloq.* 1918. [?] *intr.* To give *out*, fail or show signs of failing.

Connexion. 1. b. *Electr.* The taking up of electric current by contact; a device for effecting this 1832.

Conning, *vbl. sb.*[2]

c. tower, (also) of a submarine.

Consociation. 1. b. *Bot.* A subdivision of an association dominated by one of the codominants of the association.

Consumer. *Consumers'* or **Consumption** *goods*: things which directly satisfy human needs and desires, e.g. food and clothing 1892.

Contact, *sb.* **1. b.** *Electr.* The touching or uniting of points or surfaces of conductors to permit the flow of electric current; a device for effecting this 1915.

attrib. [cf. next]: **c. man,** an intermediary in a transaction 1939.

Contact, *v. trans.* To get into contact with (orig. *U.S.*) 1929.

Container. A vessel designed to contain or store articles 1925.

This van collects all empty containers 1944.

Contemptible, *a.* **1,** as sb. in *The Old C-s*, Sir John French's army of 1914 (in World War I), with ref. to the German Emperor's alleged description of the British expeditionary force as 'French's contemptible little army'.

Co·ntent, *sb.*[1] **1. b.** Amount of (a constituent) contained or yielded 1901.

Context, *sb.* **5.** *Bot.* The sterile part of the fruit body of a fungus.

Contract, *sb.*[1] **1. b.** An undertaking (*colloq.*, orig. *U.S.*) 1881. **c.** A season railway ticket 1899. **d.** *Bridge.* An undertaking to make so many tricks 1908. Also *c. bridge.*

Contract, *v.* **2. b.** *To c. out*: to make an arrangement not to come under certain conditions; so *to c. in* 1894.

Contrail (kǫ·ntrēl). 1940. [f. *con-*, short for *condensation* + TRAIL *sb.*] A vapour trail.

Contraprop (kǫ·ntrăprǫp). 1941. [f. CONTRA- + first part of PROPELLER.] A coaxial oppositely rotating airscrew.

Control, *sb.* **3.** *spec.* A means adopted for the regulation of prices and consumption of goods.

Mod. Yielding to vested interests over the continuation of c-s essential to the transition period from war to peace.

Conurbation (kǫnɒ̆ɪbē·ʃən). 1937. [f. CON- + L. *urb-*, *urbs* city + -ATION.] An aggregation of urban districts.

Convenience, *sb.* A structure (as in a public place) containing a urinal, with or without a lavatory and water closet.

Convertible, *a.* **4. b.** *Finance.* Of currency, balance, etc.: That can be freely converted (into gold or dollars) at a fixed price.

Coolant (kū·lănt). 1939. [f. COOL *v.* + -ANT.] A liquid applied to the edge of a cutting-tool to cool the tool and the work-piece; in a motor, a cooling medium for the cylinders.

Coon. 2. c. *U.S.* A negro 1887.

Coon-can (kūnkæ·n). 1889. [ad. Mex. Sp. *conquian*, ad. Sp. *con quien* with whom?] A card game, originating in Mexico, the main object of which is to secure sequences.

Cootie (kū·ti), *sb.*[2] *Army slang.* 1917. [?] A body louse.

Cop, *sb.*[5] *slang.* 1889. [f. COP *v.*[2]] **1.** Capture. **2.** Acquisition, 'catch' 1919.

1. Prisoner remarked it was 'a fair c.' 1889. 2. Doesn't look much c. now 1919.

Cop, *v.*[2] **b.** *To c. it*: to catch it, get into trouble (*slang*) 1886.

Cope, *v.* **2. b.** *absol.* To deal (competently) with a situation (*colloq.*).

He would c., without fuss or self-importance 1932.

Copec (kōu·pek). 1924. f. initials of *Con*ference *o*n Christian *P*olitics, *E*conomics, and *C*itizenship.

Copy-cat (kǫ·pikæt). 1896. [COPY *v.*, CAT *sb.*[1]] **1. a.** An imitator of another. **b.** One who copies another's (written) work, e.g. at school. **2.** An apparatus for making exact copies of written or printed work patented by the Miles Aircraft Co. 1945. Hence as vb.

You don't want to go through life copy-catting me, do you? 1932.

Corgi, corgy (kǭ·ɪgi). 1926. [W.] A small Welsh breed of dog.

Corner, *sb.* **2.** In slang or colloq. phr. *Round the c.*: (*a*) at or to a neighbouring public house, public lavatory, etc.: (*b*) *fig.* very near or close, about to be accomplished, almost in sight.

(*b*) Peace seemed to be just round the c. (*mod.*).

Corona. 6. d. *Biol.* The trochal disk of a rotifer 1898. **8.** *Electr.* The luminous discharge from a conductor 1906.

Coronary, *a.* **3.** Also, pertaining to or affecting the coronary artery of the heart, as *c. thrombosis.*

Corporative, *a.* **b.** *C. State* (It. *stato corporativo*): the state as organized in Fascist Italy on the basis of collective labour relations 1927.

Corridor. 4. Also, a passage in a railway carriage upon which the compartments open 1892.

Cortisone (kǭ·ɪtizōᵘn). 1949. [Coined in Feb. 1949 by E. C. Kendall, of the Mayo Foundation, Minnesota, from *17-hydroxy-11-dehydro-corticosterone*; see CORTEX, *STERONE.] A steroidal hormone ($C_{21}H_{28}O_5$) found in the cortex of the adrenal glands, and prepared synthetically for use as an anti-inflammatory agent in rheumatoid arthritis, etc.; Kendall's Compound E.

Corvette. b. Revived in World War II to designate: A small fast naval escort vessel 1941.

Cosh (kǫʃ), *sb.*[1] 1874. [Of unkn. origin.] *slang.* A short, heavy bludgeon consisting of a length of metal, rubber, etc. used as a weapon; *locally*, a school cane. Also *attrib.* as in *c. boy, c. gang.* Hence **Cosh** *v.*, *trans.*, to strike with a cosh 1896.

Cosh (kǫsē·ɪtʃ), *sb.*[2] *Math.* Abbreviation for *hyperbolic cosine.* Cf. SINH.

Coslettize (kǫ·zlĕtəiz), *v.* 1908. [f. *Coslett*, inventor's name + -IZE.] *trans.* To treat (a steel frame, etc.) with a rust-preventing process.

Cosmic, *a.* **3. b.** *C. rays*: radiations having a shorter wave length and greater penetrative power than any previously investigated: so called because their source seems to be in interstellar spaces 1925. So *c. radiation.*

Costing (kǫ·stiŋ), *vbl. sb.* of COST *v.* 1884. Estimation of the cost of production; (often *pl.*) the costs of production.

Costume, *sb.* **5.** The appearance of an animal proper to a particular season.

Smooth Newt (male) in breeding c. 1950.

Cough, *sb.*

c.-drop, (*a*) a lozenge for easing a cough 1851; (*b*) a person or thing of pungent quality, a 'cure', 'caution' (*slang*) 1895; **c. mixture**, a medicinal concoction or linctus for the alleviation of a cough 1856.

Count, *sb.*[1] **1. b.** *Boxing.* The counting of ten seconds, the limit of time allowed to a fallen boxer to rise and resume the fight or accept defeat (phr. *to take the c.*) 1913.

County[2]. Used adj. in the sense 'having the social status of a c. family'.

Mod. Determined to become 'County'.

Coupon. *spec.* A form used by an advertiser of an article to be filled up by an intending user or purchaser and forwarded in exchange for goods 1906; one of a series of tickets entitling the holder to a ration of food 1918. **b.** Also *attrib.*, as *c. candidate, election, majority.*

Court, *sb.*[1] **IV. 3.** See also HIGH COURT.

Coventrate (kǫ·vĕntrēɪt), *v.* [f. *Coventr*(*y* + -ATE[3], after G. *coventrieren.*] *trans.* To attack and devastate (an area) by aerial bombing for the purpose of reducing the output of war materials, as the Luftwaffe did Coventry on 14–15 Nov. 1940.

Cover, *sb.* **1. b.** Protection from attack (e.g. *cloud c.*); a force of aircraft detailed to protect a land or sea operation (*air c., fighter c.*).

c. girl, a girl or young woman whose portrait illustrates the c. of a periodical magazine.

Cover, *v.*[1] **III. 4.** orig. *U.S.* To take charge of the report of (a meeting, trial, etc.) 1893. Hence **Co·verage** 1931.

That the Press coverage of the forthcoming European invasion be adequate 1944.

Covetious (kɒ·vitʃəs), *a.* Vulgar var. of COVETOUS. Cf. *GRIEVIOUS, *MISCHIEVIOUS.

Crack, *sb.* **I. 5.** *U.S. colloq.* A sharp or cutting remark 1903. Cf. WISE CRACK.

Crack, *v.* **II. 7. b.** To decompose (petroleum, etc.) by the application of heat and pressure so as to produce lighter hydrocarbons 1868.

Crackers (kræ·kəɪz). *slang.* [f. CRACKED 5, *crack-brained*, etc. (see CRACK-).] 'Cracked', 'not all there'.

Crackpot (kræ·kpǫt). *colloq.* or *vulgar.* [For *cracked pot*: i.e. CRACKED *ppl. a.*, POT *sb.*[1] 1.] A crazy creature.

Crash, *sb.*[1] **1. b.** Violent percussion, concussion, or breakage 1918.

c.-dive, a sudden dive made by a submarine when surprised or in danger 1922. Also as vb. **c. helmet**, a helmet designed for the protection of the head in a crash (e.g. of a motor cyclist) 1923.

Create, *v.* **4. b.** *absol.* To make a fuss or to-do (*slang* or *vulgar*) 1919.

Crepe (krēɪp). Anglicization of CRÊPE, as in **c. rubber**, india-rubber made into sheets with a corrugated surface, used e.g. for the soles of boots and shoes 1907.

Crew. *attrib.*

c.-cut, a closely cropped style of hair-cut; short for *air-c.-cut*, a close hair-cut adopted by the crews of aircraft for comfort's sake; also called *combat crop.*

Light-brown hair with a 'crew' cut 1953.

‖**Criblé** (kri·blē). 1911. [F., pa. pple. of *cribler* to riddle with small holes, f. *crible* sieve.] *Wood-engraving.* A kind of stippling in white to produce the effect of light and dark.

When a more advanced kind of wood engraving had become prevalent the *c.* was no longer used for general purposes 1911.

Crisp, *sb.* **4.** *pl.* Thin slices of potato fried and dried, usu. sold in packets 1929.

Croak, *v.* **4.** (*a*) To die, (*b*) to kill (*slang*).

Croc, colloq. abbrev. of CROCODILE 1935.

Cro-Magnon (krǫmæ·nyoṅ). 1808. Name of a cave in Dordogne, France, the site of prehistoric remains, applied to a prehistoric European people of mesolithic or neolithic age.

Croo·kedness. 1843. [-NESS.] Dishonesty, sharp dealing.

Crooner (krū·nəɪ). [f. CROON *v.* + -ER[1].] One who croons or sings in low tones; now *spec.* a public singer of highly sentimental songs in subdued tones.

Cross, *v.* **7.** phr. *To cross the T, the t's*: see T. 1 b, *b.

Cross-. 2, 3.

c.-blown flute, c. flute: a flute played with the lips against a hole on one side (F. *flûte traversière*, It. *flauto traverso*, G. *traversflöte, querflöte*, L. *tibia obliqua*, Gr. πλαγίαυλος); **c.-connect**, to interchange the connexions of (electric wires) 1875; **c.-counter** *Boxing*, a blow at the head delivered across an opponent's lead-off with the other hand 1889; **c.-nibbed** *a.*, having the points of the nib crossed; **c.-section**, a section made by a plane cutting a thing transversely (cf. G. *querschnitt*) 1884; *fig.* a composite representation of the elements of a thing in their relations, as *a c. of society, the electors*, etc.; **c. talk**, (*a*) interference between adjacent telephone circuits resulting in the overhearing of conversation; (*b*) altercation, back-chat; **c.-tie**, a transverse connecting piece (of timber, etc.) 1849.

Cross-road. 2. b. *pl.* in fig. phr. *at the c-s*: at a critical turning-point in one's or its career or history 1898.

[He had met with four cross-roads, and he knew not which to follow 1852.] Germany at the c-s 1932.

Crotal, var. of CROTTLE, used *attrib.* = of the colour of lichen, golden-brown 1904.

‖**Croûton** (krū·toṅ). 1816. [F., f. *croûte* CRUST.] *Cookery.* A small piece of toasted or fried bread used with soups and to garnish stewed dishes and minces.

Crown, *sb.* **II. 1.** *C. and anchor*: a gambling game played with dice marked with crowns, anchors, hearts, etc. on a board similarly marked 1927.

Cruck (krɒk). ME. [prob. local variant of CROOK *sb.*, pronounced krǫk, krök, or krɒk.] One of a pair of curved timbers made from the trunk of a tree, forming with other pairs the framework of a house.

[Two great twisted beams called] crokkes [25 feet in length] 1278 in SALZMAN *Building.* Furcas videlicet crockis 1325 *Ibid.* Ye Croks of a house LEVINS 1570. *Crookes*, two crooked timbers forming a Gothic arch 1828. *Cruks*, the arched oaken timbers which support the roofs of some old houses 1890; *attrib.* in **c. house.**

Crude, *a.* **1. b.** *C. oil*: natural mineral oil 1896; also subst. for this (*U.S.*) 1916.

Cruiser.

attrib. **c. tank**, a tank of intermediate weight designed for rapid movement 1940.

Crump, *sb.*[2] The sound of a heavy shell or bomb exploding; **c.-hole**, a shell crater 1914.

Crumple, *v.* **1. b.** *To c. up*: to give way, collapse (under hostile pressure or attack) 1898.

Crush, *sb.* **2. b.** phr. *To have* or *get a c. on*: to be enamoured of or infatuated by, take a strong fancy to (orig. *U.S.*) 1914. **4.** A body of troops; a crowd of people (*colloq.*) 1916.

Crystal. 5. b. *U.S.* The glass or plastic cover of a watch face 1856.

Crystal-clear (kri·stăl,klī·ɪ), *a.* c 1500. [f. CRYSTAL + CLEAR *a.*] As clear or transparent as crystal; perfectly plain or distinct. (Much affected in recent usage since c 1890.)

Now the soule is taken the body fro Thy rekenynge is crystall clere *Everyman* 898.

Cttee, short for COMMITTEE.

Cubism presents nature as a cubic pattern, eliminates curves, and emphasizes the three-dimensional mass and structure of objects.

Cuckoo, *a.* orig. *U.S. slang.* 1923. [f. the sb.] Crazy.

Cuff, *sb.*[1] **2.** colloq. phr. *Off the c.*: 'as if from notes made on the shirt cuff', extempore, on the spur of the moment.

Cup, *sb. One's c. of tea*: what suits one 1934.

Cup, *sb.* **I. 4. b.** *Golf.* A depression in the ground causing the balls to lie badly. (Cf. CUPPY.)

Cuppa (kʊ·pă). *slang.* Short for *cuppa cha* (kʊpətʃā·), i.e. cup o' tea (see CHA).

Cupper[2] (kʊ·pəɪ). 1903. [f. *CUP-TIE + -ER[6].] *Oxford Univ. slang.* A series of inter-collegiate matches played for a cup.

Cup-tie (kʊ·ptəi). 1893. A tie, i.e. a match or contest between victors in previous contests (see TIE *sb.* 10 b) played for a cup (see CUP *sb.* I. 2 b).

Curfew. **1. c.** In extended use: A restriction imposed upon the movements of the inhabitants of an area for a specified period.

‖**Cursus.** **c.** Any of the regular varying cadences which mark the end of sentences and clauses, esp. in Greek and Latin prose 1904.

Curtain, *sb.* Short for *IRON *curtain.*

Both sides of the Curtain, by Sir Maurice Peterson 1950.

3. b. *Mil.* In full *c. of fire, c. fire*: a concentration of gun-fire to prevent the advance or the retreat of troops or to clear the way for an advance by the firing body; a similar concentration to block the progress of aircraft 1918.

attrib. **c. call,** a call for an actor or author to appear before the audience after the fall of the curtain.

Curved (kɒ̄ɪvd), *ppl. a.* *C. fire*: gun-fire with an angle of elevation or departure exceeding that of direct fire 1883.

Cusec. Abbreviation used by engineers of '*cu*bic feet per *sec*ond' 1913.

Cusp. **1.** Also, latterly, the middle of a 'house'.

Custard.

attrib. **c. powder,** a powder from which custard is made.

Cutie (kiū·ti). Also **cutey.** *U.S. slang.* 1921. [f. CUTE *a.* 2 + -IE, -Y[6].] A young woman.

Cut-out. *gen.* Something cut out; *spec.* a piece of paper, etc. cut out in a certain design 1851.

Mod. Show-cards—cut-outs and displays.

Cutter, *sb.*[1] **4.**

attrib. **c.-lid,** the lid of a tin provided with a device for cutting the top of the container 1943.

Cutthroat. **5. c.-razor** (also *ellipt.* **c.**): a razor consisting of a blade set in a handle ('scales'), as distinguished from a safety razor (*colloq.*).

Cybernetics (səibəɪne·tiks), *sb. pl.* 1947. [f. Gr. κυβερνήτης steersman (f. κυβερνᾶν to steer, GOVERN) + -ICS; invented by Norbert Wiener, of the Massachusetts Institute of Technology.] The theory of control and communication in the animal and the machine.

Cycle, *sb.* **9. b.** *Biol.* A series of changes viewed as going back to the starting-point.

A. HUGHES (*title*) The mitotic cycle 1952.

¶In sense 11 prop. a distinct word.

Cyclic, *a.* **6.** *Org. Chem.* Characterized by ring formation: opp. to *ALIPHATIC 1913.

Cyclotron (səi·klǫtrǫn). 1932. [f. CYCLO- + *tron* of ELECTRON[2].] *Physics.* An apparatus by means of which ions are accelerated by making them follow a spiral path through an electric field.

Cymo- (səi·mo, səimǫ·), comb. form of Gr. κῦμα wave, in names of instruments for measuring or detecting waves in wireless telegraphy; **Cymo·meter** 1918, **Cy·moscope** 1906.

D. III.

3 D = three-dimensional; D = Distinguished C(onduct) M(edal), F(lying) C(ross), F(lying) M(edal), S(ervice) C(ross), and S(ervice) M(edal), S(ervice) O(rder); D.A.H. = disordered action of the heart; D.A.Q.M.G. = Deputy Assistant Quartermaster General; D.C., d.c. = direct current; D.D.T. = dichlor-diphenyl-trichlorethane, an insecticide 1944; D.F. = direction-finder, -finding; D.L. = Deputy Lieutenant; D.N.I. = Director of Naval Intelligence; D.P. = displaced person (see *DISPLACED); D.R. = dead reckoning; D.(B.)S.T. = double (British) summer time; d.w., D/W, d/w = dust wrapper. See also *D-DAY.

Daily, *sb.* *ellipt.* for *d. maid, woman,* etc.: A non-resident servant who is engaged by the day 1920.

Da·mping, *vbl. sb.* of DAMP *v.*

d. off, the decay of seedlings or cuttings due to excessive damp.

Dandy, *a.* **B. 2.** Fine, splendid, first-rate (*U.S. colloq.*) 1794.

Dash, *sb.*[1] *Dash-and-dot*: see *dot-and-dash,* s.v. DOT *sb.*[1] *Comb.*

Date, *sb.*[2]

d.-lined *pa. pple.*, having a certain date-line.

Another story date-lined from Cairo 1944. A message date-lined Zurich 1944.

Day, *sb.* *To call it a d.*: to consider that a day's work or occupation has been completed (*colloq.*) 1926.

D-Day [*D* for *day*], the day (6 June 1944) of the invasion of the Continent by British and American forces. (*D+x day,* the xth day after this date.)

‖**De.** **2.**

de son tort, by his own wrongdoing; *executor de son tort,* one who, being neither executor nor administrator, intermeddles with the goods of the deceased.

Dead, *a.* **III. 5.** 'A ball is said to "fall dead" when it pitches with hardly any run' (*Encycl. Brit.* 1910).

Comb. **d.-pan,** *attrib.* expressionless (*U.S.*) 1929.

He made the announcement in almost dead-pan fashion 1952.

Dead-line. **2.** Also *gen.*, a line beyond which one may not or cannot go 1917.

Dead man. **4.** *pl.* 'The concrete, plate, or other anchorage for land ties' (*Chambers's Techn. Dict.*).

d.-man's handle: in electrically driven vehicles, a form of handle so devised that, if the driver releases his pressure on the handle, as through illness, the current is interrupted and the brakes are applied.

Deadwood. *fig.* A useless, unprofitable, or obstructive person or thing; also *attrib.* (*U.S.*) 1887.

D. people who did no work 1947.

Deal, *sb.*[2] **2.** After 'game' add: or a hand.

3. *New D.*, (U.S.) a new arrangement with a view to reform and betterment 1834; the programme of social and economic reform in U.S.A. planned by the Roosevelt administration of 1932 onwards. Hence **New Dea·ler,** an advocate of this 1876.

I pledge you—and I pledge myself—to a new deal for the American people F. D. ROOSEVELT *at Chicago Convention* 1932. Franklin D. Roosevelt, chief of the New Dealers 1936.

Decibar (de·sibāɪ): see *BAR *sb.*[4]

Decibel (de·sibel). [f. L. *decem* TEN + *BEL.] Used as a measure of response in an electrical communication circuit.

Declare, *v.* **5. b.** *Cricket.* The full expression is 'to declare the innings at an end' (1889), i.e. to close the innings voluntarily before all the batsmen on the declaring side have batted, when the number of runs scored makes it possible to win a match that would otherwise probably result in a drawn game.

Decompre·ssion. 1910. [DE- II. 1.] Relief or release of compression.

d. chamber, a chamber in which abnormal pressure can be reduced by degrees to atmospheric pressure.

Decontaminate (dīkǫntæ·minēᵉt), *v.* 1936. [DE- II. 1.] *trans.* To remove from (a person or an object) the liquid or vapour with which he or it has been contaminated by poison gas. So **De:contamina·tion** (attrib., as *d. squad*).

Dedication. **1. c.** The title under which a church, etc. is dedicated.

Deepie (dī·pi). 1952. *colloq.* [f. DEEP *a.* + *-ie,* as in *talkie.*] A three-dimensional film.

Defatted (dīfæ·tėd), *a.* 1923. [f. DE- II. 1 + FAT *sb.*[2] + -ED[1].] Deprived or destitute of fat or fats.

Deficiency. *attrib.*

d. disease, disease caused by the lack of an essential or important element in the diet.

Definitely, *adv.* In loose colloq. use: Certainly, yes 1924.

Degauss (dīgau·s, dīgǭ·s), *v.* 1940. [f. DE- II. 1 + GAUSS.] *trans.* To protect (a ship) against magnetic mines by encircling it with an electrically charged cable so as to demagnetize it.

Degrade (dīgrēᵉ·d), *sb.* [f. DEGRADE *v.*] = DEGRADATION[1] 4 c.

Degrade in oak logs due to 'ambrosia' beetles 1953.

De-icer (dīəi·səɪ). 1940. [f. DE- II. 1 + ICE *sb.* + -ER[1].] A device for removing ice deposited on aircraft.

‖**Dekko** (de·ko). orig. *Army slang.* 1894. [a. Hind. *dekho,* imper. of *dekhnā* to look.] A look; also as vb. (Earlier *deck.*)

Demantoid (dемæ·ntoid). 1892. [f. G. *demant* diamond + -OID.] *Min.* Green garnet.

‖**Dementi** (dемаṅtī). 1918. [F., f. *démentir* to give the lie, f. *dé-* DE- II. 1 + *mentir* to tell lies:—L. *mentiri.* Cf. DEMENTIE.] An official contradiction of a published statement.

Demnition (demni·ʃən). 1838. *U.S.* Repr. a minced pronunc. of DAMNATION.

Demob (dīmǫ·b), colloq. abbrev. of DEMOBILIZE 1920. Also *attrib.* as in **d. suit,** a suit issued to a soldier when demobilized after World War II.

Democratic, *a.* **1.** In loose extended use: Pertaining to, characteristic of, or suited to the conditions, resources, etc. of the average citizen or of all without distinction.

That price has increased fivefold since the series began, in 1906, at what was called 'the democratic price of one shilling' (*Advt.*). The imminent sense of death is on the land, that d. doom which all men share NOYES 7 Feb. 1952.

Demote (dīmōu·t), *v.* orig. *U.S.* 1890. [f. DE- II. 1 + *-mote* of PROMOTE.] *trans.* To reduce in rank or grade.

Denominator. **2.** *Common d.*: (the lowest) multiple of the denominators of two or more fractions; also *fig.*

dep. (in time-tables) = departs.

Derrick. **3.** The main part of the rig of an oil well, consisting of four tall uprights resting on foundations 1902.

Derris (derris). 1934. [mod.L., ad. Gr. δέρρις leather covering.] A liquid or powder prepared from species of the genus *Deguelia* (also *Derris*) of woody vines, and used as an insecticide and a poison.

I..destroyed with d. powder 13 wasps' nests 1944.

Desert, *sb.*[2] *attrib.*

d. rat *colloq.*, a soldier of the 7th (British) armoured division, whose divisional sign was the figure of a jerboa, and which took part in the desert campaign in N. Africa (1941–2).

As we stewed our tea—desert rat style 1944.

Desiccate (de·sikēᵉt, dī-), *sb.* [ad. L. *desiccatus,* pa. pple. of *desiccare* DESICCATE.] A desiccated or dried product, etc.

Negative results with tumour d-s.

Destroyer. **b.** After World War II destroyers of the 'Hunt' class of 1000 to 1050 tons were classified as frigates.

Detainee (dītēᵉnī·). [f. DETAIN *v.* + -EE[1].] A person detained in custody under No. 18 of the Defence Regulations of 1939.

Detention.

d. barrack, a military prison 1906; **d. camp,** in World War I a camp in which aliens and other suspects were kept under restraint.

Determinant, *sb.* **4.** *Biol.* In Weismann's theory of heredity, a secondary unit of germplasm supposed to determine the character of a cell or group of cells (*determinate*) in the organism 1893.

Deuterium (diutīᵊ·riǒm). 1934. [mod.L., f. Gr. δεύτερος second + -IUM.] *Chem.* An isotope of hydrogen (symbol D, atomic number 1, atomic weight 2·013). So **Deuteron** (diū·tərǫn) [n. of Gr. δεύτερος]. *Physics.* The nucleus of a deuterium atom.

Deviation. **3. d.** Departure from the exact line of conduct required by an ideology or party system, esp. communism. Hence **Devia·tionism, Devia·tionist.**

Devil, *sb.* **11. b.** More fully *dust d.*: a dust-storm in S. Africa 1897.

Dial, *sb.* **4. b.** *fig.* The face (*slang*) 1811.

Dial (dəi·ăl), *sb.*[2] [G.; abbrev.] Diallylbarbituric acid, $C_{10}H_{12}O_3N_2$, a white crystalline powder, used as a hypnotic.

Dialectical (dəiăle·ktikăl), *a.*

d. materialism, the theory propagated by Karl Marx and Friedrich Engels according to which history and political facts are to be interpreted as the conflict of social forces produced by the operation of economic causes, that is, man's material needs. (The notion was taken over from Hegel's dialectic as applied to the process thesis and antithesis succeeded by synthesis; see DIALECTIC *sb.*[1] 2.)

Didgerydoo (di:dʒəridū·). An Australian aboriginal musical instrument.

Dig, *v.* **I. 3.** [Back-formation from *diggings* (see DIGGING 4).] *intr.* To have one's digs or diggings (in a certain place) 1914.

d. out, to obtain, get hold of, or get out by search or effort 1864.

Digs (digz), *sb. pl. slang.* 1893. Diggings (see prec.).

Dilutee (dəiliutī·). 1918. [irreg. f. DILUTE *v.* + -EE [1].] An unskilled worker who is introduced among skilled workers in an industry. So **Dilu·tion.**

Dim, *a.* **3. b.** *fig.* Not 'bright' intellectually or distinguished in manner; insipid, colourless (*slang*) 1928.

He 's pretty dim. A dim sort of joke. (*mod.*)

Dim, *v.*

d.-out, a modified form of *BLACK-OUT 1941. Dim-out roads less safe 1944. So **Dimmed-out.**

‖**Dinar.** Also (Serb, etc.), the monetary unit of Jugoslavia 1924.

Dinkum (di·ŋkəm). *Austral.* 1888. [?] **A.** *sb.* Work. **B.** *adj.* Genuine, real (*d. oil,* the honest truth) 1916.

Dip, *sb.* **10.** *Pros.* An unstressed element in a line of alliterative verse. (G. *Senkung.*) Cf. *LIFT.

Diphthong. Often vulgarly pronounced (di·pþɒŋ).

Dipper. 6. *Big d.*: a switchback (as at a fair or the like).

Direction. *Comb.*

d.-finder, an apparatus for determining the bearing of a transmitting station 1913. So **Dire·ctional** *a.* and *sb.*, a signal giving the direction from which the message comes 1914.

Directive. 4. b. A general instruction for the conduct of military or other operations; also *transf.* 1911.

Dis., abbrev. of DISCOUNT.

Disaffiliate (disăfi·liět), *v.* 1949. [DIS- 8.] *trans.* To remove from affiliation.

Disgust, *sb.* **2.** (Formerly in milder use: Distaste, repugnance.)

Disince·ntive. 1951. [DIS- 9.] An act, a measure, etc. which tends to discourage production.

Disinfla·tion. 1947. [DIS- 9.] The reversal of a state of monetary inflation; the return to a state of equilibrium from an inflationary state. Hence **Disinfla·tionary** *a.*

Disi·nterested, *ppl. a.* **1.** (This sense ('uninterested') has latterly become frequent in illiterate usage.)

Displaced (displē¹·st), *ppl. a. D. person,* one who has been removed from his native or home land by military force or civil pressure (abbrev. D.P.) 1946.

Dis-saving, *vbl. sb.* [DIS- 9.] The reverse of saving. So **Dis-spe·nding.**

Nothing has been allowed for dis-saving, which must loom ever larger as increasing supplies of goods create opportunities for spending *Economist* 13 Apr. 1946.

Dissociated (dis(s)ōu·ʃiētĕd), *ppl. a.* [DIS- 6.] *Psychol.* Characterized by the disjunction of mental connexions; esp. of a state of mind in which two or more personalities exist in the same person 1911.

Distortion. 4. The uneven frequency response of electrical apparatus, usu. causing bad reproduction 1914.

Distributary. B. *sb.* **2.** A river branch which flows away from the main stream without returning towards it 1863.

Distribu·tional, *a.* [See -AL 1.] Pertaining to or depending upon the results of distribution.

Systems of bidding were evolved which took into account not merely honours strength but d. and playing trick values 1950.

Ditch, *sb.* **2.** *The D.* (a) *Naval slang.* The sea; (b) *R.A.F. slang.* The English Channel or the North Sea 1940. Hence vb. to make a forced landing on or plunge into the sea.

As I was spittin' into the Ditch aboard o' the *Crocodile* KIPLING. We ditched successfully and waited for help 1943.

Dither, *v.* In gen. colloq. use with sense: To vacillate.

Dive, *sb.* **1. b.** *Aviation.* A steep descent with the nose down 1914. So **Dive** *v.* 1908; also of a submarine: To submerge.

d.-bomb *v.*, to attack with bombs at a low level after diving; so **d.-bomber** (= G. *sturzkampfflugzeug*) 1938.

Diviner. 3. See *water-diviner* s.v. WATER *sb.* (p. 2392/3) 1896.

Divvy (di·vi), colloq. abbrev. of DIVIDEND, with ending assim. to -Y[6] 1883. Also **Di·vi.**

Doctor, *sb.* **6.**

doctor's mandate, in parliamentary practice, a commission to carry on government in circumstances of difficulty or uncertainty, authority being given to the existing administration to prescribe whatever remedies were thought fit.

The National Government [of 1931], appealing for 'a d.'s mandate', had an overwhelming success 1953.

Documentary, *sb.* A film in which natural characters or objects are used for educational or instructional purposes.

Dog, *sb.* **1. e.** *The dogs*: greyhound racing; a greyhound race meeting (*colloq.*).

Dog-fight. 1. A fight between dogs 1656. **2.** A general shindy or mêlée 1913. **3.** A 'scrap' between aircraft 1917.

Dominion. 2. b. Formerly applied spec. to Wales.

1645 (*title*) Two ordinances of the Lords and Commons..for the speedie demolishing of all organs.. throughout the Kingdom of England and Dominion of Wales.

Don, *sb.*[1] **4.** Also more widely, a senior resident member of a college at Oxford or Cambridge.

Donor. b. *spec.* One who gives his blood for transfusion 1931.

Doodle, *sb.* **2.** An aimless scrawl made by a person while his attention is engaged 1937. Hence **Doodle** *v.*, esp. in gerund and pr. pple.

Doodle-bug (dū·d'lbɒg). **1.** *U.S.* A tiger beetle or its larva 1876. **2.** A P-plane, flying-bomb (*colloq.*) 1944. Also abbrev. *doodle.*

Dormy. Add: [Of unknown origin.]

Dorothy Perkins (dǫ·rəþi pō·ɹkinz). Add: introduced by the Jackson and Perkins Nursery, Newark, N.Y., in 1901 (*Dict. Americanisms*).

Dot, *sb.*[1] **8.** colloq. phr. *On the dot*: at the precise moment.

Dot, *v.* **5.** To hit, strike (*slang*) 1896.

Dotted, *ppl. a.* **1.** *D. line*: on a document, one to carry the signature of a party to its contents; hence *to sign on the d. l.*, to acquiesce without demur or hesitation.

Double, *a.* **C. 1.**

Comb. **d.-fronted,** (of a building) having two fronts or sections flanking the main front entrance; **d.-jointed** *a.*, having joints of such a kind that parts of the body can be flexed with extraordinary mobility.

Double, *v. To d. up*: to occupy the same set of rooms, as in a residential college.

In favour of giving students a reasonable spell of living in college, without making them 'd. up' on the staircases 1952.

Double-u (dɒ·b'lyu). *Vulgar colloq.* Short for *double-u c* (*W.C.*) (dɒ·b'lyusī·).

Dover's powder (dōu·vəɹz pau·dəɹ). A preparation of opium and ipecacuanha prescribed by Dr. Thomas *Dover* (1660–1742) as an anodyne diaphoretic 1854.

Draft, *v.* **1. c.** *U.S.* To conscript in a fighting force. Hence **Draft** *sb.*, a body of persons conscripted 1917; **Draftee·** [see -EE [1]], a conscripted person 1867.

Drag, *sb.* **6. b.** The total resistance of an aeroplane along its line of flight.

Dragon. A powerful armoured tractor 1926.

dragon's teeth, (*b*) a series of concrete anti-tank defences the appearance of which suggests a comparison with teeth pointing upwards (*colloq.*) 1939.

Drain, *sb.* **1.** colloq. phr. *To go down the d.*: to disappear, vanish, get lost.

His romance had gone down the d. 1920.

Dram. pers., abbrev. of *dramatis personæ* (dræ·mătis pəɹsōᵘ·nī), characters of the play.

Drawing room. 1. More recently in restricted use as applied to a principal reception room.

Dressage (dre·sĕdʒ). 1934. [ad. F., f. *dresser* to train, DRESS *v.*: see -AGE.] Systematic training for the production of a good riding-horse and rider.

Drink, *sb.* **1. b.** R.A.F. slang. *The d.*, the sea 1940.

Driver. 3. f. *Golf.* 'The longest driving club, used when the ball lies very well and a long shot is needed' (*Encycl. Brit.*).

Drogue. 3. A canvas cone open at both ends with a hoop at the larger end, used as an anchor by seaplanes; a lighter form of this towed by an aeroplane to serve for target practice by aircraft or anti-aircraft guns.

Drome (drōᵘm). Also **'drome.** 1915. Short for AERODROME.

Drop-.

d.-foot, a condition in which it is difficult to raise the front part of the foot from the ground or in which the foot hangs limp; **d.-wrist,** a condition in which the hand droops from the wrist.

Drunk, *ppl. a. D. and disorderly, d. and incapable* (see INCAPABLE *a.* I. 5): police-court descriptions of the state of offenders charged 1874.

Dry, *a.*

d.-clean *v.*, to clean (cloth, etc.) without using water, e.g. with spirit 1818; **d. goods** *U.S.*, clothing 1851; **d. run** *U.S.A.A.F.*, a practice mission.

Dubbing, *vbl. sb.* **5.** *Cinema.* In sound-films, the re-recording of sound tracks and their mixing, as in the provision of sub-titles (e.g. in translation), music, etc.; also *dubbing-in* 1940.

One has the uneasy feeling of watching a film in a foreign language, without benefit of sub-titles or the 'dubbing-in' of English voices 1953.

Dublin (dɒ·blin). The name of the capital of the Irish Free State, formerly of Ireland; *attrib.* in **D. prawn,** the small lobster *Nephrops norvegicus.*

‖**Duce** (dū·tʃe). 1922. [It., 'leader'.] *Il* or *The Duce*: title assumed by Benito Mussolini as creator and leader of the Fascist revolution and state in Italy.

Duck, *sb.*[4] Evolved from DUKW, code name of: An amphibious landing craft, first used in World War II.

Due, *a.* **7. b.** (*U.S. colloq.*) On the point of 1921. **B.** *advb.* In loose colloq. use, *Due to*: owing to (see OWING *ppl. a.* 3 b).

Pathologically a urine might be opalescent, due to bacteria 1938.

‖**Dulag** (dū·lag). G.; abbrev. of *Durchgangslager* transit camp (for prisoners of war).

Dunkirk (dɒnkō·ɹk). Used typically for: The (scene of the) evacuation of a defeated army by sea like that performed by the British from Dunkirk in May 1940. Hence *gen.* A desperate situation from which escape is possible only by heroic measures.

As in all Dunkirks, the heavy material had had to be left behind 1943.

Dunno (dɒ·no, dǒnōᵘ·). 1842. Denoting careless pronunc. of (*I*) *don't know.*

Dust, *sb.*

d. wrapper (abbrev. d.w., D/W): a paper jacket to protect the binding of a book.

Dusty, *a.* **4.**

Ah, what a dusty answer gets the soul When hot for certainties in this our life! MEREDITH.

Dutch, *a.* **4.** slang or colloq. *D. treat*: one at which each participant provides his or her share 1887. So *to go D.*: to pay for oneself (instead of being treated).

E. III.

E = English or Egyptian, as £E 1,225; E.A.M. = Ethnikon Apeleftherotikon Metopon ('National Liberation Front'); E.C.A. = Economic Cooperation Administration; ECOSOC = Eco|nomic and Soc|ial Council (of the United Nations); E.D.C. = European Defence Community; E.D.D. = English Dialect Dictionary; E.E.G. = electro-encephalograph; E.E.T.S.

= Early English Text Society; E.L.A.S. = Ethnikos Laïkos Apeleftherotikos Stratos ('National Popular Liberation Army'); E.N.S.A. (see *ENSA); E.P.D., E.P.T. = Excess Profits Duty, Tax; E.R. = East Riding, Edwardus Rex (King Edward), Elizabetha Regina (Queen Elizabeth); E.R.P. = European Recovery Programme; E.T.A. = Estimated Time of Arrival; E.T.O. = European Theatre of Operations; E.T.U. = Electrical Trades Union; E.V.W. = European Voluntary Workers. See also *E-BOAT.

Each, *a.* **1. c.** *E. way*: a racing term denoting that a horse has been backed for a win and a place 1869.

Early, *a.*

e. door, a theatre door which is opened earlier than the ordinary door and at an enhanced price 1901.

Early, *adv.* *Earlier on* [after *later on*]: at an earlier stage. So *early on.*

Ease, *v.* **7.** To move gently or gradually 1850. Also *fig.*

There have been many precedents in the Soviet satellites for easing prominent Communist leaders into jail by incessive steps 1951.

Easter. *attrib.*

E. egg, now commonly an imitation egg; **E. offering,** a voluntary offering of money made by parishioners to the incumbent at Easter.

Eastward. B. *E. position,* the position of the celebrant facing towards the east in the Anglican Communion Service 1873.

||**Eau.**

E. de Nil: a pale green colour supposed to resemble that of the river Nile 1870.

E-boat (ī·bōᵘt). For *Enemy-boat*: a German motor torpedo-boat 1940.

Echoic (ekōᵘ·ik), *a.* 1880 (J. A. H. Murray). [f. ECHO *sb.* + -IC.] Of the nature of an echo: applied to words that echo the sound which they are intended to denote or symbolize.

Economic. A. 2. b. *spec.* Utilitarian in practice or use, with reference to the satisfaction of man's material needs, as *e. botany, e. geography, zoology* 1882.

-ectomy (e·ktŏmi), repr. Gr. ἐκτομή excision, in surgical terms denoting an operation for the removal of a part, as HYSTERECTOMY, *LOBECTOMY.

Edge, *sb.* **2.** *On e.,* (also) in an excited, irritable, or nervous state 1900.

Edgy, *a.* **3.** Having the nerves on edge 1837.

Edh, Eth (eð). Name of the letter Ð, ð.

Edwardine, *a.* *spec.* Pertaining to or characteristic of the Books of Common Prayer of the reign of Edward VI.

-eer[1]. The spelling *-eer,* replacing older *-ier,* became freq. in 17th c., as in *mountaineer.*

-eer[2], repr. Du. *-eeren,* ad. F. inf. ending *-er,* as in COMMANDEER, DOMINEER.

Efficiency. 3. The ratio of useful work performed to the total energy expended 1879.

Effort. 2. b. Something accomplished involving special exertion or activity (*colloq.*) 1871.

This e. was torn up in despair 1871.

Effusive, *a.* **1. b.** *Geol.* Of an igneous rock: Poured out in a state of fusion and afterwards solidified; so *e. period* 1895.

Egeria (idʒī·riă). 1621. [Name of a nymph, the fabled instructress of Numa Pompilius, king of ancient Rome.] (One's) tutelary divinity.

Egg, *sb.* **1. c.** *R.F.C. slang.* A high-explosive bomb dropped by aircraft 1917.

¶ See also *POWER *egg.*

Ego. b. *Psycho-analysis.* That part of the psychic outfit that responds to the outside world, mediating between the id and the environment.

Egocentric (egose·ntrik), *a.* 1897. [f. EGO + CENTRE, after *geocentric,* etc.] Centred in the ego, (pop.) self-centred, egoistic.

Egomania. Delete '*joc.*' Now a recognized term of psychology. Hence **Egoma·niac** 1890.

||**Eigen-** (ai·gən), G. *eigen* OWN, proper, in adoptions or partial anglicizations of G. compounds, as *eigenfunction, eigenperiod, eigenton*; so *eigensolution, eigenvalue*; see quots.

eigenperiod, eigenton..frequencies at which acoustic resonance is experienced in rectangular chambers, because of continued reflections between opposite walls (*Chambers's Techn. Dict.*).

Approximate Eigensolutions...The reason why we choose *a* as the known parameter and *b* as the eigenvalue...The eigenfunction of a bound state 1951.

Eight. B. 1. b. phr. *To have one over the e.*: to get rather drunk (*slang*) 1925.

Eighteen. B. 3. b. *pl.* A sheet of eighteen pages 1683.

Eightsome (ēi·tsəm), *a.* and *sb.* [-SOME [2].] *E.* (*reel*): a Scottish reel for eight dancers 1843.

Eis wool (əis wul). 1882. [G. *eis* ice.] A fine glossy worsted wool.

Either. B. *Either-or*: indicating a necessary choice between alternatives.

Too much rigid logic of the black-and-white either-or variety 1953.

Eka- (ī·kă). *Chem.* prefix, repr. Skr. *eka* one, used by Mendeléeff to denote a predicted element that should occupy the next lower position to that so qualified in the same group in the periodic system.

Elect, *v.* **3.** In the University of Cambridge, a person is elected *into* a fellowship, etc.; cf. *INTO 2.

Electra (ĭle·ktră). In ancient Gr. Myth., name of the daughter of Agamemnon and Clytemnestra, used *attrib.* in *E. complex,* Freudian psycho-analyst's term for a daughter's attraction for her father and hostility to her mother 1920.

Electro-.

electroca·rdiograph, a record of the heart's motions taken electrically by cardiograph; **electroence·phalograph,** a machine for recording the minute electrical impulses transmitted inside the brain (abbrev. E.E.G.).

Electrocute, -cution. *transf.* of any death caused by the shock of an electric current 1909.

Electronic (elĕktrǫ·nik), *a.* [f. ELECTRON [2] (*-on* from ION) + -IC.] Pertaining to or involving electrons. Hence **Electro·nics** [see -ICS], the study and application of phenomena involving the movement of electrons, as in wireless telegraphy, television, etc. 1942; also, apparatus or equipment for such application. So **Electro·nic** *a.,* pertaining to, skilled in, etc. electronics, as *e. engineer.*

Element, *sb.* **I. 4. c.** *U.S.A.A.F.* A formation of aeroplanes.

Eleven. A. 2. b. *E. o'clock* (U.S. and dial.), *e. hours* (Sc.), a lunch taken about 11 o'clock 1808. So (orig. dial.) **Ele·vens(es)** 1819.

Eleventh. phr. *E. hour*: the hour preceding midnight, as symbolizing the last available opportunity. Also *attrib.*

In response to John's eleventh-hour prayers 1897. An eleventh-hour alteration 1904. The dark eleventh hour Draws on and sees us cold To every evil power We fought against of old 1912 KIPLING *Ulster.*

Elijah (ĕlai·dʒă). Used in allusions to the mantle of the prophet E. falling from him and being taken up by Elisha (2 Kings ii. 13, 14).

The mass of material left warrants an Elisha to his Elijah 1942.

Elk. *attrib.*

e. hound, a dog of Scandinavian origin esp. adapted to elk-hunting, having a grey coat and thick tail curved over the back 1878.

Emma (e·mə), used for *m* in telephonic communications and oral transliteration of messages in code 1919. Cf. *ACK, *PIP.

Empire, *sb.* *The E.*: (*c*) the rule of Napoleon Bonaparte as Emperor of the French, 1804–14, or the period of this 1830. *E.* is used attrib. to denote styles of furniture, etc. characteristic of this period 1879.

E. Marketing Board, a body set up to superintend and promote the marketing in Great Britain of the produce of the Dominions 1927.

-en, *suffix* [6], the ending of the pa. pple. of many strong vbs., as *broken, eaten, given, sunken, taken.* OE. *-en,* OS., OHG. *-an* (Du., G. *-en*), ON. *-enn, -inn,* Goth. *-ans* :—OTeut. *-enaz, *-anaz :—Indo-Eur. *-énos, *-ónos.

Enabling, *ppl. a.*

e. act (1) *U.S.* an act making legal something that is otherwise unlawful 1856: an act of 1906 prescribing the conditions in which a territory may be admitted into the United States; (2) *gen.* an enactment empowering a person or corporation to take certain action.

Let Congress pass an e. act for that Territory 1873.

End, *sb.*

phr. **e.-to-e.,** from one end of a country to the other, esp. of races from John o' Groats to Land's End 1908.

attrib. **e. leaf,** a (usually blank) leaf inserted at one or other end of a bound book; so **e. paper(s)**; **e. rhyme,** *Pros.* rhyme occurring at the end of a line.

Endowment.

e. assurance (insurance), life insurance by which an e. or fixed sum is paid to the insured person at a specified date, or to his representatives on his death, if that occurs before.

Endres, endris, vars., with advb. **-s,** of †*ender* recently past (as in *this ender day, night, year*), f. ON. *endr* formerly, *endranær* at some other time; latterly become familiar from the text of 15th-c. carols.

Enemy. B. 2. Delete 'Now *rare*'.

An e. world 1891. E. territory 1915. Destroyed by e. action (*mod.*).

Engram (e·ngræm). 1914. [ad. F. *engramme* (Semon, *Mneme*), f. Gr. ἐν IN *prep.,* EN-[2] + γράμμα letter.] A permanent change in the nucleus of a cell, due to stimulus, which is transferred to the germ-cells and thus becomes heritable. So **Engraphy** (e·ngrăfi), action resulting in this; whence **Engra·phic** *a.*

||**Enjamb(e ment.** Also pronounced as F. (aṅʒaṅbmaṅ). Applied also less restrictedly to the carrying over of a sentence from one line to the next.

||**Enosis** (e·nŏsis). 1952. [mod. Gr. ἕνωσις, f. ἐν-, εἷς one.] The (proposed) union of Cyprus with Greece.

Ensa (e·nsă). f. initials of *Entertainment National Service Association,* an organization for entertaining the fighting services 1939.

Ensign. In the navy pronounced (e·ns'n).

Entanglement. 3. *Mil.* An extensive barrier arranged so as to obstruct an enemy's movements; an abatis formed of trees and branches or an obstruction consisting of stakes and barbed wire *c* 1840.

Entertain, *v.* **4.** The sense 'to engage, employ' survived in Indian official use.

It is not clear when a military guard was first entertained at the factory 1912.

Enthuse, *v.* 1827 (*Dict. Amer. Eng.*).

Entrain, *v.*[2] *intr.* To go on board a train 1890.

||**Entrecôte** (aṅtrəkōt). 1841. [F., 'between-rib'.] Steak cut off the ribs.

Environme·ntal, *a.* [See -AL.] Relating to the environment of a situation.

E. matters of fact 1953.

-eous. For abnormal examples see BEAUTEOUS (1440), DUTEOUS (1593), GORGEOUS (1561), PLENTEOUS (1526), RIGHTEOUS (1526).

||**Épée** (e·pe). 1889. [F., 'sword'.] The sharp-pointed sword used in duelling and (blunted) in fencing.

Equerry. The pronunc. for an officer of the Royal Household is (ĭkwe·ri).

Ergatocracy (ɜɪgătǫ·krăsi). [f. Gr. ἐργάτης workman, f. ἐργάζεσθαι, f. ἔργον WORK: see -OCRACY.] Government by 'the workers'.

Eros. 2. *Astron.* An asteroid discovered in 1898.

Erotogenic (ĕrōᵘtodʒe·nik), *a.* [f. Gr. ἐρωτο-, ἔρως love + -γενης -GEN + -IC.] Producing sexual pleasure.

The erotogenic zones are not all equally capable of yielding enjoyment...The kiss..consists of the union of two erotogenic mouth zones 1922.

||**Ersatz** (ɜ̄·ɪzæts, ||ɛ̄·rzats). 1919. [G., 'compensation, replacement'.] A substitute or imitation, usu. inferior to the real article. Also *attrib.* or *adj.*

Even when the blood-stained hand had been concealed in a glove of e. velvet 1944.

Escalator. 1900. ['A trade-mark made from *escalade* and *elevator*', *Dict. Americanisms.*]

Escape, *sb.* **1. b.** *fig.* Mental or emotional distraction from the realities of life. Hence **Esca·pism,** the tendency to seek or practice of seeking such distraction. **Esca·pist.**

Escape clause, a clause that allows avoidance of some condition.

Escapee (eskēˡpī·). 1865. [f. ESCAPE *v.* + -EE, after F. *échappé,* subst. use of pa. pple. of *échapper.*] One who has escaped, e.g. from captivity or confinement.

Escapology (eskeˡpǫ·lŏdʒi). [f. ESCAPE +

-OLOGY.] The methods and technique of escaping from captivity.

‖**Escudo** (eskū·dǫ). 1915. [Sp., Pg. :—L. *scutum* shield; cf. ÉCU.] A Spanish and Portuguese silver coin.

-ese. On the model of derivs. from authors' names were formed JOURNALESE (1882), NEWSPAPERESE (1889).

Eskimo (e·skimo). 1744. [ad. Da. *Eskimo*, ad. F. *Esquimaux* pl., corruption of an Amer. Indian word meaning 'eaters of raw flesh'.] A member of a N. American Indian race inhabiting the Arctic coast from Greenland to Alaska. Often uninflected for the pl.

The east Siberian Eskimo are especially noted for this art...Some Eskimo..have taken up foreign.. techniques with considerable success 1950.

Essence, *sb.* phr. *Of the e. of* (cf. F. *de l'essence de*): (that is) an essential or vital element of.

Stipulations as to time [not] deemed to be..of the e. of such contracts 1871.

Eta (ī·tă). **e. patch:** a fan-shaped patch of fabric attached to the envelope of a balloon to secure the rigging 1940.

Eternity. *attrib.* **e. ring,** a finger ring which has a continuous setting of stones.

Eth (eð), var. of *EDH.

Thorkelin..shows a certain carelessness in his treatment of thorn and eth 1954.

Ethiopian, *a.* and *sb.* Used since *c* 1935 for: Abyssinian.

The Pope has to consider whether such action would do anything to help the Ethiopians or to stop the war 1935. For more than 1,500 years the head of the Ethiopian Church has been a Copt 1944.

‖**Étude** (etü·d). 1876. [F., 'study'.] A short musical composition, often used as a beginner's exercise.

Eu-. b. *Bot.* Denoting 'whole', 'complete', 'in which all stages of the life cycle occur'.

Eumyce·tes, fungi having a perfect (sexual) and an imperfect (asexual) stage.

Eucharistic, *a.* *E. Congress*: an international meeting of Roman Catholics held regularly in honour of the Eucharist, instituted 1908.

Eunuchoid (yū·nyukoid), *a.* 1906. [f. EUNUCH + -OID.] Having characteristics of a eunuch.

In true e. conditions it [*sc.* testosterone] has the power of restoring male characteristics.

Eupad (yū·pæd). 1915. [f. initials of *Edinburgh University Pathological Department* (where the mixture was invented) with joc. ref. to EU- and PAD *sb.*³, quasi 'good pad'.] *Pharm.* A mixture of calcium chloride and boric acid used as an antiseptic dry dressing.

‖**Euphoria** (yufǫ·riă). 1943. [ad. Gr. εὐφορία, f. εὖ EU- + φορ-, φέρειν to BEAR.] A state of well-being or contentment. Cf. EUPHORY.

Eurovision (yūᵊrovi·ʒən). 1954. [f. *Eur*|*ope* + *-vision*, of TELEVISION.] Television of European range.

Eutectic (yūte·ktik), *a.* [f. EU- + Gr. τηκτός melted, f. τήκειν to melt + -IC.] *Chem.* Denoting or pertaining to an alloy or mixture of which the melting-point is lower than that of others having the same ingredients.

Evacuate, *v.* **7.** In recent use, to remove (inhabitants of an area liable to aerial bombing) *to* safer surroundings. So [after F. *évacué*] **Evacuee·,** a person so evacuated 1939.

Even, *a.* **14. b.** *E. money*, not laying or taking odds 1892.

Ever, *adv.* After a superl. used ellipt. for 'that ever was', or the like; e.g. *the biggest e.* (orig. *U.S.*) 1930.

Every, *a.* **1.** *E. time*, on all occasions, without exception (orig. *U.S. colloq.*) 1864.

Everyman (e·v'rimæn). [EVERY *a.*, MAN *sb.*; taken up from the 15th-century morality of which the colophon reads 'Thus endeth this morall playe of euery man', and in which Everyman is the leading character.] The typical man or ordinary human being, common humanity.

E.'s Library 1906. Now might we escape the fall of Ev'ryman R. BRIDGES. (*Advt.*) Good morning, Mr. E.

Everything. colloq. phr. *To have e.*: to possess every kind of attraction.

Exclusive, *sb.* An article, etc. contributed exclusively to a journal; an exclusive film 1901.

Executive. B. 3. A person or body of persons holding an e. position (orig. *U.S.*) 1923.

Exeter Hall (e·ksĕtəɪ hǫl). A building in the Strand, London, built 1830–1, used for religious and philanthropic assemblies until 1907; often used to typify a form of evangelicalism.

The vanishing of E. H. from the world of Evangelicalism 1907.

‖**Ex gratia** (eks grēⁱ·ʃiᵊ). 1920. [L. 'from favour'.] (Done) as a favour.

Existentialism (egziste·nʃăliz'm). 1944. [ad. F. *existentialisme*: see EXISTENTIAL, -ISM.] *Philos.* A doctrine that concentrates on the existence of the individual, who, being free and responsible, is held to be what he makes himself by the self-development of his essence through an act of the will (which, in the Christian form of the theory, leads to God). Hence **Existe·ntialist**; also *attrib.*

Expanded, *ppl. a.*

e. metal, sheet metal slit and stretched into a lattice, to form screens and to reinforce concrete 1891.

Expectant, *a.* **A. 1.** *E. mother*, a woman who is expecting to become a mother; so *e. father* 1862.

Expellee (ėkspe·lī). [f. EXPEL + -EE ¹.] One who has been expelled, esp. from his country.

1949 (*title*) Some facts about expellees in Germany.

Expendable, *a.* Liable to be wasted, i.e. killed or lost, and so deliberately sacrificed, as in a military operation 1943. Also as *sb.*

'We were told before we set out that we were "expendable" on this trip, a young corporal from Georgia told me. That the North Koreans and Chinese had treated South Korean prisoners as 'slaves and expendables' 1953.

Experience, *sb.*

e. table, a table showing the expectation of life computed from the e. of life-insurance offices 1879.

Extra, *sb.* An extra item in a dance programme 1900; an extra hand in a performance.

Extrapolate (ėkstræ·pŏlēⁱt). 1874. [f. EXTRAPOLATION, by back-formation; see -ATE ³.] *trans.* To obtain by extrapolation; also *absol.*

Used in 1831 by W. E. Gladstone for 'to put outside a sequence'.

Extraversion. 2. *Psychol.* [after Jung's *Extraversion*] The fact of having the thoughts and activities directed to or satisfied by things outside the self 1916. So **E·xtravert** *sb.*, one who is characterized by extraversion; **E·xtraverted** *ppl. a.*, said of a person, his activities, etc. Also **E·xtroversion, -vert** (1918), **-verted,** alterations of these, after *INTROVERT.

Those individuals whose motivations are mainly conditioned by the outward object..those who allow themselves to be determined principally by the subject. I [*sc.* Jung] have designated the first group as extraverted, the latter as introverted 1928. Re-education must include stimulation of their emotional, ethical, and intellectual powers, particularly in the direction of extraversion 1934.

Eye, *sb.*¹ **I. 3. d.** *E-s and no e-s*: used to express the difference between an observant and an unobservant person; so, said of or to one who fails to observe 1795.

e. rhyme *Pros.*, a rhyme that is not phonetically exact but makes an appeal to the eye only, e.g. English *good*|*flood*, which, like many rhymes of this sort, were orig. exact rhymes (OE. *gōd*|*flōd*); **e.-wash** *fig.* (*slang*), something that is intended to interfere with clear vision, something said or done to give the impression that everything is as it should be 1884; hence **e.-washing.**

The professions of those who offered them, with 'art for art's sake' as an eye-washing accompaniment L. HOUSMAN 1937.

III. 4. b. The central area of calm in a tropical cyclone.

F. III.

F.B.A., F.C.A., F.G.S., F.L.S., F.R.G.S., F.R.P.S., F.R.S.(L.), F.Z.S. = Fellow of the British Academy, Chartered Accountants, the Geological Society, the Linnean Society, the Royal Geographical Society, the Royal Photographic Society, the Royal Society (of Literature), the Zoological Society; F.A. = Football Association; F.A.A. = Fleet Air Arm 1924; F.A.N.Y. = First Aid Nursing Yeomanry; F.A.O. = Food and Agriculture Association; f.a.q./s. = free alongside quay/ship; f.o.r./t. = free on rail/truck; F.B.I. = Federation of British Industries, (*U.S.*) Federal Bureau of Investigation; f.f.i. = free from infection; F.F.I. = Forces Françaises de l'Intérieur, French Forces of the Interior; F.F.(V.) = member of one of the first families of Virginia (*U.S.*); F/Lt = Flight Lieutenant; F.M. = Field Marshall, field magnet, frequency modulation; F.O. = Foreign Office; F/O = Flying Officer; F.S., f.s. = foot-second. **b.** *Photogr.* F. = focal length.

Face, *sb.* *Comb.*

f.-lifting, the operation of tightening the skin of the face and eliminating its wrinkles in order to impart a more youthful appearance 1922.

‖**Facile princeps** (fæ·sili pri·nseps). 1834. [L.] Easily first; acknowledged leader or chief.

Facility. 2. *pl.*, esp. with qualifying word, as *customs, engineering, playing, transport facilities.*

‖**Façon de parler** (fasoṅ d parle). 1806. [F.] A manner of speaking; a mere phrase or formula.

Fact. 3. (*And*) *that's a f.*: emphatic addition to a statement stressing its truth 1834 (*U.S.*).

Comb. **f.-finding** [FIND *v.* II], discovery and establishing of facts; also *pple.*

A fact-finding commission...Fact-finding in Tokio 1939.

Factor. *F. of safety*: the ratio between the load which a structure or material is capable of supporting and the load which it is required to support 1858.

Fair Isle (fēᵊ·rəil). 1852. Name of one of the Shetland Islands used *attrib.* to designate woollen articles of characteristic pattern.

Faith, *sb.* **II. 3.** Also *in f. whereof* [tr. F. *en foi de quoi*]: as an assurance of the performance of which.

Falangist (fălæ·ndʒist). Also **Ph-.** 1937. [f. Sp. *falange* PHALANX + -IST.] A member of the *Falange Española* 'Spanish Phalanx'; a Spanish Fascist.

[The counter-revolutionary terrorism, the employment by the *Falange Española* of gunmen and thugs to destroy 'Bolshevism'. *Ann. Register for 1936*, 247.]

Fa·ll-out. 1954. [f. phr. *fall out.*] Radioactive refuse of an atomic bomb explosion.

Family. 3. *Happy families*: a game played with a pack of cards on each of which is depicted a member of a family of four, the aim of each player being to make as many complete families as he can 1865. **6. b.** *Family* has superseded *Natural Order* (see ORDER *sb.* 7) in botanical use.

f. allowance, allowance paid to employees in proportion to the size of their families 1928; **f. house,** the house which is the chief dwelling-place of a family; **f. portrait,** a portrait of a member of a family, in whose possession it often remains as a relic.

Fan, *v.* **6. b.** *intr.* with *out*, esp. of forces in the field spreading out, e.g. after a break-through. Hence **Fa·n-out** *sb.*

Far East. 1894. [FAR *a.* 1 a, EAST *sb.*] The extreme eastern regions of the Old World, esp. China and Japan.

Far-flung (fā·ɪ₁flvŋ), *a.* 1896. [FAR *adv.* 3 a, pa. pple. of FLING *v.*] 'Flung', i.e. extended, to a great distance.

Lord of our f. battle-line KIPLING.

Faro. Earlier *Farroon* (1713).

Fascist. Also *transf.* One of a similar body in other countries than Italy, e.g. *British Fascists* (1926). Also in It. form ‖**Fascista** (faʃi·sta), pl. ‖**Fasci·sti** (*-i*).

Fauve (fōᵘv). The F. word *fauve* 'wild beast', designating an advanced school of painting orig. associated with Henri Matisse (called *chef des Fauves*), and characterized by subtle harmonies or dissonances of colour and a pattern reduced to a minimum of outline independent of its relation to nature, in which a large amount of distortion might be introduced. Hence **Fau·vism,** the practice of this style of painting, **Fau·vist,** an adherent of Fauvism; after F. *fauvisme, fauviste.*

Symbolism and Fauvism *Encycl. Brit.* (1922) III. 6/1. The application of the *fauviste* recipe to the painting of fashionable Parisian society *Ibid.* 6/2. Matisse..the leader of the 'Fauve' movement *Chamb. Encycl.* (1950) IX. 160/2.

fc(a)p., contr. of FOOLSCAP.

Feather-bed (feðəɪbe·d), *v.* 1950. [f.

FEATHER-BED *sb.*] *trans.* To provide with advantages or conveniences, as if with the soft and yielding support of a feather bed.

Feature, *sb.* In combs. = forming a special f. in a magazine, etc.

Three or four f. stories about authors 1928.

Fedora (fĭdō·ră). 1899. [f. *Fédora*, name of the heroine of Victorien Sardou's play so named, popular in U.S.A. in 1883.] In full *f. hat*: A man's soft low-crowned hat.

Feed, *sb.* **6.** *Theatr.* [f. FEED *v.* 6.] A performer who supplies cues 1929.

Feeder. = *f. line* 1858.

f. line, a branch line of a railway or the like 1895.

Fellow, *sb.* *attrib.* **f. traveller,** one who travels along with another; *transf.* one who is ostensibly a member of a party but actually supports another (esp. the Communist party) 1942. (The equiv. Russ. *popútchik* (Trotsky) was used of non-communist writers sympathizing with the Revolution.)

Ferry, *v.* **2. c.** To fly (an aircraft) from one place to another, as from a factory to an aerodrome. So *f. pilot, pool.* 1917.

Few. **2. b.** In colloq. phr. *quite a few*: a fairly large number.

‖**Fianna Fail** (fĭ·ənə fǫil). [Ir.: *fianna*, pl. of *fian* band of warriors; gen. of *Fál* Ireland.] Eamon de Valera's party, which took the oath and entered the Dail Eireann in August 1927.

‖**Fibrosis** (fəibrōu·sis). 1873. [mod.L., f. L. *fibra* FIBRE; see -OSIS.] *Path.* Development in an organ of fibrous tissue, fibroid degeneration. Hence **Fi·brosed** *ppl. a.*, **Fi·brosing** *vbl. sb.* and *ppl. a.*, characterized by, formation of, developing fibrous tissue; ‖**Fibrositis** (fəibrosəi·tis), inflammatory hyperplasia of the white fibrous tissue, muscular rheumatism 1910.

Fiddle, *sb.* **6.** *slang.* A cheat, swindle. (Cf. FIDDLE *v.* 3.)

Fido (fəido). 1945. A word made up from the initials of *F*og *I*nvestigation *D*ispersal *O*perations.

Field, *sb.*

f. grey [G. *feldgrau*], the regulation colour of the uniform of a German infantryman.

‖**Fiesta** (fie·stă). 1882. [Sp., FEAST. Cf. FESTA, FÊTE.] A (religious) festival, *spec.* in Sp. America.

Fi. fa., abbrev. of FIERI FACIAS.

Fifth, *a.*

F. Column, orig. the column of supporters which General Mola declared himself to have in Madrid, when he was besieging it in the Spanish civil war of 1937–9, in addition to the four columns of his army outside the city; hence (allusively), a body of one's supporters in an attacked or occupied foreign country, or of the enemy's supporters in one's own country 1940. Hence **F.-Co·lumnist.**

The danger of what were called 'Fifth Column' activities in England... South-West Africa, at the outbreak of the war, had been a happy hunting ground for Nazi agents and Fifth Columnists 1940.

Fighter. **3.** A high-speed aeroplane designed for aerial combat 1928. Also **F.-bomber,** such a machine used as a bomber.

Fighting, *vbl. sb.*

f. chance, orig. *U.S.*, an opportunity of gaining something by fighting or struggle 1889; **f.-drunk** *a.*, drunk to a state of quarrelsomeness; **f.-fit** *a.*, fit to fight; **f. line** [LINE *sb.*[2] III. 3], that part of an armed force which is engaged in direct combat with the enemy; **f.-top,** a circular platform placed high up on a ship's mast to take guns and armed men 1896.

Figural, *a.* **3.** (In present techn. use.)

Sculptures of a monumental figural character are quite different from those of a decorative or ornamental nature 1952.

File, *v.*[3] **1. b.** *To f.* (one's petition) *in bankruptcy.* **4. b.** (*U.S.*) To march *upon* so as to occupy (vacant land) 1871.

Film, *sb.*

f. pack, an assemblage of flat photographic films fitted in a case or holder for daylight loading and changing 1903; **f. test,** a photographic test of an aspirant to film-acting.

Final. **B.** *sb.* **2. d.** The edition of a newspaper that is published latest in the day (*colloq.*).

Finalize (fəi·nălaiz), *v.* 1942. [f. FINAL *a.* + -IZE.] *trans.* To give final form to.

Fine, *adv.* **b.** With a very slight margin of time or space, e.g. *to cut* or *run f.* (colloq.) 1890. **c.** *Naut.* Close to the fore-and-aft line of the ship, e.g. *f. on the starboard bow.*

‖**Fine champagne** (fīn ʃanpanʸ). 1868. [F., short for 'eau de vie *fine* de la *Champagne*' fine brandy of Champagne.] Old liqueur brandy. Abbrev. **Fine.**

Finger, *sb.*

f.-mark *v.* (also) *intr.*, to take f.-marks.

Finsen (fi·nsən), name of Niels R. *Finsen* (1860–1904), Danish physician, designating treatment of skin diseases by actinic rays and the apparatus used therein, e.g. *F.('s) light* 1902.

Fire, *sb.* *attrib.* and *Comb.*

f. brat, baker's name for an insect allied to the silver fish, *Thermobia domestica*, which frequents hot places, e.g. ovens 1894; **f. control,** the direction and regulation of the firing of guns from a centre 1886; **f.-fighter,** one of a squad of people organized to deal with outbreaks of fire resulting from aerial bombing; so **f.-watcher,** one who detects or reports such fires 1940; later **f. guard** 1943; **f. risk,** (*a*) the risk of loss by fire; (*b*) the obligation of a fire-insurance company to make good loss by fire; **f. service,** a national, municipal, etc. organization for dealing with outbreaks of fire; **f. squad,** a body of fire-fighters working independently of the regular fire brigades 1941; **f. step** *Mil.*, a board or ledge in a trench on which soldiers stand to fire 1915; **f. top,** the place of fire control on board ship; **f. trench** *Mil.*, a deep and narrow trench from which firing takes place; **f.-walk(ing),** walking on hot coals, stones, etc. as an ordeal or as a religious rite 1898; also **f.-walker.**

Firing, *vbl. sb.*

f. party, a squad detailed to fire volleys at a funeral or to carry out a military execution 1859; **f. step** = **fire step* 1916.

First. **I. 1.** *The f. thing*: the elements or rudiments, esp. in phr. *not to know the f. thing about.* (*To put*) *f. things f.*: a catch phr. used to denote a policy of giving the first place to the most important things.

Special collocation. **f. name,** orig. *U.S.*, (one's) personal name, Christian name 1839.

Fission. **3.** *spec.* in *Physics.* Splitting (of an atom). Hence **Fissionable** (fi·ʃənăb'l), *a.*, that may be subjected to fission.

Fitter. **2. b.** *Tailoring.* One who supervises the cutting, fitting, and alteration of garments 1858. **c.** One who fits metal or machine parts together 1888.

Fit-up (fi·tɒp). *Theatr.* 1883. [f. phr. *to fit up* (FIT *v.*[1] IV).] Temporary or portable stage and stage-fittings; (in full *fit-up company*) a travelling theatrical company carrying scenery and properties to be fitted up for the occasion.

Five.

f.-year plan, the scheme (*piatilyetka*), begun in 1928, for the economic development of the U.S.S.R. over a period of f. years.

Fix, *sb.* **3.** A position determined by means of bearings or astronomical observations 1902. *Radio f.*, the position of a vessel or aircraft found by radio.

Fixation. **2. c.** *Psycho-analysis.* A mental state that occurs when an individual refuses to take the step forward in life that normal development requires 1919. **d.** The concentration of the gaze upon an object for a given time with the intention of holding the retinal image upon the area of direct vision.

Fixed, *ppl. a.*

f. focus *Photogr.*, applied to a camera having a non-adjustable lens 1892.

Fixer (fi·ksəɹ). [f. FIX *v.* + -ER [1].] **1.** A sheep-dog capable of controlling sheep by fixing them with its eyes. **2.** *U.S. slang.* One who arranges or adjusts matters (illicitly) 1889.

1. A f. at work on a Cumberland farm 1952. **2.** Five alleged fixers were indicted..on bribery and conspiracy charges 1951.

Flail, *sb.* *attrib.*

f. tank, a machine for clearing a mine-field, consisting of a 'tank' having a steel cylinder projecting in front equipped with chain-whips, which whirl in flail-like fashion and detonate land-mines in its path 1944.

‖**Flak** (flæk). 1940. [G., f. initials of the elements of F*l*iegerabwehr*k*anone 'aeroplane-defence-gun'.] Anti-aircraft fire. *F. ship*, a German anti-aircraft vessel.

Flaming, *ppl. a.* **1. b.** *F. onions*: an anti-aircraft projectile consisting of balls of fire shot upwards in succession, suggesting a resemblance to ropes of onions 1917.

‖**Flammenwerfer** (fla·mənvęrfər). 1915. [G., f. *flamme* FLAME *sb.* + *werfer*, agent-n. of *werfen* to throw.] A machine of war consisting essentially of a reservoir from which a long spray of flame can be ejected. Anglicized **Fla·me-thrower** 1917.

Flanders.

F. poppy, used as emblem of the soldiers of the Allies who fell in World War I; an artificial poppy made for sale in aid of Earl Haig's British Legion Appeal Fund 1921.

Flap, *sb.* Add: phr. *In a flap*: agitated, excited (*slang*).

Flapjack. **3.** A vanity case for face powder.

Flare, *sb.*[1] **2.** Also, a mass of combustible material fired in order to illuminate a target area.

f. path, a line of lights to guide aircraft in taking off or landing 1940.

Flash, *sb.*[2] **I. 8.** *Cinema.* The exposure of a scene. Also **Fla·shback,** the recapitulation of an earlier scene; hence, a revival of the memory of past events in a pictorial or written presentation 1918 (*U.S.*).

Fleet, *sb.*[1] **1.** *F. Air Arm*, the air force borne in ships of the Royal Navy 1924.

Fleet Street (flīt strīt). [FLEET *sb.*[2]] A street in London in which there are many establishments for the production of periodical journals; *allusively*, the journals themselves, London journalism.

J. R. ROBINSON *Fifty years of F. S.* 1904.

Flight, *sb.* *attrib.*

f. deck, the deck of an aircraft-carrier for the taking-off and landing of aircraft 1940.

Flint, *sb.* **2. b.** In an automatic petrol lighter, a piece of alloy of rare-earth metals used to produce the spark.

Float, *sb.*

f. (sea)plane, an aeroplane fitted with floats 1928.

Flop, *sb.* **3.** *fig.* A sudden failure or collapse (*slang*) 1893. So **Flop** *v.* 1919.

Fluffer (flʊ·fəɹ). [f. FLUFF *sb.* + -ER [1].] A worker on a railway system employed to clear the track of refuse.

Flutter, *sb.* **1. c.** *Aerodynamics.* Defective up-and-down movement or oscillation of a wing or other part of an aeroplane 1929.

Antisymmetrical f. of a large transport aeroplane 1953.

Fly, *sb.*[2] **II. 2. a.** *attrib.*

f. button, any of the buttons covered by the fly on the opening of the front of trousers; hence **flies** *pl.*, fly-buttons.

Flying, *ppl. a.*

f. boat, a form of seaplane having a boat-like fuselage 1913; **f. bomb** = *P-PLANE 1944 (also **fly-bomb**); **f. corps,** a unit of aircraft for military purposes (the Royal Flying Corps was the precursor of the Royal Air Force) 1913; **f. dustbin** *Service slang*, a high explosive shell thrown by A.V.R.E.; **f. machine,** a machine capable of being controlled in the air, now usu. a heavier-than-air aircraft 1848; **f. officer,** the next but lowest commissioned rank in the Royal Air Force 1918; **f. saucers,** disk-like objects, thought to resemble saucers in shape, reported since 1947 as appearing in the sky but having no hitherto ascertainable identity or origin; **f. squad,** a detachment of the police force organized for swift movement 1927.

Fly-past (fləi·past). 1914. [f. FLY *v.* + PAST *adv.*, after *march-past.*] An organized flight of aircraft past a certain point or over a certain area on a particular occasion.

Fold, *sb.*[2] **4. b.** *Geol.* The folding or curvature of strata 1863.

Follow, *sb.* **4.** A supplementary portion of a course at a restaurant 1910.

Follow, *v.*

f.-me-lads, curls or ribbons hanging loosely over the shoulder (regarded as attractions for the male sex) 1872.

Following (fǫ·loui̇ŋ), *pres. pple.* of FOLLOW *v.* loosely used as quasi-prep.: As a sequel to, in succession to (an event), after.

F. his ordination, the Reverend Mr Henry Edward Manning intends to go to Rome for the purpose of commencing his ecclesiastical studies 1851 *Tablet* (reported). F. our conversation this afternoon, I should like to note that [etc.] GEORGE V, 1914.

Follow-up. [f. *to follow up* (FOLLOW *v.*).] The action of following up; the pursuit or prosecution of something begun or attempted.

‖**Fons et origo** (fǫnz et ŏrai·gǫ). 1897. [L.] The source and origin (*of*).

Food, *sb.*

f. card, a card used in f.-rationing to indicate the amount allowed for a period; **f.-controller,** an official having control of f. supplies; **f. values,** the relative nourishing power ascribed to foods.

Foot, *sb.* **III. 1. b.** The amount of coal-gas contained in one cubic foot of space 1838.

(*To catch*) *on the wrong f.*: (to take) in a state of unpreparedness. *My foot!*: a vulgar excl. expressing scornful contradiction or incredulity.

f.-second, the speed necessary to travel one foot per second.

Force, *sb.* *Third F.* [after F. *Troisième Force*], a political party making a third party to two main others so as to check extreme action; often used loosely of any third body or power.

Forced, *ppl. a.* **2.**

f. landing, the unpremeditated landing of an air-craft as the result of its being out of control 1916. Hence **Force-land** *v.*, to make a forced landing.

Foreign, *a.* **2. b.** Of railways: Belonging to another company 1897.

Form, *sb.* **I. 11.** *A matter of f.*: a point of formal procedure; *colloq.* a merely formal affair or procedure 1787. *For f.'s sake*: as a matter of form, 'pro forma'.

Formate (fǭmēⁱt), *v.* *U.S.* [Back-formation from FORMATION* 4 b.] *intr.* Of aircraft: To fly into formation.

Formation. **4. b.** A number of aircraft associated in an exercise or operation 1917.

Foul, *a.* **II. 1. b.** Revolting, disgusting (*slang*) 1911.

f. brood [after G. *faulbrut*], a disease of bees in which the young brood die and rot in the cells.

‖**Foulé** (fū·leⁱ, ‖*fule*). [F. 'pressed' (of cloth), pa. pple. of *fouler* FULL *v.*[2]] A light woollen dress material with a glossy surface.

Four, *num. adj.*

f. flush *U.S.*, [FLUSH *sb.*[3]] in poker, a flush containing only f. (instead of five) cards; hence *attrib.* lacking in genuineness 1887; **f.-flusher,** a pretender, humbug 1910.

Fourth, *num. adj.*

f. dimension, a hypothetical dimension additional to length, breadth, and thickness 1904: hence **f.-dimensional** (*fig.* superhuman, extraordinary).

Foussa (fū·sā). Also **fossa.** Native name of a cat- or civet-like mammal of Madagascar, *Cryptoprocta ferox.*

Fox, *sb.*

f. hole, a hole in the ground used by a fighting man for protection from missiles or as a firing station 1942.

(This compound is found in early local designations, e.g. in Domesday Book, and is represented in mod. *Foxhall*, in Staffordshire.)

Fragmentation.

f. bomb, one designed to disintegrate into small fragments on explosion.

Frame, *sb.* **III. 4. b.** *Cinema.* Any of the individual pictures of a film; also, a single complete image in television.

f. aerial, an aerial composed of a rectangle or loop of wire, adapted for directional reception 1921.

Frame-up (frēⁱ·m,ɒp). orig. *U.S.* [f. phr. *frame up*; see FRAME *v.* 8 e.] A prearranged or concocted affair, esp. with sinister intent; a plot for the purpose of incriminating a person on false evidence.

Fratting (fræ·tiŋ). 1945. [Short for *fraternizing*, vbl. sb. of FRATERNIZE. Cf. U.S. *frat*, short for *fraternity.*] *joc. slang.* Friendly relations between British and American soldiers and German women in the occupied parts of Western Germany.

Fraunhofer (frau·nhǭfər). 1863. Name of Joseph von *Fraunhofer* (1787–1826), Bavarian physicist; chiefly in *F. lines* (of the spectrum).

Freedom.

Four freedoms: f. of speech, f. of religion, f. from fear, f. from want, propounded by President Franklin D. Roosevelt, 6 Jan. 1941.

Freeze, *v.* **II. 4.** To make (assets, etc.) unrealizable (cf. FROZEN *ppl. a.* 1 b). **5.** To fix (wages) at a stated level 1949. Hence **Freeze,** *sb.* in these senses.

In the first twelve months since the end of the so-called f., wage rates have increased by 10 per cent. 1951.

Freighter. **4.** A freight-carrying aircraft 1945.

Fresh, *a.* **3.** *F. air*, attrib. In U.S.A. designating organizations for providing country outings.

The work of the F. Air Fund 1887 (*Dict. Amer. Eng.*). The library was unwarmed, and the 'f. air craze' had not yet developed 1931.

Friday (frai·di). The name of the native man who was found by Robinson Crusoe on a Friday (as he thought) and became his devoted servant; hence used (often *Man F.*) as a type of faithful or servile attendant.

Fridge, frige (fridʒ). *colloq.* Abbrev. of REFRIGERATOR 1935.

Friesian (frī·ziăn), var. of FRISIAN used esp. of a breed of Friesland cattle.

Frigate. **2. c.** In recent use, a large *CORVETTE.

Frit (frit), widespread dial. and illiterate pa. pple. of FRIGHT *v.*, to frighten 1801.

Froebelism (frǭ·bəliz'm). [f. name of F. W. A. *Froebel*, German educationalist (1782–1852) + -ISM.] The KINDERGARTEN system of education. So **Froebelian** (-ī·liăn) *a.* and *sb.*

Frog [1].

attrib. **f. man,** a man having a close-fitting rubber suit with a helmet, and flippers, and a supply of oxygen, to enable him to swim and operate under water; so **f. woman.**

Front, *sb.* **II. 1. e.** The space in width occupied by a fighting force; e.g. *advancing on a f. of 70 miles.* **f.** *transf.* and *fig.* Applied with epithet to an organized body or department of activity regarded as an offensive or defensive element in the national life; e.g. *labour f.* (cf. G. *arbeitsfront*), *POPULAR *f.*; *home f.*, *kitchen f.*, *money f.*; *peace f.* 1933. **3. e.** *The f.*: the promenade of a seaside resort, often with gardens adjoining. **f.** *Meteorology.* A surface of discontinuity separating two dissimilar air masses.

f. line = II. 1; also *attrib.* 1915; **f. page,** the first outside page of a newspaper; often *attrib.* to indicate news of paramount importance 1930; **f.-page** *v.*, to display on the f. p.; **f. rank,** the first or foremost rank; also *attrib.* 1899; hence **f.-ranker.**

Frontality (frɒntæ·lĭti). 1905. [f. FRONTAL + -ITY, after Du. *frontaliteit.*] A principle in sculpture according to which the figure is carved or moulded as viewed from the full front.

Froth, *sb.*

f.-blower *joc.*, a beer-drinker: adopted as the title of a certain charitable organization 1905.

‖**Führer, Fuehrer** (fū·rər). 1934. [G., 'leader'.] The title assumed by Adolf Hitler as head of the German Reich, after *DUCE.

Fulbright (fu·lbrəit). The name of Senator William *Fulbright*, of Arkansas, U.S.A., designating the *Fulbright* Act (Public Law 584 of the 79th Congress), of 1 August 1946, which authorized agreements with foreign countries by which local currencies acquired by the American government from the sale of surplus war property might be used for financing higher learning; hence applied to persons holding positions by virtue of such agreements, as *F. Professor.*

Full, *a.* **A.**

f. hand *Poker* = *FULL HOUSE 2; **f. pitch,** without the ball having first touched the ground 1895; **f. score** *Mus.*, a score in which the parts for all voices and instruments are given on separate staves 1876; **f. time,** the complete tale of hours normally allotted to work or school attendance 1898.

Full house. **1.** An assembly that fills the building intended for it 1828. **2.** *Poker.* A hand containing three of a kind and a pair 1887.

Fully, *adv.*

f.-fashioned, (of stockings) seamed and shaped to the leg.

Funeral. **B. 1.** phr. *None of your f.*: no affair of yours. *Your* (etc.) *f.*: your (etc.) concern. orig. *U.S. slang.* 1854.

Furan (fiūə·răn). Earlier **-ane.** 1906. *Chem.* abbrev. of FURFURAN.

Furfural (fɒ̄·ɹfiŭræl). 1879. [f. L. *furfur* bran + *-al* of *aldehyde.*] *Chem.* = FURFUROL. Also called **Furfura·ldehyde.**

Furfuran (fɒ̄·ɹfiŭræn). Earlier **-ane.** 1895. [ad. G. *furfuran*, f. L. *furfur* bran; see -ANE.] *Chem.* A liquid, C_4H_4O, obtained from wood tar.

Furfuryl (fɒ̄·ɹfiŭril, -əil). 1885. [f. L. *furfur*; see prec. and -YL.] *Chem.* The radical of which furfuran is the hydride.

Futurity.

f. stakes *U.S.*, stakes to be raced for at some future time, often long after the entries or nominations are made; so **f. race** 1886.

G. III. a.

= Grand, in the titles of rank in various orders, as G.C.I.E., G.C.M.G. (Commander of the Indian Empire, of St. Michael and St. George); G.C. = Grand Chaplain, Grand Chapter, George Cross; G.I.: see below. G.M. = George Medal; G.O.M. = Grand Old Man (W. E. Gladstone); G.O.P. = Grand Old Party (the Republican party in U.S.A.). **b.** = General, in G.A.T.T. (see *GATT); G.H.Q. (headquarters); G.P. (practitioner); G.P.I. (parlaysis of the insane); G.P.O. (post office); G.P.U. = OGPU; G.R. = Georgius Rex (King George). **c.** G.M.T. = Greenwich Mean Time.

Gag, *sb.*[1] *attrib.*

g.-man *U.S.*, one who makes up jokes for the stage 1928; also **g.-writer.**

Gaga (ga·ga, gæ·gă), *a.* *slang.* 1921. [ad. F. *gaga*, imitative of the babbling of the senile.] Exhibiting senile decay, 'dotty'.

Gallery, *sb.* **5.** A room, usu. longer than it is broad, in an important house or mansion, used for work or recreation, or to contain objects of art; often particularly *the long g.* **b.** More fully *shooting g.* (1836): A long narrow room for indoor target practice.

Gallipoli (gălī·pŏli). 1842. Name of a seaport in Italy designating a kind of olive oil.

Gallup poll (gæ·ləp pǭl). [f. name of George Horace *Gallup*, American statistician, POLL *sb.*[1] II.] An organization for ascertaining popular opinion on current topics by taking the votes of sections of the public.

Game, *sb.* **6. d.** *To be on* or *off one's g.*: to be playing well or badly, be in or out of form 1891.

Garden. **1.** phr. *To lead up the g.* or *g. path*: to lead astray, mislead (*slang*) 1926.

Garn (gām), *int.* 1886. Cockney and vulgar contr. of slang *Go on!* (cf. GO *v.* VII, *Go on* j), used to express disbelief in or ridicule of a statement.

If he used such words as 'garn' or 'struth' 1925.

Gas, *sb.*

g.-mask 1917; earlier *anti-(poison-) g.-mask* 1915; **g.-proof, -tight** *a.*, impermeable to (poison-) g. 1938; **g. turbine,** a turbine in which is used for its motive power a gas produced by burning or exploding fuel 1941.

Gastro-.

ga:stroentero·logy, the branch of medicine dealing with the stomach and the intestines.

Gatt (gæt). 1952. Formed from the initials of *General Agreement on Tariffs and Trade*, a convention concerning international trade.

Appeals will..be made to the guarantees afforded by GATT against backslidings towards protectionism 1952.

‖**Gauleiter** (gau·laitər). [G., f. *gau* district + *leiter* leader.] A political official controlling a district under the Nazi régime.

Gay, *a.* **1. b.** Forward, impertinent, 'fresh' (*U.S. slang*) 1899.

Gay-Pay-Oo (gēⁱpēⁱū·). 1927. Intended as a phonetic rendering of G.P.U. (see *G).

Gear, *v.* **4. b.** *fig.* To adjust the working of (an industry, etc.) *to.*

Geiger (gəi·gəɹ). 1943. Name of Hans *Geiger* (1882–), German physicist, in **G. counter** [COUNTER *sb.*[2] 3], a metal tube containing an electrode which detects the penetration of any ionizing particle. Hence **Geiger count.**

Geissler (gai·sləɹ). 1863. [Name of Heinrich *Geissler* (1814–79), German physicist.] **G.('s) tube:** a sealed tube filled with rarefied gas which becomes incandescent when an electric current is passed through it.

Gen (dʒen). *Service slang.* [abbrev. of *general* in the official phr. 'for the general information of all ranks'.] Information for operational use 1940; *transf.* correct information.

General, *sb.* **II. 2.**

G. Winter, the winter season regarded as a military factor in a campaign. So **G. Mud.**

[Cf. Russia has two generals in which she can confide—Generals Janvier and Février. 1853.]

General, *a.*

g. hospital [after F. *hôpital général*], (*a*) a hospital that is not restricted to those suffering from a particular disease 1737; (*b*) a military hospital receiving patients from field hospitals 1899.

Geneticist (dʒĕne·tisist). 1913. [f. GENETICS + -IST.] A student of genetics.

Genocide (dʒe·nǫsəid). 1944. [irreg. f. Gr. γένος race (cf. GENUS) + -CIDE [2]. Coined by Dr. Raphael Lemkin.] Extermination of a race or community by killing or imposing conditions unfavourable to survival. Also **Ge·nocide** [-CIDE[1]], one who carries out such methods; hence **Ge·nocidal** *a.*

Genotype [1] (dʒe·nǫtəip). 1897. [irreg. f. Gr. γένος GENUS + TYPE; coined by Schucherl.] *Biol.* The type-species of a genus.

Genotype [2] (dʒe·nǫtəip). 1910. [irreg. f. GENE + TYPE.] *Biol.* The combination of genes possessed by a race or an organism; a race or group of organisms having the same combinations of genes. Hence **Genoty·pic(al)** *adjs.*, **-ty·pically** *adv.*

‖**Genro** (ge·nrǫ). 1921. [Jap., f. *gen* root, *ro* old.] The 'elder statesmen' of Japan, who directed the development of the country for the re-establishment of the Mikado to the end of the 19th century.

Gentleman. *pl. Gentlemen*, designation of a public convenience for male persons.

A big ganglion of trains and bus lines, a large Gentlemen and Ladies [etc.] *Characters of England* 1947.

Geopo·litics. [GEO-.] The politics of a country as determined by its geographical position.

George. **II. 5.** An automatic pilot of aircraft. *R.A.F. slang.* 1936.

G. Cross, G. Medal, decorations for gallantry instituted by King George VI, 23 Sept. 1940.

Georgian, *a.*[1] **1.** Also, (one) belonging to the reign of George V 1910.

There is something melancholy in having seen the end of the Georges, the Georgian age having been in part the happiest, in part the most splendid, and altogether the most momentous age of our history SOUTHEY 1830. Georgian Poetry 1911–1912 (*title*). The critical eye of Edwardian and Georgian enlightenment 1927.

Geriatry (dʒe·riætri). [f. Gr. γέρων old man + ἰατρος physician + -Y [3].] The medical treatment of old age. Also **Geria·tric** *a.*, **Geria·trics** [see -ICS].

German, *a.* *G. band* [BAND *sb.*[3] 4]: an instrumental company of street musicians, (properly) of German extraction 1881.

Gerontic, *sb. pl.* [See -ICS.] = *GERONTOLOGY.

Gerontology (dʒerǫntǫ·lǒdʒi). [f. Gr. γεροντο-, γέρων old man + -LOGY.] The department of medical science dealing with old age and the aged.

‖**Gestalt** (gəʃta·lt). 1924. [G.,'form, shape'.] *Psychol* A shape or structure which, as an object of perception, forms a specific whole incapable of expression simply in terms of its parts. Chiefly attrib., as *g. psychology, theory.*

‖**Gestapo** (gestā·pǫ). [G., f. initial letters of Ge*heime* Sta*ats*-Po*lizei* 'secret state police'.] The secret police of the Nazi régime in Germany.

Get, *v.* **I. b.** To grasp (a thing, what is said, etc.); hence with the speaker as obj., e.g. *Do you get me?* (U.S. colloq.) 1907.

To get off with: to become friendly with one of the other sex, esp. with amorous intentions 1925. *To get on to*: to succeed in getting hold of (orig. *U.S.*) 1895.

Get, *v.* **V.** *To get busy* (U.S. colloq.): to start work or operations, become active 1904. *To get left* (U.S. colloq.): to be left behind or in the lurch 1882. **VII. G. together**: to come together for conference, assemble in (friendly) consultation.

Ge·t-out. **1.** U.S. colloq. phr. (*as*) . . *as get out, like all get-out*, denoting an extreme state or condition 1837. **2.** An escape from a difficult or awkward position 1909.

Get-rich-quick, *adj. phr.* 1905. [GET V. 3, QUICK *adv.*] *U.S. colloq.* Characterized by the desire to attain wealth rapidly.

Get-toge·ther. orig. *U.S. colloq.* [f. phr. *get together*.] A coming together for consultation or conference 1911.

Ghost, *sb.* **II.** In favourable use: One who works as assistant or deputy to a professional man, as a writer, doctor, etc.

A versatile 'ghost' edits/writes Biographies, Histories, Stories, Speeches, Brochures, etc. (*Advt.*). Britain's 'ghost' doctors—young men and women who work as salaried assistants in big practices 1952.

G.I., GI (dʒī əi). [Initials of G*eneral* I*ssue* or G*overnment* I*ssue*.] *attrib.* Designed or provided for members of the armed forces of the U.S.A.; *sb.* An enlisted member of a U.S. armed force.

Gibson (gi·bsən). Name of C. Dana *Gibson* (1867–1944), an American artist and illustrator of magazines, used attrib. to designate a type of feminine beauty and costume popularized by him *c* 1900–10.

G. girl 1901. G. pleats 1905.

Gift, *sb.* *attrib.*

g. coupon, a coupon issued with certain commodities, a certain number of which entitles the holder to a free g. 1931.

Gila (hī·lă). 1877. [Name of a river in New Mexico and Arizona.] *G. monster*, a large venomous lizard, *Heloderma suspectum*.

Gilbert (gi·lbəɹt). 1911. [Name of William *Gilbert* (1544–1603), 'father of electric and magnetic science'.] The unit of magnetomotive force in the C.G.S. system.

Gilt, *ppl. a.* *Gilt-edge(d) securities, stocks*, usu. investments of the highest reliability such as trustees prefer or are restricted to; so *gilt-edge* sb.

Gimmick (gi·mik). *U.S. slang.* 1928. [Of unkn. origin.] A device used in performing a trick; a mechanical dodge, tricky contrivance.

Gippo [1] (dʒi·pǫ). Var. of dial. *gipper, jipper*, meat juice, gravy, stew, (hence) vb. to baste.

Not fit to jipper a joint with him 1822 (SCOTT).

Gippo [2] (dʒi·pǫ). 1902. [f. *gip-, gyp-*, first syll. of GIPSY. Cf. *Gippy* (1) Egyptian *c* 1890; (2) gipsy 1913.] A gipsy.

Girl, *sb.* **4.** *G. clerk* 1901; **g. friend,** a favourite female companion or sweetheart (orig. *U.S.*); **G. Guide** (see GUIDE *sb.* I. 2 d), in U.S. **G. Scout** 1920. Hence **Gi·rly** *a.* [-Y[1]], girlish; **Girly-girly** *a.*, girlish in an exaggerated or affected manner 1891.

Give, *v.*[1] *To g.* (a person) *best*: to admit the superiority of, give way to (*colloq.*) 1883.

Glad, *a.* **4. c.** *G. hand*: the hand of welcome (*U.S. colloq.*) 1896.

Glagolitic (glægǫli·tik), *a.* 1845. [ad. mod. L. *glagoliticus* (F. *-itique*, G. *-itisch*), after Russ. *glagolicheskiy*, f. *glagól* word.] Name of the alphabet (derived from the Greek) in which early Slavonic translations of the Bible and liturgical texts are written.

Gleep (glīp). [f. initials of *graphite low energy experimental pile*.] A kind of atomic pile.

Glide, *sb.* **1. b.** *Cricket.* A stroke by which the ball is deflected towards long leg by the turned blade of the bat 1888.

Global, *a.* **2. b.** Involving the whole world, world-wide.

Glomerule. Hence **Glomerular** (glǫme·rⁱŭlăɹ), *a.* Comb.-form **Glome·rulo-**, as in *glome:rulosclero·sis*.

Glottal, *a.* *G. stop*: a sound produced by the opening or shutting of the glottis with emission of breath or voice 1888 (H. Sweet).

Glove, *sb.* **2.** phr. *To take the gloves off*: to set to in earnest; so advb. phr. *with gloves off* (orig. *U.S.*).

G-man (dʒī·mæn). *U.S.* 1935. [*G.* = Government.] A Federal criminal investigation officer.

Go, *v.* **IV. 2.** *To go it alone* (U.S.): to act by oneself or without support 1855. **V. Go to —**: to set about vigorously, e.g. *Go to it!* 1918.

Goa (gōᵘ·ă). [Name of Pg. settlement in India.] *G. powder*: araroba powder, a drug derived from the tree *Andira Araroba* 1910.

Goalee, -ie (gōᵘ·li). 1921. *colloq.* [f. GOAL- + -EE [2], -IE.] A goal-keeper.

Gob, *sb.*[5] *U.S. slang.* 1919. [Short for *gobby* coastguardsman (1890), f. GOB *sb.*[1] expectoration + -Y [6].] A sailor, seaman.

Gobbet, *sb.* **4.** *Univ. slang.* A selected piece of a text set for translation or comment in an examination 1912.

Gobbledygook (gǫ·b'ldiguk). *U.S. slang.* [repr. a turkey-cock's gobble; invented by Maury Maverick, of Texas.] Official verbiage or jargon.

Gold, *sb.*

g. brick *U.S. slang*, something having only a surface appearance of value, fraud, sham 1887; **g.-digger,** (*a*) one who digs for gold 1831; (*b*) a girl or woman who attaches herself to a man merely for gain (orig. *U.S. slang*) 1925.

Gong (gǫŋ), *v.* [f. GONG [2].] *trans.* Of traffic police: To call upon (a driver) to stop by striking a gong.

Goodish, *a.* **2.** Fairly ample or plentiful, e.g. *a g. quantity* 1836.

Gorget [1].

g. patch, a distinguishing piece of material on the collar of a military, police, etc. uniform 1917.

‖**Gorsedd** (gǭ·ɹseð). 1794. [W., 'throne, tribunal, session'.] A meeting of Welsh bards and druids, esp. preparatory to the eisteddfod.

Go-slow (gōᵘ:slōᵘ·). 1930. [f. GO *v.* + SLOW *adv.*] A policy of working at a slow pace with deliberate limitation of output. Cf. CA'CANNY.

Big go-slow threat to industry 1953.

Gothic, *a.*

G. line [G. *Gotenlinie*], a fortified line constructed by the Germans in Italy in 1944, extending from Pesaro westwards.

Gouda (gau·dă). 1885. A flat round cheese made at Gouda in Holland.

‖**Goum** (gūm). 1910. [F., ad. Arab. *gūm*, dial. var. of *qūm* band, troop.] A contingent of Algerian soldiers.

Government. A frequent pronunc. is (gɒ·vəmənt), evidenced in the 16th c., is recorded as (ˈgʌvmmənt) by D. Jones *Eng. Pronouncing Dict.* 1922.

Grace, *sb.* **III. 3.** *The G.*: the prayer beginning 'The Grace of our Lord Jesus Christ, and the Love of God . . .', used at the conclusion of Morning and Evening Prayer, the Litany, and the Burial of the Dead, in the Book of Common Prayer.

Grade, *sb.* **9. d.** *To make the g.*: to reach the proper standard (orig. *U.S.*) 1930.

Grand, A. *adj.* *Comb* **b.**

The extended use of *g.* to designate the second degree in descent of relationship is recorded from the late sixteenth century

‖**Grand Guignol** (grañ gi·nʸol). 1920. [F., 'Great Punch', name of a theatre in Paris.] A dramatic entertainment in which short pieces of a sensational or horrific kind are played successively.

‖**Grand mal** (grañ mal). 1941. [F., 'great disease'.] *Path.* General convulsive epilepsy with loss of consciousness, epilepsis gravior. Cf. *PETIT MAL.

‖**Grando** (græ·ndǫ). A hand of a certain content at skat (see quot.).

The highest 'solo', still higher than clubs, is 'grando'. In this game only the four knaves are trumps. If the hand playing grando thinks he can make all the tricks, he declares open grando—*i.e.* shows his hand. *Encycl. Brit.* XXV (1910) 166/2.

Graves (grāv). 1630. [F. (pl.), name for gravelly sandy parts of the Bordeaux country.] A light (usu. white) wine of the Graves district.

Greasy, *a.* (Some speakers make a distinction in the use of the two pronunciations grī·si, grī·zi, applying the first to the presence of grease on a surface, and the second to a slippery condition such as is caused by grease.)

Great, *a.*

G. Dane: see DANE. **G. Spirit** [tr. Ojibway *kitchi manitou*], the deity of the N. American Indians 1805; **G. War,** (*a*) the war which began with the outbreak of hostilities between Great Britain and France in 1793 and lasted till the Treaty of Paris, May 1814; (*b*) the war which began on 28 July 1914 with hostilities between Austria-Hungary and Serbia and finally involved the majority of the nations of the world, suspended by armistice 11 Nov. 1918. Cf. *WORLD *war*.

Green, *a.* *Comb.* **2.**

g. light, a green-coloured lamp or reflector used as a signal that the line is clear for traffic to proceed; *to give the g. l.*, to give the signal for proceeding on a course.

Gremlin (gre·mlin). 1941. *R.A.F. slang.* [?] A mischievous sprite imagined to frequent aeroplanes and to cause mishaps.

Gretna Green (gre·tnă grīn). A village in Dumfriesshire just across the Scottish Border, where runaway couples were married (by a blacksmith) according to Scots Law.
It was my impression Gretna marriages were quite matters of the past 1852.
Greycing (grē¹·siŋ), contr. of *greyhound racing* 1928.
Grid, *sb.* **5.** For def. read: A squared network of lines on a loose sheet in an atlas for finding places on a map 1918.
Grievious (grī·viəs), *a.* Variant, now vulgar, of GRIEVOUS. Cf. *MISCHIEVIOUS.
1683 [see s.v. GRIEVOUS, p. 831, col. 3].
Griff (grif), *sb.* 1891. *slang.* Short for *GRIFFIN.
He's got the straight g. for something NAT. GOULD.
Griffin (gri·fin). 1889. *slang.* [Of unkn. origin.] A tip, as in betting; a hint; a piece of information. phr. *To give the straight g.*
And then we got the hard g. The enemy was on the run 1944.
Gri·zzle, *v.*² *local.* [?] **1.** *intr.* To grin, snarl 1746. **2.** To fret, cry in a whining or whimpering fashion 1842.
Ground, *sb.* **III. 1. e.** *On the g.*: engaged in servicing aircraft on an air-field. So *g. crew, g. staff*, also *groundsman* (1923).
g. speed, the horizontal component of an aircraft's velocity relative to the earth 1917.
Ground, *v.* **9. d.** To keep 'on the ground', prevent (aircraft, etc.) from taking off 1939.
Grouper² (grū·pəɪ). 1933. [f. GROUP *sb.* + -ER¹.] An adherent of the Group Movement, a Buchmanite.
Growler. 3. A small iceberg 1912.
Grummet. d. 'Hemp and red-lead putty mixed as a jointing material for water-tightness' (*Chambers's Techn. Dict.*).
Guag (gwæg). *Mining.* 'The space left after the mineral has been exhausted. Also called *gunis*' (*Chambers's Techn. Dict.*).
Guarani (gwărā·ni). 1797. Name of one of the two main divisions of the Tupi-Guarani, a widespread ethnic and linguistic group of South American Indians; also, the language. **b.** A currency unit (established 4 November 1943), symbolized by a crossed G, replacing the peso fuerte at the rate of 1 guarani = 100 pesos, and 1·75 guaranies = 1 gold peso. Hence Guara·nian *a.* and *sb.*
Guard, *sb.*
g. book, a book containing guards for the reception of additional leaves 1903.
Guayule (gwayū·l). 1906. A rubber substitute derived from a Mexican tree so named (*Parthenium argentatum*).
Guess, *sb.* **1.** *By g. and by God*: (to steer) at hazard 1909. Hence gen.
Guest house. 3. A superior boarding-house, sometimes having a programme of entertainments, sports, etc. 1925.
Guff (gvf). 1888. [?] *U.S. slang.* Nonsense, blarney.
Gug (gvg). 'A self-acting inclined railway in a coal-mine' (*Chambers's Techn. Dict.*).
Guide, *sb.*
g. rope, a rope used for guiding an object, e.g. as it ascends or descends ME.; a long rope hung from a balloon or airship so as to trail on the ground and maintain altitude automatically; one of a number of ropes used to steady an airship before flight 1838.
Guildhall. As used of the hall of the Corporation and City of London it is not qualified by the definite article.
Gullery (gv·ləri). [f. GULL *sb.*¹ + -ERY.] A colony of seagulls; a place where seagulls collect.
Few Londoners..suspect that they have..so large a g. almost on their doorsteps 1952.
Gum (gvm), *sb.*⁵ *Mining.* = DUFF *sb.*² 3.
Gunner. 1. *Master g.*: in mod. use, a warrant officer in the Royal Artillery having charge of the stores and equipment in a fort.
Gup (gvp), *sb. slang* (orig. *Anglo-Indian*). (1617), 1806. [Hind. *gap.*] Gossip. **b.** Silly talk 1883.
Gurkha (gūᵊ·ɹkă, gv̄·ɹkă). 1848. A member of one of the dominant races of Nepal, India, of Hindu descent and Sanskritic speech and specially famed for prowess in fighting.

Gyro-.
gyropilot, a gyro-compass used to steer a vessel without human agency 1923; **gyroplane,** a flying-machine supported in the air by a rapidly rotating screw propeller operating in a horizontal plane 1907.
Gyroscope. [F. *gyroscope* was coined by Jean Bernard Léon Foucault 1854.]
H.
H.G. = Home Guard; H.H. = heavy hydrogen; hhd. = hogshead; H.M.I.(S.) = His or Her Majesty's Inspector (of Schools).
H-bomb, hydrogen bomb; **H-Hour,** the hour at which an operation is to begin. Cf. *D-DAY.
Hair, *sb.* **1. c.** *To get by the short h–s*: to hold so that escape is painful, have complete control over (*slang*) 1899.
h. slide, a horn, tortoiseshell, or metal clip for keeping the hair in place 1895; **h.-styling,** dressing the hair in a particular style.
Hair-do (hēᵊ·ɹdū). 1943. [f. HAIR *sb.* + DO *sb.*] **a.** A way or style of dressing the hair (orig. *U.S.*). **b.** A cutting and setting of the hair.
Hairy, *a. Comb.*
h.-heeled *a. slang*, deficient in breeding or manners; f. phr. *h. at (about, in) the heel (fetlocks)* 1899.
Half-.
h.-blue, colours awarded to a player or competitor chosen as a second choice to a full blue or to a representative in minor sports, a player so distinguished 1908; **h. nelson** *Wrestling*, a hold in which one arm is thrust from the back through the corresponding arm of the opponent and the hand placed on the back of his neck 1889; **h. shot** *Golf*, a shot played with something less than a full swing; **h.-staff** *U.S.*, half-mast; **h.-title,** (*b*) the title of a section of a book printed on the recto of the leaf preceding it.
Half-deck. In a merchant ship, the accommodation assigned to cadets and apprentices.
Half-tone. 3. An illustration printed from a block produced by photography in which lights and shades are represented by dots 1895.
Halide (hæ·ləid). 1927. [f. Gr. ἅλς SALT + -IDE.] *Chem.* A term including bromides, chlorides, fluorides, and iodides.
Hallstatt (ha·lʃtat). 1900. [Name of a village in Upper Austria, where the remains were discovered.] *Archæol.* Denoting finds representing a phase of the early Iron Age.
Halve, *v.* **1. b.** *Golf.* Of opposing sides: To reach, accomplish, or finish in the same number of strokes or with the same number of holes.
Hammer, *sb.*
h. lock *Wrestling*, a position in which a wrestler is held with one arm bent behind his back 1897.
Hand, *sb.* **I. 1. f.** *A (good) h.*, applause (*U.S.*) 1890.
****To put* (one's) *hand(s) on*: to lay hands on, get hold of 1535.
Hand, *v.* *To h. off* (Rugby football), to push (a tackler) off with the hand. *To h. it to*: to acknowledge the superiority of (*U.S.*) 1916.
Handedness (hæ·ndėdnės). [f. HANDED + -NESS.] The condition of using only or preferably one hand or the other by natural tendency.
Handedness and cerebral dominance 1951.
Hand-out. 1887. [f. HAND *v.* + OUT *adv.*] **1.** What is handed out, e.g. alms (*U.S.*). **2.** Matter handed out to the newspaper press 1929.
Handwrite (hæ·nd,rəit). *Sc.* and *U.S.* 1617. [f. HAND *sb.* + WRITE *sb.*¹ 4. Cf. †*hand-writ* and *hand of writ(e.)*] Handwriting.
Hanging, *ppl. a.* [-ING².] *Golf.* 'Said of a ball that lies on a slope inclining downwards in regard to the direction in which it is wished to drive' (*Encycl. Brit.* 1910).
Hang-over. b. Unpleasant after-effects of dissipation (*slang*) 1912. Also *gen.*
Hanky (hæ·ŋki). 1895 (*handky*). Familiar colloquialism for HANDKERCHIEF (hæ·ŋkəɹtʃif); see -Y⁶.
Happen, *v.* **1. b.** With a vague subject (e.g. *anything, something*), said of some serious thing (e.g. death) coming *to* a person 1829.
Happy, *a.* **4.** phr. *Happy ship*, primarily referring to the harmonious working of a ship's crew, thence used gen. of the conduct of any organization. **b.** As the second element of a compound (orig. *U.S. colloq.*): In a state of excitement or nervousness, in respect of the object, event, use or practice of the action, etc. denoted by the first element; e.g. *bomb-h., slap-h., trigger-h.*
A branch or a department may be a theoretical monstrosity and yet be a 'h. ship'; and traditionally a 'h. ship' is the only efficient ship 1950.
Harbour, *sb.* **3. b.** *transf.* of a tank depot.
I passed some of our own tanks returning to h. 1943.
Hard, *a.* **I. 1. b.** Of a lawn tennis court: Made of asphalt or other hard material 1895.
h. case, a sailing-ship on which conditions are rough 1920; **h. core,** (*a*) heavy material forming the foundation of a road, (*b*) an irreducible nucleus or residuum; **h. currency,** the currency of a country in relation to another country with which it has an adverse balance of payments on current transactions that has to be settled in gold or dollars; **h.-lying money,** for *h.-line money* [see LINE *sb.*² I. 6], an allowance in compensation for hard conditions on board ship; **h.-pad,** a form of distemper in dogs.
‖**Haute école** (ot ekol). [F., 'high school'.] The more advanced exercises of equitation.
Have, *v.* phr. *To h. it (nothing) on* (U.S.), to have the (no) advantage over 1909. *To h. on*: to puzzle intentionally, tease (*colloq.*) 1867.
Have-not (hæ·vnɒt). 1836. [HAVE *v.*, NOT *adv.*] One who has no possessions, or very few in comparison with others; esp. of those nations that are considered not to have a due share of territory or material resources (1937).
The Rich and the Poor—the Havenots and the Haves LYTTON. There are..German experts who consider the German Empire as the only genuine 'have-not' in the world 1939.
Hay, *sb.*¹
haywire *U.S.*, anything tangled, involved, or confused 1905; phr. *to go haywire*, to become excited or distracted 1929.
Haymaker. 4. A swinging blow (*slang*) 1914.
Head, *sb.*
h. resistance = *DRAG *sb.* 6 b.
Headache. 3. *transf.* A troublesome or annoying thing; a trouble, trial (*slang* or *colloq.*); orig. *U.S.* 1939.
Headline. 2. d. *pl.* A caption in large letters in a newspaper; the summary of a B.B.C. news broadcast. *To make* or *hit the headlines*: to be news of the first importance 1867 (orig. *U.S.*).
Head-on, *adv.* and *a.* orig. *U.S.* **A.** *adv.* (*head-o·n*) With the head or front pointed directly towards something. **B.** *adj.* (*hea·d-on*) Involving the direct meeting of the front of a vehicle with another object 1904.
Health. 1. phr. *Not for one's h.* (orig. *U.S.*): for one's material advantage or interest 1900.
Hearty, *sb.* **C. b.** *Univ. slang.* An athletic non-studious man 1928.
Heat, *sb.* **8.** fig. phr. *To turn on the h.*: to apply extreme pressure in order to extract a response (*colloq.*).
Heaviside (he·visaid). Name of Oliver *Heaviside* (1850–1925) used to denote a layer of the atmosphere which reflects wireless waves and causes them to follow the contour of the earth 1913.
Heavy, *a.*¹
h. chemicals, bulk chemicals used in industry or agriculture; **h. hydrogen** = *DEUTERIUM (symbol D); so **h. water,** the oxide of deuterium, D_2O; **h. oxygen,** the oxygen isotope of atomic-weight 18 (also 17); **h. oil,** the last fraction obtained before the pitch point in the distillation of coal tar; creosote oil 1910.
B. *sb. pl.* Heavy bombers, a quantity lifted at one time.
Heck (hek). *dial.* and *U.S.* 1887. Euphemistic alteration of HELL. (*Hecky* is earlier *dial.*)
A h. of a big pile 1944. The three, working with a h. of timber 1954.
Hedge, *sb.*
h. hop, the action of an airman in flying at low levels so as to suggest hopping over hedges 1939.
Hedgehog. 1. b. A fortified position 'bristling' with guns pointing in all directions.
Heebie-jeebies (hī·bi,dʒī·biz), *sb. pl. slang.* 1926. A dance resembling the blues; also, blues, jim-jams.
Heliolithic (hī:lio̦li·þik), *a.* 1915. [f. HELIO-, after *eolithic*, etc.] Designating a civilization characterized by megaliths and sun-worship.
Hell, *sb.* Slang phr. *To give* (a person) *h.*:

to give him 'a bad time', trounce 1863. *To knock, blast*, etc. *h. out of*: to pound heavily. *Like h.*: (*a*) recklessly, desperately; very much 1855; (*b*) *ironically*, not at all, on the contrary.

Hereford (he·rĕfə̆d). 1844. Name of a West-of-England county, designating a breed of cattle. Also **He·refordshire** 1834.

Het (het), *pa. pple.* late ME. [pa. pple. of HEAT *v.*] Heated; now *dial.* and *U.S.* (with *up*: excited 1902).

Heterocyclic (he:tĕrosəi·klik), *a.* [f. HETERO- + CYCLE *sb.* + -IC.] *Chem.* Pertaining to or containing a ring made up of various kinds of atoms.

Heterosexual (he:tĕrose·ksiuăl), *a.* 1901. [f. HETERO-, after HOMOSEXUAL.] Pertaining to or characterized by the normal relations between the sexes. Also as *sb.*

Hide, *v.*[1]

h.-out, orig. *U.S. colloq.*, a hiding-place 1895 (f. phr. *to h. out*: to go into hiding 1885). So **Hi·dy-hole** (həi·dihōul) *Sc.* and *U.S.* 1828. [Alteration of *hiding-hole.*]

High, *a.*

h.-ranking *a.*, of high rank; so **h.-ranker.**

High altar. late ME. [HIGH *a.* II. 3.] The principal altar of a church.

Highlight (həi·ləit), *v.* [f. HIGH LIGHT.] *trans.* To turn the high lights upon, give full prominence to.

It is not a popularized glimpse, highlighting the more sensational, but finally less valuable, discoveries 1952.

High-up (həi·ʊp). *colloq.* 1868. In a high or exalted position, chiefly *fig.* (cf. HIGH *a.* II. 1); *sb.*, an exalted personage. So **Hi·gher-up** *sb.*

Hike, *sb.* 1865. orig. *dial.* and *U.S.* [f. HIKE *v.*] A vigorous walk; a tramp. So **Hi·ker** 1927. See also *HITCH *v.*

Hippocratic (hipokræ·tik), *a.* [f. *Hippocrates*, name of a Greek physician (460?–357 B.C.), called 'the father of medicine' + -IC.] Pertaining to or characteristic of Hippocrates; esp. *H. oath*, an oath comprising the obligations and professional conduct of physicians, taken by those entering upon medical practice.

Hippodrome. 3. A theatre used for various stage entertainments.

Histogram (hi·stǫgræm). 1903. [f. Gr. ἱστός web + -GRAM.] A form of graph or graphic representation involving a web-like pattern.

Historicism (histǫ·risiz'm). [After F. *historisme*, G. *historismus*.] The conception of phenomena in the historical process as the outcome of human activity. Also **Histo·ricist** (*attrib.*). So **Hi·storism.**

Hitch, *v.* 4. b. To tramp. Also **h.-hike** *v.*, to travel by means of lifts in vehicles; hence **h.-hiker** (orig. *U.S.*) 1925 (*Dict. Americanisms*).

Hitlerian (hitlī·riăn), *a.* 1930. Pertaining to (the policy of) Adolf *Hitler*, the German Führer. So **Hitlerism** (hi·tlĕriz'm), Nazism. **Hi·tlerite** *a.* and *sb.* See -IAN, -ISM, -ITE[1].

Hoar-frost. Now distinguished by meteorologists from *rime* as: Frozen-water vapour deposited in clear still weather on lawns and such-like surfaces.

Hock (hǫk), *sb.*[5] *U.S. slang.* 1859. [ad. Du. *hok* hutch, prison, credit, debt.] *In h.*: (*a*) in the act (of gambling), (*b*) in prison, (*c*) in pawn, (*d*) in debt.

Hold, *v.* **H. down.** b. *U.S.* To continue to occupy (a place or post); to retain (a job) 1891.

Holding, *vbl. sb.* **II. 1.** See also *small h.* s.v. SMALL *a.* ad fin.

Holy, *a.* compar. *holier* (hōu·liəɪ) in colloq. phr. *holier-than-thou*: characterized by an attitude of superior sanctity.

We didn't want a preachy 'holier-than-thou' lecture 1950.

Home, *v.* 4. *trans.* To bring in (an aircraft) by radio. Hence **Ho·ming** *vbl. sb.* attrib. in **homing device**, an automatic device for guiding aircraft and missiles.

Home Guard. a. *U.S.* A member of a local volunteer force 1861. b. The Territorial Forces of England 1909; since 1940 applied to the Local Defence Volunteers organized for the defence of the country.

Homo[2] (hǫ·mou, hōu·mou), *colloq.* Short for HOMOSEXUAL *sb.*

‖**Honved** (hǫ·nveid). 1854. [Magyar; f. *hon* home + *vēd* defence.] The Hungarian army in the Revolution of 1848–9; later, the militia reserve.

Hoodoo. 3. A malignant spell; a thing that causes ill-luck; also *attrib.* 1881. 4. A fantastically shaped pinnacle or column of rock, formed as by erosion, occurring in the Western U.S. 1879 (*Dict. Americanisms*).

Hooey (hū·i). *U.S. slang.* 1924. [?] Nonsense, humbug.

Hook, *sb.* 10. b. [f. HOOK *v.* 8d.] *Boxing.* A swinging blow with the elbow bent 1898.

h. worm, a nematoid worm having hook-like spines, which infests the intestines of animals 1903.

Hook(e)y (hu·ki). *U.S.* [?] **1.** *To play h.*: to play truant 1848. **2.** *Blind h.*: a gambling game at cards, in which players make guesses concerning the bottom card of each packet into which the pack of cards is divided 1840.

Hook-up (hu·kʊp). orig. *U.S. colloq.* 1903. [f. phr. *hook up*, HOOK *v.* 4.] A combination of apparatus, etc., esp. of broadcasting equipment; *gen.* a connexion, an alliance.

Hoop, *sb.*[1] **1. b.** A hoop, often with paper stretched across it, through which acrobats, etc. leap 1793. *To go* (*put*) *through the hoop*(*s*: to undergo (subject to) an ordeal or trial 1919.

Hooray (hurē̆ⁱ·), var. of HURRAY (HURRAH).

Hoover (hū·vəɪ). A vacuum cleaner (patented 1927) manufactured by *Hoover* Ltd. Hence **Hoover** *v. trans.*, to clean with a h. (or, by extension, any vacuum cleaner).

Hopping, *vbl. sb.*[1] and *ppl. a.* Of aircraft: Passing over physical features in a series of movements resembling hops, as *cloud-*, *HEDGE-, *wave-hopping.*

Hot, *a.* **2.** colloq. phr. *H. under the collar*: feeling anger or resentment (cf. 5, 6). **6. e.** (of a hit, etc.) difficult to deal with 1882; (of a competitor) strongly expected or fancied to win. **7. d.** Applied to jazz music having a strong extempore element, as opp. to *straight* or *sweet jazz*; also applied to the performer.

7. d. The greatest of all h. musicians 1938.

h. dog *U.S.*, a h. sausage sandwiched in a roll of bread; **h. war** (opp. to *cold war*), war with arms and shooting.

House, *sb.*[1] **4.** *The H.*, Christ Church, Oxford: from the Latin title *Ædes Christi* 'House of Christ'. **d.** *To keep a h.*: to ensure that there is always a sufficient attendance of members in the House of Commons to form a quorum and to secure support for the chosen speakers of a party. Also *to make a h.* (see MAKE *v.* II. 7). **g.** Also, a performance at a particular time in a theatre, e.g. *first, second h.* **10.** *Army slang.* Lotto 1900. (Also **Housie** hau·si.)

h. arrest, detention in one's house in protective custody; **h.-proud** *a.*, (of a woman) giving intense or excessive attention to the upkeep and outward appearance of the house.

Hoverplane (hǫ·vəɪplē̆ⁱn). [f. HOVER *v.* + PLANE *sb.* III. 1 e (*b*).] A helicopter.

How, *adv.* **II.** *And h.!*: excl. used to indicate that the effect of something is difficult to describe = And no mistake, Very much so! (*U.S. slang*) 1932. *Here's h.!*: a familiar toasting formula 1890.

Hoyle (hoil). Name of Edmond *Hoyle* (1672–1769), author of several works on card-games (the earliest, on whist, dated 1742); often cited typically for an authority on card-playing.

Hubby (hʊ·bi). 1688. Familiar colloquialism for HUSBAND; see -Y[6].

‖**Hubris** (hiū·bris). 1884. [Engl. pronunc. of Gr. ὕβρις.] Wanton arrogance or insolence.

Huddle, *sb.* 4. A close or secret conference (*colloq.*).

Human, *a.* **4. b.** Belonging or relating to man as distinguished from the lower animals, machinery and mechanism, or mere objects or events 1847.

Humanism. 3. b. A theory of the life of man in the world as a responsible being behaving independently of any revelation or of præternatural powers.

Hunk (hʊŋk), *a.* *U.S.* 1847. [ad. Du. *honk* goal, home (in a game).] Safe, all right. So **Hu·nky** *a.* 1861; **Hu·nky-do·ry, -do·rum** 1868. (See *Dict. Americanisms.*)

Hut, *sb.* *attrib.*

h. circle, a circle of earth or stones indicating the circumference of a previously existing hut 1865.

Hydrogen. For line 9 read: Symbol H; atomic number 1; atomic weight 1·0078.

h. bomb, a bomb of which the explosive power is derived from the fission of hydrogen atoms 1950.

Hydroponics (həidrǫpǫ·niks), *sb. pl.* 1938. [f. Gr. ὕδωρ HYDRO- + πόνος labour + -ICS.] Cultivation of plants by means of water impregnated with salts and without soil.

Hyper-.

Hyperemesis (həipəre·mĕsis), extreme vomiting, as in pregnancy. **Hyperte·nsion**, extreme tension 1906.

I. III.

I. = Island(s); I.A. = Indian Army; I.A.T.A. = International Air Transport Association; I.C.I. = Imperial Chemical Industries; I.L.O. = International Labour Organization; I.O.G.T. = International Order of Good Templars; I.(O.)W. = Isle of Wight; I.Q. = intelligence quotient; I.T.A. = Independent Television Authority; I.W.W. = Industrial Workers of the World.

Ichabod (i·kăbǫd). 1901. Name given by Eli's daughter-in-law to her son; used as an excl. of regret, in allusion to 1 Sam. iv. 21 (She named the child Ichabod, saying, 'The glory is departed from Israel').

Icing, *vbl. sb.* 3. The formation of ice on aircraft; also with *up.*

Id[2] (id). 1924. [L. *id* it, as tr. G. *es* (Groddock, *Das Buch vom Es*, 1923).] *Psycho-analysis.* The inherited instinctive impulses of the individual.

Iddy-umpty (i:di|ʊ·mpti). 1906. Conventional verbal representation of the dots and dashes of the Morse code.

Idea, *sb.* **I. 4.** *The big* or *great i.*, the grand plan or scheme (esp. iron.; orig. *U.S.*) 1923.

Ideology. 3. More particularly, the ideas forming the basis of an economic or political theory or system.

Idle, *v.* **1. b.** Of an internal-combustion engine: To revolve slowly with throttle closed.

‖**Ilag** (ī·læg). 1940. G., abbrev. of *Internierten*lager, a camp for internees.

Ill-feeling (ilfī·liŋ). [ILL *a.*, FEELING *vbl. sb.*] Malevolent, hostile, or unfriendly feeling or disposition.

The ill-feeling against the foreign residents 1868.

Ill(-)hea·lth. 1732. [ILL *a.* 8.] Disordered condition of the body; a physical state characterized by the presence of disease or imperfect functioning.

Ill(-)trea·tment. 1713. [ILL *a.* 2.] Bad, harsh, or rough treatment or handling. Cf. ILL-TREAT *v.*

Imaging (i·mĕdʒiŋ), *vbl. sb.* [f. IMAGE *v.* + -ING[1].] Production of an image.

Not just occurrences, neither i-s, nor anything else H. H. PRICE *Thinking & Experience* (1953) 236.

I·magism. 2. *Philos.* The theory that thinking consists in operating with mental images. So **I·magist**, one who holds the doctrine of imagism; also *attrib.*, as *imagist theory.* **I·magy** [-Y[1]], of the nature of an image.

H. H. PRICE *Thinking and Experience* (1953).

Immersion. *attrib.*

i. heater, an electric heating apparatus fitted in a hot-water tank.

Immunology (imiūnǫ·lŏdʒi). 1916. [f. IMMUN(ITY + -OLOGY.] The branch of medicine dealing with immunity from disease, immunization, and the methods used for this. Hence **Immunolo·gic, -lo·gical** *adjs.*, **-ally** *adv.*, **Immuno·logist.** So **Immu·no-**, used as comb. form in terms relating to this, as *immuno-chemical* adj., *-chemistry, -reaction, -toxin, -transfusion.*

Imperial, *sb.* 6. [The appearance of this sense much earlier than the date (1852) at which Louis Napoleon became emperor makes the current derivation improbable.]

1839 S. WARREN *Ten Thousand a Year* i, An i.—i.e. a dirt-coloured tuft of hair..1841 *Knickerbocker Mag.* XVII. 460..Two wigs, moustaches, an i. 1843 THACKERAY *Irish Sk. Bk.* i.

Importune, *v.* 5. *spec.*, mostly in pres. pple. and gerund: To solicit persons for an unlawful purpose.

Improver. 1. b. An emigrant to an English colony. Now *Hist.*

The two vessels moored off Blackwall and about to sail in a day or two for Port Nicholson with improvers 1841 *Times* 18 Sept.

In, *adv.* II. 2. h. Gathered in, garnered.

When the harvest was well in 1942.

attrib. **in-tray,** a tray in which are placed correspondence and documents that have arrived in an office to be dealt with. So *out-tray.*

A habit of having secret papers placed in 'In' or 'Out' trays on the desks of important officers 1943. One has the impression that these two Italian bosses never really cleared their in-trays W. S. CHURCHILL 1947.

‖**In,** L. prep.

20. **in vitro** ['in glass']: said of physiological reaction taking place in test tubes, etc., or of cultures grown in the laboratory; 21. **in vivo** ['in the living (subject)']: said of cultures and reactions taking place within a living organism.

Ina·ctivate, *v. trans.* To render inactive.

Inc., U.S. abbrev. of INCORPORATED 1909.

Incendiary, *a.* 1. b. *esp.* of a type of aerial bomb; also as *sb.* 1940.

Incessive (inse·siv), *a.* [f. L. *incess-*, ppl. stem of *incedere* go forward + -IVE.] Proceeding by stages.

Precedents..for easing prominent Communist leaders into jail by i. steps 1951.

‖**Incommunicado** (i:nkǫmūnikā·dǫ). 1844. [Sp., pp. of *incomunicar* to deprive of communication; see IN-³, COMMUNICATE.] Having no means of communication; in solitary confinement.

Indamine (i·ndămīn). 1940. [f. IND(IGO + AMINE.] *Chem.* Any of a series of organic compounds that form bluish or greenish salts.

Index.

i. **number** *Statistics*, a number used in comparing the value of an attribute at a certain time with its value at a standard time.

Indicane (i·ndikēⁱn). 1940. [f. L. *indicum* INDIGO + -ANE.] *Chem.* A glucoside occurring in plants yielding indigo.

Indicate, *v.* 1. b. *pass.* To be shown or appear to be desirable or necessary 1907.

Induct, *v.* 3. *U.S.* To bring or introduce into military service.

United Nations truce delegates charged yesterday that the Communists had 'forcibly inducted a sizable bloc' of the 50,000 Republic of Korea troops listed as missing 1951.

Indulge, *v.* II. 3. To partake (too) freely of intoxicants (*colloq.*)

Industry. 4. b. The activities (considered collectively) which are concerned with the winning and manipulation of natural resources, and the production (and distribution) of goods.

[The funds destined for the maintenance of i. are much greater..in proportion than they were two or three centuries ago ADAM SMITH 1776.] The Leaders of I...are virtually the Captains of the World CARLYLE 1843.

Inferiority (infiᵊriǫ·rĭti). 1599. [f. INFERIOR + -ITY.]

i. **complex** [COMPLEX *sb.* 6], a state of mind arising from a person's real or supposed inferiority; *colloq.* an excessively modest estimate of oneself.

Infra-red, *a.* 1881. [INFRA-.] Applied to invisible rays beyond the red end of the spectrum.

Inhibition. 3. *Physiol.* A reduction of activity or excitement. 4. *Psychol.* The blocking of a process by another; also *colloq.* in looser use, an inner hindrance to conduct or activity.

Injun, dial. U.S. var. of INDIAN *sb.* 2. 1812. *Honest I.*: honour bright; perh. orig. an assurance of good faith extracted from American Indians 1876. *To play I.*: to act like an Indian, avoid being seen or captured 1918.

Injunctive (indʒʊ·ŋktiv), *a.* 1624. [f. ppl. stem of L. *injungere* to ENJOIN; see -IVE.] Having the quality of enjoining; *Gram.* applied to a form of a verb having secondary personal endings and expressing injunction.

Innards (i·nəɹdz), dial. and vulgar pronunc. of *inwards* (see INWARD *a.* B. *sb.*), freq. used joc. by cultured speakers 1787.

Inner, *a.*

i. **reserve,** a secret reserve not disclosed in a balance sheet and due to understatement of capital assets 1930; i. **tube,** the separate inflatable tube inside the cover of a pneumatic tire 1902.

Inoperable (inǫ·părăb'l), *a.* 1886. [ad. F. *inopérable*; see IN-³ and OPERABLE.] That cannot be operated upon.

Inseminate, *v.* b. To impregnate with semen, spec. by artificial means. So **Insemina·tion, Inse·minator.**

Inside, *sb.* 1. e. *The inside*: the inner history, the real facts (*colloq.*) 1904; *adj.* d. Confined in prison, imprisoned, incarcerated (*slang*).

inst. = instant (i.e. of the current calendar month).

Instantiate (instæ·nʃiēⁱt), *v.* [f. L. *instantia* INSTANCE *sb.* + -ATE ³.] *trans.* To represent by an instance. So **Instantiation** (instænʃiēⁱ·ʃən), representation by an instance.

Everything about the universal which distinguishes its instantiation in one case from its instantiation in another must be itself particular...This universal is clearly not instantiated by either apple 1951.

‖**Instar** (i·nstāɹ). 1895. [L., = form, figure, likeness.] *Zool.* Any one of the periods of an insect's life between two successive ecdyses.

Instinctual (insti·ŋktiuăl), *a.* [f. L. *instinctus* INSTINCT + -AL ¹.] Of or pertaining to, involving or depending upon, instinct.

Insurance. 4. d. For 'the Acts of 1911 and 1920' read 'the Acts of 1911, 1920, and 1946'.

Intake, *sb.* 1. b. A person or thing taken in or admitted.

When new intakes arrive and..are interviewed 1943.

Intelligence.

i. **quotient** *Psychol.*, a number intended to express the ratio of a given person's i. to the normal or the average; so i. **test.** 1921.

Inter. (i·ntəɹ), abbrev. of *Intermediate* (*Examination*), often used colloq. for this.

‖**Inter,** L. prep.: *inter vivos*, among persons living.

In 1931 decedent had created a large inter vivos trust 1947.

Interceptor. *spec.* An aeroplane having the task of intercepting enemy raiders 1940.

Intercom (i·ntəɹkǫm). [abbrev.] A system of intercommunication in aircraft.

Interdiction. 4. *U.S.* The interruption of transport operations, as by aerial bombing.

Interlocutor ¹. c. The compère of a nigger minstrel troupe 1909.

Intermediate, *sb.* 3. *Chem.* A compound which is manufactured from a substance obtained directly from raw materials, and which is used as a basis for the synthesis of another product.

International. B. b.

The Revived I. On Saturday, June 30th, 1951..the Socialist I. was reconstructed, at a meeting held in Frankfurt-on-Main *Political Quarterly* XXII (1951) 335. The founders of the Labour and Socialist I. of 1923 *Ibid.*

Internship (intō·ɹnʃip). *U.S.* 1924. [f. INTERN + -SHIP.] The condition of an intern; the period of such condition.

I·nterphase. [INTER- II. 1.] An intervening phase.

I·nterphone. *U.S.* [f. INTER- II. 3 + PHONE *sb.*²] A telephone system connecting offices or departments in an establishment.

Interpol (i·ntəɹpǫl). 1923. International Criminal Police Commission.

Interpo·se, *v.* 1. *Chess.* To move (a piece) so as to protect one that is threatened; also *intr.* of the piece 1761.

Into, *prep.* 4. c. Used with *elect*, †*choose*, and the like. (The customary usage in the University of Cambridge.)

Last night we chose Mr. Vesey into our club JOHNSON 3 April 1773.

Intri·guing, *ppl. a.* In sense of INTRIGUE *v.* I. b. 1909.

Introjection (introdʒe·kʃən). [f. INTRO- + -*jection* of *injection*, etc.] *Psycho-analysis.* The unconscious process by which an image representing an external object is incorporated into the psychic equipment of a person.

Intruder. 3. An aeroplane (or its pilot) that invades the enemy's aerodromes to interfere with his operations. Also *attrib.*, as *i. raid.* So **Intru·ding** *ppl. a.*, **Intru·sion** 1940.

Inveigle, *v.* Add pronunciation (invēⁱ·g'l).

inv. et del., abbrev. of L. *invenit et delineavit* 'designed and drew', identifying the artist of an engraving or etching.

Invoice, *v.* To send an invoice to.

Mod. I. me on despatch of the volume at the special pre-publication price of 6 guineas.

Inwards, *sb. pl.*: see INWARD *a.*, B. *sb.* Cf. *INNARDS.

Ionium (əiˌōᵘ·niŭm). 1907. [f. ION + -IUM.] *Chem.* A radioactive element obtained from uranium and notable for its ionization of the surrounding air.

Ionosphere (əiˌǫ·nosfīəɹ). 1932. [f. ION + -O- + SPHERE *sb.*] The region above the surface of the earth in which ionization takes place. Hence **Ionosphe·ric** *a.*

Ipsilateral (ipsilæ·tĕrăl), *a.* 1913. [irreg. f. L. *ipse* self + LATERAL.] *Physiol.* Belonging to the same side.

‖**Ipsissima verba** (ipsi·simă vō·ɹbă). 1807. [L., n. pl. of *ipsissimus*, superl. of *ipse* the same, and pl. of *verbum* word.] The very identical words.

Iron, *sb.*¹

i. **curtain,** a curtain of i. which can be lowered in order to prevent passage or communication or for protection. The utility of an i. curtain and a reservoir of water in case of fire 1794; *fig.* of an impenetrable barrier, (spec. with caps.) that preventing free course of information and intercourse between communist-controlled countries and the rest of the world. [On the 19th November we crossed the river Betwah, and as if an i. curtain had dropt between us and the avenging angel, the deaths diminished EARL OF MUNSTER *Jrnl.* 1817.] That an i. curtain had dropped between him and the outer world 1904. [At Petrograd] We were behind the 'i. curtain' at last MRS. SNOWDEN 1920. [(Goebbels in *Das Reich*:) If the German people lay down their arms, the whole of eastern and south-eastern Europe, together with the Reich, would come under Russian occupation. Behind an i. screen, mass butcheries of peoples would begin *Times* (1945) 28 Feb.] In the east the i. curtain behind which.. the work of destruction goes on is moving steadily forward *Ibid.* (1945) 3 May. The I. Curtain of Bolshevism has come down across Europe *Ibid.* (1946) 17 Aug. The peasantry..became a depressed class indeed; the i. curtain descended on their activities VAUGHAN WILLIAMS, 1948.

i. **lung,** an i. case fitted over the body of a patient (leaving the head free), used for the prolonged administration of artificial respiration by means of mechanical pumps; i. **ration,** an emergency ration of tinned food (and biscuits) 1876.

Irradiate, *v.* I. c. *trans.* To subject to the action of X-rays, ultra-violet rays, or the like. So **Irradia·tion.** 1903.

Irredeemable, *sb.* An irredeemable stock.

Prices of most stocks stood at their lowest for twenty years, with irredeemables offering flat yields ranging up to..4⅝ per cent. 1952.

‖**Ischæmia** (iskī·miă). 1866. [mod.L., f. Gr. ἴσχαιμος, f. ἰσχειν to hold or keep back, staunch + αἷμα blood.] *Path.* Bloodlessness (of some part of the body). Hence **Ischæ·mic** *a.*

-ish ². b. Extended irreg. in *aamonish, distinguish, extinguish, relinquish.*

Island, *sb.* 2. d. *Naut.* A ship's superstructure, bridge, etc.

Isle of Wight (əiləvwəi·t). 1908. Name of the island off the coast of Hampshire designating a form of microsporidiosis infecting bees.

Isolationist (əisǒlēⁱ·ʃənist). 1899. [See -IST.] One who favours a policy of (political or national) isolation, esp. in U.S. So **Isola·tionism.**

Issue, *sb.* V. d. Widely used for: Problem, question, object or matter of inquiry, subject of discussion, or the like.

If the re-shuffling of the world goes on producing new 'issues' 1933.

Issue, *v.* II. 5. Also without *with.*

Before we were i-d our heavy trench shoes 1930. We were i-d instructions not to say 'i-d with' (*mod.*).

It, *pron.* II. 5. *slang* or *colloq.* Sexual congress.

Fretiller..lust to be at it COTGRAVE 1611. [Cf. Lady Wishfort in Congreve's *The Way of the World*, 1700.]

It [2] (it). Short for *It(alian vermouth)*; e.g. *a gin and it.*

I was sipping my gin-and-it before lunch 1932.

Italic, *a.* Pertaining to the older Latin version of the Bible known as Vetus Itala.

The Old Italic Version forms the basis of the one on which St. Jerome wrote the *Commentarium ad Paulum et Eustochium* 1861.

Ivory.

i. tower [tr. F. *tour d'ivoire* (used by Sainte-Beuve concerning Alfred de Vigny)]: a condition of seclusion or separation from the world, (gen.) protection or shelter from the crudities of life 1917 (Henry James). Also applied trivially to the teeth.

J. III.

J.A. = Justice of Appeal; J.A.(G.) = Judge Advocate (General); J.T.C. = Junior Training Corps.

Jaffa (dʒæ·fă). 1897. [mod. (Arabic) name of *Joppa*, ancient seaport of Palestine.] In full, *J. orange*, one of the kind grown in the gardens east of Joppa.

Jam, *sb.*[1] **1.** *spec.* An accumulation of logs, driftwood, etc. in a river 1805; *transf.* an awkward situation, fix (*slang*).

Jam, *sb.*[1] or *sb.*[2] *attrib.* **j. music,** music simultaneously extemporized by all taking part. Also *j. session.* 1938.

Janeite (dʒē·nəit). [f. *Jane*, Christian name of Jane Austen (1775–1817), English novelist + -ITE[1] **1.**] A devotee of Jane Austen and her writings.

Now Dr. Chapman places 'Janeites' even more deeply in his debt *Ann. Register for 1933*, 32.

Jaspe (dʒɑsp), **Jaspé** (dʒɑ·spe). 1851. [orig. F. *jaspé*, pa. pple. of *jasper* to marble.] Of variegated, mottled, or 'shot' colour or design.

Jean. 2. *pl.* Overalls, (latterly) slacks 1879.

Jeep (dʒīp). 1942. [Said to have been f. *g p* (dʒī pī), initials of *general purposes.*] A small utility motor truck.

Jehovah. *J.'s Witnesses*: 'International Bible Students', a religious sect which rejects institutional religion, recognizing the authority of Jehovah alone and refusing to acknowledge the claims of the State when in conflict with their principles.

Jellygraph (dʒe·ligrɑf). 1900. [f. JELLY *sb.* + -GRAPH.] A copying apparatus, of which the essential part is a sheet of jelly. Also as vb.

Jeminy (dʒe·mini), var. of GEMINI **3.**

Jerk, *sb.*[1] **2. c.** (*Physical*) *j-s*, the motions practised in physical training (*colloq.*) 1919.

Jerry. By association with *German* used in the British Army in World War I as a joc. designation of the German soldier.

Jerusalem. *The New J.*: the Heavenly City, the abode of God and the Saints (see Rev. xxi. 2).

Jesse (dʒe·sĭ). *U.S.* 1840. [perh. from a joc. perversion of 'There shall come forth a *rod* out of the stem of *Jesse*' (*Isa.* xi. 1).] *To give* (a person) *J.*: to handle him severely; also *to get jesse.*

Jet, *sb.*[3] Applied to the propulsion of aircraft by means of the discharge from a nozzle of a volume of compressed air and fuel vapour without the use of an airscrew; e.g. *jet-engine, -engined, -fighter, -propelled, -propulsion* 1936. Also ellipt. for jet aircraft.

Jetted (dʒe·tėd), *ppl. a.* 1923. [f. JET *v.*[2] + -ED[1].] *Tailoring.* Of a pocket: Having no flap, but an outside seam on either edge, called the Je·tting.

‖**Jeune premier** (ʒön prəmye). 1852. [F., 'first young man'.] An actor who plays the part of the principal lover or young hero. So the fem. ‖Jeune première.

‖**Jeunesse dorée** (ʒönęs dore). 1837. [F., 'gilded youth'.] orig. In France, a group of fashionable counter-revolutionaries; later, young men of wealth and fashion.

Jig, *sb.* **5. d.** An appliance that holds a piece of work and guides the tools operating upon it 1913.

Jigger, *sb.*[1] **5.** A woman's short outdoor coat.

Jimmy. *J. the One* (Naval slang): the First Lieutenant 1916.

Jimp, *a.* Special collocation:

j.-pin, a small pin-shaped nail for tacking.

Jinx (dʒiŋks). *U.S.* 1911. [perh. var. spelling of JYNX (in the sense 'charm, spell').] A person or thing that brings bad luck.

Jitney. *U.S. attrib.* or as *adj.* Cheap 1916.

Jitter (dʒi·təɹ), *v.* orig. *U.S.* [?] *intr.* To be nervous, act nervously. *Comb.* **Ji·tterbug,** (*a*) a person who dances to hot-rhythm music; (*b*) a nervous person. So **Ji·tters** *sb. pl.*, extreme nervousness 1931; **Ji·ttery** *a.* [-Y[1]], nervy, jumpy.

Jive (dʒəiv). 1946. A very fast and noisy type of syncopated instrumental music.

Job, *sb.*[1] **4. b.** A paid position of employment, 'situation' (*colloq.*) 1861.

Job, *v.*[2] **8.** To sell at a scrap price stock of a book to a bookseller, who sells it as he can.

Jock (dʒǫk). 1508. [Sc. var. of JACK.] **1.** By-form for *John*; a man, esp. of the common people. **b.** *Army slang.* A Scotch soldier 1931. **2.** A countryman, rustic 1568.

Jodhpur (dʒǫ·dpŭɹ). 1899. [Native state in Rajputana, India.] Name of a kind of riding-breeches combining breeches and gaiters in one piece.

Joe, *sb.*[2] **1. b.** phr. *Not for Joe*, not on any account.

[I have had seven invitations to public meetings this week..Not for Joseph! Jos. CHAMBERLAIN 1877.]

‖**Joie de vivre** (ʒwa d vīvr). 1901. [F., 'joy of living'.] A feeling of healthy enjoyment of life.

Jonathan. b. An American variety of dessert apple 1842.

Jordanian (dʒǫɹdē·niăn), *a.* [-IAN.] Of or pertaining to the territory of Jordan.

The refugees..aided by Jordanian and Egyptian officials 1953.

Josh (dʒǫʃ), *sb.* *U.S. slang.* 1896. [?] Banter, bandinage. So **Josh** *v.* 1887.

Judder (dʒʊ·dəɹ), *sb.* 1946 (F. C. Field-Hyde). [Imitative.] *Music.* Action consisting of rapid changes of intensity in the emission of a tone.

Judo (dʒū·do). 1892. [Jap., f. *jiu, jū* (a. Chinese *jéu, jou* soft) + *dō* (a. Chinese *tao* way.)] A form of ju-jitsu.

There is at least one jûdô society in London 1931.

Juice, *sb.* **5. b.** Electricity, electric current 1896 (*Dict. Americanisms*).

Jump, *v.* **1. c.** *To j. to it*: to take active measures. **10.** *To j. the gun*: to anticipate the firing of a pistol which starts a race; hence *fig.* to act before the permitted or agreed time.

Justice, *sb.* **II.** *High Court of J.*: see HIGH COURT.

K. IV.

= *KELVIN. K.E. = kinetic energy; K.O., k.o. = knock(ed) out; K.S.K. = Ethyl iodoacetate, CH_2I. COO Et. (a lachrymator); kW = kilowatt(s). **b.** In names of regiments = King's.

Kabyle (kăbəi·l). 1818. [Arab. *qabā'il*, pl. of *qabīlah* (tribal name).] A Berber of Algeria or Tunis.

‖**Kadir** (kā·dəɹ). 1879. (The alluvial deposit of) a river bed in India.

Kalmuck (kæ̆·lmək). (A member of) a Tatar race living on the Caspian Sea.

‖**Kamerad** (kæ·mərād, ‖kamərā·t). 1914. [G., ad. F. *camarade* COMRADE.] The exclamation used as an appeal for quarter by a German-speaking soldier on surrendering. Hence *transf.* (usu. *joc.*) as a plea for mercy; also as *v. intr.* to say 'kamerad', surrender.

Kamptulicon. Trade name of a floor covering patented by E. Galloway in 1844.

Kanarese, var. of *CANARESE.

‖**Kaput** (kapu·t), *a.* (in predic. use). *slang.* [G.] Finished, done for.

Karma, karmic. 'Some theosophists pronounce 'kəːmə, 'kəːmik, thus distinguishing these words from *kama, kamic*' (D. Jones, *English Pronouncing Dict.*).

Karri-cot (kæ·rikǫt). [*Karri-* for CARRY *v.*] Proprietary name for a portable child's cot.

Karst (kāɹst). The name of a barren limestone plateau between Carniola and the Adriatic, marked by abrupt ridges, caverns, sinks, and underground streams; *Geol.* applied to a region or scenery of similar type.

The k.-forms of the glaciers of the Austrian Alps 1895.

Kation (kæt,əi·ǫ̆n), var. of CATION.

Keel, *sb.*[1] **3. b.** In aircraft, a vertical fin which extends longitudinally underneath in order to give directional stability 1907.

Keep, *v.* **II. 6.** *To k. wicket*: to act as wicket-keeper (see WICKET 2) 1887.

‖**Keeshond** (kē·shǫnd). Also **-hound.** 1927. [Du., f. *Kees* Cornelius + *hond* HOUND.] A Dutch barge dog.

Kelt: see CELT [1].

Kelvin (ke·lvin). 1892. [Name of Sir William Thomson, Lord *Kelvin* (1824–1907).] The kilowatt-hour, the ordinary commercial unit of electric energy.

Kerb, *sb.* **3.** *U.S. Stock Exchange.* 'The street' 1894.

Kerry (ke·ri). [Name of a county in S.W. Ireland.] **1.** A breed of cows raised in K. 1880. **2.** *K. Blue (terrier)*, a breed of Irish terrier with a blue-grey coat 1922.

Keto (kī·tou), comb. form of KETONE, as in *keto-compound, -enol, -form*; *ketoge·nic* adj. 1891.

Key, *sb.* **II. 4.** *Chess.* In full, *k. move*: the first move in a problem game 1878.

Key, *v.* **5.** To distinguish (an advertisement) by some device of wording, etc. intended to identify answers to it (orig. *U.S.*) 1905.

‖**Khor** (kǭɹ). [a. Arab. *khurr, khorr.*] A water-course, ravine.

Kid, *sb.*[1] **3. b.** Also *attrib.*, as in phr. *with k. gloves*: with mild treatment 1864.

Kill, *sb.*[1] **2. b.** The destruction or putting out of action of a submarine, aircraft, etc.

Killer. 4. A murderous ruffian. *U.S.* 1885.

Kilo-. Kilo(gram) calorie, the great, large, or major CALORIE 1899.

Kimmeridge. Hence **Kimmeri·dgian** *a.* 1863.

Kissage (ki·sedʒ). *nonce-wd.* [f. KISS *v.* + -AGE.] Kissing.

Favouritism governed k. KIPLING.

Kite, *sb.* **3. b.** A proposal, suggestion, or experiment made in order to test personal or public feeling 1902. Cf. *BALLON D'ESSAI. **5. b.** *R.A.F. slang.* An aeroplane 1917.

Klondyke, -dike (klǫ·ndəik). 1897. [Name of a district in Yukon, N.W. Canada, the scene of a gold rush in the years following 1896.] **1.** *fig.* A 'mine' or 'quarry' of valuable material 1897. **2.** An American card game 1908. **3.** The herring fishery off the W. coast of Scotland 1909. Hence **Klo·ndyke** *v.*, to export (fresh herring) by fast steamer to the Continent 1923.

Knee, *sb.* *Comb.* **k.-high** *a.* *U.S.*, of such a height as to reach to the knee 1799; also in *k.-high to a duck, frog*, etc., comparisons indicating the youthfulness of those so described.

‖**Kne·sset(h).** The Israeli parliament.

Knife-and-fork. *attrib.* Applied to a meal for which a knife and fork are provided or are necessary.

Knob, *sb.* **1.** phr. *With k-s on*: joc. slang phr. indicating the speaker's mock approval of something that has been said; only more so.

Knock, *sb.* **1.** *To take the k.*: to be hard hit financially (*slang*) 1890.

Know, *v.* **III.** colloq. phr. *Don't you know*, a variant of *you know* 1896. *I want to know*: Well, well! Is it possible? *U.S.* 1840. *What do you know (about that)?*: Isn't that amazing!, Well I never! *U.S.* 1914.

Know-how (nōu·hau). 1857. (*Dict. Americanisms*).

Knut (k(ə)nʊt). Fanciful var. of NUT *sb.* I. 6.

He, Timothy Gray, bhoy, lad, knut. *Granta* (1911) 136.

Kolinsky (kǫli·nski). 1851. [Russ., f. *Kola*, a district in N.W. Russia.] The fur of the Siberian mink.

‖**Ko·lkhoz.** [Russ.] A collective farm.

Krilium (kri·liǫ̆m). 1952. [f. *-cryl-* of *acrylonitile* + -IUM.] Proprietary name of a synthetic powder, obtained from acrylonitile, used to condition soil for the reception of nutrients.

‖**Kulak** (kū·læk). 1886. [Russ., 'fist, tight-fisted person'.] A well-to-do Russian peasant, farmer, or trader; under the Soviet régime, a peasant-proprietor working for his own profit.

‖**Kuomintang** (kwomiŋdaŋ). 1912. [Chinese, 'national people's party'.] The nationalist radical party in China.

L. III.

L on a plate or card affixed to a motor vehicle indicating that the driver is a *l*earner; L.C.(T.) = Landing Craft (Tank); L.C.C. = London County Council; L.D.V. = Local Defence Volunteers (which became the Home Guard) 1940; L.P.T.B. = London Passenger Transport Board; L.S.I. = Labour and Socialist International; L.T., l.t. = low tension.

‖**Laager,** *sb.* **b.** A park for armoured vehicles.

Labour, *sb.* **2. c.** The labouring classes as a political force, party, or organization; representatives of these, e.g. in parliament, considered as a body. Also *attrib.* passing into *adj.*: Belonging to the Labour Party or holding opinions favourable to their (political) claims or aspirations. 1870.

Mod. What is Labour going to do? He has been Labour ever since he attained manhood. Hence **La·bourite,** a supporter of the interests of L. 1887.

Lachrymator (læ·krimēitəɹ). 1938. Also lacrim-. [f. L. *lacrima* tear + *-ATOR.] Lachrymatory poison gas, tear gas.

Ladder, *sb.* **2.** Delete 'recently' and add the following quotation:

He had been diverted by observing a fracture (or what a sempstress would term a *ladder*) in the back part of His Majesty's black silk stockings. MRS. MATTHEWS *Mem. Charles Matthews* II (1838) 246.

Ladin (lædī·n). 1879. [Rumansch; ad. L. *Latinus* LATIN.] The Rhæto-Romanic language spoken in the Engadine in Switzerland.

Lady, *sb.* **4.** pl. *Ladies,* designation of a public convenience for female persons. (Cf. *GENTLEMAN.)

Lallans (læ·lənz). 1785. [Sc. var. of *Lowlands* (see LOWLAND A. 2.)] Lowland Scottish; the vernacular speech of the Lowlands of Scotland, latterly in respect of its status as a literary language.

They..spak their thochts in plain braid Lallans BURNS *Ep. Wm. Simpson of Ochiltree.* Thochts anent Lallans prose D. YOUNG in *New Alliance and Sc. Rev.* Apr. 1947.

Lambeth walk (læ·mbeþ wǭk). 1938. Name of a London street on the south side of the Thames, used to designate a dance marked by a walk and gestures held to be characteristic of this part of London.

Laminate, *sb.* [subst. use of LAMINATE *a.*] A laminated structure (see LAMINATE *v.* 4), e.g. *engineering l-s.*

Land, *sb.*

l.-mine, (*a*) an explosive mine used on land 1918; (*b*) pop. a parachute mine; **l.-plane,** an aeroplane designed to take off from and alight on dry land 1923.

Land, *v.* **I. 1. b.** To place (aircraft, passengers, etc.) on the ground again; to bring to earth from the air 1918.

Landfall. 1. c. The act of reaching land after an air voyage over water 1908.

Landing-place. 1. b. A place for the landing of aircraft 1902.

‖**Langur** (lɒ·ŋguəɹ). 1826. [Hindī; cf. Skr. *lāṅgūlin* tailed.] A long-tailed monkey of India, e.g. the entellus.

Lanosterol (lănǫ·stĕrǫl). 1929. [f. irreg. comb. form of L. *lana* wool + STEROL.] *Chem.* One of the sterols occurring in wool grease, formerly called *isocholesterol.*

Lapse, *sb.*

l. rate *Meteorol.,* the rate of fall of temperature with height 1928.

Large, *a.,* etc. **C. At l.:** (also) in full, in unabridged form 1569.

A Chronicle at l. and meere History of the affayres of England 1569. The whole volume of the Statutes at l. 1587. Trials at L. (A. Thistlewood) 1817.

Laryngeal (lări·ndʒĭăl). **b.** *Philology.* A hypothetical phonetic element of a laryngeal quality supposed to have existed in Proto-Indo-European and to have left traces in the vocalic features of extant Indo-European languages.

I reconstruct in terms of the so-called 'laryngeal theory', here, however, without committing myself to the number of laryngeals necessarily to be assumed at a given time 1952.

La·sh-up. [f. phr. *lash-up*; see LASH *v.*² 2.] A temporary connexion of apparatus for experiment or in an emergency.

Last, *a.* **1.** *L. across*: a children's game consisting in trying who shall be the last to cross a road safely in front of an approaching vehicle 1904.

‖**Lat** (læt). [First syll. of *Latvija.*] A unit of gold currency established in Latvia in 1912.

Latin, *a.* *L. square,* a square conceived as consisting of n letters, $a, b, c, \ldots, n$, arranged in a square lattice of n^2 compartments, all the compartments being occupied so that no letter occurs twice in the same row or in the same column.

The 1951 experiments in which five varieties were planted on the same date in a L.-square layout 1952.

A. 4. b, B. *L. American*: of or pertaining to (a national of) *L. America,* the designation of those parts of Central and South America in which Spanish or Portuguese is the dominant language 1903.

Lay·-out. 2. *U.S.* A set, party, gang 1809.

Lead, *sb.*¹

l. wool [WOOL *sb.* 2 b], lead in a fibrous state used for jointing water-pipes.

Lead, *v.*¹ **I. 5. b.** To ply (a witness) with leading questions.

Lea·d-in. 1913. [LEAD *v.*¹ 8.] *Wireless.* The wire or other conductor connecting an aerial to a receiver.

Leading, *ppl. a.*

l. edge, (*a*) the forward edge of the blade of a screw-propeller 1877; (*b*) the foremost edge of the wing, tailplane, or fin of an aeroplane 1912.

Leap-frog. Used to describe movements of troops passing through and replacing those of the same side exhausted in the fighting 1918.

Lease-lend. [LEASE *v.*³, LEND *v.*¹] Applied orig. in 1941 to an arrangement whereby material aid was to be leased or lent by the U.S.A. to nations at war with Germany and Italy; later extended to similar assistance given to other countries and to the mutual assistance of the United Nations. Also as *v.*, and in the (later) reversed form **Lend-lease,** and attrib.

The passage through the United States Congress of the Lease and Lend Bill [11 March] *Ann. Reg. 1941.*

‖**Lebensraum** (lē·bənzraum). 1939. [G., f. genit. of *leben* life + *raum* space, ROOM.] The area claimed by the Germans for their due development; also *transf.*

Leftism (le·ftiz'm). 1920. [-ISM.] The political views of 'the left'. Hence **Le·ftist.** So **Le·ftish** *a.,* inclined to 'the left'.

Left-wing (see LEFT A. 2); frequent in attrib. use, as *l. element, member, view* 1922. Hence **Le·ft-wi·ngism.**

Le·ft-wi·nger. [f. prec. + -ER¹.] **1.** A player on the left wing in games. **2.** A left-wing politician.

‖**Legionnaire** (līdʒənēə·ɹ). 1927. [ad. F. *légionnaire,* f. *légion* LEGION 1 b.] A member of the American, British, Foreign, or other Legion.

Lemma². **2.** *Bot.* The lower palea of an inflorescence.

Length, etc. Add to pronuncs. (leŋkþ), (le·ŋkþ'n), etc.

length-man, a railway employé charged with the maintenance of a section of the permanent way 1927.

Leninism (le·niniz'm). 1919. [f. *Lenin,* assumed name of Vladimir Ilyich Ulianov (1870–1924), a leader in the Russian Revolution of 1917.] The principles or policy of Lenin.

Lenition (līni·ʃən). 1913. [f. L. *lenis* smooth + -ITION, after G. *lenierung.*] *Philol.* The soft mutation in Welsh; the aspiration in Irish. So **Lenited** (lī·nəitėd) *ppl. a.,* having been subjected to lenition; also **U·nlenited** *a.*

Continental scholars use 'Lenition' as a term embracing the Welsh 'soft mutation' and the corresponding Irish 'aspiration' 1913. Non-syllabic sounds between two vowels..were lenited 1937. Prepositions and conjunctions which appear sometimes in their radical, sometimes in their lenited, form 1948. A soft mutation (lenition) of the plosives *p, t, k* which change to *b, d, g* 1951.

Lepper (le·pəɹ). Local var. of LEAPER, freq. in hunting parlance.

Lesbian, *sb.* [*Lesbos* was the birthplace of Sappho.] = SAPPHIST. Hence **Le·sbianism.**

Lethality. (Delete *rare.*)

The new fighters being introduced into the R.A.F. will in due course be equipped with powerful air-to-air guided weapons which will increase their lethality by perhaps four times. *White Paper on Defence* 18 Feb. 1954.

Letter, *sb.* *attrib.* and *Comb.* **2.**

l.-box 1772 (*Dict. Amer. Eng.*).

Leucotomy (lūkǫ·tŏmi). [f. Gr. λευκός white + -TOMY.] *Surg.* Incision into the frontal lobe of the brain.

‖**Lev** (lef). Pl. **leva** (lē·va). 1908. [Bulg. *lev* lion.] The monetary unit of Bulgaria.

Level, *sb.* **I. 2. b.** *On the l.*: (in a) fair, honest, or straightforward (way); honestly speaking (*U.S. colloq.*) 1875.

4. Also, a plane or status in respect of rank or authority, e.g. *consultation at cabinet l., action taken at the highest l., a system of high-l. consultations* 1951.

How long it takes to get even a simple low-l. decision *Economist* 20 Sept. 1952.

Lewis gun (lū·is gɒn). 1916. [f. name of the inventor, Col. Isaac Newton *Lewis,* of the U.S. army.] A light magazine-fed gas-operated and air-cooled machine gun.

Lewisite (lū·isəit). 1937. [f. name of W. J. *Lewis*; see -ITE¹.] A blister gas (chlorovinyl dichlorarsine) for use in chemical warfare.

Ley (lēi), var. of LEA *sb.*², established in agriculturists' use, e.g. *l.-farming.*

Liaise (liē·z), *v.* *Service slang.* [Back-formation from LIAISON.] *intr.* To make liaison *with.*

Liberal, *a.* **3. c.** Not rigidly or precisely observed or defined; not to be taken or interpreted strictly; (at such a time, etc.) or thereabouts.

Breakfasted at nine—a l. nine TROLLOPE 1867. (*Mod. colloq.*) What time is tea? Oh, a l. four o'clock. So **Li·berally** *adv.,* not strictly, precisely, or rigidly.

Liberate, *v.* **b.** In the language of World War II, to free (an occupied country) of the enemy; also *ironically,* to subject to a new tyranny. So **Liberation.**

Liberty (li·bəɹti). 1888. [Name of a London drapery firm.] (With cap. *L.*) Designation of materials, etc. sold by Messrs. L. & Co.

‖**Libido** (libəi·do, libī·do). 1913. [L., 'desire, lust'.] *Psychol.* An emotion prompting a human (esp. sexual) activity.

Lib-Lab (li·blæ·b), abbrev. of *Liberal-Labour,* denoting a member of the Labour party who has affiliations with the Liberals 1906.

Lickety-split (li·kəti,spli·t), *adv.* 1859. *U.S.* At full speed, 'full lick', headlong.

‖**Lido** (lī·do). 1930. [Venetian It. *lido*:—L. *litus* shore.] Name of a bathing-place near Venice, used gen. for: A public open-air swimming-pool.

Lie, *sb.*² **1. b.** *Golf.* The angle of the club-head with the shaft, e.g. *a flat l., an upright l.* (Encycl. Brit. 1910).

Life. Phrases. *Not on your l.*: not on any account, by no means 1905. (*You*) *bet your l.,* you can be sure 1852. *To save one's l.,* for the life of one 1863. *Such is l.,* an expression signifying acquiescence in whatever happens 1849. *Life-and-death,* attrib. phr.: involving life and death, vitally important 1863.

Lift, *sb.*² **I. 1.** Transport by air (cf. **air-lift*); a number of persons or an amount of supplies so transported.

That the United Kingdom will provide the troop-lift, troops..and shipping.. Transports..with a lift of 52,000 men 1942.

5. *Pros.* An element of high intensity in an alliterative measure, marked by stress or tone 1894. = G. *Hebung.*

Light, *sb.* **5.** Mil. *Lights out*: the last bugle-call of the day, being the signal for all lights to be put out 1868.

Lighter, *sb.*² **b.** *spec.* An instrument for producing a light, consisting usu. of a reservoir containing fuel which is ignited by friction of a steel wheel on a flint.

Like, *adv.* **5.** Golf. *Like as we lie*: applied to the position when both sides have played the same number of strokes.

Limburger (li·mbɔ̄ːɹgəɹ). 1887. [Du., G.] A soft cheese made in the province of Limburg.

Limehouse (ləi·mhaus), *v.* 1913. [f. name of a district of E. London.] *intr.* To make fiery political speeches as Mr. David Lloyd George did at Limehouse in 1909.

Lime-juicer (ləi·mdʒūːsəɹ). 1859. [f. *lime juice* (LIME *sb.*[2]) + -ER [1].] **a.** *Austral.* One who has lately made a voyage from England. **b.** *U.S.* A British sailor or ship, so called because in the British Navy the consumption of lime juice is enforced 1884.

Limp, *v.*[2] **b.** Of a vessel, etc.: To proceed slowly and with difficulty because of damage.

Line, *sb.*[1] **II. 6.** *To get (give) a l. on*: to gain (provide with) a direction or clue to 1903.

Line, *sb.*[2] **V. 1. d.** *Golf.* 'The direction in which the hole towards which the player is progressing lies with reference to the present position of the ball' (*Encycl. Brit.* 1910).

Liner [1]. **2. d.** A removable metal lining to prevent wear and tear in guns or machinery.

Liner [2]. **II. 2. c.** An aeroplane belonging to a regular line, esp. for passenger transport; an air-liner.

Lining, *vbl. sb.*[2]

l.-out, the reading out of each line of a hymn by the minister, precentor, or clerk, before it is sung by the congregation.

Li·nk-up. The act or result of linking up (see LINK *v.* 3).

Lipase (li·pēiz). 1897. [f. Gr. λίπος fat + *-ASE.] *Biochemistry.* A ferment which causes the decomposition of fats and oils. So **Lipid** (li·pid), any of a group of organic compounds that constitute the fats and analogous substances; **Lipoid** (li·poid) *a.*, fat-like; *sb.*, any of a group of fatty substances such as waxes, lecithins. See -ID [4], -OID.

Lipoid changes in the gonads of wild birds *Nature* (1952) 16 Feb. 261.

Liquidate, *v.* **6.** [After Russ. *likvidírovat'*.] To put an end to, abolish, stamp out, wipe out. So **Liquida·tion.**

List, *sb.*[5] colloq. phr. *on the l.*: among the number to be dealt with or treated.

Listen, *v.* **3.** *U.S. colloq.* To sound (in a specified way) 1912.

How does it l. to you? 1921.

Lit, *ppl. a.* *L.-up*, rather drunk (*slang*) 1921.

Lit. Hum. (lit hɒm), abbrev., with corresponding pronunc., of *Literæ Humaniores* 'the more humane letters', title of a final honour school in the University of Oxford, colloq. called *Greats* (see GREAT C. II. 4).

Live, *v.* **8, 9.** phr. *To l. and let l.*, used to typify an attitude or policy of independence combined with tolerance; so *l.-and-let-l.* in attrib. use.

A live-and-let-live individualism 1947.

Liveyer, -ere (li·vyiəɹ). 1901. [f. phr. *live here.*] A permanent inhabitant of the Labrador coast.

Livid, *a.* **b.** Furiously angry, as if pale with rage (*colloq.*).

Living, *vbl. sb.* *L.-space*, tr. of *LEBENSRAUM.

Lloyd's. Also *Lloyd's Books*, 'two enormous ledger-like volumes raised on desks at right and left of the entrance to Lloyd's Room' (Brewer's *Reader's Handbook*); *Lloyd's List*, sc. of shipping, from 1726; *Lloyd's News*, a weekly bulletin of shipping news, from 1696.

Lo, *sb.*[2] *U.S.* 1874. [joc. perversion of '*Lo*, the poor Indian...' (Pope *Essay on Man* I. 99).] An American Indian. Also *Mr.* and *Mrs. Lo.*

Load, *sb.* **4. c.**

l.-shedding, reduction of the supply of electric current over a specific area, esp. with a view to adjustment of consumption.

Lobectomy (lo^u^be·ktŏmi). 1941. [f. LOBE + *-ECTOMY.] *Surg.* The operation of cutting out a lobe of a lung.

Lobo (lōu·bo). 1854. [a. Sp., 'wolf'.] *U.S.* The grey or timber wolf, *Canis griseus.*

Lobotomy (lo^u^bǫ·tŏmi). [f. comb. form of LOBE + -TOMY.] = *LEUCOTOMY.

Local, *sb.*[2] **2.** *The l.*: the public house in the immediate neighbourhood 1934.

Locarno (lokā·ɹno). Name of a town in Switzerland used to designate treaties and pacts made in October 1925 between Germany and several other European countries for the preservation of peace and the continuation of existing territorial boundaries; also *transf.* and *gen.*

Location. **7.** *Cinematography.* A place outside the studio where a film is made 1908.

Loco (lōu·ko), *a.* *U.S.* 1887. [a. Sp.; cf. LOCO [1].] Insane, crazy, 'cracked'.

Lodging (lǫ·dʒiŋ), *vbl. sb.* of LODGE *v.* *attrib.*

l. turn, an occasion or period for which a railway employé has to lodge at his place of destination before returning to his place of departure 1949.

Logical, *a.*

l. positivism *Philos.*, a form of positivism in which symbolic logic is applied (cf. G. *logistischer positivismus*, Åke Petzäll), originating in 'der Wiener Kreis'. Hence **l. positivist.**

Lolly (lǫ·li). *slang.* [Short for LOLLIPOP.] Money.

Lone, *sb.* phr. *by* or *on one's lone(s)*: by oneself (itself), all alone 1902 (Kipling).

Long, *a.* phr. *l. in the tooth*: see TOOTH.

Special collocation **l. arm,** a pole fitted with a hook, shears, etc. for lifting objects, cutting branches, etc. at or to a height beyond the ordinary reach of the arm 1890; **l. distance,** applied to a telephone service between distant places 1884; **l. letter** *Typogr.*, a letter carrying a 'long mark'; **l. pull** (see PULL *sb.* I. 2 f); **l.-short (story),** a short story of more than an average length 1929; **l. shot** *Cinematography*, a shot which includes figures or scenery at a distance; **l. suit** (SUIT *sb.* V. 3), the suit of which one holds the longest run of cards; *fig.*, one's speciality, a thing in which one excels, **l.-term,** used attrib. of a plan, policy, or the like designed to meet the circumstances of a long time ahead.

‖**Longueur** (loṅgör). 1821. [F., 'length'.] An over-lengthy tedious passage in a book, etc.; a long tedious stretch (of time).

Unnecessary *l-s* which disfigure the narrative 1887.

Lonk (lǫŋk). 1828. [var. of *Lank*, short for *Lancashire* (county of England).] A breed of sheep belonging to the moorlands of N. Lancashire and the W. Riding of Yorkshire.

Look, *sb.* **2.** *spec.* in *new l.* (see *NEW *a.*)

Looker. **1.** = *VIEWER. 1953.

Loo·k-see. [f. LOOK *v.*, SEE *v.*] Also **2.** *slang.* A telescope; a periscope 1925.

Loopy (lū·pi), *a.* *slang.* 1932. [?] Crazy, 'cracked'.

Loose, *a.*

l. change, an amount of money kept or left unsecured for casual use (orig. *U.S.*) 1827.

Lounge, *sb.*

l. hall, the hall of a house in which the amenities characteristic of a lounge are installed.

Lousy, *a.* **1. b.** 'Swarming' *with*; abundantly supplied *with* money, etc. (orig. *U.S.*) 1850.

The German lines were l. with guns (*mod.*).

Lovely, *sb.* A woman or girl of glamorous loveliness, esp. one who takes part in an entertainment or 'show'.

Lubber, *sb.*

l.'s line, mark, point, a vertical line inside a compass case, indicating the direction of the ship's head; **l.'s hole,** a hole in the platform of a ship's top to save climbing through the futtock shrouds 1772.

Lucca (lʋ·kă). 1906. [Name of a city of N. Italy.] *L. oil*, a superior quality of olive oil.

‖**Luftwaffe** (lu·ftvafə). 1936. [G., 'air-arm'.] The German air force.

‖**Lulag** (lū·læg). 1940. [G., f. *luft* air, LIFT *sb.*[1] + abbrev. of *lager* camp.] A German P. O. W. camp primarily for airmen.

Luminal (li̯ū·minæl). 1928. [ad. G., f. L. *lumin-*, *lumen* light (as a rendering of PHEN(O)-) + -AL [2].] *Chem.* Phenobarbitone or phenylethylbarbituric acid, used as a sedative.

Lusatian (li̯usēi·ʃiăn), *a.* and *sb.* 1555. [f. med.L. *Lusatia*, name of two districts (Upper and Low L.) in Germany.] Of or pertaining to, a native of, Lusatia; Wendish, a Wend.

Lutetium (li̯ūtī·ʃiɒm). 1911. [mod.L. (Urbain, 1907), f. *Lutecia* L. name of Paris + -IUM.] *Chem.* An element of the rare-earth group. Symbol Lu; atomic weight 175; atomic number 71.

‖**Lux** (lɒks). 1911. [L., 'light'.] *Physics.* The illumination produced by a light of unit intensity on a white surface at a distance of unit length.

Lyo- (ləi·o, ləiǫ·), used as comb. form of Gr. λύειν to loosen, solve, in the sense of 'solvent', as **Lyophilic** (-fi·lik) *a.*, of a colloid which is readily dispersed in an appropriate medium, **Lyophobic** (-fǫ·bik) *a.*, that resists solvents.

Lyric, *sb.* poet. applied to a singing bird.

The morning lark.. Feather'd lyric! warbling high W. THOMPSON 1757.

M. III.

m. = million (£300 m. = three hundred million pounds); M. & B. = May & Baker, style of a firm of drug-makers, used to designate their products; M.A.P. = Ministry of Aircraft Production; M.C. (*U.S.*) = Member of Congress; M.E.F. = Middle East Forces; M.G.B. = motor gunboat; M.I. = Mounted Infantry, Military Intelligence; M.O. = Medical Officer; M.O.I., M.o.I. = Ministry of Information; M.P. = military police (*U.S. pl.* MPs); m.p. = melting-point; m.p.g. = miles per gallon; m.p.h. = miles per hour; M.Q. = metol-quinol (a photographic developer); MRA = Moral Re-Armament (i.e. Buchmanism); M.S.A. = Mutual Security Agency; M.T.(C.) = Mechanical Transport (Corps); M.T.B. = motor torpedo boat; M.V.D. = *Ministerstvo Vnutrennikh Del*, Soviet Ministry of Internal Affairs; M.Y. = motor yacht.

McCoy (məkoi·). *The real M.*: the real thing, the genuine article. *U.S. slang.*

‖**Machan** (mătʃā·n). [Hind. *macān* :—Skr. *mañca(ka)*.] In India, an observation platform used in tiger-hunting.

Machine, *sb.* **4. b.** An aeroplane (short for *flying-m.*) 1909; *U.S.* a fire-engine 1859.

Mae West (mēi west). *R.A.F. slang.* [Professional name of an American film actress and entertainer 1940.] An airman's inflatable life-saving jacket.

Magdalenian (mægdălī·niăn), *a.* and *sb.* 1885. [f. MAGDALEN (for F. *Madeleine*) + -IAN.] *Archæol.* (A human being) belonging to the palæolithic period represented by remains found at La Madeleine, France

Maginot (ma·ʒino). Name of a French general, André *Maginot* (1877–1932), who designed the line of fortifications (*M. line*) extending along the eastern borders of France from Montmédy to Belfort, and in which the French placed exaggerated confidence. Hence **M.-mi·nded** *a.*, obsessed with the inviolability of the M. line; so *M. mentality.*

Maglemose (mæ·gləmōuzə). 1915. [f. *Maglemose*, Da. place-name.] Designating an early culture of which remains were found at M. So **Maglemo·sian** *a.*

Magnalium (mægnēi·liɒm). 1900. [f. MAGN(ESIUM + AL(UMINIUM + -IUM.] An alloy of magnesium and aluminium, used for articles in which lightness and rigidity are required.

Magnetic, *a.* *M. mine*, a submarine mine which is detonated by the approach of a mass of magnetic material, e.g. that of a ship 1940.

Magneto-.

m.-chemistry, that branch of science which treats of the relation of magnetic to chemical phenomena; hence **m.-chemical** *a.*

Magneton (mæ·gnētǫn). 1914. [ad. F. *magnéton*, f. *magnétique* MAGNETIC.] *Physics.* A unit of magnetic moment.

Magnetron (mæ·gnētrǫn). 1934. [f. MAGNET + *tron* of ELECTRON [2].] *Physics.* A thermionic tube containing an anode and a heated cathode, the flow of electrons from cathode to anode being controlled by an externally applied magnetic field.

Maid. **1. b.** In tailors' and dressmakers' parlance, *maids'* garments are distinguished from *women's.*

Mail, *sb.*[1]

m. order, an order for goods to be sent by post 1905; also attrib. *m. order business, firm, house.*

Mainpast (mēi·npast). 1895. [ad. AF. *meynpast*, ad. med.L. *manupastus*, f. L. *manu* abl. of *manus* hand + *pastus*, pa. pple. of *pascere* to feed (cf. PASTURE).] *Old Law.* A man's household.

Major, *a.* *M. suit* (at Bridge), spades or

hearts 1919. B. *sb.* In universities of the U.S.A., a subject to which special attention is given in a course of study 1890; hence as vb.

Make, *v.* VIII. 2. b. *To m. do* (see Do *v.* II. 5): to get along or manage *with* what is available, esp. an inferior substitute. *M. do and mend*: an economy slogan of World War II. Hence **Make-do** *attrib.* characterized by such contrivance 1923; also **Makee-do·** (*Naval slang*).

Making, *vbl. sb. pl.* (*U.S.*) paper and tobacco for rolling a cigarette 1907.

Mala-, malemute (mæ·ləmiūt). 1908. [Name of an Alaskan Eskimo tribe.] An Eskimo species of dog.

‖**Mal de mer** (mal də mɛ̄r). 1778. [F., 'malady of sea'.] Seasickness.

‖**Mali** (mā·li), var. of MALLEE¹.

Mamba (mæ·mbă). 1890. [ad. Kaffir *m'namba.*] Any of the venomous African tree snakes of the genus *Dendraspis.*

Mammato- (mæmē·to), comb. form of L. *mammatus* (f. MAMMA²) in meteorological terms descriptive of clouds resembling rounded festoons, as *m.-ci·rrus, -cu·mulus* 1880.

Man, *sb.*

m.-hour, an hour spent in working by a labouring man or artisan taken as a measure of output.

Managerial (mænĕdʒī·riăl), *a.* 1767. [f. MANAGER + -IAL.] Of or pertaining to a manager, now spec. a salaried manager of a business, industrial enterprise, or organization, who is responsible for its conduct and policy.

BURNHAM (*title*) The m. revolution, 1953.

Manhattan (mænhæ·tən). 1890. [Name of an island on which the older part of New York is situated.] A cocktail made of vermouth and whisky with a dash of bitters.

Manic (mæ·nik), *a.* c 1890. [ad. Gr. μανικός, f. μανία MANIA; see -IC.] *Psychiatry*, etc. Relating to, characteristic of, or characterized by, mania.

m.-depressive *a.*, characterized by alternation of mania and mental depression.

Manœuvrable (mănū·vrăb'l), *a.* 1926. [f. MANŒUVRE *v.* + -ABLE.] Capable of being (easily) manœuvred: esp. of aircraft. Hence **Manœuvrabi·lity.**

Map, *sb.* 1. phr. *To put on the m.*: to establish the position or vogue of.

I dare say you remember the signature tune that helped to put us on the map 1954.

‖**Maquis** (ma·ki). 1944. [F., 'brushwood, scrub', ad. Corsican It. *macchia.*] A secret army of patriots in France, so named from their being conceived as hiding in undergrowth; also, one of them. Hence ‖**Maquisard** (makizār), a member of this.

Marathon (mæ·răþŏn). 1896. [Greek place-name.] *M.* (*race*), a long-distance foot-race introduced at the revived Olympic Games at Athens: so named from the feat of the Greek runner who brought the news of the battle of M. to Athens 490 B.C. Hence used *attrib.* to denote a performance or feat of long duration and needing extraordinary endurance.

The House of Commons finally went home..after sitting through a m. session of 20 hours and 20 minutes 1951.

‖**Marcobrunner** (mā·ɹkobrunəɹ). 1825. [G., f. *Marcobrunn*, name of a vineyard in the Rheingau, Germany.] A Rhenish wine.

Marge² (māɹdʒ). Colloq. abbrev. of MARGARINE, pronounced (māɹdʒărī·n).

‖**Marijuana** (mærihwā·nă). 1923. Also -**huana.** [Amer.-Sp.] Indian hemp, *Cannabis sativa*; the dried leaves and flowers of this used in cigarettes as a narcotic.

Mark (māɹk). [ad. G. *marke* label, brand.] A designation coupled with a numeral (e.g. *Mark IV tank*) of a brand of weapon, piece of equipment, or the like.

Marker. 5. A flare used above cloud (*sky m.*) or a bomb (*ground m.*) dropped to mark out the pattern of a raid 1943.

m. bomb, a bomb emitting a coloured light dropped in a raid so as to serve as a point of direction 1944.

Market, *sb.* phr. *Buyer's m.*: a state of purchasing in favour of the buyer; so *seller's m.*

‖**Marlag** (mā·ɹlæg). 1940. [G., abbrev. of *Marinenlager* 'sailors' camp'.] A German P. o. W. camp for sailors of the Royal Navy; also coupled with ‖**Milag** (mī·læg), a P. o. W. camp for sailors of the Merchant Navy.

Marmite (mā·ɹməit). 1912. [ad. F., 'stock-pot'.] Proprietary term for an extract made from fresh brewer's yeast.

Marshal, *sb.* 3. See also FIELD-MARSHAL. c. In the R.A.F., *Air* (*Chief, Vice-*) *M., M. of the R.A.F.* 1918.

Marshal, *v.* Hence vbl. sb., used attrib. in *marshalling yard*, a railway yard in which trains are assembled and distributed 1880.

Marshall (mā·ɹʃăl). Name of George C. *Marshall*, Secretary of State in U.S.A., in **M. aid,** financial assistance given to certain Western European countries to further their recovery after World War II, according to the plan (**M. Plan**) initiated by him on 5 June 1947.

Martini (māɹtī·ni). 1894. A cocktail made from gin, French vermouth, orange bitters, etc.

Mascara (mæskā·ră). [Name of a town in Oran, Algiers.] A preparation for dyeing eyelashes, etc.

Masher². Appears to be orig. *U.S.* (1875 in *Dict. Americanisms*); so MASH *v.*² (1879).

Mass, *sb.*²

m. observation, the study and record of the social habits of people (taken in the mass) 1938; **m. raid,** a raiding operation by a large number of aircraft 1939.

‖**Mastaba(h)** (mæ·staba). [Arabic.] Among Moslems, an outdoor stone platform attached to a dwelling.

Master, *sb.*¹ I. 5. *The m.*: a designation used by servants for the head of the household; similarly *the young m.* for the son or eldest son of the family. 7. *One's own m.*: having control or command of one's actions or movements; similarly *one's own mistress* (see MISTRESS I. 3).

Match, *sb.*¹ II. 2.

m.-point, the state of a game when one side needs only one point to win the m.; the point itself 1921.

Maternity. 3.

m. home, premises to be used for the reception and delivery of pregnant women or of women immediately after childbirth (1926 *Act 16 & 17 Geo. V* c. 32).

Matriculability (mătri:kiulăbi·lĭti). 1927. [f. MATRICULATE + *-ability.*] Fitness for matriculation.

Maxwell (mæ·kswĕl). 1911. [Name of James Clerk *Maxwell* (1831–79), British physicist.] The unit of magnetic flux in the C.G.S. system.

Mean, *sb.* II. 4. Now more esp. in phr. like *man of means.*

Meanie, meany (mī·ni). *colloq.* [f. MEAN *a.*¹ + -IE, -Y⁶.] A mean-minded creature.

Medium. B.

m. bomber, a bomber (*BOMBER 2) intermediate between the heavy and the light.

Mega-. b. *megacycle, -watt.*

Megaloblast. Hence **Me:galobla·stic** *a.*

L. J. DAVIS & A. BROWN (*title*) The Megaloblastic Anæmias 1953.

Megger (me·gəɹ). Trade name patented by Messrs. Evershed and Vignoles Ltd., London, to designate an apparatus for measuring electrical insulation resistance. So **Meg,** a smaller apparatus of this kind.

Meline (mī·ləin), *a.* [ad. L. *melinus* (mod. L., sb. fem. pl. *Melinæ*), f. *meles, melis* (Pliny): see -INE¹.] Of or pertaining to the subfamily Melinæ of Mustelidæ, consisting of the badgers and skunks. Cf. *MUSTELINE.

Melon. *Comb.*

m.-cutting *Stock Exchange slang*, the dividing up or sharing of profits 1908.

Mentalism (me·ntăliz'm). 1926. [f. MENTAL *a.*¹ + -ISM.] Theory or practice concerned with the mental (as opposed to the mechanical) aspects of a matter, i.e. with features involving mind, thought, idea, or concept. Hence **Mentali·stic** *a.*

Bloomfield rules out the philosophical, logical, and mentalistic approach to the facts 1941.

Mercy, *sb. attrib.* passing into *adj.* Administered or performed out of mercy or pity in order to put a suffering person out of pain or distress; e.g. *m. drug, m. killing* (so *m. killer*).

Mescal. *attrib.* **m. buttons,** the button-shaped tops of mescal which are dried and used as an intoxicant. Hence **Me·scaline** [-INE⁵], an alkaloid derived from them.

Meson (me·sǫn, mī·sǫn). [n. of Gr. μέσος MIDDLE.] = MESOTRON.

Charged scalar meson fields and nucleons 1951.

Mesotron (me·sǫtrǫn). [f. MESO- + *tron* of ELECTRON².] *Physics.* A transitory particle observed as a result of cosmic radiation.

Met. (met). orig. *R.A.F. slang.* [abbrev. of METEOROLOGICAL.] The staff of meteorological experts who furnish reports for the R.A.F., a department of the Air Ministry; *attrib.* metman (me·tmæn), a meteorological officer; so met-flight.

The metman's miseries 1954.

Metropolitan, *a.* 3. With reference to France: Pertaining to the home country; serving in home waters; home-.

M.I. 5 (eməifəi·v). The section of Military Intelligence which deals with matters of state security.

Mickey Mouse (mi·ki maus). [Name of a mouse-like character in a series of film cartoons designed by Walt Disney.] *R.A.F. slang.* An electrical distributor which releases bombs from aircraft.

Microcard (məi·krokāɹd). [Proprietary term f. MICRO- + CARD *sb.*] Any of a series of cards on which the text of a book, periodical, etc. is microphotographically reproduced; they are read by means of a machine (*m. reader*).

Microfilm (məi·krofilm). 1938. [MICRO-.] Proprietary name of a photographic film (FILM *sb.* 3) of a manuscript, etc. on a small scale.

Microphone. Add: *spec.* An instrument for converting sound waves into electrical energy, which may be reconverted into sound after transmission by wire or by wireless, e.g. the transmitter of a telephone or the mouth-piece used in broadcasting (colloq. abbrev. *MIKE).

Mi·crowave. 1940. [MICRO-.] An electro-magnetic wave (WAVE *sb.* 5) having a wave-length of less than 20 centimetres.

Micrurgy (məi·krɒ̄ɹdʒi). 1950. [f. MICRO- + *-urgy* (Gr. -ουργία work).] The art or science of dissection and injection under a microscope. Hence **Micru·rgical** *a.*

Middle East. 1902. The countries of the East extending from Egypt to Iran (Persia) inclusive.

Mike (məik), slang abbrev. of *MICROPHONE 1929.

‖**Milag**: see *MARLAG.

Militia. 3. *spec.* The British conscript army formed in 1939. So **Mili·tiaman.**

Milk, *sb.*

m. run *U.S.A.A.F.*, a frequently repeated mission; **m. shake** *U.S.*, a glass of milk or milk and egg, flavoured and shaken up.

Millibar (mi·libāɹ): see *BAR *sb.*⁴

Mills bomb (milz bǫm). 1916. [Name of the inventor, Sir William *Mills* (1856–1932).] A kind of hand-grenade.

‖**Milreis.** The cruzeiro was substituted for the m. at par (i.e. 1 cruzeiro = 1 milreis) in October 1942.

Mine, *sb.* 3. Also, a receptacle containing explosive placed in or on the ground as a weapon of war.

m. field, an area sown with mines. So **Mine** *v.*

‖**Minenwerfer** (mī·nənvɛrfəɹ). 1915. [G., f. *mine* MINE *sb.* + *werfer*, f. *werfen* to throw.] A mine-thrower (see MINE *sb.*).

Miniature. B. b. Of a type manufactured or designed on a small scale.

The Sopwith 'miniature' biplane 1913. A m. camera 1925.

Minnie (mi·ni). 1915. *slang.* Soldier's abbrev. of *MINENWERFER with suffix -IE, simulating a hypocoristic form.

Minor, *a.* *M. suit*, (at Bridge) diamonds or clubs 1919.

Misch(i)evious (mistʃī·viəs), dial. and vulgar var. of MISCHIEVOUS *a.*, dating from the 16th century; sometimes used joc.

Wells..friendly with everybody, mischevious, quick-thinking, nonsensically inventive 1952.

Mishit (mishi·t), *sb.* 1882. Also erron.

miss-. [MIS-¹ 4.] A faulty or bad hit. So **Mishi·t** *v. trans.* 1930.

Miss, *sb.*¹ **III. 1.** *To give* (a thing) *a m.*: to pass by, leave alone (*colloq.*) 1918.

Mission, *sb.* **2. b.** *U.S.A.A.F.* The dispatch of aircraft on an operational flight.

Mix, *v.* **4. c.** *To m. in*: to join in fighting; also *to m. it* (orig. *U.S. colloq.*) 1912.

I think they [*sc.* the Germans] learned at Dieppe that to come and mix it again was going to be expensive 1944. So **Mi·x-in** *sb.* 1912.

Mixer. In sound films, etc., the apparatus that controls the contributions of various microphones 1929.

Mixture. **3. d.** In internal combustion engines, the gas or vaporized fuel mixed with air which forms the material for the explosive charges 1894.

Mi·x-up. [f. phr. *to mix up.*] A confused fight or contest, mêlée.

-mo (mōᵘ), the final syllable of terms derived from the abl. sing. masc. of L. ordinal numerals which denote book sizes by the number of leaves into which the sheet of paper has been folded, as in *quarto, octavo*; e.g. *duodecimo, sextodecimo*, which are read as *12mo, 16mo*; so *thirty-twomo, 32mo.*

Mobile (mōᵘ·bəil), *sb.*³ 1952. [subst. use of MOBILE *a.*] *pl.* A form of decoration consisting of abstract designs in metal, plastic, etc. contrived (as by suspension) so as to be mobile.

Mo·ck-up. [f. MOCK *v.* with *up*, after *make up, set up.*] The stage of design preceding the model that is adopted for production.

An exact model or 'mock-up' of the big boats on a scale of 75 to 1,000. 1941.

Mode. II. 2. b. *Statistics.* That value of a character or graded quality at which the instances are most numerous 1900.

Model(l)ist (mǫ·d'list). 1674. [f. MODEL *sb.* or *v.* + -IST.] One who makes a model.

‖**Moki**¹ (mōᵘ·ki). 1857. [Maori.] The Blue Cod (*Perses colias*) and the Bastard Trumpeter (*Latris ciliaris*), N.Z. fishes.

‖**Moki**² (mōᵘ·ki). 1840. [Maori.] A kind of Maori raft.

‖**Moko** (mōᵘkǫ). 1855. [Maori *amoko.*] The Maori system or pattern of tattooing.

Molotov (mǫ·lǫtǫf). Name of Vaycheslav Mikhailovich *Molotov*, People's Minister for Foreign Affairs, U.S.S.R., in: *M. bread-basket*, a container carrying high explosive and scattering incendiary bombs; *M. cocktail*, an anti-tank inflammatory hand-grenade 1940.

Monitor, *sb.* **2. b.** One who is appointed to listen to and report on foreign broadcasts.

Monitor, *v.* **2. a.** To regulate the volume or intensity of (sound records) 1929. **b.** To act as monitor of broadcasts, *trans.* and *intr.*

b. Radio intelligence department m-ing units 1944.

Monniker (mǫ·nikəɹ). Also **mon(n)aker, -eker, -ick(er), -arch(er).** 1851. [Of unkn. origin.] *slang.* A name.

Monolith. A. 2. *Building* and *Civil Engin.* A mass of concrete, masonry, or brick-work forming a solid element in a structure. **3.** [after Russ. монолит; cf. монолитность monolithic unity of the party] A political or social structure presenting an indivisible or unbroken unity. So **Monoli·thic** *a.*, unified and homogeneous; not exhibiting deviation or minority interests.

Dock walls may take several forms..(1) mass-concrete walls, (2) monolith walls, (3) walls built up of caissons... Walls composed of monoliths are usually constructed at sites where a mass wall is impracticable owing to the unstable qualities of the substrata *Chambers's Encycl.* 1950. Nationalization of monolithic monopolies which do not yield to other methods of control 1951. Herr Grotewohl and his monolithic Socialist Unity Party are democratic 1952. All that we can guess is that the 'monolith' of Soviet power is stirring 1953.

Monotonic (mǫnǫtǫ·nik), *a.* **b.** *Math.* Of a sequence: Such that all members of it either do not increase or do not decrease 1938.

Monovalent (mǫnovē¹·lənt, mǭnǫ·vălənt), *a.* [f. MONO- 2 + *-valent* of *equivalent.*] *Chem.* Having a valency of 1; capable of combining with one atom of hydrogen or its equivalent.

‖**Montage** (mǫ·ntāʒ). [F., f. *monter* to MOUNT.] The selection and adjustment of cinematographic shots.

Montenegrin (mǫntǐnī·grin), *a.* and *sb.* 1813 (earlier †-nerin). [ad. F. *monténégrin*, ad. It. *montenegrino*, f. *Montenegro*, f. *monte* MOUNT *sb.*¹ + (Venetian) *negro*, var. of *nero* :—L. *nigrum, niger* black. The It. name renders native *Tzrnagora* (*tzrna* black, *gora* mountain), so called from the dark aspect of Mt. Lovchen. So G. *Montenegriner, -grinisch* (adj.).] Pertaining to (a native of) Montenegro.

Montessori (mǫntĕsōᵊ·ri). 1912. Name of Dr. Maria *Montessori* (of Rome), designating a system of educating the young by the direction of natural activities without direct control.

‖**Montrachet** (moṅtraʃe, moṅraʃe). Name of a wine-growing district of the Côte d'Or, France, celebrated for its white wines.

Monument, *sb.* **4. c.** Applied, like mod.F. *monument*, to outstanding survivals of an early literature.

Specimens of the oldest m–s of the Latin language ANDREWS' FREUND'S *Lat. Lex.* App. I. 1853.

Monumental, *a.* *M. mason*, a tombstone-maker.

Moon, *sb.*

m. lighting, modified street lighting comparable to illumination by the moon.

Moot, *sb.* **5.** Revived (since 1925) in other inns of court and in legal centres elsewhere.

Mop, *sb.*¹ **1. Mrs. Mop(p),** joc. title of, hence a gen. appellation for, a charwoman 1944.

A great deal of the welfare..of a boarding school depends upon the unsung 'warrant officers and N.C.O.s', from the school messenger to Mrs. Mop 1948.

Moroccoette (mŏrǫ·koet). [f. MOROCCO + -ETTE.] A bookbinding material resembling morocco.

Morpheme (mǭ·ɹfīm). [ad. F. *morphème* (1905), f. Gr. μορφή form, after *phonème* PHONEME.] *Philol.* A morphological element considered in respect of its functional relations in a linguistic system.

Morrison (mǫ·risən). Name of Herbert S. *Morrison*, Secretary of State for Home Affairs and Home Security (1940–5): *M. shelter*, a portable indoor steel table-shaped air-raid shelter.

Mortar, *v.*² 1944. [f. MORTAR *sb.*¹] *trans.* To fire upon with mortars.

Mortician (mǭɹti·ʃăn). *U.S.* 1895. [irreg. f. L. *mort-, mors* death, after *physician*; cf. *BEAUTICIAN.] An undertaker.

Moth, *sb.*

m. ball, a ball of naphthaline used to keep moths away from fabrics 1907; fig. in attrib. use in **mothball fleet,** a fleet laid up in reserve.

Mother, *sb.*¹ *attrib.*, as *m. fixation.*

m. lodge, (*a*) the masonic lodge in which one was initiated, (*b*) the oldest lodge of a province; **m. ship,** (also) a ship having charge of submarines or aeroplanes 1909.

The dangers of m. fixation had not been discovered 1937.

Motivate (mōᵘ·tivē¹t), *v.* 1930. [f. MOTIVE *sb.* + -ATE 3.] *trans.* To provide with a motive, give a basis for. Hence **Motiva·tion,** whence **Motiva·tional** *a.*

‖**Mot juste** (mo ʒüst). [F., *mot* word (see MOT ²), *juste* exact (JUST).] The precisely appropriate expression.

Mouldy, *sb.* 1920. *Navy slang.* A torpedo.

Mouldy, *a.* **2.** Unsound, unsatisfactory; worthless, 'rotten' (*colloq.*) 1876.

Mount, *v.* **5. f.** *Mil.* To set (an offensive) in motion.

Mounty² (mau·nti). 1924. [f. MOUNTED + -Y ⁶.] *colloq.* A member of the Royal Canadian Mounted Police.

Mouse, *sb.* **I. 2. b.** A timid or shy person.

Mousetrap (mau·stræp). A trap for catching mice; *attrib.* in **m.-cheese,** cheese such as is used as bait in mousetraps; *joc.* (also with ellipsis of *cheese*) an inferior or unpalatable make of cheese.

Mulberry (mɒ·lbĕri). With cap.: Code name of the prefabricated harbour used in the invasion on *D-DAY.

Mule². **2. b.** A heelless slipper 1930.

Multilateral, *a.* **b.** *spec.* Applied to a condition in which trade is carried on between many or all countries without the necessity of balancing trade or payments between them; so **Multila·teralism,** with such spec. reference. Cf. *BILATERAL.

Multiplier. 2. b. *Economics.* The proportion of an increment of a consumer's income to the consequent increment of saving.

Munich (miū·nik). Anglicization of G. *München*, name of the capital of Bavaria, which was the scene of a meeting of representatives of Germany, Great Britain, France, and Italy on 29 Sept. 1938, when (by what is known as the *M. agreement* or *M. pact*) the Sudetenland was ceded to Germany; with allusion to this pact, taken as a typical example of dishonourable appeasement. Hence **Munichee·r** [see -EER ¹], **Mu·nichite** [see -ITE], one who conforms to such a policy of appeasement (so **Mu·nichism**).

Muscle, *sb.* *Comb.*

m.-bound *a.*, having the muscles stiff and enlarged, esp. owing to excessive exercise 1902.

Museum.

m. piece, (in derogatory sense) a person or thing regarded merely as an antiquated survival or curiosity.

Mushy, *a.* **2.** *fig.* Weakly sentimental, 'soppy' (*slang*) 1874.

Musical, *sb.* **b.** A film or a theatrical piece (not opera or operetta) of which music is an essential element.

Musical, *a.*

m. comedy (or **farce**), a light dramatic piece, consisting of dialogue, songs, and dancing, connected by a slight plot 1890.

Muskeg (mɒ·skeg). 1865. [Cree Indian.] A level swampy or boggy area in regions of Canada.

Must, *sb.*³ **b.** Something that must be done, possessed, considered, etc.; something imperative or obligatory (*colloq.*).

'Inside' [a book on prison life] is a must for people who care 1953.

Mustard. b. *fig.* That which adds piquancy or zest (*U.S. slang*) 1891.

m. gas, (read) dichlorodiethyl sulphide, an oily liquid the vapour of which is one of the blister gases.

Musteline. A. *adj.* Of, pertaining to, or characteristic of the weasels or the subfamily Mustelinæ (weasels and martens) of Mustelidæ.

Mycotrophy (məikǫ·trǒfi). 1940. [f. Gr. μύκης mushroom + τροφή nourishment.] *Bot.* The state of a plant living in symbiosis with a fungus. Hence **Mycotro·phic** *a.*

‖**Mystique** (mistī·k). [sb. use of F. *mystique* MYSTIC.] The esoteric and quasi-supernatural character of a person, institution, etc., esp. as deriving from a concentration upon it of popular devotion and veneration.

The 'mystique' built up around him [*sc.* Stalin] has become a genuine outlet for the Russian religious instinct 1951. A funeral in Predappio shrine will re-habilitate Fascism, and may well revive the whole Mussolini 'mystique' 1952. P. BLACK (*title*) The m. of modern monarchy 1953.

Myxomatosis (mi:ksǒmătōᵘ·sis). [mod.L., f. MYXOMA + -OSIS.] A disease characterized by the presence of myxomata, a contagious infection of rabbits.

As a means of eliminating the rabbit the Commonwealth Scientific and Industrial Research Organisation is now experimenting with *myxomatosis*, a virus disease which is spread amongst rabbits by mosquitoes 1952.

N. II.

N.A.A.F.I. = Navy Army and Air Force Institutes (see *NAFFY); N.A.T.O. = North Atlantic Treaty Organization (cf. *NATO); N.A.T.S.O.P.A. = National Society for Operative Printers and Assistants; N.B.G., n.b.g. = no bloody good; N.C.B. = National Coal Board; N.E.I. = Netherlands East Indies; N.F.S. = National Fire Service; N.F.U. = National Farmers' Union; N.G., n.g. = no good 1840; N.K.V.D. (People's Commissariat for Internal Affairs, U.S.S.R.), superseded by *M.V.D.; n.p. = (*c*) net personalty; n.p. or d. = no place or date; N.T.P. = normal temperature and pressure; N.U.J. = National Union of Journalists.

Naffy (næ·fi). 1939. A canteen in the charge of the *N.A.A.F.I.

Nagana (năgā·nă). 1895. [Zulu *nakane.*] Tsetse-fly disease.

Nancy (næ·nsi). *slang.* [Pet-form of the female name *Ann.*] An effeminate man or boy; a homosexual. Also as adj.

But he isn't one of them..Not a bit n. 1933.

Nanny. Also **Nannie.**

A Nannie must enter into her kingdom when the baby is a month old 1947.

Napalm (nēⁱ·pām). 1942. [f. initial syllables of na*phthenate* and palm*itate*, aluminium salts of naphthenic and palmitic acids respectively.] A jellied fuel used for incendiary bombs and flame-throwers, derived from a mixture of aluminium soaps of some fatty acids.

Nappy, *sb.*[2] *Nursery colloq.* [f. first syll. of NAPKIN + -Y[6].] A baby's napkin.

Nardoo (nāɹdū·, nā·ɹdū). [Native name, also given as *ngárdū* and *ardoo.*] (Sporocarp of) the Australian plant *Marsilea quadrifolia*, used as food.

Nark (nāɹk). *slang.* 1859. [ad. Romany *nāk* nose. Cf. NOSE *sb.* 5.] More fully *copper's n.*: A spy or informer in contact with the police. Hence **Nark** *v. trans.*, to spy or inform upon; *intr.*, to act as a spy or informer.

Nasmyth (nei·smiþ, nei·z-). Name of James *Nasmyth* (1808–90), Scottish engineer, applied to inventions of his.

Mr. N.'s steam-hammer *Encycl. Brit.* IX (1879) 413/1. A planing-machine ('N. steam-arm') *Ibid.* XXXI (1902) 76/2. [The helve] was used by the ironworkers and [the Oliver] by the smiths until displaced by the N. hammer and its extensive progeny *Ibid.* XXVII. 38/1. A friend whose mind I used to compare to a N.'s hammer, which can weld a ton of iron or crack a nut without crushing the kernel BRIDGES *Coll. Papers H. Bradley* (1928) 43. N. pile-driver *Chambers's Techn. Dict.* (1940).

Nasty, *a.* 3. slang phr. *a n. piece* (or *bit*) *of work*: an ill-conditioned person.

He was what is called 'a n. piece of work' G. B. GRUNDY *Fifty-five years at Oxford* 87.

National Insurance: see *INSURANCE.

National Socialist. 1929. [G. *Nationalsozialist.*] = NAZI.

Native, *a.* III. 3. *N. State*: a territory ruled by an Indian prince.

Nato (nēⁱ·tou). f. N.A.T.O.; see *N.

It is right that a certain secrecy should surround Nato's diplomatic and military discussions 1952.

Natter (næ·təɹ), *v.* 1829. [var. of earlier *gnatter* (1806–7).] 2. *slang*, orig. *dial.* To grumble, scold, nag; in gen. colloq. use, to nag loquaciously, chatter persistently.

Navicert (næ·visəɹt), *sb.* [f. L. *navis* ship + *cert-* of CERTIFICATE *sb.*] A consular certificate granted to a neutral ship testifying that her cargo is correctly described according to the manifest: first put into operation 16 March 1916. Hence as *v. trans.* to authorize with a n.

The 'Navicert System', as it was called [apparently in 1915], from the code word employed FAYLE *Seaborne Trade*, 1923. (See also H. RITCHIE *The 'Navicert' System during the World War*, 1938.) Any consignment not navicerted..will be liable to seizure 1940.

Navy. *attrib.*

n. cut, cake tobacco finely sliced.

‖**Nazi.** Loosely used for: A German. Hence (in the political sense) **Na·zidom** 1934, **Na·zify, -fica·tion** 1938, **Na·z(i)ism** 1933.

Near, *a.* 6. *N. miss*, not a hit but aimed close enough to damage the target.

Near, *adv.*[2] III. as prep. with sbs., passing into adj.: That is closely similar to, that is all but (what is qualified) 1902. Also with adjs.

The first illustration to a Shakespearian, or rather a near Shakespearian play, came in 1633 T. S. R. BOASE, 1945.

Necrophily (nėkrǫ·fili). 1897. [f. Gr. νεκρός dead body + -φιλία; see -PHILOUS.] A morbid attraction to corpses. Also ‖**Necrophi·lia, Necro·philism** 1864, **Ne:crophili·stic** *a.* 1924.

Needle, *sb.* I. 3. d. In gramophones and similar instruments, the stylus used in recording and playing 1902. *attrib.* **n. contest, fight, match,** a contest, etc. that arouses much interest and excitement 1922.

Neon. *attrib.*

n. lamp, n. light, forms of illumination provided by a mixture of gases in which neon is predominant.

‖**Neoplasia** (nīoplēⁱ·ʒiă). [mod.L., f. Gr. νέος NEO- + πλάσσειν to form; see -IA[1].] *Path.* = NEOPLASM.

NEP (nep). [f. initials of N*ew* E*conomic* P*olicy.*] A programme initiated in the Soviet Union in 1921 for the revival of the wage system and private ownership of industry. Hence **Ne·pman,** one engaged in this programme.

Neptunium (neptiū·niŏm). [f. NEPTUNE (as being the eighth planet in order from the sun) + -IUM.] *Chem.* A radioactive element produced by the neutron bombardment of Uranium 238.

Nerts (nōɹts). U.S. pronunc. of *nuts* (see *NUT *sb.* 5 b).

Nerve, *sb.* III. 1. b. *War of nerves*: a campaign against an enemy consisting of intimidation, propaganda intended to undermine morale, or the like 1939.

The British public..did not allow the 'war of nerves' organized by the Nazi Government to interfere..with its August holiday *Ann. Register for 1939*, 81.

Network. 2. c. A broadcasting system, e.g. the American Forces N. in the European theatre of operations.

Neuro-. Also *neuropsychiatry, -surgery.*

Never-never (ne:vəɹne·vəɹ). Colloq. (joc.) description of a system of paying for articles by periodical instalments (on which defaults often occur).

Mod. Weekly payments on the n. (system).

New, *a.* Special collocations.

N. Deal (see *DEAL *sb.*[2]); **n. look,** a new style of female costume introduced in Britain in 1947, characterized by a more ample allowance of material; also *transf.* a new appearance or aspect of a thing or an innovation in procedure, behaviour, or policy; **N. Order** [G. *die neue Ordnung*], Adolf Hitler's plan for the reconstitution of the states of Europe on the basis of a National-Socialist régime.

Further obstacles in the way of Hitler's New Order in Europe were the three remaining neutral States, Sweden, Switzerland, and Portugal 1941. His [*sc.* Lysenko's] case represents an extreme example of the Soviet new look *Observer* 30 May 1954.

Newscast (niū·zkɑst). [f. NEWS + *-cast*, of BROADCAST.] A wireless broadcast of news. So **New·sca:ster, -ca:sting.**

Graham MacNamee, the newscaster of our American newspaper newsreel *Observer* 28 Sept. 1930.

Newsman. *U.S.* A newspaperman.

Newspeak (niū·spīk). joc. formation on NEW and SPEAK, used derogatorily for: A reformed version of a language.

Mr. [Bernard] Shaw's N. *Economist* 7 April 1951.

New Year. *N. Y. honours*: titles of honour conferred by the Sovereign on New Year's Day.

‖**Niersteiner** (nīə·ɹʃtəinəɹ). 1829. [G.] Hock produced at Nierstein, near Mainz, Germany.

Nifty (ni·fti), *a.* 1869. *U.S. slang.* [?] Attractively smart or spruce. Also **Niffy** (ni·fi), 'said by Bret Harte to be fr[om] *magnificat*' (Webster's Dict.).

Night, *sb. attrib.* and *Comb.*

n.-flier, aircraft flying by night; so **n.-flying** 1907; **n. office** *Liturg.*, matins and lauds 1767.

Nineteenth, *a.* *N. hole*: the refreshment bar on a golf course (the full course being of eighteen holes); also *transf.*

1943 V. CONNELL (*title*) The n. hole in Europe.

Nip, slang shortening of NIPPON, Japanese.

The Nip pilots 1942 *R.A.F. Jrnl.* 31 Oct. 13.

Nippon (ni·pǫn). Japan; prop. the name ('origin of the sun') of the main island. Hence **Nipponian** (nipǭu·niăn) *a.* Japanese 1909.

‖**Nirvana.** In etym. read: *nirvāṇa* extinction, f. *nirvā* to be extinguished.

Nissen (ni·s'n). [Name of the inventor, Lt.-Col. Peter Norman *Nissen* (1871–1930).] *N. hut*: a tunnel-shaped hut made of corrugated iron with a cement floor.

Niton (nəi·tǫn). 1912. [f. L. *nitere* to shine.] *Chem.* W. Ramsay's name for RADON.

Nitro-.

n.-chalk, a fertilizer consisting of a mixture of calcium carbonate and ammonium nitrate.

Nitwit (ni·twit). *slang.* 1928. [perh. f. NIT + WIT *sb.*] A person of no intelligence.

Nix (niks). *slang*, orig. *U.S.* 1844. [ad. G. *nichts* nothing.] Nothing.

No, *a.* I. 1. *No trumps*: at Bridge, a declaration or bid involving playing without a trump suit 1901.

No. b. *No. 1* (nɒ·mbəɹ wɒ·n): of the first rank or quality 1843.

Mod. Public enemy No. 1. Britain's No. 1 oil town. Cf. *A. No. 1* (U.S.) = A 1.

Nod, *sb.* Colloq. phr. *On the n.*: with a merely formal assent.

Noise, *sb.* 3. *Noises off*: sounds, usu. loud or confused, produced off the stage but heard by the audience at the performance of a play; also *allus.*

The recovery..was temporarily reversed by the rumblings from the Prime Minister, but got well under way as soon as the end-July debate had shown them to be merely extraneous noises-off 1952.

Non-. 1. *Non-aggression* 1934; *Non-cooperation* 1795, (in India) 1920. 3. *Non-belligerent* (*-ence*) 1939; *non-incentive* 1947; *non-representational.*

Nordic, *a.* In transf. use, applied to an alleged race of Germanic type having distinctive qualities that are held to give it superiority over all others: often identified with *Germanic* or *Aryan.*

Norm. b. In the U.S.S.R., a standard unit of work prescribed.

Stakhanovite women miners in the Donetz basin are performing four, nine, and eleven n-s each 1952.

Nose, *v.* 5. *To n. over*: (of aircraft) to fall nose forward.

Nostalgia. *transf.* Regret or sorrowful longing *for* the conditions of a past age; regretful or wistful memory or recall of an earlier time.

The n. of the heathen past 1923. [Payton's] n. for a deceased chivalry 1945. A nostalgia for the nursery age of printing has been characteristic in particular of 'fine' printing 1947. So **Nosta·lgic** *a.* We rarely find a strong nostalgic sense of tradition 1949.

Not, *adv.* *Not too*, phr. indicating a fairly good or adequate standard of performance or condition. So *Not so good*: inferior.

Nothing. A. I. *To have n. on* (U.S. slang): see *HAVE. b. As *adv.* or *int.* Nothing of the kind; not at all, in no respect (*U.S. colloq.*) 1888.

‖**Nouveau riche** (nū:vou rī·ʃ). 1828. [pseudo-F., f. *nouveau* new, *riche* rich; after F. *nouveau marié* newly married, etc.] A wealthy parvenu.

Novocaine (nǭu·vokēⁱn). 1906. [f. L. *novus* NEW + second syll. of COCAINE.] Trade-name of a local anæsthetic obtained from coal-tar.

Nuclear (niū·kliăɹ), *a.* 1. b. *fig.* Fundamental, essential. c. *Physics* and *Chem.*, e.g. *n. charge, fission, physics, structure, theory.* Hence *n. weapon*, one derived from n. fission.

The n. fault underlying all this writing 1912.

Nuclease (niū·klīēⁱs). [f. NUCLEIC + -ASE.] *Chem.* An enzyme which induces hydrolysis of nucleic acid.

That the 'nuclease test' could not be used as a reliable index of the presence of chromatin 1952.

Nucleic (niū·klī̆ik). [f. NUCLEIN + -IC.] Chem. *N. acid*: an acid composed of the non-protein portion of nucleoproteins (the group of proteins which are constituents of the nuclei of cells).

The n. acid of fish-eggs 1952.

Nucleon (niū·klīǫn). [f. NUCLEUS with ending from *neutron, proton.*] *Physics.* The proton or neutron of an atomic nucleus. Hence **Nucleo·nics** *sb. pl.* [see -ICS], the branch of physics which treats of nucleons or the nucleus.

Nucleus. 3. b. *Physics* and *Chem.* The internal core of an atom, surrounded by electrons and containing the positive electricity of the atom 1914 (E. Rutherford).

Nuff (nɒf). In U.S., colloq. phr. *nuf(f) said* (*sed, ced*), short for 'enough (has been) said', (hence) 'that's all right' 1841.

Nullo (nɒ·lo). In skat; see quots.

If one of the players holds such cards as to enable him to force his opponents to take all the tricks, he can declare n...In n., the knaves are regarded as colour, *i.e.* are not trumps 1910.

Nurse, *sb.*[1] 1. Without article in reference to the nurse in charge of a patient.

N. looked at the silent bedstead 1937.

Nurse, *v.* 5. b. (With an injury as object.)

The..pilot was safely at his home..nursing only a slight scratch on his nose *N.Y. Times* 11 Dec. 1951.

Nut, *sb.* 5. b. *pl.* (a) Used as a derisive retort; (b) *adj.* Crazy; so **Nu·tty** *a.* (*U.S. slang*).

n.-butter, a substitute for butter, obtained from nuts 1907.

Nutriture (niū·tritʃ(u)əɹ, -tiuəɹ). Delete † and add: **1. b.** The state or condition resulting from nutrition 1948 (H. M. Sinclair).

Nutty, *a.* **5.** Of coal slack: Containing nuts (see NUT *sb.* III. 3).

Nylon (nəi·lǫn). 1932. [Proprietary name.] A synthetic fibre, similar to rayon, derived from coal-tar, water, and ammonia, and as a glue-like fluid passed through minute holes to form filament for the manufacture of brushes, material for garments, parachutes, etc. Also *attrib.*, as *n. stockings*, and *sb. pl.* for this.

O. II.

O.C.T.U. (see *OCTU); O.E.E.C. = Organization for European Economic Co-operation; O.P. = Order of Preachers, Ordo Prædicatorum (i.e. Dominicans); O.P., o.p., O.Pip. = observation post; O/S = outsize; O.U.(A.C., etc., P.) = Oxford University (Athletic Club, etc., Press); O.V.R.A.: see *OVRA.

-o (ou), the final syllable of an abbreviated form, as in *hippo, photo*; an addition to a word or the first part of a word forming a colloq. or slang equiv., as in *ammo, beano, compo*; a meaningless ending, as in *blotto, doggo, (like) billy-o, cheerio, right(y)-o.*

Oat. 1. b. *To feel one's oats*: to feel important, display self-importance (*U.S.*) 1833.

Object, *sb.* **I. 5. b.** *No o.*, orig. alteration of *not the o.* or *not an o.*: (orig.), not the end in view or aimed at; (hence), not a thing to be taken into account, forming no obstacle or hindrance. (See Tract xxxvi of The Society for Pure English.)

A Gentlewoman..wishes to superintend the Family of a single Gentleman or Lady..salary will be no o. 1782. The expense..could be no o. to the country 1796. Expense no o. 1855. *Mod. Advt.* The City Window-cleaning Co., Height no object.

Oblique. B. *sb.* **2.** A sloping VIRGULE.

Obscene, *a.* **2. b.** *transf.* Repulsive, highly offensive (*colloq.*).

That diversity of o. knick knacks 1936.

Observer. *attrib.*

(Royal) O. Corps, a body of persons whose business is to observe, report, and plot the movements of aircraft, etc.

Octu (ǫ·ktiu). 1940. From the initials of *Officer Cadet Training Unit.*

Odds. 4. Hence (esp. *U.S.*), preponderance of chances or probabilities, as in phr. *by all o.*, in all probability.

This is by all o. the best collection of sermons that you have gathered together BP. F. J. SHEEN 1952.

Oerlikon (ö·ɹlikǫn). 1940. [Swiss place-name.] Cannon used for anti-aircraft defence, on aeroplanes, etc.

Oersted (ö·ɹsted). 1903. [Name of Hans Christian *Oersted* (1777–1851), Danish physicist.] A unit of magnetic reluctance.

Offensive, *sb.* **b.** *transf.* Aggressive action or movement directed to any end, e.g. *peace o.*

‖**Oflag** (ǫ·flæg). 1940. G., abbrev. of *Offizierlager* officers' (P. o. W.) camp.

‖**Ogpu.** In etym. read: *Obedinénnoe Gosudárstvennoe Politícheskoe Upravlyénie* United State Political Administration.

O.K. (ōukēi·). For the tracing of this to the initials of *Old Kinderhook*, birthplace of Martin Van Buren (near Albany), Democratic candidate in New York in 1840, and its further history, see A. W. Read in *Saturday Review of Literature* 19 July 1941.

Old, *a.* **III. 2. b.** *O. school tie*: the necktie of characteristic pattern as worn by former members of a particular (public) school; used symbolically to denote extreme loyalty to a traditional mode of thought or behaviour 1939.

‖**Oleum** (ōu·liŏm). 1919. [L., 'oil'.] *Chem.* Fuming (or Nordhausen) sulphuric acid, $H_2SO_4xSO_3$, a solution of sulphur trioxide in sulphuric acid.

-ology (ǫ·lŏdʒi) is added directly to some sbs., as in *sexology, thyroidology*. So **-olo·gic(al), -o·logist**; cf. -LOGIC, -LOGICAL, -LOGIST.

On, *adv.* **13. e.** *To be on to*: to be aware of (the intentions of). orig. *U.S.* 1888.

One, *a.* **VII. 2.**

o.-track *a.*, (of a mind) that is concentrated on only one line of thought or action 1935.

Oner. 1. c. A big lie (*slang*) 1918.

Onion, *sb.* **5.** *pl.* Flaming rockets used against hostile aircraft (usu. **flaming o–s*) 1917.

Oomph (ŭmf). *U.S. slang.* [?] Sex appeal.

Op. (ǫp), abbrev. of (1) OPERATION, (2) OPUS, (3) OPERATOR (e.g. *wireless op.*).

Open, *v.*

O. out. f. *trans.* and *intr.* To open the throttle of a motor engine, accelerate 1906. **O. up. c.** *intr.* To begin firing *on, upon.*

Operative, *a.* **2.** *spec.* in legal use, applied to those words in a deed which express the intention to effect the transaction concerned.

Something to prevent that should be put into the o. part of the treaty 1951.

Opposite, *prep.* **b.** *To play o.*: to have (a specified actor or actress) as one's leading man or lady.

Order, *sb.* **I. 4. b.** Ellipt. for *o. of magnitude* (1897): Grade or position in a series or system based on quantity or size 1903. **IV. 3. e.** *O. to view*: a requisition from a house or estate agent to an occupier to allow a client to inspect his premises.

I. 4. b. The accuracy of spectroscopic measurements (of the order of one in a million) 1927.

Oropesa (ǫrŏpī·zä). 1940. [prob. so called from its use on a trawler of that name engaged in mine-sweeping in 1916; name of a town and a cape in Spain.] In full *O. float* or *sweep*: a form of paravane used in mine-sweeping.

Orthoptic, *a.* **3.** *Ophthalmology.* Pertaining to or concerned with the right or normal use of the eyes. **Ortho·ptics,** the theory or practice of remedial measures for the ocular muscles. Hence **Ortho·ptist,** an expert in orthoptic training.

Until the visual axis can be held continuously in the normal position without the aid of o. instruments 1940.

Oscar (ǫ·skăɹ). [Arbitrary use of the Christian name.] A gold-plated statuette awarded by the Academy of Motion Picture Arts and Sciences, of Hollywood, U.S.A., for the highest achievement of the year in film production; also used loosely for similar awards.

Oso-berry. For [? Amer. Ind.] substitute [f. Sp. *oso* bear (:—L. *ursus*) + BERRY.]

Oto-.

o:tolaryngo·logy, the branch of medicine concerned with the ears and the larynx 1949.

Otter. 3. b. An apparatus to keep wires at the required depth in mine-sweeping 1919.

Out, *sb.* **7.** A way out, way of escape 1845.

Out, *adv.* **I. **6. c.** *Boxing.* Unable to put up a defence, e.g. *out for the count* (i.e. the counting of seconds from one to ten). **II. 1.** *To be o. for*: to have one's interests or energies directed to, be intent on (orig. *U.S.*) 1889.

Outsize, *sb.* and *a.* 1883. [OUT *a.*[4], SIZE *sb.*[1]] **A.** *sb.* A person or thing larger than the normal, *esp.* a ready-made article of dress larger than a standard size. **B.** *adj.* Larger than the average or stock size.

fig. Our own age is so inured to the monstrous and o. in destruction 1944.

Over, *adv.* **2. b.** phr. (*That is*) *So-and-so all o.*: exactly what one might expect of him or her 1916.

Over, *prep.* **I. 1.** *O. one's head*: without consulting or informing one 1902. **II. 3. e.** *To be all o.* (a person): to ply with attentions.

Over-all, overall. As a fully-developed adj.: Which includes or covers all features or aspects; inclusive of everybody and/or everything.

Overall Report of the U.S. Strategic Bombing Survey 1945. A small over-all scale reduction has been applied to each map 1951. The deficiency can be made up only by increasing the overall supply of women teachers 1953.

Overlord. b. In the British government of 1951–3, a member of the House of Lords appointed to supervise and co-ordinate two or more ministries.

‖**Ovra** (ǫ·vră). f. *O.V.R.A.*, initials of It. *Opera di vigilanza e di repressione dell' antifascismo* organization for security and repression of antifascism, the secret police of the Fascist régime in Italy.

Ownable (ōu·năb'l), *a.* [f. OWN *v.* + -ABLE.] That may be owned.

Things ownable, but unowned, are res nullius... Passing over things ownable, but unowned in fact,.. all things which are not unownable as common, or unownable as public R. W. LEE 1915.

Oxer (ǫ·ksəɹ). *local.* 1896. [app. f. OX + -ER [1].] A post and a rail alongside a fence to keep cattle off it.

Oxford.

O. accent, a style of pronouncing English popularly supposed to be particularly characteristic of members of the University of Oxford and to be marked by affected utterance. **O. bags,** a style of trousers very wide at the ankles. **O. blue,** a blue of very low brilliance. **O. group (movement), O. groups:** see GROUP *sb.* 3. **O. unit** *Biochemistry*, a unit of penicillin.

Oxfordian (ǫksfǭ·ɹdiăn), *a.* and *sb.* [-IAN.] **1.** Pertaining to Oxford; *Geol.* of the lower division of the Oxford oolite 1885. **2.** Pertaining to, an adherent of, the view that the works attributed to William Shakespeare were written by Edward de Vere, 17th earl of *Oxford* (a theory initiated by J. Thomas Looney, 1920).

P. II.

P.A.Y.E. = Pay-as-you-earn (see *PAY *v.*); P.B.I. = poor bloody infantry; *transf.* with allusion to the function of the infantry as that part of an army which bears the brunt of an action in the field; p.e. = personal estate; P.E.N. (Club) = Poets, Playwrights, Essayists, Editors, Novelists; P.E.P. = Political and Economic Planning; P.F.F. = Pathfinder Force; P.G. = paying guest; P.I.A.T. = Projector Infantry Anti-Tank; P.M. = Provost Marshal, Prime Minister; p.m. = post mortem; P/O = Pilot Officer; P.O.P. = printing-out paper; P.O.S.B. = Post Office Savings Bank; P. o. W., P.W. (*U.S.*) = prisoner of war; P.P.P. = People's Progressive Party (in British Guiana); P.U.P. = People's United Party (in British Honduras); P.W.D. = Public Works Department. See also *P-PLANE.

Procedural remedies are being sought, mostly by back-benchers—the 'P.B.I.' of Parliament 1952.

Pack, *sb.*[1] **5. c.** (also *wolf-pack*) An organized group of U-boats.

Pack, *v.*[1] **I. 1. c.** *To p. up*: to retire from the fight, contest, active life, etc. 1915. **6. c.** *trans.* To contain a full measure of, be crammed with or chock-full of.

Packet, *sb.* **1. c.** A considerable sum of money (esp. lost or won) 1916; a load (*lit.* and *fig.*); *to get, catch, stop a p.*, to be (mortally) hit by a bullet, etc. (*colloq.*).

Paiforce (pəi·fǭɹs). [f. initials of *Persia and Iraq* + FORCE *sb.*] The Persia–Iraq Command in World War II.

The men of P. went out in May 1941.

Pakistan (pākistā·n). 1933. [Earlier *Pakstan*, f. initials of *Punjab, Afghan Frontier, Kashmir, (Iran), Sind*, and the last three letters of *Baluchistan*, names of parts of India where Moslems predominated.] *Indian politics.* Moslem autonomy; a separate Moslem state (officially set up as a separate dominion 15 Aug. 1947). Hence **Pakista·ni** (-ī) *a.*, *sb.*, pertaining to, a native of, Pakistan.

The partition of India by the Moslem League scheme of Pakistan *Ann. Register for 1942*, 145. The principle of the Pakistan plan *Ibid.*

Palatogram (pæ·lătogræm), a record of the use made of the palate in producing a sound.

Pale, *a.* **1. d.**

p. ale, ale of a pale colour often bottled.

Panache. 2. *fig.* Display, swagger (*colloq.*) 1934.

Pansy. In full *p. boy*: An effeminate youth, homosexual (*colloq.*) 1934. Cf. *NANCY.

‖**Panzer** (pæ·nzəɹ, ‖pa·ntsər). 1939. [G., 'mail, coat of mail'.] Properly used *attrib.* = armoured, as *p. forces, p. division*; also *sb. pl.* = *p. forces*

‖**Papillon** (păpi·lʸǫn). [F., 'butterfly'.] A breed of toy dog having ears that suggest the form of a butterfly.

Para-[1].

Parami·litary *a.*, having a function or status ancillary to that of military forces, though not professedly a military unit 1935.

Parachute, *sb.* *attrib.* '(To be) dropped by parachute', as *p. flare, mine, troops. P. troops* is contr. to Pa·ratroops, for which *paratroopers* is also used. **Parachu·tist,** one who descends from a balloon, etc. in a parachute 1888; also, an air-borne soldier.

Parade, *sb.* **2.** or **3. b.** *transf.* A serial display or recital of events, etc. (e.g. *programme* *p.* of the B.B.C.). 5. Often in the names of streets, e.g. *North P.*, *South P.*

Partisan, *sb.*[1] 2. b. In World War II, *spec.* a member of a nation whose country is occupied by enemy forces and who takes part in resistance to them. (So Russ. *partizán*, etc.)

Pash, *sb.*[3], abbrev. of PASSION (*slang*, esp. girls') 1922.

Pashto, preferred spelling of PUSHTU.

Pass, *v.*

P. out. a. To die 1899; to become unconscious from shock, etc. 1918. **P. up.** *U.S.* To refuse to have further dealings with; to give up, abandon 1896.

Paste, *v.* 3. Also, to 'plaster' with aerial bombs: often in *vbl. sb.* (*colloq.*)

Pastedown (pē·stdaun). 1904. [f. PASTE *v.* + DOWN *adv.*] An outer blank leaf of a book pasted on to the cover; a piece of paper or parchment from a manuscript or printed book pasted on the inside of the binding of a book for the protection of an end leaf.

Pat, *adv.* and *a.*: see also STAND *v.* I. 10.

Patch, *sb.*[1] 3. *To strike a bad p.*: to have a period of bad luck 1928.

p. pocket, a pocket consisting of a piece of cloth sewn on like a patch 1908.

‖**Patella** (păte·lă). 2. *spec.* in *Anat.* The knee-cap.

Patent, *a.* 3. c. Applied to proprietary foods and medicines 1871.

Path, *sb.*

p.-finder, (*b*) an aeroplane (or its pilot) sent on ahead of air-raiders to mark out the path to be followed by them 1943; cf. *P.F.F.

Pathogen (pæ·þodʒen). [f. Gr. πάθος suffering, disease (PATHOS) + -GEN.] A disease-producing agent.

Patriot, *sb.* 2. d. *spec.* applied in World World II to loyal inhabitants of a country overrun by the enemy, esp. when organized in bands of resistance.

Pattern, *sb.* 8. *fig.* The form and order followed in action or procedure, e.g. *p. of behaviour, life, movement.*

p. bombing, bombing of an area from aircraft according to a prescribed pattern.

Patulin (pæ·tiulin). 1943. [f. L. *patulus* open, broad, spreading, f. *patere* to be open; see -IN[1].] A therapeutic drug obtained from the mould *Penicillium patulum.*

Pay, *v.*[1] 6. phr. *To put paid to*: to settle the affair of (*colloq.*).

p.-as-you-earn, applied to a method of collecting income tax by deducting at the source as the income is earned 1943; abbrev. P.A.Y.E.

Pay-. 1.

p.-bed, a bed in a hospital for the use of which payment is made.

An increase in the maximum fees which can be charged by specialists giving treatment in pay-beds to their private patients 1953.

p.-packet, the packet containing an employé's wages due for a particular period.

Pedology (soil-science). [ad. Russ. *pedologiya.*]

Peep, *v.*[2] *Comb.*

p.-toe(d), designating a type of shoe which allows the toes to be seen.

Peg, *sb.*[1] *Off the p.*: said of the purchase of ready-made clothes from the peg on which they hang in a shop 1931. *To put on the p.*: to bring before the C.O. for an offence (*Army slang*).

Peg, *v.* I. 1. c. Similarly, to fix (payments, e.g. wages) at a certain figure or level.

Pekin(g). *P. man*: a prehistoric type of man, *Sinanthropus pekinensis*, represented by remains found at P., China 1928.

‖**Pelorus** (pėlōə·rŏs). [Appellative use of the reputed name of Hannibal's pilot on his leaving Italy.] *Navigation.* A form of steering apparatus.

Pen, *sb.*[1] 2. e.g. *submarine p.*

Penalty. 2. c. *Bridge.* A number of points added to the opponents' score when the declarer fails to make his contract, or to the declarer's score when his call is doubled and he makes his contract 1908.

‖**Pengö** (pe·ŋgö). [Magyar, pres. pple. of *peng* to sound.] The monetary unit of Hungary current from 1925 to 1946.

Penicillin (penisi·lin). 1929. [f. mod.L. *Penicillium* (generic name), f. L. *penicillus* painter's brush, PENCIL; so named from the brush-like sporangia of the mould; see -IN[1].] A therapeutic drug obtained from the mould *Penicillium notatum.*

To avoid the repetition of the rather cumbersome phrase 'Mould broth filtrate', the name 'penicillin' will be used 1929 (A. FLEMING). Hence **Penici·llinase** [see *-ASE], the enzyme of p.

Peninsula. b. *The P.*: (also) in World War I, Gallipoli.

Pep, *sb.* (Earlier date 1912.) Also *attrib.*, as *p. talk.* Hence **Pep** *v.*, to fill with energy or vigour, ginger *up* 1925. **Peppy** (pe·pi) *a.*, full of p. 1926.

Perfect, *a.* 4. *A p. day*: one that has been without flaw and thoroughly enjoyed.

When you come to the end of a p. day 1909 (CARRIE JACOBS-BOND).

Perfectly (pɔ̄·ɹfėktli), *adv.* ME. [f. PERFECT *a.* + -LY[2].] 1. Completely, thoroughly. 2. With perfect correctness, to perfection. 3. To the fullest extent, quite 1555. †b. Exactly (e.g. *p. alike* 1753).

Perimeter. *attrib.*

p. track *U.S.*, a concrete roadway encircling an aerodrome.

Periodic, *a.*[1] 2. *P. table*: a table of the chemical elements illustrating the p. law 1919.

Perpend, var. of PARPEN(T.

Personal, *a.* I. *P. equation* (see EQUATION 2); often *fig.* that element in an action or movement which depends on personal or individual qualities; (hence) individual prejudice or prepossession.

The scientific genealogists of the more advanced school, who settle the problem off-hand, often in accordance with their p. e. 1881.

‖**Personnel.** Vulgarly pronounced (pəɹsǫ·nəl) in the fighting forces, etc. during and since World War II.

Perspex (pɔ̄·ɹspeks). 1937. [irreg. f. *perspect-*, ppl. stem of L. *perspicere* to look through.] Trade name of a plastic material much lighter than glass, used for wind-screens and transparent parts of aircraft.

‖**Pessimum** (pe·simŏm). [neut. sing. of L. *pessimus* worst, rel. to *pejor* worse (cf. PEJORATIVE).] The worst or most unfavourable condition, amount, or degree.

Pesticide (pe·stisəid). 1950. [f. L. *pestis* PEST + -CIDE[1].] A substance for destroying pests, esp. insects.

‖**Petit mal** (pəti mal). [F., 'little disease'.] *Path.* Epileptic seizure in which convulsions are absent and only transient phenomena occur, epilepsis mitior. Cf. *GRAND MAL.

Petting, *vbl. sb.* (s.v. PET *v.*[1]).

p. party, a gathering of young people of both sexes at which fondling and kissing are indulged in (*U.S.*) 1925.

Peyote (pē·yǫtĭ), **Peyotl** (pē·yǫt'l). 1909. [Sp. *peyote*, Nahuatl *peyotl.*] A cactus, *Lophophora Williamsi*, prized by Mexican Indians for yielding a narcotic.

Pharmaceutic(al), *sb.* A p. drug.

Fertilisers, pharmaceutics, and many other products 1927. Exports to China of certain pharmaceuticals which would be of value to the maintenance of large military forces 1953.

Phenoba·rbitone. [See PHENO-, *BARBITONE.] Phenylethylbarbituric acid used as a hypnotic and sedative. Cf. *LUMINAL.

Phon (fǫn). 1936. [ad. Gr. φωνή sound.] *Physics.* A unit used in measuring a noise.

-phone, terminal element, repr. Gr. φωνή voice, sound, used in the names of instruments for transmitting, reproducing, or amplifying sound, as GRAMOPHONE, MEGAPHONE, MICROPHONE, RADIOPHONE, TELEPHONE.

Phoneme. (The variants of a phoneme as conditioned by differences of enunciation or articulation (e.g. the point and flat varieties of *l*, the trilled and uvular varieties of *r*) are normally represented by the same symbol, or an accepted equivalent, and do not constitute distinctions between words otherwise identical.) Hence **Phonematic** (-æ·tik), **Phonemic** (-ī·mik, -e·mik) *adjs.*, **Phone·micist,** a student of phonemes.

Phonofilm, Photostat are trade names.

Phospho-.

phospholipid, a lipid containing phosphorus or phosphoric acid.

Photo-. p.-finish, the finish of a race in which competitors are so close that the result has to be determined by reference to a photograph of the situation 1944; **p.-grammetry,** the process of making surveys or geodetic measurements by photography; **p.-mechanical** *a.*, pertaining to the production of pictures by mechanical printing from a photographic plate; **p.-mural,** a wall decoration consisting of a photographic enlargement of a subject; **p. receptor** (rĭse·ptǫɹ), *Physiol.*, a sensory nerve-end that receives light stimuli.

Photogenic, *a.* 2. In more recent use: Of a person who is a good subject for photography, esp. from an æsthetic aspect.

Phreatic (friæ·tik), *a.* [f. Gr. φρέατ-, nom. φρέαρ well, tank + -IC.] *Geol.* Applied to gases of atmospheric or oceanic origin which, coming into contact with ascending magma, may set off volcanic eruptions.

Physical, *a.*

p. chemistry, the study of the properties and behaviour of chemical substances in the light of the laws of physics; **p. therapy,** treatment of disease by physical and mechanical methods, e.g. the use of light, heat, water, etc., massage and exercise; so **Phy:sicothe·rapy** 1903, **Phy:siothe·raphy** 1905.

Phyto-.

phytotoxin, a toxin produced by a plant; hence **phytotoxic** *a.*

The factors influencing the selective action of phytotoxic compounds 1954.

Pianistic (piăni·stik), *a.* [f. PIANIST + -IC.] Pertaining to or adapted for playing on a piano.

The same 12-bar pattern..serves as a basis for the 'Boogie-Woogie', a typically p. species 1950.

Piat (pī·ət). 1944. [See *P.] A mortar for use against tanks.

Pickled, *ppl. a.* 2. Drunk (*slang*) 1934.

Picksome (pi·ksŏm), *a. colloq.* 1867. [f. PICK *v.*[1] + -SOME[1].] Given to picking and choosing, fastidious.

The Committee should be very p. and particular 1899.

Pick-up. I. b. A man or girl 'picked up', e.g. in the street (*colloq.*) 1895. d. Capacity for recovering speed, power to accelerate 1909.

Picquet, the common form of PIQUET.

‖**Pictura** (piktiūə·ră). 1886. [L., 'painting', PICTURE.] *Ornith.* The pattern of coloration of a particular part, e.g. a feather.

Pidgin, pigeon. 2. *One's p.*: one's particular concern 1925.

Pie, *sb.*[2] I. (A pie may be open, i.e. uncovered, as *potato pie.*) 3. slang phr. *p. in the sky*, a heavenly or paradisiacal state.

Piffer (pi·fəɹ). [f. initials of designation + -ER[1].] A member of the Punjab Irregular Frontier Force.

Pile, *sb.*[2] 6. More specifically *atomic p.*, *chain-reaction p.*: in nuclear physics, an arrangement of uranium and other fissile material, as for the production of plutonium by the action of neutrons 1945.

Pilot, *sb.* I. b. Now, one who operates the flying controls of an aircraft. c. Also applied to an automatic device for maintaining an aeroplane in flight 1934.

p. officer, lowest commissioned rank in the R.A.F.

Piltdown (pi·ltdaun). 1913. Name of a hamlet in Sussex, England, applied to remains of a pretendedly prehistoric human skull, and other objects, found there.

Pin, *sb. attrib.*

p.-point, the point of a p.; *transf.* or *fig.* as a type of something minute; used attrib. of precision bombing or bombardment concentrated on a small target; hence as vb.; **p.-tuck,** a narrow ornamental tuck.

Pincers. *attrib.*

pincer movement, an operation involving the convergence of two forces on an enemy position like the jaws of a pair of pincers.

Pine-apple. 3. A bomb or hand-grenade (*slang*) 1916.

Pi·n-up. [f. phr. *to pin up* (PIN *v.*).] A picture (e.g. of a celebrity or favourite) pinned up on a wall, post, etc.

‖ **Piou-piou** (pyupyu). 1900. [F.] The typical French private soldier.

Pip, *sb.*[5] 1937. [Echoic.] A high-pitched momentary sound, usu. produced mechanically.
The six 'pips' of the time-signal 1937.

Pip, *v.*[2] **2.** intr. *To p. out*: to die (*slang*) 1920.

Pip, *sb.*[4]; *o. pip* = observation post. Cf. *ACK, *EMMA, and TOC H.

Pipe, *sb.*[1] *attrib.*
p.-dream, (in wider application) a fantastic conception, notion, story, etc.; **p. line,** a line of piping for the conveyance across country of oil, gas, or water; also *transf.*, a channel of transmission or distribution 1879.

Pipe, *v.*[1] **IV.** *To p. down*: to be less insistent or confident (*colloq.*).

Pit, *sb.* **I. g.** A place for the inspection and repair of motor vehicles 1931.

Pituitrin (pitiū·itrin). 1910. [irreg. f. PITUITARY + -IN[1].] *Physiol.* A hormone produced by the pituitary body; a solution of this used medicinally.

Pixillated (pi·ksileʼtėd), *a.* *U.S.* 1848. [perh. alteration of dial. *pixy-laid, -laden, -led,* assoc. w. *-ated* (-ATE[2], -ATE[3]).] Bewildered, confused, crazy.

Plait, the normal U.S. form of PLEAT.

Plant, *sb.* **II. 4.** In U.S. use also *spec.*, a factory, workshop, the premises or building equipment of an institution (e.g. the p. of a college).

Plaster, *v.* **I. d.** To cover all over, 'smother' *with* (*colloq.*).
Mod. Bread and butter plastered with honey. The town was plastered with bombs.

Plastic. B. Synthetic resin or other substance that can be moulded into any form 1923.

Plate, *sb.* **III.** *On a p.*: ready to be taken without asking or seeking (*colloq.*).

Platinum. *attrib.*
p. blonde (orig. *U.S.*), a girl or woman having gold-grey hair.

Play, *sb.* *attrib.*
p. box, a box in which children keep books, toys, food, etc. at school 1852; **p. boy,** orig. *U.S.* an ostensibly wealthy pleasure-loving man of irresponsible (and often disorderly) habits; **p. pen,** an enclosure in which a young child may play 1931.
J. M. SYNGE (*title*) The Playboy of the Western World 1907.

Play, *v.* **III. 8. b.** *To p.* (a person) *up*: to make sport of, tease, irritate (*slang*) 1924. **VI. 8.** *To p. up*: to make the most of, exploit 1926; similarly *to p. down.*

Pleat, *sb.* (Pleats are placed by hand, paper pattern, or machine, and are set in position by heat or steam. For *accordion p., knife p.* see PLEAT *v.*)

Pled: see PLEAD *v.*

Plough, *v.*
Phrases. *To p. back*: to bury (grass, vegetation) in the soil by ploughing; *fig.* to invest (earnings or profits) in the business in which they have been made. *To p. a lonely furrow*: to carry on alone.

Plug, *v.* **5.** *trans.* To endeavour to popularize (a song, etc.) by having it performed often; to present over and over again for advertisement 1927. Hence *sb.*

Pluto[1] (plū·to). [a. L. *Pluto*, Gr. Πλούτων.] **1.** *Gr. Myth.* The god of the underworld ME. **2.** *Astron.* A planet more remote than Neptune, discovered by Clyde Tombaugh at the Lowell Observatory, U.S.A., in 1930.

Pluto[2] (plū·to). 1945. A word made up from the initials of P*ipe* l*ine* u*nder* t*he* o*cean* (laid for the conveyance of fuel stores under the English Channel in the invasion of France).

Plu:to-demo·cracy. [f. *pluto-* as in PLUTOCRACY.] A derisory term for the democracies of western Europe with reference to their alleged organization on the basis of wealth.
'The western pluto-democracies have always hampered the march of the Italian people,' he [*sc.* Mussolini] thundered 1940.

Plutonium (plūtōu·niŏm). [f. *PLUTO[1] 2 + -IUM.] *Chem.* A radioactive element derived from *NEPTUNIUM.

Pneumo-, before a vowel **Pneum-,** as in **Pneume·ctomy** 1895, excision of part of the lung, also **Pneumone·ctomy.**

Pocket, *sb.* **5. f.** An isolated area occupied by troops in a battlefield; the troops themselves. **8. b.** *P. battleship*: a ship equipped and armoured like a battleship but on a small scale 1933.

Point, *sb.* **III.** A unit of value in rationing; *on points*, rationed on a basis of such units.

Point, *sb.*[1] **V. 3.** In generalized use, as in *debating p., talking p.*, a matter or subject suitable or proposed for discussion. **P. of view**: now always *from*, formerly often *in, a p. of v.* [cf. F. *de* and *dans ce point de vue*].

‖ **Pointillé** (pwanti·lʸe). [F., pa. pple. of *pointiller*, f. *point* dot, POINT *sb.*[1]] = POINTILLISM.

Poison, *sb.* *One's p.*, one's particular drink (*slang*).
p. pen, an anonymous writer of malignant, libellous, or scurrilous letters to a private individual.

Pol. Econ. (pǫlɪ·kǫ·n), **Pol. Sci.** (pǫlskəi·). Univ. slang abbrevs. of *Political Economy, Political Science.*

Police, *sb.* *attrib.*
p. dog, a dog trained and employed by police to track criminals 1908; **p. state,** a state regulated by means of a national p. having secret supervision and control of the activities of citizens.

Polio (pǫ·lio, pōu·lio), colloq. shortening of POLIOMYELITIS. orig. *U.S.* 1931.

Political, *a.* **1.** *P. science* = POLITIC *sb.* 3.

‖ **Politico** (pǒli·tiko). [Sp., sb. use of the adj. (POLITIC).] A political agent, officer, or resident.
'Your Highness,' said the officious p., 'it's got Chartreuse in it' AGA KHAN in *Daily Mail* 5 May 1954.

Polka. *attrib.*
p. dot, a round dot or spot as one of a regular series forming a pattern in a textile fabric 1883; also *attrib.*; hence **p.-dotted** *a.*

Polly[2] (pǫ·li). *slang.* Aphetic and short for *Apollinaris water*, a mineral water produced at Apollinarisburg, near Bonn, Germany 1893.

Poly-. In various pathological terms.
Po:lychroma·sia, -chromatophi·lia [see CHROMO- 2, -PHILY], an abnormal reaction of red blood corpuscles in which they show affinities with all kinds of stains. **Po:lycythæ·mia** [Gr. κύτος cell, αἷμα blood], excess of red corpuscles in the blood. **Polydi·psia** [Gr. δίψα thirst], excessive thirst, as in diabetes. **Po:lyneuri·tis,** inflammatory condition of the nerves in various parts. **Polyu·ria,** voiding of urine in excessive quantity.

Polygraph. 3. b. An apparatus for making simultaneous recordings of the pulse in different parts of the circulation at one time.

Pommy (pǫ·mi). 1916. [Of unkn. origin.] In Australia and New Zealand, an emigrant from Britain.

Pool, *sb.*[2] **6. b.** Hence, a common stock of a commodity, article of commerce, or the like. So **Pool** *v.*[2] *gen.* to share in common.
Hart and Kenrick pooled friends 1927.

Poop (pūp), *sb.*[2] *slang.* 1919. Short for NINCOMPOOP.

Poplarism (pǫ·plăriz'm). 1922. The policy of giving generous or (as was alleged) extravagant outdoor relief, like that practised by the Board of Guardians of *Poplar*, London, in 1919 and later; also *transf.*

Popular, *a.* **2.** *P. front* [tr. Sp. *frente popular*, whence F. *front populaire*]: a political party or organized group representing 'left' elements 1936.

Pork, *sb.* *attrib.*
p. pie (hat), a round hat with a flat low crown.
The bullfighter's hat known in England as the 'pork pie' 1891.

Portal (pō·ɹtăl). Name of Wyndham Raymond *Portal*, baron Portal, Minister of Works and First Commissioner of Works and Public Buildings 1942–4, applied to types of prefabricated houses of standardized pattern introduced in 1944.

Portion, *sb.* **1. b.** The amount of a dish served to a person at a restaurant 1884.

Posish (pǒzi·ʃ). 1862. U.S. colloq. abbrev. of POSITION.

Positron (pǫ·zitrǫn). 1934. [f. POSI(TIVE ELEC)TRON.] *Physics.* A positive electron.

Possessed, *ppl. a.* U.S. phr. *Like all p.*: with unrestrained force or vehemence 1833.

Possible. B. *sb.* **3.** A possible candidate, winner, member, etc. 1923.

Postscript. c. A talk on a selected subject at the end of a B.B.C. news bulletin.

Potential, *sb.* **3. b.** *fig.* The resources that can be employed for an undertaking.
The whole war p. of the German Reich 1943.

Poult, short for POULT-DE-SOIE 1952.

Power, *sb.* *attrib.*
p.-dive, (of aircraft) a dive made without shutting off the motor power; also as vb.; **p. egg,** an engine with its auxiliaries compacted into one removable unit 1940; **p. politics** [tr. G. *machtpolitik*], international policy based on or backed by the threat of force.

P-plane (pī·plēin). 1944. [P for *pilotless*; PLANE *sb.*[3] 1 e (*b*).] An explosive-carrying reaction-propelled crewless aeroplane.

Prairie. *attrib.*
p. schooner *U.S.*, an emigrant's waggon used in crossing the prairies 1845.

Prang, *v.* *R.A.F. slang.* [Supposed to be echoic in origin.] *trans.* To bomb (a target) hard from the air; also, to crash (aircraft).

Pre-. A. I. Pre-ca·st *ppl. a.*, of concrete which is cast in blocks before being used in construction 1927; **Pre-co·nscious** *a. Psychol.*, not present in consciousness; *sb.*, *the p.*, personality as represented in infancy and childhood; **Pre-coo·l** *v.* 1904; **Pre-hea·t** *v.* 1898; **Pre-igni·tion,** too early ignition in an internal combustion engine 1903; **Pre-sele·ctive** *a.* (of a gear) that can be selected and set in advance 1936; **Pre-view·,** a view of a picture, film, etc., arranged before it is open to public view 1926.

Precision. *attrib.* Designed for or concerned with precise work or action, as *p. bombing, machine* (1909), *tool.*

Predictor (prĭdi·ktǫɹ). 1940. [f. PREDICT *v.* + -OR 2.] An instrument that enables the observer to estimate the course and speed of hostile aircraft.

Pre-emptive, *a.*
p. bid, in auction bridge, a bid made with the expectation that it is high enough to prevent opponents from bidding and so obtaining information 1913.

Prefabricate (prīfæ·brikeʼt), *v.* 1943. [f. PRE- A. I. 1 + FABRICATE *v.*] *trans.* To manufacture the component parts of (a building or other structure) in preparation for their assembly on a site. So **Pre:fabrica·tion.**

‖ **Presidium** (prĭsi·diŏm). 1924. [Russ. *prezidium*, ad. L. *præsidium*, garrison, f. *præsidēre* (see PRESIDE).] The presiding body or standing committee in a communistic organization.

Press, *v.*[1] **III. 2. b.** *Golf.* To attempt to hit harder than can be done with accuracy (*Encycl. Brit.* 1910).

Pressure, *sb.* *attrib.*
p. cooker, an apparatus for cooking under high p. at high temperature; **p. group,** a group or body of people which exerts p. upon the legislature or public policy, etc. by concerted agitation, propaganda, and the like; **p. mine,** a mine that is detonated by p.
The disgust felt by returning soldiers at 'pressure group politics' 1944.

Pressurize (pre·ʃərəiz), *v.* [f. PRESSURE + -IZE.] *trans.* To maintain normal pressure in an aircraft during flights at high levels.

Pre-war (prī·wǭɹ), *a.* [PRE-, WAR *sb.*] Existing, current, or active before the war (*spec.* World War I or II). Also *colloq.* as *adv.* (e.g. 'That was the case pre-war').

Pricked (prikt), *ppl. a.* [f. PRICK *v.* + -ED[1].] Of a bird: That has been slightly wounded by shot but not 'winged'.

Primary, *a.* *Gram.* Of verbal forms: Based on the present stem. Cf. HISTORIC *a.* 4.

Prime, *v.*[1] **2. b.** To pour water into (a pump) to cause the sucker to swell and so bring up water. **c.** To inject petrol into (the cylinder or carburettor of an internal-combustion engine).

Prince Albert (prins æ·lbəɹt). *U.S.* [Named after Prince Consort *Albert* (died 1861) or Prince *Albert* Edward, afterwards Edward VII (who visited U.S.A. in 1860).] †**1.** A variety of potato 1867 (*Dict. Americanisms*). **2.** In full *P. A. coat*: a long double-breasted frock coat 1884 (*Ibid.*).

Priority. 3. Also *gen.* An interest having a prior claim to consideration; often with qualification, as *first p., top p.*
Homes for soldiers will be priority No. 1. 1944.

Prism. *attrib.*
p. binoculars, binoculars in the construction of

which two pairs of triangular prisms are so introduced as to shorten the length of the barrel.

Procedural (prosī·diŭrăl). 1919. [f. PROCEDURE + -AL[1].] orig. *U.S.* Pertaining to, concerning, or involving procedure.

Profile, *sb.* **1. b.** In journalistic use, a biographical sketch of a subject, usu. accompanied by a portrait.

Programme. (Standard British usage favours this spelling.)

p. music [G. *programmusik*, F. *musique à programme*], music based on a scheme of literary ideas or mental pictures which are intended to be recalled or evoked by means of sound; **p. picture,** a cinematographic film forming part, but not the main feature, of a p. 1928.

Proleta:rianiza·tion. 1920. [f. PROLETARIAN + -IZATION.] The process of reducing or condition of being reduced to a proletarian level.

There has been a sort of p. of taste both in language and literature GILBERT MURRAY 1950.

Proliferate, *v.* **1.** *gen.* To increase vastly in numbers, grow prolifically.

Promotion. 2. c. *Book-trade.* In *sales p.*, the activities involved in the distribution of published books exclusive of advertising in the press and the actual selling 1928.

Prontosil (prǫ·ntǫsil). 1935. [Proprietary name.] One of the *SULPHONAMIDE group.

Proparoxytone (prǫpărǫ·ksitōun). See PRO-[2] 1.

Proportional, *a.* **2.**

p. representation, a method of parliamentary representation designed to allow the various political parties to be represented in proportion to their size and characterized by the use of the transferable vote, i.e. the filling up of seats, where a quota is not secured by first choices, by the transference of votes from second choices, and so on 1884.

Prosopography (prǫsoupǫ·grăfi). [ad. mod. L. *prosopographia*, f. Gr. πρόσωπον face, countenance, person; see -GRAPHY.] Description of an individual's personality and career. Hence **Prosopo·grapher, Prosopogra·phical** *a.*

The numerous prosopographical studies of Münzer, Groag, and Stein SYME *Roman Revol.* (1939) viii. Most of these [names] will be unfamiliar to any but a hardened prosopographer *Ibid.* ix.

Prosthetic, *a.* **3.** *Biochemistry.* Of a group or radical of a different kind added or substituted in a compound. **b.** *sb. pl.* = PROSTHESIS 2. 1911.

Protective, *a.*

p. custody, detention of a person in order to protect the State from his (real or supposed) hostile activities.

Protocol. 4. b. Rigid prescription or observance of precedence and deference to rank as in diplomatic and military services.

He punctuates his work with a gay laugh..and a first-name informality with colleagues...Not that p. is in danger. For behind his exuberance is a tough grasp of ceremonial and what is due 1952.

Proven (prū·v'n), *pa. pple.* orig. Sc. (prō·v'n), and surviving as a technicality in Sc. law, this form has been in southern use since the early 19th c., and is much affected in journalistic and similar usage for *proved.*

Her promise the years had p. past all speech KIPLING 1911. The wisdom that he taught us Is proven prophecy — *The Holy War* 1917.

Psycho-.

p.-catharsis = *ABREACTION 1934; **p.-neurosis,** a functional disorder of the nervous system characterized by some mental impairment without any ascertainable organic disease; **p.-somatic** *a.* [Gr. σῶμα, -ατ- body], pertaining to physical disorder due to the emotional state of the patient.

Pub. *attrib.*

p. crawl, a perambulation from one public house to another with partaking of drink.

Pull, *v.* **II. 1. b.** *U.S.* To draw (a revolver or pistol) for the purpose of firing 1883.

P. in, out. *intr.* To draw into, out of (a position) 1902. **P. round.** *intr.* To recover from sickness, a swoon, etc. 1891.

III. 4. b. Slang phr. *To p. one's punches* [PUNCH *sb.*[2]]: to use less than the force of which one is capable, hold oneself in.

Comb. **p.-in,** an entry, recess, etc. where a vehicle may p. in; **p.-out,** a folded leaf or plate in a book that can be pulled out for reference; **p.-up,** a house of call, where travellers may p. up.

[House] with natural pull-in 1952.

Pulpit, *sb.* **4.** The cockpit of an aeroplane (*R.A.F. slang*).

Punch, *sb.*[2] *Comb.*

p.-drunk *a.*, stupefied through being severely punched; (*gen.*) dazed, groggy; *sb.* a morbid condition in pugilists, marked by muscular failure and mental confusion, and resulting from repeated head concussions caused by punches 1928.

Punk[2]. **1. b.** Worthless stuff, rubbish, nonsense (*U.S.*) 1900.

Purge, *v.* **3.** *spec.* (in more recent use) To dismiss or expel from a party or community as being suspected of disloyalty or deviation. Similarly *sb.*, an act of purging.

The Munich bomb..furnished a welcome pretext for a new p. on the model of June 30, 1934 *Ann. Register for 1939*, 204.

Push, *sb.* **1. d.** Slang phr. *To give* (*get*) *the p.*, to dismiss (be dismissed) 1930.

Push-.

p.-over, orig. *U.S. slang*, a pugilist who is easily pushed over; *fig.* a thing easily overcome.

Pussyfoot, *v.* (For 1862- read 1862–1945.)

Put, *v.*[1] **II.** *To put* (a thing) *past* (a person): to consider him not incapable of (*slang*).

Put, *v.* **P. across** = *p. over* 1925.

‖**Putsch** (putʃ). 1921. [Swiss G., 'thrust, blow'.] A revolutionary attempt.

Py·ramid, *v.* 1902. [f. PYRAMID *sb.*] *U.S. Stock Exchange.* To increase the amount of (stock held) by selling at favourable times and applying the proceeds to the purchase of more stock.

‖**Pyrethrum. 3. b.** (The powder is prepared also from *Chrysanthemum cinerariifolium.*)

Q. II. 2.

Mil. as *adj.* = Pertaining to the duties of a quartermaster, as *Q. side, Q. work.*

Quads (kwǫdz), abbrev. of QUADRUPLETS.

‖**Quantum.**

q. mechanics, mechanics of phenomena to which the q. theory may be applied; so **q. dynamics, q. physics** 1927.

Quarrel, *sb.* phr. *At q.*: quarrelling.

They would be at q. the moment they were let out 1926.

Quechua, Quichua (ke·tʃwă, ki·tʃwă). Also **kechua, k(h)etschua, kichua.** [Sp. forms (*Que-, Qui-*) based on a native name.] (An Indian of) a tribe of this name inhabiting areas of Peru; also, their language, Incan. Hence **Que·chuan, Qui·chuan** *a.* and *sb.*

Queensberry (kwī·nzbĕri). Name of the eighth marquess of *Queensberry*, under whose supervision a code of laws for boxing (*Q. Rules*) was drawn up in 1867, which govern all glove contests in Great Britain.

Queer, *a.*[1] used as *sb.* A homosexual (*slang*).

Quick, *a.* **III. 7.** *A q. one*: a q. drink.

The studied taste that could refuse The golf-house quick one and the rector's tea W. H. AUDEN.

Quickie (kwi·ki). [f. QUICK *a.* + *-ie*, -Y[6].] A thing hastily done, made up, or performed, esp. a film so produced (1936).

The primary objective of the Board of Trade was the complete extirpation of the 'quota quickie' 1936 *Economist* 456/2.

Quinine, *v.* [f. QUININE.] *trans.* To dose with quinine.

I am much better..having been quinined up 1870.

Quins (kwinz), abbrev. of QUINTUPLETS.

Quirk, *sb.*[2] 1916. [?] A beginner or apprentice in the Air Service.

Quisling (kwi·zliŋ). 1940. Surname of Major Vidkun *Quisling*, a Norwegian who collaborated with the Germans when they invaded Norway in 1940, used allusively for: A collaborationist, traitor to one's country. Hence **Qui·slingite** [-ITE[1]]; **Quisle** (kwi·z'l) *v. joc.*, to play the q.

Quiz, *sb.*[2] **b.** A form of entertainment in which a series of questions is put to a team, e.g. *Round-Britain q., Transatlantic q.*

Quote. Used in dictation to introduce quoted words. Cf. *UNQUOTE.

R. II.

R.A.C. = Royal Armoured Corps, Royal Automobile Club; R.A.E. = Royal Aircraft Establishment; R.A.A.F., R.C.A.F. = Royal Australian, Canadian Air Force; R.A.F.(V.R.) = Royal Air Force (Volunteer Reserve); R.A.O.C. = Royal Army Ordnance Corps; R.C.S. = Royal Corps of Signals; R.D.C. = Rural District Council; R.D.F. = Radio-Direction-Finding; R.E.M.E. = Royal Electrical and Mechanical Engineers 1942; R.F.C. = Rugby Football Club; R.I. = Rex Imperator ('King Emperor'), Regina Imperatrix ('Queen Empress'); R.N.(V.)R. = Royal Naval (Volunteer) Reserve; R.O.C. = Royal Observer Corps; R.O.K. = Republic of Korea; R.P. = rocket projectile; R.T.C.(R.) = Royal Tanks Corps (Regiment).

Racialism (rēi·ʃiăliz'm). 1907. Used esp. of antagonistic or provocative emphasis on race.

The violent r. to be found in Europe today is a symptom of Europe's exaggerated nationalism 1939.

Racism (rēi·siz'm). 1942. [ad. It. *razzismo*, f. *razza* RACE *sb.*: see -ISM.] The theory that fundamental characteristics of race are preserved by an unchanging tradition.

Radar (rēi·dāɹ). orig. *U.S.* 1942. [f. RAD(IO and the initial letters of *a*nd *r*anging.] A radio system by which the motion, direction, and altitude of objects out of sight or hearing are detected by means of a scanning beam.

Radio. (Suggested as the mark of wireless telegrams according to the Radio Convention drawn up in Berlin in 1906 and adopted by U.S. Congress in 1912.)

b. Matter adapted for production by radio.

The feature programme now is pure radio, a new instrument for the creative writer and producer 1950.

Radio-.

r.-direction-finding (abbrev. R.D.F.), the detection by means of r. devices of the position and course of aircraft, etc.; **ra:diogonio·meter,** an apparatus for discovering the direction from which electromagnetic impulses are coming 1908; **ra:diothe·rapy** [see THERAPY], **-therapeu·tics,** the treatment of disease by X-rays or other forms of radiation 1903.

Radiolocation (rēi:diolǒkēi·ʃən). 1941. Radio-direction-finding.

Rag, *sb.*[1] *attrib.*

r.-book, a book for children made of untearable cloth 1905.

Rah (rā), *int.* (*sb.*) 1877. Clipped form of HURRAH used in cheering by colleges in U.S.A.

Rail, *sb.*[2] *attrib.*

railhead, (*a*) the furthest point reached by a railway under construction 1896; (*b*) *Mil.* the point on a railway at which road transport of supplies begins.

Rain, *sb.* *attrib.* and *Comb.*

r. day, a day on which the recorded rainfall is not less than 0·01 inch 1903; so **r.-spell,** a period of fifteen or more such days; **r.-proof** *a.*, impervious to rain 1831.

Rake, *v.*[1] *To r. down*: to win (money) at cards (*U.S. slang*) 1846.

Rake-off (rēi·kǫf). *U.S.* 1899. [f. phr. *to rake off* (RAKE *v.*[1]).] Percentage of profits allowed to or taken by another for a share in a transaction.

Raman (rā·măn). Name of Sir Chandrasekhara Venkata *Raman*, Indian physicist, used to designate phenomena observed by him in 1928; **R. effect,** the appearance of additional lines (**R. lines**) in the spectrum of light when scattered by the molecules of a substance; **R. spectrum,** the spectrum so obtained.

Ranger. 3. b. U.S. equiv. of *COMMANDO.

‖**Rara avis.** Also of things: A very unusual or exceptional occurrence.

A perfect day with us is something of a *r. a.* 1884.

Rare, *a.*

r. earth, any of the oxides of certain metallic elements found in a few rare minerals.

‖**Ratine** (rătī·n). 1922. [F.; see RATTEEN.] A fabric of rough open texture resembling sponge-cloth.

Raw, *a.* *R. deal*: the worse of a transaction, bad or harsh treatment 1934.

R-boat (ā·ɹbōut). 1944. [G. *R-boot*, for *Räumboot*, f. *räumen* to clear away, f. *raum* space, ROOM.] A German motor mine-sweeper.

Reaction. 3. b. In pop. use, the mental or moral response to a statement, event, etc.

Reactor. 3. Also *nuclear r.*: *PILE *sb.*[2] 6.

‖**Realpolitik** (reā·lpolitīk). [G., 'material politics'.] The policy of putting the material greatness of one's own country before other considerations.

Recap (rī·kæp). Shortening (orig. *U.S.*) of RECAPITULATE, -ATION.

Recco (re·kǫ). *Service slang.* Abbreviation of RECONNAISSANCE. So **Recce** (re·ki), reconnaissance corps.

'Recce' men were 'thin red line' of Anzio 1944.

Receptor (rǐse·ptǫɹ). 1898. [ad. L. *receptor*, agent-n. f. *recipere* to RECEIVE.] A receiving apparatus; a receiver; *Physiol.*, an organ or a part that receives stimuli, etc.

Recession. **2. b.** *spec.* A temporary decline or setback in industrial or economic activity or prosperity (*U.S.*).

Early in that year [1949], the signs of a r. in the United States [etc.]. . The Chancellor made explicit his fears of a r. of trade 1952.

Recessive, *a.* **b.** *Philol.* Of an accent or stress: That results from transference to or towards the first syllable 1887.

Record, *sb.* **II. 2.** *Off the r.*: not official or officially (*U.S.*).

Recorder[2]. Delete '*Obs.* exc. *Hist.*' (There has been a widespread revival of the recorder since the late 1920's, beginning in England with the work of Arnold Dolmetsch.)

Recourse. **4. b.** *Without r.*: formula used by the indorser of a bill, etc. to indicate that he declines responsibility for non-payment. Cf. *sans recours* s.v. *SANS.

Red, *a.* **I. 9. b.** *spec.* Of the extreme left wing, communistic; = SOVIET *attrib.*

He is. . the reddest of Red Republicans 1854. The new 'Red' Army of Soviet Armenia 1925.

II.

r. light, (gen.) a signal warning of danger as given by means of a r. lamp; phr. *to see the r. l.*, to be apprehensive of coming disaster.

Redbrick (re·dbrik). [RED *a.*, BRICK *sb.*] Applied *attrib.* to denote a university of modern foundation the official buildings of which are conceived as being built of red brick (in contrast to the stone of the ancient universities); also *collect.* such universities in general.

Re-di·scount, *v.* [RE- 5 a.] *trans.* To discount again. Hence as *sb.*; also *attrib.* in *r. rate*, 'the published rate at which the Federal Reserve banks will rediscount commercial paper for member banks, or lend to member banks' (*Webster's Dict.*).

The rise in the Bank of England rediscount rate from 2 to 2½ per cent. 1951.

Redouble, *sb.* [f. REDOUBLE *v.*[2]] *Bridge.* An instance of redoubling.

Reefer[2] (rī·fəɹ). 1946. [f. REEF *sb.*[1] (in the generalized sense of 'something rolled') + -ER[1].] A marijuana cigarette.

Reel, *sb.* **3. b.** *Cinema.* The standard length of a r. is 1,000 feet; films are designated as *two-*, *three-*, *four-*, etc. *reelers.*

Referred (rǐfə̄·ɹd), pa. pple. of REFER *v.*, applied to pain that is felt at a point in a sensory system remote from the actually affected part 1893.

Reflex, *a.* **8.** *R. camera*: a hand camera in which, by means of a pivoted mirror, the reflected image can be seen and focused up to the moment of exposure.

Refugee. *attrib.* or as *adj.* That has taken refuge in another country from an invading army or other oppressive conditions.

‖**Reich.** Also, a period or stage of the German Empire: *the First R.*, the Holy Roman Empire, A.D. 962–1806; *the Second R.*, 1871–1918; *the Third R.*, the Nazi régime, 1933–1945.

The terrible fate of the Jews in the Third R. 1933.

‖**Reichswehr** (rai·ksvēr). [G., f. genit. of *reich* empire + *wehr* defence.] The German defence force first organized in 1919.

Relocation. **3.** *U.S.* Internment (camp).

The Japanese r. centre near Denver, Colorado 1944.

Reme (rī·mi). *colloq.* f. R.E.M.E.: see *R.

Remote, *a.*

r.-control, controlled from a distance.

Responsible for operating the r.-c. 'tanks' 1944.

Renter. **4.** A distributor of films to exhibitors 1927.

Repatriate (rǐpæ·triēᵗt), *sb.* 1943. [ad. late L. *repatriātus*; see the vb.] One who has been repatriated.

Repeater. **5. c.** Also *gen.*, one who repeats an indictable offence.

As regards the 'repeaters', if a child sees his name in the papers it may well be an incentive. . to future wrongdoing 1954.

Reportage (rǐpǭ·ɹtėdʒ). 1939. [ad. F. *reportage*, f. *reporteur*, ad. REPORTER.] The reporting of events for the press, esp. with reference to style.

Reportedly (rǐpōᵊ·ɹtėdli), *adv.* *U.S.* [f. pa. pple. of REPORT *v.* + -LY[2].] According to report.

Reporter. **2. c.** In the title of periodical publications, as *The Cambridge University R.*

The R., or the General Observer (*title*) 1797.

Re-proo·f, *v.* 1922. [RE- 5 a.] *trans.* To render (a coat, etc.) waterproof again.

Reservation. **I. 3. c.** *U.S.* The engaging of a seat, room, place, etc. in advance; a seat, etc. so reserved 1907.

Reserve, *sb.* **1. b.** *spec.* (in reference to joint stock companies) That part of the profit which is not distributed to shareholders, but is added to the capital of the company. (*Hidden r.*: part of the profit concealed in the balance sheet by the device of assessing the value of assets below its true level); (in reference to banks) that part of the assets held in the form of cash, i.e. gold, coin, notes, or a deposit with the central bank; (in reference to central banks) that part of the assets held in the form of gold or foreign exchange.

Resistance. **1. b.** In World War II; after F. *Résistance*, an organized underground movement in a country occupied by enemy forces carried on with the assistance of armed fighters for the purpose of frustrating and damaging the occupying power.

Poets of the Resistance *French Studies* 1947.

Responsions. **3.** (Exemption from passing Responsions is granted on certain conditions.)

Retarded (rǐtā·ɹdėd), *ppl. a.* 1810. [pa. pple. of RETARD *v.*] That is or has been kept back or delayed; now often with respect to education or mental development.

Retro-. **Re:trobu·lbular** *a. Path.* applied to inflammation of the optic nerve behind the eyeball; **Re:tropharyngeal** *a. Path.* applied to an abscess in the cellular tissue behind the throat; **Re:tropu·lsion,** (*b*) *Path.*, the involuntary running backwards of one suffering from paralysis agitans.

Revenue. *attrib.*

r. cutter [CUTTER *sb.*[2]], a cutter-built vessel (also, one of other build) used by the customs authorities for the detection of smuggling, etc. 1790.

Reverse, *sb.* **5.** *In r.* **c.** With the positions reversed, the other way round.

Mod. Lease-lend in r. Italy is Dunkirk in r.

Rexist (re·ksist). 1935. [f. (*Christus*) *Rex* (Christ) the King; see -IST.] A member of a party founded in Belgium by Léon Degrelle, of Fascist tendencies.

Rheology (rǐ,ǫ·lŏdʒi). 1933. [f. RHEO- + -LOGY.] The science dealing with the flow and deformation of matter.

‖**Rhesus.** **2.** In full, *R. factor*: a substance contained in the red blood cells of many human and other higher animals (as in the rhesus monkey, in which it was first observed); abbrev. **Rh.** (Subjects in which this substance is present/absent are termed *Rh-positive*/*Rh-negative*, respectively.)

Rhode Island (rōᵘ·d əi·lənd). [Name of a N. Atlantic state.] *R.I.Red*: an American breed of domestic poultry having reddish plumage.

Rhyming, *vbl. sb.* [-ING[1].]

r. dictionary, one in which the words of a language are arranged according to the sounds of their terminal elements 1775.

‖**Ria** (rī·ă). 1898. [Sp.] A river mouth formed by the submergence of a valley or valleys.

‖**Rickettsia** (rike·tsiă). [mod.L., f. name of H. T. *Ricketts*, Amer. pathologist (1871–1910) + -IA[1].] Any member of the genus so named of small parasitic micro-organisms.

The rickettsiæ are primarily intestinal parasites of arthropod blood-sucking insects. . but some half-dozen species have become adapted to invade the animal body and cause disease 1951.

Ride, *sb.* **1.** *To take for a r.*: to take (a person) away in a motor car in order to murder him (*U.S. slang*) 1931.

Riff (rif). 1902. [f. *Rîf*, a district of Morocco.] A Berber of the Rîf. Also **Ri·ffian** *a.* and *sb.*

Rig (rig), *sb.*[5] late ME. (Lydgate). [prob. based on RIG *sb.*[1] back (ad. ON. *hryggr* = OE. *hrycg* back, RIDGE), the popular notion being that one testicle has remained in the back. Also with dims. *riggald*, *riggot*, and parallel forms in *-dg-*, viz. *ridgel*, *ridgling*; all from the 16th c.] An imperfectly developed or partially castrated male animal.

Ring, *sb.*[1] **II.** colloq. phr. *To make rings round*: to outdo in achievement, production, or performance, be greatly superior to.

Ring, *sb.*[2] **3. b.** [f. RING *v.*[2] II. 5 b.] A call on the telephone, e.g. *give me a r.*

Ring, *v.*[2] **II. 1. b.** colloq. phr. *To r. the bell*: (*a*) to achieve complete success 1925 [from the use of a bell in machines for trials of strength, in which a successful performer causes it to ring]; (*b*) to strike a sympathetic or responsive note.

Ripple, *sb.*[2] Applied to a method of firing torpedoes in succession 1940.

Ripple, *v.*[3] In vbl. sb. attrib. **rippling rhythm,** *U.S.*, applied to orchestras which include blowing through a straw into a glass of water.

Riproaring (ri·prōᵊːriŋ), *a.* 1830. *U.S. slang.* [f. RIP *sb.*[2], *v.* + pres. pple. of ROAR *v.*] Riotously vigorous, wildly noisy. So **Riproa·rious** *a.*

River, *sb.*[1] *attrib.*

r. scape [after LANDSCAPE], a picture depicting a river with adjoining scenery 1903.

‖**Riviera** (riviēᵊ·ră, pop. rivīᵊ·ră). With *the*: The maritime region of the departments of Alpes Maritimes (France) and Liguria (Italy); *transf.* applied to regions having a similar climate and scenery, e.g. *The Cornish Riviera.* (The French R. is called Côte d'Azur.)

Riz (†*ris*, †*rys*), widespread Eng. dial. and U.S. var. of the pa. pple. of RISE *v.*

The Philistines Were rys again LYDGATE. As though another day were newly ris G. FLETCHER. A batch o' bread that hain't riz LOWELL. A frish gineration had riz TENNYSON. Should I have riz to what Potipher is? KIPLING.

Road, *sb.* *attrib.*

r. fund, a fund established by the Roads Act of 1920 (Act 10 & 11 Geo. V, c. 72) to meet provisions therein specified relating to roads and vehicles used on roads; **r. house,** a public house of refreshment situated on a main road in a country district.

Roadable (rōᵘ·dăb'l), *a.* 1943. [f. ROAD *sb.* + -ABLE.] That is designed for travelling on a road.

R. airplane designed for businessmen needing a light lorry for air deliveries 1943. So **Roadabi·lity,** suitable for travelling on a road 1928.

Robot. **c.** *R. bomb* = *FLYING *bomb* 1944.

Rocket, *sb.*[2] **b.** More fully *r. engine*, *r. motor*: An engine used for the propulsion of shells, bombs, aeroplanes, etc., operated on the same principle as the pyrotechnic rocket and consisting essentially of a combustion chamber and an exhaust. Hence, a r.-propelled missile, etc.

Earlier in the year (in May) it was reported from America that the r. plane Bell XS-1 had been flown faster than sound. This was the first piloted flight at supersonic speed *Ann. Register for 1948*, 416.

r. (-firing) plane, an aeroplane fitted with an apparatus for firing rockets; **r. propulsion,** propulsion by means of a jet of gas at high velocity expelled backward from the r.; so **r.-propelled.**

Rocket, *v.* **2. c.** Of prices, etc.: To 'soar' to a great height.

Rococo. **2.** By extension applied to excessively florid or tastelessly ornate style in the visual arts generally and in literature.

Roneo (rōᵘ·nǐo). 1914. Proprietary term for a kind of duplicating machine.

Roof, *sb.* *attrib.*

r. spotter, an observer on the top of a building to spot hostile aircraft 1940.

Rooter[2]. 1894 (*Dict. Americanisms*). [See ROOT *v.*[2] 1 c.] An enthusiastic supporter, e.g. of an athletic team.

The rivalry between Mexican and Spanish fans is as traditional as, and far more bitter than, that between r–s for the Brooklyn Dodgers and the New York Giants *N. Y. Times* 3 Mar. 1953.

Rotatable (rōᵘtēᵗ·tăb'l), *a.* [f. ROTATE *v.* + -ABLE.] That can be rotated. Hence **Rota·tably** *adv.* 1947.

Round, *sb.*[1] **I. 5. a.** *In the r.*: (fig.) with all the features or elements fully displayed.

ö (Ger. Köln). ǭ (Fr. peu). ü (Ger. Müller). ü (Fr. dune). ɒ̄ (curl). ē (ēᵊ) (there). ē (ēⁱ) (rein). ɛ̄ (Fr. faire). ə̄ (fir, fern, earth).

Round, *a.* colloq. phr. *To bring up with a r. turn*: to check abruptly.

Round, *prep.*

r.-the-clock *attrib. phr.*, continuing throughout the twenty-four hours of the day.

Rout(e)ing (rū·tiŋ), *vbl. sb.* of ROUTE *v.* Direction according to a prescribed route.

All waste of time..scientific management methods endeavour to eliminate by 'routeing' 1924. Against this we devised a new kind of routeing 1947 A. HARRIS *Bomber Offensive* 188.

Roving, *vbl. sb.* [ROVE *v.*[1]]

r. commission, authority granted by the Admiralty to the officer in command of a vessel to cruise wherever he may think fit 1846; *transf.* and *gen.* authority given to pursue an inquiry or investigation in whatever quarters it may be considered necessary.

Ru·bicon, *v.* [f. RUBICON 3.] *trans.* (See quot.)

Rubicon Bézique. Four packs are used. Nine cards are dealt by three to each player...The loser is 'rubiconed' if he does not score 1000 points *Encycl. Brit.* (1910) III. 842.

‖**Rudbeckia** (rɒdbe·kiă). 1921. [mod.L., f. Olaus *Rudbeck*, surname of two professors at Upsala before Linnæus.] A herbaceous flowering plant of a genus native to N. America.

Rule, *sb.* 5. *To work to r.*: to work according to the rules laid down by the trade union to which the workman belongs.

Rum, *sb.*[1]

r. row [Row *sb.*[1]], *U.S.* a place where r.-running ships gather outside the prohibited areas 1927; **r.-runner** [see RUN *v.* II. 12c], one engaged, during the period of prohibition in the U.S.A. (1920–1933) in bringing alcoholic liquor into the country.

‖**Rumba** (rɒ·mbă). 1937. A Cuban negro dance; a ball-room dance imitative of this.

Run, *sb.* 4. **d.** The flight (of aircraft) on an even course preparatory to or during the dropping of bombs on the target. Also **R.-i·n, -u·p.**

Run, *v.* II. 18. **e.** To have as an ailment or a symptom (*colloq.*).

The President..is now running a temperature 1944.

r.-off, (*a*) something, e.g. rain, that runs off a surface; (*b*) a deciding final contest (cf. *r. off* g); **r.-on line** *Pros.*, a line of verse of which the syntax is carried on to the following line.

Runcible (rɒ·nsĭb'l), *a.* 1870. [Presumably fanciful alteration of ROUNCIVAL, which has been used in many senses of obscure origin and connexion.] Used by Edward Lear as a nonsense word (*r. cat, r. hat, r. spoon*) and established in **r. spoon,** a kind of fork used for pickles, etc., curved like a spoon and having three broad prongs of which one has a sharp edge.

Runnable (rɒ·năb'l), *a.* 1884. [f. RUN *v.* + -ABLE.] Proper for the chase.

He was a r. deer, that is, of age and size sufficient for the chase JEFFERIES.

Running, *vbl. sb.*

r. board, (earliest sense) a narrow gangway on either side of a boat 1817 (*Dict. Americanisms*).

Running, *ppl. a.* IV. 2. *R. commentary*: a continuous commentary on a text 1858; an oral description of events that are taking place.

Runway. 1. The earliest application is to the customary track of deer (*deer r.*, 1835 in *Dict. Americanisms*). 2. **b.** A specially prepared surface in an airfield for the taking-off and landing of aircraft.

Ruralization (rūə:rălɔizē¹·ʃən). 1946. [f. RURALIZE + -ATION.] The rendering of a place rural or rustic.

Ruritania (rūəritē¹·niă). [Name of the scene of Anthony Hope's novels 'The Prisoner of Zenda' (1894) and 'Rupert of Hentzau' (1898); f. L. *ruri-, rus* country + *-tania*, as in *Lusitania*.] An imaginary kingdom of Central Europe: used typically for a scene of court romance and intrigue in a modern setting, or for a petty state. Hence **-a·nian** *a., sb.*

One cannot expect every Ruritania to maintain an air arm equal to that of the Germans 1939.

Rush, *sb.*[2] Used *attrib.* in the sense 'prepared or produced in a hurry or with the least possible delay' 1901.

Rybat (rəi·băt). *Sc.* 1554 (*rebatt*). [perh. var. of RABBET, REBATE *sb.*[2], or ad. OF. source of these.] A polished stone reveal for windows, doors, etc.

S. 4.

S = (Air Raid) Shelter; S.A. = G. *Sturm Abteilung* 'storm division' (Nazi party army); S.C. = Special Constable; S.C.M. = Students' Christian Movement; S.C.R. = Senior Common Room (Oxford University); S/Ld = Squadron Leader; S/O = Section Officer; S.P. = (*b*) sparking plug, (*c*) Service Police, (*d*) stirrup pump; S.P.Q.R. = (*a*) Senatus Populusque Romanus 'the senate and people of Rome'; (*b*) *joc.* small profits quick returns; S.S. = G. *Schutz Staffel* 'protection squad' (Nazi Black Guards); S.T.C. = (*a*) Senior Training Corps; (*b*) Short Title Catalogue; S.W. = static water; S.W.G., s.w.g. = Standard Wire Gauge.

's. 4. colloq. = *does*; e.g. *What's he say?*

‖**Sadhu** (sā·du). 1845. [Skr., 'holy man'.] In India, a holy man or sage.

Sadism. Also loosely, (morbid) enjoyment of the infliction of cruelty or suffering, esp. in the adj. **Sadistic** (sădi·stik).

Preoccupation with the more sadistic elements of life 1952.

Safety. *attrib.*

s. belt, zone, an area round the Americas in which warlike activities were to be proscribed 1939; **s. film,** slow-burning film specially prepared for cinematograph work 1928; **s. man,** a man engaged to guard a temporarily disused pit in readiness for the resumption of work 1928.

Saga. 3. A series of stories dealing with the history of a family; e.g. 'The Forsyte Saga' (1906–28) of John Galsworthy.

Sale, *sb.* *attrib.*

sales resistance, the unwillingness of the prospective customer to be overcome by salesmanship.

Saloon. 4. **c.** A compartment (upper or lower) of a public passenger vehicle.

Salvo. 2. A number of bombs or parachutists released from an aircraft at one time.

‖**Sanad** (sɒ·nɒd), var. of SUNNUD.

‖**Sanctorale** (sæŋktŏrē¹·li). *Liturg.* 1872. [med.L., f. L. *sanctus* SAINT, after *temporale*.] That part of the breviary and the missal containing the proper of saints.

‖**Sans.** (Late example.)

For life *sans* matter man will seek in vain J. M. THOMPSON 1949.

sans prendre, in the game of ombre, without drawing new cards; **sans recours** *Law*, 'without recourse (to me)' an endorsement on a bill of exchange absolving the endorser or any other party from liability as such party under the Bills of Exchange Act 1882, §16.

If the second player passes, the dealer in his turn may ask to play *sans prendre*. *Encycl. Brit.* XX. (1911) 101/2.

Sate (sē¹t), pa. t. of SIT *v.*, regular from late ME. till mid-19th c., now obs. exc. as a rare archaism; as pa. pple. from 16th c., now obs. †**Satest** (sē¹·tĕst), 2nd pers. sing. pa. t. (used by R. Bridges).

‖**Satrangi** (sətrɒ·ndʒi). Also **sitringee.** 1621. [Bengali, f. Skr. *caturaṅga* chess (played by four).] An Indian cotton carpet.

Saturate, *v.* 4. **c.** To bomb (a target) from the air so thoroughly that the anti-aircraft defences are rendered powerless 1942. So SATURATION.

A 'saturation shelling' of advanced enemy positions *N.Y. Herald Tribune* 22 Nov. 1951.

‖**Satyagraha** (satyā·graha). 1921. [Skr., f. *satya* true, sincere, *āgraha* obstinacy.] Passive resistance.

Save, *sb.* **b.** *Bridge.* Action taken to avoid heavy loss 1927.

Sax (sæks), abbrev. of SAXOPHONE.

Say, *v.*[1] 1. Phrases. *Says you*: dial. or vulgar for *you say*; cf. *SEZ. *To s. a few words*: to make a short (usu. extempore) speech 1930.

Arrah, why, says you, couldn't he manage it? JOYCE.

Sayer[1]. So **Sayee·** [see -EE[1]], one to whom a thing is said.

It takes two people to say a thing—a sayee as well as a sayer...The belief on A's part that he had a *bonâ fide* sayee in B. saves his speech *quâ* him, but it has been barren and left no fertile issue S. BUTLER.

Scads (skædz), *sb. pl.* *U.S. colloq.* [?] **a.** Dollars, money 1809. **b.** 'Lots', 'heaps' 1869.

Scan, *v.* 8. In radar, to cause (a particular region) to be traversed by a controlled beam.

Scanner (skæ·nəɹ). [f. SCAN *v.* + -ER[1].] One who scans. **b.** *Television.* An instrument which scans pictures; so *scanning disc* (1928); see SCAN *v.* 7.

The Time-Springdale electronic s...was used to make, from an Ektachrome transparency, the negatives needed for the colour reproduction 1952.

Scanties (skæ·ntiz), *sb. pl. colloq.* [f. SCANT *a.*, after *frillies* (1900), *panties* (1926).] Abbreviated panties.

Scenarist (sī·nərist). *U.S.* 1937. A composer of SCENARIO.

‖**Schnauzer** (ʃnau·zəɹ). [G., f. *schnauzen* to snarl, snap.] A German breed of house dog with a close wiry coat.

‖**Schnörkel** (ʃnö·rkəl) [G., 'spiral ornament']: see SNORKEL.

Scorched, *ppl. a.* 1. **b.** *S. earth*: applied to a policy of destroying all means of sustenance or supply in a country that might be of use to an invading enemy 1941.

Scout, *sb.*[2] 2. **c.** An A.A. or R.A.C. patrol man 1909.

Scram (skræm). *U.S. slang.* 1936. [perh. shortening of synon. dial. *scramble*.] Be off!

Scramble, *v.* 1. **c.** *trans.* with advs. To deal with in a hasty manner 1869. 4. **b.** To mingle (wave-lengths) of different kinds so as to make a message unintelligible when heard; to treat (a message) in this way 1929.

Scratchy, *a.* 2. **b.** *fig.* Inclined to be cattish 1928.

Screen, *sb.* 1. **d.** *spec.* (in full *silver s.*), the surface on which moving pictures are projected 1882; *transf.* (usu. with def. art.), moving pictures collectively; *the* cinema, *the* films 1928.

Screen, *v.* 4. **b.** *transf.* and *fig.* To scrutinize so as to detect defect or failure, esp. disloyalty, in (persons). orig. *U.S.* 1946.

Script, *sb.* 5. **b.** The text of a broadcaster's announcement or talk. 6. An examinee's written answers.

5. b. His characteristic script of 'Germany speaking' and 'Views on the News' is being read by one of his stooges 1944.

Scrum. *attrib.*

s. half, the half-back who puts the ball into the s.

Sea, *sb.* *attrib.*

s. lane [LANE *sb.* II. 1], the course prescribed for ocean steamers.

Seabees (sī·bīz). 1941. [f. initials *CB* + pl. ending *s*.] Construction battalions of the U.S. navy.

S.E.A.C., SEAC, Seac (sī·æk). 1944. Initials of *South East Asia Command*.

Seal, *v.*[1] II. 6. *To s. off*: to cut off (an area) so that troops within it have no escape 1942.

Sea power. 1. A nation or state having international power or influence on the sea 1883. 2. The efficiency of a nation (or of nations) for maritime warfare; *gen.* ability to control and make successful use of the sea 1883.

Search, *v.* 3. **b.** *S. me!*: used to imply that the speaker has no knowledge of some fact or no idea what course to take (*U.S.*) 1901.

S.E.A.T.O., SEATO (sīē¹·to). 1953. f. initials of (a proposed) *South East Asia Treaty Organization*, after *NATO.

An alternative designation (August 1954) is S.E.A.D.O., with D for *Defence* instead of T.

Secondment (sĭkǫ·ndmĕnt). [f. SECOND *v.*[2] + -MENT.] Being seconded (*from* a position or employment).

Security. A body of people charged with the oversight of persons (e.g. in government employment) in respect of their reliability, and of official establishments.

Until the Fuchs trial he did not think it worth while raising the matter with s...S. were well aware of Pontecorvo's departure 1952.

attrib. **S. Council,** a body consisting of certain members of the United Nations charged with the settlement of disputes and (in general) with preventive and enforcement action.

Seep, *v.* Delete '*dial.* and *U.S.*' and add: Also *transf.* and *fig.*

Through the closed doors there seeped out a great babble of conversation 1925.

Seg(h)olate (sĭgō͡u·lē¹t), *a.* *Heb. Grammar.* [ad. mod.L. *seg(h)olatus*, f. Aram. *sĕghōl* bunch of grapes; see -ATE[2].] Characterized by *seg(h)ōl*, the vowel ֶ = (e) or (ē); *sb.* a noun of two syllables with a long vowel in the first and segol in the second syllable.

A popular conception of the word to 'EQEBH, i.e. to the segolate pattern 1946.

‖**Seiche** (sēʃ). 1882. [Swiss F.] The oscillation of lake waters due to variation of barometric pressure.

Selectivity (sĭlekti·vĭti). 1903. [f. SELECTIVE + -ITY.] *Wireless Telegr.* Power to select a particular wave-length or frequency.

Self-. 1. d. *self-doubt.*

The steps that must be taken to meet it will not be clouded by self-doubts 1951.

3. b. **self-sealing,** (*ppl.*) *a.*, having a device for filling up a hole in the framework or structure caused by shot, etc. 1940.

Self-rai·sing, (*ppl.*) *a.* orig. *U.S.* (1854 in *Dict. Americanisms*).

Semanteme (sĭmæ·ntīm). [ad. F. *sémantème*, f. *sémantique* SEMANTIC, after *phonème* PHONEME, *morphème* *MORPHEME.] *Philol.* An element of a language that expresses or denotes an image or idea.

Sense, *sb.* *attrib.*

s.-datum, an element of experience due to the stimulation of a sense organ.

These s.-data are said to have the 'presentative function' of making us conscious of material things 1951.

‖**Sensum** (se·nsŏm). *Philos.* Pl. **sensa** (se·nsă). [mod.L., neut. pa. pple. of L. *sentire* to feel, perceive (cf. SENTENCE, SENTIMENT).] A sense-datum.

It is only because Russell and Joad *first* knew that there are external objects that they are able to *infer* that there are private sensa 1937.

Sentimentalization (sentime:ntăləizē¹·ʃən). [f. SENTIMENTALIZE + -ATION.] The making sentimental.

Later 19th-century s. of church music 1938.

Septic, *a.* b. Of a tank in which the decomposition of organic matter in sewage is effected through the agency of anaerobic bacteria 1902.

Sequence. 8. *Cinema.* A film scene 1929.

Serum. *attrib.*

s. eruption, sickness, manifestations that follow upon an injection of serum, as a skin eruption, fever, or swelling of the joints 1909.

Servian[2] (sō·ɹviăn), *a.* Pertaining to *Servius* Tullius, the sixth of the legendary kings of Rome, e.g. *S. constitution*, *S. wall* (surrounding the group of the seven hills of Rome).

Service, *sb.*[1] V. 4. b. Provision or supply of what is necessary for the due maintenance of a thing or an operation 1925. Also *attrib.*, as *s. department, depot, station.*

s. area *Wireless*, that area surrounding a broadcasting station within which reception is assured 1927; **s. dress,** ordinary uniform (opp. to *full dress*); **s. hatch,** one through which dishes are passed to the dining-room; **s. pipe,** one conveying water or gas from the main to a building; **s. road,** a road constructed and situated for the convenient service of houses, etc. lying off the main road.

Service, *v.* 1893. [f. SERVICE *sb.*[1]] *trans.* To give one's services to, supply with service (*rare*). b. To provide service for (a car, etc.); see *SERVICE *sb.*[1] V. 4 b. Often in *vbl. sb.*

Servofeed (sō·ɹvoufīd). 1931. [f. *servo-* as in SERVOMOTOR + FEED *sb.* 5 b.] A mechanism that feeds a gun with ammunition, etc. So **Servome·chanism.**

Se:squicente·nnial, *a.*, *sb.* *U.S.* 1880. (Pertaining to) a hundred-and-fiftieth anniversary.

Set, *sb.*[1] III. 9. = *set scene* (SET *ppl. a.*) 1861. b. The setting, stage furniture, etc. used in a theatre or in the production of films 1918.

Set-.

set-up, (*c*) the structure or arrangement of an organization, or the like (orig. *U.S. colloq.*).

Sex, *sb.* *attrib.*

a. In many modern scientific terms relating to the origin, transmission, and functions of sex, as *sex chromosome, control, determination, factor, limitation, linkage, ratio, reversal*; b. **sex appeal,** (abbrev. (S.A.), the appeal to emotion exercised through sexual attraction 1926.

Sexology (seksǫ·lŏdʒi). 1902. (*Dict. Americanisms.*) [f. SEX + -OLOGY.] Study of the relations of the sexes or of sexual life. Hence **Sexolo·gical** *a.*, **Sexo·logist.**

Sexy (se·ksi), *a.* 1928. [f. SEX *sb.* + -Y[1].] Immoderately concerned or engrossed with sex or its manifestations.

‖**Seym** (sē¹m). 1920. The Polish parliament.

Sez, phonetic representation of *says* in *says you* (see *SAY *v.*[1]), used joc. as an ironical formula to express incredulity on the part of the speaker (*U.S. colloq.*) 1932.

Shadow, *sb.*

s. cabinet, a cabinet the prospective members of which are at present in opposition; so **s. minister** 1926; **s. factory,** a factory erected (sometimes duplicating an existing one) as a provision for future production (esp. of war materials) 1936.

Dan [Breen]..knew that the Dail might go on to the crack of doom passing secret resolutions, appointing shadow ministers, holding courts in camera..without anybody being a bit the better or a bit the worse 1926. The 'shadow' industry (for engines) consequently now consists of Austin, Daimler, Rootes, Rover, Standard and Bristol 1936. The 's.' aircraft and munitions factories, mainly extensions of existing plant 1937.

Also in extended use, as in:

So that the whole 'shadow' organization [of A.R.P.] should be in a position to function as soon as an emergency arose *Ann. Register for 1939*, 20.

S.H.A.E.F., SHAEF, Shaef (ʃē¹f). 1944. Initials of *Supreme Headquarters Allied Expeditionary Force.*

Shaggy, *a.* 1.

s. dog story, a tediously detailed story of an inconsequential series of events, supposed to be amusing but actually uninteresting.

Shake-up (ʃē¹·kˌɒp). Chiefly *U.S.* [f. phr. *shake up*, SHAKE *v.* ad fin.] An act of shaking up or being shaken up, or the result of this: a. A hastily or roughly made article 1873. b. A thorough or drastic change or rearrangement 1887 (*Dict. Americanisms*).

Officials close to Mr. Slausky, some of whom disappeared after the shakeup in September 1951.

Shamble, *sb.*[1] 5. (*pl.*) In loose pop. use: A scene of ruin, devastation, or disorder.

Shape, *sb.* 11. Also, in wider use, with ref. to condition of health, as *in good, bad,* or *poor s.*

S.H.A.P.E., SHAPE (ʃē¹p). 1951. Initials of *Supreme Headquarters Allied Powers Europe.*

The SHAPE insignia worn by a member of the SHAPE forces 1951.

Share, *sb.*[2] *Comb.*

s.-pusher *colloq.*, one who peddles shares by circular or advertisement instead of selling them on the market 1914.

Share, *v.*[2] 6.

In the language of Buchmanism, to communicate to others one's spiritual experiences 1933.

Sheer, *a.* 3. Also as *sb.*, a sheer or diaphanous textile material; similarly **Semi-sheer.**

Mod. advt. A semi-service semi-sheer for day and evening wear..a very sheer for evening and special occasions.

Shell-out (ʃe·laut). *Billiards.* 1866. [f. phr. *shell out* (see SHELL *v.*)] The game of pyramids played by three or more persons.

Shelta (ʃe·ltă). 1876 (-*er*). [?] A cryptic jargon used by tinkers, composed partly of Irish and Gaelic words disguised.

Ship, *sb.*[1] 4. b. An aircraft (esp. *U.S. Air Force*) 1928.

Shoe, *sb.* *attrib.*

s.-string, in allusion to the sudden snapping of a s.-lace used in phr. referring to the possibility of a breakdown or collapse.

I am aware..the Minister is working on a financial s.-string 1953.

Shoot, *v.* III. 3. b. To give vent or utterance to; also *absol.* in imper. (*U.S. slang*) say what you have to say, fire away, spit it out. IV. 3. *To s. up*: to assail with indiscriminate or continuous shooting (orig. *U.S.*) 1901.

III. 3. At shooting the smart stuff, Miss Blakeney has the world well beaten 1930.

Shop, *sb.* *attrib.*

s. assistant, a salesman or saleswoman in a retail shop or store.

Shore, *sb.* *Comb.*

s.-based *a.*, operating from a base on s., as *s.-b. aircraft* 1937.

Short, *a.* *Comb.*

s. head *v.*, to beat by a s. head 1922; **s. list,** a list of selected candidates for a post from which it is intended to make a final selection 1927; hence **s.-list** *v.*, to put on a s. list; **s.-staffed** *a.*, not adequately provided with staff; **s. story,** a story with a fully worked-out motive but of much smaller compass and less elaborate form than a novel 1887; **s. time,** the condition of working fewer than the regular number of hours per day or days per week 1908.

Short-fall (ʃǭ·ɹtfǫl). *colloq.* 1949. [f. phr. *fall short* (FALL *v.* VII. 2.)] A falling short or failure to reach a standard or degree of production.

Shot, *sb.*[1] II. 5. An injection (of morphia, etc.) 1929. 6. A dram (of spirits) 1928.

attrib. **s. effect, s. noise,** a noise which is produced in the anode current of a thermionic valve, caused by the fact that the current consists of a series of pulses which give the effect of firing a machine-gun; also called *small-s. effect* 1938.

Sho·t-bag. 1638. [SHOT *sb.*[1]] A bag or pouch for carrying shot.

Show, *sb.* 7, 8. In trivial exclam. *Good show!* = an excellent performance or production!, fine!, splendid!

Shuttle, *sb.*[1] *attrib.*

Denoting an out-and-back course, as in *s. car, train, service*; *s. bombing, raid.*

Shy, *a.* 3. As an element of comps. = frightened (of), averse (to), as GUN-SHY (1884), *work-s.* (1904); cf. G. *feuerscheu, arbeitscheu.*

Siamese, *a.* *S. cat*: a cat of a cream- or buff-coloured short-haired breed with chocolate markings and a tapering tail 1910.

Sicel (si·sĕl). 1836. Also **Si·kel.** [ad. Gr. Σικελός.] One of an ancient race who settled in Sicily and gave it its name. Also *adj.* So **Sice·lian, Sike·lian,** and **Si·culan, Sicu·lian** [f. L. *Siculus*]. **Sice·liot, Sik·** [see -OT[2]], an ancient Greek colonizer (also, an inhabitant) of Sicily.

Sick, *a.* III. 4. b. *S. benefit* (see BENEFIT *sb.* 4 d) 1909.

Siegfried (sī·gfrīd, ‖zī·kfrīt). Name of the German line of fortifications along the western border of Germany from Cleves to Basle; fanciful use of that of the Germanic hero.

The French in the Maginot line and the Germans in the S. line 1940.

Sighting, *vbl. sb.* 1. b. *transf.* An object sighted.

‖**Sigla.** Used esp. for editorial designations of the sources of an edition of a text.

Sign, *sb.* II. 1. (*b*) *Theol.* In sacramental ordinances, the outward or visible part which symbolizes the inward or spiritual part 1553. c. *Path.* An objective evidence or indication of disease 1885.

Sign, *v.*[1] I. 5. *spec.* To make an undertaking 1903; also with *up*. 6. b. Also with *up.*

5. She also s-d up for evening classes 1926. 6. b. Seversky..s-d the violinist up for his broadcast 1932.

Si:gnifica·tional, *a.* [See -AL[1].] Pertaining to or involving signification.

Our question concerning the 'tied' (as opposed to 'free') character of significational thinking 1953.

Silva, Silvi-: the more usual forms of SYLVA, SYLVI-.

Simp (simp). 1916. U.S. colloq. abbrev. of SIMPLETON.

Sin, *sb.* 2. colloq. phr. *in sin*: in a state of free sexual union or adultery 1912.

‖**Sinanthropus** (səinænþrō̆u·pŏs). [f. SIN(O + Gr. ἄνθρωπος man.] = *PEKIN *man.*

‖**Sinfonia** (sinfonī·ă). 1884. [It., 'SYMPHONY'.] In early Italian operas, the overture.

‖**Singh** (siŋg). 1623. *Indian.* [Hind., a. Skr. *sinhá* 'the powerful one', lion.] A great warrior: title of warrior castes, as Rajputs and Sikhs.

Single, *sb.* and *a.* (II. 3). Of a railway (etc.) ticket available for the outward journey only.

Sino-.

Sinoma·nia, a passion for the Chinese or their beliefs, civilization, etc. 1933; **Si·nophile,** one who approves of the Chinese and their ways 1900; **Si·nophobe,** (one who is) hostile to the Chinese 1920.

Sinsyne (si·nsəin), *adv.* *Sc.* 1657 (earlier *sensyne*). [See SIN, SYNE *advs.*] Since then.

Sinter, *v.* [f. the sb.] *intr.* and *trans.* To become or cause to become a solid mass.

‖**Siomio** (ʃō̆u·miǫ). 1727. [ad. Jap. *shōmiyō*, f. Chinese *hsiao* small + *ming* name, title.] One of the inferior nobles of Japan, who were vassals of the Shogun.

-sion (ʃən, ʒən), repr. (often through F.) L. *-sio(n-)*, f. pa. ppl. stems ending in *s* + *-io(n-)* -ION, as in *ascension, mansion, tension,* and *fusion, lesion, occasion.*

Siren. 5. c. An instrument for giving warning of air-raids; the warning itself 1939.

attrib. **s. suit,** a suit of overalls to be put on when the siren gives warning of an air-raid.

Sit-do·wn. 1861. [f. phr. *to sit down*: see

SIT *v.* III. 1.] An act or period of sitting down. As *adj.* At which people sit down 1837.

s. strike, one in which strikers refuse to leave the place where they are employed.

Sitka (si·tkă). 1889. The name of a town in Alaska used *attrib.* to denote trees growing in its neighbourhood, as *S. cypress, spruce, willow.*

Sitter. 3. (At end for 1908 read 1898).

s.-in, one who sits in with a child or family of children while the parents or guardians are absent.

Situational (sitiuē·ʃənăl), *a.* 1903. [f. SITUATION + -AL 1.] Pertaining to situation as in a novel or drama.

Sixth, *a.*

s. day, Friday (with the Society of Friends); s. sense, a supposed faculty by which a person perceives facts and regulates action without the direct use of any of the five senses 1837.

‖**Skat** (skæt). 1864. [ad. G. *skat*, ad. It. *scarto* discard, f. *scartare* to DISCARD.] A three-handed card game in which 32 cards are used.

Ski, *sb.* b. The launching-ramp of a flying-bomb, the form of which suggested the lateral outline of a ski 1944.

Skip, *v.* 6. b. To cause (a bomb) to ricochet from a surface towards the target. Hence S.-bombing.

Skipper, *sb.*2 1. b. *U.S.A.A.F.* The captain of an aircraft.

Skirt, *sb.* I. 1. b. Also *bit of s.*

Skit, *sb.*2 *slang.* 1925. [?] A number, crowd; *pl.* 'lots', 'heaps' (= *SCADS) 1925.

Sky, *sb.*

s. army, men, troops, air-borne troops 1944; s. marker, a parachute flare dropped by a raiding aeroplane to mark the target area 1943.

Slap.

s. and tickle *colloq.*, boisterous or knockabout entertainment.

He hoped that the cultural side [of the Festival Gardens] as well as 'the slap and tickle' would be considered 1951.

Sleeve, *sb.* 4. b. (*a*) = *WIND-*sock* 1937; (*b*) = *DROGUE.

Slip, *sb.*3 III. 2. e. The back-current generated by the propeller of an aircraft; also *s.-stream* 1916.

Slip, *v.*1 II. 1. c. *To s. up*: to make a mistake or error. *slang* or *colloq.* (orig. *U.S.*) 1854.

Slip-.

s. case, a close-fitting case in which a book is issued and from or into which it can be readily slipped.

Mod. advt. 2 vols., buckram, in slip case.

Slipped (slipt), *ppl. a.* [f. SLIP *v.* + -ED 1.] Path. *S. disk*: an intervertebral disk that has slipped from its place.

Slit, *sb.*

s. trench, a narrow trench made to accommodate a soldier or a weapon.

Slum, *sb.*2 [Cf. G. *schlamm.*] 1. = SLIME *sb.* 4. 1875. 2. The non-lubricating part of crude oil; the gummy residue formed in lubricating oil during use.

Slumber, *sb. attrib.*

s. wear, (in shop usage) night-clothes 1916.

Smart, *a. S. Aleck* (also *Alec, Alick*): depreciatory expression for a would-be clever person who knows everything about everything 1873. Also *attrib.* orig. *U.S.* [*Aleck* is a pet-form of *Alexander*, but the allusion is unkn.] Hence Smart-a·lecism.

All sorts of 'smart alecisms' HERBERT MORRISON (*Camb. Rev.*) 18 Oct. 1952.

Smarty, *a.* Also as *sb.*, e.g. *a young s.*

Smashing (smæ·ʃiŋ), *ppl. a.* [f. SMASH *v.*1 + -ING 2.] Overwhelmingly fine, impressive, or the like (*colloq.*).

Smaze (smēⁱz). 1953. Blend of SMOKE *sb.* and HAZE *sb.*, after *SMOG.

Smear, *v.* 3. c. To coat over (floor, etc.) with a mixture of cow-dung and water 1839. 7. To sully the good name or reputation of (*U.S. colloq.*). So Smear *sb.*

Smee 2 (smī). Name of Alfred *Smee* (1818–77) used to designate an electric cell and battery invented by him in 1852.

Smile, *v.* I. 1. phr. *To come up smiling*, to recover from a bout in a contest (e.g. boxing) and face what is to come cheerfully 1886.

Smog (smǫg). 1905. ['Portmanteau' word, f. SMOKE *sb.* + FOG *sb.*] Fog intensified by smoke.

Smoke, *sb.* 6. b. A break in working hours to allow workers to smoke. In Australia and New Zealand Smoko (smōu·ko).

Snafu (snăfū·). *U.S. slang.* 1942. [1. initials of *s*ituation *n*ormal, *a*ll *f*ouled *u*p.] *adj.* Confused. *sb.* Confusion.

Snap, *v.* II. 5. *intr.* To move or proceed quickly, as in *to s. into it, out of it.* So *to make it snappy*, to be quick about it (*U.S.*).

Snarl, *v.*1 2. *transf.* and *fig.* To confuse and trammel the movement of (*U.S.*).

Heaviest Snowfall in 3 Years Snarls Traffic in New York *N. Y. Herald Tribune* 3 Mar. 1952. Surprise rail strike snarls midwest *Ibid.* 10 Mar.

Sneak-, (also) *s.-raid, -raider, -raiding.*

Sned: see SNEAD.

Snip, *sb.* II. 5. Something easily won; a sure thing, certainty (orig. *Sporting slang*) 1894.

‖**Snoek** (snūk). 1853. [Du. *snook* pike: cf. SNOOK.] At the Cape of Good Hope, the common name of the fish *Thyrsites Atun.*

Snooks. Chiefly in phr. *to cock s.* (see COCK *v.*1 3).

Snooper (snū·pəɹ). 1891. [f. SNOOP *v.* + -ER 1.] One who pries into people's doings in order to discover infractions of the law or offences of any kind.

Snooty (snū·ti), *a. U.S. slang.* [?] Superciliously contemptuous.

Snorkel, alteration of *SCHNÖRKEL.

Snort (snǭɹt), *sb.*2 [Substituted for *SCHNÖRKEL, *SNORKEL.] A tubular contrivance in a submarine containing a pipe for the intake of air and one for the expulsion of gases, that can be maintained above the level of the surface of the water. Hence Snort *v.*2 *intr.* (of a submarine) to be submerged so that the snort is at the surface; whence Snorting *vbl. sb.*, esp. *attrib.* as in *snorting depth, practice.*

The possibility that the snort mast snapped while she was snorting 1951.

Snowman (snōu·mæn). *Abominable Snowman*: an animal (human or subhuman) alleged to have been seen in the Nepal area, India. Cf. *YETI.

Snurge (snɔ̄ɹdʒ). *School slang.* [Of unkn. origin, app. based on SNEAK.] A sneak or informer. So Snurge *v.*

He's probably only a kid. He may be a perfect little s. 1933.

So, *adv.* II. 4. phr. *So what?*: a retort made to a serious assertion implying that the problem expressed or implicit has no immediate interest or obvious solution.

The tragedy of the 'So what?' generation 1953.

‖**Sobranje** (sobrā·nye). [Bulg., 'assembly'.] The national assembly of Bulgaria under the Constitution of 1879.

Social, *a.* 7. *S. science*: a science that deals with the elements and conditions of human society, sociology. Hence *S. scientist*, a student of or expert in this.

Socialism. (An earlier instance in the sense of SOCIALITY 1 occurs 1831.)

‖**Sociétaire** (sosyetę̄ɹ). 1889. [Fr., f. *société* SOCIETY + *-aire* -ARY.] An actor-member of the Comédie Française, Paris.

Society. 3. d. *Bot.* A plant community forming part of a consociation.

‖**Socius** (sōu·ʃiəs). 1701. [L.] 1. An associate, colleague, companion. 2. *Philos.* Applied to God as the 'Great Companion' of man.

Sockeye (sǫ·kəi). 1887. [ad. Amer. Indian *sukai* 'fish of fishes'.] = NERKA.

Soften, *v.* 4. b. To reduce the strength of (a defended position) by bombing or bombardment. Also with *up.* Often in *gerund* or *vbl. sb.* (and attrib., as *softening process*).

‖**Soigné**(e (swa·nʸe). 1921. [pa. pple. of F. *soigner* to care for, f. *soin* care.] Dressed or adorned with great care.

Soil, *sb.*1

s. science = PEDOLOGY.

Soilless (soi·llės), *a.* 1828. [SOIL *sb.*1] Devoid of soil; *spec.* of the cultivation of plants (cf. *HYDROPONICS).

S. growth of plants 1938. S. gardening 1940.

Solubilize (sǫ·liŭbiləiz), *v.* [f. L. *solubilis* SOLUBLE + -IZE.] *trans.* To render soluble. Also So·lubiliza·tion.

The problems of hydrotropy, solubilization, emulsification, and blending 1950.

Soluble, *a.*

s. glass = WATER-GLASS 5.

Solutionist (sǒliū·ʃənist). 1885. [-IST.] One who finds a solution, *esp.* (latterly) a solver of cross-word puzzles.

Some. A. 3. *And then s.*: and a good deal or a great many in addition (*U.S. slang*) 1908.

Son. 6. d. *U.S.* in the names of societies, e.g. *The Sons of America, of Liberty* (1766), *of Temperance.*

Sonantal (soᵘnæ·ntăl), *a.* 1891. [f. SONANT + -AL 1.] Pertaining to or of the nature of a sonant, esp. of one forming a syllable.

Song, *sb.* 3. *Nothing to make a s. about*: nothing to boast of, of slight or no importance.

Sonic (sǫ·nik), *a.* 1926. [f. L. *sonus* SOUND *sb.*2 + -IC.] Pertaining to or involving the use of the reflexion of an audible sound; (of a mine) set off by sound vibrations.

S. depth soundings 1926.

Sonnet, *sb.*

s. sequence, a set of sonnets connected in theme 1881 (D. G. ROSSETTI).

Sore, *a.*1 II. 4. Now in U.S. colloq. use: Displeased, vexed 1886.

Sorption (sǭ·ɹpʃən). 1909. [Extracted from *absorption* and *adsorption.*] *Phys. Chem.* The combined action of absorption and adsorption (J. W. McBain).

Sortie. 3. An operational flight by an aeroplane 1940.

Sousaphone (sū·zăfōᵘn). [f. name of John Philip *Sousa*, U.S. bandmaster (died 1932) + *-phone* of SAXOPHONE.] A variety of bass tuba common in brass bands.

Soused (saust), *ppl. a.* [SOUSE *v.*1] 1. Pickled (*dial.*) 1550. 2. Soaked in liquor 1613; (*mod. slang*) drunk 1902. Cf. *PICKLED 2.

Soviet. (The Russian designation of Russia, abbrev. CCCP, is literally: Union of Soviet Socialist Republics.) Also *attrib.* or as *adj.*, e.g. *S. Russia, S. Union, S. literature, S. sport.* Hence Sovietic (soᵘvye·tik) *a.*

Space, *sb. attrib.*

s. ship, an aircraft conceived as practicable in the future for interstellar travel in space.

Spam (spæm). [Proprietary term f. initial and final letters of *sp*iced h*am*.] Tinned meat manufactured by Geo. A. Hormel & Co., U.S.A.

Spaniol(e (spænyōᵘ·l). [ad. Sp. *Español.*] A Spanish dialect used by Jews in the Balkans and Asia Minor.

Spa·stic, *sb.* [subst. use of the adj.] *Path.* A spastic subject.

Spe·ctrophoto·meter. [See SPECTRO-.] An instrument for comparing the brightness of the corresponding colours of two spectra. Hence Spe·ctrophoto·metry.

Speed, *sb.* II. 1. *At s.* (delete †).

Both aircraft are highly manœuvrable at speed (*mod.*).

Spee·d-up. [f. *to speed up*, SPEED *v.* II. 2 d.] Increase of the rate of work, production, movement, etc.

Spiel 1 (spīl). 1824. [See BONSPIEL.] A curling match.

Spiel 2 (spīl). *U.S. slang.* 1896. [ad. G. *spiel* game, play.] A talk, speech 1894. Hence as vb. To speak (*trans.* and *intr.*). Spie·ler, a talker, 'barker'.

Spiral, *sb.* 3. f. A progressive rising movement, in which two or more levels (as of costs, wages, etc.) mount successively one above another, e.g. *the vicious s. of rising wages and prices* 1940.

Spirit, *sb.* V. 3.

s. of salt, spirits of salts, commercial name of hydrochloric (or muriatic) acid 1651.

Spit, *v.*2 II. 5. *Spit-and-polish*: phr. used subst., often derogatorily, to characterize undue or excessive attention to outward appearance.

Spiv (spiv). *slang.* 1939. [Of unkn. origin.] A man who makes a living by his wits without working. (The orig. sense is said to be: A bookmaker's runner or assistant.) Hence Spivvery (spi·vəri), the characteristic activities of a spiv.

Splash, *sb.* 1. c. A small quantity of soda-water, etc. added to a glass of spirits (*colloq.*) 1929.

attrib. Applied to an item in a newspaper or journal set on the page with a wide display, e.g. *a front-page s. story.*

Splinter, *sb.* **1. c.** Applied to the very small parts into which (political) groups or parties may split up.

More marked..than any net transfer between the major parties was the rejection of their lesser rivals and of the 'splinter groups' *Ann. Register for 1950*, 74.

Split, *ppl. a.*

s. second, (also *transf.*) a very brief moment of time 1912.

Besides posing no comparable problem for s.-second skill 1947.

Spoken, *ppl. a.* **1.** *Well-s.* c 1440.

Spotter. 4. b. One who practises aircraft recognition 1939.

Spread, *sb.* **2. c.** *U.S.* = SPAN *sb.*¹ 5 (see quot.). 1894. **5. a.** *slang.* Butter 1812. **b.** Jam, paste, etc. spread on bread, e.g. *chocolate s.* 1886.

Sprinkled (spri·ŋk'ld), *ppl. a.* [pa. pple. of SPRINKLE *v.*] Applied *spec.* to the decoration of the edges of printed books with scattered particles of colour.

Square, *sb.* *To be on the s.*, to be a freemason 1896.

Square, *a.* **1.**

s. dance, a dance in which the partners are arranged in a square or similar set form, e.g. the lancers, the quadrille. So **s. dancer, s. dancing.**

Squeeze, *sb.* **1. d.** The compression of armed forces within an area as a tactical move. So **Squeeze** *v.*

Squit (skwit). *dial.* and *slang.* 1825. [perh. rel. to SQUITTER.] A mean insignificant person.

Stable, *sb.* *attrib.*

stablecraft, the craft or art of tending stables and s. animals.

G. BROOKE (*title*) Introduction to Riding and Stablecraft 1953.

Staff, *sb.*¹ **I. 6. b.** A token given to an engine-driver on a single-line railway as an authority to proceed over a given section of the line; also *attrib.*, as *s. system.*

Stakhanovite (stăkā·nǫvəit). [f. name of a Russian coal-miner, A. G. *Stakhanov*, with whom the practice originated + -ITE.] A (Russian) worker who is awarded recognition with special privileges for extraordinary output. Also *attrib.* Hence **Stakha·novism,** the efficiency system under which such competition and awards are current.

Stakhanovite women miners in the Donetz basin are performing four, nine, and eleven norms each 1952.

‖**Stalag** (stā·læg, stæ·læg, ‖ʃtā·lag). 1940. [G., f. *stamm* STEM *sb.*¹ (used for 'of the main stock') + *lager* camp, LEAGUER *sb.*¹ 1.] A German prison camp primarily for non-commissioned officers and privates.

Stalk, *sb.*¹ **4. b.** A cylindrical length of metal attached to the carrier of a depth-charge and fitting into the barrel of the thrower 1940.

Stand, *v.*

S. down, to go off duty; hence **Stand-down** *sb.* 1915; **S. to,** †(*a*) to be present 1540; to set to work, fall to 1605; (*b*) *Mil.* to take up a position in preparation for an attack (see To *adv.* 5) 1916.

Star, *sb.* *attrib.* and *Comb.*

s. lighting, modified street lighting comparable to illumination by the stars 1940; **s. stream,** either of two systematic drifts of stars one of which comprises the stars nearest to the solar system and moves towards Orion 1894; so **s.-streaming** 1905.

Stardom (stā·ɹdəm). 1865. [f. STAR *sb.* + -DOM.] The status of a theatrical or other star; the realm or sphere of such stars.

Starry, *a.* **3.** *Comb.*

s.-eyed *a.* (*colloq.*), having the stars (the height of one's ambition) reflected in one's eyes.

Statal (stei·tăl). 1862. orig. *U.S.* [f. STATE *sb.* + -AL¹ 1.] Pertaining to a state or states.

Political citizenship..s. or national 1862. Three great s. groups [in India] 1949.

State, *sb.* **IV. 6.**

S. Department, Department of S. *U.S.*, the federal department, the head of which is the **Secretary of S.**, and which deals with foreign affairs 1790 (*Dict. Americanisms*).

Static, *a.* **3. c.** Applied to a store of water in a tank, etc. having no pressure of its own and requiring to be pumped.

Statism (stēⁱ·tiz'm). [f. STATE *sb.* + -ISM.] State administration and control of social and economic affairs.

S., syndicalism, fabianism, all mingle in the British Socialist specific 1948.

Stay, *v.*¹ *Comb.*, f. phr. with advs.

s.-in, (of miners) **s.-down strike,** one in which strikers remain in the place in which they are employed. Cf. *SIT-DOWN.

Steeled (stīld), *a.* [f. STEEL *sb.* + -ED².] *Her.* Having the steel point (of a certain colour).

Gould on a bend sable a speare of the first the poynt steeled proper 1596 (Shakespeare's arms).

Stegophilist (stegǫ·filist). 1952. [f. Gr. στέγος roof + -PHIL(E) + -IST.] One who practises building-climbing.

Sten (gun). 1942. [f. *S*, *T*, initials of the inventors + *en*, as in *BREN.] A type of light machine-gun.

Step, *v.* **1.** *To s. on the gas*: see GAS *sb.*²; hence *to s. on it*, to hurry 1930.

Sterling. B. 1. b. Recently applied to balances (and debts) repayable in sterling.

Sternutator (stə̄·rniutēⁱtǫɹ). 1938. [f. L. *sternutare* (see STERNUTATION) + agent-suffix *-ator.*] A poison gas that acts as a nose irritant.

stg., abbrev. of STERLING.

Stick, *sb.*¹ A number of aerial bombs released in close succession, or of parachute troops from an aircraft.

Stické, stikké (sti·ki). 1903. [f. second half of *sphairistike* (1874), the earliest name of lawn tennis.] A game combining features of squash rackets and lawn tennis, played in an enclosed court with a central net.

Sticky, *a.* **1.** Also, covered with adhesive or 'tacky' foreign matter 1870. **2.** Extremely disagreeable and painful (*slang*) 1915. **3.** Very critical, particular, or captious (*slang*) 1920.

1. s. bomb, a grenade which sticks to the object that it hits. **2.** A s. time in the trenches 1915. [To] come to a s. end 1915.

Stiff, *sb.* **4.** An intractable or incorrigible person (orig. *U.S.*) 1896.

Sting, *v.* **2. d.** *pass.* To be heavily charged or involved in expense, be swindled (orig. *U.S. slang*) 1903. Also *actively.*

Stinker. 4. Something rousing, irritating, or offensive, as a pungent speech (*slang*) 1919.

Stirrup, *sb.* *attrib.*

s. pump, a pump having a foot-plate and fitted with a tube having a nozzle for producing a jet or spray to extinguish a fire or incendiary bombs 1938.

Stock, *sb.*¹ **V.** *Geol.* A body of igneous rock intruded upwards into an older formation.

Tertiary intrusive sheets and stocks of part of the Klingkang Range, Sarawak 1953.

Stockholm (stǫ·khōᵘm). Name of the capital of Sweden: *attrib.* in **S. pitch,** pitch yielded by **S. tar,** a variety of tar prepared from resinous pinewood and used in shipbuilding 1867.

Stockpile (stǫ·kpəil). [f. STOCK *sb.*¹ VI. 10 + PILE *sb.*², *v.*²] A reserve stock of raw materials, etc. that are not or may not be available in adequate quantity from the purchasing country's own resources; *transf.* and *gen.* a reserve supply of indispensable or essential material. Hence as vb. and **Sto·ckpi:ling** *vbl. sb.*

Stoic (stōᵘ·ik), *sb.*² [f. *Stowe* (Buckinghamshire) + -IC, with assim. to *sb.*¹] An alumnus of Stowe school.

Stone, *sb.* **I. 12.** *To give a s. and a beating to*: to outrun or surpass easily (orig. *Racing slang*) 1885

Stonk (stǫŋk), *v.* 1944. [Cf. dial. *stonk* (game of marbles).] *trans.* To bombard with artillery. Hence as sb.

Stooge (stūdʒ), *sb.* *slang.* (orig. *U.S.*) 1913. [Of unkn. origin.] A butt, foil, esp. for a comedian; *transf.* a deputy in difficult or strange circumstances. Hence **Stooge** *v.*, to move, travel, esp. to fly *about, around* in aircraft 1942.

Straddle, *v.* **7.** Also, to drop shot or bombs across (a target), beginning on one side or end and finishing on the other 1917. Hence **Straddle** *sb.*, an instance of this action.

Strass² (stræs). 1875. [ad. F. *strasse*, ad. It. *straccio.*] **1.** Silk refuse. **2.** Waved straw with a silky appearance, used for dress trimmings, etc. 1926.

Strategic, *a.* **b.** *S. bombing*: bombing designed to disrupt the enemy's internal economy, to destroy morale, and the like: opp. to *tactical bombing.* **c.** Of materials: Essential to the provision of munitions of war, as *s. metals, ores.*

Stratfordian (strætfǭ·ɹdiăn). 1908. [-IAN.] One who believes that William Shakespeare of *Stratford*-upon-Avon was the author of the works generally attributed to him. Also *adj.*

Stratosphere. The pronunc. (stræ·tǒsfiəɹ) is now usual.

Stray, *a.* **3. b.** Occurring or met with casually or unexpectedly, as a *s. instance, remark, customer* (colloq.).

Street. 2. *The S.*, (also) Fleet Street as a centre of journalism in London 1932.

Strength, etc. Add the pronunciations (streŋkþ), etc.

Streptomycin (streptǒməi·sin). [f. *Streptomyces* (see STREPTO-, MYCETE) + -IN¹.] An antibiotic produced by the soil micro-organism *Streptomyces griseus* and used against tularæmia and other diseases.

Strepyan (stre·piăn), *a.* [-AN.] *Archæol.* Of the stage of palæolithic culture represented by the remains at *Strépy*, Belgium.

Stressed (strest), pa. pple. of STRESS *v.*

s. skin, applied to aircraft construction in which the loads are taken chiefly by the skin 1936.

String, *sb.* **II. 1. b.** A condition attached *to* an agreement, etc. (orig. *U.S.*) 1888. **2. c.** The horses in training at a stable.

attrib.

s. alphabet, a reading contrivance for the use of the blind by which words are denoted by means of knots of various kinds in a string 1841.

Strip, *v.*¹

s.-tease, an entertainment in which a woman divests herself of her garments one by one before an audience.

Strip, *sb.*² **1. c.** A narrow section of the paper of a periodical publication carrying a series of (usu. comic) drawings, esp. *comic strip* (orig. *U.S.* 1920).

attrib. **s. cartoon,** a cartoon printed in a comic s.; **s. lighting,** illumination by electric light encased in a length of glass tubing.

Stripe, *sb.*² **1. b.** *pl.* A tiger (*colloq.*) 1885.

Stro·ng(-)point. 1922. [tr. G. *feste stellung*; see STRONG *a.* 8, POINT IV. 2.] *Mil.* A specially fortified position in a defence system.

To destroy trenches, 'pill-boxes', strong points 1930.

Strophanthin (strofæ·nþin). *Chem.* 1877. [f. STROPHANTHUS + -IN¹.] A bitter white crystalline poisonous compound obtained from species of *Strophanthus*, used as a heart tonic.

Stuff, *sb.* **III. 2.** phr. *To do one's s.*: to perform one's tricks, do what one is required or expected to do (orig. *U.S.*) 1933. Also *to know one's s.*

Stuffed (stvft), *ppl. a.*

s. shirt *U.S.*, a man of imposing or self-important exterior but of inferior abilities.

While Pompey was a competent soldier, politically he was to prove pretty much a s. shirt 1942.

Stu·ltified, *ppl. a.* *S. triple*: a three-barred gate in which one or two of the bars are inclined diagonally.

Sub, *sb.* Short for SUBMARINE *sb.* 1917.

Sub-. 5. b. *Sub-machine-gun*: a machine-gun of inferior calibre and weight.

20. h. Add *subtotally.*

Subtotally (95 %) Pancreatotomized Male Rats Treated with Thyroid Powder 1948.

Su·b-assembly. 1940. [SUB- 7.] A part of an assembly of machinery.

Su:bstitutabi·lity. [-ITY.] The condition of being substitutable; an instance of this.

The marginal substitutabilities of the factors 1950.

Subversive, *sb.* A subversive person 1953.

Sudbury (sv·dbəri). 1874. Name of a town in Ontario, Canada, used to designate mineral deposits, etc. of that area; *transf.* a place having an extraordinary wealth of such deposits. Also **Sudburian** (-biūᵊ·riăn) *a.*

Sudden, *a.* **3. b.** Colloq. phr.

s. death: (*a*) decision by a single toss (not the best of three) 1834; (*b*) *Anglo-Indian*, a spatchcocked fowl 1886; (*c*) decision of a level set at lawn tennis by the result of the next game 1927.

Sugar, *sb.*

s.-daddy *U.S. slang*, an elderly man who lavishes gifts on a young woman.

Sulphite. 3. *U.S. slang.* An unconventional person who thinks for himself. Cf. BROMIDE 2.

Sulphonamide (sɒlfǭnæ·məid). [I. SULPHONE + AMIDE.] *Chem.* Any of a group of drugs having a strong bacteriostatic action, used in the treatment of infections, e.g. prontosil, prontosil album (sulphanilamide).

Summer time. 2. *Double s. t.*, the standard time, two hours in advance of Greenwich mean time, first adopted in May 1941.

Super, *sb.* = *s.-film* (see SUPER- II. 3).

Super-ego (siūpərе·gōu). 1923. [f. SUPER- I. 3 + EGO.] *Psych.* The development of the ego in the direction of self-criticism and moral conscience.

Superintendent. 1. b. A police officer above the rank of inspector.

Supersonic, *a.* **2.** Exceeding the speed of sound; (of aircraft) flying at s. speed 1945: *sb. pl.* high-frequency sound waves; the study of or the department of science dealing with these.

Supply, *sb.* **I. 4.** *In short s.*: of which the s. is short of what is required.

Supply-, SUPPLY *sb.* or *v.* in comb. = (*a*) having charge of or carrying the supplies of an army, etc. as *s. column, officer, ship, train,* (*b*) supplying water, oil, etc. to an apparatus, etc., as *s.-pipe, -pump, -roller* 1840.

Suppo·rting, *ppl. a.* 1610. [-ING [2].] That supports (*spec.* in techn. senses). *S. film*: a less important film following the chief item of a programme.

Suppose, *v.* **8.** *pass.* Used to express the fact that the subject is (not) expected by the conditions of his employment or occupation, etc. *to do* or *to be* so-and-so (*colloq.*).

Officers..were not 's-d' to keep a scrap log 1911.

Suppressed (sǒpre·st), *ppl. a.* **1. b.** *Med.* Applied to a disease that is checked in its normal course.

Symptoms..known as..'suppressed', 'anomalous', or 'latent' gout 1897.

Sure, *a.* **IV. 1.** *S. thing*: a certainty 1836; advb. Certainly 1896 (*Dict. Americanisms*).

Surface, *sb.* **1.** *spec.* The surface of the sea, as in **s. mail**, mail carried by sea (or, in U.S.A., by land), **s. craft, s.-raider, s.-ship** (as opp. to submarine) 1904.

Surface, *v.* **3.** *intr.* To come to the surface. Also in ppl. adj., as *a s-d U-boat.*

‖**Surra** (sū·ra, sɒ·rǎ). 1890. [Marathi.] A disease of horses and other domestic animals in India, China, etc.

‖**Sursum corda** (sǒ·ɹsǒm kǭ·ɹdǎ). 1559. [L., 'up hearts'.] In the Latin Mass, one of the priest's exhortations to the people preceding the Preface; the corresponding versicle ('Lift up your hearts') in the Communion Office of the Book of Common Prayer. Also *transf.* of appeals to fervour, lofty aspiration, courageous action, or the like.

A fine speech ended on the s. c. note 1917.

Surtax. Also, since 1929–30, a graduated tax on annual incomes above £2,000 in addition to the ordinary income tax, in place of supertax.

Swastika. Used from 1933 as the emblem of the Nazi party and régime.

The lighting of S. fires and the daring hoisting of forbidden S. banners under the eyes of the police *Ann. Register for 1933*, 179.

Sweep, *v.* *Comb.*

s.-back, the angle between the lateral axis and the wing axis of an aeroplane. So **swept-back** *a.* (of the wings or tail of aircraft); also shortened to **swept,** as in **swept-wing.**

Swim, *v.* *Comb.*

s.-suit, a bathing costume.

Swing, *sb.*[1]

Applied from *c.* 1935 to jazz music consisting of a harmonic basis supplied by various instruments and marked by strong rigid rhythms with a superposed melodic part assigned to a single instrument and characterized by a free rubato. So **Swinging** *vbl. sb.*

Switch, *sb.* **6.** *fig.* Diversion of activity, effort, or production 1915. Also **Switch-over.**

Switch, *v.* **6. b.** To exchange (racehorses) after entering them for a race (with intent to defraud).

Jailed..for conspiring to cheat and defraud by switching the horses 1951.

Swither (swi·ðəɹ), *v.* *Sc.* 1501. [?] *intr.* To hesitate, be uncertain. Hence **Swi·ther** *sb.*, 1719.

Swiz(z) (swiz). *slang.* 1932. [Of unkn. origin.] A swindle.

Syllabic. A. *adj.* **1. d.** Based on or determined by number of syllables. **B.** *sb.* **3.** *pl.* Syllabic verses.

A. Neither s., nor quantitative, but simply accentual 1923. B. Neo-Miltonic Syllabics 1921 (R. BRIDGES).

Sylva, Sylvan, Sylvi-. (These spellings are now uncommon.)

Symphonic, *a.* **3.**

s. ballet, a ballet such as may be danced to a symphony; **s. dance,** an orchestral piece in dance rhythm and style but not necessarily intended for dancing.

Symphony. 3. (Now in revived use for: Harmony, consonance.)

UMBGROVE (*title*) Symphony of the Earth 1950.

Synchro- (si·nkrǫu), incorrectly **Syncro-,** abbrev. of *synchronized* used in combs.

Synchromesh, more correct f. SYNCROMESH.

Synchrotron (si·ŋkrotrǫn). 1945. [f. SYNCHRO(NIZE + *-tron* of ELECTRON [1].] An adaptation of the cyclotron designed for the high acceleration of particles (electrons, etc.) combined with a low-frequency magnetic field.

Syncretism. 2. *Philol.* The merging of two or more case-forms in one 1901.

Syncrophone (si·ŋkrǫfǭun). 1943. [Proprietary name; f. *syncro-*, as in SYNCRO-MESH + *-phone*, as in RADIOPHONE.] A combination of a radiogram and pictorial charts, on which illustrations are shown as the talk proceeds.

T. I. 1. b. *Crossing the T* (Naut.), a manœuvre in which a fleet or squadron crosses the line of advance of another and is thus able to concentrate all its guns on the enemy's leading ships, while the latter can use only bow guns. **3. b. T-shirt,** a man's short-sleeved shirt, so cut that when spread out flat its shape suggests the letter T.

II.

T.A.F. = Tactical Air Force; T.B.S. = Talks Between Ships 1943; T.D. = Territorial (Officer's) Decoration; t.e.g. = top edges gilt; T.G.W.U. = Transport and Gas Workers' Union; T.S.R. = Torpedo-Spotter-Reconnaissance; T.T. = teetotal(ler), tuberculin-tested; T.V., t.v. = terminal velocity; TWA = Trans World Airways. See also *TV.

Tab, *sb.* **II.** Also *to keep tabs on* 1904.

Table, *sb.*

III. 1. *T. of Kindred and Affinity*, a list of the degrees of relationship by blood and by marriage within which marriage may not take place according to church law. Also *T. of Affinity, T. of Prohibited* or *Forbidden Degrees* 1846.

Tactical, *a.* **1.** *T. bombing*, aerial bombing carried out in immediate support of naval or military operations. So *T. Air Force.*

‖**Tædium vitæ** (tī·diǒm vəi·tī). 1811. [L.] Weariness of life.

‖**Tahsil** (tɒsī·l). 1849. [Urdu; see TAHSILDAR.] A territorial division in India for revenue administration.

Tail, *sb.*[1] **2.** The rear part of a flying or gliding machine 1909. **3. b.** *Tails*: evening dress with tail coat (*colloq.*).

attrib. **t. rhyme** = TAILED *rhyme.*

Tailor-made, *a.* *transf.* Perfectly designed and finished 1939.

Take, *v.* **III. 2.** *To t. it*: to endure punishment, affliction, etc. with fortitude (*colloq.*).

‖**Talayot** (tǎlā·yǫt). 1872. [Mallorca Sp., f. Sp. *atalaya*, ad. Arab. *talī ah* (with prefixed article) sentinel.] A prehistoric stone tower of the Balearic Islands.

Talking, *vbl. sb.* *Comb.*

t. point, a topic suitable for or inviting discussion or argument.

Tam-tam: see TOM-TOM *sb.* Applied strictly to the metal gongs of the Far East, which are flat disks with a shallow rim (*Encycl. Brit.*, 1911, XXVI. 1064/2).

Tank [1]. *attrib.*

t. farm, an area used for the storage of petroleum in tanks; **t. farming,** growing plants in tanks of water without soil 1937. (Cf. *HYDROPONICS.)

Tank [2]. *T.-buster*: see *BUSTER.

Tape, *sb.* *attrib.*

t. recorder, a machine which records and afterwards reproduces sounds that are registered on a tape.

Target, *sb.* **2. d.** A result (e.g. a figure, sum of money) aimed at; also *attrib.*, as *t. date, t. figure.* The free use of this word for any contemplated goal (figure, total, etc.) has led to illogical expressions such as *beating, exceeding, outstripping, realizing, smashing the t., a higher* or *lower t.*

A total collection of 162,015,869 *l.* (the t. set was 150,000,000 *l.*) *Ann. Reg. for 1943*, 305. I got a different t. figure into their heads 1943. The t. set in war is made deliberately too high...The t. set in peace should be lower than that of war BEVERIDGE 1944. We should be prudent to fix October 1, 1945, as the probable t. date 1944. Targets to be revised 1947.

Task, *sb.*[1] *attrib.*

t. force *U.S.*, an armed force organized for operations under a unified command.

‖**Tass** (tæs). [f. initials of Russ. T*elegraphnoye Agentstvo* SSSR.] The telegraphic news agency of the Soviet Union.

Technicolor (te·knikɒləɹ). *Cinematography.* 1944. [f. TECHNI(CAL + COLOUR *sb.*] Colour photography in which the colours are separately but simultaneously recorded and then transferred to a single positive print. (Trade name.)

Teddy (te·di). Pet-form of the Christian name *Edward*, used *attrib.* in *T. boy*, colloq. description of a youth who affects a style of dress held to be characteristic of Edward VII's reign.

Teen-age (tī·nēᶦdʒ), *a.* 1940. [f. TEENS + AGE *sb.*] Pertaining to or characteristic of young people in their teens, e.g. *t. delinquency.* Hence **Tee·n-a·ger** [see -ER [1]], a person in his or her teens.

Tele-.

Telea·rchics *sb. pl.* [Gr. ἀρχικός governing]: wireless control of aircraft from a distance; **Te·leprinter,** a telegraphic transmitter having a typewriter keyboard and a type-printing receiver (cf. *teletype*).

b. The first element of TELEVISION, as in **Te·lecast,** a televised broadcast; hence **Te·lecaster.**

Tell, *v.* **I. 7.**

You're telling me!: there is no need to tell me, I'm well aware of that (orig. *U.S. colloq.*).

When he declares that 'over-nutrition has its dangers'..the layman is inclined to reply 'You're telling me' *Times* 16 July 1954.

Teller mine (te·ləɹ məin). 1943. [G.] A disk-shaped German anti-tank mine containing TNT.

‖**Tempo.** *transf.* Rate of movement, activity, or progress 1918.

'T.' is reduced by the huge rise in the export of timber 1931.

‖**Temporale** (tempǒrēᶦ·lī). *Liturg.* 1872. med.L., sb. use of n. of L. *temporalis* TEMPORAL.] That part of the breviary and the missal containing the proper for the ecclesiastical seasons.

Temporo-. Also *t.-mandibular.*

(*title*) The Temporo-mandibular Joint edited by B. G. SARNAT 1952.

Tenderize (te·ndərəiz), *v.* *U.S.* [f. TENDER *a.* + -IZE.] *trans.* To make (meat) tender.

Tense, *v.* *pass.* To be in a state of tension.

Highlanders and British Grenadiers are tensed for General Eisenhower's final order (*mod. newspaper*).

Tenth. B. 1. c. Used in stating the extent by which an area is covered by cloud (*ten-tenths* = total). Later replaced by a notation by eighths.

Five-tenths to eight-tenths cloud 1944. Cloud over the target was 10-10ths 1944.

Terraced (te·rēst), *a.* 1644. [f. TERRACE *sb.* + -ED.] Formed into or furnished with a terrace or terraces; arranged in terrace form.

‖**Tertium quid. b.** The third party of 'the eternal triangle'.

Once upon a time there was a Man and his Wife and a Tertium Quid. KIPLING.

‖**Tertius gaudens** (tǒ·ɹʃiǒs gǫ·denz). [L. *tertius* third, *gaudens*, pres. pple. of *gaudere* to rejoice.] A third party who is outside the dispute and is pleased in his contemplation of it.

Fomenting of quarrels in which Germany should be spectator and *tertius gaudens* SPENDER *60 years in England* (1933) 126.

Terylene (te·rilīn). 1954. Trade name of a dress fabric derived from a linear polyester of *ter*ephthalic acid and eth*ylene* glycol.

Tesla (te·slǎ). Name of Nikola *Tesla*,

æ (man). ɑ (pass). ɑu (loud). ɒ (cut). ɛ (Fr. chef). ə (ever). əi (*I, eye*). ə (Fr. eau de vie). i (sit). i (Psyche). ǫ (what). ǫ (got).

American electrician and physicist, designating apparatus invented by him and phenomena associated therewith 1902 (*T. coil*).

Testosterone (testǫste·rōun). 1906. [f. *testo-*, irreg. comb. form of TESTIS + Gr. στέρεος solid + *-one* of HORMONE.] *Physiol.* The male sex hormone secreted by the testicles.

Test-tube. Also *attrib.*, as *t. baby*, one produced by artificial insemination.

The, *dem. adj.* ¶Relics of the dative singular and plural are seen in several place-names, e.g. Noke (OE. *æt þǣm ācum* at the oaks), Rea (*æt þǣre ēa* at the river).

Theme, *sb.* *attrib.*

t. song, a recurrent melody in a musical play or a film 1928.

-therapy (þe·răpi), terminal element (see THERAPY) of words denoting cure by means expressed by the first element, as *actino-, chemo-, psycho-, radio-, röntgentherapy.*

Thermo-.

t.-nuclear *a.*, pertaining to the use of nuclear fission at very high temperatures.

Thing, *sb.*[1] 4. *Dear old t.*: an expression of affection applied to an elderly person 1852. *Old t.*, a joc. or highly affectionate term addressed to an intimate 1919.

Think, *v.*[2]

T. up: to devise, invent, contrive, or produce by thought or cogitation. (*U.S. colloq.*) 1855.

Thinkable, *sb.* A thinkable thing.

In the form of an occurrent 'thinkable' or 'thought-content' 1953.

Third, *a.*

t. force (see *FORCE); **t. programme,** a B.B.C. programme, the third of the normal daily series, having a predominant cultural character or interest; often used allusively to qualify what is intellectually superior or 'highbrow'.

We stand accused, at once, of third-programme standoffishness 1954.

Thirty.

Thirty-nine Articles, Articles of Religion agreed upon by the Archbishops and Bishops and the whole clergy of the Church of England in 1562.

Thoraco-.

tho·racopla:sty [see -PLASTY] *Surg.*, the remodelling of the thorax as by removing one or more ribs.

Three, *a.*

T. Hours (Service), a devotion lasting from 12 to 3 o'clock of Good Friday afternoon, designed to cover the three hours of our Lord's Passion 1898; **t. star,** a high-quality French brandy 1879.

Through. A. *prep.* **5. c.** esp. *U.S.* To the end of (a prescribed period), e.g. *Monday t. Tuesday, 17th t. 19th July.* **B.** *adv.* **1. b.** (To be) in connexion with one's interlocutor on the telephone.

Through-put (þrū·put). 1922. [f. THROUGH *adv.*, after OUTPUT.] Production and distribution (of oil), the quantity so treated.

Throw, *v.* **II. 10. b.** *slang.* To give (a party, dance, etc.) 1936.

Throw out. a. phr. *To t. out the baby with the bath* (*water*): to discard what is valuable along with what is waste or useless 1928.

Thrower. 3. An apparatus for throwing a depth-charge 1940.

Thumb, *v.* **5. a.** *To t. one's nose*: to 'make a long nose' (*U.S.*) 1916. **b.** To make a request for (a ride in a vehicle) by pointing with a thumb in the direction one wishes to go.

Tick, *v.*[1] **2.** phr. *To t. over*: (of an internal combustion engine) to run slowly with the propeller or gears disconnected 1916.

Tie, *v.*

Tie up. g. Also, to be closely connected or allied *with* 1903 (*Dict. Americanisms*).

Tiger. 4. b. A formidable opponent in a game (esp. lawn tennis): opp. to RABBIT *sb.* 2.

Tightwad (təi·twǫd). *U.S. slang.* 1900. [TIGHT *a.*, WAD *sb.*[1] 2 b.] One who keeps his wad of paper money tightly rolled, a close-fisted person.

Time, *sb.* *attrib.*

t. bomb, a bomb the mechanism of which is so adjusted that it will explode after a predetermined interval, delayed-action bomb 1941.

Timology (təimǫ·lŏdʒi). 1929. [f. Gr. τιμή value + -(O)LOGY.] *Philos.* The doctrine of values.

Tip, *v.*[1] *To tip off*: (*a*) to give a warning or hint of 1896 (*U.S.*); (*b*) to 'bump off' 1928. **t.-and-run** *attrib.*, of a raid, etc. marked by hasty attack and immediate withdrawal from the scene 1918.

Titoism (tī·touiz'm). [f. *Tito*, the official designation of Josip Broz, premier of Jugoslavia since 1945.] Adherence to the political system of Marshal Tito in its deviation from the U.S.S.R.

Toc (tǫk). Telephonist's and signaller's name for the letter T. Cf. TOC H.

Toff, *v.* 1928. [f. the sb.] *trans.* To dress *up* like a 'toff'; esp. *refl.* and *pass.*

Toilet. *attrib.*

t. powder, a form of dusting-powder used in making the toilet 1895; **t. roll,** a roll of t. paper.

Toke. *vulgar.* 1859. [?] Food, *spec.* bread.

Token, *sb.* *attrib.*

t. estimate, vote, an estimate, vote of an arbitrary (small) sum of money, proposed for the purpose of enabling a public discussion to take place 1915.

Tolerance. c. *Bot.* (*a*) The ability of a plant to endure unfavourable conditions of environment such as drought or lack of sunlight. (*b*) The ability of a plant to suffer the development of a parasite without manifesting serious disease.

Tom[2] (tǫm). 1920. Gardener's and tradesman's abbrev. of TOMATO.

Tommy gun (tǫ·mi gʊn). orig. *U.S.* 1929. [f. first syll. of the name of the inventor, General J. T. *Thompson* (1861–1940), assim. to TOMMY.] A type of sub-machine-gun. (Registered name.)

-ton (tən), terminal element of many town-names (repr. unstressed development of OE. *tūn* TOWN), and consequently in many surnames, e.g. *Longton, Somerton,* whence extended to form designations of persons and things, as *simpleton, singleton.* Cf. -BY *suffix* 2 and RUDESBY.

Tonic, *a.* **4.** *T. stem*: the stem carrying the tone, accent, or stress; e.g. L. *próbat* (whence OF. *preuve*, ME. *preve*), as against *probáre* (whence OF. *prover*, mod.F. *prouver*, Eng. *prove*).

Too, *adv.* Colloq. phr. *not too*: rather less than, only moderately, not very, e.g. *His health is not too good*; *He hasn't done too badly.*

Tooth, *sb.* **I. c.** phr. *To have teeth in it*: to contain stringent provisions or stipulations. So *to put teeth into.*

To 'put teeth' into the Charter of the United Nations *Economist* 10 May 1947. It is well that President Truman should have made quite clear, not only that the Atlantic Pact is meant to have teeth in it, but also what sort of teeth *Ibid.* 16 April 1949.

Top, *sb.* **IV. 5. b. (The) tops** (used predicatively): (a person or thing) of supreme quality or standing. **6.** *Bridge. pl.* The two highest cards of a suit. **VI. t. secret:** of the highest secrecy in official circles.

Topology (tǫpǫ·lŏdʒi). 1942. [ad. G. *topologie* (1934), f. Gr. τόπος place + -λογία -LOGY.] *Math.* Analysis situs; that branch of mathematics of which the subject-matter is the properties of spaces (sets of points) in respect of their being one connected piece and of forming a boundary, independently of shape and size. Also *attrib.* Hence **Topolo·gical** *a*, **Topolo·gically** *adv.*, **Topo:logiza·tion,** topological analysis. **Topo·logist,** a student of or expert in topology.

The notion of continuity..fundamental to analysis situs, follows naturally from the topologization of space *Chambers's Encyclopaedia* I (1950), 398. *Ibid.* Connectedness furnishes an example of a property of spaces which is an invariant of the topology type. *Ibid.* A topologically invariant definition.

‖**Torii** (tōu·riəi). 1727. [Jap.] The gateway of a Shinto temple.

Originally designed as a perch for fowls which sang to the deities at daybreak, this t. came to be subsequently regarded as a gateway characteristic of the Shinto shrine 1910.

Total, *a.* **1. b.** *T. war*, war in which all available resources, material and immaterial, are employed without reserve 1943.

Touch, *v.*

T. down. b. To alight on the ground from the air. **T. off. b.** *fig.* To give the impulse to, start off.

Tourism. b. More recently, the management of tours and tourists as a business, the conduct of touring parties, e.g. as an official activity. Cf. F. *tourisme, -iste*, G. *tourist*, Russ. *turizm.*

Tourist. Hence **Touri·stic(al)** adjs.; **Tou·ristry** [see -RY], touring, tourists collectively.

Tracer. 2. b. An artificially produced radioactive isotope introduced into the human body and capable of being traced in its course by the radiations it produces.

Radiation characteristics of t. atoms..T. isotopes of halogens 1951.

Track, *sb.* **I. 6. d.** The transverse distance between the wheels of a vehicle 1918.

attrib. **t. suit,** a garment worn by runners and other athletes during their training on the track.

Trade, *sb.* **I. 4.** *To be in t.*: to be a retailer, keep a shop. **5.** *The t.*: the submarine service (*Naval colloq.*) 1916.

Trade, *v.* **8.** *gen.* To exchange (*U.S.*).

Insults Traded in Commons In 20-Hour 20-Minute Session *N. Y. Herald Tribune* 29 Nov. 1951.

Traffic, *sb.* *attrib.*

t. lights, a series of lights (usu. red, amber, and green) used for the automatic control of traffic in a street, e.g. at cross roads.

Trafficator (træ·fikeⁱtəɹ). [f. TRAFFIC + -ATOR, after *indicator.*] A device attached to the side of a motor vehicle to be manipulated so as to show the proposed direction of its course.

Trailer. 9. *Cinema.* A set of short extracts from a film advertising it in advance.

attrib. **t. pump,** a mobile pump for use in fire-fighting drawn along by a vehicle 1940.

Trainee (trē̆nī·). 1944. [f. TRAIN *v.* + -EE.] One who is being trained (for an occupation).

Trans-.

transuranic (-yuræ·nik) *a. Chem.*, having a higher atomic number than uranium 238.

Transducer (trænzdiū·səɹ). [f. L. *transducere*, f. *trans* TRANS + *ducere* to lead + -ER[1].] *Physics.* A device or apparatus conveying power from a system and supplying it to another.

Trap, *sb.*[1] **4. b.** In greyhound racing, the compartment in which a dog is placed and from which it is released at the start of a race 1928.

Trek, *sb.* *transf.* and *gen.* Movement of people in large numbers from one place to another, as on a holiday journey.

The great holiday t. begins 1953.

Tremendious, Tremenduous, Tremenjous (trime·ndiəs, -diuəs, -dʒəs), *a.* Vulgar variants of TREMENDOUS. Cf. *COVETIOUS.

Triangle. 1. c. *The eternal t.*: a man, his wife, and a third party 1907.

Tribophysics (triboufi·ziks). 1954. [f. *tribo-* (see TRIBOMETER).] The physics of friction.

Tricar (trəi·kāɹ). [f. TRI- 1 + CAR *sb.*] A three-wheeled motor car.

Tricoline (tri·kǒlin). 1923. Trade name of: A fine cotton poplin resembling silk.

Trip, *sb.*[1] *attrib.* and *Comb.*

t.-dial, in a cyclometer, a dial on which the mileage of each trip is registered 1907; **tripcock,** in a railway system, a device fixed to a signal which automatically applies the brakes on any train passing a signal set at danger; **t. (valve)-gear,** a valve-gear in which the steam is cut off by the tripping of a lever which holds open the steam valve.

Triplex, *sb.* **b.** Trade name of: Unsplinterable glass consisting of two sheets of glass with a celluloid sheet between 1910.

Tritium (tri·tiǒm, tri·ʃiǒm). [mod.L., f. Gr. τρίτος third + -IUM.] *Chem.* An isotope of hydrogen (atomic weight 3, symbol H^3 or T).

Trivial. A. 3. Also *Min.*

Names of colour- and other 'trivial' varieties 1950.

‖**Trizonia** (trəizōu·niă). [f. TRI-, after BIZONIA.] The combination of the British, U.S., and French zones of occupation in Germany after World War II. Also anglicized **Tri·zone.** Hence **Tri·zonal** *a.*

Expellees in the Trizonal Area 7,554,000. 1949.

Troop, *sb.* *Comb.* See *CARRIER.

Tropacocaine (trōu:păkokē̆·n). 1902. [ad. G. *tropakokain*; see TROPINE, COCAINE.] *Pharm.* Benzoyl-pseudo-tropeine, used as a local anæsthetic.

Trypanosomiasis (tri:pănosoumai·ăsis). [f. TRYPANOSOMA + *-iasis*, after *psoriasis.*] *Med.* Any of a group of diseases caused by parasites of the genus *Trypanosoma.*

‖**Tsunami** (tsunā·mi). [Jap., 'storm wave'.] A sea wave caused by disturbance of the ocean floor or seismic movement.

Tuck, *sb.*[1] *Comb.*
t.-pointing [POINTING *vbl. sb.* 3], coloured mortar, a central groove which has a filling of fine white lime putty, which is allowed to project slightly 1881; hence **t.-point** *v.*, **-pointer.**

Tuffet (tʊ·fėt), dial. var. of TUFT *sb.*, grassy mound or hillock, familiar in the nursery rhyme 'Little Miss Muffet Sat on a tuffet' (1805).

Tularæmia (tiŭlărī·miă). 1921. [f. *Tulare* Co., California (region overgrown with tules) + Gr. αἷμα blood + -IA [1].] *Med.* A disease caused by *Bacterium tularense.*

Tumbrel. **2.** *spec.* The cart in which condemned persons were conveyed to execution during the French Revolution (*le tombereau des condamnés, le fatal tombereau*).

Tung-tree (tʊ·ŋtrī). 1921. [Chinese *yu t'ung.*] **a.** The Chinese tree *Aleurites corduta.* **b.** The E. Indian genus *Dipterocarpus.* So **Tung-oil**: see *wood-oil* s.v. WOOD *sb.* III. *Comb.*

Turbo-. Also **t.-jet engine; t.-propeller engine,** also **t.-prop (jet) engine.**
The Sea Mew [*sc.* an anti-submarine plane] has a Mamba t.-prop engine 1953.

Turf, *v.* **4.** To throw or 'kick' *out* 1923.

Turn, *sb.* **V. 1. b.** Time, season, occasion: always in *this t.* (chiefly *dial.*) 1796.

Turn, *v.*
T. round. b. (*b*) Of a ship: To enter a port, discharge cargo, and leave; also said of motor transport. Hence **Tu·rn-round,** the process involved in this.

Tu·rn-away. [f. phr. *turn away*, TURN *v.* p. 2268/1.] The action or an act of turning away from a course.
The British battle fleet turned away two points to port..This was the 'turn-away' which has given rise to considerable controversy 1921.

TV (tīvī·). Initials of the two elements of TELE|VISION. Also *attrib.*, as *T.V. viewer.*

Twee (twī), *a.* For *tweet*, infantile or affected pronunc. of SWEET.

Twerp (twə̄ɪp). *slang.* 1925. [?] A despicable fellow.

Twin, *a.* and *sb.* *Comb.*
t. set, a jumper with cardigan.

Two-way, *a.* **3.** That may be used in either of two stated ways.
Mod. A t. Proxy card is enclosed with this letter. By signing and returning this card, you will not be precluded from attending and voting in person at the Meeting should you find it possible to be present.

Tycoon. *transf.* One who is highly placed or in a dominant position in some sphere. orig. *U.S.* (app. first applied to Abraham Lincoln).

Typewriter: patented 1868 (*Dict. Americanisms*).

U. II.
U = *UTILITY; U.D.C. = Urban District Council; U.N.A.(C.) = United Nations Association (Command); U.S.(A.)A.F. = United States (Army) Air Force; U.S.A.F.E. = United States Armed Forces in Europe; U.S.P. = United States Pharmacopœia; U.S.S. = Under Secretary of State.

Ugro-Finn (yū·grofi·n). 1862. [f. comb. f. of *Ugria* + FINN.] A Finn of the Ugrian stock. So **Ugro-Fi·nnic, -Fi·nnish** *adjs.* (cf. *FINNO-UGRIAN).

Ultra-.
1. b. *U.-red*, earlier term for *INFRA-RED 1870. *U.-violet* 1875. **4.** Applied to instruments adapted for very minute measurements or observations, as *u.-micrometer, -microscope* 1910.

Ultrasonic (ʊltrăsǫ·nik), *a.* [f. ULTRA- 2 + L. *sonus* SOUND *sb.*[2] + -IC.] *Physics.* Pertaining to vibrations and waves of a frequency higher than those which affect the human ear. Cf. SUPERSONIC. Also *sb. pl.*, the department of physics concerned with these.

Umbrella. **4. b.** A screen of fighter aircraft or (in full, *u. barrage*) a curtain of fire put up as protection against hostile aircraft.

U.N. (yū e·n). United Nations (see below).

Unadopted, *ppl. a.* **b.** Of roads: Not taken over for maintenance by the local authority.

Un-American, *a.* Unfavourable to the U.S.A. and its interests.
U. Activities Committee *Ann. Register for 1948*, 206.

Under-belly (ʊ·ndəɪbe:li). †**1.** A bag under the belly (as in the kangaroo) 1607. **2.** The lower part of the belly.
2. The soft u. of the Axis [*sc.* Italy] 1942 (W. S. CHURCHILL).

U·nderca:rriage. **b.** The landing-gear of an aeroplane 1917.

Undercover (ʊ·ndəɪkʊ:vəɪ). [See COVER *sb.*[1] 2.] Used *attrib.* to denote a person who occupies a position in an organization for the purpose of illicitly obtaining confidential information.
The city is teeming with German u. men 1943.

Underline, *sb.* **2. c.** Descriptive line(s) beneath a picture, illustration, etc.

U·ndershoot, *v.* 1939. [f. UNDER-[1] III. 1 c + SHOOT *v.*] Of an aircraft: To land short of the runway.

Unemployment. *attrib.*
u. benefit, payment made to an unemployed person under an insurance act 1928.

U.N.E.S.C.O., UNESCO, Unesco (yune·skoᵘ). Initials of *U*nited *N*ations *E*ducational, *S*cientific, and *C*ultural *O*rganization.

U.N.I.C.E.F., UNICEF, Unicef (yū·nisef). Initials of *U*nited *N*ations *I*nternational *C*hildren's *E*mergency *F*und.

Unionist, *sb.* **1. c.** (The name remained the official designation of the alliance of Liberal Unionists and Conservatives until 15 January 1922, when the Irish Free State was established.)

United, *ppl. a.*
U. Nations, in World War II, the nations united against the Axis powers, developed into an international organization on the basis of a charter, April–June 1945. Also **U. Nation,** any one of these.

Univalent. Also (yūnivēⁱ·lěnt).

University. *attrib.*
u. college, a college having university connexions but not competent to grant degrees; **u. test act,** the act of 1871 abolishing subscription to the Thirty-nine Articles as a condition of graduation in a university.

Unknowable, *a.* Also *sb.* **1.** With *a.* and *pl.* An u. thing 1725. **2.** With *the*: That which cannot be known 1823.

Unlenited: see *LENITION.

U.N.O., UNO, Uno (yū·noᵘ). Initials of *U*nited *N*ations *O*rganization.

Unplanned (ʊnplæ·nd), *ppl. a.* [UN-[1] 2.]
Planning itself was u. *Economist* 26 Apr. 1952.

U·nquote. [UN-[2].] Used in dictation to indicate the end of a quotation. Cf. *QUOTE.

U.N.R.R.A., UNRRA, Unrra (ʊ·nrā). 1943. Initial letters of *U*nited *N*ations *R*elief *a*nd *R*ehabilitation *A*dministration.

Unscra·mble, *v.* [UN-[2].] *trans.* To interpret (a scrambled message: see *SCRAMBLE 4 b).

Unspru·ng, *ppl. a.* 1928. [UN-[1], pa. pple. of SPRING *v.*[2]] Not provided with springs.

Unstick (ʊnsti·k), *v.* 1706. **1.** *trans.* To remove so that it does not stick. **2.** *intr.* Of aircraft, esp. seaplanes: To take off 1913.

Unstuck (ʊnstʊ·k), *pa. pple.* [UN-[2].] Colloq. phr. *To come u.*, to come to grief 1931.

Untaken, *ppl. a.*
F. G. ORDISH (*title*) U. Harvest: Man's Loss of Crops from Pest, Weed, and Disease.

Up, *sb.* **2. d.** *On the up-and-up*: (*a*) continually improving; (*b*) on the level, honest (*U.S. colloq.*).

Up, *adv.*[2] **II. 4. d.**
A player is said to be 'one up', 'two up', &c., when he is so many holes to the good of his opponent *Encycl. Brit.* XII (1910) 224/1 (*Golf*).

Up Jenkins (ʊp dʒe·nkinz). [Of unkn. origin.] A parlour game in which a coin is passed from one to another of a group of players who are summoned to hold up their hands, palms outward, with the coin held between the fingers in such a manner as to conceal it.

Uprush, *sb.* **b.** *Psychol.* The sudden emergence of ideas from the subconscious or unconscious 1906.

Urease (yūᵊ·rīēⁱz). [f. UREA + *-ASE.] *Chem.* The enzyme which changes urea into ammonium carbonate in the ammoniacal fermentation of urine.

Use, *v.* **III. 3.** Surviving in informal language in contexts like the following:
'Taint what it usto be 1931. I usen't [= used not] to feel it, but I do now 1934. Did Aunt Dorothea use to clean it up? 1949.

‖**Usque** (ʊ·skwī) **ad nauseam:** see *AD NAUSEAM.

U.S.S.R. (yū:esesā·ɪ): see U II. 1.

Utility. **5. c.** Applied to clothes, furniture, etc. made in standardized form in accordance with the official allowance of material 1942.

V.
V. = Victory 1941, F. *Victoire*, Du. *Vrijheid* (freedom); V.A. = Vicar Apostolic, Vice-Admiral; V.A.D. = Voluntary Aid Detachments; V and A = Victoria and Albert (Museum); V.D. = volunteer decoration; venereal disease; V.D.H. = valvular disease of the heart; VE/VJ = victory in Europe/Japan (Day); V.H.F. = very high frequency; V.I.P. = very important person; V.L.R. = very-long-range (aircraft); V.R. = Volunteer Reserve; **V. sign** = a sign made to represent the letter *V* (for *victory*) by the first and second fingers spread apart, the others being held down together by the thumb.
In **V 1** (the *P-PLANE), **V 2** (the rocket bomb) = G. *Vergeltungswaffe* 'reprisal weapon'.

Value, *sb.* **I. 5.** The quality of a thing considered in respect of its power or validity for a particular (specified) end, purpose, or effect 1909. **6.** *pl.* One's judgements of things in respect of their value 1919.
5. News v. 1892. Flaws and interruptions destroy the museum v. of a mineral 1893. The exploitation by the Romantics of pictorial and evocative v. in vocabulary 1933. Until these..aerial toys..acquired what in these days has come to be known as weapon-v. 1941. *Mod.* Energy, nuisance, propaganda, scarcity, survival v. **6.** *Mod.* His v-s are all wrong.

Vapour, *sb.* *attrib.*
v. trail, pattern: cf. *VORTEX.

Variate (vēᵊ·riět), *sb.* 1889. [ad. pa. pple. of L. *variare* to VARY; see -ATE 1.] *Statistics.* The size or value of a particular character in one specimen.

Vector, *v.* 1940. [f. the sb.] *trans.* To direct (an aeroplane) on a course.

Veleta (vělī·tă). A three-time waltz-like dance.
Barn-dance and slow veleta, polka hop *Punch* 15 Oct. 1952.

Ventifact (ve·ntifækt). 1940. [f. L. *ventum* WIND *sb.*[1] + *factus*, pa. pple. of *facere* to make.] *Geol.* A stone shaped or altered by wind-blown sand.

Verbalist. Hence **Verbali·stic** *a.*, pertaining to or characterized by verbalism.
No sillier than the purely V. theory which is at present fashionable H. H. PRICE 1953.

‖**Verglas** (vɛ̄rgla). [F., perh. f. OF. *verglacier* to make a surface of frozen rain.] A silver thaw.

‖**Vers de société** (vɛ̄r də sosyete). 1803. [F., 'verses of society'.] Verse that treats of topics provided by polite society.

Versy (və̄·ɪsi), *a.* [f. VERSE *sb.* + -Y [1].] Having the character of verse.
Rhapsodial v. prose, harmonizing with the literary cults of the day [*sc.* of Hazlitt] 1929.

Vesicant. **A. b.** A blister gas 1938.

Vest, *sb.* *attrib.*
v.-pocket *attrib.*, of small articles, e.g. hand cameras, of a size suitable for the pocket.

Viable, *a.* **1. b.** Capable of living in certain conditions. **2.** Capable of developing or germinating.

Vic (vik). [Signaller's name for the letter V.] V-shaped formation of aircraft.

‖**Video** (vi·dīoᵘ). *U.S.* [L. *video* I see.] Television. Also *attrib.* or as *adj.*
V. and Radio *N. Y. Times* 1 Oct. 1950. Coast-to-Coast V. Network starts Operation in the U.S. *N. Y. Her. Tribune* 5 Sept. 1951.

Viewer. **1. b.** One who watches television.

Vintage. **1.** Also *transf.* from the use in *v. wine*, e.g. *v. verse.*

‖**Virement** (vī·rmaṅ, vīᵊ·ɪmənt). 1902. [F. (e.g. *virement de fonds*), f. *virer* to turn (cf. VEER *v.*[2]); see -MENT.] *Finance.* The application of resources intended for one end to the purposes of another.

Virgil (və̄·ɪdʒĭl). 1938. [f. the name of the inventor, A. K. *Virgil.*] *Virgil (practice) clavier*: a piano keyboard without sound-producing mechanism, except for a click made by the descent or the ascent of the key.
A virgil silent clavier, 8 octave, folding legs..adjustment for any weight of key 1950 (*Advt.*).

Virgule. Also, a short slanting line used to mark the place of line or word division, or an alternative (as *and/or*).

Viscount. Also, a courtesy title of an earl, and used by his eldest son.

Visé, superseded by VISA.

Vision, *sb.* **2. b.** Without article or pl.: Power of discerning future conditions in some sphere; sagacity in planning for these.

Vortex. 4. b. A trail of vapour, often of a whirling form, left in the sky by the exhaust of an aeroplane or by surface contacts.

W. 3.

W = (Air-Raid) Warden; W.A.C. = Women's Army Corps (U.S. equiv. of A.T.S.); W.A.F. = with all faults (in booksellers' parlance); W/Cdr = Wing Commander; W.E.U. = Western European Union; W.H.O. = World Health Organization; W.I. = Women's Institute; W.L.A. = Women's Land Army; W/O = Warrant Officer; W.O.C.C.I. = War Office Central Card Index; W.R.A.F. = Women's Royal Air Force; W.V.S. = Women's Voluntary Service.

Waaf (wæf). *colloq.* [Initial-formed.] A member of the *Women's Auxiliary Air Force* (1939); see *WRAF.

Wafdist (wɑ·fdist), *a.* and *sb.* 1926. [f. *Wafd*, the political organization supporting the Egyptian nationalist leader Zaghlul Pasha + -IST.] Pertaining to, a supporter of, the Wafd.

Waffle [2] (wǫ·f'l). 1888. *slang.* [?] Continuous rapid talk, twaddle. Also as vb.

Waggon, *sb.* **I.** *On the w.*: = *on the water-w.* (see WATER *sb.*), teetotal 1917.

Walk, *v.*[1] **3. k.** *To w. out on*: to forsake, desert, leave in the lurch (*U.S. slang*) 1896.

Walker, *sb.*[1] **6.** An apparatus for assisting infirm persons to walk.

A 'walker' which can be employed for re-education of the arthritic patient in walking 1953.

Walkie-talkie (wǭ·kitǭ:ki). Also **walky-talky.** [f. WALK *v.*, TALK *v.* + -IE repeated.] A radio transmitting and receiving set carried on the person to provide two-way communication while perambulating an area.

Walk-out. 1888. [f. *to walk out*; see WALK *v.*[1] I. 3 j.] A cessation of work by employees without notice.

The w. in the steel mills 1944.

War, *sb.* *War of nerves*: the use of hostile or subversive propaganda to influence morale and cause confusion and uncertainty.

attrib. **w.-head,** the explosive head of a torpedo or similar weapon 1898; **w. work,** work undertaken in consequence of or directly concerned with a war 1915.

Wash-out. I. b. The washing-out of a cavity of the body, the result of this.

Waste, *sb.* **III. I.** The waste products of industrial processes in respect of their disposal and treatment.

W. treatment information for chemists, engineers, municipal officials 1952.

Waterbury (wǭ·təɹberi). Name of a low-priced watch manufactured by the Waterbury Clock Co., Waterbury, Conn., U.S.A. 1896 (*Dict. Americanisms*).

Wave (wēⁱv), *sb.*[2] A member of the W.A.V.E.S. (see next).

Waves (wēⁱvz). f. initials of *Women Accepted for Volunteer Emergency Service* (Women's Reserve, U.S. Naval Reserve) 1942; corresponding to British Wrens.

Wavy, *a.*

The W. Navy: the Royal Naval Volunteer Reserve, so nicknamed in allusion to the w. line of the insignia of rank on the sleeve (*colloq.*).

Way, *sb.* **II. 4.** Colloq. phr. *On the way out*: about to disappear, fail, or perish.

Weather, *sb.* *attrib.*

w. bureau, a meteorological department, as of the U.S. Department of Commerce, established 1890.

Weave, *v.*[2] **I. b.** To take evasive action in the air (*R.A.F. slang*). Also *transf.* in *to get weaving*, to 'get a move on'.

‖**Wehrmacht** (vē·rmaχt). [G., 'defence force'.] The German armed forces organized for war from 8 February 1938.

Weight, *sb.* *Comb.*

w.-lifting, lifting weights as an athletic exercise. The London W.-lifting Club 1896.

Weimaraner (vai·mar[illegible]ānəɹ). 1954. [G. suffix *-aner*, as in *Lutheraner*, etc.] A pointer that finds and retrieves game from land and water, belonging to a hunting breed which was the private possession of the Grand Dukes of *Weimar*, Germany.

Welfare. *spec.* The condition of sustenance and maintenance of members of a group or community in a state of well-being and satisfaction, esp. as provided for and organized by legislation or social effort; often *attrib.* as in *w. centre* (1917), *w. economics, w. manager* (1904), *w. officer, w. policy* (1905), *w. service, w. work, w. worker*; **w. state,** a polity so organized that every member of the community is assured of his due maintenance, with the most advantageous conditions possible for all (1945).

The home of 'the w. policy' is the City of Dayton, Ohio 1905.

West. D. *W. wall* [G. *Westwall*]: the line of defences erected by the Germans for the protection of their western borders.

French advance towards the Westwall *Flight* 21 Sept. 1939. The gigantic defensive zone called 'West Wall', stretching from Bergen to Biarritz 1942.

Westminster. b. *Old W.*: a past pupil of W. School 1773.

What, *pron.* Colloq. phrasal sb. *and/or what-have-you*: and/or anything else that there may be or that one can think of.

Various other buildings, bridges, laboratories and what-have-you 1952.

Whisker. 5. c. A star-shaped contrivance fitted to the nose of a torpedo to ensure that the torpedo explodes without glancing off the target 1940.

Whistle, *sb.* *attrib.*

w. stop *U.S.*, a small town on a railway line at which trains stop when a signal is given on a whistle; *transf.* applied to organized stops on a (political) candidate's tour of the country 1934.

White man. phr. *The w. m.'s burden*: the task of civilizing coloured peoples.

Take up the W. M.'s burden KIPLING 1899.

Whodunit (hūdʊ·nit). *slang.* 1930 ('coined by Donald Gordon in *American News of Books*', Webster's Dict.). [= *Who done it?*, vulgar for *Who did it?*, i.e. 'Who committed the crime?'.] A detective story.

Willies (wi·liz), *sb. pl.* *U.S. slang.* 1896. [Of unkn. origin.] A nervous feeling of misery and/or fright.

Win, *v.* **3.** *transf.* in the catch-phr. *to win the peace.*

The question of post-war reconstruction at home—the problem, as it was called, of 'winning the peace' *Ann. Register for 1943*, 89.

Wind, *sb.*[1]

w.-sock, a canvas tube flown from an aerodrome mast to show the direction of the wind.

Wing, *sb.* *attrib.*

w. ship *U.S.A.A.F.*, either of the bombers that fly on each side of an element leader.

Winkle, *v.* 1943. [f. WINKLE *sb.*] *To w. out*: to extract, eject (as a winkle from its shell with a pin).

Winterize (wi·ntərəiz), *v.* [f. WINTER *sb.* + -IZE.] *trans.* To adapt for operations in winter or cold weather.

Wisdom.

W. books or **literature,** collective name for the biblical books of Job, Proverbs, Ecclesiastes, The Wisdom of Solomon, Ecclesiasticus, and the Epistle of St. James.

Wishful, *a.* **2. c.** *W. thinking*, an illusory state of mind towards events which is coloured by one's wishes concerning the future, esp. as to what one hopes will happen.

Witan. See also WITENAGEMOT.

Witch, *sb.* *attrib.*

w.-hunt, (orig. *U.S.*) the search for a victim or victims in order to justify accusations of disloyalty, etc.; by extension, (defamatory) harassing of supporters of opposite opinions, or the like.

Wiz (wiz). orig. *U.S. slang.* 1915. [abbrev. of WIZARD *sb.*] A 'wonderful' person.

Wizard, *a.* **2. b.** Marvellous, wonderful (*colloq.*) 1934.

Wo·rkbook. Chiefly *U.S.* [f. WORK *sb.* + BOOK *sb.*] **a.** A book containing a guide to or an outline of method of work, study, etc. **b.** A book containing a record of work done or planned.

Plant Ecology W. by J. T. CURTIS (Wisconsin University) 1950.

Working, *ppl. a.*

w. party, a body consisting of employers and workers in a particular industry or occupation, together with independent members, appointed to advise upon methods for improving output or performance 1945.

World. *attrib.*

The First World War, World War I, the war of 1914–18; **The Second World War, World War II,** the war of 1939–45.

When I came to the Institute after World War No. I WIENER 1948. 1949 W. S. CHURCHILL (*title*) The Second World War.

Worming (wɒ̄·ɹmiŋ), *vbl. sb.* [f. WORM *v.* + -ING [1].] The production of worm-holes in books.

Wraf (ræf). [Initial-formed.] A member of the W.R.A.F. (s.v. *W); superseded *WAAF.

Wrap, *v.* *To w.* (*up*) *in* (*a*) *mystery*: to conceal by a pretence of unknown or mysterious origin; esp. joc. with spurious pp. (*wrop* or *wropt in mystry*).

My ma wrapped up my buth [*i.e.* birth] in mistry THACKERAY *Yellowplush Papers* i.

Wrist. *attrib.* **w.-shot,** in golf, a shot shorter than a half-shot, but longer than a putt (*Encycl. Brit.* 1910).

Write, *v.*

W. off. c. To reckon as lost. Hence **W.-off,** cancellation, amount cancelled, dead loss 1905.

Xenophobia (zenofōᵘ·biă). 1919. [See XENO-, -PHOBIA.] Morbid dread or dislike of foreigners. Hence **Xe·nophobe** [see -PHOBE].

Y. *attrib.*

Y-gun, a gun with two firing-arms for discharging depth-bombs.

-y [6]. Examples of the extended application of this prefix (also in the form *-ie*, occas. *-ey*) in its addition to abbreviated forms are: *baccy, bookie, cabby, gutty, hanky, hubby, nighty, pin-n(e)y, toady, tummy.*

Yedda (ye·dă). 1918. A kind of straw grown in Italy, Japan, and the Philippine Islands, used for hats.

Yeti (yē·ti). 1951. Native (Sherpa) name of the animal supposed to leave tracks in the snow on the higher Himalaya mountains and known as 'the abominable *SNOWMAN'.

Yogic (yōᵘ·gik), *a.* [f. YOGA or YOGI + -IC.] Pertaining to or involving yoga.

S. MUZUMDAR (*title*) Y. Exercises for the Fit and the Ailing.

Yorkie (yǭ·ɹki). *Naut.* A name for the main trysail. (Cf. SPENCER [2].)

Yours. *What's y.?*: What will you have to drink? 1931.

Yourself. b. *Be y.*: Collect yourself, pull yourself together (*U.S. colloq.*).

Youth. *attrib.*

y. hostel, a lodging specially provided where young travellers or hikers can put up for the night 1929. (So G. *jugendherberge.*)

Yperite (əi·pərəit). [ad. F., f. *Ypres*, name of a Belgian town; see -ITE.] Mustard gas.

Z. *attrib.*

Z.-gun, a kind of anti-aircraft rocket gun 1944; **Z-man,** an army reservist.

Zadkiel (zæ·dkiəl). Pseudonym of Richard James Morrison (1795–1874), English astrologer, used in the title *Zadkiel's Almanac* (formerly *The Herald of Astrology*), containing predictions of the events of the coming year.

Zebra. Used *attrib.* to designate a street crossing for pedestrians marked by parallel black and white bands suggesting the markings of a zebra's coat.

A woman killed on a z. crossing 1951.

Zee (zī). 1677. (Now *U.S.*) The letter Z.

Zero. 6. c. *At z.*: (to fly) below 500 feet.

‖**Zloty** (zwǫ·ti). 1923. [Pol., f. *zloto* gold.] The Polish monetary unit having a par value of about 25 to the pound sterling.

Zombie (zǫ·mbi). In the West Indies, a corpse said to be revived by witchcraft; *transf.* one who has been brought out of a state of inactivity (for the Canadian use see quot.).

Canada has conscription for home defence, but hitherto only volunteers have been sent abroad; and 'Zombies' are conscripts who have not volunteered to leave the Dominion 1944.

Zoom, *sb.* 1917. [f. ZOOM *v.* 2.] A steep climb (of aircraft).

Zulu. 4. A rough conical straw hat.